CASES AND MATERIALS

ON

CONTRACTS

FIFTH EDITION

By

E. ALLAN FARNSWORTH
Alfred McCormack Professor of Law
Columbia University

WILLIAM F. YOUNG
James L. Dohr Professor of Law
Columbia University

Westbury, New York
THE FOUNDATION PRESS, INC.
1995

615 Merrick Ave.
Westbury, N.Y. 11590–6607
(516) 832–6950

Library of Congress Cataloging-in-Publication Data
Farnsworth, E. Allan (Edward Allan), 1928–
    Cases and materials on contracts   /   by E. Allan Farnsworth, William
F. Young. — 5th ed.
        p.   cm. — (University casebook series)
    Includes index.
    Cover title: Contracts—cases and materials.
    ISBN 1–56662–242–5 (hard cover)
    1. Contracts—United States—Cases.   I. Young, William Franklin,
1925–   . II. Title. III. Title: Contracts—cases and materials
IV. Series.
KF801.A7F37   1995
346.73'02—dc20
[347.3062]   95–12179

 TEXT IS PRINTED ON 10% POST CONSUMER RECYCLED PAPER

2nd Reprint — 1998

PREFACE

The course in Contracts serves a twofold purpose. It is the law school's first course in commercial law and so must provide the necessary foundation for advanced courses and seminars in this area, and ultimately for professional practice. In addition, it has a more ambitious function, for law teachers have long believed—rightly we think—that contract law offers a body of precepts and problems exceptionally well suited to development of the student's "legal mind": respect for sources, skepticism toward easy generalizations, and disciplined creativity in the use of legal materials. We have tried to take account of both objectives.

Notes draw connections among cases and present other situations for comparison. They call attention to relevant statutes (notably the Uniform Commercial Code), and to the formulations of the common law contained in the Restatement of Contracts. They also prompt reflection, suggest alternate solutions, and ask students to consider how counseling and drafting may avoid later litigation.

We have tried to ease the task of learning. Each chapter and section is introduced with a brief survey. Occasionally we have provided an opinion with an Introductory Note providing students with historical background or with the business setting. Some topics are presented in text, especially those dominated by legislation or by commercial practices.

But this, like its predecessors, is still essentially a casebook-with-notes rather than a professor's notebook-with-cases. A law school casebook is not a treatise and is designed for very different purposes. Although we have tried to indicate recurring questions of policy, no effort has been made to provide approved answers. We have tried to caution against the false assumption, to which beginning law students may be inclined, that questions of policy are somehow extrinsic and "nonlegal." In contracts, as elsewhere in the legal order, law and policy are inextricable.

Our indebtedness to scores of distinguished scholars in Contracts (including especially E.W. Patterson, a progenitor of this book), will be evident. We have profited immeasurably, over the years, from the responses of a host of imaginative and energetic students. More particularly, we express gratitude to our student assistants for this edition, Christopher Clark, Nichole Duncan, and Bradley Finkelstein—and to Brenda Fox for patient, efficient secretarial help.

E. ALLAN FARNSWORTH
WILLIAM F. YOUNG

New York
June, 1995

*

iii

INTRODUCTION

This is a book about legally enforceable promises, or what lawyers call "contracts." What function do contracts serve in our society? What needs are met by private agreements among its members?

As a beginning, imagine taking an inventory of all the contracts made on a typical business day in a city with which you are familiar. How many businesses were sold? How many buildings? Cars? Television sets? How many people got jobs? Rented apartments or videos? Opened bank accounts? What other transactions should be counted? As these questions suggest, the institution of contract is a vehicle through which the daily needs of ordinary people for goods and services are met. It is also, of course, a vehicle for mammoth enterprises in which governments and their agencies and great corporate bodies engage. Indeed, a large share of the wealth of any developed nation is embodied in contract rights.

The name "contract" is shared by printed forms distributed at counters (e.g., travel and insurance papers), and by agreements negotiated at arm's length by parties taking advice of counsel at every step. Countless contracts are formed daily by telephone, hand signal, or other informal means. The subjects of contracts, and the objects they advance, are even more diverse, if possible, than the means of their creation. Sometimes they are used to settle disputes. Sometimes they are used to establish long-term arrangements under which thousands of individual transactions are to be conducted. Sometimes they are used to vary the effects that certain rules of law would otherwise have on the parties and their dealings. And it is largely through contracts that interests in property are created and altered.

What does this diversity signify about the character of the law of contracts? A first inference might be that the law is largely instrumental. Much of it consists of specifying means for unstated and undetermined ends. To what purposes the power to contract will be put is left very largely to the choice of those who exercise it. Within the domain of contract, as it has been said, "the liberties recognized by law block out a sphere of social life which is left to be controlled, in the absence of further group action, by the process of *autonomous legal ordering*." [a] When organized commercial activity takes place within this sphere, it is commonly described as a "market." The law of contracts has a vital supporting function in relation to markets, as has been described by a distinguished American legal historian, Professor Willard Hurst, in the context of a study of the lumber industry in nineteenth-century Wisconsin: "Because marketing cannot go on save in a context of reasonably assured expectations, the legal order as a whole was, of course, indispensable to the exis-

---

a. H. Hart & A. Sacks, The Legal Process 132 (W. Eskridge & P. Frickey, eds. 1994). See also Jones, The Jurisprudence of Contracts, 44 U.Cin.L.Rev. 43 (1975).

tence of a market. But it was the law of contract which supplied the assurances and the procedures and tools necessary for the immediate operation and steadily expanding energy of the institution. . . . Law did not bring the market into being. But law provided essential conditions for its existence. . . . For the timber industry as for other business, contract law provided a framework of reasonably assured expectations within which men might plan and venture. The availability of the forms and procedures of contract thus helped the expansion of the market. . . . [The law] provided a framework of delegated power within which private decisions might operate. . . . The nature of contract was to disperse decision making widely. . . ." [b]

As the character and institutions of a society change, the functions of contract making and enforcement change with it. The dispersion of decision making power in private hands may lose its attractiveness as an ideal, in competition either with anarchy or with more official forms of decision making.[c] Even if it does not, conditions may change so that contracts become instruments of concentrating power in large business units. The backing of legal force given to private agreements by contract law shows to best advantage in a community, market, or society, in which bargaining power is rather widely and evenly distributed. Professor Kessler expressed the point this way: "The individualism of our rules of contract law, of which freedom of contract is the most powerful symbol, is closely tied up with the ethics of free enterprise capitalism and the ideals of justice of a mobile society of small enterprisers, individual merchants and independent craftsmen." [d]

Well before the present century it was perceived that "enterprisers" of this type were sometimes overmatched in bargaining power by firms in monopoly positions. Then, and increasingly in this century, the law has responded with restraints on the process of private ordering. Lately such restraints have been addressed especially to the position of consumers, as they have become increasingly involved in consensual transactions. Their participation in contract making commonly takes the form of routine assent, or "adhesion," to a standard form contract, whether in dealings with great corporations or in dealings with neighborhood merchants. Many contract forms are like

b. W. Hurst, Law and Economic Growth: The Legal History of the Lumber Industry in Wisconsin 1836–1915, 285, 294, 297, 333 (1964).

c. Would it not be possible to dispense with contracts entirely by dispensing with the need for private ordering? An attempt was made in the Soviet Union in the early revolutionary years to administer the economy without the institution of contract, to base centralized distribution of wealth on administrative norms. The experiment ended in failure, and Lenin wrote in 1921 that "we must now admit . . . if we do not want to hide our heads under our wings . . . [that] the private market proved to be stronger than we and . . .

we ended up with ordinary purchase and sale, trade." Contracts were reintroduced and contract law was codified, largely along traditional lines. Loeber, Plan and Contract Performance in Soviet Law in LaFave (ed.), Law in the Soviet Society 128–29 (1965). You may take it from this that contract is at least a durable institution and it is a safe generalization that few societies have been able to develop far without recognizing at least some promises as enforceable. See Farnsworth, The Past of Promise: A Historical Introduction to Contract, 69 Colum. L.Rev. 576, 578–82 (1969).

d. Kessler, Contracts of Adhesion—Some Thoughts About Freedom of Contract, 43 Colum.L.Rev. 629, 640 (1943).

statutes, having uniform application to large classes of persons. Through such forms, the drafter may exercise positions of authority, in the name of contract, without the necessity of debate and democratic validation that limits legislation. So exercised, it often appears oppressive. Under what circumstances should the law refuse to allow the dominant party to invoke official sanctions for the breach of such agreements? Through statutes and judicial decisions, the law of contracts has moved to answer this question by placing new controls on the manner of contracting and the allowable terms of agreement. It is coming to place a higher value on what Professor Patterson called the freedom *from* contract.[e]

No one imagines that, when promises are kept, it is ordinarily because the promisor is conscious of the rules of contract law. Far from it: both social and business engagements are generally kept for other reasons, including the sense of honor and the concern for community standing. The standards of mutual assistance that apply in conscience and in the market place are sometimes higher, sometimes lower, than those that contract law attaches to a bargain. On the other hand, painstaking attention is regularly paid to contract rules in setting out the terms of a business transaction. There is a skill in drafting agreements that ranks high in legal accomplishments, and you should attempt in this course to grasp it.

It has already been suggested that contract law is useful for supporting market transactions. But its value runs beyond this, in a way hard to measure. Contract is the principal mechanism for allocating and distributing financial risks. This is the object of guarantee and insurance contracts, in particular. If agreements could not be defined with some degree of precision, as a skilled drafter can do, the costs of uncertainty would stifle many an enterprise, and the affliction of insecurity would be uncontrolled. In addition, if there were no means of enforcing promises, those who keep them for reasons of conscience might be at such a disadvantage, as compared with the unscrupulous, that few of us would be willing and able to pay the price of honoring our undertakings.

The foregoing observations are chiefly practical ones. But they lead into issues of ultimate purpose. In response to the questions, What promises should be legally enforceable?, and How should they be enforced?, several answers are possible. One might say that the object is to enhance the wealth of society, broadly conceived, by encouraging activities (including the making of commitments) that gratify individual needs and wants. From that perspective it is possible to work out an appraisal of Contract law on economic grounds. Or one might say that the object is to express the obligation of respect that a community asserts on behalf of each member against the others. From that perspective it is possible to appraise Contract law on social grounds. Other vantage points—including that of simple fairness—are possible.

The materials in this book provide ample occasions for making these appraisals, and for comparing decisions that they dictate.

e. Patterson, An Apology for Consideration, 58 Colum.L.Rev. 929, 949 (1958).

INTRODUCTION

Organization. The first four chapters of this book are concerned with the law relating to the enforceability of promises. Chapter 1 begins by asking what we mean by "enforceability" and then examines possible bases for determining enforceability, concluding (not surprisingly in the light of the excerpt from Hurst) that bargained-for exchange is still the principal basis in our law. Chapter 2 explores the bargaining process through the traditional analysis of offer and acceptance. Chapter 3 deals with when a writing is necessary to the enforceability of a promise. Chapter 4 concerns the restraints that are placed on the terms of bargains and on the bargaining process to prevent social evils such as overreaching and sharp practice.

Chapter 5 turns to a different theme. It is concerned with the remedies available to the aggrieved party when, assuming that there is a contract, the other party does not perform it.

The next four chapters are concerned with the nature and extent of the parties' obligations under the contract. As drafters of documents, lawyers have played a major part in this aspect of private ordering. In the words of Professor Llewellyn: "It was . . . the lawyer who devised the mortgage, who made possible the giving of security in goods or land, while leaving the beneficial use of the borrower during the period for which the security was needed; made possible, therefore, the secured production loan whereby a debtor had the chance of financing a new venture out of whose own profits he might hope to meet the debt. . . . It was the lawyer who devised the long-term lease for real estate improvement, and the collateral trust for real estate financing, or for financing new equipment for a mortgaged railroad. And, greatest perhaps of any single line of growth within our law, it was the lawyer who from the outset has shaped the thousand uses of the law of trusts. . . ." [f] Some of the materials in this book are designed to help you develop the skills in drafting that are essential to this facet of professional activity. Chapter 6 inquires into the processes, notably that of interpretation, that define the parties' obligations and repair deficiencies in their expressions, when courts are required to give them effect. Chapter 7 takes up the effects of one party's failure of performance, or prospective failure, on the other party's obligations. Chapter 8 deals with when mutual mistake, impracticability of performance, or frustration of purpose relieves a party of an obligation.

The concluding chapters address the interests of third parties in relation to contracts. In Chapter 9 it is seen that a contract may institute rights against a party in favor of one who is not a party. Chapter 10 looks at contract rights as a kind of property, and treats of their transfer.

---

f. Llewellyn, The Bramble Bush 146–47 (1960).

SUMMARY OF CONTENTS

*

TABLE OF CONTENTS

TABLE OF CONTENTS

TABLE OF CONTENTS

*

TABLE OF CASES

Principal cases are in italic type. Cases cited or discussed are in roman type. References are to Pages.

TABLE OF CASES

xvi

CASES AND MATERIALS

ON

CONTRACTS

NOTE ON EDITING

The editors' restatements of facts and insertions within opinions are enclosed in brackets. Footnotes in opinions and quoted texts have sometimes been omitted and the remaining ones renumbered in sequence. Footnotes inserted by the editors are lettered rather than numbered.

When a problem is accompanied by a reference to a case, the facts presented are sometimes abbreviated from those before the court, but may be markedly different. In any event, the reference is only intended to support a line of thought, or an analogy, and not to supply "the answer" to the problem.

In citation, the Restatement of Contracts (1932) and the Restatement Second of Contracts (1980) are referred to simply as "Restatement" and "Restatement Second." The Uniform Commercial Code is cited as "UCC." A. Corbin on Contracts (1950–1964) is cited as "Corbin," A. Corbin on Contracts (rev ed. by J. Perillo 1993–   ) as "Corbin rev.," E.A. Farnsworth on Contracts (1990) as "Farnsworth," S. Williston on Contracts (3d ed. by W. Jaeger 1957–1979) as "Williston 3d," and S. Williston on Contracts (4th ed. by R. Lord 1990–   ) as "Williston 4th."

This casebook is accompanied by a volume of Selections for Contracts, with material from the Code, the Restatement Second, the Vienna Convention, and other sources. It is sometimes referred to simply as "Selections."

Chapter 1

BASIS FOR ENFORCING PROMISES

SECTION 1. THE MEANING OF "ENFORCE"

Books on the law of contracts often begin by explaining what lawyers mean by the word "contract." Sometimes they use the word, as it is used in common speech, simply to refer to a writing containing terms on which the parties have agreed. But they often use "contract" in a more technical sense to mean a *promise,* or a set of promises, that the law will *enforce* or at least recognize in some way. See Restatement Second § 1. (Sections of the Restatement Second, together with an introduction, can be found in Selections for Contracts.)

Some idea of what the word "contract" means in practice can be gathered from the cotton cases of 1973. That year saw a spectacular rise in the price of cotton on the American market. The causes were said to include large shipments to China, high water and flood conditions in the cotton belt, late plantings forced by heavy rains, and the devaluation of the dollar. In the early months of the year, before planting, a cotton farmer will make a "forward" sale contract for delivery to the buyer of all cotton to be raised and harvested on a specified tract at a fixed price per pound, without guarantee of quantity or quality. The farmer can then use this contract to finance the raising of his crop. Early in 1973, cotton farmers made such contracts to sell at a price roughly equal to the price on the market at that time, some 30 cents a pound. By the time the cotton had been raised and was ready for delivery, however, the market price had risen to about 80 cents a pound. The farmers felt, as one judge later put it, "sick as an old hound dog who ate a rotten skunk." Many refused to perform the "forward" contracts that they had made at the lower price, and scores of lawsuits resulted throughout the cotton belt.[a] Not only were the farmers universally unsuccessful, but the decisions evoked little attention.

We are about to ask: What promises will the law enforce? But in answering that question it is helpful to have an idea of how courts enforce promises. For example, what remedies were available to the disappointed cotton buyers on the farmers' enforceable promises? Although the intricacies of this subject are reserved until later (see

---

a. This summary is taken largely from one of those cases, Bolin Farms v. American Cotton Shippers Ass'n, 370 F.Supp. 1353 (W.D.La.1974). Citations to cases are collected at 15 UCC Rep. 20, 28.

Chapter 5, Remedies for Breach), some insight into its fundamentals will be of use, even at this early stage.

The cases in this section expose three fundamental assumptions made by courts in enforcing promises. One of these is that the law is concerned mainly with *relief* of *promisees* to *redress breach* and not with *punishment* of *promisors* to *compel performance*. A second assumption is that the relief granted to the aggrieved promisee should generally protect the promisee's *expectation* by attempting to put the promisee in the position in which it would have been had the promise been performed. A third assumption is that the appropriate form of relief is *substitutional,* in the form of a judgment awarding money damages to be paid to the aggrieved promisee, rather than *specific,* in the form of a court order directing the promisor to perform its promise.

UNITED STATES NAVAL INSTITUTE v. CHARTER COMMUNICATIONS, INC.

United States Court of Appeals, Second Circuit, 1991.
936 F.2d 692.

KEARSE, CIRCUIT JUDGE: This case returns to us following our remand in United States Naval Institute v. Charter Communications, Inc., 875 F.2d 1044 (2d Cir.1989) ("Naval I"), ... for the fashioning of relief in favor of plaintiff United States Naval Institute ("Naval") against defendant Charter Communications, Inc., and Berkley Publishing Group (collectively "Berkley"), for breach of an agreement with respect to the publication of the paperback edition of The Hunt For Red October ("Red October" or the "Book"). On remand, the district court awarded Naval $35,380.50 in damages [and] $7,760.12 as profits wrongfully received by Berkley.... Naval appeals from so much of the judgment as failed to award a greater amount as profits.... Berkley cross-appeals from the judgment as a whole and from such parts of it as awarded moneys to Naval. For the reasons below, we reverse the award of profits; we affirm the award of damages....

RIGHTS *Transferred to*

I. Background

... Naval, as the assignee of the author's copyright in Red October, entered into a licensing agreement with Berkley in September 1984 (the "Agreement"), granting Berkley the exclusive license to publish a paperback edition of the Book "not sooner than October 1985." Berkley shipped its paperback edition to retail outlets early, placing those outlets in position to sell the paperback prior to October 1985. As a result, retail sales of the paperback began on September 15, 1985, and early sales were sufficiently substantial that the Book was near the top of paperback bestseller lists before the end of September 1985.

Naval commenced the present action when it learned of Berkley's plans for early shipment, and it unsuccessfully sought a preliminary injunction. After trial, the district judge dismissed the complaint. He

DJ. (1?) Dismiss

ruled that Berkley had not breached the Agreement because it was entitled, in accordance with industry custom, to ship prior to the agreed publication date.[a] <u>On appeal, we reversed</u>. Though we upheld the district court's finding that the Agreement did not prohibit the early shipments themselves, we concluded that if the "not sooner than October 1985" term of the Agreement had any meaning whatever, it meant at least that Berkley was not allowed to cause such voluminous paperback retail sales prior to that date, and that Berkley had therefore breached the Agreement. Naval I, 875 F.2d at 1049–51. Accordingly, we remanded for entry of a judgment awarding Naval appropriate relief.

On the remand, Naval asserted that it was entitled to recovery for copyright infringement, and it sought judgment awarding it all of Berkley's profits from pre-October 1985 sales of the Book; it estimated those profits at $724,300.... Berkley, on the other hand, [contended] that Berkley could not be held liable for copyright infringement ...; it argued that Naval therefore had at most a claim for breach-of-contract [and] argued that the profits attributed to it by Naval were inflated.... [On remand, the district judge] concluded that Naval was entitled to recover damages for copyright infringement, comprising actual damages suffered by Naval plus Berkley's profits "attributable to the infringement," 17 U.S.C. § 504(b).

The court calculated Naval's "actual damages from Berkley's wrongful pre-October 'publication'" as the profits Naval would have earned from hardcover sales in September 1985 if the competing paperback edition had not then been offered for sale. July 17 Order at 8. Noting the downward trend of hardcover sales of the Book from March through August 1985, the court found that there was no reason to infer that Naval's September 1985 sales would have exceeded its August 1985 sales. The court calculated Naval's lost sales as the difference between the actual hardcover sales for those two months, and awarded Naval $35,380.50 as actual damages.

The district judge held that Berkley's profits "attributable to the infringement" were only those profits that resulted from "sales to customers who would not have bought the paperback but for the fact it became available in September." July 17 Order at 10. He found that most of the September paperback sales were made to buyers who would not have bought a hardcover edition in September, and therefore only those September sales that displaced hardcover sales were attributable to the infringement. Berkley's profit on the displacing copies totaled $7,760.12, and the court awarded that amount to Naval....

a. The role of "industry custom," often called "trade usage," is explored in Chapter 6, Finding the Law of the Contract.

II. Discussion

. . .

A. Naval's Claim of Copyright Infringement

[The court rejected this claim because an exclusive licensee cannot be liable for infringing the copyright conveyed to it, even though it is liable for breach of contract.]

B. Contract Damages . . .

Since the purpose of damages for breach of contract is to compensate the injured party for the loss caused by the breach, 5 Corbin On Contracts § 1002, at 31 (1964), those damages are generally measured by the plaintiff's actual loss, see, e.g., Restatement (Second) of Contracts § 347 (1981). While on occasion the defendant's profits are used as the measure of damages, see, e.g., Cincinnati Siemens–Lungren Gas Illuminating Co. v. Western Siemens–Lungren Co., 152 U.S. 200, 204–07, 14 S.Ct. 523, 525–26, 38 L.Ed. 411 (1894), . . . this generally occurs when those profits tend to define the plaintiff's loss, for an award of the defendant's profits where they greatly exceed the plaintiff's loss and there has been no tortious conduct on the part of the defendant would tend to be punitive, and punitive awards are not part of the law of contract damages. See generally Restatement (Second) of Contracts § 356 comment a ("The central objective behind the system of contract remedies is compensatory, not punitive."); id. comment b (agreement attempting to fix damages in amount vastly greater than what approximates actual loss would be unenforceable as imposing a penalty); id. § 355 (punitive damages not recoverable for breach of contract unless conduct constituting the breach is also a tort for which such damages are recoverable).

Here, the district court found that Berkley's alleged $724,300 profits did not define Naval's loss because many persons who bought the paperback in September 1985 would not have bought the book in hardcover but would merely have waited until the paperback edition became available. This finding is not clearly erroneous, and we turn to the question of whether the district court's finding that Naval suffered $35,380.50 in actual damages was proper.

In reaching the $35,380.50 figure, the court operated on the premise that, but for the breach by Berkley, Naval would have sold in September the same number of hardcover copies it sold in August. Berkley challenges that premise as speculative and argues that since Naval presented no evidence as to what its September 1985 sales would have been, Naval is entitled to recover no damages. It argues alternatively that the court should have computed damages on the premise that sales in the second half of September, in the absence of Berkley's premature release of the paperback edition, would have been made at the same rate as in the first half of September. Evaluating the district court's calculation of damages under the clearly erroneous standard of review, . . . we reject Berkley's contentions.

The record showed that, though there was a declining trend of hardcover sales of the Book from March through August 1985, Naval continued to sell its hardcover copies through the end of 1985, averaging some 3,000 copies a month in the latter period. It plainly was not error for the district court to find that the preponderance of the evidence indicated that Berkley's early shipment of 1,400,000 copies of its paperback edition, some 40% of which went to retail outlets and led to the Book's rising close to the top of the paperback bestseller lists before the end of September 1985, caused Naval the loss of some hardcover sales prior to October 1985.

As to the quantification of that loss, we think it was within the prerogative of the court as finder of fact to look to Naval's August 1985 sales. Though there was no proof as to precisely what the unimpeded volume of hardcover sales would have been for the entire month of September, any such evidence would necessarily have been hypothetical. But it is not error to lay the normal uncertainty in such hypotheses at the door of the wrongdoer who altered the proper course of events, instead of at the door of the injured party. See, e.g., Lamborn v. Dittmer, 873 F.2d 522, 532–33 (2d Cir.1989); Lee v. Joseph E. Seagram & Sons, Inc., 552 F.2d 447, 455–56 (2d Cir.1977).... See generally ... Restatement (Second) of Contracts § 352 comment *a* ("Doubts are generally resolved against the party in breach."). The court was not required to use as the starting point for its calculations Naval's actual sales in the first half of September, *i.e.*, those made prior to the first retail sale of the paperback edition. Berkley has not called to our attention any evidence in the record to indicate that the sales in a given month are normally spread evenly through that month. Indeed, it concedes that "[t]o a large degree, book sales depend on public whim and are notoriously unpredictable...." (Berkley brief on appeal at 31 n. 15.) Thus, nothing in the record foreclosed the possibility that, absent Berkley's breach, sales of hardcover copies in the latter part of September would have outpaced sales of those copies in the early part of the month. Though the court accurately described its selection of August 1985 sales as its benchmark as "generous[ ]," it was not improper, given the inherent uncertainty, to exercise generosity in favor of the injured party rather than in favor of the breaching party.

In all the circumstances, we cannot say that the district court's calculation of Naval's damages was clearly erroneous. ...

Conclusion

... For the foregoing reasons, we reverse so much of the judgment as granted Naval $7,760.12 as an award of Berkley's profits. In all other respects, the judgment is affirmed.

NOTES

(1) *Defendant's Gain as Plaintiff's Loss.* If the concern is with relief of promisees to redress breach, the focus in the principal case should be on the plaintiff's loss, not the defendant's gain. In what kinds of cases would "the defendant's profits ... tend to define the plaintiff's loss," as Judge Kearse put it? Cases like *Cincinnati Siemens–Lungren,* cited as an example, have been described in the following way.

"Suppose that a seller of a business makes a valid contract not to compete with the buyer and then breaks the covenant by operating a competing business. If the buyer claims damages . . ., the court will often receive evidence of the profits that the seller made from the competing business as evidence of the profit that the buyer lost as a result of the breach. But a court will not assume that the buyer could have made the same sales that the seller did . . . ." Farnsworth, Your Loss or My Gain? The Dilemma of the Disgorgement Principle in Breach of Contract Cases, 94 Yale L.J. 1339, 1366 (1985), reprinted in 3 Farnsworth § 12.20a at 335.

(2) *Disgorgement in Non–Contract Cases.* Disgorgement of profits is not uncommon in non-contract cases. Note that the district judge "concluded that Naval was entitled to recover damages for copyright infringement, comprising actual damages suffered by Naval *plus Berkley's profits* 'attributable to the infringement.' 17 U.S.C. § 504(b)." This provision of the Copyright Act requires the infringer to disgorge the resulting profits to prevent the infringer from unfairly benefiting from a wrongful act.

Disgorgement of profits has also long been a common law remedy for breach of a fiduciary duty, such as that of a trustee or agent. Would it be desirable to impose such liability on contracting parties? Consider in this connection the case in the following Note.

(3) *The Case of the Faithless Fiduciary.* When Frank Snepp went to work for the Central Intelligence Agency, he signed an agreement that began by reciting that he was "undertaking a position of trust." In the agreement, he promised not to publish any material relating to the CIA without its "specific prior approval." After he left the CIA, Snepp published a book, Decent Interval, about CIA activities in South Vietnam without submitting it for prepublication review. The Government sued Snepp to enforce the agreement, though it conceded that the book contained no classified material. The district court found that Snepp had "willfully, deliberately and surreptitiously breached his position of trust" and, since the CIA's actual damages were unquantifiable, the court enjoined future breach. It also imposed a constructive trust [a] on Snepp's profits which, at the time of suit, included $60,000 in advance payments. On appeal, the Court of Appeals upheld the injunction, opened the possibility of punitive damages if the Government could prove tortious conduct, but held that it was error to impose a constructive trust. On review, the Supreme Court held that the injunction violated Snepp's First Amendment right to publish unclassified information. It also held that punitive damages would be "speculative and unusual" and that proof of the necessary tortious conduct "might force the Government to disclose some of the very confidences that Snepp promised to protect." But the Court, three justices dissenting, sustained the district court's imposition of a constructive trust.

"A constructive trust . . . protects both the Government and the former agent from unwarranted risks. This remedy is the natural and customary consequence of a breach of trust. It deals fairly with both parties by conforming relief to the dimensions of the wrong. If the agent secures prepublication clearance, he can publish with no fear of liability. If the agent publishes unreviewed material in violation of his fiduciary and contractual obligation, the trust remedy simply requires him to disgorge the benefits of his faithlessness.

---

a. "A constructive trust is a relationship with respect to property subjecting the person by whom the title to the property is held to an equitable duty to convey it to another on the ground that his acquisition or retention of the property is wrongful and that he would be unjustly enriched if he were permitted to retain the property." Restatement (Second) of Trusts § 1, Comment e.

Since the remedy is swift and sure, it is tailored to deter those who would place sensitive information at risk. And since the remedy reaches only funds attributable to the breach, it cannot saddle the former agent with exemplary damages out of all proportion to his gain. The decision of the Court of Appeals would deprive the Government of this equitable and effective means of protecting intelligence that may contribute to national security." Snepp v. United States, 444 U.S. 507 (1980) (per curiam).

(4) *The Requirement of Certainty as a Limit on Contract Damages.* Note that Berkley challenged as "speculative" the premise "that, but for the breach by Berkley, Naval would have sold in September the same number of hardcover copies it sold in August." This challenge, though rejected by the court, points up an important limitation on the disappointed promisee's right to contract damages: The promisee must prove damages with reasonable certainty. See Restatement Second § 352. This limitation is explored in Chapter 5, Remedies for Breach.

SULLIVAN v. O'CONNOR

Supreme Judicial Court of Massachusetts, 1973.
363 Mass. 579, 296 N.E.2d 183.

$13.5 K

KAPLAN, JUSTICE. The plaintiff patient secured a jury verdict of $13,500 against the defendant surgeon for breach of contract in respect to an operation upon the plaintiff's nose. The substituted consolidated bill of exceptions presents questions about the correctness of the judge's instructions on the issue of damages.

The declaration was in two counts. In the first count, the plaintiff alleged that she, as patient, entered into a contract with the defendant, a surgeon, wherein the defendant promised to perform plastic surgery on her nose and thereby to enhance her beauty and improve her appearance; that he performed the surgery but failed to achieve the promised result; rather the result of the surgery was to disfigure and deform her nose, to cause her pain in body and mind, and to subject her to other damage and expense. The second count, based on the same transaction, was in the conventional form for malpractice, charging that the defendant had been guilty of negligence in performing the surgery.[a] Answering, the defendant entered a general denial.

On the plaintiff's demand, the case was tried by jury. At the close of the evidence, the judge put to the jury, as special questions, the issues of liability under the two counts, and instructed them accordingly. The jury returned a verdict for the plaintiff on the contract count, and for the

a. Interviews with counsel reveal that Sullivan's lawyer thought that the contract claim "simply gave the jury an easy means of deciding the case without 'embarrassing' the doctor." O'Connor's lawyer "did not originally consider the contract count in Mrs. Sullivan's declaration seriously. It was unusual in Massachusetts at that time to include a contracts claim in a medical case (he did not know of any prior case in which it had been done), and he thought plaintiff's counsel had thrown it in as an afterthought." Later research "convinced him that liability on that count would be limited to Mrs. Sullivan's medical expenses." See R. Danzig, The Capability Problem in Contract Law 5–43 (1978), which contains extensive background material on this case.

① B. of Contract → π verdict

② Negligence → Δ verdict

defendant on the negligence count. The judge then instructed the jury on the issue of damages.

As background to the instructions and the parties' exceptions, we mention certain facts as the jury could find them. The plaintiff was a professional entertainer, and this was known to the defendant. The agreement was as alleged in the declaration. More particularly, judging from exhibits, the plaintiff's nose had been straight, but long and prominent; the defendant undertook by two operations to reduce its prominence and somewhat to shorten it, thus making it more pleasing in relation to the plaintiff's other features. Actually the plaintiff was obliged to undergo three operations, and her appearance was worsened. Her nose now had a concave line to about the mid-point, at which it became bulbous; viewed frontally, the nose from bridge to midpoint was flattened and broadened, and the two sides of the tip had lost symmetry. This configuration evidently could not be improved by further surgery. The plaintiff did not demonstrate, however, that her change of appearance had resulted in loss of employment. Payments by the plaintiff covering the defendant's fee and hospital expenses were stipulated at $622.65.

The judge instructed the jury, first, that the plaintiff was entitled to recover her out-of-pocket expenses incident to the operations. Second, she could recover the damages flowing directly, naturally, proximately, and foreseeably from the defendant's breach of promise. These would comprehend damages for any disfigurement of the plaintiff's nose—that is, any change of appearance for the worse—including the effects of the consciousness of such disfigurement on the plaintiff's mind, and in this connection the jury should consider the nature of the plaintiff's profession. Also consequent upon the defendant's breach, and compensable, were the pain and suffering involved in the third operation, but not in the first two. As there was no proof that any loss of earnings by the plaintiff resulted from the breach, that element should not enter into the calculation of damages.

By his exceptions the defendant contends that the judge erred in allowing the jury to take into account anything but the plaintiff's out-of-pocket expenses (presumably at the stipulated amount). The defendant excepted to the judge's refusal of his request for a general charge to that effect, and, more specifically, to the judge's refusal of a charge that the plaintiff could not recover for pain and suffering connected with the third operation or for impairment of the plaintiff's appearance and associated mental distress.

The plaintiff on her part excepted to the judge's refusal of a request to charge that the plaintiff could recover the difference in value between the nose as promised and the nose as it appeared after the operations. However, the plaintiff in her brief expressly waives this exception and others made by her in case this court overrules the defendant's exceptions; thus she would be content to hold the jury's verdict in her favor.

We conclude that the defendant's exceptions should be overruled.

It has been suggested on occasion that agreements between patients and physicians by which the physician undertakes to effect a cure or to bring about a given result should be declared unenforceable on grounds of public policy. See Guilmet v. Campbell, 385 Mich. 57, 76, 188 N.W.2d 601 (dissenting opinion). But there are many decisions recognizing and enforcing such contracts, see annotation, 43 A.L.R.3d 1221, 1225, 1229–1233, and the law of Massachusetts has treated them as valid, although we have had no decision meeting head on the contention that they should be denied legal sanction. Small v. Howard, 128 Mass. 131; Gabrunas v. Miniter, 289 Mass. 20, 193 N.E. 551; Forman v. Wolfson, 327 Mass. 341, 98 N.E.2d 615. These causes of action are, however, considered a little suspect, and thus we find courts straining sometimes to read the pleadings as sounding only in tort for negligence, and not in contract for breach of promise, despite sedulous efforts by the pleaders to pursue the latter theory. See Gault v. Sideman, 42 Ill.App.2d 96, 191 N.E.2d 436; annotation, supra, at 1225, 1238–1244.

It is not hard to see why the courts should be unenthusiastic or skeptical about the contract theory. Considering the uncertainties of medical science and the variations in the physical and psychological conditions of individual patients, doctors can seldom in good faith promise specific results. Therefore it is unlikely that physicians of even average integrity will in fact make such promises. Statements of opinion by the physician with some optimistic coloring are a different thing, and may indeed have therapeutic value. But patients may transform such statements into firm promises in their own minds, especially when they have been disappointed in the event, and testify in that sense to sympathetic juries.[1] If actions for breach of promise can be readily maintained, doctors, so it is said, will be frightened into practising "defensive medicine." On the other hand, if these actions were outlawed, leaving only the possibility of suits for malpractice, there is fear that the public might be exposed to the enticements of charlatans, and confidence in the profession might ultimately be shaken. See Miller, The Contractual Liability of Physicians and Surgeons, 1953 Wash.L.Q. 413, 416–423. The law has taken the middle of the road position of allowing actions based on alleged contract, but insisting on clear proof. Instructions to the jury may well stress this requirement and point to tests of truth, such as the complexity or difficulty of an operation as bearing on the probability that a given result was promised. See annotation, 43 A.L.R.3d 1225, 1225–1227.

If an action on the basis of contract is allowed, we have next the question of the measure of damages to be applied where liability is found. Some cases have taken the simple view that the promise by the physician is to be treated like an ordinary commercial promise, and accordingly that the successful plaintiff is entitled to a standard measure

---

1. Judicial skepticism about whether a promise was in fact made derives also from the possibility that the truth has been tortured to give the plaintiff the advantage of the longer period of limitations sometimes available for actions on contract as distinguished from those in tort or for malpractice. See Lillich, The Malpractice Statute of Limitations in New York and Other Jurisdictions, 47 Cornell L.Q. 339; annotation, 80 A.L.R.2d 368.

of recovery for breach of contract—"compensatory" ("expectancy") damages, an amount intended to put the plaintiff in the position he would be in if the contract had been performed, or, presumably, at the plaintiff's election, "restitution" damages, an amount corresponding to any benefit conferred by the plaintiff upon the defendant in the performance of the contract disrupted by the defendant's breach. See Restatement: Contracts § 329 and comment a, §§ 347, 384(1). Thus in Hawkins v. McGee, 84 N.H. 114, 146 A. 641, the defendant doctor was taken to have promised the plaintiff to convert his damaged hand by means of an operation into a good or perfect hand, but the doctor so operated as to damage the hand still further. The court, following the usual expectancy formula, would have asked the jury to estimate and award to the plaintiff the difference between the value of a good or perfect hand, as promised, and the value of the hand after the operation. (The same formula would apply, although the dollar result would be less, if the operation had neither worsened nor improved the condition of the hand.) If the plaintiff had not yet paid the doctor his fee, that amount would be deducted from the recovery. There could be no recovery for the pain and suffering of the operation, since that detriment would have been incurred even if the operation had been successful; one can say that this detriment was not "caused" by the breach. But where the plaintiff by reason of the operation was put to more pain than he would have had to endure, had the doctor performed as promised, he should be compensated for that difference as a proper part of his expectancy recovery. It may be noted that on an alternative count for malpractice the plaintiff in the *Hawkins* case had been nonsuited; but on ordinary principles this could not affect the contract claim, for it is hardly a defence to a breach of contract that the promisor acted innocently and without negligence. The New Hampshire court further refined the *Hawkins* analysis in McQuaid v. Michou, 85 N.H. 299, 157 A. 881, all in the direction of treating the patient-physician cases on the ordinary footing of expectancy. . . .

Other cases, including a number in New York, without distinctly repudiating the *Hawkins* type of analysis, have indicated that a different and generally more lenient measure of damages is to be applied in patient-physician actions based on breach of alleged special agreements to effect a cure, attain a stated result, or employ a given medical method. This measure is expressed in somewhat variant ways, but the substance is that the plaintiff is to recover any expenditures made by him and for other detriment (usually not specifically described in the opinions) following proximately and foreseeably upon the defendant's failure to carry out his promise. Robins v. Finestone, 308 N.Y. 543, 546, 127 N.E.2d 330. . . . This, be it noted, is not a "restitution" measure, for it is not limited to restoration of the benefit conferred on the defendant (the fee paid) but includes other expenditures, for example, amounts paid for medicine and nurses; so also it would seem according to its logic to take in damages for any worsening of the plaintiff's condition due to the breach. Nor is it an "expectancy" measure, for it does not appear to contemplate recovery of the whole difference in value between the condition as promised and the condition actually resulting from the treatment. Rather the tendency of the formulation is to put the plaintiff back in the position he occupied just before the parties entered upon the agreement, to compensate him for the detriments he suffered in reliance upon the agreement. This kind of intermediate pattern of recovery for breach of contract is discussed in the suggestive article by Fuller and Perdue, The Reliance Interest in Contract Damages, 46 Yale L.J. 52, 373, where the authors show that, although not attaining the currency of the standard measures, a "reliance" measure has for special reasons been applied by the courts in a variety of settings, including noncommercial settings. See 46 Yale L.J. at 396–401.[2]

For breach of the patient-physician agreements under consideration, a recovery limited to restitution seems plainly too meager, if the agreements are to be enforced at all. On the other hand, an expectancy recovery may well be excessive. The factors, already mentioned, which have made the cause of action somewhat suspect, also suggest moderation as to the breadth of the recovery that should be permitted. Where, as in the case at bar and in a number of the reported cases, the doctor has been absolved of negligence by the trier, an expectancy measure may be thought harsh. We should recall here that the fee paid by the patient to the doctor for the alleged promise would usually be quite disproportionate to the putative expectancy recovery. To attempt, moreover, to put a value on the condition that would or might have resulted, had the treatment succeeded as promised, may sometimes put an exceptional strain on the imagination of the fact finder. As a general consideration, Fuller and Perdue argue that the reasons for granting damages for broken promises to the extent of the expectancy are at their strongest when the promises are made in a business context, when they have to do with the production or distribution of goods or the allocation of functions in the market place; they become weaker as the context shifts from a commercial to a noncommercial field. 46 Yale L.J. at 60–63.

There is much to be said, then, for applying a reliance measure to the present facts, and we have only to add that our cases are not unreceptive to the use of that formula in special situations. We have, however, had no previous occasion to apply it to patient-physician cases.[3]

---

2. Some of the exceptional situations mentioned where reliance may be preferred to expectancy are those in which the latter measure would be hard to apply or would impose too great a burden; performance was interfered with by external circumstances; the contract was indefinite. See 46 Yale L.J. at 373–386; 394–396.

3. In Mt. Pleasant Stable Co. v. Steinberg, 238 Mass. 567, 131 N.E. 295, the plaintiff company agreed to supply teams of horses at agreed rates as required from day to day by the defendant for his business. To prepare itself to fulfill the contract and in reliance on it, the plaintiff bought two "Cliest" horses at a certain price. When the defendant repudiated the contract, the plaintiff sold the horses at a loss and in its action for breach claimed the loss as an element of damages. The court properly held that the plaintiff was not entitled to this item as it was also claiming (and recovering) its lost profits (expectancy) on the contract as a whole. Cf. Noble v. Ames Mfg. Co., 112 Mass. 492. (The loss on sale of the horses is analogous to the pain and suffering for which the patient would be disallowed a recovery in Hawkins v. McGee, 84 N.H. 114, 146 A. 641, because he was claiming and recovering expectancy damages.) The court in the *Mt. Pleasant* case referred, however, to Pond v. Harris, 113 Mass. 114, as a contrasting situation where the expectancy could not be fairly deter-

The question of recovery on a reliance basis for pain and suffering or mental distress requires further attention. We find expressions in the decisions that pain and suffering (or the like) are simply not compensable in actions for breach of contract. The defendant seemingly espouses this proposition in the present case. True, if the buyer under a contract for the purchase of a lot of merchandise, in suing for the seller's breach, should claim damages for mental anguish caused by his disappointment in the transaction, he would not succeed; he would be told, perhaps, that the asserted psychological injury was not fairly foreseeable by the defendant as a probable consequence of the breach of such a business contract. See Restatement of Contracts, § 341, and comment a. But there is no general rule barring such items of damage in actions for breach of contract. It is all a question of the subject matter and background of the contract, and when the contract calls for an operation on the person of the plaintiff, psychological as well as physical injury may be expected to figure somewhere in the recovery, depending on the particular circumstances. The point is explained in Stewart v. Rudner, 349 Mich. 459, 469, 84 N.W.2d 816. Cf. Frewen v. Page, 238 Mass. 499, 131 N.E. 475; McClean v. University Club, 327 Mass. 68, 97 N.E.2d 174. Again, it is said in a few of the New York cases, concerned with the classification of actions for statute of limitations purposes, that the absence of allegations demanding recovery for pain and suffering is characteristic of a contract claim by a patient against a physician, that such allegations rather belong in a claim for malpractice. See Robins v. Finestone, 308 N.Y. 543, 547, 127 N.E.2d 330; Budoff v. Kessler, 2 A.D.2d 760, 153 N.Y.S.2d 654. These remarks seem unduly sweeping. Suffering or distress resulting from the breach going beyond that which was envisaged by the treatment as agreed, should be compensable on the same ground as the worsening of the patient's condition because of the breach. Indeed it can be argued that the very suffering or distress "contracted for"—that which would have been incurred if the treatment achieved the promised result—should also be compensable on the theory underlying the New York cases. For that suffering is "wasted" if the treatment fails. Otherwise stated, compensation for this waste is arguably required in order to complete the restoration of the status quo ante.[4]

mined. There the defendant had wrongfully revoked an agreement to arbitrate a dispute with the plaintiff (this was before such agreements were made specifically enforceable). In an action for the breach, the plaintiff was held entitled to recover for his preparations for the arbitration which had been rendered useless and a waste, including the plaintiff's time and trouble and his expenditures for counsel and witnesses. The context apparently was commercial but reliance elements were held compensable when there was no fair way of estimating an expectancy. See, generally, annotation, 17 A.L.R.2d 1300. A noncommercial example is Smith v. Sherman, 4 Cush. 408, 413–414, suggesting that a conventional recovery for breach of promise of marriage included a recompense for various efforts and expenditures by the plaintiff preparatory to the promised wedding. . . .

4. Recovery on a reliance basis for breach of the physician's promise tends to equate with the usual recovery for malpractice, since the latter also looks in general to restoration of the condition before the injury. But this is not paradoxical, especially when it is noted that the origins of contract lie in tort. See Farnsworth, The Past of Promise: An Historical Introduction to Contract, 69 Col.L.Rev. 576, 594–596; Breitel, J. in Stella Flour & Feed Corp. v. National City Bank, 285 App.Div. 182, 189,

In the light of the foregoing discussion, all the defendant's exceptions fail: the plaintiff was not confined to the recovery of her out-of-pocket expenditures; she was entitled to recover also for the worsening of her condition,[5] and for the pain and suffering and mental distress involved in the third operation. These items were compensable on either an expectancy or a reliance view. We might have been required to elect between the two views if the pain and suffering connected with the first two operations contemplated by the agreement, or the whole difference in value between the present and the promised conditions, were being claimed as elements of damage. But the plaintiff waives her possible claim to the former element, and to so much of the latter as represents the difference in value between the promised condition and the condition before the operations.

Plaintiff's exceptions waived.

Defendant's exceptions overruled.

NOTES

(1) *Three Interests.* As was pointed out earlier, one of the fundamental assumptions in enforcing promises is that the relief granted to the aggrieved promisee should attempt to put the promisee in the position in which it would have been had the promise been performed. The promisee is often said to receive "the benefit of the bargain" and the interest that is protected in this way is called the *expectation* interest. (The promisee's injury consists in being worse off than if the promise had been performed.) Contrast the expectation interest with what the court refers to as the reliance and restitution interests. The promisee has a *reliance* interest if it has changed its position to its detriment in reliance on the promise. (The promisee may, for example, have incurred expenses in preparing to perform or have lost opportunities to make other contracts. The promisee's injury consists of being worse off than if the promise had not been made.) The law might protect this interest by putting the plaintiff back in the position in which it would have been had the promise not been made. The promisee has a *restitution* interest if it has not only relied on the promise but has conferred a benefit on the promisor. (The promisee may, for example, have rendered some performance in return for the broken promise.) The law might protect this interest by putting the promisor back in the position in which it would have been had the promise not been made. For more on the three interests, see the pioneering article cited by the court, Fuller & Perdue, The Reliance Interest in Contract Damages (pt. 1), 46 Yale L.J. 52, 53–57 (1936).

136 N.Y.S.2d 139 (dissenting opinion). A few cases have considered possible recovery for breach by a physician of a promise to sterilize a patient, resulting in birth of a child to the patient and spouse. If such an action is held maintainable, the reliance and expectancy measures would, we think, tend to equate, because the promised condition was preservation of the family status quo....

It would, however, be a mistake to think in terms of strict "formulas." For example, a jurisdiction which would apply a reliance measure to the present facts might impose a more severe damage sanction for the wilful use by the physician of a method of operation that he undertook not to employ.

5. That condition involves a mental element and appraisal of it properly called for consideration of the fact that the plaintiff was an entertainer. Cf. McQuaid v. Michou, 85 N.H. 299, 303–304, 157 A. 881 (discussion of continuing condition resulting from physician's breach).

(2) *Interests According to the Numbers.* Assign the following round numbers to Sullivan's claim: doctor's fee $300; hospital fee per operation $100; pain and suffering per operation $3,000; increase in value of appearance if enhanced as promised $20,000; loss in value of appearance due to disfigurement $10,000. What would be the amount of Sullivan's claim if based on her restitution interest? Her reliance interest? Her expectation interest? How did the trial court calculate her damages?

(3) *Choice of Expectation Interest.* The law's initial choice of the expectation interest was not inevitable. In Flureau v. Thornhill, 96 Eng.Rep. 635 (King's Bench 1776), the court chose to protect the promisee's reliance interest instead. That case announced the rule that recovery against a vendor who promised to convey land, but is unable without any bad faith to give a good title, is limited to the expense incurred by the purchaser in reliance on the promise, including any down payment. As DeGrey, C.J., stated, "I do not think that the purchaser can be entitled to any damages for the fancied goodness of the bargain, which he supposes he has lost." But the subsequent development of the law of damages did not follow this course. Although the rule has persisted in England as to contracts for the sale of land and has found its way into the law of a number of states, the tendency even in these jurisdictions has been to restrict its application. The dominant theme, then, is one of relief based on expectation.

WHITE v. BENKOWSKI

Supreme Court of Wisconsin, 1967.
37 Wis.2d 285, 155 N.W.2d 74.

[In 1962, the Whites bought a house that lacked its own water supply but was connected by pipes with a well on adjacent property occupied by the Benkowskis. The Whites made a written contract with the Benkowskis under which the Benkowskis promised to supply water to the Whites' home for ten years unless the municipality supplied it, the well became inadequate or the Whites drilled their own well. The Whites paid $400 for a new pump and an additional tank and promised to pay $3 a month and half the cost of any future repairs or maintenance. By 1964, what had begun as a friendly relationship between new neighbors had deteriorated and become hostile. In that year the Benkowskis shut off the water supply on nine occasions for periods that, according to Mrs. White's records, were well under an hour and occurred in the afternoon or early evening. Mr. Benkowski claimed that this was done either to allow accumulated sand in the pipes to settle or to remind the Whites that their use of water was excessive. The Whites sued the Benkowskis, seeking compensatory and punitive damages for breach of contract. The jury returned a special verdict that found that the Benkowskis had maliciously shut off the Whites' water supply to harass them. Compensatory damages were set at $10 and punitive damages at $2,000, but on motions after verdict the award was reduced to $1 compensatory damages and no punitive damages. The Whites appeal.]

WILKIE, JUSTICE. Two issues are raised on this appeal.

1. Was the trial court correct in reducing the award of compensatory damages from $10 to $1?

2.   Are punitive damages available in actions for breach of contract?

Reduction of Jury Award

The evidence of damage adduced during the trial here was that the water supply had been shut off during several short periods.   Three incidents of inconvenience resulting from these shut-offs were detailed by the plaintiffs.   Mrs. White testified that the lack of water in the bathroom on one occasion caused an odor and that on two other occasions she was forced to take her children to a neighbor's home to bathe them.   Based on this evidence, the court instructed the jury that:

"... in an action for a breach of contract the plaintiff is entitled to such damages as shall have been sustained by him which resulted naturally and directly from the breach if you find that the defendants did in fact breach the contract.   Such damages include pecuniary loss and inconvenience suffered as a natural result of the breach and are called compensatory damages.   In this case the plaintiffs have proved no pecuniary damages which you or the Court could compute.   In a situation where there has been a breach of contract which you find to have damaged the plaintiff but for which the plaintiffs have proven no actual damages, the plaintiffs may recover nominal damages.

"By nominal damages is meant trivial—a trivial sum of money."

Plaintiffs did not object to this instruction.   In the trial court's decision on motions after verdict it states that the court so instructed the jury because, based on the fact that the plaintiffs paid for services they did not receive, their loss in proportion to the contract rate was approximately 25 cents.   This rationale indicates that the court disregarded or overlooked Mrs. White's testimony of inconvenience.   In viewing the evidence most favorable to the plaintiffs, there was some injury.   The plaintiffs are not required to ascertain their damages with mathematical precision, but rather the trier of fact must set damages at a reasonable amount.   Notwithstanding this instruction, the jury set the plaintiffs' damages at $10.   The court was in error in reducing that amount to $1.

The jury finding of $10 in actual damages, though small, takes it out of the mere nominal status.   The award is predicated on an actual injury.   This was not the situation present in Sunderman v. Warnken.[1] Sunderman was a wrongful-entry action by a tenant against his landlord.   No actual injury could be shown by the mere fact that the landlord entered the tenant's apartment, therefore damages were nominal and no punitory award could be made.   Here there was credible evidence which showed inconvenience and thus actual injury, and the jury's finding as to compensatory damages should be reinstated.

Punitive Damages

"If a man shall steal an ox, or a sheep, and kill it, or sell it; he shall

1.   (1947), 251 Wis. 471, 29 N.W.2d 496.

restore five oxen for an ox, and four sheep for a sheep."[2]

Over one hundred years ago this court held that, under proper circumstances, a plaintiff was entitled to recover exemplary or punitive damages.[3]

Kink v. Combs[4] is the most recent case in this state which deals with the practice of permitting punitive damages. In *Kink* the court relied on Fuchs v. Kupper[5] and reaffirmed its adherence to the rule of punitive damages.

In Wisconsin compensatory damages are given to make whole the damage or injury suffered by the injured party. On the other hand, punitive damages are given

"... on the basis of punishment to the injured party not because he has been injured, which injury has been compensated with compensatory damages, but to punish the wrongdoer for his malice and to deter others from like conduct."[6]

Thus we reach the question of whether the plaintiffs are entitled to punitive damages for a breach of the water agreement.

The overwhelming weight of authority supports the proposition that punitive damages are not recoverable in actions for breach of contract. In Chitty on Contracts, the author states that the right to receive punitive damages for breach of contract is now confined to the single case of damages for breach of a promise to marry.[7]

Simpson states:

"Although damages in excess of compensation for loss are in some instances permitted in tort actions by way of punishment ... in contract actions the damages recoverable are limited to compensation for pecuniary loss sustained by the breach."[8]

Corbin states that as a general rule punitive damages are not recoverable for breach of contract.[9]

In Wisconsin, the early case of Gordon v. Brewster[10] involved the breach of an employment contract. The trial court instructed the jury that if the nonperformance of the contract was attributable to the defendant's wrongful act of discharging the plaintiff, then that would go to increase the damages sustained. On appeal, this court said that the instruction was unfortunate and might have led the jurors to suppose that they could give something more than actual compensation in a breach of contract case. We find no Wisconsin case in which breach of

---

2. Exodus 22:1.

3. McWilliams v. Bragg (1854), 3 Wis. 377 (* 424).

4. (1965), 28 Wis.2d 65, 135 N.W.2d 789.

5. (1963), 22 Wis.2d 107, 125 N.W.2d 360.

6. Malco, Inc. v. Midwest Aluminum Sales (1961), 14 Wis.2d 57, 66, 109 N.W.2d 516, 521.

7. 1 Chitty, Contracts (2d ed. 1961), p. 1339.

8. Simpson, Contracts (2d ed. Hornbook series), p. 394, sec. 195.

9. 5 Corbin, Contracts, p. 438, sec. 1077.

10. (1858), 7 Wis. 309 (* 355).

contract (other than breach of promise to marry) has led to the award of punitive damages.

Persuasive authority from other jurisdictions supports the proposition (without exception) that punitive damages are not available in breach of contract actions. This is true even if the breach, as in the instant case, is willful.

Although it is well recognized that breach of a contractual duty may be a tort, in such situations the contract creates the relation out of which grows the duty to use care in the performance of a responsibility prescribed by the contract. Not so here. No tort was pleaded or proved.

Reversed in part by reinstating the jury verdict relating to compensatory damages and otherwise affirmed. Costs to appellant.

NOTES

(1) *The Scope of Article 2 of the Code.* Suppose that the contract between the Whites and the Benkowskis had been made after the Uniform Commercial Code had gone into effect in Wisconsin (July 1, 1965). (Articles 1 and 2 of the Code, together with an introduction, can be found in Selections for Contracts.) Would Article 2 of the Code have applied to their dispute? That article "applies to transactions in goods" (UCC 2–102), and water seems to come within the definition of "goods" (UCC 2–105(1)). But Article 2 is captioned "Sales" and seems not to apply to contracts for services even if, as in the case of a contract to paint a house, a small amount of goods will be transferred.

Courts have often determined whether a contract comes within Article 2 by looking for the "predominant factor" of the contract. A leading case among many is Bonebrake v. Cox, 499 F.2d 951, 960 (8th Cir.1974), in which the court held that Article 2 applied to a contract for the sale and installation of used bowling equipment for a lump sum, even though the contract involved substantial amounts of labor. The court described the test as whether the "predominant factor . . . is the rendition of service, with goods incidentally involved (e.g., contract with artist for painting) or is a transaction of sale, with labor incidentally involved (e.g., installation of a water heater in a bathroom)." In Kirkpatrick v. Introspect Healthcare Corp., 845 P.2d 800 (N.M.1992), however, the court applied the *Bonebrake* test to conclude that a contract to create the interior design for a health care facility did not come within Article 2 even though it required the interior designer to sell furnishings to complete the designs. For an interesting aberration, see Mieske v. Bartell Drug Co., 593 P.2d 1308 (Wash. 1979) (though "article 2 is entitled 'Sales,' . . . the declared scope is more comprehensive" and includes contract to develop movie film). As for the possibility of using analogy to extend the rules of Article 2 to cases not literally within the scope of the article, see Note 3, p. 613 below.

(2) *The Scope of Article 1 of the Code.* UCC 1–106(1) says that as a general rule "penal damages" may not be had. If the contract between the Whites and the Benkowskis had been made after the Code had gone into effect, would this provision have applied to their dispute? Note that this provision is in Article 1 (General Provisions), not Article 2 (Sales). What is the scope of Article 1? The Code's preamble recites that it relates to "Certain Commercial Transactions in or regarding Property and Contracts and other Documents concerning them," including the matters described in the titles to Articles 2 through 9. It is unclear, however, whether the general provisions of Article 1 apply only to transactions within the scope of those later articles or to a broader class of

transactions that might be thought of as "commercial." If the contract between the Whites and the Benkowskis did not fall within Article 2, might it nevertheless be thought of as "commercial"?

(3) *Availability of Punitive Damages.* Punitive damages are granted for tortious conduct that is sufficiently "outrageous" to justify them. See Restatement, Second, of Torts § 908. But, as the Supreme Court of Wisconsin stated, "the overwhelming weight of authority supports the proposition that punitive damages are not recoverable in actions for breach of contract." In a leading English case that followed this proposition, however, Lord James of Hereford confessed "to some feeling of remorse, because during many years when I was a junior at the Bar, when I was drawing pleadings, I often strove to convert a breach of contract into a tort in order to recover a higher scale of damages." Addis v. Gramophone Co., [1909] A.C. 488, 492 (H.L.).

Some courts have departed from the strict rule that denies punitive damages for breach of contract when the breach is accompanied by "fraudulent" conduct or by an "independent" tort sufficiently outrageous to justify such damages. See generally Restatement Second § 355; Miller Brewing Co. v. Best Beers of Bloomington, 608 N.E.2d 975 (Ind.1993). See generally 3 Farnsworth § 12.8.

"BAD FAITH BREACH"

The trend in judicial decisions toward greater use of punitive damages has been most noticeable in connection with claims against insurers for vexatious refusal to settle insurance claims. The first cases concerned liability-insurance coverage ("third party" insurance) under which the insured is protected against liability to third parties up to a stated limit, and these cases arose when over-the-limit ("excess") claims were made against the insured. It is a feature of such "third party" coverage that the insurer must provide and can control the defense of a suit against its insured. Given a relatively large claim, the insurer's interest in making a steadfast defense, with attendant risk if the defense fails, is at odds with the insured's interest in making a settlement within the policy limit. Beginning in the late 1950s, courts led by the Supreme Court of California, created a tort of "bad faith breach" as a means of imposing liability on insurers that refused to make reasonable efforts to settle in such cases. See Communale v. Traders & Gen. Ins. Co., 328 P.2d 198 (Cal.1958). Such a breach had all the consequences of a tort, notably the availability of punitive damages.

During the 1970s, the tort of "bad faith breach" was extended to insurance in other forms ("first party" coverage), such as health insurance in which the insurer's wrong consisted in its unreasonable denial of its liability to the insured under the policy. See Vernon Fire & Cas. Ins. Co. v. Sharp, 349 N.E.2d 173 (Ind.1976).

In 1984, the Supreme Court of California suggested that the new tort of "bad faith breach" might be extended beyond the insurance cases. In Seaman's Direct Buying Service v. Standard Oil Company of California, 686 P.2d 1158 (Cal.1984), a would-be oil dealer claimed punitive damages from an oil company that had refused to honor its contract. In remanding the case for erroneous jury instructions, the court in dictum defined a new tort where a party to a contract "in addition to breaching the contract ... seeks to shield itself from liability by denying, in bad faith and without probable cause, that the contract exists." But a tort action would be available for breach of contract only where there was a "special relationship" similar to that between insurer and insured.

The suggestion that the tort of "bad faith breach" could occur outside the insurance field triggered much discussion in law reviews and much litigation in California courts. In 1988, however, a differently composed Supreme Court of California dealt a severe blow to the new tort by denouncing the "uncritical acceptance" by some California courts "of the insurance model into the employment context, without careful consideration of the fundamental policies underlying the development of tort and contract law in general or of significant differences between the insurer/insured and employer/employee relationships." The court refused to apply *Seaman's* to an employer's discharge of an employee under an employment agreement terminable at will. Foley v. Interactive Data Corp., 765 P.2d 373 (Cal.1988).[a] *Seaman's* has had little impact in other states, with the exception of Montana.

NOTE

The Case of the Tricky Tenant. When United Pacific Insurance Co. (UPI) sought larger premises for its branch office in Helena, Montana, it signed a lease agreement with Nicholson for space in a building that he was to renovate. He was to confer with UPI about the renovation and the final plans were subject to mutual approval. As work progressed over a period of several months, disputes arose, and Nicholson and his architect were constantly in contact with the UPI planner and architect. Abruptly, a day before the project was to be completed, Nicholson received a letter from UPI purporting to "rescind" the lease. Although the letter asserted that the plans were defective and the area had become blighted, it became apparent that during the renovations a "secret" UPI task force had recommended that part of the Helena office be transferred to Salt Lake City, eliminating the need for expanded facilities. Nicholson sued, alleging that UPI had not only broken the agreement but had become intransigent and thrown obstacles in his path in order to get him to break the agreement. From an award of $211,105 compensatory and $225,000 punitive damages, UPI appealed.

After discussing *Seaman's,* the court observed that the Montana cases "focus on the action of the breaching party" in determining whether there has been a breach in bad faith, that would justify punitive damages, or merely "an intentional breach or one motivated by self-interest, giving rise to only contract damages." "Where one party acts arbitrarily, capriciously or unreasonably, that conduct exceeds the justifiable expectations of the second party. The second party then should be compensated for damages resulting from the other's culpable conduct.... We hold the jury had adequate evidence on which to find the culpable conduct necessary for an award of punitive damages." Nicholson v.

a. In 1989, a Ninth Circuit opinion explained that *Foley* "solidly reaffirms the notion that the bad faith denial of the existence of contract is a cause of action wholly distinct from the breach of the covenant of good faith and fair dealing." Air–Sea Forwarders, Inc. v. Air Asia Co., 880 F.2d 176, 187 (9th Cir.1989).

United Pacific Insurance Co., 710 P.2d 1342 (Mont.1985). Five years later, however, the Supreme Court of Montana wrote: "In the typical contract case the *Nicholson* reasoning is still sound, but the *Nicholson* tort remedy is excessive." Story v. City of Bozeman, 791 P.2d 767 (Mont.1990).

Would the Supreme Court of Montana have upheld the award of punitive damages in White v. Benkowski?

THE ECONOMICS OF REMEDIES

In recent years, many scholars have brought economic analysis to bear on legal problems; no lawyer can afford to be unaware of this work. Much of the analysis has been directed at contract law, and this book summarizes at least some of it. Study in depth of economic analysis of legal problems must await a more advanced course.

The economist evaluates legal rules in terms of "efficiency." A reallocation of resources in a society is considered to be "efficient" if that reallocation will make some economic unit better off without making some other unit worse off. (Such an allocation is often called "Pareto superior.") Given a set of individual preferences, the economist argues for legal rules that will help society to achieve an efficient allocation of its resources in terms of those preferences. In doing so, the economist posits that economic units are rational and that therefore they will respond to legal rules by taking into account the legal consequences of their decisions.

Thus if a seller (S) owns a widget that S values at $90, that one buyer (B1) values at $110, and that another buyer (B2) values at $130, an efficient legal rule is one that will induce the parties to behave in such a way that B2 will get the widget at a cost of no more than $130 and S will get at least $90. A rule under which S would keep the widget would not be efficient. Nor would a rule under which B1 ended up with the widget. (However, a rule under which S sold the widget to B1 and B1 then sold the widget to B2 would be efficient.)

For the good of society, resources should be allocated efficiently at every point in time. It is therefore in society's interest that each economic unit shift its resources whenever this would be efficient. But what if that unit is bound by a contract not to shift its resources? Should it break the contract and reallocate them?

A rational party's decision whether to perform a contract or break it is affected not only by that party's preferences but also by the legal consequences that would follow from a breach of contract. According to the economist, the purpose of contract remedies is to induce both parties to act efficiently. If the remedy is the award of damages, the law could provide such a large measure of damages that reallocation through breach would seldom be advantageous. Or it could provide such a small measure of damages that reallocation through breach would usually be advantageous. Economic analysis suggests, however, that if breach is to be induced only when it is efficient the measure of damages should be the diminution in value to the injured party in terms of that party's lost expectation. Why?

If the measure of damages were less than the injured party's lost expectation, that party would be worse off as a result of the breach. If the measure of recovery were greater than the injured party's lost expectation, a party contemplating breach would be discouraged from breaking contracts that society would want broken, thus impairing the efficient allocation of resources. Since reallocation through breach will not make the injured party worse off if its expectations are protected and will, by hypothesis, make the party in breach better off, it is in society's interest that the contract be broken and the resources allocated.

Reconsider the example of S's widget. Suppose that S, who values the widget at $90, makes a contract to sell it for $100 to B1 who values it at $110. B2, who values the widget at $130, then offers S $120 for it. What should S do? Our analysis suggests that S should break the contract with B1, pay B1 damages of $10 (the difference between $110 and $100) based on B1's lost expectation, and keep the resulting $10 (the $20 difference between $120 and $100 less the $10 damage payment). If S had not made a contract with B1 an efficient rule would have been one under which B2 would have gotten the widget at a cost of no more than $130 and S would have gotten at least $90. Taking S's contract with B1 into account, an efficient rule is still one under which B2 gets the widget at a cost of no more than $130 and S gets at least $90, since B1 gets damages of $10 so that B1 will be in no worse a position than if there had been no breach. As long as S, by reallocating resources and selling to B2, will realize more than B1's expectation damages, S's breach is an "efficient" one, one that the legal rules on contract remedies should seek to induce.

The foregoing analysis has been simplified in many ways. To begin with, it has considered how the damage measure might influence only one kind of conduct—a seller's decision whether to perform or break a contract to sell goods that the seller owns. The damage measure might also affect the extent to which the promisee acts in reliance on the promise. Furthermore, other factors, such as a party's opportunity to acquire a reputation of reliability in performing contracts, may alter the effects of a damage measure. These and other aspects of economic analysis are raised throughout this book and particularly in Chapter 5.

For an excellent introduction, see Kornhauser, An Introduction to the Economic Analysis of Contract Remedies, 57 U.Colo.L.Rev. 683 (1986).

NOTES

(1) *Examples.* Does the preceding discussion of reallocation provide a convincing argument for expectation as the measure of damages against the cotton farmers described at the beginning of this section? Against Berkley? Against the Benkowskis? What does it suggest about the measure of damages for "wilful" breach? Is your answer affected by the availability to the injured party of a substitute transaction? Such a substitute, known as "cover" in the case of a buyer of goods, is discussed in connection with the opinion that follows.

(2) *The Reliance Measure and Efficient Breach.* In the example just given in connection with efficient breach, no account was taken of reliance. Suppose that B1 will have to spend $3 preparing to use the widget in reliance on the contract in order to realize a value of $110. This reliance expenditure will have no value if the widget is not delivered to B1.

If S breaks the contract and sells the widget to B2 for $120 after B1 has spent the $3, under the expectation measure of damages, S would still have to pay B1 $10, the difference between the $110 value of the widget to B1 and the $100 contract price. Unless B2 were to offer S more than $110—which would not happen unless B2 valued the widget more highly than B1—S would not be induced to break the contract.

If, B1 were only entitled to the reliance measure of damages, however, S would have to pay B1 only $3. If B2 were to offer S anything more than $103—which might happen if B2 valued the widget less than $110 but more than $103 and so less than B1—S would be induced to break the contract. The reliance measure may therefore be inefficient in inducing breach.

KLEIN v. PEPSICO

United States Court of Appeals, Fourth Circuit, 1988.
845 F.2d 76.

ERVIN, CIRCUIT JUDGE: This case turns on whether a contract was formed between Universal Jet Sales, Inc. ("UJS") and PepsiCo, Inc., ("PepsiCo") for the sale of a Gulfstream G–II corporate jet to UJS for resale to one Eugene V. Klein. If a contract was formed, the question remains whether the district court acted within his discretion by ordering specific performance of the contract. We believe the district court properly found that a contract was formed; however, we conclude that the remedy of specific performance is inappropriate. Accordingly, we affirm in part, reverse and remand in part.

I.

In March 1986, Klein began looking for a used corporate jet; specifically, he wanted a G–II. He contacted Patrick Janas, President of UJS, who provided information to Klein about several aircraft including the PepsiCo aircraft. Klein's pilot and mechanic, Mr. Sherman and Mr. Quaid, inspected the PepsiCo jet in New York. Mr. James Welsch served as the jet broker for PepsiCo.

Klein asked that the jet be flown to Arkansas for his personal inspection. On March 29, 1986, he inspected the jet. Mr. Rashid, PepsiCo Vice President for Asset Management and Corporate Service, accompanied the jet to Arkansas and met Mr. Klein. Janas also went to Arkansas. Klein gave Janas $200,000 as a deposit on the jet, and told Janas to offer $4.4 million for the aircraft.

On March 31, 1986, Janas telexed the $4.4 million offer to Welsch. The telex said the offer was subject to a factory inspection satisfactory to the purchaser, and a definitive contract. On April 1, PepsiCo counteroffered with a $4.7 million asking price. After some dickering, Welsch offered the jet for $4.6 million. Janas accepted the offer by telex on April 3. Janas then planned to sell the aircraft to Klein for $4.75 million. In Finding of Fact number 18, JA 85, Judge Williams declared that a contract had been formed at this point.

Judge Williams ruled that a contract was evidenced by Janas' confirming telex which "accepted" PepsiCo's offer to sell the jet, and noted that a $100,000 down payment would be wired. The telex also asked for the proper name of the company selling the aircraft. See JA 86 Finding of Fact number 22.

On April 3, Janas sent out copies of the Klein/UJS agreement and the UJS–PepsiCo agreement to the respective parties. Janas also sent a bill of sale to the escrow agent handling the deal on April 8. Mr. Rochoff, PepsiCo's corporate counsel, spoke with Janas about the standard contract sent by Janas to PepsiCo. He noted only that the delivery date should be changed.

On Monday, April 7, the aircraft was flown to Savannah, Georgia for the pre-purchase inspection. Quaid was present at the inspection for Klein. Archie Walker, PepsiCo's chief of maintenance, was present for the seller. Walker and Quaid discussed a list of repairs to be made to the jet. Most of the problems were cured during the inspection. However, one cosmetic problem was to be corrected in New York, and there were cracks in the engine blades of the right engine.

On April 8, a boroscopic examination conducted by Aviall revealed eight to eleven cracks on the turbine blades. Walker told Rashid that the cost of repairing the blades would be between $25,000 to $28,000. Judge Williams found in Finding of Fact numbers 34 through 37 that PepsiCo, through Walker and Rashid, agreed to pay for the repair to the engine.

On April 9, the plane was returned to New York. Rashid wanted the plane grounded; however, it was sent to retrieve the stranded PepsiCo Chairman of the Board from Dulles airport that same evening. Donald Kendall, the Chairman, on April 10, called Rashid and asked that the jet be withdrawn from the market. Rashid called Welsch who effected the withdrawal. On the 11th Janas told Klein that PepsiCo refused to tender the aircraft. The deal was supposed to close on Friday, April 11.

On April 14, Klein telexed UJS demanding delivery of the aircraft. That same day, UJS telexed PepsiCo demanding delivery and expressing satisfaction with the pre-purchase inspection. On April 15, PepsiCo responded with a telex to UJS saying that it refused to negotiate further because discussions had not reached the point of agreement; in particular, Klein was not prepared to go forward with the deal.

Judge Williams, in a lengthy opinion, made numerous findings of fact. Such findings are reviewed only for clear error. Davis v. Food Lion, 792 F.2d 1274, 1277 (4th Cir.1986). If the findings are based on determinations of witness credibility, are consistent, and are corroborated by extrinsic evidence, they are virtually never clearly erroneous. Brown v. Baltimore and Ohio R. Co., 805 F.2d 1133, 1140 (4th Cir.1986).

Judge Williams' decision to grant specific performance is reviewed only for an abuse of discretion. Haythe v. May, 223 Va. 359, 288 S.E.2d 487 (1982); Horner v. Bourland, 724 F.2d 1142, 1144–45 (5th Cir.1984). Keeping these standards in mind, we now turn to the first issue, whether the district court clearly erred in finding that a contract arose between PepsiCo and UJS.

II.

PepsiCo argues forcefully that no contract was formed between it and UJS. The soft drink dealer argues first that the parties did not intend to be bound until a complete integration was written in final form. Until that definitive written contract existed, PepsiCo maintains that no contract existed. The company argues that the March 31 and April 1 telexes explicitly stated that no contract would exist until a written agreement was executed. Because no written agreement had been executed (PepsiCo had not signed the sales agreement sent by Janas to PepsiCo) the company argues that it had the right to withdraw from the negotiations. PepsiCo cites Reprosystem, B.V. v. SCM Corp., 727 F.2d 257, 262 (2d Cir.1984), cert. denied, 469 U.S. 828, 105 S.Ct. 110, 83 L.Ed.2d 54 (1984) and Skycom Corp. v. Telstar Corp., 813 F.2d 810, 815–16 (7th Cir.1987) for the general proposition that either party can withdraw from negotiations for any reason.

Upon reviewing the facts, Judge Williams ruled that a contract was formed between the parties. He explains:

> A contract was formed between UJS and PepsiCo for the sale of the GII aircraft, Serial No. 170, for $4.6 million. The contract formation is based upon (1) UJS's April 3rd confirming telex; (2) the conduct of the parties, e.g., (a) PepsiCo's failure to communicate any objection to the terms of the April 3rd telex confirming the agreement reached between Welsch and Janas; (b) PepsiCo's directive to UJS to wire transfer a One Hundred Thousand Dollar ($100,000.00) down payment, which money was received by PepsiCo; (c) PepsiCo's communication with UJS that the Sales Agreement, which served to memorialize the contract, appeared "fine"; (d) PepsiCo's execution of the Bill of Sale for the aircraft and its sending of the Bill of Sale to the escrow agent, as called for by Janas and in the Sales Agreement; (e) PepsiCo's sending the aircraft to Savannah, Georgia, for a prepurchase inspection as called for in both the April 3rd confirming telex and the Sales Agreement; and (f) admissions of PepsiCo, through Rashid, that UJS's offer to purchase the airplane was accepted.

JA 103–04, Conclusion of Law number 6. Finally, Judge Williams expressly held that the intent to memorialize the contract in writing was not necessarily a condition to the existence of the contract itself. JA 104 (Conclusion of Law number 8).

PepsiCo offers no reason as to why Judge Williams' findings on this issue are clearly erroneous. They merely disagree with his characterizations of the facts. This court may disagree with his characterization too, but that does not amount to a firm and definite conviction that a mistake has been committed. Anderson v. City of Bessemer City, N.C., 470 U.S. 564, 105 S.Ct. 1504, 84 L.Ed.2d 518 (1985).

PepsiCo argues secondly, that no contract was formed because the condition of inspection satisfactory to the buyer had not been met. PepsiCo urges strongly that neither UJS nor Klein were willing to accept the aircraft "as is," so the condition was unsatisfied. Judge Williams ruled that when PepsiCo agreed to make the repairs, the condition was satisfied. Furthermore, the court below ruled that the condition was excused by PepsiCo's refusal to tender the aircraft so that the buyer could express his dissatisfaction.

The district court's first ruling, that the condition was satisfied by PepsiCo's offers to pay for the repairs, resolves this issue. Judge Williams ruled that based on the conversations between Walker and Rashid, the seller had agreed to make the necessary repairs to market the plane. See Finding of Fact 34–37 at JA 89–90. Again, PepsiCo offers no suggestion that Judge Williams committed any error, much less clear error. Rather, PepsiCo urges its version of the facts on this court. Without more, the company loses.

Ultimately, then, a contract exists between PepsiCo and UJS for the sale of one G–II Gulfstream aircraft.[1] Because PepsiCo failed to deliver the aircraft, the district court ordered relief in the form of specific performance. We now consider the appropriateness of the relief ordered.

III.

The Virginia Code § 8.2–716 [a] permits a jilted buyer of goods to seek specific performance of the contract if the goods sought are unique, or in other proper circumstances. Judge Williams ruled that: 1) the G–II aircraft involved in this case is unique and 2) Klein's inability to cover with a comparable aircraft is strong evidence of "other proper circumstances." JA 111–112, Conclusions of Law No. 31 and No. 32. These conclusions are not supported in the record.

We note first that Virginia's adoption of the Uniform Commercial Code does not abrogate the maxim that specific performance is inappropriate where damages are recoverable and adequate. Griscom v. Chil-

---

1. PepsiCo argues that Klein has no right to sue on the PepsiCo/UJS contract because (1) the contract violates the statute of frauds [see Chapter 3 below], (2) Klein was not an intended beneficiary of the contract [see Chapter 10 below], and (3) the Klein/UJS contract, from which Klein derives his right to sue PepsiCo, was rescinded. The district court's discussion thoroughly and ably treats these claims and rejects them. Based on the district court's reasoning, this court affirms the disposition of those issues.

a. Your editors have made no changes in state citations to the Uniform Commercial Code. Therefore you are expected to surmise that Virginia Code § 8.2–716 is the Virginia version of UCC 2–716.

dress, 183 Va. 42, 31 S.E.2d 309, 311 (1944).[b] In this case Judge Williams repeatedly stated that money damages would make Klein whole. JA 668–9, 582. Klein argued that he wanted the plane to resell it for a profit. JA 669. Finally, an increase in the cost of a replacement does not merit the remedy of specific performance. Hilmor Sales Co. v. Helen Neuschalfer Division of Supronics Corp., 6 U.C.C.Rep.Serv. 325 (N.Y.Sup.Ct.1969). There is no room in this case for the equitable remedy of specific performance.

Turning now to the specific rulings of the court below, Judge Williams explained that the aircraft was unique because only three comparable aircraft existed on the market. Therefore, Klein would have to go through considerable expense to find a replacement. JA 110. Klein's expert testified that there were twenty-one other G–II's on the market, three of which were roughly comparable. JA 838–9, 1284–88. Klein's chief pilot said that other G–II's could be purchased. JA 259. Finally, we should note that UJS bought two G–II's which they offered to Klein after this deal fell through, JA 796–7, and Klein made bids on two other G–II's after PepsiCo withdrew its aircraft from the market. JA 277, 666, 694. Given these facts, we find it very difficult to support a ruling that the aircraft was so unique as to merit an order of specific performance.

Judge Williams ruled further that Klein's inability to cover his loss is an "other proper circumstance" favoring specific performance. Klein testified himself that he didn't purchase another G–II because prices had started to rise. JA 693. Because of the price increase, he decided to purchase a G–III aircraft. As noted earlier, price increases alone are no reason to order specific performance. Because money damages would clearly be adequate in this case, and because the aircraft is not unique within the meaning of the Virginia Commercial Code, we reverse the grant of specific performance and remand the case to the district court for a trial on damages.

Affirmed in Part, Reserved and Remanded in Part.

NOTES

(1) *Deferred Questions*—PepsiCo's argument that no contract was formed because "the parties did not intend to be bound until a complete integration was written in final form" is considered in the next chapter. PepsiCo's argument "that no contract was formed because the condition of inspection satisfactory to the buyer had not been met" is addressed in Chapter 7, Performance and Breach. We are here concerned only with "the appropriateness of the relief ordered."

(2) *Avoidability as a Limit on Expectation.* The court says that "money damages would clearly be adequate in this case" and remands the case for a trial on damages. How should damages be calculated on such a trial? Recall that

b. In King Aircraft Sales v. Lane, 846 P.2d 550 (Wash.App.1993), the court upheld a decree of specific performance of a contract to sell two airplanes "even though the legal remedy of damages may have been available." The court distinguished *Klein* on the ground that prior to the adoption of the Code, Washington courts "did not always require the absence of a legal remedy" or that the goods be "absolutely 'unique.' "

Klein "argued that he wanted the plane to resell it for a profit." Should Klein be allowed to recover the profit (say $500,000) he lost on that resale? This, along with return of his payments, would seem to give Klein his expectation by putting him in the position he would have been in had PepsiCo delivered the G–II jet. But if Klein could have realized the resale profit by obtaining a substitute G–II jet on the market for a somewhat enhanced price (say $200,000 more than the $4.75 million he was to pay PepsiCo), he could have put himself in that position for only $200,000.

Under an important limitation on expectation, an aggrieved promisee is not allowed to recover loss that it could reasonably have avoided. See Restatement Second § 350. Where, as here, there is a market for goods, a buyer's damages are based on the assumption that the buyer could reasonably have avoided greater loss by obtaining substitute goods on the market. See UCC 2–713, under which "the measure of damages ... is the difference between the market price ... and the contract price" (here $200,000). This limitation on expectation, often called the "mitigation principle," is explored in Chapter 5, Remedies for Breach.[a]

(3) *Cover.* Recall that "UJS bought two G–II's which they offered to Klein after the deal fell through," but Klein decided instead to buy a G–III. Suppose, however, that he had promptly bought another G–II (say for $250,000 more than the $4.75 million he was to pay PepsiCo). Under UCC 2–712 his "reasonable purchase of ... goods in substitution for those due from the seller" would have been "cover," entitling Klein to damages based on "the difference between the cost of cover and the contract price" (here $250,000).

Note that UCC 2–712 would have afforded Klein two advantages over UCC 2–713. First, he would not have to prove market price, which would probably require expert witnesses, but could simply use his cover contract to show the cover price. Second, he could recover his actual additional cost of a substitute (here $250,000) rather than the hypothetical cost of a substitute (here $200,000) if he had obtained it on the market. Cover is dealt with in more detail in Chapter 5, Remedies For Breach.

(4) *The Automobile Cases.* After the Second World War, a number of disappointed buyers sought specific performance of their contracts to buy scarce new automobiles from automobile dealers. Most buyers lost. A typical case is McCallister v. Patton, 215 S.W.2d 701 (Ark.1948), in which the buyer sought specific performance of a contract made on about September 15, 1945, to buy a Ford super deluxe tudor sedan. (The war with Japan had ended on September 2, 1945). The buyer alleged that "new Ford automobiles have been hard to obtain" and that he had been "unable to purchase an automobile at any other place or upon the open market of the description named." The Supreme Court of Arkansas held that his complaint was properly dismissed, taking "judicial notice of the fact that large numbers of cars of the type mentioned in the alleged contract have been produced since 1945, and sold through both new and used car dealers in the open market. It is neither alleged nor contended that the car ordered has any special or peculiar qualities not commonly possessed by others of the same make so as to make it practically impossible to replace it in the market."

For a case allowing specific performance, see Boeving v. Vandover, 218 S.W.2d 175 (Mo.App.1949), relied on in the opinion that follows. There the

---

a. Another limitation, the requirement of certainty, was discussed in Note 4, p. 7 above and is also explored in Chapter 5, along with a third limitation, the requirement of foreseeability.

dealer had attempted to impose the additional requirement of a trade-in upon the buyer, and the court had found that "if [the buyer] lost his priority with [the seller] he would be forced to place his order with some other Buick Agency and await his turn, which might take from one to two years." Might the Arkansas court have allowed specific performance if additional facts had been alleged? What facts?

Would UCC 2–716(1), (2) have changed the result in the *McCallister* case? For a Code case allowing specific performance of a contract for the sale of a Corvette Pace Car, produced in a limited edition of 6,000, see Sedmak v. Charlie's Chevrolet, Inc., 622 S.W.2d 694 (Mo.App.1981).

(5) *The Case of the Cowboy's Lament.* Archie Sparrow, a cowboy, agreed to work on Chip Morris' cattle ranch for 16 weeks, in return for which Morris agreed to pay him $400 and give him a horse called Keno. When Sparrow went to work, Keno was practically unbroken, but during his spare time he trained him so that, with a little additional training, he would have been a first class roping horse. At the end of the 16 week term, Morris paid Sparrow the $400 but refused to give him the horse. Sparrow sued for specific performance. *Held:* For plaintiff. "Although it has been held that equity will not ordinarily enforce, by specific performance, a contract for the sale of chattels, it will do so where special and peculiar reasons exist which render it impossible for the injured party to obtain relief by way of damages in an action at law [citing McCallister v. Patton].... Certainly when one has made a roping horse out of a green, unbroken pony, such a horse would have a peculiar and unique value; if Sparrow is entitled to prevail, he has a right to the horse instead of its market value in dollars and cents." Morris v. Sparrow, 225 Ark. 1019, 287 S.W.2d 583 (1956).

LACLEDE GAS CO. v. AMOCO OIL CO.
United States Court of Appeals, Eighth Circuit, 1975.
522 F.2d 33.

Ross, Circuit Judge. The Laclede Gas Company (Laclede), a Missouri corporation, brought this diversity action alleging breach of contract against the Amoco Oil Company (Amoco), a Delaware corporation. It sought relief in the form of a mandatory injunction prohibiting the continuing breach or, in the alternative, damages. The district court held a bench trial on the issues of whether there was a valid, binding contract between the parties and whether, if there was such a contract, Amoco should be enjoined from breaching it. It then ruled that the "contract is invalid due to lack of mutuality" and denied the prayer for injunctive relief. The court made no decision regarding the requested damages. Laclede Gas Co. v. Amoco Oil Co., 385 F.Supp. 1332, 1336 (E.D.Mo.1974). This appeal followed, and we reverse the district court's judgment.

On September 21, 1970, Midwest Missouri Gas Company (now Laclede), and American Oil Company (now Amoco), the predecessors of the parties to this litigation, entered into a written agreement which was designed to provide central propane gas distribution systems to various residential developments in Jefferson County, Missouri, until such time as natural gas mains were extended into these areas. The agreement contemplated that as individual developments were planned the owners or developers would apply to Laclede for central propane gas systems. If Laclede determined that such a system was appropriate in any given development, it could request Amoco to supply the propane to that specific development. This request was made in the form of a supplemental form letter, as provided in the September 21 agreement; and if Amoco decided to supply the propane, it bound itself to do so by signing this supplemental form.

Once this supplemental form was signed the agreement placed certain duties on both Laclede and Amoco. Basically, Amoco was to "[i]nstall, own, maintain and operate ... storage and vaporization facilities and any other facilities necessary to provide [it] with the capability of delivering to [Laclede] commercial propane gas suitable ... for delivery by [Laclede] to its customers' facilities." Amoco's facilities were to be "adequate to provide a continuous supply of commercial propane gas at such times and in such volumes commensurate with [Laclede's] requirements for meeting the demands reasonably to be anticipated in each Development while this Agreement is in force." Amoco was deemed to be "the supplier," while Laclede was "the distributing utility."

For its part Laclede agreed to "[i]nstall, own, maintain and operate all distribution facilities" from a "point of delivery" which was defined to be "the outlet of [Amoco] header piping." Laclede also promised to pay Amoco "the Wood River Area Posted Price for propane plus four cents per gallon for all amounts of commercial propane gas delivered" to it under the agreement.

Since it was contemplated that the individual propane systems would eventually be converted to natural gas, one paragraph of the agreement provided that Laclede should give Amoco 30 days written notice of this event, after which the agreement would no longer be binding for the converted development.

Another paragraph gave Laclede the right to cancel the agreement. However, this right was expressed in the following language:

> This Agreement shall remain in effect for one (1) year following the first delivery of gas by [Amoco] to [Laclede] hereunder. Subject to termination as provided in Paragraph 11 hereof [dealing with conversions to natural gas], this Agreement shall automatically continue in effect for additional periods of one (1) year each unless [Laclede] shall, not less than 30 days prior to the expiration of the initial one (1) year period or any subsequent one (1) year period, give [Amoco] written notice of termination.

There was no provision under which Amoco could cancel the agreement. *Does this mean that contract isn't mutual?*

For a time the parties operated satisfactorily under this agreement, and some 17 residential subdivisions were brought within it by supplemental letters. However, for various reasons, including conversion to natural gas, the number of developments under the agreement had shrunk to eight by the time of trial. These were all mobile home parks.

During the winter of 1972–73 Amoco experienced a shortage of propane and voluntarily placed all of its customers, including Laclede, on an 80% allocation basis, meaning that Laclede would receive only up to 80% of its previous requirements. Laclede objected to this and pushed Amoco to give it 100% of what the developments needed. Some conflict arose over this before the temporary shortage was alleviated.

Then, on April 3, 1973, Amoco notified Laclede that its Wood River Area Posted Price of propane had been increased by three cents per gallon. Laclede objected to this increase also and demanded a full explanation. None was forthcoming. Instead Amoco merely sent a letter dated May 14, 1973, informing Laclede that it was "terminating" the September 21, 1970, agreement effective May 31, 1973. It claimed it had the right to do this because "the Agreement lacks 'mutuality.' " [1]

The district court felt that the entire controversy turned on whether or not Laclede's right to "arbitrarily cancel the Agreement" without Amoco having a similar right rendered the contract void "for lack of mutuality" and it resolved this question in the affirmative. We disagree with this conclusion and hold that settled principles of contract law require a reversal.

I.

[The court held that Laclede's power to terminate did not make its promise illusory and that the agreement was an enforceable contract for Laclede's requirements for the subdivision. The district court, therefore, erred in holding that there was no binding contract.]

II.

Since he found that there was no binding contract, the district judge did not have to deal with the question of whether or not to grant the injunction prayed for by Laclede. He simply denied this relief because there was no contract. Laclede Gas Co. v. Amoco Oil Co., supra, 385 F.Supp. at 1336.

Generally the determination of whether or not to order specific performance of a contract lies within the sound discretion of the trial court. Landau v. St. Louis Public Service Co., 364 Mo. 1134, 273 S.W.2d 255, 259 (1954). However, this discretion is, in fact, quite limited; and it is said that when certain equitable rules have been met and the contract is fair and plain "specific performance goes as a matter of right." Miller v. Coffeen, 365 Mo. 204, 280 S.W.2d 100, 102 (1955), quoting, Berberet v. Myers, 240 Mo. 58, 77, 144 S.W. 824, 830 (1912). (Emphasis omitted.)

1. While Amoco sought to repudiate the agreement, it resumed supplying propane to the subdivisions on February 1, 1974, under the mandatory allocation guidelines promulgated by the Federal Energy Administration under the Federal Mandatory Allocation Program for propane. It is agreed that this is now being done under the contract.

With this in mind we have carefully reviewed the very complete record on appeal and conclude that the trial court should grant the injunctive relief prayed. We are satisfied that this case falls within that category in which specific performance should be ordered as a matter of right. . . .

Amoco contends that four of the requirements for specific performance have not been met. Its claims are: (1) there is no mutuality of remedy in the contract; (2) the remedy of specific performance would be difficult for the court to administer without constant and long-continued supervision; (3) the contract is indefinite and uncertain; and (4) the remedy at law available to Laclede is adequate. The first three contentions have little or no merit and do not detain us for long.

There is simply no requirement in the law that both parties be mutually entitled to the remedy of specific performance in order that one of them be given that remedy by the court. . . .

While a court may refuse to grant specific performance where such a decree would require constant and long-continued court supervision, this is merely a discretionary rule of decision which is frequently ignored when the public interest is involved. . . .

Here the public interest in providing propane to the retail customers is manifest, while any supervision required will be far from onerous.

Section 370 of the Restatement of Contracts (1932) provides:

> Specific enforcement will not be decreed unless the terms of the contract are so expressed that the court can determine with reasonable certainty what is the duty of each party and the conditions under which performance is due.

We believe these criteria have been satisfied here. As discussed in part I of this opinion, as to all developments for which a supplemental agreement has been signed, Amoco is to supply all the propane which is reasonably foreseeably required, while Laclede is to purchase the required propane from Amoco and pay the contract price therefor. The parties have disagreed over what is meant by "Wood River Area Posted Price" in the agreement, but the district court can and should determine with reasonable certainty what the parties intended by this term and should mold its decree, if necessary accordingly.[3] Likewise, the fact that the agreement does not have a definite time of duration is not fatal since the evidence established that the last subdivision should be converted to natural gas in 10 to 15 years. This sets a reasonable time limit on performance and the district court can and should mold the final decree to reflect this testimony.

It is axiomatic that specific performance will not be ordered when the party claiming breach of contract has an adequate remedy at law. Jamison Coal & Coke Co. v. Goltra, 143 F.2d 889, 894 (8th Cir.), cert. denied, 323 U.S. 769, 65 S.Ct. 122, 89 L.Ed. 615 (1944). This is

---

3. The record indicates that Laclede has now accepted Amoco's interpretation and has agreed that "Wood River Area Posted Price" means Amoco's posted price for propane at its Wood River refinery.

especially true when the contract involves personal property as distinguished from real estate.

However, in Missouri, as elsewhere, specific performance may be ordered even though personalty is involved in the "proper circumstances." Mo.Rev.Stat. § 400.2–716(1); Restatement of Contracts, supra, § 361. And a remedy at law adequate to defeat the grant of specific performance "must be as certain, prompt, complete, and efficient to attain the ends of justice as a decree of specific performance." National Marking Mach. Co. v. Triumph Mfg. Co., 13 F.2d 6, 9 (8th Cir.1926). Accord, Snip v. City of Lamar, 239 Mo.App. 824, 201 S.W.2d 790, 798 (1947).

One of the leading Missouri cases allowing specific performance of a contract relating to personalty because the remedy at law was inadequate is Boeving v. Vandover, 240 Mo.App. 117, 218 S.W.2d 175, 178 (1949). In that case the plaintiff sought specific performance of a contract in which the defendant had promised to sell him an automobile. At that time (near the end of and shortly after World War II) new cars were hard to come by, and the court held that specific performance was a proper remedy since a new car "could not be obtained elsewhere except at considerable expense, trouble or loss, which cannot be estimated in advance."

We are satisfied that Laclede has brought itself within this practical approach taken by the Missouri courts. As Amoco points out, Laclede has propane immediately available to it under other contracts with other suppliers. And the evidence indicates that at the present time propane is readily available on the open market. However, this analysis ignores the fact that the contract involved in this lawsuit is for a long-term supply of propane to these subdivisions. The other two contracts under which Laclede obtains the gas will remain in force only until March 31, 1977, and April 1, 1981, respectively; and there is no assurance that Laclede will be able to receive any propane under them after that time. Also it is unclear as to whether or not Laclede can use the propane obtained under these contracts to supply the Jefferson County subdivisions, since they were originally entered into to provide Laclede with propane with which to "shave" its natural gas supply during peak demand periods.[4] Additionally, there was uncontradicted expert testimony that Laclede probably could not find another supplier of propane willing to enter into a long-term contract such as the Amoco agreement, given the uncertain future of worldwide energy supplies. And, even if Laclede could obtain supplies of propane for the affected developments through its present contracts or newly negotiated ones, it would still face considerable expense and trouble which cannot be estimated in advance in making arrangements for its distribution to the subdivisions.

Specific performance is the proper remedy in this situation, and it

4. During periods of cold weather, when demand is high, Laclede does not receive enough natural gas to meet all this demand. It, therefore, adds propane to the natural gas it places in its distribution system. This practice is called "peak shaving."

should be granted by the district court.[5]   . . .

[Reversed and remanded.]

NOTE

The Code. Comments 1 and 2 to UCC 2–716 explain: "[W]ithout intending to impair in any way the exercise of the court's sound discretion in the matter, this Article seeks to further a more liberal attitude than some courts have shown in connection with the specific performance of contracts of sale. . . .   In view of this Article's emphasis on the commercial feasibility of replacement, a new concept of what are 'unique' goods is introduced under this section. Specific performance is no longer limited to goods which are already specific or ascertained at the time of contracting. The test of uniqueness under this section must be made in terms of the total situation which characterizes the contract. Output and requirements contracts involving a particular or peculiarly available source or market present today the typical commercial specific performance situation, as contrasted with contracts for the sale of heirlooms or priceless works of art which were usually involved in the older cases.[a] However, uniqueness is not the sole basis of the remedy under this section for the relief may also be granted 'in other proper circumstances' and inability to cover is strong evidence of 'other proper circumstances.' "[b]

In the case of a long-term output or requirements contract, might the difficulty of proving damages amount to "other proper circumstances" even if there is no "particular or peculiarly available source or market"? If Laclede were limited to damages, how would its damages be calculated under the Code? In Eastern Rolling Mill Co. v. Michlovitz, 145 A. 378 (Md.1929), a five-year output contract for scrap steel was broken by the seller in the first year. Part of the court's justification for ordering specific performance was that any estimate of damages "would be speculative and conjectured, and not, therefore, compensatory. . . .   To substitute damages by guess for due performance of contract could only be because 'there's no equity stirring.' "

NORTHERN DELAWARE INDUSTRIAL DEVELOPMENT CORP. v. E.W. BLISS CO., 245 A.2d 431 (Del.Ch.1968).

[Bliss, a general contractor, contracted to modernize Phoenix Steel's plant, which was spread over a 60–acre site, for $27,500,000. Work did not progress as

---

5. In fashioning its decree the district court must take into account any relevant rules and regulations promulgated under the Federal Mandatory Allocation Program.

a. An "output contract" is one in which the quantity of goods delivered is made to depend on the quantity produced by the seller; a requirements contract is illustrated by the foregoing case. The two types are bracketed in UCC 2–306(1).

b. For an entertaining opinion dealing with uniqueness, see American Brands, Inc. v. Playgirl, Inc., 498 F.2d 947 (2d Cir.1974), in which the manufacturer of Tarryton cigarettes sought to enjoin Playgirl from breaking their contract by refusing to publish Tarryton advertisements and by publishing other advertisements on the back covers of eight issues of its magazine. The court rejected the manufacturer's contention that the back pages of other magazines of comparable circulation would not afford the manufacturer a suitable substitute, since "it would seem likely that its profits picture would be the same whether the tobacco consumers are malleable young ladies or more jaded aging males" and there "is nothing in the record . . . to indicate what segment of the populace is titillated by Playgirl and why in any event it is not susceptible to the lure of tobacco by . . . blandishment in other and more pedestrian periodicals."

rapidly as contemplated in the contract, and Phoenix sought a court order of specific performance to compel Bliss to comply with the contract by putting on the job the 300 more workmen required to make up a full second shift during the period that one of the mills had to be shut down because of the work. The court denied specific performance.]

MARVEL, VICE CHANCELLOR. . . . It is not that a court of equity is without jurisdiction in a proper case to order the completion of an expressly designed and largely completed construction contract, particularly where the undertaking is tied in with a contract for the sale of land and the construction in question is largely finished. . . . The point is that a court of equity should not order specific performance of any building contract in a situation in which it would be impractical to carry out such an order, . . . unless there are special circumstances or the public interest is directly involved. . . . I conclude that to grant specific performance . . . would be inappropriate in view of the imprecision of the contract provision relied upon and the impracticability if not impossibility of effective enforcement by the Court of a mandatory order designed to keep a specific number of men on the job at the site of a steel mill which is undergoing extensive modernization and expansion. If plaintiffs have sustained loss as a result of actionable building delays . . . , they may, at an appropriate time, resort to law for a fixing of their claimed damages. [On a motion for reargument, Phoenix argued that it sought only an order "directing the performance of a ministerial act, namely the hiring by defendant of more workers." The court denied the motion, relying on "the well established principle that performance of a contract for personal services, even of a unique nature, will not be affirmatively and directly enforced."]

NOTE

Distinctions. Consider the remark of Chancellor Walworth in denying a decree of specific performance against an opera singer: "I am not aware that any officer of this court has that perfect knowledge of the Italian language, or possesses that exquisite sensibility in the auricular nerve, which is necessary to understand and to enjoy with a proper zest the peculiar beauties of the Italian opera, so fascinating to the fashionable world." De Rivafinoli v. Corsetti, 4 Paige Ch. 263, 270 (N.Y.1833). Is this point distinguishable from that in Northern Delaware?

Courts have shown increasing willingness to order specific performance of construction contracts. In most of these cases, however, the construction was to take place on the defendant's land with a conveyance or lease to follow. See, e.g., Floyd v. Watson, 254 S.E.2d 687, 690 (W.Va.1979), where the court noted that the agreement "includes a provision for conveyance of land, and therefore specific performance is proper." Cf. City Stores Co. v. Ammerman, 266 F.Supp. 766 (D.D.C.1967), aff'd, 394 F.2d 950 (D.C.Cir.1968).

WALGREEN CO. v. SARA CREEK PROPERTY CO., 966 F.2d 273 (7th Cir.1992). [For decades, Walgreen, a "discount" chain, had operated a pharmacy in the Southgate Mall in Milwaukee. Under its lease, the landlord, Sara Creek, promised not to lease space in the mall to another store operating a pharmacy. In 1990, fearful that its "anchor [largest] tenant" was about to close its store, Sara Creek informed Walgreen that it intended to buy out that tenant and install in its place a store operated by Phar–Mor, a "deep discount" chain that would contain a pharmacy. Its entrance was to be within a couple of hundred feet of Walgreen's. Walgreen's sought an injunction against Sara Creek. After a hearing in which Sara Creek's expert witnesses testified that Walgreen's damages could be readily estimated and Walgreen's employees testified to the contrary, asserting among other reasons that those damages included intangibles such as good will, the trial judge entered a permanent injunction against Sara Creek's letting the premises to Phar–Mor until Walgreen's expired. Sara Creek appealed.]

POSNER, CIRCUIT JUDGE.[a] ... Sara Creek reminds us that damages are the norm in breach of contract as in other cases. Many breaches, it points out, are "efficient" in the sense that they allow resources to be moved into a more valuable use. ... Perhaps this is one—the value of Phar–Mor's occupancy of the anchor premises may exceed the cost to Walgreen of facing increased competition. If so, society will be better off if Walgreen is paid its damages, equal to that cost, and Phar–Mor is allowed to move in rather than being kept out by an injunction. That is why injunctions are not granted as a matter of course, but only when the plaintiff's damages remedy is inadequate. Northern Indiana Public Service Co. v. Carbon County Coal Co., 799 F.2d 265, 279 (7th Cir.1986). Walgreen's is not, Sara Creek argues; the projection of business losses due to increased competition is a routine exercise in calculation. Damages representing either the present value of lost future profits or (what should be the equivalent, ... the diminution in the value of the leasehold have either been awarded or deemed the proper remedy in a number of reported cases for breach of an exclusivity clause in a shopping-center lease. ... Why, Sara Creek asks, should they not be adequate here?

The benefits of substituting an injunction for damages are twofold. First, it shifts the burden of determining the cost of the defendant's conduct from the court to the parties. If it is true that Walgreen's damages are smaller than the gain to Sara Creek from allowing a second pharmacy into the shopping mall, then there must be a price for dissolving the injunction that will make both parties better off. Thus, the effect of upholding the injunction would be to substitute for the costly processes of forensic fact determination the less costly processes of private negotiation. Second, a premise of our free-market system, and the lesson of experience here and abroad as well, is that prices and costs are more accurately determined by the market than by government. A battle of experts is a less reliable method of determining the actual cost

a. Richard Allen Posner (1939–___), after clerking for Justice William Brennan and occupying several legal positions in the federal government, taught briefly at Stanford University Law School and then for more than a decade at the University of Chicago Law School before his appointment to the United States Court of Appeals for the Seventh Circuit. A key figure in the development of the field of law and economics, his books include the influential *Economic Analysis of Law*.

to Walgreen of facing new competition than negotiations between Walgreen and Sara Creek over the price at which Walgreen would feel adequately compensated for having to face that competition.

That is the benefit side of injunctive relief but there is a cost side as well. Many injunctions require continuing supervision by the court, and that is costly.... Some injunctions are problematic because they impose costs on third parties.... A more subtle cost of injunctive relief arises from the situation that economists call "bilateral monopoly," in which two parties can deal only with each other: the situation that an injunction creates. ... The sole seller of widgets selling to the sole buyer of that product would be an example. But so will be the situation confronting Walgreen and Sara Creek if the injunction is upheld. Walgreen can "sell" its injunctive right only to Sara Creek, and Sara Creek can "buy" Walgreen's surrender of its right to enjoin the leasing of the anchor tenant's space to Phar–Mor only from Walgreen. The lack of alternatives in bilateral monopoly creates a bargaining range, and the costs of negotiating to a point within that range may be high. Suppose the cost to Walgreen of facing the competition of Phar–Mor at the Southgate Mall would be $1 million, and the benefit to Sara Creek of leasing to Phar–Mor would be $2 million. Then at any price between those figures for a waiver of Walgreen's injunctive right both parties would be better off, and we expect parties to bargain around a judicial assignment of legal rights if the assignment is inefficient. R.H. Coase, "The Problem of Social Cost," 3 J. Law & Econ. 1 (1960).[b] But each of the parties would like to engross as much of the bargaining range as possible—Walgreen to press the price toward $2 million, Sara Creek to depress it toward $1 million. With so much at stake, both parties will have an incentive to devote substantial resources of time and money to the negotiation process. The process may even break down, if one or both parties want to create for future use a reputation as a hard bargainer; and if it does break down, the injunction will have brought about an inefficient result. All these are in one form or another costs of the injunctive process that can be avoided by substituting damages.

The costs and benefits of the damages remedy are the mirror of those of the injunctive remedy. The damages remedy avoids the cost of continuing supervision and third-party effects, and the cost of bilateral monopoly as well. It imposes costs of its own, however, in the form of diminished accuracy in the determination of value, on the one hand, and of the parties' expenditures on preparing and presenting evidence of damages, and the time of the court in evaluating the evidence, on the other.

The weighing up of all these costs and benefits is the analytical procedure that is or at least should be employed by a judge asked to enter a permanent injunction, with the understanding that if the balance is even the injunction should be withheld. The judge is not required to

b. Ronald Coase, winner of the 1991 Nobel Prize in Economics, drew attention to the importance of transaction costs.

explicate every detail of the analysis and he did not do so here, but as long as we are satisfied that his approach is broadly consistent with a proper analysis we shall affirm; and we are satisfied here. The determination of Walgreen's damages would have been costly in forensic resources and inescapably inaccurate. ... The lease had ten years to run. So Walgreen would have had to project its sales revenues and costs over the next ten years, and then project the impact on those figures of Phar–Mor's competition, and then discount that impact to present value. All but the last step would have been fraught with uncertainty. ...

   Affirmed.

NOTE

The Economics of Specific Performance: Transaction Costs. In the light of our earlier discussion of the economics of remedies, specific performance seems an inefficient remedy. Reconsider the situation of S, who has contracted to deliver the widget to B1 for $100. If B1 can compel S to deliver the widget, it might be supposed that B2 would not end up with the widget. This, however, ignores two possibilities—resale and renegotiation.

   If B1 compels S to deliver the widget, B2 can still end up with the widget by buying it from B1. If B1 sells the widget to B2 for $120, it will then be B1, who values the widget at $110, who realizes the $10. Were B1 limited to expectation damages, it would have been S who realized the $10. But since no one is worse off, it makes no difference from the point of view of efficiency whether it is S or B1 who is better off. If we ignore what it costs for S and B1 to locate B2, neither rule is more efficient than the other. If, however, it is assumed that it will cost B1 more than $10 to locate B2, then B1 will not spend that much to realize only $10 and B2 will not end up with the widget. Only if such costs, included in what are called "transaction costs," are ignored are the rules equally efficient.

   Even if B1 and B2 do not locate each other, B2 may still end up with the widget under a rule of specific performance. This is because it may be to B1's as well as S's advantage for B1 to renegotiate with S rather than to compel S to perform. If B1 compels S to perform and then does not locate B2, neither S nor B1 will realize any of the $10. But if B1 negotiates for S's release from the contract so that S can sell the widget to B2, S and B1 can share the $10. (Observe that, on this assumption, a rule of specific performance results in a sharing of the $10. The negotiations will determine the share that each gets, but the efficiency of the rule does not turn on this.) If we ignore what it costs for S and B1 to negotiate a release from the contract, neither a specific performance rule nor a damage rule is more efficient. If, however, it is assumed that it will cost more than $10 to negotiate a release under a specific performance rule, the parties will not spend that much to realize only $10, and B2 will not end up with the widget. Only if such costs, also included in what are called "transaction costs," are ignored are the rules equally efficient.

   Indeed, if transaction costs are ignored, a rule of specific performance is arguably more efficient than a rule of expectation damages. If courts systematically err in the calculation of expectation damages, the efficiency of the damage rule will suffer. If courts underestimate damages, parties will tend to break their contracts too often. If courts overestimate damages, parties will break them too infrequently. The efficiency of expectation damages is thus greater in situations in which such damages can be accurately estimated. Since the accuracy of estimation is generally greatest when there is a well-developed market on which the buyer can cover, the damage remedy is easiest to defend in situations in which there is a good cover market. Conversely, specific performance is most appealing in situations in which there is not a good cover market.

To return to the example of the widget, assuming that there is no cover market, the case for specific performance is enhanced if it will be easy for B1 and B2 to locate each other if S delivers the widget to B1. What does this suggest about the case of a cotton farmer's contract to sell cotton? Amoco's contract to sell propane? An art collector's contract to sell a Rembrandt painting? A landowner's contract to sell a country estate? A developer's contract to sell a house in a large development?

For a lively debate on the merits of specific performance, compare Kronman, Specific Performance, 45 U.Chi.L.Rev. 351 (1978) (arguing for the existing limitations), with Ulen, The Efficiency of Specific Performance: Toward a Unified Theory of Contract Remedies, 83 Mich.L.Rev. 341 (1984), and Schwartz, The Case for Specific Performance, 89 Yale L.J. 271 (1979) (both arguing for general availability of specific performance). For a summary of the debate and additional references, see Kornhauser, An Introduction to the Economic Analysis of Contract Remedies, 57 U.Colo.L.Rev. 683, 711–17 (1986). See also D. Laycock, The Death of the Irreparable Injury Rule (1991), reprinted in part in Laycock, The Death of the Irreparable Injury Rule, 103 Harv.L.Rev. 687 (1990) (arguing that specific performance is granted for reasons other than inadequacy of legal remedies).

————

HISTORICAL DEVELOPMENT OF EQUITABLE RELIEF [b]

The common law courts did not generally grant specific relief for breach of contract. The usual form of relief at common law was substitutional, and the typical judgment declared that the plaintiff recover from the defendant a sum of money. This, in effect, imposed a new obligation on the defendant for the breach of the old. This new obligation could be enforced even without cooperation on the defendant's part. If the sum was not paid, a writ of execution was issued, empowering the sheriff to seize and sell so much of the defendant's property as was required to pay the plaintiff. Of course if the promise was simply to pay a sum of money, the effect of such a judgment was to give the plaintiff specific relief. For example, if a seller had judgment for the price of goods delivered but not paid for, the seller had, in effect, specific relief. And occasionally specific relief was granted by means of proprietary actions, in which a party asserted rights as owner of the property concerned. For example, if a buyer was granted replevin of goods sold to him but not delivered, the sheriff would seize them from the seller and turn them over to the buyer, and the judgment would declare that the buyer was entitled to them. But these instances were exceptional, and even when the common law courts granted specific relief, they were unwilling to exert pressure directly on the defendant to compel performance. The judgment was seen as a mere declaration of rights as between the parties, and the process for its execution was directed, not at the defendant, but at the sheriff, ordering the sheriff to put the plaintiff in possession of real or personal property or to seize the defendant's property and sell so much of it as was necessary to satisfy a money judgment.

Promises were enforced in equity in a very different way. Under the influence of canon law—for the early chancellors were usually clerics—decrees in equity came to take the form of the chancellor's personal command to the defendant to do or not to do something. The defendant that disobeyed could be punished not only for criminal contempt, at the instance of the court, but also for civil contempt, at the instance of the plaintiff. This put into the plaintiff's hands the extreme sanction of imprisonment, which might be supplemented by fines payable to the plaintiff and by sequestration of the defendant's goods. So it was said that equity acted *in personam,* against the person of the defendant, while the law acted *in rem,* against the defendant's property. But it did not follow that the chancellor stood ready to order every defaulting promisor to perform its promise. Equitable relief was confined to special cases by both historical and practical limitations.

The most important historical limitation grew out of the circumstance that the chancellor had originally granted equitable relief in order to supply the deficiencies of the common law. Equitable remedies were therefore readily characterized as "extraordinary." When, during the long jurisdictional struggle between the two systems of courts, some means of accommodation was needed, an adequacy test was developed to prevent the chancellor from encroaching on the powers of the common law judges. Equity would stay its hand if the remedy of an award of damages at law was "adequate." To this test was added the gloss that damages were ordinarily adequate—a gloss encouraged by the philosophy of free enterprise with its confidence that a market economy ought to enable the injured party to arrange a substitute transaction. So English courts came to regard money damages as the norm and specific relief as the deviation. Only for land, which English courts regarded with particular esteem, was a general exception made, on the ground that each parcel of land was "unique" so money damages were inadequate. This strong preference of English courts for substitutional relief stands in sharp contrast to the preference of civil law systems, those derived from the Roman law, for specific relief.

A second historical limitation, or group of limitations, is based on the concept that equitable relief is discretionary. Since the chancellor was to act according to "conscience" (which prompted the notorious charge that his conscience might vary with the length of his foot), he might withhold relief if considerations of fairness or morality dictated. Gradually these equitable restrictions became more precise and hardened into rules. Some of the most renowned are embodied in equity's colorful maxims: "one who seeks equity must do equity"; "one who comes into equity must come with clean hands"; and "equity aids the vigilant." One of the most troublesome of these rules was the now discredited "mutuality of remedy" rule, under which the injured party's right to specific relief depended on whether it would have been available to the other party, had the breach been on the other side.

The practical limitations on specific relief in equity grew out of the problems inherent in coercing the defendant to perform its promise. In some cases, of course, specific relief does not require the defaulting promisor's cooperation. If, for example, the promise is to convey land, the court can transfer the title by virtue of its own decree, or it can be transferred by a deed executed by an officer of the court. But there is no such simple solution if the performance is personal in nature, and courts have bridled at coercing such performances. They will not, for example, compel a singer to perform a promise to sing, although they have been willing to order the singer not to act inconsistently with the promise, by enjoining the singer from singing elsewhere.[a] Courts have also been reluctant to order performance if difficulties of supervision or enforcement are foreseen, as may be the case under a building contract, especially if the absence of clear standards may lead to conflict and unfairness. Moreover, the practical exigencies of drafting decrees to guide future conduct under the threat of the severe sanctions available for contempt have moved courts to require that contract terms be expressed with greater certainty if specific relief is to be ordered than if damages are to be awarded.

Thus it came to be that, although the injured party can always claim damages for breach of contract, that party's right to specific relief as an alternative is much more limited. The historical development of parallel systems of law and equity may afford an adequate explanation for the reluctance of our courts to grant specific relief more widely, but it is scant justification for it. A more rational basis can today be found in the severity of the sanctions available for enforcement of equitable orders. Nevertheless, the modern trend is clearly in favor of the extension of specific relief at the expense of the traditional primacy of damages.

NOTES

(1) *The Game for Dough.* In recent decades the world of professional athletics has been more productive of litigation in this field than has the world of opera. (See Note, p. 34 above.) The availability of injunction has been enhanced by the belief that the requirement "that the player be an athlete of exceptional talent ... is met prima facie in cases involving professional athletes."[b] Nassau Sports v. Peters, 352 F.Supp. 870, 876 (E.D.N.Y.1972).

a. The classic case is Lumley v. Wagner, 42 Eng.Rep. 687 (Chancery 1952), in which the chancellor said: "It is true that I have not the means of compelling [an opera singer] to sing, but she has no cause of complaint if I compel her to abstain from the commission of an act which she has bound herself not to do, and thus possibly cause her to fulfil her engagement." See Vander-Velde, The Gendered Origins of the *Lumley* Doctrine: Binding Men's Consciences and Women's Fidelity, 101 Yale L.J. 775 (1993).

b. As one court admonished a quarterback, however, "some day your passes are going to wobble in the air, you are not going to find that receiver. If you keep ... jumping your contracts ... some day your abilities will be such that [your club] won't even send a twice disbarred attorney from Dogpatch to help you." Chicago Cardinals Football Club v. Etcheverry, (unreported) (D.N.M.1956), quoted in Detroit Football Co. v. Robinson, 186 F.Supp. 933 (E.D.La. 1960).

The requirement that "he who comes into equity must come with clean hands" has come under special scrutiny in these cases. Compare New York Football Giants, Inc. v. Los Angeles Chargers Football Club, Inc., 291 F.2d 471 (5th Cir.1961) (Giants, who had kept contract with Charles Flowers secret so he could play in Sugar Bowl, lacked "clean hands" and could not have Flowers enjoined from playing with Chargers), with Houston Oilers v. Neely, 361 F.2d 36 (10th Cir.), cert. denied, 385 U.S. 840 (1966) ("if the rule announced in [the Flowers] case was intended to apply to every instance in which a contract is entered into with a college football player before a post-season game with an understanding that it will be kept secret to permit that player to compete in the game, then we must respectfully disagree").

(2) *Problem.* Suppose that a buyer of cotton had come to you in 1973 and asked what its remedies were against a recalcitrant farmer under an enforceable contract like that described at the beginning of this section? What advice would you give?

In Mitchell–Huntley Cotton Co., Inc. v. Waldrep, 377 F.Supp. 1215 (N.D.Ala. 1974), the court granted a declaratory judgment that a buyer who was "in the business of buying cotton from producers and others and selling and delivering same to textile mills and others" was "entitled to specific performance" of its contracts with farmers and enjoined the farmers from violating them. "The cotton in question is unique and irreplaceable because of the scarcity of cotton.... The majority of all cotton to be produced in the United States in the 1973 crop year has been sold under contracts similar to those here at issue. There is no substantial carry-over of merchantable grades and classes of cotton from prior years in storage in the United States and there will be very little cotton available for purchase in the open market through the 1973 cotton season." Does it appear that the plaintiff's damage remedy was inadequate if, as the court found, "a drastic shortage of cotton developed and the price for same on the open market had increased [from an original contract price of $.30 per pound] to an amount in excess of $.80 per pound"?

For cases denying specific performance of cotton contracts, see Weathersby v. Gore, 556 F.2d 1247 (5th Cir.1977); Duval & Co. v. Malcom, 214 S.E.2d 356 (Ga.1975).

(3) *Reasons for Breach.* Why does a party fail to perform its promise? Why did Berkley? Dr. O'Connor? The Benkowskis? PepsiCo? Amoco Oil? Ask yourself the same question with respect to the cases in the next section of this chapter.

ARBITRATION

Arbitration is an alternative to the resolution of disputes in court. Typically, arbitration tribunals, commonly with one or three arbitrators, are temporarily established for each specific case. Procedure is more flexible and informal than judicial procedure and the arbitrators may give no reasons for their decisions.

Many institutions, notably trade associations and chambers of commerce, engage in the administration of arbitrations, including promulgation of rules of procedure and the appointment of arbitrators. Two of the most important of these are the International Chamber of Commerce in Paris and the American Arbitration Association in New York. In addition, the United Nations Commission on International Trade Law (UNCITRAL) has promulgated the UNCITRAL Arbitration Rules which, although unconnected with any administering institution, have found favor for international arbitrations including those of the Iran–United States Claims Tribunal in the Hague. In the United States, arbitration is the subject of both federal and state statutes.

Two kinds of issues that relate to this course arise in connection with arbitration. First, because arbitration is a process by which parties voluntarily refer their disputes to a special tribunal, an arbitration can validly take place only if the parties have agreed to use this method for the settlement of disputes. Whether the parties have so agreed is an issue that has an obvious relation to this course. It should be noted that when a court compels the parties to arbitrate it in effect orders specific performance of their agreement to arbitrate.

Second, because a decision by arbitrators is subject to only very limited review by a court,[a] arbitrators can sometimes reach decisions and give relief that a trial court cannot. The extent to which the rules that constrain a trial court when confronted with a contract dispute also apply in arbitration is another question related to this course. See generally I. Macneil, R. Speidel & T. Stipanowich, Federal Arbitration Law (looseleaf).

NOTES

(1) *AAA Standard Arbitration Clause.* The American Arbitration Association recommends the following arbitration clause for insertion in all commercial contracts:

> Any controversy or claim arising out of or relating to this contract, or the breach thereof, shall be settled by arbitration in accordance with the Commercial Arbitration Rules of the American Arbitration Association, and judgment upon the award rendered by the arbitrator(s) may be entered in any court having jurisdiction thereof.

It recommends a somewhat different clause for the submission of existing disputes.

(2) *More on the Slowdown in Steel.* Suppose that in the construction contract involved in the *Northern Delaware* case, above, Bliss and Phoenix had included the arbitration clause recommended by the American Arbitration Association. Rule 43 of the Commercial Arbitration Rules, entitled Scope of Award, provides:

> The arbitrator may grant any remedy or relief which the arbitrator deems just and equitable and within the scope of the agreement of the parties, including, but not limited to, specific performance of a contract. . . .

Would the court have enforced an arbitral award granting the relief that it refused in the actual case? See Grayson–Robinson Stores, Inc. v. Iris Constr. Corp., 168 N.E.2d 377 (N.Y.1960) (a 4–3 decision).

---

a. The federal courts have used the phrase "manifest disregard" of the law in this connection. Merrill Lynch, Pierce, Fenner & Smith v. Bobker, 808 F.2d 930 (2d Cir.1986).

(3) *More on the Whites and Benkowskis.* Suppose that in White v. Benkowski, above, the contract had included the arbitration clause recommended by the American Arbitration Association. Would the court have enforced an arbitration award granting the punitive damages that it held improper in the actual case? Compare Rodgers Builders, Inc. v. McQueen, 331 S.E.2d 726 (N.C.App.1985), with Garrity v. Lyle Stuart, Inc., 353 N.E.2d 793 (N.Y.1976), and see Mastrobuono v. Shearson Lehman Hutton, Inc., 115 S.Ct. 1212 (1995). See generally Farnsworth, Punitive Damages in Arbitration, 20 Stetson L.Rev. 395 (1991); Ware, Punitive Damages in Arbitration . . ., 63 Ford.L.Rev. 529 (1994).

————

CONTRACT REMEDIES IN PRACTICE

In providing for relief through damages, the law by and large assumes a frictionless system and ignores the cost to the claimant of obtaining that relief. It is, of course, true that, if successful, one may ordinarily recover one's rather modest court costs as well as damages and interest, and it is also true that both parties can avail themselves of machinery of justice that is largely paid for by others. But in contrast to the situation in many countries, including Great Britain, an award of costs does not traditionally include attorney's fees, and even those parties that win are left to pay their own lawyers, not to mention the many other costs, some monetary and some not, of litigation.

This helps to explain why, as we have already seen, business people often put little stock in the legal enforceability of agreements, and why so many disputes are settled out of court. Where the transaction is a substantial one between business people, the cost of litigation may not seem overwhelming in relation to the amount in dispute. But what of the typical consumer transaction in which the amount in dispute is likely to be much smaller, whether the aggrieved party is the merchant or the consumer?

The merchant is clearly in the better position to cope with this problem. The merchant has enough disputes to have them handled in bulk by specialists in collection. The merchant can provide for liquidated damages and for attorney's fees. The merchant engages the professionals who write the contract. The merchant may also be able to provide for security, e.g., by taking a deposit where goods have not been delivered or by preserving the right to repossess goods that have been delivered. Indeed, the law's concern is not that the merchant can do too little but too much.

That leaves the consumer. The consumer may not know a lawyer. The consumer adhered to the contract. The consumer could not have changed its terms or have even known what changes were desirable. The consumer may, depending on how trusting the merchant has been, be able to stop payment on a check or to refuse to pay for goods delivered on credit, but even here the consumer risks the onslaught of the merchant's specialists in collection. It is not that "The customer is always right." The customer is often wrong and sometimes a "deadbeat." The problem is that the consumer and the merchant stand on an unequal footing in attempting to show who is right.

A wide variety of solutions has been suggested and attempted in limited areas. One sort of solution is to "sweeten the pot" by increasing the successful consumer's recovery: by allowing a civil penalty, multiple (e.g., treble) damages, or attorney's fees. Another sort of solution is to give consumers support by having others subsidize their representation: by providing free or inexpensive legal services, by allowing them to join with claimants similarly situated in a class action, or by having a public agency handle the claim and distribute any recovery to the aggrieved consumers. Yet another sort of solution is to reduce the cost of litigation through special tribunals: by expanding the use of small claims courts or by instituting a system of arbitration. Since most of these solutions are essentially procedural, this is not the place to explore them in detail.

NOTES

(1) *Attorney's Fees.* Because the party that wins a lawsuit is usually not allowed to recover its attorney's fees from the losing party, contracts often provide for recovery by the winning party of its fees. A simple provision for attorney's fees will be sustained as the basis for an award of such fees as may be reasonable.

(2) *The "Work of the Law Machine at the Margin."* Professor Karl Llewellyn [a] concluded "that the real major effect of law will be found not so much in the cases in which law officials actually intervene, nor yet in those in which such intervention is consciously contemplated as a possibility, but rather in contributing to, strengthening, stiffening attitudes toward performance as what is to be expected and what 'is done'.... This work of the law machine at the margin, in helping keep the level of social practice and expectation up to where it is, as against slow canker, is probably the most vital single aspect of contract law. For in this aspect each hospital case is a case with significance for the hundreds of thousands of normal cases." Llewellyn, What Price Contract?—An Essay in Perspective, 40 Yale L.J. 704, 725 n. 47 (1931). For a discussion of the nonlegal sanctions that may encourage promisors to keep their promises, see Charny, Nonlegal Sanctions in Commercial Relationships, 104 Harv.L.Rev. 373 (1990).

SECTION 2. CONSIDERATION AS A BASIS FOR ENFORCEMENT

What promises will the law enforce? The answer to this question under early English law was closely tied to the common law actions of

a. Karl Nickerson Llewellyn (1893–1962) practiced law in New York for two years, and taught law at Yale for several years before becoming a member of the law faculty at Columbia in 1925, where he remained until he joined the law faculty at Chicago in 1951. He was well-known for his contributions to the field of jurisprudence, as one of the school of "legal realists," and also to the fields of commercial law and contracts. He was Chief Reporter of the Uniform Commercial Code, and the author of many books, including The Bramble Bush: On Our Law and Its Study, which was written especially for first-year law students.

covenant, debt and assumpsit, and even today no adequate answer can ignore this aspect of legal history.

The first of these actions, covenant, was used to enforce contracts made under seal. Once a written promise was sealed and delivered, the action of covenant was available to enforce it, and it made no difference whether the promisor had bargained for or received anything in exchange for the promise, or whether the promisee had in any way changed position in reliance on it. In medieval England, the seal was a piece of wax affixed to the document and bearing an impression identifying the person who had executed it. At first its use was confined to the nobility, but later it spread to the commonalty. With the growth of literacy and the use of the personal signature as a means of authentication, the requirement of formality was so eroded that a seal could consist of any written or printed symbol intended to serve as a seal. The word "Seal" and the letters "L.S." (*locus sigilli*) were commonly used for this purpose.

Two functions performed by such legal formalities as the seal have been described by Professor Lon Fuller [a] as "evidentiary," that is, providing trustworthy evidence of the existence and terms of the contract in the event of controversy, and "cautionary," that is, bringing home to the parties the significance of their acts—inducing "the circumspective frame of mind appropriate in one pledging his future." Fuller, Anatomy of the Law 36–37 (1968); Fuller, Consideration and Form, 41 Colum.L.Rev. 799, 800 (1941). With the erosion of the solemnity of the seal, it became doubtful that it performed either of these functions well. Consequently, the distinctive effect of the seal on the enforceability of promises has been abolished in roughly half of the states of the United States and seriously curtailed in the rest. The most recent of these assaults on the seal came in UCC 2–203, which, in the words of its draftsmen, "makes it clear that every effect of the seal which relates to 'sealed instruments' as such is wiped out insofar as contracts for sale are concerned." (Comment 1 to UCC 2–203). Where the seal still retains some effect, it is often limited to raising a rebuttable presumption of consideration or making applicable a longer period of limitations. A survey of the laws on the seal in the various states is contained in the Statutory Note at the beginning of Chapter 4, Topic 3, of the Restatement Second.

The second of the three actions, that of debt, could be used to enforce some types of unsealed promises to pay a definite sum of money, including a promise to repay money that had been loaned and a promise to pay for goods that had been delivered or for work that had been done.

a. Lon L. Fuller (1902–1978) had a long teaching career at Oregon, Illinois, Duke and, for the last three decades, at Harvard, where he taught contracts and jurisprudence. In philosophical works he presented alternatives to positivist attitudes toward law, sometimes using partly-fanciful cases in imaginary and contrasting opinions. See, e.g., Fuller, The Case of the Speluncean Explorers, 62 Harv.L.Rev. 616 (1949). His article, with one of his students, on the reliance interest in contracts prompted an extensive reexamination of the remedial side of the subject. See Note, p. 103 below.

Since these were situations in which the contemplated exchange was completed on one side, they appealed to the primitive notion that the promisor (or debtor) had something belonging to the promisee (or creditor) that the former ought to surrender. The proprietary element present in this notion is reflected in the popular expression that the depositor who is owed money by a bank *"has* money in the bank." What the promisee had given the promisor was sometimes called the *"quid pro quo"* and, as the underlying principles of contract law developed, the promisor's obligation in debt was considered to rest upon receipt of a *benefit* from the promisee.

The third and ultimately the most important action, assumpsit, grew out of cases in which the promisee sought to recover damages for physical injury to person or property on the basis of a consensual undertaking. In one such case a ferryman who undertook to carry the plaintiff's horse across a river was held liable when he overloaded the boat and the horse drowned. In another a carpenter who undertook to build the plaintiff a house was held liable when he did so unskillfully. The underlying theme of these decisions was that of misfeasance—the promisor, having undertaken (*assumpsit*) to do something, had done it in a manner inconsistent with that undertaking to the detriment of the promisee. The decisions did not go so far as to impose liability for nonfeasance—where the promisor had done *nothing* in pursuance of the undertaking—for example, where the carpenter in the case just put had failed to build the house at all. It was not until the latter half of the fifteenth century that the common law courts began to make this extension. When they did, they imposed a requirement, analogous to that in the misfeasance cases, that the promisee must have incurred a *detriment* in reliance on the promise—as where the owner had changed position by selling an old house in reliance on the carpenter's promise to build a new one.

Finally, by the end of the sixteenth century, the courts made a second major extension of the action of assumpsit and held that a party that had given only a promise in exchange for the other's promise had incurred a detriment by having its freedom of action fettered, since it was bound in turn by its own promise. By this circular argument, the common law courts began to enforce exchanges of promises. Here is the opinion in what is said to be the earliest case recognizing that a promise, not even partly performed, could be consideration for a return promise:

> Note, That a promise against a promise will maintain an action upon the case, as in consideration that you do give me £10 on such a day, I promise to give you £10 such a day after.

Strangborough v. Warner, 4 Leo. 3 (Queen's Bench 1588). See Holdsworth, Debt, Assumpsit and Consideration, 11 Mich.L.Rev. 347, 351 (1913).

Eventually, for reasons that need not be gone into here, the action of assumpsit was allowed to supplant that of debt for the enforcement of promises that would previously have been enforced in the latter action. Thus, by the beginning of the seventeenth century, the common law courts had succeeded in developing the action of assumpsit as a general basis for the enforcement of promises. By the same time, the term "consideration" had come to be used as a word of art to express the sum of the conditions necessary for such an action to lie. It was therefore a tautology that a promise, if not under seal, was enforceable only where there was "consideration," for this was to say no more than that it was enforceable only where the action of assumpsit would lie. Bound up in the concept of consideration were several elements. Most important, from the *quid pro quo* of debt came the idea that there must have been an exchange arrived at by way of bargain. To the extent that debt inspired the concept of consideration, there was the notion that there must be a *benefit* to the promisor. To the extent that assumpsit inspired it, there was the notion that there must be a *detriment* to the promisee. *EITHER* The interplay of these elements can be judged from the cases that follow and from Restatement Second § 71. They lend at least some support to the claim of the English legal historian, F.W. Maitland, that "The forms of action we have buried, but they still rule us from their graves." Maitland, The Forms of Action at Common Law 2 (1936 ed.). For a thorough treatment of this historical background, see A.W.B. Simpson, A History of the Common Law of Contract (1975). See also P. Atiyah, The Rise and Fall of Freedom of Contract (1979); Farnsworth, The Past of Promise: An Historical Introduction to Contract, 69 Colum.L.Rev. 576 (1969).

NOTE

Pace of Development. How could England have reached the end of the sixteenth century before giving, in Strangborough v. Warner, legal recognition to exchanges of promises that were not partly performed? Apparently this development was even slower in coming in America. According to one legal historian, "the primitive state of eighteenth century American contract law is underscored by the surprising fact that some American courts did not enforce executory contracts where there had been no part performance.... The pressure to enforce such contracts would not be great in a pre-market economy where contracts for future delivery were rare...." Horwitz, The Historical Foundations of Modern Contract Law, 87 Harv.L.Rev. 917, 929–30 (1974), reprinted in M. Horwitz, The Transformation of American Law, 1780–1860, 169 (1977). See generally 1 Farnsworth §§ 1.5, 1.6.

Restatement 2nd 71

HAMER v. SIDWAY

Court of Appeals of New York, 1891.
124 N.Y. 538, 27 N.E. 256.

Appeal from an order of the general term of the supreme court in the fourth judicial department, reversing a judgment entered on the decision of the court at special term in the county clerk's office of Chemung county on the 1st day of October, 1889. The plaintiff presented a claim to the executor of William E. Story, Sr., for $5,000 and interest from the 6th day of February, 1875. She acquired it through several mesne assignments from William E. Story, 2d. The claim being rejected by the executor, this action was brought.

It appears that William E. Story, Sr., was the uncle of William E. Story, 2d; that at the celebration of the golden wedding of Samuel Story and wife, father and mother of William E. Story, Sr., on the 20th day of March, 1869, in the presence of the family and invited guests, he promised his nephew that if he would refrain from drinking, using tobacco, swearing, and playing cards or billiards for money until he became 21 years of age, he would pay him the sum of $5,000. The nephew assented thereto, and fully performed the conditions inducing the promise. When the nephew arrived at the age of 21 years, and on the 31st day of January, 1875, he wrote to his uncle, informing him that he had performed his part of the agreement, and had thereby become entitled to the sum of $5,000. The uncle received the letter, and a few days later, and on the 6th day of February, he wrote and mailed to his nephew the following letter:

Buffalo, Feb. 6, 1875.

"W.E. STORY, JR.:

"DEAR NEPHEW—Your letter of the 31st ult. came to hand all right, saying that you had lived up to the promise made to me several years ago. I have no doubt but you have, for which you shall have five thousand dollars as I promised you. I had the money in the bank the day you was 21 years old that I intend for you, and you shall have the money certain. Now, Willie, I do not intend to interfere with this money in any way till I think you are capable of taking care of it and the sooner that time comes the better it will please me. I would hate very much to have you start out in some adventure that you thought all right and lose this money in one year. The first five thousand dollars that I got together cost me a heap of hard work.... It did not come to me in any mysterious way, and the reason I speak of this is that money got in this way stops longer with a fellow that gets it with hard knocks than it does when he finds it. Willie, you are 21 and you have many a thing to learn yet. This money you have earned much easier than I did besides acquiring good habits at the same time and you are quite welcome to the money; hope you will make good use of it. I was ten long years getting this together after I was your age. Now, hoping this will be satisfactory, I stop....

Truly Yours,
"W.E. STORY.

"P.S.—You can consider this money on interest."

The nephew received the letter and thereafter consented that the money should remain with his uncle in accordance with the terms and conditions of the letters. The uncle died on the 29th day of January,

1887, without having paid over to his nephew any portion of the said $5,000 and interest.[a]

PARKER, J. The question which provoked the most discussion by counsel on this appeal, and which lies at the foundation of plaintiff's asserted right of recovery, is whether by virtue of a contract defendant's testator William S. Story became indebted to his nephew William E. Story, 2d, on his twenty-first birthday in the sum of five thousand dollars. The trial court found as a fact that "on the 20th day of March, 1869, ... William E. Story agreed to and with William E. Story, 2d, that if he would refrain from drinking liquor, using tobacco, swearing, and playing cards or billiards for money until he should become 21 years of age, then he, the said William E. Story, would at that time pay him, the said William E. Story, 2d, the sum of $5000 for such refraining, to which the said William E. Story, 2d, agreed," and that he "in all things fully performed his part of said agreement."

The defendant contends that the contract was without consideration to support it, and, therefore, invalid. He asserts that the promisee by refraining from the use of liquor and tobacco was not harmed but benefited; that that which he did was best for him to do independently of his uncle's promise, and insists that it follows that unless the promisor was benefited, the contract was without consideration, a contention which, if well founded, would seem to leave open for controversy in many cases whether that which the promisee did or omitted to do was, in fact, of such benefit to him as to leave no consideration to support the enforcement of the promisor's agreement. Such a rule could not be tolerated, and is without foundation in the law. The Exchequer Chamber, in 1875, defined consideration as follows: "A valuable consideration in the sense of the law may consist either in some right, interest, profit, or benefit accruing to the one party, or some forbearance, detriment, loss, or responsibility given, suffered, or undertaken by the other." Courts "will not ask whether the thing which forms the consideration does in fact benefit the promisee or a third party, or is of any substantial value to any one. It is enough that something is promised, done, forborne, or suffered by the party to whom the promise is made as consideration for the promise made to him." Anson's Prin. of Con. 63.

"In general, a waiver of any legal right at the request of another party is a sufficient consideration for a promise." Parsons on Contracts, 444.

a. The opinion of the Supreme Court, from which this appeal was taken, recites further interesting facts: the uncle had long planned to make a gift of $5,000 to young William; the uncle later loaned $2,500 to William, who went into bankruptcy along with his father and listed no claim against his uncle among his assets; the uncle subsequently gave $11,000 worth of goods to William and his father, taking promissory notes and a general release from both that was broad enough to cover this claim; but it was claimed by the plaintiff on trial that, prior to William's bankruptcy, he had already assigned the $5,000 claim to his wife, so that it was no longer one of his assets and was not later affected by the release. See Hamer v. Sidway, 64 N.Y.Sup. Ct. (57 Hun.) 229, 11 N.Y.S. 182 (1890).

"Any damage, or suspension or forbearance of a right, will be sufficient to sustain a promise." Kent, Vol. 2, 465, 12th Ed.[b]

Pollock, in his work on contracts, page 166, after citing the definition given by the Exchequer Chamber already quoted, says: "The second branch of this judicial description is really the most important one. Consideration means not so much that one party is profiting as that the other abandons some legal right in the present or limits his legal freedom of action in the future as an inducement for the promise of the first."

Now, applying this rule to the facts before us, the promisee used tobacco, occasionally drank liquor, and he had a legal right to do so.[c] That right he abandoned for a period of years upon the strength of the promise of the testator that for such forbearance he would give him $5000. We need not speculate on the effort which may have been required to give up the use of those stimulants. It is sufficient that he restricted his lawful freedom of action within certain prescribed limits upon the faith of his uncle's agreement, and now having fully performed the conditions imposed, it is of no moment whether such performance actually proved a benefit to the promisor, and the court will not inquire into it, but were it a proper subject of inquiry, we see nothing in this record that would permit a determination that the uncle was not benefited in a legal sense. Few cases have been found which may be said to be precisely in point, but such as have been support the position we have taken.

In Shadwell v. Shadwell, 9 C.B.N.S. 159, an uncle wrote to his nephew as follows:

"MY DEAR LANCEY—I am so glad to hear of your intended marriage with Ellen Nicholl, and as I promised to assist you at starting, I am happy to tell you that I will pay you 150 pounds yearly during my life and until your annual income derived from your profession of a chancery barrister shall amount to 600 guineas, of which your own admission will be the only evidence that I shall require.

"Your affectionate uncle,
"CHARLES SHADWELL."

b. James Kent (1763–1847) began practice after three years as an apprentice and was active in Federalist politics. Hamilton introduced him to the writings of European authors on the civil law, which were to influence his later work. In 1793, largely through his Federalist connections, he was made Professor of Law in Columbia College. He attracted few students, and soon resigned to become a judge on the New York Supreme Court, then the highest court in the state. In 1814 he became Chancellor. Upon his retirement in 1823, he lectured again at Columbia for three years. Out of these lectures grew the "Commentaries on American Law," in four volumes, which became the most important American law book of the century. (It is the source of the quotation above.) Kent lived to prepare six editions; subsequent ones were revised by others. For his work on the Court of Chancery, he has been called the creator of equity in the United States.

c. The opinion of the trial court, which is unreported, adds that he "on one occasion ... refused to use the same when suffering from fever and ague in the West."

It was held that the promise was binding and made upon good consideration.

In Lakota v. Newton, an unreported case in the Superior Court of Worcester, Mass., the complaint averred defendant's promise that "if you (meaning plaintiff) will leave off drinking for a year I will give you $100," plaintiff's assent thereto, performance of the condition by him, and demanded judgment therefor. Defendant demurred on the ground, among others, that the plaintiff's declaration did not allege a valid and sufficient consideration for the agreement of the defendant. The demurrer was overruled.

In Talbott v. Stemmons, 89 Ky. 222, the step-grandmother of the plaintiff made with him the following agreement: "I do promise and bind myself to give my grandson, Albert R. Talbott, $500 at my death, if he will never take another chew of tobacco or smoke another cigar during my life from this date up to my death, and if he breaks this pledge he is to refund double the amount to his mother." The executor of Mrs. Stemmons demurred to the complaint on the ground that the agreement was not based on a sufficient consideration. The demurrer was sustained and an appeal taken therefrom to the Court of Appeals, where the decision of the court below was reversed. In the opinion of the court it is said that "the right to use and enjoy the use of tobacco was a right that belonged to the plaintiff and not forbidden by law. The abandonment of its use may have saved him money or contributed to his health; nevertheless, the surrender of that right caused the promise, and having the right to contract with reference to the subject-matter, the abandonment of the use was a sufficient consideration to uphold the promise." Abstinence from the use of intoxicating liquors was held to furnish a good consideration for a promissory note in Lindell v. Rokes, 60 Mo. 249. The cases cited by the defendant on this question are not in point. . . .

[In an omitted part of the opinion the court held that the action was not barred by the statute of limitations because under the uncle's letter he held the money in trust and not merely as a debtor.] Order reversed and judgment of special term affirmed.

NOTES

(1) *Benefit and Detriment.* On what ground did the Court of Appeals hold that the uncle's promise was enforceable? Under the finding of the trial court, what was the consideration for that promise? Was the consideration arguably a benefit to the uncle? A detriment to the nephew? Did the Court of Appeals conclude that it was a benefit or a detriment? Did the circumstances under which the promise was made and the fact that it was reaffirmed play any role in that court's thinking?

(2) *"Bargain Theory" of Consideration.* What role do benefit and detriment play under Restatement Second §§ 71, 79? Was there consideration for the uncle's promise under the Restatement Second? Holmes,[d] an early advocate of

d. Oliver Wendell Holmes (1841–1935) practiced law in Boston, served briefly as professor of law at Harvard, and then for twenty years as justice and later chief jus-

the "bargain theory" of consideration espoused by the Restatement, spoke of the "reciprocal conventional inducement": "It is said that consideration must not be confounded with motive. It is true that it must not be confounded with what may be the prevailing or chief motive in actual fact. A man may promise to paint a picture for five hundred dollars, while his chief motive may be a desire for fame. A consideration may be given and accepted, in fact, solely for the purpose of making a promise binding. But, nevertheless, it is the essence of a consideration, that, by the terms of the agreement, it is given and accepted as the motive or inducement of the promise. Conversely, the promise must be made and accepted as the conventional motive or inducement for furnishing the consideration. The root of the whole matter is the relation of reciprocal conventional inducement, each for the other, between consideration and promise." O.W. Holmes, The Common Law 293–94 (1881). "[T]he promise and the consideration must purport to be the motive each for the other, in whole or at least in part. It is not enough that the promise induces the detriment or that the detriment induces the promise if the other half is wanting." Holmes, J., in Wisconsin & Michigan Railway Co. v. Powers, 191 U.S. 379 (1903). Compare Restatement Second § 71(2) with § 81(1).

(3) *"Sufficiency" of Consideration.* The term "sufficient consideration" appears at several points in Hamer v. Sidway. The first Restatement embodied a concept of the "sufficiency" of consideration. Although consideration did not have to be "adequate," it had to be "sufficient." See first Restatement §§ 76–81. The Restatement Second abandons this concept. Under its terminology the question is simply whether there is "consideration," with no qualifying adjective. See Restatement Second § 79.

(4) *Problem.* Thomas Hurley has worked as general superintendent for Marine Contractors for eight years, during which time Marine has made annual payments into an Employee Retirement Plan and Trust Fund, a legally separate entity whose sole trustee is also the president of Marine. Hurley now plans to leave Marine, and is entitled under the terms of the trust to payment of his vested share after a five year waiting period. Marine wants Hurley to make a binding promise to Marine not to compete with it after he leaves its employ. In return, Marine's president, as trustee, is willing to have the trust pay Hurley his vested share immediately. Will payment by the trust to Hurley be consideration for Hurley's promise to Marine? Does the answer depend on whether you are looking for a benefit, a detriment or a bargain? See Marine Contractors Co., Inc. v. Hurley, 310 N.E.2d 915 (Mass.1974).

GRATUITOUS PROMISES

Suppose that the uncle had given the nephew $5,000 in cash at the golden wedding anniversary and had told him that it was a gift which he could keep on condition that he refrained from drinking, smoking, swearing and gambling until he was twenty-one. Surely the nephew, having met the condition, could have kept the money if the uncle's executor had attempted to get it back. Why, if the law recognizes

tice of the Supreme Judicial Court of Massachusetts. In 1902 he was appointed an associate justice of the United States Supreme Court, where the quality of his dissenting opinions won him the title of the "Great Dissenter." He resigned because of his great age in 1932. His most famous work is The Common Law (1881), based on a series of lectures.

gratuitous transfers, should it not recognize gratuitous promises? Why did the court have to find that there was consideration? Is it arguable that gratuitous promises serve no useful economic function? That they raise dangers as to proof? What sorts of rules would you suggest if it were thought desirable to enable promisors, in appropriate cases, to make enforceable gratuitous promises? To what extent should those rules take account of such factors as the promisor's motives, the social utility of the promise, the formality with which it was made, and the availability of alternative means of making gifts? These questions will be considered again in Section 5, in connection with reform of the doctrine of consideration.

Every human society relies to some extent upon cooperation among its members to achieve social purposes. To what extent do the notion of consideration and the resulting unenforceability of gratuitous promises comport with the view that this cooperation can best be achieved by a system of "free enterprise"? Consider in this regard, and in connection with the following cases, these words of Adam Smith, written in 1776: "[M]an has almost constant occasion for the help of his brethren, and it is vain for him to expect it from their benevolence only. He will be more likely to prevail if he can interest their self-love in his favour, and shew them that it is for their own advantage to do for him what he requires of them. Whoever offers to another a bargain of any kind, proposes to do this: Give me that which I want, and you shall have this which you want, is the meaning of every such offer; and it is in this manner that we obtain from one another the far greater part of those good offices which we stand in need of.... We address ourselves, not to their humanity but to their self-love, and never talk to them of our own necessities but of their advantages. Nobody but a beggar chooses to depend chiefly upon the benevolence of his fellow-citizens." A. Smith, An Inquiry into the Nature and Causes of the Wealth of Nations 11 (1811 ed., bk. 1, ch. II). Is it significant that a bargained-for exchange may serve the function of coordinating the use of economic resources, while a gratuitous promise merely changes the distribution of wealth?

NOTES

(1) *Economics of Gratuitous Promises.* In an analysis of the economics of gratuitous promises, Professor (now Judge) Richard Posner asked why "economic man" would ever make a promise without receiving in exchange something of value from the promisee. He answered that "a gratuitous promise, to the extent it actually commits the promisor to the promised course of action ..., creates utility for the promisor over and above the utility to him of the promised performance ... by increasing the present value of an uncertain future stream of transfer payments.

"To illustrate, suppose A promises to give $1000 a year for the next 20 years to the B symphony orchestra. The value of the gift to B is the discounted present value of $1000 to be paid yearly over a 20–year period in the future. Among the factors that will be used by B in discounting these expected future receipts to present value is the likelihood that at some time during the 20–year period A will discontinue the annual payments. Depending on B's estimation of A's fickleness, income prospects, etc., the present value of the gift of $1000 a year may be quite small; it may not be much more than $1000. But suppose the gift is actually worth more to B because A is certain to continue the payments throughout the entire period, though this fact is not known to B. If A can make a binding promise to continue the payments in accordance with his intention, B will revalue the gift at its true present worth. The size of the gift (in present-value terms) will be increased at no cost to A. Here is a clear case where the enforcement of a gratuitous promise would increase net social welfare.

"This can be seen even more clearly by considering A's alternatives if his promise is not enforceable. One possibility would be for A to promise a larger gift, the discounted value of which to B would equal the true value as known to A. The higher cost of the gift to A would be a measure of the social cost of the unenforceability of his promise. Another possibility would be for A to substitute for the promised series of future transfers a one-time transfer the present value of which would be the same as that of the series of enforceable future transfers. However, the fact that A preferred making a future gift to a present one suggests that they are not perfect substitutes; there are many reasons (including tax and liquidity considerations) why they might not be. Consequently, if A cannot bind himself to make a series of future gifts, he may be led to substitute a one-time transfer, the present value of which is less than that of the series of future gifts, although greater than that of a declared but unenforceable intention to make a series of future gifts. Thus, non-enforceability of gratuitous promises could tend to bias transfers excessively toward immediacy." [a] Posner, Gratuitous Promises in Economics and Law, 6 J. Legal Stud. 411, 411–13 (1977), reprinted in A. Kronman & R. Posner, The Economics of Contract Law 46–47 (1979). See generally Eisenberg, Donative Promises, 47 U.Chi.L.Rev. 1 (1979); Kull, Reconsidering Gratuitous Promises, 21 J. Legal Stud. 39 (1992); Shavell, An Economic Analysis of Altruism and Deferred Gifts, 20 J.Legal Stud. 401 (1991).

(2) *Consideration as Form.* Under the bargain theory of consideration, can a gratuitous promise be made enforceable by a mere token payment, arranged by the parties for the sole purpose of satisfying the requirement of consideration? Holmes concluded that since courts would not in general "inquire into the amount of such consideration ..., consideration is as much a form as a seal." Krell v. Codman, 28 N.E. 578 (Mass.1891). (The term "peppercorn" is often used to deride consideration that is of trifling value.) Will such a device be given effect?

There is some authority, most of it old, that it will be. E.g., Thomas v. Thomas, 2 Q.B. 851, 114 Eng.Rep. 330 (1842). Illustration 1 to the first Restatement § 84 reads:

> A wishes to make a binding promise to his son B to convey to B Blackacre, which is worth $5,000. Being advised that a gratuitous promise is not binding, A writes to B an offer to sell Blackacre for $1. B accepts. B's promise to pay $1 is sufficient consideration.

The Restatement Second takes the opposite view. Illustration 5 to § 71 reads:

> A desires to make a binding promise to give $1,000 to his son B. Being advised that a gratuitous promise is not binding, A offers to buy from B for $1,000 a book worth less than $1. B accepts the offer knowing that the purchase of the book is a mere pretense. There is no consideration for A's promise to pay $1,000.

a. Copyright © 1977 by the University   All rights reserved.
of Chicago and reproduced with permission.

For a case in support of this illustration, see Fischer v. Union Trust Co., 101 N.W. 852 (Mich.1904).

FIEGE v. BOEHM

Court of Appeals of Maryland, 1956.
210 Md. 352, 123 A.2d 316.

DELAPLAINE, JUDGE. This suit was brought in the Superior Court of Baltimore City by Hilda Louise Boehm against Louis Gail Fiege to recover for breach of a contract to pay the expenses incident to the birth of his bastard child and to provide for its support upon condition that she would refrain from prosecuting him for bastardy.

Plaintiff alleged in her declaration substantially as follows: (1) that early in 1951 defendant had sexual intercourse with her although she was unmarried, and as a result thereof she became pregnant, and defendant acknowledged that he was responsible for her pregnancy; (2) that on September 29, 1951, she gave birth to a female child; that defendant is the father of the child; and that he acknowledged on many occasions that he is its father; (3) that before the child was born, defendant agreed to pay all her medical and miscellaneous expenses and to compensate her for the loss of her salary caused by the child's birth, and also to pay her ten dollars per week for its support until it reached the age of 21, upon condition that she would not institute bastardy proceedings against him as long as he made the payments in accordance with the agreement; (4) that she placed the child for adoption on July 13, 1954, and she claimed the following sums: Union Memorial Hospital, $110; Florence Crittenton Home, $100; Dr. George Merrill, her physician, $50; medicines $70.35; miscellaneous expenses, $20.45; loss of earnings for 26 weeks, $1,105; support of the child, $1,440; total, $2,895.80; and (5) that defendant paid her only $480, and she demanded that he pay her the further sum of $2,415.80, the balance due under the agreement, but he failed and refused to pay the same.

Defendant demurred to the declaration on the ground that it failed to allege that in September, 1953, plaintiff instituted bastardy proceedings against him in the Criminal Court of Baltimore, but since it had been found from blood tests that he could not have been the father of the child, he was acquitted of bastardy.[b] The Court sustained the demurrer with leave to amend.

Plaintiff then filed an amended declaration, which contained the additional allegation that, after the breach of the agreement by defendant, she filed a charge with the State's Attorney that defendant was the father of her bastard child; and that on October 8, 1953, the Criminal Court found defendant not guilty solely on a physician's testimony that "on the basis of certain blood tests made, the defendant can be excluded

b. Such a demurrer was known at com-   mon law as a "speaking demurrer."

as the father of the said child, which testimony is not conclusive upon a jury in a trial court."

Defendant also demurred to the amended declaration, but the Court overruled that demurrer.

Plaintiff, a typist, now over 35 years old, who has been employed by the Government in Washington and Baltimore for over thirteen years, testified in the Court below that she had never been married, but that at about midnight on January 21, 1951, defendant, after taking her to a moving picture theater on York Road and then to a restaurant, had sexual intercourse with her in his automobile. She further testified that he agreed to pay all her medical and hospital expenses, to compensate her for loss of salary caused by the pregnancy and birth, and to pay her ten dollars per week for the support of the child upon condition that she would refrain from instituting bastardy proceedings against him. She further testified that between September 17, 1951, and May, 1953, defendant paid her a total of $480.

Defendant admitted that he had taken plaintiff to restaurants, had danced with her several times, had taken her to Washington, and had brought her home in the country; but he asserted that he had never had sexual intercourse with her. He also claimed that he did not enter into any agreement with her. He admitted, however, that he had paid her a total of $480. His father also testified that he stated "that he did not want his mother to know, and if it were just kept quiet, kept principally away from his mother and the public and the courts, that he would take care of it."

Defendant further testified that in May 1953, he went to see plaintiff's physician to make inquiry about blood tests to show the paternity of the child; and that those tests were made and they indicated that it was not possible that he could have been the child's father. He then stopped making payments. Plaintiff thereupon filed a charge of bastardy with the State's Attorney.

The testimony which was given in the Criminal Court by Dr. Milton Sachs, hematologist at the University Hospital, was read to the jury in the Superior Court. In recent years the blood-grouping test has been employed in criminology, in the selection of donors for blood transfusions, and as evidence in paternity cases. The Landsteiner blood-grouping test is based on the medical theory that the red corpuscles in human blood contain two affirmative agglutinating substances, and that every individual's blood falls into one of the four classes and remains the same throughout life. According to Mendel's law of inheritance, this blood individuality is an hereditary characteristic which passes from parent to child, and no agglutinating substance can appear in the blood of a child which is not present in the blood of one of its parents. The four Landsteiner blood groups, designated as AB, A, B, and O, into which human blood is divided on the basis of the compatibility of the corpuscles and serum with the corpuscles and serum of other persons, are characterized by different combinations of two agglutinogens in the red blood cells and two agglutinins in the serum. Dr. Sachs reported that Fiege's blood group was Type O, Miss Boehm's was Type B, and the infant's was Type A. He further testified that on the basis of these tests, Fiege could not have been the father of the child, as it is impossible for a mating of Type O and Type B to result in a child of Type A.

Although defendant was acquitted by the Criminal Court, the Superior Court overruled his motion for a directed verdict. In the charge to the jury the Court instructed them that defendant's acquittal in the Criminal Court was not binding upon them. The jury found a verdict in favor of plaintiff for $2,415.80, the full amount of her claim.

Defendant filed a motion for judgment n.o.v. or a new trial. The Court overruled that motion also, and entered judgment on the verdict of the jury. Defendant appealed from that judgment.

Defendant contends that, even if he entered into the contract as alleged, it was not enforceable, because plaintiff's forbearance to prosecute was not based on a valid claim, and hence the contract was without consideration. . . .

It was originally held at common law that a child born out of wedlock is *filius nullius,* and a putative father is not under any legal liability to contribute to the support of his illegitimate child, and his promise to do so is unenforceable because it is based on purely a moral obligation. . . .

However, where statutes are in force to compel the father of a bastard to contribute to its support, the courts have invariably held that a contract by the putative father with the mother of his bastard child to provide for the support of the child upon the agreement of the mother to refrain from invoking the bastardy statute against the father, or to abandon proceedings already commenced, is supported by sufficient consideration. Jangraw v. Perkins, 77 Vt. 375, 60 A. 385; Beach v. Voegtlen, 68 N.J.L. 472, 53 A. 695; Thayer v. Thayer, 189 N.C. 502, 127 S.E. 553, 39 A.L.R. 428.

In Maryland it is now provided by statute that whenever a person is found guilty of bastardy, the court shall issue an order directing such person (1) to pay for the maintenance and support of the child until it reaches the age of eighteen years, such sum as may be agreed upon, if consent proceedings be had, or in the absence of agreement, such sum as the court may fix, with due regard to the circumstances of the accused person; and (2) to give bond to the State of Maryland in such penalty as the court may fix, with good and sufficient securities, conditioned on making the payments required by the court's order, or any amendments thereof. Failure to give such bond shall be punished by commitment in the jail or the House of Correction until bond is given but not exceeding two years. Code Supp.1955, art. 12, § 8.

Prosecutions for bastardy are treated in Maryland as criminal proceedings, but they are actually civil in purpose. . . . Accordingly a contract by the putative father of an illegitimate child to provide for its support upon condition that bastardy proceedings will not be instituted is a compromise of civil injuries resulting from a criminal act, and not a contract to compound a criminal prosecution, and if it is fair and reasonable, it is in accord with the Bastardy Act and the public policy of the State. [c]

Of course, a contract of a putative father to provide for the support of his illegitimate child must be based, like any other contract, upon sufficient consideration....

In 1867 the Maryland Court of Appeals, in the opinion delivered by Judge Bartol in Hartle v. Stahl, 27 Md. 157, 172, held: (1) that forbearance to assert a claim before institution of suit, if not in fact a legal claim, is not of itself sufficient consideration to support a promise; but (2) that a compromise of a doubtful claim or a relinquishment of a pending suit is good consideration for a promise; and (3) that in order to support a compromise, it is sufficient that the parties entering into it thought at the time that there was a *bona fide* question between them, although it may eventually be found that there was in fact no such question.

We have thus adopted the rule that the surrender of, or forbearance to assert an invalid claim by one who has not an honest and reasonable belief in its possible validity is not sufficient consideration for a contract. 1 Restatement, Contracts, sec. 76(b). We combine the subjective requisite that the claim be *bona fide* with the objective requisite that it must have a reasonable basis of support. Accordingly a promise not to prosecute a claim which is not founded in good faith does not of itself give a right of action on an agreement to pay for refraining from so acting, because a release from mere annoyance and unfounded litigation does not furnish valuable consideration.

Professor Williston [d] was not entirely certain whether the test of reasonableness is based upon the intelligence of the claimant himself, who may be an ignorant person with no knowledge of law and little sense as to facts; but he seemed inclined to favor the view that "the claim forborne must be neither absurd in fact from the standpoint of a reasonable man in the position of the claimant, nor, obviously unfounded in law to one who has an elementary knowledge of legal principles." 1 Williston on Contracts, Rev.Ed., sec. 135. We agree that while stress is placed upon the honesty and good faith of the claimant, forbearance to prosecute a claim is insufficient consideration if the claim forborne is so lacking in foundation as to make its assertion incompatible with honesty and a reasonable degree of intelligence. Thus, if the mother of a bastard knows that there is no foundation, either in law or fact, for a charge against a certain man that he is the father of the child, but that man

---

c. This act was replaced in 1963 by the Paternity Act, which substituted a civil rather than a criminal procedure.

d. Samuel Williston (1861–1963) joined the faculty of the Harvard Law School in 1890, after practicing law for a short period in Boston, and taught there until his retirement in 1938. His principal fields were contracts and sales. His multi-volume work, A Treatise on the Law of Contracts, was first published in 1920 and became one of the most widely used legal treatises in the United States. He was the Reporter for the Restatement of Contracts and the draftsman of several uniform laws, including the Uniform Sales Act. On Williston's travails, see Boyer, Samuel Williston's Struggle with Depression, 42 Buff.L.Rev. 1 (1994).

promises to pay her in order to prevent bastardy proceedings against him, the forbearance to institute proceedings is not sufficient consideration.

On the other hand, forbearance to sue for a lawful claim or demand is sufficient consideration for a promise to pay for the forbearance if the party forbearing had an honest intention to prosecute litigation which is not frivolous, vexatious, or unlawful, and which he believed to be well founded. Snyder v. Cearfoss, 187 Md. 635, 643, 51 A.2d 264; Pullman Co. v. Ray, 201 Md. 268, 94 A.2d 266. Thus the promise of a woman who is expecting an illegitimate child that she will not institute bastardy proceedings against a certain man is sufficient consideration for his promise to pay for the child's support, even though it may not be certain whether the man is the father or whether the prosecution would be successful, if she makes the charge in good faith. . . .

Another analogous case is Thompson v. Nelson, 28 Ind. 431. There the plaintiff sought to recover back money which he had paid to compromise a prosecution for bastardy. He claimed that the prosecuting witness was not pregnant and therefore the prosecution was fraudulent. It was held by the Supreme Court of Indiana, however, that the settlement of the prosecution was a good consideration for the payment of the money and it could not be recovered back, inasmuch as it appeared from the evidence that the prosecution was instituted in good faith, and at that time there was reason to believe that the prosecuting witness was pregnant, although it was found out afterwards that she was not pregnant. [The court's summary of a similar decision on similar facts in Illinois is here omitted. Heaps v. Dunham, 95 Ill. 583, 590.]

In the case at bar there was no proof of fraud or unfairness. Assuming that the hematologists were accurate in their laboratory tests and findings, nevertheless plaintiff gave testimony which indicated that she made the charge of bastardy against defendant in good faith. For these reasons the Court acted properly in overruling the demurrer to the amended declaration and the motion for a directed verdict.

[The court's discussion of alleged errors in the trial court's charge to the jury is here omitted.]

As we have found no reversible error in the rulings and instructions of the trial court, we will affirm the judgment entered on the verdict of the jury.

Judgment affirmed, with costs.

NOTES

(1) *The Objective Requisite.* What was the consideration for Fiege's promise? Boehm's forbearance to press a claim that later turned out to be invalid? According to the first Restatement § 76, "forbearance to assert an invalid claim . . . by one who has not an honest and reasonable belief in its possible validity" is not consideration. Examine Restatement Second § 74(1). What has happened to the requirement of the first Restatement that the forbearing party have a reasonable belief in its position? On a close reading of the main case, does it

appear that the new Restatement rule is substantially identical to the rule of the case?

It is a commonplace observation in judicial opinions that the law favors private settlements of disputed claims, both to alleviate discord and to eliminate sources of uncertainty. One way to favor settlements, illustrated in Fiege v. Boehm, is to hold the person (Fiege) who promises to pay in settlement of the claim bound to that promise. Another way is taken up at page 371 below.

(2) *Other Questions.* Did Boehm fail to disclose any important fact at the time Fiege made his promise? Is it arguable that her failure amounted to a misrepresentation? Misrepresentation by non-disclosure is dealt with at page 374 below. Could Boehm have enforced such promises against two men?

If Fiege had promised to pay for 21 years in consideration of Boehm's forbearance for that period of time, he might have argued that he could renege on his promise at any time before she had given *all* the consideration, that is, had foreborne for 21 years. (Could William E. Story have reneged on his promise at any time before his nephew turned 21?) This argument is considered in connection with the topic of precontractual liability in Chapter 2, Section 6. Note, however, that Boehm's lawyer avoided this argument by alleging, in effect, that Fiege promised to pay her for 21 years in consideration of her forbearance for "as long as he made the payments in accordance with the agreement." If that was his promise, she had given all of the consideration as of May, 1953, when he stopped making the payments.

(3) *The Case of the Church's Immunity.* Ralston suffered injuries, as she alleged, in a fall on a church stairway, which resulted from its negligence. An adjuster for the church's insurance company called on her and promised that it would pay all her expenses if she would refrain from suing the church or the insurer. Not being paid, she sued the insurer on its promise. The trial court sustained its demurrer to the plaintiff's petition alleging these facts, and she appealed. *Held:* Reversed. The insurer based its argument on holdings of the court that churches and charitable organizations are immune from liability for their torts. Referring to other holdings, however, the court concluded that a claim by the plaintiff, based on negligence, would not have been "obviously invalid or frivolous." If it promised to pay the plaintiff, the court said, the insurer was hardly in a position to make that contention. Ralston v. Mathew, 250 P.2d 841 (Kan.1952).

Was the decision in this case parallel to that in Fiege v. Boehm? Of course there was this difference: the challenge to Boehm's claim was based on its factual weakness, whereas Ralston's claim was questioned on a legal ground. Should this make a difference in the standard applied? Should the viewpoint of a layman or that of a lawyer be used to answer the question whether or not a claim was "obviously invalid" in law? Do you see any harmful result for the law of *torts* that may result from a decision like Ralston v. Mathew?

REFORM OF THE DOCTRINE OF CONSIDERATION

The doctrine of consideration has been subjected to attacks for more than two centuries. As long ago as 1765, Lord Mansfield [a] declared that

a. William Murray, first Earl of Mans- field (1705–1793), was a rival of the elder   Pitt in school, in Parliament and in politics. He favored strict measures with the Ameri-

"The ancient notion about the want of consideration was for the sake of evidence only: for when it is reduced into writing ... there was no objection to the want of consideration.... In commercial cases amongst merchants, the want of consideration is not an objection." Pillans and Rose v. Van Mierop and Hopkins, 3 Burr. 1663, 97 Eng.Rep. 1035 (K.B.1765). His rule was short lived, for three years later it was rejected by the House of Lords, which concluded that, "All contracts are, by the laws of England, distinguished into agreements by specialty [i.e., agreements under seal], and agreements by parol; nor is there any such third class as some of the counsel have endeavored to maintain, as contracts in writing. If they be merely written and not specialties, they are parol, and a consideration must be proved." Rann v. Hughes, 7 T.R. 350n, 101 Eng.Rep. 1014n (1778). Mansfield's heresy did not, however, remain quiescent. The view that the formality of putting a promise in writing should operate as an alternative to consideration continued to have appeal, and gained new vitality—particularly in connection with gratuitous promises—when the abolition of the seal raised the doctrine of consideration to even greater prominence.

The civil law countries (those whose legal systems are derived from Roman law) commonly have procedures involving the appearance of the promisor before a notary (a lawyer who holds an appointment from the state and who has no counterpart in common law countries), by which irrevocable gratuitous promise may be made. See von Mehren, Civil Law Analogues to Consideration: An Exercise in Comparative Analysis, 72 Harv.L.Rev. 1009, 1057–62 (1959). A few states have general statutes that facilitate the making of binding gratuitous promises by recognizing some form of writing as a substitute for a seal. One such statute, the Model Written Obligations Act, proposed by the National Conference of Commissioners on Uniform State Laws, provides:

A written release or promise hereafter made and signed by the person releasing or promising shall not be invalid or unenforceable for lack of consideration, if the writing also contains an additional express statement, in any form of language, that the signer intends to be legally bound.

Only Pennsylvania has adopted this act, and a 1937 recommendation of the English Law Revision Commission that a similar statute be adopted in that country has not been followed.[b] A New Mexico statute provides:

can rebels. His friend Alexander Pope helped him practice advocacy and later praised his eloquence in verse. Dr. Johnson said of him, "much can be made of a Scot if caught young." Mansfield achieved greatness as a judge, being Lord Chief Justice from 1756 to 1788. One of his chief services was in rationalizing mercantile law. In commercial cases he made effective use of special "juries" of merchants, whose advice about their practices was sometimes instrumental in transforming custom into law.

b. See the 1937 Report of the [English] Law Revision Committee on the Statute of Frauds and the Doctrine of Consideration (Sixth Interim Report, Cmd. No. 5449 (1937).) This fourteen-member Committee concurred in a Report on Consideration, which took the bargain concept as the meaning of "consideration," and then gave an historical summary of the doctrine which reflected the highly critical attitude of Holdsworth. Thus it was stated that the origin of consideration was "more or less" fortuitous and that the reasons which gave rise to the requirement have "ceased to be

Every contract in writing hereafter made shall import a consideration in the same manner and as fully as sealed instruments have heretofore done. (N.M.Stat.Ann. § 20–2–8 (1953).)

A more common variety of general legislation is typified by a California statute that makes a writing "presumptive evidence of consideration" (Cal.Civ.Code § 1614 (West 1954)). The specific provisions of the Uniform Commercial Code and of New York statutes, none of which applies to the simple promise of a gift, will be dealt with later at appropriate points.

Professor John Dawson has written, "A remarkable feature of the extensive literature on the requirement of consideration is the intensity and depth of the hostility it has inspired.... Yet even in the last hundred years little disposition has appeared to change the solutions in a basic way.... [E]ven in the literature of protest, denouncing the doctrine of consideration, a deeper involvement in gift transactions, either to enforce or undo them, has not been strongly urged." J. Dawson, Gifts and Promises 197, 224 (1980).[c]

SECTION 3. THE PROBLEM OF ACTION IN THE PAST

(a) "Past" Consideration and "Moral Obligation"

FEINBERG v. PFEIFFER CO.

Saint Louis Court of Appeals, Missouri, 1959.
322 S.W.2d 163.

Action on alleged contract by defendant to pay plaintiff a specified monthly amount upon her retirement from defendant's employ. The Circuit Court, City of St. Louis, rendered judgment for plaintiff, and defendant appealed.

of importance at the present day." The Committee's conclusion in principle was as follows:

"If the view is accepted that all that is necessary in order to render an agreement enforceable is that there should be evidence that the parties intend to create a relationship binding in law, then it seems to follow that this requirement can be satisfied equally well either by consideration regarded as evidence of that intention or by some other evidence of that intention. On this basis, it becomes possible to frame proposals which will carry into effect this purpose, and will, while doing as little violence as

possible to any long-established theories, remove hardships arising from the technical applications of the doctrine which have crept into the law of contracts."

c. For recent proposals of bases for enforcement, see Barnett, A Consent Theory of Contract, 86 Colum.L.Rev. 269 (1986); Farber & Matheson, Beyond Promissory Estoppel: Contract Law and the "Invisible Handshake," 52 U.Chi.L.Rev. 903 (1985); Kostritsky, A New Theory of Assent–Based Liability Emerging Under the Guise of Promissory Estoppel: An Explanation and a Defense, 33 Wayne L.Rev. 895 (1987).

DOERNER, COMMISSIONER. This is a suit brought in the Circuit Court of the City of St. Louis by plaintiff, a former employee of the defendant corporation, on an alleged contract whereby defendant agreed to pay plaintiff the sum of $200 per month for life upon her retirement. A jury being waived, the case was tried by the court alone. Judgment below was for plaintiff for $5,100, the amount of the pension claimed to be due as of the date of the trial together with interest thereon, and defendant duly appealed.

The parties are in substantial agreement on the essential facts. Plaintiff began working for the defendant, a manufacturer of pharmaceuticals, in 1910, when she was but 17 years of age. By 1947 she had attained the position of bookkeeper, office manager, and assistant treasurer of the defendant, and owned 70 shares of its stock out of a total of 6,503 shares issued and outstanding. Twenty shares had been given to her by the defendant or its then president, she had purchased 20, and the remaining 30 she had acquired by a stock split or stock dividend. Over the years she received substantial dividends on the stock she owned, as did all of the other stockholders. Also, in addition to her salary, plaintiff from 1937 to 1949, inclusive, received each year a bonus varying in amount from $300 in the beginning to $2,000 in the later years.

On December 27, 1947, the annual meeting of the defendant's Board of Directors was held at the Company's offices in St. Louis, presided over by Max Lippman, its then president and largest individual stockholder. The other directors present were George L. Marcus, Sidney Harris, Sol Flammer, and Walter Weinstock, who, with Max Lippman, owned 5,007 of the 6,503 shares then issued and outstanding. At that meeting the Board of Directors adopted the following resolution, which, because it is the crux of the case, we quote in full:

"The Chairman thereupon pointed out that the Assistant Treasurer, Mrs. Anna Sacks Feinberg, has given the corporation many years of long and faithful service. Not only has she served the corporation devotedly, but with exceptional ability and skill. The President pointed out that although all of the officers and directors sincerely hoped and desired that Mrs. Feinberg would continue in her present position for as long as she felt able, nevertheless, in view of the length of service which she has contributed provision should be made to afford her retirement privileges and benefits which should become a firm obligation of the corporation to be available to her whenever she should see fit to retire from active duty, however many years in the future such retirement may become effective. It was, accordingly, proposed that Mrs. Feinberg's salary which is presently $350.00 per month, be increased to $400.00 per month, and that Mrs. Feinberg would be given the privilege of retiring from active duty at any time she may elect to see fit so to do upon a retirement pay of $200.00 per month for life, with the distinct understanding that the retirement plan is merely being adopted at the present time in order to afford Mrs. Feinberg security for the future and in the hope that her active services will continue with the corporation for many years to come. After due discussion and consideration, and upon motion duly made and seconded, it was—

"Resolved, that the salary of Anna Sacks Feinberg be increased from $350.00 to $400.00 per month and that she be afforded the privilege of retiring from active duty in the corporation at any time she may elect to see fit so to do upon retirement pay of $200.00 per month, for the remainder of her life."

At the request of Mr. Lippman his sons-in-law, Messrs. Harris and Flammer, called upon the plaintiff at her apartment on the same day to advise her of the passage of the resolution. Plaintiff testified on cross-examination that she had no prior information that such a pension plan was contemplated, that it came as a surprise to her, and that she would have continued in her employment whether or not such a resolution had been adopted. It is clear from the evidence that there was no contract, oral or written, as to plaintiff's length of employment, and that she was free to quit, and the defendant to discharge her, at any time.

Plaintiff did continue to work for the defendant through June 30, 1949, on which date she retired. In accordance with the foregoing resolution, the defendant began paying her the sum of $200 on the first of each month. Mr. Lippman died on November 18, 1949, and was succeeded as president of the company by his widow. Because of an illness, she retired from that office and was succeeded in October, 1953, by her son-in-law, Sidney M. Harris. Mr. Harris testified that while Mrs. Lippman had been president she signed the monthly pension check paid plaintiff, but fussed about doing so, and considered the payments as gifts. After his election, he stated, a new accounting firm employed by the defendant questioned the validity of the payments to plaintiff on several occasions, and in the Spring of 1956, upon its recommendation, he consulted the Company's then attorney, Mr. Ralph Kalish. Harris testified that both Ernst and Ernst, the accounting firm, and Kalish told him there was no need of giving plaintiff the money. He also stated that he had concurred in the view that the payments to plaintiff were mere gratuities rather than amounts due under a contractual obligation, and that following his discussion with the Company's attorney plaintiff was sent a check for $100 on April 1, 1956. Plaintiff declined to accept the reduced amount, and this action followed. Additional facts will be referred to later in this opinion....

Appellant's next complaint is that there was insufficient evidence to support the court's findings that plaintiff would not have quit defendant's employ had she not known and relied upon the promise of defendant to pay her $200 a month for life, and the finding that, from her voluntary retirement until April 1, 1956, plaintiff relied upon the continued receipt of the pension installments. The trial court so found, and, in our opinion, justifiably so. Plaintiff testified, and was corroborated by Harris, defendant's witness, that knowledge of the passage of the resolution was communicated to her on December 27, 1947, the very day it was adopted. She was told at that time by Harris and Flammer, she stated, that she could take the pension as of that day, if she wished.

She testified further that she continued to work for another year and a half, through June 30, 1949; that at that time her health was good and she could have continued to work, but that after working for almost forty years she thought she would take a rest. Her testimony continued:

"Q. Now, what was the reason—I'm sorry. Did you then quit the employment of the company after you—after this year and a half? A. Yes.

"Q. What was the reason that you left? A. Well, I thought almost forty years, it was a long time and I thought I would take a little rest.

"Q. Yes. A. And with the pension and what earnings my husband had, we figured we could get along.

"Q. Did you rely upon this pension? A. We certainly did.

"Q. Being paid? A. Very much so. We relied upon it because I was positive that I was going to get it as long as I lived.

"Q. Would you have left the employment of the company at that time had it not been for this pension? A. No.

"Mr. Allen: Just a minute, I object to that as calling for a conclusion and conjecture on the part of this witness.

"The Court: It will be overruled.

"Q. (Mr. Agatstein continuing): Go ahead, now. The question is whether you would have quit the employment of the company at that time had you not relied upon this pension plan? A. No, I wouldn't.

"Q. You would not have. Did you ever seek employment while this pension was being paid to you—A. (interrupting): No.

"Q. Wait a minute, at any time prior—at any other place? A. No, sir.

"Q. Were you able to hold any other employment during that time? A. Yes, I think so.

"Q. Was your health good? A. My health was good."

It is obvious from the foregoing that there was ample evidence to support the findings of fact made by the court below.

We come, then, to the basic issue in the case. While otherwise defined in defendant's third and fourth assignments of error, it is thus succinctly stated in the argument in its brief: "... whether plaintiff has proved that she has a right to recover from defendant based upon a legally binding contractual obligation to pay her $200 per month for life."

It is defendant's contention, in essence, that the resolution adopted by its Board of Directors was a mere promise to make a gift, and that no contract resulted either thereby, or when plaintiff retired, because there was no consideration given or paid by the plaintiff. It urges that a promise to make a gift is not binding unless supported by a legal consideration; that the only apparent consideration for the adoption of the foregoing resolution was the "many years of long and faithful service" expressed therein; and that past services are not a valid consideration for a promise. Defendant argues further that there is nothing in the resolution which made its effectiveness conditional upon plaintiff's continued employment, that she was not under contract to work for any length of time but was free to quit whenever she wished, and that she had no contractual right to her position and could have been discharged at any time.

Consideration Plaintiff concedes that a promise based upon past services would be without consideration, but contends that there were two other elements which supplied the required element: First, the continuation by plaintiff in the employ of the defendant for the period from December 27, 1947, the date when the resolution was adopted, until the date of her retirement on June 30, 1949. And, second, her change of position, i.e., her retirement, and the abandonment by her of her opportunity to continue in gainful employment, made in reliance on defendant's promise to pay her $200 per month for life.

We must agree with the defendant that the evidence does not support the first of these contentions. There is no language in the resolution predicating plaintiff's right to a pension upon her continued employment. She was not required to work for the defendant for any period of time as a condition to gaining such retirement benefits. She was told that she could quit the day upon which the resolution was adopted, as she herself testified, and it is clear from her own testimony that she made no promise or agreement to continue in the employ of the defendant in return for its promise to pay her a pension. Hence there was lacking that mutuality of obligation which is essential to the validity of a contract....

Consideration for a promise has been defined in the Restatement of the Law of Contracts, Section 75, as: *What about 2nd contention?*

"(1) Consideration for a promise is
    (a) an act other than a promise, or
    (b) a forbearance, or
    (c) the creation, modification or destruction of a legal relation, or
    (d) a return promise,

bargained for and given in exchange for the promise."

As the parties agree, the consideration sufficient to support a contract may be either a benefit to the promisor or a loss or detriment to the promisee....

[The rest of the opinion in this case, dealing with Feinberg's second contention, is at p. 104, below.]

NOTES

(1) *The Missing Ingredient.* Feinberg conceded "that a promise based on past services would be without consideration." Why was it so clear to everyone

that her 37 years of service, prior to the resolution of December 27, 1947, could not be consideration for Pfeiffer's promise?

(2) *Counselling.* Suppose that Max Lippman had called in his lawyer in December, 1947, and said, "I want you to draw up a resolution that will make it sure that Mrs. Feinberg will get a pension of $200 a month as long as she lives." Would it have helped to have reworded the resolution to include the words, "*in consideration of* her many years of long and faithful service"? See Perreault v. Hall, 49 A.2d 812 (N.H.1946).

_____ $ for expenses incurred

MILLS v. WYMAN, 3 Pick. 207 (Mass.1825). [Levi Wyman, age 25, fell ill on his return from a sea voyage and, being poor and in distress, was cared for by Daniel Mills for about two weeks. A few days later, after all Mills's expenses had been incurred, Seth Wyman, Levi's father, wrote Mills promising to pay those expenses. When Seth Wyman decided not to pay, Mills sued him. From a direction of nonsuit, Mills appealed.]

PARKER, C.J. General rules of law established for the protection and security of honest and fair-minded men, who may inconsiderately make promises without any equivalent, will sometimes screen men of a different character from engagements which they are bound *in foro conscientiae* to perform. This is a defect inherent in all human systems of legislation. The rule that a mere verbal promise, without any consideration, cannot be enforced by action, is universal in its application, and cannot be departed from to suit particular cases in which a refusal to perform such a promise may be disgraceful.

Time Separate.

The promise declared on in this case appears to have been made without any legal consideration. The kindness and services towards the sick son of the defendant were not bestowed at his request. The son was in no respect under the care of the defendant. He was twenty-five years old, and had long left his father's family. On his return from a foreign country, he fell sick among strangers, and the plaintiff acted the part of the good Samaritan, giving him shelter and comfort until he died. The defendant, his father, on being informed of this event, influenced by a transient feeling of gratitude, promised in writing to pay the plaintiff for the expenses he had incurred. But he has determined to break this promise, and is willing to have his case appear on record as a strong example of particular injustice sometimes necessarily resulting from the operation of general rules....

A deliberate promise in writing, made freely and without any mistake, one which may lead the party to whom it is made into contracts and expenses, cannot be broken without a violation of moral duty. But if there was nothing paid or promised for it, the law, perhaps wisely, leaves the execution of it to the conscience of him who makes it. It is only when the party making the promise gains something, or he to whom it is made loses something, that the law gives the promise validity....

[Judgment ordered on the nonsuit.]

Law will not intervene; moral duty is broken.

NOTES

(1) *The Case Against "Moral Obligation."* Mills v. Wyman accurately reflects the traditional common law view that a promise made in recognition of a "moral obligation" arising out of a benefit previously received is not enforceable. A benefit conferred before a promise is made can hardly be said to have been given in "exchange" for the promise. Williston says: "However much one may wish to extend the number of promises which are enforceable by law, it is essential that the classes of promises which are so enforceable shall be clearly defined. The test of moral consideration must vary with the opinion of every individual. Indeed, as has been said, since there is a moral obligation to perform every promise, it would seem that if morality was to be the guide, every promise would be enforced and if the existence of a past moral obligation is to be the test, every promise which repeats or restates a prior gratuitous promise would be binding." Williston § 148.

(2) *Recognized Exceptions.* In some exceptional situations the common law does enforce a promise on the ground that it was made in recognition of what could be viewed as a "moral obligation." Two leading examples are a promise to pay a debt that is no longer legally enforceable because of the running of the period of limitations and a promise by an adult to perform a duty imposed by a promise that the adult made as an infant and could have avoided on that ground. In Mills v. Wyman the court mentioned and distinguished these cases, saying, "the principle is preserved by looking back to the origin of that transaction, where an equivalent is to be found." It said the same of a promise to pay a debt that has been discharged in bankruptcy. See Restatement Second §§ 82, 83.[a]

(3) *Reaffirmation of Debt Discharged in Bankruptcy.* The enforceability of a promise to pay a debt that is no longer legally enforceable because of the discharge of the promisor in bankruptcy proceedings is now subject to additional requirements under the Bankruptcy Code.[1] Congress was advised that reaffirmations had often been procured by creditors' threats. One of the complex provisions on the subject requires that, if the debtor is advised by a lawyer in negotiating the reaffirmation, the lawyer must report the agreement to be a "fully informed and voluntary" one. Another provision requires that, as to certain consumer debts, the court must inform the debtor of the legal effect of a reaffirmation. Should the debtor wish to repay a discharged debt "voluntarily," however, the Code permits the debtor to do so without regard to the requirements for reaffirmation.[2]

WEBB v. McGOWIN
Court of Appeals of Alabama, 1935.
27 Ala.App. 82, 168 So. 196.
Certiorari denied 232 Ala. 374, 168 So. 199 (1936).

Action by Joe Webb against N. Floyd McGowin and Joseph F. McGowin, as executors of the estate of J. Greeley McGowin, deceased. From a judgment of nonsuit; plaintiff appeals.

BRICKEN, PRESIDING JUDGE. This action is in assumpsit. The complaint as originally filed was amended. The demurrers to the complaint

---

a. In 1782 Lord Mansfield, whose earlier bout with the doctrine of consideration is discussed at p. 60 above, derived from such exceptions the dictum, "Where a man is under a moral obligation, which no Court of Law or Equity can inforce, and promises, the honesty and rectitude of the thing is a consideration." Hawkes v. Saunders, 98 Eng.Rep. 1091 (King's Bench 1782). The dictum never became the law.

1. 11 U.S.C. § 524(c), (d).

2. Id. § 524(f).

as amended were sustained, and because of this adverse ruling by the court the plaintiff took a nonsuit, and the assignment of errors on this appeal are predicated upon said action or ruling of the court.

A fair statement of the case presenting the questions for decision is set out in appellant's brief, which we adopt.[b]

"On the 3d day of August, 1925, appellant while in the employ of the W.T. Smith Lumber Company, a corporation, and acting within the scope of his employment, was engaged in clearing the upper floor of Mill No. 2 of the company. While so engaged he was in the act of dropping a pine block from the upper floor of the mill to the ground below; this being the usual and ordinary way of clearing the floor, and it being the duty of the plaintiff in the course of his employment to so drop it. The block weighed about 75 pounds.

"As appellant was in the act of dropping the block to the ground below, he was on the edge of the upper floor of the mill. As he started to turn the block loose so that it would drop to the ground, he saw J. Greeley McGowin, testator of the defendants, on the ground below and directly under where the block would have fallen had appellant turned it loose. Had he turned it loose it would have struck McGowin with such force as to have caused him serious bodily harm or death. Appellant could have remained safely on the upper floor of the mill by turning the block loose and allowing it to drop, but had he done this the block would have fallen on McGowin and caused him serious injuries or death. The only safe and reasonable way to prevent this was for appellant to hold to the block and divert its direction in falling from the place where McGowin was standing and the only safe way to divert it so as to prevent its coming into contact with McGowin was for appellant to fall with it to the ground below. Appellant did this, and by holding to the block and falling with it to the ground below, he diverted the course of its fall in such way that McGowin was not injured. In thus preventing the injuries to McGowin appellant himself received serious bodily injuries, resulting in his right leg being broken, the heel of his right foot torn off and his right arm broken. He was badly crippled for life and rendered unable to do physical or mental labor.

"On September 1, 1925, in consideration of appellant having prevented him from sustaining death or serious bodily harm and in consideration of the injuries appellant had received, McGowin agreed with him to care for and maintain him for the remainder of appellant's life at the rate of $15 every two weeks from the time he sustained his injuries to

---

b. We are grateful to counsel for the McGowin estate for the following version of the controversy. After Webb's injury, he received workmen's compensation payments from the company. When these benefits ran out, McGowin, as president, had the company continue the payments "purely out of the kindness of his heart." (It was therefore the estate's position that McGowin never made the promise alleged in Webb's complaint.) By the time the controversy arising from the demurrer was decided by the Alabama Supreme Court, the estate was ready for final settlement and to avoid further expense and delay, the executors agreed to settle the claim. Counsel later concluded that, in view of the notoriety achieved by the decision, "it would probably have been better to have had the record clarified by following up the case after reversal and requiring the plaintiff to prove the averments of his complaint."

and during the remainder of appellant's life; it being agreed that McGowin would pay this sum to appellant for his maintenance. Under the agreement McGowin paid or caused to be paid to appellant the sum so agreed on up until McGowin's death on January 1, 1934. After his death the payments were continued to and including January 27, 1934, at which time they were discontinued. Thereupon plaintiff brought suit to recover the unpaid installments accruing up to the time of the bringing of the suit.

"The material averments of the different counts of the original complaint and the amended complaint are predicated upon the foregoing statement of facts." . . .

The action was for the unpaid installments accruing after January 27, 1934, to the time of the suit. . . .

1. The averments of the complaint show that appellant saved McGowin from death or grievous bodily harm. This was a material benefit to him of infinitely more value than any financial aid he could have received. Receiving this benefit, McGowin became morally bound to compensate appellant for the services rendered. Recognizing his moral obligation, he expressly agreed to pay appellant as alleged in the complaint and complied with this agreement up to the time of his death; a period of more than 8 years.

Had McGowin been accidentally poisoned and a physician, without his knowledge or request, had administered an antidote, thus saving his life, a subsequent promise by McGowin to pay the physician would have been valid. Likewise, McGowin's agreement as disclosed by the complaint to compensate appellant for saving him from death or grievous bodily injury is valid and enforceable.

Where the promisee cares for, improves, and preserves the property of the promisor, though done without his request, it is sufficient consideration for the promisor's subsequent agreement to pay for the service, because of the material benefit received. . . .

In Boothe v. Fitzpatrick, 36 Vt. 681, the court held that a promise by defendant to pay for the past keeping of a bull which had escaped from defendant's premises and been cared for by plaintiff was valid, although there was no previous request, because the subsequent promise obviated that objection; it being equivalent to a previous request. On the same principle, had the promisee saved the promisor's life or his body from grievous harm, his subsequent promise to pay for the services rendered would have been valid. Such service would have been far more material than caring for his bull. Any holding that saving a man from death or grievous bodily harm is not a material benefit sufficient to uphold a subsequent promise to pay for the service, necessarily rests on the assumption that saving life and preservation of the body from harm have only a sentimental value. The converse of this is true. Life and preservation of the body have material, pecuniary values, measurable in dollars and cents. Because of this, physicians practice their profession charging for services rendered in saving life and curing the body of its ills, and surgeons perform operations. The same is true as to the law of

[handwritten: Promisor received A benefit]

negligence, authorizing the assessment of damages in personal injury cases based upon the extent of the injuries, earnings, and life expectancies of those injured.

In the business of life insurance, the value of a man's life is measured in dollars and cents according to his expectancy, the soundness of his body, and his ability to pay premiums. The same is true as to health and accident insurance.

It follows that if, as alleged in the complaint, appellant saved J. Greeley McGowin from death or grievous bodily harm, and McGowin subsequently agreed to pay him for the service rendered, it became a valid and enforceable contract.

2. It is well settled that a moral obligation is a sufficient consideration to support a subsequent promise to pay where the promisor has received a material benefit, although there was no original duty or liability resting on the promisor. [Cases cited.]

The case at bar is clearly distinguishable from that class of cases where the consideration is a mere moral obligation or conscientious duty unconnected with receipt by promisor of benefits of a material or pecuniary nature. .... Here the promisor received a material benefit constituting a valid consideration for his promise.

3. Some authorities hold that, for a moral obligation to support a subsequent promise to pay, there must have existed a prior legal or equitable obligation, which for some reason had become unenforceable, but for which the promisor was still morally bound. This rule, however, is subject to qualification in those cases where the promisor having received a material benefit from the promisee, is morally bound to compensate him for the services rendered and in consideration of this obligation promises to pay. In such cases the subsequent promise to pay is an affirmance or ratification of the services rendered carrying with it the presumption that a previous request for the service was made....

4. The averments of the complaint show that in saving McGowin from death or grievous bodily harm, appellant was crippled for life. This was part of the consideration of the contract declared on. McGowin was benefited. Appellant was injured. Benefit to the promisor or injury to the promisee is a sufficient legal consideration for the promissor's agreement to pay....

5. Under the averments of the complaint the services rendered by appellant were not gratuitous. The agreement of McGowin to pay and the acceptance of payment by appellant conclusively shows the contrary....

From what has been said, we are of the opinion that the court below erred in the ruling complained of; that is to say in sustaining the demurrer, and for this error the case is reversed and remanded.

Reversed and remanded.

SAMFORD, JUDGE (concurring). The questions involved in this case are not free from doubt, and perhaps the strict letter of the rule, as stated by judges, though not always in accord, would bar a recovery by plaintiff, but following the principle announced by Chief Justice Marshall in Hoffman v. Porter, Fed.Cas. No. 6,577, 2 Brock. 156, 159, where he says, "I do not think that law ought to be separated from justice, where it is at most doubtful," I concur in the conclusions reached by the court.

[Part of the short opinion of the Supreme Court of Alabama, denying certiorari, is set out below.]

FOSTER, JUSTICE. . . . The opinion of the Court of Appeals here under consideration recognizes and applies the distinction between a supposed moral obligation of the promisor, based upon some refined sense of ethical duty, without material benefit to him, and one in which such a benefit did in fact occur. We agree with that court that if the benefit be material and substantial, and was to the person of the promisor rather than to his estate, it is within the class of material benefits which he has the privilege of recognizing and compensating either by an executed payment or an executory promise to pay. The cases are cited in that opinion. The reason is emphasized when the compensation is not only for the benefits which the promisor received, but also for the injuries either to the property or person of the promisee by reason of the service rendered.

Writ denied.

NOTES

(1) *The Case for "Moral Obligation."* "Courts have frequently enforced promises on the simple ground that the promisor was only promising to do what he ought to have done anyway. These cases have either been condemned as wanton departures from legal principle, or reluctantly accepted as involving the kind of compromise logic must inevitably make at times with sentiment. I believe that these decisions are capable of rational defense. When we say the defendant was morally obligated to do the thing he promised, we in effect assert the existence of a substantive ground for enforcing the promise. . . . The court's conviction that the promisor ought to do the thing, plus the promisor's own admission of his obligation, may tilt the scales in favor of enforcement where neither standing alone would be sufficient. If it be argued that moral consideration threatens certainty, the solution would seem to lie, not in rejecting the doctrine, but in taming it by continuing the process of judicial exclusion and inclusion already begun in the cases involving infants' contracts, barred debts, and discharged bankrupts." Fuller, Consideration and Form, 41 Colum.L.Rev. 799, 821, 822 (1941). For an economic justification, see Posner, Gratuitous Promises in Economics and Law, 6 J.Legal Stud. 411, 419 (1977), reprinted in A. Kronman and R. Posner, The Economics of Contract Law 52–53 (1979). See also Grosse, Moral Obligation as Consideration in Contracts, 17 Vill.L.Rev. 1 (1971); Henderson, Promises Grounded in the Past: The Idea of Unjust Enrichment and the Law of Contracts, 57 Va.L.Rev. 1115 (1971); Thel & Yorio, The Promissory Basis of Past Consideration, 78 Va.L.Rev. 1045 (1992).

(2) *The Case of the Spared Spouse.* Lee Taylor assaulted his wife in Lena Harrington's house, where she had taken refuge from a previous assault. The wife knocked him down with an axe, and was about to cut his head open when Lena Harrington deflected the axe, mutilating her hand badly but saving Lee Taylor's life. Later, he orally promised to pay her damages, but paid only a

small sum. She sued him on his promise. *Held:* for defendant. "[H]owever much the defendant should be impelled by common gratitude to alleviate the plaintiff's misfortune, a humanitarian act of this kind, voluntarily performed, is not such consideration as would entitle her to recover at law." Harrington v. Taylor, 36 S.E.2d 227 (N.C.1945).

To the extent that consideration for a promise may be required to support the belief that the promise was in fact made, does consideration seem more necessary in this case than in Webb v. McGowin? More necessary than in Mills v. Wyman?

(3) *Reform by Statute.* New York law does not recognize "moral obligation" as an equivalent of consideration, but a New York statute enacted in 1941 and now found in General Obligations Law § 5–1105 provides: "A promise in writing and signed by the promisor or by his agent shall not be denied effect as a valid contractual obligation on the ground that consideration for the promise is past or executed, if the consideration is expressed in the writing and is proved to have been given or performed and would be a valid consideration but for the time when it was given or performed."

How would this statute have affected the results in the preceding cases? Would the common recital "for value received" satisfy the New York statute? Would you favor the adoption of that statute by other states? Would you favor the adoption of a statute enacting Restatement, Second § 86? [a] What kind of active support would you expect such proposals for reform to muster?

THE "ZEALOUS" ADVOCATE AND "TECHNICAL" DEFENSES

Is any ethical question raised when a lawyer is asked to represent a client who has a "technical" defense to the legal enforcement of a "moral" obligation?

An extreme position on the zeal of the advocate is reflected in the notorious assertion of Lord Brougham in his defense of Queen Caroline before the House of Lords, in the case of her divorce from George IV. According to Lord Brougham, "the highest and most unquestioned" of an advocate's duties to a client is to "save that client by all expedient means, to protect that client at all hazards and costs, . . . and he must not regard the alarm, the suffering, the torment, the destruction which he may bring upon any other." [1]

Contemporary ethical codes, consistent with a notion of neutral partisanship, suggest that it is up to the client to decide whether to assert a lawful claim or defense. The preamble of the American Bar Association's Model Rules of Professional Conduct says that "when an opposing party is well represented, a lawyer can be a zealous advocate on

a. The Reporter who drafted Restatement Second § 86 expressed the belief that "this statement of principle is more useful than the statutory formula drafted by the New York Law Revision Commission. . . . [The latter] is too broad in scope and too restrictive in formal requirements; it does not seem to have had any significant effect." Braucher, Freedom of Contract and the Second Restatement, 78 Yale L.J. 598, 605 (1969).

1. For a fascinating account of Brougham's defense of Queen Caroline and of his fidelity "to his own somewhat peculiar conception of an advocate's duty," see 1 J.B. Atlay, The Lives of the Victorian Chancellors, chs. 10, 11 (1906).

behalf of a client and at the same time assume that justice is being done." However, Ethical Consideration 7–8 of the same Association's older Code of Professional Responsibility says that in assisting a client, "to make a proper decision, it is often desirable for a lawyer to point out those factors which may lead to a decision that is morally just as well as legally permissible."

Critics of neutral partisanship place a heavier burden on the advocate. According to Professor Kenny Hegland, for example, in civil matters it should be "unprofessional conduct for a lawyer to assert any legal doctrine or rule on behalf of a client unless the lawyer has a good faith belief that the assertion of the doctrine or rule in the particular case will further a policy behind the doctrine or rule." Hegland, Quibbles, 67 Tex.L.Rev. 1491, 1494 (1989). But see Sutton, Outlawing Unjust Rules of Law: A Response to *Quibbles,* 67 Tex.L.Rev. 1517, 1522 (1989), objecting that this would leave it to "each lawyer on his own . . . to make the decision concerning fairness and justness."

What position should a lawyer take as to a client's defense of lack of consideration for the client's promise to perform a moral obligation?

NOTE

Ethics in Practice. "Most cases are settled; in the smaller percentage going to trial, each lawyer generally feels that the other party is at least seeking more than is justly due, if not making a wholly unjustified claim or defense. Probably the answer implicit in prevailing practice is that it is permissible to use any legally supportable ground of claim or defense, though it is a surprise move, to uphold a position you believe just, whatever the basis of your belief may be." R. Keeton, Trial Tactics and Methods 5 (2d ed. 1973).

(b) Restitution as an Alternative Basis for Recovery

To this point, we have been concerned with the enforcement of promises. We turn now to an entirely different basis of recovery— recovery based not on a promise at all but on the principle of preventing unjust enrichment. The subject of restitution to prevent unjust enrichment is too vast to be covered here. But since restitution problems are often inseparable from contract problems, a few basics are indispensable.

Suppose, for example, that two parties negotiate but never reach agreement. Can one recover from the other for benefits conferred in the course of those negotiations?[a] Or suppose that the parties do reach agreement but the agreement is unenforceable. Can one recover from the other for benefits conferred under the unenforceable agreement?

---

a. Consider, for example, the benefit to PepsiCo from the inspection by Klein's mechanic during the negotiations described in Klein v. PepsiCo, p. 22 above. If the negotiations had failed, might Klein have recovered for that?

Or suppose that the agreement is enforceable. In the event of breach, can the injured party recover for benefits conferred under the contract if this recovery would exceed recovery under the contract itself? Can the party in breach recover for benefits conferred on the injured party? And if there is no breach but both parties are excused from completing performance because of a supervening event, can either party recover for benefits already conferred on the other?

We begin by considering claims to recover for benefits voluntarily conferred. Courts have, with reason, regarded such claims with suspicion. The Restatement of Restitution § 112, Comment a, gives this rather obvious illustration:

> During A's absence and in the belief that A will be willing to pay for the work, B improves A's land, which is worth and is offered for sale at $5000, to such an extent that upon A's return he sells the land for $8000. B is not entitled to restitution from A.

Forced Sale

It has been suggested that the proposition "that no one should be required to pay for benefits that were 'forced' upon him ... is often stated with more than the needed vigor, perhaps in an effort to neutralize the beguiling effect of the unjust enrichment principle, which postulates that gains produced through another's loss are unjust and should be restored." [b] The following cases pose difficult problems in drawing the line between the "officious intermeddler" or the "volunteer" and the deserving claimant. The subject of restitution is explored in detail in the four-volume work, G. Palmer, Law of Restitution (1978).

NOTE

The Suggestion Box. Claims of liability for appropriation of ideas have provided fertile ground for the development of the law relating to unjust enrichment. Courts have dealt with such claims in terms of both contract implied in fact and restitution to prevent unjust enrichment.

Schott v. Westinghouse Electric Corp., 259 A.2d 443 (Pa.1969), is illustrative. Schott, an employee of Westinghouse, twice submitted a suggestion concerning the construction of circuit breaker panels pursuant to a program under which Westinghouse invited its employees to submit suggestions for cash awards from $5.00 up to $15,000. On the suggestion form, above the line for the employee's signature, appeared the stipulation, "I agree that the decision of the local Suggestion Committee on all matters pertaining to this suggestion ... will be final." The Committee twice rejected Schott's suggestion, stating that it would require heavy preliminary expenditures but would be reconsidered if circuit breaker redesign was undertaken for other reasons. Schott sued Westinghouse alleging that it had appropriated his idea by making the suggested change within the next year but had refused to pay him, giving the excuse that it had been made as "the result of independent action taken without knowledge of your suggestion."

He pleaded causes of action both in contract and for unjust enrichment, but the trial court dismissed the complaint. The Supreme Court of Pennsylvania reversed as to the cause of action for unjust enrichment. The stipulation on the

---

b. Dawson, The Self–Serving Intermeddler, 87 Harv.L.Rev. 1409 (1974).

form precluded a claim in contract, but the allegations that the use of his "basic idea" resulted in savings to Westinghouse stated a cause of action for unjust enrichment since it did not appear that he "expected no payment or intended to confer a gratuity, nor in the context of the suggestion program ... that the benefit was conferred officiously." Schott's case was distinguished from those in which recovery had been denied on the ground that "the 'idea' ... was neither concrete in form nor novel in nature." Two judges concurred on the ground that Schott had stated a cause of action in contract, but had relinquished any claim for unjust enrichment when he signed the form, and one judge dissented.

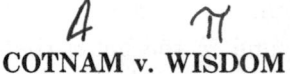

COTNAM v. WISDOM

Supreme Court of Arkansas, 1907.
83 Ark. 601, 104 S.W. 164.

Appeal from Circuit Court, Pulaski County; R.J. Lea, Judge.

Action by F.L. Wisdom and another against T.T. Cotnam, administrator of A.M. Harrison, deceased, for services rendered by plaintiffs as surgeons to defendant's intestate. Judgment for plaintiffs. Defendant appeals. Reversed and remanded.

Instructions 1 and 2, given at the instance of plaintiffs, are as follows: "(1) If you find from the evidence that plaintiffs rendered professional services as physicians and surgeons to the deceased, A.M. Harrison, in a sudden emergency following the deceased's injury in a street car wreck, in an endeavor to save his life, then you are instructed that plaintiffs are entitled to recover from the estate of the said A.M. Harrison such sum as you may find from the evidence is a reasonable compensation for the services rendered. (2) The character and importance of the operation, the responsibility resting upon the surgeon performing the operation, his experience and professional training, and the ability to pay of the person operated upon, are elements to be considered by you in determining what is a reasonable charge for the services performed by plaintiffs in the particular case."

HILL, C.J. (after stating the facts).... The first question is as to the correctness of [the first] instruction. As indicated therein the facts are that Mr. Harrison, appellant's intestate, was thrown from a street car, receiving serious injuries which rendered him unconscious, and while in that condition the appellees were notified of the accident and summoned to his assistance by some spectator, and performed a difficult operation in an effort to save his life, but they were unsuccessful, and he died without regaining consciousness. The appellant says: "Harrison was never conscious after his head struck the pavement. He did not and could not, expressly or impliedly, assent to the action of the appellees. He was without knowledge or will power. However merciful or benevolent may have been the intention of the appellees, a new rule of law, of contract by implication of law, will have to be established by this court in order to sustain the recovery." Appellant is right in saying that the recovery must be sustained by a contract by implication of law, but is not right in saying that it is a new rule of law, for such contracts are almost as old as the English system of jurisprudence. They are usually called "implied contracts." More properly they should be called "quasi contracts" or "constructive contracts." [c] See 1 Page on Contracts, sec. 14; also 2 Page on Contracts, sec. 771.

The following excerpts from Sceva v. True, 53 N.H. 627, are peculiarly applicable here: "We regard it as well settled by the cases referred to in the briefs of counsel, many of which have been commented on at length by Mr. Shirley for the defendant, that an insane person, an idiot, or a person utterly bereft of all sense and reason by the sudden stroke of an accident or disease may be held liable, in assumpsit, for necessaries furnished to him in good faith while in that unfortunate and helpless condition. And the reasons upon which this rests are too broad, as well as too sensible and humane, to be overborne by any deductions which a refined logic may make from the circumstances that in such cases there can be no contract or promise, in fact, no meeting of the minds of the parties. The cases put it on the ground of an implied contract; and by this is not meant, as the defendant's counsel seems to suppose, an actual contract—that is, an actual meeting of the minds of the parties, an actual, mutual understanding, to be inferred from language, acts, and circumstances by the jury—but a contract and promise, said to be implied by the law, where, in point of fact, there was no contract, no mutual understanding, and so no promise. The defendant's counsel says it is usurpation for the court to hold, as a matter of law, that there is a contract and a promise, when all the evidence in the case shows that there was not a contract, nor the semblance of one. It is doubtless a legal fiction, invented and used for the sake of the remedy. If it was originally usurpation, certainly it has now become very inveterate, and firmly fixed in the body of the law. Illustrations might be multiplied, but enough has been said to show that when a contract or promise implied by law is spoken of, a very different thing is meant from a contract in fact, whether express or tacit. The evidence of an actual contract is generally to be found either in some writing made by the parties, or in verbal communications which passed between them, or in their acts and conduct considered in the light of the circumstances of each particular case. A contract implied by law, on the contrary, rests upon no evidence. It has no actual existence. It is simply a mythical creation of the law. The law says it shall be taken that there was a promise, when in point of fact, there was none. Of course this is not good logic, for the obvious and sufficient reason that it is not true. It is

---

c. "Quasi contract" is a useful term for describing a ground for recovering money in an action at common law, when the claim is not based either on principles of tort law or on a true contract but instead seeks redress for unjust enrichment. "Restitution" is a broader term, propagated by American scholars in this century, to embrace all of the remedies, including subrogation and equitable liens, having that function. It refers also to the theory on which they are based. "Quantum meruit" (as much as he deserved) is an older term, narrower, and less useful in current discourse about contract law. It describes a form of action, or short-form pleading, used for centuries in enforcing duties of payment for services. A related action for the worth of goods was "quantum valebant" (as much as they were worth).

Inexact uses of these terms are common. In particular, the term "quantum meruit" is often used interchangeably with "quasi-contract."

a legal fiction, resting wholly for its support on a plain legal obligation, and a plain legal right. If it were true, it would not be a fiction. There is a class of legal rights, with their correlative legal duties, analogous to the obligations quasi ex contractu of the civil law which seem to lie in the region between contracts on the one hand, and torts on the other, and to call for the application of a remedy not strictly furnished either by actions ex contractu or actions ex delicto. . . ."

In its practical application it sustains recovery for physicians and nurses who render services for infants, insane persons, and drunkards. . . . And services rendered by physicians to persons unconscious or helpless by reason of injury or sickness are in the same situation as those rendered to persons incapable of contracting, such as the classes above described. . . . The court was therefore right in giving the instruction in question. . . .

There was evidence in this case proving that it was customary for physicians to graduate their charges by the ability of the patient to pay, and hence, in regard to that element, this case differs from the Alabama case [Morrissett v. Wood, 123 Ala. 384, 26 So. 307]. . . . This could not apply to a physician called in an emergency by some bystander to attend a stricken man whom he never saw or heard of before; and certainly the unconscious patient could not, in fact or in law, be held to have contemplated what charges the physician might properly bring against him. In order to admit such testimony, it must be assumed that the surgeon and patient each had in contemplation that the means of the patient would be one factor in determining the amount of the charge for the services rendered. While the law may admit such evidence as throwing light upon the contract and indicating what was really in contemplation when it was made, yet a different question is presented when there is no contract to be ascertained or construed, but a mere fiction of law creating a contract where none existed in order that there might be a remedy for a right. This fiction merely requires a reasonable compensation for the services rendered. The services are the same be the patient prince or pauper, and for them the surgeon is entitled to fair compensation for his time, service, and skill. It was therefore error to admit this evidence, and to instruct the jury in the second instruction that in determining what was a reasonable charge they could consider the "ability to pay of the person operated upon." [d]

It was improper to let it go to the jury that Mr. Harrison was a bachelor and that his estate was left to nieces and nephews. This was relevant to no issue in the case, and its effect might well have been prejudicial. While this verdict is no higher than some of the evidence would justify, yet it is much higher than some of the other evidence would justify, and hence it is impossible to say that this was a harmless error.

Judgment is reversed, and cause remanded.

    d. For a case rejecting Cotnam v. Wisdom on this point, see In re Agnew's Estate, 231 N.Y.S. 4 (Surrogate's Ct.1928).

BATTLE and WOOD, JJ., concur in sustaining the recovery, and in holding that it was error to permit the jury to consider the fact that his estate would go to collateral heirs; but they do not concur in holding that it was error to admit evidence of the value of the estate, and instructing that it might be considered in fixing the charge.

NOTES

(1) *Question.* Would the result have been different if Dr. Wisdom had treated Harrison in response to a call from Harrison's daughter, who had said, "Give him the best care you can and I will pay you for it"?

(2) *Gratuitousness.* Where one's life or property is imperiled by storm, fire, accident or other casualty, and another renders assistance, the law presumes, in accordance with the mores of our society, that the services were intended to be gratuitous. Thus if a passing motorist finds an injured pedestrian on the highway, administers first aid and takes the injured person to a hospital, there is a presumption of gratuity which will ordinarily bar recovery. However, the presumption may be rebutted if the services are excessively expensive or burdensome to the person rendering them, as when one goes out of one's way a hundred miles to take an injured person to a hospital, or when one's services continue for days or weeks. The presumption that services rendered in an emergency are gratuitous may also be overturned if the person rendering them does so in a business or professional capacity, as where a passing ambulance removes the injured person to the hospital or when, as in Cotnam v. Wisdom, a passing physician treats the injured person.

(3) *Webb v. McGowin Revisited.* Recall the court's argument in Webb v. McGowin that saving life has "material, pecuniary" value, supported by the fact that "physicians practice their profession charging for services rendered in saving life." Would Webb have had a claim against McGowin on the authority of cases like Cotnam v. Wisdom?

Recall, too, the Alabama court's reliance on Boothe v. Fitzpatrick, the case of the promise "to pay for the past keeping of a bull which had escaped ... and been cared for." Would the keeper of the bull have had a claim against the owner of the bull had there been no promise? Might the keeper's *belief* in such a claim have helped to justify enforcement of the owner's promise to pay a reasonable amount? Might Webb's *belief* in a claim against McGowin (even if he had no such claim) help to justify enforcement of McGowin's promise to pay $15 every two weeks? See Fiege v. Boehm, p. 55 above.

(4) *Amount of Recovery.* What is the proper measure of restitutionary recovery? In Hill v. Waxberg Construction Co., 237 F.2d 936 (9th Cir.1956), the court gave the following answer: "An 'implied in fact' contract is essentially based on the intentions of the parties. It arises where the court finds from the surrounding facts and circumstances that the parties intended to make a contract but failed to articulate their promises and the court merely implies what it feels the parties really intended. It would follow then that the general contract theory of compensatory damages should be applied. Thus, if the court can in fact imply a contract for services, the compensation therefor is measured by the going contract rate. An 'implied in law' contract, on the other hand, is a fiction of the law which is based on the maxim that one who is unjustly enriched at the expense of another is required to make restitution to the other. The intentions of the parties have little or no influence on the determination of the proper measure of damages. In the absence of fraud or other tortious conduct on the part of the person enriched, restitution is properly limited to the value of

the benefit which was acquired. The distinction is based on sound reason, too, for where a contract is all but articulated, the expectations of the parties are very nearly mutually understood, and the Court has merely to protect those expectations as men in the ordinary course of business affairs would expect them to be protected, whereas in a situation where one has acquired benefits, without fraud and in a non-tortious manner, with expectations so totally lacking in such mutuality that no contract in fact can be implied, the party benefited should not be required to reimburse the other party on the basis of such party's losses and expenditures, but rather on a basis limited to the benefits, which the benefited party has actually acquired.''

CALLANO v. OAKWOOD PARK HOMES CORP.

Superior Court of New Jersey, 1966.
91 N.J.Super. 105, 219 A.2d 332.

COLLESTER, J.A.D.   Defendant Oakwood Park Homes Corp., (Oakwood) appeals from a judgment of $475 entered in favor of plaintiffs Julia Callano and Frank Callano in the Monmouth County District Court.

The case was tried below on an agreed stipulation of facts. Oakwood, engaged in the construction of a housing development, in December 1961 contracted to sell a lot with a house to be erected thereon to Bruce Pendergast, who resided in Waltham, Massachusetts. In May 1962, prior to completion of the house, the Callanos, who operated a plant nursery, delivered and planted shrubbery pursuant to a contract with Pendergast. A representative of Oakwood had knowledge of the planting.

Pendergast never paid the Callanos the invoice price of $497.95. A short time after the shrubbery was planted Pendergast died. Thereafter, on July 10, 1962 Oakwood and Pendergast's estate cancelled the contract of sale. Oakwood had no knowledge of Pendergast's failure to pay the Callanos. On July 16, 1962 Oakwood sold the Pendergast property, including the shrubbery located thereon, to Richard and Joan Grantges for an undisclosed amount.

The single issue is whether Oakwood is obligated to pay plaintiffs for the reasonable value of the shrubbery on the theory of *quasi*-contractual liability. Plaintiffs contend that defendant was unjustly enriched when the Pendergast contract to purchase the property was cancelled and that an agreement to pay for the shrubbery is implied in law. Defendant argues that the facts of the case do not support a recovery by plaintiffs on the theory of *quasi*-contract.

Contracts implied by law, more properly described as *quasi* or constructive contracts, are a class of obligations which are imposed or created by law without regard to the assent of the party bound, on the ground that they are dictated by reason and justice. They rest solely on a legal fiction and are not contract obligations at all in the true sense, for there is no agreement; but they are clothed with the semblance of contract for the purpose of the remedy, and the obligation arises not from consent, as in the case of true contracts, but from the law or natural equity.　Courts employ the fiction of *quasi* or constructive contract with caution.　17 C.J.S. Contracts § 6, pp. 566–570 (1963).

In cases based on *quasi*-contract liability, the intention of the parties is entirely disregarded, while in cases of express contracts and contracts implied in fact the intention is of the essence of the transaction.　In the case of actual contracts the agreement defines the duty, while in the case of *quasi*-contracts the duty defines the contract.　Where a case shows that it is the duty of the defendant to pay, the law imparts to him a promise to fulfill that obligation.　The duty which thus forms the foundation of a *quasi*-contractual obligation is frequently based on the doctrine of unjust enrichment.　It rests on the equitable principle that a person shall not be allowed to enrich himself unjustly at the expense of another, and on the principle of whatsoever it is certain a man ought to do, that the law supposes him to have promised to do.　St. Paul Fire, etc., Co. v. Indemnity Ins. Co. of No. America, 32 N.J. 17, 22, 158 A.2d 825 (1960).

The key words are *enrich* and *unjustly*.　To recover on the theory of *quasi*-contract the plaintiffs must prove that defendant was enriched, *viz.,* received a benefit, and that retention of the benefit without payment therefor would be unjust.

It is conceded by the parties that the value of the property, following the termination of the Pendergast contract, was enhanced by the reasonable value of the shrubbery at the stipulated sum of $475.　However, we are not persuaded that the retention of such benefit by defendant before it sold the property to the Grantges was inequitable or unjust.

Quasi-contractual liability has found application in a myriad of situations.　See Woodruff, Cases on Quasi–Contracts (3d ed. 1993).　However, a common thread runs throughout its application where liability has been successfully asserted, namely, that the plaintiff expected remuneration from the defendant, or if the true facts were known to plaintiff, he would have expected remuneration from defendant, at the time the benefit was conferred.　See Rabinowitz v. Mass. Bonding & Insurance Co., 119 N.J.L. 552, 197 A. 44 (E. & A. 1937); Power–Matics, Inc. v. Ligotti, 79 N.J.Super. 294, 191 A.2d 483 (App.Div.1963); Shapiro v. Solomon, 42 N.J.Super. 377, 126 A.2d 654 (App.Div.1956).　It is further noted that *quasi*-contract cases involve either some direct relationship between the parties or a mistake on the part of the person conferring the benefit.

In the instant case the plaintiffs entered into an express contract with Pendergast and looked to him for payment.　They had no dealings with defendant, and did not expect remuneration from it when they provided the shrubbery.　No issue of mistake on the part of plaintiffs is involved.　Under the existing circumstances we believe it would be inequitable to hold defendant liable.　Plaintiffs' remedy is against Pendergast's estate, since they contracted with and expected payment to be made by Pendergast when the benefit was conferred.... A plaintiff is not entitled to employ the legal fiction of *quasi*-contract to "substitute one promisor or debtor for another." Cascaden v. Magryta, 247 Mich. 267, 225 N.W. 511, 512 (Sup.Ct.1929).

Plaintiffs place reliance on De Gasperi v. Valicenti, 198 Pa.Super. 455, 181 A.2d 862 (Super.Ct.1962), where recovery was allowed on the theory of unjust enrichment. We find the case inapposite. It is clear that recovery on *quasi*-contract was permitted there because of a fraud perpetrated by defendants. There is no contention of fraud on the part of Oakwood in the instant case.

Recovery on the theory of *quasi*-contract was developed under the law to provide a remedy where none existed. Here, a remedy exists. Plaintiffs may bring their action against Pendergast's estate. We hold that under the facts of this case defendant was not unjustly enriched and is not liable for the value of the shrubbery.

Reversed.

NOTES

(1) *The Case of Contractor's Claim.* Paschall's built a bathroom onto the Doziers' house at the request and on the credit of their daughter, Mrs. Best, who lived with them, and with the knowledge and consent of the Doziers. Paschall's was unsuccessful in collecting from Mrs. Best, who was subsequently adjudicated a bankrupt, and sued the Doziers on a theory of restitution. The trial court sustained the Doziers' demurrer and dismissed the complaint, and Paschall's appealed. *Held:* Reversed and remanded "to the trier of facts to determine whether or not the defendant has been so unjustly enriched at the detriment of the complainant so as to require him to make compensation therefore." The court granted that it may be "the general rule" that "an implied undertaking cannot arise against one benefitted by the work performed, where the work is done under a special contract with another. . . . However, the situation is dissimilar where a person furnishes materials and labor under a contract for the benefit of a third party, and that contract becomes unenforceable or invalid. . . . [W]e think that before recovery can be had against the landowner on an unjust enrichment theory, the furnisher of the materials and labor must have exhausted his remedies against the person with whom he had contracted, and still has not received the reasonable value of his services." Paschall's, Inc. v. Dozier, 407 S.W.2d 150 (Tenn.1966). See also Idaho Lumber, Inc. v. Buck, 710 P.2d 647 (Idaho Ct.App.1985).

Can this case be distinguished from the *Callano* case? One writer suggests: "Where benefit is conferred on a stranger through performance of one's own contract various intermediate solutions could be thought of. The most plausible would be to permit restitution of the benefit to the stranger when the remedy of the gain-producer against his own obligor had failed or was certain to fail. Restitution would then serve as a surrogate, being held in reserve to insure the gain-producer against deficits in the return promised him." Dawson, The Self–Serving Intermeddler, 87 Harv.L.Rev. 1409, 1457–58 (1974). To what extent are the *Callano* and *Paschall's* cases consistent with this suggestion? For an analysis in economic terms, see A. Kronman & R. Posner, The Economics of Contract Law 59–64 (1979).

Restatement of Restitution § 110 provides: "A person who has conferred a benefit upon another as the performance of a contract with a third person is not entitled to restitution from the other merely because of the failure of performance by the third person." Does the *Paschall's* case support this rule? Does the *Callano* case reject it?

(2) *Measure of Recovery (Reprise).* If recovery is allowed in cases like the *Callano* and *Paschall's* cases, how should it be measured? By "the reasonable value to the [defendant] of what he received in terms of what it would have cost him to obtain it from a person in the claimant's position"? Or by "the extent to which the [defendant's] property has increased in value or his other interests advanced"? See Restatement Second § 371. If Harrison's life had been saved, how would Dr. Wisdom's recovery have been measured?

(3) *Subcontractors and Mechanics' Liens.* An application of the problem considered in the preceding case that is of great practical importance concerns the rights of subcontractors on construction jobs. Typically two separate contracts are involved, one between the owner and the general contractor, and another between the general contractor and the subcontractor. It is clear that if, after the subcontractor has performed, the subcontractor is not paid by the general contractor, the subcontractor has no contractual rights against the owner. It is also clear, under reasoning like that in the *Callano* case, that even though the subcontractor has benefited the owner by improving property, the subcontractor cannot recover in restitution. "If he has not availed himself of his lien rights under the statutes, and is unable to now collect from the general contractor, the loss must be borne by him and not by the owner, who has the right to rely upon his agreement with the principal contractor." Gebhardt Brothers, Inc. v. Brimmel, 143 N.W.2d 479, 482 (Wis.1966).[a]

The statutes to which the court refers in the preceding quotation provide for what are historically known as "mechanics' liens." Now in effect in all states, these statutes began to be enacted in the late eighteenth century to spur construction in a young and growing country. They protect laborers, materialmen, subcontractors, contractors and the like, who make improvements on real property by giving them a lien, i.e., a security interest, in that property to secure payment for those improvements. Public property is generally exempt. The subcontractor's lien is limited to the reasonable value of what the subcontractor has done, and in some states it may not exceed the amount then due from the owner to the general contractor. Typically the lien must be perfected by serving notice on the owner and filing a statement in a public office within prescribed times. Although the lien does not create any personal obligation from the owner to the subcontractor, it is enforceable through sale of the owner's property in foreclosure proceedings, with the debt owed by the general contractor to the subcontractor payable out of the proceeds.[b]

(4) *Living Together I.* When two people who have lived together, whether in or out of wedlock, terminate their relationship, it is not uncommon for one of them to make a claim to restitution for services rendered in the home. Restitutionary claims between spouses have usually failed because the services are presumed to be gratuitous. As the Supreme Court of North Carolina put it, the

---

a. But see Flooring Systems, Inc. v. Radisson Group, Inc., 772 P.2d 578 (Ariz. 1989) (where owner's agent had obtained subcontractor's bid before general contractor was chosen, subcontractor might have unjust enrichment claim against owner for amount retained when general contractor became bankrupt).

b. Why did not the Callanos and Paschall's have liens? The New Jersey stat-ute provides for a lien on property for improvements including "planting thereon any shrubs," but only for "debts contracted by the owner" of the property. N.J.Stat. Ann. § 2A:44–66(g). Oakwood, not Pendergast, was the "owner" of the property. Similarly, the Tennessee statute provides for a lien where improvements have been made on a house but only by "contract with the owner or his agent." Tenn.Code Ann. §§ 66–11–102(a).

rule that restitution will not be granted for a benefit conferred gratuitously "is particularly applicable where a husband makes improvements to his wife's land because of the presumption that the improvements constitute a gift." [c] Wright v. Wright, 289 S.E.2d 347 (N.C.1982).

In Pyeatte v. Pyeatte, 661 P.2d 196 (Ariz.App.1982), however, the court upheld an award to a wife who had conferred benefits on her husband by "financial subsidization of [his] legal education—with the agreement and expectation that she would be compensated therefor by his reciprocal efforts after his graduation and admission to the Bar." The court concluded that restitution between spouses might be appropriate for "an extraordinary or unilateral effort by one spouse which inures solely to the benefit of the other by the time of dissolution." See Note 4, p. 285 below.

A restitutionary claim may take on greater importance if the couple is "living together without marriage ceremony and the benefit of legal principles that apply to the financial affairs and property interests of married couples." Mason v. Rostad, 476 A.2d 662 (D.C.1984). In Watts v. Watts, 405 N.W.2d 303 (Wis.1987), the Supreme Court of Wisconsin held "that unmarried cohabitants may raise claims based upon unjust enrichment following the termination of their relationship where one of the parties attempts to retain an unreasonable amount of the property acquired through the efforts of both." The court also held that it was sufficient to allege "that the defendant, knowing that the plaintiff expected to share in the property accumulated, 'accepted the services rendered to him by the plaintiff' and that it would be unfair under the circumstances to allow him to retain everything while she receives nothing."

SECTION 4. THE PROBLEM OF UNSOLICITED ACTION

(a) Reliance and the Requirement of Bargain

In Note 2, p. 67 above, you were asked whether it would have made a difference if Pfeiffer Co.'s resolution had been reworded to include the words *"in consideration of* [Mrs. Feinberg's] many years of faithful service." Could the resolution have been reworded to make it consideration that she continue her employment? That she retire? How would you have drafted the resolution to accomplish either result? Consider the following cases.

KIRKSEY v. KIRKSEY
Supreme Court of Alabama, 1845.
8 Ala. 131.

The plaintiff was the wife of defendant's brother, but had for some time been a widow, and had several children. In 1840, the plaintiff

---

c. In response to the husband's argument based on the Equal Protection Clauses of the federal and state constitutions, the court noted that "the same presumption of gift should apply whichever spouse furnishes improvements on the other spouse's land."

resided on public land, under a contract of lease, she had held over, and was comfortably settled, and would have attempted to secure the land she lived on. The defendant resided in Talladega County, some sixty or seventy miles off. On the 10th October, 1840, he wrote to her the following letter:

"Dear Sister Antillico,—Much to my mortification, I heard that brother Henry was dead, and one of his children. I know that your situation is one of grief and difficulty. You had a bad chance before, but a great deal worse now. I should like to come and see you, but cannot with convenience at present.... I do not know whether you have a preference on the place you live on or not. If you had, I would advise you to obtain your preference, and sell the land and quit the country, as I understand it is very unhealthy, and I know society is very bad. If you will come down and see me, I will let you have a place to raise your family, and I have more open land than I can tend; and on account of your situation, and that of your family, I feel like I want you and the children to do well."

Within a month or two after the receipt of this letter, the plaintiff abandoned her possession, without disposing of it, and removed with her family, to the residence of the defendant, who put her in comfortable houses, and gave her land to cultivate for two years, at the end of which time he notified her to remove, and put her in a house, not comfortable, in the woods, which he afterwards required her to leave.

A verdict being found for the plaintiff, for $200, the above facts were agreed, and if they will sustain the action, the judgment is to be affirmed, otherwise it is to be reversed.

ORMOND, J. The inclination of my mind is that the loss and inconvenience which the plaintiff sustained in breaking up and moving to the defendant's, a distance of sixty miles, is a sufficient consideration to support the promise to furnish her with a house, and land to cultivate, until she could raise her family. My brothers, however, think that the promise on the part of the defendant was a mere gratuity, and that an action will not lie for its breach. The judgment of the court below must therefore be reversed, pursuant to the agreement of the parties.

NOTES

(1) *Characterization of "If" Clauses.* How did the court read the words, "If you will come down and see me, I will let you have a place to raise your family"? As words of bargain for an exchange or of condition to a gratuitous promise of a gift? Was not the benefit to the brother-in-law comparable to the benefit to the uncle in Hamer v. Sidway, p. 47 above?

(2) *Problem.* A father and a daughter became estranged after the mother had divorced the father, and the daughter refused to see the father. The father then wrote to his daughter: "If you will meet me at Tiffany's next Monday at noon, I will buy you the emerald ring advertised in this week's New Yorker." The daughter came to Tiffany's at the time specified, and met her father there,

but he failed to buy her the promised ring. Bargained-for exchange or conditional gratuitous promise?

Williston put this case: "If a benevolent man says to a tramp, 'If you go around the corner to the clothing shop there, you may purchase an overcoat on my credit,' no reasonable person would understand that the short walk was requested as the consideration for the promise; rather, the understanding would be that in the event of the tramp going to the shop the promisor would make him a gift." 1 Williston 4th § 112. Is the situation of the daughter distinguishable from that of the tramp?

(3) *Problem.* Steve Jennings, a prisoner in Texas, was a faithful listener to radio station KSCS, which regularly broadcast that it played "at least three-in-a-row, or we pay you $25,000. No bull, more music on KSCS." Jennings sued KSCS, alleging that each time it played "five-in-a-row" it played only three songs, followed by a brief commercial, and then only *two* songs, but that when he notified KSCS on specific occasions of this they refused to pay him $25,000. He also alleged that he then stopped listening to KSCS. KSCS has moved to dismiss on the ground that there was no consideration for its promise. What decision? See Jennings v. Radio Station KSCS, 96.3 FM, Inc., 708 S.W.2d 60 (Tex.App. 1986).[a]

CENTRAL ADJUSTMENT BUREAU, INC. v. INGRAM

Supreme Court of Tennessee, 1984.
678 S.W.2d 28.

DROWOTA, JUSTICE. This appeal ... involves non-competition clauses in employment contracts. It raises an issue regarding the consideration necessary to support such a covenant when it is entered into after employment has begun. In addition, the Court addresses the issue of whether a covenant not to compete, the geographic and time limitations of which are unnecessarily broad, can be judicially modified so as to make the covenant reasonable and enforceable.

I

The plaintiff-employer, Central Adjustment Bureau, a Texas corporation whose home office is in Dallas, Texas, is qualified to do business in Tennessee as a collector of past-due debts. It has 25 branch offices throughout the United States, including a branch in Nashville, Tennessee. The defendants are former employees who left Central Adjustment Bureau (hereinafter CAB) in 1979 to form Ingram & Associates, a company which competed directly with CAB. All of the defendants had signed covenants not to compete with CAB. After the defendants left, CAB brought suit in Chancery Court seeking both compensatory and injunctive relief. According to CAB's allegations, the defendants were liable in tort and for breach of the non-competition covenants.

The Chancellor found that the non-competition covenants were unreasonably broad with regard to geographical and time limitations.

---

a. For more on this case, see Radio Station KSCS v. Jennings, 750 S.W.2d 760 (Tex.1988), reversing 745 S.W.2d 97 (Tex. App.1988).

The Chancellor, however, modified these restrictions enforcing them as modified by injunctive relief. In addition, the Chancellor awarded the plaintiff $80,000.00 in damages for the breach of the covenants and for the torts of unfair competition and breach of the duty of loyalty.

The Court of Appeals reversed the Chancellor on the issue of the covenant not to compete, holding that the covenants were unenforceable for lack of consideration. As an additional ground for its decision, it held, without discussing the issue of modification, that the covenants were unenforceable because they were unreasonably broad in their geographic and time limitations. The Court of Appeals affirmed the defendants' liability in tort, though it remanded the case for reconsideration of damages. The defendants' tort liability is not disputed before this Court.

II

The collection industry with approximately 8,000 agencies nationwide is highly competitive. Agencies operate essentially in the same manner regardless of size. Salespersons contact businesses and solicit past-due accounts for collection. Collectors then contact the debtors and attempt to collect the money owed. The agency receives a fee consisting of a percentage of the amount recovered. This percentage is generally set by agreement between the salesperson and the client.

Most clients use more than one collection agency. The primary factor in choosing an agency is the rate of return to the client, although the rate charged the client, the services available from the agency and the personal contact between a client and the agency salesperson are also factors.

CAB's business is national in scope, covering 48 states including Hawaii. It specializes in national accounts such as hospital holding companies, universities, major oil companies, credit card companies and financial institutions.

Defendant Henry Preston Ingram was hired on March 1, 1970, by CAB as a salesman in North Carolina with a base salary of $600.00 monthly plus commissions. A week after he began working, CAB informed him that he must sign a covenant not to compete. Ingram initially refused to sign, but under threat of termination, he signed two weeks later.

In June, 1972, CAB promoted Ingram to manager of the Nashville district. Ingram was promoted in June, 1977, to manager of the northern region of CAB. CAB is divided into three regions nationwide. The northern region which was headquartered in Nashville included Kentucky and Tennessee as well as most of the states in the midwestern, northeastern and mid-Atlantic areas of the United States. As a regional manager, Ingram was employed in the highest corporate position outside that of an officer.

Ingram resigned from CAB on February 22, 1979. At that time, he was the fifth highest paid employee at CAB. In 1978, he received more than $59,000.00 in compensation.

Defendant Richard B. Goostree was hired as a collector in the Nashville office on March 6, 1972, at a base salary of $500.00 monthly plus commissions. Prior to beginning employment, he was not informed that he would be required to sign a covenant not to compete. It was presented to him and signed on March 7, 1972.

Goostree received a promotion to collections manager in April, 1973. In June, 1977, he was promoted to district manager of the Nashville office.

Defendant James Bjorkholm was hired as a salesman for the Nashville office on May 5, 1977, at a base salary of $750.00 a month plus commissions and an automobile allowance. He signed a non-competition covenant three weeks later. This agreement was lost, however, and another was signed on August 8, 1977. Bjorkholm received one $50.00 raise in his base salary while at CAB, but no promotions.

The covenant was identical in each case, providing as follows:

"I, /s/ _____, the undersigned, during the term of my employment with Central Adjustment Bureau, Inc., and/or its wholly-owned subsidiaries, and at any time within two years of termination thereof, shall not compete within the United States, either directly or indirectly, with the corporation (1) by owning, operating, managing, being employed by, having a proprietary interest of any kind in, or extending financial credit to any person, enterprise, firm or corporation which is engaged in any business in which the corporation is engaged or directly or indirectly competes with the corporation in any manner; (2) by divulging any information pertaining to the business, trade secrets, and/or confidential data of the corporation, or make any use whatsoever of the same; or (3) by contacting any client or customer of the corporation who has been a client or customer of the corporation during the term of employment.

"I fully understand that the corporation will rely on this covenant in employing me, and I agree that in the event of any breach of this covenant that the corporation's damages are irreparable and that the corporation shall be entitled to injunctive relief, in addition to such other and further relief as may be proper. It is further agreed that if at any time it shall be determined that this covenant is unreasonable as to time or area, or both, by any court of competent jurisdiction, the corporation shall be entitled to enforce this covenant for such period of time and within such area as may be determined to be reasonable by such court. In the event of breach of this covenant, I agree to pay all costs of enforcement of the said covenant, including, but not limited to, reasonable attorney's fees."

On January 26, 1979, Ingram filed a charter of incorporation with the State of Tennessee for a corporation by the name of Ingram Associates, Inc., the purposes of which included engaging in the debt collection business. In January or early February, 1979, Ingram applied for a license in both Kentucky and Tennessee to operate a collection agency; he opened bank accounts for Ingram & Associates in Nashville and Louisville; and he began to collect master client lists and other information from other CAB offices around the country to use in his own business.

Ingram resigned from CAB on February 22, 1979; Goostree and Bjorkholm resigned in March, 1979. On March 10, 1979, Ingram, Goostree and Bjorkholm of the Nashville CAB office met with Kathleen Garrison, David Powers and Anthony Schweitzer to finalize the formation of Ingram & Associates. Ingram was to hold sixty per cent of the outstanding stock with Powers, Bjorkholm, Garrison and Goostree each holding ten per cent.[1]

On or about March 22, 1979, Ingram & Associates began actively functioning in the collection agency business. Both prior and subsequent to this date, the new venture solicited CAB customers, making use of personal contacts gained by the defendants while employed by CAB.

The Chancellor found that the defendants

"... utilized valuable knowledge and personal contacts gained and developed while they were CAB employees. They know which potential customers are likely to be profitable, and how to secure, retain and service customers. They have been able to profit from the personal relationships they developed with CAB customers...."

The record amply supports the findings. It is undisputed that defendant Ingram made plans and took actions prior to his resignation to acquire a proprietary interest in a collection agency, which was intended to operate in direct competition with CAB. For instance, prior to leaving CAB, defendant Ingram obtained from various CAB branch officers client information sheets deemed confidential by CAB. These sheets set forth information valuable to any competitor of CAB, including the names of the client contacts, collection, legal, accounting and special requirements of each client as well as the commission charged each client by CAB. Through its access to this and similar information, Ingram & Associates was able to make proposals to major CAB clients which undercut the CAB rate of commission. Other documents indicate that Ingram & Associates in its effort to attract clients made extensive use of the good will and personal contacts developed by the defendants while working for CAB.

III

As a general rule, restrictive covenants in employment contracts will be enforced if they are reasonable under the particular circumstances. Allright Auto Parks, Inc. v. Berry, 219 Tenn. 280, 409 S.W.2d 361 (1966). The rule of reasonableness applies to consideration as well as to other

---

1. CAB also sued Ingram, Garrison, Powers and Schweitzer in Kentucky. The Kentucky Court of Appeals held that the covenant was enforceable against the defendants. Central Adjustment Bureau v. Ingram, etc., 622 S.W.2d 681 (Ky.App.1981). For the reasoning of the Kentucky court, see [the discussion later in] this opinion.

matters such as territorial and time limitations. Di Deeland v. Colvin, 208 Tenn. 551, 554, 347 S.W.2d 483, 484 (1961). Whether there is adequate consideration to support a non-competition covenant signed during an on-going employment relationship depends upon the facts of each case. Davies & Davies Agency, Inc. v. Davies, 298 N.W.2d 127 (Minn.1980).

The first question before us is whether future employment of an at-will employee constitutes consideration for a non-competition covenant.[a] In Ramsey v. Mutual Supply Co., 58 Tenn.App. 164, 427 S.W.2d 849 (1968), Ramsey agreed to a non-competition covenant with his employer, Mutual Supply Company, "at the time of such employment." 427 S.W.2d at 850. Ramsey's employment lasted nearly two and a half years before he left to work for a competitor. When Mutual Supply brought suit to enforce the covenant, Ramsey argued that employment was not sufficient consideration. The court rejected that argument, holding

"that employment, even for an indefinite period of time, subject to termination at the option of the employer is sufficient consideration to support such a contract." Id. 427 S.W.2d at 852.

Ramsey is thus authority for the proposition that employment is sufficient consideration for a covenant which is part of the original employment agreement. The contention is made, however, that the employee must be informed of the covenant during employment negotiations before beginning employment. It is argued that if the covenant is not presented to the employee until the first day at work or shortly thereafter, the covenant is not the subject of free bargaining.

Such an argument, if accepted, threatens to vitiate any agreement between an employee already working and his or her employer. See McQuown v. Lakeland Window Cleaning Co., 136 So.2d 370 (Fla.App. 1962). We hold that a covenant signed prior to, contemporaneously with or shortly after employment begins is part of the original agreement, and that therefore, under *Ramsey,* it is supported by adequate consideration.

For this reason, we find that there is adequate consideration to support defendant Goostree's covenant. According to an exhibit filed by CAB, Goostree began working for CAB on March 6, 1972. He signed the covenant not to compete on March 7, 1972. Under these circumstances, the covenant was clearly part of the original employment agreement.[2]

Even when the covenant is not signed until after employment has begun, courts in the following states have found continued employment to be sufficient consideration: Alabama, Connecticut, Florida, Georgia, Iowa, Kentucky, Massachusetts, Mississippi, Missouri, New Hampshire, New Jersey and Texas. See generally Annot. 51 A.L.R.3d 825 (1973).

a. During the nineteenth century, it became firmly established that, absent agreement to the contrary, employment was terminable "at will" by either employer or employee. This rule came to be known as "Wood's rule" after Horace Gray Wood, who proclaimed it in his treatise in 1877.

See H. Wood, Master and Servant § 134 (1877).

2. In so holding, we view the record in the light most favorable to the defendant. The covenant itself is dated March 3, 1972. Goostree's testimony suggests that he began working on that same day.

Some of these courts reason that the mutual promises of the parties as to continued employment form a binding bilateral contract with the promise of employment constituting sufficient consideration. See, e.g. Sherman v. Pfefferkorn, 241 Mass. 468, 135 N.E. 568 (1922); Reed, Roberts Associates, Inc. v. Bailenson, 537 S.W.2d 238 (Mo.App.1976). Other courts, however, regard the mere promise of continued employment as not binding on the employee where the employment is one at-will. They nevertheless regard the covenant as binding if there is actual performance of the promise of continued employment.

In Thomas v. Coastal Industrial Services, 214 Ga. 832, 108 S.E.2d 328 (1959), the court stated its reasoning as follows:

> "Though a promise may be *nudum pactum* when made because the promisee is not bound, it becomes binding when he subsequently furnishes the consideration contemplated by doing what he was expected to do." Id. 108 S.E.2d at 329.

The court thus held that although there was no mutuality or consideration to bind the employer when an employee, already employed, signed a non-competition covenant, performance under the contract supplied the mutuality and consideration necessary to make the contract binding. The Kentucky Court of Appeals relied on Thomas v. Coastal Industrial Services, Inc., in holding that a covenant is enforceable "provided the employer continues to employ the employee for an appreciable length of time after he signs the covenant, and the employee severs his relationship with his employer by voluntarily resigning." CAB v. Ingram, supra, 622 S.W.2d at 685....

The defendant contends, however, that Tennessee has rejected this reasoning, adhering instead to the rule that the mere fact of continued employment will not support a non-competition covenant signed subsequent to employment, relying on Associated Dairies, Inc. v. Ray Moss Farms, Inc., et al., 205 Tenn. 268, 326 S.W.2d 458 (1959). In *Ray Moss,* the non-competition covenant signed by the defendant employee was not part of the original agreement, although the opinion does not state how long the employee, Ralph Byrum, had worked for Associated Dairies when he signed the covenant. In consideration for the covenant, Associated Dairies agreed only to retain Byrum in employment at will. The Court held that there was no consideration since Associated Dairies was not bound by the agreement to retain Byrum for even a single day.

We disagree with the defendants' interpretation of *Ray Moss.* The court there decided only the question of whether the *promise* of continued employment standing alone is sufficient consideration for a non-competition covenant signed after employment has begun. It did not address the issue of consideration when employment has in fact continued for an appreciable period of time. Indeed, the opinion does not indicate how long Byrum remained with Associated Dairies after he signed the covenant.

Thus, if there has been actual performance in the form of continued employment, the inquiry must move beyond *Ray Moss.* In Hoyt v. Hoyt, 213 Tenn. 117, 372 S.W.2d 300 (1963), this Court stated:

"The authorities are uniform in holding that where there has been full or substantial performance by one party to a bilateral contract, originally invalid for want of mutuality of obligation, the other party cannot refuse performance after receiving the promised benefits. [Citations omitted] ... Williston and Corbin contend that once performance is made of the counter-promise (Appellee's here) the other promise (Appellant's promise) becomes binding as sufficient consideration has been received for it. By this view a binding unilateral contract is forged out of a former, invalid bilateral contract."

Id. at 128–29, 372 S.W.2d at 305.

We are persuaded that the doctrine stated in *Hoyt* should be applied in cases involving non-competition covenants. Such an approach is in agreement with the decisions of our sister state courts cited above. Moreover, it does not require that we overrule *Ray Moss;* rather, *Ray Moss* remains good law when the only consideration is the promise of continued employment.

Whether performance is sufficient to support a covenant not to compete depends upon the facts and circumstances of each case. The requirement that consideration for a non-competition covenant be reasonable remains. Di Deeland v. Colvin, supra. It is possible, for instance, that employment for only a short period of time would be insufficient consideration under the circumstances. See, e.g., Frierson v. Sheppard Building Supply Co., 247 Miss. 157, 154 So.2d 151, 154 (1963) ("If appellant had been discharged shortly after signing the agreement, this Court would probably hold the agreement was not supported by consideration"). Another factor affecting reasonableness is the circumstances under which an employee leaves. Although an at-will employee can be discharged for any reason without breach of the contract, a discharge which is arbitrary, capricious or in bad faith clearly has a bearing on whether a court of equity should enforce a non-competition covenant. Id., 154 So.2d at 155; Gibson's Suits in Chancery § 18 (6th ed. 1982).

We find that because of the length of employment of each defendant, the covenant is binding against them. Defendants Ingram and Goostree remained with CAB for seven years after signing the covenants while defendant Bjorkholm was employed for two years. Each defendant left voluntarily; there is no evidence that CAB acted in bad faith or with unclean hands. It is unnecessary at this time to say how long employment must continue before there is substantial performance under the doctrine of Hoyt v. Hoyt discussed above. The length of employment of each defendant in this case is sufficient to constitute substantial performance.

In addition, we note that defendant Ingram received numerous salary increases while employed at CAB. Beginning as a salesman, Ingram advanced until at the time of his resignation, he occupied one of the highest positions in the company. Defendant Goostree also received numerous salary increases as well as two promotions. He had risen to the position of Nashville district manager at the time he resigned from CAB in order to compete with it in the Nashville area.

Some courts which have required additional consideration other than continued employment have held that a beneficial change in an employee's status constitutes sufficient consideration to support a restrictive covenant agreed to after the initial taking of employment.... In Davies & Davies Agency, Inc. v. Davies, 298 N.W.2d 127 (Minn.1980), the employee signed the covenant after his employment began. In enforcing the covenant, the court found decisive the fact that because he had signed the covenant, he had advanced to a responsible selling position in his ten years with the firm, and had in effect taken over one aspect of the firm's business which had become identified with him.

As in *Davies & Davies*, defendants Ingram and Goostree received additional benefits above and beyond continued employment which they would not have received had they not signed the covenants. The fact of these additional benefits shows the extent to which CAB performed under its contracts with Ingram and Goostree. For this additional reason, we hold that the covenants are supported by sufficient consideration.

IV

[The rest of the opinion in this case, dealing with the Chancellor's decision to enforce the covenant as modified, is at p. 461 below.]

The judgment of the Court of Appeals as to all defendants is reversed and the judgment of the Chancellor is affirmed. Costs are taxed against the defendants.

COOPER, C.J., and HARBISON, J., concur. FONES and BROCK, JJ., dissent in separate opinion.

BROCK, JUSTICE, dissenting.... In Associated Dairies, Inc. v. Ray Moss Farms, Inc., 205 Tenn. 268, 326 S.W.2d 458 (1959), this Court held that continued employment is no consideration for a restrictive covenant imposed after an employment relationship has begun. In *Ray Moss,* a competitor of the employer, who was in the dairy business, allegedly began to hire the employer's sales drivers and to use those drivers to solicit the employer's business. In response, the employer required its drivers, including the defendant, to sign a non-competition agreement. In refusing to enforce the agreement, this Court found as follows:

> "In the case at bar there was no agreement that the complainant would retain the defendant for as much as one day.... In these circumstances there was no consideration to sustain the contract which purports to restrain the defendant from engaging in the solicitation of business for another." Id., 205 Tenn. at 275, 326 S.W.2d at 461.

Thus, if the terms of the original employment agreement do not include a covenant not to compete, any subsequent covenant must be supported by some consideration other than mere continued employment under a contract terminable at will....

Ray Moss is supported by the following reasoning in Pemco Corp. v. Rose, 163 W.Va. 420, 257 S.E.2d 885, 890 (1979):

"The argument that the employer's consideration for the non-competition covenant is the forbearance of the legal right of discharge we find unavailing but not without logical support.... Common law principles governing employment contracts should not be employed to supply consideration for a non-competition covenant where such a provision was not freely bargained for by the parties."

In the instant case, CAB did not present the covenants to the defendants until after they had terminated their previous employment and begun work for CAB. Although the covenants were presented to the defendants as soon as or shortly after they began working, at that point the covenants were no longer the subject of free bargaining. As the Court of Appeals observed, "[e]ven if he [the employee] is notified of the restrictive covenant on the first day of his new employment, he has foreclosed his other options at that point and has little choice but to sign."

The *Ray Moss* rule that an employee's anticompetitive covenant executed after the commencement of his employment is unenforceable because without consideration is followed in a number of other states.... We are urged to hold in this case that consideration may be found to have consisted of promotions and increases in compensation granted to the defendants-employees over the years of their employment with the appellant. Davies & Davies Agcy., Inc. v. Davies, Minn., 298 N.W.2d 127 (1980) is cited as authority for such a holding. I decline this invitation because of the fundamental doctrine that in order for an act to constitute consideration for a promise it must have been "bargained for and given in exchange for that very promise." Section 75, Restatement of Contracts, American Law Institute. There is simply no indication in this record whatever for a conclusion that promotions and increases in compensation, given years after the covenants not to compete were executed, were bargained for and given in exchange for those covenants. The covenants not to compete in the instant case were not bargained for at all but were merely imposed upon the employees after their employment began. I would hold that these covenants fail for lack of consideration. The majority finds consideration where there is none....

NOTES

(1) *Possible Distinctions.* Although the covenants signed by the defendants were identical, the circumstances of their signing and the defendants' subsequent employment histories were not. As to which defendant did CAB have the strongest case in your opinion: Ingram, Goostree, or Bjorkholm?

(2) *Contrary Authority.* With which opinion do you agree? Courts have divided on whether continued employment is consideration for a promise not to compete. For example, the Supreme Court of Minnesota has held that "where no raises or promotions resulted, where other employees with similar access were not asked to sign, the mere continuation of employment ... is not enough." Jostens, Inc. v. National Computer Systems, Inc., 318 N.W.2d 691, 703–04 (Minn.1982).

Some of these decisions seem to reflect judicial hostility to promises not to compete. As the Supreme Court of Minnesota wrote only a few months after it decided the case just cited, "We look upon restrictive covenants with disfavor, carefully scrutinizing them because they are agreements in partial restraint of trade." National Recruiters, Inc. v. Cashman, 323 N.W.2d 736, 740 (Minn.1982). Judicial limitations on such agreements are discussed in connection with the topic of illegality in Chapter 4, Section 5.

(3) *Problem.* Richard Mettille was a loan officer at the Pine River State Bank whose employment was terminable at will by either Mettille or the bank. E.A. Griffith, president of the bank, prepared and distributed a printed Employee Handbook with information on the bank's employment policies including "job security" and "disciplinary policy." A year later Griffith fired Mettille for what Griffith called "serious" deficiencies involving loans totalling over $600,000, but Griffith failed to follow the rules of the Handbook relating to "disciplinary policy." Does Mettille have a claim against the bank for breach of contract? Would it make a difference if Mettille had never read the handbook? Would it make a difference if Mettille had never thought of leaving his job? How does Mettille's situation differ from that of CAB? See Pine River State Bank v. Mettille, 333 N.W.2d 622 (Minn.1983). See also the following case.

IN RE CERTIFIED QUESTION (BANKEY v. STORER BROAD-CASTING CO.), 443 N.W.2d 112 (Mich.1989). [After working for Storer Broadcasting Company for 13 years, Kenneth Bankey was fired on March 23, 1981. Bankey sued Storer in a federal court and proved that his employment had been governed by a 1980 employee handbook that stated that "an employee may be ... discharged for cause." In January, 1981, however, Storer had revised its handbook to eliminate the "for cause" requirement and to make employment "at the will of the company." When the case reached the federal Court of Appeals, it certified to the Supreme Court of Michigan the question: "may the employer ... unilaterally change [its] written policy statements by adopting a generally applicable policy and alter the employment relationship of existing employees to one at the will of the employer in the absence of an express notification to the employees from the outset that the employer reserves the right to make such a change?" The Supreme Court answered in the affirmative.]

GRIFFIN, JUSTICE.... An employer may, without an express reservation of the right to do so, unilaterally change its written policy from one of discharge for cause to one of termination at will, provided that the employer gives affected employees reasonable notice of the policy change....

Without rejecting the applicability of unilateral contract theory in other situations, we find it inadequate as a basis for our answer to the question as worded and certified by the United States Court of Appeals. We look, instead, to the analysis employed in [Toussaint v. Blue Cross & Blue Shield of Michigan, 292 N.W.2d 880 (Mich.1980).] which focused upon the benefit that accrues to an employer when it establishes desirable personnel policies. Under *Toussaint,* written personnel policies are not enforceable because they have been "offered and accepted" as a unilateral contract; rather, their enforceability arises from the benefit the employer derives by establishing such policies.

"While an employer need not establish personnel policies or practices, where an employer chooses to establish such policies and practices and makes them known to its employees, the employment relationship is presumably enhanced. The employer secures an orderly, cooperative and loyal work force, and the employee the peace of mind associated with job security and the conviction that he will be treated fairly. No pre-employment negotiations need take place and the parties' minds need not meet on the subject; nor does it matter that the employee knows nothing of the particulars of the employer's policies and practices *or that the employer may change them unilaterally.* It is enough that the employer chooses, presumably in its own interest, to create an environment in which the employee believes that, whatever the personnel policies and practices, they are established and official *at any given time,* purport to be fair, and are applied consistently and uniformly to each employee. The employer has then created a situation 'instinct with an obligation.'" Toussaint, supra, 408 Mich. p. 613, 292 N.W.2d 880 (emphasis added).

Under the *Toussaint* analysis, an employer who chooses to establish desirable personnel policies, such as a discharge-for-cause employment policy, is not seeking to induce each individual employee to show up for work day after day, but rather is seeking to promote an environment conducive to collective productivity. The benefit to the employer of promoting such an environment, rather than the traditional contract-forming mechanisms of mutual assent or individual detrimental reliance, gives rise to a situation "instinct with an obligation." When, as in the question before us, the employer changes its discharge-for-cause policy to one of employment-at-will, the employer's benefit is correspondingly extinguished, as is the rationale for the court's enforcement of the discharge-for-cause policy. . . .

Furthermore, it is important to recognize that even though an employment policy is revocable, the *Toussaint* approach to employer obligation promotes stability in employment relations in two significant ways: by holding employees accountable for personnel policies that "are established and official at any given time," and by requiring that such policies be "applied consistently and uniformly to each employee." *Toussaint* holds that an employee may "legitimately expect" that his employer will uniformly apply personnel policies "in force at any given time." . . .

NOTES

(1) *Questions.* Is the court's answer to the certified question consistent with the decisions in *Kirksey, Feinberg,* and *Ingram:* In terms of Restatement Second § 71(2), was the issue whether what was given by the promisee "sought by the promisor in exchange for his promise" or "given by the promisee in exchange for that promise"?

(2) *The Case of Virtue as Its Own Reward.* Sheriff Ledbetter had offered a $500 reward for the recapture and return to the Dallas County jail of Vann, an escaped prisoner. Broadnax sued for the reward and Ledbetter demurred on the ground that Broadnax had not alleged that he knew of the offer of the reward when he captured and returned the prisoner. The Supreme Court of Texas upheld the demurrer on the ground that such an offer "may be accepted by anyone who performs the service called for when the acceptor knows that it has been made and acts in performance of it, but not otherwise." Broadnax v. Ledbetter, 99 S.W. 1111 (Tex.1907). Put in terms of Restatement Second § 71(2), the service that Broadnax rendered was not given by Broadnax in exchange for Ledbetter's promise because Broadnax did not know of that promise. (Although the details of offer and acceptance are not taken up until the next chapter, it may help to know now that it is often possible to express the same principle either in terms of "consideration" or of "offer and acceptance." [a])

Could Broadnax have recovered if he had captured Vann while ignorant of the reward but had learned of it before returning him to jail? Is his solution to release the criminal and capture him again? See Restatement Second § 51. Could Broadnax have recovered if he had known of the reward but had captured Vann and turned him in because he was a close friend and wished to save him from mob violence? See Restatement Second § 81(2). Could he have recovered if he had said, when he turned Vann in, that he did not want the reward? See Corbin § 58. For an interesting reward case, see Taft v. Hyatt, 180 P. 213 (Kan.1919). *Yes. Capture and "return"*

In some legal systems, including the German, a promise of reward is treated, "not as an offer which would require acceptance in order to ripen into a contract, but as a unilateral jural act which as such is effective and binding without acceptance." 1 R. Schlesinger (ed.), Formation of Contracts: A study of the Common Core of Legal Systems 101–02 (1968). Would such a concept be a desirable one in our law? See Choice v. City of Dallas, 210 S.W. 753 (Tex.Civ. App.1919). Does the *Certified Question* case support it?

(3) *The Case of the Unsolicited Surcease.* George Whitten, a Massachusetts contractor, and Shirley Shaw had engaged in an intermittent extra-marital affair for eight years. When Whitten was at his Bermuda home with friends, expecting to be joined by his wife, Shaw came to the home uninvited to demand that, as Whitten put it, "I see her or she would come up and raise hell with my friends" and embarrass him in front of his wife. Whitten signed a one-page typewritten document, prepared by Shaw, in which he promised to pay her $500 per month for an indeterminate period, make major repairs to the house she lived in, pay for any medical needs, take one trip and supply her with one piece of jewelry per year, and visit and phone her at stated intervals. It contained the statement that "under no circumstances will there be any calls made to my homes or offices without prior permission from me." When Shaw sought to enforce the writing, the trial court held that it lacked consideration and Shaw appealed. Held: Affirmed.

---

a. According to Professor A.W.B. Simpson, an English legal historian, until the nineteenth century there was no notion "that acceptance made a promise binding— it was consideration which did that.... All this changed in nineteenth-century law, when a doctrine of offer and acceptance was superimposed upon the sixteenth-century requirement of consideration and made to perform some of the same functions and some new ones generated principally by the problem of written contracts by correspondence." Simpson, Innovation in Nineteenth Century Contract Law, 91 L.Q.Rev. 247, 258 (1975).

"[A]lthough [Shaw's] promise to forbear could constitute consideration, it cannot if it was not sought after by [Whitten], and motivated by his request that [Shaw] not disturb him.... Of this there was no evidence whatsoever. This clause, the only one that operates in [Whitten's] favor, was only included in the contract by [Shaw], because, she asserts, she felt [Whitten] should get something in exchange for his promises. Clearly, this clause was not 'bargained for' by [Whitten], and not given in exchange for his promises, and as such cannot constitute the consideration necessary to support a contract." [b] Whitten v. Greeley–Shaw, 520 A.2d 1307 (Me.1987).

It should thus be evident that, as we see it here, the doctrine of consideration does not enable courts to police bargains to assure fairness, or at least the absence of unfairness, of the exchange. The doctrines under which courts do police bargains are explored in Chapter 4, Policing the Bargain.

(4) *Problem.* Diamond Jim III, a rock fish, was tagged and placed in the Chesapeake Bay on June 19 by the American Brewery in connection with its Third Annual American Beer Fishing Derby. Under the Derby's well-publicized rules, the person who caught Diamond Jim III would receive a cash prize of $25,000. On August 6, William Simmons set out to go fishing in the Bay. He had heard of the contest, but did not have it in mind on that day. He caught Diamond Jim III, and although he at first took little notice of the tag, he realized upon reexamining it a half hour later that he had caught the prize fish. Is Simmons legally entitled to the prize? See Simmons v. United States, 308 F.2d 160 (4th Cir.1962).

* * *

(b) Reliance as an Alternative Basis for Enforcement

RICKETTS v. SCOTHORN

Supreme Court of Nebraska, 1898.
57 Neb. 51, 77 N.W. 365.

SULLIVAN, J. In the District Court of Lancaster county, the plaintiff, Katie Scothorn, recovered judgment against the defendant, Andrew D. Ricketts, as executor, of the last will and testament of John C. Ricketts, deceased. The action was based upon a promissory note, of which the following is a copy: "May the first, 1891. I promise to pay to Katie Scothorn on demand, $2,000 to be at 6 per cent. per annum. J.C. Ricketts." In the petition the plaintiff alleges that the consideration for the execution of the note was that she should surrender her employment as bookkeeper for Mayer Bros., and cease to work for a living. She also alleges that the note was given to induce her to abandon her occupation, and that, relying on it, and on the annual interest, as a means of support, she gave up the employment in which she was then engaged. These allegations of the petition are denied by the administrator.

b. Note that it is Shaw's *promise* to forbear and not her *forbearance* that is held not to have been consideration. Whether a *promise* to do or to forbear from doing something (as distinguished from the act or forbearance itself) is consideration is examined in Section 5, below.

The material facts are undisputed. They are as follows: John C. Ricketts, the maker of the note, was the grandfather of the plaintiff. Early in May—presumably on the day the note bears date—he called on her at the store where she was working. What transpired between them is thus described by Mr. Flodene, one of the plaintiff's witnesses: "A. Well, the old gentleman came in there one morning about nine o'clock, probably a little before or a little after, but early in the morning, and he unbuttoned his vest, and took out a piece of paper in the shape of a note; that is the way it looked to me; and he says to Miss Scothorn, 'I have fixed out something that you have not got to work any more.' He says, 'none of my grandchildren work, and you don't have to.' Q. Where was she? A. She took the piece of paper and kissed him, and kissed the old gentleman, and commenced to cry." It seems Miss Scothorn immediately notified her employer of her intention to quit work, and that she did soon after abandon her occupation. The mother of the plaintiff was a witness, and testified that she had a conversation with her father, Mr. Ricketts, shortly after the note was executed, in which he informed her that he had given the note to the plaintiff to enable her to quit work; that none of his grandchildren worked, and he did not think she ought to. For something more than a year the plaintiff was without an occupation, but in September, 1892, with the consent of her grandfather, and by his assistance, she secured a position as bookkeeper with Messrs. Funke & Ogden. On June 8, 1894, Mr. Ricketts died. He had paid one year's interest on the note, and a short time before his death expressed regret that he had not been able to pay the balance. In the summer or fall of 1892 he stated to his daughter, Mrs. Scothorn, that if he could sell his farm in Ohio he would pay the note out of the proceeds. He at no time repudiated the obligation.

We quite agree with counsel for the defendant that upon this evidence there was nothing to submit to the jury, and that a verdict should have been directed peremptorily for one of the parties. The testimony of Flodene and Mrs. Scothorn, taken together, conclusively establishes the fact that the note was not given in consideration of the plaintiff pursuing, or agreeing to pursue, any particular line of conduct. There was no promise on the part of the plaintiff to do, or refrain from doing, anything. Her right to the money promised in the note was not made to depend upon an abandonment of her employment with Mayer Bros., and future abstention from like service. Mr. Ricketts made no condition, requirement, or request. He exacted no quid pro quo. He gave the note as a gratuity, and looked for nothing in return. So far as the evidence discloses, it was his purpose to place the plaintiff in a position of independence, where she could work or remain idle, as she might choose. The abandonment by Miss Scothorn of her position as bookkeeper was altogether voluntary. It was not an act done in fulfillment of any contract obligation assumed when she accepted the note.

The instrument in suit, being given without any valuable consideration, was nothing more than a promise to make a gift in the future of the sum of money therein named. Ordinarily, such promises are not enforceable, even when put in the form of a promissory note.... But it has often been held that an action on a note given to a church, college, or other like institution, upon the faith of which money has been expended or obligations incurred, could not be successfully defended on the ground of a want of consideration.... In this class of cases the note in suit is nearly always spoken of as a gift or donation, but the decision is generally put on the ground that the expenditure of money or assumption of liability by the donee on the faith of the promise constitutes a valuable and sufficient consideration. It seems to us that the true reason is the preclusion of the defendant, under the doctrine of estoppel, to deny the consideration....

Under the circumstances of this case, is there an equitable estoppel which ought to preclude the defendant from alleging that the note in controversy is lacking in one of the essential elements of a valid contract? We think there is. An estoppel in pais is defined to be "a right arising from acts, admissions, or conduct which have induced a change of position in accordance with the real or apparent intention of the party against whom they are alleged." ... According to the undisputed proof, as shown by the record before us, the plaintiff was a working girl, holding a position in which she earned a salary of $10 per week. Her grandfather, desiring to put her in a position of independence, gave her the note, accompanying it with the remark that his other grandchildren did not work, and that she would not be obliged to work any longer. In effect, he suggested that she might abandon her employment, and rely in the future upon the bounty which he promised. He doubtless desired that she should give up her occupation, but, whether he did or not, it is entirely certain that he contemplated such action on her part as a reasonable and probable consequence of his gift. Having intentionally influenced the plaintiff to alter her position for the worse on the faith of the note being paid when due, it would be grossly inequitable to permit the maker, or his executor, to resist payment on the ground that the promise was given without consideration. The petition charges the elements of an equitable estoppel, and the evidence conclusively establishes them. If errors intervened at the trial, they could not have been prejudicial. A verdict for the defendant would be unwarranted. The judgment is right, and is

Affirmed.

NOTES

(1) *Kirksey Revisited.* Would the reasoning of the court in the principal case support a recovery by the plaintiff promisee in Kirksey v. Kirksey, above?

(2) *Estoppel: New Wine in an Old Bottle.* Decisions like the one in the principal case involve far more than routine application of established estoppel theory. The conventional estoppel case concerns a representation of fact made by one party and relied on by the other; the estopped party is prohibited from alleging or proving facts that would contradict the truth of his own earlier representation if the other party has taken action in reliance on that representation. Cases like Ricketts v. Scothorn concern not a factual representation but a promise, and the estoppel idea is used affirmatively as the legal basis of a claim.[a]

a. That the claimant has no right to a trial by jury of such a claim because "the doctrine of promissory estoppel is essentially equitable in nature," see C & K Engi-

(3) *Bargained–For Exchange as an Alternative.* Might another court have found a bargained-for exchange in the principal case, and so have enforced the note to Katie Scothorn as a promise supported by consideration? Compare, particularly, Hamer v. Sidway, p. 47 above.

"PROMISSORY ESTOPPEL" *→ Diff 4 then*
classical contract △

Holmes said, "It would cut up the doctrine of consideration by the roots, if a promisee could make a gratuitous promise binding by subsequently acting in reliance on it." Commonwealth v. Scituate Savings Bank, 137 Mass. 301, 302 (1884). Nevertheless, Ricketts v. Scothorn is one of a number of cases that, even prior to the promulgation of the Restatement of Contracts in 1932, recognized reliance as a basis for the enforcement of promises. For the most part, these cases fall into four categories.

1. *Family Promises.* One category consisted of cases, like Ricketts v. Scothorn itself, in which the promise was made by one member of a family to another. Is there a possible connection between the growth of this category and the fact that the pattern of bargained-for exchange, so common in a commercial setting, ordinarily seems out of place in a family setting? Contrast Ricketts v. Scothorn with Hamer v. Sidway, p. 47 above.

2. *Promises to Convey Land.* Another category consisted of cases involving promises to convey land on which the promisee had relied by moving onto the land and making improvements. An early example is Freeman v. Freeman, 43 N.Y. 34 (1870). Would the facts in Kirksey v. Kirksey, above, have brought that case within this category?

3. *Promises Coupled With Gratuitous Bailments.* A third category was made up of cases in which a bailor sought to enforce a promise made by the bailee in connection with a gratuitous bailment. The leading case is Siegel v. Spear & Co., 138 N.E. 414 (N.Y.1923). Siegel bought furniture on credit from Spear, giving Spear a mortgage on it and agreeing not to remove it from his apartment in New York City without Spear's consent until it was paid for. When he decided to leave the city for the summer, he saw Spear's credit man, McGrath, who agreed to store it free of charge. McGrath then said, "You had better transfer your insurance policy over to our warehouse," to which Siegel answered that he had no insurance but would get some through his agent. McGrath replied, "That won't be necessary to get that from him; I will do it for you; it will be a good deal cheaper; I handle lots of insurance; when you get the next bill—you can send a check for that with the next installment." In May, Siegel sent the furniture to Spear's storehouse. About a month later it was destroyed by fire. It had not been insured. Siegel sued Spear, had judgment, and Spear appealed. The Court of Appeals affirmed. Although the gratuitous bailment itself imposed no

neering Contractors v. Amber Steel Co.,
Inc., 587 P.2d 1136 (Cal.1978).

duty on Spear to insure the furniture, such a duty arose from McGrath's promise followed by the delivery of the furniture by Siegel. The court distinguished an old New York case, Thorne v. Deas, 4 Johns. 84 (N.Y.Sup.Ct.1809), in which the court had refused to hold one of two joint owners of a ship to his promise made to the other owner to insure the ship, when he had failed to do so and the ship had been lost. There, in contrast to Siegel, the promisee "parted with nothing ... gave up possession of none of his property" to the promisor. This category will be considered further in connection with the next case.

4. *Charitable Subscriptions.* The fourth category of cases involves charitable subscriptions. The enforceability of such gratuitous promises may be regarded as particularly desirable as a means of allowing decisions about the distribution of wealth to be made at an individual level. See the discussion of gratuitous promises at p. 52 above. As one court put it, "This promise was made to a charitable corporation, and for that reason we are not confined to the same orthodox concepts which once were applicable to every situation arising within a common law jurisdiction. There can be no denying that the strong desire on the part of the American courts to favor charitable institutions has established a doctrine which once would have been looked upon as legal heresy." Danby v. Osteopathic Hospital Ass'n of Delaware, 104 A.2d 903 (Del.Ch.1954). It is sometimes possible to enforce such a promise by finding an exchange among subscribers of promises for the benefit of (and enforceable by) the charitable organization, particularly where one subscriber appears as the "bellwether" of the flock and promises a large sum on condition that other subscribers raise a specified amount. See Congregation B'Nai Sholom v. Martin, 173 N.W.2d 504 (Mich.1969). (How could you draft a pledge form to help your favorite charity take advantage of this possibility?) It is also sometimes possible to enforce such a promise by finding that the charity has done or has promised to do something in exchange for the subscriber's promise.

It is perhaps curious that the most widely known and influential decision on charitable subscriptions goes off on this last ground and contains only dictum concerning the effect of reliance. It is Allegheny College v. National Chautauqua County Bank of Jamestown, 159 N.E. 173 (N.Y.1927). Mary Yates Johnston promised to pay $5,000 to Allegheny College by a writing denoted an "Estate Pledge" that stipulated that "this gift shall be known as the Mary Yates Johnston memorial fund, the proceeds from which shall be used to educate students preparing for the ministry." The sum was not payable until 30 days after her death, but $1,000 was paid while she was alive and set aside by the college for the specified purpose. She later repudiated her promise, and on the expiration of 30 days following her death the college brought an action against her executor for the unpaid balance. Chief Judge Cardozo,[a] writing for the New York Court of Appeals, found consideration for

---

a. Benjamin Nathan Cardozo (1870– 1938) practiced in New York City after law school. He served as judge and later chief judge of the Court of Appeals of New York, and was appointed an associate justice of the Supreme Court of the United States in 1932 to fill the vacancy left by Holmes. Cardozo's best known jurisprudential work

her promise in the return promise of the college to set up the memorial
fund which arose "by implication" from its acceptance of the $1,000.
"The college could not accept the money and hold itself free thereafter
from personal responsibility to give effect to the condition." But in the
course of his opinion, Cardozo went out of his way to speak to the effect
of reliance. "[T]here has grown up of recent days a doctrine that a
substitute for consideration or an exception to its ordinary requirements
can be found in what is styled 'a promissory estoppel'.... Whether the
exception has made its way in this state to such an extent as to permit
us to say that the general law of consideration has been modified
accordingly, we do not now attempt to say. Cases such as Siegel v.
Spear & Co. ... may be signposts on the road. Certain, at least, it is
that we have adopted the doctrine of promissory estoppel as the equivalent of consideration in connection with our law of charitable subscriptions." For an account of the *Allegheny College* case, see Konefsky, How
to Read, or at Least Not Misread, Cardozo in the *Allegheny College* Case,
36 Buffalo L.Rev. 645 (1987).

Restatement § 90. Cardozo's dictum in the *Allegheny College* case
was surely influenced by what was to become first Restatement § 90, the
text of which had been considered at the annual meeting of the American Law Institute in 1926. It reads:

§ 90. Promise Reasonably Inducing Definite and Substan-
tial Action

A promise which the promisor should reasonably expect to
induce action or forbearance of a definite and substantial character on the part of the promisee and which does induce such
action or forbearance is binding if injustice can be avoided only
by enforcement of the promise.

Although it avoids the use of the term "promissory estoppel," it states in
general terms the principle that had been applied in the four categories
of cases just described. Its remarkable impact is suggested by its role in
the following cases.

NOTE

Measure of Recovery. During the discussion of first Restatement § 90 on
the floor of the American Law Institute, Professor Williston, as Reporter, made
the following statement: "Either the promise is binding or it is not. If the
promise is binding it has to be enforced as it is made. As I said to Mr. Coudert, I
could leave this whole thing to the subject of quasi contracts so that the promisee
under those circumstances shall never recover on the promise but he shall
recover such an amount as will fairly compensate him for any injury incurred;
but it seems to me you have to take one leg or the other. You have either to say
the promise is binding or you have to go on the theory of restoring the status
quo." 4 American Law Institute Proceedings, Appendix, 103–04 (1926).

Does not the etymology of "promissory estoppel" (although neither version
of § 90 uses that term) support Williston? For an influential attack on Williston's position, see Fuller & Perdue, The Reliance Interest in Contract Damages

is a series of lectures entitled The Nature of
the Judicial Process (1921).

(pt. 2), 46 Yale L.J. 373, 401–06 (1937). For a different view, see Yorio & Thel, The Promissory Basis of Section 90, 101 Yale L.J. 111 (1991), criticized in Feinman, The Last Promissory Estoppel Article, 61 Fordham L.Rev. 303 (1992). See also Slawson, The Role of Reliance in Contract Damages, 76 Cornell L.Rev. 197 (1990).

FEINBERG v. PFEIFFER CO.
Saint Louis Court of Appeals, Missouri, 1959.
322 S.W.2d 163.

[The facts and the first part of the opinion in this case are at p. 66 above. The court there rejected Mrs. Feinberg's contention that her continuation in the employ of Pfeiffer Co. from December 27, 1947, the date of the resolution, until the date of her retirement, June 30, 1949, was consideration for Pfeiffer's promise to pay her $200 per month for life upon her retirement. In the portion of the opinion below, the court considers Mrs. Feinberg's second contention, that the promise was enforceable because of her reliance on it, "i.e., her retirement, and the abandonment by her of her opportunity to continue in gainful employment."]

DOERNER, COMMISSIONER. . . . But as to the second of these contentions we must agree with plaintiff. By the terms of the resolution defendant promised to pay plaintiff the sum of $200 a month upon her retirement.

[The court quoted first Restatement, § 90.] Was there such an act on the part of plaintiff, in reliance upon the promise contained in the resolution, as will estop the defendant, and therefore create an enforceable contract under the doctrine of promissory estoppel? We think there was. One of the illustrations cited under Section 90 of the Restatement is: "2. A promises B to pay him an annuity during B's life. B thereupon resigns a profitable employment, as A expected that he might. B receives the annuity for some years, in the meantime becoming disqualified from again obtaining good employment. A's promise is binding." This illustration is objected to by defendant as not being applicable to the case at hand. The reason advanced by it is that in the illustration B became "disqualified" from obtaining other employment *before* A discontinued the payments, whereas in this case the plaintiff did not discover that she had cancer and thereby became unemployable until *after* the defendant had discontinued the payments of $200 per month. We think the distinction is immaterial. The only reason for the reference in the illustration to the disqualification of A is in connection with that part of Section 90 regarding the prevention of injustice. The injustice would occur regardless of when the disability occurred. Would defendant contend that the contract would be enforceable if the plaintiff's illness had been discovered on March 31, 1956, the day before it discontinued the payment of the $200 a month, but not if it occurred on April 2nd, the day after? Furthermore, there are more ways to become disqualified for work, or unemployable, than as the result of illness. At the time she retired plaintiff was 57 years of age. At the time the payments were discontinued she was over 63 years of age. It is a matter of common knowledge that it is virtually impossible for a woman of that age to find satisfactory employment, much less a position comparable to that which plaintiff enjoyed at the time of her retirement.

The fact of the matter is that plaintiff's subsequent illness was not the "action or forbearance" which was induced by the promise contained in the resolution. As the trial court correctly decided, such action on plaintiff's part was her retirement from a lucrative position in reliance upon defendant's promise to pay her an annuity or pension. [The court quoted from Ricketts v. Scothorn, supra.]

The Commissioner therefore recommends, for the reasons stated, that the judgment be affirmed.

PER CURIAM. The foregoing opinion by DOERNER, C., is adopted as the opinion of the court. The judgment is, accordingly, affirmed.

NOTES

(1) *Case Comparison.* How would the court that decided the principal case have decided the case of Kirksey v. Kirksey, above?

(2) *Feinberg Distinguished.* In Hayes v. Plantations Steel Co., 438 A.2d 1091 (R.I.1982), the court confronted a claimant who relied on *Feinberg.* In January, 1972, Edward J. Hayes announced his intention to retire from Plantations Steel the following July after 25 years of continuous service. About a week before his retirement, he had a conversation with a Plantations Steel officer who said that, though he was not eligible for a pension, the company "would take care" of him. Hayes retired and sought no other employment, and the company paid him $5,000 a year through 1976. When payments were discontinued, Hayes sued and the trial judge held the company liable for breach of an implied contract to pay a pension for life. The Supreme Court of Rhode Island reversed, deciding that there was no consideration for the company's promise and that the theory of promissory estoppel was not applicable. The court took pains to distinguish *Feinberg.* Although Hayes contended that "he retired voluntarily while expecting to receive a pension" and "would not have otherwise retired," the court concluded that "the record indicates that he made the decision on his own initiative"—that the conversation a week before he left his employment "cannot be said to have induced his decision to leave" because he "had reached that decision long before." How do we know that Feinberg, unlike Hayes, would not have retired without the promise of a pension?

RESTATEMENT SECOND § 90

In view of the great influence that § 90 of the first Restatement has had, § 90 of the Restatement Second set out below, merits a particularly careful reading. Note the addition of the second sentence of Subsection (1). Comment *d* to § 90 suggests that in some situations, relief may be "measured by the extent of the promisee's reliance rather than by the terms of the promise." In what kinds of situations would this be appropriate? Note too the deletion in the first sentence of the requirement that the reliance be of "a definite and substantial character." Is this change related to the addition of the second sentence? Finally, note the liberalization in Subsection (2) of the rule as to charitable subscriptions.[a]

§ 90. Promise Reasonably Inducing Action or Forbearance

(1) A promise which the promisor should reasonably expect to induce action or forbearance on the part of the promisee or a third person and which does induce such action or forbearance is binding if injustice can be avoided only by enforcement of the promise. The remedy granted for breach may be limited as justice requires.

(2) A charitable subscription or a marriage settlement is binding under Subsection (1) without proof that the promise induced action or forbearance.

NOTES

(1) *Measure of Recovery (Reprise).* Assuming that each of the following plaintiffs had been allowed to recover under the rule stated in Restatement Second § 90, which of them might appropriately have been limited to recovery based on the reliance interest? Katie Scothorn? Anna Feinberg? Antillico Kirksey? Why?

How much should the nephew then recover the following hypothetical case?

An uncle promises his nephew $1,000 as a gift. The nephew decides to go into business, and, reserving the promised sum for use in paying his rent, spends a large sum of money laying in a stock of goods. The uncle declines to perform his promise; the nephew is forced to abandon his plans, and sells his stock of goods at a sacrifice of $2,000.

Fuller & Perdue, The Reliance Interest in Contract Damages (pt. 1), 46 Yale L.J. 52, 80 (1936).

(2) *Rewards (Reprise).* Does the rule of Restatement Second § 90(2) on charitable subscriptions afford a helpful analogy for the proposition that a promise of a reward ought to be enforceable by one who does the requested act in ignorance of the promise? See Note 2, p. 97 above.

(3) *Detriment.* In discussing Section 90, courts often speak of "detriment," as if reliance were not sufficient. Does Section 90 mention "detriment"?

In Vastoler v. American Can Co., 700 F.2d 916 (3d Cir.1983), Vastoler sued his employer for breach of a promise of greater pension benefits on which he claimed he had relied in taking a promotion from an hourly lithographer to a salaried supervisor. The trial court granted summary judgment for the employ-

---

a. Not all courts have followed § 90(2). Congregation Kadimah Toras–Moshe v. De-Leo, 540 N.E.2d 691 (Mass.1989), is of particular interest because it was decided by the court of the late Justice Robert Braucher, the Reporter who drafted § 90(2). In holding unenforceable an oral promise to give a synagogue $25,000, the court said: "Assuming without deciding that this court would apply § 90, we are of the opinion that in this case there is no injustice in declining to enforce the decedent's promise. Although § 90 dispenses with the absolute requirement of consideration or reliance, the official comments illustrate that these are relevant considerations. Restatement (Second) of Contracts, ... at § 90 comment f. The promise to the Congregation is entirely unsupported by consideration or reliance. Furthermore, it is an oral promise sought to be enforced against an estate. To enforce such a promise would be against public policy."

er on the ground that, because the promotion had been to Vastoler's financial advantage, there was a "complete absence of any detriment, let alone a substantial one." The Court of Appeals reversed, concluding that there was "a genuine issue of material fact ... concerning Vastoler's detrimental reliance upon the Company's promise." The court noted that Vastoler "asserted that he remained with [the] Company because of his pension benefits." It also found "that the trial judge erred in failing to recognize that absorption of the stress and anxiety inherent in supervisory positions could be one of the factors that constitutes detrimental reliance." This explains, the court said, "why some qualified people do not want to be President of Fortune 500 corporations, nominee for the Presidency of the United States, or foreman of their plants."

Was the court, in effect, applying a rule similar to that of Restatement Second § 90(2)? See Farber & Matheson, Beyond Promissory Estoppel: Contract Law and the "Invisible Handshake," 52 U.Chi.L.Rev. 903 (1985).

(4) *"The Death of Contract."* In a little book with the provocative title "The Death of Contract," Professor Grant Gilmore [b] described the "decline and fall" of "the general theory of contract," as espoused by Langdell, Holmes and Williston. He referred to "the Restatement's schizophrenia" and quoted from the first Restatement § 75 (in Feinberg v. Pfeiffer Co. at p. 66 above) and § 90 (p. 103 above).

"Perhaps what we have here is Restatement and anti-Restatement or Contract and anti-Contract.... The one thing that is clear is that these two contradictory propositions cannot live comfortably together: in the end one must swallow the other up.... Clearly enough the unresolved ambiguity in the relationship between [the two sections] has now been resolved in favor of the promissory estoppel principle of § 90 which has, in effect, swallowed up the bargain principle of § 75. The wholly executory exchange where neither party has yet taken any action would seem to be the only situation in which it would be necessary to look to § 75—and even there, as the Comment somewhat mysteriously suggests, the 'probability of reliance' may be a sufficient reason for enforcement without inquiring into whether or not there was any 'consideration.' ... Speaking descriptively, we might say that what is happening is that 'contract' is being reabsorbed into the mainstream of 'tort.' " G. Gilmore, The Death of Contract 61–65, 72, 87 (1974).

Gilmore's remark about the "wholly executory exchange where neither party has yet taken any action" has not gone unnoticed. An English contracts scholar, Professor Patrick Atiyah, has argued that the case for enforcing such exchanges is not compelling and that "there are signs of an increasing reluctance to impose liability in wholly executory contracts, that is, on promises which have neither been paid for, nor relied upon." P. Atiyah, Promises, Morals and Law 5–6 (1981). Can you find any of those signs? See Eisenberg, The Bargain Principle and Its Limits, 95 Harv.L.Rev. 741 (1982).

———

COHEN v. COWLES MEDIA COMPANY, 479 N.W.2d 387 (Minn. 1992) (en banc). [Dan Cohen, an associate of a gubernatorial candidate,

b. Grant Gilmore (1910–1982), once a teacher of French, practiced law in New York for two years before teaching law at Yale and for some years at Chicago. He was the principal architect of Article 9 of the Uniform Commercial Code, which deals with secured transactions, and wrote a two-volume work on that subject as well as shorter works on admiralty, contracts and legal history.

informed reporters for the Minneapolis Star and the Pioneer Press Dispatch of the arrests for unlawful assembly and the conviction for shoplifting of the opposing candidate for lieutenant governor. Although the reporters promised to keep Cohen's identity confidential, the newspapers' editors overruled these promises. When the stories were published, Cohen was fired by his advertising firm, and he sued the publishers of the papers for breach of contract.

The jury awarded Cohen $200,000 in compensatory damages, but the Supreme Court of Minnesota held that, though the papers may have had a moral and ethical commitment to keep their source anonymous, the parties were not thinking in terms of a legally binding contract. It also held that to allow Cohen to recover under the doctrine of promissory estoppel would violate the papers' First Amendment rights. The United States Supreme Court granted certiorari and held that the First Amendment was not offended by use of the doctrine to enforce confidentiality agreements because it had only "incidental effects" on news gathering and reporting. It remanded the case to the Supreme Court of Minnesota.

After citing Restatement Second § 90(1), that court affirmed the jury's $200,000 verdict on promissory estoppel grounds, concluding that the promise must "be enforced to prevent an injustice."]

SIMONETT, JUSTICE. . . . It is perhaps worth noting that the test is not whether the promise should be enforced to do justice, but whether enforcement is required to prevent an injustice. As has been observed elsewhere, it is easier to recognize an unjust result than a just one, particularly in a morally ambiguous situation. Cf. Edmond Cahn, The Sense of Injustice (1964). The newspapers argue it is unjust to be penalized for publishing the whole truth, but it is not clear this would result in an injustice in this case. For example, it would seem veiling Cohen's identity by publishing the source as someone close to the opposing gubernatorial ticket would have sufficed as a sufficient reporting of the "whole truth."

Cohen, on the other hand, argues that it would be unjust for the law to countenance, at least in this instance, the breaking of a promise. We agree that denying Cohen any recourse would be unjust. What is significant in this case is that the record shows the defendant newspapers themselves believed that they generally must keep promises of confidentiality given a news source. The reporters who actually gave the promises adamantly testified that their promises should have been honored. The editors who countermanded the promises conceded that never before or since have they reneged on a promise of confidentiality. A former Minneapolis Star managing editor testified that the newspapers had "hung Mr. Cohen out to dry because they didn't regard him very highly as a source." The Pioneer Press Dispatch editor stated nothing like this had happened in her 27 years in journalism. The Star Tribune's editor testified that protection of sources was "extremely important." Other experts, too, stressed the ethical importance, except on rare occasions, of keeping promises of confidentiality. It was this long-standing journalistic tradition that Cohen, who has worked in journalism, relied upon in asking for and receiving a promise of anonymity.

Neither side in this case clearly holds the higher moral ground, but in view of the defendants' concurrence in the importance of honoring promises of confidentiality, and absent the showing of any compelling need in this case to break that promise, we conclude that the resultant harm to Cohen requires a remedy here to avoid an injustice. In short, defendants are liable in damages to plaintiff for their broken promise. . . .

NOTES

(1) *Questions.* The court explains that in *Cohen I* it concluded that though "the newspapers may have had a moral and ethical commitment to keep their sources anonymous, ... this was not a situation where the parties were thinking in terms of a legally binding commitment." So they were not liable on traditional contract theory. Do you agree? A dissenting judge in *Cohen I* argued that "the news media should be compelled to keep their promises like anyone else" and should therefore be liable "on either a contract or promissory estoppel theory." If, as the majority suggested in *Cohen I,* the newspapers commitment was only "moral and ethical," was Cohen justified in relying on it?

(2) *Problem.* Samuel White, a building contractor, had discussed with the firm of Corlies & Tift the possibility of renovating their offices according to specifications that he had furnished the firm. He received from the firm a fax that read:

> If you will promise to renovate our offices according to specifications and complete the job within two weeks from date, you can begin at once.

White made no reply but immediately bought lumber and, on his own premises, cut it to the sizes required for the firm's offices. Has White done something rash? (The opinion in White v. Corlies & Tift, at p. 184 below, gives somewhat similar but not identical, facts.)

(3) *Problem.* In 1977, the Township of Ypsilanti, Michigan, created an *READ* industrial development district for General Motors' Willow Run plant and subsequently gave it a series of property tax abatements. Prior to the 1988 abatements, Harvey Williams, the plant manager, made the following statement as part of General Motors' presentation.

> Good evening, my name is Harvey Williams and I am the plant manager of the Buick Oldsmobile Cadillac group's Willow Run plant. We are pleased to have this opportunity to appear before the Ypsilanti Township Board of Trustees. This application for an industrial facilities exemption certificate is for an investment totalling $75,000,000.00 for machinery and equipment. This will enable our plant to assemble a new full size car in the 1991 model year. This new rear wheel drive car is substantially larger than our current model. And specifically it will generate major booth, oven and conveyor changes in the paint shop and assembly line process, changes in the body, trim and chassis department. This change will also provide additional flexibility at our assembly plant. Essentially we would now have the capability to produce either front or rear wheel drive cars with minimum modifications to our facility. Upon completion of this project and favorable market demand, it will allow Willow Run to continue production and maintain continu-

ous employment for our employees. I would like to introduce Russell Hughes, our controller, who will review pertinent charts pertaining to our request.

In 1991, General Motors announced that, because of record losses, it had decided to consolidate the work done at Willow Run with that done at Arlington, Texas and to close the Willow Run plant. The Township sought and obtained an injunction barring General Motors from transferring production from the Willow Run plant, and General Motors appealed.

How would you argue the case for the Township? For General Motors? See Charter Township of Ypsilanti v. General Motors Corp., 506 N.W.2d 556 (Mich. App.1993).

Judgment for →

D & G STOUT, INC. v. BACARDI IMPORTS, INC.

United States Court of Appeals, Seventh Circuit, 1991.
923 F.2d 566.

CUDAHY, CIRCUIT JUDGE. D & G Stout, Inc., operating at all relevant times under the name General Liquors, Inc. (General), was distributing liquor in the turbulent Indiana liquor market in 1987. When two of its major suppliers jumped ship in early 1987, General faced a critical dilemma: sell out at the best possible price or continue operating on a smaller scale. It began negotiating with another Indiana distributor on the terms of a possible sale. Bacardi Imports, Inc. (Bacardi), was still one of General's remaining major suppliers. Knowing that negotiations were ongoing for General's sale, Bacardi promised that General would continue to act as Bacardi's distributor for Northern Indiana. Based on this representation, General turned down the negotiated selling price it was offered. One week later, Bacardi withdrew its account. Realizing it could no longer continue to operate, General went back to the negotiating table, this time settling for an amount $550,000 below the first offer. The question is whether General can recover the price differential from Bacardi on a theory of promissory estoppel. The district court believed that as a matter of law it could not, and entered summary judgment for defendant Bacardi. We disagree, and so we remand for trial.

I.

General was (and D & G Stout, Inc., is) an Indiana corporation with its main place of business in South Bend. Bacardi is a corporation organized in New York and doing business primarily in Miami, Florida. General served at Bacardi's will as its wholesale distributor in Northern Indiana for over 35 years. During the 1980s, liquor suppliers in Indiana undertook an extensive effort to consolidate their distribution, the effect of which was to reduce the number of distributors in the state from approximately twenty in 1980 to only two in 1990.

General weathered the storm until April 1987, when two of its major suppliers withdrew their lines, taking with them the basis of more than fifty percent of General's gross sales. By June, General recognized that it must choose between selling out and scaling back operations in order to stay in business. Despite the recent setbacks, General calculated that remaining operational was possible as long as it held on to its continuing two major suppliers, Bacardi and Hiram Walker.

About this time (and probably in connection with the same forces concentrating distribution) Bacardi lost its distributor in Indianapolis and southern Indiana. Bacardi decided to convene a meeting on July 9, 1987, of applicants for the open distributorship. General's president, David Stout, attended the meetings as an observer, with no designs on the new opening. Stout did intend to seek assurances from Bacardi about its commitment to General in Northern Indiana. While in Indianapolis, Stout was approached by National Wine & Spirits Company (National), which expressed an interest in buying General. Stout agreed to begin negotiations the following weekend. Stout also received the assurances from Bacardi he sought: after listening to Stout's concerns and hearing about his contemplated sale of General, Bacardi emphatically avowed that it had no intention of taking its line to another distributor in Northern Indiana. This promise was open-ended—no one discussed how long the continuing relationship might last.

During the ensuing two weeks, General carried on negotiations with National to reach a price for the purchase of General's assets. Bacardi kept in close contact with General to find out whether it would indeed sell. The negotiations yielded a final figure for Stout to consider. On July 22 and again on July 23—with negotiations concluded and only the final decision remaining—Stout again sought assurances from Bacardi. The supplier unequivocally reconfirmed its commitment to stay with General, and Stout replied that, as a result, he was going to turn down National's offer and would continue operating. Later on the 23rd, Stout rejected National's offer. That same afternoon, Bacardi decided to withdraw its line from General.

General learned of Bacardi's decision on July 30. The news spread quickly through the industry, and by August 3, Hiram Walker had also pulled its line, expressing a belief that General could not continue without Bacardi on board. By this time, sales personnel were abandoning General for jobs with the two surviving distributors in Indiana (one of which was National). General quickly sought out National to sell its assets, but National's offer was now substantially reduced. The ensuing agreement, executed on August 14 and closed on August 28, included a purchase price $550,000 lower than the one National offered in mid-July. Stout's successor company brought suit under the diversity jurisdiction against Bacardi, claiming that the supplier was liable by reason of promissory estoppel for this decline in the purchase price. Judge Miller entered summary judgment for Bacardi, holding that the promises plaintiff alleged were not the type upon which one may rely under Indiana law. Plaintiff appeals.

II.

We have generally stated General's version of the facts, many of which are undisputed. On appeal, Bacardi does not argue the facts and is apparently willing to rest on Judge Miller's legal analysis. Both parties also agree with Judge Miller that Indiana law governs this case and we do not question this conclusion. Before us then is the legal question whether the plaintiff has alleged any injury which Indiana's law of promissory estoppel redresses.

Indiana has adopted the Restatement's theory of promissory estoppel:

> A promise which the promisor should reasonably expect to induce action or forbearance on the part of the promisee and a third person and which does induce such action or forbearance is binding if injustice can be avoided only by the enforcement of the promise. The remedy for breach may be limited as justice requires.

Restatement (Second) of Contracts § 90(1) (1981); Eby v. York–Division, Borg–Warner, 455 N.E.2d 623, 627 (Ind.App.1983); Pepsi–Cola General Bottlers, Inc. v. Woods, 440 N.E.2d 696, 698 (Ind.App.1982). The district judge dismissed the complaint on the ground that Bacardi's alleged promise was not one on which it should reasonably have expected General to rely.

The district court first noted that the relationship between General and Bacardi had always been terminable at will. Because Bacardi's promises that it would continue to use General as its distributor contained no language indicating that they would be good for any specific period,[1] the court reasoned that the relationship remained terminable at will. It then concluded that the promise was not legally enforceable, and thus was not one on which General reasonably might rely. We agree with each of these conclusions but the last. Notwithstanding the continuation of an at-will relationship between Bacardi and General, the promises given between July 9 and July 23 were not without legal effect.

In Indiana, as in many states, an aspiring employee cannot sue for lost wages on an unfulfilled promise of at-will employment. Pepsi–Cola, 440 N.E.2d 696; accord Ewing v. Board of Trustees of Pulaski Memorial Hosp., 486 N.E.2d 1094, 1098 (Ind.App.1985) (employment contract for indefinite tenure is unenforceable for future employment). Because the employer could have terminated the employee without cause at any time after the employment began, the promise of a job brings no expectation of any determinable period of employment or corresponding amount of wages. The promise is therefore unenforceable under either a contract or a promissory estoppel theory in an action for lost wages. Nevertheless, lost wages are not the only source of damages flowing from a broken promise of employment, enforceable or not. Indiana courts acknowledge certain damages as recoverable when the employer breaks a promise of employment, even if the employment is to be terminable at will. For example, in Eby v. York–Division, Borg–Warner, 455 N.E.2d at 627, a plaintiff who gave up a job and moved from Indiana to Florida on

---

1. Given the context of the promise, we see a plausible argument that the promise was one for a term, namely that Bacardi would stay on at least until the rush toward consolidation passed. But the district judge found differently, and we need not question his factual conclusion in light of our legal analysis.

a promise of employment sued for recovery of preparation and moving expenses incurred on the basis of the promise.   The Indiana appellate court reversed the lower court's summary judgment for the defendant employer, holding that the plaintiff employee had stated a cause of action for promissory estoppel.   The court found that the defendant could have expected the plaintiff and his wife to move in reliance on the promise of employment and therefore might be liable for reneging.   See also Pepsi–Cola, 440 N.E.2d 696; accord Lorson v. Falcon Coach, 214 Kan. 670, 522 P.2d 449 (1974).

Our review of Indiana law thus leaves us a simple if somewhat crude question: are the damages plaintiff seeks here more like lost future wages or like moving expenses?   We can better answer the question if we determine why Indiana draws this distinction.   Unlike lost wages, moving expenses represent out-of-pocket losses; they involve a loss of something already possessed.   It would be plausible, although not very sophisticated, to distinguish between the loss of something yet to be received and the loss of something already in hand.   But this is not precisely where Indiana draws the distinction, nor where we would draw it if it were our choice to make.   *Eby* itself involved not only moving expenses, but wages lost at plaintiff's old job during the few days plaintiff was preparing to move.   455 N.E.2d at 625.   Those wages were not out-of-pocket losses: plaintiff had no more received those wages than he had received wages from his promised employment.

In fact, the line Indiana draws is between expectation damages and reliance damages.   In future wages, the employee has only an expectation of income, the recovery of which promissory estoppel will not support in an at-will employment setting.   In wages forgone in order to prepare to move, as in moving expenses themselves, the employee gave up a presently determinate sum for the purpose of relocating.   Both moving expenses and forgone wages were the hopeful employee's costs of positioning himself for his new job; moving expenses happen to be out-of-pocket losses, while forgone wages are opportunity costs.   Both are reliance costs, not expectancy damages.

Thus, the question has become whether the loss incurred from the price drop was attributable to lost expectations of future profit or resulted from an opportunity forgone in reliance on the promise.   At first blush, the injury might seem more like the loss of future wages. Bacardi was a major supplier whose business was extremely valuable to General.   While the loss of this "asset" might cause a decline in General's market value as measured by the loss of future income from the sale of Bacardi's products, this loss is not actionable on a promissory estoppel theory.   Those damages would presumably be measured by the present value of General's anticipated profit from the sale of Bacardi's products, and Indiana will not grant relief based on promissory estoppel to compensate an aggrieved party for such expectancy damages.   Lost future income expected from an at-will relationship, whether from wages or from profits, is not recoverable on a theory of promissory estoppel, and neither is the present value of such losses.

But the fact is that recovery of lost profits is not a question before us. Bacardi's account was never an "asset" that National could acquire by purchasing General. As counsel for the defendant candidly but carefully explained, National never assumed that it would retain the Bacardi account by buying General; in fact, National assumed the opposite. Bacardi's major competitor in the rum distilling business distributed through National, and the two top distillers in a given category of liquor would not choose the same distributor. Both before and after Bacardi decided to withdraw its products, all National wanted from General were its assets other than the Bacardi account. But Bacardi's repudiation of its promise ostensibly affected the price of General's business so drastically because, as everyone in the industry understood, General's option to stay in business independently was destroyed by Bacardi's withdrawal of its account. Thus, through its repudiation, Bacardi destroyed General's negotiating leverage since General no longer had the alternative of continuing as an independent concern. Presumably, after Bacardi's withdrawal General's only alternative to selling to National was to liquidate. Thus, Bacardi's repudiation turned General's discussions with National from negotiations to buy a going concern into a liquidation sale. Instead of bargaining from strength, knowing it could reject a junk-value offer and carry on its business, General was left with one choice: sell at any price.

Under these facts, General had a reliance interest in Bacardi's promise. General was in lively negotiations with National and it repeatedly informed Bacardi of this fact. A price was agreed upon, and based on that figure, Stout had to decide whether to close his doors or continue operating. General had a business opportunity that all parties knew would be devalued once Bacardi announced its intention to go elsewhere. The extent of that devaluation represents a reliance injury, rather than an injury to General's expectation of future profit. The injury is analogous to the cost of moving expenses incurred as a result of promised employment in *Eby* and *Pepsi–Cola*.

Nor were these promises merely meaningless restatements of an understood at-will relationship. With its current business opportunity, General stood at a crossroads. Circumstances foreshadowed a costly demise for the company, but it was able to negotiate an alternative. Far from confirming the obvious, Bacardi wrote its assurances on a clean slate with full knowledge that General was just as likely to reject the offered relationship as embrace it. That this was the situation is indicated most clearly by Bacardi's repeated calls to check on Stout's impending decision. Bacardi reassured Stout of its commitment in full knowledge that he planned to reject National's offer and with the reasonable expectation that an immediate pull out would severely undermine General's asking price. Like the plaintiffs in *Eby* who moved based on the promise of a job, General incurred a cost in rejecting the deal that was non-recoverable once Bacardi's later decision became known.

There may always exist the potential for a quandary in a promissory estoppel action based on a promise of at-will employment. When could Bacardi terminate the relationship with General without fear of liability for reliance costs, once it made the assurances in question? Obviously we do not hold that General and Bacardi had formed a new, permanent employment relationship. How long an employee can rely on the employer's promise is not a matter we can decide here. The issue is one of reasonable reliance, and to the extent that there might be questions, they should be for trial.

III.

We have, of course, reviewed this case in the posture of summary judgment. General's allegations still must be proven at trial. However, under Indiana law, we think that Bacardi's promise was of a sort on which General might rely, with the possibility of damages for breach. For that reason the judgment of the district court is

Reversed and remanded.

NOTES

(1) *Outcome on Remand.* Judge Cudahy recites General's claim that "Bacardi emphatically avowed that it had no intention of taking its line to another distributor in Northern Indiana." On remand, however, the district court found as a fact that Bacardi's promise had been "contingent on future events" since it was "subject to the conditions that General would continue to meet Bacardi's expectation in sales and no market changes would occur." Nevertheless, the district court held that "the conditional nature of Bacardi's commitment does not make General's reliance unreasonable." The court awarded General "damages incurred in reliance on Bacardi's promise" equal to "the difference between National's initial offer and the final sale price"—a total of $394,050.

(2) *Reliance on "At–Will" Promises.* Judge Cudahy explained that "In Indiana, as in many states, an aspiring employee cannot sue for lost wages on an unfulfilled promise of at-will employment." Consider the seminal, if somewhat mysterious, case of Goodman v. Dicker, 169 F.2d 684 (D.C.Cir.1948), in which a disappointed applicant for a franchise to sell Emerson radios sued Emerson's local distributors on the ground that they had, as the trial court found, "by their representations and conduct induced [the applicant] to incur expenses in preparing to do business under the franchise, including employment of salesmen and solicitation of orders for radios." The local distributors argued that even if the franchise had been granted, "it would have been terminable at will and would have imposed no duty upon the manufacturer to sell or [the applicant] to buy any fixed number of radios." The court upheld an award to damages in the amount of $1,150 which the applicant "expended in preparing to do business under the promised dealer franchise." [a] It explained, "Justice and fair dealing require that one who acts to his detriment on the faith of conduct of the kind revealed here should be protected by estopping the party who has brought about the situation from alleging anything in opposition to the natural consequences of his own course of conduct."

It is arguable that this case turned on a misrepresentation of fact by the local distributors rather than on a promise by them. The trial court found, among other things, that the local distributors "represented that the application *had been* accepted" and "that the franchise *would be* granted." (emphasis

---

a. The court held that it was error, however, to award $350 for loss of profits on radios promised under an initial order. "The true measure of damages is the loss sustained by expenditures made in reliance upon the assurance of a dealer franchise."

added). The opinion does not cite the first Restatement § 90 but instead quotes from a case involving "equitable estoppel." Nevertheless, the case was seized upon by advocates of expanded promissory liability and was made the basis of Illustration 8 of Restatement Second § 90.

SECTION 5. PROMISE FOR PROMISE

We have already seen how, in the historical development of the action of assumpsit as a general basis for the enforcement of promises, courts came to recognize that the consideration for a promise could be found in a return promise, even if not even partly performed (see p. 46 above). But what rationale lies behind the enforcement of a promise when it has not been shown that the promisee has conferred a benefit upon the promisor or done anything in reliance on the promise? If one of the parties to an exchange of promises has second thoughts about the transaction the instant after the exchange has occurred, why should not that party be allowed to retract its promise without liability?

Consider this simple example. W.O. Lucy met with A.H. Zehmer and his wife Ida and arranged for the sale to Lucy of a farm owned by the Zehmers. The Zehmers promised to convey the farm, and Lucy promised to pay $50,000. When the Zehmers refused to convey, Lucy sued for specific performance. The Zehmers claimed that, before Lucy had left after making the agreement, A.H. had said, "I don't want to sell my farm. I want my son to have it." But before Lucy went out the door, he said, "Zehmer, you have sold your farm." Lucy claimed that the Zehmers had not told him this until three days after the agreement, and that in the meantime he had arranged to raise half of the money from his brother and had employed an attorney to examine the title. The Supreme Court of Appeals of Virginia held that Lucy was entitled to specific performance. Since there had been a bargained-for exchange of promises, the Zehmers' refusal came too late even on their version of the facts. (The opinion, which gives other salient facts, appears at p. 140 below.)

Why should Lucy be allowed to enforce a promise when the Zehmers had in no way benefited and Lucy had, on the Zehmers' version of the facts, in no way relied to his detriment? Would it not be better to require Lucy to prove that his version of the facts was correct and that he had relied upon the Zehmers' promise? How much reliance would you require? Would it be enough if Lucy had testified, without contradiction, that he would have made an offer on another farm had the Zehmers not agreed to sell him theirs, and that the other farm had been sold before they told him that they would not perform? Would promisees such as Lucy be as safe in relying on promises if those promises were enforceable only on proof of reliance? For some answers to these questions, see Fuller and Perdue, The Reliance Interest in Contract Damages, 46 Yale L.J. 52, 61–62 (1936).

When general counsels of corporations were asked whether a party who had not yet relied on a contract should nevertheless be entitled to recover its expected profit, 68.3% of respondents answered "yes." Weintraub, A Survey of Contract Practice and Policy, 1991 Wis.L.Rev. 1, 30–35.

Restatement Second § 71 makes it clear that the consideration for a promise can be found in a return promise. With some exceptions, "a promise which is bargained for is consideration if, but only if, the promised performance would be consideration." The following cases explore the exceptions.

NOTES

(1) *Unilateral and Bilateral Contracts.* A distinction between "unilateral" and "bilateral" contracts has long had currency. In a unilateral contract only one party makes promises; in a bilateral contract both parties make promises. The relationships between the parties in the two types of contract can be analyzed in terms of *right* and *duty*.

A is said to have a *right* that B shall do an act when, if B does not do the act, A can initiate legal proceedings against B, and B in such a situation is said to have a *duty* to do the act. *Right* and *duty* are therefore correlatives. In this strict sense there can never be a *right* without a *duty*, nor a *duty* without a *right*. The *right-duty* relationship is one between two parties. The *right* describes the relationship from one end and the *duty* from the other. Since, in a "unilateral" contract there is a promise on one side only, there is a *duty* on one side only, and a *right* on the other side; and since in a "bilateral" contract there is a promise on each side, there is a *right* and a *duty* on each side. The Restatement Second abandons the use of the terms "unilateral" and "bilateral," "because of doubt as to the utility of the distinction, often treated as fundamental, between the two types." Reporter's Note to Restatement Second § 1.

For the precise use of terms such as *right* and *duty* the legal profession is indebted to the work of Professor Wesley Newcomb Hohfeld,[a] whose system of "Hohfeldian terminology" is set forth in Hohfeld, Fundamental Legal Conceptions (1923). In this terminology the offeree has, before the contract is made, a *power* to create a contract by means of acceptance. A *power* is the capacity to change a legal relationship.

(2) *Conditional Promises.* A promisor, such as Lucy, who seeks the other party's promise in return is not, to be sure, unconcerned with the other party's performance of the return promise. The difference between Lucy's situation and that of a promisor such as Ledbetter in Broadnax v. Ledbetter (Note 2, p. 97 above) is that Lucy wants a return promise in *addition* to that performance. Both Ledbetter and Lucy want some assurance that they will get something for

---

a. Wesley Newcomb Hohfeld (1879–1918) practiced law briefly in San Francisco before joining the Stanford law faculty in 1905. In 1914 he left Stanford to teach at Yale until his death at the age of thirty-nine. He made a lasting contribution to legal literature through his development of the eight terms of "Hohfeldian terminology" in his book Fundamental Legal Conceptions. Corbin wrote, "He was a severe taskmaster, requiring his students to master his classification of 'fundamental conceptions' and to use accurately the set of terms by which they were expressed. They found this, in the light of the usage of the other professors [at Yale], almost impossible." Their resistance resulted in a petition to the President of Yale that Hohfeld's appointment not be extended. The petition was ignored and generations of law students have continued to master Hohfeld's terms.

their money. Ledbetter's assurance that he will not have to pay the reward unless Vann is captured follows from the doctrine of consideration itself: his promise to pay the reward is not enforceable unless Vann is captured. If Lucy's promise to pay for the Zehmer's farm becomes enforceable merely on the Zehmer's making their promise in return, how is Lucy assured that he will not have to pay the price unless he gets the farm? [b] The solution to this problem involves aspects of the performance, as distinguished from the formation, of a contract and will not be considered in detail until Chapter 7, Performance and Breach. However, a brief discussion of the solution may be helpful, even at this early stage.

The solution involves the concept of a *condition*. Even though a promise is enforceable, it may still be conditional in that its performance will become due only if a particular event, known as a "condition," occurs. This does not mean that the promise is not enforceable until the event occurs, but only that the event must occur before the promisor must perform. Suppose that a home owner pays $1,000 to an insurance company in return for the company's promise to pay the owner $100,000 if house is destroyed by fire. If the house burns, performance of the company's promise to pay becomes due. If it does not burn, performance does not become due. The burning of the house was not the acceptance of an offer: there was a contract—an enforceable promise by the company—before the house burned. The burning of the house was a condition of the company's promise to pay, an event that had to occur before performance of that promise was due. Consider again the agreement between the Whites and the Benkowskis (p. 14 above). Can you find three explicit conditions of the Benkowskis' ongoing duty to supply water?

Where a party makes a promise in exchange for a return promise, it can be protected by making its own promise conditional on performance by the other party, so that it is under no duty to perform until the other party has performed. Even if the contract does not so provide, the court may impose such "constructive conditions of exchange" by implication. (See Wood v. Lucy, Lady Duff–Gordon, p. 133 below.) In the case of the contract for the sale to Lucy of the Zehmers' farm, since both parties could perform simultaneously,[c] a court would protect both parties by making it a condition of Lucy's duty to pay that the Zehmers tender a deed and a condition of the Zehmers' duty to tender a deed that Lucy tender the price.[d] May the Benkowskis' ongoing duty to supply water have been subject to a constructive condition? And what of the White's duty to pay? Further discussion is left to Chapter 7, Performance and Breach.

(3) *Dominance of Bilateral Contracts.* Bilateral contracts are much more common and much more economically significant than unilateral contracts. Why do you suppose this is?

b. It is clear that if he paid the price and did not get the farm he would have a claim for damages against the Zehmers for breach of contract and probably, since the subject of the contract is land, one for specific performance as well. But such claims may not be as satisfactory to Lucy as a right to withhold payment until he gets a deed to the farm.

c. If simultaneous performance is not possible or is contrary to the agreement of the parties, the promise of the party who is to perform later is regarded as conditional on earlier performance by the other party. If a house owner promises a painter to pay $1,000 in return for the painter's promise to paint the house, it will be assumed in the absence of a contrary agreement that the painter is to go first so that painting the house is a condition of the owner's duty to pay.

d. It is generally regarded as enough if a party makes an offer to perform, accompanied with manifested present ability to make it good, even if the party does not go so far as to actually tender what is to be delivered by holding it out. See Comment *b* to Restatement Second § 238; UCC 2–503(1).

(4) *The Case of the Settlement Agreement.*　Halstead sued Murray, a neighbor who was building on his lot on Lake Winnipesaukee, to force Murray to comply with a town ordinance.　To settle the action, Halstead and Murray made an agreement under which Murray was to sell the lot to Halstead.　After Halstead had paid for a title examination and incurred other costs in reliance on the agreement, Murray refused to perform, offering to reimburse Halstead for his costs.　Halstead declined and sought specific performance.

Is there more or less reason to enforce this agreement than the one in Lucy v. Zehmer?　Would it affect your answer if the town had rescinded the ordinance just after the settlement agreement was made?　See Halstead v. Murray, 547 A.2d 202 (N.H.1988) (page 318 below).

———

STRONG v. SHEFFIELD

Court of Appeals of New York, 1895.
144 N.Y. 392, 39 N.E. 330.

[Action on a promissory note.　A judgment for plaintiff, Benjamin B. Strong, against defendant, Louisa A. Sheffield, was reversed by the General Term of the Supreme Court.]

ANDREWS, C.J.　The contract between a maker or endorser of a promissory note and the payee forms no exception to the general rule that a promise, not supported by a consideration, is nudum pactum. The law governing commercial paper which precludes an inquiry into the consideration as against bona fide holders for value before maturity, has no application where the suit is between the original parties to the instrument.　It is undisputed that the demand note upon which the action was brought was made by the husband of the defendant and endorsed by her at his request and delivered to the plaintiff, the payee, as security for an antecedent debt owing by the husband to the plaintiff. The debt of the husband was past due at the time, and the only consideration for the wife's endorsement, which is or can be claimed, is that as part of the transaction there was an agreement by the plaintiff when the note was given to forbear the collection of the debt, or a request for forbearance, which was followed by forbearance for a period of about two years subsequent to the giving of the note.　There is no doubt that an agreement by the creditor to forbear the collection of a debt presently due is a good consideration for an absolute or conditional promise of a third person to pay the debt or for any obligation he may assume in respect thereto.　Nor is it essential that the creditor should bind himself at the time to forbear collection or to give time.　If he is requested by his debtor to extend the time, and a third person undertakes in consideration of forbearance being given to become liable as surety or otherwise, and the creditor does in fact forbear in reliance upon the undertaking, although he enters into no enforceable agreement to do so, his acquiescence in the request, and an actual forbearance in consequence thereof for a reasonable time, furnishes a good consideration for the collateral undertaking.　In other words, a request followed by performance is sufficient, and mutual promises at the time are not essential unless it was the understanding that the promisor was not to be bound, except on condition that the other party entered into an immediate and reciprocal obligation to do the thing requested.... The note in question did not in law extend the payment of the debt. It was payable on demand, and although being payable with interest it was in form consistent with an intention that payment should not be immediately demanded, yet there was nothing on its face to prevent an immediate suit on the note against the maker or to recover the original debt....

In the present case the agreement made is not left to inference, nor was it a case of request to forbear, followed by forbearance, in pursuance of the request, without any promise on the part of the creditor at the time. The plaintiff testified that there was an express agreement on his part to the effect that he would not pay the note away, nor put it in any bank for collection, but (using the words of the plaintiff) "I will hold it until such time as I want my money, I will make a demand on you for it." And again: "No, I will keep it until such time as I want it." [a] Upon this alleged agreement the defendant endorsed the note. It would have been no violation of the plaintiff's promise if, immediately on receiving the note, he had commenced suit upon it. Such a suit would have been an assertion that he wanted the money and would have fulfilled the condition of forbearance. The debtor and the defendant, when they became parties to the note, may have had the hope or expectation that forbearance would follow, and there was forbearance in fact. But there was no agreement to forbear for a fixed time or for a reasonable time, but an agreement to forbear for such time as the plaintiff should elect. The consideration is to be tested by the agreement, and not by what was done under it. It was a case of mutual promises, and so intended. We think the evidence failed to disclose any consideration for the defendant's endorsement, and that the trial court erred in refusing so to rule.

The order of the General Term reversing the judgment should be affirmed, and judgment absolute directed for the defendant on the stipulation with costs in all courts.

Ordered accordingly.[b]

---

a. The record on appeal indicates that Benjamin Strong was Louisa Sheffield's uncle. He had sold his business on credit to Louisa's husband, Gerardus, and then sought Gerardus' note with Louisa's endorsement as security for the debt. Louisa was reluctant to endorse her husband's note because she had her own successful business and did not want to hurt her credit by having it known that she had undertaken a debt of her husband. Strong testified that he told Gerardus at a gymnasium, "Rard, I will give you my word as a man ... that if you will give me a note, with your wife's endorsement, as further security for what you owe me, that I will not pay that note away; I will not put it in any bank for collection, but I will hold it until

such time as I want my money, I will make a demand on you for it." Strong also testified that when Gerardus turned over the note, Gerardus asked, "You won't pay this note away?" and Strong replied, "No, I will keep it until such time as I want it." Record pp. 12–13.

b. The precise rule of this case is reversed by UCC 3–408, and may have been reversed by the enactment of the Negotiable Instruments Law, soon after the decision. See First National City Bank v. Valentine, 306 N.Y.S.2d 227 (Sup.Ct.1969), rearg. denied, 309 N.Y.S.2d 563 (Sup.Ct. 1970). However, inasmuch as these statutes purport to apply only to negotiable instruments, the principle of the case is

NOTES

(1) *Questions.* The Restatement Second § 77 mentions the "illusory" or "apparent" promise as a type that is not consideration. Did the plaintiff, Strong, make any promise of substance to the Sheffields, or either of them? Was his promise alternative in any sense? See the Restatement section cited.

Suppose Louisa Sheffield had written to Strong: "I will be responsible for my husband's debt if you will not bother him about it for two years." Would she have been accountable to Strong if he had done nothing about the note for that period? What difference is there between this situation and the case as it stands? Is the reasoning in Ingram consistent in this respect with that in Strong?

(2) *Problem.* When Nancy and Gerald were divorced, Gerald got the farm under a property settlement and Nancy took mortgages on the farm to secure payments that Gerald was to make to her. When Gerald later had financial difficulties in farming and sought to refinance previous bank loans, he found that he could not do so because of Nancy's mortgages. Nancy agreed to give up her right to payment and to satisfy the mortgages in return for Gerald's promise to make a will leaving the farm to their son Ronn, reserving the right to convey a portion of the land in order to continue farming if "future economic exigencies require." (Because Gerald had remarried and was expecting a child, Nancy feared that Ronn would not inherit the farm.) Gerald made a will and obtained refinancing, but Nancy, nevertheless, began foreclosure proceedings. She argued that Gerald's promise was illusory because Gerald had reserved a right to convey the farm. Is Nancy right? See Harrington v. Harrington, 365 N.W.2d 552 (N.D.1985).

MATTEI v. HOPPER

Supreme Court of California, 1958.
51 Cal.2d 119, 330 P.2d 625.

SPENCE, JUSTICE. Plaintiff brought this action for damages after defendant allegedly breached a contract by failing to convey her real property in accordance with the terms of a deposit receipt which the parties had executed. After a trial without a jury, the court concluded that the agreement was "illusory" and lacking in "mutuality." From the judgment accordingly entered in favor of defendant, plaintiff appeals.

Plaintiff was a real estate developer. He was planning to construct a shopping center on a tract adjacent to defendant's land. For several months, a real estate agent attempted to negotiate a sale of defendant's property under terms agreeable to both parties. After several of plaintiff's proposals had been rejected by defendant because of the inadequacy of the price offered, defendant submitted an offer. Plaintiff accepted on the same day.

The parties' written agreement was evidenced on a form supplied by the real estate agent, commonly known as a deposit receipt. Under its terms, plaintiff was required to deposit $1,000 of the total purchase price

presumably still viable in the absence of
such an instrument.

of $57,500 with the real estate agent, and was given 120 days to "examine the title and consummate the purchase." At the expiration of that period, the balance of the price was "due and payable upon tender of a good and sufficient deed of the property sold." The concluding paragraph of the deposit receipt provided: "Subject to Coldwell Banker & Company obtaining leases satisfactory to the purchaser." This clause and the 120–day period were desired by plaintiff as a means for arranging satisfactory leases of the shopping center buildings prior to the time he was finally committed to pay the balance of the purchase price and to take title to defendant's property.

Plaintiff took the first step in complying with the agreement by turning over the $1,000 deposit to the real estate agent. While he was in the process of securing the leases and before the 120 days had elapsed, defendant's attorney notified plaintiff that defendant would not sell her land under the terms contained in the deposit receipt. Thereafter, defendant was informed that satisfactory leases had been obtained and that plaintiff had offered to pay the balance of the purchase price. Defendant failed to tender the deed as provided in the deposit receipt.

Initially, defendant's thesis that the deposit receipt constituted no more than an offer by her, which could only be accepted by plaintiff notifying her that all of the desired leases had been obtained and were satisfactory to him, must be rejected. Nowhere does the agreement mention the necessity of any such notice. Nor does the provision making the agreement "subject to" plaintiff's securing "satisfactory" leases necessarily constitute a condition to the existence of a contract. Rather, the whole purchase receipt and this particular clause must be read as merely making plaintiff's performance dependent on the obtaining of "satisfactory" leases. Thus a contract arose, and plaintiff was given the power and privilege to terminate it in the event he did not obtain such leases. (See 3 Corbin, Contracts (1951), § 647, pp. 581–585.) This accords with the general view that deposit receipts are binding and enforceable contracts. (Cal.Practice Hand Book, Legal Aspects of Real Estate Transactions (1956), p. 63.)

However, the inclusion of this clause, specifying that leases "satisfactory" to plaintiff must be secured before he would be bound to perform, raises the basic question whether the consideration supporting the contract was thereby vitiated. When the parties attempt, as here, to make a contract where promises are exchanged as the consideration, the promises must be mutual in obligation. In other words, for the contract to bind either party, both must have assumed some legal obligations. Without this mutuality of obligation, the agreement lacks consideration and no enforceable contract has been created.... Or, if one of the promises leaves a party free to perform or to withdraw from the agreement at his own unrestricted pleasure, the promise is deemed illusory and it provides no consideration.... Whether these problems are couched in terms of mutuality of obligation or the illusory nature of a promise, the underlying issue is the same—consideration....

While contracts making the duty of performance of one of the parties conditional upon his satisfaction would seem to give him wide latitude in avoiding any obligation and thus present serious consideration problems, such "satisfaction" clauses have been given effect. They have been divided into two primary categories and have been accorded different treatment on that basis. First, in those contracts where the condition calls for satisfaction as to commercial value or quality, operative fitness, or mechanical utility, dissatisfaction cannot be claimed arbitrarily, unreasonably, or capriciously ..., and the standard of a reasonable person is used in determining whether satisfaction has been received.... However, it would seem that the factors involved in determining whether a lease is satisfactory to the lessor are too numerous and varied to permit the application of a reasonable man standard as envisioned by this line of cases. Illustrative of some of the factors which would have to be considered in this case are the duration of the leases, their provisions for renewal options, if any, their covenants and restrictions, the amounts of the rentals, the financial responsibility of the lessees, and the character of the lessees' businesses.

This multiplicity of factors which must be considered in evaluating a lease shows that this case more appropriately falls within the second line of authorities dealing with "satisfaction" clauses, being those involving fancy, taste, or judgment. Where the question is one of judgment, the promisor's determination that he is not satisfied, when made in good faith, has been held to be a defense to an action on the contract.... Although these decisions do not expressly discuss the issues of mutuality of obligation or illusory promises, they necessarily imply that the promisor's duty to exercise his judgment in good faith is an adequate consideration to support the contract. None of these cases voided the contracts on the ground that they were illusory or lacking in mutuality of obligation. Defendant's attempts to distinguish these cases are unavailing, since they are predicated upon the assumption that the deposit receipt was not a contract making plaintiff's performance conditional on his satisfaction. As seen above, this was the precise nature of the agreement. Even though the "satisfaction" clauses discussed in the above-cited cases dealt with performances to be received as parts of the agreed exchanges, the fact that the leases here which determined plaintiff's satisfaction were not part of the performance to be rendered is not material. The standard of evaluating plaintiff's satisfaction—good faith—applies with equal vigor to this type of condition and prevents it from nullifying the consideration otherwise present in the promises exchanged.

Moreover, the secondary authorities are in accord with the California cases on the general principles governing "satisfaction" contracts.... "A promise conditional upon the promisor's satisfaction is not illusory since it means more than that validity of the performance is to depend on the arbitrary choice of the promisor. His expression of dissatisfaction is not conclusive. That may show only that he has become dissatisfied with the contract; he must be dissatisfied with the performance, as a performance of the contract, and his dissatisfaction must be genuine." (Restatement, Contracts (1932), § 265, comment *a*.)

If the foregoing cases and other authorities were the only ones relevant, there would be little doubt that the deposit receipt here should not be deemed illusory or lacking in mutuality of obligation because it contained the "satisfaction" clause. However, language in two recent cases led the trial court to the contrary conclusion. The first case, Lawrence Block Co. v. Palston, 123 Cal.App.2d 300, 266 P.2d 856, 858, stated that the following two conditions placed in an offer to buy an apartment building would have made the resulting contract illusory: "O.P.A. Rent statements to be approved by Buyer" and "Subject to buyer's inspection and approval of all apartments." These provisions were said to give the purchaser "unrestricted discretion" in deciding whether he would be bound to the contract and to provide no "standard" which could be used in compelling him to perform. 123 Cal. App.2d at pages 308–309, 266 P.2d at pages 861–862. However, this language was not necessary to the decision....

The other case, Pruitt v. Fontana, 143 Cal.App.2d 675, 300 P.2d 371, 377, presented a similar situation. The court concluded that the written instrument with a provision making the sale of land subject to the covenants and easements being "approved by the buyers" was illusory. It employed both the reasoning and language of *Lawrence Block Co.* in deciding that this clause provided no "objective criterion" preventing the buyers from exercising an "unrestricted subjective discretion" in deciding whether they would be bound. 143 Cal.App.2d at pages 684–685, 300 P.2d at page 377. But again, this language was not necessary to the result reached. The buyers in *Pruitt* refused to approve all of the easements of record, and the parties entered into a new and different oral agreement. The defendant seller was held to be estopped to assert the statute of frauds against this subsequent contract, and the judgment of dismissal entered after the sustaining of demurrers was reversed.

While the language in these two cases might be dismissed as mere dicta, the fact that the trial court relied thereon requires us to examine the reasoning employed. Both courts were concerned with finding an objective standard by which they could compel performance. This view apparently stems from the statement in *Lawrence Block Co.* that "The standard 'as to the satisfaction of a reasonable person' does not apply where the performance involves a matter dependent on judgment." 123 Cal.App.2d at page 309, 266 P.2d at page 862. By making this assertion without any qualification, the court necessarily implied that there is no other standard available. Of course, this entirely disregards those cases which have upheld "satisfaction" clauses dependent on the exercise of judgment. In such cases, the criterion becomes one of good faith. Insofar as the language in *Lawrence Block Co.* and *Pruitt* represented a departure from the established rules governing "satisfaction" clauses, they are hereby disapproved.

We conclude that the contract here was neither illusory nor lacking in mutuality of obligation because the parties inserted a provision in their contract making plaintiff's performance dependent on his satisfaction with the leases to be obtained by him.

The judgment is reversed.

NOTES

(1) *Satisfaction With What?* If, after signing the deposit receipt, the real estate developer had thought better of the deal, could he have avoided liability by saying that he was "dissatisfied"? Would the landowner have been bound if the real estate developer had inserted a clause permitting him to do this? The meaning of "good faith" is explored further in Chapter 6, Finding the Law of Contract, and Chapter 7, Performance and Breach.

After negotiations, parties often leave some matters for their lawyers. Do you see a difference in legal effect between a provision that says "subject to my lawyer's approval of our agreement" and one that says "subject to my lawyer's approval of documents tendered when the deal is closed"? Compare Southern Bell Telephone & Telegraph Co. v. John Hancock Mutual Life Insurance Co., 579 F.Supp. 1065 (N.D.Ga.1983), with Zelazny v. Pilgrim Funding Corp., 244 N.Y.S.2d 810 (Dist.Ct.1963).

(2) *The Concealed Offer.* Note the "defendant's thesis that the deposit receipt constituted no more than an offer by her." The possibility that an offer is concealed in such an exchange of promises should not be ignored.

Suppose, for example, that Seller promises to fill at a stated price all the orders for aviation fuel that Buyer cares to send and Buyer promises to pay for any aviation fuel ordered. Although there is no contract because Buyer's promise is illusory, if Buyer orders a million gallons of aviation fuel before Seller retracts its promise or it lapses, there is a contract for that quantity. What the parties may have thought was a contract did at least amount to a standing offer by Seller.

Why did not this line of argument help the buyer in Mattei v. Hopper?

EASTERN AIR LINES, INC. v. GULF OIL CORPORATION

United States District Court, Southern District of Florida, 1975.
415 F.Supp. 429.

JAMES LAWRENCE KING, DISTRICT JUDGE. Eastern Air Lines, Inc., hereafter Eastern, and Gulf Oil Corporation, hereafter Gulf, have enjoyed a mutually advantageous business relationship involving the sale and purchase of aviation fuel for several decades.

This controversy involves the threatened disruption of that historic relationship and the attempt, by Eastern, to enforce the most recent contract between the parties. On March 8, 1974 the correspondence and telex communications between the corporate entities culminated in a demand by Gulf that Eastern must meet its demand for a price increase or Gulf would shut off Eastern's supply of jet fuel within fifteen days.

Eastern responded by filing its complaint with this court, alleging that Gulf had breached its contract and requesting preliminary and permanent mandatory injunctions requiring Gulf to perform the contract in accordance with its terms. By agreement of the parties, a preliminary injunction preserving the status quo was entered on March 20, 1974, requiring Gulf to perform its contract and directing Eastern to pay in accordance with the contract terms, pending final disposition of the case.

Gulf answered Eastern's complaint, alleging that the contract was not a binding requirements contract, was void for want of mutuality, and, furthermore, was "commercially impracticable" within the meaning of Uniform Commercial Code § 2–615; Fla.Stat. §§ 672.614 and 672.615.

The extraordinarily able advocacy by the experienced lawyers for both parties produced testimony at the trial from internationally respected experts who described in depth economic events that have, in recent months, profoundly affected the lives of every American.

THE CONTRACT

On June 27, 1972, an agreement was signed by the parties which, as amended, was to provide the basis upon which Gulf was to furnish jet fuel to Eastern at certain specific cities in the Eastern system. Said agreement supplemented an existing contract between Gulf and Eastern which, on June 27, 1972, had approximately one year remaining prior to its expiration.

The contract is Gulf's standard form aviation fuel contract and is identical in all material particulars with the first contract for jet fuel, dated 1959, between Eastern and Gulf and, indeed, with aviation fuel contracts antedating the jet age. It is similar to contracts in general use in the aviation fuel trade. The contract was drafted by Gulf after substantial arm's length negotiation between the parties. Gulf approached Eastern more than a year before the expiration of the then-existing contracts between Gulf and Eastern, seeking to preserve its historic relationship with Eastern. Following several months of negotiation, the contract, consolidating and extending the terms of several existing contracts, was executed by the parties in June, 1972, to expire January 31, 1977.

The parties agreed that this contract, as its predecessor, should provide a reference to reflect changes in the price of the raw material from which jet fuel is processed, i.e., crude oil, in direct proportion to the cost per gallon of jet fuel.

Both parties regarded the instant agreement as favorable, Eastern, in part, because it offered immediate savings in projected escalations under the existing agreement through reduced base prices at the contract cities; while Gulf found a long term outlet for a capacity of jet fuel coming on stream from a newly completed refinery, as well as a means to relate anticipated increased cost of raw material (crude oil) directly to the price of the refined product sold. The previous Eastern/Gulf contracts contained a price index clause which operated to pass on to Eastern only one-half of any increase in the price of crude oil. Both parties knew at the time of contract negotiations that increases in crude oil prices would be expected, were "a way of life", and intended that those increases be borne by Eastern in a direct proportional relationship of crude oil cost per barrel to jet fuel cost per gallon.

Accordingly, the parties selected an indicator (West Texas Sour); a crude which is bought and sold in large volume and was thus a reliable indicator of the market value of crude oil. From June 27, 1972 to the fall of 1973, there were in effect various forms of U.S. government imposed price controls which at once controlled the price of crude oil generally, West Texas Sour specifically, and hence the price of jet fuel. As the government authorized increased prices of crude those increases were in turn reflected in the cost of jet fuel. Eastern has paid a per gallon increase under the contract from 11 cents to 15 cents (or some 40%).

The indicator selected by the parties was "the average of the posted prices for West Texas sour crude, 30.0–30.9 gravity of Gulf Oil Corporation, Shell Oil Company, and Pan American Petroleum Corporation". The posting of crude prices under the contract "shall be as listed for these companies in Platts Oilgram Service—Crude Oil Supplement ..."

"Posting" has long been a practice in the oil industry. It involves the physical placement at a public location of a price bulletin reflecting the current price at which an oil company will pay for a given barrel of a specific type of crude oil. Those posted price bulletins historically have, in addition to being displayed publicly, been mailed to those persons evincing interest therein, including sellers of crude oil, customers whose price of product may be based thereon, and, among others, Platts Oilgram, publishers of a periodical of interest to those related to the oil industry.

In recent years, the United States has become increasingly dependent upon foreign crude oil, particularly from the "OPEC" nations most of which are in the Middle East. OPEC was formed in 1970 for the avowed purpose of raising oil prices, and has become an increasingly cohesive and potent organization as its member nations have steadily enhanced their equity positions and their control over their oil production facilities. Nationalization of crude oil resources and shutdowns of production and distribution have become a way of life for oil companies operating in OPEC nations, particularly in the volatile Middle East. The closing of the Suez Canal and the concomitant interruption of the flow of Mid–East oil during the 1967 "Six–Day War", and Libya's nationalization of its oil industry during the same period, are only some of the more dramatic examples of a trend that began years ago. By 1969 "the handwriting was on the wall" in the words of Gulf's foreign oil expert witness, Mr. Blackledge.

During 1970 domestic United States oil production "peaked"; since then it has declined while the percentage of imported crude oil has been steadily increasing. Unlike domestic crude oil, which has been subject to price control since August 15, 1971, foreign crude oil has never been subject to price control by the United States Government. Foreign crude oil prices, uncontrolled by the Federal Government, were generally lower than domestic crude oil prices in 1971 and 1972; during 1973 foreign prices "crossed" domestic prices; by late 1973 foreign prices were generally several dollars per barrel higher than controlled domestic prices. It was during late 1973 that the Mid–East exploded in another war, accompanied by an embargo (at least officially) by the Arab oil-producing nations against the United States and certain of its allies. World prices for oil and oil products increased.

Mindful of that situation and for various other reasons concerning the nation's economy, the United States government began a series of controls affecting the oil industry culminating, in the fall of 1973, with the implementation of price controls known as "two-tier." In practice "two-tier" can be described as follows: taking as the bench mark the number of barrels produced from a given well in May of 1972, that number of barrels is deemed "old" oil. The price of "old" oil then is frozen by the government at a fixed level. To the extent that the productivity of a given well can be increased over the May, 1972, production, that increased production is deemed "new" oil. For each barrel of "new" oil produced, the government authorized the release from price controls of an equivalent number of barrels from those theretofore designated "old" oil. For example, from a well which in May of 1972, produced 100 barrels of oil; all of the production of that well would, since the imposition of "two-tier" in August of 1973, be "old" oil. Increased productivity to 150 barrels would result in 50 barrels of "new" oil and 50 barrels of "released" oil; with the result that 100 barrels of the 150 barrels produced from the well would be uncontrolled by the "two-tier" pricing system, while the 50 remaining barrels of "old" would remain government price controlled.

The implementation of "two-tier" was completely without precedent in the history of government price control action. Its impact, however, was nominal, until the imposition of an embargo upon the exportation of crude oil by certain Arab countries in October, 1973. Those countries deemed sympathetic to Israel were embargoed from receiving oil from the Arab oil producing countries. The United States was among the principal countries affected by that embargo, with the result that it experienced an immediate "energy crises".

Following closely after the embargo, OPEC (Oil Producing Export Countries) unilaterally increased the price of their crude to the world market some 400% between September, 1973, and January 15, 1974. Since the United States domestic production was at capacity, it was dependent upon foreign crude to meet its requirements. New and released oil (uncontrolled) soon reached parity with the price of foreign crude, moving from approximately $5 to $11 a barrel from September, 1974 to January 15, 1974.

Since imposition of "two-tier", the price of "old oil" has remained fixed by government action, with the oil companies resorting to postings reflecting prices they will pay for the new and released oil, not subject to government controls. Those prices, known as "premiums", are the subject of supplemental bulletins which are likewise posted by the oil companies and furnished to interested parties, including Platts Oilgram.

Platts, since the institution of "two-tier" has not published the posted prices of any of the premiums offered by the oil companies in the United States, including those of Gulf Oil Corporation, Shell Oil Company and Pan American Petroleum, the companies designated in the agreement. The information which has appeared in Platts since the implementation of "two-tier" with respect to the price of West Texas Sour crude oil has been the price of "old" oil subject to government control.

Under the court's restraining order, entered in this cause by agreement of the parties, Eastern has been paying for jet fuel from Gulf on the basis of the price of "old" West Texas Sour crude oil as fixed by government price control action, i.e., $5 a barrel. Approximately 40 gallons of finished jet fuel product can be refined from a barrel of crude.

Against this factual background we turn to a consideration of the legal issues.

I

THE "REQUIREMENTS" CONTRACT

Gulf has taken the position in this case that the contract between it and Eastern is not a valid document in that it lacks mutuality of obligation; it is vague and indefinite; and that it renders Gulf subject to Eastern's whims respecting the volume of jet fuel Gulf would be required to deliver to the purchaser Eastern.

The contract talks in terms of fuel "requirements".[1] The parties have interpreted this provision to mean that any aviation fuel purchased by Eastern at one of the cities covered by the contract, must be bought from Gulf. Conversely, Gulf must make the necessary arrangements to supply Eastern's reasonable good faith demands at those same locations. This is the construction the parties themselves have placed on the contract and it has governed their conduct over many years and several contracts.

In early cases, requirements contracts were found invalid for want of the requisite definiteness, or on the grounds of lack of mutuality. Many such cases are collected and annotated at 14 A.L.R. 1300.

As reflected in the foregoing annotation, there developed rather quickly in the law the view that a requirements contract could be binding where the purchaser had an operating business. The "lack of mutuality" and "indefiniteness" were resolved since the court could determine the volume of goods provided for under the contract by reference to objective evidence of the volume of goods required to operate the specified business. Therefore, well prior to the adoption of the Uniform Commercial Code, case law generally held requirements contracts binding. See 26 A.L.R.2d 1099, 1139.

---

1. "Gulf agrees to sell and deliver to Eastern, and Eastern agrees to purchase, receive and pay for their requirements of Gulf Jet A and Gulf Jet A–1 at the locations listed...."

The Uniform Commercial Code, adopted in Florida in 1965, specifically approves requirements contracts in F.S. 672.306 (U.C.C. § 2–306(1)).

"(1) A term which measures the quantity by the output of the seller or the requirements of the buyer means such actual output or requirements as may occur in good faith, except that no quantity unreasonably disproportionate to any stated estimate or in the absence of a stated estimate to any normal or otherwise comparable prior output or requirements may be tendered or demanded."

The Uniform Commercial Code Official Comment interprets § 2–306(1) as follows:

"2. Under this Article, a contract for output or requirements is not too indefinite since it is held to mean the actual good faith output or requirements of the particular party. Nor does such a contract lack mutuality of obligation since, under this section, the party who will determine quantity is required to operate his plant or conduct his business in good faith and according to commercial standards of fair dealing in the trade so that his output or requirements will approximate a reasonably foreseeable figure. Reasonable elasticity in the requirements is expressly envisaged by this section and good faith variations from prior requirements are permitted even when the variation may be such as to result in discontinuance. A shut-down by a requirements buyer for lack of orders might be permissible when a shut-down merely to curtail losses would not. The essential test is whether the party is acting in good faith. Similarly, a sudden expansion of the plant by which requirements are to be measured would not be included within the scope of the contract as made but normal expansion undertaken in good faith would be within the scope of this section. One of the factors in an expansion situation would be whether the market price has risen greatly in a case in which the requirements contract contained a fixed price. Reasonable variation of an extreme sort is exemplified in Southwest Natural Gas Co. v. Oklahoma Portland Cement Co., 102 F.2d 630 (C.C.A. 10, 1939)."

Some of the prior Gulf–Eastern contracts have included the estimated fuel requirements for some cities covered by the contract while others have none. The particular contract contains an estimate for Gainesville, Florida requirement.

The parties have consistently over the years relied upon each other to act in good faith in the purchase and sale of the required quantities of aviation fuel specified in the contract. During the course of the contract, various estimates have been exchanged from time to time, and, since the advent of the petroleum allocations programs, discussions of estimated requirements have been on a monthly (or more frequent) basis.[2]

---

2. A requirements contract under the U.C.C. may speak of "requirements" alone, or it may include estimates, or it may contain maximums and minimums. In any

The court concludes that the document is a binding and enforceable requirements contract.

II

BREACH OF CONTRACT

[The court determined that Eastern's performance under the contract "did not constitute a breach of its agreement with Gulf" and was "consistent with good faith and commercial practices as required by U.C.C. § 2–306." See p. 613 below.]

III

COMMERCIAL IMPRACTICABILITY

[The court concluded that Gulf was not excused on the ground of commercial impracticability. See p. 823 below.]

IV

REMEDY

Having found and concluded that the contract is a valid one, should be enforced, and that no defenses have been established against it, there remains for consideration the proper remedy.

The Uniform Commercial Code provides that in an appropriate case specific performance may be decreed. This case is a particularly appropriate one for specific performance. The parties have been operating for more than a year pursuant to a preliminary injunction requiring specific performance of the contract and Gulf has stipulated that it is able to perform. Gulf presently supplies Eastern with 100,000,000 gallons of fuel annually or 10 percent of Eastern's total requirements. If Gulf ceases to supply this fuel, the result will be chaos and irreparable damage.

Under the U.C.C. a more liberal test in determining entitlement to specific performance has been established than the test one must meet for classic equitable relief. U.C.C. § 2–716(1)....

It has previously been found and concluded that Eastern is entitled to Gulf's fuel at the prices agreed upon in the contract. In the circumstances, a decree of specific performance becomes the ordinary and natural relief rather than the extraordinary one. The parties are before the court, the issues are squarely framed, they have been clearly

case, the consequences are the same, as Official Comments 2 and 3 indicate. Comment 2 is set out in the text above. Comment 3 provides:

"3. If an estimate of output or requirements is included in the agreement, no quantity unreasonably disproportionate to it may be tendered or demanded. Any minimum or maximum set by the agreement shows a clear limit on the intended elasticity. In similar fashion, the agreed estimate is to be regarded as a center around which the parties intend the variation to occur."

resolved in Eastern's favor, and it would be a vain, useless and potentially harmful exercise to declare that Eastern has a valid contract, but leave the parties to their own devices. Accordingly, the preliminary injunction heretofore entered is made a permanent injunction and the order of this court herein.

NOTES

(1) *Price Fluctuations.* Under a fixed price requirements contract, the seller runs a risk that if the market price rises, the buyer's requirements will escalate. (Part II of the court's opinion discusses the limited protection that the concept of good faith affords against this risk.) Does the Code suggest any drafting techniques that a seller might use to reduce this risk? For an example of successful drafting under a fixed price requirements contract for fuel oil, see Orange & Rockland Utilities, Inc. v. Amerada Hess Corp., 397 N.Y.S.2d 814 (App.Div.1977). Did Gulf succeed in avoiding this risk by making a flexible price requirements contract?

(2) *Fuel v. Glue.* Peter Cooper's Glue Factory wrote to a jobber in glue, agreeing to supply "your requirements of 'Special BB' glue for the year 1916, price to be 9¢ per lb." The jobber was misleadingly named Schlegel Manufacturing Company; in fact it had no manufacturing business in which glue was used. During 1916 the jobber ordered about five times as much glue as it had ordered in any of the preceding five years. The Glue Factory supplied less than half of the amount ordered, and Schlegel sued it. From a judgment for the plaintiff, the defendant appealed. *Held:* Reversed. The court remarked: "The price of glue having risen during the year 1916 from nine to twenty-four cents per pound, it is quite obvious why orders for glue increased correspondingly." In ruling that consideration was lacking for the defendant's promise, the court made these observations about the agreement: "there is no standard mentioned by which the quantity of glue to be furnished can be determined with any approximate degree of accuracy.... [T]here was no obligation on the part of the plaintiff to sell any of the defendant's glue, to make any effort towards bringing about such sale, or not to sell other glues in competition with it." Schlegel Manufacturing Co. v. Cooper's Glue Factory, 132 N.E. 148 (N.Y.1921).

In what respects was the glue agreement like the aviation fuel agreement in the main case? In what respects different? How should the glue case be decided under the Code?

(3) *Output Contracts.* In contrast to a "requirements" contract, an "output" contract is one that calls on the seller to deliver and the buyer to take all of the goods, or all of a certain sort, that may be produced by the seller. A contract for the sale of all of the cotton to be raised and harvested on a specified tract of land (see p. 1 above) is an output contract. Output contracts are often bracketed with requirements contracts in discussion as presenting common problems. What is said here about requirements contracts may be understood as bearing on output contracts.

WOOD v. LUCY, LADY DUFF–GORDON

Court of Appeals of New York, 1917.
222 N.Y. 88, 118 N.E. 214.

Appeal from Supreme Court, Appellate Division, First Department.

Action by Otis F. Wood against Lucy, Lady Duff–Gordon. From a judgment of the Appellate Division (177 App.Div. 624, 164 N.Y.Supp. 576), which reversed an order denying defendant's motion for judgment on the pleading, and which dismissed the complaint, plaintiff appeals. Reversed.

CARDOZO, J. The defendant styles herself "a creator of fashions." Her favor helps a sale. Manufacturers of dresses, millinery, and like articles are glad to pay for a certificate of her approval. The things which she designs, fabrics, parasols, and what not, have a new value in the public mind when issued in her name.[a] She employed the plaintiff to help her to turn this vogue into money. He was to have the exclusive right, subject always to her approval, to place her indorsements on the designs of others. He was also to have the exclusive right to place her own designs on sale, or to license others to market them. In return she was to have one-half of "all profits and revenues" derived from any contracts he might make. The exclusive right was to last at least one year from April 1, 1915, and thereafter from year to year unless terminated by notice of 90 days. The plaintiff says that he kept the contract on his part, and that the defendant broke it. She placed her indorsement on fabrics, dresses, and millinery without his knowledge, and withheld the profits. He sues her for the damages, and the case comes here on demurrer.[b]

The agreement of employment is signed by both parties. It has a wealth of recitals. The defendant insists, however, that it lacks the elements of a contract. She says that the plaintiff does not bind himself to anything. It is true that he does not promise in so many words that he will use reasonable efforts to place the defendant's indorsements and market her designs. We think, however, that such a promise is fairly to

---

a. For an entertaining account of Lady Duff–Gordon's life and of her remarkable impact on the fashions of her times, see M. Etherington–Smith & J. Pilcher, The "It" Girls (1986). "Her arrival in New York [in 1910] was a triumph—she was met with placards on street corners informing the crowds that the '*Titled Dressmaker and Her Golden Girls Arrive Today to Show Americans How to Dress.*'" Id. at 129.

b. In dismissing the complaint, the Appellate Division explained that "the plaintiff by this contract promises to collect the revenues derived from the indorsements, sales and licenses and to pay the cost of collecting them of his half thereof and to account to the defendant each month. But this promise on his part is not binding on him unless he places indorsements, makes sales or grants licenses, and nowhere in the contract has he bound himself to get these indorsements, or make the sales or grant the licenses. . . . It is quite apparent that in this respect the defendant gives everything and the plaintiff nothing and there is a lack of mutuality in the contract. . . . In fact the plaintiff in the nature of the case could not perform any of his various dependent agreements unless he placed indorsements, made sales or granted licenses to manufacture. And as the contract did not bind him to do any of these things, there is no provision of the contract which the defendant could enforce against him." 164 N.Y.S. at 577.

be implied. The law has outgrown its primitive stage of formalism when the precise word was the sovereign talisman, and every slip was fatal. It takes a broader view today. A promise may be lacking, and yet the whole writing may be "instinct with an obligation," imperfectly expressed (Scott, J., in McCall Co. v. Wright, 133 App.Div. 62, 117 N.Y.S. 775; Moran v. Standard Oil Co., 211 N.Y. 187, 198, 105 N.E. 217). If that is so, there is a contract.

The implication of a promise here finds support in many circumstances. The defendant gave an exclusive privilege. She was to have no right for at least a year to place her own indorsements or market her own designs except through the agency of the plaintiff. The acceptance of the exclusive agency was an assumption of its duties. Phoenix Hermetic Co. v. Filtrine Mfg. Co., 164 App.Div. 424, 150 N.Y.S. 193; W.G. Taylor Co. v. Bannerman, 120 Wis. 189, 97 N.W. 918; Mueller v. Mineral Spring Co., 88 Mich. 390, 50 N.W. 319. We are not to suppose that one party was to be placed at the mercy of the other. Hearn v. Stevens & Bro., 111 App.Div. 101, 106, 97 N.Y.S. 566; Russell v. Allerton, 108 N.Y. 288, 15 N.E. 391. Many other terms of the agreement point the same way. We are told at the outset by way of recital that:

"The said Otis F. Wood possesses a business organization adapted to the placing of such indorsements as the said Lucy, Lady Duff–Gordon, has approved."

The implication is that the plaintiff's business organization will be used for the purpose for which it is adapted. But the terms of the defendant's compensation are even more significant. Her sole compensation for the grant of an exclusive agency is to be one-half of all the profits resulting from the plaintiff's efforts. Unless he gave his efforts, she could never get anything. Without an implied promise, the transaction cannot have such business "efficacy, as both parties must have intended that at all events it should have." Bowen, L.J., in The Moorcock, 14 P.D. 64, 68. But the contract does not stop there. The plaintiff goes on to promise that he will account monthly for all moneys received by him, and that he will take out all such patents and copyrights and trademarks as may in his judgment be necessary to protect the rights and articles affected by the agreement. It is true, of course, as the Appellate Division has said, that if he was under no duty to try to market designs or to place certificates of indorsement, his promise to account for profits or take out copyrights would be valueless. But in determining the intention of the parties the promise has a value. It helps to enforce the conclusion that the plaintiff had some duties. His promise to pay the defendant one-half of the profits and revenues resulting from the exclusive agency and to render accounts monthly was a promise to use reasonable efforts to bring profits and revenues into existence. For this conclusion the authorities are ample....

The judgment of the Appellate Division should be reversed, and the order of the Special Term affirmed, with costs in the Appellate Division and in this court.

CUDDEBACK, McLAUGHLIN, and ANDREWS, JJ., concur. HISCOCK, C.J., and CHASE and CRANE, JJ., dissent.

NOTES

(1) *Rationale.* What is the rationale for the implication of a promise? To what extent is it an application of the maxim *ut res magis valeat quam pereat* (that the thing may rather have effect than be destroyed)? To what extent does it turn on the fact that Lady Duff–Gordon gave Wood "an exclusive privilege"? To what extent does it turn on other of the "many circumstances" referred to by Cardozo? What answers are suggested by the statement of the rule in UCC 2–306(2)?

(2) *Corbin and Llewellyn on Cardozo.* Professor Arthur Linton Corbin [c] wrote this of Cardozo: "It cannot be said that he made any extensive changes in the existing law of contract. To state the facts of the cases, the decision, and the reasoning of the opinion will not show the overthrow of old doctrine or the establishment of new. Instead, it will show the application of existing doctrines with wisdom and discretion; an application that does not leave those doctrines wholly unaffected, but one that carries on their evolution as is reasonably required by the new facts before the court. When Cardozo is through, the law is not exactly as it was before, but there has been no sudden shift or revolutionary change." Corbin, Mr. Justice Cardozo and the Law of Contracts, 39 Colum.L.Rev. 56, 56–57, 52 Harv.L.Rev. 408, 408–09, 48 Yale L.J. 426, 426–27 (1939).

Professor Karl Llewellyn used Wood v. Lucy to illustrate Cardozo's mastery in presenting the facts of a case. "You must remember that Cardozo was a truly great advocate, and the fact that he became a great judge didn't at all change the fact that he was a great advocate. And if you will watch, in the very process of your listening to the facts, you will find two things happening. The one is that ... you arrive at the conclusion that the case has to come out one way. And the other is, that it fits into a legal frame that says, 'How comfortable it will be, to bring it out that way. No trouble at all. No trouble at all.'" Llewellyn quoted the first five sentences of the opinion, noting how the defendant "is subtly made into a nasty person," and went on: "Does this sound ... like a business deal? Does a business deal sound like a legally enforceable view? Nothing is being said about that. But watch it grow on you. And if I hadn't stopped to tell you about it, it would have grown until you just took it, without a word." Llewellyn, A Lecture on Appellate Advocacy, 29 U.Chi.L.Rev. 627, 637–38 (1962). Can you give a similar reading to other parts of the opinion?

––––––––

TERMINATION CLAUSES

Contracting parties often use termination clauses to reduce the risks that they assume by contracting. If a termination clause is read as giving a party the power to terminate at any time at will, without more,

c. Arthur Linton Corbin (1874–1967) practiced law in Colorado for four years after his graduation from law school in 1899. He taught at the Yale Law School from 1903 until his retirement in 1943, and became a leading authority on the law of contracts. His eight-volume treatise, Corbin on Contracts, which began to appear in 1950, ranks as one of the great legal treatises in any field of law in this country. He also served as Special Advisor and as Reporter for the Chapter on Remedies for the Restatement of Contracts.

the party's promise will be held to be illusory. For example, a license agreement for the manufacture of Orange Crush gave the licensee the exclusive right and the duty to manufacture the soft drink in a specified territory, but it provided that the licensee could at any time terminate the contract. In a suit by the licensee against the licensor, it was held that the licensee's promise was not consideration for the licensor's because the licensee "did not promise to do anything and could at any time cancel the contract." Miami Coca–Cola Bottling Co. v. Orange Crush Co., 296 Fed. 693 (5th Cir.1924). If, however, the provision is read as requiring the party to give notice some period of time before the termination becomes effective, the promise will not be held to be illusory. Here is what the court in the Laclede case, p. 28 above, said on this point:

"A bilateral contract is not rendered invalid and unenforceable merely because one party has the right to cancellation while the other does not. There is no necessity 'that for each stipulation in a contract binding the one party there must be a corresponding stipulation binding the other.' James B. Berry's Sons Co. v. Monark Gasoline & Oil Co., 32 F.2d 74, 75 (8th Cir.1929).

. . .

"The important question in the instant case is whether Laclede's right of cancellation rendered all its other promises in the agreement illusory so that there was a complete *failure* of consideration. This would be the result had Laclede retained the right of immediate cancellation at any time for any reason. 1 S. Williston, Law of Contracts § 104, at 400–401 (3d ed. 1957). However, Professor Williston goes on to note:

Since the courts ... do not favor arbitrary cancellation clauses, the tendency is to interpret even a slight restriction on the exercise of the right of cancellation as constituting such legal detriment as will satisfy the requirement of sufficient consideration; for example, where the reservation of right to cancel is for cause, or by written notice, or after a definite period of notice, or upon the occurrence of some extrinsic event, or is based on some other objective standard.

Id. § 105, at 418–419 (footnotes omitted). Professor Corbin agrees and states simply that when one party has the power to cancel by notice given for some stated period of time, 'the contract should never be held to be rendered invalid thereby for lack of "mutuality" or for lack of consideration.' 1A A. Corbin, Corbin on Contracts § 164 at 83 (1963). The law of Missouri appears to be in conformity with this general contract rule that a cancellation clause will invalidate a contract only if its exercise is *unrestricted*. . . .

"Here Laclede's right to terminate was neither arbitrary nor unrestricted. It was limited by the agreement in at least three ways. First, Laclede could not cancel until one year had passed after the first delivery of propane by Amoco. Second, any cancellation could be effective only on the anniversary date of the first delivery under the agreement. Third, Laclede had to give Amoco 30 days written notice of termination.

These restrictions on Laclede's power to cancel clearly bring this case within the rule."

NOTES

(1) *A Way Out.* Suppose that Laclede could have terminated at will at any time before the end of the first week after delivery began. Would its promise then have been illusory? Would Amoco have been bound before the end of that week? Would it affect your answer if Laclede could have terminated at will at any time before the end of the first month rather than the first week? See Sylvan Crest Sand & Gravel Co. v. United States, 150 F.2d 642 (2d Cir.1945).

(2) *The Code.* UCC 2–309(3) requires "reasonable notification" for termination, except on the happening of an agreed event. What if a termination clause explicitly negates any duty of notification? As to this, Comment 8 to UCC 2–309 says: "An agreement dispensing with notification or limiting the time for the seeking of a substitute arrangement is, of course, valid under this subsection unless the results of putting it into operation would be the creation of an unconscionable state of affairs." Termination clauses will be considered again in Chapter 4, Policing the Bargain, and Chapter 6, Finding the Law of the Contract.

(3) *Voidable Promises.* A person who makes a contract before reaching the age of majority (today commonly 18) can disaffirm that contract and avoid being bound. Can such a person's promise be consideration? In Holt v. Ward Clarencieux, 93 Eng.Rep. 954 (King's Bench 1732), the court answered in the affirmative, sustaining an action for breach of promise of marriage brought on behalf of a young woman who had been a girl of 15 at the time of the agreement. "[W]e are all of opinion that this contract is not void but only voidable at the option of the infant.... And no dangerous consequence can follow from this determination, because our opinion protects the infant even more than if we rule the contract to be absolutely void." The capacity of minors to make contracts is dealt with in Chapter 4, Policing the Bargain.

Chapter 2

THE BARGAINING PROCESS

SECTION 1. THE NATURE OF ASSENT

What kind of assent to a bargain is necessary to bind a party? Different answers are given by two contrasting theories of contract, commonly described as "objective" and "subjective." They are illustrated by these excerpts from Judge Learned Hand [a] and his colleague Judge Jerome Frank,[b] concurring in a case in which Hand wrote the opinion of the court.

According to Hand: "A contract has, strictly speaking, nothing to do with the personal, or individual, intent of the parties. A contract is an obligation attached by the mere force of law to certain acts of the parties, usually words, which ordinarily accompany and represent a known intent. If, however, it were proved by twenty bishops that either party when he used the words intended something else than the usual meaning which the law imposes upon them, he would still be held, unless there were some mutual mistake or something else of the sort." Hotchkiss v. National City Bank of New York, 200 F. 287, 293 (S.D.N.Y.1911).

According to Frank: "In the early days of this century a struggle went on between the respective proponents of two theories of contracts, (a) the 'actual intent' theory—or 'meeting of the minds' [c] or 'will' theory—and (b) the so-called 'objective' theory.[1] Without doubt, the

a. Learned Hand (1872–1961) was admitted to the practice of law in New York in 1897, appointed to the United States District Court for the Southern District of New York in 1909 and to the United States Court of Appeals for the Second Circuit in 1924. He retired in 1951, after having sat on the bench longer than any other federal judge. Justice Cardozo called him "the greatest living American jurist," and he was so regarded by many of his contemporaries. His extrajudicial utterances may be sampled in The Spirit of Liberty (1952) and The Bill of Rights (1958).

b. Jerome New Frank (1889–1957) practiced in Chicago and New York for more than twenty years before going to Washington in 1933, where he served first as a government lawyer and then as a member and later chairman of the Securities and Exchange Commission. In 1941 he was appointed to the United States Court of Appeals for the Second Circuit. He also lectured at the Yale Law School and was associated with the philosophy of law known as "legal realism." One of his best known books is Law and the Modern Mind (1930).

c. For the curious origin of the term "meeting of the minds," see Farnsworth, "Meaning" in the Law of Contracts, 76 Yale L.J. 939, 943–44 (1967). It has remained a popular metaphor, e.g., "Any greater 'meeting of the minds' would require them to bump their heads together." Turner v. Worth Insurance Co., 472 P.2d 1 (Ariz. 1970).

1. "The 'actual intent' theory, said the objectivists, being 'subjective' and putting too much stress on unique individual motivations, would destroy that legal certainty and stability which a modern commercial

138

first theory had been carried too far: Once a contract has been validly made, the courts attach legal consequences to the relation created by the contract, consequences of which the parties usually never dreamed—as, for instance, where situations arise which the parties had not contemplated. As to such matters, the 'actual intent' theory induced much fictional discourse which imputed to the parties intentions they plainly did not have.

"But the objectivists also went too far. They tried (1) to treat virtually all the varieties of contractual arrangements in the same way, and (2), as to all contracts in all their phases, to exclude, as legally irrelevant, consideration of the actual intention of the parties or either of them, as distinguished from the outward manifestation of that intention. The objectivists transferred from the field of torts that stubborn anti-subjectivist, the 'reasonable man'; so that, in part at least, advocacy of the 'objective' standard in contracts appears to have represented a desire for legal symmetry, legal uniformity, a desire seemingly prompted by aesthetic impulses. Whether (thanks to the 'subjectivity' of the jurymen's reactions and other factors) the objectivists' formula, in its practical workings, could yield much actual objectivity, certainty, and uniformity may well be doubted. At any rate, the sponsors of complete 'objectivity' in contracts largely won out in the wider generalizations of the Restatement of Contracts and in some judicial pronouncements." Ricketts v. Pennsylvania R. Co., 153 F.2d 757 (2d Cir.1946).

Does either theory adequately explain the decision in the following case? For a discussion of the two theories, see Kabil Developments Corp. v. Mignot, 566 P.2d 505 (Or.1977).

NOTES

(1) *Mistake in Transmission.* Suppose that a seller sends an offer by telegram and the telegraph company makes an error in transmitting it so that it reads "fifty thousand" boxes rather than "fifteen thousand" as the seller instructed it. There is authority that the seller is bound by a contract for fifty thousand. Ayer v. Western Union Telegraph Co., 10 A. 495 (Me.1887). Contra: Western Union Telegraph Co. v. Cowin & Co., 20 F.2d 103 (8th Cir.1927).

Does this carry the objective theory too far? Can the imposition of the risk on the sender of the telegram be justified on the ground that the sender has a contractual relationship with the telegraph company?

(2) *Relief for Mistake.* The possibility that a party may be relieved of a contractual obligation on the ground that its assent was the result of mistake is considered at several points in this book. See, in particular, pp. 795–804, below.

---

society demands. They depicted the 'objective' standard as a necessary adjunct of a 'free enterprise' economic system. In passing, it should be noted that they arrived at a sort of paradox. For a 'free enterprise' system is, theoretically, founded on 'individualism'; but, in the name of economic individualism, the objectivists refused to consider those reactions of actual specific individuals which sponsors of the 'meeting-of-the-minds' test purported to cherish. 'Economic individualism' thus shows up as hostile to real individualism. This is nothing new: The 'economic man' is of course an abstraction, a 'fiction.' "

*Reasonable
Belief in
Contract formation*

LUCY v. ZEHMER

Supreme Court of Appeals of Virginia, 1954.
196 Va. 493, 84 S.E.2d 516.

BUCHANAN, JUSTICE. This suit was instituted by W.O. Lucy and J.C. Lucy, complainants, against A.H. Zehmer and Ida S. Zehmer, his wife, defendants, to have specific performance of a contract by which it was alleged the Zehmers had sold to W.O. Lucy a tract of land owned by A.H. Zehmer in Dinwiddie county containing 471.6 acres, more or less, known as the Ferguson farm, for $50,000. J.C. Lucy, the other complainant, is a brother of W.O. Lucy, to whom W.O. Lucy transferred a half interest in his alleged purchase.

The instrument sought to be enforced was written by A.H. Zehmer on [Saturday,] December 20, 1952, in these words: "We hereby agree to sell to W.O. Lucy the Ferguson Farm complete for $50,000.00, title satisfactory to buyer," and signed by the defendants, A.H. Zehmer and Ida S. Zehmer.[a]

*4 had
no intention
of selling*

The answer of A.H. Zehmer admitted that at the time mentioned W.O. Lucy offered him $50,000 cash for the farm, but that he, Zehmer, considered that the offer was made in jest; that so thinking, and both he and Lucy having had several drinks, he wrote out "the memorandum" quoted above and induced his wife to sign it; that he did not deliver the memorandum to Lucy, but that Lucy picked it up, read it, put it in his pocket, attempted to offer Zehmer $5 to bind the bargain, which Zehmer refused to accept, and realizing for the first time that Lucy was serious, Zehmer assured him that he had no intention of selling the farm and

a.   Here is a photostat from the record:

DE LUXE CABINS	STEAM HEATED	HOTEL ROOMS
YE OLDE VIRGINNIE RESTAURANT		
GARAGE - SERVICE STATION		
25 MILES SOUTH OF PETERSBURG		
U. S. No. 1		McKENNEY, VA.

SERVER	GUESTS	TABLE	CHECK
			25216

PLEASE PAY CASHIER

[Front]

[Back]

that the whole matter was a joke. Lucy left the premises insisting that he had purchased the farm.

Depositions were taken and the decree appealed from was entered holding that the complainants had failed to establish their right to specific performance, and dismissing their bill. The assignment of error is to this action of the court. . . .

The defendants insist that the evidence was ample to support their contention that the writing sought to be enforced was prepared as a bluff or dare to force Lucy to admit that he did not have $50,000; that the whole matter was a joke; that the writing was not delivered to Lucy and no binding contract was ever made between the parties.

It is an unusual, if not bizarre, defense. When made to the writing admittedly prepared by one of the defendants and signed by both, clear evidence is required to sustain it.

In his testimony Zehmer claimed that he "was high as a Georgia pine," and that the transaction "was just a bunch of two doggoned drunks bluffing to see who could talk the biggest and say the most." That claim is inconsistent with his attempt to testify in great detail as to what was said and what was done. It is contradicted by other evidence as to the condition of both parties, and rendered of no weight by the testimony of his wife that when Lucy left the restaurant she suggested that Zehmer drive him home. The record is convincing that Zehmer was not intoxicated to the extent of being unable to comprehend the nature and consequences of the instrument he executed, and hence that instrument is not to be invalidated on that ground. C.J.S. Contracts, § 133, b., p. 483; Taliaferro v. Emery, 124 Va. 674, 98 S.E. 627. It was in fact conceded by defendants' counsel in oral argument that under the evidence Zehmer was not too drunk to make a valid contract.

The evidence is convincing also that Zehmer wrote two agreements, the first one beginning "I hereby agree to sell." Zehmer first said he could not remember about that, then that "I don't think I wrote but one out." Mrs. Zehmer said that what he wrote was "I hereby agree," but that the "I" was changed to "We" after that night. The agreement that was written and signed is in the record and indicates no such change. Neither are the mistakes in spelling that Zehmer sought to point out readily apparent.

The appearance of the contract, the fact that it was under discussion for forty minutes or more before it was signed; Lucy's objection to the first draft because it was written in the singular, and he wanted Mrs. Zehmer to sign it also; the rewriting to meet that objection and the signing by Mrs. Zehmer; the discussion of what was to be included in the sale, the provision for the examination of the title, the completeness of the instrument that was executed, the taking possession of it by Lucy with no request or suggestion by either of the defendants that he give it back, are facts which furnish persuasive evidence that the execution of the contract was a serious business transaction rather than a casual, jesting matter as defendants now contend. . . .

If it be assumed, contrary to what we think the evidence shows, that Zehmer was jesting about selling his farm to Lucy and that the transaction was intended by him to be a joke, nevertheless the evidence shows that Lucy did not so understand it but considered it to be a serious business transaction and the contract to be binding on the Zehmers as well as on himself. The very next day he arranged with his brother to put up half the money and take a half interest in the land. The day after that he employed an attorney to examine the title. The next night, Tuesday, he was back at Zehmer's place and there Zehmer told him for the first time, Lucy said, that he wasn't going to sell and he told Zehmer, "You know you sold that place fair and square." After receiving the report from his attorney that the title was good he wrote to Zehmer that he was ready to close the deal.

 Not only did Lucy actually believe, but the evidence shows he was warranted in believing, that the contract represented a serious business transaction and a good faith sale and purchase of the farm.

In the field of contracts, as generally elsewhere, "We must look to the outward expression of a person as manifesting his intention rather than to his secret and unexpressed intention. 'The law imputes to a person an intention corresponding to the reasonable meaning of his words and acts.' " First Nat. Exchange Bank of Roanoke v. Roanoke Oil Co., 169 Va. 99, 114, 192 S.E. 764, 770.

At no time prior to the execution of the contract had Zehmer indicated to Lucy by word or act that he was not in earnest about selling the farm. They had argued about it and discussed its terms, as Zehmer admitted, for a long time. Lucy testified that if there was any jesting it was about paying $50,000 that night. The contract and the evidence show that he was not expected to pay the money that night. Zehmer said that after the writing was signed he laid it down on the counter in front of Lucy. Lucy said Zehmer handed it to him. In any event there had been what appeared to be a good faith offer and a good faith acceptance, followed by the execution and apparent delivery of a written contract. Both said that Lucy put the writing in his pocket and then offered Zehmer $5 to seal the bargain. Not until then, even under the defendants' evidence, was anything said or done to indicate that the matter was a joke. Both of the Zehmers testified that when Zehmer asked his wife to sign he whispered that it was a joke so Lucy wouldn't hear and that it was not intended that he should hear.

The mental assent of the parties is not requisite for the formation of a contract. If the words or other acts of one of the parties have but one reasonable meaning, his undisclosed intention is immaterial except when an unreasonable meaning which he attaches to his manifestations is known to the other party. Restatement of the Law of Contracts, Vol. I, § 71, p. 74. . . .

An agreement or mutual assent is of course essential to a valid contract but the law imputes to a person an intention corresponding to the reasonable meaning of his words and acts. If his words and acts, judged by a reasonable standard, manifest an intention to agree, it is immaterial what may be the real but unexpressed state of his mind. C.J.S. Contracts, § 32, p. 361; 12 Am.Jur., Contracts, § 19, p. 515.

So a person cannot set up that he was merely jesting when his conduct and words would warrant a reasonable person in believing that he intended a real agreement. . . .

Whether the writing signed by the defendants and now sought to be enforced by the complainants was the result of a serious offer by Lucy and a serious acceptance by the defendants, or was a serious offer by Lucy and an acceptance in secret jest by the defendants, in either event it constituted a binding contract of sale between the parties. . . .

The complainants are entitled to have specific performance of the contract sued on. The decree appealed from is therefore reversed and the cause is remanded for the entry of a proper decree requiring the defendants to perform the contract in accordance with the prayer of the bill.

Reversed and remanded.

NOTE

Jesting and Bluffing. What result if the price had been $50 rather than $50,000? See Note 2, p. 54 above. In Keller v. Holderman, 11 Mich. 248 (1863), Holderman, as a "frolic and banter," gave Keller a $300 check for a watch worth about $15. Holderman had no money in the bank and intended to insert a condition in the check rendering him not liable. This he neglected to do. Keller sued Holderman on the check and had judgment. Holderman appealed. *Held:* Reversed. "When the Court below found as a fact that 'the whole transaction between the parties was a frolic and a banter, the plaintiff not expecting to sell, nor the defendant intending to buy the watch at the sum for which the check was drawn,' the conclusion should have been that no contract was ever made by the parties. . . ."

[margin note: mutual understanding]

Note that the Zehmers, in addition to contending that "the whole matter was a joke," contended that the writing "was prepared as a bluff or dare to force Lucy to admit that he did not have $50,000." What result if the offer had been so intended by the Zehmers and if Lucy, knowing this, had "called their bluff" by raising the money from his brother through transferring a half interest to him? Should a distinction be made between jesting and bluffing in this situation?

LASERAGE TECHNOLOGY CORP. v. LASERAGE LABORATORIES, INC.

United States Court of Appeals, Seventh Circuit, 1992.
972 F.2d 799.

ESCHBACH, SENIOR CIRCUIT JUDGE. The central question in this appeal is whether the district court erred in concluding that the parties had reached a binding settlement of three related lawsuits. We conclude that the district court properly enforced the parties' settlement agreement and affirm for the reasons that follow.

I.

The trilogy of cases underlying this appeal arose out of related disputes arraying Laserage Technology Corporation ("Laserage") and its principal shareholder, Arthur O. Capp against James E. Byrum and the two corporations he controls, Laserage Laboratories, Inc. and Laserage Technology West, Inc. For form's sake, we refer to each side collectively as "LTC" and "Labs–West," respectively. The underlying disputes stemmed from a business relationship gone sour (Mr. Byrum is also a minority shareholder in Laserage), and contained various and over-lapping claims for breach of contract, breach of fiduciary duties, trade-mark infringement, and misappropriation of trade secrets. LTC and Labs–West engaged in extensive and often acrimonious discovery from 1987 to 1990, making several unsuccessful attempts to settle their disputes along the way. Finally, on February 26, 1990, LTC and Labs–West appeared before Judge (now Chief Judge) Moran and reported that they had reached a settlement agreement resolving their disputes that provided for LTC's buy-out of Mr. Byrum's minority interest in Laserage. That settlement agreement was embodied in a series of correspondence that LTC and Labs–West had exchanged during the previous thirty days.

When LTC and Labs–West began to reduce their settlement agreement to a formal document, however, they encountered a snag as to a term concerning security for LTC's purchase of Mr. Byrum's shares in Laserage. LTC contended that the settlement agreement contemplated that Mr. Byrum would retain none of his shareholder rights during the gradual buy-out of his shares by LTC. Conversely, Labs–West contend-ed that it had agreed that Mr. Byrum would relinquish voting rights for all his shares in Laserage, but would retain, as security, other sharehold-er rights in Laserage for those shares not yet purchased by LTC.[1] When the parties reported this snag to Judge Moran, he suggested that they resolve their purported differences through a mediator; that effort failed. Labs–West then moved to enforce the settlement agreement with LTC. After considering documentary evidence submitted by both LTC and Labs–West, Judge Moran granted Labs–West's motion, deciding that LTC and Labs–West had entered into a binding settlement agreement that included the retention of Mr. Byrum's shareholder rights (other than voting rights). LTC sought reconsideration of the district court's order. After again considering LTC's arguments and documentary sub-missions, Judge Moran denied LTC's motion by again concluding that LTC's position could not be reconciled with the contemporaneous corre-spondence and the representations made to the court in February. [Following other rulings by the district court, LTC appealed.]

II.

LTC asserts that the district court erred in concluding that it had reached a binding settlement agreement with Labs–West that allowed

---

1. Mr. Byrum's retention of shareholder rights other than voting rights is significant because, among other things, it preserves his access to the books and records of La-serage and his ability to monitor Laserage's management during the time he is depen-dent on Laserage's profitability for his stock payments.

Mr. Byrum to retain his shareholder rights. Principally, LTC believes that no enforceable agreement was reached because there was no "meeting of the minds" as to this security term. We believe that LTC misconstrues the often-deceptive "meeting of the minds" metaphor.[2] "A settlement agreement is a contract and as such, the construction and enforcement of settlement agreements are governed by principles of local law applicable to contracts generally. Air Line Stewards and Stewardesses Assoc. v. Trans World Airlines, Inc., 713 F.2d 319, 321 (7th Cir.1983). Here, we look to Illinois contract law for guidance. In interpreting a contract under Illinois law, "the paramount objective is to give effect to the intent of the parties as expressed by the terms of the agreement." International Minerals & Chemical Corp. v. Liberty Mutual Insurance Co., 522 N.E.2d 758, 764 (Ill.App.1988). Consequently, in assessing LTC's and Labs-West's intent, their "[s]ecret hopes and wishes count for nothing" because the "status of a document as a contract depends on what the parties express to each other and to the world, not on what they keep to themselves." Skycom Corp. v. Telstar Corp., 813 F.2d 810, 814–15 (7th Cir.1987) (reversing summary enforcement of settlement agreement where record did not reveal an existing, complete bargain). That is, Illinois follows the objective theory of intent. See Air Line Stewards, supra; ... As a result, whether LTC and Labs-West had a "meeting of the minds" as to security for the purchase of Mr. Byrum's Laserage shares is determined by references to what the parties expressed to each other in their writings, not by their actual mental processes. See Skycom, 813 F.2d at 814 (determination of "intent does not invite a tour through Walter's cranium, with Walters as the guide.").

We believe that the district court correctly determined that on the evidence available, a jury could reach but one conclusion about the binding quality of LTC's and Labs-West's settlement agreement and its provision to allow Mr. Byrum to retain shareholder rights (other than voting rights). Anderson v. Liberty Lobby, Inc., 477 U.S. 242, 250–52, 106 S.Ct. 2505, 2511–12, 91 L.Ed.2d 202 (1986); Skycom, 813 F.2d at 817.[3] Because of the district court's extensive treatment of this issue,[a] we highlight but a few of the factors that we believe conclusively supports the district court's decision. First, it was LTC that restarted the parties toward settlement on January 26 by proposing that Mr. Byrum relinquish his voting rights, but not his other shareholder rights, in Laserage.[4] LTC consistently refused to provide Mr. Byrum a more

2. See Farnsworth, Contracts § 3.6, at 118: "Discussions of this topic would be improved if this much-abused metaphor were abandoned. Its origins appear to go back to faulty etymology, under which it was wrongly supposed that the word 'agreement' was derived from *agregatio mentium,* a meeting of the minds."

3. While a more deferential standard of review may be warranted, ..., we have chosen to apply the de novo summary judgment standard because even under that

more rigorous standard we conclude that the district court properly enforced LTC's and Labs-West's settlement agreement....

a. References in the opinion to the record in the case are omitted throughout.

4. This proposal incorporated what the parties called an "amended arbitration agreement." The amended arbitration agreement consists of interlineations originally made by Labs-West to a draft arbitration agreement proposed by LTC. As

traditional form of security (such as a letter of credit) for the purchase of his Laserage shares. Second, on February 6, Labs–West specifically accepted LTC's January 26 proposal as to the security term. The next day, LTC responded to Labs–West, noting that it might "pay [Mr. Byrum] off quicker [than required] just to get rid of him." It makes little sense for LTC to have an incentive to "get rid of" Mr. Byrum if it understood at this juncture that he had absolutely no shareholder rights. Without those rights, Mr. Byrum was simply an unsecured creditor.

Third, and perhaps most significantly, Labs–West's next response (February 9) to LTC explicitly refers to the "amended arbitration agreement attached to your January 26, 1990 proposal." Thus, at this point it was apparent to all the world, including LTC, that Labs–West believed it was agreeing to allow Mr. Byrum to retain his shareholder rights other than voting rights. Despite that clarity, however, LTC's next communication with Labs–West did not repudiate Labs–West's clearly expressed understanding. Rather, LTC merely noted that "there will be no security, other than what we have set forth in our prior arbitration agreement for security on the payment of the stock" as it was summing up the settlement terms previously agreed upon at the end of its letter. At this point, if LTC had desired to revert to a security arrangement other than as provided in the amended arbitration agreement, it was incumbent on LTC to say so.[5] LTC's claim that there was no "meeting of the minds" on this security term fails because it had every "reason to know the meaning attached" to this term by Labs–West. See Restatement of Contracts § 20 (bargain will not fail for lack of assent where one party knows or has reason to know the meaning attached to a term by the other party). Moreover, as noted above, LTC refused to provide Mr. Byrum any security other than the retention of his shareholder rights. Thus, it would defy common sense to say "no security other than" if there was no security! As Judge Learned Hand noted, "there is a critical breaking point ... beyond which no language can be forced." Eustis Mining Co. v. Beer, Sondheimer & Co., 239 F. 976, 982 (S.D.N.Y.1917).

LTC's remaining arguments on this issue require only brief discussion. First, LTC mistakenly contends that United States v. Orr Construction Co., 560 F.2d 765 (7th Cir.1977), requires that we find the parties' settlement agreement unenforceable. In *Orr,* the parties conditioned settlement on receiving "proper legal releases from all parties," but then could not agree on what legal releases were proper. We decided that the attempted settlement agreement was unenforceable because the "phrase 'proper legal releases' could have any number of

amended, the agreement required Mr. Byrum to relinquish his voting rights in Laserage, but allowed him to retain his other shareholder rights. LTC attached this amended arbitration agreement to its January 26 proposal and specifically referred to the amended version in its proposal.

5. Similarly, LTC's argument that its January 26 proposal was a "stand alone" proposal, or that its February 14 correspondence represented a "radically different proposal" fails by this same logic. While LTC had every right to make a "stand alone" proposal or to propose "radically different terms" during a counter-offer, it had to manifest that intention. There is no evidence in the record that LTC did so; unexpressed intentions do not count.

meanings depending on the view of the person interpreting it" making it "impossible to attach a definite meaning" to the agreement." Id. at 770, 772. In this case, however, there are no terms that present such vagueness or indefiniteness problems. Perhaps if LTC and Labs–West had simply agreed that Labs–West would receive "proper legal security" for the payment of his Laserage stock, and left it at that, then this case would be closer to the situation we faced in *Orr*. *Orr* does not advance LTC's case.

. . .

In sum, we have fully considered all of LTC's properly presented arguments and we are convinced that the district court correctly concluded, based on the undisputed documentary record before it, that the parties' objective manifestations of intent all pointed to a desire to be bound by a settlement agreement providing that Mr. Byrum could retain his shareholder rights other than voting rights. The parties' correspondence reveals an existing, complete bargain; there is nothing in the record to indicate otherwise. See *Skycom*, 813 F.2d at 816. We affirm the district court's decision to enforce LTC's and Labs–West's settlement agreement.

. . .

NOTE

Case Comparisons. Compare the function of the objective theory as applied in this case with its function in Lucy v. Zehmer, above. In *Lucy* the court used it to help arrive at the conclusion that a binding agreement had been made. Was that the issue in this case? Or was it the issue—granting that a settlement agreement existed—what effect the agreement was to have on Byrum's shareholder rights? (Issues like the latter are examined in detail in Chapter 6, Finding the Law of the Contract.) If you discern separate uses that the theory has, which would you expect to occur the more often?

In Sullivan v. O'Connor, now to be reconsidered, the court mentioned optimistic medical opinions, saying: "patients may transform such statements into firm promises in their own minds. . . ." When that happens, is there a use for objective theory?

SULLIVAN v. O'CONNOR
Supreme Judicial Court of Massachusetts, 1973.
363 Mass. 579, 296 N.E.2d 183.

[For the report of this case see p. 7 above.]

NOTES

(1) *Statute.* In Guilmet v. Campbell, 188 N.W.2d 601 (Mich.1971), the Supreme Court of Michigan affirmed a judgment for damages for breach of contract against a surgeon who, according to his patient's testimony, had said before a stomach operation, "After this operation, you can throw your pillbox away," "No, there is no danger at all in this operation," and "Once you have an operation it takes care of all your troubles."

In 1974 the Michigan legislature enacted a statute providing that an "agreement promise, contract, or warranty of cure relating to medical care or treatment" is void unless evidenced by a signed writing.   31 Mich.Comp.L.Ann. § 566–132(g).   Would you favor enactment of such a statute in Massachusetts?

(2) *Problem.*   Father consulted Doctor about an operation to remove scar tissue from Son's hand which had resulted from a severe burn nine years before. Father asked Doctor, "How long will the boy be in the hospital," and Doctor replied, "Three or four days, not over four; then the boy can go home and it will be just a few days when he will go back to work with a good hand."   Son's hand was not healed for a month after the operation.   Is Doctor liable to Father for breach of contract?   Would your answer be different if Doctor added, "I will guarantee to make the hand a hundred percent perfect hand"?   How much would Father recover if Doctor were liable?   See Hawkins v. McGee, 146 A. 641 (N.H.1929).

(3) *Counsels of Perfection.*   "A good legal rule as to the enforceability of promises should make contracting available to nonlawyers who will take the pains to clarify their ideas as to what they want to contract about; yet it should not make contracting so easy that it hooks the unwary signer or the casual promisor.   The first may be called freedom *to* contract, the second, freedom *from* contract.   These are, of course, counsels of perfection."   Patterson, An Apology for Consideration, 58 Colum.L.Rev. 929, 958 (1959).

Be watchful, in proceeding through this Chapter, for instances in which courts have suppressed one of these freedoms.   What instances have been encountered so far?

"GENTLEMEN'S AGREEMENTS"

Can the parties to an agreement, by express provision, prevent the machinery of government from enforcing their promises?   Consider this question in connection with two significant situations where such "gentlemen's agreements" have been used.

One arises in "firm-commitment underwriting" of corporate stock, a transaction in which the corporate issuer sells an entire issue of stock outright to a group of underwriters, who in turn sell to a larger group of dealers, who then sell to the public.   Under the Securities Act of 1933, a registration statement containing specified information about the stock, the issuer and the underwriters must be filed with the Securities and Exchange Commission before the stock is offered to either the dealers or the public.   Before going to the substantial trouble and expense of preparing and printing a registration statement, the issuer wants some assurance of the availability of the underwriters.   The underwriters, however, are not willing to make an enforceable promise to purchase the stock, since that would subject them to the risk of an adverse change in the market during the time before the registration statement takes effect.   The solution has been found in having the underwriters write to the issuer a "letter of intent," which is then signed by the issuer, and which sets out, often in considerable detail, the terms of the proposed underwriting, but states that "no liability or obligation of any nature whatsoever is intended to be created as between any of the parties hereto." Such a clause was given effect in Dunhill Securities Corp. v. Microthermal Applications, Inc., 308 F.Supp. 195 (S.D.N.Y.1969).

Bonus and death benefit plans afford a second situation in which "gentlemen's agreements" are used. The employer may want to disclose the plan in order to take advantage of the resulting incentive, but may want to keep its administration within his uncontrolled discretion. In Mabley & Carew Co. v. Borden, 195 N.E. 697 (Ohio 1935), an employer gave an employee a certificate promising that a specified death benefit would be paid to her designated beneficiary if she was still employed at the time of her death, but stating that "it carries no legal obligation whatsoever or assurance or promise of future employment, and may be withdrawn or discontinued at any time by this Company." The court held that, in spite of this language, the employer was liable to the beneficiary. Why should this language be treated differently from that of the "letter of intent"? Cf. Spooner v. Reserve Life Ins. Co., 287 P.2d 735 (Wash.1955), distinguishing bonus plans from death benefit plans. See generally Holmes, The Freedom Not to Contract, 60 Tul.L.Rev. 751 (1986).

NOTES

(1) *Living Together II.* Note 4, p. 83 above, suggested the possibility of a claim for restitution when two persons who have lived together break up a relationship. Such a claim is often coupled with a claim based on a promise.

In Balfour v. Balfour, [1919] 2 K.B. 571 (Court of Appeal), the court denied a wife recovery on her husband's promise to pay her an allowance of £30 a month on the ground that such promises "are not contracts because the parties did not intend that they should be attended by legal consequences," and "it would be of the worst possible example to hold that agreements such as this resulted in legal obligations which could be enforced in the Courts.... In respect of these promises each house is a domain into which the King's writ does not seek to run, and to which his officers do not seek to be admitted." This strict traditional view persists in a reluctance to enforce agreements between husband and wife, but it has been relaxed considerably. As for unmarried couples, one court has said that "[o]rdinary contract principles are not suspended ... for unmarried persons living together, whether or not they engage in sexual activity." Boland v. Catalano, 521 A.2d 142 (Conn.1987).

A particularly difficult question arises if one party seeks recovery based on a promise inferred from conduct—a promise "implied in fact." As was seen in Note 4, p. 83 above, services rendered within a family have traditionally been taken to be gratuitous. This presumption was examined critically in this connection in Gibson v. McCraw, 332 S.E.2d 269 (W.Va.1985). The question has also proved troublesome when the parties are unmarried. Compare Morone v. Morone, 413 N.E.2d 1154 (N.Y.1980) ("major difficulty with implying a contract from the rendition of services for one another by persons living together is that it is not reasonable to infer an agreement to pay for the services rendered when the relationship of the parties makes it natural that the services were rendered gratuitously."), with Marvin v. Marvin, 557 P.2d 106 (Cal.1976) ("nonmarital partner may recover in quantum meruit for the reasonable value of household services rendered less the reasonable value of support received if he can show that he rendered services with the expectation of monetary reward").

(2) *Dining Together*. Would you expect a court to enforce a promise made in a social setting, such as a promise to be a guest at a dinner party? Would it make a difference if the host had gone to considerable expense to make elaborate preparations? [a]

"FORMAL CONTRACT CONTEMPLATED"

Not infrequently, particularly following complex negotiations, parties agree on what they consider to be the essential terms of a contract and leave details to be worked out, often by their lawyers, in connection with the preparation of a formal document that they expect to sign. If one of the parties refuses to sign the formal document, can the other enforce their agreement?

Whether or not the parties intended to conclude an agreement earlier is often a question. As to that, and how to determine their intent, see Consarc Corporation v. Marine Midland Bank, N.A., 996 F.2d 568 (2d Cir.1993). "The tension between the concepts—contract arises upon meeting of the minds, no binding contract absent a writing—has resulted in courts struggling to resolve these inherently conflicting notions. From this judicial effort have evolved two widely-accepted common law principles: (a) that absent an expressed intent that no contract shall exist, mutual assent between the parties, even though oral or informal, to exchange acts or promises is sufficient to create a binding contract; and (b) that to avoid the obligation of a binding contract, at least one of the parties must express an intention not to be bound until a writing is executed."

In Winston v. Mediafare Entertainment Corp., 777 F.2d 78 (2d Cir.1985), the court listed "several factors that help determine whether the parties intended to be bound in the absence of a document executed by both sides." These factors are: "(1) whether there has been an express reservation of the right not to be bound in the absence of a writing; (2) whether there has been partial performance of the contract; (3) whether all of the terms of the alleged contract have been agreed upon; and (4) whether the agreement at issue is the type of contract that is usually committed to writing." In spite of such guidance, cases involving this question are frequently before the courts.

NOTES

(1) *More About Laserage*. In Laserage Technology Corp. v. Laserage Laboratories, above, LTC argued that it had not intended to be bound prior to the

---

a. Such disputes seldom reach the courts. A rare exception is Horsley v. Chesselet, decided in the Municipal Court of San Francisco in 1978 (Small Claims Action No. 346278), in which Mr. Horsley sued Miss Chesselet for $32 "that he expended ... for gasoline and for theatre tickets in order to perform his promise to escort Defendant for an evening at the the- atre." The court found "that the promise to engage in a social relationship for one evening" was unenforceable and ordered returned to plaintiff his "Exhibit 'A' for identification, a cardboard object in the shape of a broken heart, ... with the Court mindful of Lord Byron's admonition, 'Maid of Athens, ere we part, Give, oh give me back my heart!'"

execution of a formal written agreement. LTC made that argument, the court said, in "further support" of its position that the parties' settlement agreement was unenforceable. How do the factors quoted from *Winston* above bear on the argument?

Does this further information about *Laserage* affect your answer to the questions in the Note following that case? (The court refused to consider the argument because LTC had not presented it to the district court.)

(2) *Open Terms.* For a "contextual" treatment of the factors in *Winston,* see Teachers Ins. and Annuity Ass'n v. Tribune Co., 670 F.Supp. 491 (S.D.N.Y. 1987). The court distinguished two types of binding agreements, yet to be memorialized: one in which the terms are fully settled, and another in which there are both agreed and open terms. The latter requires that the parties "negotiate the open terms in good faith toward a final contract incorporating the agreed terms." How does this distinction affect the third factor listed in *Winston?* Some courts have sought to distinguish between open terms that are "deal breakers" and those that are not. See A/S Apothekernes Laboratorium v. I.M.C. Chemical, 873 F.2d 155 (7th Cir.1989). How might a party make certain, throughout negotiations, that every open term is a deal breaker? See Budget Marketing, Inc. v. Centronics Corp., 927 F.2d 421 (8th Cir.1991).

(3) *Tortious Interference.* A party who withdraws from a contractual relation, disappointing the other party, sometimes does so as a result of finding a more attractive partner. Because the law recognizes interference with a contract as tortious in some cases, a breach of contract claim may be coupled with a tort claim against a third party. Thus, for example, an employer's breach of contract action against an employee may be coupled with an action for tortious interference against the employer who hired the employee away.

Moreover, a tort claim for interference may lie when a contract claim for breach would not. Thus there may be tort liability for inducing the breach of a contract that is unenforceable for want of a writing required by the Statute of Frauds. See UCC 2–201, Comment 4. And there may even be tort liability for causing negotiations to miscarry when the parties have not reached the point of contract. See Restatement, Second, of Torts § 766B as to the liability of one who "intentionally and improperly interferes with another's prospective contractual relation."

The matter of "impropriety" in the third party's conduct is a sensitive one. Courts are understandably concerned lest the threat of tort liability inhibit desirable competition. Thus a merchant who entices patrons away from a competitor with goods and services of high quality is not thought of as a tortfeasor.[a] Furthermore, according to the Torts Restatement, if a contractual relation is only "prospective" or an agreement is "terminable at will," there is a broad privilege to interfere with a competitor—as long as one's purpose is "at least in part to advance his interest in competing" with the competitor. Id. § 768(1).

The law of restitution also provides a remedy against a merchant who tortiously pirates a customer from another. The third party's profit from the tort can be recovered even though the injured party would itself have made no

---

a. In Youst v. Longo, 729 P.2d 728 (Cal. 1987), the court compared various forms of unfair competition, including falsehoods in election campaigns and crimes by bookmakers in "fixing" sporting contests. The court concluded that it should not entertain a complaint about a driver's conduct in a harness race, emphasizing the chanciness that the claimant would have won a larger prize if his horse had not been forced to "break stride."

profit from the contract with the customer. (Is this consistent with the concept of efficient breach?)

(4) *Of Oil and Honor.* The most celebrated of the cases about "formal contract contemplated" concerned a so-called handshake deal between the Pennzoil Company and the Getty Oil Company. Getty, having negotiated a sale of stock to Pennzoil, refused to perform and sold the stock to Texaco, Inc. Pennzoil's first legal sally, in Delaware, was an attempt to charge Getty with breach of contract. That having failed, Pennzoil shifted its ground to Texas, suing Texaco there for interfering with the alleged Getty contract. This action produced a verdict against Texaco for $10.53 billion and (after much maneuvering, including a reduction of $2 billion in the jury's punitive-damage award and a visit to the United States Supreme Court) led to Texaco's bankruptcy. Its bankruptcy petition was designed to effectuate an agreement between the parties to a $3 billion settlement. For a description of the Pennzoil–Getty dealings see Texaco, Inc. v. Pennzoil Co., 729 S.W.2d 768 (Tex.App.1987). See also T. Petzinger, Oil and Honor: The Texaco–Pennzoil Wars (1987).

(5) *Ethics in Educating a Client.* How to ascertain a client's state of mind at a particular earlier time is the subject of certain precepts of attorney conduct. It is popular wisdom that what a client reports on that subject may be influenced by what the client knows of the law's requirements. Hence there are situations in which it is at least questionable for a lawyer to give legal advice "to assist his client in developing evidence relevant to the [client's] state of mind." Precepts issued by the American Bar Association emphasize, however, that a lawyer may properly assist a client in that way, and "may discuss the legal consequences of any proposed course of conduct with a client." See Code of Professional Responsibility (Ethical Consideration 7–6) [source of the first quotation in this Note]; and Rule 1.2(d) of the Model Rules of Professional Conduct [source of the second]. For an ongoing colloquy on the question "whether it is proper to give your client legal advice when you have reason to believe that the knowledge you give him will tempt him to commit perjury," see Freedman, Professional Responsibility of the Criminal Defense Lawyer: The Three Hardest Questions, 64 Mich.L.Rev. 1469, 1478–82 (1966); Noonan, The Purposes of Advocacy and the Limits of Confidentiality, 64 Mich.L.Rev. 1485, 1488 (1966); and M. Freedman, Lawyers' Ethics in an Adversary System 73, 75 (1975). In his book, Dean Freedman conceded, responding to criticism, that there comes a point where "nothing less than 'brute rationalization' can purport to justify a conclusion that the lawyer is seeking in good faith to elicit truth rather than actively participating in the creation of perjury."

The problem has drawn attention chiefly in connection with defense preparations in criminal matters, in which intent, malice, and the like are often critical facts. Does it have a bearing on the formulation of rules about contract formation? The question is pursued further in a Note at p. 219 below.

Whether or not a contract has been formed often depends on choosing between conflicting accounts of a conversation. Examples appearing above are Sullivan v. O'Connor and Lucy v. Zehmer. Do the decisions in those cases ease or intensify qualms that lawyers may have about educating their clients about contract law?

SECTION 2.　THE OFFER

The process by which the parties arrive at a bargain will vary widely according to the circumstances.　It is common to assume that it involves two distinct steps: first, an offer by one party and, second, an acceptance by the other.　A discussion of whether this is inevitably the case can be deferred until later.　It is helpful to begin, at least, with this assumption.

What is an offer?　Corbin gives this answer: "An offer is ... an act whereby one person confers upon another the power to create contractual relations between them....　[T]he act of the offeror operates to create in the offeree a power ...; thereafter the voluntary act of the offeree alone will operate to create the new relations called a contract....　What kind of act creates a power of acceptance and is therefore an offer?　It must be an expression of will or intention.　It must be an act that leads the offeree reasonably to believe that a power to create a contract is conferred upon him....　It is on this ground that we must exclude invitations to deal or acts of mere preliminary negotiation, and acts *evidently* done in jest or without intent to create legal relations.　All these are acts that do not lead others reasonably to believe that they are empowered 'to close the contract.' "　Corbin, Offer and Acceptance, and Some of The Resulting Legal Relations, 26 Yale L.J. 169, 181–82 (1917).　See also Restatement Second § 24.

NOTE

Agreement Without Offer and Acceptance?　"[H]owever suited these rules [of offer and acceptance] may have been to the measured cadence of contracting in the nineteenth century, they have little to say about the complex processes that lead to major deals today....　During the negotiation of such deals there is often no offer or counter-offer for either party to accept, but rather a gradual process in which agreements are reached piecemeal in several 'rounds' with a succession of drafts....　When the ultimate agreement is reached, it is often expected that it will be embodied in a document or documents that will be exchanged by the parties at a closing....　[I]f the negotiations fail and no documents are signed and exchanged, a number of questions may arise that the classic rules of offer and acceptance do not address: May a disappointed party have a claim against the other party for having failed to conform to a standard of fair dealing?　If so, what is the meaning of fair dealing in this context?　And may the disappointed party get restitution?　Be reimbursed for out-of-pocket expenses?　Recover for lost opportunities?"　Farnsworth, Precontractual Liability and Preliminary Agreements: Fair Dealing and Failed Negotiations, 87 Colum.L.Rev. 217, 219 (1987).

OWEN v. TUNISON

Supreme Judicial Court of Maine, 1932.
131 Me. 42, 158 A. 926.

Action by W.H. Owen against R.G. Tunison for breach of contract.

BARNES, J. This case is reported to the law court, and such judgment is to be rendered as the law and the admissible evidence require.

Plaintiff charges that defendant agreed in writing to sell him the Bradley block and lot, situated in Bucksport, for a stated price in cash, that he later refused to perfect the sale, and that plaintiff, always willing and ready to pay the price, has suffered loss on account of defendant's unjust refusal to sell, and claims damages.

From the record it appears that defendant, a resident of Newark N.J., was, in the fall of 1929, the owner of the Bradley block and lot.

With the purpose of purchasing, on October 23, 1929, plaintiff wrote the following letter:

"Dear Mr. Tunison:

"Will you sell me your store property which is located on Main St. in Bucksport, Me. running from Montgomery's Drug Store on one corner to a Grocery Store on the other, for the sum of $6,000.00?"

Nothing more of this letter need be quoted.

On December 5, following, plaintiff received defendant's reply apparently written in Cannes, France, on November 12, and it reads:

"In reply to your letter of Oct. 23rd which has been forwarded to me in which you inquire about the Bradley Block, Bucksport, Me.

"Because of improvements which have been added and an expenditure of several thousand dollars it would not be possible for me to sell it unless I was to receive $16,000.00 cash.

"The upper floors have been converted into apartments with baths and the b'l'dg put into first class condition.

"Very truly yours,

"[Signed] R.G. Tunison."

Whereupon, and at once, plaintiff sent to defendant, and the latter received, in France, the following message:

"Accept your offer for Bradley block Bucksport Terms sixteen thousand cash send deed to Eastern Trust and Banking Co Bangor Maine Please acknowledge."

Four days later he was notified that defendant did not wish to sell the property, and on the 14th day of January following brought suit for his damages.

Granted that damages may be due a willing buyer if the owner refuses to tender a deed of real estate, after the latter has made an offer in writing to sell to the former, and such offer has been so accepted, it remains for us to point out that defendant here is not shown to have written to plaintiff an offer to sell.

There can have been no contract for the sale of the property desired, no meeting of the minds of the owner and prospective purchaser, unless there was an offer or proposal of sale. It cannot be successfully argued that defendant made any offer or proposal of sale.

No offer

In a recent case the words, "Would not consider less than half" is held "not to be taken as an outright offer to sell for one-half." Sellers v. Warren, 116 Me. 350, 102 A. 40, 41.

Where an owner of millet seed wrote, "I want $2.25 per cwt. for this seed f.o.b. Lowell," in an action for damages for alleged breach of contract to sell at the figure quoted above, the court held: "He [defendant] does not say, 'I offer to sell to you.' The language used is general, and such as may be used in an advertisement, or circular addressed generally to those engaged in the seed business, and is not an offer by which he may be bound, if accepted, by any or all of the persons addressed." Nebraska Seed Co. v. Harsh, 98 Neb. 89, 152 N.W. 310, 311, and cases cited in note L.R.A. 1915F, 824.

Defendant's letter of December 5 in response to an offer of $6,000 for his property may have been written with the intent to open negotiations that might lead to a sale. It was not a proposal to sell.

Holding

Judgment for defendant.

NOTES

(1) *Analysis of Communications.* Did Tunison by his letter of November 12 indicate an intention to empower Owen "to close the contract"? Or did he indicate that he expected the offer to come from Owen? A useful technique in analyzing the language used by the parties is to redraft it twice, staying as faithful to the original as possible, so that it would clearly require a decision, first for one party, then for the other. Take, for example, the language "it would not be possible for me to sell it unless I was to receive $16,000 cash." What result if Tunison had said instead, "I will sell for $16,000"? What result if he had said, "I will not entertain an offer for less than $16,000"? Which comes closer to the meaning of the language that he used? Is the fact that there is a considerable disparity between $6,000 and $16,000 relevant? The interpretation of contract language is the subject of Chapter 6, Section 2. On how this differs from the interpretation of communications to determine whether a contract exists in the first place, see Note 2, p. 584 below.

(2) *Problem.* In May, Joseph Oliver spoke to several neighbors about his plans to dispose of his ranch. On June 13, one of them, J.W. Southworth, asked Oliver if his plans for selling "continued to be in force," to which he responded that he expected soon to be able to put a price on the property. Southworth then said that he had the money available, that Oliver "didn't have to worry," and that "everything was ready to go." Four days later, Oliver sent a letter to four neighbors, including Southworth, enclosing "the information that I had discussed with you," as follows:

Selling [ranch as described] at the assessed market value of ... $324,-419. Terms available—29% down—balance over 5 years at 8% interest. Negotiate sale date for December 1, 1976 or January 1, 1977....

Has Oliver made an offer to sell his ranch? See Southworth v. Oliver, 587 P.2d 994 (Or.1978).

———

HARVEY v. FACEY, [1893] A.C. 552 (Privy Council) (Jamaica). [Harvey and another, solicitors in Kingston, were interested in a piece of property known as Bumper Hall Pen. Facey, the owner, had been engaged in negotiations for its sale to the town of Kingston for £900. Harvey telegraphed Facey, who was on a journey, "Will you sell us Bumper Hall Pen? Telegraph lowest cash price—answer paid." Facey replied by telegram, "Lowest price for Bumper Hall Pen £900." Harvey answered, "We agree to buy Bumper Hall Pen for the sum of nine hundred pounds asked by you." Harvey sued for specific performance of this agreement and for an injunction to restrain the town of Kingston from taking a conveyance of the property. The trial court dismissed the action on the ground that the agreement did not disclose a concluded contract; the Supreme Court of Jamaica reversed; the defendants appealed to the Judicial Committee of the Privy Council.]

LORD MORRIS.... [T]heir Lordships concur in the judgment of Mr. Justice Curran that there was no concluded contract between the appellants and L.M. Facey to be collected from the aforesaid telegrams. The first telegram asks two questions. The first question is as to the willingness of L.M. Facey to sell to the appellants [i.e. Harvey]; the second question asks the lowest price, and the word "telegraph" is in its collocation addressed to that second question only. L.M. Facey replied to the second question only, and gives his lowest price. The third telegram from the appellants treats the answer of L.M. Facey stating his lowest price as an unconditional offer to sell to them at the price named. Their Lordships cannot treat the telegram from L.M. Facey as binding him in any respect, except to the extent it does by its term, viz., the lowest price. Everything else is left open, and the reply telegram from the appellants cannot be treated as an acceptance of an offer to sell to them; it is an offer that required to be accepted by L.M. Facey. The contract could only be completed if L.M. Facey had accepted the appellants' last telegram. It has been contended for the appellants that L.M. Facey's telegram should be read as saying "yes" to the first question put in the appellants' telegram, but there is nothing to support that contention. L.M. Facey's telegram gives a precise answer to a precise question, viz., the price. The contract must appear by the telegrams, whereas the appellants are obliged to contend that an acceptance of the first question is to be implied. Their Lordships are of opinion that the mere statement of the lowest price at which the vendor would sell contains no implied contract to sell at that price to the persons making the inquiry.... [Reversed and the judgment of the trial court restored.]

NOTES

(1) *More Analysis of Communications.* Redraft Facey's telegram so that it clearly would have required a decision for Harvey. Redraft it so that it clearly would have required a decision for Facey. Which seems closer to the meaning of the language that he used? Is it significant that Harvey presumably knew that he was not the only potential buyer for Bumper Hall Pen? Could Harvey's first telegram have been more skillfully drafted? What result if it had read, "What is the lowest price at which you will sell me Bumper Hall Pen?" See, in criticism of Harvey v. Facey, Russell, 1 Can.Bar Rev. 392, 398–403 (1923); in approval, MacLeod, 1 Can.Bar Rev. 694 (1923); and in rejoinder, Russell, 1 Can.Bar Rev. 713 (1923).

(2) *The Case of the Green Mountains.* The Nature Conservancy, acting in part as agent for the State of Vermont, attempted several times, without success, to buy a large parcel of land adjacent to a state forest. A sale to another party was imminent. The trustee for the owners declined, when the State's governor telephoned, to defer the sale, but confirmed the price ($1.2 million) the State would have to match. With only a day remaining, the governor called again and read the text of a legislative resolution she was prepared to support, looking to a purchase by the State. At the trustee's suggestion, she inserted a reference to $1.2 million. They exchanged two other messages that day. According to the trustee, the governor was "off the hook for another week"; as the governor later recalled, the trustee agreed to give the State that long to commit to a purchase. Six days later the trustee declared his intention not to sell to the State. In the meanwhile, the Conservancy had faxed to him a signed purchase agreement and the legislature had passed a joint resolution expressing its intention to appropriate $750,000 for the purchase. (The remainder was to be raised by the Conservancy.)

In an action brought by the State for specific performance, the trial court granted summary judgment for the defendant. The State appealed. *Held:* Affirmed. State v. Delaney, 598 A.2d 138 (Vt.1991). "In this case, defendant ... indicated how much time the State had to put together an offer. The governor, in her affidavit, states that defendant told her he would rather sell to the State and that the State must 'commit to the purchase of the property' before February 8, 1989. These facts establish, at best, that defendant was inviting the State to make an offer." (More of the court's reasoning is reported at p. 215 below.)

What could the governor have said, in her second telephone call, that might have led the court to conclude that the defendant was making an offer to the State?

(3) *Problem.* In Hopper v. All Pet Animal Clinic, 861 P.2d 531 (Wyo.1993), it appears that the following letter was written by Dr. Johnson, president of the Clinic, to Dr. Hopper, an employee:

> I have learned that you are considering leaving us to take over the small animal part of Dr. Meeboer's practice in Laramie.
>
> When we negotiated the terms of your employment, we agreed that you could leave upon 30 days' notice, but that you would not practice small animal medicine within five miles of Laramie for a three-year period.
>
> I am willing to release you from the non-competition agreement in return for a cash buy-out. I have worked back from the proportion of the income of All–Pet which you contribute and have decided that a reasonable figure would be $40,000, to compensate the practice for the loss of business

which will happen if you practice small-animal medicine elsewhere in Laramie.

If you are willing to approach the problem in the way I suggest, please let me know and I will have the appropriate paperwork taken care of.

How would you argue that this letter was an offer? That it was not?

———

FAIRMOUNT GLASS WORKS v. GRUNDEN–MARTIN WOODENWARE CO.

Court of Appeals of Kentucky, 1899.
106 Ky. 659, 51 S.W. 196.

Action by the Crunden–Martin Woodenware Company against the Fairmount Glass Works to recover damages for breach of contract. Judgment for plaintiff, and defendant appeals. Affirmed.

HOBSON, J. On April 20, 1895, appellee wrote appellant the following letter:

"St. Louis, Mo., April 20, 1895. Gentlemen: Please advise us the lowest price you can make us on our order for ten car loads of Mason green jars, complete, with caps, packed one dozen in a case, either delivered here, or f.o.b. cars your place, as you prefer. State terms and cash discount. Very truly, Crunden–Martin W.W. Co."

To this letter appellant answered as follows:

"Fairmount, Ind. April 23, 1895. Crunden–Martin Wooden Ware Co., St. Louis, Mo.—Gentlemen: Replying to your favor of April 20, we quote you Mason fruit jars, complete, in one-dozen boxes, delivered in East St. Louis, Ill.: Pints, $4.50, quarts, $5.00, half gallons, $6.50 per gross, for immediate acceptance, and shipment not later than May 15, 1895; sixty days' acceptance,[a] or 2 off, cash in ten days. Yours truly, Fairmount Glass Works.

"Please note that we make all quotations and contracts subject to the contingencies of agencies or transportation delays or accidents beyond our control."

For reply thereto, appellee sent the following telegram on April 24, 1895:

"Fairmount Glass Works, Fairmount, Ind.: Your letter twenty-third received. Enter order ten car loads as per your quotation. Specifications mailed. Crunden–Martin W.W. Co."

In response to this telegram, appellant sent the following:

"Fairmount, Ind., April 24, 1895. Crunden–Martin W.W. Co., St. Louis, Mo.: Impossible to book your order. Output all sold. See letter. Fairmount Glass Works."

a. In this context the word "acceptance" means an instrument used to assure payment in sixty days.

Appellee insists that, by its telegram sent in answer to the letter of April 23d, the contract was closed for the purchase of 10 car loads of Mason fruit jars. Appellant insists that the contract was not closed by this telegram, and that it had the right to decline to fill the order at the time it sent its telegram of April 24. This is the chief question in the case. The court below gave judgment in favor of appellee, and appellant has appealed, earnestly insisting that the judgment is erroneous.

We are referred to a number of authorities holding that a quotation of prices is not an offer to sell, in the sense that a completed contract will arise out of the giving of an order for merchandise in accordance with the proposed terms. There are a number of cases holding that the transaction is not completed until the order so made is accepted. 7 Am. & Eng.Enc.Law (2d Ed.) p. 138; Smith v. Gowdy, 8 Allen, Mass., 566; Beaupre v. Telegraph Co., 21 Minn. 155. But each case must turn largely upon the language there used. In this case we think there was more than a quotation of prices, although appellant's letter uses the word "quote" in stating the prices given. The true meaning of the correspondence must be determined by reading it as a whole. Appellee's letter of April 20th, which began the transaction, did not ask for a quotation of prices. It reads: "Please advise us the lowest price you can make us on our order for ten carloads of Mason green jars.... State terms and cash discount." From this appellant could not fail to understand that appellee wanted to know at what price it would sell ten car loads of these jars; so when, in answer, it wrote: "We quote you Mason fruit jars ... pints $4.50, quarts $5.00, half gallons $6.50, per gross, for immediate acceptance; ... 2 off, cash in ten days,"—it must be deemed as intending to give appellee the information it asked for. We can hardly understand what is meant by the words "for immediate acceptance," unless the latter was intended as a proposition to sell at these prices if accepted immediately. In construing every contract, the aim of the court is to arrive at the intention of the parties. In none of the cases to which we have been referred on behalf of appellant was there on the face of the correspondence any such expression of intention to make an offer to sell on the terms indicated.... The expression in appellant's letter, "for immediate acceptance," taken in connection with appellee's letter, in effect, at what price it would sell it the goods, is, it seems to us, much stronger evidence of a present offer, which, when accepted immediately, closed the contract. Appellee's letter was plainly an inquiry for the price and terms on which appellant would sell it the goods, and appellant's answer to it was not a quotation of prices, but a definite offer to sell on the terms indicated, and could not be withdrawn after the terms had been accepted.

It will be observed that the telegram of acceptance refers to the specifications mailed. These specifications were contained in the following letter: "St. Louis, Mo., April 24, 1895. Fairmount Glass–Works Co., Fairmount, Ind.—Gentlemen: We received your letter of 23rd this morning, and telegraphed you in reply as follows: 'Your letter 23rd received. Enter order ten car loads as per your quotation. Specifications mailed,'—which we now confirm. We have accordingly entered this contract on our books for the ten cars Mason green jars, complete, with caps and rubbers, one dozen in case, delivered to us in East St. Louis at $4.50 per gross for pint, $5.00 for quart, $6.50 for one-half gallon. Terms, 60 days' acceptance, or 2 per cent. for cash in ten days, to be shipped not later than May 15, 1895. The jars and caps to be strictly first-quality goods. You may ship the first car to us here assorted: Five gross pint, fifty-five gross quart, forty gross one-half gallon. Specifications for the remaining 9 cars we will send later. Crunden–Martin W.W. Co." It is insisted for appellant that this was not an acceptance of the offer as made; that the stipulation, "The jars and caps to be strictly first-quality goods," was not in their offer; and that, it not having been accepted as made, appellant is not bound. But it will be observed that appellant declined to furnish the goods before it got this letter, and in the correspondence with appellee it nowhere complained of these words as an addition to the contract. Quite a number of other letters passed, in which the refusal to deliver the goods was placed on other grounds, none of which have been sustained by the evidence. Appellee offers proof tending to show that these words, in the trade in which parties were engaged, conveyed the same meaning as the words used in appellant's letter, and were only a different form of expressing the same idea. Appellant's conduct would seem to confirm this evidence.

Appellant also insists that the contract was indefinite, because the quantity of each size of the jars was not fixed, that ten car loads is too indefinite a specification of the quantity sold, and that appellee had no right to accept the goods to be delivered on different days. The proof shows that "ten car loads" is an expression used in the trade as equivalent to 1,000 gross, 100 gross being regarded as a car load. The offer to sell the different sizes at different prices gave the purchaser the right to name the quantity of each size, and, the offer being to ship not later than May 15th, the buyer had the right to fix the time of delivery at any time before that.... The petition, if defective, was cured by the judgment, which is fully sustained by the evidence.

Judgment affirmed.

NOTES

(1) *The Fairmount Letter.* Suppose that Fairmount's letter of April 23 had not been in response to a preliminary letter from Crunden–Martin. Would the result have been the same? What significance should be attached to the use of the expression "we quote you" in the Fairmount letter? What facts make "quote" mean "offer"?

Can you construct an argument in support of the court's characterization, based on the second paragraph of Fairmount's letter?

(2) *The Salt–Trade Case.* Consider the foregoing questions in relation to the decision in Moulton v. Kershaw, 18 N.W. 172 (Wis.1884). Kershaw wrote this to Moulton:

In consequence of a rupture in the salt trade we are authorized to offer Michigan fine salt in full car load lots of 80 to 95 barrels, delivered at your city at 85 cents per barrel to be shipped per C. & N.W.R.R. Co. only. At this price it is a bargain as the price in general remains unchanged. Shall be pleased to receive your order.

Moulton immediately wired Kershaw, "Your letter of yesterday received and noted. You may ship me two thousand barrels Michigan fine salt as offered in your letter." Kershaw failed to ship the salt, and Moulton sued for breach of contract. The trial court overruled Kershaw's demurrer and Kershaw appealed. *Held:* Reversed. "The language is not such as a business man would use in making an offer to sell ... a definite amount of property." Moulton v. Kershaw, 18 N.W. 172 (Wis.1884). Suppose Kershaw's communication to Moulton had read, "we are authorized to offer two thousand barrels Michigan fine salt," etc. Would the result have been different? What would be the objection to construing Kershaw's communication as an offer to sell any reasonable quantity of salt—say one to twenty-five car load lots—leaving it to the offeree to name the precise quantity? Has not Kershaw committed himself in advance to supply any reasonable quantity? What result if Kershaw's communication had read, "we are authorized to offer you all the Michigan fine salt you will order," etc.?

THE "BATTLE OF THE FORMS"

Opening Skirmish

A commercial contract for a sale of goods is often the result, as in the foregoing case, of an exchange of several messages rather than a single document signed by both parties. In routine transactions most of these messages are standardized printed forms with blanks filled in to fit the particular transaction. A characteristic sequence includes a "request for quotation," answered by a "quotation" form. (Compare the letters exchanged in *Fairmount Glass Works*.) The ensuing steps might be a "purchase order" and a "sales acknowledgment." If all goes well, the goods will be shipped, received, and paid for.

The exchange goes awry in a distinct minority of cases; but many kinds of mishap occur. One large class of disputes is associated with the widespread use of standard forms. Each party strives to make a contract on the terms of its own form. A mismatch of terms is altogether likely. Problems so caused are taken up in Section 5 below, on the "battle of the forms."

The immediate problem is whether or not a given message should be characterized as an offer. The letter sent by Fairmount Glass Works on April 23 presented a problem of that kind.

NOTE

The Case of the Power–Krug Combat. Power Engineering & Mfg. v. Krug International, 501 N.W.2d 490 (Iowa 1993), provides an illustration of the battle of the forms. Each party—Power as seller and Krug as buyer—was evidently intent on establishing its own terms as those governing the sale of a gear box to be manufactured by Power. Parts of messages that the parties exchanged are as follows. All the parts reproduced, except the description of the item and the price, were printed. Power sent the first message and received the second.

QUOTATION

Thank you for the opportunity to quote. We offer the following for your consideration.

AD–6 Speed reducing gear box Quantity 1 $149,700.

ONLY NON-CANCELLABLE ORDERS ACCEPTED

[*reverse*]

TERMS AND CONDITIONS

1. Acceptance: No contract of purchase and sale shall arise until the Seller shall have acknowledged and accepted in writing at its home office, a written purchase order from the Purchaser for the material based on the terms and provisions quoted. Quotations are subject to change without notice and shall be void after stated date....

. . .

9. Cancellation: Orders will not be subject to cancellations or modifications, either in whole or in part, without the Seller's written consent....

PURCHASE ORDER

AD–6 Gear Box $149,700

Supplier shall provide a biweekly status report starting 6/18/90.

Krug has the right to cancel this order at any time and will pay for only work completed.

No modification of this contract shall be binding upon buyer unless made in writing and signed by buyer's authorized representative.

This purchase order which constitutes an offer includes the terms and conditions on the front and reverse sides hereof. Please read them carefully.

The "quotation" indicates an intention of Power Engineering not to be an offeror. What advantage might a seller anticipate from receiving, rather than making, offers? What possible disadvantage?

Is there anything in the quotation that can fairly be compared with the expression "for immediate acceptance" in the Fairmount letter of April 23?

Krug's "purchase order" purported to be an offer. In answer to it, Power sent a "purchase order acknowledgment." This form contained the printed legend, "This order is non-cancellable." Do you see how it might be said that— in the terms of the argument made by Fairmount Glass Works—this was not an acceptance of the offer as made? (If the acknowledgment was not an acceptance, possibly it was an offer, despite the term about Acceptance in Power's Quotation, above.) The force of that argument is considered further in Section 5.

ADDRESSEE OF OFFER

Generally, an offer can be accepted only by one whom it invites to furnish the consideration. One might expect this principle to have frequent application, owing to mistakes made in addressing offers to the "wrong" persons or firms. (The fact that a business has been incorporated, or that an enterprise has changed its corporate identity, may not be widely publicized.) In point of fact, however, there are few cases exemplifying the principle. Why might that be so?

An offer is sometimes addressed to a very wide audience. Reward offers are an example; see Broadnax v. Ledbetter, Note 2, p. 97 above. Whether or not an announcement to the public of a price for goods the owner wishes to sell is an offer is considered in the next main case.

NOTE

The Case of the Pipe Hose. In a 19th–century case it appeared that Boulton, the foreman and manager of a leather "pipe hose" business, had bought out the owner, Brocklehurst. Later on the same day a regular customer named Jones, who had had a running account with Brocklehurst, sent him an order for merchandise. Boulton received the order and supplied the goods without notifying Jones of the change of ownership. When Jones refused to pay, Boulton sued for the price. *Held:* for Jones. "When a contract is made, in which the personality of the contracting party is or may be of importance, as a contract with a man to write a book, or the like, or where there might be a setoff, no other person can interpose and adopt the contract." Boulton v. Jones, 157 Eng.Rep. 232 (1857) (Exchequer Chamber; Bramwell, B.).

Possibly Boulton had a remedy that he did not pursue. There being no contract, if Jones had sold or otherwise disposed of the goods he would have converted them. That being so, Boulton could have "waived the tort" and recovered in quasi contract. See D. Dobbs, Handbook on the Law of Remedies 238 (1973). But the amount recoverable would not have been the price at which the goods were ordered; more likely it would have been their reasonable value. Jones might also have converted the goods by refusing to relinquish them upon a proper demand by Boulton, which would also have led to a reasonable-value recovery.

CRAFT v. ELDER & JOHNSTON CO.

Court of Appeals of Ohio, Montgomery County, 1941.
38 N.E.2d 416.

[Action by Craft against Elder & Johnston Co. for alleged breach of contract. From a judgment of dismissal plaintiff appeals.]

BARNES, JUDGE.... On or about January 31, 1940, the defendant, the Elder & Johnston Company, carried an advertisement in the Dayton Shopping News, an offer for sale of a certain all electric sewing machine for the sum of $26 as a "Thursday Only Special". Plaintiff in her petition, after certain formal allegations, sets out the substance of the above advertisement carried by defendant in the Dayton Shopping News. She further alleges that the above publication is an advertising paper distributed in Montgomery County and throughout the city of Dayton; that on Thursday, February 1, 1940, she tendered to the defendant company $26 in payment for one of the machines offered in the advertisement, but that defendant refused to fulfill the offer and has continued to so refuse. The petition further alleges that the value of the machine offered was $175 and she asks damages in the sum of $149 plus interest from February 1, 1940....

The trial court dismissed plaintiff's petition as evidenced by a journal entry, the pertinent portion of which reads as follows: "Upon consideration the court finds that said advertisement was not an offer which could be accepted by plaintiff to form a contract, and this case is therefore dismissed with prejudice to a new action, at costs of plaintiff."

Within statutory time plaintiff filed notice of appeal on questions of law and thus lodged the case in our court....

It seems to us that this case may easily be determined on well-recognized elementary principles. The first question to be determined is the proper characterization to be given to defendant's advertisement in the Shopping News....

"It is clear that in the absence of special circumstances an ordinary newspaper advertisement is not an offer, but is an offer to negotiate—an offer to receive offers—or, as it is sometimes called, an offer to chaffer." Restatement of the Law of Contracts, Par. 25, Page 31.

Under the above paragraph the following illustration is given, " 'A', a clothing merchant, advertises overcoats of a certain kind for sale at $50. This is not an offer but an invitation to the public to come and purchase."

"Thus, if goods are advertised for sale at a certain price, it is not an offer and no contract is formed by the statement of an intending purchaser that he will take a specified quantity of the goods at that price. The construction is rather favored that such an advertisement is a mere invitation to enter into a bargain rather than an offer. So a published price list is not an offer to sell the goods listed at the published price." Williston on Contracts, Revised Edition, Vol. 1, Par. 27, Page 54.

"The commonest example of offers meant to open negotiations and to call forth offers in the technical sense are advertisements, circulars and trade letters sent out by business houses. While it is possible that the offers made by such means may be in such form as to become contracts, they are often merely expressions of a willingness to negotiate." Page on the Law of Contracts, 2d Ed., Vol. 1, Page 112, Par. 84.

"Business advertisements published in newspapers and circulars sent out by mail or distributed by hand stating that the advertiser has a certain quantity or quality of goods which he wants to dispose of at certain prices, are not offers which become contracts as soon as any person to whose notice they may come signifies his acceptance by notifying the other that he will take a certain quantity of them. They are merely invitations to all persons who may read them that the advertiser is ready to receive offers for the goods at the price stated." Corpus Juris 289, Par. 97....

We are constrained to the view that the trial court committed no prejudicial error in dismissing plaintiff's petition.

The judgment of the trial court will be affirmed and costs adjudged against the plaintiff-appellant.

NOTES

(1) *Advertisements as Offers.* If advertisements such as that in the *Craft* case were held to be offers, what would be the position of the store if the demand were to exceed its supply? Would it arise if "first come, first served" were read into every advertisement? This last approach appears to be that of French law, under which "the great majority of authorities consider such a proposal to be an offer, even if it can be accepted only by one of those to whom it is addressed. But such an offer is subject to the condition, as to each offeree, that it has not already been accepted by a quicker-acting offeree." 1 R. Schlesinger (ed.), Formation of Contracts: A Study of the Common Core of Legal Systems 359 (1968). Can you see any difficulties that might arise under this approach? What if the personal qualities (e.g., integrity) of the other party will play an important role under the contract?

(2) *Consumer Protection.* In Geismar v. Abraham & Strauss, 439 N.Y.S.2d 1005 (Dist.Ct.1981), a disappointed shopper sued a department store that had advertised in a newspaper a set of china dishes regularly priced at $280 for only $39.95, but had refused to sell them at that price. The court held that since the advertisement was not an offer, there was no breach of contract. But it went on to hold that she could recover $50 under a New York statute providing that any person "injured" by advertising "which is misleading in a material respect" is entitled to recover actual damages or $50, whichever is greater.

Many other states also have laws dealing with false advertising. Ohio, where the Craft case was decided, now has the Uniform Deceptive Trade Practices Act. Ohio Rev.Code Ann. ch. 4165. In addition to state laws, Section 5 of the Federal Trade Commission Act (15 U.S.C. § 45) declares "unfair or deceptive acts or practices" to be unlawful, and the Commission may promulgate rules to this end. The Commission's rule on misleading advertising by grocery stores is in 16 C.F.R. § 424.1.

LEFKOWITZ v. GREAT MINNEAPOLIS SURPLUS STORE, 86 N.W.2d 689 (Minn.1957). [The Great Minneapolis Surplus Store published the following advertisement in a Minneapolis newspaper:

SATURDAY 9 A.M.
2 BRAND NEW PASTEL
MINK 3–SKIN SCARFS
Selling for $89.50
Out they go
SATURDAY, EACH $1.00

1 BLACK LAPIN STOLE ...
Beautiful,
worth $139.50 ..... $1.00
FIRST COME
FIRST SERVED [a]

a. This text appeared as one of a number of boxed items in a full-page ad featuring widely varying type sizes. A snippet from the page, somewhat reduced in size, is as follows:

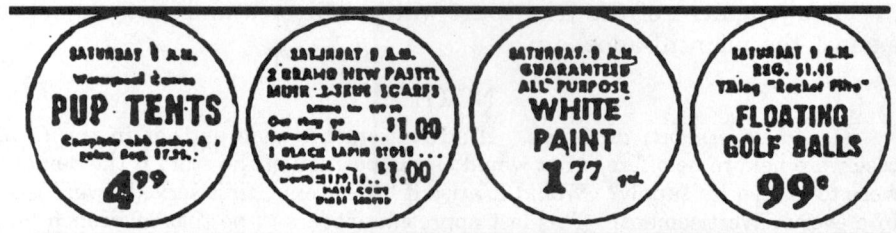

Lefkowitz was the first to present himself on Saturday and demanded the Lapin stole for one dollar. The store refused to sell to him because of a "house rule" that the offer was intended for women only. Lefkowitz sued the store and was awarded $138.50 as damages. The store appealed.]

MURPHY, JUSTICE.... The defendant relies principally on Craft v. Elder & Johnston Co.... On the facts before us we are concerned with whether the advertisement constituted an offer, and, if so, whether the plaintiff's conduct constituted an acceptance. There are numerous authorities which hold that a particular advertisement in a newspaper or circular letter relating to a sale of articles may be construed by the court as constituting an offer, acceptance of which would complete a contract.... The test of whether a binding obligation may originate in advertisements addressed to the general public is "whether the facts show that some performance was promised in positive terms in return for something requested." 1 Williston, Contracts (rev. ed.) § 27. The authorities above cited emphasize that, where the offer is clear, definite and explicit, and leaves nothing open for negotiation, it constitutes an offer, acceptance of which will complete the contract.... Whether in any individual instance a newspaper advertisement is an offer rather than an invitation to make an offer depends on the legal intention of the parties and the surrounding circumstances.... We are of the view on the facts before us that the offer by the defendant of the sale of the Lapin fur was clear, definite, and explicit, and left nothing open for negotiation.... The defendant contends that the offer was modified by a "house rule" to the effect that only women were qualified to receive the bargains advertised. The advertisement contained no such restriction. This objection may be disposed of briefly by stating that, while an advertiser has the right at any time before acceptance to modify his offer, he does not have the right, after acceptance, to impose new or arbitrary conditions not contained in the published offer....

Affirmed.[b]

b. The advertisement set out above was actually the second one by the Store to which Lefkowitz had responded. The first, published a week earlier, was: "3 Brand New Fur Coats Worth to $100.00/First Come First Served/$1 Each." To Lefkowitz's claim based on that ad the court answered that the ad was not an offer because the word "to" made the value of the coats "speculative and uncertain." This ruling is criticized in Ayres & Gertner, Filling Gaps in Incomplete Contracts: An Economic Theory of Default Rules, 99 Yale L.J. 87, 105–106 (1989).

On the first occasion the Store had also refused to sell to Lefkowitz, saying that by

NOTES

(1) *Rationale.* On what grounds might the *Craft* and *Lefkowitz* cases be distinguished? The decision in *Craft*, it is said, might have been based on the ground that the advertised price was an obvious misprint. 1 Corbin rev. 117. Was there an obvious misprint? (As to errors in offers see Note 3, p. 178 below.)

Is there another way to distinguish the cases? In what respect was the advertisement in *Lefkowitz* more "clear, definite and explicit" than that in *Craft?* Were the words "First Come First Served" significant?

(2) *Problem.* Is the following notice, appearing in a newspaper, an offer? If so, how might it be accepted?

"$50,000 REWARD. Tiffany & Co. offer a reward of up to $50,000 for information leading to the recovery of jewelry and watches stolen from Tiffany on the night of September 4th, 1994. Payment will be made solely at the discretion of the insurers of Tiffany & Co., subject to recovery, arrest and conviction of the criminals." [c]

(3) *Competitive Bidding.* A contracting party may fix the contract price, leave it to private negotiation, or determine it by competitive bidding. A party who chooses to determine it by competitive bidding may invite open bids at an auction, as is often done in the sale of goods or land, or may invite sealed bids, as is common in the letting of building contracts.

If a party invites competitive bids, is this an offer to be accepted by the highest bidder when the bid is made? Or is it merely an invitation for offers by bids that can then be accepted or rejected by the one who has invited them? The law has taken the latter view, that it is the bidder who makes the offer. Can you see why?

This is the general rule stated in UCC 2–328 with respect to the sale of goods by auction. Under that section the auctioneer may, however, make an offer by advertising the sale to be "without reserve." Note that if the sale is "without reserve," the auctioneer is bound not to withdraw after a bid is made, but the bidder is not similarly bound. Local statutes may also govern auction sales.

The rather elaborate provisions of UCC 2–328 are, of course, expressly applicable only to the sale of goods. UCC 2–102. Might they be extended by analogy to the sale of land? Comment 1 to UCC 1–102 speaks of the possibility of reasoning from the Code by analogy: "[Courts] have recognized the policies embodied in an act as applicable in reason to subject-matter which was not expressly included in the language of the act.... They have done the same where reason and policy so required, even where the subject-matter had been intentionally excluded from the act in general.... Nothing in this Act stands in the way of the continuance of such action by the courts." See Chevalier v. Town of Sanford, 475 A.2d 1148 (Me.1984), a land auction case in which the court reasoned by analogy to UCC 2–328.

(4) *The Case of the Winner's Complaint.* A firm providing business news by electronic means (FNN) filed a bankruptcy petition as part of its performance of a contract to dispose of the firm's media assets. On the morning set for opening bids, the bankruptcy court received rival offers from two firms, one of them

a "house rule" the offer was intended for women only; sales would not be made to men. Considering this additional fact, do you agree with the court's decision that he

could recover under the second advertisement?

c. Excerpted from The New York Times, Sept. 9, 1994, p. B2.

being Consumer News (CN). It appeared initially that the rival bid was slightly more attractive than CN's. CN attempted to improve its prospects by "clarifying" its bid. The court objected that CN was attempting to "change a closed bid." But on the following day the court accepted a revised offer from each bidder. CN having offered additional consideration of more than $5 million, it was declared the winner. From an order to that effect CN appealed, seeking a "rebate" of the additional amount. The appeal was unsuccessful. In re Financial News Network Inc., 980 F.2d 165 (2d Cir.1992).

What consideration, other than desiring a speedy resolution, might have persuaded the bankruptcy court to refuse to reopen the bidding?

MISTAKEN BIDS

COMMENT, THE SUBCONTRACTOR'S BID: AN OPTION CONTRACT ARISING THROUGH PROMISSORY ESTOPPEL, 34 Emory L.J. 421, 425–28 (1985).[a]—A typical bidding sequence involves most or all of the following steps. The owner first determines, according to some formal or informal financial analysis, that he desires to have a certain project built at a certain location if he can get it built within a given budget. He then employs an architect to design the project with that budget in mind, while he sets about securing and rezoning the property. When the owner is satisfied with the architect's preliminary plan, the architect employs various engineers, and together they prepare detailed plans and specifications covering all facets of the project including site work, structural, architectural, electrical, plumbing, mechanical, hardware and finish schedules, and landscaping. Multiple sets of these plans and specifications are then distributed to selected general contractors who are invited to submit bids for the total project at a given day and hour. Bids may also be invited through advertising, or be accepted from general contractors who learn of the project through the industry media or grapevine. Subcontractors obtain copies of the portions of the plans and specifications that pertain to their trades, either from a friendly general contractor or at [a] facility where sets are available to subcontractors who wish to bid the project. Equipment suppliers and materialmen whose products have been specified, or who believe their products are equivalent to those specified, similarly will obtain the portions of the plans which pertain to them. Each bidder (general contractor, subcontractor, supplier) will carefully check, measure and count each and every item on that section of the plans that pertains to him, and will calculate a price for which he is willing to guarantee performance of that portion of the work and which he believes will (1) be lower than other bids for the same work, and (2) result in a satisfactory profit to him.

By "bid day," considerable time, energy, and money has been invested by all involved, and each participant will want to ensure his ultimate opportunity to do the work he bid by having his bid included in the winning general contractor's bid. To accomplish that, each materialman and equipment supplier will try to submit his bid to each appropriate subcontractor and each subcontractor will try to submit his bid to each general contractor. Likewise, each general contractor will want access to each subcontractor's bid so that the lowest and best for each category of work can be included in his own bid. Only by including low subcontractor bids can the general contractor hope to assemble the lowest total bid, upon which the award of the prime contract will probably be based.[1]

Complications enter the bidding process as each participant weighs the likelihood that each other participant can and will perform. This involves assessing financial strengths and weaknesses, abilities and moral fiber, histories of cooperation and discord, volume of other work, and miscellaneous other factors. These assessments frequently must be made very quickly and on the basis of little or no objective data. Other complications enter as materialmen and subcontractors place qualifying restrictions on their bids. Sub X will bid one price for both plumbing and heating, and will not perform either part of the work without the other. Sub Y will bid the plumbing but will not include the gas piping or water meter. Sub Z will bid a substitute brand of cooling equipment that is considerably cheaper and which he claims is an acceptable equivalent of the equipment specified, and he will require $3,000 front money and progress payments every Friday. The general contractor has no such leeway to modify his own bid because he risks disqualification if he varies from the specified contract terms in any way.[2] He is faced with the ultimate contract of adhesion. He can bid the contract as specified or not bid it at all—no bargaining!

Subcontractor and supplier bidders may fear that their bids will be undercut by their competition, so they often wait to submit their bids until the last hour or two before the general contractor's bid is due. Frequently, a subcontractor or materialman will discover after submitting his bid that he has made a mistake,[3] perhaps because one of the general contractors informs him that he is either substantially higher or substantially lower than other bidders. He must then frantically review

1. Having the lowest overall bid will not guarantee the general contractor that he will be awarded the prime contract. Frequently even the lowest bid will be over budget and no award will be made. Similarly, some inadequacy may be perceived in the qualifications of the low bidder or his subcontractors, causing the owner to reject the bid. Bid documents usually reserve to the owner the right to reject any or all bids. [But if the owner is a governmental entity, as in the next case, it may be required by law to award the job to the lowest qualified bidder. Eds.]

2. Typically, the exact wording of the contract that the owner intends to sign will be included in the bid documents. If the general contractor submits a bid that varies the contract wording in any particular, his bid may be deemed unresponsive and may be disqualified. The purpose of specifying the exact contract language is to facilitate comparison of the various general contractors' bids by assuring that each general contractor is bidding exactly the same job and will agree to exactly the same contract terms. Comparison can then be made exclusively on the basis of price.

3. Mistakes come in a variety of flavors. There may be mistakes in construing the language of the plans and specifications, in estimating quantities required, in unit pricing, in multiplying quantities by unit prices, in transferring data from one work-sheet to another, in typing the bid form, and many others.

the plans (if he still has access to them), correct his mistake, and telephone his corrected price to all concerned.

While this last-minute subcontractor bidding is being received, the general contractor is collating and comparing the prices and the qualifying restrictions that he has received, adding in factors for his own workforce and supervision, and adjusting the total as later prices are received by phone. His final bid will probably be typed on the bid form while he stands impatiently over the typewriter with car keys in hand, hoping that traffic will not delay him on his way to the bid opening. When he arrives at the appointed place with his sealed bid envelope, he may make a quick call to his office to learn whether any substantial price cuts were received after he left. If any were, he will have to decide quickly whether he can risk using the lower price (Is it a mistake? Does he believe the subcontractor can perform?), or whether he can still be competitive if he decides not to use the lower price. If he decides to use it, he may write on the outside of his bid envelope "Deduct X dollars" and he will be bound by that writing as a reduction of the enclosed bid.

When the bids are opened, if his is found to be low, the general contractor may have $5 or $500,000 "left on the table," [4] but he is bound (and probably bonded) to perform for the bid he has submitted. The owner, however, is not bound to give him the contract. Typical provisions of the bid documents allow the owner to reject any or all bids, to negotiate further with any or all of the bidders, and to add, delete, or change portions of the work with or without corresponding changes in the base bid.[5] These post-bid negotiations in no way change the obligation of the general contractor to contract according to his bid if the owner so chooses. The post-bid negotiations may or may not require consultation and negotiation with the subcontractor bidders relating to their portions of the work. At the end of this process, the owner signs the prime contract with the general contractor of his choice. That general contractor then makes contracts with the subcontractors of his choice.

The general contractor is bound to perform his prime contract even if one or more of his selected subcontractors refuses to perform. If that happens, the general contractor must seek others to do that part of the work, usually subcontractors who bid higher than the defaulting subcontractors or who did not bid at all. The difference between the performing subcontractor's price and the defaulting subcontractor's price may be substantial. Since the general contractor cannot pass the increase to the

---

4. In construction idiom, if my $100,000 bid is lowest, and your $105,000 bid is next lowest, I have left $5,000 on the table.

5. At this point the parties behave as if the owner had an option, despite the fact that he has given no consideration. The owner is free to accept or reject the contractor's offer, and the offer may not be withdrawn for some specified (or reasonable) period of time. Negotiations and counteroffers do not operate to cancel the offer. The bid bond, if any, guarantees this result. For unbonded bids, the informal sanctions within the industry usually accomplish this result. For contracts on public projects, the limits and effects of post-bid negotiations are frequently regulated by statute. [See footnote 1 above and Note 1, p. 177 below.]

owner, the result may be a lawsuit to recover the difference from the defaulter.

NOTE

"Bid Shopping." The preceding excerpt suggests the possibility that the general contractor may shop around among the subbidders to secure a lower price. The construction industry regards such "bid shopping" with opprobrium, whether it occurs before or after the award. Subcontractors regard it with particular distaste when it occurs after the successful general contractor's bargaining position has been strengthened by the award.

It is objected, on the one hand, that bid shopping results in an undesirable decrease in competition, because subcontractors will pad their bids so that they can lower them later when bid shopping occurs, inflating the general contractor's bid to the ultimate disadvantage of the owner. Is this objection convincing if, as the excerpt suggests, there is a countervailing tendency among general contractors to discount their estimates on subcontractor's bids in anticipation of bid shopping?

It is objected, on the other hand, that bid shopping results in an undesirable increase in competition—that subcontractors will be driven to bid so low that they will be "operating at a loss" and tempted to use substandard work and materials, again to the ultimate disadvantage of the owner. Is this risk greater in the construction industry than in other areas of the economy?

The owner may combat post-award bid shopping by requiring that general contractors list their prospective subcontractors in their bids. This requirement is more common, however, in government than in private contracts. Why do not more private owners require listing if bid shopping is to their ultimate disadvantage? Subcontractors, whose self-interest is clearer, have attempted to combat bid shopping by organizing themselves into "bid depositories," although such concerted efforts raise problems under the antitrust laws. They have also tried to combat pre-award bid shopping by waiting until the last possible moment to submit their bids. The resulting haste with which the general contractor must then prepare his own bid may, of course, cause him to make the kinds of errors that gave rise to the next case. For more background, see Schultz, The Firm Offer Puzzle: A Study of Business Practice in the Construction Industry, 19 U.Chi.L.Rev. 237 (1952), an illuminating study of bidding practices in the construction industry in Indiana, based on questionaires returned by eighty general contractors and ninety-three subcontractors. For a similar survey in Virginia, see Note, 53 Va.L.Rev. 1720 (1967).

ELSINORE UNION ELEMENTARY SCHOOL DISTRICT v. KASTORFF

Supreme Court of California, 1960.
54 Cal.2d 380, 6 Cal.Rptr. 1, 353 P.2d 713.

SCHAUER, JUSTICE. Defendants, who are a building contractor and his surety,[a] appeal from an adverse judgment in this action by plaintiff

a. The standard form of bid bond promulgated by the American Institute of Architects obligates the surety to pay "the difference not to exceed the penalty hereof [i.e., the amount of the bond] between the amount specified in said bid and such larger

school district to recover damages allegedly resulting when defendant Kastorff, the contractor, refused to execute a building contract pursuant to his previously submitted bid to make certain additions to plaintiff's school buildings. We have concluded that because of an honest clerical error in the bid and defendant's subsequent prompt rescission he was not obliged to execute the contract, and that the judgment should therefore be reversed.

Pursuant to plaintiff's call for bids, defendant Kastorff secured a copy of the plans and specifications of the proposed additions to plaintiff's school buildings and proceeded to prepare a bid to be submitted by the deadline hour of 8 p.m., August 12, 1952, at Elsinore, California. Kastorff testified that in preparing his bid he employed work sheets upon which he entered bids of various subcontractors for such portions of the work as they were to do, and that to reach the final total of his own bid for the work he carried into the right-hand column of the work sheets the amounts of the respective sub bids which he intended to accept and then added those amounts to the cost of the work which he would do himself rather than through a subcontractor; that there is "a custom among subcontractors, in bidding on jobs such as this, to delay giving ... their bids until the very last moment"; that the first sub bid for plumbing was in the amount of $9,285 and he had received it "the afternoon of the bid-opening," but later that afternoon when "the time was drawing close for me to get my bids together and get over to Elsinore" (from his home in San Juan Capistrano) he received a $6,500 bid for the plumbing. Erroneously thinking he had entered the $9,285 plumbing bid in his total column and had included that sum in his total bid and realizing that the second plumbing bid was nearly $3,000 less than the first, Kastorff then deducted $3,000 from the total amount of his bid and entered the resulting total of $89,994 on the bid form as his bid for the school construction. Thus the total included no allowance whatsoever for the plumbing work.

Kastorff then proceeded to Elsinore and deposited his bid with plaintiff. When the bids were opened shortly after 8 p.m. that evening, it was discovered that of the five bids submitted that of Kastorff was some $11,306 less than the next lowest bid. The school superintendent and the four school board members present thereupon asked Kastorff whether he was sure his figures were correct. Kastorff stepped out in to the hall to check with the person who had assisted in doing the clerical work on the bid, and a few minutes later returned and stated that the figures were correct. He testified that he did not have his worksheets or other papers with him to check against at the time. The board thereupon, on August 12, 1952, voted to award Kastorff the contract.

The next morning Kastorff checked his worksheets and promptly discovered his error. He immediately drove to the Los Angeles office of the firm of architects which had prepared the plans and specifications for

amount for which the Obligee may in good faith contract with another party to per-   form the Work covered by said bid."

plaintiff, and there saw Mr. Rendon. Mr. Rendon testified that Kastorff "had his maps and estimate work-sheets of the project, and indicated to me that he had failed to carry across the amount of dollars for the plumbing work. It was on the sheet, but not in the total sheet. We examined that evidence, and in our opinion we felt that he had made a clerical error in compiling his bill.... In other words, he had put down a figure, but didn't carry it out to the 'total' column when he totaled his column to make up his bid.... He exhibited ... at that time ... his work-sheets from which he had made up his bid." That same morning (August 13) Rendon telephoned the school superintendent and informed him of the error and of its nature and that Kastorff asked to be released from his bid. On August 14 Kastorff wrote a letter to the school board explaining his error and again requesting that he be permitted to withdraw his bid. On August 15, after receiving Kastorff's letter, the board held a special meeting and voted not to grant his request. Thereafter, on August 28, *written notification* was given to Kastorff of award of the contract to him.[1] Subsequently plaintiff submitted to Kastorff a contract to be signed in accordance with his bid, and on September 8, 1952, Kastorff returned the contract to plaintiff with a letter again explaining his error and asking the board to reconsider his request for withdrawal of his bid.

Plaintiff thereafter received additional bids to do the subject construction; let the contract to the lowest bidder, in the amount of $102,900; and brought this action seeking to recover from Kastorff the $12,906 difference between that amount and the amount Kastorff had bid.[2] Recovery of $4,499.60 is also sought against Kastorff's surety under the terms of the bond posted with his bid.

Cause of Action

Defendants in their answer to the complaint pleaded, among other things, that Kastorff had made an honest error in compiling his bid; that "he thought he was bidding, and intended to bid, $9500.00 more making a total of $99,494.00 as his bid"; that upon discovering his error he had promptly notified plaintiff and rescinded the $89,994 bid. The trial court found that it was true that Kastorff made up a bid sheet, which was introduced in evidence; that the subcontractor's bids thereupon indicated were those received by Kastorff; that he "had 16 subcontracting bids to ascertain from 31 which were submitted"; and that Kastorff had neglected to carry over from the left-hand column on the bid sheet to the right-hand column on the sheet a portion of the plumbing (and heating) subcontractor's bid. Despite the uncontradicted evidence related hereinabove, including that of plaintiff's architect and of its school superintendent, both of whom testified as plaintiff's wit-

1. On the bid form, provided by plaintiff, the bidder agreed "that if he is notified of the acceptance of the proposal within forty-five (45) days from the time set for the opening of bids, he will execute and deliver to you within five (5) days after having received *written notification* a contract as called for in the 'Notice to Contractors.'" (Italics added.)

2. Plaintiff's original published call for bids contained the following statement: "No Bidder may withdraw his bid for a period of forty-five (45) days after the date set for the opening thereof." Whether upon Kastorff's rescission for good cause prior to expiration of the 45 day period plaintiff could have accepted the next lowest bid is not an issue before us.

nesses, the court further found, however, that "it is not true that the right hand column of figures was totaled for the purpose of arriving at the total bid to be submitted by E.J. Kastorff.... It cannot be ascertained from the evidence for what purpose the total of the right hand column of figures on the bid sheet was used nor can it be ascertained from the evidence for what purpose the three bid sheets were used in arriving at the total bid." And although finding that "on or about August 15, 1952," plaintiff received Kastorff's letter of August 14 explaining that he "made an error of omitting from my bid the item of Plumbing," the court also found that "It is not true that plaintiff knew at any time that defendant Kastorff's bid was intended to be other than $89,994.00.... It is not true that the plaintiff knew at the time it requested the execution of the contract by defendant Kastorff that he had withdrawn his bid because of an honest error in the compilation thereof. It is not true that plaintiff had notice of an error in the compilation of the bid by defendant Kastorff and tried nevertheless to take advantage of defendant Kastorff by forcing him to enter a contract on the basis of a bid he had withdrawn.... It is not true that it would be either inequitable or unjust to require defendant Kastorff to perform the contract awarded to him for the sum of $89,994.00, and it is not true that he actually intended to bid for said work the sum of $99,494.00" [3] Judgment was given for plaintiff in the amounts sought, and this appeal by defendants followed.

In reliance upon M.F. Kemper Const. Co. v. City of Los Angeles (1951), 37 Cal.2d 696, 235 P.2d 7, and Lemoge Electric v. County of San Mateo (1956), 46 Cal.2d 659, 662, 664, 297 P.2d 638, defendants urged that where, as defendants claim is the situation here, a contractor makes a clerical error in computing a bid on a public work he is entitled to rescind.

In the *Kemper* case one item on a worksheet in the amount of $301,769 was inadvertently omitted by the contractor from the final tabulation sheet and was overlooked in computing the total amount of a bid to do certain construction work for the defendant city. The error was caused by the fact that the men preparing the bid were exhausted after working long hours under pressure. When the bids were opened it was found that plaintiff's bid was $780,305, and the next lowest bid was $1,049,592. Plaintiff discovered its error several hours later and immediately notified a member of defendant's board of public works of its mistake in omitting one item while preparing the final accumulation of figures for its bid. Two days later it explained its mistake to the board and withdrew its bid. A few days later it submitted to the board evidence which showed the unintentional omission of the $301,769 item. The board nevertheless passed a resolution accepting plaintiff's errone-

---

3. Other findings that Kastorff "in the company of his wife and another couple left San Juan Capistrano for Elsinore ... at 6:00 P.M. on August 12, 1952, a distance of 34 miles by way of California State Highway ... Kastorff had ample time and opportunity after receiving his last subcontractor's bid to extend the figures on his bid sheet from one column to the other, to check and recheck his bid sheet figures and to take his papers to Elsinore and to check them there prior to close of receipt of bids at 8:00 P.M."

ous bid of $780,305, and plaintiff refused to enter into a written contract at that figure. The board then awarded the contract to the next lowest bidder, the city demanded forfeiture of plaintiff's bid bond, and plaintiff brought action to cancel its bid and obtain discharge of the bond. The trial court found that the bid had been submitted as the result of an excusable and honest mistake of a material and fundamental character, that plaintiff company had not been negligent in preparing the proposal, that it had acted promptly to notify the board of the mistake and to rescind the bid, and that the board had accepted the bid with knowledge of the error. The court further found and concluded that it would be unconscionable to require the company to perform for the amount of the bid, that no intervening rights had accrued, and that the city had suffered no damage or prejudice.

On appeal by the city this court affirmed, stating the following applicable rules (at pages 700–703 of 37 Cal.2d, at pages 10, 11 of 235 P.2d):

"Once opened and declared, the company's bid was in the nature of an irrevocable option, a contract right of which the city could not be deprived without its consent unless the requirements for rescission were satisfied. ... [T]he city had actual notice of the error in the estimates before it attempted to accept the bid, and knowledge by one party that the other is acting under mistake is treated as equivalent to mutual mistake for purposes of rescission.... Relief from mistaken bids is consistently allowed where one party knows or has reason to know of the other's error and the requirements for rescission are fulfilled....

"Rescission may be had for mistake of fact if the mistake is material to the contract and was not the result of neglect of a legal duty, if enforcement of the contract as made would be unconscionable, and if the other party can be placed in statu quo.... In addition, the party seeking relief must give prompt notice of his election to rescind and must restore or offer to restore to the other party everything of value which he has received under the contract....

"Omission of the $301,769 item from the company's bid was, of course, a material mistake.... [E]ven if we assume that the error was due to some carelessness, it does not follow that the company is without remedy. Civil Code section 1577, which defines mistake of facts for which relief may be allowed, describes it as one not caused by 'the neglect of a legal duty' on the part of the person making the mistake. It has been recognized numerous times that not all carelessness constitutes a 'neglect of a legal duty' on the part of the person making the mistake. It has been recognized numerous times that not all carelessness constitutes a 'neglect of legal duty' within the meaning of the section.... On facts very similar to those in the present case, courts of other jurisdictions have stated that there was no culpable negligence and have granted relief from erroneous bids.... The type of error here involved is one which will sometimes occur in the conduct of reasonable and cautious businessmen, and, under all the circumstances, we cannot say as a matter of law that it constituted a neglect of legal duty such as would bar the right to equitable relief.

"The evidence clearly supports the conclusion that it would be unconscionable to hold the company to its bid at the mistaken figure. The city had knowledge before the bid was accepted that the company had made a clerical error which resulted in the omission of an item amounting to nearly one third of the amount intended to be bid, and, under all the circumstances, it appears that it would be unjust and unfair to permit the city to take advantage of the company's mistake. There is no reason for denying relief on the ground that the city cannot be restored to status quo. It had ample time in which to award the contract without readvertising, the contract was actually awarded to the next lowest bidder, and the city will not be heard to complain that it cannot be placed in statu quo because it will not have the benefit of an inequitable bargain.... Finally, the company gave notice promptly upon discovering the facts entitling it to rescind, and no offer of restoration was necessary because it had received nothing of value which it could restore.... We are satisfied that all the requirements for rescission have been met."

In the *Lemoge* case (Lemoge Electric v. County of San Mateo (1956), supra, 46 Cal.2d 659, 662, 664), 297 P.2d 638, the facts were similar to those in *Kemper*, except that plaintiff Lemoge did not attempt to rescind but instead, after discovering and informing defendant of inadvertent clerical error in the bid, entered into a formal contract with defendant on the terms specified in the erroneous bid, performed the required work, and then sued for reformation. Although this court affirmed the trial court's determination that plaintiff was not, under the circumstances, entitled to have the contract reformed, we also reaffirmed the rule that "Once opened and declared, plaintiff's bid was in the nature of an irrevocable option, a contract right of which defendant could not be deprived without its consent unless the requirements for rescission were satisfied. ... Plaintiff then had the right to rescind, and it could have done so without incurring any liability on its bond." ...

Further, we are persuaded that the trial court's view, as expressed in the finding set forth in the margin,[4] that "Kastorff had ample time and opportunity after receiving his last subcontractor's bid" to complete and check his final bid, does not convict Kastorff of that "neglect of legal duty" which would preclude his being relieved from the inadvertent clerical error of omitting from his bid the cost of the plumbing. (See Civ.Code, § 1577; M.F. Kemper Const. Co. v. City of Los Angeles (1951), supra, 37 Cal.2d 696, 702[6], 235 P.2d 7.) Neither should he be denied relief from an unfair, inequitable, and unintended bargain simply because, in response to inquiry from the board when his bid was discovered to be much the lowest submitted, he informed the board, after checking with his clerical assistant, that the bid was correct....

If the situations of the parties were reversed and plaintiff and Kastorff had even executed a formal written contract (by contrast with

4.   See footnote 3, supra.

the preliminary bid offer and acceptance) calling for a fixed sum payment to Kastorff large enough to include a reasonable charge for plumbing but inadvertently through the *district's* clerical error omitting a mutually intended provision requiring Kastorff to furnish and install plumbing, we have no doubt but that the district would demand and expect reformation or rescission. In the case before us the district expected Kastorff to furnish and install plumbing; surely it must also have understood that he intended to, and that his bid did, include a charge for such plumbing. The omission of any such charge was as unexpected by the board as it was unintended by Kastorff. Under the circumstances the "bargain" for which the board presses (which action we, of course, assume to be impelled by advice of counsel and a strict concept of official duty) appears too sharp for law and equity to sustain.

Plaintiff suggests that in any event the amount of the plumbing bid omitted from the total was immaterial. The bid as submitted was in the sum of $89,994, and whether the sum for the omitted plumbing was $6,500 or $9,285 (the two sub bids), the omission of such a sum is plainly material to the total. In *Lemoge* (Lemoge Electric v. County of San Mateo (1956), supra, 46 Cal.2d 659, 661–662, 297 P.2d 638) the error which it was declared would have entitled plaintiff to rescind was the listing of the cost of certain materials as $104.52, rather than $10,452, in a total bid of $172,421. Thus the percentage of error here was larger than in *Lemoge*, and was plainly material.

The judgment is reversed.[b]

NOTES

(1) *Revocability.* Ordinarily a general contractor's bid on a construction contract is an offer that is revocable before acceptance. Where, however, the owner is a state or local government, statutes or ordinances usually provide that the general contractor may not withdraw its bid after the bids have been opened. Where the owner is the federal government, the same result has been reached on the basis of federal regulation. See Keys, Consideration Reconsidered—The Problem of the Withdrawn Bid, 10 Stan.L.Rev. 441, 448–53 (1958).

(2) *Restatement Second.* Courts have traditionally been less willing than the California court to grant relief to mistaken bidders. The Reporter's Note to Restatement Second § 153 states that that section "liberalizes the rule stated in

b. In 1971, California enacted a statute under which:

A bidder [on a public contract] shall not be relieved of the bid unless by consent of the awarding authority nor shall any change be made in the bid because of mistake, but the bidder may bring an action against the public entity in a court of competent jurisdiction in the county in which the bids were opened for the recovery of the amount forfeited, without interest or costs.

The bidder shall establish to the satisfaction of the court that:

(a) A mistake was made.

(b) He or she gave the public entity written notice within five days after the opening of the bids of the mistake, specifying in the notice in detail how the mistake occurred.

(c) The mistake made the bid materially different than he or she intended it to be.

(d) The mistake was made in filling out the bid and not due to error in judgment or to carelessness in inspecting the site of the work, or in reading the plans or specifications.

Cal. Public Contract Code §§ 5101, 5103.

former § 503 ... to take account of the trend of allowing avoidance although only one party has been mistaken." [c] Courts that have granted bidders relief for mistake have often characterized the mistake as "clerical" rather than as one in "judgment." What is the justification for such a distinction? See Restatement Second § 154 and Illustration 6. It has been argued that from the bidder's standpoint "his mistake is far more inexcusable when it is in computation rather than judgment. School boys have been disciplined for stupidity in that field." Carter, J., dissenting in M.F. Kemper Constr. Co. v. City of Los Angeles, 235 P.2d 7, 15 (Cal.1951).

(3) *Knowledge of Mistake.* All courts agree that if the offeree knows or has reason to know of the offeror's material mistake at the time of acceptance, the offeror is not bound. "One cannot snap up an offer or bid knowing that it was made in mistake." Tyra v. Cheney, 152 N.W. 835 (Minn.1915). Difficulty arises when the offeror claims that the magnitude of the mistake was such that it should have been apparent from the face of the offer.

Heifetz Metal Crafts, Inc. v. Peter Kiewit Sons' Co., 264 F.2d 435 (8th Cir.1959), is a good example. There Kiewit was preparing a bid for the construction of a hospital and Heifetz offered to do the kitchen work for $99,500, $52,000 less than Kiewit's next lowest quotation. Kiewit lowered its bid by $52,000, which made it $17,942,200, the lowest by $9,000. After Kiewit was awarded the contract and had accepted the Heifetz offer, Heifetz discovered that in preparing its quotation it had overlooked some subsidiary kitchen installations required by the plans. It sought rescission and argued that since its quotation was one-third less than the next lowest, Kiewit should have realized that there had been a mistake. The court rejected this contention and held that the contract was enforceable. It relied upon testimony by Kiewit's employees that they were ignorant of the mistake, upon Kiewit's lack of familiarity with the kitchen equipment field, and upon "testimony indicating that at times some contractor would have a special reason for desiring to obtain a particular job and would submit a figure controlled by that consideration." It noted that "the figures submitted by subcontractors on the electrical work for the project has varied from $1,400,000 to $1,850,000 and on the lathing and plastering work from $672,000 to $1,028,000; and the 'mechanical spread' had been between $3,647,000 and $6,000,000."

Is it of any significance that a general contractor will sometimes pass over a low bid to accept one from a subcontractor with which the general contractor has a personal or business connection, and that subcontractors sometimes deliberately make losing bids to break up such combinations? Is it of any significance that subcontractors sometimes bid low in the expectation that changes will later be made to provide for profitable extra work?

(4) *Problem.* Lee Calan Imports instructed the Chicago Sun–Times to advertise a used Volvo for sale at $1,795. The Sun–Times, by mistake, advertised it for $1,095. O'Brien went to look at the car and said that he wanted to buy it for $1,095. The salesman refused to sell it at the erroneous price. Is Lee Calan liable to O'Brien? Is the Sun–Times liable to Lee Calan? See O'Keefe v. Lee Calan Imports, 262 N.E.2d 758 (Ill.App.1970).

---

c. It has, however, been argued that "The proof of whether he has made a mistake is so completely within his control and power that the [Owner] is helpless to refute it." Carter, J., dissenting in M.F. Kemper Construction Co. v. City of Los Angeles, 235 P.2d 7, 13 (Cal.1951).

SECTION 3. THE ACCEPTANCE

———

What is an acceptance? Corbin gives this answer: "An acceptance is a voluntary act of the offeree whereby he exercises the power conferred upon him by the offer, and thereby creates the set of legal relations called a contract. What acts are sufficient to serve this purpose? We must look first to the terms in which the offer was expressed, either by words or by other conduct. . . . The offeror has, in the beginning, full power to determine the acts that are to constitute acceptance. After he has once created the power, he may lose his control over it, and may become disabled to change or to revoke it; but the fact that, in the beginning, the offeror has full control of the immediately succeeding relation called a power, is the characteristic that distinguishes contractual relations from non-contractual ones. After the offeror has created the power, the legal consequences thereof are out of his hands, and he may be brought into numerous consequential relations of which he did not dream, and to which he might not have consented. These later relations are nevertheless called contractual." Corbin, Offer and Acceptance, and Some of the Resulting Legal Relations, 26 Yale L.J. 169, 199 (1917).

Assuming that there has been an offer, the offeree by exercising the power of acceptance "thereby creates," as Corbin puts it, "the set of legal relations called a contract." One of the most important consequences of this "set of legal relations" is that the offeror is no longer free to change its mind and withdraw from the relationship without incurring liability. By what means, then, may the offeree exercise this power of acceptance? If, as Corbin says, the offeror has "full power to determine the acts that are to constitute acceptance," the first step in answering this question is to look at the offer to see what sort of acceptance it invited.

We already know from Chapter 1 that the offeror may have been bargaining either for a performance or for a promise. As will be seen more clearly from the cases that make up the bulk of this book, the economically significant transactions in our society usually involve the latter sort of bargain, in which the offeror seeks the assurance of another promise in return for its own. Contrast the bargaining for performances in Hamer v. Sidway and in Broadnax v. Ledbetter, pp. 47 and 97 above. Why, in the usual commercial transaction, would an offeror want a promise as the acceptance, rather than a performance? When a promise is sought, when can it be inferred from conduct of the offeree? Can mere silence ever count? This Section considers these and related questions.

———

INTERNATIONAL FILTER CO. v. CONROE GIN, ICE & LIGHT CO.
Commission of Appeals of Texas, 1925.
277 S.W. 631.

Action by the International Filter Company against the Conroe Gin, Ice & Light Company.   Judgment for defendant was affirmed in 269 S.W. 210, and plaintiff brings error.   Reversed and remanded.

NICKELS, J.   Plaintiff in error, an Illinois corporation, is a manufacturer of machinery, apparatus, etc., for the purification of water in connection with the manufacture of ice, etc., having its principal office in the city of Chicago.   Defendant in error is a Texas corporation engaged in the manufacture of ice, etc., having its plant, office, etc., at Conroe, Montgomery county, Tex.

On February 10, 1920, through its traveling solicitor, Waterman, plaintiff in error at Conroe, submitted to defendant in error, acting through Henry Thompson, its manager, a written instrument, addressed to defendant in error, which (with immaterial portions omitted) reads as follows:

"Gentlemen: We propose to furnish, f.o.b. Chicago, one No. two Junior (steel tank) International water softener and filter to purify water of the character shown by sample to be submitted. . . .   Price: Twelve hundred thirty ($1,230.00) dollars. . . .   This proposal is made in duplicate and becomes a contract when accepted by the purchaser and approved by an executive officer of the International Filter Company, at its office in Chicago.   Any modification can only be made by duly approved supplementary agreement signed by both parties.

"This proposal is submitted for prompt acceptance, and unless so accepted is subject to change without notice.

"Respectfully submitted,

> "International Filter Co.
> "W.W. Waterman."

On the same day the "proposal" was accepted by defendant in error through notation made on the paper by Thompson reading as follows:

"Accepted Feb. 10, 1920.

> "Conroe Gin, Ice & Light Co.,
> "By Henry Thompson, Mgr."

The paper as thus submitted and "accepted" contained the notation, "Make shipment by Mar. 10."   The paper, in that form, reached the Chicago office of plaintiff in error, and on February 13, 1920, P.N. Engel, its president and vice president, indorsed thereon: "O.K. Feb. 13, 1920, P.N. Engel."   February 14, 1920, plaintiff in error wrote and mailed, and in due course defendant in error received, the following letter:

"Feb. 14, 1920.

"Attention of Mr. Henry Thompson, Manager.

"Conroe Gin, Ice & Light Co., Conroe, Texas—Gentlemen: This will acknowledge and thank you for your order given Mr. Waterman for a No. 2 Jr. steel tank International softener and filter, for 110 volt, 60 cycle, single phase current—for shipment March 10th.

"Please make shipment of the sample of water promptly so that we may make the analysis and know the character of the water before shipment of the apparatus. Shipping tag is inclosed, and please note, the instructions to pack to guard against freezing.

"Yours very truly,

"International Filter Co.
"M.B. Johnson."

By letter of February 28, 1920, defendant in error undertook to countermand the "order," which countermand was repeated and emphasized by letter of March 4, 1920. By letter of March 2, 1920 (replying to the letter of February 28th), plaintiff in error denied the right of countermand, etc., and insisted upon performance of the "contract." The parties adhered to the respective positions thus indicated, and this suit resulted.

Plaintiff in error sued for breach of the contract alleged to have been made in the manner stated above. The defense is that no contract was made because: (1) Neither Engel's indorsement of "O.K.," nor the letter of February 14, 1920, amounted to approval "by an executive officer of the International Filter Company, at its office in Chicago." (2) Notification of such approval, or acceptance, by plaintiff in error was required to be communicated to defendant in error; it being insisted that this requirement inhered in the terms of the proposal and in the nature of the transaction and, also, that Thompson, when he indorsed "acceptance" on the paper stated to Waterman, as agent of plaintiff in error, that such notification must be promptly given; it being insisted further that the letter of February 14, 1920, did not constitute such acceptance or notification of approval, and therefore defendant in error, on February 28, 1920, etc., had the right to withdraw or countermand, the unaccepted offer. Thompson testified in a manner to support the allegation of his statement to Waterman. There are other matters involved in the suit which must be ultimately determined, but the foregoing presents the issues now here for consideration.

The case was tried without a jury, and the judge found the facts in favor of defendant in error on all the issues indicated above, and upon other material issues. The judgment was affirmed by the Court of Civil Appeals, 269 S.W. 210.

We agree with the honorable Court of Civil Appeals upon the proposition that Mr. Engel's indorsement of "O.K." amounted to an approval "by an executive officer of the International Filter Company, at its office in Chicago," within the meaning of the so-called "proposal" of February 10th. The paper then became a "contract," according to its definitely expressed terms, and it became then, and thereafter it remained, an enforceable contract, in legal contemplation, unless the fact of approval by the filter company was required to be communicated to the other party and unless, in that event, the communication was not made.

We are not prepared to assent to the ruling that such communication was essential. There is no disposition to question the justice of the general rules stated in support of that holding, yet the existence of contractual capacity imports the right of the offerer to dispense with notification; and he does dispense with it "if the form of the offer," etc., "shows that this was not to be required." 9 Cyc. 270, 271; Carlill v. Carbolic Smoke Ball Co., 1 Q.B. 256 (and other references in note 6, 9 Cyc. 271). . . .

The Conroe Gin, Ice & Light Company executed the paper for the purpose of having it transmitted, as its offer, to the filter company at Chicago. It was so transmitted and acted upon. Its terms embrace the offer, and nothing else, and by its terms the question of notification must be judged, since those terms are not ambiguous.

The paper contains two provisions which relate to acceptance by the filter company. One is the declaration that the offer shall "become a contract . . . when approved by an executive officer of the International Filter Company, at its Chicago office." The other is thus stated: "This proposal is submitted for prompt acceptance, and unless so accepted is subject to change without notice." The first provision states "a particular mode of acceptance as sufficient to make the bargain binding," and the filter company (as stated above) followed "the indicated method of acceptance." When this was done, so the paper declares, the proposal "became a contract." The other provision does not in any way relate to a different method of acceptance by the filter company. Its sole reference is to the time within which the act of approval must be done; that is to say, there was to be a "prompt acceptance," else the offer might be changed "without notice." The second declaration merely required the approval thereinbefore stipulated for to be done promptly; if the act was so done, there is nothing in the second provision to militate against, or to conflict with, the prior declaration that, thereupon, the paper should become "a contract."

A holding that notification of that approval is to be deduced from the terms of the last-quoted clause is not essential in order to give it meaning or to dissolve ambiguity. On the contrary, such a construction of the two provisions would introduce a conflict, or ambiguity, where none exists in the language itself, and defeat the plainly expressed term wherein it is said that the proposal "becomes a contract . . . when approved by an executive officer." There is not anything in the language used to justify a ruling that this declaration must be wrenched from its obvious meaning and given one which would change both the locus and time prescribed for the meeting of the minds. The offerer said that the contract should be complete if approval be promptly given by the executive officer at Chicago; the court cannot properly restate the offer so as to make the offerer declare that a contract shall be made only when the approval shall have been promptly given at Chicago and that fact shall have been communicated to the offerer at Conroe. In our opinion, therefore, notice of the approval was not required.

The letter of February 14th, however, sufficiently communicated notice, if it was required.... Here the fact of acceptance in the particular method prescribed by the offerer is established aliunde the letter—Engel's "O.K." indorsed on the paper at Chicago did that. The form of notice, where notice is required, may be quite a different thing from the acceptance itself; the latter constitutes the meeting of the minds, the former merely relates to that pre-existent fact. The rules requiring such notice, it will be marked, do not make necessary any particular form or manner, unless the parties themselves have so pre-scribed. Whatever would convey by word or fair implication, notice of the fact would be sufficient. And this letter, we think, would clearly indicate to a reasonably prudent person, situated as was the defendant in error, the fact of previous approval by the filter company. If the Gin, Ice & Light Company had acted to change its position upon it as a notifica-tion of that fact, it must be plain that the filter company would have been estopped to deny its sufficiency....

We recommend that the judgment of the Court of Civil Appeals be reversed, and that the cause be remanded to that court for its disposition of all questions not passed upon it by it heretofore and properly before it for determination.

CURETON, C.J.[a] Judgment of the Court of Civil Appeals reversed, and cause remanded to the Court of Civil Appeals for further consideration by that court, as recommended by the Commission of Appeals.

NOTES

(1) *Forms to Compare.* Refer to the Case of the Power–Krug Combat, Note, p. 161 above. What similarities are there between the quotation of Power Engineering and the "proposal" of International Filter?

(2) *Control of Representatives.* If a seller is a large organization with salespersons who are expected to use a carefully prepared standard form for all contracts, there is a risk that the salespersons will make written changes on the form itself during their negotiations with customers. Does that suggest a use for a home-office-approval clause?[b] (Allowing time to check a buyer's credit is one function the clause may have.)

(3) *Notice.* Can you distinguish the position of International Filter from that of the offeree who merely says "I accept" to itself? See Restatement Second §§ 54, 56. For a case holding that the mere signing of the contract by the offeree was not acceptance even though the contract said that it would be binding "when ... signed by both parties," see Kendel v. Pontious, 261 So.2d 167 (Fla.1972).

a. Chief Justice of the Supreme Court of Texas.

b. See Restatement, Second, of Agency § 167 as to the effect of such language as:

"No agent of seller has authority to change the terms hereof."

In the opinion below, the Court of Civil Appeals reasoned that International Filter's letter of February 14 "did not constitute an acceptance of appellee's proposal, nor a notification of the acceptance made by Mr. Engel in Chicago." International Filter Co. v. Conroe Gin, Ice & Light Co., 269 S.W. 210, 215 (1925). It relied on Courtney Shoe Co. v. E.W. Curd & Son, 134 S.W. 146 (Ky.1911). In that case a manufacturer wrote, "Your order ... is at hand and will receive our prompt and careful attention," but sent a second letter eight days later rejecting the order on the ground that the salesman had made the sale without authority. It was held that this was not an acceptance.[c] Do you agree with the Court of Civil Appeals?

WHITE v. CORLIES & TIFT

Court of Appeals of New York, 1871.
46 N.Y. 467.

Appeal from judgment of the General Term of the first judicial district, affirming a judgment entered upon a verdict for plaintiff.

The action was for an alleged breach of contract.

The plaintiff was a builder, with his place of business in Fortieth Street, New York City.

The defendants were merchants at 32 Day Street.

In September, 1865, the defendants furnished the plaintiff with specifications for fitting up a suite of offices at 57 Broadway, and requested him to make an estimate of the cost of doing the work.

On September 28th, the plaintiff left his estimate with the defendants, and they were to consider upon it, and inform the plaintiff of their conclusions.

On the same day the defendants made a change in their specifications, and sent a copy of the same, so changed, to the plaintiff for his assent under his estimate, which he assented to by signing the same and returning it to the defendants.

On the day following the defendants' bookkeeper wrote the plaintiff the following note:

c. For a different result, see Hill's Inc. v. William B. Kessler Inc., 246 P.2d 1099 (Wash.1952). On May 16 a Seattle retailer ordered men's fall suits through the manufacturer's salesman on a printed form, supplied by the salesman, providing that the manufacturer was not bound until acceptance by one of its officers in New Jersey. On May 23 the manufacturer, by form letter advised the retailer that, "You may be assured of our very best attention to this order."

On July 18, however, after the time for placing orders for fall suits had passed, and at the instigation of one of the retailer's large competitors in Seattle, the manufacturer wrote to "cancel" the order. The retailer sued the manufacturer and had judgment in the trial court, which found that the manufacturer's form letter had been an acceptance. The Supreme Court of Washington affirmed. Are the cases distinguishable?

"New York, September 29.

"Upon an agreement to finish the fitting up of offices 57 Broadway in two weeks from date, you can begin at once.

"The writer will call again, probably between 5 and 6 this p.m.

"W.H.R.
For J.W. Corlies & Co.,
32 Dey St."

No reply to this note was ever made by the plaintiff; and on the next day the same was countermanded by a second note from the defendants.

Immediately on receipt of the note of September 29th, and before the countermand was forwarded, the plaintiff commenced a performance by the purchase of lumber and beginning work thereon.

And after receiving the countermand, the plaintiff brought this action for damages for a breach of contract.[a]

The court charged the jury as follows: "From the contents of this note which the plaintiff received, was it his duty to go down to Dey Street (meaning to give notice of assent), before commencing the work?

In my opinion it was not. He had a right to act upon this note and commence the job, and that was a binding contract between the parties."

To this defendants excepted. . . .

FOLGER, J. We do not think that the jury found, or that the testimony shows, that there was any agreement between the parties, before the written communication of the defendants of September 30th was received by the plaintiff. This note did not make an agreement. It was a proposition, and must have been accepted by the plaintiff before either party was bound, in contract, to the other. The only overt action which is claimed by the plaintiff as indicating on his part an acceptance of the offer, was the purchase of the staff necessary for the work, and commencing work, as we understand the testimony, upon that stuff.

We understand the rule to be, that where an offer is made by one party to another when they are not together, the acceptance of it by that other must be manifested by some appropriate act. It does not need that the acceptance shall come to the knowledge of the one making the offer before he shall be bound. But though the manifestation need not be brought to his knowledge before he becomes bound, he is not bound, if that manifestation is not put in a proper way to be in the usual course of events, in some reasonable time communicated to him. Thus a letter received by mail containing a proposal may be answered by letter by

---

a. Some additional facts, taken from the record on appeal of White's testimony may be helpful. Corlies' initial request was to have the office done in black walnut, a hard wood, within 21 days. White replied that he could not do the job in a hard wood in that time. Corlies then requested an estimate for white pine, a soft wood. White left the estimate on September 28, but did not indicate the time within which he would finish. Corlies made a change in the specifications to which White assented. There followed the letter of September 29 from Corlies. The countermand from Corlies said that it had decided to do the office in black walnut and requested an estimate for that in place of pine. Record, pp. 7–12.

mail, containing the acceptance. And in general, as soon as the answering letter is mailed, the contract is concluded. Though one party does not know of the acceptance, the manifestation thereof is put in the proper way of reaching him.

In the case in hand, the plaintiff determined to accept. But a mental determination not indicated by speech, or put in course of indication by act to the other party, is not an acceptance which will bind the other. Nor does an act, which in itself, is no indication of an acceptance, become such, because accompanied by an unevinced mental determination. Where the act uninterpreted by concurrent evidence of the mental purpose accompanying it, is as well referable to one state of facts as another, it is no indication to the other party of an acceptance, and does not operate to hold him to his offer.

Conceding that the testimony shows that the plaintiff did resolve to accept this offer, he did no act which indicated an acceptance of it to the defendants. He, a carpenter and builder, purchased stuff for the work. But it was stuff as fit for any other like work. He began work upon the stuff, but as he would have done for any other like work. There was nothing in his thought, formed but not uttered, or in his acts that indicated or set in motion an indication to the defendants of his acceptance of their offer, or which could necessarily result therein.

But the charge of the learned judge was fairly to be understood by the jury as laying down the rule to them, that the plaintiff need not indicate to the defendants his acceptance of their offer; and that the purchase of stuff and working on it after receiving the note, made a binding contract between the parties. In this we think the learned judge fell into error.

Judgment reversed, and new trial ordered.

NOTES

(1) *Means of Acceptance.* One who wants a contractor to do work ordinarily seeks a promise from the contractor. Can you see why? Assuming that Corlies's offer sought a promise, what means of acceptance by promise did it invite? What does the language of the offer and the nature of the transaction suggest? What answer if Corlies had written, "If you want to do the work, let me know by return mail and you can begin work at once"? See Restatement Second §§ 30, 50, 60, 62.

In argument on appeal, counsel for Corlies argued that "the defendants did not instruct the plaintiff to go to work *upon the receipt of the note;* but to go to work upon *an agreement to finish* the work in two weeks from date.... The question of time had not been agreed upon.... [T]he defendants had a right to put the question of assent at rest by demanding an agreement ... and thus avoid the doubts and difficulties of spelling out an assent from the acts of the plaintiff...." They also argued that "in case the plaintiff had broken off the performance after purchasing lumber, the defendants could have no redress...., as Mr. White could show that the purchase of lumber by him was a daily occurrence." (Appellant's Brief, pp. 3–4.) How much of this argument was accepted by the court?

(2) *Problem.* As a shopper in a supermarket was lifting a soft drink bottle from the shelf to place it in a shopping cart, the bottle exploded, seriously injuring the shopper. Was there a "contract for . . . sale" giving rise to an implied warranty of merchantability under UCC 2–314? See Barker v. Allied Supermarket, 596 P.2d 870 (Okla.1979).

EVER–TITE ROOFING CORPORATION v. GREEN, 83 So.2d 449 (La.App.1955). [The Greens wished to have Ever–Tite Roofing re-roof their residence, and signed a document that set out the work in detail and the price in monthly installments. This document was also signed by Ever–Tite's sales representative who, however, had no authority to bind Ever–Tite. The document contained a provision that, "This agreement shall become binding only upon written acceptance hereof, by the principal or authorized officer of the Contractor, or upon commencing performance of the work." As the Greens knew, since the work was to be done entirely on credit, it was necessary for Ever–Tite to get credit reports and obtain the approval of the lending institution that was to finance the contract. When this was accomplished, about nine days after execution of the agreement, Ever–Tite loaded two trucks and sent them with its workmen some distance to the Green's residence. Upon their arrival they found that others had been engaged two days before, and they were not permitted to work. Ever–Tite sued the Greens for breach of contract. From a judgment for defendant, plaintiff appealed.]

AYRES, JUDGE. . . . The basis of the judgment appealed was that defendants had timely notified plaintiff before "commencing performance of work". The trial court held that notice to plaintiff's workmen upon their arrival with the materials that defendants did not desire them to commence the actual work was sufficient and timely to signify their intention to withdraw from the contract. With this conclusion we find ourselves unable to agree. . . . Defendants evidently knew this work was to be processed through plaintiff's Shreveport office. The record discloses no unreasonable delay on plaintiff's part in receiving, processing or accepting the contract or in commencing the work contracted to be done. No time limit was specified in the contract within which it was to be accepted or within which the work was to be begun. It was nevertheless understood between the parties that some delay would ensue before the acceptance of the contract and the commencement of the work, due to the necessity of compliance with the requirements relative to financing the job through a lending agency. The evidence as referred to hereinabove shows that plaintiff proceeded with due diligence.[a] . . . [S]ince the contract did not specify the time within which it was to be accepted or within which the work was to have been com-

---

a. In an omitted part of the opinion the court set out several articles of the Louisiana Civil Code. Under article 1809, the most relevant here, the offeror "may therefore revoke his offer or proposition before such acceptance, but not without allowing such reasonable time as from the terms of the offer he has given, or from the circumstances of the case he may be supposed to have intended to give to the party to communicate his determination."

menced, a reasonable time must be allowed therefor in accordance with the facts and circumstances and the evident intention of the parties. A reasonable time is contemplated where no time is expressed. What is a reasonable time depends more or less upon the circumstances surrounding each particular case. The delays to process defendants' application were not unusual. The contract was accepted by plaintiff by the commencement of the performance of the work contracted to be done. This commencement began with the loading of the trucks with the necessary materials in Shreveport and transporting such materials and the workmen to defendants' residence. Actual commencement or performance of the work therefore began before any notice of dissent by defendants was given plaintiff. The proposition and its acceptance thus became a completed contract.

[Reversed.]

NOTE

Questions. Why did Ever–Tite use a home-office-approval clause? What was the purpose of the words "or upon commencing performance of the work"? Could the court have read this language more favorably to the Greens?

NOTICE IN UNILATERAL CONTRACTS

As White v. Corlies & Tift suggests, if an offeror proposes a "bilateral" contract and invites acceptance by means of a promise, it is ordinarily understood that the offeree must at least take steps to see that the promise is, in the words of the opinion in that case, "in some reasonable time communicated" to the offeror. See also Restatement Second § 56. (Can the *International Filter* and *Ever–Tite* cases be reconciled with this rule?)

The necessity of giving notice is less obvious if the offer proposes a "unilateral" contract and invites acceptance by means of performance and not a promise. A celebrated case is Carlill v. Carbolic Smoke Ball Co., [1893] 1 Q.B. 256 (Court of Appeal 1892). It arose out of the following advertisement: "£100 reward will be paid by the Carbolic Smoke Ball Company to any person who contracts the increasing epidemic influenza, colds or any disease caused by taking cold, after having used the ball three times daily for two weeks according to the printed directions supplied with each ball. £1000 is deposited with the Alliance Bank, Regent Street shewing our sincerity in the matter. . . ." On the faith of this advertisement, Carlill used one of the balls as directed. When she contracted influenza, she sued the Company and was awarded £100 damages. The Company's appeal was dismissed. As Lindley, L.J., explained, the advertisement was not "a mere puff" but an offer under which "the reward is offered to any person who contracts the epidemic or other disease within a reasonable time after having used the smoke ball." The fact that she had not notified the Company of her acceptance was not fatal to her claim.[a] According to Bowen, L.J., "One cannot doubt that, as an ordinary rule of law, an acceptance of an offer made ought to be notified to the person who makes the offer, in order that the two minds may come together.... But there is this clear gloss to be made upon that doctrine, that as notification of acceptance is required for the benefit of the person who makes the offer, the person who makes the offer may dispense with notice to himself, if he thinks it desirable to do so, and I suppose there can be no doubt that where a person in an offer made by him to another person, expressly or impliedly intimates a particular mode of acceptance as sufficient to make the bargain binding, it is only necessary for the other person to whom such offer is made to follow the indicated method of acceptance; and if the person making the offer, expressly or impliedly intimates in his offer that it will be sufficient to act on the proposal without communicating acceptance of it to himself, performance of the condition is a sufficient acceptance without notification.... Now, if that is the law, how are we to find out whether the person who makes the offer does intimate that notification of acceptance will not be necessary in order to constitute a binding bargain? In many cases you look to the offer itself. In many cases you extract from the character of the transaction that notification is not required, and in the advertisement cases it seems to me to follow as an inference to be drawn from the transaction itself that a person is not to notify his acceptance of the offer before he performs the condition, but that if he performs the condition notification is dispensed with. It seems to me that from the point of view of common sense no other idea could be entertained." [b]

NOTES

(1) *A Guaranty Case.* A leading American case on the necessity of notice of acceptance of a unilateral offer is Bishop v. Eaton, 37 N.E. 665 (Mass.1894). In that case Frank Eaton, in Nova Scotia, had written to Bishop, in Illinois, that if he would help his brother, Harry Eaton, to get money, "I will see that it is paid." Bishop did help Harry get money by signing his note as surety when he got a loan. When Harry did not repay the loan, Bishop did, and sued Frank on his promise. The court thought that this was a case in which notice should have been given, since the loan was made in Illinois and Frank was in Nova Scotia. "Ordinarily there is no occasion to notify the offeror of the acceptance of such an offer, for the doing of the act is a sufficient acceptance, and the promisor knows that he is bound when he sees that action has been taken on the faith of his offer. But if the act is of such a kind that knowledge of it will not quickly come

a. Was the acceptance of the Carbolic Smoke Ball Company's offer: (1) the purchase of the smoke ball; (2) its use in accordance with directions; (3) the plaintiff's contracting influenza; or (4) all three? Which of these acts was bargained for? Recall that a promise may be conditional, so that its performance becomes due only if a specified event occurs. See Note 2, p. 117 above. Was there a conditional promise in the Carbolic Smoke Ball case?

b. For the background of the Carbolic Smoke Ball case, including pictures of the advertisement, the smoke ball, and Mrs. Carlill, see Simpson, Quackery and Contract Law: The Case of the Carbolic Smoke Ball, 14 J.Legal Stud. 345 (1985). The author notes that Mrs. Carlill "died on March 10, 1942, at the age of ninety-six years, principally, as her death certificate records, of old age. The other cause noted by her medical man, Dr. Joseph M. Yarman, was influenza." Id. at 389.

to the promisor, the promisee is bound to give him notice of his acceptance within a reasonable time after doing that which constitutes the acceptance." However, the court concluded that notice had been given.

(2) *Consequence of the Requirement.* Would notice have been required in these two cases under the rule stated in Restatement Second § 54? What is the consequence of a requirement of notice? Take the facts of Bishop v. Eaton. Such a requirement can be framed so that Bishop does not accept Frank's offer until he both signs Harry's note and sends the notice to Frank. Or it can be framed so that Bishop accepts Frank's offer when he signs the note, but Frank's obligation is discharged if Bishop does not send a notice within a reasonable time. Would it make any difference? Suppose (putting the case in a modern context) that the day after Bishop signs the note, and before he has sent the notice to Frank, Frank telephones Bishop and tells him that he revokes. Is the revocation effective? See Restatement Second § 54; UCC 2–206(2); Dole, Notice Requirements of Guaranty Contracts, 62 Mich.L.Rev. 57 (1963).

Introductory Note to *Allied Steel*

The following case concerns an "indemnity" provision in a purchase order issued by the Ford Motor Company. An indemnity agreement is one whereby a party undertakes contingent liability for a loss threatening another. Agreements of this kind are commonplace, as illustrated here and elsewhere in this book.[a] They are regularly enforced, even when the loss envisaged is one attributable to fault on the part of the promisee (indemnitee). Often it is difficult, when one or both parties to a contract incurs a liability by a third party, to ascribe the loss to one party or the other. If they have effectively agreed on indemnification, it may not be necessary to address that problem. Moreover, to concentrate anticipated liabilities on one of the parties may reduce the aggregate cost of risk management: it may be enough, for example, for the indemnitor to insure against the liability rather than for both parties to buy insurance.

ALLIED STEEL AND CONVEYORS, INC. v. FORD MOTOR CO.

United States Court of Appeals, Sixth Circuit, 1960.
277 F.2d 907.

[On August 19, 1955, Ford ordered machinery from Allied on Ford's printed form, Purchase Order No. 15145, which provided that if Allied

a. The following term appeared in the "quotation" sent by Power Engineering, partly set out on p. 162 above):

15. INDEMNITY: Purchaser agrees to defend, protect, indemnify and hold harmless Seller, its agents, successors and assigns, against any and all claims for personal injury, property, consequential or special damages arising from or resulting from the manner or location of installation of Seller's product by Purchaser in Purchaser's equipment, defects in equipment in which Seller's product is installed by Purchaser, or installation in equipment exceeding product's design, speed, and load specifications, or the use of any of Seller's products in combination with unsuitable goods or products not furnished by Seller, or from unauthorized modification or alteration of Seller's products, including all costs of defense and attorney's fees.

was required to perform work of installation on Ford's premises, Allied would be responsible for all damages caused by the negligence of its own employees. Attached to and made a part of the Purchase Order was another printed form, Form 3618, which included a much broader indemnity provision requiring Allied to assume full responsibility not only for the negligence of its own employees, but also for the negligence of Ford's employees in connection with Allied's work, but this provision was marked "VOID." The Purchase Order was accepted by Allied and the contract performed.

Subsequently, on July 26, 1956, Ford submitted to Allied Amendment No. 2 to Purchase Order 15145, by which Ford proposed to purchase additional machinery. The Amendment provided:

> This purchase order agreement is not binding until accepted. Acceptance should be executed on acknowledgment copy which should be returned to buyer.

The copy of Ford's Form 3618 attached to the Amendment was identical to that attached to Purchase Order No. 15145, but the broad indemnity provision of Form 3618 was not marked "VOID." The acknowledgment copy of the Amendment was executed by Allied on November 10 and reached Ford on November 12, 1956. At that time Allied had already begun installation and on September 5, 1956, Hankins, an employee of Allied, had sustained personal injuries as a result of the negligence of Ford's employees in connection with Allied's work. Hankins later brought suit against Ford and Ford in turn impleaded Allied, relying on the indemnity provision of Form 3618. The trial resulted in a verdict for Hankins against Ford and for Ford against Allied. Allied's motion for judgment notwithstanding the verdict was denied and judgment was entered against it. Allied appealed.]

MILLER, DISTRICT JUDGE... Allied first says that the contractual provisions evidenced by Amendment No. 2 were not in effect at the time of the Hankins injury because it had not been accepted at that time by Allied in the formal manner expressly required by the amendment itself. It argues that a binding acceptance of the amendment could be effected only by Allied's execution of the acknowledgment copy of the amendment and its return to Ford.

With this argument we cannot agree. It is true that an offeror may prescribe the manner in which acceptance of his offer shall be indicated by the offeree, and an acceptance of the offer in the manner prescribed will bind the offeror. And it has been held that if the offeror prescribes an exclusive manner of acceptance, an attempt on the part of the offeree to accept the offer in a different manner does not bind the offeror *in the absence of a meeting of the minds on the altered type of acceptance.* Venters v. Stewart, Ky.App., 261 S.W.2d 444, 446; Shortridge v. Ghio, Mo.App., 253 S.W.2d 838, 845. On the other hand, if an offeror merely suggests a permitted method of acceptance, other methods of acceptance are not precluded. Restatement, Contracts, Sec. 61; Williston on Contracts, Third Ed. Secs. 70, 76. Moreover, it is equally well settled that if the offer requests a return promise and the offeree without making the promise actually does or tenders what he was requested to promise to do, there is a contract if such performance is completed or tendered within the time allowable for accepting by making a promise. In such a case a tender operates as a promise to render complete performance. Restatement, Contracts, Sec. 63; Williston on Contracts, Third Ed. Sec. 75.[a]

Applying these principles to the case at bar, we reach the conclusion, first, that execution and return of the acknowledgment copy of Amendment No. 2 was merely a suggested method of acceptance and did not preclude acceptance by some other method; and, second, that the offer was accepted and a binding contract effected when Allied, with Ford's knowledge, consent and acquiescence, undertook performance of the work called for by the amendment. The only significant provision, as we view the amendment, was that it would not be binding until it was accepted by Allied. This provision was obviously for the protection of Ford, Albright v. Stegeman Motorcar Co., 168 Wis. 557, 170 N.W. 951, 952, 19 A.L.R. 463, and its import was that Ford would not be bound by the amendment unless Allied agreed to all of the conditions specified therein. The provision for execution and return of the acknowledgement copy, as we construe the language used, was not to set forth an exclusive method of acceptance but was merely to provide a simple and convenient method by which the assent of Allied to the contractual provisions of the amendment could be indicated. The primary object of Ford was to have the work performed by Allied upon the terms prescribed in the amendment, and the mere signing and return of an acknowledgment copy of the amendment before actually undertaking the work itself cannot be regarded as an essential condition to completion of a binding contract.

It is well settled that acceptance of an offer by part performance in accordance with the terms of the offer is sufficient to complete the contract....

Other authorities are to the effect that the acceptance of a contract may be implied from acts of the parties. Malooly v. York Heating & Vent. Corp., 270 Mich. 240, 253, 258 N.W. 622; and may be shown by proving acts done on the faith of the order, including shipment of the goods ordered, Petroleum Products Distributing Co. v. Alton Tank Line, 165 Iowa 398, 403, 146 N.W. 52. Cf. Texas Co. v. Hudson, 155 La. 966, 971, 99 So. 714, 716. It would seem necessarily to follow that an offeree who has unjustifiably led the offeror to believe that he had acquired a contractual right, should not be allowed to assert an actual intent at variance with the meaning of his acts.

---

a. It is curious that the court relies, even as an alternative ground, on the rule that full performance or a tender of full performance may operate as an acceptance of an offer that invites acceptance by a promise only. Allied had not fully performed and could not, since its performance was to extend over a substantial period of time, have tendered full performance. This rule is, perhaps fortunately, of limited practical importance and is not carried forward by the Restatement Second (see §§ 53(1), 62). See Note, 52 So.Cal.L.Rev. 1917 (1979). Of course the offer may give the offeree a choice between acceptance by promise and acceptance by performance, but that is not what the court suggests here.

It has been argued on behalf of Allied, by way of analogy, that Ford could have revoked the order when Allied began installing the machinery without first having executed its written acceptance. If this point should be conceded, cf. Venters v. Stewart, supra, it would avail Allied nothing. For, after Allied began performance by installing the machinery called for, and Ford acquiesced in the acts of Allied and accepted the benefits of the performance, Ford was estopped to object and could not thereafter be heard to complain that there was no contract. Sparks v. Mauk, 170 Cal. 122, 148 P. 926....

Affirmed.

NOTES

(1) *Case Comparison.* Can the *Ever–Tite* and *Allied Steel* cases be distinguished from White v. Corlies & Tift? What is the critical language of the offer in each case? What reason did Ford have for putting the clause on its form? See the Note, p. 161 above, on the "Battle of the Forms." Consider, in this connection, the 1970 revision of Ford's purchase order, which reads:

ACCEPTANCE—Unless otherwise provided herein, it is understood and agreed that the written acceptance by Seller of this purchase order or the commencement of any work or the performance of any services hereunder by Seller (including the commencement of any work or the performance of any services with respect to samples) shall constitute acceptance by Seller of this purchase order and of all of its terms and conditions, and that such acceptance is expressly limited to such terms and conditions.

(2) *Tying One's Tongue.* Refer to the Case of the Power–Krug Combat, p. 161 above. In that case Krug's purchase order contained additional language much like that of Ford's revised "acceptance" term—although it said: "We prefer that you accept this order by signing the acknowledgement copy and returning it to us...." Krug continued by saying that any reference it might make to a communication by Power "shall not be deemed to be an acceptance of any terms and conditions therein...." Effective move? Would it have been possible for Power to counter it by inserting similar language in its quotation?

(3) *Boulton v. Jones—Reprise.* Consider again this case, stated in the Note at p. 163 above. If Boulton had sent with the goods a notice that he had bought out Brocklehurst's inventory, and Jones had taken delivery of the goods, would Jones have been estopped to say that there was no contract? How else might one argue that Boulton could recover the price?

(4) *The Case of the Church's Counteroffer.* An insurance company providing coverage for church properties wants to collect as much as possible from a customer owing premiums for policies that have expired or have been cancelled. It is willing to reinstate another policy ("multi-peril"), but only if it receives a premium payment of $292.75 on that policy by July 20. The insurer has so notified the customer, the Mount Calvary Baptist Church ("MC"). "Uncertified personal checks will *not* be accepted," the notice said. On July 18 the insurer receives MC's uncertified check for $292.75. Is it possible for the insurer to use the check to pay for expired policies, without granting multi-peril coverage? This question was addressed in Church Mutual Ins. Co. v. Mount Calvary Baptist Church, 172 B.R. 880 (N.D.Ill.1994).

Further facts in the case are as follows. On the day the check was received the insurer's billing supervisor, Kleinschmidt, deposited the check and sent a letter to MC indicating that coverage under the multi-peril policy would not be provided. Kleinschmidt must have known, "or at the very least suspected," (it was later found) that the check was meant to pay for the multi-peril policy.[a] On the 20th, when MC called to protest, it was told that nothing could be done to change the outcome. Must the insurer pay for fire damage to MC's building, occurring soon after that? Two judges ruling on this question reached opposing conclusions.

Might it matter that Kleinschmidt deposited the check just before she wrote to MC, rather than the reverse?

(5) *Problem.* The Chicago Medical School distributed a bulletin for prospective students stating that it selected applicants "on the basis of scholarship, character, and motivation," after evaluation "on the basis of academic achievement" and the like. Robert Steinberg received a bulletin, applied for admission, and paid the School a $15 fee. He has been rejected and wants to sue on the ground that in breach of a contract with him the School failed to evaluate his application according to the stated criteria. Assuming that the School evaluates applicants according to its expectation of large donations, can you state a theory of contract liability? Who made the offer? See Steinberg v. Chicago Medical School, 371 N.E.2d 634 (Ill.1977).

SHIPMENT OF GOODS AS ACCEPTANCE

Is a seller's shipment of goods, in response to a buyer's order, an acceptance? The question usually arises when the buyer attempts to revoke an order after the seller has placed the goods on board a carrier in response to the order. UCC 2–206(1)(b) provides that such an order "for prompt or current shipment shall be construed as inviting acceptance either by a prompt promise to ship or by the prompt or current shipment of conforming or non-conforming goods." Under the Code the buyer's revocation comes too late if the seller has promptly shipped.

But the question can arise in another way. Suppose that the seller ships non-conforming goods. Has the seller bound itself to deliver goods that conform to the buyer's order? The answer under the Code must be that the seller has. This is clear from the provision that the seller can avoid this result if it "seasonably notifies the buyer that the shipment is offered only as an accommodation to the buyer." If the seller follows this course, shipment is not an acceptance of the buyer's offer but is a counter-offer to the buyer. What means of acceptance does that counter-offer invite? See generally Restatement Second §§ 32, 62, which are not limited to contracts for the sale of goods.

NOTES

(1) *Preparation for Shipment of Goods as Acceptance.* What if a buyer attempts to revoke an order when the seller has incurred expense in preparing to

---

a. In point of fact, the check was larger than $292.75; it included charges for two other policies that the insurer had offered to continue. According to the trial court, if Kleinschmidt had called up the MC account on her computer screen, and had done a simple addition, she would have seen a "miraculous" correspondence between the amount of the check and the cost of the three policies.

ship the goods but has not actually shipped them? In Doll & Smith v. A & S Sanitary Dairy Co., 211 N.W. 230 (Iowa 1926), the buyer, through the seller's agent, ordered advertising material from the seller. After the seller had paid its agent his commission and had incurred some expense, the buyer sent the seller a cancellation of the order. The court held that since the seller had not sent the buyer an acceptance of the order, the revocation was effective. Can this decision be reconciled with the *Ever–Tite* case, above?

(2) *Problem.* Filter Company, in Chicago, sends to Southern Sales, Inc. (SS) a proposed agreement that would make SS the exclusive distributor of Filter's water softeners, for a time, in a designated area. One paragraph reads: "This Agreement is subject to acceptance at Filter's home office in Chicago." A representative of each party signs the document. Although the agent signing for Filter has authority to bind it to such a contract, no signing occurs in Chicago. Assume that the agreement is ineffective. As support for that conclusion see Wells, Waters & Gases, Inc. v. Air Products & Chemicals, Inc., 19 F.3d 157 (4th Cir.1994). Assume also, however, that after the signing Filter ships to SS a quantity of water softeners and that SS takes delivery. When sending a check for the goods, SS announces its objection to a provision of the agreement about inventory shortages. If Filter wants to have SS for a distributor and to bind SS to the inventory-shortage term, what would you advise it to do? Sign the proposed agreement at its home office? Return the check?

Taking a cue from *Allied Steel,* above, you may suppose that a further signing is unnecessary. In *Wells, Waters & Gases,* above, on facts much like those assumed, the trial court took its cue from UCC 2–206(1)(b). Was that wrong? The appellate court rejected that basis for decision, but agreed with the trial court's conclusion that the distributor (Wells, Waters) was bound by the terms of the agreement.

(3) *Notice as a Condition.* Even where the offeree's performance, in whole or in part, amounts in itself to acceptance, the offeree may be expected to notify the offeror of acceptance. UCC 2–206(2) imposes such a requirement, stating that the consequence of the requirement is that the "offeror who is not notified of acceptance within a reasonable time may treat the offer as having lapsed before acceptance." A more conventional formulation of the consequence is that notice within a reasonable time is an implied condition of the offeror's duty to perform under the contract that is formed by the acceptance. If the offeree does not give notice within a reasonable time, the offeror's performance under the contract does not become due and the offeror's duty is discharged. Note that notice is not part of the acceptance under either formulation, so that the offeror is bound even before notice is given, as long as it is subsequently given within a reasonable time.

SILENCE NOT ORDINARILY ACCEPTANCE

The general rule is that silence alone is not acceptance. "So fundamental is the tenet ... that, even as the master of the offer, the offeror is powerless to alter the rule." 1 Farnsworth § 3.15. The offeror who appends to an offer, "Unless I hear from you within 48 hours, you will be deemed to have accepted my offer," cannot hold the offeree who fails to reject. The rule, along with some real or apparent exceptions to it, is stated in Restatement Second § 69.

In Hobbs v. Massasoit Whip Co., 33 N.E. 495 (Mass.1893), however, the court concluded that a silent retention amounted to an acceptance. A seller sued for $108.50, the price of 2,350 eelskins that he had sent to the buyer, a manufacturer of whips. Holmes wrote: "The plaintiff was not a stranger to the defendant, even if there was no contract between them. He had sent eelskins in the same way four or five times before, and they had been accepted and paid for.... [S]ending them [imposed] on the defendant a duty to act about them; and silence on its part, coupled with a retention of the skins for an unreasonable time, might be found by the jury to warrant the plaintiff in assuming that they were accepted, and thus to amount to an acceptance." What, beyond mere silence, was there in this case?

But what if the parties are reversed and it is the *buyer* who asserts that the seller has accepted by silent retention of *the buyer's order*? American Bronze Corp. v. Streamway Products, 456 N.E.2d 1295 (Ohio App.1982), is such a case. For over twenty years Streamway had called in orders to American by telephone and followed them up with written purchase orders, at which time American would begin production. When American refused to fill three orders, Streamway claimed damages and, from a denial of its claim, appealed. The Ohio Court of Appeals reversed and remanded, citing UCC 2–204(1). "The filling of these orders in this manner as a regular practice constituted a valid acceptance and thus created a binding contract.... Absent a notice of rejection Streamway would be justified in believing that American had indeed begun production." What, beyond mere silence, was there in this case?

NOTES

(1) *The Case of the Bean Buyer's Silence.* Jacks Bean Company stores, buys, and processes beans delivered to it by growers. For storage it makes a per diem charge. All the beans in Jacks's bins are considered stored unless a grower has, within 30 days of making delivery, made a sale-price agreement with Jacks. The processing of beans goes forward in any event. The prices Jacks will pay are posted at least once a day and distributed as news for farmers.

During September of 1987 the plaintiff-grower (Heiting) delivered twelve loads of beans to Jacks, receiving receipts ("scale tickets") showing the goods to be of top grade. On September 30, in a telephone conversation with a Jacks representative, Heiting was given to understand (he said) that the beans were sold at the then per-bag price of $19. But the firm's local manager told Heiting (he said) only that he would "call in" Heiting's direction to the firm's headquarters in Colorado, and that there was limited buying.

By October, when Heiting had discovered that Jacks had not bought the beans, the price was $18. Heiting made no attempt to sell at that price. The beans were later sold for $15 a bag.

The Heiting partners sued Jacks for breach of contract. The trial court gave summary judgment for Jacks, and Heiting appealed. *Held:* Reversed. Joseph Heiting and Sons v. Jacks Bean Co., 463 N.W.2d 817 (Neb.1990) (the case settled). The court said that the partnership had "offered to sell its beans at the posted price on September 30, 1987. Mr. Heiting was never informed of acceptance or rejection of the offer. When Heiting eventually did sell its beans to Jacks in March 1988, the purchase was not verified. Heiting was not informed of the acceptance or rejection of the offer. Thus, in March, the acceptance was by silence. Whether the offer was accepted in September by silence or inaction is an issue of material fact as to the existence of the alleged oral contract...." Does the rule of this case differ from that of Hobbs v. Massasoit Whip Co., above? If so, how?

(2) *Review Problem.* In the foregoing case the court said that Jacks's posting of a price on its grading-room wall was not an offer, but was "merely an offer to negotiate directed at the bean growers." Would that necessarily be so if Jacks had repeatedly and consistently paid the posted price when growers gave it "sell" signals?

(3) *Unsolicited Merchandise.* A persistent consumer complaint concerns the practice of sending unsolicited merchandise, often coupled with the suggestion that the recipient will be liable for the price if it is not returned. As you might suppose, this suggestion is not the law. Although the recipient who lays the merchandise on a shelf and does not use it incurs no liability, the practice is at best irritating and at worst deceptive. A number of states have enacted statutes dealing with it. See, e.g., N.Y.Gen.Bus.L. § 396–2a. Federal laws regulating the mails also restrict such practices.

Marketing programs of the book-club type depend on a subscriber's agreement that merchandise not specifically ordered will be paid for in the absence of a direction to the contrary. Is it significant that these arrangements "typically provide some up-front benefits to the offeree," such as an introductory bonus, and place mailing costs on the offeror?[a] See Katz, The Strategic Structure of Offer and Acceptance: Game Theory and the Law of Contract Formation, 89 Mich.L.Rev. 215, 264–65, 271–72 (1990).

(4) *The Rationale.* Professor Katz suggests, in the article just cited, an efficiency argument for the offeree's "right to be let alone." More simply, it might be thought that freedom *from* contract is a more important ideal than is freedom *of* contract. See in Patterson, An Apology for Consideration, 58 Colum.L.Rev. 929, 948ff (1958). See also Sheets v. Teddy's Frosted Foods, p. 645 below ("private persons have the right not to enter into contracts").

(5) *The Case of the Velvet Glove.* In City of Calhoun v. North Georgia Electric Membership Corp., 443 S.E.2d 469 (Ga.1994), the court concluded that the City had the authority to impose a charge on North Georgia for continuing to use the streets of the City to serve customers with electric power. The City had, by ordinance, proposed a street-franchise fee: 4% of sales. The ordinance granted the utility 90 days within which to give its written acceptance of the franchise and fee, "so as to form a contract" between it and the City. North Georgia announced that it would never pay the fee; but it continued to serve customers through its lines on city streets. When sued by the City, North Georgia contended that the City had no authority to impose a franchise fee on it. North Georgia won a summary judgment and the City appealed. *Held:* Affirmed. The City had no contract claim, owing to its requirement of an express acceptance. Nor did it have a quasi-contract claim: "The City cannot rely upon its own unilateral act of continuing to allow its streets to be used and occupied as evidence of an enforceable implied promise ... to pay a franchise fee which [North Georgia] has expressly rejected." Was the City's loss of revenue a suitable sanction for its error of law?

a. See Use of Negative Option Plans by Sellers in Commerce, 16 C.F.R. § 425.1 (1973), for a regulation requiring that subscribers be given at least ten days in which to instruct the seller not to mail the offered merchandise.

Compare Brophy v. City of Joliet, 144 N.E.2d 816 (Ill.App.1957). In that case the City received Brophy's proposal to purchase an issue of the City's bonds, concluding with a space for the mayor's signature, under a line reading (as abridged): "Accepted for the City by a resolution passed this _____ day of _____, 195__, which is hereby acknowledged." The city council passed a resolution authorizing the mayor to sign the plaintiff's "contract"; but at a later meeting, before the mayor signed, the council voted to sell the bonds to another firm. Judgment was given for the City in Brophy's action against it. On appeal, *held:* Affirmed.

SECTION 4.   TERMINATION OF THE POWER OF ACCEPTANCE

After a party has made an offer, conferring on another the power of acceptance, that power can be terminated (1) by lapse of the offer, (2) by its revocation, (3) by its rejection, or (4) by the offeror's death or incapacity. (Note that it is *offerors* who revoke offers; it is *offerees* who either accept or reject them.)

This Section begins with lapse—the expiration of the period within which an offer can be accepted. Instances are given of offers that declare a limit of time for acceptance. If, however, the offeror neglects to state a period for acceptance, when does it become too late for the offeree to accept?

Revocation and rejection are to be considered next. The primary rules, in common-law countries are that (a) an offeror can terminate an ordinary offer, at any time before it has been accepted, by revoking it; and (b) a rejection puts an end to an ordinary offer.

Attention then turns to option contracts and "firm offers," as distinguished from ordinary offers. These arrangements embody offers that are—for a time—not subject to revocation. An irrevocable offer is the defining characteristic of an option contract. (The effect of a rejection of such an offer is to be considered.)

Two further topics round out the Section: death and incapacity as terminating events, and the timing of an acceptance that is dispatched by mail, messenger, or electronic means.

LAPSE OF AN OFFER

After some period of time, an offer lapses. If no period is specified in the offer, it lapses after a reasonable time. What is a reasonable time depends, of course, on the circumstances. Take an offer to buy or sell. If the subject matter undergoes rapid fluctuation in price, as is often the case for goods, this will shorten the time. If the subject matter does not undergo rapid fluctuations in price, as is generally the case for land, this will lengthen the time. The following two cases illustrate some other factors used in determining what is a reasonable time for this purpose.

In Akers v. J.B. Sedberry, 286 S.W.2d 617 (Tenn.App.1955), Akers, while in a conference with his employer, Sedberry, orally offered to resign. Sedberry ignored his offer and continued the conference. A few days later she wired her acceptance. He sued for breach of contract, and a decree in his favor was affirmed. "Ordinarily, an offer made by one to another in a face to face conversation is deemed to continue only to the close of their conversation, and cannot be accepted thereafter." But cf. Caldwell v. E.F. Spears & Sons, 216 S.W. 83 (Ky.1919).

In Loring v. City of Boston, 7 Metc. (Mass.) 409 (1844), the City of Boston had run in the daily papers an advertisement offering a $1,000 reward for the apprehension and conviction of any person setting fire to any building within the city limits. The advertisements continued for about a week in May, 1837, and did not appear again. In January, 1841, there was a fire in Boston, and Loring, with the reward in mind, pursued the incendiary to New York, arrested him, returned him to Boston, had him indicted and prosecuted, produced evidence that convicted him, and then sued the city for the reward. There was evidence that fire alarms had been frequent before the advertisements but much less so from that time until the end of 1841. Loring sued to recover the reward. The Supreme Judicial Court of Massachusetts denied recovery. Since the purposes of such an offer are to excite the vigilance of the public and, perhaps, to alarm offenders, the offer of the reward must be notorious in order to be effective. Three years and eight months was not a reasonable time under the circumstances. "In that length of time, the exigency under which it was made having passed, it must be presumed to have been forgotten by most of the officers and citizens of the community, and cannot be presumed to have been before the public as an actuating motive to vigilance and exertion on this subject; nor could it justly and reasonably have been so understood by the plaintiffs." But cf. Carr v. Mahaska County Bankers Ass'n, 269 N.W. 494 (Iowa 1936).

NOTES

(1) *Problem.* On behalf of a motorist (M) and M's auto insurance company, A submits an offer to B, in writing. A is the attorney for the company. B is the attorney for C, who suffered a road injury and claims that M's negligence caused it. The offer is to pay C $25,000 in full satisfaction of C's claim against M.

Negotiations over this claim have continued for many months. Indeed, if the claim is not brought to court within a month it seems likely that C will be barred from suing by a statute of limitations. Six weeks elapse without a response to the offer. Then B, acting for C, sends a mailgram to A which purports to accept the offer. What might lead one to think the "acceptance" is too late?

In a contract action based on facts much like these the trial court gave summary judgment for the claimant. Appealing, the insurer referred to a two-year period of limitation for bringing personal-injury actions. But the court observed that such a period is not inflexible: excusing circumstances may justify a later suit.[a]   The court relied on comment b to Restatement Second § 41: "In general, the question is what time would be thought satisfactory to the offeror by a reasonable man in the position of the offeree."   On that basis, what result? See Vaskie v. West American Ins. Co., 556 A.2d 436 (Pa.Super.1989).   (What suggestions might be made to the attorneys—A and B—about their professional conduct? [b])

(2) *Counting the Offers.*   In the case last cited the offer to pay $25,000 was not a fresh one.   The insurer had made an earlier written offer of that amount. The message that the plaintiff's attorney responded to followed further fruitless telephone negotiations, and took the form, "offer will remain $25,000."   Considering the entire sequence of events, how many offers do you count—one?   two? more?

In Newman v. Schiff, 778 F.2d 460 (8th Cir.1985), the plaintiff was a tax lawyer who claimed $100,000 for supplying citations to the Internal Revenue Code in response to a challenge made on a TV call-in show.   The challenge had been made in the evening, on "Nightwatch"; the plaintiff had learned of it from watching a brief segment that was rebroadcast on CBS Morning News.   (He called a number at CBS different from the one announced on Nightwatch for call-ins.)   If the plaintiff thought that two offers had been made, how good was he at counting offers?   Would the problem have been different if he had seen the challenge on a VCR tape made at his home?

(3) *Questions.*   What is the effect of an expression of acceptance that arrives too late to operate as an acceptance?   Can the offeror choose simply to disregard the delay and treat the message as an acceptance?   Or is it a counter-offer, so that no contract eventuates unless the original offeror, in turn, expresses acceptance?

Consider these questions in relation to the problem in Note 1, assuming that the "acceptance" came too late.   Assume also that the claimant sued the motorist for (say) $50,000—somehow overcoming the statute-of-limitations defense—and that the defense was based on a supposed settlement at $25,000.

REVOCATION AND REJECTION

Revocation.   Grotius, the great seventeenth-century Dutch jurist, favored the rule that prevails at the common law: an offer is freely revocable.   But the opposing rule has its adherents.   In Germany and some other civil-law countries an offer is irrevocable for a reasonable time unless the offeror expresses a different intention.   See 1 Schlesinger (ed.), Formation of Contracts: A Study of the Common Core of Legal Systems 780–83 (1968).   Which rule seems preferable?   One disadvantage of the German rule is that during the period of irrevocability, the offeree can take advantage of changing economic conditions to speculate at the expense of the offeror.   Although Germany and the other countries that have this rule have experienced much greater economic upheavals than has the United States, they have been able to live with the

---

a. See, for example, Prudential–LMI Commercial Ins. v. Superior Court, 798 P.2d 1230 (Cal.1990).

⟩me circumstantial detail about e R. Summers & R. Hillman,

Contract and Related Obligation (2d ed. 1992) 416–17.   The company's attorney, we are told, recommended that settlement offers thereafter include terminal dates.

rule, at least in part, because it can easily be avoided by expressly reserving the power to revoke or providing that the communication is not an offer at all. The extent to which the offeror in the United States can avoid the common law rule by expressly relinquishing the power to revoke is discussed at p. 209 below.

When is a communication a revocation? In Hoover Motor Express Co. v. Clements Paper Co., 241 S.W.2d 851 (Tenn.1951), Hoover had made an offer to Clements to buy real estate. Although the offer had been made on November 19 and Williams, Clements' vice-president, had been authorized in December to accept it, he had not done so by January 13. On that day Williams telephoned Hoover and "told him that we were ready to go through with it and I would like to discuss it with him." Hoover replied, "Well, I don't know if we are ready. We have not decided, we might not want to go through with it." Clements later sent an acceptance, but the court held that it was too late. Hoover's remark on the telephone "brought home to Williams that Hoover no longer consented to the transaction."

Compare the court's treatment of the claimed revocation in this case with the courts' treatment of the claimed offers in Owen v. Tunison and in Harvey v. Facey, above. Are they consistent?

Rejection. There is no doubt that rejection of an offer by the offeree terminates the power of acceptance so that the offeree cannot thereafter accept the offer. But why should this be so? It can be argued that it would be unjust to allow an offeree who has rejected an offer to reconsider and accept if the offeror has already substantially relied on the rejection. But how can this explain the application of the rule where no reliance by the offeror has been shown? Does the discussion of the enforceability of exchanges of promises at p. 116 above suggest an answer?

OPTION CONTRACTS—I

The opinion that follows speaks of an "option" held by a tenant in a shopping mall—Toys, Inc., the plaintiff—to renew a five-year lease. A promise made by an offeror that effectively limits the offeror's power to revoke is called an option, or "option contract." Usually an option contract expresses, directly or indirectly, a fixed period within which the offeree must exercise, or "pick up," the option. (What is often called *exercising* an option is very nearly the same as accepting an offer, as the opinion shows.) The option contract between Toys, Inc. and the shopping-mall owner required, as will be seen, that Toys act within four years of the inception of the lease.

Financial news media report daily the prices of many option contracts, privileging the holders to buy corporate stocks (a hundred shares per contract), exercisable over periods as long as twenty months. The prices are volatile. On a day when the market price of a stock increases by only 2%, the price of a short-term option to purchase ("call") the shares might easily double.[a] The *stock* purchase price named in the contract may be close to the price of the underlying shares when the contract is issued, yet may come to seem very costly, or the reverse, from time to time thereafter. It is known as the "strike price." The reciprocal of a purchase option, which confers the power to sell at a strike price, is a "put".

Options relating to frequently traded assets such as securities and commodities are classified in financial markets (along with so-called forward contracts) as "derivatives." It is a matter of public debate to what extent banks and other firms incur financial risks, rather than abate other risks,[b] in their use of derivatives.

A tenant's option to renew a lease is not a financial instrument, of course. It may, as in the following case, contemplate further negotiations between the parties. Yet the expiration date of any option contract is a principal element in determining its value. On the importance of requiring punctuality in the exercise of an option, as opposed to making allowance, in equity, for slight tardiness, see Western Sav. Fund, Etc. v. Southeastern, Etc., 427 A.2d 175 (Pa.Super.1981).

4
TOYS, INC. v. F.M. BURLINGTON COMPANY
Supreme Court of Vermont, 1990.
155 Vt. 44, 582 A.2d 123.

DOOLEY, J. F.M. Burlington Company, defendant below and appellant here, moved for summary judgment in this contract action pursuant to V.R.C.P. 56. The trial court not only denied the motion but awarded summary judgment on the issue of liability to plaintiff in the action, Toys, Inc. V.R.C.P. 56(c) ("Summary judgment, when appropriate, may be rendered against the moving party."). We agree with defendant that plaintiff should not have been awarded a summary judgment on all liability issues and reverse on that basis. We conclude, however, that the court was correct in awarding plaintiff summary judgment on the issue of whether a valid lease renewal option existed between the parties and also conclude that neither party is entitled to summary judgment on the remaining issues. Accordingly, we remand for trial.

On November 1, 1979, the parties entered into a lease for space in a shopping mall owned by defendant. The lease was for an initial five-year term, April 1, 1980 through February 28, 1985, and plaintiff was

---

a. "Only in 1973 did two American financial economists, Myron Scholes and Fischer Black, provide a plausible answer to the pricing problem by devising a mathematical model with several inputs, the most important of which was the volatility of the price of the underlying asset." The Economist May 14, 1994, p. 22.

̇vatives can insulate end-users ̇ous risks—a derivative that ris-

es in value if oil prices fall could protect a sheikdom, while one that rises along with oil prices will insulate an airline." Hu, Misunderstood Derivatives: The Causes of Informational Failure and the Promise of Regulatory Incrementalism, 102 Yale L.J. 1457, 1466 (1993) (footnote omitted). For some complex types see id. at 1479–80.

given an option to renew for five additional years. The option provision in the lease is as follows:

> Tenant shall be provided one option to extend the lease for five years, provided that tenant was not in default of the lease at any time during the initial term upon the same terms and conditions except:
>
> (a) there shall be no further right to renew;
>
> (b) the fixed minimum rental shall be renegotiated to the then prevailing rate within the mall.

Should the tenant wish to renew, tenant shall give one year's written notice of intention to exercise the option. On February 7, 1984, Toys Inc. wrote to F.M. Burlington, pursuant to the lease, and said, "Please be advised that Toys, Inc. hereby notifies F.M. Burlington Company of its intent to exercise its option to renew." F.M. Burlington responded on February 24, 1984. In that letter defendant confirmed that plaintiff was exercising its option to renew and then stated the prevailing rate per square foot in the mall.

On March 1, 1984, plaintiff responded. This letter stated that "Toys, Inc.'s notice of intent to renew was premised on a substantially different understanding of the prevailing rate." It described a conversation with defendant's leasing agent that involved the quotation of a prevailing rental rate well below that stated in defendant's letter of February 24th and included the understanding that "we would be completely free to renegotiate the issue of a fixed minimum rent without being bound to a prevailing rate." The letter concluded, "I trust ... that in the coming months we will be able to renegotiate a mutually agreeable rent structure." On March 2, 1984, defendant responded by letter stating:

> You are of course completely free to renegotiate the rate without reference to the prevailing rate. However, as far as the rights of the Tenant under the option are concerned, the prevailing rate ... is $10.00 [per square foot]. The prevailing rate is subject to change until such time as an agreement for renewal is reached.

On July 17, 1984, the parties met and seemed to come to an understanding as to a rent structure for the renewal term. The new rent structure was not significantly different from that specified by defendant in February, except that the first-year rent was lower than the prevailing rate and the last-year rent was higher than the prevailing rate. Over the five-year period, the new rent averaged to the prevailing rate. Defendant wrote to plaintiff the next day describing the terms and stated "if this offer is accepted, please have a copy of this letter executed and returned to me. *This offer is valid through August 1, 1984.*" (Emphasis added.) Plaintiff responded with a request for more time to consider the offer and was given until August 15, 1984. On August 15, 1984, plaintiff wrote to defendant:

It is necessary for my clients at this time to ask for an <u>additional two (2) week extension</u> from [August 15, 1984], in which to accept your offer as set forth in your July 18, 1984 correspondence.

Please let me know if there is a problem with the above request.

<u>Defendant did not respond, and plaintiff did not accept or reject the "offer" of July 17, 1984.</u> During this time, plaintiff was seeking an alternative location for its toy store in case negotiations with defendant did not work out.

Sometime in the later summer or early fall, plaintiff began pursuing the purchase of a building in which to locate its store. In October, a loan application was submitted to a financing source for funds to purchase the building. The next communication between the parties to this action was a letter from defendant dated November 1, 1984 and informing plaintiff that "Burlington Square is listing store no. 20 for lease effective March 1, 1985." On November 9, 1984, plaintiff wrote to defendant:

> On February 7, 1984, my clients informed you in writing of their intention to exercise the option to renew in the above matter. At this time we would like to be advised of the prevailing rate so that a lease can be signed as soon as possible.

> In reference to your November 1, 1984, letter, we would consider any attempt on your part to lease store No. 20 to any party other than Toys, Inc., a breach of our lease.

Although the paper jousting continued, negotiations between the parties ceased. Defendant took the position that plaintiff had failed to accept the prevailing rate in February and that they had let the July offer lapse. Plaintiff stated that it had exercised the option to renew with the February 7th letter and defendant was bound at its prevailing rate. <u>Plaintiff left the mall and purchased the building for which it earlier sought financing.</u> <u>Plaintiff then sued for breach of contract.</u>

After discovery and based generally on the facts set forth above, defendant moved for summary judgment, arguing that: (1) the option provision in the lease is actually an unenforceable agreement to agree; (2) even if a valid option existed, it was never effectively exercised by plaintiff; (3) if plaintiff had a right of renewal, it waived it through its conduct. The trial court found that the lease provision created a binding option, that plaintiff exercised the option by letter on February 7, 1984, and that plaintiff never waived its acceptance of the renewal. Accordingly, it awarded summary judgment to the plaintiff. Defendant renews its same arguments here, urging that we grant it summary judgment or, alternatively, remand for trial.

. . .

We agree with the trial court that summary judgment for plaintiff was appropriate on the first issue raised by defendant. . . . Even if we give defendant the benefit of all inferences and reasonable doubt, we find no genuine issue of fact bearing on whether there was an enforceable option to renew and hold as a matter of law that a valid option existed.

Defendant's second argument is that even if a valid renewal option existed, plaintiff did not properly exercise its option. An option is merely an agreement to hold open a specific offer to a specific party for a stated time. Harden v. Vermont Dep't of Taxes, 134 Vt. 122, 125, 352 A.2d 685, 687 (1976). The essence of the option must be accepted according to its terms in order to generate a binding contract. Bricker v. Walker, 139 Vt. 361, 364, 428 A.2d 1129, 1130 (1981); Buchannon v. Billings, 127 Vt. 69, 74–75, 238 A.2d 638, 642 (1968) (terms of the option "must be strictly complied with by the optionee"). The determination of whether an acceptance meets the terms of an offer is described in Ackerman v. Carpenter, 113 Vt. 77, 81, 29 A.2d 922, 924–25 (1943), as follows:

> We agree with the defendants' contention that an acceptance which varies from the offer will not conclude a contract. But the reply may go beyond the terms of the proposal without qualifying the acceptance. The addition may be such as fairly to import a request instead of a condition. In determining what one party intended and the other ought to have understood, regard must be had to the situation and purpose of the parties, the subject matter and course of the negotiations. The question whether there was a contract between the parties does not depend alone upon the specified facts found but also upon the reasonable inferences to be drawn from them.

(Citations omitted.) While the basic facts in this action are clear and undisputed, we cannot say the same for the "situation and purpose of the parties" and the "reasonable inferences to be drawn from" the facts, two critical factors set forth in *Ackerman.*

Plaintiff's theory is that both it and defendant were bound as of February 7, 1984 as a result of the initial letter. While this is one interpretation of the facts, it is not the only one. The letter can be construed as an expression of intent only with the necessary action to await the determination of the prevailing rental rate. Indeed, the March 1 letter, which stated that the earlier notice of intent to renew was based on a substantially different understanding of the prevailing rate, is consistent with this view. It is difficult to reconcile plaintiff's theory with its actions in July when it refused to agree to terms that were slightly more favorable to it than those it says it became bound to in February. When we consider the overall course of dealings between the parties, their evident purposes, and the inferences to be drawn from the facts, we cannot say as a matter of law that plaintiff accepted the option according to its terms. It was error to award summary judgment to plaintiff on this issue.

While we do not believe it was appropriate to award summary judgment to plaintiff on this issue, we do not conclude that summary judgment for defendant would be appropriate. When we give plaintiff the benefit of all reasonable doubts and inferences, we cannot say as a matter of law that plaintiff failed to accept the option according to its terms. The question must be left to the factfinder.

The third issue is whether the actions of plaintiff subsequent to the purported exercise of the option constituted a waiver of that acceptance. As with the second issue, we find that this issue is not appropriate for summary judgment for either party. We have defined waiver of a contract right as:

> the intentional relinquishment or abandonment of a known right, and the act of waiver may be evidenced by express words as well as by conduct. Unlike an estoppel, it involves the act or conduct of one party to the contract only, and involves both knowledge and intent on the part of the waiving party. A waiver does not necessarily imply that one has been misled to its prejudice or into an altered position.

Lynda Lee Fashions, Inc. v. Sharp Offset Printing, Inc., 134 Vt. 167, 170, 352 A.2d 676, 677 (1976) (citations omitted).

Defendant argues that plaintiff's conduct subsequent to its initial letter exercising the option was so inconsistent with the intent to renew that plaintiff waived the taking of the option. It cites to the prolonged and inconclusive negotiations between the parties, the failure of plaintiff to respond to an overture to arbitrate the dispute, and plaintiff's active pursuit of real estate outside of the mall as evidence of this waiver. Plaintiff responds that it did nothing directly inconsistent with the February 7, 1984 renewal and that it was free to, and encouraged by defendant to, renegotiate its rent outside of the terms of the option, without impairing its acceptance of the option. See Ackerman, 113 Vt. at 81, 29 A.2d at 925 (reply to option may go beyond the terms of the proposal without qualifying the acceptance).

Again, the basic facts are clear but the inferences to be drawn from the facts and the intentions and purposes of the plaintiff are not clear. A factfinder could find a waiver based on this record, but that conclusion is not commanded as a matter of law. Summary judgment was in error.

Reversed and remanded.

NOTES

(1) *Second Issue: Exercise of Option.* With respect to the defendant's second argument—that the plaintiff had failed to exercise its option—what question of fact remains to be decided? Is there a question about the meaning of Toys' February–7 letter? About the meaning of the lease term, "notice of intention to exercise the option"? Or is there a question whether or not the parties later agreed on a withdrawal of Toys' notice of intention?

Consider two meanings that might be assigned to the landlord's letter of March 2: "completely free to renegotiate the rate." Should this be understood to mean that, though both parties were bound to a renewal lease, the minimum rental remained to be determined? Or only that nothing prevents a contracting party from proposing an alteration in the terms of the contract?

(2) *The Price of Parley.* Is there a lesson in *Toys, Inc.* for a lessor who, while the lessee is considering renewal, is invited to negotiate about increasing or

decreasing the space allotted to the lessee? Might the lessor find the price of a parley to be excessive? Is there a lesson for the owner of a small corporation who, having granted an option to buy some fraction of its shares, is invited to negotiate about changing that fraction? Possibly the mistake made by the shopping-mall owner was failing to remind its tenant, from time to time, of the importance of dates: first, March 31; and later August 1. If so, does promissory estoppel provide the best basis for the tenant's claim?

(3) *Third Issue: Waiver.* The court alluded to a standard definition of "waiver": an intentional relinquishment of a known right. (Waivers are further considered below, in connection with Performance and Breach—Chapter 7.) Would it have been rational for Toys, Inc. to waive a right to renew the lease on the landlord's stated terms ($10 a square foot) if it could retain a right to renew at a lower rate upon showing that the landlord had inflated the "prevailing rate"?

A waiver by a contracting party of one of its own rights does not usually abrogate a right of the other. If the landlord was entitled, after February, to have Toys, Inc. for a tenant for another term, it may be that the landlord waived that right. Possibly the case is one of a "double waiver." (A more usual characterization of that would be *rescission* of the contract.)

What can the court have meant in speaking of a waiver by Toys, Inc. of its *acceptance*?

(4) *Disposition.* On retrial, a jury found (a) that an option existed in favor of the plaintiff, and (b) that the plaintiff had exercised that option, but (c) that plaintiff had intentionally relinquished the rights it asserted.

(5) *Terminal Dates in Offers.* In a case described above (Note 4, p. 119), the defendant caused his attorney to make this offer, concerning a lot on Lake Winnepesaukee:

> Mr. Murray will accept $115,000 for the purchase of his lot. This offer will remain open until January 1, 1986....

This letter was written in November, 1985. In December, the attorney wrote again, saying:

> Mr. Murray stands firm as to his offer of $115,000.... I should also point out that my client's offer expires at the end of the year and he is firm about this.

Do these letters say the same thing about the duration of the offer? Would it have been possible for the recipient to accept the offer on December 31st if Murray had attempted to withdraw it before then?

In *Toys, Inc.,* observe the letter written on July 18, 1984, by Burlington to Toys, Inc.: "This offer is valid through August 1." Which of the two letters written by Murray's attorney does this one most nearly resemble?

OPTION CONTRACTS—II

In Dickinson v. Dodds, 2 Ch.Div. 463 (1876), it appeared that John Dodds had made an offer to sell a property at Croft, including "dwelling-houses, garden ground, stabling, and outbuildings thereto belonging": "I hereby agree to sell to Mr. George Dickinson [the property] for the sum of £800." The offer was signed, and contained this postscript, also signed:

> P.S.—This offer to be left over until Friday, 9 o'clock a.m. J.D. (the twelfth), 12th June, 1874.

It was delivered to Dickinson on Wednesday, the 10th. On Thursday afternoon Dickinson learned from one Berry (who acted as an agent for Dickinson) that Dodds had been "offering or agreeing" to sell the property to someone else—Thomas Allan.

> Thereupon Dickinson made strenuous efforts to reach Dodds with a notice of acceptance of the offer. On Friday, at about 7 a.m., Dickinson handed Dodds the notice, having found him at a railway station. But Dodds declined to receive it, saying: "You are too late. I have sold the property."

Dickinson sued Dodds for specific performance (joining Allan as a defendant). The Lord Justices concluded that what Berry told Dickinson on Thursday had the same effect as an attempt by Dodds to withdraw the offer. They dismissed the suit. Excerpts from the opinions are as follows:

> Mellish, L.J. . . . [A]lthough it is said that the offer is to be left open until Friday morning at 9 o'clock, that did not bind Dodds. He was not in point of law bound to hold the offer over until 9 o'clock on Friday morning. He was not so bound either in law or in equity.

> James, L.J. . . . There was no consideration given for the undertaking or promise, to whatever extent it may be considered binding, to keep the property unsold until 9 o'clock on Friday morning; but apparently Dickinson was of opinion, and probably Dodds was of the same opinion, that he (Dodds) was bound by that promise, and could not in any way withdraw from it, or retract it, until 9 o'clock on Friday morning, and this probably explains a good deal of what afterwards took place. But it is clear settled law, on one of the clearest principles of law, that this promise, being a mere *nudum pactum*, was not binding, and that at any moment before a complete acceptance by Dickinson of the offer, Dodds was as free as Dickinson himself.

The decisions in Dickinson v. Dodds and in cases following it have brought the law of consideration into ridicule, it has been said.[a]

a. "Until the nineteenth century was well advanced there seems to have been no serious concern over means for making offers 'firm.' . . . [Then in 1876] an English court concluded with great confidence that a time limit fixed by the offeror could not prevent revocation before the time limit had expired, for in the absence of consideration any restriction on the power to revoke was simply *nudum pactum*. American decisions have dutifully followed this line ever since and thereby made the consideration test a still more prominent target of public ridicule . . . The difficulties were all manufactured by treating offers as a subordinate form of promise." J. Dawson, Gifts and Promises 211–13 (1980).

"The very term 'option' creates a reasonable expectation of irrevocability, consideration, in the context of option contracts, being merely an obsolescent historical blot on our legal system." 1 Corbin rev. 294. (This is said, however, in the context of

In the early common law an option contract could be made by making the promise under seal. Upon the abolition of the seal, the doctrine of consideration became the exclusive means to this end. What would have been the result if Dickinson had paid Dodds £1 and the postscript had been changed to read, "In consideration of £1 paid, this offer is left over...."?

The technique of exchange may be adequate for offers of deals about real property, where the parties might be expected to foresee the possibility of revocation and deal with it in this rather elaborate way. It is less satisfactory for more informal transactions such as those for the sale of goods, where the offeror is less likely to clothe a promise in the trappings of consideration. Hence the Uniform Commercial Code contains an important provision that enables an offeror to make an irrevocable offer by means of a signed writing: section 2–205, "Firm Offers". (The section title is less than ideal, for the term is often used in and out of court to differentiate an ordinary offer from a non-offer occurring in negotiations.)

NOTES

(1) *Questions.* In *Toys, Inc.*, what consideration supported the option held by that firm? Apart from an option for which money is paid, and an option forming part of a more comprehensive exchange, the courts have been reluctant to characterize action of the offeree as a bargained-for exchange. See Friedman v. Tappan Development Corp., 126 A.2d 646 (N.J.1956), and Bard v. Kent, 122 P.2d 8 (Cal.1942).

(2) *Merchants Under the Code.* Note that only a "merchant" can make a firm offer under UCC 2–205. Is this provision available to a roofer like Ever–Tite, in the case at p. 187?

The section is one of several in which the Code lays down special rules for merchants. Another is considered in the following Section.

The definition of "merchant" in UCC 2–104(1) includes not only "a person who deals in goods of the kind" but also one who "by his occupation holds himself out as having knowledge or skill peculiar to the practices or goods involved in the transaction." Can one who does not deal in goods of the kind make a firm offer? Consider, for example, a manufacturer making an exceptional purchase of a new piece of factory equipment or an exceptional sale of a used piece of factory equipment. Would such a manufacturer hold "himself out as having knowledge or skill peculiar to the practices ... involved in the transaction"? What practices? (According to Comment 2, professional status "may be based upon specialized knowledge as to the goods, specialized knowledge as to business practices, or specialized knowledge as to both and which kind of specialized knowledge may be sufficient ... is indicated by the nature of the provisions.")

Compare the use of the term "merchant" in UCC 2–205 with its use in UCC 2–314(1). Would such a manufacturer impliedly warrant the merchantability of the used piece of factory equipment?

(3) *New York Statute.* In addition to UCC 2–205, New York has the following comprehensive statute, first enacted in 1941 (along with the statute on

action in reliance on a promise as a basis
for enforcing the promise.)

"moral obligation" in Note 3, p. 73 above), and later amended to take account of the Code:

> Except as otherwise provided in section 2–205 of the uniform commercial code with respect to an offer by a merchant to buy or sell goods, when an offer to enter into a contract is made in a writing signed by the offeror, or by his agent, which states that the offer is irrevocable during a period set forth or until a time fixed, the offer shall not be revocable during such period or until such time because of the absence of consideration for the assurance of irrevocability. When such a writing states that the offer is irrevocable but does not state any period of time of irrevocability, it shall be construed to state that the offer is irrevocable for a reasonable time. (New York General Obligations Law § 5–1109.)

Is this statute available to a roofer like Ever–Tite, in the case at p. 187, if the roofer is doing its business in New York?

(4) *Recitals.* If a sum of money is paid as consideration for an option, this fact is usually recited. What is the effect of such a recital if no payment is made? Some courts have held it to be of no effect. Others have held that it makes the offer irrevocable, either as a binding acknowledgement of payment or as a promise to pay. Restatement Second § 87 favors the latter view, with the qualifications that the recital be in a signed writing and that the proposed exchange be fair. Comment *b* to that section explains, "The signed writing has vital significance as a formality, while the ceremonial manual delivery of a dollar or a peppercorn is an inconsequential formality."

THE FRAGILITY OF OFFERS

In Dickinson v. Dodds, Lord Mellish supported the decision with this argument: "If a man makes an offer to sell a particular horse in his stable, and says, 'I will give you until the day after tomorrow to accept the offer,' and the next day goes and sells the horse to somebody else, and receives the purchase money from him, can the person to whom the offer was originally made then come and say, 'I accept,' so as to make a binding contract ...?" And he answered: "[P]arting with the property has very much the same effect as the death of the owner, for it makes the performance of the offer impossible."

This passage was dictum; and it is not the law. (*News* of the horse sale would be a different matter.) See 1 Farnsworth § 3.16. Holmes said, in the 19th century, that it would be monstrous to restrict an offer that way. Brauer v. Shaw, 46 N.E. 617, 618 (Mass.1897). *Questions:* What assumptions make it "monstrous"? The assumption that the mails might have to be used by an offeree who wishes to verify the current wishes of the offeror? The assumption that arranging option contracts is burdened with high transaction costs?

The first Restatement acceded grudgingly to the decision in *Dickinson,* that an offer might be revoked by news of inconsistent behavior by the offeror, emanating from some source other than the offeror. See Corbin, The Restatement of the Common Law by the American Law Institute, 15 Iowa L.Rev. 19, 36 (1929). Section 43 of the Restatement Second states a somewhat more expansive rule about "indirect communication of revocation." Both formulations require that the offeree receive reliable information about the offeror's behavior. They leave open the possibility that information—such as what Berry told Dickinson—might be "reliable," though false.

NOTES

(1) *The Case of the Telex Too Soon.* Transoil (Jersey) Ltd. v. Belcher Oil Co., 950 F.2d 1115 (5th Cir.), cert. denied, 113 S.Ct. 90 (1992), concerned a dispute between buyer and seller about a cargo of oil. The buyer, having inspected the oil and found excessive impurities, proposed a settlement: the price to be reduced by some $285,000. The seller sought better terms at first, but four days later signalled its acceptance. Minutes before that, however, the buyer had sent the seller a telex asserting its right not to pay for the oil. (As to a buyer's right to "reject" nonconforming goods, see UCC 2–602.) The settlement therefore failed.

What can be said in support of a system in which the existence of a contract depends on the exact sequence of "acceptance" and "revocation"? When offeror and offeree meet at a railway station, is it absurd that their legal relations can depend on who speaks first? See Farnsworth, Mutuality of Obligation in Contract Law, 3 Dayton L.Rev. 271 (1978).

(2) *Revocation of General Offers.* In the case of a general offer, such as one addressed to the general public by an advertisement, it will ordinarily be impossible for the offeror actually to communicate a revocation to all of the persons who are aware of the offer. Illustrative are the offers in the *Broadnax* case, Note 2, p. 97 above, and the *Lefkowitz* case, p. 165. The offeror can, of course, be required to give a notice of revocation publicity equal (and usually similar) to that given the offer. But having done this, is the offeror nevertheless bound by the acceptance of an offeree who was aware of the offer but missed the notice of revocation? The answer is that the offeror is not bound, in spite of the general requirement that a revocation be actually communicated to the offeree. See Restatement Second § 46. How would you revoke an offer of a reward posted on a bulletin board? Would taking it down be sufficient? When would the revocation take effect? See Carr v. Mahaska County Bankers Ass'n, 269 N.W. 494 (Iowa 1936). For an entertaining example of revocation by publication involving a reward issued by Secretary of War Stanton for Suratt, one of Booth's accomplices in the assassination of President Lincoln, see Shuey v. United States, 92 U.S. 73 (1875).

(3) *Problem.* A offered in writing to sell B Greenacre for $1,000, offer to remain open five days. On the fourth day B received information from the county recorder of deeds that the recorder had received for recording a deed of Greenacre from A to C. This information being reliable, B believed it, but thinking there might be some chance for error, notified A of acceptance on the fifth day. The information given by the recorder proved to be erroneous, but A refused to perform. Contract?

RAGOSTA v. WILDER

Supreme Court of Vermont, 1991.
156 Vt. 390, 592 A.2d 367.

PECK, JUSTICE. Defendant appeals from a judgment ordering him to convey to plaintiffs a piece of real property known as "The Fork Shop." Defendant argues that the court improperly found that a binding contract existed and that it misapplied the doctrine of equitable estoppel. He also contends that the ruling cannot be upheld under promissory estoppel principles since the court failed to examine the extent to which enforcement of defendant's promise to sell was required to prevent injustice. Because the trial court's ruling cannot stand on contract or equitable estoppel grounds and because the court's analysis of promissory estoppel is inextricably bound in its contractual analysis, we reverse and remand the cause for further proceedings consistent with the principles expressed herein.

In 1985, plaintiffs became interested in purchasing "The Fork Shop" from defendant, but preliminary negotiations between the parties were fruitless. In 1987, plaintiffs learned that defendant was again considering selling the "The Fork Shop," mailed him a letter offering to purchase the property along with a check for $2,000 and began arrangements to obtain the necessary financing. By letter dated September 28, 1987, defendant returned the $2,000 check explaining that he had two properties "up for sale" and that he would not sign an acceptance to plaintiffs' offer because "that would tie up both these properties until [there was] a closing." In the letter, he also made the following counter-offer:

> I will sell you the Fork Shop and its property as listed in book 35, at page 135 of the Brookfield Land Records on 17 April 1972, for $88,000.00 (Eighty-eight thousand dollars), at anytime up until the 1st of November 1987 that you appear with me at the Randolph National Bank with said sum. At which time they will give you a certified deed to this property or to your agent as directed, providing said property has not been sold.

On October 1st, the date plaintiffs received the letter, they called defendant. The court found that during the conversation plaintiffs told defendant that "the terms and conditions of his offer were acceptable and that they would in fact prepare to accept the offer." Defendant assured plaintiffs that there was no one else currently interested in purchasing "The Fork Shop."

On October 6th, plaintiffs informed defendant that they would not close the sale on October 8th as discussed previously but that they would come to Vermont on October 10th. On October 8th, defendant called plaintiffs and informed them that he was no longer willing to sell "The Fork Shop." The trial court found that, at that time, defendant was aware plaintiffs "had processed their loan application and were prepared to close." Plaintiffs informed defendant that they would be at the

Randolph National Bank at 10:00 a.m. on October 15th with the $88,000 purchase price and in fact appeared. Defendant did not. Plaintiffs claim they incurred $7,499.23 in loan closing costs.

Plaintiffs sued for specific performance arguing that defendant had contracted to sell the property to them. They alleged moreover that defendant knew they would have to incur costs to obtain financing for the purchase but assured them that the sale would go through and that they relied on his assurances.

The trial court concluded that defendant "made an offer in writing which could only be accepted by performance prior to the deadline." It concluded further that defendant could not revoke his offer on October 8th because plaintiffs, relying on the offer, had already begun performance and that defendant should be estopped from revoking the offer on a theory of equitable estoppel. It ordered defendant to convey to plaintiffs "The Fork Shop" for $88,000. This appeal followed.

No Consideration by D

I.

Plaintiffs claim that defendant's letter of September 28, 1987 created a contract to sell "The Fork Shop" to them unless the property was sold to another buyer. Rather, defendant's letter contains an offer to sell the property for $88,000, which the trial court found could only be accepted "by performance prior to the deadline," and a promise to keep the offer open unless the property were sold to another buyer. Defendant received no consideration for either promise. In fact, defendant returned plaintiffs' check for $2,000 which would have constituted consideration for the promise to keep the offer open, presumably because he did not wish to make a firm offer. Thus, the promise to keep the offer to sell open was not enforceable and, absent the operation of equitable estoppel, defendant could revoke the offer to sell the property at any time before plaintiffs accepted it. See Buchannon v. Billings, 127 Vt. 69, 75, 238 A.2d 638, 642 (1968) ("An option is a continuing offer, and *if supported by a consideration,* it cannot be withdrawn before the time limit.") (emphasis added).

Plaintiffs argue that the actions they undertook to obtain financing, which were detrimental to them, could constitute consideration for the promise to keep the offer to sell open. Their argument is unconvincing. Although plaintiffs are correct in stating that a detriment may constitute consideration, they ignore the rule that "[t]o constitute consideration, a performance or a return promise must be bargained for." Restatement (Second) of Contracts § 71(1) (1981). "A performance or return promise is bargained for if it is sought by the promisor in exchange for his promise and is given by the promisee in exchange for that promise." Id. at § 71(2). Plaintiffs began to seek financing even before defendant made a definite offer to sell the property. Whatever detriment they suffered was not in exchange for defendant's promise to keep the offer to sell open.

The trial court ruled that the offer to sell "The Fork Shop" could only be accepted by performance but concluded that in obtaining financing plaintiffs began performance and that therefore defendant could not revoke the offer to sell once plaintiffs incurred the cost of obtaining financing. Section 45 of the Restatement (Second) of Contracts provides that "[w]here an offer invites an offeree to accept by rendering a performance and does not invite a promissory acceptance, an option contract is created when the offeree tenders or begins the invited performance or tenders a beginning of it." However, "[w]hat is begun or tendered must be part of the actual performance invited in order to preclude revocation under this Section." Id. at comment f.

Here, plaintiffs were merely engaged in preparation for performance. The court itself found only that "plaintiffs had changed their position in order to tender performance." At most, they obtained financing and assured defendant that they would pay; plaintiffs never tendered to defendant or even began to tender the $88,000 purchase price. Thus, they never accepted defendant's offer and no contract was ever created. See Multicare Medical Center v. State Social & Health Services, 114 Wash.2d 572, 584, 790 P.2d 124, 131 (1990) ("under a unilateral contract, an offer cannot be accepted by promising to perform; rather, the offeree must accept, if at all, by performance, and the contract then becomes executed").*

II.

Defendant claims next that the court was not justified in applying equitable estoppel in this case. We agree.

One who invokes the doctrine of equitable estoppel has the burden of establishing each of its constituent elements. Four essential elements must be established: first, the party to be estopped must know the facts; second, the party being estopped must intend that his conduct shall be acted upon or the acts must be such that the party asserting the estoppel has a right to believe it is so intended; third, the latter must be ignorant of the true facts; and finally, the party asserting the estoppel must rely on the conduct of the party to be estopped to his detriment.

Fisher v. Poole, 142 Vt. 162, 168, 453 A.2d 408, 411–12 (1982) (citations omitted).

Equitable estoppel is inapplicable here because there were no facts known to defendant but unknown to plaintiffs. Plaintiffs cannot have acted on an understanding that defendant would definitely convey the property to them. On its face, defendant's offer stated only that he would convey the property to plaintiffs if he did not convey it to another party first. The trial court acknowledged that if defendant had sold "The Fork Shop" to another party plaintiffs would not have been entitled to relief. Thus, plaintiffs had no assurance that defendant would definitely convey the property to them even if on October 1st

---

* Because defendant specified that the manner of acceptance would be performance, plaintiffs' argument that they accepted defendant's offer over the telephone must fail. In fact, plaintiffs admitted in their depositions that they were very worried that the property would be sold to someone else prior to closing. Thus, they should have understood that they had no enforceable contract until closing.

defendant told them that there was no one else interested in buying the property at that time. Moreover, plaintiffs engaged in obtaining financing for the purchase even before defendant made any offer to them whatsoever. They understood, at the time they obtained financing for the transaction, that they were assuming a risk that they would be unable to purchase the property in question. Since the plaintiffs had not tendered performance and did not establish the elements for the application of equitable estoppel, defendant was entitled to withdraw his offer when he did.

III.

[This part of the opinion, dealing with promissory estoppel, appears at p. 266, below.]

NOTE

The Case of the Green Mountains—Reprise. In State v. Delaney—a case stated in Note 2, p. 157 above—the Vermont court recited its holding in the foregoing case and said: "An argument analogous to the State's argument was made, and rejected, in Ragosta v. Wilder. . . . This case is governed by *Ragosta* and is less compelling. Defendant told the State on several occasions that he was interested only in a 'solid, viable contract.' The joint resolution did not appropriate any money; it merely expressed an 'intention to proceed with the State's appropriation,' . . . . The remainder of the purchase price was to be raised privately by the Nature Conservancy during the spring and summer of 1989. Thus, the resolution could not constitute the beginning of performance. . . . The evidence discloses, at best, an attempt by the State to convince defendant that it was serious about acquiring the property. In the absence of extraordinary circumstances, not present here, efforts to obtain financing will not constitute part performance of a unilateral offer to sell real estate." 598 A.2d 138, 141–42.[a]

ACCEPTANCE VARYING OFFER

This topic has been introduced in a Note in Section 2 above (p. 161): "The Battle of the Forms." There it was assumed that the parties use standard forms to express offers and acceptances. In the case considered here, they did not.

In 1879 the letters and telegrams below passed between a railway company and a rolling-mill company. The messages of the railway, who initiated the correspondence, are lettered a, c, and e.

(a) Dec. 5: Please quote me prices for 500 to 3,000 tons 50 lb. steel rails, and for 2,000 to 5,000 tons 50 lb. iron rails, March 1880 delivery.

(b) Dec. 8: Your favor of the 5th inst. at hand. We do not make steel rails. For iron rails, we will sell 2,000 to 5,000 tons of 50

---

a. But, the court said, the State's contractual theories were not frivolous, "particularly given the sparsity of Vermont law on them at the time this suit was prosecuted. *Ragosta* . . . was issued after oral argument in this case."

lb. rails for fifty-four ($54.00) dollars per gross ton for spot cash,
F.O.B. cars at our mill, March delivery. If our offer is accepted,
shall expect to be notified of same prior to Dec. 20th.

(c) Dec. 16: PLEASE ENTER OUR ORDER FOR TWELVE HUNDRED TONS
RAILS, MARCH DELIVERY, AS PER YOUR FAVOR OF THE EIGHTH. PLEASE REPLY.

(d) Dec. 18: WE CANNOT BOOK YOUR ORDER AT PRESENT AT THAT PRICE.

(e) Dec. 19: PLEASE ENTER AN ORDER FOR TWO THOUSAND TONS RAILS,
AS PER YOUR LETTER OF THE EIGHTH. PLEASE FORWARD WRITTEN CONTRACT.
REPLY.

At the end of the day the rolling-mill denied the existence of a contract.
In an action against it by the railway, judgment was entered for the
defendant, on a jury verdict. On appeal, *held:* Affirmed. Minneapolis
& St. Louis Railway Co. v. Columbus Rolling–Mill Co., 119 U.S. 149
(1886). "A proposal to accept, or an acceptance, upon terms varying
from those offered, is a rejection of the offer, and puts an end to the
negotiation, unless the party who made the original offer renews it, or
assents to the modification suggested. The other party having once
rejected the offer, cannot afterwards revive it by tendering an acceptance
of it."

NOTES

(1) *Questions: Counting.* How many offers do you identify among the five
messages set out above? How many rejections?

(2) *Drafting.* Can you draft a substitute for message (c) that would have
been an offer to buy 1,200 tons of rails but not a rejection of the rolling mill's
offer? See Restatement Second §§ 38, 39.

(3) *Problem.* Suppose that message (d) had been this: "Cannot reduce
quantity. We cannot book your order at present at that price." Can you make
an argument that the result in the case should have been different? See
Livingston v. Evans, [1925] 4 D.L.R. 769 (Alberta Sup.Ct.).

(4) *More Drafting.* In Caldwell v. Cline, 156 S.E. 55 (W.Va.1930), an owner
of land wrote a letter offering to sell it, in which he said: "will give you eight
days in which to accept." Compare the last sentence of (b), the rolling-mill's
letter of December 8. In what way is the rolling-mill's treatment of the matter
superior? As will shortly appear, many letter-offers are open to acceptance by
the *mailing* of a letter of acceptance. In light of that fact, is the "eight days"
letter doubly artless?

(5) *The Case of the Bride's Acceptance.* Moonlight Designs, Inc. (Moonlight), a dealer in bridal gowns, sought advertising space in *Elegant Bride,* a
magazine. The advertising salesperson for the magazine, Deluca, inserted price
terms and some other performance terms, already agreed upon, in a standard-
form contract and sent a copy by fax to Moonlight's president, Chin. Believing,
apparently, that still other terms had been agreed upon—a circulation guarantee,
for example—Chin typed them in, signed the form, and faxed it back. Deluca
responded: "extremely pleased that you have decided to join our list of advertisers." Chin's insertions were not discussed. Some of the expected advertising
was published. But Moonlight cancelled other pages and the magazine's owner
sued it for breach. The trial court awarded a recovery, but in an amount less
than was prescribed by a provision of the standard-form contract. In its view,

though the parties eventually arrived at an "implied contract," the faxed messages did not create a contractual relation because they did not quite match.

On an appeal by Moonlight, the court found another reason to affirm. It said, however, that the trial court's theory was "slightly off the mark." The court characterized Chin's fax as a counteroffer, and Deluca's response as an acceptance. "It is of course true," the court said, "that there needs to be mutual assent. But ... [t]here is no requirement that parties discuss a contract's every term in order to be bound by it—indeed, such a rule would reward parties for their failure to read what they sign, hardly an incentive that contract law would seek to create." Pace Communs., Inc. v. Moonlight Design, Inc., 31 F.3d 587 (7th Cir.1994).

REJECTION OF AN IRREVOCABLE OFFER

It is doubtful that the holder of a power to accept under an option contract puts an end to the power by rejecting the "offer." See Restatement Second § 37.

The authorities are sparse. In one of them, Humble Oil & Refining Co. v. Westside Investment Corp., 428 S.W.2d 92 (Tex.1968), Humble held an option contract to acquire some subdivision lots, fixed to expire on June 4. Early in May it wrote to the owner: "Humble ... hereby exercises its option.... The contract of sale is hereby amended to provide that Seller shall extend all utility lines to the property before the date of closing." Twelve days later it wrote again: "The exercise of said option is not qualified and you may disregard the proposed amendment...." Later, Humble sued on a supposed contract of sale. What decision? How different would the case be if Humble had first written: "We have decided not to purchase your property"?

Recall that in Toys, Inc. v. F.M. Burlington Company, Toys Inc. wrote on March 1, 1984, that its earlier notice of intent to renew had been "premised on a substantially different understanding of the prevailing rate." Did that letter present the same problem that Humble's first letter did?

NOTES

(1) *Firm Offers.* It would be possible to distinguish between the *Humble Oil* and *Toys, Inc.* cases, in which the defendants received consideration for the option contracts, and one in which an offer is irrevocable as a "firm offer" under UCC 2–205. (Imagine that the Columbus Rolling–Mill had added to its December 8 letter: "Offer firm until then—Dec. 20th.") Is there any reason to make the distinction?

(2) *Problem.* To vary the facts of the iron-rails case, suppose that Railway, holding a firm offer from Rolling–Mill to sell 2,000 tons of rails for March delivery, rejects the offer on December 16th, but purports to accept it on the 18th. In the meanwhile, however, Rolling–Mill has committed all its March output to another customer. How would you explain that Rolling–Mill is under no obligation to Railway? Promissory estoppel?

DEATH OF AN OFFEROR

Restatement Second § 48 sets out the generally accepted rule in this country that an offeree's power of acceptance is terminated by the offeror's death or supervening incapacity. Corbin said of this rule that there is not "any compelling necessity for its existence. It may be said that you cannot contract with a dead man; but neither can you force a dead man to pay his debts contracted before his death. Yet the law has no difficulty, in the latter case, in creating legal relations with the dead man's personal representative, and there would be no greater difficulty in declaring the power of acceptance to survive as against the offeror's representative or in favor of the offeree's representative." Corbin, Offer and Acceptance, and Some of the Resulting Legal Relations, 26 Yale L.J. 169, 198 (1917).

Jordan v. Dobbins, 122 Mass. 168 (1877), illustrates the rule. In February, Jordan, Marsh & Co. had Dobbins guarantee the prompt payment of all sums owed by Moore to Jordan, Marsh as a result of sales of merchandise that Jordan, Marsh might make to Moore. In August Dobbins died. From the following January through May, Jordan, Marsh sold Moore merchandise in ignorance of Dobbins's death. When Moore did not pay, Jordan, Marsh sued Dobbins's estate. The Supreme Judicial Court of Massachusetts denied recovery. "The agreement which the guarantor makes with the person receiving the guaranty is not that I now become liable to you for anything, but that if you sell goods to a third person, I will then become liable to pay for them if such third person does not.... Such being the nature of a guaranty, we are of opinion that the death of the guarantor operates as a revocation of it, and that the person holding it cannot recover against his executor or administrator for goods sold after the death.... It is no hardship to require traders, whose business it is to deal in goods, to exercise diligence so far as to ascertain whether a person upon whose credit they are selling is living."

Under the original draft of the first Restatement, as written by Professor Williston and his advisers, the unknown death of the offeror did not revoke the offer, but the Council of the American Law Institute changed the rule. Professor Williston concluded that "though the amount of actual authority is not impressive, there is a very general opinion among lawyers that death, even though unknown, does revoke an offer and does revoke an agency," and it was vital that the Restatement rule for contracts coincide with that for agency. 3 Proceedings of the American Law Institute 198 (1925). The Restatement Second preserves the rule, admitting that it "seems to be a relic of the obsolete view that a contract requires a 'meeting of the minds,' and it is out of harmony with the modern doctrine that a manifestation of assent is effective without regard to actual mental assent.... In the absence of legislation, [however,] the rule remains in effect." Comment *a* to Restatement Second § 48. Should the application of the rule be limited to situations in which the offeree has not relied on the assumed contract in ignorance of the fact of the offeror's death?

Death or incapacity of the offeree has the same effect as that of the offeror under Restatement Second § 48. The death or incapacity of the offeror does not terminate the offeree's power of acceptance under an option contract.

NOTE

Problem. You are a Philadelphia lawyer. A client, Benjamin Earle, comes to see you with the following story. "About four years ago I had a conversation with my aunt, Mary Dewitt, who lived in Massachusetts, and she said to me something like this, as best I can remember: 'Ben there are few left to come to my funeral. I have thought a great deal of you for coming to your uncle's funeral and bringing that large box of flowers in the terrible snowstorm we had, when our friends could not reach here from Boston, and you coming from Philadelphia. I want you to attend my funeral, Ben, if you outlive me, and I think you will, and I will pay all expenses and I will give you five thousand dollars. I want you to come.' I replied that I would come if I was living and if they informed me in time to get there and if I was able. We talked about it a little more on the occasion of my mother's funeral two years later. Aunt Mary died a few months ago and I went to Massachusetts for her funeral. Soon after the funeral, I received in the mail this paper, bearing the date of our conversation and signed by Aunt Mary." The paper reads, "If Benjamin A. Earle should come to my funeral, I order my executor to pay him the sum of five thousand dollars. Mary Dewitt." The executor has refused to pay and Mr. Earle wants to know whether he has a claim against the estate for $5,000 and his expenses.[a] Advise him.

You may need more facts. What recollections by Earle of events in years past would help to support his claim? In Note 5, p. 152 above, you have been cautioned about prefacing your questions to Earle with an exposition of contract law; according to the Model Rules, a lawyer "shall not ... counsel or assist a witness to testify falsely." Rule 3.4(b). Compare this, from the Freedman book, Lawyers' Ethics ...:

> It is not the lawyer's function to prejudice his client as a perjurer. He cannot presume that the client will make unlawful use of his advice.... Before [a client] begins to remember essential facts, the client is entitled to know what his own interests are ... To decide otherwise would ... penalize the less well-educated defendant.

This does not mean, does it, that in advising Earle you should take account of his level of education?

———

THE "MAILBOX RULE": CONTRACTS BY CORRESPONDENCE

How do the rules for the bargaining process apply when the parties are at a distance and bargain by correspondence? Suppose, for example, that one party has sent the other an offer, and that the offeree has dispatched an acceptance which has not yet been received by the offeror. Is it too late for the offeror to change its mind and revoke the offer? Is it too late for the offeree to change its mind and reject the offer? And is

a. These facts are drawn from Earle v. Angell, 32 N.E. 164 (Mass. 1892).

there a contract if the acceptance is lost and is never received by the offeror?

As will be seen, the tendency of the common law has been to answer these questions on the assumption that dispatch of the acceptance is ordinarily the crucial point at which the contract is made—after which the offeror's power to revoke is terminated, the offeree's power to reject is ended, and the risks of transmission are on the offeror. Because the early cases involved acceptance by post, this came to be known as the "mailbox rule."

In the celebrated case of Adams v. Lindsell, 106 Eng.Rep. 250 (K.B.1818), the Court of King's Bench held that a firm of wool dealers that had made an offer by post to sell "eight hundred tods of wether fleeces" could not revoke the offer after the offeree, a firm of woolen manufacturers, had put a letter of acceptance in the post. The overwhelming weight of authority in the United States supports the "mailbox rule" of Adams v. Lindsell.[a] See Restatement Second § 63 and Comment a, which gives this explanation:

> It is often said that an offeror who makes an offer by mail makes the post office his agent to receive the acceptance, or that the mailing of a letter of acceptance puts it irrevocably out of the offeree's control. Under United States postal regulations, however, the sender of a letter has long had the power to stop delivery and reclaim the letter. A better explanation of the rule that the acceptance takes effect on dispatch is that the offeree needs a dependable basis for his decision whether to accept. In many legal systems such a basis is provided by a general rule that an offer is irrevocable unless it provides otherwise. [See p. 200 above.] The common law provides such a basis through the rule that a revocation of an offer is ineffective if received after an acceptance has been properly dispatched.[b]

A revocation, however, is generally held to be effective only on receipt, not on dispatch. See Restatement Second § 42.

It has generally been assumed that the "mailbox rule," laid down by Adams v. Lindsell in connection with the termination of the offeror's power to revoke, applies as well in connection with the termination of the offeree's power to reject. In other words, once the offeree has dispatched an acceptance, it is too late for the offeree to reject the offer. See Restatement Second § 63. This is, of course, not a necessary assumption, since it would be possible to frame a rule that would deprive the offeror of its power to revoke the offer upon dispatch of the acceptance by the offeree, but leave the offeree free to reject the offer, at

a. In Cushing v. Thomson, 386 A.2d 805 (N.H.1978), the Supreme Court of New Hampshire upheld the trial court's reliance on evidence of the offeree's "customary office procedure for the letters to be sent out the same day that they are placed in the office outbox" together with an affidavit that the letter of acceptance had been placed in the outbox, as evidence that the acceptance had been mailed.

b. Restatement Second § 63 makes the mailbox rule applicable only if the acceptance is "made in a manner and by a medium invited by [the] offer." It would not, therefore, ordinarily apply to acceptance by mail of an offer made by telegram, and such an acceptance would be effective only on receipt.

least as long as the offeror receives the rejection before receiving the acceptance. The two rules can best be contrasted by considering the case of the overtaking rejection.

Suppose that on Monday Buyer receives by mail an offer from Seller of goods. On Tuesday Buyer mails Seller a letter of acceptance which arrives on Friday. On Wednesday Buyer calls Seller to explain that it wants to revoke its acceptance and reject the offer. If the "mailbox rule" is applied, it is too late for Buyer to reconsider and Seller can hold Buyer to a contract. If the other rule is applied, Buyer remains free to change its mind while the letter is in transit, and Seller cannot hold Buyer to a contract. The disadvantage of this rule is that while the letter is in transit, although Seller is unable to revoke, Buyer is free to watch the market and speculate, having in effect an "option contract" for that period.

But does not the "mailbox rule" also have a disadvantage? Suppose that the rejection does not mention the letter of acceptance, as where Buyer on Wednesday send an overtaking telegram which is received on Thursday and says simply, "Reject your offer." May not application of the "mailbox rule" to find a contract in such a case prejudice Seller if it relies on the telegram of rejection and sells the goods to another buyer before receiving the letter of acceptance on Friday? Might Buyer be estopped to enforce the contract in such a case? See Comment *c* and Illustration 7 to Restatement, Second § 63.

The third problem that the mailbox rule has called upon to solve concerns the risks of transmission of the acceptance.[c] Who should bear the risk, the offeror or the offeree? Dean Langdell[d] concluded that the offeree should, arguing that the hardship of "making one liable on a contract which he is ignorant of having made" is greater than the hardship of "depriving one of the benefit of a contract which he supposes he has made" and that it is easier for the sender to provide against the possible miscarriage of a letter. Langdell, Summary of the Law of Contracts 21 (2d ed. 1880). Professor Llewellyn, however, concluded that the offeror should bear the risk, arguing that "the ingrained usage of business is to answer letters which look toward deals, but the usage is not so clear about acknowledging letters which close deals. The absence of an answer to a letter of offer is much more certain to lead to inquiry than is the absence of an answer to a letter of acceptance, so that the party bitten by the mischance has under our rule a greater likelihood of being aware of uncertainty and of speedily discovering his difficulty." Llewellyn, Our Case–Law of Contract: Offer and Acceptance (pt. 2), 48 Yale L.J. 779, 795 (1939). The Restatement Second takes the same view, but with some diffidence: "In the interest of simplicity and clarity,

c. On the risks of transmission of the offer, see Note 1, p. 139 above.

d. Christopher Columbus Langdell (1826–1906) was a New York lawyer who became professor of law at Harvard Law School in 1870. His principal achievement as professor and later dean was the intro-duction of the case method of instruction through the publication in 1871 of his case-book on contracts. He believed that in-struction should be of such a character that the students "might at least derive a great-er advantage from attending it than from devoting the time to private study."

the rule has been extended to cases where an acceptance is lost or delayed in the course of transmission. The convenience of the rule is less clear in such cases than in cases of attempted revocation of the offer, however, and the language of the offer is often properly interpreted as making the offeror's duty of performance conditional upon receipt of the acceptance." Comment *b* to Restatement Second § 63.

NOTES

(1) *The Electronic Highway.* A number of statutes ascribe some consequence to a communication without specifying whether dispatch or receipt is what counts. In one case a court was especially concerned about the burdens that its choice would impose on the courts. It thought that about the same number of disputes would arise under either rule; but the qualitative difference disposed the court in favor of the dispatch rule. Although that rule necessarily involves questions about the reasonableness of the sender's choice of a means of communication, the receipt rule would entail "conceptually difficult disputes concerning what constitutes receipt."

The technology of telexing worried the court. The message in question had been sent by telex; but the recipient's machine was apparently shut down overnight. "[D]id the electrons that made up the message proceed along the wires and enter [his] machine and wait there until the next morning?" In re Marin Motor Oil, Inc., 740 F.2d 220, 228 (3d Cir.1984). Does the case suggest that the "mailbox rule" has a merit today that it did not have at its origin?

(2) *Different Questions, Different Answers.* In a leading English case a judge put these questions by way of protest against the mailbox rule: "Suppose a man has paid his tailor by cheque or bank note [currency], and posts a letter containing a cheque or bank note to his tailor, which never reaches, is the tailor paid? If he is, would he be if he had never been paid before in that way? Suppose a man is in the habit of sending cheques and bank notes to his banker by post, and posts a letter containing cheques and bank notes, which never reaches. Is the banker liable? Would he be if this was the first instance of a remittance of the sort? In the cases I have supposed, the tailor and banker may have recognized this mode of remittance by sending bank receipts and putting the money to the credit of the remitter. Are they liable with that? Are they liable without it?"

The judge (Bramwell, L.J.) added that, if there is a general rule equating the mailing of a letter of acceptance to communicating with the offeror, "it is equally applicable to all communications that may be made by post." Household Fire & Carriage Acc. Ins. Co. v. Grant, 4 Ex.D. 216 (Eng.C.A.1879), dissent at 232, 234. That, Bramwell evidently thought, would be intolerable. In Laredo Hides Co. v. H & H Meat Products Co., 513 S.W.2d 210 (Tex.App.1974), the court said: "where [a] creditor expressly directs that the money owed be mailed to him, payment of such debt is made when a letter containing the agreed remittance . . . is deposited in the mail."

But it is generally understood that, while the mailbox rule applies to problems about the formation of a contract, it does not apply (absent an agreement to the contrary) to performance problems. So, if a contract requires payment to a tailor by November 1, the customer's payment must ordinarily arrive by that date. If it is mailed then (or earlier), and is lost in the mail, the customer has not performed.

(3) *Option Contracts.* Suppose a firm offer by mail to sell goods, under UCC 2–205, in which the offeror writes: "I will give you ten days in which to accept." If the offer is dated the first day of the month, mailed on the second, and received on the third, would you expect the final day for informing the offeror of acceptance to be the 11th? The 12th? The 13th? Other?

The Pennsylvania Acadamy of Fine Arts (PAFA) held a lease on a parking lot that was to expire on July 31, 1989. The lease contained an option to purchase, and this provision: "All notices hereunder shall be in writing and shall be delivered or mailed by certified mail or registered mail." The option was, according to the lease, to be exercised at least six months before the expiration of the lease. On January 30, PAFA prepared a letter to the lessor giving notice of its intent to purchase, and a check for a deposit. The letter, with check enclosed, was sent on the 31st by certified mail, return receipt requested. The lessor returned the check, saying that because she did not receive the letter until February 3 she considered the notice invalid.

In an action by PAFA to enforce the lease, it was granted summary judgment; the lessor appealed. *Held*: Affirmed. Pa. Academy of Fine Arts v. Grant, 590 A.2d 9 (Pa.Super.1991).[a] Is this decision consistent with Restatement Second § 63(b)?

————

SECTION 5.　ACCEPTANCE VARYING OFFER: THE "BATTLE OF THE FORMS"

————

The pattern of communications in a typical contract for the sale of goods has been described briefly above: see "The Battle of the Forms," p. 161.　Here is a more extensive description by Professor Stewart Macaulay, based on a study of Wisconsin businessmen.　In reading the cases that follow, consider what account, if any, should be taken of such findings in formulating legal rules applicable to the transactions described.

MACAULAY, NON-CONTRACTUAL RELATIONS IN BUSINESS: A PRELIMINARY STUDY, 28 Am.Sociological Rev. 55, 57–59 (1963).—A firm will have a set of terms and conditions for purchases, sales, or both printed on the business documents used in these exchanges.　Thus the things to be sold and the price may be planned particularly for each transaction, but standard provisions will further elaborate the performances and cover the other subjects of planning.　Typically, these terms and conditions are lengthy and printed in small type on the back of the forms.　For example, 24 paragraphs in eight point type are printed on the back of the

a. For what it is worth, it may be noted that the Acadamy acquired the lease, by assignment, on the January 30.

purchase order form used by the Allis Chalmers Manufacturing Company. . . .

In larger firms such "boiler plate" provisions are drafted by the house counsel or the firm's outside lawyer. In smaller firms such provisions may be drafted by the industry trade association, may be copied from a competitor, or may be found on forms purchased from a printer. In any event, salesmen and purchasing agents, the operating personnel, typically are unaware of what is said in the fine print on the back of the forms they use. Yet often the normal business patterns will give effect to this standardized planning. For example, purchasing agents may have to use a purchase order form so that all transactions receive a number under the firm's accounting system. Thus, the required accounting record will carry the necessary planning of the exchange relationship printed on its reverse side. If the seller does not object to this planning and accepts the order, the buyer's "fine print" will control. If the seller does object, differences can be settled by negotiation.

This type of standardized planning is very common. . . . [However], standardized planning can break down. In the example of such planning previously given, it was assumed that the purchasing agent would use his company's form with its 24 paragraphs printed on the back and that the seller would accept this or object to any provisions he did not like. However, the seller may fail to read the buyer's 24 paragraphs of fine print and may accept the buyer's order on the seller's own acknowledgment-of-order form. Typically this form will have ten to 50 paragraphs favoring the seller, and these provisions are likely to be different from or inconsistent with the buyer's provisions. The seller's acknowledgment form may be received by the buyer and checked by a clerk. She will read the *face* of the acknowledgment but not the fine print on the back of it because she has neither the time nor ability to analyze the small print on the 100 to 500 forms she must review each day. The face of the acknowledgment—where the goods and the price are specified—is likely to correspond with the face of the purchase order. If it does, the two forms are filed away. At this point, both buyer and seller are likely to assume they have planned an exchange and made a contract. Yet they have done neither, as they are in disagreement about all that appears on the back of their forms. This practice is common enough to have a name. Law teachers call it "the battle of the forms." [b]

NOTE

Buyer as Offeror. In analyzing what Professor Macaulay refers to as "the battle of the forms," it is helpful to keep in mind that the most common situation is the one that he discusses in which the buyer is the offeror and the seller is the offeree. Why is this more common than the situation in the

b. See also Northrop Corp. v. Litronic Industries, 29 F.3d 1173 (7th Cir.1994): " 'Battle of the forms' refers to the not uncommon situation in which one business firm makes an offer in the form of a preprinted form contract and the offeree responds with its own form contract."

Fairmount Glass Works case, p. 158 above, in which the seller was the offeror and the buyer was the offeree?

———

THE "MIRROR IMAGE" RULE

Traditional contract doctrine insists that an acceptance must be on the terms proposed by the offer without the slightest variation. Anything else is a counter offer and a rejection of the original offer. See the *Columbus Rolling Mill* case, described at pp. 215–16 above. The offeror, "as master of his offer," thus enjoys freedom from contract except on the offeror's own terms. In Ardente v. Horan, 366 A.2d 162 (R.I.1976), a prospective buyer who had received an offer of residential property signed an agreement, which his lawyer returned with a check and a letter that said: "My clients are concerned that the following items remain with the real estate: a) dining room set and tapestry wall covering in dining room; b) fireplace fixtures throughout; c) the sun parlor furniture. I would appreciate your confirming that these items are a part of the transaction, as they would be difficult to replace." When the offerors refused to convey the land, the offeree sought specific performance. He lost on the ground that an acceptance "must be definite and unequivocal. . . . An acceptance which is equivocal or upon condition or with a limitation is a counteroffer and requires acceptance by the original offeror before a contractual relationship can exist." It is sometimes said that the acceptance must be the "mirror image" of the offer.

The rigors of the rule that an acceptance must be the "mirror image" of the offer may be mitigated in practice. First, a court may decide that what seemed to be an additional or different term in the acceptance was an "implied term" in the offer, so that language that at first appeared to vary the terms of the offer did not really do so. An example is the court's treatment of the buyer's addition, "the jars and caps to be strictly first-quality goods," near the end of the opinion in the *Fairmount Glass Works* case, above. Second, a court may conclude that the language of the acceptance relating to an additional or different term is only "precatory." Might not the court have read the language in Ardente v. Horan, described above, in this manner? This would have resulted in a contract on the terms of the offeror, who could then have decided whether or not to modify that contract by accepting the offeree's additional proposal. Even where neither of these mitigating techniques is available and no contract has been made, parties often act on the assumption that their promises are binding and the transaction is carried out without incident. Disputes tend to rise in two kinds of cases.

In the first kind of case, one party claims that no contract was made while the other maintains the contrary. This was the situation in Ardente v. Horan, where sellers of land seized on the variation to justify their refusal to convey. When the market rises, sellers are tempted to find such pretexts for getting out of their bargains, and when the market falls buyers are so tempted. The more rigorous the application of the "mirror image" rule, the more readily available will be such pretexts.

In the second kind of case, some performance has taken place and it is clear that a contract has been made, but a dispute arises with respect to performance and the parties differ as to which terms control. Each party insists that a contract was made on its own terms. Under the "mirror image" rule, the party that sent the last form before performance began usually prevailed. This was because each later form operated as a rejection of any earlier offer by the other party and as a counter-offer. When the recipient of this last counter-offer performed, that was taken as an acceptance of that counter-offer. This made it advantageous to fire the "last shot" before performance began. In the typical contract for the sale of goods, it was the buyer that, by its purchase order, made the initial offer and the seller that, by its varying acknowledgement, fired the "last shot," rejecting the buyer's offer and making a counter-offer. When the buyer accepted the goods, it was taken to have accepted the seller's counter-offer and was bound by the seller's terms.

NOTES

(1) *Back-and-Forth Firing.* Given that the last-shot rule applies, the question sometimes arises which of the parties was the last to fire before performance commenced. See Mechanical Plant Services, Inc., v. Dresser–Rand Company, 1997 U.S. App. LEXIS 15890 (4th Cir.1997), where the parties had been at loggerheads over the terms of a services contract.

(2) *Flexible Tests of Acceptance.* In Stonewood Hotel v. Seven Seas, Inc., 452 N.W.2d 94 (N.D.1990), negotiations between a landlord and tenant for a long-term lease had arrived at Draft 4, which was submitted for the landlord, by its attorney, to the attorney for the tenant. After a conversation between the attorneys, the latter prepared Draft 5, containing some changes, had it executed by the tenant and sent it to the landlord's attorney. Thereupon the landlord purported to withdraw its offer of a long-term lease. In an eviction action, the trial court concluded that Draft 5 was a counter-offer. On appeal, *held:* Reversed and remanded. "It does not appear to us," the court said, "that the trial court considered whether the new proposals may have constituted an acceptance not dependent on [the landlord's] assent to the added terms, in accordance with Restatement (Second) of Contracts § 61 ...."[a] The tenant's possession and partial performance, the court said, "render application of flexible tests of acceptance ... all the more appropriate for determining if parties have agreed to a lease even though they have not signed a lease, rather than application of the mirror-image offer-and-acceptance-rule. . . .

THE UNIFORM COMMERCIAL CODE:
ADDITIONAL AND DIFFERENT TERMS

The Code made a marked shift in the common law associated with offer and acceptance in relation to sales of goods. That much can be

---

a. Id. at 95, quoting from Stonewood Hotel Corp., Inc. v. Davis Development, Inc., 447 N.W.2d 286, 291 (N.D.1989). The court referred also to § 9–03–21 of the North Dakota Civil Code.

observed from the first subsection of the provision titled "Additional Terms in Acceptance or Confirmation" (UCC 2–207):

> A definite and seasonable expression of acceptance or a written confirmation which is sent within a reasonable time operates as an acceptance even though it states terms additional to or different from those offered and agreed upon, unless acceptance is expressly made conditional on assent to the additional terms.

The provision goes on to specify, in an elaborate way, what constitute the terms of a contract when the writings exchanged by the parties diverge.

A remarkable feature of the provision is that it contemplates situations in which the terms of the contract as initially constituted may change over time. There is, for example, the possibility that an "additional term" will become part of the contract at the juncture when, after receiving notice of it, the offeror lets a reasonable time elapse without having given "notification of objection" to the additional term. (But materiality matters: "If a term offered by the offeree in his acceptance works a material alteration of the offer, the acceptance is still effective, but the term is not: that is, the contract is enforceable minus the term the offeree tried to add." Union Carbide Corp. v. Oscar Mayer Foods Corp., 947 F.2d 1333 (7th Cir.1990).)

Scope of the section. Professor Macaulay described the battle of the forms by reference to two firms, both of which use standardized forms containing boilerplate provisions. Is it clear that UCC 2–207 applies *only* in a case of that kind? Arguments based on the section are sometimes made when the facts are quite different; but these arguments are not always accepted. See ProCD, Inc. v. Zeidenberg, 86 F.3d 1447 (7th Cir.1996), concerning the sale of a software database package. Upon installation, the software flashed a message by which the compiler sought to restrict remarketing of the product. The buyer cited UCC 2–207 in attempting to circumvent the restriction. But the attempt was unsuccessful. "Our case has only one form," the court said; "UCC 2–207 is irrelevant."[1] Compare the Case of the Bride's Acceptance, Note 5, p. 216 above (not a case governed by UCC Article 2).

NOTES

(1) *More on scope.* What language in the section limits its application to discordant terms in standard forms?

The section is irrelevant, it has been said, once the parties have reached an agreement; it "only applies to the *formation* of a contract." Besicorp Group, Inc. v. Thermo Electron Corp., 931 F.Supp. 86, 98 (N.D.N.Y.1997). If that proposition

---

1. The court that decided this case reaffirmed its ruling in a later case: Hill v. Gateway 2000, Inc., 105 F.3d 1147 (1997). *Hill* concerned the sale to a consumer of a PC, and terms of sale wrapped in the packaging. The earlier case could not be distinguished, the court said, on the ground that the buyer there acted as a merchant in purchasing the software: he did not.

Representatives of consumers' interests have protested against "in-the-box" contract terms, in deliberations about revising the UCC.

is right, is it another reason for binding a software buyer to the terms of an end-use license, as in *ProCD*?

(2) *An Agenda*. The complexity of UCC 2–207 makes it useful to have a brief agenda of significant problems to consider. In reading the following materials, try to apply them to variations, as described below, on a situation in which the buyer sends a purchase order, followed by the seller's acknowledgment. Take four cases, as follows, each entry describing the sole difference between the terms of the documents.

(a) the acknowledgment contains a disclaimer of warranties that the purchase order does not;

(b) the acknowledgment contains an arbitration clause that the purchase order does not;

(c) the acknowledgment imposes a requirement that any claims be made within one month of the date of delivery;

(d) the acknowledgment changes the delivery date from April 1 to May 1.

UCC 2–207: TEXT ANALYSIS

Materiality of terms. When a response to an offer contains terms "additional" to those of the offer, but operates as an acceptance under subsection (1) of UCC 2–207, much may depend on whether or not these terms materially alter the offer, in the sense of subsection (2)(b). As explained in Comment 3, if they do not alter the original bargain, "they will be incorporated unless notice of objection has already been given or is given within a reasonable time." Useful examples of terms that do and do not amount to material alterations are given in Comments 4 and 5.[a]

Acceptance "expressly made conditional. . . . " It happens occasionally that the recipient of an offer responds with conscious reference to the proviso in subsection (1), answering in the manner, "I will not accept your offer unless you assent to the following: . . . " (See, for example, C. Itoh & Co. v. Jordan Int'l Co., below.) A response so expressed is sometimes described as a conditional acceptance, as in the opinion that follows. Although it is somewhat anomalous to speak of an acceptance that does not conclude a contract, the description is a convenient shorthand. The scope of the proviso has been frequently debated: is any particular form of words required? Many a litigant has contended that its response to an offer, though not written with conscious reference to the proviso, amounted to a counteroffer. These arguments have met with mixed success, as indicated in the Notes below.

There is, in some situations, a distinct advantage to an offeree in *preventing* the application of the proviso; do you see what it is?

Contrasting cases. Consider again the two kinds of case described earlier, one in which there has been some performance indicative of a contract, and one in which all that has occurred, before a dispute arises

---

a. For indications that an addition "material" under the law of one state may be immaterial under the law of another—both having enacted UCC 2–207—see Avedon Engineering, Inc. v. Seatex, 126 F.3d 1279 (10th Cir.1997).

between the parties, is that they have exchanged messages. Cases of the latter sort are far less frequent. (For an instance see Note 2, below.) Notice that subsection (3) of UCC 2–207 has no obvious bearing on that sort of case.

Is it important, when deciding whether or not an exchange of discordant messages constituted a contract, to consider the materiality of the differences? Apparently not, according to a straightforward reading of subsection (1); for subsection (2) of UCC 2–207 assumes the existence of a contract. But the statute is not always given a straightforward reading. For an explanation of how the issue of materiality might figure in the application of subsection (1), see Note 2 below.

NOTES

(1) *Problem*. Let it be supposed that S, having received a purchase order from B, responds with a standard-form confirmation of sale, together with a cover note to B as follows: "You must make any complaint about the quality of the goods within one month after receiving them. Unless you assent to this requirement, the enclosed 'confirmation' is a rejection of your purchase order; see subsection (1) of UCC 2–207, final clause." Thereafter, S ships part of the goods ordered, and B adds them to its inventory. (The case is one within the first set described above.) How might it be argued that there is a contract between the parties and that it incorporates S's one-month term?

The following Note shows how the last-shot rule has been applied to cases in which a supplier of goods was less explicit than S was.

(2) *A Discarded Precedent*. In a case decided soon after the Code was promulgated, the court considered a seller's acknowledgment that disclaimed all warranties. In an action by the buyer for breach of warranty, brought after it had accepted and used the goods, the court approved a verdict directed for the seller. The decision was widely reprobated. Much later it was reconsidered in the same court. The earlier case is Roto–Lith, Ltd. v. F.P. Bartlett & Co., 297 F.2d 497 (1st Cir.1962); the later one is Ionics, Inc. v. Elmwood Sensors, Inc., 110 F.3d 184 (1st Cir.1997). The rule of *Roto-Lith* (as stated in *Ionics*), was this:

> [A] response which states a condition materially altering the obligation solely to the disadvantage of the offeror is an "acceptance ... expressly conditional on assent to the additional ... terms." This holding took the case outside of section 2–207 by applying the exception after the comma in subsection (1).[b]

The *Ionics* court concluded that *Roto-Lith* had "outlived its usefulness" as a precedent.[c]

(3) *"Counteroffer" as an Acceptance*. The opinion in *Ionics* addresses a further issue: the word "counteroffer" appeared in the seller's response to the buyer's order; and that—the seller thought—ought to make its terms control. Not so, the court ruled: "The form ... is labelled an 'Acknowledgment' [and]

---

b. Sentences quoted out of sequence.

c. "Our decision," the court said, "brings this circuit in line with the majority view on the subject and puts to rest a case that has provoked considerable criticism from courts and commentators alike." (foot-note omitted). For adverse comment see Gardner Zemke Co. v. Dunham Bush, Inc., 850 P.2d 319 (N.M.1993) (*Roto-Lith* "almost uniformly criticized ... as an aberration in Article 2 jurisprudence").

taken as a whole, appears to contemplate an order's confirmation rather than an order's rejection in the form of a counteroffer."[d]

(4) *Readings.* The literature on the "battle of the forms" is voluminous. Some representative items are: Baird & Weisberg, Rules, Standards, and the Battle of the Forms: A Reassessment of § 2–207, 68 Va.L.Rev. 1217 (1982) (asserting merits in "formal rules of offer and acceptance," as exemplified in the mirror-image rule, in contrast to "open-textured standards," as exemplified in § 2–207); Murray, The Chaos of the "Battle of the Forms": Solutions, 39 Vand.L.Rev. 1307 (1986); and Wladis, U.C.C. Section 2–207 ..., fn. b above.

STEP–SAVER DATA SYSTEMS, INC. v. WYSE TECHNOLOGY

United States Court of Appeals, Third Circuit, 1991.
939 F.2d 91.

WISDOM, Circuit Judge: The "Limited Use License Agreement" printed on a package containing a copy of a computer program raises the central issue in this appeal. The trial judge held that the terms of the Limited Use License Agreement governed the purchase of the package, and, therefore, granted the software producer, The Software Link, Inc. ("TSL"), a directed verdict on claims of breach of warranty brought by a disgruntled purchaser, Step–Saver Data Systems, Inc. We disagree with the district court's determination of the legal effect of the license, and reverse and remand the warranty claims for further consideration.

[In the spring of 1986 Step–Saver obtained several copies of Wyse Technology's program "Advanced Multilink", which it tested with a view to incorporating it into a multi-user electronic system ("the system"). It decided to do so.] From August of 1986 through March of 1987, Step–Saver purchased and resold 142 copies of the Multilink Advanced program. Step–Saver would typically purchase copies of the program in the following manner. First, Step–Saver would telephone TSL and place an order. (Step–Saver would typically order twenty copies of the program at a time.) TSL would accept the order and promise, while on the telephone, to ship the goods promptly. After the telephone order, Step–Saver would send a purchase order, detailing the items to be purchased, their price, and shipping and payment terms. TSL would ship the order promptly, along with an invoice. The invoice would contain terms essentially identical with those on Step–Saver's purchase order: price, quantity, and shipping and payment terms. No reference was made during the telephone calls, or on either the purchase orders or the invoices with regard to a disclaimer of any warranties.

Printed on the package of each copy of the program, however, would be [form language purporting to express the complete agreement between the parties (the "box-top license"), including] five terms relevant to this action:

d. The court reconsidered the rule of *Roto-Lith* only after rejecting the seller's argument on this point. For debate about the significance of "confirmation" see Echo, Inc. v. Whitson Co., 121 F.3d 1099 (7th Cir.1997).

(1) The box-top license provides that the customer has not purchased the software itself, but has merely obtained a personal, non-transferable license to use the program.

(2) The box-top license, in detail and at some length, disclaims all express and implied warranties except for a warranty that the disks contained in the box are free from defects.

. . .

(5) The box-top license states: "Opening this package indicates your acceptance of these terms and conditions. If you do not agree with them, you should promptly return the package unopened to the person from whom you purchased it within fifteen days from date of purchase and your money will be refunded to you by that person."

Step–Saver began marketing the system in November of 1986, and sold one hundred forty-two systems mostly to law and medical offices before terminating sales of the system in March of 1987. Almost immediately upon installation of the system, Step–Saver began to receive complaints from some of its customers. At least twelve of Step–Saver's customers filed suit against Step–Saver because of the problems with the multi-user system.

[Efforts by the parties having failed to resolve the problems, Step–Saver brought an action against TSL, charging it with breaches of warranties and seeking indemnity for costs in resolving the customers' suits. Wyse Technology, a manufacturer of terminals, also a defendant, was exonerated in the trial court and on appeal.]

The district court, without much discussion, held, as a matter of law, that the box-top license was the final and complete expression of the terms of the parties' agreement. Because the district court decided the questions of contract formation and interpretation as issues of law, we review the district court's resolution of these questions *de novo*.

Step–Saver contends that the contract for each copy of the program was formed when TSL agreed, on the telephone, to ship the copy at the agreed price.[3] The box-top license, argues Step–Saver, was a material alteration to the parties' contract which did not become a part of the contract under UCC § 2–207.[4] . . .

A. *Does UCC § 2–207 Govern the Analysis?*

As a basic principle, we agree with Step–Saver that UCC § 2–207 governs our analysis. We see no need to parse the parties' various actions to decide exactly when the parties formed a contract. TSL has shipped the product, and Step–Saver has accepted and paid for each copy

---

3. See UCC § 2–206(1)(b) and comment 2. Note that under UCC § 2–201, the oral contract would not be enforceable in the absence of a writing or part performance because each order typically involved more than $500 in goods. However, courts have typically treated the questions of formation and interpretation as separate from the question of when the contract becomes enforceable. See, e.g., C. Itoh & Co. v. Jordan Int'l Co., [p. ___ below].

4. Section 2–207 provides: [quotation omitted].

of the program. The parties' performance demonstrates the existence of
a contract. The dispute is, therefore, not over the existence of a
contract, but the nature of its terms.[5] When the parties' conduct
establishes a contract, but the parties have failed to adopt expressly a
particular writing as the terms of their agreement, and the writings
exchanged by the parties do not agree, UCC § 2–207 determines the
terms of the contract.

... Under the common law of sales, and to some extent still for
contracts outside the UCC,[6] an acceptance that varied any term of the
offer operated as a rejection of the offer, and simultaneously made a
counteroffer.[7] ... [T]he terms of the party who sent the last form,
typically the seller, would become the terms of the parties' contract.
This result was known as the "last shot rule".

The UCC, in § 2–207, rejected this approach. Instead, it recognized
that, while a party may desire the terms detailed in its form if a dispute,
in fact, arises, most parties do not expect a dispute to arise when they
first enter into a contract. As a result, most parties will proceed with
the transaction even if they know that the terms of their form would not
be enforced.[8] The insight behind the rejection of the last shot rule is
that it would be unfair to bind the buyer of goods to the standard terms
of the seller, when neither party cared sufficiently to establish expressly
the terms of their agreement, simply because the seller sent the last
form.... In the absence of a party's express assent to the additional or
different terms of the writing, section 2–207 provides a default rule that
the parties intended, as the terms of their agreement, those terms to
which both parties have agreed,[9] along with any terms implied by the
provisions of the UCC.

The reasons that led to the rejection of the last shot rule, and the
adoption of section 2–207, apply fully in this case....

B. *Application of § 2–207*

. . .

1. Was the contract sufficiently definite?

TSL argues that ... several critical terms could only be determined
by referring to the box-top license. [It argued, for example, that the
warranties available to Step–Saver were essential and were defined only
in the box-top license. The court rejected this argument. It said

---

5. See McJunkin Corp. v. Mechanicals,
Inc., 888 F.2d 481, 488 (6th Cir.1989).

6. See, e.g., Learning Works, Inc. v.
Learning Annex, Inc., 830 F.2d 541, 543
(4th Cir.1987).

7. See, e.g., Diamond Fruit Growers,
Inc., 794 F.2d at 1443; J. White & R. Summers, Handbook of the Law Under the Uniform Commercial Code, § 1–2 at 34 (2d ed.
1980).

8. As Judge Engel has written:

Usually, these standard terms mean little, for a contract looks to its fulfillment

and rarely anticipates its breach. Hope
springs eternal in the commercial world
and expectations are usually, but not always, realized.

McJunkin Corp. v. Mechanicals, Inc., 888
F.2d at 482.

9. The parties may demonstrate their
acceptance of a particular term either "orally or by informal correspondence", UCC 2–
207, comment 1, or by placing the term in
their respective form.

(quoting) that the terms in question were not "gaping holes in a multi-million dollar contract that no one but the parties themselves could fill." [10] In that connection the court quoted UCC 2–204(3).] [T]he UCC provides for express and implied warranties if the seller fails to disclaim expressly those warranties.[11]   Thus, even though warranties are an important term left blank by the parties, the default rules of the UCC fill in that blank.

We hold that contract was sufficiently definite without the terms provided by the box-top license.

2.   The box-top license as a counter-offer?

TSL advances two reasons why its box-top license should be considered a conditional acceptance under UCC § 2–207(1). First, TSL argues that the express language of the box-top license, including ... the phrase "opening this product indicates your acceptance of these terms", made TSL's acceptance "expressly conditional on assent to the additional or different terms".[13]   Second, TSL argues that the box-top license, by permitting return of the product within fifteen days if the purchaser[14] does not agree to the terms stated in the license (the "refund offer"), establishes that TSL's acceptance was conditioned on Step–Saver's assent to the terms of the box-top license, citing Monsanto Agricultural Products Co. v. Edenfield.[15]   While we are not certain that a conditional acceptance analysis applies when a contract is established by performance,[16] we assume that it does and consider TSL's arguments.

To determine whether a writing constitutes a conditional acceptance, courts have established three tests. [The court described various applications that courts have given to the concluding phrase in subsection (1) of UCC 2–207, and recited some further facts about the dealings between the parties.]

Based on these facts, we conclude that TSL did not clearly express its unwillingness to proceed with the transactions unless its additional terms were incorporated into the parties' agreement. The box-top license did not, therefore, constitute a conditional acceptance under UCC § 2–207(1).

10.   488 A.2d at 591.

11.   See UCC § 2–312, 2–313, 2–314, & 2–315.

13.   UCC § 2–207(1).

14.   In the remainder of the opinion, we will refer to the transaction as a sale for the sake of simplicity, but, by doing so, do not mean to resolve the sale-license question.

15.   426 So.2d 574 (Fla.Dist.Ct.App. 1982).

16.   Even though a writing is sent after performance establishes the existence of a contract, courts have analyzed the effect of such a writing under UCC § 2–207. See Herzog Oil Field Serv. v. Otto Torpedo Co., 391 Pa.Super. 133, 570 A.2d 549, 550 (Pa.Super.Ct.1990); McJunkin Corp. v. Me-

chanicals, Inc., 888 F.2d at 487. The official comment to UCC 2–207 suggests that, even though a proposed deal has been closed, the conditional acceptance analysis still applies in determining which writing's terms will define the contract.

2. Under this Article a proposed deal which in commercial understanding has in fact been closed is recognized as a contract. Therefore, any additional matter contained in the confirmation or in the acceptance falls within subsection (2) and must be regarded as a proposal for an added term *unless the acceptance is made conditional on the acceptance of the additional or different terms.*

3. Did the parties's course of dealing establish that the parties had excluded any express or implied warranties associated with the software program?

TSL argues that because Step–Saver placed its orders for copies of the Multilink Advanced program with notice of the terms of the box-top license, Step–Saver is bound by the terms of the box-top license. Essentially, TSL is arguing that, even if the terms of the box-top license would not become part of the contract if the case involved only a single transaction, the repeated expression of those terms by TSL eventually incorporates them within the contract.

... While one court has concluded that terms repeated in a number of written confirmations eventually become part of the contract even though neither party ever takes any action with respect to the issue addressed by those terms,[17] most courts have rejected such reasoning.[18]

... [W]e are not convinced that TSL's unilateral act of repeatedly sending copies of the box-top license with its product can establish a course of dealing between TSL and Step–Saver that resulted in the adoption of the terms of the box-top license.

With regard to more specific evidence as to the parties' course of dealing or performance, it appears that the parties have not incorporated the warranty disclaimer into their agreement. First, there is the evidence that TSL tried to obtain Step–Saver's express consent to the disclaimer and limitation of damages provision of the box-top license. Step–Saver refused to sign the proposed agreements. Second, when first notified of the problems with the program, TSL spent considerable time and energy attempting to solve the problems identified by Step–Saver.

Course of conduct is ordinarily a factual issue. But we hold that the actions of TSL in repeatedly sending a writing, whose terms would otherwise be excluded under UCC § 2–207, cannot establish a course of conduct between TSL and Step–Saver that adopted the terms of the writing.

[The court rejected arguments of public policy advanced by TSL.]

C. *The Terms of the Contract*

Under section 2–207, an additional term detailed in the box-top license will not be incorporated into the parties' contract if the term's addition to the contract would materially alter the parties' agreement.[19] Step–Saver alleges that several representations made by TSL constitute express warranties, and that valid implied warranties were also a part of the parties' agreement. Because the district court considered the box-top license to exclude all of these warranties, the district court did not consider whether other factors may act to exclude these warranties.

---

17. See Schulze & Burch Biscuit Co. v. Tree Top, Inc., 831 F.2d 709, 714–15 (7th Cir.1987). [The court gave reasons to doubt the authority of this case.]

18. See, e.g., Trans–Aire Int'l v. Northern Adhesive Co., 882 F.2d at 1262–63 & n. 9; Diamond Fruit Growers, Inc., 794 F.2d at 1445; Tuck Industries v. Reichhold Chemicals, Inc., 542 N.Y.S.2d 676, 678, 151 A.D.2d 566 (N.Y.App.Div.1989); Southeastern Adhesives Co., 366 S.E.2d at 507–08.

19. UCC § 2–207(2)(b).

The existence and nature of the warranties is primarily a factual question that we leave for the district court,[20] but assuming that these warranties were included within the parties' original agreement, we must conclude that adding the disclaimer of warranty and limitation of remedies provisions from the box-top license would, as a matter of law, substantially alter the distribution of risk between Step–Saver and TSL.[21] Therefore, under UCC § 2–207(2)(b), the disclaimer of warranty and limitation of remedies terms of the box-top license did not become a part of the parties' agreement.[22]

... [T]he box-top license should have been treated as a written confirmation containing additional terms.[23] Because the warranty disclaimer and limitation of remedies terms would materially alter the parties' agreement, these terms did not become a part of the parties' agreement. We remand for further consideration the express and implied warranty claims against TSL.

NOTES

(1) *Questions and Answers. Step-Saver* was a battle-of-the-forms case, it has been said, because the court had to choose between incompatible terms proposed by the parties. Would the analysis have been different if there had been no purchase orders, and shipments—with the seller's terms attached—had followed directly on the telephone agreements? And would it matter that the seller's terms had been enclosed in the packaging?

To the first question the answer has been given, Yes. ProCD, Inc. v. Zeidenberg, 86 F.3d 1447 (7th Cir.1996) ("Our case has only one form; UCC 2–207 is irrelevant.") As to the second question, a decision of the same court has provoked an intense debate over "in the box" limitations on warranties. For the court's answer (no) see Hill v. Gateway 2000, Inc., 105 F.3d 1147 (1997) ("The difference is functional, not legal.")

(2) *The "Columbia" Deal.* As part of the projected sale of an auto dealership to a firm named Columbia, the owner proposed to transfer "all saleable new Hyundai vehicles." This term appeared in the last of several draft agreements of sale. Columbia signed and returned the proposal, but only after interlining "current year" after "saleable." The owner advised Columbia that its "counter-

20. For example, questions exist as to: (1) whether the statements by TSL were representations of fact, or mere statements of opinion; (2) whether the custom in the trade is to exclude warranties and limit remedies in contracts between a software producer and its dealer; (3) whether Step–Saver relied on TSL's alleged representations, or whether these warranties became a basis of the parties' bargain; and (4) whether Step–Saver's testing excluded some or all of these warranties. From the record, it appears that most of these issues are factual determinations that will require a trial, as did the warranty claims against Wyse. But we leave these issues open to the district court on remand.

21. See Valtrol, Inc. v. General Connectors Corp., 884 F.2d 149, 155 (4th Cir. 1989); Trans–Aire Int'l v. Northern Adhe-

sive Co., 882 F.2d at 1262–63; UCC § 2–207, official comment 4.

22. The following recent cases reach a similar conclusion concerning indemnity or warranty disclaimers contained in writings exchanged after the contract had formed: McJunkin Corp., 888 F.2d at 488–89; Valtrol, Inc. v. General Connectors Corp., 884 F.2d at 155; Trans–Aire Int'l v. Northern Adhesive Co., 882 F.2d at 1262–63; Bowdoin, 817 F.2d at 1545–46; Diamond Fruit Growers, Inc., 794 F.2d at 1445; Tuck Industries, 542 N.Y.S.2d at 678; Southeastern Adhesives Co., 366 S.E.2d at 507–08.

23. See Idaho Power Co., 596 F.2d at 925–27 (applying UCC § 2–207 despite presence of integration clause in written confirmation).

offer" was rejected. On facts like these, tried before a jury, Columbia sought to have the jury directed that a contract for sale existed; but the judge accepted a verdict to the contrary. How might the verdict be justified, according to UCC 2–207? See Columbia Hyundia v. Carll Hyundia, 484 S.E.2d 468 (S.C.1997).[a]

Compare the Case of the Bride's Acceptance, Note 5, p. 216 above (not a case governed by UCC Article 2). Is that an objectionable application of the last-shot rule?

(3) *Another Seller Unhorsed.* In Northrop Corporation v. Litronic Industries, p. ___ fn.b above, the parties were a major defense contractor (Northrop) and a supplier of electronic components for weapons systems (Litronic). Northrop sued to recover the price it had paid, having sought—long after delivery—to return the goods as defective. Litronic had declined the return by reference to a term in its offer to sell: rejection permitted only within 90 days of delivery. That term was held to be inoperative. Northrop had agreed to the sale by telephone and letter, both times referring to a forthcoming purchase order in a form with which Litronic was familiar; that form required a warranty of indefinite duration. Litronic argued that, as a much smaller firm, it would have been unlikely to make such a burdensome warranty. But it was a "curious suggestion," the court said, "that little fellows are more likely than big ones to get their way in negotiations between firms of disparate size."

Comparing the documents, the court said that any limitation on the length of the warranty as specified by Northrop would be a materially different term. (Further particulars of this case are given below.)

PROPOSALS FOR REFORM

UCC 2–207 has engendered much dissatisfaction; there is common consent that the statute should be recast. The sponsors of the Code have found it difficult, however, to satisfy themselves with draft revisions. None of the proposals would revert to the mirror-image rule.[6] A committee draft, circulated for comment in 1997, had the following features:

- Reducing the prospect that a consumer will be bound by a "non-negotiated" term;[7]

- Requiring, on occasion, "conspicuous" language to effect a conditional acceptance; and

- Otherwise, placing increased reliance on the intent of the parties, and on their having reached an agreement.[8]

a. The owner failed to argue, at trial, that the sale of a business does not involve "goods." In any event, the court said, "the majority view is that the sale of a business is treated as the sale of 'goods' under the UCC." Id. at 469 n.3.

6. But see Hyland, Draft, 97 Col.L.Rev. 1343 (1997), suggesting repeal.

7. Subject to some qualifications, the draft stated the following rule about consumers:

[A]ny non-negotiated term that a reasonable consumer in a transaction of this type would not reasonably expect to be in the record is excluded from the contract, unless the consumer had knowledge of the term before agreeing to the record.

("Record" to be defined so as include information electronically stored.)

8. The provisions referred to appear in a draft revision of Article 2. Particulars appear there in §§ 2–203, 2–205, and 2–206, as well as in 2–207.

In submitting the draft, the Reporters indicated reservations about it: "not satisfied with this version."

Another proposal for reform is described in Note 4, p. 247 below.

NOTE

International Sale-of-Goods Convention. A provision comparable to § UCC 2–207 appears as Article 19 of the Convention on Contracts for the International Sale of Goods (Vienna Convention; see the Selections). Among additional terms that are considered "materially" to alter the terms of an offer, under that provision, are those relating to "the extent of one party's liability to the other or the settlement of disputes." Does this expression embrace all terms that "substantially alter the distribution of risk" between the parties? if so, and if the step–saver case had been governed by the convention, would the result have been the same? The convention is based, it is said, on "the assumption that boilerplate terms and conditions are important so that no contract can exist until both parties agree to the terms." But that is said to be a theoretical difference, having "little practical effect." Gabriel, the Battle of the Forms: A Comparison of the [Convention] and the Uniform Commercial Code, 49 Bus.Law. 1053, 1063 (1994).[a]

Consider the effect of the Convention on the two following cases, in light of its reference to settlement-of-dispute terms.

DORTON v. COLLINS & AIKMAN CORP.

United States Court of Appeals, Sixth Circuit, 1972.
453 F.2d 1161.

CELEBREZZE, CIRCUIT JUDGE. [Dorton and his partners did business in Tennessee as "The Carpet Mart." Collins & Aikman was a Delaware corporation having its principal place of business in New York. Over a three-year period, in 55 transactions, The Carpet Mart bought carpets from Collins & Aikman. Ultimately it brought an action against the seller in a Tennessee court, claiming damages for fraud and misrepresentation about the quality of the carpets.] The Carpet Mart maintains that in May, 1970, in response to a customer complaint, it learned that not all of the carpets were manufactured from 100% Kodel polyester fiber but rather some were composed of a cheaper and inferior carpet fiber. After the cause was removed to the District Court on the basis of diversity of citizenship, Collins & Aikman moved for a stay pending arbitration, asserting that The Carpet Mart was bound to an arbitration agreement which appeared on the reverse side of Collins & Aikman's printed sales acknowledgment forms. Holding that there existed no binding arbitration agreement between the parties, the District Court denied the stay. For the reasons set out below, we remand the case to the District Court for further findings. . . .

[The court described the dealings between the parties. Upon receiving an order telephoned to the Collins & Aikman order department in Dalton, Georgia, and after a report from its credit department, Collins & Aikman typed the information concerning the particular order on one of

a. The Convention has only limited application, be it noted, to sales of goods   bought for personal, family or household use. See Article 2(a).

its printed acknowledgment forms. One legend or another on the face specified when the order "shall become a contract," e.g.,

> (a) when signed and delivered by Buyer to Seller and accepted in writing by Seller or (b) when Buyer has received and retained this order for ten days without objection, or (c) when Buyer has accepted delivery of any part of the merchandise ..., or when Buyer has otherwise indicated acceptance of the terms hereof.

Also:

> ... acceptance (or "order") subject to all of the terms and conditions on the face and reverse side hereof....]

The small print on the reverse side of the forms provided, among other things, that all claims arising out of the contract would be submitted to arbitration in New York City.... Absent a delay in the mails ... The Carpet Mart always received the acknowledgment forms prior to receiving the carpets. In all cases The Carpet Mart took delivery of and paid for the carpets without objecting to any terms contained in the acknowledgment form.

In holding that no binding arbitration agreement was created between the parties through the transactions above, the District Court relied on T.C.A. § 47–2–207 [UCC § 2–207]. [The court] found that Subsection 2–207(3) controlled the instant case ... [and it] concluded that the arbitration clause on the back of Collins & Aikman's sales acknowledgment had not become a binding term in the 50–odd transactions with The Carpet Mart.

In reviewing this determination by the District Court, we are aware of the problems which courts have had in interpreting Section 2–207. [The court proceeded by describing the general purpose of the provision and reviewing its provisions.]

With the above analysis and purposes of Section 2–207 in mind, we turn to their application in the present case....

[The court considered two possibilities: that the defendant's forms were "acceptances" and that they were "confirmations." For resolving this, the court directed that the trial court determine "whether oral agreements were reached between the parties prior to the sending of Collins & Aikman's acknowledgment forms." In an affidavit by a partner in The Carpet Mart there was testimony indicating that they were.

[In either event, the court suggested, the plaintiff's oral orders may have embodied an arbitration provision, such that in this respect the defendant's forms were not "additional to or different from" the orders: "we believe that a specific finding on this point will be required on remand."[1]

---

1. It is not inconceivable that a buyer might request that all claims be submitted to arbitration, see Universal Oil Products v. S.C.M. Corp., 313 F.Supp. 905 (D.Conn. 1970), or that a buyer might orally submit to the seller's known policy of arbitration in order to facilitate acceptance of the offer.

[The court next addressed the question whether or not, if "additional or different," the defendant's forms were within the proviso of UCC 2–207(1): . . . acceptance expressly made conditional on assent to the additional or different terms.] . . . Although Collins & Aikman's use of the words "subject to" suggests that the acceptances were conditional to some extent . . . we believe that [the proviso] was intended to apply only to an acceptance which clearly reveals that the offeree is unwilling to proceed with the transaction unless he is assured of the offeror's assent to the additional or different terms therein. See 1 Hawkland, [A Transactional Guide to the Uniform Commercial Code (1964)] § 1.090303, at 21. That the acceptance is predicated on the offeror's assent must be "directly and distinctly stated or expressed rather than implied or left to inference." Webster's Third International Dictionary (defining "express").

Although the UCC does not provide a definition of "assent," it is significant that Collins & Aikman's printed acknowledgment forms specified at least seven types of action or inaction on the part of the buyer which—sometimes at Collins & Aikman's option—would be deemed to bind the buyer to the terms therein. These ranged from the buyer's signing and delivering the acknowledgment to the seller—which indeed could have been recognized as the buyer's assent to Collins & Aikman's terms—to the buyer's retention of the acknowledgment for ten days without objection—which could never have been recognized as the buyer's assent to the additional or different terms where acceptance is expressly conditional on that assent.[2]

To recognize Collins & Aikman's acceptances as "expressly conditional on [the buyer's] assent to the additional . . . terms" therein, within the proviso of Subsection 2–207(1), would thus require us to ignore the specific language of that provision.[3] Such an interpretation is not justified in view of the fact that Subsection 2–207(1) is clearly designed to give legal recognition to many contracts where the variance between the offer and acceptance would have precluded such recognition at common law.

Because Collins & Aikman's acceptances were not expressly conditional on the buyer's assent to the additional terms within the proviso of Subsection 2–207(1), a contract is recognized under Subsection (1), and

---

2. The common law has never recognized silence or inaction as a mode of acceptance. See 1 W. Hawkland, supra, § 1.090301, at 17. Under the counter-offer approach which Section 2–207 was designed to modify, the offeror had to take receipt of and pay for the goods without objection before he was deemed to have accepted the terms of the counter-offer. And although Subsection 2–207(2)(c) provides that certain additional terms can be accepted by the offeror's failure to object, nothing in the Code suggests that silence or inaction can be recognized as an offeror's assent in the present context.

3. We are aware that at least two Courts of Appeals have not chosen to read the Subsection 2–207(1) proviso as strictly as we do here. See Roto–Lith, Ltd. v. F.P. Bartlett & Co., 297 F.2d 497, 499–500 (1st Cir.1962); Construction Aggregates Corp. v. Hewitt–Robins, Inc., 404 F.2d 505, 509 (5th Cir.1969) (dictum). But see Matter of Doughboy Industries, Inc., and Pantasote Co., 17 A.D.2d 216, 233 N.Y.S.2d 488 (1962). We believe, however, that the approach adopted here is dictated by both the language of the proviso and the purpose of Subsection 2–207(1).

the additional terms are treated as "proposals" for addition to the contract under Subsection 2–207(2).[4] Since both Collins & Aikman and The Carpet Mart are clearly "merchants" as that term is defined in Subsection 2–104(1), the arbitration provision will be deemed to have been accepted by The Carpet Mart under Subsection 2–207(2) unless it materially altered the terms of The Carpet Mart's oral offers. T.C.A. § 47–2–207(2)(b) [UCC § 2–207(2)(b)].[5] We believe that the question of whether the arbitration provision materially altered the oral offer under Subsection 2–207(2)(b) is one which can be resolved only by the District Court on further findings of fact in the present case.[6] If the arbitration provision did in fact materially alter The Carpet Mart's offer, it could not become a part of the contract "unless expressly agreed to" by The Carpet Mart. T.C.A. § 47–2–207 [UCC § 2–207], Official Comment No. 3.

We therefore conclude that if on remand the District Court finds that Collins & Aikman's acknowledgments were in fact acceptances and that the arbitration provision was additional to the terms of The Carpet Mart's oral orders, contracts will be recognized under Subsection 2–207(1). The arbitration clause will then be viewed as a "proposal" under Subsection 2–207(2) which will be deemed to have been accepted by The Carpet Mart unless it materially altered the oral offers.

[Next the court considered the possibility that the acknowledgment forms were not acceptances but rather were confirmations of prior oral

---

4. Apparently believing that Collins & Aikman's acknowledgments were acceptances "expressly . . . conditional on assent to the additional or different terms" under the Subsection 2–207(1) proviso, the District Court recognized contracts between the parties under Subsection 2–207(3) since the subsequent performance by both parties clearly recognized the existence of a contract. Absent our conclusion that Collins & Aikman's acknowledgments do not fall within the Subsection 2–207(1) proviso, we believe that the District Court correctly applied Subsection 2–207(3) to Collins & Aikman's "acceptances" notwithstanding the fact that some of the language of that Subsection appears to refer to the typical situation under Section 2–207 where there exist both a written offer and a written acceptance. Although we recognize the value that writings by both parties serve in sales transactions, where Subsection 2–207(3) is otherwise applicable we do not believe the purposes of that Subsection should be abandoned simply because the offeror chose to rely on his oral offer. In such a case, we believe that the District Court's comparison of the terms of the oral offer and the written acceptance under Subsection (3) would have been correct.

5. The parties do not dispute the fact that The Carpet Mart made no objections to the terms embodied in Collins & Aikman's

acknowledgments. Therefore, Subsection 2–207(2)(c) is not relevant in the present case. And although it is not inconceivable that an oral offer could "expressly [limit] acceptance to the terms of the offer" under Subsection 2–207(2)(a), The Carpet Mart has never asserted that this was the nature of its offers to Collins & Aikman. We are therefore concerned with only Subsection 2–207(2)(b).

6. While T.C.A. § 47–2–207 [UCC § 2–207], Official Comment Nos. 4 and 5 provide examples of terms which would and would not materially alter a contract, an arbitration clause is listed under neither. Although we recognize the rule "that the agreement to arbitrate must be direct and the intention made clear, without implication, inveiglement or subtlety," Matter of Doughboy Industries, Inc., and Pantasote Co., 17 A.D.2d 216, 218, 233 N.Y.S.2d 488, 492 (1962) (indicating in dictum that an arbitration clause would materially alter a contract under 2–207(2)(b)), we believe the question of material alteration necessarily rests on the facts of each case. See American Parts Co. v. American Arbitration Ass'n, 8 Mich.App. 156, 171, 154 N.W.2d 5, 14 (1967).

agreements between the parties. It said that "an application of Section 2–207 similar to that above will be required."]

... Assuming that the District Court finds that the arbitration provision was not a term of the oral agreements between the parties, the arbitration clause will be treated as a "proposal" for addition to the contract under Section 2–207(2).... Regardless of whether the District Court finds Collins & Aikman's acknowledgment forms to have been acceptances or confirmations, if the arbitration provision was additional to, and a material alteration of, the offers or prior oral agreements, The Carpet Mart will not be bound to that provision absent a finding that it expressly agreed to be bound thereby....

For the reasons set forth above, the case is remanded to the District Court for further findings consistent with this opinion.

NOTES

(1) *More on Conditional Acceptance.* For a spectrum of views about how to apply the proviso in UCC 2–207(1), placing *Dorton* at one extreme and Roto–Lith v. F.P. Bartlett & Co. (Note 2, p. ___ above) at the other, see Diatom, Inc. v. Pennwalt Corp., 741 F.2d 1569 (10th Cir.1984).

(2) *More on Materiality of Terms.* The "additional terms" that can become part of a contract under subsection (2) of UCC are, it is said, "only those to which the offeror would be unlikely to object, because they fill out the contract in an expectable fashion....." Also: "An alteration is material if consent to it cannot be presumed. That is our gloss; the cases more commonly speak of "unreasonable surprise,".... But it comes to the same thing. What is expectable, hence unsurprising, is okay; what is unexpected, hence surprising, is not." Union Carbide Corp. v. Oscar Mayer Foods Corp., 947 F.2d 1333 (7th Cir.1990).

Following the decision in *Dorton* the New York Court of Appeals had occasion to say that "the inclusion of an arbitration agreement materially alters a contract for the sale of goods.... " Marlene Industries Corp. v. Carnac Textiles, Inc., 380 N.E.2d 239, 242 (N.Y.1978). Although that proposition may have been qualified somewhat by subsequent decisions,[a] it has been taken to mean, at the least, that in New York "the burden is on the proponent of arbitration to establish that arbitration is not a material alteration." Avedon Engineering, Inc. v. Seatex, p. ___ fn.a above, at 1285 n.15. But according to more "typical" analysis, the court said, "the burden of showing that arbitration is a material alteration is on the party opposing its inclusion.... "[b]

Aside from provisions for arbitration, and about warranty limitations—commonplace occasions for considering materiality—the issue has arisen in connection with provisions about what state's law is to govern, about where an action for breach may be brought, about the time for delivery, and for payment.[c]

a. See Tupman Thurlow Co. v. Woolf Intern. Corp., 682 N.E.2d 1378 (Mass.App. 1997).

b. Id. at 1284, 1285.

c. Choice of law: see Ionics, Inc. v. Elmwood Sensors, Inc., Note 2, p. ___ above. Choice of forum: M.K.C. Equipment Company v. M.A.I.L. Code, Inc., 843 F.Supp. 679 (D.Kan.1994). Time for delivery: Southern Idaho Pipe & Steel v. Cal–Cut Pipe, 567 P.2d 1246 (Idaho 1977). Time for payment: St. Paul Structural Steel Co. v. ABI Contracting, Inc., 364 N.W.2d 83 (N.D.1985).

See also Rangen, Inc. v. Valley Trout Farms, Inc., 658 P.2d 955 (Idaho 1983) (finance charges on overdue accounts; immaterial; divided court); 1995 U.S. Dist. LEXIS 7686 (finance charge); and Note 2, p. 844 below ("acts of God," etc., as excusing performance).

(3) *Problem*. Suppose that The Carpet Mart had telephoned only one order to Collins & Aikman, and had taken delivery of none of its carpets. Instead, upon receiving the acknowledgment of its first telephone order, Mart had immediately answered: "Owing to your insistence on arbitration, we deny the existence of a contract between us." Might it nevertheless be found that Mart was bound to accept and pay for the carpets ordered?—and was liable for having repudiated a contract? (Presumably Mart could not be forced into arbitration unless an arbitration term was implicit in its order: see subsection (2)(c) of the governing provision.) What other conclusion is possible under subsection (1)?

BOILERPLATE CONTENT

When the meaning of a contract term is in doubt, a court may prefer one interpretation over another because that interpretation promotes a general policy of the law. This is apparent in many cases concerning the scope of arbitration clauses. A doubt about the range of issues that the clause commits to arbitration is to be resolved, it is often said, in light of a policy in favor of the arbitration of disputes.[a] (Questions of contract interpretation are examined chiefly in Chapter 6, below.) Should the law's favor or disfavor of the content of a boilerplate term also affect a decision about whether or not a party gave effective assent to it?

The fact that arbitration terms are in widespread use sometimes contributes to the conclusion that a particular term was assented to. In Pervel Industries, Inc. v. TM Wallcovering, Inc., 871 F.2d 7 (2d Cir. 1989), the court said:

> Where, as here, a manufacturer has a well established custom of sending purchase order confirmations containing an arbitration clause, a buyer who has made numerous purchases over a period of time, receiving in each instance a standard confirmation form which it either signed and returned or retained without objection, is bound by the arbitration provision.... This is particularly true in industries such as fabrics and textiles where the specialized nature of the product has led to the widespread use of arbitration clauses and knowledgeable arbitrators.

Conversely, the fact that a term diverges from trade usage and the like may be a reason to doubt that it was assented to. Business persons, it is said, "do not consider the boilerplate printed on the reverse side of their forms to be part of the deal unless it coincidentally reflects some aspect of custom, usage, course of dealing, or practice that they understand as implicit in the resulting transactional relationship." McCarthy, An Introduction: The Commercial Irrelevancy of the "Battle of the Forms," 49 Bus.Law. 1019, 1026 (1994). If this is correct, how far should the courts consult custom, usage, and the like, for indications that a given term was *not* assented to?

A contrast has sometimes been drawn between "neutral" and "one-sided" terms. A seller's disclaimer of liability is one-sided in the sense

---

a. An example is the trial-court opinion   in the case next cited.

that it is burdensome only to the buyer; whereas an arbitration term might be desired by both parties. (This distinction was a mainspring of the decision in *Roto-Lith,* Note 2, p. ___) When a seller relies on a boilerplate term that would work systematically to the advantage of sellers, should the courts be especially reluctant to find that the buyer assented to it?

———

C. ITOH & CO. (AMERICA) INC. v. JORDAN INT'L CO., 552 F.2d 1228 (7th Cir.1977). [Itoh sent Jordan a purchase order for steel coils. Jordan sent back its acknowledgement form, which contained the following provision:

> Seller's acceptance is, however, expressly conditional on Buyer's assent to the additional or different terms and conditions set forth below and printed on the reverse side. If these terms are not acceptable, Buyer should notify Seller at once.

One of the provisions on the reverse side of Jordan's form was an arbitration clause that had no counterpart in Itoh's purchase order. After the steel had been delivered and paid for, Itoh sued Jordan claiming that the steel was defective and had been delivered late. Jordan moved to stay the proceedings pending arbitration. From a denial of its motion, Jordan appealed.]

SPRECHER, CIRCUIT JUDGE. ... The instant case ... involves the classic "battle of the forms". . . . [Since] it is clear that the statement contained in Jordan's acknowledgement form comes within the Section 2–207(1) proviso . . ., the exchange of forms between Jordan and Itoh did not result in the formation of a contract under Section 2–207(1), and Jordan's form became a counteroffer. Thus, "[s]ince ... [Itoh's] purchase order and ... [Jordan's] counter-offer did not in themselves create a contract, Section 2–207(3) would operate to create one because the subsequent performance by both parties constituted 'conduct by both parties which recognizes the existence of a contract.' " Construction Aggregates [Corp. v. Hewitt–Robins, 404 F.2d 505 (7th Cir.1968), cert. denied, 395 U.S. 921 (1969)], at 509.

What are the terms of a contract created by conduct under Section 2–207(3) rather than an exchange of forms under Section 2–207(1)? ... The second sentence of Section 2–207(3) provides that where, as here, a contract has been consummated by the conduct of the parties, "the terms of the particular contract consist of those terms on which the writings of the parties agree, together with any supplementary terms incorporated under any other provisions of this Act." Since it is clear that the Jordan and Itoh forms do not "agree" on arbitration, the only question which remains *under the Code* is whether arbitration may be considered a supplementary term incorporated under some other provision of the Code.

We have been unable to find any case authority shedding light on the question of what constitutes "supplementary terms" within the meaning of Section 2–207(3) and the Official Comments to Section 2–207 provide no guidance in this regard. We are persuaded, however, that the disputed additional terms (i.e., those terms on which the writings of the parties do not agree) which are necessarily excluded from a Subsection (3) contract by the language, "terms on which the writings of the parties agree," cannot be brought back into the contract under the guise of "supplementary terms." ... Accordingly, we find that the "supplementary terms" contemplated by Section 2–207(3) are limited to those supplied by the standardized "gap-filler" provisions of Article Two.... Since provision for arbitration is not a necessary or missing term which would be supplied by one of the Code's "gap-filler" provisions unless agreed upon by the contracting parties, there is no arbitration term in the Section 2–207(3) contract which was created by the conduct of Jordan and Itoh in proceeding to perform even though no contract had been established by their exchange of writings.

We are convinced that this conclusion does not result in any unfair prejudice to a seller who elects to insert in his standard sales acknowledgement form the statement that acceptance is expressly conditional on buyer's assent to additional terms contained therein. Such a seller obtains a substantial benefit under Section 2–207(1) through the inclusion of an "expressly conditional" clause. If he decides after the exchange of forms that the particular transaction is not in his best interest, Subsection (1) permits him to walk away from the transaction without incurring any liability so long as the buyer has not in the interim expressly assented to the additional terms. Moreover, whether or not a seller will be disadvantaged under Subsection (3) as a consequence of inserting an "expressly conditional" clause in his standard form is within his control. If the seller in fact does not intend to close a particular deal unless the additional terms are assented to, he can protect himself by not delivering the goods until such assent is forthcoming. If the seller does intend to close a deal irrespective of whether or not the buyer assents to the additional terms, he can hardly complain when the contract formed under Subsection (3) as a result of the parties' conduct is held not to include those terms. Although a seller who employs such an "expressly conditional" clause in his acknowledgement form would undoubtedly appreciate the dual advantage of not being bound to a contract under Subsection (1) if he elects not to perform and of having his additional terms imposed on the buyer under Subsection (3) in the event that performance is in his best interest, we do not believe such a result is contemplated by Section 2–207. Rather, while a seller may take advantage of an "expressly conditional" clause under Subsection (1) when he elects not to perform, he must accept the potential risk under Subsection (3) of not getting his additional terms when he elects to proceed with performance without first obtaining buyer's assent to those terms. Since the seller injected ambiguity into the transaction by inserting the "expressly conditional" clause in his form, he, and not the buyer, should bear the consequence of that ambiguity under Subsection (3)....

Affirmed.

NOTE

Performance as Assent. Why did not Itoh's acceptance of and payment for the steel constitute assent to Jordan's "additional or different terms"? (Recall that in Dorton v. Collins & Aikman, above, the court observed that "the UCC does not provide a definition of 'assent'.")

————

THE "KNOCKOUT" DOCTRINE

"The Uniform Commercial Code ... does not say what the terms of the contract are if the offer and acceptance contain different terms, as distinct from cases in which the acceptance merely contains additional terms to those in the offer." Northrop Corporation v. Litronic Industries, p. 224 fn.b above. A test case may be supposed as follows.

A user of pipe addresses a purchase order to a supplier, in which delivery is required to be made not later than April 1. The supplier answers with a confirmation on terms that are the same, except that the final delivery date is stated to be May 1. Neither the purchase order nor the confirmation contains language indicating objection to a variant term. Part of the pipe ordered is delivered, and paid for, by May 1; but the user refuses to take delivery of pipe shipped to it later in May. Each party asserts that the other is in breach.

It may be possible to doubt that anything in UCC 2–207 applies in this situation. See Note 2, p. ___ above; and compare p. ___ fn.b above. (The section was applied, however, in the case that suggested the foregoing facts.[13]) Laying that doubt aside, what is to be made of these facts?

One answer is indicated by the so-called *knockout* doctrine. As applied to the facts supposed, the doctrine signifies that the parties are bound by a contract which expresses *no controlling date* for final delivery. Hence the following rule applies:

> The time ... for delivery ... shall be a reasonable time.—UCC 2–309(1).

Does that make sense? What other solution would be better?

The idea of the doctrine is that the opposing delivery-date provisions cancel one another out, so that the decision is governed by a supplementary term derived from Article 2 of the Code. According to *Northrop Corporation*:[14]

> [T]he discrepant terms in both the nonidentical offer and the acceptance drop out, and default terms found elsewhere in the Code fill the resulting gap.... [The parties' terms] are replaced by a suitable UCC gap-filler.... The idea behind [this] view is that the presence of different terms in the acceptance suggests that the

---

13. Southern Idaho Pipe & Steel v. Cal– Cut Pipe, p. ___ fn.c above. Loosely analogous facts were the premise of Northrop Corporation.

14. Pp. 1175, 1178.

offeree didn't really accede to the offeror's terms, yet both parties wanted to contract, so why not find a neutral term to govern the dispute that has arisen between them?

Technically, the doctrine is usually supported by reference to subsection (3) of UCC 2–207 ("Conduct by both parties which recognizes the existence of a contract.... ").

In *Northrop Corporation* the court gave thoughtful consideration to the knockout doctrine. A majority of the court expressed their disapproval of the doctrine.[15] On the facts supposed above, they would presumably have given effect to the delivery date as stated in the buyer's offer (April 1). Yet they applied the knockout rule as the leading doctrine, surmising that it represented the law of Illinois and was therefore binding on the court.[16] "Our own preferred view," the court said, "has as yet been adopted by only one state, California."[17]

NOTES

(1) *Scope of Subsection (3).* The facts supposed above differ from those in *C. Itoh & Co.* in that Itoh's purchase order was made "expressly conditional on Buyer's assent.... " If the knockout doctrine is justifiable in one of these situations and not the other, which is that situation? A third situation is one in which an offeror makes advance objection to any variant terms.

If the knockout doctrine were not applied in *any* of these situations, it would be difficult to envisage a case to which subsection (3) of UCC 2–207 applies. In *Northrop Corporation*, the majority conceded that it would apply in the third situation.[a] An apparent example is Ionics v. Elmwood Sensors, Note 2 p. ___ above.[b] Deciding to disregard the seller's terms in those circumstances, the court reasoned that, otherwise, "virtually any response that added to or altered the terms of the offer would be a rejection and a counteroffer."

Is it possible that subsection (3) is limited to an exceptional situation such as that in *Ionics*, or in *C. Itoh*?—assuming that these *are* exceptional situations.[c]

---

15. The judges (Posner, C.J., writing) conceded that their view "may tempt the offeror to spring a surprise on the offeree, hoping the latter won't read the fine print." Moreover—though an offeree might protect itself with a conditional acceptance—"it may be unrealistic to expect offerees to protect themselves in this way. The offeror goes first and therefore has a little more time for careful specification of the terms.... "

16. Judge Ripple, concurring, thought the court should not have taken an "institutional position as a [federal] court" on the preferable understanding of UCC 2–207.

17. As noted above, *Northrop Corporation* was a breach-of-warranty case. As to the default rule about the time for returning defective goods see UCC 2–309 and 2–601.

a. "[S]ubsection (3) comes into play only when the parties have by their conduct manifested the existence of a contract, as where the offeror, having specified that the acceptance must mirror the offer yet having received an acceptance that deviates from the offer, nonetheless goes ahead and performs as if there were a contract." Id. at 1179. (emphasis supplied)

b. Orders by buyer: "No terms ... additional to or different from those herein set forth shall ... in any way control the terms and conditions herein set forth."

c. In *Northrop Corporation* it appears that Litronic's offer provided that its terms would "take precedence over terms and conditions of the buyer, unless specifically negotiated otherwise." Litronic did not make an argument based on this provision.

(2) *Different Terms* vs. *Additional Terms*. What has been called the "notorious distinction between 'different' and 'additional' terms"[d] appears upon comparing subsections (1) and (2) of UCC 2–207. According to the opinion in *Northrop Corporation*: "Mischief lurks in the words 'additional to or different from' "; and it is hair-splitting to make a distinction. "[A]ll different terms are additional and all additional terms are different." That is, any distinction is best ignored, so that "the terms in the offer prevail over the different terms in the acceptance only if the latter are materially different."[e]

Question: Would it help to justify the knockout doctrine to draw a significant distinction between additional terms and different ones?

(3) *Fairness and the Knockout Doctrine*. The overriding goal of Article 2 is, according to one court, "to discern the bargain struck by the contracting parties. However, there are times where the conduct of the parties makes realizing that goal impossible. In such cases, we find guidance in the Code's commitment to fairness, good faith, and conscionable conduct." Gardner Zemke Co. v. Dunham Bush, Inc., fn. b, p. ___ above. What treatment of discordant forms of buyers and sellers most conduces to the Code's "commitment to fairness?

Broadscale applications of subsection (3) of UCC 2–207 tend, it may be noticed, to enhance the importance of "gap-fillers" provided by other sections in Article 2—notably the warranty sections—generally to the advantage of buyers. Is that a benign effect? Some observers think so: "Sellers should not be permitted, by surreptitious manipulation of section 2–207, to obtain contract terms that cannot be obtained either through statutory amendment of U.C.C. gap-filler provisions or by negotiation with the buyer. If warranty, remedy, and arbitration terms are so important to sellers, then those terms are and must be negotiated.... [I]f the seller 'is not willing to sacrifice the time and effort that this requires, then he should be willing to abide by the rules of Article 2." Roszkowski & Wladis, Revised U.C.C. Section 2–207: Analysis and Recommendations, 49 Bus.Law. 1065, 1070 (1994).[f]

Other observers are not so sure. According to one, the warranty of merchantability stated in UCC 2–314 is "a very broad, subjective standard that juries can interpret to mean that buyer is entitled to relief if buyer is dissatisfied in virtually any way with the product." For a seller to escape it may require expensive and time-consuming negotiation. "Simply stated, sellers may prefer ... to use the battle of the forms to avoid the effect of Article 2 gap fillers, which they believe unreasonably favor buyers."[g]

(4) *The "Best Shot" Rule*. Professor Victor Goldberg has criticized the knockout rule, proposing instead a "best shot" rule. He would require a court, faced with discordant terms in standard-form exchanges, to enforce all the terms in one of the forms, choosing between the two with reference to overall fairness. The knockout rule, he observed, "produces some anomalous results, knocking out terms that would yield the same result in a particular case and replacing them with a default rule yielding a different outcome." Professor Goldberg's solution would, he believes, enhance the incentive of each party, when devising its form, to take account of the concerns of the other. See Goldberg, The "Battle of the Forms": Fairness, Efficiency, and the Best–Shot Rule, 76 Ore.L.Rev. 155

---

d. Pace Communs., Inc. v. Moonlight Design, Inc., 31 F.3d 587 (7th Cir.1994).

e. Id. at 1174, 1175, 1178. But see Davenport, To Paraphrase Mark Twain ..., 28 U.C.C.L.J. 231 (1996), to the effect that the variation was deliberate.

f. Internal quotation from attorney's letter.

g. Id. at 1068, 1069 (sequence reversed). The first quotation is from an attorney's letter.

(1997). For a contrasting economic perspective see Ostas & Darr, Redrafting U.C.C. Section 2–207 . . ., 73 Denver U.L.Rev. 903 (1996).

STRATEGY IN THE "BATTLE"

How should parties draft their documents to win the "battle of the forms"? Is it better to be the offeror or the offeree? What clauses might a seller insert in forms entitled "quotation" or "sales acknowledgment"? What might a buyer insert in a form entitled "request for quotation" or "purchase order"?

One possibility, when the parties have a continuing relationship, is to negotiate an overriding agreement to govern all their dealings. Would a weak bargaining position make that unattractive to one of them? Still another possibility is for a trade association to work out standard terms to which its members can agree. Electronic data interchange (EDI) is espoused as a means of reducing sale terms to an agreed "transaction set." A committee of the American National Standards Institute has contributed to the preparation of a model agreement for use among trading partners. See McCarthy, An Introduction: The Commercial Irrelevancy of the "Battle of the Forms," 49 Bus.Law. 1019, 1024–27 (1994).

NOTE

The Case of the Beseeching Buyer. One firm's purchase-order form included a detachable acknowledgment for the use of suppliers, saying in large print on the front: WE [SELLER] ACKNOWLEDGE YOUR PURCHASE ORDER NO. __ AND AGREE TO ALL TERMS AND CONDITIONS ON FACE AND BACK THEREON. According to the back: "Notwithstanding any provision in any documents submitted by the Seller, Buyer reserves its rights to assert any claim against the Seller based on any express or implied warranty provided for by the Uniform Commercial Code or any other state or federal law."

What admonition to the firm about using this document would be in order from the attorney who devised it? (It backfired.[a])

SECTION 6. PRECONTRACTUAL LIABILITY

According to orthodox contract doctrine, neither party to contractual negotiations is bound until an offer has been accepted. Until then, neither party is safe in acting in reliance on the prospect of a contract. A court has, to be sure, some discretion in determining from all the circumstances whether there has been an acceptance, and it may use this discretion in a borderline case to find an acceptance and thus protect a party who has relied.

Furthermore, a party whose reliance has conferred a benefit on the other may have a claim to restitution to prevent unjust enrichment even

---

   a. See Plymouth Rubber Co. v. Uniroy-al, Inc., 1992 WL 93223 (D.Mass), especially p. 11 n. 2.

though no contract has resulted. To take a simple example, the prospective buyer of land who makes a down payment during negotiations that fail to result in a contract is entitled to the return of any down payment. But unjust enrichment is often harder to show. So in Cronin v. National Shawmut Bank, 27 N.E.2d 717 (Mass.1940), National Shawmut Bank invited brokers to submit proposals for fire and theft insurance on specified property, involving premiums of about $850,000 and broker's commissions of between $30,000 and $40,000. Cronin submitted a proposal and, at the request of McCarthy, one of the bank's officers, he revised it several times until it was "the precise proposal that McCarthy wanted." The bank then gave the contract to another firm that submitted a proposal identical to Cronin's except for the names of the broker and the insurer, because a partner in that firm was a friend of one of McCarthy's superiors. Cronin sued the bank, including a claim in restitution. The Supreme Judicial Court of Massachusetts affirmed judgment for the bank. The bank "never actually availed itself of any proposal made by the plaintiff." The contract made was with a different insurer and serviced by a different broker. "To be sure the defendant got the benefit of the rates proposed by the plaintiff, and this may have been important; but what the rates would have been if they had not been the plaintiff's rates remains speculative. It has been held in a number of cases that deriving benefit from the broker's work does not lead to liability where there has been no employment." See also Gould v. American Water Works Service Co., 245 A.2d 14 (N.J.1968), cert. denied, 394 U.S. 943 (1969).

A contrasting case on restitution is Hill v. Waxberg, 237 F.2d 936 (9th Cir.1956). Hill asked Waxberg, a contractor, to help him make preparations for the construction of a building on Hill's lot in Fairbanks, Alaska. It was understood that if the financing could be arranged through the Federal Housing Authority as contemplated, Waxberg would be awarded the building contract. Waxberg then made several trips to Seattle at Hill's request to confer with the architects, hired a third party to secure a drill log on the property, surveyed the property, and was instrumental in getting the data for the F.H.A. He expected to be compensated for this out of the profits from the contemplated contract. When the F.H.A. issued the commitment, Hill and Waxberg began negotiations for the building contract, but were unable to agree. Hill then made a contract with another contractor, and Waxberg sued to recover the reasonable value of his services and the expenditures made by him. The evidence showed that Waxberg's plans, ideas and efforts were of some value to Hill, and the trial court entered judgment for him on a jury verdict for $11,167.46. On Hill's appeal the Court of Appeals explained that it is a general principle of Anglo–American jurisprudence that "something in the nature of an implied contract results where one renders services at the request of another with the expectation of pay therefor, and in the process confers a benefit on the other.... It makes no difference whether the pay expected is in the form of an immediate cash payment, or in the form of profits to be derived from a contract, the consummation of which would or should be anticipated by reasonable

men, and it follows *a fortiori* that such a rule obtains where the contract
is in fact contemplated by *both* parties." The contract may be "implied
in fact," in which case the general contract theory of compensatory
damages applies, compensation for services being measured at "the
going contract rate." Or it may be "implied in law," in which case a
restitution measure of damages applies and recovery is limited to "the
value of the benefit which was acquired." (This portion of the opinion is
quoted in full in Note 4, p. 79 above.) Because the trial judge did not
adequately instruct the jury on this distinction, its judgment was reversed, unless the parties should agree to a reduction in its amount to
$5,896.88, the asserted reasonable value of Waxberg's services plus his
claimed expenses. Would not this court's reasoning have required a
decision for Cronin on his claim against the bank? If so, for how much?
Are the two cases distinguishable?

A claim to restitution, however, leaves the claimant uncompensated
for reliance that resulted in no benefit to the other party. To what
extent might such reliance afford an independent ground for recovery?
The following cases deal with this question.

Before turning to those cases, however, consider a notorious hypothetical put by Professor Wormser early in this century: "Suppose A
says to B, 'I will give you $100 if you walk across the Brooklyn
Bridge'.... B starts to walk across the Brooklyn Bridge and has gone
about one-half of the way across. At that moment A overtakes B and
says to him, 'I withdraw my offer.' Has B then any rights against A?
Again, let us suppose that after A has said, 'I withdraw my offer,' B
continues to walk across the Brooklyn Bridge and completes the act of
crossing. Under these circumstances, has B any rights against A?"
Wormser concluded that he had none. "What A wanted from B, what A
asked for, was the act of walking across the bridge. Until that was done,
B had not given to A what A had requested. The acceptance by B of A's
offer could be nothing but the act on B's part of crossing the bridge. It
is elementary that an offeror may withdraw his offer until it has been
accepted. It follows logically that A is perfectly within his rights in
withdrawing his offer before B has accepted it by walking across the
bridge—the act contemplated by the offeror and the offeree as the
acceptance of the offer." Wormser, The True Conception of Unilateral
Contracts, 26 Yale L.J. 136–137 (1916).

Restatement Second § 45 states a rule, based on former Restatement § 45 [a] and couched in language of "option contract," that supports
a different result. It is set out below. (It is helpful in reading this
section to understand that one cannot "tender" a performance that is to
extend over a period of time, such as the crossing of the Brooklyn

**a. § 45. Revocation of Offer for
Unilateral Contract; Effect of Part
Performance or Tender**

If an offer for a unilateral contract is
made, and part of the consideration requested in the offer is given or tendered by
the offeree in response thereto, the offeror
is bound by a contract, the duty of immediate performance of which is conditional on
the full consideration being given or tendered within the time stated in the offer, or,
if no time is stated therein, within a reasonable time.

Bridge.) Indeed, thirty-four years after Wormser first wrote of the Brooklyn Bridge hypothetical, he admitted: "Since that time I have repented, so that now, clad in sackcloth, I state frankly, that my point of view has changed. I agree, at this time, with the rule set forth in the Restatement...." Book Review, 3 J.Legal Ed. 145 (1950).

Restatement Second § 45. Option Contract Created by Part Performance or Tender

(1) Where an offer invites an offeree to accept by rendering a performance and does not invite a promissory acceptance, an option contract is created when the offeree tenders or begins the invited performance or tenders a beginning of it.

(2) The offeror's duty of performance under any option contract so created is conditional on completion or tender of the invited performance in accordance with the terms of the offer.

NOTES

(1) *Objections to "Option Contract."* Are there any objections to the "option contract" notion? May it not, in a rapidly fluctuating market, give the offeree an unfair chance to speculate during the time when the offeror is bound but the offeree is not? Judging from the kinds of situations in which the problem of the Brooklyn Bridge hypothetical actually arises, how great is this danger likely to be?

Would there be any advantage in limiting recovery by B in the Brooklyn Bridge hypothetical to damages based on B's reliance rather than B's expectation interest? See Fuller and Perdue, The Reliance Interest in Contract Damages: 2, 46 Yale L.J. 373, 410–17 (1937).

(2) *The Case of the Move to Maine.* Mrs. Hodgkin was a widow who lived alone on her farm in Lewiston, Maine. On February 8, 1915, she wrote Mrs. Brackenbury, one of her six children, in Independence, Missouri. She offered the Brackenburys the use and income of the farm if they would move to Maine and take care of Mrs. Hodgkin there during her life. The letter closed, "you to have the place when I have passed away." The Brackenburys moved to Maine late in April and began performance. But after a few weeks trouble developed, relations between the parties grew most disagreeable, and a suit was brought to force the Brackenburys to leave. They in turn sued to enforce their rights and prevailed in the trial court. *Held:* Affirmed. "The offer was the basis, not of a bilateral contract, requiring a reciprocal promise, a promise for a promise, but of a unilateral contract requiring an act for a promise.... The plaintiffs here accepted the offer by moving from Missouri to the mother's farm in Lewiston and entering upon the performance of the specified acts, and they have continued performance since that time so far as they have been permitted by the mother to do so. The existence of a completed and valid contract is clear." Brackenbury v. Hodgkin, 102 A. 106 (Me.1917).[b]

§45

b. It is reported that even after this litigation, the Brackenburys and Mrs. Hodgkin continued to live together until Mrs. Hodgkin's death in January, 1921, that "the relations were unpleasant to the end," and that Mr. Brackenbury obtained a transcript of the record in the case and "would, from time to time, read from it to the old lady." J. Dawson, W. Harvey & S. Henderson, Cases on Contracts 384 (5th ed. 1987).

(3) *Is Promise or Performance Sought?* The whole problem can be avoided, of course, if the offer seeks a promise as acceptance and either a promise is given in so many words or one can be spelled out from the offeree's conduct. (Suppose, for example, that Mrs. Hodgkin's letter had read: "If you will agree to move to Lewiston and care for me on the home place....") In Davis v. Jacoby, 34 P.2d 1026 (Cal.1934), the court held that an offer somewhat similar to that in Brackenbury v. Hodgkin invited a promise as acceptance, relying in part on the offeror's language: "Will you let me hear from you as soon as possible...." In case of doubt, Restatement Second § 32 gives the offeree an opportunity to treat the offer as inviting a promise as acceptance and thus to avoid Professor Wormser's argument simply by giving a promise. Would such an opportunity have been of any advantage to the Brackenburys? What if Mrs. Hodgkin had died after they had sold their home and liquidated their business in Missouri and begun the journey to Maine?

Are there circumstances in which an offeree might find an offer that invites a promise as acceptance *less* appealing than one which invites performance as acceptance? Suppose that the offeree's risk of failure is considerable, e.g., that A is seeking to get B to climb a flagpole rather than cross the Brooklyn Bridge. (Consider also the offer of a reward.) How might an offeror frame an offer to make it appealing to the offeree under circumstances involving *both* substantial preparation for performance by the offeree *and* considerable risk of failure on the offeree's part, e.g., calling for the offeree to deliver a piece of technologically sophisticated equipment which the offeree might not be able to develop according to the required specifications?

RELIANCE ON AN OFFER THAT SEEKS A PROMISE

In the discussion of the Brooklyn Bridge hypothetical, it was assumed that if A's offer sought B's promise, as distinguished from B's performance, B's power to accept by promising before doing anything in reliance on A's offer gave B adequate protection. Thus in White v. Corlies & Tift, p. 184 above, White should have given his promise—his "agreement to finish the fitting up of offices"—before he "purchased stuff for the work" and "began work on the stuff." In such situations there is scant reason to give the offeree protection like that afforded by Restatement Second § 45. See Ragosta v. Wilder, p. 266 below.

Consider, however, a general contractor, such as Kastorff in the case at page 171, that receives bids from subcontractors, such as the plumbing subcontractor in that case, and uses those bids in making up its own bid. Suppose that Kastorff had properly calculated his bid using the $6,500 plumbing bid, and after Kastorff had submitted his bid the plumbing subcontractor had attempted to withdraw the $6,500 bid on the ground that it was the result of a clerical error and should have been $9,500. Could the plumbing subcontractor justify withdrawal of the bid on the ground that the offer sought a promise from Kastorff and, no promise having been given, the offer could be revoked?

In James Baird Co. v. Gimbel Bros., 64 F.2d 344 (2d Cir.1933), Learned Hand gave the orthodox response. The subcontractor could withdraw its bid because "an offer for an exchange is not meant to become a promise until a consideration has been received, either a counter-promise or whatever is stipulated. To extend it would be to hold the offeror regardless of the stipulated condition of his offer." The subcontractor's offer could impose a duty to render a performance only when the general contractor "promised to take and pay for it. There is no room in such a situation for the doctrine of 'promissory estoppel.'" Hand also noted that contractors have "a ready escape from their difficulty by insisting upon a contract before they used the figures; and in commercial transactions it does not in the end promote justice to seek strained interpretations in aid of those who do not protect themselves."

DRENNAN v. STAR PAVING CO.

Supreme Court of California, In Bank, 1958.
51 Cal.2d 409, 333 P.2d 757.

General contractor brought action against paving subcontractor to recover damages because of refusal of subcontractor to perform paving according to bid which subcontractor submitted to general contractor. The Superior Court, Kern County, William L. Bradshaw, J., entered judgment adverse to the subcontractor, and the subcontractor appealed.

TRAYNOR, JUSTICE.[a] Defendant appeals from a judgment for plaintiff in an action to recover damages caused by defendant's refusal to perform certain paving work according to a bid it submitted to plaintiff.

On July 28, 1955, plaintiff, a licensed general contractor, was preparing a bid on the "Monte Vista School Job" in the Lancaster school district. Bids had to be submitted before 8:00 p.m. Plaintiff testified that it was customary in that area for general contractors to receive the bids of subcontractors by telephone on the day set for bidding and to rely on them in computing their own bids. Thus on that day plaintiff's secretary, Mrs. Johnson, received by telephone between fifty and seventy-five subcontractors' bids for various parts of the school job. As each bid came in, she wrote it on a special form, which she brought into plaintiff's office. He then posted it on a master cost sheet setting forth the names and bids of all subcontractors. His own bid had to include the names of subcontractors who were to perform one-half of one per cent or more of the construction work, and he had also to provide a bidder's bond of ten per cent of his total bid of $317,385 as a guarantee that he would enter the contract if awarded the work.

Late in the afternoon, Mrs. Johnson had a telephone conversation with Kenneth R. Hoon, an estimator for defendant. He gave his name and telephone number and stated that he was bidding for defendant for the paving work at the Monte Vista School according to plans and specifications and that his bid was $7,131.60. At Mrs. Johnson's request he repeated his bid. Plaintiff listened to the bid over an extension

---

a. Roger Traynor (1900–1983) was a member of the law faculty of the University of California at Berkeley from 1930 to 1940 and specialized in tax law. He served from 1940 to 1964 as associate justice of the Supreme Court of California and from 1964 to 1970 as its chief justice. Some of his opinions on contract law are discussed in Macaulay, Mr. Justice Traynor and the Law of Contracts, 13 Stan.L.Rev. 812 (1961).

telephone in his office and posted it on the master sheet after receiving the bid form from Mrs. Johnson. Defendant's was the lowest bid for the paving. Plaintiff computed his own bid accordingly and submitted it with the name of defendant as the subcontractor for the paving. When the bids were opened on July 28th, plaintiff's proved to be the lowest, and he was awarded the contract.

On his way to Los Angeles the next morning plaintiff stopped at defendant's office. The first person he met was defendant's construction engineer, Mr. Oppenheimer. Plaintiff testified: "I introduced myself and he immediately told me that they had made a mistake in their bid to me the night before, they couldn't do it for the price they had bid, and I told him I would expect him to carry through with their original bid because I had used it in compiling my bid and the job was being awarded them. And I would have to go and do the job according to my bid and I would expect them to do the same."

Defendant refused to do the paving work for less than $15,000. Plaintiff testified that he "got figures from other people" and after trying for several months to get as low a bid as possible engaged L & H Paving Company, a firm in Lancaster, to do the work for $10,948.60.

The trial court found on substantial evidence that defendant made a definite offer to do the paving on the Monte Vista job according to the plans and specifications for $7,131.60, and that plaintiff relied on defendant's bid in computing his own bid for the school job and naming defendant therein as the subcontractor for the paving work. Accordingly, it entered judgment for plaintiff in the amount of $3,817.00 (the difference between defendant's bid and the cost of the paving to plaintiff) plus costs.

Defendant contends that there was no enforceable contract between the parties on the ground that it made a revocable offer and revoked it before plaintiff communicated his acceptance to defendant.

There is no evidence that defendant offered to make its bid irrevocable in exchange for plaintiff's use of its figures in computing his bid. Nor is there evidence that would warrant interpreting plaintiff's use of defendant's bid as the acceptance thereof, binding plaintiff, on condition he received the main contract, to award the subcontract to defendant. In sum, there was neither an option supported by consideration nor a bilateral contract binding on both parties.

Plaintiff contends, however, that he relied to his detriment on defendant's offer and that defendant must therefore answer in damages for its refusal to perform. Thus the question is squarely presented: Did plaintiff's reliance make defendant's offer irrevocable?

Section 90 of the Restatement of Contracts states: "A promise which the promisor should reasonably expect to induce action or forbearance of a definite and substantial character on the part of the promisee and which does induce such action or forbearance is binding if injustice can be avoided only by enforcement of the promise." This rule applies in this state....

Defendant's offer constituted a promise to perform on such conditions as were stated expressly or by implication therein or annexed thereto by operation of law. (See 1 Williston, Contracts [3rd ed.], § 24A, p. 56, § 61, p. 196.) Defendant had reason to expect that if its bid proved the lowest it would be used by plaintiff. It induced "action . . . of a definite and substantial character on the part of the promisee."

Had defendant's bid expressly stated or clearly implied that it was revocable at any time before acceptance we would treat it accordingly. It was silent on revocation, however, and we must therefore determine whether there are conditions to the right of revocation imposed by law or reasonably inferable in fact. In the analogous problem of an offer for a unilateral contract, the theory is now obsolete that the offer is revocable at any time before complete performance. Thus section 45 of the Restatement of Contracts provides: "If an offer for a unilateral contract is made, and part of the consideration requested in the offer is given or tendered by the offeree in response thereto, the offeror is bound by a contract, the duty of immediate performance of which is conditional on the full consideration being given or tendered within the time stated in the offer, or, if no time is stated therein, within a reasonable time." In explanation, comment b states that the "main offer includes as a subsidiary promise, necessarily implied, that if part of the requested performance is given, the offeror will not revoke his offer, and that if tender is made it will be accepted. Part performance or tender may thus furnish consideration for the subsidiary promise. Moreover, merely acting in justifiable reliance on an offer may in some cases serve as sufficient reason for making a promise binding (see § 90)."

Whether implied in fact or law, the subsidiary promise serves to preclude the injustice that would result if the offer could be revoked after the offeree had acted in detrimental reliance thereon. Reasonable reliance resulting in a foreseeable prejudicial change in position affords a compelling basis also for implying a subsidiary promise not to revoke an offer for a bilateral contract.

The absence of consideration is not fatal to the enforcement of such a promise. It is true that in the case of unilateral contracts the Restatement finds consideration for the implied subsidiary promise in the part performance of the bargained-for exchange, but its reference to section 90 makes clear that consideration for such a promise is not always necessary. The very purpose of section 90 is to make a promise binding even though there was no consideration "in the sense of something that is bargained for and given in exchange." (See 1 Corbin, Contracts 634 et seq.) Reasonable reliance serves to hold the offeror in lieu of the consideration ordinarily required to make the offer binding. In a case involving similar facts the Supreme Court of South Dakota stated that "we believe that reason and justice demand that the doctrine [of section 90] be applied to the present facts. We cannot believe that by accepting this doctrine as controlling in the state of facts before us we will abolish the requirement of a consideration in contract cases, in any different sense than an ordinary estoppel abolishes some legal requirement in its application. We are of the opinion, therefore, that the defendants in executing the agreement [which was not supported by consideration] made a promise which they should have reasonably expected would induce the plaintiff to submit a bid based thereon to the Government, that such promise did induce this action, and that injustice can be avoided only by enforcement of the promise." Northwestern Engineering Co. v. Ellerman, 69 S.D. 397, 408, 10 N.W.2d 879, 884; see also, Robert Gordon, Inc., v. Ingersoll–Rand Co., 7 Cir., 117 F.2d 654, 661; cf. James Baird Co. v. Gimbel Bros., 2 Cir., 64 F.2d 344.

When plaintiff used defendant's offer in computing his own bid, he bound himself to perform in reliance on defendant's terms. Though defendant did not bargain for this use of its bid neither did defendant make it idly, indifferent to whether it would be used or not. On the contrary it is reasonable to suppose that defendant submitted its bid to obtain the subcontract. It was bound to realize the substantial possibility that its bid would be the lowest, and that it would be included by plaintiff in his bid. It was to its own interest that the contractor be awarded the general contract; the lower the subcontract bid, the lower the general contractor's bid was likely to be and the greater its chance of acceptance and hence the greater defendant's chance of getting the paving subcontract. Defendant had reason not only to expect plaintiff to rely on its bid but to want him to. Clearly defendant had a stake in plaintiff's reliance on its bid. Given this interest and the fact that plaintiff is bound by his own bid, it is only fair that plaintiff should have at least an opportunity to accept defendant's bid after the general contract has been awarded to him.

It bears noting that a general contractor is not free to delay acceptance after he has been awarded the general contract in the hope of getting a better price. Nor can he reopen bargaining with the subcontractor and at the same time claim a continuing right to accept the original offer. See, R.J. Daum Const. Co. v. Child, Utah, 247 P.2d 817, 823. In the present case plaintiff promptly informed defendant that plaintiff was being awarded the job and that the subcontract was being awarded to defendant.

Defendant contends, however, that its bid was the result of mistake and that it was therefore entitled to revoke it. It relies on the rescission cases of M.F. Kemper Const. Co. v. City of Los Angeles, 37 Cal.2d 696, 235 P.2d 7, and Brunzell Const. Co. v. G.J. Weisbrod, Inc., 134 Cal. App.2d 278, 285 P.2d 989. See also, Lemoge Electric v. San Mateo County, 46 Cal.2d 659, 662, 297 P.2d 638. In those cases, however, the bidder's mistake was known or should have been known to the offeree, and the offeree could be placed in status quo. Of course, if plaintiff had reason to believe that defendant's bid was in error, he could not justifiably rely on it, and section 90 would afford no basis for enforcing it. Robert Gordon, Inc. v. Ingersoll–Rand, Inc., 7 Cir., 117 F.2d 654, 660. Plaintiff, however, had no reason to know that defendant had made a mistake in submitting its bid, since there was usually a variance of 160 per cent between the highest and lowest bids for paving in the desert around Lancaster. He committed himself to performing the main contract in reliance on defendant's figures. Under these circumstances defendant's mistake, far from relieving it of its obligation, constitutes an additional reason for enforcing it, for it misled plaintiff as to the cost of doing the paving. Even had it been clearly understood that defendant's offer was revocable until accepted, it would not necessarily follow that defendant had no duty to exercise reasonable care in preparing its bid. It presented its bid with knowledge of the substantial possibility that it would be used by plaintiff; it could foresee the harm that would ensue from an erroneous underestimate of the cost. Moreover, it was motivated by its own business interest. Whether or not these considerations alone would justify recovery for negligence had the case been tried on that theory (see Biakanja v. Irving, 49 Cal.2d 647, 650, 320 P.2d 16), they are persuasive that defendant's mistake should not defeat recovery under the rule of section 90 of the Restatement of Contracts. As between the subcontractor who made the bid and the general contractor who reasonably relied on it, the loss resulting from the mistake should fall on the party who caused it.

Leo F. Piazza Paving Co. v. Bebek & Brkich, 141 Cal.App.2d 226, 296 P.2d 368, 371, and Bard v. Kent, 19 Cal.2d 449, 122 P.2d 8, 139 A.L.R. 1032, are not to the contrary. In the Piazza case the court sustained a finding that defendants intended, not to make a firm bid, but only to give the plaintiff "some kind of an idea to use" in making its bid; there was evidence that the defendants had told plaintiff they were unsure of the significance of the specifications. There was thus no offer, promise, or representation on which the defendants should reasonably have expected the plaintiff to rely. The *Bard* case held that an option not supported by consideration was revoked by the death of the optionor. The issue of recovery under the rule of section 90 was not pleaded at the trial, and it does not appear that the offeree's reliance was "of a definite and substantial character" so that injustice could be avoided "only by the enforcement of the promise."

There is no merit in defendant's contention that plaintiff failed to state a cause of action, on the ground that the complaint failed to allege that plaintiff attempted to mitigate the damages or that they could not have been mitigated. Plaintiff alleged that after defendant's default, "plaintiff had to procure the services of the L & H Co. to perform said asphaltic paving for the sum of $10,948.60." Plaintiff's uncontradicted evidence showed that he spent several months trying to get bids from other subcontractors and that he took the lowest bid. Clearly he acted reasonably to mitigate damages. In any event any uncertainty in plaintiff's allegation as to damages could have been raised by special demurrer. Code Civ.Proc. § 430, subd. 9. It was not so raised and was therefore waived. Code Civ.Proc. § 434.

The judgment is affirmed.

NOTES

(1) *Preparing to Cross the Brooklyn Bridge.* The rationale of the *Drennan* case is reflected in Restatement Second § 87(2). Would this rule protect B in the Brooklyn Bridge hypothetical, p. 250 above, if B had spent time and money in preparing to cross the bridge but had not begun to cross it when A revoked?

Would you advise B, in such a situation, to cross the bridge in spite of the revocation?

(2) *Problems.* Suppose that after receiving Star Paving's bid on July 28, Drennan had telephoned Star Paving and asked if it "could shave it a little," that Star Paving had said it would "have to think it over," and that Star Paving's bid had then been used without further inquiry. Same result? Compare Jaybe Constr. Co. v. Beco, Inc., 216 A.2d 208 (Conn.Cir.1965), with State ex rel. Sorenson v. Wisner State Bank, 250 N.W. 89 (Neb.1933).

Suppose that this telephone conversation had taken place after the award to Drennan but before Star Paving had discovered its mistake, and that before any further discussion could be had it had discovered its mistake and told Drennan of its unwillingness to perform. Same result? Compare N. Litterio & Co. v. Glassman Constr. Co., 319 F.2d 736 (D.C.Cir.1963), with Crook v. Mortenson–Neal, 727 P.2d 297 (Alaska 1986). See Note, Rejection of an Irrevocable Offer, p. 217 above.

(3) *Statutory Reform.* In California there is a variation of UCC 2–205. In 1980 this additional provision [a] was added:

"Notwithstanding [the Official Text], when a merchant renders an offer, oral or written, to supply goods to a [licensed [b]] contractor ... and the merchant has actual or imputed knowledge that the contractor is so licensed, and that the offer will be relied upon by the contractor in the submission of its bid for a construction contract with a third party, the offer relied upon shall be irrevocable, notwithstanding lack of consideration, for 10 days after the awarding of the contract to the prime contractor, but in no event for more than 90 days after the date the bid or offer was rendered by the merchant; except that an oral bid or offer, when for a price of two thousand five hundred dollars ($2,500) or more, shall be confirmed in writing by the contractor or his or her agent within 48 hours after it is rendered. Failure by the contractor to confirm such offer in writing shall release the merchant from his or her offer. Nothing in this subdivision shall prevent a merchant from providing that the bid or offer will be held open for less than the time provided for herein."

If the facts of *Drennan* were now to recur would this provision have any effect on the decision? If not, what reason might be given for the failure of the legislature to address those facts? If a would-be supplier were to make a written offer otherwise governed by the provision, could the supplier nullify its effect by stamping the offer "revocable"?

So far as the statute is applicable, does it affect your answers to the problems in the foregoing Note?

(4) *Questions.* Under the rule in the *Drennan* case, would it make a difference if the bid in question were much lower than the bids of other subcontractors? (Would the fact that the general contractor had asked the subcontractor to check its bid affect your answer?) Would it make a difference if the subcontractor could show that "bid shopping" and "bid chopping" were

---

a. Subdivision (b).

b. Passage following "contractor", elided here: "... licensed pursuant to the provisions of Chapter 9 (commencing with Section 7000) of Division 3 of the Business and Professions Code or a similar contractor's licensing law of another state".

From § 7026 of the provisions referred to: "Contractor defined": "... synony-

mous with the term 'builder' and ... a contractor is any person, who ... submits a bid to ... construct, alter, repair, add to, subtract from, improve, move, wreck or demolish any building, highway ... or other structure, project, development or improvement.... The term contractor includes subcontractor...."

widespread in the industry? If the subcontractor could show that the general contractor had, after receiving the award, been successful in making contracts with most of its other subcontractors and suppliers at prices lower than the bids on which the general contractor had based its own bid? If the subcontractor could show that the general contractor had, after receiving the award, used the subcontractor's bid in an unsuccessful attempt at "bid shopping"? See Saliba–Kringlen Corp. v. Allen Engineering Co., 92 Cal.Rptr. 799 (Ct.App.1971); Constructors Supply Co. v. Bostrom Sheet Metal Works, Inc., 190 N.W.2d 71 (Minn.1971).

———

HOLMAN ERECTION CO. v. ORVILLE E. MADSEN & SONS, INC., 330 N.W.2d 693 (Minn.1983). [Holman, a steel erection subcontractor, telephoned sub-bids to seven general contractors who were bidding on a wastewater treatment project for the City of Moorhead. One of them, Madsen, used Holman's sub-bid and listed Holman. When Madsen was awarded the contract, it made subcontracts with other subcontractors but did not contact Holman. Instead, Madsen eventually awarded the steel erection subcontract to Van Knight, after requesting information on its status as a minority business. (Madsen's contract with the city required that an effort be made to use minority businesses for part of the work, pursuant to federal regulations.) When Holman learned from another general contract bidder that Madsen had listed Holman and had been awarded the contract, Holman sued Madsen alleging that Madsen had accepted its sub-bid. The trial court held that no contract had been made between the parties and granted summary judgment for Madsen. Holman appealed.]

YETKA, JUSTICE. . . . Holman argues that listing Holman as a subcontractor, as required by the awarding authority, constitutes an acceptance because: 1) there is no other reasonable explanation for the act; 2) it is unfair to bind Holman to its bid without binding Madsen to use it; and 3) Madsen knew the general bid was public record pursuant to statutes. Since Madsen knew Holman could discover that Holman had been listed in the general bid, Holman argues that the inference can be drawn that Madsen intended to accept Holman's offer and communicated the assent by listing Holman in the general bid.

Appellant's argument flies in the face of a large body of precedent holding that no contract is formed by the listing of a subcontractor in a general contractor's bid. There is no case in Minnesota that deals precisely with the issue presented. This court has held, however, that the subcontractor may be bound to his bid as submitted to the general contractor by operation of promissory estoppel. See Constructors Supply Co. v. Bostrom Sheet Metal Works, Inc., 291 Minn. 113, 190 N.W.2d 71 (1971). . . .

Holman attempts to distinguish the vast authority that holds in opposition to its position by pointing to factual differences between those cases and the instant case. While mistake, inadvertence, and other distinguishing facts are present in the cases, the courts' decisions did not turn on these elements. The holdings applied the general law of contracts, not resting on the types of facts highlighted by appellant. In the present case, the subcontractor has shown no reliance, additional communications or detriment stemming from the substitution of a different subcontractor. Further, Madsen had a legitimate reason for substituting a different subcontractor for Holman, that is, complying with federal Minority Business Enterprise (MBE) regulations. The mere absence of mistake, fraud or incapability of the subcontractor has no determinative effect on the resolution of the contract formation issue.

While commentators have urged that a general contractor be bound to a listed subcontractor upon the mere listing or use of the subcontractor's bid in the general bid on several theories, we do not adopt the reasoning. . . . One theory requires a factual inquiry into the circumstances surrounding the relationship of the general contractor and subcontractor. It would find that a contract exists unless: 1) the subbid is not responsive to the plans and specifications embodied in the overall project; or 2) the subcontractor is shown to be unreliable or incapable of performing his side of the bargain without unreasonably complicating the general's position. This approach rests on a supposedly objective and realistic examination of construction industry bidding practices and emphasizes "factual realities."

The dominant policy justification is said to be the avoidance of bid-shopping while not unnecessarily restricting the freedom of general contractors.

A second analysis rests on an analogy to the Uniform Commercial Code. The UCC provides a more liberal standard for formation of contracts than does the common law of contracts and allows any reasonable manner of acceptance to bind both promisor and promisee. See Minn.Stat. § 336.2–206 (1982). It is argued that the court must look to the "fulcrum point of agreement" to determine when the parties are bound. The factual context of general/subcontractor agreements is said to compel the conclusion that since the parties consider themselves bound at the time the general utilizes the subcontractor's bid, this intent should be enforceable.

The broad policy justifications advanced for binding the general to the subcontractor upon utilization or listing of the subcontractor in the general bid include:

1) limiting bargaining to the pre-award stage to put the general and the sub on equal footing as to any subsequent negotiation or modification of the initial agreement;

2) providing certainty in the industry;

3) avoiding bid-shopping;

4) providing formality and allowing the commercial context to supply the necessary fact basis; and

5) allowing for necessary negotiation on open terms, the only binding terms being the price and the nature of the work bid on.

Underlying all of the above justifications is a superficial equity notion. In Minnesota, as well as most other jurisdictions, the subcontractor may be obligated to perform by application of promissory estoppel. The general, however, remains free to avoid the listed subcontractor and negotiate with other subcontractors. This one-sided arrangement seems, on its face, unfair. Why should one party be bound and other not? A close examination of the construction business and the nature of the bidding process, however, reveals several justifications for the unequal treatment of generals and subcontractors.

First, the reason a subcontractor is bound by its bid is the existence of justifiable reliance by the general on the subcontractor's price for specified work. The general makes his bid after gathering and evaluating a number of subcontract bids. Once the general wins the prime contract from the awarding authority, he is bound to his own bid. For the subcontractor to be able to refuse to perform would subject the general to a financial detriment....

In contrast, the subcontractor does not rely on the general and suffers no detriment. A subcontractor submits bids to all or most of the general contractors that it knows are bidding on a project. The subcontractor receives invitations to bid from some generals and submits bids to others without invitation. The time and expense involved in preparing the bid is not segregated to any particular general. The total cost is part of the overhead of doing business. The same bid is submitted to each general. Thus, whether or not any particular general wins the contract is of little or no concern to the subcontractor. The subcontractor engages in the same work and expense in preparing its bid regardless of who wins the general contract and whether the subcontractor wins the contract on which it bid. No further expense is incurred until a formal agreement is reached with the general and actual work commences. Clearly, the promissory estoppel concept is not applicable in this situation. *Bostrom* bound the subcontractor to his bid not on the basis of a contract, but on the basis of estoppel. With no detrimental reliance, there can be no estoppel claim. Ample justification exists for binding the subcontractor and not binding the general. The two situations are very different.

Second, the nature of the bidding process compels allowing the general sufficient leeway to maintain its flexibility in executing subcontracts and selecting the subcontractors it will hire for a project. Typically, subcontractors submit their bids only a few hours before the general bid must be submitted to the awarding authority. The general's representatives take the bids over the telephone and hurriedly compile their own bid. This period of time is hectic and complex. The bids received consist of the contract price and a listing of work included. Specifics are left for future negotiation and clarification.

The last-minute procedure is designed to prevent bid-shopping. This court has recognized the undesirable nature of bid-shopping, ... and the last-minute bidding process seems well entrenched in the construction industry....

The bidding process puts the subcontractor and the general in very different positions as to the content of the subcontract. The subcontractors have the luxury of preparing their bids on their own timetable, subject only to the deadline for submitting their bids to the general contractors. The same bid goes to all the general contractors and covers the same work. The generals, on the other hand, are dealing with all the various construction aspects of the project and with numerous potential subcontractors. They compile their bids, as the various subcontractor bids are received, within a few hours of the deadline for submission of the prime bid. Specifics are necessarily given less than thorough consideration and are left for future negotiations. Finally, the lowest dollar amount bidder is not always the one chosen to do the work or the one listed as the potential subcontractor. Reliability, quality of work, and capability to handle the job are all considerations weighed by the general in choosing subcontractors. MBE regulations requiring an effort to use a percentage of minority contractors are another potential consideration.

Binding general contractors to subcontractors because a particular bid was listed in the general bid or was utilized in making the bid would remove a considerable degree of needed flexibility. The present case illustrates the consequences quite well. Because the project involved was a public project, MBE regulations required that an effort be made to use minority contractors. When Madsen began to put the specifics of the project together, it was forced to juggle the subcontracts in order to comply with the MBE regulations. Van Knight, the subcontractor chosen instead of Holman, qualified as a minority business and offered to supply materials and supplies not included in Holman's bid. Despite a slightly higher cost, Madsen selected Van Knight as the steel erection subcontractor.

If Madsen was bound to the bids listed in its prime bid, there is a possibility that the contract would have been lost due to failure to comply with MBE regulations. The next highest qualifying bidder would then have been selected, to the awarding authority's greater expense and to Madsen's detriment. Such a result imposes a greater cost on the project and a loss to the general contractor. The result under the prevailing law in most jurisdictions, and which we adopt here, would not impose any additional expenses on the rejected subcontractor.

A decision in favor of the subcontractor on this issue would place Minnesota in a minority position as perhaps the sole state to hold that a contract is formed by the mere listing of a subcontractor in a general contractor's bid to the awarding authority. Although supplying some certainty and symmetry to the construction industry, such a decision would also impose a rigidity on the process and result in greater cost to awarding authorities and potential detriment to general contractors. If such a change is to take place, it is one properly brought before the legislature....

[Affirmed.]

NOTE

The Case of the Contractor Caught in the Act. Page & Wirtz, a general contractor, was preparing a bid for construction on the Western Plaza Shopping Center, and already had a subcontractor's bid of about $214,000 on the masonry from Southwestern Bricklaying. At 11:00 a.m., a few hours before the 2:00 p.m. deadline for general contractors' bids, Van Doran, another subcontractor, left his bid of $204,395 with Walter Wirtz after discussing it. Van Doran was still in the building talking to Wirtz' son Jack, when Wirtz came out of his office and told Page to get Southwestern on the telephone immediately. When Wirtz turned around and saw that Van Doran had overheard him, there was "an atmosphere of embarrassment," particularly because Van Doran had accused other general contractors of bid shopping in the past. At 1:00 p.m. Southwestern submitted a second bid, $1,595 under the Van Doran bid. Page & Wirtz submitted its own bid based on Van Doran's figures by 2:00 p.m. At 4:00 p.m. Van Doran telephoned Walter Wirtz, who said "this morning I made the biggest bust I ever made in my life" and "under existing conditions, I can do nothing but give you the job." Van Doran replied, "Well, Walter, now, as I understand it, if you get this job, I've got a job," and Wirtz said "Yes." Page & Wirtz was awarded the contract and awarded the masonry contract to Southwestern. Van Doran sued Page & Wirtz for breach of contract, claiming loss of prospective profits. From a judgment for $25,000, defendant appealed. *Held:* Reversed. "Van Doran admitted throughout his testimony to numerous conditions of the contract between it and Wirtz which would have to be later negotiated." These related to lien rights, a two-year guarantee, an escalator clause, and arrangements that would have to be made if the owners refused to use the standard contract conditions of the American Institute of Architects. "It is clear in the record that before Van Doran's bid was submitted the [owners] were insisting on the conditions just related and Van Doran and Wirtz had discussed the fact that efforts would be made by Wirtz to secure modifications thereof to conform to Van Doran's bid." Page & Wirtz Const. Co. v. Van Doran Bri–Tico Co., 432 S.W.2d 731 (Tex.Ct.App. 1968).

LIABILITY FOR FAILED NEGOTIATIONS

Although the law governing the formation of contracts is usually analyzed in terms of the classic rules of offer and acceptance, these rules have little to say about the complex processes that lead to major deals today. Major contractual commitments are typically set out in a lengthy document, or set of documents, signed by the parties in multiple copies and often exchanged at a closing. The terms are arrived at by negotiations that are a far cry from the simple bargaining envisioned by the classic rules of offer and acceptance.

But what if the negotiations fail and no documents are signed and exchanged? May a disappointed party have a claim against the other? Of course if one party has conferred a benefit on the other during the course of the negotiations, the recipient of the benefit may be required to make restitution. See Hill v. Waxberg, Note 4, p. 79 above. But restitution will not compensate the disappointed party for losses that did not result in a benefit to the other party.

Restitution aside, courts have traditionally accorded parties the freedom to negotiate without risk of precontractual liability. Under the classic rules of offer and acceptance, there is no contractual liability until a contract is made by the acceptance of an offer; prior to acceptance the offeror is free to back out by revoking the offer. This "freedom from contract" is enhanced by a judicial reluctance to read a proposal as an offer in the first place. The assumption is that a party entering negotiations in the hope of the gain that will result from agreement bears the risk of whatever loss results if the other party breaks off the negotiations. The following materials deal with the extent to which disappointed parties have succeeded in making inroads into this assumption.

A seminal, if somewhat mysterious, case is Goodman v. Dicker, 169 F.2d 684 (D.C.Cir.1948), in which a disappointed applicant for a franchise to sell Emerson radios sued Emerson's local distributors on the ground that they had, as the trial court found, "by their representations and conduct induced [the applicant] to incur expenses in preparing to do business under the franchise, including employment of salesmen and solicitation of orders for radios." The local distributors argued that even if the franchise had been granted, "it would have been terminable at will and would have imposed no duty upon the manufacturer to sell or [the applicant] to buy any fixed number of radios." The court upheld an award of damages in the amount of $1,150 which the applicant "expended in preparing to do business under the promised dealer franchise." [a] It explained, "Justice and fair dealing require that one who acts to his detriment on the faith of conduct of the kind revealed here should be protected by estopping the party who has brought about the situation from alleging anything in opposition to the natural consequences of his own course of conduct."

It is arguable that this case turned on a misrepresentation of fact by the local distributors rather than on a promise by them. The trial court found, among other things, that the local distributors "represented that the application *had been* accepted" and "that the franchise *would be* granted." (emphasis added). The opinion does not cite the first Restatement § 90 but instead quotes from a case involving "equitable estoppel." Nevertheless, the case was seized upon by advocates of expanded promissory liability and was made the basis of Illustration 8 of Restatement Second § 90.

NOTES

(1) *The Case of Miller High Life.* In October, 1963, Prince, an established beer distributor, undertook the Miller High Life distributorship in East Harris County, Texas, although he knew that the area had been poorly serviced in the past and that it would be two or three years before he would realize a profit. The contract provided, "Either of us can terminate this relationship at any time without incurring liability to the other." Miller terminated in June, 1965

a. The court held that it was error, however, to award $350 for loss of profits on radios promised under an initial order. "The true measure of damages is the loss sustained by expenditures made in reliance upon the assurance of a dealer franchise."

because it had become involved in a lawsuit with a corporation that Prince controlled. Prince had just begun to make a profit, after having sustained losses of over $20,000, not including his own time and effort and that of his wife. Miller then appointed another distributor, whose operation showed a continued and substantial increase in sales volume. Prince sued Miller for the money he had spent in preparation for and operation of the distributorship and for reasonable compensation for his services. The trial court directed a verdict for the defendant and the plaintiff appealed. *Held:* Affirmed. "It is appellant's contention that where a manufacturer and a distributor enter into an arrangement whereby the distributor is to develop a market for and sell the manufacturer's products, and it is contemplated by both parties that expenditures of time and money by the distributor are necessary to build up his distributorship, though the relationship be one terminable at will, the law will not allow the manufacturer to exercise its rights of cancellation with impunity, but will imply an obligation on its part to respond in damages sufficient to compensate the distributor for his expenditures made and losses incurred in reliance upon the agreement if the manufacturer terminates the distributorship before the distributor is afforded a reasonable time to recoup his losses.... This statement of the law is supported by respectable authority.... [However], each of these cases presented situations where the contract was oral, of indefinite duration, or void, and were considered cancellable at will as a matter of law. There was no specific written agreement authorizing cancellation without liability.... In Wheeler v. White [Note 3, p. 271 below], the Supreme Court recognized the case of Goodman v. Dicker.... In this case, however, there is a legally sufficient contract.... Appellant cannot disregard the contract and sue for his reliance damage. Because of the valid contract the theory of promissory estoppel is not applicable." Prince v. Miller Brewing Co., 434 S.W.2d 232 (Tex.App.1968).

What result if Prince had been able to show that Miller had terminated the contract in order to let a close personal friend of one of its officers have a profitable franchise? In Goodman v. Dicker, would Dicker have had any recourse if Emerson had granted him a franchise and then terminated it immediately? Would the wording of the termination clause affect your answer? What answer if it read, "Either of us can terminate this relationship at any time"? See Lockewill v. United States Shoe, p. 642 below, and Gellhorn, Limitations on Contract Termination Rights—Franchise Cancellations, 1967 Duke L.J. 465 (1967).

✱ (2) *The Case of Grouse's Grouse.* John Grouse, who worked as a pharmacist at Richter Drug in Minneapolis, applied for a job with Group Health Plan in the same city. When he was offered a position by Cyrus Elliott, Group Health's Chief Pharmacist, Grouse told Elliott that he had to give Richter two week's notice, which he did. The same day, Grouse received an offer from a Veteran's Administration Hospital in Virginia, but rejected it because of Group Health's offer. Sometime in the next few days, Elliott was told by Donald Shoberg, Group Health's General Manager, that the company required a favorable written reference, a background check, and Shoberg's approval. Two of Grouse's former teachers declined to give references, as did several of his employers for part time work. (Grouse had asked that Richter not be contacted.) Shoberg then hired someone else. Grouse had difficulty regaining full time employment and sued for damages. The trial judge dismissed his complaint. The Supreme Court of Minnesota reversed and remanded for a new trial on the issue of damages.

"The parties focus their arguments on whether an employment contract which is terminable at will can give rise to an action for damages if anticipatorily repudiated.... Group Health contends that recognition of a cause of action on these facts would result in the anomalous rule that an employee who is told not to report to work the day before he is scheduled to begin has a remedy while an employee who is discharged after the first day does not. We cannot agree since under appropriate circumstances we believe section 90 would apply even after employment has begun. When a promise is enforced pursuant to section 90 "[t]he remedy granted for breach may be limited as justice requires." Relief may be limited to damages measured by the promisee's reliance.

"The conclusion we reach does not imply that an employer will be liable whenever he discharges an employee whose term of employment is at will. What we do hold is that under the facts of this case the appellant had a right to assume he would be given a good faith opportunity to perform his duties to the satisfaction of respondent once he was on the job. He was not only denied that opportunity but resigned the position he already held in reliance on the firm offer which respondent tendered him. Since, as respondent points out, the prospective employment might have been terminated at any time, the measure of damages is not so much what he would have earned from respondent as what he lost in quitting the job he held and in declining at least one other offer of employment elsewhere." Grouse v. Group Health Plan, Inc., 306 N.W.2d 114 (Minn.1981). How should Grouse's damages be calculated on a new trial?

RAGOSTA v. WILDER
Supreme Court of Vermont, 1991.
156 Vt. 390, 592 A.2d 367.

[The facts and the first part of the opinion in this case are at p. 212 above.]

PECK, J. In the course of analyzing the case under part performance and equitable estoppel theories,[a] the trial court cited promissory estoppel principles. It noted, "Plaintiffs relied on the conduct of the Defendant to their detriment when they prepared for and tendered performance" and concluded that defendant's conduct induced plaintiffs to begin performance by obtaining financing. [Here the court set out Restatement Second § 90(1).] This principle is distinct from part performance since the action or forbearance involved need not constitute part performance. While the court's order cannot be upheld under a part performance theory, its ruling may be appropriate on promissory estoppel grounds. We cannot affirm the order on those grounds, however, because the trial court, in ruling that the promise must be enforced, erroneously relied on a part performance theory. Cf. Price v. Price, 149 Vt. 118, 122, 541 A.2d 79, 82 (1987) (order must be reversed and remanded where court may have relied on inappropriate considerations for its ruling). Under promissory estoppel, plaintiffs are entitled to enforcement of defendant's promise only if the promise induced them to take action "of a definite and substantial character," and if "injustice [*can*] *be avoided only* by enforcement of the promise." Stacy v. Mer-

---

a. As to equitable estoppel, see the description of conventional estoppel theory in Note 2, p. 100 above.

chants Bank, 144 Vt. 515, 521, 482 A.2d 61, 64 (1984) (emphasis added) (citing Restatement (Second) of Contracts § 90).

On remand the court shall consider the case under promissory estoppel only and determine what remedy, if any, is necessary to prevent injustice. In making this determination the court should consider the fact that plaintiffs incurred the expense of obtaining financing although they could not be certain that the property would be sold to them.

Because we reverse, we do not address defendant's claim that specific performance was an inappropriate remedy or plaintiffs' claim that they are entitled to the interest which has accrued on the purchase price since the date of the trial court's decision.

Reversed and the cause remanded for further proceedings consistent with the principles expressed herein.

NOTES

(1) *Questions.* Consider again the Note, Reliance on an Offer, p. 252 above, especially the concluding quotation from Learned Hand. Is the decision above a "strained interpretation" in favor of the Ragostas? If they had cited Drennan v. Star Paving, above, and the court had wished to distinguish that case, how might it have done so?

(2) *Problem.* Suppose a difference in the facts of *Ragosta,* as follows. Instead of writing letters and telephoning to one another, the parties met on October 1 and signed this document:

> I, Allen Wilder, hereby agree to sell The Fork Shop to Louis and Sylvia Ragosta, the purchase price to be $88,000. Deed to be given and price paid on November 1.

In Heinzel v. Backstrom, 794 P.2d 775 (Or.1990), a document much like this was held to be an offer only. Do you agree? If so, does the form of the offer affect your judgment about the justice of permitting Wilder to revoke?

In the case cited there was a finding that, while the prospective buyers (one more than the other) were sophisticated in real-estate matters, the owner had had little experience of them, if any. Should that matter? The owner's attorney, being consulted about the effect of the document, said that it was probably binding until the date named, advised her not to communicate with the prospective purchasers, and procured an offer from another purchaser (to whom she later conveyed). Can the attorney's conduct be faulted?

(3) *The Case of the Adversary's Secret.* A tenant, upon receiving an eviction notice from the landlord, telephones several attorneys, seeking representation. One of them is A, to whom the tenant discloses some important and confidential information about the tenancy. The tenant selects another attorney. A undertakes to represent the landlord. The tenant's attorney, B, moves to have A disqualified. Should the motion be denied on the ground that there was never a contract between A and the tenant? See New York University v. Simon, 498 N.Y.S.2d 659 (City Ct.1985). As to the confidentiality of information "relating to the representation of a client," see Rule 1.6 of the ABA Model Code of Professional Responsibility.

HOFFMAN v. RED OWL STORES

Supreme Court of Wisconsin, 1965.
26 Wis.2d 683, 133 N.W.2d 267.

[Hoffman and his wife owned and operated a bakery in Wautoma, Wisconsin. In November, 1959, he contacted Red Owl, which operated a supermarket chain, seeking to obtain a franchise for a Red Owl store in Wautoma. He mentioned that he had only $18,000 to invest and was assured that this would be sufficient. In February, 1961, on the advice of Red Owl's representative, Lukowitz, he acquired a small grocery store as a means of gaining experience. After three months, the store was operating at a profit, and Lukowitz advised him to sell it, assuring him that Red Owl would find him a larger store elsewhere. Hoffman did so in June, 1961, although he was reluctant to lose the summer tourist business. He was again assured that $18,000 would suffice to obtain a franchise. In September, on Lukowitz' advice, Hoffman put $1,000 down on a lot in Chilton selected by Red Owl. Later in September, after meeting with Hoffman to prepare a financial statement, Lukowitz told him, "[E]verything is ready to go. Get your money together and we are set." Lukowitz then told Hoffman to sell his bakery, which Hoffman did in November for $10,000, a loss of $2,000. He paid a month's rent of $125 on a house in Chilton, and they spent $140 in moving his family to Neenah where Red Owl suggested that he get experience by working at their store near there. When that job did not materialize, he went to work on the night shift at an Appleton bakery.

[By this time, Lukowitz and Hoffman had considered a variety of arrangements under which Red Owl would get some third party to acquire the Chilton lot, build the building, and lease it to Hoffman, and had agreed on some of the terms of a ten-year lease, with an option in Hoffman to renew the lease or purchase the property. Late in November they met with Red Owl's credit manager and drew up a proposed financing statement showing Hoffman contributing $24,100 of which $4,600 was an actual cash contribution, and another $7,500 was to be borrowed from his father-in-law. A week or two later, Lukowitz said that according to the home office, if Hoffman could get another $2,000 for promotion, the deal could go through for $26,000. Hoffman got his father-in-law to agree to put up $13,000 if he could come in as a partner. The home office, however, insisted that the father-in-law sign an agreement that the $13,000 was either a gift or a loan subordinate to all general creditors. Early in February, 1962, the negotiations collapsed when Hoffman refused to accede to a proposed financial statement that showed his contribution as $34,000, including $13,000 from his father-in-law as an outright gift. The Hoffmans sued Red Owl and the jury gave a special verdict, assessing damages as $16,735 for the sale of the Wautoma store, $2,000 for the sale of the bakery, $1,000 for taking up the option on the Chilton lot, $140 for moving expenses to Neenah, and $125 for house rental in Chilton. The trial court confirmed the verdict, except for the figure of $16,735 for the sale of the Wautoma store, as to which it ordered a new trial.]

CURRIE, CHIEF JUSTICE.... The record here discloses a number of promises and assurances given to Hoffman by Lukowitz in behalf of Red Owl upon which plaintiffs relied and acted upon to their detriment.... There remains for consideration the question of law raised by defendants that agreement was never reached on essential factors necessary to establish a contract between Hoffman and Red Owl. Among these were the size, cost, design, and layout of the store building; and the terms of the lease with respect to rent, maintenance, renewal, and purchase options. This poses the question of whether the promise necessary to sustain a cause of action for promissory estoppel must embrace all essential details of a proposed transaction between promisor and promisee so as to be the equivalent of an offer that would result in a binding contract between the parties if the promisee were to accept the same.

Originally the doctrine of promissory estoppel was invoked as a substitute for consideration rendering a gratuitous promise enforceable as a contract. See Williston, Contracts (1st ed.), p. 307, sec. 139. In other words, the acts of reliance by the promisee to his detriment provided a substitute for consideration. If promissory estoppel were to be limited to only those situations where the promise giving rise to the cause of action must be so definite with respect to all details that a contract would result were the promise supported by consideration, then the defendants' instant promises to Hoffman would not meet this test. However, sec. 90 of Restatement, 1 Contracts, does not impose the requirement that the promise giving rise to the cause of action must be so comprehensive in scope as to meet the requirements of an offer that would ripen into a contract if accepted by the promisee. Rather the conditions imposed are:

(1) Was the promise one which the promisor should reasonably expect to induce action or forbearance of a definite and substantial character on the part of the promisee?

(2) Did the promise induce such action or forbearance?

(3) Can injustice be avoided only by enforcement of the promise? [1]

We deem it would be a mistake to regard an action grounded on promissory estoppel as the equivalent of a breach of contract action. As Dean Boyer points out, it is desirable that fluidity in the application of the concept be maintained. 98 University of Pennsylvania Law Review (1950), 459, at page 497. While the first two of the above listed three requirements of promissory estoppel present issues of fact which ordinarily will be resolved by a jury, the third requirement, that the remedy can only be invoked where necessary to avoid injustice, is one that involves a policy decision by the court. Such a policy decision necessarily embraces an element of discretion.

1. See Boyer, 98 University of Pennsylvania Law Review (1950), 459, 460. "Enforcement" of the promise embraces an award of damages for breach as well as decreeing specific performance.

We conclude that injustice would result here if plaintiffs were not granted some relief because of the failure of defendants to keep their promises which induced plaintiffs to act to their detriment....

[With regard to damages, all of the items properly represented losses that he had reasonably sustained in reliance on Red Owl's promises except for the $16,735 for the sale of the Wautoma store. This should have been] limited to the difference between the sales price received and the fair market value of the assets sold, giving consideration to any goodwill attaching thereto by reason of the transfer of a going business. There was no direct evidence presented as to what this fair market value was on June 6, 1961. The evidence did disclose that Hoffman paid $9,000 for the inventory, added $1,500 to it and sold it for $10,000 or a loss of $500. His 1961 federal income tax return showed that the grocery equipment had been purchased for $7,000 and sold for $7,955.96. Plaintiffs introduced evidence of the buyer that during the first eleven weeks of operation of the grocery store his gross sales were $44,000 and his profit was $6,000 or roughly 15 percent. On cross-examination he admitted that this was gross and not net profit. Plaintiffs contend that in a breach of contract action damages may include loss of profits. However, this is not a breach of contract action.

The only relevancy of evidence relating to profits would be with respect to proving the element of goodwill in establishing the fair market value of the grocery inventory and fixtures sold. Therefore, evidence of profits would be admissible to afford a foundation for expert opinion as to fair market value.

Where damages are awarded in promissory estoppel instead of specifically enforcing the promisor's promise, they should be only such as in the opinion of the court are necessary to prevent injustice. Mechanical or rule of thumb approaches to the damage problem should be avoided....

At the time Hoffman bought the equipment and inventory of the small grocery store at Wautoma he did so in order to gain experience in the grocery store business. At that time discussion had already been had with Red Owl representatives that Wautoma might be too small for a Red Owl operation and that a larger city might be more desirable. Thus Hoffman made this purchase more or less as a temporary experiment. Justice does not require that the damages awarded him, because of selling these assets at the behest of defendants, should exceed any actual loss sustained measured by the difference between the sales price and the fair market value.

Since the evidence does not sustain the large award of damages arising from the sale of the Wautoma grocery business, the trial court properly ordered a new trial on this issue.

Order affirmed....

NOTES

(1) *Impact of Red Owl.* Although the *Red Owl* case has been cited in other situations involving promissory estoppel, it seems to have spawned few suits

involving facts similar to its own. Exceptions are Werner v. Xerox Corp., 732 F.2d 580 (7th Cir.1984); Vigoda v. Denver Urban Renewal Authority, 646 P.2d 900 (Colo.1982). The Supreme Court of Wisconsin has since refused to extend the doctrine of promissory estoppel to protect an employee who enters into an employment agreement that is terminable at will. Forrer v. Sears, Roebuck & Co., 153 N.W.2d 587 (Wis.1967).

(2) *An Academic Point.* Not all courts have been as averse to damages based on lost profits as was the Wisconsin Supreme Court. In Walters v. Marathon Oil Co., 642 F.2d 1098 (7th Cir.1981), the Walterses sued Marathon Oil when, as a result of the Iranian revolution and the uncertainty of oil supplies, Marathon refused to sign an agreement to provide them with gasoline. The Walterses had purchased the station "and continued to make improvements upon it, based upon promises made, and the continuing negotiations with representatives" of Marathon. The trial court held Marathon liable "on the theory of promissory estoppel" and awarded damages of $22,200 based on lost profits for the first year. The Court of Appeals affirmed, noting that "in reliance upon [Marathon's] promise to supply gasoline supplies to them, [the Walteres] purchased the station, and invested their funds and their time," and in addition "they had foregone the opportunity to make the investment elsewhere." It did not cite Hoffman v. Red Owl.

Professor Jay Feinman cited this case for the proposition that "the typical damage remedy applied in promissory estoppel cases is measured by the expectation interest," adding that courts may "recognize that, in business cases, expectation recovery may better reflect opportunity losses than would reliance recovery." Feinman, Promissory Estoppel and Judicial Method, 97 Harv.L.Rev. 678, 687–88 (1984). Professor Robert Birmingham took issue with Feinman, arguing that the *Marathon* court did not seem, in the language quoted earlier, to be speaking of the expectation interest. "The court protected the reliance interest, but gave just what it would have given had it been protecting the expectation interest.... Feinman (I think wrongly) calls 'protecting the expectation interest' what I call 'protecting the reliance interest' if the damages awarded are the same." Birmingham, Notes on the Reliance Interest, 60 Wash.L.Rev. 217, 237 (1985).

Is this a purely academic point? As long as the Walterses get their lost profits, why do we care what their "interest" is called? When might it make a difference in practice?

(3) *The Case of the Uncertain Loan.* Wheeler owned a tract of land in Port Arthur, Texas, on which he wanted to build a commercial structure. He made a written agreement with White, under which White was to either make or obtain a loan of $70,000, payable in monthly installments over 15 years at not more than 6%, to finance the project and to receive a $5,000 fee for obtaining the loan and a 5% commission on all rentals from tenants that he procured. Later White assured Wheeler that he would make the loan himself if the money was unobtainable elsewhere, and urged him to proceed with the demolition of the existing buildings, which had a value of $58,500 and a rental value of $400 a month. After Wheeler had razed the old buildings and begun to prepare the site, White refused to perform. When Wheeler was unable to obtain a loan himself, he sued White. From judgment dismissing Wheeler's complaint, Wheeler appealed. *Held:* Reversed. "[T]he pleaded contract did not contain essential elements to its enforceability in that it failed to provide the amount of monthly installments, the amount of interest due upon the obligation, how much interest would be computed, [and] when such interest would be paid...." The court then discussed Goodman v. Dicker, p. 264 above. "We agree with the reasoning

announced in those jurisdictions that, in cases such as we have before us, where there is actually no contract the promissory estoppel theory may be invoked, thereby supplying a remedy which will enable the injured party to be compensated for his foreseeable, definite and substantial reliance. Where the promisee has failed to bind the promisor to a legally sufficient contract, but where the promisee has acted in reliance upon a promise to his detriment, the promisee is to be allowed to recover no more than reliance damages measured by the detriment sustained." Wheeler v. White, 398 S.W.2d 93 (Tex.1965). How should those damages be calculated when the case goes back for trial? Does this case go beyond Goodman v. Dicker? Beyond Hoffman v. Red Owl?

CHANNEL HOME CENTERS, DIVISION OF GRACE RETAIL CORP. v. GROSSMAN

United States Court of Appeals, Third Circuit, 1986.
795 F.2d 291.

BECKER, CIRCUIT JUDGE. This diversity case presents the question whether, under Pennsylvania law, a property owner's promise to a prospective tenant, pursuant to a detailed letter of intent, to negotiate in good faith with the prospective tenant and to withdraw the lease premises from the marketplace during the negotiation, can bind the owner for a reasonable period of time where the prospective tenant has expended significant sums of money in connection with the lease negotiations and preparation and where there was evidence that the letter of intent was of significant value to the property owner. We hold that it may. We therefore vacate and reverse the district court's determination that there was no enforceable agreement, and remand the case for trial.

Appellant Channel Home Centers ("Channel"), a division of Grace Retail Corporation, operates retail home improvement stores throughout the Northeastern United States, including Philadelphia and its suburbs. Appellee Frank Grossman, a real estate broker and developer, with his sons Bruce and Jeffrey Grossman, either owns or has a controlling interest in appellees Tri–Star Associates ("Tri–Star"), Baker Investment Corporation ("Baker"), and Cedarbrook Associates, a Pennsylvania Limited Partnership ("Cedarbrook").

Between November, 1984 and February, 1985, the Grossmans, through Baker, were in the process of acquiring ownership of Cedarbrook Mall ("the mall") located in Cheltenham Township, Pennsylvania, a northern suburb of Philadelphia. During these months, Baker was the equitable owner of the mall, Tri–Star was acting as the mall's leasing agent, and legal title was in Equitable Life Assurance Society. It was anticipated that, upon closing in February, 1985, Baker would become both legal and equitable owner of the mall. The Grossmans intended to revitalize the mall, which had fallen on hard times prior to their acquisition, through an aggressive rehabilitation and leasing program.

In the third week of November, 1984, Tri–Star wrote to Richard Perkowski, Director of Real Estate for Channel, informing him of the availability of a store location in Cedarbrook Mall which Tri–Star believed Channel would be interested in leasing. Perkowski expressed some interest, and met the Grossmans on November 28, 1984. After Perkowski was given a tour of the premises, the terms of a lease were discussed. Frank Grossman testified that "we discussed various terms, and these terms were, some were loose, some were more or less terms." App. at 364a, 496a–497a.

In a memorandum dated December 7, 1984, to S. Charles Tabak, Channel's senior vice-president for general administration, Perkowski outlined the salient lease terms that he had negotiated with the Grossmans. On or about the same date, Tabak and Leon Burger, President of Channel, visited the mall site with the Grossmans. They indicated that Channel desired to lease the site. Frank Grossman then requested that Channel execute a letter of intent that, as Grossman put it, could be shown to "other people, banks or whatever." Tabak testified that the Grossmans wanted to get Channel into the site because it would give the mall four "anchor" stores. Apparently, Frank Grossman was anxious to get Channel's signature on a letter of intent so that it could be used to help Grossman secure financing for his purchase of the mall.

On December 11, 1984, in response to Grossman's request, Channel prepared, executed, and submitted a detailed letter of intent setting forth a plethora of lease terms which provided, *inter alia,* that

> [t]o induce the Tenant [Channel] to proceed with the leasing of the Store, you [Grossman] will withdraw the Store from the rental market, and only negotiate the above described leasing transaction to completion.

> Please acknowledge your intent to proceed with the leasing of the store under the above terms, conditions and understanding by signing the enclosed copy of the letter and returning it to the undersigned within ten (10) days from the date hereof.

App. at 31a.

Frank Grossman promptly signed the letter of intent and returned it to Channel. Grossman contends that Perkowski and Tabak also agreed orally that a draft lease be submitted within thirty (30) days. Perkowski and Tabak denied telling Grossman that a lease would be forthcoming within 30 days or any finite period of time.

Thereafter, both parties initiated procedures directed toward satisfaction of lease contingencies. The letter of intent specified that execution of the lease was expressly subject to each of the following: (1) approval by Channel's parent corporation, W.R. Grace & Company ("Grace"), of the essential business terms of the lease; (2) approval by Channel of the status of title for the site; and (3) Channel's obtaining, with Frank Grossman's cooperation, all necessary permits and zoning variances for the erection of Channel's identification signs. ...

On December 14, 1984, Channel directed the Grace legal department to prepare a lease for the premises. Channel's real estate committee approved the lease site on December 20, 1984. Channel planning representatives visited the premises on December 21, 1984, to obtain measurements for architectural alterations, renovations and related construction. Detailed marketing plans were developed, building plans drafted, delivery schedules were prepared and materials and equipment deemed necessary for the store were purchased. The Grossmans applied to the Cheltenham Township building and zoning committee for permission to erect commercial signs for Channel and other tenants of the mall.

On January 11, 1985, Frank Shea, Esquire, of the Grace legal department sent to Frank Grossman two copies of a forty-one (41) page draft lease and, in a cover letter, requested copies of several documents to be used as exhibits to the lease. On January 16, 1985, Frank Shea received the following letter from Bruce Grossman:

Dear Mr. Shea:

As you requested, enclosed please find the following documents:

1) A copy of a recent title report for the Cedarbrook Mall (the "Mall"),

2) A legal description of the Mall,

3) A site plan of the Mall, and

4) A description of the Landlord's construction.

As we discussed, we have commenced work on the Channel location at the Mall and would, therefore, appreciate your assistance in expediting the execution of the Channel lease.

I look forward to hearing from you soon.

Very truly yours,

BAKER INVESTMENT CORPORATION

/s/ Bruce S. Grossman,

Executive Vice President

App. at 16a. On January 21, 1985, Frank Shea received a copy of a letter from Frank Grossman to Richard Perkowski dated January 17, 1985. It provided:

At Frank Shea's request, enclosed is a site plan for the Cedarbrook Mall and also a copy of the proposed pylon sign design.

We look forward to executing the lease agreement in the very near future. If you have any questions, please feel free to call me.

App. at 46a.

Bruce Grossman called Shea on January 23, 1985 to discuss the lease. The only item Grossman could recall discussing pertained to the "use" clause in the lease, specifically whether Channel could use the site for warehouse facilities at some future point. Apparently, Grossman then related other areas of concern and Shea suggested that a telephone conference be arranged with all parties the following week. Grossman agreed. According to Grossman, Shea was supposed to initiate the conference call; however, when the call was not forthcoming, Grossman did not attempt to reach Shea or anyone else at Channel. Shea understood that the Grossmans were going to discuss the lease among themselves and get back to him.

On or about January 22, 1985, Stephen Erlbaum, Chairman of the Board of Mr. Good Buys of Pennsylvania, Inc. ("Mr. Good Buys"), contacted Frank Grossman. Like Channel, Mr. Good Buys is a corporation engaged in the business of operating retail home improvement centers; it is a major competitor of Channel, in the Philadelphia area. Erlbaum advised Grossman that Mr. Good Buys would be interested in leasing space at Cedarbrook Mall, and sent Grossman printed information about Mr. Good Buys.

On January 24, 1985, construction representatives from Channel met at the mall site to go over building alterations and designs. The next day, January 25, 1985, Erlbaum and other representatives from Mr. Good Buys met with the Grossmans and toured Channel's proposed lease location. When Erlbaum expressed an interest in leasing this site, lease terms were discussed.

On February 6, 1985, Frank Grossman notified Channel that "negotiations terminated as of this date" due to Channel's failure to submit a signed and mutually acceptable lease for the mall site within thirty days of the December 11, 1984 letter of intent. (This was the first and only written evidence of the purported thirty-day time limit. The letter of intent contained no such term. . . .) On February 7, 1985, Mr. Good Buys and Frank Grossman executed a lease for the Cedarbrook Mall. Mr. Good Buys agreed to make base-level annual rental payments which were substantially greater than those agreed to by Channel in the December 11, 1984 letter of intent. Channel's corporate parent, Grace, approved the terms of Channel's proposed lease on February 13, 1985. . . .

[Channel contends on appeal] that the district court erred in holding that the letter of intent was unenforceable and did not bind the parties to any obligation. Channel argues that the letter, coupled with the surrounding circumstances, constitutes a binding agreement to negotiate in good faith. Appellees rejoin that a promise to negotiate in good faith or to use best efforts to reduce to formal writing an agreement between the parties is enforceable only if the parties have in fact reached agreement on the underlying transaction. Because it is conceded that the letter of intent did not constitute a final agreement between the parties, appellees contend that it is merely evidence of preliminary negotiations and, as such, is unenforceable at law. Appellees further argue that even if the agreement were an otherwise enforceable contract, the letter of intent and any promises contained therein are unenforceable by virtue of Channel's lack of consideration.[1] The parties agree that Pennsylvania law applies to the case.

---

1. The district court also rejected Channel's additional contention that the letter of intent should be enforced under the doctrine of promissory estoppel. In light of our disposition on appeal, we need not reach the propriety of the district court's determinations that neither a unilateral contract analysis nor the doctrine of promissory estoppel is applicable to the instant case. [Footnote transposed. Eds.]

It is hornbook law that evidence of preliminary negotiations or an agreement to enter into a binding contract in the future does not alone constitute a contract.... Appellees believe that this doctrine settles this case, but, in so arguing, appellees misconstrue Channel's contract claim. Channel does not contend that the letter of intent is binding as a lease or an agreement to enter into a lease. Rather, it is Channel's position that this document is enforceable as a mutually binding obligation *to negotiate in good faith.*[2] By unilaterally terminating negotiations with Channel and precipitously entering into a lease agreement with Mr. Good Buys, Channel argues, Grossman acted in bad faith and breached his promise to "withdraw the Store from the rental market and only negotiate the above-described leasing transaction to completion."
. . .

Under Pennsylvania law, the test for enforceability of an agreement is whether both parties have manifested an intention to be bound by its terms and whether the terms are sufficiently definite to be specifically enforced.... Additionally, of course, there must be consideration on both sides.... Consideration "confers a benefit upon the promisor or causes a detriment to the promisee and must be an act, forbearance or return promise bargained for and given in exchange for the original promise." Curry v. Estate of Thompson, 332 Pa.Super. 364, 371, 481 A.2d 658, 661 (1984).

Although no Pennsylvania court has considered whether an agreement to negotiate in good faith may meet these conditions, the jurisdictions that have considered the issue have held that such an agreement, if otherwise meeting the requisites of a contract, is an enforceable contract. See, e.g., Thompson v. Liquichimica of America, Inc., 481 F.Supp. 365, 366 (E.D.N.Y.1979) ("Unlike an agreement to agree, which does not constitute a closed proposition, an agreement to use best efforts [or to negotiate in good faith] is a closed proposition, discrete and actionable."); . . . see generally Kessler and Fine, *Culpa in Contrahendo*, Bargaining in Good Faith, and Freedom of Contract; a Comparative Study, 77 Harv.L.Rev. 401 (1964).[3] We are satisfied that Pennsylvania would follow this rule. Applying Pennsylvania law, then, we must ask (1) whether both parties manifested an intention to be bound by the agreement; (2) whether the terms of the agreement are sufficiently definite to be enforced; and (3) whether there was consideration.

In determining the parties' intentions concerning the letter of intent, we must examine the entire document and the relevant circum-

---

2. Because Channel does not argue that the letter of intent is enforceable as a lease between the parties, appellees' reliance upon the district court's conclusion that the letter of intent is insufficient to satisfy the Pennsylvania Statute of Frauds for Leases, Pa.Stat.Ann. tit. 68, §§ 250.202–203 (Purdon 1965 & Supp.1986), is misplaced. The district court therefore erred in holding that the letter of intent was insufficient to satisfy the Statute of Frauds for leases.

3. Good faith in the bargaining or formation stages of the contracting process is distinguishable from the common law duty to perform in good faith. See Restatement of Contracts (Second) § 205 (1979) ("Every contract imposes upon each party a duty of good faith and fair dealing in its performance and its enforcement.").....

stances surrounding its adoption.... The letter of intent, signed by both parties, provides that "[t]o induce the Tenant [Channel] to proceed with the leasing of the Store, you [Grossman] will withdraw the Store from the rental market, and only negotiate the above described leasing transaction to completion." ... The agreement thus contains an unequivocal promise by Grossman to withdraw the store from the rental market and to negotiate the proposed leasing transaction with Channel to completion.

Evidence of record supports the proposition that the parties intended this promise to be binding. After the letter of intent was executed, both Channel and the Grossmans initiated procedures directed toward satisfaction of lease contingencies. Channel directed its parent corporation to prepare a draft lease; Channel planning representatives visited the lease premises to obtain measurements for architectural alterations, renovations, and related construction. Channel developed extensive marketing plans; delivery schedules were prepared and material and equipment deemed necessary for the store were purchased. The Grossmans applied to the township zoning committee for permission to erect Channel signs at various locations on the mall property. Channel submitted a draft lease on January 11, 1985, and the parties, through correspondence and telephone conversations and on-site visits, exhibited an intent to move toward a lease as late as January 23, 1985.... Accordingly, the letter of intent and the circumstances surrounding its adoption both support a finding that the parties intended to be bound by an agreement to negotiate in good faith.

We also believe that Grossman's promise to "withdraw the Store from the rental market and only negotiate the above described leasing transaction to completion," viewed in the context of the detailed letter of intent (which covers most significant lease terms ...), is sufficiently definite to be specifically enforced, provided that Channel submitted sufficient legal consideration in return.

Appellees argue that "[n]o money or thing of value was paid, either at the time of the letter or at any other time that would convert an agreement to negotiate into some enforceable type of contract." Brief of Appellees at 16. We disagree. It seems clear that the execution and tender of the letter of intent by Channel was of substantial value to Frank Grossman. At the time the letter of intent was executed, Grossman was in the process of obtaining financing for his purchase of the mall. When it became apparent to Grossman that Channel—a major corporate tenant—was seriously interested in leasing the mall site, he requested that Channel sign a letter of intent which, as Grossman put it, could be shown to "other people, banks or whatever with a view to getting permanent financing." App. at 366a–367a. Fully aware of Grossman's desire to obtain financing, Channel sought to solidify its bargaining position by requesting that Grossman also sign the letter of intent and promise to "withdraw the store from the rental market and only negotiate the above-described leasing transaction to completion." There being evidence that value passed from each party to the other, we conclude that the record would support a finding that Channel's execution and tender of the letter of intent conferred a bargained for benefit on Grossman which was valid consideration for Grossman's return promise to negotiate in good faith.

In sum, we agree with Channel that the record contains evidence that supports a finding that the parties intended to enter into a binding agreement to negotiate in good faith. We further hold that the agreement had sufficient specificity to make it an enforceable contract if the parties so intended, and that consideration passed between the parties. We will therefore remand this case to the district court for trial.

At least two significant issues must be resolved at trial. First, although our review of the record reveals that there is sufficient evidence to support a finding that the parties intended to be bound by the letter of intent, we do not hold that the evidence requires this conclusion. At trial, evidence will presumably be brought to light that will aid the trier of fact in deciding this issue.

As noted above, there is also some dispute over whether there was a time limit on the negotiations that was not specified in the letter of intent. Because the district court erroneously concluded that the letter of intent was unenforceable as a matter of law, it made no factual findings with regard to this critical term. If, as appellees suggest, Channel orally agreed to forward a draft lease within 30 days of the date on which the letter of intent was executed, Channel's failure to do so could have terminated the agreement. Alternatively, if, as Channel argues, the parties did not fix a definite time for the duration of negotiations, then a reasonable time would be applicable ..., and a determination must be made as to what constitutes a reasonable time under all the circumstances.

The judgment of the district court will therefore be reversed, and the case remanded for further proceedings consistent with this opinion.

NOTES

(1) *Culpa in Contrahendo.* Channel's argument was based on Grossman's promise to "withdraw the Store from the rental market and only negotiate the above-described leasing transaction to completion." Might an obligation to negotiate in good faith arise from the mere fact of prolonged negotiations, even without such explicit language?

Note that the court cites with approval an article by Kessler and Fine dealing with *culpa in contrahendo* (fault in contractual negotiation). This term was introduced in 1861 by the German jurist Rudolf von Jhering, who advanced the thesis that parties to precontractual negotiations are bound to observe the "necessary diligentia," and a party who commits a breach of this obligation is liable for reliance damages. Although Jhering's thesis has received some acceptance in Europe, American courts have been unwilling to impose such an obligation on negotiating parties. See Farnsworth, Precontractual Liability and Preliminary Agreements: Fair Dealing and Failed Negotiations, 87 Colum.L.Rev. 217, 239–43 (1987).

(2) *Measure of Damages.* How would Channel's damages for breach be measured? In terms of its expectation? In terms of its reliance? If Channel could show that it had passed up other opportunities to lease premises in reliance

on Grossman's promise to negotiate, would damages based on those lost opportunities be recoverable? Is the *Grouse* case, above, relevant?

(3) *Negotiation Without Intent to Contract.* In Heyer Products Co. v. United States, 140 F.Supp. 409 (Ct.Cl.1956), Heyer, a disappointed bidder on a contract with the Army Ordnance Corps, sued the government alleging that, although its bid had been the lowest, the government had awarded the contract to another bidder in order to retaliate against Heyer for having testified against the Ordnance Corps at a Senate hearing. The court held that while the government "could accept or reject an offer as it pleased, and no contract resulted until an offer was accepted," it was "an implied condition of the request for offers that each of them would be honestly considered," and the government was under an "obligation to honestly consider [the bid] and not to wantonly disregard it." It would therefore be liable to Heyer for its expense in preparing its bid if "bids were not invited in good faith." The rule must be regarded with caution, since it was framed in the particular circumstances of an invitation to bid on a government contract where, it will be remembered, the bidder's power to revoke its bid is restricted. See Note 1, p. 177 above. Nevertheless, one writer has hailed the decision as a unique one "in which a court has recognized, in the absence of a statutory or contractual duty to negotiate, that a cause of action exists against a party who negotiates without serious intent to contract." Summers, "Good Faith" in General Contract Law and the Sales Provisions of the Uniform Commercial Code, 54 Va.L.Rev. 195, 221 (1968). Might liability for negotiation without intent to contract be based on misrepresentation? Is Goodman v. Dicker, page 264 above, relevant? [a]

SECTION 7. THE REQUIREMENT OF DEFINITENESS

In the *Channel Home Centers* case, the court asked first "whether both parties manifested an intention to be bound by the agreement" and second "whether the terms of the agreement are sufficiently definite to be enforced." The preceding sections of this chapter have explored the question: Did both parties *assent* to be bound? This section explores the question: Is there agreement *definite* enough to be enforced? Both questions must be answered in the affirmative for there to be a contract.

The requirement of definiteness is implicit in the principle that the promisee's expectation interest is to be protected. In calculating the damages that will put the promisee in the position in which it would have been had the promise been performed, a court must determine the scope of that promise with some precision. In the less usual case where the court orders specific performance or enjoins a threatened breach, it must know the scope of the promise with even greater precision to frame a decree because failure to obey subjects the promisor to the court's contempt power. If recovery on a broken promise were limited to the promisee's restitution or reliance interest, it would often be unnecessary

---

a. For an interesting case in which it was claimed that negotiations were "a ruse," see Skycom Corp. v. Telstar Corp., 813 F.2d 810 (7th Cir.1987). A claim based on fraud failed, however, because not pleaded with particularity.

to inquire into the scope of the promise, as long as it was clear that the promise had been broken. See the statements of the requirement of definiteness in UCC 2–204(3) and in Restatement Second § 33.

The impact of the requirement of definiteness can be seen from Varney v. Ditmars, 111 N.E. 822 (N.Y.1916), in which an architectural draftsman sued his employer on the employer's promise to pay "a fair share of my profits" in addition to a stated salary. The court denied recovery of profits on the ground that their amount was a matter of "pure conjecture" and "may be any amount from a nominal sum to a material part according to the particular views of the person whose guess is considered. Such an executory contract must rest for performance upon the honor and good faith of the parties making it."

Before concluding that an agreement is too indefinite to enforce, however, a court must first interpret it. Often it can piece together enough terms to satisfy the requirement from preliminary negotiations, including prior communications, from references to external sources of terms, including trade and other standard terms, or from usages to which the parties are subject, a course of dealing between the parties prior to the transaction, or a course of performance between them after their agreement. Indefiniteness may also be cured by the addition of such implied terms as will be supplied by law, in the same manner in which the duty to use reasonable efforts was supplied in Wood v. Lucy, p. 133 above. The processes by which language is interpreted and such terms are supplied are explored in detail in Chapter 6.

Terms such as "reasonable efforts" are regarded as sufficiently definite if their content can be determined by reference to some external standard. This would have been done in Wood v. Lucy had it been necessary, in an action by Lady Duff–Gordon against Otis Wood, to have determined what efforts would have been reasonable in his circumstances. Corthell v. Summit Thread Co., 167 A. 79 (Me.1933), is an extreme case. There an employer promised its employee "reasonable recognition" in return for his promise to turn over rights to his future inventions. The court held that the employer was liable under the agreement even though it had taken the precaution of going on to provide "the basis and amount of recognition to rest entirely 'with the employer, the agreement' to be interpreted in good faith on the basis of what is reasonable and intended and not technically." [a] Contrast Varney v. Ditmars, above. Courts have also generally found "good faith" to be sufficiently definite under similar reasoning. The meaning of "reasonable efforts" and "good faith" is taken up in detail in Chapter 6, Section 3.

Furthermore, it is enough if the agreement provides the means for making its terms sufficiently definite by the time that performance is called for. For example, in the cotton cases of 1973, discussed at p. 1

---

a. For another exceptional case, see Rutcosky v. Tracy, 574 P.2d 382 (Wash. 1978), cert. denied, 439 U.S. 930 (1978), in which, when the plaintiff asked for extra compensation in the form of a percentage of the revenue from a program he was to develop, he was told merely that he would be "taken care of."

above, the quantity of cotton was not determined until the cotton was harvested, but the agreements were not unenforceable on that ground. The same is true of output and requirements contracts generally. For another example, in the *Fairmount Glass* case, p. 158 above, the seller argued "that the contract was indefinite, because the quantity of each size of the jars was not fixed," but the court held that the agreement was not unenforceable on this ground because the buyer had "the right to name the quantity of each size" before shipment. The same is true of contracts that have particulars of performance to be specified by one of the parties. See UCC 2–311. (Note that in the *Fairmount Glass* case the buyer, who was to specify the particulars, was the injured party. Would the agreement have been sufficiently definite if the buyer had been the party in breach and had refused not only to take and pay for the jars but even to make a specification?)

NOTES

(1) *Causes of Indefiniteness.* Why are parties not more precise in setting out the terms of their agreements? Consider the following possible answers.

(a) They do not want to take the time or trouble to do so, but prefer to rely on the terms that a court will supply in case a dispute arises.

(b) They are reluctant to raise difficult issues for fear that the deal may fall through.

(c) They do not foresee the problem that happens to arise.

Are there other answers? Might the answer in a particular case affect the court's willingness to overlook some indefiniteness?

(2) *Question.* Review Note 1, p. 121 above. Suppose that Louisa Sheffield had written to Strong: "I will be responsible for my husband's debt if you will not bother him about it for a reasonable time." Would she have been accountable to Strong if he had done nothing about the note for two years? See Baker v. Citizens State Bank of St. Louis Park, 349 N.W.2d 552 (Minn.1984); Farmers Union Oil Co. of New England v. Maixner, 376 N.W.2d 43 (N.D.1985).

(3) *"Complete Contingent" and "Relational" Contracts.* The terms "complete contingent contracts" and "relational contracts" have come into vogue in recent years. Professor Charles Goetz and Robert Scott provide the following description.

"Parties in a bargaining situation are presumed able, at minimal cost, to allocate explicitly the risks that future contingencies may cause one or the other to regret having entered into an executory agreement.... Once the underlying rules policing the bargaining process have been specified, contract rules serve as standard or common risk allocations that can be varied by the individual agreement of particular parties. These rules serve the important purpose of saving most bargainers the cost of negotiating a tailor-made arrangement.... All relevant risks thus can be assigned optimally—either by legal rule or through individualized agreement—because future contingencies are not only known and understood at the time the bargain is struck, but can also be addressed by efficacious contractual responses.

"In a complex society, however, many contractual arrangements diverge so markedly from the classical model that they require separate treatment. Parties frequently enter into continuing, highly interactive contractual arrangements. For these parties, a complete contingent contract may not be a feasible contracting mechanism [and therefore such parties] seek specially adapted contractual devices. The resulting 'relational contracts' encompass most generic agency relationships, including distributorships, franchises, joint ventures, and employment contracts.... A contract is relational to the extent that the parties are incapable of reducing important terms of the arrangement to well-defined obligations." Goetz & Scott, Principles of Relational Contracts, 67 Va.L.Rev. 1089, 1089–91 (1981).

The term "relational exchanges," in contradistinction to "discrete exchanges," was popularized by Professor Ian Macneil. See Macneil, Contracts: Adjustment of Long–Term Economic Relations Under Classical, Neoclassical, and Relational Contract Law, 72 Nw.U.L.Rev. 854 (1978).

(4) *Offers of Job Security.* In Sayres v. Bauman, 425 S.E.2d 226 (W.Va. 1992), the plaintiffs were apparently related to the owners of the firm for which they worked. When the firm was about to change hands they were told, according to one of the plaintiffs, "you won't lose your job because a new company is buying us out." The plaintiffs continued in their jobs for more than a year under the new ownership, but were then discharged. Might the statement attributed to the former owners be construed as an offer to the employees of job security—one that the employees accepted by continuing on their jobs? In an action by the employees, charging wrongful discharge, the court reversed a judgment for the plaintiffs, saying: "an oral promise which has as its effect the alteration of an 'at will' employment relationship must contain terms that are both ascertainable and definitive in nature to be enforceable."

Statements of company policies, announced in handbooks or manuals for employees, have often been found to be incorporated in the terms of employment for personnel already in place, as well as for new recruits. The "handbook" cases frequently permit employees to escape the rigors of the doctrine of at-will employment. (See Note 3, p. 95 above. Restrictions on that doctrine are considered in Chapter 6, Finding the Law of the Contract.) In Berube v. Fashion Centre, Ltd., 771 P.2d 1033 (Utah 1989), according to the lead opinion, the defendant employer had "created and distributed a disciplinary action policy which was read and understood by the plaintiff," and so had limited the grounds on which it could discharge her. On these facts, was an offer any more evident than in *Sayres* ? The court reversed a judgment for the employer and ordered a retrial on the theory of an implied-in-fact contract.

According to some cases, Berube might have based a claim on the employer's statement even if it had not been distributed to her and she had known nothing of it. See In re Certified Question, p. 95 above, and the case quoted there. On what ground can that be justified? See 1 Farnsworth § 3.15a.

(5) *Restitution.* A party who has performed under an agreement that is unenforceable for indefiniteness is entitled to restitution. For example, in Varney v. Ditmars, above, the court suggested that if the architectural draftsman's work was worth more than his salary he would have had a right to restitution measured by the difference.

TOYS, INC. v. F.M. BURLINGTON COMPANY

Supreme Court of Vermont, 1990.
155 Vt. 44, 582 A.2d 123.

[handwritten: Language is definite b/c formula (prevailing mall rate) has been given.]

[The facts and part of the opinion in this case are at p. 202 above.]

DOOLEY, J. ... We agree with the trial court that summary judgment for plaintiff was appropriate on the first issue raised by defendant. The lease provision created a valid option for plaintiff to renew for an additional five years. Defendant characterizes the lease renewal provision as merely an agreement to agree and therefore not enforceable. If defendant's construction were correct, the lease provision would not create an enforceable option. See Reynolds v. Sullivan, 136 Vt. 1, 3, 383 A.2d 609, 611 (1978). In *Reynolds* we held that a preliminary option agreement that was vague and uncertain in its terms "would be an impossibility to enforce." Id. The test is whether the option agreement contains "all material and essential terms to be incorporated in the subsequent document." Id. The agreement in *Reynolds* was labeled as preliminary and specifically provided that the parties "agree to enter an agreement for an option" and that "more specific terms will be stated in the option to purchase." Id. at 2, 383 A.2d at 610.

It is not necessary under *Reynolds* that the option agreement contain all the terms of the contract as long as it contains a practicable, objective method of determining the essential terms. See Krupinsky v. Birsky, 129 Vt. 400, 405, 278 A.2d 757, 760 (1971) (option contract valid even though it "did not fix a price certain" where "it did appoint a mode of determining the price"); Restatement (Second) of Contracts § 33 comment a, § 34(1) (1981) ("The terms of a contract may be reasonably certain even though it empowers one or both parties to make a selection of terms in the course of performance."). We must construe the option agreement in a way to give it binding effect if possible. See Agway, Inc. v. Marotti, 149 Vt. 191, 194, 540 A.2d 1044, 1046 (1988) (before voiding a contract for vagueness, indefiniteness or uncertainty of expression, Court must attempt to construe the contract to avoid the defect). We are also mindful that defendant drafted the language of the option clause and that a doubtful provision in a written instrument is construed against the party responsible for drafting it. See Trustees of Net Realty v. AVCO Financial Services, 147 Vt. 472, 475–76, 520 A.2d 981, 983 (1986).

The option agreement states that "the fixed minimum rental shall be renegotiated to the then prevailing rate within the mall." We believe that this language sets forth a definite, ascertainable method of determining the price term for the lease extension. Within days after plaintiff stated its original intent to exercise its option, defendant replied by quoting the "prevailing rate within the mall" at that time. Neither defendant nor plaintiff have disputed the accuracy of this calculation.

Defendant puts much emphasis on the use of the term "renegotiate" in the renewal clause, as showing an intent to reach a future agreement.

While the choice of wording could have been more precise, we agree with the plaintiff that the term means that the then-existing "prevailing rate" would be determined by agreement, and does not mean that the parties would start from a clean slate in renegotiating a rent term. Even if we give defendant the benefit of all inferences and reasonable doubt, we find no genuine issue of fact bearing on whether there was an enforceable option to renew and hold as a matter of law that a valid option existed.

NOTES

(1) *Open Price Term.* Would you expect a similar result if the option provision had been: "Tenant shall be provided one option to extend the lease for five years at annual rentals to be agreed upon"? See Joseph Martin, Jr., Delicatessen, Inc. v. Schumacher, 417 N.E.2d 541 (N.Y.1981). A contract for the sale of goods can be concluded—"if [the parties] so intend"—even though they leave the price term "open." UCC 2–305. Why might the law be more indulgent of indefiniteness in buyer-seller agreements than in landlord-tenant agreements?

(2) *The Case of the Business Opportunity.* In Lee v. Joseph E. Seagram & Sons, Inc., 552 F.2d 447 (2d Cir.1977), a jury found that when Seagram contracted in writing to buy a wholesale liquor distributorship (Capitol City), it had orally agreed with some of its owners to provide them, within a reasonable time, with a Seagram distributorship in another city, in a location acceptable to them, "whose price would require roughly an amount equal to the capital obtained by [those owners] for the sale of their interest in Capitol City." In an action by the promisees, a judgment was entered on the verdict. Seagram appealed, contending in part that the oral agreement was so vague and indefinite as to be unenforceable. *Held:* Affirmed. The plaintiffs had testified about the financial record of Capitol City and produced expert testimony about the industry standard for valuing a liquor distributorship.

Why do you suppose the parties were not more precise in defining their obligations with respect to the new distributorship? What answer can be given to Seagram's further point that the oral agreement was illusory, owing to the promisees' "unbridled discretion" to accept or to reject any new situation that Seagram might proffer? Suppose that the promisee had been an investor negotiating to buy Capitol City, and that Seagram had persuaded the investor to break off negotiations by making a comparable promise. Same result?

(3) *Flexible Pricing.* Suppose that over a long term a seller wants to be assured of an outlet for a fixed quantity of a product and that a buyer wants to be assured of a source of supply for the same quantity. But neither wants to take the risk of a shift in the market: the seller does not want the risk of a rise in prices before delivery, and the buyer does not want the risk of a fall. How can they make an agreement that will be legally enforceable and yet will allow the price of the goods to fluctuate?

One possibility is to leave the price term open, so that under UCC 2–305 the price will then be "a reasonable price at the time for *delivery.*" The opportunities for dispute over what is "reasonable" may make this solution unattractive.[a]

a. That a market price is not necessarily a "reasonable" price, see Spartan Grain & Mill Co. v. Ayers, 517 F.2d 214 (5th Cir. 1975) ("Spartan's prices [for chicken feed] were not necessarily unreasonable simply because they were higher than those charged by the other sellers, since it also

(Would it be useful to designate a third party to fix the price if the parties disagreed? See UCC 2–305.) Another possibility is to use an "escalator clause" under which the price will be fixed according to a formula tied in some way to the market. Would it be easier to draft such an agreement if there were an ascertainable market price for the raw materials required by the seller to produce his product? An ascertainable market price for the product itself? (On ascertainable market price, see UCC 2–723, 2–724.) Would prices charged by competing sellers or to competing buyers be useful?[b] Helpful analogies can be found in clauses in leases tied to gross profits, in clauses in collective bargaining agreements tied to the cost of living, and in clauses in construction contracts tied to costs ("cost-plus" contracts).[c]

(4) *Living Together III.* Note 1, above, discussed the enforceability of agreements between persons living together. An additional barrier to enforceability may be the requirement of definiteness.

In Pyeatte v. Pyeatte, 661 P.2d 196 (Ariz.App.1982), for example, the court refused on that ground to enforce a husband's oral promise that, in return of his wife's putting him through law school without having to work, he would put her through her master's degree without having to work. The court found the agreement too indefinite as to "the time when [she] would attend graduate school," as to the "place of education," including the necessity of relocation, and as to "the cost of the program." "Such a loosely worded agreement can hardly be said to have fixed [his] liability with certainty." But though the court found that the agreement "failed to meet the requirements of an enforceable contract, the agreement still has importance in considering [her] claim for unjust enrichment because it both evidences [her] expectation of compensation and the circumstances which make it unjust to allow [her husband] to retain the benefits of her extraordinary efforts." The court held that restitution was appropriate. See Note 4, p. 83 above.

committed itself to purchase" all the buyers' eggs).

b. The impact of the antitrust laws on this question must be left for a later course.

c. Such clauses may, particularly in an inflationary period, have an adverse effect on the economy. (Is this necessarily so, if the clause is a substitute for a higher initial price?) Should this be of concern to the lawyer drafting an agreement for his client?

An interesting variant is patterned after the "most favored nation" clause found in treaties. See, for example, Reynolds Metals Co. v. United States, 438 F.2d 983 (Ct.Cl. 1971), in which the United States promised Reynolds to amend their contract "if later agreements with the Aluminum Company of America and/or the Kaiser Aluminum and Chemical Company are, in your opinion, more favorable than the agreement which has been executed with you."

Chapter 3

THE REQUIREMENT OF A WRITING
FOR ENFORCEABILITY: THE
STATUTE OF FRAUDS

SECTION 1. INTRODUCTION

In this chapter we shall examine some principal types of agreement that are unenforceable because they are oral, considering versions of the Statute of Frauds that were enacted by legislatures in the United States—and have been modified and supplemented from time to time. We shall also examine judicial doctrines by which the courts have prevented much of this legislation from having literal effect. The subject is controversial. "Real and honest contracts," one judge has said, "will not be enforced because of the statute of frauds; honest men will lose the benefits of their bargains because they neglected to reduce them to writing." [a]

What is usually designated as "the Statute of Frauds" is a set of provisions derived, with local variations, from one of two sections of a 17th–century enactment. The name given by Parliament to the whole was "An Act for the Prevention of Frauds and Perjuries." [b] One section of this act (XVII) imposed a writing requirement on certain contracts for the sale of goods. Another section (IV) embraced contracts of rather miscellaneous types, all of them reflected in current versions of the Statute. Legislation over the years has tended to enlarge this family of enactments, as they are collected in the statute books. Scattered provisions requiring that a contract of a given type be in writing are to be found in great number. Although these are not placed with the progeny of the ancestral act, one of them is frequently called "a statute of frauds."

Section 2–201 of the Uniform Commercial Code (Formal Requirements; Statute of Frauds) is the contemporary version of the initial provision about sale-of-goods contracts. For a quarter of a century this complex section has been a dominant provision about oral contracts, a major factor in commercial affairs, and a focus of innumerable cases. In this Chapter, nevertheless, the section is treated largely in text and notes. The reason is that the revisers of Article 2 propose to delete the section, eliminating any formal bar to the enforcement of oral sale-of-

---

a. Paterson, J., dissenting, in Lovely v. Dierkes, 347 N.W.2d 752 (Mich.App.1984).

b. 29 Charles II, c. 3.

goods contracts as such. No more dramatic alteration in Article 2 can well be imagined.[c]

Upon enactment of the revision, there will remain in force everywhere in this country a Statute of Frauds derived from Section IV of the statute of Charles II. A representative version, that of New Jersey, is set out just below, and another in the footnote following that, as examples. As compared with UCC 2–201, these provisions are generally older, are less detailed, and resemble the ancient statute more closely.

Agreements of each of the following types are dealt with in the various statutes:

• Suretyship contracts;

• Contracts concerning interests in land; and

• Agreements not to be performed within a year of their making.

Note, in addition, parts of the California statute (footnote f below) which were not derived from the ancestral statute. The brokerage provision (d) represents comparable statutes generally prevailing in this country.

NOTES

(1) *The History.* In Halstead v. Murray, the case concerning an agreement about a lot on Lake Winnepesuakee (Note 4, p. 119), the following historical passage appears:

"The original Statute of Frauds has an interesting history which is worthy of a brief review. The English Parliament first enacted the statute in 1677 to prevent ' "many fraudulent practices, which are commonly endeavored to be upheld by perjury and subornation of perjury." ' Note, The Doctrine of Equitable Estoppel and the Statute of Frauds, 66 Mich.L.Rev. 170 (1967). At that time, under English trial practice, parties to a lawsuit were deemed to be incompetent witnesses and hence barred from testifying. The statute thus was aimed at making virtually all contracts of significance unenforceable unless they had been reduced to writing. The statute, of course, sometimes produced harsh results, and the English courts soon developed exceptions, such as the rule that partial performance of the contract took the agreement out of the requirements of the statute. Since that time, all of the States of this country have adopted some portion of the original Statute of Frauds. Id. at 170–71. However, they have done so with full knowledge that the Statute of Frauds has been judicially interpreted in such a way as to attempt to prevent fraud rather than to promote it." (For the opinion in the case, omitting this passage, see p. 318 below.)

(2) *Economic Muscle.* Are there parties who should be excused from having their contracts in writing because they do not have the bargaining power to insist on a writing? A realtors' association has argued that a broker's reliance on an oral fee contract should be protected: "disparity of bargaining power is most common in the commercial real estate market." In response, the court cited a survey of firms that showed strong support for the Statute of Frauds.[d]

---

c. Article 2A of the Code (Leases), which concerns leases of goods, and which became part of the Code in 1987, contains a section closely modelled on § 2–201: UCC 2A–201.

d. Comment, 66 Yale L.J. 1030 (1957). Also: "The business community's preference for written contracts was stated most colorfully in the memorable malaprop attributed to motion picture producer Samuel

The court also depicted the broker's-fee statute as a protection for parties to sales of homes, and listed ten types of consumer contracts now required to be in writing.   Phillippe v. Shapell Industries, Inc., 743 P.2d 1279 (Cal.1987).

(3) *Security Agreements.*   An agreement whereby property of a debtor is to stand as security for the debt is ineffective, broadly speaking, if it is not in writing.   An oral mortgage on the debtor's home, or other real property, is subject to the usual Statute of Frauds.   An agreement conferring a security interest in the debtor's car, or in other personal property, is likely to be unenforceable "against the debtor or third parties," under a provision of UCC Article 9.[e]   (But the provision does not require a writing as to collateral in the creditor's possession, pursuant to agreement.)

Oral security agreements might be disfavored on the grounds that, as a class, creditors are in a position to insist on formalities when dealing with debtors and are exceptionally well-informed of the law.   Are there other grounds?

A STATUTE OF FRAUDS

No action shall be brought upon any of the following agreements or promises, unless the agreement or promise, upon which such action shall be brought or some memorandum or note thereof, shall be in writing, and signed by the party to be charged therewith, or by some other person thereunto by him lawfully authorized:

a.   A special promise of an executor or administrator to answer damages out of his own estate;

b.   A special promise to answer for the debt, default or miscarriage of another person;

c.   An agreement made upon consideration of marriage;

d.   A contract for sale of real estate, or any interest in or concerning the same;   or

e.   An agreement that is not to be performed within one year from the making thereof.   (N.J.Stat.Ann. § 25:1-5 (West).)[f]

Goldwyn: 'An oral contract isn't worth the paper it's written on.' "

e.   UCC 9-203(1).

f.   Statute of frauds [California]

The following contracts are invalid, unless the same, or some note or memorandum thereof, is in writing and subscribed by the party to be charged or by his agent:

(a) An agreement that by its terms is not to be performed within a year from the making thereof.

(b) A special promise to answer for the debt, default, or miscarriage of another, except in the cases provided for in Section 2794 [stating, in six subdivisions, "original obligations which need not be in writing"].

(c) An agreement for the leasing for a longer period than one year, or for the sale of real property, or of an interest therein; such an agreement, if made by an agent of the party sought to be charged, is invalid, unless the authority of the agent is in writing, subscribed by the party sought to be charged.

(d) An agreement authorizing or employing an agent, broker, or any other person to purchase or sell real estate, or to lease real estate for a longer period than one year, or to procure, introduce, or find a purchaser or seller of real estate or a lessee or lessor of real estate where the lease is for a longer period than one year, for compensation or a commission.

(e) An agreement which by its terms is not to be performed during the lifetime of the promisor.

This Chapter calls attention to problems of the following kinds: What contracts are within the Statute? For those contracts, what are the requirements of writing and signing? What circumstances will lead a court to dispense with those requirements, despite the wording of the Statute?

Before taking up these questions in turn, however, it will be useful to glance at some general features of the law generated by the Statute. First, the fact that the parties have *expressed* an agreement in a signed writing is no assurance that they have *contracted* about the matter. A party seeking to enforce the agreement will fail if it can be shown that the writing does not represent an otherwise enforceable agreement.[g] Second, the Statute is sometimes a "one-way street": Party One can enforce the agreement against Party Two (who has signed a required writing); but Party Two cannot enforce it (since Party One has not).[h]

In Section 2 it will be seen that the courts have shown disfavor toward the Statute by narrowing the classes of contract that must satisfy its formal requirements. A notable example is an oral contract for services that will in all probability require more than one year to perform. This contract is enforceable, by the prevailing rule, if there is some *possibility* that it can be performed within a year. In applying this rule a court is unlikely to be influenced by the fact that, more than a year after the contract was made (when the dispute arose), part of it remained to be performed. Whether or not the one-year clause applies is determined by the prospects as they existed at the time of contracting.

Section 3 concerns the content of a writing required to satisfy the Statute, and the requirement of "signing." For a sale-of-goods contract within UCC 2–201, the content requirement is minimal: "some writing sufficient to indicate that a contract for sale has been made between the parties ... but the contract is not enforceable ... beyond the quantity of goods shown in such writing." More is required to satisfy other clauses of the statute; the omission of a material term (such as the price) may well disqualify the writing.

In Section 4 it will be seen that the effect of the Statute is minimized, in varying degrees, by court-made doctrines. An example is the doctrine of part performance, whereby a contract may become enforceable, though it would not have been enforceable at the outset, through a party's conduct in complying with it. More recent inroads have been made on the Statute in the name of "action in reliance." This development is generalized in Restatement Second § 139 (see Note 3, p. 307 below).

(f) An agreement by a purchaser of real property to pay an indebtedness secured by a mortgage or deed of trust upon the property purchased, unless assumption of the indebtedness by the purchaser is specifically provided for in the conveyance of the property. (Cal.Civ.Code § 1624.)

g. See Scheck v. Francis, 260 N.E.2d 493 (N.Y.1970), concerning an apparent contract with the singer Connie Francis which, however, was intended to take effect only when authenticated by the parties.

h. "The operation of the [Statute] is often lopsided and partial." British Law Revision Committee, Sixth Interim Report, Cmd. No. 5449, pp. 6–7 (1937).

NOTE

UCC 2–201. According to subsection (3)(c) of this provision, a contract that the provision would otherwise make unenforceable (but that is valid in other respects) "is enforceable with respect to goods for which payment has been made or accepted or which have been received and accepted." In view of this partial codification of the part-performance doctrine, in what situation are the expectations of a buyer or seller most likely to be defeated by § 2–201?

The observation that the Statute of Frauds is a "one-way street" is subject to qualification in light of subsection (2) of UCC 2–201—the so-called "merchants' exception." Further attention is given to that provision in the Note at p. 300 below.

SECTION 2. PROBLEMS OF STATUTORY SCOPE

Identifying the contracts that are subject to two provisions of the Statute of Frauds is an especially vexing matter; that is the subject of this section.

(a) The Suretyship Clause

This clause covers agreements to "answer for" another's debt or other obligation, as surety or guarantor.[a] A suretyship promise in writing is illustrated by Strong v. Sheffield, p. 119 above. Although in that case the promise was unenforceable for want of consideration, it illustrates the class of cases most certainly within the Statute: a promise by a relative or friend of the primary debtor (Mr. Sheffield in this case) made with the benevolent purpose of enabling that person to get credit, or to get a further extension of credit. Consider how easy it may be for a creditor, now faced with the insolvency of this debtor, to "remember" that a person of means—someone well disposed toward the debtor—gave an advance assurance to the creditor that the debt would be repaid. A false recollection to that effect is facilitated if the creditor made inquiries about the credit-worthiness of the primary debtor before making a loan to it or providing it with property or services on credit, and got encouraging responses that figured in the inquirer's decision to do so.

The parties' interest in the suretyship clause is most intense when the primary obligor is insolvent. If that party has the means to pay or perform all its obligations, one who has been compelled to perform as surety can get reimbursement from the primary obligor.

---

a. As to the distinction between a contract of suretyship and one of guaranty, see General Motors Acceptance Corp. v. Daniels, 492 A.2d 1306 (Md.1985).

LANGMAN v. ALUMNI ASSOCIATION OF THE UNIVERSITY OF VIRGINIA, 442 S.E.2d 669 (Va.1994).

BARBARA MILANO KEENAN, JUSTICE. The primary issue in this appeal is whether a deed containing a mortgage assumption clause was repudiated by the grantee.

[Dr. M.W. Langman, a psychologist, and Caleb Stowe, a real-estate broker, wished to make gifts to the University of Virginia. They were the owners, in common, of "Ferdinand's Arcade," a commercial property in Maryland. Late in 1986, on the advice of University development officers, they conveyed the property to the Alumni Association. The property had been appraised earlier that year at $775,000. The deed to the Association recited that the property was subject to a lien, securing a debt of $600,000 that Langman and Stowe had incurred in purchasing the property. The deed continued: "The Grantee does hereby assume payment of such obligation and agrees to hold the Grantors harmless from further liability on such obligation." The Association did not sign. It acknowledged the gift, however, and had the deed recorded.

[Before long the loan charges and expenses of operating the Arcade outran the income it produced. For some time Stowe, who continued to manage the property, made up the shortfall. He wrote off the difference as a gift. But he discontinued payments on the loan in the summer of 1989, following a business failure. The lender [b] demanded payments from Langman. She cured the default and sued the Association, contending that it was obliged to reimburse her under the debt-assumption term in the deed. The trial court received evidence of circumstances attending and following the transfer.]

In its letter opinion, the trial court held that the Alumni Association "did not knowingly accept the gift with contractual conditions," that the assumption clause was mistakenly placed in the deed by an unknown draftsman, and that by its disavowal of the obligation sought to be enforced, the Alumni Association had "sufficiently rejected the gift to require a finding by the court that the conveyance is ineffective." The trial court held that the assumption clause was unenforceable and the attempted conveyance a nullity....[c] [Langman appealed and the Supreme Court of Virginia reversed, saying:] the trial court's findings are unsupported by the evidence, since they are based on erroneously admitted parol evidence....[d]

b. Actually, a successor to the defunct savings and loan association that had made the loan.

c. As recited on appeal, the trial court's rulings included these: that "the Alumni Association had no clear understanding of the deed's contents; that the deed contained contractual provisions that were contrary to the parties' intentions, as shown by their discussions leading up to the conveyance; and that there was no meeting of the minds between the grantors and grantee of the deed."

But the court rejected contentions of the Association that the mortgage assumption clause was unenforceable on the basis of actual or constructive fraud, of mutual mistake, or of unilateral mistake induced by inequitable conduct, or by reason of failure of consideration. These rulings were sustained on appeal.

d. On this topic see Chapter 6, Section 1, on determining the subject matter of a contract.

A grantee who accepts a deed becomes contractually bound by its provisions, and becomes liable to perform any promise or undertaking imposed by the deed on the grantee, including a promise to assume an existing mortgage. . . .

We also disagree with the Alumni Association's contention that the trial court erred in holding that the statute of frauds does not bar enforcement of a mortgage assumption clause that is not signed by the grantee.

Code § 11-2 provides, in material part:

Unless a promise, contract, agreement, representation, assurance, or ratification, or some memorandum or note thereof, is in writing and signed by the party to be charged or his agent, no action shall be brought in any of the following cases: . . .

4. To charge any person upon a promise to answer for the debt, default, or misdoings of another[.]

The Alumni Association argues that the "suretyship" provision of the statute of frauds, Code § 11-2(4), required the Alumni Association to sign a written agreement to assume the mortgage. Citing Lawson v. States Construction Co., 69 S.E.2d 450, 453 (Va.1952), the Alumni Association contends that this Court has held that any "collateral" promise to answer for the debts of another must comply with Code § 11-2(4). The Alumni Association asserts that, because Langman would remain secondarily liable to Dominion Federal on the mortgage debt even after an effective assumption of the debt, the Alumni Association's agreement to assume the mortgage was a "collateral" promise falling within the scope of Code § 11-2(4). We disagree.

A grantee who assumes an existing mortgage is not a surety. The grantee makes no promise to the mortgagee to pay the debt of another, but promises the grantor to pay to the mortgagee the debt the grantee owes to the grantor. This is an original undertaking. Blanton v. Keneipp, 155 Va. 668, 678, 156 S.E. 413, 416 (1931). . . .

A collateral undertaking to which Code § 11-2(4) applies is one in which the promisor is merely a surety or guarantor, receives no direct benefit, and is liable only if the debtor defaults. Colonial Ford Truck Sales, Inc. v. Schneider, 325 S.E.2d 91, 93-94 (Va.1985). Here, the Alumni Association received a direct benefit and did not merely act as surety for the grantors. Therefore, we conclude that the trial court did not err in ruling that the statute of frauds does not bar enforcement of the mortgage assumption clause.

NOTES

(1) *Original or Collateral?* According to Williston, "A promise which is within the Statute is often said to be 'collateral'; if not within the Statute, it is called 'original.' . . . 'The terms collateral or original promise did not occur in

the Statute, and have been introduced by courts of law to explain its objects and expound its true interpretation.' [e]

"Although the terms 'original' and 'collateral' do not obviate the difficulty of determining the ultimate question as to whether a promise is or is not within the Statute, they afford a convenient mode of expression for distinguishing between the cases within and those not within the Statute...." 3 Williston § 463.

Brad Ragan, Inc. v. Callicutt Enterprises, Inc., 326 S.E.2d 62 (N.C.App. 1985), concerned a sale of tires, followed by a sale of trucks. The seller of tires was the Carolina Tire Company; the buyer was Callicutt Enterprises. Callicutt mounted the tires on trucks, which it sold to Bobby Lewis. In buying the trucks, Lewis orally promised Callicutt that he would pay Carolina for the tires. Not being paid, Carolina sued Lewis on his promise. Does the suretyship clause afford a defense for Lewis? (Do you see why he has no defense under UCC 2–201?)

The price that Callicutt received for the trucks, in relation to their value, might provide some confirmation that Lewis did agree to pay Carolina for the tires, or might tend to refute the evidence that he did. If this source of evidence is a reason for treating his promise as an "original" one, is it also a reason for treating the Virginia Alumni Association's promise as an "original" one?

(2) *An Exception.* Many oral suretyship promises are enforceable because they fall within an exception to the suretyship clause, judicially created, known as the *main-purpose* or *leading-object* rule. "The doctrine applies when the pecuniary interests of a promisor in a commercial contract context replace the gratuitous elements often present in suretyship." White Stag Mfg. Co. v. Wind Surfing, Inc., 679 P.2d 312 (Or.App.1984). A natural case for its application is one in which a major investor in a firm, or a major customer, has helped it to continue operations by giving an unwritten guarantee to a creditor putting pressure on the firm. As to the "original" nature of an insider's promise see Garland Co., Inc. v. Roofco Co., 809 F.2d 546 (8th Cir.1987).

A possible justification for the exception is the thought that the self-interest of the promisor tends to confirm the fact that the promise was made. Another is that, in a case of benefit for the promisor, "in respect to which the promise was made," justice requires that the promisor be charged with (at least) its reasonable value. See Tore, Ltd. v. Church, 772 P.2d 1281 (Nev.1989).

(3) *Problem.* The holder of a mortgage on "Isabella's Arcade" objects to a transfer of the property by the owner. The owner wishes to convey the property to her college as a gift, continuing to pay the mortgage from other assets. In order to obviate the mortgagee's objection, the college gives the mortgagee an oral undertaking that it will satisfy the donor's debt if she fails to do so. The mortgagee withdraws its objection and the gift is made. The donor defaults on the mortgage. Does the suretyship clause bar enforcement of the college's promise? Or does the main-purpose exception apply?

What answer is indicated by the "justifications" for the main-purpose rule described in the foregoing Note?

(4) *Cases for Comparison.* Consider again the hypothetical case of a daughter's unwritten promise to a physician, stated in Note 1, p. 79 above. Compare this case: Buddy makes an oral promise to buy a set of tires, to fit Buddy's car, from a tire dealer. The tires are to be delivered to a used-car dealer's lot where

e. Quoting from Story, J., in D'Wolf v. Rabaud, 26 U.S. 476, 499 (1828).

the car is. The dealer has contracted to buy the car if Buddy will provide new tires for it.

Neither the daughter's promise to the physician nor Buddy's promise to the tire dealer is affected by the suretyship clause, is it? (But there is UCC 2–201 to think of in the latter case.)

(b) Contracts Not to Be Performed Within One Year

The New York statute on this subject speaks of an agreement, promise, or undertaking that "[b]y its terms is not to be performed within one year from the making thereof." [a] A criticism of the one-year limitation is as follows: It is "apparently founded on a concern with the tendency of evidence to go stale with the passage of time, but the foundation is weak because the limitation applies even if the promise is broken the day after it is made and suit on it is brought immediately." Goldstick v. ICM Realty, 788 F.2d 456 (7th Cir.1986).[b] Does any other foundation for the one-year rule occur to you?

A contract for lifetime, or "permanent", employment is not within the one-year clause, by the prevailing view.[c] Owing to the possibility of the employee's death within a year of its making, it cannot be said—at the time of contracting—that performance will necessarily require more than a year.[d]

When a large-scale development is planned, a contract for the work may require a writing even though the work might be completed within a year by extraordinary effort. According to one court, "[t]here must be a reasonable possibility of performance within a year.... We see [none], and certainly not within the intention of the parties." Dean v. Myers, 466 So.2d 952 (Ala.1985). But the rule generally applied is different: "Courts tend to take the concept of 'capable of full performance' quite literally. See Farnsworth [Contracts (2d ed. 1990)] § 6.4. They do this because they find the one-year limitation irksome.... Some promises, for example a promise to work for an employer for five years, really cannot be performed within a year. But a promise to pay $250,000 over 10 years can be—by paying the full $250,000 the first

---

a. N.Y.Gen.Oblig.L. § 5–701, subd. a, par. 1.

In measuring the one-year period, a fraction of a day is commonly disregarded. Hence, for example, an oral contract of employment for one year, beginning "tomorrow", might be enforced. But not one requiring the employee to begin work the day after. (See Schwartzreich v. Bauman–Basch, Inc., stated at p. 354 below.)

b. The opinion in this case makes many points of interest.

c. A contract of employment "for life or until the employee decides to retire" is not within the one-year clause. Price v. Mercu-

ry Supply Co., 682 S.W.2d 924 (Tenn.App. 1984). And if a contract is for indefinite employment, but the employer cannot terminate it except for "just cause," it is not within the clause. Weiner v. McGraw–Hill, Inc., 443 N.E.2d 441, 33 A.L.R.4th 110 (N.Y.1982).

d. For a full-dress rehearsal of the problems of long-term employment, see Hodge v. Evans Financial Corp., 823 F.2d 559 (D.C.Cir.1987), where a dissenting judge read the evidence to show a contract that was to last for at least a specified term. Compare Finley v. Aetna Life and Cas. Co., 520 A.2d 208 (Conn.1987).

year." [e] Trovese v. O'Meara, 493 N.W.2d 221 (S.D.1992), is a case in which the distinction was applied—leading to the dismissal of the action. The plaintiff's claim was that she had been engaged, on August 12, 1990, to manage a fast-food store. According to her testimony, she was to begin work eight days later, and was to have a year thereafter to "turn the operation around." The court observed that the contract was not one for employment simply for an indefinite term. As for the possibility that the plaintiff might die within a year of the 12th, the court said, her death would " 'defeat' rather than 'complete' the express terms of the contract."

As already observed, if a person contracts for lifetime employment, the contract is performable *by its terms* within a year. A contrasting case is one in which A agrees to work for B for five years. For that case a writing is required even though the contract will be at an end—given that it requires A's personal services—upon A's death. [f] Broadly speaking, the distinction is that between full performance as agreed upon—for a lifetime—and the discharge of duties of performance by death, or "operation of law."

> Compare, however, this more expansive application of the Statute:
>
> [I]f the disputed contract was not in fact performed within one year by the plaintiff, there should be clear and convincing evidence that the contract in fact exists before the court submits the claim to a jury.

Teays Farms Owners Ass'n v. Cottrill, 425 S.E.2d 231 (W.Va.1992) (quoting). This passage represents a decision to avoid an "entirely mechanical application of the 'capable of performance' exception" to the Statute.

Occasionally the distinction has proved difficult to apply. Consider, for example, these two problematical cases:

(1) A agrees to work for B for five years, if A lives that long; and

(2) A agrees to work for B for five years, but if A dies the contract is to be terminated.

Is a writing required, in either case? [g]

---

e. Goldstick v. ICM Realty, 788 F.2d 456 (7th Cir.1986).

See also opinions of Justices Jones and Embry, dissenting, in Kitsos v. Mobile Gas Service Corp., 404 So.2d 40, 42 (Ala.1981). Justice Jones spoke disapprovingly of authorities that "grasp for every conceivable exception in order to narrow the Statute's field of operation." But see D & N Boening, Inc. v. Kirsch Beverages, Inc., 472 N.E.2d 992 (N.Y.1984).

f. The contract would be discharged, as a case of impossibility of performance; see Chapter 8 (Impracticability of Performance and Frustration of Purpose).

According to some decisions, "a contract containing a covenant not to compete for a period longer than a year does not run afoul of the Statute of Frauds, while a contract containing a term of employment for such a period would do so." Wyatt v. Dishong, 469 N.E.2d 608 (Ill.App.1984). What is the difference between the effect of death in the one case and the other? (For a contrary view see Reagan Outdoor Advertising, Inc. v. Lundgren, 692 P.2d 776 (Utah 1984).)

g. See Silverman v. Bernot, 239 S.E.2d 118 (Va.1977).

NOTES

(1) *Power to Terminate.* A and B contract for performances over five years, agreeing, however, that either can terminate if its performance is hindered by a strike, epidemic, "Act of God," or another condition "beyond the affected party's control." Such an agreement was held to be unenforceable in the absence of a memorandum. See Jillcy Film Enterprises, Inc. v. Home Box Office, Inc., 593 F.Supp. 515 (S.D.N.Y.1984). Is this decision simply a special application of the rule that no writing is required for a contract of indefinite duration?

Consider again the employment agreements in the paragraph preceding this Note. What solutions are suggested by the holding in *Jillcy Film*? Consult the agreement in White v. Benkowski, p. 14 above. Does the holding indicate that the agreement would have been unenforceable in the absence of a writing?

In cases of oral employment for more than a year, in which the contract permits one party to terminate at will on (say) a month's notice, divergent views exist. One view is that the contract is enforceable by one party but not the other.[h]

(2) *Part Performance.* A contract that is initially within the one-year clause may be "taken out," according to most courts, by the fact that the person seeking to enforce it though not the other has completed performance.[i] A minority view on the point is represented by Montgomery v. Futuristic Foods, Inc., 411 N.Y.S.2d 371 (App.Div.1978).

PROBLEMS

(a) Reconsider Hamer v. Sidway, p. 47 above, in light of the one-year clause. In that case there was of course a writing signed by the uncle. (Nothing in the Statute requires that the memorandum be contemporaneous with the agreement.) Can you think of one or two reasons why the contract there might be enforceable in the absence of a writing?

(b) Carl Coan, a first-year law student, entered into an oral agreement with Victor Orsinger, under which Coan was to be resident manager of an apartment development owned by Orsinger "until [Coan] completed his law studies as a student duly matriculated in Georgetown University Law Center, Washington, D.C. or was obliged to discontinue these studies." Five weeks after Coan undertook his duties, he was fired. Does the Statute of Frauds bar recovery by Coan? See Coan v. Orsinger, 265 F.2d 575 (D.C.Cir.1959).

Could complete studies w/in 1 year!

SECTION 3. REQUISITES OF WRITING AND SIGNING

As to contracts within the Statute—other than UCC 2–201—it has been said that the writing must contain "substantially the whole agreement and all its material terms and conditions, so that one reading it can

h. Hopper v. Lennen & Mitchell, 146 F.2d 364, 161 A.L.R. 282 (9th Cir.1944).

i. Some courts would say so only if the performance has been completed within a year of the making of the contract. But see Lampousis v. Johnston, 657 P.2d 358 (Wyo. 1983) (performance within any period).

understand from it what the agreement is," [j] or contain the "essential elements of a specific, consummated agreement." [k]   The attitude of courts toward this requirement is suggested by the opinion of Cardozo in Marks v. Cowdin, 123 N.E. 139 (N.Y.1919), in which he said: "The statute must not be pressed to the extreme of a literal and rigid logic.... The memorandum which it requires, like any other memorandum, must be read in the light of reason."

Marks went to work as sales manager for Cowdin's ribbon business, under a contract that ran from 1911 to 1913.   Cowdin sent out notices to salesmen describing him as "sales-manager."   In 1913 the contract was orally renewed for three years, at a larger compensation.   Later that year, after a disagreement with Cowdin, Marks asked for and received a memorandum signed by Cowdin and reciting that the arrangement made earlier that year for Marks's employment at a salary of $15,000 per year plus a stated share of gross profits "continues in force until Jan. 1st, 1916," but omitting any mention of his title or duties.   When, in 1914, Cowdin told Marks that he was to work under a new sales manager, McLaren, Marks refused and was fired.   Marks sued Cowdin, who raised the one-year provision of the Statute as a defense.   The Court of Appeals rejected this defense.   The contract had been made in January; the memorandum had been signed the following December.   "It assumes the existence of a position that the plaintiff is then filling.   It says that the employment shall be continued for a term and at a salary prescribed....   We are not left to gather the relation between the parties from executory promises.   We are informed that the relation existing is the one to be maintained....   In this case the plaintiff does not need the aid of one spoken word of promise to identify his place.   His first contract was for two years, from January 1, 1911, to January 1, 1913.   During that period, writings subscribed by the defendants attest the nature of his position.   The memorandum exacted by the statute does not have to be in one document.   It may be pieced together out of separate writings, connected with one another either expressly or by the internal evidence of subject matter and occasion."

NOTES

(1) *Sets of Papers.*   Many contracts are expressed in multiple, detached documents.   If only one of them is signed, it is well to incorporate the others by reference.   Absent that, "there is basic disagreement as to what constitutes a sufficient connection permitting the unsigned papers to be considered as part of the statutory memorandum."   Marks v. Cowdin, quoted above.   The matter is illustrated by a case in which Elizabeth Arden, as president of a sales corporation, agreed to a two-year term for an employee, but did not honor the

j. Mentz v. Newwitter, 25 N.E. 1044, 1046 (N.Y.1890).

k. Seaman's Direct Buying Serv., Inc. v. Standard Oil, 686 P.2d 1158 (Cal.1984). (In applying the Code, however, the court was satisfied as to the expression of quantity by an "obvious implication" that the seller would supply as much fuel as the buyer required.)

It has been held that a tenant's option to renew a lease "at a rental to be negotiated" is enforceable.   Family Med. Bldg., Inc. v. Department of Social & Health Serv., 702 P.2d 459 (Wash.1985).   Compare Restatement Second § 131 (must state "with reasonable certainty the essential terms of the unperformed promises").

agreement. The employee's problem was that the period ("2 years to make good") was referred to only in an unsigned salary memo prepared by Miss Arden's secretary. Later, however, payroll cards were prepared, signed or initialled by officers of the firm, in which identical salary figures and other job particulars appeared. In an action by the employee, the firm denied the alleged agreement and relied on the Statute of Frauds. The plaintiff got a judgment and the firm appealed. *Held:* Affirmed. Crabtree v. Elizabeth Arden Sales Corp., 110 N.E.2d 551 (N.Y.1953). The court said:

> The danger of fraud and perjury, generally attendant upon the admission of parol evidence, is at a minimum in a case such as this. None of the terms of the contract are supplied by parol. All of them must be set out in the various writings presented to the court, and at least one writing, the one establishing a contractual relationship between the parties, must bear the signature of the party to be charged, while the unsigned document must on its face refer to the same transaction as that set forth in the one that was signed. . . . If [parol] testimony does not convincingly connect the papers, or does not show assent to the unsigned paper, it is within the province of the judge to conclude, as a matter of law, that the statute has not been satisfied.

The court acknowledged that more rigorous requirements had been applied.

(2) *Missing Papers.* One observation about the "signed writing" requirements may occasion some surprise—although it is not clear that it should. The requirement may be met by proof that a sufficient writing could have been produced except that it has been destroyed, or lost, or stolen. Can this apparent weakness in the Statute be discounted by supposing that a fact-finder would look with suspicion on evidence to this effect, given by a party who cannot produce a paper critical to his case?

Questions

(a) In a written contract of employment, is the single word "consultant" a sufficient description of the employee's duties to comply with the Statute of Frauds? See Gittes v. Cook International, 598 F.Supp. 717 (S.D.N.Y.1984) (quoting: "The concept of essentiality is relative.")

(b) Should a word-processing file ever be regarded as the equivalent of a "writing", for the purposes of the Statute of Frauds? Some courts have held that a tape recording can count.[a]

UCC 2–201: Subsection (1)

A major reform effected by the Uniform Commercial Code was a relaxation of the requirements for a "writing" that the Statute of Frauds necessitated. According to Comment 1 to UCC 2–201:

> The required writing need not contain all the material terms of the contract. . . . The price, time and place of payment or delivery, the general quality of the goods, or any particular warranties may all [*sic*] be omitted. All that is required is that the writing afford a

---

a. See Londono v. City of Gainesville, 768 F.2d 1223 (11th Cir.1985). For a contrary ruling see Sonders v. Roosevelt, 476 N.E.2d 996 (N.Y.1985). (The defendant's statement in that case, relied on as part of a lifetime support contract, was as follows: "Do you want me to buy you a car? All right I'll buy you a car." What do the facts of the case suggest about the purposes of requiring a writing?)

basis for believing that the offered oral evidence rests on a real transaction.... The only term which must appear is the quantity term....[b]

Moreover, according to the statute, a writing is not insufficient because it incorrectly states a term agreed upon. (If the quantity is understated, however, "recovery is limited to the amount stated." [c])

A question of interest can be made of a telegram about a purchase of iron rails, sent by the Minneapolis (etc.) Railway Company to the Columbia Rolling–Mill Company. This telegram is quoted as message (c) in the Note, Acceptance Varying Offer, p. 215 above: "Please enter our order for twelve hundred tons rails...." If the telegram had been sent in response to an offer, in writing, to sell that quantity of rails, would it have been a "writing sufficient to indicate that a contract for sale [was] made between the parties"?

The fact that the sender (Railway Company) did not sign the telegram in script, or via keyboard, would not preclude a finding that the writing was "signed" by it or by its authorized agent: the word *signed* "includes any authorization which identifies to the party to be charged." [d] One way to discern a sufficient writing is to say that an *offer* to buy, in a signed writing, satisfies the statute, *in an action against the buyer* (and that an offer to sell does so in an action against the seller). In Benya v. Stevens and Thompson Paper Co., Inc., 468 A.2d 929 (Vt.1983), the court said: "a written offer that is orally accepted may constitute a sufficient memorandum of the contract provided the offeror is the party to be charged." (The case did not concern a transaction in goods.) But on that point the courts are divided. See 1 Farnsworth 132 fn. 16 ("unfortunate" if more required). What language in UCC 2–201(1) casts doubt on the proposition?

If a written offer can satisfy the statute, would the statute also be satisfied by a memorandum containing the terms of a projected sale that was prepared by the sales manager of a firm and sent to its president for approval? See Wells, Waters & Gases v. Air Products & Chemicals, 19 F.3d 157, 161–63 (4th Cir.1994), for a three-fold classification of "pre-contractual writings."

In the supposed case of the iron rails, a safer way to discern a sufficient writing is to treat the buyer's telegram as one part—together with the offer it responded to—of a writing expressive of a contract.

In the actual iron-rails case there was no prior offer to sell 1,200 tons of rails. Hence the telegram would not have created an enforceable contract even if it had read "We accept your offer to sell twelve hundred tons rails." But that expression ought certainly to suffice, under UCC

b. Sentences transposed in this excerpt.

c. Comment 1.

d. Ibid. See also UCC 1–201(39).

The printed name of a firm, appearing in the letterhead at the top of a writing, is a sufficient signature if it is adopted by the firm with the intention of authenticating the writing. Merrill Lynch, Pierce, Fenner & Smith, Inc. v. Cole, 457 A.2d 656 (Conn. 1983). As to a telegram as a signed document see Hansen v. Hill, 340 N.W.2d 8 (Neb.1983).

2–201, to indicate that a contract for sale had been made between the parties, and so to make enforceable an oral agreement upon the quantity, if there had been one. See Howard Const. Co. v. Jeff–Cole Quarries, Inc., 669 S.W.2d 221 (Mo.App.1983): "The words 'as per our agreement,' 'in confirmation of,' or 'sold to buyer,' would indicate that the parties had reached an agreement."

NOTES

(1) *Problems.* Each of two railway companies receives this letter, signed by a manufacturer of rails: "This acknowledges your telephone order for 3,000 tons of iron rails, and our acceptance." Each company responds immediately, in a signed writing. Company One answers: "The quantity of rails we agreed to buy is 2,000 tons, not 3,000." Company Two answers: "Don't ship rails ordered; we have decided to look elsewhere."

Has Company One given notice of objection to the contents of the manufacturer's letter? Company Two?

In an action by the manufacturer against Company Two, the question may not matter; for that company's answer might suffice under subsection (1) of UCC 2–201 as a writing permitting enforcement. See Louisville Asphalt Varnish Co. v. Lorick, 8 S.E. 8 (S.C.1888).

In an action against Company One, however, the question of "objection" plainly matters. Do you see why?

(2) *Distributorship Agreements.* Refer again to the Case of the Wallpaper Orders, Note 1, p. 242 above, concerning an agreement for distributing wallcovers and particular sale agreements. Distributorship agreements are frequently classified as "UCC contracts" in the sense that they are governed by UCC Article 2. See Monetti, S.P.A. v. Anchor Hocking Corp., 931 F.2d 1178, 1184 (7th Cir.1991). Does it follow that UCC 2–201 required the wallcovers distributorship agreement to be memorialized in a writing? If so, would a series of purchase orders and confirmations suffice to make enforceable an oral agreement for an exclusive distributorship?

The opinion in *Monetti* considers the possibility that the provision "does not cover every transaction that is otherwise within the scope of Article 2." The opinion also broaches the possibility of applying the provision "flexibly" to situations that do not make a smooth fit with UCC 2–201.

UCC 2–201: Subsection (2)

This provision, referred to above as the "merchants' exception," is one of the most remarkable features of UCC 2–201. When it applies, it makes a writing efficacious against a *non-signer*. It proceeds on the principle that a regular player in the commercial world will not stand silent upon the receipt of a message indicating its assent to an agreement that it did not make. It is expected, rather, that the recipient will shortly give "written notice of objection to [the] contents" of such a message. The consequence of failing to do so—the only consequence—is to "take away from the party who fails to answer the defense of the Statute of Frauds." [e]

The reach of the subsection is closely circumscribed. The message to which an objection is expected is one—only—that is "sufficient against the sender." This phrase is a reference back to subsection (1). It requires asking the hypothetical question whether or not, if the parties were reversed, and the sender were being charged with breach, the recipient could overcome a Statute-of-Frauds defense by producing the message. Moreover, the subsection applies only if the message (signed writing) amounts to one "in confirmation" of the alleged contract. Not only so, but the non-signer's receipt of the writing must have occurred "within a reasonable time"—counting, presumably, from the time of the parties' agreement. (Recall that if there has been no agreement, actual or manifested, no writing whatever could sustain the sender's claim.)

According to its terms, the subsection applies only "between merchants." Hence, for as long as the Code incorporates § 2–201, the Statute of Frauds will afford a defense for firms of most kinds, and for most individuals, who might receive and simply ignore a telegram reading "Confirming sale to you of twelve hundred tons rails. /Signed: Rolling Mill." If, however, the recipient is a railroad company, there is a certain peril in letting the matter ride. [f]

NOTES

(1) *Problem.* S, a producer of plastic products, has received two messages from B, a distributor of "hula hoops." The first was a purchase order for 30,000 hoops. The second was a letter, sent three days later, as follows:

> As per our phone conversation of today kindly enter our order for 60,000 hoops [specifying colors and other particulars, and giving packing instructions]: 39¢ each.

> It is our understanding that these will be produced upon completion of the present order for 30,000 hoops.

> Very truly yours, "B"

Ten days elapsed after S's receipt of the letter, during which S made no attempt to communicate with B. Having failed to receive any of the larger quantity of hoops, B sues S for damages. S's defenses are (a) that it did not make the alleged oral agreement, and (b) that the alleged contract is anyway unenforceable for want of a writing signed by S. As to subsection (2) of UCC 2–201, S contends that B's letter cannot count as a "confirmation": it would have been incumbent on S to object to its contents only if the letter referred to a sale, a contract, or an agreement.

e. Comment 3 to UCC 2–201.

f. See Gateway Co. v. Charlotte Theatres, Inc., 297 F.2d 483, 486 (1st Cir.1961): "The advice of Wm. Randolph Hearst, 'Throw [it] in the wastebasket. Every letter answers itself in a couple of weeks.' ... is not a safe principle."

Can you construct an argument to overcome the Statute of Frauds defense? Does it matter that the word "order" appeared twice in B's letter? See Harry Rubin & Sons v. Consolidated Pipe Co., 153 A.2d 472 (Pa.1959).

What revision of the letter would have made the Statute of Frauds a frivolous defense? See Dura–Wood Treating Co. v. Century Forest Industries, Inc., 675 F.2d 745 (5th Cir.), cert. denied, 459 U.S. 865 (1982). Would you have advised B to add: "This letter serves as a confirmation under UCC 2–201(2)"?

(2) *"Reasonable Time" for Confirming.* In Serna, Inc. v. Harman, 742 F.2d 186 (5th Cir.1984), a seller of cattle waited for the whole of a Spring season before sending an invoice to the buyer, confirming their unwritten agreement for sale. In sustaining the trial court's finding that the delay was not unreasonable, the court said: "there was no showing of any prejudice to defendant [the buyer] because of plaintiff's delay of approximately three and one-half months in sending a written confirmation." Does this observation seem to put an unfair burden on the buyer of showing prejudice? If the market price of the cattle had fluctuated considerably during the Spring, would that have indicated prejudice? Might the decision have been different if the plaintiff had been a "merchant" other than a cattle-grower, for whom springtime is not so busy a season?

(3) *Overlap of Clauses.* Would the repeal of UCC 2–201 affect the operation of other provisions of the Statute of Frauds? Consider the contract reported in Eastern Air Lines v. Gulf Oil Corporation, p. 125 above, for the sale of jet fuel over a period of 4½ years. If there had been no memorandum representing that contract, there are two reasons for doubting that it was enforceable, as the law stands. On the other hand, there is a remarkable decision that a contract within UCC 2–201 is exempt from the requirement of a writing as imposed by the one-year clause. Roth Steel Products v. Sharon Steel Corp., 705 F.2d 134 (6th Cir.1983). (Cases can easily be supposed in which a writing would satisfy the former requirement, but not the latter.) It is a nice question whether or not the authority of *Roth Steel* would survive a revision of Article 2 lopping off the branch of the Statute of Frauds appearing there.

Contrary to *Roth Steel*, it has generally been held that a single contract can be subject to cumulative requirements imposed by multiple provisions—such as the sale-of-goods clause and the land-sale clause. See Fort Howard Paper Co. v. William D. Witter, Inc., 787 F.2d 784 (2d Cir.1986) (suretyship and finder's-fee provisions).

UCC 2–201: Subsection (3)

Unlike UCC 2–201, the other statutory offspring of the historic Statute of Frauds can be satisfied only by writings, and not (so far as the usual text goes) by either part performance or by an admission. Clauses (a) and (b) of this subsection are Code innovations.

NOTES

(1) *Custom Goods.* What explains the enforceability rule of subsection (3)(a)? It is easy to imagine a producer-seller who has acted under an oral contract in such a way that, if the contract is unenforceable, the seller will suffer hardship. (The product is "custom" goods, such as a Palladian-style doghouse, say.) Moreover, the seller's conduct supplies some evidence that the contract asserted is a genuine one. Note that when the clause applies *either* party can

enforce the contract: why the buyer? Does this rule throw any light on the purpose of the provision?

(2) *Admission in Proceedings.* S writes out and signs the terms of an agreement with B by which S is to supply and B is to buy all B's requirements of fuel oil over a period of years. B says (without signing), "We've got a deal," and the parties shake hands. In an action by S against B, based on the agreement, may B move for dismissal *without asserting that B did not consent to the "deal"*? Or may B confess making the agreement and justify a failure to perform by reference to the Statute of Frauds? One court has spoken to the point as follows: "to enforce an oral contract against a party merely because he or she admitted to its existence and substance, against his or her own interest, is likely to promote perjury. Instead of admitting to the contract, the breaching party would be tempted to deny the agreement in order to escape liability." Darby v. Johnson, 477 So.2d 322 (Ala.1985).

But see subsection (3)(b) of UCC 2–201. If B may move for dismissal without denying the agreement, is this provision simply vacuous? See Boylan v. G.L. Morrow Co., 468 N.E.2d 681 (N.Y.1984).[a]

(3) *The Lawyer's Conscience.* In a thoughtful article, Dean Robert Stevens pointed out that it is "probably a prevailing practice automatically to plead the Statute of Limitations to a stale claim and the Statute of Frauds when there is known to be no writing signed by the defendant, or his agent, evidencing the contract sued upon. The statutes are there, they supply the defenses, and the attorney would not be giving full and competent service to his client if he did not advise him of them and advance them for him." As to the Statute of Frauds, Dean Stevens saw a problem of ethics in which "the lawyer's conscience may be in conflict, not merely with a custom of the profession habitually to plead the defense, as in the case of the Statute of Limitations, but with judge-made law, that is all but unanimously adopted, to the effect that the defendant can admit an honest obligation and yet defeat its enforcement by pleading that the agreement was only oral.... In the conflict between conscience and judicially approved practice, what is the lawyer to do? Conscience tells him that the practice is wrong, but the literature from insurance companies reminds him of liability for malpractice." Ethics and the Statute of Frauds, 37 Cornell L.Q. 355 (1952).

What effect does UCC 2–201(3)(b) have upon this problem?

SECTION 4. DISPENSING WITH THE REQUIREMENT OF A WRITING

MONARCO v. LO GRECO

Supreme Court of California, 1950.
35 Cal.2d 621, 220 P.2d 737.

TRAYNOR, JUSTICE. Natale and Carmela Castiglia were married in 1919 in Colorado. Carmela had three children, John, Rosie and Christie,

---

a. Concerning UCC 8–319(d); note the reference there to quantity and price. A dissenting opinion in this case cites authori- ties looking each way and reviews the literature extensively.

by a previous marriage. Rosie was married to Nick Norcia. Natale had one grandchild, plaintiff Carmen Monarco, the son of a deceased daughter by a previous marriage. Natale and Carmela moved to California where they invested their assets, amounting to approximately $4,000, in a half interest in agricultural property. Rosie and Nick Norcia acquired the other half interest. Christie, then in his early teens, moved with the family to California. Plaintiff remained in Colorado. In 1926, Christie, then 18 years old, decided to leave the home of his mother and stepfather and seek an independent living. Natale and Carmela, however, wanted him to stay with them and participate in the family venture. They made an oral proposal to Christie that if he stayed home and worked they would keep their property in joint tenancy so that it would pass to the survivor who would leave it to Christie by will except for small devises to John and Rosie. In performance of this agreement Christie remained home and worked diligently in the family venture. He gave up any opportunity for further education or any chance to accumulate property of his own. He received only his room and board and spending money. When he married and suggested the possibility of securing some present interest to support his wife, Natale told him that his wife should move in with the family and that Christie need not worry, for he would receive all the property when Natale and Carmela died. Natale and Carmela placed all of their property in joint tenancy and in 1941 both executed wills leaving all their property to Christie with the exception of small devises to Rosie and John and $500 to plaintiff. Although these wills did not refer to the agreement, their terms were agreed upon by Christie, Natale and Carmela. The venture was successful, so that at the time of Natale's death his and Carmela's interest was worth approximately $100,000. Shortly before his death Natale became dissatisfied with the agreement and determined to leave his half of the joint property to his grandson, the plaintiff. Without informing Christie or Carmela he arranged the necessary conveyances to terminate the joint tenancies and executed a will leaving all of his property to plaintiff. This will was probated and the court entered its decree distributing the property to plaintiff. After the decree of distribution became final, plaintiff brought these actions for partition of the properties and an accounting. By cross-complaint Carmela asked that plaintiff be declared a constructive trustee of the property he received as a result of Natale's breach of his agreement to keep the property in joint tenancy. On the basis of the foregoing facts the trial court gave judgment for defendants and cross-complainant, and plaintiff has appealed.

The controlling question is whether plaintiff is estopped from relying upon the statute of frauds (Civil Code § 1624; Code Civ.Proc. § 1973) to defeat the enforcement of the oral contract.[a] The doctrine of estoppel to assert the statute of frauds has been consistently applied by the courts of this state to prevent fraud that would result from refusal to enforce oral contracts in certain circumstances. Such fraud may inhere in the unconscionable injury that would result from denying enforce-

a. See the lifetime provision set out in fn. f, p. 288 above.

ment of the contract after one party has been induced by the other seriously to change his position in reliance on the contract, ... or in the unjust enrichment that would result if a party who has received the benefits of the other's performance were allowed to rely upon the statute.... In many cases both elements are present. Thus, not only may one party have so seriously changed his position in reliance upon, or in performance of, the contract that he would suffer an unconscionable injury if it were not enforced, but the other may have reaped the benefits of the contract so that he would be unjustly enriched if he could escape its obligations....

In this case both elements are present. In reliance on Natale's repeated assurances that he would receive the property when Natale and Carmela died, Christie gave up any opportunity to accumulate property of his own and devoted his life to making the family venture a success. That he would be seriously prejudiced by a refusal to enforce the contract is made clear by a comparison of his position with that of Rosie and Nick Norcia. Because the Norcias were able to make a small investment when the family venture was started, their interest, now worth approximately $100,000, has been protected. Christie, on the other hand, forbore from demanding any present interest in the venture in exchange for his labors on the assurance that Natale's and Carmela's interest would pass to him on their death. Had he invested money instead of labor in the venture on the same oral understanding, a resulting trust would have arisen in his favor. Byers v. Doheny, 105 Cal.App. 484, 493–495, 287 P. 988; see, Restatement, Trusts, § 454, comment j. illus. 12. His twenty years of labor should have equal effect. On the other hand, Natale reaped the benefits of the contract. He and his devisees would be unjustly enriched if the statute of frauds could be invoked to relieve him from performance of his own obligations thereunder.

It is contended, however, that an estoppel to plead the statute of frauds can only arise when there have been representations with respect to the requirements of the statute indicating that a writing is not necessary or will be executed or that the statute will not be relied upon as a defense. This element was present in the leading case of Seymour v. Oelrichs, 156 Cal. 782, 108 P. 88, 134 Am.St.Rep. 154, and it is not surprising therefore that it has been listed as a requirement of an estoppel in later cases that have held on their facts that there was or was not an estoppel.... Those cases, however, that have refused to find an estoppel have been cases where the court found either that no unconscionable injury would result from refusing to enforce the oral contract, ... or that the remedy of quantum meruit for services rendered was adequate.... In those cases, however, where either an unconscionable injury or unjust enrichment would result from refusal to enforce the contract, the doctrine of estoppel has been applied whether or not plaintiff relied upon representations going to the requirements of the statute itself.... Likewise in the case of partly performed oral contracts for the sale of land specific enforcement will be decreed whether or not there have been representations going to the requirements of the statute, because its denial would result in a fraud on the plaintiff who has gone into possession or made improvements in reliance on the contract.... In reality it is not the representation that the contract will be put in writing or that the statute will not be invoked, but the promise that the contract will be performed that a party relies upon when he changes his position because of it. Moreover, a party who has accepted the benefits of an oral contract will be unjustly enriched if the contract is not enforced whether his representations related to the requirements of the statute or were limited to affirmations that the contract would be performed.

It is settled that neither the remedy of an action at law for damages for breach of contract nor the quasi-contractual remedy for the value of services rendered is adequate for the breach of a contract to leave property by will in exchange for services of a peculiar nature involving the assumption or continuation of a close family relationship.... The facts of this case clearly bring it within the foregoing rule....

The judgments are affirmed.

NOTES

(1) *Christie's Case and Kenneth's Case.* For about 28 years after Virginia M. Davis was widowed, her son Kenneth lived on and operated a ranch that had been left to her. According to him, he expended some $400,000 in improvements. Then his mother conveyed it to her other children. Kenneth brought an action against his mother and his siblings for specific performance of an alleged oral promise by his mother to convey the ranch to him. The consideration, he alleged, was his payment of a $12,000 mortgage on the ranch. Which of the following facts, if established, best differentiates this case from *Monarco?* [a]—(i) Other than the mortgage payments, Kenneth paid nothing for his use of the property; (ii) As to the alleged agreement, Mrs. Davis testified, "I can't remember. I can't remember"; (iii) Over the years, she maintained title to the property despite repeated requests by Kenneth that she sell it to him. See Davis v. Davis, 855 P.2d 342 (Wyo.1993).

(2) *Reliance Unreasonable.* In Wilma Corp. v. Fleming Foods, Inc., 613 So.2d 359 (Ala.1993), a shopping-center developer, as plaintiff, charged the defendant with fraud, upon being faced with a Statute-of-Frauds defense to a contract claim. An agent for the defendant had signed a paper expressing all the essential terms of a projected 15–year lease. According to the developer, the agent had said, on signing, that the transaction was a "done deal"; and in reliance on that the developer (Wilma Corporation) had torn down two buildings in anticipation of constructing a new one for lease as a Piggly Wiggly store.

The claim failed. In affirming a summary judgment for the defendant, the court said that both parties were "corporate entities engaging in a business transaction.... This case does not involve a consumer transaction, but an arm's-length transaction between two corporations whose agents knew or should have known of the requirements of the Statute of Frauds. Because Wilma Corporation deals in property development and leasing, it either knew or should have known that the Statute of Frauds prohibits an agent from entering into a contract for the lease of land on a principal's behalf without written authority

---

a. For a discussion of *Monarco,* see the case described in Note 2, p. 287 above.

from the principal." A claim of fraudulent misrepresentation could not be made out in the absence of justifiable reliance.

(3) *Reliance Reasonable?* Can a promisee have a reasonable expectation that performance will be forthcoming even though the promisee knows that, under the Statute of Frauds, the promise is unenforceable? Might the answer depend on a close relation between the parties, such as mother and son? On the fact that the promisor is a firm whose success depends on providing reliable services? See Lehman v. Dow Jones & Co., Inc., 783 F.2d 285 (2d Cir.1986).

Restatement Second § 139 is an adaptation of promissory estoppel in relation to the Statute of Frauds. The section, it has been observed, "complements Restatement Second of Contracts § 90." Warder & Lee Elevator, Inc. v. Britten, 274 N.W.2d 339 (Iowa 1979). Subsection (2) states five circumstances as "significant," in determining whether or not injustice can be avoided only by enforcement of the promise. One is the reasonableness of the action or forbearance induced by the promise. Another is the extent to which it was foreseeable by the promisor.

A circumstance of special interest is the tendency of a party's action or forbearance to corroborate the making and terms of the promise—or "the extent to which ... the making and terms are otherwise established by clear and convincing evidence." Is Monarco v. Lo Greco a good illustration of that element in § 139?

(4) *Estoppel Confined.* In some courts there are exacting requirements for an estoppel to assert the Statute of Frauds. In particular, reliance on a promise of performance, as such, may not suffice. If, however, the promise was made with the intent not to perform, the Statute may be circumvented by the fraud. (In *Wilma Corporation,* above, the court acknowledged that it would enforce a contract on that basis, describing it as "inherent fraud.") Perhaps the most secure basis for an estoppel is a representation that the speaker has signed a designated writing, where the writing would have satisfied the Statute but has not been signed. See Ozier v. Haines, 103 N.E.2d 485 (Ill.1952), expressing a restrictive view: "It is true that harsh results ... may occur where one has changed his position in reliance on the oral promise of another, but it is a result which is invited and risked when the agreement is not reduced to writing in the manner prescribed by law." Otherwise, the court said, the Statute would be rendered "useless and unmeaning."

(5) *Unjust Enrichment.* A party who has conferred a valuable performance on another, under an unenforceable contract between the parties, and has not enjoyed offsetting benefits, can generally get restitution if the other party refuses to perform. See Restatement Second §§ 141 and 375.[b] Why was a quasi-contract claim not a suitable remedy for Christie Lo Greco?

When a plaintiff seeks to circumvent the Statute of Frauds through estoppel, is it a critical issue whether or not the defendant would be unjustly enriched in the absence of enforcement? Or should the emphasis be placed on detriment to

b. An interesting way in which the "other party" might escape restitution liability is to sign a memorandum making the contract enforceable. See Note 5, p. 735 below.

A given statute may preclude restitution. See Cal.Civ. Code § 1624(d), fn. f, p. 288 above. How would the reasonable value of the broker's services to the principal, if the broker were allowed restitution, differ from the amount provided in the unenforceable contract? On the assumption that it would differ little, if at all, it is usually held that the broker cannot get restitution because it would circumvent the statute. See, for example, American Intern. Enterprises, Inc. v. F.D.I.C., 3 F.3d 1263, 1270 (9th Cir.1993).

the plaintiff? See Atlantic Wholesale Co., Inc. v. Solondz, 320 S.E.2d 720 (S.C.App.1984).

(6) *Reliance Loss.* While Farash, the owner of a commercial building, had it under renovation, a firm agreed, orally, to enter into a lease for two years' use of the building. As part of the agreement Farash undertook to complete the renovation and to make certain modifications, expediting the work. "Timing is critical," said the prospective tenant. "Don't worry about the lease, it will be signed and the work should not wait for the actual signing...." Farash completed the work, but the other party reneged. The owner had no right to contract damages against the other. So it was held in Farash v. Sykes Datatronics, Inc., 452 N.E.2d 1245 (N.Y.1983). The applicable statute provides that a lease for so long a period is "void" if not expressed in a signed writing.[c]

In the *Farash* case, however, the owner made a claim against the prospective tenant for the value of the work done on the building in reliance on the defendant's promises, and at its request. This claim, the court held, was not one barred by the Statute of Frauds. "This is not an attempt to enforce an oral lease, but is in disaffirmance of the void contract.... That defendant did not benefit from plaintiff's efforts does not require dismissal; plaintiff may recover for those efforts that were to his detriment and that thereby placed him in a worse position." [d]

Does it seem that every kind of interest protected by an *enforceable* contract (restitution, reliance, expectancy) can also be vindicated under an *unenforceable* contract?

CHEVRON U.S.A. INC. v. SCHIRMER
United States Court of Appeals, Ninth Circuit, 1993.
11 F.3d 1473.

FLETCHER, CIRCUIT JUDGE: Chevron U.S.A. Inc. ("Chevron") appeals the entry of summary judgment in favor of W. Scott Schirmer ("Schirmer") on Chevron's suit for specific performance of an option contract to purchase real property. Schirmer appeals the entry of summary judgment for Chevron on his counterclaim for damages sustained from Chevron's recording of notice of lis pendens on the property.[e] Both sides appeal the denial of their requests for attorneys' fees. We affirm the summary judgment against Chevron denying specific performance and the denial of its fee request, but reverse the summary judgment against Schirmer on his counterclaim. We also reverse the denial of Schirmer's fee request, and remand for the determination of reasonable fees.

I. Facts

In 1987, Schirmer Properties[1] owned a 37.8 acre tract of land in Peoria, Arizona, a small community near Phoenix. On May 14, 1987,

c. Gen.Oblig.L. § 5–703, subd. 2.

d. As to this, two judges dissented.

e. A plaintiff's filing of a notice of "litigation pending" concerning real property, as authorized by statute, will show up on a search of the defendant's title, and so will impede the defendant in attempting to sell the property, or to borrow against it.

1. Schirmer is the successor in interest to Schirmer Properties by virtue of a property settlement agreement with his ex-wife

the partnership entered into an option contract with Chevron to sell it a 200′ × 200′ corner parcel of that tract, upon which Chevron intended to build a service station and convenience store. The option provided, in relevant part, that on or before the 13th day of November, 1987, Buyer [Chevron] may exercise this Real Estate Purchase Option (hereinafter called "Option") by mailing or delivering to Seller (or any one of them if more than one Seller) at c/o Scott Schirmer [address], a copy of this Option signed on behalf of Buyer. If Buyer exercises this Option by mail, such exercise shall be deemed valid and effective upon mailing.

Upon exercise of this Option by Buyer, all the terms and conditions set forth herein shall constitute the contract of Seller to sell and the contract of Buyer to buy the Property. Chevron failed to exercise the option before it expired.[2]

The record does not definitively reveal why Chevron failed to simply sign the option and timely deliver it to Schirmer, thereby binding the parties to the contract. Zoning and permit issues, for example, were seemingly covered by the option:

> Notwithstanding any other provision of this Option to the contrary, Buyer shall have no obligation to pay the balance of the purchase price until ten (10) days after obtaining all necessary rezoning and permits. If the necessary rezoning and permits cannot be obtained or if they are available only upon terms and conditions which are unsatisfactory to Buyer, Buyer may rescind the exercise of this Option and the Deed deposited in escrow by Seller shall be returned to Seller.

One possibility is that Chevron badly miscalculated the option expiration date. (An internal Chevron memorandum suggests the author's confidence that "we can receive all necessary permits prior to our *December 21, 1987* expiration of option") (emphasis added).

The record reveals that the passing of the expiration date did not bring a halt to either side's efforts to secure the necessary governmental permits, a quest aided by Schirmer's real estate agent, Robert Broyles. Chevron characterizes the continuing effort and other instances of continued interaction as evidence that the parties "at all relevant times recognized that there existed an agreement between them for Chevron to buy the Property," that Schirmer "never denied or expressed doubt as to the existence of such an agreement" and indeed made "renewed promises to Chevron to perform [his] obligations under the agreement." Complaint Par. 10. Schirmer argues that both sides benefitted by following through on the permit process after the option expired— Chevron because its interest in the property was conditioned on its being suitably zoned, and Schirmer because any such permits would be ob-

---

(the other general partner in Schirmer Properties).

2. There is some dispute as to the option's expiration date. This dispute, however, is irrelevant, since there is no conten-

tion that Chevron exercised the option prior to November 21, 1987, the date it represents as the "more accurate[ ]" expiration date. Blue Brief at 9.

tained in his name, thereby enhancing the value of the property to other potential buyers.

On March 11, 1988, Chevron delivered to an escrow agent what it considered to be sufficient funds to complete the transaction; some time prior to March 11, it had mailed to Broyles a copy of the option (unsigned), along with a copy of the instruction letter to the escrow agent, dated March 4. Schirmer refused to convey the property. On November 14, 1988, Chevron filed a diversity action in the District of Arizona seeking specific performance.

On July 26, 1989, Schirmer filed an amended answer and counterclaim alleging that, inter alia, the notice of lis pendens recorded by Chevron on the property when it filed its suit was (and was known by it to be) "groundless, improper and invalid." Schirmer asked for treble damages under Arizona Revised Statute § 33–420.

On March 6, 1990, the district court granted Schirmer's motion for summary judgment against Chevron on its complaint. The court subsequently permitted Chevron to amend its complaint to allege, inter alia, that in February 1988 it had entered into a new, oral agreement with Schirmer for the purchase of the property and that this oral agreement had been partially performed. On August 29, 1991, the court entered summary judgment against Chevron on its amended complaint, and summary judgment against Schirmer on his counterclaim.

II. Analysis

A. Chevron's Suit for Specific Performance

Chevron concedes that there is little or no dispute about the "objective events as to which the parties offered evidence." First Brief at 3. It argues, however, that the district court erred in resolving in Schirmer's favor the "substantial dispute as to what inferences should be drawn from these events." Id.

Our review of the trial court's summary judgment decision is de novo. Jones v. Union P.R.R., 968 F.2d 937, 940 (9th Cir.1992). We must ascertain, viewing the evidence in the light most favorable to Chevron (the nonmoving party), whether there are any genuine issues of material fact and whether the district court correctly applied the relevant substantive law....

There is no dispute that Chevron attempted to exercise the option at (in its words) "a time when according to its original written terms, it had expired." First Brief at 3. It contends, nonetheless, that because the parties' words and conduct both before and after the option expiration date were consistent with an inference that an agreement between them still existed, summary judgment in Schirmer's favor was inappropriate. This is contrary to Arizona law....[3] Exact compliance with an

---

3. To the extent that Texas or Utah law may be different with respect to options, see Broady v. Mitchell, 572 S.W.2d 36, 40 (Tex.Ct.App.1978); Coombs v. Ouzounian, 24 Utah 2d 39, 465 P.2d 356, 358 (Utah 1970), Chevron offers no argument that Arizona would adopt such a posture and overturn its long-standing law.

option contract's terms is stringently enforced because an optionor like Schirmer is strictly bound to those terms, while an optionee like Chevron may freely accept or reject the terms as it chooses. Id.[4]

Here, Chevron did not comply with the option's terms and conditions. The district court correctly held that "once the option had expired, it could no longer be modified." [The court rejected an argument made by Chevron based on discussions it had held with Broyles shortly before the option expiration date.]

Chevron contends, alternatively, that the parties entered into a new option agreement after the expiration of the original option. Arizona's Statute of Frauds provisions require an option agreement for real property to be in writing. Ariz.Rev.Stat.Ann. § 44–101(6); see also Bass Inv. Co. v. Banner Realty, Inc., 103 Ariz. 75, 436 P.2d 894, 898 (Ariz. 1968). Chevron points to no writing that evidences a second option agreement. The December 23, 1988 letter from Schirmer to the bank holding his mortgage on the property is not, as Chevron characterizes it, a document "memorializing the parties' unwritten agreement." This letter stated only Schirmer's belief that "the Chevron sale ... is still available" as one way to raise money to pay his debt to the bank; it was not a confirmation, for purposes of the Statute of Frauds, that Schirmer had granted Chevron another option.

Neither of the two exceptions to the Statute of Frauds identified by Chevron applies in this case. One possibility argued by Chevron is waiver. At her deposition, Schirmer's ex-wife, Kandi Schirmer Kaufman (a partner in Schirmer Properties and one of the original defendants), related that it was her "understanding" that Schirmer "had simply verbally extended [the option] for—I don't know—several months. I don't know. Maybe—you know, it was—it wasn't anything like a year or anything like that. It was maybe three, four months, I don't remember what it was. I don't remember the specifics." A party may not rely on a Statute of Frauds defense if it testifies to the terms of an oral agreement, but such testimony must be more specific than Kandi Schirmer Kaufman's indefinite and inconclusive recitation of vague terms she believed someone else had agreed to. See Anchorage–Hynning & Co. v. Moringiello, 225 U.S.App.D.C. 114, 697 F.2d 356, 362–63 (D.C.Cir.1983) (Statute of Frauds defense barred when party deemed to have admitted to specific payment terms, delivery dates, and conditions of lease).

Chevron's second suggested exception, part performance, "is inapplicable in a suit where only money damages are sought." Trollope v. Koerner, 106 Ariz. 10, 470 P.2d 91, 98 (Ariz.1970); William Henry Brophy College v. Tovar, 127 Ariz. 191, 619 P.2d 19, 23 (Ariz.Ct.App. 1980). Schirmer's bank foreclosed on the entire 37.8–acre tract and conducted a sheriff's sale, meaning, among other things, that specific

---

4. Purchase contracts are treated differently than option contracts. Compare, e.g., Kammert Bros. Enters., Inc. v. Tanque Verde Plaza Co., 102 Ariz. 301, 428 P.2d 678, 682 (Ariz.1967) (oral extension of time to make contract payments valid) with, e.g., *Rogers,* 613 P.2d at 846 (option contracts strictly construed).

performance is not an available form of relief. But even if Schirmer still owned the property, " 'part performance necessary to take an oral contract out of the statute of frauds must be unequivocably [sic] referable to the contract.' " MH Inv. Co. v. Transamerica Title Ins. Co., 162 Ariz. 569, 785 P.2d 89, 94 (Ariz.Ct.App.1989) (quoting Gene Hancock Constr. Co. v. Kempton & Snedigar Dairy, 20 Ariz.App. 122, 510 P.2d 752, 755 (Ariz.Ct.App.1973)). Here, the district court ruled that the most likely explanation for the parties' conduct after the alleged February 1988 oral agreement was that it was "simply in line with the continuing negotiations." CR 296, at 8. That conduct was not unequivocally referable to the alleged contract—conduct that would not have been undertaken unless the option was in existence.

Chevron's amended complaint also contained various tort claims against Schirmer. The district court correctly found that these claims were predicated on a promise to agree in the future; Arizona law prohibits basing a misrepresentation claim on such a promise. See Walters v. First Fed. Sav. & Loan Ass'n, 131 Ariz. 321, 641 P.2d 235, 239 (Ariz.1982).

B. Schirmer's Counterclaim

Pursuant to Arizona Revised Statute § 12–1191(A), Chevron recorded notice of lis pendens on November 14, 1988, effectively announcing that it had initiated legal action "affecting title to real property." The thrust of that part of Schirmer's counterclaim at issue on appeal is that Chevron recorded this notice of lis pendens knowing it to be "groundless." Such action would constitute a violation of Arizona Revised Statute § 33–420. . . . [According to this provision, a violation by the person recording notice entails liability to the owner for damages, and for reasonable attorney fees and costs of the action.]

[The trial court's summary judgment for Chevron on the counterclaim rested on its finding that its action had "some basis."] [W]e must conclude that the district court erred in not finding that Chevron's notice of lis pendens was groundless. First, there is no dispute that Chevron knew its option contract with Schirmer had expired at the time it filed its complaint and notice of lis pendens. It also knew, or certainly should have known, that once the option contract expired, it could not be modified by Schirmer's oral representations or other conduct. Arizona law requires option contracts to be in writing, Ariz.Rev.Stat.Ann. § 44–101(6), and is "crystal clear" that they will be strictly construed. Rogers, 613 P.2d at 846. Under Arizona's Statute of Frauds, there is no plausible argument that Schirmer and Chevron entered into a new, oral option agreement. In sum, Chevron knew or should have known it had no "arguable basis" under Arizona law for asserting that its action for specific performance would affect Schirmer's property. Its notice of lis pendens was thus groundless under Arizona Revised Statute § 33–420.

· · ·

III.

We affirm the summary judgment against Chevron and the denial of its fees request. We reverse the summary judgment entered against Schirmer on his counterclaim. We also reverse the denial of his fees request, and remand for a determination of reasonable fees.[b]

Affirmed, in part, reversed in part and remanded.

REINHARDT, J., concurring and dissenting: ...

In my opinion, the majority's otherwise fine analysis goes astray when it concludes that "under Arizona's Statute of Frauds, there is *no plausible argument* that Schirmer and Chevron entered into a new, oral option agreement." (emphasis added). The record clearly shows that a *plausible* argument exists that Schirmer and Chevron entered into an enforceable oral agreement to extend the expiration date of the original option contract, notwithstanding the Arizona Statute of Frauds, Ariz. Rev.Stat. § 44–101(6).

Under Arizona law, an oral agreement can fall outside the scope of the statute of frauds under a theory of estoppel. "Where one has acted to his detriment solely in reliance on an oral agreement, an estoppel may be raised to defeat the defense of the statute of frauds." Waugh v. Lennard, 69 Ariz. 214, 222, 211 P.2d 806, 814 (1949). In my opinion, Chevron has adduced sufficient evidence to give rise to a plausible argument regarding a theory of estoppel.

There is evidence that Chevron "acted to [its] detriment solely in reliance on an oral agreement" and that Schirmer was therefore estopped from raising the statute of frauds. Chevron continued to make efforts to obtain a conditional use permit, health permits, and various other operating permits well after the original exercise date had expired and well after the time when Chevron contends it had entered into an alleged oral agreement to extend the option contract.[1] After the time of the alleged oral agreement, Chevron incurred expenses in its efforts to obtain those permits and to close the deal. It incurred building, fire, health, grading, and other permit expenses exceeding $44,000.00. It tied up over $725,000.00 in escrow. Chevron might not have acted in this manner unless it believed that the option contract had been extended.

---

b. Schirmer's fee request may be compared with a motion made by the defendant in the Case of the Green Mountains, in the Note at p. 215 above. The motion was to impose a sanction on the State of Vermont for pressing the action without having made reasonable inquiry into the facts, and for the State's "continued pursuit of the action after it should have realized that defendant had never signed a writing that would satisfy the Statute of Frauds." The motion was based on Rule 11 of the Vermont Rules of Civil Procedure (tracking Fed.R.Civ.P. 11) which provides, in part, that the signature of a party or an attorney on a pleading constitutes a certificate by the signer that "to the best of the signer's knowledge, information, and belief formed after reasonable inquiry [the pleading] is well grounded in fact and is warranted by existing law or a good faith argument for extension, modification, or reversal of existing law."

The motion was denied; and the defendant's appeal from that ruling was unsuccessful.

1. The original exercise date expired on November 13, 1987. According to Chevron, the parties agreed to extend the option contract prior to November 13, 1987. Chevron alleged that it relied on the extension agreement until at least March 11, 1988, when it delivered to an escrow agent sufficient funds to complete the transaction.

Accordingly, Chevron can argue that it acted to its detriment solely in reliance on Schirmer's representations that the option agreement had been extended.[2] ...

In all other respects, I generally agree with the majority opinion and the decisions it reaches....

NOTES

(1) *Part Performance of Land Contracts.* "Taking possession of property pursuant to an oral contract, together with making improvements or paying a substantial part of the purchase price, is generally sufficient to avoid the bar of the statute of frauds." Pearl Brewing Co. v. McNaboe, 495 A.2d 238 (R.I.1985). But the requirements differ from state to state. The requirement of conduct "unequivocally" or "exclusively" referable to the alleged contract (or at least to a contract much like the one alleged) is commonplace. See Anostario v. Vichinanzo, 450 N.E.2d 215 (N.Y.1983) ("unintelligible or at least extraordinary, explainable only with reference to the oral agreement").

In the Restatement Second the exception for part performance is reshaped into an exception for cases of reliance—although an evidentiary element is said to be part of the rationale. See § 129 and Comment *d*.

In Wilma Corporation v. Fleming Foods, Note 2, p. 306 above, the plaintiff did not assert the exception for part performance, possibly because it claimed money damages. Would it ever be possible for tearing down a building to count as part performance? What reason can be given for restricting the exception to cases in which equitable relief is sought, and not money damages only?

(2) *Law* vs. *Equity.* In the concluding paragraph of Monarco v. Lo Greco, above, the court explained why, although Christie might have succeeded in claiming a money award, he had properly invoked the power of equity to award specific performance (in the form of imposing a constructive trust).

In Merex A.G. v. Fairchild Weston Systems, Inc., 29 F.3d 821 (2d Cir.1994), the plaintiff sought a money judgment, either the value of its services in finding a business opportunity or a commission to be paid for the services under an alleged oral contract. The trial judge applied a provision of the New York Statute of Frauds and gave judgment for the defendant. In doing so she disregarded the verdict of a jury she had impanelled, treating the verdict as advisory only. On the appeal, the court had to decide whether or not, in a federal-court action based on the doctrine of promissory estoppel, a jury trial is required by the Constitution. The Seventh Amendment requires that the right of trial by jury be preserved only in "suits at common law"—not in equity suits.

The court distinguished between two functions of promissory estoppel. It said that this "protean doctrine ... eludes classification as either entirely legal or entirely equitable." Citing Restatement Second § 90, the court said that "where a plaintiff sues for contract damages and uses detrimental reliance as a substitute for consideration, the analogy to actions in assumpsit (law) is compelling." But in this case the plaintiff had used promissory estoppel, instead, to "avoid a draconian application of the Statute of Frauds." When promissory

2. The fact that under the original agreement Chevron could have exercised its option and then rescinded this action if it did not receive the permits does not affect my conclusion. The oral agreement allowed Chevron to seek the permits without committing itself to any firm contractual obligation. Moreover, even if the distinction is more legal than practical in this particular case, it is still sufficient to justify a finding of the requisite "minimal arguable basis."

estoppel is utilized in this manner, the court said, "the claim is more equitable than promissory in nature." *Held:* Affirmed.

The plaintiff's claim, the court acknowledged, comprised its expectation interest. "[W]hile we recognize the legal nature of expectation damages generally, we remain unpersuaded that [the plaintiff's] prayer for money damages outweighs the undeniably equitable nature of the promissory estoppel claim as a whole, particularly where, as here, the measure of damages plaintiff seeks is inappropriate."

(3) *Option for Goods.* Suppose a signed option contract for a sale of specified goods, written so as to expire at the end of the month. Might the holder of the option exercise it effectively in the following month, upon showing that the expiration date was intended to be the end of the year? Consider the second sentence of UCC 2–201: "A writing is not insufficient because it ... incorrectly states a term agreed upon...." Aside from this question, the application of the section to option contracts—and more especially to firm offers (UCC 2–205)—is uncertain.

(4) *Problem.* To change the facts of Chevron v. Schirmer, suppose that Chevron had made an oral promise to Schirmer, in September, that it would purchase Schirmer's property. Suppose further that, in October, Schirmer had received an offer from the XON Oil Company to purchase the property, and—relying on Chevron's promise—had rejected that offer. Upon Chevron's breach of its promise, what remedy, if any, might be available to Schirmer?

See Restatement Second § 139 (Note 3, p. 307 above). One circumstance of "action or forbearance" induced by a promise that is said to be significant is "the definite and substantial character of the action or forbearance *in relation to the remedy sought* " (emphasis supplied). See also Note 6, p. 308 above.

(5) *The Resort to Tort.* C.F. Huber II played a part in the merger of a Wisconsin paper company and the Maryland Cup Corporation. Not receiving a fee for his services, he made a claim against Maryland Cup whose chairman (he alleged) had assured him that Maryland Cup would pay his fee if the paper company failed to do so. Because this promise was not in writing, the enforcement of it would be barred under the New York statute about promises to "answer for the debt ... of another person." But the promise, Huber alleged, was fraudulently made. From the dismissal of his fraud claim, Huber appealed. "Surely," he argued, the policy of the Statute is "not so omnivorous that it swallows up claims based on independent fraudulent representations." *Held:* Reversed. For the court an important element in the case was the New York rule for measuring damages in fraud cases: rather than allowing the benefit of the bargain, it allows only out-of-pocket loss. (For this reason, in part, the court chose to apply New York law rather than the contrasting law of Wisconsin.) Fort Howard Paper Co. v. William D. Witter, Inc., 787 F.2d 784 (2d Cir.1986).[a]

a. In some states, but not in others, an oral contract for a commission, payable to a broker for finding a business that the other party acquires by purchase or merger, is unenforceable. See, for example, N.Y.Gen. Oblig.L. § 5–701a subd. 10. (As to the world-wide significance of this statute see Bushkin Associates, Inc. v. Raytheon Co., 473 N.E.2d 662 (Mass.1985).) This was the provision principally discussed in Huber's case. In point of fact, he preferred the application of Wisconsin law, which would have permitted him to enforce a commission contract with the paper company.

Given an oral contract that might be governed by the law of either of two states, and a decisive variation in their Statutes of Frauds, a number of courts have shown an inclination to prefer the law of the state where the Statute is not an impediment to enforcement. See, for example, William J. Conlon & Sons, Inc. v. Wanamaker, 583 F.Supp. 212 (E.D.N.Y.1984). What is there about a Statute of Frauds that might dis-

As to the tort of misrepresenting an intention, in making a promise, see Note 1, p. 384 below.

————

ESTOPPEL AND UCC 2–201

The formulation of the Statute of Frauds applicable to sale-of-goods contracts in the Uniform Commercial Code is considerably more detailed than the usual provisions requiring writings for other types of contracts. In particular, it contains qualifications relating both to part performance (subsection (3)(c)) and to some circumstances in which reliance on an oral contract would entail prejudice if the contract were denied enforcement (subsection (3)(a)). These features of UCC 2–201, and others, provide a footing for an argument that the statute does not license the courts to grant relief on grounds of part performance, benefits received, or detrimental reliance, other than relief based on the text of the statute.

Courts are sharply at odds about the force of this argument. For one view of the statute, see Lige Dickson Co. v. Union Oil Co., 635 P.2d 103 (Wash.1981). In that case a paving contractor, faced with a Statute-of-Frauds defense by a supplier of liquid asphalt, relied on Restatement Second § 139: Enforcement by Virtue of Action in Reliance. (See Note 3, p. 307 above.) The asphalt buyer's argument was rejected:

> [W]e must hold that promissory estoppel cannot be used to overcome the statute of frauds in a case which involves the sale of goods.... [W]e cannot help but foresee increased litigation and confusion as being the necessary result of the eroding of the U.C.C. if [§ 139] is adopted in this case.

Elsewhere in the Code, it will be recalled, provision is made for supplementing the text with principles of law and equity (unless "displaced" by particular provisions). UCC 1–103. One of the "general principles" mentioned there as being available for application, in an appropriate case, is estoppel. But that section begins: "Unless displaced by the particular provisions of this Act ..."

NOTES

(1) *The Rigorous View.* The opening phrase of § 2–201 has been relied on as reinforcement for the view represented by *Lige Dickson,* with the following emphasis: "Except as otherwise provided *in this section*...." See Reynoldson, C.J., dissenting, in Warder & Lee Elevator, Inc. v. Britten, 274 N.W.2d 339 (Iowa 1979), at 344. In part, Justice Reynoldson reasoned as follows:

> It is a rare case when either promisor in a bilateral contract does not rely on the contract.... Most situations in which such an oral contract is breached result in injustice.
>
> But [UCC 2–201] obviously is designed to suffer these injustices in isolated oral contract cases in favor of the general public policy to reduce fraud and perjury, curtail litigation and controversy, and encourage written contracts in sales of goods for a price of $500 or more.... It is significant

pose a court to avoid its application when possible?

that by trial time the plaintiff corporation in the case at bar was using written sales contracts with its customers.

The following Note indicates how the plaintiff in that case did business before the defendant, a customer, disappointed it.

(2) *The Relaxed View.*   The opinion of the majority in *Warder & Lee Elevator* relied on § 139 of the Restatement Second.   The court approved a recovery of cover damages, claimed by Elevator against a grower of corn and beans, J.W. Britten.   Elevator had contracted with Britten for a quantity of these goods, for fall delivery, on July 4, 1974.   The agreement was unwritten: Britten had made similar sales to Elevator for years, and had never defaulted. In fact, none of its suppliers had refused to perform an oral agreement.   But after July 4, grain prices increased substantially.   On the 29th, Britten called the deal off.   In the meanwhile, however, Elevator had committed itself to deliver identical quantities of corn and beans to a regional buyer, for a few cents more per bushel.[a]

Of UCC 2–201 the court said that it "does not purport to eliminate equitable and legal principles traditionally applicable in contract actions. . . .   If [it] were construed as displacing principles otherwise preserved in [UCC 1–103], it would mean that an oral contract coming within its terms would be unenforceable despite fraud, deceit, misrepresentation, dishonesty or any other form of unconscionable conduct by the party relying upon the statute.   No court has taken such an extreme position."

According to one court, the issue embodies a "philosophical conflict [that] implicates principles of statutory construction, fundamental fairness, and certainty in the law which have been the subject of legal debate in the English common law system since the Middle Ages."   B & W Glass, Inc. v. Weather Shield Mfg., Inc., 829 P.2d 809, 812 (Wyo.1992).   See also, Monetti, S.P.A. v. Anchor Hocking Corp., 931 F.2d 1178, 1186 (7th Cir.1991); Edwards, The Statute of Frauds of the Uniform Commercial Code and the Doctrine of Estoppel, 62 Marquette L.Rev. 205 (1978).

(3) *Opportunity Cost.*   A contractor proposing to build a dam requires a turbine for the job.   The contractor gets Alpha's oral agreement to supply the turbine for $900,000.   When Alpha fails to do so, the contractor pays $999,000 to Beta for the cheapest available substitute.   When the contractor sues Alpha, and is faced with the Statute of Frauds as a defense, it appears that if Alpha had supplied the turbine as promised, the contractor would have made a profit of $100,000 on the job.   As matters stand, the contractor has barely broken even.

Is this a case of what is called "unconscionable injury" in Monarco v. Lo Greco, above?   From an opinion by one judge (East) in C.R. Fedrick, Inc. v. Borg–Warner Corp., 552 F.2d 852 (9th Cir.1977), it appears that he thought not. He relied on other California cases for this proposition: the "mere" fact that a buyer has lost a bargain is not enough to estop a seller from relying on the Statute of Frauds.   Are there situations to which the proposition can be applied, without agreeing with Judge East's conclusion?   See the dissenting opinion in *C.R. Fedrick.*   (No two of the three judges in the case could agree on the ground for decision: one judge voted with Judge East on taking the "rigorous view" of UCC 2–201.)

How would Judge East have solved the problem in Note 4, p. 315 above?

a.   For a discussion of hedging contracts made by elevators, and the effect of market moves on growers' telephone contracts, see Note, 1977 Utah L.Rev. 59.

(4) *Questions.* Consider the concluding sentence in Restatement Second § 139(1) ("The remedy granted for breach is to be limited as justice requires") and see Note 5, p. 307 above. How does this bear on the turbine-sale problem stated in the foregoing Note?

Consider the possibility of recovery for deceit in making a promise that is unenforceable under the Statute of Frauds, but would otherwise be enforceable: Note 5, p. 315 above. How does this bear on the turbine-sale problem?

(5) *Problem.* Refer to James Baird Co. v. Gimbel Bros., stated at pp. 252–53 above. In that case the proposal by Gimbel, the "sub", was to supply linoleum to Baird. If a court were disposed to sustain Baird's claim, on these facts, but Gimbel's bid were oral, should relief be denied on the ground of UCC 2–201? See Edward Joy Co. v. Noise Control Products, Inc., 443 N.Y.S.2d 361 (Sup.Ct. 1981).

HALSTEAD v. MURRAY

Supreme Court of New Hampshire, 1988.
130 N.H. 560, 547 A.2d 202.

JOHNSON, JUSTICE. The plaintiff, Kirk Halstead, appeals from the denial of his motion to enforce settlement of an agreement entered into between his attorney and the attorney representing the defendant Stewart Murray. The Superior Court (Wyman, J.) approved the report of the Master (Charles T. Gallagher, Esq.) recommending that the agreement be found unenforceable because it failed to comply with the New Hampshire Statute of Frauds. We reverse and remand.

The parties own abutting property on Lake Winnipesaukee in Moultonborough. In April, 1984, the plaintiff filed petitions for declaratory and injunctive relief in the superior court seeking to enjoin Murray from constructing a building which Halstead alleged was in violation of the Moultonborough setback ordinance. The Town of Moultonborough was joined as a defendant. After the litigation had commenced, the individual parties engaged in settlement negotiations through their respective counsel.

[In November, 1985, and again in December, defendant's counsel, Robert Schroeder, wrote to the plaintiff's attorney, Philip T. McLaughlin, transmitting an offer by Murray—"take it or leave it"—to sell his lot to Halstead for $115,000. "The worst that can happen to my client is that he will be forced to remove part of the foundation...." Each letter indicated that a copy was sent to Murray. In December, McLaughlin wrote as follows to Schroeder:]

"Mr. Murray's $115,000 offer is accepted. I suggest you give me a Purchase & Sale Agreement signed by Mr. Murray, $115,000; closing on or before February 1, 1986; subject to title search; usual provisions; no financing contingencies.

On receipt I will Federal Express the Purchase & Sale Agreement to Mr. Halstead in New Jersey for his signature."

It is not contested that, upon Murray's direction, Murray's counsel prepared and forwarded to Halstead's attorney a purchase and sale agreement that called for the sale of the Murray property to Halstead and stated that "[t]he purchase price is $115,000." The contract was then forwarded to Halstead by his counsel, and Halstead executed the agreement as presented. Murray, however, had not signed the purchase and sale contract prior to its being forwarded to Halstead's counsel.

On February 3, 1986, Murray's counsel notified Halstead's counsel that Murray had decided not to go forward with the agreed sale. Shortly thereafter, Murray's counsel informed Halstead's counsel that Murray would consummate the sale if Halstead would pay the sum of $130,000 for the real estate. On February 13, 1986, Halstead filed a motion to enforce settlement with the superior court setting forth facts which were undisputed. Murray's counsel filed an objection, contending that the Statute of Frauds (RSA 506:1) had not been satisfied by the writings set forth above. However, Murray in his objection, offered to reimburse Halstead for "costs of title examination and other costs in reliance upon a proposed settlement." After a brief hearing before the master, in which the above correspondence and a copy of the purchase and sale agreement were entered into evidence, the master concluded that there had not been compliance with the statute and that he "must reluctantly recommend" that Halstead's motion be denied. This appeal followed.

... The New Hampshire version of the Statute of Frauds relating to the sale of land is contained in RSA 506:1. The statute reads as follows:

> "*Sale of Land.* No action shall be maintained upon a contract for the sale of land unless the agreement upon which it is brought, or some memorandum thereof, is in writing and signed by the party to be charged, or by some person authorized by him in writing."

. . .

We begin our analysis by determining whether there was an enforceable contract for the sale of land but for RSA 506:1. This court has indicated that an exchange of correspondence, such as that which occurred in this case, may create a binding contract for the sale of land where the necessary elements for such a contract have been set forth. Estate of Younge v. Huysmans, 127 N.H. 461, 465–66, 506 A.2d 282, 284–85 (1965)....

It is thus undisputed that the settlement agreement was a contract for the sale of land. The New Hampshire statute, on its face, would therefore require that Murray either have signed an agreement for the sale of the land in question or given written authorization to his attorney to contract in writing for the sale of the land. As Murray did neither of these, we must consider whether this case should fall within an exception to the Statute of Frauds....

We have said that RSA 506:1 "is intended to promote certainty and to protect from frauds and perjuries in land transactions." Weale v. Massachusetts Gen. Housing Corp., 117 N.H. 428, 431, 374 A.2d 925, 928 (1977). Further, we have said that "a strict enforcement of the statute can produce frustration on the one hand, and unethical conduct on the other. Hence the law seeks to alleviate the harshness of the statute when some operating facts, such as fraud, part performance or other equitable considerations, are present." Id. (citations omitted).

The authority of Murray's counsel to enter into settlement negotiations is not in dispute. Counsel for Murray, at the motion hearing, said, "It's a very difficult matter. In fact, I feel myself there was fully a settlement reached. There's no question as to my authority to make the offer." Further, Murray's counsel also had "no quarrel" with the statement of Halstead's counsel that the original settlement amount was $115,000, and that "Mr. Murray would adhere to the settlement now if the number were 130,000." Hence in this case the effect of the Statute of Frauds would apparently be to allow a party to escape the consequences of a bargain fairly made, not to protect him from the loss of property through fraud of another. There is thus reason to consider whether an exception to the Statute of Frauds is warranted.

There can be no question that the law favors the settlement of a dispute. McIsaac v. McMurray, 77 N.H. 466, 471, 93 A. 115, 118 (1915). . . .

We have also said that "[o]ur rule regarding the power of an attorney to bind his client by settlement is, perhaps, the most liberal in the country." Ducey v. Corey, 116 N.H. 163, 164, 355 A.2d 426, 427 (1976). The reason for this liberal rule is clear. "The authority of attorneys to make [settlement] agreements is in practice never questioned. It is essential to the orderly and convenient dispatch of business, and necessary for the protection of the rights of the parties." Beliveau v. Amoskeag Co., 68 N.H. 225, 226, 40 A. 734, 734 (1894).

In Perley v. Bailey, 89 N.H. 359, 199 A. 570 (1938), this court affirmed its dedication to upholding settlement agreements between counsel. In that case we enforced an oral agreement between counsel for the conveyance of land that was made before a master and was incorporated into his report. We found that this oral settlement agreement was not intended to be covered by the Statute of Frauds because the agreement of the parties was made under the "supervision . . . of the court's representative." Id. at 360, 199 A. at 571. We thus enforced the oral agreement for the conveyance of land to settle a dispute. . . .

The liberal rule of New Hampshire in enforcing agreements of counsel is grounded upon our recognition of the special relationship that exists between counsel and their clients. See Ducey v. Corey, 116 N.H. 163, 355 A.2d 426; Beliveau v. Amoskeag Co., 68 N.H. 225, 40 A. 734. Justice Oliver Wendell Holmes, then a member of the Massachusetts Supreme Judicial Court, spoke of this relationship as one "of the unity of person between attorney and client" in a case involving an oral settlement made by counsel in open court. Savage v. Blanchard, 148 Mass. 348, 350, 19 N.E. 396, 397 (1888).

We hold that because there is such a special relationship between the attorney and his client, our Statute of Frauds does not require the client to authorize his attorney, in writing, to settle an action involving a land dispute through sale of the subject property. The last clause of RSA 506:1, relating to an agent, was not intended to cover an attorney under such circumstances. A written settlement contract signed by a client's attorney with full authorization, and agreeing to convey the land which is the subject of the action in which the attorney represents the client, satisfies our Statute of Frauds and is binding on the client.

A client should not be allowed, on the one hand, to assert a special relationship with his lawyer, such that his confidential communications cannot be revealed, and, on the other hand, to assert that his lawyer is nothing more than an agent of the same status as a real estate broker. A client receives great privileges when dealing with his lawyer, and he must assume burdens commensurate with such privileges.

In deciding this case we emphasize that we limit our decision to those cases in which the client has authorized the attorney to settle a pending case involving land by the sale of the land which is the subject of the suit. If the client is able to prove, in subsequent litigation, that he did not authorize the attorney to settle the dispute or that he was not adequately informed of the terms of settlement, then the client may have recourse to suit against the attorney for breach of his fiduciary duty zealously to protect the interest of his client. Of course, a lawyer in any case must have authorization from his client in order to settle a dispute for money damages or for any other consideration. Here, the record would indicate that all necessary conditions have been met. We, of course, make no factual finding as to whether the client indeed authorized his lawyer to settle the case, nor do we make factual findings as to whether copies of the letters between counsel, which constitute the contract for the sale of land in settlement of the pending case, were in fact sent to the client as the facial record would indicate.

Reversed and Remanded.

THAYER, J., dissenting: ... While I agree with the plaintiff that the Statute of Frauds may not be used to perpetrate a fraud, and that defendant Murray's actions in increasing the settlement amount or refusing to sign the purchase and sale agreement are suggestive of bad faith, we do not, upon the record before us, have facts sufficient to establish fraudulent behavior on the part of Murray. This court has previously held that mere refusal to sign a purchase and sale agreement does not, by itself, constitute fraud. Weale v. Massachusetts Gen. Housing Corp., 117 N.H. 428, 431, 374 A.2d 925, 928 (1977); Clark v. Lovelace, 102 N.H. 97, 99, 151 A.2d 224, 225 (1959)....

The majority cites one case in support of their holding that an oral agreement for the conveyance of land may be enforced, Perley v. Bailey, 89 N.H. 359, 199 A. 570. However, as stated earlier, the enforcement of the agreement in *Perley* was based on the fact that the oral stipulation was reached in court and incorporated in the master's report. As part of a court order, the agreement was outside the Statute of Frauds. In the present case, the agreement was not made in court, nor was it incorporated into a court decree.

In their quest to find some justification for their disregard of the plain meaning of RSA 506:1, and the exceptions previously approved by the court, the majority draw upon Justice Oliver Wendell Holmes to establish the proposition that the relationship between lawyers and their clients is one "of the unity of person...." ... The majority view of such "unity" is that the lawyer is not representing the client. As the majority opinion states it, the lawyer is not an agent for his client because the lawyer is one with the client and has a unique relationship to the court. The inconsistency presented by this unity theory is that a lawyer, because of his relationship to the court, can bind the client without conforming to the Statute of Frauds, while the client, if he appeared *pro se,* would not be bound to an agreement unless he conformed with the statute.

Aware that this new exception to the statute has the potential of forcing clients to convey property based on agreements reached by their lawyers, my brothers comprising the majority state that clients may have recourse by suing their lawyers. This, I point out to them, is the same type of litigation that is eliminated when the party authorizing another to act for him does so in writing. The majority opinion will result in attorneys having to require written authorization from their clients in matters involving the sale of land, if for no other reason than self-protection.

SOUTER, J., joins in the dissent.

NOTES

(1) *Questions.* Compare the lease case described in Note 2, p. 306 above. If the lease had been designed as part of the settlement of a dispute between the developer and the prospective tenant, might the case have been decided differently? If the agent of a corporation that deals in real property should know of the requirements of the Statute of Frauds, should an attorney handling a real-estate matter also know of them?

(2) *Coda: Decay of the Ancestral Statute.* In 1954 Parliament repealed most of the 1677 Statute. In parts of the Commonwealth as well the Statute of Frauds has been severely restricted in scope. The parts generally retained are the suretyship clause and those concerning transfers of interests in land. (What special merits do these provisions have?) The Law Revision Committee of Great Britain concluded in 1937 that the conditions prevailing when the Statute was enacted "have long passed away." [a] Some of the former conditions mentioned had to do with modes of trial: parties in interest were not permitted to testify; jurors were permitted to determine facts on the basis of their personal knowledge; subornation and perjury were rife. Another was the political turmoil of the 17th century. Also, it was said, "contemporaries were, by modern standards,

a. Sixth Interim Report, Cmd. 5449, 1937, at 6, 7. See also Background Paper No. 12 (Statute of Frauds), Institute of Law Research and Reform, The University of Alberta (1979).

extremely litigious, so that opportunities to bring groundless suits were likely to be taken.... Litigation indeed came close to a form of sanctioned aggression...." [b] How notable do you think the change of circumstances has been, in relation to the United States?

---

b. A.W.B. Simpson, A History of the Common Law of Contract 599 (1975).

Chapter 4

POLICING THE BARGAIN

In some exchanges, the assent of a party is more apparent than real. That is evidently so when the offer takes the form, "Your money or your life." When a promise is exacted through lawless threat or through fraud, one would expect the courts not to enforce it. Naturally, many offenses committed in bargaining processes are somewhat less egregious than these. Bargaining abuses take many subtle forms in commercial societies, and the means of abating them are correspondingly varied, some curative, some prophylactic. We treat these means under the title, "policing the bargain."

One sort of policing measure attends chiefly to the *status* of the parties. In its strongest form, this method disqualifies certain classes of persons from committing themselves by contract: minors and married women are among the historic classes. (See Section 1.) Another attends chiefly to the *behavior* of the parties—how they bargained in fact. The treatment of fraud and duress illustrates this method. A third sort of policing measure attends to the *substance* of the bargain in question. As we have seen, exchanges of highly unequal advantage are commonly enforced. Yet the courts have found ways to discountenance them. This is the mainspring, more or less overt, of certain applications of the doctrine of consideration.

A great chancellor of the 18th century expressed concern for inequality "apparent from the intrinsic nature and subject of the bargain itself; such as no man in his senses ... would make." [a] For such a bargain Lord Hardwicke's opprobrium was "fraud"—a name for bad behavior. But his concern (only modestly veiled) was about substance. The policing of bargains by the courts still proceeds both in ancient forms, such as rescission for fraud, and in veiled forms, such as the strict construction of harsh terms. (Sections 2 and 3 depict the background of conventional controls over unequal bargains and misconduct in bargaining.) Yet in this century the rapid production of new means of policing (illustrated in Section 4) has somewhat eclipsed the old, and has perhaps reduced the dependence of courts on "covert tools" for attacking abuses.

One reading of the courts' performance in policing bargains is that they are moved by moral conviction, including a "rights theory" of contract.[b] Another, now strongly influenced by economic thought, is

a. Earl of Chesterfield v. Janssen, 28 Eng.Rep. 82, 100 (Chancery 1751).

b. "Contract theory either does not recognize, or characterizes as voidable, arrangements between parties who lack ade-

324

that they are deterred by certain social inutilities from investing in the enforcement of bargains that have special anomalies—such as mistaken premises. However that may be, no one now believes that the courts can go it alone. The discriminating powers of legislatures and administrative agencies have increasingly come to bear in setting the proper conditions for effective bargaining. Much of their effort is directed to consumer protection. In this matter it is a special challenge to disentangle concerns about behavior, about status, and about substance: the shifts of focus in the courts and elsewhere are sometimes obtrusive, sometimes not.

In a final section, the chapter deals with illegal bargains, which threaten interests of the public at large. Here again the direction is partly set by legislation and hard questions arise about coordinating the judicial and the legislative functions.

SECTION 1. CAPACITY

What classes of persons are considered by the law to have less than full power to contract? Since the materials in this section are confined to the two important classes of infants and insane persons, some words may here be in order concerning others.

As to intoxicated persons, a common standard of capacity is stated in Lucy v. Zehmer, p. 140 above: "Zehmer was not intoxicated to the extent of being unable to comprehend the nature or consequences of the instrument he executed." An older case puts the test this way: "To render a transaction voidable on account of the drunkenness of a party to it, the drunkenness must have been such as to have drowned reason, memory, and judgment, and to have impaired the mental faculties to such an extent as to render the party non compos mentis for the time being." Martin v. Harsh, 83 N.E. 164 (Ill.1907).[c]

The common-law incapacities of married women have also been alluded to. They were largely removed, in this country, by statutes during the nineteenth century—long before women were given the vote.

Another important class consists of corporations, on which limited powers are conferred by charter. The extent to which ultra vires acts of

----

quate bargaining power.... Contract obligations are enforceable as a matter of 'right,' and contract theory is based on the intention of parties who possess the freedom to agree or disagree." Boggs v. Blue Diamond Coal Co., 590 F.2d 655 (6th Cir. 1979).

c. As to a transaction effected by a drunkard in a sober interval, see Olsen v. Hawkins, 408 P.2d 462 (Idaho 1965) (change of insurance beneficiary).

In First State Bank of Sinai v. Hyland, 399 N.W.2d 894 (S.D.1987), the court overturned a trial court finding of incapacity by drunkenness, saying that the defendant had not been shown to have been "entirely without understanding."

a corporation—acts beyond its powers—may be effective is best left to a course in corporations.

MINORS' CONTRACTS

A minor is permitted to disaffirm a contract not only during minority but also within a reasonable time after reaching the age of majority. That age is generally 18, under legislation enacted relatively recently.[d] "[H]e who deals with a minor does so at his own peril and with the attendant risk that the minor may at his election disaffirm the transaction because of his minority." [e] The purpose is to protect the minor from "at least some of his childish foibles." [f] A characteristic transaction is one in which a youthful person purchases a car on credit. If the subject of the purchase is goods or services that are "necessaries," disaffirmance is not permitted. (In what circumstances should a vehicle be regarded as a necessary item?)

A period of time within which a person may disaffirm after reaching majority may be many months; but there is said to be "no hard and fast rule as to just what constitutes a 'reasonable' time within which the infant may disaffirm." Keser v. Chagnon, 410 P.2d 637 (Colo.1966).

Upon disaffirming a car-purchase contract, the buyer must restore the vehicle to the seller. Upon doing so, the buyer can get restitution of payments earlier made to the seller. The requirement of restoration serves to prevent unjust enrichment of the buyer. It does not, however, prevent loss to the seller. What kinds of loss can you envisage?

Standard-form contracts used by car dealers contain a statement above the buyer's signature that the buyer is not below the age of majority. This lays a predicate for an action by the seller for deceit, in the event of disaffirmance. When Chagnon bought a used Edsel from Keser he signed such a statement. When Chagnon returned the car and sued for payments he had made to Keser, Keser claimed and won an offset for damages. The trial court was directed, on remand, to determine the amount of the setoff by reference to the value of the car when it was returned.

NOTES

(1) *Should Appearances Count?* If Keser reasonably believed Chagnon when he lied about his age, why should Chagnon be allowed to rely upon his infancy? Does not this clash with the objective standard advanced in Lucy v. Zehmer, p. 140 above? Why was not Chagnon estopped to deny his representation of age? Can it be argued that every agreement a minor makes, otherwise effective as a contract, ought to be taken as implying a representation that he is competent to contract? Are there differences among infancy, mental incapacity and intoxication in this regard?

(2) *Voidable Not Void.* In many statutes and cases the promise of a person without capacity is said to be "void." As the discussion of disaffirmance in the

---

d. On the minimum ages for selected activities, see The Book of States 476 (1994–95 ed.).

e. Keser v. Chagnon, cited in the text below.

f. Id.

Keser case suggests, it is more accurate to regard it as "voidable." In Holt v. Ward Clarencieux, 2 Strange 937, 93 Eng.Rep. 954 (King's Bench 1732), the court sustained an action for a breach of promise of marriage brought on behalf of a young woman, who had been a girl of 15 at the time of the agreement. "[W]e are all of opinion that this contract is not void, but only voidable at the option of the infant.... And no dangerous consequences can follow from this determination, because our opinion protects the infant even more than if we rule the contract to be absolutely void."

Protect
minors

KIEFER v. FRED HOWE MOTORS, INC.
Supreme Court of Wisconsin, 1968.
39 Wis.2d 20, 158 N.W.2d 288.

[Steven Kiefer bought a five-year-old Willys station wagon from Fred Howe Motors when he was married, the father of a child, working, and a few months short of 21 years. The contract that he signed stated: "I represent that I am 21 years of age or over and recognize that the dealer sells the above vehicle upon this representation." He had difficulty with the car which he claimed had a cracked block, and after becoming of age, he sought to return it, and later sued to recover the price. From judgment for plaintiff, defendant appealed.]

WILKIE, J. ... The law governing agreements made during infancy reaches back over many centuries. The general rule is that " ... the contract of a minor, other than for necessaries, is either void or voidable at his option." The only other exceptions to the rule permitting disaffirmance are statutory or involve contracts which deal with duties imposed by law such as a contract of marriage or an agreement to support an illegitimate child. The general rule is not affected by the minor's status as emancipated or unemancipated.

Appellant does not advance any argument that would put this case within one of the exceptions to the general rule, but rather urges that this court, as a matter of public policy, adopt a rule that an emancipated minor over eighteen years of age be made legally responsible for his contracts.

The underpinnings of the general rule allowing the minor to disaffirm his contracts were undoubtedly the protection of the minor. It was thought that the minor was immature in both mind and experience and that, therefore, he should be protected from his own bad judgments as well as from adults who would take advantage of him. The doctrine of the voidability of minors' contracts often seems commendable and just. If the beans that the young naive Jack purchased from the crafty old man in the fairy tale "Jack and the Bean Stalk" had been worthless rather than magical, it would have been only fair to allow Jack to disaffirm the bargain and reclaim his cow. However, in today's modern and sophisticated society the "infancy doctrine" seems to lose some of its gloss.

Paradoxically, we declare the infant mature enough to shoulder arms in the military, but not mature enough to vote; mature enough to marry and be responsible for his torts and crimes, but not mature enough to assume the burden of his own contractual indiscretions. In Wisconsin, the infant is deemed mature enough to use a dangerous instrumentality—a motor vehicle—at sixteen, but not mature enough to purchase it without protection until he is twenty-one.

No one really questions that a line as to age must be drawn somewhere below which a legally defined minor must be able to disaffirm his contracts for nonnecessities. The law over the centuries has considered this age to be twenty-one. Legislatures in other states have lowered the age. We suggest that the appellant might better seek the change it proposes in the legislative halls rather than this court. A recent law review article in the Indiana Law Journal explores the problem of contractual disabilities of minors and points to three different legislative solutions leading to greater freedom to contract. The first approach is one gleaned from the statutes of California and New York, which would allow parties to submit a proposed contract to a court which would remove the infant's right of disaffirmance upon a finding that the particular contract is fair. This suggested approach appears to be extremely impractical in light of the expense and delay that would necessarily accompany the procedure. A second approach would be to establish a rebuttable presumption of incapacity to replace the strict rule. This alternative would be an open invitation to litigation. The third suggestion is a statutory procedure that would allow a minor to petition a court for the removal of disabilities. Under this procedure a minor would only have to go to court once, rather than once for each contract as in the first suggestion.

Undoubtedly, the infancy doctrine is an obstacle when a major purchase is involved. However, we believe that the reasons for allowing that obstacle to remain viable at this point outweigh those for casting it aside. Minors require some protection from the pitfalls of the market place. Reasonable minds will always differ on the extent of the protection that should be afforded. For this court to adopt a rule that the appellant suggests and remove the contractual disabilities from a minor simply because he becomes emancipated, which in most cases would be the result of marriage, would be to suggest that the married minor is somehow vested with more wisdom and maturity than his single counterpart. However, logic would not seem to dictate this result especially when today a youthful marriage is oftentimes indicative of a lack of wisdom and maturity.

[The court went on to rule that the dealer had not established deceit. The recital in the contract should have been supplemented by evidence of intent to defraud on the part of Kiefer, and of justifiable reliance on the part of the dealer.]

[Affirmed.]

HALLOWS, CHIEF JUSTICE (dissenting) . . . The magical age limit of 21 years as an indication of contractual maturity no longer has a basis in fact or in public policy. [Furthermore,] an automobile to this respondent was a necessity and therefore the contract could not be disaffirmed. . . . Automobiles for parents under 21 years of age to go to and from work in our current society may well be a necessity, and I think in this case the record shows it is. . . .

NOTES

(1) *Benefit or Burden.* Some of those whose capacity was limited under the common law, such as infants and married women, were described as "favorites" of the law. Is lack of capacity a benefit or a burden to the "favorite"? Would married women applaud revival of the old rules that made them "favorites"? Would they refuse to take advantage of analogous rules if they were made generally applicable to all "consumers"?

Lack of capacity can obviously be a serious burden to the person who is underage and who seeks to buy a substantial item, such as an automobile, on credit. For some items the burden is avoided by the exception that makes an infant liable for "necessaries." What sort of assurances might satisfy a prospective creditor where "necessaries" are not involved?

But lack of capacity was obviously a significant benefit to Kiefer when he became dissatisfied with the performance of his Willys station wagon. What would his situation have been if he had not had his infancy as an ace up his sleeve? It has been suggested that the refuge of nonage may no longer be needed, as laws are progressively developed to protect *all* the public from unscrupulous dealings.[a]

(2) *Department of Higher Education.* For a provision that youthful persons eligible for state-funded student loans are deemed to have full legal capacity, see N.Y.Ed.L. § 681. Can this be regarded as a boon to young people?

(3) *Problem.* An employer loaned money to a youthful employee for the purpose of paying tuition while training for greater responsibilities. The employee got the job through the services of an employment agency, for which he promised it a fee. He completed the course and attained majority at the same time, and promptly repudiated his undertakings both to the employer and the agency. Is he liable to either of them? See Gastonia Personnel Corp. v. Rogers, 172 S.E.2d 19 (N.C.1970).

ORTELERE v. TEACHERS' RETIREMENT BD.

New York Court of Appeals, 1969.
25 N.Y.2d 196, 250 N.E.2d 460.

[Grace Ortelere was a 60–year–old New York City schoolteacher, who had suffered a nervous breakdown diagnosed as involving "involutional psychosis, melancholia type," and was on leave for mental illness.

a. See Navin, The Contracts of Minors Viewed from the Perspective of Fair Exchange, 50 N.C.L.Rev. 517 (1972), and Note, 41 Ind.L.J. 140 (1965).

This note also invites speculation that the age of capacity should be increased because of the academic seclusion of modern young people and the growing complexity of commercial affairs. It is thought that early English law may have responded to technological advances by increasing the age of maturity from 15 to 21 when the introduction of chain mail armor made military service unduly burdensome for older boys.

Her psychiatrist also suspected that she suffered from cerebral arteriosclerosis. Her husband of 38 years had quit his job as an electrician to stay home and care for her. She had a reserve of $70,925 in the public retirement system in which she had participated for over 40 years. In 1965, without telling her husband she borrowed from the system the maximum possible, $8,760, and made an irrevocable election to take maximum retirement benefits of $450 a month during her lifetime. This revoked an earlier election under which she would have received only $375 a month but her husband would have taken the unexhausted reserve on her death, and it left him and their two grown children with no benefits in the event of her death. Two months later she died of cerebral arteriosclerosis. Her husband sued to set aside her 1965 election on the ground of mental incompetence. Her psychiatrist testified that she was incapable of making a decision of any kind and that victims of involutional melancholia "can't think rationally.... They will even tell you ... 'I don't know whether I should get up or whether I should stay in bed.' ... Everything is impossible to decide." From a judgment for the plaintiff, the defendant appealed to the Appellate Division, which reversed and dismissed the complaint. The plaintiff appealed.]

BREITEL, JUDGE.[a] ... Traditionally, in this State and elsewhere, contractual mental capacity has been measured by what is largely a cognitive test.... Under this standard the "inquiry" is whether the mind was "so affected as to render him wholly and absolutely incompetent to comprehend and understand the nature of the transaction".... A requirement that the party also be able to make a rational judgment concerning the particular transaction qualified the cognitive test.... Conversely, it is also well recognized that contractual ability would be affected by insane delusions intimately related to the particular transaction....

These traditional standards governing competency to contract were formulated when psychiatric knowledge was quite primitive. They fail to account for one who by reason of mental illness is unable to control his conduct even though his cognitive ability seems unimpaired. When these standards were evolving it was thought that all the mental faculties were simultaneously affected by mental illness.... This is no longer the prevailing view....

Of course the greatest movement in revamping legal notions of mental responsibility has occurred in the criminal law. The nineteenth century cognitive test embraced in the *M'Naghten* rules has long been criticized and changed by statute and decision in many jurisdictions (see *M'Naghten's Case,* 10 Clark & Fin. 200; 8 Eng.Rep. 718 [House of Lords, 1843]; Weihofen, Mental Disorder as a Criminal Defense [1954],

a. Charles D. Breitel (1908–1991) was appointed to the New York Supreme Court in 1950 after law practice in New York City and service with Thomas E. Dewey, first on his staff when Dewey was district attorney and later as his counsel when Dewey was governor. He was elevated to the Appellate Division in 1952 and to the Court of Appeals in 1967, serving as Chief Judge from 1974 to 1978. He also taught jurisprudence as an adjunct professor at Columbia.

pp. 65–68; British Royal Comm. on Capital Punishment [1953], ch. 4; A.L.I. Model Penal Code, § 4.01, supra; cf. Penal Law, § 30.05).

It is quite significant that Restatement, 2d, Contracts, states the modern rule on competency to contract.... Thus, the new Restatement section reads: "(1) A person incurs only voidable contractual duties by entering into a transaction if by reason of mental illness or defect ... (b) he is unable to act in a reasonable manner in relation to the transaction and the other party has reason to know of his condition." (Restatement, 2d, Contracts [T.D. No. 1, April 13, 1964], § 18C.) [renumbered 15]....[b]

The system was, or should have been, fully aware of Mrs. Ortelere's condition. They, or the Board of Education, knew of her leave of absence for medical reasons and the resort to staff psychiatrists by the Board of Education. Hence, the other of the conditions for avoidance is satisfied.

Lastly, there are no significant changes of position by the system other than those that flow from the barest actuarial consequences of benefit selection.

Nor should one ignore that in the relationship between retirement system and member, and especially in a public system, there is not involved a commercial, let alone an ordinary commercial, transaction. It is not a sound scheme which would permit 40 years of contribution and participation in the system to be nullified by a one-instant act committed by one known to be mentally ill. This is especially true if there would be no substantial harm to the system if the act were avoided. Of course, nothing less serious than medically classified psychosis should suffice or else few contracts would be invulnerable to some kind of psychological attack. As noted earlier, the trial court's finding and perhaps some of the testimony attempted to fit into the rubrics of the traditional rules. For that reason rather than reinstatement of the judgment at Trial Term there should be a new trial under the proper standards frankly considered and applied.

[Reversed (5–2).]

JASEN, JUDGE (dissenting). [The dissent set out the full text of a letter from Grace to the Retirement System prior to her election, in which she put eight questions typified by the following (No. 6): "If I take a loan of $5,000 before retiring and select option four-a on both the pension and annuity, what would my allowance be?"] It seems clear that this detailed, explicit and extremely pertinent list of queries reveals a mind fully in command of the salient features of the Teachers' Retirement System. Certainly, it cannot be said the decedent could possess sufficient capacity to compose a letter indicating such a comprehensive understanding of the retirement system, and yet lack the capacity to understand the answers.

b. The section was approved in Krasner v. Berk, 319 N.E.2d 897 (Mass.1974), in an opinion by Mr. Justice Braucher. As Professor Braucher he was the Reporter for this portion of the Restatement Second.

As I read the record, the evidence establishes that the decedent's election to receive maximum payments was predicated on the need for a higher income to support two retired persons—her husband and herself. Since the only source of income available to decedent and her husband was decedent's retirement pay, the additional payment of $75 per month which she would receive by electing the maximal payment was a necessity. . . .   Under these circumstances, an election of maximal income during decedent's lifetime was not only a rational, but a necessary decision. . . .   Moreover, there is nothing in the record to indicate that the decedent had any warning, premonition, knowledge or indication at the time of retirement that her life expectancy was, in any way, reduced by her condition.

The generally accepted test of mental competency to contract which has thus evolved . . . represents a balance struck between policies to protect the security of transactions between individuals and freedom of contract on the one hand, and protection of those mentally handicapped on the other hand.   In my opinion, this rule has proven workable in practice and fair in result. . . .   As in every situation where the law must draw a line between liability and nonliability, between responsibility and nonresponsibility, there will be borderline cases, and injustices may occur by deciding erroneously that an individual belongs on one side of the line or the other.   To minimize the chances of such injustices occurring, the line should be drawn as clearly as possible. . . .[c]

NOTES

(1) *Question.*   Can you envisage any adverse consequences for a pension plan offering a choice among various modes of benefit, if the choice made by a large number of participants proved to be revocable after death? See Kennedy v. New York City Employees Retirement System, 381 N.Y.S.2d 79, (App.Div.1976), aff'd, 362 N.E.2d 259 (N.Y.1977).

(2) *Scope of the Precedent.*   How expansible is the *Ortelere* decision? Might it apply to increase the income of a surviving spouse when the decedent has failed to make *any* choice among benefit plans—except to leave in place the "default" arrangement that the plan specifies in the absence of a participant's contrary selection? See Tomasino v. New York State Employees' Retirement System, 440 N.E.2d 1330 (N.Y.1982).

Soon after the *Ortelere* decision was announced the principle was naturally invoked in an ordinary business setting. In Fingerhut v. Kralyn Enterprises, 337 N.Y.S.2d 394 (Sup.Ct.1971), aff'd, 335 N.Y.S.2d 926 (App.Div.1972), the seller of a golf course met resistance from the buyer who, he claimed, had been in the manic phase of a psychosis when he agreed to pay $3 million for it.[d]

c. Under the Employee Retirement Income Security Act [ERISA], 29 U.S.C. §§ 1001 et seq., a person in Mrs. Ortelere's position could not now, except in some cases of exigency, elect a lifetime annuity and deprive her or his spouse of a survivor's annuity, without the spouse's written consent, given before a witness. (Consent is not required to reduce the survivor's annuity to half the amount payable while both live.) For details see §§ 1002(2) and 1055 [especially subsections (a), (c), (d), and (f).]

As it happens, however, since the particular plan providing for Mrs. Ortelere's pension was a "governmental" one, ERISA would not have applied to her. See § 1003(b)(1).

d. What degree of competence is required for a patient to consent to psychiatric treatment? For a view of *Ortelere* taken

Is the *Ortelere* rule limited to cases in which the employee has had psychiatric or similar consultation before making an election? How significant was it that "the system was, or should have been, fully aware of Mrs. Ortelere's condition"? Many employers fund their pension plans through professional insurers, who are not likely to know of an employee's psychosis. Should the knowledge of such an employer be attributed to the insurer? Why should it matter whether or not *either* was aware of the employee's condition? Does it matter under Restatement Second § 15? See Pentinen v. Retirement System, 401 N.Y.S.2d 587 (App.Div.1978).

(3) *Testamentary Capacity.* Farnum v. Silvano, 540 N.E.2d 202 (Mass.App. 1989), was an action for the rescission of the sale of a home, brought by the nephew and guardian of the seller. The purchaser, defendant, had paid about 56% of the fair market value of the home, it was found. At the same time, he obtained a mortgage loan on the property for more than the amount he paid. The seller, a woman of 90 years, sometimes exhibited distressing illusions (e.g., that her house had a second story). The purchaser was a young man who had kept up her lawn and who had her confidence. The nephew had "warned" him not to proceed with the purchase. The trial court, a probate judge, concluded that the seller had conveyed her home during a lucid interval and ruled for the defendant. On appeal, *held:* Reversed, and rescission ordered. The court cited *Ortelere,* and said: "Acting during a lucid interval can be the basis for executing a will.... Competence to enter into a contract presupposes something more than a transient surge of lucidity."

"The test of mental capacity [to make a will] is whether one possesses sufficient mental capacity to retain in the memory, without prompting, the extent and condition of one's property and to comprehend how one is disposing of it and to whom." Taylor v. Edoe, Inc., 574 S.W.2d 894 (Ark.1978). But more is required for making a contract. Is this because death is compulsory, whereas contracting is not? What other reason can you think of?

(4) *A Criminal Case.* Attorney (A) contracts to represent client (C) in a prosecution of C for embezzlement. A's fee is fixed by a note that C gives A, secured by a mortgage on C's home. A attempts to establish that C is not guilty by reason of insanity. C is convicted and appeals. Should the conviction be reversed on the ground that A and C had a "conflict of interest"? See People v. Kinion, 435 N.E.2d 533 (Ill.App.1982), cert. denied, 460 U.S. 1014 (1983).

CUNDICK v. BROADBENT

United States Court of Appeals, Tenth Circuit, 1967.
383 F.2d 157.

[Darwin Cundick was a 59–year–old sheep rancher who had sometimes sold his lamb crop to J.R. Broadbent. At a meeting between the two men in September, 1963, they signed a one-page contract in longhand by which Cundick agreed to sell all of his ranching properties to Broadbent. Mr. and Mrs. Cundick then took the contract to their lawyer, who refined and amplified it into an eleven-page document,

by a psychiatrist, see Alexander & Szasz, Santa Clara L.Rev. 537 (1973). From Contract to Status Via Psychiatry, 13

which the parties signed in his office. In October, 1963, the agreement was amended, again with a lawyer's aid, so as to increase the price to Cundick and in another respect favorable to him. Under the amended agreement, more than 2,000 acres of range land went for about $40,000. (An expert later valued it at $89,000.) Also included was Cundick's interest in a development company of which Broadbent was a director, at a price of $46,750. (A witness for Cundick later valued this at $184,000, and one for Broadbent at $73,743.) As late as February, 1964, he was executing documents to carry out the sale. In March, 1964, when the price had been paid and the sale was almost completed, Cundick sought to rescind. His wife, who had been appointed his guardian ad litem, for the purpose of suing, brought an action against Broadbent to set aside the agreement. She asserted that her husband had been mentally incompetent to contract, and that in any event he was mentally infirm and that Broadbent had knowingly overreached him. The evidence showed that Cundick had psychiatric treatment in 1961. Thereafter his family doctor saw him many times about various ailments, but nothing was said or done about a mental condition until suit was commenced. The court ordered examinations in 1964, which disclosed premature arteriosclerosis. Two neurosurgeons and a psychologist testified that he had been incapable, the previous September, of transacting important business affairs, that he was a "confused and befuddled man with very poor judgment." There was no medical evidence to the contrary. The trial court nevertheless found: "The acts and conduct of Cundick between September 2, 1963, and the middle of February, 1964, were the acts, conduct and behavior of a person competent to manage his affairs and cognizant of the effect of his actions." It also found that the contract was not unconscionable, unfair or inequitable. From a dismissal of the action, the plaintiff appealed.]

MURRAH, CHIEF JUDGE.... At one time, in this country and in England, it was the law that since a lunatic or non compos mentis had no mind with which to make an agreement, his contract was wholly void and incapable of ratification. But, if his mind was merely confused or weak so that he knew what he was doing yet was incapable of fully understanding the terms and effect of his agreement, he could indeed contract, but such contract would be voidable at his option.... But in recent times courts have tended away from the concept of absolutely void contracts toward the notion that even though a contract be said to be void for lack of capacity to make it, it is nevertheless ratifiable at the instance of the incompetent party. The modern rule, and the weight of authority, seems to be [that] "... the contractual act by one claiming to be mentally deficient, but not under guardianship, absent fraud, or knowledge of such asserted incapacity by the other contracting party, is not a void act but at most only voidable at the instance of the deficient party; and then only in accordance with certain equitable principles." Rubenstein v. Dr. Pepper Co., 8 Cir., 228 F.2d 528....

In recognition of different degrees of mental competency the weight of authority seems to hold that mental capacity to contract depends upon whether the allegedly disabled person possessed sufficient reason to enable him to understand the nature and effect of the act in issue. Even average intelligence is not essential to a valid bargain.... "Mere weakness of body or mind, or of both, do not constitute what the law regards as mental incompetency sufficient to render a contract voidable.... A condition which may be described by a physician as senile dementia may not be insanity in a legal sense." Kaleb v. Modern Woodmen of America, 51 Wyo. 116, 64 P.2d 605, 607. Weakmindedness is, however, highly relevant in determining whether the deficient party was overreached and defrauded....

There was, to be sure, evidence of a change in his personality and attitude toward his business affairs during [the period between his mental examinations in 1961 and 1964]. But the record is conspicuously silent concerning any discussion of his mental condition among his family and friends in the community where he lived and operated his ranch. Certainly, the record is barren of any discussion or comment in Broadbent's presence. It seems incredible that Cundick could have been utterly incapable of transacting his business affairs, yet such condition be unknown on this record to his family and friends, especially his wife who lived and worked with him and participated in the months-long transaction which she now contends was fraudulently conceived and perpetrated....

The narrated facts of this case amply support the trial court's finding to the effect that Broadbent did not deceive or overreach Cundick.... [Although] there is positive evidence that the property was worth very much more than what Broadbent paid for it, ... there was evidence to the effect that after the original contract was signed and some complaint made about the purchase price, the parties agreed to raise the price and the contract was so modified.

[Affirmed.]

HILL, CIRCUIT JUDGE (dissenting): .... The evidence relied upon by the majority is actually trivial and inconsequential as compared with the undisputed medical testimony.... It is inconceivable to me that any mentally competent person, with a lifetime of experience as a successful rancher and stockman, would dispose of his ranch interests at a price equal to less than one-half of the actual value....[a]

NOTES

(1) *Orientation.* Are the *Ortelere* and *Cundick* cases distinguishable? At p. 324 above mention was made of status, behavior and substance orientation. To what extent do the differences among the majority and dissenting opinions in those cases reflect different orientations? For a discussion of mental illness and contracts, see Note 57 Mich.L.Rev. 1020 (1959).

(2) *Supervision.* Guardians and conservators may be appointed for persons of mental debility, as authorized by statutes. In California there is a procedure for the judicial appointment of conservators for persons who, for specified

a. Compare Bliss v. Rhodes, 384 N.E.2d 512 (Ill.App.1978), concerning a comparable contract, in which the evidence was that the seller's life was disordered before and after the sale, that he was then depressed and sometimes intoxicated, and that the fair market value of his farm was greater than the contract price.

reasons, are "likely to be deceived or imposed upon by artful or designing persons." See Board of Regents of State University, State of Wisconsin v. Davis, 533 P.2d 1047 (Cal.1975). What virtues and hazards do you see in the process?

(3) *Of Minors Again.* Professor Navin has noted some elements that figure in rulings about mental competence to contract—the degree of impairment, the claimant's means of knowing of it, and the fairness of the exchange—and has compared them favorably with the less flexible rules about minors' contracts. (Some undertakings by "older minors," he believes, should be enforced.) Should the rules about minors' contracts be made more amenable to assessments of individual circumstances? Or are they adaptable enough by reason of looseness in the notions of "necessaries" and "ratification"? See Navin, The Contracts of Minors Viewed from the Perspective of Fair Exchange, 50 N.C.L.Rev. 517 (1972).

SECTION 2. UNFAIRNESS: CONVENTIONAL CONTROLS

In this section we turn attention to inequality of exchange, as manifested in the terms of a bargain. Is it the proper business of a court to calculate the advantages of a contract for each party, and see to it that neither of them suffers a disproportionate loss or enjoys a disproportionate gain? Put in that form the question has an obvious answer, supported by a powerful tradition. "Parties of sufficient mental capacity for the management of their own business," it is said, "have the right to make their own bargains." [a] We have seen that the core idea of consideration is the fact of a bargain, and the law on that subject contains an implicit judgment that a promise should be enforced whether or not something of equal value was given for it. "If the requirement of a consideration is met, there is no additional requirement of ... equivalence in the values exchanged." [b] As the materials to follow will show, that judgment is supported by substantial reasons of policy.

Nevertheless, a number of limiting principles serve to prevent the routine enforcement of unequal bargains. Some of them have long been fixed in the law. They are the subject of this section. The less traditional means that courts have developed in recent years to police against unfairness in the substance of an exchange are explored in Section 4, below.

The function of policing has always been something of a specialty of equity courts. Relying on the element of discretion, or grace, associated with granting specific performance, they have refused that remedy in cases where the exchange appeared highly disproportionate. In cases "at law," by contrast, the means of policing have had to be either more direct, or more devious, depending on the circumstances. A direct measure is to pronounce a public policy by which a particularly overbearing provision of a contract may be disregarded. That course is excep-

---

a. Hardesty v. Smith, 3 Ind. 39 (1851).   **b.** Restatement Second § 79(b).

tional. More commonly, the courts have manipulated the doctrine of consideration to serve the ideal of fairness. It will be seen in this section that that ideal plays a part in determining whether or not any "bargain" at all has been effected.

NOTE

Good Faith. According to the Restatement Second, "Every contract imposes upon each party a duty of good faith and fair dealing in its performance and its enforcement." Section 205. This "rule" has no predecessor in the original Restatement; but see UCC 1–203. According to a comment, neither § 205 nor the Code provision deals with good faith in the *formation* of a contract.

Is it useful to draw a sharp distinction between the formation and performance stages of contracting? Why is there no recognition of a generalized duty of good faith in negotiation in the Code or the Restatement? In going through the chapter, you should consider how many of the problems could helpfully be approached in terms of such a duty. See fn. 3, p. 276 above.

McKINNON v. BENEDICT

Supreme Court of Wisconsin, 1968.
38 Wis.2d 607, 157 N.W.2d 665.

[In 1960 Roderick McKinnon, the owner of a home on Mamie Lake, Wisconsin, amid more than a thousand acres, gave help to Mr. and Mrs. Roy Benedict in buying a resort known as Bent's Camp. It consisted of a lodge and some cabins on about 80 acres that were enclosed by the lake and McKinnon's property. McKinnon promised some help in getting business and in other minor respects, but his principal contribution was in making a loan of $5,000. The Benedicts used the advance as part of a down payment on a land purchase contract with the previous owners of the camp. The Benedicts promised McKinnon to cut no trees between the camp and his property, and to make no improvements "closer to [his] property than the present buildings." The term of these restrictions was 25 years. They did not affect all the resort tract, but did affect all the most desireable portion.

The resort business did not prosper, after the Benedicts bought it, although they repaid the loan in about seven months. In 1964 they decided to add a trailer park and tent camp. In the fall and following spring they invested some $9,000 in bulldozing and installing utilities. The summer of 1965 brought McKinnon from Arizona, where he spent the winters, and brought also a suit against the Benedicts. The trial court enjoined them from continuing with their projected improvements, and they appealed.]

HEFFERNAN, JUSTICE. . . . No action at law has been commenced for damages by virtue of the breach of the restrictions; and, in fact, the plaintiffs in their complaint claim that they have no adequate remedy at law. [The court expounded some "ancient principles of equity," and quoted the Restatement of Contracts § 367.[a]]

Coupled with the general equitable principle that contracts that are oppressive will not be enforced in equity is the principle of public policy that restrictions on the use of land "are not favored in the law" (Mueller v. Schier (1926), 189 Wis. 70, 82, 205 N.W. 912, 916), and that restrictions and prohibitions as to the use of real estate should be resolved, if a doubt exists, in favor of the free use of the property. Stein v. Endres Home Builders, Inc. (1938) 228 Wis. 620, 629, 280 N.W. 316....

The great hardship sought to be imposed upon the Benedicts is apparent. What was the consideration in exchange for this deprivation of use? The only monetary consideration was the granting of a $5,000 loan, interest free, for a period of seven months. The value of this money for that period of time, if taken at the same interest rate as the 5 percent used on the balance of the land contract, is approximately $145; and it should be noted that this was not an unsecured loan, since McKinnon took a mortgage on the cottage property of the Benedicts in Michigan. In addition, McKinnon stated that he would "help you try" to reach a solution of the problem posed by Mrs. Vair's occupancy of one of the cottages on a fifty-year lease at $5 per year. His one attempt, as stated above, was a failure; and McKinnon's promise to generate business resulted in an occupancy by only one group for less than a week. For this pittance and these feeble attempts to help with the operational problems of the camp, the Benedicts have sacrificed their right to make lawful and reasonable use of their property.

In oral argument it was pointed out that the value of the $5,000 loan could not be measured in terms of the interest value of the money, since, without this advance, Benedict would have been unable to purchase the camp at all. To our mind, this is evidence of the fact that Benedict was not able to deal at arm's length with McKinnon, for his need for these funds was obviously so great that he was willing to enter into a contract that results in gross inequities. Lord Chancellor Northington said "necessitous men are not, truly speaking, free men." Vernon v. Bethell (1762), 2 Eden 110, 113.

We find that the inadequacy of consideration is so gross as to be unconscionable and a bar to the plaintiffs' invocation of the extraordinary equitable powers of the court.

While there is no doubt that there are benefits from this agreement to McKinnon, they are more than outweighed by the oppressive terms that would be imposed upon the Benedicts. McKinnon testified that he and his wife spend only the summer months on their property. Undoubtedly, these are the months when it is most important that there be no disruption of the natural beauty or the quiet and pleasant enjoyment

---

a. Specific enforcement of a contract may be refused if

  (a) The consideration for it is grossly inadequate or its terms are otherwise unfair, or

  (b) its enforcement will cause unreasonable or disproportionate hardship or loss to the defendant or to third persons, or

  (c) it was induced by some sharp practice, misrepresentation, or mistake.

of the property, nevertheless, there was testimony that the trailer camp could not be seen from the McKinnon home, nor could the campsite be seen during the summer months of the year, when the leaves were on the trees. Thus, the detriment of which the McKinnons complain, that would be cognizable in an equity action, is minimal,[1] while the damage done to the Benedicts is severe.

Considering all the factors—the inadequacy of the consideration, the small benefit that would be accorded the McKinnons, and the oppressive conditions imposed upon the Benedicts—we conclude that this contract failed to meet the test of reasonableness that is the *sine qua non* of the enforcement of rights in an action in equity.

5A Corbin, Contracts, sec. 1164, p. 219, points out that, although a contract is harsh, oppressive, and unconscionable, it may nevertheless be enforceable at law; but, in the discretion of the court, equitable remedies will not be enforced against one who suffers from such harshness and oppression.

A fair reading of the transcript indicates no sharp practice, dishonesty, or overreaching on the part of McKinnon. However, there was a wide disparity between the business experience of the parties. McKinnon was a man of stature in the legal field, an investment counsellor, a former officer of a major corporation, and had held posts of responsibility with the United States government, while, insofar as the record shows, Benedict was a retail jeweler and a man of limited financial ability. He no doubt overvalued the promises of McKinnon to assist in getting the operation "well organized" and to solve the lease problem and to "generate business." These factors, in view of Benedict's financial inability to enter into an arms-length transaction, may be explanatory of the reason for the agreement, but the agreement viewed even as of the time of its execution was unfair and based upon inadequate consideration. We, therefore, have no hesitancy in denying the plaintiffs the equitable remedy of injunction. . . .

[Reversed.[b]]

NOTES

(1) *Questions.* Has it been decided that the Benedicts may bulldoze on their property and make improvements wherever they please? If the Benedicts had begun their new business immediately after making the agreement of 1960, would the court have given McKinnon the relief then that he is now denied?

(2) *Specific Performance and Damages.* In a sense it is extraordinary for a contract claimant to be entitled to specific performance, in English and American law. See pp. 25–41 above.

1. McKinnon testified that the value of his property had depreciated in the amount of $50,000. That testimony was properly admissible, but its probative value was slight, especially since plaintiff's expert real estate witness stated that he was unable to testify to the amount of the depreciated value.

b. Except insofar as the trial court had given relief on a separate cause of action for trespass.

By tradition, a decree of specific performance is not a matter of right in the same sense as damages are, but may be withheld in the court's discretion. Specific performance is often denied because the bargain was procured by sharp practice or was affected by a mistake. If the remedy seems oppressive simply because the exchange is grossly unequal, the result may be the same; but the issue has been debated.[c]

In denying specific performance to a claimant, the courts sometimes take comfort in the thought, as many opinions show, that the decision does not deprive the claimant of all remedy, but only remits it to the more perfunctory one of damages. But that may be an empty justification in a case like McKinnon v. Benedict. Perhaps there was no effective remedy available to the McKinnons other than specific performance: notice their allegation that they had no adequate remedy at law. What reasons can be given for accepting this assertion? (Remedies for breach of contract are dealt with in more detail in the following chapter.) The thought that courts of law are less sensitive than courts of equity to issues of fairness is repulsive to some. It has been described as a "moral curtain that, heavy with the mold of centuries, still hangs across our law." Newman, The Rennaissance of Good Faith in Contracting in Anglo–American Law, 54 Cornell L.Rev. 553, 554 (1969). This writer observes that the dual standard may have ceased to exist in practice, though it continues to be repeated. Only two cases have been found, it seems, in which specific performance was denied and damages awarded (and in one of these the judgment was set aside for an error in calculating it).[d]

One way to eliminate the "dual standard" would be for equity courts to rescind or cancel contracts for unfairness, using the same standards as they apply in specific performance cases. In McKinnon v. Benedict, if the Benedicts had sought to have the restrictions on their use of the property cancelled, does it appear that they would have been successful? The power to cancel has not been freely exercised. This fact may mean that damage claims are more readily available to parties who fail to get specific performance than the reported cases happen to show. "One suspects that the Chancellors thought there was a real remedy at law, and that the litigants did too; else the actions for cancellation and the judges' agonizing over them make little sense."[e]

(3) *Problem.* Refer to Note 2, p. 121 above. Should Gerald's claim against Nancy for specific performance have been denied? According to the opinion: "Courts have neither the authority nor competence to rectify all perceived injustices or right all asserted wrongs."

(4) *Certainty.* In going through the cases in this chapter, you should consider whether or not certainty in commercial affairs has been overvalued or undervalued. "There does come a point where the additional costs of having

c. As to inadequacy of price, Lord Eldon said that unless it is "such as shocks the conscience, and amounts in itself to conclusive and decisive evidence of fraud in the transaction it is not in itself a sufficient ground for refusing a specific performance." Coles v. Trecothick, 32 Eng.Rep. 592 (1804). But this is a proposition on which very great men have differed, it has

been said. Savage, C.J., dissenting, in Seymour v. Delancey, 3 Cowen 445 (N.Y.1824).

d. See also Frank and Endicott, Defenses in Equity and "Legal Rights," 14 La. L.Rev. 380 (1954).

e. Leff, Unconscionability and the Code—The Emperor's New Clause, 115 U.Pa.L.Rev. 485, 541 n. 237 (1967).

personalized transactions may be too great; a little injustice may be a social good." [f]

TUCKWILLER v. TUCKWILLER [g]
Supreme Court of Missouri, 1967.
413 S.W.2d 274.

[John and Ruby Tuckwiller lived on the Hudson family farm in Missouri, and John farmed it as a renter. Almost half of the property— 160 acres—was owned by Mrs. Metta Hudson Morrison, John's aunt. When she was about 70 years of age, Mrs. Morrison contracted Parkinson's disease, and at about the same time she gave up her residence in New York. She had been educated at Columbia and other schools, had been a teacher for many years, and had held other jobs. After leaving New York she travelled extensively, but early in 1963 she returned to the Hudson farm, where some rooms were reserved for her use. In April she was hospitalized for about a week, as a result of dizziness and falling. She was thought then to have had a "stroke," and showed some mental confusion. But at the first of May her doctor and a friend found her mentally clear—"clear as a bell." She knew, the doctor said, that Parkinsonism is a progressive disease, leaving the victim ultimately dependent entirely on outside care.

[Before the April incident, Mrs. Tuckwiller had been urged by Mrs. Morrison to quit a job she held and care for her for the rest of her life, and the subject was discussed again after Mrs. Morrison's release from the hospital. The two were quite congenial. On May 3, a Saturday, when she was with the Tuckwillers, Mrs. Morrison signed the following paper, written by Mrs. Tuckwiller:

My offer to Aunt Metta is as follows

I will take care of her for her lifetime; by that I mean provide her 3 meals per day—a good bed—do any possible act of nursing and provide her every pleasure possible.

In exchange she will will me her (Corum) farm at her death keeping all money made from it during her life. She will maintain expense of her medicine.

On May 6 Mrs. Tuckwiller resigned her job, and Mrs. Morrison made an appointment with a lawyer to change her will. Later that day, however, she fainted and fell. She was taken to the hospital, where, except for four days, she remained until her death on June 14. She was 73 at that time. Mrs. Tuckwiller spent much time at the hospital during Mrs. Morrison's final illness, assisting as she could, but Mrs. Morrison was attended by special nurses.

[Before leaving for the hospital on May 6, Mrs. Morrison had the date put on the paper set out above, and obtained the signatures of the

---

f. Leff, Injury, Ignorance and Spite— The Dynamics of Coercive Collection, 80 Yale L.J. 1, 42 (1970).

g. Marion Tuckwiller, Executor of the Estate of Flora Metta Morrison.

two ambulance attendants as witnesses. Her will, dated in 1961, was never changed. It provided for the sale of the farm, the proceeds to be used for a student loan fund at Davidson College. The farm had an "inventory value" of $34,400.

[Mrs. Tuckwiller brought a bill for specific performance of the contract, which was resisted by the College and Mrs. Morrison's executor. The trial court granted the relief, and the defendants appealed.]

WELBORN, COMMISSIONER.... [I]n determining whether or not a contract is so unfair or inequitable or is unconscionable so as to deny its specific performance, the transaction must be viewed prospectively, not retrospectively. The same rule applies with respect to sufficiency of consideration.... Viewed in this light, we find that plaintiff gave up her employment with which she was well satisfied and undertook what was at the time of the contract an obligation of unknown and uncertain duration, involving duties which, in the usual course of the disease from which Mrs. Morrison suffered, would have become increasingly onerous.... Viewed from the standpoint of Mrs. Morrison, the contract cannot be considered unfair. She was appreciative of the care and attention which plaintiff had given her prior to the agreement. Although, as defendants suggest, such prior services cannot provide the consideration essential to a binding contract, such prior services and the past relation of the parties may properly be considered in connection with the fairness of the contract and adequacy of the consideration. 5A Corbin on Contracts, § 1165, p. 227. Aware of her future outlook and having no immediate family to care for her, Mrs. Morrison was understandably appreciative of the personal care and attention of plaintiff and concerned with the possibility of routine impersonal care over a long period of time in a nursing home or similar institution. Having no immediate family which might be the object of her bounty, she undoubtedly felt more free to agree to dispose of the farm without insisting upon an exact quid pro quo. Her insistence that the contract be witnessed prior to her hospitalization is clear evidence of her satisfaction with the bargain as was her unsuccessful effort to change her will to carry out her agreement....

Properly viewed from the standpoint of the parties at the time of the agreement, we find that the contract was fair, not unconscionable, and supported by an adequate consideration. Although not conceding that such conclusion is correct, defendants argue, in effect, that in view of the obviously brief duration of plaintiff's services and their value in comparison with the value of the farm, plaintiff should be obliged to accept the offered payment of the reasonable value of her services and denied the relief of specific performance. Defendants point out that the trial court found that valuing the services which plaintiff rendered might be "possible." That conclusion is undoubtedly correct and unquestionably the monetary value of plaintiff's services would have been a quite small proportion (perhaps one percent) of the value of the farm. Once, however, the essential fairness of the contract and the adequacy of the consideration are found, the fact that the subject of the contract is real estate answers any question of adequacy of the legal remedy of monetary damages. "Whenever a contract concerning real property is in its nature and incidents entirely unobjectionable—that is, when it possesses none of those features which . . . appeal to the discretion of the court—it is as much a matter of course for a court of equity to decree a specific performance of it, as it is for a court of law to give damages for the breach of it." Pomeroy's Specific Performance of Contracts (3d ed.), § 10, p. 23.[a]

[Affirmed.]

NOTES

(1) *Question.* Part of the plaintiff's evidence was that the life expectancy of a 73–year–old person is about nine years. Do you see any reason to discount this evidence?

(2) *Professional Services.* In Gladding v. Langrall, Muir & Noppinger, 401 A.2d 662 (Md.1979),[b] the court rejected a claim of "unconscionability" in reliance on the principle that a bargain is to be evaluated by reference to the situation existing at the time it was struck. Is this principle of special importance to lawyers who spend many "billable hours" on claims of questionable value?[c] To lawyers who contract for contingent fees?

Would you expect the principle to be equally reliable for an attorney and for an accountant, working for a contingent fee? In *Gladding* the court spoke of "the broader judicial interest in attorney-client contracts, which exist only because of the attorney's status as an officer of the court." The claimant was an accounting firm. It recovered a fee of more than $30,000 (in addition to a retainer of $10,000) for seventeen hours of professional services.[d]

(3) *Equitable Discretion.* "Within the ambit of those factors of contract-producing behavior which would result in a denial of specific performance, a bewildering number of permutations work to inform the chancellor's discretion. In these cases one runs continually into the old, the young, the ignorant, the necessitous, the illiterate, the improvident, the drunken, the naive and the sick, all on one side of the transaction, with the sharp and hard on the other. Language of quasi-fraud and quasi-duress abounds. Certain whole classes of presumptive sillies like sailors[e] and heirs and farmers and women continually wander on and off stage. Those not certifiably crazy, but nonetheless pretty peculiar, are often to be found. And in most of the cases, of course, several of these factors appear in combination. . . . Almost without exception, actions for specific performance were (and are) brought with respect to transactions involving real property." Leff, Unconscionability and the Code—the Emperor's New Clause, 115 U.Pa.L.Rev. 485, 531–34 (1967).

---

a. The court rejected the defendants' "hint that the contract was unfair because of evidence of mental confusion of Mrs. Morrison at her hospitalization in April and again on May 6." At the time of agreement, it said, it appeared from the evidence that she was "mentally alert and fully aware of what she was doing."

b. Citing Mortgage Investors v. Citizens Bank & Trust Co., 366 A.2d 47, 50–52 (Md. 1976), for a discussion of the role of the court in regulating attorneys and their fees.

c. See Cetenko v. United California Bank, 638 P.2d 1299, 34 A.L.R.4th 657 (Cal.

1982). Compare Brobeck, Phleger & Harrison v. Telex Corp., 602 F.2d 866 (9th Cir. 1979), in which a law firm recovered a million dollars for filing a petition for certiorari.

d. The fee was a percentage of tax savings effected for the firm's clients through a settlement with the Internal Revenue Service.

e. As to safeguards for seamen, see Davis v. American Commercial Lines, Inc., 823 F.2d 1006 (6th Cir.1987).

(4) *Problem*. George A. Shea contracted to sell twenty acres of land, worth $24,000, and a badly used Cadillac, to Dr. Joseph Hodge for $4,000 and a "new $6600 Coupe DeVille Cadillac." Shea was a man of means, but badly in need of cash to pay taxes. After accepting the car, he refused to convey. On these facts alone, should specific performance be granted at the instance of the doctor? Which of the following circumstances, if any, should tip the scales against the plaintiff? (a) Shea was 75 years old at the time. (b) He was fatuously fond of new Cadillacs. (c) He was an inebriate of long standing, and afflicted with grievous chronic illnesses. (d) He had been the plaintiff's patient for many years. See Hodge v. Shea, 168 S.E.2d 82 (S.C.1969).

BLACK INDUSTRIES, INC. v. BUSH

United States District Court, D. New Jersey, 1953.
110 F.Supp. 801.

FORMAN, CHIEF JUDGE. The plaintiff, Black Industries, Inc., a citizen of Ohio, is suing the defendant, George F. Bush, a citizen of New Jersey doing business as G.F. Bush Associates, for breach of a contract. The defendant has moved for a summary judgment in its favor.

The complaint alleges as a first cause of action that the plaintiff, a manufacturer of drills, machine parts and components thereof and a purchaser of subcontract work from other suppliers, obtained an invitation to bid upon certain contracts with The Hoover Company upon three parts known as anvils, holder primers and plunger supports. The plaintiff assumed the task of obtaining a supplier of these parts and on about March 22, 1951, the defendant reached an agreement with the plaintiff to manufacture 1,300,000 anvils at a price of $4.40 per thousand; 750,000 holder primers at $11.50 per thousand and 700,000 plunger supports at a price of $12 per thousand, all of which were to be made in accordance with government specifications and in conformity with certain drawings. The plaintiff agreed to "service the contract", be responsible for all dealings with The Hoover Company and would be entitled to the difference between the defendant's quotations and the ultimate price. The Hoover Company agreed to purchase the parts from the plaintiff at a rate of $8.10 per thousand anvils, $16 per thousand holder primers and $21.20 per thousand plunger supports.

The complaint further alleges that after undertaking performance of this contract, the defendant failed to complete the order, which caused a loss of $14,625 to the plaintiff, for which sum, together with interest, the plaintiff demands judgment.

[As a second cause of action the plaintiff alleges "understandings" between these parties whereby the defendant agreed to manufacture other quantities of plunger supports and anvils, for which plaintiff made a re-sale contract with Standby Products Company; and that defendant's failure to comply with this undertaking caused plaintiff a loss of $4,460.95, for which plaintiff seeks judgment. To each cause of action defendant pleads various defenses not here relevant, and then alleges that the contract set forth in the complaint is void as against public

A → Void b/c of Public Policy

policy. The defendant, on this last ground, now moves for summary judgment.

[The contract alleged in the first count was evidenced by a letter of April 13, 1951, from plaintiff's Gepfert to defendant Bush, and signed as "agreed to" by the latter. In this letter Gepfert stated that he had "spent considerable time, effort and money in developing the contract" to the point where The Hoover Company issued a purchase order. The letter continued as follows: "The purchase order, when received, will run directly to George F. Bush and Associates ... Your company is to ship the material directly to The Hoover Co. ... Your company, however, is not to bill The Hoover Co. All shipping invoices, documents of transfer and title are to be forwarded to me, and I shall have the exclusive right to bill, upon (your) billing forms and receive payment therefor in your behalf ... It is understood that I shall have the right to receive payment, cash checks made payable to your company under The Hoover Co. contract; and to remit to you (retaining sums) as compensation due me." The compensation stipulated by Gepfert "for my services" was to be the difference between Bush's price to Black and Black's price to Hoover. The products to be purchased both by Hoover and by Standby Products were to be used by them to fulfill United States government contracts in aid of "the defense effort," i.e., the Korean War of 1950–53. Defendant then alleges that plaintiff was to receive a "profit" of 84.09% on anvils, 39.13% on holder primers and 68.33% on plunger supports under the Hoover contract, and similar percentages under the Standby contract. Defendant further alleges that these contracts are void as against public policy because these "profits" of Black were passed on to the government and the public in the form of increased prices; and cites two Federal laws intended to prevent excessive profits on war contracts: Renegotiation Act, 50 U.S.C.A. Appendix, § 1211, and 41 U.S.C.A. § 51.]

In order to declare a contract, entered by the parties freely and without evidence of fraud, void as against public policy, the contract must be invalid on the basis of recognized legal principles. [In an omitted passage, the court quotes from Muschany v. United States, 324 U.S. 49, 66–67 (1945), as follows: "It is a matter of public importance that good faith contracts of the United States should not be lightly invalidated." Then it discusses three types of illegal contracts, as indicated in the following paragraph.]

The contract in the present case, however, does not fall in any of these categories. It is not a contract by the defendant to pay the plaintiff for inducing a public official to act in a certain manner; it is not a contract to do an illegal act; and it is not a contract which contemplates collusive bidding on a public contract. It should be noted that the first and third categories of cases, upon which the defendant relies most heavily, involve agreements which directly impinge upon government activities. In the case at hand, the contract's only effect on the government was that ultimately the government was to buy the product of which defendant's goods were to be a component. Neither the defendant nor the plaintiff had any dealings with the United States on account of this contract, and therefore the profit accruing to the plaintiff was not to have been earned as a result of either inducing government action or interfering with the system of competitive bidding. This contract cannot, therefore, be declared void as against public policy on the basis of the precedents cited by the defendant.

It is quite possible that the plaintiff was to have received a very high profit on the sale of the parts, either because The Hoover Company agreed to pay too high a price or because the defendant quoted too low a price. Further proof would be required to establish this as a fact. Even if it were proved that the plaintiff was to have received a far greater profit than the defendants for a much smaller contribution, the defendant would nevertheless be bound by his agreement by the familiar rule that relative values of the consideration in a contract between business men dealing at arm's length without fraud will not affect the validity of the contract. The Coast National Bank v. Bloom, 113 N.J.L. 597, 174 A. 576, 95 A.L.R. 528 (E. & A. 1934); Restatement of the Law of Contracts § 81 (1932).

Argument The fact that the government is the ultimate purchaser of the product in which defendant's parts are used is cited by the defendant as a reason to hold that this contract is void as against public policy. To so hold would necessitate either ruling that all contracts are void if they provide for compensation for middlemen, such as Black Industries, between producer and purchaser of goods which ultimately are incorporated in products sold to the government, a result which is not supported by precedent and which would defy the realities of our economic life, or deciding in every case involving such a contract whether the compensation paid a middleman such as the plaintiff here who locates purchasers and assists the producer in other ways, is reasonable. This latter course would, in effect, impose price regulatory functions on the court. There are other and more effective methods of insuring that the government does not pay an unreasonable price for its supplies. The manufacturer selling directly to the United States must conform to procedures such as bidding designed to protect the government, and which should, in conjunction with the ordinary considerations of profits and loss, insure that prime contractors do not pay outlandish prices for the products they buy in order to fulfill a government contract. The contract may be subject to renegotiation. 50 U.S.C.A. Appendix, § 1211 et seq. I do not believe that it is the function of the court to interfere by determining the validity of a contract between ordinary business men on the basis of its beliefs as to the adequacy of the consideration. Consequently, I hold that, assuming the facts to be as stated by the defendant, the contract sued on in this case is not void as against public policy and the defendant's motion for a summary judgment will, therefore, be denied.

Let an order be submitted in accordance with this opinion.

NOTES

(1) *"Adequacy" of Consideration.* The arguments against courts' inquiring into the "relative value of the consideration in a contract between business men dealing at arm's length without fraud" have been summarized as follows: "(1)

The efficient administration of the law of contracts requires that courts shall not be required to prescribe prices. (2) The test of enforceability should be certain and should not be beclouded by such vague terms as 'fair' or 'reasonable' as tests of validity. (3) There is still the somewhat old-fashioned theory that persons of maturity and sound mind should be free to contract imprudently as well as prudently." Patterson, An Apology for Consideration, 58 Colum.L.Rev. 929 (1958).

Does it appear that courts of equity, in specific performance actions, have undertaken price regulatory functions? Does the dispensing power exercised in McKinnon v. Benedict invite litigation in a large proportion of contracts about land? If so, it may tend to impair the value of such contracts as the Tuckwillers made with Mrs. Morrison, in Tuckwiller v. Tuckwiller. Should the courts be cautious, on that account, in attempting supervision over the values exchanged?

(2) *"Middlemen."* The court acknowledges the possibility that Black might have stood to receive a "far greater profit" than Bush "for a much smaller contribution." What is the nature of the "contribution" of a middleman such as Black?

He may perform an "informational" function, by bringing together buyers and sellers who would otherwise be ignorant of each other's needs. (See the following Note.) He may also perform a "risk-shifting" function, by taking on himself risks of market fluctuations that would otherwise have to be borne by buyers or sellers. Both of these functions are highly developed in well organized markets, such as commodities exchanges, where brokers clearly perform both an "informational" function by facilitating transactions between buyers and sellers and a "risk-shifting" function through stabilizing foreseeable market fluctuations. See Samuelson, Economics, Appendix to Chap. 22 (12th ed. 1985).

Does it appear that Black's "contribution" involved either an "informational" or a "risk-shifting" function? If it involved the former, did Black supply Hoover with enough information about available suppliers to merit the compensation he received? Why did not Hoover contact Bush directly? Why did not Bush contact Hoover directly? Would Bush have been able to charge Black more if he had known how much Hoover was paying Black?

We have already spent some time on an important type of middleman, the general contractor in the construction industry. At one extreme, the contractor may be little more than a broker between owner and subcontractors, maintaining only a small office with supervisory personnel and contracting out substantially all the work. It has been suggested that the evils of bid shopping can be avoided if the owner bypasses the general contractor and makes separate contracts directly with the subcontractors, leaving their supervision to an architect. Can you see any disadvantages to this? See Note, 39 N.Y.U.L.Rev. 816, 828–29 (1964).

(3) *An Economist's View.* George Stigler, an economist, has written of the phenomenon of "search," by which, in a market economy, buyers (or sellers) canvass various sellers (or buyers). If the dispersion of prices quoted "is at all large (relative to the cost of search), it will pay, on average, to canvass several sellers." Thus the optimal amount of search varies directly with the dispersion of prices in a market and inversely with the cost of search. In markets with search the low-price sellers will attract more buyers than the high-price sellers, which will tend to force the latter out of business and decrease the dispersion. Once the dispersion is known to be low, the system becomes stable. Stigler, The Economics of Information, 69 J.Political Economy 213 (1961). See also Stigler, Information in the Labor Market, 70 J.Political Economy (Supp.) 94 (1962).

What does this have to say about the merits of the decision in Black v. Bush?

(4) *Excessive Profits in Contracts With the Government.* Should the courts, as a matter of public policy, deny enforcement to a military procurement contract or other contract with the United States, when it is demonstrable that the contractor's profits have been or will be exorbitant? The leading case is U.S. v. Bethlehem Steel Corporation, 315 U.S. 289 (1952), in which counsel for the government contended that a contract for building war vessels during World War I had yielded such great profits that it should be treated as having been induced by "duress" on the United States. But the Court, over strenuous dissenting opinions, held that the contract had not been induced by duress. In World War II, a number of legislative and administrative devices were used to limit profits on war contracts. These devices included: (1) compulsory renegotiation of procurement contracts so as to reduce the contractor's profits to reasonable margins; (2) administrative price regulation and priority control of scarce materials; (3) a sharply graduated "excess profits" tax; and (4) elimination of the cost-plus-percentage-of-cost contract in government procurement.

One of Bush's arguments was that Black's profits were passed on to the government and the public in the form of excessive prices, contrary to "public policy." If Bush had been granted the relief that he sought, what would have been the probable impact on prices paid by the government in similar transactions?

SECTION 3. OVERREACHING: CONVENTIONAL CONTROLS

Under the leadership, again, of equity, the courts have traditionally been insistent that no advantage should be gained through gross unfairness in the process of bargaining. The means reprobated in classical equity are fraud, mistake, and duress. The ordinary remedy, when a contract is found to be subject to one of these infirmities, is to rescind or avoid it, at the instance of the victim. Not only fraud, in the more shameful sense, but an innocent misrepresentation made in the bargaining process may be a ground for avoiding a contract. Indeed, it is sometimes required that a party possessed of information material to the exchange either disclose it or refrain from imposing on the ignorance of the other. What privilege of exploiting superior knowledge for a bargaining advantage should be recognized? How should the risks of inaccuracy in statements and of errors of fact be allocated between the parties? What pressures may conscientiously be exerted by one party on another to gain assent to a bargain or the settlement of a dispute? These are questions examined here.

Some further aspects of the doctrine of consideration are also presented. The doctrine has sometimes been extended to prevent overreaching in bargaining. Is it too blunt an instrument for that purpose? If so, how should it be reshaped?

The subject of this section has a complex relation to the problems of capacity and of unfairness in the substance of bargains, presented above. If the parties are fully competent to contract, and the bargaining process is cleansed of overreaching, is there any need for the courts to concern themselves with possible imbalances in the resulting exchange? Should all of these elements be considered together, from case to case? Or is it important, for purposes of predictability, that when a court declines to enforce a contract it specify a single deficiency of the bargain, or in the capacity of a party? Do you find instances of each method?

NOTE

Law and Equity. As the successors to equity powers, virtually all courts in which contract litigation is conducted are now competent to avoid a contract without requiring an independent proceeding for rescission. (The procedure of the court may reflect the origin in equity of these defenses, however; notably, it may not be necessary to submit them to juries. Courses in civil procedure examine this difference.) Quite apart from equity "jurisdiction," there are instances of fraud, mistake and duress that serve as invalidating causes in contract law: the contract affected is said to be "void."

(a) Pressure in Bargaining

When a person has used compulsion on another to obtain a benefit, the other can sometimes compel restoration. Money paid and property transferred under duress may be recovered; if assent to a contract is obtained by duress it may not be enforced against the victim. At p. 364 below an example is given of duress in a contemporary form. In early English cases from which the current doctrine stems, relief was confined to situations in which imprisonment and threats of confinement or bodily harm were the instruments of coercion. Threats of purely economic injury became a ground for relief when "duress of goods" was recognized. In comparatively recent times, duress has been recognized in a greatly enlarged range of situations, and the general conception of "economic coercion" or "business compulsion" has won a place as a sort of junior partner of duress in redressing oppression.[a]

These developments have not yet made duress a commonplace defense in contract actions. Freehanded applications of the doctrine are still prevented by a number of policy considerations, as well as some surviving technical obstacles. A mention of these will be useful as a prelude to the materials that follow.

In some courts a reasonable degree of temerity in the face of a threat is insisted on. This requirement serves to restrict relief for duress by denying it to persons who yield to pressure too readily. As

---

a. See McCubbin v. Buss, 144 N.W.2d 175 (Neb.1966); King Enterprises v. Man-   chester Water Works, 453 A.2d 1276 (N.H. 1982).

one court puts it, duress consists of "restraint or danger, either actually inflicted or impending, which is sufficient in severity or apprehension to overcome the mind of a person of ordinary firmness." [b] Some expressions of the courts imply an even stricter test: it is duress, as they describe it, to deprive a person of free choice,[c] or to destroy a person's volition,[d] or to obtain consent only in form.[e] Such expressions, often somewhat metaphorical, appear largely in cases where relief was *granted,* and it has often been granted where no such total mastery existed. A classical passage rejecting the "no will" conception of duress is this from Holmes:

> It always is for the interest of a party under duress to choose the lesser of two evils. But the fact that a choice was made according to interest does not exclude duress. It is the characteristic of duress properly so called.[f]

On the other hand, it is regularly acknowledged that a perfectly honorable agreement may be made with a person who must either accede to it or face some repugnant alternative.[g] "The question is one of degree." [h]

Duress is sometimes associated with unlawful conduct. In a recent case the court detected a "marked shift in emphasis from the subjective effect of a threat to the nature of the threat itself." [i] One who yields to a threat of criminal or tortious injury may be given relief on this ground. On cognate reasoning, it has been held that a threat of lawful action cannot be wrongful. "It is not duress to threaten to do what there is a legal right to do." [j]

Such reasoning has particular application to cases in which a dispute is compromised under a threat of suit.[k] As it is not unlawful to institute legal proceedings, a party threatened with suit may not buy its way out and thereafter complain of the bargain: such is a usual argument in support of settlements. Yet it is not now accepted as a general proposition that one may rightfully threaten any kind of rightful act. "An unjust and inequitable threat is wrongful, although the threatened act would not be a violation of duty in the sense of an independent

b. Carrier v. William Penn Broadcasting Co., 233 A.2d 519 (Pa.1967).

c. Joannin v. Ogilvie, 52 N.W. 217 (Minn.1892); Raymundo v. Hammond Clinic Ass'n, 449 N.E.2d 276 (Ind.1983) (free exercise of will).

d. See Konsuvo v. Netzke, 220 A.2d 424 (N.J.Super.1966); cf. Kaplan v. Kaplan, 182 N.E.2d 706 (Ill.1962).

e. See United States v. Huckabee, 16 Wall. (83 U.S.) 414 (1873) (alleged duress by a rebel government); Gerber v. First Nat. Bank, 332 N.E.2d 615, 79 A.L.R.3d 592 (Ill.App.1975) ("bereft of the quality of mind essential to the making of a contract").

f. Union Pacific R. Co. v. Public Service Comm., 248 U.S. 67 (1918) (duress by a state agency).

g. Tidwell v. Critz, 282 S.E.2d 104 (Ga. 1981).

h. Hellenic Lines, Ltd. v. Louis Dreyfus Corp., 372 F.2d 753 (2d Cir.1967) (valuable discussion).

i. Food Fair Stores, Inc. v. Joy, 389 A.2d 874 (Md.1978).

j. This proposition, in one form or another, is relied on in a mass of American cases. In Chouinard v. Chouinard, 568 F.2d 430 (5th Cir.1978), the court said that a lawful demand, or insistence on a legal right, even as against a necessitous person, is not duress.

k. See Dunbar v. Dunbar, 429 P.2d 949 (Ariz.1967): "It is not duress to declare an intention to resort to the courts for the purpose of insisting on what one believes are one's legal rights."

actionable wrong in the law of crimes, torts, or contracts." [1] This view is illustrated in cases of benefit that an employer exacts from an employee, under threat of discharge, where the employment contract is terminable at will.[m]

Professor Dawson has pointed out that preventing unjust enrichment is a principal function of the doctrines of duress, and that the limitations on relief mentioned above tend to obscure that function.[n] These limitations have been considerably relaxed, at least in some situations.[o] Instances are given at a later point in this chapter, following materials on related topics.

NOTES

(1) *Duress by Threat of Suit.* When a party seeks relief from a contract on the ground of coercion, it is not uncommon to find that that party is itself adept at coercive practices. An example is Undersea Eng. & Const. Co. v. International Tel. & Tel. Corp., 429 F.2d 543 (9th Cir.1970). In that case the plaintiff, Undersea, had been a subcontractor on a job for which the defendant, ITT, was the general contractor. Disputes between them led to extended negotiations, and to a settlement which the plaintiff later sought to void. The defendant was depicted as a billion-dollar corporation having elephantine power over the plaintiff. The court observed, however, that before the settlement "Undersea was using every threat of economic and moral pressure to coerce and force ITT to settle rather than face a law suit with threatened world-wide publicity."

If a settlement of a disputed claim does not put a period to the dispute, the claimant may usually begin second-round negotiations with the valuable advantage that it has already been paid a portion of its claim. If it were the rule that a settlement *never* puts an end to a dispute, the rule might put an end to settlements.

(2) *Restitution.* Duress is a ground not only for avoiding an agreement or settlement, but also for recovering a payment exacted by lawless compulsion. The fountainhead case on the law of restitution is Moses v. Macferlan, 97 Eng.Rep. 676 (K.B. 1760), which speaks to the point. In that case Lord Mansfield said that an action for money had and received lies "for money got through imposition (express or implied); or extortion; or oppression; or an undue advantage taken of the plaintiff's situation, contrary to laws made for the protection of persons under those circumstances."

(3) *Question.* Is it possible, in dealing with a remorseful person, to exact harsh terms through playing on the sense of guilt, such that the ensuing transaction with that person would be voidable for coercion? Consider the facts of Fiege v. Boehm, p. 55 above. Compare Stauffer v. Stauffer, 351 A.2d 236 (Pa.1976), where the court said: "weakness, whether real or apparent, can be a source of power over one who feels a sense of guilt."

l. McCubbin v. Buss, fn. a, above. See also Silsbee v. Webber, 50 N.E. 555 (Mass. 1898): "When it comes to the question of obtaining contracts by threats, it does not follow that, because you cannot be made to answer for the act, you may use the threat."

m. See Laemmar v. J. Walter Thompson Company, 435 F.2d 680 (7th Cir.1970);

Gerber v. First Nat. Bank, 332 N.E.2d 615, 79 A.L.R.3d 592 (Ill.App.1975).

n. Dawson, Economic Duress—An Essay in Perspective, 45 Mich.L.Rev. 253, 282 ff. (1947). See also Patterson, Compulsory Contracts in the Crystal Ball, 43 Colum.L.Rev. 731, 741 (1943).

o. See Hellenic Lines, Ltd. v. Louis Dreyfus Corp., fn. h, above.

(4) *The Case of the Parents' Concern.* A farm couple mortgaged their property to a bank for the purpose (they said) of preventing their son from going to prison. Glen, the son, had been found to have defrauded creditors of his business, a farm-implement dealership. The president of the bank, to which the parents gave a guarantee of debt, and the mortgage, testified that no threats were made to induce the execution of these papers. But a trial court found otherwise and rescinded the agreement. On the bank's appeal, the court found it incredible that the parents would hazard the fruits of fifty years of toil to try to bail out a business "which was in debt to the extent of $628,000 plus, absent the threat and concern that the son might go to prison."

Before the guarantee was given, Glen's father had consulted a lawyer (and had disregarded his advice) and Glen's mother had berated the bank president for lending him so much money. Should the trial court's decree be reversed? Would it matter that Glen implored his parents to sign? What if the bank had relied on the guaranty by purchasing the claims of other creditors of Glen's business? See Haumont v. Security State Bank, 374 N.W.2d 2 (Neb.1985).

THE PRE–EXISTING–DUTY RULE

"Performance of a legal duty owed to a promisor which is neither doubtful nor the subject of honest dispute is not consideration...." Restatement Second § 73. This is a recent version of an old rule that has given rise to some dissatisfaction. Professor Edwin W. Patterson [a] observed that it is, "on the whole, that adjunct of the doctrine of consideration which has done most to give it a bad name." Patterson, An Apology for Consideration, 58 Colum.L.Rev. 929, 936 (1958). On the other hand, some decisions that can be referred to the rule are generally applauded. In such cases there is commonly an element of coercion, as illustrated in the following well-known case.

A group of workmen had individually signed contracts to work on Alaska Packers' ship during the salmon canning season, from San Francisco to Pyramid Harbor, Alaska, and return, for a specified compensation. Upon arrival at the canning factory in Alaska, they presented a demand to Alaska Packers' superintendent for a very substantial increase in compensation, and they refused to work any further unless this demand was agreed to. Since it was impossible to get substitute workers the superintendent signed an agreement to pay the larger amount. Upon the return of the men to San Francisco at the end of the season, Alaska Packers paid them in accordance with the first agreement, and the employees sued in admiralty to recover the additional compensation. From judgment for the libelants, the defendant appealed. *Held:* Reversed. The agreement to pay the increased compensation was without consideration and was induced by the coercion of libelants' unjustified refusal to perform their contracts. Alaska Packers Ass'n v. Domenico, 117 Fed. 99 (9th Cir.1902).

a. Edwin W. Patterson (1889–1965) practiced for four years in Kansas City and then taught at Texas, Colorado, Iowa and Columbia. Among his writings are books on contracts, insurance and jurisprudence, including four editions of the predecessor of this casebook. He was one of the Advisers for the Restatement of Restitution.

In some states the pre-existing duty rule has been largely rejected by judicial decision. In Alabama, for example, the rule is that "an executory contract may be modified by the parties without any new consideration other than mutual consent." [b]   For contrast see Rosellini v. Banchero, 517 P.2d 955 (Wash.1974).

For a statutory modification of the rule, see UCC 2–209(1).

NOTES

(1) *New York Statute.*   How would the Alaska Packers case have been decided under the following provision of New York law? [c]

Written agreement for modification or discharge.   An agreement, promise or undertaking to change or modify, or to discharge in whole or in part, any contract, obligation, or lease, or any mortgage or other security interest in personal or real property, shall not be invalid because of the absence of consideration, provided that the agreement, promise or undertaking changing, modifying, or discharging such contract, obligation, lease, mortgage or security interest, shall be in writing and signed by the party against whom it is sought to enforce the change, modification or discharge, or by his agent.

(2) *Duress?*   Might a modifying agreement that is within UCC 2–209(1) or the New York statute quoted above still be voidable for duress where it was induced by one party's threat to break the contract?   Comment 2 to UCC 2–209 states, in part, that "modifications made thereunder must meet the test of good faith imposed by this Act ... and the extortion of a 'modification' without legitimate commercial reason is ineffective as a violation of the duty of good faith."   See Farnsworth, Good Faith Purchase and Commercial Reasonableness Under the Uniform Commercial Code, 30 U.Chi.L.Rev. 666, 675–76 (1963).

A thoughtful review of the pre-existing duty rule by Professor Hillman concludes that it has been dismissed too summarily in the Code provision.   He recommends that the person relying on a concession under certain modifying agreements be put to proof that it was not unfairly coerced.   Does the rule of Restatement Second § 89, make a satisfying balance of the opposing considerations?   See Policing Contract Modifications under the UCC: Good Faith and the Doctrine of Economic Duress, 64 Iowa L.Rev. 849 (1979).   *Question:* Would you expect the definition of "good faith" in UCC 1–201(19) or that in UCC 2–103(1)(b) to be the more decisive in this connection?

(3) *Work–Reduction Problem.*   Refer again to Ever–Tite Roofing Corp. v. Green, p. 187 above.   Suppose the following situation: Ever–Tite's workmen arrived at the Greens' residence and found no other roofer engaged.   They advised the Greens that, though new gutters were called for in the signed agreement, Ever–Tite had discontinued gutter work.   They then persuaded the Greens to initial an amendment to the agreement, "gutter installation eliminated."   Would it be possible for the Greens, on changing their minds, to repudiate the amendment?   See Engle v. Shapert Constr. Co., 443 F.Supp. 1383 (M.D.Pa. 1978).   Would it matter whether or not the court considers that Article 2 of the Code applies to a sale and installation of roofing materials?

(4) *Firm–Offer Problems.*   In October A makes a firm offer to sell a widget to B for $100, not to be revoked before the end of the year.   (See UCC 2–205.)

---

b.   Winegardner v. Burns, 361 So.2d 1054 (Ala.1978).

For an extensive recital of cases see Brody, Performance of a Pre–Existing Contractual Duty as Consideration, 52 Denver L.J. 433 (1975).

c.   N.Y.Gen.Oblig.L., § 5–1103.   See also Mich.Comp.L.Ann. § 566.1.

In November B promises A not to buy a widget from anyone else before the end of the year. B's promise, like A's offer, is in writing. Is that promise enforceable?

If, in October, B had made a similar promise to A in exchange for the same "firm offer," would B's promise be enforceable? Cf. Electrical Const. & Maint. Co., Inc. v. Maeda Pacific Corp., 764 F.2d 619 (9th Cir.1985), concerning a bid by a would-be subcontractor that may have become irrevocable by reason of the prime contractor's reliance.

Introductory Note to Arzani v. People

In this case a paving subcontractor (Arzani) ran into trouble in performing his side of the bargain. According to him, he laid the problem before the general contractors, who agreed to increase the price of the paving. They might, instead, have insisted on performance at the agreed price: "you are not obliged to become an altruist toward the other party and relax the terms if he gets into trouble in performing his side of the bargain." Fasolino Foods Co. v. Banca Nazionale del Lavoro, 961 F.2d 1052 (2d Cir.1992).[a] Whether or not the promise of additional pay was enforceable was the issue. Because it was oral, the New York statute set out in Note 1 on the preceding page did not apply.

But Arzani relied on a case decided well before the enactment of that statute: Schwartzreich v. Bauman–Basch, Inc., 131 N.E. 887 (N.Y. 1921). In that case Schwartzreich had contracted in writing to work for a year, as a clothing designer, for the salary of $90 a week. The employer was Bauman–Basch. During the period before this employment was to begin, Schwartzreich received an offer of $115 a week to do similar work elsewhere. When he informed Bauman–Basch of this development, it suggested that it would pay him at the weekly rate of $100 if he would reject the offer. The parties prepared and signed a new contract just like the earlier one, except for the pay rate. At the same time the parties' signatures were torn off the earlier contract—the "August contract." Schwartzreich began work in November, as scheduled; in December he was discharged. A jury awarded him damages based on the $100 rate. The trial court set aside the verdict; but it was reinstated on appeal.

According to the appellate court in *Schwartzreich,* the situation was one in which "an existing contract is terminated by consent of both parties and a new one executed in its place and stead." The court quoted this from Williston:

A rescission followed shortly afterwards by a new agreement in regard to the same subject-matter would create the legal obligations provided in the subsequent agreement.

a. Quoting from Market Street Assocs. Ltd. Partnership v. Frey, 941 F.2d 588 (7th Cir.1991), at 594.

"Very little difference may appear," the court said, "in a mere change of compensation in an existing and continuing contract and a termination of one contract and the making of a new one for the same time and work, but at an increased compensation. There is, however, a marked difference in principle."

In a study for the New York Law Revision Commission,[b] leading to the enactment of the statute mentioned above, *Schwartzreich* was said to be a source of uncertainty. Jury determinations would be unpredictable, it was thought, about whether—in the words of Watkins & Son v. Carrig, p. 357 below—"the contract was rescinded with a new one to take its place or whether it remained in force with a modification of its terms." Consider whether or not *Schwartzreich* was successfully distinguished in Arzani's case.

ARZANI v. PEOPLE, 149 N.Y.S.2d 38 (Sup.Ct.1956). [The State of New York let a contract for the reconstruction of a highway to Kranz and Martin, as general contractors. They entered into a written subcontract with Victor Arzani, by which he agreed to do part of the work, including contract paving. After doing it, and being paid $106,000, Arzani brought suit against Kranz and Martin (including the State as a defendant) for an unpaid balance. After adjusting for various charges and credits, the court gave judgment for Arzani, in the amount of $19,520.62. It rejected Arzani's claim for an additional amount of some $1,500, based on an oral promise made to him by Kranz.]

GORMAN, JUSTICE.... The proposal issued by the State listed the minimum wage for laborers as $1.95 per hour, which amount was in effect when the plaintiff commenced work on his subcontract. A few days later, the union representative demanded an increase of twenty cents per hour or he would call a strike and shut down the job. The plaintiff says that he then told the defendant Kranz that he, himself, would pull off the job if Kranz did not agree to pay one-half of the additional labor cost, and that Kranz agreed. This testimony is uncontradicted. The plaintiff further stated on cross-examination that it constituted the entire conversation with Kranz and was not reduced to writing. The proof showed that the plaintiff thereafter paid his laborers the sum of $3,003.40 over the amount he would have paid at the lesser rate, and that the work proceeded to a satisfactory conclusion.

It is the contention of the defendant contractors that there is no enforceable contract between the interested parties as to this item because of failure of consideration. It is competent for the parties to a contract to abandon it or to substitute another in its place. Merger of the rescission and promise into one transaction does not destroy them as elements composing the transaction. See Schwartzreich v. Bauman–Basch, Inc.... But there must be a new consideration, and there is general acceptance in this state that where A is under a contract with B,

b. N.Y.Law Rev.Com., Second Annual Report 255 (Leg.Doc. No. 65, 1936).

a promise made by one to the other to induce performance is void. Consideration is not necessary to an act of rescission, waiver, release or discharge, but rather to the enforceability of executory promises. But it is necessary that there be a valid abrogation of the existing contract, and this by mutual agreement. This fact has not been established, whether the test be factual or legal.

It is true that this is not a situation where coercion or expediency has been utilized by the plaintiff in a mere attempt to exact more money. The conceded circumstances might spell out factually a mutual acceptance of immediate danger to the completion of one of interrelated contracts. But termination is not shown. The most that the plaintiff shows beyond the promise is his reliance upon his capacity to breach the contract, and his statement that he would do so if the excess labor cost was not shared. See McGowan & Connolly Co., Inc. v. Kenny–Moran Co., Inc., 202 N.Y.S. 513 (App.Div.1924). Judged from the standpoint of ordinary business morality, the situation of the promisor contractor may well be less defensible than that of the plaintiff. But termination is not presumed. It must be proved and upon this record the plaintiff has failed to sustain his burden.[a]

NOTES

(1) *Questions.* In Schwartzreich v. Bauman–Basch, was it possible to find three contracts between the parties, or only two? What was the significance, if any, of the ceremony in which the signatures were torn off the original employment contract? Would the decision have been different if the signatures had not been torn off the old contract until after the parties had signed the new one?

(2) *The Role of an Attorney.* The owners of a farm became dissatisfied with the price they had agreed to accept for it. The buyers agreed to an increase when the sellers' attorney told them that his clients were willing to go to court to get out of the initial agreement, and that they would find litigation expensive. (These facts are taken from Recker v. Gustafson, 279 N.W.2d 744 (Iowa 1979).)

Are there circumstances in which you, as attorney for the sellers, would have declined to negotiate for them in the manner stated? If so, would your decision turn on whether or not the buyers also had a legal adviser? Would it matter that the initial agreement was afflicted (as it was in the case cited) with problems such as definiteness and the Statute of Frauds?

If an attorney *for the buyers* had advised them to agree to the price increase, would that attorney be at liberty, later, to question the consideration for it? See Rickett v. Doze, 603 P.2d 679 (Mont.1979).

(3) *The Restatement.* In the Restatement Second, the facts of *Schwartzreich* are used as an illustration to § 89. Should the job offer at $115 a week be regarded as a circumstance not anticipated when the contract was made, such that a $10 raise was "fair and equitable"? Would the decision in *Arzani* have been different under the rule of that section?

In the Iowa case cited in the foregoing Note, the court reviewed some of its earlier opinions about the pre-existing-duty rule, concluding that they "digressed" from it without sound reasoning and blurred the distinction between

a. Part of the opinion—"Judged from the standpoint of ordinary business morali- ty ..."—is an unacknowledged excerpt from Corbin's writing.

the modification and the rescission of a contract. Taking note of the Restatement position—section 89(a)—the court called it interesting, but inapplicable. The court directed specific performance of the initial agreement.

(4) *The Sheep and the Goats.* It has been urged that the courts should endeavor "to separate the sheep from the goats" by enforcing the new promise in favor of the honest contractor and refusing to enforce it in favor of the dishonest or extortionate contractor. Corbin, Does a Preexisting Duty Defeat Consideration?, 27 Yale L.J. 362, 373 (1918). What facts, provable in court, can provide the basis for separating "the sheep from the goats"? How would the plaintiff in the present case be characterized, as "sheep" or "goat"? Is it clear that he used no coercion to secure the agreement about labor costs?

"The traditional rationale employed in support of the pre-existing duty doctrine is that it prevents overreaching and blackmail. See Williston, Successive Promises of the Same Performance, 8 Harv.L.Rev. 27 (1894). As Professor Fried notes, however, the modern trend is toward recognition of promises whose legitimacy the strict consideration doctrine placed in doubt, so long as the sincerity of the obligation is clear and the commitment freely made. C. Fried [Contract as Promise (1981)], at 39." Hoffa v. Fitzsimmons, 673 F.2d 1345, 1359 n. 34 (D.C.Cir.1982).

(5) *Avoiding the Rule.* Speaking of the pre-existing-duty rule, one court has said: "any consideration for the new undertaking, however insignificant, satisfies this rule. For instance, an undertaking to pay part of the debt before maturity, or at a place other than that where the obligor was legally bound to pay, or to pay in property, regardless of its value, or to effect a composition with creditors by the payment of less than the sum due, has been held to constitute a consideration sufficient in law." [b] The same thought was expressed by Lord Coke, in Pinnel's Case: "by no possibility, a lesser sum can be satisfaction to the plaintiff for a greater sum: but the gift of a horse, hawk or robe, etc. in satisfaction is good." [c]

What modern equivalent of a "horse, hawk or robe" might suitably be used to make a creditor's concession to a debtor irreversible? In Restatement Second § 73 it is said that a performance "similar" to that owing "is consideration if it differs from what was required ... in a way which reflects more than a pretense of a bargain." Does the concluding phrase encourage lawyers to make a pioneering search for trivial new objects of bargaining?

WATKINS & SON v. CARRIG

Supreme Court of New Hampshire, 1941.
91 N.H. 459, 21 A.2d 591, 138 A.L.R. 131.

Assumpsit for work done. By a written contract between the parties the plaintiff agreed to excavate a cellar for the defendant for a stated price. Soon after the work was commenced solid rock was encountered. The plaintiff's manager notified the defendant, a meeting between them was held, and it was orally agreed that the plaintiff should remove the rock at a stipulated unit price about nine times greater than

b. Levine v. Blumenthal, 186 A. 457 (N.J.L.1936), aff'd on opinion of Supreme Court, 189 A. 54 (N.J.L.Err. & App.1937).

c. See fn. a, p. 362 below.

the unit price for excavating upon which the gross amount to be paid according to the written contract was calculated. The rock proved to constitute about two-thirds of the space to be excavated.

A referee found that the oral agreement "superseded" the written contract, and reported a verdict for the plaintiff based on the finding. To the acceptance of the report and an order of judgment thereon the defendant excepted. Further facts appear in the opinion. Transferred by Burque, C.J.

ALLEN, CHIEF JUSTICE. When the written contract was entered into, no understanding existed between the parties that no rock would be found in the excavating. The plaintiff's manager made no inquiry or investigation to find out the character of the ground below the surface, no claim is made that the defendant misled him, and the contract contains no reservations for unexpected conditions. It provides that "all material" shall be removed from the site, and its term that the plaintiff is "to excavate" is unqualified. In this situation a defence of mutual mistake is not available. A space of ground to be excavated, whatever its character, was the subject matter of the contract, and the offer of price on that basis was accepted. Leavitt v. Dover, 67 N.H. 94, 32 A. 156, 68 Am.St.Rep. 640. If the plaintiff was unwise in taking chances, it is not relieved, on the ground of mistake, from the burden incurred in being faced with them. The case differs from that of King Co. v. Aldrich, 81 N.H. 42, 121 A. 434, in which the parties did not contract for the property delivered in purported performance of the contract actually made.

The referee's finding that the written contract was "superseded" by an oral contract when the rock was discovered is construed to mean that the parties agreed to rescind the written contract as though it had not been made and entered into an oral one as though it were the sole and original one. The defendant either thought that the contract did not require the excavation of rock on the basis of the contract price or was willing to forego his rights under the contract in respect to rock. It was important to him that the work should not be delayed, and other reasons may have contributed to induce him to the concession he made. In any event, he consented to a special price for excavating rock, whatever his rights under the contract. The plaintiff on the strength of the promise proceeded with the work.

But the defendant contends that the facts do not support a claim of two independent and separate transactions, one in rescission of the written contract as though it were nugatory, and one in full substitution of it. All that is shown, as he urges, is one transaction by which he was to pay more for the excavating than the written contract provided, with that contract otherwise to remain in force. And upon the basis of this position he relies upon the principle of contract law that his promise to pay more was without consideration, as being a promise to pay the plaintiff for performance of its obligation already in force and outstanding. Whether the contract was rescinded with a new one to take its place or whether it remained in force with a modification of its terms, is not important. In the view of a modification, the claim of a promise unsupported by consideration is as tenable as under the view of a rescission. A modification involves a partial rescission.

In the situation presented the plaintiff entered into a contractual obligation. Facts subsequently learned showed the obligation to be burdensome and the contract improvident. On insistent request by the plaintiff, the defendant granted relief from the burden by a promise to pay a special price which overcame the burden. The promise was not an assumption of the burden; the special price was fair and the defendant received reasonable value for it.

The issue whether the grant of relief constituted a valid contract is one of difficulty. The basic rule that a promise without consideration for it is invalid leads to its logical application that a promise to pay for what the promisor already has a right to receive from the promise is invalid. The promisee's performance of an existing duty is no detriment to him, and hence nothing is given by him beyond what is already due the promisor. But the claim is here made that the original contract was rescinded, either in full or in respect to some of its terms, by mutual consent, and since any rescission mutually agreed upon is in itself a contract, the claim of a promise to pay for performance of a subsisting duty is unfounded. The terms of the contract of rescission are of course valid if the rescission is valid. The defendant's answer to this claim is well stated in this quotation from Williston, Contr., 2d Ed., § 130a: "But calling an agreement an agreement for rescission does not do away with the necessity of consideration, and when the agreement for rescission is coupled with a further agreement that the work provided for in the earlier agreement shall be completed and that the other party shall give more than he originally promised, the total effect of the second agreement is that one party promises to do exactly what he had previously bound himself to do, and the other party promises to give an additional compensation therefor."

With due respect for this eminent authority, the argument appears to clothe consideration with insistence of control beyond its proper demands. With full recognition of the legal worthlessness of a bare promise and of performance of a subsisting duty as a void consideration, a result accomplished by proper means is not necessarily bad because it would be bad if the means were improper or were not employed.

It is not perceived that the requirement of consideration is necessarily disregarded in spite of the net result of a promise to pay more for less, without additional obligation of the promisee. If the process in reaching such a result is inoffensive to the doctrine of consideration, the result does not become a naked promise. If in analysis of the transaction compliance with the elements of a valid contract may be found, it is hardly a perversion of principle to give the steps taken recognition. The result being reasonable, the means taken to reach it may be examined to determine their propriety.

In common understanding there is, importantly, a wide divergence between a bare promise and a promise in adjustment of a contractual promise already outstanding. A promise with no supporting consideration would upset well and long-established human interrelations if the law did not treat it as a vain thing. But parties to a valid contract generally understand that it is subject to any mutual action they may take in its performance. Changes to meet changes in circumstances and conditions should be valid if the law is to carry out its function and service by rules conformable with reasonable practices and understandings in matters of business and commerce.

Rescission in full or in modification being intended, it should be effective although the result benefits only one party and places a burden only on the other. It is the fact of rescission rather than the effect of it that determines its legal quality. The difference between a rescission unrelated to a new contract and one interdependent with a new contract, with the result the same in each case, signifies no failure of consideration in the latter case. The result, whatever it may be, is indecisive of the contractual character of the transaction. The steps taken being pointed out by the law, the result should not be held an idle one. Merger of the rescission and promise into one transaction does not destroy them as elements composing the transaction....

... The case is one of a simple relinquishment of a right pertaining to intangible personalty.[a] The defendant intentionally and voluntarily yielded to a demand for a special price for excavating rock. In doing this he yielded his contract right to the price it provided. Whether or not he thought he had the right, he intended, and executed his intent, to make no claim of the right. The promise of a special price for excavating rock necessarily imported a release or waiver of any right by the contract to hold the plaintiff to the lower price the contract stipulated. In mutual understanding the parties agreed that the contract price was not to control. The contract right being freely surrendered, the issue of contract law whether the new promise is valid is not doubtful. If the totality of the transaction was a promise to pay more for less, there was in its inherent makeup a valid discharge of an obligation. Although the transaction was single, the element of discharge was distinct in precedence of the new promise.

The foregoing views are considered to meet the reasonable needs of standard and ethical practices of men in their business dealings with each other. Conceding that the plaintiff threatened to break its contract because it found the contract to be improvident, yet the defendant yielded to the threat without protest, excusing the plaintiff, and making a new arrangement. Not insisting on his rights but relinquishing them, fairly he should be held to the new arrangement. The law is a means to the end. It is not the law because it is the law, but because it is adapted

---

a. In a passage preceding this sentence, the court intimated that the defendant might have made an informal transfer to the plaintiff of a portion of the defendant's entitlement under the written contract. A consideration is not essential to the effectiveness of a transfer (assignment) of a con-tract right. The passage is omitted here, however, because the court did not press the point strongly. "[W]hen a creditor releases his debtor," the court said, "without full payment of the debt, no assignment is involved."

and adaptable to establish and maintain reasonable order. If the phrase justice according to law were transposed into law according to justice, it would perhaps be more accurately expressive. In a case like this, of conflicting rules and authority, a result which is considered better to establish "fundamental justice and reasonableness" (Cavanaugh v. Boston & M. Railroad, 76 N.H. 68, 72, 79 A. 694, 696), should be attained. It is not practical that the law should adopt all precepts of moral conduct, but it is desirable that its rules and principles should not run counter to them in the important conduct and transactions of life.

Exceptions overruled.[b]

NOTES

(1) *Presumption of Duress.* Professor Hillman urges the courts to apply a presumption against a modifying agreement—that it was "a product of unlawful means"—if the effect of it is a material net loss in the value of the contract to the party making the concession. Hillman, Policing ..., 64 Iowa L.Rev. 849, 883 (1979). Do you find a case on the topic pre-existing duty in which this presumption would not apply?

(2) *The Hawaiian Housing Case.* Richards contracted to build housing in Hawaii for the Marine Air Corps, using a subcontractor's bid for the metal work by the Air Conditioning Company (AC). By error, AC had calculated its bid on the assumption that galvanized sheet metal would be used, rather than zinc alloy. When AC informed Richards that it would not do the work for the bid price, Richards "blew up." Over the next two months, hard bargaining ensued, during which Richards insisted that AC was bound by its bid price. At length, Richards and AC executed a contract for the metal work at $62,000. (The AC bid had been less than $49,000). After paying some $50,000 as the work progressed, Richards refused to pay more. In fact, Richards never intended to pay the agreed price. When sued for the remainder, Richards relied on the pre-existing duty rule, and cited Alaska Packers Ass'n v. Domenico. (See brief of the case at p. 352 above.) From judgment for the plaintiff, the defendant appealed. *Held:* Affirmed. Richards Constr. Co. v. Air Conditioning Co. of Hawaii, 318 F.2d 410 (9th Cir.1963).

Was the Alaska Packers case easily distinguishable? Was Richards in a good position to assert the rule, having retreated from the position that AC was bound by its bid?

An additional fact in the case was that AC did not inform Richards of its error for about a month after it had learned of the award of the main contract, and after it had discovered the error. What conclusion does this suggest? Another fact was that the second lowest bid was $83,000.[c] What conclusion does this suggest?

SCOPE OF THE PRE–EXISTING–DUTY RULE

One of the parties in the next main case, the Loral Corporation, made a counterclaim against Austin Instrument, Inc. and charged Austin

----

b. For a very similar case relying on Restatement Second § 89, see Brian Constr. & Development Co., Inc. v. Brighenti, 405 A.2d 72 (Conn.1978).

c. Richards' architect had estimated the cost of the metal work at $16,000. One of the bids it received was for more than $173,000.

with having forced a price hike of more than $20,000 after having contracted to produce some goods for Loral. Loral sought to recover this amount on the ground of duress. Why (one might wonder) did not Loral base its claim on the pre-existing-duty rule? How was its position different from that of the employer of the cannery workers in Alaska Packers Ass'n v. Domenico, stated at p. 352 above?

Consideration is only a test of the enforceability of an executory promise, it has been said. Angel v. Murray, 322 A.2d 630 (R.I.1974). At the least this seems to mean that when a payment has been made, or some other performance given, the recipient cannot be required to make restitution on the simple ground that nothing was given in exchange. There is little reason to doubt this proposition.

The Foakes v. Beer Problem. A controversial application of the pre-existing-duty rule concerns cases in which part of a debt has been paid as part of an agreement for forgiving the rest. Does the rule prevent enforcement by the debtor of the creditor's forgiveness agreement?

The leading case is Foakes v. Beer, 9 App.Cas. 605 (H.L.1884). In that case the creditor (Mrs. Beer) had obtained a judgment against her debtor (Dr. Foakes). She then agreed to forego interest on her judgment; and Dr. Foakes paid the principal amount of it in installments. Still later, she was allowed to recover the unpaid interest. The law lords found a controlling precedent in Pinnel's Case, decided by Lord Coke in 1602.[a] There it was said that "payment of a lesser sum on the day [i.e., on or after the due date of a money debt] cannot be any satisfaction of the whole." In agreeing to pay the judgment, Dr. Foakes did no more than he was obliged to do in any event.

The rule of Foakes v. Beer has often been doubted or denounced. One eminent judge called it a relic of antique law, and "evidence of the former capacity of lawyers and judges to make the requirement of consideration an overworked shibboleth rather than a logical and just standard of accountability." Stone, J., in Rye v. Phillips, 282 N.W. 459 (Minn.1938).[b] Do you agree?

NOTES

(1) *Questions.* (i) How was the problem in Foakes v. Beer different from that in Watkins & Son v. Carrig, above? (ii) In one state the rule of Foakes v. Beer is said to apply, with the exception that if the debtor is a "known insolvent" the debtor's agreed part payment can absolve it of further liability.

---

a. Cited as 5 Coke's Rep. 117a (in Vol. 3, Part V), 77 Eng.Rep. 237 (Common Pleas).

Some of the justices doubted that the operative document purported to foreclose Mrs. Beer's interest claim. Others did not acquiesce in the authority of Pinnel's Case. But there was a majority ruling as stated in the text.

For an assault on the rule of the case see Comment, 11 Ariz.L.Rev. 344 (1969).

b. Taking broader ground, some scholars have challenged the general rule about pre-existing duty, as it affects the modification of contracts. One thoughtful appraisal is that of Patterson, in An Apology for Consideration, 58 Colum.L.Rev. 929, 936–38 (1958), concluding: "The nineteenth century, striving to bring unity out of diversity, included too many different ideas under the general heading of consideration."

Prather v. Citizens Nat. Bank of Dallas, 582 S.W.2d 903 (Tex.App.1979), writ ref. n.r.e. What merit do you see in this rule?

(2) *The Case of the Endowed Bride.* Four days before the wedding of Blanche Schweizer to an Italian nobleman, the groom and the bride's parents entered into articles of agreement conferring on her an annual payment for as long as Blanche and her fiancee should live. Her father expressed his promise of the annuity in a sentence beginning:

> Whereas, Miss Blanche Josephine Schweizer ... is now affianced to and is to be married to the above said Count Oberto Giacomo Giovanni Frances-co Maria Gullinelli: Now in consideration of all that is herein set forth the said Mr. Joseph Schweizer promises....[c]

The first payment ($2,500) was made on the wedding day. After the tenth payment, no more were made. The couple assigned their rights in the contract to Attilio De Cicco, and he sued the father-in-law, J. Schweizer.[d]

When the case reached the New York Court of Appeals, Cardozo wrote for the court. De Cicco v. Schweizer, 117 N.E. 807 (N.Y.1917). He first stated the defendant's contention: "that Count Gulinelli was already affianced to Miss Schweizer, and that the marriage was merely the fulfillment of an existing legal duty." Turning to the law, he accepted the premise of the defendant's argument: "The courts of this state are committed to the view that a promise by A. to B. to induce him not to break his contract with C. is void." He then developed at length a distinction, showing that Schweizer's promise was not of that character. Instead, he reasoned, it was a promise to induce the Count not to join with Blanche in a voluntary rescission of their engagement. Although neither could rightfully withdraw without the other's consent, *together* they were free to terminate the engagement or postpone the marriage. The consideration, then, for Schweizer's promise was that they did not do so.[e]

In some beautifully articulated paragraphs the opinion seeks to make this reading plausible: "It does not seem a far-fetched assumption [in relation to contracts to marry] that one will release where the other has repented ... one does not commonly apply pressure to coerce the will and action of those who are anxious to proceed. The attempt to sway their conduct by new inducements is an implied admission that both may waver.... The springs of conduct are subtle and varied. One who meddles with them must not insist upon too nice a measure of proof that the spring which he released was effective to the exclusion of all others." And in a final paragraph, Cardozo took higher ground, appealing to "those considerations of public policy which cluster about contracts that touch the marriage relation."[f]

(3) *On the Road.* Is the principle of De Cicco v. Schweizer usable in any situation that does not involve a marriage? In Arzani v. People, would it have been plausible for the plaintiff to cite De Cicco v. Schweizer? If not, what change in the facts would make the two cases comparable?

c. Translated; the agreement was in Italian.

Mrs. Schweizer covenanted to continue the payments in the event of her husband's death, and there were testamentary provisions as well.

d. The court assumed, properly, that De Cicco's right to enforce the contract was as good as that of either Blanche or the Count. It did not indicate which of them might have enforced it, or when the assignment was given, or for what consideration, if any.

e. Along the way, Cardozo rejected the contention that Schweizer had only made a promise of a gift: "One does not commonly pledge one's self to generosity in the language of a covenant."

f. One judge concurred in a separate opinion.

In a later opinion, Cardozo cited De Cicco v. Schweizer as a "signpost on the road" toward general acceptance of the doctrine of promissory estoppel. See Allegheny College v. National Chautauqua County Bank, referred to at pp. 101–103 above. Do you see a connection between the case and that doctrine? See also Restatement Second § 90, Illustration 8.

(4) *The Jockey's Case.* Mike McDevitt was a jockey who had accepted employment from Shaw to drive a mare named Grace in the Kentucky Futurity. Stokes owned "relatives" of the mare, and stood to gain if she should win. Stokes promised McDevitt a bonus of $1,000 for riding in and winning the race. McDevitt won, but Stokes refused to pay, and McDevitt sued him. From judgment for the defendant on a demurrer to the plaintiff's complaint, the plaintiff appealed. *Held:* Affirmed. "To hold that [plaintiff] would not have won the race with Grace but for the agreement of [defendant] to pay him the $1,000 . . . would be to say that he would have been recreant to the obligation arising out of his employment by Shaw . . ." McDevitt v. Stokes, 192 S.W. 681 (Ky.1917). Does this case illustrate (to use Cardozo's words) "a promise by A. to B. to induce him not to break his contract with C."?

AUSTIN INSTRUMENT, INC. v. LORAL CORPORATION

Court of Appeals of New York, 1971.
29 N.Y.2d 124, 272 N.E.2d 533.

FULD, CHIEF JUDGE.[g]   The defendant, Loral Corporation, seeks to recover payment for goods delivered under a contract which it had with the plaintiff Austin Instrument, Inc., on the ground that the evidence establishes, as a matter of law, that it was forced to agree to an increase in price on the items in question under circumstances amounting to economic duress.

In July of 1965, Loral was awarded a $6,000,000 contract by the Navy for the production of radar sets. The contract contained a schedule of deliveries, a liquidated damages clause applying to late deliveries and a cancellation clause in case of default by Loral. The latter thereupon solicited bids for some 40 precision gear components needed to produce the radar sets, and awarded Austin a subcontract to supply 23 such parts. That party commenced delivery in early 1966.

In May, 1966, Loral was awarded a second Navy contract for the production of more radar sets and again went about soliciting bids. Austin bid on all 40 gear components but, on July 15, a representative from Loral informed Austin's president, Mr. Krauss, that his company would be awarded the subcontract only for those items on which it was low bidder. The Austin officer refused to accept an order for less than all 40 of the gear parts and on the next day he told Loral that Austin would cease deliveries of the parts due under the existing subcontract unless Loral consented to substantial increases in the prices provided for

g. Stanley H. Fuld (1903–_____) practiced law in New York City from 1926 to 1935 when he became assistant district at-   torney. In 1946 he was appointed to the New York Court of Appeals. He became chief judge in 1967 and served until 1974.

by that agreement—both retroactively for parts already delivered and prospectively on those not yet shipped—and placed with Austin the order for all 40 parts needed under Loral's second Navy contract. Shortly thereafter, Austin did, indeed, stop delivery. After contacting 10 manufacturers of precision gears and finding none who could produce the parts in time to meet its commitments to the Navy,[1] Loral acceded to Austin's demands; in a letter dated July 22, Loral wrote to Austin that "We have feverishly surveyed other sources of supply and find that because of the prevailing military exigencies, were they to start from scratch as would have to be the case, they could not even remotely begin to deliver on time to meet the delivery requirements established by the Government.... Accordingly, we are left with no choice or alternative but to meet your conditions."

Loral thereupon consented to the price increases insisted upon by Austin under the first subcontract and the latter was awarded a second subcontract making it the supplier of all 40 gear parts for Loral's second contract with the Navy.[2] Although Austin was granted until September to resume deliveries, Loral did, in fact, receive parts in August and was able to produce the radar sets in time to meet its commitments to the Navy on both contracts. After Austin's last delivery under the second subcontract in July, 1967, Loral notified it of its intention to seek recovery of the price increases.

On September 15, 1967, Austin instituted this action against Loral to recover an amount in excess of $17,750 which was still due on the second subcontract. On the same day, Loral commenced an action against Austin claiming damages of some $22,250—the aggregate of the price increases under the first subcontract—on the ground of economic duress. The two actions were consolidated and, following a trial, Austin was awarded the sum it requested and Loral's complaint against Austin was dismissed on the ground that it was not shown that "it could not have obtained the items in question from other sources in time to meet its commitment to the Navy under the first contract." A closely divided Appellate Division affirmed (35 A.D.2d 387, 316 N.Y.S.2d 528, 532). There was no material disagreement concerning the facts; as Justice Steuer stated in the course of his dissent below, "[t]he facts are virtually undisputed, nor is there any serious question of law. The difficulty lies in the application of the law to these facts." (35 A.D.2d 392, 316 N.Y.S.2d 534.)

The applicable law is clear and, indeed, is not disputed by the parties. A contract is voidable on the ground of duress when it is established that the party making the claim was forced to agree to it by means of a wrongful threat precluding the exercise of his free will.... The existence of economic duress or business compulsion is demonstrated by proof that "immediate possession of needful goods is threatened" ... or, more particularly, in cases such as the one before us, by proof

---

1. The best reply Loral received was from a vendor who stated he could commence deliveries sometime in October.

2. Loral makes no claim in this action on the second subcontract.

that one party to a contract has threatened to breach the agreement by withholding goods unless the other party agrees to some further demand.... However, a mere threat by one party to breach the contract by not delivering the required items, though wrongful, does not in itself constitute economic duress. It must also appear that the threatened party could not obtain the goods from another source of supply and that the ordinary remedy of an action for breach of contract would not be adequate.

We find without any support in the record the conclusion reached by the courts below that Loral failed to establish that it was the victim of economic duress. On the contrary, the evidence makes out a classic case, as a matter of law, of such duress.[3]

It is manifest that Austin's threat—to stop deliveries unless the prices were increased—deprived Loral of its free will. As bearing on this, Loral's relationship with the Government is most significant. As mentioned above, its contract called for staggered monthly deliveries of the radar sets, with clauses calling for liquidated damages and possible cancellation on default. Because of its production schedule, Loral was, in July, 1966, concerned with meeting its delivery requirements in September, October and November, and it was for the sets to be delivered in those months that the withheld gears were needed. Loral had to plan ahead and the substantial liquidated damages for which it would be liable, plus the threat of default, were genuine possibilities. Moreover, Loral did a substantial portion of its business with the Government, and it feared that a failure to deliver as agreed upon would jeopardize its chances for future contracts. These genuine concerns do not merit the label " 'self-imposed, undisclosed and subjective' " which the Appellate Division majority placed upon them. It was perfectly reasonable for Loral, or any other party similarly placed, to consider itself in an emergency, duress situation.

... [T]he parts needed for the October schedule were delivered in late August and early September. Even so, Loral had to "work ... around the clock" to meet its commitments. Considering that the best offer Loral received from the other vendors it contacted was commencement of delivery sometime in October, which, as the record shows, would have made it late in its deliveries to the navy in both September and October, Loral's claim that it had no choice but to accede to Austin's demands is conclusively demonstrated.

We find unconvincing Austin's contention that Loral, in order to meet its burden, should have contacted the Government and asked for an extension of its delivery dates so as to enable it to purchase the parts from another vendor. Aside from the consideration that Loral was anxious to perform well in the Government's eyes, it could not be sure when it would obtain enough parts from a substitute vendor to meet its

---

3. The suggestion advanced that we are precluded from reaching this determination because the trial court's findings of fact have been affirmed by the Appellate Division ignores the question to be decided. That question, undoubtedly one of law (see Cohen and Karger, Powers of the New York Court of Appeals [1952], § 115, p. 492), is, accepting the facts found, did the courts below properly apply the law to them.

commitments. The only promise which it received from the companies it contacted was for *commencement* of deliveries, not full supply, and, with vendor delay common in this field, it would have been nearly impossible to know the length of the extension it should request. It must be remembered that Loral was producing a needed item of military hardware. Moreover, there is authority for Loral's position that nonperformance by a subcontractor is not an excuse for default in the main contract. (See, e.g., McBride & Wachtel, Government Contracts, § 35.10, [11].) In light of all this, Loral's claim should not be held insufficiently supported because it did not request an extension from the Government.

Loral, as indicated above, also had the burden of demonstrating that it could not obtain the parts elsewhere within a reasonable time, and there can be no doubt that it met this burden. The 10 manufacturers whom Loral contacted comprised its entire list of "approved vendors" for precision gears and none was able to commence delivery soon enough.[4] As Loral was producing a highly sophisticated item of military machinery requiring parts made to the strictest engineering standards, it would be unreasonable to hold that Loral should have gone to other vendors, with whom it was either unfamiliar or dissatisfied, to procure the needed parts. As Justice Steuer noted in his dissent, Loral "contacted all the manufacturers whom it believed capable of making these parts" (35 A.D.2d at p. 393, 316 N.Y.S.2d at p. 534), and this was all the law requires.

It is hardly necessary to add that Loral's normal legal remedy of accepting Austin's breach of the contract and then suing for damages would have been inadequate under the circumstances, as Loral would still have had to obtain the gears elsewhere with all the concomitant consequences mentioned above. In other words, Loral actually had no choice, when the prices were raised by Austin, except to take the gears at the "coerced" prices and then sue to get the excess back.

Austin's final argument is that Loral, even if it did enter into the contract under duress, lost any rights it had to a refund of money by waiting, until July, 1967, long after the termination date of the contract, to disaffirm it. It is true that one who would recover moneys allegedly paid under duress must act promptly to make his claim known. . . . In this case, Loral delayed making its demand for a refund until three days after Austin's last delivery on the second subcontract. Loral's reason— for waiting until that time—is that it feared another stoppage of deliveries which would again put it in an untenable situation. Considering Austin's conduct in the past, this was perfectly reasonable, as the possibility of an application by Austin of further business compulsion still existed until all of the parts were delivered.

In sum, the record before us demonstrates that Loral agreed to the price increases in consequence of the economic duress employed by

---

4. Loral, as do many manufacturers, maintains a list of "approved vendors," that is, vendors whose products, facilities, techniques and performance have been inspected and found satisfactory.

Austin. Accordingly, the matter should be remanded to the trial court for a computation of its damages.

The order appealed from should be modified, with costs, by reversing so much thereof as affirms the dismissal of defendant Loral Corporation's claim and, except as so modified, affirmed.

BERGAN, JUDGE (dissenting).

Whether acts charged as constituting economic duress produce or do not produce the damaging effect attributed to them is normally a routine type of factual issue.

Here the fact question was resolved against Loral both by the Special Term and by the affirmance at the Appellate Division. It should not be open for different resolution here. . . .

When the testimony of the witnesses who actually took part in the negotiations for the two disputing parties is examined, sharp conflicts of fact emerge. Under Austin's version the request for a renegotiation of the existing contract was based on Austin's contention that Loral had failed to carry out an understanding as to the items to be furnished under that contract and this was the source of dissatisfaction which led both to a revision of the existing agreement and to entering into a new one.

This is not necessarily and as a matter of law to be held economic duress. On this appeal it is needful to look at the facts resolved in favor of Austin most favorably to that party. Austin's version of events was that a threat was not made but rather a request to accommodate the closing of its plant for a customary vacation period in accordance with the general understanding of the parties.

Moreover, critical to the issue of economic duress was the availability of alternative suppliers to the purchaser Loral. . . .

Austin asserted and Loral admitted on cross-examination that there were many suppliers listed in a trade registry but that Loral chose to rely only on those who had in the past come to them for orders and with whom they were familiar. It was, therefore, at least a fair issue of fact whether under the circumstances such conduct was reasonable and made what might otherwise have been a commercially understandable renegotiation an exercise of duress.

The order should be affirmed.

BURKE, SCILEPPI and GIBSON, JJ., concur with FULD, C.J.

BERGAN, J., dissents and votes to affirm in a separate opinion in which BREITEL and JASEN, JJ., concur.

NOTES

(1) *Questions.* Suppose that Loral had renounced its agreement with Austin a year before it did, shortly after acceding to Austin's demands. Laying aside the problem of duress, would it have been justified in renouncing the price increases? Would it have been justified in renouncing the purchase order under the second Navy contract? What is the answer to these questions under the

New York Gen.Oblig.L. § 5–1103, p. 353 above? What is the answer apart from such a statute?

If Loral had consented to Austin's demand for price increases without protesting as it did in the letter of July 22, but had not meant to pay as agreed, would that have been an instance of bad faith on Loral's part? See United States for Use and Benefit of Crane Co. v. Progressive Enterprises, Inc., 418 F.Supp. 662 (E.D.Va.1976).

(2) *Objective Standard?* Does the court apply the test for duress that the danger must have been sufficient to "overcome the mind of a person of ordinary firmness?" See Note, pp. 349–51 above. Holmes once remarked that to apply a requirement of ordinary courage in duress cases is "an attempt to apply an external standard of conduct in the wrong place." Silsbee v. Webber, 50 N.E. 555 (Mass.1898). And Holmes was usually insistent on objective criteria in the law.

(3) *Self-help.* Reconsider Watkins & Son v. Carrig, above. By making a concession to the excavator, as the defendant-promisee did, and contesting it later, the defendant got what has been called a "self-help specific performance remedy." Narasimhan, Modification ..., 97 Yale L.J. 61 (1987). "In general," Professor Narasimhan argues, "the promisee may justify her self-help remedy by showing either that she would have been entitled to specific performance or that specific performance, while theoretically preferable [to damages], would be unavailable for reasons of administrative limitation." Id. at 95. Otherwise the promisee under pressure should (as the law of duress sometimes requires) be expected to resist and claim damages.

If you accept this view, would you take issue with the decision in *Watkins & Son?* With that in *Austin Instrument?* With UCC 2–209?

(4) *Problem.* In wartime, when the national interest requires a program of rapid production of ships for the government, a large shipbuilding firm drives a hard bargain for its services, yielding immense profits. The government seeks later to reclaim part of its cost, charging the firm with duress. Is there a common-law remedy? Apart from making a one-sided bargain, what responses to the pressure might the government have made? Should the courts pass judgment on its choice of responses? When it seeks a judicial remedy for duress, is there any way for the courts to avoid passing such a judgment? See United States v. Bethlehem Steel Corp., 315 U.S. 289 (1952).

VICTIM'S OPTIONS

Some threats are so empty ("last opportunity to buy at this low price") that they cannot well amount to duress in a legal sense. In most cases where an issue of duress is fairly arguable, it has to be asked whether the victim of the threat was opportunistic in yielding to it, or might have resisted it and found a reasonably satisfactory remedy for any resulting injury. In the leading case on duress of goods, the defendant, a pawnbroker, argued that the plaintiff borrower might have gone to law to regain the property being wrongfully withheld from him. (Instead, he overpaid his debt to get it.) But the court said, "plaintiff might have had such an immediate want of his goods that an action of trover would not do his business." [a] Since then, allowance has regularly been made for the delay attendant on legal proceedings.[b]

If the threat is one to sue for a money judgment, the obvious mode of resistance is to make a defense. Some legal proceedings, however, such as mortgage foreclosure and body seizure, commonly put the debtor in a situation of greater urgency. Even so, the debtor may have recourse to injunctive relief, or to damages for abuse of legal process. To forego such a remedy, in favor of a settlement, is naturally prejudicial to the debtor in making a subsequent complaint of duress. Should the law insist on its preference that wrongful threats be met by resort to the courts? Professor Dawson observes that if the "freedom to litigate" is prized, to control abuses of it by injunction or tort recoveries impairs that freedom more directly than to do so through relief for duress. "The most that is sought," in the latter form, "is judicial review of a settlement, after surrender to the pressure. The object is neither to transfer nor to prevent losses but to cancel out the gain." [c]

NOTE

Financial Stress. The company building the Alyeska pipeline let a contract to a newly-formed corporation to barge pipe from Houston to Alaska. Impediments were met in loading and sailing, which caused long delays, wrangling between the parties, and finally termination of the contract. Now the goods were offloaded at Long Beach. Now the carrier has presented bills for services of several hundreds of thousands of dollars. Prompt payment is required; the carrier's president believes that its creditors' demands will otherwise cause bankruptcy. Officials of Alyeska have negotiated with the carrier's attorney, and are prepared to offer it $100,000 in full settlement. If you were counsel to Alyeska, would you advise it that the carrier may not accept such a settlement and thereafter make a triable claim for further payment? See Totem Marine Tug & Barge v. Alyeska Pipeline Service Co., 584 P.2d 15 (Alaska, 1978) (summary judgment for Alyeska reversed). What distinctions are there between this case and Austin Instrument v. Loral Corp.?

For an economic analysis of duress see Selmer Co. v. Blakeslee–Midwest Co., 704 F.2d 924 (7th Cir.1983), sustaining a settlement agreement between a contractor and a subcontractor. The financial difficulties of the sub, it was held, did not present a factual issue of duress. "The fundamental issue in a duress case is ... whether the statement that induced the promise is the kind of offer to deal that we want to discourage, and hence that we call a 'threat.' ... If contractual protections are illusory, people will be reluctant to make contracts. Allowing contract modifications to be avoided in circumstances such as those in *Alaska Packers' Ass'n* [p. 352 above] assures prospective contract parties that

---

a. Astley v. Reynolds, 2 Str. 915, 93 Eng.Rep. 939 (K.B.1732).

b. E.g., Ross Systems v. Linden Dari–Delite, 173 A.2d 258 (N.J.1961) ("no immediate and adequate remedy in the courts"). See also Silsbee v. Webber, 50 N.E. 555 (Mass.1898), as to the shortfall in the law of its own aspirations.

In a somewhat related connection, it has been said that "the notion of the arms' length transaction still requires that the 'arm' hold a boxing glove, rather than a mace." Roberts, J., dissenting in Fratto v. New Amsterdam Cas. Co., 252 A.2d 606, 609, 610 (Pa.1969).

c. Dawson, Duress Through Civil Litigation: I, 45 Mich.L.Rev. 571, 577 (1947).

signing a contract is not stepping into a trap, and by thus encouraging people to make contracts promotes the efficient allocation of resources."

"PAYMENT IN FULL" CHECKS

Some of the law affecting claim settlements has been illustrated above (e.g., Fiege v. Boehm, p. 55 above) and other instances are presented below. At this point we examine an aspect of the subject closely related to the materials of this section: the tender by a debtor of a payment that the debtor designates as conclusive settlement of the account between the parties. In some circumstances, if the creditor accepts the tender of payment the account is effectively settled and the debtor is discharged of further liability on the account. In some cases that result is indicated by the common law, and in others by a relatively new provision of the Uniform Commercial Code, § 3–311 (Accord and Satisfaction by Use of Instrument).

Section 3–311 alludes to two problems that the transaction may generate: Was there an effective agreement between the parties? and Did the debtor give consideration for the discharge? Section 3–311 addresses only situations in the amount of the claim in question was "unliquidated" was "subject to a bona fide dispute." According to a comment, other law applies to "cases in which a debtor is seeking discharge of a liquidated, undisputed amount by paying less than the amount owed." Comment 4.

A "full payment" problem arose in Kibler v. Frank L. Garrett & Sons, Inc., 439 P.2d 416 (Wash.1968). In that case Kibler sent a bill for $826 to Garrett & Sons for harvesting wheat. In return, Kibler received a check for $444. He noticed the typed notation on it, "Harvesting Wheat Washington Ranch." He did not notice the statement, in fine print, "By endorsement this check when paid is accepted in full payment of the following account." Kibler deposited the check and received payment. He then brought an action for the difference between the amount of his bill and the amount of the check. His action was dismissed. On appeal, *held:* Reversed. The court seemed to be concerned chiefly about the matter of agreement. It said: "while the claim was disputed, there was no showing that the defendant manifested to the plaintiff his intention to pay no more than the amount which he remitted." [a] More or less similar facts have been litigated countless times.

Three phases of the governing law can be identified. *Kibler* is an example of common-law rulings. An additional complication arose upon the enactment of the Code; and some precedents have been affected by two Code amendments (including the addition of UCC 3–311).

The general principle of the common law was expressed in a leading case as follows:

---

[a]. Curiously, the attorney for Garrett & Sons was apparently unaware of the fine print until it was called to his attention at the trial.

A debtor paying his own money may couple the payment with such conditions as he pleases.... From this the rule has grown up in connection with the satisfaction of unliquidated demands that one who sends a check to another upon a condition explicitly declared, that the demand shall be extinguished or the check sent back unused, may hold the creditor to the condition, however embarrassing the choice.

This was a statement by Cardozo of New York law, made in 1932.[b] In one case illustrating the rule, the payee of a check sought to evade the choice by erasing a "payment in full" legend before depositing the check. Toledo Edison Co. v. Roberts, 197 N.E. 500 (Ohio App.1934). The attempt failed.

A provision of the Uniform Commercial Code, as initially enacted, added complexity to the problem. Section 1–207 was construed, by a number of courts, so as reduce the utility of a full-payment check. As it stood then, the section suggested that even a payee who (unlike Kibler) faced a condition "explicitly declared" might both collect the check and thereafter assert a further payment right by the means of making an "explicit reservation of rights." Illustrations of an explicit reservation are given in the statute: "Such words as 'without prejudice', 'under protest' or the like are sufficient." (The initial version of the section contained only the part that later became subsection (1).) In New York, for example, the Court of Appeals concluded that the Code altered the rule quoted above.[c] The Vermont court agreed, finding "increasing evidence that the common-law outcome is harsh and arbitrary and does not comport with modern commercial needs and realities." [d]

Other courts disagreed. Section 1–207 and its Official Comment did not make specific reference to the payment-in-full check. Moreover, these courts were loyal to the policy underlying the common-law rule. "If we were to decide," one court said, "that a creditor can reserve his rights on a payment in full check, it would seriously circumvent what has been universally accepted in the business community as a convenient means for the resolution of disagreements." Pillow v. Thermogas Co. of Walnut Ridge, 644 S.W.2d 292 (Ark.App.1982).

Taking note of the division of authority, the UCC sponsors proposed an addition to § 1–207 in 1990, in conjunction with a proposed revision of Article 3 of the Code (Negotiable Instruments). The addition—new subsection (2)—makes the provision inapplicable when "an accord and satisfaction is attempted by tender of a negotiable instrument." Comment 3. In that situation, then, either UCC 3–311 applies and a discharge results, or it does not and "the issue ... is determined by the law of contract." Ibid.

b. Hudson v. Yonkers Fruit Company, 179 N.E. 373, 80 A.L.R. 1052 (N.Y.1932).

c. Horn Waterproofing Corp. v. Bushwick Iron & Steel Co., 488 N.E.2d 56 (N.Y. 1985).

d. Frangiosa v. Kapoukranidis, 627 A.2d 351 (Vt.1993) (with a full-payment check a debtor "seeks to pressure a creditor into choosing between an inadequate, but immediate, payment and litigation").

One requirement for the application of § 3–311 is that the claimant have obtained payment of an "instrument" (e.g., check) tendered as full satisfaction of the claim.   Other particulars of § 3–311 are noticed below.   The 1990 revisions have yet to be enacted in a number of states. New York is among them.

NOTES

(1) *Comparing Cases; Contrasting Views.*   The utility of payment-in-full checks is a subject of ongoing debate.   To some extent the debate turns on the character of the underlying claim.   Consider these cases:

(i) A homeowner is billed for remodelling work done under a "cost-plus" contract.   Believing the bill is excessive, the homeowner answers, enclosing a check, "I am sending you 80% of your bill.   By cashing this check you will release me from any further claim for your remodelling work." [e]

(ii) An insurance company receives a claim that it believes to be unfounded. It tenders a check for 5% of the claim, indicating a desire to settle for the nuisance value of the claim.

Are the cases fairly comparable?   Consider the following general observations:

"Offering a check for less than the contract amount, but 'in full settlement' inflicts an exquisite form of commercial torture on the payee." [f]

"Perhaps one should balance against [that], the exquisite pleasure that the rule of the conditioned check has afforded to many aggrieved consumers." [g]

(2) *Problems.*   In Kibler v. Frank L. Garrett & Sons, described above, the fine-print legend was on a "form check, presumably used in the payment of all of the defendant's accounts."   How might this fact be used in stating an argument for Kibler?

If the case were to arise under the Uniform Commercial Code as revised, would § 3–311 apply?   According to subsection (a), the section applies only when an instrument has been "in good faith tendered ... as full satisfaction."   See Comment 4 as to that case, and to one of a disproportionately small check sent by an insurer to a "necessitous" claimant.

(3) *UCC 3–311.*   Section 3–311 of revised Article 3 distinguishes between a claimant that is a government, corporation, or another "organization", and a claimant that is not.   As to the former, Comment 7 gives the instance of a small bill received by the customer of a chain store, and a response ("payment in full") directed to the store's chief executive officer.   Whether or not collection of the check effects a settlement depends in part on whether or not that officer gives personal attention to the payment, and on directions the store may have given the customer about how to protest a charge.

If the payee is not an "organization", however, the factors of decision under § 3–311 are somewhat different.   According to Comment 3, the differences are "minor variations" reflecting "modern business conditions....   The section is not designed to favor either the individual or the business organization."

e. These facts are suggested by Marton Remodeling v. Jensen, 706 P.2d 607 (Utah 1985).

f. R. Summers & J. White, The Uniform Commercial Code § 13–21 (2d ed. 1980).

g. Rosenthal, Discord and Dissatisfaction ..., 78 Colum.L.Rev. 48, 56 (1978).

In a case governed by the section, an organization that has not taken specified steps for channelling communications to it about disputed debts, and any individual, has a period of 90 days following payment within which to nullify a condition on payment, by making a tender of repayment.

Would you say that, while § 3–311 has much to say about the quality of a creditor's assent to the terms of a check, it is reticent about the problem of consideration?

(4) *Payment by Fiduciary.* Suppose this case: A lawyer has agreed to attempt collection of a client's claim, for a "reasonable" fee. Having collected the claim, the lawyer forwards a check to the client for 75% of the amount collected. In a cover letter the lawyer states that 25% is the usual charge and directs the client not to deposit the check if it considers the fee unreasonable. May the client deposit the check and call the attorney to account for any additional amount?

In Hudson v. Yonkers Fruit Company (fn. b, p. 372 above) the defendant company had effected a sale of apples owned by Hudson, at his request. The company sent Hudson a check for 90% of the price along with a statement indicating a deduction of 10% as a commission. Hudson sued for the balance, contending that the company had agreed to find a buyer without charge, as a friendly accommodation. In affirming a judgment for Hudson the court said: "The defendant was not merely a debtor, paying its own money, which it would have been free to retain or to disburse according to its pleasure. It was an agent, a fiduciary, accounting for money belonging to its principal.... The law will not suffer an agent to withhold moneys collected for a principal's account by the pressure of a threat that no part of the moneys will be remitted to the owner without the approval of deductions beneficial to the agent. Such conduct is a flagrant abuse of the opportunities and powers of a fiduciary position."

(5) *Payment of an Undisputed Part.* As to an ordinary debt, part of which is certainly due, it has been said: "the condition is unlawful when what is paid is no more than must certainly be due." Hudson v. Yonkers Fruit Company, above. But other cases indicate that the payment of an admitted part of a claim can, if suitably conditioned, effect a discharge of the whole. See, e.g., Marton Remodeling v. Jensen, fn. e above.

(b) Concealment and Misrepresentation

According to Chancellor Kent: "Cicero de Officiis, lib. 3. sec. 12–17, states the case of a corn merchant of Alexandria arriving at Rhodes in a time of great scarcity, with a cargo of grain, and with knowledge that a number of other vessels, with similar cargoes, had already sailed from Alexandria for Rhodes, and whom he had passed on the voyage. He then puts the question, whether the Alexandrine merchant was bound in conscience to inform the buyers of that fact, or to keep silence, and sell his wheat for an extravagant price; and he answers it by saying, that, in his opinion, good faith would require of a just and candid man, a frank disclosure of the fact." [a]

What is the requirement that the law makes, as opposed to the demand of conscience, for disclosing facts in a bargaining context? Many courts have said that they will not insist on the degree of disclosure that a person of exceptional scruple might make. On the other hand, in allowing bargaining advantages to be secured by persons of little scruple, the law may attach a competitive disadvantage to conscientious conduct.

NOTES

(1) *Expert Knowledge.* Should there be special rules about information derived from research, training, and experience? It is generally understood that dealers in certain types of merchandise, such as antiques and rare coins, for example, trade on their expertness, and they are not expected to disclose to their customers all the elements that enter into their evaluations. The expense of acquiring such expertness would not be justified if it did not yield bargaining advantages.   To some extent the same consideration affects the degree of disclosure required in most commercial exchanges. Compare the market expertness of middlemen, mentioned in Note 2, p. 347 above.

The next main case is a suit in tort, for deceit, rather than in contract. It demonstrates, however, the wide extent of the privilege commonly allowed to keep silent about material facts in the bargaining process.

(2) *The Kidd Creek Strike.* The discovery of an extremely valuable ore deposit near Timmins, Ontario, touched off an immense number of trades. The finder, Texas Gulf Sulphur Company, detected the deposit through aerial searches for electromagnetic "anomalies." Having found one, it purchased mineral rights and options from landowners in the vicinity. When the deposit was verified, but not publicly announced, officers of the firm made purchases of its stock. Some of the officers were successfully charged with violations of the securities laws, for wrongful use of "inside" information.[b] One of the landowners sued the firm for wrongful use of its information in dealing with him: it had failed to disclose "an unusually promising indication of economic mineralization on [his] property." A justification for enforcing the option is given in Kronman, Mistake, Disclosure, Information, and the Law of Contracts, 7 J.Leg. Studies 1 (1978).[c]

Certain information, Dean Kronman has argued, is "in essence a property right," at least when produced by a "deliberate search for socially useful information." The law tends (he said) to recognize such a right, and "not to

a. 2 Kent's Commentaries 491 * n. c (3d ed. 1836). Kent cited Grotius, Puffendorf, and Pothier for the contrary opinion, but he added, "It is a little singular, however, that some of the best ethical writers under the Christian dispensation, should complain of the moral lessons of Cicero, as being too austere in their texture, and too sublime in speculation, for actual use."

b. See S.E.C. v. Texas Gulf Sulphur Co., 446 F.2d 1301 (2d Cir.1971), cert. denied, 404 U.S. 1005, reh. denied, 404 U.S. 1064.

And the company itself was held accountable to former stockholders for its mismanagement of the news. Mitchell v. Texas Gulf Sulphur Co., 446 F.2d 90 (10th Cir. 1971), cert. denied, 404 U.S. 1004, reh. denied, 404 U.S. 1064.

c. The "landowner" was actually the corporate representative of a trust. For an account of the suit see M. Shulman, The Billion Dollar Windfall, Ch. 7 (1969). The case was settled, Dean Kronman reported.

recognize it where the information has been casually acquired"—so enhancing efficiency in resource allocation. Id. at 33.

SWINTON v. WHITINSVILLE SAV. BANK

Supreme Judicial Court of Massachusetts, 1942.
311 Mass. 677, 42 N.E.2d 808, 141 A.L.R. 965.

QUA, JUSTICE. The declaration alleges that on or about September 12, 1938, the defendant sold the plaintiff a house in Newton to be occupied by the plaintiff and his family as a dwelling; that at the time of the sale the house "was infested with termites, an insect that is most dangerous and destructive to buildings"; that the defendant knew the house was so infested; that the plaintiff could not readily observe this condition upon inspection; that "knowing the internal destruction that these insects were creating in said house", the defendant falsely and fraudulently concealed from the plaintiff its true condition; that the plaintiff at the time of his purchase had no knowledge of the termites, exercised due care thereafter, and learned of them about August 30, 1940; and that, because of the destruction that was being done and the dangerous condition that was being created by the termites the plaintiff was put to great expense for repairs and for the installation of termite control in order to prevent the loss and destruction of said house.

There is no allegation of any false statement or representation, or of the uttering of a half truth which may be tantamount to a falsehood. There is no intimation that the defendant by any means prevented the plaintiff from acquiring information as to the condition of the house. There is nothing to show any fiduciary relation between the parties, or that the plaintiff stood in a position of confidence toward or dependence upon the defendant. So far as appears the parties made a business deal at arm's length. The charge is concealment and nothing more; and it is concealment in the simple sense of mere failure to reveal, with nothing to show any peculiar duty to speak. The characterization of the concealment as false and fraudulent of course adds nothing in the absence of further allegations of fact. Province Securities Corp. v. Maryland Casualty Co., 269 Mass. 75, 92, 168 S.E. 252.

If this defendant is liable on this declaration every seller is liable who fails to disclose any nonapparent defect known to him in the subject of the sale which materially reduces its value and which the buyer fails to discover. Similarly it would seem that every buyer would be liable who fails to disclose any nonapparent virtue known to him in the subject of the purchase which materially enhances its value and of which the seller is ignorant. See Goodwin v. Agassiz, 283 Mass. 358, 186 N.E. 659. The law has not yet, we believe, reached the point of imposing upon the frailties of human nature a standard so idealistic as this. That the particular case here stated by the plaintiff possesses a certain appeal to the moral sense is scarcely to be denied. Probably the reason is to be found in the facts that the infestation of buildings by termites has not been common in Massachusetts and constitutes a concealed risk against which buyers are off their guard. But the law cannot provide special rules for termites and can hardly attempt to determine liability according to the varying probabilities of the existence and discovery of different possible defects in the subjects of trade. The rule of nonliability for bare nondisclosure has been stated and followed by this court in [seven cases cited]. It is adopted in the American Law Institute's Restatement of Torts, § 551. See Williston on Contracts, Rev.Ed., §§ 1497, 1498, 1499.

The order sustaining the demurrer is affirmed, and judgment is to be entered for the defendant. Keljikian v. Star Brewing Co., 303 Mass. 53, 55–63, 20 N.E.2d 465.

So ordered.

NOTES

(1) *Questions.* Does it follow from this holding that the plaintiff could not have rescinded the sale, on establishing the facts he alleged? If the decision had been to the contrary, overruling the demurrer, would it follow that the plaintiff *could* have rescinded the sale? (An answer to this question is suggested by the next main case.) If the sale had not been executed, and the seller had brought an action against the buyer for specific performance, would it have succeeded?

(2) *Latent Defects: Caveat Emptor?* For a statute requiring that sellers of homes disclose defects known to them—unless the property is sold "as is"—see Va.Code §§ 55–517 et seq. (1994). Apart from statute, some courts require that dangerous conditions be disclosed. Some impose a warranty, in cases of sales by builders, that a home is fit for habitation. Given one or more of these measures in favor of buyers, would you expect the courts to be confirmed in the general rule of *caveat emptor* so far as they do not apply? See Hydro–Manufacturing, Inc. v. Kayser–Roth Corp., 640 A.2d 950, 954–57 (R.I.1994) (negligence claim against polluter—not the plaintiff's vendor).

In a case like *Swinton,* some courts start with the proposition that a seller of a home should disclose to the buyer a so-called latent defect—a deleterious condition, known to the seller, that is not readily observable. "[W]e are certain," the New Jersey court has said, that *Swinton* "does not represent our sense of justice or fair dealing." Weintraub v. Krobatsch, 317 A.2d 68 (N.J. 1974). Another court contrasted the sale of a simple farm home with the sale of a modern residence of complex construction. While the ancient rule of *caveat emptor* "may have had some merit in the agrarian society in which it was applied," the court thought, it is "no longer an expression of American mores." Holcomb v. Zinke, 365 N.W.2d 507 (N.D.1985). But see Boyd, C.J., dissenting, in Johnson v. Davis, 480 So.2d 625 (Fla.1985): although it "sounds progressive, high-minded, and idealistic," a decision to blur the distinction between misrepresentation and nondisclosure can be expected to distort the real-estate market. Id. at 629, 631.

What justification might be given for imposing a broad disclosure requirement in connection with the sale of a new home by the builder, and otherwise adhering to the *Swinton* rule? Compare Compass Point Condominium Owners Ass'n v. First Federal Sav. & Loan Ass'n, 641 So.2d 253 (Ala.1994), with Hill v. Jones, 725 P.2d 1115 (Ariz.App.1986) (termite case). In the case of a builder-vendor, is an implied warranty more suitable, as protection for the buyer, than a disclosure requirement?

(3) *Remedies.* A considerable array of remedies are suggested by the authorities cited in the foregoing Note. In *Weintraub*, the buyers were sued initially for specific performance and countered with a rescission claim. (The seller abandoned her claim for specific performance.) In *Johnson*, the sellers were required to repay the amounts they had received from the buyers, with interest. In *Holcomb* (as in *Weintraub*), the court ordered rescission of the contract. It charged the sellers for the buyers' expenses in curing defects, but charged the buyers with the reasonable rental value of the home. In *Compass Point*, the buyers claimed punitive damages. In the Virginia statute, one of the remedies provided for a buyer is recovery of the "actual damages suffered" as a result of an undisclosed defect.

What might a buyer hope to recover in a breach-of-warranty action against the seller? If that action is available to a buyer, should the buyer be permitted to choose rescission instead?

(4) *A Change of Career.* A religious congregation employed a man of the cloth to provide spiritual and educational leadership on the strength of two services he conducted, some conversations, and a sparse resume ("references on request"). Thereafter it transpired that he had been convicted for scheming to defraud an insurance company and had been disbarred as an attorney for bribing a police officer. In an action by the employer for rescission of the contract, summary judgment was granted for the plaintiff. See Jewish Center of Sussex County v. Whale, 397 A.2d 712 (N.J.Super.1978) (concealment), aff'd, 432 A.2d 521 (N.J.1981) (misrepresentation).

(5) *Problem.* In connection with the sale of S's home to B, S is required to provide a "termite-inspection report." A firm employed by S to make the report gives S an envelope containing two documents: a letter reporting no current infestation, and a "graph" showing signs of a prior infestation. S extracts the graph and delivers the letter to B. After the sale is completed, B learns of the graph. B would have resisted paying for the home if S had delivered both documents. Is any relief available to B? See Soniat v. Johnson–Rast & Hays, 626 So.2d 1256 (Ala.1993).

KANNAVOS v. ANNINO
Supreme Judicial Court of Massachusetts, 1969.
356 Mass. 42, 247 N.E.2d 708.

[In 1961 or 1962, Mrs. Carrie Annino bought a one-family dwelling in Springfield: No. 11, Ingersoll Grove.[a] She converted it into a multi-family building with eight apartments, without obtaining a building permit, and in knowing violation of the city zoning ordinance. The house was in a "Residence A" district, where multi-family uses were prohibited. In 1965 a real-estate broker was employed to try to sell the property. He placed newspaper ads, of which the following is an example: "Income gross $9,600 yr. in lg. single house, converted to 8 lovely, completely furn. (includ. TV and china) apts. 8 baths, ideal for couple to live free with excellent income. By apt. only. Foote Realty."

a. Throughout the transactions described, Mrs. Annino acted as the authorized agent for the Annino Realty Trust. Her co-defendants, not mentioned hereafter, were Samuel Annino and Joseph Santospirito.

[Apostolos Kannavos read one of the ads, and got in touch with the broker, Foote. Foote showed him the house, and gave him income and expense figures supplied by Mrs. Annino. Without the aid of a lawyer, Kannavos contracted to buy the property, and did so, borrowing money from a bank for the purpose, and giving it a mortgage. At the closing, attorneys for the seller and for the mortgagee were present, and the latter prepared the papers. Mrs. Annino and Foote knew that Kannavos's reason for buying was to rent the apartments. He was unaware of any zoning or building permit violation, and would not have purchased the property if he had known of any such violation. It was worth substantially less if operated only as a single-family dwelling than it was as an apartment building.

[Soon after the sale, the city started legal proceedings to abate the non-conforming use of the building.[b] Kannavos brought a bill in equity against Mrs. Annino to rescind the purchase. The trial court overruled a demurrer, and granted rescission on the basis of findings by a master. Mrs. Annino appealed.

[It appeared that Kannavos had immigrated from Greece in 1957, when he was about thirty years old. In this country he had learned English, and become a self-employed hairdresser. It was found that he made no inquiry of anyone about zoning or building permits before or during the closing, and that no statements were made to him on these subjects. Everything that was said to him by or on behalf of the seller was substantially true.]

CUTTER, JUSTICE.... We assume that, if the vendors had been wholly silent and had made no references whatsoever to the use of the Ingersoll Grove houses, they could not have been found to have made any misrepresentation. See Swinton v. Whitinsville Sav. Bank, 311 Mass. 677, 678–679, 42 N.E.2d 808, 141 A.L.R. 965,[1] where this court affirmed an order sustaining a demurrer to a declaration in an action of tort brought by a purchaser of a house.... The court (p. 679) indicated that it was applying a long standing "rule of nonliability for *bare nondisclosure*" (emphasis supplied).

As in the *Swinton* case, the parties here were dealing at arm's length, the vendees were in no way prevented from acquiring information, and the vendors stood in no fiduciary relationship to the vendees. In two aspects, however, the present cases differ from the *Swinton* case: viz. (a) The vendees themselves could have found out about the zoning violations by inquiry through public records, whereas in the *Swinton* case the purchaser would have probably discovered the presence of

---

b. As to other, similar properties that Kannavos (and an associate) also bought from Mrs. Annino, the city also asserted violations of the building code, but the opinion does not make it clear whether or not No. 11 was in question on this score.

1. The *Swinton* case may not represent the law elsewhere. See Restatement 2d: Torts, § 551 (Tent. Draft No. 11, April 15, 1965), p. 43; Prosser, Torts (3d ed.), § 101,

p. 711. Cf. discussions of situations in landlord and tenant cases like Cutter v. Hamlen, 147 Mass. 471, 474, 18 N.E. 397, 1 L.R.A. 429; Stumpf v. Leland, 242 Mass. 168, 172–174, 136 N.E. 399; Cooper v. Boston Housing Authy., 342 Mass. 38, 40, 172 N.E.2d 117. For general consideration of silence as misrepresentation, see Restatement: Restitution, § 8; Williston, Contracts (2d ed.) § 1497.

termites only by retaining expert investigators; and (b) there was something more here than the "bare nondisclosure" of the seller in the *Swinton* case.

(a) We deal first with the affirmative actions by the vendors, their conduct, advertising, and statements. Was enough said and done by the vendors so that they were bound to disclose more to avoid deception of the vendees and reliance by them upon a half truth? In other words, did the statements made by the vendors in their advertising and otherwise take the cases out of the "rule of nonliability for bare nondisclosure" applied in the *Swinton* case?

Although there may be "no duty imposed upon one party to a transaction to speak for the information of the other ... if he does speak with reference to a given point of information, voluntarily or at the other's request, he is bound to speak honestly and to divulge all the material facts bearing upon the point that lie within his knowledge. Fragmentary information may be as misleading ... as active misrepresentation, and half-truths may be as actionable as whole lies...." See Harper & James, Torts, § 7.14. See also Restatement: Torts, § 529; Williston, Contracts (2d ed.) §§ 1497–1499. The existence of substantially this principle was assumed in the *Swinton* case, 311 Mass. 677, 678, 42 N.E.2d 808, 141 A.L.R. 965, in the first sentence of the passage from that case quoted above. Massachusetts decisions have applied this principle. See Kidney v. Stoddard, 7 Metc. 252, 254–255 (a father represented that his son was entitled to credit but failed to disclose that the son was a minor; statement treated as a fraudulent representation); Burns v. Dockray, 156 Mass. 135, 137, 30 N.E. 551 (assertion that title was good [see Lyman v. Romboli, 293 Mass. 373, 374, 199 N.E. 916] but omitting to refer to the possible insanity of one whose incompetence might cloud title); Van Houten v. Morse, 162 Mass. 414, 417–419, 38 N.E. 705, 26 L.R.A. 430 (partial disclosure by a woman to her fiance about a prior divorce). See also ... Boston Five Cents Sav. Bank v. Brooks, 309 Mass. 52, 55–56, 34 N.E.2d 435, 437 ("Deception need not be direct.... Declarations and conduct calculated to mislead ... which ... do mislead one ... acting reasonably are enough to constitute fraud"). Cf. Wade v. Ford Motor Co., 341 Mass. 596, 597–598, 171 N.E.2d 282.

The master's report provides ample basis for treating the present cases as within the decisions just cited. The original advertisements in effect offered the houses as investment properties and referred to them as single houses converted to apartments. The investment aspect of the houses was emphasized by Foote's action in furnishing income and expense figures. There was an express assertion that 11 Ingersoll Grove was "being rented to the public for multi-family purposes" and that Kannavos and Bellas "could continue to operate ... [the other properties] as multi-dwelling property." The master's conclusions indicate that this statement applied to all the properties.[2] The buildings were

---

2. In any event some discussions with respect to all these properties in the same　　neighborhood were going on about the same time and the later transaction appears to

divided into apartments. The sales included refrigerators, stoves, and other furnishings appropriate for apartment use as well as real estate. The vendors knew that the vendees were planning to continue to use the buildings for apartments, and yet the vendors still failed to disclose the zoning and building violations. We conclude that enough was done affirmatively to make the disclosure inadequate and partial, and, in the circumstances, intentionally deceptive and fraudulent.

(b) The second difference between these cases and the *Swinton* case is the character of the defect not disclosed.

In the *Swinton* case, the presence of predatory insects threatened the structure sold. In the absence of any seller's representations whatsoever, there was no duty to disclose this circumstance, even though doubtless it would have been difficult to discover. In the present cases, the defect in the premises related to a matter of public regulation, the zoning and building ordinances. Its applicability to these premises could have been discovered by these vendees or by the vendees' counsel if, acting with prudence, they had retained counsel, which they did not. The bank mortgagee's counsel presumably was looking only to the protection of the bank's security position. Nevertheless, where there is reliance on fraudulent representations or upon statements and action treated as fraudulent, our cases have not barred plaintiffs from recovery merely because they "did not use due diligence . . . [when they] could readily have ascertained from . . . records" what the true facts were. See Yorke v. Taylor, 332 Mass. 368, 373, 124 N.E.2d 912. There this court allowed rescission because of the negligent misrepresentation, innocent but false, of the current assessed value of the property being sold. Here the representations made by the advertising and the vendors' conduct and statements in effect were that the property was multi-family housing suitable for investment and that the housing could continue to be used for that purpose. Because the vendors did as much as they did do, they were bound to do more. Failing to do so, they were responsible for misrepresentation. We think the situation is comparable to that in Yorke v. Taylor, 332 Mass. 368, 374, 124 N.E.2d 912, even though there the misrepresentation was "not consciously false" and here it was by half truth.

We hold that the vendors' conduct entitled the vendees to rescind. See Yorke v. Taylor, 332 Mass. 368, 371–372, 374, 124 N.E.2d 912; Restatement: Contracts, §§ 472, 489; Restatement: Restitution, § 28; Williston, Contracts (2d ed.) §§ 1497–1500. There was, in our opinion, much more than "bare nondisclosure" as in the *Swinton* case. Cf. Spencer v. Gabriel, 328 Mass. 1, 2, 101 N.E.2d 369; Donahue v. Stephens, 342 Mass. 89, 92, 172 N.E.2d 101.

[The court affirmed the decree below overruling the demurrer. However, it reversed the final decree so that there might be further

have been commenced either before or about the time the earlier one was completed.

consideration of the relief, in view of a fire that had occurred at No. 11 after that decree.]

NOTES

(1) *Question.* Does it follow from this decision that Kannavos could have maintained an action in deceit against Mrs. Annino? The requisites of that action, and the remedy it affords, are dealt with in detail in courses on torts. It should be noted, however, that contract remedies are not the only guarantees of minimum decencies in the bargaining process.

(2) *Sales Talk.* Consider the following cases, briefly sketched, as problems in assigning responsibility for a buyer's disappointment to the seller. How would the Massachusetts court have decided them?

(a) Answering a dealer's ad, C bought a used car after a test drive. The salesman had told him it was air-conditioned (repeating a statement in the ad), "and that Chrysler was a nice car and all that jazz." Contract voidable by C when he learns that the knobs marked "air" are for ventilation only? See Williams v. Rank & Son Buick, Inc., 170 N.W.2d 807 (Wis.1969) (fraud action; 4–3 decision).

(b) A grower of cattle discussed with a potential buyer sales that had occurred earlier in the day at a local sales barn. The buyer had attended. The grower contracted to sell 360 head at $60 a hundredweight. Now he knows—as the buyer knew earlier—that some cattle had been sold at the barn for as much as $62 a hundredweight. Contract voidable? See Kanzmeier v. McCoppin, 398 N.W.2d 826 (Iowa 1987).

(3) *The Case of the Reforming Hand.* John Hand sued his former employer (D–H) for breach of contract and age discrimination after his job as an attorney was eliminated. D–H moved for summary judgment on the ground that Hand had released it from these claims. Upon firing Hand, D–H had offered him $38,000 for a general release of any claim he might have against it. The release form was given to Hand for study. He conceived a "clever scheme" for turning the tables (as he put it) on D–H. He retyped the document so as to mimic the original, but inserted the term, "except as to claims of age discrimination and breach of contract." Not suspecting the change, D–H executed the copy and paid Hand $38,000. Assuming that Hand's conduct was fraudulent, and that D–H's failure to read the copy was excusable, should Hand be permitted to return the amount paid him and maintain his claims? Or should he be bound by the release as D–H understood it? For opinions on reformation to conform a writing to an agreement to which one of the parties did not assent, see Hand v. Dayton-Hudson, 775 F.2d 757 (6th Cir.1985).

————

MISREPRESENTATION

Misrepresentation is a ground for rescinding a contract, closely related to concealment. As a predicate for a tort action, it may be necessary for the plaintiff to establish that the defendant made the misrepresentation knowing it to be false, or at least with reckless disregard for its truth. This element in deceit actions is known as *scienter.* The requirement was insisted on in 19th century English cases, and remains influential in many courts. In contract law it generally has never had the same force, owing partly to the equitable character of rescission. See Halpert v. Rosenthal, 267 A.2d 730 (R.I. 1970), a "termite case" making the distinction. As a rule, a party to a contract may avoid it if the other party obtained its assent by an innocent misrepresentation, i.e., one that the party making it believed to be true. What difference between the functions of tort and contract law might explain this difference in sensitivity to the nature of a falsehood?

In both tort and contract law relief for misrepresentation is restricted in some ways that merit at least a mention. (To the extent that they are distinctive, the principles of tort law will not be pursued here.)

It has sometimes been held that a misrepresentation of law is innocuous. The same thought underlies the view that *mistake* of law is not a ground for relief: everyone should know the law. Apart from the general discredit that has fallen on such reasoning, its influence on misrepresentation cases has been limited in practice. One reason is that the author of a misrepresentation of law is frequently one better placed to know the law than the victim of it is: a lawyer speaking to a client, an insurance agent to a customer, and so on. In such cases the inequality of competence is perceived as a reason for giving relief.

A misrepresentation of opinion, as opposed to one of fact, is not a ground for relief, by tradition. Doubtless the distinction retains considerable force as it affects ordinary "puffing" of the style, "This property is worth every cent I am asking for it." Yet the distinction has lost much of its clarity, as witness a case in which the seller's statement was: "these are good, sound buildings and they will make you a good investment." Maser v. Lind, 148 N.W.2d 831, 22 A.L.R.3d 965 (Neb.1967). Again, the relative positions of the parties may influence the decision more than the form of words that was used. See, for example, Ward Development Co. v. Ingrao, 493 A.2d 421 (Md.App.1985), in which the court approved a recovery against a seller of homes for negligence in stating an *estimate* of an expense the buyers should expect: "the homeowners relied on Ward ... as knowledgeable in the field of real estate."

The misrepresentation must be a material one. This requirement is prominent in insurance litigation, where a misrepresentation by a policy buyer relating to health is a commonplace ground for rejecting a claim. A policy of medical expense insurance, for example, was voidable because the application for it omitted reference to various prior occasions of hospital treatment, including one for angina pectoris. As to the applicant's prior treatment for an infected toenail, however, the judges thought that the misrepresentation was immaterial.[a] Various standards of materiality have been expressed, and none of them is applied uniformly. They serve the common function, however, of justifying a certain control by judges over the more volatile behavior of juries.

When a contract is enforced in favor of a party who made a misrepresentation, a reason sometimes given is that the other party was negligent in relying on it. Naturally, the degree of diligence required in

a. Delaney v. Prudential Ins. Co., 139 N.W.2d 48 (Wis.1966).

detecting a falsehood is a function partly of the victim's capacities, partly of the nature of the transaction, and partly of the plausibility of the representation. The question of diligence should be distinguished from the question whether any credence was placed in the representation at all. If it was not relied upon in that sense, no legal consequences follow from a misrepresentation. There can be no complaint about a statement by one who heard it and proceeded to investigate its accuracy: "reliance and verification are incompatible." [b] There is a necessary dimension in a complaint about misrepresentation, however, that goes beyond the fact of reliance. In the currently preferred formulation, the complainant must show *justifiable* reliance.

Other limitations on relief for misrepresentation mentioned above, notably those having to do with statements of law and statements of opinion, have been considerably relaxed, if not subsumed entirely under the issue last mentioned. There is a plain tendency to consider the character of the statement in question as only one aspect of the broader issue whether or not the complainant justifiably relied upon it.

NOTES

(1) *Promissory Fraud.* According to Hoffman v. Red Owl Stores, p. 268 above, in a passage omitted there, a tort action for misrepresentation "cannot be predicated on unfulfilled promises unless the promisor possessed the present intent not to perform." The tort requires a misrepresentation of *fact,* that is. But a promise can be interpreted as including the (factual) representation, "I do not mean to default." On this understanding of the tort, can there be liability for negligent promising, as opposed to "promissory fraud"?

The law is shot through with the distinction between promises made without the intent to perform and promises that are simply not performed. Whether or not a contract obligation is discharged in a bankruptcy often depends, for example, on an application of the distinction. For a case in which a tort judgment was reversed because of the jury's disregard of the precept that "fraud cannot be predicated upon the mere fact that a promise has been broken," see International Travel Arrangers v. NWA, Inc., 991 F.2d 1389 (8th Cir.1993). See also Moore, Owen, Thomas & Co. v. Coffey, 992 F.2d 1439, 1447 (6th Cir.1993)— in which, however, exceptions and limitations are described.

(2) *Post–Contract Misrepresentations.* Consider again the facts in Lucy v. Zehmer, p. 140 above, assuming that Zehmer was as serious about selling the Ferguson farm as Lucy was about buying it. Assume also that on the day following the restaurant transaction, Lucy had asked Zehmer about the prior year's income from the farm. If Zehmer had answered with an inflated figure, would the contract have been voidable *by Lucy?* In considering this question, what weight might be placed on the further fact that Lucy proceeded later to arrange financing and have the title examined?

On these facts, would you have scruples about representing Zehmer in the suit *Zehmer v. Lucy?* Should the matter be left to Zehmer's "interior forum, as the tribunal of conscience has been aptly called?" (quotation from Mills v. Wyman, p. 67 above.) Would you expect a court to reject a specific performance

---

b. Hayat Carpet Cleaning Co., Inc. v. Northern Assur. Co., 69 F.2d 805 (2d Cir. 1934) (L. Hand).

claim for Zehmer, even if it would award damages? Compare McKinnon v. Benedict, p. 337 above.

"It would be contrary to all notions of fairness and justice," according to one case, "for this Court to place its stamp of approval on an affirmative misrepresentation . . . just because it was made after the signing of the executory contract when all of the necessary elements for actionable fraud are present." Johnson v. Davis, 480 So.2d 625 (Fla.1985). But the precedents are divided.

(3) *What the Document Means.* "A representation as to the legal effect of a document is regarded as a statement of opinion rather than of fact and will not ordinarily support an action for fraud." Fina Supply, Inc. v. Abilene Nat. Bank, 726 S.W.2d 537 (Tex.1987).

In this case a bank (defendant) had given a formal assurance to a customer (plaintiff) that the customer could require the bank to pay certain obligations of a third party. The customer, Fina, dealt in large quantities of oil. The document expressing the bank's assurance had been amended from time to time. In litigation between Fina and the bank about the scope of the bank's assurance, Fina charged that a bank employee had misled it about the effect of the amendments. Fina charged the bank with fraud and sought reformation of the document (letter of credit) expressing the bank's undertaking.

From a judgment for Fina, the bank appealed. *Held:* Reversed. See the sentence quoted above. The court also said: "where the parties are in an equal bargaining position with equal access to legal advice, there is no room for application of the doctrine that misrepresentations of points of law will be considered misrepresentations of fact if they were so intended and understood."

CONFIDENTIAL RELATIONS

In attempting to avoid contracts on the ground of overreaching, the key to success often lies in establishing that a relation of trust and confidence existed between the parties, so that the bargain was not an arm's length transaction. In the absence of such a relation, it is said, fraud must be affirmatively shown, and will not be presumed. Furthermore, it is the tradition derived from equity practice that the evidence required to establish fraud must be "clear and convincing"—meeting a more exacting standard than that applied to most issues in civil litigation.

By contrast, when a confidential relation existed, and the party asserting rights under the contract is the one in whom confidence was reposed, the claimant is required to show that the bargain was "fair, conscientious, and beyond the reach of suspicion." Young v. Kaye, 279 A.2d 759 (Pa.1971). In this case, representative of many like it, an elderly man was imposed upon by an ex-convict who provided him services and won his confidence as a "tax consultant." As examples of confidential relations, the court mentioned guardian and ward, principal and agent, attorney and client. Beyond such routine entries, however, the list is not pre-determined. A "confidential relation" does not necessarily attend a friendship, or even a marriage; [a] yet an automobile dealer and a customer have been found to be in that relation, with respect to an arcane feature of their dealings.[b] "It is not restricted to any specific association ... but is deemed to exist whenever the relative position of the parties is such that one has power and means to take advantage of or exert undue influence over the other." [c]

NOTE

The Case of the Confiding Clerk. Some factors of particular relevance in identifying a confidential relationship are said to be "disparity of age, education and business experience between the parties." These were found to exist when Peter Roberts, a minor, assigned to Sears, Roebuck & Company all rights in an invention of his for a royalty not to exceed $10,000. Roberts relied on Sears' advice about the value of the invention, and on the advice of an attorney who (without informing Roberts) also accepted employment from Sears. There was evidence that in less than two years Sears made "an incremental profit of $44,032,082 from the sales of its wrenches with Roberts' quick release feature." When negotiating with him, Sears "downgraded" the value of the invention, though it had formed a high opinion of its merit.[d]

In a suit by Roberts, jury verdicts were held to justify relief against Sears. (What relief seems suitable)? Both parties appealed from a judgment for a million dollars. *Held:* Reversed in part, and remanded. Roberts v. Sears, Roebuck & Co., 573 F.2d 976 (7th Cir.1978), cert. denied, 439 U.S. 860. In approving the jury's finding of a confidential relationship, the court thought it significant that Roberts had submitted his idea to Sears while working for it as a sales clerk. (Sears' negotiating attorney, it seems, may not have been aware of that).

What changes in Sears' procedure with ideas would you suggest? Should it have disclosed to Roberts that it anticipated sales which would more than recapture its royalty costs in one year?

SECTION 4. UNCONSCIONABILITY AND PROBLEMS OF ADHESION CONTRACTS

In the preceding sections of this Chapter a number of familiar principles aimed at preserving the decencies of bargaining have been

a. Eaton v. Sontag, 387 A.2d 33 (Me. 1978); Francois v. Francois, 599 F.2d 1286 (3d Cir.1979).

b. Browder v. Hanley Dawson Cadillac, 379 N.E.2d 1206 (Ill.App.1978).

c. Young v. Kaye, above.

For a celebrated case in which an heiress alleged that she had been induced, through the abuse of a confidential relation, to support a religious organization over a period of years, and got restitution of assets worth several millions, see In re The Bible Speaks, 869 F.2d 628 (1st Cir.1989), cert. denied, 493 U.S. 816 (1989). (The claimant's family name was Dayton, as in "Dayton–Hudson.")

d. Some of the facts recited here are drawn from an opinion in the case on remand: Roberts v. Sears, Roebuck and Co., 471 F.Supp. 372 (N.D.Ill.1979). For later developments, a discussion of patent law, and drawings, see Roberts v. Sears, Roebuck & Co., 723 F.2d 1324 (7th Cir.1983).

seen at work, both limiting and supplementing the process. In this section some newly established or newly expanded ones are presented. The notion of unconscionability in contracts is by no means new, but it has taken on new life since it was embodied as a test of enforceability in the Uniform Commercial Code; a substantially new body of case law has formed about it, and there has been an explosion of literature on the subject. Also, the "contract of adhesion" has emerged in this century as a type of agreement requiring distinctive treatment. The principles mentioned thus far have been developed largely through judicial decisions. In this section it will be seen that legislative and administrative measures have an important and developing role in policing bargains. The question arises whether or not these are better means for dealing with overreaching by contract than any remedies the courts can devise.

In the policing rules to be illustrated, elements of status, behavior, and substance are often combined. That being so, it is perhaps inevitable that the rules are largely undefined. The notions of unconscionability and adhesion have not yet become fixed quantities in the law. Is it desirable that they should be? Would they cease to be useful as agents for the law's renewal if they were rigorously defined? Or do they cause needless uncertainty and confusion?

NOTES

(1) *Strict Construction.* It is often objected that courts introduce uncertainty and confusion by interpreting and construing agreements in accordance with their predispositions. The opinion that follows speaks of "strict construction" of provisions in leases whereby landlords attempt to immunize themselves from liability for negligence to their tenants. In reading the case, it will be well to have in mind the fact that a court's idea of fairness between the parties can sometimes be imposed on them by a purposive reading of their agreement. Many examples might be given, but one must suffice here: Galligan v. Arovitch, 219 A.2d 463 (Pa.1966). The plaintiff was a tenant in an apartment building who suffered injury in a fall on the lawn. She sued the owner, charging that he was accountable for negligence in maintenance. Judgment was given for the defendant on the pleadings. The plaintiff's lease excluded liability of the owner for injury arising from her use of the hallways and six other common areas, including sidewalks. On appeal, the judgment was reversed. One judge declared the provision violative of public policy, and another expressed serious doubt on that score. The opinion of the court, however, was based on the location of the injury—the lawn was not mentioned in the lease. "A lawn and a sidewalk are clearly different locations." [a] Two judges dissented. Might the decision have been based on a better ground? [b] Consider the view of Professor Llewellyn:

a. Compare Ultimate Computer Services, Inc. v. Biltmore Realty Co., Inc., 443 A.2d 723, 30 A.L.R.4th 963 (N.J.Super.1982), certif. denied, 450 A.2d 522 (N.J. 1982).

b. In Spallone v. Siegel, 362 A.2d 263 (Pa.Super.1976), five of seven judges concluded that an exculpatory clause in an apartment lease failed of effect because it did not apply, on the doctrine of strict construction, to the place of injury. One of

these, Judge Spaeth, developed another ground for the decision: "We do not wish to base our holding solely on [that] doctrine.... The courts of this state have too long used this circuitous route to avoid the harsh result of exculpatory clauses in leases.... [W]here such clauses appear in standard form leases they are presumptively invalid." None of his colleagues cared to join in these remarks; some of them ob-

"A court can 'construe' language into patently not meaning what the language is patently trying to say. It can find inconsistencies between clauses and throw out the troublesome one. It can even reject a clause as counter to the whole purpose of the transaction.... Indeed, the law of agreeing can be subjected to diverse modes of employment, to make the whole bargain or a clause stick or not stick according to the status of the party claiming under it.... The difficulty with these techniques of ours is threefold. First, since they all rest on the admission that the clauses in question are permissible in purpose and content, they invite the draftsman to recur to the attack. Give him time, and he will make the grade. Second, since they do not face the issue, they fail to accumulate either experience or authority in the needed direction: that of marking out for any given type of transaction what the *minimum decencies* are which a court will insist upon as essential to an enforceable bargain of a given type, or as being inherent in a bargain of that type. Third, since they purport to construe, and do not really construe, nor are intended to, but are instead tools of intentional and creative misconstruction, they seriously embarrass later efforts at true construction, later efforts to get at the true meaning of those wholly legitimate contracts and clauses which call for their meaning to be got at instead of avoided. The net effect is unnecessary confusion and unpredictability, together with inadequate remedy, and evil persisting that calls for remedy. Covert tools are never reliable tools." Llewellyn, Book Review, 52 Harv.L.Rev. 700, 702 (1939). See also Kessler, Contracts of Adhesion—Some Thoughts About Freedom of Contract, 43 Colum.L.Rev. 629, 631 (1943).

(2) *A Meaning Test.* "CONSENT FOR MEDICAL CARE ... I therefore release Dr. E.R. from all liabilities to me, including all claims and complaints by me or by other members of my family." Can this be read, as signed by a person about to take a course of treatment, as relating *only* to claims based on advice given earlier? See Schneider v. Revici, 817 F.2d 987 (2d Cir.1987).

O'CALLAGHAN v. WALLER & BECKWITH REALTY CO.

Supreme Court of Illinois, 1958.
15 Ill.2d 436, 155 N.E.2d 545.

SCHAEFER, JUSTICE.[c] This is an action to recover for injuries allegedly caused by the defendant's negligence in maintaining and operating a large apartment building. Mrs. Ella O'Callaghan, a tenant in the building, was injured when she fell while crossing the paved courtyard on her way from the garage to her apartment. She instituted this action to recover for her injuries, alleging that they were caused by defective pavement in the courtyard. Before the case was tried, Mrs. O'Callaghan died and her administrator was substituted as plaintiff. The jury returned a verdict for the plaintiff in the sum of $14,000, and judgment was entered on the verdict. Defendant appealed. The Appellate Court

served that the legislature had the issue before it.

Problems of interpreting agreements are dealt with in detail in Chapter 6, Section 2, below.

c. Walter V. Schaefer (1904–1986) practiced law and served in a variety of govern-

mental posts in Chicago between 1928 and 1940, when he became a professor of law at Northwestern University. From 1951 to 1976 he was a member of the Illinois Supreme Court. He was one of the Advisers for the Restatement Second.

[handwritten: enforced unless contrary to public policy]

held that the action was barred by an exculpatory clause in the lease that Mrs. O'Callaghan had signed, and that a verdict should have been directed for the defendant.   15 Ill.App.2d 349, 146 N.E.2d 198.   It therefore reversed the judgment and remanded the cause with directions to enter judgment for the defendant.   We granted leave to appeal.

In reaching its conclusion the Appellate Court relied upon our recent decision in Jackson v. First National Bank, 415 Ill. 453, 114 N.E.2d 721.   There we considered the validity of such an exculpatory clause in a lease of property for business purposes.   We pointed out that contracts by which one seeks to relieve himself from the consequences of his own negligence are generally enforced "unless (1) it would be against the settled public policy of the State to do so, or (2) there is something in the social relationship of the parties militating against upholding the agreement."   415 Ill. at page 460, 114 N.E.2d at page 725.   And we held that there was nothing in the public policy of the State or in the social relationship of the parties to forbid enforcement of the exculpatory clause there involved.

[handwritten: No liability]

[handwritten: LEASE] The exculpatory clause in the lease now before us clearly purports to relieve the lessor and its agents from any liability to the lessee for personal injuries or property damage caused by any act or neglect of the lessor or its agents.   It does not appear to be amenable to the strict construction to which such clauses are frequently subjected.   See 175 A.L.R. 8, 89.   The plaintiff does not question its applicability, and she concedes that if it is valid it bars her recovery.   She argues vigorously, *[handwritten: Argument]* however, that such a clause is contrary to public policy, and so invalid, in a lease of residential property.

Freedom of contract is basic to our law.   But when that freedom expresses itself in a provision designed to absolve one of the parties from the consequences of his own negligence, there is danger that the standards of conduct which the law has developed for the protection of others may be diluted.   These competing considerations have produced results that are not completely consistent.   This court has refused to enforce contracts exculpating or limiting liability for negligence between common carriers and shippers of freight or paying passengers (Chicago and Northwestern Railway Co. v. Chapman, 133 Ill. 96, 24 N.E. 417, 8 L.R.A. 508), between telegraph companies and those sending messages (Tyler, Ullman & Co. v. Western Union Telegraph Co., 60 Ill. 421), and between masters and servants (Campbell v. Chicago, Rock Island and Pacific Railway Co., 243 Ill. 620, 90 N.E. 1106).   The obvious public interest in these relationships, coupled with the dominant position of those seeking exculpation, were compelling considerations in these decisions, which are in accord with similar results in other jurisdictions.   See 175 A.L.R. 8.

On the other hand, as pointed out in the *Jackson* case, the relation of lessor and lessee has been considered a matter of private concern. Clauses that exculpate the landlord from the consequences of his negligence have been sustained in residential as well as commercial leases.... There are intimations in other jurisdictions that run counter to the current authority.   See Kuzmiak v. Brookchester, Inc., 1955, 33

N.J.Super. 575, 111 A.2d 425; Kay v. Cain, 1946, 81 U.S.App.D.C. 24, 154 F.2d 305. The New Hampshire court applies to exculpatory clauses in all leases its uniform rule that any attempt to contract against liability for negligence is contrary to public policy. Papakalos v. Shaka, 1941, 91 N.H. 265, 18 A.2d 377. But apart from the Papakalos case we know of no court of last resort that has held such clauses invalid in the absence of a statute so requiring.

A contract shifting the risk of liability for negligence may benefit a tenant as well as a landlord. See Cerny–Pickas & Co. v. C.R. Jahn Co., 7 Ill.2d 393, 131 N.E.2d 100. Such an agreement transfers the risk of a possible financial burden and so lessens the impact of the sanctions that induce adherence to the required standard of care. But this consideration is applicable as well to contracts for insurance that indemnify against liability for one's own negligence. Such contracts are accepted, and even encouraged. See Ill.Rev.Stat.1957, chap. 95½, pars. 7–202(1) and 7–315.

The plaintiff contends that due to a shortage of housing there is a disparity of bargaining power between lessors of residential property and their lessees that gives landlords an unconscionable advantage over tenants. And upon this ground it is said that exculpatory clauses in residential leases must be held to be contrary to public policy. No attempt was made upon the trial to show that Mrs. O'Callaghan was at all concerned about the exculpatory clause, that she tried to negotiate with the defendant about its modification or elimination, or that she made any effort to rent an apartment elsewhere. To establish the existence of a widespread housing shortage the plaintiff points to numerous statutes designed to alleviate the shortage (see Ill.Rev.Stat.1957, chap. 67½, *passim*) and to the existence of rent control during the period of the lease. 65 Stat. 145 (1947), 50 U.S.C.A. Appendix, § 1894.

Unquestionably there has been a housing shortage. That shortage has produced an active and varied legislative response. Since legislative attention has been so sharply focused upon housing problems in recent years, it might be assumed that the legislature has taken all of the remedial action that it thought necessary or desirable. One of the major legislative responses was the adoption of rent controls which placed ceilings upon the amount of rent that landlords could charge. But the very existence of that control made it impossible for a lessor to negotiate for an increased rental in exchange for the elimination of an exculpatory clause. We are asked to assume, however, that the legislative response to the housing shortage has been inadequate and incomplete, and to augment it judicially.

The relationship of landlord and tenant does not have the monopolistic characteristics that have characterized some other relations with respect to which exculpatory clauses have been held invalid. There are literally thousands of landlords who are in competition with one another. The rental market affords a variety of competing types of housing accommodations, from simple farm house to luxurious apartment. The use of a form contract does not of itself establish disparity of bargaining power. That there is a shortage of housing at one particular time or place does not indicate that such shortages have always and everywhere existed, or that there will be shortages in the future. Judicial determinations of public policy cannot readily take account of sporadic and transitory circumstances. They should rather, we think, rest upon a durable moral basis. Other jurisdictions have dealt with this problem by legislation. McKinney's Consol.Laws of N.Y.Ann., Real Property Laws, sec. 234, Vol. 49, Part I; Ann.Laws of Mass., Vol. 6, c. 186, sec. 15. In our opinion the subject is one that is appropriate for legislative rather than judicial action.

The judgment of the Appellate Court is affirmed.

BRISTOW, JUSTICE, and DAILY, CHIEF JUSTICE (dissenting). We cannot accept the conclusions and analysis of the majority opinion, which in our judgment not only arbitrarily eliminates the concept of negligence in the landlord and tenant relationship, but creates anomalies in the law, and will produce grievous social consequences for hundreds of thousands of persons in this State.

According to the undisputed facts in the instant case, this form lease with its exculpatory clause, was executed in a metropolitan area in 1947, when housing shortages were so acute that "waiting lists" were the order of the day, and gratuities to landlords to procure shelter were common. (U.S.Sen.Rep.1780, Committee on Banking & Currency, vol. II, 81st Cong., 2nd Sess. (1950), p. 2565 et seq.; Cremer v. Peoria Housing Authority, 399 Ill. 579, 589, 78 N.E.2d 276.) While plaintiff admittedly did not negotiate about the exculpatory clause, as the majority opinion notes, the record shows unequivocally that the apartment would not have been rented to her if she had quibbled about any clause in the form lease. According to the uncontroverted testimony, "If a person refused to sign a [form] lease in the form it was in, the apartment would not be rented to him."

Apparently, the majority opinion has chosen to ignore those facts and prevailing circumstances, and finds instead that there were thousands of landlords competing with each other with a variety of rental units. Not only was the element of competition purely theoretical—and judges need not be more naive than other men—but there wasn't even theoretical competition, as far as the exculpatory clauses were concerned, since these clauses were included in all form leases used by practically all landlords in urban areas. Simmons v. Columbus Venetian Stevens Building, Inc., Ill.App., 155 N.E.2d 372; 1952 Ill.L.Forum, 321, 328. This meant that even if a prospective tenant were to "take his business elsewhere," he would still be confronted by the same exculpatory clause in a form lease offered by another landlord.

Thus, we are *not* construing merely an isolated provision of a contract specifically bargained for by one landlord and one tenant, "a matter of private concern," as the majority opinion myoptically [sic] views the issue in order to sustain its conclusion. We are construing, instead, a provision affecting thousands of tenants now bound by such provisions, which were foisted upon them at a time when it would be pure fiction to state that they had anything but a Hobson's choice in the matter. Can landlords, by that technique, immunize themselves from liability for negligence, and have the blessings of this court as they destroy the concept of negligence and standards of law painstakingly evolved in the case law? That is the issue in this case, and the majority opinion at no time realistically faces it.

In resolving this issue, it is evident that despite the assertion in the majority opinion, there is no such thing as absolute "freedom of contract" in the law. West Coast Hotel Co. v. Parrish, 300 U.S. 379, 392, 57 S.Ct. 578, 582, 81 L.Ed. 703. As Mr. Justice Holmes stated, "pretty much all law consists in forbidding men to do some things that they want to do, and contract is no more exempt from law than other acts." Dissent, Adkins v. Children's Hospital of District of Columbia, 261 U.S. 525, 568, 43 S.Ct. 394, 405, 67 L.Ed. 785. Thus, there is no freedom to contract to commit a crime; or to contract to give a reward for the commission of a crime; or to contract to violate essential morality; or to contract to accomplish an unlawful purpose, or to contract in violation of public policy. 12 I.L.P. Contracts §§ 151, 154.

In the instant case we must determine whether the exculpatory clause in the lease offends the public policy of this State. We realize that there is no precise definition of "public policy" or rule to test whether a contract is contrary to public policy, so that each case must be judged according to its own peculiar circumstances. First Trust & Savings Bank of Kankakee v. Powers, 393 Ill. 97, 102, 65 N.E.2d 377. None would dispute, however, that there is a recognized policy of discouraging negligence and protecting those in need of goods or services from being overreached by those with power to drive unconscionable bargains.

Even the majority opinion recognizes this policy as a possible limitation on the concept of "freedom of contract" in its statement, "when that freedom expresses itself in a provision designed to absolve one of the parties from the consequences of his own negligence, there is danger that the standards of conduct which the law has developed for the protection of others may be diluted." Diluted? As applied in the instant case, the word is "destroyed." When landlords are no longer liable for failure to observe standards of care, or for conduct amounting to negligence by virtue of an exculpatory clause in a lease, then such standards cease to exist. They are not merely "diluted." Negligence cannot exist in abstraction. The exculpatory clause destroys the concept of negligence in the landlord-tenant relationship, and the majority opinion, in sustaining the validity of that clause, has given the concept of negligence in this relationship a "judicial burial."

This court, however, has refused to countenance such a destruction of standards of conduct and of the concept of negligence in other relationships. We have invalidated such exculpatory clauses as contrary to our public policy in contracts between common carriers and shippers or paying passengers ...; between telegraph companies and those sending messages ..., and between employers and employees....

By what logic and reasoning can you hold that such clauses are void and contrary to public policy in an employer-employee contract, but valid in contracts between landlords and tenants, as the majority opinion does? If the criterion for invalidating exculpatory clauses is the presence of "monopolistic characteristics" in the relationship, as the majority opinion suggests, then do employers have a greater monopoly on the labor market than landlords have on the tenant market? Is there less competition among employers for employees than among landlords for tenants? The facts defy any such reasoning. Nor are there any other cogent grounds for distinguishing between these categories....

The basis of voiding exculpatory clauses is that they are contrary to the public policy of discouraging negligence and protecting those in need of goods or services from being overreached by those with power to drive unconscionable bargains. Bisso v. Inland Waterways Corp., 349 U.S. 85, 91, 75 S.Ct. 629, 99 L.Ed. 911. In determining whether such clauses should be deemed void, the courts have weighed such factors as the importance which the subject has for the physical and economic well-being of the group agreeing to the release; their bargaining power; the amount of free choice actually exercised in agreeing to the exemption; and the existence of competition among the group to be exempted. (Williston, Contracts, vol. 6, p. 4968; "The Significance of Bargaining Power in the Law of Exculpation," 37 Col.L.Rev. 248; 175 A.L.R. 8, 48; 15 Univ.Pitt.L.Rev. 493.) Adjudged by such criteria, it is evident that the subject matter of the exculpatory clause herein—shelter—is indispensable for the physical well being of tenants; that they have nothing even approaching equality of bargaining power with landlords and no free choice whatever in agreeing to the exemption, since they will be confronted with the same clause in other form leases if they seek shelter elsewhere. Although the majority opinion claims that such clauses may also benefit tenants, it is hard for us to envisage a tenant on a waiting list for an apartment, insisting that the lease include a provision relieving him from liability for his negligence in the maintenance of the premises. Consequently, in our judgment, every material ground for voiding the exculpatory clause exists in the lease involved in the instant case....

NOTES

(1) *Current Law.* In most states, by statute, a provision in a residential lease exculpating the landlord from liability to the tenant for negligence is ineffective. In several others decisional rules have a similar effect. In some other states variant statutory rules prevail. In Maine, for example, a tenant may accept in writing "specified conditions which violate the warranty of fitness for human habitation in return for a stated reduction in rent or other fair consideration." [a] In Texas certain waivers by a tenant of a landlord's responsibilities are effective, subject to requirements of form. The waiver must be made "knowingly, voluntarily, and for consideration." [b] Are there situations in which a residen-

a. Me.Rev.Stat.Ann.Tit.   14   §§ 6021 (4)(B), (5) and 6026(5).

b. Tex.Prop.Code § 92.006(c), (e)(4)(D).

tial tenant might prefer, with full information, to exculpate a landlord from liability for negligence? What situations occur to you?

In several states there are statutory limitations on exculpatory provisions in commercial as well as residential leases. (Illinois is one of these.[c]) What differences between residential and commercial leasing might justify a difference in treatment?

(2) *Abusive Drafting?* A landlord asks you, his attorney, to prepare for his use a waiver of tenants' rights that you know to be unenforceable. What procedure would you follow in dealing with the situation? It is said that "many tenants give credence to lease provisions even if they are unenforceable." Note, 64 Corn.L.Q. 522, 526 (1979). To the extent that they do, whatever public policy supports their rights is naturally thwarted. In responding to your client, would it matter to you what that policy is? What if you did not know, but only suspected, the suggested provision to be unenforceable? The Note cited suggests some legislative and administrative means for dealing with the problem of credulous and unadvised tenants. If effective means were in place, would that affect your conduct? For a partial answer to these questions see Opinions on Professional Ethics, No. 435, Committee, Association of the Bar of the City of New York (1956).

(3) *Exculpation and Insurance.* In New Hampshire, where "naked exculpatory provisions" are disfavored, the court has approved exculpatory terms included in a construction contract as "part of a larger comprehensive approach to indemnifying the parties involved ..., allocating the risks involved, and spreading the costs of different types of insurance." Chadwick v. CSI, Ltd., 629 A.2d 820, 825 (N.H.1993).

Backlund v. Bd. of Commissioners of King County, 724 P.2d 981 (Wash. 1986), appeal dism'd, 481 U.S. 1034 (1987), reports on the difficulties of a hospital-staff physician who had a conscientious objection to purchasing malpractice-liability insurance. He said he had the consent of his patients to the omission. But, the court said, "with some exceptions, one may not contract against one's own negligence."

STANDARD FORM CONTRACTS

Standard form contracts have become a commonplace aspect of daily life. Their use in business affairs is so prevalent that they provide a vehicle for every move in the dealings of consumers with merchants and others.[d] Take, for example, a person who buys a car "on time." The contract of sale will be on a standard form prepared by a finance

---

c. Ill.Ann.Stat., ch. 765, para. 705/1.

d. A study of 500 contracts cases reported in 1951 revealed that written contracts were involved in 341, and that of these 187 seemed to have been the product of bargaining and negotiation, 123 to have been printed form contracts, with the remainder uncertain. Shepherd, Contracts in a Prosperity Year, 6 Stan.L.Rev. 208, 212 (1954). In another study, "Requests for copies of business documents used in buying and selling were sent to approximately 6,000 manufacturing firms which do business in Wisconsin. Approximately 1,200 replies were received and 850 companies used some type of standardized planning. With only a few exceptions, the firms that did not reply and the 350 that indicated they did not use standardized planning were very small manufacturers such as local bakeries, soft drink bottlers and sausage makers." Macaulay, Non–Contractual Relations in Business: A Preliminary Study, 28 Am.Sociological Rev. 55, 58 (1963).

company. The car will be insured under a standard form prepared by an insurance company. The check used for the down payment will be drawn on an account governed by a standard form prepared by a bank. And so it goes. Sometimes such items as quantity, quality and price will be open to actual bargain; sometimes they will not.

Mass production of contracts, like mass production of goods, may serve the interests of all parties. Among the advantages claimed for the use of standard form contracts are these: it takes advantage of the lessons of experience and enables a judicial interpretation of one contract to serve as an interpretation of all contracts; it reduces uncertainty and saves time and trouble; it simplifies planning and administration and makes the skill of the draftsman available to all personnel; it makes risks calculable and "increases that real security which is the necessary basis of initiative and the assumption of foreseeable risks." Cohen, The Basis of Contract, 46 Harv.L.Rev. 553, 558 (1933). Professor Kessler has discussed some of these advantages more fully:

"The development of large scale enterprise with its mass production and mass distribution made a new type of contract inevitable—the standardized mass contract. A standardized contract, once its contents have been formulated by a business firm, is used in every bargain dealing with the same product or service. The individuality of the parties which so frequently gave color to the old type of contract has disappeared. The stereotyped contract of today reflects the impersonality of the market. It has reached its greatest perfection in the different types of contracts used on the various exchanges. Once the usefulness of these contracts was discovered and perfected in the transportation, insurance, and banking business, their use spread into all other fields of large scale enterprise, into international as well as national trade, and into labor relations. It is to be noted that uniformity of terms of contracts typically recurring in a business enterprise is an important factor in the exact calculation of risks. Risks which are difficult to calculate can be excluded altogether. Unforeseeable contingencies affecting performance, such as strikes, fire, and transportation difficulties can be taken care of. The standard clauses in insurance policies are the most striking illustrations of successful attempts on the part of business enterprises to select and control risks assumed under a contract. The insurance business probably deserves credit also for having first realized the full importance of the so-called 'juridical risk', the danger that a court or jury may be swayed by 'irrational factors' to decide against a powerful defendant. Ingenious clauses have been the result. Once their practical utility was proven, they were made use of in other lines of business.... Standardized contracts have thus become an important means of excluding or controlling the 'irrational factor' in litigation. In this respect they are a true reflection of the spirit of our time with its hostility to irrational factors in the judicial process, and they belong in the same category as codifications and restatements." Kessler, Contracts of Adhesion—Some Thoughts About Freedom of Contract, 43 Colum.L.Rev. 629, 631–32 (1943).

But there are dangers inherent in standardized contract as well, for it may be the means by which one party imposes its will upon another unwilling or even unwitting party. Such contracts have come to be known generally as "contracts of adhesion" [e] but courts and writers have not always been careful to articulate precisely the means of the imposition. There are at least three distinct possibilities, which often appear in combination. First, bargaining over terms may not be between equals. The standardized contract may be used by an enterprise with such disproportionately strong economic power that it can dictate its terms to the weaker party. Second, there may be no opportunity to bargain over terms at all. The standardized contract may be a take-it-or-leave-it proposition in which the only alternatives are adherence or outright rejection. Third, one party may be completely, or at least relatively, unfamiliar with the terms. The standardized contract may be used by a party who has had the advantage of time and expert advice in preparing it while the other party may have no real opportunity to scrutinize it. This may be compounded by the use of fine print and convoluted clauses.

NOTE

Status to Contract, and Back. One of the great generalizations about social history is the thesis of Sir Henry Maine that the history of progressive societies may be described as a movement from status to contract. His influential book, Ancient Law, developing this thesis, was published in 1864. More recently, some writers have detected a reverse tendency in the law. Curiously, a high regard for freedom of contract may be seen as providing a climate for the reverse movement. The prevalence of standard form contracts is conducive to a regime of status, as the argument goes, and they are implemented in the name of freedom to contract. The following excerpts represent these views:

(a) Maine, Ancient Law 163–65: "The movement of the progressive societies has been uniform in one respect. Through all its course it has been distinguished by the gradual dissolution of family dependency and the growth of individual obligation in its place. The individual is steadily substituted for the Family, as the unit of which civil laws take account.... Nor is it difficult to see what is the tie between man and man which replaces by degrees those forms of reciprocity in rights and duties which have their origin in the Family. It is Contract. Starting, as from one terminus of history, from a condition of society in which all the relations of Persons are summed up in the relations of Family, we seem to have steadily moved towards a phase of social order in which all these relations arise from the free agreement of individuals.... All the forms of Status taken notice of in the Law of Persons were derived from, and to some extent are still coloured by, the powers and privileges anciently residing in the Family. If then we employ Status, agreeably with the usage of the best writers,

---

e. The term "contract of adhesion" was first used in the United States by Patterson, The Delivery of a Life–Insurance Policy, 33 Harv.L.Rev. 198, 222 (1919). It was coined by Raymond Saleilles as "contrat d'adhésion" to describe contracts "in which one predominant unilateral will dictates its law to an undetermined multitude rather than to an individual ... as in all employ-ment contracts of big industry, transportation contracts of big railroad companies and all those contracts which, as the Romans said, resemble a law much more than a meeting of the minds." Saleilles, De la Declaration de Volonté 229 (1901). It has been popularized in the United States by scholars who were educated in Europe and who later taught in this country.

to signify these personal conditions only, and avoid applying the term to such conditions as are the immediate or remote result of agreement, we may say that the movement of the progressive societies has hitherto been a movement *from Status to Contract.*"

(b) Kessler, op. cit. supra, 640: "With the decline of the free enterprise system due to the innate trend of competitive capitalism towards monopoly, the meaning of contract has changed radically. Society, when granting freedom of contract, does not guarantee that all members of the community will be able to make use of it to the same extent. On the contrary, the law, by protecting the unequal distribution of property, does nothing to prevent freedom of contract from becoming a one-sided privilege. Society, by proclaiming freedom of contract, guarantees that it will not interfere with the exercise of power by contract. Freedom of contract enables enterprisers to legislate by contract and, what is even more important, to legislate in a substantially authoritarian manner without using the appearance of authoritarian forms. Standard contracts in particular could thus become effective instruments in the hands of powerful industrial and commercial overlords enabling them to impose a new feudal order of their own making upon a vast host of vassals.... Thus the return back from contract to status which we experience today was greatly facilitated by the fact that the belief in freedom of contract has remained one of the firmest axioms in the whole fabric of the social philosophy of our culture."

EXCULPATION TERMS AND STATUTORY PROBLEMS

Two cases concerning identical statutes illustrate variations in the judicial views of agreements by which a person accepts the risk of bodily harm caused by the negligence of another. In the first case (in California) Hugo Tunkl had signed a paper containing a "release" when he entered a hospital.[a] The document purported to release the hospital "from any and all liability for the negligent or wrongful acts or omissions of its employees, if the hospital has used due care in selecting its employees." Later Tunkl sued the hospital, alleging negligence on the part of physicians in its employ. From a judgment for the defendant, based on a jury verdict that sustained the release, the plaintiff appealed.[b]

In the second case (in Montana) Linda Miller sued her husband's employer for injuries she suffered when thrown from a truck. Her husband, Cecil, was the driver. Mrs. Miller sought to charge his employer, the PreFab Transit Company, with vicarious liability, based on Cecil's careless driving. Earlier Mrs. Miller had applied to PreFab for permission to accompany her husband on his trips, which was granted. The form she signed purported to "waive any rights whatsoever" on account of such an injury.[c] Mrs. Miller appealed from a summary judgment against PreFab.

a. The Medical Center of the University of California at Los Angeles.

b. Tunkl died and his widow, as executrix, was substituted as plaintiff.

c. Also: "I hereby ... agree that Pre-Fab Transit Co., its agents, employees and contractors are to be held harmless in all respects by virtue of my being a passenger in said vehicle."

For present purposes, it may be assumed that the company owned the truck and that Cecil Miller was its employee, although the

In each case the court construed a statute as follows: "All contracts which have for their object, directly or indirectly, to exempt anyone from responsibility for his own fraud, or willful injury to the person or property of another, or violation of law, whether willful or negligent, are against the policy of the law." [d] The California Supreme Court reversed the judgment against Tunkl.[e] The course of the statute had been a troubled one, the court observed. "In one respect, [however,] the decisions are uniform. The cases have consistently held that the exculpatory provision may stand only if it does not involve 'the public interest.'" After describing the character of the patient-hospital transaction, the court said:

> While obviously no public policy opposes private, voluntary transactions in which one party, for a consideration, agrees to shoulder a risk which the law would otherwise have placed upon the other party, the above circumstances pose a different situation.... [W]e think that the <u>hospital-patient contract clearly falls within the category of agreements affecting the public interest.</u>"

What circumstances can you suggest in support of this conclusion?

The Montana Supreme Court also reversed the judgment against Miller, saying, "Nothing in the statute limits its application to contracts which involve the public interest." [f] Two justices dissented:

> The majority opinion points out ... that the [Montana] statute was adopted verbatim from California in 1895. The majority then concludes that the interpretation of the statute ... in *Tunkl* is persuasive.... Clearly the present case does not set forth facts justifying the application of the public interest rule under *Tunkl*.... I conclude that negligent torts were not contemplated by [the statute].

The dissenters invited the attention of the legislature to the decision, "in order that it may determine if it approves."

NOTES

(1) *Public Policy and Unconscionability Compared.* The marks of unconscionability in a contract, it has been said, include "an absence of meaningful choice on the part of one of the parties together with contract terms which are unreasonably favorable to the other party." Williams v. Walker–Thomas Furniture Co., p. 416 below. Did the transaction in Miller's case fit this description? The transaction in Tunkl's case? In that case the court gave a "rough outline" of the type of transaction in which a provision exculpating a party will be held invalid. One entry in the outline is this: "In exercising a superior bargaining power the party confronts the public with a standardized adhesion contract of exculpation, and makes no provision whereby a purchaser may pay additional reasonable fees and obtain protection against negligence."

court described him as an "independent truck driver."

d. In Tunkl's case, Cal.Civ.Code § 1668; in Miller's case, Mont.Code Ann. § 28–2–702.

e. Tunkl v. Regents of University of California, 383 P.2d 441 (Cal.1963).

f. Miller v. Fallon County, 721 P.2d 342 (Mont.1986).

From this part of the *Tunkl* opinion does it seem that the court drew on the idea of unconscionability in construing a statute about "the policy of the law"?

(2) *Questions.* Did PreFab give consideration for the release it exacted from Mrs. Miller? If she had sued PreFab for negligence in maintaining the brakes on the truck, would her claim have been more appealing? If so, why?

TICKETS, PASSES AND STUBS

Printed slips and tickets are issued to their customers by firms offering services of many kinds: laundries, parking lot operators, and firms storing and carrying baggage, for examples. It is common to find a provision on such a ticket that purports to limit the liability of the issuer for injury or loss. To what extent are these provisions effective? It is difficult to find current authority that a provision of this type, appearing in an unsigned paper incident to an everyday transaction, is effective to curtail the issuer's liability for negligence. What language or procedure would you suggest to achieve that effect?

In one well-known case the ticket reproduced next was issued by a firm offering a checking service to the public.

H. & M. PARCEL ROOM, INC.
BROADWAY & 33rd ST., HUDSON TUNNELS
OPEN 7:00 A. M. - CLOSE 1:00 A. M.
(E. S. Time Except When Another Time Is In Effect)

■ **CONTRACT** ■

THIS **CONTRACT** IS MADE ON THE FOLLOWING CONDITIONS AND IN CONSIDERATION OF THE LOW RATE AT WHICH THE SERVICE IS PERFORMED, AND ITS ACCEPTANCE BY THE DEPOSITOR. EXPRESSLY BINDS BOTH PARTIES TO THE CONTRACT.
CHARGE—10 CENTS FOR EVERY 24 HOURS OR FRACTION THEREOF, FOR EACH PIECE COVERED BY THIS CONTRACT
LOSS OR DAMAGE—NO CLAIM SHALL BE MADE IN EXCESS OF $25.00 FOR LOSS OR DAMAGE TO ANY PIECE.
UNCLAIMED ARTICLES REMAINING AFTER 90 DAYS MAY BE SOLD AT PUBLIC OR PRIVATE SALE TO SATISFY ACCRUED CHARGES.
PHONE PEnnsylvania 6-2467 ·H. & M. PARCEL ROOM, INC.

34--971

[C 1224]   *Bailment*

One Ellis, acting for a patron, left a package for storage at the parcel room and received the ticket but did not read it. Two days later, when the patron went to reclaim the package, he was told that it had been delivered to someone else by mistake. He sued the storage firm for the alleged value of the contents: $1,000. The trial court gave judgment for nearly that amount. On successive appeals, the judges were in disagreement, some believing that the recovery should be limited to $25. One judge holding that view wrote as follows: "The parcel check ... had conspicuously printed the word 'Contract' on the face thereof near the top in bold face type, clearly legible in red ink.... The whole form was exceptionally brief.... Plaintiffs ... had ample opportunity to read the notice on the check stub ... The package, alleged to contain valuable furs, was tied up with a piece of cord in a brown paper parcel. The charge for checking was the trivial sum of ten cents." [a]

The court affirmed the trial court's judgment, however. An excerpt from the opinion is as follows: " 'The coupon was presumptively intended as between the parties to serve the special purpose of affording a means of identifying the parcel left by the bailor. In the mind of the bailor the little piece of cardboard . . . did not arise to the dignity of a contract by which he agreed that in the event of the loss of the parcel, even through the negligence of the bailee itself, he would accept therefor a sum which, perhaps, would be but a small fraction of its actual value.' . . . While the defendant bailee should be protected in its legal right to limit its responsibility, the public should also be safeguarded against imposition. If the bailee wishes to limit its liability for negligence, it must at least show that it has given adequate notice of the special contract and that it has received the assent thereto of those with whom it transacts business." Klar v. H. & M. Parcel Room, Inc., 61 N.Y.S.2d 285 (App.Div.1946), aff'd mem. 73 N.E.2d 912 (N.Y.1947).

Would the parcel-room case have been decided differently if the defendant had posted a placard, plainly visible to customers, stating the limitation on its liability? Would it have been decided differently if the customer had read the ticket when he deposited the package? If he had not read the ticket, but had previously read this note?

The Restatement Second deals with the problem in § 211. What distinction does it make between persons who read the tickets handed to them and those who do not?

NOTES

(1) *Bargaining Process.* In Klar v. Parcel Room and similar cases, it may be said that the courts have policed against overreaching in contracts by manipulating the principles of contract formation. What are the limits of this method? Specialized conceptions of offer and acceptance doubtless have something to contribute to substantive fairness in enforcing contracts, as these cases show. See also the note on knowledge of mistake, p. 178, above. Are the ticket cases based on the principle stated there?

(2) *Case for Comparison.* In Parton v. Mark Pirtle Oldsmobile–Cadillac–Isuzu, Inc., 730 S.W.2d 634 (Tenn.App.1987), the owner of a car entrusted it to a dealer for repair and *signed* a document purporting to exculpate the dealer from liability for loss of the car. Following a theft of the car from the dealer's premises, the owner sued the dealer for negligence. The exculpation provision

---

a. The relation between Ellis and the plaintiff is not known.

A conceivable one is suggested by the following report: "Public lockers in Penn Station. Locked trunks in parked cars. This is where the contraband is hidden, deposited there surreptitiously by one party and picked up quietly by another. Is it narcotics, jewels, gold bullion? No, it is furs, or, more accurately, parts of fur garments, awaiting sewing so that the complete garment can be made available for sale. The lined skins are placed in lockers or car-trunks by fur-garment producers willing to use nonunion contractors, usually a one-man sewing shop or a shop with a few workers. After picking up the garments at their convenience, the contractors sew them for 50 per cent less than a unionized shop would. They then return the garments via the same conduits to their unionized clients. Although outlawed in labor-management contracts, the increasing use of such contractors has produced consternation in an already-troubled industry."—The New York Times, March 26, 1972, Business Section, p. 1.

was held to be ineffectual. Compare the parcel-room case. If that case had been decided for the bailee, what might be said to distinguish *Parton?* If *Parton* had been decided for the dealer, what might be said to distinguish the decision in the parcel-room case?

(3) *Sport Cases.* Releases of anticipated claims for personal injury permeate the world of sports, from sky- to scuba-diving. The release forms are sometimes amateurishly made, and in the nature of the case the signers are often youthful and eager for the day's diversion. Yet injured sportsmen of every description turn up as plaintiffs: neophyte aeronauts, skiers well-versed in college tournament rules, and gasoline-propelled golfers. In a characteristic case the defendant is an instructor, sponsor, or supplier of equipment connected with the sport. Being sued for negligence, the defendant produces the plaintiff's "release" and moves for summary judgment.[a]

One judge protested against a ruling unfavorable to a student of parachuting, as follows: "I wonder how comfortable this court and others will feel with such a rule when it is invoked in favor of day care centers, youth activity organizations . . . or any of a myriad of activities to which this concept logically can be extended." Thomas, C.J., dissenting in Schutkowski v. Carey, 725 P.2d 1057, 1063 (Wyo.1986).[b]

Are you content with trusting judges to know the difference between discretionary, high-risk conduct and the rest of life's activities? Is that in fact what they *purport* to know?

(4) *Problem.* William Jones, 17 years old, contracted with a sport aviation company (Free Flight, Inc.) for facilities for parachute jumping. He would not have been allowed to engage in the activity if he had not signed its standard form contract. It purported to exempt Free Flight from liability arising out of injury to Jones while so engaged. He was injured in the crash of a plane furnished by Free Flight, caused (he alleges) by its negligence. At that time he was 18 years and 10 months of age. In an action by Jones against the company, centering on the contract, what arguments occur to you to make on each side? See Jones v. Dressel, 623 P.2d 370 (Colo.1981).

(5) *Limited Liability.* Firms offering certain services—alarm services, for example—characteristically attempt to avoid heavy liabilities for faulty performance through contract terms that limit the amount a disappointed customer may recover. See Corral v. Rollins Protective Services, 732 P.2d 1260 (Kan. 1987), where the defendant sought to cap its potential liability at the greater of $250 or 10% of a year's service charge. Publishers of "Yellow Pages" use comparable provisions. (What do they have in common with alarm-service providers?) The validity of such provisions has often been questioned, with mixed results. As to publishers' errors see Discount Fabric House v. Wisconsin Telephone Company, 345 N.W.2d 417 (Wis.1984) (trade name omitted from display ad: "The courts have historically treated yellow page advertising as . . . a matter of private contract. . . ."). For a spirited justification of a limited-liability provision in a burglar-alarm-system contract see Fireman's Fund American

---

a. For suggestions about immunizing a resort operator from liability for skiing tragedies see Passero v. Killington, Ltd., 1993 WL 8722 (E.D.Pa.1993).

As to the scope of a statute about sporting-event injuries and exculpation see Lago v. Krollage, 575 N.E.2d 107 (N.Y.1991) (stock-car racing).

b. According to the majority: "Private recreational businesses generally do not qualify as services demanding a special duty to the public, nor are their services of a special, highly necessary nature."

Insurance Cos. v. Burns Electronic Security Services, Inc., 417 N.E.2d 131 (Ill.App.1981). (The plaintiff was the subscriber's insurer, claiming by right of subrogation.)

Courts have differed about whether a limitation that is otherwise effective should be disregarded in a case of "gross negligence" in maintaining an alarm system. *Questions:* Is it helpful to make distinctions turning on degrees of fault? (For an instance of a "colossal blunder" see Ostalkiewicz v. Guardian Alarm, 520 A.2d 563 (R.I.1987).) In the case of an alarm system that fails, what defense might be made if the subscriber claims restitution for all the installation and other charges it has paid?

HENNINGSEN v. BLOOMFIELD MOTORS, INC.

Supreme Court of New Jersey, 1960.
32 N.J. 358, 161 A.2d 69, 75 A.L.R.2d 1.

[Claus Henningsen purchased a new Plymouth automobile from Bloomfield Motors. His wife Helen was injured when the steering mechanism failed while she was driving it ten days after it had been delivered. They both sued Bloomfield Motors and the manufacturer, Chrysler Corporation, for breach of an implied warranty of merchantability imposed by the Uniform Sales Act. The defendants contended that the warranty had been disclaimed, as permitted by the Act, and relied upon a provision contained on the back of the purchase contract, among eight and a half inches of fine print, which purported to limit liability for breach of warranty to replacement of defective parts for the period of 90 days after delivery or 4,000 miles of driving, whichever was shorter.[a] The provisions on the back of the purchase contract were referred to on the front, above the signature elements, in language printed in six point type, as follows, although most of the language on the front was in twelve point type:[b]

"The front and back of this Order comprise the entire agreement affecting this purchase and no other agreement or understanding of any

a. It is expressly agreed that there are no warranties, express or implied, made by either the dealer or the manufacturer on the motor vehicle, chassis, or parts furnished hereunder except as follows:

"The manufacturer warrants each new motor vehicle (including original equipment placed thereon by the manufacturer except tires), chassis or parts manufactured by it to be free from defects in material or workmanship under normal use and service. Its obligation under this warranty being limited to making good at its factory any part or parts thereof which shall, within ninety (90) days after delivery of such vehicle to the original purchaser or before such vehicle has been driven 4,000 miles, whichever event shall first occur, be returned to it with trans-portation charges prepaid and which its examination shall disclose to its satisfaction to have been thus defective; this warranty being expressly in lieu of all other warranties expressed or implied, and all other obligations or liabilities on its part, and it neither assumes nor authorizes any other person to assume for it any other liability in connection with the sale of its vehicles...."

b. The cases in this book are set in 10 point type, the notes in 9 point type, and the footnotes in 8 point type. To a considerable extent, however, the readability of type depends not only on its size but also upon the width of the column, a point that is humorously made in "A Contract with Cunard," The New Yorker magazine, February 4, 1961, p. 36.

nature concerning same has been made or entered into, or will be recognized. I hereby certify that no credit has been extended to me for the purchase of this motor vehicle except as appears in writing on the face of this agreement.

"I have read the matter printed on the back hereof and agree to it as a part of this order the same as if it were printed above my signature. I certify that I am 21 years of age, or older, and hereby acknowledge receipt of a copy of this order."

[From judgment for the plaintiffs the defendant appealed.]

FRANCIS, J.[c] ... In assessing [the disclaimer's] significance we must keep in mind the general principle that, in the absence of fraud, one who does not choose to read a contract before signing it, cannot later relieve himself of his burdens. . . . And in applying that principle, the basic tenet of freedom of competent parties to contract is a factor of impor-tance. But in the framework of modern commercial life and business practices, such rules cannot be applied on a strict, doctrinal basis. . . . The traditional contract is the result of free bargaining of parties who are brought together by the play of the market, and who meet each other on a footing of approximate economic equality. In such a society there is no danger that freedom of contract will be a threat to the social order as a whole. But in present-day commercial life the standardized mass contract has appeared. It is used primarily by enterprises with strong bargaining power and position. "The weaker party, in need of the goods or services, is frequently not in a position to shop around for better terms, either because the author of the standard contract has a monopo-ly (natural or artificial) or because all competitors use the same clauses. His contractual intention is but a subjection more or less voluntary to terms dictated by the stronger party, terms whose consequences are often understood in a vague way, if at all." Kessler, "Contracts of Adhesion—Some Thoughts About Freedom of Contract," 43 Co-lum.L.Rev. 629, 632 (1943); Ehrenzweig, "Adhesion Contracts in the Conflict of Laws," 53 Colum.L.Rev. 1072, 1075, 1089 (1953). Such standardized contracts have been described as those in which one predominant party will dictate its law to an undetermined multiple rather than to an individual. They are said to resemble a law rather than a meeting of the minds. Siegelman v. Cunard White Star, 221 F.2d 189, 206 (2 Cir.1955). . . .

The warranty before us is a standardized form designed for mass use. It is imposed upon the automobile consumer. He takes it or leaves it, and he must take it to buy an automobile. No bargaining is engaged in with respect to it. In fact, the dealer through whom it comes to the buyer is without authority to alter it; his function is ministerial—simply to deliver it. The form warranty is not only standard with Chrysler but, as mentioned above, it is the uniform warranty of the Automobile Manufacturers Association. Members of the Association are: General

---

c. The official report of this case fills   here to save space.
sixty pages. It has been severely edited

quasi-
monopoly
No bargaining
Power

Motors, Inc., Ford, Chrysler, Studebaker–Packard, American Motors (Rambler), Willys Motors, Checker Motors Corp., and International Harvester Company. Automobile Facts and Figures (1958 Ed., Automobile Manufacturers Association) 69. Of these companies, the "Big Three" (General Motors, Ford, and Chrysler) represented <u>93.5%</u> of the passenger-car production for 1958 and the independents 6.5%. Standard & Poor (Industrial Surveys, Autos, Basic Analysis, June 25, 1959) 4109. And for the same year the "Big Three" had 86.72% of the total passenger vehicle registrations. Automotive News, 1959 Almanac (Slocum Publishing Co., Inc.) p. 25.

The gross inequality of bargaining position occupied by the consumer in the automobile industry is thus apparent. There is no competition among the car makers in the area of the express warranty. Where can the buyer go to negotiate for better protection? Such control and limitation of his remedies are inimical to the public welfare and, at the very least, call for great care by the courts to avoid injustice through application of strict common-law principles of freedom of contract. Because there is no competition among the motor vehicle manufacturers with respect to the scope of protection guaranteed to the buyer, there is no incentive on their part to stimulate good will in that field of public relations. Thus, there is lacking a factor existing in more competitive fields, one which tends to guarantee the safe construction of the article sold. Since all competitors operate in the same way the urge to be careful is not so pressing. See "Warranties of Kind and Quality," 57 Yale L.J. 1389, 1400 (1948).

Although the courts, with few exceptions, have been most sensitive to problems presented by contracts resulting from gross disparity in buyer-seller bargaining positions, they have not articulated a general principle condemning, as opposed to public policy, the imposition on the buyer of a skeleton warranty as a means of limiting the responsibility of the manufacturer. They have endeavored thus far to avoid a drastic departure from age-old tenets of freedom of contract by adopting doctrines of strict construction, and notice and knowledgeable assent by the buyer to the attempted exculpation of the seller. 1 Corbin, supra, 337; 2 Harper & James [Law of Torts], 1590; Prosser, "Warranty of Merchantable Quality," 27 Minn.L.Rev. 117, 159 (1932). Accordingly to be found in the cases are statements that disclaimers and the consequent limitation of liability will not be given effect if "unfairly procured," ... International Harvester Co. of America v. Bean, 159 Ky. 842, 169 S.W. 549 (Ct.App.1914); if not brought to the buyer's attention and he was not made understandingly aware of it ... or if not clear and explicit....

The rigid scrutiny which the courts give to attempted limitations of warranties and of the liability that would normally flow from a transaction is not limited to the field of sales of goods. Clauses on baggage checks restricting the liability of common carriers for loss or damage in transit are not enforceable unless the limitation is fairly and honestly negotiated and understandingly entered into. If not called specifically to the patron's attention, it is not binding. It is not enough merely to show the form of a contract; it must appear also that the agreement was understandingly made. . . .   The same holds true in cases of such limitations on parcel check room tickets . . . and on storage warehouse receipts . . .; on automobile parking lot or garage tickets or claim checks . . .; as to exculpatory clauses in leases releasing a landlord of apartments in a multiple dwelling house from all liability for negligence where inequality of bargaining exists, see Annotation, 175 A.L.R. 8 (1948).   And the validity of release clauses in orders signed by a depositor directing a bank to stop payment of his check, exonerating the bank from liability for negligent payment, has been seriously questioned on public policy grounds in this State. . . .   Elsewhere they have been declared void as opposed to public policy. . . .

It is true that the rule governing the limitation of liability cases last referred to is generally applied in situations said to involve services of a public or semi-public nature.   Typical, of course, are the public carrier or storage or parking lot cases.   Kuzmiak v. Brookchester, 33 N.J.Super. 575, 111 A.2d 425 (App.Div.1954); Annotation, supra, 175 A.L.R. at pp. 14–17.   But in recent times the books have not been barren of instances of its application in private contract controversies. . . .

Basically, the reason a contracting party offering services of a public or *quasi*-public nature has been held to the requirements of fair dealing, and, when it attempts to limit its liability, of securing the understanding consent of the patron or consumer, is because members of the public generally have no other means of fulfilling the specific need represented by the contract.   Having in mind the situation in the automobile industry as detailed above, and particularly the fact that the limited warranty extended by the manufacturers is a uniform one, there would appear to be no just reason why the principles of all of the cases set forth should not chart the course to be taken here.

It is undisputed that the president of the dealer with whom Henningsen dealt did not specifically call attention to the warranty on the back of the purchase order.   The form and the arrangement of its face, as described above, certainly would cause the minds of reasonable men to differ as to whether notice of a yielding of basic rights stemming from the relationship with the manufacturer was adequately given.   The words "warranty" or "limited warranty" did not even appear in the fine print above the place for signature, and a jury might well find that the type of print itself was such as to promote lack of attention rather than sharp scrutiny.   The inference from the facts is that Chrysler placed the method of communicating its warranty to the purchaser in the hands of the dealer.   If either one or both of them wished to make certain that Henningsen became aware of that agreement and its purported implications, neither the form of the document nor the method of expressing the precise nature of the obligation intended to be assumed would have presented any difficulty.

But there is more than this.   Assuming that a jury might find that the fine print referred to reasonably served the objective of directing a buyer's attention to the warranty on the reverse side, and, therefore, that he should be charged with awareness of its language, can it be said that an ordinary layman would realize what he was relinquishing in return for what he was being granted? Under the law, breach of warranty against defective parts or workmanship which caused personal injuries would entitle a buyer to damages even if due care were used in the manufacturing process. Because of the great potential for harm if the vehicle was defective, that right is the most important and fundamental one arising from the relationship. Difficulties so frequently encountered in establishing negligence in manufacture in the ordinary case make this manifest. 2 Harper & James, supra, §§ 28.14, 28.15; Prosser, supra, 506. Any ordinary layman of reasonable intelligence, looking at the phraseology, might well conclude that Chrysler was agreeing to replace defective parts and perhaps replace anything that went wrong because of defective workmanship during the first 90 days or 4,000 miles of operation, but that he would not be entitled to a new car. It is not unreasonable to believe that the entire scheme being conveyed was a proposed remedy for physical deficiencies in the car. *In the context* of this warranty, only the abandonment of all sense of justice would permit us to hold that, as a matter of law, the phrase "its obligation under this warranty being limited to making good at its factory any part or parts thereof" signifies to an ordinary reasonable person that he is relinquishing any personal injury claim that might flow from the use of a defective automobile. Such claims are nowhere mentioned. The draftsmanship is reflective of the care and skill of the Automobile Manufacturers Association in undertaking to avoid warranty obligations without drawing too much attention to its effort in that regard. No one can doubt that if the will to do so were present, the ability to inform the buying public of the intention to disclaim liability for injury claims arising from breach of warranty would present no problem. . . .

The task of the judiciary is to administer the spirit as well as the letter of the law. On issues such as the present one, part of that burden is to protect the ordinary man against the loss of important rights through what, in effect, is the unilateral act of the manufacturer. The status of the automobile industry is unique. Manufacturers are few in number and strong in bargaining position. In the matter of warranties on the sale of their products, the Automobile Manufacturers Association has enabled them to present a united front. From the standpoint of the purchaser, there can be no arms length negotiating on the subject. Because his capacity for bargaining is so grossly unequal, the inexorable conclusion which follows is that he is not permitted to bargain at all. He must take or leave the automobile on the warranty terms dictated by the maker. He cannot turn to a competitor for better security.

Public policy is a term not easily defined. Its significance varies as the habits and needs of a people may vary. It is not static and the field of application is an ever increasing one. A contract, or a particular provision therein, valid in one era may be wholly opposed to the public policy of another. . . . Courts keep in mind the principle that the best interests of society demand that persons should not be unnecessarily restricted in their freedom to contract. But they do not hesitate to declare void as against public policy contractual provisions which clearly tend to the injury of the public in some way. . . .

[Affirmed.]

NOTES

(1) *Questions.* If the accident in *Henningsen* had occurred four months after the car had been delivered, would the disclaimer have been effective to bar recovery? Is there any indication that the Henningsens were concerned about their warranty protection? Was there an agreement among the American automobile manufacturers, at the time of the case, to follow the language proposed by the Association?

Within a few years after the decision they began to jockey for competitive advantage by extending and advertising their warranties. More recently car buyers have been offered still further protection against defects, in the form of term contracts for repair, sold for a separate price. Do these developments seriously undercut the court's reasoning? [a]

(2) *Legal Developments.* In New Jersey the Code was adopted in 1961 (effective in 1963). Mr. Henningsen bought his Plymouth in 1955. If the Code had been in effect then, would it have been sufficient for the court's purposes to cite UCC 2–719(3)? Compare UCC 2–316(2). See Matthews v. Ford Motor Co., 479 F.2d 399 (4th Cir.1973).

(3) *Contracts Compared.* What factors distinguish the main case from *O'Callaghan,* p. 388 above? Is a standard-form apartment lease any less a contract of adhesion than a new-car purchase contract? On the uses—and limitations—of unconscionability in relation to landlord-tenant relations, see Berger, Hard Leases Make Bad Law, 74 Colum.L.Rev. 791 (1974).

How do the contracts in these cases compare with an appliance-dealership contract? Which is most like a gasoline service-station lease? See Jordan, Unconscionability at the Gas Station, 62 Minn.L.Rev. 813 (1978). Or a community-home and lifetime care contract? See Onderdonk v. Presbyterian Homes of New Jersey, 410 A.2d 252 (N.J.Super.1979).[b]

(4) *Problem.* In Royal Indemnity Co. v. Westinghouse Electric Corp., 385 F.Supp. 520 (S.D.N.Y.1974), a complaint was made against the manufacturer of a ten-million-dollar generator in that it had limited its liability for breakdown— unconscionably, the plaintiff charged. Which of the following circumstances is most significant in such a case?—(a) the buyer had insured itself against the mishap; (b) it was a utility, having some power to pass through its costs to customers; (c) only two manufacturers were capable of supplying the item; (d) other.

(5) *Reconstruction.* For a proposed extension of the law relating to "invisible terms," see Rakoff, Contracts of Adhesion: An Essay in Reconstruction, 96 Harv.L.Rev. 1174 (1983). Professor Rakoff depicts such contracts as "circumstances intimately linked to the specific organizational form in which mass production and distribution most typically occur in our society." Id. at 1229. "My broad conclusion is that . . . the form terms present in contracts of adhesion ought to be considered presumptively (although not absolutely) unenforceable."

a. "The experience proved beyond doubt that consumers do care enough about warranties to make their selections felt competitively *if they are sufficiently in-* *formed to do so.*" Slawson, Standard Form Contracts, 84 Harv.L.Rev. 529, 548 (1971).

b. Aff'd in part and rev'd in part, 425 A.2d 1057 (N.J.1981).

A necessary step in evaluating a form term is to "estimate the degree to which [it] was included for its direct commercial utility and the degree to which it was designed merely to gain power over the other party." Id. at 1176, 1263. Professor Rakoff offers examples of how that calculation might be made.

(6) *The Meaning of "Adhesion"*. "The attack on contracts of adhesion rests upon an unstated conception of distributive fairness; though often overlooked, it is this conception that gives the attack its appeal. Many contracts are contracts of adhesion in the general sense that one party is able to dictate terms to the other, but this alone does not make an agreement objectionable. Suppose, for example, that my neighbor owns a painting I happen to covet. I offer him $5000 for it. He responds, '$10,000 and no warranties regarding its authenticity. Take it or leave it.' Clearly, the fact that I lack bargaining power and must adhere to the terms he proposes does not by itself justify a judicial or legislative effort to tip the balance in my favor. The imbalance in this case, which stems from the fact that he owns the painting and I do not, is unobjectionable because we do not care how control over the painting is distributed.

"We feel differently about the distribution of control over society's available housing stock. . . . The distribution of housing matters more to us than the distribution of paintings: Only the first is likely to seem important from the standpoint of most theories of distributive justice. Those contracts of adhesion that disturb us do so, then, because they reflect an underlying distribution of power or resources that offends our conception of distributive fairness; when distributive concerns are weak or nonexistent, contracts of adhesion are less troubling and the concept of adhesion itself loses meaning." Kronman, Paternalism and the Law of Contracts, 92 Yale L.J. 763, 771–2 (1983).

LEGISLATIVE MARKET INTERVENTION

This Note illustrates some methods used by legislatures and by governmental agencies in attempting to improve the conditions in which goods, services, and credit are made available to consumers. Countless enactments could be used to illustrate each method. In the main the enactments mentioned here are relatively recent; they were preceded by the drafting of the Uniform Commercial Code, which contains only minor provisions directed specifically to consumer markets. Many older ones exist, especially statutes and administrative rules concerning "regulated industries," such as common carriers and the insurance business.

Two federal statutes have unusually wide effects: the Consumer Credit Protection Act of 1968 [a] and the "Magnuson–Moss Warranty Act" of 1975.[b] Much earlier, Congress created the Federal Trade Commission and charged it with implementing this statutory declaration:

Unfair methods of competition in or affecting commerce, and unfair or deceptive acts or practices in or affecting commerce, are declared unlawful.[c]

a. 15 U.S.C. § 1601 et seq.

b. Title I of the Magnuson–Moss Warranty–FTC Improvement Act: 15 U.S.C. §§ 2301–2312.

c. 15 U.S.C. § 45(a)(1).

State legislatures, as well as Congress, have continuously intervened in consumer markets, both with broad enactments and with statutes targeted on particular market segments. Many states have enacted provisions modelled on the FTC Act—so-called "little FTC Acts." Other models for state legislation are the Uniform Consumer Credit Code (the "U–Triple–C") and the Uniform Consumer Sales Practices Act,[d] although these models are followed closely in only a few states.

The measures in this field can be grouped loosely into types, illustrated below, as follows: (1) controls over the terms of exchange, prompted by concern about either the fairness of particular terms or the fairness of the exchange as a whole; (2) provisions about remedies, premised on the belief that consumers suffer systematic handicaps in the effective enforcement of their rights; and (3) disclosure requirements, designed to enhance information available to consumers.

Disclosure rights are exemplified by state "plain language" statutes. The New York version[e] requires that an agreement affected[f] be

1. Written in a clear and coherent manner using words with common and every day meanings;

2. Appropriately divided and captioned by its various sections.

Other plain-language statutes make use of objective tests of comprehensibility. These draw heavily on the work of the linguist Rudolf Flesch, who devised a system for scoring the "readability" of texts.[g]

NOTES

(1) *Plain Language in Application.* If the contract in the *Henningsen* case had been subject to a plain-language statute, might the decision have been based on the statute? A characteristic remedy provided for the violation of such a statute is a modest monetary claim, perhaps augmented by an attorney's fee. The New York statute allows recovery of "any actual damages sustained"; but it also provides that a violation does not affect the enforceability of an agreement.

Suppose that the contract in *Henningsen* had complied with an applicable plain-language statute. Would that have required the court to modify its opinion in any way?

(2) *Truth in Lending.* The Act of this name is Title I of the Consumer Credit Protection Act. Its avowed purpose is to facilitate shopping for favorable credit terms by users of consumer credit. A central requirement is early disclosure by financers of an annual percentage rate (APR), which expresses a ratio between the "finance charge" and the "amount financed"—interest and principal in common parlance. Much technicality is hidden in these expressions.

---

d. See 7A Uniform Laws Ann. 1 et seq.

e. Gen.Oblig.L. § 5–702.

f. A written residential lease, and a written agreement "to which a consumer is a party and the money, property or service which is the subject of the transaction is primarily for personal, family or household purposes." A qualification is made for agreements "involving amounts in excess of fifty thousand dollars."

g. Counting the syllables in words, the words in sentences, and the sentences in paragraphs is the core of the "Flesch test." For musings on this method by a stylist see E.B. White, The Second Tree From the Corner 166 (1954). A later work by Flesch is How to Write Plain English: A Book for Lawyers and Consumers (1979).

(3) *The Magnuson–Moss Warranty Act.* This Act is a bravura effort by Congress to improve marketing practices in consumer products and to make the rights and remedies of consumers under warranties more effectual. The most striking technique of the Act is that it builds on the impulse of manufacturers and dealers to provide warranties in writing for promoting consumer sales. Any "supplier" who yields to that impulse incurs elaborate obligations, some of them substantive and others relating to disclosure and remedies. One may resist simply by failing to provide a "written warranty"; and in that event neither the Act nor the rules of the Federal Trade Commission that supplement it [h] have any application. Given a written warranty, the Act requires that it carry a conspicuous designation, as either a FULL or a LIMITED warranty. The Act specifies the content of an express warranty only in some particular ways. But the following dictate is difficult for a merchant to avoid: "[I]mplied warranties may be limited in duration to the duration of a written warranty *of reasonable duration,* if such limitation is *conscionable . . .*" [i]

(4) *Beyond Damages.* To state an appropriate set of remedies for substandard performance by a seller of goods is a major challenge in market regulation. Magnuson–Moss provides for a wide array of remedies, official and private, including class actions and (sometimes) suit costs. Given a "full" warranty, it provides that a customer may insist on a replacement or a refund after the merchant has made a reasonable number of unsuccessful attempts to repair a defect. A similar provision appears in the widespread statutes known as "lemon laws," designed for the protection of new-car buyers. These laws require the manufacturer to replace the vehicle or refund the price after a specified number of failures to repair a serious defect.

The Uniform Commercial Code provides, for buyers of goods in general, a restitution-like remedy in the circumstances stated in § 2–608. Some observers have thought that, as between a supplier of non-conforming goods and a *merchant*-buyer, the choice between repair, replacement, and refund ought to lie with the supplier. Unlike a typical consumer, often a merchant-buyer is "able to resell defective or subgrade goods . . . at a cost equal to that of the seller," so that a damage remedy (or a price allowance) is "more likely to minimize costs." Priest, Breach and Remedy . . . : An Economic Approach, 91 Harv.L.Rev. 960, 971 (1978). Lemon laws provide a remedy, it is said, "similar to revocation of acceptance under 2–608, but applicable to manufacturers rather than sellers." White, Retail Sellers and the Enforcement of Manufacturer Warranties . . . , 32 Wayne L.Rev. 1045, 1062 (1986).

If a damages remedy entails special costs in resolving disputes, are disappointed consumers especially justified in seeking additional remedies? What justification is there for focussing car-buyers' complaints on manufacturers, rather than on sellers? Given that lemon laws differ from state to state, what untoward effects might they have?

(5) *The Procedure of Sanctions.* A fair and effective system of enforcement is an elusive goal in consumer-protection legislation. If a government official is to be authorized to move against an objectionable marketing practice, it is a major policy issue whether or not the official's action should be filtered through a judicial proceeding. Whether or not a *class* action can be maintained on behalf of the consumers affected is another momentous issue. In Vasquez v. Superior

---

h. Title I of the Magnuson–Moss Warranty–FTC Improvement Act of January 5, 1975: 15 U.S.S.C. §§ 2301–2312.

i. " . . . and is set forth in clear and unmistakable language and prominently displayed on the face of the warranty." (emphasis supplied)

Court of San Joaquin County, 484 P.2d 964 (Cal.1971), concerning a fraud charge against a firm selling food freezers, the court supposed that a class action by consumers "produces several salutary by-products." What might those be?

Each of these issues is connected with the question whether a "prophylactic" remedy (such as an injunction) is appropriate—one that attaches a sanction to a given offense in the absence of a showing that someone was misled or injured by the offense. What sorts of offense call for a prophylactic remedy? Are private and official claimants equally well situated to assert that kind of remedy?

(6) *UCC Question.* A state's attorney general brings an action against a retailer that makes exorbitant charges for its merchandise. The relief sought is an award of damages to customers who have overpaid and an injunction. Is UCC 2–302 a sufficient basis for this action? [a]

GENERAL PROBLEMS OF POLICING

Recognizing that serious problems attend the use of standard form contracts, the decision what to do about them remains a difficult one. What combination of judicial, legislative, and administrative remedies promises the best result? Professor Llewellyn thought that the courts had the solution to problems of standard form contracts ready at hand. Essentially it is to recognize a distinction between "dickered" terms and boiler-plate clauses, to the specifics of which no assent is asked or given. Building on that distinction, he wrote, "the true answer to the whole problem seems, amusingly, to be one which could occur to any court or any lawyer, at any time...." He was not sanguine about an approach through legislation, "which seems to be dubious, uncertain, and likely to be both awkward in manner and deficient or spotty in scope." [b]

Another thoughtful scholar has observed, however, that "the courts have neither the equipment nor the materials for resolving the basic conflicts of modern society over ... the limits to be set to the use, or misuse, of economic power." Dawson, Economic Duress—An Essay in Perspective, 45 Mich.L.Rev. 253, 289 (1947). See also Hale, Bargaining, Duress, and Economic Liberty, 43 Colum.L.Rev. 603 (1943). In like vein, the doctrine of unconscionability, at least in some formulations, is criticized as a cover for smuggling notions of distributive justice into the judicial process. That is an improper use of it: "The unequal bargaining power concept should be abandoned." [c] Some scholars, whether or not they profess that view, have urged the courts to take wide liberties with the terms of standard form contracts and have proposed models of judicial activity more elaborate than anything Llewellyn suggested. [d]

a. See Kugler v. Romain, 279 A.2d 640, 650–54 (N.J.1971), applying the state's Consumer Fraud Act.

b. The Common Law Tradition: Deciding Appeals 370 (1960).

c. Schwartz, Seller Unequal Bargaining Power and the Judicial Process, 49 Ind.L.J. 367, 396 (1974).

d. See Oldfather, Toward a Usable Method of Judicial Review of the Adhesion Contractor's Lawmaking, 16 U.Kan.L.Rev. 303 (1968); Slawson, Standard Form Contracts and Democratic Control of Lawmaking Power, 84 Harv.L.Rev. 529 (1971). Automobile manufacturers, Professor Slawson observes, "make more warranty law in a

Statutory measures. Legislation is, of course, the traditional means of curbing abuses of economic power. Congress has addressed an imbalance of bargaining power, for example, in laws that favor the massing of employees' bargaining power. Anti-trust laws may also have an incidental effect by helping to preserve a party's opportunity to choose among firms open to bargaining.

Legislation more specific to standard-form contracts takes the form sometimes of prohibiting the use of a particular term, sometimes of requiring the use of a term, and sometimes of prescribing virtually all the (non-dickered) terms of a contract. A standard form of fire insurance is generally set out in state statutes or in insurance-department regulations; and the terms of ocean bills of lading are set out in the federal Carriage of Goods by Sea Act (COGSA). Less sweeping control of terms is exemplified by statutes about exculpation clauses in leases, referred to above. Another illustration is UCC 2–318, forbidding a provision by which a buyer's family or guests might be deprived of the benefit of the seller's warranties. More generally, the Code prohibits disclaimers of "the obligations of good faith, diligence, reasonableness and care prescribed by this Act." UCC 1–102(3).

Other legislation works off the assumption that consumers can best improve their position through well-informed shopping, which leads to disclosure requirements. The firm-offer rule of UCC 2–205 contains one of these, requiring that a "term of assurance" on a form supplied by the offeree be separately signed by the offeree. Many disclosure requirements are addressed to selected markets, such as one about statements of mileage in connection with sales of vehicles.[e]

Administrative measures. There is hope of avoiding some of the disadvantages associated with legislation, such as inflexibility, if control over contract terms is given to an administrative agency. The statutory mandate for many agencies has more to do with setting the price that a given firm (a public utility, say) may charge than with language in the firm's contracts. Yet these agencies have on occasion used their powers so as to exert control over contract language as well as rates. In many business areas—notably insurance—official surveillance over contract terms is a main part of an agency's mandate. Sometimes an agency acts in a quasi-judicial way, as when the Federal Trade Commission charges a merchant with a deceptive practice.

NOTES

(1) *Llewellyn on Boiler–Plate.*[f] Professor Llewellyn repeatedly addressed problems of standard form contracts. One statement of his influential views is as follows:

"The answer, I suggest, is this: Instead of thinking about 'assent' to boiler-plate clauses, we can recognize that so far as concerns the specific, there is no

day than most legislatures or courts make in a year." Id. at 530.

   e. The Motor Vehicles Information and Cost Savings Act: 15 U.S.C. § 1984.

   f. For a thoughtful definition of "boiler-plate," see The Leff Dictionary of Law: A Fragment, 99 Yale.L.J. 1855, 2186 (1985).

assent at all. What has in fact been assented to, specifically, are the few dickered terms, and the broad type of the transaction, and but one thing more. That one thing more is a blanket assent (not a specific assent) to any not unreasonable or indecent terms the seller may have on his form, which do not alter or eviscerate the reasonable meaning of the dickered terms. The fine print which has not been read has no business to cut under the reasonable meaning of those dickered terms which constitute the dominant and only real expression of agreement, but much of it commonly belongs in . . . ." Llewellyn, The Common Law Tradition: Deciding Appeals 370–71 (1960).

(2) *Judicial vs. Legislative Action.* The following excerpts suggest some arguments about the relative merits of efforts in the courts and in legislatures to deal with standard form contracts.

"It is hard to prove the factual justification of laissez faire capitalism; it is also hard to disprove it. In practical politics, in disputes about the wisdom of particular legislation, the issue is framed differently. The immediate effects of restrictive legislation, in mitigating or removing certain evils, can often be measured with as much precision as the value of the conclusions requires. On the contrary, the effects of such a restriction in diminishing the beneficent effects of freedom of enterprise often cannot be measured at all. The economic evaluation of compulsory contract vs. freedom of enterprise is thus a weighing of ponderables against imponderables." Patterson, Compulsory Contracts in the Crystal Ball, 43 Colum.L.Rev. 731, 746 (1943).

"[Legislation] has a serious disadvantage. It does away with the flexibility without which only very few trades can do. It enlarges the business man's risk and does not allow him to take measures against its increase, measures which only he can devise and which must be applied rapidly. Legislative compulsion works best where a trade has grown into a quasi-governmental function, as, e.g., insurance or traffic; it is almost impossible in all other branches." Prausnitz, The Standardization of Commercial Contracts in English and Continental Law 145 (1937).

THE DUTY TO READ AND THE RIGHT TO UNDERSTAND

One who signs a contract document without reading it runs a risk. It has been said (with some exaggeration): "The whole panoply of contract law rests on the principle that one is bound by the contract which he voluntarily and knowingly signs." National Bank of Washington v. Equity Investors, 506 P.2d 20, 36 (Wash.1973). The rule may be thought of as an aspect of the objective theory of contract law (see Note, p. 138 above). However, it is older than that general theory and it has limitations based on duress, mistake and the like, also very old. The rule is also subject to some new qualifications created both by courts and by legislatures. A statutory example already noted is the rule that an "assurance" creating a firm offer under the Code, which is on a form supplied by the offeree, is ineffective unless it is "separately signed" by the offeror. UCC 2–205. This rule will usually—not always—operate on a document designed to produce a standard form contract.

Presenting a standard form contract to a consumer for assent entails a certain obligation to make it intelligible. This general proposition, though not yet fully defined, is exemplified by widespread decisions, statutes, and regulations, quite various in detail. The use of red ink for certain terms is required; more commonly requirements about captions and size of type are imposed. The Code is free of such provisions, but it occasionally demands that a provision be "conspicuous," and other legislation has followed suit. For some purposes it is required in the Code that the recipient of a writing have "reason to know its contents." See, e.g., UCC 2–201(2). On a simpler level, there is the requirement in a New York statute on retail installment sale contracts that they include this admonition to buyers: "Do not sign this agreement until you read it." Pers.Prop.L. § 402.

The courts' efforts for clarity are also diverse. As already indicated, they include "ameliorating" interpretations of standard form contracts. One judicial remedy for a person who—excusably—accedes to a form without understanding it is to deny any enforcement of the agreement as written. If the difficulty lies in part of the writing only, a court may deny enforcement of that part.

The Restatement Second provides, in § 211(3), that where a party effectively manifests assent to a standardized expression of agreement, and the other party has reason to believe that he would not have done so if he had known that it contained a particular term, "the term is not part of the agreement."

The impact of that provision is illustrated by Darner Motor Sales v. Universal Underwriters, 682 P.2d 388 (Ariz.1984). Darner Motor Sales, the claimant, was in the business of selling and leasing cars. It held contracts insuring against various risks, and supposed, erroneously, that an "umbrella" policy enhanced the limited amount of insurance provided by a basic one. Darner had occasion to claim insurance in the higher amount, which the insurer denied. In an action against the insurer, Darner alleged that, before the loss occurred, it had been told by the insurer's soliciting agent "not to worry" about the basic limit: "the umbrella policy would provide additional coverage." From a summary judgment for the insurer, Darner appealed. *Held:* Reversed. In a wide-ranging opinion, accompanied by a sharp dissent, the court sought a rule applicable to the use of "standardized forms which, because of the nature of the enterprise, customers will not be expected to read and over which they have no real power of negotiation." Id. at 399. The court subscribed to the Restatement rule quoted above.

The failure of a signer to appreciate the effect of a writing is not such a mistake as will ordinarily excuse compliance with it. (One who cannot read can express binding consent to a written agreement.[a]) Yet the requirements of a relievable mistake have been loosened; and to that may now be added an even looser exception for unconscionability.

---

a. "The general rule is that, in the absence of fraud, one who signs a written agreement is bound by its terms whether he read and understood it or not, or whether he can read or not." Cohen v. Santoianni, 112 N.E.2d 267, 271 (Mass.1953).

As for protecting "the non-English speaker" see Comment, 30 Baylor L.Rev. 765 (1978).

Certainly in situations where other marks of unconscionability may appear, one who devises a standard form contract without troubling to make it intelligible has weakened the signer's duty to read. See Calamari, Duty to Read—A Changing Concept, 43 Fordham L.Rev. 341 (1974).[b]

In the materials to follow you will find instances of both the duty to read and the right to understand.

NOTES

(1) *Types of Relief.* In *Darner Motor Sales* the court suggested relief for Darner that seems to go beyond the prescription of Restatement Second § 211(3) ("the term is not part of the agreement") and to treat the policies as if they contained *different* terms concerning the disputed matter. It suggested reformation of the policy as a possible ground of recovery. Would reformation of the policy make it needless to rely on the Restatement rule? If Darner's claim could be sustained by reference to that rule, would reformation be inappropriate? Similar questions may be asked about other grounds of recovery suggested by the court, including equitable estoppel.

(2) *The Case of the Air–Force Maneuver.* In Fraass Surgical Mfg. Co., Inc. v. United States, 571 F.2d 34 (Ct.Cl.1978), an Air Force procurement contract assigned a risk to the supplier which, in previous contracts between the same parties, had been assigned to the government. If the government had known that the supplier was unaware of the change, an appropriate remedy would have been to reform the document so as to assign the risks as before.[c] That knowledge was not proved, however. The testimony of the supplier's president was that he did not read the contract "because contracts that he had signed in 1963 and 1960 had contained the other clause." The court found this testimony unacceptable: "He is an experienced businessman and should know better."

What best differentiates this case from Darner Motor Sales v. Universal Underwriters? How would you compare the principle of this case with that of Laserage Technology Corp. v. Laserage Laboratories, p. 143 above?

(3) *Disclosure for Naught?* The utility of disclosure requirements is intrinsically limited, and especially so as to groups who suffer most from an imbalance of bargaining power. The following comment makes the point in relation to low-income consumers: "In sum, the new wave of informational legislation will be of little help to the poor because it presupposes values, motivation and knowledge which do not generally exist among them. The actual problem is not just a shortage of a narrowly defined sort of information—such as the price per pound of prepackaged food—but a total breakdown in the function the consumer is supposed to play in the market. 'Bad buys' are the rule and price and quality competition the exception. As one merchant in New York put it: 'People do not *shop* in this area.... It is just up to who catches him.'" Note, Consumer Legislation and the Poor, 76 Yale L.J. 745, 754 (1967).

(4) *UCC 2–316: Conspicuous.* Curtailment of the implied fitness warranty must, according to subsection (2), be "conspicuous". Is an exception to that

---

b. For an analysis of the duty to read in relation to a structured set of legal policies, see Macaulay, Private Legislation and the Duty to Read, 19 Vand.L.Rev. 1051 (1966). For an amusing discussion of methods employed to prevent the written word from conveying any message, see Mellinkoff, How to Make Contracts Illegible, 5 Stan.L.Rev. 418 (1953).

c. See Restatement Second § 166, Comment *a*.

requirement to be found in subsection (3)? See Smith v. Sharpensteen, 521 P.2d 394, 73 A.L.R.3d 244 (Okl.1974).

The Code defines "conspicuous" with reference to what "a reasonable person against whom it is to operate ought to have noticed." UCC 1–201(10). In Avenell v. Westinghouse Electric Corp., 324 N.E.2d 583 (Ohio App.1974), a finding of conspicuousness was made—and approved on appeal—for the reason, among others, that the buyer was a "prominent, sophisticated entity": the Toledo Edison Company. Is there a difference between this case and one in which the buyer is an "average Joe," but happens to know of the disclaimer? See Annot., 73 A.L.R.3d at 273, 299–300 (1976). What reason might there be for refusing to recognize a distinction?

(5) *Squinting in the Courtroom.* For an opinion excoriating the typography of a services contract see McCarthy Well Co. v. St. Peter Creamery, Inc., 410 N.W.2d 312 (Minn.1987): "difficult, exceedingly tedious, and even physically painful" to read. "This is not a case of unconscionability as that concept is usually understood. . . . Rather, this is a case where a party is not able to know what the contract terms are because they are unreadable. As a matter of law, the exculpatory clause will not be enforced."

INSURANCE MARKETING

Long ago it was suggested that the typography of an insurance policy presented a triable issue of a "fraudulent plot" on the part of the insurer. De Lancey v. Rockingham Farmers' Mut. Fire Insurance Co., 52 N.H. 581 (1873) ("Seldom has the art of typography been so successfully diverted from the diffusion of knowledge to the suppression of it.") The courts use a variety of tactics to ameliorate the difficulties that complex, standard-form policies pose for insurance buyers.

The "doctrine of reasonable expectations" has a considerable following. The chief influence on its formulation is the scholarly writing of Professor (now Judge) Robert E. Keeton. See R. Keeton & A. Widiss, Insurance Law § 6.3 (Prac. ed. 1988). The subject is canvassed extensively in *Darner Motor Sales,* p. 414 above. In brief, the principle is that, when insurance is sold in circumstances that discourage detailed inquiries, the reasonable expectations of the buyer should be honored even though the policy terms do not support them.[a]

One small set of cases giving impetus to the doctrine concern air-travel insurance sold through vending machines. An example is Steven v. Fidelity and Casualty Co. of New York, 377 P.2d 284 (Cal.1962). The plaintiff's husband had paid $2.50 for a policy covering his round trip, for the plaintiff's benefit. A close reading might have excluded an injury suffered during travel via a "non-scheduled" air carrier. The carrier for one leg of Mr. Steven's journey cancelled his flight; and its agent helped him arrange an air-taxi charter. Steven suffered a fatal injury in the

---

a. "In general, courts will protect the reasonable expectations of applicants, insureds, and intended beneficiaries regarding the coverage afforded . . . even though a careful examination of the policy provisions indicates that such expectations are contrary to the expressed intention of the insurer." Keeton & Widiss, op. cit. supra at 633.

crash of the chartered craft. He had mailed the policy to his wife in an envelope provided by the machine. On an appeal by the plaintiff from an adverse judgment, the court said:

> In this type of standardized contract . . . the insured may reasonably expect coverage for the whole trip which he inserted in the policy, including reasonable substituted transportation necessitated by emergency. If the insurer did not propose such coverage, it should have plainly and clearly brought to the attention of the purchaser such limitation of liability.

By a 4–3 vote the court reversed and directed judgment for the plaintiff.[b]

Should a buyer of automobile insurance get coverage according to an ordinary buyer's reasonable expectations, notwithstanding a policy exclusion? See Powers v. Detroit Auto. Inter–Insurance Exchange, 398 N.W.2d 411 (Mich.1986) ("It is fatuous to suppose the policy owner had any part in the language of the policy besides filling in the blanks. . . . The common wisdom is that very few insurance policy purchasers read all or even substantially all of the purchased contract, and it is not guaranteeable that they would understand it if they did.")[c]

In *Steven* the court relied also on an alternate ground: that the policy was ambiguous. "The rule of resolving ambiguities against the insurer does not serve as a mere tie-breaker," the court said, "it rests upon fundamental considerations of policy." This rule has support in all courts. It is not, however, uniformly applied. In some cases the search for ambiguity has been pressed beyond the limits of common sense. "The conclusion is inescapable that courts have sometimes invented ambiguity where none existed, then resolving the invented ambiguity contrary to the plainly expressed terms of the contract document." R. Keeton, Insurance Law (Basic Text) 356 (1971).[d]

NOTES

(1) *Alternative Grounds.* Another case in which the ambiguity of an insurance policy was one ground of decision is C & J Fertilizer, Inc. v. Allied Mut. Ins. Co., 227 N.W.2d 169, 86 A.L.R.3d 839 (Iowa 1975) (5–4 decision). There the court denounced a limitation of coverage in a burglary policy, intended to preclude recovery for "inside jobs." Another ground of decision was that the limitation was unconscionable. A minority of the court would also have imposed a warranty on the insurer that the policy was fit for its intended purpose;

b. See also Mutual of Omaha Ins. Co. v. Russell, 402 F.2d 339, 29 A.L.R.3d 753 (10th Cir.1968), cert. denied, 394 U.S. 973 (1969) ("Does the speed of the modern jet age and the restless, irrepressible, increased tempo of all who are in its vortex impose on a flight insurer the obligation toward prospective policy buyers of explaining the distinctive differences of the several available coverages?").

c. See also Sparks v. St. Paul Ins. Co., 495 A.2d 406 (N.J.1985): ". . . courts have a special responsibility to prevent the mar-keting of policies that provide unrealistic and inadequate coverage."

d. What Judge Keeton has called "false ambiguity" cases have provided support for the doctrine of reasonable expectations. This doctrine is less widely accepted as a basis for insurers' liability than the rule of resolving ambiguities against the insurer.

For an opinion canvassing various formulations of the doctrine see Allen v. Prudential Prop. & Cas. Ins. Co., 839 P.2d 798 (Utah 1992).

compare UCC 2–315. For a comparable decision, grounded directly in public policy, see Note 2, p. 696 below.

What circumstances make one or another of these grounds the preferable one for disregarding a policy limitation? To what extent do these grounds overlap one another?

(2) *Overservice by the Profession.* "The lawyer who serves his client without regard to the public welfare, though he succeed in getting the decision in a particular case, in the long run does his client no real service, and, if you want an illustration, let me briefly refer to the extraordinary service which insurance lawyers rendered the insurance business in years gone by, in exaggerating warranties to the point where they were almost one hundred per cent protection against claims, only to develop a public atmosphere resulting in judicial decision and legislation which puts the insurer under his contract in a worse position today than is any other contracting party. That is overservice by the profession." Parkinson, Are the Law Schools Adequately Training for the Public Service?, 8 Am.Law School Rev. 291, 294 (1935).

(3) *The Red–Letter Auto Policy.* An insurer doing business in Maine proposed to issue an automobile liability policy containing this warning, in red letters, on its cover: "This is not a Standard Automobile Policy .. [and] in general does not cover operation of the insureds' automobiles by others." The Insurance Commissioner disapproved the form, one of his findings being (in summary) as follows: "it is so limited as to be beyond the reasonable comprehension of the average policyholder, who through the years, has been educated to a broadening of coverages under liability policies insuring his automobile."

The insurer appealed against the Commissioner's action, and observed that the charge for the policy would be less than that for more conventional coverages. The action was based on a statute prohibiting the use of forms found to be illegal, misleading, or "capable of a construction which is unfair to the assured or the public."

The appeal was allowed in part. Most of the Commissioner's specific objections were unwarranted, except in the opinion of one justice. The court observed that affording the coverage might induce more motorists to insure themselves, particularly those in the "less endowed financial group." American Fidelity Co. v. Mahoney, 174 A.2d 446 (Me.1961).

UNCONSCIONABLE CONTRACTS UNDER
THE UNIFORM COMMERCIAL CODE

One of the most widely debated sections of the Uniform Commercial Code is UCC 2–302, which authorizes a court to refuse enforcement or to limit the application of a contract or clause that it determines to have been "unconscionable." The comment to that section reads in part:

"This section is intended to make it possible for the courts to police explicitly against the contracts or clauses which they find to be unconscionable. In the past such policing has been accomplished by adverse construction of language, by manipulation of the rules of offer and acceptance or by determinations that the clause is contrary to public policy or to the dominant purpose of the contract.... The principle is one of the prevention of oppression and unfair surprise (Cf. Campbell

Soup Co. v. Wentz, 172 F.2d 80, 3d Cir.1948) and not of disturbance of allocation of risks because of superior bargaining power."

Professor Llewellyn, the Chief Reporter of the Code, defended the section at the hearings of the New York Law Revision Commission in 1954 in these words:

"Business lawyers tend to draft to the edge of the possible. Any engineer makes his construction within a margin of safety, and a wide margin of safety, so that he knows for sure that he is getting what he is gunning for. The practice of business lawyers has been, however—it has grown to be so in the course of time—to draft, as I said before, to the edge of the possible.

"Let me rapidly state that I do not find that this is desired by the business lawyers' clients.... The only doubt that comes up in regard to unconscionability is, if you start drafting to the absolute limit of what the law can conceivably bear. At that point you run into what they run into now, and what you run into now is, the court kicks it over." Report of the New York State Law Revision Commission for 1954, N.Y.Leg.Doc. (1954) No. 65, pp. 177–78.

Campbell Soup Co. v. Wentz concerned a standard-form canner-grower contract. The defendant had committed his entire crop of carrots to Campbell for a price of not more than $30 a ton. By the time for delivery a scarcity had developed, goods of the kind were virtually unobtainable, and their price had risen to at least $90 a ton. Campbell's suppliers began to sell some of their crops to others; and it brought an action to enjoin further sales elsewhere, and for specific performance. The court of appeals found several provisions of the contracts to be objectionable and refused to grant equitable relief. It said that the contract was obviously "drawn by skilful draftsmen with the buyer's interests in mind," and was "too hard a bargain to entitle the plaintiff to relief in a court of conscience." Also:

[W]e are not suggesting that the contract is illegal. Nor are we suggesting any excuse for the grower in this case who has deliberately broken an agreement.

The case is the basis for Illustration 1 to Restatement Second § 208, which states a rule in virtually the same terms as UCC 2–302(1). The section is without parallel in the original Restatement.

The *Campbell Soup* case is cited in Comment 1 to UCC 2–302. Does the decision support the Code rule? See Hillman, Debunking Some Myths About Unconscionability: A New Framework for U.C.C. Section 2–302, 67 Cornell.L.Q. 1 (1981).

NOTES

(1) *Code Drafting.* For an illuminating and amusing account of the development, in successive Code drafts, of what became UCC 2–302, see Leff, Unconscionability and the Code—The Emperor's New Clause, 115 U.Pa.L.Rev. 485 (1967). Early drafts focussed on improprieties in bargaining, or the absence of it. Then the focus shifted: at one stage there was a comment condemning a "lopsided bargain," though deliberately entered into, with full knowledge and awareness.

By Professor's Leff's account, the element of "naughty bargaining conduct" proved impossible to formulate, and a prohibition on lopsided terms proved unacceptable to important backers of the Code. "Thus faced with a dilemma, the difficulty of the first alternative and the unpopularity of the second, the draftsmen opted for a third solution. They fudged." Id. at 501.

(2) *Equal Treatment.* Should a particular term in a standardized insurance policy, harshly restricting the insurer's liability, be unenforceable against a large majority of those who purchase the policy, but enforceable against the minority who have reason to know of it and appreciate its effect? (See, for example, subsection (3) of Restatement Second § 211.) One expert in insurance law regards this situation as objectionable: one policyholder's premium money ought to go as far as another's, it might be said. Hence it would be "unconscionable" to enforce the term in question even against the minority. See R. Keeton, Insurance Law (Basic Text) 358–60 (1971). Is this conception of unconscionability different from that of Restatement Second § 208? For a less dramatic response to the problem see subsection (2) of § 211.

UNCONSCIONABILITY: TWO VIEWS

Excerpts from two wide-ranging essays on the subject of unconscionability, as developed in the courts, will indicate the differing degrees of welcome it has received.[a]

(a) When the concept of unconscionability was first made explicit by the Uniform Commercial Code, the initial effort was to reconcile it with the bargain principle. A major step in this direction was a distinction, drawn in 1967 by Arthur Leff, between "procedural" and "substantive" unconscionability. Leff defined procedural unconscionability as fault or unfairness in the bargaining *process;* substantive unconscionability as fault or unfairness in the bargaining *outcome*—that is, unfairness of terms. The effect (if not the purpose) of this distinction, which influenced much of the later analysis,[1] was to domesticate unconscionability by accepting the concept insofar as it could be made harmonious with the bargain principle (that is, insofar as it was "procedural"), while rejecting its wider implication that in appropriate cases the courts might review bargains for fairness of terms. Correspondingly, much of the scholarly literature and case law concerning unconscionability has emphasized the element of unfair surprise, in which a major underpinning of the bargain principle—knowing assent—is absent by hypothesis.

Over the last fifteen years, however, there have been strong indications that the principle of unconscionability authorizes a review of elements well beyond unfair surprise, including, in appropriate cases, fairness of terms. For example, comment *c* to section 208 of the Restatement (Second) of Contracts states that "[t]heoretically it is possible for a contract to be oppressive taken as a whole, even though there is no weakness in the bargaining process and no single term which

a. Most footnotes omitted.   **1.** See, e.g., Epstein, Unconscionability: A Critical Reappraisal [source of the following excerpt].

is in itself unconscionable." [b]   ... [A] basic thesis of this Article is that unconscionability is a paradigmatic concept that can never be exhaustively described.   It is, however, a major purpose [here] to suggest a methodology by which specific unconscionability norms should be developed.   Three general propositions underlie the methodology, and should be stated at the outset: (1) Since the bargain principle rests on arguments of fairness and efficiency, it is appropriate to develop and apply a specific unconscionability norm whenever a class of cases can be identified in which neither fairness nor efficiency support the bargain principle's application.   (2) The development and application of specific unconscionability norms is closely related to the manner in which the relevant market deviates from a perfectly competitive market.   (3) The distinction between procedural and substantive unconscionability is too rigid to provide significant help in either the development or the application of such norms.—Eisenberg, The Bargain Principle and Its Limits, 95 Harv. L.Rev. 741, 752–54 (1982).[c]

(b) [This paper offers a defense] against modern attacks [on] the principle of freedom of contract which was central to the classical common law.   Properly understood, that position does not require a court to enforce every contract brought before it.   It does, however, demand that the reasons invoked for not enforcing the contract be of one of two sorts.   Either there must be proof of some defect in the process of contract formation (be it duress, fraud or undue influence); or there must be, but only within narrow limits, some incompetence of the party against whom the agreement is to be enforced.   The doctrine of unconscionability is important in both these respects because it can, if wisely applied, allow the courts to police these two types of problems, and thereby improve the general administration of the contract law.   Yet when the doctrine of unconscionability is used in its substantive dimension, be it in a commercial or consumer context, it serves only to undercut the private right of contract in a manner that is apt to do more social harm than good.   The result of the analysis is the same even if we view the question of unconscionability from the lofty perspective of public policy.   "[I]f there is one thing which more than another public policy requires, it is that men of full age and competent understanding shall have the utmost liberty of contracting, and that their contracts when entered into freely and voluntarily shall be held sacred and shall be enforced by Courts of justice." [1]—Epstein, Unconscionability: A Critical Reappraisal, 18 J.Law & Econ. 293, 315 (1975).[d]

NOTES

(1) *Problem.*   A statute attaches sanctions to unconscionable conduct and defines such conduct as

b. The comment continues: "Ordinarily, however, an unconscionable contract involves other factors as well as overall imbalance."

c. © 1982, Harvard Law Review Association.

1. Printing and Numerical Registering Co. v. Sampson, L.R. 19 Eq. 462, 465 (1875).

d. Reprinted by permission of the Journal of Law & Economics, © 1975 by the University of Chicago. All rights reserved.

[A]n act or practice which, to a person's detriment: (A) takes advantage of the lack of knowledge, ability, experience, or capacity of a person to a grossly unfair degree; or (B) results in a gross disparity between the value received and consideration paid, in a transaction ... involving transfer of consideration.

An attorney claims relief under the statute after purchasing an office copier. The trial court grants relief on findings that the sales agent took "grossly unfair" advantage of the plaintiff's lack of knowledge to a "grossly unfair degree," and that there was a "glaring and flagrant" difference between the price charged to the plaintiff and the value received. On appeal by the seller, should the judgment be reversed? How important is it to know what relief the statute authorizes? See Tri–Continental Leasing v. Law Office, 710 S.W.2d 604 (Tex.App.1985), writ ref. n.r.e.

(2) *The Case of the Off–Color Yarn.* The firms "Wilson Trading" and "Ferguson" were parties to a contract for the sale of yarn. When Wilson Trading sued Ferguson for the price, Ferguson alleged that the yarn was not "good merchantable yarn," as the contract required (¶ 4). Ferguson claimed that the existence of the defect could not have been discovered until it had cut the yarn and knitted it into sweaters: when the sweaters were washed, they were vari-colored owing to "shading" of the yarn. The trial court entered summary judgment for Wilson, relying on this other provision of the contract (¶ 2):

No claims relating to ... quality or shade shall be allowed if made after weaving, knitting, or processing, or more than 10 days after receipt of shipment.... The buyer shall within 10 days of [receipt] examine the merchandise for any and all defects.

On appeal, *held:* Reversed. Wilson Trading Corp. v. David Ferguson, Ltd., 244 N.E.2d 685 (N.Y.1968).

One judge would have had the trial court determine at trial whether or not the limitation of time was "manifestly unreasonable," referring to UCC 1–204. But the other judges directed the trial court to determine whether or not there were latent shading defects that were not "reasonably discoverable" before the yarn was processed. If there were, the court said, the purport of ¶ 2 was to eliminate every remedy for those defects. The situation would then bring UCC 2–719(2) into play: "Where circumstances cause an exclusive or limited warranty to fail of its essential purpose, remedy may be had as provided in this Act."

The court considered an alternate function for ¶ 2, not related to remedies: that of modifying the substance of ¶ 4. On that view, however, the warranty language of ¶ 4 would prevail over the "negation or limitation" of ¶ 2: see UCC 2–316(1).

The court's reasoning has not been well received. On one view it is unduly favorable to *sellers* by offering them alternative means for curtailing the effect of a warranty. On another view the court should not have relied on the Code section quoted above: section 2–719(2) supposes circumstances that change after the contract is made. See Note, Warranty Liability Limitation, 63 Va.L.Rev. 791 (1977); Brook, Contractual Disclaimers and Limitation of Liability ..., 49 Brooklyn L.Rev. 1 (1982). As to the "metaphysics" of UCC 2–719(2) see Eddy, On the "Essential" Purpose of Limited Remedies ..., 65 Calif.L.Rev. 23 (1977).

(3) *Unconscionability.* In *Wilson Trading* the court avoided deciding whether or not the seller's time limitation (¶ 2) was unconscionable. Suppose that the seller rewrote the provision so as to state a "modification" of its warranties that

would be effective under UCC 2–316. Can it be supposed that the provision would be condemned as ineffective under UCC 2–302? One critic, Professor Leff, thought that incredible. But see Martin v. Joseph Harris Co., Inc., 767 F.2d 296 (6th Cir.1985), and Ellinghaus, In Defense of Unconscionability, 78 Yale L.J. 757 (1969).

Note that UCC 2–316(4) makes a cross-reference to UCC 2–719, which embodies a test of unconscionability. What inference should be drawn from that? See Leff, Unconscionability and the Code—The Emperor's New Clause, 115 U.Pa.L.Rev. 485, 520–32 (1967).

WARRANTIES AND LOSS LIMITATIONS

Buyers of cars, appliances, equipment, and other "hard goods" regularly receive express warranties against defects. In a common form, the warranty commits the manufacturer, dealer, or both, to repair or replace the item, or parts of it, in certain circumstances. The Code gives its blessing to agreements making this the limit of the buyer's remedies: UCC 2–719(1)(a). However, beginning in the late 60's it became a flourishing industry to break through the limitation in the courts. Owing to post-Code legislation it is now virtually impossible to preclude a consumer buyer from all remedies other than repair or replacement, as against a dealer. Moreover, the Code itself provides for overriding the limitation in certain cases; note the opening phrase of section 2–719(1): "Subject to the provisions [cited]."

The allowance of consequential damages is illustrated by an action against a manufacturer. The plaintiffs had bought a Ford truck that proved to be seriously defective (twisted and diamonded frame). "As required by Ford's warranty, Mr. and Mrs. Mayes returned the truck to the selling dealer, North City, seven or eight times for major repairs. The problems were never corrected. When the trouble was finally diagnosed ... Ford would not extend the duration of the warranty...." After returning the truck, the buyers sued under a Consumer Protection Act [a] and got a judgment including amounts for gas and mileage expenses, time lost from work, an attorney's fee, and punitive damages. On an appeal by Ford, most of these recoveries survived. The sale warranty disclaimed responsibility for "loss of use of the vehicle, loss of time, inconvenience, commercial loss or consequential damages."

Although the court conceded that the disclaimer was not unconscionable on its face, it said:

> Ford's warranty policy was unconscionable as applied to Mr. and Mrs. Mayes. [I]t acted "unconscionably" when it insisted that [they] had no remedy other than to allow Ford and its dealer to continue indefinitely in their efforts to correct the problem.

Many courts have reached a like conclusion on comparable facts. What is usually at stake is "consequential" damages. These are to be distin-

----

a. Kentucky Act of 1972: K.R.S. 367.110–.300. The case report is Ford Mo-tor Co. v. Mayes, 575 S.W.2d 480 (Ky.App. 1978).

guished from "direct" damages, such as the difference between the price and the value of the defective item (see Chapter 5, on Remedies for Breach, for elaboration). Some courts would have awarded consequential damages to the truck buyers on the ground that the remedy as limited in the contract failed of its essential purpose. Alternatively, it might be said that the failure to keep a warranty amounts to a repudiation of it and that the repudiator may not assert provisions of the warranty beneficial to it.

For a contrasting case see S.M. Wilson & Co. v. Smith Int'l, Inc., 587 F.2d 1363 (9th Cir.1978). See also In re Chateaugay Corp., 162 B.R. 949, 961 (Bankr.S.D.N.Y.1994) (New York law), examining the question whether or not, if a "repair, replacement or credit" remedy for a buyer fails of its essential purpose, the seller's damage-limitation provisions also fall. "Even if the former falls," the court said, "the latter will still be enforced, at least where the seller has acted in good faith and the buyer retains a minimum adequate remedy such as damages." Also: "It is extremely rare for a court to find an unconscionable limitation on consequential damages in a contract between experienced businessmen arising in a commercial setting."

Owing to decisions like these, limited to the facts at hand, and to some avowed differences of opinion, the law on the point is unsettled. Many decisions can be reconciled by distinguishing between commercial and consumer goods. (*S.M. Wilson* concerned a tunnel-boring machine, designed and built by the seller for more than half a million dollars.) [b] However, one court has refused to distinguish between the purchase of an automobile and the purchase of a commercial laser: "not that different." [c] Does UCC 2–719(2) admit of the distinction? [d] What others might be made? Should anything turn on the conscientiousness of the seller's efforts at repair? On whether the loss in question occurred before or after a reasonable time for making repairs had elapsed?

b. As the seller knew, the buyer meant to use it to drive a coal-mine shaft. Owing to poor performance of the machine, there was a long delay in the project. In suing the seller, the buyer alleged damages of more than $1.8 million, all related to its use of the machine. The contract purported to limit the seller's obligation to the repair and replacement of certain parts and to exclude liability for the losses claimed. After delivery, the seller made repeated efforts to put the machine in good working order, but never succeeded. (Late in the day it was discovered that important elements of the machine had been installed backward, through the seller's fault.) The trial court gave summary judgment for the seller, and it was affirmed on appeal. No issue of unconscionability was presented; but the buyer invoked UCC 2–719(2).

The court noted that the seller "did not ignore his obligation to repair; he simply was unable to perform it. This is not enough to require that the seller absorb losses the buyer plainly agreed to bear. Risk shifting is socially expensive and should not be undertaken in the absence of a good reason.... The default of the seller is not so total and fundamental as to require that its consequential damage limitation be expunged from the contract."

"Each case must stand on its own facts."

c. AES Technology Systems, Inc. v. Coherent Radiation, 583 F.2d 933 (7th Cir. 1978).

d. See Comment, 64 Corn.L.Rev. 30, 235–39 (1978); Samuels, The Unconscionability of Excluding Consequential Damages, etc., 43 U.Pitt.L.Rev. 197 (1981).

NOTES

(1) *A Blow-Out Case.* A tire manufacturer warrants its products against defects. In addition, it wishes to provide a buyer with a replacement or refund if its tire fails during the first two years of normal use. (In that event the buyer is to be charged with a fraction of the price of a new tire, determined with reference to the unexpired portion of that period.) The manufacturer does *not* wish to pay for other physical damage or for personal injury that a blow-out may cause. How would you draft a provision about warranties to achieve these purposes?

In Collins v. Uniroyal, Inc., 315 A.2d (16 N.J.1974), a tire manufacturer was adjudged liable for death and other injuries, resulting from the blow-out of a tire, on a jury verdict. For purposes of the appeal the jury findings were understood to mean that there was no defect in the tire, and no liability in tort. The tire had been sold with a guarantee of repair or replacement and the liability was pitched on that. In light of this ruling, would you give up the effort to draft an express warranty and limit the remedy to refund and the like? If so, would that be a disservice to consumers? Justice Clifford, dissenting in *Collins,* argued that manufacturers would be discouraged by the decision from offering "extra" protection (i.e., more than buyers are entitled to under implied warranties and the like). The court said: "We deem this position not consonant with the commercial and human realities."

The contract in *Collins* recited: "This Guarantee does not cover consequential damages." Was this clearly unconscionable? Another court has said: "to give what looks like relief in the form of an express warranty, but is not, is unconscionable as a surprise limitation and therefore against public policy." [e] Does that beg the question? The same court observed that under the Code it is "very difficult" to create an express warranty and limit the remedy; and it remarked on the anomaly that UCC 2–316 permits warranties to be disclaimed altogether. Do you find the anomaly in the Code or in the decisions?

For a discriminating criticism of the *Collins* case—and of UCC 2–713(3)—see Note, 50 N.Y.U.L.Rev. 146 (1975).

(2) *Problem.* A manufacturer of commercial aircraft has had this experience: Two days after delivering a craft to a customer, the nose wheel malfunctioned, causing damage to the hull. The manufacturer was compelled to pay for that damage. For the future, is it possible for the manufacturer to restrict its liability in such a case by agreeing to replace the wheel only? See Delta Air Lines, Inc. v. Douglas Aircraft Co., 47 Cal.Rptr. 518 (Cal.App.1965). (In that case the head of the manufacturer's legal department testified that customers frequently asked that a remedy-limitation clause be removed, to which the normal reply was, "We will take it out only at an increase in price.")

(3) *A Lost Life.* A couple named Mieske kept a home-movie record of their wedding and their family life over many years thereafter. Wishing to have the films spliced into four reels, Mrs. Mieske delivered them to the Bartell Drug Co. for transmittal to a processor. She said, "Don't lose these. They are my life." At the same time she was handed a receipt (which she did not read) containing the language, "We assume no responsibility beyond retail cost of film unless otherwise agreed to in writing." The films being lost, the Mieskes sued Bartell Drug and the processor for $7,500. Each of them admitted negligence.

Assume that the plaintiffs' recovery depends upon establishing unconscionability in the receipt. If the court finds the facts only as stated above, may it

e. Tuttle v. Kelly–Springfield Tire Co.,
585 P.2d 1116 (Okla.1978).

direct the jury that the limitation of liability is not binding? Or must it consider further evidence if offered by the defendant? If the court may not take judicial notice of the "commercial setting, purpose, and effect" of the agreement, what sort of evidence might the defendant suitably offer?

The trial court entered judgment for the plaintiff in the amount claimed, and Bartell Drug appealed. For the appellate disposition see Mieske v. Bartell Drug Co., 593 P.2d 1308 (Wash.1979). As to problems of interpreting a comparable document see Carr v. Hoosier Photo Supplies, Inc., 441 N.E.2d 450 (Ind.1982).

WILLIAMS v. WALKER–THOMAS FURNITURE CO.

United States Court of Appeals, District of Columbia Circuit, 1965.
350 F.2d 445, 18 A.L.R.3d 1297.

J. SKELLY WRIGHT, CIRCUIT JUDGE. Appellee, Walker–Thomas Furniture Company, operates a retail furniture store in the District of Columbia. During the period from 1957 to 1962 each appellant in these cases purchased a number of household items from Walker–Thomas, for which payment was to be made in installments. The terms of each purchase were contained in a printed form contract which set forth the value of the purchased item and purported to lease the item to appellant for a stipulated monthly rent payment. The contract then provided, in substance, that title would remain in Walker–Thomas until the total of all the monthly payments made equaled the stated value of the item, at which time appellants could take title. In the event of a default in the payment of any monthly installment, Walker–Thomas could repossess the item.

The contract further provided that "the amount of each periodical installment payment to be made by (purchaser) to the Company under this present lease shall be inclusive of and not in addition to the amount of each installment payment to be made by (purchaser) under such prior leases, bills or accounts; *and all payments now and hereafter made by (purchaser) shall be credited pro rata on all outstanding leases, bills and accounts* due the Company by (purchaser) at the time each such payment is made." (Emphasis added.) The effect of this rather obscure provision was to keep a balance due on every item purchased until the balance due on all items, whenever purchased, was liquidated. As a result, the debt incurred at the time of purchase of each item was secured by the right to repossess all the items previously purchased by the same purchaser, and each new item purchased automatically became subject to a security interest arising out of the previous dealings.

On May 12, 1962, appellant Thorne purchased an item described as a Daveno, three tables, and two lamps, having total stated value of $391.10. Shortly thereafter, he defaulted on his monthly payments and appellee sought to replevy all the items purchased since the first transaction in 1958. Similarly, on April 17, 1962, appellant Williams bought a stereo set of stated value of $514.95.[1] She too defaulted shortly thereafter, and appellee sought to replevy all the items purchased since December, 1957. The Court of General Sessions granted judgment for appellee. The District of Columbia Court of Appeals affirmed, and we granted appellants' motion for leave to appeal to this court.

Appellants' principal contention, rejected by both the trial and the appellate courts below, is that these contracts, or at least some of them, are unconscionable and, hence, not enforceable. In its opinion in Williams v. Walker–Thomas Furniture Company, 198 A.2d 914, 916 (1964), the District of Columbia Court of Appeals explained its rejection of this contention as follows:

"Appellant's second argument presents a more serious question. The record reveals that prior to the last purchase appellant had reduced the balance in her account to $164. The last purchase, a stereo set, raised the balance due to $678. Significantly, at the time of this and the preceding purchases, appellee was aware of appellant's financial position. The reverse side of the stereo contract listed the name of appellant's social worker and her $218 monthly stipend from the government. Nevertheless, with full knowledge that appellant had to feed, clothe and support both herself and seven children on this amount, appellee sold her a $514 stereo set.

"We cannot condemn too strongly appellee's conduct. It raises serious questions of sharp practice and irresponsible business dealings. A review of the legislation in the District of Columbia affecting retail sales and the pertinent decisions of the highest court in this jurisdiction disclose, however, no ground upon which this court can declare the contracts in question contrary to public policy. We note that were the Maryland Retail Installment Sales Act, Art. 83 §§ 128–153, or its equivalent, in force in the District of Columbia, we could grant appellant appropriate relief. We think Congress should consider corrective legislation to protect the public from such exploitive contracts as were utilized in the case at bar."

We do not agree that the court lacked the power to refuse enforcement to contracts found to be unconscionable. In other jurisdictions, it has been held as a matter of common law that unconscionable contracts are not enforceable.[2] While no decision of this court so holding has been found, the notion that an unconscionable bargain should not be given full enforcement is by no means novel. In Scott v. United States, 79 U.S. (12 Wall.) 443, 445, 20 L.Ed. 438 (1870), the Supreme Court stated:

"... If a contract be unreasonable and unconscionable, but not void for fraud, a court of law will give to the party who sues for its

---

1. At the time of this purchase her account showed a balance of $164 still owing from her prior purchases. The total of all the purchases made over the years in question came to $1,800. The total payments amounted to $1,400.

2. Campbell Soup Co. v. Wentz, 172 F.2d 80 (3d Cir.1948); Indianapolis Morris Plan Corp. v. Sparks, 132 Ind.App. 145, 172 N.E.2d 899 (1961); Henningsen v. Bloomfield Motors, Inc., 32 N.J. 358, 161 A.2d 69, 84–96, 75 A.L.R.2d 1 (1960). Cf. 1 Corbin, Contracts Section 128 (1963).

breach damages, not according to its letter, but only such as he is equitably entitled to...."

Since we have never adopted or rejected such a rule, the question here presented is actually one of first impression.

Congress has recently enacted the Uniform Commercial Code, which specifically provides that the court may refuse to enforce a contract which it finds to be unconscionable at the time it was made. [Section 2–302] The enactment of this section, which occurred subsequent to the contracts here in suit, does not mean that the common law of the District of Columbia was otherwise at the time of enactment, nor does it preclude the court from adopting a similar rule in the exercise of its powers to develop the common law for the District of Columbia. In fact, in view of the absence of prior authority on the point, we consider the congressional adopting of Section 2–302 persuasive authority for following the rationale of the cases, from which the section is explicitly derived.[3] Accordingly, we hold that where the element of unconscionability is present at the time a contract is made, the contract should not be enforced.

Unconscionability has generally been recognized to include an absence of meaningful choice on the part of one of the parties together with contract terms which are unreasonably favorable to the other party. Whether a meaningful choice is present in a particular case can only be determined by consideration of all the circumstances surrounding the transaction. In many cases the meaningfulness of the choice is negated by a gross inequality of bargaining power.[4] The manner in which the contract was entered is also relevant to this consideration. Did each party to the contract, considering his obvious education or lack of it, have a reasonable opportunity to understand the terms of the contract, or were the important terms hidden in a maze of fine print and minimized by deceptive sales practices? Ordinarily, one who signs an agreement without full knowledge of its terms might be held to assume the risk that he has entered a one-sided bargain.[5] But when a party of

---

3. See Comment, Sec. 2–302, Uniform Commercial Code (1962). Compare Note, 45 Va.L.Rev. 583, 590 (1959), where it is predicted that the rule of Sec. 2–302 will be followed by analogy in cases which involve contracts not specifically covered by the section. Cf. 1 State of New York Law Revision Commission, Report and Record of Hearings on the Uniform Commercial Code 108–110 (1954) (remarks of Professor Llewellyn).

4. See Henningsen v. Bloomfield Motors, Inc., supra Note 2, 161 A.2d 69 at 86, and authorities there cited. Inquiry into the relative bargaining power of the two parties is not an inquiry wholly divorced from the general question of unconscionability, since a one-sided bargain is itself evidence of the inequality of the bargaining parties. This fact was vaguely recognized in the common law doctrine of intrinsic fraud, that is, fraud which can be presumed from the grossly unfair nature of the terms of the contract. See the oft-quoted statement of Lord Hardwicke in Earl of Chesterfield v. Janssen, 28 Eng.Rep. 82, 100 (1751):

"... (Fraud) may be apparent from the intrinsic nature and subject of the bargain itself; such as no man in his senses and not under delusion would make ..."

5. See Restatement, Contracts Sec. 70 (1932); Note, 63 Harv.L.Rev. 494 (1950). See also Daley v. People's Building, Loan & Savings Ass'n, 178 Mass. 13, 59 N.E. 452, 453 (1901), in which Mr. Justice Holmes, while sitting on the Supreme Judicial Court of Massachusetts, made this observation:

"... Courts are less and less disposed to interfere with parties making such contracts as they choose, so long as they

little bargaining power, and hence little real choice, signs a commercially unreasonable contract with little or no knowledge of its terms, it is hardly likely that his consent, or even an objective manifestation of his consent, was ever given to all the terms. In such a case the usual rule that the terms of the agreement are not to be questioned[6] should be abandoned and the court should consider whether the terms of the contract are so unfair that enforcement should be withheld.[7]

In determining reasonableness or fairness, the primary concern must be with the terms of the contract considered in light of the circumstances existing when the contract was made. The test is not simple, nor can it be mechanically applied. The terms are to be considered "in the light of the general commercial background and the commercial needs of the particular trade or case."[8] Corbin suggests the test as being whether the terms are "so extreme as to appear unconscionable according to the mores and business practices of the time and place." 1 Corbin, op. cit. supra Note 2.[9] We think this formulation correctly states the test to be applied in those cases where no meaningful choice was exercised upon entering the contract.

Because the trial court and the appellate court did not feel that enforcement could be refused, no findings were made on the possible unconscionability of the contracts in these cases. Since the record is not sufficient for our deciding the issue as a matter of law, the cases must be remanded to the trial court for further proceedings.

So ordered.

DANAHER, CIRCUIT JUDGE (dissenting): The District of Columbia Court of Appeals obviously was as unhappy about the situation here presented as any of us can possibly be. Its opinion in the *Williams* case, quoted in the majority text, concludes: "We think Congress should consider corrective legislation to protect the public from such exploitive contracts as were utilized in the case at bar."

My view is thus summed up by an able court which made no finding that there had actually been sharp practice. Rather the appellant seems to have known precisely where she stood.

There are many aspects of public policy here involved. What is a luxury to some may seem an outright necessity to others. Is public

interfere with no one's welfare but their own.... It will be understood that we are speaking of parties standing in an equal position where neither has any oppressive advantage or power...."

6. This rule has never been without exception. In cases involving merely the transfer of unequal amounts of the same commodity, the courts have held the bargain unenforceable for the reason that "in such a case, it is clear, that the law cannot indulge in the presumption of equivalence between the consideration and the promise." 1 Williston, Contracts Sec. 115 (3d ed. 1957).

7. See the general discussion of "Boiler–Plate Agreements" in Llewellyn, The Common Law Tradition 362–371 (1960).

8. Comment, Uniform Commercial Code Sec. 2–307.

9. See Henningsen v. Bloomfield Motors, Inc., supra Note 2; Mandel v. Liebman, 303 N.Y. 88, 100 N.E.2d 149 (1951). The traditional test as stated in Greer v. Tweed ..., 13 Abb.Pr., N.S. (N.Y.1872), at 429, is "such as no man in his senses and not under delusion would make on the one hand, and as no honest or fair man would accept, on the other."

oversight to be required of the expenditures of relief funds? A washing machine, e.g., in the hands of a relief client might become a fruitful source of income. Many relief clients may well need credit, and certain business establishments will take long chances on the sale of items, expecting their pricing policies will afford a degree of protection commensurate with the risk. Perhaps a remedy when necessary will be found within the provisions of the "Loan Shark" law, D.C.Code Sections 26–601 et seq. (1961).

I mention such matters only to emphasize the desirability of a cautious approach to any such problem, particularly since the law for so long has allowed parties such great latitude in making their own contracts. I dare say there must annually be thousands upon thousands of installment credit transactions in this jurisdiction, and one can only speculate as to the effect the decision in these cases will have.[10]

I join the District of Columbia Court of Appeals in its disposition of the issues.[a]

NOTES

(1) *Effect of Repossession.* The contract provision authorizing the seller to repossess one item for the buyer's failure to pay for another is known as a cross-collateral, or "dragnet" provision. Is it clear that the furniture company would be overpaid by the enforcement of this provision? If the repossessed items are resold for less than the buyer's indebtedness, the seller is entitled to a deficiency judgment for the difference, plus certain expenses. (The right to such a judgment is curtailed, however, in some consumer credit legislation, such as section 5.103 of the Uniform Consumer Credit Code.) If they are resold for more than is due, the seller must account to the buyer for the surplus. What is the likelihood of a surplus, on a resale of second-hand consumer goods? On the subject of enforcing security interests, Article 9, Part 5, of the Uniform Commercial Code may be consulted, but the subject must be pursued in a course concerning security interests in personal property.

(2) *Questions.* If the furniture company's contracts had not contained a cross-collateral provision, would there have been anything offensive about them? Should Mrs. Williams have been permitted to keep the stereo set without paying for it? To keep it on paying part of the price? To return it and keep the other furniture she had bought? Do your answers depend in part on what you know of her financial position? Note the remarks of the lower court on the subject. Do they contain a patronizing implication that storekeepers may decide who can and who cannot afford their merchandise?

(3) *Reform Measures.* Mrs. Williams was represented by the legal assistance office of the bar association.[b] "The Legal Assistance Office was willing to concede that the store could repossess the stereo record player for nonpayment, but what stirred them to action was that the seller sought to scoop up all that it

---

10. However the provision ultimately may be applied or in what circumstances, D.C.Code Sec. 28–2–302 (Supp. IV, 1965) did not become effective until January 1, 1965.

a. The case is the basis for illustration 5 after Restatement Second § 208, referring especially to the clause, "all payments . . .

shall be credited pro rata on all outstanding . . . accounts." The Illustration concludes: "It may be determined that either the quoted clause or the contract as a whole was unconscionable when made."

b. In addition, the court of appeals appointed amicus curiae.

had ever sold to Ora.... The store's records showed that of a combined total claim of $444 as of December 26, 1962, Ora still owed 25¢ on item 1, purchased December 23, 1957 (price $45.65); 3¢ on item 2, purchased December 31, 1957 (price $13.21); ... and similarly for subsequent purchases...." Skilton and Helstad, Protection of the Installment Buyer of Goods under the UCC, 65 Mich.L.Rev. 1465 (1967).[c] Mrs. Williams had made payments of more than $1,000. Apparently the store applied each payment in the proportion that the outstanding balances on the several items bore to one another at the time of the payment.

Another way to apportion a payment is in relation to the *original* debt for each item. If the store had applied Mrs. Williams' payments that way, she would evidently have paid in full for about a dozen of the 16 items she bought from the store. Could the store have been compelled to reallocate her payments in that manner, as a plausible reading of the contract?

The manner of apportioning payments has been widely prescribed by legislation on retail installment sales, so as to forestall the problem faced in the *Williams* case. See UCCC 3.303(1). More recently, however, the apportionment problem has been finessed by a broader consumer-protection rule of the Federal Trade Commission. As applied to the *Williams* case, the regulation would have limited the furniture company to reserving an interest in any items sold so as to secure only the unpaid price of the item or items subject to that transaction. That is, it could require that the stereo be collateral for the unpaid price of the stereo; it could *not* secure that debt by items sold at other times, nor could it provide that the stereo was security for the price of other items. (Only a "purchase money" security interest in household goods is permitted.) [d]

The specific legislation germane to the *Williams* case, and many concrete prohibitions on particular practices, suggest some questions: Is a court less likely to declare a contract unconscionable by reason of the fact that the legislature has placed contracts of its type in a straitjacket of exact proscriptions designed to protect one of the parties? That is, does statutory control of contract terms, as it grows, limit the range of unconscionability doctrine? If so, is this a good thing?

(4) *The Lawyer's Role.* As a legal precedent, the court's ruling on unconscionability is more significant for consumers generally than any victory Mrs. Williams could have won on the basis of interpretation of her contract. Sometimes a client's interest is better served by seeking relief on a narrow basis than by treating the problem as a test case on a broader principle, such as unconscionability. In this situation, what is the duty of the lawyer? Legal-aid lawyers report that they can commonly settle complaints of consumer debtors on favorable terms, with little effort. Should they urge such a client to forego settlement in the hope of obtaining a landmark ruling? What are the ethical considerations? For a legal-aid lawyer, who is not compensated by individual clients, is it necessary to enlist in general causes more than for a lawyer charging fees? Permissible?

c. Of many comments on the *Williams* case, this is an outstanding one.

d. "In connection with the extension of credit to consumers in or affecting commerce, as commerce is defined in the Federal Trade Commission Act, it is an unfair act or practice within the meaning of Section 5 of that Act for a lender or retail installment seller directly or indirectly to take or receive from a consumer an obligation that . . .

"(4) Constitutes or contains a nonpossessory security interest in household goods other than a purchase money security interest." Credit Practices Rule: 16 C.F.R. § 444.2 (1984). (Certain items in this excerpt are defined in § 444.1.)

(5) *Unconscionability and Incapacity.* Should the principle of unconscionability be regarded as defining a new class of persons lacking the capacity to
contract? An analogy between unconscionability cases and those on capacity has
been drawn by Professor Leff. As he saw it, the notion of *Williams* is that the
poor should be discouraged from frill-buying, and is comparable to the premise in
infancy. Both of them illustrate a tendency toward stereotyping of parties. He
wrote: "One can see it enshrined in the old English equity courts' jolly
treatment of English seamen as members of a happy, fun-loving race (with, one
supposes, a fine sense of rhythm), but certainly not to be trusted to take care of
themselves. What effect, if any, this had upon the sailors is hidden behind the
judicial chuckles as they protected their loyal sailor boys, but one cannot help
wondering how many sailors managed to get credit at any reasonable price. In
other words, the benevolent have a tendency to colonize, whether geographically
or legally." [e]

Is this fair criticism of the *Williams* case? Should new conceptions of
capacity to contract be framed as a solution to consumer credit problems, or
should the focus remain on the characteristics of the credit *transactions*?

JONES v. STAR CREDIT CORP., 298 N.Y.S.2d 264 (N.Y.Sup.Ct.
1969).

WACHTLER, J. On August 30, 1965 the plaintiffs, who are welfare
recipients, agreed to purchase a home freezer unit for $900 as the result
of a visit from a salesman representing Your Shop At Home Service, Inc.
With the addition of the time credit charges, credit life insurance, credit
property insurance, and sales tax, the purchase price totalled $1,234.80.
Thus far the plaintiffs have paid $619.88 toward their purchase. The
defendant claims that with various added credit charges paid for an
extension of time there is a balance of $819.81 still due from the
plaintiffs. The uncontroverted proof at the trial established that the
freezer unit, when purchased, had a maximum retail value of approximately $300. The question is whether this transaction and the resulting
contract could be considered unconscionable within the meaning of
Section 2–302 of the Uniform Commercial Code....

[The court mentioned a concern for "the uneducated and often
illiterate individual who is the victim of gross inequality of bargaining
power, usually the poorest members of the community."]

---

e. Leff, Unconscionability and the
Code—The Emperor's New Clause, 115
U.Pa.L.Rev. 485, 556–58 (1967). Professor
Leff regarded the *Williams* case as an example of certain decisions which have relied
on UCC 2–302 as a way of escape from
difficult policy judgments. (He regarded
the opinion in *Henningsen* with favor: "it
is most significant that the court did *not*
have § 2–302 to work with."). See also
Schwartz, A Reexamination of Nonsubstan-
tive Unconscionability, 63 Va.L.Rev. 1053
(1977).

With these views compare Ellinghaus, In
Defense of Unconscionability, 78 Yale L.J.
757, 766–67, 773 (1969): "nothing could be
more misconceived"; "Just because the
contract I signed was proffered to me by
Almighty Monopoly Incorporated does not
mean that I may subsequently argue exemption from any or all obligation: at the
very least, some element of deception or
substantive unfairness must presumably be
shown."

Concern for the protection of these consumers against overreaching by the small but hardy breed of merchants who would prey on them is not novel. The dangers of inequality of bargaining power were vaguely recognized in the early English common law when Lord Hardwicke wrote of a fraud, "which may be apparent from the intrinsic nature and subject of the bargain itself; such as no man in his senses and not under delusion would make." The English authorities on this subject were discussed in Hume v. United States, 132 U.S. 406, 10 S.Ct. 134, 33 L.Ed. 393 (1889) where the United States Supreme Court characterized these as "cases in which one party took advantage of the other's ignorance of arithmetic to impose upon him, and the fraud was apparent from the face of the contracts."

The law is beginning to fight back against those who once took advantage of the poor and illiterate without risk of either exposure or interference. From the common law doctrine of intrinsic fraud we have over the years, developed common and statutory law which tells not only the buyer but also the seller to beware. This body of laws recognizes the importance of a free enterprise system but at the same time will provide the legal armor to protect and safeguard the prospective victim from the harshness of an unconscionable contract.

Section 2–302 of the Uniform Commercial Code enacts the moral sense of the community into the law of commercial transactions.... It permits a court to accomplish directly what heretofore was often accomplished by construction of language, manipulations of fluid rules of contract law and determinations based upon a presumed public policy.

There is no reason to doubt, moreover, that this section is intended to encompass the price term of an agreement. In addition to the fact that it has already been so applied ... the statutory language itself makes it clear that not only a clause of the contract, but the contract in toto, may be found unconscionable as a matter of law. Indeed, no other provision of an agreement more intimately touches upon the question of unconscionability than does the term regarding price.

Fraud, in the instant case, is not present; nor is it necessary under the statute. The question which presents itself is whether or not, under the circumstances of this case, the sale of a freezer unit having a retail value of $300 for $900 ($1,439.69 including credit charges and $18 sales tax) is unconscionable as a matter of law. The court believes it is.

Concededly, deciding the issue is substantially easier than explaining it. No doubt, the mathematical disparity between $300, which presumably includes a reasonable profit margin, and $900, which is exorbitant on its face, carries the greatest weight. Credit charges alone exceed by more than $100 the retail value of the freezer. These alone, may be sufficient to sustain the decision. Yet, a caveat is warranted lest we reduce the import of Section 2–302 solely to a mathematical ratio formula. It may, at times, be that; yet it may also be much more. The very limited financial resources of the purchaser, known to the sellers at the time of the sale, is entitled to weight in the balance. Indeed, the value disparity itself leads inevitably to the felt conclusion that knowing advantage was taken of the plaintiffs. In addition, the meaningfulness of choice essential to the making of a contract, can be negated by a gross inequality of bargaining power. (Williams v. Walker–Thomas Furniture Co., 121 U.S.App.D.C. 315, 350 F.2d 445.)

There is no question about the necessity and even the desirability of instalment sales and the extension of credit. Indeed, there are many, including welfare recipients, who would be deprived of even the most basic conveniences without the use of these devices. Similarly, the retail merchant selling on instalment or extending credit is expected to establish a pricing factor which will afford a degree of protection commensurate with the risk of selling to those who might be default prone. However, neither of these accepted premises can clothe the sale of this freezer with respectability.

Support for the court's conclusion will be found in a number of other cases already decided. . . . [I]n Frostifresh Corp. v. Reynoso [274 N.Y.S.2d 757, aff'd, 281 N.Y.S.2d 964], the sale of a refrigerator costing the seller $348 for $900 plus credit charges of $245.88 was unconscionable as a matter of law. . . .

Having already paid more than $600 toward the purchase of this $300 freezer unit, it is apparent that the defendant has already been amply compensated. In accordance with the statute, the application of the payment provision should be limited to amounts already paid by the plaintiffs and the contract be reformed and amended by changing the payments called for therein to equal the amount of payment actually so paid by the plaintiffs.

NOTES

(1) *The Question of Remedies.* If Mr. and Mrs. Jones had paid $1,000 before complaining of the contract, would the court have permitted them to recover a part of it? If they had paid only $300, would the court have required them to pay more? What is the rationale of stopping the payments at $619.88?

The case last mentioned by the court, Frostifresh Corp. v. Reynoso, was an action by the seller of a freezer for the unpaid balance of the price. The Reynosos had made only one payment, of $32. The plaintiff had paid $348 for the appliance. The trial court made a simple deduction, and gave judgment for $316. On appeal, the judgment was reversed, and the trial court was directed to give judgment for the "net cost for the refrigerator-freezer, plus a reasonable profit, in addition to trucking and service charges necessarily incurred and reasonable finance charges." Two comments on the case are as follows:

"This case means that sellers can charge the most exorbitant rates, secure in the knowledge that at the worst they will be able to recover a reasonable profit plus all their expenses." Narral, interview, in The Law and the Low Income Consumer 330 ff. (Katz, ed., 1968).

"It must be recognized that even in the poverty situations, putting aside the cases of fraud and high pressure in home sales, the buyers do want the goods. Even in the famous *Frostifresh* case, the question of remedies was complicated by the fact that the Spanish-speaking people deceived into buying a home freezer at a high price *chose to keep the freezer.* Thus we cannot adopt restrictions on remedies so punitive as to put the credit sellers in the poverty areas, and their financers, out of business. Despite the present high social cost, they serve a social purpose." Kripke, Consumer Credit Regulation: A Creditor–Oriented Viewpoint, 68 Colum.L.Rev. 455, 478 ff. (1968).

Appeals have been made against price unconscionability, with success, not only by buyers of food freezers and of home improvements (as the foregoing opinion shows) but also by buyers of Oriental jade carvings for a price of some $67,000. Vom Lehn v. Astor Art Galleries, Ltd., 380 N.Y.S.2d 532 (N.Y.Sup.Ct. 1976). What divers things might the doctrine mean, in relation to such differing consumers?

(2) *The Case of the Literate Lessee.* In KPC Corp. v. Book Press, Inc., 636 A.2d 325 (Vt.1993), a landlord sued a tenant for a rent increase that had been provided for in the lease. The tenant answered that the provision was unconscionable, and that in the circumstances the application of the provision subjected the tenant to unfair surprise. According to the lease, a sustained default by the tenant in paying the base rent, or repeated underpayments, would lead (in addition to a charge for interest) either to termination of the lease or to a 10% increase in the rent over the remainder of the lease term. For several months the tenant had, by error, underpaid the rent. The increase claimed by the landlord amounted to a considerable sum of money, the court said: nearly $1.5 million. (The lease term extended to the year 2005.) But the court affirmed a judgment for the landlord, saying: "the lease has been in existence since 1980, and the increase provision has never been altered. Absent poor education or hidden terms or lack of opportunity to read the lease, none of which are asserted by Book Press [the tenant], we cannot say that the effect of the provision, however shocking to Book Press, was unfair or a surprise."

What relief for the tenant would have been suitable if the contested provision had been found to be unconscionable?

PRICE UNCONSCIONABILITY

How may a court determine that the price charged for goods is so high that the contract is unconscionable, if there is no other element of overreaching? Must the court be prepared to say what the "intrinsic" value of the goods is? Must it be prepared to say what costs of doing business the seller may reasonably incur? What would be a reasonable profit? Can it be maintained that a price is unconscionable if it yields the seller "a greater profit than similarly situated sellers ordinarily receive"? See Note, 67 Mich.L.Rev. 1248, 1259 (1969).

The Uniform Consumer Credit Code (not widely adopted) puts the focus on what is too much for the buyer to pay, rather than on what is too much for the seller to charge. It directs that a comparison be made between the for-credit price agreed to by the buyer (of property or services) and the value "measured by the price at which similar property or services are readily obtainable in credit transactions by like consumers...." If gross disparity exists, that is one of several stated factors to be considered in determining whether or not an agreement is unconscionable.[a]

---

a. Section 5.108. The Code authorizes injunctive relief at the behest of a consumer and also of a public official.

See also the Uniform Consumer Sales Practices Act § 4(c).

To some observers the conceptions "like buyers" and "similarly situated sellers" appear to be fatally undefined. But see Kugler v. Romain, 279 A.2d 640 (N.J.1971).

If sales are made through home solicitations, is the relevant market the universe of such sales or the universe of sales (of like merchandise) both in-store and door-to-door? As will be seen, the judgment has been made that door-to-door selling is so distinctive as to warrant special legislative treatment. One of the premises is that selling costs are exceptionally high, yet the statutes on the subject do *not* preclude pricing to cover those costs.[b] In Jones v. Star Credit Corp., above, is it implicit that exceptional selling costs ought not to be countenanced? In that case reference is made to taking advantage of "the poor and illiterate." In a comparable case the court noted that the buyer had to claim welfare benefits while paying for the goods.[c] Do these observations suggest any appropriate basis for classifying buyers?

A classification of sellers was attempted in an FTC survey of retailing in the District of Columbia. Two groups were identified: those catering primarily to low-income customers and those catering to a more general market. The former used comparatively high markups and prices, it was found; but their costs appeared to be correspondingly high: their "net profit on sales ... was only slightly higher and net profit return on net worth was considerably lower when compared to general market retailers."[d] For low-income market retailers, what elements of cost would you expect to be above average? Presumably the residents of low-income neighborhoods are relatively poor credit risks, as a class. If that fact imposes a special cost on such a resident who would otherwise qualify for favorable credit terms (why should it?), and the cost takes the form of a high markup, does it follow that the price is unconscionable as to that person?

NOTES

(1) *Trial Tactics.* On the difficulties of procedure, and delaying tactics, in maintaining an action for consumer relief on grounds of fraud and unconscionability, see Schrag, Bleak House 1968: A Report on Consumer Test Litigation, 44 N.Y.U.L.Rev. 115 (1969). A bare allegation of price unconscionability is not enough, it has been held, to require the seller to respond to disclosure proceedings aimed at ascertaining his costs.[e] If seller insists that its prices, though relatively high, are warranted by exceptional costs, what reply can be made? It has been suggested that a price exceeding the "average" by 100% be deemed prima facie unconscionable. Speidel, Unconscionability, Assent and Consumer

b. On the significance of high costs, see Note, 20 Me.L.Rev. 159 (1968).

c. Toker v. Westerman, 274 A.2d 78 (N.J.Dist.Ct.1970). The court reasoned, in part, that a dealer using door-to-door salesmen "would have less overhead expense than a dealer maintaining a store or showroom."

d. Federal Trade Commission, Economic Report on Installment Credit and Retail Sales Practices of District of Columbia Retailers (1968).

e. Patterson v. Walker–Thomas Furniture Co., 277 A.2d 111 (D.C.App.1971).

Protection, 31 U.Pitt.L.Rev. 359, 372–73 (1970).   Would it be better to focus attention on the mark-up of an item than on its price? [f]

Under UCC 2–302 the issue of unconscionability is not to be submitted to a jury.   Why this reservation?

(2) *Poverty and Price.*   Urban rioting in the 1960s prompted the formation of a National Advisory Committee on Civil Disorders, whose report included a section on "Exploitation of Disadvantaged Consumers By Retail Merchants." While acknowledging that "higher prices are not necessarily exploitative in themselves," the report enumerated tactics by which "a special kind of merchant" take advantage of inner-city residents who have low and unstable incomes and little understanding of the "pitfalls of credit buying."   See Report, 274–76 (Bantam ed. 1968).   At about that time the Federal Trade Commission made a few charges, against District-of-Columbia merchants, of unfair or deceptive practices.   "[I]t is manifestly unfair," the agency concluded, "to adopt a marketing policy which has the effect of luring unsophisticated customers into entering contractual obligations which in all likelihood they have little understanding of, convincing them that the credit is 'easy' and prices are low and at the same time following a rigid collection policy resulting in default judgments and garnishments being levied against their meager wages."   On the basis of that and other findings, the FTC entered a cease-and-desist order.   Leon A. Tashof, No. 8714 (F.T.C.1986), CCH Trade Reg.Rep. ¶ 18,606, aff'd, Tashof v. F.T.C., 437 F.2d 707 (D.C.Cir.1970).

Various remedial measures for improving the quality of the marketing process described here have been attempted or proposed, including buyers' strikes and consumer education programs.   One of the most elaborate is a joint industry-government program designed to make property insurance available to inner-city merchants.

(3) *Gender and Color and Price.*   A study of sale tactics in Chicago-area auto showrooms indicated that shoppers who are male, and white, find it easier than others do to arrive at the dealer's reservation price.   What the researchers identified as a dealer's "final offer" was exceptionally high for black women shoppers.   But the data provided weak support for bigotry as an explanation: "each class of testers received its best treatment from salespeople of a different race and gender and, in many cases, the worst treatment from salespeople of the same race and gender."   It appeared, as a tentative conclusion, that the differences reflected the sellers' perception of the opportunity for gain.   Ayres, Fair Driving: Gender and Race Discrimination in Retail Car Negotiations, 104 Harv.L.Rev. 817 (1991).   (The research sought to neutralize impressions of credit-worthiness: the testers volunteered that they could finance their purchases independently.)

Professor Ayres surmised that, from the dealer's viewpoint, white male shoppers, especially, are amenable to the bargaining process and are adept at discerning overpricing.   "[R]evealing that a tester had already taken a test drive reduced the seller's final offer by $319, and revealing that a tester did not own a car increased the final offer by $337."   Id. at 848.   Ayres favors, at least for the new-car market, a requirement that price stickers include information about the dealer's markup.   See Ayres & Miller, "I'll Sell it to You at Cost" ..., 84 Nw.L.Rev. 1047 (1990).

(4) *In Practice.*   The focus of reported consumer-grievance litigation has shifted, in recent years, away from common-law doctrines of overreaching, and

f.   See Remco Enterprises, Inc. v. Houston, 677 P.2d 567 (Kan.App.1984).

rules about unconscionability, toward claims under statutes about unfair and deceptive trade practices. One possible explanation is the complexity and detail of some of those statutes. For another, many of them provide for the recovery of attorneys' fees and of punitive damages. See Macaulay, Bambi Meets Godzilla...., 26 Houston L.Rev. 575 (1989).

HELL–OR–HIGH–WATER CLAUSES

This Note introduces legislative measures addressed to provisions of a type often found in consumer credit contracts—measures that include part of the UCC and an FTC rule. In Jones v. Star Credit Corp., the home-freezer contract was a "consumer credit contract," as defined in the rule. So were the "leases" involved in Williams v. Walker–Thomas Furniture Company.

It is a common practice for a merchant extending credit to assign (transfer) its payment rights to a bank or other financer, permitting the merchant immediately to realize the agreed (discounted) value of the rights. In anticipation of the assignment, the contract that the consumer is asked to execute may well provide that the consumer will not assert against an assignee—the financer—any claim or defense that the consumer may have against the seller. If effective, the term may require a consumer to continue making payments after learning that the goods are seriously defective, that the merchant misrepresented their quality, or that for another reason the *merchant* could not have required payment. Hence the popular name: consumer will pay "come hell or high water." (The consumer might sometimes recoup a payment to the financer, of course, by suing the merchant for any fraud or breach of warranty.)

For cases that do *not* involve consumers, UCC 9–206(1) makes the term enforceable, though it may operate harshly. A case presented in Chapter 10 (Assignments), below, applied the statute in favor of a bank and against a law firm that was disappointed with telephone equipment it had purchased on credit. Because the equipment was not consumer goods, the case was not one within a qualification that introduces the UCC rule: "Subject to any statute or decision which establishes a different rule for buyers or lessees of consumer goods...."

Consumer credit contracts are required by the FTC rule mentioned above to contain this legend:

> ANY HOLDER OF THIS CONSUMER CREDIT CONTRACT IS SUBJECT TO ALL CLAIMS AND DEFENSES WHICH THE DEBTOR COULD ASSERT AGAINST THE SELLER OF GOODS OR SERVICES OBTAINED [*PURSUANT HERETO OR*] WITH THE PROCEEDS HEREOF....

A failure to include the legend amounts, when it is required by the rule, to an unfair or deceptive act. The rule is generally understood to nullify any hell-or-high water clause appearing in a consumer credit contract, whether or not the contract includes the legend. It is therefore a "different rule" for buyers or lessees of consumer goods—a rule "expressly designed to compel creditors to either absorb seller misconduct costs or seek reimbursement of those costs from sellers." Tinker v. De Maria Porsche Audi, Inc., 459 So.2d 487 (Fla.App.1985). A buyer is likely to find the rule especially advantageous when the seller's insolvency makes it unable to pay a judgment for "misconduct costs."

NOTES

(1) *Problem.* The FTC legend appeared in a services contract considered in In re Arnold, 147 B.R. 435, 440 (Bankr.N.D.Ill.1992). (The FTC rule—though not the UCC rule—applies to some contracts for services, calling for installment payments, as well as sale-of-goods contracts.) Arnold sought to avoid paying for work done by a repair firm, over two weeks, on her five-unit "apartment complex," including a few hours' work in the unit she occupied. The contract required Arnold to make installment payments. Arnold made complaints about the work as it proceeded. But in the end she signed a "completion statement" reciting that the work agreed upon had been done to her satisfaction. On the same day the repair firm sold its payment rights to the First Credit Corporation, showing it Arnold's statement. She also assured First Credit of her satisfaction in a telephone call she received.

Thereafter, when First Credit sought to enforce the contract, Arnold resisted on grounds of misconduct by the repair firm. Supposing that the firm had obtained the contract by fraud, or had violated the contract, should the "FTC legend" prevent its enforcement by First Credit? How might one explain disregarding the legend? If the repair contract was not a "consumer credit contract," should the legend be disregarded because no law required its inclusion?

(2) *Unconscionable?* To vary the facts of Arnold's case (Note 1), suppose that her building-repair contract was in a standard form, containing a hell-or-high-water clause, and that the clause was not called to her attention. Assume also that the contract did not contain the FTC legend, and (because it was not a "consumer credit contract") was not required to contain it. If Arnold were to contest the clause on the ground that it was unconscionable, how should that contention be evaluated? In answering this question, consider the possible bearing of UCC 9–206(1).

HOME SOLICITATION SALES AND "COOLING OFF" PERIODS

Since 1963, following the lead of Parliament, a number of American legislatures have enacted statutes directed at door-to-door selling, and providing what is known as a cooling-off period. A representative one, embodied in the Uniform Consumer Credit Code, is quoted below. There is a federal provision of this character, in the Consumer Credit Protection Act of 1968. It applies to most home-improvement loan contracts.[a] There are significant variances in the state statutes, both as to scope and as to the mechanics of cancellation.

a. In explaining why "uncommon emphasis" on disclosure of the borrower's entitlement under this statute is warranted, one court observed that it is "an important and novel right in the history of contract law, for under the Act a customer may rescind for no more reason than a 'change of heart.'" Reed v. Washington Trailer Sales, Inc., 393 F.Supp. 886 (M.D.Tenn. 1974).

The basic rule of the UCCC is stated in section 3.502:

(1) Except as provided in subsection (5),[b] in addition to any right otherwise to revoke an offer, the buyer may cancel a home solicitation sale [c] until midnight of the third business day after the day on which the buyer signs an agreement or offer to purchase which complies with this Part.

The power to cancel cannot be terminated until the end of the statutory period *following* the time when the buyer signs a document containing this statement:

BUYER'S RIGHT TO CANCEL [d]

If you decide you do not want the goods or services, you may cancel this agreement by mailing a notice to the seller. The notice must say that you do not want the goods or services and must be mailed before midnight of the third business day after you sign this agreement. The notice must be mailed to: _____.

(insert name and mailing address of seller)

NOTES

(1) *Questions.* Would it be well to extend the principle of this legislation to in-store sales? It is a well-known practice in some stores to let customers take merchandise out of stock "on approval," or virtually so. If it could be shown that this practice is least prevalent among merchants catering to poor persons, would the distinction seem invidious?

(2) *Borrowing Under Pressure.* A separation agreement provided that a woman in the process of being divorced would pay her husband for his interest in their home. To get the money, she granted a lender a second mortgage on the home. The loan proved to be imprudent: before long she defaulted and lost the property. Thereafter she brought an action against the lender under a statute proscribing unfair and deceptive conduct. The trial court gave summary judgment for the lender, and the plaintiff appealed. In part she contended that—as the lender knew—the "exigencies and pressures of the divorce proceedings placed her under duress to proceed with the loan, whatever the terms." Is this argument foreclosed by the fact that she had had a three-day cooling-off period within which to reconsider and rescind the loan? See Hogan v. Riemer, 619 N.E.2d 984 (Mass.App.1993). Compare the court's reading of the transaction ("Any person who arrives at a loan closing generally has fiscal needs which act as a powerful force to go through with the transaction") with that of Justice Brown, dissenting ("consistent with the all too familiar trend in which women experience a significant drop in their standard of living after divorce"; lender's conduct denounced).

b. According to subsection (5), the buyer may not cancel in certain circumstances, if he "requests the seller to provide goods or services without delay" in an emergency.

c. The definition of "home solicitation sale" embraces most consumer credit sales "in which the seller or a person acting for him personally solicits the sale, and the buyer's agreement or offer to purchase is given to the seller or a person acting for him, at a residence." Section 3.501.

d. This caption must be conspicuous. The Code definition of "conspicuous" is derived in part from UCC 1–201(10).

Section 3.503(2)(b). An alternative—(a)—is compliance with an applicable FTC rule.

For an application of unconscionability doctrine to a real-estate transaction see In re Davis, 169 B.R. 285, 303–304 (E.D.N.Y.1994). Credit terms extended in that case to a family in need, by a "group of real estate sophisticates," were said to be so onerous that the family was sure to lose its home.

(3) *Cooling–Off and Incapacity.* Dean Kronman has pointed out that the law of minors' contracts allows them an extended period for "cooling off" about the deals they make. Paternalism and the Law of Contracts, 92 Yale.L.J. 763 (1983). Do the statutes that provide cooling-off periods suggest a sensible reform of the law of incapacity?

————

Introductory Note to *Carnival Cruise Lines*

In the following case the Court considered the enforceability of a "forum selection" clause in Carnival's contracts with customers for cruises. The clauses purported to restrict the customers, in bringing suits on their contracts, to actions in the courts of Florida; they preferred to sue at their home, the State of Washington. In this case, and in others on the subject, consideration has been given to the reasonableness of the contract provision and to possibilities of over-reaching.

There is, however, an initial question about the enforceability of *any* choice-of-forum provision. Courts have expressed hostility by saying that the parties cannot "oust" a court of jurisdiction over a dispute properly presented to it. A shift of attitude is reflected in the Restatement (Second) of Conflict of Laws § 80, where it is said that a choice-of-forum provision "will be given effect unless it is unfair and unreasonable." The question may be further considered in a course on the conflict of laws.

————

CARNIVAL CRUISE LINES, INC. v. SHUTE
United States Supreme Court, 1991.
499 U.S. 585, 111 S.Ct. 1522, 113 L.Ed.2d 622.

JUSTICE BLACKMUN delivered the opinion of the Court.

In this admiralty case we primarily consider whether the United States Court of Appeals for the Ninth Circuit correctly refused to enforce a forum-selection clause contained in tickets issued by petitioner Carnival Cruise Lines, Inc., to respondents Eulala and Russel Shute.

I

The Shutes, through an Arlington, Wash., travel agent, purchased passage for a 7–day cruise on petitioner's ship, the *Tropicale*. Respondents paid the fare to the agent who forwarded the payment to petitioner's headquarters in Miami, Fla. Petitioner then prepared the tickets and sent them to respondents in the State of Washington. The face of each ticket, at its left-hand lower corner, contained this admonition:

"SUBJECT TO CONDITIONS OF CONTRACT ON LAST PAGES **IMPORTANT**! PLEASE READ CONTRACT—ON LAST PAGES 1, 2, 3"

The following appeared on "contract page 1" of each ticket:

"TERMS AND CONDITIONS OF PASSAGE CONTRACT TICKET

. . .

"3. (a) The acceptance of this ticket by the person or persons named hereon as passengers shall be deemed to be an acceptance and agreement by each of them of all of the terms and conditions of this Passage Contract Ticket.

. . .

"8. It is agreed by and between the passenger and the Carrier that all disputes and matters whatsoever arising under, in connection with or incident to this Contract shall be litigated, if at all, in and before a Court located in the State of Florida, U.S.A., to the exclusion of the Courts of any other state or country."

The last quoted paragraph is the forum-selection clause at issue.

II

Respondents boarded the *Tropicale* in Los Angeles, Cal. The ship sailed to Puerto Vallarta, Mexico, and then returned to Los Angeles. While the ship was in international waters off the Mexican coast, respondent Eulala Shute was injured when she slipped on a deck mat during a guided tour of the ship's galley. Respondents filed suit against petitioner in the United States District Court for the Western District of Washington, claiming that Mrs. Shute's injuries had been caused by the negligence of Carnival Cruise Lines and its employees.

Petitioner moved for summary judgment, contending that the forum clause in respondents' tickets required the Shutes to bring their suit against petitioner in a court in the State of Florida. Petitioner contended, alternatively, that the District Court lacked personal jurisdiction over petitioner because petitioner's contacts with the State of Washington were insubstantial. The District Court granted the motion, holding that petitioner's contacts with Washington were constitutionally insufficient to support the exercise of personal jurisdiction.

The Court of Appeals reversed. Reasoning that "but for" petitioner's solicitation of business in Washington, respondents would not have taken the cruise and Mrs. Shute would not have been injured, the court concluded that petitioner had sufficient contacts with Washington to justify the District Court's exercise of personal jurisdiction. 897 F.2d 377, 385–386 (CA9 1990).

Turning to the forum-selection clause, the Court of Appeals acknowledged that a court concerned with the enforceability of such a clause must begin its analysis with The Bremen v. Zapata Off–Shore Co.,

407 U.S. 1 (1972), where this Court held that forum-selection clauses, although not "historically ... favored," are "prima facie valid." Id., at 9–10. See 897 F.2d, at 388. The appellate court concluded that the forum clause should not be enforced because it "was not freely bargained for." Id., at 389. As an "independent justification" for refusing to enforce the clause, the Court of Appeals noted that there was evidence in the record to indicate that "the Shutes are physically and financially incapable of pursuing this litigation in Florida" and that the enforcement of the clause would operate to deprive them of their day in court and thereby contravene this Court's holding in *The Bremen*. 897 F.2d, at 389.

We granted certiorari to address the question whether the Court of Appeals was correct in holding that the District Court should hear respondents' tort claim against petitioner. 498 U.S. 807–808 (1990). Because we find the forum-selection clause to be dispositive of this question, we need not consider petitioner's constitutional argument as to personal jurisdiction. . . .

III

We begin by noting the boundaries of our inquiry. First, this is a case in admiralty, and federal law governs the enforceability of the forum-selection clause we scrutinize. . . . Second, we do not address the question whether respondents had sufficient notice of the forum clause before entering the contract for passage. Respondents essentially have conceded that they had notice of the forum-selection provision. Brief for Respondents 26 ("The respondents do not contest the incorporation of the provisions nor [sic] that the forum selection clause was reasonably communicated to the respondents, as much as three pages of fine print can be communicated"). Additionally, the Court of Appeals evaluated the enforceability of the forum clause under the assumption, although "doubtful," that respondents could be deemed to have had knowledge of the clause. See 897 F.2d, at 389, and n. 11.

Within this context, respondents urge that the forum clause should not be enforced because, contrary to this Court's teachings in *The Bremen*, the clause was not the product of negotiation, and enforcement effectively would deprive respondents of their day in court. Additionally, respondents contend that the clause violates the Limitation of Vessel Owner's Liability Act, 46 U.S.C.App. § 183c. We consider these arguments in turn.

IV

A

Both petitioner and respondents argue vigorously that the Court's opinion in *The Bremen* governs this case, and each side purports to find ample support for its position in that opinion's broad-ranging language. This seeming paradox derives in large part from key factual differences between this case and *The Bremen*, differences that preclude an automatic and simple application of *The Bremen* 's general principles to the facts here.

In *The Bremen,* this Court addressed the enforceability of a forum-selection clause in a contract between two business corporations. An American corporation, Zapata, made a contract with Unterweser, a German corporation, for the towage of Zapata's oceangoing drilling rig from Louisiana to a point in the Adriatic Sea off the coast of Italy. The agreement provided that any dispute arising under the contract was to be resolved in the London Court of Justice. After a storm in the Gulf of Mexico seriously damaged the rig, Zapata ordered Unterweser's ship to tow the rig to Tampa, Fla., the nearest point of refuge. Thereafter, Zapata sued Unterweser in admiralty in federal court at Tampa. Citing the forum clause, Unterweser moved to dismiss. The District Court denied Unterweser's motion, and the Court of Appeals for the Fifth Circuit, sitting en banc on rehearing, and by a sharply divided vote, affirmed. In re Complaint of Unterweser Reederei, GmBH, 446 F.2d 907 (1971).

This Court vacated and remanded, stating that, in general, "a freely negotiated private international agreement, unaffected by fraud, undue influence, or overweening bargaining power, such as that involved here, should be given full effect." 407 U.S., at 12–13 (footnote omitted). The Court further generalized that "in the light of present-day commercial realities and expanding international trade we conclude that the forum clause should control absent a strong showing that it should be set aside." Id., at 15. The Court did not define precisely the circumstances that would make it unreasonable for a court to enforce a forum clause. Instead, the Court discussed a number of factors that made it reasonable to enforce the clause at issue in *The Bremen* and that, presumably, would be pertinent in any determination whether to enforce a similar clause.

In this respect, the Court noted that there was "strong evidence that the forum clause was a vital part of the agreement, and [that] it would be unrealistic to think that the parties did not conduct their negotiations, including fixing the monetary terms, with the consequences of the forum clause figuring prominently in their calculations." Id., at 14 (footnote omitted). Further, the Court observed that it was not "dealing with an agreement between two Americans to resolve their essentially local disputes in a remote alien forum," and that in such a case, "the serious inconvenience of the contractual forum to one or both of the parties might carry greater weight in determining the reasonableness of the forum clause." Id., at 17. The Court stated that even where the forum clause establishes a remote forum for resolution of conflicts, "the party claiming [unfairness] should bear a heavy burden of proof." Ibid.

In applying *The Bremen,* the Court of Appeals in the present litigation took note of the foregoing "reasonableness" factors and rather automatically decided that the forum-selection clause was unenforceable because, unlike the parties in *The Bremen,* respondents are not business persons and did not negotiate the terms of the clause with petitioner. Alternatively, the Court of Appeals ruled that the clause should not be enforced because enforcement effectively would deprive respondents of an opportunity to litigate their claim against petitioner.

The Bremen concerned a "far from routine transaction between companies of two different nations contemplating the tow of an extremely costly piece of equipment from Louisiana across the Gulf of Mexico and the Atlantic Ocean, through the Mediterranean Sea to its final destination in the Adriatic Sea." Id., at 13. These facts suggest that, even apart from the evidence of negotiation regarding the forum clause, it was entirely reasonable for the Court in *The Bremen* to have expected Unterweser and Zapata to have negotiated with care in selecting a forum for the resolution of disputes arising from their special towing contract.

In contrast, respondents' passage contract was purely routine and doubtless nearly identical to every commercial passage contract issued by petitioner and most other cruise lines. See, e.g., Hodes v. S.N.C. Achille Lauro ed Altri–Gestione, 858 F.2d 905, 910 (CA3 1988), cert. dism'd, 490 U.S. 1001 (1989). In this context, it would be entirely unreasonable for us to assume that respondents—or any other cruise passenger—would negotiate with petitioner the terms of a forum-selection clause in an ordinary commercial cruise ticket. Common sense dictates that a ticket of this kind will be a form contract the terms of which are not subject to negotiation, and that an individual purchasing the ticket will not have bargaining parity with the cruise line. But by ignoring the crucial differences in the business contexts in which the respective contracts were executed, the Court of Appeals' analysis seems to us to have distorted somewhat this Court's holding in *The Bremen*.

In evaluating the reasonableness of the forum clause at issue in this case, we must refine the analysis of *The Bremen* to account for the realities of form passage contracts. As an initial matter, we do not adopt the Court of Appeals' determination that a nonnegotiated forum-selection clause in a form ticket contract is never enforceable simply because it is not the subject of bargaining. Including a reasonable forum clause in a form contract of this kind well may be permissible for several reasons: First, a cruise line has a special interest in limiting the fora in which it potentially could be subject to suit. Because a cruise ship typically carries passengers from many locales, it is not unlikely that a mishap on a cruise could subject the cruise line to litigation in several different fora. See *The Bremen,* 407 U.S., at 13, and n. 15; *Hodes,* 858 F.2d, at 913. Additionally, a clause establishing ex ante the forum for dispute resolution has the salutary effect of dispelling any confusion about where suits arising from the contract must be brought and defended, sparing litigants the time and expense of pretrial motions to determine the correct forum and conserving judicial resources that otherwise would be devoted to deciding those motions. See Stewart Organization, [Inc. v. Ricoh Corp., 487 U.S. 22 (1988)] 487 U.S., at 33 (concurring opinion). Finally, it stands to reason that passengers who purchase tickets containing a forum clause like that at issue in this case benefit in the form of reduced fares reflecting the savings that the cruise line enjoys by limiting the fora in which it may be sued.   Cf. Northwestern Nat. Ins. Co. v. Donovan, 916 F.2d 372, 378 (CA7 1990).

We also do not accept the Court of Appeals' "independent justification" for its conclusion that *The Bremen* dictates that the clause should not be enforced because "there is evidence in the record to indicate that the Shutes are physically and financially incapable of pursuing this litigation in Florida."   897 F.2d, at 389.   We do not defer to the Court of Appeals' findings of fact.   In dismissing the case for lack of personal jurisdiction over petitioner, the District Court made no finding regarding the physical and financial impediments to the Shutes' pursuing their case in Florida.   The Court of Appeals' conclusory reference to the record provides no basis for this Court to validate the finding of inconvenience.   Furthermore, the Court of Appeals did not place in proper context this Court's statement in *The Bremen* that "the serious inconvenience of the contractual forum to one or both of the parties might carry greater weight in determining the reasonableness of the forum clause."   407 U.S., at 17.   The Court made this statement in evaluating a hypothetical "agreement between two Americans to resolve their essentially local disputes in a remote alien forum."   Ibid.   In the present case, Florida is not a "remote alien forum," nor—given the fact that Mrs. Shute's accident occurred off the coast of Mexico—is this dispute an essentially local one inherently more suited to resolution in the State of Washington than in Florida.   In light of these distinctions, and because respondents do not claim lack of notice of the forum clause, we conclude that they have not satisfied the "heavy burden of proof," ibid., required to set aside the clause on grounds of inconvenience.

It bears emphasis that forum-selection clauses contained in form passage contracts are subject to judicial scrutiny for fundamental fairness.   In this case, there is no indication that petitioner set Florida as the forum in which disputes were to be resolved as a means of discouraging cruise passengers from pursuing legitimate claims.   Any suggestion of such a bad-faith motive is belied by two facts: Petitioner has its principal place of business in Florida, and many of its cruises depart from and return to Florida ports.   Similarly, there is no evidence that petitioner obtained respondents' accession to the forum clause by fraud or overreaching.   Finally, respondents have conceded that they were given notice of the forum provision and, therefore, presumably retained the option of rejecting the contract with impunity.   In the case before us, therefore, we conclude that the Court of Appeals erred in refusing to enforce the forum-selection clause.

B

Respondents also contend that the forum-selection clause at issue violates 46 U.S.C.App. § 183c.   [The statute makes it unlawful for the owner of a passenger vessel to employ an agreement purporting to limit its liability for death or bodily injury arising from the negligence or fault of the owner "or his servants," or purporting "to lessen, weaken, or avoid the right of any claimant to a trial by court of competent jurisdiction on the question of liability for such loss or injury, or the measure of damages therefor."]

By its plain language, the forum-selection clause before us does not . . . contravene the explicit proscription of § 183c. [The Court cited legislative history suggesting that "this provision was enacted in response to passenger-ticket conditions purporting to limit the shipowner's liability for negligence or to remove the issue of liability from the scrutiny of any court by means of a clause providing that 'the question of liability and the measure of damages shall be determined by arbitration.' "] There was no prohibition of a forum-selection clause. Because the clause before us allows for judicial resolution of claims against petitioner and does not purport to limit petitioner's liability for negligence, it does not violate § 183c.

V

The judgment of the Court of Appeals is reversed.

JUSTICE STEVENS, with whom JUSTICE MARSHALL joins, dissenting.

The Court prefaces its legal analysis with a factual statement that implies that a purchaser of a Carnival Cruise Lines passenger ticket is fully and fairly notified about the existence of the choice of forum clause in the fine print on the back of the ticket. Even if this implication were accurate, I would disagree with the Court's analysis. But, given the Court's preface, I begin my dissent by noting that only the most meticulous passenger is likely to become aware of the forum-selection provision. I have therefore appended to this opinion a facsimile of the relevant text, using the type size that actually appears in the ticket itself. A careful reader will find the forum-selection clause in the 8th of the 25 numbered paragraphs.

Of course, many passengers, like the respondents in this case, will not have an opportunity to read paragraph 8 until they have actually purchased their tickets. By this point, the passengers will already have accepted the condition set forth in paragraph 16(a), which provides that "the Carrier shall not be liable to make any refund to passengers in respect of . . . tickets wholly or partly not used by a passenger." Not knowing whether or not that provision is legally enforceable, I assume that the average passenger would accept the risk of having to file suit in Florida in the event of an injury, rather than canceling—without a refund—a planned vacation at the last minute. The fact that the cruise line can reduce its litigation costs, and therefore its liability insurance premiums, by forcing this choice on its passengers does not, in my opinion, suffice to render the provision reasonable. Cf. Steven v. Fidelity & Casualty Co. of New York, 58 Cal.2d 862, 883, 377 P.2d 284, 298 (1962) (refusing to enforce limitation on liability in insurance policy because insured "must purchase the policy before he even knows its provisions").[a]

---

a. For a brief of this case see the Note,
Insurance Marketing, p. 416 above.

Even if passengers received prominent notice of the forum-selection clause before they committed the cost of the cruise, I would remain persuaded that the clause was unenforceable under traditional principles of federal admiralty law and is "null and void" under the terms of Limitation of Vessel Owner's Liability Act, ch. 521, 49 Stat. 1480, 46 U.S.C.App. § 183c, which was enacted in 1936 to invalidate expressly stipulations limiting shipowners' liability for negligence.

Exculpatory clauses in passenger tickets have been around for a long time. These clauses are typically the product of disparate bargaining power between the carrier and the passenger, and they undermine the strong public interest in deterring negligent conduct. For these reasons, courts long before the turn of the century consistently held such clauses unenforceable under federal admiralty law....

Clauses limiting a carrier's liability or weakening the passenger's right to recover for the negligence of the carrier's employees come in a variety of forms. Complete exemptions from liability for negligence or limitations on the amount of the potential damage recovery, requirements that notice of claims be filed within an unreasonably short period of time, provisions mandating a choice of law that is favorable to the defendant in negligence cases, and forum-selection clauses are all similarly designed to put a thumb on the carrier's side of the scale of justice.[b]

Forum-selection clauses in passenger tickets involve the intersection of two strands of traditional contract law that qualify the general rule that courts will enforce the terms of a contract as written. Pursuant to the first strand, courts traditionally have reviewed with heightened scrutiny the terms of contracts of adhesion, form contracts offered on a take-or-leave basis by a party with stronger bargaining power to a party with weaker power. Some commentators have questioned whether contracts of adhesion can justifiably be enforced at all under traditional contract theory because the adhering party generally enters into them without manifesting knowing and voluntary consent to all their terms. See, e.g., Rakoff, Contracts of Adhesion: An Essay in Reconstruction, 96 Harv.L.Rev. 1173, 1179–1180 (1983); Slawson, Mass Contracts: Lawful Fraud in California, 48 S.Cal.L.Rev. 1, 12–13 (1974); K. Llewellyn, The Common Law Tradition 370–371 (1960).

The common law, recognizing that standardized form contracts account for a significant portion of all commercial agreements, has taken a less extreme position and instead subjects terms in contracts of adhesion to scrutiny for reasonableness. Judge J. Skelly Wright set out the state of the law succinctly in Williams v. Walker–Thomas Furniture Co., 121 U.S.App.D.C. 315, 319–320, 350 F.2d 445, 449–450 (1965) (footnotes omitted):

"Ordinarily, one who signs an agreement without full knowledge of its terms might be held to assume the risk that he has entered a one-sided bargain. But when a party of little bargaining power, and hence little real choice, signs a commercially unreasonable contract

b. Footnotes in this paragraph omitted.

with little or no knowledge of its terms, it is hardly likely that his consent, or even an objective manifestation of his consent, was ever given to all of the terms. In such a case the usual rule that the terms of the agreement are not to be questioned should be abandoned and the court should consider whether the terms of the contract are so unfair that enforcement should be withheld."

See also *Steven*, 58 Cal.2d, at 879–883, 377 P.2d, at 295–297; Henningsen v. Bloomfield Motors, Inc., 32 N.J. 358, 161 A.2d 69 (1960).

The second doctrinal principle implicated by forum-selection clauses is the traditional rule that "contractual provisions, which seek to limit the place or court in which an action may ... be brought, are invalid as contrary to public policy." See Dougherty, Validity of Contractual Provision Limiting Place or Court in Which Action May Be Brought, 31 A.L.R.4th 404, 409, § 3 (1984).... A forum-selection clause in a standardized passenger ticket would clearly have been unenforceable under the common law before our decision in *The Bremen,* see 407 U.S., at 9, and n. 10, and, in my opinion, remains unenforceable under the prevailing rule today.

[Mr. Justice Stevens discussed the Court's decision in *The Bremen,* and gave reasons for a "liberal reading" of the statute relied on by the Shutes.]

The Courts of Appeals, construing an analogous provision of the Carriage of Goods by Sea Act, 46 U.S.C.App. § 1300 et seq., have unanimously held invalid as limitations on liability forum-selection clauses requiring suit in foreign jurisdictions.... The forum-selection clause here does not mandate suit in a foreign jurisdiction, and therefore arguably might have less of an impact on a plaintiff's ability to recover. See Fireman's Fund American Ins. Cos. v. Puerto Rican Forwarding Co., 492 F.2d 1294 (CA1 1974). However, the plaintiffs in this case are not large corporations but individuals, and the added burden on them of conducting a trial at the opposite end of the country is likely proportional to the additional cost to a large corporation of conducting a trial overseas.[1]

Under these circumstances, the general prohibition against stipulations purporting "to lessen, weaken, or avoid" the passenger's right to a trial certainly should be construed to apply to the manifestly unreasonable stipulation in these passengers' tickets. Even without the benefit of the statute, I would continue to apply the general rule that prevailed prior to our decision in *The Bremen* to forum-selection clauses in passenger tickets.

I respectfully dissent.

NOTES

(1) *Innocents Abroad.* How would the Shutes have fared if (a) they had contracted for their cruise with a Greek ship owner, (b) their travel agent had

---

1. The Court does not make clear whether the result in this case would also apply if the clause required Carnival passengers to sue in Panama, the country in which Carnival is incorporated.

dealt with a New York firm as the ship's agent, (c) the contract had restricted actions to the courts of Athens, and (d) the Shutes had brought the action in New York? See Effron v. Sun Line Cruises, Inc., 857 F.Supp. 1079 (S.D.N.Y. 1994). For arguments opposing the enforcement against a consumer of any forum-selection clause in a form contract, see Goldman, My Way and the Highway: The Law and Economics of Choice of Forum Clauses in Consumer Form Contracts, 86 Nw.L.Rev. 700 (1992).

In 1992 Congress responded to *Carnival Cruise Lines* by amending the statute addressed there. The word "any" was inserted before "court" in the line quoted at the foot of p. 446, above. What might be said for a broader reform? A narrower one? See Sturley, Forum Selection Clauses in Cruise Line Tickets: An Update ..., 24 J.Mar.L. & Com. 399 (1993). The statute does not affect cruises wholly outside U.S. waters.

If each party to a contract in which a foreign forum is chosen is American, should that matter? (Lloyd's, the defendant in Hugel's action, is a London institution.) In Pearcy Marine, Inc. v. Seacor Marine, Inc., 847 F.Supp. 57 (S.D.Tex.1993), it appeared that the defendant, a Louisiana firm, had induced the plaintiff, a Texas firm, to agree to London-only litigation. Disapproving that provision, the court observed that nothing relevant to the case was in England. It also observed that the Texas firm was undergoing reorganization in bankruptcy when it made the contract, that it had employed attorneys for the suit on a contingent-fee contract, and that contingent-fee contracts are unlawful in England. In this case, and in *Hugel,* the term in question provided also that English law should govern disputes relating to the contract. Should that matter?[a]

If the amount in dispute is relatively small, should that matter? See Indussa Corporation v. S.S. Ranborg, 377 F.2d 200 (2d Cir.1967).

(2) *Review Question.* A supplier of goods telephones its assent to a purchase order it has received from out of state. Thereafter it sends the buyer a confirmation of the agreement containing, among other printed provisions, one requiring the buyer to bring any action on the contract in the supplier's home state. Whether or not that provision is enforceable might depend on UCC 2–207. If it does, should the provision be considered a material alteration of the terms of the purchase order? See M.K.C. Equipment Company v. M.A.I.L. Code, Inc., 843 F.Supp. 679 (D.Kan.1994).

(3) *Alternative Dispute Resolution.* The Westinghouse Electric Corporation won a contract to provide and install equipment in the New York City subway system. Disputes about the performance and termination of the contract led Westinghouse to sue the City's Transit Authority. The Authority's chief electrical officer, functioning as its superintendent, had earlier rejected Westinghouse's claims. A federal court in which the case was lodged sought the views of the New York Court of Appeals about an "alternative dispute resolution" (ADR) provision in the contract.

The provision precluded Westinghouse from presenting to a court any dispute related to the contract before submitting the dispute to the Authority's superintendent; and the court's review was "limited to the question of whether or not the Superintendent's determination is arbitrary, capricious or [so?] grossly erroneous [as?] to evidence bad faith...." The question was whether or not the ADR provision "imposes a procedure for dispute resolution by a functionary

---

a. A provision for applying English law, appearing in a steamship ticket issued to an American passenger, was considered in Siegelman v. Cunard White Star, 221 F.2d 189 (2d Cir.1955). The case is notable for an impassioned dissent, by Judge Frank, reviewing literature about contracts of adhesion.

inseparable from one of the parties [and] fosters a predisposed adjudication process, which is contrary to New York public policy."

The court observed that "powerful municipalities ... enjoy a virtual monopolistic-kind of power" in the bidding process leading to public-works jobs. "But that does not make those contracts adhesion agreements." Westinghouse had accepted the contract terms with its "business eyes open," the court said. The court answered the question No, saying that the contrary answer would have "destabilizing commercial-law consequences." Westinghouse Electric Corp. v. New York City Transit Authority, 623 N.E.2d 531 (N.Y.1993).

(4) *Add-on Arbitration Agreements.* A bank decides that it prefers arbitration, rather than trial, as a mode of resolving some types of dispute it may have with its customers. To holders of accounts in the bank (holders of credit cards, as well as depositors) it mails an announcement on the subject along with the bank's regular monthly statements. Each depositor has signed a signature card, upon opening an account, which incorporates a statement of the bank's rules and charges, in the form of a booklet handed at that time to the depositor. According to the booklet, the bank may from time to time alter its rules upon giving notice to customers. The announcement refers to that provision, specifies an arbitration procedure, and states that either party to a dispute thereafter arising about charges and credits to an account may require arbitration. In a class action brought against the bank on behalf of its depositors for a declaratory judgment that the rule change is ineffective, what should the ruling be?

Compare the action of a firm of securities brokers that has a similar agreement with its customers about altering account agreements. In a special mailing, the firm sends them a statement of various amendments, including one about arbitration (paragraph 17). According to the statement, it is "mandatory" that a customer sign and return the statement. Is paragraph 17 binding on customers who sign? On those who do not? Would it matter that the paragraph is in conspicuous print?

FRANCHISE RELATIONS

"The franchise system is a method of selling products and services identified by a particular trade name which may be associated with a patent, a trade secret, a particular product design or management expertise. The franchisee usually purchases some products from the franchisor ... and makes royalty payments on the basis of units sold, in exchange for the right to offer products for sale under the trademark. The franchise agreement establishes the relationship between the parties and usually regulates the quality of the product, sales territory, the advertising and other details; and it usually requires that certain supplies be purchased from the franchisor." [a]

The complex contract relations between a franchisor and a franchise holder are a fruitful source of disputes. Either party may be aggrieved by self-interested action by the other: on the part of the franchisor, for example, it may be contended that the franchisee has provided substandard service, damaging to the reputation of the product or services on which the royalties depend; and on the part of the franchisee it may be

a. Kosters v. Seven–Up Co., 595 F.2d 347 (6th Cir.1979).

contended that the franchisor has skimped on advertising or has si-
phoned off revenues through a competing franchisee.

Many franchise agreements are in a standard form prepared by the
franchisor, containing terms that are not open to negotiation and are
strikingly favorable to the franchisor. In particular, a franchisor may
reserve the power of termination on short notice, "at any time for any
reason." [b] It may be said, in justification of this power, that it serves to
discipline a franchisee who might be tempted by free-ride possibilities.
Comparable levels of energy, skill, and investment are required of all
franchisees in order to maximize the returns not only of the franchisor
but also of other franchisees using the same trade name, whose interests
the franchisor represents.

Might a termination power, or another provision harsh on a franchisee, be regarded as unconscionable, and so unenforceable? A lease and
dealership agreement between the Shell Oil Company and a service-
station operator was the occasion for what is possibly the most notable
setback that franchisors have suffered in the name of the common law.
The operator sought and got relief from termination of these arrangements, as provided for in the parties' contracts, on short notice. Among
the facts deemed "significant" by the trial court were:

> the gross disparity in bargaining power between Shell and Marinel-
> lo, resulting in Shell's ability to dictate the terms of the agreements;
> the grossly unfair contractual provisions at issue; and the clear
> tendency to injure the public.[c]

The New Jersey Supreme Court expressed full agreement with the
"basic determination ... that Shell had no legal right to terminate its
relationship with Marinello except for good cause...." It cited also
"the public policy of this State affecting such [a] relationship." [d] Might
a decision like this be based on UCC 1–203 ("obligation of good faith")?
See Burton, Breach of Contract and the Common Law Duty to Perform
in Good Faith, 94 Harv.L.Rev. 369 (1980).[e] On principles of equity?
See Overhead Door Co. of Reno, Inc. v. Overhead Door Corp., 734 P.2d
1233 (Nev.1987). On franchises generally, see Hadfield, Problematic
Relations: Franchising and the Law of Incomplete Contracts, 42 Stan.
L.Rev. 927 (1990).

The relations between franchisors and franchisees are increasingly
governed by statutes and regulations, as indicated below.[f] (A curiosity
about Shell Oil v. Marinello is that it was decided after the legislature

---

b. Such a term was the subject of construction in Corenswet, Inc. v. Amana Refrigeration, Inc., 594 F.2d 129 (5th Cir.
1979), cert. denied, 444 U.S. 938 (1979).

c. Schultze v. Chevron Oil Co., 579 F.2d
776 (3d Cir.1978), cert. denied, 439 U.S.
985 (1978).

d. Shell Oil Co. v. Marinello, 307 A.2d
598 (N.J.1973), cert. denied, 415 U.S. 920
(1974).

e. Compare Corenswet, Inc. v. Amana
Refrigeration, Inc., fn. b above, with Rich-
ard Short Oil Co., Inc. v. Texaco, Inc., 799
F.2d 415 (8th Cir.1986).

f. These include the various bodies of
antitrust law (federal and state), the mandate of the FTC Act that the Commission
prevent "unfair methods of competition and
unfair or deceptive acts or practices," and
the Lanham Act (trademark protection), 15
U.S.C. § 1055 et seq.

had acted to curb powers of termination—though not with respect to franchise agreements already in place.)

NOTES

(1) *Legislation.* A number of state fair-practices acts are directed particularly to franchising, either in general or in specified lines of business. There have also been notable initiatives at the federal level.

A federal statute of 1956, the Automobile Dealers' Day in Court Act,[g] proved to be a bellwether for comparable state legislation. It imposed on the automobile manufacturers a duty of good faith "in performing or complying with any of the terms or provisions of [a dealer's] franchise, or in terminating, canceling, or not renewing the franchise."[h] Note that the statute does not purport to restrict the grounds on which a franchise may be terminated. (The failure of a *dealer* to act in good faith may serve as a defense when it charges the manufacturer with a violation of the statute.[i])

The Petroleum Marketing Practices Act of 1978,[j] substantially preempted state regulation of the termination and renewal of franchise relationships between motor-fuel dispensers and their suppliers, in an attempt to "level the playing field." See Simmons v. Mobil Oil Corp., 29 F.3d 505 (9th Cir.1994). A notable feature of the statute is that it deals only in an indirect way with the terms of particular franchises, such as rents charged by major oil companies to service-station operators. It does, however, affect terminations. Periods of notice and knowledge figure prominently in the statute. It contains an open-ended list of events justifying termination: "events relevant to the franchise relationship" causing termination, or nonrenewal, to be "reasonable."[k]

In 1979, by rule, the FTC established a minimum federal standard of disclosure applicable to all "franchise and business opportunity offerings." 16 C.F.R. § 436. (A number of state disclosure requirements are also operative.)

Statutes that restrict the grounds for termination by a franchisor have come to be known as "good cause" legislation. In this matter the states have led the way. "The fundamental thrust of good cause legislation is to confirm the franchisee's ownership of the business of his own which was granted by the franchisor.[l] In Remus v. Amoco Oil Co., 794 F.2d 1238 (7th Cir.1986), cert. dism'd 479 U.S. 925 (1987), Judge Posner said, with reference to the Wisconsin Fair Dealership Act, that its main purpose "is to give dealers a kind of tenure—like federal judges, or teachers, or workers in establishments covered by collective bargaining contracts."

(2) *Questions.* How would you compare the unrestricted power of a franchisor to terminate a contract with the power of an employer to discharge an

g. 15 U.S.C. §§ 1221 et seq.

h. Id. at § 1222.

The definition of the critical term *good faith* is "the duty of each party to any franchise, and all officers, employees, or agents thereof to act in a fair and equitable manner toward each other so as to guarantee the one party freedom from coercion, intimidation, or threats of coercion or intimidation from the other party: Provided, That recommendation, endorsement, exposition, persuasion, urging or argument shall not be deemed to constitute a lack of good faith." Id. at § 1221(e).

For an interpretation, and a contrast with a state motor vehicle franchise act, see Carroll Kenworth Truck Sales, Inc. v. Kenworth Truck Co., 781 F.2d 1520 (11th Cir. 1986). For an extensive discussion of the federal act see S. Macaulay, Law and the Balance of Power (1966).

i. Id. at § 1222.

j. 15 U.S.C. §§ 2801–2806.

k. Section 2802(c).

l. H. Brown, Franchising: Realities and Remedies 201 (1978).

employer "at will"? How would you compare the interest of a franchisee with that of an employee in continuing the relation with the other party?

Do statutes that restrict a franchisor's power to terminate to occasions of good cause, or of particular causes, tend to enhance or to reduce efficiencies in marketing? Does your answer depend on whether or not the statute permits the franchisor to terminate a franchise in order to maintain its competitive position in the market? [m]

Should a statute regulating "dealership" relations apply in the circumstances of Goodman v. Dicker, described at p. 264 above? It might be sound policy for a legislature, one court has suggested, in enacting a good-cause statute, to suspend the requirement for "fledgling" arrangements, comparable to the untenured stages of government and professional employments. See R.W. Intl. Corp. v. Welchs Food, Inc., 13 F.3d 478 (1st Cir.1994). (But the court ruled that the statute in question applied to a "dealer's contract" that had not yet been fully negotiated.) What merits are there in the court's suggestion?

SECTION 5. ILLEGALITY

In the preceding sections our concern was with protecting one party to an agreement against imposition by the other party. In this section our concern is with protecting the public at large against imposition by both parties. When will a court refuse to enforce an agreement, fairly and freely entered into by both parties, on the ground that to enforce it would contravene "public policy"?

To begin with, where do courts get their notions of public policy? In some cases they formulate them for themselves, or rely on prior formulations by other courts. In other cases they derive them from legislation. Rarely, however, do statutes proscribing conduct speak to the enforceability of contracts involving such conduct. (The main exceptions are the usury and gambling statutes which characteristically state that contracts in violation of them are "void.") But courts often look to statutes as sources of public policy, even when they are silent on enforceability itself. This phenomenon is not, of course, peculiar to the law of contracts, but is merely one aspect of the broader problem of adjusting the body of existing law to take account of statutory directions. A comparable phenomenon can be seen in the law of torts when conduct in violation of a criminal statute is held to constitute negligence per se.

It may at first seem strange that the impact of public policy upon the enforceability of agreements is relegated to a single section at the end of this chapter. The explanation lies in the fact that most of the conduct that society finds objectionable (e.g., pollution, discrimination, crime in the streets) involves private agreement only peripherally or not at all. In discouraging such conduct, the threat of the conventional

---

m. As to that ground for termination under the Wisconsin Fair Dealership Act   see Ziegler Co., Inc. v. Rexnord, Inc., 433 N.W.2d 8 (Wis.1988).

criminal sanctions of fine and imprisonment is far mcre likely to be effective than is the threat of the unenforceability of private agreement. Even where the conduct (e.g., usury, gambling, restraint of competition) is more intimately connected with private agreement, the relative efficacy of the threat of unenforceability may be questionable. In short, policing the bargain in the interests of society is not likely to be a very effective way of furthering those interests.

The illegality of an agreement often precludes not only enforcement of it but also restitutionary claims associated with it. When public policy forecloses all remedies, it can produce what appear to be striking injustices in individual cases.

NOTES

(1) *The Sex Part.* A "meretricious relation" between the parties to an agreement is sometimes a ground for refusing to enforce it. But most courts, it is said, have "attempted ... to enforce legitimate business expectations whenever the business part of a contract between cohabiting or romantically attached partners can be separated from the personal part." Thomas v. LaRosa, 400 S.E.2d 809, 813 (W.Va.1990).

In this case the trial court inquired whether or not certain support agreements between non-marital partners are enforceable. The plaintiff, Karen Thomas, alleged a promise by J.D. LaRosa of lifetime financial security, made in return for substantial business advice and consultation. She sought to bring her case within the orbit of the leading "palimony" case, Marvin v. Marvin, 557 P.2d 106 (Cal.1976) (see Note 1, p. 149 above). But here the parties' relation was adulterous. The court observed that the damages Thomas claimed were "exactly those to which a faithful wife would be entitled upon the dissolution of a valid marriage"; and it said that recovery would inevitably be injurious to LaRosa's wife (although he was alleged to be a man of immense wealth). The court rejected authority taking a lighter view of marriage—"a central secular institution in this society"; it rejected also authority denying recovery for domestic services "inextricably interwoven with the sexual relationship."

Ms. Thomas's claim apparently suffered because she had presented herself as "Mrs. LaRosa". Except for the fact that the defendant was married, that fact would have helped her establish a common-law marriage in some states. But the court made a point of the fact that common-law marriage is not part of the law of West Virginia. The court rephrased the certified question, making it: "whether moral standards have changed sufficiently ... that a man can now be married to two women at the same time." And it answered with "an emphatic 'no.'"

Compare Boland v. Catalano, 521 A.2d 142 (Conn.1987), where an implicit sharing agreement between unmarried partners was alleged. In *Marvin*, the court attributed some rulings against recovery to an ascription of prostitution; and it said: "To equate the nonmarital relationship of today to such a subject matter is to do violence to an accepted and wholly different practice."

(2) *Surrogate–Parentage Contracts.* Johnson v. Calvert, 851 P.2d 776 (Cal. 1993), concerned a "gestational surrogacy" contract. The contestants were a woman (Johnson) who bore a child and the child's genetic parents (the Calverts). Each sought to establish a parent-child relation. Johnson had agreed to accept $10,000 for implantation of the zygote, produced by the Calverts, and for

carrying the fetus. The Calverts relied on a finding by the State's legislature, in support of a bill, that surrogate-parenting contracts were consistent with public policy. But the State's governor had vetoed the bill. ("The full moral and psychological dimensions of this practice are not yet clear.") The court decided to draw no conclusion about State policy from the passage of the bill, or from its veto.

The majority wrote at some length about constitutional and policy issues. One observation:

> The argument that a woman cannot knowingly and intelligently agree to gestate and deliver a baby for intending parents carries overtones of the reasoning that for centuries prevented women from attaining equal economic rights and professional status under the law.

Justice Arabian, concurring, refrained from a pronouncement of public policy: "The implications of addressing the general soundness of surrogacy contracts are vast and profound." All the justices regretted the absence of a legislative pronouncement.

Compare In re Baby M, 537 A.2d 1227 (N.J.1988), a widely publicized case in which the "birth mother" was a genetic parent. The agreement she had made with the father recited that his wife was infertile. In disregard of the agreement, the court concluded that custody should be assigned according to the best interest of the child. (It awarded custody to Mr. Stern, in preference to Mrs. Whitehead.) In discounting the trial court's reliance on the agreement, the court said: "There are, in a civilized society, some things that money cannot buy."

Justice Kennard, dissenting in *Johnson*, would have determined the issue by reference to the best interest of the child. On this criterion, might the wealth or attainments of the contestants be influential? How else might these factors count? (The majority observed that Anna Johnson was a licensed nurse, and had previously borne a child.) "[C]ommon sense suggests," according to the court, "that women of lesser means serve as surrogate mothers more often than to wealthy women...."—a point also made in *Baby M*. But the court doubted that surrogacy contracts exploit poor women "to any greater degree than economic necessity in general exploits them...."

(3) *Problem.* On learning that his unmarried daughter, D, was pregnant, F changed his will so as to favor F's son. F told D, however, that he would again revise the will, if she should terminate the pregnancy without giving birth, so that D would get a half share of F's estate. D complied with F's wish and so informed him. F said he would honor his promise; but he died without having done so. Is there a ground of public policy by which a court might refuse to enforce F's promise? See L.G. v. F.G.H., 729 S.W.2d 634 (Mo.App.1987).

HOPPER v. ALL PET ANIMAL CLINIC
Supreme Court of Wyoming, 1993.
861 P.2d 531.

TAYLOR, JUSTICE. [For three years following her education as a veterinarian, Dr. Glenna Hopper worked—part-time at first—at the All Pet Animal Clinic, Inc., in Laramie, Wyoming. She and her employer executed an agreement, effective in March of 1989, containing this provision:

This agreement may be terminated by either party upon 30
days' notice to the other party. Upon termination, Dr. Hopper
agrees that she will not practice small animal medicine for a period
of three years from the date of termination within 5 miles of the
corporate limits of the City of Laramie, Wyoming. Dr. Hopper
agrees that the duration and geographic scope of that limitation is
reasonable.[a]

Later the president of All Pet, Dr. R.B. Johnson, heard a rumor that Dr.
Hopper was investigating the purchase of a competing practice and
suggested that she buy her way out of the covenant about competition.
In her response she said that she could do anything she wanted.
Thereupon she was discharged. In July, 1991, having purchased the
other practice, she began operating the Gem City Veterinary Clinic. In
November, All Pet sued for an injunction, claiming also damages. (An
additional plaintiff was the Alpine Animal Clinic, Inc., in which Dr.
Hopper and Dr. Johnson had also been associated.) The case came to
trial in the following year, more than two years after Hopper was
discharged. The plaintiffs did not seek a temporary injunction.

[It appeared that slightly more than half of Hopper's gross income
was derived from small-animal practice, and the evidence showed a
substantial overlap of clientele in her former and current practices.]

[The trial court granted an injunction, but concluded that the
amount of the plaintiff's damages was too speculative to be allowed.
Both parties appealed.]

A. *The Enforceability of a Covenant Not to Compete*

The common law policy against contracts in restraint of trade is one
of the oldest and most firmly established. Restatement (Second) of
Contracts §§ 185–188 (1981) (Introductory Note at 35). See Dutch Maid
Bakeries v. Schleicher, 58 Wyo. 374, 131 P.2d 630, 634 (1942). The
traditional disfavor of such restraints means covenants not to compete
are construed against the party seeking to enforce them.... The initial
burden is on the employer to prove the covenant is reasonable and has a
fair relation to, and is necessary for, the business interests for which
protection is sought. Tench v. Weaver, 374 P.2d 27, 29 (Wyo.1962).

Two principles, the freedom to contract and the freedom to work,
conflict when courts test the enforceability of covenants not to compete.
Ridley v. Krout, 63 Wyo. 252, 180 P.2d 124, 128 (1947). There is general
recognition that while an employer may seek protection from improper
and unfair competition of a former employee, the employer is not
entitled to protection against ordinary competition. See, e.g. Duffner v.
Alberty, 19 Ark.App. 137, 718 S.W.2d 111, 112 (1986) and American Sec.
Services, Inc. v. Vodra, 222 Neb. 480, 385 N.W.2d 73, 78 (1986). The
enforceability of a covenant not to compete depends upon a finding that
the proper balance exists between the competing interests of the employ-

---

a. This term was part of the first written agreement between Hopper and the
Clinic, executed in December, 1989, but was
antedated to the preceding March, when
Hopper had begun work.

er and the employee. See Restatement (Second) of Agency § 393 cmt. e (1958) (noting that without a covenant not to compete, an agent, employee, can compete with a principal despite past employment and can begin preparations for future competition, such as purchasing a competitive business, before leaving present employment).

Wyoming adopted a rule of reason inquiry from the Restatement of Contracts testing the validity of a covenant not to compete. *Dutch Maid Bakeries*, 131 P.2d 634 (citing Restatement of Contracts §§ 513–515 (1932)); *Ridley,* 180 P.2d at 127. The present formulation of the rule of reason is contained in Restatement (Second) of Contracts, supra § 188: ... See also Restatement (Second) of Contracts, supra, §§ 186–187.[b] An often quoted reformulation of the rule of reason inquiry states that "[a] restraint is reasonable only if it (1) is no greater than is required for the protection of the employer, (2) does not impose undue hardship on the employee, and (3) is not injurious to the public." Harlan M. Blake, Employee Agreements Not to Compete, 73 Harv.L.Rev. 625, 648–49 (1960).

A valid and enforceable covenant not to compete requires a showing that the covenant is: (1) in writing; (2) part of a contract of employment; (3) based on reasonable consideration; (4) reasonable in durational and geographical limitation; and (5) not against public policy. A.E.P. Industries, Inc. v. McClure, 308 N.C. 393, 302 S.E.2d 754, 760 (1983). See *Tench,* 374 P.2d at 29; *Ridley,* 180 P.2d at 128; *Dutch Maid Bakeries,* 131 P.2d at 634; and Wyo.Stat. § 1–23–105 (1988). The reasonableness of a covenant not to compete is assessed based upon the facts of the particular case and a review of all of the circumstances. American Sec. Services, Inc., 385 N.W.2d at 79....

Wyoming has never determined whether a promise not to compete made during the employment relationship is supported merely by the consideration of continued employment or must be supported by separate contemporaneous consideration.... [The court observed that the parties had agreed to an "Addendum" to their agreement, on June 1, 1990, whereby Dr. Hopper's pay was raised by $550 a month. At the same time a bonus provision was deleted.] This agreement restates, by incorporation, the terms of the covenant not to compete. We hold that the Addendum to Agreement, with its pay raise, represented sufficient separate consideration supporting the reaffirmation of the covenant not to compete....

... [W]e turn to the rule of reason inquiry....

b. According to § 187, "A promise to refrain from competition that imposes a restraint that is not ancillary to an otherwise valid transaction or relationship is unreasonably in restraint of trade."

Comment *b* to the section contains these observations: "The promisee's interest ... may arise out of a relation between himself as employer or principal and the promisor as employee or agent.... In order for a restraint to be ancillary to a transaction or relationship the promise that imposes it must be made as part of that transaction or relationship. A promise made subsequent to the transaction or relationship is not ancillary to it. In the case of an ongoing transaction or relationship, however, it is enough if the promise is made before its termination, as long as it is supported by consideration and meets the other requirements of enforceability."

The special interests of All Pet and Alpine identified by the district court as findings of fact are not clearly erroneous. Dr. Hopper moved to Laramie upon completion of her degree prior to any significant professional contact with the community. Her introduction to All Pet's and Alpine's clients, client files, pricing policies, and practice development techniques provided information which exceeded the skills she brought to her employment. While she was a licensed and trained veterinarian when she accepted employment, the additional exposure to clients and knowledge of clinic operations her employers shared with her had a monetary value for which the employers are entitled to reasonable protection from irreparable harm. See Reddy [v. Community Health Foundation of Man, 171 W.Va. 368, 298 S.E.2d 906 (1982)] at 912–14 (discussing the economic analysis applied to restrictive covenants). The proven loss of 187 of All Pet's and Alpine's clients to Dr. Hopper's new practice sufficiently demonstrated actual harm from unfair competition.

The reasonableness, in a given fact situation, of the limitations placed on a former employee by a covenant not to compete are determinations made by the court as a matter of law. See, e.g. Jarrett v. Hamilton, 179 Ga.App. 422, 346 S.E.2d 875, 876 (1986). Therefore, the district court's conclusions of law about the reasonableness of the type of activity, geographic, and durational limits contained in the covenant are subject to *de novo* review.

. . . [I]n Cukjati [v. Burkett, 772 S.W.2d 215 (1989)] at 216, 218, the Court of Appeals of Texas held a covenant not to compete was unreasonable because it limited a veterinarian from practicing within twelve miles of his former employer's clinic in North Irving, a community within the Dallas–Fort Worth metropolitan area. Because evidence from that proceeding disclosed that Dallas area residents are unlikely to travel more than a few miles for pet care, the court found the restriction unreasonable. Id. at 218. The number of veterinarians and the demands upon their services obviously varies between Laramie, Wyoming and metropolitan Dallas, Texas, creating a different usage pattern. We believe the reasonableness of individual limitations contained in a specific covenant not to compete must be assessed based upon the facts of that proceeding. *Ridley*, 180 P.2d at 131.

. . .

Enforcement of the practice restrictions Dr. Hopper accepted as part of her covenant not to compete does not create an unreasonable restraint of trade. While the specific terms of the covenant failed to define the practice of small animal medicine the parties' trade usage provided a conforming standard of domesticated dogs and cats along with exotic animals maintained as household pets. As a veterinarian licensed to practice in Wyoming, Dr. Hopper was therefore permitted to earn a living in her chosen profession without relocating by practicing large animal medicine, a significant area of practice in this state. The restriction on the type of activity contained in the covenant was sufficiently limited to avoid undue hardship to Dr. Hopper while protecting the special interests of All Pet and Alpine. . . .

The public will not suffer injury from enforcement of the covenant....

The geographical limit contained in the covenant not to compete restricts Dr. Hopper from practicing within a five mile radius of the corporate limits of Laramie. As a matter of law, this limit is reasonable in this circumstance. The evidence presented at trial indicated that the clients of All Pet and Alpine were located throughout the county. Despite Wyoming's rural character, the five mile restriction effectively limited unfair competition without presenting an undue hardship. Dr. Hopper could, for example, have opened a practice at other locations within the county.

A durational limitation should be reasonably related to the legitimate interest which the employer is seeking to protect. Restatement (Second) of Contracts, supra, § 188 cmt. b....

A one year durational limit sufficiently secures All Pet's and Alpine's interest in pricing policies and practice development information. Pricing policies at All Pet and Alpine were changed yearly, according to Dr. Johnson, to reflect changes in material and service costs provided by the clinics as well as new procedures. Practice development information, especially in a learned profession, loses its value quickly as technological change occurs and new reference material become [sic] available. We hold, as a matter of law, that enforcement of a one year durational limit is reasonable and sufficiently protects the interest of All Pet and Alpine without violating public policy.... Because we hold that the covenant's three year durational term imposed a partially unreasonable restraint of trade, we remand for a modification of the judgment to enjoin Dr. Hopper from unfair competition for a duration of one year from the date of termination.

B. *Damages for Violation of a Covenant Not to Compete*

[The court rejected the calculations of damages suggested by the plaintiffs, all of which were "based on figures for gross profits."]

The finding of the district court that the amount of damages suffered was speculative and unproven by a preponderance of the evidence is not clearly erroneous....

CARDINE, JUSTICE, dissenting.

Glenna Hopper has beaten the system. Just prior to being terminated, Dr. Hopper informed Dr. Johnson that "the [covenant] isn't worth the paper it's written on." And she was right....

The court has now decided as a matter of law that a one-year noncompetition restriction is reasonable, and a longer period is unreasonable....

... I would require that appellant be enjoined from that part of the practice of veterinary medicine specified in the covenant not to compete from the date the trial court, on remand, enters its modified judgment for at least the one-year period which this court now finds reasonable.

NOTES

(1) *A Statute.* In Oregon, for a time, an employee's agreement not to compete with the employer was made unenforceable unless it was entered into upon the initial employment. See Pacific Veterinary Hosp. v. White, 696 P.2d 570 (Or.App.1985). The statute to that effect has been amended, however, to allow for enforcement if the agreement is accompanied by a "subsequent bona fide advancement of the employee." See Or.Rev.Stat. § 653.259 (dealing also with "bonus restriction agreements").

In Hopper's case Dr. Johnson testified that her employment was conditioned on her agreement to a covenant not to compete, the "details" of which were not discussed. Hopper received no advancement when the employment contract was put in writing, apparently. (See footnote a above.) The writing contained this recital, however:

> When we negotiated the terms of your employment, we agreed that you could leave upon 30 days' notice, but that you would not practice small animal medicine within five miles of Laramie for a three-year period.

As it would apply to the initial written contract between Hopper and the Clinic, is the Oregon statute too restrictive? As to supplementing an employment agreement with a covenant against competition see Liebman & Nathan, The Enforceability of Post–Employment Noncompetition Agreements Formed After At–Will Employment Has Commenced: The "Afterthought" Agreement, 60 So.Cal.L.Rev. 1465, 1516–17 (1987).

(2) "*. . . And/or Dentistry*". In Karpinski v. Ingrasci, 268 N.E.2d 751 (N.Y.1971), the court directed that an injunction be issued against the practice of oral surgery by a former employee of the plaintiff; the defendant had contracted not to practice oral surgery "and/or" dentistry in the vicinity of Ithaca. The court said that since "there are 'powerful considerations of public policy which militate against sanctioning the loss of a man's livelihood,' the courts will subject a covenant by an employee not to compete with his former employer to an 'overriding limitation of "reasonableness" '."

Dr. Karpinski sued also to enforce a $40,000 note issued to him by Dr. Ingrasci, and payable if Ingrasci violated the covenant. Ingrasci resisted the injunction on the ground, apparently, that the employment agreement provided him with a choice between paying and practicing. Could that argument have been forestalled by a simple provision in the agreement? As to enforcing the note the court said: "it would be grossly unfair to grant the plaintiff, in addition to an injunction, the full amount . . . which the parties apparently contemplated for a total breach of the covenant, since the injunction will halt any further violation." (*Actual* damages might be allowed, the court suggested.)

CENTRAL ADJUSTMENT BUREAU, INC. v. INGRAM
Supreme Court of Tennessee, 1984.
678 S.W.2d 28.

[The facts and the first part of the opinion in this case are at p. 86 above.]

DROWOTA, JUSTICE. In Allright Auto Parks, Inc. v. Berry, 219 Tenn. 280, 409 S.W.2d 361 (1966) this Court held that "the time and territorial limits involved must be no greater than is necessary to protect the business interests of the employer." In the instant case the Chancellor found that Central Adjustment Bureau had a legitimate business interest to be protected by the noncompetition covenants and that the defendants' competition damaged that interest. The record supports that finding.

The Chancellor held that although Central Adjustment Bureau had such a legitimate business interest to protect, the covenants sought to be enforced were unreasonably broad. He found that the two year limitation was unreasonable but enforced a one year limitation. He based this upon a finding that when clients of a collection agency change agencies in order to maintain a relationship with a former employee, they do so immediately and that customers seldom use only one collection agency and frequently and regularly re-evaluate their agencies.

The Chancellor further found that the restriction prohibiting contact with any customer which was a client of Central Adjustment Bureau during the defendants' entire terms of employment, was also unreasonable. He, therefore, limited the prohibition to those CAB customers who were customers as of January 1, 1979, and that, as thus altered, the covenant was reasonable and enforceable.

Finally, the Chancellor concluded that the nationwide scope of the restrictions here imposed was too broad but that, since the defendants were competing with CAB in the very area in which they had worked previously, the defendants had no cause to complain.

We agree with both the Chancellor and the Court of Appeals that the restrictions were unreasonably broad. As enforced by the Chancellor, however, the covenants were reasonable. The question before this Court is whether the Chancellor had the authority to modify a covenant not to compete which is otherwise unreasonably broad. Tennessee courts have not previously addressed this question. As a case of first impression, therefore, it is appropriate to look for guidance to decisions by courts having considered this question....

At one time the majority of courts employed the "all or nothing at all" rule. See Ehlers v. Iowa Warehouse Co., 188 N.W.2d 368 (Iowa 1971). Under this rule, a court either enforces the contract as written or rejects it altogether. A covenant containing a term greater than necessary to protect the employer's interest is void in its entirety. Courts employing this rule reason that partial enforcement delegates to courts, when the covenants prove excessive, power to make private agreements.

The recent trend, however, has been away from the all or nothing at all rule in favor of some form of judicial modification. Several courts have explicitly overruled their own prior case law and adopted judicial modification. See, e.g., Ehlers v. Iowa Warehouse Co., supra; Solari Industries, Inc. v. Malady, 55 N.J. 571, 264 A.2d 53 (1970). Our research indicates some form of judicial modification has now been adopted by the majority of jurisdictions.... We think that under appropriate circumstances, some form of judicial modification should be permitted, especially when, as in the case before us, the covenant specifically provides for modification.

Courts have taken one of two approaches in modifying restrictive covenants. The "blue pencil" rule provides that an unreasonable restriction against competition may be modified and enforced to the extent that a grammatically meaningful reasonable restriction remains after the words making the restriction unreasonable are stricken. Solari Industries, Inc. v. Malady, supra, 264 A.2d at 57. For example, in a restriction on soliciting business clients in "Toledo, Ohio, and the United States" the court would "blue pencil" or mark out "Ohio, and the United States" leaving the covenant enforceable in Toledo. See, Briggs v. Butler, 140 Ohio St. 499, 45 N.E.2d 757 (1942).

The blue pencil rule has the advantage of simplicity and prevents a court from actually rewriting private agreements. On the other hand, the contract still fails if the offending provision cannot be stricken. Often a divisible term contains an integral part of the agreement so that "blue penciling" the provision emasculates the contract. Raimonde v. Van Vlerah, 42 Ohio St.2d 21, 325 N.E.2d 544 (1975). The rule has been criticized as emphasizing form over substance. Bess v. Bothman, 257 N.W.2d 791 (Minn.1977). It has been rejected as against the weight of authority and criticized by writers such as Williston and Corbin. See, Restatement (Second) of Contracts § 184 reporter's note; 6A Corbin on Contracts, §§ 1390 and 1394 (1968); 14 Williston on Contracts, § 1647B, 1647C (3d ed. 1972).

The most recent trend, therefore, has been to abandon the "blue pencil" rule in favor of a rule of reasonableness.... This rule provides that unless the circumstances indicate bad faith on the part of the employer, a court will enforce covenants not to compete to the extent that they are reasonably necessary to protect the employer's interest "without imposing undue hardship on the employee when the public interest is not adversely affected." Ehlers v. Iowa Warehouse Co., supra, at 370.

We are persuaded that the rule of reasonableness is the better rule. It is consistent with and an extension of the rule of reasonableness set forth in Allright Auto Parks v. Berry, supra. In adopting it, we do not intend a retreat from the general rule precluding courts from creating new contracts for parties. See, Bob Pearsall Motors, Inc. v. Regal Chrysler–Plymouth, Inc., 521 S.W.2d 578 (Tenn.1975). We are guided instead by the special nature of covenants not to compete already discussed. Further, as noted by two leading commentators on contracts:

> "This is not making a new contract for the parties; it is a choice among the possible effects of the one that they made, establishing the one that is the most desirable for the contractors and the public at large. Partial enforcement involves much less of a variation from the effects intended by the parties than total nonenforcement would. If the arguments in favor of partial enforcement are convincing, no court need hesitate to give them effect." Williston & Corbin, On the Doctrine of Beit v. Beit, 23 Conn.B.J. 40, 49–50 (1949).

We recognize the force of the objection that judicial modification could permit an employer to insert oppressive and unnecessary restrictions into a contract knowing that the courts can modify and enforce the covenant on reasonable terms. Especially when the contract allows the employer attorney's fees, the employer may have nothing to lose by going to court, thereby provoking needless litigation. See, Rector–Phillips–Morse, Inc. v. Vroman, supra, 489 S.W.2d at 5. If there is credible evidence to sustain a finding that a contract is deliberately unreasonable and oppressive, then the covenant is invalid. Ehlers v. Iowa Warehouse Co., supra, at 374. Even in the absence of evidence sufficient to support a finding of invalidity, a court may well find in the course of determining reasonableness that a contractual provision for attorney's fees is unreasonable either in whole or in part.

In the instant case, we hold that the Chancellor acted properly in enforcing the contract on reasonable terms against the defendants. We further find no credible evidence to sustain a finding of bad faith on the part of CAB or to warrant invalidation of the contractual provision on attorney's fees.

BROCK, JUSTICE, dissenting.... I agree with both the Chancellor and the Court of Appeals that the restrictions in these covenants were unreasonably broad. But, we are urged to uphold the reasonableness of the covenants as they have been altered by the Chancellor.... I continue to adhere to the rule that the courts of this state have no business in creating new contracts for the parties.... Our proper role is to enforce a contract as written, or, if it be invalid, to reject it altogether.

The policy whereby unreasonable covenants not to compete are to be modified by the courts and, as thus modified, enforced, will permit an employer to insert oppressive and unnecessary restrictions into such covenants, knowing that the courts will modify and enforce the covenants on reasonable terms. And, when such covenants contain a provision for the employer to recover attorney's fees, as they often do, the employer will have nothing to lose by going to court, thereby provoking needless litigation....

I would hold that the Chancellor erred in his attempt to so modify the unreasonable provisions of these covenants not to compete as to render them reasonable and to enforce the altered "covenants."

NOTES

(1) *Analysis in Stages.* In a West Virginia case (*Reddy*) cited in the foregoing opinion, the court directed a two-step analysis. Whether or not the employee's covenant is reasonable on its face is the first inquiry. On deciding that it is, a court should pare down any overbreadth so that the covenant "conforms to the actual requirements of the parties." The court followed economic arguments about an employer's sunk costs connected with a break-in period for an employee, and concluded that courts should (except in an extreme case) enforce a covenant that "operates purposely as a hardship in order to encourage the employee to remain with his employer until [the employer's] investment is recouped...." Does *Reddy* support the decision in the main case?

By statute in Wisconsin, an employee's covenant restricting competition with an employer is unenforceable unless the restrictions are "reasonably necessary." A covenant that imposes an unreasonable restraint is unenforceable "even as to so much of the covenant or performance as would be a reasonable restraint." Wis.Stat.Ann. § 103.465.[a]

(2) *The "Blue Pencil".* Consider the decision in Karpinski v. Ingrasci, Note 2, p. 461 above: was it an instance of blue-pencilling? What might be said for the rule that "we do not blue pencil in employment cases, but do so in sale of business cases"? See White v. Fletcher/Mayo/Associates, 303 S.E.2d 746 (Ga. 1983).

(3) *Restatement Second.* The rule of the Restatement Second is more tolerant of far-reaching restrictions than the blue-pencil rule. See Illustration 3 and the Reporter's Note to § 184. The rule resembles the position taken by the Iowa court: if an employee's agreement results from the employer's "taking unconscionable advantage" of the employee, it will not be enforced even in part. What circumstances would indicate that undue advantage was taken? See Tasco, Inc. v. Winkel, 281 N.W.2d 280 (Iowa 1979); Smith, Batchelder & Rugg v. Foster, 406 A.2d 1310 (N.H.1979).

(4) *The Drafter's Problem.* Does the Restatement rule invite abuses by drafters of no-compete clauses? Given the blue-pencil rule, how may the drafter go to the limit of what the law allows? By expressing the prohibited activities and areas as the aggregate of numerous small units?

If a court is prepared to "pare down any overbreadth" in a no-compete clause, how might it curb the drafter's temptation to draft an extreme prohibition?

(5) *The Litigator's Problem.* In Peripheral Dynamics, Inc. v. Holdsworth, 385 A.2d 1354 (Pa.Super.1978), the plaintiff sought to prevent its former sales manager from working for a competitor. The plaintiff's attorney could not have been pleased with the testimony of its president, who said that Tibet and the North Pole were the only places where he would be content to let the defendant pursue his career.

What is an effective and ethical way for an attorney to deal with the damaging emotions of a client? (The president's testimony was not ruinous. The court quoted this observation: "A man who wildly claims that he owns all the cherry trees in the country cannot be denied protection of the orchard in his back yard.")

EX–EMPLOYEE BENEFITS

Norton Sarnoff was one of 400 employees of the American Home Products Corporation to whom incentive awards of corporate shares

a. The statute was a response to the decision in Fullerton Lumber Co. v. Torborg, 70 N.W.2d 585 (Wis.1955). For an account by Professor Stewart Macaulay of the engrossing misadventures of the parties in this case see R. Danzig, The Capability Problem in Contract Law (1978).

For an entertaining account of litigation in several courts about shifts among the managements of three department-store chains (Neiman Marcus; Federated; Macy) see The New York Times: Aug. 9, 1993 (p. D1) and Oct. 23, 1993 (p. 37). The reporter detected "subtle differences" between (i) an action *against Federated* for acquiring a CEO from a firm (the plaintiff) that had no agreement with its former employee about competition, and (ii) an action by Federated *against an employee* who had covenanted not to compete with it.

were promised, delivery to be made in ten annual installments commencing at the end of their employment. By the terms of the awards, shares not yet delivered would be withheld from a recipient who entered a competing business. After Sarnoff quit that job, on inquiry the company determined that he was one of 13 former employees, all recipients of awards, who had broken the condition. He sued the company for an order that it issue him the full 600 shares promised. The company appealed from a summary judgment adverse to it. *Held:* Reversed and remanded for a determination whether or not the company had acted unreasonably in concluding that Sarnoff had violated the condition. Sarnoff v. American Home Products Corp., 798 F.2d 1075 (7th Cir.1986). For the decision see id., 666 F.Supp. 137 (N.D.Ill.1987).

As to the difference between the condition in the incentive award and a covenant not to compete, the court said that the latter prevents the promisor from competing "unless he buys back the covenant from his former employer, whereas the condition gives him a choice between competing and receiving compensation for not competing—a choice, it might appear, between a cushion and a soft place." Although the court was uncertain that a differentiation would be made under applicable law,[a] it concluded that the condition was enforceable without regard to its reasonableness.

NOTES

(1) *Effect on Competition?* In Sarnoff's case the court observed that, whether a covenant or a condition was the arrangement, "the parties, because there are only two of them (so that the costs of transacting should not be prohibitive), will be able to bargain their way to the position that maximizes their joint wealth. See Coase, The Problem of Social Cost, 3 J.Law & Econ. 1 (1960). Hence the amount of competition should not be affected. The only difference—but an important one given the paternalistic thinking that has been so prominent from the start in judicial thinking about covenants not to compete, see, e.g., Mitchel v. Reynolds, 1 P.Wms. 181, 24 Eng.Rep. 347 (K.B. 1711)—is that at the moment when the employee must make the decision that will trigger the covenant or condition, he has a more limited set of choices under the former than under the latter."

(2) *Practicing Law: A Special Case?* "Should an attorney who leaves a law firm be free to compete with that firm?" That was the question in Howard v. Babcock, 863 P.2d 150 (Cal.1993), as put by Justice Kennard, dissenting (at p. 161).

In that case the plaintiffs and defendants, partners in a law firm, had agreed that any of them withdrawing from the firm would receive a share of the firm's net profit for a period following the withdrawal, but would do so only at the discretion of the remaining partners if that person should engage in a designated type of competitive practice. When three partners withdrew, and the limitation was invoked against them, they sought a recovery of profits and a declaration that the limitation was unenforceable. From a judgment favoring the defendants, the plaintiffs appealed once, with limited success, and sought further

---

a. The law of New York ("not a legal backwater"), according to a choice-of-law   term in the agreement.

review. *Held:* Reversed. Howard v. Babcock, 863 P.2d 150 (Cal.1993). Citing changes in "law firm culture," the court said that "the general rules and habits of commerce have permeated the legal profession." Many other courts have "interpreted the rules of professional conduct of their states ... as prohibiting all agreements restricting competition among lawyers, including those that merely assess a cost for competition.... Upon reflection [however], we have determined that these courts' steadfast concern to assure the theoretical freedom of each lawyer to choose whom to represent and what kind of work to undertake, and the theoretical freedom of any client to select his or her attorney of choice is inconsistent with the reality that both freedoms are actually circumscribed."

One of the decisions disapproved by the California court was Jacob v. Norris, McLaughlin & Marcus, 607 A.2d 142 (N.J.1992). In that case the court condemned part of an inter-attorney agreement as a "penalty designed to protect the former law firm's turf." But part of the agreement survived, as severable; and the court added: "we recognize that if a partner's departure will result in a decrease in the probability of a client's return and a consequent decrease in prospective earnings, that departure may decrease the value of the firm's goodwill. It would not be inappropriate therefore for law partners to take that specific effect into account in determining the shares due a departing partner." What formula could be used to "take that specific effect into account"?

INDUCING OFFICIAL ACTION

Influence peddling is a common subject of judicial denunciation, but lawyers above all should be aware that services in procuring favorable official action are worthy of a price. Contracts to pay lobbyists are by no means condemned as such. The proper line has been stated as follows: "The authorities very generally hold that a contract to pay for services to be performed in the endeavor to obtain or defeat legislation by other means than the use of argument addressed to the reason of the legislators, such as, for example, for the exertion of personal or political influence apart from the appeal to reason as applied to the consideration of the merits or demerits of the legislation in question, is an illegal contract." Campbell County v. Howard & Lee, 112 S.E. 876 (Va.1922). The consequence of stepping over the line is illustrated in Ewing v. National Airport Corporation, 115 F.2d 859 (4th Cir.1940), cert. denied, 312 U.S. 705 (1941).

In the latter case the court said: "Contingent fees for services in securing the passage of legislation are especially regarded with disfavor by the courts." Why should this be? Tort litigation in this country is customarily conducted by lawyers for claimants under contracts for contingent fees. It has been said that in such cases, "Because of the very fact that [the contingent fee] does insure the most humble citizen equal justice under law, while at the same time preserving the lawyer's independence of judgment and action, it serves the highest public interest." Cohen, Book Review, 24 Vand.L.Rev. 433, 441 (1971). Is it significant that in some courts there are disclosure requirements and regulations designed to control immoderate contingent fees for lawyers, and that there are schedules and ceilings for the compensation of lawyers pressing certain types of claims?

NOTES

(1) *Chutzpah Illustrated.* Being offered a bribe, a judge consulted the state's attorney and was advised to accept the money. It became evidence in criminal proceedings against the payor, who was imprisoned. He then moved for the return of the money by the state, and that was ordered (by another judge). The state appealed. The court considered the case under the aspect of failure of consideration, or breach by the "bribed" judge. *Held:* Reversed. The court opened its opinion with a definition of "chutzpah". It went on to say that the courts will not order damages for breach of a contract to commit a crime. "Parties of that ilk are left where they are found, to stew in their own juice." State v. Strickland, 400 A.2d 451 (Md.App.1979).

(2) *Problem.* An electrical contractor (S–1) gave a bid to a general contractor (G) who was in competition for a sizeable government contract. G's chief estimator said it was "very interesting," and S–1 asked, "Do we have a job if you have one?" The answer was that G would like some "protection". This was understood to mean that S–1 would submit higher bids to G's competitors so that G would have the lowest electrical costs. S–1 told G he would give what was asked: "we are banking on you getting the job and we are willing to gamble on you and you only." G's estimator made a commitment to S–1, including the promise, "I am not going to tell anybody else what your number is." In spite of that, he telephoned another electrical contractor with whom G had often done business (S–2) and asked if it could beat S–1's bid. At the last moment before the general contractors' bids were opened G recast its bid on the basis of a figure supplied by S–2. G won the contract and sublet the electrical work to S–2. Does S–1 have a claim against G? See Premier Electrical Constr. Co. v. Miller–Davis Co., 291 F.Supp. 295 (N.D.Ill.1968), aff'd, 422 F.2d 1132 (7th Cir.), cert. denied, 400 U.S. 828 (1970).

Introductory Note to *McConnell*

Some background propositions for the case that follows, and related ones, are these: "[I]t is well settled both in law and in equity that the courts will not aid either party to an illegal agreement. The law leaves the parties where it found them. Except in some cases where the parties are not in pari delicto, the rule applies even though both parties were party to the illegal contract. While it may not always seem an honorable thing to do, a party to an illegal agreement is permitted to set up the illegality as a defense even though the party may be alleging his or her own turpitude." Early Detection Center, Inc. v. Wilson, 811 P.2d 860, 867 (Kan.1991).

The opinion that follows refers to a much earlier decision on somewhat different facts and says, "There cannot be any difference in principle between that situation and the present one. . . ." Consider the facts of the earlier case: Sirkin v. Fourteenth Street Store, 108 N.Y.S. 830 (App.Div.1908).

McGuinness was the Store's purchasing agent. The plaintiff, Sirkin, had promised to pay McGuinness 5% of the price of all goods that he ordered, for the Store, from Sirkin. Not being paid for some goods that Sirkin had delivered to the Store, he sued it for the purchase price: $1,555. The Store alleged as a defense that Sirkin had paid McGuinness $75 for the sale transaction. The trial court directed a verdict for Sirkin, reasoning that the Store could not retain the goods and decline to pay. On appeal, *held:* Reversed. Under the state's penal code, it was a misdemeanor for a seller to offer a commission, discount, or bonus to a purchasing agent, and for the agent to receive it. The stated sanctions were a fine of not more than $500 and imprisonment for not more than a year.

Nothing could be more effective than denying recovery, the court said, in stopping the spread of "this corrupting and now criminal custom." Also: "it is the duty of the court to be guided [by the Legislature] in administering the law." The court acknowledged other remedies that might have been open to the Store: counterclaiming for damages, if there were any; rescinding the purchase contract for fraud; and requiring McGuinness to account for the $75. But it said that the case was not one of ordinary fraud, in which no "general public policy" is involved. (Two justices dissented, saying: "It is no part of our duty to assume legislative power and prescribe an additional punishment....")

Note the references to this decision in *McConnell.*

McCONNELL v. COMMONWEALTH PICTURES CORP.

Court of Appeals of New York, 1960.
7 N.Y.2d 465, 166 N.E.2d 494.

DESMOND, CHIEF JUDGE. The appeal is by defendant [Commonwealth Pictures] from so much of an Appellate Division, First Department, order as affirmed that part of a Special Term order which struck out two defenses in the answer.

Plaintiff sues for an accounting. Defendant had agreed in writing that, if plaintiff should succeed in negotiating a contract with a motion-picture producer whereby defendant would get the distribution rights for certain motion pictures, defendant would pay plaintiff $10,000 on execution of the contract between defendant and the producer, and would thereafter pay plaintiff a stated percentage of defendant's gross receipts from distribution of the pictures. Plaintiff negotiated the distribution rights for defendant and defendant paid plaintiff the promised $10,000 but later refused to pay him the commissions or to give him an accounting of profits.

Defendant's answer contains, besides certain denials and counterclaims not now before us, two affirmative defenses the sufficiency of which we must decide. In these defenses it is asserted that plaintiff, without the knowledge of defendant or of the producer, procured the distribution rights by bribing a representative of the producer and that plaintiff agreed to pay and did pay to that representative as a bribe the $10,000 which defendant paid plaintiff. The courts below (despite a strong dissent in the Appellate Division) held that the defenses were insufficient to defeat plaintiff's suit. Special Term's opinion said that, since the agreement sued upon—between plaintiff and defendant—was not in itself illegal, plaintiff's right to be paid for performing it could not be defeated by a showing that he had misconducted himself in carrying it out. The court found a substantial difference between this and the performance of an illegal contract. We take a different view. Proper and consistent application of a prime and long-settled public policy closes the doors of our courts to those who sue to collect the rewards of corruption.

New York's policy has been frequently and emphatically announced in the decisions. " 'It is the settled law of this State (and probably of every other State) that a party to an illegal contract cannot ask a court of law to help him carry out his illegal object, nor can such a person plead or prove in any court a case in which he, as a basis for his claim, must show forth his illegal purpose', Stone v. Freeman, 298 N.Y. 268, 271, 82 N.E.2d 571, 572, 8 A.L.R.2d 304, citing the leading cases. The money plaintiff sues for was the fruit of an admitted crime and 'no court should be required to serve as paymaster of the wages of crime'. Stone v. Freeman, supra, 298 N.Y. at page 271, 82 N.E.2d at page 572. And it makes no difference that defendant has no title to the money since the court's concern 'is not with the position of the defendant' but with the question of whether 'a recovery by the plaintiff should be denied for the sake of public interests', a question which is one 'of public policy in the administration of the law'. Flegenheimer v. Brogan, 284 N.Y. 268, 272, 30 N.E.2d 591, 592, 132 A.L.R. 613. That public policy is the one described in Riggs v. Palmer, 115 N.Y. 506, 511–512, 22 N.E. 188, 190, 5 L.R.A. 340: 'No one shall be permitted to profit by his own fraud, or to take advantage of his own wrong, or to found any claim upon his own iniquity, or to acquire property by his own crime. These maxims are dictated by public policy, have their foundation in universal law administered in all civilized countries, and have nowhere been superseded by statutes' " (Carr v. Hoy, 2 N.Y.2d 185, 187, 158 N.Y.S.2d 572, 574–575, 139 N.E.2d 531, 533).

We must either repudiate those statements of public policy or uphold these challenged defenses. It is true that some of the leading decisions (Oscanyan v. Arms Co., 103 U.S. 261, 26 L.Ed. 539; Stone v. Freeman, 298 N.Y. 268, 82 N.E.2d 571, 8 A.L.R.2d 304) were in suits on intrinsically illegal contracts but the rule fails of its purpose unless it covers a case like the one at bar. Here, as in Stone v. Freeman and Carr v. Hoy (supra), the money sued for was (assuming the truth of the defenses) "the fruit of an admitted crime." To allow this plaintiff to collect his commissions would be to let him "profit by his own fraud, or to take advantage of his own wrong, or to found [a] claim upon his own iniquity, or to acquire property by his own crime" (Riggs v. Palmer, 115 N.Y. 506, 511, 22 N.E. 188, 190, 5 L.R.A. 340). The issue is not whether the acts alleged in the defenses would constitute the crime of commercial bribery under section 439 of the Penal Law, Consol.Laws, c. 40, although it appears that they would. "A seller cannot recover the price of goods sold where he has paid a commission to an agent of the purchaser (Sirkin v. Fourteenth Street Store, 124 App.Div. 384, 108 N.Y.S. 830); neither could the agent recover the commission, even at common law and before the enactment of section 384–r of the Penal Law (now section 439)" (Judge Crane in Reiner v. North American Newspaper Alliance, 259 N.Y. 250, 261, 181 N.E. 561, 565, 83 A.L.R. 23). The *Sirkin* opinion . . . has been cited with approval by this court. . . . In unmistakable terms it forbids the courts to honor claims founded on commercial bribery.

We are not working here with narrow questions of technical law. We are applying fundamental concepts of morality and fair dealing not to be weakened by exceptions. So far as precedent is necessary, we can rely on *Sirkin* . . . and Reiner v. North American Newspaper Alliance, 259 N.Y. 250, 181 N.E. 564, 83 A.L.R. 23, supra. *Sirkin* is the case closest to ours and shows that, whatever be the law in other jurisdictions, we in New York deny awards for the corrupt performance of contracts even though in essence the contracts are not illegal. . . . There cannot be any difference in principle between that situation and the present one where plaintiff (it is alleged) contracted to buy motion-picture rights for defendant but performed his covenant only by bribing the seller's agent. In the *Reiner* case (supra), likewise, the plaintiff had fully performed the services required by his agreement with the defendant but was denied a recovery because his performance had involved and included "fraud and deception" practiced not on defendant but on a third party. It is beside the point that the present plaintiff on the trial might be able to prove a prima facie case without the bribery being exposed. On the whole case (again assuming that the defenses speak the truth) the disclosed situation would be within the rule of our precedents forbidding court assistance to bribers.

It is argued that a reversal here means that the doing of any small illegality in the performance of an otherwise lawful contract will deprive the doer of all rights, with the result that the other party will get a windfall and there will be great injustice. Our ruling does not go as far as that. It is not every minor wrongdoing in the course of contract performance that will insulate the other party from liability for work done or goods furnished. There must at least be a direct connection between the illegal transaction and the obligation sued upon. Connection is a matter of degree. Some illegalities are merely incidental to the contract sued on. . . . We cannot now, any more than in our past decisions, announce what will be the results of all the kinds of corruption, minor and major, essential and peripheral. All we are doing here is labeling the conduct described in these defenses as gross corruption depriving plaintiff of all right of access to the courts of New York State. Consistent with public morality and settled public policy, we hold that a party will be denied recovery even on a contract valid on its face, if it appears that he has resorted to gravely immoral and illegal conduct in accomplishing its performance.[a]

Perhaps this application of the principle represents a distinct step beyond *Sirkin* and *Reiner* (supra) in the sense that we are here barring recovery under a contract which in itself is entirely legal. But if this be an extension, public policy supports it. We point out that our holding is limited to cases in which the illegal performance of a contract originally valid takes the form of commercial bribery or similar conduct and in which the illegality is central to or a dominant part of the plaintiff's whole course of conduct in performance of the contract. . . .

The sufficiency of defendant's counterclaim (for the return of its $10,000) was litigated below but it is not before us on this appeal.

The order appealed from should be reversed, with costs, the certified question answered in the negative, and plaintiff's motion, insofar as it attacks the sufficiency of the two separate defenses, should be denied.

FROESSEL, JUDGE (dissenting). This is not a case where the contract *sued upon* is intrinsically illegal (cf. Stone v. Freeman, 298 N.Y. 268, 82 N.E.2d 571, 8 A.L.R.2d 304; Reiner v. North American Newspaper Alliance, 259 N.Y. 250, 181 N.E. 561, 83 A.L.R. 23); or was *procured* by the commission of a crime (Sirkin v. Fourteenth Street Store, 124 App.Div. 384, 108 N.Y.S. 830); or where a beneficiary under a will murdered his ancestor in order to obtain the speedy enjoyment of his property (Riggs v. Palmer, 115 N.Y. 506, 22 N.E. 188, 5 L.R.A. 340). In the *Sirkin* case, so heavily relied upon by the majority, the plaintiff obtained the very contract he was seeking to enforce by paying secret commissions to defendant's own purchasing agent. In Merchants' Line v. Baltimore & Ohio R. Co., 222 N.Y. 344, 347, 118 N.E. 788, we pointed out that in *Sirkin* "the plaintiff reached and bribed the man who made *the contract under which he was seeking to recover* " (emphasis supplied). In Morgan Munitions Supply Co. v. Studebaker Corp., 226 N.Y. 94, 99, 123 N.E. 146, 147, we likewise cited the *Sirkin* case for the proposition that "a contract *procured by* the commission of a crime is unenforceable even if executed" (emphasis supplied).

In the instant case, the contract which plaintiff is seeking to enforce is perfectly valid, and it was not intended or even contemplated that plaintiff would perform the contract by illegal or corrupt means. Having received and retained the full benefits of plaintiff's performance, defendant now seeks to "inject into" its contract with plaintiff, "which was fair and legal in itself, the illegal feature of the other independent transaction" Messersmith v. American Fidelity Co., 187 App.Div. 35, 37, 175 N.Y.S. 169, 170, affirmed 232 N.Y. 161, 133 N.E. 432, 19 A.L.R. 876. This court is now adopting a rule that a party may retain the benefits of, but escape his obligations under, a wholly lawful contract if the other

a. In Jaclyn, Inc. v. Edison Bros. Stores, Inc., 406 A.2d 474 (N.J.Super.1979), the court observed: "Prior to *McConnell* courts probed the record in search of an independent legal consideration which would sustain the contract notwithstanding a periph- eral element of wrongdoing. By contrast, courts in recent years have focused upon 'the extent and seriousness of the illegal conduct and its relationship to the contract at issue' before denying recovery."

party commits some illegal act not contemplated nor necessary under the contract....

The majority opinion seeks to distinguish between "major" and "minor" illegality and "direct" and "peripheral" corruption. It decides this case on the ground that the manner in which plaintiff performed his admittedly valid contract with defendant was "gravely immoral and illegal." Such distinctions are neither workable nor sanctioned by authority. If a contract was lawfully made, and did not contemplate wrongdoing, it is enforcible; if, on the other hand, it was *procured* by the commission of a crime, or was in fact for the performance of illegal services, it is not enforcible. These are the criteria distinguishing enforcible from unenforcible contracts—not "nice" distinctions between degrees of illegality and immorality in the performance of lawful contracts, or whether the illegal act of performance was "directly" or "peripherally" related to the main contract.

    ... [T]he contract between plaintiff and defendant was perfectly legal, and defendant is seeking to avoid its obligations under the contract—of which it has reaped the benefits for some 12 years—by asserting the illegality of a *different* and subsequent agreement between plaintiff and a third party. This it should not be permitted to do....

VAN VOORHIS, JUDGE (dissenting). Public morals and fair dealing are likely to be advanced by limiting rather than by enlarging the rule that is being extended to the facts of this case. This rule is grounded on considerations of public policy. Courts will not intervene between thieves to compel them to divide the spoils. But in a situation like the present, it seems to me that the effect of this decision will not be to restrain the corrupt influencing of agents, employees or servants but to encourage misappropriation of funds and breaches of faith between persons who do not stand in corrupt relationships with one another. The public interest is not served best by decisions which put a premium on taking unconscionable advantage of such situations, or which drive the enforcement of obligations of this kind underground. I concur in the dissenting opinion by Judge Froessel.

NOTES

(1) *Beneficiary of the Bribe.* In both *Sirkin* and *McConnell* it might be said that some "surplus" was realized by persons who were not parties—those who took the bribes. In *Sirkin* the court said: "The servant would be accountable to his master or employer for any moneys thus received...." Presumably the employer could have gotten that relief *in addition* to retaining the goods without paying for them. Compare a solution proposed in the Restatement Second for McDevitt v. Stokes, Note 4, p. 364 above: the jockey's driving in the race is consideration for the promise of a bonus; but his employer is entitled to the bonus. See Illustration 12 to § 73.

Other dispositions of a like surplus have been proposed, though not as yet (in U.S. law) adopted. See H. Berman, Justice in the U.S.S.R. 141 (1963) (forfeit to the state), and Seavey, Problems in Restitution, 7 Okla.L.Rev. 257, 259 (1954). Compare the "chutzpah" case, Note 1, p. 468 above, and the trial court's use of a constructive trust in Rush v. Curtiss–Wright Export Co., 31 N.Y.S.2d 550 (App.Div.1941), aff'd, 43 N.E.2d 712 (N.Y.1943).

(2) *Cases for Comparison.* Not long before it decided *McConnell,* the New York court had ruled that a "mere agent or depository of the proceeds of an illegal transaction will not be permitted to assert the defense of illegality in an action to recover the proceeds by a party to the illegal transaction." Southwestern Shipping Corp. v. National City Bank, 160 N.E.2d 836 (N.Y.1959). In that case the defendant bank sought to escape the consequences of an error in dealing with a credit on its books; its defense—which proved to be unavailing—was that the credit had been established as a subterfuge, unknown to it, for a violation of international exchange controls. In a paragraph of the *McConnell* opinion omitted above, the court said: "There is no pertinence here of the rule which makes such defenses unavailable to one who is a mere depository or escrowee...." In his dissent in *McConnell,* Judge Froessel argued that the decision there was "contrary to the spirit, if not the letter, of our holding in *Southwestern Shipping....* Here, the contract between plaintiff and defendant was perfectly legal, and defendant is seeking to avoid its obligations under the contract—of which it has reaped the benefits for some 12 years—by asserting the illegality of a *different* and subsequent agreement between plaintiff and a third party. This it should not be permitted to do."

Judge Froessel gave this case as an illustration of the untoward effects of *McConnell:* "an owner may thus avoid paying his contractor for the cost of erecting a building because the contractor gave an inspector a sum of money to expedite an inspection." How would the majority have decided that case? Compare Tocci v. Lembo, 92 N.E.2d 254 (Mass.1950).

✳ (3) *Degrees of Involvement.* In selling goods, Holmes indicated, a merchant may safely exhibit an "understood indifference" to the buyer's intended use of the goods. Graves v. Johnson, 60 N.E. 383 (Mass.1901). For an application of the principle see Fineman v. Faulkner, 93 S.E. 384 (N.C.1917), in which the plaintiff had made a credit sale of a phonograph. The defendant, administrator of the buyer's estate, sought to avoid paying by showing that the plaintiff had known "by general reputation" that the buyer was a prostitute by vocation. In *Graves,* also, the plaintiffs had neither sought nor received information that the goods would be used in a lawless venture.

> [A] sale otherwise lawful is not connected with subsequent unlawful conduct by the mere fact that the seller correctly divines the buyer's unlawful intent, closely enough to make the sale unlawful.... Of course the [buyer-defendant] was free to change his mind, and there was no communicated desire of the plaintiffs to co-operate with the defendant's present intent.... [T]he decisions tend more and more to agree that the connection with the unlawful act in cases like the present is too remote.

The buyer was unsuccessful in relying on his intention to resell the goods in question (liquor) in another state, in violation of its laws.

Apparently there is still some force, however, in a distinction drawn in old English cases about smugglers' liability to their suppliers. This statement from Hull v. Ruggles, 56 N.Y. 424 (1874), is still referred to: If a supplier "has so packed the goods as to facilitate the smuggling, he is regarded as particeps criminis and cannot recover." In that case a buyer of candies meant to market them in violation of the statute against lotteries. The seller (plaintiff) cooperated by boxing, in a fifth of the candy boxes, cards designating items of silverware.

Compare the statement in *McConnell:* "There must at least be a direct connection between the illegal transaction and the obligation sued upon."

(4) *Problem.* *R* and *M* had a joint arrangement for selling Irish sweepstakes tickets and for their efforts received two tickets for every twenty they sold. On each bonus ticket one or the other put his name, but only on the agreement that they would share any winnings. A penal statute in their state makes it unlawful to promote a lottery (although the state conducts one). *R* has collected a "super prize" on a bonus ticket bearing his name. Does *M* have a claim against *R*? See Miller v. Radikopf, 228 N.W.2d 386 (Mich.1975).[a]

LICENSING LAWS

In Sirkin v. Fourteenth St. Store, stated at p. 469 above, the court said that "one who is required by law to procure a license to conduct any trade, calling, or profession may not recover for services rendered or property sold, without first obtaining such license." That statement goes too far. When the purpose of a licensing requirement is ascertained to be raising public revenue, and not the protection of the public's welfare—health, morals or the like—a claimant's want of a license is generally not a bar.

If a person whose vocation is related to the construction industry, such as an architect or a mechanical engineer, performs services without having a mandated license or certification, should the services go uncompensated? What is the purpose of licensing such persons? If a dealer in goods of a particular kind is required to be licensed as part of a statutory system for the economic regulation of the market in those goods, how should the "welfare *vs.* revenue" distinction apply? Should this distinction be abandoned, and consideration be given to matters such as the quality of the services and the hardship entailed by denying recovery?

The decisions bearing on these questions are far from uniform.

NOTES

(1) *Line Drawing.* In Town Planning & Engineering Associates, Inc. v. Amesbury Specialty Co., 342 N.E.2d 706 (Mass.1976), concerning the plaintiff's want of a certification as an engineer, the court considered the possibility of confining the plaintiff's recovery to "a quantum meruit less than the contract price." It concluded, however, that a "vector of considerations" pointed toward recovery of the contract price. One consideration was whether or not "the characteristics which gave the plaintiff's act its value to the defendant [were] the same as those which made it a violation" of law.[b] Contrast Kansas City Community Center v. Heritage Industries, Inc., 972 F.2d 185 (8th Cir.1992) (architect). For a useful distinction between a claim made by an unlicensed contractor in its capacity as a contractor and one made by an unlicensed contractor in its capacity as a joint venturer, see In re Lake Providence Properties, Inc., 168 B.R. 876 (W.D.N.C.1994).

a. Private wager contracts are unlawful in most of the United States—although the common law had no generalized objection. As to an attempt to exploit local variations in the law of wagers, see Intercontinental Hotels Corp. (P.R.) v. Golden, 203 N.E.2d 210 (N.Y.1964).

b. Quotation by the court from Gardner, An Inquiry into the Principles of the Law of Contracts, 46 Harv.L.Rev. 1, 37 (1932).

As to licenses required of dealers, compare John E. Rosasco Creameries, Inc. v. Cohen, 11 N.E.2d 908 (N.Y.1937) (plaintiff a milk dealer), with Carmine v. Murphy, 35 N.E.2d 19 (N.Y.1941) (dealer in liquor).

(2) *Two Views.* In 1692 Lord Holt expressed the following influential view: "every contract made for or about any matter or thing which is prohibited and made unlawful by any statute, is a void contract, though the statute itself doth not mention that it shall be so, but only inflicts a penalty on the offender, because a penalty implies a prohibition, though there are no prohibitory words in the statute." Bartlett v. Vinor, 20 Eng.Rep. 750 (King's Bench). (Whether or not a private action can be derived from a statutory proscription is of course another matter. See Cort v. Ash, 422 U.S. 66 (1975).)

In 1936 Professor Gellhorn wrote: "The judges are not bound to regard as void every contract which seems in some way to fall within the general aura of the criminal law, but only those whose enforcement, they are persuaded, after respectfully studying the 'public policy' involved, will disserve the general interest as it has been indicated by the legislature." Contracts and Public Policy, 35 Colum.L.Rev. 679, 686 (1936). Compare the oft-quoted observation of Burrough, J., in Richardson v. Mellish, 130 Eng.Rep. 294, 303 (Common Pleas, 1824), that public policy "is a very unruly horse, and when once you get astride it you never know where it will carry you."

IN PARI DELICTO

In circumstances of equal fault, the position of the defendant is the more compelling (*in pari delicto potior est conditio defendantis*). Arguing from that baseline, many a claimant has occasion to contend that the parties are *not* equally culpable. If both parties have knowingly attempted a violation of law, in what situations is that contention plausible?

One was thought to have occurred in Schneider v. Schneider, 644 A.2d 510 (Md.1994), where specific performance of a promise of support was sought. The promise was part of an agreement, the claimant alleged, under which she and her husband had colluded in perjury to get a quickie divorce. Reversing the ruling below, the majority of the court said that dismissing the complaint would do little to suppress the evil, and would "neuter" the obligation of support contracted for by an economically dependent spouse.

The case of "Amateur *vs.* Professional" is another such situation. As Professor Wade wrote, "Courts are loath to see a professional profiting from his iniquitous business. . . ." Restitution of Benefits Acquired Through Illegal Transactions, 95 U.Pa.L.Rev. 261, 277 (1947). For a striking instance see Watts v. Malatesta, 186 N.E. 210 (N.Y.1933), in which a bookie and a patron made claims against one another. The court construed a statute so as to restore the patron's losses, but not the bookie's (much larger) ones. Even more striking, perhaps, is Goldberg v. Sanglier, 639 P.2d 1347 (Wash.1982), an action between former partners in an auto dealership that had been acquired by deceit. The trial court gave a judgment for the plaintiffs. On an appeal, this judgment was approved, partly in reliance on a finding that the plaintiffs had "had no prior experience in the automobile business, and relied on the experience and knowledge of the defendants." Is it experience in a lawful business, or experience in deceit, that should count?

In *Goldberg* the court approved an award by the trial court that included the appreciation in value, enjoyed by the defendants, of assets the defendants had fraudulently acquired from the plaintiffs. This relief exemplified, the court said, flexibility in "shaping a full range of remedies to parties not in pari delicto."

The doctrine *in pari delicto* has a standard meaning that, exceptionally, restitutionary relief is available to a party who joined another, the defendant, in wrongdoing. The doctrine alleviates harshness that would result if it were the invariable rule that the parties to an illegal contract are "left where they are found, to stew in their own juice" (see Note 1, p. 468 above). According to the Restatement Second, restitution is available to a party "who would otherwise suffer a forfeiture that is disproportionate in relation to the contravention of public policy involved." Section 197, Comment *b*.

NOTES

(1) *Restitution, and Beyond.* In Goldberg v. Sanglier, above, the intermediate court had said that the plaintiffs were limited to "disaffirming their agreement and recovering the funds they paid under it." The high court disagreed. The defendants, it said, as the "primary transgressors" of the law, "will be justly required to disgorge profits accruing to them from their improper behavior." The remedy, imposing a constructive trust, was (like that in *Watts*) restitutionary in kind. The doctrine *in pari delicto* is sometimes invoked in support of a remedy of another kind, naturally, although that use is contrary to the usual understanding. Schneider v. Schneider is an example.

Suppose that in Sirkin v. Fourteenth Street Store, p. 469 above, the sale contract had been (for some reason) unlawful, but that the parties were not *in pari delicto*. Would the reasoning in *Goldberg* support a recovery of the contract price? See City of Damascus v. Bivens, 726 S.W.2d 677 (Ark.1987) ("not error to base the unjust enrichment award on the contract price").

(2) *Seriousness of the Offense.* In *Goldberg* the investor-plaintiffs had apparently joined a defendant in practicing concealment, when the dealership was acquired, of their stake in the enterprise. (Subsequently—as might have been anticipated—the defendant practiced fraud on the plaintiffs in buying out their interest.) Considered as a "contravention of public policy," should the concealment count for more or less than the parties' imposition on the divorce court in Schneider v. Schneider, above?

(3) *The Law-of-Nature Case.* In Liebman v. Rosenthal, Justice Hooley denied a motion by the defendant for summary judgment on a claim alleged as follows: Fleeing the German armies through France in 1941, Liebman met Rosenthal and turned over to him jewelry worth $28,000. Rosenthal had represented that by bribing a Portuguese consul, his friend, he could get visas for Liebman and his family. Rosenthal absconded with the jewelry. The two next met in New York City. Liebman brought this action for the value of the jewelry, having demanded its return without success.

On Rosenthal's appeal, *held:* Affirmed. Liebman v. Rosenthal, 59 N.Y.S.2d 148 (App.Div.1945) (cryptic opinion). Justice Adel, dissenting, wrote: "There is no authority for the holding that urgency of motive provides an excuse for entering into an illegal engagement." The trial court's opinion [a] made reference to the executory character of the contract and denied that the parties were in pari delicto. Further: "There is no question of public policy involved in a case like this where a man is attempting to save himself from an enemy who has violated all the laws of civilization. Protection of one's self and one's family is among the first laws of nature.... Rather it may be said that public policy should not permit the defendant to profit by what plaintiff maintains happened here."

X.L.O. CONCRETE CORP. v. RIVERGATE CORP.

New York Court of Appeals, 1994.
83 N.Y.2d 513, 634 N.E.2d 158.

CIPARICK, J. The question presented in this action for breach of contract, account stated, and unjust enrichment is whether interposition of an antitrust illegality defense under the Donnelly Act (General Business Law §§ 340 et seq.) prevents enforcement of the contract between these parties as a matter of law....

The parties, plaintiff X.L.O. Concrete Corp., as subcontractor, and defendant Rivergate Corporation, as general contractor, entered into a written contract on May 12, 1983 for construction of the concrete superstructure and fills of a project located in Manhattan. Plaintiff fully performed its obligations under the contract and sought payment of $844,125.07, the balance due and owing. Defendant refused to pay on the ground that the contract was an integral feature of an extortion and labor bribery operation known as the "Club".

The "Club" was an arrangement between the "Commission" of La Cosa Nostra, a ruling body comprised of four of the five New York City organized crime family bosses, and seven concrete construction companies operating in New York City, and the District Council of Cement and Concrete Workers, Laborers International Union of North America (see United States v. Salerno, 868 F.2d 524, 528–529, cert. denied 493 U.S. 811 [describing the Club and its workings in fuller detail]). The Commission decided which concrete companies would be permitted to undertake construction jobs in New York City worth more than two million dollars; contractors who took jobs over two million were required to pay the Commission two percent of the contract price for guaranteed "labor peace". The Commission not only approved which companies got which jobs, but also rigged the bidding to ensure that the designated company would submit the lowest bid. The Commission enforced compliance through threatened or actual labor unrest or violence. In May 1981, plaintiff became the last concrete contractor doing business in New York City to join the Club.[b]

---

a. 57 N.Y.S.2d 875 (Sup.Ct.1945).

b. On the vicissitudes of a City program designed to lower construction costs and

"kick the Mafia out of the concrete industry," see The New York Times, Sept. 3, 1994, p. 21. The program entailed a re-

The Rivergate project was allocated to plaintiff by the Commission on the assumption that it would not exceed $15 million. Plaintiff's principal, James Costigan, paid the 2% "labor peace" fee to Ralph Scopo, the Commission's representative and the business manager and president of the District Council of Cement and Concrete Workers. Plaintiff then negotiated the terms of the contract with defendant. The parties agreed on a figure of $16,300,000 (later adjusted to $16,544,125.07).

The contract price exceeded the amount approved by the Commission, and Scopo, acting on behalf of the Commission, approached Costigan and requested that his company abandon the project. Costigan refused, arguing that the Commission had not allocated his company any work in over 18 months. Scopo carried Costigan's message back to the Commission and the Commission decided to permit plaintiff to work on the project. Costigan subsequently gave Scopo a $50,000 "gift" for speaking favorably on plaintiff's behalf to the Commission.

The record indicates that defendant negotiated the contract with full knowledge of the Club and its rules. Plaintiff completed the work agreed upon under the contract and, upon defendant's refusal to pay, commenced this action. [The Supreme Court dismissed the complaint, and certain counterclaims; the Appellate Division modified the judgment to the extent of reinstating the complaint, and in certain other respects.]

The interposition of antitrust defenses in contract actions is not favored (see Kelly v. Kosuga, 358 U.S. 516, 518, 3 L.Ed.2d 475, 79 S.Ct. 429). The concern is that "successful interposition of antitrust defenses is too likely to enrich parties who reap the benefits of a contract and then seek to avoid the corresponding burdens" (Viacom International, Inc. v. Tandem, 526 F.2d 593, 599). Nevertheless, antitrust defenses will be upheld in cases where a court's judgment would result in enforcement of the "precise conduct made unlawful by the Act" (Kelly v. Kosuga, 358 U.S. 516, 520, 3 L.Ed.2d 475, 79 S.Ct. 429 ...). Beyond that point, however, "courts are to be guided by the overriding general policy ... 'of preventing people from getting other people's property for nothing when they purport to be buying it' " (id. at 520–521 [quoting Continental Wall Paper Co. v. Louis Voight & Sons Co., 212 U.S. 227, 271, 53 L.Ed. 486, 29 S.Ct. 280] [Holmes, J., dissenting]). Thus, a contract which is legal on its face and does not call for unlawful conduct in its performance is not voidable simply because it resulted from an antitrust conspiracy (see, *Kelly,* supra; ...; but see *Continental Wall Paper,* supra ...).

This Court has held that the Donnelly Act, having been modelled on the Federal Sherman Act of 1890, "should generally be construed in light of Federal precedent and given a different interpretation only where State policy, differences in the statutory language or the legislative history justify such a result" (see People v. Rattenni, 81 N.Y.2d 166, 171, 597 N.Y.S.2d 280, 613 N.E.2d 155 [quoting Anheuser–Busch, Inc. v.

quirements contract for Manhattan, and subsidies for a concrete plant at the foot of West 57th Street.

Abrams, 71 N.Y.2d 327, 335, 525 N.Y.S.2d 816, 520 N.E.2d 535]).
Indeed, courts which have considered interposition of antitrust defenses
in contract actions have followed the rule and rationale of *Kelly* (supra)
(see, e.g., . . .; Columbia Broadcasting System, Inc. v. Roskin Distributors, Inc., 31 A.D.2d 22, 25, 294 N.Y.S.2d 804, affd in part, dismissed in
part 28 N.Y.2d 559, 319 N.Y.S.2d 449, 268 N.E.2d 128 [Sherman and
Clayton Acts "may not be pleaded in defense of an action for goods sold
and delivered or services rendered"]).

    . . . [T]he critical question is whether the contract is so integrally
related to the agreement, arrangement or combination in restraint of
competition that its enforcement would result in compelling performance
of the precise conduct made unlawful by the antitrust laws (id. at 520).
This question we cannot answer on the record before us. Whether the
contract was an indivisible, effectuating component of an illegal arrangement that would be consummated by granting the judgment sought in
this action is a question that requires further development at trial.

    The extent to which the contract price is excessive and discriminato-
ry and fails to reflect fair market value at the contract date because of an
unlawful attempt to stifle competition is an important issue requiring
development. The unlawful use of market power to inflate the contract
price, and the resulting anti-competitive effects, must be assessed in
determining whether granting the judgment sought "would be to make
the courts a party to the carrying out of one of the very restraints
forbidden by the [antitrust laws]" (*Kelly*, 358 U.S., at 520, 79 S.Ct., at
432, . . .).

    Additionally, the equities of the parties must be examined. Courts
should avoid upholding antitrust defenses in contract cases where doing
so would work a substantial forfeiture on one party while unjustly
enriching the other (see *Kelly* . . .; see also Comment, The Defense of
Antitrust Illegality in Contract Actions, 27 U.Chi.L.R. 758, 768–769 [the
strongest fear held by courts in contract actions involving antitrust
illegality defenses is the possibility of forfeiture and unjust enrich-
ment]). A relevant consideration is whether sustaining the illegality
defense would render the contract void in its entirety or whether
recovery could still be had on a quantum meruit basis. Additionally, the
relative culpability, bargaining power, and knowledge of the parties to
the contract should also be considered in assessing the possibility of
unjust enrichment.

    Finally, the public policy in favor of frustrating or discouraging
unlawful schemes such as the Club must not be deprecated. However,
such a danger is reduced where statutory remedies exist and the State
Attorney General can directly attack the alleged antitrust violations.

    In light of our analysis, the Court rejects defendant's remaining
contention that the contract should be held per se illegal under the
Donnelly Act. . . .

    Order affirmed, with costs, and certified question answered in the
affirmative.

NOTES

(1) *Statutory Remedies.* The Attorney General of New York State filed a brief, as amicus curiae, opposing the result in this case. Among the forms of relief available to the Attorney General for antitrust violations are injunctions and prosecutions. Treble damages and other recoveries may be awarded to an entity that is injured, whether public or private. (The statute does not restrict the right of "workingmen to combine.")

(2) *Questions.* Were the parties *in pari delicto?* Did the court decide that further findings in the trial court might warrant a recovery for unjust enrichment, but not of the balance due under the contract? That they might warrant a recovery in excess of the defendant's enrichment?

(3) *Case Comparisons.* In Jered Contr. Corp. v. New York City Trans. Auth., 239 N.E.2d 197 (N.Y.1968), the court ruled that a public authority need pay nothing for painting services it had received under a contract if it could show that, as the authority later learned, the painting firm had procured the contract by fraudulent and collusive bidding practices. The same court has indicated, moreover, that the firm could have been required to refund any payments it had received for the work. (The case might be different, however, if the authority had received goods under the contract that it could return.) See S.T. Grand, Inc. v. City of New York, 298 N.E.2d 105 (N.Y.1973). Does the court's opinion in *X.L.O. Concrete* cast doubt on the views it expressed in the earlier cases?

What accounts for the fact that the court did not cite its decision in McConnell v. Commonwealth Pictures Corp., above? Is it that the plaintiff's infraction of the Donnelly Act did not contravene "fundamental concepts of morality and fair dealing"? Is it that the Rivergate Corporation "negotiated the contract with full knowledge of the Club and its rules"? What is the best way to distinguish the cases?

CLEAN HANDS

Courts of equity exhibit a special sense of delicacy when confronted with unsavory claims and claimants. Suits for equitable remedies such as specific performance and rescission are sometimes disposed of on the colorful maxim, "He who comes into equity must come with clean hands." Consider how this principle might have applied to the case in Note 3, p. 477 above, if Liebman had sought a constructive trust or another equitable remedy.

Is there a difference between the thought of the maxim and the thought that a court of equity should avoid sullying *its* hands? In North Pacific Lumber Co. v. Oliver, 596 P.2d 931 (Or.1979), the court said that the clean-hands doctrine "is designed to protect the court's integrity by permitting it to avoid sullying its hands with the enforcement of a corrupt bargain"—not to punish or reward a party. The court also said: "Even equity does not require saintliness. Perhaps more importantly, the misconduct must bear a certain kind of relationship to the subject matter of the suit before a court will consider it."

NOTES

(1) *Problem.* In the case last cited the company, a wholesaler, relied on its employees to spy on one another by unlawful monitoring of telephone calls. It also profited by settlement practices that deceived its suppliers and its customers. As an employee, Oliver had shared knowingly in the profits and had conducted some spying. When he resigned to work for another firm the company sued to enforce a covenant he had made not to compete with it. Was the company eligible for injunctive relief?

(2) *Shades of Cleanliness.* The sellers of a business committed a "serious offense" through attempting to conceal a feature of the sale from the tax authorities. Agents of the buyer, purporting to have expertness in taxation, advised the sellers that a full statement of the transaction would jeopardize certain lawful tax advantages. The chairman of the buyer's board assured the sellers that the board members—"honorable men"—would agree to rescission if the tax advantages did not materialize. When this assurance was not honored, the sellers sued to recover the property they had sold. On an appeal from a judgment in their favor, *held;* Affirmed. West Los Angeles Institute for Cancer Research v. Mayer, 366 F.2d 220 (9th Cir.1966), cert. denied, 385 U.S. 1010 (1967). The plaintiffs' motive, the court said, was not to circumvent the tax laws, but to exclude "an extraneous fact which might improperly influence the [Internal Revenue Service]. The parties were not in pari delicto. The agents [of the buyer] stood in a superior position. They were the active parties.... And the forfeiture ... if relief were denied would be extreme."

(3) *Question:* Does it appear from the foregoing cases that the clean-hands maxim is shaped by the same factors that affect courts of "law" in dealing with illegal agreements? (As to the relevance of the maxim in a law action, see Gratreak v. North Pacific Lumber Co., 609 P.2d 375 (Or.App.1980).)

Chapter 5

REMEDIES FOR BREACH

SECTION 1. MEASURING EXPECTATION

We have already seen that the usual goal of the law of contract remedies is to give the injured party relief based on that party's expectation interest, as measured by the net gain that it would have enjoyed had the contract been performed. This is commonly done by awarding a sum of damages that will, to the extent that money can, put the injured party in the position in which it would have been had the promise been performed.

In principle, the expectation interest is that of the injured party itself, quite without regard to that of a hypothetical reasonable person, and depends on its own particular circumstances or those of its enterprise. Where the injured party's expected advantage consists largely or exclusively of the realization of profit, as is the case for most commercially significant exchanges, the expectation interest can be expressed in money with some assurance. A breach may affect the injured party in four ways.

First, it may cause the injured party a loss by depriving that party, at least to some extent, of the expected return performance. The difference between the value to the injured party of the performance that should have been received and the value to that party of what, if anything, actually was received is the injured party's *loss in value*.[a]

Second, the breach may cause the injured party loss other than *loss in value*, such as physical harm to that party's person or property or expenses incurred in an attempt to salvage the transaction after breach. This residual category is injured party's *other loss*.

A breach may result in *loss in value* and in *other loss* regardless of whether the injured party chooses to continue performing or to stop performing and treat the contract as terminated. If the injured party chooses to treat the contract as terminated, the breach may affect that party in a third and fourth way.

Third, then, the breach may have a beneficial effect on the injured party by saving that party further expense that would have been

a. But see Clydebank Engineering & Shipbuilding Co. v. Yzquierdo y Castaneda, [1905] A.C. 6, 13 (House of Lords 1904) (contention that if warships had been delivered to Spanish government on time they would have been sunk with rest of Spanish armada was "utterly absurd").

incurred had performance continued. This saving is the injured party's *cost avoided*.

Fourth, the breach may have a further beneficial effect on the injured party by allowing that party to avoid some loss by salvaging and reallocating some or all of the resources that otherwise it would have had to devote to performance of the contract. The saving that results is the injured party's *loss avoided*.[b]

The general measure of damages is then the sum of these two positive and two negative components, which gives Formula A.

(A) *damages = loss in value + other loss − cost avoided − loss avoided*

Since, in most agreements, one of the parties (here called the "recipient") is required to pay money, the estimation of *loss in value* and *cost avoided* usually poses problems only in connection with the performance of the other party (here called the "supplier"), who may be required, for example, to furnish goods, land, or services in return. Where the supplier is the injured party, and the breach consists of the recipient's promise to pay, the difficulty lies in the determination of the supplier's *cost avoided*, since its *loss in value* is simply the amount of money that the recipient has failed to pay. Where the recipient is the injured party, and the supplier is in breach, the difficulty lies in the determination of the recipient's *loss in value*, since its *cost avoided* is simply the amount of money that it has not yet paid.

The building contract cases afford a simple illustration. Suppose that Builder contracts with Owner to construct a factory on Owner's land for $1,000,000 payable on completion. If the recipient (Owner) is the party in breach and the supplier (Builder) has used the breach to excuse further performance, the controversy will center on the *cost avoided* by Builder in not having to complete construction of the factory. The *loss in value* to Builder will be simply the amount remaining unpaid. If, for example, Builder can show that it would have cost $400,000 more to complete the job, recovery under Formula A (ignoring *other loss* and *loss avoided*) would be $1,000,000 less $400,000 or $600,000. Builder will often calculate *cost avoided* by determining the cost already incurred in reliance on the contract. Assuming that this sum is $500,000, the *cost of complete performance* would be the total of the *cost of reliance* and the *cost avoided*, that is $500,000 plus $400,000, or $900,000. In other words:

cost avoided = cost of complete performance − cost of reliance.

Substituting the right hand side of this equation for *cost avoided* in Formula A, and remembering that the difference between *loss in value*

b. It may help in understanding the distinction between *cost avoided* and *loss avoided* to imagine a contract for the sale of two widgets to be manufactured by the seller. Suppose that the buyer repudiates after the seller has already manufactured one of the widgets. The saving that results when the seller stops production of the second widget is the seller's *cost avoided*. The saving that results when the seller sells the first widget to another buyer is the seller's *loss avoided*.

and *cost of complete performance* is Builder's expected *profit,* we get Formula B as the equivalent of Formula A.[c]

(B) *damages = cost of reliance + profit − loss avoided + other loss*

In the illustration given, Builder's recovery under Formula B (ignoring *other loss* and *loss avoided*) would be $500,000 plus $100,000 or $600,-000, just as under Formula A. How should items of overhead be treated under either Formula A or Formula B?

NOTES

(1) *More on the Lost Life.* In the case described in Note 3, p. 425 above, the court affirmed a judgment for $7,500 with this explanation. "The fact that damages are difficult to ascertain and measure does not diminish the loss to the person whose property has been destroyed. Indeed, the very statement of the rule suggests the opposite. If one's destroyed property has a market value, presumably its equivalent is available on the market and the owner can acquire that equivalent property. However, if the owner cannot acquire the property in the market or by replacement or reproduction, then he simply cannot be made whole.

"The problem is to establish the value to the owner. Market and replacement values are relatively ascertainable by appropriate proof. Recognizing that value to the owner encompasses a subjective element, the rule has been established that compensation for sentimental or fanciful values will not be allowed.... That restriction was placed upon the jury in this case by the court's damages instruction.

"What is sentimental value? The broad dictionary definition is that sentimental refers to being 'governed by feeling, sensibility or emotional idealism....' Webster's Third New International Dictionary (1963). Obviously that is not the exclusion contemplated by the statement that sentimental value is not to be compensated. If it were, no one would recover for the wrongful death of a spouse or a child. Rather, the type of sentiment which is not compensable is that which relates to 'indulging in feeling to an unwarranted extent' or being 'affectedly or mawkishly emotional ...' Webster's Third New International Dictionary (1963).

"Under these rules, the court's damages instruction was correct. In essence it allowed recovery for the actual or intrinsic value to the plaintiffs but denied recovery for any unusual sentimental value of the film to the plaintiffs or a fanciful price which plaintiffs, for their own special reasons, might place thereon." [d]

(2) *The Economics of Remedies (Reprise).* In the earlier discussion of the economics of remedies, at p. 20 above, we considered a buyer's remedies for breach of contract in the event that the seller received a better offer from another prospective buyer. Much the same analysis applies to the buyer's remedies in the event that the seller discovers that it will cost more to produce the goods.

---

c. For the sake of simplicity, it is assumed that Builder has not received any payment from Owner. If Builder has, the amount of the payment must be subtracted in applying Formula B.

d. Oenophiles will want to consult Bowes v. Fox–Stanley Photo Products, 379 So.2d 844 (La.App.1980).

Suppose that a seller, believing that it can produce a custom-made widget for $90, contracts to sell the widget for $100 to a buyer that values the widget at $110. The seller later discovers that it will cost $120 to produce the widget, so that performance will result in a loss of $20 ($120 − $100). If, as under Formula A, the buyers damages are $10 ($110 − $100), it will be in the seller's interest to refuse to perform, pay the buyer the $10 as damages, and save $10 of the $20 loss that would result from performance.

SULLIVAN v. O'CONNOR

Supreme Judicial Court of Massachusetts, 1973.
363 Mass. 579, 296 N.E.2d 183.

[For the report of this case, see p. 7 above.]

NOTES

(1) *Questions.* How would Sullivan's expectation interest be calculated under Formula A? If she had been allowed to recover her expectation interest, which elements would have been most difficult to prove? See generally Cooter & Eisenberg, Damages for Breach of Contract, 73 Calif.L.Rev. 1432, 1434–44 (1985).

(2) *Efficient Reliance.* We have already considered (at p. 20 above) the impact of the damage measure on efficient breach of contract. For an argument that the expectation measure, though efficient in inducing breach, may be inefficient in inducing reliance, see A. Polinsky, An Introduction to Law and Economics 34–37 (2d ed. 1989).

VITEX MANUFACTURING CORP. v. CARIBTEX CORP.

United States Court of Appeals, Third Circuit, 1967.
377 F.2d 795.

STALEY, CHIEF JUDGE. This is an appeal by Caribtex Corporation from a judgment of the District Court of the Virgin Islands finding Caribtex in breach of a contract entered into with Vitex Manufacturing Company, Ltd., and awarding $21,114 plus interest to Vitex for loss of profits. The only substantial question raised by Caribtex is whether it was error for the district court, sitting without a jury, not to consider overhead as part of Vitex's costs in determining the amount of profits lost. We conclude that under the facts presented, the district court was not compelled to consider Vitex's overhead costs, and we will affirm the judgment.

Before discussing the details of the controversy between the parties, it will be helpful to briefly describe the peculiar legal setting in which this suit arose. At the time of the events in question, there were high tariff barriers to the importation of foreign wool products. However, under § 301 of the Tariff Act of 1930, 19 U.S.C.A. § 1301a, repealed but the provision continued under Revised Tariff Schedules, 19 U.S.C.A. § 1202, note 3(a)(i)(ii) (1965), if such goods were imported into the

Virgin Islands and were processed in some manner so that their finished value exceeded their importation value by at least 50%, then the high tariffs to importation into the continental United States would be avoided. Even after the processing, the foreign wool enjoyed a price advantage over domestic products so that the business flourished. However, to keep the volume of this business at such levels that Congress would not be stirred to change the law, the Virgin Islands Legislature imposed "quotas" on persons engaging in processing, limiting their output. 33 V.I.C. § 504 (Supp.1966).

Vitex was engaged in the business of chemically shower-proofing imported cloth so that it could be imported duty-free into the United States. For this purpose, Vitex maintained a plant in the Virgin Islands and was entitled to process a specific quantity of material under the Virgin Islands quota system. Caribtex was in the business of importing cloth into the islands, securing its processing, and exporting it to the United States.

In the fall of 1963, Vitex found itself with an unused portion of its quota but no customers, and Vitex closed its plant. Caribtex acquired some Italian wool and subsequently negotiations for a processing contract were conducted between the principals of the respective companies in New York City. Though the record below is clouded with differing versions of the negotiations and the alleged final terms, the trial court found upon substantial evidence in the record that the parties did enter into a contract in which Vitex agreed to process 125,000 yards of Caribtex's woolen material at a price of 26 [25?] cents per yard.

Vitex proceeded to re-open its Virgin Islands plant, ordered the necessary chemicals, recalled its work force and made all the necessary preparations to perform its end of the bargain. However, no goods were forthcoming from Caribtex, despite repeated demands by Vitex, apparently because Caribtex was unsure that the processed wool would be entitled to duty-free treatment by the customs officials. Vitex subsequently brought this suit to recover the profits lost through Caribtex's breach.

Vitex alleged, and the trial court found, that its gross profits for processing said material under the contract would have been $31,250 and that its costs would have been $10,136, leaving Vitex's damages for loss of profits at $21,114. On appeal, Caribtex asserted numerous objections to the detailed computation of lost profits. While the record below is sometimes confusing, we conclude that the trial court had substantial evidence to support its findings on damages. It must be remembered that the difficulty in exactly ascertaining Vitex's costs is due to Caribtex's wrongful conduct in repudiating the contract before performance by Vitex. Caribtex will not be permitted to benefit by the uncertainty it has caused. Thus, since there was a sufficient basis in the record to support the trial court's determination of substantial damages, we will not set aside its judgment. Stentor Elec. Mfg. Co. v. Klaxon Co., 115 F.2d 268 (C.A.3, 1940), rev'd other grounds 313 U.S. 487, 61 S.Ct.

1020, 85 L.Ed. 1477 (1941); 5 Williston, Contracts § 1345 (rev. ed. 1937).

Caribtex first raised the issue at the oral argument of this appeal that the trial court erred by disregarding Vitex's overhead expenses in determining lost profits. In general, overhead "... may be said to include broadly the continuous expenses of the business, irrespective of the outlay on a particular contract." Grand Trunk W.R.R. Co. v. H.W. Nelson Co., 116 F.2d 823, 839 (C.A.6, 1941). Such expenses would include executive and clerical salaries, property taxes, general administration expenses, etc.[1] Although Vitex did not expressly seek recovery for overhead, if a portion of these fixed expenses should be allocated as costs to the Caribtex contract, then under the judgment of the district court Vitex tacitly recovered these expenses as part of its damages for lost profits, and the damages should be reduced accordingly. Presumably, the portion to be allocated to costs would be a pro rata share of Vitex's annual overhead according to the volume of business Vitex would have done over the year if Caribtex had not breached the contract.

Although there is authority to the contrary, we feel that the better view is that normally, in a claim for lost profits, overhead should be treated as a part of gross profits and recoverable as damages, and should not be considered as part of the seller's costs. A number of cases hold that since overhead expenses are not affected by the performance of the particular contract, there should be no need to deduct them in computing lost profits. E.g., Oakland California Towel Co. v. Sivils, 52 Cal. App.2d 517, 520, 126 P.2d 651, 652 (1942); Jessup & Moore Paper Co. v. Bryant Paper Co., 297 Pa. 483, 147 A. 519, 524 (1929); Annot., 3 A.L.R.3d 689 (1965) (collecting cases on both sides of the controversy). The theory of these cases is that the seller is entitled to recover losses incurred and gains prevented in excess of savings made possible, Restatement, Contracts § 329 (made part of the law of the Virgin Islands, 1 V.I.C. § 4); since overhead is fixed and nonperformance of the contract produced no overhead cost savings, no deduction from profits should result.

The soundness of the rule is exemplified by this case. Before negotiations began between Vitex and Caribtex, Vitex had reached a lull in business activity and had closed its plant. If Vitex had entered into no other contracts for the rest of the year, the profitability of its operations would have been determined by deducting its production costs and overhead from gross receipts yielded in previous transactions. When this opportunity arose to process Caribtex's wool, the only additional expenses Vitex would incur would be those of re-opening its plant and the direct costs of processing, such as labor, chemicals and fuel oil. Overhead would have remained the same whether or not Vitex and Caribtex entered their contract and whether or not Vitex actually processed Caribtex's goods. Since this overhead remained constant, in

---

1. Caribtex could not be referring to overhead expenses as including labor costs and the like, because the trial judge did charge as costs all the expenses directly associated with the reactivation of Vitex's plant, and the actual processing of Caribtex's goods according to the terms of the contract.

no way attributable-to or affected-by the Caribtex contract, it would be improper to consider it as a cost of Vitex's performance to be deducted from the gross proceeds of the Caribtex contract.

However, Caribtex may argue that this view ignores modern accounting principles, and that overhead is as much a cost of production as other expenses. It is true that successful businessmen must set their prices at sufficient levels to recoup all their expenses, including overhead, and to gain profits. Thus, the price the businessman should charge on each transaction could be thought of as that price necessary to yield a pro rata portion of the company's fixed overhead, the direct costs associated with production, and a "clear" profit. Doubtless this type of calculation is used by businessmen and their accountants. Pacific Portland Cement Co. v. Food Mach. & Chem. Corp., 178 F.2d 541 (C.A.9, 1949). However, because it is useful for planning purposes to allocate a portion of overhead to each transaction, it does not follow that this allocate share of fixed overhead should be considered a cost factor in the computation of lost profits on individual transactions.

First, it must be recognized that the pro rata allocation of overhead costs is only an analytical construct. In a similar manner one could allocate a pro rata share of the company's advertising cost, taxes and/or charitable gifts. The point is that while these items all are paid from the proceeds of the business, they do not normally bear such a direct relationship to any individual transaction to be considered a cost in ascertaining lost profits.

Secondly, even were we to recognize the allocation of overhead as proper in this case, we should uphold the tacit award of overhead expense to Vitex as a "loss incurred." Conditioned Air Corp. v. Rock Island Motor Transit Co., 253 Iowa 961, 114 N.W.2d 304, 3 A.L.R.3d 679, cert. denied, 371 U.S. 825, 83 S.Ct. 46, 9 L.Ed.2d 64 (1962). By the very nature of this allocation process, as the number of transactions over which overhead can be spread becomes smaller, each transaction must bear a greater portion or allocate share of the fixed overhead cost. Suppose a company has fixed overhead of $10,000 and engages in five similar transactions; then the receipts of each transaction would bear $2000 of overhead expense. If the company is now forced to spread this $10,000 over only four transactions, then the overhead expense per transaction will rise to $2500, significantly reducing the profitability of the four remaining transactions. Thus, where the contract is between businessmen familiar with commercial practices, as here, the breaching party should reasonably foresee that his breach will not only cause a loss of "clear" profit, but also a loss in that the profitability of other transactions will be reduced. Resolute Ins. Co. v. Percy Jones, Inc., 198 F.2d 309 (C.A.10, 1952); Cf. In re Kellett Aircraft Corp., 191 F.2d 231 (C.A.3, 1951). Therefore, this loss is within the contemplation of "losses caused and gains prevented," and overhead should be considered to a compensable item of damage.

Significantly, the Uniform Commercial Code, adopted in the Virgin Islands, 11A V.I.C. § 1–101 et seq., and in virtually every state today, provides for the recovery of overhead in circumstances similar to those presented here. Under 11A V.I.C. § 2–708, the seller's measure of damage for non-acceptance or repudiation is the difference between the contract price and the market price, but if this relief is inadequate to put the seller in as good position as if the contract had been fully performed, "... then the measure of damages is the *profit (including reasonable overhead)* which the seller would have made from full performance by the buyer...." 11A V.I.C. § 2–708(2). (Emphasis added.) While this contract is not controlled by the Code, the Code is persuasive here because it embodies the foremost modern legal thought concerning commercial transactions. Indeed, it may overrule some of the cases denying recovery for overhead. E.g., Wilhelm Lubrication Co. v. Brattrud, 197 Minn. 626, 632, 268 N.W. 634, 636, 106 A.L.R. 1279 (1936).

Caribtex also argued that the contract should not be enforced because it was unconscionable. While Vitex was to make a large profit on the processing and Caribtex did bear the risk of failure to meet customs standards, the contract was freely entered-into, after much negotiation, between parties of apparently equal bargaining strength. This was not a contract of adhesion—Vitex was not the only processor in the Virgin Islands and Caribtex's bargaining strength was evidenced by the successive and substantial price reductions it wrested from Vitex during the negotiations. Compare, Campbell Soup Co. v. Wentz, 172 F.2d 80 (C.A.3, 1948); Henningsen v. Bloomfield Motors, Inc., 32 N.J. 358, 161 A.2d 69, 75 A.L.R.2d 1 (1960).

The judgment of the district court will be affirmed.

NOTE

Overhead. Vitex's *loss on the bargain* was the difference between *loss in value* and *cost avoided* (see Formula A). Did the trial court include "overhead" costs in *cost avoided?* Should it have? Or, from a different perspective, Vitex's *loss on the bargain* was the sum of *cost of reliance* and *profit* (see Formula B). Did the trial court include "overhead" costs in *cost of reliance* and in *profit?* Should it have?

LAREDO HIDES CO., INC. v. H & H MEAT PRODUCTS CO., INC.

Court of Civil Appeals of Texas, 1974.
513 S.W.2d 210.

BISSETT, JUSTICE. This is a breach of contract case. Laredo Hides Company, Inc., the buyer, sued H & H Meat Products Company, Inc., the seller, to recover damages for breach of a written contract for the sale of cattle hides. Trial was to the court without a jury. A take nothing judgment in favor of defendant was rendered. Plaintiff has appealed.

The controlling facts of the case are undisputed. H & H Meat Products Company, Inc. (H & H) is a meat processing and packing corporation, located in Mercedes, Texas. It sells cattle hides as a by-product of its business. Laredo Hides Company, Inc. (Laredo Hides) is a corporation, located in Laredo, Texas. It purchases cattle hides from various meat packers in the United States and ships them to tanneries in Mexico.

A written contract dated February 29, 1972, was executed whereby Laredo Hides agreed to buy H & H's entire cattle hide production during the period March through December, 1972.... [After two deliveries of hides, a $9,000 check sent by Laredo Hides to H & H in payment for the second shipment was delayed in the mail. Before it arrived, H & H gave Laredo Hides an ultimatum demanding payment within a few hours. When the demand was not met, H & H notified Laredo Hides on March 30, 1972, that H & H regarded this as a breach justifying cancellation of the contract and that it would deliver no more hides. In an omitted part of the opinion, the court held that H & H's precipitous action was unjustified, that its refusal to deliver more hides was itself a breach by repudiation of the contract that relieved Laredo Hides of tendering performance during the remaining months of the contract, and that the trial court's disposition of the case was error.]

why?

Laredo Hides, on March 3, 1972, had contracted with a Mexican tannery for the sale of all the hides which it expected to purchase from H & H under the February 29, 1972, contract. Following the cancellation by H & H of the contract, Laredo Hides, in order to meet the requirements of its contract with the tannery, was forced to purchase hides on the open market in substitution for the hides which were to have been delivered to it under the contract with H & H.

H & H's total production during the months April through December, 1972, was 17,218 hides. Under the contract with H & H, the price was $9.75 per hide for bull, steer and heifer hides, and $9.75 per hide for cow hides if the shipment was under 5% cow hides. In the event the shipment was more than 5% cow hides, the price on the excess of cow hides over 5% was reduced to $7.50 per cow hide. The market price for hides steadily increased following the execution of the contract in question. By December 31, 1972, the average cost of bull hides was about $33.00 each and the average cost of cow, heifer and steer hides was about $22.00 each. The total additional cost to Laredo Hides of purchasing substitute hides from other suppliers was $142,254.48. The additional costs (transportation and handling charges) to Laredo Hides which resulted because of the purchases from third parties amounted to $3,448.95....

Since this case must be reversed, we now confront the issue of damages. The guidelines for determining a buyer's remedies in a case where there is a breach of a contract for the sale of goods by a seller are found in Chapter 2 of the Texas Business and Commerce Code. Among other remedies afforded by the Code, when there is a repudiation of the contract by the seller or a failure to make delivery of the goods under contract, the buyer may cover under § 2.711. He may have damages under § 2.712 "by making in good faith and without unreasonable delay any reasonable purchase of or contract to purchase goods in substitution for those due from the seller", and "may recover from the seller as damages the difference between the cost of cover and the contract price together with any incidental or consequential damages" provided by the chapter; or, he may, under § 2.713, have damages measured by "the difference between the market price at the time when the buyer learned of the breach and the contract price together with any incidental and consequential damages" provided by the chapter.

Laredo Hides instituted suit in May, 1972, and filed its amended petition (its trial pleading) on October 24, 1972, when performance was still due by H & H under the contract. It prayed for specific performance, or in the alternative "... damages at least in the amount of one hundred thousand dollars ($100,000), the same being the damages proximately caused by defendant's breach of the contract ..." There was never a trial amendment of this petition. There were no exceptions by H & H to Laredo Hides' pleadings. Trial commenced on February 28, 1973, was recessed on March 2, 1973, resumed on May 15, 1973, and ended May 16, 1973. Judgment was signed and rendered on August 6, 1973.

Laredo Hides offered uncontroverted evidence of the hide production of H & H from April to December, 1972. It also established the price for the same number of hides which it was forced to buy elsewhere. There was testimony that purchases had to be made periodically throughout 1972 since Laredo Hides had no storage facilities, and the hides would decompose if allowed to age. Furthermore, White, a C.P.A., testified as to statistical summaries which he made showing the cost of buying substitute hides. These summaries were made from invoices which are also in evidence. All of this evidence was admitted without objection. Clearly, Laredo Hides elected to pursue the remedy provided by § 2.712 of the Code, and by its pleadings and evidence brought itself within the purview of the "cover" provisions contained therein.

It is not necessary under § 2.712 that the buyer establish market price. Duesenberg and King, Sales and Bulk Transfers under the U.C.C. § 14.04 Matthew Bender (1974). Where the buyer complies with the requirements of § 2.712, his purchase is presumed proper and the burden of proof is on the seller to show that "cover" was not properly obtained. Spies, Sales, Performance and Remedies, 44 Tex.L.Rev. 629, 638 (1966). There was no evidence offered by H & H to negate this presumption or to "establish expenses saved in consequence of the seller's breach", as permitted by § 2.712.

The difference between the cover price and the contract price is shown to be $134,252.82 for steer hides and $8,001.66 for bull hides, or a total of $142,254.48. In addition, Laredo Hides offered evidence of increased transportation costs of $1,435.77, and increased handling charges of $2,013.18. These are clearly recoverable as incidental damages where the buyer elects to "cover". §§ 2.715(a); 2.712(b)....

There is no evidence that Laredo Hides, in any manner, endeavored to increase its damages sustained when H & H refused to deliver any more hides to it. Laredo Hides, in purchasing the hides in substitution of the hides which should have been delivered under the contract, acted promptly and in a reasonable manner. The facts of this case regarding the issue of liability of H & H and the issues pertaining to damages suffered by Laredo Hides, have been fully and completely developed in the court below. The facts upon which judgment should have been rendered for Laredo Hides by the trial court are conclusively established. It, therefore, becomes the duty of this Court to render judgment which the trial court should have rendered. . . .

Applying the rules announced by the above cited cases and authorities to the instant case, we hold that the record does not support the findings of fact made by the trial judge and there is no legal justification for the conclusion of law reached by the court. Accordingly, the judgment of the trial court is reversed, and judgment is here rendered for Laredo Hides in the amount of $152,960.04, together with interest thereon at the rate of 6% per annum from August 6, 1973, the date judgment was rendered by the trial court, until paid.

Reversed and rendered.

NOTES

(1) *Substitute Transactions.* Often, following breach, the injured party arranges a substitute transaction and claims damages based on that transaction rather than on one of the damage formulas set out earlier. Laredo Hides did this by arranging substitute purchases of hides and basing its damages on the cover price in those transactions under UCC 2–712. The rule on cover in UCC 2–712 is a Code innovation. It has no antecedent in prior law. Had this case arisen before the Code, Laredo Hides would have had to prove damages based on the difference between market price and contract price under the common law rule which in Texas was the antecedent of UCC 2–713. What disadvantages would that have had for Laredo Hides? See Note 3, p. 27 above.

(2) *What Is Cover?* Note that although Laredo Hides' contract with H & H was for a term of ten months, its substitute purchases were on the "spot" market. What statutory language justified the court in treating these purchases as cover? What result if the hides purchased on the spot market had been of a better quality than those that H & H had contracted to supply? Would it make a difference if other hides of the quality contracted for were available on the spot market?[a] Recall the discussion (in Note 3, p. 27 above) of Klein's purchase of a G–III jet. If Laredo Hides had been denied recovery under UCC 2–712, to what relief would it have been entitled?[b]

(3) *Supplier as Injured Party.* If the seller is the injured party, the Code accords a similar remedy of reselling the goods and basing damages on the resale price in that transaction under UCC 2–706. The use of a substitute transaction as the basis of a claim for damages is not, however, confined to suppliers of

---

a. See Handicapped Children's Education Board v. Lukaszewski, 332 N.W.2d 774 (Wis.1983) (school board's damages based on higher salary it paid to hire replacement teacher with greater experience where no other qualified person applied); see also Cives Corp. v. Callier Steel Pipe & Tube, Inc., 482 A.2d 852 (Me.1984) (steel tube buyer's own manufacture of tubes using more expensive steel was "cover" where

"thorough search for an alternative supplier" failed).

b. See Martella v. Woods, 715 F.2d 410 (8th Cir.1983) (heifer buyer's purchase of better heifers was not "cover" and buyer's damages were governed by UCC 2–713); see also McGinnis v. Wentworth Chevrolet Co., 668 P.2d 365 (Or.1983) (car buyer's rental of car was not "cover" and buyer's damages were governed by UCC 2–713).

goods. If an employee is fired in breach of a contract and does other work as a result of being freed from that contract, the employee's damages are based on the salary that would have been earned under the broken contract less that earned by doing the other work. In State ex rel. Schilling v. Baird, 222 N.W.2d 666 (Wis.1974), Schilling, a deputy sheriff who was wrongfully suspended, argued that he was not required to deduct his earnings from other work because they were not made between midnight and eight in the morning, the shift to which he was assigned as a deputy. "With this conclusion the Court cannot agree. It lends itself to an almost absurd result. Under this interpretation all Schilling had to do was to refrain from getting a third shift job and could then earn as much as he wanted or was fortunate enough to earn and would not be required to deduct any of it." [c]

(4) *What Is a Substitute?* As the case in the preceding note suggests, it is sometimes no simple matter to decide whether another comparable opportunity accepted by the injured party after breach should be treated as a "substitute" in calculating damages. Often a seller or other supplier claims that a subsequent transaction *was not* a substitute in order to have not only the benefit of that transaction but also damages based on profits lost on the original transaction.

This claim will not succeed in the case of an injured party who was to supply personal services under a contract of full-time employment. Other employment taken after breach is viewed as a substitute transaction since "No one can serve two masters" and the employee could not have taken advantage of the second opportunity had not the first contract been broken. But an injured party who was to supply services that are not personal, under a contract for construction of a building for example, is regarded differently. In this situation, another comparable opportunity is not ordinarily viewed as a substitute. Rather, it is assumed that the contractor could have expanded its business to undertake additional jobs so that the breach of the original contract resulted in "lost volume" that could not be recaptured by a second similar contract. On this assumption, the second contract is not a substitute for the first and the amount earned on the second contract should not be subtracted in calculating the damages for breach of the first. The materials that follow explore the borderline of this distinction.

(5) *Problem.* Star Paving subcontracted with Drennan to do for $15,000 the paving required under Drennan's contract to build a school for the Lancaster School District. Drennan wrongfully ordered Star to stop work at a time when it would have cost Star $5,000 to complete it. Star at once made a contract with the Lancaster School District to do the same work to finish the job at a price of $7,000. Star demands $10,000 ($15,000 minus $5,000) from Drennan. Drennan offers to pay $8,000 ($15,000 minus $7,000). Who is right? See Olds v. Mapes–Reeve Construction Co., 58 N.E. 478 (Mass.1900). Would it make a difference if some of the terms of the second contract (e.g., on liability in the event of breach) were significantly different from those of the first?

R.E. DAVIS CHEMICAL CORP. v. DIASONICS, INC.
United States Court of Appeals, Seventh Circuit, 1987.
826 F.2d 678.

CUDAHY, CIRCUIT JUDGE. Diasonics, Inc. appeals from the orders of the district court denying its motion for summary judgment and grant-

[c]. Courts have divided over whether an employee must deduct sums received from a "collateral source," such as unemployment compensation and similar benefits. See 3 Farnsworth § 12.9 n. 9.

ing R.E. Davis Chemical Corp.'s summary judgment motion. Diasonics also appeals from the order dismissing its third-party complaint against Dr. Glen D. Dobbin and Dr. Galdino Valvassori. We affirm the dismissal of the third-party complaint, reverse the grant of summary judgment in favor of Davis and remand for further proceedings.

I.

Diasonics is a California corporation engaged in the business of manufacturing and selling medical diagnostic equipment. Davis is an Illinois corporation that contracted to purchase a piece of medical diagnostic equipment from Diasonics. On or about February 23, 1984, Davis and Diasonics entered into a written contract under which Davis agreed to purchase the equipment. Pursuant to this agreement, Davis paid Diasonics a $300,000 deposit on February 29, 1984. Prior to entering into its agreement with Diasonics, Davis had contracted with Dobbin and Valvassori to establish a medical facility where the equipment was to be used. Dobbin and Valvassori subsequently breached their contract with Davis. Davis then breached its contract with Diasonics; it refused to take delivery of the equipment or to pay the balance due under the agreement. Diasonics later resold the equipment to a third party for the same price at which it was to be sold to Davis.

Davis sued Diasonics, asking for restitution of its $300,000 down payment under section 2–718(2) of the Uniform Commercial Code (the "UCC" or the "Code"). . . . Diasonics counterclaimed. Diasonics did not deny that Davis was entitled to recover its $300,000 deposit less $500 as provided in section 2–718(2)(b). However, Diasonics claimed that it was entitled to an offset under section 2–718(3). Diasonics alleged that it was a "lost volume seller," and, as such, it lost the profit from one sale when Davis breached its contract. Diasonics' position was that, in order to be put in as good a position as it would have been in had Davis performed, it was entitled to recover its lost profit on its contract with Davis under section 2–708(2) of the UCC. . . .

Diasonics subsequently filed a third-party complaint against Dobbin and Valvassori, alleging that they tortiously interfered with its contract with Davis. Diasonics claimed that the doctors knew of the contract between Davis and Diasonics and also knew that, if they breached their contract with Davis, Davis would have no use for the equipment it had agreed to buy from Diasonics.

The district court dismissed Diasonics' third-party complaint for failure to state a claim upon which relief could be granted, finding that the complaint did not allege that the doctors intended to induce Davis to breach its contract with Diasonics. The court also entered summary judgment for Davis. The court held that lost volume sellers were not entitled to recover damages under 2–708(2) but rather were limited to recovering the difference between the resale price and the contract price along with incidental damages under section 2–706(1). . . . . Davis was awarded $322,656, which represented Davis' down payment plus pre-judgment interest less Diasonics' incidental damages. Diasonics appeals the district court's decision respecting its measure of damages as well as the dismissal of its third-party complaint.

II.

We consider first Diasonics' claim that the district court erred in holding that Diasonics was limited to the measure of damages provided in 2–706 and could not recover lost profits as a lost volume seller under 2–708(2). Surprisingly, given its importance, this issue has never been addressed by an Illinois court, nor, apparently, by any other court construing Illinois law. Thus, we must attempt to predict how the Illinois Supreme Court would resolve this issue if it were presented to it. Courts applying the laws of other states have unanimously adopted the position that a lost volume seller can recover its lost profits under 2–708(2). Contrary to the result reached by the district court, we conclude that the Illinois Supreme Court would follow these other cases and would allow a lost volume seller to recover its lost profit under 2–708(2).

We begin our analysis with 2–718(2) and (3). Under 2–718(2)(b), Davis is entitled to the return of its down payment less $500. Davis' right to restitution, however, is qualified under 2–718(3)(a) to the extent that Diasonics can establish a right to recover damages under any other provision of Article 2 of the UCC. Article 2 contains four provisions that concern the recovery of a seller's general damages (as opposed to its incidental or consequential damages): 2–706 (contract price less resale price); 2–708(1) (contract price less market price); 2–708(2) (profit); and 2–709 (price). The problem we face here is determining whether Diasonics' damages should be measured under 2–706 or 2–708(2). To answer this question, we need to engage in a detailed look at the language and structure of these various damage provisions.

The Code does not provide a great deal of guidance as to when a particular damage remedy is appropriate. The damage remedies provided under the Code are catalogued in section 2–703, but this section does not indicate that there is any hierarchy among the remedies. One method of approaching the damage sections is to conclude that 2–708 is relegated to a role inferior to that of 2–706 and 2–709 and that one can turn to 2–708 only after one has concluded that neither 2–706 nor 2–709 is applicable.[1] Under this interpretation of the relationship between 2–

---

1. Evidence to support this approach can be found in the language of the various damage sections and of the official comments to the UCC. See § 2–709(3) ("a seller who is held not entitled to the price under this Section shall nevertheless be awarded damages for non-acceptance under the preceding section [§ 2–708]"); UCC comment 7 to § 2–709 ("[i]f the action for the price fails, the seller may nonetheless have proved a case entitling him to damages for non-acceptance [under § 2–708]"); UCC comment 2 to § 2–706 ("[f]ailure to act properly under this section deprives the seller of the measure of damages here provided and relegates him to that provided in Section 2–708"); UCC comment 1 to § 2–704 (describes § 2–706 as the "primary remedy" available to a seller upon breach by the buyer); see also Commonwealth Edison Co. v. Decker Coal Co., 653 F.Supp. 841, 844 (N.D.Ill.1987) (statutory language and case law suggest that "§ 2–708 remedies are available only to a seller who is not entitled to the contract price" under § 2–709); Childres & Burgess, Seller's Reme-

706 and 2–708, if the goods have been resold, the seller can sue to recover damages measured by the difference between the contract price and the resale price under 2–706. The seller can turn to 2–708 only if it resells in a commercially unreasonable manner or if it cannot resell but an action for the price is inappropriate under 2–709. The district court adopted this reading of the Code's damage remedies and, accordingly, limited Diasonics to the measure of damages provided in 2–706 because it resold the equipment in a commercially reasonable manner.

The district court's interpretation of 2–706 and 2–708, however, creates its own problems of statutory construction. There is some suggestion in the Code that the "fact that plaintiff resold the goods [in a commercially reasonable manner] does *not* compel him to use the resale remedy of § 2–706 rather than the damage remedy of § 2–708." Harris, A Radical Restatement of the Law of Seller's Damages: Sales Act and Commercial Code Results Compared, 18 Stan.L.Rev. 66, 101 n. 174 (1965) (emphasis in original). Official comment 1 to 2–703, which catalogues the remedies available to a seller, states that these "remedies are essentially cumulative in nature" and that "[w]hether the pursuit of one remedy bars another depends entirely on the facts of the individual case." See also State of New York, Report of the Law Revision Comm'n for 1956, 396–97 (1956).[2]

Those courts that found that a lost volume seller can recover its lost profits under 2–708(2) implicitly rejected the position adopted by the district court; those courts started with the assumption that 2–708 applied to a lost volume seller without considering whether the seller was limited to the remedy provided under 2–706. None of those courts even suggested that a seller who resold goods in a commercially reasonable manner was limited to the damage formula provided under 2–706. We conclude that the Illinois Supreme Court, if presented with this

dies: The Primacy of UCC 2–708(2), 48 N.Y.U.L.Rev. 833, 863–64 (1973). As one commentator has noted, 2–706

> is the Code section drafted specifically to define the damage rights of aggrieved reselling sellers, and there is no suggestion within it that the profit formula of section 2–708(2) is in any way intended to qualify or be superior to it.

Shanker, The Case for a Literal Reading of UCC Section 2–708(2) (One Profit for the Reseller), 24 Case W.Res. 697, 699 (1973).

2. UCC comment 2 to 2–708(2) also suggests that 2–708 has broader applicability than suggested by the district court. UCC comment 2 provides:

> This section permits the recovery of lost profits in all appropriate cases, which would include all standard priced goods. The normal measure there would be list price less cost to the dealer or list price less cost to the dealer or list price less manufacturing cost to the manufacturer.

The district court's restrictive interpretation of 2–708(2) was based in part on UCC comment 1 to 2–704 which describes 2–706 as the aggrieved seller's primary remedy. The district court concluded that, if a lost volume seller could recover its lost profit under 2–708(2), every seller would attempt to recover damages under 2–708(2) and 2–706 would become the aggrieved seller's residuary remedy. This argument ignores the fact that to recover under 2–708(2), a seller must first establish its status as a lost volume seller. . . .

The district court also concluded that a lost volume seller cannot recover its lost profit under 2–708(2) because such a result would negate a seller's duty to mitigate damages. This position fails to recognize the fact that, by definition, a lost volume seller cannot mitigate damages through resale. Resale does not reduce a lost volume seller's damages because the breach has still resulted in its losing one sale and a corresponding profit. See Autonumerics, 144 Ariz. at 192, 696 P.2d at 1341.

question, would adopt the position of these other jurisdictions and would conclude that a reselling seller, such as Diasonics, is free to reject the damage formula prescribed in 2–706 and choose to proceed under 2–708.

Concluding that Diasonics is entitled to seek damages under 2–708, however, does not automatically result in Diasonics being awarded its lost profit. Two different measures of damages are provided in 2–708. Subsection 2–708(1) provides for a measure of damages calculated by subtracting the market price at the time and place for tender from the contract price.[3] The profit measure of damages, for which Diasonics is asking, is contained in 2–708(2). However, one applies 2–708(2) only if "the measure of damages provided in subsection (1) is inadequate to put the seller in as good a position as performance would have done...."
... Diasonics claims that 2–708(1) does not provide an adequate measure of damages when the seller is a lost volume seller.[4] To understand Diasonics' argument, we need to define the concept of the lost volume seller. Those cases that have addressed this issue have defined a lost volume seller as one that has a predictable and finite number of customers and that has the capacity either to sell to all new buyers or to make the one additional sale represented by the resale after the breach. According to a number of courts and commentators, if the seller would have made the sale represented by the resale whether or not the breach occurred, damages measured by the difference between the contract price and market price cannot put the lost volume seller in as good a position as it would have been in had the buyer performed.[5] The breach effectively cost the seller a "profit," and the seller can only be made whole by awarding it damages in the amount of its "lost profit" under 2–708(2).

We agree with Diasonics' position that, under some circumstances, the measure of damages provided under 2–708(1) will not put a reselling seller in as good a position as it would have been in had the buyer performed because the breach resulted in the seller losing sales volume. However, we disagree with the definition of "lost volume seller" adopted by other courts. Courts awarding lost profits to a lost volume seller have focused on whether the seller had the capacity to supply the breached units in addition to what it actually sold. In reality, however,

---

3. There is some debate in the commentaries about whether a seller who has resold the goods may ignore the measure of damages provided in 2–706 and elect to proceed under 2–708(1). Under some circumstances the contract-market price differential will result in overcompensating such a seller. See J. White & R. Summers, Handbook of the Law under the Uniform Commercial Code § 7–7, at 271–73 (2d ed. 1980); Sebert, Remedies under Article Two of the Uniform Commercial Code: An Agenda for Review, 130 U.Pa.L.Rev. 360, 380–83 (1981). We need not struggle with this question here because Diasonics has not sought to recover damages under 2–708(1).

4. This is also the position adopted by those courts that have held that a lost volume seller can recover its lost profits under 2–708(2)....

5. According to one commentator,

Resale results in loss of volume only if three conditions are met: (1) the person who bought the resold entity would have been solicited by plaintiff had there been no breach and resale; (2) the solicitation would have been successful; and (3) the plaintiff could have performed that additional contract.

Harris, supra, at 82 (footnotes omitted).

the relevant questions include, not only whether the seller could have produced the breached units in addition to its actual volume, but also whether it would have been profitable for the seller to produce both units. Goetz & Scott, Measuring Sellers' Damages: The Lost–Profits Puzzle, 31 Stan.L.Rev. 323, 332–33, 346–47 (1979). As one commentator has noted, under

> the economic law of diminishing returns or increasing marginal costs[,] ... as a seller's volume increases, then a point will inevitably be reached where the cost of selling each additional item diminishes the incremental return to the seller and eventually makes it entirely unprofitable to conclude the next sale.

Shanker, supra n. 1, at 705. Thus, under some conditions, awarding a lost volume seller its presumed lost profit will result in overcompensating the seller, and 2–708(2) would not take effect because the damage formula provided in 2–708(1) does place the seller in as good a position as if the buyer had performed. Therefore, on remand, Diasonics must establish, not only that it had the capacity to produce the breached unit in addition to the unit resold, but also that it would have been profitable for it to have produced and sold both. Diasonics carries the burden of establishing these facts because the burden of proof is generally on the party claiming injury to establish the amount of its damages; especially in a case such as this, the plaintiff has easiest access to the relevant data....[6]

One final problem with awarding a lost volume seller its lost profits was raised by the district court. This problem stems from the formulation of the measure of damages provided under 2–708(2) which is "the profit (including reasonable overhead) which the seller would have made from full performance by the buyer, together with any incidental damages provided in this Article (Section 2–710), due allowance for costs reasonably incurred and due credit for payments or *proceeds of resale*." ... (emphasis added). The literal language of 2–708(2) requires that the proceeds from resale be credited against the amount of damages awarded which, in most cases, would result in the seller recovering nominal damages. In those cases in which the lost volume seller was awarded its lost profit as damages, the courts have circumvented this problem by concluding that this language only applies to proceeds realized from the resale of uncompleted goods for scrap. See, e.g., Neri [v. Retail Marine Corp., 30 N.Y.2d 393, 399 & n. 2, 334 N.Y.S.2d 165, 169 & n. 2, 285 N.E.2d 311, 314 & n. 2 (1972)]; *see also* J. White & R. Summers, Handbook of the Law under the Uniform Commercial Code § 7–13, at 285 ("courts should simply ignore the 'due credit' language in lost volume cases") (footnote omitted). Although neither the text of 2–708(2) nor the official comments limit its application to resale of goods for scrap, there is evidence that the drafters of 2–708 seemed to have had this more limited application in mind when they proposed amending 2–

---

6. As some commentators have pointed out, the cost of calculating a loss of profit may be very high. Goetz & Scott, supra, at 353 ("the complexity of the lost-volume problem suggests that the information costs of exposing an overcompensatory rule are relatively high").

708 to include the phrase "due credit for payments or proceeds of resale."[7] We conclude that the Illinois Supreme Court would adopt this more restrictive interpretation of this phrase rendering it inapplicable to this case.

We therefore reverse the grant of summary judgment in favor of Davis and remand with instructions that the district court calculate Diasonics' damages under 2–708(2) if Diasonics can establish, not only that it had the capacity to make the sale to Davis as well as the sale to the resale buyer, but also that it would have been profitable for it to make both sales. Of course, Diasonics, in addition, must show that it probably would have made the second sale absent the breach.

[In an omitted part of the opinion, the court went on to uphold dismissal of the third-party complaint.]

NOTES

(1) *Appeal after Remand.* On remand, after a three-day bench trial, the district judge concluded that Diasonics had adequately established damages for lost profits amounting to $453,050 and entered judgment for that sum less the $300,000 deposit retained by Diasonics. On appeal by Davis, the Court of Appeals upheld this conclusion as not clearly erroneous. "The evidence is undisputed that Diasonics possessed the capacity to manufacture one more MRI. Diasonics also demonstrated that it was ... 'beating the bushes for all possible sales.' ... Diasonics was still a young company struggling to acquire business in an extremely competitive market.... The mere fact that Diasonics was unable to specify the particular unit Davis contracted to buy and trace the exact resale buyer for that unit ... should not foreclose it from recovering lost profits." R.E. Davis Chemical Corp. v. Diasonics, Inc., 924 F.2d 709, 711–12 (7th Cir.1991).

(2) *Lost Volume.* Many hundreds of pages of economic analysis have been devoted to the subject of sellers' claims of lost volume resulting from buyers' breaches. Two helpful articles are Cooter & Eisenberg, Damages for Breach of Contract, 73 Calif.L.Rev. 1432, 1444–77 (1985); Goldberg, An Economic Analysis of the Lost–Volume Retail Seller, 57 So.Cal.L.Rev. 283 (1984).

In practice, the outcome may turn on who has the burden of proof on the issue of lost volume. Courts have generally placed the burden of proof on the seller. Famous Knitwear Corp. v. Drug Fair, Inc., 493 F.2d 251 (4th Cir.1974). But in Islamic Republic of Iran v. Boeing Co., 771 F.2d 1279 (9th Cir.1985), cert. dismissed, 479 U.S. 957 (1986), the court rejected the argument that to take advantage of UCC 2–708(2) a seller must prove that the market is one "in which supply exceeds demand." "We will not ... impose rigid and complex burdens of proof on this section.... Most other jurisdictions have held that to qualify as a 'lost volume' seller under section 2–708(2), the seller needs to show only that it *could have* supplied both the breaching purchaser and the resale purchaser."

---

7. In explaining its recommendation that 2–708 be amended to include the requirement that due credit be given for resale, the Enlarged Editorial Board stated that its purpose was "to clarify the privilege of the seller to realize junk value when it is manifestly useless to complete the operation of manufacture." Supplement No. 1 to the 1952 Official Draft (1955), quoted in Harris, supra, at 98.

LOSING CONTRACTS

Suppose that in the simple example given at the beginning of the chapter (p. 484 above) Owner can show that it would have cost Builder $600,000 more to have completed the job. The contract was then a losing contract, on which it would have cost Builder $500,000 plus $600,000, or $1,100,000, to do work for which he would have been paid only $1,000,000, for a loss of $100,000. Using either Formula A or Formula B, Builder's damages come to only $400,000, or $100,000 less than the $500,000 cost already incurred in reliance on the contract. Should this be the limit of Builder's recovery?

NOTES

(1) *The Hard Line.* For a case applying Formula A in such a situation, see Millen v. Gulesian, 118 N.E. 267 (Mass.1918). For a defense of expectation-based recovery in such cases, see Mather, Restitution as a Remedy for Breach of Contract: The Case of the Partially Performing Seller, 92 Yale L.J. 14 (1982).

(2) *Burden of Proof.* Consider the following as a possible solution. "In cases where the venture would have proved profitable to the promisee, there is no reason why he should not recover his expenses. On the other hand, on those occasions in which the performance would not have covered the promisee's outlay, such a result imposes the risk of the promisee's contract upon the promisor. We cannot agree that the promisor's default in performance should under this guise make him an insurer of the promisee's venture; yet it does not follow that the breach should not throw upon him the duty of showing that the value of the performance would in fact have been less than the promisee's outlay. It is often very hard to learn what the value of the performance would have been; and it is a common expedient, and a just one, in such situations to put the peril of the answer upon that party who by his wrong has made the issue relevant to the rights of the other. On principle therefore the proper solution would seem to be that the promisee may recover his outlay in preparation for the performance, subject to the privilege of the promisor to reduce it by as much as he can show that the promisee would have lost, if the contract had been performed." Learned Hand in L. Albert & Son v. Armstrong Rubber Co., 178 F.2d 182, 189 (2d Cir.1949).

The case just quoted from involved material delay by a seller of machines to be used by the buyer to reclaim old rubber during World War II. The buyer did not ask for loss of profits when the delay caused this speculative venture to fall through, but did claim expenses in reliance on the seller's promise to deliver on time, including the cost of laying foundations for the machines. It was this claim to which Hand spoke. Note that in the example of Builder and Owner the profit in question was profit to be made from the transaction between the parties, while here the profit in question was profit to be made from *other* transactions which were to be made possible by the one between the parties. Similarly, in the preceding cases the reliance in question was reliance in performing or at least in preparing to perform in the transaction between the parties, while here the reliance was in preparing to perform in *other* transactions which were to be made possible by this transaction. Should this make a difference?

(3) *Problem.* Buyer made a $5,000 payment on a contract for the sale of flour for a total price of $14,000. Seller broke the contract by failing to deliver the flour, although the market price of the flour had dropped to $11,000 by the

time of delivery. Is Buyer entitled to restitution of $5,000 from Seller? See Bush v. Canfield, 2 Conn. 485 (1818).

UNITED STATES v. ALGERNON BLAIR, INC.

United States Court of Appeals, Fourth Circuit, 1973.
479 F.2d 638.

CRAVEN, CIRCUIT JUDGE. May a subcontractor, who justifiably ceases work under a contract because of the prime contractor's breach, recover in quantum meruit the value of labor and equipment already furnished pursuant to the contract irrespective of whether he would have been entitled to recover in a suit on the contract? We think so, and, for reasons to be stated, the decision of the district court will be reversed.

The subcontractor, Coastal Steel Erectors, Inc., brought this action under the provisions of the Miller Act, 40 U.S.C.A. § 270a et seq., in the name of the United States against Algernon Blair, Inc., and its surety, United States Fidelity and Guaranty Company. Blair had entered a contract with the United States for the construction of a naval hospital in Charleston County, South Carolina. Blair had then contracted with Coastal to perform certain steel erection and supply certain equipment in conjunction with Blair's contract with the United States. Coastal commenced performance of its obligations, supplying its own cranes for handling and placing steel. Blair refused to pay for crane rental, maintaining that it was not obligated to do so under the subcontract. Because of Blair's failure to make payments for crane rental, and after completion of approximately 28 percent of the subcontract, Coastal terminated its performance. Blair then proceeded to complete the job with a new subcontractor. Coastal brought this action to recover for labor and equipment furnished.

The district court found that the subcontract required Blair to pay for crane use and that Blair's refusal to do so was such a material breach as to justify Coastal's terminating performance. This finding is not questioned on appeal. The court then found that under the contract the amount due Coastal, less what had already been paid, totaled approximately $37,000. Additionally, the court found Coastal would have lost more than $37,000 if it had completed performance. Holding that any amount due Coastal must be reduced by any loss it would have incurred by complete performance of the contract, the court denied recovery to Coastal. While the district court correctly stated the " 'normal' rule of contract damages," we think Coastal is entitled to recover in quantum meruit.

In United States for Use of Susi Contracting Co. v. Zara Contracting Co., 146 F.2d 606 (2d Cir.1944), a Miller Act action, the court was faced with a situation similar to that involved here—the prime contractor had unjustifiably breached a subcontract after partial performance by the subcontractor. The court stated:

> For it is an accepted principle of contract law, often applied in the case of construction contracts, that the promisee upon breach has the option to forego any suit on the contract and claim only the reasonable value of his performance.

146 F.2d at 610.... Quantum meruit recovery is not limited to an action against the prime contractor but may also be brought against the Miller Act surety, as in this case. Further, that the complaint is not clear in regard to the theory of a plaintiff's recovery does not preclude recovery under quantum meruit. Narragansett Improvement Co. v. United States, 290 F.2d 577 (1st Cir.1961). A plaintiff may join a claim for quantum meruit with a claim for damages from breach of contract.

In the present case, Coastal has, at its own expense, provided Blair with labor and the use of equipment. Blair, who breached the subcontract, has retained these benefits without having fully paid for them. On these facts, Coastal is entitled to restitution in quantum meruit.

> The "restitution interest," involving a combination of unjust impoverishment with unjust gain, presents the strongest case for relief. If, following Aristotle, we regard the purpose of justice as the maintenance of an equilibrium of goods among members of society, the restitution interest presents twice as strong a claim to judicial intervention as the reliance interest, since if A not only causes B to lose one unit but appropriates that unit to himself, the resulting discrepancy between A and B is not one unit but two.

Fuller & Perdue, The Reliance Interest in Contract Damages, 46 Yale L.J. 52, 56 (1936).

The impact of quantum meruit is to allow a promisee to recover the value of services he gave to the defendant irrespective of whether he would have lost money on the contract and been unable to recover in a suit on the contract. Scaduto v. Orlando, 381 F.2d 587, 595 (2d Cir.1967). The measure of recovery for quantum meruit is the reasonable value of the performance, Restatement of Contracts § 347 (1932); and recovery is undiminished by any loss which would have been incurred by complete performance. 12 Williston on Contracts § 1485, at 312 (3d ed. 1970). While the contract price may be evidence of reasonable value of the services, it does not measure the value of the performance or limit recovery. Rather, the standard for measuring the reasonable value of the services rendered is the amount for which such services could have been purchased from one in the plaintiff's position at the time and place the services were rendered.

Since the district court has not yet accurately determined the reasonable value of the labor and equipment use furnished by Coastal to Blair, the case must be remanded for those findings.[1] When the amount has been determined, judgment will be entered in favor of Coastal, less

---

1. Under the view of the case taken by the district court it was unnecessary to precisely appraise the value of services and materials rendered; an approximation was thought to suffice because the hypothetical loss had the contract been fully performed was greater in amount.

payments already made under the contract. Accordingly, for the reasons stated above, the decision of the district court is

Reversed and remanded with instructions.

NOTES

(1) *Measure of Restitution Interest.* What recovery for Builder under the losing contract according to *Algernon Blair?* What is the court's justification for measuring Coastal's restitution interest by "the reasonable value of the performance"? Is this a proper measure of the "benefits" that Blair "retained without having fully paid for"? How does it differ from Coastal's reliance interest? See Restatement Second § 371. The conclusion that "the property owner is enriched by each stroke of the hammer or the paint brush" is characterized as "Pickwickian" in Patterson, The Scope of Restitution and Unjust Enrichment, 1 Mo.L.Rev. 223, 230 (1936).[a]

Reconsider *Snepp* (Note 3, p. 6 above). Under *Algernon Blair,* could the United States have required Snepp to disgorge his royalties on a breach of contract theory, without any fiduciary relationship?

(2) *Contract Price as a Ceiling.* An injured party who has fully performed and then been refused payment can not recover more than the contract price. Should an injured party who has not fully performed be allowed to recover "the reasonable value of the performance" even if it exceeds the contract price? Using the contract price as a ceiling on recovery in such a case will not entirely avoid problems of measurement of the benefit conferred on the party in breach, since that benefit must, at least in principle, be measured before it can be known whether the ceiling has been reached. On the other hand, not using the contract price as a ceiling on recovery may result in a more generous recovery for part performance than would have been allowed for full performance.

For authority that the contract price is a ceiling, see Johnson v. Bovee, 574 P.2d 513 (Colo.App.1978). For authority that it is not, see Southern Painting Co. v. United States, 222 F.2d 431 (10th Cir.1955).

(3) *A Pro Rata Result.* In Kehoe v. Rutherford, 27 A. 912 (N.J.L.1893), a contractor was to grade a street for a municipality for 65 cents per running foot or $2,743 for the entire 4,220 feet. When the municipality defaulted, the contractor sued and proved that the cost of reliance had been $3,153 and that his cost avoided was $1,891, giving a cost of complete performance of $5,044. The court held that the contractor was entitled to such a proportion of $2,743 as $3,153 bears to $5,044, or $1,715. Since he had already been paid $1,850 he could recover nothing.

What result in the example of Builder's losing contract under *Kehoe?* (*Kehoe* has not gained much of a following.) Is this result justifiable?

(4) *The Case of the Royalty Restored.* Bausch & Lomb ("B & L") paid Sonomed $500,000 as a nonrefundable "prepaid royalty" under an Agreement that gave B & L exclusive distributorship rights for approximately five years to certain ophthalmic diagnostic instruments. After several years, a dispute arose

---

a. For a case allowing recovery for expenditures prior to the making of the contract, see Anglia Television Ltd. v. Reed, 3 All.E.R. 690 (Court of Appeal 1971). When an actor repudiated his contract to play the lead role for a studio, the studio abandoned the film and sued for expenditures including those incurred before contracting with him. Lord Denning explained that this sum was recoverable since "it was such as would reasonably be in the contemplation of the parties as likely to be wasted if the contract was broken." Can such recovery be justified?

and B & L sued Sonomed for breach of contract. The trial court found that Sonomed had broken the contract by selling in B & L's territory, but denied B & L's claims for lost profits on these sales because B & L offered no evidence linking the sales to profits lost by B & L. But the trial court awarded B & L $500,000, the amount of the "prepaid royalty." On Sonomed's appeal, *held,* reversed and remanded. If the $500,000 was awarded as expectation damages, the trial court erred because there was "simply no evidence connecting this $500,000 to any profit that B & L would have received had Sonomed fully performed." If the $500,000 was awarded as reliance damages, the trial court also erred because it "did not address the 'losing contract' limitation upon awards of reliance damages"—there having been support for Sonomed's contention "that the Agreement was a losing contract for B & L, entitling Sonomed to an offset of all or part of the $500,000 payment under a reliance theory." (The court cited L. Albert & Son v. Armstrong Rubber Co., discussed in Note 2, p ___ above.) But B & L might "be entitled to a damage award by way of restitution, a remedies doctrine not addressed by the district court." Although the Agreement made the $500,000 nonrefundable, its terms "do not control an award of restitution." But B & L was not entitled to the entire $500,000 because the Agreement had been partially performed and B & L's "several years of distribution rights constitute a benefit the value of which must be offset against the $500,000 paid." Since "the contract may provide probative evidence of the value of the benefit," it might be appropriate for the trial court to pro-rate the $500,000 over the approximately five years the Agreement was to run. Bausch & Lomb Inc. v. Bressler, 977 F.2d 720 (2d Cir.1992).

(5) *Problem.* Security Stove in Kansas City had developed a furnace which it was anxious to exhibit at a trade association convention in Atlantic City, although it was not yet on the market. Since it was too late to ship it by freight, Security Stove made a contract for its shipment with Express Company, explaining its need, asking that it be shipped to arrive by October 8, and reminding Express Company of the urgency shortly before the date for shipment. Express Company picked up the shipment of 21 numbered packages, but the package containing the gas manifold, the most important part of the exhibit, was mislaid and did not arrive until the convention closed. Security Stove sues to recover from Express Company for express charges to Atlantic City, freight charges back to Kansas City, travel and hotel expenses and salaries for its employees who went to the convention to exhibit the furnace, and rental for the booth. What decision? See Security Stove & Mfg. Co. v. American Ry. Express Co., 51 S.W.2d 572 (Mo.App.1932).

SECTION 2. LIMITATIONS ON DAMAGES

(a) Avoidability

In Virtue v. Bird, 84 Eng.Rep. 1000, 86 Eng.Rep. 200 (King's Bench 1678), a quaint case from three centuries ago, the plaintiff contracted to carry goods to Ipswich and to deliver them to a place to be appointed by the defendant. When the plaintiff arrived in Ipswich, however, "the defendant delayed by the space of six hours the appointment of the place; insomuch that his horses being so hot . . . and standing in aperto aere, they died soon after." The court denied him recovery of this loss on the ground that "it was the plaintiff's folly to let the horses stand," for he "might have taken his horses out of the cart, or have laid down the [goods] any where in Ipswich." Although it is sometimes said that in such cases the injured party is under a "duty" to mitigate damages, the injured party incurs no liability to the party in breach for a failure to mitigate. Recovery is the same regardless of whether the injured party takes steps in mitigation or not. The injured party is simply precluded from recovering for loss that it could reasonably have avoided. See Restatement Second § 350.

ROCKINGHAM COUNTY v. LUTEN BRIDGE CO.

United States Circuit Court of Appeals, Fourth Circuit, 1929.
35 F.2d 301, 66 A.L.R. 735.

[Action at law, instituted in the district court, to recover an amount alleged to be due under a contract for the construction of a bridge in North Carolina. The contract was entered into by the Board of County Commissioners on January 7, 1924; but there was considerable public opposition to the building of the bridge, and on February 21, 1924, the board notified the plaintiff not to proceed any further under the contract, which it refused (unjustifiably, as the court found) to recognize as valid.[a] At that time plaintiff had expended about $1900 for labor done and material on the ground. Despite this notice from the county commissioners, plaintiff continued to build the bridge in accordance with the terms of the contract. The present action is brought to recover $18,301.07, the amount alleged to be due plaintiff for work done before November 3, 1924. The trial court directed a verdict for plaintiff for this sum. Defendant appealed.]

PARKER, CIRCUIT JUDGE. . . . Coming, then, to the third question—i.e., as to the measure of plaintiff's recovery—we do not think that, after the county had given notice, while the contract was still executory, that it did not desire the bridge built and would not pay for it, plaintiff could proceed to build it and recover the contract price. It is true that the

---

a. The vote of the commissioners had been three to two in favor of the contract, but on February 11 one of the commissioners who had voted in favor sent his resignation to the clerk, who immediately accepted it. Later the same day this commissioner attempted to withdraw his resignation, but the clerk ignored this and appointed another person to succeed him. The three commissioners who had voted in favor attended no further meetings, but the new commissioner together with the two who had voted against met frequently and, on February 21, unanimously adopted a resolution asserting that the contract was not valid and directing the clerk to so notify Luten, which he did. On April 7, the board passed a resolution reciting that it had been informed that one of its members was privately insisting that the bridge be built and repudiating this action by the member. In September it passed a resolution stating that it would pay no bills for the bridge.

county had no right to rescind the contract, and the notice given plaintiff amounted to a breach on its part; but, after plaintiff had received notice of the breach, it was its duty to do nothing to increase the damages flowing therefrom. If A enters into a binding contract to build a house for B, B, of course, has no right to rescind the contract without A's consent. But if, before the house is built, he decides that he does not want it, and notifies A to that effect, A has no right to proceed with the building and thus pile up damages. His remedy is to treat the contract as broken when he receives the notice, and sue for the recovery of such damages as he may have sustained from the breach, including any profit which he would have realized upon performance, as well as any other losses which may have resulted to him. In the case at bar, the county decided not to build the road of which the bridge was to be a part, and did not build it. The bridge, built in the midst of the forest, is of no value to the county because of this change of circumstances. When, therefore, the county gave notice to the plaintiff that it would not proceed with the project, plaintiff should have desisted from further work. It had no right thus to pile up damages by proceeding with the erection of a useless bridge.

The contrary view was expressed by Lord Cockburn in Frost v. Knight, L.R. 7 Ex. 111, but, as pointed out by Prof. Williston (Williston on Contracts, vol. 3, p. 2347), it is not in harmony with the decisions in this country. The American rule and the reasons supporting it are well stated by Prof. Williston as follows:

"There is a line of cases running back to 1845 which holds that, after an absolute repudiation or refusal to perform by one party to a contract, the other party cannot continue to perform and recover damages based on full performance. This rule is only a particular application of the general rule of damages that a plaintiff cannot hold a defendant liable for damages which need not have been incurred; or, as it is often stated, the plaintiff must, so far as he can without loss to himself, mitigate the damages caused by the defendant's wrongful act. The application of this rule to the matter in question is obvious. If a man engages to have work done, and afterwards repudiates his contract before the work has been begun or when it has been only partially done, it is inflicting damage on the defendant without benefit to the plaintiff to allow the latter to insist on proceeding with the contract. The work may be useless to the defendant, and yet he would be forced to pay the full contract price. On the other hand, the plaintiff is interested only in the profit he will make out of the contract. If he receives this it is equally advantageous for him to use his time otherwise." ...

Judgment reversed.

NOTE

The Code. Under UCC 2–704(2), a seller who is to manufacture goods may proceed to complete their manufacture upon the buyer's repudiation, instead of halting manufacture and salvaging them while in process, "in the exercise of reasonable commercial judgment for the purposes of avoiding loss and of effective realization." The seller who does so may then base recovery on the goods as completed, even if the "reasonable commercial judgment" turned out to be wrong. Is the manufacturer's situation in any way distinguishable from that of the Luten Bridge Co.?

Introductory Note to Shirley MacLaine's Case

It is one thing to say that the injured party cannot recover for cost that could have been avoided by simply stopping performance. It is another to say that the injured party cannot recover for loss that could have been avoided by taking affirmative steps to arrange a substitute transaction. In Gandell v. Pontigny, 171 Eng.Rep. 119 (1816), the court refused to take this second step. A merchant was sued by his clerk, whom he had wrongfully discharged in the middle of a quarter. The clerk was allowed to recover the agreed compensation for the entire quarter, including the part when he had not worked, on Lord Ellenborough's reasoning that:

> Having served a part of the quarter and being willing to serve the residue, in contemplation of law he may be considered to have served the whole.

In Howard v. Daly, 61 N.Y. 362 (1875), a leading American case, Dwight [a] rejected this doctrine of "constructive service" as

> so wholly irreconcilable to that great and beneficent rule of law, that a person discharged from service must not remain idle, but must accept employment elsewhere if offered, that we cannot accept it.... The doctrine of "constructive service" is not only at war with principle but with the rules of political economy, as it encourages idleness and gives compensation to men who fold their arms and decline service, equal to those who perform with willing hands their stipulated amount of labor.

The case that follows is premised on that rejection.

PARKER v. TWENTIETH CENTURY–FOX FILM CORP.
Supreme Court of California, 1970.
3 Cal.3d 176, 474 P.2d 689.

Burke, Justice. Defendant Twentieth Century–Fox Film Corporation appeals from a summary judgment granting to plaintiff the recovery

---

a. Theodore William Dwight (1822–1892) served as a professor of law at Hamilton College, and then as a professor of law and later as warden of the law school at Columbia from 1858 to 1891. His principal field was contracts. His method of teaching involved interrogation of his students on an assigned text, and it is reported that, "He could so cross-examine a dunce that the dunce would come off amazed at his own unconscious cerebration." From 1873 to 1875 he was a member of the New York Commission of Appeals, which had been created to help the Court of Appeals dispose of its backlog of undecided cases. It was said that his sixty-eight opinions were "monographs, exhausting the particular subject," and it was doubted "whether in any reports a greater amount of learning is anywhere condensed into an equal number of pages."

of agreed compensation under a written contract for her services as an actress in a motion picture. As will appear, we have concluded that the trial court correctly ruled in plaintiff's favor and that the judgment should be affirmed.

Plaintiff is well known as an actress,[a] and in the contract between plaintiff and defendant is sometimes referred to as the "Artist." Under the contract, dated August 6, 1965, plaintiff was to play the female lead in defendant's contemplated production of a motion picture entitled "Bloomer Girl." The contract provided that defendant would pay plaintiff a minimum "guaranteed compensation" of $53,571.42 per week for 14 weeks commencing May 23, 1966, for a total of $750,000. Prior to May 1966 defendant decided not to produce the picture and by a letter dated April 4, 1966, it notified plaintiff of that decision and that it would not "comply with our obligations to you under" the written contract.

By the same letter and with the professed purpose "to avoid any damage to you," defendant instead offered to employ plaintiff as the leading actress in another film tentatively entitled "Big Country, Big Man" (hereinafter, "Big Country"). The compensation offered was identical, as were 31 of the 34 numbered provisions or articles of the original contract.[1] Unlike "Bloomer Girl," however, which was to have been a musical production, "Big Country" was a dramatic "western type" movie. "Bloomer Girl" was to have been filmed in California; "Big Country" was to be produced in Australia. Also, certain terms in the proffered contract varied from those of the original.[2] Plaintiff was

---

a. Mrs. Parker may be better known to the reader under her professional name, Shirley MacLaine. The following listing from Who's Who in America (1970–1971) may be of interest in connection with the case. "Broadway plays include Me and Juliet, 1953, Pajama Game, 1954; actress movies The Trouble With Harry, 1954, Artists and Models, 1954, Around the World in 80 Days, 1955–56, Hot Spell, 1957, The Matchmaker, 1957, The Sheepman, 1957, Some Came Running, 1958 (Fgn. Press award 1959), Ask Any Girl, 1959 (Silver Bear award as best actress Internat. Berlin Film Festival 1959), Career, 1959, Can-Can, 1959, The Apartment, 1959 (best actress prize Venice Film Festival 1960); Two for the Seesaw, 1962; Irma La Douce, 1963; What A Way to Go! 1964; The Yellow Rolls Royce, 1964; John Goldfarb Please Come Home, 1965; Gambit [1966]; Woman Times Seven [1967]."

1. Among the identical provisions was the following found in the last paragraph of Article 2 of the original contract: "We [defendant] shall not be obligated to utilize your [plaintiff's] services in or in connection with the Photoplay hereunder, our sole obligation, subject to the terms and conditions of this Agreement, being to pay you the guaranteed compensation herein provided for."

2. Article 29 of the original contract specified that plaintiff approved the director already chosen for "Bloomer Girl" and that in case he failed to act as director plaintiff was to have approval rights of any substitute director. Article 31 provided that plaintiff was to have the right of approval of the "Bloomer Girl" dance director, and Article 32 gave her the right of approval of the screenplay.

Defendant's letter of April 4 to plaintiff, which contained both defendant's notice of breach of the "Bloomer Girl" contract and offer of the lead in "Big Country," eliminated or impaired each of those rights. It read in part as follows: "The terms and conditions of our offer of employment are identical to those set forth in the 'BLOOMER GIRL' Agreement, Articles 1 through 34 and Exhibit A to the Agreement, except as follows:

"1. Article 31 of said Agreement will not be included in any contract of employment regarding 'BIG COUNTRY, BIG MAN' as it is not a musical and it thus will not need a dance director.

"2. In the 'BLOOMER GIRL' agreement, in Articles 29 and 32, you were given certain director and screenplay approvals and you had preapproved certain matters.

given one week within which to accept; she did not and the offer lapsed. Plaintiff then commenced this action seeking recovery of the agreed guaranteed compensation.

The complaint sets forth two causes of action. The first is for money due under the contract; the second, based upon the same allegations as the first, is for damages resulting from defendant's breach of contract. Defendant in its answer admits the existence and validity of the contract, that plaintiff complied with all the conditions, covenants and promises and stood ready to complete the performance, and that defendant breached and "anticipatorily repudiated" the contract. It denies, however, that any money is due to plaintiff either under the contract or as a result of its breach, and pleads as an affirmative defense to both causes of action plaintiff's allegedly deliberate failure to mitigate damages, asserting that she unreasonably refused to accept its offer of the leading role in "Big Country."

Plaintiff moved for summary judgment under Code of Civil Procedure section 437c, the motion was granted, and summary judgment for $750,000 plus interest was entered in plaintiff's favor. This appeal by defendant followed. . . .

The general rule is that the measure of recovery by a wrongfully discharged employee is the amount of salary agreed upon for the period of service, less the amount which the employer affirmatively proves the employee has earned or with reasonable effort might have earned from other employment. . . . However, before projected earnings from other employment opportunities not sought or accepted by the discharged employee can be applied in mitigation, the employer must show that the other employment was comparable, or substantially similar, to that of which the employee has been deprived; the employee's rejection of or failure to seek other available employment of a different or inferior kind may not be resorted to in order to mitigate damages. . . .

In the present case defendant has raised no issue of *reasonableness of efforts* by plaintiff to obtain other employment; the sole issue is whether plaintiff's refusal of defendant's substitute offer of "Big Country" may be used in mitigation. Nor, if the "Big Country" offer was of employment different or inferior when compared with the original "Bloomer Girl" employment, is there an issue as to whether or not plaintiff acted reasonably in refusing the substitute offer. Despite defendant's arguments to the contrary, no case cited or which our research has discovered holds or suggests that reasonableness is an element of a wrongfully discharged employee's option to reject, or fail to

Since there simply is insufficient time to negotiate with you regarding your choice of director and regarding the screenplay and since you already expressed an interest in performing the role in 'BIG COUNTRY, BIG MAN,' we must exclude from our offer of employment in 'BIG COUNTRY, BIG MAN' any approval rights as are contained in said Articles 29 and 32; however, we shall consult with you respecting the di-rector to be selected to direct the photoplay and will further consult with you with respect to the screenplay and any revisions or changes therein, provided, however, that if we fail to agree . . . the decision of . . . [defendant] with respect to the selection of a director and to revisions and changes in the said screenplay shall be binding upon the parties to said agreement."

seek different or inferior employment lest the possible earnings there-from be charged against him in mitigation of damages.[3]

Applying the foregoing rules to the record in the present case, with all intendments in favor of the party opposing the summary judgment motion—here, defendant—it is clear that the trial court correctly ruled that plaintiff's failure to accept defendant's tendered substitute employment could not be applied in mitigation of damages because the offer of the "Big Country" lead was of employment both different and inferior, and that no factual dispute was presented on that issue. The mere circumstance that "Bloomer Girl" was to be a musical review calling upon plaintiff's talents as a dancer as well as an actress, and was to be produced in the City of Los Angeles, whereas "Big Country" was a straight dramatic role in a "Western Type" story taking place in an opal mine in Australia, demonstrates the difference in kind between the two employments; the female lead as a dramatic actress in a western style motion picture can by no stretch of imagination be considered the equivalent of or substantially similar to the lead in a song-and-dance production. Additionally, the substitute "Big Country" offer proposed to eliminate or impair the director and screenplay approvals accorded to plaintiff under the original "Bloomer Girl" contract (see fn. 2, ante), and thus constituted an offer of inferior employment. No expertise or judicial notice is required in order to hold that the deprivation or infringement of an employee's rights held under an original employment contract converts the available "other employment" relied upon by the employer to mitigate damages, into inferior employment which the employee need not seek or accept. (See Gonzales v. Internat. Assn. of Machinists, supra, 213 Cal.App.2d 817, 823–824, 29 Cal.Rptr. 190; and fn. 3, ante.) . . .

In view of the determination that defendant failed to present any facts showing the existence of a factual issue with respect to its sole defense—plaintiff's rejection of its substitute employment offer in mitigation of damages—we need not consider plaintiff's further contention that for various reasons, including the provisions of the original contract

---

3. Instead, in each case the reasonableness referred to was that of the *efforts* of the employee to obtain other employment that was not different or inferior; his right to reject the latter was declared as an unqualified rule of law. Thus, Gonzales v. Internat. Assn. of Machinists, supra, 213 Cal.App.2d 817, 823–824, 29 Cal.Rptr. 190, 194, holds that the trial court correctly instructed the jury that plaintiff union member, a machinist, was required to make "such *efforts* as the average [member of his union] desiring employment would make at that particular time and place" (italics added); but, further, that the court *properly rejected* defendant's *offer of proof* of the *availability of other kinds of employment* at the same or higher pay than plaintiff usually received and all outside the jurisdiction of his union, as plaintiff could not be required to accept different employment or a nonunion job.

In Harris v. Nat. Union, etc., Cooks and Stewards, supra, 116 Cal.App.2d 759, 761, 254 P.2d 673, 676, the issues were stated to be, inter alia, whether comparable employment was open to each plaintiff employee, and if so whether each plaintiff made a *reasonable effort* to secure such employment. It was held that the trial court *properly sustained an objection to an offer to prove a custom of accepting a job in a lower rank* when work in the higher rank was not available, as "The duty of mitigation of damages . . . does not require the plaintiff 'to seek or to accept other employment of a different or inferior kind.'" (p. 764[5], 254 P.2d p. 676.)

set forth in footnote 1, ante, plaintiff was excused from attempting to mitigate damages.

The judgment is affirmed.

SULLIVAN, ACTING CHIEF JUSTICE (dissenting).... Over the years the courts have employed various phrases to define the type of employment which the employee, upon his wrongful discharge, is under an obligation to accept. Thus in California alone it has been held that he must accept employment which is "substantially similar" (Lewis v. Protective Security Life Ins. Co. (1962) 208 Cal.App.2d 582, 584, 25 Cal.Rptr. 213; De La Falaise v. Gaumont–British P. Corp. (1940), 39 Cal.App.2d 461, 469, 103 P.2d 447); "comparable employment" (Erler v. Five Points Motors, Inc. (1967) 249 Cal.App.2d 560, 562, 57 Cal.Rptr. 516; Harris v. Nat. Union, etc., Cooks and Stewards (1953) 116 Cal.App.2d 759, 761, 254 P.2d 673); employment "in the same general line of the first employment" (Rotter v. Stationers Corporation (1960) 186 Cal.App.2d 170, 172, 8 Cal.Rptr. 690, 691); "equivalent to his prior position" (De Angeles v. Roos Bros., Inc. (1966) 244 Cal.App.2d 434, 443, 52 Cal.Rptr. 783); "employment in a similar capacity" (Silva v. McCoy (1968) 259 Cal.App.2d 256, 260, 66 Cal.Rptr. 364); employment which is "not ... of a different or inferior kind...." (Gonzales v. Internat. Assn. of Machinists (1963) 213 Cal. App.2d 817, 822, 29 Cal.Rptr. 190, 193.)

For reasons which are unexplained, the majority cite several of these cases yet select from among the various judicial formulations which contain one particular phrase, "Not of a different or inferior kind," with which to analyze this case. I have discovered no historical or theoretical reason to adopt this phrase, which is simply a negative restatement of the affirmative standards set out in the above cases, as the exclusive standard. Indeed, its emergence is an example of the dubious phenomenon of the law responding not to rational judicial choice or changing social conditions, but to unrecognized changes in the language of opinions or legal treatises. However, the phrase is a serviceable one and my concern is not with its use as the standard but rather with what I consider its distortion.

The relevant language excuses acceptance only of employment which is of a *different kind*.... It has never been the law that the mere existence of *differences between two jobs in the same field* is sufficient, as a matter of law, to excuse an employee wrongfully discharged from one from accepting the other in order to mitigate damages. Such an approach would effectively eliminate any obligation of an employee to attempt to minimize damage arising from a wrongful discharge. The only alternative job offer an employee would be required to accept would be an offer of his former job by his former employer.

Although the majority appear to hold that there was a difference "in kind" between the employment offered plaintiff in "Bloomer Girl" and that offered in "Big Country", an examination of the opinion makes crystal clear that the majority merely point out differences between the two *films* (an obvious circumstance) and then apodictically assert that these constitute a difference in the *kind of employment*. The entire rationale of the majority boils down to this: that the *"mere circumstances"* that "Bloomer Girl" was to be a musical review while "Big Country" was a straight drama "demonstrates the difference in kind" since a female lead in a western is not "the equivalent of or substantially similar to" a lead in a musical. This is merely attempting to prove the proposition by repeating it. It shows that the vehicles for the display of the star's talents are different but it does not prove that her employment as a star in such vehicles is of necessity different *in kind* and either inferior or superior.

I believe that the approach taken by the majority (a superficial listing of differences with no attempt to assess their significance) may subvert a valuable legal doctrine.[1] The inquiry in cases such as this should not be whether differences between the two jobs exist (there will always be differences) but whether the differences which are present are substantial enough to constitute differences in the *kind* of employment or, alternatively, whether they render the substitute work employment of an *inferior kind....*

I remain convinced that the relevant question in such cases is whether or not a particular contract provision is so significant that its omission create employment of an inferior kind. This question is, of course, intimately bound up in what I consider the ultimate issue: whether or not the employee acted reasonably. This will generally involve a factual inquiry to ascertain the importance of the particular contract term and a process of weighing the absence of that term against the countervailing advantages of the alternate employment. In the typical case, this will mean that summary judgment must be withheld....[a]

NOTE

Same Employer. The court lays no stress on the fact that the offer of substitute employment came from the employer who had broken the contract in suit. Might this fact ever be significant? Would this be affected by the circumstances of the breach? Would it make a difference if the offer of substitute employment were conditioned on the injured party's surrender of rights under the old contract?

1. The values of the doctrine of mitigation of damages in this context are that it minimizes the unnecessary personal and social (e.g., nonproductive use of labor, litigation) costs of contractual failure. If a wrongfully discharged employee can, through his own action and without suffering financial or psychological loss in the process, reduce the damages accruing from the breach of contract, the most sensible policy is to require him to do so. I fear the majority opinion will encourage precisely opposite conduct.

a. One writer notes that Amelia Bloomer was a "mid-nineteenth century feminist,

suffragist, and abolitionist" and observes that perhaps "a film entitled 'Bloomer Girl' was related in some way to the radical effort feminists in the last century made to achieve more freedom of movement and control over what they wore by reforming their dress." If so, the writer suggests, the role in the film might have had "personal significance for the actress ... even if the film treated women's issues in the light-hearted fashion typical of musical comedy." Frug, Re–Reading Contracts: A Feminist Analysis of a Contracts Casebook, 34 Am. U.L.Rev. 1065, 1116 (1985). Could an answer to the dissent have been constructed along these lines?

In Voorhees v. Guyan Machinery Co., 446 S.E.2d 672, 679 (W.Va.1994), the court explained that "an offer of reemployment by an employer will not diminish the employee's recovery if the offer is not accepted if circumstances are such as to render further association between the parties offensive or degrading to the employee." The court went on to observe that the former employer's offer of reemployment came after it had caused the employee to lose his job with his new employer and after he had sued his former employer, and concluded that expecting him to return to work for his former employer "in such circumstances would be tantamount to expecting that Sulla and Gaius Marius might form a productive working relationship after Sulla's march on Rome."

Problem. Suppose that in the *Diasonics* case, p. 494 above, a company affiliated with Davis had offered to buy the equipment if Davis did not, so that Davis would not lose its deposit. What result if Diasonics had ignored the offer? See Schiavi Mobile Homes, Inc., v. Gironda, 463 A.2d 722 (Me.1983).

CONTRACTS FOR THE SALE OF GOODS

The limitation of avoidability is of particular importance in connection with contracts for the sale of goods since, in a free enterprise economy, it is assumed that the injured party generally has available a market on which to arrange a substitute transaction. If the seller fails to deliver goods, the assumption is that the buyer can go into the market and "cover" by obtaining substitute goods, so that the buyer's damages should be based on the difference between a presumably greater price that the buyer will have to pay on the market and the lesser contract price. See UCC 2–712. If the buyer fails to take and pay for goods, the assumption is that the seller can go into the market and resell to a substitute buyer, so that the seller's damages should be based on the difference between the presumably greater contract price and a lesser price it will receive on the market. See UCC 2–706.

For the injured party who fails to take advantage of the availability of a substitute transaction on the market, the limitation of avoidability results in a formula based on the difference between the contract price and the market price at which it could have arranged a hypothetical substitute transaction. If, when the seller fails to deliver goods, the buyer fails to go into the market and "cover," its damages are based on "the difference between the market price ... and the contract price." UCC 2–713. If, when the buyer fails to take and pay for goods, the seller fails to go into the market and resell, its damages are based on "the difference between the market price ... and the unpaid contract price." UCC 2–708. On proof of market price, see UCC 2–723, 2–724.

The details of the Code rules in this area have occasioned confusion and criticism. A common criticism of the Code rules is that in some circumstances they seem to give the injured party a "windfall" by allowing that party to recover more than its actual loss, in disregard of the goal stated in UCC 1–106(1) of putting that party "in as good a position as if the other party had fully performed."

Suppose, for example, that the injured party has arranged an actual substitute transaction for a price *more* favorable than the market price. Can the injured party recover damages based on market price even though they exceed that party's actual loss? Comment 5 to UCC 2–713 suggests that a buyer cannot do so by explaining that that section "provides a remedy which is completely alternative to cover ... and applies only when and to the extent that the buyer has not covered." See also UCC 2–703, 2–711. But the Code nowhere suggests that a seller is subject to a similar restriction after a resale for more than market price. Should the Code be read as giving a "windfall" to a seller but not to a buyer? To neither? To both? See Sebert, Remedies Under Article Two of the Uniform Commercial Code: An Agenda for Review, 130 U.Pa.L.Rev. 360 (1981).

Other examples of situations in which it might be argued that the injured party may receive a "windfall" appear in the following problems. (Consideration of the Code's rules as they apply to a repudiation before the time for performance, as distinguished from a breach by nonperformance, will be postponed until the topic of anticipatory repudiation is reached in Chapter 7, Performance and Breach.)

NOTES

(1) *Specific Relief.* The possibility of specific relief for the buyer in the form of a decree of specific performance under UCC 2–716(1) has already been discussed in Chapter 1, Section 1. In some circumstances the buyer may also obtain specific relief through an action to replevy the goods under UCC 2–716(3). Can the buyer do so if it can cover? What would you advise an aggrieved buyer to do following breach in order to lay the foundation for a possible action for replevin under this section?

In some circumstances the seller may also obtain what amounts to specific relief through an action for the price under UCC 2–709(1)(b). Can the seller do so if it can resell? What would you advise an aggrieved seller to do following breach in order to lay the foundation for a possible action for the price under this section?

(2) *Lost Volume (Reprise).* A seller that could have arranged a substitute transaction to dispose of the goods elsewhere, but has not done so, may still argue that recovery should not be limited to damages based on market price but should include lost profit on the ground that such a sale would have resulted in lost volume. See UCC 2–708(2). Issues raised by such a contention have already been discussed in connection with the *Diasonics* case, p. 494 above, in the context of the seller that actually makes such a sale and then claims lost profit on the ground that that sale resulted in lost volume. See Note 2, p. 500 above. Is a seller that has not arranged a substitute transaction likely to have more trouble in proving lost volume than a seller that has arranged such a transaction?

(3) *Problem.* Seller contracts to sell Buyer goods for $100,000. Buyer then makes a contract to resell the goods to another purchaser at $125,000. Seller fails to deliver. The market price of similar goods at and immediately after the delivery date is $110,000. Since Buyer's resale contract does not require delivery for six months, Buyer waits and does not go into the market for six months, by which time the market price has dropped to $90,000. How much should Buyer recover? Would $10,000 give Buyer a "windfall"? (Suppose that the market

price had risen to $120,000 during Buyer's delay. How much should Buyer recover?) Is the applicable section UCC 2–712 or 2–713?

TONGISH v. THOMAS, 840 P.2d 471 (Kan.1992). [Tongish, a farmer, made a contract with the Coop Association under which he was to grow 116.8 acres of sunflower seeds, to be purchased by Coop at $13 per hundredweight for large seeds and $8 per hundredweight for small seeds, delivery to be in thirds by December 31, 1988, March 31, 1989, and May 31, 1989. Coop had a contract to deliver the seeds to Bambino Bean & Seed for the same price it paid Tongish less a 55 cent per hundredweight handling fee, Coop's only anticipated profit. Owing to a short crop, bad weather, and other factors, the market price of sunflower seeds in January 1989 had risen to double that in the Tongish contract. Tongish notified Coop that he would make no more deliveries and sold the balance of his crop to Danny Thomas for about $20 per hundredweight or $14,714, which was $5,153 more than the Coop contract price. Coop sued Tongish and recovered $455 in damages, based on its loss of handling charges. Coop appealed and the Court of Appeals reversed for determination of damages based on market price under UCC 2–713. Tongish appealed, arguing that under UCC 1–106 the trial court was correct.]

McFARLAND, JUSTICE: This case presents the narrow issue of whether damages arising from the nondelivery of contracted-for sunflower seeds should be computed on the basis of K.S.A. 84–1–106 or K.S.A. 84–2–713.... The analyses and rationale of the Court of Appeals utilized in resolving the issue are sound and we adopt the following portion thereof: ...

"There is authority for appellee's position that K.S.A. 84–2–713 should not be applied in certain circumstances. In Allied Canners & Packers, Inc. v. Victor Packing Co., 162 Cal.App.3d 905, 209 Cal.Rptr. 60 (1984), Allied contracted to purchase 375,000 pounds of raisins from Victor for 29.75 cents per pound with a 4% discount. Allied then contracted to sell the raisins for 29.75 cents per pound expecting a profit of $4,462.50 from the 4% discount it received from Victor. 162 Cal. App.3d at 907–08 [209 Cal.Rptr. 60].

"Heavy rains damaged the raisin crop and Victor breached its contract, being unable to fulfill the requirement. The market price of raisins had risen to about 80 cents per pound. Allied's buyers agreed to rescind their contracts so Allied was not bound to supply them with raisins at a severe loss. Therefore, the actual loss to Allied was the $4,462.50 profit it expected, while the difference between the market price and the contract price was about $150,000. 162 Cal.App.3d at 908–09 [209 Cal.Rptr. 60].

"The California appellate court, in writing an exception, stated: 'It has been recognized that the use of the market-price contract-price formula under section 2–713 does not, absent pure accident, result in a

damage award reflecting the buyer's actual loss. [Citations omitted.]'
162 Cal.App.3d at 912 [209 Cal.Rptr. 60]. The court indicated that
section 2–713 may be more of a statutory liquidated damages clause and,
therefore, conflicts with the goal of section 1–106. The court discussed
that in situations where the buyer has made a resale contract for the
goods, which the seller knows about, it may be appropriate to limit 2–713
damages to actual loss. However, the court cited a concern that a seller
not be rewarded for a bad faith breach of contract. 162 Cal.App.3d at
912–14 [209 Cal.Rptr. 60].

"In *Allied*, the court determined that if the seller knew the buyer
had a resale contract for the goods, and the seller did not breach the
contract in bad faith, the buyer was limited to actual loss of damages
under section 1–106. 162 Cal.App.3d at 915 [209 Cal.Rptr. 60].

"The similarities between the present case and *Allied* are that the
buyer made a resale contract which the seller knew about. (Tongish
knew the seeds eventually went to Bambino, although he may not have
known the details of the deal.) However, in examining the breach itself,
Victor could not deliver the raisins because its crop had been destroyed.... Victor had no raisins to sell to any buyer, while Tongish
took advantage of the doubling price of sunflower seeds and sold to
Danny Thomas. Although the trial court had no need to find whether
Tongish breached the contract in bad faith, it did find there was no valid
reason for the breach. Therefore, the nature of Tongish's breach was
much different than Victor's in *Allied*.

"Section 2–713 and the theories behind it have a lengthy and
somewhat controversial history. In 1963, it was suggested that 2–713
was a statutory liquidated damages clause and not really an effort to try
and accurately predict what actual damages would be. Peters, Remedies
for Breach of Contracts Relating to the Sale of Goods Under the Uniform
Commercial Code: A Roadmap for Article Two, 73 Yale L.J. 199, 259
(1963).

"In 1978, Robert Childres called for the repeal of section 2–713.
Childres, Buyer's Remedies: The Danger of Section 2–713, 72 Nw.
U.L.Rev. 837 (1978). Childres reflected that because the market
price/contract price remedy 'has been the cornerstone of Anglo–American damages' that it has been so hard to see that this remedy 'makes no
sense whatever when applied to real life situations.' 72 Nw.U.L.Rev. at
841–42.

"In 1979, David Simon and Gerald A. Novack wrote a fairly objective analysis of the two arguments about section 2–713 and stated:

'For over sixty years our courts have divided on the question of
which measure of damages is appropriate for the supplier's breach of his
delivery obligations. The majority view, reinforced by applicable codes,
would award market damages even though in excess of plaintiff's loss.
A persistent minority would reduce market damages to the plaintiff's
loss, without regard to whether this creates a windfall for the defendant.
Strangely enough, each view has generally tended to disregard the
arguments, and even the existence, of the opposing view.' Simon and

Novack, Limiting the Buyer's Market Damages to Lost Profits: A Challenge to the Enforceability of Market Contracts, 92 Harv.L.Rev. 1395, 1397 (1979).

"Although the article discussed both sides of the issue, the authors came down on the side of market price/contract price as the preferred damages theory. The authors admit that market damages fly in the face 'of the familiar maxim that the purpose of contract damages is to make the injured party whole, not penalize the breaching party.' 92 Harv. L.Rev. at 1437. However, they argue that the market damages rule discourages the breach of contracts and encourages a more efficient market. 92 Harv.L.Rev. at 1437.

"The *Allied* decision in 1984, which relied on the articles cited above for its analysis to reject market price/contract price damages, has been sharply criticized. In Schneider, UCC Section 2–713: A Defense of Buyers' Expectancy Damages, 22 Cal.W.L.Rev. 233, 266 (1986), the author stated that *Allied* 'adopted the most restrictive [position] on buyer's damages. This Article is intended to reverse that trend.' Schneider argued that by following section 1–106, 'the court ignored the clear language of section 2–713's compensation scheme to award expectation damages in accordance with the parties' allocation of risk as measured by the difference between contract price and market price on the date set for performance.' 22 Cal.W.L.Rev. at 264.

"Recently in Scott, The Case for Market Damages: Revisiting the Lost Profits Puzzle, 57 U.Chi.L.Rev. 1155, 1200 (1990), the *Allied* result was called 'unfortunate.' Scott argues that section 1–106 is 'entirely consistent' with the market damages remedy of 2–713. 57 U.Chi.L.Rev. at 1201. According to Scott, it is possible to harmonize sections 1–106 and 2–713. Scott states, 'Market damages measure the expectancy ex ante, and thus reflect the value of the option; lost profits, on the other hand, measure losses ex post, and thus only reflect the value of the completed exchange.' 57 U.Chi.L.Rev. at 1174. The author argues that if the nonbreaching party has laid off part of the market risk (like Coop did) the lost profits rule creates instability because the other party is now encouraged to breach the contract if the market fluctuates to its advantage. 57 U.Chi.L.Rev. at 1178.

"We are not persuaded that the lost profits view under *Allied* should be embraced. It is a minority rule that has received only nominal support. We believe the majority rule or the market damages remedy as contained in K.S.A. 84–2–713 is more reasoned and should be followed as the preferred measure of damages. While application of the rule may not reflect the actual loss to a buyer, it encourages a more efficient market and discourages the breach of contracts." Tongish v. Thomas, 16 Kan.App.2d at 811–17 [829 P.2d 916].

At first blush, the result reached herein appears unfair. However, closer scrutiny dissipates this impression. By the terms of the contract Coop was obligated to buy Tongish's large sunflower seeds at $13 per hundredweight whether or not it had a market for them. Had the price of sunflower seeds plummeted by delivery time, Coop's obligation to purchase at the agreed price was fixed. If loss of actual profit pursuant to K.S.A. 84–1–106(1) would be the measure of damages to be applied herein, it would enable Tongish to consider the Coop contract price of $13 per hundredweight plus 55 cents per hundredweight handling fee as the "floor" price for his seeds, take advantage of rapidly escalating prices, ignore his contractual obligation, and profitably sell to the highest bidder. Damages computed under K.S.A. 84–2–713 encourage the honoring of contracts and market stability....

[Judgment of the Court of Appeals affirmed.]

NOTES

(1) *Questions.* If Coop had gone into the market after Tongish's repudiation and bought seeds to deliver to Bambino for $14,714, could it have recovered $5,153 from Tongish under UCC 2–712? If Coop bought no seeds to deliver to Bambino and therefore had to pay damages to Bambino, could Coop recover those damages from Tongish? Note that Allied's buyers had agreed to rescind their contracts. Should the result in *Tongish* be different if Bambino had agreed to rescind its contract with Coop? Compare Iron Trade Products v. Wilkoff, p. 747 below, with H–W–H Cattle Co. v. Schroeder, 767 F.2d 437 (8th Cir.1985). Should the result in *Tongish* be different if Coop had protected itself by reserving the power to cancel on breach by Tongish? See Farnsworth, Legal Remedies for Breach of Contract, 70 Colum.L.Rev. 1145, 1190 n. 189 (1970).

(2) *Problem.* Seller contracts to sell Buyer goods for $100,000. Seller then makes a contract to purchase the goods from a supplier for $90,000. The market price for similar goods then falls to $75,000, and Buyer repudiates the contract. (The market price then remains constant through the delivery date.) Seller has neither received the goods from its supplier nor resold them to another buyer. How much should Seller recover? Would $25,000 give Seller a "windfall"? Does UCC 2–708(2) apply if a seller will be overcompensated by UCC 2–708(1)? Compare Nobs Chemical, U.S.A., Inc. v. Koppers Co., Inc., 616 F.2d 212 (5th Cir.1980), with Trans World Metals, Inc. v. Southwire Co., 769 F.2d 902 (2d Cir.1985), and see Scott, The Case for Market Damages: Revisiting the Lost Profits Puzzle, 57 U.Chi.L.Rev. 1155, 1175–79 (1990).

AVOIDABILITY AND COST TO REMEDY DEFECT

Cases of defective, as distinguished from merely incomplete, performance may raise difficult problems of avoidability. If the breach consists merely of incomplete performance, the injured party can usually arrange to have someone else complete the work at less than the loss in value to the injured party. The limitation of avoidability then has the effect of restricting the injured party to damages based on that lesser cost to complete the work rather than on the loss in value. Suppose, for example, that a builder breaks a contract to construct a factory by failing to finish the roof, making the factory unusable. The owner cannot recover the relatively enormous loss resulting from the inability to use the factor but is relegated to the relatively small amount that it will cost to get another builder to finish the roof.

Trouble may arise, however, if the performance is defective rather than merely incomplete. In that case, part of the cost to remedy the defect and complete performance as agreed will probably be the cost of undoing some of the work already done. The total cost to remedy the defect may then exceed the loss in value to the injured party so that an award based on that cost would to that extent be a windfall.

The following case involves this situation. In reading it you should focus on the issue in the fifth paragraph of Cardozo's opinion, going to "the measure of the allowance." The issue dealt with in the third and fourth paragraphs and in the dissent will be taken up later, for the reasons given in Note 1 below.

NOTE

The Case of the Inapposite Analogy. Freund made a contract with Washington Square Press under which the Press was to publish his book on modern drama on a royalty basis. Freund was paid a nonreturnable $2,000 "advance." After Freund delivered his manuscript, the Press merged with another publisher and refused to publish his book. Freund sued the Press and recovered $10,000 as the amount that publication would have cost Freund. *Held:* Damages reduced from $10,000 to six cents, with costs to the plaintiff. "[T]he analogy ... to the construction contract situation was inapposite. In the typical construction contract, the owner agrees to pay money or other consideration to a builder and expects, under the contract, to receive a completed building in return. The value of the promised performance to the owner is the properly constructed building. In this case, unlike the typical construction contract, the value to plaintiff of the promised performance—publication—was a percentage of sales of the books published and not the books themselves. Had the plaintiff contracted for the printing, binding and delivery of a number of hardbound copies of his manuscript, to be sold or disposed of as he wished, then perhaps the construction analogy, and measurement of damages by the cost of replacement or completion, would have some application. Here, however, the specific value to plaintiff of the promised publication was the royalties he stood to receive from defendant's sales of the published book." Since the amount of royalties was not proved with sufficient certainty, the plaintiff could recover only nominal damages. Freund v. Washington Square Press, 314 N.E.2d 419 (N.Y.1974).

Do you agree that the analogy was inapposite? If the court believed that the $10,000 cost of publication exceeded the most optimistic forecast of Freund's royalties, could the decision be defended on another ground?

JACOB & YOUNGS v. KENT
Court of Appeals of New York, 1921.
230 N.Y. 239, 129 N.E. 889, 23 A.L.R. 1429.

CARDOZO, J. The plaintiff built a country residence for the defendant at a cost of upwards of $77,000, and now sues to recover a balance of $3,483.46, remaining unpaid. The work of construction ceased in June, 1914, and the defendant then began to occupy the dwelling. There was no complaint of defective performance until March, 1915. One of the specifications for the plumbing work provides that "all wrought iron pipe must be well galvanized, lap welded pipe of the grade known as 'standard pipe' of Reading manufacture." The defendant learned in March, 1915, that some of the pipe, instead of being made in Reading, was the product of other factories. The plaintiff was accordingly direct-ed by the architect to do the work anew. The plumbing was then encased within the walls except in a few places where it had to be exposed. Obedience to the order meant more than the substitution of other pipe. It meant the demolition at great expense of substantial parts of the completed structure. The plaintiff left the work untouched, and asked for a certificate that the final payment was due. Refusal of the certificate was followed by this suit.[a]

The evidence sustains a finding that the omission of the prescribed brand of pipe was neither fraudulent nor willful. It was the result of the oversight and inattention of the plaintiff's sub-contractor. Reading pipe is distinguished from Cohoes pipe and other brands only by the name of the manufacturer stamped upon it at intervals of between six and seven feet. Even the defendant's architect, though he inspected the pipe upon arrival, failed to notice the discrepancy. The plaintiff tried to show that the brands installed, though made by other manufacturers, were the same in quality, in appearance, in market value and in cost as the brand stated in the contract—that they were, indeed, the same thing, though manufactured in another place. The evidence was excluded, and a verdict directed for the defendant. The Appellate Division reversed, and granted a new trial.

We think the evidence, if admitted, would have supplied some basis for the inference that the defect was insignificant in its relation to the project. The courts never say that one who makes a contract fills the measure of his duty by less than full performance. They do say, however, that an omission, both trivial and innocent, will sometimes be atoned for by allowance of the resulting damage, and will not always be the breach of a condition to be followed by a forfeiture (Spence v. Ham, 163 N.Y. 220, 57 N.E. 412; Woodward v. Fuller, 80 N.Y. 312; Glacius v. Black, 67 N.Y. 563, 566; Bowen v. Kimbell, 203 Mass. 364, 370, 89 N.E. 542.) The distinction is akin to that between dependent and indepen-dent promises, or between promises and conditions (Anson on Contracts,

a. The record on appeal indicates that, under the contract, payments were to be made monthly as the work progressed, on the certificate of the architect in an amount which "in his judgment" represented the amount due less 15% to be withheld. The specifications attached to the contract pro-vided that where "any particular brand of manufactured article is specified, it is to be considered as a standard," and that a con-tractor "desiring to use another shall first make application in writing to the Architect ... and obtain their written approval of the change. The specifications made the archi-tect's decision "as to the character of any material or labor furnished by the Contrac-tor ... final and conclusive." Further-more, "Any work furnished by the Contrac-tor, the material or workmanship of which is defective or which is not fully in accor-dance with the drawings and specifications, in every respect, will be rejected and is to be immediately torn down, removed and remade or replaced in accordance with the drawings and specifications, whenever dis-covered.... The Owner will have the op-tion at all times to allow the defective or improper work to stand and to receive from the Contractor a sum of money equivalent to the difference in value of the work as performed and as herein specified." Rec-ord pp. 98–108. For the contract terms and much useful background, see R. Danzig, The Capability Problem in Contract Law 108–28 (1978).

Corbin's Ed., sec. 367: 2 Williston on Contracts, sec. 842). Some promises are so plainly independent that they can never by fair construction be conditions of one another. (Rosenthal Paper Co. v. Nat. Folding Box & Paper Co., 226 N.Y. 313, 123 N.E. 766; Bogardus v. N.Y. Life Ins. Co., 101 N.Y. 328, 4 N.E. 522.) Others are so plainly dependent that they must always be conditions. Others, though dependent and thus conditions when there is departure in point of substance, will be viewed as independent and collateral when the departure is insignificant (2 Williston on Contracts, secs. 841, 842; Eastern Forge Co. v. Corbin, 182 Mass. 590, 592, 66 N.E. 419; Robinson v. Mollett, L.R., 7 Eng. & Ir.App. 802, 814; Miller v. Benjamin, 142 N.Y. 613, 37 N.E. 631). Considerations partly of justice and partly of presumable intention are to tell us whether this or that promise shall be placed in one class or another. The simple and the uniform will call for different remedies from the multifarious and the intricate. The margin of departure within the range of normal expectation upon a sale of common chattels will vary from the margin to be expected upon a contract for the construction of a mansion or a "skyscraper." There will be harshness sometimes and oppression in the implication of a condition when the thing upon which labor has been expended is incapable of surrender because united to the land, and equity and reason in the implication of a like condition when the subject-matter, if defective, is in shape to be returned. From the conclusions that promises may not be treated as dependent to the extent of their uttermost minutiae without a sacrifice of justice, the progress is a short one to the conclusion that they may not be so treated without a perversion of intention. Intention not otherwise revealed may be presumed to hold in contemplation the reasonable and probable. If something else is in view, it must not be left to implication. There will be no assumption of a purpose to visit venial faults with oppressive retribution.

Those who think more of symmetry and logic in the development of legal rules than of practical adaptation to the attainment of a just result will be troubled by a classification where the lines of division are so wavering and blurred. Something, doubtless, may be said on the score of consistency and certainty in favor of a stricter standard. The courts have balanced such considerations against those of equity and fairness, and found the latter to be the weightier. The decisions in this state commit us to the liberal view, which is making its way, nowadays, in jurisdictions slow to welcome it (Dakin & Co. v. Lee, 1916, 1 K.B. 566, 579). Where the line is to be drawn between the important and the trivial cannot be settled by a formula. "In the nature of the case precise boundaries are impossible" (2 Williston on Contracts, sec. 841). The same omission may take on one aspect or another according to its setting. Substitution of equivalents may not have the same significance in fields of art on the one side and in those of mere utility on the other. Nowhere will change be tolerated, however, if it is so dominant or pervasive as in any real or substantial measure to frustrate the purpose of the contract (Crouch v. Gutmann, 134 N.Y. 45, 51, 31 N.E. 271). There is no general license to install whatever, in the builder's judgment, may be regarded as "just as good" (Easthampton L. & C., Ltd. v.

Worthington, 186 N.Y. 407, 412, 79 N.E. 323). The question is one of degree, to be answered, if there is doubt, by the triers of the facts (Crouch v. Gutmann; Woodward v. Fuller, supra), and, if the inferences are certain, by the judges of the law (Easthampton L. & C. Co., Ltd. v. Worthington, supra). We must weigh the purpose to be served, the desire to be gratified, the excuse for deviation from the letter, the cruelty of enforced adherence. Then only can we tell whether literal fulfillment is to be implied by law as a condition. This is not to say that the parties are not free by apt and certain words to effectuate a purpose that performance of every term shall be a condition of recovery. That question is not here. This is merely to say that the law will be slow to impute the purpose, in the silence of the parties, where the significance of the default is grievously out of proportion to the oppression of the forfeiture. The willful transgressor must accept the penalty of his transgression (Schultze v. Goodstein, 180 N.Y. 248, 251, 73 N.E. 21; Desmond–Dunne Co. v. Friedman–Doscher Co., 162 N.Y. 486, 490, 56 N.E. 995). For him there is no occasion to mitigate the rigor of implied conditions. The transgressor whose default is unintentional and trivial may hope for mercy if he will offer atonement for his wrong (Spence v. Ham, supra).

In the circumstances of this case, we think the measure of the allowance is not the cost of replacement, which would be great, but the difference in value, which would be either nominal or nothing. Some of the exposed sections might perhaps have been replaced at moderate expense. The defendant did not limit his demand to them, but treated the plumbing as a unit to be corrected from cellar to roof.[b] In point of fact, the plaintiff never reached the stage at which evidence of the extent of the allowance became necessary. The trial court had excluded evidence that the defect was unsubstantial, and in view of that ruling there was no occasion for the plaintiff to go farther with an offer of proof. We think, however, that the offer, if it had been made, would not of necessity have been defective because directed to difference in value. It is true that in most cases the cost of replacement is the measure (Spence v. Ham, supra). The owner is entitled to the money which will permit him to complete, unless the cost of completion is grossly and unfairly out of proportion to the good to be attained. When that is true, the measure is the difference in value. Specifications call, let us say, for a foundation built of granite quarried in Vermont. On the completion of the building, the owner learns that through the blunder of a subcontractor part of the foundation has been built of granite of the same quality quarried in New Hampshire. The measure of allowance is not the cost of reconstruction. "There may be omissions of that which could not afterwards be supplied exactly as called for by the contract without taking down the building to its foundations and at the same time the omission may not affect the value of the building for use or otherwise, except so slightly as to be

---

b. In a brief per curiam opinion on a motion for reargument, the Court of Appeals later said that it "did not overlook the specification which provides that defective work shall be replaced" (see footnote a above). But for the promise to replace, as for the promise to install, the law "restricts the remedy to damages." 130 N.E. 933 (1921).

hardly appreciable" (Handy v. Bliss, 204 Mass. 513, 519, 90 N.E. 864. Cf. Foeller v. Heintz, 137 Wis. 169, 178, 118 N.W. 543; Oberlies v. Bullinger, 132 N.Y. 598, 601, 30 N.E. 999; 2 Williston on Contracts, sec. 805, p. 1541). The rule that gives a remedy in cases of substantial performance with compensation for defects of trivial or inappreciable importance, has been developed by the courts as an instrument of justice. The measure of the allowance must be shaped to the same end.

The order should be affirmed, and judgment absolute directed in favor of the plaintiff upon the stipulation, with costs in all courts.

McLAUGHLIN, J. (dissenting). I dissent. The plaintiff did not perform its contract. Its failure to do so was either intentional or due to gross neglect which, under the uncontradicted facts, amounted to the same thing, nor did it make any proof of the cost of compliance, where compliance was possible....[c]

I am of the opinion the trial court was right in directing a verdict for the defendant. The plaintiff agreed that all the pipe used should be of the Reading Manufacturing Company. Only about two-fifths of it, so far as appears, was of that kind. If more were used, then the burden of proving that fact was upon the plaintiff, which it could easily have done, since it knew where the pipe was obtained. The question of substantial performance of a contract of the character of the one under consideration depends in no small degree upon the good faith of the contractor. If the plaintiff had intended to, and had complied with the terms of the contract except as to minor omissions, due to inadvertence, then he might be allowed to recover the contract price, less the amount necessary to fully compensate the defendant for damages caused by such omissions. Woodward v. Fuller, 80 N.Y. 312; Nolan v. Whitney, 88 N.Y. 648. But that is not this case. It installed between 2,000 and 2,500 feet of pipe, of which only 1,000 feet at most complied with the contract. No explanation was given why pipe called for by the contract was not used, nor was any effort made to show what it would cost to remove the pipe of other manufacturers and install that of the Reading Manufacturing Company. The defendant had a right to contract for what he wanted. He had a right before making payment to get what the contract called for. It is no answer to this suggestion to say that the pipe put in was just as good as that made by the Reading Manufacturing Company, or that the difference in value between such pipe and the pipe made by the Reading Manufacturing Company would be either "nominal or nothing." Defendant contracted for pipe made by the Reading Manufacturing Company. What his reason was for requiring this kind of pipe is of no importance. He wanted that and was entitled to it.... The rule, therefore, of substantial performance, with damages for unsubstantial omissions, has no application. (Crouch v. Gutmann, 134 N.Y. 45, 31 N.E. 271; Spence v. Ham, 163 N.Y. 220, 57 N.E. 412.) ...

---

c. An omitted part of the dissent explains that on the first delivery of pipe Jacob & Youngs's superintendent examined the pipe to make certain it was of Reading manufacture, the subcontractor's foreman simply left word at its shop that he wanted a certain number of feet without specifying the manufacture, and there was no examination before installation.

HISCOCK, CH. J., HOGAN and CRANE, JJ., concur with CARDOZO, J.; POUND and ANDREWS, JJ., concur with MCLAUGHLIN, J.

NOTES

(1) *Substantial Performance.* Kent promised to pay Jacob & Youngs if it built him a house as specified. Building the house as specified was therefore a condition of Jacob & Youngs' right to recover from Kent on that promise. In the first part of the opinion, Cardozo explains why Jacob & Youngs can recover from Kent on that promise in spite of the fact that it did not strictly fulfill that requirement. As to this, three judges dissent. This notion of substantial, as opposed to strict, performance and the law of conditions in general are taken up in Chapter 7, Performance and Breach. For present purposes, we are concerned only with the second part of Cardozo's opinion, in which he considers how much, if anything, should be deducted from that recovery as Kent's damages. (To remove the problem of substantial performance from the picture, assume that Kent had paid Jacob & Youngs in full and was suing them for damages.)

(2) *Relevance of Diminution in Value.* Diminution in market price is useful in fixing a lower limit for recovery, since the value of property to its owner is usually no less than the net price at which the owner could sell it. Similarly, cost to remedy the defect is useful in fixing an upper limit for recovery since, even if that cost is less than the loss in value to the owner, the lesser sum will enable the owner to complete and avoid any loss in value.

"An owner's recovery is not necessarily limited to diminution in value whenever that figure is less than the cost of repair. It is true that in a case where the cost of repair exceeds the damages under the value formula, an award under the cost of repair measure may place the owner in a better economic position than if the contract had been fully performed, since he could pocket the award and then sell the defective structure. On the other hand, it is possible that the owner will use the damage award for its intended purpose and turn the structure into the one originally envisioned. He may do this for a number of reasons, including personal esthetics or a hope for increased value in the future. If he does this his economic position will equal the one he would have been in had the contractor fully performed. The fact finder is the one in the best position to determine whether the owner will actually complete performance, or whether he is only interested in obtaining the best immediate economic position he can. In some cases, such as where the property is held solely for investment, the court may conclude as a matter of law that the damage award can not exceed the diminution in value. Where, however, the property has special significance to the owner and repair seems likely, the cost of repair may be appropriate even if it exceeds the diminution in value." Advanced, Inc. v. Wilks, 711 P.2d 524, 527 (Alaska 1985).

(3) *Proving Diminution in Value.* Do you agree that the "difference in value" *to Kent* "would be either nominal or nothing"? It may be that the difference between the *market price* of a house with Reading pipe and one with Cohoes pipe is zero, because buyers of houses consider the two kinds of pipe to be of equal value *to them.* But why should *Kent's* recovery be limited by this?[c]

c. "If a proud householder, who plans to live out his days in the home of his dreams, orders a new roof of red barrel tile and the roofer instead installs a purple one, money damages for the reduced value of his house may not be enough to offset the strident offense to aesthetic sensibilities, continuing over the life of the roof." Gory Associated Industries v. Jupiter Roofing & Sheet Metal, 358 So.2d 93, 95 (Fla.Ct.App.1978).

The problem of determining loss in value is most acute when, as in the principal case, there is great disparity between the minimum of diminution in market price and the maximum of cost to remedy the defect. Which better approximates loss in value? Although the opinion gives us no insight into why Kent might have specified Reading rather than some other brand of pipe, it does suggest one reason for the disparity between the maximum and minimum. Does that reason suggest which better approximates loss in value? (If a very large fraction of the disparity represents the cost of undoing and redoing the work, how large a fraction represents the loss in value to Kent?) Who should have the burden with respect to diminution in value?

One court has said that if the builder "thought that the cost of repairs was an unreasonable measure of damages given what it believed to be the relatively small decrease in value resulting from the breach, it clearly had the burden to present evidence from which the jury could find the diminution in value." [d] But the builder could do this simply by presenting evidence of market price.

Another court has said that, as plaintiff, the owner "had the burden of producing evidence that afforded the jury a reasonable basis to measure" the owner's loss. But that court went on to say, "It is undisputed that homeowners are qualified to testify as to their personal opinion regarding the value, or diminution in value, of their properties." This is so even though the homeowner may rely in part on the cost of repairs in forming that opinion. The appropriate vehicle for challenging such an opinion is cross-examination.[e]

Could Kent's lawyer have done more?

GROVES v. JOHN WUNDER CO.

Supreme Court of Minnesota, 1939.
205 Minn. 163, 286 N.W. 235.

STONE, J. Action for breach of contract. Plaintiff got judgment for a little over $15,000. Sorely disappointed by that sum, he appeals.

In August, 1927 S.J. Groves & Sons Company, a corporation (hereinafter mentioned simply as Groves), owned a tract of 24 acres of Minneapolis suburban real estate. It was served or easily could be reached by railroad trackage. It is zoned as heavy industrial property. But for lack of development of the neighborhood its principal value thus far may have been in the deposit of sand and gravel which it carried. The Groves company had a plant on the premises for excavating and screening the gravel. Nearby defendant owned and was operating a similar plant.

In August, 1927, Groves and defendant made the involved contract. For the most part it was a lease from Groves, as lessor, to defendant, as lessee; its term seven years. Defendant agreed to remove the sand and gravel and to leave the property "at a uniform grade, substantially the same as the grade now existing at the roadway . . . on said premises, and that in stripping the overburden . . . it will use said overburden for the purpose of maintaining and establishing said grade."

---

d. Advanced, Inc. v. Wilks, quoted in Note 2, above at 526.

e. Tessmann v. Tiger Lee Construction Co., 634 A.2d 870, 873 (Conn.1993).

Under the contract defendant got the Groves screening plant. The transfer thereof and the right to remove the sand and gravel made the consideration moving from Groves to defendant, except that defendant incidentally got rid of Groves as a competitor. On defendant's part it paid Groves $105,000. So that from the outset, on Groves' part the contract was executed except for defendant's right to continue using the property for the stated term. (Defendant had a right to renewal which it did not exercise.)

Defendant breached the contract deliberately. It removed from the premises only "the richest and best of the gravel" and wholly failed, according to the findings, "to perform and comply with the terms, conditions, and provisions of said lease . . . with respect to the condition in which the surface of the demised premises was required to be left." Defendant surrendered the premises, not substantially at the grade required by the contract "nor at any uniform grade." Instead, the ground was "broken, rugged and uneven." Plaintiff sues as assignee and successor in right of Groves.

As the contract was construed below, the finding is that to complete its performance 288,495 cubic yards of overburden would need to be excavated, taken from the premises, and deposited elsewhere. The reasonable cost of doing that was found to be upwards of $60,000. But, if defendant had left the premises at the uniform grade required by the lease, the reasonable value of the property on the determinative date would have been only $12,160. The judgment was for that sum,[a] including interest, thereby nullifying plaintiff's claim that cost of completing the contract rather than difference in value of the land was the measure of damages. The gauge of damage adopted by the decision was the difference between the market value of plaintiff's land in the condition it was [in] when the contract was made and what it would have been if defendant had performed. The one question for us arises upon plaintiff's assertion that he was entitled, not to that difference in value, but to the reasonable cost to him of doing the work called for by the contract which defendant left undone.

1. Defendant's breach of contract was wilful. There was nothing of good faith about it. Hence, that the decision below handsomely rewards bad faith and deliberate breach of contract is obvious. That is not allowable. Here the rule is well settled, and has been since Elliott v. Caldwell, 43 Minn. 357, 45 N.W. 845, 9 L.R.A. 52, that, where the contractor wilfully and fraudulently varies from the terms of a construction contract, he cannot sue thereon and have the benefit of the equitable doctrine of substantial performance. That is the rule generally. See Annotation, "Wilful or intentional variation by contractor from terms of contract in regard to material or work as affecting measure of damages," 6 A.L.R. 137.

a. This was on the assumption that the land as it was left could not have been sold on the market.

Jacob & Youngs, Inc. v. Kent, 230 N.Y. 239, 243, 244, 129 N.E. 889, 891, 23 A.L.R. 1429, is typical. It was a case of substantial performance of a building contract. (This case is distinctly the opposite.) Mr. Justice Cardozo, in the course of his opinion, stressed the distinguishing features. "Nowhere," he said, "will change be tolerated, however, if it is so dominant or pervasive as in any real or substantial measure to frustrate the purpose of the contract." Again, "the willful transgressor must accept the penalty of his transgression."

2. In reckoning damages for breach of a building or construction contract, the law aims to give the disappointed promisee, so far as money will do it, what he was promised. 9 Am.Jur. Building and Construction Contracts, sec. 152. It is so ruled by a long line of decisions in this state beginning with Carli v. Seymour, Sabin & Co., 26 Minn. 276, 3 N.W. 348, where the contract was for building a road. There was a breach. Plaintiff was held entitled to recover what it would cost to complete the grading as contemplated by the contract. For our other similar cases, see 2 Dunnell, Minn.Dig., 2 Ed. & Supp., secs. 2561, 2565.

Never before, so far as our decisions show, has it even been suggested that lack of value in the land furnished to the contractor who had bound himself to improve it [gave] any escape from the ordinary consequences of a breach of the contract. . . .

Even in case of substantial performance in good faith, the resulting defects being remediable, it is error to instruct that the measure of damage is "the difference in value between the house as it was and as it would have been if constructed according to contract." The "correct doctrine" is that the cost of remedying the defect is the "proper" measure of damages. Snider v. Peters Home Building Co., 139 Minn. 413, 414, 416, 167 N.W. 108.

Value of the land (as distinguished from the value of the intended product of the contract, which ordinarily will be equivalent to its reasonable cost) is no proper part of any measure of damages for wilful breach of a building contract. The reason is plain.

The summit from which to reckon damages from trespass to real estate is its actual value at the moment. The owner's only right is to be compensated for the deterioration in value caused by the tort. That is all he has lost.[1] But not so if a contract to improve the same land has been breached by the contractor who refuses to do the work, especially where, as here, he has been paid in advance. The summit from which to reckon damages for that wrong is the hypothetical peak of accomplishment (not value) which would have been reached had the work been done as demanded by the contract.

The owner's right to improve his property is not trammeled by its small value. It is his right to erect thereon structures which will reduce its value. If that be the result, it can be of no aid to any contractor who

1. So also in condemnation cases, where the owner loses nothing of promised con- tractual performance.

declines performance. As said long ago in Chamberlain v. Parker, 45 N.Y. 569, 572: "A man may do what he will with his own, ... and if he chooses to erect a monument to his caprice or folly on his premises, and employs and pays another to do it, it does not lie with a defendant who has been so employed and paid for building it, to say that his own performance would not be beneficial to the plaintiff." To the same effect is Restatement, Contracts, sec. 346, p. 576, Illustrations of Subsection (1), par. 4.

Suppose a contractor were suing the owner for breach of a grading contract such as this. Would any element of value, or lack of it, in the land have any relevance in reckoning damages? Of course not. The contractor would be compensated for what he had lost, i.e., his profit. Conversely, in such a case as this, the owner is entitled to compensation for what he has lost, that is, the work or structure which he has been promised, for which he has paid, and of which he has been deprived by the contractor's breach.

To diminish damages recoverable against him in proportion as there is presently small value in the land would favor the faithless contractor. It would also ignore and so defeat plaintiff's right to contract and build for the future. To justify such a course would require more of the prophetic vision than judges possess. This factor is important when the subject matter is trackage property in the margin of such an area of population and industry as that of the Twin Cities....

The genealogy of the error pervading the argument contra is easy to trace. It begins with Seely v. Alden, 61 Pa. 302, 100 Am.Dec. 642, a tort case for pollution of a stream. Resulting depreciation in value of plaintiff's premises, of course, was the measure of damages. About 40 years later, in Bigham v. Wabash–Pittsburg T. Ry., 223 Pa. 106, 72 A. 318, the measure of damages of the earlier tort case was used in one for breach of contract, without comment or explanation to show why....

It is at least interesting to note Morgan v. Gamble, 230 Pa. 165, 79 A. 410, decided two years after the *Bigham* case. The doctrine of substantial performance is there correctly stated, but plaintiff was denied its benefit because he had deliberately breached his building contract. It was held that: "Where a building contractor agrees to lay an extra strong lead water pipe, and he substitutes therefor an iron pipe, he will be required to allow to the owners in a suit upon the contract, not the difference [in value] between the iron and lead pipes, but the cost of laying a lead pipe as provided in the agreement."

To show how remote any factors of value were considered, it was also held that: "Where a contractor of a building agrees to construct two gas lines, one for natural gas, and one for artificial gas, he will not be relieved from constructing both lines, because artificial gas was not in use in the town in which the building was being constructed."

The objective of this contract of present importance was the improvement of real estate. That makes irrelevant the rules peculiar to damages to chattels, arising from tort or breach of contract.... In tort, the thing lost is money value, nothing more. But under a construction contract, the thing lost by a breach such as we have here is a physical structure or accomplishment, a promised and paid for alteration in land. That is the "injury" for which the law gives him compensation. Its only appropriate measure is the cost of performance.

It is suggested that because of little or no value in his land the owner may be unconscionably enriched by such a reckoning. The answer is that there can be no unconscionable enrichment, no advantage upon which the law will frown, when the result is but to give one party to a contract only what the other has promised; particularly where, as here, the delinquent has had full payment for the promised performance.

3. It is said by the Restatement, Contracts, sec. 346, comment b: "Sometimes defects in a completed structure cannot be physically remedied without tearing down and rebuilding, at a cost that would be imprudent and unreasonable. The law does not require damages to be measured by a method requiring such economic waste. If no such waste is involved, the cost of remedying the defect is the amount awarded as compensation for failure to render the promised performance."

The "economic waste" declaimed against by the decisions applying that rule has nothing to do with the value in money of the real estate, or even with the product of the contract. The waste avoided is only that which would come from wrecking a physical structure, completed, or nearly so, under the contract. The cases applying that rule go no further. Illustrative are Buchholz v. Rosenberg, 163 Wis. 312, 156 N.W. 946; Burmeister v. Wolfgram, 175 Wis. 506, 185 N.W. 517. Absent such waste, as it is in this case, the rule of the Restatement, Contracts, sec. 346, is that "the cost of remedying the defect is the amount awarded as compensation for failure to render the promised performance." That means that defendants here are liable to plaintiff for the reasonable cost of doing what defendants promised to do and have wilfully declined to do.

It follows that there must be a new trial. The initial question will be as to the proper construction of the contract. Thus far the case has been considered from the standpoint of the construction adopted by plaintiff and acquiesced in, very likely for strategic reasons, by defendants. The question has not been argued here, so we intimate no opinion concerning it, but we put the question whether the contract required removal from the premises of any overburden. The requirement in that respect was that the overburden should be used for the purpose of "establishing and maintaining" the grade. A uniform slope and grade were doubtless required. But whether, if it could not be accomplished without removal and deposit elsewhere of large amounts of overburden, the contract required as a condition that the grade everywhere should be as low as the one recited as "now existing at the roadway" is a question for initial consideration below.

The judgment must be reversed with a new trial to follow.

So ordered.

[JULIUS J. OLSON, J., dissenting in an opinion in which HOLT, J. concurred, urged that the diminished value rule be applied in the absence of evidence to show that the completed product was to satisfy the personal taste of the promisee, and denied that the wilfulness of the breach should affect the measure of damages. HILTON and LORING, JJ., took no part.]

NOTES

(1) *Explanation.* In 1927, when the parties were bargaining over the terms of their contract, they would surely not knowingly have agreed to have Wunder assume such a burdensome task if it would have been of so slight a benefit to Groves. What is the explanation for the circumstances that, after seven years, Wunder's task was so burdensome and Groves' benefit was apparently so slight? That Wunder had underestimated the burden? That Groves had overestimated the benefit? That the cost of Wunder's performance had risen? That the amount of the benefit to Groves had fallen? That Wunder's performance would not have been so burdensome if it had done the restoration as the work progressed? That the actual benefit to Groves would have been greater than that reflected in the market price of the land? Some combination of these? Which of these possible explanations would justify the court's decision?

According to one critic, "not enforcing the contract would have given the defendant a windfall. But enforcing the contract gave the plaintiff an equal and opposite windfall: a cushion, which almost certainly the parties had not intended, against the impact of the Depression on land values." R. Posner, Economic Analysis of Law 121 (4th ed. 1992).

After the decision in Groves, Wunder paid Groves $55,000 to settle the claim. The land was left until 1951, when some grading was done on a portion at a cost of $6,000, and in 1953 this portion was sold for $45,000 to a buyer who planned to use it for a factory. J. Dawson, W. Harvey & S. Henderson, Cases on Contracts 17–18 (5th ed. 1987). Does this suggest anything about the proper measure of recovery?

(2) *Economics of Breach (Reprise).* If you had been counsel for Wunder and had been asked by your client whether it should perform its promise to do the grading at a cost of $60,000 if the benefit to Groves would be under $13,000, what advice would you have given?

(3) *"Wilfulness."* The court says that Wunder's "breach of contract was wilful." [a] What does "wilful" mean in this connection? If Wunder had refused to perform as a result of your advice (see Note 2 above), would its breach have been "wilful"?

Holmes said, "If a contract is broken the measure of damages generally is the same, whatever the cause of the breach." Globe Refining Co. v. Landa Cotton Oil Co., 190 U.S. 540, 544 (1903). Is the *Groves* case an exception? If Wunder must pay over $47,000 more in damages if its breach is "wilful," is this not a penalty for "wilfulness"? Is that consistent with the goals of contract remedies?

---

a. In H.P. Droher & Sons v. Toushin, 85 N.W.2d 273 (Minn.1957), the court distinguished Groves on the ground that, "The majority opinion is based, at least in part, on the fact that the breach of the contract was wilful and in bad faith".

PEEVYHOUSE v. GARLAND COAL & MINING CO., 382 P.2d 109 (Okla.1962), cert. denied, 375 U.S. 906 (1963). [In 1954 Willie and Lucille Peevyhouse leased their farm for five years to Garland Coal & Mining Co. to strip mine coal. In addition to the usual covenants, Garland agreed to perform specified restorative and remedial work at the end of the lease. It failed to do this work, which would have involved the moving of many thousands of cubic yards of dirt at a cost of about $29,000. Had the work been done, the market price of the farm would have been increased by only $300. The Peevyhouses sued for $25,000 in damages. The trial court gave judgment on a verdict for $5,000. Both parties appealed.]

JACKSON, JUSTICE. . . . On appeal, the issue is sharply drawn. Plaintiffs contend that the true measure of damages in this case is what it will cost plaintiffs to obtain performance of the work that was not done because of defendant's default. Defendant argues that the measure of damages is the cost of performance "limited, however, to the total difference in the market value before and after the work was performed". It appears that this precise question has not heretofore been presented to this court. . . .

Plaintiffs rely on Groves v. John Wunder Co., 205 Minn. 163, 286 N.W. 235, 123 A.L.R. 502. In that case, the Minnesota court, in a substantially similar situation, adopted the "cost of performance" rule as opposed to the "value" rule. The result was to authorize a jury to give plaintiff damages in the amount of $60,000, where the real estate concerned would have been worth only $12,160, even if the work contracted for had been done.

It may be observed that Groves v. John Wunder Co., supra, is the only case which has come to our attention in which the cost of performance rule has been followed under circumstances where the cost of performance greatly exceeded the diminution in value resulting from the breach of contract. Incidentally, it appears that this case was decided by a plurality rather than a majority of the members of the court. . . .

We do not think [that] either [the] analogy [of a "building and construction" or a "grading and excavation" contract] is strictly applicable to the case now before us. The primary purpose of the lease contract between plaintiffs and defendant was neither "building and construction" nor "grading and excavation". It was merely to accomplish the economical recovery and marketing of coal from the premises, to the profit of all parties. The special provisions of the lease contract pertaining to remedial work were incidental to the main object involved.

Even in the case of contracts that are unquestionably building and construction contracts, the authorities are not in agreement as to the factors to be considered in determining whether the cost of performance rule or the value rule should be applied. The American Law Institute's Restatement of the Law, Contracts, Volume 1, Sections 346(1)(a)(i) and (ii) submits the proposition that the cost of performance is the proper measure of damages "if this is possible and does not involve *unreasonable economic waste*"; and that the diminution in value caused by the breach is the proper measure "if construction and completion in accordance with the contract would involve *unreasonable economic waste*". (Emphasis supplied.) In an explanatory comment immediately following the text, the Restatement makes it clear that the "economic waste" referred to consists of the destruction of a substantially completed building or other structure. Of course no such destruction is involved in the case now before us.

On the other hand, in McCormick, Damages, Section 168, it is said with regard to building and construction contracts that "... in cases where the defect is one that can be repaired or cured without *undue expense*" the cost of performance is the proper measure of damages, but where "... the defect in material or construction is one that cannot be remedied without *an expenditure for reconstruction disproportionate to the end to be attained*" (emphasis supplied) the value rule should be followed. The same idea was expressed in Jacob & Youngs, Inc. v. Kent, 230 N.Y. 239, 129 N.E. 889, 23 A.L.R. 1429, as follows: "The owner is entitled to the money which will permit him to complete, unless the cost of completion is grossly and unfairly out of proportion to the good to be attained. When that is true, the measure is the difference in value."

It thus appears that the prime consideration in the Restatement was "economic waste"; and that the prime consideration in McCormick, Damages, and in Jacob & Youngs, Inc. v. Kent, supra, was the relationship between the expense involved and the "end to be attained"—in other words, the "relative economic benefit"....

We ... hold that where, in a coal mining lease, lessee agrees to perform certain remedial work on the premises concerned at the end of the lease period, and thereafter the contract is fully performed by both parties except that the remedial work is not done, the measure of damages in an action by lessor against lessee for damages for breach of contract is ordinarily the reasonable cost of performance of the work; however, where the contract provision breached was merely incidental to the main purpose in view, and where the economic benefit which would result to lessor by full performance of the work is grossly disproportionate to the cost of performance, the damages which lessor may recover are limited to the diminution in value resulting to the premises because of the non-performance....

[Judgment reduced to $300 and affirmed (4–3).]

Irwin, Justice (dissenting).... Although the contract speaks for itself, there were several negotiations between the plaintiffs and defendant before the contract was executed. Defendant admitted in the trial of the action, that plaintiffs insisted that the above provisions be included in the contract and that they would not agree to the coal mining lease unless the above provisions were included....

[I]n my opinion, the plaintiffs were entitled to specific performance of the contract and since defendant has failed to perform, the proper measure of damages should be the cost of performance. Any other measure of damage would be holding for naught the express provisions of the contract; would be taking from the plaintiffs the benefits of the contract and placing those benefits in defendant which has failed to perform its obligations; would be granting benefits to defendant without a resulting obligation; and would be completely rescinding the solemn obligation of the contract for the benefit of the defendant to the detriment of the plaintiffs by making an entirely new contract for the parties. . . .

NOTES

(1) *Groves and Peevyhouse.* Are *Groves* and *Peevyhouse* distinguishable? Is it clear that the loss in value to the Peevyhouses was not $5,000? Did Garland get a "windfall"? See Farnsworth, Your Loss or My Gain? The Dilemma of the Disgorgement Principle in Breach of Contract, 94 Yale L.J. 1339 (1985). What result in these cases under Restatement Second § 348(2)? For the background of *Peevyhouse*, see Maute, *Peevyhouse v. Garland Coal Co.* Revisited: The Ballad of Willie and Lucille, 89 Nw.U.L.Rev. ___ (1995).

(2) *"Economic Waste."* The first Restatement, we are told by the court in *Peevyhouse*, speaks of "economic waste" in the sense of destruction of a substantially completed structure. If Kent had been awarded damages measured by the cost to replace the pipe with Reading pipe, would he then have been required to replace it? Does it seem likely that he would have done so? In what sense is there "economic waste" if he is awarded damages measured by the cost to complete? See Comment *c* to Restatement Second § 348.

(b) Foreseeability

Until the nineteenth century, judges left the assessment of damages for breach of contract largely to the discretion of the jury. It was no accident that the development of rules to curb this discretion and the "outrageous and excessive" verdicts that resulted coincided with the end of the industrial revolution and with a consequent solicitude for burgeoning enterprise.[a] Hadley v. Baxendale is the leading case in this development.

HADLEY v. BAXENDALE
Court of Exchequer, 1854.
9 Ex. 341, 156 Eng.Rep. 145.

[Plaintiffs, who operated a mill at Gloucester, sued defendants, who were common carriers, for damages for breach of a contract of carriage. The declaration contained two counts, but prior to the trial plaintiffs

---

a. An analogy may be drawn from these restrictions on the extent of liability in terms of the amount for which a promisor may be held liable to restrictions on the extent of liability in terms of the persons to whom a promisor may be held liable. The latter is explored in Chapter 9, Third Party Beneficiaries.

entered a *nolle prosequi* as to the first. In the second count plaintiffs alleged that they were forced to shut their mill down because the crank shaft of the steam engine, by which their mill was operated, became broken; that they arranged with W. Joyce & Co., of Greenwich, the manufacturers of the engine, to make a new shaft from the pattern of the old one; that they delivered the broken shaft to defendants who, in consideration of the payment of their charges, promised to use due care to deliver it to W. Joyce & Co. within a reasonable time but that defendants failed to do so; that by reason of defendants' negligence the completion of the new shaft and the reopening of plaintiffs' mill were delayed five days longer than would otherwise have been the case; and that during that period plaintiffs were compelled to pay wages and lost profits aggregating 300£ for which amount plaintiffs sought judgment. Defendants pleaded that they had paid 25£ into court in satisfaction of plaintiffs' claim; plaintiffs replied that this sum was insufficient for that purpose; and issue was joined upon this replication.]

At the trial before Crompton, J., at the last Gloucester Assizes, it appeared that the plaintiffs carried on an extensive business as millers at Gloucester; and that, on the 11th of May, their mill was stopped by a breakage of the crank shaft by which the mill was worked. The steam-engine was manufactured by Messrs. Joyce & Co., the engineers at Greenwich, and it became necessary to send the shaft as a pattern for a new one to Greenwich. The fracture was discovered on the 12th, and on the 13th the plaintiffs sent one of their servants to the office of the defendants, who are the well known carriers trading under the name of Pickford & Co., for the purpose of having the shaft carried to Greenwich. The plaintiffs' servant told the clerk that the mill was stopped, and that the shaft must be sent immediately; and in answer to the inquiry when the shaft would be taken, the answer was, that if it was sent up by twelve o'clock any day, it would be delivered at Greenwich on the following day. On the following day the shaft was taken by the defendants, before noon, for the purpose of being conveyed to Greenwich, and the sum of 2£ 4s. was paid for its carriage for the whole distance; at the same time the defendants' clerk was told that a special entry, if required, should be made to hasten its delivery. The delivery of the shaft at Greenwich was delayed by some neglect; and the consequence was, that the plaintiffs did not receive the new shaft for several days after they would otherwise have done, and the working of their mill was thereby delayed, and they thereby lost the profits they would otherwise have received.

On the part of the defendants, it was objected that these damages were too remote, and that the defendants were not liable with respect to them. The learned Judge left the case generally to the jury, who found a verdict with 25£ damages beyond the amount paid into Court.

Whateley, [for defendants], in last Michaelmas Term, obtained a rule nisi for a new trial, on the ground of misdirection. * * *

ALDERSON, B. We think that there ought to be a new trial in this case; but, in so doing, we deem it to be expedient and necessary to state explicitly the rule which the Judge, at the next trial, ought, in our opinion, to direct the jury to be governed by when they estimate the damages.

It is, indeed, of the last importance that we should do this; for, if the jury are left without any definite rule to guide them, it will, in such cases as these, manifestly lead to the greatest injustice. The Courts have done this on several occasions; and, in Blake v. Midland Railway Company, 21 L.J., Q.B. 237, the Court granted a new trial on this very ground, that the rule had not been definitely laid down to the jury by the learned judge at Nisi Prius.

"There are certain established rules," this Court says, in Alder v. Keighley, 15 M. & W. 117, "according to which the jury ought to find." And the Court, in that case, adds: "and here there is a clear rule, that the amount which would have been received if the contract had been kept is the measure of damages if the contract is broken."

Now we think the proper rule in such a case as the present is this: Where two parties have made a contract which one of them has broken, the damages which the other party ought to receive in respect of such breach of contract should be such as may fairly and reasonably be considered either arising naturally, i.e., according to the usual course of things, from such breach of contract itself, or such as may reasonably be supposed to have been in the contemplation of both parties, at the time they made the contract, as the probable result of the breach of it. Now, if the special circumstances under which the contract was actually made were communicated by the plaintiffs to the defendants, and thus known to both parties, the damages resulting from the breach of such a contract, which they would reasonably contemplate, would be the amount of injury which would ordinarily follow from a breach of contract under these special circumstances so known and communicated. But, on the other hand, if these special circumstances were wholly unknown to the party breaking the contract, he, at the most, could only be supposed to have had in his contemplation the amount of injury which would arise generally, and in the great multitude of cases not affected by any special circumstances, from such a breach of contract. For, had the special circumstances been known, the parties might have specially provided for the breach of contract by special terms as to the damages in that case; and of this advantage it would be very unjust to deprive them. Now the above principles are those by which we think the jury ought to be guided in estimating the damages arising out of any breach of contract. It is said, that other cases, such as breaches of contract in the nonpayment of money, or in the not making a good title to land, are to be treated as exceptions from this, and as governed by a conventional rule. But as, in such cases, both parties must be supposed to be cognizant of that well-known rule, these cases may, we think, be more properly classed under the rule above enunciated as to cases under known special circumstances, because there both parties may reasonably be presumed to contemplate the estimation of the amount of damages according to the conventional rule. Now, in the present case if we are to apply the principles above laid down, we find that the only circumstances here communicated by the plaintiffs to the defendants at the time the contract was made, were, that the article to be carried was the broken shaft of a mill, and that the plaintiffs were the millers of that mill. But how do these circumstances show reasonably that the profits of the mill must be stopped by an unreasonable delay in the delivery of the broken shaft by the carrier to the third person? Suppose the plaintiffs had another shaft in their possession put up or putting up at the time, and that they only wished to send back the broken shaft to the engineer who made it; it is clear that this would be quite consistent with the above circumstances, and yet the unreasonable delay in the delivery would have no effect upon the intermediate profits of the mill. Or, again, suppose that, at the time of the delivery to the carrier, the machinery of the mill had been in other respects defective, then, also, the same results would follow. Here it is true that the shaft was actually sent back to serve as a model for a new one, and that the want of a new one was the only cause of the stoppage of the mill, and that the loss of profits really arose from not sending down the new shaft in proper time, and that this arose from the delay in delivering the broken one to serve as a model. But it is obvious that, in the great multitude of cases of millers sending off broken shafts to third persons by a carrier under ordinary circumstances, such consequences would not, in all probability, have occurred; and these special circumstances were here never communicated by the plaintiffs to the defendants. It follows, therefore, that the loss of profits here cannot reasonably be considered such a consequence of the breach of contract as could have been fairly and reasonably contemplated by both the parties when they made this contract. For such loss would neither have flowed naturally from the breach of this contract in the great multitude of such cases occurring under ordinary circumstances, nor were the special circumstances, which, perhaps, would have made it a reasonable and natural consequence of such breach of contract, communicated to or known by the defendants. The Judge ought, therefore, to have told the jury that, upon the facts then before him, they ought not to take the loss of profits into consideration at all in estimating the damages. There must therefore be a new trial in this case.

Rule absolute.

NOTES

(1) *Rule of Hadley v. Baxendale.* Do you think that in Hadley v. Baxendale the court applied the rule which it formulated correctly or incorrectly? Cf. Victoria Laundry (Windsor) Ltd. v. Newman Industries Ltd., 2 K.B. 528, 537 (1949): "In considering the meaning and application of these rules, it is essential to bear clearly in mind the facts on which Hadley v. Baxendale proceeded. The head-note is definitely misleading in so far as it says that the defendant's clerk, who attended at the office, was told that the mill was stopped and that the shaft must be delivered immediately. The same allegation figures in the statement of facts which are said on page 344 to have 'appeared' at the trial before Crompton J. If the Court of Exchequer had accepted these facts as established, the court must, one would suppose, have decided the case the other way round.... But it is reasonably plain from Alderson B.'s judgment that the court rejected this evidence, for on page 355 he says: 'We find that the only circumstances here

communicated by the plaintiffs to the defendants at the time when the contract was made were that the article to be carried was the broken shaft of a mill and that the plaintiffs were the millers of that mill.' ..." Compare the rule laid down in *Hadley v. Baxendale* with the formulations of Restatement Second § 351 and UCC 2–715(2)(a).

(2) *Limitation of Risk.* "The rule of Hadley v. Baxendale is an attempt to restrict the promisor's liability for breach of promise to those consequences, the risk of which he knew about, or must be taken to have known about, when he made the contract. The scope of damage for breach of contract is much narrower than the 'proximate consequence' rule which prevails in actions to recover for a tort. If we may assume that the defaulting promisor is usually an *entrepreneur,* a business man who has undertaken a risky enterprise, the law here manifests a policy to encourage the *entrepreneur* by reducing the extent of his risk below that amount of damage which, it might be plausibly argued, the promisee has actually been caused to suffer." Patterson, The Apportionment of Business Risks Through Legal Devices, 24 Colum.L.Rev. 335, 342 (1924).[b] For advocacy of a rule of proximate cause, see Eisenberg, The Principle of *Hadley v. Baxendale,* 80 Calif.L.Rev. 563 (1992). For a thorough discussion of the background of Hadley v. Baxendale, see Danzig, *Hadley v. Baxendale:* A Study in the Industrialization of the Law, 4 J.Legal Stud. 249 (1975). Compare Restatement Second § 351 with Restatement, Second, of Torts § 435; compare UCC 2–715(2)(a) with (2)(b).[c]

(3) *Consequential Damages.* Damages that, in Baron Alderson's words, would not be considered as "arising naturally" but only as a result of "the special circumstances under which the contract was actually made" are often called "consequential" damages. The Code has given special significance to this term by providing in UCC 2–712(2) for buyer's recovery of "any incidental or consequential damages" while providing in UCC 2–708(1) for seller's recovery of only "any incidental damages." In addition, UCC 2–715 refers to both "inciden-

b. Thus in British Columbia Saw Mill Co. v. Nettleship, L.R., 3 C.P. 499 (1868), Willes, J., criticized the result reached in an old case "said to have been decided two centuries ago where a man going to be married to an heiress, his horse having cast a shoe on the journey, employed a blacksmith to replace it, who did the work so unskilfully that the horse was lamed, and the rider not arriving in time, the lady married another; and the blacksmith was held liable for the loss of the marriage."

But cf. Coppola v. Kraushaar, 92 N.Y.S. 436 (App.Div.1905), in which a disappointed suitor whose betrothed broke their engagement after their wedding was delayed, sued to recover five hundred dollars, expended uselessly on the wedding, from the defendant, whose failure to deliver two gowns, ordered for the bride, had caused the postponement of the wedding. "Before the defendant can be held to these alleged damages ... I think that the parties must have had in contemplation that the wedding would never occur if the defendant failed to furnish the 'two dresses' on the day before the appointed time.... While such a

disappointment would naturally be keen to any prospective bride, it was hardly to be contemplated, in the absence of specific warning, that she would forever refuse to wed if those 'two dresses' were not forthcoming before the day set for the ceremony. The damages are too remote."

c. In Globe Refining Co. v. Landa Cotton Oil Co., 190 U.S. 540 (1903), Justice Holmes declared that "the extent of liability ... should be worked out on terms which it fairly may be presumed he would have assented to if they had been presented to his mind.... [It] depends on what liability the defendant fairly may be supposed to have assumed consciously, or to have warranted the plaintiff reasonably to suppose that it assumed, when the contract was made.... [M]ere notice to a seller of some interest or probable action of the buyer is not enough."

This "tacit agreement" test has not, however, found favor. According to Comment 2 to UCC 2–715, "The 'tacit agreement' test for the recovery of consequential damages is rejected."

tal" and "consequential" damages "resulting from seller's breach," while UCC 2–710 speaks only of "incidental damages to an aggrieved seller."

Courts have read the Code as precluding recovery by sellers of consequential damages, a reading that has resulted in attempts by sellers to characterize claims such as those for additional interest costs resulting from breach as "incidental" rather than "consequential" and therefore allowable under UCC 2–710. In an omitted part of the opinion in the St. Paul Structural Steel case, p. 206 above, the court accepted St. Paul's argument that "interest payments incurred as a result of a buyer's breach of a sales agreement do constitute incidental damages." Can you justify such a distinction between buyers and sellers?

Disputes over the meaning of "consequential" also arise when the contract contains a provision precluding recovery of "consequential damages." See, for example, Article X–B of the General Electric form in the Supplement. For a recent case involving such a clause, see Reynolds Metals Co. v. Westinghouse Electric Corp., 758 F.2d 1073 (5th Cir.1985), holding that where seller of transformer failed to provide competent engineer to install it, buyer was limited to "difference-in-value losses" based on fee that competent engineer would have charged for services that seller had failed to render and could not recover consequential damages for cost of repairing damage to transformer caused by breach.[d]

SPANG INDUSTRIES, INC. v. AETNA CAS. & SURETY CO.
United States Court of Appeals, Second Circuit, 1975.
512 F.2d 365.

MULLIGAN, CIRCUIT JUDGE. [In September 1969, Torrington Construction Co. was the successful bidder with the New York State Department of Transportation on a highway reconstruction job in northern New York. Torrington made a subcontract with Fort Pitt Bridge, a division of Spang Industries, for the structural steel to be used for a bridge over the Battenkill River. One of the terms was "Delivery to be mutually agreed upon."

On November 3, 1969, Torrington advised that it would need the steel in late June 1970. Fort Pitt replied that it was tentatively scheduling delivery accordingly. However, on January 29, 1970, Fort Pitt advised that it could not meet the June date because of an expansion program in which it was engaged and because of "unforeseen delays caused by weather, delivery from suppliers, etc." On May 20, 1970, Fort Pitt promised to ship the steel in August 1970, but most of the steel did not arrive until mid-September. This delayed the pouring of the concrete until the end of October. The danger of freezing temperatures then required that the concrete be poured on a crash basis in a single

---

d. See Western Industries, Inc. v. Newcor Canada Ltd., 739 F.2d 1198 (7th Cir. 1984), holding that it was error to exclude "evidence that the custom of the specialty welding machine trade is not to give a disappointed buyer his consequential damages but just to allow him either to return the machines and get his money back or (for example if the breach consists in delivering them late) keep the machines and get the purchase price reduced to compensate for the costs of delay."

day, which entailed additional costs for Torrington including overtime pay and extra equipment.

When Fort Pitt sued for the unpaid balance of the price, Torrington claimed damages of $23,290.81 for the delay. From a judgment that gave Torrington damages of $7,653.57, Fort Pitt appealed.]

While the damages awarded Torrington are relatively modest ($7,653.57) in comparison with the subcontract price ($132,274.37), Fort Pitt urges that an affirmance of the award will do violence to the rule of Hadley v. Baxendale, 156 Eng.Rep. 145 (Ex.1854), and create a precedent which will have a severe impact on the business of all subcontractors and suppliers.

While it is evident that the function of the award of damages for a breach of contract is to put the plaintiff in the same position he would have been in had there been no breach, Hadley v. Baxendale limits the recovery to those injuries which the parties could reasonably have anticipated at the time the contract was entered into. If the damages suffered do not usually flow from the breach, then it must be established that the special circumstances giving rise to them should reasonably have been anticipated at the time the contract was made.

There can be no question but that Hadley v. Baxendale represents the law in New York and in the United States generally.... There is no dispute between the parties on this appeal as to the continuing viability of Hadley v. Baxendale and its formulation of the rule respecting special damages, and this court has no intention of challenging or questioning its principles, which Chief Judge Cardozo characterized to be, at least in some applications, "tantamount to a rule of property," Kerr S.S. Co. v. Radio Corporation of America, 245 N.Y. 284, 291, 157 N.E. 140, 142 (1927).

The gist of Fort Pitt's argument is that, when it entered into the subcontract to fabricate, furnish and erect the steel in September, 1969, it had received a copy of the specifications which indicated that the total work was to be completed by December 15, 1971. It could not reasonably have anticipated that Torrington would so expedite the work (which was accepted by the State on January 21, 1971) that steel delivery would be called for in 1970 rather than in 1971. Whatever knowledge Fort Pitt received after the contract was entered into, it argues, cannot expand its liability, since it is essential under Hadley v. Baxendale and its Yankee progeny that the notice of the facts which would give rise to special damages in case of breach be given at or before the time the contract was made. The principle urged cannot be disputed.... We do not, however, agree that any violence to the doctrine was done here.

Fort Pitt also knew from the same specifications that Torrington was to commence the work on October 1, 1969. The Fort Pitt letter of September 5, 1969, which constitutes the agreement between the parties, specifically provides: "Delivery to be mutually agreed upon." On November 3, 1969, Torrington, responding to Fort Pitt's inquiry, gave "late June 1970" as its required delivery date and, on November 12, 1969, Fort Pitt stated that it was tentatively scheduling delivery for that time. Thus, at the time when the parties, pursuant to their initial agreement, fixed the date for performance which is crucial here, Fort Pitt knew that a June, 1970 delivery was required. It would be a strained and unpalatable interpretation of Hadley v. Baxendale to now hold that, although the parties left to further agreement the time for delivery, the supplier could reasonably rely upon a 1971 delivery date rather than one the parties later fixed. The behavior of Fort Pitt was totally inconsistent with the posture it now assumes. In November, 1969, it did not quarrel with the date set or seek to avoid the contract. It was not until late January, 1970 that Fort Pitt advised Torrington that, due to unforeseen delays and its expansion program, it could not meet the June date. None of its reasons for late delivery was deemed excusable according to the findings below, and this conclusion is not challenged here. It was not until five months later, on May 20, 1970, after Torrington had threatened to cancel, that Fort Pitt set another date for delivery (early August, 1970) which it again failed to meet, as was found below and not disputed on this appeal.

We conclude that, when the parties enter into a contract which, by its terms, provides that the time of performance is to be fixed at a later date, the knowledge of the consequences of a failure to perform is to be imputed to the defaulting party as of the time the parties agreed upon the date of performance. This comports, in our view, with both the logic and the spirit of Hadley v. Baxendale. Whether the agreement was initially valid despite its indefiniteness or only became valid when a material term was agreed upon is not relevant. At the time Fort Pitt did become committed to a delivery date, it was aware that a June, 1970 performance was required by virtue of its own acceptance. There was no unilateral distortion of the agreement rendering Fort Pitt liable to an extent not theretofore contemplated.

Having proceeded thus far, we do not think it follows automatically that Torrington is entitled to recover the damages it seeks here; further consideration of the facts before us is warranted. Fort Pitt maintains that, under the Hadley v. Baxendale rubric, the damages flowing from its conceded breach are "special" or "consequential" and were not reasonably to be contemplated by the parties. Since Torrington has not proved any "general" or "direct" damages, Fort Pitt urges that the contractor is entitled to nothing. We cannot agree. It is commonplace that parties to a contract normally address themselves to its performance and not to its breach or the consequences that will ensue if there is a default. . . . As the New York Court of Appeals long ago stated:

> [A] more precise statement of this rule is, that a party is liable for all the direct damages which both parties to the contract would have contemplated as flowing from its breach, if at the time they entered into it they had bestowed proper attention upon the subject, and had been fully informed of the facts. [This] may properly be called the fiction of law . . .

Leonard v. New York, Albany & Buffalo Electro–Magnetic Telegraph Co., 41 N.Y. 544, 567 (1870). It is also pertinent to note that the rule does not require that the direct damages must necessarily follow, but only that they are likely to follow; as Lord Justice Asquith commented in Victoria Laundry, Ltd. v. Newman Industries, Ltd., [1949] 2 K.B. 528, 540, are they "on the cards"? We believe here that the damages sought to be recovered were also "in the cards." [a]

It must be taken as a reasonable assumption that, when the delivery date of June, 1970 was set, Torrington planned the bridge erection within a reasonable time thereafter. It is normal construction procedure that the erection of the steel girders would be followed by the installation of a poured concrete platform and whatever railings or superstructure the platform would require. Fort Pitt was an experienced bridge fabricator supplying contractors and the sequence of the work is hardly arcane. Moreover, any delay beyond June or August would assuredly have jeopardized the pouring of the concrete and have forced the postponement of the work until the spring. The work here, as was well known to Fort Pitt, was to be performed in northern New York near the Vermont border. The court below found that continuing freezing weather would have forced the pouring to be delayed until June, 1971. Had Torrington refused delivery or had it been compelled to delay the completion of the work until the spring of 1971, the potential damage claim would have been substantial. Instead, in a good faith effort to mitigate damages, Torrington embarked upon the crash program we have described. It appears to us that this eventuality should have reasonably been anticipated by Fort Pitt as it was experienced in the trade and was supplying bridge steel in northern climes on a project requiring a concrete roadway.

Torrington's recovery under the circumstances is not substantial or cataclysmic from Fort Pitt's point of view. It represents the expenses of unloading steel from the gondola due to Fort Pitt's admitted failure to notify its erection subcontractor, Syracuse Rigging, that the steel had been shipped, plus the costs of premium time, extra equipment and the cost of protecting the work, all occasioned by the realities Torrington faced in the wake of Fort Pitt's breach. In fact, Torrington's original claim of $23,290.81 was whittled down by the court below because of Torrington's failure to establish that its supervisory costs, overhead and certain equipment costs were directly attributable to the delay in delivery of the steel. . . .

In this case, serious or catastrophic injury was avoided by prompt, effective and reasonable mitigation at modest cost. Had Torrington not acted, had it been forced to wait until the following spring to complete the entire job and then sued to recover the profits it would have made had there been performance by Fort Pitt according to the terms of its agreement, then we might well have an appropriate setting for a classical Hadley v. Baxendale controversy. As this case comes to us, it hardly presents that situation. We therefore affirm the judgment below permitting Torrington to offset its damages against the contract price. . . .

a. "On the cards" was, however, severely disapproved as excessively liberal, and other tests, such as "a real danger" and "a serious possibility," were suggested by the noble lords in The Heron II, [1967] 3 All E.R. 686 (House of Lords).

NOTES

(1) *Availability of Cover.* Courts have often assumed that in our market economy there is ordinarily a market on which an injured buyer can cover. They have therefore concluded that losses resulting from the buyer's inability to cover do not follow from the breach in the ordinary course and are foreseeable by the seller only if the seller was aware of facts making the buyer's inability to cover foreseeable. See Marcus & Co. v. K.L.G. Baking Co., 3 A.2d 627 (N.J.1939). Does UCC 2–715(2)(a) dispense with the requirement that the buyer's inability to cover be foreseeable?

(2) *The Case of the Double Chopper Folder.* Bockman Printing was in the business of mailing advertising material for its customers. Baldwin–Gregg contracted to design and build for Bockman by February 1983 a "double chopper folder," a machine that would fold pages at the same speed as they came off the press. In December 1983, Baldwin–Gregg advised Bockman that they could not design such a machine. Bockman sued, claiming that it had made contracts with its customers on the assumption that it would have the more efficient "double chopper folder" by April 1983 and, when the machine was not delivered, Bockman had incurred additional expenses to meet those commitments. On appeal from the award of overtime expenses and the cost of an additional employee, *held,* reversed. Baldwin–Gregg "had no reason to believe that plaintiff would make quotes and enter contracts based on defendants' promise to design and build a double chopper folder by February 1983.... Reasonable skepticism based upon past experience and good business practice would require plaintiff to wait until some initial indicia of success was demonstrated.... The record does not indicate that defendants knew or could reasonably expect plaintiff to enter into contracts months prior to the anticipated delivery date." Bockman Printing & Services, Inc. v. Baldwin–Gregg, Inc., 572 N.E.2d 1094, 1101 (Ill.App.1991).

(3) *Problem.* Federal contracted to sell 75,000 tons of sugar to Czarnikow, to be delivered directly to Czarnikow's customers. In the contracts that Czarnikow then made in turn with its customers, it described the sugar as "Federal" brand, but this was not known to Federal. When the sugar delivered by Federal turned out to be defective, Czarnikow spent $340,000 in the settlement of claims and the defense of law suits brought by its customers, an amount that was inflated because Czarnikow's obligations to them could not be met by delivery of sugar from other suppliers, which it might have obtained on the market. Is Federal liable for $340,000? Czarnikow–Rionda Co. v. Federal Sugar Refining Co., 173 N.E. 913 (N.Y.1930).

Assuming that Federal is liable for $340,000, could Czarnikow recover an additional $100,000 by showing that it had lost this much in profits when its volume dropped because it was deprived of $340,000 in capital? See Lewis v. Mobil Oil Corp., 438 F.2d 500 (8th Cir.1971).

(4) *Jury Instructions.* Because the issue of foreseeability is often one for the jury, it is of interest to see how judges instruct juries on the issue. In Redgrave v. Boston Symphony Orchestra, Inc., 602 F.Supp. 1189 (D.Mass.1985), the actress Vanessa Redgrave sued the Boston Symphony Orchestra for breach of a contract under which she was to appear as narrator in the Orchestra's centenary performances of Stravinsky's opera-oratorio Oedipus Rex, claiming, among other things, damages for harm to her professional career. She alleged that the Orchestra had cancelled the performances in retaliation for her public expressions on political issues, and the Orchestra argued that it had done so because Redgrave's statements in support for the Palestine Liberation Organization

caused it to fear a disruption of the performances. Here is the judge's instruction on the issue of foreseeability.[b]

Damages are allowed for consequential harm to her professional career only if the harm was a foreseeable consequence within the contemplation of the parties to the contract when it was made.

By the phrase "harm that is a foreseeable consequence within the contemplation of the parties" we mean harm of a kind within one or more of the following groups:

(1) harm of a kind that was referred to in communications between the parties while they were negotiating at or before the time the contract was made; (2) any other harm of a kind foreseeable as sufficiently likely to result from cancellation that it would have been taken into account in the exercise of reasonable care in assessing the possible costs and benefits of the proposed contract and in deciding whether or not to enter into the contract. The test of foreseeable harm is an objective one based on what a party to the contract, at the time of making the contract, knew or had reason to foresee or had reason to know or ought to have known would be harm which could result from the breach of the contract. To be within the contemplation of the parties, the harm must be of a kind that either was foreseen or else was foreseeable by a reasonable person in the position of the party now being sued, taking into account the facts and circumstances that party or its agents knew, as well other facts and circumstances, if any, which a reasonable person in that position would have known through the exercise of reasonable care. Thus, in order to find that consequential harm was within the contemplation of both parties in this case, you must find that BSO's agents knew or should have known, when the contract was made, that there was a substantial likelihood that a cancellation would be likely to cause Vanessa Redgrave to lose other professional work.

The plaintiffs have the burden of proving by a preponderance of the evidence that the harm was a foreseeable consequence within the contemplation of the parties. You are not allowed to speculate on this question.

The jury found that harm to Redgrave's professional career was foreseeable and awarded $100,000 in consequential damages. The trial judge concluded that this award was supported by the evidence but that, on principles analogous to the law of defamation, Redgrave could not recover for such harm on the facts of the case. Therefore, he limited Redgrave's recovery to $27,500, the amount she was to be paid for the performances less expenses that she would have incurred to perform the contract. The Court of Appeals held that it was error so to limit damages but concluded that, though the quoted instruction was "appropriate," Redgrave's evidence was sufficient to support only some $12,000 in consequential damages. Redgrave v. Boston Symphony Orchestra, Inc., 831 F.2d 339 (1st Cir.1987).

EMOTIONAL DISTURBANCE

Courts have been reluctant to allow damages for emotional disturbance resulting from breach of contract. See Restatement Second § 353. Why should this be so? Sometimes emotional disturbance is not foresee-

---

b. The judge was Robert E. Keeton, an author of a leading textbook on insurance, R. Keeton & A. Widiss, Insurance Law (1988).

able. Even if emotional disturbance is foreseeable, the resulting dam-
ages are often particularly difficult to establish and to measure. See
Goldberg, Emotional Distress Damages and Breach of Contract: A New
Approach, 20 U.C.Davis L.Rev. 57 (1986).

Furthermore, some courts have likened the award to damages for
emotional disturbance to the award of punitive damages. In Brown v.
Fritz, 699 P.2d 1371 (Idaho 1985), for example, the court overturned an
award of $15,000 for the emotional disturbance of a home buyer when
she discovered that the sellers had fraudulently represented the property. When the buyer learned that the sellers had previously sold part of
the property to another and that the sewage system malfunctioned,
causing raw sewage to accumulate beneath the house, she resold the
property and "suffered severe emotional distress which manifested itself
in physical symptoms, including the need for substantial hospitalization."

The court noted that in a decision five years earlier it had said that
"the commercial nature of the contract" was relevant but not decisive,
indicating a distinction between commercial contracts and " 'non-commercial' contracts, such as to perform a caesarean section, to bury a
body, or to deliver a bride's trousseau." The court also noted that in a
decision two years earlier it had said that punitive damages "should be
awarded only in the most unusual and compelling circumstances" and
"will be sustained on appeal only when it is shown that the defendant
acted in a manner that was 'an extreme deviation from reasonable
standards of conduct, and that the act was performed by the defendant
with an understanding of or disregard for its likely consequences.' "

The home buyer's emotional disturbance "resulted from the negotiations for and the consummation of a contract to convey real property"
and not "from an 'independent' tort involving a physical or a constructive contact between two parties who were not in a contractual relationship." Observing "the close parallel between allowable damages for
breach of contract under the terminology of 'emotional distress' and for
punitive damages," the court held that "when damages are sought for
breach of a contractual relationship, there can be no recovery for
emotional distress suffered by the plaintiff. If the conduct of a defendant has been sufficiently outrageous, we view the proper remedy to be
in the realm of punitive damages."

NOTES

(1) *The Case of the "Whole Damned Business."* Mrs. Lamm employed the
Shingletons, undertakers, to inter her first husband, Mr. Waddell, in a vault
guaranteed to be watertight. About three months later, during a heavy rain, the
vault rose above the ground, and the Shingletons undertook to reinter the body.
In her presence, they raised the vault and found that the casket was wet. The
sight "caused her considerable shock and made her extremely nervous as a result
of which she became a nervous wreck." One of the Shingletons said he would
not get the mud out of the vault and "to hell with the whole damned business,
it's no concern of mine." This made her "so nervous she could hardly stand
up." She sued for breach of contract and, from judgment that she take nothing,

she appealed. *Held:* Reversed. Although "as a general rule," damages for mental anguish are not recoverable in a contract action, the law is "in a state of flux. . . . Where the contract is personal in nature and the contractual duty or obligation is so coupled with matters of mental concern or solicitude, or with the sensibilities of the party to whom the duty is owed, that a breach of that duty will necessarily or reasonably result in mental anguish or suffering, and it should be known to the parties from the nature of the contract that such suffering will result from its breach, compensatory damages therefor may be recovered. . . . The contract was predominantly personal in nature and no substantial pecuniary loss would follow its breach." Lamm v. Shingleton, 55 S.E.2d 810 (N.C.1949).[a]

(2) *The Case of the Designer Dress.* The purchaser of a custom-made wedding dress sued "the high fashion designer . . . known to the cognoscenti simply as Halston" for "mental anguish" caused because the dress was allegedly improperly made and could not be worn by the purchaser's daughter at her wedding. *Held:* Cause of action dismissed. Levin v. Halston Ltd., 398 N.Y.S.2d 339 (N.Y.City Ct.1977).

(c) Certainty

According to the opinion in a leading New York case decided in 1858, damages for breach of contract must "be shown, by clear and satisfactory evidence, to have been actually sustained" and "be shown with certainty, and not left to speculation or conjecture." Griffin v. Colver, 16 N.Y. 489, 491 (1858). Contemporary formulations, however, insist only on "reasonable certainty" rather than on "certainty" itself. Restatement Second § 352, for example, precludes recovery "for loss beyond an amount that the evidence permits to be established with reasonable certainty." Comment 1 to UCC 1–106 explains that damages need not "be calculable with mathematical accuracy," are "at best approximate," and "have to be proved with whatever definiteness and accuracy the facts permit, but no more." Nevertheless, it is clear that in this regard the injured party has a more onerous burden than that imposed by the ordinary requirement that that party make out its case by the "preponderance of evidence." What does this mean in practice? Are there similarities between the operation of this requirement and that of foreseeability?

NOTES

(1) *The Value of a Chance.* In Collatz v. Fox Wisconsin Amusement Corp., 239 Wis. 156, 300 N.W. 162 (1941), the plaintiff, one of two finalists in a quiz

a. For an unusual case granting recovery for "mental anguish" resulting from the defective construction of a new home, see B & M Homes v. Hogan, 376 So.2d 667 (Ala.1979). The court noted that the "largest single investment the average American family will make is the purchase of a home" and concluded that "any reasonable builder could easily foresee that an individual would undergo extreme mental anguish if their newly constructed house contained defects as severe as those shown to exist in this case." For a contrary and more traditional view, see Ostrowe v. Darensbourg, 377 So.2d 1201 (La.1979).

contest held at the defendant's theater, claimed a half interest in the automobile offered as a prize, on the ground that it had been arbitrarily awarded to the other finalist before completion of the contest. The court held for the defendant. The plaintiff "suffered no damage because of the defendant's breach of the contract, for it cannot be assumed nor is it susceptible of proof that had the contest proceeded to a proper finish he would have become the winner." The classic case to the contrary is Chaplin v. Hicks, [1911] 2 K.B. 786, in which the winner of a preliminary round in a beauty contest prevailed. Accord: Wachtel v. National Alfalfa Journal Co., 176 N.W. 801 (Iowa 1920). See Restatement Second § 348(3).

(2) *The Right to Work.* In Shirley MacLaine's case, p. 508 above, could she have recovered more than $750,000? Would not starring in "Bloomer Girl" have enhanced her reputation as an actress? [a] A few courts have favored recovery for lost reputation. See e.g., Herbert Clayton & Jack Waller, Ltd. v. Oliver [1930] A.C. 209, in which the court said: "Here both parties knew that as flowing from the contract the plaintiff would be billed and advertised as appearing at the Hippodrome, and in the theatrical profession this is a valuable right." American courts, however, have generally denied recovery for lost reputation on grounds of either uncertainty or unforeseeability. Cases are discussed in Vanessa Redgrave's case, Note 4, p. 453 above. The court there noted that she did not claim that "her general reputation as a professional actress has been tarnished" but rather "that a number of specific movie and theater performances that would have been offered to her in the usual course of events were not offered to her." How did Redgrave's situation differ from MacLaine's?

(3) *Nominal Damages.* The plaintiff who proves a breach of contract but fails to prove damages is traditionally awarded nominal damages (six cents or one dollar). Such an award may serve as a declaration of the plaintiff's rights and may also carry with it an award of court costs.

FERA v. VILLAGE PLAZA, INC.
Supreme Court of Michigan, 1976.
396 Mich. 639, 242 N.W.2d 372.

T.G. KAVANAGH, CHIEF JUSTICE. Plaintiffs received a jury award of $200,000 for loss of anticipated profits in their proposed new business as a result of defendants' breach of a lease. The Court of Appeals reversed.... We reverse and reinstate the jury's award.

FACTS

On August 20, 1965 plaintiffs and agents of Fairborn–Village Plaza executed a ten-year lease for a "book and bottle" shop in defendants' proposed shopping center. This lease provided for occupancy of a specific location at a rental of $1,000 minimum monthly rent plus 5% of annual receipts in excess of $240,000. A $1,000 deposit was paid by plaintiffs.

After this lease was executed, plaintiffs gave up approximately 600 square feet of their leased space so that it could be leased to another

a. Compare the discussion of sentimental value in Note 1, p. 485 above.

tenant. In exchange, it was agreed that liquor sales would be excluded from the percentage rent override provision of the lease.

Complications arose, including numerous work stoppages. Bank of the Commonwealth received a deed in lieu of foreclosure after default by Fairborn and Village Plaza. Schostak Brothers managed the property for the bank.

When the space was finally ready for occupancy, plaintiffs were refused the space for which they had contracted because the lease had been misplaced, and the space rented to other tenants. Alternative space was offered but refused by plaintiffs as unsuitable for their planned business venture.

Plaintiffs initiated suit in Wayne Circuit Court, alleging *inter alia* a claim for anticipated lost profits. The jury returned a verdict for plaintiffs against all defendants for $200,000.

The Court of Appeals reversed and remanded for new trial on the issue of damages only, holding that the trial court "erroneously permitted lost profits as the measure of damages for breach of the lease." 52 Mich.App. 532, 542, 218 N.W.2d 155, 160.

In Jarrait v. Peters, 145 Mich. 29, 31–32, 108 N.W. 432 (1906), plaintiff was prevented from taking possession of the leased premises. The jury gave plaintiff a judgment which included damages for lost profits. This Court reversed:

> "It is well settled upon authority that the measure of damages when a lessor fails to give possession of the leased premises is the difference between the actual rental value and the rent reserved. 1 Sedgwick on Damages (8th Ed.) par. 185. Mr. Sedgwick says:
>
> " 'If the business were a new one, since there could be no basis on which to estimate profits, the plaintiff must be content to recover according to the general rule.'
>
> "The rule is different where the business of the lessee has been interrupted. . . .
>
> "The evidence admitted tending to show the prospective profits plaintiff might have made for the ensuing two years should therefore have been excluded under the objections made by defendant, and the jury should have been instructed that the plaintiff's damages, if any, would be the difference between the actual rental value of the premises and the rent reserved in the lease."

Six years later, in Isbell v. Anderson Carriage Co., 170 Mich. 304, 318, 136 N.W. 457, 462 (1912), the Court wrote:

> "It has sometimes been stated as a rule of law that prospective profits are so speculative and uncertain that they cannot be recognized in the measure of damages. This is not because they are profits, but because they are so often not susceptible of proof to a reasonable degree of certainty. Where the proof is available, prospective profits may be recovered, when proven, as other damages.

But the jury cannot be asked to guess. They are to try the case upon evidence, not upon conjecture."

These cases and others since should not be read as stating a rule of law which prevents every new business from recovering anticipated lost profits for breach of contract. The rule is merely an application of the doctrine that "[i]n order to be entitled to a verdict, or a judgment, for damages for breach of contract, the plaintiff must lay a basis for a reasonable estimate of the extent of his harm, measured in money". 5 Corbin on Contracts, § 1020, p. 124. The issue becomes one of sufficiency of proof. "The jury should not [be] allowed to speculate or guess upon this question of the amount of loss of profits." Kezeli v. River Rouge Lodge IOOF, 195 Mich. 181, 188, 161 N.W. 838, 840 (1917)....

The rule was succinctly stated in Shropshire v. Adams, 40 Tex.Civ. App. 339, 344, 89 S.W. 448, 450 (1905):

"Future profits as an element of damage are in no case excluded merely because they are profits but because they are uncertain. In any case when by reason of the nature of the situation they may be established with reasonable certainty they are allowed."

It is from these principles that the "new business"/"interrupted business" distinction has arisen.

"If a business is one that has already been established a reasonable prediction can often be made as to its future on the basis of its past history. * * * If the business * * * has not had such a history as to make it possible to prove with reasonable accuracy what its profits have been in fact, the profits prevented are often but not necessarily too uncertain for recovery." 5 Corbin on Contracts, § 1023, pp. 147, 150–151. Cf. Jarrait v. Peters, supra.

The Court of Appeals based its opinion reversing the jury's award on two grounds: First, that a new business cannot recover damages for lost profits for breach of a lease. We have expressed our disapproval of that rule. Secondly, the Court of Appeals held plaintiffs barred from recovery because the proof of lost profits was entirely speculative. We disagree.

The trial judge in a thorough opinion made the following observations upon completion of the trial.

"On the issue of lost profits, there were days and days of testimony. The defendants called experts from the Michigan Liquor Control Commission and from Cunningham Drug Stores, who have a store in the area, and a man who ran many other stores. The plaintiffs called experts and they, themselves, had experience in the liquor sales business, in the book sales business and had been representatives of liquor distribution firms in the area.

"The issue of the speculative, conjectural nature of future profits was probably the most completely tried issue in the whole case. Both sides covered this point for days on direct and cross-examination. The proofs ranged from no lost profits to two hundred and seventy thousand dollars over a ten-year period as the highest in the testimony. A witness for the defendants, an expert from Cunningham Drug Company, testified the plaintiffs probably would lose money. Mr. Fera, an expert in his own right, testified the profits would probably be two hundred and seventy thousand dollars. The jury found two hundred thousand dollars. This is well within the limits of the high and the low testimony presented by both sides, and a judgment was granted by the jury.

. . .

"The Court cannot invade the finding of fact by the jury, unless there is no testimony to support the jury's finding. There is testimony to support the jury's finding. We must realize that witness Stein is an interested party in this case, personally. He is an officer or owner in Schostak Brothers. He may personally lose money as a result of this case. The jury had to weigh this in determining his credibility. How much credibility they gave his testimony was up to them. How much weight they gave to counter-evidence was up to them. . . .

"The Court must decide whether or not the jury had enough testimony to take this fact from the speculative-conjecture category and find enough facts to be able to make a legal finding of fact. This issue [damages for lost profits] was the most completely tried issue in the whole case. Both sides put in testimony that took up days and encompassed experts on both sides. This fact was adequately taken from the category of speculation and conjecture by the testimony and placed in the position of those cases that hold that even though loss of profits is hard to prove, if proven they should be awarded by the jury. In this case, the jury had ample testimony to make this decision from both sides. . . ."

As Judge Wickens observed, the jury was instructed on the law concerning speculative damages. The case was thoroughly tried by all the parties. Apparently, the jury believed the plaintiffs. That is its prerogative.

The testimony presented during the trial was conflicting. The weaknesses of plaintiffs' specially prepared budget were thoroughly explored on cross-examination. Defendants' witnesses testified concerning the likelihood that plaintiffs would not have made profits if the contract had been performed. There was conflicting testimony concerning the availability of a liquor license. All this was spread before the jury. The jury weighed the conflicting testimony and determined that plaintiffs were entitled to damages of $200,000.

As we stated in Anderson v. Conterio, 303 Mich. 75, 79, 5 N.W.2d 572, 574 (1942):

"The testimony . . . is in direct conflict, and that of plaintiff . . . was impeached to some extent. However, it cannot be said as a matter of law that the testimony thus impeached was deprived of all probative value or that the jury could not believe it. The credibility of witnesses is for the jury, and it is not for us to determine who is to be believed."

The trial judge, who also listened to all of the conflicting testimony, denied defendants' motion for a new trial, finding that the verdict was justified by the evidence. We find no abuse of discretion in that decision. . . .

While we might have found plaintiffs' proofs lacking had we been members of the jury, that is not the standard of review we employ. "As a reviewing court we will not invade the fact finding of the jury or remand for entry of judgment unless the factual record is so clear that reasonable minds may not disagree." Hall v. Detroit, 383 Mich. 571, 574, 177 N.W.2d 161, 163 (1970). This is not the situation here.

The Court of Appeals is reversed and the trial court's judgment on the verdict is reinstated. . . .

COLEMAN, JUSTICE (concurring in part, dissenting in part). Although anticipated profits from a new business may be determined with a reasonable degree of certainty such was not the situation regarding loss of profits from liquor sales as proposed by plaintiffs.

First, plaintiffs had no license and a Liquor Control Commission regional supervisor and a former commissioner testified that the described book and bottle store could not obtain a license. Further, the proofs of possible profits from possible liquor sales—if a license could have been obtained—were too speculative. The speculation of possible licensing plus the speculation of profits in this case combine to cause my opinion that profits from liquor sales should not have been submitted to the jury.

I agree with Judge O'Hara in his Court of Appeals dissent and would have allowed proof of loss from the bookstore operation to go to the jury, but not proof of loss from liquor sales. His remedy is also approved. I would affirm the trial court judgment conditioned upon plaintiffs' consenting within 30 days following the release of this opinion, to "remitting that portion of the judgment in excess of $60,000. Otherwise, the judgment should be reversed and a new trial had". Plaintiffs are also entitled to the $1,000 deposit.

NOTES

(1) *New Businesses.* For a stricter view, see Evergreen Amusement Corp. v. Milstead, 112 A.2d 901 (Md.1955), an action against a contractor for damages for delay in the opening of a drive-in theater from June 1 to mid-August. The operator of the theater proffered a witness who had built a majority of the drive-in theaters in the area and who would have testified as to reasonably anticipated profits for the months in question by comparison with the theater's profits for the same months of the following year. The court held that it was not error to refuse to hear the witness. "[T]he general rule clearly is that loss of profit is a definite element of damages in an action for breach of contract or in an action for harming an established business which has been operating for a sufficient length of time to afford a basis of estimation with some degree of certainty as to the probable loss of profits, but that, on the other hand, loss of profits from a

business which has not gone into operation may not be recovered because they are merely speculative and incapable of being ascertained with the requisite degree of certainty.... While this Court has not laid down a flat rule (and does not hereby do so), nevertheless, no case has permitted recovery of lost profits under comparable circumstances."

(2) *Royalties From Artistic Creations.* The requirement of reasonable certainty has plagued plaintiffs whose claims are based on lost royalties on artistic creations. In Freund v. Washington Square Press, Inc., discussed in Note, p. 520 above, for example, the author of a book on modern drama sued his publisher for breach of its contract to publish and pay royalties on the book. The court held that he was properly denied recovery for his lost royalties. "His expectancy interest in the royalties—the profit he stood to gain from the sale of the published book—while theoretically compensable, was speculative. Although this work is not plaintiff's first, at trial he provided no stable foundation for a reasonable estimate of royalties he would have earned had defendant not breached its promise to publish."

The plaintiff fared somewhat better, however, in Contemporary Mission, Inc. v. Famous Music Corp., 557 F.2d 918 (2d Cir.1977), in which New York law was applied. There a group of Roman Catholic priests who wrote musical compositions and recordings sued Famous Music for breach of its contract to make and sell records on a royalty basis from the master tape recording of their rock opera "Virgin." It was held that the trial court erred in excluding a statistical analysis, together with expert testimony, in order to prove how successful the most successful of the opera's single recordings, "Fear No Evil," would have been. The court acknowledged, citing the Freund case, that the requirement of certainty "operates with particular severity in cases involving artistic creations such as books, ... movies, ... and, by analogy, records." Nevertheless, at the time of the breach, "the record was real, the price was fixed, the market was buying and the record's success, while modest, was increasing. Even after the promotional efforts ended, the record was withdrawn from the marketplace, it was carried, as a result of its own momentum, to an additional 10,000 sales and to a rise from approximately number 80 on the "Hot Soul Singles' chart of Billboard magazine to number 61." The court, however, rejected the plaintiff's "domino theory" of projected damages under which, if "Fear No Evil" had become a "hit," it would have generated opportunities for concert and theatrical tours and similar benefits on the ground that "these additional benefits are too dependent upon taste or fancy to be considered anything other than speculative and uncertain."

(3) *Good Will.* The requirement of certainty is likely to be particularly troublesome to a claimant that seeks to recover for loss of business reputation, or what is commonly termed "good will." For many years, Pennsylvania refused to allow recovery for loss of good will on the ground that "damages of this nature would be entirely too speculative". Harry Rubin & Sons v. Consolidated Pipe Co., 153 A.2d 472, 476 (Pa.1959) (wholesaler's loss of good will due to manufacturer's failure to deliver hula hoops). In 1990, however, Pennsylvania joined the overwhelming majority of states by overruling such cases "to the extent they prohibit a plaintiff from alleging a claim for damage to good will as a matter of law." AM/PM Franchise Ass'n v. Atlantic Richfield Co., 584 A.2d 915, 926 (Pa.1990) (gasoline franchisee's loss of good will due to franchisor's breach of warranty).

SECTION 3. "LIQUIDATED DAMAGES" AND "PENALTIES"

———

At the beginning of this book, it was pointed out that our law's concern is directed at relief of promisees to redress breach rather than at punishment of promisors to compel performance, and that for this reason punitive damages are not ordinarily awarded for breach of contract. See White v. Benkowski, p. 14 above. The *promisee*, however, may be concerned with compulsion of the promisor. Consider the following explanation, given by a bridge engineer for the California Division of Highways, of the completion assessment—the per-day assessment for each day the contractor overruns the specified contract time. "The sole purpose of a completion assessment is to assure that the contract work will be done within the time specified, ... to threaten the Contractor with sufficient monetary loss so that he will find it advantageous to apply sufficient men and equipment to the work to get it done on time. Whereas moderate liquidated damages such as $100 per day may well be used to insure the completion of a normal project having no special urgency, higher amounts are used to force faster work on jobs which must be finished in less than a normal construction time. High assessments may be used to emphasize the need for haste and should be of sufficient size to make it economically desirable that the contractor expedite his work by the use of multiple shifts or additional equipment." Elliott, A Study of Liquidated Damages on Highway Contracts 5 (1956). Should courts lend their aid to the enforcement of such penalties where the parties have bargained for and agreed to them?

NOTES

(1) *Penalties in Other Legal Systems.* Are there reasons of public policy that justify a limitation on freedom of contract with respect to penalties? Are terms providing for penalties more onerous than other terms? Some insights may be gained from a look at other legal systems.

According to article 1152 of the French Civil Code: "When the agreement provides that the party who fails to carry it out shall pay a certain sum as damages, no larger or smaller amount can be awarded to the other party." In 1975, however, following a recommendation that there be judicial control over penal clauses in leases, this article was amended by adding: "However, the judge may reduce or increase the penalty that has been agreed upon if it is plainly excessive or ridiculously low. No effect will be given to an agreement to the contrary." What might have prompted these changes?

(2) *Penalties in California.* In 1977 California enacted a statute under which "a provision in a contract liquidating the damages for the breach of the contract is valid unless the party seeking to invalidate the provision establishes that the provision was unreasonable under the circumstances existing at the time the contract was made." Cal.Civil Code § 1671. The statute does not apply against a consumer and in some other situations.

———

WASSERMAN'S INC. v. TOWNSHIP OF MIDDLETOWN

Supreme Court of New Jersey, 1994.
137 N.J. 238, 645 A.2d 100.

POLLOCK, J. Pursuant to a public advertisement for bids, plaintiff Wasserman's Inc. (Wasserman's) and defendant, Township of Middletown (the Township or Middletown), entered into a commercial lease for a tract of municipally-owned property. The agreement contained a clause providing that if the Township cancelled the lease, it would pay the lessee, Wasserman's, a pro-rata reimbursement for any improvement costs and damages of twenty-five percent of the lessee's average gross receipts for one year. In 1989, the Township cancelled the lease and sold the property, but refused to pay the agreed damages. On cross-motions for summary judgment, the Law Division held that the lease and the cancellation clause were enforceable. It subsequently required the Township to pay damages in the amount of $346,058.44 plus interest. In an unreported opinion, the Appellate Division affirmed. We granted certification, 134 *N.J.* 478, 634 A.2d 525 (1993), and now affirm the judgment on liability but reverse and remand for a plenary trial on damages. We conclude that the lease is enforceable. We affirm the award of renovation costs and remand to the Law Division the issue of the enforceability of the stipulated damages clause.

I

The Township owned a parcel of approximately 20,500 square feet in a commercial area at 89 Leonardville Road, in the Belford section of the Township. From 1948 to 1968, Wasserman's leased the property from the Township for a 3,200–square–foot general store. In 1969, the Township advertised for bids to lease the property, which the Township evaluated at $47,500. Wasserman's submitted the sole bid. After rejecting Wasserman's bid, the Township again advertised in May 1970. Once again, Wasserman's submitted the only bid. Subsequent negotiations resulted in the Township adopting a resolution approving the lease on September 22, 1970. The parties signed the lease on May 21, 1971.

At the center of the dispute is the cancellation clause in the lease. The bid specifications provided that if the Township cancelled the lease, it would pay the tenant a pro-rata reimbursement of improvement costs. Consistent with the specifications, the clause provides in part for reimbursement: "payment to be made shall be (1.) total value of all improvements made by lessee at time of construction × (multiplied by) years remaining in Lease term ÷ (divided by) total number of years in Lease term." More controversial is the second half of the clause, the terms of which were not included in the original specifications. That provision requires the Township to pay "(2.) twenty-five percent of the lessee[']s average gross receipts for one year (to be computed by + (adding) the lessee[']s total gross receipts for the lessee[']s three full fiscal years immediately preceding the time of cancellation of the lease and ÷ (dividing by) 12 (twelve) [ )]." The lease also provided for a fixed monthly rental of $458.33, with no escalation for the entire thirty-year term.

Wasserman's made the agreed improvements, spending $142,336.01 in 1971 on the expansion and renovation of the store, which now is approximately 5,600 square feet. In August 1973, Wasserman's sold "the business," presumably the corporate assets, and sublet the premises to Rocco Laurino doing business as Jo–Ro, Inc. (Jo–Ro). The sublease provided that Jo–Ro was to pay Wasserman's a monthly rent of $1,850. Wasserman's and Jo–Ro, jointly described as "plaintiffs," provided for an allocation of any payments made by the Township if it cancelled the lease.

In 1977, Samuel Krawet and Arnold Kornblum purchased from Laurino all of the Jo–Ro stock for $95,000. In connection with the sale, Laurino executed an affidavit, representing that the lease between Middletown and Wasserman's was in full force and effect. Additionally, the Township sent a letter to Wasserman's stating that the Township would permit subletting the property to Jo–Ro.

By letter dated December 7, 1987, the Township cancelled the lease effective December 31, 1988. Krawet and Kornblum vacated the premises, leaving them without a place for their business. In June 1989, the Township, after advertising the property at public auction, sold it for $610,000, nearly thirteen times the value of the property at the time the Township had leased it to Wasserman's in 1971. . . .

II

Plaintiffs sued for breach of contract, seeking in part damages under the terms of the lease. The Township filed an answer and counterclaim seeking a declaration of invalidity of that part of the cancellation clause that required the Township to pay as damages twenty-five percent of the lessee's gross receipts. Originally the Township also disputed its obligation to reimburse Wasserman's for a pro-rata portion of the cost of renovations, but it now concedes the validity of that provision. The parties filed cross-motions for summary judgment.

The Law Division initially granted plaintiffs a partial summary judgment according "full force and effect" to the lease and the cancellation clause. On a subsequent motion, the court awarded plaintiffs damages of $346,058.44 plus ten-percent prejudgment interest. The trial court calculated damages as follows:

$142,336.01 (construction costs) multiplied by 11.75 (remaining years) divided by 30 years (term of lease) for a total of $55,748.27.

$3,483,722.25 (Jo–Ro's gross receipts for the years 1985, 1986, 1987) divided by 12 equalling $290,310.18.

Construction compensation	$ 55,748.27
Gross receipts compensation	+ 290,310.18
Total amount due	$346,058.45

III

[In an omitted part of the opinion the court rejected the Township's argument that the lease did not meet the requirements for a valid public contract.]

IV

The provision in the termination clause providing for damages based on the lessee's gross receipts presents a more difficult issue. The issue is whether that provision is an enforceable liquidated damages provision or is an enforceable penalty clause.

Disapproval of penalty clauses originated at early common law when debtors bound themselves through sealed penalty bonds for twice the amount of their actual debts. Charles J. Goetz & Robert E. Scott, Liquidated Damages, Penalties and the Just Compensation Principle: Some Notes on an Enforcement Model and a Theory of Efficient Breach, 77 Colum.L.Rev. 554, 554 (1977) (hereinafter Goetz & Scott). Because clauses in penalty bonds "carried an unusual danger of oppression and extortion," equity courts refused to enforce them. Id. at 555. "This equitable rule, designed to prevent overreaching and to give relief from unconscionable bargains, was later adopted by courts of law." John D. Calamari & Joseph M. Perillo, The Law of Contracts, § 14–31 at 639 (3d ed. 1987) (hereinafter Calamari & Perillo). In a sense, judicial reluctance to enforce penalty clauses is a product of history.

For more than five centuries, courts have scrutinized contractual provisions that specify damages payable in the event of breach. Wassenaar v. Panos, 111 Wis.2d 518, 331 N.W.2d 357, 362 (1983); Goetz & Scott, supra, 77 Colum.L.Rev. at 554. The validity of these "stipulated damage clauses" has depended on a judicial assessment of the clauses as an unenforceable penalty or as an enforceable provision for "liquidated damage." Thus, " '[l]iquidated damages' and 'penalties' are terms used to reflect legal conclusions as to the enforceability or nonenforceability, respectively, of stipulated damage clauses." Kenneth W. Clarkson et al., Liquidated Damages v. Penalties: Sense or Nonsense?, 1978 Wis.L.Rev. 351, 351 n. 1 (hereinafter Clarkson).

Thirty years ago, the Appellate Division distinguished liquidated damages and penalty clauses:

> *Liquidated damages* is the sum a party to a contract agrees to pay if he breaks some promise, and which, having been arrived at by a good faith effort to estimate in advance the actual damages that will probably ensue form the breach, is legally recoverable as agreed damages if the breach occurs. A *penalty* is the sum a party agrees to pay in the event of a breach, but which is fixed, not as a preestimate of probable actual damages, but as a punishment, the threat of which is designed to prevent the breach.

Parties to a contract may not fix a penalty for its breach. The settled rule in this State is that such a contract is unlawful.

[Westmount Country Club v. Kameny, 82 N.J.Super. 200, 205,
197 A.2d 379 (1964) (citations omitted).]

Stating the distinction, however, has been easier than describing its
underlying rationale. " '[T]he ablest judges have declared that they felt
themselves embarrassed in ascertaining the principle on which the
decisions [distinguishing penalties from liquidated damages] were founded.' " E. Allan Farnsworth, Contracts § 12.18 at 937 (2d ed. 1990)
(alterations in original) (quoting Cotheal v. Talmage, 9 N.Y. 551, 553
(1854))....

As the law has evolved, a stipulated damage clause "must constitute
a reasonable forecast of the provable injury resulting from breach;
otherwise, the clause will be unenforceable as a penalty and the non-
breaching party will be limited to conventional damage measures."
Goetz & Scott, supra, 77 Colum.L.Rev. at 554. So viewed, "reasonableness" emerges as the standard for deciding the validity of stipulated
damages clauses. See Wassenaar, supra, 331 N.W.2d at 361 (noting that
"[t]he overall single test of validity is whether the clause is reasonable
under the totality of circumstances").

The reasonableness test has developed as a compromise between two
competing viewpoints concerning stipulated damages clauses. The Wisconsin Supreme Court has described the policy considerations underlying
these viewpoints:

> Enforcement of stipulated damages clauses is urged because the
> clauses serve several purposes. The clauses allow the parties to
> control their exposure to risk by setting the payment for breach in
> advance. They avoid the uncertainty, delay, and expense of using
> the judicial process to determine actual damages. They allow the
> parties to fashion a remedy consistent with economic efficiency in a
> competitive market, and they enable the parties to correct what the
> parties perceive to be inadequate judicial remedies by agreeing upon
> a formula which may include damage elements too uncertain or
> remote to be recovered under rules of damages applied by the courts.
> In addition to these policies specifically relating to stipulated dam-
> ages clauses, considerations of judicial economy and freedom of
> contract favor enforcement of stipulated damages clauses.

> A competing set of policies disfavors stipulated damages clauses,
> and thus courts have not been willing to enforce stipulated damages
> clauses blindly without carefully scrutinizing them. Public law, not
> private law, ordinarily defines the remedies of the parties. Stipu-
> lated damages are an exception to this rule. Stipulated damages
> allow private parties to perform the judicial function of providing
> the remedy in breach of contract cases, namely, compensation of the
> nonbreaching party, and courts must ensure that the private remedy
> does not stray too far from the legal principle of allowing compensa-
> tory damages. Stipulated damages substantially in excess of injury
> may justify an inference of unfairness in bargaining or an objection-
> able *in terrorem* agreement to deter a party from breaching the

contract, to secure performance, and to punish the breaching party if the deterrent is ineffective.

[Wassenaar, supra, 331 N.W.2d at 362.]

Consistent with the principle of reasonableness, New Jersey courts have viewed enforceability of stipulated damages clauses as depending on whether the set amount "is a reasonable forecast of just compensation for the harm that is caused by the breach" and whether that harm "is incapable or very difficult of accurate estimate." Westmount Country Club, supra, 82 N.J.Super. at 206, 197 A.2d 379....

Uncertainty or difficulty in assessing damages is best viewed not as an independent test, Calamari and Perillo, supra, § 14–31 at 641; Goetz & Scott, supra, 77 Colum.L.Rev. at 559 (stating, "liquidated damages provisions have seldom been voided solely because the damages were easy to estimate"), but rather as an element of assessing the reasonableness of a liquidated damages clause, Wassenaar, supra, 331 N.W.2d at 363. Thus, "[t]he greater the difficulty of estimating or proving damages, the more likely the stipulated damages will appear reasonable." *Ibid.*

Some courts in other jurisdictions have also considered whether the parties intended the clause to be one for liquidated damages. Clarkson, supra, 1978 Wis.L.Rev. at 353. Even those courts recognize that "subjective intent has little bearing on whether the clause is objectively reasonable." Wassenaar, supra, 331 N.W.2d at 363. For the past eighty years, New Jersey courts have relied on the "circumstances of the case and not on the words used by the parties" in determining the enforceability of stipulated damages clauses. Gibbs v. Cooper, 86 N.J.L. 226, 227–28, 90 A. 1115 (E. & A.1914); see also Farnsworth, supra, § 12.18 at 939 ("the parties' own characterization of the sum as 'liquidated damages' or as a 'penalty' is not controlling"); Clarkson, supra, 1978 Wis.L.Rev. at 353 (same)....

Although the Appellate Division has indicated that courts should determine the enforceability of a stipulated damages clause as of the time of the making of the contract. Westmount Country Club, supra, 82 N.J.Super. at 206, 197 A.2d 379, the modern trend is towards assessing reasonableness either at the time of contract formation or at the time of the breach. Calamari & Perillo, supra, § 14–31 at 642 (stating, "there are two moments at which the liquidated damages clause may be judged rather than just one").

Actual damages, moreover, reflect on the reasonableness of the parties' prediction of damages. "If the damages provided for in the contract are grossly disproportionate to the actual harm sustained, the courts usually conclude that the parties' original expectations were unreasonable." Wassenaar, supra, 331 N.W.2d at 364; see 5A Corbin on Contracts § 1063 (1951) (Corbin) ("It is to be observed that hindsight is frequently better than foresight, and that, in passing judgment upon the honesty and genuineness of the pre-estimate made by the parties, the court cannot help but be influenced by its knowledge of subsequent events."). Determining enforceability at the time either when the contract is made or when it is breached encourages more frequent enforcement of stipulated damages clauses. Calamari & Perillo, supra, § 14–31 at 642.

Two of the most authoritative statements concerning liquidated damages are contained in the Uniform Commercial Code and the Restatement (Second) of Contracts, both of which emphasize reasonableness as the touchstone. Farnsworth, supra, § 12.18 at 938. Thus, section 2–718 of the Uniform Commercial Code, adopted in New Jersey as N.J.S.A. 12A:2–718, provides:

> (1) Damages for breach by either party may be liquidated in the agreement but only at an amount which is reasonable in the light of the anticipated or actual harm caused by the breach, the difficulties of proof of loss, and the inconvenience or nonfeasibility of otherwise obtaining an adequate remedy.

Similarly, the Second Restatement of Contracts provides:

> Damages for breach by either party may be liquidated in the agreement but only at an amount that is reasonable in the light of the anticipated or actual loss caused by the breach and the difficulties of proof of loss. A term fixing unreasonably large liquidated damages is unenforceable on grounds of public policy as a penalty.

> [Restatement (Second) of Contracts § 356(1) (1981).]

Consistent with the trend toward enforcing stipulated damages clauses, the Appellate Division has recognized that such clauses should be deemed presumptively reasonable and that the party challenging such a clause should bear the burden of proving its unreasonableness.... Similarly, most courts today place the burden on the party challenging a stipulated damages clause....

In commercial transactions between parties with comparable bargaining power, stipulated damage provisions can provide a useful and efficient remedy. See Priebe & Sons v. United States, 332 U.S. 407, 411–13, 68 S.Ct. 123, 126, 92 L.Ed. 32, 38–39 (1947) (observing that "[t]oday the law does not look with disfavor upon 'liquidated damages' provisions in contracts[ ] [w]hen they are fair and reasonable attempts to fix just compensation for anticipated loss caused by breach"). Sophisticated parties acting under the advice of counsel often negotiate stipulated damages clauses to avoid the cost and uncertainty of litigation. Such parties can be better situated than courts to provide a fair and efficient remedy. Absent concerns about unconscionability, courts frequently need ask no more than whether the clause is reasonable. We do not reach the issue of the enforceability of liquidated damage clauses in consumer contracts. Notwithstanding the presumptive reasonableness of stipulated damage clauses, we are sensitive to the possibility that, as their history discloses, such clauses may be unconscionable and unjust....

V

The purpose of a stipulated damages clause is not to compel the promisor to perform, but to compensate the promisee for non-performance. Farnsworth, supra, § 12.18 at 936. Accordingly, provisions for liquidated damages are enforceable only if "the amount so fixed is a reasonable forecast of just compensation for the harm that is caused by the breach." Westmount Country Club, supra, 82 N.J.Super. at 206, 197 A.2d 379; see also Restatement (Second) of Contracts, supra, § 356 comment a (stating, "The parties to a contract may effectively provide in advance the damages that are to be payable in the event of breach as long as the provision does not disregard the principle of just compensation."). One injured by a breach of contract is entitled only to just and adequate compensation. McDaniel Bros. Constr. Co. v. Jordy, 195 So.2d 922, 925 (Miss.1967). Thus, the subject cancellation clause is unreasonable if it does more than compensate plaintiffs for their approximate actual damages caused by the breach.

Whether measured from the time of execution of the contract or from the termination of the lease, see Westmount Country Club, supra, 82 N.J.Super. at 206, 197 A.2d 379, damages based on gross receipts run the risk of being found unreasonable. Generally speaking, gross receipts do not reflect actual losses incurred because of the cancellation. Gross receipts, unlike net profits, do not account for ordinary expenses; nor do they account for the expenses specifically attributable to the breach. Here, we cannot determine whether the stipulated amount was based on damages that would likely flow from a breach or whether it is an arbitrary figure unrelated to any such damages....

Courts also have disapproved the use of gross receipts as a measure of damages apart from stipulated damages clauses.... Evaluating damages based on gross income is problematic partly because such damages would be too speculative or uncertain. Furthermore, basing damages on gross profits could award the plaintiff a windfall....

We cannot determine from plaintiffs' gross receipts the losses they sustained because of the Township's cancellation of the lease. The subject clause requires the Township to pay damages of twenty-five percent of the lessee's average gross receipts for one year. Under the lease, average gross receipts are calculated by taking an average of the lessee's total gross receipts for three fiscal years immediately preceding the cancellation. So calculated, Jo–Ro's average yearly gross was $1,161,240.75. Twenty-five percent of this figure amounts to $290,-310.18.

This amount, however, does not necessarily reflect plaintiffs' actual losses on considering operating expenses or relocation costs and other expenses attributable to defendant's breach. As reflected in Jo–Ro's income-tax returns, Jo–Ro earned a net profit of $3,649 in 1985, $414 in 1986, and sustained a loss of $323 in 1987. We recognize the difference between tax losses and actual losses. Yet, to the extent that tax returns reflect actual profit or loss, they demonstrate the unreasonableness of damages exceeding $290,000, which were calculated on the basis of gross receipts.

The decision whether a stipulated damages clause is enforceable is a question of law for the court.... Although the question is one of law, it may require resolution of underlying factual issues....

On balance, we believe we should remand this matter to the trial court to consider the reasonableness of the clause in light of this opinion. In resolving that issue, the court should consider, among other relevant considerations, the reasonableness of the use of gross receipts as the measure of damages no matter when the cancellation occurs; the significance of the award of damages based on twenty-five percent of one year's average gross receipts, rather than on some other basis such as total gross receipts computed for each year remaining under the lease; the reasoning of the parties that supported the calculation of the stipulated damages; the lessee's duty to mitigate damages; and the fair market rent and availability of replacement space. We leave to the sound discretion of the trial court the extent to which additional proof is necessary on the reasonableness of the clause. Because stipulated damages clauses are presumptively reasonable, supra at 252–253, 645 A.2d at 108, the burden of production and of persuasion rests on the Township.

To summarize, we affirm the judgment of the Appellate Division that the Township is liable to plaintiffs for terminating the lease.... We also affirm the judgment of the Appellate Division awarding plaintiffs damages of $55,748.27 for renovation costs. We remand to the Law Division the issue whether the clause requiring payment of stipulated damages based on the lessee's gross receipts is a valid liquidated damages clause.

The judgment of the Appellate Division is affirmed in part, reversed in part, and the matter is remanded to the Law Division.

NOTES

(1) *Arguments on Remand.* If you were the lawyer for Wasserman's on remand, what arguments and evidence would you use to meet the "burden" of challenging the clause? If you were the lawyer for the Township, how would you counteract Justice Pollock's critical remarks on gross receipts as a standard?

(2) *Time of Formation or Time of Breach?* Note that Justice Pollock reports that "the modern trend is towards assessing reasonableness either at the time of contract formation or at the time of the breach." This echoes the language of UCC 2–718, which speaks of the "anticipated or actual harm." But Article 2A of the Code, added in 1987 to deal with leases of goods, departs from the language of Article 2 and speaks of only the "anticipated harm." UCC 2A–504(1). The comments say that this section is intended to give "greater flexibility" than UCC 2–718 and that whether common formulae used in leases "are enforceable will be determined in the context of each case by applying a standard of reasonableness in light of the harm anticipated when the formula was agreed to." Does Article 2A's deletion of the reference to "actual harm" give "greater flexibility?" Does it reflect the "modern trend" referred to by Judge Pollock?

(3) *Similarities and Dissimilarities.* Reconsider the Case of the Literate Lessee (Note 2, p. 435 above), where you encountered a clause dealing with the

consequences of a lessee's failure to pay rent. Was that a penalty clause? In what ways did it differ from that in Wasserman's lease?

(4) *Arbitration and Liquidated Damages.* Suppose that Wasserman's lease had included the arbitration clause recommended by the American Arbitration Association. See Note 1, p. 42 above. Would the court have enforced an arbitration award granting damages under the clause even if the court had considered it a penalty clause? See Matter of Associated General Contractors, 335 N.E.2d 859 (N.Y.1975). How does the question differ from that in Note 3, p. 43 above?

(5) *Problem.* Seller contracts to deliver to Buyer a machine that is readily available on the market for $1,000 more than the contract price. If Seller fails to deliver, what are the rights of the parties under each of the following provisions?

(a) "In the event of Seller's failure to deliver, Seller shall pay Buyer a penalty of $10,000."

(b) "In the event of Seller's failure to deliver, Seller shall be liable to Buyer for $10,000 in liquidated damages."

(c) "Seller hereby agrees, at Seller's option, to either deliver the machine to Buyer or to pay Buyer $10,000."

(d) "In the event of Seller's failure to deliver, Buyer shall be entitled to keep the $10,000 deposit that Seller has made to secure performance of this contract."

DAVE GUSTAFSON & CO. v. STATE, 156 N.W.2d 185 (S.D.1968) [Gustafson surfaced a new state highway that paralleled an older road that remained open during and after the construction. From the $530,-724.14 due for the work, the state withheld $14,070 that it claimed as liquidated damages for a delay of 67 days. The contract provided a graduated scale of "liquidated damages per day" under which damages of $210 per day were fixed for a contract in an amount of over $500,000 but not more than $1,000,000. This daily damage multiplied by 67 gave $14,070. When Gustafson sued, the trial court upheld the state's claim and Gustafson appealed.]

HANSON, PRESIDING JUDGE. . . . [As this court said in an earlier case,] "A provision for payment of a stipulated sum as a liquidation of damages will ordinarily be sustained if it appears that at the time the contract was made the damages in the event of a breach will be incapable or very difficult of accurate estimation, that there was a reasonable endeavor by the parties as stated to fix fair compensation, and that the amount stipulated bears a reasonable relation to probable damages and not disproportionate to any damages reasonably to be anticipated."

This case reflects the modern tendency not to "look with disfavor upon 'liquidated damages' provisions in contracts. When they are fair and reasonable attempts to fix just compensation for anticipated loss caused by breach of contract, they are enforced . . . They serve a particularly useful function when damages are uncertain in nature or amount or are unmeasurable, as is the case in many government contracts." Priebe & Sons v. United States, 332 U.S. 407, 68 S.Ct. 123, 92 L.Ed. 32. . . .

Judged in this light and by the standards established in Anderson v. Cactus Heights Country Club, 80 S.D. 417, 125 N.W.2d 491, the provision in question must be considered to be one for liquidated damages rather than a penalty for the following reasons: I. Damages for delay in constructing a new highway are impossible of measurement. II. The amount stated in the contract as liquidated damages indicates an endeavor to fix fair compensation for the loss, inconvenience, added costs, and deprivation of use caused by delay. Daily damage is graduated according to total amount of work to be performed. It may be assumed that a large project involves more loss than a small one and each day of delay adds to the loss, inconvenience, cost and deprivation of use.... For the same reasons we must conclude the amount stipulated in the contract bears a reasonable relation to probable damages and is not, as a matter of law, disproportionate to any and all damage reasonably to be anticipated from the unexcused delay in performance.

Affirmed.

NOTES

(1) *What the Traffic Will Bear.* How much should the drafter ask for in preparing a liquidated damage clause? As much as the traffic will bear, consistent with the cases? Or are there practical limitations as well? Consider the following analysis. "High liquidated damages have a tendency to make the contractors jittery. A fear of the high cost of delay will cause an involuntary rise in bid prices. All of the bidders' thinking on prices must inevitably be colored by the specter of the high damages lurking in the background. This only emphasizes the need to use this specialized treatment and high liquidated damages only on those projects where the urgency really exists. Otherwise the State will be paying extra for expediting jobs which do not need the hurry and will not justify the higher cost. High liquidated damages make a contractor susceptible to considerable labor pressure. When a contractor is working under high liquidated damages, it gives the unions a powerful lever to force compliance with demands which may or may not be justified. The contractor is forced to give in because he cannot afford a delaying argument or strike. This pressure also may have a widespread effect. When labor unions make an advance by this sort of a squeeze play against the contractor working under high liquidated damages, other contractors in the area find that they too must give the same benefits or face considerable trouble." Elliott, A Study of Liquidated Damages on Highway Contracts 21–22 (1956).

(2) *Subterfuge.* Can not a party by the use of subterfuge accomplish the same purpose that a penalty would accomplish? Instead of providing a penalty of $10,000 a day for each day's delay in construction beyond June 1, up to a maximum of $100,000, an owner might provide a bonus of $10,000 a day for each day's early completion before June 10, up to a maximum of $100,000.

Another possibility is suggested by the circumstance that the proscription of penalties is not carried over to alternative performances. Instead of having an employee promise not to compete or pay a penalty of $100,000, an employer might have the employee promise either not to compete or, in the alternative, pay $100,000. Is this a "subterfuge" or a different sort of agreement? See Note 3 below.

(3) *Equitable Relief.* Should a valid liquidated damages clause bar equitable relief that would otherwise be available? See Karpinski v. Ingrasci, Note 2, p.

461 above; Bowen v. Carlsbad Insurance & Real Estate, Inc., 724 P.2d 223 (N.M.1986).

Can parties by explicit provision bar equitable relief that would otherwise be available? Can parties by explicit provision make equitable relief available where it would not be otherwise?

What is the effect of the following provision of the NFL Player Contract, used in the National Football League?

> Player represents that he has special, exceptional and unique knowledge, skill, ability, and experience as a football player, the loss of which cannot be estimated with any certainty and cannot be fairly or adequately compensated by damages. Player therefore agrees that Club will have the right, in addition to any other right which Club may possess, to enjoin Player by appropriate proceedings from playing football or engaging in football-related activities other than for Club or from engaging in any activity other than football which may involve a significant risk of personal injury.

For a case holding that specific performance was available against farmers who had contracted to sell the cotton that they produced where at trial "the parties stipulated that the cotton involved was unique," see R.L. Kimsey Cotton Co., Inc. v. Ferguson, 214 S.E.2d 360 (Ga.1975).

(4) *Problem.* Suppose that in the Dave Gustafson case the state highway had connected with a bridge that was also under construction, but by a different contractor. Would the result have been the same if, because of a delay by that contract, the bridge had also been closed for 67 days so that the highway could not have been used even if it had been completed on time? Would it affect your answer if the contractor responsible for the bridge had had a similar clause stipulating damages and had argued that it was invalid because the delay in the highway would have prevented the use of the bridge even if it had been completed on time? Compare Massman Constr. Co. v. City Council of Greenville, 147 F.2d 925 (5th Cir.1945), with California & Hawaiian Sugar Co. v. Sun Ship, Inc., 794 F.2d 1433 (9th Cir.1986), and Southwest Engineering Co. v. United States, 341 F.2d 998 (8th Cir.1965).

(5) *Questionable Categories.* As this Chapter has suggested, an injured party may have difficulty in recovering for loss that falls in a variety of categories. These include sentimental value, value of a chance, emotional disturbance, lost volume, loss of reputation, and loss of good will. To what extent will loss in these categories, if not recoverable in the absence of agreement, serve to support the enforceability of a clause stipulating damages? See Wassenaar v. Panos, 331 N.W.2d 357 (Wis.1983), discussed in *Wasserman's,* above.

Chapter 6

FINDING THE LAW OF THE CONTRACT

———

Much of what we think of as "contract law" consists of the legal framework within which parties may create their own rights and duties. Thus far this book has been largely concerned with this framework—with enforceability and enforcement. And yet in many contract disputes the disagreement relates not to such matters but rather to the nature and extent of the rights and duties that have been created. These disputes, over what are commonly called the "interpretation" and "construction" of contracts, are representative of a hefty and growing fraction of contract disputes. They are referred to here as disputes over the "law of the contract," to distinguish them from disputes over "contract law."

The purpose of this chapter is to introduce some of the problems encountered and the techniques used by the courts in finding the law of the contract. At the same time it would be well to remember that many potential disputes of this kind do not arise at all because the language of the contract is clear, and that many actual disputes would not have arisen had the language of the contract been clearer. It would not, therefore, be amiss to ask yourself how the parties, or their lawyers, in each case might have drafted a contract which would have avoided litigation.

———

SECTION 1. DETERMINING THE SUBJECT MATTER TO BE INTERPRETED

———

A threshold problem goes to the limitations on the sources that a court may consider in finding the law of the contract. Our initial concern is with a rule, or complex of rules, that goes under the name of "the parol evidence rule." Typically it is called into play where a contract has been reduced to writing after oral or written negotiations during which the parties have given assurances, made promises, or reached understandings. In the event of litigation, one of them may seek to introduce evidence of the negotiations in order to establish that the terms of the contract are other than as shown in the writing. Here that party will be met with the parol evidence rule which, where the parties have embodied their agreement in writing, may preclude reliance on such extrinsic evidence as negotiations.

Professor Thayer said of the parol evidence rule that, "Few things are darker than this, or fuller of subtle difficulties," and it is not purposed to explore it fully here. Certain it is that, in spite of its name, it is not limited to oral agreements; it also operates to exclude writings, such as letters or telegrams. There is also a general consensus that it is not, strictly speaking, a rule of evidence (such as the hearsay rule), which bars the use of some types of evidence to prove an ultimate matter of fact but which permits that fact to be established in a different way; rather it is a rule of "substantive" law, which precludes any showing of the ultimate matter of fact itself, that is, that the terms of the contract are other than as expressed in the writing. So much for what the rule is not. It is more difficult to state what it is.

NOTES

(1) *Rule of Substantive Law.* Characterization of the parol evidence rule as "substantive" has some important practical consequences. For example, in our adversary trial system it is traditionally incumbent upon the aggrieved party to make timely objection to the admission of evidence in order to give the trial judge an opportunity to rule on its admissibility. Under an exclusionary rule of evidence, failure to object at trial is ordinarily a waiver of any ground of complaint against admission, and the evidence becomes part of the proof in the case. That this is not the case under the parol evidence rule, see Gajewski v. Bratcher, 221 N.W.2d 614 (N.D.1974).

To take another example, in our federal court system, under the Erie doctrine, federal courts sitting in diversity cases are bound to apply state rather than federal law to matters that are "substantive." That a federal court sitting in a diversity case is bound to apply the parol evidence rule of the state in question, see Betz Laboratories, Inc. v. Hines, 647 F.2d 402 (3d Cir.1981).

(2) *Wisdom of Rule.* Controversy has raged over the wisdom of the parol evidence rule. In England, for example, the Law Commission wrote: "It is a technical rule of uncertain ambit which, at best, adds to the complications of litigation without affecting the outcome and, at worst, prevents the courts from getting at the truth. We accordingly make the provisional recommendation that it should be abolished." [a]

Judge Richard Posner, however, has defended the rule. "The parol evidence rule is maligned in some circles as the vestige of an era when judges were hostile to plaintiffs and mistrusted juries, and thus as an arbitrary barrier to getting at the truth. But it has stubbornly refused to die ..., and in fact it serves an important social purpose.... Not all parties to contracts want to entrust their fate to the vagaries of juries unversed in the usages of business...." [b]

GIANNI v. R. RUSSELL & CO., INC.

Supreme Court of Pennsylvania, 1924.
281 Pa. 320, 126 A. 791.

Action by Frank Gianni against R. Russell & Co., Inc. From judgment for plaintiff, defendant appeals.

a. The [English] Law Commission, Law of Contract, The Parol Evidence Rule 25, Working Paper No. 70 (1976).

b. Olympia Hotels Corp. v. Johnson Wax Development Corp., 908 F.2d 1363, 1373 (7th Cir.1990).

Reversed, and judgment entered for defendant.

SCHAFFER, J.   Plaintiff had been a tenant of a room in an office building in Pittsburgh wherein he conducted a store, selling tobacco, fruit, candy and soft drinks.   Defendant acquired the entire property in which the storeroom was located, and its agent negotiated with plaintiff for a further leasing of the room.   A lease for three years was signed.   It contained a provision that the lessee should "use the premises only for the sale of fruit, candy, soda water," etc., with the further stipulation that "it is expressly understood that the tenant is not allowed to sell tobacco in any form, under penalty of instant forfeiture of this lease." The document was prepared following a discussion about renting the room between the parties and after an agreement to lease had been reached.   It was signed after it had been left in plaintiff's hands and admittedly had been read over to him by two persons, one of whom was his daughter.

Plaintiff sets up that in the course of his dealings with defendant's agent it was agreed that, in consideration of his promises not to sell tobacco and to pay an increased rent, and for entering into the agreement as a whole, he should have the exclusive right to sell soft drinks in the building.   No such stipulation is contained in the written lease. Shortly after it was signed defendant demised the adjoining room in the building to a drug company without restricting the latter's right to sell soda water and soft drinks.   Alleging that this was in violation of the contract which defendant had made with him, and that the sale of these beverages by the drug company had greatly reduced his receipts and profits, plaintiff brought this action for damages for breach of the alleged oral contract, and was permitted to recover.   Defendant has appealed.

Plaintiff's evidence was to the effect that the oral agreement had been made at least two days, possibly longer, before the signing of the instrument, and that it was repeated at the time he signed; that, relying upon it, he executed the lease.   Plaintiff called one witness who said he heard defendant's agent say to plaintiff at a time admittedly several days before the execution of the lease that he would have the exclusive right to sell soda water and soft drinks, to which the latter replied if that was the case he accepted the tenancy.   Plaintiff produced no witness who was present when the contract was executed to corroborate his statement as to what then occurred.   Defendant's agent denied that any such agreement was made, either preliminary to or at the time of the execution of the lease.

Appellee's counsel argues this is not a case in which an endeavor is being made to reform a written instrument because of something omitted as a result of fraud, accident, or mistake, but is one involving the breach of an independent oral agreement which does not belong in the writing at all and is not germane to its provisions.   We are unable to reach this conclusion.

"Where parties, without any fraud or mistake, have deliberately put their engagements in writing, the law declares the writing to be not only the best, but the only evidence of their agreement." Martin v. Berens, 67 Pa. 459, 463; Irvin v. Irvin, 142 Pa. 271, 287, 21 A. 816.

"All preliminary negotiations, conversations and verbal agreements are merged in and superseded by the subsequent written contract, . . . and 'unless fraud, accident, or mistake be averred, the writing constitutes the agreement between the parties, and its terms cannot be added to nor subtracted from by parol evidence.'" Union Storage Co. v. Speck, 194 Pa. 126, 133, 45 A. 48, 49; Vito v. Birkel, 209 Pa. 206, 208, 58 A. 127.

The writing must be the entire contract between the parties if parol evidence is to be excluded, and to determine whether it is or not the writing will be looked at, and if it appears to be a contract complete within itself, "couched in such terms as import a complete legal obligation without any uncertainty as to the object or extent of the engagement, it is conclusively presumed that the whole engagement of the parties, and the extent and manner of their undertaking, were reduced to writing." Seitz v. Brewers' Refrigerating Machine Co., 141 U.S. 510, 517, 12 S.Ct. 46, 48, 35 L.Ed. 837.

When does the oral agreement come within the field embraced by the written one? This can be answered by comparing the two, and determining whether parties, situated as were the ones to the contract, would naturally and normally include the one in the other if it were made. If they relate to the same subject-matter, and are so interrelated that both would be executed at the same time and in the same contract, the scope of the subsidiary agreement must be taken to be covered by the writing. This question must be determined by the court.

In the case at bar the written contract stipulated for the very sort of thing which plaintiff claims has no place in it. It covers the use to which the storeroom was to be put by plaintiff and what he was and what he was not to sell therein. He was "to use the premises only for the sale of fruit, candy, soda water," etc., and was not "allowed to sell tobacco in any form." Plaintiff claims his agreement not to sell tobacco was part of the consideration for the exclusive right to sell soft drinks. Since his promise to refrain was included in the writing, it would be the natural thing to have included the promise of exclusive rights. Nothing can be imagined more pertinent to these provisions which were included than the one appellee avers.

In cases of this kind, where the cause of action rests entirely on an alleged oral understanding concerning a subject which is dealt with in a written contract it is assumed that the writing was intended to set forth the entire agreement as to that particular subject.

"In deciding upon this intent [as to whether a certain subject was intended to be embodied by the writing], the chief and most satisfactory index . . . is found in the circumstance whether or not the particular element of the alleged extrinsic negotiation is dealt with at all in the writing. If it is mentioned, covered, or dealt with in the writing, then presumably the writing was meant to represent all of the transaction on that element, if it is not, then probably the writing was not intended to embody that element of the negotiation." Wigmore on Evidence, 2d Ed., vol. 5, p. 309.

As the written lease is the complete contract of the parties, and since it embraces the field of the alleged oral contract, evidence of the latter is inadmissible under the parol evidence rule.

"The [parol evidence] rule also denies validity to a subsidiary agreement within [the] scope [of the written contract] if sued on as a separate contract, although except for [that rule], the agreement fulfills all the requisites of a valid contract." 2 Williston, Contracts, 1222; Penn Iron Co. v. Diller, 1 Sad., Pa., 82, 1 A. 924; Krueger v. Nicola, 205 Pa. 38, 54 A. 494; Wodock v. Robinson, 148 Pa. 503, 24 A. 73.

There are, of course, certain exceptions to the parol evidence rule, but this case does not fall within any of them. Plaintiff expressly rejects any idea of fraud, accident, or mistake, and they are the foundation upon which any basis for admitting parol evidence to set up an entirely separate agreement within the scope of a written contract must be built. The evidence must be such as would cause a chancellor to reform the instrument, and that would be done only for these reasons (Pioso v. Bitzer, 209 Pa. 503, 58 A. 891) and this holds true where this essentially equitable relief is being given, in our Pennsylvania fashion, through common-law forms.

We have stated on several occasions recently that we propose to stand for the integrity of written contracts.... We reiterate our position in this regard.

The judgment of the court below is reversed, and is here entered for defendant.[a]

NOTE

Rationale. What is the reason behind the parol evidence rule? According to Corbin: "Any contract ... can be discharged or modified by subsequent agreement of the parties.... If the foregoing is true of antecedent contracts that were once legally operative and enforceable, it is equally true of preliminary negotiations that were not themselves mutually agreed upon or enforceable at law. The new agreement is not a discharging contract, since there were no legal relations to be discharged; but the legal relations of the parties are now governed by the terms of the new agreement." 3 Corbin § 574. See Restatement Second § 213 for a reflection of this view.

Many of the older cases, however, suggested a different rationale, reflected in the explanation of Professor McCormick, an expert on the law of evidence, that "usually the one who sets up the spoken against the written word is economically the under-dog," and jurors would tend to favor that party in spite of the unreliability of evidence of spoken words when given months or years later, even by a disinterested witness and particularly by a party. C. McCormick, Handbook of the Law of Evidence § 210 (1954). Does this explain why the

a. See Mellon Bank Corp. v. First Union Real Estate Equity & Mortgage Invs., 951 F.2d 1399, 1405 (3d Cir.1991) ("Pennsylvania courts still rely upon *Gianni*'s definitive statement of Pennsylvania's parol evidence rule").

rule bars prior *written* negotiations and does not bar *subsequent* oral ones? See generally, 2 Farnsworth § 7.2.

MASTERSON v. SINE

Supreme Court of California, 1968.
68 Cal.2d 222, 436 P.2d 561.

TRAYNOR, CHIEF JUSTICE. Dallas Masterson and his wife Rebecca owned a ranch as tenants in common. On February 25, 1958, they conveyed it to Medora and Lu Sine by a grant deed. "Reserving unto the Grantors herein an option to purchase the above described property on or before February 25, 1968" for the "same consideration as being paid heretofore plus their depreciation value of any improvements Grantees may add to the property from and after two and a half years from this date." Medora is Dallas' sister and Lu's wife. Since the conveyance Dallas has been adjudged bankrupt. His trustee in bankruptcy and Rebecca brought this declaratory relief action to establish their right to enforce the option.

The case was tried without a jury. Over defendants' objection the trial court admitted extrinsic evidence that by "the same consideration as being paid heretofore" both the grantors and the grantees meant the sum of $50,000 and by "depreciation value of any improvements" they meant the depreciation value of improvements to be computed by deducting from the total amount of any capital expenditures made by defendants grantees the amount of depreciation allowable to them under United States income tax regulations as of the time of the exercise of the option.

The court also determined that the parol evidence rule precluded admission of extrinsic evidence offered by defendants to show that the parties wanted the property kept in the Masterson family and that the option was therefore personal to the grantors and could not be exercised by the trustee in bankruptcy.

The court entered judgment for plaintiffs, declaring their right to exercise the option, specifying in some detail how it could be exercised, and reserving jurisdiction to supervise the manner of its exercise and to determine the amount that plaintiffs will be required to pay defendants for their capital expenditures if plaintiffs decide to exercise the option.

Defendants appeal. They contend that the option provision is too uncertain to be enforced and that extrinsic evidence as to its meaning should not have been admitted. The trial court properly refused to frustrate the obviously declared intention of the grantors to reserve an option to repurchase by an overly meticulous insistence on completeness and clarity of written expression.... It properly admitted extrinsic evidence to explain the language of the deed ... to the end that the consideration for the option would appear with sufficient certainty to permit specific enforcement.... The trial court erred, however, in excluding the extrinsic evidence that the option was personal to the grantors and therefore nonassignable.

When the parties to a written contract have agreed to it as an "integration"—a complete and final embodiment of the terms of an agreement—parol evidence cannot be used to add to or vary its terms.... When only part of the agreement is integrated, the same rule applies to that part, but parol evidence may be used to prove elements of the agreement not reduced to writing....

The crucial issue in determining whether there has been an integration is whether the parties intended their writing to serve as the exclusive embodiment of their agreement. The instrument itself may help to resolve that issue. It may state, for example, that "there are no previous understandings or agreements not contained in the writing," and thus express the parties' "intention to nullify antecedent understandings or agreements." (See 3 Corbin, Contracts (1960) § 578, p. 411.) Any such collateral agreement itself must be examined, however, to determine whether the parties intended the subjects of negotiation it deals with to be included in, excluded from, or otherwise affected by the writing. Circumstances at the time of the writing may also aid in the determination of such integration....

California cases have stated that whether there was an integration is to be determined solely from the face of the instrument and that the question for the court is whether it "appears to be a complete ... agreement...." (See Ferguson v. Koch (1928) 204 Cal. 342, 346, 268 P. 342, 344, 58 A.L.R. 1176; ...) Neither of these strict formulations of the rule, however, has been consistently applied. The requirement that the writing must appear incomplete on its face has been repudiated in many cases where parol evidence was admitted "to prove the existence of a separate oral agreement as to any matter on which the document is silent and which is not inconsistent with its terms"—even though the instrument appeared to state a complete agreement.... Even under the rule that the writing alone is to be consulted, it was found necessary to examine the alleged collateral agreement before concluding that proof of it was precluded by the writing alone. (See 3 Corbin, Contracts (1960) § 582, pp. 444–446.) It is therefore evident that "The conception of a writing as wholly and intrinsically self-determinative of the parties' intent to make it a sole memorial of one or seven or twenty-seven subjects of negotiation is an impossible one." (9 Wigmore, Evidence (3d ed. 1940) § 2431, p. 103.) For example, a promissory note given by a debtor to his creditor may integrate all their present contractual rights and obligations, or it may be only a minor part of an underlying executory contract that would never be discovered by examining the face of the note.

In formulating the rule governing parol evidence, several policies must be accommodated. One policy is based on the assumption that written evidence is more accurate than human memory.... This policy, however, can be adequately served by excluding parol evidence of agreements that directly contradict the writing. Another policy is based on the fear that fraud or unintentional invention by witnesses interested in the outcome of the litigation will mislead the finder of facts. (... Mitchill v. Lath (1928) 247 N.Y. 377, 388, 160 N.E. 646, 68 A.L.R. 239....) ... McCormick has suggested that the party urging the spoken as against the written word is most often the economic underdog, threatened by severe hardship if the writing is enforced. In his view the parol evidence rule arose to allow the court to control the tendency of the jury to find through sympathy and without a dispassionate assessment of the probability of fraud or faulty memory that the parties made an oral agreement collateral to the written contract, or that preliminary tentative agreements were not abandoned when omitted from the writing. (See McCormick, Evidence (1954) § 210.) He recognizes, however, that if this theory were adopted in disregard of all other considerations, it would lead to the exclusion of testimony concerning oral agreements whenever there is a writing and thereby often defeat the true intent of the parties. (See McCormick, op. cit. supra, § 216, p. 441.)

Evidence of oral collateral agreements should be excluded only when the fact finder is likely to be misled. The rule must therefore be based on the credibility of the evidence. One such standard, adopted by section 240(1)(b) of the Restatement of Contracts, permits proof of a collateral agreement if it "is such an agreement as might *naturally* be made as a separate agreement by parties situated as were the parties to the written contract." (Italics added; see McCormick, Evidence (1954) § 216, p. 441; see also 3 Corbin, Contracts (1960) § 583, p. 475, § 594, pp. 568–569; 4 Williston, Contracts (3d ed. 1961) § 638, pp. 1039–1045.) The draftsmen of the Uniform Commercial Code would exclude the evidence in still fewer instances: "If the additional terms are such that, if agreed upon, they would *certainly* have been included in the document in the view of the court, then evidence of their alleged making must be kept from the trier of fact." (Com. 3, § 2–202, italics added.) [1]

The option clause in the deed in the present case does not explicitly provide that it contains the complete agreement, and the deed is silent on the question of assignability. Moreover, the difficulty of accommodating the formalized structure of a deed to the insertion of collateral agreements makes it less likely that all the terms of such an agreement were included.... The statement of the reservation of the option might well have been placed in the recorded deed solely to preserve the grantors' rights against any possible future purchasers and this function could well be served without any mention of the parties' agreement that the option was personal. There is nothing in the record to indicate that the parties to this family transaction, through experience in land trans-

---

1. Corbin suggests that, even in situations where the court concludes that it would not have been natural for the parties to make the alleged collateral oral agreement, parol evidence of such an agreement should nevertheless be permitted if the court is convinced that the unnatural actually happened in the case being adjudicated. (3 Corbin, Contracts, § 485, pp. 478, 480; cf. Murray, The Parol Evidence Rule: A Clarification (1966) 4 Duquesne L.Rev. 337, 341–342.) This suggestion may be based on a belief that judges are not likely to be misled by their sympathies. If the court believes that the parties intended a collateral agreement to be effective, there is no reason to keep the evidence from the jury.

actions or otherwise, had any warning of the disadvantages of failing to put the whole agreement in the deed.   This case is one, therefore, in which it can be said that a collateral agreement such as that alleged "might naturally be made as a separate agreement." A *fortiori,* the case is not one in which the parties "would certainly" have included the collateral agreement in the deed.

It is contended, however, that an option agreement is ordinarily presumed to be assignable if it contains no provisions forbidding its transfer or indicating that its performance involves elements personal to the parties. . . .   The fact that there is a written memorandum, however, does not necessarily preclude parol evidence rebutting a term that the law would otherwise presume. . . .

In the present case defendants offered evidence that the parties agreed that the option was not assignable in order to keep the property in the Masterson family.   The trial court erred in excluding that evidence.

The judgment is reversed.

PETERS, TOBRINER, MOSK, and SULLIVAN, JJ., concur.

BURKE, JUSTICE (dissenting).   I dissent.   The majority opinion:

(1) Undermines the parol evidence rule as we have known it in this state since at least 1872 by declaring that parol evidence should have been admitted by the trial court to show that a written option, absolute and unrestricted in form, was intended to be limited and nonassignable;

(2) Renders suspect instruments of conveyance absolute on their face;

(3) Materially lessens the reliance which may be placed upon written instruments affecting the title to real estate; and

(4) Opens the door, albeit unintentionally to a new technique for the defrauding of creditors.

The opinion permits defendants to establish by parol testimony that their grant to their brother (and brother-in-law) of a written option, absolute in terms, was nevertheless agreed to be nonassignable by the grantee (now a bankrupt), and that therefore the right to exercise it did not pass, by operation of the bankruptcy laws, to the trustee for the benefit of the grantee's creditors.

And how was this to be shown?   By the proffered testimony of the bankrupt optionee himself!   Thereby one of his assets (the option to purchase defendants' California ranch) would be withheld from the trustee in bankruptcy and from the bankrupt's creditors.   Understandably the trial court, as required by the parol evidence rule, did not allow the bankrupt by parol to so contradict the unqualified language of the written option.

The court properly admitted parol evidence to explain the intended meaning of the "same consideration" and "depreciation value" phrases of the written option to purchase defendants' land, as the intended meaning of those phrases was not clear.   However, there was nothing ambiguous about the *granting* language of the option and not the slightest suggestion in the document that the option was to be nonassignable. Thus, to permit such words of limitation to be added by parol is to *contradict* the absolute nature of the grant, and to directly violate the parol evidence rule.

Just as it is unnecessary to state in a deed to "lot X" that the house located thereon goes with the land, it is likewise unnecessary to add to "I grant an option to Jones" the words *"and his assigns"* for the option to be assignable. As hereinafter emphasized in more detail, California statutes expressly declare that it *is* assignable, and only if I add language in writing showing my intent to withhold or restrict the right of assignment may the grant be so limited. Thus, to seek to restrict the grant by parol is to *contradict* the written document in violation of the parol evidence rule.

The majority opinion arrives at its holding via a series of false premises which are not supported either in the record of this case or in such California authorities as are offered....

At the outset the majority in the present case reiterate that the rule against contradicting or varying the terms of a writing remains applicable when only part of the agreement is contained in the writing, and parol evidence is used to prove elements of the agreement not reduced to writing. But having restated this established rule, the majority opinion inexplicably proceeds to subvert it....

Options are property, and are widely used in the sale and purchase of real and personal property. One of the basic incidents of property ownership is the right of the owner to sell or transfer it.... These rights of the owner of property to transfer it, are elementary rules of substantive law and not the mere disputable presumptions which the majority opinion in the present case would make of them. Moreover, the right of transferability applies to an option to purchase, unless there are words of limitation in the option forbidding its assignment or showing that it was given because of a peculiar trust or confidence reposed in the optionee....

The right of an optionee to transfer his option to purchase property is accordingly one of the basic rights which accompanies the option unless limited under the language of the option itself. To allow an optionor to resort to parol evidence to support his assertion that the written option is not transferable is to authorize him to limit the option by attempting to restrict and reclaim rights with which he has already parted. A clearer violation of two substantive and basic rules of law— the parol evidence rule and the right of free transferability of property— would be difficult to conceive....

[D]espite the law which until the advent of the present majority opinion has been firmly and clearly established in California and relied upon by attorneys and courts alike, that parol evidence may *not* be employed to vary or contradict the terms of a written instrument, the majority now announce that such evidence "should be excluded only when the fact finder is *likely to be misled,*" and that "The rule must therefore be based on the *credibility of the evidence.*" (Italics added.) But was it not, inter alia, to avoid misleading the fact finder, and to further the introduction of only the evidence which is most likely to *be* credible (the written document), that the Legislature adopted the parol evidence rule as a part of the substantive law of this state?

Next, in an effort to implement this newly promulgated "credibility" test, the majority opinion offers a choice of two "standards": one, a "certainty" standard, quoted from the Uniform Commercial Code, and the other a "natural" standard found in the Restatement of Contracts, and concludes that at least for purposes of the present case the "natural" viewpoint should prevail.

This new rule, not hitherto recognized in California, provides that proof of a claimed collateral oral agreement is admissible if it is such an agreement as might *naturally* have been made a separate agreement by the parties under the particular circumstances. I submit that this approach opens the door to uncertainty and confusion. Who can know what its limits are? Certainly I do not. For example, in its application to this case who could be expected to divine as "natural" a separate oral agreement between the parties that the assignment, absolute and unrestricted on its face, was intended by the parties to be limited to the Masterson family?

Or, assume that one gives to his relative a promissory note and that the payee of the note goes bankrupt. By operation of law the note becomes an asset of the bankruptcy. The trustee attempts to enforce it. Would the relatives be permitted to testify that by a separate oral agreement made at the time of the execution of the note it was understood that should the payee fail in his business the maker would be excused from payment of the note, or that, as here, it was intended that the benefits of the note would be *personal* to the payee? I doubt that trial judges should be burdened with the task of conjuring whether it would have been "natural" under those circumstances for such a separate agreement to have been made by the parties. Yet, under the application of the proposed rule, this is the task the trial judge would have, and in essence the situation presented in the instant case is no different.

Under the application of the codes and the present case law, proof of the existence of such an agreement would not be permitted, "natural" or "unnatural." But conceivably, as loose as the new rule is, one judge might deem it natural and another judge unnatural. And in each instance the ultimate decision would have to be made ("naturally") on a case-by-case basis by the appellate courts.

In an effort to provide justification for applying the newly pronounced "natural" rule to the circumstances of the present case, the majority opinion next attempts to account for the silence of the writing in this case concerning assignability of the option, by asserting that "the difficulty of accommodating the formalized structure of a deed to the insertion of collateral agreements makes it less likely that all the terms of such an agreement were included." What difficulty would have been involved here, to add the words "this option is nonassignable"? The asserted "formalized structure of a deed" is no formidable barrier....

Comment hardly seems necessary on the convenience to a bankrupt of such a device to defeat his creditors. He need only produce parol testimony that any options (or other property, for that matter) which he holds are subject to an oral "collateral agreement" with family members (or with friends) that the property is nontransferable "in order to keep the property in the family" or in the friendly group. In the present case the value of the ranch which the bankrupt and his wife held an option to purchase has doubtless increased substantially during the years since they acquired the option. The initiation of this litigation by the trustee in bankruptcy to establish his right to enforce the option indicates his belief that there is substantial value to be gained for the creditors from this asset of the bankrupt. Yet the majority opinion permits defeat of the trustee and of the creditors through the device of an asserted collateral oral agreement that the option was "personal" to the bankrupt and nonassignable "in order to keep the property in the family"! ...

I would hold that the trial court ruled correctly on the proffered parol evidence, and would affirm the judgment.

McComb, J., concurs.

NOTES

(1) *"Integrated" Agreements and the Restatement.* According to the Restatement Second, where a writing has been adopted by the parties as "a final expression of one or more terms of an agreement" that writing is known as an "integrated agreement," and "evidence of prior agreements or negotiations is not admissible in evidence to contradict a term of the writing." Restatement Second §§ 209, 215. Where the writing has been "adopted by the parties as a complete and exclusive statement of the terms of the agreement," it is known as a "completely integrated agreement," and not even evidence of "a consistent additional term is admissible to explain or supplement" it. Restatement Second §§ 210, 216. Such evidence is, however, admissible if the writing is only a "partially integrated agreement."

Are Gianni v. Russell and Masterson v. Sine distinguishable? How would the writings in those cases be characterized in Restatement Second terms? Who characterized them? See Restatement Second § 209(2). On the basis of what evidence were they characterized? See Restatement Second § 214. For what purpose did Gianni and the Sines seek to introduce extrinsic evidence? What rationale for the parol evidence rule was relied on in reaching each decision?

The Code's version of the parol evidence rule is found in UCC 2–202. It does not, of course, apply to transactions like those in the preceding two cases. Are its provisions consistent with the results in those cases?

(2) *Test of Complete Integration.* Chief Justice Traynor refers to the "strict formulations of the rule" under which "whether there was an integration is to be determined solely from the face of the instrument and . . . the question for the court is whether it 'appears to be a complete . . . agreement.'" This was Williston's view, and many courts, particularly in cases like *Gianni*, decided in the first half of this century, agreed. See 4 Williston 3d § 633.

Corbin led the opponents of this view, arguing that "The writing cannot prove its own completeness and accuracy." Corbin, The Parol Evidence Rule, 53 Yale L.J. 603, 630 (1944), reprinted in 3 Corbin § 582. The trend clearly favors Corbin. As Comment *b* to Restatement Second § 210 phrases it, "a writing cannot of itself prove its own completeness, and wide latitude must be allowed for inquiry into circumstances bearing on the intention of the parties."

(3) *Merger Clauses.* Chief Justice Traynor observed that the "instrument may help to resolve" the issue of whether the agreement is completely integrated. It is a common practice to include in written contracts a clause known as a "merger" or "integration" clause, which may read somewhat as follows: "There are no promises, verbal understandings, or agreements of any kind, pertaining to this contract other than specified herein." Since integration is a matter of the parties' intention, such clauses have usually been given effect, in situations like those in the two preceding cases, to show complete integration. But in Franklin v. White, 493 N.E.2d 161 (Ind.1986), while giving effect to a merger clause, the court explained that "there are rules adequately protecting against the unconscionable use of integration clauses." The court added that such a clause "is only some evidence of the parties' intentions" so that "rather than operating to exclude evidence" it is "merely probative of the parties' intentions." Is this consistent with Corbin's view in Note, p. 569 above? For a case holding a merger clause not unconscionable since in "other circumstances, the clause might as easily have benefited plaintiffs as it now does defendants," see Smith v. Central Soya of Athens, Inc., 604 F.Supp. 518 (E.D.N.C.1985).

How does the function of a merger clause compare with that of a home-office-approval clause with regard to the control of representatives? See Note 2, p. 183 above.

(4) *"Collateral Agreements."* The fact that the parties have adopted a writing as an integration of one agreement has, of course, no effect on another entirely separate agreement. Note that Chief Justice Traynor speaks of a "collateral agreement" in Masterson v. Sine. What was that agreement? What was its consideration? Does the notion of a "collateral agreement," as he uses it, differ from that of "partial integration"?

He cites Mitchill v. Lath, 160 N.E. 646 (N.Y.1928). In that case the buyer of land under a written contract attempted to show a prior agreement by the seller to remove an unsightly ice house from a nearby tract. The court held that the parol evidence rule precluded such a showing. For evidence of a contemporaneous oral agreement to be admissible: "(1) The agreement must in form be a collateral one; (2) it must not contradict express or implied provisions of the written contract; (3) it must be one that parties would not ordinarily be expected to embody in the writing." The court thought that "an inspection of this contract shows a full and complete agreement, setting forth in detail the obligations of each party. On reading it, one would conclude that the reciprocal obligations of the parties were fully detailed."

(5) *A Case of Seagram's (Reprise).* In Lee v. Joseph E. Seagram & Sons, part of which appears in Note 2, p. 284 above, the court distinguished Mitchill v. Lath and rejected Seagram's contention that "the oral agreement was 'part and parcel' of the subject-matter of the sales contract and that failure to include it in the written contract barred proof of its existence." The court noted that "the written agreement does not contain the customary integration clause" and that there was not "an identity of parties" in the writing and the asserted oral agreement. The court pointed out that "although it would have been physically possible to insert a provision dealing with only the shareholders of a 50%

interest, the transaction itself was a *corporate* sale of assets. Collateral agreements which survive the closing of a corporate deal, such as employment agreements for particular shareholders of the seller or consulting agreements, are often set forth in separate agreements." Because of the "close relationship of confidence and friendship over many years between two old men, Harold Lee and Yogman, ... it would not be surprising that a handshake for the benefit of Harold's sons would have been thought sufficient."

BOLLINGER v. CENTRAL PENNSYLVANIA QUARRY STRIPPING AND CONSTRUCTION CO.

Supreme Court of Pennsylvania, 1967.
425 Pa. 430, 229 A.2d 741.

Musmanno, Justice. Mahlon Bollinger and his wife, Vinetta C. Bollinger, filed an action in equity against the Central Pennsylvania Quarry Stripping Construction Company asking that a contract entered into between them be reformed so as to include therein a paragraph alleged to have been omitted by mutual mistake and that the agreement, as reformed, be enforced.

The agreement, as executed, provided that the defendant was to be permitted to deposit on the property of the plaintiffs, construction waste as it engaged in work on the Pennsylvania Turnpike in the immediate vicinity of the plaintiffs' property. The Bollingers claimed that there had been a mutual understanding between them and the defendant that, prior to depositing such waste on the plaintiffs' property, the defendant would remove the topsoil of the plaintiffs' property, pile on it the waste material and then restore the topsoil in a way to cover the deposited waste. The Bollingers averred that they had signed the written agreement without reading it because they assumed that the condition just stated had been incorporated into the writing.

When the defendant first began working in the vicinity of the plaintiffs' property, it did first remove the topsoil, deposited the waste on the bare land, and then replaced the topsoil. After a certain period of time, the defendant ceased doing this and the plaintiffs remonstrated. The defendant answered there was nothing in the written contract which required it to make a sandwich of its refuse between the bare earth and the topsoil. It was at this point that the plaintiffs discovered that that feature of the oral understanding had been omitted from the written contract. The plaintiff husband renewed his protest and the defendant's superintendent replied he could not remove the topsoil because his equipment for that operation had been taken away. When he was reminded of the original understanding, the superintendent said, in effect, he couldn't help that.

The plaintiffs then filed their action for reformation of the contract, the Court granted the requested relief, and the defendant firm appealed. We said in Bugen v. New York Life Insurance Co., 408 Pa. 472, 184 A.2d 499: "A court of equity has the power to reform the written evidence of a contract and make it correspond to the understanding of the parties.... However, the mistake must be mutual to the parties to the contract." The fact, however, that one of the parties denies that a mistake was made does not prevent a finding of mutual mistake. Kutsenkow v. Kutsenkow, 414 Pa. 610, 612, 202 A.2d 68.

Once a person enters into a written agreement he builds around himself a stone wall, from which he cannot escape by merely asserting he had not understood what he was signing. However, equity would completely fail in its objectives if it refused to break a hole through the wall when it finds, after proper evidence, that there was a mistake between the parties, that it was real and not feigned, actual and not hypothetical.

The Chancellor, after taking testimony, properly concluded: "We are satisfied that plaintiffs have sustained the heavy burden placed upon them. Their understanding of the agreement is corroborated by the undisputed evidence. The defendant did remove and set aside the topsoil on part of the area before depositing its waste and did replace the topsoil over such waste after such depositing. It follows it would not have done so had it not so agreed. Further corroboration is found in the testimony that it acted similarly in the case of plaintiffs' neighbor Beltzner."

After the Court handed down its Decree Nisi, the defendant petitioned for a rehearing on the ground of after-discovered evidence. Even assuming, without so deciding, that the so-called after-discovered evidence qualified as such, it is not clear that it was sufficiently material or relevant to bring about a change in the result reached by the Chancellor, and he so stated in his Opinion. We are satisfied that the proffered evidence would not be inconsistent with the Chancellor's findings.

Decree affirmed, costs on the appellant.

NOTES

(1) *Reformation for Mistake.* How did the situation of the Bollingers differ from that of Gianni? What would he have had to show in order to bring himself within the rule of the *Bollinger* case? See Palmer, Reformation and the Parol Evidence Rule, 65 Mich.L.Rev. 833 (1967), reprinted in 3 G. Palmer, The Law of Restitution §§ 13.10, 13.11 (1978).

(2) *Validity of Written Agreement.* It is generally held that, since the parole evidence rule proceeds on the assumption that there is a written agreement, it does not bar extrinsic evidence to show that the written agreement is not valid. It does not, for example, preclude the use of such evidence to show that the writing was a sham not intended to be enforced (see Note, p. 143 above) or that a recital of a performance as consideration, (e.g., "in consideration of the payment of $10, receipt of which is hereby acknowledged") is false (see Note 4, p. 210 above). See Restatement Second § 214(d). (However, the rule does apply if the consideration is a promise rather than a performance.)

(3) *Fraud.* For the reason suggested in the preceding note, it is also generally held that the parol evidence rule does not preclude the use of extrinsic evidence to show fraud. Is the rule the same under UCC 2–202? For an affirmative answer, see Associated Hardware Supply Co. v. Big Wheel Distribut-

ing Co., 355 F.2d 114 (3d Cir.1965). What language of UCC 2–202 supports such a result? Is UCC 1–103 relevant?

The exception for fraud has been held applicable to promissory fraud, where a promisor makes a promise not intending to perform it. Lovejoy Electronics, Inc. v. O'Berto, 873 F.2d 1001 (7th Cir.1989) (Posner, J.). But see Alling v. Universal Manufacturing Corp., 7 Cal.Rptr.2d 718, 734 (App.1992) (fraud exception does not apply unless "the false promise is either independent of or consistent with the written instrument").

Would a merger clause preclude the use of extrinsic evidence to show fraud? See Restatement Second § 214.[a]

NO–ORAL–MODIFICATION CLAUSES

Suppose that one of the parties seeks to prove that the provisions of a carefully drafted written contract were varied by a conversation between the parties *after* the contract was made. The parol evidence rule does not speak to this problem. Yet to the party who seeks to exclude such proof it is not dissimilar from the problems to which the rule does speak. If one wants to do business on the basis of the written word (preferably one's own), to the exclusion of oral agreements, one has as much interest in excluding subsequent as in excluding prior oral agreements. The owner under a construction contract has a particularly strong interest in preventing claims by the builder for extra work allegedly done under oral modifications by the owner's representative on the site. A typical clause reads:

> No extra work or changes from plans and specifications under this contract will be recognized or paid for, unless agreed to in writing before the extra work is started or the changes made.[b]

Is such a clause effective? The common law answer has been that it is not effective. The reasoning goes that any prior agreement, including the no-oral-modification clause itself, can be modified by a later agreement. In the baroque prose of Justice Michael Musmanno, "The most ironclad written contract can always be cut into by the acetylene torch of parol modification supported by adequate proof.... The hand that pens a writing may not gag the mouths of the assenting parties." Wagner v. Graziano Construction Co., 136 A.2d 82, 83–84 (Pa.1957).

Moreover, the party that seeks to escape the effect of the oral modification clause can often show reliance on the oral modification. As the Supreme Court of Pennsylvania concluded in such a case, "When an owner requests a builder to do extra work, promises to pay for it and watches it performed knowing that it is not authorized in writing, he

---

a. See also Keller v. A.O. Smith Harvestore Products, Inc., 819 P.2d 69, 73 (Colo. 1991) ("general integration clause does not effect a waiver of a claim of negligent misrepresentation not specifically prohibited by the terms of the agreement").

b. This clause is taken from Wagner v. Graziano Construction Co., 136 A.2d 82

(Pa.1957), where it appeared in a contract between a general contractor and a subcontractor. As to the desirability of extra work from the builder's point of view, see Note 3, p. 178 above.

cannot refuse to pay on the ground that there was no written change order." Universal Builders, Inc. v. Moon Motor Lodge, Inc., 244 A.2d 10, 16 (Pa.1968).

The Uniform Commercial Code changes the common law rule. Under UCC 2–209, "A signed agreement which excludes modification or rescission except by a signed writing cannot be otherwise modified or rescinded...." Note, however, that under subsection (3), what may fail to be effective as a modification or rescission may nevertheless be effective as a waiver. And under subsection (4), a material change of position in reliance on the waiver may prevent its retraction. The difficulties in interpreting these subsections are illustrated by the conflicting opinions in Wisconsin Knife Works v. National Metal Crafters, 781 F.2d 1280 (7th Cir.1986) (Posner, J.; Easterbrook, J. dissenting). On no-oral-modification clauses, see 2 Farnsworth § 7.6.

NOTES

(1) *The Vienna Sales Convention.* Article 29(2) of the Vienna Convention provides that a written contract "which contains a provision requiring any modification or termination by agreement to be in writing may not be otherwise modified or terminated by agreement." Note that this provision, evidently designed to change the rule in common law countries, makes an exception for cases of reliance.

(2) *Drafting.* What circumstances might make it desirable or undesirable to limit the terms of the contract to those contained in a writing and to exclude prior, contemporaneous and subsequent oral agreements? Draft a clause to accomplish this result for a contract for the sale of water filters that will be serviced by the seller after installation.[c] (To what extent is the clause analogous to a home-office-approval clause? See Note 2, p. 183 above.)[d]

(3) *"Private Statutes of Frauds."* It is sometimes suggested that UCC 2–209(2) allows the parties to set up a "private statute of frauds." Would a writing that satisfies UCC 2–201(1) necessarily satisfy a no-oral-modification clause? See Marlowe v. Argentine Naval Commission, 808 F.2d 120 (D.C.Cir. 1986).

SECTION 2.   INTERPRETING CONTRACT LANGUAGE

" 'When *I* use a word,' Humpty Dumpty said, in rather a scornful tone, 'it means just what I choose it to mean—neither more nor less.'

" 'The question is,' said Alice, 'whether you *can* make words mean so many different things.'

c. New York has a statute similar to UCC 2–209(2) that applies to contracts generally. N.Y.General Obligations L. § 15–301.

d. Here, too, a clause limiting the power of the seller's representatives in the field to bind him might be considered, but this raises questions of the law of agency that are beyond the scope of this course. See footnote b, p. 183 above.

" 'The question is,' said Humpty Dumpty, 'which is to be master—
that's all.' " Lewis Carroll, Through the Looking Glass, Chapter VI.

As this suggests, the problem of interpretation of language is not
peculiar to the law. However, language is commonly involved in social
control through law, and the interpretation of this language may have
consequences of great practical moment. The critical language may
come from one of a variety of sources, such as a constitution, a statute,
an administrative regulation, a will, a deed, or a contract. We are
concerned with contracts.

Scholars less boastful than Humpty Dumpty have cautioned us on
what Professor Chafee called "the disorderly conduct of words." There
is no "lawyers Paradise" where, in Professor Thayer's language, "all
words have a fixed, precisely ascertained meaning, . . . and where, if the
writer has been careful, a lawyer, having a document referred to him
may sit in his chair, inspect the text, and answer all questions without
raising his eyes." As Justice Holmes put it, "A word is not a crystal,
transparent and unchanged, it is the skin of a living thought and may
vary greatly in color and content according to the circumstances and the
time in which it is used." Towne v. Eisner, 245 U.S. 418 (1918). One of
the most perceptive of these scholars, Professor Willard van Orman
Quine, has emphasized a distinction between *vagueness* and *ambiguity*.
See Quine, Word and Object (1960).

According to Quine, a word, such as "green," is vague to the extent
that its applicability in marginal situations is uncertain. The parties,
for example, contract for the removal of "all the dirt" on a given tract.
May sand from a stratum of subsoil be taken?[a]

A word may also have two entirely different connotations so that it
may be at the same time both appropriate and inappropriate, as the
word "light" may be when applied to dark feathers. Such a word is
ambiguous.[b] Ambiguities may be classified into those of term and those
of syntax.

Ambiguities of term are relatively rare in contract cases. A contract
specifies "tons." Are they to be long or short tons?[c] Ambiguity of
syntax is, in the strictest sense, an ambiguity of grammatical structure,
of what is syntactically connected to what. It is more common a cause of
contract disputes than is ambiguity of term. A health insurance policy
excludes any "disease of organs of the body not common to both sexes."
Does the policy cover a fibroid tumor (which can occur in any organ) of
the uterus?[d]

a. See Highley v. Phillips, 5 A.2d 824
(Md.1939) (held: yes).

b. Since "ambiguous" is often used to
comprehend vague, as well as ambiguous in
the narrow sense, some writers prefer to
use "equivocal" for this purpose.

c. Compare Chemung Iron & Steel Co.
v. Mersereau Metal Bed Co., 179 N.Y.S. 577
(Sup.1920) (short tons), with Higgins v.
California Petroleum & Asphalt Co., 52 P.
1080 (Cal.1898) (long tons).

d. Business Men's Assur. Ass'n v. Read,
48 S.W.2d 678 (Tex.Civ.App.1932) (held:
yes).

A useful technique in describing disputes about language is to state the issue in terms of the contract language, much as an issue arising under a statute is stated in terms of the statutory language. It should be framed so that it can be answered "yes" or "no," as a court ordinarily must do. It should be framed so that it contains the controlling language of the contract, with such emphasis as is helpful. And it should be framed so that it recognizes that different meanings are attached to words in different contexts. For example:

Is a fibroid tumor of the uterus a "*disease* of *organs* of the body *not common to both sexes* " within the insured's contract of insurance?

A second technique is to redraft the language twice, staying as faithful to the original as possible, so that it would clearly require a decision, first for one party, then for the other. (See Note 1, p. 155 above.) For example:

(For insured) "disease of organs of the body that is not common to both sexes"

(For insurer) "disease of organs of the body that are not common to both sexes"

Try, in each of the following problems: (1) to describe the problem in Quine's terms; (2) to state the issue in terms of the contract language; and (3) to redraft the contract language, first for one party and then for the other. (Consider, also, what additional information would be useful in answering the problems.)

(a) A contract for the sale of a photography studio provides that the seller will not compete with the buyer "for the school photography work in any school in Grant County, with the exception of Marion High School and Bennett High School." May the seller compete with the buyer for the photography of Marion College students? See Lawrence v. Cain, 245 N.E.2d 663 (Ind.App.1969).

(b) A contract for the sale of a grocery store provides that the seller will not engage in a similar business "within a radius of five city blocks from the above mentioned premises." May the seller establish a grocery four blocks north and two blocks east of his old store before the five years are up? See Kunin v. Weller, 145 A. 719 (Pa.1929).

(c) A construction contract provides that "All domestic water piping and rainwater piping installed above finished ceilings under this specification shall be insulated." Must the contractor insulate domestic water piping installed below finished ceilings? See Paul W. Abbott v. Axel Newman Heating & Plumbing, 166 N.W.2d 323 (Minn.1969).

The cases that follow are concerned with how to answer questions like those raised in these problems. A threshold problem is posed by the fact that unlike a will, which expresses the intention of a single testator, or even a statute, which expresses the collective intention of a single legislature, a contract involves *two* parties who may attach very different meanings to language and have very different expectations. The next cases deal with this problem. On vagueness and ambiguity in contracts, see generally 2 Farnsworth § 7.8.

NOTES

(1) *Care in Drafting.* One of the most common results of carelessness in drafting is a conflict between different parts of the contract. For an example, see Robinhorne Construction Corp. v. Snyder, 265 N.E.2d 670 (Ill.1970), in which Justice Schaefer wrote: "This is the kind of case that has been described as 'one where no principle of law is involved, but only the meaning of careless and slovenly documents.' ... The parties used a standard cost-plus contract form. They modified it to specify a maximum contract price, but they failed to modify the termination provision. The conditions that they attached had been prepared for use with a lump-sum contract." For another example, see Schauerman v. Haag, 416 P.2d 88 (Wash.1966) ("Glaziers should glaze and lawyers should scriven, and neither ought do the other; for, when glaziers write and lawyers glaze, they are apt to make porous contracts and drafty windows.").

(2) *Interpretation in the Agreement Process.* We have already encountered problems of interpretation in the agreement process. See, for example, Owen v. Tunison, p. 154 above, and Harvey v. Facey, p. 156 above. Consider in this connection the remarks of Judge Medina in United States v. Braunstein, 75 F.Supp. 137 (S.D.N.Y.1947): "It is true that there is much room for interpretation once the parties are inside the framework of a contract, but it seems that there is less in the field of offer and acceptance. Greater precision of expression may be required, and less help from the court given, when the parties are merely at the threshold of a contract." This view was echoed in Henry Simons Lumber Co. v. Simons, 44 N.W.2d 726 (Minn.1950): "Because of strict rules governing offer and acceptance, which require that an acceptance be in terms of the offer, we are reluctant to follow by analogy rules laid down with respect to contracts already formed. In passing upon questions of offer and acceptance, courts may wisely require greater exactitude than when they are trying to salvage an existing contract. Where no contract has been completed and neither party has acted to his detriment, there is no compulsion on a court to guess at what the parties intended."

(3) *Intentional Vagueness.* Are there reasons why a drafter may intentionally leave language vague? Consider such Code terms as "good faith," "best efforts" and "reasonable time." Are there contract analogues?

(4) *Drafting Problem.* Tomayne, Inc., furnishes cafeteria service to business firms. It is about to employ your client Claiborne Craig as manager of its cafeteria operation at the Kent Data Processing plant under a two-year contract. The draft contains the following restrictive covenant:

> For one year after my employment with you ends, I will not participate in the management of any cafeteria operated by any firm who shall have been your client within the period of one year prior to the termination of my employment or with whom you may have been negotiating during my employment with you if I have participated in such negotiations or had contact with that firm in the course of my employment with you.

Do you see any important ambiguity in this clause? How can it be corrected? (Suppose that Craig leaves Tomayne at the end of two years and takes a job managing a cafeteria for a firm with which he has had no previous connection but which had been Tomayne's client three months earlier, before deciding to operate its own cafeteria?)   See Servomation Mathias, Inc. v. Englert, 333 F.Supp. 9 (M.D.Pa.1971).

FRIGALIMENT IMPORTING CO. v. B.N.S. INTERNATIONAL SALES CORP.

United States District Court, S.D.N.Y., 1960.
190 F.Supp. 116.

FRIENDLY, CIRCUIT JUDGE.[a]   The issue is, what is chicken?[b]   Plaintiff says "chicken" means a young chicken, suitable for broiling and frying. Defendant says "chicken" means any bird of that genus that meets contract specifications on weight and quality, including what it calls "stewing chicken" and plaintiff pejoratively terms "fowl".   Dictionaries give both meanings, as well as some others not relevant here.   To support its, plaintiff sends a number of volleys over the net; defendant essays to return them and adds a few serves of its own.   Assuming that both parties were acting in good faith, the case nicely illustrates Holmes' remark "that the making of a contract depends not on the agreement of two minds in one intention, but on the agreement of two sets of external signs—not on the parties' having *meant* the same thing but on their having *said* the same thing."   The Path of the Law, in Collected Legal Papers, p. 178.   I have concluded that plaintiff has not sustained its burden of persuasion that the contract used "chicken" in the narrower sense.

The action is for breach of the warranty that goods sold shall correspond to the description, New York Personal Property Law, McKinney's Consol.Laws, c. 41, § 95.   Two contracts are in suit.   In the first, dated May 2, 1957, defendant, a New York sales corporation, confirmed the sale to plaintiff, a Swiss corporation, of

> "US Fresh Frozen Chicken, Grade A, Government Inspected,
> Eviscerated
> 2½–3 lbs. and 1½–2 lbs. each
> all chicken individually wrapped in cryovac, packed in secured
> fiber cartons or wooden boxes, suitable for export
> 75,000 lbs. 2½–3 lbs....................................$33.00

a. Henry J. Friendly (1903–1986) clerked for Brandeis and then practiced law in New York for thirty years before becoming a judge, and later chief judge, on the United States Court of Appeals, Second Circuit. He was admired for his keen mind and the breadth of his learning. He advocated a drastic pruning of the diversity jurisdiction of federal courts but would have retained jurisdiction over suits between aliens and United States citizens (as in the principal case) owing to their "possible effect on international relations." H. Friendly, Federal Jurisdiction: A General View 150 n. 42 (1973).

b. In the 1940's, American chicken producers began to differentiate chickens raised for meat from those raised for eggs, and started using "assembly-line" techniques for the former, giving rise to a new consumer product, the "broiler chicken." Production grew phenomenally, prices dropped correspondingly, and exports to Europe increased sharply. Between 1956 and 1962, German chicken consumption went from 136 million pounds (of which 2.5 million or 1% was exported from the United States) to 716 million pounds (of which 169.6 million or 26% was exported from the United States).

25,000 lbs. 1½–2 lbs.....................................$36.50
per 100 lbs. FAS New York
scheduled May 10, 1957 pursuant to instructions from Penson
& Co., New York."

The second contract, also dated May 2, 1957, was identical save that only 50,000 lbs. of the heavier "chicken" were called for, the price of the smaller birds was $37 per 100 lbs., and shipment was scheduled for May 30. The initial shipment under the first contract was short but the balance was shipped on May 17. When the initial shipment arrived in Switzerland, plaintiff found, on May 28, that the 2½–3 lbs. birds were not young chicken suitable for broiling and frying but stewing chicken or "fowl"; indeed, many of the cartons and bags plainly so indicated. Protests ensued. Nevertheless, shipment under the second contract was made on May 29, the 2½–3 lbs. birds again being stewing chicken. Defendant stopped the transportation of these at Rotterdam.

This action followed. Plaintiff says that, notwithstanding that its acceptance was in Switzerland, New York law controls under the principle of Rubin v. Irving Trust Co., 1953, 305 N.Y. 288, 305, 113 N.E.2d 424, 431; defendant does not dispute this, and relies on New York decisions. I shall follow the apparent agreement of the parties as to the applicable law.

Since the word "chicken" standing alone is ambiguous, I turn first to see whether the contract itself offers any aid to its interpretation. Plaintiff says the 1½–2 lbs. birds necessarily had to be young chicken since the older birds do not come in that size, hence the 2½–3 lbs. birds must likewise be young. This is unpersuasive—a contract for "apples" of two different sizes could be filled with different kinds of apples even though only one species came in both sizes. Defendant notes that the contract called not simply for chicken but for "US Fresh Frozen Chicken, Grade A, Government Inspected." It says the contract thereby incorporated by reference the Department of Agriculture's regulations, which favor its interpretation; I shall return to this after reviewing plaintiff's other contentions.

The first hinges on an exchange of cablegrams which preceded execution of the formal contracts. The negotiations leading up to the contracts were conducted in New York between defendant's secretary, Ernest R. Bauer, and a Mr. Stovicek, who was in New York for the Czechoslovak government at the World Trade Fair. A few days after meeting Bauer at the fair, Stovicek telephoned and inquired whether defendant would be interested in exporting poultry to Switzerland. Bauer then met with Stovicek, who showed him a cable from plaintiff dated April 26, 1957, announcing that they "are buyer" of 25,000 lbs. of chicken 2½–3 lbs. weight, Cryovac packed, grade A Government inspected, at a price up to 33¢ per pound, for shipment on May 10, to be confirmed by the following morning, and were interested in further offerings. After testing the market for price, Bauer accepted, and Stovicek sent a confirmation that evening. Plaintiff stresses that, although these and subsequent cables between plaintiff and defendant, which laid the basis for the additional quantities under the first and for all of the second contract, were predominantly in German, they used the English word "chicken"; it claims this was done because it understood "chicken" meant young chicken whereas the German word, "Huhn," included both "Brathuhn" (broilers) and "Suppenhuhn" (stewing chicken), and that defendant, whose officers were thoroughly conversant with German, should have realized this. Whatever force this argument might otherwise have is largely drained away by Bauer's testimony that he asked Stovicek what kind of chickens were wanted, received the answer "any kind of chickens," and then, in German, asked whether the cable meant "Huhn" and received an affirmative response....

Plaintiff's next contention is that there was a definite trade usage that "chicken" meant "young chicken." Defendant showed that it was only beginning in the poultry trade in 1957, thereby bringing itself within the principle that "when one of the parties is not a member of the trade or other circle, his acceptance of the standard must be made to appear" by proving either that he had actual knowledge of the usage or that the usage is "so generally known in the community that his actual individual knowledge of it may be inferred." 9 Wigmore, Evidence (3d ed. 1940) § 2464. Here there was no proof of actual knowledge of the alleged usage; indeed, it is quite plain that defendant's belief was to the contrary. In order to meet the alternative requirement, the law of New York demands a showing that "the usage is of so long continuance, so well established, so notorious, so universal and so reasonable in itself, as that the presumption is violent that the parties contracted with reference to it, and made it a part of their agreement." Walls v. Bailey, 1872, 49 N.Y. 464, 472–473.

Plaintiff endeavored to establish such a usage by the testimony of three witnesses and certain other evidence. Strasser, resident buyer in New York for a large chain of Swiss cooperatives, testified that "on chicken I would definitely understand a broiler." However, the force of this testimony was considerably weakened by the fact that in his own transactions the witness, a careful businessman, protected himself by using "broiler" when that was what he wanted and "fowl" when he wished older birds. Indeed, there are some indications, dating back to a remark of Lord Mansfield, Edie v. East India Co., 2 Burr. 1216, 1222 (1761), that no credit should be given "witnesses to usage, who could not adduce instances in verification." 7 Wigmore, Evidence (3d ed. 1940) § 1954; see McDonald v. Acker, Merrall & Condit Co., 2d Dept.1920, 192 App.Div. 123, 126, 182 N.Y.S. 607. While Wigmore thinks this goes too far, a witness' consistent failure to rely on the alleged usage deprives his opinion testimony of much of its effect. Niesielowski, an officer of one of the companies that had furnished the stewing chicken to defendant, testified that "chicken" meant "the male species of the poultry industry. That could be a broiler, a fryer or a roaster," but not a stewing chicken; however, he also testified that upon receiving defendant's inquiry for "chickens," he asked whether the desire was for "fowl or frying chickens" and, in fact, supplied fowl, although taking the precaution of asking defendant, a day or two after plaintiff's acceptance of the contracts in suit, to change its confirmation of its order from "chickens," as defendant had originally prepared it, to "stewing chickens." Dates, an employee of Urner–Barry Company, which publishes a daily market report on the poultry trade, gave it as his view that the trade meaning of "chicken" was "broilers and fryers." In addition to this opinion testimony, plaintiff relied on the fact that the Urner–Barry service, the Journal of Commerce, and Weinberg Bros. & Co. of Chicago, a large supplier of poultry, published quotations in a manner which, in one way or another, distinguish between "chicken," comprising broilers, fryers and certain other categories, and "fowl," which, Bauer acknowledged, included stewing chickens. This material would be impressive if there were nothing to the contrary. However, there was, as will now be seen.

Defendant's witness Weininger, who operates a chicken eviscerating plant in New Jersey, testified "Chicken is everything except a goose, a duck, and a turkey. Everything is a chicken, but then you have to say, you have to specify which category you want or that you are talking about." Its witness Fox said that in the trade "chicken" would encompass all the various classifications. Sadina, who conducts a food inspection service, testified that he would consider any bird coming within the classes of "chicken" in the Department of Agriculture's regulations to be a chicken. The specifications approved by the General Services Administration include fowl as well as broilers and fryers under the classification "chickens." Statistics of the Institute of American Poultry Industries use the phrases "Young chickens" and "Mature chickens," under the general heading "Total chickens." and the Department of Agriculture's daily and weekly price reports avoid use of the word "chicken" without specification.

Defendant advances several other points which it claims affirmatively support its construction. Primary among these is the regulation of the Department of Agriculture, 7 C.F.R. §§ 70.300–70.370, entitled, "Grading and Inspection of Poultry and Edible Products Thereof." and in particular § 70.301 which recited:

Chickens. The following are the various classes of chickens:

    (a) Broiler or fryer ...

    (b) Roaster ...

    (c) Capon ...

    (d) Stag ...

    (e) Hen or stewing chicken or fowl ...

    (f) Cock or old rooster ...

Defendant argues, as previously noted, that the contract incorporated these regulations by reference. Plaintiff answers that the contract provision related simply to grade and Government inspection and did not incorporate the Government definition of "chicken," and also that the definition in the Regulations is ignored in the trade. However, the latter contention was contradicted by Weininger and Sadina; and there is force in defendant's argument that the contract made the regulations a dictionary, particularly since the reference to Government grading was already in plaintiff's initial cable to Stovicek.

Defendant makes a further argument based on the impossibility of its obtaining broilers and fryers at the 33¢ price offered by plaintiff for the 2½–3 lbs. birds. There is no substantial dispute that, in late April, 1957, the price for 2½–3 lbs. broilers was between 35 and 37¢ per pound, and that when defendant entered into the contracts, it was well aware of this and intended to fill them by supplying fowl in these weights. It claims that plaintiff must likewise have known the market since plaintiff had reserved shipping space on April 23, three days before plaintiff's cable to Stovicek, or, at least, that Stovicek was chargeable with such knowledge. It is scarcely an answer to say, as plaintiff does in its brief, that the 33¢ price offered for the 2½–3 lbs. "chickens" was closer to the prevailing 35¢ price for broilers than to the 30¢ at which defendant procured fowl. Plaintiff must have expected defendant to make some profit—certainly it could not have expected defendant deliberately to incur a loss.

Finally, defendant relies on conduct by the plaintiff after the first shipment had been received. On May 28 plaintiff sent two cables complaining that the larger birds in the first shipment constituted "fowl." Defendant answered with a cable refusing to recognize plaintiff's objection and announcing "We have today ready for shipment 50,000 lbs. chicken 2½–3 lbs. 25,000 lbs. broilers 1½–2 lbs.," these being the goods procured for shipment under the second contract, and asked immediate answer "whether we are to ship this merchandise to you and whether you will accept the merchandise." After several other cable exchanges, plaintiff replied on May 29 "Confirm again that merchandise is to be shipped since resold by us if not enough pursuant to contract chickens are shipped the missing quantity is to be shipped within ten days stop we resold to our customers pursuant to your contract chickens grade A you have to deliver us said merchandise we again state that we shall make you fully responsible for all resulting costs." Defendant argues that if plaintiff was sincere in thinking it was entitled to young chickens, plaintiff would not have allowed the shipment under the second contract to go forward, since the distinction between broilers and chickens drawn in defendant's cablegram must have made it clear that the larger birds would not be broilers. However, plaintiff answers that the cables show plaintiff was insisting on delivery of young chickens and that defendant shipped old ones at its peril. Defendant's point would be highly relevant on another disputed issue—whether if liability were established, the measure of damages should be the difference in market value of broilers and stewing chicken in New York or the larger difference in Europe, but I cannot give it weight on the issue of interpretation. Defendant points out also that plaintiff proceeded to deliver some of the larger birds in Europe, describing them as "poulets"; defendant argues that it was only when plaintiff's customers complained about this that plaintiff developed the idea that "chicken" meant "young chicken." There is little force in this in view of plaintiff's immediate and consistent protests.

When all the evidence is reviewed, it is clear that defendant believed it could comply with the contracts by delivering stewing chicken in the 2½–3 lbs. size. Defendant's subjective intent would not be significant if this did not coincide with an objective meaning of "chicken." Here it did coincide with one of the dictionary meanings, with the definition in the Department of Agriculture Regulations to which the contract made at least oblique reference, with at least some usage in the trade, with the realities of the market, and with what plaintiff's spokesman had said. Plaintiff asserts it to be equally plain that plaintiff's own subjective intent was to obtain broilers and fryers; the only evidence against this is the material as to market prices and this may not have been sufficiently brought home. In any event it is unnecessary to determine that issue. For plaintiff has the burden of showing that "chicken" was used in the narrower rather than in the broader sense, and this it has not sustained.

This opinion constitutes the Court's findings of fact and conclusions of law. Judgment shall be entered dismissing the complaint with costs.

NOTES

(1) *"What is Chicken"?* Judge Friendly says that "The issue is, what is chicken?" [a] Is this the issue that the court had to decide? He also says that the case "nicely illustrates Holmes' remark 'that the making of a contract depends . . . not on the parties' having *meant* the same thing but on their having *said* the same thing.'" Does it? Would the result have been the same if *both* parties had *meant* broilers although they had *said* "chicken"? Is there any reason to hold the parties to a meaning that *neither* attached to their language? [b]

(2) *Incorporation by Reference.* Are there any special problems that arise in the interpretation of terms, such as the regulations of the Department of Agriculture, that have been incorporated in a contract by reference? Cf. Wilcox v. Wilcox, 406 S.W.2d 152 (Ky.1966), involving a divorce settlement in which the husband agreed to make maintenance payments until his daughter reached "the age of majority." The court held that the husband's obligation continued until the child reached 21, the statutory age of majority at the time of the agreement, even though the statutory age had subsequently been lowered to 18.

(3) *Problem.* Fredrick Hamann, who taught at the Garden City Community Junior College, wanted a year's leave to take a teacher training course. The college regulations incorporated by reference in his contract of employment provided:

Professional employees granted leaves will, if possible, be reinstated in positions that are similar to the position held when granted the leave.

a. See also Shrum v. Zeltwanger, 559 P.2d 1384 (Wyo.1977) ("What is a 'cow'?").

b. Since both parties were corporations, the notion that either "meant" anything or had any "intention" may seem somewhat strained. It would seem even more strained if other persons, including lawyers, had participated in the negotiations along with Bauer and Stovicek. Courts have not been greatly troubled by the problems of finding a collective "intention" in such cases. (For example, Judge Friendly states that B.N.S. "was only beginning in the poultry trade." Would it have been significant if Bauer had been hired by B.N.S. because of his long experience in that trade?) For a rare instance where such a problem was raised, see Franklin Life Insurance Co. v. Mast, 435 F.2d 1038 (9th Cir.1970), where the court said, "Whatever may have been the secret intent of Mast, it is clear that the intent of his attorney in fact, Attorney Lohse, was to enter into a bona fide agreement."

When he was offered a leave, he knew that the college interpreted this to mean that they would not be required to re-hire him unless there was a similar position open when he re-applied. However, he consulted a lawyer, who advised that in his judgment the provision should be interpreted to mean that the college was required to re-hire him even though a similar position might not be open. Secure in this knowledge, Hamann said nothing and accepted the leave. When he sought to return, the college told him that he could not do so because there was no similar position available. What do you think of the lawyer's advice? See Hamann v. Crouch, 508 P.2d 968 (Kan.1973).

OBJECTIVE AND SUBJECTIVE THEORIES
OF CONTRACT INTERPRETATION

Just as the objective and subjective theories have influenced the law of contract formation (see p. 138 above), they have also influenced the law of contract interpretation. There would be little disagreement with the proposition that, where the parties have in fact attached different meanings to their language, an objective standard should determine which meaning will prevail. But the objectivists argue that, even where the parties have in fact attached the same meaning to their language, an objective standard should determine the meaning, which might be different from their shared meaning. Hand, for example, said: "It is quite true that we commonly speak of a contract as a question of intent, and for most purposes it is a convenient paraphrase, accurate enough, but, strictly speaking, untrue. It makes not the least difference whether a promisor actually intends that meaning which the law will impose upon his words. The whole House of Bishops might satisfy us that he had intended something else, and it would make not a particle of difference in his obligation. That obligation the law attaches to his act of using certain words, provided, of course, the actor be under no disability." Eustis Mining Co. v. Beer, Sondheimer & Co., 239 F. 976 (S.D.N.Y.1917). The currency of this view can be judged from the following cases. See Restatement Second § 201.

NOTE

The Case of John's Other Wife. In 1921, Ira Soper penned several suicide notes to Adeline, his wife of ten years, parked his car containing his hat and some clothing by a canal, and left Louisville, Kentucky, without a trace, for Minneapolis, Minnesota, where he began a new life under the name of John W. Young. There he married Gertrude Whitby, took out a $5,000 insurance policy on his own life, payable to a trust company, and made an "escrow" agreement with his partner Karstens and the trust company by which the company would pay the proceeds to "the wife" of the insured. In 1932 he actually did commit suicide, and the trustee paid the proceeds to Gertrude as his surviving wife. Several months later Adeline appeared and brought suit against Gertrude for the proceeds. From a judgment for defendant, plaintiff appealed. *Held:* Affirmed. Although Gertrude was not the legal wife of the deceased, evidence was admissible to show that she was intended as beneficiary. "Were we to award the insurance fund to plaintiff Adeline, it is obvious that we would thereby be doing violence to the contract.... That agreement points to no one else than

Gertrude as Young's 'wife'. To hold otherwise is to give the word 'wife' 'a fixed symbol,' as 'something inherent and objective, not subjective and personal'.... The trust agreement has become 'susceptible of construction' because 'ambiguity appears when attempt is made to operate the contract.' " One judge dissented, arguing: "A man can have only one wife.... The contract in this case designates the 'wife' as the one to whom the money was to be paid. I am unable to construe this word to mean anyone else than the only wife of Soper then living." In re Soper's Estate (Cochran v. Whitby), 264 N.W. 427 (Minn.1935). But cf. State Farm Mutual Automobile Ins. Co. v. Thompson, 372 F.2d 256 (9th Cir.1967).

Introductory Note to Raffles v. Wichelhaus

The next case, Raffles v. Wichelhaus, pushes these theories to their limits. In an extensive discussion of the case and its background, the case is characterized as "one of the best known old chestnuts of the common law.... No student of the law of contract could regard his education as complete without either reading the case in the reports themselves, or, more commonly, acquiring some acquaintance with the case from one of the abbreviated, and sometimes garbled, accounts which appear in the legal casebooks or hornbooks." At least some of the case's fascination is due to the circumstances that "the judges ... thought the solution to the problem presented to them to be so obvious that they gave judgment for the defendants without troubling to give any reasons for their decision." [c] This circumstance permits a variety of explanations of their decision. What is yours?

RAFFLES v. WICHELHAUS
Court of Exchequer, 1864.
2 H. & C. 906, 159 Eng.Rep. 375.

Declaration. For that it was agreed between the plaintiff and the defendants, to wit, at Liverpool, that the plaintiff should sell to the defendants, and the defendants buy of the plaintiff, certain goods, to wit, 125 bales of Surat cotton, guaranteed middling fair merchant's Dhollorah, to arrive ex Peerless from Bombay; and that the cotton should be taken from the quay, and that the defendants would pay the plaintiff for the same at a certain rate, to wit, at the rate of 17¼d. per pound, within a certain time then agreed upon after the arrival of the said goods in England. Averments: that the said goods did arrive by the said ship from Bombay in England, to wit, at Liverpool, and the plaintiff was then and there ready and willing and offered to deliver the said goods to the defendants, etc. Breach: that the defendants refused to accept the said goods or pay the plaintiff for them.

Plea. That the said ship mentioned in the said agreement was meant and intended by the defendants to be the ship called the Peerless,

---

c. Simpson, Contracts for Cotton to Arrive: The Case of the Two Ships *Peerless*, 11 Cardozo L.Rev. 287, 287–88 (1989).

which sailed from Bombay, to wit, in October; and that the plaintiff was not ready and willing, and did not offer, to deliver to the defendants any bales of cotton which arrived by the last-mentioned ship, but instead thereof was only ready and willing, and offered to deliver to the defendants 125 bales of Surat cotton which arrived by another and different ship, which was also called the Peerless, and which sailed from Bombay, to wit, in December.

Demurrer, and joinder therein.

MILWARD in support of the demurrer. The contract was for the sale of a number of bales of cotton of a particular description, which the plaintiff was ready to deliver. It is immaterial by what ship the cotton was to arrive, so that it was a ship called the Peerless. The words "to arrive ex Peerless," only mean that if the vessel is lost on the voyage, the contract is to be at an end. [Pollock, C.B. It would be a question for the jury whether both parties meant the same ship called the Peerless.] That would be so if the contract was for the sale of a ship called the Peerless; but it is for the sale of cotton on board a ship of that name. [Pollock, C.B. The defendant only bought that cotton which was to arrive by a particular ship. It may as well be said that if there is a contract for the purchase of certain goods in warehouse A that is satisfied by the delivery of goods of the same description in warehouse B.] In that case there would be goods in both warehouses; here it does not appear that the plaintiff had any goods on board the other Peerless. [Martin, B. It is imposing on the defendant a contract different from that which he entered into. Pollock, C.B. It is like a contract for the purchase of wine coming from a particular estate in France or Spain, where there are two estates of that name.] The defendant has no right to contradict by parol evidence a written contract good upon the face of it. He does not impute misrepresentation or fraud, but only says that he fancied the ship was a different one. Intention is of no avail, unless stated at the time of the contract. [Pollock, C.B. One vessel sailed in October and the other in December.] The time of sailing is no part of the contract.

MELLISH (Cohen with him) in support of the plea. There is nothing on the face of the contract to show that any particular ship called the Peerless was meant; but the moment it appears that two ships called the Peerless were about to sail from Bombay there is a latent ambiguity, and parol evidence may be given for the purpose of showing that the defendant meant one Peerless and the plaintiff another. That being so, there was no consensus ad idem, and therefore no binding contract. He was then stopped by the court.

PER CURIAM. There must be judgment for the defendants.

Judgment for the defendants.

NOTES

(1) *The Meaning of "Peerless."* Can the result be explained only on the subjective theory? Holmes thought not: "By the theory of our language, while other words may mean different things, a proper name means one person or

thing and no other.... In theory of speech your name means you and my name means me, and the two names are different. They are different words.... In the use of common names and words a plea of different meaning from that adopted by the court would be bad, but here the parties have said different things and never have expressed a contract." Holmes, The Theory of Legal Interpretation, 12 Harv.L.Rev. 417, 418 (1899).

(2) *Simpson v. Gilmore* Professor Grant Gilmore wrote that "the celebrated case of Raffles v. Wichelhaus ... is to the ordinary run of case law as the recently popular theater of the absurd is to the ordinary run of theater." He noted that if the ship which sailed first had also arrived first and if the market price had broken between the two arrival dates, the buyer would presumably have pleaded these facts, and since he did not "we may ... safely assume that there was no such issue to be raised." There was therefore merit to Milward's argument that it was "immaterial by what ship the cotton was to arrive, so [long as] it was a ship called the Peerless." But "the judges, no doubt mistakenly, believed that the identity of the carrying ship was important." G. Gilmore, The Death of Contract 35–39 (1974).

Professor Brian Simpson concluded otherwise in a detailed examination of the background of the contract, which was made in 1862 during the cotton famine created by the blockade of the southern states during the Civil War. The famine made cotton prices high and volatile and caused English spinners to look to India. Speculators were attracted to "arrival" contracts, under which the buyer purchased cotton in transit for forward delivery. Although the time of arrival was of paramount importance to the buyer, it was not common for the contract to specify this time because of the uncertainties involved. One technique that made it possible for the buyer to at least estimate the approximate date of arrival was to name the ship and sometimes the port of departure. The contract in the principal case was such a "ship named" and "port named" contract.

Simpson concludes that Gilmore's "speculations as to the background are inevitably misconceived, being unrelated to evidence," and that "it is perfectly plain that in arrival contracts where ship and port were named, the identity of the carrying vessel was of central importance" because "that fixed the time of arrival and delivery." Simpson, Contracts for Cotton to Arrive: The Case of the Two Ships *Peerless,* 11 Cardozo L.Rev. 287, 324 (1989).

How might the outcome of this debate affect the value of the case as a precedent?

OSWALD v. ALLEN, 417 F.2d 43 (2d Cir.1969). [Dr. Oswald, a coin collector from Switzerland, arranged to see Mrs. Allen's collection of Swiss coins in Newburgh, New York, where two of her collections, referred to as the Swiss Coin Collection and the Rarity Coin Collection, were located in separate bank vaults. After examining the coins in the Swiss Coin Collection, he was shown several valuable Swiss coins from the Rarity Coin Collection, although he later testified that he did not know that they were in a separate "collection." During the drive back to New York City, Dr. Oswald, who spoke very little English, arranged with the help of his brother to buy for $50,000 what Mrs. Allen thought was her Swiss coin collection and what Dr. Oswald thought were all her

Swiss coins.   He later wrote her to "confirm my purchase of all your Swiss coins (gold, silver and copper) at the price of $50,000" and she wrote back that she had arranged to go to Newburgh with Dr. Oswald's agent.   When Dr. Oswald was informed that she would not go through with the sale because of her children's wishes, he sued for specific performance.   From a judgment dismissing his complaint after trial, he appealed.]

MOORE, CIRCUIT JUDGE. . . .   In such a factual situation the law is settled that no contract exists.   The Restatement of Contracts in section 71(a) adopts the rule of Raffles v. Wichelhaus, 2 Hurl. & C. 906, 159 Eng.Rep. 375 (Ex.1864).   Professor Young states that rule as follows: "when any of the terms used to express an agreement is ambivalent, and the parties understand it in different ways, there cannot be a contract unless one of them should have been aware of the other's understanding."   Young, Equivocation in Agreements, 64 Colum.L.Rev. 619, 621 (1964).   Even though the mental assent of the parties is not requisite for the formation of a contract (see Comment to Restatement of Contracts § 71 (1932)), the facts found by the trial judge clearly place this case within the small group of exceptional cases in which there is "no sensible basis for choosing between conflicting understandings."   Young, at 647.   The rule of Raffles v. Wichelhaus is applicable here.

[The court also held that the exchange of letters did not satisfy the Statute of Frauds.]

Affirmed.

NOTE

Another View.   In the article quoted by Judge Moore, Professor Young writes: "Roughly speaking, the rule is restricted to differences of understanding which have their source in the ambivalence or 'double meaning' of an expression. Neither the courts nor the logicians have succeeded, so far as I am aware, in establishing a criterion by which we can readily decide whether or not a particular expression has a 'double meaning.'   Holmes's formulation [in Note, p. 593 above] would have limited the application of the Peerless rule too narrowly. The Restatement test [now stated in Restatement Second § 20] is too broad." Young, Equivocation in the Making of Agreements, 64 Colum.L.Rev. 619, 646–47 (1964).

FUNCTION OF JUDGE AND JURY

A detailed consideration of the respective roles of judge and jury, where trial is had by jury, in matters of contract interpretation is best left to a course in evidence or procedure.   Nevertheless, a few elementary generalizations may be in order.   It is clear that the meaning of language is, strictly speaking, a question of fact.   Yet the interpretation of written agreements, as to which there is no dispute over the words used by the parties, has often been withdrawn from the jury by calling it a question of "law" for the judge, rather than a question of "fact" for the jury.   This has been done for a variety of reasons, including a distrust of unsophisticated, uneducated, and—at least at one time—illiterate jurors, and a desire for consistency in interpretation of some kinds of contracts, such as standard insurance policies.

The difficulty in drawing a line between the province of the judge and that of the jury is suggested by this dictum of Justice Story: [a] "It is certainly true, as a general rule, that the interpretation of written instruments properly belongs to the court, and not to the jury. But there certainly are cases in which, from the different senses of the words used, or their obscure and indeterminate reference to unexplained circumstances, the true interpretation of the language may be left to the consideration of the jury for the purpose of carrying into effect the real intention of the parties." Williams & James Brown & Co. v. McGran, 39 U.S. (14 Pet.) 479, 493 (1840). A similar view has been more recently expressed by Chief Justice Traynor, who wrote, "It is . . . solely a judicial function to interpret a written instrument unless the interpretation turns upon the credibility of extrinsic evidence." Parsons v. Bristol Development Co., 402 P.2d 839, 842 (Cal.1965).

But Judge Friendly has pointed out: "With the courts' growing appreciation of Professor Corbin's lesson that words are seldom so 'plain and clear' as to exclude proof of surrounding circumstances and other extrinsic aids to interpretation, . . . the exception bids fair largely to swallow the supposed general rule. . . . Whether determination of meaning be regarded as a question of fact, a question of law, or just itself, reliance on the jury to resolve ambiguities in the light of extrinsic evidence seems quite as it should be, save where the form or subject-matter of a particular contract outruns a jury's competence. . . ." Meyers v. Selznick Co., 373 F.2d 218, 222 (2d Cir.1966).

If a particular question of interpretation is one for the judge and not for the jury, what is the scope of review of the judge's decision on appeal? In Ram Construction Co., Inc. v. American States Insurance Co., 749 F.2d 1049 (3d Cir.1984), the court reasoned that in matters of interpretation the traditional distribution of functions between judge and jury "rests on outdated common law policy considerations, such as jury illiteracy and lack of respect for writings, as well as such continuing concerns as a judicial desire for uniformity. . . . In instances of contract interpretation, therefore, assignment to judge or jury does not of itself determine the standard of review to be applied on appeal. Interpretation by a trial court of a factual matter is reviewable on a clearly erroneous basis, rather than as a plenary one." [b]

a. Joseph Story (1779–1845) was appointed to the United States Supreme Court in 1811. In 1829, while retaining his seat on the Court, he became a professor of law at the Harvard Law School, where he reorganized the curriculum and revitalized the school. From his lectures developed his nine commentaries on subjects ranging from the Constitution to conflict of laws, which played an important role in promoting uniformity in the development of American law during the first half of the nineteenth century.

b. Compare Paragon Resources, Inc. v. National Fuel Gas Distribution Corp., 695 F.2d 991 (5th Cir.1983) ("[T]he clearly erroneous rule applies when extrinsic evidence is used to interpret an *ambiguous* contract, and ambiguity is a question of law." Therefore the appellate court "must first review the decision that the contract terms are ambiguous." If it agrees with

NOTE

"What is Chicken"? (Reprise). At the end of the *Frigaliment* case, Judge Friendly said that "the burden of showing that 'chicken' was used in the narrower rather than in the broader sense" was on the buyer. Its action for breach of warranty therefore failed. See UCC 2–607(4). Suppose, however, that immediately after the contracts were made, the buyer had told the seller that it would accept nothing but broilers, and the seller had treated this as a repudiation and sued for damages. Would not the burden of showing that "chicken" was used in the broader sense have then been on the seller? Is it possible that the seller might have failed to sustain this burden?

In a case like Raffles v. Wichelhaus, is it possible that the seller might fail to meet the burden of showing that "Peerless" was used in the sense of the ship sailing in December and that the buyer might also fail to meet the burden of showing that "Peerless" was used in the sense of the ship sailing in October? Do the preceding excerpts on the function of judge and jury suggest that interpretation is a question of "fact" as to which a party can be said to have a "burden"?

PACIFIC GAS & ELECTRIC CO. v. G.W. THOMAS DRAYAGE & RIGGING CO.

Supreme Court of California, 1968.
69 Cal.2d 33, 69 Cal.Rptr. 561, 442 P.2d 641.

TRAYNOR, CHIEF JUSTICE. Defendant appeals from a judgment for plaintiff in an action for damages for injury to property under an indemnity clause of a contract.

In 1960 defendant entered into a contract with plaintiff to furnish the labor and equipment necessary to remove and replace the upper metal cover of plaintiff's steam turbine. Defendant agreed to perform the work "at [its] own risk and expense" and to "indemnify" plaintiff "against all loss, damage, expense and liability resulting from . . . injury to property, arising out of or in any way connected with the performance of this contract." Defendant also agreed to procure not less than $50,000 insurance to cover liability for injury to property. Plaintiff was to be an additional named insured, but the policy was to contain a cross-liability clause extending the coverage to plaintiff's property.

During the work the cover fell and injured the exposed rotor of the turbine. Plaintiff brought this action to recover $25,144.51, the amount it subsequently spent on repairs. During the trial it dismissed a count based on negligence and thereafter secured judgment on the theory that the indemnity provision covered injury to all property regardless of ownership.

the trial court that they are, it must "accord 'clearly erroneous' deference to its interpretation of that contract in light of extrinsic evidence.").

As to the effect of such a decision under the doctrine of *stare decisis,* see South Hampton Co. v. Stinnes Corp., 733 F.2d 1108, 1115 n. 5 (5th Cir.1984) ("[D]etermination of ambiguity, like other fact questions, will sometimes be a question to be answered by the judge and not the jury. . . . The determination, however, does not become imbued with *stare decisis* effect just because a judge made it.").

Defendant offered to prove by admissions of plaintiff's agents, by defendant's conduct under similar contracts entered into with plaintiff, and by other proof that in the indemnity clause the parties meant to cover injury to property of third parties only and not to plaintiff's property. Although the trial court observed that the language used was "the classic language for a third party indemnity provision" and that "one could very easily conclude that ... its whole intendment is to indemnify third parties," it nevertheless held that the "plain language" of the agreement also required defendant to indemnify plaintiff for injuries to plaintiff's property. Having determined that the contract had a plain meaning, the court refused to admit any extrinsic evidence that would contradict its interpretation.

When a court interprets a contract on this basis, it determines the meaning of the instrument in accordance with the "... extrinsic evidence of the judge's own linguistic education and experience." (3 Corbin on Contracts (1960 ed.) [1964 Supp. § 579, p. 225, fn. 56].) The exclusion of testimony that might contradict the linguistic background of the judge reflects a judicial belief in the possibility of perfect verbal expression. (9 Wigmore on Evidence (3d ed. 1940) § 2461, p. 187.) This belief is a remnant of a primitive faith in the inherent potency [1] and inherent meaning of words.[2]

The test of admissibility of extrinsic evidence to explain the meaning of a written instrument is not whether it appears to the court to be plain and unambiguous on its face, but whether the offered evidence is relevant to prove a meaning to which the language of the instrument is reasonably susceptible....

A rule that would limit the determination of the meaning of a written instrument to its four-corners merely because it seems to the court to be clear and unambiguous, would either deny the relevance of the intention of the parties or presuppose a degree of verbal precision and stability our language has not attained.

Some courts have expressed the opinion that contractual obligations are created by the mere use of certain words, whether or not there was any intention to incur such obligations.[3] Under this view, contractual

---

1. E.g., " 'The elaborate system of taboo and verbal prohibitions in primitive groups; the ancient Egyptian myth of Khern, the apotheosis of the word, and of Thoth, the Scribe of Truth, the Giver of Words and Script, the Master of Incantations; the avoidance of the name of God in Brahmanism, Judaism and Islam; totemistic and protective names in mediaeval Turkish and Finno–Ugrian languages; the misplaced verbal scruples of the 'Precieuses'; the Swedish peasant custom of curing sick cattle smitten by witchcraft, by making them swallow a page torn out of the psalter and put in dough...." from Ullman, The Principles of Semantics (1963 ed.) 43. (See also

Ogden and Richards, The Meaning of Meaning (rev. ed. 1956) pp. 24–47.)

2. " 'Rerum enim vocabula immutabilia sunt, homines mutabilia,' " (Words are unchangeable, men changeable) from Dig. XXXIII, 10, 7 § 2, de sup. leg. as quoted in 9 Wigmore on Evidence, op. cit. supra, § 2461, p. 187.

3. "A contract has, strictly speaking, nothing to do with the personal, or individual, intent of the parties. A contract is an obligation attached by the mere force of law to certain acts of the parties, usually words, which ordinarily accompany and represent a known intent." (Hotchkiss v. National City Bank of New York (S.D.N.Y.1911) 200 F. 287, 293....)

obligations flow, not from the intention of the parties but from the fact that they used certain magic words. Evidence of the parties' intention therefore becomes irrelevant.

In this state, however, the intention of the parties as expressed in the contract is the source of contractual rights and duties. A court must ascertain and give effect to this intention by determining what the parties meant by the words they used. Accordingly, the exclusion of relevant, extrinsic evidence to explain the meaning of a written instrument could be justified only if it were feasible to determine the meaning the parties gave to the words from the instrument alone.

If words had absolute and constant referents, it might be possible to discover contractual intention in the words themselves and in the manner in which they were arranged. Words, however, do not have absolute and constant referents. "A word is a symbol of thought but has no arbitrary and fixed meaning like a symbol of algebra or chemistry,...." (Pearson v. State Social Welfare Board (1960) 54 Cal.2d 184, 195, 5 Cal.Rptr. 553, 559, 353 P.2d 33, 39.) The meaning of particular words or groups of words varies with the "... verbal context and surrounding circumstances and purposes in view of the linguistic education and experience of their users and their hearers or readers (not excluding judges).... A word has no meaning apart from these factors; much less does it have an objective meaning, one true meaning." (Corbin, The Interpretation of Words and the Parol Evidence Rule (1965) 50 Cornell L.Q. 161, 187.) Accordingly, the meaning of a writing "... can only be found by interpretation in the light of all the circumstances that reveal the sense in which the writer used the words. The exclusion of parol evidence regarding such circumstances merely because the words do not appear ambiguous to the reader can easily lead to the attribution to a written instrument of a meaning that was never intended. [Citations omitted.]" (Universal Sales Corp. v. Cal. Press Mfg. Co., supra, 20 Cal.2d 751, 776, 128 P.2d 665, 679 (concurring opinion);....)

Although extrinsic evidence is not admissible to add to, detract from, or vary the terms of a written contract, these terms must first be determined before it can be decided whether or not extrinsic evidence is being offered for a prohibited purpose. The fact that the terms of an instrument appear clear to a judge does not preclude the possibility that the parties chose the language of the instrument to express different terms. That possibility is not limited to contracts whose terms have acquired a particular meaning by trade usage, but exists whenever the parties' understanding of the words used may have differed from the judge's understanding.

Accordingly, rational interpretation requires at least a preliminary consideration of all credible evidence offered to prove the intention of the parties.[4] (Civ.Code, § 1647; Code Civ.Proc., § 1860; see also 9 Wigmore

4. When objection is made to any particular item of evidence offered to prove the intention of the parties, the trial court may not yet be in a position to determine wheth- er in the light of all of the offered evidence, the item objected to will turn out to be admissible as tending to prove a meaning of which the language of the instrument is

on Evidence, op. cit. supra, § 2470, fn. 11, p. 227.) Such evidence includes testimony as to the "circumstances surrounding the making of the agreement ... including the object, nature and subject matter of the writing ..." so that the court can "place itself in the same situation in which the parties found themselves at the time of contracting." (Universal Sales Corp. v. Cal. Press Mfg. Co., supra, 20 Cal.2d 751, 761, 128 P.2d 665, 671.) If the court decides, after considering this evidence, that the language of a contract, in the light of all the circumstances, is "fairly susceptible of either one of the two interpretations contended for...." (Balfour v. Fresno C. & I. Co. (1895) 109 Cal. 221, 225, 44 P. 876, 877; ...) extrinsic evidence relevant to prove either of such meanings is admissible.[5]

In the present case the court erroneously refused to consider extrinsic evidence offered to show that the indemnity clause in the contract was not intended to cover injuries to plaintiff's property. Although that evidence was not necessary to show that the indemnity clause was reasonably susceptible of the meaning contended for by defendant, it was nevertheless relevant and admissible on that issue. Moreover, since that clause was reasonably susceptible of that meaning, the offered evidence was also admissible to prove that the clause had that meaning and did not cover injuries to plaintiff's property.[6] Accordingly, the judgment must be reversed....

The judgment is reversed.

NOTES

(1) *Extrinsic Evidence in California.* The preceding opinion followed by only four months that in Masterson v. Sine, p. 570 above. Six months later the California Supreme Court decided Delta Dynamics, Inc. v. Arioto, 446 P.2d 785 (Cal.1968), which arose out of an exclusive distributorship contract under which Delta was to supply trigger locks for firearms to Pixey Distributing for five years. Pixey agreed to sell a minimum of 50,000 units during the first year and 100,000 units in each of the following four years. If Pixey failed to meet the minimum, the agreement was "subject to termination." In case of breach by either party,

reasonably susceptible or inadmissible as tending to prove a meaning of which the language is not reasonably susceptible. In such case the court may admit the evidence conditionally by either reserving its ruling on the objection or by admitting the evidence subject to a motion to strike. (See Evid.Code, § 403.)

5. Extrinsic evidence has often been admitted in such cases on the stated ground that the contract was ambiguous (e.g., Universal Sales Corp. v. Cal.Press Mfg. Co., supra, 20 Cal.2d 751, 761, 128 P.2d 665). This statement of the rule is harmless if it is kept in mind that the ambiguity may be exposed by extrinsic evidence that reveals more than one possible meaning.

6. The court's exclusion of extrinsic evidence in this case would be error even under a rule that excluded such evidence when the instrument appeared to the court to be clear and unambiguous on its face. The controversy centers on the meaning of the word "indemnify" and the phrase "all loss, damage, expense and liability." The trial court's recognition of the language as typical of a third party indemnity clause and the double sense in which the word "indemnify" is used in statutes and defined in dictionaries demonstrate the existence of an ambiguity. (Compare Civ.Code, § 2772, "Indemnity is a contract by which one engages to save another from a legal consequence of the conduct of one of the parties, or of some other person," with Civ.Code, § 2527, "Insurance is a contract whereby one undertakes to indemnify another against loss, damage, or liability, arising from an unknown or contingent event.")

"the party prevailing in any action for damages or enforcement of the terms of this Agreement shall be entitled to reasonable attorneys' fees." When Pixey took only 10,000 locks during the first year, Delta terminated and sued Pixey for damages. Pixey contended that Delta's exclusive remedy for Pixey's failure to meet the minimum was to terminate the contract. The trial court excluded extrinsic evidence offered by Pixey to prove this meaning, and Pixey appealed from a judgment for Delta. *Held:* Reversed. Chief Justice Traynor considered the contract language "reasonably susceptible" to Pixey's contention. "It does not render meaningless the provision for the recovery of attorney's fees in the event of an action for damages for breach of the contract, for the attorneys' fees provision would still have full effect with respect to other breaches of the contract." Three of seven judges dissented, Justice Mosk lamenting that the court was adopting "a course leading toward emasculation of the parol evidence rule. During this very year Masterson v. Sine ... and Pacific Gas & Elec. Co. v. G.W. Thomas Drayage & Rigging Co. ... have contributed toward that result. Although I had misgivings at the time, I must confess to joining the majority in both of those cases. Now, however, ... the trend has become so unmistakably ominous that I must urge a halt."

(2) *Extrinsic Evidence in the Ninth Circuit.* Two decades after the decision in *Pacific Gas,* the United States Court of Appeals for the Ninth Circuit applied that precedent with a vengeance to a contract made in 1983 for a $56 million commercial loan from Connecticut General to Trident. The promissory note given by Trident provided that it "shall not have the right to repay the principal amount hereof in whole or in part before January 1996." In 1987, when interest rates began to drop, Trident sought a declaration that it was entitled to prepay the note before 1996 and sought unsuccessfully to introduce extrinsic evidence to support its interpretation. It argued that the quoted language was ambiguous because another clause in the note providing that "[i]n the event of a prepayment resulting from a default ... prior to January 10, 1996, the prepayment fee will be ten percent." Judge Kozinski rejected Trident's argument that this clause gave it the option of prepaying the loan if it was willing to incur the prepayment fee, explaining that whether to accelerate repayment of the loan in the event of default was entirely Connecticut General's decision.

Nevertheless, after stating that Trident's interpretation was "one to which the contract, as written is not reasonably susceptible," Judge Kozinski explained that in *Pacific Gas* the California Supreme Court

> turned its back on the notion that a contract can ever have a plain meaning discernible by a court without resort to extrinsic evidence.... Under *Pacific Gas,* it matters not how clearly a contract is written, nor how completely it is integrated, nor how carefully it is negotiated, nor how squarely it addresses the issue before the court; the contract cannot be rendered impervious to attack by parol evidence. If one side is willing to claim that the parties intended one thing but the agreement provides for another, the court must consider extrinsic evidence of possible ambiguity. If that evidence raises the specter of ambiguity where there was none before, the contract language is displaced and the intention of the parties must be divined from self-serving testimony offered by partisan witnesses whose recollection is hazy from passage of time and colored by their conflicting interest. *See* Delta Dynamics, Inc. v. Arioto, ... (Mosk, J., dissenting) ...

Be that as it may. While we have our doubts about the wisdom of *Pacific Gas,* we have no difficulty understanding its meaning, even without extrinsic evidence to guide us. As we read the rule in California, we must reverse and remand to the district court in order to give plaintiff an opportunity to present extrinsic evidence as to the intention of the parties in drafting the contract. It may not be a wise rule we are applying, but it is a rule that binds us. Erie R.R. Co. v. Tompkins . . . .

Trident Center v. Connecticut General Life Insurance Co., 847 F.2d 564, 568–69 (9th Cir.1988).

A few months later, a different panel of judges on the Ninth Circuit, in the course of an opinion in another case, cast doubt on the "broad language in Trident [that] suggests that under California law courts must always admit extrinsic evidence to determine the meaning of disputed language." A. Kemp Fisheries, Inc. v. Castle & Cooke, Inc., 852 F.2d 493, 496–97 n. 2 (9th Cir.1988).

Do you agree with the reading given in *Trident* to *Pacific Gas?* See generally 2 Farnsworth § 7.12.

(3) *Variation by Contract.* Could the parties, by a provision in their contract, prevent the court from admitting extrinsic evidence that it would otherwise admit as an aid to interpretation? In Garden State Plaza Corp. v. S.S. Kresge Co., 189 A.2d 448 (N.J.Super.Ct.1963), the court held void as against public policy a clause providing that no "previous negotiations, arrangements, agreements and understandings . . . shall be used to interpret or construe this lease." The clause would, the court said, have it construe the contract "wearing judicial blinders. We are requested to conform to a private agreement mandating our performance of a judicial function in a manner which, under our precedents, is not the path to justice in arriving at the binding meaning of a contract." Do you agree? Would it make a difference if the language in question were "plain"?

(4) *Private Conventions or Codes.* Holmes wrote that he did "not suppose that you could prove, for purposes of construction . . . for instance, that the parties to a contract orally agreed that when they wrote five hundred feet it should mean one hundred inches, or that Bunker Hill Monument should signify Old South Church." [a] Holmes, The Theory of Legal Interpretation, 12 Harv. L.Rev. 417, 420 (1899). But consider the following case.

Ward contracted in writing to furnish crushed stone at $2.75 per cubic yard to Smith, the general contractor for the construction of a state highway. Shortly thereafter they orally agreed that each of Ward's trucks, fully loaded, contained four cubic yards of crushed stone. Ward was paid for 12,955 cubic yards, figured on this basis. He sued Smith for $24,432, claiming that the quantity actually delivered was 21,538 cubic yards, and introduced, over objection, the testimony of a civil engineer that by a more accurate method of measurement Ward had delivered the larger amount. From judgment for plaintiff, defendant appealed. *Held:* Reversed. "When a contract specifies the mode of measurement to be adopted such mode should be followed." Ward v. Smith, 86 S.E.2d 539 (W.Va. 1955). Was the case rightly decided? Under Holmes' view?

STEUART v. McCHESNEY, 444 A.2d 659 (Pa.1982). [In 1968, the Steuarts gave the McChesneys a right of first refusal on a farm under which "should said Steuarts obtain a Bona Fide Purchaser for Value, the said McChesneys may exercise their right to purchase said premises at a

---

a. " 'That's a great deal to make one word mean,' Alice said in a thoughtful tone. 'When I make a word do a lot of work like that,' said Humpty Dumpty, 'I always pay it extra.' " Lewis Carroll, Through the Looking Glass, Chapter VI.

value equivalent to the market value of the premises according to the assessment rolls as maintained by the County of Warren." In 1977, a broker appraised the farm at a market value of $50,000. Later that year, the Steuarts received two offers of $35,000 and $30,000 for the farm, and the McChesneys sought to exercise their right by tendering $7,820, the assessed market value according to the County's tax rolls. The Steuarts rejected the tender, arguing that the agreement should be read to require that the exercise price be that of the third party offer or fair market value determined independently of assessed value. The McChesneys sought specific performance but lost in the Court of Common Pleas, which held, after hearing testimony, that "market value" was intended as "a mutual protective minimum price" and not "the controlling price without regard to a market third party offer." It therefore interpreted the agreement as giving the McChesneys a preemptive right to purchase the farm for $35,000, the amount of the first offer received. From a decision of the Superior Court, reversing the trial court and holding that the plain language of the agreement required that assessed market value alone determine the exercise price, the Steuarts appealed.]

FLAHERTY, JUSTICE.... It is well established that the intent of the parties to a written contract is to be regarded as being embodied in the writing itself, and when the words are clear and unambiguous the intent is to be discovered only from the express language of the agreement....

Application of the plain meaning rule of interpretation has, however, been subjected to criticism as being unsound in theory. "The fallacy consists in assuming that there is or ever can be *some one real* or absolute meaning." 9 Wigmore, Evidence § 2462 (Chadbourn rev. 1981). "[S]ome of the surrounding circumstances always must be known before the meaning of the words can be plain and clear; and proof of the circumstances may make a meaning plain and clear when in the absence of such proof some other meaning may also have seemed plain and clear." 3 Corbin, Contracts § 542 (1960)....

Nevertheless, the rationale for interpreting contractual terms in accord with the plain meaning of the language expressed is multifarious, resting in part upon what is viewed as the appropriate role of the courts in the interpretive process: "[T]his Court long ago emphasized that '[t]he parties [have] the right to make their own contract, and it is not the function of this Court to re-write it, or to give it a construction in conflict with ... the accepted and plain meaning of the language used.' Hagarty v. William Akers, Jr. Co., 342 Pa. 236, 20 A.2d 317 (1941)." ...

In addition to justifications focusing upon the appropriate role of the courts in the interpretive process, the plain meaning approach to construction has been supported as generally best serving the ascertainment of the contracting parties' mutual intent.... "In determining what the parties intended by their contract, the law must look to what they clearly expressed. Courts in interpreting a contract do not assume that its language was chosen carelessly." Moore v. Stevens Coal Co., 315 Pa. at

568, 173 A. at 662. Neither can it be assumed that the parties were ignorant of the meaning of the language employed. . . .

Accordingly, the plain meaning approach enhances the extent to which contracts may be relied upon by contributing to the security of belief that the final expression of *consensus ad idem* will not later be construed to import a meaning other than that clearly expressed. Cf. McCormick, The Parol Evidence Rule as a Procedural Device for Control of the Jury, 41 Yale L.J. 365, 365–366 (1932). Likewise, resort to the plain meaning of language hinders parties dissatisfied with their agreement from creating a myth as to the true meaning of the agreement through subsequently exposed extrinsic evidence. Absent the plain meaning rule, nary an agreement could be conceived, which, in the event of a party's later disappointment with his stated bargain, would not be at risk to having its true meaning obfuscated under the guise of examining extrinsic evidence of intent. Even if the dissatisfied party in good faith believed that the agreement, as manifest, did not express the *consensus ad idem,* his post hoc judgment would be inclined to be colored by belief as to what should have been, rather than what strictly was, intended. Hence, the plain meaning approach to interpretation rests upon policies soundly based, and the judiciousness of that approach warrants reaffirmation.

In the instant case, the language of the Right of First Refusal, viewed in context, is express and clear and is, therefore, not in need of interpretation by reference to extrinsic evidence. The plain meaning of the agreement in question is that if, during the lifetime of the appellant, a bona fide purchaser for value should be obtained, the appellees may purchase the property "at a value equivalent to the market value of the premises according to the assessment rolls as maintained by the County of Warren and Commonwealth of Pennsylvania for the levying and assessing of real estate taxes." Indeed, a more clear and unambiguous expression of the Right of First Refusal's exercise price would be onerous to conceive. By conditioning exercise of the Right of First Refusal upon occurrence of the triggering event of there being obtained a bona fide offer, protection was afforded against a sham offer, made not in good faith, precipitating exercise of the preemptive right. The clear language of the agreement, however, in no manner links determination of the exercise price to the magnitude of the bona fide offer received through that triggering mechanism.

. . . In holding that an ambiguity is present in an agreement, a court must not rely upon a strained contrivancy to establish one; scarcely an agreement could be conceived that might not be unreasonably contrived into the appearance of ambiguity. Thus, the meaning of language cannot be distorted to establish the ambiguity. . . .

[Affirmed.]

ROBERTS, JUSTICE, dissenting. [It would appear that the property was last assessed in 1972, when the assessed market value was increased by only $810.]

Here, where appellant received bona fide offers of $30,000, $35,000, and $50,000 for her property, there can be no doubt that the actual value of appellant's property in 1977 was at least four times greater than the value according to the outdated assessment on the Warren County tax rolls. It is the height of unfairness to grant appellees' requested decree for specific performance at a price based on a valuation which took place in 1972. In effect, appellees are receiving a substantial windfall simply because Warren County has apparently failed to maintain accurate assessments "according to the actual value" of appellant's property, as required by law.

In these circumstances, I would remand this case to the Court of Common Pleas of Warren County for a determination of what the proper assessed value of appellant's property would have been on October 25, 1977, the "date of valuation," with directions to enter a decree of specific performance in favor of appellees at a "market value" based upon that determination.

[LARSON, J., joined in the dissent.]

NOTES

(1) *Questions.* Was the language in question ambiguous? Was it, as the court put it in *Pacific Gas,* "reasonably susceptible of the meaning contended for" by the Steuarts? How would you have decided the case?

(2) *Extrinsic Evidence in Pennsylvania.* When Sonia and Merle Kohn were divorced, they signed a separation agreement that provided for the payment of "alimony". Less than a year later, Merle got custody of the children and refused to make any more payments, claiming that they were solely for support of the children. In Kohn v. Kohn, 364 A.2d 350 (Pa.Super.1976), the court held that the trial court erred in excluding extrinsic evidence to support Merle's contention that "alimony" meant "child support." "[A]lthough a word is generally used for its ordinary meaning, the context of the instrument may indicate it was used in a different sense.... According to Black's Law Dictionary there is no clear meaning of the word alimony which, in a broad sense, also means child support.... In this case there are several provisions of the separation agreement which indicate that tax consequences prompted the parties' use of the term 'alimony' while intending child support." [a] Three of seven judges dissented.[b]

(3) *Wisdom of Rule (Reprise).* Judge Richard Posner, whose views on the parol evidence rule were quoted earlier (Note 2, p. 566 above), had this to say in defense of the plain meaning rule. "The older view, sometimes called the 'four corners' rule,[c] which excludes extrinsic evidence if the contract is clear 'on its

---

a. The court cited provisions of the Internal Revenue Code that "permit the husband to deduct alimony payments for income tax purposes even though the parties to the agreement intend the payments as child support."

b. In a case applying Pennsylvania law, the court gave this example: "extrinsic evidence may be used to show that 'Ten Dollars paid on January 5, 1980,' meant ten Canadian dollars, but it would not be allowed to show the parties meant twenty

dollars." Mellon Bank, N.A. v. Aetna Business Credit, Inc., 619 F.2d 1001 (3d Cir. 1980). Does this help to explain the Pennsylvania cases?

c. Although it is common to refer to the plain meaning rule, as both Traynor and Posner do, as a "four corners" rule, the rule properly understood does not exclude evidence of surrounding circumstances (other than prior negotiations). See SAPC v. Lotus Development Corp., 921 F.2d 360, n. 2 (1st Cir.1990) ("parol evidence rule

face,' is not ridiculous. (There is ancient wisdom as well as ancient prejudice.) The rule tends to cut down on the amount of litigation, in part by reducing the role of the jury; for it is the jury that interprets contracts when interpretation requires consideration of extrinsic evidence. Parties to contracts may prefer, ex ante (that is, when negotiating the contract, and therefore before an interpretive dispute has arisen), to avoid the expense and uncertainty of having a jury resolve a dispute between them, even at the cost of some inflexibility in interpretation." Federal Deposit Insurance Corp. v. W.R. Grace & Co., 877 F.2d 614, 621 (7th Cir.1989).

What impact might the plain meaning rule have on pre-trial discovery? Does this help to distinguish the rule as applied to contracts from the rule as applied to legislation?

(4) *And/or?* Employees signed benefit plan agreements under which all accrued benefits were forfeited if the employee "competes with the Employer within three years of termination of employment; commits theft, fraud or embezzlement with respect to the Employer; and discloses to third parties the Employer's trade secrets." The employer contends that an employee who merely competes within three years of termination forfeits benefits under this provision. Is the word "and" plain enough to bar extrinsic evidence under a plain meaning rule? See Noell v. American Design, Inc., Profit Sharing Plan, 764 F.2d 827 (11th Cir.1985).

(5) *Reformation and Interpretation.* As the *Bollinger* case, p. 578 above, indicates, if by mistake the parties have omitted an agreed term from a writing, a court, exercising its equity powers, will decree reformation to include it. It is sometimes assumed that where the parties have used words in an unclear way, reformation is also appropriate to clarify their meaning for the purpose of enforcement. Is not there an adequate remedy "at law" in such cases, through interpretation? See 3 Corbin § 540.

RULES IN AID OF INTERPRETATION

The Statutory Analogy. There is an obvious similarity between the interpretation of contracts and that of statutes. To what extent is the analogy a valid one? For example, are the policies for or against the use of legislative history as an aid to statutory interpretation similar to those for or against the use of negotiations ("transactional history") as an aid to contract interpretation?

Purpose Interpretation. Is there an analogy to what is known as "purpose interpretation" in the field of statutory interpretation? According to the formulation in Heydon's Case, 3 Coke 7a, 76 Eng.Rep. 637 (Ex.1584), it involves these steps: examination of the law before enactment of the statute; ascertainment of the "mischief or defect" for which the law did not provide; analysis of the remedy provided by the legislature to "cure the disease"; determination of the "true reason of the

does not preclude consideration of background facts that explain the context in which the agreement was made"). For a case holding that the rule does not exclude dictionary definitions, see Matter of Envirodyne Indus., Inc., 29 F.3d 301 (7th Cir. 1994) (Posner, C.J.: "dictionaries, treatises, articles, and other publications created by strangers to the dispute ... are ... entirely appropriate for use in contract cases as interpretative aids").

remedy"; and then application of the statute so as to "suppress the mischief, and advance the remedy." Can you formulate an analogous technique for contract interpretation?

In the case of a statute, purpose interpretation does not depend on the availability of legislative history, and the court may even find a helpful statement of the purpose of enactment set forth in the preamble or purpose clause of the statute itself. Similarly, it is not uncommon for written contracts to begin with a series of recitals of the surrounding circumstances and of the objectives of the parties. Usually prefixed by the word "whereas," contract recitals are not ordinarily drafted as promises or conditions, and their proper rule in the interpretation of the main body of the contract has been a source of bafflement to many a judge and lawyer. Courts in this country have frequently repeated with approval Lord Esher's "three rules": "If the recitals are clear and the operative part is ambiguous, the recitals govern the construction. If the recitals are ambiguous, and the operative part is clear, the operative part must prevail. If both the recitals and the operative part are clear, but they are inconsistent with each other, the operative part is to be preferred." Ex parte Dawes, 17 Q.B.D. 275, 286 (1886). But these, like many rules of interpretation, are easier of statement than of application.

Maxims. Many of the same rules of thumb that are used in the interpretation of statutes are also used in the interpretation of contracts. Maxims such as "ejusdem generis" and "expressio unius est exclusio alterius" are as popular here as they are there. See J.E. Faltin Motor Transportation, Inc. v. Eazor Express, Inc., 273 F.2d 444 (3d Cir.1960). Their reliability is also as questionable here as it is there.

Some of the maxims of contract interpretation are not used in statutory interpretation. One of the most time-honored maxims of contract interpretation is that a contract is to be interpreted *contra proferentem*—against its author ("profferer"). In North Gate Corp. v. National Food Stores, Inc., 140 N.W.2d 744 (Wis.1966), the court applied this to a clause in a printed shopping center lease prepared by the lessee for use by its retail food stores throughout the country. "Where various meanings can be given a term, the term is to be strictly construed against the draftsman of the contract." Why? To carry out the intention of the parties? To penalize sloppy drafters? To encourage careful drafters? Has this maxim no statutory analogue? In many of the instances where the rule has been applied, the party who chose the contract language also had superior bargaining power. Consider in this connection the problems raised in Chapter 4, Policing the Bargain.[c]

Should it make a difference if the party who proffered the contract invited suggestions for change from the other party? See Acme Markets

---

c. That the rule applies to government contracts, see WPC Enterprises, Inc. v. United States, 323 F.2d 874 (Ct.Cl.1963). But see Shedd, Resolving Ambiguities in Interpretation of Government Contracts, 36 Geo.Wash.L.Rev. 1, 21 (1967), where the author concludes, "The rule of interpreting against the drafter, if not discarded entirely, should be relegated to a rule of last resort in contract interpretation...." For dispute in the Supreme Court of the United States over the application of the rule, see United States v. Seckinger, 397 U.S. 203 (1970).

v. Dawson Enterprises, 251 A.2d 839 (Md.1969), in which the court noted that the other party had kept the contract for sixty days before signing it, that its president was a member of the bar, and that it had, at least earlier in the negotiations, been represented by "a member of a prominent Washington law firm." The court quoted with approval its suggestion in an earlier case that "perhaps [the *contra proferentem* rule] should have but slight force in a situation where both parties are represented by counsel."

Public Interest. In the *North Gate* case, above, the court pointed out that "the intent of the provision in question"—which prohibited the owner of the shopping center from leasing to other retail food stores— was "to restrict trade and the use of land. Such provisions are to be strictly construed." In Chapter 4, Policing the Bargain, we saw that contracts involving performance that would be in violation of some strongly rooted public interest, often expressed in a statute, may be held to be unenforceable. As the *North Gate* case shows, public interest may also affect interpretation and construction of contracts.

In State ex rel. Youngman v. Calhoun, 231 S.W. 647 (Mo.App.1921), a physician sold his practice, agreeing not to "establish [himself] as a practicing physician and surgeon within a radius of five miles" of his former office. The court held that he was not precluded from making calls within this area or treating patients from this area who might call at his office outside the area. "The contract in question is clearly one in restraint of trade and personal liberty, and as such should not be construed to extend beyond its fair import." Why? Because of the intention of the parties? [d]

NOTES

(1) *"Woe Unto You, Lawyers."* Should it make a difference, in interpreting a contract, whether the parties were represented by lawyers? In Weiland Tool & Mfg. Co. v. Whitney, 251 N.E.2d 242 (Ill.1969), the court wrote: "In interpreting the letter ... we have taken into consideration not only that inferences from ambiguous language must be resolved against its author ..., but also that he is a lawyer with a number of years of trial experience and experience as a legal adviser in commercial transactions. He must have had the ability to express [his intention] in concise and clear English ... if that were his intention. Since he did not do so, we are further persuaded that this was not his intention." See also Gulf Oil Corp. v. American Louisiana Pipe Line Co., 282 F.2d 401 (6th Cir.1960) (fact that both parties were represented by lawyers suggested that difference in language between two sections of contract was not inadvertent).

(2) *Problem.* Following a dispute between a general contractor and a subcontractor, in which each claims damages for breach of contract by the other, they sign a writing in which the subcontract "is hereby cancelled without prejudice by mutual agreement." Do the words "without prejudice" mean that claims to damages arising out of the subcontract survive or that they do not?

---

d. See also Sun Oil Co. v. Vickers Refining Co., 414 F.2d 383 (8th Cir.1969), in which the court remarked, in rejecting Sunray's interpretation under which the contract would have been void because of a violation of the antitrust laws: "Sunray's attorneys, experienced in antitrust work, approved the contract without any question of antitrust consequences."

Might it make a difference whether the parties were represented by lawyers when they signed the writing? See Copeland Process Corp. v. Nalews, Inc., 312 A.2d 576 (N.H.1973).

HURST v. W.J. LAKE & CO., 16 P.2d 627 (Or.1932). [Hurst contracted to sell Lake 350 tons of horse meat scraps at $50 a ton. The specifications stated "minimum 50% protein" and the contract provided that if any of the scraps "analyzes less than 50% of protein" Lake was to have a discount of $5.00 a ton. Lake paid only $45 a ton for 140 tons that contained protein varying from 49.53 to 49.96 per cent. Hurst sued to recover the balance of $5 a ton, alleging that both parties were members of a group of traders in horse meat scraps and that the defendant was aware of a usage, prevalent among that group, under which the terms "minimum 50% protein" and "less than 50% protein" required the buyer to accept all scraps containing 49.5 per cent protein or more and pay for them at the rate provided for scraps containing 50% protein. The trial court entered judgment on the pleadings for the defendant and the plaintiff appealed.]

ROSMAN, J. . . . [T]he language of the dictionaries is not the only language spoken in America. For instance, the word "thousand" as commonly used has a very specific meaning . . ., but the language of the various trades and localities has assigned to it meanings quite different from that just mentioned. Thus in the bricklaying trade a contract which fixes the bricklayer's compensation at "$5.25 a thousand" does not contemplate that he need lay actually 1,000 bricks in order to earn $5.25, but that he should build a wall of a certain size. Brunold v. Glasser, 25 Misc. 285, 52 N.Y.S. 1021; Walker v. Syms, 118 Mich. 183, 76 N.W. 320. In the lumber industry a contract requiring the delivery of 4,000 shingles will be fulfilled by the delivery of only 2,500 when it appears that by trade custom two packs of a certain size are regarded as 1,000 shingles, and that hence the delivery of eight packs fulfills the contract, even though they contain only 2,500 shingles by actual count. Soutier v. Kellerman, 18 Mo. 509. And, where the custom of a locality considers 100 dozen as constituting a thousand, one who has 19,200 rabbits upon a warren under an agreement for their sale at the price of 60 pounds for each thousand rabbits will be paid for only 16,000 rabbits. Smith v. Wilson, 3 Barn. & Adol. 728. Numerous other instances could readily be cited showing the manner in which the meaning of words has been contracted, expanded, or otherwise altered by local usage, trade custom, dialect influence, code agreement, etc. . . .

The defendant cites numerous cases in many of which the courts held that, when a contract is expressed in language which is not ambiguous upon its face the court will receive no evidence of usage, but will place upon the words of the parties their common meaning; in other words, in those decisions the courts ran the words of the parties through a judicial sieve whose meshes were incapable of retaining anything but the common meaning of the words, and which permitted the meaning which the parties had placed upon them to run away as waste material. Surely those courts did not believe that words are always used in their orthodox sense. The rulings must have been persuaded by other considerations. The rule which rejects evidence of custom has the advantage of simplicity; it protects the writing from attack by some occasional individual who will seek to employ perjured testimony in proof of alleged custom; and, if one can believe that the parol evidence rule is violated when common meaning is rejected in favor of special meaning, then the above rule serves the purpose of the parol evidence rule. Without setting forth the manner in which we came to our conclusion, we state that none of these reasons appeals to us as sufficient to exclude evidence of custom and assign to the words their common meaning only, even though the instrument is nonambiguous upon its face. . . .

[Reversed.]

NOTES

(1) *Questions.* State the issue in Hurst v. Lake in terms of the contract language. How will usage help resolve that issue at the trial? How can Hurst prove usage? Why did the buyer fail in his attempt to prove usage in the *Frigaliment* case, above? Would he have succeeded under the Code? See UCC 1–205. Under the Code, what is the difference between a usage and a course of dealing? How would a party like Hurst prove a course of dealing?

What impact does UCC 1–205 have on the plain meaning rule? See also UCC 2–202.[a]

(2) *Knowledge of Usage.* Under UCC 1–205 would the buyer have been bound by the usage if the buyer had been unaware of the usage? Recall that in the *Frigaliment* case, above, the seller had no knowledge of the usage claimed by the buyer. If the buyer had succeeded in proving that usage, would the seller, who "was only beginning in the poultry trade," have been bound by it? Compare Foxco Industries, Ltd. v. Fabric World, Inc., 595 F.2d 976 (5th Cir. 1979) (buyer bound by usage of trade association as to meaning of "first quality," though it was not a member and did not know of industry usage), with Flower City Painting Contractors, Inc., v. Gumina Construction Co., 591 F.2d 162 (2d Cir.1979) ("neophyte minority painting contractor" with first substantial subcontract did not have reason to know of trade usage).

(3) *Problem.* Williams, a Georgia resident who sells produce grown by others, contracted to sell all of the "slaw cabbage" grown on 30 acres to Curtin, a New York resident who buys cabbage for processing into cole slaw. Both parties had federal licenses to buy and sell perishable agricultural commodities in interstate commerce. Curtin was to send trucks for the cabbage. Because of the weather, most of the cabbage did not grow to the desired size and the market price for cabbage increased dramatically. Williams, claiming that according to a usage of trade in Georgia "slaw cabbage" meant large cabbage, delivered only the large cabbage to Curtin and sold the rest on the risen market. Curtin, claiming that according to a usage of trade in the interstate cole slaw market,

---

a. Even Holmes endorsed usage, as distinguished from private codes or conventions. After the passage quoted in Note 4, p. 602 above, he continued: "On the other hand, when you have the security of a local or class custom or habit of speech, it may be presumed that the writer conforms to the usage of his place or class when that is what a normal person in his situation would do." Does this give some insight into Holmes' reasons for espousing the objective theory?

"slaw cabbage" meant all cabbage suitable for making cole slaw, seeks damages for breach of contract. If both usages can be established, which applies? Williams v. Curtin, 807 F.2d 1046 (D.C.Cir.1986).[b]

SECTION 3.　FILLING GAPS

Thus far we have concerned ourselves with finding the law of the contract by interpreting its language. But what is the law of the contract if the language, when interpreted, does not cover the case at hand—what if it is an omitted case? Will a court fill the gap in the contract? As we have already seen as far back as in Wood v. Lucy, p. 133 above, a court may supply a term in such a situation by using a process called "implication." See Restatement Second § 204 (a section that has no counterpart in the first Restatement).

But when will a court imply a term in a contract? Justice Holmes wrote: "Behind the logical form lies a judgment as to the relative worth and importance of competing legislative grounds, often an inarticulate and unconscious judgment, it is true, and yet the very root and nerve of the whole proceeding. You can give any conclusion a logical form. You can always imply a condition in a contract. But why do you imply it? It is because of some belief as to the practice of the community or of a class, or because of some opinion as to policy, or, in short, because of some attitude of yours upon a matter not capable of exact quantitative measurement, and therefore not capable of founding exact logical conclusions. Such matters really are battle grounds where the means do not exist for determinations that shall be good for all time, and where the decision can do no more than embody the preference of a given body in a given time and place." Holmes, The Path of the Law, 10 Harv.L.Rev. 457, 466 (1897); also in O.W. Holmes, Collected Legal Papers 167, 181 (1920).

Some of the most significant applications of this process of dealing with omitted cases arise in connection with the next two chapters. In Chapter 7, Performance and Breach, we consider how the process is used to secure the expectations of the parties during performance. In Chapter 8, Basic Assumptions: Mistake, Impracticability and Frustration, we consider how it is used in coping with extraordinary circumstances that are contrary to the parties' assumptions at the time they made the

---

b. Hibernians may be interested in Ermolieff v. R.K.O. Radio Pictures, Inc., 122 P.2d 3 (Cal.1942), in which a usage of the motion picture industry was admitted to establish that the term "The United Kingdom," as used in an agreement granting movie rights, included Eire, the Irish Free State. Devotees of detective stories in general and of Sam Spade in particular may be interested in an entertaining case in which the court, in construing a contract, took judicial notice that it "has long been common practice among detective-fiction writers to make use of the same central and supporting characters in subsequent works." Warner Bros. Pictures v. Columbia Broadcasting System, 102 F.Supp. 141 (S.D.Cal.1951), affirmed as to this point but reversed in part in 216 F.2d 945 (9th Cir. 1954).

contract. As an introduction to the process itself, however, we shall focus on applications that are both more familiar and less complex—the obligations to use "good faith" and "best efforts" that, as we have already seen, are often implied in contracts.[a]

NOTES

(1) *Implied Terms.* We are speaking here of terms that are "implied in law" rather than "implied in fact." Corbin explained that difference in this way: "When a promise is said to be 'implied in fact' we are describing one that is found by interpretation of a promisor's words or conduct. When a promise is said to be 'implied in law,' we are declaring the existence of legal duty created otherwise than by assent and without any words or conduct that are interpreted as promissory." 3 Corbin § 561. Corbin's distinction found its way into the Uniform Commercial Code, which defines "agreement" as "the bargain of the parties in fact" and "contract" as "the total legal obligation which results." Compare UCC 1–201(3) with (11).

(2) *Default Rules.* Most implied terms are subject to agreement by the parties. In recent years it has become popular in academic circles to refer to these as "default rules," a term adapted from computer terminology.[b] The subject of default rules has spawned a rich scholarly literature, too extensive to be summarized here.

By way of example, Professors Ayres and Gertner fault prior theorists for arguing "that parties leave gaps in contracts because the cost of writing additional terms outweighs the benefit," leading those theorists to suggest "that courts should simply fill in the gap with the term the parties 'would have wanted.'" Ayres and Gertner argue that sometimes contractual incompleteness results because, "when one party to a contract knows more than another, the knowledgeable party may strategically decide not to contract around even an inefficient default. Because the process of contracting around a default can reveal information, the knowledgeable party may purposefully withhold information to get a larger piece of the smaller contractual pie. This possibility of strategic incompleteness leads us to embrace more diverse forms of default rules. In particular, lawmakers may be able to undercut the incentives for this strategic rent-seeking by establishing penalty defaults that encourage the better informed parties to reveal their information by contracting around the default." Ayres &

---

a. Although the words "interpretation" and "construction" are often used interchangeably, attempts have been made to give them distinct meanings. Professor Corbin proposed the following distinction: "By 'interpretation of language' we determine what ideas that language induces in other persons. By 'construction of the contract,' as that term will be used here, we determine its legal operation—its effect upon the action of courts and administrative officials." 3 Corbin § 534.

Corbin succeeded in popularizing the term "constructive condition," to refer to conditions implied *in law,* in order to distinguish them from conditions implied *in fact.* 3A Corbin §§ 632, 653: Corbin, Conditions in the Law of Contract, 28 Yale L.J. 739, 743–44 (1919). Its analogue, "constructive promise," is not used, however, and lawyers speak, somewhat inconsistently, of *"implied promises"* and *"constructive* conditions." For more on conditions, see Chapter 7, Performance and Breach.

b. Lawyers from civil law systems tend not to think of specific terms "implied" in the particular case but of generalized rules which apply to all such cases unless the parties provide otherwise. In France these rules, here often called default rules, are called *suppletive* rules, in contrast to *imperative* rules, which the parties are powerless to alter. Perhaps the happiest English equivalents are "suppletory" and "mandatory." Since civil law lawyers are accustomed to finding such rules spelled out in a code in advance of controversy, they are less tempted to attribute them to the supposed "intentions" of the parties.

Gertner, Filling Gaps in Incomplete Contracts: An Economic Theory of Default Rules, 99 Yale L.J. 87, 127 (1989).

For other discussions of default rules, see Barnett, The Sound of Silence: Default Rules and Contractual Consent, 78 Va.L.Rev. 821 (1992); Gillette, Commercial Relationships and the Selection of Default Rules for Remote Risks, 19 J.Legal Stud. 535 (1990); Scott, A Relational Theory of Default Rules for Commercial Contracts, 19 J.Legal Stud. 597 (1990).

(3) *Implied Warranties.* Perhaps the most noted of the many terms that courts have supplied for omitted cases are the warranties implied in contracts for the sale of goods. See UCC 2–314, 2–315. They have, however, been creatures of statute for so long that it is easy to lose sight of their judicial origins. Of greater current interest is the question of the extent to which similar implied warranties will be imposed in other fields. The Supreme Court of New Jersey has provided some striking examples. In just over five years, it handed down leading decisions imposing implied warranties, by analogy to those in the sale of goods, in the lease of personal property (a truck), the sale of real property (a development house), the lease of real property (both commercial and residential), and the furnishing of goods in connection with a contract for services (a permanent wave).[c]

(4) *Question.* Review Note 2, p. 281 above. Suppose that Louisa Sheffield, in the case at p. 119 above, had written to Strong: "I will be responsible for my husband's debt if you will not bother him about it." Would she have been accountable to Strong if he had done nothing about the note for two years?

EASTERN AIR LINES, INC. v. GULF OIL CORPORATION

United States District Court, Southern District of Florida, 1975.
415 F.Supp. 429.

[The facts and part of the opinion in this case are at page 125 above.]

JAMES LAWRENCE KING, DISTRICT COURT JUDGE. . . . Gulf suggests that Eastern violated the contract between the parties by manipulating its requirements through a practice known as "fuel freighting" in the airline industry. Requirements can vary from city to city depending on whether or not it is economically profitable to freight fuel. This fuel freighting practice in accordance with price could affect lifting from Gulf stations by either raising such liftings or lowering them. If the price was higher at a Gulf station, the practice could have reduced liftings there by lifting fuel in excess of its actual operating requirements at a prior station, and thereby not loading fuel at the succeeding high price Gulf station. Similarly where the Gulf station was comparatively cheaper, an aircraft might load more heavily at the Gulf station and not load at other succeeding non-Gulf stations.

---

c. Cintrone v. Hertz Truck Leasing & Rental Service, 212 A.2d 769 (N.J.1965) (lease of truck); Schipper v. Levitt & Sons, 207 A.2d 314 (N.J.1965) (sale of development house); Reste Realty Corp. v. Cooper, 251 A.2d 268 (N.J.1969) (lease of offices); Marini v. Ireland, 265 A.2d 526 (N.J.1970) (lease of apartment); Newmark v. Gimbel's Inc., 258 A.2d 697 (N.J.1969) (furnishing of permanent wave solution). For a discussion of the implied warranty of habitability in the construction and sale of a new home, see McDonald v. Mianecki, 398 A.2d 1283 (N.J.1979).

The court however, finds that Eastern's performance under the contract does not constitute a breach of its agreement with Gulf and is consistent with good faith and established commercial practices as required by U.C.C. § 2–306.

"Good Faith" means "honesty in fact in the conduct or transaction concerned" U.C.C. § 1–201(19). Between merchants, "good faith" means "honesty in fact and the observance of reasonable commercial standards of fair dealing in the trade"; U.C.C. § 2–103(1)(b) and Official Comment 2 of U.C.C. § 2–306. The relevant commercial practices are "courses of performance," "courses of dealing" and "usages of trade." [1]

Throughout the history of commercial aviation, including 30 years of dealing between Gulf and Eastern, airlines' liftings of fuel by nature have been subject to substantial daily, weekly, monthly and seasonal variations, as they are affected by weather, schedule changes, size of aircraft, aircraft load, local airport conditions, ground time, availability of fueling facilities, whether the flight is on time or late, passenger convenience, economy and efficiency of operation, fuel taxes, into-plane fuel service charges, fuel price, and, ultimately, the judgment of the flight captain as to how much fuel he wants to take.

All these factors are, and for years have been, known to oil companies, including Gulf, and taken into account by them in their fuel contracts. Gulf's witnesses at trial pointed to certain examples of numerically large "swings" in monthly liftings by Eastern at various Gulf stations. Gulf never complained of this practice and apparently accepted it as normal procedure. Some of the "swings" were explained by the fueling of a single aircraft for one flight, or by the addition of one schedule in mid-month. The evidence establishes that Eastern, on one occasion, requested 500,000 additional gallons for one month at one station, without protest from Gulf, and that Eastern increased its requirements at another station more than 50 percent year to year, from less than 2,000,000 to more than 3,000,000 gallons, again, without Gulf objection.

The court concludes that fuel freighting is an established industry practice, inherent in the nature of the business. The evidence clearly demonstrated that the practice has long been part of the established courses of performance and dealing between Eastern and Gulf. As the practice of "freighting" or "tankering" has gone on unchanged and

---

1. U.C.C. § 2–208(1) defines "course of performance" as those "repeated occasions for performance by either party with knowledge of the nature of the performance and opportunity for objection to it by the other."

U.C.C. § 1–205(1) defines "course of dealing" as "a sequence of previous conduct between the parties to a particular transaction which is fairly to be regarded as establishing a common basis of understanding for interpreting their expressions and other conduct."

U.C.C. § 1–205(2) defines "usage of trade" as "any practice or method of dealing having such regularity of observance in a place, vocation or trade as to justify an expectation that it will be observed with respect to the transaction in question."

U.C.C. § 2–208(2) provides that "express terms shall control course of performance and course of performance shall control both course of dealings and usage of trade."

unchallenged for many years accepted as a fact of life by Gulf without complaint, the court is reminded of Official Comment 1 to U.C.C. § 2–208:

> "The parties themselves know best what they have meant by their words of agreement and their action under that agreement is the best indication of what that meaning was."

From a practical point of view, "freighting" opportunities are very few, according to the uncontradicted testimony, as the airline must perform its schedules in consideration of operating realities. There is no suggestion here that Eastern is operating at certain Gulf stations but taking no fuel at all. The very reason Eastern initially desired a fuel contract was because the airline planned to take on fuel, and had to have an assured source of supply.

If a customer's demands under a requirements contract become excessive, U.C.C. § 2–306 protects the seller and, in the appropriate case, would allow him to refuse to deliver unreasonable amounts demanded (but without eliminating his basic contract obligation); similarly, in an appropriate case, if a customer repeatedly had no requirements at all, the seller might be excused from performance if the buyer suddenly and without warning should descend upon him and demand his entire inventory, but the court is not called upon to decide those cases here.

Rather, the case here is one where the established courses of performance and dealing between the parties, the established usages of the trade, and the basic contract itself all show that the matters complained of for the first time by Gulf after commencement of this litigation are the fundamental given ingredients of the aviation fuel trade to which the parties have accommodated themselves successfully and without dispute over the years.

> "The practical interpretation given to their contracts by the parties to them while they are engaged in their performance, and before any controversy has arisen concerning them, is one of the best indications of their true intent, and courts that adopt and enforce such a construction are not likely to commit serious error."

Manhattan Life Ins. Co. of New York v. Wright, 126 F. 82, 87 (8th Cir.1903). Accord, Spindler v. Kushner, 284 So.2d 481, 484 (Fla.App. 1973).

The court concludes that Eastern has not violated the contract.

NOTE

Obligation of Good Faith. UCC 1–203 provides that "Every contract or duty within this Act imposes an obligation of good faith in its performance or enforcement." "Good faith" is generally defined in the Code to mean only "honesty in fact in the conduct or transaction concerned," a purely subjective test. UCC 1–201(19). But the Sales Article, Article 2, contains a special definition of "good faith" which "in the case of a merchant means honesty in fact and the observance of reasonable commercial standards of fair dealing in the trade." UCC 2–103(1)(b). What sort of evidence might parties adduce to define "good faith"?

The notion of an obligation of good faith in the performance of contract duties is a familiar one to civil law systems, most notably the German. Article 242 of the German Civil Code imposes an obligation of "performance according to the requirements of good faith [*Treu and Glauben*], common habits being duly taken into consideration." It is a novel one to the common law, and the Code provisions have already occasioned considerable discussion. See Burton, Breach of Contract and the Common Law Duty to Perform in Good Faith, 94 Harv.L.Rev. 369 (1980); Farnsworth, Good Faith Performance and Commercial Reasonableness under the Uniform Commercial Code, 30 U.Chi.L.Rev. 666 (1963); Summers, "Good Faith" in General Contract Law and the Sales Provisions of the Uniform Commercial Code, 54 Va.L.Rev. 195 (1968).

WOOD v. LUCY, LADY DUFF–GORDON

Court of Appeals of New York, 1917.
222 N.Y. 88, 118 N.E. 214.

[For the report of this case, see p. 133 above.]

NOTES

(1) *The Code.* Comment 5 to UCC 2–306, which lays down a similar rule, has this to say: "Subsection (2), on exclusive dealing, makes explicit the commercial rule embodied in this Act under which the parties to such contracts are held to have impliedly, even when not expressly, bound themselves to use reasonable diligence as well as good faith in their performance of the contract.... An exclusive dealing agreement brings into play all of the good faith aspects of the output and requirement problems of subsection (1)." Why?

(2) *Showing Implied Terms and the Parol Evidence Rule.* What is the impact of the parol evidence rule on an attempt to show an implied term? Assuming, as seems likely, that the agreement in Wood v. Lucy was completely integrated, why did not the parol evidence rule prevent Wood from showing his "promise to use reasonable efforts"? What evidence did he need to show his promise? See Hadjiyannakis, The Parol Evidence Rule and Implied Terms: The Sounds of Silence, 54 Fordham L.Rev. 35 (1985).

(3) *Derogating from Implied Terms and the Parol Evidence Rule.* What is the impact of the parol evidence rule on an attempt to derogate from a term that would otherwise be implied? In Hayden v. Hoadley, 111 A. 343 (Vt.1920), the parties signed a written "memorandum of agreement" reciting the exchange of their properties and a promise on one side to make stated repairs. The agreement was signed on May 2, and no time was fixed for the repairs. When suit was brought for failure to make the repairs, the defendant sought to show that it had been orally agreed at the time the writing was signed that they should have until October 1 to make them. The court decided that this evidence was properly excluded. "The legal effect of the contract before us—it being silent as to the time of performance—was to require the repairs specified to be completed within a reasonable time.... To admit the testimony offered by the defendants to the effect that the parties agreed upon October 1 as the limit of time given for the repairs would be to allow the plain legal effect of the written contract to be controlled by oral evidence. That is not permissible."

The court noted that the evidence "was not offered on the ground that it was admissible on the question of what was a reasonable time under the circumstances, so we give that question no attention." If, before offering the evidence, the attorney for the defendant had stated that it was being offered to show what was a reasonable time for performance, would the evidence have been admissible? Should the admissibility of the evidence turn upon the inference it is to support?

PERCENTAGE LEASES

An example of flexible pricing (see Note 3, p. 284 above) that is especially favored by retailers is the percentage lease, which fixes the rent as a stated percentage of the lessee's receipts or profits. Under such a lease the lessor has a useful hedge against inflation and also shares to some extent the lessee's risk of success or failure. Although a wide variety of formulas is possible, the most common is based, for obvious reasons of accounting convenience, on the lessee's gross receipts.

Use of gross receipts may, however, bring the parties' interests into sharp conflict. Under such a formula, it is in the lessor's interest that the lessee maximize its gross receipts, while it is in the lessee's own interest that it maximize its net profit. When these goals become markedly inconsistent, as may happen if the profit margin dwindles, trouble is the likely result. The extreme case arises when the lessee finds that it is operating at a loss and wants to go out of business.

If the situation is viewed through the optic of Wood v. Lucy, it would appear that, since the lessor has given the lessee the exclusive use of the land in return for a percentage of gross receipts, the lessee would be under a duty to use best efforts. Although the law in this field has developed with surprisingly little regard to cases such as Wood v. Lucy, it has nevertheless reached results that are in harmony with those cases.

A representative statement of the law was occasioned by a percentage lease to a physical therapist who, when the business of physical therapy turned out to be unprofitable, abandoned it and paid no rent. In holding that this was a breach, the court said: "The lessee obligated herself to pay rent at the rate of 5% of the gross receipts of the business. No minimum rent was reserved. Under these circumstances we are of the opinion that the lease must be construed as including an implied covenant to continue the business.... Any other construction would excuse the plaintiff from the obligation to pay any rent to the defendants and would, therefore, defeat the defendants' purpose in entering into the lease." Prins v. Van Der Vlugt, 337 P.2d 787, 796 (Or.1959). Accord: Lippman v. Sears, Roebuck & Co., 280 P.2d 775 (Cal.1955).

The court's observation that there was no minimum rental suggests a simple way of dealing with the problem. By inserting a provision for a minimum rental in a percentage lease, the lessor can eliminate some of the risk that it would otherwise face. If the lessor chooses this kind of protection is the lessee still under a duty to use best efforts? The next case addresses this problem.

NOTE

Maximum Rental. Just as the lessor may want to fix a minimum rental, the lessee may want to fix a maximum rental. The final result is, of course, the result of the negotiations between the parties.

DICKEY v. PHILADELPHIA MINIT–MAN CORP.

Supreme Court of Pennsylvania, 1954.
377 Pa. 549, 105 A.2d 580.

HORACE STERN, CHIEF JUSTICE.... Plaintiff, Samuel Dickey, in 1947 leased to defendant, Philadelphia Minit–Man Corporation, a vacant piece of land in Millbourne, Delaware County, for a term of ten years with an option to the lessee of an additional ten-year term. The lease provided that the premises were to be occupied by the lessee "in the business of washing and cleaning automobiles within the scope of the business of the Philadelphia Minit–Man Corporation, ... and for no other purpose." As rent the lessee was to pay a sum equal to 12½% on the amount of the annual gross sales but a minimum of $1,800 per year; the term "gross sales" was to include the sales price of all merchandise sold and also all charges for services performed by the lessee in the course of the business conducted on the premises. The lessee agreed to erect and place on the premises the buildings and equipment needed to carry on the business; all buildings and fixtures erected by the lessee were to become the property of the lessor as and when the lease agreement should expire for any reason whatever. If default were made in the observance or performance of any of the conditions or agreements the lessor was to have the right to terminate the lease and reenter the premises.

Defendant erected the buildings, installed the necessary equipment, and washed and cleaned cars until August, 1952, when it discontinued that feature of its business except as incidental to simonizing and polishing, and it so notified the public. Defendant never failed to pay at least the minimum rental, but in September, 1953, plaintiff filed the present action in ejectment seeking recovery of possession of the property on the ground that defendant had defaulted by discontinuing the business specified in the lease. Defendant filed preliminary objections in the nature of a demurrer to the complaint; the court below sustained the objections and dismissed the action. Plaintiff appeals.

The question involved is whether there was any implied obligation on the part of the lessee to continue to conduct the business on the premises of washing and cleaning cars if its failure to do so resulted in a diminution of rental payable to the lessor.

Generally speaking, a provision in a lease that the premises are to be used only for a certain prescribed purpose imports no obligation on the part of the lessee to use or continue to use the premises for that purpose; such a provision is a covenant against a noncomplying use, not a covenant to use. Plaintiff urges, however, that in a lease such as that here involved, in which the amount of rental to be paid is based upon the lessee's gross sales, there arises an implied obligation on his part to continue the business on the premises to the fullest extent reasonably possible. Defendant, on the other hand, contends that, where such an obligation is intended, it must be expressly inserted in the lease, and that the raising of an implied covenant is never justified except where obviously necessary to effectuate the intention of the parties and so clearly within their contemplation that they deemed it unnecessary to express it, and that this is especially true where a substantial minimum rental is provided the obvious purpose of which is to protect the lessor from any unfavorable circumstances that might subsequently arise whether caused by voluntary conduct of the lessee or by events beyond his control. . . .

If an implied covenant, as claimed by plaintiff, should be held to arise in such cases what would be the extent of the restriction thereby imposed upon the lessee? Would it extend to each and every act on his part that might serve to reduce the extent of his business and thereby the percentage rental based thereon? Would it forbid him, for example, if operating a retail store, from keeping it open for a fewer number of hours each day than formerly? Would it forbid him from dismissing salesmen whereby his business might be reduced in volume? Would it forbid him from discontinuing any department of his business even though he found it to be operating at a loss? It would obviously be quite unreasonable and wholly undesirable to imply an obligation that would necessarily be vague, uncertain and generally impracticable.

. . . Defendant has not moved any part of its business to another location nor deliberately sought to decrease the percentage of rent payable in order to induce plaintiff to declare a termination of the lease; on the contrary, it is seeking to maintain the lease. Nor is there anything in the present case to indicate that defendant's action in discontinuing the washing and cleaning of cars except as incidental to simonizing and polishing was taken other than in good faith and in the exercise of legitimate business judgment. In our opinion it was not forbidden by any implied obligation in the lease.

The decree is affirmed and judgment is here entered for defendant.

NOTES

(1) *Questions.* Chief Justice Stern pointed out that there was no indication that the lessee had acted "other than in good faith and in the exercise of legitimate business judgment." What did he mean by "good faith"? How could Dickey have shown "bad faith"? What result if Minit–Man had moved part of its business to another location?

(2) *Substantial Minimum Rental.* In deciding whether there is "any implied obligation on the part of the lessee to continue to conduct the business on the premises," many courts have, like that in the principal case, taken account of whether "a substantial minimum rental is provided." Why should this be influential? How can a court determine whether a minimum rental is "substantial" or not? Was it significant that Minit–Man was to build the necessary buildings? Might the result have been different if the lease had required Dickey to build the buildings? The opinion does not disclose the extent, if any, by which

the rental during the first five years of operation exceeded the minimum. Would it be interesting to know? To what extent could the parties have avoided the dispute by careful drafting?

(3) *Reducing One's Requirements and Good Faith.* At the end of the principal case, the court observed that there was nothing "to indicate that defendant's action ... was taken other than in good faith and in the exercise of legitimate business judgment." Was it up to Dickey to show Philadelphia Minit–Man's *bad* faith? What will suffice to show good faith in reducing one's requirements?

After a sharp rise in gasoline prices in 1979 and 1980, American Bakeries, which had a fleet of more than 3,000 vehicles, decided to convert to propane as fuel. It contracted to buy from Empire Gas "approximately three thousand (3,000) [conversion] units, more or less depending on requirements," along with propane, for four years. Apparently, within days after signing the contract, it decided not to convert to propane, but gave no reason. Here is what Judge Richard Posner said.

"If no reason at all need be given for scaling back one's requirements even to zero, then a requirements contract is from the buyer's standpoint just an option to purchase up to (or slightly beyond, i.e., within the limits of reasonable proportionality) the stated estimate on the terms specified in the contract, except that the buyer cannot refuse to exercise the option because someone offers him better terms. This is not an unreasonable position, but it is not the law.... Empire Gas put in evidence, uncontested and incontestable, showing that American Bakeries had not got rid of its fleet of trucks and did have the financial wherewithal to go through with the conversion process. After this evidence came in, American Bakeries could avoid a directed verdict only by introducing some evidence concerning its reasons for reducing its requirements. It not only introduced no evidence, but as is plain from counsel's remarks at argument it has no evidence that it would care to put before the jury—no reasons that it would care to share with either the district court or this court. It disagrees with the standard of good faith, believing that so long as it did not buy conversion units elsewhere or want to hurt Empire Gas it was free to reduce its requirements as much as it pleased. It does not suggest that it has a case under the standard we have adopted, which requires at a minimum that the reduction of requirements not have been motivated solely by a reassessment of the balance of advantages and disadvantages under the contract to the buyer." Empire Gas Corp. v. American Bakeries Co., 840 F.2d 1333, 1339, 1341 (7th Cir.1988).

What sort of reasons would have sufficed?

(4) *The Case of the Tailored Woman's Furs.* The Tailored Woman, a retail store, had a percentage lease on the lower floors of a Fifth Avenue building. Later it acquired from the same landlord a fixed rental lease on the fifth floor, where it opened a custom-made dress department. When this venture failed, it moved its fur department from the second to the fifth floor. The landlord sued for additional rental based on a percentage of sales of furs on the fifth floor. From an adverse judgment, the landlord appealed. *Held:* Affirmed. "In deciding this case as we do, we are not moving away from the good old rule that there is in every contract an implied covenant of fair dealing.... Defendant, as we see it, was merely exercising its rights." There was no "unconscionable diversion of business from percentage-lease premises to others." Two judges dissented. Mutual Life Ins. Co. v. Tailored Woman, 128 N.E.2d 401 (N.Y.1955).

MARKET STREET ASSOCIATES v. FREY, 941 F.2d 588 (7th Cir.1991). [J.C. Penney, the retail chain, entered into a sale and leaseback arrangement with General Electric Pension Trust in order to finance Penney's growth. Under paragraph 34, the pension trust agreed to give reasonable consideration to requests by Penney for the financing of additional improvement. It went on to provide, in effect, that if the average annual appreciation in the property exceeded 6 percent, a breakdown in the negotiations over the financing of improvements would entitle Penney to buy back the property for less than its market value.

[Twenty years later, Market Street Associates, Penney's successor under one of the leases, sought to buy back the property it leased from the pension trust in order to use the property to get financing elsewhere. When Erb of the pension trust, who was responsible for the property, was slow in responding, Orenstein of Market Street Associates then sent two letters to Erb formally requesting $4 million financing but not mentioning paragraph 34. Erb responded to the first by saying that the amount requested was below the pension trust's $7 million minimum. Over a month later, Orenstein wrote Erb that Market Street was exercising its option under paragraph 34, which had evidently become advantageous to it.

[When the pension trust refused to sell, Market Street Associates sought specific performance. The district judge granted summary judgment for the pension trust, holding that Market Street Associates had violated the duty of good faith. The judge emphasized a statement in Orenstein's deposition that it had occurred to him that Erb might not know about paragraph 34. The judge inferred that Market Street Associates did not want financing from the pension trust but just wanted an opportunity to buy the property at a bargain price and hoped that the pension trust would not realize the implications of turning down the request for financing. Market Street Associates appealed.]

POSNER, J.... [T]he judge emphasized a statement by Orenstein in his deposition that it had occurred to him that Erb mightn't know about paragraph 34, though this was unlikely (Orenstein testified) because Erb or someone else at the pension trust would probably check the file and discover the paragraph and realize that if the trust refused to negotiate over the request for financing, Market Street Associates, as Penney's assignee, would be entitled to walk off with the property for (perhaps) a song. The judge inferred that Market Street Associates didn't want financing from the pension trust—that it just wanted an opportunity to buy the property at a bargain price and hoped that the pension trust wouldn't realize the implications of turning down the request for financing. Market Street Associates should, the judge opined, have advised the pension trust that it was requesting financing pursuant to paragraph 34, so that the trust would understand the penalty for refusing to negotiate....

So we must consider the meaning of the contract duty of "good faith." The Wisconsin cases are cryptic as to its meaning though emphatic about its existence, so we must cast our net wider.... The particular confusion to which the vaguely moralistic overtones of "good faith" give rise is the belief that every contract establishes a fiduciary relationship. A fiduciary is required to treat his principal as if the principal were he, and therefore he may not take advantage of the principal's incapacity, ignorance, inexperience, or even naïveté....

But it is unlikely that Wisconsin wishes, in the name of good faith, to make every contract signatory his brother's keeper, especially when the brother is the immense and sophisticated General Electric Pension Trust, whose lofty indifference to small ($= < \$7$ million) transactions is the signifier of its grandeur. In fact the law contemplates that people frequently will take advantage of the ignorance of those with whom they contract, without thereby incurring liability.... The duty of honesty, of good faith even expansively conceived, is not a duty of candor. You can make a binding contract to purchase something you know your seller undervalues.... That of course is a question about formation, not performance, and the particular duty of good faith under examination here relates to the latter rather than to the former. But even after you have signed a contract, you are not obliged to become an altruist toward the other party and relax the terms if he gets into trouble in performing his side of the bargain.... Otherwise mere difficulty of performance would excuse a contracting party—which it does not....

But it is one thing to say that you can exploit your superior knowledge of the market—for if you cannot, you will not be able to recoup the investment you made in obtaining that knowledge—or that you are not required to spend money bailing out a contract partner who has gotten into trouble. It is another thing to say that you can take deliberate advantage of an oversight by your contract partner concerning his rights under the contract. Such taking advantage is not the exploitation of superior knowledge or the avoidance of unbargained-for expense; it is sharp dealing....

The essential issue bearing on Market Street Associates' good faith was Orenstein's state of mind, a type of inquiry that ordinarily cannot be concluded on summary judgment, and could not be here. If Orenstein believed that Erb knew or would surely find out about paragraph 34, it was not dishonest or opportunistic to fail to flag that paragraph, or even to fail to mention the lease, in his correspondence and (rare) conversations with Erb, especially given the uninterest in dealing with Market Street Associates that Erb fairly radiated. To decide what Orenstein believed, a trial is necessary....

Reversed and remanded.

NOTE

Opinion on Remand. After a trial on remand, the district judge held that Market Street Associates was not entitled to specific performance. "While Orenstein initially assumed that the Trust would review the lease and make its determination as to whether it should provide financing to Market Street in light of paragraph 34, he subsequently recognized that the Trust was not operating under paragraph 34. While Orenstein knew this fact, he did not bring the matter to the Trust's attention, and continued to write ambiguous letters, until he wished to utilize the purchase option, thereby purchasing the property at a discounted cost. By so doing, this court concludes that Orenstein breached his duty to use good faith in his dealings with the Trust, and Market Street is not entitled to specific performance." Market Street Associates v. Frey, 817 F.Supp. 784, 788 (E.D.Wis.1993).

BLOOR v. FALSTAFF BREWING CORP.
United States Court of Appeals, Second Circuit, 1979.
601 F.2d 609.

FRIENDLY, CIRCUIT JUDGE: This action, wherein federal jurisdiction is predicated on diversity of citizenship, 28 U.S.C. § 1332, was brought in the District Court for the Southern District of New York, by James Bloor, Reorganization Trustee of Balco Properties Corporation, formerly named P. Ballantine & Sons (Ballantine), a venerable and once successful brewery based in Newark, N.J. He sought to recover from Falstaff Brewing Corporation (Falstaff) for breach of a contract dated March 31, 1972, wherein Falstaff bought the Ballantine brewing labels, trademarks, accounts receivable, distribution systems and other property except the brewery. The price was $4,000,000 plus a royalty of fifty cents on each barrel of the Ballantine brands sold between April 1, 1972 and March 31, 1978. Although other issues were tried, the appeals concern only two provisions of the contract. These are:

8. *Certain Other Covenants of Buyer.*

(a) After the Closing Date the [Buyer] will use its best efforts to promote and maintain a high volume of sales under the Proprietary Rights.

2(a)(v) [The Buyer will pay a royalty of $.50 per barrel for a period of 6 years], provided, however, that if during the Royalty Period the Buyer substantially discontinues the distribution of beer under the brand name "Ballantine" (except as the result of a restraining order in effect for 30 days issued by a court of competent jurisdiction at the request of a governmental authority), it will pay to the Seller a cash sum equal to the years and fraction thereof remaining in the Royalty Period times $1,100,-000, payable in equal monthly installments on the first day of each month commencing with the first month following the month in which such discontinuation occurs....

Bloor claimed that Falstaff had breached the best efforts clause, 8(a), and indeed that its default amounted to the substantial discontinuance that would trigger the liquidated damage clause, 2(a)(v). In an opinion that interestingly traces the history of beer back to Domesday Book and beyond, Judge Brieant upheld the first claim and awarded damages but dismissed the second. Falstaff appeals from the former ruling, Bloor from the latter. Both sides also dispute the court's measurement of damages for breach of the best efforts clause.

We shall assume familiarity with Judge Brieant's excellent opinion, 454 F.Supp. 258 (S.D.N.Y.1978), from which we have drawn heavily, and will state only the essentials. Ballantine had been a family owned business, producing low-priced beers primarily for the northeast market, particularly New York, New Jersey, Connecticut and Pennsylvania. Its sales began to decline in 1961, and it lost money from 1965 on. On June 1, 1969, Investors Funding Corporation (IFC), a real estate conglomerate with no experience in brewing, acquired substantially all the stock of Ballantine for $16,290,000. IFC increased advertising expenditures, levelling off in 1971 at $1 million a year. This and other promotional practices, some of dubious legality, led to steady growth in Ballantine's sales despite the increased activities in the northeast of the "nationals" [1] which have greatly augmented their market shares at the expense of smaller brewers. However, this was a profitless prosperity; there was no month in which Ballantine had earnings and the total loss was $15,500,000 for the 33 months of IFC ownership.

After its acquisition of Ballantine, Falstaff continued the $1 million a year advertising program, IFC's pricing policies, and also its policy of serving smaller accounts not solely through sales to independent distributors, the usual practice in the industry, but by use of its own warehouses and trucks—the only change being a shift of the retail distribution system from Newark to North Bergen, N.J., when brewing was concentrated at Falstaff's Rhode Island brewery. However, sales declined and Falstaff claims to have lost $22 million in its Ballantine brand operations from March 31, 1972 to June 1975. Its other activities were also performing indifferently, although with no such losses as were being incurred in the sale of Ballantine products, and it was facing inability to meet payrolls and other debts. In March and April 1975 control of Falstaff passed to Paul Kalmanovitz, a businessman with 40 years experience in the brewing industry. After having first advanced $3 million to enable Falstaff to meet its payrolls and other pressing debts, he later supplied an additional $10 million and made loan guarantees, in return for which he received convertible preferred shares in an amount that endowed him with 35% of the voting power and became the beneficiary of a voting trust that gave him control of the board of directors.

Mr. Kalmanovitz determined to concentrate on making beer and cutting sales costs. He decreased advertising, with the result that the Ballantine advertising budget shrank from $1 million to $115,000 a year.[2] In late 1975 he closed four of Falstaff's six retail distribution centers, including the North Bergen, N.J. depot, which was ultimately replaced by two distributors servicing substantially fewer accounts. He also discontinued various illegal practices that had been used in selling Ballantine products.[3] What happened in terms of sales volume is shown

1. Miller's, Schlitz, Anheuser–Busch, Coors and Pabst.

2. This was for cooperative advertising with purchasers.

3. There were two kinds of illegal practices, the testimony on both of which is, unsurprisingly, rather vague. Certain "national accounts", i.e. large draught beer buyers, were gotten or retained by "black

bagging", the trade term for commercial bribery. On a smaller scale, sales to taverns were facilitated by the salesman's offering a free round for the house of Ballantine if it was available ("retention"), or the customer's choice ("solicitation"). Both practices seem to have been indulged in by many brewers, including Falstaff before Kalmanovitz took control.

in plaintiff's exhibit 114 J, a chart which we reproduce in the margin.[4]
With 1974 as a base, Ballantine declined, 29.72% in 1975 and 45.81% in
1976 as compared with a 1975 gain of 2.24% and a 1976 loss of 13.08%
for all brewers excluding the top 15.   Other comparisons are similarly
devastating, at least for 1976.[5]   Despite the decline in the sale of its own
labels as well as Ballantine's, Falstaff, however, made a substantial
financial recovery.   In 1976 it had net income of $8.7 million and its
year-end working capital had increased from $8.6 million to $20.2
million and its cash and certificates of deposit from $2.2 million to $12.1
million.

Seizing upon remarks made by the judge during the trial that
Falstaff's financial standing in 1975 and thereafter "is probably not
relevant" and a footnote in the opinion, 454 F.Supp. at 267 n. 7,[6]
appellate counsel for Falstaff contend that the judge read the best efforts
clause as requiring Falstaff to maintain Ballantine's volume by any sales
methods having a good prospect of increasing or maintaining sales or, at
least, to continue lawful methods in use at the time of purchase, no
matter what losses they would cause.   Starting from this premise,
counsel reason that the judge's conclusion was at odds with New York
law, stipulated by the contract to be controlling, as last expressed by the
Court of Appeals in Feld v. Henry S. Levy & Sons, Inc., 37 N.Y.2d 466,
373 N.Y.S.2d 102, 335 N.E.2d 320 (1975).   The court was there dealing
with a contract whereby defendant agreed to sell and plaintiff to purchase all bread crumbs produced by defendant at a certain factory.
During the term of the agreement defendant ceased producing bread
crumbs because production with existing facilities was "very uneconomical", and the plaintiff sued for breach.   This case was governed by § 2–

4. Percentage Increase or Decline in
Sales Volume of Ballantine Beer, Falstaff
Beer and Comparable Brewers for Years
Ending December 31, 1972–1976

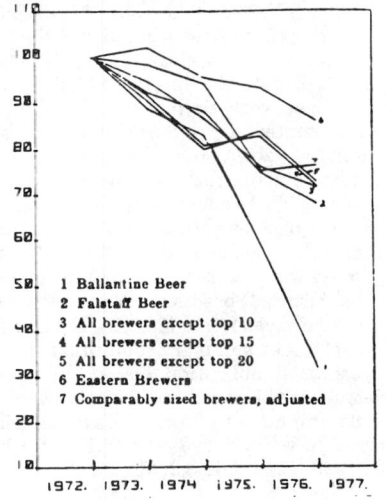

1 Ballantine Beer
2 Falstaff Beer
3 All brewers except top 10
4 All brewers except top 15
5 All brewers except top 20
6 Eastern Brewers
7 Comparably sized brewers, adjusted

1972. 1973. 1974 1975. 1976. 1977.

5. Falstaff argues that a trend line pro-
jecting the declining volume of Ballantine's
sales since 1966, before IFC's purchase,
would show an even worse picture.   We
agree with plaintiff that the percentage figures since 1974 are more significant; at
least the judge was entitled to think so.

6. "Even if Falstaff's financial position
had been worse in mid–1975 than it actually was, and even if Falstaff had continued
in that state of impecuniosity during the
term of the contract, performance of the
contract is not excused where the difficulty
of performance arises from financial difficulty or economic hardship.   As the New
York Court of Appeals stated in 407 E. 61st
Garage, Inc. v. Savoy Corp., 23 N.Y.2d 275,
281, 296 N.Y.S.2d 338, 344, 244 N.E.2d 37,
41 (1968):

'[W]here impossibility or difficulty of performance is occasioned only by financial
difficulty or economic hardship, even to
the extent of insolvency or bankruptcy,
performance of a contract is not excused.'
(Citations omitted.)"

306 of the Uniform Commercial Code [which the opinion quoted].

Affirming the denial of cross-motions for summary judgment, the court said that, absent a cancellation on six months' notice for which the contract provided:

> defendant was expected to continue to perform in good faith and could cease production of the bread crumbs, a single facet of its operation, only in good faith. Obviously, a bankruptcy or genuine imperiling of the very existence of its entire business caused by the production of the crumbs would warrant cessation of production of that item; the yield of less profit from its sale than expected would not. Since bread crumbs were but a part of defendant's enterprise and since there was a contractual right of cancellation, good faith required continued production until cancellation, even if there be no profit. In circumstances such as these and without more, defendant would be justified, in good faith, in ceasing production of the single item prior to cancellation only if its losses from continuance would be more than trivial, which, overall, is a question of fact.

37 N.Y.2d 471–72, 373 N.Y.S.2d 106, 335 N.E.2d 323.[7] Falstaff argues from this that it was not bound to do anything to market Ballantine products that would cause "more than trivial" losses.

We do not think the judge imposed on Falstaff a standard as demanding as its appellate counsel argues that he did. Despite his footnote 7, see note 6 supra, he did not in fact proceed on the basis that the best efforts clause required Falstaff to bankrupt itself in promoting

---

7. The text of the Feld opinion did not refer to the case cited by Judge Brieant in the preceding footnote, 407 East 61st Garage, Inc. v. Savoy Fifth Avenue Corporation, 23 N.Y.2d 275, 296 N.Y.S.2d 338, 244 N.E.2d 37 (1968), which might suggest a more onerous obligation here. The Court of Appeals there reversed a summary judgment in favor of the defendant, which had discontinued operating the Savoy Hilton Hotel because of substantial financial losses, in alleged breach of a five-year contract with plaintiff wherein the defendant had agreed to use all reasonable efforts to provide the garage with exclusive opportunity for storage of the motor vehicles of hotel guests. Although the court did use the language quoted by Judge Brieant, the actual holding was simply that "an issue of fact is presented whether the agreement did import an implied promise by Savoy to fulfill its obligations for an entire five-year period." 23 N.Y.2d at 281, 296 N.Y.S.2d at 343, 244 N.E.2d at 41.

Other cases suggest that under New York law a "best efforts" clause imposes an obligation to act with good faith in light of one's own capabilities. In Van Valkenburgh v. Hayden Publishing Co., 30 N.Y.2d 34, 330 N.Y.S.2d 329, 281 N.E.2d 142 (1972), the court held a publisher liable to an author when, in clear bad faith after a contract dispute, he hired another to produce a book very similar to plaintiff's and then promoted it to those who had been buying the latter. On the other hand, a defendant having the exclusive right to sell the plaintiff's product may sell a similar product if necessary to meet outside competition, so long as he accounts for any resulting losses the plaintiff can show in the sales of the licensed product. Parev Products Co. v. I. Rokeach & Sons, 124 F.2d 147 (2 Cir.1941). A summary definition of the best efforts obligation, cited by Judge Brieant, 454 F.Supp. at 266, is given in Arnold Productions, Inc. v. Favorite Films Corp., 176 F.Supp. 862, 866 (S.D.N.Y.1959), aff'd 298 F.2d 540 (2 Cir.1962), to wit,

Ballantine products or even to sell those products at a substantial loss. He relied rather on the fact that Falstaff's obligation to "use its best efforts to promote and maintain a high volume of sales" of Ballantine products was not fulfilled by a policy summarized by Mr. Kalmanovitz as being:

We sell beer and you pay for it....

We sell beer, F.O.B. the brewery. You come and get it.

—however sensible such a policy may have been with respect to Falstaff's other products. Once the peril of insolvency had been averted, the drastic percentage reductions in Ballantine sales as related to any possible basis of comparison, see fn. 5, required Falstaff at least to explore whether steps not involving substantial losses could have been taken to stop or at least lessen the rate of decline. The judge found that, instead of doing this, Falstaff had engaged in a number of misfeasances and nonfeasances which could have accounted in substantial measure for the catastrophic drop in Ballantine sales shown in the chart, see 454 F.Supp. at 267–72. These included the closing of the North Bergen depot which had serviced "Mom and Pop" stores and bars in the New York metropolitan area; Falstaff's choices of distributors for Ballantine products in the New Jersey and particularly the New York areas, where the chosen distributor was the owner of a competing brand; its failure to take advantage of a proffer from Guinness–Harp Corporation to distribute Ballantine products in New York City through its Metrobeer Division; Falstaff's incentive to put more effort into sales of its own brands which sold at higher prices despite identity of the ingredients and were free from the $.50 a barrel royalty burden; its failure to treat Ballantine products evenhandedly with Falstaff's; its discontinuing the practice of setting goals for salesmen; and the general Kalmanovitz policy of stressing profit at the expense of volume. In the court's judgment, these misfeasances and nonfeasances warranted a conclusion that, even taking account of Falstaff's right to give reasonable consideration to its own interests, Falstaff had breached its duty to use best efforts as stated in the *Van Valkenburgh* decision, supra, 30 N.Y.2d at 46, 330 N.Y.S.2d at 334, 281 N.E.2d at 145.

Falstaff levels a barrage on these findings. The only attack which merits discussion is its criticism of the judge's conclusion that Falstaff did not treat its Ballantine brands evenhandedly with those under the Falstaff name. We agree that the subsidiary findings "that Falstaff but not Ballantine had been advertised extensively in Texas and Missouri" and that "[i]n these same areas Falstaff, although a 'premium' beer, was sold for extended periods below the price of Ballantine," while literally

performing as well as "the average prudent comparable" brewer.

The net of all this is that the New York law is far from clear and it is unfortunate that a federal court must have to apply it.

true, did not warrant the inference drawn from them.   Texas was Falstaff territory and, with advertising on a cooperative basis, it was natural that advertising expenditures on Falstaff would exceed those on Ballantine.   The lower price for Falstaff was a particular promotion of a bicentennial can in Texas, intended to meet a particular competitor.

However, we do not regard this error as undermining the judge's ultimate conclusion of breach of the best efforts clause.   While that clause clearly required Falstaff to treat the Ballantine brands as well as its own, it does not follow that it required no more.   With respect to its own brands, management was entirely free to exercise its business judgment as to how to maximize profit even if this meant serious loss in volume.   Because of the obligation it had assumed under the sales contract, its situation with respect to the Ballantine brands was quite different.   The royalty of $.50 a barrel on sales was an essential part of the purchase price.   Even without the best efforts clause Falstaff would have been bound to make a good faith effort to see that substantial sales of Ballantine products were made, unless it discontinued under clause 2(a)(v) with consequent liability for liquidated damages.   Cf. Wood v. Duff–Gordon, 222 N.Y. 88, 118 N.E. 214 (1917) (Cardozo, J.).   Clause 8 imposed an added obligation to use "best efforts to promote and maintain a *high* volume of sales...."   (emphasis supplied).   Although we agree that even this did not require Falstaff to spend itself into bankruptcy to promote the sales of Ballantine products, it did prevent the application to them of Kalmanovitz' philosophy of emphasizing profit *über alles* without fair consideration of the effect on Ballantine volume. Plaintiff was not obliged to show just what steps Falstaff could reasonably have taken to maintain a high volume for Ballantine products.   It was sufficient to show that Falstaff simply didn't care about Ballantine's volume and was content to allow this to plummet so long as that course was best for Falstaff's overall profit picture, an inference which the judge permissibly drew.   The burden then shifted to Falstaff to prove there was nothing significant it could have done to promote Ballantine sales that would not have been financially disastrous.

Having correctly concluded that Falstaff had breached its best efforts covenant, the judge was faced with a difficult problem in computing what the royalties on the lost sales would have been.   There is no need to rehearse the many decisions that, in a situation like this, certainty is not required; "[t]he plaintiff need only show a 'stable foundation for a reasonable estimate of royalties he would have earned had defendant not breached'".   Contemporary Mission, Inc. v. Famous Music Corp., 557 F.2d 918, 926 (2 Cir.1977), quoting Freund v. Washington Square Press, Inc., 34 N.Y.2d 379, 383, 357 N.Y.S.2d 857, 861, 314 N.E.2d 419, 421 (1974).   After carefully considering other possible bases, the court arrived at the seemingly sensible conclusion that the most nearly accurate comparison was with the combined sales of Rheingold and Schaefer beers, both, like Ballantine, being "price" beers sold primarily in the northeast, and computed what Ballantine sales would have been if its brands had suffered only the same decline as a composite of Rheingold and Schaefer....

We also reject plaintiff's complaint on his cross-appeal that the court erred in not taking as its standard for comparison the grouping of all but the top 15 brewers, Ballantine having ranked 16th in 1971. The judge was entirely warranted in believing that the Rheingold–Schaefer combination afforded a better standard of comparison. [Finally, the court rejected plaintiff's contention that Falstaff's actions triggered the liquidated damage clause.]

The judgment is affirmed. Plaintiff may recover two-thirds of his costs.

NOTES

(1) *Scope of Duty.* How can a court determine what standard is imposed by a duty of "best efforts" in a particular case? Courts have often looked to the behavior of others engaged in like activities. See the reference near the end of footnote 7 to the performance of " 'the average prudent comparable' brewer."

Professors Goetz and Scott propose a more sophisticated test. They note that "best efforts" contracts are often used instead of vertical integration in a single firm and argue that such contracts "can most sensibly be construed as requiring the level of effort necessary to maximize the joint net product flowing from the contractual relationship. This joint-maximization criterion ... produces the largest possible net product for ultimate division between the parties." They admit, however, that it is hard to tell from damage computations in cases like *Bloor* what standard of performance has been applied. In *Bloor,* damages were "projected from the behavior of 'comparable' brands that were marketed by integrated non-royalty-paying firms. Thus, the 'comparable brand' volume behavior could be regarded as a good proxy for the joint-maximization outcome for the Ballantine–Falstaff contractual combination. There is, however, no real indication in the decision that the use of integrated firms as comparable entities was understood or intended in this way." Goetz & Scott, Principles of Relational Contracts, 67 Va.L.Rev. 1089, 1149–50, 1123 (1981). See also Gergen, The Use of Open Terms in Contracts, 92 Colum.L.Rev. 997 (1992).

(2) *Exclusivity.* Does a promise to use best efforts imply exclusivity? (Would Otis Wood have broken his contract with Lady Duff Gordon if he had handled the fashions of another designer at the same time?)

In Van Valkenburgh, Nooger & Neville, Inc. v. Hayden Publishing Co., 281 N.E.2d 142 (N.Y.), cert. denied, 409 U.S. 875 (1972), cited by Judge Friendly, the court concluded that a publisher's undertaking to use efforts to promote an author's works "does not close off the right of a publisher to issue books on the same subject, to negotiate with and pay authors to write such books and to promote them fully according to the publisher's economic interests, even though those later publications adversely affect the contracting author's sales.... Although a publisher has a general right to act on its own interests in a way that may incidentally lessen an author's royalties, there may be a point where that activity is so manifestly harmful to the author, and must have been seen by the publisher to be so harmful, as to justify the court in saying there was a breach of the covenant to promote the author's work."

This qualification of a party's "general right to act on its own interests" is illustrated by Joyce Beverages of New York, Inc. v. Royal Crown Cola Co., 555 F.Supp. 271 (S.D.N.Y.1983), in which Joyce had agreed to "devote its best efforts ... so as to achieve maximum distribution and sale [of Royal Crown] beverages within the territory." The court held that undertaking to distribute Seven–Up beverages was a breach. "A best efforts clause is not *per se* breached by a mere undertaking of a competitive product line ...; it depends on the circumstances.... [But here the] entire pattern of industry practice since the beginning of the soft drink industry has been for distributors to distribute only one cola. This best efforts clause is properly read in terms of the trade practice and usage." In addition, "Seven–Up's national advertising campaign denigrates the content of Royal Crown cola products. Seven–Up's slogan is 'You don't need caffeine and neither does your cola.'"

(3) *The Case of the "Fritos" and "Fandangos."* Frito–Lay and So Good Potato Chip Company agreed that So Good was to be licensed to manufacture and distribute corn chips made by Frito–Lay's secret process within a prescribed area under the trademark "Fritos." The contract provided that Frito–Lay "will neither authorize nor permit the use of its trademark 'FRITOS' on corn chips by anyone other than Licensee." It also prohibited So Good from engaging "directly or indirectly ... in the manufacture and/or sale of corn chips or similar products" other than "Fritos." When Frito–Lay introduced "Doritos," "Fandangos" and "Intermission" corn chips in the licensed territory, So Good sought an injunction. From an adverse judgment, So Good appealed. *Held:* Affirmed. "[T]he parties here have expressly touched on the point in controversy.... A covenant cannot be implied if the parties have either expressly dealt with the matter in the contract or have left the agreement intentionally silent on the point.... [T]he franchise agreement expressly deals with the sale of products by Frito–Lay in the franchised territory, and thus precludes any implied covenant." So Good Potato Chip Co. v. Frito–Lay, Inc., 462 F.2d 239 (8th Cir.1972).

ZILG v. PRENTICE–HALL, INC.

United States Court of Appeals, Second Circuit, 1983.
717 F.2d 671.
Certiorari denied, 466 U.S. 938 (1984).

WINTER, CIRCUIT JUDGE: Prentice–Hall, Inc. ("P–H") appeals from a judgment entered after a bench trial before Judge Brieant ordering it to pay damages of $24,250 plus pre-judgment interest to the plaintiff, Gerard Colby Zilg, for breach of contract. Zilg cross-appeals the judgment in favor of E.I. DuPont de Nemours & Co., Inc. ("DuPont Company") on his claim of tortious interference with contract. We reverse as to Zilg's breach of contract claim against P–H and affirm the judgment in favor of the DuPont Company.

BACKGROUND

Gerard Colby Zilg is the author of DuPont: Behind the Nylon Curtain, an historical account of the role of the DuPont family in American social, political and economic affairs. Early in 1972, after one partially successful and several unsuccessful efforts to find a publisher for his proposed book, Zilg's agent introduced him to Bram Cavin, a senior editor in P–H's Trade Book Division. Cavin expressed interest in the book, and he and Zilg submitted a formal proposal to John Kirk, P–H's Editor-in-Chief at that time. Kirk approved the proposal.... As it passed through the editorial and corporate hierarchy, the proposal received a notation from P–H's publicity director that the book's potential for radio and television coverage was "slight to non-existent unless matter in [the] book is highly controversial and print [media] says so first."

P–H and Zilg executed a form contract which provided in relevant part:

3. The manuscript ... will be delivered ... by the AUTHOR to the PUBLISHER in final form and content acceptable to the PUBLISHER....

4. When the manuscript has been accepted and approved for publication by the PUBLISHER ... it will be published at the PUBLISHER'S own expense....

12. The PUBLISHER shall have the right: (1) to publish the work in such style as it deems best suited to the sale of the work; (2) to fix or alter the prices at which the work shall be sold; (3) to determine the method and means of advertising, publicizing, and selling the work, the number and destination of free copies, and all other publishing details, including the number of copies to be printed, if from plates or type or by other process, date of publishing, form, style, size, type, paper to be used, and like details.

Zilg submitted the first half of his completed manuscript to Cavin in November, 1972, and the remainder a year later. Cavin authorized acceptance of the work on behalf of P–H, apparently without the participation of Peter Grenquist, who had become president of P–H's Trade Book Division sometime after execution of the contract but before submission of the manuscript. P–H's legal division scrutinized the manuscript for libelous content and concluded that, if a libel action were brought, P–H "would ultimately prevail" because the subject matter of the work was constitutionally privileged and the plaintiffs would have to prove actual malice. The division's opinion noted, however, that litigation against the DuPonts would be very costly.

A decision was made to accept the manuscript which was distributed to selected wholesalers, reviewers, and booksellers. Copies were also sent to the editorial director of the Book of the Month Club ("BOMC"). Although BOMC decided not to offer the book as a selection of its main club, a subsidiary, the Fortune Book Club, which appealed to a readership composed largely of business executives, did choose it as a selection.

A committee of various P–H department representatives, including the book's editor, met on March 28, 1974 to discuss production plans. The sales estimates of committee members varied from 12 to 15 thousand copies for the first year although by May two members were predicting sales of only 10 thousand. Estimates of from 15 to 20 thousand sales over a five year period were also made. Cavin, an ardent supporter of the book, made estimates of 20 to 25 thousand in the first year and 25 to 35 thousand over five years. The committee decided on a first printing of 15,000 copies at a retail price of $12.95 per copy. At a later meeting, the committee decided to devote roughly $15,000 to advertising.

Although the literary or scholarly merits of the book are not our concern, its nature, tone and marketability among various audiences are key facts in this litigation, for they bear upon the book's prospects for commercial success and illuminate the negative reactions which later set in at P–H. The book is a harshly critical portrait of the DuPont family and their role in American social, political and economic history. Indeed, it is a harshly critical portrait of that history itself. The reactions of readers and reviewers in the record indicate that the book is polarizing, the difference in viewpoint depending in no small measure upon the politics of the beholder. A significant number of readers regard the book as a strident caricature, drawing every conceivable inference against the DuPont family and firms with which members of the family were or are associated. One judge at BOMC, for example, described it as "300,000 words of pure spite." On the other hand, the book has a loyal band of admirers. It received a favorable review in many newspapers, including the *New York Times* Book Review section. Its comprehensiveness and the extensive research on which it was based were frequently noted. The book also has some appeal to another audience, namely readers with a taste for gossip about the rich and powerful, particularly readers in Delaware. Indeed, it was once first in non-fiction sales in that state.

In the American market, the book's appeal is somewhat limited by the fact that it is not a work critical of business on grounds that reform of capitalism is necessary in order to save it, a viewpoint with mainstream appeal. Rather, it presents a Marxist view of history. Also weighing against its overall marketability were its size (586 pages of text, 2 inches thick, three and one-half pounds), complexity (almost 200 family members with the surname DuPont and 170 years of American history) and price ($12.95 in 1974 dollars).

Prior to June, 1974, Grenquist appears not to have been aware of the nature and tone of the book, of the intensity of negative feeling it might arouse in some readers or of evidence of serious inaccuracies. He may have been reassured partly by Cavin's enthusiasm and partly by the book's selection by the Fortune Book Club. That selection itself remains something of a mystery since the Club's inside reader concluded it was "a bad book, politically crude and cheaply journalistic." However, instead of accepting his recommendation that it "be fed back to the author page by page," BOMC contracted with P–H to have it adopted by the Fortune Book Club.

In June, 1974, a chain of events was set in motion which apprised Grenquist of the negative aspects of Zilg's work. A member of the DuPont family obtained an advance copy of the manuscript from a bookseller and, predictably outraged, turned it over to the Public Affairs Department of the DuPont Company. [A representative of the Company contacted the Fortune Book Club and BOMC to protest the "scurrilous" nature of the book. F. Harry Brown, Editor-in-Chief of BOMC] "spent a horrible two days reading" the book and decided it was an unsuitable selection for the Fortune Book Club. He later stated he felt no pressure from the DuPont Company in reaching this decision. In view of the nature of the book and the Club's audience of business executives, his decision seems an inevitable result of his reading the book. BOMC immediately notified P–H of its decision not to distribute the book. The reason given was BOMC's belief that the book was malicious and had an objectionable tone.

P–H's own detailed examination of the manuscript may also have introduced or heightened skepticism on Grenquist's part. A toning down was found to be necessary even after the book was in page proof. Mistakes of fact, such as a statement that Irving S. Shapiro (DuPont's Chief Executive Officer) had served as an Assistant District Attorney in Queens County, New York, were discovered. More serious matters also came to light. The original manuscript attacked Judge Harold R. Medina for matters irrelevant to the DuPonts and in a fashion which the district court characterized as libelous. Zilg admitted at trial that there was no factual foundation for this attack. Some eyebrows at P–H may well have been raised when this passage was discovered and deleted, since it was not only unfounded but also irrelevant.

P–H continued to correct and tone down the book, hoping to reverse BOMC's decision not to offer it through the Fortune Book Club. A certain defensiveness also began to creep into P–H's attitude toward the book. On August 2, Grenquist circulated a memorandum which noted that questions had arisen regarding both the tone of the book and Zilg's approach and recommended that the adjective "polemical" henceforth be used because "[t]he book is a polemical argument and no pretense is made that it is anything else." More importantly, he also cut the first printing from 15,000 copies to 10,000, stating that 5,000 copies were no longer needed for BOMC. The proposed advertising budget was also slashed from $15,000 to $5,500....

As to P–H, Judge Brieant found that the publishing contract required the publisher to "exercise its discretion in good faith in planning its promotion of the Book, and in revising its plans." This obligation required that Prentice–Hall use "its best efforts . . . to promote the Book fully and fairly." He held that P–H breached this obligation because it had no "sound" or "valid" business reason for reducing the first printing by 5,000 volumes and the advertising budget by $9,500, which allowed the book to go briefly out of stock (although wholesalers had ample copies) just as it gained sales momentum. He expressly found that since BOMC did its own printing of club selections, the first printing cut could not be attributed to the cancellation of the BOMC order. He also found that the book would have sold 25,000 copies had P–H not taken these actions.

Having concluded that P–H had no sound or valid business reason for reducing the first printing and advertising budget, Judge Brieant held that P–H "privished" Zilg's book on the basis of the testimony of plaintiff's expert, William Decker. Decker testified that publishers often mount a wholly inadequate merchandising effort after concluding that a book does not meet prior expectations in either quality or marketability. Such "privishing" is intended to fulfill the technical requirements of the contract to publish but to avoid adding to one's losses by throwing "good money after bad."

DISCUSSION

We agree with Judge Brieant that DuPont did not tortiously interfere with Zilg's beneficial commercial relationships. We disagree, however, with his conclusion that P–H breached its contract with Zilg and reverse that judgment. [The discussion of tortious interference is omitted.]

Judge Brieant read the contract in question to oblige P–H "to use its best efforts ... to promote the Book fully...." and found that the decision to cut the first printing and original advertising budget resulted in a loss of sales momentum when the book was briefly out of stock. These actions by P–H, he held, breached its agreement with Zilg because they lacked a sound or valid business reason.

Putting aside for the moment P–H's motive in slashing the first printing and advertising budget, we note that Zilg neither bargained for nor acquired an explicit "best efforts" or "promote fully" promise, much less an agreement to make certain specific promotional efforts. The contract here thus contrasts with that in issue in Contemporary Mission, Inc. v. Famous Music Corp., 557 F.2d 918 (2d Cir.1977), which contained specific promotional obligations with regard to a musical group. While P–H obligated itself to "publish" the book once it had accepted it, the contract expressly leaves to P–H's discretion printing and advertising decisions. Working as we must in the context of a surprising absence of caselaw on the meaning of this not uncommon agreement, we believe that the contract in question establishes a relationship between the publisher and author which implies an obligation upon the former to make certain efforts in publishing a book it has accepted notwithstanding the clause which leaves the number of volumes to be printed and the advertising budget to the publisher's discretion. This obligation is derived both from the common expectations of parties to such agreements and from the relationship of those parties as structured by the contract. See generally Goetz and Scott, Principles of Relational Contracts, 67 Va.L.Rev. 1089 (1981).

Zilg, like most authors, sought to take advantage of a division of labor in which firms specialize in publishing works written by authors who are not employees of the firm. Under contracts such as the one before us, publishing firms print, advertise and distribute books at their own expense. In return for performing these tasks and for bearing the risk of a book's failure to sell, the author gives a publisher exclusive rights to the book with certain reservations not important here. Such contracts provide for royalties on sales to the author, often on an escalating basis, i.e., higher royalties at higher levels of sales.

While publishers and authors have generally similar goals, differences in perspective and resulting perceptions are inevitable. An author usually has a bigger stake in the success or failure of a book than a publisher who may regard it as one among many publications, some of which may lose money. The author, whose eggs are in one basket, thus has a calculus of risk quite different from the publisher so far as costly promotional expenditures are concerned. The publisher, of course, views the author's willingness to take large risks as a function of the fact that it is the publisher's money at peril. Moreover, the publisher will inevitably regard his or her judgment as to marketing conditions as greatly superior to that of a particular author.

One means of reconciling these differing viewpoints is "up-front" money—$6,500 in Zilg's case—which provides a token of the publisher's seriousness about the book. Were such sums not bargained for, acquisition of publishing rights would be virtually costless and firms would acquire those rights without regard to whether or not they had truly decided to publish the work.

However, up-front money alone cannot fully reconcile the conflicting interests of the parties. Uncertainty surrounds the publication of most books and publishers must be cautious about the size of up-front payments since they increase the already considerable economic risks they take by printing and promoting books at their own expense. Negotiating such matters as the number of volumes to be printed and the level of advertising efforts might be possible but such bargaining in the case of each author and each book would be enormously costly. There is never a guarantee of ultimate agreement, and if a set of negotiations fails over these issues, the bargaining must begin again with another publisher. Moreover, publishers must also be wary of undertaking obligations to print a certain number of volumes or to spend fixed sums on promotion. They will strongly prefer to have flexibility in reacting to actual marketing conditions according to their own experience.

The contract between Zilg and P–H was a printed form with formal and negotiated matters—e.g., the parties' names and the amount of the advance to the author—typed in. Under the terms of the printed form, once P–H accepted the manuscript it was obliged to publish the book but had discretion to determine the number of volumes to be printed and the level of advertising expenditures. These clauses are, of course, interrelated and the extent to which the language regarding promotional efforts and the promise to publish modify each other is the central issue before us. In resolving it, we must attempt to preserve the major interests of both parties. Sharon Steel Corp. v. Chase Manhattan Bank, 691 F.2d 1039 (2d Cir.1982).

Once P–H had accepted the book, it obtained the exclusive right to publish it. Were the clause empowering the publisher to determine promotional expenses read literally, the contract would allow a publisher to refuse to print or distribute any copies of a book while having exclusive rights to it. In effect, authors would be guaranteed nothing but whatever up-front money had been negotiated, and the promise to publish would be meaningless. We think the promise to publish must be given some content and that it implies a good faith effort to promote the book including a first printing and advertising budget adequate to give the book a reasonable chance of achieving market success in light of the subject matter and likely audience. See Contemporary Mission, Inc. v. Famous Music Corp.; cf. Van Valkenburgh Nooger & Neville, Inc. v. Hayden Publishing Co., 30 N.Y.2d 34, 281 N.E.2d 142, 330 N.Y.S.2d 329 (1972) (publication of competing works may be so foreseeably harmful to author's royalties as to breach covenant to promote the book).

However, the clause empowering the publisher to decide in its discretion upon the number of volumes printed and the level of promotional expenditures must also be given some content. If a trier of fact is free to determine whether such decisions are sound or valid, the publisher's ability to rely upon its own experience and judgment in marketing books will be seriously hampered. We believe that once the obligation to undertake reasonable initial promotional activities has been fulfilled, the contractual language dictates that a business decision by the publisher to limit the size of a printing or advertising budget is not subject to second guessing by a trier of fact as to whether it is sound or valid.

The line we draw reconciles the legitimate conflicting interests of publisher and author as reflected in the contractual language, for it compels the publisher to make a good faith effort to promote the book initially whether or not it has had second thoughts while relying upon the profit motive thereafter to create the incentive for more elaborate promotional efforts. Once the initial obligation is fulfilled, all that is required is a good faith business judgment. This is not an interpretation harmful to authors. Were courts to impose rigorous requirements as to promotional efforts, publishers would of necessity undertake to publish fewer books with unpredictable futures.

Given the line we draw, a breach of contract might be proven by Zilg in two ways. First, he might demonstrate that the initial printing and promotional efforts were so inadequate as not to give the book a reasonable chance to catch on with the reading public. Second, he might show that even greater printing and promotional efforts were not undertaken for reasons other than a good faith business judgment. Because he has shown neither, we reverse the judgment in his favor.

As to P–H's initial obligation, Zilg has not shown that P–H's efforts on behalf of his book did not give it a reasonable chance to catch on with the reading public. It printed or reprinted 13,000 volumes (3,000 over the volume of sales at which the highest royalty was triggered), authorized an advertising budget of $5,500 (1974 purchasing power), distributed over 600 copies to reviewers, purchased ads in papers such as the New York Times and Wall Street Journal, and made reasonable efforts to sell the paperback rights. The documentary record shows that Grenquist took a continued interest in marketing the book, made suggestions as to promoting it effectively and ordered that "rave reviews" be sent to BOMC as late as January, 1975.

The fact that initial decisions as to promotional efforts were trimmed is of no relevance absent evidence that the actual efforts made were so inadequate that the book did not have a reasonable chance to catch on with the reading public. The record is barren of such evidence. P–H's estimates of first year sales made at the peak of the book's standing within the firm were only 12,000–15,000. By May, before the BOMC reversal, the low estimate was 10,000. It can hardly be contended that an initial printing of 10,000 and reprinting of 3,000 is so low that it breaches the obligation to give the book a reasonable chance to sell. Plaintiff's expert, Decker, himself testified that these efforts were "perfectly adequate," although they were "routine" and P–H "did not follow through as they might have."

Judge Brieant found only that an "unexplained" reduction in the first printing and advertising budget caused the book to go out of stock for a brief period of time and prevented the exploitation of growing sales momentum. He thus did not find that P–H's promotional efforts gave the book no reasonable chance to sell. Rather, he found that sales momentum was generated but not adequately exploited because the book was briefly out of stock. That situation, however, was not an inevitable outcome of the size of the first printing since a timely reprinting would have prevented it. Indeed, Grenquist ordered a reprinting when over 10% of the original volumes were still in stock and a delivery delay in that reprinting led to the three week out of stock situation. Moreover, the book was always available from wholesalers although, as Judge Brieant found, book sellers prefer to buy from publishers who provide a discount.

The district court read the contract as imposing on P–H a continuing obligation to use "its best efforts . . . to promote the Book fully and fairly" and as empowering a trier of fact to second guess a publisher's judgments as to the soundness of the decisions made. We disagree. So long as the initial promotional efforts are adequate under the test we outline above, a publisher's printing and advertising decisions do not breach a contract such as that before us unless the plaintiff proves that the motivation underlying those decisions was not a good faith business judgment. Zilg failed to produce such evidence. His case was based on the theory that economic coercion by the DuPont Company caused P–H to reduce its promotional efforts. Judge Brieant found against him on this issue and, for reasons stated above, we affirm this determination.

This district court's finding that the reduction of promotional efforts was not based on a sound or valid business reason thus does not support the conclusion that the contract was breached. The district court took a different view of the legal obligations imposed by the contract and its conclusion was based on its highly optimistic opinion of the marketability of Zilg's book. Even at the peak of the book's standing within P–H, at a time when the Fortune Book Club was going to offer it as a selection and before the problems of tone and accuracy had come into focus, no one at P–H save Cavin thought the book would be as successful as the district court later found. P–H's March, 1974, estimate for five year sales, for example, was 15,000 to 20,000, the low estimate being closer to actual sales than the high estimate is to Judge Brieant's finding. Indeed, Judge Brieant's view of the book's potential is entirely inconsistent with Decker's definition of privishing—not throwing "good money after bad"—for he in essence found that P–H had managed to avoid a small bonanza by breaching its contract.

As explained above, we think the contract between P–H and Zilg left the decisions in question to the business judgment of the publisher, the author's protection being in the publisher's experience, judgment and quest for profits. P–H's promotional efforts were, in Decker's words, "adequate," notwithstanding the reduction of the first printing and the initial advertising budget. Indeed, those reductions, coming on the heels of BOMC's decision not to distribute the book, appear to be a rational reaction to that news. Decker himself testified that the Fortune Book Club selection was an important barometer of marketability since it was an independent judgment that the book had an audience. Zilg's contract with P–H did not compel the publisher to ignore the implications of BOMC's change of heart.

Affirmed in part, reversed in part.

NOTE

Questions. What would have been the outcome under Prentice–Hall's form contract had it not contained paragraph 12?

Introductory Note to *Bak–A–Lum* and *Lockewill*

Distributorship and franchise agreements are usually explicit as to duration and termination. If they are not, courts have generally held that they are terminable at will by either party. This can work hardship if the distributor or franchisee has not had an opportunity to recoup its initial investment or has not been given time to arrange a substitute relationship. In the two following cases, courts consider possible modification of the at-will rule in such cases.

BAK–A–LUM CORP. OF AMERICA v. ALCOA BLDG. PRODUCTS, INC.
Supreme Court of New Jersey, 1976.
69 N.J. 123, 351 A.2d 349.

CONFORD, P.J.A.D., Temporarily Assigned. Plaintiff corporation ("BAL" hereinafter) sued defendant ("ALCOA" hereinafter) for an injunction and damages for alleged breach of an exclusive distributorship of aluminum siding and related products manufactured by ALCOA. It was denied an injunction but awarded damages for breach of contract; at the same time the trial court granted defendant judgment on a counterclaim for merchandise sold to plaintiff, together with interest thereon. Plaintiff appealed on the ground the damages awarded were inadequate; the defendant cross-appealed, asserting its conduct was not actionable. The Appellate Division affirmed. We granted plaintiff's petition for certification and defendant's cross-petition. . . .

We find the record to support the trial court's finding of fact that in or about 1962 or 1963 BAL entered into a verbal agreement with

ALCOA whereby BAL would be exclusive distributor in Northern New Jersey for ALCOA's aluminum siding and certain related products. Although the agreement did not preclude BAL handling other lines of siding, the understanding was that it would maintain an adequate organization and exert its best efforts to promote the sales of the ALCOA products, and the evidence and trial findings were that BAL produced to the satisfaction of ALCOA, even meeting fixed quotas of sales set by ALCOA during the latter phase of the relationship.

ALCOA terminated the "exclusive" in January 1970 by appointing four additional distributors to share the North Jersey territory with plaintiff, thereby precipitating the controversy that gave rise to this action. The trial court, although refusing a request for a preliminary injunction against the termination of the exclusive distributorship, held after trial that there was a binding agreement between the parties terminable only after a reasonable period of time and on reasonable notice. It found that a reasonable period of time had passed before termination but that a reasonable period of notice of termination would be seven months. It established plaintiff's damages at $5,000 per month and entered judgment in plaintiff's favor for $35,000 together with interest from September 1, 1970.

In addition to a complaint that it established losses in sales profits as a result of the termination of the exclusive at a rate of $10,000 per month rather than at the $5,000 rate determined by the court, plaintiff's major grievance is that in the Spring of 1969, at a time when defendant had already decided upon the termination of the distributorship but was secreting that plan from plaintiff, the latter undertook a major expansion of its warehouse facilities at substantial added operating expense. Plaintiff asserts that defendant knew of and encouraged this step, leading plaintiff to believe it was well warranted in view of the expected enlargement of the business of both of the contracting parties. On the basis of defendant's concealment of its intentions in the face of plaintiff's incurrence of a five year lease obligation for the new space, plaintiff asserts it is entitled to additional damages from defendant for the excess of its expense for the period of the lease over its operating expenses in its former headquarters—a loss allegedly attributable directly to defendant's breach of contract.

The trial court found that if ALCOA's decision, made in January or February of 1969, to enlarge the number of North Jersey distributors, had been promptly communicated to BAL's president, "it is unlikely that he would have signed the lease [for the new quarters] in April [1969] without first getting from [ALCOA] the assurance of continuance of the distributorship which he sought to get after the lease was signed". The court further found that all the circumstances surrounding the defendant's attitude to and treatment of plaintiff preceding and attending the disruption of the contractual arrangement "bespeak a certain hypocrisy as well as ruthlessness on the part of [ALCOA] toward its distributor of many years". The court further "surmised" that the reason defendant had concealed during the year 1969 its intention to terminate plaintiff's exclusive even though it had arrived at that intent before plaintiff entered into the new lease in 1969 was "that the men at [ALCOA] in charge of sales thought a period of secrecy ending with a sudden announcement to Mr. Diamond [plaintiff's president] of the accomplished fact of new distributors would avoid any risk of cooling plaintiff's interest in selling ALCOA products during the several months before the new distributors were named and made ready to go". Indeed, defendant's salesman induced plaintiff in January 1970, just before the announcement of the termination of the exclusive, to order $150,000 worth of merchandise—a very heavy order for that time of year.

In fixing seven months as a reasonable period of notice of termination of the exclusive agreement the trial court stated that the criterion for such a period of notice is the amount of time the notified party needs to make adjustments and to plan and arrange for business activities to replace those which are to be eliminated. However, the court apparently placed little if any weight on the circumstances of the new lease as an element going to the reasonableness of the period for notice of termination, although it stated that the lease was a "factor" for consideration. It pointed out that the decision to undertake the lease was plaintiff's and that plaintiff was able to use the space to store merchandise other than that purchased from defendant as well as defendant's lines.

Our review of the record leads us to concur in the trial court's holding that there was a valid distributorship agreement terminable only on reasonable notice.... Plaintiff's contention that the agreement was not terminable at all without "cause" based on the recent holding of this court in Shell Oil Co. v. Marinello, 63 N.J. 402, 307 A.2d 598 (1973) [Note 1, p. 439 above], is without merit. The "franchise" agreement here is in no sense comparable with that which produced the holding of non-terminability in *Shell.*

However, we are constrained to differ with the trial court's assessment of seven months as an adequate period for notice of termination of this agreement. It may be true that defendant ordinarily would be under no strictly legal obligation to inform plaintiff that it was about to terminate its exclusive distributorship although it knew that in all probability plaintiff was enlarging its plant upon an assumption of the continuation of the business arrangement for the indefinite future. However, we have been at pains recently to point out that "[i]n every contract there is an implied covenant that 'neither party shall do anything which will have the effect of destroying or injuring the right of the other party to receive the fruits of the contract; in other words, in every contract there exists an implied covenant of good faith and fair dealing.' " Association Group Life, Inc. v. Catholic War Vets. of U.S., 61 N.J. 150, 153, 293 A.2d 382, 384 (1972)....

While the contractual relation of manufacturer and exclusive territorial distributor continued between the parties an obligation of reciprocal good-faith dealing similarly persisted between them. In such circumstances defendant's selfish withholding from plaintiff of its intention seriously to impair its distributorship although knowing plaintiff was embarking on an investment substantially predicated upon its continuation constituted a breach of the implied covenant of dealing in good faith of which we have spoken. As such it must be given substantial weight in determining the reasonableness of a period of notice of termination of the distributorship.

We cannot, however, agree with plaintiff that the period should encompass the remaining 4½ years of the lease as of the date of breach. The evidence justifies the conclusion that the prospects were fair for ultimate utilization to a substantial extent of the expanded warehouse space for new business plaintiff was able to obtain after defendant's breach or for other means of mitigating that phase of the damage attributable to defendant's conduct.

Exercising our original fact finding jurisdiction in order to bring this litigation to a close, it is our determination that a reasonable period of notice of termination of the distributorship, under all the circumstances, would have been 20 months.

Moreover, we find unwarranted the trial court's determination of plaintiff's monthly losses of profits of sales at $5,000 in the face of apparently unchallenged proofs by plaintiff, accepted by the court, that the damage figures were about $10,000 monthly....

On defendant's appeal the judgment is affirmed, with costs. On plaintiff's appeal the judgment is modified in accordance with this opinion, with costs to plaintiff.

NOTES

(1) *Questions.* How does the problem raised in this case differ from that in Shell Oil Co. v. Marinello, discussed at p. 452 above? From that in the case of *Miller Brewing Co.,* Note 1, p. 264 above? Could Alcoa have protected itself by providing for termination on 30-days notice? For termination at will?

How should a franchisee's damages be figured if, because the franchisor fails to give reasonable notice, the franchisee suffers delay in obtaining a substitute franchise? On the profit that the franchisee would have made under the original franchise had it continued until the end of the reasonable time? Or on the (presumably smaller) profit that the franchisee would have made under the substitute franchise had there been no delay in obtaining it? (Is the breach the early termination or the failure to give notice?)

(2) *The Case of the Bad Faith Order.* Massachusetts Gas & Electric Light Supply, a distributor of appliances, had a distributorship agreement with V–M, a manufacturer, cancellable by V–M on 30 days' notice. In June, Massachusetts learned that V–M was about to cancel and on June 28 it ordered 892 units, its estimated need for the rest of the year, although its normal inventory was about 100 units. V–M cancelled and refused to fill the order, but offered to fill a part of it. Massachusetts took the position that it wanted the whole order or nothing, and sued. From judgment for the defendant, the plaintiff appealed. *Held:* Affirmed. "The agreement was a distributorship and not a mere sales agreement, and it was the disclosed intention that when plaintiff ceased to be a distributor it should, at least shortly, cease to carry defendant's goods.... [T]he maximum June 28 order which defendant should have had to respect was to maintain an appropriate inventory through July. Plaintiff's order was not a good faith attempt to accomplish this, see U.C.C. §§ 1–203, 2–103(1)(b), 2–306,

but an effort to nullify the termination clause." Massachusetts Gas & Electric Light Supply Corp. v. V–M Corp., 387 F.2d 605 (1st Cir.1967).

———

LOCKEWILL, INC. v. UNITED STATES SHOE CORP., 547 F.2d 1024 (8th Cir.1976), cert. denied, 431 U.S. 956 (1977). [In 1965, Grant Williams, a man experienced in the shoe business, made an oral agreement with Pappagallo, Inc., a distributor of fashionable women's shoes that then sold only through small stores, each known as "The Shop for Pappagallo." Under the agreement, Williams was to open such a shop in the St. Louis area and purchase shoes in reasonable volume, in return for the exclusive right to market Pappagallo products in that area. Nothing was said about duration or termination. When Williams asked about the propriety of a written contract, Maurice Bandler, the sole owner of Pappagallo and a lawyer, said that none was necessary and that their handclasp was sufficient. Williams organized a corporation to run the shop, invested about $100,000 in the venture and sold Pappagallo products for years. During this time, however, United States Shoe Corp. bought out Bandler's interest in Pappagallo, and in the summer of 1973 an arrangement was made under which Stix, Baer & Fuller, a large St. Louis department store would be allowed to sell Pappagallo shoes in competition with Williams' shop. In September, 1973, Williams' lawyer wrote a letter to Pappagallo protesting this and, when, in February 1974, Stix, Baer & Fuller began selling Pappagallo shoes, suit was brought against Pappagallo and United States Shoe for breach of the exclusivity provision of the 1965 distributorship agreement. From a judgment awarding the plaintiff $150,000 in damages, the defendants appealed.]

HENLEY, CIRCUIT JUDGE.... The law of Missouri, which we are undertaking to apply in this case, appears to be that where the parties to a franchise or exclusive agency or distributorship agreement which is silent as to duration and which does not deal specifically with termination begin to perform thereunder, the agreement is construed to be terminable at the will of either party. See ... Beebe v. Columbia Axle Co., 233 Mo.App. 212, 117 S.W.2d 624 (1938).

That general rule, however, is subject to an important limitation which was expressed in *Beebe*, supra, in the following language (117 S.W.2d at 629): "The limitation is that, in any case of an indefinite agency where it is revoked by the principal, if it appears that the agent, induced by his appointment, has in good faith incurred expense and devoted time and labor in the matter of the agency without having had a sufficient opportunity to recoup such from the undertaking, the principal will be required to compensate him in that behalf; for the law will not permit one thus to deprive another of value without awarding just compensation. The just principle acted upon by the courts in the circumstances suggested requires no more than that, in every instance, the agent shall be afforded a reasonable opportunity to avail himself of the primary expenditures and efforts put forth to the end of executing the authority conferred upon him and that, if such opportunity is denied him, the principal shall compensate him accordingly. (Citations omitted.)" In a case to which the limitation of the general rule is applicable, the agent is entitled to recoupment or to compensation on a quantum meruit basis rather than by way of ordinary damages for breach of contract.... Applying to this case the principles of Missouri law that have been mentioned, we hold that apart from any question of the statute of frauds, which was pleaded by the defendants, the agreement between plaintiff and Pappagallo was binding, at least quasi-contractually, on Pappagallo and later on U.S. Shoe for a reasonable time after plaintiff had opened its shop in May, 1965, to the end that plaintiff might have a reasonable opportunity to recover its initial investment and expenses. During that period of time Pappagallo and U.S. Shoe were required to supply goods to the plaintiff and to refrain from interfering with his exclusive distributorship in the St. Louis area.

However, we are convinced that reasonable men could not differ on the proposition that by late 1973 and early 1974 such a reasonable time or period had expired, and that U.S. Shoe and Pappagallo had the right to terminate their contractual relations with plaintiff entirely, which they did not do, or to cancel the exclusivity feature of plaintiff's distributorship, which they did do when they permitted SBF to open Shops for Pappagallo in its stores.

And, we are convinced that plaintiff suffered no legal wrong when U.S. Shoe and Pappagallo finally implemented a change in marketing policy which had evidently been in contemplation for some years.

It is true that plaintiff was not given any formal or written notice of what the defendants intended to do. However, it is evident that at least by late September, 1973 plaintiff had received actual notice of what was in the wind, and there is nothing to indicate that plaintiff sustained any loss or damage by the fact that it was not given formal notice. It will be remembered that the contract said nothing about termination and naturally there was no requirement of formal notice of cancellation....

[Reversed.]

NOTES

(1) *Agreements Without End.* Agreements that involve continuing performance but fail to provide for the period over which that performance is to take place have proved troublesome for courts. Here are two cases.

In 1881, Dr. J.J. Lawrence granted J.W. Lambert the exclusive commercial use of the secret formula for an antiseptic known as Listerine for which Lambert bound himself and his successors "to pay monthly to the said Dr. J.J. Lawrence his heirs, executors or assigns, the sum of twenty dollars for each and every gross of said Listerine hereafter sold by myself, my heirs, executors or assigns." There was no termination date. Although the amount of the royalties was later reduced, royalties rose to a million and a half dollars a year. Gradually the formula unavoidably became a matter of public knowledge, so that by the middle of the twentieth century the same antiseptic could be produced by anyone. Warner–Lambert sought a declaratory judgment that it was no longer required to pay royalties, but the court refused "gratuitously to rewrite the contract" and held that Warner–Lambert "is obligated to make the periodic payments called for

... as long as it continues to sell the preparation described ... as Listerine." Warner–Lambert Pharmaceutical v. John J. Reynolds, Inc., 178 F.Supp. 655 (S.D.N.Y.1959), aff'd, 280 F.2d 197 (2d Cir.1960). See also Lichnovsky v. Ziebart International Corp., 324 N.W.2d 732 (Mich.1982).

Tanner supplied promotional materials to radio stations, taking in part payment advertising air time, or "spots," that it then sold to advertisers. Its contracts with the stations provided that the spots were "valid until used." In William B. Tanner Co., Inc. v. Sparta–Tomah Broadcasting Co., Inc., 716 F.2d 1155 (7th Cir.1983), the court observed that similar contracts with such language had "turned out to be a significant boon to the legal profession," prompting "a raft of cases across the country where courts have struggled to discern exactly what was intended" by "words of somewhat astonishing imprecision." The court declined to follow decisions relied on by Tanner, holding that the words "valid until used" meant that the station's commitment was of "potentially infinite duration," noting that the reluctance of courts "to interpret contracts providing for some perpetual or unlimited contractual right unless the contract clearly states that that is the intention of the parties." It found that the contract was "incomplete with respect to the duration of the validity of the spots" and remanded the case for a determination of a "reasonable time" to limit validity.

(2) *A Dispute Over Discharge.* In 1924, the City of New York and two upstate communities made an agreement, designed to keep untreated sewage out of a reservoir of the city's water supply system, under which the city agreed to construct and maintain a sewage system and to extend the sewer lines when "necessitated by future growth and building constructions of the respective communities." The plant began operation in 1928. After almost fifty years, the demand exceeded the plant's capacity so that it would have to be enlarged or a new one built. When the city refused, an action was brought against it for injunctive and declaratory relief. The lower court ruled that, while the contract did not call for perpetual performance, the city was bound to construct additional facilities until the communities were legally obligated to maintain a sewage system. *Held:* Order modified. "We conclude that the city is presently obligated to maintain the existing plant but is not required to expand that plant or construct any new facilities to accommodate ... increased demands on the sewage system.... [I]t is reasonable to infer from the circumstances of the 1924 agreement that the parties intended the city to maintain the sewage disposal facility until such time as the city no longer needed or desired the water, the purity of which the plant was designed to insure. The city argues that it is no longer obligated to maintain the plant because State law now prohibits persons from discharging raw sewage.... However, the parties did not contemplate the passage of environmental control laws.... Thus, the city agreed to assume the obligation of assuring that its water supply remained unpolluted and it may not now avoid that obligation for reasons not contemplated by the parties when the agreement was executed, and not within the purview of their intent, expressed or implied.... [However the] city should not be required to extend the lines ... if to do so would overload the system and result in its inability to properly treat sewage." Haines v. City of New York, 364 N.E.2d 820 (N.Y.1977).

In its opinion, the court also mentioned that the "compelling policy reasons" that applied to employment contracts "do not obtain here." What are those reasons? See also In re Miller's Estate, 447 A.2d 549 (N.J.1982) (involving royalties from the Glenn Miller Orchestra).

Introductory Note to *Sheets*

For roughly a century, courts honored "Wood's rule" (see fn. a, p. 90 above) by showing a strong preference for termination at will in employment agreements. Courts resolutely ignored contrary indications such as description of the employment as "permanent" or "lifetime." Thus the statement that "so long as you do your job you can be here until you're a hundred" was held "insufficient as a matter of law" to vary the at-will rule.[a]

In the mid–1970's, however, a revolution began with decisions that qualified the employer's power to terminate under employment agreements.[b] Since then, there has been a remarkable outpouring of cases and commentary. There is general agreement that a plainly opportunistic discharge is actionable. Thus, if an employee is discharged without good cause "the obligation of good faith and fair dealing imposed on an employer requires that the employer be liable for the loss in compensation that is ... clearly related to an employee's past service," such as commissions earned by that service.[c] Many courts have gone beyond this and fashioned a public policy exception. The case that follows is one of these. See generally 2 Farnsworth § 7.17.

SHEETS v. TEDDY'S FROSTED FOODS

Supreme Court of Connecticut, 1980.
179 Conn. 471, 427 A.2d 385.

PETERS, ASSOCIATE JUSTICE.[d] The issue in this case is whether an employer has a completely unlimited right to terminate the services of an employee whom it has hired for an indefinite term. The plaintiff, Emard H. Sheets, filed a complaint that as amended alleged that he had been wrongfully discharged from his employment as quality control director and operations manager of the defendant, Teddy's Frosted Foods, Inc. The defendant responded with a motion to strike the complaint as legally sufficient. The plaintiff declined to plead further when that motion was granted. From the consequent rendering of judgment for the defendant, the plaintiff has appealed to this court.

... The complaint alleges that for a four-year period, from November 1973 to November 1977, the plaintiff was employed by the defendant, a producer of frozen food products, as its quality control director

a. Mursch v. Van Dorn Co., 851 F.2d 990, 996 (7th Cir.1988).

b. The seminal case was Monge v. Beebe Rubber Co., 316 A.2d 549 (N.H. 1974), involving a worker fired because she resisted her foreman's sexual advances.

c. Gram v. Liberty Mut. Ins. Co., 429 N.E.2d 21, 29 (Mass.1981).

d. Peters. Ellen Ash Peters (1930–___) was a member of the faculty of the Yale Law School for over two decades, teaching and writing in the fields of contracts and commercial law and serving as an Adviser for the Restatement Second of Contracts. In 1978 she was appointed an associate justice of the Connecticut Supreme Court, becoming Chief Justice in 1984. For discussion of her decisions involving the Uniform Commercial Code, 21 Conn.L.Rev. 753 (1989).

and subsequently also as operations manager. In the course of his employment, the plaintiff received periodic raises and bonuses. In his capacity as quality control director and operations manager, the plaintiff began to notice deviations from the specifications contained in the defendant's standards and labels, in that some vegetables were substandard and some meat components underweight. These deviations meant that the defendant's products violated the express representations contained in the defendant's labeling; false or misleading labels in turn violate the provisions of General Statutes § 19–222,[1] the Connecticut Uniform Food, Drug and Cosmetic Act. In May of 1977, the plaintiff communicated in writing to the defendant concerning the use of substandard raw materials and underweight components in the defendant's finished products. His recommendations for more selective purchasing and conforming components were ignored. On November 3, 1977, his employment with the defendant was terminated. Although the stated reason for his discharge was unsatisfactory performance of his duties, he was actually dismissed in retaliation for his efforts to ensure that the defendant's products would comply with the applicable law relating to labeling and licensing.

The plaintiff's complaint alleges that his dismissal by his employer was wrongful in three respects. He claims that there was a violation of an implied contract of employment, a violation of public policy, and a malicious discharge. On this appeal, the claim of malice has not been separately pursued, and we are asked to consider only whether he has stated a cause of action for breach of contract or for intentionally tortious conduct. On oral argument, it was the tort claim that was most vigorously pressed, and it is upon the basis of tort that we have concluded that the motion to strike was granted in error.

The issue before us is whether to recognize an exception to the traditional rules governing employment at will so as to permit a cause of action for wrongful discharge where the discharge contravenes a clear mandate of public policy. In addressing that claim, we must clarify what is not at stake in this litigation. The plaintiff does not challenge the general proposition that contracts of permanent employment, or for an indefinite term, are terminable at will.... Nor does he argue that contracts terminable at will permit termination only upon a showing of just cause for dismissal. Some statutes, such as the Connecticut Franchise Act, General Statutes § 42–133e through 42–133h, do impose limitations of just cause upon the power to terminate some contracts; see § 42–133f; but the legislature has recently refused to interpolate such a requirement into contracts of employment. See H.B. No. 5179, 1974 Sess.[2] There is a significant distinction between a criterion of just cause and what the plaintiff is seeking. "Just cause" substantially limits employer discretion to terminate, by requiring the employer, in all

---

1. Section 19–222 provides in relevant part: "MISBRANDED FOOD. A food shall be deemed to be misbranded: (a) If its labeling is false or misleading in any particular."

2. Some statutes of course expressly forbid retaliatory discharge. See, e.g., Public Acts 1979, No. 79–599, and 29 U.S.C. § 660(c)(1) (1976)....

instances, to proffer a proper reason for dismissal, by forbidding the employer to act arbitrarily or capriciously.... By contrast, the plaintiff asks only that the employer be responsible in damages if the former employee can prove a demonstrably *improper* reason for dismissal, a reason whose impropriety is derived from some important violation of public policy.

The argument that contract rights which are inherently legitimate may yet give rise to liability in tort if they are exercised improperly is not a novel one. Although private persons have the right not to enter into contracts, failure to contract under circumstances in which others are seriously misled gives rise to a variety of claims sounding in tort. See Kessler & Fine, "Culpa in Contrahendo," 77 Harv.L.Rev. 401 (1964). The development of liability in contract for action induced by reliance upon a promise, despite the absence of common-law consideration normally required to bind a promisor; see Restatement (Second), Contracts § 90 (1973); rests upon principles derived at least in part from the law of tort. See Gilmore, The Death of Contract 8–90 (1974). By way of analogy, we have long recognized abuse of process as a cause of action in tort whose gravamen is the misuse or misapplication of process, its use "in an improper manner or to accomplish a purpose for which it was not designed." Varga v. Pareles, 137 Conn. 663, 667, 81 A.2d 112, 115 (1951); Schaefer v. O.K. Tool Co., 110 Conn. 528, 532–33, 148 A. 330 (1930); Restatement (Second), Torts § 682 (1977); Wright & Fitzgerald, Connecticut Law of Torts § 163 (1968); Prosser, Torts § 121 (1971).

It would be difficult to maintain that the right to discharge an employee hired at will is so fundamentally different from other contract rights that its exercise is never subject to judicial scrutiny regardless of how outrageous, how violative of public policy, the employer's conduct may be. Cf. General Statutes § 31–126 (unfair employment practices). The defendant does not seriously contest the propriety of cases in other jurisdictions that have found wrongful and actionable a discharge in retaliation for the exercise of an employee's right to: (1) refuse to commit perjury; ... (2) file a workmen's compensation claim; ... (3) engage in union activity; ... (4) perform jury duty.... While it may be true that these cases are supported by mandates of public policy derived directly from the applicable state statutes and constitutions, it is equally true that they serve at a minimum to establish the principle that public policy imposes some limits on unbridled discretion to terminate the employment of someone hired at will.... No case has been called to our attention in which, despite egregiously outrageous circumstances, the employer's contract rights have been permitted to override competing claims of public policy, although there are numerous cases in which the facts were found not to support the employee's claim....

The issue then becomes the familiar common-law problem of deciding where and how to draw the line between claims that genuinely involve the mandates of public policy and are actionable, and ordinary disputes between employee and employer that are not. We are mindful that courts should not lightly intervene to impair the exercise of managerial discretion or to foment unwarranted litigation. We are, however, equally mindful that the myriad of employees without the bargaining power to command employment contracts for a definite term are entitled to a modicum of judicial protection when their conduct as good citizens is punished by their employers.

The central allegation of the plaintiff's complaint is that he was discharged because of his conduct in calling to his employer's attention repeated violations of the Connecticut Uniform Food, Drug and Cosmetic Act. This act prohibits the sale of mislabeled food. General Statutes §§ 19–213, 19–222. The act, in § 19–215, imposes criminal penalties upon anyone who violates § 19–213; subsection (b) of § 19–215 makes it clear that criminal sanctions do not depend upon proof of intent to defraud or mislead, since special sanctions are imposed for intentional misconduct. The plaintiff's position as quality control director and operations manager might have exposed him to the possibility of criminal prosecution under this act. The act was intended to "safeguard the public health and promote the public welfare by protecting the consuming public from injury by product use and the purchasing public from injury by merchandising deceit...." General Statutes § 19–211.

It is useful to compare the factual allegations of this complaint with those of other recent cases in which recovery was sought for retaliatory discharge. In Geary v. United States Steel Corporation, [456 Pa. 171, 319 A.2d 174 (1974)], in which the plaintiff had disputed the safety of tubular steel casings, he was denied recovery because, as a company salesman, he had neither the expertise nor the corporate responsibility to "exercise independent, expert judgment in matters of product safety." Id., 319 A.2d 178. By contrast, this plaintiff, unless his title is meaningless, did have responsibility for product quality control. Three other recent cases in which the plaintiff's claim survived demurrer closely approximate the claim before us....

In the light of these recent cases, which evidence a growing judicial receptivity to the recognition of a tort claim for wrongful discharge, the trial court was in error in granting the defendant's motion to strike. The plaintiff alleged that he had been dismissed in retaliation for his insistence that the defendant comply with the requirements of a state statute, the Food, Drug and Cosmetic Act. We need not decide whether violation of a state statute is invariably a prerequisite to the conclusion that a challenged discharge violates public policy. Certainly when there is a relevant state statute we should not ignore the statement of public policy that it represents. For today, it is enough to decide that an employee should not be put to an election whether to risk criminal sanction or to jeopardize his continued employment.

There is error and the case is remanded for further proceedings.

In this opinion BOGDANSKI and HEALEY, JJ., concurred.

COTTER, CHIEF JUSTICE (dissenting). I cannot agree that, on the factual situation presented to us, we should abandon the well-established principle that an indefinite general hiring may be terminated at the will of either party without liability to the other.... The majority by seeking to extend a "modicum" of judicial protection to shield employees from retaliatory discharges instead offers them a sword with which to coerce employers to retain them in their employ. In recognizing an exception to the traditional rules governing employment at will and basing a new cause of action for retaliatory discharge on the facts of this case, the majority is necessarily led to the creation of an overly broad new cause of action whose nuisance value alone may impair employers' ability to hire and retain employees who are best suited to their requirements. Other jurisdictions which have recognized a cause of action for retaliatory discharge have done so on the basis of a much clearer and more direct contravention of a mandate of public policy.

. . . [T]he purposes of the statute the majority would rely on, . . . can only be considered as, at most, marginally affected by an allegedly retaliatory discharge of an employee who observed the supposed sale of shortweight frozen entrees and the use of U.S. Government Certified "Grade B" rather than "Grade A" vegetables. A retaliatory discharge in the present case would not necessarily thwart or inhibit the Connecticut Uniform Food, Drug and Cosmetic Act's purpose of protecting the consumer. The plaintiff, if he desired to protect the consumer, could have communicated, even anonymously, to the commissioner of consumer affairs his concerns that his employer was violating the Food, Drug and Cosmetic Act so as to invoke the statute's enforcement mechanisms. See General Statutes §§ 19–214 through 19–217. To further and comply with the public policy expressed in Connecticut's Uniform Food, Drug and Cosmetic Act and to avoid the exceedingly remote possibility of criminal sanctions, the plaintiff need not have jeopardized his continued employment. There is no indication that the plaintiff has either, before or after his discharge, informed or even attempted to inform the commissioner of consumer protection of violations the plaintiff claims to have first noted in his fourth year as the defendant's quality control director and fourth month as its operations manager. Unlike those cases where an employer allegedly discharged employees for engaging in union activities or filing workmen's compensation claims and the discharge itself contravened a statutory mandate, in the present case the discharge itself at most only indirectly impinged on the statutory mandate.

Consequently, the majority seemingly invites the unrestricted use of an allegation of almost any statutory or even regulatory violation by an employer as the basis for a cause of action by a discharged employee hired for an indefinite term. By establishing a cause of action, grounded upon "intentionally tortious conduct," for retaliatory discharges which do not necessarily in and of themselves directly contravene statutory mandates, the majority is creating an open-ended arena for judicial policy making and the usurpation of legislative functions. To base this new cause of action on a decision as to whether an alleged reason for discharge "is derived from some important violation of public policy" is not to create adequate and carefully circumscribed standards for this new cause of action but is to invite the opening of a Pandora's box of unwarranted litigation arising from the hope that the judicial estimate of derivation, importance, and public policy matches that of the plaintiff. . . .

Finally, it should be reiterated that the minority of jurisdictions which have created a cause of action for retaliatory discharges have done so with caution and when the employee termination contravenes a clear mandate of public policy. It is because the majority abandons that caution and for the reason that the factual situation before us does not demonstrate a "wrongful discharge where the discharge contravenes a clear mandate of public policy" that I feel compelled to dissent.

In this opinion LOISELLE, J., concurred.

NOTES

(1) *Discharge for Cause.* Courts have been reluctant to hold that an employer is under a duty of good faith performance that allows discharge only for good cause. They "have generally rejected the invitation" to imply such a limitation, "voicing the concern that to do so would place undue restrictions on management and would infringe the employer's 'legitimate exercise of management discretion.'" Wagenseller v. Scottsdale Memorial Hospital, 710 P.2d 1025, 1039 (Ariz.1985). For an argument "that courts are reacting wisely to the issues litigants present to them" in employment termination cases, see Schwab, Life–Cycle Justice: Accommodating Just Cause and Employment at Will, 92 Mich. L.Rev. 8, 61 (1993).

(2) *Economic Effects.* A study of the economic effects of increased employer liability, both by judicial modification of the at-will doctrine and by employer undertakings in handbooks and the like, reached some startling conclusions. It estimated "that the indirect effects of wrongful-termination doctrines are 100 times more costly than the direct legal costs of jury awards, settlements, and attorney fees" and "that, after states adopt the most liberal tort versions of the covenant of good faith and fair dealing and the broad public policy exceptions to employment at will ... [a]ggregate employment drops by 2 to 5 percent." J. Dertouzos & L. Karoby, Labor–Market Responses to Employer Liability xiii, 62 (1991). If you were Justice Peters, would evidence to that effect cause you to reach a different decision?

Consider, in this connection, the arguments of Judge Easterbrook, in dissent, for the importance of giving employers the ability to decide who shall work for them. "It is easy for a jury to mistake a pest, a busybody, for a champion of the law. Firms need to prune their work forces of persons who create more trouble than they are worth; time diverted from business means lower efficiency and higher prices for consumers, undermining still another public policy. Employers fearing litigation—with high legal fees and the risk of punitive damages—will keep troublesome and inefficient employees on the payroll. Everyone loses when that happens." Belline v. K–Mart Corp., 940 F.2d 184, 191 (7th Cir.1991).

Introductory Note to *Nanakuli*

UCC 1–205(3) provides that a course of dealing or a usage of trade may not only "give particular meaning to ... terms of an agreement," but may also "supplement or qualify" those terms. In the *Frigaliment* (p. 585) and *Hurst* (p. 609) cases, we saw how usage could give meaning to contract language. The two following cases are concerned with how usage and course of dealing may supplement or qualify contract language.

NANAKULI PAVING & ROCK CO. v. SHELL OIL CO.
United States Court of Appeals, Ninth Circuit, 1981.
664 F.2d 772.

HOFFMAN, DISTRICT JUDGE. . . . Nanakuli, the second largest asphaltic paving contractor in Hawaii, had bought all its asphalt requirements from 1963 to 1974 from Shell under two long-term supply contracts; its suit charged Shell with breach of the later 1969 contract. The jury returned a verdict of $220,800 for Nanakuli on its first claim, which is that Shell breached the 1969 contract in January, 1974, by failing to price protect Nanakuli on 7200 tons of asphalt at the time Shell raised the price for asphalt from $44 to $76. Nanakuli's theory is that price-protection, as a usage of the asphaltic paving trade in Hawaii, was incorporated into the 1969 agreement between the parties, as demonstrated by the routine use of price protection by suppliers to that trade, and reinforced by the way in which Shell actually performed the 1969 contract up until 1974. Price protection, appellant claims, required that Shell hold the price on the tonnage Nanakuli had already committed because Nanakuli had incorporated that price into bids put out to or contracts awarded by general contractors and government agencies. The District Judge set aside the verdict and granted Shell's motion for judgment n.o.v., which decision we vacate. We reinstate the jury verdict because we find that, viewing the evidence as a whole, there was substantial evidence to support a finding by reasonable jurors that Shell breached its contract by failing to provide protection for Nanakuli in 1974. Quichocho v. Kelvinator Corp., 546 F.2d 812, 813 (9th Cir.1976). We do not believe the evidence in this case was such that, giving Nanakuli the benefit of all inferences fairly supported by the evidence and without weighing the credibility of the witnesses, only one reasonable conclusion could have been reached by the jury. Cockrum v. Whitney, 479 F.2d 84, 85–86 (9th Cir.1973).

Nanakuli offers two theories for why Shell's failure to offer price protection in 1974 was a breach of the 1969 contract. First, it argues, all material suppliers to the asphaltic paving trade in Hawaii followed the trade usage of price protection and thus it should be assumed, under the U.C.C., that the parties intended to incorporate price protection into their 1969 agreement. This is so, Nanakuli continues, even though the written contract provided for price to be "Shell's Posted Price at time of delivery," F.O.B. Honolulu. . . . The U.C.C. looks to the actual performance of a contract as the best indication of what the parties intended those terms to mean. Nanakuli points out that Shell had price protected it on the two occasions of price increases under the 1969 contract other than the 1974 increase. In 1970 and 1971 Shell extended the old price for four and three months, respectively, after an announced increase. . . .[1]

Nanakuli's second theory for price protection is that Shell was obliged to price protect Nanakuli, even if price protection was not incorporated into their contract, because price protection was the commercially reasonable standard for fair dealing in the asphaltic paving trade in Hawaii in 1974. . . .

Shell presents three arguments for upholding the judgment n.o.v. or, on cross appeal, urging that the District Judge erred in admitting certain evidence. First, it says, the District Court should not have denied Shell's motion *in limine* to define trade, for purposes of trade usage evidence, as the sale and purchase of asphalt in Hawaii, rather than expanding the definition of trade to include other suppliers of materials to the asphaltic paving trade. Asphalt, its argument runs, was the subject matter of the disputed contract and the only product Shell supplied to the asphaltic paving trade. Shell protests that the judge, by expanding the definition of trade to include the other major suppliers to the asphaltic paving trade, allowed the admission of highly prejudicial evidence of routine price protection by all suppliers of aggregate. Asphaltic concrete paving is formed by mixing paving asphalt with crushed rock, or aggregate, in a "hot-mix" plant and then pouring the mixture onto the surface to be paved. Shell's second complaint is that the two prior occasions on which it price protected Nanakuli, although representing the only other instances of price increases under the 1969 contract, constituted mere waivers of the contract's price term, not a course of performance of the contract. A course of performance of the contract, in contrast to a waiver, demonstrates how the parties understand the terms of their agreement. . . . Shell's final argument is that, even assuming its prior price protection constituted a course of performance and that the broad trade definition was correct and evidence of trade usages by aggregate suppliers was admissible, price protection could not be construed as reasonably consistent with the express price term in the contract, in which case the Code provides that the express term controls.

We hold that the judge did not abuse his discretion in defining the applicable trade, for purposes of trade usages, as the asphaltic paving trade in Hawaii, rather than the purchase and sale of asphalt alone. . . . Additionally, we hold that, under the facts of this case, a jury could reasonably have found that Shell's acts on two occasions to price protect Nanakuli were not ambiguous and therefore indicated Shell's understanding of the terms of the agreement with Nanakuli rather than being a waiver by Shell of those terms.

Lastly we hold that, although the express price terms of Shell's posted price of delivery may seem, at first glance, inconsistent with a trade usage of price protection at time of increases in price, a closer

---

1. Price protection was practiced in the asphaltic paving trade by either extending the old price for a period of time after a new one went into effect or charging the old price for a specified tonnage, which represented work committed at the old price. In addition, several months' advance notice was given of price increases.

reading shows that the jury could have reasonably construed price protection as consistent with the express term....

Trade Usage Before and After 1969

The key to price protection being so prevalent in 1969 that both parties would intend to incorporate it into their contract is found in one reality of the Oahu asphaltic paving market: the largest paving contracts were let by government agencies and none of the three levels of government—local, state, or federal—allowed escalation clauses for paving materials. If a paver bid at one price and another went into effect before the award was made, the paving company would lose a great deal of money, since it could not pass on increases to any government agency or to most general contractors. Extensive evidence was presented that, as a consequence, aggregate suppliers routinely price protected paving contractors in the 1960's and 1970's, as did the largest asphaltic supplier in Oahu, Chevron. Nanakuli presented documentary evidence of routine price protection by aggregate suppliers as well as two witnesses.... Both testified that price protection to their knowledge had always been practiced.... Such protection consisted of advance notices of increases, coupled with charging the old price for work committed at that price or for enough time to order the tonnage committed. The smallness of the Oahu market led to complete trust among suppliers and pavers.... None of the aggregate companies had a contract with Nanakuli expressly stating price protection would be given....

Shell's Course Of Performance Of The 1969 Contract

The Code considers actual performance of a contract as the most relevant evidence of how the parties interpreted the terms of that contract. In 1970 and 1971, the only points at which Shell raised prices between 1969 and 1974, it price protected Nanakuli by holding its old price for four and three months, respectively, after announcing a price increase....

Scope Of Trade Usage

The validity of the jury verdict in this case depends on four legal questions. First, how broad was the trade to whose usages Shell was bound under its 1969 agreement with Nanakuli: did it extend to the Hawaiian asphaltic paving trade or was it limited merely to the purchase and sale of asphalt, which would only include evidence of practices by Shell and Chevron? Second, were the two instances of price protection of Nanakuli by Shell in 1970 and 1971 waivers of the 1969 contract as a matter of law or was the jury entitled to find that they constituted a course of performance of the contract? Third, could the jury have construed an express contract term of Shell's posted price at delivery as reasonably consistent with a trade usage and Shell's course of performance of the 1969 contract of price protection, which consisted of charging the old price at times of price increases, either for a period of time or for specific tonnage committed at a fixed price in non-escalating contracts? Fourth, could the jury have found that good faith obliged

Shell to at least give advance notice of a $32 increase in 1974, that is, could they have found that the commercially reasonable standards of fair dealing in the trade in Hawaii in 1974 were to give some form of price protection? ...

The Code defines usage of trade as "any practice or method of dealing having such regularity of observance in a *place, vocation or trade* as to justify an expectation that it will be observed with respect to the transaction in question." Id. § 490:1–205(2) (emphasis supplied)....
[A] usage need not necessarily be one practiced by members of the party's own trade or vocation to be binding *if* it is so commonly practiced in a locality that a party should be aware of it.... A party is always held to conduct generally observed by members of his chosen trade because the other party is justified in so assuming unless he indicates otherwise. He is held to more general business practices to the extent of his actual knowledge of those practices or to the degree his ignorance of those practices is not excusable: they were so generally practiced he should have been aware of them.

No U.C.C. cases have been found on this point, but the court's reading of the Code language is similar to that of two of the best-known commentators on the U.C.C.:

> Under pre-Code law, a trade usage was not operative against a party who *was not a member of the trade unless* he actually knew of it or *the other party could reasonably believe he knew of it.*

J. White & R. Summers, Uniform Commercial Code, § 12–6 at 371 (1972) (emphasis supplied).... White and Summers add (emphasis supplied):

> This view has been carried forward by 1–205(3).... [U]sage of the trade is only binding on *members of the trade* involved *or persons* who know or *should know about it.* Persons who should be aware of the trade usage doubtless *include those who regularly deal with members of the relevant trade,* and also members of a second trade that commonly deals with members of a relevant trade (for example, farmers should know something of seed selling).

White & Summers, supra, § 12–6 at 371. Using that analogy, even if Shell did not "regularly deal" with aggregate supplies, it did deal constantly and almost exclusively on Oahu with one asphalt paver. It therefore should have been aware of the usage of Nanakuli and other asphaltic pavers to bid at fixed prices and therefore receive price protection from their materials suppliers due to the refusal by government agencies to accept escalation clauses. Therefore, we do not find the lower court abused its discretion or misread the Code as applied to the peculiar facts of this case in ruling that the applicable trade was the asphaltic paving trade in Hawaii. An asphalt seller should be held to the usages of trade in general as well as those of asphalt sellers and common usages of those to whom they sell. Certainly, under the unusual facts of this case it was not unreasonable for the judge to extend trade usages to include practices of other material suppliers toward Shell's primary and perhaps only customer on Oahu. He did exclude, on Shell's motion *in limine,* evidence of cement suppliers. He only held Shell to routine practices in Hawaii by the suppliers of the two major ingredients of asphaltic paving, that is, asphalt and aggregate. Those usages were only practiced towards two major pavers. It was not unreasonable to expect Shell to be knowledgeable about so small a market. In so ruling, the judge undoubtedly took into account Shell's half-million dollar investment in Oahu strictly because of a long-term commitment by Nanakuli, its actions as partner in promoting Nanakuli's expansion on Oahu, and the fact that its sales on Oahu were almost exclusively to Nanakuli for use in asphaltic paving. The wisdom of the pre-trial ruling was demonstrated by evidence at trial that Shell's agent in Hawaii stayed in close contact with Nanakuli and was knowledgeable about both the asphaltic paving market in general and Nanakuli's bidding procedures and economics in particular.

Shell argued not only that the definition of trade was too broad, but also that the practice itself was not sufficiently regular to reach the level of a usage and that Nanakuli failed to show with enough precision how the usage was carried out in order for a jury to calculate damages. The extent of a usage is ultimately a jury question. The Code provides, "The existence and scope of such a usage are to be proved as facts." Haw. Rev.Stat. § 490:1–205(2). The practice must have "such regularity of observance ... as to justify an expectation that it will be observed...." Id. The Comment explains:

> The ancient English tests for "custom" are abandoned in this connection. Therefore, it is not required that a usage of trade be "ancient or immemorial," "universal" or the like.... [F]ull recognition is thus available for new usages and for usages currently observed by the great majority of decent dealers, even though dissidents ready to cut corners do not agree.

Id., Comment 5. The Comment's demand that "not universality but only the described 'regularity of observance' " is required reinforces the provision only giving "effect to usages of which the parties 'are or should be aware'...." Id., Comment 7. A "regularly observed" practice of protection, of which Shell "should have been aware," was enough to constitute a usage that Nanakuli had reason to believe was incorporated into the agreement.

Nanakuli went beyond proof of a regular observance. It proved and offered to prove that price protection was probably a universal practice by suppliers to the asphaltic paving trade in 1969.... Shell did not point in rebuttal to one instance of failure to price protect by any supplier to an asphalt paver in Hawaii before its own 1974 refusal to price protect Nanakuli. Thus, there clearly was enough proof for a jury to find that the practice of price protection in the asphaltic paving trade existed in Hawaii in 1969 and was regular enough in its observance to rise to the level of a usage that would be binding on Nanakuli and Shell....

Waiver or Course of Performance

Course of performance under the Code is the action of the parties in carrying out the contract at issue, whereas course of dealing consists of relations between the parties prior to signing that contract. Evidence of the latter was excluded by the District Judge; evidence of the former consisted of Shell's price protection of Nanakuli in 1970 and 1971. Shell protested that the jury could not have found that those two instances of price protection amounted to a course of performance of its 1969 contract, relying on two Code comments. First, one instance does not constitute a course of performance. "A single occasion of conduct does not fall within the language of this section...." Haw.Rev.Stat. § 490:2–208, Comment 4. Although the Comment rules out one instance, it does not further delineate how many acts are needed to form a course of performance. The prior occasions here were only two, but they constituted the only occasions before 1974 that would call for such conduct. In addition, the language used by a top asphalt official of Shell in connection with the first price protection of Nanakuli indicated that Shell felt that Nanakuli was entitled to some form of price protection. On that occasion in 1970 Blee, who had negotiated the contract with Nanakuli and was familiar with exactly what terms Shell was bound to by that agreement, wrote of the need to "bargain" with Nanakuli over the extent of price protection to be given, indicating that some price protection was a legal right of Nanakuli's under the 1969 agreement.

Shell's second defense is that the Comment expresses a preference for an interpretation of waiver.

> 3. Where it is difficult to determine whether a particular act merely sheds light on the meaning of the agreement or represents a waiver of a term of the agreement, the preference is in favor of "waiver" whenever such construction, plus the application of the provisions on the reinstatement of rights waived ..., is needed to preserve the flexible character of commercial contracts and to prevent surprise or other hardship.

Id., Comment 3. The preference for waiver only applies, however, where acts are ambiguous. It was within the province of the jury to determine whether those acts were ambiguous, and if not, whether they constituted waivers or a course of performance of the contract. The jury's interpretation of those acts as a course of performance was bolstered by evidence offered by Shell that it again price protected Nanakuli on the only two occasions of post–1974 price increases, in 1977 and 1978.

Express Terms as Reasonably Consistent With Usage in Course of Performance

Perhaps one of the most fundamental departures of the Code from prior contract law is found in the parol evidence rule and the definition of an agreement between two parties. Under the U.C.C., an agreement goes beyond the written words on a piece of paper. " 'Agreement' means the bargain of the parties in fact as found in their language or by implication from other circumstances including course of dealing or usage of trade or course of performance as provided in this chapter (sections 490:1–205 and 490:2–208)." Id. § 490:1–201(3). Express terms, then, do not constitute the entire agreement, which must be sought also in evidence of usages, dealings, and performance of the contract itself.... Course of dealings is more important than usages of the trade, being specific usages between the two parties to the contract. "[C]ourse of dealing controls usage of trade." Id. § 490:1–205(4)....

A commercial agreement, then, is broader than the written paper and its meaning is to be determined not just by the language used by them in the written contract but "by their action; read and interpreted in the light of commercial practices and other surrounding circumstances. The measure and background for interpretation are set by the commercial context, which may explain and supplement even the language of a formal or final writing." Id., Comment 1. Performance, usages, and prior dealings are important enough to be admitted always, even for a final and complete agreement; only if they cannot be reasonably reconciled with the express terms of the contract are they not binding on the parties. "The express terms of an agreement and an applicable course of dealing or usage of trade shall be construed wherever reasonable as consistent with each other; but when such construction is unreasonable express terms control both course of dealing and usage of trade and course of dealing controls usage of trade." Id. § 490:1–205(4)....

Our study of the Code provisions and Comments, then, form the first basis of our holding that a trade usage to price protect pavers at times of price increases for work committed on nonescalating contracts could reasonably be construed as consistent with an express term of seller's posted price at delivery. Since the agreement of the parties is broader than the express terms and includes usages, which may even add terms to the agreement, and since the commercial background provided by those usages is vital to an understanding of the agreement, we follow the Code's mandate to proceed on the assumption that the parties have included those usages unless they cannot reasonably be construed as consistent with the express terms....

Some guidelines can be offered as to how usage evidence can be allowed to modify a contract. First, the court must allow a check on usage evidence by demanding that it be sufficiently definite and widespread to prevent unilateral post-hoc revision of contract terms by one party. The Code's intent is to put usage evidence on an objective basis....

Although the Code abandoned the traditional common law test of nonconsensual custom and views usage as a way of determining the parties' probable intent, ... thus abolishing the requirement that common law custom be universally practiced, trade usages still must be well settled.... Here the evidence was overwhelming that all suppliers to the asphaltic paving trade price protected customers under the same types of circumstances. Chevron's contract with H.B. was a similar long-term supply contract between a buyer and seller with very close relations, on a form supplied by the seller, covering sales of asphalt, and setting the price at seller's posted price, with no mention of price protection....

[In addition, here] the express price term was "Shell's Posted Price at time of delivery." A total negation of that term would be that the buyer was to set the price. It is a less than complete negation of the term that an unstated exception exists at times of price increases, at which times the old price is to be charged, for a certain period or for a specified tonnage, on work already committed at the lower price on nonescalating contracts. Such a usage forms a broad and important exception to the express term, but does not swallow it entirely. Therefore, we hold that, under these particular facts, a reasonable jury could have found that price protection was incorporated into the 1969 agreement between Nanakuli and Shell and that price protection was reasonably consistent with the express term of seller's posted price at delivery.

Good Faith in Setting Price

Nanakuli offers an alternative theory why Shell should have offered price protection at the time of the price increases of 1974. Even if price protection was not a term of the agreement, Shell could not have exercised good faith in carrying out its 1969 contract with Nanakuli when it raised its price by $32 effective January 1 in a letter written December 31st and only received on January 4, given the universal practice of advance notice of such an increase in the asphaltic paving trade. The Code provides, "A price to be fixed by the seller or by the buyer means a price for him to fix in good faith," Haw.Rev.Stat. § 490:2–305(2). For a merchant good faith means "the observance of reasonable commercial standards of fair dealing in the trade." Id. 490:2–103(1)(b). The comment to Section 2–305 explains, "[I]n the normal case a 'posted price' ... satisfies the good faith requirement." Id., Comment 3. However, the words "in the normal case" mean that, although a posted price will usually be satisfactory, it will not be so under all circumstances. In addition, the dispute here was not over the amount of the increase—that is, the price that the seller fixed—but over the manner in which that increase was put into effect. It is true that Shell, in order to observe the good faith standards of the trade in 1974, was not bound by the practices of aggregate companies, which did not labor under the same disabilities as did asphalt suppliers in 1974. However, Nanakuli presented evidence that Chevron, in raising its price to $76, gave at least six weeks' advance notice, in accord with the long-time usage of the asphaltic paving trade. Shell, on the other hand, gave absolutely no notice, from which the jury could have concluded that Shell's manner of carrying out the price increase of 1974 did not conform to commercially reasonable standards. In both the timing of the announcement and its refusal to protect work already bid at the old price, Shell could be found to have breached the obligation of good faith imposed by the Code on all merchants. "Every contract or duty within this chapter imposes an obligation of good faith in its performance or enforcement," id. § 490:1–203, which for merchants entails the observance of commercially reasonable standards of fair dealing in the trade. The Comment to 1–203 reads:

> This section sets forth a basic principle running throughout this Act. The principle involved is that in commercial transactions good faith is required in the performance and enforcement of all agreements or duties. Particular applications of this general principle appear in specific provisions of the Act.... It is further implemented by Section 1–205 on course of dealing and usage of trade.

Id. § 490:1–203, Comment. Chevron's conduct in 1974 offered enough relevant evidence of commercially reasonable standards of fair dealing in the asphalt trade in Hawaii in 1974 for the jury to find that Shell's failure to give sufficient advance notice and price protect Nanakuli after the imposition of the new price did not conform to good faith dealings in Hawaii at that time.

Because the jury could have found for Nanakuli on its price protection claim under either theory, we reverse the judgment of the District Court and reinstate the jury verdict for Nanakuli in the amount of $220,800, plus interest according to law.

KENNEDY, CIRCUIT JUDGE, concurring specially: The case involves specific pricing practices, not an allegation of unfair dealing generally. Our opinion should not be interpreted to permit juries to import price protection or a similarly specific contract term from a concept of good faith that is not based on well-established custom and usage or other objective standards of which the parties had clear notice. Here, evidence of custom and usage regarding price protection in the asphaltic paving trade was not contradicted in major respects, and the jury could find that the parties knew or should have known of the practice at the time of making the contract. In my view, these are necessary predicates for either theory of the case, namely, interpretation of the contract based on the course of its performance or a finding that good faith required the seller to hold the price. With these observations, I concur.

NOTES

(1) *Questions.* Is this a case in which usage is used, in the words of UCC 1–205(3) to "give particular meaning to ... terms of an agreement"? To "supplement" those terms? To "qualify" them? (If the purpose is interpretation, what language is being interpreted?)

Would the "reasonable commercial standards of fair dealing in the trade" under UCC 2–103(1)(b) be those of the time of the making of the contract, or those of the time of its performance? Would your answer be the same for a "usage of trade" under UCC 1–205?

In answer to Shell's objection to the trial court's admission of evidence of usage after 1969, the Court of Appeals, in an omitted footnote, said that it did "not need to decide whether usage evidence after a contract was signed is admissible to show that a party's reliance on a given usage was justifiable, given its continuation, because part of that evidence dealing with asphalt prices was admissible to show the reasonable commercial standards of fair dealing prevalent in the trade in 1974 and the part dealing with the continuation of price protection by aggregate suppliers, after 1969 was not so extensive as to be prejudicial to Shell."

(2) *Usage and Omitted Cases.* Look back at the *Drennan* case, p. 253 above. Could a general contractor use usage of trade to show that a subcontractor's bid, which was silent as to revocability, was irrevocable? What facts would be sufficient to establish such a usage? See Albert v. R.P. Farnsworth & Co., 176 F.2d 198 (5th Cir.1949); cf. Industrial Electric–Seattle v. Bosko, 410 P.2d 10 (Wash.1966).

(3) *The Case of the Cantor Who Wouldn't.* Fisher, an orthodox Jewish cantor, contracted in writing with an orthodox congregation to officiate as cantor. At that time the congregation observed the orthodox practice of separate seating of men and women. The contract, however, was silent as to the orthodox character of the congregation and its seating practices. Shortly thereafter, on the eve of moving into a new synagogue, the congregation determined to modify its practice of separate seating by setting aside the first four rows for men, the next four rows for women, and the remainder for mixed seating. When Fisher was informed of this, he refused to officiate because to do so would be a violation of his beliefs. When the congregation refused to change its decision, he sued for breach of contract. Three rabbis testified on his behalf that orthodox Judaism required the separation of the sexes in the synagogue and that an orthodox cantor could not conscientiously officiate in a synagogue that violated this law. From judgment for the plaintiff, the defendant appealed. *Held:* Affirmed. "[T]he ancient provision of the Hebrew law relating to separate seating is read into the contract only because implicit in the writing as to the basis—according to the evidence—upon which the parties dealt.... In our law the provision became a part of the written contract under a principle analogous to the rule applicable to the construction of contracts in the light of custom or immemorial and invariable usage." Fisher v. Congregation B'Nai Yitzhok, 110 A.2d 881 (Pa.Super.1955).[a]

(4) *The Case of the Cantor Who Couldn't.* Richard Tucker, the renowned opera singer and cantor, was engaged to conduct the 1964 Passover Seder at the Eden Roc Hotel in Miami Beach under a standard American Guild of Variety Artists form for the first Seder Service, with the typewritten provision: "If second Seder service to be held, same price as first night." He performed the first service but, although the second service had been advertised nationally and he had hired a choir and turned down other engagements, he was told by a waiter at the end of the first service and without further explanation that there would be no second service. He sued for breach of contract and was denied recovery for the second night. He appealed. *Held:* Affirmed. The court quoted "the Passover Haggadah itself—'Wherein is this night different from all other nights?' For purposes of our legal analysis, this may be paraphrased to be: Wherein is a contract for the performance of a Passover Seder different from all other contracts? ... Although Tucker testified that in the Orthodox Jewish religion two Sedarim are always held, the period of observance is, for us at least, a problematical one. Owing to the unsettled state of the Jewish calendar in olden times, Passover was celebrated for seven days in Palestine and eight days

a. In Congregation B'Nai Sholom v. Martin, 173 N.W.2d 504 (Mich.1969), the court held that persons who had signed pledge cards in connection with a fund-raising drive to build a new synagogue "should have been permitted to assert, as a defense, their claim as to the custom of their religion which requires disputes between the synagogue and its members over religious matters to be resolved according to Jewish law," including a prohibition on a law suit in a nonreligious court before resort is had to a religious court.

elsewhere. This meant that those outside of Palestine (now Israel) conducted two Sedarim, while those in Palestine conducted only one. The Reform Jews in America today have adopted the latter procedure and observe but one Seder. It appears that while Tucker may have been Orthodox in his observance, the Eden Roc had traditionally followed the Reform view and had only one Seder in each year prior to 1964. We cannot therefore treat the instant agreement as different from any other agreement, and must look to the common, every day principles of law to resolve the dispute." The court decided that the trial court had not erred in concluding that there was no legally binding contract for the second Seder. Tucker v. Forty–Five Twenty–Five, 199 So.2d 522 (Fla.App.1967).

COLUMBIA NITROGEN CORP. v. ROYSTER CO., 451 F.2d 3 (4th Cir.1971). [Royster manufactured and sold mixed fertilizers, the principal components of which are nitrogen, phosphate and potash. Columbia was primarily a producer of nitrogen, although it also manufactured some mixed fertilizer for several years. Royster had been a major buyer from Columbia, but Columbia had never been a significant buyer from Royster. In the fall of 1966, Royster built a phosphate production facility and, to dispose of what it did not need, negotiated a contract to sell to Columbia a minimum of 31,000 tons of phosphate a year for three years, with an option to extend. The contract stated the price per ton subject to an escalation clause dependent on production costs. It set the quantities under the heading "Products Supplied Under Contract Minimum Tonnage Per Year" and contained a merger clause.

When phosphate prices plunged precipitously, Columbia was unable to resell competitively and ordered less than one tenth of the scheduled tonnage during the first contract year. Royster sold the unaccepted phosphate below the contract price and sued for damages. Columbia sought to show by witnesses with long experience in the trade that because of uncertain crop and weather conditions, farming practices and government agricultural programs, express price and quantity terms in the mixed fertilizer industry are mere projections to be adjusted according to market forces. Columbia also sought to show that in its business dealings with Royster during the previous six years—mainly nitrogen sales to Royster—there was repeated and substantial deviation from stated amount or price. The district court excluded this evidence on the ground that "custom and usage or course of dealing are not admissible to contradict the express, plain, unambiguous language of a valid written contract, which by virtue of its detail negates the proposition that the contract is open to variances in its terms." From a $750,000 judgment for Royster, Columbia appealed on the ground that the proffered evidence was improperly excluded.]

BUTZNER, CIRCUIT JUDGE. . . . There can be no doubt that the Uniform Commercial Code restates the well established rule that evidence of usage of trade and course of dealing should be excluded whenever it cannot be reasonably construed as consistent with the terms of the contract. . . . Royster argues that the evidence should be excluded as inconsistent because the contract contains detailed provisions regarding the base price, escalation, minimum tonnage, and delivery schedules. The argument is based on the premise that because a contract appears on its face to be complete, evidence of course of dealing and usage of trade should be excluded. We believe, however, that neither the language nor the policy of the Code supports such a broad exclusionary rule. Section 8.2–202 expressly allows evidence of course of dealing or usage of trade to explain or supplement terms intended by the parties as a final expression of their agreement. When this section is read in light of Va.Code Ann. § 8.1–205(4), it is clear that the test of admissibility is not whether the contract appears on its face to be complete in every detail, but whether the proffered evidence of course of dealing and trade usage reasonably can be construed as consistent with the express terms of the agreement. . . .

For the following reasons it is reasonable to construe this evidence as consistent with the express terms of the contract:

The contract does not expressly state that course of dealing and usage of trade cannot be used to explain or supplement the written contract.

The contract is silent about adjusting prices and quantities to reflect a declining market. It neither permits nor prohibits adjustment, and this neutrality provides a fitting occasion for recourse to usage of trade and prior dealing to supplement the contract and explain its terms.

Minimum tonnages and additional quantities are expressed in terms of "Products Supplied Under Contract." Significantly, they are not expressed as just "Products" or as "Products Purchased Under Contract." The description used by the parties is consistent with the proffered testimony.

Finally, the default clause of the contract refers only to the failure of the buyer to pay for delivered phosphate.[a] During the contract negotiations, Columbia rejected a Royster proposal for liquidated damages of $10 for each ton Columbia declined to accept. On the other hand, Royster rejected a Columbia proposal for a clause that tied the price to the market by obligating Royster to conform its price to offers Columbia received from other phosphate producers. The parties, having rejected both proposals, failed to state any consequences of Columbia's refusal to take delivery—the kind of default Royster alleges in this case. Royster insists that we span this hiatus by applying the general law of contracts permitting recovery of damages upon the buyer's refusal to take delivery according to the written provisions of the contract. This solution is not what the Uniform Commercial Code prescribes. Before allowing damages, a court must first determine whether the buyer has in fact defaulted. It must do this by supplementing and explaining the agreement with evidence of trade usage and course of dealing that is consis-

---

a. "*Default*—If Buyer fails to pay for any delivery under this contract within 30 days after Seller's invoice to Buyer and then if such invoice is not paid within an additional 30 days after the Seller notifies the Buyer of such default, then after that time the Seller may at his option defer further deliveries hereunder or take such action as in their judgment they may decide including cancellation of this contract. Any balances carried beyond 30 days will carry a service fee of ¾ of 1% per month."

tent with the contract's express terms. Va.Code Ann. §§ 8.1–205(4), 8.2–202. Faithful adherence to this mandate reflects the reality of the marketplace and avoids the overly legalistic interpretations which the Code seeks to abolish....

Nor can we accept Royster's contention that the testimony should be excluded under the contract clause: "No verbal understanding will be recognized by either party hereto; this contract expresses all the terms and conditions of the agreement, shall be signed in duplicate, and shall not become operative until approved in writing by the Seller." Course of dealing and trade usage are not synonymous with verbal understandings, terms and conditions. Section 8.2–202 draws a distinction between supplementing a written contract by consistent additional terms and supplementing it by course of dealing or usage of trade. Evidence of additional terms must be excluded when "the court finds the writing to have been intended also as a complete and exclusive statement of the terms of the agreement." Significantly, no similar limitation is placed on the introduction of evidence of course of dealing or usage of trade. Indeed the official comment notes that course of dealing and usage of trade, unless carefully negated, are admissible to supplement the terms of any writing, and that contracts are to be read on the assumption that these elements were taken for granted when the document was phrased.[1] Since the Code assigns course of dealing and trade usage unique and important roles, they should not be conclusively rejected by reading them into stereotyped language that makes no specific reference to them....

[Judgment vacated and case remanded.]

NOTE

Specific Reference to Usage. Would the result have been different if the merger clause had begun: "No verbal understanding, usage of trade or course of dealing will be recognized by either party hereto...."?

---

1. Va.Code Ann. § 8.2–202, Comment 2 states:

"Paragraph (a) [of § 8.202] makes admissible evidence of course of dealing, usage of trade and course of performance to explain or supplement the terms of any writing stating the agreement of the parties in order that the true understanding of the parties as to the agreement may be reached. Such writings are to be read on the assumption that the course of prior dealings between the parties and the usages of trade were taken for granted when the document was phrased. Unless carefully negated they have become an element of the meaning of the words used. Similarly, the course of actual performance by the parties is considered the best indication of what they intended the writing to mean." ...

Chapter 7

PERFORMANCE AND BREACH

An exchange of promises will lead to an exchange of performances, in the ordinary course of affairs. One who has committed oneself in exchange for a return performance is entitled, as stated in Comment 1 to UCC 2–609, to "a continuing sense of reliance and security that the promised performance will be forthcoming when due." Much detail in the law of contract is understandable only with reference to this principle that a party's fair expectation of return performance deserves protection.

One means of protection is to afford an immediate remedy for breach when that expectation is seriously impaired, and in this chapter we pursue further the matter of damages. But there are other means of at least equal importance for assuring a party's expectations, such as permitting the party to defer or withhold its own performance when a threat of a certain order arises that it will not receive what was promised in exchange. Protection in this form is generally described in the language of condition.

Section 1 considers what a party may do to establish a condition by language in the agreement. It will be seen that the parties have wide liberties both to shape their commitments and to protect their expectations through suitable use of the language of conditions. Section 2 introduces the idea of constructive (implied) conditions of exchange. It shows how constructive conditions in a contract are determined according to the order of the performances required by the contract and how this may afford one party some assurance that the other will perform as agreed. Section 3 examines three ways that courts mitigate the harsh results of conditions where constructive conditions are involved: substantial performance, divisibility, and restitution. Section 4 deals with problems that arise when breach occurs during the course of performance, notably the question of materiality of breach. Finally, Section 5 concerns prospective, as distinguished from actual, nonperformance. Here we consider repudiation and the right to demand assurance of a promised performance.

SECTION 1.   CONDITIONS

———

(a) Effects of Conditions

———

Thus far, this book has been largely concerned with the imposition and enforcement of *duties*. What follows deals mainly with how duties are qualified by being subjected to the occurrence of *conditions*. According to Restatement Second § 224, "A condition is an event, not certain to occur, which must occur, unless its nonoccurrence is excused, before performance under a contract becomes due."[a] Our present interest is with the interpretation of language relating to such events.[b]

———

LUTTINGER v. ROSEN

Supreme Court of Connecticut, 1972.
164 Conn. 45, 316 A.2d 757.

LOISELLE, ASSOCIATE JUSTICE. The plaintiffs contracted to purchase for $85,000 premises in the city of Stamford owned by the defendants and paid a deposit of $8500. The contract was "subject to and conditional upon the buyers obtaining first mortgage financing on said premises from a bank or other lending institution in an amount of $45,000 for a term of not less than twenty (20) years and at an interest rate which does not exceed 8½ per cent per annum." The plaintiffs agreed to use due diligence in attempting to obtain such financing. The parties further agreed that if the plaintiffs were unsuccessful in obtaining financing as provided in the contract, and notified the seller within a specific time, all sums paid on the contract would be refunded and the contract terminated without further obligation of either party.

In applying for a mortgage which would satisfy the contingency clause in the contract, the plaintiffs relied on their attorney who applied at a New Haven lending institution for a $45,000 loan at 8¼ percent per annum interest over a period of twenty-five years. The plaintiffs' attorney knew that this lending institution was the only one which at that time would lend as much as $45,000 on a mortgage for a single-

---

a. Comment *a* to § 224 adds that sometimes the word "is used to refer to a term ... in an agreement that makes an event a condition, or more broadly to refer to any term in an agreement (e.g., 'standard conditions of sale')."

b. If the event is fortuitous, i.e., not within the power of the parties, the promise is sometimes said to be "aleatory."

family dwelling. A mortgage commitment was obtained for $45,000 with "interest at the prevailing rate at the time of closing but not less than 8¾%." Since this commitment failed to meet the contract requirement, timely notice was given to the defendants and demand was made for the return of the down payment. The defendants' counsel thereafter offered to make up the difference between the interest rate offered by the bank and the 8½ percent rate provided in the contract for the entire twenty-five years by a funding arrangement, the exact terms of which were not defined. The plaintiffs did not accept this offer and on the defendants' refusal to return the deposit an action was brought. From a judgment rendered in favor of the plaintiffs the defendants have appealed.

The defendants claim that the plaintiffs did not use due diligence in seeking a mortgage within the terms specified in the contract. The unattacked findings by the court establish that the plaintiffs' attorney was fully informed as to the conditions and terms of mortgages being granted by various banks and lending institutions in and out of the area and that the application was made to the only bank which might satisfy the mortgage conditions of the contingency clause at that time. These findings adequately support the court's conclusion that due diligence was used in seeking mortgage financing in accordance with the contract provisions. Brauer v. Freccia, 159 Conn. 289, 293, 268 A.2d 645. The defendants assert that notwithstanding the plaintiffs' reliance on their counsel's knowledge of lending practices, applications should have been made to other lending institutions. This claim is not well taken. The law does not require the performance of a futile act. Vachon v. Tomascak, 155 Conn. 52, 57, 230 A.2d 5; Tracy v. O'Neill, 103 Conn. 693, 699, 131 A. 417; Janulewycz v. Quagliano, 88 Conn. 60, 64, 89 A. 897.

The remaining assignment of error briefed by the defendants is that the court erred in concluding that the mortgage contingency clause of the contract, a condition precedent, was not met and, therefore, the plaintiffs were entitled to recover their deposit. "A condition precedent is a fact or event which the parties intend must exist or take place before there is a right to performance." Lach v. Cahill, 138 Conn. 418, 421, 85 A.2d 481, 482. If the condition precedent is not fulfilled the contract is not enforceable. Lach v. Cahill, supra; Bialeck v. Hartford, 135 Conn. 551, 556, 66 A.2d 610. In this case the language of the contract is unambiguous and clearly indicates that the parties intended that the purchase of the defendants' premises be conditioned on the obtaining by the plaintiffs of a mortgage as specified in the contract. From the subordinate facts found the court could reasonably conclude that since the plaintiffs were unable to obtain a $45,000 mortgage at no more than 8½ percent per annum interest "from a bank or other lending institution" the condition precedent to performance of the contract was not met and the plaintiffs were entitled to the refund of their deposit. Any additional offer by the defendants to fund the difference in interest payments could be rejected by the plaintiffs. See Lach v. Cahill, supra, 138 Conn. 420, 85 A.2d 481. There was no error in the court's exclusion of testimony relating to the additional offer since the offer was obviously irrelevant.

There is no error.

NOTES

(1) *Questions.* Why was the buyer's promise made conditional? What was the event on which it was conditioned? Why did not the mortgage commitment at 8¾% together with the seller's offer to make up the difference in interest rates amount to occurrence of that event? [a]

(2) *Financing Conditions.* Note the specificity of the clause in Luttinger v. Rosen. A poll of Wisconsin lawyers and brokers on such clauses is reported in Raushenbush, Problems and Practices with Financing Conditions in Real Estate Purchase Contracts, 1963 Wis.L.Rev. 566. According to the responses: such clauses are in widespread use, general language like "subject to financing" was not favored by most of the respondents, and a majority of them felt unable to say what would be a "reasonable loan" for a buyer. Would an agreement "contingent upon the purchaser's obtaining the proper amount of financing" have been enforceable? See Gerruth Realty Co. v. Pire, 115 N.W.2d 557 (Wis.1962).

(3) *The Case of the Treatment of Time.* Kakalik contracted to buy real estate from the Bernardos, conditional on his ability to obtain a conventional 30–year mortgage at 8.75 percent interest plus one point. The contract further provided that the mortgage commitment "shall be obtained not later than April 23, 1975 or this agreement shall become null and void and deposit money returned to Buyer." The date was not separately negotiated but represented a real estate broker's estimate of the average period of time normally required to obtain a mortgage commitment. Kakalik applied for a mortgage loan from the New Haven Savings Bank, which approved the loan on April 23, and a letter of commitment was mailed to Kakalik in Maine on April 24. The Bernardos were informed of approval on April 23 but indicated unwillingness to consummate the sale on the ground that they had received no written confirmation of the commitment from Kakalik by April 23. They had in fact changed their minds for personal reasons. Kakalik sued for specific performance, which was ordered, and the Bernardos appealed. *Held:* Affirmed.

"The rule that time is ordinarily not of the essence in transactions involving real property applies to the occurrence of a contractual condition as well as to the performance of a contractual duty.... There was ample evidence to support the trial court's finding that time was not of the essence in the procurement of the mortgage commitment under this contract. The contract contains no clause expressly making time of the essence or expressly requiring notification of the defendants on or before the designated date.... [W]e deem it unnecessary to decide whether the mortgage commitment clause would have been satisfied by the mortgagee's oral notification of the parties on April 23, 1975, or its written notification to the plaintiff on April 24, 1975. By the 24th, it was clear that the defendants were refusing to proceed with the contract, and the plaintiff was thereafter excused from completing mortgage arrangements...." One judge disagreed with the conclusion that time was not of the essence, noting that the situation was not one "where the buyer would suffer some extreme forfeiture which would justify excusing the nonperformance of a condition," but concurred in the result on the ground that "the mortgage commitment condition, in the sense contemplated by the parties, was met once the loan committee ...

a. As to the effect of an offer of a purchase money mortgage by the seller himself, compare Simms Co. v. Wolverton, 375 P.2d 87 (Or.1962), with Kovarik v. Vesely, 89 N.W.2d 279 (Wis.1958).

approved the mortgage loan application ... on April 23." Kakalik v. Bernardo, 439 A.2d 1016 (Conn.1981).

What result if the contract had provided "time is of the essence"?

INTERNATIO–ROTTERDAM, INC. v. RIVER BRAND RICE MILLS, INC.

United States Court of Appeals, Second Circuit, 1958.
259 F.2d 137.
Certiorari denied, 358 U.S. 946 (1959).

HINCKS, CIRCUIT JUDGE. Appeal from the United States District Court, Southern District of New York, Walsh, Judge, upon the dismissal of the complaint after plaintiff's case was in.

The defendant-appellee, a processor of rice, in July 1952 entered into an agreement with the plaintiff-appellant, an exporter, for the sale of 95,600 pockets of rice. The terms of the agreement, evidenced by a purchase memorandum, indicated that the price per pocket was to be "$8.25 F.A.S. Lake Charles and/or Houston, Texas"; that shipment was to be "December, 1952, with two weeks call from buyer" and that payment was to be by "irrevocable letter of credit to be opened immediately payable against" dock receipts and other specified documents.[a] In the fall, the appellant, which had already committed itself to supplying this rice to a Japanese buyer, was unexpectedly confronted with United States export restrictions upon its December shipments and was attempting to get an export license from the government. December is a peak month in the rice and cotton seasons in Louisiana and Texas, and the appellee became concerned about shipping instructions under the contract, since congested conditions prevailed at both the mills and the docks. The appellee seasonably elected to deliver 50,000 pockets at Lake Charles and on December 10 it received from the appellant instructions for the Lake Charles shipments. Thereupon it promptly began ship-

---

a. A letter of credit is a binding undertaking by a bank that is used in the following manner. Seller in Neartown and Buyer in Farville agree upon the sale of goods, but Seller is reluctant to rely upon the promise of a distant merchant. If Buyer should fail to pay after the shipment had reached Farville, Seller might sustain a substantial loss, even though it might still have the right to the goods. This would be particularly true if they were not readily resaleable or if the market price should drop so that their resale would bring little. Furthermore, suit against a buyer on its home ground is not an attractive possibility for a seller. These difficulties for a seller are of course compounded in international trade, to which letters of credit are an indispensable adjunct.

Seller may, therefore, require Buyer to obtain a letter of credit from a Farville bank. The bank, by issuing its letter of credit at Buyer's request, undertakes with Seller that it will pay against Seller's orders in an amount equal to the purchase price, on condition that the orders, known as "drafts" or "bills of exchange," are accompanied by documents affording control over the goods. The documents specified are commonly bills of lading, issued by a carrier. Less commonly they may be documents of other sorts, such as the dock receipts in the present case, that also carry with them power over the goods. When Seller ships the goods, it forwards to the Farville bank its draft together with the specified document covering the goods. The bank then pays the draft and takes up the document. As soon as Buyer reimburses the bank, it may have the document and use it to obtain the goods from the carrier.

ments to Lake Charles which continued until December 23, the last car at Lake Charles being unloaded on December 31. December 17 was the last date in December which would allow appellee the two week period provided in the contract for delivery of the rice to the ports and ships designated. Prior thereto, the appellant had been having difficulty obtaining either a ship or a dock in this busy season in Houston. On December 17, the appellee had still received no shipping instructions for the 45,600 pockets destined for Houston. On the morning of the 18th, the appellee rescinded the contract for the Houston shipments, although continuing to make the Lake Charles deliveries. It is clear that one of the reasons for the prompt cancellation of the contract was the rise in market price of rice from $8.25 per pocket, the contract price, to $9.75. The appellant brought this suit for refusal to deliver the Houston quota.

The trial court, in a reasoned but unreported opinion which dealt with all phases of the case, held that New York would apply Texas law. Auten v. Auten, 308 N.Y. 155, 124 N.E.2d 99, 50 A.L.R.2d 246. We think this ruling right, but will not discuss the point because it is conceded that no different result would follow from the choice of Louisiana law.

The area of contest is also considerably reduced by the appellant's candid concession that the appellee's duty to ship, by virtue of the two-week notice provision, did not arise until two weeks after complete shipping instructions had been given by the appellant. Thus on brief the appellant says: "[w]e concede (as we have done from the beginning) that on a fair interpretation of the contract appellant had a duty to instruct appellee by December 17, 1952 as to the place to which it desired appellee to ship—at both ports, and that, being late with its instructions in this respect, appellant could not have demanded delivery (at either port) until sometime after December 31, 1952." This position was taken, of course, with a view to the contract provision for shipment "December, 1952": a two-week period ending December 31 would begin to run on December 17. But although appellant concedes that the two weeks' notice to which appellee was entitled could not be shortened by the failure to give shipping instructions on or before December 17, it stoutly insists that upon receipt of shipping instructions subsequent to December 17 the appellee thereupon became obligated to deliver within two weeks thereafter. We do not agree.

It is plain that a giving of the notice by the appellant was a condition precedent to the appellee's duty to ship. Corbin on Contracts, Vol. 3, § 640. Id. § 724. Obviously, the appellee could not deliver free alongside ship, as the contract required, until the appellant identified its ship and its location. Jacksboro Stone Co. v. Fairbanks Co., 48 Tex.Civ. App. 639, 107 S.W. 567; Fortson Grocery Co. v. Pritchard Rice Milling Co., Tex.Civ.App., 220 S.W. 1116. Thus the giving of shipping instructions was what Professor Corbin would classify as a "promissory condition": the appellant promised to give the notice and the appellee's duty to ship was conditioned on the receipt of the notice. Op. cit. § 633, p. 523, § 634, footnote 38. The crucial question is whether that condition was performed. And that depends on whether the appellee's duty of shipment was conditioned on notice *on or before December 17,* so that the appellee would have two weeks wholly within December within which to perform, or whether, as we understand the appellant to contend, the appellant could perform the condition by giving the notice later in December, in which case the appellee would be under a duty to ship within two weeks thereafter. The answer depends upon the proper interpretation of the contract: if the contract properly interpreted made shipment *in December* of the essence then the failure to give the notice on or before December 17 was nonperformance by the appellant of a condition upon which the appellee's duty to ship in December depended.

In the setting of this case, we hold that the provision for December delivery went to the essence of the contract. In support of the plainly stated provision of the contract there was evidence that the appellee's mills and the facilities appurtenant thereto were working at full capacity in December when the rice market was at peak activity and that appellee had numerous other contracts in January as well as in December to fill. It is reasonable to infer that in July, when the contract was made, each party wanted the protection of the specified delivery period; the appellee so that it could schedule its production without undue congestion of its storage facilities and the appellant so that it could surely meet commitments which it in turn should make to its customers. There was also evidence that prices on the rice market were fluctuating. In view of this factor it is not reasonable to infer that when the contract was made in July for December delivery, the parties intended that the appellant should have an option exercisable subsequent to December 17 to postpone delivery until January. United Irr. Co. v. Carson Petroleum Co., Tex.Civ.App., 283 S.W. 692; Steiner v. United States, D.C., 36 F.Supp. 496. That in effect would have given the appellant an option to postpone its breach of the contract, if one should then be in prospect, to a time when, so far as could have been foreseen when the contract was made, the price of rice might be falling. A postponement in such circumstances would inure to the disadvantage of the appellee who was given no reciprocal option. Further indication that December delivery was of the essence is found in the letter of credit which was provided for in the contract and established by the appellant. Under this letter, the bank was authorized to pay appellee only for deliveries "during December, 1952." It thus appears that the appellant's interpretation of the contract, under which the appellee would be obligated, upon receipt of shipping instructions subsequent to December 17, to deliver in January, would deprive the appellee of the security for payment of the purchase price for which it had contracted.[b]

Since, as we hold, December delivery was of the essence, notice of shipping instructions *on or before December 17* was not merely a "duty" of the appellant—as it concedes: it was a condition precedent to the performance which might be required of the appellee. The nonoccurrence of that condition entitled the appellee to rescind or to treat its

---

b. For critical comment on this passage, see Childres, Conditions in the Law of Con- tracts, 45 N.Y.U.L.Rev. 33, 56–57 (1970).

contractual obligations as discharged. Corbin on Contracts, §§ 640, 724 and 1252; Williston on Sales, §§ 452, 457; Restatement, Contracts, § 262; ... On December 18th the appellant [appellee?] unequivocally exercised its right to rescind. Having done so, its obligations as to the Houston deliveries under the contract were at an end. And of course its obligations would not revive thereafter when the appellant finally suc-ceeded in obtaining an export permit, a ship and a dock and then gave shipping instructions; when it expressed willingness to accept deliveries in January; or when it accomplished a "liberalization" of the outstand-ing letter of credit whereby payments might be made against simple forwarder's receipts instead of dock receipts.[1]

The appellant urges that by reason of substantial part performance on its part prior to December 17th, it may not be held to have been in default for its failure sooner to give shipping instructions. The conten-tion has no basis on the facts. As to the Houston shipments the appellant's activities prior to December 17th were not in performance of its contract: they were merely preparatory to its expectation to perform at a later time. The mere establishment of the letter of credit was not an act of performance: it was merely an arrangement made by the appellant for future performance which as to the Houston deliveries because of appellant's failure to give shipping instructions were never made. From these preparatory activities the appellee had no benefit whatever.

The appellant also maintains that the contract was single and "indivisible" and that consequently appellee's continuing shipments to Lake Charles after December 17 constituted an election to reaffirm its total obligation under the contract. This position also, we hold untena-ble. Under the contract, the appellee concededly had an option to split the deliveries betwixt Lake Charles and Houston. The price had been fixed on a per pocket basis, and payment, under the letter of credit, was to be made upon the presentation of dock receipts which normally would be issued both at Lake Charles or Houston at different times. The fact that there was a world market for rice and that in December the market price substantially exceeded the contract price suggests that it would be more to the appellants' advantage to obtain the Lake Charles delivery than to obtain no delivery at all. The same considerations suggest that by continuing with the Lake Charles delivery the appellee did not deliberately intend to waive its right to cancel the Houston deliveries. Conclusions to the contrary would be so greatly against self-interest as to be completely unrealistic. The only reasonable inference from the totality of the facts is that the duties of the parties as to the Lake Charles shipment were not at all dependent on the Houston shipments. We conclude their duties as to shipments at each port were paired and reciprocal and that performance by the parties as to Lake Charles did not preclude the appellee's right of cancellation as to Houston. Cf.

---

1. The appellee was not informed that the letter of credit had "liberalized" until after it had rescinded. Moreover, even the liberalized letter did not call for payment of deliveries not made until January.

Corbin on Contracts §§ 688, 695; Simms—Wylie Co. v. City of Ranger, Tex.Civ.App., 224 S.W.2d 265.

Finally, we hold that the appellant's claims of estoppel and waiver have no basis in fact or in law.

Affirmed.

NOTES

(1) *How to Assert Rights Upon Breach by the Other Party.* There is some hazard for an aggrieved party in declaring a "rescission" of the contract. Do you see what it is? See Plunkett v. Comstock–Cheney Co., 208 N.Y.S. 93 (App.Div. 1925). Compare such an announcement with what was said by the injured sellers in the rice case and the bean case. For obvious reasons it is better to announce a *default* than to announce a *rescission.* But see UCC 2–720. The meaning of rescission is discussed in Corbin §§ 1236–1237.

(2) *When Time Is of the Essence.* "Courts of equity have treated stipulations as to time as subsidiary and of comparatively little importance, unless either the language of the parties or the nature of the case imperatively indicated that the date of performance was vital. In courts of common law, however, and especially in mercantile contracts, it is held that time is of the essence of the contract." Williston 3d § 845. The reference to equity has special application to land sale contracts, specific performance of which may be granted, to prevent injustice, in spite of "considerable delay" on the part of the plaintiff, either buyer or seller, in tendering performance. Restatement Second, § 242, Comment c. General statements that "time is of the essence," even in reference to mercantile contracts, and even when so provided in the agreement, need not be taken at face value. See Fairchild Stratos Corp. v. Lear Siegler, Inc., 337 F.2d 785 (4th Cir.1964). "By the blind eye of the common law, it would seem, 'time' is read as a master word in the contract jungle, absolute and uncompromising in its significance and power. It can be asserted with confidence that never were the common law judges so blind as this.... [T]here is no absolute and universal rule." Corbin § 713.

(b) Problems of Interpretation

CONDITION, DUTY, OR BOTH?

Suppose that two parties are negotiating a contract and one, who expects to undertake a duty, wants to make sure that the other will do something in return. The two most common contractual devices by which an obligor may attempt to induce an obligee to do an act are, first, by having the obligee undertake a duty to do it and, second, by making the obligee's doing of the act a condition of the obligor's duty.[a] Here is

---

a. They are not the only devices used for this purpose. Another is the "unilateral" offer in which, for example, A attempts to induce B to walk across the Brooklyn Bridge by saying, "I will give you $100 if you walk across the Brooklyn Bridge." See p. 250 above. It would, to be sure, be possible to call walking across the bridge a "condition" of A's promise, even though it is also the acceptance of A's offer, but the

an example based on the venerable case of Constable v. Cloberie, 81 Eng.Rep. 1141 (King's Bench 1626).

A cargo owner desires a ship owner to sail from England to Cadiz and back carrying his cargo. This the ship owner agrees to do in return for the cargo owner's promise to pay freight. In addition, the cargo owner wants the ship owner to sail with the next wind. To induce the ship owner to do this, he can have the ship owner undertake a duty to sail with the next wind, or can make sailing with the next wind a condition of his own duty to pay the freight, or can do both. The consequences will, however, be different in each case.

Suppose that he has the ship owner undertake a duty to sail with the next wind. If the ship owner delays in sailing, the cargo owner can recover any damages caused by the ship owner's breach of duty, but will not be excused from his own duty to pay the freight.[b]

Suppose that he makes sailing with the next wind a condition of his own duty to pay the freight. If the ship owner delays in sailing, the cargo owner cannot recover damages but will be excused from his own duty to pay the freight.

Suppose that he does both.[c] If the ship owner delays in sailing, the cargo owner can recover damages caused by the ship owner's breach of duty *and* will be excused from his own duty to pay the freight. (In calculating damages, however, the court will have to take account of the fact that the cargo owner will not have to pay the freight. See p. 483 above.)

What are the relative advantages to the cargo owner of these three solutions? Plainly the third, which gives him the advantages of both the first two, would be the best. But how much better is it, assuming that freight rates vary according to the relative disadvantage to the ship owner? As between the first two solutions, what are the relative advantages to the cargo owner?

NOTES

(1) *Drafting.* Assume that the contract begins: "In consideration of Ship Owner's promise to sail to Cadiz and return with cargo, Cargo Owner promises to pay freight at [a specified rate]." Draft clauses to follow which would make sailing with the next wind: (1) a duty of Ship Owner; (2) a condition of Cargo Owner's duty; (3) both a duty of Ship Owner and a condition of Cargo Owner's duty.[d]

term is not ordinarily used in this broad sense. According to Comment *c* to Restatement, Second § 224: "Events which must occur before there is a contract, such as offer and acceptance, are ... excluded under the definition in this section. It is not customary to call such events conditions.... For the most part, they are required by law and may not be dispensed with by the parties, while conditions are the result of, or at least subject to, agreement."

b. This ignores the impact of the doctrine of "constructive conditions of exchange," which is taken up in the next section.

c. Corbin uses the term "promissory condition" to describe this case. 3A Corbin § 633.

d. Those with a penchant for law French may find assistance in the facts of the actual case. The cargo owner covenanted to pay freight "si le niefe [ship] va le

(2) *Preference in Interpretation.* If the language that you prepare in response to the preceding note is unclear, a court will prefer an interpretation that makes sailing with the next wind only a duty to Ship Owner. As Comment d to Restatement Second § 227(1) puts it, "The preferred interpretation avoids the harsh results that might otherwise result from the non-occurrence of a condition and still gives adequate protection to the obligor under the rules ... relating to promises for an exchange of performances." In the next section, we examine those rules.

PEACOCK CONSTRUCTION CO. v. MODERN AIR CONDITIONING, INC.

Supreme Court of Florida, 1977.
353 So.2d 840.

BOYD, ACTING CHIEF JUSTICE. We issued an order allowing certiorari in these two causes because the decisions in them of the District Court of Appeal, Second District, conflict with the decision in Edward J. Gerrits, Inc. v. Astor Electric Service, Inc., 328 So.2d 522 (Fla.3d DCA 1976). The two causes have been consolidated for all appellate purposes in this Court because they involve the same issue. That issue is whether the plaintiffs, Modern Air Conditioning and Overly Manufacturing, were entitled to summary judgments against Peacock Construction Company in actions for breaches of identical contractual provisions.

Peacock Construction was the builder of a condominium project. Modern Air Conditioning subcontracted with Peacock to do the heating and air conditioning work and Overly Manufacturing subcontracted with Peacock to do the "rooftop swimming pool" work. Both written subcontracts provided that Peacock would make final payment to the subcontractors,

> "within 30 days after the completion of the work included in this sub-contract, written acceptance by the Architect and full payment therefor by the Owner."

Modern Air Conditioning and Overly Manufacturing completed the work specified in their contracts and requested final payment. When Peacock refused to make the final payments the two subcontractors separately brought actions in the Lee County Circuit Court for breach of contract. In both actions it was established that no deficiencies had been found in the completed work. But Peacock established that it had not received from the owner[1] full payment for the subcontractors' work. And it defended on the basis that such payment was a condition which, by express term of the final payment provision, had to be fulfilled before it

---

intended voyage [to Cadiz], & retorn." The ship owner covenanted that his ship would go with "le prochien vent," and the cargo owner denied that it did so, and refused to pay the freight. The ship owner sued, and the cargo owner's plea was held bad on demurrer, "car le substance del covenant ... est que le niefe vaera le voyage, & ceo fuit primary intention del parties." Sailing with the next wind was not a condition to the plaintiff's right to the freight. The case is discussed in 3A Corbin § 633.

1. The owner, a corporation, had entered proceedings in bankruptcy.

was obligated to perform under the contract. On motions by the plaintiffs, the trial judges granted summary judgments in their favor. The orders of judgment implicitly interpreted the contract not to require payment by the owner as a condition precedent to Peacock's duty to perform.

The Second District Court of Appeal affirmed the lower court's judgment in the appeal brought by Peacock Construction Company. In so doing it adopted the view of the majority of jurisdictions in this country that provisions of the kind disputed here do not set conditions precedent but rather constitute absolute promises to pay, fixing payment by the owner as a reasonable time for when payment to the subcontractor is to be made. When the judgment in the *Overly Manufacturing* case reached the Second District Court, *Modern Air Conditioning* had been decided and the judgment, therefore, was affirmed on the authority of the latter decision. These two decisions plainly conflict with *Gerrits,* supra.

In *Gerrits,* the Court had summarily ordered judgment for the plaintiff/subcontractor against the defendant/general contractor on a contractual provision for payment to the subcontractor which read,

> The money to be paid in current funds and at such times as the General Contractor receives it from the Owner. Id. at 523.

In its review of the judgment, the Third District Court of Appeal referred to the fundamental rule of interpretation of contracts that it be done in accordance with the intention of the parties. Since the defendant had introduced below the issue of intention, a material issue, and since the issue was one that could be resolved through a factual determination by the jury, the Third District reversed the summary judgment and remanded for trial.

Peacock urges us to adopt *Gerrits* as the controlling law in this State. It concedes that the Second District's decisions are backed by the weight of authority. But it argues that they are incorrect because the issue of intention is a factual one which should be resolved after the parties have had an opportunity to present evidence on it. Peacock urges, therefore, that the causes be remanded for trial. If there is produced no evidence that the parties intended there be condition precedents, only then, says Peacock, should the judge, by way of a directed verdict for the subcontractors, be allowed to take the issue of intention from the jury.

The contractual provisions in dispute here are susceptible to two interpretations. They may be interpreted as setting a condition precedent or as fixing a reasonable time for payment. The provision disputed in *Gerrits* is susceptible to the same two interpretations. The questions presented by the conflict between these decisions, then, are whether ambiguous contractual provisions of the kind disputed here may be interpreted only by the factfinder, usually the jury, or if they should be interpreted as a matter of law by the court, and if so what interpretation they should be given.

Although it must be admitted that the meaning of language is a factual question, the general rule is that interpretation of a document is a question of law rather than of fact. 4 Williston on Contracts, 3rd Ed., § 616. If an issue of contract interpretation concerns the intention of parties, that intention may be determined from the written contract, as a matter of law, when the nature of the transaction lends itself to judicial interpretation. A number of courts, with whom we agree, have recognized that contracts between small subcontractors and general contractors on large construction projects are such transactions. Cf. Thos. J. Dyer Co. v. Bishop International Engineering Co., 6 Cir., 303 F.2d 655 (1965). The reason is that the relationship between the parties is a common one and usually their intent will not differ from transaction to transaction, although it may be differently expressed.

That intent in most cases is that payment by the owner to the general contractor is not a condition precedent to the general contractor's duty to pay the subcontractors. This is because small subcontractors, who must have payment for their work in order to remain in business, will not ordinarily assume the risk of the owner's failure to pay the general contractor. And this is the reason for the majority view in this country, which we now join.

Our decision to require judicial interpretation of ambiguous provisions for final payment in subcontracts in favor of subcontractors should not be regarded as anti-general contractor. It is simply a recognition that this is the fairest way to deal with the problem. There is nothing in this opinion, however, to prevent parties to these contracts from shifting the risk of payment failure by the owner to the subcontractor. But in order to make such a shift the contract must unambiguously express that intention. And the burden of clear expression is on the general contractor.

The decisions of the Second District Court of Appeal to affirm the summary judgments were correct. We adopt, therefore, these two decisions as the controlling law in Florida and we overrule *Gerrits,* to the extent it is inconsistent with this opinion.

The orders allowing certiorari in these two causes are discharged. It is so ordered.

NOTES

(1) *Condition or Not?* Can you draft a clause that would "unambiguously" shift to the subcontractor the risk of the owner's failure to pay? Would it suffice to add the following sentence? "Under no circumstances shall General Contractor be required to make payment to Subcontractor until the funds have been paid by Owner to General Contractor." See Gulf Construction Co., Inc. v. Self, 676 S.W.2d 624 (Tex.App.1984).

(2) *Fact or Law?* As to the court's decision to treat the question of interpretation as "a matter of law," recall the discussion at p. 595 above. Thirteen years later, in DEC Electric, Inc. v. Raphael Construction Corp., 558 So.2d 427 (Fla.1990), the same court had certified to it a question "of great public importance":

Must all payment provisions in contracts between contractors and subcontractors or suppliers that concern a condition or time of payment provision be construed as a matter of law?

Answering in the affirmative, the court explained that if the provision "is clear and unambiguous, it is interpreted as setting a condition precedent," but if it "is ambiguous it is interpreted as fixing a reasonable time for the general contractor to pay.... Once a judge decides that a provision is ambiguous there is nothing for the jury to decide or interpret."

(3) *Brokers and Conditions.* In Amies v. Wesnofske, 174 N.E. 436 (N.Y. 1931), a seller of land made a contract with the brokers who had arranged its sale. Under this contract the seller agreed "to pay for their services in bringing about such sale the sum of Five Thousand ($5,000) Dollars, one-half of which is paid this date and the balance to be paid on the closing of title." When the buyers failed to go through with the sale because of lack of funds, the seller kept $10,000 that the buyer had already paid on the total price of $124,000, but refused to pay the brokers the remaining $2,500. In holding that the seller was not obligated to do so, the court stated: "The employment of such words as 'when,' 'after,' or 'as soon as,' clearly indicate that a promise is not to be performed except upon a condition.... We think that reason and authority compel the conclusion that we have here a promise to pay a broker upon a condition which has not been fulfilled." [a]

Is the situation of the broker distinguishable from that of the subcontractor?

(4) *Effect of Ignorance.* If the nonoccurrence of a condition would otherwise entitle an obligor to suspend its performance or treat its duty as discharged, does it have the same effect even though the obligor is ignorant of the fact that the condition has not occurred? The prevailing view is that it does. Thus in Johnson v. Honeywell Information Systems, Inc., 955 F.2d 409, 413 (6th Cir. 1992), the court concluded that "the Michigan Supreme Court would hold that just cause for termination of employment may include facts unknown to an employer at the time of dismissal, though obviously such facts would be neither the actual nor inducing cause for the discharge." [b]

MATTEI v. HOPPER
Supreme Court of California, 1958.
51 Cal.2d 119, 330 P.2d 625.

[For the report of this case, see p. 121 above.]

NOTES

(1) *Conditions of Satisfaction.* Provisions like that in Mattei v. Hopper play an important role in allowing parties to contract even though one party wants to

a. If the decision is that the broker may not claim the commission from the seller, what are the chances of collecting it from the buyer? In Professional Realty Corp. v. Bender, 222 S.E.2d 810 (Va.1976), there was a sale contract executed by the brokerage firm as well as the sellers and the buyers. In it the sellers, who had employed the broker, promised it a commission. The sale was not consummated because the buyer defaulted. In an action by the broker against the buyers, the court gave summary judgment for the defendants. On appeal, the broker urged the court to adopt the rule that, in these circumstances, "the buyer's promise to purchase implies a promise to pay the commission if he defaults on his contract with the seller." The court affirmed. "We decline to adopt such a rule."

b. This and similar cases are reviewed in Massey v. Trump's Castle Hotel & Casino, 828 F.Supp. 314 (D.N.J.1993).

reserve some discretion to itself. Suppose that Mattei, the developer, had refused to go through with the purchase of the tract on the ground that the leases were not satisfactory to him and that Hopper had sued Mattei. If trial were before a jury, what sort of instruction would have been appropriate on the issue of satisfaction under the standard used by the Supreme Court of California? Under the "standard of a reasonable person"?

Consider the following description of real estate financing. "The determination of adequate security for a particular loan is highly subjective. Each lender will evaluate differently the chances that it will be able to realize upon the security if the borrower defaults on the loan. A multitude of factors and their interrelationship must be evaluated in determining whether the risk is one which the lender is willing to take.... The good faith requirement thus appears to be more appropriate when dealing with loan commitments since it is all but impossible to judge reasonable satisfaction." Draper, Tight Money and Possible Substantive Defenses to Enforcement of Future Mortgage Commitments, 50 N.D.Law. 603, 610 (1975).

(2) *The Case of the Cheaper Chips.* Cornett and Moore, potato farmers, contracted to sell twelve loads of chipping potatoes to Neumiller Farms, which brokered potatoes to makers of potato chips. The contract fixed the price at $4.25 per hundredweight and required that the potatoes be United States Grade No. 1 and "chips to buyer satisfaction." Neumiller accepted three loads while the market price remained at $4.25 per hundredweight but, when the market price declined to $2.00, rejected the last nine loads claiming that the potatoes would not chip satisfactorily. The farmers had samples tested by an expert from the county Cooperative Extension Service, who found them entirely satisfactory. After unsuccessful negotiations—during which Neumiller's agent said "I can buy potatoes all day for $2.00"—the farmers sued Neumiller. From a judgment for the farmers on a $17,500 jury verdict, Neumiller appealed. *Held:* Affirmed.

"The law requires such a claim of dissatisfaction to be made in good faith, rather than in an effort to escape a bad bargain.... Buyer ... is a broker who deals in farm products as part of its occupation and, therefore, is a 'merchant' with respect to its dealings in such goods [under UCC 2–104. UCC 2–103] requires '... honesty in fact and the observance of reasonable commercial standards of fair dealing in the trade.' A claim of dissatisfaction by a merchant-buyer ... must be evaluated using an objective standard to determine whether the claim is made in good faith. Because there was evidence that the potatoes would 'chip' satisfactorily, the jury was not required to accept Buyer's subjective claim to the contrary." Neumiller Farms, Inc. v. Cornett, 368 So.2d 272 (Ala.1979).

Would the farmers necessarily have lost under the standard used in Mattei v. Hopper?

(3) *The Case of the Cheaper Cherries.* International contracted to sell Devoine, a candy manufacturer, 400 50–gallon barrels of cherries in syrup, "quality satisfactory." After accepting 97 barrels, Devoine refused to take more, and International sued. It introduced evidence to show: that the standards it used were up to the highest known to the trade; that Devoine had made no complaint about the first 97 barrels and had once written a letter expressing its satisfaction; that Devoine had subsequently explained that its own sales had slackened and later that it had an arrangement for putting up its own supply of cherries and therefore could not use the balance under the contract; and that finally Devoine had sent a letter stating that, as International had previously

been informed, Devoine found the cherries unsatisfactory. From a judgment for International on a jury verdict, Devoine appealed. *Held:* Affirmed.

Even if "the decision of the other party ... is final ... it is only the decision contracted for that is final.... And ... if the person to whom it is referred decides, not on the question submitted, but on some question of interest or advantage not made the basis of rights or obligations of the contract, the decision is outside of the contract and is given no effect by it.[a] ... [T]he seller was at liberty to prove if he could that his goods were rejected not because the quality was unsatisfactory, but because the buyer had found a cheaper source of supply.... [International's evidence] was sufficient, no matter how strong the evidence of the Devoine Company may have been to the contrary, to require submission to the jury of the question of good faith...." Devoine Co. v. International Co., 136 A. 37 (Md.1927).

Would Devoine have been entitled to reject the cherries if it had both been dissatisfied with International's cherries and found a cheaper source of supply? See Columbia Christian College, Inc. v. Commonwealth Properties, Inc., 594 P.2d 401 (Or.1979).

(4) *Conditions "Precedent" and "Subsequent"*. "Parties sometimes provide that the occurrence of an event, such as the failure of one of them to commence an action within a prescribed time, will extinguish a duty after performance has become due, along with any claim for breach. Such an event has often been called a 'condition subsequent' while an event of the kind defined in this section has been called a 'condition precedent.' " Comment *e* to Restatement Second § 224. The Restatement Second abandons the term "condition subsequent" and deals with such events in § 230, Event That Terminates a Duty. It calls a "condition precedent" simply a "condition."

The terms "condition precedent" and "condition subsequent" have a significance in the law of procedure that is independent of their significance, or lack of it, in the law of contracts. This significance is best left for the treatment of burdens of pleading and burdens of proof in a course in civil procedure.

GIBSON v. CRANAGE

Supreme Court of Michigan, 1878.
39 Mich. 49.

Marston, J. Plaintiff in error brought assumpsit to recover the contract price for the making and execution of a portrait of the deceased daughter of defendant. It appeared from the testimony of the plaintiff that he at a certain time called upon the defendant and solicited the privilege of making an enlarged picture of his deceased daughter. He says "I was to make an enlarged picture that he would like, a large one from a small one, and one that he would like and recognize as a good picture of his little girl, and he was to pay me."

The defendant testified that the plaintiff was to take the small photograph and send it away to be finished, "and when returned if it

---

a. "The promisor may in fact be satisfied with the performance, but not with the bargain." Learned Hand, J., in Thompson– Starrett Co. v. La Belle Iron Works, 17 F.2d 536 (2d Cir.1927).

was not perfectly satisfactory to me in every particular, I need not take it or pay for it. I still objected and he urged me to do so. There was no risk about it; if it was not perfectly satisfactory to me I need not take it or pay for it."

There was little if any dispute as to what the agreement was. After the picture was finished it was shown to defendant who was dissatisfied with it and refused to accept it. Plaintiff endeavored to ascertain what the objections were, but says he was unable to ascertain clearly, and he then sent the picture away to the artist to have it changed.

On the next day he received a letter from defendant reciting the original agreement, stating that the picture shown him the previous day was not satisfactory and that he declined to take it or any other similar picture, and countermanded the order. A further correspondence was had, but it was not very material and did not change the aspect of the case. When the picture was afterwards received by the plaintiff from the artist, he went to see defendant and to have him examine it. This defendant declined to do, or to look at it, and did not until during the trial, when he examined and found the same objections still existing.

We do not consider it necessary to examine the charge in detail, as we are satisfied it was as favorable to plaintiff as the agreement would warrant.

The contract (if it can be considered such) was an express one. The plaintiff agreed that the picture when finished should be satisfactory to the defendant, and his own evidence showed that the contract in this important particular had not been performed. It may be that the picture was an excellent one and that the defendant ought to have been satisfied with it and accepted it, but under the agreement the defendant was the only person who had the right to decide this question. Where parties thus deliberately enter into an agreement which violates no rule of public policy, and which is free from all taint of fraud or mistake, there is no hardship whatever in holding them bound by it.

Artists or third parties might consider a portrait an excellent one, and yet it prove very unsatisfactory to the person who had ordered it and who might be unable to point out with clearness or certainty the defects or objections. And if the person giving the order stipulates that the portrait when finished must be satisfactory to him or else he will not accept or pay for it, and this is agreed to, he may insist upon his right as given him by the contract. McCarren v. McNulty, 7 Gray, 141; Brown v. Foster, 113 Mass., 136; 18 Amer., 465.

The judgment must be affirmed with costs.

NOTES

(1) *Questions.* Would the result have been the same if Cranage had refused to look at the portrait at all?

Would the result have been the same if Gibson's promise had been to paint the exterior of Cranage's barn? Does a satisfaction clause impose different risks on a seller of land, a painter of a portrait, and a painter of a barn? [a]

Can you draft language that would make an objective test applicable to the painting of a portrait? That would make a subjective test applicable to the painting of a barn?

Note that the court said that Gibson "agreed that the picture when finished should be satisfactory" to Cranage. Did the court hold that Gibson was under a duty to furnish a picture satisfactory to Cranage? Could Cranage have recovered damages from Gibson for his failure to do so?

(2) *Effect of Forfeiture.* It should be apparent that the law of conditions has a draconian quality. If Gibson's portrait does not satisfy Cranage, Gibson gets nothing for his efforts and is left with a painting that is of no value to him. (Should we assume that Gibson was himself the artist?) Comment b to Restatement Second § 227 explains that "forfeiture" is used in that Restatement to refer to "the denial of compensation" that results if the non-occurrence of a condition causes to obligee "to lose his right to the agreed exchange as by preparation or performance." Gibson's risk of forfeiture if Cranage was not satisfied was thus greater than Hopper's risk of forfeiture if Mattei was not satisfied.

(3) *Of Pigs and Paintings.* In Morin Building Products Co., Inc. v. Baystone Construction, Inc., 717 F.2d 413 (7th Cir.1983), the court, by Posner, J., reasoned that if a requirement of reasonableness is read into a condition of satisfaction, it is "not to protect the weaker party but to approximate what the parties would have expressly provided with respect to a contingency that they did not foresee if they had foreseen it.... Suppose the manager of a steel plant rejected a shipment of pig iron because he did not think the pigs had a pretty shape. The reasonable-man standard would be applied even if the contract had an 'acceptability shall rest strictly with the [buyer]' clause, for it would be fantastic to think that the iron supplier would have subjected his contract rights to the whimsey of the buyer's agent. At the other extreme would be a contract to paint a portrait," like that in Gibson v. Cranage.

Is it necessary to apply a reasonableness standard in the case of the pigs to avoid rejection for their want of "a pretty shape"?

DOUBLEDAY & CO., INC., v. CURTIS, 763 F.2d 495 (2d Cir.1985), cert. dismissed, 474 U.S. 912 (1985). [In 1976, the actor Tony Curtis made a two-novel contract with Doubleday on a standard industry form. Doubleday was to pay royalties on hardcover sales and a share of the proceeds from the sale of paperback rights if Curtis delivered within a specified time final manuscripts "satisfactory to Publisher in content and form." Doubleday published the first novel, which was generally acknowledged to have been a joint effort by Curtis and Larry Jordan, a Doubleday editor. The contract was then renegotiated to give Curtis a $100,000 advance against royalties on the second novel, half paid when the contract was signed on September 7, 1977, and the balance due on "acceptance of complete satisfactory manuscript" to be produced by October 1, 1978. Doubleday then negotiated with New American Li-

---

a. If Gibson had painted Cranage's barn, a question of unjust enrichment might arise. Such questions are taken up in Section 3(c) below.

brary (NAL) a contract for the paperback rights in which NAL agreed to pay $200,000 for those rights if Doubleday accepted the manuscript for publication.

[In April 1980, Curtis delivered a partial first draft of Starstruck, a rags-to-riches story of a lascivious Hollywood starlet. Doubleday, ignoring the deadline, had the manuscript reviewed by Zackheim, an editor, who sent Curtis a seven-page letter containing both criticism and encouragement. Curtis declined Zackheim's offer to review revisions piecemeal, and, when Curtis submitted the completed draft, Zackheim was appalled. Drew, Zackheim's superior, concluded that it was "junk, pure and simple" and could not be edited into shape or even rewritten into shape. When Curtis's literary agent rejected Doubleday's suggestion that Curtis submit the manuscript to a "novel doctor," Doubleday terminated the contract in November 1981. (The extended deadline under Doubleday's contract with NAL was December 31, 1981.) Doubleday sued for return of its $50,000 advance and Curtis counterclaimed for $150,000 damages for breach of contract. The trial court dismissed Curtis's counterclaim on the ground that, although it was not clear whether New York law imposed on Doubleday a duty to provide editorial services, Doubleday had performed such a duty and was therefore not liable for breach. The court also dismissed Doubleday's complaint on the ground that it had waived its right to return of the advance. Both parties appealed.]

IRVING R. KAUFMAN, CIRCUIT JUDGE. . . . We note at the outset that Curtis has never defended his August 1981 manuscript as a work of publishable quality. Rather, Curtis maintains that but for Doubleday's inability and unwillingness to provide adequate editorial assistance, Starstruck would have met the "satisfactory to publisher" condition. Curtis concedes that his proposed interpretation is not supported by a literal reading of the 1977 agreement. On its face, the document is completely silent regarding any obligation on Doubleday's part to ensure that Curtis's rough drafts are transformed, through the company's affirmative efforts, into a polished novel.

Our task, then, is to delineate the extent to which New York law requires us to infer such an obligation from the agreement. Because New York's appellate courts have not yet addressed this question, we must attempt to divine the likely response of our state brethren.

The 1977 agreement expressly granted Doubleday the right to terminate the contract if it deemed Curtis's manuscript to be unsatisfactory. In similar circumstances—where the satisfactory performance of one party is to be judged by another party—New York courts have required the party terminating the contract to act in good faith. . . . This principle—that a contract containing a "satisfaction clause" may be terminated only as a result of honest dissatisfaction—would seem especially appropriate in construing publishing agreements. To shield from scrutiny the already chimerical process of evaluating literary value would render the "satisfaction" clause an illusory promise, and place authors at the unbridled mercy of their editors.

A corollary of this duty to appraise a writing honestly is an obligation on the part of the publisher not to mislead an author deliberately regarding the work required for a given project. A willful failure to respond to a request for editorial comments on a preliminary draft may, in many instances, work no less a hardship than would an unjustifiable rejection of a final manuscript. A publisher's duty to exercise good faith in its dealings toward an author exists at all stages of the creative process.

Although we hold that publishers must perform honestly, we decline to extend that requirement to include a duty to perform skillfully. The possibility that a publisher or an editor—either through inferior editing or inadvertence—may prejudice an author's efforts is a risk attendant to the selection of a publishing house by a writer, and is properly borne by that party. To imply a duty to perform adequate editorial services in the absence of express contractual language would, in our view, represent an unwarranted intrusion into the editorial process. Moreover, we are hesitant to require triers of fact to explore the manifold intricacies of an editorial relationship. Such inquiries are appropriate only where contracts specifically allocate certain creative responsibilities to the publisher.[1]

Accordingly, we hold that a publisher may, in its discretion, terminate a standard publishing contract, provided that the termination is made in good faith, and that the failure of an author to submit a satisfactory manuscript was not caused by the publisher's bad faith....

Evaluating the Doubleday–Curtis relationship in light of these principles, we are convinced that Starstruck's failure was not attributable to any dishonesty, willful neglect or any other manifestations of bad faith on the part of Doubleday. The factual landscape illustrates the complete frustration experienced by Doubleday's editors, who were forced to harmonize an inferior manuscript, a lucrative reprint agreement and a recalcitrant author. Zackheim sincerely endeavored to assist Curtis in the completion of his manuscript. Although Zackheim's suggested revisions may have been offered somewhat belatedly, the evidence indicates that he extended numerous offers to discuss the novel with Curtis, as well as to review portions of the second draft. Indeed, it was Curtis who refused these renderings of assistance. That Zackheim's editing was perhaps inadequate is beside the point, as is any comparison with Larry

---

1. Our views comport with the principles we previously articulated in interpreting a standard publishing contract under New York law. In Zilg v. Prentice–Hall Inc., 717 F.2d 671 (2d Cir.1983), we reversed a judgment entered against a publisher for failing to promote a book adequately. In that case, the contract left the number of copies to be printed and the level of advertising expenses within the unfettered discretion of the publisher. Accordingly, we required only that the publisher make an initial good faith effort to promote the book and exercise good faith business judgment in evaluating promotional decisions. Id. at 680. Any greater obligation, we cautioned, would hamper the "publisher's ability to rely upon its own experience and judgment in marketing books." Id.

The concerns expressed in *Zilg* are no less compelling with respect to standard "satisfactory to the publisher" clauses. Clearly, such agreements are drafted with the intention of foreclosing the possibility that a publisher's editorial decision could be later questioned by a disgruntled writer or be "subject to second guessing ... as to whether it ... [was] sound or valid." Id.

Jordan. Curtis neither alleged, nor does the record support a finding that Doubleday deliberately or even recklessly assigned Starstruck to an editor unfit or unsuited for the project.[2]

Admittedly, the selection of an editor is a matter of paramount importance to a writer, but we note once again that the power to control this decision—like all aspects of the publication process—could have been reserved to Curtis in his contract.[3]

Turning our attention to the actual termination of the contract, we believe the district court's finding that Doubleday rejected Starstruck in good faith is amply supported by the record before us. Zackheim and Drew were in complete agreement that no amount of in-house editing could save the project. Moreover, the suggestion that Curtis consult a "novel doctor"—though perhaps somewhat humiliating—appears to have been made sincerely, rather than as a strategem for avoiding the responsibilities attendant to a difficult editing job.[4]

Curtis argues with some force that Doubleday terminated his contract in November 1981 primarily because of the impending NAL deadline. Although we agree the two events were not unconnected, we choose to characterize the relationship between them quite differently. Were it not for the extremely lucrative arrangement with NAL, it is likely that Doubleday would have abandoned Starstruck without hesitation, and perhaps at a much earlier date. Only the prospect of a commercially profitable reprint deal prevented Zackheim from rejecting the August 1981 manuscript immediately. Doubleday's decision to sacrifice financial reward for "ethics," as Zackheim's superior Drew framed the choice, can hardly be said to constitute an act of bad faith....

[Dismissal of Curtis's counterclaims affirmed. Since the issue of waiver was not properly before the court, however, dismissal of Doubleday's complaint reversed and cause remanded for entry of $50,000 judgment in its favor.]

2. We pause briefly to comment on the false optimism generated by Zackheim and expressed to Curtis, concerning the likelihood that Starstruck would be accepted for publication. We recognize that an editor might inhibit a propitious working relationship by emphasizing the failings of a particular manuscript—particularly in an early draft—and warning the author of possible rejection. Nevertheless, it would be perverse if outright prevarication were insufficient to demonstrate bad faith. In any event, we need not dwell on Zackheim's overly encouraging communications to Curtis, because there is no indication that they prejudiced the author's efforts. In fact, they may well have inspired Curtis to persevere.

3. Indeed, Curtis's own expert witness at trial admitted that an author's desire to work with a particular editor is often achieved by making that preference an explicit condition of the publishing contract.

4. Curtis relies on two district court decisions that denied publishers recovery of their advances after rejecting manuscripts as "unsatisfactory." Dell Publishing Co. v. Whedon, 577 F.Supp. 1459 (S.D.N.Y.1984); Harcourt Brace & Jovanovich v. Goldwater, 532 F.Supp. 619 (S.D.N.Y.1982). Although both decisions appear to recognize a duty on the part of publishers to provide adequate editorial services, the results reached in those cases are consistent with the framework we have adopted. In marked contrast to the supervision Zackheim offered Curtis on Starstruck, the authors in *Whedon* and *Goldwater* received no response to their requests for guidance and assistance in the preparation and revision of their manuscripts.

NOTES

(1) *Scope of Duty.* In what circumstances would a publisher's disapproval be in bad faith? What kinds of explicit provisions might an author ask to have inserted in a contract with a publisher in order to get greater protection? See generally Fowler, The "Satisfactory Manuscript" Clause in Book Publishing Contracts, 10 Colum.–VLA J.L. & Arts 119 (1985); House, Good Faith Rejection and Specific Performance in Publishing Contracts: Safeguarding the Author's Reasonable Expectations, 51 Brooklyn L.Rev. 95 (1984).

(2) *Change of Mind.* Suppose that Mattei had told Hopper that he was not satisfied with the leases obtained but the next day, still within the 120–day period, had changed his mind and said he was satisfied. Would Hopper have been bound? Is the discussion on p. 217 above, helpful in answering this question? See Beverly Way Associates v. Barham, 276 Cal.Rptr. 240 (Cal.App. 1990).

ARCHITECTS' CERTIFICATES

Some of the problems inherent in making a party's duty conditional on its own satisfaction can be eliminated by making its duty conditional instead on the satisfaction of an independent third party, usually an expert of some kind. Widespread use is made of such terms in construction contracts, where the owner's duty to pay the contractor is often conditional on satisfaction of the architect.[a] The next case arises in this setting.

LAUREL RACE COURSE, INC. v. REGAL CONSTRUCTION CO.

Court of Appeals of Maryland, 1975.
274 Md. 142, 333 A.2d 319.

LEVINE, JUSTICE. [Laurel Race Course, Inc. aspired to reconstruct its race track to make it "the best track in the United States." Laurel made a contract with Watkins & Associates, a Kentucky firm that had designed "all-weather" tracks throughout the world, for Watkins to design a plan for the reconstruction of the track and the installation of a drainage system and to supervise the work.

[On July 3, 1972, Laurel made a contract with Regal Construction, the lowest bidder, which declared that it had fully examined the site and agreed to do the work "in strict accordance with the terms and conditions," to "substantially complete all work" by September 1, 1972, "and to finish the job by September 15, 1972." The contract made time of the essence. It allowed Laurel to retain ten percent of progress payments "until final completion and acceptance." It defined Watkins's status as the "Engineer," to "have general inspection and direction of the work" as Laurel's representative. The contract contained the following provisions (emphasis added by the Court):

a. It is also possible to make the architect's approval conclusive on the owner, that is, to make his approval the sole condition of the owner's duty. As to such provisions see Note 2, p. 707 below.

Subsection 2:

The Engineer shall have general inspection and direction of the work as the authorized representative of the Owner. He shall have authority to stop the work whenever such action may be necessary to insure the proper execution of the contract. He shall also have authority *to reject work and materials which do not conform* to the plans, specifications and contract documents, to direct the place or places where work shall be prosecuted, and to have the Contractor's force increased or decreased as in his judgment is required. *He shall decide all engineering questions* which arise in the *execution* of the work.

The Engineer shall *also interpret* the meaning and requirements of the plans, specifications and contract documents, and *decide all disputes* that arise. The Engineer's decisions on *these* matters shall be final and binding on both the Contractor and the Owner unless both parties agree to submit the dispute to arbitration or either party resorts to *legal action* for settlement.

Subsection 24:

Upon notice that the work is ready for final inspection and acceptance, the Engineer shall make such inspection; and *when he finds the work acceptable* under the Contract and *the Contract fully performed,* he shall promptly issue a 'Final Certificate' over his signature stating in effect that the work provided for in the Contract has been satisfactorily completed and recommending its acceptance by the Owner.

The balance due the Contractor, including the percentage retained during the construction period, *will then be paid* to the Contractor by the Owner. This final payment will be made within sixty days after date of the Engineer's 'Final Certificate', and said final payment shall evidence the Owner's acceptance of work unless it is accepted in writing prior to said final payment.

[Performance was neither substantially completed by September nor fully completed by September 15. After "turning over" the track to Laurel on the 25th, Regal received on September 28 a "punch list" of 18 deficiencies needing its attention. In late November, after Regal claimed that it had remedied these deficiencies, Watkins refused to issue a "Final Certificate" and recommended to Laurel that payment be withheld because Regal had "permitted a large amount of rock and oversize material to become mixed with the clay and sand." Laurel refused to pay the unpaid balance of $110,931.91 on the total contract price of $786,401.35, and Regal brought suit against Laurel in February 1973. By the time of trial in April 1974, payments by Laurel had reduced the amount claimed to $40,648.

[At the trial, experts testified for Laurel that, among other problems, oversize stones were "coming out of" the soil base and working their way to the top. At the end of the trial, with conflicting testimony, the court said with respect to the stones: "I hold every body responsible for that: the contractor, the racetrack owner and the engineers." The trial judge therefore refused to recognize the presence of the stones as a deviation from contract performance. As to the engineer's refusal to furnish the certificate, the trial judge held that Regal "had performed substantially" and allowed the entire $49,648 claimed. Laurel appealed, arguing that the trial court erred in awarding judgment because the engineer's final certificate was "a condition precedent to Laurel's liability" and that, in any event, the trial court erred in awarding judgment for the full contract balance on a finding of only substantial performance.]

LEVINE, JUDGE. Almost a century ago, our predecessors held in Gill v. Vogler, 52 Md. 663, 666 (1879), where work was "to be done ... to the satisfaction of the City Commissioner [of Baltimore]," and payments during the progress of the work were to be made only in accordance with his "monthly estimates," that those estimates were a condition precedent to recovery of such payments, absent bad faith or collusion.

From that holding has emerged the general rule, followed uniformly by decisions of this Court, that where payments under a contract are due only when the certificate of an architect or engineer is issued, production of the certificate becomes a condition precedent to liability of the owner for materials and labor in the absence of fraud or bad faith.... Apart from fraud or bad faith, the only other exceptions to this rule are waiver or estoppel....

The durability of this rule may be more readily appreciated when one considers the emphasis with which it was enunciated by our predecessors. For example, in Lynn v. B. & O. R.R. Co., 60 Md. 404 (1883), Judge Miller said for this Court:

"... So, in the case before us, it was not enough that the jury might believe from the evidence that Legge *unreasonably* rejected the ice, or that he was *grossly* wrong in his judgment ...; they must go further, and actually infer and find fraud or bad faith. By this contract, which is perfectly lawful, the parties expressly agreed to submit the question whether the ice to be supplied was 'good, clear, and solid,' to the judgment of this third party, and his judgment, *no matter how erroneous or mistaken it may be, or how unreasonable it may appear to others, is conclusive* between the parties, unless it be tainted with fraud or bad faith. To substitute for it the opinions and judgments of other persons, whether judge, jury or witnesses, would be to annul the contract, and make another in its place." 60 Md. at 415 (emphasis added).

There is no question but that under subsection 24 of the General Conditions, payment of the "balance due ... including the percentage retained during the construction period" is expressly conditioned upon production of the engineer's " 'Final Certificate.' " It is equally clear that the amount awarded by the trial court ... was the alleged "balance due ... including the percentage retained." Nor is there any contention advanced by Regal that any of the exceptions to the general rule—fraud, bad faith, waiver or estoppel—were established here.

The argument interposed by Regal to the applicability of the general rule rests exclusively on the second paragraph of subsection 2 of the General Conditions. It draws upon this language for the contention that the condition precedent in subsection 24 is dispensed with once "either party resorts to legal action." Otherwise stated, the argument is that the engineer's certificate is controlling—a condition precedent to payment—only until the parties reach the courthouse; but once they do so, the engineer's decision that the specifications have not been met is reviewable by a judge or jury. Thus, under this view, if the trier of fact were to determine that the specifications had been met, the absence of the engineer's certificate would not bar recovery by the contractor under the written contract.

Although Regal's argument purports to rest on the last several words of subsection 2, "either party resorts to legal action," it is necessarily keyed to the final phrase in the immediately preceding sentence of that paragraph, "and decide all disputes that arise." Under the construction advocated by Regal, this specific phrase alone not only refers to disputes under the first part of that sentence—concerning the engineer's interpretation—but applies to all disputes arising under the contract. Hence, Regal would say, the binding effect of the engineer's decisions on all disputes—whether arising out of interpretation or performance—is subject to the "legal action" clause. In sum, the engineer's decisions on all disputes of whatever nature, arising under the contract, would be binding only until there is a "legal action."

The difficulty we encounter with this argument is that it completely ignores paragraph 1 of subsection 2 and the manifest intention of the parties. While this intent is readily discernible from the clear and unambiguous language of these provisions, we nevertheless think it appropriate to stress that the intention of the parties to an agreement must be garnered from the terms considered as a whole, and not from the clauses considered separately. . . .

The engineer, pursuant to paragraph 1 of subsection 2, possesses the "authority to reject work and materials *which do not conform* to the plans, specifications and contract documents," and to "*decide* all engineering questions which arise in the *execution* of the work." (emphasis added). In accordance with this paragraph, decisions of the engineer on questions pertaining to performance and execution of the work are controlling and unqualified. Paragraph 2, however, is confined to disputes arising out of the engineer's role as an interpreter of the technical provisions contained in the various documents. The words "these matters," to which the "legal action" exception applies, pertain solely to such disputes. In this limited respect only are the engineer's decisions, though otherwise final, subject to the "legal action" exception.

At first blush, perhaps, one might question whether the positioning of the comma immediately preceding the words, "and decide all disputes that arise," was intended to mean that this phrase should refer to disputes under the first paragraph as well, and hence, whether the "legal action" exception should not apply to decisions under both paragraphs.

This construction, however, would permit a simple comma to alter what we regard as the clear intent of the agreement. "The authorities make it plain that punctuation cannot control or alter the effect of language that is plain in its meaning." Illian v. Northwestern Ins. Co., 215 Md. 507, 516, 138 A.2d 884, 888 (1958).

It is uncontroverted that the disputes under the written contract all relate to the rejection of "work and materials which do not conform to the plans, specifications and contract documents ..." within the contemplation of the first paragraph of subsection 2. Regal claimed at the trial that its performance did conform and Laurel insisted that it did not. Nowhere in the testimony is there a conflict over an interpretation of the "meaning and requirements of the plans, specifications and contract documents." Therefore, the "legal action" clause is not applicable.

As we see it, therefore, the supremacy of the engineer's certificate on all matters pertaining to conformance and execution survived the resort to "legal action," and should not have been ignored, absent a finding of bad faith, fraud, waiver or estoppel. No such finding was made here. Hence, production of the engineer's certificate was a condition precedent to the liability of Laurel.... It is fundamental that where a contractual duty is subject to a condition precedent, whether express or implied, there is no duty of performance and there can be no breach by nonperformance until the condition precedent is either performed or excused.... Here, the condition precedent was neither performed nor excused; therefore, no judgment should have been rendered against Laurel under the written contract.

This holding makes it unnecessary for us to reach the question whether the court erred in awarding judgment for the full contract balance despite its holding that Regal had rendered only substantial performance....

NOTES

(1) *A.I.A. Provisions.* An American Institute of Architects form of General Conditions for an owner-contractor agreement is contained in the Selections for Contracts. It contains elaborate provisions on the role of the architect. Under Article 10, he "will provide administration of the Contract and will be the Owner's representative ... during construction [and] until final payment is due." He "will interpret and decide matters concerning performance under and requirements of the Contract Documents." His "decisions in matters relating to aesthetic effect will be final if consistent with the intent expressed in the Contract Documents." Other decisions of his "shall be subject to arbitration." "Based on the Architect's observations and evaluations of the Contractor's Applications for Payment, the Architect will review and certify the amounts owing to the Contractor and will issue Certificates for Payment in such amounts." Under Article 15, "When the Architect agrees that the Work is substantially complete, he will issue a Certificate of Substantial Completion." Final payment by the owner is to be made, under Article 5, when "a final Certificate for Payment has been issued by the Architect."

What would have been the result in the preceding case if these provisions had been applicable? See NSC Contractors, Inc. v. Borders, 564 A.2d 408 (Md.1989).

(2) *Satisfaction in New York.* New York courts have tended to read "satisfaction" to mean "reasonable satisfaction." An early example is Duplex Safety Boiler Co. v. Garden, 4 N.E. 749 (N.Y.1886), in which an owner of boilers agreed to pay for repairs only if "satisfied that the boilers, as changed, were a success." The Court of Appeals concluded that it "cannot be presumed" that the parties supposed that the owner was "to be sole judge in [his] own cause." This tendency carries over into cases involving architects' certificates.

In the leading case of Nolan v. Whitney, 88 N.Y. 648 (1882), a contractor, who had agreed to do masonry work to the satisfaction of the architect, sued for a $2,700 final payment on the total price of $11,700, although the architect had refused to give a certificate for that payment. The Court of Appeals affirmed a judgment for the contractor for the $2,700 less a $200 deduction for trivial defects in the plastering. "[W]hen he had substantially performed his contract, the architect was bound to give him the certificate, and his refusal to give it was unreasonable, and it is held that an unreasonable refusal on the part of an architect in such a case to give the certificate dispenses with its necessity." [a]

(3) *The Case of the Refusal Without Reason.* Rizzolo, a contractor, sued Stahl, the owner, who defended on the ground that Rizzolo had not procured an architect's certificate. Rizzolo's complaint alleged "fraud on the part of the architect." Judgment of the trial court for Rizzolo was reversed on appeal, and Rizzolo appealed. *Held:* Reversed and judgment of trial court affirmed. "It is inferable from the architect's own testimony that he was ready to issue the certificate, but that the defendants wished to cut down the final payment by several hundred dollars on account of a counterclaim which the architect refused to recognize or support except for a much smaller sum; that he advised the plaintiff to 'get after them and get his money'; and that when plaintiff asked for the certificate, it was on the day before suit was begun, after plaintiff had retained counsel, and that he then refused it because he 'did not want it to appear that he was issuing a certificate for a case.' Such a reason was, of course, no reason at all, and led the judge very naturally to inquire of the witness whether he did not think that he had assumed responsibilities not belonging to his duties as architect.... [H]is refusal under such circumstances was fraudulent.... It is claimed that, to constitute such fraud, the owner must be a participant. If this were the rule, a corrupt architect would be greatly aided in extorting money from the contractor as a condition of awarding a certificate that was fully earned." Rizzolo v. Poysher, 99 A. 390 (N.J.1916).

For a case in which certification by a city engineer was made a condition and the engineer, who was not obligated to do so, refused to exercise his judgment, see Grenier v. Compratt Construction Co., 454 A.2d 1289 (Conn.1983).

HICKS v. BUSH, 180 N.E.2d 425 (N.Y.1962). [Frederick Hicks executed a completely integrated written agreement with shareholders of the Clinton G. Bush Company under which the parties were to merge their corporate interests into a single "holding" company, Bush–Hicks Enterprises. Each party was to subscribe to a specified number of shares of this new company, transferring to it shares representing his existing corporate interest. Hicks transferred his stock, but the others did not, and the merger did not take place. When Hicks sued the others for specific performance, they set up as an affirmative defense that the written agreement was executed "upon a parol condition" that it "was

a. Does this help to explain why the failure of Jacob & Youngs to obtain the architect's certificate troubled neither Cardozo for the majority nor McLaughlin for the dissenters in Jacob & Youngs v. Kent, p. 520 above?

not to operate" as a contract and that the merger was not "to become effective" until "equity expansion funds" of $672,500 were first raised and they had not been raised. At the trial the evidence showed that this sum was essential to the successful operation of the merger and that the parties had agreed that the entire merger deal was subject to the condition that the sum be raised, the writing not to become effective as a binding contract until the specified equity expansion funds were obtained. As one witness said, the understanding was "Get the money or no deal." [1] From an adverse judgment, Hicks appealed.

FULD, JUDGE. . . . The applicable law is clear, the relevant principles settled. Parol testimony is admissible to prove a condition precedent to the legal effectiveness of a written agreement . . . if the condition does not contradict the express terms of such written agreement.[a] . . . A certain disparity is inevitable, of course, whenever a written promise is, by oral agreement of the parties, made conditional upon an event not expressed in the writing. Quite obviously, though, the parol evidence rule does not bar proof of every orally established condition precedent, but only of those which in a real sense contradict the terms of the written agreement. . . . Upon the present appeal, our problem is to determine whether there is such a contradiction.[b] . . .

There is here no direct or explicit contradiction between the oral condition and the writing; in fact, the parol agreement deals with a matter on which the written agreement, as in some of the cases cited . . ., is silent. The plaintiff, however, contends that, since the written agreement provides in terms that the obligations of the parties were to be terminated if the merged corporation failed to accept any of their stock subscriptions within 25 days, the additional oral condition—that the writing "was [not] to become operative" and that the merger was "not to become effective" until the expansion funds had been raised—is irreconcilable with the written agreement.

As already indicated, and analysis confirms it, the two conditions may stand side by side. The oral requirement that the writing was not

---

1. Hicks, however, testified that he was "absolutely positive" that nothing was said about such a condition at the time of the signing and that "to the best of my knowledge no such language was ever used at any time let alone on the day of the signing." Record at pp. 410, 434.

a. The classic case is Pym v. Campbell, 119 Eng.Rep. 903 (Queen's Bench 1856). Pym, an inventor, was negotiating with Campbell and his associates for the sale to them of Pym's invention. The parties prepared a written agreement containing the terms of the proposed sale and were awaiting an opinion from Abernathie, an engineer. In order to avoid having to meet again, they signed the agreement on the oral understanding that it would be an agreement only if Abernathie approved of the invention. When Pym sued on the agreement, Campbell and his associates prevailed at the trial by proving that Aber-

nathie had not approved. The reasoning of the court in upholding this decision is suggested by Earle, J.: "The distinction in point of law is that evidence to vary the terms of an agreement in writing is not admissible, but evidence to show that there is not an agreement at all is admissible."

b. The court distinguished Fadex Foreign Trading Corp. v. Crown Steel Corp., 79 N.E.2d 739 (N.Y.1948), in which a seller of goods was barred from showing a contemporaneous oral agreement that its duty to deliver was conditioned on its ability to obtain the goods within a month. The court there concluded that the claimed agreement was "contradictory of" and would "actually annul the express terms of the writing," which contained a merger clause and stated that the goods were "Ready now" and that delivery was to be "Prompt" and "Within 4 to 6 weeks, if possible earlier."

to take effect as a contract until the equity expansion funds were obtained is simply a further condition—a condition added to that requiring the acceptance of stock subscriptions within 25 days—and not one which is contradictory. If both provisions had been contained in the written agreement, it is clear that the defendants would not have been under immediate legal duty to transfer the stock in their companies to Bush–Hicks Enterprises until both conditions had been fulfilled and satisfied. And it is equally clear that evidence of an oral condition is not to be excluded as contradictory or "inconsistent" merely because the written agreement contains other conditions precedent....

In short, the parties in the case before us intended that their respective rights and duties with respect to the contemplated transfers of stock in the operating companies to the holding company be subject to two conditions, each independent of the other—the acceptance of the stock subscription within a specified period and the procuring of expansion funds of $672,500. As the courts below found, the parties did not contemplate performance of the written agreement until such funds were first received. In other words, it was their desire and understanding that the merger was to be one of proposal only and that, even though the formal preliminary steps were to be taken, the writing was not to become operative as a contract or the merger effective until $672,500 was raised. It is certainly not improbable that parties contracting in these circumstances would make the asserted oral agreement; the condition precedent at hand is the sort of condition which parties would not be inclined to incorporate into a written agreement intended for public consumption. The challenged evidence was, therefore, admissible and, since there was ample proof attesting to the making of the oral agreement, the trial court was fully warranted in holding that no operative or binding contract ever came into existence....

[Affirmed.]

NOTES

(1) *Conditions and the Parol Evidence Rule.* Were the defendants attempting to show that the writing was not to have any effect until the funds were procured or that the obligations of the parties under the instrument were conditional on the procurement of the funds? If the former, was there an integrated agreement? If the latter, does the case stand for the proposition that the parol evidence rule does not apply to conditions precedent? That it does not apply to conditions like those in *Luttinger* and *Laurel Race Course*, above? See Luria Bros. & Co. v. Pielet Bros. Scrap Iron & Metal, Inc., 600 F.2d 103 (7th Cir.1979).

(2) *The Code.* What would have been the result in Hicks v. Bush if UCC 2–202 had been applicable? See Hunt Foods & Industries v. Doliner, 270 N.Y.S.2d 937 (App.Div.1966).

(3) *Merger Clauses and Conditions.* In Kryl v. Mechalson, 47 N.W.2d 899 (Wis.1951), the court held that an oral condition to the contract could be established in spite of the following language: "It is understood that this contract is complete in itself, and that the party of the first part is not bound by any other terms or agreements other than are herein contained." Can you draft

a clause which would be more likely to be effective? See Edward T. Kelly Co. v. Von Zakobiel, 171 N.W. 75 (Wis.1919).

Review the clause that you drafted in response to Note 2, p. 581 above. Can you improve it in the light of Hicks v. Bush?

(c) Mitigating Doctrines

PREVENTION AND CONDITIONS

One who prevents the occurrence of a condition of one's own duty may be precluded from later asserting the non-occurrence of that condition. The duty of good faith performance that is usually imposed requires at least that one do nothing to prevent the occurrence of such a condition.

Questions of prevention often arise in cases involving real-estate brokers. Recall Note 3, p. 677 above, which dealt with the right of a broker whose commission was payable, in part, "on the closing of title." If a broker's right is so conditioned, can the broker nevertheless recover the commission if the sale is not consummated because the *seller,* rather than the *buyer,* backs out? For an affirmative answer, see Drake v. Hosley, 713 P.2d 1203 (Alaska 1986), in which the court held that the condition was excused by the seller's "frustrating conduct" in selling the property to a third party.

NOTES

(1) *A Coup at the NRA.* At the annual meeting of the National Rifle Association in May 1977 the organization was "taken over" by dissident members. Earlier, the decision had been taken to move its headquarters to Colorado and sell its site in the District of Columbia. Indeed, the president had signed a contract of sale to a purchaser procured by Shear, as broker, "subject to the approval of the Board." His $150,000 commission was confirmed early in May, before the takeover, under an agreement making it "contingent on settlement." After the takeover, the Management Committee, which had earlier selected the purchaser, declined to recommend the sale to the Board. Moreover, the Association by-laws were amended to prohibit changing the headquarters and to strip the Board of Directors of power to approve the sale.

All the foregoing "facts" were alleged by Shear in suing the Association for breach of contract. From a dismissal of his complaint, he appealed. *Held:* Reversed. The court discussed an exception for what it called "assumption of risk," to the effect that the prevention doctrine does not apply if the contract authorizes prevention. But it ruled that the doctrine of prevention and not the exception applied. "Actually," the court said, "it is somewhat inaccurate to call the assumption of risk rule ... an 'exception' to the prevention doctrine." Prevention, as defined, is a breach of contract. "A corollary of this definition is that there is no prevention when the contract authorizes a party to prevent a condition from occurring.... Shear did not assume the risk that the Management Committee would refuse to recommend the contract, or that the Board would be deprived . . . of authority to approve the contract." Shear v. National Rifle Association, 606 F.2d 1251 (D.C.Cir.1979).

The court also rejected the Association's contention that "nothing but abject speculation could show that 'the condition [settlement] would have occurred'." [a]

(2) *The Case of the School Board's Lesson.* The New York City Board of Education let a contract for work on a school building, containing a condition that the agreement should be binding only if "the comptroller shall indorse hereon his certificate" that appropriated and unexpended funds were on hand to meet the estimated expense. After the contractor had done some preliminary work, the Board "rescinded" the contract. Although it did not question that the required funds were available, it justified its action by the comptroller's failure to certify the contract. He had withheld certification at the Board's request. The contractor sued the Board. From a judgment for the defendant, the plaintiff appealed. *Held:* Reversed. The Board's action could not be justified by the comptroller's failure to certify the contract. "The general rule is, as it has been frequently stated, that a party to a contract cannot rely on the failure of another to perform a condition precedent where he has frustrated or prevented the occurrence of the condition." Kooleraire Serv. & Inst. Corp. v. Board of Ed., 268 N.E.2d 782 (N.Y.1971).

WAIVER, ESTOPPEL, AND ELECTION

A requirement that a condition occur may be eliminated by agreement between the parties. After a contract is made, an obligor whose duty is conditional may promise to perform despite the nonoccurrence of a condition or despite a delay in its occurrence. See Restatement Second § 84. Such a promise is commonly termed a *waiver*. Although it is often said that a waiver is "the intentional relinquishment of a known right," this is misleading. What is involved is not the relinquishment of a right and the termination of the reciprocal duty but rather the excuse of the nonoccurrence of a condition of a duty. The creditor who discharges a debt by release or renunciation does not "waive" the debt in the strict sense of that word.[a] However, as Corbin said, the word is one "of indefinite connotation" that, "like a cloak, . . . covers a multitude of sins."[b]

A party that, without consideration, has waived a condition that is within the other party's control *before* the time for occurrence of the condition can retract the waiver and reinstate the requirement that the condition occur unless the other party has relied to such an extent that retraction would be unjust. See Restatement Second § 84(2); UCC 2–

---

a. Shear also alleged that when he signed his contingent-on-settlement agreement the NRA official who signed for it knew of the impending coup, and that he (Shear) would not have signed if he had known of it. What sort of claim does this allegation support?

a. Note, however, that UCC 1–107 does not use the word in the strict sense. What of the title to UCC 2–605?

b. Corbin, Conditions in the Law of Contracts, 28 Yale L.J. 739, 754 (1919).

209(5). If there has been such reliance, *estoppel* will preclude retraction. However, a party that has waived a condition *after* the time for occurrence of the condition is subject to a dramatically different rule under which the waiver cannot be retracted, even in the absence of reliance. See Restatement Second § 84(1). Such waivers smack of election.

The word *election* signifies a choice, one that is often binding on the party that makes it. When the time for occurrence of a condition has expired, the party whose duty is conditional has a choice between, on the one hand, taking advantage of the nonoccurrence of the condition and treating the duty as discharged or, on the other hand, disregarding the nonoccurrence of the condition and treating the duty as unconditional. Under the rule just stated, a party that chooses to disregard the nonoccurrence of a condition is bound by an election to treat the duty as unconditional. The parties that have most often been bound by such election waivers are insurers.

NOTES

(1) *The Case of the Porsche Procrastination.* Early in 1990, Dr. Jerry Morgan bought a 1984 Porsche "on time" from Riverside Motors, which assigned its rights to Mercedes–Benz Credit Corporation (MBCC). Morgan, who was to make 48 monthly payments, was late in making payments, and in 1991 MBCC exercised its right to repossess the Porsche. After repossession, Morgan brought his account current and sued MBCC in conversion. As the Supreme Court of Arkansas explained, "Dr. Morgan made only one timely payment of the fourteen monthly payments required prior to MBCC having repossessed Morgan's automobile. The thirteen late payments ranged from a few days to more than thirty days delinquent from the due date required under the parties' agreement. MBCC's personnel had contacted Morgan concerning his delinquent payments, but no one at MBCC ever informed Morgan that MBCC intended to commence strict enforcement of its rights under their contract. The record shows that shortly before it repossessed Morgan's Porsche on April 8, 1991, MBCC had again accepted another late payment (March) on April 1, 1991, and it also accepted Morgan's delinquent April payment on April 11, 1991. In fact, MBCC even tendered the car's return to Morgan when Morgan became current on his account."

The court concluded: "Clearly, a jury ... could have found that (1) MBCC, by its course of dealing, had waived its right to repossession based on its having repeatedly accepted late payments, and (2) in order to reinstate its right under the parties' contract, MBCC was required to give Morgan notice that MBCC expected strict compliance in future dealings. If MBCC failed to give such notice in these circumstances, it would then not have the right to declare a default and repossess its collateral." Mercedes–Benz Credit Corp. v. Morgan, 850 S.W.2d 297 (Ark.1993).

(2) *The Case of the Delayed Defense.* Burglars cut their way into a retail store operated by Ross Jewelers, Inc., and made off with merchandise worth more than $60,000, all but about $10,000 of which was taken from a vault in the store. The vault had a protective alarm system, as required by insurance on the goods, but the manager's habit was to leave the key in the lock. The policy also required the insured to maintain a "detailed and itemized inventory" of its property. A report to the insurer's home office stated that "a detailed and

itemized inventory was not kept," "the internal control over the stock was inadequate," and "the detail stock records were not up to date." A week later the insurer wrote that nothing would be paid for contents of the vault, but authorizing a settlement offer for the remainder of the loss. The offer was declined. In a suit brought by Ross Jewelers on the policy, the insurer disclaimed liability altogether, relying on the inventory provision. The trial court gave judgment for the plaintiff for the merchandise lost both from the vault and elsewhere. The insurer appealed.

The Court of Appeals said: "We are in agreement with the district court's holding that the denial of liability by Phoenix upon the sole ground that Ross Jewelers had breached the condition that it would maintain the protective devices . . . operated as a waiver of the defense of the failure of Ross Jewelers to maintain an inventory." Although the writer of the letter testified that he had prepared it in haste, without thought of the inventory question, intention may be inferred from conduct. Judgment was reversed, however, to redetermine the amount so as to eliminate the contents of the vault. Phoenix Ins. Co. v. Ross Jewelers, Inc. 362 F.2d 985 (5th Cir.1966).

(3) *Anti–Waiver Clauses.* A party may have a better chance to fend off a claim of waiver if the contract contains an anti-waiver clause. Such a clause typically states that no action or inaction by that party shall amount to a waiver of any condition of any duty of that party. However, such clauses are not always honored by courts. See Connecticut Fire Ins. Co. v. Fox, 361 F.2d 1 (10th Cir.1966), holding that a "non-waiver" agreement providing that the insurer's investigation would not waive any conditions of the policy did not prevent waiver of the proof of loss requirement by an adjuster on whom the insureds relied "to know what they must do to recover their loss."

(4) *Waiver or Course of Performance.* It is often argued that conduct results in a waiver. Recall that in *Eastern Airlines* (p. 613 above) conduct resulted in a course of performance under UCC 2–208. How do these two effects of conduct differ? As one court has pointed out, in contrast to course of dealings, "the conduct of the parties in *performing* an agreement may be relevant to show a modification or waiver of a provision inconsistent with their conduct in the performance of that agreement." J.R. Hale Contracting Co. v. United New Mexico Bank, 799 P.2d 581, 587 (N.M.1990). According to Comment 3 to UCC 2–208, "Where it is difficult to determine whether a particular act merely sheds light on the meaning of the agreement or represents a waiver of a term of the agreement, the preference is in favor of 'waiver' whenever such construction, plus the application of the provisions on the reinstatement of rights waived (see Section 2–209), is needed to preserve the flexible character of commercial contracts and to prevent surprise or other hardship."

McKENNA v. VERNON, 101 A. 919 (Pa.1917). [The plaintiff undertook to build a moving picture theatre in Philadelphia for the defendant. The contract price, $8,750, was to be paid in installments of 80% of the work set in place, and the final installment within 30 days after completion of the work. The work was to be done under the direction of an architect, whose certificate of work done was to be the condition of each payment by the defendant. The plaintiff received several payments, amounting in all to $6,000, and brought this action for the remainder of the contract price. The defendant asserted that the work was defective; but the architect testified that there were no unauthorized departures from the specifications, and the plaintiff received a judgment for $2,500. The defendant appealed on the theory that no right of action existed in the absence of a certificate from the architect of final completion of the building. *Held:* Affirmed.]

STEWART, JUSTICE.... All payments were to be made only on certificate of the architect, and yet with a single exception each of the seven payments made as the work progressed was made without a certificate being asked for. With such constant and repeated disregard on the part of the owner to exact compliance with this provision in the contract, it is too late now for him to insist that failure on the part of the plaintiff to secure such certificate before suit defeats his right of action.... If he waived it repeatedly, as he did here, during the progress of the work, he cannot complain if he be held to have waived it when he seeks to defend against a final payment for work shown to have been honestly and substantially performed, especially when almost daily he has had the work under his own observation, without remonstrance or complaint at any time with respect to either the work done or materials employed....

NOTE

The Rationale. How many payments might the defendant have made before losing, as to the future, the right to insist that the architect's certificates be given? Is it clear that the decision was not based on facts creating an estoppel? If the plaintiff had asked for and received, early in the course of performance, the defendant's promise that he would not insist on compliance with the condition, enforcement of the promise would present an obvious problem of consideration. Was there any problem of consideration on the facts of McKenna v. Vernon?

INTERPRETATION AND FORFEITURE

Courts have traditionally preferred interpretations of contract language that avoid forfeiture. (See Note 2, p. 674 above.) Language making a promise conditional may be interpreted in such a way that the condition has occurred, as where a condition of satisfaction is taken to be reasonable satisfaction. (See Note 2, p. 678 above.) Language that does not clearly make a promise conditional may be interpreted as not imposing a condition at all, as in the Peacock Construction case.

Interpretation cannot prevent forfeiture if the drafter of the contract has taken pains to make clear that forfeiture is intended. Even in such a case, the second Restatement asserts that in some circumstances a condition may be excused to avoid "disproportionate forfeiture." Restatement Second § 229. For a rare case overtly excusing a condition on grounds of forfeiture, see Holiday Inns of America, Inc. v. Knight, 450 P.2d 42 (Cal.1969). Courts have, for the most part, preferred more traditional methods, sometimes bordering on subterfuge, to avoid forfeiture.

NOTES

(1) *The Case of Constructive Fraud.* A contract for the construction of low-rent housing required the Wilmington Housing Authority to extend the time for

completing the work "when in its judgment the findings of fact of the [Authority's] Contracting Officer justify such an extension, and his findings of fact thereon shall be final and conclusive upon the parties." The contractor gave notice of a delay resulting from a shortage of plumbers, and the officer found that a delay of 15 days was justifiable on this account. In an action against the Authority, the contractor complained that the officer had arrived at the figure of 15 days by taking 8% of the actual delay of 182 days because the plumbing cost was only that percentage of the cost of the entire contract. The Authority moved for summary judgment. *Held:* Summary judgment denied. The officer's finding may be set aside, and the issue of allowable delay presented to a jury.

"It is unfortunate that a finding of constructive fraud must be made in so many words when, in fact, we are actually dealing with serious errors in calculations. However, the decisions refer to such miscalculations as constructive fraud and I find it necessary to pin that label upon the contracting officer's erroneous findings here although, actually, there is no hint of bad faith, dishonesty or deliberate wrongful conduct upon the part of the contracting officer or the Authority. I am sure that these errors were the product of inexperience and mistaken judgment." Anthony P. Miller, Inc. v. Wilmington Housing Authority, 179 F.Supp. 199 (D.Del.1959). See Illustration 8 to Restatement Second § 227. Is a contracting officer the same sort of third party as an architect?

(2) *The Case of the Evidentiary Condition.* Ferguson, who ran a drugstore, had an insurance policy under which Phoenix Assurance promised to pay $1,000 for loss by safe burglary, which was defined, under the heading "CONDITIONS," so as to require "felonious entry ... provided such entry shall be made by actual force and violence, of which force and violence there are visible marks made by tools, explosives, electricity or chemicals upon the exterior of ... all of said doors of such vault or such safe and any vault containing the safe, if entry is made through such doors." Ferguson's safe was opened by a thief who took $400 after opening the outer locked door by manipulating its combination lock and the inner locked door by punching out the lock. When Phoenix denied liability Ferguson sued and recovered. Phoenix appealed. *Held:* Affirmed.

"The reason for such restrictions, quite obviously, is to protect the companies from what are commonly known as 'inside jobs,' and from frauds that would inevitably result, but for such protection.... The recital that there be visible marks upon the exterior of all of the doors to the safe has reference only to evidence of the force and violence used in making the felonious entry into the safe. In other words, the substantive condition of the proviso is that entry into the safe be made by actual force and violence. The further condition that there be visible marks upon the exterior of all doors to the safe, if entry is made through such doors is merely evidentiary to show an entry into the safe by actual force and violence.... We hold that where a rule of evidence is imposed by a provision in an insurance policy, as here, the assertion of such rule by the insurance carrier, beyond the reasonable requirements necessary to prevent fraudulent claims against it in proof of the substantive conditions imposed by the policy, contravenes the public policy of the state." Ferguson v. Phoenix Assur. Co., 370 P.2d 379 (Kan.1962).

See Note 1, p. 417 above.

SECTION 2.   CONSTRUCTIVE CONDITIONS OF EXCHANGE

This section introduces problems of performance and non-performance that do not turn on express conditions. Two main instruments of the law's development in this connection are the conception of "constructive conditions" [a] and "material breach." As the Restatement Second indicates, a party's failure to *render* a performance—or in some cases its failure to *offer* a performance—is a possible excuse for the non-performance of a duty undertaken by the other party. Moreover, a *prospective* failure to perform may have that effect. A traditional way of affirming these effects is to say that the commitments exchanged by the parties are "dependent covenants." (And a way of denying these effects is to speak of "independent covenants.") The first case in the section, Kingston v. Preston, is a cornerstone of the law of constructive conditions, reasoned in terms of such dependency.

Kingston v. Preston was regarded in its own time as a notable advance in the doctrine of dependency of covenants, and has been so referred to ever since. To speak in current terms, it is regarded as the chief inspiration for constructive conditions. The views expressed by Lord Mansfield have been commonly seen as modifying an attitude of the common law that was centuries old. Although the dependency of promises was neither invented nor finally resolved in that case, it is the most celebrated of a long series on the subject.

The impact of Kingston v. Preston is suggested by a case in which a seller of an interest in land sued the buyer for a sum stipulated to be paid if either party failed to perform. The issue presented by the pleadings was whether or not the plaintiff might recover without having made any move to convey the property. According to Lord Kenyon (who succeeded Mansfield as Chief Justice), the claim would be good under "the old cases," but he said that they "outrage common sense." [b] Some hypothetical "old cases" were stated in 1500.[c] One of them concerned a father who covenants to transfer an estate to his daughter and her husband-to-be, as part of a marriage settlement between the two men. According to the old text, if the latter is faithless—"if I marry another woman"—nevertheless the father can be compelled to convey. That result represents in an extreme degree the principle that mutual covenants are independent unless expressed to be otherwise; in current terms we might say that the marriage is not a constructive condition of the father's undertaking. (The result is otherwise, says the note, if the father's covenant refers to the marriage promise in a certain way, being made "for the same cause.")

a. This expression is preferred—at least by some commentators such as Corbin and Patterson—as being more precise than "implied condition." The first Restatement employed the term in black-letter rules; see § 253. The Restatement Second incorpo-rates the idea, but not in such rules; see §§ 204 and 237 (especially Comment a).

b. Goodisson v. Nunn, 4 T.R. 761, 100 Eng.Rep. 1288 (King's Bench 1792).

c. Y.B.Trin. 15 Hen. 7, f. 10, pl. 17 (1500).

The defendant in Kingston v. Preston was in business as a silk mercer, and the plaintiff had entered his business as a "covenant servant," or apprentice. The articles of indenture provided that after a year and a quarter the defendant would retire from the business. Thereafter it was to be carried on by the plaintiff and a partner—either a nephew of the defendant or someone else nominated by the defendant. The plaintiff was to pay for his share of the business in monthly installments of 250£. (The payments were to represent the value of the inventory, or stock in trade, which was to be fixed at a fair valuation.) For assuring these payments, the plaintiff agreed to give the defendant "good and sufficient security," approved of by him, "at and before the sealing and delivery of the deeds" conveying the business.

All this was alleged by the plaintiff, and further that he had performed and been ready to perform his covenants, but that the defendant had refused to surrender the business at the appointed time. The defendant pleaded that the plaintiff did not give sufficient security for the payments. To this the plaintiff demurred, and arguments ensued as reported below.

KINGSTON v. PRESTON
King's Bench, 1773.
Lofft 194, 2 Doug. 689, 99 Eng.Rep. 437.

On the part of the plaintiff, the case was argued by Mr. Buller, who contended that the covenants were mutual and independent, and therefore a plea of the breach of one of the covenants to be performed by the plaintiff was no bar to an action for a breach by the defendant of one which he had bound himself to perform, but that the defendant might have his remedy for the breach by the plaintiff in a separate action. On the other side, Mr. Gross insisted that the covenants were dependent in their nature, and therefore performance must be alleged: the security to be given for the money was manifestly the chief object of the transaction, and it would be highly unreasonable to construe the agreement so as to oblige the defendant to give up a beneficial business, and valuable stock-in-trade, and trust to the plaintiff's personal security (who might, and, indeed was admitted to be worth nothing), for the performance of his part.

In delivering the judgment of the Court, Lord Mansfield expressed himself to the following effect: There are three kinds of covenants: 1. Such as are called mutual and independent, where either party may recover damages from the other for the injury he may have received by a breach of the covenants in his favor, and where it is no excuse for the defendant to allege a breach of the covenants on the part of the plaintiff. 2. There are covenants which are conditions and dependent, in which the performance of one depends on the prior performance of another, and, therefore, till this prior condition is performed, the other party is not liable to an action on his covenant. 3. There is also a third sort of covenants, which are mutual conditions to be performed at the same time; and in these, if one party was ready and offered to perform his part, and the other neglected or refused to perform his, he who was ready and offered has fulfilled his engagement, and may maintain an action for the default of the other; though it is not certain that either is obliged to do the first act. His Lordship then proceeded to say, that the dependence or independence of covenants was to be collected from the evident sense and meaning of the parties, and that, however transposed they might be in the deed, their precedency must depend on the order of time in which the intent of the transaction requires their performance. That, in the case before the Court, it would be the greatest injustice if the plaintiff should prevail: the essence of the agreement was, that the defendant should not trust to the personal security of the plaintiff, but, before he delivered up his stock and business, should have good security for the payment of the money. The giving such security, therefore, must necessarily be a condition precedent. Judgment was accordingly given for the defendant, because the part to be performed by the plaintiff was clearly a condition precedent.

NOTES

(1) *An Example.* Jacob & Youngs v. Kent, p. 520 above, was an action for the unpaid price of building a residence for the defendant. The defendant sought to justify his failure to pay on the ground that the plaintiff had violated a promise on its part to install Reading pipe. The premise of this defense was that a relation of "dependency" existed between the promises exchanged by the parties. According to Restatement Second § 232 the existence of this relation is presumed to exist when a contract includes an exchange of promises, "unless a contrary intention is clearly manifested."

(2) *The Move to Dependency.* Compare the "three kinds of covenants" enumerated by Lord Mansfield with the distinctions made by Cardozo in Jacob & Youngs v. Kent: promises "plainly independent"; some "so plainly dependent that they must always be conditions"; and others that, "though dependent and thus conditions when there is departure in point of substance, will be viewed as independent and collateral when the departure is insignificant." (See pp. 521–22 above.) The historical sequence from Mansfield to Cardozo to the Second Restatement can be read to mean that the category of independent covenants is on its way to extinction, to be replaced by a two-fold distinction between a party's *material* failure to render a promised performance and an *immaterial* (insignificant) breach.

Examine the cases presented in Section 1 of this chapter in light of the dependency of promises. Does it appear that the doctrine would supply a satisfactory "off the rack" solution to problems that the parties sought to solve with the language of conditions? In Luttinger v. Rosen, p. 665 above, the purchasers agreed to use diligence in a search for financing. If they had failed to do so, but the contract were not expressly qualified as it was ("subject to . . ."), would the sellers have been bound to convey the house? To repay the deposit? In Gibson v. Cranage, p. 679 above, might the doctrine of dependency have protected the interest of the defendant if the only evidence of the agreement was the testimony of the plaintiff as quoted in the first paragraph of the opinion?

(3) *Opportunism and Its Answers.* The doctrine of constructive conditions is one counterweight to self-interested conduct on the part of a contracting party. The doctrine permits a promisor (A) to withhold performance if the other party (B) has not given—or tendered—a performance promised by B in exchange. If A

could not withhold performance, B might capture the benefit of A's performance and yet withhold B's own return performance. (Whether B would be tempted to do this or not might depend on other factors, such as a cost in reputation that B might suffer through breach of contract.)

Self-interested conduct of this kind is often referred to as "opportunism." Although the word suggests predatory behavior, in economic discourse the word has little or no moral flavor and the phenomenon is considered pervasive among contracting parties. A party to an exchange of promises can therefore be expected to take protective measures. One possibility is to require the other party to "go first," so as to have the protection afforded by the doctrine of constructive conditions. Another is to require the other party to furnish a guarantee of performance by a reliable third party.

What protective measures might have been feasible for the plaintiffs in White v. Benkowski, p. 14 above? In Bloor v. Falstaff Brewing Corp., p. 623 above? Compare the protection provided by a right to assurance of due performance (Section 5(b), below.)

(4) *Drafting (Reprise)*. Refer again to the drafting problem in Note 1 at p. 673 above, especially the direction to draft a clause making "sailing with the next wind" the subject of a duty alone. Do you see a difficulty in doing this, not apparent till now?

STEWART v. NEWBURY

Court of Appeals of New York, 1917.
220 N.Y. 379, 115 N.E. 984.

CRANE, J. [Plaintiff, a builder, offered to do the excavation work for defendant's new foundry building at 65 cents per cubic yard, to furnish labor and forms for the concrete work at $2.05 per cubic yard, and to furnish labor to put in re-enforcing (of the concrete) at $4.00 per ton. The defendant accepted this offer. Other necessary facts are stated in the opinion. In the trial court judgment was entered upon a verdict for the plaintiff; this judgment was affirmed in the Appellate Division, and the defendant appealed by permission.]

Nothing was said in writing about the time or manner of payment. The plaintiff, however, claims that after sending his letter and before receiving that of the defendant he had a telephone communication with Mr. Newbury and said: "I will expect my payments in the usual manner," and Newbury said, "All right, we have got the money to pay for the building." This conversation over the telephone was denied by the defendants.

The custom, the plaintiff testified, was to pay 85 per cent every thirty days or at the end of each month, 15 per cent being retained till the work was completed.

In July the plaintiff commenced work and continued until September 29th, at which time he had progressed with the construction as far as the first floor. He then sent a bill for the work done up to that date for $896.35. The defendants refused to pay the bill and work was discontinued.

The plaintiff claims that the defendants refused to permit him to perform the rest of his contract, they insisting that the work already done was not in accordance with the specifications. The defendants claimed upon the trial that the plaintiff voluntarily abandoned the work after their refusal to pay his bill.

On October 5, 1911, the defendants wrote the plaintiff a letter containing the following: "Notwithstanding you promised to let us know on Monday whether you would complete the job or throw up the contract, you have not up to this time advised us of your intention.... Under the circumstances we are compelled to accept your action as being an abandonment of your contract and of every effort upon your part to complete your work on our building. As you know, the bill which you sent us and which we declined to pay is not correct, either in items or amount, nor is there anything due you under our contract as we understand it until you have completed your work on our building."

To this letter the plaintiff replied the following day. In it he makes no reference to the telephone communication agreeing, as he testified, to make "the usual payments," but does say this: "There is nothing in our agreement which says that I shall wait until the job is completed before any payment is due, nor can this be reasonably implied.... As to having given you positive date as to when I should let you know what I proposed doing, I did not do so; on the contrary I told you that I would not tell you positively what I would do until I had visited the job, and I promised that I would do this at my earliest convenience...."

The defendant Herbert Newbury testified that the plaintiff "ran away and left the whole thing." And the defendant F.E. Newbury testified that he was told by Mr. Stewart's man that Stewart was going to abandon the job; that he thereupon telephoned Mr. Stewart, who replied that he would let him know about it the next day, but did not.

In this action, which is brought to recover the amount of the bill presented as the agreed price and $95.68 damages for breach of contract, the plaintiff had a verdict for the amount stated in the bill, but not for the other damages claimed, and the judgment entered thereon has been affirmed by the Appellate Division.

The appeal to us is upon exceptions to the judge's charge. The court charged the jury as follows: "Plaintiff says that he was excused from completely performing the contract by the defendant's unreasonable failure to pay him for the work he had done during the months of August and September.... Was it understood that the payments were to be made monthly? If it was not so understood the defendant's only obligation was to make payments at reasonable periods, in view of the character of the work, the amount of work being done and the value of it. In other words, if there was no agreement between the parties respecting the payments, the defendants' obligation was to make payments at reasonable times.... But whether there was such an agreement or not, you may consider whether it was reasonable or unreasonable for him to exact payment at that time and in that amount."

The court further said, in reply to a request to charge:

"I will say in that connection, if there was no agreement respecting the time of payment, and if there was no custom that was understood by both parties, and with respect to which they made the contract, then the plaintiff was entitled to payments at reasonable times."

The defendants' counsel thereupon made the following request, which was refused: "I ask your Honor to instruct the jury that if the circumstances existed as your Honor stated in your last instruction, then the plaintiff was not entitled to any payment until the contract was completed."

The jury was plainly told that if there were no agreement as to payments, yet the plaintiff would be entitled to part payment at reasonable times as the work progressed, and if such payments were refused he could abandon the work and recover the amount due for the work performed.

This is not the law. Counsel for the plaintiff omits to call our attention to any authority sustaining such a proposition and our search reveals none. In fact the law is very well settled to the contrary. This was an entire contract. (Ming v. Corbin, 142 N.Y. 334, 340, 341, 37 N.E. 105.) Where a contract is made to perform work and no agreement is made as to payment, the work must be substantially performed before payment can be demanded. . . .

This case was also submitted to the jury upon the ground that there may have been a breach of contract by the defendants in their refusal to permit the plaintiff to continue with his work, claiming that he had departed from the specifications, and there was some evidence justifying this view of the case, but it is impossible to say upon which of these two theories the jury arrived at its conclusion. The above errors, therefore, cannot be considered as harmless and immaterial. . . . As the verdict was for the amount of the bill presented and did not include the damages for a breach of contract, which would be the loss of profits, it may well be presumed that the jury adopted the first ground of recovery charged by the court as above quoted and decided that the plaintiff was justified in abandoning work for nonpayment of the installment.

The judgment should be reversed, and a new trial ordered, costs to abide the event.

NOTES

(1) *Questions.* If the jury believed Stewart's evidence about the telephone conversation with Newbury, does it follow that he was justified in abandoning the work? Would it matter whether this conversation occurred before or after the contract was concluded? If it occurred before, how might Stewart's case be affected by the parol evidence rule? If it occurred afterward, what was the consideration for Newbury's promise to pay "in the usual manner"?

(2) *Work Before Pay.*   Because of the doctrine of constructive conditions, fixing the time for performance under a contract has the effect of allocating the credit risk—the risk that one party (here Stewart) will do the required work but not be paid.   "When the performance of a contract consists in doing (faciendo) on one side, and in giving (dando) on the other side, the doing must take place before the giving.   (Langdell's Summary of Law of Contracts, sec. 125 [2d ed. 1880].)"   Kellogg, J., in Coletti v. Knox Hat Co., Inc., 169 N.E. 648, 649–650 (N.Y.1930).   "Centuries ago, the principle became settled that where work is to be done by one party and payment is to be made by the other, the performance of the work must precede payment, in the absence of a showing of a contrary intention.   It is sometimes supposed, that this principle grew out of employment contracts, and reflects a conviction that employers as a class are more likely to be responsible than are workmen paid in advance.   Whether or not the explanation is correct, most parties today contract with reference to the principle, and unless they have evidenced a contrary intention it is at least as fair as the opposite rule would be."   Restatement Second § 234, Comment *e.*

For repair work on buildings and chattels, and similar modest jobs, payment is commonly withheld until completion.   But for sizable construction work it is well-nigh universal practice to agree upon periodic progress payments, or "draws," in favor of the contractor.   As security for completion, the owner retains a fraction (usually 10–20%) of the amount earned each month by the contractor, and the sums withheld (sometimes called the "retent") are payable only upon completion.   Does this practice indicate that contractors are dissatisfied with the rule in Stewart v. Newbury?   Is it a reason for discarding the rule?

CONCURRENT CONDITIONS AND TENDER

In Kingston v. Preston, Mansfield spoke of promises "which are mutual conditions to be performed at the same time; and in these, if one party was ready and offered to perform his part, and the other neglected or refused to perform his, he who was ready and offered has fulfilled his engagement, and may maintain an action for the default of the other; though it is not certain that either is obliged to do the first act."

The Court of Kings Bench applied this analysis in Morton v. Lamb, 101 Eng.Rep. 890 (Kings Bench 1797), several years after Mansfield's death.   When a buyer of grain alleged that the seller had failed to deliver the grain, although the buyer was ready to receive it, the court upheld the seller's objection that the buyer had failed to allege that he was ready to pay for the grain.   "[W]here two concurrent acts are to be done, the party who sues the other for non-performance must aver that he has performed, or was ready to perform, his part of the contract."

Courts still apply this rule to contracts for the sale of goods where there is no provision for credit or other means of payment.   Courts express the mutual dependency of the parties' promises by saying that tender of the goods by the seller and tender of the price by the buyer are "concurrent conditions."   "Tender of delivery is a condition to the buyer's duty to accept the goods and ... to pay for them" (UCC 2–507(1)), and "tender of payment is a condition to the seller's duty to tender and complete any delivery" (UCC 2–511(1)).

"A formal tender is seldom made in business transactions," it is said, "except to lay the foundation for subsequent assertion in a court of justice of rights which spring from refusal of the tender." [a] Courts are not often called on to say what is or is not a formal tender of performance under a contract. Partly for that reason, perhaps, as the word "tender" is commonly used it suggests a degree of punctilio in conduct that is seldom achieved. Paradoxically, the strict sense of the word is supported by a set of rules dispensing with the necessity of tender in ordinary contract litigation.

The Code states the requisites, under contracts for the sale of goods, for a seller's tender of delivery (UCC 2–507) and for a buyer's tender of payment (UCC 2–511). A comment after the former section identifies two senses of the word "tender." In the stricter sense, it "contemplates an offer coupled with a present ability to fulfill all the conditions resting on the tendering party and must be followed by actual performance if the other party shows himself ready to proceed." But the comment indicates that something less than this will suffice to put the other party in default, "if he fails to proceed in some manner."

If a buyer has not made an arrangement with the seller for credit, must he proffer payment in money—i.e., "legal tender"? The Code recognizes that it is commercially normal to accept a check from a "seemingly solvent party," and states a rule designed to avoid "commercial surprise." Tendering a check is commonly sufficient under this rule, "unless the seller demands payment in legal tender and gives any extension of time reasonably necessary to procure it." UCC 2–511(2).

NOTES

(1) *The Case of the Procrastinating Purchaser.* In Lawrence v. Miller, 86 N.Y. 131 (1881), a contract for the sale of land had fallen through, and the buyer sought to recover an initial payment of $2,000. The buyer contended that the seller could retain the money only if he had put the buyer in default by making tender of a deed, and that he had not done so. The court said: "it may be taken that by the term tender is generally meant the actual physical production of the deed, and the reaching it out, with words of offer of it, to the vendee." But the court ruled that the buyer had been put in default without such a ceremony; "the requirement of the law is not cast in a rigid mould...." It appeared that the parties had met twice "with a view to perform." Each time the seller had laid the deed on the table, and the buyer had asked for more time. On the second occasion the seller refused to allow another day. The court's opinion can be understood as saying either that the seller's conduct was a sufficient tender, or that a perfect tender was excused by the buyer's conduct. An exact definition of the word, if it could be achieved, would not be decisive in many cases.

(2) *Specific Performance.* In actions for specific performance, and especially those based on land-sale contracts, constructive conditions of exchange sometimes do not operate with the same effect as in ordinary damage actions. Because the remedy takes the form of an *order,* a court can insert a condition that effectively secures the receipt by the defendant of the plaintiff's promised performance.

a. Lehman, J., dissenting, in Petterson   Compare Crowder v. Aurora Co-op. Ele-
v. Pattberg, 161 N.E. 428 (N.Y.1928).   vator Co., 393 N.W.2d 250 (Neb.1986).

In McMillan v. Smith, 363 S.W.2d 437 (Tex.1962), the plaintiffs, purchasers of a ranch, were uncertain what the per-acre price amounted to, in the aggregate. Upon making a deposit into court, they alleged their ability and willingness to pay "such further sum as the Court may order." The court accepted this invitation, saying: "Historically, in a suit for specific performance, the question as to the necessity for a tender of performance by a purchaser has been determined according to equitable rules rather than to those applicable to an action at law. The latter requires the purchaser, as a condition precedent, to tender performance. Courts of equity, on the other hand have not been bound by strict and inflexible rules."

———

SECTION 3. MITIGATING DOCTRINES

———

(a) Substantial Performance

———

JACOB & YOUNGS v. KENT

[For the report of this case, see p. 520 above.]

NOTES

(1) *Question.* Would it have been possible for the parties, using a tightly-drawn provision in the contract, to preclude a recovery by the contractor such as this? Consider the provisions that the contract contained, set out in footnote a, p. 521 above. How could they have been improved upon, as a means of protecting the defendant?

In American Continental Life Ins. Co. v. Ranier Const. Co., 607 P.2d 372 (Ariz.1980), a builder's arguments of prevention, substantial performance, and waiver failed to overcome the condition of an architect's final certificate for payment (requirement not "procedural chaff").

(2) *Conclusiveness of Certificate.* A contractor who agrees to procure the certificate of an architect or an engineer as a condition of payment may want to take care lest the provision on the subject be read as leaving the certificate inconclusive when it is issued, so that the contractor remains exposed to a claim that its performance was defective. The other party may wish, naturally, to retain such a claim notwithstanding the issuance of a certificate. What language would you suggest to avert the risk for the contractor? What language to have the opposite effect? How would you interpret the language in footnote a, p. 521 above?

———

SUBSTANTIAL PERFORMANCE IN CONTEXT

The rule of substantial performance is commonly associated with building and improvement contracts. It is applied sporadically, however, in litigation over other types of contracts. Indeed, the origin of the rule has been traced to a decision by Mansfield about the sale of a plantation in the West Indies. Boone v. Eyre, 126 Eng.Rep. 160, Note (Kings Bench 1777). A leading English case on the subject concerned an indenture of apprenticeship. Ellen v. Topp, 155 Eng.Rep. 609 (Exchequer 1851). Nevertheless, the rule has found its chief proving ground in suits on construction contracts.

Why should this be so? Several considerations suggest the answer. As for employment contracts, it is usual for an employer to pay wages at short intervals, and to reserve the power of termination at will. Leases of real property have traditionally been regarded as exempt from the usual contract rules of constructive conditions. As for contracts for the sale of goods, the party who is denied a remedy does not suffer an investment loss, ordinarily, in the same degree as a builder whose earnings prove uncollectible. As for land sale contracts, enforcement is regularly sought in a court of equity, in which there are specialized rules serving some of the same objects as the doctrine of substantial performance. But neither party to a construction contract has access to specific performance as a remedy, ordinarily.

"Through the doctrine of substantial performance," it is said, "the judges installed themselves as administrators of the execution and discharge of contracts. They freed themselves from rigid rules and adopted a broad standard under which they could apply a policy of making contract effective." [a] This must not be understood to mean that the courts will directly administer the performance of a contract; it means that practical judgments about performance figure in their decisions about money claims. Should the courts undertake a more active role as to construction contracts? Having become "administrators of execution" indirectly, would they find it a short and easy step beyond to order the correction of defective work?

NOTES

(1) *Preference in Interpretation (Reprise).* How does the doctrine of substantial performance, which applies only to constructive and not express conditions, relate to the preference in interpretation mentioned in Note 2, p. 674 above.

(2) *Willful Breach.* What cases of a builder's deviation from the plans agreed upon should be regarded as intentional or willful misconduct? The use of inferior materials for the purpose of filching a profit?

Professor Corbin has objected to the use of the word *willful* on the ground that it "indicates a childlike faith in the existence of a plain and obvious line between the good and the bad, between unfortunate virtue and unforgivable sin.... [T]he enrichment of even an injured man may become unjust." [b] What word is better than "willful" to describe conduct of a builder that will bar him from claiming on the theory of substantial performance? In Restatement Second § 241, the absence of that word is noteworthy. But does subsection (e) bring the sense of it in by the back door? See Comment *f.*

a. J. Corry, Law and Policy 41–43 (1959).

b. Section 1123; cf. § 1254. And see Shapiro, Inc. v. Bencich, 101 A.2d 890 (D.C.Mun.App.1954) (petty vengeance).

What if the builder departs from the plans for the purpose of enhancing the value of the structure? To meet unforeseen construction problems? What if it is *impossible* to follow the plans literally? Compare a builder who cannot pay all his laborers and materialmen, as the contract requires him to do, because he lacks funds.

It has been generally held—or at least said—that a "willful" or "intentional" deviation from the terms of the contract will always preclude a finding of substantial performance.[c] (This is often said when the facts seem to show a deviation that would be material in any case.)

Restatement Second § 241 takes a different view, under which the pertinent inquiry is not simply whether the breach was "wilful" but whether the behavior of the party in default "comports with standards of good faith and fair dealing." Even an adverse conclusion on this point is not decisive but is to be weighed with other factors, such as the extent to which the owner will be deprived of a reasonably expected benefit and the extent to which the builder may suffer forfeiture, in deciding whether there has been substantial performance.

(3) *Producing Evidence.* In a substantial-performance action, where a builder claims the unpaid price (subject to allowances for deficiencies), some courts require the owner to produce evidence of damages resulting from defects in the builder's work. But see Vance v. My Apartment Steak House, Etc., 677 S.W.2d 480 (Tex.1984), requiring the builder, as plaintiff, to establish the cost of remedying defects. A minority of the justices here thought it "anomalous" to require that the plaintiff provide support for the defendant's position.

Who is in a better position to establish the loss to the defendant? Does the answer depend on the question how that loss is measured?

(4) *The Case of the "Independent Covenant".* On acquiring the business of Don Hanks, an insurance adjuster, GAB Business Services made a first payment of $28,000 and agreed to make two further payments of $33,500 each, at yearly intervals. Hanks worked for GAB for about a year, but a dispute arose after GAB had made the first $33,500 payment and Hanks quit and began to compete with GAB in violation of a five-year restrictive covenant. GAB then refused to make the final payment. The Supreme Court of Texas held that Hanks was entitled to recover $33,500 less $1,200 damages for GAB's loss resulting from Hanks's competition.

" '[W]hen a covenant goes only to part of the consideration on both sides and a breach may be compensated for in damages, it is to be regarded as an independent covenant, unless this is contrary to the expressed intent of the parties.' The covenant not to compete in the Hanks/GAB contract only goes to part of the contract. The contract covers numerous items and the parties had bargained for a value of $5,000 to be assigned to the covenant not to compete, although the value assigned was admittedly for tax reasons. Further, there is no express language in the contract that indicates the parties intended the covenants to be mutually dependent.... In this case, Hanks' breach may be adequately compensated by damages." Hanks v. GAB Business Services, Inc., 644 S.W.2d 707 (Tex.1982).

On the facts of this case, what "covenant" (i.e., promise) was "independent" of what other "covenant" (i.e., promise)? Would the result have been the same

---

c. In Samuel J. Creswell I. Wks. v. Housing Auth. of Camden, 449 F.2d 557 (3d Cir.1971), a vice-president of the plaintiff contractor testified that it did not intend to comply with the specifications of the contract when bidding for it; the plaintiff was held to be "estopped" from asserting substantial performance.

if Hanks had begun to compete with GAB immediately after selling his business? (Assume that GAB offered to return what it had received.) If not, would the decision in the actual case be better explained by saying that Hanks's breach was not a material one?

(5) *Problem.* Contractor installed a heating system in a building, and did such poor work that he is accountable to Owner for his loss of $25,000, calculated on the "diminished value" rule. The misperformance was willful. Owner has withheld $15,000 of the contract price, and Contractor believes it should be held liable only for the difference, $10,000. Should the unpaid price be allowed as a credit upon his liability? See Kirk Reid Company v. Fine, 139 S.E.2d 829 (Va.1965). Compare Di Mare v. Capaldi, 146 N.E.2d 517 (Mass.1957). Willfulness aside, if the cost of correcting the work is greater than $25,000, Jacob & Youngs v. Kent is not an authority for limiting the contractor's liability to that amount, is it? See Bellizzi v. Huntley Estates, 143 N.E.2d 802 (N.Y.1957).

PLANTE v. JACOBS

Supreme Court of Wisconsin, 1960.
10 Wis.2d 567, 103 N.W.2d 296.

[Eugene Plante contracted with Frank and Carol Jacobs to furnish the materials and construct a house upon their lot in Brookfield, in accordance with plans and specifications, for the sum of $26,765. During the course of construction Plante was paid $20,000. Disputes arose between the parties, the Jacobs refused to continue payment, and Plante did not complete the house. He sued to establish a lien on the property as a way of recovering the unpaid balance of the contract price, plus extras. The owners—who are the appellants—answered with allegations of faulty workmanship and incomplete construction.]

HALLOWS, JUSTICE. The defendants argue the plaintiff cannot recover any amount because he has failed to substantially perform the contract. The plaintiff conceded he failed to furnish the kitchen cabinets, gutters and downspouts, sidewalk, closet clothes poles, and entrance seat amounting to $1,601.95. This amount was allowed to the defendants. The defendants claim some 20 other items of incomplete or faulty performance by the plaintiff and no substantial performance because the cost of completing the house in strict compliance with the plans and specifications would amount to 25 or 30 per cent of the contract price. The defendants especially stress the misplacing of the wall between the living room and the kitchen, which narrowed the living room in excess of one foot. The cost of tearing down this wall and rebuilding it would be approximately $4,000. The record is not clear why and when this wall was misplaced, but the wall is completely built and the house decorated and the defendants are living therein. Real estate experts testified that the smaller width of the living room would not affect the market price of the house.

The defendants rely on Manitowoc Steam Boiler Works v. Manitowoc Glue Co., 1903, 120 Wis. 1, 97 N.W. 515, for the proposition there can be no recovery on the contract as distinguished from *quantum meruit* unless there is substantial performance. This is undoubtedly the correct rule at common law. For recovery on *quantum meruit,* see Valentine v. Patrick Warren Construction Co., 1953, 263 Wis. 143, 56 N.W.2d 860. The question here is whether there has been substantial performance. The test of what amounts to substantial performance seems to be whether the performance meets the essential purpose of the contract. In the Manitowoc case the contract called for a boiler having a capacity of 150 per cent of the existing boiler. The court held there was no substantial performance because the boiler furnished had a capacity of only 82 per cent of the old boiler and only approximately one-half of the boiler capacity contemplated by the contract. In Houlahan v. Clark, 1901, 110 Wis. 43, 85 N.W. 676, the contract provided the plaintiff was to drive pilings in the lake and place a boat house thereon parallel and in line with a neighbor's dock. This was not done and the contractor so positioned the boat house that it was practically useless to the owner. Manthey v. Stock, 1907, 133 Wis. 107, 113 N.W. 443, involved a contract to paint a house and to do a good job, including the removal of the old paint where necessary. The plaintiff did not remove the old paint, and blistering and roughness of the new paint resulted. The court held that the plaintiff failed to show substantial performance. The defendants also cite Manning v. School District No. 6, 1905, 124 Wis. 84, 102 N.W. 356. However, this case involved a contract to install a heating and ventilating plant in the school building which would meet certain tests which the heating apparatus failed to do. The heating plant was practically a total failure to accomplish the purposes of the contract. See also Nees v. Weaver, 1936, 222 Wis. 492, 269 N.W. 266, 107 A.L.R. 1405 (roof on a garage).

Substantial performance as applied to construction of a house does not mean that every detail must be in strict compliance with the specifications and the plans. Something less than perfection is the test of specific [substantial?] performance unless all details are made the essence of the contract. This was not done here. There may be situations in which features or details of construction of special or of great personal importance, if not performed, would prevent a finding of substantial performance of the contract. In this case the plan was a stock floor plan. No detailed construction of the house was shown on the plan. There were no blueprints. The specifications were standard printed forms with some modifications and additions written in by the parties. Many of the problems that arose during the construction had to be solved on the basis of practical experience. No mathematical rule relating to the percentage of the price, of cost of completion, or of completeness can be laid down to determine substantial performance of a building contract. Although the defendants received a house with which they are dissatisfied in many respects, the trial court was not in error in finding the contract was substantially performed.

The next question is what is the amount of recovery when the plaintiff has substantially, but incompletely, performed. For substantial performance the plaintiff should recover the contract price less the damages caused the defendant by the incomplete performance. Both parties agree. Venzke v. Magdanz, 1943, 243 Wis. 155, 9 N.W.2d 604, states the correct rule for damages due to faulty construction amounting to such incomplete performance, which is the difference between the value of the house as it stands with faulty and incomplete construction and the value of the house if it had been constructed in strict accordance with the plans and specifications. This is the diminished-value rule. The cost of replacement or repair is not the measure of such damage, but is an element to take into consideration in arriving at value under some circumstances. The cost of replacement or the cost to make whole the omissions may equal or be less than the difference in value in some cases and, likewise, the cost to rectify a defect may greatly exceed the added value to the structure as corrected. The defendants argue that under the Venzke rule their damages are $10,000. The plaintiff on review argues the defendants' damages are only $650. Both parties agree the trial court applied the wrong rule to the facts.

The trial court applied the cost-of-repair or replacement rule as to several items, relying on Stern v. Schlafer, 1943, 244 Wis. 183, 11 N.W.2d 640, 12 N.W.2d 678, wherein it was stated that when there are a number of small items of defect or omission which can be remedied without the reconstruction of a substantial part of the building or a great sacrifice of work or material already wrought in the building, the reasonable cost of correcting the defect should be allowed. However, in Mohs v. Quarton, 1950, 257 Wis. 544, 44 N.W.2d 580, the court held when the separation of defects would lead to confusion, the rule of diminished value could apply to all defects.

In this case no such confusion arises in separating the defects. The trial court disallowed certain claimed defects because they were not proven. This finding was not against the great weight and clear preponderance of the evidence and will not be disturbed on appeal. Of the remaining defects claimed by the defendants, the court allowed the cost of replacement or repair except as to the misplacement of the living-room wall. Whether a defect should fall under the cost-of-replacement rule or be considered under the diminished-value rule depends upon the nature and magnitude of the defect. This court has not allowed items of such magnitude under the cost-of-repair rule as the trial court did. Viewing the construction of the house as a whole and its cost we cannot say, however, that the trial court was in error in allowing the cost of repairing the plaster cracks in the ceilings, the cost of mud jacking and repairing the patio floor, and the cost of reconstructing the non-weight-bearing and nonstructural patio wall. Such reconstruction did not involve an unreasonable economic waste.

The item of misplacing the living-room wall under the facts of this case was clearly under the diminished-value rule. There is no evidence that defendants requested or demanded the replacement of the wall in the place called for by the specifications during the course of construction. To tear down the wall now and rebuild it in its proper place would involve a substantial destruction of the work, if not all of it, which was put into the wall and would cause additional damage to other parts of the house and require replastering and redecorating the walls and ceilings of at least two rooms. Such economic waste is unreasonable and unjustified. The rule of diminished value contemplates the wall is not going to be moved. Expert witnesses for both parties, testifying as to the value of the house, agreed that the misplacement of the wall had no effect on the market price. The trial court properly found that the defendants suffered no legal damage, although the defendants' particular desire for specified room size was not satisfied. For a discussion of these rules of damages for defective or unfinished construction and their application see Restatement, 1 Contracts, pp. 572–573, sec. 346(1)(a) and illustrations. . . .

　　Judgment affirmed.

NOTES

　　(1) *Question.* In what ways does the New York version of the substantial performance rule appear to differ from the Wisconsin court's approach in Plante v. Jacobs?

　　(2) *Problem.* Suppose this case: Once the owners have complained about the situation of the living-room wall, Plante hires another builder to put it in the proper place, for the contract price of $4,500. Plante goes about his other work. When he comes to inspect the new wall at the Jacobs home he finds that it has been moved about *two* feet—contrary to his directions. The living room is larger, but the kitchen is now narrower than it should have been. That does not affect the market price of the house. What, if anything, must Plante pay for having the wall relocated? If your answer is "nothing", how do you explain that so minor a point as the misplacement of a wall by one foot could matter so greatly to Plante?

　　(3) *Limitations on the Rule.* Real or apparent exceptions to the rule of substantial performance are abundant. In builders' cases, however, none of them seems to command general assent. A short list is as follows:

　　(a) "The doctrine is essentially a rule of damages . . . [I]ts purpose is not to compel the unwilling acceptance of tendered work that fails to meet contract specifications." Ballou v. Basis Constr. Co., 407 F.2d 1137, 1140 (4th Cir.1969).

　　(b) "[S]ubstantial performance relates to the degree of completion rather than the date of completion." Todd Shipyards Corp. v. Jasper Electric Service Co., 414 F.2d 8 (5th Cir.1969).

　　(c) The rule does not temporize with "structural defects." See Spence v. Ham, 57 N.E. 412 (N.Y.1900), in which the size and placement of girders was faulty, affecting the solidity of the building: these were "deviations from the general plan of so essential a character that they cannot be remedied without partially reconstructing the building, and hence do not come within the rule of substantial performance. . . ." Compare Kizziar v. Dollar, 268 F.2d 914 (10th Cir.1959) ("standard and adequate" foundation for the building, though not equal to that specified).

　　(d) "Under ordinary circumstances . . . a failure to perform 10 percent of the contract price will not admit of the claim of substantial performance." Rochkind v. Jacobson, 110 N.Y.S. 583 (App.Div.1908). But see Jardine Estates v. Donna Brook Corp., 126 A.2d 372 (N.J.Super.1956) ("The matter is not to be determined on a percentage basis, for the cost of remedying defects may sometimes even exceed the outlay for original construction.").

(4) *Seriatim Objections.* A builder has put up a dwelling, under contract with the owner of the lot, and considers that he has complied with all the specifications, leaving no defects. If, however, the owner disagrees, the builder means to do corrective work. The builder wishes to do all such work at one time, before moving its crew and equipment away. How can the builder elicit a definitive list of the owner's objections?

In Cawley v. Weiner, 140 N.E. 724 (N.Y.1923), the owners of a new bungalow moved in before the builder had stopped work, and handed him a list of 17 items that they considered necessary by way of change in or addition to the structure. For about a week after that, apparently, the builder continued work. Not being paid in full, he brought suit against the owners for the price. At the trial, they offered to prove three particulars, not specified in the earlier list, in which the plaintiff had failed of performance. The trial court excluded the evidence on grounds of waiver and estoppel, and gave the plaintiff judgment for virtually the whole amount he claimed. On appeal by the owners, *held:* Reversed. "Unless the plaintiff were in some way harmed by the action of these defendants in furnishing him with a list of the defects, how are they estopped from showing the departures from the plans and specifications?" Can you reconcile this decision with that in McKenna v. Vernon, p. 696 above?

MOULTON CAVITY & MOLD, INC. v. LYN–FLEX INDUSTRIES, INC.

Supreme Judicial Court of Maine, 1979.
396 A.2d 1024.

DELAHANTY, JUSTICE. Defendant, Lyn–Flex Industries, Inc., appeals from a judgment entered after a jury trial by the Superior Court, York County, in favor of plaintiff, Moulton Cavity & Mold, Inc. The case concerns itself with an oral contract for the sale of goods which, as both parties agree, is governed by Article 2 of the Uniform Commercial Code, 11 M.R.S.A. §§ 2–101 et seq. For the reasons set forth below, we agree with defendant that the presiding Justice committed reversible error by instructing the jury that the doctrine of substantial performance applied to a contract for the sale of goods. We do not agree, however, that based on the evidence introduced at trial defendant is entitled to judgment in its favor as a matter of law. The appeal is therefore sustained and the case remanded for a new trial.

An examination of the record discloses the following sequence of events: On March 19, 1975, Lynwood Moulton, president of plaintiff, and Ernest Sturman, president of defendant, orally agreed that plaintiff would produce, and defendant purchase, twenty-six innersole molds capable of producing saleable innersoles. The price was fixed at $600.00 per mold. Whether or not a time for delivery had been established was open to question. In his testimony at trial, Mr. Moulton admitted that he was fully aware that defendant was in immediate need of the molds, and he stated that he had estimated that he could provide suitable molds in about five weeks' time. Mr. Sturman testified that "I conveyed the urgency to [Mr. Moulton] and he said 'within three weeks I will begin showing you molds and by the end of five weeks you will have [the entire order].' ''

In apparent conformity with standard practice in the industry, plaintiff set about constructing a sample mold and began a lengthy series of tests. These tests consisted of bringing the sample mold to defendant's plant, fitting the mold to one of defendant's plastic-injecting machines, and checking the innersole thus derived from the plaintiff's mold to determine if it met the specifications imposed by defendant. After about thirty such tests over a ten-week period, several problems remained unsolved, the most significant of which was "flashing," that is, a seepage of plastic along the seam where the two halves of the mold meet. Although characterized by plaintiff as a minor defect, Mr. Moulton admitted that a flashing mold could not produce a saleable innersole.

It was plaintiff's contention at trial, supported by credible evidence, that at one point during the testing period officials of defendant signified that in their judgment plaintiff's sample mold was turning out innersoles correctly configured so as to fit the model last supplied by defendant's customer. Allegedly relying on this approval, plaintiff went ahead and constructed the full run of twenty-six molds.

For its part, defendant introduced credible evidence to rebut the assertion that it had approved the fit of the molds. It also noted that Moulton's allegation of approval extended only to the fit of the mold; as Moulton conceded, defendant had never given full approval since it considered the flashing problem, among others, unacceptable.

On May 29, some ten weeks after the date of the oral agreement and five weeks after the estimated completion date, Mr. Sturman met with plaintiff's foreman at the Moulton plant. A dispute exists regarding the substance of the ensuing conversation. Plaintiff introduced evidence tending to show that at that time, Mr. Sturman revoked defendant's prior approval of the fit of the sample mold and demanded that plaintiff redesign the molds to fit the last. Testimony introduced by defendant tended to show that it had never approved the fit of the molds to begin with and that on the date in question, May 29, plaintiff's foreman indicated that plaintiff simply would not invest any more time in conforming the molds to the contract. Mr. Sturman met the next day with Mr. Moulton, and Moulton ratified the position taken by his foreman. Thereupon, Mr. Sturman immediately departed for Italy and arranged to have the molds produced by the Plastak Corporation, an Italian mold-making concern, at a cost of $650.00 per mold. Plaintiff later billed defendant for the contract price of the molds, deducting an allowance for "flashing and shut-off adjustments." Upon defendant's refusal to pay, plaintiff brought this action for the price less adjustments. Defendant counterclaimed for its costs in obtaining conforming goods to the extent that they exceeded the contract price.

At trial, plaintiff's basic theory of recovery was that it had received approval with regard to the fit of the sample mold, that in reliance on that approval it had constructed a full run of twenty-six molds, and that defendant had, in effect, committed an anticipatory breach of contract within the meaning of Section 2–610 by demanding that the fit of the molds be completely redesigned. On its counterclaim, and in response to plaintiff's position, defendant advanced the theory that plaintiff had breached the contract by failing to tender conforming goods within the five-week period mentioned by both parties.

After the presiding Justice had charged the jury, counsel for plaintiff requested at side bar that the jury be instructed on the doctrine of substantial performance. Counsel for defendant entered a timely objection to the proposed charge which objection was overruled. The court then supplemented its charge as follows:

> The only point of clarification that I'll make, ladies and gentlemen, is that I've referred a couple of times to performance of a contract and you, obviously, have to determine no matter which way you view the contract to be, and there might even be a possible third way that I haven't even considered, whether the contract whatever it is has been performed and there is a doctrine that you should be aware of in considering that. That is the doctrine of substantial performance.
>
> It is not required that performance be in any case one hundred percent complete in order to entitle a party to enforcement of their contractual rights. That is not to say within the confines of this case that the existence of flashing would be excused or not be excused. It is just a recognition on the part of the law when we talk about performance, probably if we took any contract you could always find something of no substance that was not completed one hundred percent. It is for you to determine that whether it has been substantially performed or not and what in fact constitutes substantial performance.
>
> In your consideration, and as I say in this case, that's not to intimate that something like flashing is to be disregarded or to be considered. It's up to you based upon facts.

The jury returned a verdict in favor of plaintiff in the amount of $14,480.82.

I

In Smith, Fitzmaurice Co. v. Harris, 126 Me. 308, 138 A. 389 (1927), a case decided under the common law, we recognized the then-settled rule that with respect to contracts for the sale of goods the buyer has the right to reject the seller's tender if in any way it fails to conform to the specifications of the contract. We held that "[t]he vendor has the duty to comply with his order in kind, quality and amount." *Id*. at 312, 138 A. at 391. Thus, in *Smith,* we ruled that a buyer who had contracted to purchase twelve dozen union suits could lawfully refuse a tender of sixteen dozen union suits. Various provisions of the Uniform Sales Act, enacted in Maine in 1923, codified the common-law approach. R.S. (1954) ch. 185, §§ 11, 44. The so-called "perfect tender" rule came under considerable fire around the time the Uniform Commercial Code was drafted. No less an authority than Karl Llewellyn, recognized as the *primum mobile* of the Code's tender provisions, (see, e.g., W. Twining, Karl Llewellyn and the Realist Movement 270–301 (1973); Carroll, Harpooning Whales, of Which Karl N. Llewellyn is the Hero of the Piece; or Searching for More Expansion Joints in Karl's Crumbling Cathedral, 12 B.C.Indus. & Comm.L.Rev. 139, 142 (1970)), attacked the rule principally on the ground that it allowed a dishonest buyer to avoid an unfavorable contract on the basis of an insubstantial defect in the seller's tender. Llewellyn, On Warranty of Quality and Society, 37 Colum.L.Rev. 341, 389 (1937). Although Llewellyn's views are represented in many Code sections governing tender,[1] the basic tender provision, Section 2–601, represents a rejection of Llewellyn's approach and a continuation of the perfect tender policy developed by the common law and carried forward by the draftsmen of the Uniform Sales Act. See Official Comment, § 2–106; Priest, Breach and Remedy for the Tender of Nonconforming Goods Under the Uniform Commercial Code: An Economic Approach, 91 Harv.L.Rev. 960, 971 (1978). Thus, Section 2–601 states that, with certain exceptions not here applicable, the buyer has the right to reject "if the goods or the tender of delivery fail *in any respect* to conform to the contract ..." (emphasis supplied). Those few courts that have considered the question agree that the perfect tender rule has survived the enactment of the Code. Ingle v. Marked Tree Equipment Co., 244 Ark. 1166, 428 S.W.2d 286 (1968); Maas v. Scoboda, 188 Neb. 189, 195 N.W.2d 491 (1972); Bowen v. Young, 507 S.W.2d 600 (Tex.Civ.App.1974). We, too, are convinced of the soundness of this position.

In light of the foregoing discussion, it is clear that the presiding Justice's charge was erroneous and, under the circumstances, reversibly so. The jury was informed that "[i]t is not required that performance be in any case one hundred percent complete in order to entitle a party to enforcement of their contractual rights." Under this instruction, the jury was free to find that although plaintiff had not tendered perfectly conforming molds within the agreed period (assuming the jury found that the parties had in fact agreed on a specific time period for completion) it had nevertheless substantially performed the contract within the agreed time frame and was merely making minor adjustments when defendant backed out of the deal. Had the jury been instructed that plaintiff was required to tender perfectly conforming goods—not just substantially conforming goods—within the period allegedly agreed to and had they been instructed that, under Section 2–711, the buyer has the absolute right to cancel the contract if the seller "fails to make delivery," a different verdict might have resulted. Indeed, the supplemental instruction tended to encourage the jury to resolve the question by deciding whether "flashing" was or was not a substantial defect:

> It is not required that performance be in any case one hundred percent complete in order to entitle a party to enforcement of their contractual rights. That is not to say within the confines of this

---

1. See, e.g., §§ 2–508 (seller's limited right to cure defects in tender), 2–608 (buyer's limited right to revoke acceptance), and 2–612 (buyer's limited right to reject nonconforming tender under installment contract).

case that the existence of flashing would be excused or not be excused.... It is for you to determine ... whether [the contract] has been substantially performed or not and what in fact constitutes substantial performance.

We find unpersuasive plaintiff's argument that the presiding Justice's instruction merely informed the jury that if it found that defendant had committed an anticipatory breach of the contract then plaintiff was not thereafter required to complete its performance as a condition precedent to recovery under the contract. Such an instruction might well have been appropriate and would certainly have been supportable under the applicable law. Dehahn v. Innes, Me., 356 A.2d 711, 719 (1976) ("When the other party has already repudiated the agreement, a tender would be a futile act and is not required by law."); §§ 2–610, 2–704. However, an examination of the passage of the charge in question leads us to reject plaintiff's interpretation. Without informing the jury that it must first find that defendant had committed an anticipatory repudiation, the presiding Justice, without qualification, stated that "performance [need not] be ... one hundred percent complete in order to entitle a party to enforcement of their contractual rights." Furthermore, the court drew a distinction between substantial and insubstantial defects, a distinction which, on these facts and under plaintiff's interpretation of the charge, would have been completely irrelevant. Finally, both the presiding Justice and counsel for plaintiff referred to the instruction at side bar as an explanation of the "substantial performance" doctrine. In legal parlance, that doctrine requires a buyer, under certain circumstances, to accept something less than a perfectly conforming tender. See, e.g., Rockland Poultry Co. v. Anderson, 148 Me. 211, 216, 91 A.2d 478, 480 (1952) (construction contract); Jacob & Youngs, Inc. v. Kent, 230 N.Y. 239, 129 N.E. 889 (1921) (Cardozo, J.) (construction contract). As such, it has no application to a contract for the sale of goods, and the jury should not have been permitted to consider it.

II

In his testimony at trial, Mr. Moulton indicated that he was aware that to defendant time was a critical factor. He also stated that he had given defendant an estimated delivery date of five weeks from the date the contract was formed. On appeal, defendant takes the position that the parties agreed on a five-week time period for delivery and that plaintiff's failure to tender conforming goods after ten weeks constitutes a breach as a matter of law and precludes plaintiff from recovering under the contract.

We disagree. While on the one hand Mr. Sturman testified that Mr. Moulton had told him that the goods would be delivered in five weeks, on the other hand Mr. Moulton testified that it was clear that he was merely making an estimate. The testimony thus left the jury at liberty to decide the factual question of whether the five-week time period was an agreed delivery date and thus a term of the contract or merely an estimate. While the interpretation of unambiguous language in a written contract falls within the province of the court, Blue Rock Industries v. Raymond International, Inc., Me., 325 A.2d 66 (1974), questions of fact concerning the terms of an oral agreement are left to the trier of fact, Carter v. Beck, Me., 366 A.2d 520 (1976).

The entry is: Appeal sustained. New trial ordered.

NOTES

(1) *The Code's Retention of the Perfect Tender Rule.* In its influential study of the proposed Uniform Commercial Code, the New York State Law Revision Commission recommended that "the right of rejection as stated in Section 2–601 be limited to material breach." In declining to accept this recommendation, the Editorial Board responsible for revising the Code following the New York study relied on two grounds: "first, . . . the buyer should not be required to guess at his peril whether a breach is material; second, . . . proof of materiality would sometimes require disclosure of the buyer's private affairs such as secret formulas or processes." [a]

(2) *The Code's Softening of the Perfect Tender Rule.* While retaining the perfect tender rule, the Code softens it in several ways. First, UCC 2–508 gives a seller the power to cure a defective tender "if the time for performance has not yet expired"—and, in some situations, even if that time has expired. Second, UCC 2–608 allows a buyer who has already accepted goods to revoke that acceptance (and return the goods to the seller) only if the "non-conformity substantially impairs [their] value to him." Third, UCC 2–612 similarly allows a buyer under a contract for delivery of goods in installments to reject an installment only if a non-conformity as to the goods "substantially impairs the value of that installment" and to claim a breach of the whole contract only for a breach that "substantially impairs the value of the whole contract."

(3) *The Vienna Convention's Abandonment of the Perfect Tender Rule.* The Vienna Convention abandons the perfect tender rule in favor of a rule of "fundamental breach." Article 25 defines that term as a breach that "results in such detriment to the other party as substantially to deprive him of what he is entitled to expect under the contract, unless the party in breach did not foresee, and a reasonable person of the same kind in the same circumstances would not have foreseen, such a result." Is this an improvement on the test in UCC 2–601? Is it a better formulation than those in UCC 2–608 and 2–612?

(4) *The Case of the Off-Color Books.* The Supermind Publishing Company paid a deposit to a printing firm under a contract for the production of a book. In an action to recover the deposit, a witness for Supermind, as plaintiff, testified that the books tendered were gray, whereas the defendant's newsprint sample was white; there was also evidence of other defects. On a jury finding that the books failed to conform to the contract, the plaintiff got judgment for the deposit, and the defendant appealed. *Held:* Affirmed. Printing Center of Texas, Inc. v. Supermind Publishing Co., Inc., 669 S.W.2d 779 (Tex.Ct.App.1984).

In dictum the court said that if Supermind had carried the burden of showing that "the buyer's motivation in rejecting the goods was to escape the bargain," this would have established a breach of the duty of good faith. But there was no evidence that "its primary motivation in rejection of the books was to escape a bad bargain." Such a finding, the court said, might be warranted by

a. R. Braucher & E. Sutherland, Commercial Transactions—Text, Cases and   Problems 41 (3d ed. 1964).

evidence of rejection on account of a minor defect, in a falling market. The court cited UCC 1–203 and 2–103(1)(b).[b] *Questions:* What is the relation of these provisions to UCC 2–601? How would the court's reasoning have been different if the contract had required that the quality of the books be satisfactory to the plaintiff?

(b) Divisibility

GILL v. JOHNSTOWN LUMBER CO.

Supreme Court of Pennsylvania, 1892.
151 Pa. 534, 25 A. 120.

[Assumpsit for driving logs under a written contract, the terms of which are set forth in the opinion. Plaintiff agreed to drive some four million feet of logs, and to begin driving at once, "if sufficient natural water, or by the use of splash dams." The trial court directed a verdict for defendant on the ground that the contract was "entire" and that plaintiff had defaulted in that a flood had carried a considerable proportion of the logs past defendant's boom.[a] Plaintiff appeals.]

HEYDRICK, J. The single question in this cause is whether the contract upon which the plaintiff sued is entire or severable. If it is entire it is conceded that the learned court below properly directed a verdict for the defendant; if severable, it is not denied that the cause ought to have been submitted to the jury. The criterion by which it is to be determined to which class any particular contract shall be assigned is thus stated in 1 Parsons on Contracts, 29–31: "If the part to be performed by one party consists of several and distinct items, and the price to be paid by the other is (1) apportioned to each item to be performed, or (2) is left to be implied by law, such a contract will generally be held to be severable.... But if the consideration to be paid is single and entire the contract must be held to be entire, although the subject of the contract may consist of several distinct and wholly independent items." The rule thus laid down was ... applied in Ritchie v. Atkinson, 10 East, 295, a case not unlike the present. There the master and freighter of a vessel of four hundred tons mutually agreed that the ship should proceed to St. Petersburg, and there load from the freighter's factors a complete cargo of hemp and iron and deliver the same to the freighter at London on being paid freight for hemp £5 per ton, for iron 5s. per ton, and certain other charges, one half to be paid on

---

b. Although the court relied on the Code, it expressed grave doubt that the contract was governed by Article 2.

a. On May 31, 1889, ten days after the date of the contract, the then-largest earthen dam, above Johnstown, broke. More than 2,000 lives were lost. That and other flooding in the area, caused by a great rain, carried log booms estimated at many millions of feet of timber into the Potomac River and the Chesapeake Bay. R. O'Connor, Johnstown—The Day the Dam Broke (1957).

delivery and the other at three months. The vessel proceeded to St. Petersburg, and when about half loaded was compelled by the imminence of a Russian embargo upon British vessels to leave, and returning to London deliver to the freighter so much of the stipulated cargo as had been taken on board. The freighter, conceiving that the contract was entire and the delivery of a complete cargo a condition precedent to a recovery of any compensation, refused to pay at the stipulated rate for so much as was delivered. Lord Ellenborough said: "The delivery of the cargo is in its nature, divisible, and therefore I think it is not a condition precedent; but the plaintiff is entitled to recover freight in proportion to the extent of such delivery; leaving the defendant to his remedy in damages for the short delivery."

Applying the test of an apportionable or apportioned consideration to the contract in question, it will be seen at once that it is severable. The work undertaken to be done by the plaintiff consisted of several items, viz., driving logs, first, of oak, and second of various other kinds of timber, from points upon Stony creek and its tributaries above Johnstown to the defendant's boom at Johnstown, and also driving cross-ties from some undesignated point or points, presumably understood by the parties, to Bethel in Somerset county, and to some other point or points below Bethel. For this work the consideration to be paid was not an entire sum, but was apportioned among the several items at the rate of one dollar per thousand feet for the oak logs; seventy-five cents per thousand feet for all other logs; three cents each for cross-ties driven to Bethel, and five cents each for cross-ties driven to points below Bethel. But while the contract is severable, and the plaintiff entitled to compensation at the stipulated rate for all logs and ties delivered at the specified points, there is neither reason nor authority for the claim for compensation in respect to logs that were swept by the flood to and through the defendant's boom, whether they had been driven part of the way by the plaintiff or remained untouched by him at the coming of the flood. In respect to each particular log the contract in this case is like a contract of common carriage, which is dependent upon the delivery of the goods at the designated place, and if by casus the delivery is prevented the carrier cannot recover pro tanto for freight for part of the route over which the goods were taken: Wharton, Law of Contracts, sec. 714. Indeed this is but an application of the rule already stated. The consideration to be paid for driving each log is an entire sum per thousand feet for the whole distance and is not apportioned or apportionable to parts of the drive.

The judgment is reversed and a venire facias de novo is awarded.

NOTES

(1) *Question.* Into how many parts was the contract divisible? Two parts: one for logs and one for cross-ties? Four parts? One part for each log and cross-tie properly delivered? If some of the oak logs had been driven half way, might the plaintiff have recovered at the rate of 50¢ per thousand feet for them? Why was the contract not divisible by distances?

(2) *Pay Periods.* Work done under a contract of employment for a term may go uncompensated if the employee abandons the job, or is justifiably discharged, before the end of the term. (Quasi-contractual recovery is granted by some courts: see Subsection (c), below.) The doctrine of divisibility, liberally applied, would tend to alleviate such losses by permitting the employee to enforce partial payments for units of the work done—so much per week, for instance—prior to the end of the term. But findings of divisibility were not readily obtained, in the early cases: a reference in the agreement to weekly or monthly pay periods might not count. The problem rarely arises in contemporary litigation. Several reasons have been suggested; one is "the passage in many jurisdictions of wage statutes which inexorably clamp divisibility down upon large classes of employment contracts ..." McGowan, The Divisibility of Employment Contracts, 21 Iowa L.Rev. 50, 67 (1935).

PENNSYLVANIA EXCHANGE BANK v. UNITED STATES, 170 F.Supp. 629 (Ct.Cl.1959). [The United States Army Signal Corps contracted to pay certain sums to Joseph Lerner & Son, Inc., under an "Industrial Preparedness Contract." Lerner's obligation was to equip itself for the production, in volume, of an item called a microwave magic tee. The work was to be done in four steps. Steps I and II entailed acquiring information about and making plans for production, subject to approval, making a pilot run, and going through "all production processes short of procuring tooling and materials and short of actual volume manufacture." Step III required Lerner to acquire certain equipment for which it spent about $38,000.

These steps were substantially completed by October 1, 1953, and the Government had paid Lerner about $128,000. Step IV, which was to be taken only in case of a national emergency, and after receipt of an order from the Government, required "volume production in accordance with previously planned schedules." Lerner was obligated to maintain a status of readiness for this over a six-year period in anticipation of a national emergency. On October 1 Lerner transferred all its assets to assignees for the benefit of creditors, as an alternative to bankruptcy. The assignees sued the Government for about $45,000, the sum owed for completing steps I–III, and the Government counterclaimed for damages.]

WHITAKER, JUDGE. [The court considered the purpose of the contract, as stated in a Signal Corps procurement specification, and said that Steps I, II, and III were] merely incidental to Step IV, which was the ultimate objective. . . . The duty to stand by and be ready to perform Step IV was the essential element of the bargain. The contract was not divisible. . . .

The assignment for the benefit of creditors operates as a present and total breach of the contract, for it is an implied condition in every contract that the promisor will not permit itself, through insolvency or acts of bankruptcy, to be disabled from making performance. . . .

[The Government's motion for summary judgment was granted.]

NOTE

Insolvency Proceedings. Assignments for the benefit of creditors, and ordinary ("straight") bankruptcy proceedings, are arrangements for the expeditious liquidation of a debtor's business and other assets, and the distribution of the proceeds among his creditors. Therefore the assignees for Joseph Lerner & Son could not well have undertaken complete performance of its "industrial preparedness" contract. However, the Bankruptcy Code (title 11, U.S.C.) makes provision for preserving the going-concern value of an enterprise, through reorganization. When that is undertaken, usually under Chapter 11, the bankruptcy trustee or a manager having like powers may well wish to keep the firm's gainful contracts in force. (With some important exceptions, the trustee may reject its executory contracts that are burdensome, subject to the court's approval. Rejection will usually give rise to a claim against the bankruptcy estate.) The Bankruptcy Code contains elaborate provisions both to protect and to restrict the trustee's right to "assume" a contract: 11 U.S.C. § 365. If the debtor has already committed a default, the trustee may yet assume the contract, but only when giving certain assurances.

THE USES OF DIVISIBILITY

Reconsider the "rice" case (Internatio–Rotterdam, Inc. v. River Brand Rice Mills, Inc.), p. 668 above. What argument did the buyer try to combat by maintaining that the contract was not divisible? Compare the plaintiff's claim in that case and the defendant's contention in Gill v. Johnstown Lumber Co. Does it seem that the doctrine of divisibility has various uses? Corbin listed fourteen questions which have been answered by reference to the distinction between entirety and divisibility, concluding that they cannot be answered by "the application of some simple and uniform test." Corbin § 695.

In the rice case would the seller have been *justified* in withholding further shipments to Lake Charles after December 17th? If it had done so, how would you compare the merits of the buyer's claim with that in Gill v. Johnstown Lumber Company? With the claim in Pennsylvania Exchange Bank v. United States?

NOTE

The Case of the House Divided. The home of Mr. and Mrs. M stands in the center of their 320–acre farm, which they wish to sell. Mr. and Mrs. O contract to buy the house and farm. The parties' lawyers advise them that income taxes can be saved on each side if they report the sale of the house and environs as a separate transaction. Hence the contract allocates $288,000 of the price to the farm and $50,000 to the residence, and provides for the latter sum to be paid first (the remainder to be paid in installments). But it also provides that, "although the aforesaid acreages are divisible by nature, and divisible by purchase allocation amounts, a single deed shall be delivered ... in conveyance of both said tracts."

After the payment of more than $50,000, Mr. O dies and the payments cease. The sellers give notice of forfeiture to Mrs. O. Thereupon she sues for a deed to the residence portion of the farm. What result if the contract does not describe the boundaries of the "home" tract? What result if it does? See May v. Oakley, 407 N.W.2d 569 (Iowa 1987).

(c) Restitution

We have seen a variety of situations in which restitution may be available. It is sometimes available as between persons who have not dealt with one another (see Chapter 1, Section 3(b)). Sometimes restitutionary claims arise from negotiations that fall short of a contract (see Chapter 2, Section 6). As between the parties to an agreement, it is sometimes granted when their agreement proves to be unenforceable for one reason or another: because of the Statute of Frauds (see Chapter 3, Section 4); or because the contract is illegal (see Chapter 4, Section 5).

When there is a breach of an enforceable agreement, *the aggrieved party* may prefer restitution to other forms of relief, and it is commonly available (see Chapter 5, Section 1). It is often available also when an agreement has become unenforceable by reason of mistake, impracticability of performance or frustration of purpose (see Chapter 8).

But what of restitution for *a party in breach* of an enforceable agreement? If that party has performed in part, and is unable to enforce the contract because it has failed to complete performance, may it nevertheless get restitution? Such claims have met serious resistance, especially when the plaintiff's breach may be characterized as "willful." The following remarks, written over a century ago by the court in Lawrence v. Miller (Note 1, p. 706 above), represent a traditional response:

> It would be an alarming doctrine, to hold, that the plaintiffs might violate the contract, and because they chose to do so, make their own infraction of the agreement the basis of an action for money had and received.... To allow a recovery of this money would be to sustain an action by a party on his own breach of his own contract, which the law does not allow.... That would be ill doctrine.

Some other responses are shown in this section. The next main case is a watershed.

NOTE

Officious Performance. A builder was given notice of cancellation of his contract, prompted by his unreasonable delay on the job constituting a material breach. Nevertheless he continued with his work and subsequently made a restitutionary claim against his employer for its value. In denying recovery, the court observed that such a claim does not lie in favor of one who is guilty of willful breach. Trachsel v. Barney, 503 P.2d 696 (Or.1972).

BRITTON v. TURNER

Supreme Court of Judicature of New Hampshire, 1834.
6 N.H. 481.

Assumpsit, for work and labor, performed by the plaintiff, in the service of the defendant, from March 9, 1831, to December 27, 1831.

The declaration contained the common counts, and among them a count in quantum meruit, for the labor, averring it to be worth $100.

At the trial in the C.C. Pleas, the plaintiff proved the performance of the labor as set forth in the declaration.

The defense was that it was performed under a special contract; that the plaintiff agreed to work one year, from some time in March, 1831, to March, 1832, and that the defendant was to pay him for said year's labor the sum of $120; and the defendant offered evidence tending to show that such was the contract under which the work was done. Evidence was also offered to show that the plaintiff left the defendant's service without his consent, and it was contended by the defendant that the plaintiff had no good cause for not continuing in his employment. There was no evidence offered of any damage arising from the plaintiff's departure, farther than was to be inferred from his nonfulfillment of the entire contract.

The court instructed the jury that, if they were satisfied from the evidence that the labor was performed under a contract to labor a year, for the sum of $120, and if they were satisfied that the plaintiff labored only the time specified in the declaration, and then left the defendant's service, against his consent, and without any good cause, yet the plaintiff was entitled to recover, under his quantum meruit count, as much as the labor he performed was reasonably worth, and under this direction the jury gave a verdict for the plaintiff for the sum of $95.

The defendant excepted to the instructions thus given to the jury.

PARKER, J., delivered the opinion of the court. It may be assumed that the labor performed by the plaintiff, and for which he seeks to recover a compensation in this action, was commenced under a special contract to labor for the defendant the term of one year, for the sum of $120, and that the plaintiff has labored but a portion of that time, and has voluntarily failed to complete the entire contract.

It is clear, then, that he is not entitled to recover upon the contract itself, because the service, which was to entitle him to the sum agreed upon, has never been performed.

But the question arises: Can the plaintiff, under these circumstances, recover a reasonable sum for the service he has actually performed, under the count in quantum meruit? Upon this, and questions of a similar nature, the decisions to be found in the books are not easily reconciled.

It has been held, upon contracts of this kind for labor to be performed at a specified price, that the party who voluntarily fails to fulfill the contract by performing the whole labor contracted for, is not entitled to recover anything for the labor actually performed, however much he may have done towards the performance, and this has been considered the settled rule of law upon this subject. [Citations of Massachusetts, New York and English cases omitted.]

That such rule in its operation may be very unequal, not to say unjust, is apparent. A party who contracts to perform certain specified labor, and who breaks his contract in the first instance, without any attempt to perform it, can only be made liable to pay the damages which the other party has sustained by reason of such non-performance, which in many instances may be trifling; whereas a party who in good faith has entered upon the performance of his contract, and nearly completed it, and then abandoned the further performance, although the other party has had the full benefit of all that has been done, and has perhaps sustained no actual damage, is in fact subjected to a loss of all which has been performed, in the nature of damages for the non-fulfillment of the remainder, upon the technical rule, that the contract must be fully performed in order to [sustain] a recovery of any part of the compensation.

By the operation of this rule, then, the party who attempts performance may be placed in a much worse situation than he who wholly disregards his contract, and the other party may receive much more, by the breach of the contract, than the injury which he has sustained by such breach, and more than he could be entitled to were he seeking to recover damages by an action.

The case before us presents an illustration. Had the plaintiff in this case never entered upon the performance of his contract, the damage could not probably have been greater than some small expense and trouble incurred in procuring another to do the labor which he had contracted to perform. But having entered upon the performance, and labored nine and a half months, the value of which labor to the defendant as found by the jury is $95, if the defendant can succeed in this defense, he in fact receives nearly five-sixths of the value of a whole year's labor, by reason of the breach of contract by the plaintiff, a sum not only utterly disproportionate to any probable, not to say possible damage which could have resulted from the neglect of the plaintiff to continue the remaining two and a half months, but altogether beyond any damage which could have been recovered by the defendant, had the plaintiff done nothing towards the fulfillment of his contract.

Another illustration is furnished in Lantry v. Parks, 8 Cow., N.Y., 63. There the defendant hired the plaintiff for a year, at ten dollars per month. The plaintiff worked ten and a half months, and then left saying he would work no more for him. This was on Saturday—on Monday the plaintiff returned, and offered to resume his work, but the defendant said he would employ him no longer. The court held that the refusal of the defendant [plaintiff?] on Saturday was a violation of his contract, and that he could recover nothing for the labor performed.

There are other cases, however, in which principles have been adopted leading to a different result.

It is said, that where a party contracts to perform certain work, and to furnish materials, as, for instance, to build a house, and the work is done, but with some variations from the mode prescribed by the contract, yet if the other party has the benefit of the labor and materials he should be bound to pay so much as they are reasonably worth. 2 Stark.Ev. 97, 98; Hayward v. Leonard, 7 Pick., Mass., 181....

A different doctrine seems to have been holden in Ellis v. Hamlen, 3 Taunt. 52, and it is apparent, in such cases, that if the house has not been built in the manner specified in the contract, the work has not been done. The party has no more performed what he contracted to perform, than he who has contracted to labor for a certain period, and failed to complete the time.

It is in truth virtually conceded in such cases that the work has not been done, for, if it had been, the party performing it would be entitled to recover upon the contract itself, which it is held he cannot do.

Those cases are not to be distinguished, in principle, from the present, unless it be in the circumstance, that where the party has contracted to furnish materials, and do certain labor, as to build a house in a specified manner, if it is not done according to the contract, the party for whom it is built may refuse to receive it—elect to take no benefit from what has been performed—and therefore, if he does receive, he shall be bound to pay the value; whereas in a contract for labor, merely, from day to day, the party is continually receiving the benefit of the contract under an expectation that it will be fulfilled, and cannot, upon the breach of it, have an election to refuse to receive what has been done, and thus discharge himself from payment.

But we think this difference in the nature of the contracts does not justify the application of a different rule in relation to them. The party who contracts for labor merely, for a certain period, does so with full knowledge that he must, from the nature of the case, be accepting part performance from day to day, if the other party commences the performance, and with knowledge also that the other may eventually fail of completing the entire term. If under such circumstances he actually receives a benefit from the labor performed, over and above the damage occasioned by the failure to complete, there is as much reason why he should pay the reasonable worth of what has thus been done for his benefit, as there is when he enters and occupies the house which has been built for him, but not according to the stipulations of the contract, and which he perhaps enters, not because he is satisfied with what has been done, but because circumstances compel him to accept it such as it is, that he should pay for the value of the house.

Where goods are sold upon a special contract as to their nature, quality, and price, and have been used before their inferiority has been discovered, or other circumstances have concurred which have rendered it impracticable or inconvenient for the vendee to rescind the contract in toto, it seems to have been the practice formerly to allow the vendor to recover the stipulated price, and the vendee recovered by a cross-action damages for the breach of the contract. "But according to the later and more convenient practice, the vendee in such case is allowed, in an action for the price, to give evidence of the inferiority of the goods in reduction of damages, and the plaintiff who has broken his contract is not entitled to recover more than the value of the benefits which the defendant has actually derived from the goods; and where the latter has derived no benefit, the plaintiff cannot recover at all." 2 Stark.Ev. 640, 642; Okell v. Smith, 1 Starkie's Rep. 107. . . .

There is a close analogy between all these classes of cases, in which such diverse decisions have been made.

If the party who has contracted to receive merchandise takes a part and uses it, in expectation that the whole will be delivered, which is never done, there seems to be no greater reason that he should pay for what he has received than there is that the party who has received labor in part, under similar circumstances, should pay the value of what has been done for his benefit.

It is said that in those cases where the plaintiff has been permitted to recover there was an acceptance of what had been done. The answer is that where the contract is to labor from day to day, for a certain period, the party for whom the labor is done in truth stipulates to receive it from day to day, as it is performed, and although the other may not eventually do all he has contracted to do, there has been, necessarily, an acceptance of what has been done in pursuance of the contract, and the party must have understood when he made the contract that there was to be such acceptance.

If, then, the party stipulates in the outset to receive part performance from time to time, with a knowledge that the whole may not be completed, we see no reason why he should not equally be holden to pay for the amount of value received, as where he afterwards takes the benefit of what has been done, with a knowledge that the whole which was contracted for has not been performed. In neither case has the contract been performed. In neither can an action be sustained on the original contract. In both the party has assented to receive what is done. The only difference is that in the one case the assent is prior, with a knowledge that all may not be performed; in the other it is subsequent, with a knowledge that the whole has not been accomplished.

We have no hesitation in holding that the same rule should be applied to both classes of cases, especially as the operation of the rule will be to make the party who has failed to fulfill his contract liable to such amount of damages as the other party has sustained, instead of subjecting him to an entire loss for a partial failure, and thus making the amount received in many cases wholly disproportionate to the injury. 1 Saund. 320, c; 2 Stark.Ev. 643. It is as "hard upon the plaintiff to preclude him from recovering at all, because he has failed as to part of his entire undertaking," where his contract is to labor for a certain period, as it can be in any other description of contract, provided the defendant has received a benefit and value from the labor actually performed.

We hold, then, that where a party undertakes to pay upon a special contract for the performance of labor, or the furnishing of materials, he is not to be charged upon such special agreement until the money is earned according to the terms of it, and where the parties have made an express contract the law will not imply and raise a contract different from that which the parties have entered into, except upon some farther transaction between the parties.

In case of a failure to perform such special contract, by the default of the party contracting to do the service, if the money is not due by the terms of the special agreement he is not entitled to recover for his labor, or for the materials furnished, unless the other party receives what has been done, or furnished, and upon the whole case derives a benefit from it. Taft v. Montague, 14 Mass. 282; 2 Stark.Ev. 644.

But if, where a contract is made of such a character, a party actually receives labor, or materials, and thereby derives a benefit and advantage, over and above the damage which has resulted from the breach of the contract by the other party, the labor actually done, and the value received, furnish a new consideration, and the law thereupon raises a promise to pay to the extent of the reasonable worth of such excess. This may be considered as making a new case, one not within the original agreement, and the party is entitled to "recover on his new case, for the work done, not as agreed, but yet accepted by the defendant." 1 Dane's Abr. 224.

If on such failure to perform the whole, the nature of the contract be such that the employer can reject what has been done, and refuse to receive any benefit from the part performance, he is entitled so to do, and in such case is not liable to be charged, unless he has before assented to and accepted of what has been done, however much the other party may have done towards the performance. He has in such case received nothing, and having contracted to receive nothing but the entire matter contracted for, he is not bound to pay, because his express promise was only to pay on receiving the whole, and having actually received nothing the law cannot and ought not to raise an implied promise to pay. But where the party receives value—takes and uses the materials, or has advantage from the labor, he is liable to pay the reasonable worth of what he has received. Farnsworth v. Garrard, 1 Camp. 38. And the rule is the same whether it was received and accepted by the assent of the party prior to the breach, under a contract by which, from its nature, he was to receive labor, from time to time until the completion of the whole contract, or whether it was received and accepted by an assent subsequent to the performance of all which was in fact done. If he received it under such circumstances as precluded him from rejecting it afterwards, that does not alter the case—it has still been received by his assent.

In fact, we think the technical reasoning—that the performance of the whole labor is a condition precedent, and the right to recover anything dependent upon it; that, the contract being entire, there can be no apportionment; and that, there being an express contract, no other can be implied, even upon the subsequent performance of service— is not properly applicable to this species of contract, where a beneficial service has been actually performed; for we have abundant reason to believe, that the general understanding of the community is that the hired laborer shall be entitled to compensation for the service actually performed, though he do not continue the entire term contracted for, and such contracts must be presumed to be made with reference to that understanding, unless an express stipulation shows the contrary.. . .

It is easy, if parties so choose, to provide by an express agreement that nothing shall be earned, if the laborer leaves his employer without having performed the whole service contemplated, and then there can be no pretense for a recovery if he voluntarily deserts the service before the expiration of the time.

The amount, however, for which the employer ought to be charged, where the laborer abandons his contract, is only the reasonable worth, or the amount of advantage he receives upon the whole transaction (Wadleigh v. Sutton, 6 N.H. 15), and, in estimating the value of the labor, the contract price for the service cannot be exceeded.. . .

If a person makes a contract fairly, he is entitled to have it fully performed; and, if this is not done, he is entitled to damages. He may maintain a suit to recover the amount of damage sustained by the non-performance. The benefit and advantage which the party takes by the labor, therefore, is the amount of value which he receives, if any, after deducting the amount of damage; and if he elects to put this in defense he is entitled so to do, and the implied promise which the law will raise, in such case, is to pay such amount of the stipulated price for the whole labor, as remains after deducting what it would cost to procure a completion of the residue of the service and also any damage which has been sustained by reason of the nonfulfillment of the contract. If in such case it be found that the damages are equal to or greater than the amount of the labor performed, so that the employer, having a right to the full performance of the contract, has not upon the whole case received a beneficial service, the plaintiff cannot recover.. . .

Applying the principles thus laid down, to this case, the plaintiff is entitled to judgment on the verdict. The defendant sets up a mere breach of the contract in defense of the action, but this cannot avail him. He does not appear to have offered evidence to show that he was damnified by such breach, or to have asked that a deduction should be made upon that account. The direction to the jury was therefore correct, that the plaintiff was entitled to recover as much as the labor performed was reasonably worth, and the jury appear to have allowed a pro rata compensation, for the time which the plaintiff labored in the defendant's service.

As the defendant has not claimed or had any adjustment of damages, for the breach of the contract, in this action, if he has actually sustained damage he is still entitled to a suit to recover the amount.. . .

Judgment on the verdict.

NOTES

(1) *Restitution for an Employer.* Melbourne Henry studied for a graduate degree with the financial aid of his former employer, a non-profit medical agency. The parties to the "loan" agreed that Henry would resume the employment at the end of his studies, that the agency would provide him with an appropriate position, and that the advances would be repaid through a specified payroll deduction. On concluding his studies Henry took a job elsewhere, and the agency sued for its advances. The jury returned a verdict for the defendant, finding that the agency had broken the contract by offering him only a subordinate position. The agency appealed from a judgment for Henry. *Held:* Reversed. Appalachian Regional Hospitals, Inc. v. Henry, 597 P.2d 1247 (Or. 1979). The trial court had improperly failed to instruct, as requested by the plaintiff, that it was entitled to the amount loaned less the defendant's damages—even if the plaintiff's breach went to the essence of the contract. "The reason plaintiff is not barred is the same as that underlying equitable rules against the enforcement of penalties and forfeitures. . . ." *Question:* How is this ruling different from a decision that the covenants in the contract were independent ones?

(2) *References.* Each time the American Law Institute has taken up the subject it seems to have moved somewhat in advance of the cases at large, in favor of restitution. According to the first Restatement § 357, a plaintiff was barred from restitution if his breach or non-performance was "wilful and deliberate." For the present position, assimilating the rule to the law of liquidated damages, see Restatement Second § 374. Examine the cases in this section with a view to finding those affected by the change.

In 1978 Professor Palmer reported that the doctrine of Britton v. Turner was still a minority position. 1 G. Palmer, Law of Restitution § 5.13 (1978). The conflicting but rather faded precedents are reviewed in Birmingham, Breach of Contract, Damage Measures, and Economic Efficiency, 24 Rutgers L.Rev. 273, 286–89 (1970). The author approves the ruling, with qualifications, as conducive to "proper functioning of the market mechanism."

(3) *Lawyer–Client Relations.* Begovich was charged with murder. He retained Murphy to defend him and paid $2,500. Later Murphy was paid another $4,000 as an advance for legal services to be rendered for Begovich. He consulted with his client, and made two appearances in his behalf, these services not being worth more than $2,500. At that point Begovich committed suicide. The administrator of the estate sued Murphy for $4,000, and Murphy demurred. What decision? See Begovich v. Murphy, 101 N.W.2d 278 (Mich.1960).

For an interesting question of compensation for a lawyer who quit (i.e., refused to conduct litigation to a conclusion by refusing to handle an appeal as he had agreed), see Moore v. Fellner, 325 P.2d 857 (Cal.1958). Part of an intermediate court's opinion in this case was as follows: "The question is whether an attorney who undertakes to render an entire service may quit when an important part of the work remains undone and deserve to be paid for partial performance. As well might a surgeon claim compensation when he had quit in the middle of an operation, or a barber when he had shaved half of a customer's face." The judgment of this court was reversed on the reasoning that the parties "contemplated that the attorney's services should be divisible into those rendered (1) in the superior court, and (2) any appeal from a superior court judgment."

KIRKLAND v. ARCHBOLD

Court of Appeals of Ohio, Cuyahoga County, 1953.
113 N.E.2d 496.

[The plaintiff contracted to make alterations and repairs on a dwelling house owned by the defendant. Paragraph 20 of the contract provided: "The Owner agrees to pay the Contractor, as follows: $1,000 when satisfactory work has been done for ten days; an additional $1,000 when twenty days work has been completed; an additional $1,000 when thirty days work has been completed, and $1,000 on completion of the contract. $2,000 shall be paid within thirty days after the completion of the contract." After the plaintiff had worked for two months on the job he was prevented from proceeding further. He claims that he and his sub-contractors had reasonably expended $2,985 at that point; he has been paid only $800; and he sues for damages in the amount of the difference.

The trial court found that the plaintiff was in default in attempting to plaster the house over wood lath instead of rock lath, and without the use of rock wool. Paragraph 4 of the contract provided: "All outside walls are to be lined with rock wool and rock lathe, superimposed thereon." Thus the defendant was within her rights in preventing the plaintiff from proceeding. However, the court held that her payment of $800 was an admission that the first installment of the price was earned, and gave the plaintiff judgment for $200. The plaintiff appealed.]

SKEEL, PRESIDING JUDGE.... The court committed error prejudicial to the rights of plaintiff in holding that the provisions of the contract were severable. The plaintiff agreed to make certain repairs and improvements on the defendant's property for which he was to be paid $6,000. The total consideration was to be paid for the total work specified in the contract. The fact that a schedule of payments was set up based on the progress of the work does not change the character of the agreement. Newman Lumber Co. v. Purdum, 41 Ohio St. 373.

The court found that the plaintiff and not the defendant breached the agreement, leaving the job without just cause, when the work agreed upon was far from completed. In fact, the plaintiff by his pleadings and evidence does not attempt to claim substantial performance on his part. The question is, therefore, clearly presented on the facts as the court found them to be, as to whether or not the plaintiff being found in default can maintain a cause of action for only part performance of his contract.

The earlier case law of Ohio has refused to permit a plaintiff to found an action on the provisions of a contract where he himself is in default. The only exception to the rule recognized is where the plaintiff has substantially performed his part of the agreement....

The result of decisions which deny a defaulting contractor all right of recovery even though his work has enriched the estate of the other party to the contract is to penalize the defaulting contractor to the extent of the value of all benefit conferred by his work and materials upon the property of the other party. This result comes from unduly emphasizing the technical unity and entirety of contracts. Some decisions permit such result only when the defaulting contractor's conduct was wilful or malicious.

An ever-increasing number of decisions of courts of last resort now modify the severity of this rule and permit defaulting contractors, where their work has contributed substantial value to the other contracting party's property, to recover the value of the work and materials expended on a quantum meruit basis, the recovery being diminished, however, to the extent of such damage as the contractor's breach causes the other party. These decisions are based on the theory of unjust enrichment. The action is not founded on the broken contract but on a quasi-contract to pay for the benefits received, which cannot be returned, diminished by the damages sustained because of the contractor's breach of his contract.

The leading case supporting this theory of the law is Britton v. Turner, 6 N.H. 481, 26 Am.Dec. 713. . . .

Williston on Contracts, Vol. 5, p. 4123, par. 1475, says: "The element of forfeiture in wholly denying recovery to a plaintiff who is materially in default is most strikingly exemplified in building contracts. It has already been seen how, under the name of substantial performance, many courts have gone beyond the usual principles governing contracts in allowing relief in an action on the contract. But many cases of hardship cannot be brought within the doctrine of substantial performance, even if it is liberally interpreted; and the weight of authority strongly supports the statement that a builder, whose breach of contract is merely negligent, can recover the value of his work less the damages caused by his default; but that one who has wilfully abandoned or broken his contract cannot recover. The classical English doctrine, it is true, has denied recovery altogether where there has been a material breach even though it was due to negligence rather than wilfulness; and a few decisions in the United States follow this rule, where the builder has not substantially performed. But the English court has itself abandoned it and now holds that where a builder has supplied work and labor for the erection or repair of a house under a lump sum contract, but has departed from the terms of the contract, he is entitled to recover for his services and materials, unless (1) the work that he has done has been of no benefit to the owner; (2) the work he has done is entirely different from the work which he has contracted to do; or (3) he has abandoned the work and left it unfinished. The courts often do not discuss the question whether one who has intentionally abandoned the contract did so merely to get out of a bad bargain or whether he acted in a mistaken belief that a just cause existed for the abandonment. Where the latter situation exists, however, it would seem that the defaulter might properly be given recovery for his part performance. It seems probable that the tendency of decisions will favor a builder who has not been guilty of conscious moral fault in abandoning the contract or in its performance."

The drastic rule of forfeiture against a defaulting contractor who has by his labor and materials materially enriched the estate of the other party should in natural justice, be afforded relief to the reasonable value of the work done, less whatever damage the other party has suffered....

We conclude, therefore, that the judgment is contrary to law as to the method by which the right to judgment was determined....

For the foregoing reasons the judgment is reversed and the cause is remanded for further proceedings.

NOTES

(1) *Divisibility.* Can the court's holding that the contract was not severable, or divisible, be reconciled with the decision in *Internatio–Rotterdam*, p. 668 above? Would the trial court's treatment of the contract in *Kirkland* as divisible have been justified if the *defendant* had broken the contract rather than the plaintiff? See Fuller v. United Electric Co., 273 P.2d 136 (Nev.1954). The Electric Company sued Fuller for 80% of the contract price of doing the wiring in his new home, which became payable "on the completion of rough-in and inspection thereof." Fuller unjustifiably replaced the Electric Company with another contractor at that point, and apparently the cost of completing the work was well above 20% of the contract price. *Held:* The damages must be ascertained upon the entire contract. "The breach was a total breach and was so treated by plaintiff. The contract was thereby terminated."

(2) *Substantial Performance and Quasi Contract.* The function of the rule of substantial performance, as Cardozo explains it, is to "mitigate the rigor of implied conditions." That is also the function of quasi contract, as applied in cases like Kirkland v. Archbold. What is the difference in effect between applying the one remedy or the other? In some cases it is difficult to tell whether the court is proceeding on the basis of substantial performance or of quasi contract, in giving relief to a defaulting plaintiff. Should the problems in all cases of deviating builders be allowed to "blend into one problem with but one answer?" See Nordstrom & Woodland, Recovery by Building Contractor in Default, 20 Ohio St.L.J. 193, 217 (1959). In some cases the builder's measure of recovery seems to be more generous if the builder has failed of substantial performance than if the builder has achieved it. Does that make any sense?

(3) *Sales of Goods.* The Code provision about a seller's right to retain a buyer's prepayment, upon breach by the buyer, was examined in R.E. Davis Chemical Corporation v. Diasonics, Inc., p. 494 above. For some history behind UCC 2–718 see Amtorg Trading Corp. v. Miehle Printing Press & Mfg. Co., 206 F.2d 103 (2d Cir.1953).

If a seller delivers part of the goods contracted for, and defaults as to the rest, and has received no payment, is the seller entitled to the price fixed by the contract for the goods delivered, or to the amount by which the buyer is enriched? See UCC 2–607(1).

(4) *Sales of Land.* The traditional rule that denies restitution to a party in breach has been particularly tenacious in connection with down payments by purchasers of land. In 1986, the New York Court of Appeals declined to overrule its century-old decision in Lawrence v. Miller (quoted at p. 724 above). "The rule permitting a party in default to seek restitution for part performance has much to commend it in its general applications. But as applied to real estate down payments approximating 10% it does not appear to offer a better or more workable rule than the long-established 'usage' in this State with respect to the

seller's right to retain a down payment upon default." In a footnote, however, the court emphasized that it expressed no view as to payments in excess of 10%. Maxton Builders, Inc. v. Lo Galbo, 502 N.E.2d 184, 188–89 (N.Y.1986).

The Supreme Court of Connecticut arrived at a similar result from the opposite direction. In Vines v. Orchard Hills, Inc., 435 A.2d 1022, 1027, 1029 (1980), the court began by explaining "that a purchaser whose breach is not willful has a restitutionary claim to recover moneys that unjustly enrich his seller." But it concluded that the seller was entitled to retain the buyer's down payment of 10%, which had been designated in the contract as liquidated damages, because a "liquidated damages clause allowing the seller to retain 10 percent of the contract price as earnest money is presumptively a reasonable allocation of the risks associated with default." The presumption is a rebuttable one.

How do the New York and Connecticut rules differ? Could a 15% down payment be retained in either state? Should it make a difference in Connecticut if nothing is said about liquidated damages?

(5) *Statute of Frauds.* "A makes an oral contract to buy a tract of land from B for $100,000.... Payment is to be made in $10,000 installments, conveyance to be made on the payment of the third installment. A pays $10,000 and then refuses to pay any more and sues B to recover in restitution the $10,000 that he has paid. If B signs a sufficient memorandum, A's refusal to pay is a defense to his action ... and A cannot get restitution.... If B refuses to sign a sufficient memorandum, A's refusal to pay is not a defense ... and A can get restitution." Restatement Second § 375, Illustration 4.

Should A be put in a better position, with respect to restitution, than he would have been in if the contract had been in writing? Does the Restatement rule do that? For variant positions see 2 G. Palmer, The Law of Restitution, § 6.2 (1978).

SECTION 4.   BREACH IN THE COURSE OF PERFORMANCE

WALKER & CO. v. HARRISON

Supreme Court of Michigan, 1957.
347 Mich. 630, 81 N.W.2d 352.

SMITH, JUSTICE. This is a suit on a written contract. The defendants are in the dry-cleaning business. Walker & Company, plaintiff, sells, rents, and services advertising signs and billboards. These parties entered into an agreement pertaining to a sign. The agreement is in writing and is termed a "rental agreement." It specifies in part that:

"The lessor agrees to construct and install, at its own cost, one 18' 9" high × 8' 8" wide pylon type d.f. neon sign with electric clock and flashing lamps.... The lessor agrees to and does hereby lease or rent unto the said lessee the said SIGN for the term, use and rental and under the conditions, hereinafter set out, and the lessee agrees to pay said rental. . . .

"(a) The term of this lease shall be 36 months. . . .

"(b) The rental to be paid by lessee shall be $148.50 per month for each and every calendar month during the term of this lease; . . . .

"(d) Maintenance. Lessor at its expense agrees to maintain and service the sign together with such equipment as supplied and installed by the lessor to operate in conjunction with said sign under the terms of this lease; this service is to include cleaning and repainting of sign in original color scheme as often as deemed necessary by lessor to keep sign in first class advertising condition and make all necessary repairs to sign and equipment installed by lessor. . . ."

At the "expiration of this agreement," it was also provided, "title to this sign reverts to lessee." This clause is in addition to the printed form of agreement and was apparently added as a result of defendants' concern over title, they having expressed a desire "to buy for cash" and the salesman, at one time, having "quoted a cash price."

The sign was completed and installed in the latter part of July, 1953. The first billing of the monthly payment of $148.50 was made August 1, 1953, with payment thereof by defendants on September 3, 1953. The first payment was also the last. Shortly after the sign was installed, someone hit it with a tomato. Rust, also, was visible on the chrome, complained defendants, and in its corners were "little spider cobwebs." In addition, there were "some children's sayings written down in here." Defendant Herbert Harrison called Walker for the maintenance he believed himself entitled to under subparagraph (d) above. It was not forthcoming. He called again and again. "I was getting, you might say, sorer and sorer. . . . Occasionally, when I started calling up, I would walk around where the tomato was and get mad again. Then I would call up on the phone again." Finally, on October 8, 1953, plaintiff not having responded to his repeated calls, he telegraphed Walker that:

"You Have Continually Voided Our Rental Contract By Not Maintaining Signs As Agreed As We No Longer Have A Contract With You Do Not Expect Any Further Remuneration."

[Walker answered by letter, pointing out that the telegram did not "make any specific allegations as to what the failure of maintenance comprises," and concluding:]

"We would like to call your attention to paragraph G in our rental contract, which covers procedures in the event of a Breach of Agreement. In the event that you carry out your threat to make no future monthly payments in accordance with the agreement, it is our intention to enforce the conditions outlined under paragraph G[1]. . . . Unless we

---

1. "(g) Breach of Agreement. Lessee shall be deemed to have breached this agreement by default in payment of any installment of the rental herein provided for; abandonment of the sign or vacating premises where the sign is located; termination or transfer of lessee's interest in the premises by insolvency, appointment of a

receive both the September and October payments by October 25th, this entire matter will be placed in the hands of our attorney for collection in accordance with paragraph G which stipulates that the entire amount is forthwith due and payable."

No additional payments were made and Walker sued in assumpsit for the entire balance due under the contract, $5,197.50, invoking paragraph (g) of the agreement. Defendants filed answer and claim of recoupment, asserting that plaintiff's failure to perform certain maintenance services constituted a prior material breach of the agreement, thus justifying their repudiation of the contract and grounding their claim for damages. The case was tried to the court without a jury and resulted in a judgment for the plaintiff. The case is before us on a general appeal.

Defendants urge upon us again and again, in various forms, the proposition that Walker's failure to service the sign, in response to repeated requests, constituted a material breach of the contract and justified repudiation by them. The legal proposition is undoubtedly correct. Repudiation is one of the weapons available to an injured party in event the other contractor has committed a material breach. But the injured party's determination that there has been a material breach, justifying his own repudiation, is fraught with peril, for should such determination, as viewed by a later court in the calm of its contemplation, be unwarranted, the repudiator himself will have been guilty of material breach and himself have become the aggressor, not an innocent victim.

What is our criterion for determining whether or not a breach of contract is so fatal to the undertaking of the parties that it is to be classed as "material"? There is no single touchstone. Many factors are involved. They are well stated in section 275 of Restatement [first] of Contracts in the following terms:

receiver for lessee's business; filing of a voluntary or involuntary petition in bankruptcy with respect to lessee or the violation of any of the other terms or conditions hereof. In the event of such default, the lessor may, upon notice to the lessee, which notice shall conclusively be deemed sufficient if mailed or delivered to the premises where the sign was or is located, take possession of the sign and declare the balance of the rental herein provided for to be forthwith due and payable, and lessee hereby agrees to pay such balance upon any such contingencies. Lessor may terminate this lease and without notice, remove and repossess said sign and recover from the lessee such amounts as may be unpaid for the remaining unexpired term of this agreement. Time is of the essence of this lease with respect to the payment of rentals herein provided for. Should lessee after lessor has declared the balance of rentals due and payable, pay the full amount of rental here-

in provided, he shall then be entitled to the use of the sign, under all the terms and provisions hereof, for the balance of the term of this lease. No waiver by either party hereto of the nonperformance of any term, condition or obligation hereof shall be a waiver of any subsequent breach of, or failure to perform the same, or any other term, condition or obligation hereof. It is understood and agreed that the sign is especially constructed for the lessee and for use at the premises now occupied by the lessee for the term herein provided; that it is of no value unless so used and that it is a material consideration to the lessor in entering into this agreement that the lessee shall continue to use the sign for the period of time provided herein and for the payment of the full rental for such term."

[Is the provision in the third sentence, for recovery of unpaid amounts, enforceable? See Note 3, p. 561 above. Eds.]

"In determining the materiality of a failure fully to perform a promise the following circumstances are influential:

"(a) The extent to which the injured party will obtain the substantial benefit which he could have reasonably anticipated;

"(b) The extent to which the injured party may be adequately compensated in damages for lack of complete performance;

"(c) The extent to which the party failing to perform has already partly performed or made preparations for performance;

"(d) The greater or less hardship on the party failing to perform in terminating the contract;

"(e) The wilful, negligent or innocent behavior of the party failing to perform;

"(f) The greater or less uncertainty that the party failing to perform will perform the remainder of the contract."

We will not set forth in detail the testimony offered concerning the need for servicing. Granting that Walker's delay (about a week after defendant Herbert Harrison sent his telegram of repudiation Walker sent out a crew and took care of things) in rendering the service requested was irritating, we are constrained to agree with the trial court that it was not of such materiality as to justify repudiation of the contract, and we are particularly mindful of the lack of preponderant evidence contrary to his determination. Jones v. Eastern Michigan Motorbuses, 287 Mich. 619, 283 N.W. 710. The trial court, on this phase of the case, held as follows:

"Now Mr. Harrison phoned in, so he testified, a number of times. He isn't sure of the dates but he sets the first call at about the 7th of August and he complained then of the tomato and of some rust and some cobwebs. The tomato, according to the testimony, was up on the clock; that would be outside of his reach, without a stepladder or something. The cobwebs are within easy reach of Mr. Harrison and so would the rust be. I think that Mr. Bueche's argument that these were not materially a breach would clearly be true as to the cobwebs and I really can't believe in the face of all the testimony that there was a great deal of rust seven days after the installation of this sign. And that really brings it down to the tomato. And, of course, when a tomato has been splashed all other (sic) your clock, you don't like it. But he says he kept calling their attention to it, although the rain probably washed some of the tomato off. But the stain remained, and they didn't come. I really can't find that that was such a material breach of the contract as to justify rescission. I really don't think so."

Nor, we conclude, do we. There was no valid ground for defendants' repudiation and their failure thereafter to comply with the terms of the contract was itself a material breach, entitling Walker, upon this record, to judgment.

The question of damages remains. [The court's discussion of this question is omitted.] Judgment was, therefore, rendered for the cash price of the sign, for such services and maintenance as were extended and accepted, and interest upon the amount in default.   There was no error.

Affirmed.   Costs to appellee.

NOTES

(1) *Counselling Problems.*   If Harrison had consulted you before sending the telegram, what would you have advised him to do?   How might the telegram have been drafted in order to put pressure on Walker without risking liability for the price of the sign?   (The right of a party that has become insecure about the other party's performance to demand assurance of due performance is dealt with in Section 5(b) below.)

Suppose that on Harrison's second or third call about the sign Walker had said: "You might try wiping the sign with ammonia or look for a cleaning service in the Yellow Pages."   Would that have justified Harrison in telegraphing as he did?   See Central Garment Co., Inc. v. United Refrigerator Co., 341 N.E.2d 669 (Mass.1976).

If Harrison had consulted you before signing the agreement, what proposals would you have made for changes in its terms?

(2) *Condition v. Promise.*   Maintenance of the sign by the plaintiff with some diligence, and in some degree of respectability, was of course a constructive condition of the defendant's duty to keep up the rental payments.   The plaintiff's duty of maintenance, as stated in paragraph (d), would not be met by anything less than punctilious performance.   But the condition resting on the plaintiff need not be so stringent.   Obviously there is some softening effect, or "play", in the process of deriving a condition from a promise.   Compare the effect the paragraph might have had if it had been written in terms of an express condition.   At the extreme, it might have been written so as to excuse the lessee from all further duties upon any shortcoming in the maintenance services.

(3) *Question of Law or Fact?*   Did the court make its own judgment whether or not Walker's conduct amounted to a material breach?   Or did it accept the trial judge's determination as a permissible finding on the evidence?   Should the issue of materiality of a breach ever be submitted to a jury?   And if so, should they be directed to balance the factors mentioned in Restatement Second § 241, or in some similar list?   What merit or demerit do you find in treating the issue as a "question of law"? [a]

(4) *Restatement Second.*   Under the scheme of the Restatement Second, the most serious consequences of non-performance of a contract promise are that (a) it "discharges the injured party's remaining duties" and (b) it "gives rise to a claim for damages for total breach."   In general the second of these consequences cannot occur unless the breach entails the first, in a case like Walker & Co. v. Harrison.   Restatement Second § 243(1).   In that case, be it noted, there remained performances to be exchanged when the parties reached an impasse.   Can a breach have the first consequence but not the second?   What is the Restatement answer?   Compare § 242 with § 243.

One goal of the Restatement Second's scheme is to avoid rupture of the sort in Walker & Co. v. Harrison by encouraging cure.   Note the word "uncured" in

---

a.   For a case in which a jury's opinion was taken on the issue of materiality of breach by a pro football player, who had flirted with a club in competition with the one entitled to his services, see McLean v. Buffalo Bills Football Club, Inc., 301 N.Y.S.2d 872 (App.Div.1969).

§ 237. Compare UCC 2–508. In the Restatement, according to the Reporter's Note, the term *cure* is used in a broader sense than in the Code, "to include performance by one party before the other party's remaining duties of performance have been discharged, even though the other party has a claim for damages for partial breach because of the delay." While awaiting cure of a material breach, the injured party may *suspend* its own performance. Would Harrison have been safe in doing this? For an analysis in Restatement Second terms, see 2 Farnsworth §§ 8.16, 8.17, 8.18.

(5) *Delay Under the Vienna Convention.* Recall that the Vienna Convention abandons the "perfect tender" rule in favor of a rule of "fundamental breach" (Note 3, p. 719 above). If a seller delays delivery of the goods under a contract that does not make time "of the essence," how can the buyer know how much delay will make the seller's breach "fundamental"?

Article 47(1) empowers the buyer to "Fix an additional period of time of reasonable length for performance by the seller of his obligations." If the seller fails to deliver the goods within this additional period, article 49(1)(b) provides that the buyer may declare the contract avoided, regardless of whether the failure amounts to a "fundamental breach." Articles 63(1) and 64(1)(b) set out comparable rules for the seller in the event of a breach by buyer.

These provisions of the Vienna Convention were inspired by the *Nachfrist* provisions of German law. Under German law, however, failure to give a *Nachfrist* notice may preclude termination, whereas under the Convention it gives an alternative ground for avoidance. See J. Honnold, Uniform Law for International Sales under the 1980 United Nations Convention paras. 27, 287–90, 301–54 (2d ed. 1990).

Reconsider the questions in Note 1 above. Do these provisions of the Vienna Convention give you any ideas for changes in the terms of Harrison's agreement with Walker?

(6) *A Soybean Case.* A contract for the sale of about five carloads of soybeans was made on September 14, 1950. The seller was Simpson Feed Company, the buyer Continental Grain Company. Delivery was to be made at any time Simpson named during October or November. As the beans were loaded, Continental was to furnish shipping instructions. On the last day of October the second car was loaded and Simpson called for shipping instructions. Simpson received them some 48 hours later. It thereupon notified Continental that no more beans would be shipped. (Simpson was under pressure from the railroad either to move the car or to unload it. According to Continental, it was having trouble getting "clearance" from New Orleans, where it meant to send the beans for export.)

In an action by Continental for breach, the court assumed that the plaintiff had broken the contract by its delay. But it concluded "as a matter of law" that the breach was insubstantial; that "neither party was in a particular hurry;" and that Simpson "simply seized upon what was at most an inconsequential breach" as an excuse from performing a disadvantageous contract. (The price of soybeans rose steadily from the date of the contract to the end of November.) Continental Grain Co. v. Simpson Feed Co., 102 F.Supp. 354 (E.D.Ark.1951), aff'd, 199 F.2d 284 (8th Cir.1952). The court relied on the first Restatement § 275, quoted in Walker & Company v. Harrison.

"The vendor who fails to receive payment of an installment on the very day that it is due may sue at once for the price. But it does not follow that he may be equally precipitate in his election to declare the contract at an end. . . . We must know the cause of the default, the length of the delay, the needs of the vendor, and the expectations of the vendee."

Is this case distinguishable from *Internatio–Rotterdam*, p. 668 above? How would it be decided under the Code?

K & G CONSTRUCTION CO. v. HARRIS
Court of Appeals of Maryland, 1960.
223 Md. 305, 164 A.2d 451.

[A case was stated for appeal in an action by a Contractor against a Subcontractor, and the following facts were given. K & G Construction Company was the owner and general contractor for a housing subdivision project. Harris and Brooks contracted with it to do excavating and earth-moving work on the project. Certain provisions of the agreement were as follows:

"Section 4.   (b) Progress payments will be made each month during the performance of the work. Subcontractor will submit to Contractor, by the 25th of each month, a requisition for work performed during the preceding month. Contractor will pay these requisitions, less a retainer equal to ten per cent (10%), by the 10th of the months in which such requisitions are received.[1]

"(c) No payments will be made under this contract until the insurance requirements of Sec. 9 hereof have been complied with.

. . .

"Section 8. . . .   All work shall be performed in a workmanlike manner, and in accordance with the best practices.

"Section 9. Subcontractor agrees to carry, during the progress of the work, . . . liability insurance against . . . property damage, in such amounts and with such companies as may be satisfactory to Contractor and shall provide Contractor with certificates showing the same to be in force."

While in the course of his employment by the Subcontractor on the project, a bulldozer operator drove his machine too close to Contractor's house while grading the yard, causing the immediate collapse of a wall and other damage to the house. Contractor was generally satisfied with Subcontractor's work and progress as required by the contract until September 12, 1958, with the exception of the bulldozer accident which occurred on August 9. The Subcontractor and its insurance carrier refused to repair damage or compensate Contractor for damage to the house, claiming that there was no liability on the part of the Subcontractor.

For work done prior to July 25, the Subcontractor submitted a requisition payable under the terms of the contract on or before August

----

1. This section is not a model for clarity.

10. Contractor refused to pay it because the bulldozer damage had not been repaired or paid for. Subcontractor continued to work on the project until September 12, when it discontinued work because of Contractor's refusal to pay the said requisition, but notified Contractor by registered letter of its willingness to return to the job upon payment. Contractor later requested it to return and complete work, which Subcontractor refused to do because of nonpayment of work requisitions of July 25 and thereafter. Contractor had another excavating concern complete the work, for which it paid $450 above the contract price.

Contractor's suit against Subcontractor contained two counts: (1) for the bulldozer damage, alleging negligence, and (2) for $450 as damages for breach of contract. Subcontractor filed a counterclaim for work done and not paid for and for profit it lost by not being permitted to finish the job, totalling $2,824.50. The bulldozer damage claim was submitted to a jury, who found in favor of Contractor in the amount of $3,400, and that judgment has been paid. The other claims were submitted to the trial judge, who allowed the Subcontractor's claim in full. Contractor appealed from this determination.]

PRESCOTT, JUDGE.... The vital question, more tersely stated, remains: Did the contractor have a right, under the circumstances, to refuse to make the progress payment due on August 10, 1958?

The answer involves interesting and important principles of contract law. Promises and counter-promises made by the respective parties to a contract have certain relations to one another, which determine many of the rights and liabilities of the parties. Broadly speaking, they are (1) independent of each other, or (2) mutually dependent, one upon the other. They are independent of each other if the parties intend that *performance* by each of them is in no way conditioned upon *performance* by the other. 5 Page, The Law of Contracts, ¶ 2971. In other words, the parties exchange promises for promises, not the *performance* of promises for the *performance* of promises. 3 Williston, Contracts (Rev. Ed.), ¶ 813, n. 6. A failure to perform an independent promise does not excuse non-performance on the part of the adversary party, but each is required to perform his promise, and, if one does not perform, he is liable to the adversary party for such non-performance. (Of course, if litigation ensues questions of set-off or recoupment frequently arise.) Promises are mutually dependent if the parties intend *performance* by one to be conditioned upon *performance* by the other, and, if they be mutually dependent, they may be (a) precedent, i.e., a promise that is to be performed before a corresponding promise on the part of the adversary party is to be performed, (b) subsequent, i.e., a corresponding promise that is not to be performed until the other party to the contract has performed a precedent covenant, or (c) concurrent, i.e., promises that are to be performed at the same time by each of the parties, who are respectively bound to perform each. Page, op. cit., ¶¶ 2941, 2951, 2961....

In the early days, it was settled law that covenants and mutual promises in a contract were *prima facie* independent, and that they were to be so construed in the absence of language in the contract clearly showing that they were intended to be dependent. Williston, op. cit., ¶ 816; Page, op. cit., ¶¶ 2944, 2945. In the case of Kingston v. Preston, 2 Doug. 689, decided in 1774, Lord Mansfield, contrary to three centuries of opposing precedents, changed the rule, and decided that performance of one covenant might be dependent on prior performance of another, although the contract contained no express condition to that effect. Page, op. cit., ¶ 2946; Williston, op. cit., ¶ 817. The modern rule, which seems to be of almost universal application, is that there is a presumption that mutual promises in a contract are dependent and are to be so regarded, whenever possible. Page, op. cit., ¶ 2946; Restatement, Contracts, ¶ 266. Cf. Williston, op. cit., ¶ 812. . . .

. . . It would, indeed present an unusual situation if we were to hold that a building contractor, who has obtained someone to do work for him and has agreed to pay each month for the work performed in the previous month, has to continue the monthly payments, irrespective of the degree of skill and care displayed in the performance of work, and his only recourse is by way of suit for ill-performance. If this were the law, it is conceivable, in fact, probable, that many contractors would become insolvent before they were able to complete their contracts. As was stated by the Court in Measures Brothers Ltd. v. Measures, 2 Ch. 248: "Covenants are to be construed as dependent or independent according to the intention of the parties and the good sense of the case."

We hold that when the subcontractor's employee negligently damaged the contractor's wall, this constituted a breach of the subcontractor's promise to perform his work in a "workmanlike manner, and in accordance with the best practices." Gaybis v. Palm, 201 Md. 78, 85, 93 A.2d 269; Johnson v. Metcalfe, 209 Md. 537, 544, 121 A.2d 825; 17 C.J.S. Contracts § 515; Weiss v. Sheet Metal Fabricators, 206 Md. 195, 203, 110 A.2d 671. And there can be little doubt that the breach was material: the damage to the wall amounted to more than double the payment due on August 10. Speed v. Bailey, 153 Md. 655, 661, 662, 139 A. 534. 3A Corbin, Contracts, § 708, says: "The failure of a contractor's [in our case, the subcontractor's] performance to constitute 'substantial' performance may justify the owner [in our case, the contractor] in refusing to make a progress payment. . . . If the refusal to pay an installment is justified on the owner's [contractor's] part, the contractor [subcontractor] is not justified in abandoning work by reason of that refusal. His abandonment of the work will itself be a wrongful repudiation that goes to the essence, even if the defects in performance did not." See also Restatement, Contracts, § 274; . . . and compare Williston, op. cit., §§ 805, 841 and 842. Professor Corbin, in § 954, states further: "The unexcused failure of a contractor to render a promised performance when it is due is always a breach of contract. . . . Such failure may be of such great importance as to constitute what has been called herein a 'total' breach. . . . For a failure of performance constituting such a 'total' breach, an action for remedies that are appropriate thereto is at once maintainable. Yet the injured party is not required to bring such action. He has the option of treating the nonperformance as a 'partial' breach only...." In permitting the subcontractor to proceed with work on the project after August 9, the contractor, obviously, treated the breach by the subcontractor as a partial one. As the promises were mutually dependent and the subcontractor had made a material breach in his performance, this justified the contractor in refusing to make the August 10 payment; hence, as the contractor was not in default, the subcontractor again breached the contract when he, on September 12, discontinued work on the project, which rendered him liable (by the express terms of the contract) to the contractor for his increased cost in having the excavating done—a stipulated amount of $450. Cf. Keystone Engineering Corp. v. Sutter, 196 Md. 620, 628, 78 A.2d 191....

[Defendant also contended] that the contractor had no right to refuse the August 10 payment, because the subcontractor had furnished the insurance against property damage, as called for in the contract. There is little, or no, merit in this suggestion. The subcontractor and his insurance company denied liability. The furnishing of the insurance by him did not constitute a license to perform his work in a careless, negligent, or unworkmanlike manner; and its acceptance by the contractor did not preclude his assertion of a claim for unworkmanlike performance directly against the subcontractor.

Judgment against the appellant reversed; and judgment entered in favor of the appellant against the appellees for $450, the appellees to pay the costs.

NOTES

(1) *Questions.* Did the contractor withhold the payment due on August 10 because the subcontractor "did his work in a careless, negligent or unworkmanlike manner"? Or because the insurer denied liability? (It is a customary condition in liability insurance policies that the insured shall not assume any obligation in connection with an accident, except at its own cost.) If the subcontractor and its insurer had conceded liability at once, reserving only the question how much damage was done, would the contractor have been justified in withholding the August payment? Or if the subcontractor had promised at once to repair the damage?

Did the court overlook a clear implication in the contract (§§ 4(c) and 9) that the contractor's duty to pay was *independent* of isolated acts of carelessness by the subcontractor? What may the subcontractor include in its next contract that would alter the foregoing result?

Would the court's reasoning have been simpler if it had said that the contractor was entitled to set off the bulldozer damage against the requisition payable August 10th? Sound? With respect to the sale of goods, see UCC 2–717.

(2) *Wrongful Refusal to Make Progress Payments.* If the jury had found that the bulldozer damage was not due to the subcontractor's fault, would the trial court's judgment have been affirmed? The subcontractor discontinued work on September 12, and the last payment it had received was presumably made on July 10. It is not uncommon for disputes to arise about the amount due as a progress payment, leading to a wrongful withholding of all or part of it. If the builder discontinues work, what are its rights?

In one such case where a builder brought an action against the other party for damages, the defendant requested an instruction that "The delay of defendant to make payments on estimates, in the absence of a positive refusal to pay anything, was not ground for a rescission or termination of the contract by plaintiff," and that plaintiff's remedy was to recover interest on the deferred payments. Instead, the court instructed the jury that if defendant failed to make payments on account as called for by the contract—"a substantial failure, amounting substantially to the withholding of the whole payment, not necessarily the whole payment, but the bulk of the payment"—such failure constituted a breach on the part of defendant justifying plaintiff in stopping work and entitling it to recover damages (including lost profits) from defendant. A judgment for the builder was affirmed by the Supreme Court, saying: "As is usually the case with building contracts, it evidently was in the contemplation of the parties that the contractor could not be expected to finance the operation to completion without receiving the stipulated payments on account as the work progressed. In such cases a substantial compliance as to advance payments is a condition precedent to the contractor's obligation to proceed." Guerini Stone Co. v. P.J. Carlin Constr. Co., 248 U.S. 334 (1919).

For a somewhat divergent view, see Palmer v. Watson Const. Co., 121 N.W.2d 62 (Minn.1963): "We are committed . . . to the rule that non-payment of installment obligations is not in and of itself such prevention of performance as will make possible suit for loss of profits even though the party entitled to payment may lack working capital."

(3) *Breach of a Separate Contract.* "Neither the Uniform Commercial Code nor general contract law gives either party to a contract the right to refuse performance because the other has breached a separate contract between them." Northwest Lumber Sales, Inc. v. Continental Forest Products, Inc., 495 P.2d 744, 749 (Or.1972). Does this suggest that a party expecting to deal with another on multiple occasions or subjects should consider whether to consolidate the transactions into a single contract or to enter into multiple contracts? Would it make a difference if the single contract were divisible?

HINDRANCE AND PREVENTION

Recall Gulf's contention, in the *Eastern Airlines* case (pages 125, 613 above), that "fuel freighting" by Eastern was a breach of its duty of good faith performance. If Gulf had prevailed, it might have been justified in terminating the contract. (Would this have been so if the breach was not material?)

As Gulf's contention suggests, a party's breach of the duty of good faith performance may have the same effect as any other breach under the doctrine of constructive conditions. Moreover, a party's interference with the other party's performance may well be such a breach. See Restatement Second, Comment *d* to § 205. Consider United States v. Peck, 102 U.S. 64 (1880), described this way in the case that follows: "Peck contracted to sell the government a certain quantity of hay for the Tongue River station, and the trial court found it was mutually understood the hay was to be cut on government lands called 'the Big Meadows,' in the Yellowstone valley, which was the only available source of supply, also that thereafter the government caused all of that hay to be cut for it by other parties, in view of which Peck was relieved from his contract." The Supreme Court of the United States held that "the conduct of one party to a contract which prevents the other from performing his part is an excuse for nonperformance." [a]

When will hindrance short of prevention have the same effect? Compare the effect of prevention in the case of express conditions, discussed at p. 690 above.

NOTES

(1) *Cooperation.* In many situations a contracting party is responsible for taking affirmative steps to cooperate with the other party, even though the parties have not troubled to express such a duty in their agreement. This is likely to be so if it can be shown that such cooperative effort is essential to the other party's performance.

This principle is frequently applied in construction cases: under building contracts it is understood that a contractor, or subcontractor, cannot proceed effectively until a site is provided, prepared in a way appropriate for the work.[b] In the Restatement Second, an illustration from sales law is given:

> A contracts with B to manufacture and deliver 100,000 plastic containers for a price of $100,000. The colors of the containers are to be selected by B from among those specified in the contract. B delays in making his selection for an unreasonable time, holding up their manufacture and causing A loss. B's delay is a breach. His duty of good faith and fair dealing (§ 205) includes a duty to make his selection within a reasonable time. [§ 235, illus. 3].

This illustration is based on Kehm Corp. v. United States, 93 F.Supp. 620 (Ct.Cl.1950), in which the Government was held accountable for a supplier's delays in producing concrete bombs for practice in the Navy. Owing to delays by the Government in providing tail assemblies, Kehm's casting work was extended, sporadic, and costly. (In truth, the Navy had lost interest in the concrete bomb program.) Speaking of Kehm as the promisor, the court said: "The promisor's undertaking normally gives rise to an implied complementary obligation on the part of the promisee: He must not only not hinder his promisor's performance, he must do whatever is necessary to enable him to perform.... The implied obligation is as binding as if it were spelled out. Wood v. Lucy [p. 133 above]."

a. "The older common law did not uniformly require the promisor to refrain from actively preventing the promisee from performing the condition of the promise. In one early case the defendant had given his penal bond to pay the plaintiff eighty pounds unless the defendant should procure a marriage to take place between the plaintiff and one Bridget Palmer, before a certain day. The defendant pleaded that before that day the plaintiff addressed Bridget in such vile and insulting language that the defendant could not bring about the marriage. The plea was adjudged bad on the ground that the defendant should show that he used due diligence to bring about the marriage. [Blandford v. Andrews, 78 Eng.

Rep. 930 (King's Bench 1599)] ... These decisions show that the implication of a condition of non-prevention was by no means inevitable." Patterson, Constructive Conditions in Contracts, 42 Colum.L.Rev. 903, 931–32 (1942).

b. See R.G. Pope Constr. Co., Inc. v. Guard Rail of Roanoke, Inc., 244 S.E.2d 774 (Va.1978) (contractor vs. subcontractor, with counterclaim: "the defendant's performance of the duty to install guardrail was subject to certain conditions, the most important of which was the implied condition that a site would be available for such installation"). See Goldberg, The Owner's Duty to Coordinate Multi–Prime Construction Contractors, 28 Emory L.J. 377 (1979).

Naturally there are contracting parties who, in a spirit of self-pity or worse, demand more than their fair share of cooperation. There is a countervailing principle that "enthusiasm is not required in performing contractual obligations." Esmieu v. Hzieh, 580 P.2d 1105 (Wash.App.1978).

(2) *Influences in Cooperation Cases.* Patterson, Constructive Conditions in Contracts, 42 Colum.L.Rev. 903 (1942), gives an historical and critical survey of the requirement of cooperation at pp. 928–42. "While not every act or omission by the obligor which may expedite performance by the obligee (of his promise or of a condition) is required, the acts or omissions which are clearly within the obligor's control and which are the normal or obvious means of the obligee's performance, are presumably required of the obligor, or he assumes the risk of their non-occurrence. The justifiable reliance by the obligee, the usages of the trade or activity, the mores of the community, are obviously influential in determining what co-operation is required in a particular transaction. Judicial opinions reveal these influences. The moral notions of carelessness or diligence, malice or inadvertence, have sporadic influence. The avoidance of unjust enrichment seems also influential." Id., pp. 937–38. How many of these "influences" would be relevant in applying Restatement Second § 205?

IRON TRADE PRODUCTS CO. v. WILKOFF CO.

Supreme Court of Pennsylvania, 1922.
272 Pa. 172, 116 A. 150.

WALLING, J. In July, 1919, plaintiff entered into a written contract with defendant for the purchase of 2,600 tons of section relaying rails, to be delivered in New York harbor at times therein specified for $41 a ton. Defendant failed to deliver any of the rails, and plaintiff brought this suit, averring, by reason of such default, it had been compelled to purchase the rails elsewhere (2,000 tons thereof at $49.20 per ton and 600 tons at $49 per ton), also that the market or current price of the rails at the time and place of delivery was approximately $50 per ton, and claiming as damages the difference between what it had been compelled to pay and the contract price. Defendant filed an affidavit of defense and a supplement thereto, both of which the court below held insufficient and entered judgment for plaintiff, from which defendant brought this appeal.

In effect, the affidavit of defense avers the supply of such rails was very limited, there being only two places in the United States (one in Georgia and one in West Virginia) where they could be obtained in quantities to fill the contract, and that pending the time for delivery defendant was negotiating for the required rails when plaintiff announced to the trade its urgent desire to purchase a similar quantity of like rails, and in fact bought 887 tons and agreed to purchase a much larger quantity from the parties with whom defendant had been negotiating, further averring this conduct on behalf of plaintiff reduced the available supply of relaying rails and enhanced the price to an exorbitant sum, rendering performance by defendant impossible. The affidavit, however, fails to aver knowledge on part of plaintiff that the supply of rails was limited or any intent on its part to prevent, interfere with, or embarrass defendant in the performance of the contract; and there is no suggestion of any understanding, express or implied, that defendant was to secure the rails from any particular source, or that plaintiff was to refrain from purchasing other rails; hence it was not required to do so. The true rule is stated in Williston on Contracts, p. 1308, as quoted by the trial court, viz.:

"If a party seeking to secure all the merchandise of a certain character which he could entered into a contract for a quantity of the required goods, and subsequently made performance of the contract by the seller more difficult by making other purchases which increased the scarcity of the available supply, his conduct would furnish no excuse for refusal to perform the prior contract."

Mere difficulty of performance will not excuse a breach of contract. Corona C. & C. Co. v. Dickinson, 261 Pa. 589, 104 A. 741; Janes v. Scott, 59 Pa. 178, 98 Am.Dec. 328; 35 Cyc. 245. Defendant relies upon the rule stated in United States v. Peck, 102 U.S. 64, 26 L.Ed. 46, that—

"The conduct of one party to a contract which prevents the other from performing his part is an excuse for nonperformance."

The cases are not parallel. Here plaintiff's conduct did not prevent performance by defendant, although it may have added to the difficulty and expense thereof. There is no averment that plaintiff's purchases exhausted the supply of rails, and the advance in price caused thereby is no excuse. The *Peck* Case [p. 745 above] stands on different ground....

The affidavit "denies that there was any market or market price or current price for such relaying rails" at any time from the date of the contract to the beginning of this suit, but other statements therein amount to an admission of a market price. For example, it speaks of "the trade in Pittsburgh, New York, and other centers of such trade"; also of "the very small quantity of such rails in the market." The affidavit further states that—

"After making the said contract with the plaintiff the defendant began negotiations with the persons from whom the said rails in Georgia and West Virginia might be purchased; and in each of the two cases referred to such negotiations had proceeded so far that defendant could have purchased 2,600 tons of such rails either in Georgia or West Virginia at some such price as that contracted to the plaintiff, or less, or not greatly in excess thereof.

"In fact, the plaintiff bought a quantity of such rails, to wit, 887 tons, and at one time had contracted for the purchase of a much larger quantity thereof, from the same persons with whom the defendant had been negotiating for the same, and at higher prices than had been offered to the defendant by the same persons within the terms of the said contract.

"And affiant, while denying, as aforesaid, that the plaintiff was compelled to purchase the said rails or any of them, avers that, if the plaintiff was so compelled, it was only as the result of plaintiff's own interference with the defendant's performance of the said contract, and avers that but for the said interference the defendant would have made full performance of its said contract."

The above and the admitted facts that plaintiff actually bought the 2,600 tons and had previously resold the same indicate a market value, and the specific averment thereof, in the statement of claim is not sufficiently denied in the affidavit. An affidavit of defense must be considered as a whole, and therein a general denial is of no avail against an admission of the same fact. An affidavit that is contradictory or equivocal is insufficient. See Noll v. Royal Exchange Assurance Corp., 76 Pa.Super.Ct. 510.

The supplemental affidavit avers that when the contract in suit was made plaintiff, to the knowledge of defendant, had resold the 2,600 tons of rails at $42.25 per ton, and, furthermore, that the purchaser at such resale released plaintiff from all claim for damages under the contract.... The fact that a vendee has resold the goods contracted for is of no moment unless made a part of the contract; for, if not, he is entitled to the benefit of his bargain, regardless of the disposition he may intend to make of the property involved. To hold otherwise would inject collateral issues in trials for breaches of such contracts.

The assignments of error are overruled, and the judgment is affirmed.

NOTES

(1) The *Case of the Underbidding Supplier.* John Alice had been invited by the General Services Administration to bid for a contract to supply uniforms to the Government. He then made a contract to purchase shirts and trousers for the uniforms from the Robett Company: 3500 shirts at $4 each and the trousers at $3 each. Alice told Robett that its price would be the basis for his bid to GSA. About ten days later Robett made its own bid, offering to supply the uniforms to the Government for $7.78 each; and the Government accepted. Alice sued Robett for breach. On defendant's motion for summary judgment, *held:* granted. The court rejected the plaintiff's contention that "an offer from a manufacturer, to a supplier who is bidding for resale over to a third party contains an implied term prohibiting the manufacturer from submitting its own bid directly to the third party, in competition with the supplier." Alice v. Robett Mfg. Co., 328 F.Supp. 1377 (N.D.Ga.1970), aff'd, 445 F.2d 316 (5th Cir.1971).

Comparing this case with the main case, is Alice's case distinctive because Robett's bid to the GSA was apparently prompted by information that Alice supplied? (On the market value of information see Black Industries, Inc. v. Bush, p. 344 above, and the notes following.) Or is *Iron Trade Products* the more distinctive case because there the plaintiff's rail purchases might have forced the defendant into a breach of contract?

(2) *The Case of the Overbidding Buyer.* Some houses in Brooklyn were about to be offered for sale in a foreclosure proceeding. Patterson was in a favorable position to buy them at the public sale, and Mrs. Meyerhofer was interested in owning them. Therefore they entered into an ordinary sale contract whereby Mrs. Meyerhofer agreed to pay Patterson $23,000 for the property. No mention was made of the fact that he did not own it. When Patterson attended the foreclosure sale Mrs. Meyerhofer was also there, and whenever he made a bid she bid higher. The four houses in question were

struck down to her for $22,380. Patterson sued for damages, and it was said that on these facts he was entitled to $620. "In the case of every contract there is an implied undertaking on the part of each party that he will not intentionally and purposely do anything to prevent the other party from carrying out the agreement on his part." Patterson v. Meyerhofer, 97 N.E. 472 (N.Y.1912). *Question:* What differentiates this case from *Iron Trade Products?*

(3) *Damages (Reprise).* In Note 1, p. 519 above, which dealt with Buyer's damages against Seller, you were asked about the effect if Buyer's purchaser on resale released Buyer. Note that the court in *Iron Trade Products* declines to consider the assertion "that the purchaser at such resale released plaintiff from all claim for damages under the contract." If one takes the contract price as $41 per ton, the price under Iron Trade Products contract for resale as $42.25 per ton, the price at which Iron Trade Products purchased other rails as $49 per ton, and the market price as $50 per ton, what should Iron Trade Products' damages be?

(4) *Anti–Waiver Clauses (Reprise).* Recall the discussion of anti-waiver clauses in the context of express conditions (Note 3, p. 696 above). Such clauses are also frequently invoked in the context of constructive conditions of exchange. But, again, courts have not always honored such clauses. See Dillingham Commercial Co. v. Spears, 641 P.2d 1 (Alaska 1982), in which the court held that, in spite of an anti-waiver clause, a landlord's "long acquiescence" in late rental payments "constituted a waiver of her right to claim a default for [her tenant's] late payments."

(5) *Imprisonment of Language?* A contract for the sale of a home required the purchaser to make periodic payments of the price and keep the premises in repair. The sellers placed a deed in escrow, awaiting full payment. The purchaser allowed the home to deteriorate and defaulted on payments. The sellers sent a "notice of default" to the purchaser, stating that the purchaser's interest would be "cancelled and terminated" in thirty days. Although the purchaser failed to cure defaults within that period, the sellers decided to claim the unpaid balance of the price (the value of the property had fallen below that amount). The trial court granted a motion by the purchaser for summary judgment. On appeal, the court considered one basis for the judgment at length:

> Election of remedies is an ancient doctrine created by the courts. It requires a plaintiff to choose between inconsistent remedies for redress of a single injury. The doctrine originated as a means to prevent double recovery and to limit potential harassment of defendants.... Commentators have criticized the election doctrine, calling it a "delusion," a "judicial weed," and an "anachronism." ... Its historic purposes ... now are served by other principles.... [C]lose examination reveals that the doctrine exists in name only.... The election doctrine has become a form of estoppel.

> We believe the time has come to escape the imprisonment of obsolete language. Where the term "election of remedies" has no substantive meaning apart from the principles of satisfaction, claim preclusion or estoppel, it should not be invoked as a separate doctrine. If a plaintiff is said to have "elected" a remedy, through certain acts or statements prior to litigation, the proper inquiry should be whether the defendant has relied upon such acts or statements prior to litigation and, therefore, would be unfairly prejudiced by assertion of a different, inconsistent remedy.

Held: Reversed. Keesee v. Fetzek, 681 P.2d 600 (Idaho App.1984).[a]

a. For a subsequent appeal, applying "quasi-estoppel" against the seller, see Id., 723 P.2d 904 (Idaho App.1986) ("Quasi- estoppel, unlike equitable estoppel, does not require misrepresentation by one party or actual reliance by the other").

If you had been asked by the purchaser to provide language that would bar the sellers from changing course as they did, what would you have suggested? (The court examined several terms of the contract and concluded that none of them had that effect.) If your effort were to succeed, would "Election-of-remedies Clause" be a good name for your provision? What better?

NEW ENGLAND STRUCTURES, INC. v. LORANGER

Supreme Judicial Court of Massachusetts, 1968.
354 Mass. 62, 234 N.E.2d 888.

CUTTER, JUSTICE. In one case the plaintiffs, doing business as Theodore Loranger & Sons (Loranger), the general contractor on a school project, seeks to recover from New England Structures, Inc., a subcontractor (New England), damages caused by an alleged breach of the subcontract. Loranger avers that the breach made it necessary for Loranger at greater expense to engage another subcontractor to complete work on a roof deck. In a cross action, New England seeks to recover for breach of the subcontract by Loranger alleged to have taken place when Loranger terminated New England's right to proceed. The actions were consolidated for trial. A jury returned a verdict for New England in the action brought by Loranger, and a verdict for New England in the sum of $16,860.25 in the action brought by New England against Loranger. The cases are before us on Loranger's exceptions to the judge's charge.

Loranger, under date of July 11, 1961, entered into a subcontract with New England by which New England undertook to install a gypsum roof deck in a school, then being built by Loranger. New England began work on November 24, 1961. On December 18, 1961, New England received a telegram from Loranger which read, "Because of your ... repeated refusal ... or inability to provide enough properly skilled workmen to maintain satisfactory progress, we ... terminate your right to proceed with work at the ... school as of December 26, 1961, in accordance with Article ... 5 of our contract. We intend to complete the work ... with other forces and charge its costs and any additional damages resulting from your repeated delays to your account." New England replied, "Failure on your [Loranger's] part to provide ... approved drawings is the cause of the delay." The telegram also referred to various allegedly inappropriate changes in instructions.

The pertinent portions of art. 5 of the subcontract are set out in the margin.[1] Article 5 stated grounds on which Loranger might terminate New England's right to proceed with the subcontract.

---

1. "The Subcontractor agrees to furnish sufficient labor, materials, tools and equipment to maintain its work in accordance with the progress of the general construction work by the General Contractor. Should the Subcontractor fail to keep up with ... [such] progress ... then he shall work overtime with no additional compensation, if directed to do so by the General Contractor. If the Subcontractor should be

There was conflicting evidence concerning (a) how New England had done certain work; (b) whether certain metal cross pieces (called bulb tees) had been properly "staggered" and whether joints had been welded on both sides by certified welders, as called for by the specifications; (c) whether New England had supplied an adequate number of certified welders on certain days; (d) whether and to what extent Loranger had waived certain specifications; and (e) whether New England had complied with good trade practices. The architect testified that on December 14, 1961, he had made certain complaints to New England's president. The work was completed by another company at a cost in excess of New England's bid. There was also testimony (1) that Loranger's job foreman told one of New England's welders "to do no work at the job site during the five day period following the date of Loranger's termination telegram," and (2) that, "if New England had been permitted to continue its work, it could have completed the entire subcontract ... within five days following the date of the termination telegram."

The trial judge ruled, as matter of law, that Loranger, by its termination telegram confined the justification for its notice of termination to New England's "repeated refusal ... or inability to provide enough properly skilled workmen to maintain satisfactory progress." He then gave the following instructions: "If you should find that New England ... did not furnish a sufficient number of men to perform the required work under the contract within a reasonable time ... then you would be warranted in finding that Loranger was justified in terminating its contract; and it may recover in its suit against New England.... [T]he termination ... cannot, as ... matter of law, be justified for any ... reason not stated in the telegram of December 18 ... including failure to stagger the joints of the bulb tees or failure to weld properly ... or any other reason, unless you find that inherent in the reasons stated in the telegram, namely, failure to provide enough skilled workmen to maintain satisfactory progress, are these aspects. Nevertheless, these allegations by Loranger of deficiency of work on the part of New England Structures may be considered by you, if you find that Loranger was justified in terminating the contract for the reason enumerated in the telegram. You may consider it or them as an element of damages sustained by Loranger...." [2] Counsel for Loranger claimed exceptions

adjudged a bankrupt ... or if he should persistently ... fail to supply enough properly skilled workmen ... or ... disregard instructions of the General Contractor or fail to observe or perform the provisions of the Contract, then the General Contractor may, by at least five ... days prior written notice to the Subcontractor without prejudice to any other rights or remedies, terminate the Subcontractor's right to proceed with the work. In such event, the General Contractor may ... prosecute the work to completion ... and the Subcontractor shall be liable to the General Contractor for any excess cost occasioned ... thereby ..." (emphasis supplied).

2. The judge also instructed, "[I]f you find that on the day following the sending of this telegram ... employees of New England ... were refused permission to continue that work, then you may consider that as a breach of the contract by Loranger, for Loranger's telegram terminated the contract ... as of December 26th [by] the giving of five days notice.... [I]f you find that [employees of] New England ... reported for work and were only informed that they were to call their office and were not prevented from working then ... you would be warranted in finding that this was not a refusal on the part of Loranger to permit them to work for the period between

to the portion of the judge's charge quoted above in the body of this opinion.[3]

1.   Some authority supports the judge's ruling, in effect, that Loranger, having specified in its telegram one ground for termination of the subcontract, cannot rely in litigation upon other grounds, except to the extent that the other grounds may directly affect the first ground asserted. See Railway Co. v. McCarthy, 96 U.S. 258, 267–268, 24 L.Ed. 693 ("Where a party gives a reason for his conduct and decision touching ... a controversy, he cannot, after litigation has begun, change his ground, and put his conduct upon ... a different consideration. He is not permitted thus to mend his hold. He is *estopped* from doing it by a settled principle of law" [emphasis supplied]).... In each of these cases, there is reference to estoppel or "waiver" as the legal ground behind the principle.

Our cases somewhat more definitely require reliance or change of position based upon the assertion of the particular reason or defence before treating a person, giving one reason for his action, as estopped later to give a different reason. See Bates v. Cashman, 230 Mass. 167, 168–169, 119 N.E. 663, 664. There it was said, "The defendant is not prevented from setting up this defense. Although he wrote respecting other reasons for declining to perform the contract, he expressly reserved different grounds for his refusal.[4] While of course one cannot fail in good faith in presenting his reasons as to his conduct touching a controversy he is not prevented from relying upon one good defense among others urged simply because he has not always put it forward, when it does not appear that he has acted dishonestly or that the other party has been misled to his harm, or that he is estopped on any other ground." See Brown v. Henry, 172 Mass. 559, 567, 52 N.E. 1073; St. John Bros. Co. v. Falkson, 237 Mass. 399, 402–403, 130 N.E. 51; Moss v. Old Colony Trust Co., 246 Mass. 139, 150, 140 N.E. 803; Sheehan v. Commercial Travelers Mut. Acc. Assn. of America, 283 Mass. 543, 551–553, 186 N.E. 627, 88 A.L.R. 975; Restatement: Contracts, § 304; Williston, Contracts (3d ed.) § 742 (and also §§ 678, 679, 691); Corbin, Contracts, §§ 762, 1218, 1266 (and also §§ 265, 721, 727, 744, 756). See also Randall v. Peerless Motor Car Co., 212 Mass. 352, 376, 99 N.E. 221.

We think Loranger is not barred from asserting grounds not mentioned in its telegram unless New England establishes that, in some manner, it relied to its detriment upon the circumstance that only one ground was so asserted. Even if some evidence tended to show such reliance, the jury did not have to believe this evidence. They should

---

the receipt of the telegram and the date of the termination, December 26th."

3. No exception appears to have been claimed to the portion of the charge (see fn. 2) relating to whether Loranger prevented New England from performing work on the subcontract during the period from December 19 to December 26.

4. The original papers show (record, p. 22) that the reservation was, "The state-

ment of the foregoing [reason] is not to be taken as waiving any other reason for ... Cashman's refusal to proceed further with the agreement." This distinction from the present case, in our opinion, does not affect the principle that any estoppel to assert a different reason must rest on actual reliance.

have received instructions that they might consider grounds for termination of the subcontract and defences to New England's claim (that Loranger by the telegram had committed a breach of the subcontract), other than the ground raised in the telegram, unless they found as a fact that New England had relied to its detriment upon the fact that only one particular ground for termination was mentioned in the telegram.

2. As there must be a new trial, we consider whether art. 5 of the subcontract (fn. 1) afforded New England any right during the five-day notice period to attempt to cure its default, and, in doing so, to rely on the particular ground stated in the telegram ... Although the intention of the notice provision of art. 5 is obscure, we interpret it as giving New England no period in which to cure continuing defaults, but merely as directing that New England be told when it must quit the premises and as giving it an opportunity to take steps during the five-day period to protect itself from injury. Nothing in art. 5 suggests that a termination pursuant to its provisions was not to be effective in any event at the conclusion of the five-day period, even if New England should change its conduct.

If Loranger in fact was not justified by New England's conduct in giving the termination notice, it may have subjected itself to liability for breach of the subcontract. The reason stated in the notice, however, for giving the notice cannot be advanced as the basis of any reliance by New England in action taken by it to cure defaults. After the receipt of the notice, as we interpret art. 5, New England had no further opportunity to cure defaults.

Exceptions sustained.

NOTE

Golden Silence. "When a party believes it is entitled to terminate a contract at will, it often will refrain from stating its reasons. The party may also refrain from undertaking a complete (and possibly costly) investigation of possible grounds for termination. Should it turn out that the contract was not terminable at will, it would be unfair, without some additional showing, to preclude the party from asserting legitimate grounds for termination." First Commodity Traders, Inc. v. Heinold Commodities, Inc., 591 F.Supp. 812, 822 (N.D.Ill.1984), aff'd, 766 F.2d 1007 (7th Cir.1985).

If this is good policy, does it follow that it is wise for a land-purchaser, believing there is a defect in the seller's title, to withdraw without giving a reason? For a buyer of goods to reject a tender without giving a reason? See UCC 2–605(1).

SECTION 5.   PROSPECTIVE NONPERFORMANCE

(a) Anticipatory Repudiation

In Phillpotts v. Evans, 5 M. & W. 475, 151 Eng.Rep. 200 (Exchequer 1839), a seller sued on a contract for the sale of "wheat." The buyer had refused to take delivery. Some time before the seller was required to make delivery, the buyer had given him notice that it would not be accepted. The market price had dropped between then and the last day when the seller could have made a proper tender. The question was whether the damages should be calculated with reference to the market price at the time of the buyer's repudiation, or to the price at the later time. Naturally, the buyer preferred the earlier date. The same issue was presented in Roehm v. Horst, 178 U.S. 1 (1900), which is perhaps the leading American case on anticipatory breach of contract.

In the Restatement Second the term "anticipatory breach" is called an elliptical expression for a "breach by anticipatory repudiation, because it occurs before there is any breach by non-performance." Section 253, Comment *a*. By the better usage, an anticipatory repudiation occurs when a promisor wrongfully signifies, in advance of the time for that party's performance, that it will not be forthcoming. The notice given by the buyer in Phillpotts v. Evans was a repudiation in this sense. See also UCC 2–609(4); Restatement Second, § 251.

What are the effects of an anticipatory repudiation? This is the question to be considered next. Sometimes it is assumed that if an anticipatory repudiation has one effect similar to that of a breach it must have other consequences as well. The leading case on the subject, Hochster v. De la Tour, has been criticized for reasoning in that way. After reading the opinion, which follows, consider whether or not the criticism is a fair one.

In any event, the problem of calculating damages that was raised in Phillpotts v. Evans is separable from other issues relating to anticipatory repudiation. More recent materials addressing that problem are presented below.

NOTE

Definitions. Repudiation has been defined as an " 'overt communication of intention' not to perform (UCC 2–610, Comment 2); a positive and unequivocal announcement of an intention not to perform." Tenavision, Inc. v. Neuman, 379 N.E.2d 1166 (N.Y.1978). Compare the definition in Restatement Second § 250.

How was the word used in Walker & Co. v. Harrison, p. 735 above. Compare UCC 2–106(4).

HOCHSTER v. DE LA TOUR
Queen's Bench, 1853.
2 E. & B. 678, 118 Eng.Rep. 922.

[Action of assumpsit.]   Declaration: "for that, heretofore, to wit, on 12th April 1852, in consideration that plaintiff, at the request of defendant would agree with the defendant to enter into the service and employ of the defendant in capacity of a courier, on a certain day then to come, to wit, the 1st day of June, 1852, and to serve the defendant in that capacity, and travel with him on the continent of Europe as a courier for three months certain from the day and year last aforesaid, and to be ready to start with the defendant on such travels on the day and year last aforesaid, at and for certain wages or salary, to wit," £10 per month of such service, "the defendant then agreed with the plaintiff, and then promised him, that he, the defendant, would engage and employ the plaintiff in the capacity of a courier on and from the said 1st day of June, 1852, for three months" on these terms; "and to start on such travels with the plaintiff on the day and year last aforesaid, and to pay the plaintiff" on these terms.   [Further averments of the plaintiff were that he did make the agreement, "confiding in" the defendant's promise, and that—as the defendant always knew—from that time until the defendant broke his promise the plaintiff was "always ready and willing" to start travels with the defendant on the day aforesaid and would have entered the defendant's service on that day but for the defendant's breach.   "(Y)et the defendant, not regarding the said agreement ... before the said 1st June, 1852, wrongfully wholly refused" to employ the plaintiff for the three months agreed upon, or for any other time, and then "absolved" the plaintiff from performance of the agreement and from "being ready and willing to perform," and put an end to the engagement, to the plaintiff's damage.]   The writ was dated on the 22d of May, 1852.

Pleas: 1.   That defendant did not agree or promise in manner, and form, & c.: conclusion to the country.   Issue thereon.

2.   That plaintiff did not agree with defendant in manner and form, & c.: conclusion to the country.   Issue thereon.

3.   That plaintiff was not ready and willing, nor did defendant absolve, exonerate, or discharge plaintiff from being ready and willing, in manner and form, & c.: conclusion to the country.   Issue thereon.

4.   That defendant did not refuse or decline, nor wrongfully absolve, exonerate, or discharge, nor wrongfully break, put an end to or determine, in manner and form, & c.: conclusion to the country.   Issue thereon.

On the trial before Erle, J., at the London sittings in last Easter term, it appeared that plaintiff was a courier, who in April, 1852, was engaged by defendant to accompany him on a tour, to commence on 1st June, 1852, on the terms mentioned in the declaration.   On the 11th May, 1852, defendant wrote to plaintiff that he had changed his mind, and declined his services. He refused to make him any compensation. The action was commenced on 22d May. The plaintiff, between the commencement of the action and the 1st of June, obtained an engagement with Lord Ashburton, on equally good terms, but not commencing till 4th July. The defendant's counsel objected that there could be no breach of the contract before the 1st of June. The learned judge was of contrary opinion, but reserved leave to enter a nonsuit on this objection. The other questions were left to the jury, who found for plaintiff.

LORD CAMPBELL, C.J.,[a] now delivered the judgment of the court:

On this motion in arrest of judgment, the question arises whether if there be an engagement between A. and B. whereby B. engages to employ A. on and from a future day for a given period of time, to travel with him into a foreign country as a courier, and to start with him in that capacity on that day, A. being to receive a monthly salary during the continuance of such service, B. may, before the day, refuse to perform the agreement and break and renounce it, so as to entitle A. before the day to commence an action against B. to recover damages for breach of the agreement, A. having been ready and willing to perform it, till it was broken and renounced by B. The defendant's counsel very powerfully contended that, if the plaintiff was not contented to dissolve the contract, and to abandon all remedy upon it, he was bound to remain ready and willing to perform it till the day when the actual employment as courier in the service of the defendant was to begin; and that there could be no breach of the agreement, before that day, to give a right of action. But it cannot be laid down as a universal rule that, where by agreement an act is to be done on a future day, no action can be brought for a breach of the agreement till the day for doing the act has arrived. If a man promises to marry a woman on a future day, and before that day marries another woman, he is instantly liable to an action for breach of promise of marriage. Short v. Stone, 8 Q.B. 358. If a man contracts to execute a lease on and from a future day for a certain term, and, before that day, executes a lease to another for the same term, he may be immediately sued for breaking the contract. Ford v. Tiley, 6 B. & C. 325. So if a man contracts to sell and deliver specific goods on a future day, and before the day he sells and delivers them to another he is immediately liable to an action at the suit of the person with whom he first contracted to sell and deliver them. Bowdell v. Parsons, 10 East, 359. One reason alleged in support of such an action is, that the defendant has, before the day, rendered it impossible for him to perform the contract at the day; but this does not necessarily follow; for, prior to

a. John Campbell (1779–1861), a Scotsman of ancient lineage, matriculated at St. Andrews University at the age of eleven. Upon entering the English bar he predicted that he would become Lord Chancellor. His name is associated with a number of law reform statutes which he pressed as a member of Parliament, as Attorney General, and in the House of Lords. As a reward for his services to the government, he was made the first Baron Campbell. He won literary fame with his "Lives of the Lord Chancellors," followed by the "Lives of the Chief Justices." These works are full of good stories, inaccuracies, and harsh judgments; it was said that they had added a new sting to death. He held judicial office briefly as Lord Chancellor of Ireland, where he was not popular, and as Chief Justice of England from 1850 to 1859. Then he became Lord Chancellor of England, at the age of eighty.

the day fixed for doing the act, the first wife may have died, a surrender of the lease executed might be obtained, and the defendant might have repurchased the goods so as to be in a situation to sell and deliver them to the plaintiff. Another reason may be that, where there is a contract to do an act on a future day, there is a relation constituted between the parties in the meantime by the contract, and that they impliedly promise that in the meantime neither will do anything to the prejudice of the other inconsistent with that relation. As an example, a man and woman engaged to marry are affianced to one another during the period between the time of the engagement and the celebration of the marriage. In this very case of traveller and courier, from the day of the hiring till the day when the employment was to begin, they were engaged to each other; and it seems to be a breach of an implied contract if either of them renounced the engagement. This reasoning seems in accordance with the unanimous decisions of the Exchequer Chamber in Elderton v. Emmens, 6 C.B. 160, which we have followed in subsequent cases in this court. The declaration in the present case, in alleging a breach, states a great deal more than a passing intention on the part of the defendant which he may repent of, and could only be proved by evidence that he had utterly renounced the contract, or done some act which rendered it impossible for him to perform it. If the plaintiff has no remedy for breach of the contract unless he treats the contract as in force, and acts upon it down to the 1st June, 1852, it follows that, till then, he must enter into no employment which will interfere with his promise "to start with the defendant on such travels on the day and year," and that he must then be properly equipped in all respects as a courier for a three months' tour on the continent of Europe. But it is surely much more rational, and more for the benefit of both parties, that, after the renunciation of the agreement by the defendant, the plaintiff should be at liberty to consider himself absolved from any future performance of it, retaining his right to sue for any damage he has suffered from the breach of it. Thus, instead of remaining idle and laying out money in preparations which must be useless, he is at liberty to seek service under another employer, which would go in mitigation of the damages to which he would otherwise be entitled for a breach of the contract. It seems strange that the defendant, after renouncing the contract, and absolutely declaring that he will never act under it, should be permitted to object that faith is given to his assertion, and that an opportunity is not left to him of changing his mind. If the plaintiff is barred of any remedy by entering into an engagement inconsistent with starting as a courier with the defendant on the 1st June, he is prejudiced by putting faith in the defendant's assertion; and it would be more consistent with principle if the defendant were precluded from saying that he had not broken the contract when he declared that he entirely renounced it. Suppose that the defendant, at the time of his renunciation, had embarked on a voyage for Australia, so as to render it physically impossible for him to employ the plaintiff as a courier on the continent of Europe in the months of June, July and August, 1852; according to decided cases, the action might have been brought before the 1st June; but the renunciation may have been founded on other facts, to be given in evidence, which would equally have rendered the defendant's performance of the contract impossible. The man who wrongfully renounces a contract into which he has deliberately entered cannot justly complain if he is immediately sued for a compensation in damages by the man whom he has injured; and it seems reasonable to allow an option to the injured party, either to sue immediately, or to wait till the time when the act was to be done, still holding it as prospectively binding for the exercise of this option, which may be advantageous to the innocent party, and cannot be prejudicial to the wrongdoer. An argument against the action before the 1st of June is urged from the difficulty of calculating the damages; but this argument is equally strong against an action before the 1st of September, when the three months would expire. In either case, the jury in assessing the damages would be justified in looking to all that happened, or was likely to happen, to increase or mitigate the loss of the plaintiff down to the day of trial. We do not find any decision contrary to the view we are taking of this case. Leigh v. Paterson, 8 Taunt, 540, only shows that upon a sale of goods to be delivered at a certain time, if the vendor before the time gives information to the vendee that he cannot deliver them, having sold them, the vendee may calculate the damages according to the state of the market when they ought to have been delivered. . . .

If it should be held that, upon a contract to do an act on a future day, a renunciation of the contract by one party dispenses with a condition to be performed in the meantime by the other, there seems no reason for requiring that other to wait till the day arrives before seeking his remedy by action; and the only ground on which the condition can be dispensed with seems to be, that the renunciation may be treated as a breach of contract.

Upon the whole, we think that the declaration in this case is sufficient. It gives us great satisfaction to reflect that, the question being on the record, our opinion may be reviewed in a Court of Error. In the meantime, we must give judgment for the plaintiff.

    Judgment for plaintiff.

NOTES

(1) *The Victim's Option.* The implication of the opinion seems to be that the victim of a repudiation may treat it as a breach, or not, at will: "the renunciation may be treated as a breach." The element of choice appears in many anticipatory breach cases. Sometimes it is said that the injured party has an election, sometimes that the repudiation amounts to an "offer" of breach.

If the injured party disregards the repudiation altogether, will the rights of the parties later be determined as if it had never occurred? Frost v. Knight, an English decision of 1872, contains reasoning by Lord Cockburn that is well-known in this country, and indicates that they will. However, that reasoning has also been rejected, at least where it would permit the injured party to pile up damages by proceeding with performance. See Rockingham County v. Luten Bridge Co., p. 506 above, where Frost v. Knight is criticized.

Nevertheless, it is a persistent idea that the injured party has a choice, upon receiving a repudiation, and may "keep the contract alive," to use Lord Cockburn's expression, for the benefit of both parties.   To the effect that no acceptance is requisite for a breach by anticipatory repudiation, see Stefanowicz Corp. v. Harris, 373 A.2d 54 (Md.Ct.App.1977); and to the contrary effect see William B. Tanner Co., Inc. v. WIOO, Inc., 528 F.2d 262 (3d Cir.1975).   Compare Stauth v. Brown, 734 P.2d 1063 (Kan.1987).

(2) *Retraction.*   An offer to contract and an anticipatory repudiation have virtually nothing in common, except this: each may be withdrawn.   In the case of an offer, the appropriate word is "revoke"; in the case of a repudiation the appropriate word is "retract".   See UCC 2–611.   Inasmuch as a present breach of contract cannot be undone, the view has been expressed that the conception of breach by anticipatory repudiation is anomalous, and cannot be accounted for on "normal contract analysis."   G.E.J. Corp. v. Uranium Aire, Inc., 311 F.2d 749, 754 n. 3 (9th Cir.1963).   In the case of an ordinary breach of contract, nothing the defaulting party may do can deprive the injured party of a right of action— although the breach may be so slight that only nominal damages would be granted.

The matter of retraction will be further considered below.

(3) *Laredo Hides Rebuffed.*   Laredo Hides Co. v. H & H Meat Products Co., p. 490 above, reports that a seller of cattle hides gave an "ultimatum" to the buyer about payment for hides that had been delivered.   Liborio Hinojosa acted for H & H, the seller, in this matter.   The deadline he set for payment (March 21) passed without action satisfactory to him, and he refused payment when it was later tendered.   The following delivery of hides was scheduled under the contract for Saturday, April 1.   On the Thursday before that (March 30), an agent for Laredo Hides, the buyer, telephoned Hinojosa to ask if Saturday's shipment would be ready for pickup.   "Hinojosa unequivocally told him that he was not going to sell him any more hides, and further advised that it was useless for him to send a truck for the hides, since at 4:30 p.m., Tuesday, March 21st, he had made up his mind to terminate the contract."   The suit by Laredo Hides followed.

When the plaintiff appealed from the trial court judgment against it, the point seems to have been made, on behalf of H & H, that Laredo Hides had taken no further action in performance of the contract.   Before confronting the issue of damages, the court disposed of that point briefly, as follows:

"An anticipatory breach of the entire contract exists if one party thereto, either before the time for performance, or after partial but before full performance, in positive and unconditional terms, refuses to perform further thereunder.   Where one of the parties repudiates the contract and absolutely refuses to perform the duties and obligations required of him, the other party need not go through the useless act of tendering performance.   Under the record before us, H & H repudiated the contract with Laredo Hides on March 30, 1972.   That repudiation relieved Laredo Hides of itself tendering performance during the remaining months covered by the contract.   It would have been useless and futile for Laredo Hides to have made such a tender twice in each of the months remaining."   Was anything more than this decided in Hochster v. De la Tour?

(4) *Jarbeau's Case.*   In Bernstein v. Meech, 29 N.E. 255 (N.Y.1891), a party charged with repudiation was permitted to recover on the contract because the other party had "elected" to disregard the plaintiff's apparent misconduct.   The plaintiff represented a performing troupe, the Jarbeau Comedy Company.   It had incurred expenses for the purpose of appearing at the Buffalo Academy of Music, but was not allowed to appear.   The agreement was for a period in December, and called for an equal division of the gross receipts.   The plaintiff's offense,

committed in August, was to send a draft contract increasing his share: he could not think of playing for less than 60%, he said. The defendants returned the contract unsigned "for the reason that we have a contract signed by you and do not need any other for the appearance of Vernona Jarbeau and company at our Academy." On November 17 the plaintiff wrote again, sending advertising material and saying, "Please keep Miss Jarbeau before the public as much as possible. I want to see her turn them away in your town." Owing to the itinerant habits of both parties, the plaintiff did not receive the defendants' response for about a month. It expressed surprise that Miss Jarbeau intended to play the Academy; the house was booked to other performers. The plaintiff's damage action produced a judgment favorable to him, and the defendants appealed. The Court of Appeals affirmed. For one thing, the court reasoned, it was open to the jury to conclude that the plaintiff's August letter did not justify the defendants in treating the contract as at an end and acting on that assumption. In addition, however that might be, the defendants' answer "disposed of that question."

> By this it appeared that the defendants elected to keep the contract in force for the purposes for which it was made. This operated alike upon the rights of both parties, and the plaintiff was justified in so understanding it. In that view the contract was kept alive until the time arrived for performance....

The court quoted Lord Cockburn in Frost v. Knight.

PHELPS v. HERRO, 137 A.2d 159 (Md.1957). [In 1955 Herro contracted to sell interests in realty and corporate stock, to Phelps for $37,500. Phelps agreed to pay $5,000 by January 1, 1956, and to give a promissory note for the remainder. This note was to be payable in $5,000 installments, with interest, on the first of each succeeding year until paid in full. The first $5,000 was paid, and in September of 1956 Herro made the transfers called for in the contract. Later he was notified that the rest of the price would not be paid. He had never received the note. On December 7, 1956, he sued for $32,500. From judgment for Herro, Phelps appealed.

PRESCOTT, JUDGE.... We think the proper rule is that the doctrine of anticipatory breach of a contract has no application to money contracts, pure and simple, where one party has fully performed his undertaking, and all that remains for the opposite party to do is to pay a certain sum of money at a certain time or times, and, under the circumstances of this case, this is as far as we need to rule, although some of the cases cited hold that the doctrine of anticipatory breach has no application whatsoever in unilateral contracts, or bilateral contracts that have become unilateral by full performance on one side....

[Reversed.]

HAMMOND, JUDGE (dissenting).... I could not bring myself ... to saddle Maryland needlessly with what I consider to be illogical and unsound law—a doctrine that is more apparent than real, and one that has been repudiated by the ablest judges and scholars. [Judge Hammond conceded that Williston favored an exception to the doctrine of anticipatory breach—"perhaps because of his dislike of the doctrine." However, he quoted from Corbin and others to sustain his view.]

NOTES

(1) *The Rose Bowl Affair.* Diamond v. University of Southern California, 89 Cal.Rptr. 302 (App.1970), was an action brought by an attorney in his capacity as a football fan, threatened with exclusion from the Rose Bowl. In affirming a summary judgment for the University, the court said that "the doctrine of anticipatory repudiation does not apply to contracts which are unilateral in their inception or have become so by complete performance by one party." *Question:* How does that rule differ from the one applied in Phelps v. Herro?

The court expressed qualms about the principle ("technical exception;" "not universally admired"), and seems to have used it as a convenient way of avoiding problems about class actions.[a]

(2) *The Restatement.* The American Law Institute has vacillated over the effect of full performance on one side. See Comment and Reason for Changes in Restatement of the Law, 1948 Supplement 252–53 (1949). What is the difference between the rule of Phelps v. Herro and the present Institute position? See Restatement Second, §§ 243(3), 253.

(3) *The Code.* It has been suggested that the Code "demands discontinuance of the artificial distinction between contracts which have been fully performed by one party and those which are completely executory." Taylor, The Impact of Article 2 of the U.C.C. on the Doctrine of Anticipatory Repudiation, 9 Bost.Coll.Ind. & Comm.L.Rev. 917, 926–27 (1968). What Code sections are incompatible with the distinction? Do any Code sections support it?

PERIODIC INSURANCE PAYMENTS

Limitations on the doctrine of anticipatory breach reflect, in part, the reluctance of courts to enter judgments based on the present (discounted)[b] value of a stream of expectable income. The reluctance is especially marked as to contracts of indefinite term. Two prominent examples are contracts for lifetime (permanent) disability payments, and annuity contracts. In litigation over such contracts the claimant is usually the holder, or beneficiary, of an "insurance" contract; the other party may be called the issuer.

As to contracts of this type, it may be observed that the uncertainty of the duration of an individual's life makes it unusually speculative to determine the present value of the recipient's expected income.[c] More-

---

a. The plaintiff, holder of a season ticket to the "Trojan" football games, brought a class action on behalf of himself and other fans, based on alleged contracts by the University to provide them with Rose Bowl tickets. (After the suit was brought, the University had a "sudden affluence in the matter of tickets.")

b. As to discounting anticipated benefits so as to arrive at a judgment for an amount currently due see Republic Bankers Life

Ins. Co. v. Jaeger, 551 S.W.2d 30 (Tex. 1976).

c. "Damages are not to be based upon mere conjecture or speculation, and we think plaintiff cannot be heard to claim serious physical permanent disability on one hand, which condition existed at the time the alleged agreement was made, and at the same time to claim damages based on a normal life expectancy. Suppose he were to die a year or two from now." Mabery v.

over, a definitive judgment of the claimant's entitlement is especially likely to be respected by the issuer. (A vocational insurer is invariably regulated by a state insurance authority, and is likely to have a substantial interest in its reputation for promise-keeping.)

These considerations have assisted insurers in resisting claims based on anticipatory repudiation. A well-known example is New York Life Ins. Co. v. Viglas, 297 U.S. 672 (1936), in which Cardozo addressed a claim by a policyholder for nearly $16,000. Viglas asserted that he had been permanently disabled from performing any work, and so had met a condition on benefits under the policy. He had received some twenty monthly payments from the insurer. Thereafter, he alleged, it had committed a "repudiation and denunciation of the entire contract" by declaring that he was not continuously and totally disabled. The insurer demurred, asserting that the amount in controversy was only the benefits in issue at the time of suit: $98. The Supreme Court accepted review on the question whether or not the amount required for federal jurisdiction was in controversy.[d]

Justice Cardozo condemned the "loose practice" of speaking of an *anticipatory* breach in cases like this, where, if there was a breach at all, the defendant had already defaulted. Although the defendant may have declared the contract at an end, for nonpayment of premiums, it had not declared the contract a nullity. At worst, the defendant had denied that Viglas was excused from paying premiums: it "did not disclaim the intention or the duty to shape its conduct in accordance with the provisions of the contract. Repudiation there was none as the term is known to the law."[e]

Moreover, Viglas "does not need redress in respect of unmatured instalments in order to put himself in a position to shape his conduct for the future. [A]n annuitant or a creditor exacting payment from a debtor, may be compelled to wait for the instalments as they severally mature, just as a landlord may not accelerate the rent for the residue of the term because the rent is in default for a month or for a year."[f] Generally, the case in which "justice requires that, irrespective of repudiation or abandonment, the sufferer from the breach shall be relieved of a duty to treat the contract as subsisting or to hold himself in readiness to perform it in the future" is one in which the contract is "a bilateral one with continuing obligations.... With the aid of this analysis, one discovers the rationale of the cases which have stated at times, though with needless generality, that by reason of the subject-matter of the undertaking the rule applicable to contracts for the payment of money is not the same as that applicable for the performance of services or the delivery of merchandise."[g]

Western Casualty & Surety Co., 250 P.2d 824 (Kan.1952).

d. The trial court had given judgment for the defendant, and the Circuit Court of Appeals had reversed.

e. At this point and some others in this note, quotations from the Viglas opinion are given out of sequence.

f. Compare Note 3 below.

g. But see Fanning v. Guardian Life Ins. Co., 366 P.2d 207 (Wash.1961), one of many cases limiting recovery to accrued

The opinion contains a reservation as to payments "contumaciously" withheld: "The law will be able to offer appropriate relief.... The declaration in the case at hand ... does not make a showing of a breach so wilful and material as to make acceleration of future benefits essential to the attainment of present reparation."

NOTES

(1) *Contumacious Nonpayment.* In a case following *Viglas* the court said: "The verdict and the decision of the trial court amounts to a determination that the plaintiff is entitled to the monthly payments as specified in the insurance policies so long as he is totally and permanently disabled.... Should the defendants fail in the future to make payment in accordance with the terms of the policies without just cause or excuse and the plaintiff is compelled to file another action for delinquent installments, the court at that time should be able to fashion such relief as will compel performance." Greguhn v. Mutual of Omaha Ins. Co., 461 P.2d 285 (Utah 1969). Aside from a possible award of attorneys' fees and punitive damages, exactly what does this pronouncement portend?

To some extent the courts' concern has since been addressed by statutes and decisions concerning fair practices in the adjustment of insurance claims. See also Sarchett v. Blue Shield of California, 729 P.2d 267 (Cal.1987).

(2) *Specific Performance.* "A contract for the payment of money in installments is not ordinarily specifically enforceable, the common law remedies being regarded as adequate." 5A Corbin § 1147. But in a few courts an order may be granted for periodic future payments. Corbin argues for more flexibility in this regard, especially in favor of an insured person claiming by right of disability.

Compare Quick v. American Steel & Pump Corp., 397 F.2d 561 (2d Cir. 1968), as to the "usual rule that contracts to pay money in installments are breached one installment at a time."

(3) *Leases.* A repudiation by a tenant of realty may not give the landlord the usual remedies for anticipatory breach, owing to a long-held view that a lease effects full performance by the lessor. A lease was asserted to be "essentially a conveyance, rather than a contract." 2 R. Powell, The Law of Real Property 179 (1986). But this view has steadily eroded. "Particularly with regard to business or commercial leases, the contractual aspects of the landlord-tenant relationship have become increasingly important." Id. at 187. See, for example, Schneiker v. Gordon, 732 P.2d 603 (Colo.1987), where the court went so far as to quote from a Code comment on anticipatory repudiation.

KANAVOS v. HANCOCK BANK & TRUST CO.

Supreme Judicial Court of Massachusetts, 1985.
395 Mass. 199, 479 N.E.2d 168.

WILKINS, JUSTICE. This appeal presents two basic questions. First, if, for valid consideration, the owner of stock in a corporation has agreed to give A the opportunity to purchase that stock at the price at which the

installments by following the rule stated in Phelps v. Herro. (And in this case the company denied the existence of the contract.)

owner intends to sell it to another in the future (a right of first refusal) but the owner instead sells the stock to a third party without giving A the opportunity to match the third party's offer and thus acquire the stock, does A's right to recover in an action for breach of contract in any way depend on whether A had the financial ability to purchase the stock during the relevant time? Second, if A's right does so depend, as we conclude it does, does A have the burden of proving his financial ability to perform or is the burden on the repudiating former stockholder to prove A's inability to perform?

The plaintiff Harold J. Kanavos (Kanavos) is A in the example given, an individual to whom the defendant Hancock Bank & Trust Company (bank) gave the right to acquire all the stock of 1025 Hancock, Inc., before the bank sold the stock to anyone else on the same terms. This corporation owned a fourteen-story apartment building, known as Executive House, on Hancock Street in Quincy. The corporation was a G.L. c. 121A limited dividend corporation, and the first mortgage was guaranteed by the Federal Housing Administration of the Department of Housing and Urban Development. On July 16, 1976, James M. Brown, then executive vice president of the bank, gave Kanavos a letter in which the bank agreed to pay him $40,000 for surrendering an option to purchase the stock and further gave Kanavos "the option to match the price of sale of said property to extend for a 60 day period from the time our offer is received." In November, 1976, the bank entered into a purchase and sale agreement to sell the stock for $760,000 to a third person and, early in December, the bank sold the stock accordingly without giving Kanavos notice and the opportunity to purchase the stock.

For the purpose of determining Kanavos's contract damages, apart from the $40,000 to be paid for the surrender of his option, the parties and the trial judge treated the value of the stock as equal to the value of the equity in the apartment building. The balance on the first mortgage was $2,500,000 at the relevant times. When the jury, in response to a special verdict question, concluded that the apartment complex was worth $4,000,000, contract damages were determined by subtracting from $4,000,000 the balance due on the mortgage ($2,500,000) and the sale price of the stock ($760,000). That damage figure ($740,000) equaled the amount by which the fair market value of the stock exceeded the price at which it was sold. The $40,000 option surrender payment was then added to arrive at a final judgment of $780,000.

The judge presented the case to the jury seeking a special verdict.... The bank's only challenge to the special verdict and resulting judgment is that the judge failed to instruct the jury (and give them an associated special verdict question) that the plaintiff had to be ready, willing, and able, pursuant to the letter creating the right of first refusal, to pay the bank $760,000 (i.e., within the sixty days, to match the offer the bank received and accepted).

The judge ruled, over objection, that Kanavos's ability to pay $760,-000 was not material to this case. This is the first issue we stated above in the abstract. We conclude that Kanavos's financial ability was material because he should not recover contract damages, even from a repudiating promisor, under an agreement to sell stock unless he could have complied with his concurrent obligation to pay for the stock (or, as is not the case here, unless the bank's conduct substantially prevented Kanavos from being able to meet his obligation).

When the bank received an offer for the stock that it was prepared to accept, the bank was obliged to give Kanavos the right to match that offer. At that point, Kanavos had an option to purchase the stock on the same terms, although, of course, in this case he was unaware that such an offer (and hence the option) existed. He could have exercised his option by tendering the purchase price, and the bank would have been obliged to deliver the shares of stock. In the circumstances of this case, Kanavos was not obliged to make a meaningless tender of the purchase price. The stock had already been sold. However, one party's repudiation of a bilateral contract containing simultaneous obligations does not normally make immaterial the question whether the other party could perform his obligation. "It is the general rule 'that when performance under a contract is concurrent, one party cannot put the other in default unless he is ready, able, and willing to perform and has manifested this by some offer of performance' although a tender of performance is not necessary 'if the other party has shown that he cannot or will not perform.'" Mayer v. Boston Metropolitan Airport, Inc., 355 Mass. 344, 354, 244 N.E.2d 568 (1969), quoting Leigh v. Rule, 331 Mass. 664, 668, 121 N.E.2d 854 (1954).

The weight of authority in this country is that the financial ability of a prospective buyer of property is a material issue in his action for damages against a repudiating defendant for breach of an agreement to sell that property for an established price. See 5 S. Williston, Contracts § 699, at 352–353 (Jaeger ed. 1961), and 6 S. Williston, Contracts § 882, at 394 (Jaeger ed. 1962); 4 A. Corbin, Contracts § 978, at 924–925 (1951); Restatement (Second) of Contracts § 254, comment a (1981) (the duty of a repudiating party "to pay damages is discharged if it subsequently appears that there would have been a total failure of performance by the injured party"); Farnsworth, The Problems of Nonperformance in Contract, 17 New Eng.L.Rev. 249, 306 (1982) (If a seller repudiates an option to sell land, "[a]lthough the holder of the option is under no duty to pay the price of the land, his payment of the price is a condition of the seller's repudiated duty"); Taylor, The Impact of Article 2 of the U.C.C. on the Doctrine of Anticipatory Repudiation, 9 B.C.Indus. & Com.L.Rev. 917, 927 (1967)[1].... We have taken the view that, even where promises were not concurrent, a plaintiff could only recover nominal or small damages against a defendant who repudiated a contract, where it would have been impossible for the plaintiff to perform a

---

1. "Under general contract law there was, however, a twist: If the nonrepudiating party was not in a position to perform either at the time of repudiation or at sometime thereafter prior to the date for performance, he had no remedy. The fact that the repudiation may have been unjustified did not change this result, and the burden of proving the necessary ability to perform was on the nonrepudiating plaintiff." Id.

contractual obligation arising shortly after the defendant's breach. See Randall v. Peerless Motor Car Co., 212 Mass. 352, 382, 99 N.E. 221 (1912).

Here, the bank's obligation to sell the shares and Kanavos's obligation to pay for them were concurrent obligations. If neither could perform, even if the bank repudiated the contract, neither could recover. 6 S. Williston, supra § 882, at 389–391. Kanavos did not have to show that he was ready, willing, and able to purchase the stock on the day the bank repudiated its agreement with him by selling the stock. Thomas v. Christensen, 12 Mass.App.Ct. 169, 177, 422 N.E.2d 472 (1981). That principle does not mean, however, that his ability to purchase the stock during the option period is irrelevant.

Kanavos relies, as the trial judge apparently did, on a statement in Lowe v. Harwood, 139 Mass. 133, 135, 29 N.E. 538 (1885), that, when a seller repudiates a purchase and sale agreement by selling land to a third person, the inability of the plaintiff to pay the purchase price according to the contract terms is unimportant in an action for breach of contract.[2] The *Lowe* opinion cites no relevant authority for the proposition that a repudiating seller is liable in damages to a buyer who could not have carried out his end of the bargain. That principle ... appears now to be extinct.... There is no compelling reason to adopt such a rule at this time.[3]

If, as we have concluded, Kanavos's ability to match the offer which the bank accepted is material to his right to recover, the question then is whether the burden of proof should be placed on Kanavos to show his ability or on the bank to show his lack of ability. The general rule is that the plaintiff must prove his ability to perform his obligations under a contract of the type involved here. See Wolbarsht v. Donnelly, 302 Mass. 568, 570–571, 20 N.E.2d 415 (1939); 5 S. Williston, supra § 699, at 352–353; 4 A. Corbin, supra § 978, at 925; Taylor, 9 B.C.Indus. & Com.L.Rev. supra at 927 ("the burden of proving the necessary ability to perform was on the nonrepudiating plaintiff"). Cf. Restatement (Second) of Contracts § 245, comment b (1981) (where an express condition of the defendant's liability has not occurred but the defendant has already repudiated the contract, the repudiating defendant has the

---

2. The relevant language of the opinion is as follows: "It is suggested that it does not appear that the plaintiff was able to pay the money which he was to pay. But he was personally bound for it, and the degree of his ability at any moment before he was called on to pay was no concern of the defendant's. The way for the defendant to test that was to tender performance on his side conditionally upon the plaintiff's performing his part of the agreement. See Brown v. Davis, 138 Mass. 458."

3. We perceive no reason why Kanavos's ability to purchase the stock should be any less significant than the ability of a person who had the right to buy property under a

purchase and sale agreement or of a person who held an option to purchase property. Once the bank determined that it would sell the property to a third person, Kanavos's rights were substantially equivalent to an option to buy. Once the bank repudiated its obligation to Kanavos by selling the stock to a third person, Kanavos's rights and his burden of proof were the same as they would have been if he had been a buyer under a repudiated purchase and sale or option agreement. The bank's repudiation of the agreement giving Kanavos a right of first refusal did not estop the bank from arguing that Kanavos lacked the ability to pay for the stock.

burden of proving that the condition would not have occurred). There is not, however, a unanimity of view in this country on the placing of the burden of proof in such a case. . . .

The burden was on Kanavos to prove his ability to finance the purchase of the stock. The fact of his ability to do so was an essential part of establishing the defendant's liability. Circumstances concerning his ability to raise $760,000 for the stock were far better known to him than to the bank. It is, of course, true that the bank created the problem by selling the stock to another in violation of its contractual obligation, and one could argue that, therefore, it should take the risk of failing to establish Kanavos's inability to purchase the stock. Such an argument, however, has not been generally accepted, for to do so would in effect place on the defendant the burden of disproving a fact essential to the plaintiff's case.

There was evidence from which the jury would have been warranted in finding that Kanavos had the ability to finance the purchase of the stock. Although he admitted that he was in financial difficulty during the relevant times, he had connections with people who might have assisted him. He testified that he could have purchased the stock if the bank had given him timely notice of his rights. Moreover, the jury found that the apartment complex was worth $1,500,000 more than the principal balance of the first mortgage, and thus $780,000 more than Kanavos would have had to have paid the bank for the stock (the sale price of $760,000 less the $40,000 the bank owed him). This differential suggests that financing was not an impossibility for Kanavos. Considering Kanavos's admitted financial difficulties at that time, the question of his ability to purchase the stock (or to sell his rights to another) may depend on whether the earnings of the apartment complex were sufficient to support some arrangement to finance the acquisition within the various limitations applicable under the federally guaranteed first mortgage (assuming it were not to be discharged in the process).

The question of Kanavos's ability to purchase the stock should have been submitted to the jury. We see no reason, however, for a retrial of those issues already decided by the jury. We remand the case for a retrial on the question whether, if he had had proper notice of his right to purchase the stock, Kanavos would have been ready, willing, and able to do so during the option period.

So ordered.

NOTES

(1) *Analogy to Express Conditions.* The first question addressed by the court is analogous to one that arises in the case of an express condition. In Shear v. National Rifle Association, discussed in Note 1, p. 693 above, the NRA argued that, even if the Management Committee had recommended the sale and even if the by-laws had not been amended, "nothing but abject speculation could show that 'the condition [settlement] would have occurred.'" The court rejected this argument, noting that "almost all cases in which prevention is alleged will involve speculation as to what would have happened had the defendant's conduct not taken place." 606 F.2d at 1257.

(2) *Question.* Suppose that the bank had told Kanavos, *before it was approached by any competing buyer,* that it would not honor the contract with him. Anticipatory breach? See Brauer v. Hobbs, 391 N.W.2d 482 (Mich.App. 1986).

McCLOSKEY & CO. v. MINWELD STEEL CO.

United States Court of Appeals, Third Circuit, 1955.
220 F.2d 101.

Suit by contractor against subcontractor alleging anticipatory breach of three contracts entered into by parties. The United States District Court for the Western District of Pennsylvania, Joseph P. Willson, J., granted defendant's motion for judgment on ground that plaintiff had not made out prima facie case, and entered order denying plaintiff's motion for findings of fact, to vacate judgments and for new trial, and plaintiff appealed....

Order affirmed.

McLaughlin, Circuit Judge. Plaintiff-appellant, a general contractor, sued on three contracts alleging an anticipatory breach as to each. At the close of the plaintiff's case the district judge granted the defense motions for judgment on the ground that plaintiff had not made out a cause of action.

By the contracts involved the principal defendant,[1] a fabricator and erector of steel, agreed to furnish and erect all of the structural steel required on two buildings to be built on the grounds of the Hollidaysburg State Hospital, Hollidaysburg, Pa. and to furnish all of the long span steel joists required in the construction of one of the two buildings. Two of the contracts were dated May 1, 1950 and the third May 26, 1950. By Article V of each of the contracts "Should the Sub–Contractor [the defendant herein] ... at any time refuse or neglect to supply a sufficiency ... of materials of the proper quality, ... in and about the performance of the work required to be done pursuant to the provisions of this agreement ..., or fail, in the performance of any of the agreements herein contained, the Contractor shall be at liberty, without prejudice, to any other right or remedy, on two days' written notice to the Sub–Contractor, either to provide any such ... materials and to deduct the cost thereof from any payments then or thereafter due the Sub–Contractor, or to terminate the employment of the Sub–Contractor for the said work and to enter upon the premises...."

There was no stated date in the contracts for performance by the defendant subcontractor. Article VI provided for completion by the subcontractor of its contract work "by and at the time or times hereafter stated to-wit:

---

1. The Travelers Indemnity Co., which posted performance bonds on two of the contracts, is a co-defendant in No. 11,422.

"Samples, Shop Drawings and Schedules are to be submitted in the quantities and manner required by the Specifications, for the approval of the Architects, immediately upon receipt by the Sub–Contractor of the contract drawings, or as may be directed by the Contractor. All expense involved in the submission and approval of these Samples, Shop Drawings and Schedules shall be borne by the Sub–Contractor.

"All labor, materials and equipment required under this contract are to be furnished at such times as may be directed by the Contractor, and in such a manner so as to at no time delay the final completion of the building.

"It being mutually understood and agreed that prompt delivery and installation of all materials required to be furnished under this contract is to be the essence of this Agreement."

Appellee Minweld Steel Co., Inc., the subcontractor, received contract drawings and specifications for both buildings in May, 1950. On June 8, 1950, plaintiff McCloskey & Co. wrote appellee asking when it might "expect delivery of the structural steel" for the buildings and "also the time estimated to complete erection." Minweld replied on June 13, 1950, submitting a schedule estimate of expecting to begin delivery of the steel by September 1, and to complete erection approximately November 15. On July 20, 1950 plaintiff wrote Minweld threatening to terminate the contracts unless the latter gave unqualified assurances that it had effected definite arrangements for the procurement, fabrication and delivery within thirty days of the required materials. On July 24, 1950 Minweld wrote McCloskey & Co. explaining its difficulty in obtaining the necessary steel. It asked McCloskey's assistance in procuring it and stated that "We are as anxious as you are that there be no delay in the final completion of the buildings or in the performance of our contract, ..."[2]

---

2. This letter in full is as follows:

Minweld Steel Company
Incorporated
Shaler and Wabash Streets
Pittsburgh 20, Pa.
      July 24, 1950.

McClosky & Company
1620 Thompson Street
Philadelphia 21, Penna.

In re: New Hospital Buildings
      Hollidaysburg State Hospital
      Hollidaysburg, Pennsylvania

Attention of J.C. McCloskey,
      Vice President
Dear Sir:

This will acknowledge receipt of your letter of July 20th, 1950, which was received by us today.

Upon receipt of the architect's specifications, we completed the engineering and erection plans on the said specifications.

Immediately after those details were available, we attempted to place orders for the steel with the Bethlehem Steel Company. Our order was held in the offices of the Bethlehem Steel Company for two weeks before we were notified that it could not be supplied. Since that time, we have tried the U.S. Steel Corporation and Carnegie Illinois, both companies informing us that they were under contract for approximately one year and could not fulfill the order.

The recent directive by the President of the United States, with which we assume you are familiar, has further tightened up the steel market so that at the present writing we cannot give you any positive promise as to our ability to obtain the steel or delivery dates.

In view of the directive from Washington and the tightening up of the entire steel industry, we solicit your help and that of the General State Authority in aiding us to obtain the steel for these contracts.

Plaintiff-appellant claims that by this last letter, read against the relevant facts, defendant gave notice of its positive intention not to perform its contracts and thereby violated same.[3] Some reference has already been made to the background of the July 24th letter. It concerned Minweld's trouble in securing the steel essential for performance of its contract. Minweld had tried unsuccessfully to purchase this from Bethlehem Steel, U.S. Steel and Carnegie–Illinois. It is true as appellant urges that Minweld knew and was concerned about the tightening up of the steel market.[4] And as is evident from the letter it, being a fabricator and not a producer, realized that without the help of the general contractor on this hospital project particularly by it enlisting the assistance of the General State Authority,[5] Minweld was in a bad way for the needed steel. However, the letter conveys no idea of contract repudiation by Minweld. That company admittedly was in a desperate situation. Perhaps if it had moved earlier to seek the steel its effort might have been successful. But that is mere speculation for there is no showing that the mentioned producers had they been solicited sooner would have been willing to provide the material.

Minweld from its written statement did, we think, realistically face the problem confronting it. As a result it asked its general contractor for the aid which the latter, by the nature of the construction, should have been willing to give. Despite the circumstances there is no indication in the letter that Minweld had definitely abandoned all hope of otherwise receiving the steel and so finishing its undertaking. One of the mentioned producers might have relented. Some other supplier might have turned up. It was McCloskey & Co. who eliminated whatever chance there was. That concern instead of aiding Minweld by urging its plea for the hospital construction materials to the State Authority which represented the Commonwealth of Pennsylvania took the position that the subcontractor had repudiated its agreement and then moved quickly to have the work completed. Shortly thereafter, and without the slightest trouble as far as appears, McCloskey & Co. procured the steel

We are as anxious as you are that there be no delay in the final completion of the buildings or in the performance of our contract, but we have nowhere else to turn at the present time for the supply of steel necessary under said contracts, unless through your aid and assistance, and that of the General State Authority, a supplier can be induced to give us the materials needed.

The U.S. Steel Corporation informs us that you have discussed this matter with them and are presently aware of our present difficulties.

If steel is to be supplied to these hospital buildings by governmental directive, we feel that the steel should be supplied to us for completion under our contract.

Very truly yours,
Minweld Steel Company, Inc.
J.A. Roberts
Sales Manager

JAR/fs

c/c Travelers Indemnity Co.,
Hartford, Conn.
General State Authority,
Harrisburg, Penna.

3. Plaintiff cancelled the contracts on July 26, 1950 on the ground that the July 24th letter constituted an admission of defendant's inability to perform the required work.

4. The Korean War broke out on June 24, 1950.

5. The Pennsylvania state agency which represented and owned the Hollidaysburg State Hospital.

from Bethlehem [6] and brought in new subcontractors to do the work contemplated by the agreement with Minweld.

Under the applicable law Minweld's letter was not a breach of the agreement. The suit is in the federal court by reason of diversity of citizenship of the parties. Though there is no express statement to that effect the contracts between the parties would seem to have been executed in Pennsylvania with the law of that state applicable. In McClelland v. New Amsterdam Cas. Co., 1936, 322 Pa. 429, 433, 185 A. 198, 200, the Pennsylvania Supreme Court held in a case where the subcontractor had asked for assistance in obtaining credit, "In order to give rise to a renunciation amounting to a breach of contract there must be an absolute and unequivocal refusal to perform or a distinct and positive statement of an inability to do so." Minweld's conduct is plainly not that of a contract breaker under that test. See also Dingley v. Oler, 1886, 117 U.S. 490, 6 S.Ct. 850, 29 L.Ed. 984. Restatement of Contracts, Comment (i) to Sec. 318 (1932) speaks clearly on the point saying:

"Though where affirmative action is promised mere failure to act, at the time when action has been promised, is a breach, failure to take preparatory action before the time when any performance is promised is not an anticipatory breach, even though such failure makes it impossible that performance shall take place, and though the promisor at the time of the failure intends not to perform his promise." See Williston on Contracts, Vol. 5, Sec. 1324 (1937), Corbin on Contracts, Vol. 4, Sec. 973 (1951).

Appellant contends that its letter of July 20, requiring assurances of arrangements which would enable appellee to complete delivery in thirty days, constituted a fixing of a date under Article VI of the contracts. The short answer to this is that the thirty day date, if fixed, was never repudiated. Appellee merely stated that it was unable to give assurances as to the preparatory arrangements. There is nothing in the contracts which authorized appellant to demand or receive such assurances.

The district court acted properly in dismissing the actions as a matter of law on the ground that plaintiff had not made out a prima facie case.

The order of the district court of July 14, 1954 denying the plaintiff's motion for findings of facts, to vacate the judgments and for new trials will be affirmed.

NOTES

(1) *A Pair of Newer Rules.* According to Restatement Second § 251(2), a possible consequence of a justified demand by an obligee for assurance of due performance by the obligor is this: "The obligee may treat as a repudiation the obligor's failure to provide within a reasonable time such assurance of due

---

6. Bethlehem had originally submitted a bid in competition with Minweld. Its new proposals were dated July 28, 1950 and were finally accepted by McCloskey & Co. on August 7, 1950. The long span steel joists required by the third contract were procured from the Frederick Grundy Iron Works.

performance as is adequate in the circumstances of the particular case." Compare UCC 2–609.

Under the Restatement Second rule, is there necessarily a repudiation if the obligor fails to provide "adequate assurance" when it is properly demanded?

Under either that rule or the Code, would McCloskey's letters of June 8 and July 20 be regarded as demands for assurance of due performance? If so, would the responses be regarded as adequate?

Does the contract in the main case lie clearly in the sphere of general contract law, as opposed to that of the Code?

(2) *Indubitable Repudiation.* "In order to constitute a repudiation, a party's language must be sufficiently positive to be reasonably interpreted to mean that the party will not or cannot perform.... [L]anguage that under a fair reading 'amounts to a statement of intention not to perform except on conditions which go beyond the contract' constitutes a repudiation. Comment 2 to Uniform Commercial Code § 2–610." Restatement Second § 250, Comment b. See also Comment d as to a party's insistence on a minor enhancement of his contract rights. And see again the Note, p. 755 above.

(3) *Questionable Repudiation.* Can you envisage a repudiation by a party who is content with the bargain and willing to perform it? See Philadelphia Eagles, Inc. v. Armstrong, [1952] 1 D.L.R. 332 (Manitoba).[a] Can you envisage a communication that would be called a repudiation if made in bad faith, and not otherwise? Consider the remarks of Cardozo, as reported at p. 763, above. Do you see a reason not to require a party receiving a disclaimer to judge whether or not it was made in good faith? Compare Williston 3d § 1323, and Corbin § 973, on this point. Can you envisage a repudiation that does no more than express doubt about a party's ability or willingness to perform? See J.K. Welding Co. v. W.J. Halloran Steel Erection Co., 178 F.Supp. 584 (D.R.I.1959).[b]

If the test for determining what is a repudiation is an objective one, it is surely no better to say "I cannot perform the contract" than to say "I will not perform it." Is it any better to say, "I will try to perform, though I see no prospect of succeeding?"[c] How does that differ from what Minweld wrote to McCloskey, in the main case?[d]

In formulating tests for repudiation, what bearing might it have that a party having grounds to expect a breach by the other may (if he may) demand assurance of due performance?

(4) *Problem.* Refer to the facts in Stewart v. Newbury, p. 702 above. Assuming that the plaintiff did not abandon the job, did he repudiate the contract at any time? By sending the bill on September 29? By writing the letter of October 5? Compare Menako v. Kassien, 61 N.W.2d 332 (Wis.1953).

(5) *Forcing the Issue.* A party who is delinquent in performance, or threatened with inability, can surely plead with the other for leniency without being guilty of a repudiation. If pressed, one may hope to skirt a repudiation with

---

a. Compare Campos v. Olson, 241 F.2d 661 (9th Cir.1957), another sporting case.

b. This court, applying Massachusetts law, conceived of an expression of doubt which warrants rescission by the recipient, but not a damage claim. The Restatement Second appears to reject this conception; see § 253. (But see § 243(4).) What are the merits?

c. Compare Avery v. Bowden, 119 Eng. Rep. 647 (Queen's Bench 1855), aff'd, 119 Eng.Rep. 1119 (Exchequer Chamber 1856).

d. For an unusual attempt to "manufacture" a sizeable claim for damages by seizing on a supposed anticipatory repudiation, see Bowes v. Saks & Co., 397 F.2d 113 (7th Cir.1968).

cautiously written letters, perhaps drafted with the aid of counsel. How may the other party force the issue? Would it be easier to do so in a face-to-face encounter than by correspondence? Which party is likely to call for a conference? See Plunkett v. Comstock–Cheney Co., 208 N.Y.S. 93 (App.Div.1925).

————

BILL'S COAL CO. v. BOARD OF PUBLIC UTILITIES, 682 F.2d 883 (10th Cir.1982), cert. denied, 459 U.S. 1171 (1983). [The electric power authority for Springfield, Missouri, had contracted to buy its requirements of coal from Bill's Coal Company (Coal), but hoped to replace Coal with a lower-cost supplier. The contract permitted Coal to state a new price each year and allowed the utility three months to search for another supplier. Upon getting a bid lower than Coal's price by at least 15%, the utility was permitted to notify Coal of termination, effective one year later.[a] The contract was unclear about the method of price comparison: on one interpretation the utility was required to compare Coal's price at its mine ("f.o.b.") with the cost of a competitor's coal delivered at Springfield. Naturally, on this reading the power of termination was sharply curtailed. The utility preferred to compare product costs as delivered (including Coal's products); Coal asserted the former reading.

The utility gave notice of termination and sued Coal for a declaratory judgment that the notice was rightful. The pleadings framed an issue of contract interpretation. The trial court concluded that a comparison of delivery prices was required. Thereupon the pleadings were amended. Coal asserted that the contract was ambiguous; and the utility charged Coal with having repudiated the contract (with the effect of releasing the utility of any further performance).

The trial court ruled for the utility, finding that Coal's interpretation was the result of bad faith, and was not honestly held by Coal.[b] Thereupon the court dissolved an injunction, previously entered, that compelled performance by the utility. Coal appealed, arguing that even if it acted in bad faith, "when the bad faith is limited to espousing an interpretation of the circumstances under which the other party can terminate the contract and does not interfere with the performance either party owes under the contract, that bad faith interpretation does not give to other contracting party a right to cancel the contract."]

LOGAN, CIRCUIT JUDGE.... A repudiation is a party's manifestation that it is not going to [perform an obligation] due at some future date.... The bad faith urging of a particular interpretation of a termination clause is neither a failure to perform contract obligations (breach) nor an indication those obligations will not be performed in the future (repudiation).... If a seller's interpretation of a termination

---

a. The year's delay was not required if the utility got a bid as much as 25% below Bill's stated price.

b. By inadvertence, discovery proceedings put a document in the hands of the utility, disclosing a "plan" devised by an attorney for Coal for taking advantage of the misleading expression of the termination power, which had been detected on the very day it was drafted.

clause is ludicrous, the buyer should ignore it; if the interpretation might prevail in a court of law, the seller has a right to urge it. If the party that wishes to invoke the termination clause is unsure of the merits of the other party's interpretation, it can either accept that interpretation, rely on its own interpretation, or obtain a declaratory judgment as to the meaning of the contract language.[c]

[Judge Barrett, dissenting, quoted Corbin as follows: "Where the two contracting parties differ as to the interpretation of a contract . . . an offer to perform in accordance with his own interpretation . . . [will] constitute such a breach, [if] the offer . . . be accompanied by a clear manifestation of intention not to perform in accordance with any other interpretation."] [d]

NOTES

(1) *What is a Repudiation?* In REA Express, Inc. v. Interway Corp., 538 F.2d 953, 955 (2d Cir.1976), the court said that "insistence on terms which are not contained in a contract constitutes an anticipatory repudiation." This is consistent with the traditional view that a party's good faith will not prevent a statement from amounting to a repudiation. Can *Bill's Coal* be reconciled with the traditional view?

(2) *Problem.* A buyer of iron rails to be delivered in installments complained that the first two shipments were short, and expressed the wish to be absolved from the contract. The seller answered by letter asking "to know definitely what is your intention." The buyer answered: "You ask us to determine whether we will or will not object to receive further shipments because of past defaults. We tell you we will if we are entitled to do so, and will not if we are not entitled to do so. We do not think you have the right to compel us to decide a disputed question of law to relieve you from the risk of deciding it yourself. You know quite as well as we do what is the rule and its uncertainty of application." On receiving this letter, how should the seller act? See Norrington v. Wright, 115 U.S. 188 (1885).

COSDEN OIL & CHEMICAL COMPANY v. KARL O. HELM AKTIENGESELLSCHAFT

United States Court of Appeals, Fifth Circuit, 1984.
736 F.2d 1064.

REAVLEY, CIRCUIT JUDGE: We must address one of the most difficult interpretive problems of the Uniform Commercial Code—the appropriate time to measure buyer's damages where the seller anticipatorily repudiates a contract and the buyer does not cover. The district court applied

c. The court also said: "We can envision situations in which bad faith conduct might be actionable: for instance, if the Utility solicited bids from competing coal companies and Bill's Coal in some way coerced competitors into not submitting bids. That might constitute such a breach of Bill's Coal's good faith obligation as to allow the Utility to cancel the contract."

The case was remanded for findings on other points.

d. Id. at 685 F.2d 360, 362.

the Texas version of Article 2[1] and measured buyer's damages at a commercially reasonable time after seller's repudiation. We affirm, but remand for modification of damages on another point.

I. CASE HISTORY

This contractual dispute arose out of events and transactions occurring in the first three months of 1979, when the market in polystyrene, a petroleum derivative used to make molded products, was steadily rising. During this time Iran, a major petroleum producer, was undergoing political turmoil. Karl O. Helm Aktiengesellschaft (Helm or Helm Hamburg), an international trading company based in Hamburg, West Germany, anticipated a tightening in the world petrochemical supply and decided to purchase a large amount of polystyrene. Acting on orders from Helm Hamburg, Helm Houston, a wholly-owned subsidiary, initiated negotiations with Cosden Oil & Chemical Company (Cosden), a Texas-based producer of chemical products, including polystyrene.

. . . Negotiating over the telephone and by telex, the parties agreed to the purchase and sale of 1250 metric tons[2] of high impact polystyrene at $.2825 per pound and 250 metric tons of general purpose polystyrene at $.265 per pound. [The confirmations of these contracts gave Helm options for additional amounts of each type of polystyrene. Upon the proper exercise of these options, Helms held four confirmations, numbered 04 through 07. Numbers 04 and 06 represented the "high impact" product.

[On or about January 26 Cosden shipped 90,000 pounds of this product. After encountering difficulties described in the note,[a] Cosden notified Helm in late January that delivery under the 04 contract might be delayed. On February 6 Cosden informed Helm that it "was cancelling orders 05, 06, and 07 because two plants were 'down' and it did not have sufficient product to fill the orders." In mid-February Cosden shipped some 1,260,000 pounds under order 04. It refused, as "not possible," a request to make the final delivery under 04 by March 16; and near the end of March it cancelled the remainder of 04.

---

1. The Uniform Commercial Code is codified as Title 1 of the Business and Commerce Code, Tex.Bus. & Com.Code Ann. (Vernon 1968 & Supp.1984). All mention or citation within this opinion to "the Code" and to individual Code sections and comments are intended to refer to the Texas Business and Commerce Code, unless designated otherwise.

2. One metric ton equals approximately 2,204.5 pounds.

a. "As Helm had expected, polystyrene prices began to rise in late January, and continued upward during February and March. Cosden also experienced problems at two of its plants in late January. Normally, Cosden supplied its Calumet City, Illinois, production plant with styrene monomer, the "feed stock" or main ingredient of polystyrene, by barges that traveled from Louisiana up the Mississippi and Illinois Rivers to a canal that extended to Cosden's plant. Due to the extremely cold winter of 1978–79, however, the Illinois River and the canal froze, suspending barge traffic for a few weeks. A different problem beset Cosden's Windsor, New Jersey, production plant. A new reactor, used in the polystyrene manufacturing process, had recently been installed at the Windsor plant. A manufacturing defect soon became apparent, however, and Cosden returned the reactor to the manufacturer for repair, which took several weeks. At the time of the reactor breakdown, Cosden was manufacturing only general purpose at the Windsor plant. Cosden had planned on supplying Helm's high impact orders from the Calumet City plant."

[Meanwhile, Cosden remained unpaid for product it had delivered.[b]]

Cosden sued Helm, seeking damages for Helm's failure to pay for delivered polystyrene. Helm counterclaimed for Cosden's failure to deliver polystyrene as agreed. The jury found on special verdict that Cosden had agreed to sell polystyrene to Helm under all four orders.[c] The jury also found that Cosden anticipatorily repudiated orders 05, 06, and 07 and that Cosden cancelled order 04 before Helm's failure to pay for the second 04 delivery constituted a repudiation. The jury fixed the per pound market prices for polystyrene under each of the four orders at three different times: when Helm learned of the cancellation, at a commercially reasonable time thereafter, and at the time for delivery.

The district court ... determined that Helm was entitled to recover $628,676 in damages representing the difference between the contract price and the market price at a commercially reasonable time after Cosden repudiated its polystyrene delivery obligations and that Cosden was entitled to an offset of $355,950 against those damages for polystyrene delivered, but not paid for, under order 04.

II. TIME FOR MEASURING BUYER'S DAMAGES

Both parties find fault with the time at which the district court measured Helm's damages for Cosden's anticipatory repudiation of orders 05, 06, and 07.[3] Cosden argues that damages should be measured when Helm learned of the repudiation. Helm contends that market price as of the last day for delivery—or the time of performance—should be used to compute its damages under the contract-market differential. We reject both views, and hold that the district court correctly measured damages at a commercially reasonable point after Cosden informed Helm that it was cancelling the three orders.

Article 2 of the Code has generally been hailed as a success for its comprehensiveness, its deference to mercantile reality, and its clarity. Nevertheless, certain aspects of the Code's overall scheme have proved troublesome in application. The interplay among sections 2.610, 2.711, 2.712, 2.713, and 2.723, Tex.Bus. & Com.Code Ann. (Vernon 1968), represents one of those areas, and has been described as "an impossible legal thicket." J. White & R. Summers, Uniform Commercial Code § 6–7 at 242 (2d ed. 1980). The aggrieved buyer seeking damages for seller's

---

b. After Helm Hamburg learned of Cosden's cancellation, apparently in February, "Wolfgang Gordian, a member of Helm's executive board, sent an internal memorandum to Helm Houston outlining a strategy. Helm would urge that Cosden continue to perform under 04 and, after receiving the high impact polystyrene, would offset amounts owing under 04 against Helm's damages for nondelivery of the balance of polystyrene."

c. It found also that the four orders comprised one contract, and [according to a stipulation] Cosden was not in breach prior to March 19.

3. The damages measurement problem does not apply to Cosden's breach of order 04, which was not anticipatorily repudiated. The time Helm learned of Cosden's intent to deliver no more polystyrene under 04 was the same time as the last date of performance, which had been extended to the end of March.

anticipatory repudiation presents the most difficult interpretive problem.[4] Section 2.713 describes the buyer's damages remedy:

Buyer's Damages for Non–Delivery or Repudiation

(a) Subject to the provisions of this chapter with respect to proof of market price (Section 2.723), the measure of damages for non-delivery or repudiation by the seller is the difference between the market price *at the time when the buyer learned of the breach* and the contract price together with any incidental and consequential damages provided in this chapter (Section 2.715), but less expenses saved in consequence of the seller's breach.

(emphasis added).

Courts and commentators have identified three possible interpretations of the phrase "learned of the breach." If seller anticipatorily repudiates, buyer learns of the breach:

(1) When he learns of the repudiation;

(2) When he learns of the repudiation plus a commercially reasonable time; or

(3) When performance is due under the contract.

. . .

We would not be free to decide the question if there were a Texas case on point.... [But] no Texas case has addressed the Code question of buyer's damages in an anticipatory repudiation context....[5]

We do not doubt, and Texas law is clear, that market price at the time buyer learns of the breach is the appropriate measure of section 2.713 damages in cases where buyer learns of the breach at or after the time for performance. This will be the common case, for which section 2.713 was designed. See Peters, Remedies for Breach of Contracts Relating to the Sale of Goods Under the Uniform Commercial Code: A Roadmap for Article Two, 73 Yale L.J. 199, 264 (1963). In the relatively rare case where seller anticipatorily repudiates and buyer does not cover, see Anderson, supra, at 318, the specific provision for anticipatory repudiation cases, section 2.610, authorizes the aggrieved party to await performance for a commercially reasonable time before resorting to his remedies of cover or damages.

In the anticipatory repudiation context, the buyer's specific right to wait for a commercially reasonable time before choosing his remedy must be read together with the general damages provision of section

---

4. The only area of unanimous agreement among those that have studied the Code provisions relevant to this problem is that they are not consistent, present problems in interpretation, and invite amendment.

5. Before Texas adopted the Code, its courts applied the traditional time-of-performance measure of damages in repudiation cases. See, e.g., Henderson v. Otto Goedecke, Inc., 430 S.W.2d 120, 123–24 (Tex.Civ.App.—Tyler 1968, writ ref'd n.r.e.); Anderson, Learning of Breaches Under Section 2–713 of the Code, 40 Tex. B.J. 317, 318 & n. 7 (1977). By interpreting the time buyer learns of the breach to mean a commercially reasonable time after buyer learns of the repudiation, we depart from pre-Code law....

2.713 to extend the time for measurement beyond when buyer learns of the breach.   Comment 1 to section 2.610 states that if an aggrieved party "awaits performance beyond a commercially reasonable time he cannot recover resulting damages which he should have avoided."   This suggests that an aggrieved buyer can recover damages where the market rises during the commercially reasonable time he awaits performance. To interpret 2.713's "learned of the breach" language to mean the time at which seller first communicates his anticipatory repudiation would undercut the time that 2.610 gives the aggrieved buyer to await performance.

The buyer's option to wait a commercially reasonable time also interacts with section 2.611, which allows the seller an opportunity to retract his repudiation.   Thus, an aggrieved buyer "learns of the breach" a commercially reasonable time after he learns of the seller's anticipatory repudiation.   The weight of scholarly commentary supports this interpretation.   See J. Calamari & J. Perillo, Contracts § 14–20 (2d ed. 1977); Sebert, Remedies Under Article Two of the Uniform Commercial Code: An Agenda for Review, 130 U.Pa.L.Rev. 360, 372–80 (1981); Wallach, Anticipatory Repudiation and the UCC, 13 U.C.C.L.J. 48 (1980); Peters, supra, at 263–68.

Typically, our question will arise where parties to an executory contract are in the midst of a rising market.   To the extent that market decisions are influenced by a damages rule, measuring market price at the time of seller's repudiation gives seller the ability to fix buyer's damages and may induce seller to repudiate, rather than abide by the contract.   By contrast, measuring buyer's damages at the time of performance will tend to dissuade the buyer from covering, in hopes that market price will continue upward until performance time.

Allowing the aggrieved buyer a commercially reasonable time, however, provides him with an opportunity to investigate his cover possibilities in a rising market without fear that, if he is unsuccessful in obtaining cover, he will be relegated to a market-contract damage remedy measured at the time of repudiation.   The Code supports this view.   While cover is the preferred remedy, the Code clearly provides the option to seek damages.   See § 2.712(c) & comment 3.   If "[t]he buyer is always free to choose between cover and damages for non-delivery," and if 2.712 "is not intended to limit the time necessary for [buyer] to look around and decide as to how he may best effect cover," it would be anomalous, if the buyer chooses to seek damages, to fix his damages at a time before he investigated cover possibilities and before he elected his remedy.   See id. comment 2 & 3; Dura–Wood Treating Co. v. Century Forest Industries, Inc., 675 F.2d 745, 754 (5th Cir.), cert. denied, 459 U.S. 865, 103 S.Ct. 144, 74 L.Ed.2d 122 (1982) ("buyer has some time in which to evaluate the situation").   Moreover, comment 1 to section 2.713 states, "The general baseline adopted in this section uses as a yardstick the market in which the buyer would have obtained cover had he sought that relief."   See § 2.610 comment 1.   When a buyer chooses not to cover, but to seek damages, the market is measured at the time he could have covered—a reasonable time after repudiation. See §§ 2.711 & 2.713.

Persuasive arguments exist for interpreting "learned of the breach" to mean "time of performance," consistent with the pre-Code rule. See J. White & R. Summers, supra, § 6–7; Anderson, supra. If this was the intention of the Code's drafters, however, phrases in section 2.610 and 2.712 lose their meaning. If buyer is entitled to market-contract damages measured at the time of performance, it is difficult to explain why the anticipatory repudiation section limits him to a commercially reasonable time to await performance. See § 2.610 comment 1. Similarly, in a rising market, no reason would exist for requiring the buyer to act "without unreasonable delay" when he seeks to cover following an anticipatory repudiation. See § 2.712(a).

The interplay among the relevant Code sections does not permit, in this context, an interpretation that harmonizes all and leaves no loose ends. We therefore acknowledge that our interpretation fails to explain the language of section 2.723(a) insofar as it relates to aggrieved buyers. We note, however, that the section has limited applicability—cases that come to trial before the time of performance will be rare. Moreover, the comment to section 2.723 states that the "section is not intended to exclude the use of any other reasonable method of determining market price or of measuring damages...." In light of the Code's persistent theme of commercial reasonableness, the prominence of cover as a remedy, and the time given an aggrieved buyer to await performance and to investigate cover before selecting his remedy, we agree with the district court that "learned of the breach" incorporates section 2.610's commercially reasonable time.[6]

---

6. We note that two circuits arrived at a similar conclusion by different routes. In Cargill, Inc. v. Stafford, 553 F.2d 1222 (10th Cir.1977), the court began its discussion of damages by embracing the "time of performance" interpretation urged by Professors White and Summers. Id. at 1226. Indeed, the court stated that "damages normally should be measured from the time when performance is due and not from the time when the buyer learns of repudiation." Id. Nevertheless, the court conclude[d] that under § 4–2–713 a buyer may urge continued performance for a reasonable time. At the end of a reasonable period he should cover if substitute goods are readily available. If substitution is readily available and buyer does not cover within a reasonable time, damages should be based on the price at the end of that reasonable time rather than on the price when performance is due. Id. at 1227. The Cargill court would employ the time of performance measure only if buyer had a valid reason for not covering.

In First Nat'l Bank of Chicago v. Jefferson Mortgage Co., 576 F.2d 479 (3d Cir. 1978), the court initially quoted with approval legislative history that supports a literal or "plain meaning" interpretation of New Jersey's section 2–713. Nevertheless, the court hedged by interpreting that section "to measure damages within a commercially reasonable time after learning of the repudiation." Id. at 492. In light of the unequivocal repudiation and because cover was "easily and immediately ... available ... in the well-organized and easily accessible market," id. at 493 (quoting Oloffson v. Coomer, 11 Ill.App.3d 918, 296 N.E.2d 871 (1973)), a commercially reasonable time did not extend beyond the date of repudiation.

We agree with the First National court that "the circumstances of the particular market involved should determine the duration of a 'commercially reasonable time.'" 576 F.2d at 492; see Tex.Bus. & Com.Code § 1.204(b). In this case, however, there was no showing that cover was easily and immediately available in an organized and accessible market and that a commercially reasonable time expired on the day of Cosden's cancellation. We recognize that § 2.610's "commercially reasonable time"

. . .

VI. "COVER" AS A CEILING

At trial Cosden argued that Helm's purchases of polystyrene from other sources in early February constituted cover. Helm argued that those purchases were not intended to substitute for polystyrene sales cancelled by Cosden. Helm, however, contended that it did cover by purchasing large amounts of high impact polystyrene from other sources late in February and around the first of March. Cosden claimed that these purchases were not made reasonably and that they should not qualify as cover. The jury found that none of Helm's purchases of polystyrene from other sources were cover purchases.

Now Cosden argues that the prices of polystyrene for the purchases that Helm claimed were cover should act as a ceiling for fixing market price under section 2.713. We refuse to accept this novel argument. Although a buyer who has truly covered may not be allowed to seek higher damages under section 2.713 than he is granted by section 2.712, see § 2.713 comment 5; J. White & R. Summers, supra, § 6–4 at 233–34, in this case the jury found that Helm did not cover. We cannot isolate a reason to explain the jury's finding: it might have concluded that Helm would have made the purchases regardless of Cosden's nonperformance or that the transactions did not qualify as cover for other reasons. Because of the jury's finding, we cannot use those other transactions to determine Helm's damages.

. . .

[The jury found that Cosden was excused by commercial impracticability—UCC 2–615 [d]—from performing under orders 05 and 07, but that Cosden had failed to allocate its production as that section requires. At the trial court's direction, the jury therefore assessed damages based on the amount of general purpose polystyrene that Cosden should have allocated to Helm. On appeal, this was held to be error: owing to the misallocation, Cosden should have been allowed no credit for commercial impracticability.]

Affirmed, but, in part, reversed and remanded.

NOTES

(1) *Other Views.* Some readers of the Code suppose that an anticipatory repudiation is not a "breach," in Code terms. Do you agree? See UCC 2–610(b): party aggrieved may "resort to any remedy for breach." But see UCC

and § 2.712's "without unreasonable delay" are distinct concepts. Often, however, the two time periods will overlap, since the buyer can investigate cover possibilities while he awaits performance. See Sebert, supra, at 376–77 & n. 80.

Although the jury in the present case did not fix the exact duration of a commercially reasonable time, we assume that the jury determined market price at a time commercially reasonable under all the circumstances, in light of the absence of objection to the form of the special issue.

d. This subject is examined in Chapter 8, Basic Assumptions: Mistake, Impracticability and Frustration.

2–711(1).[e] As to the authorities, see the court's fn. 6. Observe that in the *Cargill* case, cited there, the issue was posed whether or not the buyer had a valid reason for not covering. (But see Note 3, below.) What reason might Helm have given for failing to cover?

(2) *The Reverse Case.* Suppose that the market price of polystyrene had dropped rather than risen after Cosden made its sale agreements with Helm, and that the buyer (Helm) rather than the seller had repudiated in February, 1979. For that case the Code provides (subject to certain qualifications and adjustments) that the seller may recover, as damages, the unpaid contract price less the market price *"at the time and place for tender."* UCC 2–708(1). If that rule were different, the decision in the main case would be easier to accept, would it not? What might account for the difference?

If Helm had repudiated the contract, might Cosden have claimed the remedy provided in UCC 2–706 (seller's resale)? Is it clear that the conditions stated in UCC 2–703 prevailed?

(3) *"Quick Draw"* Rules. For convenience we may say that certain rules for fixing damages in repudiation cases are "quick draw" rules—those that preclude reference to a price prevailing on or after the time fixed for performance. The foregoing case gives some reasons to believe that the Code is not committed to such rules. The Code suggests that resale is not a mandatory remedy for a seller aggrieved by a repudiation, and that cover is not mandatory for an aggrieved buyer. Indeed, it *says* that a buyer's failure to effect cover "does not bar him from any other remedy." UCC 2–712(3). Moreover, Comment 1 to that section says that cover is "the buyer's equivalent of the seller's right to resell." Yet the Code remedy provisions admit of some manipulation.

(4) *Quick–Draw Advocates.* As the main case shows, heroic efforts have been made to extract quick-draw rules from the text of the Code. In economic analysis, it has been pointed out that if an aggrieved buyer may delay cover indefinitely, the seller has more to fear from making an early repudiation than from committing a breach at the end. (That is so because, absent any cover requirement, the extent of the seller's "upside" risk is unknowable and unlimited at the time of repudiation.)[f] But the damages rule should be framed—so the argument runs—to make the seller indifferent to the time of breach: an early one may accomplish a more efficient allocation of resources. Jackson, "Anticipatory Repudiation" and the Temporal Element of Contract Law, 31 Stan.L.Rev. 69 (1978).

(5) *Anomalous Cover Contracts.* In February, when a polystyrene buyer learns that its supplier will default two months later, it buys substitute goods on the "spot" market and claims cover damages under UCC 2–712. If the buyer could have made a (forward) contract for delivery after two months, is the claim questionable? Suppose the buyer contracts for substitute goods to be delivered two months later *at the price then prevailing*, and claims cover damages.

---

e. In the first edition of their handbook, The Uniform Commercial Code 197–202 (1972), Professors White and Summers offered five "elegant" arguments for believing that a buyer cannot—in the Code sense—learn of the seller's breach before the time for tender.

f. In 1992, the Nebraska Court of Appeals, in following *Cosden,* observed: "When a performance measure is applied,

an aggrieved buyer in a rising market will speculate that prices will continue to rise. If the market falls after repudiation, the buyer will obtain the same goods at a price lower than under the contract. The effect is to overcompensate the buyer and penalize the seller." Trinidad Bean & Elevator Co. v. Frosh, 494 N.W.2d 347, 353 (Neb. App.1992).

Allowable? If so, does it make any sense to impose a quick-draw rule on buyers aggrieved by repudiation?

UNITED STATES v. SEACOAST GAS CO.

United States Court of Appeals, Fifth Circuit, 1953.
204 F.2d 709.
Certiorari denied 346 U.S. 866 (1953).

Suit against gas company and its surety on gas company's performance bond, for damages alleged to have resulted from an anticipatory breach of contract in nature of notice of intent to cancel contract as of November 15, 1947. The United States District Court for the Southern District of Georgia entered judgment in favor of gas company and surety, and plaintiff appealed. . . .

Judgment reversed, cause remanded with directions.

HUTCHESON, CHIEF JUDGE. Brought against Seacoast Gas Company and the surety on its performance bond, the suit was for damages alleged to have resulted from the anticipatory breach by the Gas Company of its contract with plaintiff to supply gas to a federal housing project during the period from April 15, 1947, to June 15, 1948. The claim was: that on October 7, 1947, while performance of the contract was in progress, Seacoast anticipatorily breached the contract by writing plaintiff unequivocally that, because of plaintiff's breach of the contract, Seacoast intended to cancel same as of November 15, 1947; that the plaintiff immediately notified Seacoast that it did not recognize any right in it to cease performance and that it proposed to advertise for bids to insure a continued supply of gas if Seacoast's breach persisted; that, thereafter, having advertised for bids and on November 6th, having received the low bid from Trion Company, it on that date notified Seacoast by letter that unless it retracted its repudiation of the contract within three days from the letter date, Trion's bid would be accepted and Seacoast and its surety would be held liable for breach of contract; and that thereafter Seacoast not having retracted within the time fixed, plaintiff on November 10, accepted Trion's bid, and, pursuant thereto, began its preparations to execute with Trion a contract for a price in excess of that provided in the Seacoast contract, and Seacoast is liable to plaintiff for this excess.

Defendant Seacoast, admitting in its pleading and its testimony that the facts were substantially as claimed by plaintiff, defended on the ground: that it had retracted its notice of repudiation and given assurance of its intention to continue to perform before the plaintiff had actually signed the new contract; and that, since, as it claimed, plaintiff had not then substantially changed its position or suffered any damages as a result of Seacoast's notice to terminate the contract and cease performance under it, the retraction was timely and healed the breach.

Upon the issue thus joined, the cause was tried to the court without a jury, and the court stating the question for decision thus, "The question in this case is as to whether Seacoast Gas Company, Inc.

withdrew its notice of cancellation of its contract prior to the rendering of the contract to the Trion Gas Company," found that it had done so. On the basis of this finding and a further finding that on November 13, two days before the termination date which Seacoast had fixed in its notice, Zell, who was president both of Seacoast and of Trion Company, to whom the new contract was awarded, notified the regional counsel for the Public Housing Authority that Seacoast admitted it had no right to cancel the contract and was rescinding its notice, the court held that the anticipatory breach had been healed and plaintiff could not recover.

Appealing from this judgment, plaintiff is here insisting that under the settled law governing anticipatory breaches not only as it is laid down in Georgia but generally, Seacoast's retraction came too late to heal the breach, and the judgment must be reversed.

Appellees, on their part, insist that the judgment appealed from was soundly based in law and in fact and must be affirmed.

We do not think so. The undisputed facts establish: that Zell, president of both companies, was present at the opening of the new bids on November 6, 1947, and upon being asked to withdraw Seacoast's notice that it would cease performing the contract, refused to do so; that on that date the Public Housing Administration regional counsel wrote Seacoast by registered mail, addressed "Attention Zell", advising of the steps the government had taken and stating that unless Seacoast retracted its repudiation within three days from the date of the letter, Trion's bid would be accepted and Seacoast and its sureties would be held liable for breach of contract; and that having received no response from Seacoast within the three days specified, and Zell again asked on November 10th, to retract the notice of repudiation having refused to do so, the government accepted Trion's bid and proceeded with the execution of the contract. The record standing thus, under settled law[1] not only of Georgia but generally elsewhere, the breach was not healed, the judgment was wrong, and it must be reversed.

A comparison of the briefs and arguments of appellant and appellees will show that the case is in quite small compass. Both agree that Seacoast's letter of October 24th [sic] operated as an anticipatory breach and that unless effectively withdrawn during the *locus poenitentiae* it operated to put Seacoast in default and to render it liable for the loss to the government of the difference in price between the old and the new contract.

Appellees, after quoting from Anson on Contracts, 6th Ed., Sec. 385, p. 444:

1. Baker v. Corbin, 148 Ga. 267, 96 S.E. 428; Bu–Vi–Bar Petroleum Corp. v. Krow, 10 Cir., 40 F.2d 488, 69 A.L.R. 1295; Finch v. Sprague, 117 Wash. 650, 202 P. 257; Parker v. King, 68 Ga.App. 672, 23 S.E.2d 575; Roehm v. Horst, 178 U.S. 1, 20 S.Ct. 780, 44 L.Ed. 953; United Press Ass'n v. National Newspaper Ass'n, 10 Cir., 237 F. 547; 12 Am.Jur., "Contracts" Sec. 392; Ballantine, Anticipatory Breach and the Enforcement of Contractual Duties, 22 Mich. L.Rev. 329; 17 C.J.S., Contracts, § 472, p. 973; Vold, Withdrawal of Repudiation after Anticipatory Breach of Contract, 5 Tex. L.Rev. 9, 10; Williston on Contracts (Rev. Ed.1936) Sec. 1323, Vol. 5, pp. 3710–3711.

"The repudiator has the power of retraction prior to any change of position by the other party, but not afterwards."

go on to say:

"So we see that the authorities seem to be unanimous that a person who gives notice of his intention not to perform a contract may withdraw such notice and offer to perform prior to the time the other party acted or relied thereon."

Based upon these premises, they insist that "the undisputed evidence is that appellant did not 'accept the bid of Trion Gas' until November 17th, which was after the notice of cancellation had been withdrawn in writing."

We think: that this statement is erroneous; that it represents the crucial difference between the parties; and that the error of the statement lies in the fact that it confuses the acceptance of the bid with the signing of the contract.

It is true that the contract was not signed until the 17th, after Seacoast had retracted its notice and if appellees were correct in its position that the date of the signing of the new contract was determinative of this case, they would be correct in their conclusion that the judgment should be affirmed.

But that position is not correct. In fact and in law, when the government took bids and notified Seacoast that unless it retracted within three days it would proceed to accept the Trion bid and award the contract to it, the *locus poenitentiae* ended with these three days. The fact that Seacoast claims that it did not receive the notice is completely immaterial both because it was not necessary for the government to give any notice or fix any time and because Zell, on November 10th, repeated to the Regional Counsel his refusal to retract.

All that is required to close the door to repentance is definite action indicating that the anticipatory breach has been accepted as final, and this requisite can be supplied either by the filing of a suit or a firm declaration, as here, that unless within a fixed time the breach is repudiated, it will be accepted.

Here, in addition to this firm declaration, the record shows the taking of bids and the awarding of the contract to the lowest bidder. The error of the district judge lies, we think, in holding that the *locus poenitentiae* was extended until the 17th, when the contract was signed, and that Seacoast having repented before the signing of the contract, had healed the breach and restored the contract to its original vitality.

Whatever of doubt there may be, and we have none with respect to this view, as a matter of strict law, there can be none with respect to the justice or equity of this determination when it is considered; that Zell, the president and practically sole owner of Seacoast, was the organizer, the president and practically sole owner of Trion; that he organized Trion for the sole purpose of the bidding; and that on the date the bids were opened and later on the date the contract was awarded, he, though requested to do so, refused to withdraw Seacoast's repudiation and continued in that refusal until a day or two before the contract was signed.

The evidence showing, as it does, without contradiction, that the signing of the contract was not delayed because of a purpose on the part of the government to extend the time for Seacoast's repentance, but because until that date Trion had not furnished his bond, we think it clear that, in entering judgment for the defendants, the court erred. The judgment is, therefore, reversed and the cause is remanded with directions to enter judgment for plaintiff for the loss Seacoast's breach of contract has caused it.

NOTES

(1) *Alternative Explanations.* The error of the trial court was in supposing that timely action by Seacoast had "healed the breach and restored the contract to its original vitality." One way of interpreting the appellate opinion is that the United States had *elected* to treat the repudiation as conclusive before Zell recanted. In the alternative, the decision may rest on a change of position by the United States such that Seacoast was *estopped* to retract its repudiation. Finally, it might have been said that Seacoast *waived* its power to retract through delay while the bidding procedure went forward. It is mildly surprising that the court did not use any of these terms to justify its ruling, for they are tempting ways to explain how expectations are altered over the life of a contract through behavior of the parties that does not amount to a fresh bargain.

(2) *The Door to Repentance.* There was a substantial change of position by the Government, was there not, on November 10 when it accepted Trion's bid? The filing of a suit against Seacoast would have been such a change of position.[a] The question remaining, then, is whether *without any such step* the Government's firm declaration "accepting" the repudiation would "close the door to repentance." Why should it? See Note 3 below.

Cases which assimilate a repudiation to an offer, in that each may be made irrevocable by acceptance, are not uncommon in this country. The other side of the coin is that a repudiation can be ignored by the innocent party: "I have never been able to understand what effect the repudiation of one party has unless the other party accepts the repudiation." (Lord Scrutton) "An unaccepted repudiation is a thing writ in water and of no value to anybody: it confers no legal rights of any sort or kind." (Lord Asquith)[b] Such expressions are not consistent with American law, however. See Note 1, p. 759 above. They overstate the difference between an "actual breach" and a breach by anticipation. For various differences between an anticipatory repudiation and an offer to rescind, see Corbin, §§ 980–81.

American cases are somewhat more compatible with the view that a repudiation puts the injured party to an election of cancelling the contract or of keeping it alive, as Lord Cockburn indicated (see the Note referred to). However, the better view is that the injured party may urge that the repudiation be withdrawn—that repentance be made—without becoming committed to further performance if it is not. If a seller of goods repudiates its obligation and then seeks

---

a. "A retraction of an anticipatory repudiation after the injured party sues for enforcement or damages comes too late." Glatt v. Bank of Kirkwood Plaza, 383 N.W.2d 473 (N.D.1986).

b. These observations were quoted and commented on in White and Carter (Councils) Ltd. v. McGregor, [1962] A.C. 413 (House of Lords), at 438 and 444.

to retract after a rise in market prices, should the buyer be privileged to disregard the retraction? [c]

What position does the Code take on these problems? See UCC 2–610(b), 2–611.

(3) *A Professor's Plaint.* Early in 1977 the new chairman of the Department of Medicine at the University of Vermont Medical College told a staff member, Dr. David Lowe, that Lowe should "plan to relocate as of July 1"; later he asked repeatedly for Lowe's resignation. Lowe had begun a two-year term as an assistant professor on July 1, 1976. Through his attorney Lowe indicated his intention to sue the University for breach of contract. He also began to look for comparable employment elsewhere. In March, 1977, the University's attorney expressed its intention to honor the two-year employment contract. In July Lowe left the University to take up private practice.

In an action by Lowe against the University (and the chairman) Lowe got a judgment based on a jury verdict; the University appealed. *Held:* Reversed. There was, the court concluded, "sufficient evidence presented to support the determination that the defendant's statements ... constituted a 'positive and unequivocal' refusal on the part of the University to perform in accordance with the terms of the contract." But the breach had been "nullified," the court said. "The testimony of the plaintiff indicates that before he received notice of the retraction by the University, he made inquiries about other similar positions in the area. Finding none available, he decided to give up his career in academic medicine and instead pursue a career in private practice. The evidence also shows that in furtherance of this decision, the plaintiff made some trips to Rhode Island and expended time and money making preliminary arrangements for this change. However, there is no evidence indicating that this was done before the plaintiff received notice of the University's retraction. Thus, the only actions taken by the plaintiff in reliance on the repudiation, and prior to the retraction, were making a few phone calls and changing his mind. These alone are insufficient as a matter of law to support a determination that the plaintiff materially changed his position in reliance on the defendant's repudiation." Lowe v. Beaty, 485 A.2d 1255 (Vt.1984).

According to a rule stated in the Restatement Second § 256, the time when the effect of a statement as constituting a repudiation can be "nullified by a retraction" comes to an end when the injured party "indicates to the other party that he considers the repudiation to be final"—apart from a change of position. Compare UCC 2–611(1). Was the decision in Lowe v. Beaty consistent with that rule? If not do you prefer the decision to the rule?

(4) *Summary.* Comment *a* to Restatement Second § 329 has this to say about repudiation and its effects: "In some cases a repudiation by one party to a contract discharges the duty of the other party; in some cases it requires the other to treat as total a breach which might otherwise be partial, or it may itself be a total breach. See Chapter 10, Third Party Beneficiaries; UCC 2–610. For these purposes repudiation includes a positive statement by [a promisor] that he will not or cannot substantially perform his duties, or any voluntary affirmative action which renders substantial performance apparently impossible. In some circumstances a statement that he doubts whether he will substantially perform, or that he takes no responsibility for performance, or even a failure to give adequate assurance of performance may have a similar effect."

c. Is the retraction some evidence that market price equals contract price? See   Goldfarb v. Campe Corp., 164 N.Y.S. 583 (City Ct.1917).

Reconsider the cases in this chapter with a view to finding support for each of these propositions. Where do you find indications that this pattern is not consistently followed?

(b) Assurance of Due Performance

"Ordinarily an obligee has no right to demand reassurance by the obligor that the latter will perform when his performance is due. However, a contract 'imposes an obligation on each party that the other's expectation of receiving due performance will not be impaired.' Uniform Commercial Code § 2–609(1). When, therefore, an obligee reasonably believes that the obligor will commit a breach by nonperformance that would of itself give him a claim for damages for total breach (§ 243), he may, under the rule stated in this Section, be entitled to demand assurance of performance." Restatement Second § 251, Comment *a*.

Section 251 had no counterpart in the first Restatement. It is a generalization from UCC 2–609, which was itself something of a legislative innovation. It remains to be seen whether or not the courts will accede to the Restatement position in cases not governed by Article 2 of the Code.

The sort of case that chiefly inspired the Code section was one in which a seller committed itself to supply goods for payment thereafter, and received signals before making delivery that the buyer was in financial distress.[a] In an extreme case of this type a supplier named Gestetner was sued by Turntables, Inc. for his failure to deliver goods on credit, as promised. It seems that Gestetner had demanded assurance of payment under UCC 2–609 after learning these facts: Turntables was in arrears in payment for goods already delivered; it had a bad credit reputation; its "Fifth Avenue Showroom" turned out to be a telephone answering service; and its "factory" turned out to be someone else's premises, to which Turntables did not have a key. (The court said that Gestetner "obviously" had reasonable grounds for insecurity.) Turntables' response to the demand for assurance was to cancel the contract and sue. Gestetner made a counterclaim for damages and obtained a judgment from which Turntables appealed. *Held:* Affirmed. Turntables, Inc. v. Gestetner, 382 N.Y.S.2d 798 (App.Div.1976).

Questions

Some of the questions relating to insecurity that are to be addressed are these:

----

a. The principal cases are cited in the Reporter's Note to Restatement Second § 252. See also United States for Use and Benefit of Industrial Instrument Corp. v. Paul Hardeman, Inc., 202 F.Supp. 124 (N.D.Tex.1962), aff'd, 320 F.2d 115 (5th Cir.1963).

(1) Suppose that a demand for assurance is made on reasonable grounds, but is not expressed in writing. Under UCC 2–609 or the Restatement Second § 251, is the demand effective? Hazardous?

(2) Suppose a demand made for "assurance" in general terms. Is the recipient justified in demanding to know from the sender what specific form of assurance would or might be satisfactory?

(3) Suppose a demand made for a specific form of assurance (e.g., a bank guarantee of payment) which is inconvenient or impossible for the recipient to give. If another form would serve the purpose equally well, is the demand effective? Hazardous?

(4) Suppose a demand made on insufficient grounds. Is the recipient entitled to treat that as a breach?

NOTES

(1) *Breach of a Separate Contract (Reprise).* Recall that the doctrine of constructive conditions cannot be invoked where there has been a breach of a separate contract. This is so even though the separate contract has been repudiated. UCC 2–610 applies only when a party "repudiates *the* contract." But might UCC 2–609 help an apprehensive party in such a situation? According to Comment 3 to UCC 2–609, "under commercial standards and in accord with commercial practice, a ground for insecurity need not arise from or be directly related to the contract in question."

(2) *Problem (Reprise).* Review the letter in Note 2, p. 775 above. Would the seller be justified in demanding assurance of due performance under UCC 2–609?

PITTSBURGH–DES MOINES STEEL CO. v. BROOKHAVEN MANOR WATER CO.

United States Court of Appeals, Seventh Circuit, 1976.
532 F.2d 572.

[At the request of the Water Company (Brookhaven), Pittsburgh–Des Moines Steel Company (PDM) submitted a revised proposal to build an elevated tank for $175,000. The original proposal called for progress payments to PDM; the revised offer called for no payment until the tank had been built and tested. After Brookhaven's acceptance, PDM heard something about a loan that Brookhaven was negotiating for. The credit manager for PDM wrote the prospective lender (copy to Brookhaven) asking for a notice that $175,000 had been put in escrow for the job, and adding: "As a matter of good business we are holding this matter in abeyance until receipt of such notification." The loan did not go through. Then the credit manager wrote the president of Brookhaven asking for his personal guarantee of payment, "to protect us between now and the time your loan is completed." The letter mentioned the escrow again, this time as a requirement. The president sent a statement of his personal worth. PDM stopped fabricating parts, and the tank was never built.

[PDM sued Brookhaven, charging repudiation of the contract, and Brookhaven entered a counterclaim. A jury returned a verdict for PDM, but the trial court entered a judgment notwithstanding the verdict, in Brookhaven's favor. PDM appealed.]

PELL, CIRCUIT JUDGE. ... PDM argues that its position was in accordance with Section 2–609 of the Uniform Commercial Code. [The court determined that the subject of the contract was goods, so that Article 2 of the Code was applicable.[a]] The question remaining is whether PDM's actions subsequent to the execution of the contract were within the protection provided by § 2–609. We hold that they were not.

The performance to which PDM was entitled was the full payment of the purchase price within a specified time after the completion of the tank. While we have a substantial question as to whether PDM made a written demand as required by the statute, in keeping with our concept that the UCC should be liberally construed, we do not desire to rest our decision on a formalistic approach. Letters were written which conveyed what PDM wanted done before they would pursue their obligations under the contract. The fundamental problem is that these letters, if they be deemed to be in the nature of a demand, demanded more than that to which PDM was entitled and the demand was not founded upon what in our opinion was an actuating basis for the statute's applicability.

We do not construe § 2–609 as being a vehicle without more for an implied term being inserted in a contract when a substantially equivalent term was expressly waived in the contract. The something more to trigger applicability of the statute is that the expectation of due performance on the part of the other party entertained at contracting time no longer exists because of "reasonable grounds for insecurity" arising. We find that PDM's actions in demanding either the escrowing of the purchase price or a personal guarantee lacked the necessary predicate of

---

a. A footnote to an omitted passage is as follows:

"In Note, A Right to Adequate Assurance of Performance in All Transactions: U.C.C. § 2–609 Beyond Sales of Goods, 48 S.Cal.L.Rev. 1358, 1375–87 (1975), the author supports a case for either judicial expansion or legislative imposition of the § 2–609 provisions as to contracts not covered by the UCC. The Note, however, concedes that other than a dictum in Berry's Sons Co. v. Monark Gasoline & Oil Co., 32 F.2d 74 (8th Cir.1929), no subsequent case has held that there would be an implied term of the contract if the parties have not expressly included such a provision."

In Schenectady Steel Co., Inc. v. Bruno Trimpoli General Constr. Co., Inc., 316 N.E.2d 875 (N.Y.1974), the trial court concluded that a contractor was justified in terminating its contract with a steel fabricator for failure to respond adequately to a demand under UCC 2–609. The Appellate Division affirmed (except as to damages), but not on that ground. It reasoned that the contract was one for work, labor and materials to which Article 2 did not apply, and said: "Of course, at common law no such duty to provide adequate assurances existed." On further appeal, the Court of Appeals also affirmed, but without approving either opinion below: "We would further indicate that on the facts of this case it is immaterial whether article 2 ... applies."

To the effect that UCC 2–609 is inapplicable to a plumbing contract see Cork Plumbing Co., Inc. v. Martin Bloom Associates, Inc., 573 S.W.2d 947 (Mo.App.1978).

reasonable grounds for insecurity having arisen.   The contract negates
the existence of any basis for insecurity at the time of the contract when
PDM was willing to wait 30 days beyond completion for payment.   The
fact that Brookhaven had not completed its loan negotiations does not
constitute reasonable grounds for insecurity when the money in question
was not to be needed for some months.   Reasonable business men prefer
in the absence of some compulsive reason not to commence paying
interest on borrowed money until the time for the use for that money is
at hand.   The credit manager's January letter that the order was being
held in abeyance until receipt of notification of escrowing was based
upon a "matter of good business," but not upon any change of condition
bearing upon Brookhaven's ability to discharge its payment obligation
under the contract.   With regard to the later request for a personal
guarantee, it is not uncommon for an individual to decline assuming
obligations of a corporation in which he is a shareholder.   Indeed, the
use of the corporate device frequently has as a principal purpose the
limitation on individual exposure to liability.   If an unfavorable risk in
dealing with a corporation exists at contracting time, good business
judgment may well indicate that an assurance be secured before contracting that there will be individual shareholder backup.   None of this
occurred and the record is silent as to any reasonable grounds for
insecurity arising thereafter. . . .

We, of course, would not deprive PDM of resort to § 2–609 if there
had been a demonstration that reasonable grounds for insecurity had
arisen.   The proof in that respect was lacking.   The comptroller and
supervisor of PDM's credit department testified that he had access to all
of the credit information that the company had regarding Brookhaven,
that he had reviewed that information, and that he was unaware of any
change in the financial condition of Brookhaven between November of
1968 and the end of 1969.[b]   . . . The fact, if it were a fact, that
Brookhaven may not have had a large amount of cash lying in the bank
in a checking account, not an unusual situation for a real estate
developer, does not support the belief that it, as a company with
substantial assets, would fail to meet its obligations as they fell due.
Section 2–609 is a protective device when reasonable grounds for insecurity arise; it is not a pen for rewriting a contract in the absence of
those reasonable grounds having arisen, particularly when the proposed
rewriting involves the very factors which had been waived by the one
now attempting to wield the pen.   The situation is made no more
persuasive for PDM when it is recalled that that company was the
original scrivener.

Brookhaven's request to put off the contract for a year clearly came
after PDM's repudiation of the contract and was indicative of nothing
more than that Brookhaven was willing to undertake a new arrangement

b. The court wrote as follows of the
trial court's ruling: "The district court apparently regarded the matter as being the
not entirely unfamiliar situation of a corporate credit department not viewing a contract of sale with the same *joie de vivre* as
did the sales department; but the court
thought that the sales department had legally committed the firm and that the credit department had gone beyond the grounds
for actuating the assurance provided by the
statute."

with PDM a year hence. Pursuant to § 2–610 of the UCC, Brookhaven was entitled to suspend its own performance by virtue of the anticipatory repudiation by PDM and to resort to available remedies, including damages pursuant to § 2–711 of the Code.[1] ...

Affirmed.

CUMMINGS, CIRCUIT JUDGE (concurring). Although I agree with the result reached in the majority opinion, I differ with the reasoning. Reasonable men could certainly conclude that PDM had legitimate grounds to question Brookhaven's ability to pay for the water tank. When the contract was signed, the parties understood that Brookhaven would obtain a loan to help pay for the project. When the loan failed to materialize, a prudent businessman would have "reasonable grounds for insecurity." I disagree that there must be a fundamental change in the financial position of the buyer before the seller can invoke the protection of UCC § 2–609. Rather, I believe that the Section was designed to cover instances where an underlying condition of the contract, even if not expressly incorporated into the written document, fails to occur. See Comment 3 to UCC § 2–609. Whether, in a specific case, the breach of the condition gives a party "reasonable grounds for insecurity" is a question of fact for the jury.

UCC § 2–609, however, does not give the alarmed party a right to redraft the contract.... The district court could properly conclude as a matter of law that these requests by PDM demanded more than a commercially "adequate assurance of due performance."

NOTES

(1) *Problem.* Your firm orders a commercial furnace. Next it learns that a furnace of the same make and model, delivered to another buyer, has systematically overheated. You write to the supplier to express concern about this problem. The supplier gives an evasive answer, but delivers the furnace. Your firm pays the purchase price, but at the same time demands (a) that the supplier extend the period for which it has warranted satisfactory performance of the furnace, and (b) that it provide a letter of credit to assure repayment of the purchase price if the warranty is broken. The supplier rejects these demands. On these facts alone, can your firm revoke its acceptance of the furnace? Compare Creusot–Loire Int'l, Inc. v. Coppus Engineering Corp., 585 F.Supp. 45 (S.D.N.Y.1983).

(2) *Drafting About Insecurity.* A firm that anticipates repeat business with another may wish to specify remedies it may invoke, in addition to demanding

---

1. We have not attempted to determine whether the parties were merchants within the meaning of subsection 2 of § 2–609 in which case the determination of the reasonableness of grounds for insecurity would be in accordance with commercial standards. There being no evidence as to what commercial standards might be applicable, we have attempted to construe the controlling phrase in accordance with what appears to us to be its plain meaning.

Further, we find no merit in PDM's argument that even if its January action could be construed as an anticipatory repudiation under § 2–610, its subsequent actions demonstrated a retraction of the anticipatory repudiation pursuant to § 2–611. That section requires a clear indication to the aggrieved party "that the repudiating party intends to perform." PDM only made it clear throughout that it intended to perform if Brookhaven gave assurances not required of it legally or contractually.

assurance of performance, if it becomes apprehensive about the reliability of the other. An example of generalized apprehension on the part of sellers, about the performances of buyers, appeared in the standard form of a trade association of lumber dealers.

> The seller shall have the right to cancel on account of any arbitrary deductions made by the buyer with respect to, or failure to comply with, contract terms in respect to any prior shipment, or on account of any transfer of or change in the buyer's business, his insolvency, suit by other creditors, failure of buyer to meet financial obligations to seller, impairment of buyer's credit information, or for unfavorable credit reports made to seller through usual channels of credit information unless the buyer shall promptly furnish to the seller's satisfaction guaranty of full payment for any shipment made or to be made. Notice of such cancellation shall be given in writing.

Analogous provisions are found in notes and other papers representing extensions of credit: the credit grantor may reserve the power to demand payment of installments scheduled for the future "if the creditor deems itself insecure." Provisions of this type are addressed in UCC 1–208, under the heading "Option to Accelerate at Will." The section reads, in part:

> A term providing that [a party] may accelerate payment or performance ... "at will" or "when he deems himself insecure" or in words of similar import shall be construed to mean that he shall have power to do so only if he in good faith believes that the prospect of payment or performance is impaired.

Is this section applicable to the trade-association term quoted above? Is there any other reason to expect that that term would not be effective as written? Consult UCC 1–102(3), which entrenches the Code obligations of good faith, diligence, reasonableness, and care, but permits the parties to specify (though not in a manifestly unreasonable way) the standards of compliance.

Can the provisions of UCC 2–609 be reinforced by a term like that quoted above? And at the other extreme, might the parties to a sale-of-goods contract "contract out" of the section?

(3) *Flaws in the Fabric Trade.* Compare the Standard Textile Salesnote ("Worth Street Rules") in the Selections for Contracts:

"[U]pon Buyer's breach or default with respect to any term or condition of this or any other contract with Seller, all sums owing under this and other contracts between Buyer and Seller, shall at the option of Seller ..., at once become due...."

This paragraph also requires current payments by Buyer in the event that net balances under all their contracts exceed Buyer's established "credit limit," and continues: "Upon failure by Buyer to make any such payment within five (5) days after demand in writing, Seller shall have the option to cancel *this and other contracts* between Buyer and Seller...."

Is this a "manifestly unreasonable" standard of performance of a seller's (non-disclaimable) duty of reasonableness prescribed in the Code? Is it a permissible variation of UCC 2–609? What does it mean if "construed with reference to that provision"?

(4) *Unwritten Demand.* It has been held that a written demand is not demanded by UCC 2–609, at least when the failure to use a writing is excusable. See AMF, Inc. v. McDonald's Corp., 536 F.2d 1167 (7th Cir.1976) (first party had

a clear understanding that "other" was awaiting assurance before proceeding).[a]
Is there any reason for requiring a writing, as the Code seems to do?

(5) *Self–Help Remedies Under the Code.* Under the doctrine of constructive conditions of exchange, an injured party may suspend performance and ultimately terminate. As long as the injured party does not claim damages, that party does not need to go to court. Suspension and termination are "self-help" remedies. The Code expands the array of such remedies available under contracts for the sale of goods. See UCC 2–609, 2–717. What might be the reason for this expansion? Do you see any drawback?

a. See also Kunian v. Development Corp. of America, 334 A.2d 427 (Conn. 1973); Toppert v. Bunge Corp., 377 N.E.2d 324 (Ill.App.1978).

Chapter 8

BASIC ASSUMPTIONS: MISTAKE, IMPRACTICABILITY AND FRUSTRATION

SECTION 1. MUTUAL MISTAKE

Sometimes one of the parties to a contract faces obstacles to its performance that result from circumstances not anticipated at the time the contract was made. In this chapter we consider whether and to what extent, such obstacles relieve a party of its duty to perform.

Often the circumstances have arisen *after* the time the contract was made. So it was in the following cases: Eastern Airlines v. Gulf Oil Corp. (p. 125 above) (subsequent price controls on oil), Gill v. Johnstown Lumber Co. (p. 720 above) (subsequent flood), McCloskey & Co. v. Minweld Steel Co. (p. 769 above) (subsequent outbreak of war), and Cosden Oil & Chemical Co. v. Karl O. Helm (p. ___ above) (subsequent freeze). Obstacles due to changes in circumstances are dealt with in Sections 2 and 3 of this chapter under the rubrics of *impracticability of performance* and *frustration of purpose*.

Sometimes, however, the circumstances existed at the time the contract was made but did not become known until later. Thus the obstacles that Watkins faced (p. 357 above) resulted from subsoil conditions that existed at the time it contracted to do the excavation. Obstacles due to existing circumstances are dealt with in this section under the rubric of *mutual mistake*. Recall that the Supreme Court of New Hampshire said of Watkins, that if it "was unwise in taking chances, it is not relieved, on the ground of mistake, from the burden incurred in being faced with them."

The court's reference to "taking chances" is apt, since the cases considered in this chapter have much to do with risk. Would you surmise that a contracting party would be more likely to be held to risks resulting from existing circumstances or from changed circumstances? Does the notion that the institution of contract is designed to enable contacting parties to plan for the future affect your answer?

NOTE

Distinctions. The cases considered here, involving what is commonly called "mutual mistake," should not be confused with those (such as *Elsinore,* p. 171 above) involving what is commonly called "unilateral mistake." Compare Restatement (Second) § 152 with § 153. Nor should they be confused with cases (such as *Bollinger,* p. 578 above) granting reformation for an error in reducing an agreement to writing or with cases (such as the *Peerless* case, p. 592 above) finding that no agreement has been reached because of a misunderstanding. What distinctions do you see among these different types of cases?

STEES v. LEONARD

Supreme Court of Minnesota, 1874.
20 Minn. 494, 20 Gil. 448.*

Appeal by defendants from an order of the district court, Ramsey county, denying a new trial.

The action was brought to recover damages for a failure of defendants to erect and complete a building on a lot of plaintiffs, on Minnesota Street, between Third and Fourth streets, in the city of St. Paul, which, by an agreement under seal between them and plaintiffs, the defendants had agreed to build, erect, and complete, according to plans and specifications annexed to and made part of the agreement. The defendants commenced the construction of the building, and had carried it to the height of three stories when it fell to the ground. The next year, 1869, they began again and carried it to the height as before, when it again fell to the ground, whereupon defendants refused to perform the contract. They claimed that in their attempts to erect the building they did the work in all respects according to the plans and specifications and that the failure to complete the building and its fall on the two occasions was due to the fact that the soil upon which it was to be constructed was composed of quicksand, and when water flowed into it, was incapable of sustaining the building. . . . The specifications annexed to the contract are very full, and provide, (among other things,) that "All the walls shall be of the following thickness: foundation walls, two feet thick, and shall have footings six inches thick, which shall run clear across walls and project six inches on each side of wall above it." The specifications contain no other provisions relating to the character of the foundation for the building. [The plaintiffs alleged that the specifications, signed by both parties to the contract, had been prepared by a firm of architects named Sheire & Bro. Two persons named Sheire were named as defendants along with Leonard.]

The plaintiffs allege . . . that the fall of the building was owing to the negligence and unskilful work of the defendants, and the poor quality of the material furnished by them. Judgment is demanded for the sum of $5,214.80, with interest, as the damages sustained by the plaintiffs; being $3,745.80 paid, pursuant to the contract, during the progress of the work, $1,000 as damages for loss of the use of the lot on which the building was to be erected, and $469, as damages, occasioned

* The statement of facts is taken in part
from the 1882 edition by Gilfillan of 20
Minnesota Reports.

by the fall of the building, to an adjacent house of plaintiffs, and property stored therein. . . .

The jury found for the plaintiffs. The defendants moved, upon a bill of exceptions, for a new trial, and appeal from the order denying their motion.

YOUNG, J. The general principle of law which underlies this case is well established. If a man bind himself, by a positive, express contract, to do an act in itself possible, he must perform his engagement, unless prevented by the act of God, the law, or the other party to the contract. No hardship, no unforeseen hindrance, no difficulty short of absolute impossibility, will excuse him from doing what he has expressly agreed to do. This doctrine may sometimes seem to bear heavily upon contractors; but, in such cases, the hardship is attributable, not to the law, but to the contractor himself, who has improvidently assumed an absolute, when he might have undertaken only a qualified, liability. The law does no more than enforce the contract as the parties themselves have made it. . . .

School Trustees v. Bennett, 3 Dutcher, N.J., 513, is almost identical, in its material facts, with the present case. The contractors agreed to build and complete a schoolhouse, and find all materials therefor, according to specifications annexed to the contract; the building to be located on a lot owned by plaintiff, and designated in the contract. When the building was nearly completed it was blown down by a sudden and violent gale of wind. The contractors again began to erect the building, when it fell, solely on account of the soil on which it stood having become soft and miry, and unable to sustain the weight of the building; although, when the foundations were laid, the soil was so hard as to be penetrated with difficulty by a pickax, and its defects were latent. The plaintiff had a verdict for the amount of the installments paid under the contract as the work progressed. The verdict was sustained by the supreme court, which held that the loss, although arising solely from a latent defect in the soil, and not from a faulty construction of the building, must fall on the contractor. . . .

In Dermott v. Jones, 2 Wall., U.S., 1, the foundation of the building sank, owing to a latent defect in the soil, and the owner was compelled to take down and rebuild a portion of the work. The contractor having sued for his pay, it was held that the owner might recoup the damages sustained by his deviation from the contract. The court refer with approval to the cases cited, and say: "The principle which controlled them rests upon a solid foundation of reason and justice. It regards the sanctity of contracts. It requires a party to do what he has agreed to do. If unexpected impediments lie in the way, and a loss ensue, it leaves the loss where the contract places it. If the parties have made no provision for a dispensation, the rule of law gives none. It does not allow a contract fairly made to be annulled, and it does not permit to be interpolated what the parties themselves have not stipulated."

Nothing can be added to the clear and cogent arguments we have quoted in vindication of the wisdom and justice of the rule which must govern this case, unless it is in some way distinguishable from the cases cited.

It is argued that the spot on which the building is to be erected is not designated with precision in the contract, but is left to be selected by the owner; that, under the contract, the right to designate the particular spot being reserved to plaintiffs they must select one that will sustain the building described in the specifications, and if the spot they select is not, in its natural state, suitable, they must make it so; that in this respect the present case differs from School Trustees v. Bennett.

The contract does not, perhaps, designate the site of the proposed building with absolute certainty; but in this particular it is aided by the pleadings. The complaint states that defendants contracted to erect the proposed building on "*a certain piece* of land, of which the plaintiffs then were, and now are, the owners in fee, fronting on Minnesota street, between Third and Fourth streets, in the city of St. Paul." The answer expressly admits that the defendants entered into a contract to erect the building, according to the plans, etc., "on that certain piece of land in said complaint described," and that they "entered upon the performance of said contract and proceeded with the erection of said building," etc. This is an express admission that the contract was made with reference to the identical piece of land on which the defendants afterwards attempted to perform it, and leaves no foundation in fact for the defendants' argument.

It is no defense to the action that the specifications directed that "footings" should be used as the foundation of the building, and that the defendants, in the construction of those footings, as well as in all other particulars, conformed to the specifications. The defendants contracted to "erect and complete the building." Whatever was necessary to be done in order to complete the building, they were bound by the contract to do. If the building could not be completed without other or stronger foundations than the footings specified, they were bound to furnish such other foundations. If the building could not be erected without draining the land, then they must drain the land, "because they have agreed to do everything necessary to erect and complete the building." (3 Dutcher, N.J., 520; and see Dermott v. Jones, supra, where the same point was made by the contractor, but ruled against him by the court.)

As the draining of the land was, in fact, necessary to the erection and completion of the building, it was a thing to be done, under the contract, by the defendants. The prior parol agreement that plaintiffs should drain the land, related therefore, to a matter embraced within the terms of the written contract, and was not, as claimed by defendants' counsel, collateral thereto. It was, accordingly under the familiar rule, inadmissible in evidence to vary the terms of the written contract, and was properly excluded.

[In the remainder of the opinion the court considered evidence offered by the defendants that *after* the work was begun the plaintiffs made promises to drain the site of the building, and that the failure to do so caused the collapse. The court held that the evidence was properly excluded because the defendants had failed to allege consideration for the promises, or justifiable reliance upon them.]

There was, therefore, no error in the exclusion of the evidence offered, and the order appealed from is affirmed.

NOTES

(1) *Loss Questions.* The opinion in *Stees* seems to proceed on the assumption that a loss traceable to a latent soil condition must fall on either the owner or the builder. If the builder discovers the difficulty when he begins work, and refuses to proceed, what kinds of loss have to be considered? One may be the additional price the owner must pay to have the work done as projected. Evidently the plaintiffs did not claim this type of loss in Stees v. Leonard. Would it have been granted, if such an amount had been proved and claimed?

(2) *Mistake.* There is authority for avoiding a construction contract that the parties made without sufficient information about soil conditions, on the ground of mutual mistake. See Restatement of Restitution § 9; but see Watkins & Son v. Carrig, p. 357 above. Is a builder that has made test borings at the site before contracting in a good position to plead mistake? Should the builder be allowed to make this defense if the agreement requires the builder to test the soil, and the builder has not done so? If the contract in Stees v. Leonard had been held voidable for mutual mistake, which elements in the plaintiffs' recovery could have been granted, if any?

(3) *Case Comparisons.* In United States v. Spearin, 248 U.S. 132, 136–37 (1918), it was said that although "one who undertakes to erect a structure upon a particular site, assumes ordinarily the risk of subsidence of the soil," nevertheless "if the contractor is bound to build according to plans and specifications prepared by the owner, the contractor will not be responsible for the consequences of defects in the plans and specifications." The Supreme Court held that where the government furnished contract plans and specifications for a sewer, this "imported a warranty that, if the specifications were complied with, the sewer would be adequate."

Were the specifications in Stees v. Leonard adequate for the construction of the building on the site specified? Compare Ridley Investment Co. v. Croll, 192 A.2d 925, 6 A.L.R.3d 1389 (Del.1963), a "soft soil" case in which the contractor prevailed. The court observed that "plans and specifications do not exist in a vacuum; they are made for a particular building at a particular place. The defect in the plans and specifications for the building in question was the failure to make provision for adequate pilings and other support for the floor; the fact that these plans and specifications might provide for an adequate building in some other place does not render the plans and specifications less defective for the location in question."

BASIS OF RELIEF FOR MISTAKE

A celebrated case of avoidance for mutual mistake is Sherwood v. Walker, 33 N.W. 919 (Mich.1887). Walker, a cattle breeder, sold to Sherwood, a banker, a cow of distinguished ancestry known as Rose 2d of Aberlone. Rose went for $80 because both parties believed that she was sterile. When Walker discovered that Rose was pregnant and therefore worth between $750 and $1,000, he refused to deliver her and

Sherwood sued in replevin. Judgment for plaintiff was reversed on appeal. The Supreme Court of Michigan explained: "If there is a difference or misapprehension as to the substance of the thing bargained for ... and intended to be sold, then there is no contract; but if it be only a difference in some quality or accident, even though the mistake may have been the actuating motive to the purchaser or seller, or both of them, yet the contract remains binding.... A barren cow is substantially a different creature than a breeding one.... She was not in fact the animal, or the kind of animal, the defendants had intended to sell or the plaintiff to buy." [a]

The court's distinction between "substance" and "quality" has not worn well. The Restatement Second speaks with disapproval of "such artificial and specious distinctions as are sometimes drawn between 'intrinsic' and 'extrinsic' mistakes or between mistakes that go to the 'identity' or 'existence' of the subject matter and those that go merely to its 'attributes,' 'quality' or 'value.'" Restatement Second § 154, Comment *a*. Section 152 asks instead whether the mistake is "as to a basic assumption on which the contract was made."

In 1982, nearly a century after it decided Sherwood v. Walker, the Supreme Court of Michigan abandoned the test of that case in favor of the Restatement Second's test in a case in which both buyer and seller of an apartment building mistakenly believed that the building was suitable for human habitation and would generate rental income. The court concluded that "the distinctions which may be drawn from *Sherwood* ... do not provide a satisfactory analysis of the nature of a mistake sufficient to invalidate a contract" and that "the better reasoned approach" is that of the Restatement Second. The court held, however, that the buyer bore the risk of this mistake because the contract contained an "as is" clause, stating that the buyer "has examined this property and agrees to accept the same in its present condition." Lenawee County Bd. of Health v. Messerly, 331 N.W.2d 203, 211 (Mich.1982).

Would the builder in Stees v. Leonard have been relieved of liability under the Restatement Second approach? Is that approach helpful in resolving the dispute in the following case? Is it clear that that dispute involves a risk resulting from existing circumstances rather than one resulting from changed circumstances?

a. There was a vigorous dissent.

Literati will want to consult Professor Brainerd Currie's ballad about Rose of Aberlone in Student Law., April 1956, 1965, p. 4, Harv.L.S.Record, March 4, 1954, p. 3. The final lines of this epic read:

> She rules the cases, she stalks the page
> Even in this atomic age.
> In radioactive tracts of land,
> In hardly collectible notes of hand,
> In fiddles of dubious pedigree,
> In releases of liability,
> In zoning rules unknown to lessors,
> In weird conceits of law professors,
> In printers' bids and ailing kings,
> In all mutations and sorts of things,
> In many a hypothetical
> With characters alphabetical,
> In many a subtle and sly disguise
> There lurks the ghost of her sad brown eyes.
> That she will turn up in some set of facts is
> Almost as certain as death and taxes:
> For students of law must still atone
> For the shame of Rose of Aberlone.

NOTES

(1) *Restatement Restrictions.* Restatement Second § 152(1) places this qualification on the power of the adversely affected party to avoid the contract: "unless he bears the risk of the mistake under the rule stated in § 154." In what circumstances would that party bear the risk of a mistake if the other requirements of § 152(1) are satisfied? Is the *Watkins* case an example? Comment *d* to § 154(c) gives this instance: it would generally be "reasonable in the circumstances" for a court to allocate the risk of mistake to a seller of farm land "who seeks to avoid the contract of sale on the ground that valuable mineral rights have been newly found."

Would it be equally plausible to say that the risk was allocated to the seller by the agreement? See § 154(a). Or that the seller was aware, in making the contract, of having limited knowledge on the subject of possible minerals, and treated that knowledge as sufficient? See § 154(b).

(2) *The Case of the One–Dollar Diamond.* Clarissa Wood found a pretty stone, about the size of a canary bird's egg. She did not know what it was. She showed it to Samuel Boynton, a jeweler, who bought it from her for a dollar, although he too did not know what it was. The stone turned out to be an uncut diamond worth an estimated $700. (Samuel had never seen an uncut diamond.) Clarissa tendered the price back and sued Samuel for rescission. Judgment for the defendant was affirmed on appeal. "There is no pretense of any mistake as to the identity of the thing sold.... When this sale was made the value of the thing sold was open to the investigation of both parties, neither knew its intrinsic value, and, so far as the evidence in this case shows, both supposed that the price paid was adequate." Wood v. Boynton, 25 N.W. 42 (Wis.1885).

In the Restatement Second, the "basic rule" for mistake of both parties "allows avoidance by the adversely affected party if the mistake was one as to a basic assumption on which the contract was made, if it had a material effect on the agreed exchange of performance, and if he does not bear the risk of the mistake." Chapter 16, Introductory Note; see also § 154. What element was missing in the diamond case? Is it possible that a *mistake* was missing? (If Clarissa and Samuel each knew that she or he did not know what the stone was, what was the mistake?) Compare Matter of Estates of Thompson, 601 P.2d 1105 (Kan.1979).

In both the diamond case and the cow case a dealer was the victor—either in claiming or in resisting relief. What reason might there be for favoring, in general, the person who is not a dealer in goods of the type concerned? That the dealer is a better risk-bearer? That the dealer has better access to information about the goods? Did any of the dealers seem to act as a *conscious* risk-taker? Any of the other parties?

(3) *Unilateral Mistake.* Is either the diamond case or the cow case difficult to square with the rule in Elsinore Union Elementary School District v. Kastorff, p. 171 above? If the jeweler had known that the stone was a diamond, and Sherwood had known that Rose was pregnant, the cases would have presented problems of unilateral mistake. Assuming those facts, would it be possible to justify a different result in either case? *Both* cases? On avoiding a contract for unilateral mistake see Restatement Second § 153.

(4) *The Bargain–Hunter's Case.* Professor Warren Seavey put the case of a second-hand book dealer who places a valuable first edition on a shelf of $5 books. He considered that a sale at that price should not be rescinded, at least if the customer was bargain hunting, and had no reason to suppose the book was

misplaced.　The case is one, he said, where the book dealer "matches his judgment against that of a purchaser."　But he added: "I would suppose that if a valuable first edition, by mistake of the bookseller's clerk, got mixed with a current cheap edition, the $5 purchaser would have to return it."　Op. cit. supra fn. d.　Problems in Restitution, 7 Okla.L.Rev. 257, 268 (1954).

THE DOVER POOL & RACQUET CLUB, INC. v. BROOKING

Supreme Judicial Court of Massachusetts, 1975.
366 Mass. 629, 322 N.E.2d 168.

BRAUCHER, JUSTICE.　On January 31, 1972, the parties entered into a written contract for the sale of real estate in Dover and Medfield.　A few days earlier, unknown to them, the planning board of Medfield had published a notice of a public hearing on a proposed amendment to the zoning by-law.　The proposed amendment would newly require a special permit for the use of the premises contemplated by both the vendor and the purchaser, and under G.L. c. 40A, § 11, the amendment if adopted would have effect retroactive to the date of publication.　The purchaser sought rescission of the contract and return of its deposit.　A judge of the Superior Court decreed rescission and return because of a mutual mistake of fact, and we affirm.

The case was referred to a master, whose report was confirmed except for its conclusions.　We summarize the master's findings.　The Brookings owned about fifty acres of land, nine acres in Medfield and the rest in Dover, used as a single family residence.　The buildings were in Dover, and the only established access was through the Medfield portion.　During negotiations with the purchaser (the Club) the Brookings were informed that the Club intended to use the property for a nonprofit tennis and swim club.

Both the Dover and the Medfield zoning by-laws permitted use of the premises as of right for a "club when not conducted for profit and not containing more than five sleeping rooms."　The parties discussed the zoning by-law of Dover.　The Brookings asked their broker about zoning, and he replied that everything would be all right under the existing Dover and Medfield by-laws.　The vice-president of the Club who signed the agreement checked both the Dover and the Medfield zoning by-laws.

The agreement, signed on January 31, 1972, provides for conveyance of "a good and clear record and marketable title thereto, free from encumbrances, except (a) Provisions of existing building and zoning laws...."　The planning board of Medfield on January 27 and February 3, 1972, published notice of a public hearing on February 14, 1972, on proposed amendments to the Medfield zoning by-law, including a requirement of a special permit for use of the Medfield portion of the premises as a "non-profit country, hunting, fishing, tennis or golf club without liquor license."　Neither of the parties was aware of the notice, but the Club's board of directors became aware of it about ten days before the agreed closing date of March 1, 1972. The parties met on the closing date, and the Brookings were prepared to deliver a deed, but the Club refused to proceed with the purchase. The proposed zoning amendment was adopted at the Medfield town meeting on March 21, 1972, and approved by the Attorney General in July, 1972.

In general building and zoning laws in existence at the time a land contract is signed are not treated as encumbrances, and the purchaser has no recourse against the vendor by virtue of restrictions imposed by such laws on the use of the property purchased.... Moreover, changes in such laws after the contract is signed have commonly been held to be part of the risk assumed by the purchaser.... In some such cases, however, specific performance at the suit of the vendor has been denied, particularly where both parties knew of the contemplated use later prohibited....

In the present case the agreement itself makes it explicit that "existing building and zoning laws" are not included in the vendor's obligation to convey "free from encumbrances." The Club argues, by contrasting the quoted exception with other exceptions,[1] that the building and zoning laws excepted are those "existing" on the date of the agreement, but we think it is clear that the reference is to laws "existing" on the date of the deed. Kares v. Covell, 180 Mass. 206, 209, 62 N.E. 244 (1902). In other words, the purchaser bore the risk of zoning laws in effect on the date of closing.

We have upheld a decree of rescission of a sale of land by reason of misrepresentations of the zoning situation by the vendors, and in doing so assumed that there would be no liability for bare nondisclosure. Kannavos v. Annino, 356 Mass. 42, 46–47, 247 N.E.2d 708 (1969) [p. 378 above].... In other States rescission has been decreed on the basis of mutual mistake of fact in circumstances like those before us.... We have long recognized that land contracts may be rescinded for mutual mistake.... But we seem not to have been called on to pass upon a mistake as to zoning.

The Medfield zoning amendment was not an "existing" zoning law at the time of the closing. It was not an encumbrance and it was not within the exception in the agreement. Yet under G.L. c. 40A, § 11, the notice published four days before the agreement was signed had a material impact on the purchaser's intended use of the premises. After the notice was published, the issuance of a building permit or the beginning of work on a building or structure would not protect the purchaser if the steps required for the adoption of the proposed amendment were taken in their usual sequence without unnecessary or unreasonable delay.... Meanwhile, no special permit could be issued under the proposed amendment before it was enacted. The agreement provides "that time is of the essence of this agreement," and the record

---

1. The agreement provides that the deed shall convey a title "free from encumbrances, except (a) Provisions of existing building and zoning laws; (b) [deleted]; (c) Such taxes for the then current year as are not due and payable on the date of the delivery of such deed; (d) Any liens for municipal betterments assessed after the date of this agreement; (e) None Other."

does not indicate any willingness by the vendor to extend the time for closing until after the town meeting which was to act on the proposed amendment. Under Harrison v. Building Inspector of Braintree, 350 Mass. 559, 561, 215 N.E.2d 773 (1966), use of the only established access to the premises might be barred if no special permit were obtained.

Thus at the time the contract was made both parties made the assumption that the zoning by-laws interposed no obstacle to the use of the premises for a non-profit tennis and swim club. That assumption was mistaken, and we think it was a basic assumption on which the contract was made. It could not yet be said that the purchaser's principal purpose had been frustrated. Cf. Restatement 2d: Contracts (Tent. Draft No. 9, April 8, 1974), § 286(2), and illustration 6.[a] But a right of vital importance to the purchaser did not exist, and as a result of the mistake enforcement of the contract would be materially more onerous to the purchaser than it would have been had the facts been as the parties believed them to be. The contract was therefore voidable by the purchaser unless it bore the risk of the mistake. The agreement does not provide for that risk, and the case is not one of conscious ignorance or deliberate risk-taking on the purchaser's part. Nor do we think there is any common understanding that purchasers take the risk of the unusual predicament in which the purchaser found itself. We therefore agree with the judge's conclusion that the contract was voidable for mutual mistake of fact.

Decree affirmed with costs of appeal.

NOTE

The Problem of the Putative Poussin. The Saint–Arromans, a French couple, inherited a painting attributed by family tradition to the great seventeenth century artist Nicolas Poussin. When they sought to sell it at auction, however, the auctioneers, after consulting an expert, concluded that it was by an unknown minor painter, not Poussin, and put it up for sale under the modest designation "school of the Carraci". At the sale, the musées nationaux, exercising their right of preemption, obtained the picture for the Louvre at the buyer's price of about $500. The painting was later authenticated as a Poussin by an expert connected with the Louvre and exhibited there as a Poussin. Other experts, however, continued to doubt this attribution, and the question remained in doubt. On these facts, can the Saint–Arromans recover the painting? See (Réunion des Musées Nationaux c/Saint–Arromans), Versailles, Jan. 7, 1987, Gaz.Pal.1987 Jur. 34—the last of six opinions which, nearly twenty years after the sale, finally resolved a dispute that, as one commentator wrote, "had caused more ink than paint to flow." Compare Firestone & Parson, Inc. v. Union League of Philadelphia, 672 F.Supp. 819 (E.D.Pa.1987).

---

a. The author of this opinion, when a professor at Harvard Law School, was Reporter for roughly half of the Restatement Second, not including the sections on mistake.

SECTION 2. IMPRACTICABILITY OF PERFORMANCE

Recall *Stees v. Leonard:* "If a man bind himself, by a positive, express contract, to do an act in itself possible, he must perform his engagement, unless prevented by the act of God, the law, or the other party to the contract. No hardship, no unforeseen hindrance, no difficulty short of absolute impossibility, will excuse him from doing what he has expressly agreed to do."

Of course there are many contractual undertakings that are not "absolute" in this sense. Take, for example, the obligations of Otis Wood and Falstaff Brewing to use reasonable efforts. In the rest of this chapter, however, we explore the limits of "absolute" undertakings. To what extent is even an "absolute" contractual undertaking affected by changed circumstances—by the occurrence of such an event after the contract is made?

English law began with the principle that agreements must be enforced—*pacta sunt servanda*. Over three centuries ago the King's Bench gave two justifications for this principle in Paradine v. Jane, Aleyn 26, 82 Eng.Rep. 897 (K.B.1647). The plaintiff sued on a lease, for three years' back rent on a place of business. The defendant's plea was that he had been dispossessed by a hostile army under Rupert—"a German prince, an alien born, enemy to the King and kingdom" [a]—and that during his ouster he could not take income from the premises. The court's conclusion was that he ought to pay his rent; the plea was bad. For one reason, the court said that, though the defendant was unable to prevent his eviction, "he might have provided against it in his contract." For another reason, the court added that "as the lessee is to have the advantage of casual profits, so he must run the hazard of casual losses." Evidently the court contemplated that some fortuitous event ("casualty") might have occurred during the term of the lease that would have increased markedly the value of the premises to the defendant. Nothing of that sort would have permitted the lessor to relet the premises, or to charge a higher rent. Hence—to draw out the court's reasoning—the contract imposed matching burdens on the parties. Both of these reasons are echoed in later cases and continue to be effective as argument, on occasion.

Paradine v. Jane has regularly been taken to mean that contract duties are "absolute," in the sense that no excuse based on change of conditions will be recognized.[b] If that was ever the rule, it has long been

a. This is a somewhat misleading characterization of Prince Rupert. The son of Frederick V of Bohemia and Elizabeth, daughter of James I of England, Rupert joined his uncle Charles I in England shortly before the outbreak of the Civil War in 1642 and later served as commander in chief of the King's armies. He was banished in 1646, the year before the decision in Paradine v. Jane, when the King surrendered, but served Charles II after he gained the throne in the Restoration of 1660.

b. Whether the case could have been understood that way when it was decided, or ever, is questionable. (See Note 1, p. 836 below.) Note that the changed circumstances did not prevent the lessee from performing, that is, paying rent, but only from using the leased property. As with

subject to some important qualifications. The scope and grounds of those qualifications are the subject of this section.

NOTE

Specific Result or Reasonable Efforts? Parties are not always explicit as to whether a duty is one to achieve a specific result or only one to use reasonable efforts to do so. The difference may be critical if changed circumstances make the achievement of the result more difficult. In City of Mounds View v. Walijarvi, 263 N.W.2d 420 (Minn.1978), the same court that decided Stees v. Leonard had this to say in rejecting the argument that an architect's undertaking was to achieve a specific result—an implied warranty that the structure was fit for its intended purpose:

"Architects, doctors, engineers, attorneys, and others deal in somewhat inexact sciences and are continually called upon to exercise their skilled judgment in order to anticipate and provide for random factors which are incapable of precise measurement. The indeterminate nature of these factors makes it impossible for professional service people to gauge them with complete accuracy in every instance. Thus, doctors cannot promise that every operation will be successful; a lawyer can never be certain that a contract he drafts is without latent ambiguity; and an architect cannot be certain that a structural design will interact with natural forces as anticipated. Because of the inescapable possibility of error which inheres in these services, the law has traditionally required, not perfect results, but rather the exercise of that skill and judgment which can be reasonably expected from similarly situated professionals."

For a different view, see Tamarac Development Co., Inc. v. Delamater, Freund & Associates, P.A., 675 P.2d 361 (Kan.1984), reasoning that the "work performed by architects and engineers is an exact science; that performed by doctors and lawyers is not."

Do professionals never undertake to achieve a specific result? See Sullivan v. O'Connor, p. 7 above. Do nonprofessionals always undertake to achieve a specific result? See Bloor v. Falstaff Brewing Corp., p. 623 above. Absent explicit provision, what factors other than professionalism might affect the classification? See Milau Associates, Inc. v. North Avenue Development Corp., 368 N.E.2d 1247 (N.Y.1977) (subcontractor that designed and installed sprinkler system not liable for breach of warranty since "those who hire experts for the predominant purpose of rendering services, relying on their special skills, cannot expect infallibility").

TAYLOR v. CALDWELL
King's Bench, 1863.
3 B. & S. 826, 122 Eng.Rep. 309.

[Action for breach of a written agreement by which defendants contracted to "let" the Surrey Gardens and Music Hall, at Newington, Surrey, to plaintiffs, for four days, for the purpose of giving four "grand concerts" and "day and night fêtes" in the hall; plaintiffs agreeing to pay £100 at the close of each day. The defendants agreed to furnish a band and certain other amusements in connection with plaintiffs' enter-

many an early text, however, its importance
resides chiefly in its interpretation.

tainments, but the plaintiffs were to have all moneys paid for entrance to the music hall and gardens. The plaintiffs alleged the defendants' breach, "Whereby the plaintiffs lost divers moneys paid by them for printing advertisements of and in advertising the concerts, and also lost divers sums expended and expenses incurred by them in preparing for the concerts and otherwise in relation thereto, and on the faith of the performance by the defendants of the agreement on their part". The defendants pleaded that the Gardens and Music Hall were accidentally destroyed by fire on June 11, 1861, without the default of the defendants or either of them. A verdict was returned for the plaintiffs, with leave reserved to enter a verdict for defendants.]

BLACKBURN, J. In this case the plaintiffs and defendants had, on the 27th May, 1861, entered into a contract by which the defendants agreed to let the plaintiffs have the use of The Surrey Gardens and Music Hall on four days then to come, viz., the 17th June, 15th July, 5th August and 19th August, for the purpose of giving a series of four grand concerts, and day and night fêtes at the Gardens and Hall on those days respectively; and the plaintiffs agreed to take the Gardens and Hall on those days, and pay £100 for each day.

[The court interpreted the agreement not to be a lease, and concluded that the entertainments provided for in the agreement could not be given without the existence of the Music Hall.]

After the making of the agreement, and before the first day on which a concert was to be given, the Hall was destroyed by fire. This destruction, we must take it on the evidence, was without the fault of either party, and was so complete that in consequence the concerts could not be given as intended. And the question we have to decide is whether, under these circumstances, the loss which the plaintiffs have sustained is to fall upon the defendants. The parties when framing their agreement evidently had not present to their minds the possibility of such a disaster, and have made no express stipulation with reference to it, so that the answer to the question must depend upon the general rules of law applicable to such a contract.

There seems no doubt that where there is a positive contract to do a thing, not in itself unlawful, the contractor must perform it or pay damages for not doing it, although in consequence of unforeseen accidents, the performance of his contract has become unexpectedly burdensome or even impossible. The law is so laid down in 1 Roll.Abr. 450, Condition (G), and in the note (2) to Walton v. Waterhouse, 2 Wms. Saund. 421a. 6th Ed., and is recognised as the general rule by all the Judges in the much discussed case of Hall v. Wright (E.B. & E. 746). But this rule is only applicable when the contract is positive and absolute, and not subject to any condition either express or implied: and there are authorities which, as we think, establish the principle that where, from the nature of the contract, it appears that the parties must from the beginning have known that it could not be fulfilled unless when the time for the fulfillment of the contract arrived some particular specified thing continued to exist, so that, when entering into the contract, they must have contemplated such continuing existence as the foundation of what was to be done; there, in the absence of any express or implied warranty that the thing shall exist, the contract is not to be construed as a positive contract, but as subject to an implied condition that the parties shall be excused in case, before breach, performance becomes impossible from the perishing of the thing without default of the contractor.

There seems little doubt that this implication tends to further the great object of making the legal construction such as to fulfil the intention of those who entered into the contract. For in the course of affairs men in making such contracts in general would if it were brought to their minds, say that there should be such a condition.

Accordingly, in the Civil law, such an exception is implied in every obligation of the class which they call obligatio de certo corpore. The rule is laid down in the Digest, lib. XLV, tit. 1, de verborum obligationibus, 1.33. "Si Stichus certo die dari promissus, ante diem moriatur: non tenetur promissor." The principle is more fully developed in 1.23. "Si ex legati causa, aut ex stipulatu hominem certum mihi debeas: non aliter post mortem ejus tenearis mihi, quam si per te steterit, quominus vivo eo eum mihi dares: quod ita fit, si aut interpellatus non dedisti, aut occidisti eum." The examples are of contracts respecting a slave, which was the common illustration of a certain subject used by the Roman lawyers, just as we are apt to take a horse; and no doubt the propriety, one might almost say necessity, of the implied condition is more obvious when the contract relates to a living animal, whether man or brute, than when it relates to some inanimate thing (such as in the present case a theatre) the existence of which is not so obviously precarious as that of the live animal, but the principle is adopted in the Civil law as applicable to every obligation of which the subject is a certain thing. The general subject is treated of by Pothier, who in his Traite des Obligations, partie 3, chap. 6, art. 3, sec. 668, states the result to be that the debtor corporis certi is freed from his obligation when the thing has perished, neither by his act, nor his neglect, and before he is in default, unless by some stipulation he has taken on himself the risk of the particular misfortune which has occurred.[a]

Although the Civil law is not of itself authority in an English Court, it affords great assistance in investigating the principles on which the law is grounded. And it seems to us that the common law authorities establish that in such a contract the same condition of the continued existence of the thing is implied by English law.

There is a class of contracts in which a person binds himself to do something which requires to be performed by him in person; and such promises, e.g. promises to marry, or promises to serve for a certain time, are never in practice qualified by an express exception of the death of the party; and therefore in such cases the contract is in terms broken if the

a. For a criticism of the Roman law authorities relied upon by Blackburn, J., see Buckland, *Casus* and Frustration in Ro- man and Common Law, 46 Harv.L.Rev. 1281, 1287–89 (1933).

promisor dies before fulfilment. Yet it was very early determined that, if the performance is personal, the executors are not liable; Hyde v. The Dean of Windsor (Cro.Eliz. 552, 553). See 2 Wms. Exors. 1560, 5th Ed., where a very apt illustration is given. "Thus," says the learned author, "if an author undertakes to compose a work, and dies before completing it, his executors are discharged from this contract: for the undertaking is merely personal in its nature, and, by the intervention of the contractor's death, has become impossible to be performed." ...

These are instances where the implied condition is of the life of a human being, but there are others in which the same implication is made as to the continued existence of a thing. For example, where a contract of sale is made amounting to a bargain and sale, transferring presently the property in specific chattels, which are to be delivered by the vendor at a future day; there, if the chattels, without the fault of the vendor, perish in the interval, the purchaser must pay the price and the vendor is excused from performing his contract to deliver, which has thus become impossible.

[In Williams v. Lloyd W. Jones, 179] the count, which was in assumpsit, alleged that the plaintiff had delivered a horse to the defendant, who promised to redeliver it on request. Breach, that though requested to redeliver the horse he refused. Plea, that the horse was sick and died, and the plaintiff made the request after its death; and on demurrer it was held a good plea, as the bailee was discharged from his promise by the death of the horse without default or negligence on the part of the defendant. "Let it be admitted," say the Court "that he promised to deliver it on request, if the horse die before, that is become impossible by the act of God, so the party shall be discharged as much as if an obligation were made conditioned to deliver the horse on request, and he died before it." [b]

It may, we think, be safely asserted to be now English law, that in all contracts of loan of chattels or bailments if the performance of the promise of the borrower or bailee to return the things lent or bailed, becomes impossible because it [sic] has perished, this impossibility (if not arising from the fault of the borrower or bailee from some risk which he has taken upon himself) excuses the borrower or bailee from the performance of his promise to redeliver the chattel.

The great case of Coggs v. Bernard (1 Smith's L.C. 171, 5th ed.; 2 L.Raym. 909) is now the leading case on the law of bailments, and Lord Holt, in that case, referred so much to the Civil law that it might perhaps be thought that this principle was there delivered direct from the civilians, and was not generally applicable in English law except in the case of bailments; but the case of Williams v. Lloyd (W. Jones, 179), above cited, shows that the same law had been already adopted by the English law as early as The Book of Assizes. The principle seems to us to be that, in contracts in which the performance depends on the

b. But at an earlier period the bailee was not excused. O.W. Holmes, The Common Law 176 et seq. (1881).

continued existence of a given person or thing, a condition is implied that the impossibility of performance arising from the perishing of the person or thing shall excuse the performance.

In none of these cases is the promise in words other than positive, nor is there any express stipulation that the destruction of the person or thing shall excuse the performance; but that excuse is by law implied, because from the nature of the contract it is apparent that the parties contracted on the basis of the continued existence of the particular person or chattel. In the present case, looking at the whole contract, we find that the parties contracted on the basis of the continued existence of the Music Hall at the time when the concerts were to be given; that being essential to their performance.

We think, therefore, that the Music Hall having ceased to exist, without fault of either party, both parties are excused, the plaintiffs from taking the gardens and paying the money, the defendants from performing their promise to give the use of the Hall and Gardens and other things. Consequently the rule must be absolute to enter the verdict for the defendants.

Rule absolute.

NOTES

(1) *The Doctrine of Implied Conditions.* A seller of jute contended that its performance had become impossible because of a wartime order prohibiting shipment. The contract provided for arbitration of "any dispute that may arise under this contract." When arbitrators were appointed, the seller brought an action for a declaration that the issue of impossibility was not within their jurisdiction.

Lord Sands of the Court of Session in Edinburgh wrote an opinion in which he observed that the House of Lords had steadily expounded the law of impossibility by reference to an express or implied condition in the contract itself. He continued as follows: "Mr. Chree [counsel for the seller] argued that this is a pious fiction—a fiction because it does not correspond with anything that was in the minds of parties at the time; pious because it seeks to do homage to a very sacred legal principle, the sanctity of contract. I confess I have some sympathy with Mr. Chree. It does seem to me somewhat far-fetched to hold that the non-occurrence of some event, which was not within the contemplation or even the imagination of the parties, was an implied term of the contract.... No doubt this theory has been developed to square with the rule of the English common law in regard to supervening impossibility. A tiger has escaped from a travelling menagerie. The milkgirl fails to deliver the milk. Possibly the milkman may be exonerated from any breach of contract; but, even so, it would seem hardly reasonable to base that exoneration on the ground that 'tiger days excepted' must be held as if written into the milk contract. But though I sympathise with Mr. Chree's difficulty I am unable to adopt his reasoning." Lord Sands concluded that a question about an implied term was one which "arose under" the contracts, so that the arbiters had jurisdiction. Scott & Sons v. Del Sel, 1922 Sess.Cas. 592, 596–97, aff'd, 1923 Sess.Cas. (H.L.) 37.

The Restatement Second approaches the matter in the following way: "An extraordinary circumstance may make performance so vitally different from what was reasonably to be expected as to alter the essential nature of that performance. In such a case the court must determine whether justice requires a departure from the general rule that the obligor bear the risk that the contract may become more burdensome or less desirable. This Chapter is concerned with the principles that guide that determination.... In recent years courts have shown increasing liberality in discharging obligors on the basis of such extraordinary circumstances." Restatement Second, Introductory Note to Chapter 11.

(2) *Death and Illness.* Just as a duty such as that in Taylor v. Caldwell may be discharged by the destruction of a thing, a duty to perform a "personal" service (one that cannot be delegated to another to perform) is usually excused when the person to perform suffers death or injury. So, in Oneal v. Colton Consolidated School District No. 306, 557 P.2d 11 (Wash.App.1976), a school teacher's duty was discharged by deterioration of his vision. Not only illness but the "apprehension" of illness may excuse. See Wasserman Theatrical Enterprise, Inc. v. Harris, 77 A.2d 329 (Conn.1950), in which Walter Huston, the actor, was excused from appearing on stage because of a minor throat ailment.

A party who wilfully disables himself or herself is, however, in no position to claim excuse. "Some day it may have to be finally determined whether a *prima donna* is excused by complete loss of voice from an executory contract to sing if it is proved that her condition was caused by her carelessness in not changing her wet clothes after being out in the rain." Viscount Simon, in Joseph Constantine Steamship Line v. Imperial Smelting Corp., [1942] A.C. 154, [1941] 2 All E.R. 165.

LOSS IN RELATION TO SALES

Suppose that goods that are the subject of a contract of sale are lost or damaged without fault. It is, of course, common to insure against such risks. But insurance aside, how does the loss affect the rights of the parties? To answer this question, it must first be determined whether risk of loss has passed from the seller to the buyer, a question that is dealt with in UCC 2–509 and 2–510 and that must be left for a later course in sales or commercial law.

If risk has passed, UCC 2–709(1)(a) generally gives the seller the right to the price, just as if the seller had performed the contract without incident. The buyer must pay for the lost or damaged goods and has no possibility of recovering damages. If risk has not passed, however, the seller has no right to the price. The buyer not only need not pay for the lost or damaged goods but has a possibility of recovering damages.

Whether the buyer can recover damages turns on whether the seller can take advantage of UCC 2–613, a provision that shows the ancestry of Taylor v. Caldwell. Note that it does not apply to the usual contract for sale of goods to be produced or procured by the seller or even of goods to be selected from a stock of merchandise. Unless the goods are "identified when the contract is made," UCC 2–613 affords no relief. It would not, then, help a seller of a carload of alfalfa seed even if a flood destroyed all the seed in the vicinity—unless, to be sure, the particular carload had been picked out when the contract was made. (As to "identification," see UCC 2–501(1).) The possible impact of UCC 2–615 can be considered in connection with the next case.

NOTE

A Visit to the Farm. Ray Colley, an experienced wheat farmer, contracted in April 1974 to deliver 25,000 bushels of wheat to Bi–State, Inc. in July or August. He believed that prices, then high, would drop by harvest time, and he expected a bumper crop from his spring planting. Both expectations failed. June was particularly hot and dry, and his deliveries fell nearly 20,000 bushels short. Bi–State had committed the wheat to an exporter, and it incurred substantial expense, including the cost of cover, to extricate itself. When Colley sued it for the price of wheat he had delivered, Bi–State counterclaimed for this expense. Its buying agent testified that he felt Colley was probably selling wheat he planned to harvest from his farm, but that he (the agent) would not agree to buy wheat grown on specified property. Farmers and grain dealers from the area testified that, "under existing custom and trade usage, such agreements were never contingent upon the success of the seller's crop." The trial court gave judgment in favor of Bi–State on the counterclaim, and it was affirmed on appeal. Colley v. Bi–State, Inc., 586 P.2d 908 (Wash.App.1978).

In another crop-failure case, Unke v. Thorpe, 59 N.W.2d 419 (S.D.1953), the contract was for the sale of 600–800 bushels of alfalfa seed. The seller-farmer offered testimony that the agreement was executed at the seller's farm, after the buyer had inspected his operations. The buyer testified to a conversation between the parties in which he insisted on a quantity term and explained that he intended to resell against the contract. Should any of this testimony be excluded? If so, how does it differ from the testimony in Colley's case? Each item might shed light on the "basic assumptions" of the contract in issue, might it not? Nevertheless, in Unke v. Thorpe, evidence of the conversation was thought to be inadmissible, at least in part, given the written agreement.

Comment 9 after UCC 2–615 is as follows: "The case of a farmer who has contracted to sell crops to be grown on designated land may be regarded as falling either within the section on casualty to identified goods or this section, and he may be excused, when there is a failure of the specific crop, either on the basis of the destruction of identified goods or because of the failure of a basic assumption of the contract." Is this assertion incompatible with the case above?

TRANSATLANTIC FINANCING CORPORATION
v. UNITED STATES

United States Court of Appeals, D.C.Circuit, 1966.
363 F.2d 312.

J. SKELLY WRIGHT, CIRCUIT JUDGE. This appeal involves a voyage charter between Transatlantic Financing Corporation, operator of the SS CHRISTOS, and the United States covering carriage of a full cargo of wheat from a United States Gulf port to a safe port in Iran. The District Court dismissed a libel filed by Transatlantic against the United States for costs attributable to the ship's diversion from the normal sea route caused by the closing of the Suez Canal. We affirm.

On July 26, 1956, the Government of Egypt nationalized the Suez Canal Company and took over operation of the Canal. On October 2, 1956, during the international crisis which resulted from the seizure, the voyage charter in suit was executed between representatives of Transatlantic and the United States. The charter indicated the termini of the voyage but not the route. On October 27, 1956, the SS CHRISTOS sailed from Galveston for Bandar Shapur, Iran, on a course which would have taken her through Gibraltar and the Suez Canal. On October 29, 1956, Israel invaded Egypt. On October 31, 1956, Great Britain and France invaded the Suez Canal Zone. On November 2, 1956, the Egyptian Government obstructed the Suez Canal with sunken vessels and closed it to traffic.

On or about November 7, 1956, Beckmann, representing Transatlantic, contacted Potosky, an employee of the United States Department of Agriculture, who appellant concedes was unauthorized to bind the Government, requesting instructions concerning disposition of the cargo and seeking an agreement for payment of additional compensation for a voyage around the Cape of Good Hope. Potosky advised Beckmann that Transatlantic was expected to perform the charter according to its terms, that he did not believe Transatlantic was entitled to additional compensation for a voyage around the Cape, but that Transatlantic was free to file such a claim. Following this discussion, the CHRISTOS changed course for the Cape of Good Hope and eventually arrived in Bandar Shapur on December 30, 1956.

Transatlantic's claim is based on the following train of argument. The charter was a contract for a voyage from a Gulf port to Iran. Admiralty principles and practices, especially stemming from the doctrine of deviation, require us to imply into the contract the term that the voyage was to be performed by the "usual and customary" route. The usual and customary route from Texas to Iran was, at the time of contract, via Suez, so the contract was for a voyage from Texas to Iran via Suez. When Suez was closed this contract became impossible to perform. Consequently, appellant's argument continues, when Transatlantic delivered the cargo by going around the Cape of Good Hope, in compliance with the Government's demand under claim of right, it conferred a benefit upon the United States for which it should be paid in *quantum meruit*.

The doctrine of impossibility of performance has gradually been freed from the earlier fictional and unrealistic strictures of such tests as the "implied term" and the parties' "contemplation." Page, The Development of the Doctrine of Impossibility of Performance, 18 Mich.L.Rev. 589, 596 (1920). See generally 6 Corbin, Contracts §§ 1320–1372 (rev. ed. 1962); 6 Williston, Contracts §§ 1931–1979 (rev. ed. 1938). It is now recognized that " 'A thing is impossible in legal contemplation when it is not practicable; and a thing is impracticable when it can only be done at an excessive and unreasonable cost.' " Mineral Park Land Co. v. Howard, 172 Cal. 289, 293, 156 P. 458, 460, L.R.A.1916F, 1 (1916). Accord, Whelan v. Griffith Consumers Company, D.C.Mun.App., 170 A.2d 229 (1961); Restatement, Contracts § 454 (1932); Uniform Commercial Code (U.L.A.) § 2–615, comment 3. The doctrine ultimately represents the ever-shifting line, drawn by courts hopefully responsive to commercial practices and mores, at which the community's interest in having contracts enforced according to their terms is outweighed by the commercial senselessness of requiring performance.[1] When the issue is raised, the court is asked to construct a condition of performance [2] based on the changed circumstances, a process which involves at least three reasonably definable steps. First, a contingency—something unexpected—must have occurred. Second, the risk of the unexpected occurrence must not have been allocated either by agreement or by custom. Finally, occurrence of the contingency must have rendered performance commercially impracticable.[3] Unless the court finds these three requirements satisfied, the plea of impossibility must fail.

The first requirement was met here. It seems reasonable, where no route is mentioned in a contract, to assume the parties expected performance by the usual and customary route at the time of contract.[4] Since the usual and customary route from Texas to Iran at the time of contract [5] was through Suez, closure of the Canal made impossible the

1. While the impossibility issue rarely arises, as it has here, in a suit to recover the cost of an alternative method of performance, compare Annot., 84 A.L.R.2d 12, 19 (1962), there is nothing necessarily inconsistent in claiming commercial impracticability for the method of performance actually adopted; the concept of impracticability assumes performance was physically possible. Moreover, a rule making nonperformance a condition precedent to recovery would unjustifiably encourage disappointment of expectations.

2. Patterson, Constructive Conditions in Contracts, 42 Colum.L.Rev. 903, 943–954 (1942).

3. Compare Uniform Commercial Code § 2–615(a), which provides that, in the absence of an assumption of greater liability, delay or non-delivery by a seller is not a breach if performance as agreed is made "impracticable" by the occurrence of a "contingency" the non-occurrence of which was a "basic assumption on which the contract was made." To the extent this limits relief to "unforeseen" circumstances, comment 1, see the discussion below, and compare Uniform Commercial Code § 2–614(1). There may be a point beyond which agreement cannot go, Uniform Commercial Code § 2–615, comment 8, presumably the point at which the obligation would be "manifestly unreasonable," § 1–102(3), in bad faith, § 1–203, or unconscionable, § 2–302. For an application of these provisions see Judge Friendly's opinion in United States v. Wegematic Corporation, 2 Cir., 360 F.2d 674 (1966).

4. Uniform Commercial Code § 2–614, comment 1, states: "Under this Article, in the absence of specific agreement, the normal or usual facilities enter into the agreement either through the circumstances, usage of trade or prior course of dealing." So long as this sort of assumption does not necessarily result in construction of a condition of performance, it is idle to argue over whether the usual and customary route is an "implied term." The issue of impracticability must eventually be met. One court refused to imply the Suez route as a contract term, but went on to rule the contract had been "frustrated." Carapanayoti & Co. Ltd. v. E.T. Green Ltd., [1959] 1 Q.B. 131. The holding was later rejected by the House of Lords. Tsakiroglou & Co. Ltd. v. Noblee Thorl G.m.b.H., [1960] 2 Q.B. 348.

5. The parties have spent considerable energy in disputing whether the "usual and customary" route by which performance was anticipated is defined as of the time of contract or of performance. If we were automatically to treat the expected route as a condition of performance, this matter would be crucial, and we would be compelled to choose between unacceptable alternatives. If we assume as a constructive condition the usual and customary course always to mean the one in use at the time of contract, any substantial diversion (we assume the diversion would have to be substantial) would nullify the contract even though its effect upon the rights and obligations of the parties is insignificant. Nor would it be desirable, on the other hand, to assume performance is conditioned on the availability of *any* usual and customary route at the time of performance. It may be that very often the availability of a customary route at the time of performance other than the route expected to be used at the time of contract should result in denial of relief under the impossibility theory; certainly if *no* customary route is available at the time of performance the contract is rendered impossible. But the same customarily used alternative route may be practicable in one set of circumstances and impracticable in another, as where the goods

expected method of performance. But this unexpected development raises rather than resolves the impossibility issue, which turns additionally on whether the risk of the contingency's occurrence had been allocated and, if not, whether performance by alternative routes was rendered impracticable.[6]

Proof that the risk of a contingency's occurrence has been allocated may be expressed in or implied from the agreement. Such proof may also be found in the surrounding circumstances, including custom and usages of the trade. See 6 Corbin, *supra*, § 1339, at 394–397; 6 Williston, *supra*, § 1948, at 5457–5458. The contract in this case does not expressly condition performance upon availability of the Suez route. Nor does it specify "via Suez" or, on the other hand, "via Suez or Cape of Good Hope."[7] Nor are there provisions in the contract from which we may properly imply that the continued availability of Suez was a condition of performance.[8] Nor is there anything in custom or trade

are unable to survive the extra journey. Moreover, the "time of performance" is no special point in time; it is every moment in a performance. Thus the alternative route, in our case around the Cape, may be practicable at some time during performance, for example while the vessel is still in the Atlantic Ocean, and impracticable at another time during performance, for example after the vessel has traversed most of the Mediterranean Sea. Both alternatives, therefore, have their shortcomings, and we avoid choosing between them by refusing automatically to treat the usual and customary route as of any time as a condition of performance.

6. In criticizing the "contemplation" test for impossibility Professor Patterson pointed out: " 'Contemplation' is appropriate to describe the mental state of philosophers but is scarcely descriptive of the mental state of business men making a bargain. It seems preferable to say that the promisee *expects* performance by [the] means ... the promisor expects to (or which on the facts known to the promisee it is probable that he will) use. It does not follow as an inference of fact that the promisee expects performance by *only* that means...." Patterson, *supra* Note 2, at 947.

7. In Glidden Company v. Hellenic Lines, Limited, 2 Cir., 275 F.2d 253 (1960), the charter was for transportation of materials from India to America "via Suez Canal or Cape of Good Hope, or Panama Canal," and the court held performance was not "frustrated." In his discussion of this case, Professor Corbin states: "Except for the provision for an alternative route, the defendant would have been discharged, for the reason that the parties contemplated an open Suez Canal as a specific condition or means of performance." 6 Corbin, *supra*, § 1339, at 399 n. 57. Appellant claims this

supports its argument, since the Suez route was contemplated as usual and customary. But there is obviously a difference, in deciding whether a contract allocates the risk of a contingency's occurrence, between a contract specifying no route and a contract specifying Suez. We think that when Professor Corbin said, "Except for the provision for an alternative route," he was referring, not to the entire *provision*—"via Suez Canal or Cape of Good Hope" etc.—but to the fact that *an alternative route* had been provided for. Moreover, in determining what Corbin meant when he said "the parties contemplated an open Suez Canal as a specific condition or means of performance," consideration must be given to the fact, recited by Corbin, that in *Glidden* the parties were specifically aware when the contract was made the Canal might be closed, and the promisee had refused to include a clause excusing performance in the event of closure. Corbin's statement, therefore, is most accurately read as referring to cases in which a route is specified after negotiations reflecting the parties' awareness that the usual and customary route might become unavailable. Compare Held v. Goldsmith, 153 La. 598, 96 So. 272 (1919).

8. The charter provides that the vessel is "in every way fitted for *the voyage*" (emphasis added), and the "P. & I. Bunker Deviation Clause" refers to "the contract voyage" and the "direct and/or customary route." Appellant argues that these provisions require implication of a voyage by the direct and customary route. Actually they prove only what we are willing to accept— that the parties expected the usual and customary route would be used. The provisions in no way condition performance upon nonoccurrence of this contingency.

usage, or in the surrounding circumstances generally, which would support our constructing a condition of performance. The numerous cases requiring performance around the Cape when Suez was closed, see e.g., Ocean Tramp Tankers Corp. v. V/O Sovfracht (The Eugenia), [1964] 2 Q.B. 226, and cases cited therein, indicate that the Cape route is generally regarded as an alternative means of performance. So the implied expectation that the route would be via Suez is hardly adequate proof of an allocation to the promisee of the risk of closure. In some cases, even an express expectation may not amount to a condition of performance.[9] The doctrine of deviation supports our assumption that parties normally expect performance by the usual and customary route, but it adds nothing beyond this that is probative of an allocation of the risk.[10]

If anything, the circumstances surrounding this contract indicate that the risk of the Canal's closure may be deemed to have been allocated to Transatlantic. We know or may safely assume that the

There are two clauses which allegedly demonstrate that time is of importance in this contract. One clause computes the remuneration "in steaming time" for diversions to other countries ordered by the charterer in emergencies. This proves only that the United States wished to reserve power to send the goods to another country. It does not imply in any way that either was in a rush about the matter. The other clause concerns demurrage and despatch. The charterer agreed to pay Transatlantic demurrage of $1,200 per day for all time in excess of the period agreed upon for loading and unloading, and Transatlantic was to pay despatch of $600 per day for any saving in time. Of course this provision shows the parties were concerned about time, see Gilmore & Black, The Law of Admiralty § 4–8 (1957), but the fact that they arranged so minutely the consequences of any delay or speedup of loading and unloading operates against the argument that they were similarly allocating the risk of delay or speed-up of the voyage.

9. Uniform Commercial Code § 2–614(1) provides: "Where without fault of either party ... the *agreed* manner of delivery ... becomes commercially impracticable but a commercially reasonable substitute is available, such substitute performance must be tendered and accepted." (Emphasis added.) Compare Mr. Justice Holmes' observation: "You can give any conclusion a logical form. You always can imply a condition in a contract. But why do you imply it? It is because of some belief as to the practice of the community or of a class, or because of some opinion as to policy...." Holmes, The Path of the Law, 10 Harv. L.Rev. 457, 466 (1897).

10. The deviation doctrine, drawn principally from admiralty insurance practice, implies into all relevant commercial instruments naming the termini of voyages the usual and customary route between those points. 1 Arnould, Marine Insurance and Average § 376, at 522 (10th ed. 1921). Insurance is cancelled when a ship unreasonably "deviates" from this course, for example by extending a voyage or by putting in at an irregular port, and the shipowner forfeits the protection of clauses of exception which might otherwise have protected him from his common law insurer's liability to cargo. See Gilmore & Black, supra Note 8, § 2–6, at 59–60. This practice, properly qualified, see id. § 3–41, makes good sense, since insurance rates are computed on the basis of the implied course, and deviations in the course increasing the anticipated risk make the insurer's calculations meaningless. Arnould, supra, § 14, at 26. Thus the route, so far as insurance contracts are concerned, is crucial, whether express or implied. But even here, the implied term is not inflexible. Reasonable deviations do not result in loss of insurance, at least so long as established practice is followed. See Carriage of Goods by Sea Act § 4(4), 49 Stat. 1210, 46 U.S.C.A. § 1304(4); and discussion of "held covered" clauses in Gilmore & Black, supra, § 3–41, at 161. Some "deviations" are required. E.g., Hirsch Lumber Co. v. Weyerhaeuser Steamship Co., 233 F.2d 791 (2d Cir.1956), cert. denied, 352 U.S. 880, 77 S.Ct. 102, 1 L.Ed.2d 80. The doctrine's only relevance, therefore, is that it provides additional support for the assumption we willingly make that merchants agreeing to a voyage between two points expect that the usual and customary route between those points will be used. The doctrine provides no evidence of an allocation of the risk of the route's unavailability.

parties were aware, as were most commercial men with interests affected by the Suez situation, see The Eugenia, supra, that the Canal might become a dangerous area. No doubt the tension affected freight rates, and it is arguable that the risk of closure became part of the dickered terms. Uniform Commercial Code § 2–615, comment 8. We do not deem the risk of closure so allocated, however. Foreseeability or even recognition of a risk does not necessarily prove its allocation.[11] Compare Uniform Commercial Code § 2–615, Comment 1; Restatement, Contracts § 457 (1932). Parties to a contract are not always able to provide for all the possibilities of which they are aware, sometimes because they cannot agree, often simply because they are too busy. Moreover, that some abnormal risk was contemplated is probative but does not necessarily establish an allocation of the risk of the contingency which actually occurs. In this case, for example, nationalization by Egypt of the Canal Corporation and formation of the Suez Users Group did not necessarily indicate that the Canal would be blocked even if a confrontation resulted.[12] The surrounding circumstances do indicate, however, a willingness by Transatlantic to assume abnormal risks, and this fact should legitimately cause us to judge the impracticability of performance by an alternative route in stricter terms than we would were the contingency unforeseen.

We turn then to the question whether occurrence of the contingency rendered performance commercially impracticable under the circumstances of this case. The goods shipped were not subject to harm from the longer, less temperate Southern route. The vessel and crew were fit to proceed around the Cape.[13] Transatlantic was no less able than the United States to purchase insurance to cover the contingency's occurrence. If anything, it is more reasonable to expect owner-operators of vessels to insure against the hazards of war. They are in the best position to calculate the cost of performance by alternative routes (and therefore to estimate the amount of insurance required), and are undoubtedly sensitive to international troubles which uniquely affect the demand for and cost of their services. The only factor operating here in appellant's favor is the added expense, allegedly $43,972.00 above and beyond the contract price of $305,842.92, of extending a 10,000 mile

---

11. See Note, The Fetish of Impossibility in the Law of Contracts, 53 Colum.L.Rev. 94, 98 n. 23 (1953), suggesting that foreseeability is properly used "as a *factor* probative of assumption of the risk of impossibility." (Emphasis added.)

12. Sources cited in the briefs indicate formation of the Suez Canal Users Association on October 1, 1956, was viewed in some quarters as an implied threat of force. See N.Y. Times, Oct. 2, 1956, p. 1, col. 1, noting, on the day the charter in this case was executed, that "Britain has declared her freedom to use force as a last resort if peaceful methods fail to achieve a satisfactory settlement." Secretary of State Dulles was able, however, to view the statement as evidence of the canal users' "dedication to a just and peaceful solution." The Suez Problem 369–370 (Department of State Pub. 1956).

13. The issue of impracticability should no doubt be "an objective determination of whether the promise can reasonably be performed rather than a subjective inquiry into the promisor's capability of performing as agreed." Symposium, The Uniform Commercial Code and Contract Law: Some Selected Problems, 105 U.Pa.L.Rev. 836, 880, 887 (1957). Dealers should not be excused because of less than normal capabilities. But if both parties are aware of a dealer's limited capabilities, no objective determination would be complete without taking into account this fact.

voyage by approximately 3,000 miles. While it may be an overstatement to say that increased cost and difficulty of performance never constitute impracticability, to justify relief there must be more of a variation between expected cost and the cost of performing by an available alternative than is present in this case,[14] where the promisor can legitimately be presumed to have accepted some degree of abnormal risk, and where impracticability is urged on the basis of added expense alone.[15]

We conclude, therefore, as have most other courts considering related issues arising out of the Suez closure,[16] that performance of this contract was not rendered legally impossible. Even if we agreed with appellant, its theory of relief seems untenable. When performance of a contract is deemed impossible it is a nullity. In the case of a charter party involving carriage of goods, the carrier may return to an appropri-

---

14. Two leading English cases support this conclusion. The Eugenia, supra, involved a time charter for a trip from Genoa to India via the Black Sea. The charterers were held in breach of the charter's war clause by entering the Suez Canal after the outbreak of hostilities, but sought to avoid paying for the time the vessel was trapped in the Canal by arguing that, even if they had not entered the Canal, it would have been blocked and the vessel would have had to go around the Cape to India, a trip which "frustrated" the contract because it constituted an entirely different venture from the one originally contemplated. The lower court agreed, but the House of Lords (see Lord Denning's admirable treatment, [1964] 2 Q.B. at 233), "swallowing" the difficulty of applying the frustration doctrine to hypothetical facts, reversed, holding that the contract had to be performed. Especially relevant is the fact that the case expressly overruled Societe Franco Tunisienne D'Armement v. Sidermar S.P.A. (The Massalia), [1961] 2 Q.B. 278, where a voyage charter was deemed frustrated because the Cape route was "highly circuitous" and cost 195s. per long ton to ship iron ore, rather than 134s. via Suez, a difference well in excess of the difference in this case.

In Tsakiroglou & Co. Ltd. v. Noblee Thorl G.m.b.H., supra Note 4, the difference to the seller under a C.I.F. contract in freight costs caused by the Canal's closure was £15 per ton instead of £7.10s. per ton—precisely twice the cost. The House of Lords found no frustration.

15. See Uniform Commercial Code § 2-615, comment 4: "Increased cost alone does not excuse performance unless the rise in cost is due to some unforeseen contingency which alters the essential nature of the performance." See also 6 Corbin, supra, § 1333; 6 Williston, supra, § 1952, at 5468.

16. Appellant seeks to distinguish the English cases supporting our view. The Eugenia, supra, appellant argues, involved a time charter. True, but it overruled The Massalia, supra Note 14, which involved a voyage charter. Indeed, when the time charter is for a voyage the difference is only verbal. See Carver, Carriage of Goods by Sea 256–257 (10th ed. 1957). More convincing is the argument that Tsakiroglou & Co. Ltd., supra Note 4, involved a contract for the sale of goods, where the seller agreed to a C.I.F. clause requiring him to ship the goods to the buyer. There is a significant difference between a C.I.F. contract and voyage or time charters. The effect of delay in the former due to longer sea voyages is minimized, since the seller can raise money on the goods he has shipped almost at once, and the buyer, once he takes up the documents, can deal with the goods by transferring the documents before the goods arrive. See Tsakiroglou & Co. Ltd., supra Note 4, [1960] 2 Q.B. at 361. But this difference is not so material that impossibility in C.I.F. contracts is unrelated to impossibility in charter parties. It would raise serious questions for a court to require sellers under C.I.F. contracts to perform in circumstances under which the sellers could be refused performance by carriers with whom they have entered into charter parties for affreightment. See The Eugenia, supra, [1964] 2 Q.B. at 241. Where the time of the voyage is unimportant, a charter party should be treated the same as a C.I.F. contract in determining impossibility of performance.

These cases certainly are not distinguishable, as appellant suggests, on the ground that they refer to "frustration" rather than to "impossibility." The English regard "frustration" as substantially identical with "impossibility." 6 Corbin, supra, § 1322, at 327 n. 9.

ate port and unload its cargo, The Malcolm Baxter, Jr., 277 U.S. 323, 48 S.Ct. 516, 72 L.Ed. 901 (1928), subject of course to required steps to minimize damages. If the performance rendered has value, recovery in *quantum meruit* for the entire performance is proper. But here Transatlantic has collected its contract price, and now seeks *quantum meruit* relief for the additional expense of the trip around the Cape. If the contract is a nullity, Transatlantic's theory of relief should have been *quantum meruit* for the entire trip, rather than only for the extra expense. Transatlantic attempts to take its profit on the contract, and then force the Government to absorb the cost of the additional voyage.[17] When impracticability without fault occurs, the law seeks an equitable solution, see 6 Corbin, supra, § 1321, and *quantum meruit* is one of its potent devices to achieve this end. There is no interest in casting the entire burden of commercial disaster on one party in order to preserve the other's profit. Apparently the contract price in this case was advantageous enough to deter appellant from taking a stance on damages consistent with its theory of liability. In any event, there is no basis for relief.

Affirmed.

NOTES

(1) *Shipment via Suez.* Suppose the charter had given the Government a right to notice of the progress of the vessel by requiring the master to send it a telegram "on passing Suez." Such a provision appeared in *The Massalia,* one of the more controversial of the Suez cases. The charter was for a voyage from India to Genoa. Note the court's reference to the case (and to its overruling) in footnotes 14 and 16.

In footnote 7 the court uses the *Glidden* case, in the Second Circuit, for support. The charter there gave the shipper power to designate a destination (on the Atlantic seaboard) "not later than on Vessel's passing Gibraltar." But a more interesting feature of this case was that the shipowner had asked for a clause excusing it in the event the Canal was closed, and that the shipper had rejected any such term. These facts, taken together, make the case a near-perfect example of the type described in the last sentence of footnote 7, do they not? Do you agree with the court that the doctrine of impossibility is better applicable in that situation than in the case before it?

As the court notes, all of these cases were rather different from the problem in *Tsakiroglou,* mentioned in footnotes 4, 14 and 16, where the contract was one of *sale*. The seller had agreed to ship groundnuts from the Sudan to Hamburg, paying the cost, insurance and freight (c.i.f.). The contract was entered into on October 4, and called for shipment in November or December. The House of Lords sustained an award of damages for failure to perform. As regards the custom of shipment via Suez, Lord Radcliffe said: "A man may habitually leave

---

17. The argument that the Uniform Commercial Code requires the buyer to pay the additional cost of performance by a commercially reasonable substitute was advanced and rejected in Symposium, supra Note 13, 105 U.Pa.L.Rev. at 884 n. 205. In Dillon v. United States, 156 F.Supp. 719, 140 Ct.Cl. 508 (1957), relief was afforded for some of the cost of delivering hay from a commercially unreasonable distance, but the suit was one in which the plaintiff had suffered losses far in excess of the relief given.

his house by the front door to keep his appointments; but, if the front door is stuck, he would hardly be excused for not leaving by the back."

(2) *Impracticability and Risk.* In Judge Friendly's opinion cited in footnote 3, he wrote that the "basic assumption" part of the Code's test "seems a somewhat complicated way of putting Professor Corbin's question of how much risk the promisor assumed." He went on: "We see no basis for thinking that when an electronics system is promoted by its manufacturer as a revolutionary breakthrough, the risk of the revolution's occurrence falls on the purchaser; the reasonable supposition is that it has already occurred or, at least, that the manufacturer is assuring the purchaser that it will be found to have when the machine is assembled.... If a manufacturer wishes to be relieved of the risk that what looks good on paper may not prove so good in hardware, the appropriate exculpatory language is well known and often used."

Note that UCC 2–615 begins with an exception where a seller has "assumed a greater obligation," recognizing that a party may assume the risk of being unable to do the impracticable—even the impossible.

———

FORESEEABILITY

Writers have disagreed on the relevance of foreseeability under UCC 2–615. Comment 8 speaks of situations in which "the contingency in question is sufficiently foreshadowed at the time of contracting to be included among the business risks which are fairly to be regarded as part of the dickered terms." Does UCC 2–615 itself mention foreseeability?

According to Restatement Second, Introductory Note to Chapter 11, "The fact that the event was unforeseeable is significant as suggesting that its nonoccurrence was a basic assumption. However, the fact that it was foreseeable, or even foreseen, does not, of itself, argue for a contrary conclusion, since the parties may not have thought it sufficiently important a risk to have made it a subject of their bargaining." The "foreseeability test" has been excoriated in academic literature. See, e.g., Smit, Frustration of Contract: A Comparative Attempt at Consolidation, 58 Colum.L.Rev. 287 (1958). One economist appears to tolerate the test, at least, as imposing a penalty on the "suboptimal use of available information." Joskow, Commercial Impossibility, the Uranium Market and the Westinghouse Case, 6 J.Legal Stud. 119, 173 (1977). Others, however, conclude that it is "nonoperational"—at least in the form usually stated—"for it fails to indicate which contracting party is the superior bearer of the foreseeable risk. The test," they say, "is disappearing, and although occasionally mentioned is seldom applied." Posner & Rosenfield, Impossibility and Related Doctrines in Contract Law: An Economic Analysis, 6 J.Legal Stud. 83, 100 (1977). But see Duesenberg, Contract Impracticability: Courts Begin to Shape § 2–615, 32 Bus.Law. 1089, 1095 (1977) (foreseeability "has been central to impossibility cases for as long as they have been around" and "is proving no less important under section 2–615"); see also the following case.

NOTE

The Case of the Foreseeable Finale. The Wolf Trap Foundation for the Performing Arts leased from the National Park Service facilities in Wolf Trap Park for summer performances. Wolf Trap then contracted with The Opera Company of Boston for opera performances on four nights in June. Wolf Trap was to pay the Opera Company $272,000 in installments and to furnish the place of performance including "lighting equipment as shall be specified by the Opera Company of Boston's lighting designer." On the day of the last performance, a severe thunderstorm caused an electrical power outage and that performance had to be cancelled. Wolf Trap refused to pay the final installment and the Opera Company sued. The trial court held that "if the contingency that occurred was one that could have been foreseen reliance on the doctrine of impossibility ... is absolutely barred" and granted judgment in favor of the Opera Company. Wolf Trap appealed. *Held:* Reversed and remanded.

"Foreseeability ... is at best but one fact to be considered in resolving first how likely the occurrence of the event in question was and, second whether its occurrence, based on past experience, was of such reasonable likelihood that the obligor should not merely foresee the risk but, because of the degree of its likelihood, the obligor should have guarded against it or provided for non-liability against the risk. This is a question to be resolved by the trial judge after a careful scrutiny of all the facts in the case."

One judge noted in dissent that "a representative of Wolf Trap who apparently negotiated the contract" had said in a statement made immediately after the cancellation that "we have experienced power outages on several occasions," that "Wolf Trap has been very lucky they did not occur during the evening," that "a far better solution ... is to have a generator of sufficient capacity" available for such an emergency, and that it was his "feeling that a theater without this capacity is incomplete." The dissenting judge added, "It would have taken only a few seconds to write into the contract a sentence which said in effect, 'If the electric power fails, Wolf Trap will not be responsible for any losses caused by the power failure.'" Opera Company of Boston, Inc. v. Wolf Trap Foundation for the Performing Arts, 817 F.2d 1094 (4th Cir.1987).

CANADIAN INDUSTRIAL ALCOHOL CO. v. DUNBAR MOLAS-SES CO., 179 N.E. 383 (N.Y.1932). [At the end of 1927 the plaintiff Alcohol Co. contracted with Dunbar to purchase a quantity of molasses, shipments to begin after the following April 1, and to be spread out during the warm weather. The goods were described as "approximately 1,500,000 wine gallons Refined Blackstrap (Molasses) of the usual run from the National Sugar Refinery, Yonkers, N.Y., to test around 60 per cent sugars." While the contract was in force, that refinery produced much less molasses than its capacity—less than half a million gallons. Dunbar shipped to the Alcohol Co. its entire allotment of the refinery's output (344,083 gallons), but failed to deliver any more molasses. Upon being sued for damages, Dunbar contended that its duty was conditioned, by an implied term, on the refinery's producing enough molasses to fill the plaintiff's order. From a judgment for the buyer, Dunbar appealed.]

CARDOZO, C.J. ... The contract, read in the light of the circumstances existing at its making, or more accurately in the light of any such circumstances apparent from this record, does not keep the defendant's duty within boundaries so narrow.... The defendant does not even show that it tried to get a contract from the refinery during the months that intervened between the acceptance of the plaintiff's order and the time when shipments were begun. It has wholly failed to relieve itself of the imputation of contributory fault (3 Williston on Contracts, sec. 1959). So far as the record shows, it put its faith in the mere chance that the output of the refinery would be the same from year to year, and finding its faith vain, it tells us that its customer must have expected to take a chance as great. We see no reason for importing into the bargain this aleatory element. The defendant is in no better position than a factor who undertakes in his own name to sell for future delivery a special grade of merchandise to be manufactured by a special mill. The duty will be discharged if the mill is destroyed before delivery is due. The duty will subsist if the output is reduced because times turn out to be hard and labor charges high....

[Affirmed.]

NOTES

(1) *Questions.* If Dunbar had made a contract with the refinery, as Cardozo suggests, would the result in the case have been different? Could Dunbar, in its contract with Alcohol Co., have relieved itself of the risk that its source of supply would fail as it did? If so, would Dunbar be expected to turn over to Alcohol Co. any rights of Dunbar against the refinery? Compare Comment 5 to UCC 2–615 with InterPetrol Bermuda Ltd. v. Kaiser Aluminum International Corp., 719 F.2d 992 (9th Cir.1983).

(2) *The Vienna Sales Convention.* Article 79 of the Vienna Convention, in paragraph (1), relieves a party from liability "for a failure to perform any of his obligations if he proves that the failure was due to an impediment beyond his control and that he could not reasonably be expected to have taken the impediment into account at the time of the conclusion of the contract or to have avoided or overcome it or its consequences." Does this test seem more or less strict than that of UCC 2–615? The article has been criticized as having a "chameleon-like character that permits it to take on that meaning that best conforms to the reader's own legal background."[a]

Consider paragraph (2) of article 79, which deals with the case where a "party's failure is due to the failure by a third person whom he has engaged to perform the whole or a part of the contract." Would that paragraph exempt Dunbar from liability if it had made a contract with the refinery, and the refinery had then curtailed its production? If the refinery had then been destroyed by fire? Would the answers to these questions be different if Dunbar had not made a contract with the refinery? If paragraph (2) does not exempt Dunbar, might paragraph (1) exempt it?

Surprisingly, it appears that paragraph (2) was not intended to apply to situations like Dunbar's but only to situations like the following.

a. Farnsworth, Perspective of Common Law Countries, in La Vendita Internazionale 3, 19 (Congress at S. Margherita Ligure 1981).

> Seller contracted to sell Buyer a machine to be built in accordance with specifications supplied by Buyer. Seller contracted with Electron to manufacture the machine. Electron had a good reputation for efficiency and responsibility but, in this case, mismanaged production so that it was unable to deliver the machine. At the time of Electron's default, Seller could not obtain the machine from another supplier and was unable to deliver the machine to Buyer.

J. Honnold, Uniform Law for International Sales Under the 1980 United Nations Convention 544 (2d ed. 1991), where it is emphasized that paragraph (2) applies only to cases where a party "has engaged a third person (Electron) 'to perform the whole or a part of the contract.' "

What result then in the case of Electron? What answers to the questions posed earlier concerning Dunbar?

(3) *"Subjective" and "Objective" Impracticability.* A distinction is sometimes drawn between "objective" impracticability ("the thing cannot be done") and "subjective" impracticability ("I cannot do it"). Financial inability ("I cannot pay.") is a classic example of the latter. The Restatement Second retains a requirement of objective impracticability in other terms, explaining that "a party generally assumes the risk of his own inability to perform his duty. Even if a party contracts to render a performance that depends on some act by a third party, he is not ordinarily discharged because of a failure by that party because this is also a risk that is commonly understood to be on the obligor." Comment *e* to § 261. See also Comment 5 to UCC 2–615: "There is no excuse under this section, however, unless the seller has employed all due measures to assure himself that his source will not fail"—citing the main case.

EASTERN AIR LINES, INC. v. GULF OIL CORPORATION

United States District Court, Southern District of Florida, 1975.
415 F.Supp. 429.

[The facts and part of the opinion in this case are at p. 125 above, and another part is at p. 613 above.]

JAMES LAWRENCE KING, DISTRICT COURT JUDGE.... Gulf's commercial impracticability defenses are premised on two sections of the Uniform Commercial Code specifically §§ 2–614 (F.S. 672.614) and 2–615 (F.S. 672.615).... The modern U.C.C. § 2–615 doctrine of commercial impracticability has its roots in the common law doctrine of frustration or impossibility and finds its most recognized illustrations in the so-called "Suez Cases", arising out of the various closings of the Suez Canal and the consequent increases in shipping costs around the Cape of Good Hope. Those cases offered little encouragement to those who would wield the sword of commercial impracticability. As a leading British case arising out of the 1957 Suez closure declared, the unforeseen cost increase that would excuse performance "must be more than merely onerous or expensive. It must be positively unjust to hold the parties bound." Ocean Tramp Tankers v. V/O Sovfracht (The Eugenia), 2 Q.B. 226, 239 (1964).... These British precedents were followed by the District of Columbia Circuit, which gave specific consideration to U.C.C.

2–615, Comment 4, in Transatlantic Financing Corp. v. United States, 124 U.S.App.D.C. 183, 363 F.2d 312, 319 (1966).

Other recent American cases similarly strictly construe the doctrine of commercial impracticability. For example, one case found no U.C.C. defense, even though costs had doubled over the contract price, the court stating, "It may have been unprofitable for defendant to have supplied the pickers, but the evidence does not establish that it was impossible. A mere showing of unprofitability, without more, will not excuse the performance of a contract." Schafer v. Sunset Packing Co., 256 Or. 539, 474 P.2d 529, 530 (1970)....

Gulf's argument on commercial impracticability has two strings to its bow. First, Gulf contends that the escalator indicator does not work as intended by the parties by reason of the advent of so-called "two-tier" pricing under Phase IV government price controls.[4] Second, Gulf alleges that crude oil prices have risen substantially without a concomitant rise in the escalation indicator, and, as a result, that performance of the contract has become commercially impracticable.[5]

The short and dispositive answer to Gulf's first argument under U.C.C. § 2–615, that the price escalation indicator (posting in Platt's Oilgram Crude Oil Supplement) no longer reflects the intent of the parties by reason of the so-called "two-tier" pricing structure, is that the language of the contract is clear and unambiguous. The contract does not require interpretation and requires no excursion into the subjective intention of the parties. The intent of the parties is clear from the four corners of the contract; they intended to be bound by the specified entries in *Platt's,* which has been published at all times material here, which is published today, and which prints the contract reference prices. Prices under the contract can be and still are calculated[6] by reference to Platt's publication.[7]

It should be noted that Platt's Oilgram Crude Oil Supplement states on its face that its postings since the advent of "two-tier" are basically comparable to the postings historically quoted in Platt's, and that postings listed in Platt's were price controlled at the time of negotiation and execution of the contract, just as they are today and have been at all times in between. In addition, Gulf's expert witness Mr. Coates testified that oil companies, including Gulf, continue to use "old oil" prices (the prices reported in Platt's) for contracts between themselves. Finally, as

---

4. One tier being "old" price-controlled oil, and the second tier being the unregulated oil.

5. The average price paid by Eastern to Gulf has risen more than 40% over the life of the contract.

6. The parties have stipulated that Eastern has been paying prices mandated by the contract terms.

7. Gulf's contention that the publication of the postings has been "suspended" and therefore that a proviso of Article II of the contract, declaring the consequences of "suspension", has been triggered, is without merit. The Proviso deals, in the clearest of terms, with *Platt's* ceasing to publish either *in toto* or in regard to the specified postings, neither of which is the case here. Furthermore, the proviso contains its own prescription for remedial action in the case of suspension, including notice and substitution of other indicators. Gulf has never attempted to follow the prescribed remedy; thus its argument fails for procedural as well as substantive reasons.

to the indicator crude (West Texas Sour) there is no showing that the Platt's postings do not reflect the market price for that oil today. The testimony is in substantial dispute but the court finds, with respect to domestic oil, some 60 percent of Gulf's 1974 domestic production was old oil. With respect to foreign crude oil, domestic prices were considerably lower than imported price at the beginning of the period in question so that the West Texas Sour Crude postings unquestionably did not reflect foreign crude oil postings. In the absence of any evidence to the contrary it may be reasonably inferred that virtually all transactions in West Texas Sour Crude Oil take place at the postings reflected in *Platt's,* since most of the production in that field is "old" oil.

With regard to Gulf's contention that the contract has become "commercially impracticable" within the meaning of U.C.C. § 2–615, because of the increase in market price of foreign crude oil and certain domestic crude oils, the court finds that the tendered defense has not been proved. On this record the court cannot determine how much it costs Gulf to produce a gallon of jet fuel for sale to Eastern, whether Gulf loses money or makes a profit on its sale of jet fuel to Eastern, either now or at the inception of the contract, or at any time in between. Gulf's witnesses testified that they could not make such a computation. The party undertaking the burden of establishing "commercial impracticability" by reason of allegedly increased raw material costs undertakes the obligation of showing the extent to which he has suffered, or will suffer, losses in performing his contract. The record here does not substantiate Gulf's contention on this fundamental issue.

Gulf presented evidence tending to show that its "costs" of crude oil have increased dramatically over the past two years.

However, the "costs" to which Gulf adverts are unlike any "costs" that might arguably afford ground for any of the relief sought here. Gulf's claimed "costs" of an average barrel of crude oil at Gulf's refineries (estimated by Gulf's witness Davis at about $10.00 currently, and about $9.50 during 1974) include intra-company profits, as the oil moved from Gulf's overseas and domestic production departments to its refining department. The magnitude of that profit was not revealed.

With respect to Gulf's foreign crude oil "costs", the record shows that at the very time Gulf was in the process of repudiating its contract with Eastern (January 1974), Gulf's profit margin on foreign crude oil brought into the United States (Cabindan and Nigerian) was approximately $4.43 to $3.88 per barrel compared with profits of $0.92 and $0.88 respectively, one year earlier.[8] That margin may now have declined, but the record discloses that Gulf's overseas subsidiaries have enjoyed substantial profits from crude oil transactions and that those profits are included in the "average" crude oil "costs" of which Gulf now complains. The "transfer" prices at which Gulf "sells" its foreign oil to its domestic subsidiaries are set by a pricing committee in Gulf's Pittsburgh home office. Intra-company profit can be and is allocated among

---

8. Gulf's international oils expert, Mr. Blackledge testified that foreign oil costs were up four-fold during 1973–74 but Gulf's profits also went up four-fold in that period.

those 400–plus corporate subsidiaries of Gulf, largely through the transfer price device, to optimize overall benefit to the corporation, as documents from the committee reveal. Internal memoranda from the pricing committee introduced into evidence showed for instance that the committee had before it the view of one of its tax experts that every $1 increase in Nigerian oil prices resulted in a 50 to 90 cent benefit to the company; other memoranda describe how profits might be assigned, through intercompany sales, to various other offshore subsidiaries to obtain favorable tax treatment for the purpose of maximizing the advantages to the corporation for the benefit of the parent corporation. Similarly, there are memoranda reflecting a policy of charging the highest prices possible to the United States.

In like manner, the "per barrel" cost calculations which Gulf introduced at trial reflect "in house" profits from Gulf's domestic production. During the discovery process, Gulf developed for Eastern certain "cost" figures. Those data show that a Gulf-produced barrel of domestic crude oil is reflected on Gulf's books at a cost of approximately $2.44 for the nine-month period ending September 30, 1974. Yet, for purposes of computing an overall average "cost" to Gulf of a barrel of crude oil for trial purposes (estimated by Gulf's economist witness Davis on the stand at about $9.50 for that period), Gulf used, not the $2.44 actual booked cost, but a "transfer" price, equal to "postings" and including intra-company profit. To the extent "old oil" postings are reflected in the domestic oil "transfer price", the intra-company profit would be on the order of $2.76 per barrel, measured against the $5.20 posting listed in *Platt's* for West Texas Sour Crude; "new" oil "transfer prices" would include an even larger profit margin. Gulf estimated that some 70 percent of domestic oil going into Gulf's refineries was its own proprietary production.

Again, these are not the kinds of "costs" against which to measure hardship, real or imagined, under the Uniform Commercial Code. Under no theory of law can it be held that Gulf is guaranteed preservation of its intra-company profits, moving from the left-hand to the right-hand, as one Gulf witness so aptly put it. The burden is upon Gulf to show what its real costs are, not its "costs" inflated by its internal profits at various levels of the manufacturing process and located in various foreign countries.

No criticism is implied of Gulf's rational desire to maximize its profits and take every advantage available to it under the laws. However, these factors cannot be ignored in approaching Gulf's contention that it has been unduly burdened by crude oil price increases.

No such hardship has been established. On the contrary, the record clearly establishes that 1973, the year in which the energy crises began, was Gulf's best year ever, in which it recorded some $800 million in net profits after taxes. Gulf's 1974 year was more than 25% better than

1973's record $1,065,000,000 profits were booked by Gulf in 1974 after paying all taxes.[9]

For the foregoing reasons, Gulf's claim of hardship giving rise to "commercial impracticability" fails.

But even if Gulf had established great hardship under U.C.C. § 2–615, which it has not, Gulf would not prevail because the events associated with the so-called energy crises were reasonably foreseeable at the time the contract was executed. If a contingency is foreseeable, it and its consequences are taken outside the scope of U.C.C. § 2–615, because the party disadvantaged by fruition of the contingency might have protected himself in his contract, Ellwood v. Nutex Oil Co., 148 S.W.2d 862 (Tex.Civ.App.1941)....

The record is replete with evidence as to the volatility of the Middle East situation, the arbitrary power of host governments to control the foreign oil market, and repeated interruptions and interference with the normal commercial trade in crude oil. Even without the extensive evidence present in the record, the court would be justified in taking judicial notice of the fact that oil has been used as a political weapon with increasing success by the oil-producing nations for many years, and Gulf was well aware of and assumed the risk that the OPEC nations would do exactly what they have done.

With respect to Gulf's argument that "two-tier" was not "foreseeable", the record shows that domestic crude oil prices were controlled at all material times, that Gulf foresaw that they might be de-controlled, and that Gulf was constantly urging to the Federal Government that they should be de-controlled. Government price regulations were confused, constantly changing, and uncertain during the period of the negotiation and execution of the contract. During that time frame, high ranking Gulf executives, including some of its trial witnesses, were in constant repeated contact with officials and agencies of the Federal Government regarding petroleum policies and were well able to protect themselves from any contingencies.

Even those outside the oil industry were aware of the possibilities. Eastern's principal contract negotiator advised his superior in recommending this contract to him:

> "While Gulf is apparently counting on crude price increases, such increases are a fact of life for the future, except as the government may inhibit by price controls, therefore all suppliers have such anticipation."

> "1975 is the year during which the full effect of energy shortages will be felt in the United States according to most estimates."

Knowing all the factors, Gulf drafted the contract and tied the escalation to certain specified domestic postings in *Platt's*. The court is of the view that it is bound thereby.

---

9. Gulf stipulated in the parties' pretrial stipulation that it had the capability to per- form the contract.

The court is further of the opinion that U.C.C. § 2–614(2) is not applicable to this case.... It is clear that this section dealing with "means or manner of payment" speaks, by way of illustration, to the blocking by governmental interference with the contemplated mode of monetary exchange (e.g., when a contract provides for payment in gold specie and the government subsequently forbids payment in gold). No such issue appears in the case at bar and U.C.C. § 2–614 is inapposite here.

NOTES

(1) *The Economics of Impracticability.* Writers have also disagreed over what economic analysis has to say about the doctrine of impracticability. Some argue that whether a promisor is excused should turn on whether the promisee is the "superior risk bearer"—after ruling out the capacity on either side to forestall the event at reasonable cost. This test arguably comes down, for most practical purposes, to a question of which party is best situated to protect against the contingency through insuring, making hedge contracts, and the like. Posner & Rosenfield, Impossibility and Related Doctrines in Contract Law: An Economic Analysis, 6 J. Legal Stud. 83 (1977). Was this the mainspring of the decision in *Transatlantic Financing Corp. v. United States,* above?

Another scholar suggests that the prevalence of flexible-pricing terms tends to give government a handle on the problem of price inflation and reasons that the use of such terms would be discouraged by free-handed applications of commercial impracticability. (Do you see why?) He argues for imposing on sellers the risk of large, general price rises associated with management—or mismanagement—of the economy (i.e., inflation). Schwartz, Sales Law and Inflations, 50 So.Cal.L.Rev. 1 (1976).

(2) *The Westinghouse Litigation.* The most widely observed litigation over UCC 2–615 arose out of long term contracts made by Westinghouse Electric to supply uranium oxide ("yellowcake") to electric utility companies in connection with sales of nuclear power plants. The price of uranium oxide rose from about $6 a pound in 1972 to about $40 a pound in 1976. Late in 1975 Westinghouse wrote seventeen utilities that it was excused because of commercial impracticability from delivering the total of some 80 million pounds that it was obligated to supply and that it would prorate among them some 15 million pounds that it could command. From this event a fountain of litigation flowed, resulting in many settlements. Most interesting is the interim decision in the Richmond case, in which the suits of several utilities were consolidated for trial.

Westinghouse arranged, with court approval, to deliver the uranium oxide at its disposal, subject to a later determination. After nine months of hearings, the judge ruled that Westinghouse was not wholly excused, but he expressed willingness to hear argument that a judicial limitation of the remedy was appropriate. Submissions on issues of damages and an "equitable adjustment" were then made. Eventually all claims were settled on terms relatively favorable to Westinghouse. For background, see Joskow, Commercial Impossibility, the Uranium Market and the Westinghouse Case, 6 J.Legal Stud. 119 (1977).[a]

---

a. For a later episode in Westinghouse's travails arising out of nuclear power contracts, see Florida Power & Light Co. v. Westinghouse Electric Corp., 826 F.2d 239 (4th Cir.1987). The court there noted a trial court finding that "while Westing-

MINERAL PARK LAND CO. v. HOWARD, 156 P. 458 (Cal.1916).
[Action for breach of contract. Defendants agreed to take from plaintiff's land all the gravel and earth necessary in the construction of a
bridge and to pay for it at a stated rate. Defendants actually used
101,000 cubic yards of earth and gravel, only 50,131 of which they took
from plaintiff's land, having procured the rest elsewhere. The court
found this was all the material on plaintiff's land which was above water
level; that defendants removed "all that could have been taken advanta-
geously to defendants, or all that was practical to take and remove from
a financial standpoint"; and ruled that this fact did not excuse defendant's failure. Defendants appealed.]

SLOSS, J. . . . The parties were contracting for the right to take earth
and gravel to be used in the construction of the bridge. When they
stipulated that all of the earth and gravel needed for this purpose should
be taken from plaintiff's land they contemplated and assumed that the
land contained the requisite quantity, available for use. . . . And, in
determining whether the earth and gravel were "available," we must
view the conditions in a practical and reasonable way. Although there
was gravel on the land, it was so situated that the defendants could not
take it by ordinary means, nor except at prohibitive cost. To all fair
intents then, it was impossible for defendants to take. . . . We do not
mean to intimate that the defendants could excuse themselves by showing the existence of conditions which would make the performance of
their obligation more expensive than they had anticipated, or which
would entail a loss upon them. But where the difference in cost is so
great as here, and has the effect, as found, of making performance
impracticable, the situation is not different from that of a total absence
of earth and gravel.

Judgment reversed.

NOTE

Mistake v. Impracticability. Recall that the statement from Stees v. Leonard, with which this chapter began, was made in imposing liability on a builder
for failure to put up a structure on what appeared to be quicksand. Recall also
the court's statement in Watkins & Son v. Carrig, p. 357 above, that though
Watkins, the excavating contractor, struck solid rock, "a defense of mutual
mistake is not available. . . . If the plaintiff was unwise in taking chances, it is
not relieved, on the ground of mistake, from the burden incurred in being faced
with them."

As the *Mineral Park Land* case shows, the doctrine of impracticability
encompasses existing as well as supervening impracticability. Unlike a party
who claims supervening impracticability, a party who claims existing impracticability may also have a claim of mistake. What difficulties would Howard have
encountered if he had based his defense on mistake? What difficulties would

house was supposedly more expert in the
field of nuclear energy, Florida was more
expert in the drafting of agreements and
that it had demonstrated this superior expertise by 'out-negotiating' Westinghouse."

Watkins have encountered if he had claimed that he was relieved on the ground of impracticability?

EASTERN AIR LINES, INC. v. McDONNELL DOUGLAS CORP., 532 F.2d 957 (5th Cir.1976). [In 1964, Eastern Airlines, the last of the major trunk carriers to make a commitment to jet aircraft, contracted with a single manufacturer, McDonnell Douglas, to purchase 99 jets. Eastern was anxious about prompt delivery, and, when the planes were delivered thousands of plane-days late, Eastern sued McDonnell Douglas for damages. The delays were due to competing demands on the manufacturer for military production for use in Vietnam during the 1966–1968 escalation of the war, but dealings between the government and the airline industry never led to a general pre-emption of civilian production. This was avoided through exhortation and other informal demands for priority known as "jawboning." The trial judge, however, took the position that only delays resulting from written government orders issued in strict compliance with procurement regulations were excusable under the following excusable delay clause.

> Seller shall not be responsible nor deemed to be in default on account of delays in performance ... due to causes beyond Seller's control and not occasioned by its fault or negligence, including but not being limited to ... any act of government, governmental priorities, allocation regulations or orders affecting materials, equipment, facilities or completed aircraft, ... failure of vendors (due to causes similar to those within the scope of this clause) to perform their contracts ..., provided such cause is beyond Seller's control.

The trial judge entered judgment on a jury verdict in Eastern's favor for $24,552,659, and McDonnell Douglas appealed.]

AINSWORTH, CIRCUIT JUDGE. ... McDonnell's first contention in this regard is that the District Court unduly narrowed the scope of this clause by instructing the jury that an excusable delay must be the result of "one or more of the listed events in the excusable delay clause of the contracts, or ... a similar cause beyond the defendant's control...." This instruction, in McDonnell's view, effectively construes the specifically listed excusable causes of delay as restricting the application of the more general phrase which exempts Douglas from liability for delays beyond its control and not due to its negligence. McDonnell feels, therefore, that its affirmative defense was unjustifiably limited to delays caused by events similar to those specifically listed when, in fact, the contracts excused all delays which were not its fault.

The trial judge's construction of the clause, moreover, affords McDonnell Douglas a narrower range of excuses than is available under the modern view of impossibility as it is codified in U.C.C. § 2–615.... Under section 2–615, the impossibility defense is available to the seller only if he has not "assumed a greater obligation" than that imposed upon him by this provision. During the trial, the court below ruled that section 2–615 was not applicable for this reason. Although the trial judge failed to explain his holding, it must have been based upon his restrictive construction of the excusable delay clause. Presumably, then, the protections of section 2–615 were deemed to have been waived because the contracts were interpreted as limiting McDonnell's impossibility defense to delays caused by events similar to those specifically provided for in the excusable delay clause.

In support of this approach, Eastern argues that the District Court correctly applied *ejusdem generis,* a canon of judicial construction limiting the application of general terms which follow specific ones to matters similar in kind or classification to those specified.... This maxim, however, "is only an instrumentality for ascertaining the correct meaning of words when there is uncertainty." ... Obviously, the application of the doctrine in this case would make superfluous the unambiguous words "including but not being limited to" which precede the specifically listed excuses for delay. It is clear, then, that by excusing delays not within McDonnell's control nor due to its negligence, "including but not being limited to" governmental acts, priorities, or orders, the parties intended to excuse all delays coming within the general description regardless of their similarity to the listed excuses. Consequently, there is no basis for the trial judge's conclusion that McDonnell waived the protections of section 2–615 and that its contract excuses are narrower than those available under the doctrine of commercial impracticability....

McDonnell also challenges the trial judge's jury instruction which limited excusable delivery delays to those resulting from events which were not "reasonably foreseeable" at the time a contract was executed. By writing a foreseeability requirement into the excusable delay clause, the District Court appeared to construe the contracts as constituting nothing more than an application of the Code's commercial impracticability rule to those particular events specified in the contracts.

Although there has been some doubt expressed as to whether the Code permits parties to bargain for exemptions broader than those available under section 2–615, this concern is ill-founded.... Comment 8 to this provision plainly indicates that parties may "enlarge upon or supplant" section 2–615.... There appear to be, however, certain strictures imposed upon judicial interpretation of such agreements. Comment 8 provides:

> Generally, express agreements as to exemptions designed to enlarge upon or supplant the provisions of this section are to be read in light of mercantile sense and reason, for this section itself sets up the commercial standard for normal and reasonable interpretation and provides a minimum beyond which agreement may not go.

While this provision could have been drafted in less vague terms, we presume that Comment 8 establishes "mercantile sense and reason" as a general standard governing our construction of agreements enlarging upon the protections of section 2–615. As we understand Comment 8, where there is doubt concerning the parties' intention, exemption clauses should not be construed as broadening the excuses available under the Code's impracticability rule. Applying this standard to the excusable delay clause, we cannot, in the absence of evidence to the contrary, hold that McDonnell is exempt from liability for any delay, regardless of its foreseeability, that is due to causes beyond its control. Exculpatory provisions which are phrased merely in general terms have long been construed as excusing only unforeseen events which make performance impracticable.... Courts have often held, therefore, that if a promisor desires to broaden the protections available under the excuse doctrine he should provide for the excusing contingencies with particularity and not in general language....

We realize, of course, that this rule of construction developed in the pre-U.C.C. era when the scope of the impossibility and frustration doctrines was unclear and varied from jurisdiction to jurisdiction. Because of the uncertainty surrounding the law of excuse, parties had good reason to resort to general contract provisions relieving the promisor of liability for breaches caused by events "beyond his control." Although the Uniform Commercial Code has ostensibly eliminated the need for such clauses, lawyers, either through an abundance of caution or by force of habit, continue to write them into contract.... Thus, even though our interpretation would render the general terms of the excusable delay clause merely duplicative of section 2–615, we will adhere to the established rule of construction because it continues to reflect prevailing commercial practices....

While we hold that the provision of the excusable delay clause exempting McDonnell from liability for delays beyond its control should be interpreted as incorporating the Code's commercial impracticability doctrine, we disagree with the trial judge's jury instruction on foreseeability insofar as it implies that the events specifically listed in the excusable delay clause in each contract must have been unforeseeable at the time the agreement was executed. The rationale for the doctrine of impracticability is that the circumstance causing the breach has made performance so vitally different from what was anticipated that the contract cannot reasonably be thought to govern.... However, because the purpose of a contract is to place the reasonable risk of performance on the promisor, he is presumed, in the absence of evidence to the contrary, to have agreed to bear any loss occasioned by an event which was foreseeable at the time of contracting.... Underlying this presumption is the view that a promisor can protect himself against foreseeable events by means of an express provision in the agreement.... Therefore, when the promisor has anticipated a particular event by specifically providing for it in a contract, he should be relieved of liability for the occurrence of such event regardless of whether it was foreseeable.

[The court went on to hold that the government's informal priority program came within the ambit of "any act of government, governmental priorities, allocations, or orders affecting materials."]

[Reversed and remanded.] [a]

NOTES

(1) *Force Majeure Clauses.* An exculpation provision written with special reference to events beyond a party's control is often called a *force majeure* provision. For examples other than the one used by McDonnell Douglas, see the clauses in Selections for Contracts used by General Electric, by buyers of cocoa, and by sellers of grain. Would you expect such a clause to be broader in scope in a seller's or a buyer's contract? In a short-term or long-term contract?

Can you suggest any improvements in the clauses you have read? Are there advantages to the use of a list of events? Are there disadvantages? Can they be overcome? Would it have been to McDonnell Douglas's advantage to have inserted language such as "in addition to any excuses provided by law"? Language such as "whether or not of the same kind"? Language such as "whether or not foreseeable"?

It has been suggested that express terms "offer two distinct options for using particularized instructions to enhance a framework of implied terms. The first of these enables one to augment or *supplement* the implied terms ('opting in')... . By contrast, parties sometimes desire to countermand or *trump* one or more of the preformulated provisions ('opting out')." Goetz & Scott, The Limits of Expanded Choice: An Analysis of the Interactions Between Express and Implied Contract Terms, 73 Calif.L.Rev. 261, 281 (1985). Did the *force majeure* clause used by McDonnell Douglas involve supplementing or trumping?

(2) *Labor Disputes.* In Mishara Construction Co., Inc. v. Transit–Mixed Concrete Corp., 310 N.E.2d 363 (Mass.1974), a general contractor sued a supplier for breach of a contract to supply ready-mixed concrete for a housing project, and the supplier defended on the ground that a picket line at the job site had made performance impracticable under UCC 2–615. The court noted that in some situations a "picket line might constitute a mere inconvenience and hardly make performance 'impracticable.' " Furthermore, "in certain industries with a long record of labor difficulties, the nonoccurrence of strikes and picket lines could not fairly be said to be a basic assumption," and, "in general, labor disputes cannot be considered extraordinary in the course of modern commerce." Nevertheless, since much "must depend on the facts known to the parties at the time of contracting with respect to the history of and prospects for labor difficulties during the period of performance of the contract, as well as the likely severity of the effect of such disputes on the ability to perform," the issue of impracticability was properly left to the jury. (According to Restatement Second, Introductory Note to Chapter 11, however, the question "is generally considered to be one of law rather than fact.") Does the *Mishara* case have anything to say about the desirability of mentioning labor disputes in a *force majeure* clause?

(3) *Other Precautions Compared.* Negotiating with a view to an unwelcome change of circumstances presents some nice choices. Take, for example, the concern of an airline that wants an assured supply of fuel over a long period of time at a terminal it hopes to serve and the concern of the supplier negotiating with it. The sorts of events covered by a *force majeure* clause may not cover all the risks that cause concern, such as the risk of a change in the market price for fuel.

---

a. After this decision a complicated settlement was reached under which Eastern returned nine older jets and leased nine newer ones at an advantageous price. Ma- caulay, Elegant Models, Empirical Pictures, and the Complexities of Contract, 11 Law & Soc.Rev. 507, 517 (1977).

One way of casting the risks sharply in favor of the airline would be to give it a power of termination or to fix a short period for duration of the contract and give the airline periodic options to renew. Other possibilities for shifting the risks in favor of the airline include setting up a requirements contract and limiting the supplier's remedies for breach by the airline. And, if the concern is only the risk of a change in market price, the parties may adopt some flexible pricing mechanism. For any of these provisions, the airline would expect a price to be exacted by the supplier. Can you think of comparable precautions that would protect the supplier?

(4) *Problem.* Mark–O–Lite made a contract with George Seitz to restore and replace a neon sign marquee on a theater that Seitz was renovating for the county arts center. Mark–O–Lite's contract contained the following clause:

> The Company shall not be liable for any failure in the performance of its obligations under this agreement which may result from strikes or acts of labor unions, fires, floods, earthquakes, or acts of God, war or other conditions or contingencies beyond its control.

Shortly after making the contract, Mark–O–Lite discovered that its expert sheet metal worker, Al Jorgenson, a diabetic, had to enter the hospital for an unknown period of time. Since he was the only employee who could do the sheet metal work on the marquee, Mark–O–Lite explained that it would be unable to do that part of the work and returned the uncashed deposit check. Seitz had City Sign Service do the work for $20,000 and sues Mark–O–Lite for the $7,200 difference between that and Mark–O–Lite's price of $12,800. What result? Seitz v. Mark–O–Lite Sign Contractors, Inc., 510 A.2d 319 (N.J.Super.1986).

SECTION 3. FRUSTRATION OF PURPOSE

KRELL v. HENRY

Court of Appeal, 1903.
2 K.B. 740.

[By a contract in writing of June 20, 1902, the defendant agreed to hire from the plaintiff a flat in Pall Mall, London, for June 26 and 27, on which days it had been officially announced that the coronation processions (i.e., to be held in connection with the coronation of Edward VII) would take place and pass along Pall Mall. The contract contained no express reference to the coronation processions, or to any other purpose for which the flat was taken. A deposit was paid when the contract was entered into. As, owing to the serious illness of the King, the processions did not take place on the days originally fixed, the defendant declined to pay the balance of the rent.]

VAUGHN WILLIAMS, L.J. The real question in this case is the extent of the application in English law of the principle of the Roman law which has been adopted and acted on in many English decisions, and notably in the case of Taylor v. Caldwell, (3 B. & S. 826).... I do not think that the principle of the civil law as introduced into the English law is limited to cases in which the event causing the impossibility of performance is the destruction or non-existence of some thing which is the subject matter of the contract or of some condition or state of things expressly specified as a condition of it. I think that you first have to ascertain, not necessarily from the terms of the contract, but, if required, from necessary inferences, drawn from surrounding circumstances recognized by both contracting parties, what is the substance of the contract, and then to ask the question whether that substantial contract needs for its foundation the assumption of the existence of a particular state of things. If it does, this will limit the operation of the general words, and in such case, if the contract becomes impossible of performance by reason of the non-existence of the state of things assumed by both contracting parties as the foundation of the contract, there will be no breach of the contract thus limited. Now what are the facts of the present case? The contract is contained in two letters of June 20 which passed between the defendant and the plaintiff's agent, Mr. Cecil Bisgood. These letters do not mention the coronation, but speak merely of the taking of Mr. Krell's chambers, or, rather, of the use of them, in the daytime of June 26 and 27, for the sum of 75*l.*, 25*l.* then paid, balance 50*l.* to be paid on the 24th. But the affidavits, which by agreement between the parties are to be taken as stating the facts of the case, show that the plaintiff exhibited on his premises, third floor, 56A, Pall Mall, an announcement to the effect that windows to view the Royal coronation procession were to be let, and that the defendant was induced by that announcement to apply to the housekeeper on the premises, who said that the owner was willing to let the suite of rooms for the purpose of seeing the Royal procession for both days, but not nights, of June 26 and 27.[a] In my judgment the use of the rooms was let and taken for the purpose of seeing the Royal procession. It was not a demise of the rooms, or even an agreement to let and take the rooms. It is a license to use rooms for a particular purpose and none other. And in my judgment the taking place of those processions on the days proclaimed along the proclaimed route, which passed 56A, Pall Mall, was regarded by both contracting parties as the foundation of the contract; and I think that it

a. Two processions were planned in connection with the coronation: that on Coronation Day, and a "Pageant" on the following day. Experience of the Diamond Jubilee (1897) provided some guidance for the pricing of space to see the processions. At that time a club-house had been "let to a speculator for £200, who realized £500 by his bargain." C. Pascoe, The Pageant & Ceremony of The Coronation 213 (1902). But there were complications in the early summer of 1902, in that the routes of the processions had not been determined. Pall Mall—"club-land of the empire"—was thought to be a certainty for the Pageant procession; but for Coronation Day two shorter routes, not including Pall Mall, were thought to be under consideration. One writer of the time estimated that prices

for the Pageant ought not to exceed those paid for Victoria's Jubilee—"that is to say, if the Route be not [curtailed]. Of course, the lesser the opportunity of seeing the Pageant, the higher will be the prices asked for accommodation." Id. at 212.

On June 22 Commons was informed that the King had just undergone an operation for appendicitis, and that the Coronation was indefinitely postponed. V. Cowles, Edward VII and His Circle 240 (1956). It was performed on August 9. Though some of the captains and the princes (kings were not invited) had departed London, the splendor of the ceremony was "scarcely dimmed." Pall Mall was on the coronation route. London Illustrated News, Aug. 14, 1902.

cannot reasonably be supposed to have been in the contemplation of the contracting parties, when the contract was made, that the coronation would not be held on the proclaimed days, or the processions not take place on those days along the proclaimed route; and I think that the words imposing on the defendant the obligation to accept and pay for the use of the rooms for the named days, although general and unconditional, were not used with reference to the possibility of the particular contingency which afterwards occurred. It was suggested in the course of the argument that if the occurrence, on the proclaimed days, of the coronation and the procession in this case were the foundation of the contract, and if the general words are thereby limited or qualified, so that in the event of the non-occurrence of the coronation and procession along the proclaimed route they would discharge both parties from further performance of the contract, it would follow that if a cabman was engaged to take someone to Epsom on Derby Day at a suitable enhanced price for such a journey, say 10*l.*, both parties to the contract would be discharged in the contingency of the race at Epsom for some reason becoming impossible; but I do not think this follows, for I do not think that in the cab case the happening of the race would be the foundation of the contract. No doubt the purpose of the engager would be to go to see the Derby, and the price would be proportionately high; but the cab had no special qualification for this particular occasion. Any other cab would have done as well.

Appeal dismissed.

NOTES

(1) *Frustration of Purpose.* The foregoing decision is the best-known example of a doctrine known as "frustration of purpose." As opposed to impossibility, the label *frustration* signifies that nothing has happened to impede performance of the defendant's undertaking. After the King's illness, as before, it was perfectly possible for the defendant to pay the agreed price—and indeed for him to occupy the rooms. Other instances of frustration claims are given below. Was the issue raised in Paradine v. Jane (p. 805 above) one of impossibility or of frustration? (As to the significance of that case and the main case see Wladis, Common Law and Uncommon Events: The Development of the Doctrine of Impossibility of Performance in English Contract Law, 75 Geo.L.J. 1575 (1987).)

(2) *Problem.* For a promise of $500 P promises to provide a wedding dress for D by June 1. D's marriage to X is scheduled for a week after that. When the dress is all but ready, X dies by accident. Is D bound to pay anything? Is P's situation distinguishable from that of the cabman on Derby Day?

SWIFT CANADIAN CO. v. BANET
United States Court of Appeals, Third Circuit, 1955.
224 F.2d 36.

Action to recover from buyer of goods, for breach of contract. In the United States District Court for the Eastern District of Pennsylvania, George A. Welsh, District Judge, each party moved for summary judgment upon stipulated facts, and the buyer's motion was granted. The seller appealed to the Court of Appeals. . . .

Judgment reversed with instructions to enter judgment for plaintiff.

GOODRICH, CIRCUIT JUDGE.[a] This is an action on the part of a seller of goods to recover against the buyer for breach of contract. In the trial court each party, following the filing of a stipulation of facts, moved for summary judgment. The court granted the motion of the defendant. Plaintiff here says that it should have had the summary judgment or, at the worst, that the case should be remanded for trial on the facts.

The one point presented is both interesting and elusive. The seller is a Canadian corporation. It entered into an agreement with defendant buyers who do business as Keystone Wool Pullers in Philadelphia. By this contract Keystone agreed to purchase a quantity of lamb pelts at a stipulated price. Part of the quantity was delivered on board railroad cars at Toronto and shipped to Keystone in Philadelphia. On or about March 12, 1952, Swift advised Keystone of its readiness to deliver the remaining pelts to the buyer on board railroad cars in Toronto for shipment to Philadelphia. The parties have stipulated that on or about that day the government of the United States by its agency, the Bureau of Animal Industry, had issued stricter regulations for the importation of lamb pelts into the United States. The parties have stipulated that "pursuant to these regulations, the importation into the United States of these lamb pelts by Keystone was prevented." They have also stipulated that for the reasons just stated Keystone then and thereafter refused to accept delivery of the pelts and the loading and shipment of the car did not occur.

From an inspection of the contract made between the parties it appears that the seller agreed to sell the pelts:

"all at $3.80 each U.S. Funds

F.O.B. Toronto."

Below this an approximate time was stipulated for shipment and then there were shipping directions in the following form:

"Note -- Frankford

Via: Buffalo—Penna. R.R. to
~~Broad & Washington Ave.~~

Freight Sta. Penna. R.R. Delivery."

Following this appears the terms and method of payment.

Two additional conditions of sale should be stated. There was a provision that neither party is to be liable for "orders or acts of any

a. Herbert F. Goodrich (1889–1962) taught law for twenty-five years at Iowa, Michigan and Pennsylvania, where he also served as dean. Beginning in 1940 he served as judge on the United States Court of Appeals for the Third Circuit, and beginning in 1947 he served as director of the American Law Institute. His best-known book is a text on the conflict of laws.

government or governmental agency ..." And there was a provision that "when pelts are sold F.O.B. seller's plant title and risk of loss shall pass to buyer when product is loaded on cars at seller's plant."

The one question in this case is the legal effect of this agreement between the parties. If the seller's obligation was performed when it delivered, or offered to deliver, the pelts to the railroad company in Toronto, we think it is entitled to recovery. If the seller did fulfill its obligation, when it did so deliver, of course it is clear that when it failed to load the pelts because the buyer had signified his refusal to accept them, the seller may assert the same rights as though he had loaded them. A party is not obligated to do the vain thing of performing, assuming that he is ready to perform, when the other party has given notice of refusal to accept performance. 3 Williston on Sales, § 586 (Rev. ed., 1948); Restatement, Contracts, §§ 280, 306; Leonard Seed Co. v. Lustig Burgerhoff Co., 1923, 81 Pa.Super. 499. See also Uniform Commercial Code, § 2–610(c); Pa.Stat.Ann. tit. 12A, § 2–610(c) (1954).

The argument for the buyer must rest on the fact that the shipping directions in the contract showed that what the parties had in mind was such kind of performance by the seller as would start the goods to the buyer in Philadelphia. This coupled with the stipulation that, in consequence of the stiffening of federal regulations, "the importation into the United States of these lamb pelts by Keystone was prevented," forms the basis for the argument that the carrying out of the agreement was prevented by governmental agency and the buyer is therefore excused.

The validity of this argument depends upon what effect we give to a provision for shipment of the goods to the buyer via Pennsylvania R.R., destination Philadelphia. We do not think that this is any more than a shipping direction which the buyer could have changed to any other destination in the world had it so desired. Suppose the buyer had found that it wanted the goods in New York, could it not have directed such a change in destination without any violation of the contract? Could the seller have insisted that it would ship to Philadelphia and nowhere else? We think that authority in general regards these shipping directions as simply inserted for the convenience of the buyer and subject to change by him. Dwight v. Eckert, 1888, 117 Pa. 490, 12 A. 32; Hocking v. Hamilton, 1893, 158 Pa. 107, 27 A. 836; Richter v. Zoccoli, 1930, 150 A. 1, 8 N.J.Misc. 289; 1 & 2 Williston on Sales, §§ 190, 457 (Rev. ed., 1948). See also Uniform Commercial Code, § 2–319(3); Pa.Stat.Ann. tit. 12A, § 2–319(3) (1954).

If the contract in this case had called for performance "F.O.B. seller's plant" a provision of the contract itself would clearly have indicated when the seller's responsibility was finished and the buyer's had begun.[1] Here the provision in the earlier part of the contract was simply "F.O.B. Toronto" and it was not specifically provided that the sale was delivery at the seller's plant. We think the provision shows what the parties meant by "F.O.B." and can see no difference, so far as

---

1. See the second additional condition of sale quoted in the text above.

this expressed meaning goes, between F.O.B. at seller's plant and F.O.B. Toronto.

The general rule on this subject is pretty clear. Williston points out that when goods are delivered "free on board" pursuant to contract the presumption is that the property passes thereupon. Williston on Sales, § 280(b) (Rev. ed., 1948). It is agreed that this is a presumption and that the phrase F.O.B. is not one of iron-clad meaning. Seabrook Farms Co. v. Commodity Credit Corp., 206 F.2d 93 (C.A.3, 1953). There is nothing in this case, however, to counteract the effect of such a presumption. When the shipper had made his delivery he was to send bill of lading and draft through a Philadelphia bank. His part of the agreement would have been fully performed when the goods were delivered F.O.B. at Toronto. We think both the risk of loss and the possibility of profit if the market advanced, were in the buyer from then on. Even if the goods could not be imported into the United States under the then existing regulations, the rest of the world was free to the buyer, so far as we know, as destination for the shipment. If he did not care to accept them under the circumstances and his expectation of a profitable transaction was disappointed, nevertheless, the seller having performed or being ready, able and willing to perform, was entitled to the value of his bargain.

[The court found that the law of Pennsylvania and that of Ontario were identical on the issue involved here, and that the seller's damages were sufficiently proved.]

The judgment of the district court will be reversed with instructions to enter judgment for the plaintiff for the difference between the contract price and the price at which the goods were sold.

NOTE

Questions. Would the decision have been different if the sale contract had provided for delivery f.o.b. Philadelphia rather than Toronto? As to the seller's obligation in that case see UCC 2–319(1)(b). If the seller failed to deliver in accordance with such a contract because of United States import regulations, would that necessarily be a breach of its duty?

If Canada had regulated the *export* of lamb pelts, so as to require a license, would the Canadian seller have borne the risk that one could not be obtained? See Amtorg Trading Corp. v. Miehle Printing Press & Mfg. Co., 206 F.2d 103 (2d Cir.1953).

Reconsider Columbia Nitrogen Corp. v. Royster Co. (p. 661 above). Might Columbia have prevailed on the alternative ground of frustration of purpose?

CHASE PRECAST CORP. v. JOHN J. PAONESSA CO.
Supreme Judicial Court of Massachusetts, 1991.
409 Mass. 371, 566 N.E.2d 603.

LYNCH, JUSTICE. This appeal raises the question whether the doctrine of frustration of purpose may be a defense in a breach of contract action in Massachusetts, and, if so, whether it excuses the defendant John J. Paonessa Company, Inc. (Paonessa), from performance.

The claim of the plaintiff, Chase Precast Corporation (Chase), arises from the cancellation of its contracts with Paonessa to supply median barriers in a highway reconstruction project of the Commonwealth. Chase brought an action to recover its anticipated profit on the amount of median barriers called for by its supply contracts with Paonessa but not produced. Paonessa brought a cross action against the Commonwealth for indemnification in the event it should be held liable to Chase. After a jury-waived trial, a Superior Court judge ruled for Paonessa on the basis of impossibility of performance.[1] Chase and Paonessa cross appealed. The Appeals Court affirmed, noting that the doctrine of frustration of purpose more accurately described the basis of the trial judge's decision than the doctrine of impossibility. Chase Precast Corp. v. John J. Paonessa Co., 28 Mass.App.Ct. 639, 554 N.E.2d 868 (1990). We agree. We allowed Chase's application for further appellate review, and we now affirm.

The pertinent facts are as follows. In 1982, the Commonwealth, through the Department of Public Works (department), entered into two contracts with Paonessa for resurfacing and improvements to two stretches of Route 128. Part of each contract called for replacing a grass median strip between the north and southbound lanes with concrete surfacing and precast concrete median barriers. Paonessa entered into two contracts with Chase under which Chase was to supply, in the aggregate, 25,800 linear feet of concrete median barriers according to the specifications of the department for highway construction. The quantity and type of barriers to be supplied were specified in two purchase orders prepared by Chase.

The highway reconstruction began in the spring of 1983. By late May, the department was receiving protests from angry residents who objected to use of the concrete median barriers and removal of the grass median strip. Paonessa and Chase became aware of the protest around June 1. On June 6, a group of about 100 citizens filed an action in the Superior Court to stop installation of the concrete median barriers and other aspects of the work. On June 7, anticipating modification by the department, Paonessa notified Chase by letter to stop producing concrete barriers for the projects. Chase did so upon receipt of the letter the following day. On June 17, the department and the citizens' group entered into a settlement which provided, in part, that no additional concrete median barriers would be installed. On June 23, the department deleted the permanent concrete median barriers item from its contracts with Paonessa.

Before stopping production on June 8, Chase had produced approximately one-half of the concrete median barriers called for by its contracts with Paonessa, and had delivered most of them to the construction

---

1. The judge also ruled that the Department of Public Works had the right to cancel the order for median barriers under its general contracts with Paonessa, particularly under subsection 4.06 of those contracts. See note 6, *infra*.

sites. Paonessa paid Chase for all that it had produced, at the contract price. Chase suffered no out-of-pocket expense as a result of cancellation of the remaining portion of barriers.

This court has long recognized and applied the doctrine of impossibility as a defense to an action for breach of contract. See, e.g., Boston Plate & Window Glass Co. v. John Bowen Co., 335 Mass. 697, 141 N.E.2d 715 (1957); ... Butterfield v. Byron, 153 Mass. 517, 27 N.E. 667 (1891). Under that doctrine, "where from the nature of the contract it appears that the parties must from the beginning have contemplated the continued existence of some particular specified thing as the foundation of what was to be done, then, in the absence of any warranty that the thing shall exist ... the parties shall be excused ... [when] performance becomes impossible from the accidental perishing of the thing without the fault of either party." Boston Plate & Window Glass Co., supra, 335 Mass. at 700, 141 N.E.2d 715, quoting Hawkes v. Kehoe, 193 Mass. 419, 423, 79 N.E. 766 (1907).

On the other hand, although we have referred to the doctrine of frustration of purpose in a few decisions, we have never clearly defined it. See Mishara Constr. Co. v. Transit–Mixed Concrete Corp., 365 Mass. 122, 128–129, 310 N.E.2d 363 (1974).... Other jurisdictions have explained the doctrine as follows: when an event neither anticipated nor caused by either party, the risk of which was not allocated by the contract, destroys the object or purpose of the contract, thus destroying the value of performance, the parties are excused from further performance. See Lloyd v. Murphy, 25 Cal.2d 48, 153 P.2d 47 (1944).

In Mishara Constr. Co., supra, 365 Mass. at 129, 310 N.E.2d 363, we called frustration of purpose a "companion rule" to the doctrine of impossibility. Both doctrines concern the effect of supervening circumstances upon the rights and duties of the parties. The difference lies in the effect of the supervening event. Under frustration, "[p]erformance remains possible but the expected value of performance to the party seeking to be excused has been destroyed by [the] fortuitous event...."[2] Lloyd v. Murphy, supra, 25 Cal.2d at 53, 153 P.2d 47. The principal question in both kinds of cases remains "whether an unanticipated circumstance, the risk of which should not fairly be thrown on the promisor, has made performance vitally different from what was reasonably to be expected." See Lloyd, supra at 54, 153 P.2d 47 (frustration); Mishara Constr. Co., supra, 365 Mass. at 129, 310 N.E.2d 363 (impossibility).

Since the two doctrines differ only in the effect of the fortuitous supervening event, it is appropriate to look to our cases dealing with impossibility for guidance in treating the issues that are the same in a

2. Clearly frustration of purpose is a more accurate label for the defense argued in this case than impossibility of performance, since, as the Appeals Court pointed out, "[p]erformance was not literally impossible. Nothing prevented Paonessa from honoring its contract to purchase the remaining sections of median barrier, whether or not the [department] would approve their use in the road construction." 28 Mass.App.Ct. 639, 644 n. 5, 554 N.E.2d 868 (1990).

frustration of purpose case.[3] The trial judge's findings with regard to those issues are no less pertinent to application of the frustration defense because they were considered relevant to the defense of impossibility.

Another definition of frustration of purpose is found in the Restatement (Second) of Contracts § 265 (1981):

"Where, after a contract is made, a party's principal purpose is substantially frustrated without his fault by the occurrence of an event the non-occurrence of which was a basic assumption on which the contract was made, his remaining duties to render performance are discharged, unless the language or the circumstances indicate the contrary."

This definition is nearly identical to the defense of "commercial impracticability," found in the Uniform Commercial Code, G.L. c. 106, § 2–615 (1988 ed.),[4] which this court, in Mishara Constr. Co., supra at 127–128, 310 N.E.2d 363, held to be consistent with the common law of contracts regarding impossibility of performance. It follows, therefore, that the Restatement's formulation of the doctrine is consistent with this court's previous treatment of impossibility of performance and frustration of purpose.

Paonessa bore no responsibility for the department's elimination of the median barriers from the projects. Therefore, whether it can rely on the defense of frustration turns on whether elimination of the barriers was a risk allocated by the contracts to Paonessa. Mishara Constr. Co., supra, 365 Mass. at 129, 310 N.E.2d 363, articulates the relevant test:

"The question is, given the commercial circumstances in which the parties dealt: Was the contingency which developed one which the parties could reasonably be thought to have foreseen as a real possibility which could affect performance? Was it one of that variety of risks which the parties were tacitly assigning to the promisor by their failure to provide for it explicitly? If it was, performance will be required. If it could not be so considered, performance is excused."

This is a question for the trier of fact. Id. at 127, 130, 310 N.E.2d 363.

Paonessa's contracts with the department contained a standard provision allowing the department to eliminate items or portions of work found unnecessary.[5] The purchase order agreements between Chase and

---

3. Those issues include the foreseeability of the supervening event, allocation of the risk of occurrence of the event, and the degree of hardship to the promisor. ...

4. That section states that performance is excused when it has been made "impracticable by the occurrence of a contingency the non-occurrence of which was a basic assumption on which the contract was made." G.L. c. 106, § 2–615.

5. The contracts contained the following provision:

"4.06 Increased or Decreased Contract Quantities.

"When the accepted quantities of work vary from the quantities in the bid schedule, the Contractor shall accept as payment in full, so far as contract items are concerned, payment at the original contract unit prices for the accepted quantities of work done.

"The Engineer may order omitted from the work any items or portions of work

Paonessa do not contain a similar provision. This difference in the contracts does not mandate the conclusion that Paonessa assumed the risk of reduction in the quantity of the barriers. It is implicit in the judge's findings that Chase knew the barriers were for department projects. The record supports the conclusion that Chase was aware of the department's power to decrease quantities of contract items. The judge found that Chase had been a supplier of median barriers to the department in the past. The provision giving the department the power to eliminate items or portions thereof was standard in its contracts. See Standard Specifications for Highways and Bridges, Commonwealth of Massachusetts Department of Public Works § 4.06 (1973). The judge found that Chase had furnished materials under and was familiar with the so-called "Unit Price Philosophy" in the construction industry, whereby contract items are paid for at the contract unit price for the quantity of work actually accepted. Finally, the judge's finding that "[a]ll parties were well aware that lost profits were not an element of damage in either of the public works projects in issue" further supports the conclusion that Chase was aware of the department's power to decrease quantities, since the term prohibiting claims for anticipated profit is part of the same sentence in the standard provision as that allowing the engineer to eliminate items or portions of work.

In Mishara Constr. Co., supra at 130, 310 N.E.2d 363, we held that, although labor disputes in general cannot be considered extraordinary, whether the parties in a particular case intended performance to be carried out, even in the face of a labor difficulty, depends on the facts known to the parties at the time of contracting with respect to the history of and prospects for labor difficulties. In this case, even if the parties were aware generally of the department's power to eliminate contract items, the judge could reasonably have concluded that they did not contemplate the cancellation for a major portion of the project of such a widely used item as concrete median barriers, and did not allocate the risk of such cancellation.[6]

Our opinion in Chicopee Concrete Serv., Inc. v. Hart Eng'g Co., 398 Mass. 476, 498 N.E.2d 121 (1986), does not lead to a different conclusion. Although we held there that a provision of a prime contract requiring city approval of subcontractors was not incorporated by reference into the subcontract, id. at 478, 498 N.E.2d 121, we nevertheless stated that, if the record had supported the conclusion that the subcontractor knew,

---

found unnecessary to the improvement and such omission shall not operate as a waiver of any condition of the Contract nor invalidate any of the provisions thereof, nor shall the Contractor have any claim for anticipated profit.

"No allowance will be made for any increased expenses, loss of expected reimbursement therefor or from any other cause."

6. The judge did not explicitly find that cancellation of the barriers was not contemplated and that the risk of their elimination was not allocated by the contracts. However, the judge's decision imports every finding essential to sustain it if there is evidence to support it. Mailer v. Mailer, 390 Mass. 371, 373, 455 N.E.2d 1211 (1983).

or at least had notice of, the approval clause, the result might have been different.   Id. at 478–479, 498 N.E.2d 121.[7]   ...

Judgment affirmed.

NOTES

(1) *Question.* What would have been the result if Chase had, in accordance with its contract, produced all of the median barriers before receiving Paonessa's letter notifying it to stop?

(2) *The Gear–Box Case: Reprise.* In Power Engineering & Manufacturing v. Krug International, the case about the sale of a "gear box" (Note, p. 161 above), the buyer, Krug, refused to take delivery after Power Engineering had manufactured the item. Krug had intended to incorporate it into an aeromedical equipment laboratory that its British subsidiary was to build for Iraqi Airways. Krug directed Power not to make shipment very shortly after the outbreak of the Gulf War and the implementation of a United Nations embargo against deliveries to Iraq. What more is needed to show that Krug's performance was excused? Might it be significant if Power Engineering had subsequently made a favorable sale of the gear box to the Mayo Clinic?

Krug's purchase order contained, in addition to the terms quoted at p. 162, a paragraph captioned "Contingencies":

> In the event of causes beyond the control of Purchaser, including but not limited to acts of God, fire, the elements, strikes or labor disputes, and accident or transportation difficulties which would make it unreasonable in Purchaser's judgment to accept delivery hereunder, Purchaser shall have the option to terminate this purchase order or to delay the delivery or completion of all or part of the items, such termination or delay being without cost to Purchaser.

The court nevertheless affirmed a judgment against Krug. The paragraph quoted was not part of the contract, the court concluded. Krug had transmitted its purchase order by fax and had not included the reverse side, on which the paragraph appeared. Not until a month later, after Power Engineering had begun production, did it receive the entire purchase order. Does Krug's carelessness about the matter of "contingencies" indicate that its performance should not be excused on the ground of changed circumstances?

(3) *Problem.* Karl Wendt Farm Equipment Company was a franchised International Harvester dealer. After a dramatic downturn in the market for farm equipment which caused International Harvester to lose $4 billion in four

---

7. This court held in John Soley & Sons v. Jones, 208 Mass. 561, 566–567, 95 N.E. 94 (1911), that, where by its terms the prime contract could be cancelled if the defendant was not making sufficient progress on the work, and the plaintiff knew of the article of cancellation, nevertheless, even if it was mutually understood that the defendant did not intend to perform unless the prime contract remained in force, the defendant was not relieved from performance on the ground of impossibility where it failed to provide for the risk of cancellation in its contract with the plaintiff. To the extent that holding is contrary to our decision in this case, we decline to follow it, and refer to our adoption in Mishara Constr. Co., supra, 365 Mass. at 130, 310 N.E.2d 363, of the following statement: "Rather than mechanically apply any fixed rule of law, where the parties themselves have not allocated responsibility, justice is better served by appraising all of the circumstances, the part the various parties played, and thereon determining liability," quoting Badhwar v. Colorado Fuel & Iron Corp., 138 F.Supp. 595, 607 (S.D.N.Y.1955), aff'd, 245 F.2d 903 (2d Cir.1957). See West Los Angeles Inst. for Cancer Research v. Mayer, 366 F.2d 220, 225 (9th Cir.1966), cert. denied, 385 U.S. 1010, 87 S.Ct. 718, 17 L.Ed.2d 548 (1967) ("foreseeability of the frustrating event is not alone enough to bar rescission if it appears that the parties did not intend the promisor to assume the risk of its occurrence").

years, it concluded that it had no alternative but to go into bankruptcy or sell off its farm implement division. It decided to do the latter, receiving for its assets from J.I. Case Co. and Tenneco, Inc., $246,700,000 in cash and $161,300,000 in Tenneco stock. Although Case did not acquire International Harvester's franchise network, it offered franchises to many of International Harvester's dealers. But because Case already had a dealer in Wendt's area, Case did not offer Wendt a franchise, and Wendt sued International Harvester for breach of contract. Does International Harvester have the defense of impracticability? Of frustration? See Karl Wendt Farm Equip. Co. v. International Harvester Co., 931 F.2d 1112 (6th Cir.1991).

(4) *Frustration and the Code.* Does the Code have a bearing on the question in *Chase Precast?* See the next case.

NORTHERN INDIANA PUBLIC SERVICE CO. v. CARBON COUNTY COAL CO.

United States Court of Appeals, Seventh Circuit, 1986.
799 F.2d 265.

POSNER, CIRCUIT JUDGE. These appeals bring before us various facets of a dispute between Northern Indiana Public Service Company (NIPSCO), an electric utility in Indiana, and Carbon County Coal Company, a partnership that until recently owned and operated a coal mine in Wyoming. In 1978 NIPSCO and Carbon County signed a contract whereby Carbon County agreed to sell and NIPSCO to buy approximately 1.5 million tons of coal every year for 20 years, at a price of $24 a ton subject to various provisions for escalation which by 1985 had driven the price up to $44 a ton.

NIPSCO's rates are regulated by the Indiana Public Service Commission. In 1983 NIPSCO requested permission to raise its rates to reflect increased fuel charges. Some customers of NIPSCO opposed the increase on the ground that NIPSCO could reduce its overall costs by buying more electrical power from neighboring utilities for resale to its customers and producing less of its own power. Although the Commission granted the requested increase, it directed NIPSCO, in orders issued in December 1983 and February 1984 (the "economy purchase orders"), to make a good faith effort to find, and wherever possible buy from, utilities that would sell electricity to it at prices lower than its costs of internal generation. The Commission added ominously that "the adverse effects of entering into long-term coal supply contracts which do not allow for renegotiation and are not requirement contracts, is a burden which must rest squarely on the shoulders of NIPSCO management." Actually the contract with Carbon County did provide for renegotiation of the contract price—but one-way renegotiation in favor of Carbon County; the price fixed in the contract (as adjusted from time to time in accordance with the escalator provisions) was a floor. And the contract was indeed not a requirements contract: it specified the exact amount of coal that NIPSCO must take over the 20 years during which the contract was to remain in effect. NIPSCO was eager to have an assured supply of low-sulphur coal and was therefore willing to guarantee both price and quantity.

Unfortunately for NIPSCO, as things turned out it was indeed able to buy electricity at prices below the costs of generating electricity from coal bought under the contract with Carbon County; and because of the "economy purchase orders," of which it had not sought judicial review, NIPSCO could not expect to be allowed by the Public Service Commission to recover in its electrical rates the costs of buying coal from Carbon County. NIPSCO therefore decided to stop accepting coal deliveries from Carbon County, at least for the time being; and on April 24, 1985, it brought this diversity suit against Carbon County in a federal district court in Indiana, seeking a declaration that it was excused from its obligations under the contract either permanently or at least until the economy purchase orders ceased preventing it from passing on the costs of the contract to its ratepayers. In support of this position it argued that the contract violated section 2(c) of the Mineral Lands Leasing Act of 1920, 30 U.S.C. § 202, because of Carbon County's affiliation with a railroad (Union Pacific), and that in any event NIPSCO's performance was excused or suspended—either under the contract's *force majeure* clause or under the doctrines of frustration or impossibility—by reason of the economy purchase orders.

On May 17, 1985, Carbon County counterclaimed for breach of contract and moved for a preliminary injunction requiring NIPSCO to continue taking delivery under the contract. On June 19, 1985, the district judge granted the preliminary injunction, from which NIPSCO has appealed. Also on June 19, rejecting NIPSCO's argument that it needed more time for pretrial discovery and other trial preparations, the judge scheduled the trial to begin on August 26, 1985. Trial did begin then, lasted for six weeks, and resulted in a jury verdict for Carbon County of $181 million. The judge entered judgment in accordance with the verdict, rejecting Carbon County's argument that in lieu of damages it should get an order of specific performance requiring NIPSCO to comply with the contract. Upon entering the final judgment the district judge dissolved the preliminary injunction, and shortly afterward the mine—whose only customer was NIPSCO—shut down. NIPSCO has appealed from the damage judgment, and Carbon County from the denial of specific performance. . . .

The contract permits NIPSCO to stop taking delivery of coal "for any cause beyond [its] reasonable control . . . including but not limited to . . . orders or acts of civil . . . authority . . . which wholly or partly prevent . . . the utilizing . . . of the coal." This is what is known as a *force majeure* clause. . . . NIPSCO argues that the Indiana Public Service Commission's "economy purchase orders" prevented it, in whole or part, from using the coal that it had agreed to buy, and it complains that the district judge instructed the jury incorrectly on the meaning and application of the clause. The complaint about the instructions is immaterial. The judge should not have put the issue of *force majeure* to the jury. It is evident that the clause was not triggered by the orders.

All that those orders do is tell NIPSCO it will not be allowed to pass on fuel costs to its ratepayers in the form of higher rates if it can buy electricity cheaper than it can generate electricity internally using Carbon County's coal. Such an order does not "prevent," whether wholly or in part, NIPSCO from using the coal; it just prevents NIPSCO from shifting the burden of its improvidence or bad luck in having incorrectly forecasted its fuel needs to the backs of the hapless ratepayers. The purpose of public utility regulation is to provide a substitute for competition in markets (such as the market for electricity) that are naturally monopolistic. Suppose the market for electricity were fully competitive, and unregulated. Then if NIPSCO signed a long-term fixed-price fixed-quantity contract to buy coal, and during the life of the contract competing electrical companies were able to produce and sell electricity at prices below the cost to NIPSCO of producing electricity from that coal, NIPSCO would have to swallow the excess cost of the coal. It could not raise its electricity prices in order to pass on the excess cost to its consumers, because if it did they would buy electricity at lower prices from NIPSCO's competitors. By signing the kind of contract it did, NIPSCO gambled that fuel costs would rise rather than fall over the life of the contract; for if they rose, the contract price would give it an advantage over its (hypothetical) competitors who would have to buy fuel at the current market price. If such a gamble fails, the result is not *force majeure*.

This is all the clearer when we consider that the contract price was actually fixed just on the downside; it put a floor under the price NIPSCO had to pay, but the escalator provisions allowed the actual contract prices to rise above the floor, and they did. This underscores the gamble NIPSCO took in signing the contract. It committed itself to paying a price at or above a fixed minimum and to taking a fixed quantity at that price. It was willing to make this commitment to secure an assured supply of low-sulphur coal, but the risk it took was that the market price of coal or substitute fuels would fall. A *force majeure* clause is not intended to buffer a party against the normal risks of a contract. The normal risk of a fixed-price contract is that the market price will change. If it rises, the buyer gains at the expense of the seller (except insofar as escalator provisions give the seller some protection); if it falls, as here, the seller gains at the expense of the buyer. The whole purpose of a fixed-price contract is to allocate risk in this way. A *force majeure* clause interpreted to excuse the buyer from the consequences of the risk he expressly assumed would nullify a central term of the contract.

The Indiana Public Service Commission is a surrogate for the forces of competition, and the economy fuel orders are a device for simulating the effects in a competitive market of a drop in input prices. The orders say to NIPSCO, in effect: "With fuel costs dropping, and thus reducing the costs of electricity to utilities not burdened by long-term fixed-price contracts, you had better substitute those utilities' electricity for your own when their prices are lower than your cost of internal generation. In a freely competitive market consumers would make that substitution;

if you do not do so, don't expect to be allowed to pass on your inflated fuel costs to those consumers." Admittedly the comparison between competition and regulation is not exact. In an unregulated market, if fuel costs skyrocketed NIPSCO would have a capital gain from its contract (assuming the escalator provisions did not operate to raise the contract price by the full amount of the increase in fuel costs, a matter that would depend on the cause of the increase). This is because its competitors, facing higher fuel costs, would try to raise their prices for electricity, thus enabling NIPSCO to raise its price, or expand its output, or both, and thereby increase its profits. The chance of this "windfall" gain offsets, on an ex ante (before the fact) basis, the chance of a windfall loss if fuel costs drop, though NIPSCO it appears was seeking a secure source of low-sulphur coal rather than a chance for windfall gains. If as is likely the Public Service Commission would require NIPSCO to pass on any capital gain from an advantageous contract to the ratepayers (which is another reason for thinking NIPSCO wasn't after windfall gains—it would not, in all likelihood, have been allowed to keep them), then it ought to allow NIPSCO to pass on to them some of the capital loss from a disadvantageous contract—provided that the contract, when made, was prudent. Maybe it was not; maybe the risk that NIPSCO took was excessive. But all this was a matter between NIPSCO and the Public Service Commission, and NIPSCO did not seek judicial review of the economy purchase orders.

If the Commission had ordered NIPSCO to close a plant because of a safety or pollution hazard, we would have a true case of *force majeure*. As a regulated firm NIPSCO is subject to more extensive controls than unregulated firms and it therefore wanted and got a broadly worded *force majeure* clause that would protect it fully (hence the reference to partial effects) against government actions that impeded its using the coal. But as the only thing the Commission did was prevent NIPSCO from using its monopoly position to make consumers bear the risk that NIPSCO assumed when it signed a long-term fixed-price fuel contract, NIPSCO cannot complain of *force majeure;* the risk that has come to pass was one that NIPSCO voluntarily assumed when it signed the contract.

The district judge refused to submit NIPSCO's defenses of impracticability and frustration to the jury, ruling that Indiana law does not allow a buyer to claim impracticability and does not recognize the defense of frustration....

Section 2–615 of the Uniform Commercial Code takes this approach. It provides that "delay in delivery ... by a seller ... is not a breach of his duty under a contract for sale if performance as agreed has been made impracticable by the occurrence of a contingency the non-occurrence of which was a basic assumption on which the contract was made...." Performance on schedule need not be impossible, only infeasible—provided that the event which made it infeasible was not a risk that the promisor had assumed. Notice, however, that the only type of promisor referred to is a seller; there is no suggestion that a buyer's performance might be excused by reason of impracticability. The reason is largely semantic. Ordinarily all the buyer has to do in order to perform his side of the bargain is pay, and while one can think of all sorts of reasons why, when the time came to pay, the buyer might not have the money, rarely would the seller have intended to assume the risk that the buyer might, whether through improvidence or bad luck, be unable to pay for the seller's goods or services. To deal with the rare case where the buyer or (more broadly) the paying party might have a good excuse based on some unforeseen change in circumstances, a new rubric was thought necessary, different from "impossibility" (the common law term) or "impracticability" (the Code term, picked up in Restatement (Second) of Contracts § 261 (1979)), and it received the name "frustration." Rarely is it impracticable or impossible for the payor to pay; but if something has happened to make the performance for which he would be paying worthless to him, an excuse for not paying, analogous to impracticability or impossibility, may be proper. See Restatement, supra, § 265, comment a....

NIPSCO is the buyer in the present case, and its defense is more properly frustration than impracticability; but the judge held that frustration is not a contract defense under the law of Indiana.... At all events, the facts of the present case do not bring it within the scope of the frustration doctrine, so we need not decide whether the Indiana Supreme Court would embrace the doctrine in a suitable case.

For the same reason we need not decide whether a *force majeure* clause should be deemed a relinquishment of a party's right to argue impracticability or frustration, on the theory that such a clause represents the integrated expression of the parties' desires with respect to excuses based on supervening events; or whether such a clause either in general or as specifically worded in this case covers any different ground from these defenses; or whether a buyer can urge impracticability under section 2–615 of the Uniform Commercial Code, which applies to this suit. Regarding the last of these questions, although the text says "seller," Official Comment 9 to the section says that in some circumstances "the reason of the present section may well apply and entitle the buyer to the exemption," and many courts have done just that.... The rub is that Indiana has not adopted the "Official Comments" to the UCC.[a] It has its own official comments, and they seem critical of Official Comment 9: "Comment 9 discusses 'exemption' for the buyer, but the text of the section is applicable only to sellers." Burns Ind.Stat. Ann. § 26–1–2–615, Ind.Comment. It may be, therefore, that buyers cannot use section 2–615 in Indiana. But it is not clear that this has substantive significance. Section 1–103 of the Uniform Commercial Code authorizes the courts to apply common law doctrines to the extent consistent with the Code—this is the basis on which NIPSCO is able to plead frustration as an alternative defense to section 2–615; and the essential elements of frustration and of impracticability are the same. With section 2–615 compare Restatement, supra, §§ 261 (impossibili-

---

a. No state adopted the Official Comments. Most states, like Indiana, have their own state comments, which have likewise not been adopted. See the Editors' Note to Uniform Commercial Code in the Supplement.

ty/impracticability) and 265 (frustration); and see id., § 265, comment a. NIPSCO gains nothing by pleading section 2–615 of the Uniform Commercial Code as well as common law frustration, and thus loses nothing by a ruling that buyers in Indiana cannot use section 2–615.

Whether or not Indiana recognizes the doctrine of frustration, and whether or not a buyer can ever assert the defense of impracticability under section 2–615 of the Uniform Commercial Code, these doctrines, so closely related to each other and to *force majeure* as well, ... cannot help NIPSCO. All are doctrines for shifting risk to the party better able to bear it, either because he is in a better position to prevent the risk from materializing or because he can better reduce the disutility of the risk (as by insuring) if the risk does occur. Suppose a grower agrees before the growing season to sell his crop to a grain elevator, and the crop is destroyed by blight and the grain elevator sues. Discharge is ordinarily allowed in such cases.... The grower has every incentive to avoid the blight; so if it occurs, it probably could not have been prevented; and the grain elevator, which buys from a variety of growers not all of whom will be hit by blight in the same growing season, is in a better position to buffer the risk of blight than the grower is.

Since impossibility and related doctrines are devices for shifting risk in accordance with the parties' presumed intentions, which are to minimize the costs of contract performance, one of which is the disutility created by risk, they have no place when the contract explicitly assigns a particular risk to one party or the other. As we have already noted, a fixed-price contract is an explicit assignment of the risk of market price increases to the seller and the risk of market price decreases to the buyer, and the assignment of the latter risk to the buyer is even clearer where, as in this case, the contract places a floor under price but allows for escalation. If, as is also the case here, the buyer forecasts the market incorrectly and therefore finds himself locked into a disadvantageous contract, he has only himself to blame and so cannot shift the risk back to the seller by invoking impossibility or related doctrines.... It does not matter that it is an act of government that may have made the contract less advantageous to one party.... Government these days is a pervasive factor in the economy and among the risks that a fixed-price contract allocates between the parties is that of a price change induced by one of government's manifold interventions in the economy. Since "the very purpose of a fixed price agreement is to place the risk of increased costs on the promisor (and the risk of decreased costs on the promisee)," the fact that costs decrease steeply (which is in effect what happened here—the cost of generating electricity turned out to be lower than NIPSCO thought when it signed the fixed-price contract with Carbon County) cannot allow the buyer to walk away from the contract....

[The court went on to hold that Carbon County was not entitled to specific performance which "would force the continuation of production that has become uneconomical." The workers and merchants where Carbon County's mine was located might suffer hardship, but they were not parties to the contract or third party beneficiaries.

[Affirmed.]

NOTE

"Take or Pay" Clauses. "Take or pay" clauses first became popular in natural gas contracts and then spread to other energy contracts. A typical natural gas transaction is described in International Minerals & Chemical Corp. v. Llano, Inc., 770 F.2d 879 (10th Cir.1985), cert. denied, 475 U.S. 1015 (1986), involving a contract by International Minerals & Chemical Corp. (IMC), which operated a potash mine and processing facility, to buy from Llano, a pipeline company, "the entire fuel requirements of Buyer's plant," subject to other provisions in the contract.

One of the other provisions was a "take or pay" clause that required IMC to take a fixed annual minimum and, if IMC did not take this minimum, to pay for it anyway. Another provision was a *force majeure* clause that excused either party if failure or delay in performance was "occasioned" by such events as fire, flood, acts of God, or interference of civil or military authorities.

When IMC's attempts to comply with a new state environmental regulation reduced its requirements for natural gas below the minimum, the court concluded that the *force majeure* clause did not relieve IMC of its duty to pay. "Since this is a 'take or pay' contract, the buyer can perform in either of two ways. It can either (1) take the minimum purchase obligation of natural gas (and pay) or (2) pay the minimum bill. It is settled law that when a promisor can perform a contract in either of two alternative ways, the impracticability of one alternative does not excuse the promisor if performance by means of the other alternative is still practicable." The *force majeure* clause "does not compel a different result; it would at most excuse IMC from its duty to 'take,' not from its duty to 'pay.'"

The court reached a different conclusion, however, under another clause that provided for an "appropriate adjustment in the minimum purchase requirements" in the event that "Buyer is unable to receive gas ... for any reason beyond the reasonable control of the parties, or in the event of *force majeure* as provided [herein]." The court reasoned that "'unable' is synonymous with 'impracticable'" and concluded that since "there was no technically suitable way for IMC to comply" with the new regulation without reducing its natural gas requirements below the minimum, "the adjustment provision ... was triggered."

SECTION 4. HALF MEASURES

What further consequences follow when a party is excused from performance on the ground of impracticability or frustration? One consequence is that, because of the operation of the concept of constructive conditions of exchange, the other party is excused from having to render any further performance. But this will not serve to compensate either party for losses incurred in reliance on the contract before the parties were excused. To what extent have courts in such situations been receptive to "half measures" [a]—to relief that stands somewhere between strict enforcement and complete excuse?

---

a. See Young, Half Measures, 81 Colum.L.Rev. 19, 20 (1981), noting "that half measure relief is equivalent to a court-imposed compromise."

If the contract can be treated as divisible, a court may hold that the parties are excused as to only part of their performances. See Gill v. Johnstown Lumber Co., p. 720 above. If the losses incurred in reliance have resulted in a benefit to the other party, restitution will be allowed. See Restatement Second § 377. Beyond this, however, courts have not been anxious to venture.

Thus no compensation has generally been allowed for reliance that has not conferred a benefit on the other party. Scholarly writers have shown occasional dissatisfaction with this state of affairs and the Restatement Second, in one of its more audacious pronouncements, states that if the traditional rules "will not avoid injustice, the court may grant relief on such terms as justice requires including protection of the parties' reliance interests." Restatement Second § 272.[b] The cases and other materials that follow examine some of the support for such an assertion.

NOTES

(1) *Measure of Benefit.* How should benefit be calculated in such cases of excuse based on changed circumstances? See Clark v. Gilbert, 26 N.Y. 279 (1863) ("the recovery in such a case cannot exceed the contract price or the rate of it for the part of the service performed"); Matter of Buccini v. Paterno Construction Co., 170 N.E. 910 (N.Y.1930) ("The question to be determined is the benefit to the owner in advancement of the ends to be promoted by the contract.")

(2) *The Case of Cutter's Contingency.* Cutter had signed on in Jamaica as second mate aboard the ship Governor Parry in return for a promise of "the sum of thirty guineas, provided he proceeds, continues and does his duty as second mate in the said ship from hence to the port of Liverpool." The ship sailed from Jamaica on August 2 with Cutter on board and arrived at Liverpool on October 9, but Cutter had died on September 20. The usual wage for a second mate on such a voyage, if fixed by the month for a round-trip voyage, was £ 4 per month, roughly a quarter of what Cutter had been promised. Cutter's administratrix sued for the thirty guineas. *Held:* judgment for defendant.

"[I]f there been no contract between these parties, all that the intestate could have recovered . . . for the voyage would have been eight pounds; whereas here the defendant contracted to pay thirty guineas provided the mate continued to do his duty as mate during the whole voyage, in which case the latter would have received nearly four times as much as if he were paid for the number of months he served. He stipulated to receive the larger sum if the whole duty were performed, and nothing unless the whole of that duty were performed; it was a kind of insurance." Cutter v. Powell, 101 Eng.Rep. 573 (King's Bench 1795).

b. Cal.Civ.Code § 1514, part of the Field Civil Code, enacted in 1872, provides for apportionment, upon excuse from performance of an obligation, "of the consideration to which [the obligor] would have been entitled upon full performance, according to the benefits" received by the other party. For proposals to apportion losses, see Trakman, Winner Take Some: Loss Sharing and Commercial Impracticability, 69 Minn.L.Rev. 471 (1985); Note, 69 Yale L.J. 1054 (1960). For a contrary view, see Posner & Rosenfield, Impossibility and Related Doctrines in Contract Law: An Economic Analysis, 6 J.Legal Stud. 83, 112–15 (1977).

Do you agree? In what sense was there "a kind of insurance"?

(3) *Temporary Impracticability or Frustration.* Particularly thorny questions arise when it is clear that the impracticability and frustration will be only temporary. Assuming that the affected party is temporarily excused from performing, when is the other party justified in terminating the contract? If the other party does not terminate the contract, is the excused party justified in refusing to perform after the impracticability or frustration has ceased?

Two leading cases reaching opposite results on the first question are Bettini v. Gye, 1 Q.B.D. 183 (1876), and Poussard v. Spiers & Pond, 1 Q.B.D. 410 (1876). Both dealt with whether an impresario is justified in terminating the contract of a performer who has become ill. A case, also from the world of entertainment, giving an affirmative answer to the second question is Autry v. Republic Productions, Inc., 180 P.2d 888 (Cal.1947), which held that the cowboy movie star Gene Autry was justified in refusing to resume performance of his contract with his studio after service in the Army in World War II.

(4) *Problem.* In response to an invitation from the Federal Reserve Board, Wegematic Corp. submitted the winning proposal for a new computing system, which Wegematic described as "a truly revolutionary system utilizing all of the latest technical advances." Delivery was to be a year later, but after delays of nearly four months, Wegematic finally announced that "due to engineering difficulties it has become impracticable to deliver the ... Computing System at this time." After another year, the Board succeeded in procuring comparable equipment from IBM. When sued by the United States, Wegematic agreed that it was excused because it was unable to achieve the revolutionary breakthrough that it had anticipated because of "basic engineering difficulties" that would have taken up to two years and a million and a half dollars to correct, with success likely but not certain.

Is mistake or impracticability *Wegematic* stronger ground for excuse? What decision on either ground? Did Wegematic make a tactical error in not asking the Board for more time? See United States v. Wegematic Corp., 360 F.2d 674 (2d Cir.1966).

YOUNG v. CITY OF CHICOPEE

Supreme Judicial Court of Massachusetts, 1904.
186 Mass. 518, 72 N.E. 63.

HAMMOND, J. This is an action to recover for work and materials furnished under a written contract providing for the repair of a wooden bridge forming a part of the highway across the Connecticut river. While the work was in progress the bridge was totally destroyed by fire without the fault of either party, so that the contract could not be performed. The specifications required that the timber and other woodwork of the carriageway, wherever decayed, should be replaced by sound material, securely fastened, so that the way should be in "a complete and substantial condition." As full compensation both for work and materials, the plaintiff was to receive a certain sum per thousand feet for the lumber used "on measurements made after laying and certified by the engineers"; or, in other words, the amount of the plaintiff's compensation was measured by the number of feet of new material wrought into the bridge. That the public travel might not be interfered with more than was reasonably necessary, the contract provided that no work should be begun until material for at least one-half of the repairs contemplated should be "upon the job." With this condition the plaintiff complied, the lumber, which, at the time of the fire had not been used, being distributed "all along the bridge" and upon the river banks. Some of this lumber was destroyed by the fire. At the trial the defendant did not dispute its liability to pay for the work done upon and materials wrought into the structure at the time of the fire (Angus v. Scully, 176 Mass. 357, 57 N.E. 674, 49 L.R.A. 562, 79 Am.St.Rep. 318, and cases there cited), and the only question before us is whether it was liable for the damage to the lumber which was distributed as above stated and had not been used. It is to be noted that there had been no delivery of this lumber to the defendant. It was brought "upon the job," and kept there as the lumber of the plaintiff. The title to it was in him, and not in the defendant. Nor did the defendant have any care or control over it. No part of it belonged to the defendant until wrought into the bridge. The plaintiff could have exchanged it for other lumber. If at any time during the progress of the work before the fire the plaintiff had refused to proceed, the defendant, against his consent, could not lawfully have used it. Indeed, had it not been destroyed, it would have remained the property of the plaintiff after the fire. Nor is the situation changed, so far as respects the question before us, by the fact that the lumber was brought there in compliance with the condition relating to the commencement of the work. This condition manifestly was inserted to insure the rapid progress of the work, and it has no material bearing upon the rights of the parties in relation to the lumber. It is also to be borne in mind in this connection that the compensation for the whole job was to be determined by the amount of lumber wrought into the bridge. The contract was entire. By the destruction of the bridge each party was excused from further performance, and the plaintiff could recover for partial performance. The principle upon which the plaintiff can do this is sometimes said to rest upon the doctrine that there is an implied contract upon the owner of the structure upon which the work is to be done that it shall continue to exist, and therefore, if it is destroyed, even without his fault, still he must be regarded as in default, and so liable to pay for what has been done. Niblo v. Binsse, 40 N.Y. 476; Whelen v. Ansonia Clock Co., 97 N.Y. 293. In Butterfield v. Byron, 153 Mass. 523, 27 N.E. 669, 12 L.R.A. 571, 25 Am.St.Rep. 654, it was said by Knowlton, J., that there was "an implied assumpsit for what has properly been done by either [of the parties], the law dealing with it as done at the request of the other, and creating a liability to pay for it its value." In whatever way the principle may be stated, it would seem that the liability of the owner in a case like this should be measured by the amount of the contract work done which at the time of the destruction of the structure had become so far identified with it as that, but for the destruction, it would have inured to him as contemplated by the contract. In the present case the defendant, in accordance with this doctrine, should be held liable for the labor and materials actually wrought into the bridge. To that extent it insured the plaintiff. But it did not insure the plaintiff against the loss of lumber owned by him at the time of the fire, which had not then come into such relations with the bridge as, but for the fire, to inure to the benefit of the defendant, as contemplated by the contract. The cases of Haynes v. Second Baptist Church, 88 Mo. 285, 57 Am.Rep. 413, and Rawson v. Clark, 70 Ill. 656, cited by the plaintiff, seem to us to be distinguishable from this case.

The exceptions therefore must be sustained, and the verdict set aside. In accordance with the terms of the statement contained in the bill of exceptions, judgment should be entered for the plaintiff in the sum of $584 damages, and it is so ordered.

NOTES

(1) *Repair v. Building.* If Young had contracted to erect a bridge from scratch, rather than to repair one, the risk of its destruction by casualty before completion would have rested entirely on him, in the absence of an agreement to the contrary. Far from recovering for part performance, he would have been accountable for breach if he did not begin again. "It is well established law that where one contracts to furnish labor and materials, and construct a chattel, or build a house, on land of another, he will not ordinarily be excused from performance of his contract by the destruction of the chattel or building without his fault before the time fixed for the delivery of it." Butterfield v. Byron, 27 N.E. 667 (Mass.1891). What, aside from the analogy of Taylor v. Caldwell, might account for this difference between construction contracts and repair contracts?

(2) *English Law Reform.* In Fibrosa Spolka Akcyjna v. Fairbairn Lawson Combe Barbour, Ltd., [1943] A.C. 32, 144 A.L.R. 1298, the House of Lords allowed a Polish buyer of textile machines to recover £1,000 that it had paid to an English seller in the summer of 1939, after the invasion of Poland made it impossible for the seller to deliver the machines as required by the contract. If the seller had done any fruitless work on the machines, however, it was said that no offset could be allowed for that.

The case suggested to Parliament that a more equitable solution might be achieved, and the response was the Law Reform (Frustrated Contracts) Act, 1943. One of its chief effects was to alter one's position if one has received an advance payment but has also incurred expenses going toward one's own performance: "the court may, if it considers it just to do so having regard to all the circumstances of the case, allow him to retain [part of the prepayment], not being an amount in excess of the expenses so incurred." Section 1(2).

In the *Fibrosa* case, how much of the prepayment could the seller justly retain, if it had expended £800 in manufacturing the machines (now unsalable) before the contract was discharged? The proponents of the Act thought he should have to repay £200. The Lord Chancellor (Simon) said, "I think that will commend itself to everybody as good sense," in giving such an example. But Professor Glanville Williams has argued that he should have to return £600, shouldering half of the unavoidable loss. "Either natural justice, on my understanding of it, is altogether silent on a case of this sort, or it decrees that the distribution of loss shall be equal. Equal division of loss is also economically sounder than the placing of loss on one party only, for each of the two parties may be able to bear half the loss without serious consequences when the whole loss might come close to ruining him." See G. Williams, Law Reform (Frustrated Contracts) Act, 35–36 (1944).

This argument assumes that the seller did not contract for the early payment of £1,000 as protection against discharge of the contract by the law of impossibility, but rather against the risk of insolvency: "It is not often that parties contemplate that performance of their contract will become impossible. If they do contemplate the latter event, their usual reaction is to take out a policy of insurance, not to provide for payment in advance." Id. at 36.

(3) *The Case of the House Halfway.* Owner contracted with Mover to have a building on Third Street relocated on First Street, at a fixed price. When Mover had gotten it about halfway, and quit work for the night, it was consumed by fire, through no fault of Mover. Owner disclaimed any liability, and Mover sued for the fair value of the services rendered in the work down to the time of the fire. Mover obtained a judgment on a jury verdict (amount unspecified), and Owner appealed. *Held:* Affirmed. Angus v. Scully, 57 N.E. 674 (Mass.1900).

(4) *Reliance–Based Recovery.* In 1936, the authors of the seminal article on the reliance interest admitted that, although "it would seem that the reliance interest should also play an important role" in cases involving changed circumstances, at that time there were, "apparently, no American or English cases expressly recognizing a recovery measured by the reliance interest as the means of accomplishing a desirable compromise between the extreme demands of no liability and liability for the full expectation interest." Fuller & Perdue, The Reliance Interest in Contract Damages (pt. 2), 46 Yale L.J. 373, 380 (1936). Two decades later a case was decided that confirmed their analysis.

John Bowen Co. was the general contractor for the construction by the Commonwealth of Massachusetts of a hospital in Boston. After subcontracts had been made and work begun, the Supreme Judicial Court of Massachusetts held that the contract between Bowen and the Commonwealth was void because Bowen had, though not in bad faith, dealt with subbids in such a way as to make its bid seem lowest when in fact it was not. Work on the hospital stopped. The same court then held that a subcontractor who had begun work was entitled to recovery based on the value of the labor and materials furnished. The court declined to justify such recovery "on the principle of unjust enrichment which underlies restitution cases wherein recovery is limited to benefits received," noting that the case was not one in which "the defendant stands fully apart, as the plaintiff does, from the circumstances which caused the unexpected destruction of the subject matter of the contract." M. Ahern Co. v. John Bowen Co., Inc., 133 N.E.2d 484 (Mass.1956).

The following year the same court passed on the claim of another subcontractor that, in contrast to the other subcontractor, had not yet begun work. The contract provided that the subcontractor would "furnish and submit all necessary or required samples, shop drawings, tests, affidavits, etc., for approval, all as ordered or specified." The court decided that the subcontractor should recover the "fair value of those acts done in conformity with the specific request of the defendant as contained in the contract," and justified the decision by reference to a "combination of circumstances peculiar to this case."

"Although the matter of denial of reliance expenditures in impossibility situations seems to have been discussed but little in judicial opinions, it has, however, been the subject of critical comment by scholars. See Fuller and Perdue, The Reliance Interest in Contract Damages, 46 Yale L.J. 52, 373, 379–383.... In England the recent frustrated contracts legislation provides that the court may grant recovery for expenditures in reliance on the contract or in preparation to perform it where it appears *'just to do so having regard to all the circumstances of the case'* (emphasis supplied). 6 & 7 George VI, c. 40." [a]

"... We are mindful that in Young v. Chicopee ... recovery of the value of materials brought to the construction site at the specific request of the defendant therein was denied. But in that case the supervening act rendering further performance impossible was a fire not shown to have been caused by the fault of either party. We are not disposed to extend that holding to a situation in which the defendant's fault is greater than the plaintiff's.

"Moreover, the acts requested here by their very nature could not be 'wrought into' the structure. In Angus v. Scully [Note 3, above], recovery for the value of services rendered by house movers was allowed although the house was destroyed midway in the moving. The present case comes nearer to the rationale of the Angus case than to that of the Young case." Albre Marble and Tile Co. v. John Bowen Co., 155 N.E.2d 437 (Mass.1959).

———

THE *ALCOA* CASE

One of the most controversial decisions dealing with changed circumstances is Aluminum Company of America v. Essex Group, Inc., 499 F.Supp. 53 (W.D.Pa.1980). Late in 1967, after more than six months of negotiations, ALCOA contracted with Essex to convert Essex's alumina into molten aluminum by a smelting process. Performance was to take place over 16 years, with an option in Essex to extend for another five years, for a flexible price. (Alan Greenspan, the economist, assisted ALCOA in devising the pricing formula.) One of the variables in the formula represented changing production costs other than labor; for this the Wholesale Price Index–Industrial Commodities (WPI) was used as a proxy. At all events the charge to Essex was limited to 65% of an aluminum market price periodically published (the "65% cap"). In each of the first six years of operations ALCOA's profit exceeded 4¢ a pound, but by the tenth year ALCOA was incurring losses that threatened to mount to more than 75 million dollars. Other than the labor cost, that of electricity is the chief outlay in converting alumina. Since energy costs are a relatively small component of the WPI, electricity rates had begun swiftly to outpace that index owing to OPEC's influence on oil prices and to anti-pollution regulations.

In litigation between ALCOA and Essex, the trial court in an opinion of some 40 pages found that though ALCOA had sought a profit of 4¢ a pound, the parties had foreseen that the profit might vary 3¢ either way, between 7¢ and 1¢ a pound, and reformed the price term so as to yield ALCOA not less than a 1¢ per pound profit (unless the 65% cap should be less). The case was settled while on appeal.

NOTES

(1) *The Ground in Alcoa.* It is unclear that the Alcoa case should be read as one involving changed circumstances. The court first concluded that the parties were mistaken as to the WPI's "capacity to work as the parties expected it to

a. This is not accurate. See Note 2, above.

work" and that this was "a matter of fact, existing at the time they made the contract" and not an error in "simple prediction of future events" (499 F.Supp. at 63, 64). The court's subsequent consideration of changed circumstances was prefaced by the explanation that the discussion of mistake above sufficed to establish that ALCOA was entitled to some kind of relief, but other theories would be examined because "the stakes in this case are large and the changes of review by higher courts are high" (id. at 70).

(2) *The Remedy in Alcoa.* Most of the comment on the Alcoa case has focused on the court's remedy of reformation. On this score, the case has played to mixed reviews. See generally Halpern, Application of the Doctrine of Commercial Impracticability: Searching for "The Wisdom of Solomon," 135 U.Pa. L.Rev. 1123 (1987).

Professor Richard Speidel has referred to it as "a trail blazer" and has written of its "new 'spirit' of contract law," although he suggests that the judge acted prematurely because "the court should not impose its own price adjustment until it has concluded that the advantaged party has acted improperly in the ex post bargaining process." Speidel, Court–Imposed Price Adjustments Under Long–Term Supply Contracts, 76 Nw.U.L.Rev. 369, 395, 416 (1981). See also Speidel, The New Spirit of Contract, 2 J.L. & Com. 193 (1983). For the results of a survey of general counsel, indicating approval of judicial price adjustment, see Weintraub, A Survey of Contract Practice and Policy, 1992 Wis.L.Rev. 1, 41–45.

Professor John Dawson, on the other hand, took issue with Speidel, finding a "strange inversion of ideas" in the case, which he described as "grotesque" and as "a lonely monument on a bleak landscape, the only instance in which an American judge has tried to dictate entirely different substantive terms (in this instance the price) in a contract that was still being actively performed.... Does anyone seriously contend that a judge ... becomes better equipped than the parties concerned to reconcile their divergent, often conflicting interests, to devise the terms that can govern a complex enterprise and ensure its future survival?" Dawson, Judicial Revision of Frustrated Contracts: The United States, 64 B.U.L.Rev. 1, 26, 35–36 (1984).

(3) *Significance of Concessions.* Although scholars have occasionally suggested that changed circumstances may place a party under an obligation to negotiate in good faith with respect to a modification,[a] courts have not been receptive to this suggestion. See, for example, L.C. Williams Oil Co., Inc. v. Exxon Corp., 625 F.Supp. 477 (M.D.N.C.1985), rejecting the argument "that Exxon was under a good faith obligation to modify the existing contract terms when Williams's circumstances changed."

This is not to say, however, that a court will ignore a party's reasonable proposal for a concession in the face of changed circumstances. See, for example, Lloyd v. Murphy, 153 P.2d 47 (Cal.1944), in which a dealer in new cars suffered from wartime restrictions and ultimately vacated his Wilshire Boulevard location. Before that, however, the landlords had offered to reduce the rent and to waive prohibitions in the lease against uses they had not consented to and against subletting. In a major statement on the law of frustration of purpose, Justice Traynor denied relief to the tenant, emphasizing the value of the landlord's concession. The inference might be that the tenant's obligation turned on how the landlords chose to refashion the terms of the lease.

---

a. See Speidel, Court–Imposed Price Adjustments Under Long–Term Supply Contracts, 76 Nw.U.L.Rev. 369 (1981), discussed in Note 2, above.

(4) *Renegotiation Clauses.* Long-term contracts, under which changed circumstances pose a significant risk, sometimes provide for renegotiation under stated conditions. The drafter of such a clause faces two challenging questions. First, what are the conditions under which renegotiation is required? Second, what are the consequences of a failure of negotiations?

The International Chamber of Commerce has promulgated "drafting suggestions" for a "hardship clause" for international contracts. The answer to the first question is that renegotiation is required on "the occurrence of events not contemplated by the parties [that] fundamentally alter the equilibrium of the present contract, thereby placing an excessive burden on one of the parties in the performance of its contractual obligations."[b] Several alternatives are suggested in answer to the second question. One possibility is that the contract will remain in force as before. Another is that the party seeking modification may ask the International Chamber of Commerce to appoint a third person whose recommendation the hardship clause may make binding or merely advisory.

OGLEBAY NORTON CO. v. ARMCO, INC.

Supreme Court of Ohio, 1990.
52 Ohio St.3d 232, 556 N.E.2d 515.

[In 1957, Armco made a long-term contract with Oglebay requiring Oglebay to have adequate shipping capacity available and requiring Armco to use that capacity for the transportation of iron ore on the Great Lakes. The contract provided for a primary and a secondary price mechanism:

> *Armco agrees to pay* ... for all iron ore transported hereunder *the regular net contract rates for the season* in which the ore is transported, *as recognized by the leading iron ore shippers* in such season for the transportation of iron ore.... *If,* in any season of navigation hereunder, *there is no regular net contract rate recognized by the leading iron ore shippers* for such transportation, *the parties shall mutually agree upon a rate* for such transportation, *taking into consideration the contract rate being charged for similar transportation* by the leading independent vessel operators engaged in transportation of iron ore from The Lake Superior District. [Emphasis supplied by the court.]

During the next 23 years the parties modified the contract four times, each time extending the time and entailing substantial capital investment by Oglebay to meet Armco's requirements. After the fourth modification, which extended the contract to the year 2010, Oglebay began a $95 million capital improvement program.

[From 1957 through 1983 the parties established the contract shipping rate by reference to a rate published in Skillings Mining Review, in

b. For a case involving a provision under which the parties to a long-term coal supply contract agreed to address revising the price on the occurrence "of material unforeseen events or changed conditions" which caused the price to be inequitable to one of the parties, see Kentucky Utilities Co. v. South East Coal Co., 836 S.W.2d 392 (Ky.1992).

accord with the contract's primary price mechanism. After a serious downturn in the iron and steel industry in 1983, Armco challenged the rate quoted by Oglebay and the parties negotiated a mutually satisfactory rate for the 1984 season. After that, however, the parties were unable to agree on a rate and, in April of 1986, Oglebay sought a declaratory judgment, asking the court to declare the contract rate to be correct rate or, in the absence of such a rate, to declare a reasonable rate. Armco denied that the rate sought by Oglebay was the "contract rate" and denied that the court had jurisdiction to declare a rate of its own accord. The parties continued to perform pending resolution of the dispute. In August of 1987, Armco filed a supplementary counterclaim seeking a declaration that the contract was no longer enforceable.

[In November of 1987, the trial court issued its declaratory judgment, fixing $6.25 as the rate for the 1986 season and holding that, if the parties were unable to agree on a rate for the upcoming seasons, they must notify the court, which would appoint a mediator and require the parties' chief executive officers to meet and "mutually agree upon a rate." The court of appeals affirmed and a motion was made to certify the record.]

PER CURIAM. This case presents three mixed questions of fact and law. First, did the parties intend to be bound by the terms of this contract despite the failure of its primary and secondary pricing mechanisms? Second, if the parties did intend to be bound, may the trial court establish $6.25 per gross ton as a reasonable rate for Armco to pay Oglebay for shipping Armco ore during the 1986 shipping season? Third, may the trial court continue to exercise its equitable jurisdiction over the parties, and may it order the parties to utilize a mediator if they are unable to mutually agree on a shipping rate for each annual shipping season? We answer each of these questions in the affirmative and for the reasons set forth below affirm the decision of the court of appeals.

I

Appellant Armco argues that the complete breakdown of the primary and secondary contract pricing mechanisms renders the 1957 contract unenforceable, because the parties never manifested an intent to be bound in the event of the breakdown of the primary and secondary pricing mechanisms. Armco asserts that it became impossible after 1985 to utilize the first pricing mechanism in the 1957 contract, i.e., examining the published rate for a leading shipper in the "Skillings Mining Review," because after 1985 a new rate was no longer published. Armco asserts as well that it also became impossible to obtain the information necessary to determine and take into consideration the rates charged by leading independent vessel operators in accordance with the secondary pricing mechanism. This is because that information was no longer publicly available after 1985 and because the trial court granted the motions to quash of non-parties, who were subpoenaed to obtain this specific information. Armco argues that since the parties never consented to be bound by a contract whose specific pricing mechanisms had failed, the trial court should have declared the contract to be void and unenforceable.

The trial court recognized the failure of the 1957 contract pricing mechanisms. Yet the trial court had competent, credible evidence before it to conclude that the parties intended to be bound despite the failure of the pricing mechanisms. The evidence demonstrated the long-standing and close business relationship of the parties, including joint ventures, interlocking directorates and Armco's ownership of Oglebay stock. As the trial court pointed out, the parties themselves contractually recognized Armco's vital and unique interest in the combined dedication of Oglebay's bulk vessel fleet, and the parties recognized that Oglebay could be required to ship up to 7.1 million gross tons of Armco iron ore per year.

Whether the parties intended to be bound, even upon the failure of the pricing mechanisms, is a question of fact properly resolved by the trier of fact.... Since the trial court had ample evidence before it to conclude that the parties did so intend, the court of appeals correctly affirmed the trial court regarding the parties' intent. We thus affirm the court of appeals on this question.

II

Armco also argues that the trial court lacked jurisdiction to impose a shipping rate of $6.25 per gross ton when that rate did not conform to the 1957 contract pricing mechanisms. The trial court held that it had the authority to determine a reasonable rate for Oglebay's services, even though the price mechanism of the contract had failed, since the parties intended to be bound by the contract. The court cited 1 Restatement of the Law 2d, Contracts (1981) 92, Section 33, and its relevant comments to support this proposition. Comment *e* to Section 33 explains in part:

" * * * Where * * * [the parties] * * * intend to conclude a contract for the sale of goods * * * and the price is not settled, the price is a reasonable price at the time of delivery if * * * (c) the price is to be fixed in terms of some agreed market or other standard as set or recorded by a third person or agency and it is not so set or recorded. Uniform Commercial Code § 2–305(1)." Id. at 94–95....

The court therefore determined that a reasonable rate for Armco to pay to Oglebay for transporting Armco's iron ore during the 1986 shipping season was $6.00 per gross ton with an additional rate of twenty-five cents per gross ton when self-unloading vessels were used. The court based this determination upon the parties' extensive course of dealing, " * * * the detriment to the parties respectively, and valid comparisons of market price which reflect [the] economic reality of current depressed conditions in the American steel industry."

The court of appeals concluded that the trial court was justified in setting $6.25 per gross ton as a "reasonable rate" for Armco to pay Oglebay for the 1986 season, given the evidence presented to the trial court concerning various rates charged in the industry and given the intent of the parties to be bound by the agreement....

III

Armco also argues that the trial court lacks equitable jurisdiction to order the parties to negotiate or in the failure of negotiations, to mediate, during each annual shipping season through the year 2010. The court of appeals ruled that the trial court did not exceed its jurisdiction in issuing such an order.

3 Restatement of the Law 2d, Contracts (1981) 179, Section 362, entitled "Effect of Uncertainty of Terms," is similar in effect to Section 33 and states:

"Specific performance or an injunction will not be granted unless the terms of the contract are sufficiently certain to provide a basis for an appropriate order."

Comment *b* to Section 362 explains:

" * * * Before concluding that the required certainty is lacking, however, a court will avail itself of all of the usual aids in determining the scope of the agreement. * * * Expressions that at first appear incomplete may not appear so after resort to usage * * * or the addition of a term supplied by law * * *." Id. at 179.

Ordering specific performance of this contract was necessary, since, as the court of appeals pointed out, " * * * the undisputed dramatic changes in the market prices of great lakes shipping rates and the length of the contract would make it impossible for a court to award Oglebay accurate damages due to Armco's breach of the contract." We agree with the court of appeals that the appointment of a mediator upon the breakdown of court-ordered contract negotiations neither added to nor detracted from the parties' significant obligations under the contract.

It is well-settled that a trial court may exercise its equitable jurisdiction and order specific performance if the parties intend to be bound by a contract, where determination of long-term damages would be too speculative. See 3 Restatement of the Law 2d, Contracts, supra, at 171–172, Section 360(a), Comment *b;* Columbus Packing Co. v. State, ex rel. Schlesinger (1919), 100 Ohio St. 285, 294, 126 N.E. 291, 293–294. Indeed, the court of appeals pointed out that under the 1962 amendment, Armco itself had the contractual right to seek a court order compelling Oglebay to specifically perform its contractual duties.

The court of appeals was correct in concluding that ordering the parties to negotiate and mediate during each shipping season for the duration of the contract was proper, given the unique and long-lasting business relationship between the parties, and given their intent to be bound and the difficulty of properly ascertaining damages in this case. The court of appeals was also correct in concluding that ordering the parties to negotiate and mediate with each shipping season would neither add to nor detract from the parties' significant contractual obligations. This is because the order would merely facilitate in the most practical manner the parties' own ability to interact under the contract. Thus we affirm the court of appeals on this question. . . .

Judgment affirmed.

NOTE

Questions. How does the third question in *Oglebay Norton* differ from the question as to the remedy in *Alcoa* (see Note 2, p. 858 above? How did the court's answer in *Oglebay Norton* differ from the court's answer in *Alcoa?*

Chapter 9

THIRD PARTY BENEFICIARIES

The modern development of third party beneficiary law, at least in this country, is usually dated from the 1859 case Lawrence v. Fox, the first in this Chapter. Long before then, however, claims on contracts had been made by persons who were not parties to them. The results were mixed. In 17th century England it was successfully argued that a promise to pay a woman £1,000 was enforceable by her, although it was made to her father, and although she gave nothing in exchange for the promise. Later this case was disapproved. According to a 19th century English judge, "It would be a monstrous proposition to say that a person was a party to the contract for the purpose of suing upon it for his own advantage, and not for the purpose of being sued." [a]

As the case law has developed in this country, it is generally accepted that an action may be maintained on a contract, in an appropriate case, by one who had no part in creating it. The contract in such a case is said to be a "third party beneficiary contract." Probably the class of these contracts most familiar to the public at large is contracts of life insurance. It is perfectly well understood that the beneficiary of a life insurance policy may enforce a right to the death benefits even though the beneficiary did not apply for it, pay for it, or have any other connection with it.

Of course, many contracts are not in this category, and often a claimant's attempt to seize an advantage under a contract between other parties meets with failure. The Restatement of Contracts has popularized the term "incidental beneficiary" for a third party who may enjoy an advantage through the performance of a contract but has no enforceable interest in its performance. A clear though admittedly unusual example may be helpful. As a sports referee, John Bain made a controversial last-minute call of foul. The contestants were teams of schools in the Big Ten Basketball Conference: Iowa and Purdue. Iowa lost. In Iowa City there was a novelty store stocked with Iowa University sports memorabilia. The store owners made a claim against Bain for losses due to his alleged incompetence as a referee; the game had destroyed Iowa's chance of a championship. One basis for the claim was an alleged contract between Bain and the Conference, requiring professional competence. The trial court granted summary judgment for Bain.

---

a. Crompton, J., in Tweddle v. Atkinson, 121 Eng.Rep. 762 (Q.B.1861).

863

On appeal, *held:* Affirmed. Bain v. Gillispie, 357 N.W.2d 47 (Iowa App.1984).[b]

A beneficiary who has an enforceable interest in performance of the contract may be variously known as a "donee beneficiary," a "creditor beneficiary," or simply as an "intended beneficiary."

Several bodies of law exist, apart from third party beneficiary law, by which a contract may create such an interest in a party who is not named or addressed in it. By the law of agency, for example, an undisclosed principal of one of the named parties may enforce a contract made on its behalf. In some situations various doctrinal ideas work in tandem to the same end. The following example is given in the Restatement Second: "the rights of employees under a collective bargaining agreement are sometimes treated as rights of contract beneficiaries, sometimes as rights based on agency principles, sometimes as rights analogous to the rights of trust beneficiaries. Or the collective bargaining agreement may be treated as establishing a usage incorporated in individual employment contracts, or as analogous to legislation." [c]

The Restatement Second also refers to certain "overriding social policies" that may determine the stake of third parties in an agreement. Such policies are beyond the scope of the Restatement and of this book. For instance, the range of warranties accompanying sales of goods is not explored here. The business of this chapter is to identify third party interests in performance, as determined by the general law of agreements, and to indicate some qualities of those interests.

Through the power of contracting parties to create rights in others many needs have been met, some commercial in nature, others not; and there are "procedural" conveniences also in recognizing third party claims in contracts. Nevertheless, there are complications and inconveniences in the law of third party beneficiaries. It will be well, in going through the chapter, to consider both aspects of the subject. When disadvantages are encountered in granting a third-party claim, it may be possible to think of an alternate arrangement that would serve the purpose better. And in many of the cases there is a challenge to skill in drafting, so as to remove doubts and to promote the objects of the agreement.

NOTES

(1) *Express Contract Terms.* When a corporation agreed to sell the assets of one of its divisions, the sale contract contained this provision:

> It is understood and agreed that Purchaser is only purchasing certain assets of Seller, that Purchaser is not intended to be a successor to Seller for any purpose unless expressly set forth herein, and that Purchaser has not assumed, and expressly denies assumption hereby of, any other liability, obligation or commitment of Seller other than as set forth above or otherwise expressly set forth herein.[d]

b. Compare Mississippi High School Activities Ass'n, Inc. v. Farris, 501 So.2d 393 (Miss.1987) (umpire trouble at home plate).

c. Chapter 14, Introductory Note.

d. See Adams v. Avondale Industries, Inc., 905 F.2d 943, 952 (6th Cir.1990).

The object must have been to forestall claims against the buyer by the seller's customers, employees, and creditors in general. Although the contract did not "bind" them as it did the parties to the contract (buyer and seller), such a term is likely to be conclusive in actions they might bring on the contract. See McKinney v. Anheuser–Busch, Inc., 951 F.2d 360 (9th Cir.1991).[e]

Some business-asset sales expressly designate obligations of the seller that are to be enforceable against the buyer.[f] A case showing the effectiveness of a term like that is presented in Note 2, p. 883 below.[g]

(2) *Express Trust.* An express trust is defined as "a fiduciary relationship with respect to property, subjecting the person by whom the property is held to equitable duties to deal with the property for the benefit of another person, which arises as a result of a manifestation of an intention to create it." The requisite to be noticed here is that there be some property—a *res*—as the subject matter of the trust. An instance that is given in the next main case is a quantity of lead: X has promised a pig of lead to A, and he entrusts lead to B who undertakes to make it into a pig and deliver it to A. In such a case A has a property interest in the lead which will be recognized and vindicated by special procedures in equity, chancery courts being the historic guardians of trusts. The property may be a bag of money as well as a pig of lead; or it may be an intangible such as a contract right. But in any event, in the case of a trust "there is always some property which is the subject matter of the trust, and which is held by the trustee for the benefit of the cestui que trust." 1 Fratcher, Scott on Trusts § 2.6 (4th ed. 1987).[h]

LAWRENCE v. FOX

Court of Appeals of New York, 1859.
20 N.Y. 268.

Appeal from the Superior Court of the City of Buffalo. On the trial before Mr. Justice Masten, it appeared by the evidence of a bystander that one Holly, in November, 1857, at the request of the defendant, loaned and advanced to him $300, stating at the time that he owed that sum to the plaintiff for money borrowed of him, and had agreed to pay it to him the then next day; that the defendant, in consideration thereof, at the time of receiving the money, promised to pay it to the plaintiff the then next day. Upon this state of facts the defendant moved for a nonsuit, upon three several grounds, viz.: That there was no proof tending to show that Holly was indebted to the plaintiff, that the agreement by the defendant with Holly to pay the plaintiff was void for

---

e. In this case, however, the court distinguished a third party's action based on the tort of interference with contract relations.

Some liabilities are so far entrenched by law that they attach to a successor firm in a business buyout, notwithstanding a provision to the contrary. Moreover, liens on *assets* of a seller are not, as a general rule, divested upon a disposition of the assets. See, e.g., UCC 9–306(2).

f. For comparable terms in model contract forms for use in the construction industry, see Eisenberg, Third Party Beneficiary Contracts, 92 Colum.L.Rev. 1358, 1392–93 (1992).

g. But see Kary v. Kary, 318 N.W.2d 334 (S.D.1982).

h. For a comparison of agency and trust relationships with those growing out of third party beneficiary contracts, see Restatement Second § 302, Comment *f.*

want of consideration, and that there was no privity between the plaintiff and defendant. The court overruled the motion, and the counsel for the defendant excepted. The cause was then submitted to the jury, and they found a verdict for the plaintiff for the amount of the loan and interest, $344.66, upon which judgment was entered, from which the defendant appealed to the Superior Court, at General Term, where the judgment was affirmed, and the defendant appealed to this court. The cause was submitted on printed argument.

H. GRAY, J. The first objection raised on the trial amounts to this: That the evidence of the person present, who heard the declarations of Holly giving directions as to the payment of the money he was then advancing to the defendant, was mere hearsay and, therefore, not competent. Had the plaintiff sued Holly for this sum of money no objection to the competency of this evidence would have been thought of; and if the defendant had performed his promise by paying the sum loaned to him to the plaintiff, and Holly had afterwards sued him for its recovery, and the evidence had been offered by the defendant, it would doubtless have been received without an objection from any source. All the defendant had the right to demand in this case was evidence which, as between Holly and the plaintiff, was competent to establish the relation between them of debtor and creditor. For that purpose the evidence was clearly competent; it covered the whole ground and warranted the verdict of the jury.

But it is claimed that notwithstanding this promise was established by competent evidence, it was void for the want of consideration. It is now more than a quarter of a century since it was settled by the supreme court of this state—in an able and painstaking opinion by the late Chief Justice Savage, in which the authorities were fully examined and carefully analyzed—that a promise in all material respects like the one under consideration was valid; and the judgment of that court was unanimously affirmed by the court for the correction of errors. Farley v. Cleveland, 4 Cow. 432, 15 Am.Dec. 387; s. c. in error, 9 Cow. 639. In that case one Moon owed Farley and sold to Cleveland a quantity of hay, in consideration of which Cleveland promised to pay Moon's debt to Farley; and the decision in favor of Farley's right to recover was placed upon the ground that the hay received by Cleveland from Moon was a valid consideration for Cleveland's promise to pay Farley, and that the subsisting liability of Moon to pay Farley was no objection to the recovery. The fact that the money advanced by Holly to the defendant was a loan to him for a day, and that it thereby became the property of the defendant, seemed to impress the defendant's counsel with the idea that because the defendant's promise was not a trust fund placed by the plaintiff in the defendant's hands, out of which he was to realize money as from the sale of a chattel or the collection of a debt, the promise although made for the benefit of the plaintiff could not inure to his benefit. The hay which Cleveland bought of Moon was not to be paid to Farley, but the debt incurred by Cleveland for the purchase of the hay, like the debt incurred by the defendant for money borrowed, was what was to be paid.

That case has been often referred to by the courts of this state, and has never been doubted as sound authority for the principle upheld by it. Barker v. Bucklin, 2 Denio 45, 43 Am.Dec. 726; Canal Co. v. Westchester County Bank, 4 Denio 97. It puts to rest the objection that the defendant's promise was void for want of consideration. The report of that case shows that the promise was not only made to Moon but to the plaintiff Farley. In this case the promise was made to Holly and not expressly to the plaintiff; and this difference between the two cases presents the question, raised by the defendant's objection, as to the want of privity between the plaintiff and defendant. . . .

But it is urged that because the defendant was not in any sense a trustee of the property of Holly for the benefit of the plaintiff, the law will not imply a promise. I agree that many of the cases where a promise was implied were cases of trusts, created for the benefit of the promisor. The case of Felton v. Dickinson, 10 Mass. 287, and others that might be cited are of that class; but concede them all to have been cases of trusts, and it proves nothing against the application of the rule to this case. The duty of the trustee to pay the cestui que trust, according to the terms of the trust, implies his promise to the latter to do so. In this case the defendant, upon ample consideration received from Holly, promised Holly to pay his debt to the plaintiff; the consideration received and the promise to Holly made it as plainly his duty to pay the plaintiff as if the money had been remitted to him for that purpose, and as well implied a promise to do so as if he had been made a trustee of property to be converted into cash with which to pay. The fact that a breach of the duty imposed in the one case may be visited, and justly, with more serious consequences than in the other, by no means disproves the payment to be a duty in both. The principle illustrated by the example so frequently quoted (which concisely states the case in hand) "that a promise made to one for the benefit of another, he for whose benefit it is made may bring an action for its breach," has been applied to trust cases, not because it was exclusively applicable to those cases, but because it was a principle of law, and as such applicable to those cases.

It was also insisted that Holly could have discharged the defendant from his promise, though it was intended by both parties for the benefit of the plaintiff, and, therefore, the plaintiff was not entitled to maintain this suit for the recovery of a demand over which he had no control. It is enough that the plaintiff did not release the defendant from his promise, and whether he could or not is a question not now necessarily involved; but if it was, I think it would be found difficult to maintain the right of Holly to discharge a judgment recovered by the plaintiff upon confession or otherwise, for the breach of the defendant's promise; and if he could not, how could he discharge the suit before judgment, or the promise before suit, made as it was for the plaintiff's benefit and in accordance with legal presumption accepted by him (Berly v. Taylor, 5 Hill, 577–584 et seq.), until his dissent was shown?

The cases cited and especially that of Farley v. Cleveland, established the validity of a parol promise; it stands then upon the footing of a written one. Suppose the defendant had given his note in which for value received of Holly, he had promised to pay the plaintiff and the plaintiff had accepted the promise, retaining Holly's liability. Very clearly Holly could not have discharged that promise, be the right to release the defendant as it may. No one can doubt that he owes the sum of money demanded of him or that in accordance with his promise it was his duty to have paid it to the plaintiff; nor can it be doubted that whatever may be the diversity of opinion elsewhere, the adjudications in this state, from a very early period, approved by experience, have established the defendant's liability; if, therefore, it could be shown that a more strict and technically accurate application of the rules applied, would lead to a different result (which I by no means concede), the effort should not be made in the face of manifest justice.

The judgment should be affirmed.

JOHNSON, CH. J., DENIO, SELDEN, ALLEN and STRONG, JJ., concurred. JOHNSON, CH. J., and DENIO, J., were of opinion that the promise was to be regarded as made to the plaintiff through the medium of his agent, whose action he could ratify when it came to his knowledge, though taken without his being privy thereto.

COMSTOCK, J. (dissenting). The plaintiff had nothing to do with the promise on which he brought this action. It was not made to him, nor did the consideration proceed from him. If he can maintain the suit, it is because an anomaly has found its way into the law on this subject. In general, there must be privity of contract. The party who sues upon a promise must be the promisee, or he must have some legal interest in the undertaking. In this case, it is plain that Holly who loaned the money to the defendant, and to whom the promise in question was made, could at any time have claimed that it should be performed to himself personally. He had lent the money to the defendant, and at the same time directed the latter to pay the sum to the plaintiff. This direction he could countermand, and if he had done so, manifestly the defendant's promise to pay according to the direction would have ceased to exist. The plaintiff would receive a benefit by a complete execution of the arrangement, but the arrangement itself was between other parties, and was under their exclusive control. If the defendant had paid the money to Holly, his debt would have been discharged thereby. So Holly might have released the demand or assigned it to another person, or the parties might have annulled the promise now in question, and designated some other creditor of Holly as the party to whom the money should be paid. It has never been claimed that in a case thus situated the right of a third person to sue upon the promise rested on any sound principle of law. We are to inquire whether the rule has been so established by positive authority....

If A. delivers money or property to B., which the latter accepts upon a trust for the benefit of C., the latter can enforce the trust by an appropriate action for that purpose. Berly v. Taylor, 5 Hill, 577. If the trust be of money, I think the beneficiary may assent to it and bring the action for money had and received to his use. If it be of something else than money, the trustee must account for it according to the terms of the trust, and upon principles of equity. There is some authority even for saying that an express promise founded on the possession of a trust fund may be enforced by an action at law in the name of the beneficiary, although it was made to the creator of the trust. Thus, in Comyn, Dig. "Action on the Case upon Assumpsit," B. 15, it is laid down that if a man promise a pig of lead to A. and his executor give lead to make a pig to B., who assumes to deliver it to A., an assumpsit lies by A. against him. The case of Delaware & H. Canal Co. v. Westchester County Bank, 4 Denio 97, involved a trust because the defendants had received from a third party a bill of exchange under an agreement that they would endeavor to collect it and would pay over the proceeds when collected to the plaintiffs. A fund received under such an agreement does not belong to the person who receives it. He must account for it specifically; and perhaps there is no gross violation of principle in permitting the equitable owner of it to sue upon an express promise to pay it over. Having a specific interest in the thing, the undertaking to account for it may be regarded as in some sense made with him through the author of the trust. But further than this we cannot go without violating plain rules of law. In the case before us there was nothing in the nature of a trust or agency. The defendant borrowed the money of Holly and received it as his own. The plaintiff had no right in the fund, legal or equitable. The promise to repay the money created an obligation in favor of the lender to whom it was made and not in favor of any one else....

The judgment of the court below should, therefore, be reversed, and a new trial granted.

GROVER, J., also dissented.

Judgment affirmed.

NOTES

(1) *English Law.* Though there were early precedents to the contrary, it seems to have become settled in the common law of England that contracts may not confer enforceable rights on third parties as such. For discussion of the rule, see Beswick v. Beswick, [1967] 2 All E.R. 1197, in which a widow sued on a promise of payments to her that the defendant had made to her husband. The House of Lords ruled that she was entitled to specific performance, in her capacity as administratrix of her husband's estate, but it was conceded that she had no claim as an individual. An American scholar has said that the English courts are "very ready to torture a contract into a trust" because they feel the injustice of denying a remedy to the beneficiary of a contract. 1 Scott on Trusts, § 14.4 (3d ed. 1967).

For a promise such as the one made to Mr. Beswick, specific performance may be especially appropriate in a suit by the promisee. Do you see why? See Restatement Second § 307, Comment d; Thorpe v. Collins, 263 S.E.2d 115 (Ga.1980).

(2) *The American Scene.* For a history of the litigation in Lawrence v. Fox see Waters, The Property in the Promise: A Study of the Third Party Beneficiary Rule, 98 Harv.L.Rev. 1109 (1985). Professor Waters's investigations led him to believe that the promisee (not "Holly" but actually one Samuel Hawley) made

the loan to Fox for the purpose of gambling, as Hawley knew. The article depicts the influence of Corbin in the development of doctrine favoring third-party contract claims. For an appraisal of the case see Eisenberg, Third Party Beneficiary Contracts, fn. f, p. 865 above, at 1362–74 (1992).

Both articles describe ensuing developments in the law. Professor Eisenberg provides also a reformulation of third-party-beneficiary principle, alternative to those of the first and second Restatements ("inadequate and indeed largely meaningless"). See especially pp. 1385–89.

(3) *Restatement Terminology.* In the diction of the first Restatement, Lawrence would be known as a "creditor beneficiary." Section 133 established a threefold classification: donee, creditor and incidental beneficiaries. "An incidental beneficiary acquires by virtue of the promise no right against the promisor or the promisee." Section 147, carried forward as Restatement Second § 315. Because the diction of the first Restatement lingers in the courts, most of the definitional section (133) is reproduced next.

Restatement Second introduces the term "intended" beneficiary to designate claimants who (like the plaintiff in Lawrence v. Fox) are permitted to enforce contracts to which they are not party. Section 302. It discards the terms "creditor" and "donee" in this connection. What is gained by the new diction is not altogether clear. The new text begins: "(1) Unless otherwise agreed between promisor and promisee, a beneficiary of a promise is an intended beneficiary if recognition of a right to performance in the beneficiary is appropriate to effectuate the intention of the parties and ... (a) the performance of the promise will satisfy an obligation of the promisee to pay money to the beneficiary...." In the new lexicon, it seems, Lawrence may be called a "subsection (1)(a) intended beneficiary."

Sometimes one encounters a third party beneficiary contract in which each of the immediate parties is a promisor and each is a promisee. For present purposes "the promisor" is the maker of the promise sought to be enforced by the third party, and "the promisee" is its recipient. A firm grip on this convention will speed the discussion of cases in this chapter.

FIRST RESTATEMENT

Because the extant cases on third party beneficiary law rely largely on the first Restatement, its chief provision on the subject is reproduced here, in part.

§ 133. Definition of Donee Beneficiary, Creditor Beneficiary, Incidental Beneficiary

(1) Where performance of a promise in a contract will benefit a person other than the promisee, that person is [exception omitted [a]]:

　　(a) a donee beneficiary if it appears from the terms of the promise in view of the accompanying circumstances that the purpose of the promisee in obtaining the promise of all or part of the

---

a. "(3) Where it appears from the terms of the promise in view of the accompanying circumstances that the purpose of the promisee is to benefit a beneficiary under a trust and the promise is to render performance to the trustee, the trustee, and not the beneficiary under the trust, is a beneficiary within the meaning of this Section."

performance thereof is to make a gift to the beneficiary or to confer upon him a right against the promisor to some performance neither due nor supposed or asserted to be due from the promisee to the beneficiary;

(b) a creditor beneficiary if no purpose to make a gift appears from the terms of the promise in view of the accompanying circumstances and performance of the promise will satisfy an actual or supposed or asserted duty of the promisee to the beneficiary, or a right of the beneficiary against the promisee which has been barred by the Statute of Limitations or by a discharge in bankruptcy, or which is unenforceable because of the Statute of Frauds;

(c) an incidental beneficiary if neither the facts stated in Clause (a) nor those stated in Clause (b) exist.

(The corresponding provision of the Restatement Second appears at p. 881 below.)

NOTES

(1) *Problem.* In Gianni v. R. Russell & Co., Inc., p. 566 above, a provision of Gianni's lease was that he would not sell tobacco in any form. It may be supposed that the owner of the office building had leased other space for tobacco sales. If so, should the lessee of that space be treated as a third party beneficiary of Gianni's lease? This case is not provided for in subsection (1)(a) of Restatement Second § 302, is it? Is it in former § 133(2)(b)?

(2) *Statute of Frauds.* Following the decision in Lawrence v. Fox, the situation appears to be this: two persons ("Holly" and Fox) are bound to pay a single debt, and as between them the person primarily accountable is Fox. This effect could have been accomplished also by an initial agreement among all three persons concerned, whereby Fox became indebted to Lawrence and Holly became *surety* for payment of the debt. Observe that for enforcing that (differing) agreement against Holly the suretyship clause of the Statute of Frauds would require that his undertaking be in writing. But the clause has no application to the agreements actually made among the three parties. See pp. 291–94 above.

In the case that follows, no section of the original Statute would be applicable. (The agreement in question was oral.) In some states, however, extensions of the statute have been enacted which would in terms preclude enforcement. New York is one: if an identical case were to arise today, a different result might be compelled.[b] Consider whether or not this is a desirable "reform" in the law.

(3) *Restitution.* Could the decision in Lawrence v. Fox have been based on quasi-contract? Does it seem that the court would have affirmed if there had been no evidence of a promise made by Fox to Holly? Compare Callano v. Oakwood Park Homes Corp., p. 80 above.

b. "Every agreement, promise or undertaking is void unless [represented in a writing] if such agreement, promise or undertaking:

　　1. By its terms is not to be performed within one year from the making thereof

or the performance of which is not to be completed before the end of a lifetime; ..." N.Y.Gen.Oblig.L. § 5–701[a](1) (emphasis supplied).

See also footnote f, p. 288 above; Redke v. Silvertrust, 490 P.2d 805 (Cal.1971).

"The underlying premise on which the third-party beneficiary doctrine is based," it has been said, "is the same as that of unjust enrichment. It must appear that one party is holding sums of money which *rightfully belong* to another party." Litton Systems, Inc. v. Frigitemp Corp., 613 F.Supp. 1377 (S.D.Miss.1985).[c] Does this statement ignore the discussion in Lawrence v. Fox of "cases of trusts"? Can it account for the decision in the following case?

SEAVER v. RANSOM

Court of Appeals of New York, 1918.
224 N.Y. 233, 120 N.E. 639, 2 A.L.R. 1187.

Action by Marion E. Seaver against Matt. C. Ransom and another, as executors, etc., of Samuel A. Beman, deceased. From a judgment of the Appellate Division (180 App.Div. 734, 168 N.Y.S. 454), affirming judgment for plaintiff, defendants appeal. Affirmed.

POUND, J. Judge Beman and his wife were advanced in years. Mrs. Beman was about to die. She had a small estate consisting of a house and lot in Malone and little else. Judge Beman drew his wife's will according to her instruction. It gave $1,000 to plaintiff, $500 to one sister, plaintiff's mother, and $100 each to another sister and her son, the use of the house to her husband for life, and remainder to the American Society for the Prevention of Cruelty to Animals. She named her husband as residuary legatee and executor. Plaintiff was her niece, 34 years old, in ill health, sometimes a member of the Beman household. When the will was read to Mrs. Beman, she said that it was not as she wanted it. She wanted to leave the house to the plaintiff. She had no other objection to the will, but her strength was waning, and, although the judge offered to write another will for her, she said she was afraid she would not hold out long enough to enable her to sign it. So the judge said, if she would sign the will, he would leave plaintiff enough in his will to make up the difference. He avouched the promise by his uplifted hand with all solemnity and his wife then executed the will. When he came to die, it was found that his will made no provision for the plaintiff.

This action was brought, and plaintiff recovered judgment in the trial court, on the theory that Beman had obtained property from his wife and induced her to execute the will in the form prepared by him by his promise to give plaintiff $6,000, the value of the house, and that thereby equity impressed his property with a trust in favor of the plaintiff. Where a legatee promises the testator that he will use property given him by the will for a particular purpose, a trust arises. O'Hara v. Dudley, 95 N.Y. 103, 47 Am.Rep. 53; Trustees of Amherst College v. Ritch, 151 N.Y. 282, 45 N.E. 876, 37 L.R.A. 305; Aherns v. Jones, 169 N.Y. 555, 62 N.E. 666, 88 Am.St.Rep. 620. Beman received nothing under his wife's will but the use of the house in Malone for life. Equity

c. As to a less direct relation between third party beneficiary law and restitution law, see Waters, op. cit. supra, Note 2, p. 869 above.

compels the application of property thus obtained to the purpose of the testator, but equity cannot so impress a trust, except on property obtained by the promise. Beman was bound by his promise, but no property was bound by it; no trust in plaintiff's favor can be spelled out.

An action on the contract for damages, or to make the executors trustees for performance, stands on different ground. Farmers' Loan & Trust Co. v. Mortimer, 219 N.Y. 290, 294, 295, 114 N.E. 389. The Appellate Division properly passed to the consideration of the question whether the judgment could stand upon the promise made to the wife, upon a valid consideration, for the sole benefit of plaintiff. The judgment of the trial court was affirmed by a return to the general doctrine laid down in the great case of Lawrence v. Fox, 20 N.Y. 268, which has since been limited as herein indicated.

Contracts for the benefit of third persons have been the prolific source of judicial and academic discussion. Williston, Contracts for the Benefit of a Third Person, 15 Harvard Law Review, 767; Corbin, Contracts for the Benefit of Third Persons, 27 Yale Law Review, 1008. The general rule, both in law and equity (Phalen v. United States Trust Co., 186 N.Y. 178, 186, 78 N.E. 943, 7 L.R.A., N.S., 734, 9 Ann.Cas. 595), was that privity between a plaintiff and a defendant is necessary to the maintenance of an action on the contract. The consideration must be furnished by the party to whom the promise was made. The contract cannot be enforced against the third party, and therefore it cannot be enforced by him. On the other hand, the right of the beneficiary to sue on a contract made expressly for his benefit has been fully recognized in many American jurisdictions, either by judicial decision or by legislation, and is said to be "the prevailing rule in this country." Hendrick v. Lindsay, 93 U.S. 143, 23 L.Ed. 855; Lehow v. Simonton, 3 Colo. 346. It has been said that "the establishment of this doctrine has been gradual, and is a victory of practical utility over theory, of equity over technical subtlety." Brantly on Contracts, 2d Ed., p. 253. The reasons for this view are that it is just and practical to permit the person for whose benefit the contract is made to enforce it against one whose duty it is to pay. Other jurisdictions still adhere to the present English Rule (7 Halsbury's Laws of England, 342, 343; Jenks' Digest of English Civil Law, sec. 229) that a contract cannot be enforced by or against a person who is not a party. Exchange Bank v. Rice, 107 Mass. 37, 9 Am.Rep. 1. But see, also, Forbes v. Thorpe, 209 Mass. 570, 95 N.E. 955; Gardner v. Denison, 217 Mass. 492, 105 N.E. 359, 51 L.R.A., N.S., 1108.

In New York the right of the beneficiary to sue on contracts made for his benefit is not clearly or simply defined. It is at present confined: First. To cases where there is a pecuniary obligation running from the promisee to the beneficiary, "a legal right founded upon some obligation of the promisee in the third party to adopt and claim the promise as made for his benefit." [Cases cited.] Secondly. To cases where the contract is made for the benefit of the wife (Buchanan v. Tilden,[a] 158

---

a. The defendant in this case was the nephew of Samuel J. Tilden, who succeeded   in "breaking" a portion of his uncle's will. He had promised to share the recovery with

N.Y. 109, 52 N.E. 724, 44 L.R.A. 170, 70 Am.St.Rep. 454; Benton v. Welch, 170 N.Y. 554, 63 N.E. 539), affianced wife (De Cicco v. Schweizer, 221 N.Y. 431, 117 N.E. 807, Ann.Cas.1918C, 816), or child (Todd v. Weber, 95 N.Y. 181, 193, 47 Am.Rep. 20; Matter of Kidd, 188 N.Y. 274, 80 N.E. 924) of a party to the contract. The close relationship cases go back to the early King's Bench case (1677), long since repudiated in England, of Dutton v. Poole, 2 Lev. 211 (s.c., 1 Ventris, 318, 332). See Schemerhorn v. Vanderheyden, 1 Johns, 139, 3 Am.Dec. 304. The natural and moral duty of the husband or parent to provide for the future of wife or child sustains the action on the contract made for their benefit. "This is the furthest the cases in this state have gone," says Cullen, J., in the marriage settlement case of Borland v. Welch, 162 N.Y. 104, 110, 56 N.E. 556.

The right of the third party is also upheld in, thirdly, the public contract cases [cases cited] where the municipality seeks to protect its inhabitants by covenants for their benefit; and, fourthly, the cases where, at the request of a party to the contract, the promise runs directly to the beneficiary although he does not furnish the consideration [cases cited]. It may be safely said that a general rule sustaining recovery at the suit of the third party would include but few classes of cases not included in these groups, either categorically or in principle.

The desire of the childless aunt to make provisions for a beloved and favorite niece differs imperceptibly in law or in equity from the moral duty of the parent to make testamentary provision for a child. The contract was made for the plaintiff's benefit. She alone is substantially damaged by its breach. The representatives of the wife's estate have no interest in enforcing it specifically. It is said in Buchanan v. Tilden that the common law imposes moral and legal obligations upon the husband and the parent not measured by the necessaries of life. It was, however, the love and affection or the moral sense of the husband and the parent that imposed such obligations in the cases cited, rather than any common-law duty of husband and parent to wife and child. If plaintiff had been a child of Mrs. Beman, legal obligation would have required no testamentary provision for her, yet the child could have enforced a covenant in her favor identical with the covenant of Judge Beman in this case. De Cicco v. Schweizer, supra. The constraining power of conscience is not regulated by the degree of relationship alone. The dependent or faithful niece may have a stronger claim than the affluent or unworthy son. No sensible theory of moral obligation denies arbitrarily to the former what would be conceded to the latter. We might consistently either refuse or allow the claim of both, but I cannot reconcile a decision in favor of the wife in Buchanan v. Tilden, based on the moral obligations arising out of near relationship, with a decision against the niece here on the ground that the relationship is too remote for equity's ken. No controlling authority depends upon so absolute a rule. In Sullivan v. Sullivan, 161 N.Y. 554, 56 N.E. 116, the grandniece

the plaintiff, who was, by adoption, a niece of Governor Tilden. The promise was made to her husband in return for arrang- ing advances for use in prosecuting the will contest.

lost in a litigation with the aunt's estate, founded on a certificate of deposit payable to the aunt "or in case of her death to her niece;" but what was said in that case of the relations of plaintiff's intestate and defendant does not control here, any more than what was said in Durnherr v. Rau [135 N.Y. 219, 32 N.E. 49], on the relation of husband and wife, and the inadequacy of mere moral duty, as distinguished from legal or equitable obligation, controlled the decision in Buchanan v. Tilden.   Borland v. Welch, supra, deals only with the rights of volunteers under a marriage settlement not made for the benefit of collaterals. Kellogg, P.J., writing for the court below, well said:

"The doctrine of Lawrence v. Fox is progressive, not retrograde. The course of the late decisions is to enlarge, not limit, the effect of that case."

The court in that leading case attempted to adopt the general doctrine that any third person, for whose direct benefit a contract was intended, could sue on it. [Next the court referred to a number of later New York precedents, some stating the doctrine in general terms, and others narrowing its application.]

But, on principle, a sound conclusion may be reached. If Mrs. Beman had left her husband the house on condition that he pay the plaintiff $6,000, and he had accepted the devise, he would have become personally liable to pay the legacy, and plaintiff could have recovered in an action at law against him, whatever the value of the house. . . .   That would be because the testatrix had in substance bequeathed the promise to plaintiff, and not because close relationship or moral obligation sustained the contract. The distinction between an implied promise to a testator for the benefit of a third party to pay a legacy and an unqualified promise on a valuable consideration to make provision for the third party by will is discernible, but not obvious. The tendency of American authority is to sustain the gift in all such cases and to permit the donee beneficiary to recover on the contract. Matter of Edmundson's Estate (1918) 259 Pa. 429, 103 A. 277. The equities are with the plaintiff, and they may be enforced in this action, whether it be regarded as an action for damages or an action for specific performance to convert the defendants into trustees for plaintiff's benefit under the agreement.

The judgment should be affirmed, with costs.

Judgment affirmed.

NOTES

(1) *A Buyer's Claim*   DeLaval Turbine, Inc. contracted to provide the Kodiak Electric Association with a unit composed of a reconditioned engine and a used generator. The contract required DeLaval to have the generator inspected, repaired as necessary, and tested, by a competent firm. Westinghouse performed these services under a contract with DeLaval. After a breakdown of the unit, Kodiak Electric sued Westinghouse for breach of that contract. The trial court dismissed the claim.[a] On appeal, *held:* Affirmed. Kodiak Elec. Ass'n, Inc. v.

a. Other claims were also made, against both DeLaval and Westinghouse.

DeLaval Turbine, Inc., 694 P.2d 150 (Alaska 1984).[b] The court relied on Restatement Second § 302. Is that section dispositive?

The same court had ruled, a year earlier, in favor of an owner as plaintiff in an action on a foundation subcontract, saying that the defendant's work was "obviously intended to benefit the owner of the building." Syndoulos Luth. Church v. A.R.C. Industries, Inc., 662 P.2d 109 (Alaska 1983). How might these decisions be reconciled?

(2) *A Medical Case.* For about 25 years no physician had practiced in the community of Booker, Texas, despite vigorous efforts by the Booker Booster Club to attract one. Ultimately the efforts had a limited success. A corporate Scholarship Fund was created and it received public subscriptions. It contributed $1,800 to help defray the expense of a medical education for Neal K. Suthers. In 1966 Suthers contracted to use his best efforts to become a licensed physician, and thereafter immediately move to Booker, and to remain in practice there for at least ten years. In breach of this agreement, he practiced for only about five weeks in Booker, during 1974, before moving from the state. Meanwhile, in 1973, the citizens of Booker voted to create a Hospital District, floated a bond issue, and built a clinic, all as "contemplated" by the 1966 agreement.

Dr. Suthers was sued by the Scholarship Fund for the amount of its subvention, together with a 50% "penalty," as prescribed by the agreement. Additional plaintiffs claimed further sums as third party beneficiaries: the Hospital District and some of its residents, claiming to represent both a class of taxpayers and a larger class of residents deprived of medical services. The trial court asked the jury, "Was the agreement [of 1966] intended for the direct benefit of the Plaintiff class of residents . . .?"; to which the jury answered Yes. The court entered judgment for the Fund, and for the other claimants awarded a sum for loss of value in the clinic ($110,000) and another thousand dollars found by the jury to represent the loss to residents at large. On appeal, *held:* Reversed as to the non-Fund claimants. Suthers v. Booker Hospital Dist., 543 S.W.2d 723 (Tex.App.1976), error ref'd, n.r.e.

If it were feasible to grant specific performance in such a case, and otherwise consistent with public interests, should the taxpayers and residents of Booker have been allowed to claim that remedy? If the drafter had provided in the contract for all the recoveries allowed by the trial court, could it fairly have been questioned on the ground of unconscionability? In Restatement Second § 302(1), what language supports the conclusion in *Suthers*?

REMARKS ABOUT INTENTION

The intention of the parties to a contract—promisor, promisee, or both—naturally play a major part in determining third party beneficiary claims. According to one court, the third party cannot prevail in the absence of an "objectively verifiable intention" on the part of the *promisor* to assume a direct obligation to the claimant.[c] Is this necessary according to Restatement Second § 302? Sufficient?

b. Reh. denied, 696 P.2d 665 (1985). Compare Computerized Design and Mfg., Inc. v. GenRad, Inc., 733 P.2d 485 (Or. 1987) (negligence claims).

c. In re New England Fish Co., 749 F.2d 1277 (9th Cir.1984).

Would it be preferable to emphasize the intent of the *promisee?* Is it necessary to make a choice? See Note 2, p. 912 below.[d]

It has been said that the motives and subjective intentions of the parties to a contract are not relevant in determining whether or not a third party can enforce it: "an objective standard is to be used which discerns the parties' intentions from the contract itself." [e] Similarly:

> If the terms of the contract *necessarily require the promisor to confer a benefit upon a third person,* then the contract, and hence the parties thereto, *contemplate a benefit to the third person....* The "intent" which is a prerequisite of the beneficiary's right to sue is "not a desire or purpose to confer a particular benefit upon him," nor a desire to advance his interests, but an intent that the promisor shall assume a direct obligation to him. In short, the motive, purpose, or desire of the parties is a quite different thing from their intention.[f]

But it has been said that "the primary focus is placed on the subjective intent of the promisee" when there is a close familial or benevolent nexus between the promisee and the beneficiary.[g]

Do you find a contradiction between any of the quotations in this Note and Lawrence v. Fox? Seaver v. Ransom? Is it possible to reconcile the quotations through analysis of the word "intention"? See Eisenberg, Third Party Beneficiary Contracts, fn. f, p. 865 above, at 1378–81 ("The term 'intent' is deeply ambiguous along at least three axes.")

A relatively objective interpretation of the word may have the consequence of licensing appellate courts to make their own determinations about who is an intended beneficiary, and who is an incidental one. What merit or demerit do you see in that?

NOTES

(1) *Parol Evidence Rule.* Professor Corbin, no friend to the parol evidence rule, thought it should permit an extrinsic showing that a written contract was intended for the benefit of a third party. But his view has been characterized as more "liberal" in that respect than that of the New York courts. Hylte Bruks Aktiebolag v. Babcock & Wilcox Co., 399 F.2d 289 (2d Cir.1968).

d. And for an intermediate view, considering extrinsic evidence in relation to the intentions of *both* parties, see American Financial Corp. v. Computer Sciences Corp., 558 F.Supp. 1182 (D.Del.1983).

e. Rieth–Riley Const. Co., Inc. v. Department of Transp., 357 N.W.2d 62, 65 (Mich.App.1984) (said with reference to a statute: Mich.Comp.L. § 600.1405).

f. Vikingstad v. Baggott, 282 P.2d 824, 825–26 (Wash.1955) (quoting from Anno., 81 A.L.R. 1271 (1932) at 1287; emphasis by the court); reiterated in Lonsdale v. Chesterfield, 662 P.2d 385 (Wash.1983), at 389–90.

In the Annotation, the first quoted sentence continues: "... and although the actual purpose motivating the parties in making the provision in question was the purely selfish one of benefiting or protecting themselves...."

g. Kary v. Kary, fn. g, p. 865 above, at 336. This was an exceptional case in which the court confronted language in the contract to the effect that the claimant was among those who might enforce the contract, as it was made for their benefit; this language did not have conclusive effect.

Suppose a writing that a husband and wife intend to be a complete and exclusive statement of an agreement between them, and a claim under the agreement made by a third party against the husband. Would it violate the rule to admit evidence that there was a "close familial or benevolent nexus" between the claimant and the wife?

(2) *Problem a.* A and B are siblings. Each owns half the shares in a family corporation; each has one child. They agree in writing that if either party decides to sell shares, that party's child will have a right of first refusal. After A's death B decides to sell shares outside the family. B's child sues B to enjoin the sale. Is it open to B to testify that the object of the agreement was to protect the parents against an unwanted business association, and not to confer benefits on the children? See Ridder v. Blethen, 166 P.2d 834 (Wash.1946); and compare Russell v. Posey County Dept. of Public Welfare, 471 N.E.2d 1209 (Ind.App. 1984). What of a claim by B to reformation of the contract for mistake? See Merrimack Mut. Fire Ins. Co. v. Allied Fairbanks Bank, 678 S.W.2d 574 (Tex. App.1984).

(3) *Problem b.* Anyone current in American letters knows that the writer J.D. Salinger (Catcher in the Rye) abhors public attention. A well-known critic, Ian Hamilton, consulted letters written by Salinger, which their owners had deposited in university libraries. After trying without success to get Salinger's cooperation in a projected biography, Hamilton nevertheless made liberal use of the letters in a book about the author. Salinger sued Hamilton for an injunction against publication of the book. In part Salinger relied on form agreements that Hamilton had signed for getting access to the letters. (Harvard required its permission to "publish the contents ... or any excerpt.") Is Salinger an intended beneficiary of the promises made by Hamilton to the universities? (In Salinger v. Random House, Inc., 811 F.2d 90 (2d Cir.1987), cert. denied, 484 U.S. 890 (1987), the court pretermitted this question.)

STATUTORY ACTIONS

In several states there are general statutory provisions recognizing third-party actions.[a] The following provision of the Virginia Code is an instance:

§ 55–22. When person not a party, etc., may take or sue under instrument.— ... [I]f a covenant or promise be made for the benefit, in whole or in part, of a person with whom it is not made, or with whom it is made jointly with others, such person, whether named in the instrument or not, may maintain in his own name any action thereon which he might maintain in case it had been made with him only and the consideration had moved from him to the party making such covenant or promise. In such action the covenantor or promisor shall be permitted to make all defenses he may have, not only against the covenantee or promisee, but against such beneficiary as well.

---

a. These include the provision in several "Field Code" states that "a contract made expressly for the benefit of a third person may be enforced by him at any time before the parties thereto rescind it." See, e.g., Cal.Civ.Code, § 1559; Idaho Code § 29–102.

Introductory Note to *Septembertide Publishing*

This case grew out of the dissolution of a publishing firm (Stein & Day) in bankruptcy. The contestants were two of the firm's creditors: Bookcrafters and Septembertide. The contest was over certain payment rights that the debtor, Stein & Day, had acquired under a contract—the "paperback agreement"—it had made with another publisher, New American Library.

The court's statement of facts, given next, explains how Bookcrafters acquired its interest in those rights: by an assignment from Stein & Day. Part III of the opinion, describing the interest of Bookcrafters, is reserved for Chapter 10, on assignments. Part II, presented here, concerns Septembertide's claim of an interest in the payment rights created in the paperback agreement.

Some information about the assignment to Bookcrafters will help to explain the importance of the court's ruling as reported here. That assignment was one governed by Article 9 ("Secured Transactions . . .") of the Uniform Commercial Code, as enacted in New York. The statute made it imperative that Bookcrafters, whose assignment made it a "secured party," place on file in a public office a notice, called a financing statement, designed to alert others that it had, or might have, an interest in the payment rights. Some of the consequences of a failure to do so, and some particulars of the Code filing system, are given in Chapter 10. For now, it is necessary only to say that the Bookcrafters interest in the payment rights would have been at grave risk if it had failed to make an Article-9 filing.

Bookcrafters took that precaution. (Part III of the opinion reports that fact.) Moreover, before giving credit to Stein & Day, Bookcrafters consulted the public records to see whether or not anyone else had filed a financing statement referring to the rights in question. (The court mentions "Bookcrafters' search of UCC filings.")

SEPTEMBERTIDE PUBLISHING, B.V. v. STEIN & DAY, INC.

United States Court of Appeals, Second Circuit, 1989.
884 F.2d 675.

CARDAMONE, CIRCUIT JUDGE: On this appeal from the United States District Court for the Southern District of New York, Richard Owen, Judge, we are required to resolve a difficult and close question involving third-party beneficiary and commercial law principles which in this case suggest different results. The author and a trade creditor each claim to be entitled to the proceeds flowing from the paperback publication of a novel. The author, an intended third-party beneficiary, claims superior rights to the funds because so often a writer has all his or her financial eggs in one basket. The secured creditor asserts that as a financier of the commercial side of publishing, it should be accorded all those rights to which a secured creditor is entitled. Yet, the resolution of this question does not rest entirely on the parties' rights, but rather on which of them has priority. The issue for us is to determine, and properly observe, priority to the disputed proceeds between the claimant parties.

FACTS AND PROCEEDINGS BELOW

Septembertide Publishing, B.V. (Septembertide or author), a corporation organized and existing under the laws of the Netherlands, is owned and controlled by one Harry Patterson, a resident of the Isle of Jersey in the Channel Islands, which are a part of the United Kingdom. S & L Enterprises (S & L), Septembertide's predecessor-in-interest, also is owned by Patterson who is the author of numerous literary works, usually under pseudonyms. He wrote the novel "Confessional" (the Work) under the pseudonym "Jack Higgins." The rights to the funds derived from the paperback edition of "Confessional" is the subject of the instant litigation.

S & L granted exclusive licensing rights to Stein & Day, a publishing house incorporated in New York with headquarters in New York City, to publish a hardcover edition of the Work in the United States. These rights were embodied in a written contract dated December 12, 1984 (Hardcover Agreement). In October 1985 Septembertide took over as successor-in-interest to S & L's rights in that contract. Under the contract's terms Stein & Day was obligated to pay an advance against future royalties of $375,000 in three equal installments of $125,000. Stein & Day was also obliged to account semi-annually, to pay royalties, and to pay its share of sublicensing income, after recouping its advances. With respect to the sublicensing income, these proceeds "from the sale or license of reprint rights" in media other than hardcover publication were to be divided two-thirds to the author Septembertide, and one-third to the publisher, Stein & Day. The first two advances were made, but the third one, due on January 15, 1986, was not paid. As of December 31, 1985 Stein & Day owed Septembertide $152,030.31. Stein & Day subsequently became insolvent and, though acknowledging its debt, was unable to make payments to Septembertide.

At the same time (actually one day earlier, December 11, 1984) that it entered into the Hardcover Agreement with Septembertide, Stein & Day entered into a contract with New American Library (New Library), giving New Library the rights to publish the paperback edition of "Confessional" (Paperback Agreement). New Library agreed to advance Stein & Day $750,000 in five installments, of which, prior to the institution of this suit on July 14, 1986, Stein & Day had received $385,500. Meanwhile, on November 20, 1985 Stein & Day had entered into a security agreement with Bookcrafters U.S.A., Inc. (Bookcrafters), assigning all its contract rights and accounts to Bookcrafters, including the paperback rights it had with New Library. Bookcrafters' search of UCC filings uncovered no evidence of Septembertide's interest in payments from New Library to Stein & Day. In a March 6, 1986 letter Septembertide terminated Stein & Day's rights in the Hardcover Agreement because the final $125,000 payment due in January had not been made. Septembertide then requested in May 1986 that New Library—as a result of Stein & Day recouping its advances—forward directly to it all future payments due Stein & Day under the Paperback Agreement. When New Library refused, Septembertide initiated this lawsuit against Stein & Day and New Library.

Septembertide's suit sought [among other things] (3) an injunction against New Library ... compelling direct payment to Septembertide of all amounts due under the Paperback Agreement or, in the alternative, damages ...; and (4) two-thirds of the proceeds of the remaining payments of the Paperback Agreement as a third-party beneficiary to that Agreement....

Bookcrafters then intervened, alleging that it had prior and superior right to the proceeds of the Paperback Agreement by virtue of its security agreement with Stein & Day. [New Library deposited into court the amount it concededly owed. The district court divided the funds one-third to Bookcrafters and two-thirds to Septembertide. Both of these parties appealed.] ...

II   *Third–Party Beneficiary*

Was Septembertide properly held to be an intended beneficiary of the Paperback Agreement? Discussion must begin with Lawrence v. Fox, 20 N.Y. 268 (1859). There, one Holly loaned $300 to defendant stating at the time that he (Holly) owed the same sum to plaintiff and, in consideration of the loan, defendant promised to repay it to plaintiff the next day. It was held that plaintiff beneficiary could maintain an action on the promise defendant made for his benefit, even though plaintiff was not a party to or aware of the promise at the time it was made. Because this intent to benefit test was difficult to apply, see, e.g., Port Chester Elec. Constr. Corp. v. Atlas, 40 N.Y.2d 652, 655, 389 N.Y.S.2d 327, 357 N.E.2d 983 (1976), New York's Court of Appeals subsequently adopted the Restatement (Second) of Contracts approach. The Restatement formulation captures the essence of New York law. See Fourth Ocean Putnam Corp. v. Interstate Wrecking Co., Inc., 66 N.Y.2d 38, 44–45, 495 N.Y.S.2d 1, 485 N.E.2d 208 (1985). Section 302 of the Restatement distinguishes between an "intended" and an "incidental" beneficiary as follows:

> (1) Unless otherwise agreed between promisor and promisee, a beneficiary of a promise is an intended beneficiary if recognition of a right to performance in the beneficiary is appropriate to effectuate the intention of the parties and either

> (a) the performance of the promise will satisfy an obligation of the promisee to pay money to the beneficiary; or

> (b) the circumstances indicate that the promisee intends to give the beneficiary the benefit of the promised performance.

> (2) An incidental beneficiary is a beneficiary who is not an intended beneficiary.

Applying New York law to the present facts, we conclude that Septembertide plainly is an intended beneficiary of the Paperback Agreement between Stein & Day and New Library. To reach that determination, we must examine the intent of the parties—as revealed in their agreement—and the surrounding circumstances. See Owens v. Haas, 601 F.2d 1242, 1250 (2d Cir.1979); Fourth Ocean, 66 N.Y.2d at 45, 495 N.Y.S.2d 1, 485 N.E.2d 208.

Septembertide's rights as a third-party beneficiary hinge on its demonstration of Stein & Day's intent to benefit it at the time the two agreements were entered into. Goodman–Marks Associates, Inc. v. Westbury Post Associates, 70 A.D.2d 145, 148, 420 N.Y.S.2d 26 (2d Dep't 1979). The timing, language, and financial obligations created by the Hardcover and Paperback Agreements shed much light on Stein & Day's intent. The former agreement, signed on December 12, 1984, was entered into virtually simultaneously with the latter. The timing of the two agreements and the mention by name of the author and his Work suggest that Stein & Day intended New Library's payments to it under the Paperback Agreement to be used to satisfy its obligation to Septembertide under the Hardcover Agreement.

The December 12 agreement—plainly referring to the Paperback Agreement of the previous day—states "[p]roceeds from the sale or license of reprint rights shall be divided two-thirds to the author [Septembertide] and one-third to the Publisher [Stein & Day]." The record reveals that Stein & Day used the first New Library advance installment to satisfy the first two $125,000 payments it owed Septembertide. Further, the district court found that since Stein & Day agreed—once its original advance had been recouped—to pay two-thirds of the paperback proceeds to the author, it owed a duty to Septembertide to transmit that share of the proceeds to it.

New Library's intent to benefit Septembertide is not quite so clear as that of Stein & Day's. Yet, Septembertide's argument that New Library is charged with some knowledge of the fact that it was to be benefitted under New Library's simultaneous contract with Stein & Day is a reasonable one. The Work and its author are identified in the Paperback Agreement. More significantly, Stein & Day acknowledged that it did not control British Commonwealth rights to softcover reprints, but would use its "best efforts" with the "author's agent" to protect New Library's softcover rights. We think this reference sufficiently alerted New Library to the fact that Septembertide had retained an interest in its Work and that Stein & Day maintained a working relationship with that author. New Library is also chargeable with knowing that it is a publishing industry practice for an author to receive a percentage of the royalty from the sublicense, particularly under the present circumstances where the two agreements were executed simultaneously.

As a consequence, Septembertide is an intended beneficiary of the promise made by Stein & Day to satisfy its obligation to Septembertide. A recognition of the author's rights to such performance was appropriate

in effectuating Stein & Day's and New Library's purposes when the
former granted a license to the latter for the rights to the paperback
publication of the Work.

. . .

Modified, and as modified, affirmed.[a]

NOTES

(1) *Questions.* From what sources did the court derive the intent of Stein &
Day to benefit Septembertide? If Bookcrafters had offered the testimony of Sol
Stein, the principal of Stein & Day, that no such intent existed, would that
testimony have had any weight? As to New Library, did the court attach any
significance to its intent (as opposed to its knowledge)?

In its discussion of Lawrence v. Fox, the court said that "this intent to
benefit test was difficult to apply." How much progress was made in the
adoption of the approach of the Restatement Second?

(2) *Additional Benefit.* It has been argued that unless someone not a party
to a contract is to get an "additional benefit" under it that person is at most an
incidental beneficiary. But this proposition can be misleading if the meaning of
benefit is misunderstood.

In 1980 Vincent Heron sold "Vince's Lounge" to the Markmil Corporation.
Markmil signed an Assumption of Obligation as follows:

> The undersigned, for ... part of the purchase price of [assets]
> known as Vince's Lounge ... do hereby agree and assume to pay, the
> obligations listed on Exhibit A which is attached ... and hold [Heron]
> Seller herein, harmless from these obligations and, further agree to
> indemnify said Heron in the event he is ever held liable for said
> obligation in any lawsuit or garnishment thereon. . . .

One of the entries on Exhibit A was a debt of $3,510, representing the unpaid
part of a loan made to Heron by one Spiklevitz in 1974.

In 1981 Spiklevitz sued Markmil. The trial court gave judgment for the
defendant, saying that a statute of limitations had run on the initial loan and
that the assumption agreement gave the plaintiff no "additional rights." On
appeal, *held:* Reversed. "Where one sells his business or other property and the
buyer undertakes to pay the seller's debts, those to be paid are creditor
beneficiaries and actions by them lie against the buyer on his promise. . . . A
person's status as a third-party beneficiary of a contract cannot be determined by
asking whether he receives additional benefit from the contract. If he is not a
beneficiary of it, he does not; if he is, he does." Spiklevitz v. Markmil Corp.,
357 N.W.2d 721 (Mich.App.1984).[b]

If the period of limitation had not run in Heron's favor when the plaintiff
brought this action, would you say that the assumption agreement conferred an
additional benefit on the plaintiff? In that case, what additional fact can you
suppose that would make it important for the plaintiff to get recognition as a
third party beneficiary?

---

a. The district court had allocated some
$3,000 to Stein & Day; as to this the Court
of Appeals modified, saying that it "belongs
instead to Bookcrafters."

b. What is here called the "trial court"
was actually a circuit court, affirming a
district-court judgment.

FINANCING BY BENEFICIARY

As trustee of a pension fund, J. Kenneth Lee, had money to invest. He loaned some of it to a firm, called P & F, which was engaged in construction and painting work as a subcontractor on an apartment project. P & F needed the money to pay workers and suppliers. Before getting the loan P & F was required to solicit a letter agreement from the general contractor, Paragon Group Contractors, Inc. An officer of Paragon wrote to Powell, of P & F, saying that as earnings became payable to P & F for its work Paragon would issue checks jointly to P & F and Lee. (The effect of naming both as payees would be to put Paragon's bank at risk if it paid a check that did not bear Lee's indorsement as well as P & F's.) The letter to Powell became known as the "March 3 letter" in litigation that ensued. P & F's contracts with Paragon had been entered into in November of the previous year.

In the following September the contracts were terminated. Lee's loan had not been repaid. He sued Paragon, alleging that it had issued checks for P & F's work to "parties unknown," in violation of the March 3 letter. Paragon resisted on the ground that the letter agreement was unenforceable, in that it constituted a modification of the subcontracts for which Paragon had received no consideration. On Paragon's motion, the action was dismissed. On appeal, *held:* Affirmed. Lee v. Paragon Group Contractors, Inc., 337 S.E.2d 132 (N.C.App.1985), rev. denied, 345 S.E.2d 383 (N.C.1986).[c]

Although the decision may seem overtechnical, it illustrates one of the hazards of basing a financing transaction on third party beneficiary law. It will be seen in the following chapter how the transaction might have been based on the law of assignments. That is, Lee might have required P & F to *transfer* to him its rights to payment under the subcontracts. Given an effective assignment, the loan would have been secured by these rights, as "collateral."

The suggested assignment would not have required Paragon's assent. On the other hand, it would not have imposed a requirement on Paragon to pay Lee until Paragon received notification of the assignment. Moreover, as indicated in the Introductory Note to *Septembertide Publishing*, the assignment would not have put Lee in a position of special advantage over other creditors of P & F unless a *public* notice (filing) step was taken. If Lee had achieved the status of third party beneficiary of the subcontracts, through a binding modification, it is not obvious that he would have been burdened with any public filing requirement—although the point is debatable. Other contrasts between the position of third party beneficiary and of transferee (assignee), with respect to a payment right, will appear when the following chapter is consulted.

c. "Consideration is the 'glue' that binds parties together, and a mere promise, without more, is unenforceable.... Generally, a promise to perform a pre-existing contractual obligation is not adequate consideration in exchange for a new promise by the other party."

NOTES

(1) *Problem.* If the original contracts between Paragon and P & F had simply *authorized* Paragon to make checks payable, jointly, to P & F and to anyone providing financing for P & F, would that have made Lee a third party beneficiary? See Wing v. Amalgamated Sugar Co., 684 P.2d 307 (Idaho App. 1984). Compare Noland Co. v. Armco, Inc., 445 A.2d 1079 (Md.App.1982).

(2) *Questions.* Assuming that Lee had effective control of the arrangements between P & F and Paragon from the outset, what suggestion can you make that would have solved the problem in the foregoing Note? What would have solved the problem of consideration that Lee faced in the actual case?

(3) *Role Reversal.* If Lee had contracted with P & G to provide it with financing and had failed to do so, causing a default by P & G on its contract with Paragon, would Paragon have had a claim as a third party beneficiary of the financing agreement? See Braten v. Bankers Trust Co., 456 N.E.2d 802 (N.Y. 1983); and see Chemical Realty v. Home Federal Sav. and Loan, 351 S.E.2d 786 (N.C.App.1987).

LUCAS v. HAMM

Supreme Court of California, 1961.
56 Cal.2d 583, 15 Cal.Rptr. 821, 364 P.2d 685, cert. denied, 368 U.S. 987 (1962).

[In a complaint against a lawyer, L.S. Hamm, some plaintiffs made the following allegations: They were designated as beneficiaries in a will prepared by the defendant for Eugene Emmick, deceased. The will had placed certain assets in trust, and specified that the plaintiffs were to have a 15% interest in it. After the will was probated, the lawyer had advised the plaintiffs that the trust provision was invalid under the California Civil Code. The plaintiffs were compelled to enter into a settlement with Emmick's blood relatives, by which they received a share of his estate that was $75,000 less than what they would have received if the will had been properly prepared. They sought recovery from the lawyer in that amount, basing the claim on his negligence, and on breach of his contract with Emmick. The action was dismissed, and the plaintiffs appealed.]

GIBSON, CHIEF JUSTICE.... It was held in Buckley v. Gray, 110 Cal. 339, 42 P. 900, 31 L.R.A. 862, that an attorney who made a mistake in drafting a will was not liable for negligence or breach of contract to a person named in the will who was deprived of benefits as a result of the error.... For the reasons hereinafter stated the case is overruled. [The court's discussion of the tort claim is omitted.]

Neither do we agree with the holding in *Buckley* that beneficiaries damaged by an error in the drafting of a will cannot recover from the draftsman on the theory that they are third-party beneficiaries of the contract between him and the testator.[1] Obviously the main purpose of

---

1. It has been recognized in other jurisdictions that the *client* may recover in a contract action for failure of the attorney to carry out his agreement. (See 5 Am.Jur. 331; 49 A.L.R.2d 1216, 1219–1221; Prosser, Selected Topics on the Law of Torts

a contract for the drafting of a will is to accomplish the future transfer of the estate of the testator to the beneficiaries named in the will, and therefore it seems improper to hold, as was done in *Buckley,* that the testator intended only "remotely" to benefit those persons. It is true that under a contract for the benefit of a third person performance is usually to be rendered directly to the beneficiary, but this is not necessarily the case. (See Rest., Contracts, § 133, com. d; 2 Williston on Contracts (3rd ed. 1959) 829.) For example, where a life insurance policy lapsed because a bank failed to perform its agreement to pay the premiums out of the insured's bank account, it was held that after the insured's death the beneficiaries could recover against the bank as third-party beneficiaries. Walker Bank & Trust Co. v. First Security Corp., 9 Utah 2d 215, 341 P.2d 944, 945 et seq. Persons who had agreed to procure liability insurance for the protection of the promisees but did not do so were also held liable to injured persons who would have been covered by the insurance, the courts stating that all persons who might be injured were third-party beneficiaries of the contracts to procure insurance. Johnson v. Holmes Tuttle Lincoln–Merc., Inc., 160 Cal. App.2d 290, 296 et seq., 325 P.2d 193; James Stewart & Co. v. Law, 149 Tex. 392, 233 S.W.2d 558, 561–562, 22 A.L.R.2d 639. Since, in a situation like those presented here and in the *Buckley* case, the main purpose of the testator in making his agreement with the attorney is to benefit the persons named in his will and this intent can be effectuated, in the event of a breach by the attorney, only by giving the beneficiaries a right of action, we should recognize, as a matter of policy, that they are entitled to recover as third-party beneficiaries. See 2 Williston on Contracts (3rd ed. 1959) pp. 843–844; 4 Corbin on Contracts (1951) pp. 8, 20.

Section 1559 of the Civil Code, which provides for enforcement by a third person of a contract made "expressly" for his benefit, does not preclude this result. The effect of the section is to exclude enforcement by persons who are only incidentally or remotely benefited. See Hartman Ranch Co. v. Associated Oil Co., 10 Cal.2d 232, 244, 73 P.2d 1163; cf. 4 Corbin on Contracts (1951) pp. 23–24. As we have seen, a contract for the drafting of a will unmistakably shows the intent of the testator to benefit the persons to be named in the will, and the attorney must necessarily understand this.

Defendant relies on language in Smith v. Anglo–California Trust Co., 205 Cal. 496, 502, 271 P. 898, and Fruitvale Canning Co. v. Cotton, 115 Cal.App.2d 622, 625, 252 P.2d 953, that to permit a third person to bring an action on a contract there must be "an intent clearly manifest-

---

(1954) pp. 438, 442.) This is in accord with the general rule stated in Comunale v. Traders & General Ins. Co., 50 Cal.2d 654, 663, 328 P.2d 198, 68 A.L.R.2d 883, that where a case sounds in both tort and contract, the plaintiff will ordinarily have freedom of election between the two actions.

[In Schirmer v. Nethercutt, 288 P. 265 (Wash.1930), S was a student of law in N's office. He employed N to draw up a will for his grandmother, for which S paid. The grandmother instructed N to provide a substantial legacy for S. N prepared the will and had it witnessed by S—thereby costing him the legacy. S recovered his loss from N.—Eds.]

ed by the promisor" to secure some benefit to the third person. This language, which was not necessary to the decision in either of the cases, is unfortunate. Insofar as intent to benefit a third person is important in determining his right to bring an action under a contract, it is sufficient that the promisor must have understood that the promisee had such intent. (Cf.Rest., Contracts, § 133, subds. 1(a) and 1(b); 4 Corbin on Contracts (1951) pp. 16–18; 2 Williston on Contracts (3rd ed. 1959) pp. 836–839.) No specific manifestation by the promisor of an intent to benefit the third person is required. The language relied on by defendant is disapproved to the extent that it is inconsistent with these views.

We conclude that intended beneficiaries of a will who lose their testamentary rights because of failure of the attorney who drew the will to properly fulfill his obligations under his contract with the testator may recover as third-party beneficiaries.

[The court went on to rule, however, that the complaint did not allege any error by Hamm that was not excusable in a well-informed lawyer. The supposed invalidity of the trust depended on rules about perpetuities and restraints on alienation—subjects which "have long perplexed the courts and the bar." In view of the state of the law, and the nature of the supposed error, "it would not be proper to hold that defendant failed to use such skill, prudence, and diligence as lawyers of ordinary skill and capacity commonly exercise." Judgment affirmed.]

NOTES

(1) *Contract vs. Tort.* Buckley v. Gray, the case overruled by Lucas v. Hamm, was cited in 1900 for the proposition that "an attorney employed to draw a will is not liable to a person who, through the attorney's ignorance or negligence in the discharge of his professional duties, was deprived of the portion of the estate which the testator instructed the attorney should be given such person by the will." Currey v. Butcher, 61 P. 631 (Or.1900). Since then, however, "many courts have reconsidered that proposition, some preferring a contract analysis, some negligence, and at least one a 'definite maybe.'" Hale v. Groce, 744 P.2d 1289, 1291 (Or.1987).

The choice between a contract and a tort analysis may determine the kind of proof required of a claimant. It may determine also the time within which an action must be brought. (Does the period of limitation begin to run when the will was prepared, or when the client died?) In California, on reconsideration, it has been said that "the crux of the action must lie in tort in any case; there can be no recovery without negligence." Heyer v. Flaig, 449 P.2d 161, 164 (Cal. 1969); see also J'Aire Corp. v. Gregory, 598 P.2d 60 (Cal.1979). The opinion in Hale v. Groce, above, is more discriminating: "A contract to prepare a will or other instrument may promise different things. It may undertake to make a particular disposition by means specified by the client ... or to accomplish the intended gift by specified means of the lawyer's choosing. Failure to do what was promised then would be a breach of contract regardless of any negligence. On the other hand, the lawyer's promise might be to use his best professional efforts to accomplish the specified result with the skill and care customary among lawyers in the relevant community." See Eisenberg, Third Party Beneficiary Contracts, fn. f, p. 865 above, at 1393–96.

(2) *Counsel to Trustees.* The will of Robin Damon set up a trust which was administered by Damon Lyons and another, for the benefit of themselves and 66 other beneficiaries. Stock in the publisher of the Salem (Massachusetts) News was the chief trust asset, by far. Lyons wanted to sell the stock when an offer was received for nearly $42 million; but his co-trustee did not. Thereafter, the value of the investment declined substantially. An action was brought by four of the beneficiaries (not including Lyons) against fifteen attorneys who had advised the trustees, including associates and former associates at major law firms. The defendants were charged with negligence, breach of third-party-beneficiary contracts, and aiding and abetting a breach of fiduciary duty. From a dismissal, the plaintiffs appealed. *Held:* Affirmed. Spinner v. Nutt, 631 N.E.2d 542 (Mass. 1994).

In connection with the negligence claim the court said: "[T]here is no similarity to cases where the beneficiaries are seeking to enforce the desires of the client. We note, also, that policy considerations present in the negligent will-drafting cases where, if beneficiaries had no standing, an attorney's negligence would be sheltered from suit are nonexistent in this situation. Here, the beneficiaries may bring an action against the trustees and the trustees, in turn, may bring an action against the attorneys if appropriate. Indeed, the [trial] judge took judicial notice of a legal action pending against the trustees in this matter."

Is it as important that there be some advocate to get redress for a breach of promise—a bargained-for promise, at least—as it is important to redress professional carelessness? For that purpose, in what cases is it necessary to recognize a third-party-beneficiary claim? Lawrence v. Fox? Seaver v. Ransom?

For the view that a third party does not necessarily become an intended beneficiary of a promise when the promisee ceases to have an interest in enforcing it, see Lake Placid Club v. Elizabethtown Builders, 521 N.Y.S.2d 165 (App.Div.1987).

(3) *Problem.* An adoption agency agrees with a pregnant woman to act as guardian for her baby from its birth until its final adoption. She has arranged for its adoption by a couple she knows. The agency is to provide her with counseling and to facilitate the termination of her parental rights. It is required by law to conduct a "home study" of the couple. They agree with the expectant mother to pay the agency's charges. The study leads the agency to the erroneous conclusion that the couple are, as members of a cult, unsuitable parents; and it withdraws from the process. The couple incur additional costs in arranging the adoption through another agency. Can they charge the first agency with these costs in a contract action? See Kennedy v. Children's Service Society of Wisconsin, 17 F.3d 980 (7th Cir.1994).

Schatz v. Rosenberg, 943 F.2d 485 (4th Cir.1991).

CHAPMAN, SENIOR CIRCUIT JUDGE. [Until the end of 1986 two firms in the bedding business—"VAMCO" and "ABC"—were owned by Ivan and Joanne Schatz, plaintiffs in this case. At that time they sold a controlling interest in each company to a firm newly created by Mark E. Rosenberg (MER Enterprises, or "MER").] As payment for their eighty percent (80%) interests in VAMCO and ABC, Mr. and Mrs. Schatz received $1.5 million in promissory notes issued by MER, which Rosenberg personally guaranteed. The plaintiffs relied on a financial statement dated March 31, 1986 and an update letter delivered at closing on December 31, 1986 which indicated that Rosenberg's net worth exceeded $7 million. These financial documents contained several misrepresentations obscuring the fact that Rosenberg's financial empire had crumbled between April and December of 1986.... The law firm of Weinberg & Green represented Rosenberg and his entities throughout this period.

The plaintiffs never received payment on their promissory notes.... To add insult to injury, Rosenberg paid Weinberg & Green's legal fees for the transaction out of VAMCO and ABC's cash reserves.... By the time Rosenberg ... filed for bankruptcy, VAMCO and ABC were essentially worthless, and plaintiffs had no control over the businesses. [In suing Rosenberg, the Shatzes included several counts against the law firm. From a dismissal of these counts, the Shatzes appealed.] ... [T]he plaintiffs never claimed that they could allege that Weinberg & Green had made any affirmative misstatements or other misrepresentations....

Plaintiffs argue that Weinberg & Green committed fraud by remaining silent even though it knew that its client, Rosenberg, was financially insolvent. [The court addressed separately plaintiffs' arguments for a duty of disclosure based on (i) public policy, (ii) federal securities laws, and (iii) Maryland law. In connection with the latter ground, plaintiffs had submitted, anonymously, a statement of the facts to the State Bar Committee on Ethics, and had obtained an opinion that attorneys situated as Weinberg & Green were should have made a disclosure or should have withdrawn from the representation.] This ethical responsibility, plaintiffs argue, establishes a legal duty to disclose....

We reject this argument. An ethical duty of disclosure does not create a corresponding legal duty under the federal securities laws. Courts have consistently refused to use ethical codes to define standards of civil liability for lawyers....

The rationale for these rulings is clear. The ethical rules were intended by their drafters to regulate the conduct of the profession, not to create actionable duties in favor of third parties. The preliminary statement to the Model Code, upon which the Maryland code is patterned, warns that the Code does not "undertake to define standards for civil liability of lawyers for professional conduct." Preliminary Statement, Model Code of Professional Responsibility. We believe this statement accurately reflects the goals and purposes of the Maryland Code of Professional Responsibility....

We also hold that Maryland common law does not impose a duty to disclose under these circumstances. In the negligence context, Maryland courts have held that a lawyer only owes a duty to his clients or third party beneficiaries of the attorney-client relationship. See Flaherty v. Weinberg, 303 Md. 116, 492 A.2d 618 (1985). Applying such rule to the facts of this case, we hold that because plaintiffs were neither clients nor third party beneficiaries of the attorney-client relationship, Weinberg & Green had no duty to disclose.

Plaintiffs rely on Crest Investment Trust, Inc. v. Comstock, 23 Md.App. 280, 327 A.2d 891 (1974), to establish a common law duty of disclosure for lawyers. However, this case says nothing about whether an attorney owes a duty of disclosure to persons who are not his clients. *Comstock* involved a lawyer who had a conflict of interest because he tried to represent both sides in a transaction, and, therefore, the lawyer owed a duty of disclosure to both sides. Thus, *Comstock* does not impose a duty of disclosure on a lawyer to a third party the lawyer does not represent. In this case, plaintiffs do not allege that Weinberg & Green represented them; in fact, plaintiffs admit that they were represented by their own chosen lawyers. Thus, the facts of *Comstock* are not analogous to this case. . . .

Affirmed.

NOTES

(1) *The Adversarial Role.* An attorney's liability to non-clients should be limited, it has been said, "for the following reasons: (1) the attorney's duty of loyalty and effective advocacy for his client; (2) the nature of the adversarial relationship between an attorney and other parties; and (3) the potential liability to an unlimited number of third parties if attorney liability to third parties is extended." Schmidt v. Frankewich, 819 P.2d 1074, 1079 (Colo.App. 1991). "In the area of legal malpractice the attorney's obligations to his client must remain paramount." Pelham v. Griesheimer, 440 N.E.2d 96, 99 (Ill.1982).

Pelham was an action by children of a client against an attorney who had procured a divorce and a property settlement for her. Considered as contract claimants, the plaintiffs were said to be "at best" incidental beneficiaries of the employment. The court distinguished cases of lawyers in less adversarial roles, such as that of drafting wills. Given that divorce proceedings are "for the most part" adversarial in nature, the court invoked a privity requirement against the plaintiffs, drawn by analogy to the law of third party beneficiaries. The court envisaged various interests of mother and child that might collide upon divorce, and said: "We refuse to create such a wide range of potential conflicts by imposing such duties upon an attorney in favor of a nonclient, unless the intent to benefit the third party is clearly evident."

Rules about lawyer's liabilities to non-clients, as asserted in Lucas v. Hamm, above, and in Schatz v. Rosenberg, were proposed to the American Law Institute in 1994, as § 73 of a proposed Restatement of "The Law Governing Lawyers." As to negligence in preparing a will, see Comment *f* of Tentative Draft # 7. In the Reporter's Notes to § 77 *Schatz* is cited as "But see. . . ." The Reporter was directed to prepare a further draft.

(2) *Other Vocations.* Should third party beneficiary law also be the pattern of liability, through negligence, of public accountants, architects, and the like, in favor of persons who do not employ them? See Raritan River Steel v. Cherry, et al., 407 S.E.2d 178 (N.C.1991) (accountant's contract to perform an audit).

HAMPTON v. FEDERAL EXPRESS CORP.

United States Court of Appeals, Eighth Circuit, 1990.
917 F.2d 1119.

RE, CHIEF JUDGE. In this diversity action, plaintiffs-appellants, Carl Jerry Hampton, individually and on behalf of his deceased son, Carl Gerome Hampton (collectively, Hampton), Missouri residents, sued defendant-appellee, Federal Express Corporation, a Delaware corporation, in the United States District Court for the Western District of Missouri, seeking a total of $3,081,000, for personal injury, wrongful death, and loss of services.

Hampton alleged that Federal Express, a common carrier, negligently failed to deliver blood samples of Carl Gerome Hampton, a cancer patient in need of a bone marrow transplant, that had to be matched with a potential bone marrow donor. Hampton appeals from judgment of the district court which granted the partial summary judgment motion of the carrier, Federal Express, limiting Hampton's recovery to $100 in damages.

The question presented is whether the district court erred in determining that the carrier, Federal Express, is entitled to partial summary judgment under the released value doctrine, limiting its liability to $100, the amount stated in the contract of carriage between it and the shipper.

Since, on the facts presented, the nature and extent of damages suffered by plaintiff Hampton were not reasonably foreseeable to the carrier, Federal Express, we affirm the judgment of the district court granting Federal Express' motion for partial summary judgment.

I. BACKGROUND

In March, 1988, Carl Gerome Hampton, a 13–year old cancer patient at Children's Memorial Hospital in Omaha, Nebraska, was awaiting a bone marrow transplant. A transplant operation was scheduled at the University of Iowa Hospital in Iowa City, Iowa, where five potential bone marrow donors had been found.

On March 21, 1988, in order to match Carl with the most suitable donor, five samples of Carl's blood were sent by the shipper, the Children's Memorial Hospital in Omaha, to Dr. Nancy Goeken, at the Veterans Administration Medical Center in Iowa City. The shipper, the Children's Memorial Hospital, entered into a contract with the carrier, Federal Express, for the transport of the blood samples.

In a paragraph entitled "Damages or Loss," the contract of carriage, set forth in the airbill, stated:

We are liable for no more than $100 per package in the event of physical loss or damage, unless you fill in a higher **Declared Value** to the left and document higher actual loss in the event of a claim. We charge 30 cents for each additional $100 of declared value up to the maximum shown in our Service Guide.

The reverse side of the airbill contains several paragraphs, entitled "Limitations On Our Liability," which state that:

> Our liability for loss or damage to your package is limited to your actual damages or $100, whichever is less, unless you pay for and declare a higher authorized value. We do not provide cargo liability insurance, but you may pay thirty cents for each additional $100 of declared value. If you declare a higher value and pay the additional charge, our liability will be the lesser of your declared value or the actual value of your package.

It is not disputed that the blood samples were never received by Dr. Goeken, that Carl Hampton, the infant cancer patient, never obtained a bone marrow transplant, and that he died on May 19, 1988.

Alleging causes of action for personal injury, wrongful death, and loss of services, Carl Jerry Hampton, individually and on behalf of his deceased son, Carl Gerome Hampton, filed suit in the United States District Court for the Western District of Missouri, seeking $3,081,000 in damages. On the basis of the released value doctrine, the district court granted Federal Express' motion for partial summary judgment, and entered judgment in favor of Hampton for $100.

II. DISCUSSION

A. *The "Released Value Doctrine"*

We have held that, under federal common law, "[a] common carrier may not exempt itself from liability for its negligence; however, a carrier may limit its liability." Hopper Furs, Inc. v. Emery Air Freight Corp., 749 F.2d 1261, 1264 (8th Cir.1984). ... This body of law, which has come to be known as the "released value doctrine" of federal common law, requires that in order to limit its liability "the carrier must present the shipper with a reasonable opportunity to declare a value for the shipment above the maximum value set by the carrier, pay an additional fee, and thereby be insured at a higher rate should the shipment go awry." Husman Constr. Co. v. Purolator Courier Corp., 832 F.2d 459, 461 (8th Cir.1987).

In this case, the contract entered into by the shipper, the Children's Memorial Hospital, with the carrier, Federal Express, clearly limited the liability of the carrier to $100, and provided the shipper with an opportunity to declare a higher value. Furthermore, it is not disputed that the shipper never declared a higher value for the blood samples. Hence, should the released value doctrine apply, the liability of the carrier, Federal Express, would be limited to $100.

There is a question, however, as to whether the released value doctrine applies in a suit brought by a plaintiff not a party to the contract of carriage. Hampton contends that his damages should not be limited by the released value doctrine since he was not the shipper of the blood samples, and, therefore, was not a party to the contract with the carrier, Federal Express....

Apart from [two lower-court cases], Hampton has failed to cite any authority in support of his position that the released value doctrine does not apply. Even if the released value doctrine does not apply, in this case, Hampton still cannot prevail under general principles of the common law.

B. *Recovery in Contract*

The arguments raised present important questions in contrasting a recovery based on contract or tort. English legal history shows that classifications and concepts that today seem absolutely distinct, were once blended and spring from a common source. Tort and contract law is an example, since the law of contracts began with the common law action of assumpsit, which traces its origins to the law of tort. See 3 W. Holdsworth, A History of English Law 428–29 (3d ed. 1923). Furthermore, in modern times, the difference between tort and contract liability "has become an increasingly difficult distinction to make." W. Keeton, Prosser and Keeton on the Law of Torts § 92 (5th ed. 1984) (hereinafter Prosser). Although it may be true that "general propositions do not decide concrete cases," Lochner v. New York, 198 U.S. 45, 76, 49 L.Ed. 937, 25 S.Ct. 539 (1905) (Holmes, J., dissenting), it is basic that, in contract law, the defendant's liability to a plaintiff arises from the contractual agreement between the parties. Tort liability, however, arises from "general obligations that are imposed by law—apart from and independent of promises made and therefore apart from the manifested intention of the parties—to avoid injury to others." Prosser at § 92.

In this case, even if it were to be assumed that Hampton may sue as a third party beneficiary of the contract between the shipper and the carrier, on the facts presented he still cannot recover in contract. See Osmond State Bank v. Uecker Grain, Inc., 227 Neb. 636, 639, 419 N.W.2d 518, 520 (1988) (under Nebraska law, the rights of a third party beneficiary depend on the liability of the promisor contained in the contract); Bridgman v. Curry, 398 N.W.2d 167, 170 (Iowa 1986) (under Iowa law, third party beneficiary must show that contract was formed for his express benefit). See also Restatement (Second) of Contracts § 302 (1981).

It is a fundamental principle of the law of damages that, in contract cases, a plaintiff can only recover for a loss which, in the ordinary course of events, would result from the defendant's breach or for a loss which was in the contemplation of the parties. In the words of the Restatement, "damages are not recoverable for loss that the party in breach did not have reason to foresee as a probable result of the breach when the contract was made." Restatement (Second) of Contracts § 351(1) (1981). This rule of damages may be traced to Hadley v. Baxendale [p. 534 above]; E. Re, Cases and Materials on Remedies 758 (2d ed. 1987).[a] See also Victoria Laundry (Windsor) Ld. v. Newman Indus., 2 K.B. 528, 539 (1949) ("In cases of breach of contract the aggrieved party is only

---

a. By the author of this opinion.

entitled to recover such part of the loss actually resulting as was at the time of the contract reasonably foreseeable as liable to result from the breach."). Hampton, in this case, cannot dispute that Federal Express had no knowledge of Hampton or of the contents of the package that it accepted for delivery. Hence, even apart from the limitation of liability provision, since the damages suffered by Hampton were not reasonably foreseeable, they would not be recoverable in a breach of contract action.

C. Recovery in Tort

The tort law of negligence, however, does not provide as clear a rule as to whether a defendant may be held liable for injuries or damages that are not reasonably foreseeable. Indeed, the wealth of literature on the subject is illustrative of the differences of opinion on the subject. [The court continued with a discussion of Palsgraf v. Long Island R.R., 162 N.E. 99 (N.Y.1928), and other authorities.]

... If Federal Express had known of the contents of the package, it might have charged a higher rate, exercised additional care, have obtained insurance, or might not have accepted the responsibility. Since Federal Express had no knowledge of the contents, and hence could not reasonably foresee the injury and damages that could be suffered, plaintiff Hampton cannot recover on its cause of action founded in tort.

[Affirmed.]

NOTES

(1) *Release from "Released Value".* In an omitted part of the court's discussion of the released-value doctrine, the court distinguished its earlier decision in Arkwright–Boston Mfrs. Mut. Ins. Co. v. Great Western Airlines, Inc., 767 F.2d 425 (8th Cir.1985), a case cited by the plaintiff. In that case a dealer in electronic goods shipped four packages of goods to a customer, TRW, via Federal Express. Federal Express issued four airbills to the dealer, and contracted with Great Western Airlines (GW) to transport the goods. The goods were destroyed in a crash of GW's airplane. They had become TRW's property when the dealer delivered them to Federal Express. The plaintiff, an insurer for TRW, paid it $99,000 for the loss and sought, as subrogee of TRW, to recover that amount from GW.

The trial court gave effect to limitations of liability in the airbills: total recovery, $400. On appeal by the plaintiff, *held:* Reversed. "Since the airbill did not expressly extend the liability limitation to a subcontractor of the carrier ... we held," the *Hampton* court said, "that, under federal common law, [GW] could not benefit from the limitation on liability contained in the airbill, which stated the contract between the parties. ... This case, however, differs from *Arkwright* since Hampton is suing the carrier, Federal Express, rather than a defendant who is not a party to the contract of carriage."

If the airbills in *Arkwright* had extended the limitation to subcontractors of Federal Express, would GW have been a third party beneficiary of the dealer/Federal Express contract? In Allied Steel v. Ford, p. 190 above, were Ford's employees third party beneficiaries?

(2) *Terms of the Promise.* The main case stands for the proposition, does it not, that the extent of the rights of a claimant, as third party beneficiary, depend on the terms of the promise—as expressed to the promisee—of which the

claimant is a beneficiary? Review Spiklevitz v. Markmil Corp., Note 2, p. 883 above. Does that case contradict the proposition, or exemplify it?

(3) *Problem.* Alpha Corporation did *not* acquire Beta Corporation, as it had planned to do. A business broker had attracted Alpha's attention to Beta as a target; and for the broker's services Beta had contracted to pay it a fee "in the event a transaction is consummated." Alpha and Beta had contracted for a merger. But Alpha withdrew from the contract without justification. In the merger agreement Alpha had agreed with Beta to pay the broker its fee in the event of consummation, "and not otherwise."

Does the broker have a claim against Alpha? See Massengale v. Transitron Electronic Corp., 385 F.2d 83 (1st Cir.1967) (When the action was brought, the target corporation—"Beta"—had already paid the plaintiff a fee for arranging the acquisition of that corporation by the Westinghouse Electric Corporation. Does that matter?).

What basis for the broker's claim against Alpha can you suggest? If Alpha and Beta had simply rescinded their merger agreement, what rights would the broker have had?

MUNICIPAL CONTRACTS AND PUBLIC SERVICES

Contracts by which private firms undertake to provide services wanted by a broad public (such as a dependable supply of electric power) often require payment by a governmental unit. If users of the service are disappointed, can they charge their losses to promisors as third party beneficiaries? A series of three New York cases illustrate the problems. In each case the court was concerned about the amounts and kinds of losses the defendant might be charged with.

The first case was an action against a waterworks that had contracted with the City of Rensselaer to supply water for homes and commercial users, and for various city purposes. It contracted, for example, to supply the city's fire hydrants, at $42.50 a year for each hydrant. The plaintiff, H.R. Moch Company, alleged that a fire had spread to its warehouse, owing to a failure of the defendant to supply enough water at the pressure needed for firefighting, and that the warehouse and its contents had been destroyed. The trial court dismissed the claim. The Court of Appeals (Cardozo, J.) approved this disposition. Distinguishing Lawrence v. Fox, above, the court said: "No legal duty rests upon a city to supply its inhabitants with protection against fire." City uses of water were the subject of separate "branches" of the contract. No intention was discernible to "assume an obligation of indefinite extension to every member of the public.... [Such an intention] is seen to be the more improbable when we recall the crushing burden that the obligation would impose." [a] The Court applied the method of analogy: "A promisor undertakes to supply fuel for heating a public building. He is not liable for breach of contract to a visitor who finds the building

a. Also: "If the plaintiff were to prevail, one who negligently omits to supply sufficient pressure to extinguish a fire started by another assumes an obligation to pay the ensuing damage, though the whole city is laid low. A promisor will not be deemed to have had in mind the assumption of a risk so overwhelming for any trivial reward."

without fuel, and thus contracts a cold." H.R. Moch Co., Inc. v. Rensselaer Water Co., 159 N.E. 896, 62 A.L.R. 1199 (N.Y.1928).[b]

In the second case, the plaintiff was the widow of a motorist who had suffered cardiac infarction, later dying, while changing a flat tire on the State Thruway on a hot August day. He and his family had waited for about two hours for assistance, after a state trooper had radioed for automotive service. The basis for the action was a contract by which the Thruway Authority enfranchised the Chevron Oil Company to sell gas on the highway. The contract required Chevron to be prepared to reach a disabled car within 30 minutes of an assignment (subject to extremes of weather and traffic). The contract specified the price of a service call and required refunds in cases of overcharge.

The widow, Mrs. Kornblut, got a judgment against Chevron for about half a million dollars. On appeal, the court described the *Authority's* interests in arranging for car service: one was attracting toll-paying users to the highway. But "there was also a personal interest of the user served by the contract," so that users were intended beneficiaries at least as to the specified charges. Even so, a suit for property damage, personal injury, or the like is "another matter." The court reversed the judgment and dismissed the complaint, saying that the plaintiff had failed to "show that the injury was one which the defendants [c] had reason to foresee as a probable result of the breach, under the ancient doctrine of Hadley v. Baxendale [p. 534 above]." [d]

The third case concerned the electric power supply for New York City, which was massively interrupted one night in 1977. The defendant was the private power supplier ("Con Ed"). The legislature of New York State had acted to provide a tax advantage to the supplier by permitting it to sell plants to a State authority; and in exchange Con Ed had undertaken to provide service of a stated quality to its customers. These included the plaintiffs: the City itself and various institutions. Their claims were based in part on the law of third party beneficiaries. To that extent the defendant moved for summary judgment, which the trial court denied. On appeal, *held:* Affirmed. The plaintiffs were "precisely the consumers for whose benefit the legislation was enacted and the agreements made...." Koch v. Consolidated Edison Co., 468 N.E.2d 1 (N.Y.1984).[e]

"To be distinguished," the court said, "are our holdings in H.R. Moch Co. v. Rensselaer Water Co. and Kornblut v. Chevron Oil Co. ... In neither of those cases did the operative contract provide that the

b. Other grounds for the claim, equally unavailing, were (a) a cause of action for a common-law tort "within MacPherson v. Buick Motor Co., 217 N.Y. 382, 111 N.E. 1050 ...," and (b) a cause of action for the breach of a statutory duty.

c. Another defendant was a gas station operator to whom Chevron had delegated some of its contract responsibilities.

d. The opinion quoted is that of Hopkins, J., in Kornblut v. Chevron Oil Co., 407 N.Y.S.2d 498, aff'd on opinion below, 400 N.E.2d 368 (N.Y.1979).

e. Cert. denied, 469 U.S. 1210 (1985).

service was to be rendered other than for the contracting party, city or authority.''

Turning to the extent of damages, however, the Court disapproved of some items, such as overtime wages for police and other City officers. Con Ed conceded that the plaintiffs could recover losses due to physical injury to persons and property directly resulting from the "blackout". As to damages resulting from looting and vandalism by rioters, the Court said: "plaintiffs have shown facts sufficient to require a trial of the factual question of whether intervention of the rioters was within the contemplation of the parties or reasonably to have been foreseen by Con Edison.''

Do the cases suggest a category of third-party claimants who are *quasi-intended* beneficiaries?

NOTES

(1) *The Case of the Blind Crossing.* A truck driver was killed at the intersection of a road and two rail lines. One was a main line of the "Chessie" Road; [a] the other was a parallel spur serving a fertilizer plant. The driver's widow brought an action against the owner of the plant, alleging that her husband's view had been obscured by railroad cars that the owner had placed on the spur within fifty feet of the crossing. The owner had contracted with the railroad not to spot cars so close to the crossing. For dictum that the decedent was not a third party beneficiary of that contract, see Justice v. CSX Transp., Inc., 908 F.2d 119, 124 (7th Cir.1990).

Should that be said even if the owner had contracted with the railroad to "be liable for injuries and damages to persons and property suffered by reason of the Owner's use of the spur or any negligence in connection therewith"? If the widow must rely on that provision alone—absent one about the location of cars— and can make no showing of negligence, should her action be dismissed? Compare Leija v. Materne Bros., Inc., 664 P.2d 527 (Wash.App.1983).

(2) *Tort Liability via Promise?* Most opinions that cite H.R. Moch v. Rensselaer Water Company do so for its elaboration on the principle of negligence law ("ancient learning," Cardozo wrote), that "one who assumes to act, even though gratuitously, may thereby become subject to the duty of acting carefully, if he acts at all." Glanzer v. Shepard, 135 N.E. 275, 276 (N.Y.1922). In the Restatement, Second, of Torts, the formulation of this principle [b] is accompanied by a *Caveat:*

> The Institute expresses no opinion as to whether . . . the making of a contract or a gratuitous promise, without in any way entering upon performance, is a sufficient undertaking to result in liability under the rule stated in this Section.[c]

As for protecting the interests of a third person, part performance of a promise may, apparently, entail a duty of care, at least if the duty "undertaken" is owed by the promisee to that person. The fact that the promisee is a municipality, and that the third person is someone entitled to its protection, tends to supply the latter requirement. Long v. District of Columbia, 820 F.2d 409 (D.C.Cir. 1987).

In this case a co-defendant, Potomac Electric Power ("Pepco"), had contracted to make emergency repairs to malfunctioning traffic signals in Washington

---

a. Once the Chesapeake & Ohio; later CSX Transportation, Inc.

b. Sections 323–324A.

c. Appended to §§ 323 and 324A (Caveat 1).

D.C., and may have deferred a repair; the plaintiff's husband had been killed in a collision at an unguarded intersection. Would liability based on this contract pose a serious risk of "crushing" Pepco?

(3) *The Case of the Bridge Collapse.* In Fort Bend County Drainage District v. Sbrusch, 818 S.W.2d 392 (Tex.1991), a municipal unit (the District) was the *promisor.* A jury found that it had been negligent in deferring the repair of a bridge it had built. Earlier, when the owner of the bridge advised the District that it was unsafe, he was promised a repair. Many months after that, when nothing had been done, the bridge collapsed under the truck of a neighboring landowner who had the right to use the bridge. He suffered personal injuries, and sued the District. From a judgment for the District, n.o.v., he appealed. *Held:* Affirmed. "[T]here was neither the slightest performance by the promisor nor reliance by the injured party." [d] Indeed, he had not been aware of the promise.

Questions: Would the plaintiff's case have been better if he had known of the owner's complaint, the District's promise, and its inaction? If the bridge had collapsed under the *promisee* (owner of the bridge), would he have had a better case? In either case, if it appeared that the owner had agreed to pay the District for the repair, would that make a crucial difference?

Would the bridge-collapse case be materially different if the promisor (defendant) had been a private bridge-building firm, rather than a municipal unit? What might be said to distinguish that case, or the actual case, from the case described in Note 1 above?

DAVIS v. UNITED AIR LINES, INC.

United States District Court, Eastern District of New York, 1983.
575 F.Supp. 677.

WEINSTEIN, CHIEF JUDGE: Plaintiff, who has a physical disability, is suing his former employer claiming wrongful dismissal from his job, allegedly in violation of section 503 of the Rehabilitation Act of 1973 as amended. 29 U.S.C. § 793. He contends that the dismissal violated the contract between his employer and the federal government. The contract, as required by section 503, incorporated an affirmative action provision in favor of physically disabled workers. He claims standing to sue as a third-party beneficiary. Plaintiff also contends that the dismissal violated the collective bargaining agreement between his union and his employer; that agreement, it is claimed, incorporated by inference the affirmative action provision. For the reasons indicated below, defendant's motion to dismiss must be granted.

I. FACTS

Starting in September 1966, the plaintiff was employed by United as a "ramp serviceman" at Kennedy Airport in New York. In 1969, he was first diagnosed as having epilepsy. United was aware of this diagnosis, as it was of the five seizures that plaintiff experienced from 1969 to 1974. From September 1974 to June 1977, United increasingly restrict-

---

d. Id. at 396.

ed plaintiff's employment.   On June 6, 1977, plaintiff was placed involuntarily on permanent unpaid sick leave and in 1980, United terminated plaintiff's employment.

It is contended that the restrictions, suspension and dismissal were not justified, as United claims, by plaintiff's disability and that United's actions violated section 503 of the Rehabilitation Act.   That section requires that all contracts over $2,500 made by the United States for property or services include a provision requiring the party contracting with the United States to take "affirmative action to employ . . . qualified handicapped individuals."   It also provides for an aggrieved handicapped individual to file a complaint with the Department of Labor and for the Department to take appropriate action if it finds a violation.

The plaintiff originally stated a cause of action directly under the statute.   The Court of Appeals, however, held that no such private right of action exists.   Davis v. United Air Lines, Inc., 662 F.2d 120 (2d Cir.1981), cert. denied, 456 U.S. 965, 102 S.Ct. 2045, 72 L.Ed.2d 490 (1982) criticized in Comment, Closing the Courthouse Door on Section 503 Complaints, 49 Bklyn.L.Rev. 1159 (1983).   An amended complaint is predicated on the view that plaintiff could sue as a third-party beneficiary of the statutorily mandated contract and for violation of the collective bargaining agreement.

II. LAW

Section 503 provides in relevant part:

(a) Any contract in excess of $2,500 entered into by any Federal department or agency for the procurement of personal property and nonpersonal services (including construction) for the United States shall contain a provision requiring that, in employing persons to carry out such contract the party contracting with the United States shall take affirmative action to employ and advance in employment qualified handicapped individuals. . . .

(b) If any handicapped individual believes any contractor has failed or refuses to comply with the provisions of his contract with the United States, relating to employment of handicapped individuals, such individual may file a complaint with the Department of Labor. The Department shall promptly investigate such complaint and shall take such action thereon as the facts and circumstances warrant, consistent with the terms of such contract and the laws and regulations applicable thereto.   29 U.S.C. § 793.

A. *Third–Party Beneficiary Claim*

Although there is little New York law on point, it appears that New York courts would, in the case of a contract mandated by a federal statute, be guided by federal contract law in deciding a third-party beneficiary claim.   Filardo v. Foley Bros., 297 N.Y. 217, 225, 78 N.E.2d 480, 484, 79 N.Y.S.2d 217 (1948), rev'd on other grounds, 336 U.S. 281, 69 S.Ct. 575, 93 L.Ed. 680 (1949). . . .

... Since New York State courts would follow federal law, federal courts must do so in an action such as this one which is now based on diversity jurisdiction. Klaxon Co. v. Stentor Elec. Mfg. Co., 313 U.S. 487, 61 S.Ct. 1020, 85 L.Ed. 1477 (1941).

Federal common law, in deciding whether a third-party beneficiary may sue, looks to the same considerations as does the Restatement of Contracts. See Restatement (Second) Section 302; Owens v. Haas, 601 F.2d 1242, 1250 (2d Cir.), cert. denied, 444 U.S. 980, 100 S.Ct. 483, 62 L.Ed.2d 407 (1979); Weinberger v. New York Stock Exchange, 335 F.Supp. 139, 143 (S.D.N.Y.1971). Under the Restatement, the relevant factors are whether "[1] recognition of a right to performance in the beneficiary is appropriate to effectuate the intention of the parties and ... [2 whether] the circumstances indicate that the promisee intends to give the beneficiary the benefit of the promised performance." Restatement (Second) Section 302.

The second part of the test is met here: The promisee, the United States, in mandating that the contractual provision in question be put into the contract, manifested an intention to benefit handicapped employees such as the plaintiff. The first part of the test, however, is not, according to the Court of Appeals in *Davis*. Under this part of the test, one looks to whether allowing the third-party beneficiary to sue is appropriate to effectuate the intention of the parties. Although whether the plaintiff has a private right of action under the statute is conceptually distinct from whether the plaintiff may sue as a third-party beneficiary of the contract mandated by the statute, the same considerations largely determine both issues.

The Second Circuit in *Davis* emphasized the comprehensive administrative scheme provided by Congress to remedy section 503 violations in concluding that it was not "consistent with the underlying purpose of the legislative scheme to infer a private right of action for the handicapped person discriminated against by his employer," 662 F.2d at 126. A private contract action would be as "inconsistent with the underlying purpose of the legislative scheme" and would interfere with the implementation of that scheme to the same extent as would a cause of action directly under the statute. Such an action would therefore not be "appropriate to effectuate the intention of the parties." This result is consistent with that reached by the two other courts that have considered the issue: Hoopes v. Equifax, Inc., 611 F.2d 134 (6th Cir.1979); Howard v. Uniroyal, Inc., 543 F.Supp. 490 (M.D.Ala.1981).

Plaintiff contends that Owens v. Haas... controls this case and compels an opposite result. In *Owens,* the court held that although the plaintiff, a federal prisoner, did not have a private right of action under a statute which authorized the United States to contract with local authorities for prisoner care, he could sue as a third-party beneficiary of the statutorily authorized contract. In *Owens,* however, the statute merely authorized the United States to make the contract. By contrast, in the instant case, the statute and the regulations under it not only mandated the inclusion of the affirmative action provision, but spelled out *in haec verba* the terms of that provision. Thus, unlike *Owens,* allowing him to sue here under the contract would be allowing him to make an "end-run" around a statute which the Court of Appeals has held did not allow him to sue.

The result is, of course, that plaintiff must forego relief, warmed only by the pleasant thought that public policy is being vindicated. As Judge Fuld noted in *Filardo,* quoting from City of Phoenix v. Drinkwater, 46 Ariz. 470, 472, 52 P.2d 1175, 1177 (1935):

> Such [is] . . . a Pyrrhic victory for the workman, consoling perhaps to his feelings, but of very little value in giving to him what the law says he has earned and is due him.

Filardo v. Foley Bros., 297 N.Y. 217, 223, 78 N.E.2d 480, 483 (1948). The result, however, follows from the Court of Appeals decision in *Davis.*

B. *Collective Bargaining Agreement Claim*

[For the plaintiff's failure properly to pursue a grievance as required by the Railway Labor Act, the court rejected this claim.]

In any event, given the Court of Appeals decision in *Davis,* there is no reason to believe that there is merit in plaintiff's substantive argument. If express incorporation as between his employer and the government does not suffice to permit a private suit, implied incorporation [through collective bargaining agreements] certainly does not.

CONCLUSION

Plaintiff's claim is dismissed without costs or disbursements.

NOTES

(1) *Across the River.* When the same issue came before a judge in the Southern District of New York (Lasker, J.), he made a like ruling. His opinion enlarged on the prior Second Circuit decision as follows: "the *Davis* Court examined the four factors set out in Cort v. Ash, 422 U.S. 66 . . . (1975): first, 'is the plaintiff "one of the class for whose *especial* benefit the statute was enacted;" ' second, 'is there any indication of legislative intent, explicit or implicit, either to create such a remedy or to deny one;' third, 'is it consistent with the underlying purposes of the legislative scheme to imply such a remedy for the plaintiff;' and fourth, 'is the cause of action one traditionally relegated to state law, in an area basically the concern of the States, so that it would be inappropriate to infer a cause of action based solely on federal law?' " Chaplin v. Consolidated Edison Co., 579 F.Supp. 1470 (S.D.N.Y.1984).

Referring to § 503, the court said: "Of course, plaintiffs' claim as third-party beneficiaries . . . is conceptually distinct from a claim based directly on the statute. As a practical matter, however, the considerations determining the validity of the former overlap to a substantial extent those determining the validity of the latter."

As to Owens v. Haas, the court said that, there, "a federal prisoner sued county prison officials and the county itself based on a severe beating he had received while housed at the county prison pursuant to a contract between the federal government and the county. . . . It is true that the outcome which we believe *Davis* mandates for plaintiffs' third-party claim may be at odds with the outcome suggested by *Owens*. A possible ground for distinguishing the two cases exists, however, in *Owens'* reliance on the fact that the United States owes a duty of care to federal prisoners independent of the contract and statute at issue there...." Compare Note, 94 Yale L.J. 875 (1985).

(2) *Affirmative Action.* Organization of Minority Vendors, Inc. v. Illinois Central Gulf Railroad, 579 F.Supp. 574 (N.D.Ill.1983), was a notable recognition of a third-party claim, in connection with federal funding, although the court said: "The law in federal courts is somewhat unsettled on the existence of third-party beneficiary rights under the many different kinds of contracts between federal agencies and recipients of federal funds." See Waters, op. cit. supra Note 2, p. 869, at 1173–1208.

In that case "the railroad defendants were required, as part of their funding agreements with the federal government under [the '4–R Act'] to formulate affirmative action plans designed to increase MBE [minority-business enterprise] participation as a goal. Those plans were incorporated into the funding agreements. The plaintiff, a group of black- and hispanic-owned MBE's, sued on a third-party beneficiary theory to enforce the affirmative action provisions of the funding agreements. They alleged that the railroads breached the funding agreements by practicing discrimination and failing to achieve 15% MBE participation and sought injunctive relief and damages." [a] A motion to dismiss was denied.

The court also found an implied private right of action under the statute. But the court alluded to difficulties the plaintiffs might encounter, on this theory, according to authority in the Supreme Court ("badly splintered").

(3) *Questions.* Is third-party-beneficiary theory a good way to solve problems of remedies that are, in good part, peculiar to the federal courts? To cure the failure of a governmental agency to fulfill its statutory mission?

The *Minority Vendors* decision followed the lead of an earlier case concerning the rights of black children, segregation in schools, and federal funding. How nearly comparable are the cases?

(4) *The Case of the County's Intentions.* A group of tenants of commercial space brought an action against their landlords. They based the claim on a lease, under which the landlords had acquired from the County of Los Angeles the right to develop the property; it provided for a "fair and reasonable" return to the landlords on their investment. In light of that, the tenants contended, the rents they had agreed to pay were "overcharges." An order dismissing this claim was affirmed on appeal. Marina Tenants Ass'n v. Deauville Marina Development Co., Ltd., 226 Cal.Rptr. 321 (App.1986). The County's lease referred to its "immediate" and its "ultimate" objects: the ultimate one was the benefit of the public; whereas the immediate one was to realize the greatest possible revenue for the County. The lease recited, touchingly, that its immediate and ultimate objects were "consistent and compatible." If this recital was a mere rhetorical flourish, might anything else in the lease be dismissed as rhetorical? Aside from public contracts, what kinds of contracts might be expected to contain recitals about motives?

---

a. Technicable Video Systems, Inc. v. Americable of Greater Miami, Ltd., 479 So.2d 810 (Fla.App.1985).

KARO v. SAN DIEGO SYMPHONY ORCHESTRA ASS'N, 762 F.2d 819 (9th Cir.1985). [Employees of the Symphony were represented by Local 325 of the American Federation of Musicians. The three-year collective bargaining agreement of September, 1979, provided for filling vacant chairs through a "blind" audition procedure. Stephen Karo, Jr., a percussionist, learned of an opening to be filled by audition in the 1981–82 season. In February, 1982, however, the Symphony and the Local modified their contract. As a result the position went, without an audition, to a "noncontract" musician who had served for six years with the Symphony. Karo brought a class action against the Symphony for its failure to conduct auditions.[a] From a dismissal, Karo appealed.]

BOOCHEVER, CIRCUIT JUDGE: ... There is nothing in the agreement which indicates that the audition procedure is for the benefit of nonemployee union members. On its face it is equally applicable to any musician seeking employment with the Symphony. Moreover, there is no indication that the provision was intended to benefit union members rather than the Symphony. But even if Karo could be considered a third party beneficiary of the 1979 agreement he still cannot prevail. The agreement was amended to provide specifically for filling positions without auditions when noncontract musicians had prior service for specified periods. Under the modified agreement Karo had no right to audition for the seat.

... The power to modify terminates when the beneficiary materially changes position in justifiable reliance on the promise before receiving notification of the modification.... Karo does not allege any such change of position. Thus, assuming that Karo could be regarded as a third party beneficiary under the 1979 contract, no rights he might have acquired thereunder had vested when the contract was modified in 1982. Accordingly the union and Symphony had the power to modify the agreement eliminating the open audition provisions when noncontract musicians had requisite experience for filling the position.

[W]e are cognizant that labor agreements involve policy considerations that sometimes make ordinary contract law inapplicable. See Lewis v. Benedict Coal Corp., 361 U.S. 459, 470, 80 S.Ct. 489, 495, 4 L.Ed.2d 442 (1960). We find no reason, however, for not following third party beneficiary principles in this case. As long as no vested rights are affected, a union and an employer should be able to modify a collective bargaining agreement under circumstances such as these. As stated in Brown v. Sterling Aluminum Products Corp., 365 F.2d 651, 657 (8th Cir.1966), cert. denied, 386 U.S. 957, 87 S.Ct. 1023, 18 L.Ed.2d 105 (1967), "for an individual to bring an action under § 301 he must be seeking to enforce a right that is personal to him and vested in him at the time of the suit." Karo has not satisfied these two requirements.

a. Karo was a member of the AFM, but not of the Local. He made a claim made against the Local as well—without success.

The claims were premised on the Labor Management Relations Act of 1947, section 301 [29 U.S.C. § 125 (1982)], which implies private rights of action. As to Karo's status as a third party beneficiary, however, the court thought it appropriate to consult state law.

. . .

Affirmed.

NOTE

Collective Interests. Beginning with Lewis v. Benedict Coal Corp., 361 U.S. 459 (1960), the Supreme Court has repeatedly differentiated collective-bargaining agreements from the "typical third-party beneficiary contract." In Schneider Moving & Storage Co. v. Robbins, 466 U.S. 364 (1984), an employer (the company) had withheld contributions to a pension fund that were claimed for certain employees, denying that these were covered employees. As plaintiffs, the trustees of the fund—one of the largest multiemployer funds in the nation—contended that the contributions were required by the company's contract with the local Teamsters' union. The trial court dismissed the action, referring to a provision in that contract requiring the arbitration of differences between the company and the union as to its meaning or application.

On appeal, the company relied on the "general rule that the promisor [company] may assert against the beneficiary [trustees] any defense that he could assert against the promisee [union] if the promisee were suing on the contract." The Court characterized that as a rule of construction only, and refused to apply it. In part, the Court relied on the interests nationwide of teamsters and their employers: "Each of the participating unions and employers has an interest in the prompt collection of the proper contributions from each employer." It relied also, in part, on enforcement provisions in the pension-trust agreements, which "protect the collective interests of the parties from the delinquence of individual employers...." [b]

Introductory Note to *Jardel Enterprises*

The United States was a third party beneficiary of a settlement agreement between Mr. and Mrs. Wood when they were divorced. The agreement awarded the marital home, and some other properties, to Mrs. Wood. It provided, however, that she would pay some of her husband's debts, including a lien that the Internal Revenue Service (IRS) had established on the properties to secure taxes that Mr. Wood had failed to pay. This arrangement was explained to the IRS. Later, however, the Woods executed an "addendum" to their agreement, purporting to relieve Mrs. Wood of the obligation to pay the IRS. (Apparently her attempt to sell the home was less successful than the parties had anticipated.) Still later, the IRS brought an action against Mrs. Wood for the taxes, and got a judgment against her for more than $126,000. She appealed. She contended that her husband, as the promisee in a "creditor-beneficiary" contract, had the power to release her from the original undertaking.

b. The decision in *Schneider Moving & Storage* may be contrasted with that in National Tax Credit Partners, L.P. v. Havlik, 20 F.3d 705 (7th Cir.1994). That was an action by investors, as promisees, for specific performance of a contract for the benefit of a third party. Because the third party was in bankruptcy, its right to performance was property of the estate. In the court's view, the remedy sought by the investors would have been an exercise of control over that asset and was therefore precluded by the Bankruptcy Code.

This position was supported by the first Restatement. But the court rejected it, saying: "the position of the Second Restatement, stating that creditors' rights vest upon their learning of the contract and assenting to it, represents the majority view...." For the purpose of rescinding a third-party benefit, the court said, there is no difference between creditor beneficiaries and donee beneficiaries. U.S. v. Wood, 877 F.2d 453 (6th Cir.1989) (affirming).

In Lawrence v. Fox, above, the next-to-last paragraph of the majority opinion addresses this problem: "how could he [Holly] ... discharge ... the promise ... made as it was for the plaintiff's benefit and in accordance with legal presumption accepted by him ...?" The problem is addressed also in the opinion that follows.

JARDEL ENTERPRISES, INC. v. TRICONSULTANTS, INC.

Colorado Court of Appeals, 1988.
770 P.2d 1301. Certiorari denied.

TURSI, JUDGE. Plaintiffs, Jardel Enterprises, Inc., Carlos De La Rosa, and Lawrence E. Jaro, (owners) appeal the summary judgment entered in favor of defendants, Tri–Consultants, Inc., James V. Laraby, James W. Rogers, and James R. Busse (subcontractors). We affirm.

To consider the propriety of the summary judgment entered, we must view the record in the light most favorable to the plaintiffs. Zalnis v. Thoroughbred Datsun Car Co., 645 P.2d 292 (Colo.App.1982).

When so viewed, the record reveals the following. The owners contracted with Brooks Western Builders, Inc., (contractor) to build a fast-food restaurant. The contract included a liquidated damages provision which provided that for each day completion was delayed, the contractor would pay the owner $100 as the reasonable estimate of the owners' loss of profit.

The contractor subcontracted with the subcontractors to stake out the foundation corners and boundary lines. The subcontractors sent an unlicensed surveyor to complete the work. He misread the building plans; consequently, the building foundation was poured 20 feet too far north. This precluded an efficient drive-through lane and parking spaces in front of the restaurant.

The owners required the contractor to remove the foundation and rebuild it in the correct location resulting in a 65–day delay in opening the restaurant. The owners received $6,500 from the contractor pursuant to the liquidated damages provision.

The contractor brought an action against the subcontractors alleging they negligently staked the restaurant foundation thereby breaching their contract. That action was settled by the subcontractors' payment of $25,000 to the contractor. In exchange, the contractor released and discharged any and all causes of actions and claims against the subcontractors arising from the services the subcontractors provided to the contractor on the restaurant. The owners were not a party to that action or settlement.

Subsequently, the owners brought this action against the subcontractors alleging claims for breach of contract and negligence and sought lost profit damages caused by the delayed opening of the restaurant. The subcontractors moved for summary judgment contending that the settlement agreement and release between the contractor and the subcontractors was a valid defense to any claims made by the owners as third-party beneficiaries of the subcontract.

The trial court entered summary judgment in favor of the subcontractors. It concluded that the general release entered into between the contractor and the subcontractor was an effective bar against the owners' action against the subcontractor as a third-party beneficiary of the contractor-subcontractor agreement. It determined that the owners' breach of contract and negligence claims were barred.

I

The owners assert the settlement agreement and release entered by the contractor and the subcontractors did not affect their right to bring this action as the third-party beneficiaries of the breached subcontract. We disagree.

A person not a party to an express contract may bring an action on the contract if the parties to the agreement intended to benefit the non-party, provided that the benefit claimed is a direct and not merely an incidental benefit of the contract. E.B. Roberts Construction Co. v. Concrete Contractors, Inc., 704 P.2d 859 (Colo.1985). However, if the third person is a creditor beneficiary, i.e., if performance of the contract satisfies an actual duty owed by one of the parties to the beneficiary, then the beneficiary's right pursuant to the contract is purely derivative of the right of the contract promisee. 2 S. Williston, Contracts §§ 356 and 397 (W. Jaeger 3rd ed. 1959).

In such circumstances, the creditor beneficiary may assert contract rights equal to but not greater than the rights of the contract promisee. The parties to the contract retain the power to discharge or modify the contractual duty to the intended beneficiary unless (1) a term of the contract provides otherwise or (2) the beneficiary, before he receives notification of the discharge or modification, materially changes his position in justifiable reliance on the promise or brings suit on it or manifests assent to it at the request of either of the parties to the contract. Restatement (Second) of Contracts § 311 (1981).

Here, it is undisputed that the owners were intended creditor beneficiaries of the subcontract since the contractor owed the owners the duty to stake the foundation corners. It is also undisputed that the contractor discharged the contractual duty before the owners brought suit on it. Nevertheless, the owners maintain that they significantly altered their position in reliance on the subcontract. However, each "change of position" they assert was part of the normal progression on the restaurant project and was not related to reliance on the subcontract.

Therefore, the subcontractors and the contractor retained the power to discharge the duty to the owners. The trial court correctly concluded that the settlement agreement and release between the subcontractors and the contractor barred the owners' derivative breach of contract claim.

II

The owners also contend that the trial court erred by determining that the settlement agreement and release barred their negligence claim against the subcontractors. While we agree that the settlement agreement and release did not bar any claim by the owner except the derivative breach of contract claim, we conclude that the owners did not have a negligence claim against the subcontractors. A correct judgment will not be disturbed on review even though the reason for the decision may be wrong. Miller v. Mountain Valley Ambulance Service, Inc., 694 P.2d 362 (Colo.App.1984).

As a general rule, no cause of action lies in tort when purely economic damage is caused by negligent breach of a contractual duty. Flintkote Co. v. Dravo Corp., 678 F.2d 942 (11th Cir.1982); Album Graphics, Inc. v. Beatrice Foods Co., 87 Ill.App.3d 338, 408 N.E.2d 1041, 42 Ill.Dec. 332 (1980). This economic loss rule prevents recovery for negligence when the duty breached is a contractual duty and the harm incurred is the result of failure of the purpose of the contract. Flintkote Co. v. Dravo Corp., supra.

When parties dealing at arms length enter into a contract, they may shape the terms of the contract as they please and restrict the remedies for breach of the contract. However, in a negligence action one may seek damages for all injuries proximately caused by the defendant's negligence. Therefore, where only economic losses are incurred by breach of a contractual duty, we reject the assertion that the non-breaching party has a negligence cause of action because to hold otherwise would permit that party to avoid the contractual limitation of remedy. See Album Graphics, Inc. v. Beatrice Foods Co., supra. A claim for economic loss on a contract should not be translatable into a tort action in order to escape some roadblock to recovery on a contract theory. W. Prosser & W. Keeton, Torts § 92 (5th ed. 1984).

This economic loss rule applies whether the plaintiff is a party to the contract or a third-party beneficiary of the contract since the duty the contract promisor owed and breached was determined by the manifested intentions of the parties to the contract and is entirely contractual. W. Prosser & W. Keeton, supra.

> "Thus, a builder or a contractor would normally be subject to liability on a contract theory only to the promisee and a third-party beneficiary for delays in construction or defects in construction that do not result in physical harm to persons and tangible things, other than the thing itself that is being constructed or repaired."

W. Prosser & W. Keeton, supra.

The rule is limited to cases that involve only economic loss and does not prevent a negligence action to recover for physical injury to property or persons because, in that case, the duty breached generally arises independent of the contract. Flintkote Co. v. Dravo Corp., supra. There is a general rule of tort law that one who acts is under a duty to exercise reasonable care to avoid physical harm to persons and tangible property of others and this general duty extends to parties to contracts. W. Prosser & W. Keeton, supra. The distinction between a contract and tort claim depends upon the nature of the duty that has been breached, which in most instances can be determined from the harm suffered. Flintkote Co. v. Dravo Corp., supra.

Here, the owners sought lost profits, which are purely economic damages, with no claim of physical harm to person or property. Furthermore, the only duty they maintain the subcontractors breached was their contractual duty to perform surveying services. Consequently, owners have no negligence cause of action since no duty independent of the contract was breached.

Judgment affirmed.

NOTES

(1) *"Creditor" Beneficiary: Vested Rights?* In U.S. v. Wood, described above, the court concluded that the government could recover not only because it had assented to Mrs. Wood's undertaking, but also because it had changed its position in reliance on statements to the IRS regarding Mrs. Wood's obligations under the initial agreement. That would be a ground for enforcing her promise on any view. Possibly the usual form of prejudice through reliance by a creditor beneficiary is the creditor's *failure* to take energetic collection measures against the promisee (e.g., taxpayer) at a time when they might have proved to be successful. Is the position of Restatement Second justifiable on the ground that that kind of prejudice is especially difficult to establish? On any other ground?

Compare the argument of the owners, in *Jardel Enterprises,* about change of position: Did the court dismiss that argument too summarily?

For a view contrary to that case, and to the Restatement rule, about modifying the rights of a creditor beneficiary, see Hickox v. Bell, 552 N.E.2d 1133 (Ill.App.1990) (alternative ground: reliance by beneficiary).

(2) *"Donee" Beneficiary: Vested Rights?* In 1979, on retiring from his firm of realty brokers, R.A. Biggins sold his interest to his partners, Shore and Guerra. The contract provided for them to make, in addition to fixed payments, a payment of $35 upon the settlement of each sale effected by the firm over a period of six years. Upon the death of Biggins within that period, payments were to continue to his wife, Marie, for her life.

After Biggins's death, in 1984, a memorandum was found in an envelope that he had handed to Guerra about two years earlier, marked "To be opened only at the death of Robert A. Biggins." According to the memorandum, his former partners had two options: either to observe the contract as made or to make somewhat scaled-down payments, over a period of three years, to St. Joseph's Preparatory School.

In an action by Marie Biggins for enforcement of the contract, the former partners contended that the contract had been modified in favor of the school. The trial court entered summary judgment for the plaintiff. On successive appeals, *held:* Affirmed. Biggins v. Shore, 565 A.2d 737 (Pa.1989). The court acknowledged that, according to § 311 of the Restatement Second, R.A. Biggins and his partners retained the power to discharge or modify the contract by subsequent agreement, in the absence of a contrary term in the contract.[a] But it subscribed, instead, to the rule of the original Restatement (§ 142): a promisor's duty to a "donee beneficiary" cannot be released by the promisee absent a permissive provision in the contract. "Pennsylvania's existing rule, unlike the Restatement (Second) position, is consistent with the concept of a gift.... To permit Biggins, from his grave, to destroy the annuity of his widow would not be equitable."[b]

How different would the case have been if (i) the initial contract had favored the school, not Mrs. Biggins, and (ii) the parties had agreed afterward to make her the beneficiary rather than the school?

If Karo v. San Diego Symphony, above, had come before the Pennsylvania court, and the percussionist plaintiff had been considered an intended beneficiary of the collective bargaining agreement, would the case have been decided differently?

(3) *A Dissenter's View.* In the view of Justice Papadakos, dissenting in *Biggins,* (i) the Restatement Second rule is the one "best suited to modern commercial and contractual expectations"; but (ii) the memorandum did not create a true option, but was on its face only an offer to the defendants, which they did not accept before Biggins's death. The Justice professed not to understand why the Restatement position was changed, but said: "The dominant idea [of] a number of the revisions ... was that of enhancing freedom of contract." In favor of the change, he said: "Requiring an express clause to make these kinds of contracts irrevocable also vivifies for the parties what the consequences are of their consensual agreement. This has traditionally been one of the reasons that for an *inter vivos* gift to be effective, actual delivery is generally required—because it vivifies for the donor what the irrevocable step is that he is taking."[c]

The Justice found further merit in the Restatement Second, in that it consolidates rules applicable to all "intended" beneficiaries, saying:

> By adopting Section 311 we would reduce the number of conceptual categories that encumber the contract law of this Commonwealth, but more importantly, we would be doing what is required by the merit and justice of the cause.[d]

a. As to distinctive rules applicable to insurance contracts see Comment c to § 311.

b. Two of the justices, concurring, thought it might be well to align Pennsylvania with the "majority of the states" embracing the rule of the Restatement Second; but they would not apply that rule to contracts already made.

c. Justice Papadakos objected to the court's appeal to the equity of the plaintiff's claim, saying, "It is wrong to pick a winner for extraneous reasons and then to adopt a rule to reach the pre-chosen result. To do so ... lends credence to the theories of 'realists' like the late Judge Jerome Frank [see biographical note, fn. b, p. 138 above], and the modern 'critical legal studies' radicals that ours is not a system of law at all, but merely one of individual preference."

d. Quotations from id. at 743, 748–49 (footnotes omitted).

The Justice concluded, finally, that the case should be remanded for a determination whether or not, on further evidence, Biggins's memorandum was effective as an instrument of gift (e.g., a will).

In Detroit Bank & Trust Co. v. Chicago Flame Hardening Co., Inc., 541 F.Supp. 1278 (N.D.Ind.1982), the court deprecated the theory, advanced on behalf of a widow, that she should be presumed to have accepted a promise that had been made to her husband for her benefit: "camouflaged application of gift theory." (In that case the testimony of the widow was laudably candid. She had known of the agreement in her favor; but when asked about long-range plans she might have made in reliance on it, she said "No, I forgot the whole thing.")

(4) *Benefits With Life and Death Contingencies.* Insurance contracts (including annuity contracts) are the most important class of agreements consciously made for the benefit of third parties. Only a small fraction of life-insurance buyers wish to make irrevocable beneficiary designations; hence most policies contain provisions for changing a designation.

Through the social-security system, and otherwise, the deferred earnings of American workers are to some extent dedicated to their surviving spouses. Notably, the military pension plan (heavily populated by male workers) presents an obstacle to a participant wishing—perhaps upon a divorce—to make an enduring commitment of benefits.

BUILDING AND REPAIR CONTRACTS:

THIRD–PARTY CLAIMS

In Jardel Enterprises v. Triconsultants, above, was it necessary for the defendant-subcontractors to concede that the plaintiffs were intended beneficiaries of the contracts to stake out the corners and lines?

Compare Chestnut Hill Development Corp. v. Otis Elevator Co., 653 F.Supp. 927 (D.Mass.1987). In that case Chestnut Hill, the developer of a condominium complex, sued the firm (Otis) that had installed the elevators, complaining of delayed work and malfunctions. The complaint alleged direct damages of $1 million and lost profits of $10 million. The plaintiff sought recognition as a third party beneficiary of the contract between the defendant and the general contractor, Vappi Construction Company. In response, Otis contended that

> it did not promise to fulfill Vappi's promise to Chestnut Hill, which was to furnish completed condominium units. Instead, Otis promised only to furnish and install the five elevators. According to Otis, Chestnut Hill is thus merely an incidental beneficiary.

What more information is required, if any, to resolve this dispute? The terms of the contract between Vappi and Chestnut Hill? What Otis knew about those terms when it contracted to install the elevators?

The court granted summary judgment for the defendant on the lost-profits claim but denied summary judgment on the direct-loss claim. Chestnut Hill and Vappi had agreed not to charge one another with any consequential losses. (In light of the suit against Otis, can you suggest a more efficient arrangement?)

The court said that what the plaintiff could not recover from the promisee—Vappi—it could not recover as third party beneficiary.[a] Is this sound as a generalization about third-party rights?

Compare also Syndoulos Luth. Church v. A.R.C. Industries, Inc., 662 P.2d 109 (Alaska 1983), an action by an owner as the supposed beneficiary of a foundation subcontract. The court said that the defendant's work was "obviously intended to benefit the owner of the building." (A year later, however, the same court decided Kodiak Elec. Ass'n v. DeLaval Turbine, described in Note 1, p. 875 above. How might these decisions be reconciled?)

Contracts related to property improvement or repair sometimes give rise to third party claims *by contractors*. As an economizing move an owner wanting improvements will sometimes dispense with a general contractor and assign the several stages of a project to different firms. In these cases, it is said, there are "multi-prime" contractors. Naturally, if there is delay by firm A in placing the foundation, say, added expense may result for other contractors; and they may be inclined to sue A as "intended" beneficiaries of A's contract with the owner. In other cases, the target of a contractor's claim is an architect or engineer employed by the owner.

In principle, all such claims might be governed by appropriate provisions in the several contracts. For example, in an action by a prime contractor against an engineering firm the following provision was held to be dispositive:

> The Contractor agrees to make no claim for damages for delay in the performance of this Contract occasioned by any act or omission to act of the District [owner] or any of its representatives . . . and agrees that any such claim shall be fully compensated for by an extension of time to complete performance of the work. . . .[b]

In the same case, two subcontractors joined the prime as plaintiffs. Their claims failed because the owner had required the prime to include a similar provision in the subcontracts. (*Question:* Would you say that the engineering firm was a third party beneficiary of the subcontracts?)

What purposes of the owner might have been served by these provisions? What might induce a project owner, using co-prime contractors, to provide that none of them should be accountable to another for defective or delayed performance?

a. The case was complicated by evidence that the plaintiff had participated actively in the selection of Otis elevators and in discussion of their installation. Moreover, the elevator contract naturally made reference to the prime contract. And that contract contained this provision:

"Each subcontract shall contain a clause by which the subcontractor agrees that the owner . . . shall have the right, prior to any termination of the subcontract, and after notice to the subcontractor, to assume the Contractor's rights and obligations in the subcontract. Nothing herein shall create any third party beneficiary or agency relationship between the Owner and any subcontractor."

b. Bates & Rogers Const. Corp. v. Greeley & Hansen, 486 N.E.2d 902 (Ill.1985).

NOTES

(1) *Multi–Prime Projects.* Compare the claim of an owner against a sub-contractor with the claim by a "prime" contractor (Moore Construction) against a fellow-prime (Kennon Construction) for expenses caused by delays in the defendant's work. Which of the plaintiffs was in a better position, when contracting, to insist on a provision supporting its claim? If the owner was, and no such provision exists, is that a reason to disfavor the owner's claim? Is there any other general ground for treating the claims differently?

As to the contractor's claim it has been said: "Unless the construction contracts involved clearly provide otherwise, prime contractors on construction contracts involving multiple prime contractors will be considered to be intended or third party beneficiaries of the contracts between the project's owner and other prime contractors." Moore Const. Co. v. Clarksville Dept. of Electricity, 707 S.W.2d 1 (Tenn.App.1985) (collecting cases). Could Moore have maintained an action against Kennon's subcontractors, as a beneficiary of the subcontracts?

(2) *A College's Claim.* A college contracted for a new roof on its Perpetual Building, to be provided by Kaller's, Inc. Kaller's subcontracted most of the work to John J. Spencer Roofing, Inc. (Spencer). This contract was not in writing. The college replaced Kaller's after a rainstorm damaged the interior and Kaller's failed to do satisfactory preventive work. In an action by the college against Spencer (as well as Kaller's), the trial court ruled that the college had no claim against Spencer based on the subcontract, and the college appealed. *Held:* Affirmed. Manor Junior College v. Kaller's Inc., 507 A.2d 1245 (Pa.Super.1986). The opinion is interesting for the questioning of Mr. Spencer by the college's attorney, as reported; all it showed, the court said, was that Spencer knew the work was to be done on the plaintiff's building.[c]

(3) *Tort Liabilities.* For the failure of an architect or engineer to use reasonable care in its work, it may be possible for a contractor to recover economic loss caused by the negligence. Consider the contract provision quoted in the text above. Should it be construed as exculpating the engineers from *tort* liability? If so, it is a provision for the benefit of a third party, is it not?

---

c. For a subsequent development in Pennsylvania law on the subject see Scarpitti v. Weborg, 609 A.2d 147 (Pa.1992).

Chapter 10

ASSIGNMENT AND DELEGATION

Most contract rights having commercial value are transferable. The proposition is, indeed, something of a truism, for commercial worth is attributable to a right largely *because* of its transferability. Broad recognition of the principle is commonly found in statutes, as for instance in § 13–101 of the New York General Obligations Law which begins, "Any claim or demand can be transferred, except in one of the following cases...." [a]

Section 1 of this Chapter presents some fundamental propositions about assignments of contract rights, including the necessity of taking certain simple steps in order to effect the transfer of such a right. The topic of non-commercial (i.e., gift) assignments is featured here. The section demonstrates the primary function of an assignment: by this means a creditor may institute a duty running directly from its debtor to a third party, the assignee.

Section 2 focusses on sales of businesses, although lessons learned from other types of transaction are brought to bear on this one. When a business is sold, the buyer commonly acquires not only its tangible properties, such as plant and equipment, but also its intangibles, including accounts receivable. In addition, the buyer commonly undertakes to perform the duties of the seller under contracts that the seller has made, but not yet performed. From the seller's point of view, this transaction amounts to a delegation of its duties, which may be to render service to its customers, or to supply goods to them, or to render some other variety of performance. Of course, the right to be paid for such a performance is also transferred to the buyer—assigned to it. With respect to an executory contract, then, a seller of a business typically makes both an assignment of the contract rights and a delegation of its duties. The section considers the limits of assignability and delegability in this context.

Section 3 concentrates on a problem loosely described as the "holder in due course" problem. May a credit sale transaction be so arranged

---

a. "1. Where it is to recover damages for a personal injury;

"2. Where it is founded upon a grant, which is made void by a statute of the state; or upon a claim to or interest in real property, a grant of which, by the transferrer, would be void by such a statute;

"3. Where a transfer thereof is expressly forbidden by a statute of the state, or of the United States, or would contravene public policy."

Cal.Civ.Code, § 1458: "A right arising out of an obligation is the property of the person to whom it is due, and may be transferred as such."

that, upon an assignment by the seller of the right to be paid, the assignee can override defenses of the buyer that would have defeated or limited a claim against it by the seller? (Not only contracts for the sale of goods, but services contracts and others present the problem.) The issue has been highly controversial, especially in relation to "consumer" transactions. Banks and finance companies provide financing for consumer credit, backed by assignments purporting to give them a specialized legal advantage. Successes and failures in this attempt are examined here.

Section 4 turns to the role of financing institutions in relation to commercial credit. Manufacturers and merchants obtain financing on the strength of assigning their accounts receivable. Farmers and contractors obtain financing through assigning their anticipated earnings. A large and complex body of law bears on the value of these assignments. In part it is case law; in part it is the Code and other state legislation; in part it is federal law, particularly the Bankruptcy Code.[b] The financer (and its counsel) have to think of multiple risks, in addition to the prospect that the person expected to pay may be financially unable to do so. For one thing, that person and the assignor may indulge in dealings without regard to the financer's interest, and prejudicial to it. For another, the payment may be intercepted by other creditors of the assignor, or a bankruptcy trustee, or someone else claiming under the assignor. These risks, and the measures available to limit them, are examined in this section.

NOTES

(1) *Evolution of Assignments.* Contract rights of many kinds, known as "choses in action," were not transferable in an early stage of English law. Legal historians have delighted in tracing the process by which this rule was overthrown. As usually recounted, it employed the device called a "power of attorney." That device is still in use to enable lawyers and collection agencies to proceed against debtors on claims turned over to them by their creditor-clients, for collection only. Characteristically the agent suing on the claim does so in the name of the client, as principal. So used, the device does not involve an assignment of a claim. There was a time, however, when the device was employed to implement assignments indirectly, apparently to circumvent the rule that a chose in action is not transferable. The critical point in this evolution was passed when the creditor, having given a power of attorney for that purpose, could no longer prevent the "agent" from suing in the agent's name. "Thus by the typically muddle-headed process of thinking known as the genius of the common law, assignments of intangibles were made effective in fact while basic theory still proclaimed them to be legal impossibilities." G. Gilmore, 1 Security Interests in Personal Property 202 (1965).

(2) *Inalienability.* Statutes often restrict the alienability of rights to payment. For an example see footnote a above.

An exceptionally important restriction on alienation appears in the Employee Retirement Income Security Act (ERISA).[c] The statute includes complex rules for protecting the interests of participants in employee retirement plans

---

b. Title 11 of the United States Code.   **c.** 29 U.S.C. ch. 18 (§§ 1001 et seq.).

and their beneficiaries. "Each pension plan shall provide that benefits provided under the plan may not be assigned or alienated," according to § 206(d)(1) of the Act.[d]

Assignments of payment rights against the United States are regulated by statutes.[e] Assignments that are not in proper form, or are not for a permitted purpose, are not fully effective. But the statutes are for the protection of the United States only, it is said; the government may choose to honor a non-complying assignment. Contrast the effect of ERISA: the fact that a pension payor accedes to an assignment by a pensioner (or pensioner-to-be) does nothing to validate the assignment. What considerations might have led Congress to frown on a robust market in pension entitlements? To restrict assignments of claims against the United States?

SECTION 1.   GENERAL PRINCIPLES

What is the effect of an assignment? Consider the following example:

> A has a right to $100 against B. A assigns his right to C. A's right is thereby extinguished, and C acquires a right against B to receive $100. (Restatement Second § 317, Illustration 1)

After reading the text that follows, consider whether or not C's right amounts to much, on the facts given, other than the power to enforce the claim without the cooperation of A.

GIFT ASSIGNMENTS

A characteristic asset subject to an assignment is a right to payment resulting from a sale of goods or the performance of services. Manufacturers and dealers commonly assign their payment rights against customers; contractors assign their rights to payment (often before doing the work for which payment is the exchange); employees sometimes assign wages, salaries, and retirement benefits. In commercial transactions the recipient nearly always gives "value" for the assignment,

d. 29 U.S.C. § 1056(d)(1). There are exceptions: certain support orders for spouses are among them. Also "a voluntary and irrevocable assignment of not to exceed 10 percent of any benefit payment." Section 201(d)(2), (3) of the Act. The Supreme Court has enforced the prohibition vigorously: a pensioner's benefits cannot be reached by his or her creditors via bankruptcy. Patterson v. Shumate, ___ U.S. ___, 112 S.Ct. 2242 (1992). See also Guidry v. Sheet Metal Workers Nat'l Pension Fund, 493 U.S. 365 (1990). But see Coar v. Kazimir, 990 F.2d 1413 (3d Cir.1993). The Court has referred to § 201(d)(1) as an "antigarnishment provision." *Guidry,* at 376. *Garnishment* is a creditor's collection device; the term "denotes a proceeding whereby a plaintiff seeks to subject to his claim property of the defendant in the hands of a third person, or money owed by a third person to the defendant." Western v. Hodgson, 494 F.2d 379, 382–83 (4th Cir. 1974).

e. See 31 U.S.C. § 3727 and 41 U.S.C. § 15.

sometimes purchasing the right assigned, sometimes making a loan secured by the assigned right as "collateral." A promise to the assignor can constitute value.[a] If the assignee receives the assignment to secure a prior loan, the assignee has given value ("antecedent debt").

This Note concerns assignments for which value is *not* given—gifts—a subject on which the Uniform Commercial Code has nothing to say. There are, however, occasional statutes on the subject, as for example this provision of the California Civil Code: [b]

> A verbal gift is not valid, unless the means of obtaining possession and control of the thing are given, nor, if it is capable of delivery, unless there is an actual or symbolical delivery of the thing to the donee.

The idea of giving the "means" of control is often illustrated by the handing over of a passbook for a bank savings deposit, where the depositor's right to make a withdrawal is conditioned on presenting the book to the bank. Many other payment rights are similarly embodied in "symbolic" documents, such as a certificate of deposit, a life-insurance policy, or a promissory note.[c]

The position of the Restatement Second is that a gratuitous (gift) assignment is not *invalid,* but that it is *revocable* unless some formality is complied with, such as a signed writing that is delivered by the assignor,[d] or the delivery of "a writing of a type customarily accepted as a symbol or as evidence of the right assigned." [e] Moreover, the assignee's right is terminated if the assignor makes a subsequent, inconsistent assignment, or if the assignor dies or simply gives a notice of revocation. Hence the recipient of an oral assignment (not for value) has a highly tenuous hold on the assigned right.[f]

The California statute quoted above was applied in an action against the Merced Stone Company by the executor of Thomas Prather. The Company had been indebted to Prather. Its president and general manager was his brother, Samuel. According to Samuel's testimony, Thomas spoke to him only two days before dying as follows: "Now, in reference to [my] account in the Merced Stone Company, I want to give you that account, all that is due me.... I don't know how just to do this, but I give it to you." The trial court found that Thomas had effectively transferred the account. On appeal, *held:* Reversed. The court acknowledged that Samuel had the power and authority to alter

---

a. UCC 1–201(44).

b. Section 1147.

c. Consider Ricketts v. Scothorn, p. 98 above. How would Katie Scothorn's position have been different if her grandfather (Ricketts) had presented her with a $2,000 note payable *to him* and signed, as maker, by a third party to whom Ricketts had made a loan?

As to symbolic documents referred to in Restatement Second § 332(1)(b), see Comment c; and see § 342(b).

d. By statute in New York, the absence of consideration does not entail the conclusion that an assignment is revocable, if it is in writing and signed by the assignor. Gen. Oblig.L. § 5–1107. Compare § 5–708(a)[9].

e. Section 332.

f. But the situation may be different if the assignee has been induced, by the assignment, into action or forbearance that the assignor should reasonably have expected. Ibid., subsection (4).

the Company's books so as to show that he, and not Thomas, had been made the owner of the account. But that did not comply with the statutory requirement that the "means [be] given." Samuel's power concerning the books "did not emanate from the decedent. [He] possessed it before the asserted gift as well as after." Adams v. Merced Stone Co., 178 P. 498, 3 A.L.R. 928 (Cal.1917).

The absence of witnesses to the conversation may have influenced the court. But perhaps it would not have been satisfied with anything less than a writing, containing the decedent's signature. "Speaking for myself," said a lord chancellor of England, "I do not look with any particular favor on these death-bed gifts." [g] Would it have mattered to the court if the conversation had occurred long before Thomas's death?

NOTES

(1) *Problem.* Suppose that Thomas Prather wishes to make the gift to his sister, Sarah. Instead of speaking to Sarah about it, Thomas says to Samuel: "I want you, as president of the Merced Stone Company, to agree that after my death the Company will pay to Sarah all that it owes me. In exchange for your promise, I will release the Company from its indebtedness to me." Samuel agrees, acting as the Company's authorized agent. After Thomas's death, may his executor (Adams) make a successful claim for the amount owing? What arguments would you make in favor of Sarah? Is there anything about the transaction that tends to remove the suspicion commonly surrounding an oral death-bed gift?

(2) *A Case of Two Wives.* After his second marriage, John Cassiday brought home from the office a folder containing two certificates of insurance on his life, and placed it in a dresser drawer. His former wife, Margaret, was named as beneficiary on these certificates, and that designation was never changed. Yet when he brought them home John said to his wife, Edytha: "the beneficiaries are changed ... and he also said he didn't want that woman [Margaret] to have any more of his money." After John died, a contest arose between the two women over the proceeds, and the insurer brought an interpleader action. From a judgment for Margaret, Edytha appealed. *Held:* Affirmed. It was found that John had made no parol assignment or gift of the two policies in question to Edytha. "He did not say: 'Edytha, I give you these policies.' He did not say: 'Edytha, these policies are yours.' ... [H]e exhibited no intention either to give or assign the policies to Edytha." Cassiday v. Cassiday, 259 A.2d 299 (Md.1969).

Even if John had said what the court suggested, Edytha's claim would probably have failed in some courts, for want of delivery of the certificates to her. On the other hand, a symbolic or a "constructive" delivery sometimes meets the requirement. In the attempt to apply these conceptions, especially to intangible assets, the courts have made some refined distinctions. See Brooks v. Mitchell, 161 A. 261, 84 A.L.R. 547 (Md.1932); Rohan, Delivery in the Law of Gifts, 38 Ind.L.J. 1 (1962), 470 (1963). If John had handed the insurance certificates to Edytha for her to place in the dresser drawer, should that be regarded as a sufficient delivery?

---

g. Ashbourne, quoted in Williston, Gifts of Rights, 40 Yale L.J. 1 (1930).

FORM OF ASSIGNMENT

For making an assignment, no particular expression or form of words is required. It may be helpful, however, to consider a formbook example:

Buyer's Assignment of Rights [a]

> I [*name of buyer*] of [*address*], hereby assign to [*name of assignee*] of [*address*], my rights to purchase [*identify goods*] for [*amount*] from [*name of seller*], of [*address*], under a contract dated _____, 19__, executed by me with him. . . .

This is an unusually succinct form of assignment in commercial affairs.

"It is essential to an assignment of a right," according to the Restatement Second,[b] "that the obligee manifest an intention to transfer the right to another person without further action or manifestation of intention." The manifestation is usually made to the "other person," but it may also be made to a third person as a representative; e.g., a borrower might make an assignment of an insurance claim to a bank by a suitable indication to the insurer. In such a case, however, special problems arise in characterizing the terms used. If obligee (A) says to obligor (B), "I direct you to pay what you owe me to C," is that an assignment? If A says, "I authorize you to discharge your debt to me by paying C," is that an assignment? The Restatement Second states that an order to pay may be an assignment, but only in special circumstances. See § 325. The following illustration is given:

> A writes to B, "Please pay to C the balance due me." This is insufficient to establish an assignment . . . But the letter would be an effective assignment if delivered to C to pay or secure a debt owed by A to C.

Assignments have often been contrasted with promises to make payments. See Christmas v. Russell, 81 U.S. 69, 84 (1871): "An agreement to pay out of a particular fund, however clear in its terms, is not an equitable assignment. . . ."

---

a. 5 West's McKinney's Forms: UCC § 2–210, Form 8 (1987). (signature line omitted)

"Comment

"Either the seller or the buyer may assign his respective rights under a contract for the sale of goods, unless the parties have otherwise agreed or unless the assignment would materially change the duty of the other party, materially increase the burden or risk imposed on him by the contract or materially impair his chance of obtaining return performance. U.C.C. § 2–210(2).

"In addition to the assignment clause set forth above, the assignee should require warranties from the assignor to the effect that the contract is valid and enforceable, is in full force and effect and has not been amended or breached, and that there are no set-offs or counterclaims against the assignor." Id.

[Reprinted with permission from West Publishing Company, McKinney's Forms, Copyright © 1987.]

Note the implication that an "otherwise" agreement may preclude an assignment by the seller of its payment rights. As to this see, however, UCC 9–318(5).

b. Section 324.

PROBLEMS

Which of the following documents most clearly effects an assignment? How would you redraft the others so as to make it clear that an assignment is being given?

(a) A sends a signed document to his tailor (C) reading: "First Bank. Pay to the order of C $100 (One Hundred) Dollars." A has a large checking account in First Bank. See UCC 3–409(1): "A check or other draft does not of itself operate as an assignment ..."

(b) Siler obtains a contract for work on a project. Before starting, he gets a bank loan and executes this document: "I, Vernon Siler, do hereby assign to the First Bank ... my right, title and interest in the funds due me from Mountain States Telephone Company on Job No. N–3–0868...." See First Nat. Bank v. Mountain States Telephone & Telegraph Co., 571 P.2d 118 (N.M.1977).

(c) A real estate broker (A) earns a commission, with the help of another (C), and before it is paid gives him this signed document: "In consideration of $1 I hereby agree with C that he is entitled to one-half of the commission earned from the sale of Greenacres." See Donovan v. Middlebrook, 88 N.Y.S. 607 (Sup.Ct.1904).

NOTE

Legal Effect Without Assignment. If any of the documents set out in the preceding note is not an assignment, it does not follow that the document is legally insignificant. It is clear, for instance, that a bank may charge the checking account of a customer upon payment of a check properly drawn and issued, and indorsed and presented by the payee. Do you find the elements of a contract in any of the transactions described above?

———

Introductory Note to *Shiro*

Most contests over assignments arise in bankruptcies or other proceedings for distributing the assets of an insolvent debtor. Particular rules for those situations are described in Section 4 of this Chapter. It will be useful, however, to consider one old but illustrative case at this point. It arose in the bankruptcy of the American Fiberlast Company.

———

SHIRO v. DREW, 174 F.Supp. 495 (D.Me.1959). The American Fiberlast Company (Fiberlast, or "the corporation") needed financing to fulfill a contract for the construction of a "radome"; the work was to be done for a firm named Hazeltine. Fiberlast got a loan of some $2,000 from Gordon Drew, and gave him a letter reading, in part:

Nov. 1, 1956

[A]ny money advanced by Mr. Drew for the specific expense of manufacturing the Radome will be paid immediately to Mr. Drew upon receipt of Hazeltine's remittance irrespective of any other demands from other creditors.

When Fiberlast became a bankrupt (now officially called a bankruptcy "debtor"), Drew found himself in a contest with Shiro, the bankruptcy trustee, over the right to Fiberlast's earnings under the radome contract. Drew contended that he had an assignment of the debtor's payment rights, indefeasible in bankruptcy, which assured him of repayment of his loan to the extent of the value of those rights. Shiro's opposing position was that the radome earnings were distributable among the creditors of Fiberlast generally (those having claims allowable in the bankruptcy). In contemporary terms, that is, Drew asserted a *security interest* in the earnings, whereas Shiro regarded him as an unsecured, "general" creditor, entitled at best to a pro-rata distribution from the bankruptcy estate.

(In point of fact, Fiberlast entered bankruptcy only after it had collected for building the radome and had paid Drew's loan. Shiro brought this action on behalf of Fiberlast's creditors to recover its payment—made nine days before the bankruptcy filing—as a "preference." Success for Shiro would have put Drew in the position of a general creditor. Certain payments made not long before a bankruptcy are recoverable under the bankruptcy statutes if they have preferential effect. A trustee's claim to recapture a payment as a preference can, however, be repelled by a showing that, if it had not been made, the recipient's claim would anyway have been fully satisfied by a distribution in the bankruptcy.[a] Hence it was incumbent on Shiro to show that Drew had no interest (or had only a defeasible one) in Fiberlast's payment right *before* the payment.)

GIGNOUX, DISTRICT JUDGE. No Maine case succinctly sets forth the requisites of a valid assignment. However, it is hornbook law that an assignment is an act or manifestation by the owner of a right which indicates his intention to transfer, without further action, that right to another.... [T]he instrument of November 1, 1956 is susceptible of only one reasonable interpretation. ... There is nothing in its terms indicative of that manifestation of present surrender of control essential to an assignment. Language of present transfer is wholly lacking. Defendant asserts that the instrument was drawn by laymen, inartistically perhaps, solely with the intention of securing future advances this defendant ... might make to attempt to save a sinking corporation. Mayhap such was the case. Unfortunately for this defendant, the Court has before it no evidence of what the parties intended save the instrument itself. Whether it was authored by laymen or lawyers, it speaks clearly in future terms and can rise to no higher legal status than a promise to pay out of a particular fund to come into existence in the future. Insofar as this record discloses, the debtor was not notified that the contract had been assigned, nor was any attempt made to limit the Corporation's control over the contract or its proceeds....

Since the November 1 instrument was neither a partial assignment nor a declaration of trust, it follows that the payment by Fiberlast to

a. Technically, would have been fully satisfied in a *liquidation* bankruptcy. Fi-berlast's assets were being liquidated; it was not being reorganized.

defendant on February 11, 1957 was a preference within the meaning of Section 60, sub. a of the Bankruptcy Act and may be avoided by the Trustee under Section 60, sub. b.

NOTE

Preferences. The current bankruptcy provision on this subject is § 547 of the Bankruptcy Code (11 U.S.C.). It states a "reachback" period of at least 90 days before the filing of the bankruptcy petition, and in some instances one year. The provision is a crucible in which—as in Shiro v. Drew—the validity of an assignment preceding a payment is tested. The particulars of preference law are addressed in courses concerning bankruptcy.

HERZOG v. IRACE

Supreme Judicial Court of Maine, 1991.
594 A.2d 1106.

BRODY, JUSTICE. Anthony Irace and Donald Lowry appeal from an order entered by the Superior Court (Cumberland County, *Cole, J.*) affirming a District Court (Portland, Goranites, J.) judgment in favor of Dr. John P. Herzog in an action for breach of an assignment to Dr. Herzog of personal injury settlement proceeds [1] collected by Irace and Lowry, both attorneys, on behalf of their client, Gary G. Jones. On appeal, Irace and Lowry contend that the District Court erred in finding that the assignment was valid and enforceable against them. They also argue that enforcement of the assignment interferes with their ethical obligations toward their client. Finding no error, we affirm.

The facts of this case are not disputed. Gary Jones was injured in a motorcycle accident and retained Irace and Lowry to represent him in a personal injury action. Soon thereafter, Jones dislocated his shoulder, twice, in incidents unrelated to the motorcycle accident. Dr. Herzog examined Jones's shoulder and concluded that he needed surgery. At the time, however, Jones was unable to pay for the surgery and in consideration for the performance of the surgery by the doctor, he signed a letter dated June 14, 1988, written on Dr. Herzog's letterhead stating:

> I, Gary Jones, request that payment be made directly from settlement of a claim currently pending for an unrelated incident, to John Herzog, D.O., for treatment of a shoulder injury which occurred at a different time.

Dr. Herzog notified Irace and Lowry that Jones had signed an "assignment of benefits" from the motorcycle personal injury action to cover the cost of surgery on his shoulder and was informed by an employee of Irace and Lowry that the assignment was sufficient to allow the firm to pay Dr. Herzog's bills at the conclusion of the case. Dr. Herzog

---

1. This case involves the assignment of proceeds from a personal injury action, not an assignment of the cause of action itself.

performed the surgery and continued to treat Jones for approximately one year.

In May, 1989, Jones received a $20,000 settlement in the motorcycle personal injury action. He instructed Irace and Lowry not to disburse any funds to Dr. Herzog indicating that he would make the payments himself. Irace and Lowry informed Dr. Herzog that Jones had revoked his permission to have the bill paid by them directly and indicated that they would follow Jones's directions. Irace and Lowry issued a check to Jones for $10,027 and disbursed the remaining funds to Jones's other creditors. Jones did send a check to Dr. Herzog but the check was returned by the bank for insufficient funds and Dr. Herzog was never paid.

Dr. Herzog filed a complaint in District Court against Irace and Lowry seeking to enforce the June 14, 1988 "assignment of benefits." The matter was tried before the court on the basis of a joint stipulation of facts. The court entered a judgment in favor of Dr. Herzog finding that the June 14, 1988 letter constituted a valid assignment of the settlement proceeds enforceable against Irace and Lowry. Following an unsuccessful appeal to the Superior Court, Irace and Lowry appealed to this court. Because the Superior Court acted as an intermediate appellate court, we review the District Court's decision directly. See Brown v. Corriveau, 576 A.2d 200, 201 (Me.1990).

. . . [W]e will set aside trial court findings based solely upon documentary evidence and stipulated facts only if clearly erroneous. . . .

Validity of Assignment

An assignment is an act or manifestation by the owner of a right (the assignor) indicating his intent to transfer that right to another person (the assignee). See Shiro v. Drew, 174 F.Supp. 495, 497 (D.Me. 1959). For an assignment to be valid and enforceable against the assignor's creditor [debtor?] (the obligor), the assignor must make clear his intent to relinquish the right to the assignee and must not retain any control over the right assigned or any power of revocation. Id. The assignment takes effect through the actions of the assignor and assignee and the obligor need not accept the assignment to render it valid. Palmer v. Palmer, 112 Me. 149, 153, 91 A. 281, 282 (1914). Once the obligor has notice of the assignment, the fund is "from that time forward impressed with a trust; it is . . . impounded in the [obligor's] hands, and must be held by him not for the original creditor, the assignor, but for the substituted creditor, the assignee." Id. at 152, 91 A. 281. After receiving notice of the assignment, the obligor cannot lawfully pay the amount assigned either to the assignor or to his other creditors and if the obligor does make such a payment, he does so at his peril because the assignee may enforce his rights against the obligor directly. Id. at 153, 91 A. 281.

Ordinary rights, including future rights, are freely assignable unless the assignment would materially change the duty of the obligor, materially increase the burden or risk imposed upon the obligor by his contract, impair the obligor's chance of obtaining return performance, or materially reduce the value of the return performance to the obligor, and unless the law restricts the assignability of the specific right involved. See Restatement (Second) Contracts § 317(2)(a) (1982). In Maine, the transfer of a future right to *proceeds* from pending litigation has been recognized as a valid and enforceable equitable assignment. McLellan v. Walker, 26 Me. 114, 117–18 (1896). An equitable assignment need not transfer the entire future right but rather may be a partial assignment of that right. Palmer, 112 Me. at 152, 91 A. 281. We reaffirm these well established principles.

Relying primarily upon the Federal District Court's decision in Shiro, 174 F.Supp. 495, a bankruptcy case involving the trustee's power to avoid a preferential transfer by assignment, Irace and Lowry contend that Jones's June 14, 1988 letter is invalid and unenforceable as an assignment because it fails to manifest Jones's intent to permanently relinquish all control over the assigned funds and does nothing more than request payment from a specific fund. We disagree. The June 14, 1988 letter gives no indication that Jones attempted to retain any control over the funds he assigned to Dr. Herzog. Taken in context, the use of the word "request" did not give the court reason to question Jones's intent to complete the assignment and, although no specific amount was stated, the parties do not dispute that the services provided by Dr. Herzog and the amounts that he charged for those services were reasonable and necessary to the treatment of the shoulder injury referred to in the June 14 letter. Irace and Lowry had adequate funds to satisfy all of Jones's creditors, including Dr. Herzog, with funds left over for disbursement to Jones himself. Thus, this case simply does not present a situation analogous to *Shiro* because Dr. Herzog was given preference over Jones's other creditors by operation of the assignment. Given that Irace and Lowry do not dispute that they had ample notice of the assignment, the court's finding on the validity of the assignment is fully supported by the evidence and will not be disturbed on appeal.

Ethical Obligations

Next, Irace and Lowry contend that the assignment, if enforceable against them, would interfere with their ethical obligation to honor their client's instruction in disbursing funds. Again, we disagree.

... The Bar Rules [of Maine] require that an attorney "promptly pay or deliver to the client, as requested by the client, the funds, securities, or other properties in the possession of the lawyer which the client is entitled to receive." M.Bar R. 3.6(f)(2)(iv). The rules say nothing, however, about a client's power to assign his right to proceeds from a pending lawsuit to third parties. Because the client has the power to assign his right to funds held by his attorney, McLellan v. Walker, 26 Me. at 117–18, it follows that a valid assignment must be honored by the attorney in disbursing the funds on the client's behalf. ... Irace and Lowry were under no ethical obligation, and the record gives no indication that they were under a contractual obligation, to honor their client's instruction to disregard a valid assignment. The

District Court correctly concluded that the assignment is valid and enforceable against Irace and Lowry.

NOTES

(1) *Questions.* What do you understand the court to mean in saying that the situation was "simply not [one] analogous to *Shiro* because Dr. Herzog was given preference over Jones's other creditors...."? Do you infer that the decision would have been different if Jones, being insolvent but having a credit of $20,000 with the attorneys, had applied to the court for directions about how to distribute that sum among his creditors?

(2) *Promissory Estoppel?* Observe the precaution that Dr. Herzog took before giving Jones treatment on credit: he got an assurance from an employee of the attorneys that the assignment was ample for his payment. Assuming that the employee was suitably authorized by the attorneys, were they accountable to Herzog irrespective of the issues presented to the court?

(3) *Partial Assignment.* At the common law, the assignment of less than the whole of a claim was regarded as creating only an equitable interest, and not a legal interest, in the part assigned. This conception has the potential of putting the assignee at risk in the event of the insolvency of the assignor. See Angeles Real Estate Co. v. Kerxton, 737 F.2d 416 (4th Cir.1984).

In that case the court acknowledged that the common-law rule once prevailed in Maryland; but it went on to say: "We think it fair to assume that Maryland now would subscribe to § 326 of the Restatement (Second) of Contracts, which provides that 'assignment of a part of a right ... is operative as to that part to the same extent and in the same manner as if the part had been a separate right.' "

ASSIGNMENTS AND UCC ARTICLE 9: PRELIMINARY VIEW

Much of the most important law about assignments is expressed in two sections of UCC Article 9 ("Secured Transactions ..."). These sections are set out in the Selections, and in a footnote here.[a] Broadly

---

a. UCC 9–318. *Defenses Against Assignee: Modification of Contract After Notification of Assignment; Term Prohibiting Assignment Ineffective; Identification and Proof of Assignment.*

(1) Unless an account debtor has made an enforceable agreement not to assert defenses or claims arising out of a sale as provided in Section 9–206 [see below] the rights of an assignee are subject to

(a) all the terms of the contract between the account debtor and assignor and any defense or claim arising therefrom; and

(b) any other defense or claim of the account debtor against the assignor which accrues before the account debtor receives notification of the assignment.

(2) So far as the right to payment or a part thereof under an assigned contract has not been fully earned by performance, and notwithstanding notification of the assignment, any modification of or substitution for the contract made in good faith and in accordance with reasonable commercial standards is effective against an assignee unless the account debtor has otherwise agreed but the assignee acquires corresponding rights under the modified or substituted contract. The assignment may provide that such modification or substitution is a breach by the assignor.

(3) The account debtor is authorized to pay the assignor until the account debtor receives notification that the amount due or to become due has been assigned and that payment is to be made to the assignee. A notification which does not reasonably identify the rights assigned is ineffective. If requested by the account debtor, the assignee must seasonably furnish reasonable

speaking, the subject-matter provisions of Article 9 identify assignments that occur in connection with commercial financing. At the core, the Article–9 rules apply to an assignment of an "account" to serve as collateral, along with a mass of other accounts, for credit given by the assignee.[b] UCC 9–106 defines *account* to mean—with two exceptions mentioned below [c]—as "any right to payment for goods sold or leased or for services rendered ... whether or not it has been earned by performance." The person required to pay is included in the defined term *account debtor*.[d]

An illustrative assignment of accounts that was governed by the Code has been given in Chapter 9: Septembertide Publishing v. Stein & Day, p. 879 above. (As to the effect of the statute on the decision, see p. 937 below.) The account debtor in that case was New American Library.

Another example appears in District of Columbia v. Thomas Funding, 593 A.2d 1030 (D.C.App.1991), in which the District was the account debtor. The assignor in that case was the Silverline Building and Maintenance Company; the assignee was Thomas Funding. The accounts subject to the assignment were Silverline's rights to payment under a contract it had with the District to perform janitorial services. Silverline notified the District of the assignment by letter and directed the District to make payments to Thomas Funding on Silverline's invoices to the District. (Doubtless Thomas Funding instigated that letter.) By this means Silverline got money to use as working capital.

These facts resemble those in Shiro v. Drew, p. 919 above. Unlike Drew, however, Thomas Funding took care to have Silverline execute a document transferring rights under the services contract. Hence *Thomas Funding* was an "Article 9 case." Shiro v. Drew would have been one also, if the Code had been enacted in Maine at the time, and if the "radome rights" had been transferred to Drew. There was, however, another important difference in the facts of the two cases, now to be noticed.

The facts of *Thomas Funding* draw attention to a singular and important feature of Article 9, having consequences not yet fully worked

---

proof that the assignment has been made and unless he does so the account debtor may pay the assignor.

(4) A term in any contract between an account debtor and an assignor is ineffective if it prohibits assignment of an account ... or requires the account debtor's consent to such assignment or security interest.

UCC 9–206. *Agreement Not to Assert Defenses Against Assignee; ...*

(1) Subject to any statute or decision which establishes a different rule for buyers or lessees of consumer goods, an agreement by a buyer or lessee that he will not assert against an assignee any claim or defense which he may have against the seller or lessor is enforceable by an assignee who takes his assignment for value, in good faith

and without notice of a claim or defense, except as to defenses of a type which may be asserted against a holder in due course of a negotiable instrument under the Article on Commercial Paper (Article 3). A buyer who as part of one transaction signs both a negotiable instrument and a security agreement makes such an agreement.

· · ·

b. Whether or not a given assignment is subject to Article 9 depends, however, on a number of statutory distinctions. Further indications of the subject matter of the Article are given in the text on Assignments Outside Article 9, at p. 931 below.

c. See fn. h below.

d. UCC 9–105(1)(a).

out. In the "subject matter" section—9–102—we are told that Article 9 applies "to any sale of accounts...." [e] In *Thomas Funding* the financer did not make an "advance" to Silverline in the manner of the advance made by Gordon Drew to the American Fiberlast Company: rather, it *bought* Silverline's payment rights. Article 9 reflects a difference between the risks in lending on accounts and those in buying accounts. (What special risk in buying occurs to you?) For present purposes, however, the point is that essential protections for both lenders and buyers depend upon compliance with precautions specified in Article 9.

In practice, according to a Code comment about the subject matter of Article 9, "the distinction between a security transfer and a sale is blurred, and a sale [of accounts] is therefore covered ... whether intended for security or not, unless excluded by Section 9–104." [f] Article 9 implements the assimilation of sales to security transfers with some artifice, especially in definitions. As one court has said, after citing the definitions, "[T]he buyer of an account is treated as a secured party, his interest in the account is treated as a security interest, and the seller of the account is a debtor, and the account sold is treated as collateral." [g]

A principal requirement of Article 9, for the enforceability of a security interest in an account, is that the debtor (assignor) have "signed a security agreement which contains a description of the collateral." That requirement, which amounts to a statute of frauds, applies also to a security transfer—though not to a sale—of important payment rights other than accounts. See Note 1, below. Absent that, the security agreement is not enforceable even against the assignor (debtor), much less third parties. (It is often feasible to have an enforceable security interest in goods and other types of collateral without a signed security agreement. An oral agreement will suffice as to collateral in the possession of the secured party. But accounts cannot be reduced to possession.)

Major elements of Article 9 relate to the rights of an assignee when the assignor has proved to be insolvent. These provisions play a large role in bankruptcies. (Shiro v. Drew was a case of an assignor's bankruptcy.) Many of the situations presented in this Chapter would not have arrived in court if the assignor were able to pay all its debts. (Is Herzog v. Irace one of those?) In general, you should consider assignment law on the assumption that either an assignee or an "account debtor" must absorb a loss arising from the insolvency of the assignor.

NOTE

(1) *Drawing the Line.* In Herzog v. Irace, was the assignment made by Gary Jones to his doctor a security transfer or a sale? The case may exemplify

e. Continuing: "... or chattel paper." For the definition of *chattel paper* see § 9–105(1)(b).

Transactions in chattel paper are not treated in this book, except incidentally. Examples appear, however, including the "lease" contracts evaluated in Williams v. Walker–Thomas Furniture Co., p. 426

above, and in Chemical Bank v. Rinden Professional Ass'n, p. 963 below.

f. Comment 2 to § 9–102. The operative provision is subsection (1)(b).

g. Octagon Gas Systems, Inc. v. Rimmer, 995 F.2d 948, 955 (10th Cir.1993) (footnote omitted).

blurring of the distinction. What facts in *Herzog* might indicate the making of a security transfer?

The asset transferred in that case was not an "account" as defined in Article 9; it was a *general intangible*.

"General intangibles" means any personal property (including things in action) other than goods, accounts, chattel paper, documents, instruments, and money.[h]

Because sales of general intangibles are not within the subject matter of Article 9—whereas security transfers are—the classification of Jones's assignment is more momentous than the classification of an assignment of accounts. (For a projected revision of Article 9, however, consideration is being given to an expansion of the article in this respect.[i])

(2) *The View from Vermont.* Twin Valley Motors, Inc. v. Morale, 385 A.2d 678 (Vt.1978), is a case for contrast with *Herzog*. In that case Morale, an attorney, represented a couple who had suffered a road injury. Expecting money from a settlement, the couple bought a new car and signed a letter directing Morale to pay some $4,000 out of the settlement to Twin Valley Motors, the seller. Later, however, at his clients' instance, Morale disbursed the settlement money through a check made payable to Twin Valley *or* the clients. Being so written, the check, delivered to the clients, enabled them to collect it without the signature of Twin Valley. A dispute arose about the new car, leading to the clients' refusal to make further payments. (The car had been damaged in another collision.) In an action by Twin Valley against the attorney, the trial court ruled for the attorney. On appeal, *held:* Affirmed.

In part, the court's reasoning was that the authority conferred on Morale by the letter was "merely executory," in that his clients were not then indebted to Twin Valley. Also:

The claim of assignment is further compromised by its obvious security nature. This is a characteristic inconsistent with the transfer of ownership ingredient essential to make an irrevocable assignment.

According to the court, the letter (not quoted) was only an agreement to pay out of a particular fund; and Morale's responsibility to his clients was an "unbroken" one, persisting beyond that agreement.

In *Herzog* the defendants relied on this decision. The court answered—in a footnote omitted here—that the Vermont decision "cuts against authority in Maine...."

(3) *General Principles.* It may be that, though a transaction is one governed by Article 9, a particular question about it is not addressed there. That being so, it is necessary to consult "general principles" of law and equity. See

---

h. UCC 9–106. This section is cited above for its definition of "account". It provides that a right to payment is not an account if it is evidenced by an *instrument* or by *chattel paper*. Checks and promissory notes usually fit the definition of "instrument" (9–105(1)(i)). As to "chattel paper" see fn. e above.

i. "It remains to be seen whether the Drafting Committee can craft a satisfactory statutory approach for including within the scope of Article 9 some, but not all, general intangibles for the payment of money. (This assumes, arguendo, that the Drafting Committee will accept the Committee's recommendations concerning general intangibles for the payment of money.)" Harris & Mooney, The Article 9 Study Committee Report: Strong Signals and Hard Choices, 29 Idaho L.Rev. 561, 572 n. 52 (1992) (by the Reporters for the Drafting Committee).

UCC 1–103. Possibly that explains the fact that, in *Herzog,* the court did not mention Article 9.[j]

(4) *Words of Grant.* If Dr. Herzog received a security transfer of Jones's payment right, it was subject to the Article–9 requirement of a signed security agreement. (It was, that is, unless it was within an exclusion stated in § 9–104. As to the exclusions see the note below, Assignments Outside Article 9.)

There is some authority requiring words of grant for a security agreement effective under the article. No such words appeared in the letter that Gary Jones signed.

Vocational financers on accounts and general intangibles are usually careful to insist that their customers (e.g., Stein & Day; Silverline Building & Maintenance) sign papers containing formal words such as "hereby assign," "transfer," "mortgage," and the like—often in combination.[k] Dr. Herzog was not a vocational financer, of course. Would you favor a requirement of more formality than Jones's letter showed, as a means of putting borrowers on guard when they are asked to make assignments? The requirement of words of grant is in general disfavor among courts and scholars.[l]

NOTIFICATION OF ACCOUNT DEBTORS

In most of the cases mentioned in the foregoing text the financer saw to it that notice of the financing was given to the party obligated to pay: in *Shiro,* Hazeltine was notified; in *Herzog,* the attorneys were notified; and in *Thomas Funding* the District of Columbia was notified. Financers of firms in the building trades who rely on the contractors' earnings for payment characteristically give notice of assignments to the obligors, such as owners and prime contractors.

Other kinds of financing on accounts are prevalent, especially in the financing of mercantile firms. Often this is "non-notification financing," which signifies that the financer does not inform the account debtor that an assignment has been made. The financer is content to bear the risk that the assignor, having collected the assigned accounts, will fail to apply the proceeds properly. That is, the financer assumes

---

j. A passage in the opinion suggests, however, that the court did not regard the assignment as one subject to Article 9. In saying that "ordinary rights are freely assignable," it cited to the Restatement, rather than to anything in the Code. If Article 9 applied, § 9–318(4) would have been a more apt citation. (Section 2–210(2) concerns only assignments of the rights of buyers and sellers.) Moreover, the court did not allude to § 9–203(1)(a); see the following note.

Why the court might have thought Article 9 did not apply is not obvious, however. See § 9–102(1)(a).

k. An example of words of grant, taken from a security agreement about shares of corporate stock, is as follows:

"The Debtor hereby *sells, assigns, transfers and conveys* unto the Secured Party

and grants to the Secured Party a Security interest in and to all of the Debtor's interest and property rights, ... including, without limitation, all moneys and claims for moneys due and to become due to the Debtor under all dividends, distributions, accounts, contract rights, voting rights and general intangibles relating to and/or due from [the issuing corporation]...." (emphasis supplied).

(A question arose about dividends paid to the debtor during his reorganization under chapter 11 of the Bankruptcy Code. In re Hastie, 2 F.3d 1042 (10th Cir.1993).

l. For a representative, though somewhat inconclusive, case see Evans v. Everett, 183 S.E.2d 109 (N.C.1971).

the risk of the assignor's dishonesty. It hopes, however, to be protected against loss in the event of the assignor's insolvency, at least to the extent of accounts not yet collected. (The financing of Stein & Day by Bookcrafters may have been an instance of non-notification financing.)

Notification is important. See the opinion in *Herzog*, above. See also subsection (3) of UCC 9–318 (footnote a above). In *Thomas Funding* the court cited that provision and said:

> Under Article 9, the account debtor is authorized to pay the assignor until the account debtor receives notification that the amount due has been assigned and that payment is to be made to the assignee. If thereafter the account debtor continues to pay the assignor, the debtor will remain liable to the assignee for the same amount. The obligation of the account debtor is not discharged by the "wrongful payment" to the assignor.[m]

This rule applies, at the common law, to assignments that are not governed by the Code, as well as to those subject to Article 9—although the notification procedure is not necessarily the same. A comparable common-law rule applies to assignments of rights to performance other than payment rights.

In some instances, although the account debtor is informed of the assignment, the financer authorizes the assignor to collect the accounts—until further notice. (Apparently that was the case in Harris v. Dial Corporation, p. 973 below.) In that event, of course, the account debtor can discharge its accounts payable by disbursements to the assignor.

NOTES

(1) *Another Explanation?* Can the "wrongful payment" rule be found in subsection (1) of UCC 9–318, as well as in subsection (3)? In part, that provision seems to limit the account debtor, in an action by an assignee, to defenses which—unless they arise from the contract between the account debtor and the assignor—accrue before notification. Consider payment to the assignor as a defense that the account debtor might raise against a claim by the assignee. Whether "wrongful" or not, this defense appears to be ruled out if notification occurred before the payment. See clause (b).

Some readers are tempted to say that the "wrongful payment" rule is not expressed in subsection (1), believing that the payment is a defense "arising from" the contract under clause (a). But that clause is better illustrated by cases such as fraud by the assignor in contracting with the account debtor and breach by the assignor of that contract.

(2) *Browne's Bank vs. Browne's Buyer.* Browne, a producer of lumber, made a series of three shipments to a lumber wholesaler, North Pacific Lumber Company (the buyer). Each time, Browne assigned his right to payment to a bank as security for advances made by the bank. The buyer was directed to make payments to the bank. After paying the bank for the first shipment, the buyer found the lumber in that shipment to have been defectively manufactured, and ordered a reinspection. Upon paying for the second shipment, the buyer deducted $1,000 from the invoice price on account of the defect in the first,

m. District of Columbia v. Thomas Funding, above, at 1034 (citations omitted).

though it did not yet know the loss in value attributable to the defect. Later it determined that loss to be $1,580.80. It therefore tendered to the bank, in payment for the third shipment, an amount less than the invoice price by $580.80. The bank rejected the tender, although it conceded that Browne was indebted to the buyer in that amount.

The Investment Service Company, as assignee of the bank, brought an action against the buyer for the amount of the third invoice. The trial court ruled for the plaintiff, and the buyer appealed. *Held:* Reversed. Investment Service Co. v. North Pacific Lumber Co., 492 P.2d 470 (Or.1972).[n] The court said:

> When the defendant purchaser overpaid the bank because it did not know that the lumber was defective, the bank became indebted to the defendant. The assignment and payment to the bank created a new relationship between the bank and the defendant. Stated simply . . . the bank now owes defendant money. For our purposes, the legal consequences are the same as if the defendant had loaned $580.80 to the bank, which the bank now owes defendant.[o]

Did the decision in this case depend on the fact that the defendant (buyer) was notified of the assignments? In choosing whether to apply clause (a) or clause (b) of UCC 9–318(1) to the case, is it important to know how many contracts Browne made with the buyer? Apparently the three lumber shipments represented three separate sale contracts rather than a single contract for three shipments.

(3) *Timing and Diction.* Given an assignment, X to Y, would you consider that Y has given notification of it upon saying to the account debtor: "You are directed to make payment of the account to me, rather than to X"? What of this statement by Y: "I intend to take an assignment from X of X's rights against you"—followed by an acknowledgment from the account debtor? Consider the Code language: "that the amount due or to become due *has been assigned* and that payment *is to be made* to the assignee." Does it suffice for Y to hand the account debtor a copy of X's assignment?

Should the Code language be read with indulgence for the assignee whose timing or diction is imperfect? The courts have shown considerable indulgence; e.g., Robert Parker's Truck & Trailer Repair, Inc. v. Speer, 722 S.W.2d 45 (Tex.App.1986).

(4) *Request for Proof.* Notice the final sentence of 9–318(3). Do you see a resemblance to UCC 9–609?

Suppose that an account debtor receives from an assignee a notification, effective under the subsection, and responds as follows: "We decline to make any payments to you until we have received written direction from our creditor (the

---

n. For a decision reaffirming this decision see Security Pacific Bank v. Haines Terminal, 869 P.2d 156 (Alaska 1994).

o. The plaintiff argued that, because the bank had a security interest in Browne's inventory of lumber as well as in the accounts, the buyer could not escape paying for the third shipment in full. To that the court's answer was: "If the bank has a claim against the defendant for taking delivery of the lumber . . ., the defendant is entitled to set off its debt of $580.80 just as it could set off such amount if the bank were making a claim against it for a loan the bank had made defendant."

The buyer also contended that its interest in the lumber was not subject to the bank's inventory security interest: according to the Uniform Commercial Code the buyer was a "buyer in ordinary course of business" who took free of that interest. For the Code provisions on this subject see UCC 1–201(9) and 9–307(1).

assignor) to do so." Does the assignee run a risk if it fails to take further action? What might it do? See The BOC Group, Inc. v. Katy National Bank, 720 S.W.2d 229 (Tex.App.1986).

ASSIGNMENTS OUTSIDE ARTICLE 9

UCC 9–105 excludes certain assignments of certain payment rights from the subject-matter of Article 9, either because the transfer is of a type excluded from the Article or because the right is not an *account*.[a]

Even if Article 9 applies, it may not provide a solution to a problem about the transfer. In that case "general principles of law and equity" may be consulted: UCC 1–103.

One of the exclusions from Article 9 is illustrated by a lawyer's action for money earned by a client who was in the painting business: Lataif v. Commercial Industrial Construction, Inc., 286 S.E.2d 159 (Va.1982). The facts are given as alleged by the lawyer, Lataif. The client, Myers, lacked cash to pay Lataif's fee and paid him by assigning his unpaid earnings from a painting job that Commercial (the debtor, or "firm") had given Myers. Lataif agreed not to give immediate notice to the firm, so as to protect Myers's business relation with it. Some weeks later, however, Lataif sent the firm a copy of the assignment; and the president assured Lataif that he would be paid. More than a month after that, Lataif wrote to the president: "I have held off taking any other action to collect this fee because of your kind agreement to disburse the funds in accordance with the assignment." The president returned the letter with this note: "Myers indicated the account has been settled, and we paid him, in full, on 13 August."

In the lawyer's action against the firm, the trial court struck the claim and Lataif appealed. *Held:* Reversed. Consider what principle of the common law might explain the lawyer's success. (Article 9 did not apply because of the following statutory exclusion: "This Article does not apply [to] a transfer of a single account to an assignee in whole or partial satisfaction of a preexisting indebtedness...."[b])

NOTES

(1) *The Lawyer's Reliance.* In reflecting on Lataif's case, you may find two observations by the court to be suggestive. First, Myers had become a debtor in bankruptcy some five months after the firm's president, Cobb, had assured Lataif he would be paid. But, second, the court said there was nothing to show that Lataif could not have collected his fee from Myers by legal proceedings at some point "during the time Lataif was relying on Cobb's assurance."

a. And is also not a *general intangible.* This is a term defined in Article 9 (UCC 9–106). Other defined terms, germane to the definition of *account* are "chattel paper" and "instrument" (UCC 9–105(1)).

The application of Article 9 to a security interest in goods, or in any personal property other than a payment right in the form of an account, is dealt with only incidentally in this book.

b. UCC 9–104(f).

(2) *Myers as a Target.* If Cobb was right about what Myers told him ("indicated the account has been settled"), Myers has obligations both to the firm and to Lataif, does he not? Restitution is a possible basis for recovery by the firm, if not fraud. But the possibility of a full recovery from Myers may have been slim. (Some fraud claims are immune to discharge in bankruptcy.)

(3) *Particular Exclusions.* In Shiro v. Drew, p. 919 above, none of the Code's exclusions would have applied if at that time the Code had been enacted in Maine. By the time of Herzog v. Irace, p. 921, the Code had been enacted there; but here again the court did not refer to Article 9. Can that be explained by the fact that the Article excludes "a transfer in whole or in part of any claim arising out of tort"?[c] See L & L Roofing Company v. Transportation Ins. Co., 15 F.3d 1086 (9th Cir.1994). A better explanation, possibly, is that the court found nothing especially helpful in the Code.

Some other exclusions were discussed in District of Columbia v. Thomas Funding, partially described at p. 925 above.

(4) *A Case in Five Acts.* In Warrington v. Dawson, 798 F.2d 1533 (5th Cir.1986), Dawson was described as a "good ol' boy." His troubles began when he was interrupted while at work on his rice farm, to be told: "Reitz, Inc. has borrowed some money from Valley Bank and put up your account receivable as collateral." Reitz was a crop-dusting firm whose services Dawson had engaged. Dawson signed a letter, on the bank's stationery, referring to its lien on the Reitz account and promising to make his checks payable to the bank as well as to Reitz. Dawson did not read the letter, however, not having his reading glasses with him. "Dawson gets on his tractor and heads back into the rice field, muttering under his breath 'What was that all about?' " (An opinion in the case is written as a five-act drama.) Thereafter, at Dawson's direction, his wife issued checks for Reitz's services that were not payable to the bank. In the last act the bank's debtor, Reitz, was in bankruptcy and the bank remained unpaid.

An action against Dawson by an assignee of the bank was dismissed, and the plaintiff appealed. *Held:* Affirmed. There was no opinion of the court. One judge, referring to the first sentence of UCC 1–201(26), said: "Waving a letter before a man in a rice field is not a reasonable way to notify him of an important change in his property rights."[d] One judge concurred in the result. The third dissented, emphasizing the second sentence of clause (26).

CREDITORS' CLAIMS AND THE ASSIGNEE

Examples have been given of firms that took assignments in the course of providing capital and made efforts to notify the nonassigning parties, so as to limit the risks of being assignees. The advantage of successful notification is apparent.

This Note calls attention to a different kind of risk that no one in the vocation of financing on assignments will willingly take. This is the risk of being ousted—or outranked—by one or more creditors of the assignee, acting through legal process to collect from the assigned right.

c. UCC 9–104(j).

d. This judge (Goldberg) concluded also that the terms of the letter were not sufficiently informative. He was further trou-bled by the fact that the bank had failed to object while, over a year or more, Dawson had made payments to Reitz of more than $50,000.

Whether or not a financing assignee attempts to give notice to the nonassigning party, it is well advised to comply with the directions of Article 9 about how to *perfect* an assignment.

Article–9 filings. The only way to make sure of durable perfection— with respect to an assignment of accounts or general intangibles, within Article 9—is to file, in a designated public office, a writing that constitutes a "financing statement." The writing is popularly known as a UCC–1; the requisites are stated in subsection (1) of UCC 9–402. Subsection (3) gives a skeletal form. The names of the assignor ("debtor") and assignee ("secured party") must appear. Filing officers index the statements according to the debtors' names. (For an instance given earlier of an Article–9 filing see p. 880 above, where it is indicated that Bookcrafters filed a UCC–1 designating "Stein & Day" as its debtor.)

The risks of failing to make a proper filing are illustrated in a case cited and partly described above at p. 925: District of Columbia v. Thomas Funding.

The "Silvermine" filing. The assignor in that case was (to repeat) the Silverline Building and Maintenance Company, which expected earnings under a contract with the District of Columbia for janitorial services. Early in 1984, not long after Silverline assigned its accounts under this contract to Thomas Funding, the assignee filed what it thought to be an effective financing statement in the appropriate office: that of the Recorder of Deeds in the District. Unfortunately for Thomas Funding, the assignor was identified in the statement as the *Silvermine* Building and Maintenance Company.

Nine months later, when Silverline was owed some $18,000 for its services during September, the Internal Revenue Service (IRS) filed a notice of levy for income taxes—more than $20,000—that Silverline had failed to pay. The District paid the IRS for those services, although it had been notified of the assignment. In an action by Thomas Funding against the District, the trial court gave summary judgment for Thomas Funding. It based the decision on two grounds, either of which would have sustained the judgment: first, the spelling error was a minor one, not seriously misleading; and second, because Silverline had transferred its payment rights under the contract it had no property in them to which a tax lien could attach.

On appeal, *held:* Reversed. The spelling error was seriously misleading; the financer's filing was ineffective; and its security interest was unperfected. "[A]n assignment that falls within the scope of Article 9 which is not perfected leaves a property interest in the assignor against which a third party lien creditor, such as the IRS, can attach a lien." [a] That being so, the federal tax-lien laws favored the IRS over the assignee.

a. District of Columbia v. Thomas Funding, 593 A.2d 1030, 1035 (D.C.App. 1991).

Priority for lien creditor. Some of the rulings in *Thomas Funding* have significance far beyond cases of tax liens. If a creditor of Silverline's other than the IRS had obtained a writ of garnishment against the District, that creditor would also have prevailed over the unfortunate assignee. In that case the governing priority rule would have been one supplied by Article 9, rather than the tax-lien statutes. As the court appreciated, the interest in the account acquired by Thomas Funding is characterized as a "security interest." (See Note 3, below.) The applicable provision is—disregarding an exception not considered here—as follows:

> ... an unperfected security interest is subordinate to the rights of ...

> (b) a person who becomes a lien creditor before the security interest is perfected.... [b]

What that person knows about the assignment, upon becoming a lien creditor, and what the account debtor knows about it, are not germane.

Bankruptcy of assignor. Hazards for a financing assignee who neglects to make a required filing, or who attempts to file and fails, are already apparent. But they are greatly magnified by two provisions of the Bankruptcy Code. One is section 544(a), known as the strong-arm clause; the other is section 547, on "preferences." If Silverline had entered bankruptcy, rather than encountering the IRS, the bankruptcy trustee would have appropriated any unpaid account that had been assigned to Thomas Funding, for pro-rata distribution—along with other assets of the debtor—among Silverline's creditors. That is an effect of the strong-arm clause, which invests the trustee with the status of a hypothetical creditor who (hypothetically) obtains a judicial lien on "all property" accessible to a creditor's judicial lien.[c] It can be taken as axiomatic that, upon the bankruptcy of an assignor, an outstanding assignment will avail the assignee nothing—nothing more than permitting the filing of a claim as a general creditor—if the assignment is one that should have been perfected under the rules of Article 9 and if the assignee has failed to perfect before the bankruptcy petition was filed.

Moreover, upon a bankruptcy the trustee might well have recovered from Thomas Funding a payment made to it by the District within the 90–day period preceding the filing of the bankruptcy petition. That is a possible effect of the section on preferences. (But ordinary-course payments are the subject of an exception: section 547(c)(2).) On the other hand, preference law is so constructed that a proper and timely

---

b. UCC 9–301(1)(b). The position of a creditor using garnishment is within the definition of "lien creditor": one who "has acquired a lien on the property involved by attachment, levy or the like...." UCC 9–301(3).

c. Literally: "a creditor that extends credit to the debtor at the time of the commencement of the case, and that ob-tains, at such time and with respect to such credit, a judicial lien on all property on which a creditor on a simple contract could have obtained such a judicial lien, whether or not such a creditor exists."—section 544(a)(1).

On the working of this provision see D. Baird, The Elements of Bankruptcy (rev. ed. 1993) 100–104.

filing made by Thomas Funding would have diminished greatly, if not obviated, the hazard of a recovery back by a bankruptcy trustee.[d]

Article–9 perfection in general. Article 9 comprehends a host of security interests in assets (personal property) other than accounts. For many types of assets—notably goods—perfection can be achieved by means other than filing a UCC–1.[e] Indeed, if the collateral is household goods (a species of "consumer goods"[f]) and the security interest has the commonplace form of a "purchase money security interest" (PMSI), perfection is automatic.

But the rule quoted above, about the priority in right of a lien creditor over an unperfected security interest, is of general application. Hence it will be understood that successful asset-based financing depends on compliance with the perfection rules of Article 9 not only when the collateral is accounts but also when it is the debtor's inventory, or equipment, or "general intangibles," or a more specialized type of asset. Combinations are customary. For merchants, inventory-and-accounts financing is popular, a filing as to both being relied upon. (For an obvious reason, Thomas Funding did not provide Silverline with inventory financing.)

NOTES

(1) *Filing Not Notification.* The indispensable contents of a financing statement (UCC–1) do little more than advise an inquirer that there is, or may be, a transaction in accounts between the assignor and the assignee. (A mechanism is provided whereby an inquirer may obtain further particulars by directing a quiz to the assignee who has filed: UCC 9–208.) The point now to be noticed is that a filing does not effect notification of the account debtor under UCC 9–318. Bank of Waunakee v. Rochester Cheese Sales, Inc., 906 F.2d 1185 (7th Cir.1990) (offset case); see Restatement Second § 338, Comment *e*.

(2) *Minor Filing Error.* "Minor errors" in a financing statement are the subject of UCC 9–402(8). Do you consider that a searcher would have required the talents of "a prognosticator or a magician" to unearth the filing by Thomas Funding ("Silvermine")? In testing for minor error, should it matter that the data base is accessible to a searcher electronically? On these questions see In re Thriftway Auto Supply, Inc., 159 B.R. 948 (W.D.Okl.1993) (trade name used: "Thriftway Auto Stores"); Hillman, What's in a Name: The U.C.C. Filing System in the Courts, 44 Okla.L.Rev. 151 (1991).

(3) *Factors and Others.* A principal issue in *Thomas Funding* had to do with what right the taxpayer (Silverline) had in the accounts when the tax lien arose. Thomas Funding contended that Silverline had no "property" in them because the assignment "effected a sale of Silverline's entire interest in the accounts rather than the creation of a security interest." In business terms, Thomas Funding acted as a factor (purchaser), rather than as a lender. When accounts are sold, without any assurance that they will prove to be collectible,

---

d. On the working of § 547 see Baird, fn. c above, Chapter 7.

e. Possession of the collateral by the secured party is a means of perfection. UCC 9–302(1)(a).

f. Goods "used or bought for use primarily for personal, family or household purposes"—UCC 9–109(1).

the assignee takes the risk that the account debtor will be unable to pay, and has no recourse in that event against the assignor.

To that contention the court gave the answer indicated in the Note above on Assignments and Article 9.[g]

(4) *A Case for Contrast.* In a case comparable to *Thomas Funding* the account debtor was General Motors. In that case, also, a delinquent taxpayer had made an assignment of earnings to a financer, and the IRS had established a tax lien on the taxpayer's assets. GM had contracted to pay the taxpayer (D) for engineering services. The financer was a bank. Some differences were these: (a) the bank had made a loan to D, secured by D's account; (b) the bank had perfected its interest by filing a financing statement in proper form;[h] and (c) GM had made payment for D's services to the assignee (bank), rather than to the IRS.

The government sought to compel GM to pay again. From a summary judgment for the government, GM appealed. *Held*: Reversed, and judgment directed for GM. The court said that, from the time when (at the latest) GM was notified by the bank of the assignment, D had "no property rights" to which the government's lien could attach.[i] U.S. v. General Motors Corp., 929 F.2d 249 (6th Cir.1991).

Despite the differences in the facts, the decision appears to be in conflict with that in *Thomas Funding*. Indeed, owing to difference (a), it is possible that each case should have been decided differently. In particular, if D had *sold* its right to payment from GM there would be much more reason to believe that GM made payment to the right party.

---

g. The court said: "Article 9 applies not only to any transaction which is intended to create a security interest in accounts, but also to any sale of accounts. The drafters of the Uniform Commercial Code expressed concern that transactions involving the sale of accounts would be indistinguishable from transactions involving accounts as security, and thus they included both types of transactions within the scope of Article 9...." The court cited UCC 9–102(1) (citation omitted here). See also UCC 1–201(39).

This passage is accurate and important. It does not necessarily follow, however, that "security agreement," as an imprint of Article 9 on a sale transaction, should govern an assignee's entitlement in relation to an interest—such as a federal tax lien—resting on a statute of the United States.

Moreover, the assimilation in Article 9 of accounts sales to security transfers need not carry over, full-blown, to the determination of the composition of a bankruptcy estate. But see *Octagon Gas Systems, Inc. v. Rimmer*, p. 926 fn. g above. The issue in that case is distinguishable from anything decided in *Thomas Funding*, although federal law affected both decisions.

h. This fact is supplied by counsel in the case; the opinion does not disclose it.

Congress has decided that its tax lien should not take a back seat to a security interest that has "attached" to an asset of the taxpayer unless the interest is also "perfected." See § 6323(h)(1) of the Internal Revenue Code (26 U.S.C.)

What is defined there as a "security interest" differs also in another way from what the term means in Article 9: "any interest in property acquired ... *for the purpose of securing payment or performance of an obligation....*" Curiously, in District of Columbia v. Thomas Funding the court seems to have overlooked this difference.

i. For a contrasting analysis see In re Philips, 882 F.2d 302 (8th Cir.1989) (concerning the capacity of an assignor to "embezzle" the proceeds of a payment right that had been assigned as collateral), and In re Contractors Equipment Supply Co., 861 F.2d 241 (9th Cir.1988) (assignor "retained an interest in the account"; proceeding in bankruptcy).

SEPTEMBERTIDE PUBLISHING, B.V. v. STEIN & DAY, INC.

United States Court of Appeals, Second Circuit, 1989.
884 F.2d 675.

[The facts and part of the opinion in this case are at p. 879 above. There the court concluded that Septembertide was a third party beneficiary of a contract between Stein & Day and New American Library. In the part of the opinion that follows the court considered the relation between Septembertide's interest and that of Bookcrafters as an assignee of Stein & Day.]

CARDAMONE, CIRCUIT JUDGE: ...

III　Security Interest

Bookcrafters argues that the district court erred in deciding that the author's rights in the Paperback Agreement were superior to its rights as an assignee with a secured interest in Stein & Day's contract rights and receivables. On Bookcrafters' motion for summary judgment for *all* payments due from New Library, the district court held that Bookcrafters was only entitled to such rights as Stein & Day could give. And, because Stein & Day was obligated to transfer to the author (Septembertide) two-thirds of the funds it received from New Library, Bookcrafters obtained rights only in the remaining one-third.

Bookcrafters urges that it is entitled to the full amount. It asserts that, under New York law, the fact that funds equal to two-thirds of the receivables from the paperback sales of "Confessional" were eventually to go to Septembertide as third-party beneficiary did not affect Stein & Day's right to grant a security interest in all of the receivables. It cites Recchio v. Manufacturers and Traders Trust Co., 55 Misc.2d 788, 286 N.Y.S.2d 390 (Sup.Ct.Genesee County 1968), rev'd on other grounds, 35 A.D.2d 769, 316 N.Y.S.2d 915 (4th Dep't 1970), for the proposition that a *bona fide* creditor in Bookcrafters' position may perfect a security interest, even when the debtor transferring the security interest does not actually own the collateral. It conducted a UCC filings search, its argument continues, and properly perfected its security interest; hence it should not be forced to bear the loss when its debtor (Stein & Day) breached a contractual obligation to a third party (Septembertide) regarding the collateral. To hold otherwise, Bookcrafters argues, would be to eviscerate the fundamental principle that secured interests are superior to unsecured interests. Contending that the security interest granted to it by the hard cover publisher is superior to Septembertide's rights as a third-party beneficiary, Bookcrafters therefore claims the right to all of the New Library payments.

We recognize that the issue of whether Septembertide's rights as a third-party beneficiary of the Paperback Agreement are superior to Bookcrafters' rights, as the secured creditor and assignee of Stein & Day, presents a difficult question of law. In resolving it, we look first to the security agreement.

In return for a $1,187,374 loan, Stein & Day executed and delivered a mortgage on certain of its real property. It also granted a security interest to Bookcrafters in tangible and intangible collateral. The tangible collateral included machinery, equipment, motor vehicles, appliances, fixtures, computers, goods, books, paper products, raw materials, files, records etc. "and all other tangible personal property owned by debtor." The intangible collateral—the subject with which we are concerned—included "all of debtor's contract rights ... subsidiary rights contracts ... all of debtor's accounts receivable ... and all rights to payments of money...." Stein & Day represented that it was "the owner of the collateral free from any prior claim, lien, security interest or encumbrance....", and that its title and interest in the intangible collateral "is not subject to any defense, offset, counterclaim or claim...." The 30–page agreement was comprehensive and thorough. Several exhibits were attached to it stating the locations where the debtor's collateral was kept and itemizing the subsidiary rights contracts, including the December 11, 1984 contract Stein & Day had with New Library regarding "Confessional," which is the contract on which Bookcrafters bases its claim.

We examine next the law of secured transactions. To create an enforceable security interest: (1) a debtor must sign a security agreement that describes the collateral; (2) value must be given; and (3) the debtor must have rights in the collateral. See NYUCC § 9–203(1) (McKinney's Supp.1988). Concededly, Stein & Day signed the security agreement that contained a thorough description of the collateral, and for which value was given.

Thus, the question is whether (3) Stein & Day had rights in the collateral that it could assign to Bookcrafters. Bookcrafters advances several arguments to support its assertion of a valid security interest in *all* of the New Library payments. For example, it contends that Stein & Day was not a mere conduit for money passing from New Library to the author, and that these funds were not earmarked or segregated for Septembertide's account. The money coming in could be commingled and used by Stein & Day as it saw fit. We agree that such accurately describes the flow of funds. Further, Septembertide granted Stein & Day the authority, under the hardcover publishing agreement, to license the paperback version and to receive payments from such license. It took the risk, so Bookcrafters urges, that these funds might become encumbered to third parties. Now that they are encumbered, it cannot take back what it bargained away.

Most importantly, Bookcrafters continues, the author could have protected its interests with a security agreement or a non-assignment provision. Its failure to do so in the face of Stein & Day's and Bookcrafters' commercially reasonable actions makes Septembertide's third-party interest subordinate to Bookcrafters' security interest in the subject funds. Bookcrafters asserts that when the true owner of property allows another party to appear as owner, and that other party assigns the property to a third party that acts in good faith, the rights of the third party may be superior to those of the true owner. See, e.g., Monroe Abstract & Title Corp. v. Giallombardo, 54 A.D.2d 1084, 1085 (4th Dep't 1976). Moreover, Bookcrafters claims that the district court erred when it focused not on the assignment of the rights in the

Paperback Agreement, but on the collateral Hardcover Agreement between the author and Stein & Day. It completes that argument by noting that defenses flowing from collateral agreements do not defeat an assignee's interest. See Bank Leumi Trust Co. v. Collins Sales Serv., Inc., 47 N.Y.2d 888, 890 (1979).

Although these contentions are seemingly persuasive, when taken together they are fundamentally flawed. Bookcrafters' assertions that Stein & Day could commingle funds and control paperback licensing rights are not in dispute, but they are largely irrelevant. What is most significant in our view is that Stein & Day assigned to Bookcrafters "all of [its] contract rights." The assignment did not purport to assign an interest in "all of the monies payable under the Paperback Agreement." The rights to the two-thirds of *those* funds had been previously transferred to Septembertide. Hence, they could not lawfully thereafter be assigned to Bookcrafters because an assignor cannot assign that which it no longer owns or controls. See International Ribbon Mills, Ltd. v. Arjan Ribbons, Inc., 36 N.Y.2d 121, 126, 365 N.Y.S.2d 808, 325 N.E.2d 137 (1975) ("It is elementary ancient law that an assignee never stands in any better position than his assignor. He is subject to all the equities and burdens which attach to the property assigned because he receives no more ... than his assignor."); Caribbean Steamship Co., S.A. v. Sonmez Denizcilik Ve Ticaret A.S., 598 F.2d 1264, 1266–67 (2d Cir. 1979). See also White & Summers, Uniform Commercial Code, § 23–4 at p. 795 (1972).

We agree with the district court that Bookcrafters' security interest was subject to Septembertide's third-party interest in the Paperback Agreement. Defenses may properly be asserted against an assignee (here Bookcrafters) that are "based on facts existing at the time of the contract." See Restatement of Contracts § 167(1). Here, of course, Septembertide's rights and its claim to two-thirds of the Paperback income from New Library derives from a contract in existence at the time of Stein & Day's assignment to Bookcrafters.

Moreover, UCC § 9–318(1)(A) provides that the rights of the assignee (Bookcrafters) are subject to "all the terms of the contract between the account debtor (New Library) and assignor (Stein & Day) and any defense or claim arising therefrom." It has always been the law in New York that an assignee stands in the shoes of its assignor and takes subject to those liabilities of its assignor that were in existence prior to the assignment. See Seibert v. Dunn, 216 N.Y. 237, 245–46, 110 N.E. 447 (1915); Arjan Ribbons, Inc., 36 N.Y.2d at 126, 365 N.Y.S.2d 808, 325 N.E.2d 137. As a consequence, Bookcrafters' rights in monies New Library owed to Stein & Day did not include the author's two-thirds share, which had vested in Septembertide upon execution of the Publishing and Paperback Agreements. Once vested, the author's third-party rights could not be assigned without its consent.

In sum, Bookcrafters possessed a valid and enforceable security interest under the UCC. But in taking a security interest in its assignor's property, it cannot claim rights in the property that were not the assignor's to give. Stein & Day's "rights in the collateral" were limited in this respect to a one-third share of the funds that New Library was free to alienate.

It seems fair to require, as between a trade creditor and an author, that the creditor-assignee prudently ascertain the actual existence of its collateral before agreeing to take a security interest in it. In this case the security interest contract was comprehensive. An examination by Bookcrafters of the publishing Hardcover Agreement, flagged by the Paperback Agreement, would quickly have revealed Septembertide's interest and the corresponding reduction in the assignor's rights in the debtor's collateral. Bookcrafters admits that its financing of Stein & Day reflected a customary assignment in the industry of a publisher's receivable. As a creditor lending to a book publisher, Bookcrafters was effectively on notice of the fact that its assignor-debtor, Stein & Day did not own (and therefore could not validly assign) the two-thirds of the paperback royalties owing to the author.

In resolving the question of priority between a secured creditor and an intended third-party beneficiary whose interests in the collateral preceded it, a first in time, first in right rule applies. It is the existence of Septembertide's earlier rights that tied Stein & Day's hands and prevented it from assigning to Bookcrafters that two-thirds share of the funds which had previously vested in Septembertide. Because Stein & Day's rights in the contract receivables were thereafter limited to a one-third share, Bookcrafters can claim no more. . . .

Modified, and as modified, affirmed.

NOTES

(1) *Reach of Article 9.* Is there a sense in which Septembertide (and its predecessor, "S & L") provided *financing* to Stein & Day? If so, a case can be made for requiring it to alert other investors, such as Bookcrafters, by filing a UCC–1 ("Bookcrafter's search of UCC filings uncovered no evidence of Septembertide's interest. . . .") One of the drafters of Article 9 is among those who have suggested its extension to third party beneficiary contracts, as well as assignments, at least when they serve a financing function. 2 G. Gilmore, Security Interests in Personal Property § 41.3 (1965).

See, in this connection, the Note, "Financing by Beneficiary," p. 884 above, and compare the role of the pension fund (in relation to P & F) with that of Septembertide (in relation to Stein & Day). If the argument for third-party-beneficiary filings is stronger in the Note case, why is it?

(2) *"What is most significant".* Might the court have decided differently if Stein & Day had made an assignment to Bookcrafters in the terms suggested by the court?—"all of the monies payable under the Paperback Agreement." Or would the decision have been no different, owing to the principle that an assignee cannot claim rights that "were not the assignor's to give"? (On the reach of that principle, see District of Columbia v. Thomas Funding, stated at p. 925 above, and the Note on Successive Assignments, below.)

(3) *Surplusage?* Perhaps it is not obvious how the court's statements in the paragraph beginning "Moreover . . ." are germane to the problem of the case. The Code section cited there—section 9–318(1)(a)—does not appear to address

rival claims such as those of Septembertide and Bookcrafters, but rather disputes between an assignee and an obligor (such as New Library). Similarly, when it is said that an assignee "stands in the shoes of its assignor," the usual context is that kind of dispute. Would the opinion benefit by the omission of this paragraph? Or is the paragraph an essential part of the reasoning?

SUCCESSIVE ASSIGNMENTS

In commercial affairs, the most important rule about priorities among parties claiming under multiple assignments from the same assignor is this: "Conflicting security interests rank according to priority in time of filing or perfection...." [a]

This rule, quoted from UCC Article 9, can be illustrated by supposing additional facts in the *Septembertide* case. Let it be supposed that Stein & Day assigned its payment rights against New Library first to a financer named "Octobertide", and thereafter to Bookcrafters. (The assignment to Bookcrafters was made in November, 1985, it will be recalled. Assume the earlier assignment to have been made in October.) As between the two financers—laying aside the rights of Septembertide—which would have priority?

Other facts are needed for applying the rule to this case. Presumably Bookcrafters made an Article–9 filing at about the time of its assignment, in November. If Octobertide made a filing in October, when taking its assignment, it would have priority. Its security interest would be the first in time of both filing and perfection. (Of course, on that assumption, Bookcrafters' search for filings would presumably have revealed the earlier one. Bookcrafters would have refused to finance Stein & Day as it did, no doubt, upon encountering an earlier filing. Possibly there would have been negotiations with Octobertide in that event.)

A more interesting case to suppose is that Bookcrafters made a filing in (say) September, in anticipation of getting a security agreement from Stein & Day in November. According to Article 9: "A financing statement may be filed before a security agreement is made or a security interest otherwise attaches." [b] On that supposition, Bookcrafters' security interest would not have priority in time of *perfection*. (Note the

----

a. UCC 9–312(5). This provision begins:

> In all cases not governed by other rules stated in this section ... priority between conflicting security interests in the same collateral shall be determined according to the following rules ...

Then follows the rule quoted in the text, designated as clause (a).

A second rule—clause (b)—is this: "So long as conflicting security interests are unperfected, the first to attach has priority." This rule is relatively insignificant because an issue of priority among conflicting security interests rarely reaches litigation before at least one of the contestants has perfected its interest.

Apart from Note 2, below, the instances in which conflicting security interests in accounts are governed by "other rules stated in this section" [UCC 9–312] are beyond the scope of this book. It may be assumed, for present purposes, that none of these instances is one of "successive assignments."

b. Section 9–402(1).

three steps listed in the *Septembertide* opinion as necessary to create an enforceable security interest. A security interest cannot be perfected until it has become enforceable—i.e., has attached.) But it would have priority in time of *filing*. Hence its security interest would have priority over that of Octobertide. (Of course, on that assumption, presumably Octobertide would have made a search, in October, for filings against Stein & Day and would have been warned off on discovering that of Bookcrafters.)

The latter illustration is a key feature of what is often called the "notice-filing system" of Article 9. As the court said in District of Columbia v. Thomas Funding (see p. 925 above), "Article 9 adopts a system of 'notice filing,' requiring only a simple notice, the financing statement, to be filed, rather than the security agreement itself." Reflection will suggest that if a firm interested in getting financing—such as Stein & Day, or the Silverline Cleaning Company—signs a UCC–1 in which the types of collateral are indicated in broad terms, its access to credit from financers other than the one designated there, the filer, may be sharply curtailed.

Although the filing of a UCC–1 may give the filer something of a "throttle hold" on the debtor, some countermoves are open to the debtor. Possibly the debtor can get advances from another financer that are sufficient in amount both to give the debtor fresh credit and to discharge the debtor's obligations to the earlier-filing financer. If so, the debtor can compel that financer to file a termination statement.[c] Or possibly that financer will accede to a subordination agreement, by which any fresh credit from another one, based on a conflicting security interest, will have priority over (at least) any new obligations the debtor may incur to the former.

(The priority rule quoted at the beginning of this Note is supplemented and qualified by Article 9 in ways not examined here. Priorities among security interests in many types of collateral—not only accounts—are regulated by Article 9.)

It is a notable fact about the priority rules of Article 9 concerning conflicting security interests, which rest on agreements with a debtor, that these rules differ systematically from those concerning security interests *vis-a-vis* judicial liens and other liens that do not depend on the debtor's consent. So, for cases like the illustrations above, the applicable set of rules is independent of the Article–9 rules concerning creditors' claims and an assignee.

NOTES

(1) *Non–Code Priority Rules.* The Restatement Second contains a complex rule for ranking conflicting assignments, while acknowledging that the rule is largely displaced by Article 9. "The subject is now largely governed by the Uniform Commercial Code, except in cases of wage claims, rights under insurance policies, deposit accounts, and certain other excluded types of transac-

c. UCC 9–404(1).

tions." [d] In general, as to an assignment of an excluded type, there is no possibility of making a useful filing in a public office.[e]

(2) *A Case of Double–Dealing.* Without regard to any of the rules mentioned above, if an assignee might have made an effective filing under Article 9, but has not attempted to do so (or has attempted to do so without success) it is exposed to some risk that an assignment thereafter made will have priority. This risk is a relatively minor one, however; the assumption is that an effective filing could *not* have been made as to the subsequent assignment.

Elements of value and "good faith" figure in the rule describing the risk. The recipient of the subsequent assignment is protected only "to the extent that he gives value without knowledge of the security interest." [f] So, for example, in District of Columbia v. Thomas Funding, described at p. 925 above, if another building-cleaning firm (the Goldmine Company, say) had taken over the contract from Silverline, without knowledge of the assignment, its right to the payments would have preempted that of Thomas Funding. (Note that a transfer of a payment right under a contract to an assignee who is also to do the performance does not generate a security interest.[g] Hence a filing by the surrogate firm would have no effect.) The undertaking by Goldmine to do the work would count as value given. A fraud by Silverline is inherent in the facts supposed.

(3) *A Question of Code Policy.* As has been indicated (p. 934 above), the Code subjects the rights of an assignee to those of a creditor of the assignor who pursues an ordinary collection process to the point of getting a lien, if the assignee has failed to make a requisite filing.[h] It does so even if the creditor has knowledge of the assignment. If that provision were deleted from the Code, financers on accounts might often dispense with filing, and those who file would have much less to fear from an error in filing. A nonfiler would bear the risk, even so, of the faithlessness of the assignor, in making a conflicting assignment. But financers generally assume that they can avoid doing business with malefactors, and consider the primary risk to be that of the assignor's insolvency. Some observers favor reversing the rule that favors lien creditors.

What would be the cost? There is this: a firm seeking ordinary (unsecured) credit, such as suppliers often grant, could not give reliable assurances that it has not burdened its ostensible wealth in the form of accounts receivable (or of inventory, equipment, and so on) with a preemptive "security interest." The suggested reform raises the question how much reliance is placed on the UCC filing system, directly or indirectly, by trade creditors and others who depend simply on the prosperity of their debtors.

At what juncture is the United States, as a tax creditor, likely to place reliance on a taxpayer's appearance of wealth, as manifested in the absence of UCC filings naming the taxpayer as a debtor?

---

d. A reference to UCC 9–104 follows this sentence. In the course of a projected revision of Article 9, active consideration is being given to reducing the list of exclusions in that section.

e. In the cases to which one of these rules applies the assignor is especially likely to be a double-dealing malefactor. In contrast, in many cases to which the Article–9 rules apply the assignor has no thought of defrauding anyone.

f. Continuing: "and before it is perfected." UCC 9–301(1)(d).

g. UCC 9–104(f).

h. UCC 9–301(1)(b).

SECTION 2. ASSIGNMENT AND DELEGATION IN CONNECTION WITH THE SALE OF A BUSINESS

———

This Section proceeds, in part, according to the several types of contracts that may generate problems of assignment and delegation. In the first item, leases of goods are considered (and, in a note, leases of real property). As to leases of goods, Article 2A of the Uniform Commercial Code is a major source of the law, although it has not yet been enacted in all states. The principal case concerned a sale of goods, as to which Article 2 is a controlling text. Contracts for services are illustrated in the notes at several points.

It should be observed that Article 9 does not apply to the topic of this Section. According to an exclusion, "This Article does not apply ... to a sale of accounts or chattel paper as part of a sale of the business out of which they arose ... or a transfer of a right to payment under a contract to an assignee who is also to do the performance under the contract...." [a]

———

PERSONAL–PROPERTY LEASES:

TWO ENGLISH CASES

Two 19th–century King's–Bench decisions are part of the backdrop of law about the delegability of duties. Both concerned the leasing of vehicles, a subject of current commercial importance. In the first case [b] the defendant, Drummond, had taken the hire of a "chariot" for five years from Sharpe. Robson, the plaintiff, who had been Sharpe's "secret partner" in the coachmaking business, acquired all the business assets when Sharpe retired. Sharpe joined with Robson in an action to enforce the hiring agreement (although he said he "had no longer any thing to do with it"). Part of the agreement was that Sharpe would keep the carriage in repair, provide new wheels as necessary, and give it one painting. The plaintiffs were nonsuited, and they appealed. The ruling was (as later stated) that

> Drummond could not be sued on the contract—by Lord Tenterden on the ground that "the defendant might have been induced to enter into the contract by reason of the personal confidence which he reposed in Sharpe, and therefore have agreed to pay money in advance, for which reason the defendant had a right to object to its being performed by any other person;" and by Littledale and Parke, JJ., on the additional ground that the defendant had a right to the

———

a. UCC 9–104(f). But see Albee v. Maverick Media, Inc., 474 N.W.2d 238 (Neb. 1991).

b. Robson v. Drummond, 109 Eng.Rep. 1156 (1831).

personal services of Sharpe, and to the benefit of his judgment and taste, to the end of the contract.

Robson v. Drummond was distinguished in The British Waggon Co. v. Lea & Co., 5 Q.B.D. 149 (1880). The defendant, Lea & Company, was a coal merchant that had entered into seven-year leases for the use of a hundred railway wagons. The agreements contained this provision:

> The owners, their executors, or administrators, will at all times during the said term ... keep the waggons in good and substantial repair and working order....

The lessor was the Parkgate Waggon Company. Before the year was out, Parkgate entered "winding up" proceedings, for liquidation under court supervision. Some time later, Parkgate's payment rights under the leases were transferred to the British Waggon Company (plaintiff), which undertook to perform Parkgate's obligations to Lea & Company. British Waggon took over the repair facilities and the staff of Parkgate that had been used in performing those obligations. In an action by British Waggon for the rent, Lea contended that Parkgate "had no right ... to substitute a third party to do the work they had engaged to perform, nor were the defendants bound to accept the party so substituted as the one to whom they were to look for performance of the contract; the contract was therefore at an end."

The court subscribed to the principle of Robson v. Drummond, for a case in which personal performance is "of the essence of the contract." But the earlier decision, the court said, "went to the utmost limit" in applying the principle.

> Much work is contracted for, which it is known can only be executed by means of subcontracts; much is contracted for as to which it is indifferent to the party for whom it is to be done, whether it is done by the immediate party to the contract, or by some on his behalf. In all these cases the maxim Qui facit per alium facit per se applies.

Rejecting the defendant's contention, the court described the repair of the wagons as "a rough description of work which ordinary workmen conversant with the business would be perfectly able to execute," and said: "we cannot suppose that ... the defendants attached any importance to whether the repairs were done by the company [Parkgate], or by any one with whom the company might enter into a subsidiary contract to do the work."

NOTES

(1) *Leasing Under the UCC.* If the facts of *Robson* or of *British Waggon* were to recur now, in the United States, they would require consideration of a complex provision of the Uniform Commercial Code: section 2A–303. That provision deals, as its title indicates, with three subjects:

—Alienability of Party's Interest Under Lease Contract or of Lessor's Residual Interest in Goods;

—Delegation of Performance; [and]

—Transfer of Rights.

Delegation of performance is the matter of immediate interest, although in each of the English cases there was also an attempt to "alienate" the lessor's interest in the goods (carriage; railway wagons) and to transfer a right (the lessor's right to rent payments).

A Comment to UCC 2A–303 refers to a distinction between a lease like those in the English cases and a ("non-operating") lease in which, once the lessee is in possession of the goods, no remaining performance under the contract is due from the lessor.

> [A] lessor can transfer the right to future payments under the lease contract
> ... if the lessor has no remaining performance....

A transfer is effective in that case, and the lessor cannot be sanctioned for making it, even if the contract purports to prohibit the transfer. But this rule would not govern the English cases:

> [T]he lessor would have "remaining performance" under a lease contract requiring the lessor to regularly maintain and service the goods or to provide "upgrades" of the equipment on a periodic basis in order to avoid obsolescence.[a]

Section 2A–303 goes beyond this. It fosters transfers of rights and interests under leases, made by either party, over an objection by the "other party," even when the transferor owes further performance to that party.

By way of qualification, however, the section refers to a transfer that "materially impairs the prospect of obtaining return performance by, materially changes the duty of, or materially increases the burden or risk imposed on" the "other party." Hence the distinction drawn in the English cases remains important in connection with equipment leasing under the Uniform Commercial Code. (Whether or not those cases applied the distinction correctly is another matter.)

(2) *"Personal Services"*. A passage often quoted in connection with assignment law is as follows:

> "All painters do not paint portraits like Sir Joshua Reynolds, nor landscapes like Claude Lorraine, nor do all writers write dramas like Shakespeare or fiction like Dickens. Rare genius and extraordinary skill are not transferable, and contracts for their employment are therefore personal, and cannot be assigned. But rare genius and extraordinary skill are not indispensable to the workmanlike digging down of a sand hill or the filling up of a depression to a given level, or the construction of brick sewers with manholes and covers, and contracts for such work are not personal, and may be assigned." Taylor v. Palmer, 31 Cal. 240, 247–248 (1866).

In Macke Co. v. Pizza of Gaithersburg, Inc., 270 A.2d 645 (Md.1970), the court made use of this passage in connection with the maintenance of vending machines that had been installed by a firm later bought out by the plaintiff.

(3) *Contracting Against Assignment.* It has been said that the law "typically respects the decisions of private parties about whether particular contract rights are assignable." D. Baird, The Elements of Bankruptcy 134 (rev. ed. 1993). But an inspection of the Uniform Commercial Code will disclose several limitations on this generality.

In Article 2, concerning sale-of-goods contracts, there is this provision (UCC 2–210(2)):

a. Comment 7.

A right to damages for breach of the whole contract or a right arising out of the assignor's due performance of his entire obligation can be assigned despite agreement otherwise.

In UCC 9–318(4), it is provided that an "account debtor" cannot effectively bargain so as to prevent the transfer of a payment right described in Article 9 as an "account". And in Article 2A, concerning leases, the effectiveness of provisions about transfers is closely regulated. (That is the source of the quotations in the foregoing Note.)

The decision in Robson v. Drummond appears to be disapproved in UCC 2A–303; see subsection (3)—"actual delegation of a material performance"—and Comment 2. (Curiously, the section is written chiefly in terms of the efficacy of default terms and other provisions that may be found in lease contracts. Provisions about termination of a lease in the event of an attempted transfer are commonplace.) The section provides that in some cases a prohibition on transfer will operate only as a covenant, leading to damages, and not as a limit on the rights of the transferee.

(4) *The Case of the Landlord's Consent.* In Julian v. Christopher, 575 A.2d 735 (Md.1990), the court considered a real-estate lease provision that the lessees could not assign the lease or sublet the premises without the consent of the lessor. According to earlier Maryland authority this meant that the lessor could withhold consent—in the words of the trial court—"for a good reason, a bad reason, or no reason at all." The Court of Appeals found reasons of public policy for changing the law. "The first is the public policy against restraints on alienation. The second is the public policy which implies a covenant of good faith and fair dealing in every contract." Id. at 738. Reversing a decision for the lessor, the court remanded for a determination whether or not he had been aware of, and had relied on, the prior rule. The court referred to the Restatement, Second, of Property § 15.2 and to the trend of decisions elsewhere.

The court gave some examples of reasonable objections to subletting that a lessor might have, and contrasted a case of withholding consent for no purpose other than to exact a rent increase.

(5) *Bankruptcy.* Owing to a mishap in the Bankruptcy Code, there is conflicting authority about whether or not a firm entering reorganization proceedings under chapter 11 can maintain its rights under an advantageous contract if, under nonbankruptcy law, the firm could not deputize another to render the performance required of it by the contract. See In re James Cable Partners, L.P., 154 B.R. 813 (M.D.Ga.1993). This much, however, is well-understood: "If Placido Domingo files a Chapter 11 petition, his contract to sing at the Metropolitan Opera never becomes property of the estate. The trustee cannot assign it to Neil Shicoff, even if the bankruptcy judge can be persuaded that Shicoff is as fine a tenor as Domingo." Baird, op. cit. supra 137.

In that case, of course, Domingo could continue to enjoy his earnings at the Met; whereas the earnings of a firm entering bankruptcy reorganization are devoted to its bankruptcy expenses and to the payment of old debts.

SALES OF GOODS

UCC 2–210 is the controlling text on the subject of the assignment of rights and the delegation of duties that are generated by sale-of-goods contracts. In an omitted part of the opinion next presented, the court quoted from the statute and from a comment, and said:

> Consideration is given to balancing the policies of free alienability of commercial contracts and protecting the obligee from having to accept a bargain he did not contract for.

Subsection (2) of UCC 2–210 is the source of language in UCC 2A–303, quoted above; and other parts of the latter are adaptations of section 2–210. Both sections were drafted with a view to Code provisions about a party's right to demand assurances of due performance: sections 2–609 and 2A–401. (Note, however, that whereas § 2–210 enlarges on that right in subsection (5), § 2A–303 does not.)

UCC 2–210 has influenced the Restatement rule about permissible assignments and delegations. With slight alterations, the phrasing of subsection (2) has been copied into Restatement Second § 317(2)(a). Also, the original Restatement standard for delegation has been made more congruent with the Code standard: see Restatement Second § 318.

NOTES

(1) *Ordering Goods.* In *British Waggon* the court said that "where goods are ordered of a particular manufacturer," someone who has succeeded to the business of that manufacturer "cannot execute the order, so as to bind the customer." The customer is entitled, the court said, "to refuse to deal with any other than the manufacturer whose goods he intended to buy. For this Boulton v. Jones ... is a sufficient authority." Boulton v. Jones is described in a Note at p. 163 above.

Compare a case in which a manufacturer has contracted to deliver a stock item and transfers the contract—along with all its other assets—to a second firm. For this simple case, assuming that the contract requires payment upon delivery, the Uniform Commercial Code provides, with near certainty, that the customer is *not* entitled to refuse to deal with the second firm. See UCC 2–210. How would you argue that the enactment of the Code did not alter the rule of Boulton v. Jones?

(2) *The Case of the Boston Buyer.* A problem almost unique to sale-of-goods cases can arise when a buyer receives goods without knowing their source. In the early case Boston Ice Co. v. Potter, 123 Mass. 28 (1877), the buyer refused to pay for ice that he had supposed, wrongly, to have been delivered by the Citizens' Ice Company. He had contracted with that company for it; but Citizens' had sold its business to Boston Ice. In an action on the contract by Boston Ice, the court sustained Potter's demurrer "on the ground that [he] had a right to choose with whom he would deal and could not have another supplier thrust upon him." It is said that modern authorities do not support this result. Macke Co. v. Pizza of Gaithersburg, 270 A.2d 645 (Md.1970) (source of the quotation above).

How would the case have been decided by the court that, three years later, decided *British Waggon*. Would an action by Boston Ice in quasi-contract have been more appealing than an action for the price? Less appealing? There was this further fact: Potter had earlier switched his ice business from Boston Ice to Citizens' Ice when he found Boston's service to be unsatisfactory. Does that fact affect your answers?

(3) *The Case of the Baltimore Buyer.* The business of W.C. Frederick was making ice cream in a "simple plant in Baltimore." The Crane Ice Cream

Company operated a similar business "upon a large and extensive scale" in Maryland and Pennsylvania. On going out of business, Frederick turned over his plant and "everything constituting his business" to Crane.

One of Frederick's assets was a three-year contract, which he assigned to Crane, for the supply of ice by the Terminal Freezing & Heating Company. (Terminal had also supplied ice to Frederick under an earlier contract similar in terms.) The contract entitled Frederick to all the ice required in his business, up to a maximum weekly delivery of 250 tons. He was to make payment on each Tuesday for the ice delivered during the preceding week, at the rate of $3.25 a ton; and he was required to buy all his ice from Terminal (unless more than 250 tons was required in a given week). The contract recited that the ice was bought by Frederick for "use in his business as an ice cream manufacturer."

When Terminal learned that Frederick's business had been absorbed by Crane, it declared the contract at an end. In an action by Crane against Terminal, the trial court sustained a demurrer by the defendant, and Crane appealed. The court mentioned that Crane "had a large capitalization, ample resources, and credit to meet any of its obligations [and] was prepared to pay cash for all ice deliverable under the contract." *Held:* Affirmed. Crane Ice Cream Co. v. Terminal Freezing & Heating Co., 128 A. 280, 39 A.L.R. 1184 (Md.1925). The court said that before the contract was made the "character, credit, and resources of Frederick had been tried and tested" by Terminal; also that Terminal must be assumed to have relied upon his "personal integrity, capacity, and management," and upon its knowledge of the average quantity of ice "probably to be needed, in the usual course of [his] business." As for Crane, the court surmised that if ice should be more costly than $3.25 in (say) Philadelphia, it might exploit the Terminal contract to the full by shifting some production to its new plant.

Consider, in relation to this case, an excerpt from Comment 4 to UCC 2–210, set out in the following Note.

(4) *Requirements Contracts, and Others.* The following passage summarizes the effect of UCC 2–210 on certain contracts: "This Article and this section are intended to clarify [the problem of assignability of rights], particularly in cases dealing with output, requirement and exclusive dealing contracts. In the first place the section on requirements and exclusive dealing removes from the construction of the original contract most of the 'personal discretion' element by substituting the reasonably objective standard of good faith operation of the plant or business to be supplied. Secondly, the section on insecurity and assurances ... frees the other party from the doubts and uncertainty which may afflict him under an assignment of the character in question by permitting him to demand adequate assurance of due performance without which he may suspend his own performance. [In subsection 5] the word 'performance' includes the giving of orders under a requirements contract. Of course, in any case where a material personal discretion is sought to be transferred, effective assignment is barred by subsection (2)." Cf. Robbins v. Hunts Food & Industries, Inc., 391 P.2d 713 (Wash.1964).

NOVATION

When an agreement is made for the substitution of one obligor for another, such that the obligee is entitled to the same performance, but the original obligor is released, the agreement is one of a class called "novation".[a]   The assent of the obligee is indispensable.   In the case described in Note 3, above, the court said that a *liability* under a contract—as opposed to a beneficial right—is not assignable.   It is not, "because any one who is bound to any performance whatever or who owes money cannot by any act of his own, or by any act in agreement with any other person than his creditor or the one to whom his performance is due, cast off his own liability and substitute another's liability."

   The assent of the person to whom the performance is due (obligee) may, of course, be inferred from that person's conduct.   As a rule, when an obligor delegates performance of a duty, and the obligee does no more than "go along" with it, the obligee is not understood as agreeing to release of the original obligor.   See Bank of Fairbanks v. Kaye, 227 F.2d 566 (9th Cir.1955).   Compare Barton v. Perryman, 577 S.W.2d 596 (Ark.1979), a case in which the plaintiffs, as creditors, took a much more active part than "going along" with transactions affecting their claim. The court was divided on the issue of novation.

NOTES

   (1) *The Case of the Dancers' Faux Pas.*   Mr. and Mrs. Philip Seale signed up with the Dale Dance Studio, a corporation, for a series of lessons, paying some $200.   They became dissatisfied, and Dale arranged for them to complete the lessons at the Bates Dance Studio, also a corporation.   At the end of this series they contracted with Bates for another series of 600 lessons.   These lessons were interrupted by illness, and when the Seales returned they found that Bates had assigned the contract to the Dale Studio which undertook to complete performance for Bates.   They were told that the entire Bates organization was transferred to Dale, and that they would have the same instructors and instruction as before.   However, the Seales found the lessons unsatisfactory and made unsuccessful complaints: the rooms were small, crowded and noisy, and the couple had to share an instructor, a Mr. Ritchie.   After some 30 sessions at the Dale Studio they stopped attending, and subsequently sued Bates and Dale to recover the cost of the lessons.   *Held:* For the defendants.

   "The argument of plaintiffs that this was a personal service contract and therefore non-assignable without their consent is valid. . . .   Had they refused to receive instruction from Dale and had they taken the position that their contract was with Bates and no other, there would be substance to their present contention that this violation justified the rescission.   [But they accepted the assignment.]   While we sympathize with Mr. Seale's preference for Miss Valie over Mr. Ritchie, we do not consider this a breach of a promise implicit in the contract. . . .   It is probable that Mrs. Seale preferred to be taught by Mr. Ritchie.   It thus appears to us that the proper remedy for this problem is an express stipulation in the contract requiring a partner of the opposite sex." Seale v. Bates, 359 P.2d 356 (Colo.1961).

   (2) *The Code.*   Consult UCC 2–210(4) in relation to the following case: "A sells and delivers an automobile to B, the price to be paid in installments, and

a. Sometimes novation is defined to embrace not only the substitution of one debtor for another, but a substitution of creditors as well, and even the substitution of a new debt or obligation for an existing one between the same parties. But it is said that in any of these situations "the old debt must be extinguished." Davenport v. Dickson, 507 P.2d 301 (Kan.1973).

assigns to C for value 'all A's rights under the contract.' After B has made all the payments, the automobile is discovered to have been stolen and is retaken by the owner. C is not liable to B for breach of warranty of title; A is." Restatement Second § 328, Illustration 3. How can it be explained, under the Code, that C is not liable to B? Note the parenthesis in the Code section. The Restatement comment, to which the illustration is appended, directs attention (via other sections) to UCC 1–201(37), the third sentence.

Introductory Note to *Sally Beauty Co.*

As this case is read, the Note above on Sales of Goods (p. 947) should be kept in mind.

There is an idea in the law that "in dealing with a corporation a party cannot rely on what may be termed the human equation in the company." New York Bank Note Co. v. Hamilton Bank Note Engraving & Printing Co., 73 N.E. 48, 52 (N.Y.1905). A reading of cases from New York courts has raised a doubt that they "would impose the same implied duty of personal service upon a contracting corporation as [they] would on an individual under the same circumstances." Arnold Productions, Inc. v. Favorite Films Corp., 298 F.2d 540 (2d Cir.1962). This might suggest that in the Case of the Baltimore Buyer, Note 3, p. 948 above, the case would have been different if the seller (Frederick) had conducted his business in corporate form. Or that the case would have been different if he had simply incorporated his business, and transferred the contract to the corporation.

In contrast, when there is a change in the membership of a professional partnership, having ongoing services contracts with clients, there is often good reason to doubt that the "new firm" may maintain the entitlements of the former partnership as of right.

Yet the decisions relating to delegation of contract obligations do not insist on a sharp dichotomy. Something of a "personal character" has been ascribed to a corporation, owing to its distinctive charter powers and the applicable laws governing the liabilities of its officers and stockholders. See the first case cited above. For partnership cases an illustration is City of North Kansas City v. Sharp, 414 F.2d 359 (8th Cir.1969). "The essence of the professional service cases," the court said, "is that the critical partner, for one reason or another, is no longer available to render those services. Here the critical partners were available and the record indicates ... that they were able to, and did, function collectively."

In the opinions that follow serious questions are raised about the degree of "personal trust and confidence" that existed in an intercorporate relation, as compared with that between, say, a lawyer and a client.

SALLY BEAUTY CO. v. NEXXUS PRODUCTS CO.

United States Court of Appeals, Seventh Circuit, 1986.
801 F.2d 1001.

CUDAHY, CIRCUIT JUDGE. [In July of 1981 the Best Barber Beauty & Supply Company was acquired by, and merged into, the Sally Beauty Company, a Dallas-based firm. Both firms were distributors of hair care and beauty products to retail stores and hair styling salons. Sally Beauty succeeded to Best's rights and interests in all of Best's contracts. One of these was a letter agreement of August 2, 1979, with Nexxus Products, a California firm founded in that year, which formulates and markets hair care products through independent distributors. The agreement provided for introducing and promoting Nexxus products in the Texas market; it made Best the exclusive distributor of these in Texas (except for El Paso). Prices to Best were specified; and Nexxus agreed to provide support, such as maintaining a technician in the territory and helping to pay for an annual seminar, with "guest artist." Nexxus agreed not to terminate the agreement except on an anniversary date, and then upon 120 days' notice and upon buying back Best's inventory of Nexxus products at cost. "[We] look forward to a long and successful business relationship," Best wrote.

[Nexxus renounced its obligations when Best was merged into Sally Beauty. Sally Beauty was a wholly-owned subsidiary of a company (Alberto–Culver) which is a major manufacturer of hair-care products and, thus, a direct competitor of Nexxus in the hair-care market: "we have great reservations about allowing our NEXXUS products to be distributed by a company which is, in essence, a direct competitor."

[Sally Beauty sued Nexxus, charging it with breach of contract and violation of the antitrust laws. Nexxus made a motion for summary judgment on the former claim.] Nexxus ... argued that the distribution agreement it entered into with Best was a contract for personal services, based upon a relationship of personal trust and confidence between Reichek and the Redding family. As such, the contract could not be assigned to Sally without Nexxus's consent.

In opposing this motion Sally Beauty argued that the contract was freely assignable because (1) it was between two corporations, not two individuals and (2) the character of the performance would not be altered by the substitution of Sally Beauty for Best....

In ruling on this motion, the district court [said]:

> ... [I]n this case the circumstances surrounding the contract's formation support the conclusion that the agreement was not simply an ordinary commercial contract but was one which was based upon a relationship of personal trust and confidence between the parties. Specifically, Stephen Redding, Nexxus's vice-president, travelled to Texas and met with Best's president personally for several days before making the decision to award the Texas distributorship to Best. Best itself had been in the hair care business for 40 years and

its president Mark Reichek had extensive experience in the industry. It is reasonable to conclude that Stephen Redding and Nexxus would want its distributor to be experienced and knowledgeable in the hair care field and that the selection of Best was based upon personal factors such as these.

. . .

We cannot affirm this summary judgment on the grounds relied on by the district court. . . .   Although it might be "reasonable to conclude" that Best and Nexxus had based their agreement on "a relationship of personal trust and confidence," and that Reicheck's participation was considered essential to Best's performance, this is a finding of fact. . . .

We may affirm this summary judgment, however, on a different ground if it finds support in the record. . . . Sally Beauty contends that the distribution agreement is freely assignable because it is governed by the provisions of the Uniform Commercial Code (the "UCC" or the "Code"), as adopted in Texas.[1]   . . .

III.

. . . Texas applies the "dominant factor" test to determine whether the UCC applies to a given contract or transaction: was the essence of or dominant factor in the formation of the contract the provision of goods or services?   . . . We are confident that a Texas court would find the sales aspect of this contract dominant and apply the majority rule that such a distributorship is a contract for "goods" under the UCC.

IV.

. . .

We are concerned here with the delegation of Best's duty of performance under the distribution agreement, as Nexxus terminated the agreement because it did not wish to accept Sally Beauty's substituted performance.[2]   . . .

In the exclusive distribution agreement before us, Nexxus had contracted for Best's "best efforts" in promoting the sale of Nexxus products in Texas. UCC § 2–306(2). . . .   It was this contractual undertaking which Nexxus refused to see performed by Sally.

. . . [We] hold that Sally Beauty's position as a wholly-owned subsidiary of Alberto–Culver is sufficient to bar the delegation of Best's duties under the agreement.

---

1. The parties agree that the contract is governed by the law of Texas. . . .

2. If this contract is assignable, Sally Beauty would also, of course, succeed to Best's rights under the distribution agreement. But the fact situation before us must be distinguished from the assignment of contract rights that are no longer executory (*e.g.,* the right to damages for breach or the right to payment of an account), which is considered in UCC section 2–210(2), Tex.Bus. & Com.Code Ann. § 2–210(b) (Vernon 1968), and in several of the authorities relied on by appellants. The policies underlying these two situations are different and, generally, the UCC favors assignment more strongly in the latter. See UCC § 2–210(2) (non-executory rights assignable even if agreement states otherwise).

We do not believe that our holding will work the mischief with our national economy that the appellants predict. We hold merely that the duty of performance under an exclusive distributorship may not be delegated to a competitor in the market place—or the wholly-owned subsidiary of a competitor—without the obligee's consent. We believe that such a rule is consonant with the policies behind section 2–210, which is concerned with preserving the bargain the obligee has struck. Nexxus should not be required to accept the "best efforts" of Sally Beauty when those efforts are subject to the control of Alberto–Culver. It is entirely reasonable that Nexxus should conclude that this performance would be a different thing than what it had bargained for. At oral argument, Sally Beauty argued that the case should go to trial to allow it to demonstrate that it could and would perform the contract as impartially as Best. It stressed that Sally Beauty is a "multi-line" distributor, which means that it distributes many brands and is not just a conduit for Alberto–Culver products. But we do not think that this creates a material question of fact in this case.[3] When performance of personal services is delegated, the trier merely determines that it is a personal services contract. If so, the duty is *per se* nondelegable. There is no inquiry into whether the delegate is as skilled or worthy of trust and confidence as the original obligor: the delegate was not bargained for and the obligee need not consent to the substitution.[4] And so here: it is undisputed that Sally Beauty is wholly owned by Alberto–Culver, which means that Sally Beauty's "impartial" sales policy is at least acquiesced in by Alberto–Culver—but could change whenever Alberto–Culver's needs changed. Sally Beauty may be totally sincere in its belief that it can operate "impartially" as a distributor, but who can guarantee the outcome when there is a clear choice between the demands of the parent-manufacturer, Alberto–Culver, and the competing needs of Nexxus? The risk of an unfavorable outcome is not one which the law can force Nexxus to take. Nexxus has a substantial interest in not seeing this contract performed by Sally Beauty, which is sufficient to bar the delegation under section 2–210.... Because Nexxus should not be forced to accept performance of the distributorship agreement by Sally, we hold that the contract was not assignable without Nexxus' consent.[5]

The judgment of the district court is AFFIRMED.

3. We do not address here the situation in which the assignee is not completely under the control of a competitor. If the assignee were only a partially-owned subsidiary, there presumably would have to be fact-finding about the degree of control the competitor-parent had over the subsidiary's business decisions.

4. Of course, the obligee makes such an assessment of the prospective delegate. If it thinks the delegated performance will be as satisfactory, it is of course free to consent to the delegation. Thus, the dissent is mistaken in its suggestion that we find it improper—a "conflict of interest"—for one competitor to distribute another competi-

tor's products. Rather, we believe only that it is commercially reasonable that the supplier in those circumstances have consented to such a state of affairs. To borrow the dissent's example, Isuzu allows General Motors to distribute its cars because it considers this arrangement attractive.

Nor is distrust of one's competitors a trait unique to lawyers (as opposed to ordinary businessmen), as the dissent may be understood to suggest.

5. This disposition makes it unnecessary to address Nexxus' argument that Sally Beauty breached the distribution agreement by not giving Nexxus 120 days' notice of the Best–Sally Beauty merger.

POSNER, CIRCUIT JUDGE, dissenting....[a] My brethren find this a simple case—as simple (it seems) as if a lawyer had undertaken to represent the party opposing his client. But notions of conflict of interest are not the same in law and in business, and judges can go astray by assuming that the legal-services industry is the pattern for the entire economy. The lawyerization of America has not reached that point. Sally Beauty, though a wholly owned subsidiary of Alberto–Culver, distributes "hair care" supplies made by many different companies, which so far as appears compete with Alberto–Culver as vigorously as Nexxus does. Steel companies both make fabricated steel and sell raw steel to competing fabricators. General Motors sells cars manufactured by a competitor, Isuzu. What in law would be considered a fatal conflict of interest is in business a commonplace and legitimate practice. The lawyer is a fiduciary of his client; Best was not a fiduciary of Nexxus.

How likely is it that the acquisition of Best could hurt Nexxus? Not very. Suppose Alberto–Culver had ordered Sally Beauty to go slow in pushing Nexxus products, in the hope that sales of Alberto–Culver "hair care" products would rise. Even if they did, since the market is competitive Alberto–Culver would not reap monopoly profits. Moreover, what guarantee has Alberto–Culver that consumers would be diverted from Nexxus to it, rather than to products closer in price and quality to Nexxus products? In any event, any trivial gain in profits to Alberto–Culver would be offset by the loss of goodwill to Sally Beauty; and a cost to Sally Beauty is a cost to Alberto–Culver, its parent. Remember that Sally Beauty carries beauty supplies made by other competitors of Alberto–Culver; Best alone carries "hair care" products manufactured by Revlon, Clairol, Bristol–Myers, and L'Oreal, as well as Alberto–Culver. Will these powerful competitors continue to distribute their products through Sally Beauty if Sally Beauty displays favoritism for Alberto–Culver products? Would not such a display be a commercial disaster for Sally Beauty, and hence for its parent, Alberto–Culver? Is it really credible that Alberto–Culver would sacrifice Sally Beauty in a vain effort to monopolize the "hair care" market, in violation of section 2 of the Sherman Act? Is not the ratio of the profits that Alberto–Culver obtains from Sally Beauty to the profits it obtains from the manufacture of "hair care" products at least a relevant consideration?

Another relevant consideration is that the contract between Nexxus and Best was for a short term. Could Alberto–Culver destroy Nexxus by failing to push its products with maximum vigor in Texas for a year? In the unlikely event that it could and did, it would be liable in damages to Nexxus for breach of the implied best-efforts term of the distribution contract. Finally, it is obvious that Sally Beauty does not have a bottleneck position in the distribution of "hair care" products, such that by refusing to promote Nexxus products vigorously it could stifle the

a. Judge Posner observed that Alberto–Culver's products "mostly are cheaper than Nexxus's, and are sold to the public primarily through grocery stores and drugstores."

distribution of those products in Texas; for Nexxus has found alternative distribution that it prefers—otherwise it wouldn't have repudiated the contract with Best when Best was acquired by Sally Beauty.

Not all businessmen are consistent and successful profit maximizers, so the probability that Alberto–Culver would instruct Sally Beauty to cease to push Nexxus products vigorously in Texas cannot be reckoned at zero. On this record, however, it is slight. And there is no principle of law that if something happens that trivially reduces the probability that a dealer will use his best efforts, the supplier can cancel the contract.... At most, so far as the record shows, Nexxus may have had grounds for "insecurity" regarding the performance by Sally Beauty of its obligation to use its best efforts to promote Nexxus products, but if so its remedy was not to cancel the contract but to demand assurances of due performance. See UCC § 2–609; Official Comment 5 to § 2–306. No such demand was made. An anticipatory repudiation by conduct requires conduct that makes the repudiating party unable to perform. Farnsworth, Contracts 636 (1982). The merger did not do this. At least there is no evidence it did. The judgment should be reversed and the case remanded for a trial on whether the merger so altered the conditions of performance that Nexxus is entitled to declare the contract broken.

NOTES

(1) *Big Fish, Little Fish.* Should a franchise holder be permitted to object to an assignment conferring rights on a new firm, as assignee, on the ground that the franchisee is a financial weakling in relation to that firm? In Schultze v. Chevron Oil Co., 579 F.2d 776 (3d Cir.1978), an industry giant (Chevron) obtained rights under a lease from a lesser firm (Morris Oil Co.). One of the judges speculated as follows on the consequences for the obligors: "If Morris' bargaining position was significantly less powerful than that of a major oil company, it would follow that the Schultzes could expect that in enforcing its right of first refusal, Morris would be forced to be more accommodating than a major oil company, since its position would not be as strong." (Adams, J., dissenting at 780, 783, fn. 20) Is this reasoning questionable on the ground that it tends to make the assets of the Morris Company less marketable?

Do you find an indication that the power, position or personality of the assignee counts, in this matter, in the provisions on assignability of the Code— UCC 2–210—or the Restatement—§ 317?

(2) *Clean Hands.* In August, 1969, the owners of the Oakland "Oaks" basketball club contracted to sell all its assets to the Washington Capitols Basketball Club, Inc. One of its assets, valued at three-quarters of a million dollars, was a contract for the services of the star player Richard "Rick" Barry. He had signed with the Oaks for a three-year term in 1967. The day after the sale, Barry contracted to play for the San Francisco "Warriors." The Washington club brought an action against him in equity, seeking an injunction against his playing for the Warriors.

One of the defenses was based on the curious events of 1967, leading up to Barry's contract with the Oaks. It appears that he had previously had a contract with the Warriors club, and that the owners of the Oaks had induced him to play for them in violation of that contract. An objection to the injunction, then, was based on the maxim: "He who comes into equity must come with clean hands." (See Note, p. 481 above.) The court granted a preliminary injunction, ruling that the suitor, Washington, should not be barred by the offense of its assignor, the Oakland Club. The relation between an assignee and his assignor is relatively remote, the court said, for purposes of the maxim. Washington Capitols Basketball Club, Inc. v. Barry, 304 F.Supp. 1193 (N.D.Cal.1969). (The court observed that the Warriors club had had Barry enjoined from playing with the Oaks in 1967–68.)

How can it be supposed that a contract so "personal" as this one was assignable at all? The opinion discusses the point.

(3) *Nexxus vs. Best Barber.* Suppose that Best Barber had not been merged into Sally Beauty, but had simply assigned the Nexxus contract to it, retaining its independent existence. And suppose that *Nexxus Products* had sued *Best Barber* for breach of their agreement. Does it follow from the decision in Sally Beauty v. Nexxus Products that that suit would be successful?

In the Case of the Baltimore Buyer, Note 3, p. 948 above, the court said that the attempted assignment by Frederick of his ice-purchase contract was a "repudiation [by him] of any future liability." That seems to mean that, in the case supposed, Nexxus Products could hold Best Barber accountable for any damages it suffered from the assignment.

However that may be, the Code rather clearly indicates a way for Nexxus Products to establish a damage claim. See UCC 2–210(5) and the final clause of UCC 2–609: ". . . is a repudiation of the contract." These sections permit the non-assigning party to demand assurances from *both* the assignee and the assignor in a proper case, do they not? If only one of them responds, but that one is unquestionably willing and able to perform, should that count as an "adequate assurance" on behalf of both?

(4) *Nexxus vs. Sally Beauty.* Did the merger of Best Barber into Sally Beauty establish Nexxus Products as a third party beneficiary of a contract between the merging parties?

DELEGATION DISPUTED

A provision of the Uniform Commercial Code addresses a problem that sometimes arises when an assignment is made of "the contract," or of "all my rights under the contract," or is made "in similar general terms". The effect is that the duties of the assignor are delegated and that the assignee's acceptance "constitutes a promise by him to perform those duties," subject to the qualification that "the language or the circumstances (as in an assignment for security) [may] indicate the contrary." See UCC 2–210(4).[a] Hence a buyer of goods, assigning "all my rights" under the contract of purchase, can readily confer on the seller a right to payment against the assignee.

a. As to the parenthetical language see BAII Banking Corp. v. UPG, Inc., 985 F.2d 685, 696 (2d Cir.1993). See also Allstate Financial Corp. v. Utility Trailer of Illinois, Inc., 1994 WL 33965 (N.D.Ill.1994) (counterclaim by customer of defunct truck-services firm against its factor: "one of the most bizarre theories advanced before this court in recent memory").

The Restatement Second contains a similar rule, adding that in appropriate circumstances the nonassigning party "is an intended beneficiary" of the assignee's (inferred) promise. See section 328(2). To that section, however, the Restatement appends the following *Caveat:*

> The [American Law] Institute expresses no opinion as to whether the rule stated in Subsection (2) applies to an assignment by a purchaser of his rights under a contract for the sale of land.[b]

More than doctrinal difficulties may be at work, however. In a current case the court said:

> [T]here can be no implied assumption of contractual liabilities in real estate transactions. Because of the complexity of these transactions, the large amounts of money that are typically involved, and the customary presumption that the only obligations are those which have been expressed, a rule that would permit the inadvertent assumption of debt is inappropriate.

Davey v. Nessan, 830 P.2d 92, 96 (Mont.1992). A leading case is Langel v. Betz, 164 N.E. 890 (N.Y.1928) (Cardozo, J.; referring to Lawrence v. Fox and Seaver v. Ransom, pp. 865 and 872 above).

NOTE

The "Continuation" Theory. It has been held that a firm acquiring the assets of another, in bulk, thereby becomes bound to a contract obligation undertaken by the predecessor firm. See, however, Carstedt v. Grindeland, 406 N.W.2d 39 (Minn.App.1987), in which the successor firm discontinued paying royalties under a licensing agreement made by its predecessor. In an action by the licensor against the successor firm, the plaintiff relied on the "mere continuation" theory to establish the defendant's liability. The trial court entered summary judgment for the defendant, and the plaintiff appealed. *Held:* Affirmed.

The court observed that the defendant could rightfully use the device that was the subject of the license (a "paper decurling device"), so far as patent law was concerned. And it said (quoting) that "the 'continuation' exception to the general rule 'refers principally to a "reorganization" of the original corporation,' usually accomplished under federal bankruptcy law or statute."

SECTION 3.　FINANCING CONSUMER CREDIT

The main topic of this Section is foreshadowed in the Note, Hell–or–High–Water Clauses, p. 438 above. This Section presents the business setting and develops the doctrines and policies affecting the topic.

---

b. The 1932 Restatement stated a rule of presumptive delegation without reference to any exception: section 164. In 1967, during deliberations over the Restatement Second, the Institute voted on the choice between the Caveat (avoiding a pronouncement on the matter) and a statement that land-sale contracts are exceptional. The Caveat won, 47–44.

Mr. John Q. Public buys a new Thunderwagen car from the Potluck Motor Company. The purchase is on "time," because John does not have cash enough to pay the full price at once. He signs a promissory note in favor of the Motor Company for the price of the car, interest, and certain other charges, less the down payment. It calls for equal monthly payments over the course of four years. At the same time both the Motor Company (as Seller) and John (as Customer) sign a "Conditional Sale Contract." The critical feature of the contract is this sentence: "Title to the car is retained by Seller until said time balance is fully paid in money to the holder hereof (meaning Seller or its assignee if this contract is assigned) when title shall pass to Customer." The contract is lengthy, and contains many clauses in rather fine print. Permission for the Seller to seize the car in the event of John's default is expressly reserved.

The Motor Company wishes to maintain a full inventory of cars. Since it has to pay cash to the manufacturer before delivery, it does not have the additional funds necessary to finance its customers. For this purpose it has a long-standing arrangement with a finance company, the Thunderwagen Acceptance Corporation (TACO). In accordance with this agreement, TACO credits the Motor Company with all of the time balance owing under the conditional sale contract, less a "discount." In return, the Motor Company executes a "Dealer's Assignment" form appearing on the back of the contract, indorses John's note, and delivers both instruments to TACO. The first sentence of the assignment form is as follows: "We hereby sell and assign the contract on the reverse side and all interest in the car ... to you ... with full power to you in your or our name to collect and discharge the same and to take all such legal or other proceedings as we might take, save for this assignment." TACO sends notice to John that he should make the monthly payments directly to it. It encloses a handy coupon book for keeping the account straight. Steps may be taken, depending on local law, to reflect the fact that the car is subject to an encumbrance, or security interest. (Ordinarily a notation to that effect would be made on the buyer's certificate of title.) When John completes his payments, he then has the car free of TACO's security interest and can obtain a suitable record of his unencumbered title.

A transaction more or less like the one described occurs in connection with most consumer purchases of cars in this country, and the volume of credit generated is enormous. Sometimes the security agreement taken by the dealer and assigned to the finance company takes the form of a chattel mortgage rather than a conditional sale contract. Not only automobile purchases, but also purchases of many kinds of durable consumer goods (furniture, appliances, etc.) are similarly financed. And so it is with the purchase of items of business equipment ranging from barber chairs to drilling rigs. Some finance companies specialize in particular lines of business—the name TACO suggests an affiliation with the manufacturer of Thunderwagen cars. Others are not specialized, and commercial banks generally engage in financing on the same basis.

NOTES

(1) *Another Version.* In a "plain language" form of John's contract with the dealer, set out in the Selections, there is no title-reservation provision, but this instead: "I am giving a security interest in the motor vehicle being purchased.... Seller intends to assign this Contract to the Assignee named below." The form is titled "Retail Installment Contract."

(2) *Dealer's Finance Agreement.* By the agreement between the Motor Company and TACO, the assignment of John's contract might be made "without recourse," so that the Motor Company would be under no liability to TACO in the event of the customer's default in making payments. However, certainly with respect to a new-car sale, it would more probably be agreed that the Motor Company would repurchase the car from TACO if it be repossessed as a result of the customer's default. The amount credited to the Motor Company in connection with the assignment of John's contract would depend on that and a number of other factors. "In automobile financing under a repurchase arrangement, the financing agency ordinarily pays into a reserve account a portion of the finance charge on paper purchased from a particular dealer. Such payments continue until the account reaches either a minimum dollar amount or, more commonly, a percentage of the dealer's outstanding paper (usually three percent). Upon default by a buyer and repossession by the financer, the dealer is obligated to repurchase the vehicle, and the unpaid balance of the note is charged to the reserve account.... Once the stipulated reserve account balance is attained, subsequent sums payable under the dealer-participation agreement are periodically distributed to the dealer. Since the dealer's share of the finance charges typically ranges from one-fifth to one-third, dealer participation constitutes a major element of his income." Warren, Regulation of Finance Charges, 68 Yale L.J. 839, 859 (1959).

(3) *Assignee's Rights.* The principal problem of this Section may be stated as follows: after the assignment, is the contract, in the hands of TACO, subject to the defenses that John might have made against the dealer? On the facts so far given, the answer is certainly "yes." When sued by the assignee, the buyer's defense is most often based on breach of warranty by the seller, or other nonperformance, or on a misrepresentation inducing the buyer to contract. All these and many other defenses are available to the buyer to the same extent they would be if the dealer itself were suing for the purchase price.

If an assignee bank or finance company finds that the contract is unenforceable by reason of the seller's conduct it will invariably have a claim against the seller. The claim may be based on an implied warranty of the assignor. Or it may be based on express warranties accompanying the assignment. For examples of such warranties see Warner v. Seaboard Finance Company, 345 P.2d 759 (Nev.1959), concerning the assignment of an installment contract for storm windows and awnings. Among other things, the dealer warranted to the finance company that the contracts he assigned would be valid and enforceable obligations of the customer, signed by him, and that "ethical and proper selling practice will be followed."

The assignee must consider the possibility, however, that the dealer will be unable to respond to such a claim, by reason of insolvency, when the time comes to enforce it. For this reason, chiefly, financing institutions have not been content to take assignments of contracts "subject to defenses" that the customer, or obligor, may have against the assignor. The law has traditionally provided means for them to "take free" of such defenses, and the efficacy of these means is to be considered in this section. In most of the cases presenting the issue there is a loss attributable to substandard performance by a dealer in goods or services, and it must be allocated either to the customer or to the financing assignee. If the dealer is available for suit, and able to pay a judgment, the problem is not an acute one. In considering the materials to follow, you should assume that that is not the case.

———

WAIVING DEFENSES AND HOLDING IN DUE COURSE

Two principal arrangements are available for permitting an assignee to take free of an obligor's defenses against the assignor. Each requires a specialized form of expression for the obligor's undertaking. One relies on the law of negotiable instruments, and the object is to give the assignee status as a "holder in due course." The other relies on a term in the assigned contract known as a waiver-of-defense clause. For consumer transactions, at least, such clauses are now more commonly used than negotiable instruments. But the issues they raise are similar to those associated with negotiability.

Both arrangements are illustrated in Unico v. Owen, 232 A.2d 405 (N.J.1967), which concerned the sale of 140 record albums, to be delivered and paid for in installments (with a "free" record player thrown in). That sale contract is the source of the following waiver-of-defense clause:

> Buyer hereby acknowledges notice that the contract may be assigned and that assignees will rely upon the agreements contained in this paragraph, and agrees that the liability of the Buyer to any assignee shall be immediate and absolute and not affected by any default whatsoever of the Seller signing this contract; and in order to induce assignees to purchase this contract, the Buyer further agrees not to set up any claim against such Seller as a defense, counterclaim or offset to any action by an assignee for the unpaid balance of the purchase price or for possession of the property.

The buyers received the record player, and 12 albums; but the remainder were never received because the seller became insolvent. The buyers stopped their monthly payments after a year, and were then sued by a finance company as assignee of their contract.

The same buyers had also signed a promissory note, negotiable in form, for the entire purchase price of the albums, payable in installments. The note had also been transferred to the finance company, and it sought to recover on the note as a holder in due course, in the technical sense. The case is unusual in that the documents were designed to give the finance company the advantages both of a waiver clause and of negotiability; but the object was the same: to deprive the buyers of defenses such as failure of consideration.

The definition and effects of negotiable instruments are now stated in Article 3 of the Uniform Commercial Code. For about half a century before the Code was drafted, the subject was governed by the Negotiable Instruments Law (NIL), the first of the "uniform laws." And for perhaps two centuries before that the essential characteristics of negotiable instruments were established in the common law.

When the obligation on the instrument takes the form of a promise, the instrument is known as a *promissory note* or simply a *note*. In order to be *negotiable,* however, the note must meet a number of other requirements: it must be signed by the maker, it must contain an unconditional promise to pay a sum certain in money, it must be payable on demand or at a definite time, and it must be payable to order or to bearer. Only if it meets these requirements is the note invested with the special characteristics of a negotiable instrument.

Chief among these characteristics is the protection of a good faith purchaser against defenses. When a negotiable instrument payable to bearer is transferred by delivery or when a negotiable instrument payable to order is transferred by a valid indorsement followed by delivery, the transfer is known as *negotiation* and the transferee is known as a *holder* of the instrument. A transferee who is a holder will, moreover, qualify as a *holder in due course* if these further conditions are met: the transferee takes the instrument for value, in good faith, and without notice that it is overdue or has been dishonored or of any defense against or claim to it. Thus in order to be a holder in due course, a transferee must show: first, that the instrument is negotiable; second, that it took by negotiation, as a holder; and third, that it took in due course. If the transferee can do all this, then its right against the maker is not subject to a defense that would be available if the transferee were enforcing a right to payment under a "simple contract."[a] (The transferee's right is, however, subject to certain exceptional defenses known as *real* defenses. These include incapacity, duress, and an unusual species of fraud.) The defenses that a holder in due course overcomes are known as *personal* defenses: they include such common matters as want of consideration, failure of condition, breach of warranty in the sale of goods, and most cases of fraud.

NOTES

(1) *Defenses of a Law Firm.* Although the case that follows is not a *consumer* financing case, it illustrates some of the problems associated with a waiver-of-defense clause. In particular, it is an application of UCC 9–206(1), set out in footnote a at p. 925 above (and in the Selections). In preparation for reading the case, see again the Note, Hell-or-High-Water Clauses, p. 438 above.

In reading this subsection, it may be helpful to see it as having three main parts. First, the section broadly validates waiver-of-defense clauses, in favor of certain assignees. Second, in the concluding sentence a transferee of a negotiable instrument is placed on at least as strong a footing as an assignee relying on a waiver-of-defense clause.[b] Third, the section begins with a curious qualification referring to non-Code law. This phrase is explained in Comment 2 as follows: "This Article takes no position on the controversial question whether a buyer of consumer goods may effectively waive defenses by contractual clause or

---

a. UCC 3–305(b) (revised text).

b. Note that the section does not require that the transferee be a holder taking the instrument by negotiation.

by execution of a negotiable note." The opinion that follows indicates some elements in that controversy.

(2) *Meaning of "Consumer".* The Uniform Commercial Code, true to its name, was meant to leave consumer-protection laws in place, for the most part.[c] It does not give special treatment to consumers, and so has no definition for the class. It does, however, embody special rules about "consumer goods" [d] as defined in section 9–109(1): "used or bought for use primarily for personal, family or household purposes." Some form of this expression is regularly used (often with qualifiers) to identify the beneficiaries of reform legislation. More artful definitions of "consumer" can readily be thought of; [e] but it has been rightly observed that "no legal definition, however sophisticated, could adequately cater for all borderline cases." [f]

CHEMICAL BANK v. RINDEN PROFESSIONAL ASSOCIATION
Supreme Court of New Hampshire, 1985.
126 N.H. 688, 498 A.2d 706.

[A firm named Intertel installed an office telephone system for a law firm (Rinden) under a lease-purchase agreement made in April, 1974. The contract required monthly payments into 1982, at which time Rinden might purchase the equipment for a dollar. Thereafter Rinden received written notice that the Chemical Bank expected to purchase from Intertel the payment rights. This document required Rinden's assent to its terms; and on June 11 Rinden's office manager, John Satterfield, read and signed it. One of its terms included this provision:

As Lessee, you ... agree as follows: (a) that your obligation to pay directly to the Assignee [bank] the amounts which come due as rentals as set forth in said Lease shall be absolutely unconditional and shall be payable whether or not the Lease is terminated [in any way] and you promise to pay the same notwithstanding any defense, set-off or counterclaim whatsoever, [by] breach or otherwise, which you may or might now or hereafter have as against the Lessor [Intertel].

After receiving the signed document, the bank paid Intertel $8,800 and received an assignment of the payment rights.

[After three years of payments to the bank, the phone system began to malfunction seriously. Rinden replaced it and refused to make further payments to the bank. A three-party lawsuit ensued, which resulted in a master's report in 1984. In the meanwhile, Intertel had gone into bankruptcy.

c. See UCC 9–201 and Comment.

d. For examples of special rules about transactions in consumer goods see UCC 9–204(2) and 9–505, as well as 9–206(1).

e. Consider such a "business" transaction as the purchase of a car by a doctor.

Because we are all consumers, it has been said, it is somewhat crass to classify any of us as such. Skilton & Helstad, Protection of the Installment Buyer of Goods Under the UCC, 65 Mich.L.Rev. 1465 (1967).

f. Exemption Clauses in Contracts, First Report of the [English] Law Commission, etc., 30–32 (1969).

[The report favored the bank. Rinden appealed, contesting a finding that the waiver clause was enforceable. In part, the objection was that the provision was unconscionable. The court rejected that contention.]

DOUGLAS, JUSTICE. . . . This case is governed by the Uniform Commercial Code (UCC) as enacted in Massachusetts. See Mass.Gen.Laws Ann. chapter 106. The version of the provision of article 9 of the UCC applicable to this case, Mass.Gen.Laws Ann. ch. 106 § 9–206(1), is entitled "Agreement Not to Assert Defenses Against Assignee; Modification of Sales Warranties Where Security Agreement Exists" and reads:

[Here the court set out the statute, identical in terms to UCC 9–206(1), except that the Massachusetts version omitted any reference to the parties to a lease. The court concluded that Article 9 applied because the "lease" fit the UCC definition of a security agreement.] [a]

. . . The requirements of a valid waiver are that there was an agreement by a buyer, who is not a consumer, to waive defenses against an assignee and that the assignment was made for value, in good faith, and without notice of a claim or defense. . . . We find that these requirements were met so that the defendant validly waived his defenses against Chemical Bank.

The master found that Rinden agreed to the waiver of defenses clause, and the evidence supports this view. . . .

The defendant does not claim that it is a consumer so as to make Mass.Gen.Laws Ann. ch. 106 § 9–206(1) inapplicable on that account. The defendant is a professional association, a law firm, not in need of special protections often provided for unwary consumers. See, e.g., Mass.Gen.Laws Ann. ch. 106 § 2–719; Mass.Gen.Laws Ann. ch. 255 § 12c; Mass.Gen.Laws Ann. ch. 93A; see also RSA 382–A:3–205–a (Supp.1983).

Next we must determine whether there is sufficient evidence to support the master's findings that Chemical Bank took the assignment for value, in good faith, and without notice of a claim or defense. As to the first issue, Chemical Bank paid Intertel over $8,800 for the assignment of Intertel's rights in the defendant's contract.

As to the next requirement, the defendant asserts that Chemical Bank is not a good faith purchaser, mainly because the plaintiff and Intertel were too closely connected. Nothing in the record indicates, however, that the relationship between Intertel and Chemical Bank was anything other than an arms-length commercial relationship.

William Tupka, the Chemical Bank employee in charge of the Intertel account, testified that Chemical Bank's course of dealing in purchasing the rights to the Rinden contract from Intertel was typical of its transactions with hundreds of other clients with which it had entered into similar agreements. Chemical Bank and Intertel were not related

a. UCC 1–201(37).

corporations, having common directors or owning shares of stock in each other. Nor was Chemical the only bank to lend to Intertel.

Finally, the facts that Chemical Bank checked Rinden's credit rating and insisted upon an insertion of a waiver of defenses clause, before it would purchase the assignment, certainly do not prove lack of good faith as Rinden claims. Both Mr. Tupka and Kenneth Barron, former president of Intertel, testified that these actions were standard procedure for a bank extending credit. Moreover, even if there was any evidence of interrelatedness, Massachusetts law appears to look with disfavor on the admission of past dealings between parties to show bad faith, absent some other indications of bad faith by the holder. See Bowling Green, Inc. v. State Street Bank and Trust Co., 425 F.2d 81, 85 (1st Cir.1970) (citing Universal C.I.T. Credit Corp. v. Ingel, 347 Mass. 119, 125, 196 N.E.2d 847, 852 (1964)).

There is also no basis to conclude that the master erred in finding that Chemical Bank took the assignment without notice of a claim or defense. Mr. Tupka testified that he came across nothing in his investigation of the Intertel account which would indicate that Rinden might have some kind of claim or defense relating to the lease agreement between it and Intertel. No evidence was introduced to contradict this testimony. . . .

The defendant next argues that even if the terms of Mass.Gen.Laws Ann. ch. 106 § 9–206(1) were complied with, the waiver of defenses is ineffective because it was given without consideration. The short answer to this is that none was required. Mass.Gen.Laws Ann. ch. 106 § 2–209(1) states that "[a]n agreement modifying a contract within this Article needs no consideration to be binding." . . .[a]

[The court rejected an argument grounded in public policy.]

We note that our decision today is in accord with the policy of the UCC in general, and of § 9–206(1) in particular, "to encourage the supplying of credit for the buying of goods by insulating the [institutional] lender from lawsuits over the quality of the goods." Massey–Ferguson Credit Corp. v. Brown, 169 Mont. 396, 402, 547 P.2d 846, 850 (1976) (quoting Massey–Ferguson, Inc. v. Utley, 439 S.W.2d 57, 60 (Ky.1969)). "A contrary holding would not only have a chilling effect on loans made by financial institutions but would mean that the law allows the plain meaning of covenants to be declared nugatory whenever a bad bargain results." B.V.D. Co. v. Marine Midland Bank–New York, 46 A.D.2d 51, 53, 360 N.Y.S.2d 901, 904 (1974). . . .

Affirmed.

NOTES

(1) *The Merchant–Financer Link.* The court's discussion of "interrelatedness" ties in with other decisions in which it has been found that a close business

---

a. The argument next devolved around the defendant's contention that a provision of Article 2, such as that last cited, is inapplicable to a transaction within Article 9 of the Code. The court concluded that "Article 2 does apply to transactions in goods which involve both a sales contract and a security agreement."

connection between a merchant and a financer deprives the latter of the benefit of a waiver of defenses. "There are, of course, commercial cases in which a court has held that the seller and the alleged holder in due course were so closely linked that the entities were indistinguishable for purposes of the holder in due course doctrine.... In those cases the manufacturer's representative either assisted or participated in the sale by the dealer, and the manufacturer's course of dealing was, to furnish blank sales contracts to its dealer and to have the dealer assign the contract routinely as soon as the sale was made." Leasing Service Corp. v. River City Const., Inc., 743 F.2d 871 (11th Cir.1984). Is a decision like that justifiable on the ground that a closely-connected financer is in a position to monitor the merchant's selling practices and the quality of its products? Is a decision like that consistent with UCC 9–206?

(2) *Alternate Rationale.* The facts given in *Rinden* suggest (as one might suppose) that while the letter sent to Rinden was signed by Intertel, it was prepared by the bank and sent either by the bank or by Intertel as the bank's agent. Suppose, in addition, that a copy was to be returned to the bank. If that was so—and certainly if Rinden had addressed its response directly to the bank— it might not be necessary to rely on Article 9 of the Code to explain the decision.

Why could the decision not rest on a direct obligation undertaken by Rinden to the bank? Section 9–206 would not apply to that obligation, would it?

There might be a question, however, about consideration: What was given in exchange for Rinden's undertaking? The bank had already made its investment in the contract, apparently. (Rinden could of course bargain with the bank for it to make an advance, or a payment, to Intertel, if the bank had not already acted.) Possibly a promise by Rinden to the bank, if one was made, could be enforced on the basis of promissory estoppel. A showing of something in the way of reliance by the bank would be required. What kind of reliance might be shown? See Lataif v. Commercial Industrial Construction, Inc., described at p. 931 above.

(3) *Expressing the Waiver.* Examine again the contract language used in *Rinden:* "you promise to pay ... notwithstanding any defense...." The risk to a financer that less-expressive language can produce is shown in Noblett v. General Electric Credit Corporation, 400 F.2d 442 (10th Cir.1968), cert. denied, 393 U.S. 935 (1968), a case concerning a lease of bowling-alley equipment. The lease provided that, if the lessor should make an assignment, "the assignee shall not be held responsible for any of the lessor's obligations," and that the obligations of the lessee should "continue in full force and effect." Moreover: "Assignee shall have no obligations of lessor under said lease."

What purposes might these terms have, other than to immunize the assignee from defenses of the lessee? A possible purpose is suggested by a (later-enacted) provision of UCC Article 2A: section 2A–303(6)—a virtual rescript of UCC 2–210(4). Yet some of the language seems superfluous, unless a waiver of defenses was intended.

(4) *Variant State Rules.* The formulation of UCC 9–206(1) was sharply debated in the councils of the Code sponsors.[a] The decision was, of course, not to strive for uniformity on the issue of consumer protection. (Does that fact suggest any attitude that should be taken toward the business buyer?)

The issue of consumer protection has also been hard-fought in the legislatures and the courts. A number of states virtually deprive waiver-of-defense

a. As to the Code's neutrality on consumer credit issues see Skilton & Helstad, Protection of the Installment Buyer of Goods under the UCC, 65 Mich.L.Rev. 1465 (1967).

clauses—and holder-in-due-course status, with respect to notes—of their efficacy in ordinary consumer transactions.[b] Other statutes provide the consumer with a limited period for raising objections against paying the assignee. (In states of this persuasion, the inception and the duration of this period are variables.)

(5) *Gaps in the Fictional Fence.* Unico v. Owen, partially stated at p. 961 above, was a notable episode in the controversy over consumer defenses. Unico, the assignee of the contract, sued Owen, the buyer, and lost in the trial court. On successive appeals, the judgment was twice affirmed. The Supreme Court of New Jersey wrote an elaborate opinion, referring to Henningsen v. Bloomfield Motors (p. 402 above) and Williams v. Walker–Thomas Furniture Co. (p. 426 above), among other cases. It summarized some of them as follows:

"The courts have recognized that the basic problem in consumer goods sales and financing is that of balancing the interest of the commercial community in unrestricted negotiability of commercial paper against the interest of installment buyers of such goods in the preservation of their normal remedy of withholding payment when, as in this case, the seller fails to deliver as agreed, and thus the consideration for his obligation fails. Many courts have solved the problem by denying to the holder of the paper the status of holder in due course where the financer maintains a close relationship with the dealer whose paper he buys. . . . Other courts have said that when the financer supplies or prescribes or approves the form of sales contract, or conditional sale agreement, or chattel mortgage as well as the installment payment note (particularly if it has the financer's name printed on the face or in the endorsement), and all the documents are executed by the buyer at one time and the contract assigned and note endorsed to the financer and delivered to the financer together (whether or not attached or part of a single instrument), the holder takes subject to the rights and obligations of the seller. The transaction is looked upon as a species of tripartite proceeding, and the tenor of the cases is that the financer should not be permitted 'to isolate itself behind the fictional fence' of the Negotiable Instruments Law, and thereby achieve an unfair advantage over the buyer."

In this case the New Jersey court also considered the effect of a negotiable note given by Mr. Owen, on which Unico asserted rights as a holder in due course.[c]

(6) *Unconscionability.* In the main case, in addition to its other arguments, Rinden contended that the waiver-of-defense clause was unconscionable. What responses can you imagine on the part of the court?

---

b. See Uniform Consumer Credit Code § 3.307 and other sections cited in the Comment. A description and compilation of retail installment sales statutes as they affect assignment law appear in Introductory Note to Chapter 15 of Restatement Second.

c. On this point see also Jones v. Approved Bancredit Corp., 256 A.2d 739 (Del. 1969), a case said to be "especially analogous" to Unico v. Owen, and Rosenthal, Negotiability—Who Needs It?, 71 Colum.L.Rev. 375, 378–80 (1971). The *Unico* case was successfully defended for the Owens by private counsel, who accepted a "small fee" for representing them in the trial court. Unico appealed to an intermediate court, and then to the state supreme court. (What would justify this expense to a finance company? Was it worth it?) The Owens could not pay for appellate representation, but their lawyers espoused their cause through both appeals, plus supplementary briefing and argument requested by the supreme court. "We, of course, did not realize what we were getting into; however, once we were involved we had no choice but to proceed to the ultimate conclusion." During the proceedings Mr. Owen died, leaving his family without means, and they moved back to their former home in another state. The foregoing incidents are as reported in a letter to the editors from counsel for the Owens.

POLICY CONSIDERATIONS

Are there distinctive considerations of policy that underlie the decision in Unico v. Owen (preceding note) and the legislation referred to before that? To some extent these rules reflect only concern about the more general problems of standard form contracts. However, there have been attempts to show that the "holder in due course problem" is a singular one, deserving of specialized treatment. The following considerations figure in the argument.

(1) Financing institutions are in a superior position, by comparison with ordinary consumers, to evaluate the responsibility of a retail merchant or firm. The prospect of disappointment in dealing with a firm is partly a function of its usual business practices, its reputation for fair dealing, and the risk of its becoming insolvent. On all these matters a bank or finance company supplying it with funds is equipped to make judgments more accurately than its ordinary customers.

(2) Customers of a retail firm are poorly situated to exercise discipline against it for substandard business practices, whereas corrective measures may readily be forced on it by a financer if its retail operations give rise to an undue number of complaints. Hence a rule imposing on financers the risk of customer disappointment will effectively engage them in the function of "policing" against irresponsible merchandising.

(3) Pooling of information is an effective means of reducing substandard performance by merchants. Financing institutions are capable of organizing exchanges of information, such that a merchant who proves unworthy of trust will be promptly foreclosed from the credit market. By contrast, information exchanges among consumers are feebly organized, so that a retail firm may maintain a certain reputation with the public even though many of its customers suffer from its delinquencies. Not only so, but it may also be able to escape th eir wrath by a change of business name, or of location. Financing institutions can more easily penetrate disguises. Furthermore, when such an institution undertakes collections for a merchant the wrath of a disappointed customer is likely to be deflected from the merchant to the assignee.[a] Hence, the argument runs, it is appropriate to align the assignee with the customer as a party aggrieved by the merchant's delinquency. That is the effect when the assignee is deprived of holder-in-due-course status, and deprived of the benefit of a waiver-of-defense clause.[b]

None of these arguments need be taken at face value, of course. What countervailing considerations are there? It has been forcefully argued that, if merchants cannot give the assurances to financing institutions described as holder-in-due-course status, they will find credit more expensive, or inaccessible, and that the cost to merchants must be reflected in retail prices. How do you appraise this argument? If a rule

a. See Leff, Injury, Ignorance and Spite—The Dynamics of Coercive Collection, 80 Yale L.J. 1, 35 (1970).

b. An extensive statement of policy arguments tending in the same direction as these appears in a paper of the Federal Trade Commission published as an addendum to the F.T.C. Rule described next: Statement of Basis and Purpose, 40 Fed. Reg. 5306 (1975).

against cutting off defenses has any such consequence, would you expect it to affect only credit prices, or cash prices as well? Suppose that the buyers in Unico v. Owen had paid cash in advance for the merchandise. What would their remedy have been? Presumably any remedy you suggest would have been available to them on the facts as they were. Do you conclude that a disappointed cash buyer never has a better prospect of relief than one who pays by a negotiable note, and often has a worse one? Does this state of affairs make any sense? You should reconsider these questions after reading further in this section.

PRESERVATION OF CONSUMERS' CLAIMS AND DEFENSES

In 1976 the Federal Trade Commission took action against financers of consumer transactions by promulgating a three-part Rule requiring a "notice" provision in certain contracts.[c] The notice is prescribed in two forms, differing slightly as will be indicated. The first form is as follows (with brackets supplied):

> ANY HOLDER OF THIS CONSUMER CREDIT CONTRACT IS SUBJECT TO ALL CLAIMS AND DEFENSES WHICH THE DEBTOR COULD ASSERT AGAINST THE SELLER OF GOODS OR SERVICES OBTAINED [*PURSUANT HERETO OR*] WITH THE PROCEEDS HEREOF. RECOVERY HEREUNDER BY THE DEBTOR SHALL NOT EXCEED THE AMOUNTS PAID BY THE DEBTOR HEREUNDER.

The second form, which does not contain the bracketed words, is for inclusion in the documentation of certain loans.[d]

The Rule would not have required using either form of the notice in the lease-purchase agreement between Intertel and the Rinden Professional Association (see p. 963 above), for the notices are required only in a "consumer credit contract." The FTC Rule defines this expression[e] so as to include evidences of debt that arise either from a "purchase money loan" or from a "financed sale." Each of these expressions is restricted, by definition,[f] to a transaction in which credit is given to "a natural person who seeks or acquires goods or services for personal, family, or household use" (defined as a *consumer*[g]). If, however, Intertel had dealt with a consumer on the terms of the lease-purchase agreement, the Rule would have required it to include the entire notice set out above.[h]

The merit of the Rule was sharply contested when it was promulgated.[i]

---

c. 40 C.F.R. § 433 (1987).

References to the Rule in this Note are to § 433.1, unless otherwise noted.

d. Section 433.2.

e. Paragraph (i).

f. Paragraphs (d), (e).

g. Paragraph (b).

h. Unless the transaction was of a certain magnitude. The operative part of the Rule is a definition ("financing a sale") which is not of moment here. The Rule itself exempts certain transactions.

i. For a Comment highly critical of the Rule see 25 UCLA L.Rev. 821 (1978). For an attempt at empirical research on "holder in due course" reform, and a comment on

NOTES

(1) *Debt Cancellation.* When should a lender forgive a loan because the borrower is disappointed in goods that the borrower purchased with the loan proceeds? This question is addressed both in the FTC Rule and in various state statutes. In all cases the answer depends on a showing, in some form, of a measure of affiliation between the lender and the seller of the goods.

The New York statute on the subject [j] states circumstances in which a lender is presumed to be "directly connected" with a consumer sale. (E.g., forms used to evidence the loan were prepared by the seller.) Given the connection, it declares, "A creditor, who made a consumer loan the proceeds of which were primarily used in a consumer sale, shall be subject to all of the defenses of a consumer arising from such consumer sale."

A branch of the FTC Rule relates to loans, and requires that a "purchase money loan" [k] contract contain a version of the notice set out above. The Rule is not designed to affect routine lending contracts, even when the borrower discloses the purpose of using the loan proceeds to buy an item from a particular merchant. It applies either when the seller refers customers to the lender or when the seller is "affiliated with the creditor by common control, contract, or business arrangement." (In a case of strong affiliation, the sale transaction is sometimes described as a "specious cash sale," reflecting the fact that a loan is integral to the sale.)

In *Bank v. Rinden,* does it appear that the bank should take note of the New York statute, or of the FTC Rule, in making a loan to a consumer for the purchase of an Intertel telephone system?

(2) *Enforcement.* For a violation of the FTC Act, the Commission may claim a civil penalty or invoke other sanctions. That is not the intended thrust of the Rule, however. The effect intended is to deprive an assignee of the power to override the buyer's defenses by virtue of either negotiability or a waiver-of-defense clause. If the required notice appears, the assignee is hardly in a position to assert the immunity provided by those mechanisms.

But what if a seller flouts the law, omits the notice, and transfers a "clean" embodiment of the debt? So far as the Rule goes, its purpose is not attained in that event.[l] The buyer seems to be remitted to whatever protection applicable state law may afford. But this prospect is probably negligible in practice. It would be unusual for a financing institution to acquire an interest in a "consumer credit contract" without recognizing it for what it is. And if the required notice does not appear, the good faith of such a transferee would be suspect, to say the least: vocational financers know the law, or should know it.

(Various considerations inhibit the Federal Trade Commission from making direct pronouncements about the enforceability of commercial paper; hence the roundabout technique of the Rule.)

(3) *Multiple–Choice Question.* You have bought a refrigerator under a credit contract containing a waiver-of-defense clause. Given this assumption, a group of laymen were asked to read the "contract" and then, without referring to it, to answer the following question:

its methodology, see Note, A Case Study, etc., 78 Yale L.J. 618 (1969).

j. Gen.Bus.L. §§ 252–255.

k. Paragraph (d).

l. Assuming that the transferee purchases "in good faith and without notice . . ."

If the seller assigns the contract to another party, say a bank, you will make your payments to the bank rather than to the seller. If, then, the refrigerator stops working and the seller wrongfully fails to honor the warranty:

(a) You will still have to make the payments to the bank.

(b) You will be excused from making payments to the bank until the seller honors the warranty.

(c) . . .

(d) Don't know/unsure.

Actually, two groups were given the test, based on different contracts. One contract—not the other—contained a notice, as mandated by the FTC (p. 969 above), indicating that (b) is the most nearly correct answer. The group that did not see the notice scored markedly better than the group that did. Davis, Protecting Consumers from Overdisclosure and Gobbledygook, 63 Va.L.Rev. 841, 884 fn. 119 (1977).[m]

ASSIGNEE AS DEFENDANT

Wayne and Jacqueline Mardis put 53,000 miles on a car they had bought, used, from Cloverleaf Lincoln–Mercury, Inc., before they discovered that it was a 1985 model. Cloverleaf had sold it to them as a later model. So they said, at least, in an action they brought against the Ford Motor Credit Company (FMCC). They had bought the car on credit; and Cloverleaf had assigned the contract to FMCC. The Mardises sought to rescind the contract and recover damages from FMCC. From a summary judgment for the defendant, the Mardises appealed. *Held:* Affirmed. "[T]he FTC regulations did not provide a basis for an affirmative action against FMCC for rescission based on allegations of wrongful conduct on the part of Cloverleaf, and the undisputed evidence shows that FMCC was not liable under the state law doctrine of respondeat superior for any fraud that may have been committed by Cloverleaf." Mardis v. Ford Motor Credit Company, 642 So.2d 701 (Ala.1994).

The court referred to an FTC release indicating that, although its Rule warrants an affirmative action against a creditor for the return of money paid, the "most typical example" would be a case in which a buyer makes a payment in advance of delivery and the seller fails to deliver the goods. "The FTC regulations further state that 'consumers will not be in a position to obtain an affirmative recovery from a creditor, unless they have actually commenced payments and received little or nothing of value from the seller' and that a 'total failure of performance' is necessary to entitle a consumer to sue an assignee/creditor for a return of money paid on account." A dissenting justice argued that the decision was counter to the plain meaning of the notice required

---

m. Professor Davis appears to conclude that the FTC has failed signally in an attempt at informing consumers of their rights. At best, however, this is only a secondary object of the notice requirement.

by the Rule: "holder ... subject to all *claims* and defenses which the debtor could assert against the seller...."

The issue in *Mardis* has been a divisive one, not only in connection with the FTC Rule, but also in connection with comparable state statutes. Should recovery be allowed at all, in an action "Buyer vs. Assignee"? If so, what factors should determine the amount? Compare the limitation in a New York statute:

> Liability not to exceed the amount owing to the assignee "at the time the defenses ... are asserted,"

with that in a California statute:

> Liability not to exceed the amount owing "at the time of the assignment."

Which of these limitations makes more sense?

NOTES

(1) *Statutory Questions.* Both of the statutes just quoted provide that the rights of the buyer "can only be asserted as a matter of defense" [a] to a claim by the assignee. If that is taken literally, what is the point of limiting the assignee's liability? Is it possible that "liability" means "amount of reduction—via recoupment or setoff—of the assignee's claim"? Is it possible that the statutes are directed only to a *breach of warranty* claim by a buyer, and not to a claim for *restitution* (such as the Mardises made)? See Vasquez v. Superior Court of San Joaquin County, 484 P.2d 964 (Cal.1971), concerning an earlier version of the California statute. There the court ruled that the language quoted in this Note did not apply in favor of an assignee who had actively participated in the sale transaction.[b] Might a personal-injury claim be maintained against an "active participant," or any other assignee?

(2) *Problem.* A homeowner makes a home-improvement contract with a builder, paying the builder $1,000 and signing a promissory note for the remainder of the price ($14,000). The builder immediately transfers the note to a bank. That is a violation of a statute prohibiting such a transfer for the period of five days following the signing of the contract. The builder fails to perform the work, never having intended to perform, and the homeowner suffers $10,000 in damages as a consequence. On these facts alone, what remedy is appropriate in an action by the homeowner against the bank? See Home Sav. Ass'n v. Guerra, 733 S.W.2d 134 (Tex.1987).

SECTION 4. FINANCING COMMERCIAL CREDIT

Introductory Note to *Harris*

A diagram of the facts in the following case might be as follows:

----

a. Or, in New York, as a setoff.

b. "Participation" being taken in the sense described in a well-known earlier case, Commercial Credit Corp. v. Orange County Machine Works, 214 P.2d 819 (Cal. 1950). Nor did the restriction apply in favor of an assignee who "has taken the contract with notice of defenses of the buyer against the assignor."

| Brewster | | Chesapeake | | Harris, |
| Plastics | → | Fin'l Corp. | → | *et al.* (plaintiffs) |

(bottles   ↑ ↓   (resin
  contract) | contract)

Dial Corp. (defendant)

The vertical arrows represent sums owing on the two contracts—assuming that there were two contracts. The plaintiff contended that there were; whereas the defendant contended that there was only a single bottle-and-resin contract.

The court does not say so, but it must be the case that Harris sued either as assignee of or as subrogee to the Chesapeake claim against Brewster. The question is, then, what is the extent of Chesapeake's right as assignee of Brewster's payment right against Dial?

(The case bears a family resemblance to that stated in Note 2, p. 929 above. You should compare the two with a view to identifying an issue they have in common.)

HARRIS v. DIAL CORPORATION

United States Court of Appeals, Fourth Circuit, 1992.
954 F.2d 990.

JOSEPH H. YOUNG, SENIOR DISTRICT JUDGE: This case arises out of a dispute between two parties claiming a right to a company's accounts receivable in satisfaction of debts owed by the company to each of the parties. The issue presented on appeal is whether the defendant has a right to offset its accounts receivable against the accounts receivable related to transactions between the defendant and the business held by the plaintiffs. The district court held that there was one agreement between the defendant and the business held by the plaintiffs, and that the defendant, therefore, had a right of set-off under the applicable section of the Uniform Commercial Code ("UCC"). Consequently, the court granted the defendant's motion for summary judgment. Finding no error, we affirm.

RELEVANT FACTS

Plaintiffs are stockholders in the Lynchburg–Phoenix Group, which in turn was a stockholder in Brewster of Lynchburg, Inc., d/b/a Brewster Plastics ("Brewster"). Brewster was a company which manufactured, among other things, plastic bottles. The defendant, Dial Corporation ("Dial") is a manufacturer of household supplies.

Dial approached Brewster in April, 1988 with a proposal that Brewster manufacture plastic bottles for use in Dial's Virginia plant. Brewster agreed, and they encapsulated their agreement in a purchase order.

However, Brewster was unable to get the resin necessary for the manufacture of the bottles. Dial had available to it an allocation of resin, so it contracted with its supplier to buy the resin and resell it to Brewster. Dial and Brewster executed a change order as an addendum to the purchase order, which included agreements pertaining to both the manufacture of bottles and the supply of resin. Dial became Brewster's largest customer as the result of this agreement. Brewster began manufacturing bottles for Dial in June or July, 1988.

Brewster, needing additional capital for its business, borrowed money from Chesapeake Financial Corporation ("Chesapeake") and also obtained a line of credit from Chesapeake. Brewster's accounts receivable and inventory served as security for the loan; the loan was guaranteed by the plaintiffs.

When Brewster fell behind in its payments to Dial for the resin in August, 1988, Dial proposed a set-off arrangement, whereby the amount Brewster owed to Dial for resin was offset against the amount Dial owed to Brewster for bottles. Brewster refused to agree to the set-off agreement and in September, 1988, Brewster and Dial implemented a payment schedule to reduce Brewster's debt to Dial; the goal of the plan was to ensure that Brewster owed Dial no more than $20,000 at any one time. Brewster complied with the payment plan for several weeks but soon fell behind in its payments.

In the meantime, Chesapeake determined that the security for the loan was jeopardized by Dial's possible interest in Brewster's accounts receivable. Brewster sought, at Chesapeake's request, an agreement by Dial not to seek set-off of accounts receivable, but Dial refused. On November 17, 1988, Chesapeake declared the loan to be in default and made demand on the guarantee of the plaintiffs. In the letter declaring the loan to be in default, Chesapeake acknowledged that Brewster's accounts receivable were subject to claims by Dial because of the contra-account arrangement between Brewster and Dial. On November 21, 1988, Brewster sent a letter to Dial stating that Brewster's accounts receivable had been assigned to Chesapeake, and that Dial was to pay Chesapeake directly for any money owed to Brewster. Brewster then ceased manufacturing bottles.

The plaintiffs brought this action claiming that Brewster owed them over $300,000 as a result of its default on the loan they guaranteed and sought to collect the money that Dial owed to Brewster in satisfaction of the amount that Brewster owed to the plaintiffs. Dial claimed that Brewster owed it more than it owed Brewster, and sought to set-off the amount it owed Brewster by the amount Brewster owed it. If the accounts receivable were offset, Brewster would still owe Dial several hundred dollars and plaintiffs would not be able to collect any money on the outstanding balance of the note they guaranteed. If the accounts receivable were not offset, Dial would have to pay the plaintiffs the amount it owed Brewster but would not be able to collect the amount Brewster owed it and the proceeds of Brewster's accounts receivable would be used to pay off the outstanding balance of the loan guaranteed by the plaintiffs. Ultimately, either the plaintiffs or Dial would lose a substantial amount of money depending on the disposition of Brewster's accounts receivable.

The district court held that there was one agreement between Brewster and Dial, and that because there was only one agreement, offsetting the accounts receivable was proper, and it granted Dial's motion for summary judgment. The plaintiffs appealed.

APPLICABLE LAW

The parties agreed in the district court that the applicable law was the UCC as adopted by Arizona. The pertinent statutory section provides:

[Here the court set out subsection (1) of UCC 9–318, as enacted in Arizona.[a] In Arizona, "(1)(a)" becomes "(A)(1)".]

ANALYSIS

The critical issue on appeal is whether there was one contract between the parties for supply of resin and manufacture of bottles, or whether these transactions were covered by two separate agreements. If there was one agreement, the rights of the plaintiffs, as assignees of Chesapeake's security interest in Brewster's accounts receivable,[1] would be subject to "[a]ll the terms of the contract between the account debtor and assignor and any defense or claim arising therefrom," including Dial's right to offset. § 47–9318(A)(1). However, if there were two agreements, Dial would only be able to claim an offset of accounts receivable to the extent that its rights accrued "before the account debtor [Dial] receives notification of the assignment." § 47–9318(A)(1).

Dial contends that the contract embodying both of the agreements (resin supply and bottle manufacture) was contained in an amended purchase order. The purchase order contains the quantity and price of bottles to be manufactured by Brewster, and explains the payment terms for the bottles. The purchase order also contains the agreement to supply resin and the price of the resin; however, it does not state the terms of payment for the resin. Dial further contends that because Brewster could not obtain resin in the open market, the resin agreement was an integral part of the bottle contract.

The plaintiffs argue that the lack of payment information regarding the resin in the purchase order, along with the lack of explicit language in the purchase order making it a contract for both resin and bottles, prevent construing the purchase order as a contract for both. They argue that resin was covered by a separate agreement between the parties, that the agreements cannot be considered a single contract, and that because Dial charged a markup on the resin it obtained from its

a. Ariz.Rev.Stat.Ann. § 47–9318(A).

1. The plaintiffs, as Brewster's assignees (via Chesapeake), have no greater rights than did Brewster. See Business Fin. Servs., Inc. v. Butler & Booth Dev. Co., 147 Ariz. 510, 711 P.2d 649 (Ct.App.1985); Valley Nat'l. Bank v. Flagstaff Dairy, 22 UCC Rep.Serv. (Callaghan) 787, 116 Ariz. 513, 570 P.2d 200 (Ct.App.1977).

supplier, the resin agreement was not an inherent part of the bottle contract.

The Restatement of Contracts, in a repo ter's comment, addresses the issue of separate contracts as opposed to a single contract.

> If there are two separate contracts, one party's performance under the first and the other party's performance under the second are not to be exchanged under a single exchange of promises, and even a total failure of performance by one party as to the first has no necessary effect on the other party's duty to perform the second.... This is not so, however, if there is a single contract under which the parties are to exchange performances, even though it is proper to regard pairs of corresponding parts of those performances as agreed equivalents.

Restatement (Second) of Contracts § 240 cmt. b (1981).

Further, the intent of the parties at the time of the agreement is to be considered in determining whether there is a single contract or whether there are two severable contracts. O'Malley Inv. & Realty Co. v. Trimble, 5 Ariz.App. 10, 422 P.2d 740, 747 (Ct.App.1967).

We hold that there was one contract covering both the resin and the bottles. Dial and Brewster initially entered into an agreement to manufacture bottles. When Brewster could not get the resin necessary for the production of the bottles on the open market, the only way Brewster could fulfill its contractual obligation was for Dial to get the resin for Brewster from its allocation from a petroleum company. The resin was only used for the bottles manufactured for Dial—it was not used for Brewster's other customers. Both the resin supply agreement and the bottle manufacturing agreement were embodied in one form— the change order. The resin agreement was inseparable from the bottle agreement because Brewster could not have made the bottles without the resin, and it could not get the resin except from Dial. If Dial had breached its agreement to supply resin, Brewster's performance of its agreement to produce bottles would have been excused. Therefore, the two agreements were inseparably intertwined, and there was only one contract between Dial and Brewster.[2]

We also reject plaintiff's contention that, even if there was only one contract, Dial's right to set-off was not a claim or defense arising from the contract within the meaning of § 47–9318(A)(1). The conclusion that there was one contract brings the offset claim within the protection of subsection (A)(1), regardless of whether the right of set-off was spelled out in the contract itself. See generally Business Fin. Servs., Inc. v. Butler & Booth Dev. Co., 147 Ariz. 510, 711 P.2d 649 (Ct.App.1985).

2. The plaintiffs also argue that this is an issue of fact, and that the case should not have been decided on summary judgment. Fed.R.Civ.P. 56(c); Anderson v. Liberty Lobby, Inc., 477 U.S. 242, 106 S.Ct. 2505, 91 L.Ed.2d 202 (1986). However, under Arizona law the divisibility of a contract is a matter of law. Leeker v. Marcotte, 41 Ariz. 118, 15 P.2d 969, 972 (1932). Therefore, the district court did not err in deciding this issue on summary judgment.

Finally, plaintiffs maintain that Dial waived its right to offset by entering into a payment plan at the time Brewster fell behind in its payments for resin. Dial claims that it rejected Brewster's suggestion, made at Chesapeake's request, that it execute a "Letter of Non Offset." Dial expressly rejected a proposal to waive its right to offset. Therefore, it cannot be held, under any logical construction, to have waived that right.

CONCLUSION

There was one agreement between Dial and Brewster regarding supply of resin and production of bottles. Further, Dial had a common law right of offset arising out of the agreement and did not waive that right. The order of the district court is

Affirmed.

NOTES

(1) *One Contract or Two?* In a 1993 case, Judge Posner of the Seventh Circuit reported on a search for cases answering this question; he found few.[a] (He did not find the main case.) As an initial proposition, relying on efficiency grounds, the court concluded that the answer should turn on the number of purchase orders. Apparently, that is, each offer-&-acceptance gives rise to a separate contract. On that theory it seems that Brewster and Dial had a bottle contract and a resin contract, rather than a single bottle-&-resin contract. But on the facts the cases may be distinguishable.

(2) *Vocabulary.* The term "recoupment" is often used to represent the netting out of two enforceable claims arising under the *same contract:* a claim by the plaintiff against the defendant, and one by the defendant against the plaintiff. In a strict sense of the term "setoff", it represents the netting out of reciprocal claims arising from separate transactions. Observe that the opinion in the *Harris* case does not make use of the distinction. Would it clarify or obfuscate the issue for you if the court had distinguished between recoupment and setoff?

(3) *Keeping the Assignee Informed.* One thing that Dial might have done when Brewster "fell behind" in its payments for resin is to send Brewster a demand for assurance of due performance of the bottle-sale contract. (See UCC 2–609.) Suppose that Dial did so, and that it had already been notified of Brewster's assignment to Chesapeake. There is authority that, in like circumstances, it is not incumbent on the account debtor to advise the assignee of the demand. See BAII Banking Corp. v. UPG, Inc., 985 F.2d 685 (2d Cir.1993).

Would you favor treating the assignee as a contract "party" so as to require that the assignee be advised? Might that requirement be drawn out of the Code as it stands?—perhaps under UCC 1–203 ("Obligation of Good Faith")?

(4) *Warranties of an Assignor.* Rules on this subject are stated in Restatement Second § 333. One who makes an assignment for value, it is said, warrants to the assignee "that he will do nothing to defeat or impair the value of the assignment and has no knowledge of any fact which would do so." (The warranty may be disclaimed.)

---

a. Coplay Cement Co. v. Willis & Paul Group, 983 F.2d 1435 (7th Cir.1993).

How would this rule affect the rights of Chesapeake Financial against Brewster?—disregarding Harris for the moment. The practical importance of this question is slight, of course. If Brewster has assets from which a judgment can be collected, Chesapeake could enforce its loan contract against them; otherwise, a warranty claim would be uncollectible. But the question might be important if there had been a *sale* of the accounts, as in District of Columbia v. Thomas Funding (see p. 925 above).

If Brewster borrowed from Chesapeake, using the bottle-sale accounts as collateral, and did not disclose the "resin addendum," that might be a breach of the warranty. (Might it also be fraud?) A comparable question would arise if the resin deal were struck after Brewster made the assignment. Would that be a breach of the warranty? The deal would seem to be an "affirmative act" impairing the value of the assignment.

The question has arisen whether or not an assignor can violate the warranty by a mere failure to act—as if Brewster had simply stopped making bottles for Dial. "No cases have been found," one court has said. "However, we see no good reason to distinguish between an affirmative act and a failure to act when as a practical matter the assignor can impair or defeat the assigned right by doing either. Our conclusion is directly in accord with the established principle of cooperation between contracting parties...." Lonsdale v. Chesterfield, 662 P.2d 385, 388 (Wash.1983).

If this reasoning is right, the next question is whether or not Brewster could go out of the bottle-making business and yet comply with the warranty by contracting for the bottles to be supplied to Dial by another firm in that business—one of good repute, say, that nevertheless defaulted. How would you answer?[b] See again the *Lonsdale* case.[c]

CONTRACT MODIFICATION

As a rule, an assignee's rights against the obligor are not impaired by the fact that the obligor, having notice of the assignment, makes a payment in disregard of the assignment. If the obligor is so unwise as to deal with the assignor after notice, the assignee may commonly require that a second payment be made of the assigned claim. See Herzog v. Irace, p. 921 above.

An important qualification on this rule is suggested by a handful of cases that may be described as involving "necessary advances." These cases are part of the legislative history of an Article–9 provision about "modification" and "substitution" respecting an assigned contract: subsection (2) of UCC 9–318.

An example is a case in which a canning company made large advances to a tomato grower, after contracting to purchase his 1952 crop. Most of the money was advanced after the company had given its

b. One might think the case supposed is an instance of a good-faith "substitution for the contract," within the meaning of UCC 9–318(2). But Comment 2 to the section suggests a different meaning for that expression.

c. If the facts supposed were to generate a breach-of-warranty claim by Chesapeake against Brewster, and if Harris and the other plaintiffs were controlling shareholders of Brewster, a claim made by the plaintiffs against Brewster on that basis might well meet with skepticism.

assent to a transaction whereby the grower assigned part of his crop earnings to a supplier of soil fumigant. (The company had accepted a "crop order" from the supplier; this was treated as a partial assignment.) The proceeds of the crop—less the advances made by the canning company—left nothing to be paid to the supplier. He sued the company, asserting that the post-crop-order advances were made in disregard of his assignment. The court accepted the view that (as an exception to the general rule), the company was entitled to credit for advances that it could show to be necessary to the grower for producing his crop. A judgment against the company was affirmed. Some of the advances in question were not allowable. (These included some advances used by the grower as living expenses.) Fricker v. Uddo & Taormina Co., 312 P.2d 1085 (Cal.1957).

In a leading English case, dealing more harshly with a buyer—and more favorably with an assignee—than the Code appears to do, a dissenting justice thought that the dealings between the buyer and the seller (assignor) ought not to be "impeded or imperilled" by the assignment, "if what they do is done bona fide and in the ordinary course of business." (How does this view compare with subsection (2) of UCC 9–318?) Speaking of the buyer and the seller, the dissenter continued: "Why may they not modify [their contract]? If they cannot modify it, it seems to me to denote a state of slavery in business that ought not to be suffered." Brett, L.J., dissenting in Brice v. Bannister, [1878] 3 Q.B.D. 569 (Ct.App.).

NOTES

(1) *The Code Applied.* For a case in which the standards of UCC 9–318(2) were applied to dealings between the parties to a requirements contract, see Madden Eng. Corp. v. Major Tube Corp., 568 S.W.2d 614 (Tenn.App.1977), cert. denied (1978). When the seller proved to be unable to supply all the buyer's needs, as promised, the buyer made certain concessions. For example, the buyer began to provide the seller with raw material—core paper—when the seller could not otherwise finance purchases of the paper. These concessions, as the trial court later observed, "diluted" the seller's earnings under the contract. The buyer had earlier consented to an assignment by the seller of its payment rights under the contract to a bank, as security for a $100,000 loan. After the seller ceased operations, the bank sued the buyer for the unpaid balance of the loan: $78,200. From a judgment for the bank, the buyer appealed. *Held:* Award reduced to some $12,000.

As to certain disbursements by the buyer, the court said, the buyer was not entitled to credit: "it does not appear that Archer made any effort to protect [the bank's] assignment." [a] As to another credit the court (Goddard, J.) referred to UCC 9–318 and said:

> As to the purchase of core paper, it is undisputed that had Archer not purchased the paper Major Tube [the seller] would have gone out of business the latter part of July rather than in November, and that it was absolutely necessary for them to have the raw material to be able to operate. Conse-

a. On petition to rehear, Archer complained that this would require it to make double payment. Conceding this, the court said it is "invariably the penalty exacted of a creditor [debtor?] who fails to protect an assignee."

quently, we find that this was a commercially reasonable modification of the contract as contemplated by subsection (2) and should be credited against any amount owed [the bank].

(2) *Harris v. Dial Corporation: Reprise.* Consider again the *Harris* case. Does subsection (2) of UCC 9–318 describe what Brewster and Dial did when they made the resin deal?—make a "modification of or substitution for" the bottle deal?

Possibly an argument can be made that UCC 9–318 describes three—not just two—kinds of defenses for an account debtor: (i) "arising therefrom" defenses under (1)(a); (ii) the "modification" defense under subsection (2); and (iii) "any other" defense under (1)(b). On that analysis, Harris's claim should have been tested, not by the one-contract/two-contract distinction, but by the standards of subsection (2): good faith and commercial reasonableness.[b] How would Dial's defense have fared under those standards?

(3) *New York Variation.* When the UCC was initially proposed in New York, subsection (2) was a serious impediment to its enactment. New York banks perceived it as a grave threat to their interests. The Law Revision Commission refused to endorse the then Official Text; and the sponsors revised it substantially. They did not retreat on the modification issue, however. As enacted in New York, subsection (2) contains this additional phrase, following the word "standards":

. . . and without material adverse effect upon the assignee's rights under or the assignor's ability to perform the contract.

How would Dial's defense have fared under this standard?

(4) *Payment via Third Party.* Not infrequently a firm buying goods on credit will ask the seller to agree that the price can be paid by debiting any account owing by the seller to one or more designated third parties—usually a firm or firms affiliated with the buyer. A term to that effect might be an unwelcome surprise to an assignee of the seller's payment rights. If the term is agreed on as part of the initial sale agreement, does it afford the buyer a defense under subsection (1)(a) of UCC 9–318? If it is agreed on thereafter, is it a modification under subsection (2)? What else might it be? See the foregoing footnote.

(5) *Restatements.* The original Restatement contains no provision comparable to UCC 9–318(2); but Restatement Second states a closely parallel rule, in § 338(2). Comment *f* after the section states: "Contrary agreement between obligor and assignee is effective." The inference is clear that a "contrary agreement" between obligor and assignor is *ineffective.* But Comment *a* after § 311 states: "The parties to a contract . . . can by agreement create a duty to a beneficiary which cannot be varied without the beneficiary's consent." How is it possible to reconcile these rules?

---

b. Compare In re Apex Oil Co., 975 F.2d 1365 (10th Cir.1992), where the court intimated that UCC 9–318 recognizes the following three kinds of defenses for an account debtor: (i) "arising therefrom" defenses under subsection (1)(a); (ii) the "payment" defense under subsection (3); and (iii) "other" defenses under subsection (1)(b). There is little to recommend this classification, it seems.

To complicate matters, an agreement for allowing an offset of an exceptional kind—an offset of debt owed by the assignor to an affiliate of the account debtor—has sometimes been regarded as only "a collateral agreement in which the method of payment [by the assignor to the affiliate] was established." See MNC Commercial Corp. v. Joseph T. Ryerson & Son, 882 F.2d 615 (2d Cir.1989).

TACTICS IN SERIAL TRANSACTIONS

When dealing repeatedly with a single supplier, a customer who anticipates that the supplier may make an assignment of payment rights against the customer is well advised to consider measures to enable it to make the best use of the "subject to" rules of UCC 9–318(1). Assuming that the customer has the bargaining power to dictate terms to the supplier, how might the customer make sure that clause (a) will apply, rather than clause (b)? Consider the two "cosmetics" cases reported as American Trade Partners, L.P. v. K Mart Corp., 1992 WL 59153 (E.D.Pa. 1992).

The Montaj Corporation assigned to a firm named American Trade Partners (ATP) its claim for the price of cosmetics sold at various times to the K Mart Corporation, a retailer. K Mart was notified of the assignment. Thereafter, Montaj accepted from K Mart the return of some unsold goods. In an action by ATP against K Mart on the assigned claims, K Mart sought a credit of $1,200 on account of the "returns." The court denied the credit, saying that it was not one arising from the terms of the contract between K Mart and Montaj pursuant to subsection (1) of UCC 9–318, and was not one that accrued before K Mart's notification of the assignment pursuant to subsection (2).

This result is striking because K Mart had attempted, in buying cosmetics from Montaj, to provide itself with offsets arising from "any other transaction" with the same supplier.[a] In an associated case concerning a different supplier, K Mart was more successful, for it had obtained from that supplier an agreement governing a series of sales: it permitted K Mart to return to the seller, for credit or a refund, all unsold items. Owing to that agreement, K Mart was able to establish certain credits under the rule of UCC 9–318(1)(a). Apparently K Mart had no such ongoing agreement with Montaj—or at most there was an oral agreement that was unenforceable under the Statute of Frauds.

NOTES

(1) *Modification by Montaj?* K Mart had a plausible claim against Montaj for $1,200, on the facts given above. The claim might be based on a tacit agreement by Montaj—one made *after* the notification, when Montaj accepted returned goods—that it would credit their price to K Mart. (As to goods received and accepted by Montaj, the Statute of Frauds would not have barred enforcement of this claim.) It is not reported that K Mart asserted such an agreement.

If K Mart had persuaded the court, when ATP sued it, that such an agreement existed, the court might have concluded that the agreement was a "modification" of the assigned contract. Would you consider it to be a modification "made in good faith and in accordance with reasonable commercial standards"?

a. In K Mart's standard purchase-order form, this provision appeared:

Any sums payable to Seller shall be subject to all claims and defenses of Buyer, whether arising from this or any other transaction or occurrence, and Buyer may set off and deduct against any such sums all present and future indebtedness of Seller to Buyer.

If, however, the returns were made pursuant to a preassignment (unenforceable) agreement, "modification" is a somewhat inexact description of what happened when the credit became enforceable.

(2) *Problem.* Drennan engages Star Paving (SP) to do paving in connection with a new school. SP assigns to a financing bank its payment rights under the contract and the bank notifies Drennan of the assignment. Drennan learns that SP is unable to provide a performance bond as required by the contract between them, and terminates the contract. Next Drennan engages Moon Building (MB) to do the work. MB makes a subcontract with SP whereby SP supplies the labor required for the paving. (Compare Note 5, p. 494 above.)

The bank asserts a right to either the earnings of MB under its contract with Drennan or the earnings of SP under its contract with MB. Is either claim supported by UCC 9–318(2) ("corresponding rights")? See Federal Deposit Ins. Corp. v. Registry Hotel Corp., 639 F.Supp. 812 (N.D.Tex.1986).

PROBLEMS OF "ACCRUAL"

In construing UCC 9–318(1)(b), one court has said that the " 'accrual' of a 'claim' ... bespeaks more than the existence of an unripened obligation. Though there is little legislative history or case law on point, the official UCC Comment says the subsection 'makes no substantial change in prior law.' "

> Thus "accrual" of the "claim"—a "cause of action" notion— necessarily involves a *breach* of an obligation rather than its mere existence.

The court referred to UCC 2–725(2): "A cause of action accrues when the breach occurs...."

The court's interpretation may have worked unfair prejudice to a firm that had bought some machine tools, the I.P.M. Precision Machinery Company. The buyer (IPM) acted as a distributor for the manufacturer. In August of 1982, IPM was notified that the invoices for these items had been sold to a French financer and was directed to make payment to that firm's U.S. agent. In September IPM incurred some expenses for exhibiting the manufacturer's products at a trade show; and when it was sued by the financer for the unpaid price of the tools bought it claimed a credit for these expenses. An agreement for sharing these expenses had been made between the manufacturer (seller) and IPM in June of 1982, while they were negotiating the sale terms. *Held:* Credit denied. Factofrance Heller v. I.P.M. Precision Machinery, 627 F.Supp. 1412 (N.D.Ill.1986).

What responsibility should the financer bear for ascertaining, when it bought the seller's payment rights, the full set of dealings between the seller and IPM? What meaning could be given to the expression "claim ... which accrues," such that the financer would have to allow to IPM the credit it claimed? (The matter was important because the manufacturer had entered bankruptcy.)

NOTES

(1) *Counselling.* In *Factofrance Heller,* does it seem that IPM could have learned something useful from studying the purchase order forms used by K Mart—as described on p. 981 above?

(2) *Problems.* Rochester Cheese Sales, Inc. had an ongoing business relation with a processor ("reprocessor") of cheeses named Waunakee Kase Haus, Inc.; each would buy from and sell to the other. A bank had made loans to Waunakee, secured by Waunakee's accounts receivable. The security agreement permitted the bank, upon the debtor's default, to notify the account debtors to make payment directly to the bank. "Until account debtors are so notified, Debtor, as agent for Bank shall make collections on the Collateral." At a time when Waunakee owed Rochester more than $97,000 for cheeses purchased, Rochester sold cheeses to Waunakee for about $122,000 (difference, about $25,000). Apparently the parties anticipated weight- and shipping-charge adjustments in these amounts. See Bank of Waunakee v. Rochester Cheese Sales, Inc., 906 F.2d 1185 (7th Cir.1990).

If, at that juncture, Waunakee had defaulted, and the bank had notified Rochester that it claimed Waunakee's accounts, how should the amount of Rochester's indebtedness to the bank be calculated?

In point of fact, before the dealer was notified, it agreed with Waunakee upon the amount of $22,643.22 as the net balance and sent a check, "payment in full," for that amount. Waunakee collected the check. Should that fact affect the calculation of Rochester's indebtedness?

MICHELIN TIRES (CANADA) LTD. v.
FIRST NAT. BANK OF BOSTON

United States Court of Appeals, First Circuit, 1981.
666 F.2d 673.

MAZZONE, DISTRICT JUDGE. This appeal is from a district court's denial of restitution to the plaintiff, a contractual obligor, of monies mistakenly paid to the defendant, an assignee of contract rights. [An engineering firm, designated "SNC" in this opinion, was retained by Michelin Tires ("Michelin") to supervise the building of a tire factory in Nova Scotia. The factory was to include a system for storing and handling carbon black. J.C. Corrigan, Inc. ("JCC") undertook to design and install the system. Between August 1970 and February 1971, Michelin made three progress payments on account of JCC's performance, as certified by SNC. These payments were made to the First National Bank of Boston ("FNB"), which held a security interest in JCC's payment rights under the Michelin contract. JCC had been financed by the bank since 1960. The amounts paid by Michelin were 90% of invoice amounts submitted by JCC to SNC, and certified by SNC to be due.] With each invoice, Michelin had the right to require JCC to submit a "Statutory Declaration," or sworn statement, stating the amount JCC owed to subcontractors, suppliers, and others in connection with the work and listing any claims that could result in liens on Michelin's property. If JCC failed to make prompt payments to subcontractors and suppliers, SNC could withhold or nullify its certification and Michelin could deduct from its progress payments to JCC the amount necessary to protect its property from liens.

[In March, 1971, Michelin learned that JCC had not been paying its subcontractors. Michelin had made a payment in response to JCC's first invoice without having received a Declaration. Thereafter it insisted on Declarations; but the ones submitted were fraudulent. Eventually JCC initiated a liquidation proceeding.]

Throughout this time, FNB maintained its lending relationship with JCC. FNB knew of JCC's financial difficulties. By early 1970, before JCC contracted with Michelin, FNB regarded its loan to JCC as a problem and was concerned about repayment. The bank knew from examining JCC's books that the company's earnings were declining, its trade debt was rising, and its customers were slow to pay. It was further evident from JCC's books that JCC was overstating its income in its reports to the bank. By late August of 1970, the bank was aware that JCC's outstanding indebtedness was greater than the agreed-upon loan ceiling of 80% of JCC's accounts receivable, and a bank officer reminded JCC that loan funds received while JCC was "over-advanced" were to be used only to meet payroll and pay taxes. FNB used the payments it received from Michelin after the assignment to reduce the outstanding amount on its loan to JCC. In October of 1970, FNB sent an inquiry to SNC to verify the accuracy of copies of invoices the bank had received from JCC, used by the bank to calculate the 80% loan ceiling. SNC replied that the invoices were "OK."

On December 22, 1970, FNB notified JCC that it would extend no further loans to JCC after March 31, 1971 and that JCC should seek financing elsewhere. It was after JCC failed to find a new lender that the company made its assignment for the benefit of creditors on April 6, 1971 and filed a petition in bankruptcy.

After discovering JCC's fraud, Michelin brought this suit to recover the payments it made to FNB, a total of $724,197.60. Michelin asserted it was entitled to restitution under two theories. First, it claimed that since its right to restitution arose from its contract with JCC, the claim could be successfully asserted against FNB, the assignee of contract rights to payment, pursuant to § 9–318(1)(a) of the Uniform Commercial Code (UCC), Mass.Gen.Laws Ann. ch. 106, § 9–318(1)(a).[1] Second,

---

1. Michelin's complaint framed this claim as one in breach of contract. On appeal, however, Michelin characterizes the claim as purely restitutionary, although "arising from" its contract with JCC. Apparently, then, Michelin is not attempting to assert that it is entitled to restitution as an alternative remedy for breach of contract. If it were, Michelin would have to show the breach was total, warranting rescission of the contract. See 5 A. Corbin, Corbin on Contracts § 1104 (1964). On the other hand, restitution of property transferred in the course of performance of a contract can be had under equitable principles without regard to the totality of the breach. See Restatement of Restitution § 28, Comment a (1937).

Given our interpretation of § 9–318(1)(a) of the UCC, we need not reach the next question—whether this claim, essentially one in equity, can nevertheless be said to "arise from" the contract.

Michelin asserted that FNB was liable because it has been unjustly enriched under traditional restitutionary principles.

The district court tried the case without a jury and upon a stipulated record. In a detailed memorandum, the court found that JCC had breached its contract with Michelin by submitting fictitious invoices and fraudulent Statutory Declarations and by failing to pay its subcontractors when payment was due. It further found that Michelin's payments to FNB had been made in reliance on the fraudulent Statutory Declarations. [It] found that FNB knew of JCC's contractual obligations to Michelin. Those obligations included prompt payment of subcontractors. FNB, however, did not know that JCC was sending false Statutory Declarations to Michelin, stating under oath that the subcontractors had been paid.[a] The district court then ruled, first, that § 9–318(1)(a) does not create a new affirmative cause of action by an account debtor as against an assignee and, second, that since FNB did not know of the fraudulent Statutory Declarations or of JCC's indebtedness to subcontractors, FNB had not been unjustly enriched at the expense of Michelin. This appeal followed.

We affirm because we believe that (1) § 9–318(1)(a) of the UCC was not intended to create a new cause of action by an account debtor against an assignee and (2) the facts the district court found were available to FNB did not put it on notice of JCC's fraud and Michelin's mistake.

I.

Michelin's first argument is that it has an independent cause of action against FNB under § 9–318 of the UCC, Mass.Gen.Laws Ann. ch. 106, § 9–318 (West Supp.1981). That section reads in pertinent part:

Defenses Against Assignee; . . .

(1) . . . [T]he rights of an assignee are subject to

(a) all the terms of the contract between the account debtor and assignor and any defense or claim arising therefrom.

In essence, Michelin contends that its restitution claim arises from its contract with JCC, and that § 9–318(1)(a) accordingly permits Michelin to recover from FNB as JCC's assignee. Although Michelin emphasizes the narrow application of this theory to the instant case, the theory rests upon a construction of § 9–318 that would impose full contract liability on assignees of contract rights. Under this view, a bank taking an assignment of contract rights as security for a loan would also receive as "security" a delegation of duties under the contract and the risk of being held liable on the contract in place of its borrower. We do not believe it was the intent of § 9–318(1)(a) to create such a result.

The key statutory language is ambiguous. That "the rights of an assignee are *subject to* . . . (a) all the terms of the contract" connotes only that the assignee's rights to recover are limited by the obligor's

a. Statement of findings rearranged.

rights to assert contractual defenses as a set-off, implying that affirmative recovery against the assignee is not intended. . . .

On the other hand, the use of the word "claim" raises the possibility that affirmative recovery was indeed contemplated. However, the section's title and the official Comment support the view that the section does not create affirmative rights. The title reads, "Defenses Against Assignee." Official Comment 1 states in pertinent part:

> Subsection (1) makes no substantial change in prior law. An assignee has traditionally been subject to defenses or set-offs existing before an account debtor is notified of the assignment.

Under prior law, an assignee of contract rights was not liable on the contract in the place of his assignor. Wright v. Graustein, 248 Mass. 205, 142 N.E. 797 (1924). Common sense requires that we not twist the "precarious security"[2] of an assignee into potential liability for his assignor's breach.

It is evident that § 9–318 has become a red herring in suits against an assignee. We note two cases that have denied account debtors the right to sue. . . . There are also cases that have allowed affirmative claims, at least in limited circumstances. Benton State Bank v. Warren, 263 Ark. 1, 562 S.W.2d 74 (1978); Farmers Acceptance Corp. v. DeLozier, 178 Colo. 291, 496 P.2d 1016 (1972); K Mart Corp. v. First Penn. Bank, 29 UCC Rep.Serv. 70 (Pa.1980).

The decisions permitting an affirmative suit all rely on the pre-UCC case of Firestone Tire and Rubber Co. v. Central Nat. Bank, 159 Ohio St. 423, 112 N.E.2d 636 (1953). There the court required the bank to return payments to an account debtor because, although the bank was innocent of the assignor's fraud, the bank had unwittingly assisted that fraud by independently requesting periodic payment from the account debtor. The bank attached invoices from the assignor to each request thereby impliedly representing that the underlying obligation was valid. The court found that the account debtor relied on the genuineness of the invoices forwarded by the bank. Id. 112 N.E.2d at 639. In the case at hand there was no such reliance. Rather, Michelin established its own system of assuring compliance, including approval of an intermediary, SNC. In addition, they required a Statutory Declaration under oath from JCC. The stipulated record indicates that FNB had no involvement in verifying JCC's performance and was completely unaware of the Statutory Declaration. . . .

---

2. This phrase was coined by Professor Gilmore in his article, The Assignee of Contract Rights and His Precarious Security, 74 Yale L.J. 217 (1964). This article has been the source of some of the confusion regarding section 9–318. In it, Professor Gilmore analyzes the early case of Firestone Tire and Rubber Co. v. Central National Bank, 159 Ohio St. 423, 112 N.E.2d 636 (1953), and concludes that account debtors should be entitled to sue for repayment of funds mistakenly transferred to assignees even if the transfer was negligent, so long as the assignee has not changed its position. With all due respect to Professor Gilmore, we disagree with this conclusion for the reasons stated in this opinion. We further note, however, that even under Gilmore's analysis, Michelin's suit would fail here since Massachusetts law suggests that a bank's crediting of a debtor's account involves a change of position. Merchants' Insurance Co. v. Abbott, 131 Mass. 397 (1881).

In each of the cases permitting an affirmative suit, with the possible exception of *DeLozier,* the assignee actively participated in the transactions to a degree not approached here. We are aware of no case that has gone beyond those we have cited and actually permitted an affirmative suit against a nonparticipating assignee like FNB. We do not anticipate that the Supreme Judicial Court would extend the law in this way and we are unwilling to do so ourselves. Given the factual distinctions between the cases discussed above and the transactions at issue here, we do not need to reach the issue of whether Massachusetts law would permit suit against an assignee who became more involved in the course of dealings.

While it is our judgment that analysis of the statutory language, taken in context, indicates that no affirmative right was contemplated and further that those cases that have permitted such a right are factually inapposite, we also believe it would be unwise to permit such suits as a matter of policy. As the dissenting justice in Benton State Bank, 562 S.W.2d 74, noted, allowing affirmative suits would "make every Banker, who has taken an assignment of accounts for security purposes, a deep pocket surety for every bankrupt contractor in the state to whom it had loaned money." Id. at 77 (Byrd, J., dissenting).

We are unwilling to impose such an obligation on the banks of the Commonwealth without some indication that this represents a considered policy choice. By making the bank a surety, not only will accounts receivable financing be discouraged, but transaction costs will undoubtedly increase for everyone. The case at hand provides a good example. In order to protect themselves, FNB would essentially be forced to undertake the precautionary measures that Michelin attempted to use, independent observation by an intermediary and sworn certifications by the assignor. FNB would have to supervise every construction site where its funds were involved to ensure performance and payment. We simply do not believe that the banks are best suited to monitor contract compliance. The party most interested in adequate performance would be the other contracting party, not the financier. Given this natural interest, it seems likely to us that while the banks will be given additional burdens of supervision, there would be no corresponding reduction in vigilance by the contracting parties, thus creating two inspections where there was formerly one. Costs for everyone thus increase, without any discernible benefit. It is also difficult to predict the full impact a contrary decision would have on the availability of accounts receivable financing in general.

Our holding, of course, is not that § 9–318 *prohibits* claims against the assignee. We hold merely that § 9–318 concerns only the preservation of defenses to the assignee's claims and, as such, is wholly inapposite in an affirmative suit against an assignee.

II.

[Next the court proceeded to discuss Michelin's asserted right to restitution from FNB. It referred to the Restatement of Restitution

(1937), especially §§ 14 and 28, which indicate that a person does not owe restitution of payments received before that person has "notice" of fraud, mistake, or another ground for restitution, if the recipient gave "value" for the payment. Much of the discussion concerned the question of "notice" to the Boston Bank. The court referred to provisions of the Uniform Commercial Code and to case law, concluding: "We believe that, under Massachusetts law, a person has notice of a fact when, from all the information at his disposal, he has reason to know of it."]

Under § 14 of the Restatement, FNB would be liable to make restitution if it had notice of Michelin's defense or mistake before giving value for the payment—i.e., if it had notice that the subcontractors had not been paid.... Michelin argues that FNB had constructive notice of this fact....

If we were to hold FNB chargeable with notice of JCC's nonpayment of subcontractors on this record, we would be imposing an affirmative duty on lenders to look out for the interests of account debtors such as Michelin. In order for FNB to have discovered JCC's failure to pay its subcontractors, FNB would have had to initiate an investigation of JCC's business practices under the Michelin contract, not aimed at determining the company's financial health for purposes of the bank's continued financing, but aimed at verifying JCC's compliance with the Michelin contract. That JCC was in monetary straits could not have indicated that subcontractors had gone unpaid without such an investigation. We are unwilling to impose such a responsibility on lenders.

Here, FNB did attempt to verify the accuracy of the copies of invoices it was receiving from JCC by contacting Michelin. Michelin's agent, SNC, responded that the invoices were "OK." Michelin's losses might have been avoided if it had required JCC to provide a performance bond [b] or if it had availed itself of its right to visit the offices of subcontractors and investigate the progress of the work. It might have demanded more vigilance from its agent, SNC. SNC was on the site and was charged with supervising the job and certifying its progress. The one area where Michelin was most vulnerable to fraud—the Statutory Declarations—was the area that it could have checked very easily and where, unfortunately, it failed to check at all. It cannot shift its loss to the bank by arguing now that the bank should have monitored JCC's compliance when it failed to do so.

Affirmed. [c]

NOTES

(1) *Restitution.* The Restatement of Restitution supports the rule of the main case on the ground that the payee is a bona fide purchaser of the money:

b. The court's statement of facts included this additional paragraph:

"Prior to signing the construction contract with JCC, neither SNC nor Michelin made inquiries concerning JCC's financial situation. Initially, SNC had requested that JCC provide a performance bond to cover its work, and JCC had requested that Michelin provide a letter of credit to cover the payments due for work performed. Michelin, or SNC, dropped its proposal that JCC be required to provide a performance bond in return for JCC's withdrawal of its request for a letter of credit for Michelin."

c. Bownes, J., dissented.

§ 14(2) ["... if the transferee made no misrepresentation and did not have notice of the defense"]. Professor Palmer prefers the reason that the payee is not unjustly enriched by the payment: 3 Palmer, Restitution, § 16.7 (1978). More generally, one might call the payments conclusive, when the competing equity is not compelling, in the interest of maintaining the security of transactions.

Are these explanations compatible with the reasoning in *Michelin Tires* about the most efficient placement of responsibility for monitoring contract compliance by the assignor? If not, which do you prefer?

(2) *"Subject to" by Contract.* Would a financer reverse the decision in the main case if it were to prepare a provision something like this, for inclusion in contracts to be assigned?—"Notice: Any holder of this contract is subject to all claims and defenses which the debtor could assert against the seller of goods or services obtained pursuant hereto or with the proceeds hereof. Recovery hereunder shall not exceed amounts paid by the debtor hereunder." Do you recognize a source for this language? See p. 969 above.

No financer whose vocation is limited to commercial credit would be likely to draft such a provision, naturally. For opposing views about its effect in a consumer case see the Note at p. 971 above.

ALLHUSEN v. CARISTO CONSTRUCTION CORP.

Court of Appeals of New York, 1952.
303 N.Y. 446, 103 N.E.2d 891, 37 A.L.R.2d 1245.

FROESSEL, JUDGE. Defendant, a general contractor, subcontracted with the Kroo Painting Company (hereinafter called Kroo) for the performance by the latter of certain painting work in New York City public schools. Their contracts contained the following prohibitory provision: "The assignment by the second party [Kroo] of this contract or any interest therein, or of any money due or to become due by reason of the terms hereof without the written consent of the first party [defendant] shall be void." Kroo subsequently assigned certain rights under the contracts to Marine Midland Trust Company of New York, which in turn assigned said rights to plaintiff. These rights included the "moneys due and to become due" to Kroo. The *contracts* were not assigned, and no question of improper delegation of contractual duties is involved. No written consent to the assignments was procured from defendant.

Plaintiff [Herman Allhusen] as assignee seeks to recover, in six causes of action, $11,650 allegedly due and owing for work done by Kroo.... Special Term dismissed the complaint, holding that the prohibition against assignments "must be given effect." The Appellate Division affirmed, one Justice dissenting on the ground that the "account receivable was assignable by nature, and could not be rendered otherwise without imposing an unlawful restraint upon the power of alienation of property." 278 App.Div. 817, 104 N.Y.S.2d 565, 566.

Whether an anti-assignment clause is effective is a question that has troubled the courts not only of this State but in other jurisdictions as well, Burck v. Taylor, 152 U.S. 634, 14 S.Ct. 696, 38 L.Ed. 578; State St. Furniture Co. v. Armour & Co., 345 Ill. 160, 177 N.E. 702, 76 A.L.R. 1298. . . .

Our courts have not construed a contractual provision against assignments framed in the language of the clause now before us. Such kindred clauses as have been subject to interpretation usually have been held to be either (1) personal covenants limiting the covenantee to a claim for damages in the event of a breach as e.g., Manchester v. Kendall, 19 Jones & Sp. 460, affirmed 103 N.Y. 638; Sacks v. Neptune Meter Co., 144 Misc. 70, 258 N.Y.S. 254, affirmed 238 App.Div. 82, 263 N.Y.S. 462, or (2) ineffectual because of the use of uncertain language, State Bank v. Central Mercantile Bank, 248 N.Y. 428, 162 N.E. 475, 59 A.L.R. 1473. But these decisions are not to be read as meaning that there can be no enforcible prohibition against the assignment of a claim; indeed, they are authority only for the proposition that, in the absence of language clearly indicating that a contractual right thereunder shall be nonassignable, a prohibitory clause will be interpreted as a personal covenant not to assign.

In the *Manchester* case, supra, it was held, 103 N.Y. at page 463, that the words, " 'This contract not to be assigned, or any part thereof, or any installments to grow due under the same' ", must be construed as an agreement not to assign, the breach of which would give rise to a claim for damages by the covenantee. The court stated, 103 N.Y. at page 463, that the quoted words "would not make the assignment void." In the clause now before us, however, it is expressly provided that the "assignment . . . shall be void." In the *State Bank* case, supra [the court said:] "The plainest words should have been chosen so that he who runs could read, in order to limit the freedom of alienation of rights and prohibit the assignment. It might have been stipulated on the face of the certificates that they should be 'nontransferable' or 'nonassignable.' "

[Other New York authorities are] in harmony with Restatement of the Law of Contracts (§ 151): "A right may be the subject of effective assignment unless . . . (c) the assignment is prohibited by the contract creating the right." See, also, 2 Williston on Contracts, § 422, pp. 1217–1218.

In the light of the foregoing, we think it is reasonably clear that, while the courts have striven to uphold freedom of assignability, they have not failed to recognize the concept of freedom to contract. In large measure they agree that, where appropriate language is used, assignments of money due under contracts may be prohibited. When "clear language" is used, and the "plainest words . . . have been chosen", parties may "limit the freedom of alienation of rights and prohibit the assignment." State Bank v. Central Mercantile Bank, supra, 248 N.Y. at page 435, 162 N.E. at page 477, 59 A.L.R. 1473. We have now before us a clause embodying clear, definite and appropriate language, which may be construed in no other way but that any attempted assignment of either the contract or any rights created thereunder shall be "void" as against the obligor. One would have to do violence to the language here employed to hold that it is merely an agreement by the subcontractor not to assign. The objectivity of the language precludes such a construction. We are therefore compelled to conclude that this prohibitory clause is a valid and effective restriction of the right to assign.

Such a holding is not violative of public policy. Professor Williston, in his treatise on Contracts, states (Vol. 2, § 422, p. 1214): "The question of the free alienation of property does not seem to be involved." The New York cases do not hold otherwise, State Bank v. Central Mercantile Bank, supra, 248 N.Y. at page 435, 162 N.E. at page 477, 59 A.L.R. 1473. Plaintiff's claimed rights arise out of the very contract embodying the provision now sought to be invalidated. The right to moneys under the contracts is but a companion to other jural relations forming an aggregation of actual and potential interrelated rights and obligations. No sound reason appears why an assignee should remain unaffected by a provision in the very contract which gave life to the claim he asserts.

Nor is there any merit in plaintiff's contention that section 41 of the Personal Property Law, Consol.Laws, c. 41,[a] requires that the prohibitory clause be denied effect. Because the statute provides that a person may transfer a claim, it does not follow that he may not contract otherwise. Countless rights granted by statutes are voluntarily surrendered in the everyday affairs of individuals. In Rosenthal Paper Co. v. National Folding Box & Paper Co., 226 N.Y. 313, 325–326, 123 N.E. 766, 770, we noted: "The general rule now prevailing ... that any property right, not necessarily personal, is assignable, *is overcome only by agreement of the contracting parties* or a principle of law or public policy. [Citing cases.] In this jurisdiction the statute, in effect, so provides [referring to the predecessor of section 41 of the Personal Property Law]." (Emphasis supplied.)

The judgment should be affirmed, with costs.

NOTES

(1) *Status of the Rule.* The Restatement Second seems to acknowledge that an assignment may be proscribed, but only in a rather grudging way: section 322. Compare Portuguese–American Bank of San Francisco v. Welles, 242 U.S. 7 (1916); Augusta Med. Complex, Inc. v. Blue Cross of Kansas, 634 P.2d 1123 (Kan.1981).

"The no assignment right is one of those peculiar legal rules which are honored almost exclusively in the breach." Gilmore, Good Faith Purchase, 63 Yale L.J. 1057, 1118 (1954). Both here and in drafting UCC comments Professor Gilmore criticized *Allhusen* as a monument to conceptualism and a throwback to ancient law. "The cases are legion in which courts have construed the heart out of prohibitory or restrictive terms and held the assignment good.... This gradual and largely unacknowledged shift in legal doctrine has taken place in response to economic need: as accounts and contract rights have become the

a. The statute referred to has been carried forward as Gen.Oblig.L., § 13–101. See p. 913 above.

collateral which secures an ever-increasing number of financing transactions, it has been necessary to reshape the law so that these intangibles, like negotiable instruments and negotiable documents of title, can be freely assigned." Comment to UCC 9–318(4).

(2) *Protection for the Obligor.* Consider some of the reasons a contracting party [R] might have for insisting upon a term prohibiting an assignment of rights by the other party [E]: (a) R anticipates equivocal action by E —a questionable notice or the like—which leaves doubt about the person to whom R's performance is due. (b) R is concerned about E's financial needs and the risk involved in meeting those needs—after notice of an assignment—with prepayments and advances. (c) R foresees circumstances that might make it desirable to modify the contract in a way affecting the interest of the assignee adversely—a hazardous course to take without the assignee's assent. Are there other possible reasons for prohibiting an assignment?

How much does the Code do to satisfy these objectives of the obligor? Is it enough to offset the rule that a prohibition on assignment is ineffective?

(3) *Problem.* Kroo Painting Company makes an assignment of its job earnings to First Bank, without Caristo's consent. Then it makes another assignment of the same earnings—fraudulently—to Second Bank, this time obtaining written consent from Caristo. When both banks claim the proceeds, Caristo interpleads them and deposits the fund into the court. Does it follow from the main case that Second Bank will prevail, because the first assignment was "void"? See Fox–Greenwald Sheet Metal Co. v. Markowitz Bros., Inc., 452 F.2d 1346 (D.C.Cir.1971), and the Note on Successive Assignments, p. 941 above.

INDEX

Notes: References are to pages. Some items are indexed not only under the usual analytic headings but also under generic headings, such as: Biographical notes; Economics of contract law; Restatement; and Specialized agreements. Except as a main heading, "Uniform Commercial Code" is usually referred to as "UCC."

†

1–56662–242–5

90000

9 781566 622424

THE STATESMAN'S YEAR-BOOK

1984–1985

Man hat behauptet, die Welt werde durch Zahlen regiert:
das aber weiss ich, dass die Zahlen uns belehren, ob sie gut
oder schlecht regiert werde.   GOETHE

Editors

Frederick Martin	1864–1883
Sir John Scott-Keltie	1883–1926
Mortimer Epstein	1911/27–1946
S. H. Steinberg	1946–1969
John Paxton	1963/69–

THE
STATESMAN'S
YEAR-BOOK

STATISTICAL AND HISTORICAL ANNUAL
OF THE STATES OF THE WORLD
FOR THE YEAR

1984–1985

EDITED BY

JOHN PAXTON

ST. MARTIN'S PRESS
NEW YORK

First published in 1864
121st edition 1984

For information, write:
ST. MARTIN'S PRESS, INC.
175 Fifth Ave., New York, N.Y. 10010

Typeset in Great Britain by
MB GRAPHIC (TYPESETTING) SERVICES
Dunstable, Bedfordshire

Printed in Great Britain by
RICHARD CLAY (THE CHAUCER PRESS), LTD
Bungay, Suffolk

Library of Congress Catalog Card No. 4–3776

ISBN 0–312–76098–1

This edition published in the United States of America in 1984

PREFACE

The 121st edition of THE STATESMAN'S YEAR-BOOK has been thoroughly revised and there are changes of a major or minor nature on every page. In the 21 years that the editor has been associated with THE STATESMAN'S YEAR-BOOK he has always hoped that the section devoted to Defence would diminish and other sections showing increase in the prosperity of countries of the world could be expanded accordingly, but this has not happened and a thorough review, and in some cases an expansion of the Defence entries has been undertaken for this edition. In addition a Chronology of the year has been added as this was thought to be of benefit to readers. In a recent market survey it was found that there was a need for details of the climate of the countries of the world and this has been added.

As usual the editor thanks his many correspondents, in all parts of the world, for their constructive advice and revisions.

The second edition of THE STATESMAN'S YEAR-BOOK WORLD GAZETTEER is available for those who need more details about individual towns.

J.P.

THE STATESMAN'S YEAR-BOOK OFFICE,
THE MACMILLAN PRESS LTD,
LITTLE ESSEX STREET,
LONDON, WC2R 3LF

WEIGHTS AND MEASURES

On 1 Jan. 1960 following an agreement between the standards laboratories of Great Britain, Canada, Australia, New Zealand, South Africa and the USA, an international yard and an international pound (avoirdupois) came into existence. 1 yard = 91·44 centimetres; 1 lb. = 453·59237 grammes.
The abbreviation 'm' signifies 'million(s)' and tonnes implies metric tons.

094814

LENGTH		DRY MEASURE	
Centimetre	0·394 inch	Litre	0·91 quart
Metre	1·094 yards	Hectolitre	2·75 bushels
Kilometre	0·621 mile		
		WEIGHT—AVOIRDUPOIS	
LIQUID MEASURE		Gramme	15·42 grains
Litre	1·75 pints	Kilogramme	2·205 pounds
Hectolitre	22 gallons	Quintal (= 100 kg)	220·46 pounds
		Tonne (= 1,000 kg)	{ 0·984 long ton / 1·102 short tons
SURFACE MEASURE		WEIGHT—TROY	
Square metre	10·76 sq. feet	Gramme	15·43 grains
Hectare	2·47 acres	Kilogramme	{ 32·15 ounces
Square kilometre	0·386 sq. mile		2·68 pounds }

BRITISH WEIGHTS AND MEASURES

LENGTH		WEIGHT	
1 foot	0·305 metre	1 ounce (= 437·2 grains)	28·350 grammes
1 yard	0·914 metre	1 lb. (= 7,000 grains)	453·6 grammes
1 mile (= 1,760 yds)	1·609 kilometres	1 cwt. (= 112 lb.)	50·802 kilo- grammes
		1 long ton (= 2,240 lb.)	1·016 tonnes
		1 short ton (= 2,000 lb.)	0·907 tonne
SURFACE MEASURE		LIQUID MEASURE	
1 sq. foot	9·290 sq. decimetres		
1 sq. yard	0·836 sq. metre	1 pint	0·568 litre
1 acre	0·405 hectare	1 gallon	4·546 litres
1 sq. mile	2·590 sq. kilometres	1 quarter	2·909 hectolitres

CONTENTS

Part I: International Organizations

Part II: Countries of the World A–Z

xii

CONTENTS

WHEAT

Countries	Area (1,000 hectares)					Production (1,000 tonnes)				
	Average 1974-76	1979	1980	1981	1982	Average 1974-76	1979	1980	1981	1982
Afghánistán	2,326	2,400*	2,192	2,600	2,585	2,845	2,663	2,750	3,000	3,008
Algeria	2,240	1,946	2,071	2,000*	2,000	1,240	1,080	1,511	1,400*	1,200*
Argentina	5,311	4,787	5,023	5,790	7,200	8,513	8,100	7,780	7,900	14,500
Australia [1]	8,606	11,153	11,283	11,840	11,500	11,721	16,483	10,856	16,372	8,600
Bulgaria [1,2]	911	958	968	1,032	1,059	3,180	3,355	3,847	4,443	4,901
Canada	9,888	10,489	11,098	12,427	12,591	17,990	17,185	19,292	24,802	27,620
Chile [1]	652	560	546	432	374	936	995	966	686	650
China [1]	27,714	29,358	29,231	28,311	27,601	45,522	62,733	55,213	59,643	63,003
Czechoslovakia [2]	1,240	1,092	1,189	1,083	1,068	4,690	3,736	5,386	4,325	4,606
Egypt [1]	583	584	557	588	577	1,960	1,856	1,796	1,938	2,017*
France	4,099	4,087	4,582	4,753	4,844	16,715	19,522	23,683	22,858	25,342
Germany, Fed. Rep. of [2]	1,611	1,627	1,668	1,632	1,578	7,159	8,061	8,156	8,313	8,632
Greece	924	991	1,012	1,063	1,030	2,216	2,407	2,970	2,780	2,992
Hungary [1,3]	1,300	1,135	1,276	1,151	1,325*	4,709	3,709	6,077	4,614	6,000
India	19,016	22,641	22,172	22,279	22,308	24,910	35,508	31,830	36,313	37,833
Iran	5,839	5,000*	5,500*	6,300	6,000	5,438	5,500*	5,700*	6,600	6,500
Iraq	1,513	1,750*	1,500*	1,200*	1,200	1,162	1,492	1,300	1,100*	900
Italy [1]	3,600	3,452	3,408	3,258	3,327	9,607	8,980	9,156	8,828	8,998
Japan [1]	87	149	191	224	228	232	541	583	587	742
Mexico	816	599	739	861	1,013	2,983	2,339	2,785	3,189	4,468
Morocco	1,843	1,656	1,715	1,647	1,699*	1,872	1,796	1,811	892	1,824*
Pakistan [1]	6,012	6,687	6,912	6,920	6,959	7,998	9,950	10,805	11,303	11,570
Poland [1]	1,892	1,549	1,609	1,418	1,456	5,787	4,187	4,175	4,203	4,476
Romania [1]	2,378	2,105	2,244	2,111	2,175*	5,530	4,676	6,427	5,310	6,460
S. Africa, Republic of	1,718	1,900*	1,620*	1,790*	1,800	1,876	2,086	1,470	2,340	2,300
Spain [2]	2,866	2,551	2,699	2,635	2,602	4,425	4,101	6,040	3,409	4,368
Turkey [2]	9,142	9,380	8,915	9,250	9,250	14,163	17,569	16,554	17,000	17,650
USSR [1]	60,376	57,682	61,475	59,232	57,278	82,340	90,207	98,182	80,000	87,000
UK	1,167	1,371	1,441	1,491	1,664	5,120	7,168	8,470	8,707	10,258
USA	27,760	25,275	28,727	32,784	31,905	54,555	58,081	64,619	76,170	76,443
Yugoslavia [2]	1,727	1,524	1,516	1,386	1,559	5,555	4,512	5,091	4,270	5,217
World total	227,465	228,972	236,873	240,089	239,412	383,122	428,777	446,107	453,705	481,050

* Unofficial figures. [1] Sown area. [2] Includes spelt. [3] Field crops and other crops.

RYE

Countries	Area (1,000 hectares)					Production (1,000 tonnes)				
	Average 1974–76	1979	1980	1981	1982	Average 1974–76	1979	1980	1981	1982
Argentina	338	225	210	162	270	303	202	155	149	244
Austria	120	106	109	101	100	391	278	383	320	348
Belgium	13	14	11	9	8*	47	51	42	35	32*
Bulgaria [1]	15	16	20	27	23	18	25	28	34	33
Canada	304	330	310	445	439	497	525	455	927	888
China	933	800	700	700	750	1,267	1,400	1,000	1,100	1,400
Czechoslovakia [2]	198	164	177	171	176	588	486	570	544	583
Denmark	56	70	56	51	53	181	257	199	208	226
Finland	59	37	53	41	16	131	77	124	64	35
France	115	116	130	117	110	312	355	408	342	323
German Demo. Rep.	610	678	678	656	633*	1,655	1,830	1,917	1,797	2,071*
Germany, Fed. Rep. of	665	564	547	484	407	2,262	2,114	2,098	1,729	1,639
Hungary [1,3]	101	69	73	74	72*	160	93	141	116	120*
Netherlands	21	12	10	7	6	69	49	39	29	26
Poland [1]	2,955	2,868	3,039	3,002	3,273	7,024	5,201	6,566	6,731	7,792
Portugal	213	209	206	199	200	151	120	138	126	118
Romania [1]	36	35*	35*	30*	35*	48	40	40*	35*	45*
Spain	233	223	217	220	212	236	220	284	212	170
Sweden	109	59	67	50	54	397	195	223	177	204
Turkey	565	470	443	410	400*	683	620	525	530	480*
USSR [1]	8,952	6,476	8,645	7,551	9,829	12,759	8,117	10,205	8,500	12,500
USA	301	352	273	286	289	409	569	419	478	529
Yugoslavia	84	59	55	54	53	108	81	79	75	86
World total	17,151	14,118	16,223	15,038	17,620	29,913	23,127	26,257	24,487	30,126

* Unofficial figures. [1] Sown area. [2] Includes mixture of wheat and rye. [3] Field crops and other crops.

BARLEY

Countries	Area (1,000 hectares)					Production (1,000 tonnes)				
	Average 1974–76	1979	1980	1981	1982	Average 1974–76	1979	1980	1981	1982
Australia [1]	2,159	2,482	2,452	2,683	2,530	2,846	3,703	2,682	3,510	1,740
Austria	320	373	374	362	340	1,177	1,129	1,514	1,220	1,437
Belgium	154	176	171	172	144*	625	842	865	824	800
Bulgaria [1]	525	468	426	382	352	1,705	1,536	1,375	1,406	1,426
Canada	4,532	3,724	4,634	5,476	5,179	9,604	8,460	11,394	13,724	14,073
Czechoslovakia	896	1,017	911	987	964	3,130	3,604	3,575	3,392	3,654
Denmark	1,453	1,622	1,577	1,541	1,489	5,308	6,662	6,044	6,044	6,388
Finland	471	633	533	570	540	1,253	1,650	1,534	1,080	1,599
France	2,753	2,803	2,581	2,579	2,391	9,303	11,196	11,423	10,231	10,026
German Demo. Rep.	889	945	969	964	981*	3,520	3,323	3,979	3,476	4,049*
Germany, Fed. Rep. of	1,719	1,989	2,002	2,044	2,021	6,835	8,184	8,826	8,687	9,460
Greece	398	384	331	303	311	943	861	950	768	853
Hungary [1,2]	252	262	246	286	290*	783	710	929	903	980*
India	2,779	1,828	1,771	1,807	1,750	2,899	2,142	1,624	2,293	2,012
Iran	1,432	1,250*	1,300	1,400	1,400	1,263	1,000*	1,100	1,300*	1,200
Ireland	250	324	332	330	312	993	1,439	1,247	1,400	1,450*
Italy	249	308	329	338	355	654	813	947	983	1,020
Japan [1]	79	116	122	122	125*	221	406	385	383	393*
Korea, South [1]	709	473	331	353	317	1,616	1,508	811	859	749
Morocco	2,026	2,193	2,150	2,228	2,046*	2,279	1,888	2,210	1,039	1,901*
Poland [1]	1,258	1,470	1,322	1,294	1,237	3,721	3,731	3,420	3,540	3,647
Romania [1]	418	773	809	917	920*	1,033	2,043	2,466	2,571	2,700
Spain	3,176	3,424	3,575	3,508	3,556	5,868	6,153	8,705	4,757	5,280
Sweden	585	704	648	681	628	2,028	2,346	2,172	2,452	2,103
Syria	960	1,102	1,210	1,346	1,350	770	396	1,587	1,406	661
Turkey	2,599	2,790	2,800	2,965	2,950*	4,243	5,240	5,300	5,900	6,000*
USSR [1]	32,624	37,005	31,583	31,781	29,706	53,185	47,954	43,450	39,000	41,000
UK	2,248	2,343	2,330	2,329	2,221	8,434	9,623	10,320	10,227	10,908
USA	3,370	3,044	2,944	3,706	3,688	7,699	8,334	7,859	10,436	11,374
World total	79,222	83,855	78,242	80,645	77,506	154,178	157,554	159,319	154,648	160,288

* Unofficial figures. [1] Sown area. [2] Field crops and other crops.

OATS

Countries	Area (1,000 hectares)					Production (1,000 tonnes)				
	Average 1974–76	1979	1980	1981	1982	Average 1974–76	1979	1980	1981	1982
Argentina	334	410	350	299	400*	430	522	433	339	524
Australia	960	1,123	1,093	1,387	1,340	1,029	1,411	1,128	1,617	800
Austria	96	95	92	92	91	293	273	316	304	325
Belgium	71	44	38	36	43*	262	178	136	142	200*
Canada	2,430	1,541	1,515	1,561	1,653	4,430	2,978	2,911	3,188	3,776
Chile	90	79	92	80	68	126	150	173	131	118
China	533	400	400	400	400	700	700	500	600	800
Czechoslovakia [2]	201	127	121	147	161	553	401	421	431	488
Denmark	110	39	40	44	43	368	163	159	176	177
Finland	558	451	448	434	459	1,379	1,283	1,258	1,008	1,320
France	653	540	534	500	520	1,796	1,845	1,927	1,774	1,804
German Demo. Rep.	219	136	155	172	218*	736	532	582	598	846*
Germany, Fed.Rep.of	876	728	691	682	723	3,141	2,994	2,658	2,678	3,113
Ireland	45	28	26	24	24	151	105	90	89	90*
Italy	237	222	226	222	218	469	432	450	422	360
Netherlands	31	21	18	21	24	142	109	94	115	136
Norway	103	95	112	118	130	309	361	428	463	501
Poland [1]	1,196	1,094	997	1,156	1,150	2,953	2,186	2,245	2,730	2,608
Spain	462	428	458	464	440	565	449	680	445	474
Sweden	450	457	452	474	483	1,409	1,524	1,567	1,816	1,559
Turkey	259	220	197	180	180*	390	370	355	325	330*
USSR [1]	11,648	12,239	11,770	12,470	11,489	15,303	15,162	15,544	14,000	14,000
UK	241	136	148	144	129	838	542	600	619	587
USA	5,056	3,917	3,501	3,810	4,274	8,613	7,643	6,652	7,391	8,955
Yugoslavia	250	209	194	194	176	347	283	294	311	269
World Total	28,285	25,949	24,853	26,368	26,270	47,863	43,658	42,760	42,916	45,278

* Unofficial figures. [1] Sown area. [2] Includes mixture of oats and barley.

MAIZE

Countries	Area (1,000 hectares)					Production (1,000 tonnes)				
	Average 1974–76	1979	1980	1981	1982	Average 1974–76	1979	1980	1981	1982
Argentina	3,107	2,800	2,490	3,394	3,170	7,818	8,700	6,400	12,900	9,600
Austria	151	188	193	189	198	925	1,347	1,293	1,374	1,446
Brazil	10,882	11,319	11,451	11,493	12,650	16,786	16,306	20,372	21,098	21,919
Bulgaria	636	666	585	563	621	2,493	3,223	2,256	2,401	3,218
Canada	645	893	958	1,136	1,112	3,345	4,983	5,753	6,673	6,383
China	18,426	20,167	20,385	19,457	20,039	48,218	60,149	62,715	59,301	64,100
Egypt	767	791	800	808	816	2,823	2,938	3,231	3,308	2,709*
France	1,755	1,995	1,757	1,570	1,617	7,511	10,413	9,358	8,956	9,833
Greece	129	123	172	175	164	484	711	1,279	1,428	1,310
Hungary	1,418	1,367	1,253	1,185*	1,200*	6,187	7,396	6,673	6,998	7,000
India	5,965	5,721	6,005	5,898	5,800	6,392	5,603	6,957	6,760	6,500
Indonesia	2,396	2,594	2,735	2,955	2,700	2,829	3,606	3,991	4,509	3,800
Italy	892	937	942	998	1,009	5,230	6,197	6,377	7,197	6,820
Kenya	1,513	1,400	939	1,124	1,300	2,450	1,800*	1,620	2,070	2,300*
Malawi	1,037	1,000	1,100	1,100*	1,100	1,127	1,200*	1,165	1,245	1,415
Mexico	6,732	5,502	6,955	8,150	6,272	8,105	8,124	12,383	14,766	12,215
Nigeria	1,508	1,665	1,710	1,746	1,800	1,258	1,500	1,550	1,580	1,650
Philippines	3,027	3,327	3,319	3,426	3,300	2,541	3,167	3,176	3,290	3,475
Portugal	379	394	377	365	367	489	506	489	419	464
Romania	3,215	3,311	3,288	3,327	3,300	9,421	12,425	11,153	11,892	12,600*
S. Africa, Republic of	5,967	5,000	6,000	7,000	6,000	9,186	8,240	10,790	14,660	8,320
Spain	472	460	455	429	412	1,777	2,205	2,314	2,157	2,284
Thailand	1,180	1,509	1,335	1,465	1,500	2,679	3,300	2,998	3,449	3,004
Turkey	605	585	583	580	590*	1,237	1,350	1,240	1,200	1,400*
USSR[1]	3,303	2,667	2,977	3,545	4,161	9,857	8,373	9,454	8,000	12,500
USA	27,591	29,300	29,555	30,230	29,604	142,511	201,655	168,787	208,330	213,302
Yugoslavia	2,331	2,251	2,202	2,297	2,220	8,842	10,084	9,317	9,807	11,137
Zimbabwe	981	800	1,146	1,330	1,416*	1,886	1,200	1,539	2,814	1,800*
World total	123,144	125,796	128,014	132,587	131,427	335,188	418,357	395,949	450,557	455,351

* Unofficial figures.
[1] For dry grain only.

RICE (Paddy)

Countries	Area (1,000 hectares)					Production (1,000 tonnes)				
	Average 1974–76	1979	1980	1981	1982	Average 1974–76	1979	1980	1981	1982
Bangladesh	10,001	10,160	10,309	10,460	10,460	17,900	19,599	20,821	20,444	21,000
Brazil	5,543	5,452	6,243	6,066	6,021	8,101	7,595	9,776	8,261	9,711
Burma	4,955	4,442	4,801	4,809	4,900	9,037	10,448	13,100	13,900	14,000
Cambodia	1,002	853	1,356*	1,350	1,600	1,312	850*	1,470*	1,160*	1,500*
China	36,604	34,594	34,517	33,927	33,667	128,435	146,959	142,993	147,042	155,111
Colombia	364	442	416	413	481*	1,571	1,932	1,798	1,799	2,070*
Egypt	446	439	408	402	411	2,322	2,517	2,384	2,236	2,287*
India	38,625	39,414	40,152	40,706	39,000	65,351	63,476	80,312	80,362	68,000
Indonesia	8,458	8,804	9,005	9,382	9,022	22,705	26,283	29,652	32,774	34,104
Iran	452	300	300	320	330	1,436	1,420	1,212	1,500	1,400
Italy	181	183	176	169	175	988	1,107	968	837	915
Japan	2,756	2,497	2,377	2,278	2,257	16,116	14,948	12,189	12,824	12,838
Korea, South	1,212	1,224	1,233	1,224	1,189	6,636	7,881	5,311	7,149	7,308
Madagascar	1,069	1,164	1,178	1,239	1,200	2,009	2,045	2,109	2,135	2,000
Malaysia	741	738	718	723	722	2,029	2,095	2,070	2,095	2,062
Mexico	196	149	132	180	175	557	500	456	644	600
Nepal	1,252	1,250	1,270	1,250	1,260	2,481	2,060	2,464	2,060	2,300
Nigeria	234	400	550*	600*	700	476	750	1,090*	1,241*	1,400
Pakistan	1,688	2,035	1,935	1,976	2,006	3,834	4,824	4,679	5,145	5,000*
Philippines	3,555	3,500	3,637	3,459	3,500	6,092	7,504	7,836	8,158	8,346
Sri Lanka	677	790	824	842	825	1,336	1,917	2,137	2,233	2,150
Thailand	7,952	8,651	9,099	9,105	9,400	14,585	15,758	17,368	17,774	17,500*
USSR	506	610	666	634	648	1,975	2,394	2,791	2,400	2,500
USA	1,056	1,161	1,340	1,535	1,316	5,390	5,985	6,629	8,289	6,995
Vietnam	5,134	5,483	5,544	5,615	5,700	11,213	10,758	11,679	12,570	13,780
World total	140,576	141,052	144,529	145,099	143,475	347,358	377,394	399,112	411,714	411,897

* Unofficial figures.

MILLET

Countries	Area (1,000 hectares)					Production (1,000 tonnes)				
	Average 1974–76	1979	1980	1981	1982	Average 1974–76	1979	1980	1981	1982
Argentina	211	238	182	187	132	241	310	188	238	154
Australia	30	32	19	27	34	28	36	14	27	39
Cameroon	433	497	450	450	455	389	414	400	400	406
Chad	959	1,140	1,150*	1,150	1,190	520	550	600	580	600
Egypt	205	171	172	173	174	786	635	635	671	633*
Ethiopia	253	249*	233	230	230	245	191*	205	200	200
Ghana	221	250	240*	230	250	140	149	66	73*	90
India	18,338	17,196	18,158	18,129	18,000	9,042	8,094	9,337	9,942	9,000
Kenya	79	81	81	82	82	128	110	130	130	130
Korea, North	413	415	420	420	415	415	440	450	450	445
Korea, South	27	3	3	4	5	27	3	4	5	5
Mali	1,212	1,400	1,400	1,420	1,454	852	922*	750	930	952
Nepal	124	121	120	120	121	140	119	122	122	122
Niger	2,150	2,883	3,072	3,038*	3,066*	828	1,246	1,364	1,305*	1,295*
Nigeria	4,800	5,000*	5,030*	5,050*	5,100	2,843	3,130*	3,130*	3,230*	3,300
Pakistan	606	561	406	559	560	295	277	215	272	265
Senegal	1,004	968	1,115	850*	850	658	521	540	736	650
Sudan	1,126	1,293	1,300	1,250	800	416	550	450	500	230
Tanzania	200	220	220	220	220	129	160	160	140	150
Togo	142	170	170	170	170	110	136	128	107	125
Uganda	498	313	279	300	330	613	481	459	480	528
USSR	2,914	2,784	2,907	2,692	2,821	2,410	1,553	1,873	1,500	2,000
Upper Volta	857	900	800	900	900	364	431	330	400*	420
Zimbabwe¹	360	400	380	395	390	173	140	180	196	190
World total	43,610	42,613	43,261	43,045	42,841	29,062	27,441	27,887	29,147	29,166

* Unofficial figures.

¹ On farms and estates.

SORGHUM

Countries	Area (1,000 hectares)					Production (1,000 tonnes)				
	Average 1974–76	1979	1980	1981	1982	Average 1974–76	1979	1980	1981	1982
Argentina	2,115	2,044	1,279	2,100	2,510	5,391	6,200	2,960	7,550	8,000*
Australia	518	469	519	658	651	1,029	1,125	922	1,204	1,317
China	4,550	3,174	2,696	2,614	2,804	8,584	7,656	6,785	6,662	8,011
Colombia	153	221	206	231	198*	366	501	431	532	517*
Ethiopia[1,2]	847	726	1,014	979	1,000	792	680	1,642	1,411	1,300
France	79	84	74	67	57	291	339	321	321	259
India	16,018	16,674	15,809	16,158	16,000	10,148	11,648	10,431	11,571	10,800
Mexico	1,284	1,456	1,579	1,767	1,340	3,778	3,917	4,812	6,296	4,956
Niger	649	716	768	982*	1,131*	253	346	368	327*	357*
Nigeria	5,793	6,000*	6,000*	6,000*	6,000	3,590	3,785*	3,800*	3,750*	3,800
S. Africa, Republic of	317	280	450	400*	350	454	354	695	545	286
Sudan	2,530	3,025	3,000	3,400	3,000	1,907	2,408	2,200	3,350	2,100
Thailand	152	230*	234	266	256	210	260*	237	274	267
Uganda	335	174	167	170	200	401	316	299	320	400
USA	5,892	5,221	5,068	5,551	5,766	17,678	20,546	14,712	22,333	21,364
Upper Volta	1,131	900	850	1,200	1,100	666	610	559	750*	700
Venezuela	48	215	265	240	210	76	429	403	386	337*
Yemen Arab Republic	1,104	673*	791	730	670	835	632*	692	635	583
World total	47,646	46,243	44,905	47,853	47,760	60,223	65,171	55,703	72,001	69,113

* Unofficial figures. [1] Includes teff. [2] Unspecified millet and sorghum.

CENTRIFUGAL RAW SUGAR
(in 1,000 tonnes)

Countries	Average 1974–76	1977	1978	1979	1980	1981	1982
Argentina	1,480	1,666	1,397	1,411	1,716	1,624	1,615*
Australia [1]	3,000	3,318	2,902	2,963	3,329	3,434	3,560
Barbados [2]	104	124*	101	114	132	94	86*
Brazil	6,867	8,760*	7,767*	7,027*	8,547*	8,393*	9,420*
Canada	141	149	123	106	107*	144*	120*
China	2,700	3,076	3,213	3,587	3,650	4,191	4,690
Cuba	6,251	6,607*	7,457	8,048	6,787	7,542*	8,280*
Czechoslovakia	717	939*	885*	910*	810*	747*	890*
Dominican Rep.	1,229	1,258	1,199	1,200	1,039*	1,063*	1,220*
Egypt	595	668	635	668	662	693	758*
France	3,049	4,268	4,065	4,332	4,253	5,576	4,800
Fiji [1]	281	362	347	473	396	470	487
German Demo. Rep.	627	780*	780*	679*	600*	747*	710*
Germany, Fed. Rep.of	2,568	3,075	2,997	3,088	2,994	3,702	3,570*
Guyana	331	253*	342	316	273	306	288
India [3]	4,712	5,261	7,018	6,367	4,191	5,596	9,170
Indonesia [4]	1,037	1,106	1,105	1,307	1,250	1,247	1,629
Italy	1,390	1,359	1,620	1,707	1,934	2,226	1,290
Jamaica	367	295	292	283	232	205*	197*
Mauritius [4]	655	705	705	730	504	610	727
Mexico	2,761	2,728	3,072	3,078*	2,765*	2,586*	2,873*
Pakistan [3]	629	800	936	663	624	928	1,410
Peru	965	926	856	716	552	493*	700*
Philippines	2,572	2,688	2,335	2,342	2,343	2,394	2,527
Poland	1,752	1,850*	1,763*	1,762	1,186	1,872	2,000
Puerto Rico	271	239	185*	174	158	137	137
S. Africa, Rep. of	1,909	2,084	2,082	2,079	1,611	2,055	2,210
Spain	984	1,213	1,143	750	972	1,111	1,106
Sweden	294	343	327	350	327	374	385
Trinidad	188	179	148*	144	114	93*	79*
USSR	7,594	8,825*	9,100*	7,700*	7,150*	6,200*	6,800*
UK	686	1,015	1,111	1,255	1,202	1,187	1,457
USA [5]	5,745	5,254	5,353	5,061	5,331	5,644	5,092
World total	79,518	89,747	90,258	88,984	84,047	92,577	101,403

[1] 94° net titre.
[2] Includes the sugar equivalent of fancy molasses.
[3] Includes sugar (raw value) refined from gur.
[4] Tel quel.
[5] Includes Hawaii.
* Unofficial figures.

WORLD ESTIMATED CRUDE OIL PRODUCTION [1]
(in 1,000 tonnes)

	1960	1970	1982	1983
North America				
USA	384,080	533,677	486,200	486,700
Canada	27,480	69,954	74,200	76,500
Caribbean Area				
Venezuela	148,690	193,209	100,175	97,500
Trinidad	6,075	7,225	9,104	8,500
Colombia	8,100	11,071	7,326	7,550
Other Latin America				
Mexico	14,125	21,877	150,390	149,000
Argentina	9,160	19,969	24,390	24,650
Brazil	390	8,009	13,355	16,500
Ecuador	2,680	191	10,688	12,150
Peru	450	3,450	9,465	8,700
Bolivia	990	1,128	1,210	1,100
Chile		1,620	2,003	2,000
Middle East				
Saudi Arabia	61,090	176,851	323,330	246,000
Iran	52,065	191,663	120,396	124,000
Iraq	47,480	76,600	49,566	46,000
Kuwait	81,860	137,397	41,615	54,000
Abu Dhabi	—	33,288	42,022	37,500
Qatar	8,210	17,257	16,033	14,000
Syria	—	4,350	8,200	8,400
Turkey	350	3,461	2,342	2,200
Bahrain	2,250	3,834	2,187	2,100
Sharjah	—	—	340	500
Africa				
Nigeria	880	53,420	63,468	60,000
Libya	—	159,201	55,167	52,000
Algeria	8,630	47,253	32,676	32,000
Gabon	850	5,460	7,835	8,000
Angola	70	5,066	6,403	8,000
Tunisia	—	4,151	5,100	5,200
Congo	—	—	4,400	4,600
Zaïre	—	—	1,055	1,150

[1] Excluding small scale production in Afghánistán, Bangladesh, Cuba, Guatemala, Israel, Mongolia, Morocco, New Zealand, Taiwan and Thailand.

WORLD ESTIMATED CRUDE OIL PRODUCTION
(contd.)

(in 1,000 tonnes)

	1960	1970	1982	1983
Western Europe				
UK	90	84	103,387	114,500
Norway	—	—	24,480	30,000
Germany, Fed. Rep. of	5,560	7,536	4,234	4,160
Austria	2,440	2,798	1,303	1,200
Spain	—	156	1,533	3,000
Netherlands	1,920	1,919	1,895	2,800
France	2,260	2,308	1,638	1,600
Italy	1,990	1,408	1,744	2,200
Denmark	—	—	1,686	2,400
Far East				
Indonesia	20,560	42,102	64,646	63,000
Australia	—	8,292	17,530	19,500
Brunei	4,690	6,916	8,015	8,750
India	440	6,809	19,712	24,000
Malaysia	—	—	15,200	18,050
Burma	530	750	1,350	1,300
Japan	510	750	398	420
Pakistan	360	486	582	600
USSR and Eastern Europe				
USSR	148,000	352,667	613,000	618,000
Romania	11,500	13,377	11,700	12,500
Yugoslavia	1,040	2,854	4,324	4,200
Albania	600	1,199	4,000	4,000
Hungary	1,215	1,937	2,026	1,950
Poland	195	424	241	250
German Dem. Rep.	—	60	60	60
Bulgaria	200	334	300	300
Czechoslovakia	140	203	89	90
China	5,000	20,000	102,120	105,000
World Total	1,090,080	2,336,153	2,755,385	2,722,687

OIL

Main Oil Producing Countries
1982

	(1,000 bbls daily)
USSR	11,921
USA	8,670
Saudi Arabia [1]	6,484
Mexico	2,749
UK	2,060
China	2,023
Iran	1,964
Venezuela	1,891
Indonesia	1,339
Nigeria	1,295

Proved Oil Reserves
1 Jan. 1983

	(1m. bbls)
Saudi Arabia [2]	167,920
Kuwait [2]	67,150
USSR	63,000
Iran	55,308
Mexico	48,300
Iraq	41,000
UAE – Abu Dhabi	30,510
USA	29,785
Libya	21,500
Venezuela	21,500

Leading Oil-Consuming Countries
1982

	(in 1,000 bbls daily)
USA	15,200
USSR	9,200
Japan	4,250
Germany, Federal Republic of	2,085
China	1,800
France	1,650
Italy	1,620
Canada	1,470
UK	1,345
Brazil	1,300

[1] Includes 50% of the Partitioned Neutral Zone production.
[2] Includes 50% of the Partitioned Neutral Zone reserves.

TERRITORIAL SEA LIMITS (IN MILES)

State	Territorial Sea	Jurisdiction over fisheries (measured from the baseline of the territorial sea)
Albania	15 (1976)	—
Algeria	12 (1963)	—
Angola	20 (1975)	200 (1975)
Antigua and Barbuda	12 (1983)	200 (1983) [1]
Argentina	200 (1967)	—
Australia	3 (1878)	200 (1979)
Bahamas	3 (1878)	200 (1977)
Bahrain	3	—
Bangladesh	12 (1974)	200 (1974) [1]
Barbados	12 (1977)	200 (1978) [1]
Belgium	3	up to median line (1978)
Belize	3 (1878)	12 (1978)
Benin	200 (1976)	—
Brazil	200 (1970)	—
Bulgaria	12 (1951)	—
Burma	12 (1968)	200 (1977) [1]
Cambodia	12 (1969)	200 (1979) [1]
Cameroon	50 (1974)	—
Canada	12 (1970)	200 (1977)
Cape Verde	12 (1978)	200 (1978) [1]
Chile	3	200 (1947–52) [1]
China	12 (1958)	—
Colombia	12 (1970)	200 (1978) [1]
Comoros	12 (1976)	200 (1976) [1]
Congo	200 (1977)	—
Costa Rica	12 (1972)	200 (1975) [1]
Cuba	12 (1977)	200 (1977) [1]
Cyprus	12 (1964)	—
Denmark (including Faroe Islands and Greenland)	3 (1966)	200 (1977)
Djibouti	12 (1971)	200 (1979) [1]
Dominica	12 (1981)	200 (1981) [1]
Dominican Republic	6 (1967)	200 (1977) [1]
Ecuador	200 (1966)	—
Egypt	12 (1958)	—
El Salvador	200 (1950)	—
Equatorial Guinea	12 (1970)	—
Ethiopia	12 (1953)	—
Fiji	12 (1976)	200 (1981) [1]
Finland	4 (1956)	12 (1975)
France	12 (1971)	200 (1977) [1] (except Mediterranean)
Gabon	100 (1972)	—
Gambia	12 (1969)	200 (1978)
German Democratic Republic	3	up to median line (1978)
Germany, Federal Republic of	In accordance with international law	200 (1977)
Ghana	200 (1977)	—
Greece	6 (1936)	—
Grenada	12 (1978)	200 (1978) [1]
Guatemala	12 (1934)	200 (1976) [1]
Guinea	12 (1980)	200 (1980) [1]
Guinea-Bissau	12 (1978)	200 (1978) [1]
Guyana	12 (1977)	200 (1977)
Haiti	12 (1972)	200 (1977) [1]
Honduras	12 (1965)	200 (1951) [1]

[1] Economic zone.

TERRITORIAL SEA LIMITS (IN MILES)—*contd.*

State	Territorial Sea	Jurisdiction over fisheries (measured from the baseline of the territorial sea)
Iceland	12 (1979)	200 (1979) [1]
India	12 (1967)	200 (1977) [1]
Indonesia	12 (1957) [2]	200 (1980) [1]
Iran	12 (1959)	[3]
Iraq	12 (1958)	—
Ireland	3 (1959)	200 (1977)
Israel	6 (1956)	—
Italy	12 (1974)	—
Ivory Coast	12 (1977)	200 (1977) [1]
Jamaica	12 (1971)	—
Japan	12 (1977)	200 (1977)
Jordan	3 (1943)	—
Kenya	12 (1969)	200 (1979) [1]
Kiribati	3 (1878)	200 (1979)
Korea (North)	12	200 (1977) [1]
Korea (South)	12 (1978)	12
Kuwait	12 (1967)	—
Lebanon	—	6 (1921)
Liberia	200 (1976)	—
Libya	12 (1959)	—
Madagascar	50 (1973)	—
Malaysia	12 (1969)	200 (1980) [1]
Maldive, Republic of	3–55 [3]	(1976) [1,4]
Malta	12 (1978)	25 (1978)
Mauritania	70 (1978)	200 (1978) [1]
Mauritius	12 (1970)	200 (1977) [1]
Mexico	12 (1969)	200 (1976) [1]
Monaco	12	
Morocco	12 (1973) [5]	200 (1981) [1]
Mozambique	12 (1976)	200 (1976) [1]
Namibia	3	12 (1964)
Nauru	12 (1971)	200 (1978) [1]
Netherlands	3	200 (1977)
New Zealand	12 (1977)	200 (1978) [1]
Nicaragua	200 (1979)	200 (1979) [1]
Nigeria	12 (1967)	200 (1978) [1]
Norway	4 (1812)	200 (1977) [1]
Oman	12 (1977)	200 (1981) [1]
Pakistan	12 (1966)	200 (1976) [1]
Panama	200 (1967)	—
Papua New Guinea	12 (1978)	200 (1978) (offshore waters)
Peru	200 (1947) [6]	200 (1947) [6]
Philippines	[7]	200 (1979) [1]

[1] Economic zone.

[2] The territorial sea of Indonesia is measured by straight lines surrounding the archipelago.

[3] Outer limits of the superjacent waters of the continental shelf. Median line in the Sea of Oman (1973).

[4] Territorial limits and economic zone defined by geographical co-ordinates.

[5] Limits with opposite or adjacent states to be fixed by agreement, failing which median line principle to apply.

[6] Sovereignty and jurisdiction over the sea, its soil and subsoil up to 200 miles (1947).

[7] The territorial sea of the Philippines is determined by straight base-lines joining appropriate points of the outermost islands forming the Philippine archipelago in accordance with Treaties of 1898, 1900 and 1930 (1961).

TERRITORIAL SEA LIMITS (IN MILES)—*contd.*

State	Territorial Sea	Jurisdiction over fisheries (measured from the baseline of the territorial sea)
Poland	12 (1977)	up to median line (1978)
Portugal	12 (1977)	200 (1977) [2]
Qatar	3	[1]
Romania	12 (1951)	—
St Christopher (St Kitts)—Nevis	3 (1878)	—
St Lucia	3 (1878)	—
St Vincent and the Grenadines	3 (1878)	—
São Tomé and Principe	12 (1978)	200 (1978) [2]
Saudi Arabia	12 (1958)	[1]
Senegal	150 (1976)	200 (1976)
Seychelles	12 (1977)	200 (1977) [2]
Sierra Leone	200 (1971)	—
Singapore	3 (1878)	—
Solomon Islands	12 (1978)	200 (1978)
Somalia	200 (1972)	—
South Africa, Republic of	12 (1977)	200 (1977)
Spain	12 (1977)	200 (1978) [2] (except Mediterranean)
Sri Lanka	12 (1971)	200 (1977) [2]
Sudan	12 (1960)	—
Suriname	12 (1978)	200 (1978) [2]
Sweden	4 (1779)	200 (1978)
Syria	35 (1981)	—
Tanzania	50 (1973)	—
Thailand	12 (1966)	200 (1982)
Togo	30 (1977)	200 (1977) [2]
Tonga	[3]	—
Trinidad and Tobago	12 (1969)	—
Tunisia	12 (1973)	—
Turkey	6 (1964)	12 (1964)
Tuvalu	3 (1878)	200 (1979)
USSR	12 (1909)	200 (1976)
United Arab Emirates	3 [4]	[5]
UK	3 (1878)	200 (1977)
USA	3 (1793)	200 (1983) [2]
Uruguay	200 (1969)	—
Vanuatu	12 (1978–82)	200 (1978–82) [2]
Venezuela	12 (1956)	200 (1978) [2]
Vietnam	12 (1977)	200 (1977) [2]
Western Samoa	12 (1977)	200 (1982)
Yemen, Peoples Dem. Rep. of	12 (1970)	200 (1978) [2]
Yemen, Republic of	12 (1967)	—
Yugoslavia	12 (1979)	—
Zaïre	12 (1974)	—

[1] Outer limits of the superjacent waters of the continental shelf (1974).
[2] Economic zone.
[3] Territorial limits defined by geographical co-ordinates (173–177° W. and 15–23° 30′ S.) (1887).
[4] Sharjah, 12 miles.
[5] Limits to be defined by agreement, failing which median line to apply (1980).

The table above, reproduced from a survey prepared by the FAO of the UN shows: *(a)* the territorial sea limit, and *(b)* jurisdiction over fisheries.

Books of Reference

Buzan, B., *Seabed Politics.* New York, 1976

Janis, M. W., *Sea Power and the Law of the Sea.* Lexington, 1977

Luard, E., *The Control of the Sea-Bed.* London, 1974

Moore, G., *Coastal State Requirements for Foreign Fishing. FAO Legislative Study No. 21.* Rev. 1. Rome, 1983

1983
April   18   Thailand. General election to the House of Representatives: Social Action Party, 92; Thai Nation Party, 73; Democratic Party, 36. Four-party government formed on 7 May.

         21   United Kingdom. £1 coin came into use.

         23   Iceland. General election to the Alþingi: Independence Party, 23; Progressives, 14; People's Alliance, 10; Social Democrats, 4; Feminists, 3.

         24   Austria. General election to the National Assembly: Socialists, 90; People's Party, 81; Freedom Party, 12.
Turkey. Ban on political parties lifted.

May   6   Finland. Coalition government formed by Kalevi Sorsa.

         17   Lebanon. Israel agreed that the state of war between itself and Lebanon had ended, and that it would withdraw Israeli forces within 8–12 weeks.
Upper Volta. Prime Minister, Capt. Thomas Sankara, arrested; his People's Salvation Council was dissolved on 27 May.

         18   Austria. Coalition government formed by Dr Fred Sinowatz.

         22   Yemen Arab Republic. President Ali Abdullah Saleh was re-elected.

         24   United Kingdom. The Criminal Justice Act came into force.
Sudan. President Jaafar Mohammed Nemery was sworn in for a further term.

         26   Iceland. Coalition government formed by Steingrímur Hermannsson.

June   8   Norway. Coalition government formed by Kaare Willoch.

         9   United Kingdom. General election to the House of Commons: Conservatives, 397; Labour, 209; Liberal-Social Democratic Alliance, 23; others, 21.
Portugal. Coalition government formed by Dr Mário Soares.

         16   USSR. Yury Andropov, First Secretary of the Soviet Communist Party, elected President of the Presidium of the Supreme Soviet.

     16–23   Poland. Visit of the Pope, who met the Prime Minister, Gen. Wojciech Jaruzelski, and the Chairman of Solidarity, Lech Walesa.

         18   China. Li Xiannian elected President of the People's Republic, and Gen. Ulanhu Vice-President. Peng Zhen was elected Chairman of the Standing Committee of the National People's Congress, and Deng Xiaoping, Chairman of the Military Commission of the Central Committee.

         23   USA. The Supreme Court ruled that Congress could not veto decisions of the President and his executive.

         24   Syria. Yassar Arafat of the PLO expelled; New PLO headquarters in Tripoli, Lebanon.

July   11–13   Nepál. The Prime Minister, Surya Bahadur Thapa, resigned and was replaced by Lokendra Bahadur Chand.

     21–22   Poland. Martial law ended at midnight.

         25   Sri Lanka. Communal violence began between Sinhalese and Tamils.

CHRONOLOGY—*contd.*

1983
Aug. 4 Italy. Coalition government formed by Bettino Craxi.
Upper Volta. Capt. Thomas Sankara overthrew President Ouedraogo.

5 Sri Lanka. The constitution amended, making it an offence to advocate a separate Tamil state.

6–27 Nigeria. General and presidential elections. President Shagari and his government re-elected.

8 Guatemala. President Ríos Montt overthrown and replaced by Gen. Mejía Victores.

9 Swaziland. Royal Wife Ntombi succeeded Royal Wife Dzeliwe as Queen Regent.

11 Chad. Northern rebels took Faya Largeau.

15 Paraguay. President Stroessner sworn in for a seventh term.

21 Philippines. The Leader of the Opposition, Benigno Aquino, murdered.

22 Cameroon. The Prime Minister, Bello Bouba, was dismissed.

29–30 Chile. State of emergency ended at midnight.

29 Kenya. President Arap Moi re-elected.

Sept. 4 Lebanon. Israeli forces withdrew south of the Awali River; fighting then broke out in the Chouf Mountains between Druze and Lebanese government forces.

9 South Africa. Parliament passed a bill creating a new constitution, subject to referendum, among the white population (held on 2 Nov.).

15 Israel. The Prime Minister, Menachem Begin, resigned.

19 St Kitts-Nevis. Independence achieved.

Oct. 10 Israel. Itshak Shamir sworn in as Prime Minister.

14 USA. William Clark appointed Interior Secretary (James Watt had resigned on 12 Sept.).
Korea. The Prime Minister, Kim Sang Hyup, replaced by Chin Iee Chong.

19 Grenada. The Prime Minister, Maurice Bishop, and others were murdered and a revolutionary military council set up.

23 Grenada. The Caribbean Community suspended Grenada's membership, and asked for military aid from the USA.

24–28 Grenada. Invasion by American-led forces, leading to the end of the revolution.
Sri Lanka. Tamil United Liberation Front Members of Parliament were declared to have lost their seats, following their boycott of parliament.

27–30 Zambia. President Kaunda re-elected; general election to the National Assembly (of a one-party state).

30 Argentina. General election to the Chamber of Deputies.

Nov. 6 Turkey. General election to the Grand National Assembly.

CHRONOLOGY—*contd.*

1983
Nov.   15   Grenada. Installation of a 9-member Advisory Council. End of the
              state of emergency.
              Cyprus. The Turkish Cypriot Federated State declared itself
              independent.

Dec.   10   Argentina. Raul Alfonsin President, and head of a new civilian
              government.

        11   Bangladesh. Lieut.-Gen. Hossain Mohammad Ershad President.

        15   Jamaica. General election to the House of Representatives, con-
              tested by one party only. Edward Seaga's government re-elected.

     20–26   Lebanon. Yasser Arafat's PLO guerillas left Tripoli, Lebanon.

        31   Brunei. The state became independent.
              Nigeria. President Shagari's government was overthrown by
              Gen. Mohammed Buhari in a *coup*.

1984
Jan.   16   Jordan. King Hussein opened the first Parliament to be summoned
              since the dissolution of the lower house in 1976.

        18   Nigeria. An 18-member cabinet was appointed, including 11 civi-
              lians.

        27   Malaysia. Sultan Idris Shah of Perak died and was succeeded by
              Sultan Azlan Shah.

        29   Tanzania. President Aboud Jumbe of Zanzibar resigned; Ali
              Hassan Mwinyi was appointed interim President on 30 Jan.

Feb.   5   Lebanon. The cabinet resigned, Chafik Wazzan remaining as a
              'caretaker' Prime Minister. The unratified military withdrawal
              agreement between Israel and Lebanon was considered null and
              void by President Gemayal.

         9   Malaysia. The sultans elected Sultan Mahmood Iskander of Johore
              to be next Yang di Pertuan Agong from 25 April.
              USSR. President Andropov died.

        13   USSR. Konstantin Chernenko elected General Secretary of the
              Soviet Communist Party.
              Poland. Parliament voted to extend its present term indefin-
              itely.
              Panama. President Espriella resigned; succeeded by Jorge
              Illueca.

        16   Angola. South Africa, Angola and the USA reached agreement on
              joint withdrawal of South African forces and of Cuban and
              SWAPO forces from southern Angola.

        20   Vanuatu. President Sokomanu resigned.

March   16   Prime Minister P. W. Botha of the Republic of South Africa and
              President Samora Machel of Mozambique signed a 'non-
              agression and good neighbourliness pact'.

        20   The Lausanne talks on Lebanon's future government ended in
              complete failure.

ADDENDA

LIBYA. On 18 Feb. 1984 Libyan students seized control of the People's Bureau in London and following a shooting incident and siege UK broke off diplomatic relations with Libya on 22 April.

GUINEA-BISSAU. Vitor Saude Maria was dismissed as Prime Minister by the President on 10 March 1984.

USSR. The city of Rybinsk was renamed Andropov in March 1984. On 11 April Konstantin Chernenko elected President of the Presidium.

NORTH KOREA. Vice-President Kim Il died on 10 March 1984.

CANADA. Pierre Trudeau announced his forthcoming retirement as Prime Minister on 29 Feb. His successor will be chosen at the convention of the Liberal Party to be held in June 1984 in Ottawa.

British High Commissioner: Derek Day.

VENEZUELA. The Cabinet on 2 Feb. 1984 was as follows: *Interior:* Octavio Lepage Barreto. *Foreign Affairs:* Isidro Morales Paúl. *Finance:* Manuel Azpurúa Arreaza. *Defence:* Gen. Humberto Alcalde Alvarez. *Development:* Héctor Hurtado Navarro. *Education:* Ruth Lerner de Almea. *Health:* Luis Manuel Manzanilla. *Agriculture and Livestock:* Felipe Gómez Alvarez. *Labour:* Simoń Antoni Paván. *Transport and Communications:* Juan Pedro del Moral. *Justice:* José Manzo González. *Energy and Mines:* Arturo Hernández Grisanti. *Environment and Renewable Resources:* Orlando José Castejón. *Urban Development:* Rafael Martín Guédez. *Information and Tourism:* Armando Durán. *Youth:* Milena Sardi de Selle. *Secretary to the Presidency:* Simón Alberto Consalvi. *President of State Planning Corporation:* Luis Raúl Matos Azócar. *President of the Venezuelan Investment Fund:* Carlos Rafael Silva. There are 4 Ministers of State.

KENYA. *High Commissioner in London:* Benjamin K. Kipkulei.

GUINEA. President Ahmed Sekou Touré died on 27 March. The interim government under Dr Lansana Beauozui fell following a military *coup* on 3 April. On 5 April a 32-member Council of Ministers was appointed with Col. Lansana Conté as President and Col. Diara Traoré as Prime Minister.

VATICAN. *US Ambassador:* William Wilson.

PERU. *Prime Minister:* Sandro Mariategui.

BANGLADESH. *Prime Minister:* Ataur Rahman Khan.

EL SALVADOR. No Presidential candidate emerged from the elections held on 25 March. The second round of elections is expected to be held on 6 May 1984.

CAMEROON. An attempted *coup* took place on 6 April 1984 but President Biya retained control after heavy loss of life by 9 April.

PART I

INTERNATIONAL ORGANIZATIONS

PART 1

INTERNATIONAL
ORGANIZATIONS

THE UNITED NATIONS

The United Nations is an association of states which have pledged themselves, through signing the Charter, to maintain international peace and security and to co-operate in establishing political, economic and social conditions under which this task can be securely achieved. Nothing contained in the Charter authorizes the organization to intervene in matters which are essentially within the domestic jurisdiction of any state.

The United Nations Charter originated from proposals agreed upon at discussions held at Dumbarton Oaks (Washington, D.C.) between the USSR, US and UK from 21 Aug. to 28 Sept., and between US, UK and China from 29 Sept. to 7 Oct. 1944. These proposals were laid before the United Nations Conference on International Organization, held at San Francisco from 25 April to 26 June 1945, and (after amendments had been made to the original proposals) the Charter of the United Nations was signed on 26 June 1945 by the delegates of 50 countries. Ratification of all the signatures had been received by 31 Dec. 1945. (For the complete text of the Charter *see* THE STATESMAN'S YEAR-BOOK, 1946, pp. xxi–xxxii.)

The United Nations formally came into existence on 24 Oct. 1945, with the deposit of the requisite number of ratifications of the Charter with the US Department of State. The official languages of the United Nations are Arabic, Chinese, English, French, Russian and Spanish.

The headquarters of the United Nations is in New York City, USA.

Flag: UN emblem in white centred on a light blue ground.

Membership. Membership is open to all peace-loving states whose admission will be effected by the General Assembly upon recommendation of the Security Council. The table on pp. 7–8 shows the member states of the United Nations.

The Principal Organs of the United Nations are: 1. The General Assembly. 2. The Security Council. 3. The Economic and Social Council. 4 The Trusteeship Council. 5. The International Court of Justice. 6. The Secretariat.

1. **The General Assembly** consists of all the members of the United Nations. Each member has only 1 vote. The General Assembly meets regularly once a year, commencing on the third Tuesday in Sept.; the session normally lasts until mid-December and is resumed for some weeks in the new year if this is required. Special sessions may be convoked by the Secretary-General if requested by the Security Council, by a majority of the members of the United Nations or by 1 member concurred with by the majority of the members. The Assembly also meets in emergency special session. The General Assembly elects its President for each session.

The first regular session was held in London from 10 Jan. to 14 Feb. and in New York from 23 Oct. to 16 Dec. 1946.

Special sessions have been held on Palestine (1947, 1948), Tunisia (1961), Financial Situation of UN (1963), South West Africa, Peace-Keeping, Postponement of Outer Space Conference (1967), Raw Materials and Development (1974), New International Economic Order (1975), Peace-keeping force in the Lebanon, Namibia, Disarmament (1978, 1982), Economic Issues (1980); Emergency Special sessions were held on Suez, Hungary (1956), Lebanon-Jordan-United Arab Republic dispute (1958), Congo (1960), Middle East (1967), Afghánistán, Palestine (1980) and Namibia (1981).

The work of the General Assembly is divided between 7 Main Committees, on which every member state is represented. These are: First committee (disarmament

3

and related international security matters); special political committee; second committee (economic and financial matters); third committee (social, humanitarian and cultural matters); fourth committee (decolonisation matters); fifth committee (administrative and budgetary matters); sixth committee (legal matters).

In addition there is a General Committee charged with the task of co-ordinating the proceedings of the Assembly and its Committees; and a Credentials Committee which verifies the credentials of the delegates. The General Committee consists of 25 members, comprising the President of the General Assembly, its 17 Vice-Presidents and the Chairmen of the 7 Main Committees. The Credentials Committee consists of 9 members, elected at the beginning of each session of the General Assembly. The Assembly has 2 standing committees—an Advisory Committee on Administrative and Budgetary Questions, and a Committee on Contributions. The General Assembly establishes subsidiary and ad hoc bodies when necessary to deal with specific matters. These include: Special Committee on Peace-keeping Operations (33 members), Commission on Human Rights (32 members), Committee on the peaceful uses of outer space (28 members), Conciliation Commission for Palestine (3 members), Committee on Disarmament (40 members), International Law Commission (25 members), Scientific Committee on the effects of atomic radiation (15 members), Special Committee on the implementation of the declaration on the granting of independence to colonial countries and peoples (24 members), Special Committee on the policies of Apartheid of the Government of the Republic of South Africa (11 members), UN Commission on International Trade Law (29 members) and Committee on the Peaceful Uses of Sea-bed and Ocean Floor Beyond the Limits of National Jurisdiction (91 members).

The General Assembly may discuss any matters within the scope of the Charter, and, with the exception of any situation or dispute on the agenda of the Security Council, may make recommendations on any such questions or matters. For decisions on important questions a two-thirds majority is required, on other questions a simple majority of members present and voting. In addition, the Assembly at its fifth session, in 1950, decided that if the Security Council, because of lack of unanimity of the permanent members, fails to exercise its primary responsibility for the maintenance of international peace and security in any case where there appears to be a threat to the peace, breach of the peace or act of aggression, the General Assembly shall consider the matter immediately with a view to making appropriate recommendations to members for collective measures, including in the case of a breach of the peace or act of aggression the use of armed force when necessary, to maintain or restore international peace and security.

The General Assembly receives and considers reports from the other organs of the United Nations, including the Security Council. The Secretary-General makes an annual report to it on the work of the Organization.

2. **The Security Council** consists of 15 members, each of which has 1 vote. There are 5 permanent and 10 non-permanent members elected for a 2-year term by a two-thirds majority of the General Assembly.

Retiring members are not eligible for immediate re-election. Any other member of the United Nations will be invited to participate without vote in the discussion of questions specially affecting its interests.

The Security Council bears the primary responsibility for the maintenance of peace and security. It is also responsible for the functions of the UN in trust territories classed as 'strategic areas'. Decisions on procedural questions are made by an affirmative vote of 9 members. On all other matters the affirmative vote of 9 members must include the concurring votes of all permanent members (in practice, however, an abstention by a permanent member is not considered a veto), subject to the provision that when the Security Council is considering methods for the peaceful settlement of a dispute, parties to the dispute abstain from voting.

For the maintenance of international peace and security the Security Council can, in accordance with special agreements to be concluded, call on armed forces, assistance and facilities of the member states. It is assisted by a Military Staff Committee consisting of the Chiefs of Staff of the permanent members of the Security Council or their representatives.

The Presidency of the Security Council is held for 1 month in rotation by the member states in the English alphabetical order of their names.

The Security Council functions continuously. Its members are permanently represented at the seat of the organization, but it may meet at any place that will best facilitate its work.

The Council has 2 standing committees of Experts and on the Admission of New Members. In addition, from time to time, it establishes *ad hoc* committees and commissions such as the Truce Supervision Organization in Palestine.

Permanent Members: China, France, USSR, UK, USA.

Non-Permanent Members: Malta, Netherlands, Nicaragua, Pakistan, Zimbabwe (until 31 Dec. 1984); Guyana, Jordan, Poland, Togo. Zaïre (until 31 Dec. 1983).

3. **The Economic and Social Council** is responsible under the General Assembly for carrying out the functions of the United Nations with regard to international economic, social, cultural, educational, health and related matters.

By Nov. 1977, 15 'specialized' inter-governmental agencies working in these fields had been brought into relationship with the United Nations. The Economic and Social Council may also make arrangements for consultation with international non-governmental organizations and, after consultation with the member concerned, with national organizations; by Sept. 1978, 231 non-governmental organizations had been granted consultative status and a further 534 were on the register.

The Economic and Social Council consists of 54 Member States elected by a two-thirds majority of the General Assembly. Nine are elected each year for a 3-year term. Retiring members are eligible for immediate re-election. Each member has 1 vote. Decisions are made by a majority of the members present and voting.

The Council nominally holds 2 sessions a year, and special sessions may be held if required. The President is elected for 1 year and is eligible for immediate re-election.

The Economic and Social Council has the following commissions:

Regional Economic Commissions: ECE (Economic Commission for Europe. Geneva); ESCAP (Economic and Social Commission for Asia and the Pacific. Bangkok); ECLA (Economic Commission for Latin America. Santiago, Chile); ECA (Economic Commission for Africa. Addis Ababa). ECWA (Economic Commission for Western Asia. Baghdad). These Commissions have been established to enable the nations of the major regions of the world to co-operate on common problems and also to produce economic information.

(1) Six functional Statistical Commissions; with subcommission on Statistical Sampling. (2) Commission on Human Rights; with subcommission on Prevention of Discrimination and Protection of Minorities; (3) Social Development Commission; (4) Commission on the Status of Women; (5) Commission on Narcotic Drugs; (6) Population Commission.

The Economic and Social Council has the following standing committees: The Economic Committee, Social Committee, Co-ordination Committee, Committee on Non-Governmental Organizations, Interim Committee on Programme of Conferences, Committee for Industrial Development, Advisory Committee on the Application of Science and Technology to Development, Committee on Housing, Building and Planning.

Other special bodies are the International Narcotics Control Board, the Interim Co-ordinating Committee for International Commodity Arrangements and the Administrative Committee on Co-ordination to ensure (1) the most effective implementation of the agreements entered into between the United Nations and the specialized agencies and (2) co-ordination of activities.

Membership: Austria, Benin, Brazil. Colombia, France, Federal Republic of Germany, Greece, Japan, Liberia, Mali, Pakistan. Portugal, Qatar, Romania, St Lucia, Swaziland, Tunisia (until 31 Dec. 1984). Argentina, Bangladesh, Burundi, Byelorussia, Cameroon, Canada, China, Denmark. Fiji, India, Kenya, Nicaragua, Norway, Peru, Poland, Sudan, USSR, UK (until 31 Dec. 1983): Algeria, Botswana,

Bulgaria, Congo, Djibouti, Ecuador, German Democratic Republic, Lebanon, Luxembourg, Malaysia, Mexico, Netherlands, New Zealand, Saudi Arabia, Sierra Leone, Suriname, Thailand, USA (until 31 Dec. 1985).

4. **The Trusteeship Council.** The Charter provides for an international trusteeship system to safeguard the interests of the inhabitants of territories which are not yet fully self-governing and which may be placed thereunder by individual trusteeship agreements. These are called trust territories.

All of the original 11 trust territories except one, the Pacific Islands (Micronesia), administered by the USA, have become independent or joined independent countries. The Trusteeship Council consists of the 1 member administering trust territories: USA; the permanent members of the Security Council that are not administering trust territories: China, France, USSR and UK. Decisions of the Council are made by a majority of the members present and voting, each member having 1 vote. The Council holds one regular session each year, and special sessions if required.

5. **The International Court of Justice** was created by an international treaty, the Statute of the Court, which forms an integral part of the United Nations Charter. All members of the United Nations are *ipso facto* parties to the Statute of the Court.

The Court is composed of independent judges, elected regardless of their nationality, who possess the qualifications required in their countries for appointment to the highest judicial offices, or are jurisconsuls of recognized competence in international law. There are 15 judges, no 2 of whom may be nationals of the same state. They are elected by the Security Council and the General Assembly of the United Nations sitting independently. Candidates are chosen from a list of persons nominated by the national groups in the Permanent Court of Arbitration established by the Hague Conventions of 1899 and 1907. In the case of members of the United Nations not represented in the Permanent Court of Arbitration, candidates are nominated by national groups appointed for the purpose by their governments. The judges are elected for a 9-year term and are eligible for immediate re-election. When engaged on business of the Court, they enjoy diplomatic privileges and immunities.

The Court elects its own President and Vice-Presidents for 3 years and remains permanently in session, except for judicial vacations. The full court of 15 judges normally sits, but a quorum of 9 judges is sufficient to constitute the Court. It may form chambers of 3 or more judges for dealing with particular categories of cases, and forms annually a chamber of 5 judges to hear and determine, at the request of the parties, cases by summary procedures. Taslim O. Elias (Nigeria) and José Sette-Camara (Brazil) are, respectively, President and Vice-President of the Court until 1985.

Competence and Jurisdiction. Only states may be parties in cases before the Court, which is open to the states parties to its Statute. The conditions under which the Court will be open to other states are laid down by the Security Council. The Court exercises its jurisdiction in all cases which the parties refer to it and in all matters provided for in the Charter, or in treaties and conventions in force. Disputes concerning the jurisdiction of the Court are settled by the Court's own decision.

The Court may apply in its decision: *(a)* international conventions; *(b)* international custom; *(c)* the general principles of law recognized by civilized nations; and *(d)* as subsidiary means for the determination of the rules of law, judicial decisions and the teachings of highly qualified publicists. If the parties agree, the Court may decide a case *ex aequo et bono*. The Court may also give an advisory opinion on any legal question to any organ of the United Nations or its agencies.

Procedure. The official languages of the Court are French and English. At the request of any party the Court will authorize the use of another language by this party. All questions are decided by a majority of the judges present. If the votes are equal, the President has a casting vote. The judgment is final and without appeal, but a revision may be applied for within 10 years from the date of the judgment on the ground of a new decisive factor. Unless otherwise decided by the Court, each party bears its own costs.

Judges. The judges of the Court, elected by the Security Council and the General Assembly, are as follows: (1) To serve until 5 Feb. 1985: Manfred Lachs (Poland), Taslim Olawale Elias (Nigeria), Hermann Mosler (Federal Republic of Germany), Shigeru Oda (Japan), Abdallah Fikri El-Khani (Syria). (2) To serve until 5 Feb. 1988: Platon D. Morozov (USSR), Roberto Ago (Italy), Bedjaoui (Algeria), José Sette-Camara (Brazil), Stephen Schwebel (USA). (3) To serve until 5 Feb. 1991: Nagendra Singh (India), José Maria Ruda (Argentina), Sir Robert Jennings (UK), Guy Ladreit de Lacharrière (France), Kéba Mbaye (Senegal).

Judges. If there is no judge on the bench of the nationality of the parties to the dispute, each party has the right to choose a judge. Such judges shall take part in the decision on terms of complete equality with their colleagues.

The Court has its seat at The Hague, but may sit elsewhere whenever it considers this desirable. The expenses of the Court are borne by the UN.

Registrar: Santiago Torres Bernárdez (Spain).

6. **The Secretariat** is composed of the Secretary-General, who is the chief administrative officer of the organization, and an international staff appointed by him under regulations established by the General Assembly. However, the Secretary-General, the High Commissioner for Refugees and the Managing Director of the Fund are appointed by the General Assembly. The first Secretary-General was Trygve Lie (Norway), 1946–53; the second, Dag Hammarskjöld (Sweden), 1953–61; the third, U. Thant (Burma), 1961–71; the fourth, Kurt Waldheim (Austria), 1972–81.

The Secretary-General acts as chief administrative officer in all meetings of the General Assembly, the Security Council, the Economic and Social Council and the Trusteeship Council.

The financial year coincides with the calendar year; accountancy is in US$. Budget for 1982–83, $1,506,241,800.

Secretary-General: Javier Perez de Cuellar (Peru), appointed 1 Jan. 1982 for a 5-year term.

The Secretary-General is assisted by Under-Secretaries-General and Assistant Secretaries-General.

MEMBER STATES OF THE UN

(as in 1983 with percentage scale of contribution)

Afghánistán	0·01	1946	Cameroon	0·01	1960
Albania	0·01	1955	Canada [1]	3·28	1945
Algeria	0·12	1962	Cape Verde	0·01	1975
Angola	0·01	1976	Central African Rep.	0·01	1960
Antigua and Barbuda	0·01	1981	Chad	0·01	1960
Argentina [1]	0·78	1945	Chile [1]	0·07	1945
Australia [1]	1·83	1945	China [1]	1·62	1945
Austria	0·71	1955	Colombia [1]	0·11	1945
Bahamas	0·01	1973	Comoros	0·01	1975
Bahrain	0·01	1971	Congo	0·01	1960
Bangladesh	0·04	1974	Costa Rica [1]	0·02	1945
Barbados	0·01	1966	Cuba [1]	0·11	1945
Belgium [1]	1·22	1945	Cyprus	0·01	1960
Belize		1981	Czechoslovakia [1]	0·83	1945
Benin	0·01	1960	Denmark [1]	0·74	1945
Bhután	0·01	1971	Djibouti	0·01	1977
Bolivia [1]	0·01	1945	Dominica	0·01	1978
Botswana	0·01	1966	Dominican Republic [1]	0·03	1945
Brazil [1]	1·27	1945	Ecuador [1]	0·02	1945
Bulgaria	0·16	1955	Egypt [1]	0·07	1945
Burma	0·01	1948	El Salvador [1]	0·01	1945
Burundi	0·01	1962	Equatorial Guinea	0·01	1968
Byelorussia [1]	0·39	1945	Ethiopia [1]	0·01	1945
Cambodia	0·01	1955	Fiji	0·01	1970

Finland	0·48	1955	Pakistan	0·07	1947	
France [1]	6·26	1945	Panama [1]	0·02	1945	
Gabon	0·02	1960	Papua New Guinea	0·01	1975	
Gambia	0·01	1965	Paraguay [1]	0·01	1945	
German Democratic Rep.	1·39	1973	Peru [1]	0·06	1945	
Germany, Federal Rep. of	8·31	1973	Philippines [1]	0·10	1945	
Ghana	0·03	1957	Poland [1]	1·24	1945	
Greece [1]	0·35	1945	Portugal	0·19	1955	
Grenada	0·01	1974	Qatar	0·03	1971	
Guatemala [1]	0·02	1945	Romania	0·21	1955	
Guinea	0·01	1958	Rwanda	0·01	1962	
Guinea-Bissau	0·01	1974	St Lucia	0·01	1979	
Guyana	0·01	1966	St Vincent and the			
Haiti [1]	0·01	1945	Grenadines	0·01	1980	
Honduras [1]	0·01	1945	Samoa, Western	0·01	1976	
Hungary	0·33	1955	São Tomé and Principe	0·01	1975	
Iceland	0·03	1946	Saudi Arabia [1]	0·58	1945	
India [1]	0·60	1945	Senegal	0·01	1960	
Indonesia	0·16	1950	Seychelles	0·01	1976	
Iran [1]	0·65	1945	Sierra Leone	0·01	1961	
Iraq [1]	0·12	1945	Singapore	0·08	1965	
Ireland	0·16	1955	Solomon Islands	0·01	1978	
Israel	0·25	1949	Somalia	0·01	1960	
Italy	3·45	1955	South Africa [1]	0·42	1945	
Ivory Coast	0·03	1960	Spain	1·70	1955	
Jamaica	0·02	1962	Sri Lanka	0·02	1955	
Japan	9·58	1956	Sudan	0·01	1956	
Jordan	0·01	1955	Suriname	0·01	1975	
Kenya	0·01	1963	Swaziland	0·01	1968	
Kuwait	0·20	1963	Sweden	1·31	1946	
Laos People's Dem. Rep.	0·01	1955	Syrian Arab Rep.[1]	0·03	1945	
Lebanon [1]	0·03	1945	Tanzania	0·01	1961	
Lesotho	0·01	1966	Thailand	0·10	1946	
Liberia [1]	0·01	1945	Togo	0·01	1960	
Libyan Arab Jamahiriya	0·23	1955	Trinidad and Tobago	0·03	1962	
Luxembourg [1]	0·05	1945	Tunisia	0·03	1956	
Madagascar	0·01	1960	Turkey [1]	0·30	1945	
Malawi	0·01	1964	Uganda	0·01	1962	
Malaysia	0·09	1957	Ukrainian Soviet			
Maldives	0·01	1965	Socialist Rep.[1]	1·46	1945	
Mali	0·01	1960	USSR [1]	11·10	1945	
Malta	0·01	1964	United Arab Emirates	0·10	1971	
Mauritania	0·01	1961	UK [1]	4·46	1945	
Mauritius	0·01	1968	USA [1]	25·00	1945	
Mexico [1]	0·76	1945	Upper Volta	0·01	1960	
Mongolia	0·01	1961	Uruguay [1]	0·04	1945	
Morocco	0·05	1956	Vanuatu	0·01	1981	
Mozambique	0·01	1975	Venezuela [1]	0·50	1945	
Nepál	0·01	1955	Vietnam	0·03	1977	
Netherlands [1]	1·63	1945	Yemen Arab Republic	0·01	1947	
New Zealand [1]	0·27	1945	Yemen, P.D.R.	0·01	1967	
Nicaragua [1]	0·01	1945	Yugoslavia [1]	0·42	1945	
Niger	0·01	1960	Zaïre	0·02	1960	
Nigeria	0·16	1960	Zambia	0·02	1964	
Norway [1]	0·50	1945	Zimbabwe	0·02	1980	
Oman	0·01	1971				

[1] Original member.

Books of Reference

Yearbook of the United Nations. New York, 1947 ff. Annual
United Nations Chronicle. Quarterly
Monthly Bulletin of Statistics
General Assembly: Official-Records: Resolutions
Reports of the Secretary-General of the United Nations on the Work of the Organization.
  1946 ff.
Documents of the United Nations Conference on International Organization, San Francisco,
  1945. 16 vols.

Charter of the United Nations and Statute of the International Court of Justice. Text in English, French, Chinese, Russian and Spanish.
Repertory of Practice of UN's Organs. 5 vols. New York, 1955
Official Records of the Security Council, the Economic and Social Council, Trusteeship Council and the Disarmament Commission
Demographic Yearbook, 1948 ff. New York, 1969
Everyman's United Nations. New York. 1958 ff. Annual
Statistical Yearbook. New York, 1947 ff.
Yearbook of International Statistics. New York, 1950 ff.
World Economic Survey. New York, 1947 ff.
Economic Survey of Asia and the Far East. New York, 1946 ff.
Economic Survey of Latin America. New York, 1948 ff.
Economic Survey of Europe. New York, 1948 ff.
Economic Survey of Africa. New York. 1960 ff.
Foote, W., *Dag Hammarskjöld—Servant of Peace.* London, 1962
Forsythe, D., *United Nations Peacemaking: The Conciliation Commission for Palestine.* Johns Hopkins Univ. Press, 1973
Hiscocks, R., *The Security Council: A Study in Adolescence.* New York, 1974
Lie, Trygve, *In the Cause of Peace.* London, 1954
Luard, E., *A History of the United Nations.* Vol. 1. London, 1982
Rikhye, I. J., Harbottle, M., Egge, B., *The Thin Blue Line.* London, 1974
Symonds, R., and Carder, M., *The United Nations and the Population Question.* London, 1973
Thant, U., *Towards World Peace.* New York, 1964
Urquhart, B., *Hammarskjöld.* London, 1973
Walters, F. P., *A History of the League of Nations.* 2 vols. London, 1952
Winton, H. N. M. (comp. and ed.), *Man and the Environment. A Bibliography of Selected Publications of the United Nations System 1946–1971.* New York, 1972
Witthauer, K., *Die Bevölkerung der Erde: Verteilung und Dynamik.* Gotha, 1958.—*Distribution and Dynamics Relating to World Population.* Gotha, 1969
Her Majesty's Stationery Office. *Sectional List 23* (currently revised) and *International Organizations Publications* contain a full list of publications on UN and Specialized Agencies, issued by HMSO.

United Nations Information Centre. 14–15 Stratford Place, London W1N 9AF

UNITED NATIONS SYSTEM

The bulk of the work of the UN, measured in terms of money and personnel, goes into programmes aimed at achieving the pledge made in Article 55 of the Charter to 'promote higher standards of living, full employment and conditions of economic and social progress and development'.

In addition to the specialized agencies, there are some 14 major United Nations programmes, funds and organizations devoted to achieving economic and social progress in the developing countries, and in providing humanitarian assistance, they include:

The *United Nations Development Programme* (UNDP) is the world's largest agency for multilateral technical and pre-investment co-operation. It is the funding source for most of the technical assistance provided by the United Nations system, and UNDP is active in almost 150 countries and territories and in virtually every economic and social sector. UNDP assistance is provided only at the request of Governments and in response to their priority needs, integrated into over-all national and regional plans.

There are more than 5,000 UNDP-supported projects currently in operation at the national, regional, inter-regional and global levels, all aimed at helping developing countries make better use of their assets, improve living standards and expand productivity. The volume of such work is over $1,700m. annually, with countries receiving UNDP assistance paying for well over half of all project costs.

UNDP also administers a number of special purpose funds and programmes, including: the United Nations Capital Development Fund, which provides grants and long-term loans for grassroots self-help activities in the world's poorest countries; the United Nations revolving Fund for Natural Resources Exploration, which helps developing countries carry out potentially high-return mineral searches that they cannot afford on their own; the United Nations Sudano-Sahelian Office; the United Nations Volunteers; and the United Nations Financing System for Science and Technology for Development.

UNDP is financed by voluntary contributions from Member States of the UN system.

Headquarters: 1 United Nations Plaza, New York, NY 10017, USA.

Administrator: Bradford Morse (USA).

The *Office of the United Nations High Commissioner for Refugees* (UNHCR) was established by the UN General Assembly with effect from 1 Jan. 1951, originally for three years. Since 1954, its mandate has been renewed for successive five-year periods. Under General Assembly resolution 37/196 adopted in Dec. 1982 the mandate of the Office was extended until 31 Dec. 1988.

The work of UNHCR is of a purely humanitarian and non-political character. The main functions of the Office are to provide international protection for refugees and to seek permanent solutions to their problems through voluntary repatriation, resettlement in other countries or integration into the country of present residence. UNHCR may also be called upon to provide emergency relief and ongoing material assistance where necessary.

UNHCR concerns itself with refugees who have been determined to come within its mandate under the Statute, and with persons in analogous circumstances whom it assists under the terms of the good offices resolutions adopted by the General Assembly.

The High Commissioner is elected by the General Assembly and follows policy directives given by the General Assembly or the Economic and Social Council. He reports to the Third Committee of the General Assembly (Social and Humanitarian Affairs), through the Economic and Social Council. The Executive Committee of the High Commissioner's Programme, which currently includes 41 States, gives the High Commissioner guidance concerning material assistance programmes and advises him at his request in the exercise of his functions under the Statute. Its annual sessions are normally held in October in Geneva. In recent years it has been customary for the High Commissioner to invite representatives of member States to meet with him informally between sessions to keep them abreast of important developments.

International protection is the primary function of UNHCR. Its main objective is to promote and safeguard the rights and interests of refugees. In so doing UNHCR devotes special attention to promoting a generous policy of asylum on the part of Governments and seeks to improve the status of refugees in their country of residence. It also helps them to cease being refugees through the acquisition of the nationality of their country of residence when voluntary repatriation is not applicable. UNHCR pursues its objectives in the field of protection by encouraging the conclusion of intergovernmental legal instruments in favour of refugees, by supervising the implementation of their provisions and by encouraging Governments to adopt legislation and administrative procedures for the benefit of refugees. The main instrument in this field is the UN 1951 Convention Relating to the Status of Refugees. It prescribes a minimum standard of treatment for refugees in such important matters as employment, social security and freedom of movement, and provides for the issuance, by contracting States, of travel documents in lieu of national passports. The most important provision of the Convention is embodied in Article 33 which forbids the forcible return of a refugee to a country where his life or liberty would be in danger because of persecution for reasons of race, religion, nationality or political opinion *(refoulement)*. A protocol relating to the status of refugees came into force in 1967 and had the effect of extending the provisions of the 1951 Convention (which applies to persons who have become refugees as a result of events prior to that date) to new groups of refugees. During 1983, El Salvador and Guatemala acceded to the 1951 Convention relating to the Status of Refugees, thus bringing the total number of States party to the Convention to 95.

The thirty-fourth session of the Executive Committee of the High Commissioner's Programme, held in Oct. 1983, noted with deep concern that an increasingly restrictive trend in the granting of asylum and refugee status by many Governments was eroding the rights of asylum-seekers in many parts of the world. It also expressed alarm at continued threats to the physical safety of refugees through military or armed attacks against refugee camps and settlements in various parts of the world and worked towards the elaboration of a statement of principles to prevent such attacks.

Throughout 1983 the numbers of refugees requiring material assistance from UNHCR remained relatively stable as there occurred no massive outflows of refugees of the kind so familiar in the late 1970's. While the magnitude and persistence of ongoing refugee problems in various parts of the world continued to cause grave concern, the comparative lack of new situations of mass influx permitted the High Commissioner to devote increased resources to the promotion of permanent solutions to refugee problems through voluntary repatriation, local integration and resettlement overseas. It is hoped that this trend can be consolidated further in 1984.

The size of the refugee population in Africa, particularly in the Horn of Africa and the Sudan, has continued to be a major cause of concern. Several positive developments have, however, occurred in the course of 1983. In Sept. 1983 a programme of voluntary repatriation from Djibouti to Ethiopia was launched and UNHCR expanded its assistance to returnees in Ethiopia accordingly. Meanwhile in Somalia, possibilities have opened up for establishing local settlements and encouraging self-reliance among the refugee caseload which is estimated by the Government at some 700,000. Consolidation of local settlements for large numbers of refugees from Ethiopia and Uganda has also continued in the Sudan. In the United Republic of Tanzania, UNHCR activities have also continued to concentrate on the local settlement of some 159,000 refugees largely of Burundi and Zaïrian origin, and on the integration of rural settlements, once self-reliant, into the country's socio-economic system. In recognition of the outstanding contribution that he and his country have made to the promotion of solutions to refugee problems in Africa, President Julius Nyerere of Tanzania was awarded the 1983 Nansen Medal.

Many African countries burdened by the presence of large numbers of refugees face serious economic and social difficulties of their own. To ensure adequate assistance both to the refugees themselves and to the often severely pressured countries of refuge, the UN General Assembly adopted in Dec. 1981 a resolution calling for a Second International Conference on Assistance to Refugees in Africa (ICARA II) which is scheduled to be held in July 1984. Extensive preparatory work has been undertaken in the course of 1983 and projects are currently being drawn up by affected countries for submission to the Conference.

According to Government estimates, the number of Afghan refugees in Pakistan reached some 3m. in 1983. As no solution is in sight, efforts have been made to encourage self-reliance and income-generating projects among the refugee population. Financial requirements for 1983 are estimated at US$69m. to assist the most needy cases totalling some 2·3m. persons. UNHCR's programme of humanitarian assistance in Pakistan remains its largest single-country programme.

The problem of refugees and displaced persons from the Indo-Chinese peninsula continued to be the main focus of attention in South-East Asia. A continuing reduction in the number of refugees arriving in the region either by boat or overland in 1983 has been largely offset by a decline in the number of resettlement places available. On 1 Oct. 1983, those awaiting resettlement in UNHCR camps mostly in Thailand, numbered some 176,000 as compared with some 200,000 one year previously. By the end of Sept. 1983, a total of 876,921 Indo-Chinese refugees had been resettled overseas, the majority in Australia (81,453), Canada (89,031), France (91,799) and the USA (514,977). In addition some 270,000 refugees have been locally integrated in the People's Republic of China with UNHCR's assistance.

By early 1983, the total refugee population in Central America and Mexico had reached 300,000 mostly from El Salvador but with considerable numbers from Guatemala and Nicaragua. The countries most concerned by these influxes were Honduras and Mexico and, to a lesser extent, Costa Rica and Nicaragua. Although progress has been achieved in the consolidation of local integration projects in various countries, mounting political tensions and widespread economic difficulties in the region have hampered the solution of refugee problems. Most notable, sizeable numbers of Salvadorian and Guatemalan refugees in Honduras and Mexico remain entirely dependent on relief assistance.

In Oct. 1983 the Executive Committee of the High Commissioner's Programme approved a revised financial target of US$348m. for UNHCR general programmes in 1983 and also approved the figure of US$368m. for projected requirements in 1984.

For its work on behalf of refugees around the world, UNHCR was awarded the Nobel Peace Prize in 1955 and again in 1981.

Headquarters: Palais des Nations, 1211, Geneva 10, Switzerland.

UK Office: 36 Westminster Palace Gardens, London, SW1P 1RR.

High Commissioner: Poul Hartling (Denmark).

SPECIALIZED AGENCIES OF THE UN

INTERNATIONAL ATOMIC ENERGY AGENCY (IAEA)

Origin. The International Atomic Energy Agency came into existence on 29 July 1957. Its statute had been approved on 26 Oct. 1956, at an international conference held at UN Headquarters, New York. A relationship agreement links it with the United Nations. The IAEA had 110 member states in 1982.

Functions. (1) To accelerate and enlarge the contribution of atomic energy to peace, health and prosperity throughout the world, and (2) to ensure that assistance provided by it or at its request or under its supervision or control is not used in such a way as to further any military purpose.

The IAEA gives advice and technical assistance to developing countries on nuclear power development (provides a series of training courses on nuclear power project planning, construction and operation), on health and safety, on radioactive waste management, on legal aspects of the use of atomic energy, and on prospecting for and exploiting nuclear raw materials; in addition it promotes the use of radiation and isotopes in agriculture, industry, medicine and hydrology through expert services, training courses and fellowships, grants of equipment and supplies, research contracts, scientific meetings and publications. Since 1958 the Agency has provided assistance totalling over $172m. More than 8,000 persons have been trained in nuclear science subjects through the award of fellowships, and over 5,800 through participation in training courses and study tours; more than 5,500 experts have been sent into the field as advisers and training course lecturers; and equipment worth more than $67m. has been provided. The IAEA has research laboratories in Austria and Monaco. At Trieste, the International Centre for Theoretical Physics was established in 1964 which is now operated jointly by UNESCO and IAEA.

The IAEA applies safeguards in 74 States pursuant to NPT and in 10 States under other agreements to 143 power reactors, 6 conversion plants, 39 fabrication plants, 4 enrichment plants, 6 reprocessing plants, 177 research reactors and critical assemblies, 24 separate storage facilities, 40 locations containing more than 1 effective kg of nuclear material, 422 locations containing 1 or less than 1 effective kg of nuclear material. The above figures include facilities safeguarded under agreement with the European Atomic Energy Community and its non-nuclear-weapon States.

Organization. The Statute provides for an annual General Conference, a Board of Governors of 34 members and a Secretariat headed by a Director-General.

Headquarters: Vienna International Centre, PO Box 100, A-1400 Vienna, Austria.

Director-General: Hans Blix (Sweden).

INTERNATIONAL LABOUR ORGANISATION (ILO)

Origin. The ILO, established in 1919 as an autonomous part of the League of

Nations, is an intergovernmental agency with a tripartite structure, in which representatives of governments, employers and workers participate. It seeks through international action to improve labour conditions, raise living standards and promote productive employment. In 1946 the ILO was recognized by the United Nations as a specialized agency. In 1969 it was awarded the Nobel Peace Prize. In 1983 it numbered 150 members.

Functions. One of the ILO's principal functions is the formulation of international standards in the form of International Labour Conventions and Recommendations. Member countries are required to submit Conventions to their competent national authorities with a view to ratification. If a country ratifies a Convention it agrees to bring its laws into line with its terms and to report periodically how these regulations are being applied. More than 5,000 ratifications of 159 Conventions had been deposited by mid-1983. Machinery is available to ascertain whether Conventions thus ratified are effectively applied.

Recommendations do not require ratification, but member states are obliged to consider them with a view to giving effect to their provisions by legislation or other action. By the end of 1983 the International Labour Conference had adopted 168 recommendations.

Organization. The ILO consists of the International Labour Conference, the Governing Body and the International Labour Office.

The Conference is the supreme deliberative organ of the ILO; it meets annually at Geneva. National delegations are composed of 2 government delegates, 1 employers' delegate and 1 workers' delegate.

The Governing Body, elected by the Conference, is the executive council. It is composed of 28 government members, 14 workers' members and 14 employers' members.

Ten governments hold permanent seats on the Governing Board because of their industrial importance, namely, Brazil, China, Federal Republic of Germany, France, India, Italy, Japan, USA, USSR and UK. The remaining 18 government seats were, at the end of 1983, held by Australia, Bahrain, Bangladesh, Barbados, Bulgaria, Colombia, Ecuador, Egypt, German Democratic Republic, Kenya, Mali, Mexico, Mozambique, Netherlands, Nigeria, Philippines, Senegal and Venezuela.

The Office serves as secretariat, operational headquarters, research centre and publishing house.

The ILO budget for 1984–85 amounted to US$254 7m.

Activities. In addition to its research and advisory activities, the ILO extends technical co-operation to governments under its regular budget and under the UN Development Programme and Funds-in-Trust in the fields of employment promotion, human resources development (including vocational and management training), development of social institutions, small-scale industries, rural development, social security, industrial safety and hygiene, productivity, etc. Technical co-operation also includes expert missions and a fellowship programme. Some $100m. was spent on technical co-operation in 1981. Projects were in progress in some 115 countries and about 900 experts involved.

Major emphasis is being given to the ILO's World Employment Programme, launched in 1969 with the purpose of stimulating national and international efforts to increase the volume of productive employment, and so to counter the problem of rising unemployment in developing countries. Employment strategy missions were carried out under the Programme in Colombia, the Dominican Republic, Egypt, Iran, Kenya, Sri Lanka, Sudan and the Philippines. The work of these missions was complemented by an ILO programme of research designed to provide policy-makers with the information to promote employment. A World Employment Conference was held in June 1976.

The International Labour Conference (Geneva, June 1982) adopted a Convention concerning the maintenance of rights in social security and a Convention and Recommendation on termination of employment at the initiative of the employer. It also revised the Plantations Convention (No. 110) and prepared the way for new Recommendations in 1983 on maintenance of rights in social security and on vocational rehabilitation of the disabled.

In 1960 the ILO established in Geneva the International Institute for Labour Studies. The Institute specializes in advanced education and research on social and labour policy. It brings together for group study experienced persons from all parts of the world—government administrators, trade-union officials, industrial experts, management, university and other specialists.

A training institution was opened by the ILO in Turin, Italy, in 1965—the International Centre for Advanced Technical and Vocational Training. The Centre provides opportunities for technical, vocational and management training for individuals who have advanced beyond the facilities available in their own countries. Courses are geared particularly to the needs of developing countries.

Headquarters: International Labour Office, CH-1211 Geneva 22, Switzerland.
Director-General: Francis Blanchard (France).
Chairman of the Governing Body: Aída Gonzales Martinez (Mexico).
London Branch Office: 96/98 Marsham St., SW1.

ILO received the Nobel Peace Prize for 1969.

The ILO has regional offices in Addis Ababa (for Africa), Bangkok (for Asia and the Pacific), Lima (for Latin America and the Caribbean) and Beirut (for Arab States).

Publications: Regular periodicals in English, French and Spanish include the *International Labour Review, Legislative Series, Bulletin of Labour Statistics, Year Book of Labour Statistics, Official Bulletin* and *Labour Education. Women at Work* and the *Social and Labour Bulletin* are issued in English and French.
   The Practice of Entrepreneurship. Workforce Reductions in Undertakings. Agrarian Policies and Rural Poverty in Africa. Workers' Management in Yugoslavia. Negotiating Development: Labour Relations in Southern Asia. Deterrence and Compensation: Legal Liability in Occupational Safety and Health. Working Conditions and Environment. Employment Opportunities and Equity in a Changing Economy: Egypt in the 1980s. International Labour Conventions and Recommendations, 1919–1981. New Technologies: Their Impact on Employment and the Working Environment. Safety and Health in the Construction of Fixed Offshore Installations in the Petroleum Industry. (All 1982).

FOOD AND AGRICULTURE ORGANIZATION OF THE UNITED NATIONS (FAO)

Origin. The UN Conference on Food and Agriculture in May 1943, at Hot Springs, Virginia, set up an Interim Commission in Washington in July 1943 to plan the Organization, which came into being on 16 Oct. 1945.

Aims and Activities. The aims of FAO are to raise levels of nutrition and standards of living; to improve the production and distribution of all food and agricultural products from farms, forests and fisheries; to improve the living conditions of rural populations; and, by these means, to eliminate hunger.

In carrying out these aims, FAO promotes investment in agriculture, better soil and water management, improved yields of crops and livestock, and the transfer of technology to, and the development of agricultural research in, developing countries. FAO promotes the conservation of natural resources and the rational use of fertilizers and pesticides. The Organization combats animal diseases, promotes the development of marine and inland fisheries, and encourages the rational use of forest resources. Technical assistance is provided in all these fields and others such as nutrition, agricultural engineering, agrarian reform, development communications, remote sensing for natural resources, and the prevention of food losses.

Special FAO programmes help countries prepare for, and provide relief in the event of, emergency food situations, in particular through the setting up of food reserves. The Global Information and Early Warning System provides current information on the world food situation and identifies countries threatened by shortages to guide potential donors. Assistance is given to set up national and regional early warning systems.

The Organization also has a major rôle in the collection, analysis and dissemination of information on natural resources and agricultural production.

FAO sponsors the World Food Programme (WFP) with the UN; WFP uses food commodities, cash and services contributed by member States of the UN to back programmes of social and economic development, as well as for relief in emergency situations.

Finance and Administration. The FAO Conference, composed of all member states, meets every other year to determine the policy and approve the budget and work programme of FAO. The Council, consisting of 49 member nations elected by the Conference, serves as FAO's governing body between Sessions of the Conference. At its 22nd Session in Nov. 1983, the Conference admitted four new member states, Antigua and Barbuda, Belize, St Kitts–Nevis–Anguilla, and Vanuatu, raising the total to 156. The Conference also approved a Regular Programme budget for the two years 1984–85 of $421m., an increase of 0·5% in real terms over the previous period. The Regular Programme, which is financed by contributions from member governments, covers the cost of the Organization's secretariat, its Technical Co-operation Programme and part of the cost of several Special Action Programmes.

FAO provides advice and assistance in the field through its Field Programmes, funded largely from external sources, such as the UN Development Programme (UNDP) and trust funds provided by governments. Funds available from UNDP have continued to fall – from $141m. in 1982 to around $120m. in 1983. The drop in funds from UNDP was partially offset by increases in trust funds and in funds available through the Technical Co-operation Programme funded from FAO's own Regular Programme budget. Trust fund delivery in 1983 was expected to be about $135m. compared with $120m. the previous year. Delivery under the Technical Co-operation Programme in 1983 was expected to reach about $20m., compared with $17m. in 1982. Total Field Programme delivery in 1983 was expected to remain close to the 1982 figure of $278m., while falling significantly in real terms.

Headquarters: Viale delle Terme di Caracalla, Rome, Italy.
Director-General: Dr Edouard Saouma (Lebanon).

FAO publications include: FAO Books in Print 1980–81; The State of Food and Agriculture (annual), 1974 ff.; *The FAO World Food Report* (annual), 1983 ff.; *Animal Health Yearbook* (annual), 1957 ff.; *Production Yearbook* (annual), 1947 ff.; *Trade Yearbook* (annual), 1947 ff.; *FAO Commodity Review* (annual), 1961 ff.; *Yearbook of Forest Products Statistics* (annual), 1947 ff.; *Yearbook of Fishery Statistics* (in two volumes). *Ceres* (bi-monthly). *Food and Nutrition* (bi-annual), *FAO Fertilizer Yearbook, FAO Plant Protection Bulletin* (quarterly), *World Animal Review* (quarterly).

UNITED NATIONS EDUCATIONAL, SCIENTIFIC AND CULTURAL ORGANIZATION (UNESCO)

Origin. A Conference for the establishment of an Educational, Scientific and Cultural Organization of the United Nations was convened by the Government of the UK in association with the Government of France, and met in London, 1–16 Nov. 1945. UNESCO came into being on 4 Nov. 1946.

Functions. The purpose of UNESCO is to contribute to peace and security by promoting collaboration among the nations through education, science and culture in order to further universal respect for justice, for the rule of law and for the human rights and fundamental freedoms which are affirmed for the peoples of the world, without distinction of race, sex, language or religion, by the Charter of the United Nations. The UNESCO budget for 1980 was $115·5m.

Activities. The education programme has four main objectives: the extension of education; the improvement of education; and life-long education for living in a world community.

To train teachers specialized in the techniques of fundamental education UNESCO is helping to establish regional and national training centres. A centre for Latin America was opened in Mexico in 1951, one for the Arab States was set up in Egypt in 1953. UNESCO seeks to promote the progressive application of the right to free and compulsory education for all and to improve the quality of education everywhere.

In the natural sciences, UNESCO seeks to promote international scientific co-operation, such as the International Hydrological Programme which began in 1966. It encourages scientific research designed to improve the living conditions of mankind. Science co-operation offices have been set up in Montevideo, Cairo, New Delhi, Nairobi and Jakarta.

In the field of communication, UNESCO endeavours, by disseminating information, carrying out research and providing advice, to increase the scope and quality of press, film and radio services throughout the world.

Organization. The organs of UNESCO are a General Conference (composed of representatives from each member state), an Executive Board (consisting of 45 government representatives elected by the General Conference) and a Secretariat. UNESCO had 153 members and 1 associate member in 1980.

National commissions act as liaison groups between UNESCO and the educational, scientific and cultural life of their own countries.

Budget for 1981: $200,133,700.

Headquarters: UNESCO House, 9 Place de Fontenoy, Paris (7ᵉᵐᵉ).
Director-General: Amadou Mahtar M'Bow (Senegal).

Periodicals. Museum (quarterly, English and French); *International Social Science Journal* (quarterly, English and French); *Impact of Science on Society* (quarterly, English and French); *Unesco Courier* (monthly, English, French and Spanish); *Fundamental and Adult Education Bulletin* (quarterly, English, French and Spanish); *Copyright Bulletin* (twice-yearly, English and French); *Unesco News* (English, French and Spanish); *Unesco Bulletin for Libraries* (monthly, English, French and Spanish).

WORLD HEALTH ORGANIZATION (WHO)

Origin. An International Conference, convened by the UN Economic and Social Council, to consider a single health organization resulted in the adoption on 22 July 1946 of the constitution of the World Health Organization. This constitution came into force on 7 April 1948.

Structure. The principal organs of WHO are the World Health Assembly, the Executive Board and the Secretariat. Each of the 158 member states and 1 Associate Member (1980) has the right to be represented at the Assembly, which meets annually usually in Geneva, Switzerland. The 30-member Executive Board is composed of technically qualified health experts designated by as many member states elected by the Assembly. The Secretariat consists of technical and administrative staff headed by a Director-General. Health activities in member countries are carried out through regional organizations which have been established in Africa (regional office, Brazzaville), South-East Asia (New Delhi), Europe (Copenhagen), Eastern Mediterranean (Alexandria) and Western Pacific (Manila). The Pan American Sanitary Bureau in Washington serves as the Regional Office of WHO for the Americas.

Functions. WHO's objective, as stated in the first article of the Constitution is 'the attainment by all peoples of the highest possible level of health'. As the directing and co-ordinating authority on international health it establishes and maintains collaboration with the UN, specialized agencies, government health administrations, professional and other groups concerned with health. The Constitution also directs WHO to assist governments to strengthen their health services, to stimulate and advance work to eradicate diseases, to promote maternal and child health, mental health, medical research and the prevention of accidents; to improve standards of teaching and training in the health professions, and of nutrition, housing, sanitation, working conditions and other aspects of environment health. The

Organization also is empowered to propose conventions, agreements and regulations and make recommendations about international health matters; to revise the international nomenclature of diseases, causes of death and public health practices; to develop, establish and promote international standards concerning foods, biological, pharmaceutical and similar substances.

Methods of work. Co-operation in country projects is undertaken only on the request of the government concerned, through the 6 regional offices of the Organization. Worldwide technical services are made available by headquarters. Expert committees whose members are chosen from the 47 advisory panels of experts meet to advise the Director-General on a given subject. Scientific groups and consultative meetings are called for similar purposes. To further the education of health personnel of all categories, seminars, technical conferences and training courses are organized and advisors, consultants and lecturers are provided. WHO awards fellowships for study to nationals of member countries.

Activities. The main thrust of WHO's activities in 1982–83 was towards promoting national, regional and global strategies for the attainment of the main social target of the Member States for the next two decades: 'Health for All by the Year 2000', or the attainment by all citizens of the world of a level of health that will permit them to lead a socially and economically productive life.

Almost all countries indicated a high level of political commitment to this goal, and guiding principles for formulating corresponding strategies and plans of action were prepared.

The 36th World Health Assembly, meeting in May 1983, adopted 'The Global Strategy for Health for All by the Year 2000'. Based on primary health care approach to health as outlined in the Declaration of Alma-Ata (named after the city in the Soviet Union where the International Conference on Primary Health Care was held in 1978), the Global Strategy reflects the national and regional strategies as seen from a global perspective and responds to the UN General Assembly Resolution concerning health as an integral part of development. It describes broad lines of action to be undertaken at policy and operational levels, nationally and internationally, in the health and other social and economic sectors to attain 'Health for All by the Year 2000'.

Member States were invited to enter into this 'contract for health' of their own volition, and to enlist the involvement of people in all walks of life, including individuals, families, communities, all categories of health workers, non-governmental organizations and other associations of people concerned. They were urged to allocate adequate resources for health and in particular for primary health care and for the supporting levels of the health system.

Among milestones set as countries strive for the goal of health for all are these: Ensuring enough of the right kind of food for all by 1985; providing essential drugs for all by 1986; providing an adequate supply of safe drinking water and basic sanitation for all by 1990; and immunizing all children against six common diseases – measles, whooping cough, tetanus, polio, tuberculosis and diptheria – also by 1990.

The Assembly invited the relevant agencies, programmes and funds of the UN system, as well as other bodies concerned, to provide financial and other support to developing countries for the implementation of national strategies to achieve health for all by the year 2000.

The Global Strategy was presented to the 1981 UN General Assembly by the Director-General of WHO. The unique role conferred on the WHO in international health work was stressed. This rôle comprises in essence the inseparable and mutually supportive functions of acting as the directing and co-ordinating authority in the field of health and of international health work, and of ensuring technical co-operation between the WHO and its Member States. These functions are essential for the attainment of health for all by the year 2000.

The Organization's working budget for 1984–85 is $520·1m.

Meeting in May 1982, the 35th World Health Assembly approved the plan of action for implementing the Global Strategy for Health for All and requested the Director-General and the Executive Board to monitor progress. It called on

Member States 'to fulfil their responsibilities as partners in the solemnly agreed Strategy for Health for All by carrying out in their countries as well as through inter-country co-operation, the activities devolving on them in the plan of action for implementing the strategy'. Once again, the Assembly emphasized that the strategy is not a 'WHO exercise', but rather an expression of individual and collective national responsibilities fully supported by WHO, which offers a unique opportunity for international co-operation in an important area of basic human needs.

The Assembly approved the Seventh General Programme of Work covering the period 1984–89 which constitutes a 'satisfactory response' of the Organization to the Global Strategy.

Patents: The Assembly decided that WHO should enter the fields of patents to encourage research in areas where it is needed and to ensure that new discoveries in the field of health are placed within reach of all. A resolution ('Policy on Patents', Resolution WHA 35/14), says that 'it shall be the policy of WHO to obtain patents, inventors' certificates or interests in patents on patentable health technology developed through projects supported by WHO, where such rights and interests are necessary to ensure development of the new technology'. This will be done to promote the 'development, production, and wide availability of health technology in the public interest'.

WHO will thus be able to induce pharmaceutical companies, for example, to develop useful drugs by helping to protect them whilst a large, potential market is assured. Also, by controlling patent rights WHO can insist that the price at which the process or product is sold remains low enough to be available to developing countries that need it most. Examples of health technology funded wholly or in part by WHO are in the field of malaria vaccine and low-dose, long-acting hormone preparations for fertility control.

Action Programme on Essential Drugs: Member States wishing to carry out national programmes aimed at making essential drugs available to all their people have been promised WHO's technical co-operation and support.

An Assembly resolution invited other agencies, programmes and funds of the UN system, bilateral agencies, non-governmental and voluntary organizations and the pharmaceutical industry to collaborate in their respective fields of interest in carrying out the Action Programme. WHO has already drawn up model lists of around 200 of the basic drugs and vaccines that are required within any one country's health services; these lists can then be adapted to the specific needs of each Member State.

Health implications of development schemes: The Assembly noted that many development projects carry major potential health hazards and dangers to the health of populations and the environment has deteriorated as a result of development projects, especially those associated with water resources. The resolution pledges WHO's total commitment to work with Member States, international and national agencies and financial institutions to incorporate the necessary preventive measures into development projects so as to minimize health and environment risks.

Marketing of breast-milk substitutes: The Assembly noted that, while many Member States had taken some measures related to improving infant and young child feeding, few countries had yet adopted and adhered to the International Code of Marketing of Breast-milk Substitutes drawn up at last year's Assembly. Member States were urged to give fresh attention to the need for national legislation, regulations or other suitable measures to give effect to the Code. Meanwhile WHO will undertake prospective surveys, including statistical data of infant and young child feeding practices in the various countries, particularly with regard to the incidence and duration of breast-feeding.

Health care of the elderly: WHO is asked to continue to collaborate closely with the UN in the field of aging, in a role that goes beyond traditional medical concerns and involves the health sector in the larger context of improving the quality of life for the elderly.

World Health Day: World Health Day, 7 April 1982, was devoted to the theme 'Add Life to Years'. The theme chosen for World Health Day 1983 is 'Health for All: the Count-down has begun!'.

New Members: Saint Lucia and Bhután were admitted to membership of the Organization, making total membership 158.

The Assembly reiterated its appeal to Member States to multiply their efforts to consolidate peace in the world, reinforce detente and achieve disarmament so as to release resources for the development of public health in the world.

Headquarters: 1211 Geneva 27. *Regional Offices:* Alexandria, Brazzaville, Copenhagen, Manila, New Delhi, Washington.

Director-General: Dr Halfdan T. Mahler (Denmark).

Basic Documents. 30th ed., 1980 (English, French, Russian, Spanish)
Handbook of Resolutions and Decisions. Vol. I, 1973 and Vol. II, 1979 (Arabic, English, French, Russian, Spanish)
WHO Chronicle (bi-monthly from 1947; English, French, Russian and Spanish)
Bulletin of WHO (quarterly, 1947–51; 6 issues a year from 1978; English and French)
International Digest of Health Legislation (quarterly, from 1948; English)
World Health, the Magazine of WHO. 1957 ff. (10 issues a year; Arabic, English, French, German, Italian, Persian, Portuguese, Russian and Spanish)
WHO Technical Report Series, 1950 ff. (English, French, Russian, Spanish)
WHO Monograph Series, 1951 ff. (English, French, Russian, Spanish)
Public Health Papers, 1959 ff. (English, French, Russian, Spanish)
World Health Statistics Annual (from 1939; English, French and Russian)
World Health Statistics Quarterly (monthly, 1947–76 then quarterly; English and French)
Weekly Epidemiological Record (from 1926; English and French)
Publications of the WHO, 1947–57; a bibliography (1958).—*1958–62* (1965).—*1963–67* (1969).—*1968–72* (1974)
World Directories:
Dental Schools, 1963 (1967); *Medical Schools, 1979; Post-Basic and Post-Graduate Schools of Nursing* (1965); *Schools of Pharmacy, 1963* (1966); *Schools of Public Health, 1971* (1972); *Venereal Disease Treatment Centres at Ports* (1972); *Veterinary Schools, 1971* (1973). *Schools for Medical Assistants, 1973* (1976); *Auxiliary Sanitarians 1973* (1978); *Dental Auxiliaries 1973* (1977); *Medical Lab. Technicians and Assistants, 1973* (1977)
The International Pharmacopoeia. 3rd. ed., 1979 (English, French and Spanish)
Manual of the International Statistical Classification of Diseases, Injuries and Causes of Death. 9th rev. (1977; English, French, Russian, Spanish)
IARC Monographs on the Evaluation of Carcinogenic Risk of Chemicals to Humans. 1967 ff. (English)
International Histological Classification of Tumours. Books and slides, from 1967, No. 25, 1980 (English, French, Russian and Spanish)
Report on the World Health Situation. 1959 ff. (English, French, Russian, Spanish); Sixth report 1973–77 (1979)

INTERNATIONAL MONETARY FUND (IMF)

The International Monetary Fund was established on 27 Dec. 1945 as an independent international organization and began operations on 1 March 1947; its relationship with the UN is defined in an agreement of mutual co-operation which came into force on 15 Nov. 1947. The first amendment to the Fund's articles creating the special drawing right (SDR) took effect on 28 July 1969 and the second amendment took effect on 1 April 1978.

The Fund is authorized under its Articles of Agreement to supplement its resources by borrowing. In Jan. 1962, a 4-year agreement was concluded with 10 industrial members (Belgium, Canada, France, Federal Republic of Germany, Italy, Japan, Netherlands, Sweden, UK, USA) who undertook to lend the Fund up to $6,000m. in their own currencies, if this should be needed to forestall or cope with an impairment of the international monetary system. Switzerland subsequently joined the group as an associate. These agreements, which have now been extended until Oct. 1985, were used to finance drawings made by the UK in 1964, 1965, 1968, 1969 and 1977, by France in 1969 and 1970 and by USA in 1978. The Fund has also borrowed from member countries and official institutions for a supplementary financing facility, and, more recently, from the Saudi Arabian Monetary Agency (SAMA).

Purposes: To promote international monetary co-operation, the expansion of international trade and exchange rate stability; to assist in the removal of exchange restrictions and the establishment of a multilateral system of payments; and to alleviate any serious disequilibrium in members' international balance of payments by making the financial resources of the Fund available to them, usually subject to conditions to ensure the revolving nature of Fund resources.

Activities. Each member of the Fund undertakes a broad obligation to collaborate with the Fund and other members to ensure the existence of orderly exchange arrangements and to promote a system of stable exchange rates. In addition, members are subject to certain obligations relating to domestic and external policies that can affect the balance of payments and the exchange rate. The Fund makes its resources available, under proper safeguards, to its members to meet short-term or medium-term payments difficulties. The first allocation of special drawing rights was made on 1 Jan. 1970 with five SDR allocations since then. SDRs in existence now total SDR 21,400m. On 24 Sept. 1978 the Fund's Interim Committee agreed on a 50% increase in quotas under the 7th general review of quotas; such reviews are required at least every five years. Total quotas now amount to SDR 61,000m., and the 8th general review of quotas is proceeding. To further enhance its balance of payments assistance to its members the Fund established a compensatory financing facility on 23 Feb. 1963, temporary oil facilities in 1974 and 1975, a trust fund in 1976, and an extended facility for medium term assistance to members with special balance of payments problems on 13 Sept. 1974 with additional financing now provided through a policy of enlarged access.

A Report on Reform of the International Monetary System was submitted to the Board of Governors at the 1972 annual meeting. During the meeting the Committee on Reform of the International Monetary System and Related Issues, generally known as the Committee of Twenty, held its first session, with the mandate to advise and report to the Board on all aspects of the international monetary system, including proposals for any amendments of the Articles of Agreement. The Committee of Twenty disbanded after submitting its final report in 1974. An Interim Committee of the Board of Governors on the International Monetary System and a Joint Ministerial Committee of the Boards of Governors of the World Bank and the Fund on the Transfer of Real Resources to Developing Countries (Development Committee) were established and held their initial meetings in Jan. 1975 and since then have met on a semi-annual basis.

Organization. The highest authority in the Fund is exercised by the Board of Governors on which each member government is represented. Normally the Governors meet once a year, although the Governors may take votes by mail or other means between annual meetings. The Board of Governors has delegated many of its powers to the executive directors in Washington, of whom there are 22, of which 6 are appointed by individual members and the other 16 elected by groups of countries. Each appointed director has voting power proportionate to the quota of the government he represents, while each elected director casts all the votes of the countries which elected him. The 6 appointed executive directors represent the US, UK, France, Federal Republic of Germany, Saudi Arabia and Japan.

The managing director is selected by the executive directors; he presides as chairman at their meetings, but may not vote except in case of a tie. His term is for 5 years, but may be extended or terminated at the discretion of the executive directors. He is responsible for the ordinary business of the Fund, under general control of the executive directors, and supervises a staff of about 1,500.

Headquarters: 700 19th St. NW, Washington, D.C., 20431. Offices in Paris and Geneva.

Managing Director: Jacques de Larosière (France).

Publications. Summary Proceedings of Annual Meetings of the Board of Governors.—Annual Report of the Executive Board.—Financial Statement (quarterly).—*International Financial Statistics* (monthly).—*IMF Survey* (bi-weekly).—*Balance of Payments Statistics.* Washington, monthly.—*IMF Staff Papers* (four times a year). Washington, from Feb. 1950.—*IMF Occasional Papers.—Annual Report on Exchange Arrangements and Exchange*

Restrictions. Washington, 1950 ff.—*Finance and Development.* Washington, from June 1964 (quarterly).—*Direction of Trade.* Washington (monthly). *World Economic Outlook.* Washington (annual). *Government Finance Statistics Yearbook.*

de Vries, M. G., *The International Monetary Fund 1966–1971.* Washington D.C., 1976

INTERNATIONAL BANK FOR RECONSTRUCTION AND DEVELOPMENT (IBRD)

Conceived at the Bretton Woods Conference, July 1944, the Bank began operations in June 1946. Its purpose is to provide funds and technical assistance to facilitate economic development in its poorer member countries.

The Bank obtains its funds from the following sources: Capital subscribed by member countries; sales of its own securities; sales of parts of its loans; repayments; and net earnings. The subscribed capital of the Bank amounted to $36,614m. at 30 June 1981. On 4 Jan. 1980, the Board of Governors adopted a resolution that increased the authorized capital stock of the Bank by 331,500 shares. This represented an increase of approximately $40,000m. The resolution provides that the paid-in portion of the shares authorized to be subscribed under it will be 75%, compared with the 10% paid-in portion of existing capital stock. Borrowing in the market had reached more than $50,000m. by 30 June 1981, of which $27,797m. was outstanding, and sales of portions of Bank loans from portfolio had totalled $2,980m. The Bank is self-supporting. Its net earnings for year ending 30 June 1980 amounted to $588m.; in addition, the Bank had reserves of $3,995m.

By 30 June 1981 the Bank had made 2,015 loans totalling $68,150·3m. in 102 of its 139 member countries. Lending was for the following purposes: Agriculture and rural development, $14,383m.; Development Finance Companies, $7,027m.; education, $2,473m.; energy, $14,535m.; industry, $5,156m.; non-project, $2,516m.; population, health and nutrition, $239m.; small-scale enterprises, $833m.; telecommunications, $1,264m.; tourism, $364m.; transportation, $13,665m.; urban development, $1,596m.; water supply and sewerage, $3,216m., and technical assistance, $91·1m. In order to eliminate wasteful overlapping of development assistance and to ensure that the funds available are used to the best possible effect, the Bank has organized consortia or consultative groups of aid-giving nations for the following countries: Bangladesh, Colombia, Egypt, Korea, Nepál, Pakistan, the Philippines, Sudan, Uganda. Zaïre and the Caribbean Group for Co-operation in Economic Development. The Bank furnishes a wide variety of technical assistance. It acts as executing agency for a number of pre-investment surveys financed by the UN Development Programme. Resident missions have been established in 23 developing member countries as well as 3 regional missions in East and West Africa and Thailand primarily to assist in the preparation of projects. The Bank helps member countries to identify and prepare projects for the development of agriculture, education and water supply by drawing on the expertise of the FAO, WHO, UNIDO and UNESCO through its co-operative agreements with these organizations. The Bank maintains a staff college, the Economic Development Institute in Washington, D.C., for senior officials of the member countries.

To help the poorest member countries the INTERNATIONAL DEVELOPMENT ASSOCIATION (IDA) was established in 1960. IDA grants development credits on a long-term, interest-free basis. By 30 June 1981 IDA had extended 1,079 credits to 73 countries, totalling $24,052m. for the same general purpose as bank loans. IDA's primary lending resources have been the subscriptions and supplementary contributions of member countries, chiefly its 21 wealthiest. The World Bank has made grants to IDA out of its net income; the Association also has a small flow of net income of its own.

Headquarters: 1818 H St., NW, Washington, D.C., 20433, USA. *European office:* 66 avenue d'Iéna, 75116 Paris, France. *London office:* New Zealand House, Haymarket, SW1Y 4TE, England. *Tōkyō office:* Kokusai Building, 1–1, Marunouchi 3-chome, Chiyoda-ku, Tōkyō 100, Japan.

President: Alden W. (Tom) Clausen (USA).

Publications. Annual Reports. 1946 ff.—*Summary Proceedings of Annual Meetings.* 1947 ff.—*The World Bank Group.* 1971.—*The World Bank Atlas.* 1967 ff.—*The World Bank, Group Policies and Operations.* 1974.—*Catalog of Publications,* 1982.—IDA, 1979.—*World Development Report.* 1978 ff.

INTERNATIONAL DEVELOPMENT ASSOCIATION (IDA)

A lending agency which came into existence on 24 Sept. 1960. Administered by the World Bank, IDA is open to all members of the Bank.

IDA concentrates its assistance on those countries with an annual *per capita* gross national product of less than $520 (1975 rate). Its resources consist mostly of subscriptions, general replenishments from its more industrialized and developed members, special contributions, and transfers from the net earnings of the Bank. IDA credits are made to Governments only. It had committed over $16,730m. for development projects by 30 June 1979.

INTERNATIONAL FINANCE CORPORATION (IFC)

The Corporation, an affiliate of the World Bank, was established in July 1956. Paid-in capital at 30 June 1983 was $547·3m., subscribed by 124 member countries. In addition, it has accumulated earnings of $203·8m. IFC supplements the activities of the World Bank by encouraging the growth of productive private enterprises in less developed member countries. Chiefly, IFC makes investments in the form of subscriptions to the share capital of privately owned companies, or long-term loans, or both. The Corporation will help finance new ventures, and it will also assist established enterprises to expand, improve or diversify their operations.

At 30 June 1983 IFC had approved investments amounting to $5,520m., in 81 countries. The total amount of loans and equity which IFC had sold or agreed to sell to other investors as of that date was $1,747m.

President: Alden W. (Tom) Clausen (USA).
Executive Vice-President: Hans A. Wuttke (Germany).

Publications. Annual Reports. 1956 ff.—*General Policies.* 1983

INTERNATIONAL CIVIL AVIATION ORGANIZATION (ICAO)

Origin. The Convention providing for the establishment of the International Civil Aviation Organization was drawn up by the International Civil Aviation Conference held in Chicago from 1 Nov. to 7 Dec. 1944. A Provisional International Civil Aviation Organization (PICAO) operated for 20 months until the formal establishment of ICAO on 4 April 1947.

The Convention on International Civil Aviation superseded the provisions of the Paris Convention of 1919, which established the International Commission for Air Navigation (ICAN), and the Pan American Convention on Air Navigation drawn up at Havana in 1928.

Functions. It assists international civil aviation by establishing technical standards for safety and efficiency of air navigation and promoting simpler procedures at borders; develops regional plans for ground facilities and services needed for international flying; disseminates air-transport statistics and prepares studies on aviation economics; fosters the development of air law conventions. As part of the UN Development Programme it provides technical assistance to States in developing civil aviation programmes.

Organization. The principal organs of ICAO are an Assembly, consisting of all members of the Organization, and a Council, which is comprised of 33 states elected by the Assembly, for 3 years, and meets in virtually continuous session. In electing these states, the Assembly must give adequate representation to: (1) states of major importance in air transport; (2) states which make the largest contribution to the provision of facilities for the international civil air navigation; (3) those states not otherwise included whose election will ensure that all major geographical areas of the world are represented. The main subsidiary bodies are: the Air Navigation Commission, composed of 15 members appointed by the Council; Air Transport

Committee, open to council members; and the Legal Committee, on which all members of ICAO may be represented. There are 151 members. Budget for 1983: $32,879,000.

Headquarters: 1000 Sherbrooke St. West, Suite 400, Montreal, Quebec, Canada H3A 2R2.
President: Dr Assad Kotaite (Lebanon).
Secretary-General: Yves Lambert (France).

Annual Report of the Council. (English, French, Russian, Spanish).

UNIVERSAL POSTAL UNION (UPU)

Origin. The UPU was established on 1 July 1875, when the Universal Postal Convention adopted by the Postal Congress of Berne on 9 Oct. 1874 came into force. The UPU was known at first as the General Postal Union, its name being changed at the Congress of Paris in 1878. In 1980 there were 158 member countries.

Functions. The aim of the UPU is to assure the organization and perfection of the various postal services and to promote, in this field, the development of international collaboration. To this end, the members of UPU are united in a single postal territory for the reciprocal exchange of correspondence.

Organization. The UPU is composed of a Universal Postal Congress which usually meets every 5 years, a permanent Executive Council consisting of 40 members, a consultative Committee, which consists of 35 members elected on a geographical basis by each Congress, and an International Bureau, which functions as the permanent secretariat.

Since 1 July 1948 the Union has been governed by the revised Convention adopted by the twelfth Congress in Paris on 5 July 1947.

Budget for 1981: $9·5m.

Headquarters: Weltpoststrasse 4, 3000, Berne 15, Switzerland.
Director-General: Mohamed Ibrahim Sobhi (Egypt).

Publications. Documents of the Lausanne Congress 1974. Bern, 1975.—*Universal Postal Convention: Paris, 5 July, 1948.* (Cmd. 7435).—*The Postal Union* (monthly, Arabic, Chinese, English, French, German, Spanish, Russian).—*The UPU: Its Foundation and Development.* Bern, 1959.

INTERNATIONAL TELECOMMUNICATION UNION (ITU)

Origin. The International Telegraph Union, founded in Paris in 1865, and the International Radiotelegraph Union, founded in Berlin in 1906, were merged by the Madrid Convention of 1932 to form the International Telecommunication Union. ITU came into being on 1 Jan. 1934. The ITU has been governed since 1 Jan. 1975 by the revised International Telecommunication Convention adopted on 23 Oct. 1973.

Functions. The ITU: (1) allocates radio frequencies and registers radio-frequency assignments; (2) seeks to establish the lowest rates possible, consistent with efficient service and taking into account the necessity for keeping the independent financial administration of telecommunication on a sound basis; (3) promotes the adoption of measures for ensuring the safety of life through telecommunicion; and (4) makes studies and recommendations and collects and publishes information for the benefit of its members.

Organization. The ITU consists of the Plenipotentiary Conference, Administrative Conferences, the Administrative Council of 36 members, the General Secretariat, the International Frequency Registration Board, and 2 international consultative committees (radio, telephone and telegraph).

Budget for 1975: $62·32m.

Headquarters: Place des Nations, Geneva, Switzerland.
Secretary-General: Mohamed Mili (Tunisia).

Publications: International Convention on Telecommunications, Malaga-Torremolinos, 1973.—Yearbook of Common Carrier Telecommunication Statistics (1964–73), 1975. —Telecommunication Journal (monthly).—Radio Regulations. 1971.

WORLD METEOROLOGICAL ORGANIZATION (WMO)

Origin. A Conference of Directors of the International Meteorological Organization (set up in 1873), meeting in Washington in 1947, adopted a Convention creating the World Meteorological Organization. The WMO Convention became effective on 23 March 1950, and WMO was formally established on 19 March 1951, when the first session of its Congress was convened in Paris. An agreement to bring WMO into relationship with the United Nations was approved by this Congress and came into force on 21 Dec. 1951 with its approval by the General Assembly of the United Nations.

Functions. (1) To facilitate world-wide co-operation in the establishment of networks of stations for the making of meteorological observations as well as hydrological or other geophysical observations related to meteorology, and to promote the establishment and maintenance of meteorological centres charged with the provision of meteorological and related services; (2) to promote the establishment and maintenance of systems for the rapid exchange of meteorological and related information; (3) to promote standardization of meteorological and related observations and to ensure the uniform publication of observations and statistics; (4) to further the application of meteorology to aviation, shipping, water problems, agriculture and other human activities; (5) to promote activities in operational hydrology and to further close co-operation between meteorological and hydrological services; and (6) to encourage research and training in meteorology and, as appropriate, to assist in co-ordinating the international aspects of such research and training.

Organization. WMO is an inter-governmental organization of 152 member states and 5 member territories responsible for the operation of their own meteorological services. Constituent bodies of WMO are the World Meteorological Congress which meets every 4 years, the executive council composed of 36 members elected in their personal capacity and including the President and 3 Vice-Presidents of the Organization, 6 regional associations of members and 8 technical commissions established by the Congress. A permanent secretariat is maintained in Geneva.

Budget for 1983: $18,108,200.

Headquarters: Case postale 5, CH-1211, Geneva 20, Switzerland.
Secretary-General: A. C. Wiin-Nielsen (Denmark).

Publications. WMO Bulletin. 1952 ff.—*Meteorological Services of the World.* 1982. —*Publications of the World Meteorological Organization, 1951–1983.*

INTERNATIONAL MARITIME ORGANIZATION (IMO)

Origin. The International Maritime Organization was established as a specialized agency of the UN by a convention drawn up at the UN Maritime Conference held at Geneva in Feb./March 1948. The Convention became effective on 17 March 1958 when it had been ratified by 21 countries, including 7 with at least 1m. gross tons of shipping each. The International Maritime Organization started operations in Jan. 1959.

Functions. To facilitate co-operation among governments on technical matters affecting merchant shipping, especially concerning safety at sea; to prevent and control marine pollution caused by ships; to encourage abolition of discriminatory and restrictive practices affecting merchant shipping. The International Maritime Organization is responsible for convening international maritime conferences and for drafting international maritime conventions.

Organization. The International Maritime Organization had 125 members (and 1 associate member) in 1983. The Assembly, composed of all member states, normally meets every 2 years. The Council of 24 member states acts as governing body between Assembly sessions. The Maritime Safety Committee deals with all technical questions. It can establish specialized sub-committees to deal with specific problems and like the Marine Environment Protection Committee, Legal Committee, Facilitation Committee and Committee on Technical Co-operation is open to all International Maritime Organization members. The Secretariat is composed of international civil servants.

The International Maritime Organization is depositary authority for the International Convention for the Safety of Life at Sea, 1960, and the Regulations for Preventing Collisions at Sea, 1948 and 1960; the International Convention for the Prevention of Pollution of the Sea by Oil, 1954, as amended in 1962 and 1969; the Convention on Facilitation of International Maritime Traffic, 1965; the International Convention on Load Lines, 1966; the International Convention on Tonnage Measurement of Ships, 1969; the International Convention relating to Intervention on the High Seas in cases of Oil Pollution Casualties, 1969; the International Convention on Civil Liability for Oil Pollution Damage, 1969; Convention on International Compensation Fund for Oil Pollution Damage, 1971; Special Trade Passenger Ships Agreement, 1971; Convention on International Regulations for Preventing Collisions at Sea, 1972; the International Convention for Safe Containers, 1972; the International Convention on Prevention of Pollution from Ships, 1973; the International Convention for the Safety of Life at Sea, 1974; Athens Convention relating to the Carriage of Passengers and their Luggage by Sea, 1974; Convention on the International Maritime Satellite Organization, 1976; Convention on Limitation of Maritime Claims, 1976; Torremolinos International Convention for the Safety of Fishing Vessels, 1977; International Convention on Standards of Training, Certification and Watchkeeping for Seafarers, 1978; International Convention on Maritime Search and Rescue, 1979.

Headquarters: 4 Albert Embankment, London SE1 7SR.
Secretary-General: C. P. Srivastava (India).
Assistant General Secretary: T. A. Mensah (Ghana).

IMO News

GENERAL AGREEMENT ON TARIFFS AND TRADE (GATT)

Origin. The General Agreement on Tariffs and Trade was negotiated in 1947 and entered into force on 1 Jan. 1948. Its 23 original signatories were members of a Preparatory Committee appointed by the UN Economic and Social Council to draft the charter for a proposed International Trade Organization. Since this charter was never ratified, the General Agreement, intended as an interim arrangement, has instead remained as the only international instrument laying down trade rules accepted by countries responsible for most of the world's trade. In Nov. 1983 there were 90 contracting parties, with a further 30 countries participating under special arrangements.

Functions. GATT functions both as a multilateral treaty that lays down a common code of conduct in international trade and trade relations and as a forum for negotiation and consultation to overcome trade problems and reduce trade barriers. Key provisions of the Agreement guarantee most-favoured-nation treatment (exceptions being granted to customs unions and free trade areas, and for certain preferences in favour of developing countries); require that protection be given to domestic industry only through tariffs (apart from specified exceptions); provide for negotiations to reduce tariffs (which are then 'bound' against subsequent increase) and other trade distortions; and lay down principles (particularly in Part IV of the Agreement, added in 1965) to assist the trade of developing countries. The Agreement also provides for consultation on, and settlement of, disputes, for 'waivers' (the grant of authorization, when warranted, to derogate from specific GATT obligations) and for emergency action in defined circumstances.

Seven 'rounds' of multilateral trade negotiations, including the Kennedy Round of 1964–67, took place in GATT up to 1979. The latest in this series, the Tōkyō

Round, although held in Geneva, was so called because it was launched at a Ministerial meeting in the Japanese capital in Sept. 1973.

Ninety-nine countries participated in the Tōkyō Round. In Nov. 1979, the negotiations were concluded with agreements covering: an improved legal framework for the conduct of world trade (which includes recognition of tariff and nontariff treatment in favour of and among developing countries as a permanent legal feature of the world trading system); non-tariff measures (subsidies and countervailing duties; technical barriers to trade; government procurement; customs valuation; import licensing procedures; and a revision of the 1967 GATT antidumping code); bovine meat; dairy products; tropical products; and an agreement on free trade in civil aircraft. The agreements contain provisions for special and more favourable treatment for developing countries.

Participating countries also agreed to reduce tariffs on thousands of industrial and agricultural products, for the most part over a period of 7 years beginning on 1 Jan. 1980. As a result of these concessions, industrialized countries will reduce the average level of their import duties on manufactures by about 34%, a cut comparable to that achieved in the Kennedy Round.

The agreements providing an improved framework for the conduct of world trade took effect in Nov. 1979. The other agreements took effect on 1 Jan. 1980, except for those covering government procurement and customs valuation, which took effect on 1 Jan. 1981, and the concessions on tropical products which began as early as 1977. Committees were established to supervise implementation of each of the Tōkyō Round agreements. Negotiations continued on the one major unresolved Tōkyō Round issue of whether to revise GATT rules on emergency safeguard action against imports.

GATT's member governments met in Geneva 24–29 Nov. 1982. The purpose of the meeting was to 'examine the functioning of the multilateral trading system, and to reinforce the common efforts of the contracting parties to support and improve the system for the benefit of all nations'. They adopted by consensus a joint Ministerial declaration which included: (i) An agreement on the problems facing the world economy and international trade; (ii) reaffirmation of the member governments' commitment to the GATT rules and to the multilateral trading system; (iii) an undertaking to refrain from taking or maintaining any trade measures inconsistent with GATT; (iv) an undertaking to ensure the effective implementation of GATT rules and provisions concerning developing countries, thereby furthering the dynamic role of these countries in international trade; (v) an undertaking to bring agriculture more fully into the multilateral trading system; to this end a Committee on Trade in Agriculture is to be established to carry out a major two-year work programme in this area; (vi) an undertaking to bring into effect quickly a comprehensive understanding on safeguards to be based on the principles of the General Agreement.

The Ministerial declaration also included decisions to improve the GATT procedures for settling trade disputes between members, to study such issues as trade in certain natural resource products, and to exchange information through GATT on international trade in services.

To assist the trade of developing countries, GATT established in 1964 the International Trade Centre (since 1968 operated jointly with the UN Conference on Trade and Development) to provide information and training on export markets and marketing techniques. Other GATT action in favour of developing countries includes training courses on trade policy questions.

Budget for 1982: Sw. Frs. 49·6m.

Headquarters: Centre William Rappard, 154 rue de Lausanne, 1211 Geneva 21, Switzerland.

Director-General: Arthur Dunkel (Switzerland).

Publications. Basic Instruments and Selected Documents. 4 vols. and 28 supplements 1952–82.—*International Trade* [i.e., annual review], 1952 ff. Annually from 1953.—*GATT, What It Is, What It Does* (1982).—*GATT Activities,* 1960 ff. Annually from 1972.—*GATT Focus.* Monthly from Feb. 1981.—*GATT Studies in International Trade.* 1971 ff. (irregular series).—*The Tokyo Round of Multilateral Trade Negotiations.* Report of the Director-General, 2 vols., 1979

Casadio, G. P., *Transatlantic Trade: USA–EEC Confrontation in the GATT Negotiations*. Farnborough, 1973
Dam, K. W., *The GATT: Law and International Economic Organization*. Chicago and London, 1970
Golt, S., *The GATT Negotiations, 1973–75: A Guide to the Issues*. London, 1974
Hudec, R. E., *The GATT Legal System and World Trade Diplomacy*. New York, 1975
Jackson, J. H., *World Trade and the Law of GATT: A Legal Analysis of the General Agreement on Tariffs and Trade*. New York, 1969

WORLD INTELLECTUAL PROPERTY ORGANIZATION (WIPO)

Origin. The Convention establishing WIPO was signed at Stockholm in 1967 by 51 countries, and entered into force in April 1970. In Dec. 1974 WIPO became a specialized agency of the UN.

Functions. To promote the protection of intellectual property throughout the world through co-operation among States and, where appropriate, in collaboration with any other international organization, and to ensure administrative co-operation among the Unions established by various treaties for the protection of intellectual property. The WIPO Convention provides expressly for the encouragement of the conclusion of international agreements designed to promote the protection of intellectual property, and for the provision of legal-technical assistance at the request of States.

Intellectual property means the legal rights which result from intellectual activity in the industrial, scientific, literary or artistic fields. The main examples are industrial property (patents and other rights in inventions, rights in trademarks and industrial designs etc.) and copyright and neighbouring rights (chiefly in literary, musical and artistic works, in films, records and broadcasts etc.) in all fields of human endeavour; scientific discoveries; industrial designs; trade-marks, service marks and commercial names and designations; protection against unfair competition and all other rights resulting from intellectual activity in the industrial, scientific, literary or artistic fields.

Membership in WIPO is open to any State which is a member of at least one of the Unions and to other States which are members of the organizations of the United Nations system, are party to the Statute of the International Court of Justice, or are invited to join by the General Assembly of WIPO. Membership of the Unions is open to any State. The total combined membership of WIPO and of the Unions on 31 Dec. 1983, was 124 states.

Organization. The bodies of WIPO are: The *General Assembly* consisting of all States members of WIPO which are members of any of the Unions. Among its other functions, the General Assembly appoints and gives instructions to the Director General, reviews and approves his reports and adopts the biennial budget of expenses common to the Unions. The *Conference*, consisting of all States members of WIPO whether or not they are members of any of the Unions. Among its other functions, the Conference adopts its biennial budget and establishes the biennial programme of legal-technical assistance. The *Co-ordination Committee*, consisting of the States members of WIPO which are members of the Executive Committees of the Paris or Berne Unions.

In addition, the Paris and Berne Unions have Assemblies and Executive Committees, with functions similar to those of the WIPO bodies in respect of the biennial and annual budgets and programmes of the Unions.

The *WIPO Permanent Committees for Development Co-operation Related to Industrial Property* and *Related to Copyright and Neighbouring Rights* plan and review activities in the said fields; the *WIPO Permanent Committee on Patent Information* is responsible for intergovernmental co-operation in patent search systems and in such matters as the classification, standardization and exchange of patent documents.

Headquarters: 34, chemin des Colombettes, 1211 Geneva 20, Switzerland.
Director General: Arpad Bogsch (USA).

Principal publications. Industrial Property (monthly, in English and French).—*Copyright* (monthly, in English and French).—*Les Marques internationales* (monthly, in French).— *Brochures of Conventions and Agreements.—Collections of Laws and Treaties.—Model Laws for Developing Countries on Inventions, on Marks Trade Names and Acts of Unfair Competition on Designs on Copyright and on Neighbouring Rights* (in Arabic, English, French and Spanish).—*Licensing Guide for Developing Countries* (in Arabic, Chinese, English, French, Portuguese and Spanish).—*Glossaries - industrial property and copyright* (multilingual).— *Guide to the Berne Convention* (in Arabic, English, French, German, Hindi, Japanese, Portuguese, Russian, Spanish).—*Guide to the Rome and Phonograms Convention* (in English, French and Spanish).

INTERNATIONAL FUND FOR AGRICULTURAL DEVELOPMENT (IFAD)

The establishment of IFAD was one of the major actions proposed by the 1974 World Food Conference. The agreement for IFAD entered into force on 30 Nov. 1977 following attainment of initial pledges of $1,000m. and the agency began its operations the following month. IFAD's purpose is to mobilise additional funds for agricultural and rural development in developing countries through projects and programmes directly benefitting the poorest rural population. In line with the Fund's focus on the rural poor, its resources are being made available in highly concessional loans.

Organization. The Governing Council, consisting of the entire membership, directs the Fund's operations. The chief executive is the President, who is also the Chairman of the 18-member Executive Board.

President: Abdelmuhsin Al-Sudeary (Saudi Arabia).
Headquarters: 107 Via del Serafico, Rome, Italy.

THE COMMONWEALTH

The Commonwealth is a free association of sovereign independent states, numbering 48 at the beginning of 1984. There is no charter, treaty or constitution; the association is expressed in co-operation, consultation and mutual assistance for which the Commonwealth Secretariat is the central co-ordinating body.

The Commonwealth was first defined by the Imperial Conference of 1926 as a group of 'autonomous communities within the British Empire, equal in status, in no way subordinate one to another in any aspect of their domestic or foreign affairs, though united by a common allegiance to the Crown, and freely associated as members of the British Commonwealth of Nations'. The basis of the association changed from one owing allegiance to a common Crown, and the modern Commonwealth was born in 1949 when the member countries accepted India's intention of becoming a republic at the same time continuing 'her full membership of the Commonwealth of Nations and her acceptance of the King as the symbol of the free association of its independent member nations and as such the Head of the Commonwealth'. There are now (1983) 18 Queen's realms, 26 republics, and 4 indigenous monarchies in the Commonwealth. All acknowledge the Queen symbolically as Head of the Commonwealth.

The Queen's legal title rests on the statute of 12 and 13 Will. III, c. 3, by which the succession to the Crown of Great Britain and Ireland was settled on the Princess Sophia of Hanover and the 'heirs of her body being Protestants'. By proclamation of 17 July 1917 the royal family became known as the House and Family of Windsor. On 8 Feb. 1960 the Queen issued a declaration varying her confirmatory declaration of 9 April 1952 to the effect that while the Queen and her children should continue to be known as the House of Windsor, her descendants, other than descendants entitled to the style of Royal Highness and the title of Prince or Princess, and female descendants who marry and their descendants should bear the name of Mountbatten-Windsor. The Royal Style and Titles of Queen Elizabeth are: In *Antigua and Barbuda* 'Elizabeth the Second, by the Grace of God, Queen of Antigua and Barbuda and of Her other Realms and Territories, Head of the

Commonwealth'. In *Australia*: 'Elizabeth the Second, by the Grace of God Queen of Australia and Her other Realms and Territories, Head of the Commonwealth'. In the *Bahamas*: 'Elizabeth the Second, by the Grace of God, Queen of the Commonwealth of the Bahamas and of Her other Realms and Territories, Head of the Commonwealth'. In *Barbados*: 'Elizabeth the Second, by the Grace of God, Queen of Barbados and of Her other Realms and Territories, Head of the Commonwealth'. In *Belize*: 'Elizabeth the Second, by the Grace of God, Queen of Belize and of Her Other Realms and Territories, Head of the Commonwealth'. In *Canada*: 'Elizabeth the Second, by the Grace of God of the United Kingdom, Canada and Her other Realms and Territories Queen, Head of the Commonwealth, Defender of the Faith'. In *Fiji*: 'Elizabeth the Second, by the Grace of God, Queen of Fiji and of Her other Realms and Territories. Head of the Commonwealth'. In *Grenada*: 'Elizabeth the Second, by the Grace of God, Queen of the United Kingdom of Great Britain and Northern Ireland and of Grenada and Her other Realms and Territories, Head of the Commonwealth'. In *Jamaica*: 'Elizabeth the Second, by the Grace of God of Jamaica and of Her other Realms and Territories Queen, Head of the Commonwealth'. In *Mauritius*: 'Elizabeth the Second, Queen of Mauritius and of Her other Realms and Territories, Head of the Commonwealth'. In *New Zealand*: 'Elizabeth the Second, by the Grace of God Queen of New Zealand and Her Other Realms and Territories, Head of the Commonwealth, Defender of the Faith'. In *Papua New Guinea*: 'Elizabeth the Second, Queen of Papua New Guinea and Her other Realms and Territories, Head of the Commonwealth'. In *Saint Christopher and Nevis*: 'Elizabeth the Second, by the Grace of God, Queen of Saint Christopher and Nevis and Her other Realms and Territories, Head of the Commonwealth'. In *Saint Lucia*: 'Elizabeth the Second, by the Grace of God, Queen of Saint Lucia and of Her other Realms and Territories, Head of Commonwealth'. In *Saint Vincent and the Grenadines*: 'Elizabeth the Second, by the Grace of God, Queen of Saint Vincent and the Grenadines and of Her other Realms and Territories, Head of the Commonwealth'. In *Solomon Islands*: 'Elizabeth the Second by the Grace of God Queen of Solomon Islands and of Her other Realms and Territories, Head of the Commonwealth'. In *Tuvalu*: 'Elizabeth the Second by the Grace of God Queen of Tuvalu and of Her other Realms and Territories, Head of the Commonwealth'. In the *United Kingdom*: 'Elizabeth the Second, by the Grace of God of the United Kingdom of Great Britain and Northern Ireland and of Her other Realms and Territories Queen, Head of the Commonwealth, Defender of the Faith'.

A number of territories, formerly under British jurisdiction or mandate did not join the Commonwealth: Egypt, Iraq, Transjordan, Burma, Palestine, Sudan, British Somaliland, South Cameroons, and Aden. Two countries, the Republic of South Africa in 1961 and Pakistan in 1972, have left the Commonwealth.

Maldives, Nauru, Tuvalu and Saint Vincent and the Grenadines are special members, with the right to participate in all functional Commonwealth meetings and activities but not to attend meetings of Commonwealth Heads of Government.

Member States. The following are the member countries, with their dates of independence, and, where appropriate, the date on which they became republics: *United Kingdom*; *Canada* 1 July 1867[1]; *Australia* 1 Jan. 1901[1]; *New Zealand* 26 Sept. 1907[1]; *India* 15 Aug. 1947 (Republic on 26 Jan. 1950); *Sri Lanka* 4 Feb. 1948 (Republic on 22 May 1972); *Ghana* 6 March 1957 (Republic on 1 July 1960); *Malaysia* 31 Aug. 1957 as Federation of Malaya, 16 Sept. 1963 as Federation of Malaysia; *Cyprus* 16 Aug. 1960 (Republic on independence; joined Commonwealth on 13 March 1961); *Nigeria* 1 Oct. 1960 (Republic on 1 Oct. 1963); *Sierra Leone* 27 April 1961 (Republic on 19 April 1971); *Tanzania*–Tanganyika 9 Dec. 1961 (Republic on 9 Dec. 1962), Zanzibar 10 Dec. 1963 (Republic on 12 Jan. 1964), United Republic of Tanganyika and Zanzibar 26 April 1964; renamed United Republic of Tanzania 29 Oct. 1964; *Western Samoa* 1 Jan. 1962 (joined Commonwealth on 28 Aug. 1970); *Jamaica* 6 Aug. 1962; *Trinidad and Tobago* 31 Aug. 1962 (Republic on 1 Aug. 1976); *Uganda* 9 Oct. 1962 (Republic 8 Sept. 1967, second republic 25 Jan. 1971); *Kenya* 12 Dec. 1963 (Republic on 12 Dec. 1964); *Malawi* 6 July 1964 (Republic on 6 July 1966); *Malta* 21 Sept. 1964 (Republic on 13 Dec. 1974); *Zambia* 24 Oct. 1964 (Republic on independence); *The Gambia* 18

Feb. 1965 (Republic on 24 April 1970); *Maldives* 26 July 1965 (Republic on independence, joined Commonwealth on 9 July 1982); *Singapore* 16 Sept. 1963 as a state in the Federation of Malaysia, 9 Aug. 1965 as an independent state and republic not part of Malaysia; *Guyana* 26 May 1966 (Republic on 23 Feb. 1970); *Botswana* 30 Sept. 1966 (Republic on independence); *Lesotho* 4 Oct. 1966; *Barbados* 30 Nov. 1966; *Nauru* 31 Jan. 1968 (Republic on independence); *Mauritius* 12 March 1968; *Swaziland* 6 Sept. 1968; *Tonga* 4 June 1970; *Fiji* 10 Oct. 1970; *Bangladesh* seceded from Pakistan as Republic 16 Dec. 1971, recognized by United Kingdom 4 Feb. 1972 (joined Commonwealth on 18 April 1972); *Bahamas* 10 July 1973; *Grenada* 7 Feb. 1974; *Papua New Guinea* 16 Sept. 1975; *Seychelles* 29 June 1976 (Republic on independence); *Solomon Islands* 7 July 1978; *Tuvalu* 1 Oct. 1978; *Dominica* 3 Nov. 1978 (Republic on independence); *Saint Lucia* 22 Feb. 1979; *Kiribati* 12 July 1979 (Republic on independence); *Saint Vincent and the Grenadines* 27 Oct. 1979; *Zimbabwe* 18 April 1980 (Republic on independence); *Vanuatu* 30 July 1980 (Republic on independence); *Belize* 21 Sept. 1981; *Antigua* and *Barbuda* 1 Nov. 1981; *Saint Christopher and Nevis* 19 Sept. 1983.

[1] These are the effective dates of independence, given legal effect by the Statute of Westminster 1931.

Dependent Territories and Associated States. There are 15 British dependent territories, 7 Australian external territories, 2 New Zealand dependent territories and 2 New Zealand associated states. A dependent territory is a territory belonging by settlement, conquest or annexation to the British, Australian or New Zealand Crown.

United Kingdom dependent territories administered through the Foreign and Commonwealth Office comprise, in the Far East: Hong Kong; in the Indian Ocean: British Indian Ocean Territory; in the Mediterranean: Gibraltar; in the Atlantic Ocean: Bermuda, Falkland Islands, Falkland Islands Dependencies, British Antarctic Territory, St Helena, St Helena Dependencies (Ascension and Tristan da Cunha); in the Caribbean: Montserrat, British Virgin Islands, Cayman Islands, Turks and Caicos Islands, Anguilla; in the Western Pacific: Pitcairn Group of Islands. The Australian external territories are: Coral Sea Islands Territory, Cocos (Keeling) Islands, Christmas Island, Heard Island and McDonald Islands, Norfolk Island, Australian Antarctic Territory and the Territory of Ashmore and Cartier Islands. The New Zealand dependent territories are: Tokelau and Ross Dependency. The New Zealand associated states are: Cook Islands and Niue.

While constitutional responsibility to Parliament for the government of the British dependent territories rests with the Secretary of State for Foreign and Commonwealth Affairs, the administration of the territories is carried out by the Governments of the territories themselves.

Brunei is a sovereign state in treaty relationship with Britain, whereby Britain is responsible for the conduct of external affairs and has a consultative responsibility for defence. It has never been a dependent territory, and in 1971 ceased to be a protected state. A Treaty of Friendship and Co-operation was signed on 7 Jan. 1979, becoming effective on 1 Jan. 1984 when Brunei assumed her full international responsibilities and Britain gave up her consultative commitment over defence matters.

British Government Department. With effect from 17 Oct. 1968, the Secretary of State for Foreign and Commonwealth Affairs is responsible for the conduct of relations with members of the Commonwealth as well as with foreign countries, and for the administration of British dependent territories.

Commonwealth Secretariat. The Commonwealth Secretariat is an international body at the service of all 48 member countries. It provides the central organization for joint consultation and co-operation in many fields. It was established in 1965 by Commonwealth Heads of Government and has observer status at the UN General Assembly.

The Secretariat disseminates information on matters of common concern, organizes and services meetings and conferences, co-ordinates many Commonwealth activities, and provides expert technical assistance for economic and social development through the multilateral Commonwealth Fund for Technical Co-operation. The Secretariat is organized in divisions and sections which correspond to its main areas of operation: International affairs, economic affairs, food production and rural development, youth, education, information, applied studies in government, science and technology, law and health. Within this structure the Secretariat organizes the biennial meetings of Commonwealth Heads of Government, annual meetings of Finance Ministers of member countries, and regular meetings of Ministers of Education, Law, Health, and others as appropriate.

To emphasize the multilateral nature of the association, meetings are held in different cities and regions within the Commonwealth. Heads of Government decided that the Secretariat should work from London as it has the widest range of communications of any Commonwealth city, as well as the largest assembly of diplomatic missions.

The Commonwealth Secretary-General, who has access to Heads of Government, is the head of the Secretariat which is staffed by officers from member countries and financed by contributions from member governments.

Headquarters: Marlborough House, Pall Mall, London, SW1Y 5HX.
Secretary-General: Shridath S. Ramphal (Guyana).

Books of Reference

Year-Book of the Commonwealth, HMSO, 1983
The Cambridge History of the British Empire. 8 vols. CUP, 1929 ff.
Economic Survey of the Colonial Territories. 7 vols. HMSO. 1952 ff.
Ball, M., *The Open Commonwealth.* Duke Univ. Press, 1971
Bradley, K. (ed.), *The Living Commonwealth.* London, 1961
Burns, Sir Alan, *In Defence of Colonies.* London, 1957
Chadwick, J., *The Unofficial Commonwealth.* London, 1982
Dale, W., *The Modern Commonwealth.* London, 1983
Garner, J., *The Commonwealth Office, 1925–1968.* London. 1978
Grierson, E., *The Imperial Dream.* London, 1972
Hailey, Lord, *An African Survey.* Rev. ed. Oxford, 1957.—*Native Administration in the British African Territories.* 5 vols. HMSO, 1951 ff.
Hall, H. D., *Commonwealth: A History of the British Commonwealth.* London and New York, 1971
Holland, R. F., *Britain and the Commonwealth Alliance 1918–39.* London, 1981
Ingram, D. T., *The Commonwealth at Work.* London, 1969.—*The Imperfect Commonwealth.* London, 1977
Keeton, G. W. (ed.), *The British Commonwealth: Its Laws and Constitutions.* 9 vols. London, 1951 ff.
McIntyre, W. D., *The Commonwealth of Nations: Origins and Impact 1869–1971.* Univ. of Minnesota Press and OUP, 1978
Mansbergh, N., *The Commonwealth Experience.* 2 vols. London, 1982
Maxwell, W. H. and L. F., *A Legal Bibliography of the British Commonwealth of Nations.* 2nd ed. London, 1956
Papadopoulos, A. N., *Multilateral Diplomacy within the Commonwealth: A Decade of Expansion.* The Hague, 1982
Roberts-Wray, K., *Commonwealth and Colonial Law.* London, 1966
Smith, A., and Sanger, C., *Stitches in Time: The Commonwealth in World Politics.* New York, 1983
Smith, T. E., *Commonwealth Migration: Flows and Policies.* London, 1981
Wade, E. C. S., and Phillips, G. G., *Constitutional Law: An Outline of the Law and Practice of the Constitution, Including Central and Local Government and the Constitutional Relations of the British Commonwealth and Empire.* 8th ed. London, 1970
Wheare, K. C., *The Statute of Westminster and Dominion Status.* 5th ed. Oxford, 1953.—*Constitutional Structure of the Commonwealth.* Oxford, 1960

WORLD COUNCIL OF CHURCHES

The World Council of Churches was formally constituted on 23 Aug. 1948, at Amsterdam, by an assembly representing 147 churches from 44 countries. By 1980 the member churches numbered nearly 300, from over 100 countries.

The basis of membership (1975) states: 'The World Council of Churches is a fellowship of Churches which confess the Lord Jesus Christ as God and Saviour according to the Scriptures and therefore seek to fulfil together their common calling to the glory of the one God, Father, Son and Holy Spirit.' Membership is open to Churches which express their agreement with this basis and satisfy such criteria as the Assembly or Central Committee may prescribe. Today 271 Churches of Protestant, Anglican. Orthodox, Old Catholic and Pentecostal confessions belong to this fellowship.

The World Council was founded by the coming together of several diverse Christian movements. These included the overseas mission groups gathered from 1921 in the International Missionary Council, the Faith and Order Movement founded by American Episcopal Bishop Charles Brent, and the Life and Work Movement led by Swedish Lutheran Archbishop Nathan Söderblom.

On 13 May 1938 at Utrecht a provisional committee was appointed to prepare for the formation of a World Council of Churches. It was under the chairmanship of William Temple, then Archbishop of York.

Assembly. The governing body of the World Council, consisting of delegates specially appointed by the member Churches. It meets every 6 or 7 years to frame policy and to consider some main theme. The Assembly has no legislative powers and depends for the implementation of its decisions upon the action of the member Churches. Assemblies have been held in Amsterdam (1948), Evanston (1954), New Delhi (1961), Uppsala (1968), and Nairobi (1975) and most recently in Vancouver, Canada in 1983 under the theme 'Jesus Christ – the Life of the World'. In between assemblies, a 134-member Central Committee meets annually to carry out the assembly mandate, with a smaller 26-member Executive Committee meeting twice a year.

Presidents. Hon. President: The Rev. Dr W. A. Visser't Hooft. *Presidium:* Dr Marga Bührig (Switzerland), Most Rev. W. P. K. Makhulu (Botswana), Dame R. Nita Barrow (Barbados), Bishop Johannes Hempel (German Democratic Republic), Dr Lois Wilson (Canada), Metropolitan Paulos Mar Gregorios (India), Patriarch Ignatios IV (Syria).

WCC programmes are organized from headquarters in Geneva, Switzerland by a staff of 300 and a range of supervisory committees drawn from member churches. The 3 programme units are:

(i) Justice and Service which includes Inter-Church Aid, Refugee and World Service (channelling over $30m. from member churches to areas of need); the Commission on the Churches' Participation in Development; the Commission of the Churches on International Affairs, the Programme to Combat Racism and the Christian Medical Commission.

(ii) Education and Renewal includes sections dealing with renewal and congregational life, women, youth, church-related education, biblical studies, family ministry and the Programme on Theological Education.

(iii) Faith and Witness includes the Commission on Faith and Order, World Mission and Evangelism, Church and Society and the sub-unit on Dialogue with People of Living Faiths and Ideologies.

A General Secretariat with a Communication Department, finance and central services co-ordinates the work of these 3 units.

Since 1975 the WCC has held several major world conferences on such diverse themes as 'Faith, Science and the Future', 'Your Kingdom Come', 'Family Power and Social Change', 'Strategies for Churches Combating Racism in the 1980's', 'The Community of Women and Men in the Church' and 'Giving an Account of the Hope that is in Us'.

Officers of the Central and Executive Committees: *Moderator:* Rev. Dr Heinz J. Held (Federal Republic of Germany). *Vice-moderators:* Dr Sylvia Ross Talbot (USA), Metropolitan Chrysostomos of Myra (Turkey). *General Secretary:* The Rev. Dr Philip A. Potter.

Office: PO Box 66, 150 route de Ferney, 1211 Geneva 20, Switzerland.

The British Council of Churches, which is an associated national council of the World Council, acts as agent for the WCC in the UK.

Books of Reference

Official Reports: The First [. . . *etc.*] *Assembly* (London, 1948, 1955, 1962, Geneva, 1968)
New Delhi to Uppsala 1961–68. Geneva, 1968
Uppsala to Nairobi 1968–75. Geneva, 1975
Official Reports of the Faith and Order Conferences at Lausanne 1927, Edinburgh 1937, Lund 1952, Montreal 1963, Meeting of Faith and Order Commission, Louvain 1971, Accra 1974, Bangalore 1978
Official Reports of the Life and Work Conferences at Stockholm 1925 and Oxford 1937; World Conference on Church and Society 1966
Minutes of the Central Committee. Geneva, 1949 to date
Howell, L., *Acting in Faith: The World Council of Churches since 1975.* London, 1982
Hudson, D., *The World Council of Churches in International Affairs.* Leighton Buzzard, 1977
Paton, D. M., *Breaking Barriers—Nairobi 1975.* London, 1976
Potter, P., *Life in all its Fullness.* Geneva, 1981
van der Bent, A. J., *What in the World is the World Council of Churches?* Geneva, 1978.—*Handbook of Member Churches of the World Council of Churches*

INTERNATIONAL TRADE UNIONISM

There are three main international trade union confederations *(i)* the International Confederation of Free Trade Unions (ICFTU) which has in membership most of the national trade union confederations in the Western industrialized countries as well as democratic organizations in Asia, Africa, and Latin America; *(ii)* the World Federation of Trade Unions (WFTU) which draws its support mainly from Eastern Europe, but which also has affiliates in France and in several developing countries; and *(iii)* the World Confederation of Labour (WCL) which has affiliates in Western Europe, Latin America and a small number of African and Asian countries. In addition, national trade unions are frequently members of international trade union federations, set up to protect the interests of working people in particular industries or trades, which are associated with the international confederations. The International Trade Secretariats (ITS) are associated with the ICFTU; Trade Union Internationals (TUI) with the WFTU; and the International Trade Federations (ITF) with the WCL.

Coldrick, A. P., and Jones, P., *International Directory of the Trade Union Movement.* London, 1979

History. The international trade union structure in 1983 was shaped mainly by developments since 1945. In that year the WFTU was set up with world-wide membership. Attempts by trade unions in Eastern Europe to turn the WFTU into an organization voicing unquestioning support for the policies of the USSR led most of the affiliates in the Western European countries to break away from the WFTU and to form the ICFTU in 1949.

EUROPEAN TRADE UNION CONFEDERATION. In Feb. 1973 the European Trade Union Confederation was formed by trade unionists in 15 Western European countries to deal with questions of interest to European working people arising inside and outside the EEC. All the founding organizations were ICFTU affiliates but subsequently they accepted into membership European WCL affiliates, the Irish Congress of Trade Unions and the Italian Communist trade union centre (CGIL) and other national organizations. The ETUC Congress meets every 3 years and the Executive Committee 6 times a year. The membership is now about 43m. from 34 centres in 20 countries.

General Secretary: Mathias Hinterscheid.
Headquarters: Rue Montagne aux Herbes Potagères 37, 1000 Brussels.

INTERNATIONAL CONFEDERATION OF FREE TRADE UNIONS.

The first congress of ICFTU was held in London in Dec. 1949. The constitution as amended provides for co-operation with the United Nations and the International Labour Organization and for regional organizations to promote free trade unionism, especially in less-developed countries.

Organization. The Congress meets every 4 years. It elects the Executive Board of 37 members nominated on an area basis for a 4-year period; the Board meets at least twice a year. Various committees cover policy *vis-à-vis* such problems as those connected with Atomic Energy and also the administration of the International Solidarity Fund. There are joint ICFTU–ITS committees for co-ordinating activities and also for women workers' problems.

Headquarters: 37–41, rue Montagne aux Herbes Potagères, Brussels 1000, Belgium.

General Secretary: John Vanderveken.

Regional organizations exist in America, offices in Mexico City and Caracas; Asia, offices in New Delhi and Singapore; and Africa.

Membership. The ICFTU has 135 affiliated organizations in 95 countries, which together represent about 83m. workers. The biggest groups were the American Federation of Labor and Congress of Industrial Organizations (13·6m.), the British Trades Union Congress (10·5m.), the Federal German Deutscher Gewerkschaftsbund (8m.), the Confederazione Italiana Sindacati Lavoratori (2·1m.), the Swedish Landsorganisationen (2·1m.), the Canadian Labour Congress (1·3m.), the Österreichischer Gewerkschaftsbund (1·7m.), the Belgian General Federation of Labour (925,000), the Indian National Trade Union Congress (3·6m.), Australian Council of Trade Unions (1·8m.), Japanese Confederation of Labour, Domei (1·4m.).

Publications (in 4 languages). *Free Labour World* (bi-monthly); *International Trade Union News* (fortnightly); *Economic and Social Bulletin* (bi-monthly).

THE WORLD FEDERATION OF TRADE UNIONS.

The WFTU formally came into existence on 3 Oct. 1945, representing trade-union organizations in more than 50 countries of the world, both Communist and non-Communist, excluding Federal Republic of Germany and Japan, as well as a number of lesser and colonial territories. Representation from the USA was limited to the Congress of Industrial Organizations, as the American Federation of Labor declined to participate.

In Jan. 1949 the British, USA and Netherlands trade unions withdrew from WFTU, which had come under complete Communist control; and by June 1951 all non-Communist trade-unions, and the Yugoslavian Federation, had left WFTU.

Organization. The Congress meets every 4 years. In between, the General Council, of 134 members (including deputies), is the governing body, meeting (in theory) at least once a year. The Bureau controls the activities of WFTU between meetings of the General Council; it consists of the President, the General Secretary and members from different continents, the total number being decided at each Congress. The Bureau is elected by the General Council.

General Secretary: I. Zakaria (Sudan).

Membership. A total membership of 180m. from 71 national centres is claimed. The biggest groups are the Soviet All-Union Central Council of Trade Unions (107m.), the German Democratic Republic Free German Trade Union Federation (8m.), the Czechoslovak Central Council of Trade Unions (6m.), the Romanian General Confederation of Labour (6·4m.), the Hungarian Central Council of Trade Unions (4·5m.) and the French Confederation of Labour (CGT, 2m.).

Publications. World Trade Union Movement (monthly, in 9 languages); *Trade Union Press* (fortnightly, in 6 languages).

WORLD CONFEDERATION OF LABOUR. The first congress of the International Federation of Christian Trade Unions (IFCTU), as the WCL was then called, met in 1920; but a large proportion of its 3·4m. members were in Italy and Germany, where affiliated unions were suppressed by the Fascist and Nazi régimes, and in 1940 IFCTU went out of existence. It was reconstituted in 1945, and declined to merge with WFTU and, later, with ICFTU. The policy of IFCTU was based on the papal encyclicals *Rerum novarum* (1891) and *Quadragesimo anno* (1931), but in 1968, when the Federation became the WCL, it was broadened to include other concepts. The WCL now has Protestant, Buddhist and Moslem members as well as its mainly Roman Catholic members.

Organization. The WCL is organized on a federative basis which leaves wide discretion to its autonomous constituent unions. Its governing body is the Congress, which meets every 4 years. The Congress appoints (or re-appoints) the Secretary-General at each 4-yearly meeting. The General Council which meets at least once a year, is composed of the members of the Confederal Board (at least 22 members, elected by the Congress) and representatives of national confederations, international trade federations, and trade union organizations where there is no confederation affiliated to the WCL. The Confederal Board is responsible for the general leadership of the WCL, in accordance with the decisions and directives of the Council and Congress. Headquarters: 71 rue Joseph II, Brussels 1040, Belgium.

Secretary-General: Jan Kulakowski.

There are regional organizations in Latin America (office in Caracas), Africa (office in Banjul, Gambia) and Asia (office in Manila) There is also a liaison centre in Montreal.

Membership. A total membership of 14m. in about 90 countries is claimed. The biggest group is the Confederation of Christian Trade Unions of Belgium (1·1m.).

Publication. Labour Press and Information (11 each year, in 5 languages).

ORGANISATION FOR ECONOMIC CO-OPERATION AND DEVELOPMENT (OECD)

History and Membership. On 30 Sept. 1961 the Organisation for European Economic Co-operation (OEEC), after a history of 14 years (*see* THE STATESMAN'S YEAR-BOOK, 1961, p. 32), was replaced by the Organisation for Economic Co-operation and Development. The change of title marks the Organisation's altered status and functions: with the accession of Canada and USA as full members it ceased to be a purely European body; while at the same time it added development aid to the list of its other activities. The member countries are now Australia, Austria, Belgium, Canada, Denmark, Federal Republic of Germany, Finland, France, Greece, Iceland, Ireland, Italy, Japan, Luxembourg, the Netherlands, New Zealand, Norway, Portugal, Spain, Sweden, Switzerland, Turkey, UK and USA. Yugoslavia participates in the Organisation's activities with a special status. The Commission of the European Communities generally takes part in OECD's work.

Objectives. To promote economic and social welfare throughout the OECD area by assisting its member governments in the formulation of policies designed to this end and by co-ordinating these policies; and to stimulate and harmonize its members' efforts in favour of developing countries.

Organs. The supreme body of the Organisation is the Council composed of one representative for each member country. It meets either at Heads of Delegations level (about once a week) under the Chairmanship of the Secretary-General, or at Ministerial level (usually once a year) under the Chairmanship of a Minister elected annually. Decisions and Recommendations are adopted by mutual agreement of all members of the Council.

The Council is assisted by an Executive Committee composed of 14 members of the Council designated annually by the latter. The major part of the Organisation's work is, however, prepared and carried out in numerous specialized committees and working parties and sub-groups, of which there exist over 200. Thus, the Organisation comprises Committees for Economic Policy; Economic and Development Review; Development Assistance (DAC); Trade; Capital Movements and Invisible Transactions; Financial Markets; Fiscal Affairs; Restrictive Business Practices; Maritime Transport; International Investment and Multinational Enterprises; Tourism; Energy Policy; Industry; Steel; Scientific and Technological Policy; Information, Computer and Communications Policy; Education; Manpower and Social Affairs; Environment; Agriculture; Fisheries, etc. Moreover there exists a High-Level Group on Commodities and a Group on North-South Economic Issues.

Four autonomous or semi-autonomous bodies also belong to the Organisation: the International Energy Agency (IEA); the Nuclear Energy Agency (NEA); the Development Centre and the Centre for Educational Research and Innovation (CERI). Each one of these bodies has its own governing committee.

The Council, the committees and the other bodies are serviced by an international Secretariat headed by the Secretary-General of the Organisation.

All member countries have established permanent Delegations to OECD, each headed by an Ambassador.

Chairman of the Council (ministerial): Elected annually.
Chairman of the Council (official level): The Secretary-General.
Chairman of the Executive Committee: Hervé Robinet (Belgium).
Secretary-General: Emile van Lennep (Netherlands).
Deputy Secretaries-General: Jacob M. Myerson (USA), Paul Lemerle (France).
Executive Director of the International Energy Agency: Ulf Lantzke (Federal Republic of Germany).
Headquarters: Château de la Muette, 2, rue André Pascal, 75775 Paris Cedex 16, France.

OECD publishes numerous reports and statistical papers. Regular features include:
Activities of OECD. Annual, from 1972
News from OECD. Monthly
Main Economic Indicators. Monthly, from 1965
The OECD Observer. Bi-monthly, from 1962
The OECD Economic Outlook. 1966 ff.
OEEC/OECD Economic Surveys of Member Countries. 1954 ff.
European Nuclear Energy Agency, Activity Report. 1959 ff.
The Flow of Financial Resources to Countries in Course of Economic Development. 1960 ff.
Development Assistance Efforts and Policies. 1962 ff.
Tourism Policy and International Tourism in OECD Member Countries. 1955 ff.
Energy Policies and Programmes of the IEA Member Countries. 1977 ff.

NORTH ATLANTIC TREATY ORGANIZATION (NATO)

Western perceptions of the political situation in Europe following World War II gave rise, in 1947, to 2 major US initiatives – the Truman Doctrine and the Marshall Plan. These policies were designed to increase the ability of Western European countries to resist outside pressure and to assist them in bringing about their economic recovery. By 1948, on the initiative of the Foreign Secretary of the UK Ernest Bevin, 5 Western European nations had also entered into a treaty of mutual assistance in which they pledged themselves to come to each other's aid in the event of armed aggression against them (Brussels Treaty, 17 March 1948). The idea of a single mutual defence system involving North America as well as the European signatories of the Brussels Treaty was put forward by the Canadian Secretary of State for External Affairs in April 1948. It led, *via* the Vandenberg Resolution which enabled the US constitutionally to participate, to the creation of the Atlantic Alliance.

On 4 April 1949 the foreign ministers of Belgium, Canada, Denmark, France, Iceland, Italy, Luxembourg, the Netherlands, Norway, Portugal, the UK and the USA met in Washington and signed a treaty, the main clauses of which read as follows:

Article 1. The parties undertake, as set forth in the Charter of the United Nations, to settle any international disputes in which they may be involved by peaceful means in such a manner that international peace and security and justice are not endangered, and to refrain in their international relations from the threat or use of force in any manner inconsistent with the purposes of the United Nations.

Article 2. The parties will contribute toward the further development of peaceful and friendly international relations by strengthening their free institutions, by bringing about a better understanding of the principles upon which these institutions are founded, and by promoting conditions of stability and well-being. They will seek to eliminate conflict in their international economic policies and will encourage economic collaboration between any or all of them.

Article 3. In order more effectively to achieve the objectives of this treaty, the parties, separately and jointly by means of continuous and effective self-help and mutual aid, will maintain and develop their individual and collective capacity to resist armed attack.

Article 4. The parties will consult together whenever, in the opinion of any of them, the territorial integrity, political independence or security of any of the parties is threatened.

Article 5. The parties agree that an armed attack against one or more of them in Europe or North America shall be considered an attack against them all and consequently they agree that, if such an armed attack occurs, each of them, in exercise of the right of individual or collective self-defence recognized by article 51 of the Charter of the United Nations, will assist the party or parties so attacked by taking forthwith, individually and in concert with the other parties, such action as it deems necessary, including the use of armed force, to restore and maintain the security of the North Atlantic area. Any such armed attack and all measures taken as a result thereof shall immediately be reported to the Security Council. Such measures shall be terminated when the Security Council has taken the measures necessary to restore and maintain international peace and security.

Article 6. For the purpose of Article 5 an armed attack on one or more of the parties is deemed to include an armed attack *(i)* on the territory of any of the parties in Europe or North America, on the Algerian Departments of France, on the territory of Turkey or on the islands under the jurisdiction of any of the parties in the North Atlantic area north of the Tropic of Cancer; *(ii)* on the forces, vessels or aircraft of any of the parties, when in or over these territories or any other area in Europe in which occupation forces of any of the parties were stationed on the date when the treaty entered into force or the Mediterranean Sea or the North Atlantic area north of the Tropic of Cancer.

Article 8. Each party declares that none of the international engagements now in force between it and any other of the parties or any third state is in conflict with the provisions of this treaty, and undertakes not to enter into any international engagement in conflict with this treaty.

Article 10. The parties may, by unanimous agreement, invite any other European state in a position to further the principles of this treaty and to contribute to the security of the North Atlantic area to accede to this treaty. Any state so invited may become a party to the treaty by depositing its instrument of accession with the government of the United States of America. The government of the United States of America will inform each of the parties of the deposit of each such instrument of accession.

Article 12. After the treaty has been in force for 10 years, or at any time thereafter, the parties shall, if any of them so requests, consult together for the purpose of reviewing the treaty, having regard for the factors then affecting peace and security in the North Atlantic area, including the development of universal as well as regional arrangements under the Charter of the United Nations for the maintenance of international peace and security.

Article 13. After the treaty has been in force for 20 years, any party may cease to be a party one year after its notice of denunciation has been given to the government of the United States of America, which will inform the governments of the other parties of the deposit of each notice of denunciation.

The treaty came into force on 24 Aug. 1949. Greece and Turkey were admitted as parties to the treaty in 1952, the Federal Republic of Germany in 1955 and Spain in 1982.

NATO is an organization of sovereign states equal in status. Decisions taken are expressions of the collective will of member governments arrived at by common consent.

The North Atlantic Council is composed of representatives of the 16 member countries. At Ministerial Meetings of the Council, member nations are represented by Ministers of Foreign Affairs. These meetings are held twice a year. The Council also meets on occasion at the level of Heads of State and Government. In permanent session, at the level of Ambassadors, the Council meets at least once a week.

The Defence Planning Committee is composed of representatives of the member countries taking part in NATO's integrated military structure. Like the Council, it meets both in permanent session at the level of Ambassadors and twice a year at Ministerial level. At Ministerial Meetings member nations are represented by Defence Ministers.

The Council and Defence Planning Committee are chaired by the Secretary General of NATO at whatever level they meet. Opening sessions of Ministerial Meetings of the Council are presided over by the President, an honorary position held annually by the Foreign Minister of one of the member nations.

Nuclear matters are discussed by the Nuclear Planning Group in which 13 countries now participate. It meets regularly at the level of Permanent Representatives (Ambassadors) and twice a year at the level of Ministers of Defence.

The Permanent Representatives of member countries are supported by the National Delegations located at NATO Headquarters. The Delegations are composed of advisors and officials qualified to represent their countries on the various committees created by the Council. The Committees are supported by the International Staff responsible to the Secretary General.

Headquarters: 1110 Brussels. Belgium.
Secretary-General: Lord Carrington (UK).
Flag: Dark blue with a white compass rose of 4 points in the centre.

The *Military Committee* is responsible for making recommendations to the Council and the Defence Planning Committee on military matters and for supplying guidance to the Allied Commanders. Composed of the Chiefs-of-Staff of all member countries except France and Iceland (which has no military forces), the Committee is assisted by an International Military Staff. It meets at Chiefs-of-Staff level at least twice a year but remains in permanent session at the level of national military representatives. Liaison between the Military Committee and the French High Command is effected through the French Mission to the Military Committee. The permanent chairman of the Military Committee is elected by the Chiefs-of-Staff for a period of 2–3 years. The present chairman is Gen. Cornelis De Jager (Netherlands), appointed July 1983.

The area covered by the North Atlantic Treaty is divided among three commands: The Atlantic Ocean Command, the European Command and the Channel Command. Defence plans for the North American area are developed by the Canada–US Regional Planning Group.

The NATO commanders are responsible for the development of defence plans for their respective areas, for the determination of force requirements and for the deployment and exercise of the forces under their command.

The *Allied Command Europe* (ACE) covers the area extending from the North Cape to the Mediterranean and from the Atlantic to the eastern border of Turkey, excluding the UK and Portugal, the defence of which does not fall under any one major NATO Command. The European area, which is subdivided into a number of subordinate commands, is under the Supreme Allied Commander Europe (SACEUR) whose Headquarters, near Mons in Belgium, are known as SHAPE (Supreme Headquarters Allied Powers Europe).

SACEUR has also under his orders the ACE Mobile Force, composed of both land and air force units from different member countries, which can be ready for action at very short notice in any threatened area. The present SACEUR is Gen. Bernard W. Rogers (USA).

Under the Supreme Allied Commander Atlantic (SACLANT) the *Atlantic Command* extends from the North Pole to the Tropic of Cancer and from the coastal waters of North America to those of Europe and Africa, but excludes the Channel and the British Isles. SACLANT, who would have the primary task in wartime of ensuring the security of the sea lanes in the whole Atlantic area, is an operational rather than an administrative commander. Under his direct command is the Standing Naval Force Atlantic (STANAVFORLANT) which is a permanent international squadron of ships drawn from NATO Navies which normally operate in the Atlantic.

The present SACLANT, whose Headquarters are in Norfolk (USA), is Admiral Wesley L. McDonald (US), appointed Sept. 1982.

The *Channel Command* covers the English Channel and the southern North Sea. Under the Allied Commander-in-Chief Channel (CINCHAN) its mission is to control and protect merchant shipping in the area, co-operating with SACEUR in the air defence of the Channel. The forces earmarked to the Command in emergency are predominantly naval but include maritime air forces. CINCHAN has also under his command the NATO Standing Naval Force Channel (STANAVFORCHAN) a permanent mine counter measures force comprising ships drawn from the navies of Belgium, the Netherlands and the UK. The present CINCHAN, with Headquarters at Northwood (UK), is Admiral Sir William Staveley (UK), appointed Oct. 1982.

The *Canada–US Regional Planning Group*, which covers the North American area, develops and recommends to the Military Committee plans for the defence of this area. It meets alternately in Washington and Ottawa.

Books of Reference

The NATO Handbook.—NATO: Facts and Figures.—The NATO Review (bi-monthly).— *Aspects of NATO.—NATO Pocket Guide.—NATO Folder.—NATO and the Warsaw Pact.—Economic and Scientific Publications.*

Henderson, N., *The Birth of NATO*. London, 1982
Hill-Norton, P., *No Soft Options: The Politico-Military Realities of NATO*. London, 1980
Kaplan, L. S., and Clawson, R. W., *NATO After Thirty Years*. Wilmington, 1981
Myers, K. A. (ed.), *NATO: The Next Twenty Years*. Boulder, 1980
Vigeveno, G., *The Bomb and European Security*. London, 1983
Yost, D. S., *NATO's Strategic Options: Arms Control and Defense*. Oxford and New York, 1981

WESTERN EUROPEAN UNION

On 17 March 1948 a 50-year treaty 'for collaboration in economic, social and cultural matters and for collective self-defence' was signed in Brussels by the Foreign Ministers of the UK, France, the Netherlands, Belgium and Luxembourg. (*See* THE STATESMAN'S YEAR-BOOK, 1954, pp. 32 f.)

On 20 Dec. 1950 the functions of the Western Union defence organization were transferred to the North Atlantic Treaty command, but it was decided that the reorganization of the military machinery should not affect the right of the Western Union Defence Ministers and the Chiefs of Staff to meet as they please to consider matters of mutual concern to the Brussels Treaty powers.

After the breakdown of the European Defence Community on 30 Aug. 1954 a conference was held in London from 28 Sept. to 3 Oct. 1954, attended by Belgium, Canada, France, the Federal Republic of Germany, Italy, Luxembourg, the Netherlands, the UK and the USA, at which it was decided to invite the Federal Republic of Germany and Italy to accede to the Brussels Treaty, to end the occupation of Western Germany and to invite the latter to accede to the North Atlantic Treaty; the Federal Republic agreed that it would voluntarily limit its arms production, and provision was made for the setting up of an agency to control the armaments of the 7 Brussels Treaty powers; the UK undertook not to withdraw from the Continent her 4 divisions and the Tactical Air Force assigned to the Supreme Allied Commander against the wishes of a majority, *i.e.*, 4 of the Brussels Treaty powers, except in the event of an acute overseas emergency.

At a Conference of Ministers held in Paris from 20 to 23 Oct. 1954 these decisions were embodied in 4 Protocols modifying the Brussels Treaty which were signed in Paris on 23 Oct. 1954 and came into force on 6 May 1955.

The *Council of WEU* consists of the Foreign Ministers of the 7 powers or their representatives; it is so organized as to be able to exercise its functions continuously. An *Assembly,* composed of representatives of the Brussels Treaty powers to the Consultative Assembly of the Council of Europe, meets twice a year, usually in Paris. An *Agency for the Control of Armaments* and a *Standing Armaments Committee* have been set up in Paris. The social and cultural activities were transferred to the Council of Europe on 1 June 1960.

After the breakdown of the negotiations for Britain's entry into the Common Market in 1963 the 6 EEC countries proposed to the UK that the WEU Council (the Six and the UK) should meet every 3 months 'to take stock of the political and economic situation in Europe'. The UK welcomed this proposal, and regular meetings took place. Following the re-opening of negotiations in 1970 which led to the signing of the Treaty of Accession in Jan. 1972 this arrangement has been discontinued.

Headquarters: 9 Grosvenor Place, London, SW1X 7HL.
Secretary-General: Edouard F. T. Longerstaey.

COUNCIL OF EUROPE

In 1948 the 'Congress of Europe', bringing together at The Hague nearly 1,000 influential Europeans from 26 countries, called for the creation of a united Europe, including a European Assembly. This proposal, examined first by the Ministerial Council of the Brussels Treaty Organization, then by a conference of ambassadors, was at the origin of the Council of Europe, which is, with its 21 member States, the widest organization bringing together all European democracies. The Statute of the Council was signed at London on 5 May 1949 and came into force 2 months later. The founder members were Belgium, Denmark, France, Ireland, Italy, Luxembourg, the Netherlands, Norway, Sweden and the UK. Turkey and Greece joined in 1949, Iceland in 1950, the Federal Republic of Germany in 1951 (having been an associate since 1950), Austria in 1956, Cyprus in 1961, Switzerland in 1963, Malta in 1965, Portugal in 1976, Spain in 1977 and Liechtenstein in 1978.

Membership is limited to European States which 'accept the principles of the rule of law and of the enjoyment by all persons within [their] jurisdiction of human rights and fundamental freedoms'. The Statute provides for both withdrawal (Art. 7) and suspension (Arts. 8 and 9). Greece withdrew from the Council in Dec. 1969 and rejoined in Nov. 1974.

Structure. Under the Statute two organs were set up: an inter-governmental *Committee of [Foreign] Ministers* with powers of decision and of recommendation to governments, and an inter-parliamentary deliberative body, the *Parliamentary Assembly* (referred to in the Statute as the *Consultative Assembly*)—both of which are served by the Secretariat. In addition, a large number of committees of experts have been established, two of them, the Council for Cultural Co-operation and the Committee on Legal Co-operation, having a measure of autonomy; on municipal matters the Committee of Ministers receives recommendations from the Conference of Local and Regional Authorities of Europe.

The Committee of Ministers meets usually twice a year, their deputies 10 times a year.

The Parliamentary Assembly normally consists of 170 parliamentarians elected or appointed by their national parliaments (Austria 6, Belgium 7, Cyprus 3, Denmark 5, France 18, Federal Republic of Germany 18, Greece 7, Iceland 3, Ireland 4, Italy 18, Liechtenstein 2, Luxembourg 3, Malta 3, Netherlands 7, Norway 5, Portugal 7, Spain 12, Sweden 6, Switzerland 6, Turkey 12, UK 18); it meets 3 times a year for approximately a week. For domestic reasons Cyprus is not at present represented in the Assembly. The work of the Assembly is prepared by parliamentary committees.

The *Joint Committee,* which acts as an organ of co-ordination and liaison between representatives of the Committee of Ministers and members of the Parliamentary Assembly and gives members an opportunity to exchange views on matters of important European interest.

The European Convention on Human Rights, signed in 1950, set up special machinery to guarantee internationally fundamental rights and freedoms. A *European Commission* investigates alleged violations of the Convention submitted to it either by States or, in most cases, by individuals. Its findings can then be examined by the *European Court of Human Rights* (set up in 1959), whose obligatory jurisdiction has been recognized by 19 States, or by the Committee of Ministers, empowered to take binding decisions by two-thirds majority vote.

For questions of national refugees and over-population, a Special Representative has been appointed, responsible to the governments collectively.In 1956 the Resettlement Fund for National Refugees and Over-Population was created on the initiative of the special representative. With 19 member countries, the main purpose of the Fund is to give financial aid, particularly in the spheres of housing, vocational training, regional planning and regional development. Since its foundation, the total amount of loans thus granted comes to over US$1,800m. at 31 Dec. 1982.

In 1970 the Council set up a European Youth Centre where young people can discuss their own approach to international co-operation. More recently, a European Youth Foundation was created, administered by the Secretary-General, and which provides money to subsidize activities by European Youth Organizations.

Aims and Achievements. Art. 1 of the Statute states that the Council's aim is 'to achieve a greater unity between its members for the purpose of safeguarding and realising the ideals and principles which are their common heritage and facilitating their economic and social progress'; 'this aim shall be pursued . . . by discussion of questions of common concern and by agreements and common action'. The only limitation is provided by Art. 1 *(d)*, which excludes 'matters relating to national defence'.

Although without legislative powers, the Assembly acts as the power-house of the Council initiating European action in key areas by making recommendations to the Committee of Ministers. As the widest parliamentary forum in Western Europe, the Assembly also acts as the conscience of the area by voicing its opinions on important current issues. These are embodied in resolutions. The Ministers' rôle is to translate the Assembly's recommendations into action, particularly as regards lowering the barriers between the European countries, harmonizing their legislation or introducing where possible common European laws, abolishing discrimination on grounds of nationality and undertaking certain tasks on a joint European basis.

In May 1976 the first plan of intergovernmental co-operation to be undertaken by the Council of Europe was adopted by the Committee of Ministers. The second one, adopted in Dec. 1980, will run until Dec. 1986, subject to a mid-term revision in 1983. The plan takes account of political developments and progress achieved, and covers 8 key areas: human rights, social and socio-economic questions, education and culture, youth, public health, environment and regional planning, local and regional government, and legal co-operation.

About 115 Conventions and Agreements have been concluded covering such matters as social security, patents, extradition, medical treatment, training of nurses, equivalence of degrees and diplomas, innkeepers' liability, compulsory motor insurance, the protection of television broadcasts, adoption of children, transportation of animals and *au pair* placement. In the legal field, of particular significance in 1977, was the adoption of the European Convention on the Suppression of Terrorism, as well as the European Convention on the Legal Status of Migrant Workers. In 1980 the Committee of Ministers adopted a European Convention for the protection of individuals with regard to the automatic processing of personal data. A Social Charter which came into force in 1965 sets out the social and economic rights which all member governments agree to guarantee to their citizens.

The official languages are English and French.

Chairman of the Committee of Ministers: (held in rotation).

President of the Parliamentary Assembly: Karl Ahrens (Federal Republic of Germany).
President of the European Court of Human Rights: Gérard J. Wiarda (Netherlands).
President of the European Commission of Human Rights: Carl Aage Nørgaard (Denmark).
Secretary-General: Franz Karasek (Austria).
Headquarters: Palais de l'Europe, 67006, Strasbourg, CEDEX, France.
Flag: Dark blue with a ring of 12 gold stars in the centre.

European Yearbook. The Hague, from 1955
Forum. Strasbourg, from 1978, 4 times a year
Guide to the Council of Europe. Strasbourg, 1982
Manual of the Council of Europe. London, 1970
Yearbook on the Convention on Human Rights. Strasbourg, from 1958
Cook, C., and Paxton, J., *European Political Facts, 1918–73.* London, 1975

EUROPEAN COMMUNITIES

In May 1950 Belgium, France, the Federal Republic of Germany, Italy, Luxembourg and the Netherlands started negotiations with the aim of ensuring continual peace by a merging of their essential interests. The negotiations culminated in the signing in 1951 of the Treaty of Paris creating the European Coal and Steel Community (ECSC). After it was found impossible to create European Communities covering Defence and Foreign Affairs, two more communities with the aims of gradually integrating the economies of the 6 nations and of moving towards closer political unity, the European Economic Community (EEC) and the European Atomic Energy Community (EAEC or Euratom) were created in 1957 by the signing of the Treaties of Rome.

On 30 June 1970 membership negotiations began between the Six and the UK, Denmark, Ireland and Norway. On 22 Jan. 1972 those 4 countries signed a Treaty of Accession, although this was rejected by Norway in a referendum in Nov. 1972. On 1 Jan. 1973 the UK, Denmark and Ireland became full members. On 28 May 1979 the Greek Treaty of Accession was signed, and Greece joined the Community on 1 Jan. 1981. Negotiations for accession were in progress in 1984 with Spain and Portugal.

The institutional arrangements of the Communities provide an independent executive with powers of proposal (the Commission), various consultative bodies, and a decision-making body drawn from the Governments (the Council). Until 1967 the 3 Communities were completely distinct, although they shared some non-decision-making bodies: from that date the executives were merged in the European Commission, and the decision-taking bodies in the Council. The institutions and organs of the Communities are as follows:

The *Commission* consists of 14 members appointed by the member states to serve for 4 years; the President and Vice-Presidents are appointed initially for 2 years, but are generally re-appointed for the rest of their term. The Commission acts independently of any country in the interests of the Community as a whole, with as its mandate the implementation and guardianship of the Treaties. In this it has the right of initiative (putting proposals to the Council for action); and execution (once the Council has decided); and can take the other institutions or individual countries before the Court of Justice (see below) should any of these renege upon its responsibilities.

President: Gaston Thorn.
Address: 200 rue de la Loi, 1049, Brussels.

The *Council of Ministers* consists of foreign ministers from the 10 national governments and represents the national as opposed to the Community interests. It is the body which takes decisions under the Treaties. Although legally most of its decisions should be made by majority, it has since 1966 sought unanimity wherever possible, using majority votes only rarely. Specialist Councils (*e.g.* the Agriculture

Council) meet to discuss matters related to individual policies. Since 1974 the Heads of State and Government have met 3 times a year as the *European Council* to discuss Community, and also Foreign Policy, affairs. The Foreign Ministers also meet in Political Co-operation to discuss Foreign Policy matters. The Presidency of the Council is held for a 6-month term in the following order: Belgium, Denmark, Federal Republic of Germany, Greece, France, Ireland, Italy, Luxembourg, Netherlands, UK.

Address: 170 rue de la Loi, 1048, Brussels.

The *European Parliament* consists of 434 members of whom all but the Greek members were elected by direct universal suffrage on 7 and 10 June 1979; the Greek elections were held on 18 Oct. 1981. France, the Federal Republic of Germany, Italy and the UK each returned 81 members, the Netherlands 25, Belgium and Greece 24, Denmark 16, Ireland 15 and Luxembourg 6. Party representation in the new Parliament was as follows in Nov. 1983: Socialists and Allies 125, European People's Party—Christian Democratic Group 117, European Democratic Group (formerly European Conservative Group) 63, Communists and Allies 48, Liberal and Democratic Group 38, European Progressive Democratic Group 22, Others and vacancies 21. Elections are due in June 1984. The Parliament has a right to be consulted on a wide range of legislative proposals, and forms one arm of the Communities' Budgetary Authority.

President: Piet Dankert.
Address: Centre européen du Kirchberg, Luxembourg.

The *Economic and Social Committee* has an advisory role and consists of 156 representatives, employers, trade unions, consumers, etc. The *Consultative Committee*, of 84 members, performs a similar role for the ECSC.

President: François Ceyrac.
Address: 2, rue Ravenstein, 1000 Brussels.

The *European Court of Justice* is composed of 11 judges and 5 advocates-general, is responsible for the adjudication of disputes arising out of the application of the treaties, and its findings are enforceable in all member countries.

President: Josse Mertens de Wilmars.
Address: Palais de la Cour de Justice, Kirchberg, Luxembourg.

The *Court of Auditors* was established by a Treaty signed on 22 July 1975 which took effect on 1 June 1977. It consists of 10 members, and replaced the former *Audit Board*. It audits all income and current and past expenditure of the European Communities.

President: Pierre Lelong.
Address: 29 Rue Aldringen, Luxembourg.

Annual Report of the Court of Auditors, from 1977

The *European Investment Bank* (EIB) was created by the EEC Treaty to which its statute is annexed. Its governing body is the Board of Governors consisting of ministers designated by member states. Its main task is to contribute to the balanced development of the common market in the interest of the Community by financing projects: developing less-developed regions; for modernizing or converting undertakings; or developing new activities, or those of common interest to several member states.

Address: 100, Boulevard Konrad Adenauer, Plateau du Kirchberg, Luxembourg.

Annual Report of the European Investment Bank

Community Law. Provisions of the Treaties and secondary legislation may be either directly applicable in Member States or only applicable after Member States have enacted their own implementing legislation. Secondary legislation consists of: regulations, which are of general application and binding in their entirety and directly applicable in all member states; directives which are binding upon each

Member State as to the result to be achieved within a given time, but leave the national authority the choice of form and method of achieving this result; decisions, which are binding in their entirety on their addressees. In addition the Council and Commission can issue recommendations and opinions, which have no binding force.

The Community's Legislative Process starts with a proposal from the Commission (either at the suggestion of its services or in pursuit of its declared political aims) to the Council. The Council generally seeks the views of the European Parliament on the proposal, and the Parliament adopts a formal Opinion, after consideration of the matter by its specialist Committees. The Council may also (and in some cases is obliged to) consult the Economic and Social Committee, which similarly delivers an opinion. When these opinions have been received, the Council will decide. Most decisions are taken on a majority basis, but will take account of reserves expressed by individual member states. The text eventually approved may differ substantially from the original Commission proposal.

Community Finances. The general budget of the European Communities for 1983 was (in ECUm.; 1EUA = US$0·85 or £0·57 on 1 Nov. 1983):

Receipts		Expenditure	
Agricultural levies	2,572	Agriculture	14,785
Import duties	7,574	Social	1,475
VAT	11,053	Regional	1,486
Miscellaneous	362	Industry, energy, research	553
	21,559	Development aid	977
		Administration and miscellaneous	2,282
			21,599

The resources of the Community (the levies and duties mentioned above, and up to a 1% VAT charge) have been surrendered to it by Treaty. The Budget is made by the Council and the Parliament acting jointly as the Budgetary Authority. The Parliament has control, within a certain margin, of non-obligatory expenditure (*i.e.*, expenditure where the amount to be spent is not set out in the legislation concerned), and can also reject the Budget totally (this has only been done once, for the 1980 Budget). Otherwise, the Council decides. ECSC operations are separately funded by a turnover levy (1983: 0·31%) on the coal and steel industries of the Community. The ECSC operating budget for 1983 was ECU268m.

THE EUROPEAN COAL AND STEEL COMMUNITY. The ECSC was the first of the 3 Communities, coming into existence on 10 Aug. 1952 following the signature of the Treaty of Paris on 18 April 1951. Its aim was to contribute towards economic expansion, growth of employment and a rising standard of living in Member States, through common action in the coal and steel sector, in a Community open to other nations. Since 1957 it has had the same membership as the other Communities.

The Common Market for Coal and Steel. This first aim of the ECSC was achieved for coal, iron ore and scrap in Feb. 1953, for steel in May 1953 and for special steels in Aug. 1954. The Common External Tariff on ECSC products is between 4-8%. Rules for fair competition within the Common Market, based on non-discrimination by nationality and the free movement of goods, have been established. The ECSC also gives readaptation and retraining grants to former workers in these industries, and makes capital grants for new industrial investment in former coal and steel areas.

The Commission has to approve take-overs and mergers of coal or steel undertakings, and has the power in the case of crisis (and with the approval of the Council) to set production quotas and minimum prices by product, with fines for non-observance. This power was first used in 1980.

THE EUROPEAN ECONOMIC COMMUNITY (EEC) or COMMON MARKET

Based on the Treaty of Rome of 25 March 1957 the EEC came into being on 1 Jan. 1958 with the same original members as the ECSC. The Treaty guarantees certain rights to the citizens of all Member States (*e.g.*, the outlawing of economic discrimination by nationality, and equal pay for equal work as between men and women) and sets out certain other areas where secondary legislation is to fill in the details. The most important policy areas are as follows:

Freedom of movement for persons, goods and capital. Under the Treaty individuals or companies from one Member State may establish themselves in another country (for the purposes of economic activity) or sell goods or services there on the same basis as nationals of that country. With a few exceptions, restrictions on the movement of capital have also been ended.

Customs Union and External Trade Relations. Goods or Services originating in one Member State have free circulation within the EEC, which implies common arrangements for trade with the rest of the world. Member States can no longer make bilateral trade agreements with third countries: this power has been ceded to the Community. The Customs Union was achieved in July 1968, with the abolition of internal customs tariffs (or equivalents) and quantitative restrictions, and the establishment of the Common External Tariff. Denmark, Ireland and the UK adopted these from July 1977; Greece is due to do so by Jan. 1986.

Following the 1973 accessions the Community made a series of agreements with the member states of EFTA to form an industrial free trade zone and to start the liberalization of agricultural trade. Association agreements which could lead to accession or customs union have been made with Cyprus, Malta and Turkey; and commercial, industrial, technical and financial aid agreements with Algeria, Egypt, Israel, Jordan, Lebanon, Morocco, Syria and Tunisia. In 1976 Canada signed a framework agreement for co-operation in industrial trade, science and natural resources.

In the *Development Aid* sector, the Community has an agreement (the Lomé Convention, originally signed in 1975 but renewed and enlarged in 1979) with some 60 African, Caribbean and Pacific countries which removes customs duties without reciprocal arrangements for most of their imports to the Community, and under which ECU5,600m. of aid will be granted between 1980–84. Negotiations for the renewal of the Convention were in progress in 1983. An economic and commercial agreement has also been signed with ASEAN.

The Common Agricultural Policy (CAP). The objectives set out in the Treaty are to increase agricultural productivity, to ensure a fair standard of living for the agricultural community, to stabilise markets, to assure supplies, and to ensure reasonable consumer prices. In Dec. 1960 the Council laid down the fundamental principles on which the CAP is based: a single market, which calls for common prices, stable currency parities and the harmonising of health and veterinary legislation; Community preference, which protects the single Community market from imports; common financing, through the European Agricultural Guidance and Guarantee Fund (EAGGF), which seeks to improve agriculture through its Guidance section, and to stabilise markets against world price fluctuations through market intervention, with levies and refunds on exports. At present common market organizations cover over 95% of EEC agricultural production. Greece will bring its agricultural prices into line with the Community over a period of up to 7 years.

Following the disappearance of stable currency parities, artificial currency levels have been applied in the CAP. This factor, together with over-production due to high producer prices, means that the CAP consumes about two-thirds of the Communities' budget.

The European Monetary System (EMS), whose immediate objective is to create a zone of monetary stability in Europe by closer monetary co-operation, began operating in March 1979. All Member States (except Greece and the UK, 1983) limit fluctuations in the exchange rates of their currencies against a central rate denominated in ECU. The Greek drachma will join the EMS by 31 Dec. 1986.

Competition. The Competition (anti-trust) law of the Community is based on 2 principles: that businesses should not seek to nullify the creation of the common market by the erection of artificial national (or other) barriers to the free movement of goods; and against the abuse of dominant positions in any market. These two principles have led among other things to the outlawing of prohibitions on exports to other Member States, of price-fixing agreements and of refusal to supply; and to the refusal by the Commission to allow mergers or take-overs by dominant undertakings in specific cases. Increasingly heavy fines are imposed on offenders.

THE EUROPEAN ATOMIC ENERGY COMMUNITY (EURATOM)

Like the EEC, Euratom came into being on 1 Jan. 1958 following a Treaty signed in Rome on 25 March 1957, and it had the same Member States as the EEC. Its task is to promote common efforts between its members in the development of nuclear energy for peaceful purposes, and for this purpose it has monopoly powers of acquisition of fissile materials for civil purposes. It is in no way concerned with military uses of nuclear power; indeed, its members are forbidden under the Treaty to use nuclear materials obtained through Euratom for such purposes.

The execution of the Treaty now rests with the European Commission, which is advised by the Scientific and Technical Committee (28 members). Major decisions rest with the Council. Euratom has 1 substantial research institute of its own, at Ispra, in Italy; it does other work in co-operation with research institutes in the Member States, or in joint and international undertakings.

A common market for nuclear materials and equipment came into force, and external tariffs were suspended, in Jan. 1959. Although a recent Court of Justice decision has confirmed that Member States have ceded to Euratom the right to make supply contracts with outside suppliers (e.g. Australia, Canada or the USA), Euratom has generally been growing less effective in recent years, and most major new nuclear energy projects within the Member States have been undertaken outside its framework.

European Community Delegation to the US: 2111 M Street NW (Suite 707), Washington DC 20037.
Head of Delegation: Sir Roy Denman.
US Delegation to the European Community: 40 Boulevard du Régent, 1000 Brussels.
Head of Delegation: George S. Vest.
European Community Delegation to the United Nations: 1 Dag Hammarskjöld Plaza, 245 East 47th Street, New York NY 10017.
Head of Delegation: Michael Hardy.

Books of Reference

Official Journal of the European Communities.—General Report on the Activities of the European Communities (annual, from 1967).—*The Agricultural Situation in the Community.* 1982.—*Twelfth Report of Competition Policy.* 1982.—*Report on the Development of the Social Situation in the Community in 1982.—Basic Statistics of the Community* (annual).—*Bulletin of the European Community* (monthly)

Europe (monthly), obtainable from the Information Office of the European Commission, 8 Storey's Gate, London, SW1P 3AT
Arbuthnott, H. and Edwards, G., (eds.), *A Common Man's Guide to the Common Market.* London, 1979
Coffey, P., *The External Economic Relations of the E.E.C.* London, 1976
Cook, C., and Francis, M., *The First European Elections.* London, 1979
Drew, J., *Doing Business with the European Community.* London, 1979
Dyas, G. P., and Thanheiser, H. T., *The Emerging European Enterprise.* London, 1976
Fennell, R., *The Common Agricultural Policy of the European Community.* London, 1979
Fitzmaurice, J., *The European Parliament.* London, 1982
Goodhart, P., *Full-hearted Consent.* London, 1976
Hallstein, W., *Europe in the Making.* London, 1973
Herman, V., and Lodge, J., *The European Parliament and the European Community.* London, 1978
Korah, V., *An Introductory Guide to EEC Competition Law and Practice.* Oxford, 1979
Mayre, R., *Postwar Europe.* London, 1983
Palmer, D. M., *Sources of Information on the European Communities.* London, 1979
Parry, A., and Hardy, S., *EEC Law.* London, 1973

Paxton, J., *The Developing Common Market.* London, 1976.—*A Dictionary of the European Communities.* 2nd ed. London, 1982
Shanks, M., *European Social Policy, Today and Tomorrow.* Oxford, 1977
Swann, D., *The Economies of the Common Market.* 4th ed. Harmondsworth, 1978
Twitchett, C. C., *Harmonisation in the EEC.* London, 1981
Wallace, W., and Herreman, I. (eds.), *A Community of Twelve?* Bruges, 1978
Walsh, A. E., and Paxton, J., *Competition Policy.* London, 1975

EUROPEAN FREE TRADE ASSOCIATION (EFTA)

The European Free Trade Association has 6 member countries: Austria, Iceland, Norway, Portugal, Sweden and Switzerland. A seventh country, Finland, is an associate member. The Stockholm Convention establishing the Association entered into force on 3 May 1960 and Finland became associated on 27 March 1961. Iceland joined EFTA on 1 March 1970 and was immediately granted duty-free entry for industrial goods exported to EFTA countries, while being given 10 years to abolish her own existing protective duties. Two founder members of EFTA, the UK and Denmark, left EFTA on 31 Dec. 1972 to join the EEC.

When the Association was created it had three objectives: to achieve free trade in industrial products between member countries, to assist in the creation of a single market embracing the countries of Western Europe, and to contribute to the expansion of world trade in general.

The first objective was achieved on 31 Dec. 1966, when virtually all inter-EFTA tariffs were removed. This was 3 years earlier than originally planned. Finland removed her remaining EFTA tariffs a year later on 31 Dec. 1967 and Iceland removed her tariffs on 31 Dec. 1979.

The fulfilment of the second aim was secured in 1972. On 22 Jan. 1972 the UK and Denmark signed the Treaty of Accession to the EEC whereby they became members of the enlarged Community from 1 Jan. 1973. On 22 July 1972, 5 other EFTA countries, Austria, Iceland, Portugal, Sweden and Switzerland signed Free Trade Agreements with the enlarged EEC. A similar agreement negotiated with Finland was signed on 5 Oct. 1973. Norway, whose intention of joining the EEC was reversed following a referendum, signed a similar agreement on 14 May 1973. Through these agreements virtually complete free trade in industrial goods was achieved in 16 Western European countries from July 1977. The free trade agreements apply also to Greece since its accession to the EEC on 1 Jan. 1981. A multilateral free trade agreement between the EFTA countries and Spain, a candidate for EEC membership, came into force on 1 May 1980 and the first tariff cuts were applied on 1 June 1980.

The third objective was to contribute to the expansion of world trade. In 1959 trade between the countries now in EFTA amounted to US$759m. and total exports from these countries were US$6,852m. In 1982 the respective figures were US$15,011m. and US$105,323m. More than half EFTA trade is with the EEC.

EFTA tariff treatment applies to those industrial products which are of EFTA origin, and these are traded freely between member countries. Each EFTA country remains free, however, to impose its own rates of duty on products entering from outside EFTA or the EEC.

Generally, agricultural products do not come under the provisions for free trade, but bilateral agreements have been negotiated to increase trade in these products.

The operation of the Convention is the responsibility of a Council assisted by a small secretariat. Each EFTA country holds the chairmanship of the Council for 6 months.

Secretary-General: Per Kleppe (Norway).

Headquarters: 9–11 rue de Varembé, 1211 Geneva 20, Switzerland.

Convention Establishing the European Free Trade Association
EFTA Bulletin (Four issues a year)
EFTA What it is, What it does
The European Free Trade Association

THE WARSAW PACT

On 14 May 1955 the USSR, Albania, Bulgaria, Czechoslovakia, the German Democratic Republic, Hungary, Poland and Romania signed, in Warsaw, a 20-year treaty of friendship and collaboration, after the USSR had (on 7 May) annulled the 20-year treaties of alliance with the UK (1942) and France (1944).

The main provisions of the treaty are as follows:

Article 4. In case of armed aggression in Europe against one or several States party to the pact by a State or group of States, each State member of the pact ... will afford to the State or States which are the object of such aggression immediate assistance ... with all means which appear necessary, including the use of armed force ... These measures will cease as soon as the Security Council takes measures necessary for establishing and preserving international peace and security.

Article 5. The contracting Powers agree to set up a joint command of their armed forces to be allotted by agreement between the Powers, at the disposal of this command and used on the basis of jointly established principles. They will also take over agreed measures necessary to strengthen their defences.

Article 9. The present treaty is open to other States, irrespective of their social or Government regime, who declare their readiness to abide by the terms of the treaty in order to safeguard peace and security of the peoples.

Article 11. In the event of a system of collective security being set up in Europe and a pact to this effect being signed—to which each party to this treaty will direct its efforts—the present treaty will lapse from the day such a collective security treaty comes into force.

It is estimated (1981) that the armed forces of the Warsaw Pact countries total 4·82m., including 3·71m. Russians, compared with 4·99m. NATO forces.

Marshal Grechko was from July 1960 to April 1967 C.-in-C. of the united Armed Forces, with headquarters in Moscow. He was succeeded by Marshal I. I. Yakubovsky in 1967 and by Marshal V. G. Kulikov in Jan. 1977.

In 1962 Albania was no longer invited to the Warsaw Pact meetings without being formally expelled.

Two Soviet divisions are stationed in Poland, 20 divisions in German Democratic Republic, 4 divisions in Hungary and 5 in Czechoslovakia.

Clawson, R. W. and Kaplan, L. S. (eds.), *The Warsaw Pact: Political Purpose and Military Means.* Wilmington, 1982
Lewis, W. J., *The Warsaw Pact: Doctrine and Strategy.* Maidenhead, 1982

COUNCIL FOR MUTUAL ECONOMIC ASSISTANCE [1]

Membership. Founder members were USSR, Bulgaria, Czechoslovakia, Hungary, Poland and Romania. Later admissions were Albania (1949; ceased participation 1961), German Democratic Republic (1950), Mongolia (1962), Cuba (1972), Vietnam (1978). In 1964 Yugoslavia concluded an agreement with CMEA whereby Yugoslavia would participate in the work of some CMEA bodies (at present 21). Afghánistán, Angola, Ethiopia, Laos, Mozambique and the People's Democratic Republic of Yemen attend CMEA sessions as observers.

External relations. There are co-operation agreements with Finland, Iraq and Mexico. Talks with the EEC at expert level on possible commercial co-operation were resumed in July 1980.

The Charter. The charter consists of a preamble and 18 articles. Extracts (in the language of the official English version) are as follows:

Article 1. Aims and Principles: 1 'The purpose of the Council is to promote, by uniting and co-ordinating the efforts of the member countries, the further extension and improvement of

---

[1] Abbreviations and Foreign Names. CMEA is the official abbreviation. Other unofficial abbreviations are COMECON and CEMA. The working language of the organization is Russian. The Russian form is *Sovet Ekonomicheskoi Vzaimopomoshchi* (SEV).

co-operation and the development of socialist economic integration, the planned development of their national economies, the acceleration of economic and technical progress in these countries, higher level of industrialization of the less industrialized countries, a continuous increase in labour productivity, a gradual approximation and equalization of economic development levels and a steady improvement in the wellbeing of the peoples. 2 The Council is based on the principles of the sovereign equality of all member countries.'

Article 2. Membership 'open to other countries which subscribe to the purposes and principles of the Council'.

Article 3. Functions and Powers to (a) 'organize all-round . . . co-operation of member countries in the most rational use of natural resources and acceleration of the development of their productive forces'; (b) 'foster the improvement of the international socialist division of labour by co-ordinating national economic development plans, and the specialization and co-operation of production in member countries'; (c) to assist in . . . carrying out joint measures for the development of industry and agriculture . . . transport . . . principal capital investments . . . [and] trade'.

Article 4. Recommendations and Decisions '. . . shall be adopted only with the consent of the interested member countries.'

The Structure. The supreme authority is the 'Session' of all members held (usually annually) in members' capitals in rotation under the chairmanship of the head of the delegation of the host country; all members must be present, and decisions must be unanimous. Delegations are usually led by prime ministers.

The *Executive Committee* is made up of 1 representative from each member state of deputy premier rank. It meets at least once every 3 months.

The administrative organ is the *Secretariat.*

Headquarters: Prospekt Kalinina, 56, Moscow, G-205.
Secretary: V. V. Sychev (appointed 1958).

There is a *Committee for Co-operation in the Field of Planning* and a *Committee for Scientific and Technical Co-operation* set up in 1971 and a *Committee for Material and Technical Supply* set up in 1974. There are *Permanent Commissions* on: Statistics, Foreign Trade, Currency and Finance, Electricity, Peaceful Uses of Atomic Energy, Geology, Coal Industry, Oil and Gas Industry, Chemical Industry, Iron and Steel Industry, Non-Ferrous Metals Industry, Engineering Industry, Radio Engineering and Electronics Industries, Light Industry, Food Industry, Agriculture, Construction, Transport, Posts and Telecommunications, Standardization, Civil Aviation, Public Health.

There are 7 *Standing Conferences:* for Legal Problems; of Ministers of Internal Trade; of Chiefs of Water Resources Authorities; of Chiefs of Patent Authorities; of Chiefs of Pricing Authorities; of Chiefs of Labour Authorities, and of Representatives of Freight and Shipping Organizations.

There are 3 semi-autonomous bodies within CMEA: The Institute of Standardization, The Bureau for the Co-ordination of Ship Freighting and The International Institute of Economic Problems of the World Socialist System.

In 1983 there were over 20 technical and economic agencies associated with CMEA.

Also associated with CMEA are:

The **International Bank for Economic Co-operation** was founded in 1963 with a capital of 300m. roubles and started operating on 1 Jan. 1964. It undertakes multilateral settlements in 'transferable roubles' (*i.e.*, used for intra-CMEA clearing accounts only) and advances credits to finance trading and other operations. The transferable *rouble* is a unit of account: gold content 0·987412 gramme.

The **International Investments Bank** was founded in 1970 and went into operation on 1 Jan. 1971 with a capital of 1,713m. roubles (70% transferable and 30% convertible or in gold).

Banking and Sources of Finance in Comecon. London, 1978
Charter of the Council for Mutual Economic Assistance. Moscow, 1980
Council for Mutual Economic Assistance: Thirty Years. Moscow, 1979
Comprehensive Programme for the Further Extension and Improvement of Co-operation and the Development of Socialist Economic Integration by the CMEA-member Countries.

Moscow, 1971 (The official English-language version. This document also frequently referred to as the *Complex Programme,* etc.)
Ekonomicheskoe Sotrudnichestvo Stran-Chlenov SEV. Moscow, monthly
Multilateral Economic Co-operation of Socialist States: A Collection of Documents. Moscow, 1977
Statistical Year Book of CMEA Member Countries. Moscow, annual
Survey of CMEA Activities. Moscow, annual
Bautina, N. V., *CMEA Today: from Economic Co-operation to Economic Integration.* Moscow, 1975
Bystrický, R., *Le Droit de l'Intégration Économique Socialiste.* Geneva, 1979
Schiavone, G., *The Institutions of Comecon.* London, 1981
Shaeffer, H. W., *Comecon and the Politics of Integration.* New York and London, 1972
Szawlowski, R., *The System of the International Organizations of the Communist Countries.* Leyden, 1976
van Brabant, J. M. P., *Essays on Planning, Trade and Integration in Eastern Europe.* Rotterdam Univ. Press, 1974
Wilczynski, J., *Technology in Comecon.* London, 1974

COLOMBO PLAN

History: Founded in 1950 to promote the development of newly independent Asian member countries, the Colombo Plan has grown from its modest beginning as a group of seven Commonwealth nations into an international organization of 26 countries.

Originally the Plan was conceived for a period of six years. Its life has since been extended from time to time, generally at five-year intervals. The Consultative Committee, the Plan's highest deliberative body, at its meeting in Jakarta in 1980, gave the Plan an indefinite span of life; its need and relevance will henceforth be examined only if considered necessary.

The Plan is multilateral in approach but bilateral in operation: multilateral in that it takes cognizance of the problems of development of member countries in the Asia and Pacific region and endeavours to deal with them in a co-ordinated way; bilateral because negotiations for assistance are made direct between a donor and a recipient country.

Aims: The aims of the Colombo Plan are: *(a)* to promote interest in and support for the economic and social development in Asia and the Pacific; *(b)* to keep under review economic and social progress in the region and help accelerate development through co-operative effort; and *(c)* to facilitate development assistance to and within the region.

Member Countries: Afghánistán, Australia, Bangladesh, Bhutan, Burma, Cambodia, Canada, Fiji, India, Indonesia, Iran, Japan, Republic of Korea, Lao People's Democratic Republic, Malaysia, Maldives, Nepal, New Zealand, Pakistan, Papua New Guinea, Philippines, Singapore, Sri Lanka, Thailand, UK and USA.

Development Assistance: Colombo Plan aid covers all fields of socio-economic development and amounted to US$3,261·4m. in 1982. It takes two principal forms:

(i) *Capital Aid* takes the form of grants and loans for national projects mainly from the six developed member countries to the developing member countries of the Plan.

The total amount of capital aid provided by the leading donors under the plan in 1982 was as follows:

	US$1m.
Japan	1,112·8
USA	827·2
Australia	386·0
Canada	256·7
UK	233·8
New Zealand	6·9
Total	2,823·4

(ii) Technical Co-operation: Technical assistance is provided in the form of services of experts and technicians, fellowships, and equipment for training and research.

During 1982, 17,936 trainees and students received training, 7,839 experts and 892 volunteers were sent out, value of equipment supplied was $22·7m. Total disbursements on technical co-operation in 1982 amounted to $438m.

Structure: There are four organs which give focus to the Plan:

Consultative Committee: The Committee consists of Ministers of member Governments who meet once in two years. The Ministerial meeting is preceded by a meeting of senior officials who are directly concerned with the operation of the Plan in various countries.

Colombo Plan Council: The Council is also a deliberative body which meets two or three times a year in Colombo, where most member countries have resident diplomatic missions, to review the economic and social development of the Asia-Pacific region and promote co-operation among member countries.

Colombo Plan Bureau: This is the only permanent organ of the Colombo Plan with headquarters in Colombo. Its functions include servicing the meetings of the Colombo Plan Council and the Consultative Committee, carrying out research, and dissemination of statistical and other information relating to activities under the Plan. Since 1973 the Bureau has been operating a Drug Advisory Programme to assist national and regional efforts to eliminate the causes and ameliorate the effects of drug abuse.

Colombo Plan Staff College: The Colombo Plan Staff College for Technician Education, located in Singapore, was opened in March 1975 to help member countries in developing their system of technician education. The College conducts training courses for senior technician educators and planners both at the College and in regional member countries.

Headquarters: Colombo Plan Bureau, 12 Melbourne Avenue, PO Box 596, Colombo 4, Sri Lanka.

The Colombo Plan (Cmd. 8080). HMSO, 1950; reprinted 1952.—*Annual Report.* HMSO 1952 to 1971 followed by Colombo Plan Bureaux, Sri Lanka, 1972 to date.
Reports of the Council for Technical Co-operation. HMSO annually until 1966–67 followed by the Colombo Plan Bureau, Sri Lanka, 1967–68 to date

ASSOCIATION OF SOUTH EAST ASIAN NATIONS (ASEAN)

History and Membership. The Association of South East Asian Nations is a regional organization formed by the governments of Indonesia, Malaysia, the Philippines, Singapore and Thailand through the Bangkok Declaration which was signed by the Foreign Ministers of ASEAN countries on 8 Aug. 1967. Brunei joined in 1984.

Objectives. The main objectives are to accelerate economic growth, social progress and cultural development, to promote active collaboration and mutual assistance in matters of common interest, to ensure the stability of the South East Asian region and to maintain close co-operation with existing international and regional organizations with similar aims. Principal projects concern economic co-operation and development, with the intensification of Intra-ASEAN trade and trade between the region and the rest of the world; joint research and technological programmes; co-operation in transportation and communications; promotion of tourism and south-east Asian studies; including cultural, scientific, educational and administrative exchanges.

Organs. The highest authority in ASEAN are the Heads of Government of the Member Countries who meet as and when necessary to give directions to ASEAN. The highest policy-making body is the Meeting of Foreign Ministers, commonly known as the Annual Ministerial Meeting, which convenes in each of the ASEAN members countries on a rotational basis in alphabetical order. The Standing Committee, comprising the Foreign Minister of the country hosting the Ministerial Meeting in that particular year and the accredited ambassadors of the other member countries, carries out the work of the Association in between the Ministerial Meetings and handles the routine matters to ensure continuity and to make decisions which can not wait for the Ministerial Meetings and submit for the consideration of the Foreign Ministers all reports and recommendations of the various ASEAN committees. There are 4 specialized committees under the Standing Committee and five others under the ASEAN Economic Ministers that recommend and draw up programmes of ASEAN co-operation. These committees are responsible for the operation and implementation of ASEAN projects in their respective fields. Each ASEAN capital has an ASEAN National Secretariat. The central secretariat for ASEAN is located in Jakarta, Indonesia, and is headed by the ASEAN Secretary General, a post that revolves among the member states in alphabetical order every 2 years. Bureau directors and other officers of the ASEAN Secretariat remain in office for 3 years.

Secretary-General: Chan Kai Yau (Singapore).

Books of Reference

Broinowski, A., *Understanding ASEAN*. London, 1982
Wawn, B., *The Economies of the ASEAN Countries*. London, 1982
Wong, J., *ASEAN Economics in Perspective*. London, 1979

ORGANIZATION OF AMERICAN STATES

On 14 April 1890 representatives of the American republics, meeting in Washington at the First International Conference of American States, established an 'International Union of American Republics' and, as its central office, a 'Commercial Bureau of American Republics', which later became the Pan American Union. This international organization's object was to foster mutual understanding and co-operation among the nations of the western hemisphere. Since that time, successive inter-American conferences have greatly broadened the scope of work of the organization.

This led to the adoption on 30 April 1948 by the Ninth International Conference of American States, at Bogotá, Colombia, of the Charter of the Organization of American States. This co-ordinated the work of all the former independent official entities in the inter-American system and defined their mutual relationships. The purposes of the OAS are to achieve an order of peace and justice, promote American solidarity, strengthen collaboration among the member states and defend their sovereignty, territorial integrity and independence. The OAS is a regional organization of the United Nations for the maintenance of peace and security.

Membership is on a basis of absolute equality. Each country has one vote in the Council of the Organization and its organs. The member countries were (1980): Antigua and Barbuda, Argentina, Bahamas, Barbados, Bolivia, Brazil, Chile, Colombia, Costa Rica, Cuba, Commonwealth of Dominica, Dominican Republic, Ecuador, El Salvador, Grenada, Guatemala, Haiti, Honduras, Jamaica, Mexico, Nicaragua, Panama, Paraguay, Peru, Saint Lucia, Saint Vincent and the Grenadines, Suriname, Trinidad and Tobago, USA, Uruguay, Venezuela.

The OAS has been concerned increasingly in recent years with programmes to promote Latin American economic and social development. The OAS provides specialized training for thousands of Latin Americans each year in a wide variety of development-related fields. It also carries out several missions projects each year in response to requests from member governments.

On 27 Feb. 1967 the Third Special Inter-American Conference in Buenos Aires approved the Protocol of Amendment to the Charter of the OAS, which contained new standards for inter-American co-operation and a number of structural changes in the Organization.

On 14 April 1967 the Declaration of the Presidents of America, signed in Punta del Este, Uruguay, expressed the commitment of the American chiefs of state to promote Latin American economic integration; to join in efforts to increase substantially Latin American foreign-trade earnings; to modernize the living conditions of the rural population and raise agricultural productivity; and to expand programmes in education, science, technology and health.

On 22 Feb. 1968, in the Resolution of Maracay, the Inter-American Cultural Council launched new regional programmes for educational development and for scientific and technological development.

On 27 Feb. 1970, by ratification of more than the mandatory two-thirds of the OAS member states, the Protocol of Buenos Aires, modifying the 1948 Charter, entered into effect.

Under the amended Charter, the OAS accomplishes its purposes by means of:

(a) The *General Assembly*, which meets annually in various countries of the member states.

(b) The *Meeting of Consultation of Ministers of Foreign Affairs*, held to consider problems of an urgent nature and of common interest.

(c) Three councils of equal rank: the *Permanent Council*, which replaces the old OAS Council; the *Inter-American Economic and Social Council*; and the *Inter-American Council for Education, Science and Culture*. Functions are to direct and co-ordinate work in the areas of their competence and render the governments such specialized services as they may request. Each council is composed of 1 representative from each member state, appointed by his government.

(d) The *Inter-American Juridical Committee* which acts as an advisory body to the OAS on juridical matters and promotes the development and codification of international law. Eleven jurists, elected every 4 years by the General Assembly, represent all the American States.

(e) The *Inter-American Commission on Human Rights* which oversees the observance and protection of human rights. Seven members represent all the OAS member states.

(f) The *General Secretariat* is the central and permanent organ of the OAS.

(g) The *Specialized Conferences*, meeting to deal with special technical matters or to develop specific aspects of inter-American co-operation.

(h) The *Specialized Organizations*, inter-governmental organizations established by multilateral agreements to discharge specific functions in their respective fields of action, such as women's affairs, agriculture, child welfare, Indian affairs, geography and history, and health.

Secretary-General: Alejandro Orfila (until 1984).

Assistant Secretary-General: Valerie McComie (Barbados).

The Secretary-General and the Assistant Secretary-General are elected by the General Assembly for 5-year terms. The General Assembly approves the annual budget for the Organization, which is financed by quotas contributed by the member governments.

General Secretariat: Washington, D.C., 20006, USA.
Flag: Light blue with the OAS seal in colour in the centre.

Books of Reference

Publications of the OAS General Secretariat include:

Charter of the Organization of American States. 1948.—As Amended by the Protocol of Buenos Aires in 1967

Americas. Illustrated monthly, from 1949 (Spanish, Portuguese and English edition)
Organization of American States, a Handbook. Rev. ed. 1977
Organization of American States. Directory. Quarterly, from 1951
Report on the Tenth Inter-American Conference, Caracas 1954. 1955
Inter-American Review of Bibliography. Quarterly, from 1951
Annual Report of the Secretary-General
Status of Inter-American Treaties and Conventions. Annual
The Alliance for Progress: The Charter of Punta del Este. 1962
The Americas in the 1980s: An Agenda for the Decade Ahead. 1982
Human Rights in the American States. 1960
Report of Inter-American Commission on Human Rights. From 1970

Publications on Latin America (*see also* the bibliographical notes appended to each country):

Revenue, Expenditure and Public Debts of the Latin American Republics. Division of
 Financial Information, US Department of Commerce. Annual
Boundaries of the Latin American Republics: An Annotated List of Documents, 1493–1943.
 Department of State, Office of the Geographer. Washington, 1944
Burgin, M. (ed.), *Handbook of Latin American Studies.* Gainesville, Fla., 1935 ff.
Hirschman, Albert O., *Latin American Issues:* [11] *Essays and Comments.* New York, 1961
Humphreys, R. A., *Latin American History: A Guide to the Literature in English.* London,
 1958
Munro, D. G., *The Latin American Republics; A History.* London, 1961
Plaza, G., *The Organization of American States: Instrument for Hemispheric Development.*
 Washington, 1969.—*Latin America Today and Tomorrow.* Washington, 1971
Steward, J. H. (ed.), *Handbook of the South American Indian.* 7 vols. Washington, 1946–59
Thomas, A. V. W. and A. J., *The Organization of American States.* Southern Methodist Univ.
 Press, 1963

LATIN AMERICAN ECONOMIC GROUPINGS

The Economic Commission for Latin America, an organ of the United Nations,
with headquarters in Santiago, Chile, has facilitated the co-operation of two groups
of countries concerning production, tariffs and trade.

Latin American Free Trade Association was concluded in Montevideo on 18 Feb.
1961 by Argentina, Boliva, Brazil, Chile, Mexico, Paraguay, Peru and Uruguay.
Colombia (3 Oct. 1961), Ecuador (20 Oct. 1961) and Venezuela (1 Sept. 1966) have
joined the ALALC/LAFTA Treaty. The permanent secretariat is at Montevideo. The
11 signatories held the 19th Extraordinary Conference at Acapulco, 16–27 June
1980. A Constitution was drawn up for a new Latin American Integration Association (LAIA) to take over after LAFTA expired on 31 Dec. 1980.

Central American Common Market (ODECA). On 13 Dec. 1960, at Managua, El
Salvador, Guatemala, Honduras and Nicaragua concluded a general treaty on
Central American integration; a protocol on the equalization of import duties and
charges; and an agreement establishing the Central American Bank for Economic
Integration. Costa Rica acceded in 1962 and in Sept. 1963 ratified the charter of the
Banco Centroamericano de Integración Económica (in Tegucigalpa), whose
capital was thereupon increased to US$20m.

The San Salvador Charter, signed on 14 Dec. 1962, expanded these provisions,
envisaging permanent political, economic, educational, defence, etc., councils.
The permanent secretariat is at Guatemala City.

Total intra-ODECA trade increased from US$8·6m. in 1960 to US$176m. in
1966. Total USA investments in the area are about $400m.

The Andean Group (Grupo Andino). On 26 May 1969 an agreement was signed
by Bolivia, Chile, Colombia, Ecuador and Peru creating the Andean Group.
Venezuela was initially actively involved but did not sign the agreement. The
Group signed a further agreement on 31 Dec. 1970 on common regulations controlling foreign investments. Under the Cartagena Agreement of 1975 the development of an integrated petrochemical industry in each of the member countries was
established.

Sistema Económico Latinoamericano (SELA) was created by 25 countries (not including USA) meeting at Panama, 17 Oct. 1975. Its Permanent Secretary is Jaime Moncayo, former Finance Minister of Ecuador. It held an 'extraordinary' technical meeting at Caracas, 5 Jan. 1976, to prepare for other activities, such as UNCTAD, at Nairobi in May 1976.

Britain and Latin America. Latin America Bureau, London (annual)

British Bulletin of Publications on Latin America, the Caribbean, Portugal and Spain. London, from June 1949 (half-yearly)

Hispanic and Luso–Brazilian Councils, Portuguese and Spanish Dictionaries. London, 1971

Instruments of Economic Integration in Latin America and the Caribbean. New York, 1975

Libre Comercio. Revista oficial de la Associación de Empresarios participantes de la ALALC. Montevideo, from June 1964 (monthly)

Committee on Latin America (COLA), *Latin American Serials.* 3 vols. London, 1969, 1973, 1977

Brooks, J. (ed.), *The South American Handbook.* Bath (Annual)

Einaudi, L., R. (ed.), *Beyond Cuba: Latin America Takes Charge of its Future.* New York, 1974

Jaguaribe, H., *Political Development: A General Theory and a Latin American Case Study.* New York, 1973

Loveman, B., and Davies, T. M., *The Politics of Antipolitics: The Military in Latin America.* Univ. of Nebraska Press, 1978

Milenky, E. S., *The Politics of Regional Organization in Latin America. The Latin American Free Trade Association.* New York, 1973

Morawetz, D., *The Andean Group: A Case Study in Economic Integration Among Developing Countries.* MIT Press, 1974

UN Economic Commission for Latin America. *The Latin America Economy.* Washington (annual)

CARIBBEAN COMMUNITY
(CARICOM)

Establishment and Functions. The Treaty establishing the Caribbean Community, including the Caribbean Common Market, and the Agreement establishing the Common External Tariff for the Caribbean Common Market, was signed by the Prime Ministers of Barbados, Guyana, Jamaica and Trinidad and Tobago at Chaguaramas, Trinidad, on 4 July 1973, and entered into force on 1 Aug. 1973. Six less developed countries of CARIFTA signed the Treaty of Chaguaramas on 17 April 1974. They were Belize, Dominica, Grenada, Saint Lucia, St Vincent and Montserrat, and the Treaty came into effect for those countries on 1 May 1974. Antigua acceded to Membership on 4 July 1974 and on 26 July the Associated State of St Kitts–Nevis–Anguilla signed the Treaty of Chaguaramas in Kingston, Jamaica, and became a member of the Caribbean Community, Bahamas became a member of the Community but not of the Common Market.

The Caribbean Community has 3 areas of activity: economic integration (that is, the Caribbean Common Market which replaces CARIFTA); co-operation in non-economic areas and the operation of certain common services; and co-ordination of foreign policies of independent member states.

The Caribbean Common Market provides for the establishment of a Common External Tariff, a common protective policy and the progressive co-ordination of external trade policies; the adoption of a scheme for the harmonization of fiscal incentives to industry; double taxation arrangements among member countries; the co-ordination of economic policies and development planning; and a special regime for the less developed countries of the community.

Membership: Antigua, Bahamas, Barbados, Belize, the Commonwealth of Dominica, Grenada, Guyana, Jamaica, Montserrat, St Kitts–Nevis, Saint Lucia, St Vincent and the Grenadines, and Trinidad and Tobago.

Structure: The *Heads of Government Conference* is the principal organ of the Community, and its primary responsibility is to determine the policy of the Community. It is the final authority of the Community and the Common Market, and for the conclusion of treaties and relationships between the Community and international organizations and States. It is responsible for financial arrangements for meeting the expenses of the Community.

The *Common Market Council* is the principal organ of the Common Market and consists of a Minister of Government designated by each member state. Decisions in both the Conference and the Council are in the main taken on the basis of unanimity.

The *Secretariat*, successor to the Commonwealth Caribbean Regional Secretariat, is the principal administrative organ of the Community and of the Common Market. The Secretary-General is appointed by the Conference on the recommendation of the Council for a term not exceeding 5 years and may be reappointed. The Secretary-General shall act in that capacity in all meetings of the Conference, the Council, and of the institutions of the Community.

Institutions of the Community, established by the Heads of Government Conference, are: Conference of Ministers responsible for Health; Standing Committees of Ministers responsible for Education, Industry, Labour, Foreign Affairs, Finance, Agriculture, Mines and Transport, respectively.

Associate Institutions: East Caribbean Common Market Council of Ministers; Organization of East Caribbean States; Caribbean Development Bank; Caribbean Examinations Council; Caribbean Investment Corporation; Council of Legal Education; University of the West Indies; University of Guyana.

Field Projects: Caribbean Agricultural and Rural Development Advisory and Training Service; Caribbean Agricultural Research and Development Institute; Caribbean Food Corporation; Caribbean Tourism Research Centre; West Indies Shipping Corporation; Small Vessel Shipping Project; LIAT 1974 Ltd. and Caribbean Aviation Training Institute.

Secretary-General: Roderick Rainford.
Deputy Secretary-General: (Vacant).
Headquarters: Bank of Guyana Building, PO Box 10827, Georgetown, Guyana.

The language of the Community is English.

Books of Reference

CARICOM Perspective. (Bi-monthly). *CARICOM Bibliography* (Bi-annual)
The Caribbean Community in the 1980's. Caribbean Community Secretariat, 1982
Axline, A. W., *Caribbean Integration: The Politics of Regionalism.* London and New York, 1979
Payne, A. J., *The Politics of the Caribbean Community 1961–79.* Manchester Univ. Press, 1980

THE LEAGUE OF ARAB STATES

Origin. The formation of the League of Arab States in 1945 was largely inspired by the Arab awakening of the 19th century. This movement sought to re-create and reintegrate the Arab community which, though for 400 years a part of the Ottoman Empire, had preserved its identity as a separate national group held together by memories of a common past, a common religion and a common language, as well as by the consciousness of being part of a common cultural heritage. The leaders of the Arab movement in the 19th century and of the Arab revolt against Turkey in the First World War sought to achieve these aims through secession from the Ottoman Empire into a united and independent Arab state comprising all the Arab countries in Asia. However the 1919 peace settlement divided the Arab world in Asia (with the exception of Saudi Arabia and the Yemen) into British and French spheres of influence and established in them a number of separate states and administrations (Syria, Lebanon, Iraq, Jordan and Palestine) under temporary mandatory control.

By 1943, however, 7 of these countries had substantially achieved their independence. An Arab conference therefore met in Alexandria in the autumn of 1944; it formulated the 'Alexandria Protocol', which delineated the outlines of the Arab League. It was found that neither a unitary state nor a federation could be achieved, but only a league of sovereign states. A covenant, establishing such a league, was signed in Cairo on 22 March 1945 by the representatives of Egypt, Iraq, Saudi Arabia, Syria, Lebanon, Jordan and Yemen. There were (1980) 21 members of the League: Algeria, Bahrain, Djibouti, Iraq, Jordan, Kuwait, Lebanon, Libya, Mauritania, Morocco, Oman, Palestine L.O., Qatar, Saudi Arabia, Somalia, Sudan, Syria, Tunisia, United Arab Emirates, P.D.R. of Yemen and Yemen Arab Republic.

Egypt's membership of the League was suspended, in accordance with a resolution passed at the Baghdad summit, in March 1979, at which time it was also agreed that the League secretariat should be moved from Cairo to Tunis. This action was taken in response to the signing of a bilateral peace treaty between Egypt and Israel.

Organization. The machinery of the League consists of a Council, a number of Special Committees and a Permanent Secretariat. On the Council each state has one vote. The Council may meet in any of the Arab capitals. Its functions include mediation in any dispute between any of the League states or a League state and a country outside the League. The Council has a Political Committee consisting of the Foreign Ministers of the Arab states.

The Permanent Secretariat of the League, under a Secretary-General (who enjoys, along with his senior colleagues, full diplomatic status), has its seat in Tunisia.

The League considers itself a regional organization within the framework of the United Nations at which its secretary-general is an observer.

Secretary-General: Chedli Klibi (Tunisia).

Flag: Dark green with the seal of the Arab League in white in the centre.

Arab Common Market. The Arab Common Market came into operation on 1 Jan. 1965. The agreement, reached on 13 Aug. 1964 and open to all the Arab League states, has been signed by Iraq, Jordan, Syria and Egypt. The agreement provides for the abolition of customs duties on agricultural products and natural resources within 5 years, by reducing tariffs at an annual rate of 20%. Customs duties on industrial products are to be reduced by 10% annually. The agreement also provides for the free movement of capital and labour between member countries, the establishment of common external tariffs, the co-ordination of economical development and the framing of a common foreign economic policy.

Books of Reference

Arab Maritime Data, 1979–80. London, 1979
Gomaa, A. M., *The Foundation of the League of Arab States.* London, 1977

ORGANIZATION OF THE PETROLEUM EXPORTING COUNTRIES

Aims. The Organization was founded in Iraq in 1960 with the following founder members, Iran, Iraq, Kuwait, Saudi Arabia and Venezuela. The principal aims are unifying the petroleum policies of member countries and determining the best means for safeguarding their interests, individually and collectively; to devise ways and means of ensuring the stabilization of prices in international oil markets with a view to eliminating harmful and unnecessary fluctuations; and to secure a steady income for the producing countries, an efficient, economic and regular supply of petroleum to consuming nations, and a fair return on their capital to those investing in the petroleum industry.

Membership (1981). Algeria, Ecuador, Gabon, Indonesia, Iran, Iraq, Kuwait, Libya, Nigeria, Qatar, Saudi Arabia, United Arab Emirates and Venezuela. Membership is open to any other country having substantial net exports of crude petroleum, which has fundamentally similar interests to those of member countries.

OPEC Fund. The Fund was established in 1976 to provide financial aid to developing countries, other than OPEC members, on advantageous terms.

Secretary-General: Dr Marc S. Nan Nguema (Gabon).
Deputy Secretary-General: Dr Fadhil J. Al-Chalabi (Iraq).

Headquarters: Obere Donaustrasse 93, A–1020 Vienna, Austria.

Books of Reference

OPEC publications include: *Annual Statistical Bulletin. Annual Report. Proceedings of the OPEC Seminar 1977. OPEC Bulletin* (monthly). *OPEC Review* (quarterly). *OPEC Papers* (bi-monthly).
Al-Chalabi, Dr F., *OPEC and the International Oil Industry: A Changing Structure.* OUP, 1980
Abolfathi, F., *The OPEC Market to 1985.* Lexington, 1977
El Mallakh, R., *OPEC: Twenty Years and Beyond.* London, 1982
Ghadar, F., *The Evolution of OPEC Strategy.* Lexington, 1977
Griffin, J., and Teece, D. J., *OPEC Behaviour and World Oil Prices.* London and Boston, 1982

ORGANIZATION OF AFRICAN UNITY

On 25 May 1963 the heads of state or government of 32 African countries, at a conference in Addis Ababa, signed a charter establishing an 'Organization of African Unity' *(Organisation de l'Unité Africaine).*

Its chief objects are the furtherance of African unity and solidarity; the co-ordination of the political, economic, cultural, health, scientific and defence policies and the elimination of colonialism in Africa.

The organs of the Organization are: (1) the assembly of the heads of state and government; (2) the council of foreign ministers; (3) the general secretariat; (4) a commission of mediation, conciliation and arbitration. Arabic, French and English are recognized as working languages.

Chairman: Mengistu Haile Mariam (Ethiopia).
Secretary-General: Dr Peter U. Onu (Nigeria).
Headquarters: Addis Ababa.
Flag: Horizontally green, white, green, with the white fimbriated yellow, and the seal of the OAU in the centre.

DANUBE COMMISSION

The Danube Commission was constituted in 1949 based on the Convention regarding the regime of navigation on the Danube, which was signed in Belgrade on 18 Aug. 1948. The Belgrade Convention reaffirmed that navigation on the Danube from Ulm to the Black Sea, with access to the sea through the Sulina arm and the Sulina Canal, is equally free and open to the nationals, merchant shipping and merchandise of all states as to harbour and navigation fees as well as conditions of merchant navigation.

The Danube Commission is composed of representatives from the countries on the Danube (1 for each of these countries), namely, Austria, Bulgaria, Hungary, Romania, Czechoslovakia, USSR and Yugoslavia. Since 1957, representatives of the Ministry of Transport from the Federal Republic of Germany have attended the meetings of the Commission as guests of the Secretariat.

The functions of the Danube Commission are to check that the provisions of the

Convention are carried out, to establish a uniform buoying system on all the Danube's navigable waterways and to establish the basic regulations for navigation on the river. The Commission co-ordinates the regulations for river, customs and sanitation control as well as the hydrometeorological service and collects statistical data concerning navigation on the Danube.

The Danube Commission enjoys legal status. It has its own seal and flag. The members of the Commission and elected officers enjoy diplomatic immunity. The Commission's official buildings, archives and documents are inviolable. French and Russian are the official languages of the Commission.

Since 1954 the headquarters of the Commission have been in Budapest.

Flag: Blue, with a red strip fimbriated white along the bottom edge, and the initials of the Commission within a wreath in the canton—Latin letters on obverse Cyrillic on reverse.

Books of Reference

Danube Commission's publications include: *Summary Records and Documents Adopted by the Sessions of the Danube Commission. Rules of Procedure of the Danube Commission. Basic Regulations for Navigation on the Danube. Reports on the Maintenance of the Navigability of the Danube. Guidebook for Sailors. Hydrological Yearbooks. Statistical Yearbooks. Mileage Chart of the Danube. Ice Control on the Danube. Collection of Internal Laws Concerning Navigation on the Danube. Collection of International Agreements Relating to Navigation on the Danube. Radio-Codes for Navigation on the Danube.*

PART II

COUNTRIES OF THE WORLD

A—Z

AFGHÁNISTÁN

De Afghanistan Democrateek Jamhuriat

Capital: Kábul
Population: 16·28m. (1981)
GNP per capita: US$168 (1982)

HISTORY. A military *coup* on 17 July 1973 overthrew the monarchy of King Záhir Sháh. The *coup* was led by the King's cousin and brother-in-law Mohammad Daoud who declared a Republic. King Záhir abdicated on 24 Aug. 1973. President Daoud was killed in a military *coup* in April 1978 which led to the establishment of a pro-Soviet government of the People's Democratic Party of Afghánistán.

AREA AND POPULATION. Afghánistán is bounded north by the USSR, east and south by Pakistan and west by Iran.

The area is 251,773 sq. miles (652,090 sq. km). Population, according to the (1979) census, is 15,551,358, of which some 2·5m. are nomadic tribes. Estimate (1981) 16,276,000 of whom 2m. are living in Pakistan and Iran as refugees. Annual population growth rate (1981) 2·6%; infant mortality rate (1979) 182 per 1,000 live births.

Census (1979), Kábul 913,164; Kandahár, 178,409; Herát, 140,323; Mazár-i-Sharif, 103,372; Jalálábád, 53,915; Kunduz, 53,251; Baghlan, 39,228; Charikar, 22,424; Shibergan, 18,955; Gardez, 9,550; Faizabad, 9,098; Qala-i-nau, 5,340; Uiback, 4,938; Meterlam, 3,987; Cheghcherán, 2,974.

The main ethnic group are the Pathans. Other ethnic groups include the Tajiks, the Hazaras, the Turkomans and the Uzbeks.

CLIMATE. The climate is arid, with a big annual range of temperature and very little rain, apart from the period Jan. to April. Winters are very cold, with considerable snowfall, which may last the year round on mountain summits. Kabul. Jan. 27°F (–2·8°C), July 76°F (24·4°C). Annual rainfall 13" (338 mm).

CONSTITUTION AND GOVERNMENT. The 1964 Constitution was abolished by Presidential decree in 1973 and on 14 Feb. 1977 a new Constitution was adopted by the *Loya-Jirgah* (Grand Assembly). The 1977 Constitution was abrogated in April 1978 by the new Head of State. Noor Mohammad Taraki. On 16 Sept. 1979 President Taraki was ousted in a *coup* and replaced by Hafizullah Amin. In Dec. 1979 Soviet troops invaded Afghánistán and Hafizullah Amin was deposed and replaced by Babrak Karmal. The pretext for the airlift of combat troops to Kábul was the Treaty of Friendship signed in Dec. 1978 between USSR and Afghánistán. In Oct. 1983 there were some 105,000 Soviet troops in Afghánistán.

President: Babrak Karmal.
Prime Minister: Sultan Ali Kishtmand.
National flag: Three equal horizontal stripes of red, black and green, with the national arms in the canton.

The official languages are Pushtu and Dari (Persian).

DEFENCE. Conscription is for a period of 3 years, with reserve liability continuing to the age of 42.

Army. The Army is organized in 3 armoured and 11 infantry divisions, 1 mechanized infantry brigade, 1 artillery brigade, 2 mountain infantry and 2 commando regiments and 1 parachute battalion. Equipment includes 50 T-34, 500 T-54/-55 and 100 T-62 battle tanks. Strength was (1984) about 40,000, but most units of the

Army, effectively under Soviet control, are well below strength, largely as a result of desertions

Air Force. The Air Force, which is Russian-equipped, has about 150 combat aircraft and 7,000 officers and men. Nominal strength comprises 1 squadron of Su-17 attack aircraft, 3 squadrons of MiG-21 interceptors (about 40 aircraft), 6 squadrons of MiG-17s and Su-7s (about 75 aircraft), 2 bomber squadrons each with about 10 twin-jet Il-28s, a helicopter attack force of at least 30 Mi-24s, a transport wing with 15 twin-turboprop An-26s, about 10 piston-engined An-2s, 30 Mi-8 and 10 Mi-4 helicopters and 1 or 2 turboprop Il-18s, and Yak-18, Aero L-39 and MiG-15UTI trainers. The main fighter station is Bagram, with facilities for the largest jet airliners and bombers. There is a bomber station at Shindand, a training station at Mazár-i-Sharif and an air academy at Sherpur. Large numbers of 'Guideline' and 'Goa' surface-to- air missiles are operational in Afghánistán. Strong Soviet forces in Afghánistán in 1983 included Su-25 attack aircraft, and large numbers of Mi-8 assault helicopters and Mi-24 helicopter gunships.

Police and Militia. In addition to the Army and Air Force there are a number of paramilitary units, including a 30,000-strong gendarmerie, secret police and 'Defence of the Revolution' forces.

INTERNATIONAL RELATIONS

Membership. Afghánistán is a member of UN and of the Colombo Plan.

ECONOMY

Planning. The 1979–84 5-year plan provides for expenditure of Afs. 105,000m. Industry and mining will receive 42% and agriculture 25%.

Budget. In 1980–81 the budget envisaged expenditure of Afs. 33,759m. and revenue of Afs. 33,759m.

Currency. The monetary system is on the silver standard. The unit is the *afghání*, weighing 10 grammes of silver 0·900 fine, which is subdivided into 100 *puls*. Rates of exchange fluctuate round Afs. 100 = £1; Afs. 50 = US$1.

Banking. The Afghán State Bank *(Da Afghánistán Bank)* is the largest of the 3 main banks and also undertakes the functions of a central bank, holding the exclusive right of note issue. Total assets of the 3 main banks were: Da Afghánistán Bánk (1981), Afs. 22,839m.; Pashtany Tejaraty Bánk (1981), Afs. 6,997m.; Bánk-i-Milli (1981), Afs. 3,087m.

Weights and Measures. Weights and measures used in Kábul are: Weights: 1 *khurd* = 0·244 lb.; 1 *pao* = 0·974 lb.; 1 *charak* = 3·896 lb.; 1 *sere* = 16 lb.; 1 *kharwár* = 1,280 lb. or 16 maunds of 80 lb. each. Long measure: 1 yard or *gaz* = 40 in. The metric system is in increasingly common use. Square measures: 1 *jaríb* = 60 × 60 kábuli yd or ½ acre; 1 *kulbá* = 40 jaríbs (area in which 2½ kharwárs of seed can be sown); 1 jaríb yd = 29 in.

Local weights and measures are in use in the provinces.

ENERGY AND NATURAL RESOURCES

Minerals. Mineral resources are scattered and little developed. Coal is mined at Karkar in Pul-i-Khumri, Ishpushta near Doshi, north of Kábul and Dar-i-Suf south of Mazar (total production, 1975–76, 150,000 tonnes). Natural gas is found in northern Afghánistán around Shiberghan and Sar-i-Pol; over 2,000m. cu. metres, about 90% of production, is piped to the USSR annually. Rich, but as yet unexploited, deposits of iron ore exist in the Hajigak hills about 100 miles west of Kábul; beryllium has been found in the Kunar valley and barite in Bamian province. Other deposits include gold; silver (now unexploited, in the Panjshir valley); lapis lazuli (in the Panjshir valley and Badakhshán); asbestos; mica; sulphur (near Maimana); chrome (in the Logar valley and near Herát); and copper (in the north).

Agriculture. Although the greater part of Afghánistán is more or less mountainous and a good deal of the country is too dry and rocky for successful cultivation, there are many fertile plains and valleys, which, with the assistance of irrigation from small rivers or wells, yield very satisfactory crops of fruit, vegetables and cereals. It is estimated that there are 14m. hectares of cultivable land in the country, of which 7,844,000 hectares are being cultivated (5·34m. hectares of this being irrigated land). Before 1979 Afghánistán was virtually self-supporting in foodstuffs (including wheat in 1973), apart from sugar. The USSR now provides wheat, sugar and other foodstuffs.

The castor-oil plant, madder and the asafœtida plant abound.

Fruit forms a staple food (with bread) of many people throughout the year, both in the fresh and preserved state, and in the latter condition is exported in great quantities. The fat-tailed sheep furnish the principal meat diet, and the grease of the tail is a substitute for butter. Wool and skins provide material for warm apparel and one of the more important articles of export. Persian lambskins (Karakuls) are one of the chief exports.

Cotton production, 1981, was estimated at 65,000 tonnes; wheat, 2·75m.; barley, 321,000; maize, 798,000; rice, 461,000.

Livestock (1982): Cattle, 3·8m.; horses, 405,000; donkeys, 1·3m.; mules, 30,000; sheep, 20m.; goats, 3m.; poultry, 20·6m.

INDUSTRY AND TRADE

Industry. At Kábul there are factories for the manufacture of cotton and woollen textiles, leather, boots, marble-ware, furniture, glass, bicycles, prefabricated houses and plastics. A large machine shop has been constructed and equipped by the USSR, with a capability of manufacturing motor spares. There is a wool factory and there are several cotton-ginning plants; a small cotton factory at Jabal-us-Seráj and a larger one at Pul-i-Khumri; a cotton-seed oil extraction plant at Lashkargah; a cotton textile factory at Gulbahar, and a cotton plant at Balkh.

An ordnance factory manufactures arms and ammunition, boots and clothing, etc. for the Army. There is a beet sugar plant at Baghlan (equipped with Soviet machinery) and a fruit-canning factory in Kandahár. Hydro-electric plants have been constructed at Sarobi, Nangarhár, Naghlu, Mahipár, Pul-i-Khumri and Kandahár; more hydro and thermal plants are projected.

Industries include cement, coalmining, cotton textiles, small vehicle assembly plants, fruit canning, carpet making, leather tanning, footwear manufacture, sugar manufacture, preparation of hides and skins, and building. Most of these are relatively small and, with the exception of hides and skins, carpets and fruits, do not meet domestic requirements.

Commerce. Trade is supervised by the Government through the Ministries of Commerce and Finance and the Da Afghánistán Bánk. The Association of Afghán Chambers of Commerce works in close liaison with the Ministry of Commerce. The Government monopoly controls the import of petrol and oil, sugar, cigarettes and tobacco, motor vehicles and consignment goods from bilateral trading countries. The principal surface routes for imports to Afghánistán are via the Soviet rail system and the border posts at Torghundi and Hairatan; and from Karachi via the border post at Torkham.

In the year ended 20 March 1982 Afghán imports totalled US$622·4m. and exports US$694·3m.

Main export commodities were karakul skins (US$18·8m.), raw cotton (US$22·6m.), dried fruit and nuts (US$174·9m.), fresh fruit (US$50·5m.) and natural gas (US$272·6m.). Main items imported were petroleum products (US$112m.), textiles (US$64·9m.).

Total trade between Afghánistán and UK (in £1,000 sterling, British Department of Trade returns):

	1979	1980	1981	1982	1983
Imports to UK	20,276	20,174	22,822	20,855	19,837
Exports and re-exports from UK	9,567	6,818	7,725	9,344	10,310

Tourism. Owing to internal political instability there has been negligible tourism since 1979.

COMMUNICATIONS

Roads. There were in 1978 over 2,812 km of asphalted road and 15,940 km of other roads. The Americans asphalted the Kandahár–Chaman and Kábul–Torkham roads. The Russians constructed a road and tunnel through the Salang pass (over 11,000 ft) which was opened in Sept. 1964 and cut 120 miles off the old road from Kábul to the north; they continued this road to Kunduz and Sherkhan Bandar (Qizil Qala) on the Oxus. In addition, the Americans in 1966 completed the road between Kábul and Kandahár and the Russians constructed a concrete road between Kandahár and Herát. In 1968 the Americans completed an asphalt road from Herát to the Iranian frontier at Islam Qala. With Soviet assistance a metalled road from Pul-i-Khumri to Mazár-i-Sharif was completed in 1969 and Mazár-i-Sharif to Shiberghán in 1971. A Soviet-built road and rail bridge across the Oxus (Amu Darya) River was opened in May 1982.

Railways. There are no railways in the country, but the Oxus bridge opened in 1982, brought Soviet Railways' track into the country. A 200 km line has been authorized from Termez to Pul-i-Khumri.

Aviation. On 29 June 1956 Afghánistán signed an agreement with the USA for the development of civil aviation, including the construction of the international airport at Kandahár, comprising a loan of $5m. and a grant of $9·56m. Kábul airport has been expanded with Russian assistance. New runways at Kábul and Kandahár airports have been completed. Provincial all-weather airports have been constructed at Herát, Qunduz, Jalálábád and Mazár-i-Sharif.

Ariana Afghan Airlines (a national airline) operates regular services to New Delhi, Tashkent and Moscow.

Bakhtar Afghan Airlines (the domestic national airline) began operations on 8 Feb. 1968 and regularly serves the main internal airfields.

Shipping. There are practically no navigable rivers in Afghánistán, and timber is the only article of commerce conveyed by water, floated down the Kunar and Kábul rivers from Chitral on rafts. A port has been built at Qizil Qala on the Oxus; barge traffic is increasing on the Oxus. Three river ports on the Amu Darya have been built at Sherkhan Bandar, Tashguzar and Hairatan, linked by road to Kábul.

Post and Broadcasting. Telephones, installed in most of the large towns, numbered 31,200 in 1978. There is telegraphic communication between all the larger towns and with other parts of the world. Kábul Radio broadcasts in Pushtu, Persian, Urdu, English, French, Russian and German. The first TV colour transmissions in Kábul began in mid-1978. An agreement was signed in 1981 under which the USSR undertook to assist with the development of communications. In 1978 there were 823,000 radio receivers and in 1982 12,000 television receivers

JUSTICE, RELIGION, EDUCATION AND WELFARE

Justice. A Supreme Court was established in June 1978. If no provision exists in the Constitution or in the general laws of the State, the courts follow the Hanafi jurisprudence of Islamic law.

Religion. The predominant religion is Islam, mostly of the Sunni sect, though there is a minority of about 1m. Shiah Moslems.

Education. There are elementary schools throughout the country, but secondary schools exist only in Kábul and provincial capitals. Both elementary and secondary education are free. In 1982 there were 1·1m. pupils (35,364 teachers) in primary education and 124,000 pupils (6,170 teachers) in secondary education. There are 3 teacher-training institutions in Kábul and 11 elsewhere; UNESCO is supporting an expansion programme. Technical, art, commercial and medical schools exist for higher education. Kábul University was founded in 1932 and has 9 faculties (medicine, science, agriculture, engineering, law and political science, letters, economics, theology, pharmacology). The University of Nangarhar in Jalálábád was founded in 1963. A Polytechnic in Kábul was completed in 1968. In

1982 there were 13,115 students in higher education, 4,427 in teacher-training schools and 1,230 in technical schools.

Health. In 1982 there were 1,215 doctors and 6,875 hospital beds. Two-thirds of the doctors and half the beds were in Kábul.

DIPLOMATIC REPRESENTATIVES

Of Afghánistán in Great Britain (31 Prince's Gate, London, SW7 1QQ)
Chargé d'Affaires: Mohammad Azam Shahim.

Of Great Britain in Afghánistán (Karte Parwan, Kábul)
Chargé d'Affaires: J. D. Garner, MVO.

Of Afghánistán in the USA (2341 Wyoming Ave., NW, Washington, D.C., 20008)
Chargé d'Affaires: Haider Rask.

Of the USA in Afghánistán (Wazir Akbar Khan Mina, Kábul)
Chargé d'Affaires: Edward Hurwitz.

Of Afghánistán to the United Nations
Ambassador: Mohammad Farid Zarif.

Books of Reference

Arnold, A., *Afghanistan: The Soviet Invasion in Perspective.* Oxford and Stanford, 1981.— *Afghanistan's Two-Party Communism.* Oxford and Santa Barbara, 1983
Bradsher, H. S., *Afghanistan and the Soviet Union.* Duke Univ. Press, 1983
Chaliand. G., *Rapport sur la résistance afghane.* Paris, 1981.—*Report from Afghanistan.* New York, 1982
Gilbertson, G. W., *Pakkhto Idiom Dictionary.* 2 vols. London, 1932
Gregorian, V., *The Emergence of Modern Afghanistan.* Stamford, 1970
Griffiths, J. C., *Afghanistan: Key to a Continent.* London, 1981
Hammond, T. T., *Red Star over Afghanistan.* Boulder, 1982
Hanifi, M. J., *Historical and Cultural Dictionary of Afghanistan.* Metuchen, 1976
Hyman, A., *Afghanistan under Soviet Domination 1964–81.* London, 1982
Male, B., *Revolutionary Afghanistan.* London, 1982
Misra, K. P., *Afghanistan in Crisis.* London, 1981
Newell, N. P. and Newell, R. S., *The Struggle for Afghanistan.* Cornell Univ. Press, 1981
Sykes, P. M., *A History of Afghanistan.* 2 vols. New York, 1975
Wilber, D. N. (ed.), *Afghanistan.* 2nd ed. New Haven, 1962.—(ed.), *Afghanistan, A Bibliography.* 2nd ed. New Haven, 1963

ALBANIA

Republika Popullore
Socialiste e Shqipërisë

Capital: Tirana
Population: 2·75m. (1982)
GNP per capita: US$840 (1979)

HISTORY. After the death of Gjergi Kastrioti Skënderbeu (Skanderbeg), Albania's national hero, in 1468 Albania passed under Turkish suzerainty until 1912. Independence was proclaimed at Vlonë on 28 Nov. 1912, and the London conference of ambassadors decided upon its frontiers and nominated as its ruler Prince William of Wied, who arrived at Durrës on 7 March 1914, but on 3 Sept. 1914 left the country, which fell into a state of anarchy. By the secret Pact of London of 26 April 1915 provision was made for the partition of Albania; but this arrangement was repudiated on 3 June 1917, when the Italian C.-in-C. in Albania proclaimed at Gjirokastër the independence of Albania. In Jan. 1925 a republic was proclaimed and on 1 Sept. 1928 a monarchy. Ahmed Beg Zogu, President since 31 Jan. 1925, reigned as King Zog till April 1939, when, on the occupation of the country by the Italians, he fled to England. After the liberation he was deposed *in absentia* on 2 Jan. 1946. During the years 1939–44 the country was overrun by Italians and Germans. The official Albanian date of the liberation is 29 Nov. 1944.

On 10 Nov. 1945 the British, US and USSR Governments recognized the Provisional Government under Gen. Enver Hoxha, on the understanding that it would hold free elections. The elections of 2 Dec. 1945 resulted in a Communist-controlled assembly, which on 11 Jan. 1946 proclaimed Albania a republic.

In 1946 Great Britain and the USA broke off relations with Albania and vetoed its admission to the United Nations. Albania was finally admitted on 15 Dec. 1955.

Because of Albania's Stalinist and pro-Chinese attitudes diplomatic relations with USSR were broken off in 1961. In 1977 Albania terminated its special relationship with China. In Dec. 1981 the Prime Minister, Mehmet Shehu committed suicide. Later Hoxha alleged that Shehu had been a foreign agent. Massive purges of Shehu's associates in the leadership took place in 1982. ·

AREA AND POPULATION. The area of the country is 28,748 sq. km (11,101 sq. miles). By the peace treaty Italy restored the island of Sazan (Saseno) to Albania. At the census of Jan. 1979 the population was, 2,590,600 (34% urban; density, 90 per sq. km). Population in 1982, 2·75m. The capital is Tirana (1978 population (in 1,000), 198); other large towns are Shkodër (Shkodra, Scutari) (62·5), Durrës (Durrsi, Durazzo) (61), Vlorë (Vlona, Vlonë, Vlora, Valona) (58·4), Korçë (Korça, Koritza) (50·9), Elbasan (50·7). Other towns (1975): Berat (30), Fier (28), Gjirokastër (Argyrocastro) (22), Lushnjë (21), Kavajë, 1971 (18), Qytet Stalin (formerly Kuçovë) (14).

There is a small Greek minority (1977 estimate, 50,000).

Vital statistics, 1980 (per 1,000): Births, 26·5; deaths, 6·4; marriages, 8·1; divorces, 0·8; natural increase, 20·1 per thousand. Population density, 93 per sq. km. Growth rate, 1945–79, 2·5%. Life expectancy in 1979 was 69 years.

The country is administratively divided into 26 districts (*rreth*, pl. *rrethët*) (*see* map in THE STATESMAN'S YEAR-BOOK, 1962. N.B. The district of Ersekë has been renamed Kolonjë). Districts are subdivided into *lokaliteteve*.

Districts	Area (sq. km)	Population (in 1,000) (1973)	Districts	Area (sq. km)	Population (in 1,000) (1973)
Berat	1,026	124·3	Gramsh	695	29·4
Dibrë	1,569	106·8	Gjirokastër	1,137	53·5
Durrës	859	182·4	Kolonjë	805	19·2
Elbasan	1,466	154·7	Korçë	2,181	175·4
Fier	1,191	171·5	Krujë	607	75·6

Districts	Area (sq. km)	Population (in 1,000) (1973)	Districts	Area (sq. km)	Population (in 1,000) (1973)
Kukës	1,564	71·4	Pukë	969	32·8
Lezhë	479	40·5	Sarandë	1,097	66·5
Librazhd	1,013	48·5	Skrapar	775	30·8
Lushnjë	712	94·1	Shkodër	2,528	178·5
Mat	1,028	53·5	Tepelenë	817	37·8
Mirditë	698	29·4	Tirana	1,222	272·0
Përmet	930	31·7	Tropojë	1,043	30·5
Pogradec	725	49·3	Vlorë	1,609	133·5

The districts are for the greater part named after their capitals; exceptions: Tropojë, chief town, Bajram Curri; Mat, Burrel; Mirditë, Rrëshen; Skrapar, Çorovodë.

The Albanian language is divided into two dialects—Gheg, north of the river Shkumbi, and Tosk in the south. Many places therefore have two forms of name: Vlonë (Gheg), Vlorë (Tosk), etc., and many are known also by an Italian name, *e.g.*, Valona. Since 1945 the official language has been based on Tosk.

CLIMATE. Mediterranean-type, with rainfall mainly in winter, but thunderstorms are frequent and severe in the great heat of the plains in summer. Winters in the highlands can be severe, with much snow. Tirana. Jan. 44°F (6·8°C), July 75°F (23·9°C). Annual rainfall 54″ (1,353 mm).

CONSTITUTION AND GOVERNMENT. The political structure derived from the Constitution of 14 March 1946 as amended in 1950, 1955, 1960 and 1963. In Dec. 1976 a new Constitution was adopted, by which Albania became a 'Socialist People's Republic'. The supreme legislative body is the single-chamber People's Assembly of 250 deputies, which meets twice a year, and delegates its day-to-day functions to a Presidium composed of a chairman, 3 deputy chairmen, a secretary and 10 members. Election to the People's Assembly is by universal suffrage (at 18) every 4 years.

In the elections of 14 Nov. 1982 a 100% turnout of the electorate of 1,627,968 was claimed to vote for the 250 candidates on the single list of the Democratic Front. (There were 8 spoiled papers and 1 vote against).

The Government consists of a prime minister (Chairman of the Council of Ministers), 2 deputy prime ministers, 15 ministers and the chairman of the State Planning Commission. Effective rule is exercised by the Albanian Labour (*i.e.*, Communist) Party, founded 8 Nov. 1941, whose governing body is the Politburo.

In 1981 the Party had 122,600 full members and candidates (in 1979 37·5% workers, 29% farmers, 27% women).

Titular Head of State: Chairman of the Presidium of the People's Assembly: Ramiz Alia, elected Nov. 1982. In March 1984 the chief Party and Government posts were filled as follows: Full members of the Politburo:

First Secretary of the Central Committee of the Party: Enver Hoxha. Adil Çarçani *(Prime Minister)*, Ramiz Alia, Hekuran Isai *(Minister of the Interior)*, Pali Miska, Manush Myftiu,[1] Rita Marko. Muho Asllani; Hajreddin Celiku *(Ministry of Industry)*; Simon Stefani; Ms. Lenka Çuko. Candidate members: Llambi Gegprifti; Qirjako Mihali *(Minister of Finance)*. Besnik Bekteshi [1]; Foto Cami Prokop Murra *(Minister of Defence)*. Not in the Politburo: *Foreign Minister:* Reis Malile. *Minister of Foreign Trade:* Shane Korbeci. *Minister of Agriculture:* Ms. Themie Thomai. *Chairman, State Planning Commission:* Harilla Papajorgji.

[1] Deputy Prime Minister.

Local Government is carried out by People's Councils at village, *lokalitet,* town and district level. Councillors are elected for 3 years.

National flag: Red, with a black double-headed eagle and a red, gold-edged 5-pointed star above it. *Mercantile flag:* red, black, red (horizontal) with a red yellow-edged star in the centre.

National anthem: Rreth Flamurit te per bashkuar (The flag that united us in the struggle).

DEFENCE. Albania withdrew from the Warsaw Pact in 1968 in protest against the invasion of Czechoslovakia. The Constitution precludes the stationing of foreign troops in Albania. Conscription is for 2 years in the Army and 3 years in the Navy, Air Force and special forces.

Army. The Army consists of 1 tank brigade, 5 infantry brigades and 4 artillery regiments. Equipment includes 70 T-34, 15 T-54 and 15 T-59 main battle tanks. Strength is 30,000 (including 20,000 conscripts) and reserves number 150,000. There are also paramilitary internal security forces (5,000 men) and frontier guards (7,500).

Navy. The Navy consists of 3 submarines, 2 fleet minesweepers, 3 patrol vessels, 4 inshore minesweepers, 44 torpedo boats, 6 fast gunboats, 11 minesweeping boats, 1 degaussing ship, 4 oilers, 2 diving tenders, 2 torpedo recovery craft, 4 tugs and 12 small auxiliaries and service tenders. Navy personnel in 1984 exceeded 3,000 officers and ratings, including 300 coastal frontier guards. Service for ratings is 3 years. There are naval bases at Durrës and Vlorë.

Air Force. The Air Force, controlled by the Army, has about 7,000 officers and men, and operates the serviceable survivors of more than 125 combat aircraft received before relations with China were broken. The original force included 20 Chinese-built MiG-21s and 36 MiG-19s, some Il-28 twin-jet light bombers and 2 ground attack squadrons of MiG-15s and MiG-17s. Transport and training types include 3 Il-14s, 10 An-2s, Mi-4 helicopters, Yak-18s and MiG-15UTIs.

INTERNATIONAL RELATIONS
Membership. Albania is a member of UN.

ECONOMY
Planning. For the first five 5-year plans *see* THE STATESMAN'S Year-BOOK, 1982–83. The sixth 5-year plan ran from 1976 to 1980. Annual average increases: national income, 5%; industrial production, 6·8%; agricultural production, 21·4%. The seventh 5-year plan covers 1981–85. Target increases: agricultural production, 32%, industrial, 34%. Emphasis is laid on industrial expansion, especially in the oil, mining and chemical industries. It is now stated that economic policy is founded on 'the revolutionary principle of self-reliance'.

Budget. Budget figures for 1983: Revenue, 8,800m. leks (8,200m. leks from enterprises and agricultural co-operatives); expenditure, 8,750m. leks (industry, 5,300m. leks; social, 2,300m. leks; defence, 910m. leks).

Currency. The monetary unit is the *lek* of 100 *qintars*. It replaced the gold franc *(franc ar)* in July 1947. In Aug. 1965 a new *lek* was introduced: 10 old *leks* = 1 new *lek*. There are 5, 10, 20 and 50 *qintar* coins and a 1 *lek* coin; notes are for 1, 3, 5, 10, 25, 50 and 100 *leks*. Exchange rates, Sept. 1983: US$1 = 6·68 *leks*; £1 = 10·14.

Banking. The Albanian State Bank was founded in 1925 with Italian aid. In 1970 savings deposits amounted to 572m. leks. In 1970 the Agricultural Bank was set up as a credit institution for agricultural co-operatives.

Weights and Measures. The metric system is in force.

ENERGY AND NATURAL RESOURCES
Electricity. Albania is rich in hydro-electric potential. Electric power production in 1973 was 1,603m. kwh., of which 1,127m. was hydro-electric. Total electrification was claimed in 1970.

Oil. The oil industry is being rapidly expanded. Output in 1973: Crude, 2,107,000 tonnes; refined, 1,596,000 tonnes. Refining capacity in 1970 was over 1m. tonnes. Oil is produced chiefly at Qytet Stalin which a pipeline connects to the port of Vlorë. Natural gas is extracted.

Minerals. The mineral wealth of Albania is considerable but is only recently being developed. In 1971 there were 8 coal, 7 chromium (1977 output 9,000 tonnes) and 6 copper mines. Ferro-nickel ores are mined and output is increasing. In 1969 extensive coal deposits were discovered at Valias, near Tirana. There is no bituminous coal. Salt is extracted near Vlorë and bitumen mined at Selenicë. Production in tonnes (1973): Chrome ore, 611,000; copper ore, 435,000; ferro-nickel ore, 384,000; brown coal, 811,000; phosphate, 110,000; nitrogenous fertilizer, 106,000; bitumen (1964), 242,000; cement (1965), 133,600.

Agriculture. The country for the greater part is rugged, wild and mountainous, the exceptions being along the Adriatic littoral and the Korçë (Koritza) Basin, which are fertile. In 1973 a programme of land reclamation and anti-erosion measures was instituted. In 1970 arable land comprised 599,000 hectares and pasture 623,000 hectares. In 1980 366,000 hectares were irrigated.

Land is held by the State (largely forests and non-agricultural), state farms (50 in 1982 averaging 3,000 hectares of arable land) and co-operatives (500 in 1983 averaging 1,100 hectares). Co-operatives are divided into 'advanced' and 'ordinary'. There is a pension scheme for collective farmers. In 1982 there were 31 machine and tractor stations. Tractors in 1980 numbered 17,300 (in 15-h.p. units).

The yield of the main crops in 1981 was (in 1,000 tonnes): Wheat, 510; sugar-beet, 270; maize, 250; potatoes, 140; fruit, 132; grapes, 62; oats, 30; sorghum, 30; cotton, 26; barley, 25; sunflower seeds, 25; wine, 23; rice, 17; beans, 16; tobacco, 15.

Livestock, 1982: Cattle, 580,000; sheep, 1·17m.; goats, 670,000; pigs, 125,000; horses and mules, 75,000; poultry, 4·4m.

Forestry. 47% of the territory of Albania is forest land, of which 38% is oak forest, 26% elm and 18% pine and birch. Timber reserves reach 44·5m. cu. metres. In 1967 forests covered 1,242,100 hectares; 6,784 hectares were afforested, 10,000 hectares improved in 1967.

Fisheries. The catch in 1964 was 3,600 tonnes.

INDUSTRY AND TRADE

Industry. All industry is nationalized down to the smallest workshop. Output is small, and the principal industries are agricultural product processing, textiles, oil products and cement. Chemical and engineering industries are being built up. The metallurgical combine at Elbasan is being extended.

Labour. In 1973, 462,900 persons worked in the socialist sector of the national economy, of whom 34·7% were employed in industry. In 1976, 46% of wage-earners were women.

Minimum wages may not fall below one-third of maximum. A new labour code was introduced in 1980 normalizing an 8-hour day and 6-day week and 12 days yearly paid holiday. Retirement age is 60 for men and 55 for women.

Commerce. Between 1954 and 1978 Chinese aid amounted to US$5,000m., but economic relations were then broken off. There are 1981–5 trade agreements with Bulgaria, Czechoslovakia, North Korea, Poland, Vietnam and Yugoslavia; and Albania also trades with Italy, France, Czechoslovakia and India. The establishment of joint companies with, and the acceptance of credits from, capitalist firms is forbidden by the constitution. In 1980 indebtedness to the West was US$100m.

Exports include crude oil, bitumen, chrome, nickel, copper, tobacco, fruit and vegetables.

Total trade between Albania and UK (British Department of Trade returns, in £1,000 sterling):

	1978	1979	1980	1981	1982	1983
Imports to UK	52	62	107	110	45	60
Exports and re-exports from UK	255	701	1,478	2,445	4,453	240

COMMUNICATIONS

Roads. There were, in 1960, 3,100 km of roads suitable for motor traffic. The mountain districts of the north are still mostly inaccessible for wheeled vehicles, and communications are still by means of pack ponies or donkeys. Registered motor vehicles in 1960: Cars, 1,900; lorries and buses, 3,400. Road traffic carried 8·6m. passengers in 1970; goods carried, 34m. tonnes.

Railways. Total length, in 1983 was 253 km. They comprise the lines Durrës–Tirana, Durrës–Kavajë–Pegin–Elbasan, Vlorë–Memaliaj, Vlorë–Milot, Perrenjas–Pogradec, Durrës–Tirana-Shkodër. In 1974 a railway was opened from Elbasan to the iron mines at Pishkash and a line is under construction from Fier to Vlorë. In 1981 the Laç–Shkodër section of the Tirana–Shkodër line opened. In April 1982 Albania and Yugoslavia signed an agreement for the construction of a line from Shkodër to Titograd to be opened in 1984 and an extension of the main line from Fiër to Vlorë is also under construction. Goods carried in 1970 amounted to 2,324,000 tonnes; passengers (1971), 6·4m.

Aviation. There are regular scheduled flights from Tirana (Rinas Airport) to Belgrade, Bucharest, Budapest and East Berlin. Olympic Airways operate a weekly flight from Athens to Tirana.

Shipping. The ports are Shëngjin, Durrës, Vlorë and Sarandë. 567,000 tonnes of freight were carried in 1970. A ferry service from Trieste to Durrës opened in Nov. 1983.

Post and Broadcasting. Number of post and telegraph offices (1970), 292; telephones (1963), 10,150. There are 17 broadcasting stations, including Tirana and Korçë. Radio Tirana operates a foreign service in 18 languages. Radio receiving sets (1978), 200,000; television sets, 5,000. Regular television broadcasting began in 1971.

Cinemas and Theatres. In 1975 there were 410 cinemas (including mobile) and in 1973 27 theatres with an attendance of 1·6m. 14 full-length films were produced in 1980.

Newspapers. In 1976 there were 25 newspapers with an annual circulation of 47m. The Party paper is *Zëri i Popullit* (Voice of the People) (daily circulation, 105,000).

JUSTICE, RELIGION, EDUCATION AND WELFARE

Justice is administered by People's Courts. Minor crimes are tried by tribunals. Judges of the Supreme Court are elected by the People's Assembly for 4-year terms. The Office of the Procurator-General oversees the administration of justice. In 1983 an Investigator's Office was set up, separate from the Ministry of the Interior and answerable to the People's Assembly.

Religion. Albania is constitutionally an atheist state. In 1967 the Government closed all mosques and churches. For details of the situation before 1967 *see* THE STATESMAN'S YEAR-BOOK, 1969–70. The population had been mainly Moslem.

Education. Primary education is free and compulsory in 8-year schools from 7 to 15 years. Secondary education is available in 12-year (general), technical-professional or lower vocational schools. Periods of productive work and military service are intermingled with full-time education. There were, in 1979–80, 2,541 kindergartens with 83,697 pupils and 3,920 teachers and in 1973–74 1,470 primary schools with 569,600 pupils and 22,686 teachers; 39 secondary schools with 32,900 pupils; 116 technical–professional schools with 69,700 pupils (the last two categories had 3,990 teachers taken together); and (in 1969–70) 36 institutes of higher education with 36,525 students and 941 teachers, including a university in Tirana (founded 1957), a polytechnic, an agricultural college, a medical school, 5 teachers' training colleges and an institute of science. In 1969–70 there were 382 teachers and 12,783 full-time students at Tirana University. An Albanian Academy was founded in 1973.

Health. Medical services are free, though medicines are charged for. In 1978 there were 763 hospitals and 3,028 outpatient clinics. In 1982 there were 4,476 doctors and dentists, and 70 hospital beds per 1,000 inhabitants. In 1982 there were 730 maternity hospitals or hospital sections.

DIPLOMATIC REPRESENTATIVE

Of Albania to the United Nations
Ambassador: Justin Papajorgji.

Books of Reference

Vjetari Statistikor (Statistical Yearbook). Tirana, irregular, 1959–72
35 vjet Shqipëri socialiste (statistical handbook). Tirana, 1979
History of the Labour Party of Albania. Tirana, 1971
History of the Labour Party of Albania 1966–1980. Tirana, 1981
Portrait of Albania. Tirana, 1982
Bertolino, J., *Albanie: la Citadelle de Staline.* Paris, 1979
Duro, I., and Hysa, R., *Albanian-English Dictionary.* Tirana, 1981
Hetzer, A., and Roman, V. S. *Albania: A Bibliographic Research Survey.* Munich, 1983
Hoxha, E., *Réflexions sur la Chine.* Paris, 1979.—*Speeches, Conversations and Articles, 1969–1970.* Tirana, 1980.—*The Khrushchevites: Memoirs.* Tirana, 1980.—*The Anglo-American Threat to Albania.* Tirana, 1982
Logoreci, A., *The Albanians: Europe's Forgotten Survivors.* London, 1977
Marmullaku, R., *Albania and the Albanians.* London, 1975
Martin, N., *La Forteresse Albanaise: un Communisme National.* Paris, 1979
Pano, N. C., *The People's Republic of Albania.* Baltimore, 1968
Pollo, S. and Arben, P., *The History of Albania.* London, 1981
Prifti, P. R., *Socialist Albania since 1944.* Cambridge, Mass., 1978
Russ, W., *Der Entwicklungsweg Albaniens.* Meisenheim-am-Glan, 1979
Schnytzer, A., *Stalinist Economic Strategy: The Case of Albania.* OUP, 1982
Tönnes, B., *Sonderfall Albanien: Enver Hoxhas 'Eigener Weg und die Historischen Ursprünge seiner Ideologie.* Munich, 1980

ALGERIA

al-Jumhuriya al-Jazairiya ad-Dimuqratiya ash-Shabiya

Capital: Algiers
Population: 20·33m. (1983)
GNP per capita: US$1,920 (1980)

HISTORY. On 1 Nov. 1954 the National Liberation Front (FLN) went over to open warfare against the French administration and armed forces. For details of history 1958–62 *see* p. 76 THE STATESMAN'S YEAR-BOOK, 1982–83. A cease-fire agreement was reached on 18 March 1962, and Gen. de Gaulle declared Algeria independent on 3 July 1962; the Republic was declared on 25 Sept. 1962.

The Government was overthrown by a junta of army officers which, on 19 June 1965, established a Revolutionary Council under Col. Houari Boumédienne.

AREA AND POPULATION. Algeria is bounded west by Morocco and Western Sahara, south-west by Mauritania and Mali, south-east by Niger, east by Libya and Tunisia, and north by the Mediterranean Sea. It has an area of 2,381,741 sq. km. Population (census 1977) 17,422,000; estimate (1983) 20,325,000.

The 31 departments are as follows:

Departments	Area (sq. km)	Population (1980)	Departments	Area (sq. km)	Population (1980)
Adrar	422,498	146,815	Médéa	8,704	511,070
al-Jazair (Algiers)	786	2,159,573	Mostaganem	7,024	791,688
Annaba (Bône)	3,489	544,519	M'Sila	19,825	477,614
Batna	14,882	633,723	Ouahran (Oran)	1,820	795,405
Béchar	306,000	156,107	Ouargla	559,234	226,728
Béjaia (Bougie)	3,444	590,979	Oum el Bouaghi	8,123	429,296
Biskra	109,728	585,403	Saida	106,177	469,348
al-Boulaida (Blida)	3,704	962,664	Sétif	10,350	1,061,161
Bouira	4,517	401,419	Sidi-Bel-Abbès	11,648	546,377
Qacentina (Constantine)	3,562	929,213	Skikda	4,748	520,359
Djelfa	22,905	722,927	Tamanrasset	556,000	60,702
al-Asnam (Orléansville)	8,677	384,694	Tébessa	16,575	403,278
Guelma	8,624	589,120	Tiaret	23,456	676,467
Jijel	3,704	529,651	Tizi-Ouzou	3,756	931,071
Laghouat	112,052	354,959	Tlemcen	9,284	618,856
Mascara	5,846	455,314			

The chief towns (estimates, 1974) are as follows: Algiers, 1,503,720; Oran, 485,139; Constantine, 350,183; Annaba, 313,174; Tizi-Ouzou, 223,702; Blida, 158,947; Sétif, 157,065; Sidi-Bel-Abbès, 151,148; Skikda, 127,968; Batna, 115,138; Tlemcen, 115,054; Al Asnam, 114,327; Bejaia, 103,996; Médéa, 102,336; Mostaganem, 101,780.

Arabic is spoken by 80·4% of the population and Berber by 18·7%.

CLIMATE. Coastal areas have a warm temperate climate, with most rain in winter, which is mild, while summers are hot and dry. Inland, conditions become more arid beyond the Atlas Mountains. Algiers. Jan. 54°F (12·2°C), July 76°F (24·4°C). Annual rainfall 30" (762 mm). Oran. Jan. 54°F (12·2°C), July 76°F (24·4°C). Annual rainfall 15" (376 mm).

CONSTITUTION AND GOVERNMENT. A new Constitution was approved by referendum on 19 Nov. 1976 and came into effect 3 days later. It provides for a single Party, the *Front de Libération Nationale,* working in parallel with state organs.

The President of the Republic is Head of State, Head of the Armed Forces, and Head of Government. He is nominated by the FLN Congress and elected by universal suffrage for 5-year terms (renewable).

Former Presidents of the Republic:

Ferhat Abbas, 25 Sept. 1962–15 Sept. 1963.

Ahmed Ben Bella, 15 Sept. 1963–19 June 1965 (deposed).

Col. Houari Boumediénne, 19 June 1965–27 Dec. 1978 (died).

Rabah Bitat (interim), 27 Dec. 1978–9 Feb. 1979.

President of the Republic, General Secretary of the FLN, Minister of Defence: Bendjedid Chadli (sworn in 9 Feb. 1979, re-elected Feb. 1984).

The President appoints a Prime Minister and other Ministers, and presides over meetings of the Council of Ministers.

The Council of Ministers, as in March 1984, consisted of:

Prime Minister: Abdelhamid Brahimi.
Foreign Affairs: Ahmed Taleb Ibrahimi. *Interior:* M'hamed Yala. *Finance:* Boualem Benhamouda. *Justice:* Boualem Baki. *Agriculture and Fisheries:* Abdellah Khalef. *Information:* Bachir Rouis. *Posts and Telecommunications:* Boualem Bessaieh. *Transport:* Salah Goudjil. *Energy, Chemical and Petrochemical Industries:* Belkacem Nabi. *Heavy Industry:* Salim Saadi. *Light Industry:* Zitouni Messaoudi. *Hydraulics, Environment and Forests:* Mohamed Rouighi. *Trade:* Abdelaziz Khelaf. *Education:* Mohamed Cherif Kherroubi. *Higher Education:* Rafik Abdelhak Brerhi. *Further Education and Labour:* Mohamed Nabi. *Youth and Sports:* Kamal Bouchama. *Public Health:* Djamal Eddine Houhou. *Social Security:* Z'hor Hounissi. *Veterans:* Djelloul Bakhti Nemiche. *Public Works:* Ahmed Benfreha. *Town Planning and Housing:* Abderrahmane Belayat. *Religious Affairs:* Abderrahmane Chibane. *Culture and Tourism:* Abdelmadjid Chibane.

Legislative power is held by the National People's Assembly, whose 261 members are elected for a 5-year term by universal suffrage from the single list of the FLN who nominate 3 candidates for each single-member seat.

National flag: Vertically green and white, a red crescent and star over all in centre.

The official language is Arabic, French being the principal foreign language.

DEFENCE. Conscription is for a period of 6 months at the age of 19.

Army. The Army had a strength of 120,000 in 1984, organized in 3 armoured, 4 mechanized and 6 motorized brigades; 3 tank, 20 infantry, 2 paratroop, 5 artillery, 11 air defence and 4 engineer battalions; and 12 companies of desert troops. Equipment includes 400 T-54/-55, 200 T-62 and 30 T-72 main battle tanks.

Navy. The Navy, largely supplied from the USSR, consists of 2 modern frigates, 2 new missile-armed corvettes, 2 fleet minesweepers, 6 patrol vessels, 22 fast missile boats, 4 torpedo boats, 2 fast gunboats, 1 logistic landing ship, 1 landing vessel, 1 diving tender, 2 training craft, 1 torpedo recovery vessel, 1 degaussing ship, 1 survey ship, 6 fishery protection craft and 18 coastguard cutters (16 Italian-built). Naval personnel in 1984 totalled 300 officers and cadets and 3,500 ratings.

There are naval bases at Algiers, Annaba and Mers el Kebir.

Air Force. Five MiG-15 jet-fighters were delivered in 1962 as the nucleus of an Algerian Air Force. Since then many more aircraft of Soviet design have followed, and the Air Force now has about 300 combat aircraft and 12,500 personnel. Training and technical assistance have been given by Egypt and the Soviet Union. There are 3 squadrons of MiG-21s, 3 squadrons of MiG-23 variable-geometry interceptors and fighter-bombers, 2 squadrons of MiG-17 fighter-bombers, 2 squadrons of Su-7 and Su-20 variable-geometry attack aircraft, 1 squadron of Il-28 twin-jet bombers, 2 squadrons with MiG-25 fighter and reconnaissance aircraft, more than 30 Mi-24 assault helicopters and gunships, 14 C-130H Hercules and 8 An-12 transports, an Il-18 and a variety of smaller transports, a wing of 4 Mi-6, 12 Mi-8, about 10 Mi-4, 5 Puma and 6 Hughes 269 helicopters, and training units equipped with CM.170 Magister armed jet counter-insurgency/trainers (26), 3 Beech Queen Air twin-engine/instrument trainers, MiG-15s and -15UTIs, and two-seat versions of operational types. Surface-to-air missile units have Soviet-built 'Guidelines', 'Goas', 'Gainfuls' and 'Gaskins'.

INTERNATIONAL RELATIONS

Membership. Algeria is a member of UN, OAU, the Arab League, OAPEC, OPEC and the Maghreb Organization.

ECONOMY

Planning. The second 4-year development plan (1974–77) envisaged investment of DA 110,000m. The third development plan (1980–84) gives priority to education, housing, water supply and agriculture.

Currency. The Algerian currency is the *dinar* (DA). There are in circulation banknotes of DA 5, 10, 50 and 100 and coins of 1, 2, 5, 20 and 50 centimes and DA 1, 5 and 10. In March 1984, £1 = 7·209 DA; US$1 = 4·826.

Budget. The budget (including extraordinary budget) was as follows in calendar years (in DA 1m.):

	1977	1978	1979	1980	1981
Revenue	33,479	36,782	46,429	59,344	68,305
Expenditure	25,472	29,946	33,514	43,214	67,788

Banking. The Banque Centrale d'Algérie is the government emission bank. Other banks operating in Algeria are Banque National d'Algérie, Crédit Populaire d'Algérie, Banque Extérieure d'Algérie, Caisse Algérienne de Développement, Banque Algérienne de Développement, Banque de l'Agriculture et du Développement.

Weights and Measures. The metric system is in use.

ENERGY AND NATURAL RESOURCES

Electricity. Production of energy in 1980 totalled 7·1m. kwh.

Oil. Two large oilfields went into production in 1957 around Edjélé and Hassi Messaoud and in 1959 at El Gassi. In 1960 about 200 wells were productive. Natural gas was discovered at Djebel Berga in 1954 and at Hassi-R'Mel in 1956. Oil pipelines from Edjélé to Skirra (Tunisia) and from Hassi Messaoud to Béjaia, and a gas pipeline from Hassi Messaoud *via* Hassi-R'Mel to Mostaganem–Oran–Algiers, have been completed. Oil production in 1981, 36·5m. tonnes. Production of natural gas in 1981 was 19,347m. cu. metres.

Minerals. Algeria possesses deposits of iron, zinc, lead, mercury, copper and antimony. Kaolin, marble and onyx, salt and coal are also found. Mineral output in 1980 (1,000 tonnes): Ferrous metals, 3,500; zinc, 7·6; copper, 0·8; lead, 2·7; phosphates, 1,025.

Agriculture. The greater part of Algeria is of limited value for agricultural purposes. In the northern portion the mountains are generally better adapted to grazing and forestry than agriculture, and a large portion of the native population is quite poor. In spite of the many excellent roads built by the Government, a considerable area of the mountainous region is without adequate means of communication and is accessible only with difficulty. There were an estimated 7·5m. hectares of agricultural land in 1978–79, of which 6·8m. hectares were arable; 200,000 hectares under vine and 31·7m. hectares pastures and brushlands.

The chief crops in 1980 were (in 1,000 tonnes): Wheat, 1,512; barley, 794; dates, 201; potatoes, 591; oranges, 281; wine, 284; tomatoes, 182; olives, 103; onions, 118; oats, 110.

Livestock, 1982: 134,000 horses, 746,000 mules and asses, 1·39m. cattle, 13·7m. sheep, 2·76m. goats and 150,000 camels.

Forestry. The greater part of the state forests are mere brushwood, but there are very large areas covered with cork-oak trees, Aleppo pine, evergreen oak and cedar. The dwarf-palm is grown on the plains, alfa on the table-land. Timber is cut for firewood, also for industrial purposes, for railway sleepers, telegraph poles, etc., and for bark for tanning. Considerable portions of the forest area are also leased for tillage, or for pasturage for cattle and sheep.

Fisheries. There are extensive fisheries for sardines, anchovies, sprats, tunny fish, etc., and also shellfish. In 1977, 692 boats were employed in fishing. Fish taken in 1980 amounted to 33,615 tonnes, value DA 311m.

INDUSTRY AND TRADE

Industry. The main industries are iron and steel, plastics and fertilizers.

Commerce. The foreign trade of Algeria was as follows (in DA 1m.):

	1977	1978	1979	1980
Imports	29,534	34,439	32,378	41,545
Exports	25,356	25,037	36,505	52,418

In 1980 imports came chiefly from France (23%), Federal Republic of Germany (14%), Italy (12%), USA (7%). Exports went mainly to USA (49%), Federal Republic of Germany (9·5%), France (15%).

Crude oil amounted to 78% and petroleum products 14%, of exports.

Total trade between Algeria and UK (British Department of Trade returns, in £1,000 sterling):

	1978	1979	1980	1981	1982	1983
Imports to UK	37,930	87,526	114,054	159,470	176,304	157,645
Exports and re-exports from UK	120,642	115,016	142,552	172,964	199,234	233,425

Tourism. In 1980, 291,000 tourists visited Algeria.

COMMUNICATIONS

Roads. There were in 1978, 19,157 km of national highway. Motor vehicles in 1980 included 472,483 passenger cars and 283,966 commercial vehicles.

Railways. In 1983 there were 3,890 km of which 2,632 km is of standard gauge (298 km electrified) and 1,258 km of 1,055mm gauge railway open for traffic. In 1981 the railways carried 2,156 tonne-km of freight.

Aviation. There are 5 international airports as well as another 65 airfields controlled by government and 135 owned by petroleum companies. Air Algeria serves the main Algerian cities, and an international network. Algeria is also served by Swissair, Royal Air Maroc and United Arab Airline. In 1980 the airports handled 2·84m. passengers and 22,479 tonnes of freight.

Shipping. In 1980, 63·2m. tonnes of goods were handled at Algerian ports.

A state shipping line, Compagnie Nationale Algérienne de Navigation, was formed in Jan. 1964.

Post and Broadcasting. There were, in 1980, 1,534 post offices; number of telephones (1982), 606,869, of which 186,312 were in Algiers and 48,428 in Oran. In 1974 there were some 3·5m. radio receivers and 500,000 TV licences issued.

Newspapers (1980). There were 4 daily newspapers, 1 in French and 3 in Arabic, with a combined circulation of 350,000.

JUSTICE, RELIGION, EDUCATION AND WELFARE

Justice. There are appeal courts at Algiers, Constantine and Oran; and in the *arrondissements* are 17 courts of first instance. There are also commercial courts and justices of the peace with extensive powers. Criminal justice is organized as in

France. The Supreme Court is at the same time Council of State and High Court of Appeal.

Religion. The overwhelming part of the population are Moslems. The Roman Catholic Church has an archbishop and 2 bishops, with some 400 officiating clergymen. Jews number about 150,000.

Education. In 1982 there were 9,263 state primary schools with 88,481 teachers and 4·6m. pupils; 1,128 secondary schools with 38,845 teachers and 1,029,884 pupils; and 71 technical and teacher-training colleges with 1,168 teachers and 12,903 students in technical education and 1,124 teachers and 13,315 students in teacher-training.

In 1981 there were 72,200 students in higher education including universities at Algiers (with 17,086 students), Oran (9,000), Constantine (8,340), Annaba (6,126), Sétif (5,800) and Boumedes. There are also Universities of Science and Technology at Algiers (11,500) and Oran (5,800) and university centres at Tlemcen, Tizi-Ouzou, Batna, Tiaret, Constantine, Mostaganem and Sidi-Bel-Abbès.

Health. There were in 1980, 182 general and specialized hospitals with together 45,160 beds; there were 6,081 doctors, 1,183 dentists, 778 pharmacists. There were also 1,422 dispensaries and consulting rooms, 747 health centres and 175 specializing centres for tuberculosis, venereal disease and trachoma.

DIPLOMATIC REPRESENTATIVES

Of Algeria in Great Britain (54 Holland Park, London, W11 3RS)
Ambassador: Redha Malek.

Of Great Britain in Algeria (Résidence Cassiopée, 7 Chemin des Glycines, Algiers)
Ambassador: M. E. Pike, CMG.

Of Algeria in the USA (2118 Kalorama Rd., NW, Washington, D.C., 20008)
Ambassador: Layachi Yaker.

Of the USA in Algeria (4 Chemin Cheikh Bachir Brahimi, Algiers)
Ambassador: Michael H. Newlin.

Of Algeria to the United Nations
Ambassador: Mohammed Sahnoun.

Books of Reference

Statistical Information: The Service de Statisque Générale (12, rue Bab-Azoun, Alger) publishes the annual *Statistique Générale de l'Algérie, Documents statistiques sur le commerce de l'Algérie* (from 1902). *Tableaux de l'économie algérienne* (1960).

Hensissart, P., *Wolves in the City: The Death of French Algeria.* New York, 1970
Horne, A., *A Savage War of Peace: Algeria 1954–1962.* London, 1977
Ministère de l'Information et de la Culture, *La Révolution Algérienne: Réalités et Perspectives,* Algiers, 1972.—*Dix années de réalisations 19 juin 1965–19 juin 1975.* Algiers, 1976.— *Statistiques 1967–78.* Algiers, 1980
Lawless, R. I., *Algeria.* [Bibliography] Oxford and Santa Barbara, 1981
Ottaway, D., *Algeria: The Politics of a Socialist Revolution.* Berkeley, 1970
Quandt, W. B., *Revolution and Political Leadership: Algeria, 1954–68.* Cambridge, Mass., 1970

ANDORRA

Capital: Andorre-la-Vieille
Population: 39,940 (1983)

Principat d'Andorra

HISTORY AND CONSTITUTION. The political status of Andorra was regulated by the *Paréage* of 1278 which placed Andorra under the joint suzerainty of the Comte de Foix and of the Bishop of Urgel. The rights vested in the house of Foix passed by marriage to that of Bearn and, on the accession of Henri IV, to the French crown. The sovereignty is exercised jointly by the President of the French Republic and the Bishop of Urgel.

The co-princes are represented in Andorra by the *'Viguier français'* and the *Viguier Episcopal'*. Each co-prince has set up a Permanent Delegation for Andorran affairs; the Prefect of the Eastern Pyrenees is the French Permanent Delegate.

The valleys pay every second year a due of 960 francs to France and 460 pesetas to the bishop.

A 'General Council of the Valleys' submits motions and proposals to the Permanent Delegations. Its 28 members are elected for 4 years; half of the council is renewed every 2 years.

The council nominates a First Syndic *(Syndic Procureur Général)* and a Second Syndic from outside its members.

In Jan. 1982 an Executive Council was appointed, following elections held in Dec. 1981, and legislative and executive powers were separated.

First Syndic: Francesc Cerqueda-Pascuet.

Head of Government: Oscar Ribas-Reig (from 14 Jan. 1982).

Public Works: Josep Vidal Marti. *Finance, Commerce and Industry:* Aleix Santuré. *Agriculture and National Patrimony:* Josep Casal Puigcernal. *Education and Culture:* Antoni Ubach.

National flag: Three vertical strips of blue, yellow, red, with the arms of Andorra in the centre.

AREA AND POPULATION. The co-principality of Andorra is situated in the eastern Pyrenees on the French–Spanish border. The country consists of gorges, narrow valleys and defiles, surrounded by high mountain peaks varying between 1,880 and 3,000 metres. Its maximum length is 30 km and its width 20 km; it has an area of 465 sq. km (190 sq. miles) and a population of (1983) 39,940, scattered in 7 villages.

Catalan is the official and spoken language.

ECONOMY

Budget. The 1979 budget balanced at 3,209m. pesetas.

Currency. French and Spanish currency are both in use.

Tourism. Tourism is the main industry, and over 6m. people visited Andorra in 1982.

COMMUNICATIONS

Roads. A good road connects the Spanish and French frontiers by way of Sant Julià, Andorre-la-Vieille, les Escaldes, Encamp, Canillo and Soldeu: it crosses the Col d'Envalira (2,400 metres). Another road connects Andorre-la-Vieille with La Massana and Ordino. Motor vehicles (1983) 24,789.

Aviation. The nearest airports are at Barcelona and Perpignan.

Post and Broadcasting. Number of telephones (1982) 17,719. Number of receivers (1977), radio, 7,000; TV, 3,000.

JUSTICE, RELIGION AND EDUCATION

Justice. Judicial power is exercised in civil matters in the first instance, according to the plaintiff's choice, by either the *Bayle Français* or the *Bayle Episcopal*, who are nominated by the respective co-princes. The judge of appeal is nominated alternately for 5 years by each co-prince; the third instance *(Tercera Sala)* is either the supreme court of Andorra at Perpignan or the supreme court of the Bishop at Urgel.

Criminal justice is administered by the *Corts* consisting of the 2 Viguiers, the judge of appeal, 2 *rahonadors* elected by the general council of the valleys, a general attorney and an attorney nominated for 5 years alternatively by each of the co-princes. The accused may be assisted by a barrister.

Religion. The prevailing religious denomination is Roman Catholic.

Education. In 1982–83 there were 1,925 pupils at infant schools, 3,453 at primary schools, 2,526 at secondary schools and 170 at technical schools.

Books of Reference

Brutails, *La Coutume d'Andorre*. Paris, 1904
Corts Peyret, J., *Geografia e Historia de Andorra*. Barcelona, 1945
Llobet, S., *El medio y la vida en Andorra*. Barcelona, 1947
Riberaygua-Argelich, B., *Les Valls d'Andorra*. Barcelona, 1946
Vidally Guitart, J. M., *Instituciones politicas y sociales de Andorra*. Madrid, 1949

ANGOLA

República Popular de Angola

Capital: Luanda
Population: 7·11m. (1983)
GNP per capita: US$470 (1980)

HISTORY. The first Europeans to arrive in Angola were the Portuguese in 1482, and the first settlers arrived there in 1491. Luanda was founded in 1575. Apart from a brief period of Dutch occupation from 1641 to 1648, Angola remained a Portuguese colony until 11 June 1951, when it became an Overseas Province of Portugal. On 11 Nov. 1975 Angola became fully independent as the People's Republic of Angola.

AREA AND POPULATION. Angola is bounded by Congo on the north, Zaïre on the north and north-east, Zambia on the east, South West Africa/Namibia on the south and the Atlantic ocean on the west. The area is 1,246,700 sq. km (481,351 sq. miles) including the 7,270 sq. km province of Cabinda, an enclave of territory separated by 30 km of Zaïre. The population at census, 1970, was 5,646,166, of whom 14% urban. Estimate (1983) 7,108,000, of whom 38% speak Umbundu, 27% Kimbundu, 13% Lunda and 11% Kikongo. Portuguese remains the official language. There were (1980) about 38,000 Cubans and 30,000 Europeans (mostly Portuguese) in Angola.

The most important towns (with 1970 populations) are Luanda, the capital (480,613, 1982, 700,000), Huambo (61,885), Lobito (59,258), Benguela (40,996), Lubango (31,674) and Malange (31,559).

CLIMATE. The climate is tropical, with low rainfall in the west but increasing inland. Temperatures are constant over the year and most rain falls in March and April. Luanda. Jan. 78°F (25·6°C), July 69°F (20·6°C). Annual rainfall 13″ (323 mm). Lobito. Jan. 77°F (25°C), July 68°F (20°C). Annual rainfall 14″ (353 mm).

CONSTITUTION AND GOVERNMENT. Under the Constitution adopted at independence, the sole legal party is the *Movimento Popular de Libertação de Angola – Partido do Trabalho.* The supreme organ of state is the unicameral National People's Assembly, whose 203 members were first elected in Aug. 1980 for a 3-year term and a further 20 members appointed by the 55-member Central Committee of the MPLA–PT. There is an executive President, who appoints a Council of Ministers to assist him.

The Council of Ministers in Sept. 1983 was as follows:

President: José Eduardo dos Santos.
Planning: Lopo Fortunato do Nascimento. *Defence:* Col. Pedro Maria Tonha (Pedalé). *Foreign Relations:* Paulo Teixeira Jorge. *Justice:* Dr Diogenes de Assis Boavida. *Education:* Augusto Lopes Teixeira (Tutu). *Health:* António José Ferreira Neto. *Finance:* Augusto Teixeira de Matos. *External Trade:* Ismael Gaspar Martins. *Internal Trade:* Adriano Perreira dos Santos Junior. *Industry:* Maj. Alberto do Carmo Bento Ribeiro. *Transport and Communications:* Fernando Faustino Muteka. *Labour and Social Security:* Horacio Perreira Brás da Silva. *Agriculture:* Artur Vidal Gomes. *State Security:* Col. Julião Mateus Paulo (Dino Matross). *Interior:* Manuel Alexandre Rodrigues (Kito). *Petroleum and Energy:* Pedro Castro Van-Dúnem (Loy). *Construction:* Jorge Henrique Varela de Melo Dias Flora. *Housing:* Lourenço Ferreira (Diandengue). *Provincial Co-ordination:* Maj. Evaristo Domingos (Kimba). *Fisheries:* Emílic Guerra. There are 6 Secretaries of State.

Flag: Horizontally red over black, with a star and an arc of cogwheel crossed by a machete, all yellow over all in the centre.

Local government: Angola is divided into 18 provinces – (Cabinda, Zaïre, Uíge, Luanda, Cuanza Norte, Cuanza Sul, Malange, Lunda Norte, Lunda Sul, Benguela, Huambo, Bié, Moxico, Cuando-Cubango, Namibe, Huíla, Cunene and Bengo) each under a Provincial Commissioner, appointed by the President and an elected legislative of from 55 to 85 members.

DEFENCE. Conscription is for a period of 2 years.

Army. The Army has 2 motorized infantry, 17 infantry, and 4 air defence brigades. Total strength (1984) 35,000. Equipment includes Soviet T-34, T-54 and PT-76 tanks.

Navy. Twenty Portuguese naval craft were transferred on independence in 1975 and 9 vessels were acquired from the Soviet Navy in 1977-79, when 8 merchant ships were taken over from local trade for naval use. There are 4 fast missile boats, 4 fast torpedo boats, 5 patrol craft, 9 coastal patrol boats, 18 landing craft, 1 survey ship and 8 auxiliary vessels. Naval personnel in 1984 totalled 1,500.

Air Force. The Angolan People's Air Force (FAPA) was formed in 1976. Combat equipment is mainly of Soviet origin, comprising about 35 MiG-21 and 25 MiG-17 fighters. FAPA also has 1 F.27 Maritime overwater reconnaissance aircraft, 1 Noratlas, 1 F.27 Friendship, 4 Nord 262, 2 L-100-20 Hercules, 15 An-26 and 3 C-47 transports, 8 Islander twin-engined light transports, 10 Do 27 and 2 Turbo-Porter liaison aircraft, 12 PC-7 Turbo Trainers, 24 L-39 jet trainers, 1 MiG-15UTI, and 27 Alouette III and 35 Mi-8 helicopters. 'Goa' surface-to-air missiles are deployed.

INTERNATIONAL RELATIONS

Membership. Angola is a member of UN and OAU.

ECONOMY

Budget. The 1981 budget balanced at 93,478m. Kwanza.

Currency. The currency is the *kwanza* divided into 100 *lwei*. Coins are of 50 *lwei*, 1, 2, 5 and 10 *kwanza*; notes are of 20, 50, 100, 500 and 1,000 *kwanza*. In March 1984, £1 = 45·4 *kwanza*; US$1 = 30·21 *kwanza.*

Banking. All banking was nationalized in 1975. The *Banco Nacional de Angola* is the central bank and bank of issue, while the *Banco Popular de Angola* handles all commercial activities throughout the country.

Weights and Measures. The metric system is in force.

ENERGY AND NATURAL RESOURCES

Electricity. Production (1977) totalled 1,360 m. kwh, mainly hydro-electricity.

Oil. Total production (1982) 6·5m. tonnes.

Minerals. The country possesses valuable diamond deposits. Production of diamonds during 1981 totalled 1·4m. carats (1978, 650,000). Production (1981) of salt, 38,900 tonnes. There has been no production of iron ore since 1975, but the mines at Kassinga were restarted in 1980 and a second project near Dondo started production in early 1981. Manganese and copper deposits exist.

Agriculture. The principal cash crops (with 1982 production, in 1,000 tonnes) were sugar-cane (410), coffee (35), bananas (280), palm oil (40), palm kernels (12), cotton (33); others include tobacco, citrus fruit and sisal. Food crops comprise cassava (1,950), maize (250), sweet potatoes (180) and beans (40).
  Livestock (1982): 3·25m. cattle, 235,000 sheep, 945,000 goats, 440,000 pigs.

Fisheries. Total catch (1981) 174,100 tonnes.

Forestry. Mahogany and other hardwoods are exported, chiefly from the tropical rain forests of the north, especially Cabinda. Production (1979) 8·56m. cu. metres.

COMMERCE. Imports (1979, in 1m. kwanza), 28,093; exports, 39,531. The chief imports are textiles, transport equipment, foodstuffs, pig-iron and steel; chief exports are crude oil, coffee, diamonds, sisal, fish, maize, palm-oil. In 1981, crude petroleum represented 74% of exports, petroleum products, 10%, coffee 5% and diamonds 10%.

Total trade between Angola and UK for calendar years (British Department of Trade returns, in £1,000 sterling):

	1980	1981	1982	1983
Imports to UK	83,125	6,388	7,368	45,732
Exports and re-exports from UK	27,811	39,507	25,781	22,847

COMMUNICATIONS

Roads. There were, in 1974, 72,323 km of roads, and in 1978, 143,100 cars and 42,600 commercial vehicles.

Railways. The length of railways open for traffic in 1982 was 2,798 km. The Benguela Railway runs from Lobito to the Zaïre border at Dilolo where it connects with the National Railways of Zaïre. Other lines link Luanda with Malange; Gunza with Gabela; and Moçâmedes with Menongue. In 1981 Angola's railways carried 7·6m. passengers and 725,000 tonnes of freight.

Aviation. Luanda has international air links to Lisbon, Rome, Paris, Moscow, Budapest, Brazzaville, Saõ Tomé, Lusaka, Maputo, Sal (Cape Verde Islands), Havana, Kinshasa, Libreville, Berlin, Tripoli, Lagos, Algiers, Niamey, Sofia, Malta, Rio de Janeiro and São Paulo.

Shipping. In 1973, 6,500 vessels of 16,256,322 net tons entered Angolan ports. In 1975, 2·85m. tonnes were discharged and 16m. tonnes loaded in Angolan ports.

Post and Broadcasting. Angola is connected by cable with east, west and south African telegraph systems. There were, in 1973, 1,808 km of telegraph lines, 77 telephone stations (with 29,796 instruments in 1978), 162 telegraph stations and 31 wireless stations.

Rádio Nacional de Angola is the largest of the 18 stations operating on medium- and short-waves. *Rádio Nacional* transmits 3 programmes as well as operating 2 regional stations. Number of radio receivers (1981)125,000 and television receivers 2,000.

Cinemas. There were, in 1972, 47 cinemas with seating capacity of 35,142.

Newspaper. The national daily newspaper is *Jornal de Angola*, with a circulation of 41,000.

RELIGION, EDUCATION AND WELFARE

Religion. Article 7 of the Constitution of the People's Republic of Angola states that: 'The People's Republic of Angola is a secular state, where there is a complete separation of religious institutions from the state. All religions will be respected.'

In 1979 46% of the population were Roman Catholic, 12% Protestant and 42% animist.

Education. In 1983 there were 2·4m. pupils in primary schools, 153,000 in secondary schools and 4,746 students in higher education. The *Universidade de Angola* (founded 1963) at Luanda with faculties at Huambo and Lubango, had 3,500 students in 1982.

Health. In 1972 there were 4 state, 14 regional and 70 rural hospitals and about 260 health centres and dispensaries, with a total of 18,011 hospital beds. In 1973 there were 383 doctors, 87 pharmacists, 284 midwives and 3,115 nursing personnel.

DIPLOMATIC REPRESENTATIVES

Of Great Britain in Angola (Rua Diogo Cao, 4, Luanda)
Ambassador: M. I. Goulding.

Of Angola to the United Nations
Ambassador: Elísio de Figueiredo.

Books of Reference

Anuário Estatistico de Angola. Luanda, from 1897

Araújo, A. Correia de, *Aspectos do desenvolvimento económico e social de Angola.* Lisbon, 1964

Bender, G. J., *Angola under the Portuguese.* London, 1979

Davidson, B., *In the Eye of the Storm.* London, 1972

Dias, G. de Sousa, *Os portugueses em Angola.* Lisbon, 1959

Klinghoffer, A. J., *The Angolan War.* Boulder, 1980

Pélissier, R., *Les guerres grises.* Montamets, 1980—*La Colonie du Minotaure.* Montamets, 1980.—*Le naufrage des coravelles.* Montamets, 1980

Wheeler, D. L., and Pélissier, R., *Angola.* London, 1971

Wolfers, M., and Bergerol., *Angola in the Frontline.* London, 1983

Zirka, A. K., *Angola Libre?* Paris, 1975

ANGUILLA

HISTORY. Anguilla was probably given its name by the Spaniards because of its eel-like shape. After British settlements in the 17th century, the territory was administered as part of the Leeward Islands. From 1825 it became more closely associated with St Kitts and ultimately incorporated in the colony of St Kitts-Nevis-Anguilla. Opposition to this association grew and finally in 1967 the island seceded unilaterally. Following direct intervention by the UK in 1969 Anguilla became *de facto* a separate dependency of Britain; and this was formalized on 19 Dec. 1980 under the Anguilla Act 1980.

AREA AND POPULATION. Anguilla is the most northerly of the Leeward Islands, some 70 miles (112 km) to the north-west of St Kitts and 5 miles (8 km) to the north of St Martin/St Maarten. The territory also comprises the island of Sombrero (on which there is an important lighthouse) and several other off-shore islets or cays. The total area of the territory is about 60 sq. miles (155 sq. km). Census population (1974) was 6,500. The capital is The Valley.

CONSTITUTION AND GOVERNMENT. The House of Assembly consists of a Speaker, 7 elected members, 2 nominated members and 2 official members.

Executive power is vested in the Governor who is appointed by HM The Queen. Apart from his special responsibilities (External Affairs, Defence, Internal Security, including the Police, and the Public Service) and his reserve powers in respect of legislation, the Governor discharges his executive powers on the advice of an Executive Council comprising a Chief Minister, 3 Ministers and 2 official members: Attorney-General and Permanent Secretary, Finance.

Governor: A. T. Baillie.
Chief Minister and Minister of Finance: James Ronald Webster.

ECONOMY

Budget. In 1983, the recurrent budget was: Expenditure EC$11,776,868; Local Revenue EC$11,061,000; Grant-in-Aid EC$715,000.

Currency. The currency is the Eastern Caribbean *dollar.*

NATURAL RESOURCES

Agriculture. Because of low rainfall agriculture potential is limited. Main crops are pigeon peas, corn and sweet potatoes. Livestock consists of sheep, goats, cattle and poultry.

Fisheries. Fishing is a thriving industry with exports to neighbouring islands.

TOURISM. There are some unpretentious hotels, guest houses and apartments. Several new hotels of international standard were completed in 1983 and others are under construction. By Dec. 1984 some 200-300 beds should be available.

COMMUNICATIONS

Roads. There are about 32 miles of tarred roads and 25 miles of secondary roads.

Aviation. There is a 3,600 ft surfaced runway at Wallblake Airport. Apart from regular air taxi and charter flights WINAIR (subsidiary of ALM) provides daily scheduled services between Juliana International Airport, St Maarten and Anguilla.

Shipping. The main seaports are Road Bay and Blowing Point, the latter serving passenger and cargo traffic to and from St Martin.

Post and Telecommunications. There is a modern internal telephone service with (1983) 1,200 exchange lines; and international telegraph, telex and telephone services, all operated by Cable & Wireless.

EDUCATION AND WELFARE

Education. There are 6 government primary schools and 1 secondary school. Tertiary education is provided at regional universities and similar institutions.

Health. There is a 24-bed cottage hospital, clinics and a modern dental clinic.

ANTIGUA AND BARBUDA

Capital: St John's
Population: 74,000 (1981)
GNP per capita: US$ 1,270 (1980)

HISTORY. Antigua was discovered by Colombus in 1493 and named by him after a church in Seville (Spain). It was first colonized by English settlers in 1632; nearby Barbuda was colonized in 1661 from Antigua. Formed part of the Leeward Islands Federation from 1871 until 30 June 1956, when Antigua became a separate Crown Colony, which was part of the West Indies Federation from 3 Jan. 1958 until 31 May 1962. It became an Associated State of the UK on 27 Feb. 1967 and obtained independence on 1 Nov. 1981.

AREA AND POPULATION. Antigua and Barbuda comprises 3 islands of the Lesser Antilles situated in the Eastern Caribbean with a total land area of 442 sq. km (171 sq. miles); it consists of Antigua (280 sq. km), Barbuda, 40 km to the north (161 sq. km) and uninhabited Redonda, 40 km to the southwest (1 sq. km).

The population at the Census of 7 April 1970 was 65,525; the latest estimate (1981) is 74,000. The chief towns are St John's, the capital on Antigua (24,000 inhabitants in 1975) and Codrington, the only settlement on Barbuda.

Vital statistics (1974): Birth rate, 18·3 per 1,000; death rate 7·1 per 1,000.

CLIMATE. A tropical climate, but drier than most West Indies islands. The hot season is from May to Nov., when rainfall is greater. Mean annual rainfall is 40″ (1,000 mm).

CONSTITUTION AND GOVERNMENT

Governor-General: Sir Wilfred Ebenezer Jacobs, KCVO, OBE, QC.

Prime Minister: Right Hon. Vere C. Bird, Sen., PC.

Flag: Red, with a triangle based on the top edge, divided horizontally black, blue, white, with a rising sun in gold on the black portion.

ECONOMY

Budget. The budget for 1982–83 envisaged revenue at EC$99·3m.

Currency. The Eastern Caribbean $. In March 1984, £1 = EC$3·98; US$1 = EC$2·70.

Banking. In government savings bank, 4,917 depositors on 31 Dec. 1971, $432,277 deposits. Barclays Bank International, Royal Bank of Canada, Canadian Imperial Bank of Commerce, the Virgin Islands National Bank, the Antilles International Trust Co. and the Bank of Nova Scotia have branches at St John's. The Antigua Co-operative Bank was opened in Jan. 1965.

AGRICULTURE. Sugar, cotton and fruits are the main crops. There were 40,000 lb. of cotton produced in 1981, 105,000 in 1980.

Livestock (1982): Cattle, 6,000; pigs, 7,000; sheep, 9,000; goats, 7,000; poultry, 70,000.

INDUSTRY AND TRADE

Commerce. Imports in 1975 amounted to EC$145·14m. (of which 19% came from the UK and 19% from the US) and exports to EC$59·92m. of which the major amount came from bunkering provided to ships.

Tourism. There were 67,412 tourists (excluding cruise passengers) in 1978.

COMMUNICATIONS

Roads. There are 600 miles of roads (150 miles main road).

Shipping. The main harbour is the St John's deep water harbour. There are 2 tugs for the berthing of ships and all modern and efficient general cargo handling equipment. The harbour can also accommodate 3 large cruise ships simultaneously.

Post and Broadcasting. Telephone lines, 720 miles; 3,104 telephones.

RELIGION, EDUCATION AND WELFARE.

Religion. The vast majority of the population are Christian, preponderantly Anglican.

Education. In 1977 there were 13,285 pupils and 477 teachers in primary schools and 6,458 pupils and 271 teachers in secondary schools.

Health. There is a general hospital (Holberton) with 215 beds, a mental hospital with 200 beds, a geriatric unit with 150 beds, 4 health centres and 16 dispensaries.

DIPLOMATIC REPRESENTATIVES

Of Antigua and Barbuda in Great Britain (10 Kensington Ct., London, W8)
High Commissioner: Dr Claudius C. Thomas, CMG.

Of Great Britain in Antigua and Barbuda (38 St Mary's St., St John's)
High Commissioner: G. L. Bullard, CMG.

Of Antigua and Barbuda in the USA (2000 N. St., NW, Washington, D.C., 20036)
Ambassador: Edmund Hawkins Lake.

Of the USA in Antigua and Barbuda
Ambassador: Milan D. Bish (resides in Bridgetown).

Of Antigua and Barbuda to the United Nations
Ambassador: Lloydston Jacobs.

ARGENTINA

República Argentina

Capital: Buenos Aires
Population: 27·95m. (1980)
GNP per capita: US$2,390 (1980)

HISTORY. In 1515 Juan Díaz de Solis discovered the Río de La Plata. In 1534 Pedro de Mendoza was sent by the King of Spain to take charge of the 'Gobernación y Capitanía de las tierras del Rio de La Plata', and in Feb. 1536 he founded the city of the 'Puerto de Santa María del Buen Aire'. In 1810 the population rose against Spanish rule, and in 1816 Argentina proclaimed its independence. Civil wars and anarchy followed until, in 1853, stable government was established.

AREA AND POPULATION. The Argentine Republic is bounded in the north by Bolivia, in the north-east by Paraguay, in the east by Brazil, Uruguay and the Atlantic Ocean and the west by Chile. The republic consists of 22 provinces, 1 federal district and the National Territories of Tierra del Fuego, the Antarctic and the South Atlantic Islands (census of 1980) as follows:

Provinces	Area: sq. km. 1960	Population: census, 1980	Capital	Population census, 1980 (1,000)
Litoral				
Federal Capital	200	2,922,829	Buenos Aires	2,908
Buenos Aires	307,804	10,365,408	La Plata	455
Corrientes	88,199	661,454	Corrientes	180
Entre Ríos	76,216	908,313	Paraná	160
Chaco	99,633	701,392	Resistencia	218
Santa Fé	133,007	2,465,546	Santa Fé	287
Formosa	72,066	295,887	Formosa	95
Misiones	29,801	588,977	Posadas	140
Norte				
Jujuy	53,219	410,008	San Salvador de Jujuy	124
Salta	154,775	662,870	Salta	260
Santiago del Estero	135,254	594,920	Santiago del Estero	148
Tucumán	22,524	972,655	San Miguel de Tucuman	497
Centro				
Córdoba	168,766	2,407,754	Córdoba	969
La Pampa	143,440	208,260	Santa Rosa	52
San Luis	76,748	214,416	San Luis	71
Andina				
Catamarca	99,818	207,717	Catamarca	88
La Rioja	92,331	164,217	La Rioja	67
Mendoza	150,839	1,196,228	Mendoza	597
San Juan	86,137	465,976	San Juan	118
Neuquén	94,078	243,850	Neuquén	90
Patagonia				
Chubut	224,686	263,116	Rawson	52
Rio Negro	203,013	383,354	Viedma	24
Santa Cruz	243,943	114,941	Rio Gallegos	43
Tierra del Fuego [2]	20,912	29,392	Ushuaia	11
Grand total	2,777,815 [1]	27,949,480		

[1] Total area claimed was 2,808,602 sq. km (1,084,120 sq. miles).

[2] The official census including the 'Antarctic Sector', and stated to comprise the 'Malvinas' (Falklands), South Orcadas (Orkneys), South Georgias, South Sandwich Islands and the 'sovereign territories of Argentina in the Antarctic': population 3,300.

Other large towns (1970 Census): Rosario (750,455), Mar del Plata (302,282), Bahia Blanca (182,158).

CLIMATE. The climate is warm temperate over the pampas, where rainfall occurs at all seasons, but diminishes towards the west. In the north and west, the climate is more arid, with high summer temperatures, while in the extreme south conditions are also dry, but much cooler. Buenos Aires. Jan. 74°F (23·3°C), July 50°F (10°C). Annual rainfall 37″ (950 mm). Bahia Blanca. Jan. 74°F (23·3°C), July 48°F (8·9°C). Annual rainfall 21″ (523 mm). Mendoza. Jan. 75°F (23·9°C), July 47°F (8·3°C). Annual rainfall 8″ (190 mm). Rosario. Jan. 76°F (24·4°C), July 51°F (10·6°C). Annual rainfall 35″ (869 mm). San Juan. Jan. 78°F (25·6°C), July 50°F (10°C). Annual rainfall 4″ (89 mm). San Miguel de Tucuman. Jan. 79°F (26·1°C), July 56°F (13·3°C). Annual rainfall 38″ (970 mm). Ushuaia. Jan. 50°F (10°C), July 34°F (1·1°C). Annual rainfall 19″ (475 mm).

CONSTITUTION AND GOVERNMENT. Military leaders supported by the Navy and Air Force staged a *coup d'état* on 27 June 1966, and the temporary Revolutionary Junta of the Commanders-in-Chief of the three Armed Services deposed Dr Illia and his Government elected in 1963. A former Commander-in-Chief of the Army, Lieut.-Gen. Ongania, was appointed President and the Junta dissolved. The previous Constitution remained in force in so far as it was consistent with the statutes and objectives of the Revolution. For details of earlier Constitutions *see* THE STATESMAN'S YEAR-BOOK, 1982–83.

Presidential, congressional and municipal elections will take place on 30 Oct. 1983 and a return to civilian rule took place on 10 Dec. 1983.

The following is a list of Presidents from 1966 onwards:

Gen. Juan Carlos Onganía. 29 June 1966–8 June 1970. (Deposed.)

Brig.-Gen. Robert Marcelo Levingston. 18 June 1970–22 March 1971. (Deposed.)

Gen. Alejandro Agustin Lanusse. 26 March 1971–May 1973.

Dr Hector Cámpora. 27 May 1973–13 July 1973.

Gen. Juan Domingo Perón. 12 Oct. 1973–1 July 1974.

Maria Estela (Isabel) Martinez Perón. 1 July 1974 (*a.i.* from 29 June 1974)–23 March 1976. (Deposed.)

Gen. Jorge Rafael Videla. 29 March 1976–29 March 1981.

Gen. Roberto Viola, 29 March–22 Dec. 1981.

Gen. Leopoldo Fortunato Galtieri, 22 Dec. 1981–17 June 1982.

Gen. Reynaldo Benito Antonio Bignone, 1 July 1982–10 Dec. 1983.

President of the Republic: Dr Raúl Alfonsín (sworn in 10 Dec. 1983).

Vice-President: Dr Víctor Martínez.

The Cabinet in March 1984 was composed as follows:

Foreign Affairs: Dante Caputto. *Interior:* Dr Antonio Tróccili. *Treasury and Finance:* Dr Bernardo Grinspun. *Labour:* Antonio Mucci. *Defence:* Raúl Borrás. *Education and Justice:* Dr Carlos Alconada Aramburú. *Public Health and Environment:* Aldo Neri. *Public Works:* Roque Carranza.

National flag: Three horizontal stripes of light blue, white and light blue, with the gold Sun of May in the centre.

National anthem: Oid, mortales, el grito sagrado Libertad (words by V. López y Planes, 1813; tune by J. Blas Parera).

Local Government. From June 1966 the governors have been appointed by the President and are responsible to him.

DEFENCE

Army. The Army is a National Militia, service in which is compulsory for all citizens from their 18th to their 45th year. Naturalized citizens are exempt for a period of 10 years. For the first 10 years the men belong to the 'active' Army, or first line. After completing 10 years in the first line the men pass to the National Guard, and serve in it for another 10 years, finishing their service with 5 years in the Territorial Guard; the latter is mobilized only in case of war. The period of continuous service, or training in the ranks with the permanent forces, is for 1 year for the Army or Air Force, and 14 months for the Navy. The reservists can be called out for training periodically.

The territory of the republic is divided into 5 military districts for administrative purposes. The Army is organized in 5 army corps; it consists of 2 armoured and 3 mechanized infantry, 2 infantry, 1 airborne, 2 mountain and 2 jungle brigades; 16 artillery, 1 aviation and 5 air defence battalions.

In 1984 the Army was 100,000 strong, of whom 80,000 were conscripts.

The trained reserve numbers about 250,000, of whom 200,000 belong to the National Guard and 50,000 to the Territorial Guard.

Navy. Principal ships of the Argentine Navy:[3]

Completed	Name	Standard displacement Tons	Aircraft	Guns	Shaft horsepower	Speed Knots
		Aircraft Carrier [1]				
1945	Veinticinco de Mayo [2]	15,892	18 fixed-wing, 4 helicopters	9 40mm	40,000	24·0

[1] The aircraft carrier *Independence*, ex-*Warrior*, purchased from the UK in 1958 was withdrawn from service in 1971.

[2] Ex-*Karel Doorman*, purchased from the Netherlands in 1968, ex-*Venerable*, purchased from UK in 1948.

[3] The cruiser *General Belgrano*, ex-*Phoenix*, purchased from the USA in 1951 was sunk by the British fleet submarine *Conqueror* in May 1982. Sister ship *Nueve de Julio* (ex-USS *Bloise*) was withdrawn from service in 1980. The cruiser *La Argentina* was stricken from the list in 1975.

There are 2 modern German-built submarines, 1 old *ex*-US submarine, 2 new German-built destroyers, 2 new British-built destroyers (Type 42), 5 old *ex*-US destroyers, 2 German-designed medium frigates, 3 new French-built small frigates, 2 old training frigates, 4 coastal minesweepers, 2 minehunters, 4 patrol vessels (armed ocean tugs), 2 fast patrol vessels, 2 torpedo boats, 6 patrol craft, 2 survey ships, 2 survey launches, 2 training ships, 5 transports, 3 oilers, 1 tank landing ship, 20 minor landing craft, 58 auxiliary amphibious craft, 2 polar ships, 20 ancillary vessels and service craft and 12 tugs.

The new construction programme includes 6 diesel-powered patrol submarines (three building and three projected), 2 destroyers and 4 fast frigates.

The submarine *Sante Fe*, ex-USS *Catfish*, was damaged and beached during the Falklands invasion in April 1982. The corvette (patrol vessel) *Comodoro Somellera* was sunk in May 1982.

The active personnel of the Navy in 1984 comprised 30,900 (2,900 officers and 28,000 men, including 12,000 conscripts). The Marine Corps numbered 6,000 including coast artillery.

The *Prefectura Naval Argentina* (PNA) for Coast Guard and rescue duties comprises five new 910-ton corvettes with helicopter and hangar, an ex-whaler of 1,000 tons, a former fleet minesweeper of 650 tons, 8 patrol vessels, 34 coastal patrol craft and a training ship.

The Naval Aviation Service, formed on 17 Oct. 1919, has some 140 fixed-wing aircraft and helicopters with 2,000 personnel, in 6 wings. Aircraft include 10 A-4Q Skyhawk attack bombers, 18 Aermacchi M.B. 326 and 7 M.B.339A light jet armed trainers, 3 P-2H Neptune and 10 S-2E ship-based Tracker anti-submarine aircraft, navalized Harvard trainers, and North American armed T-28s bought from

France, and a dozen types of training, transport and general purpose aircraft, plus 7 types of helicopters. A variable mix of Skyhawks, Trackers and Sea King and Alouette helicopters operated from the aircraft carrier.

Air Force. The Air Force, founded on 10 Aug. 1912 and autonomous since 4 Jan. 1945, is organized into Air Operations, Air Regions, Materiel and Personnel Commands. Air Operations Command, responsible for all operational flying, is made up of air brigades, each with 1 to 4 squadrons, usually operating from a single base. No. I Air Brigade is a military air transport service, with responsibility also for LADE (state airline) operations into areas of Argentina not served by civilian companies. Its equipment includes 8 C-130E/H Hercules and 10 F.27 Friendship/ Troopship turboprop transports, 2 KC-130H Hercules tanker/transports, 5 twin-turbofan F.28 Fellowship freighters, 5 Twin Otters, 15 Guarani IIs, the Presidential Boeing 707-320B and 707-320C, 2 more 707s, 2 VIP Fellowships, and many older or smaller types. No. II Air Brigade has 5 Canberra twin-jet bombers and 2 Canberra trainers; a photographic squadron with Guarani IIs. No. III Air Brigade has 2 squadrons of IA 58 Pucara twin-turboprop COIN aircraft. No. IV Air Brigade comprises 2 ground attack squadrons equipped with about 15 A-4P Skyhawks and 15 Paris light jet combat and liaison aircraft. No. V Air Brigade comprises 2 squadrons with a total of about 30 A-4P Skyhawk strike aircraft. No. VI Air Brigade has 40 Dagger (Israeli-built Mirage III) fighters, equipping 2 squadrons. No. VII Air Brigade has 2 COIN, general-purpose, and search and rescue squadrons with 12 armed Hughes 500M, 5 Lama, 5 Sikorsky S-58T/S-61, 8 Bell 212 and 9 Bell UH-1 helicopters; and a COIN/training squadron of T-34 Mentors. No. VIII Air Brigade has 1 squadron with 14 Mirage IIIE fighter-bombers and 2 Mirage IIID trainers. Recent purchases, not listed above, include more than 30 Mirage III/5 fighters. There is a flying school at Córdoba, equipped with piston-engined T-34 Mentors and Paris jets. There are about 17,500 personnel and 180 combat aircraft.

INTERNATIONAL RELATIONS

Membership. Argentina is a member of UN, OAS and LAIA (formerly LAFTA).

ECONOMY

Budget. The financial year commences on 1 Nov. Budget receipts in 1980 33,459,261m. pesos and expenditure 37,248,461m. pesos.

Currency. The monetary system is on a gold-exchange standard, the unit for foreign transactions being, nominally, the *peso oro* (gold peso) and for domestic transactions, the *peso argentino* (paper peso), legal tender for all domestic debts.

The gold peso weighs 1·6129 grammes of gold 0·900 fine; it is divided into 100 *centavos*, but gold is not in circulation. Circulation consists chiefly of paper notes (issued since 1897) ranging from 1,000 down to 10 cents. The coins actually circulating, 1984, were steel-nickel, 50, 20 and 10 centavos. In March 1984, US$1 = 28,665 *pesos*; £1 = 42,095 *pesos*.

Banking. A law promulgated 25 March 1946 nationalized the Central Bank (established in 1935), as an autonomous institution. Six decree-laws of Oct. 1957 have brought back a greater elasticity to the structure, especially as regards the deposits and loans of the private banks, which have regained their autonomy.

In 1980 there were 29 government banks, 160 private banks and 22 foreign banks. There are 6 Stock Exchanges.

Weights and Measures. Since 1 Jan. 1887 the use of the metric system has been compulsory.

ENERGY AND NATURAL RESOURCES

Electricity. Electric power production (1972) was 25,319 kwh.

Oil and gas. Crude oil production (1980) 179·8m. bbls. Investment of

US$10,000m. is envisaged by 1985 in the oil industry with the aim of achieving self-sufficiency. Natural gas production (1980) 9,900,000m. cu. metres.

Minerals. Argentina produced 726,900 tonnes of washed coal in 1979. Gold, silver and copper are worked in Catamarca, where there are also 2 tin-mines, and gold and copper in San Juan, La Rioja and the south-western territories. Iron ore (102,000 tonnes in 1972), tungsten, beryllium, mica, uranium (25 tonnes in 1972), lead (39,000 tonnes in 1972), barites, zinc (43,500 tonnes in 1972), tin (1·8m. tonnes in 1972), manganese and limestone are produced.

Agriculture. Argentina has an area of about 670,251,000 acres, of which about 41% is pasture land, 32% woodland and 11% (73·73m. acres) cultivated.

Livestock (1982): Cattle 57,882,000; sheep, 30m.; pigs, 3·9m.; horses, 3m. The Province of Buenos Aires has 38% of the cattle. Wool production, 1972, was 194,000 tonnes.

Crop statistics with area (in 1,000 hectares) and production (in 1,000 tonnes) are shown as follows:

	1976–77		1977–78 [1]		1978–79 [1]	
	Area	Output	Area	Output	Area	Output
Wheat	7,192	11,000	4,600	5,300	5,230	7,800
Linseed	722	617	950	810	900	630
Maize	2,980	8,300	3,100	9,700	3,300	9,000
Oats	1,471	530	1,480	570	1,545	676
Barley	962	650	890	353	761	554
Rye	2,300	330	2,140	170	1,722	210
Sunflower seed	1,460	900	2,200	1,600	1,745	1,270
Sugar-cane	360	16,000	356	13,600	350	14,100

[1] Provisional.

Argentina's meat exports are calculated in terms of actual weight; not 'carcase weight', as is the international practice.

Cotton, potatoes, vine, tobacco, citrus fruit, olives, rice, soya, and yerba maté (Paraguayan tea) are also cultivated. There are 36 cane-sugar mills and 1 beet-sugar factory; production, 1979, 14·12m. tonnes. Potato harvest, 1979, amounted to 1,694,000 tonnes. The area under tobacco, 1979, was 76,000 hectares; output 68,000 tonnes.

Sunflower seed, first grown by Russian immigrants in 1900, now furnishes the country's most popular edible oil. There are more than 10m. olive trees, of which 48% are in Mendoza. 672,000 tonnes of groundnuts were produced in 1979 (mainly in Córdoba). Argentina is the world's largest source of tannin.

Fisheries. Fish landings in 1979 amounted to 658,688 tonnes.

INDUSTRY AND TRADE

Industry. Production (1979 in tonnes) Paper, 39,000; sulphuric acid, 279,066; cement, 6·7m. Motor vehicles produced (1981) totalled, 172,350; television receivers, 262,000.

Commerce. Import values include charges for carriage, insurance and freight; export values are on a f.o.b. basis. Real values of foreign trade (in US$1m.), exclusive of coin and bullion:

	1974	1975	1976	1977	1978	1979	1980
Imports	3,216	3,510	2,766	4,162	3,834	6,300	10,400
Exports	3,930	2,961	3,916	5,652	6,400	7,750	8,000

Total trade between Argentina and UK (British Department of Trade returns, in £1,000 sterling):

	1978	1979	1980	1981	1982	1983
Imports to UK	153,191	145,064	114,286	136,892	58,728	194
Exports and re-exports from UK	113,826	128,278	172,830	161,192	37,349	4,472

Tourism. In 1982, 800,000 tourists visited Argentina.

COMMUNICATIONS

Roads. In 1978 there were 207,630 km of national and provincial highways. The 4 main roads constituting Argentina's portion of the Pan-American Highway were opened to traffic in 1942. In 1981 there were 3·19m. cars and 1·23m. commercial vehicles.

Railways. The system based on the 1949 amalgamation of 18 government, British and French-owned railways, comprises 6 railways with a total route-km in 1983 of 33,807 km (142 km electrified) on metre, 1,435 mm and 1,676 mm gauges. In 1981 railways carried 17·6m. tonnes of freight and 345m. passengers.

Aviation. There were (1980) 10 international airports. Commercial airlines flew a total of 94m. km in 1980, carrying 5·6m. passengers and 54,400 tonnes of freight.

Shipping. The merchant fleet, 31 Dec. 1976 (registered with Lloyd's), consisted of 1,869,662 GRT; traffic during 1971: vessels of 13·27m. GRT entered ports; 14m. tonnes of goods were unloaded and 10·6m. tonnes were loaded.

Post and Broadcasting. In 1949 the telephone service was nationalized; instruments numbered 3,041,475 in 1982. There were (1984) 122 radio stations and 4 television channels in Buenos Aires. In 1980 there were 7·5m. radio receivers and 5·6m. television receivers.

Cinemas (1972). Cinemas numbered 1,650, with seating capacity of 611,400.

Newspapers (1984). Daily newspapers numbered 297. Buenos Aires had (1984) 11 daily newspapers with a circulation of 2·5m.

JUSTICE, RELIGION, EDUCATION AND WELFARE

Justice. Justice is administered by federal and provincial courts. The former deal only with cases of a national character, or in which different provinces or inhabitants of different provinces are parties. The chief federal court is the Supreme Court, with 5 judges at Buenos Aires. Other federal courts are the appeal courts, at Buenos Aires, Bahía Blanca, La Plata, Córdoba, Mendoza, Tucumán and Resistencia. Each province has its own judicial system, with a Supreme Court (generally so designated) and several minor chambers. Trial by jury is established by the Constitution for criminal cases, but never practised, except occasionally in the provinces of Buenos Aires and Córdoba.

The death penalty was re-introduced in 1976 for the killing of government, military police and judicial officials, and for participation in terrorist activities.

The police force is centralized under the Federal Security Council.

Religion. The Roman Catholic religion is supported by the State and membership was 23·67m. in 1976.

There are several Protestant denominations with a total congregation (1983) of 500,000.

The Jewish congregation numbered 300,000 in 1983.

Education. In 1981 the primary schools had 218,294 teachers and 4,218,992 pupils; secondary schools had 191,096 teachers and 1,366,444 pupils.

There are National Universities at Buenos Aires (2), Córdoba (2), La Plata, Tucumán, Santa Fé (Litoral), Rosario, Corrientes (Nordeste,), Mendoza (Cuyo), Bahía Blanca (Sur), Catamarca, Tandil, Neuquén (Comahue), San Salvador de Jujuy, Salta, Santa Rosa (La Pampa), Mar del Plata, Comodoro Rivadavia (Patagonia), Río Cuarto, Entre Ríos, Resistencia, San Juan and Santiago del Estero. There are also private universities in Buenos Aires (6), Mendoza (3), Córdoba, Comodoro Rivadavia, La Plata, Morón, Tucumán, Salta, Santa Fé and Santiago del Estero. In 1981 universities had 525,688 students and 54,039 lecturers.

Health. Free medical attention is obtainable from public hospitals. Many trade unions provide medical, dental and maternity services for their members and dependants. A Ministry of Social Welfare was set up in 1966. In 1971 there were 2,864 hospitals with 133,847 beds and in 1975 there were 48,693 doctors.

DIPLOMATIC REPRESENTATIVES

Diplomatic links with Argentina were broken by Great Britain in April 1982 following the invasion of the Falkland Islands.

Of Argentina in the USA (1600 New Hampshire Ave., NW, Washington, 20009) *Ambassador:* Lucio Garcia del Solar.

Of the USA in Argentina (4300 Colombia, Palermo, Buenos Aires) *Ambassador:* Frank Ortiz.

Of Argentina to the United Nations *Ambassador:* Dr Carlos M. Muñiz.

Books of Reference

Boletin del comercio exterio Argentino y estadisticas económicas retrospectivas. Annual
Anuario de comercio exterior de la República Argentina. Annual
Economic Review, Banco de la Nación. Buenos Aires
Sintesis Estadistica Mensual. Dirección General de Estadistica. Buenos Aires, 1947 ff.
Boletin Internacional de Bibliografia Argentina. Ministry of Foreign Relations. Buenos Aires. Monthly
Geografia de la República Argentino. Ed. by the Sociedad Argentina de Estudios Geográficos. 7 vols. Buenos Aires. 1945–53
Bridges, E. L., *Uttermost Part of the Earth [Tierra del Fuego].* New York, 1949
Ferns, H. S., *Britain and Argentina in the 19th Century.* OUP, 1960.—*The Argentine Republic 1516–1971.* Newton Abbot, 1973
Graham-Yooll, A., *The Forgotten Colony: A History of the English-Speaking Communities in Argentina.* London, 1981
Santillán, Diego A. de (ed.), *Gran Enciclopedia Argentina.* 9 vols. 1956–64
Snow, P. G., *Political Forces in Argentina.* Rev. ed. New York and London, 1979

AUSTRALIA

Capital: Canberra
Population: 15·28m. (1982)
GNP per capita: US$9,820 (1980)

HISTORY. On 1 Jan. 1901 New South Wales, Victoria, Queensland, South Australia, Western Australia and Tasmania were federated under the name of the 'Commonwealth of Australia', the designation of 'colonies' being at the same time changed into that of 'states'—except in the case of Northern Territory, which was transferred from South Australia to the Commonwealth as a 'territory' on 1 Jan. 1911.

In 1911 the Commonwealth acquired from the State of New South Wales the Canberra site for the Australian capital. Building operations were begun in 1923 and Parliament was opened at Canberra on 9 May 1927 by HRH the Duke of York (afterwards King George VI). A further area at Jervis Bay was acquired in 1915.

Territories under the administration of Australia in Jan. 1977, but not included in it, comprise Norfolk Island, the territory of Ashmore and Cartier Islands, and the Australian Antarctic Territory (24 Aug. 1936), comprising all the islands and territory other than Adélie Land, situated south of 60° S. lat. and between 160° and 45° E. long.

The British Government transferred sovereignty in the Heard Island and McDonald Islands to the Australian Government on 26 Dec. 1947. Cocos (Keeling) Islands on 23 Nov. 1955 and Christmas Island on 1 Oct. 1958 were also transferred to Australian jurisdiction.

AREA AND POPULATION. Area and resident population (estimate), 31 Dec. 1982:

States and Territories (capitals in brackets)	Area (sq. km)	Males	Females	Total	Per 100 sq. km
New South Wales (Sydney)	801,600	2,656,900	2,675,300	5,332,200	665
Victoria (Melbourne)	227,600	1,991,700	2,021,500	4,013,200	1,763
Queensland (Brisbane)	1,727,200	1,231,300	1,218,600	2,449,900	142
South Australia (Adelaide)	984,000	660,900	673,200	1,334,100	136
Western Australia (Perth)	2,525,500	683,000	668,400	1,351,400	54
Tasmania (Hobart)	67,800	214,000	216,700	430,600	635
Northern Territory (Darwin)	1,346,200	69,700	61,600	131,400	10
Aust. Cap. Terr. (Canberra)	2,400	116,500	116,700	233,200	9,717
Total	7,682,300	7,624,000	7,652,100	15,276,100	199

Resident population (estimate) in State capitals and other major cities, 30 June 1982:

Statistical division	State	Persons
Sydney	NSW	3,310,500
Melbourne	Vic.	2,836,800
Brisbane	Qld	1,124,200
Adelaide	SA	960,000
Perth	WA	948,900
Newcastle [1]	NSW	410,300
Canberra [1] [2]	ACT	251,000
Wollongong [1]	NSW	233,700
Hobart	Tas.	178,800
Gold Coast [1] [3]	Qld	172,500
Geelong [1]	Vic.	142,900

[1] Statistical District of 100,000 persons or more.
[2] Includes Queanbeyan.
[3] Includes Tweed Heads.

The number of occupied dwellings in Australia (at 1981 census) was 4,691,425, distributed as follows: New South Wales, 1,669,596; Victoria, 1,243,453; Queensland, 703,964; South Australia, 433,841; Western Australia, 405,999;

96

Tasmania, 136,269; Northern Territory, 29,563; Australian Capital Territory, 68,740. There were also 469,742 unoccupied dwellings. Total completed new dwellings numbered 138,310 in 1981–2.

Vital statistics for 1982:

States and Territories	Marriages	Divorces	Births	Deaths	Infant deaths
New South Wales	41,955	14,378	83,489	42,352	823
Victoria	28,851	11,266	59,983	30,611	641
Queensland	18,928	6,770	40,540	18,149	432
South Australia	10,936	4,526	19,294	10,457	221
Western Australia	10,455	3,842	22,236	8,187	204
Tasmania	3,576	1,391	7,002	3,432	55
Northern Territory	818	369	2,880	573	57
Aust. Cap. Terr.	1,756	1,546	4,479	1,010	49
Total	11,275	44,088	239,903	114,771	2,482
Rate [1]	7·7	2·9	15·8	7·6	10·3 [2]

[1] Resident (estimate).
[2] Per 1,000 live births registered.

Overseas arrivals during 1982 numbered 2,409,519 and departures 2,300,708. Of these 195,202 were long-term and permanent arrivals and 92,342 were long-term and permanent departures. Of these 107,171 came to Australia intending to settle. There were 22,493 Australian residents departing permanently.

Australian Bureau of Statistics, *Australian Demographic Statistics.* Quarterly. Canberra, June 1979 to date

National Population Inquiry, Population and Australia, A Demographic Analysis and Projection. Canberra, 1975

National Population Inquiry, Population and Australia: Recent Demographic Trends and their Implications. Canberra, 1978

CLIMATE. Over most of the continent, four seasons may be recognised. Spring is from Sept. to Nov., Summer from Dec. to Feb., Autumn from March to May and Winter from June to Aug., but because of its great size there are climates that range from tropical monsoon to cool temperate, with large areas of desert as well. In Northern Australia there are only two seasons, the wet one lasting from Nov. to March, but rainfall amounts diminish markedly from the coast to the interior. Central and southern Queensland are subtropical, north and central New South Wales are warm temperate, as are parts of Victoria, Western Australia and Tasmania, where most rain falls in winter. Canberra. Jan. 68°F (20°C), July 42°F (5·6°C). Annual rainfall 23″ (584 mm). Adelaide. Jan. 73°F (22·8°C), July 52°F (11·1°C). Annual rainfall 21″ (536 mm). Brisbane. Jan. 77°F (25°C), July 58°F (14·4°C). Annual rainfall 45″ (1,135 mm). Darwin. Jan. 83°F (28·3°C), July 77°F (25°C). Annual rainfall 59″ (1,491 mm). Hobart. Jan. 62°F (16·7°C), July 46°F (7·8°C). Annual rainfall 24″ (610 mm). Melbourne. Jan. 67°F (19·4°C), July 49°F (9·4°C). Annual rainfall 26″ (653 mm). Perth. Jan. 74°F (23·3°C), July 55°F (12·8°C). Annual rainfall 35″ (881 mm). Sydney. Jan. 71°F (21·7°C), July 53°F (11·7°C). Annual rainfall 47″ (1,181 mm).

CONSTITUTION AND GOVERNMENT. *Federal Government:* Under the Australian Constitution legislative power in Australia is vested in a Federal Parliament, consisting of the Queen, represented by a Governor-General, a Senate and a House of Representatives. Under the terms of the constitution there must be a session of parliament at least once a year.

The Senate comprises 64 Senators (10 for each State voting as one electorate and as from Aug. 1974, 2 Senators respectively for the Australian Capital Territory and the Northern Territory). Senators representing the States are chosen for 6 years. The terms of Senators representing the Territories expire at the close of the day next preceding the polling day for the general elections of the House of Representatives. In general, the Senate is renewed to the extent of one-half every 3 years, but in case of disagreement with the House of Representatives, it, together with the House of Representatives, may be dissolved, and an entirely new Senate elected. The

House of Representatives consists, as nearly as practicable, of twice as many Members as there are Senators, the numbers chosen in the several States being in proportion to population as shown by the latest statistics, but not less than 5 for any original State. The numerical size of the House after the election in 1980 was 125, including the Members for Northern Territory and the Australian Capital Territory. The Northern Territory has been represented by 1 Member in the House of Representatives since 1922, and the Australian Capital Territory by 1 Member since 1949 and 2 Members since May 1974. The Member for the Australian Capital Territory was given full voting rights as from the Parliament elected in Nov. 1966. The Member for the Northern Territory was given full voting rights in 1968. The House of Representatives continues for 3 years from the date of its first meeting, unless sooner dissolved. Every Senator or Member of the House of Representatives must be a British subject, be of full age, possess electoral qualifications and have resided for 3 years within Australia. The franchise for both Houses is the same and is based on universal (males and females aged 18 years) suffrage. Compulsory voting was introduced in 1925. If a Member of a State Parliament wishes to be a candidate in a federal election, he must first resign his State seat.

Executive power in Australia is vested in the Governor-General, who is advised by an Executive Council. This is presided over by the Governor-General, and its members hold office at his pleasure. All Ministers of State, who are members of the party or parties commanding a majority in the lower House, are members of the Executive Council under summons. A record of proceedings of meetings is kept by the Secretary to the Council. At Executive Council meetings the decisions of the Cabinet are (where necessary) given legal form, appointments made, resignations accepted, proclamations, regulations and the like made.

The policy of a ministry is, in practice, determined by the Ministers of State meeting without the Governor-General under the chairmanship of the Prime Minister. This group is known as the Cabinet. The Cabinet of the Liberal–National Country Party Coalition Government comprises the 14 senior Ministers. Other Ministers attend meetings of Cabinet only when required. Meetings of the full Ministry are held when necessary. There are 11 Standing Committees of the Cabinet comprising varying numbers of Cabinet and non-Cabinet Ministers. In Labor Governments all Ministers have been members of Cabinet. Cabinet meetings are private and deliberative and records of meetings are not made public. The Cabinet does not form part of the legal mechanisms of Government; the decisions it takes have, in themselves, no legal effect. The Cabinet substantially controls, in ordinary circumstances, not only the general legislative programme of Parliament but the whole course of Parliamentary proceedings. In effect, though not in form, the Cabinet, by reason of the fact that all Ministers are members of the Executive Council, is also the dominant element in the executive government of the country.

The legislative powers of the Federal Parliament embrace trade and commerce, shipping, etc.; taxation, finance, banking, currency, bills of exchange, bankruptcy, insurance; defence; external affairs, naturalization and aliens, quarantine, immigration and emigration; the people of any race for whom it is deemed necessary to make special laws; postal, telegraph and like services; census and statistics; weights and measures; astronomical and meteorological observations; copyrights; railways; conciliation and arbitration in disputes extending beyond the limits of any one State; social services; marriage, divorce etc.; service and execution of the civil and criminal process; recognition of the laws, Acts and records, and judicial proceedings of the States. The Senate may not originate or amend money bills; and disagreement with the House of Representatives may result in dissolution and, in the last resort, a joint sitting of the two Houses. No religion may be established by the Commonwealth. The Federal Parliament has limited and enumerated powers, the several State parliaments retaining the residuary power of government over their respective territories. If a State law is inconsistent with a Commonwealth law, the latter prevails.

The Constitution also provides for the admission or creation of new States. Proposed laws for the alteration of the Constitution must be submitted to the electors, and they can be enacted only if approved by a majority of the States and by a majority of all the electors voting.

The 33rd Parliament was elected in March 1983.

The results of the elections to the House of Representatives and to the Senate held in March 1983 were not available when THE STATESMAN'S YEAR-BOOK went to press but they do appear in the ADDENDA.

Governor-General: The Rt Hon. Sir Ninian Stephen, AK, GCMG, GCVO, KBE.

The following is a list of Governors-General of the Commonwealth:

Earl of Hopetoun	1901–02	HRH the Duke of Gloucester	1945–47
Lord Tennyson	1902–04	Sir William McKell	1947–53
Lord Northcote	1904–08	Viscount Slim	1953–60
Earl of Dudley	1908–11	Viscount Dunrossil	1960–61
Lord Denman	1911–14	Viscount De L'Isle	1961–65
Viscount Novar	1914–20	Lord Casey	1965–69
Lord Forster	1920–25	Sir Paul Hasluck	1969–74
Lord Stonehaven	1925–31	Sir John Kerr	1974–77
Sir Isaac Isaacs	1931–36	Sir Zelman Cowen	1977–82
Earl Gowrie	1936–45	Sir Ninian Stephen	1982–

National flag: The British Blue Ensign with a large star of 7 points beneath the Union Flag, and in the fly 5 stars of the Southern Cross, all in white.

The cabinet of the Labour administration in Nov. 1983 was composed as follows:

Prime Minister: Robert Hawke.
Deputy Prime Minister and Minister for Trade: Lionel Bowen.
Industry and Commerce: John Button.
Social Security: Don Grimes.
Employment and Industrial Relations: Ralph Willis.
Treasurer: Paul Keating.
Immigration and Ethnic Affairs: Stewart West.
Resources and Energy: Peter Walsh.
Foreign Affairs: Bill Hayden.
Education and Youth Affairs: Susan Ryan.
Attorney-General: Gareth Evans.
Defence: Gordon Scholes.
Finance: John Dawkins.
Transport: Peter Morris.
Primary Industry: John Kerin.
Aviation: Kim Beazley.
Housing and Construction: Chris Hurford.
Sport, Recreation and Tourism, and Administrative Services: John Brown.
Health: Neal Blewett.
Science and Technology: Barry Jones.
Communications: Michael Duffy.
Home Affairs and the Environment: Barry Cohen.
Aboriginal Affairs: Clyde Holding.
Veterans' Affairs: Arthur Gietzelt.
Territories and Local Government: Tom Uren.
Defence Support: Brian Howe.

The Acts of the Parliament of the Commonwealth of Australia Passed from 1901 to 1973. 12 vols. Annual volumes, 1974 to date
The Australian Constitution Annotated. Attorney-General's Department, Canberra, 1980
Parliamentary Handbook of the Commonwealth of Australia. Canberra, 1915 to date
Commonwealth of Australia Directory [1921–1958 The Federal Guide; 1961–72 *Commonwealth Directory;* 1973–75 *Australian Government Directory*]. *Prime Minister's Department.* Canberra, 1924 to date
Crisp, L. F., *Australian National Government.* 3rd ed. Melbourne and London, 1975
Hughes, C. A., and Graham, B. D., *A Handbook of Australian Government and Politics.* Canberra, 1968

Odgers, J. R., *Australian Senate Practice.* 5th ed. Canberra, 1976 ·
Paton, Sir George (ed.), *The Commonwealth of Australia: its Laws and Constitution.* London, 1952
Pettifer, J. A., *House of Representatives Practice.* Canberra, 1981
Sawer, G., *Australian Federal Politics and Law 1901–1929, 1929–1949.* 2 vols. Melbourne, 1974.—*Australian Government To-day.* 11th ed. Melbourne, 1973
Wynes, W. A., *Executive and Judicial Powers in Australia.* 5th ed. Sydney, 1976

State Government: In each of the 6 States (New South Wales, Victoria, Queensland, South Australia, Western Australia, Tasmania) there is a State government whose constitution, powers and laws continue, subject to changes embodied in the Australian Constitution and subsequent alterations and agreements, as they were before federation. The system of government is basically the same as that described above for the Commonwealth—*i.e.*, the Sovereign, her representative (in this case a Governor), an upper and lower house of Parliament (except in Queensland, where the upper house was abolished in 1922), a cabinet led by the Premier and an Executive Council. Among the more important functions of the State governments are those relating to education, health, hospitals and charities, law, order and public safety, business undertakings such as railways and tramways, and public utilities such as water supply and sewerage. In the domains of education, hospitals, justice, the police, penal establishments, and railway and tramway operation, State government activity predominates. Care of the public health and recreative activities are shared with local government authorities and the Federal Government, social services other than those referred to above are now primarily the concern of the Federal Government, and the operation of public utilities is shared with local and semi-government authorities.

Administration of Territories. Since 1911, responsibility for administration and development of the Australian Capital Territory has been vested in Federal Ministers and Departments. In 1930, the ACT Advisory Council was established, with both elected and appointed Members, to advise the Minister on administration of the Territory.

Late in 1974 the Government replaced the ACT Advisory Council with a Legislative Assembly of eighteen Members all of whom are elected and on 29 June 1979 the Legislative Assembly became the House of Assembly. While the Assembly has been accorded the forms of a legislature, it continues to perform an advisory function for the Minister for the Capital Territory.

On 1 July 1978 the Northern Territory of Australia became a self-governing Territory with expenditure responsibilities and revenue-raising powers broadly approximating those of a State, although the Territory is not a State under the Constitution.

Under self-government the Legislative Assembly and Ministers of the Northern Territory have responsibility in the areas of insurance, banking, taxation, provision of credit and assistance; Public Service of the Territory; maintenance of law and order and the administration of Justice etc.; civil liberties; markets and marketing; inquiries and administrative reviews; consumer affairs; sales and leases of goods and supply of services etc.; prices and rent control; industry and regulation of businesses and professions; tourism; printing and publishing; labour relations and industrial safety; mining and minerals; land and land use; transport; environment protection and conservation; fire prevention; water resources; energy planning; public utilities and public works; local government; housing, education, health, welfare etc.; censorship; Supreme Court, agreements between the Territory and the Commonwealth, State or States.

Local Government. The system of municipal government is broadly the same throughout Australia, although local government legislation is a State matter.

Each State is sub-divided into areas known variously as municipalities, cities, boroughs, towns, shires or district councils, totalling about 900. Within these areas the management of road, street and bridge construction, health, sanitary and garbage services, water supply and sewerage, and electric light and gas undertakings, hospitals, fire brigades, tramways and omnibus services and harbours is generally part of the functions of elected aldermen and councillors. The scope of their duties, however, differs considerably, for in all States the State Government, either directly or through semi-government authorities, also carries out some or all of these types of services.

In some instances, *e.g.*, in New South Wales, a number of local government authorities combine to conduct a public undertaking such as the supply of water or electricity.

DEFENCE. The Minister for Defence has responsibility under legislation for the control and administration of the Defence Force. The Chief of Defence Force Staff is vested with command of the Defence Force. He is the principal military adviser to the Minister. The Secretary, Department of Defence is the Permanent Head of the Department. He is the principal civilian adviser to the Minister and has statutory responsibility for financial administration of the Defence outlay. The Chief of Defence Force Staff and the Secretary are jointly responsible for the administration of the Defence Force except with respect to matters falling within the command of the Defence Force or any other matter specified by the Minister.

The Chief of Naval Staff, the Chief of the General Staff and the Chief of the Air Staff command the Navy, Army and Air Force respectively. They have delegated authority from the Chief of Defence Force Staff and the Secretary to administer matters relating to their particular Service.

The structure of Defence is characterized by 3 organizational types: *(i)* A Central Office comprising 5 groups of functional orientated Divisions: Strategic Policy and Force Development; Supply and Support; Manpower and Financial Services; Management and Infrastructure Services; and, Defence Science and Technology; *(ii)* the 3 Armed Services of the Defence Force, each having a Service Office element in addition to the command structure; and *(iii)* a small number of outrider organizations concerned with such specialist fields as intelligence and natural disasters.

Defence Support. A separate Department of Defence Support was formally established on 7 May 1982, and draws together elements previously located in the Departments of Administrative Services, Defence, and Industry and Commerce.

The Department: Undertakes the purchase of goods and services for defence purposes; undertakes and sponsors research and deployment relevant to defence needs, supporting both the Defence Force and the defence industry base in this regard; provides technical expertise and other forms of assistance to encourage defence industry initiatives and the acquisition of modern techniques and technologies; ensures that Australian industry participates in the procurement and support of defence equipment to the maximum practical extent; administers the Australian Offsets Program so as to stimulate technological advancement and broaden the capabilities of Australian industries of significance to this country's strategic and overall manufacturing needs; manages the Government's defence oriented facilities including munitions and aircraft factories, and dockyards; and consistent with the Government's defence and foreign affairs policies, markets defence and allied products and services to help maintain industrial capabilities of strategic significance.

Army. Overall organization and financial control of the Australian Army is vested in the Chief of General Staff. Under the Defence Force Re-organisation Act, which received the Royal Assent on 9 Sept. 1975, the Military Board, which was previously the controlling body of the Army, was abolished. The Act became effective on 1 Feb. 1976. A functional command structure, Headquarters Field Force Command, Headquarters Logistic Command, and Headquarters Training Command, with Headquarters in military districts, was introduced in 1973.

The strength of the Army was 32,677 as at 30 June 1983. There is emphasis in the field force organization on the combat element and high-priority logistic units to meet the requirements for limited war and tropical warfare with light airportable formations. The Field Force is organized on the divisional structure, on the basis of 6 battalions organized in 3 brigades each with combat and logistic support.

The effective strength of the Army Reserve at 30 June 1983 was 31,620.

Training for commissioned rank is carried out at the Royal Military College and the Officer Cadet School. The Royal Military College was established in Canberra in 1911, to train young men from Australia and New Zealand for the Regular Armies of those two countries. The college, which is affiliated with the University of New South Wales, accepts young men between the ages of 17 and 20 who are qualified to enter university. The course covers 4 years and leads to the award of the university's degrees of Bachelor of Arts, Bachelor of Science and Bachelor of Engineering.

The Officer Cadet School was established at Portsea, Victoria, in 1952. The course there takes 11 months.

Staff and command training is carried out at the Command and Staff College, Queenscliff, Victoria and the Land Warfare Centre, Canungra, Queensland.

Navy. The overall control of the Royal Australian Navy is vested in the Chief of Naval Staff assisted by the Deputy Chief of Naval Staff with the Chief of Naval Personnel, the Chief of Naval Technical Services and the Chief of Naval Material. Under the Defence Re-organisation Act effective from 1 Feb. 1976 the Naval Board was abolished. The command, operation and administration of the Fleet is the responsibility of the Flag Officer Commanding HM Australian Fleet. The Flag Officer Naval Support Command, formerly the Flag Officer Commanding East Australia area, is responsible for the material support for the fleet.

The aircraft carrier Melbourne (ex-Majestic)[1], 16,000 tons, completed in 1955, was paid off to contingent reserve in 1982, and the front-line fixed-wing squadron disbanded, pending a decision on her replacement. In March 1983 the Government announced that this sole aircraft carrier would not be replaced and that subsequently fixed-wing aviation would be phased out of the RAN by mid-1984.

[1] Sister ship Sydney (ex-Terrible), completed as an aircraft carrier in 1949, converted to a fast military transport in 1961, officially announced for disposal on 20 July 1973, left Sydney for shipbreakers on 23 Dec. 1975.

There are 6 British-built 'Oberon' class submarines, Onslow, Otway, Ovens and Oxley (completed in 1967–69) and Orion and Otama (completed in 1977–78), 3 US-built guided-missile destroyers, Brisbane, Hobart and Perth (completed in 1965–68), 4 US-built guided missile frigates, Adelaide, Canberra and Sydney (completed in 1981–83) and Darwin (completing in 1984), 6 destroyer escorts or 'Type 12' fast anti-submarine frigates, 4 oceanographic research and survey ships, 1 minehunter, 1 minesweeper, a destroyer tender, 23 patrol craft, 1 landing ship, 6 landing craft, 1 fleet oiler, 20 auxiliary vessels, 8 service craft, 5 tugs and 47 workboats. HMAS Jervis Bay (formerly the ANL ro-ro vessel Australian Trader) was commissioned in 1977 as the RAN's training ship. The 'Daring' class destroyer Vampire is also used as a training ship.

The Naval dockyards at Garden Island, Sydney, and Williamstown, Victoria have been transferred to the Department of Defence Support. Naval shipbuilding is carried out at Williamstown, at Vickers Cockatoo Dockyard (VCD), Sydney, and the North Queensland Engineers and Agents (NQEA), Cairns and Carringtons, Newcastle. The main repair base and store depots are at Sydney.

The main training establishments are HMAS Cerberus in Victoria, HMAS Watson, HMAS Penguin and HMAS Nirimba at Sydney, HMAS Albatross (Naval Air Station) at Nowra, NSW, and HMAS Creswell (Royal Australian Naval College) at Jervis Bay, ACT. Training for junior recruits is at HMAS Leeuwin in Fremantle, WA, and Reserve training in all major seaboard capital cities.

The Fleet Air Arm was established in 1948. At 30 Sept. 1983 it had 67 aircraft and consisted of 4 squadrons operating Skyhawk, Tracker and HS7-18 aircraft and Sea King Wessex, Iroquois and Bell 206B helicopters. Sixteen of the fixed-wing aircraft have been placed in storage and all Trackers and Seahawks will be disposed of after 30 June 1984 when fixed wing flying, with the exception of HS 748s, is planned to cease (official, Nov. 1983).

The serving strength at 30 Sept. 1983 totalled 17,000 personnel including 1,000 WRANS.

Navy estimates 1982–83, $A1,097,566,000; 1983–84, $A1,172,744,000.

Air Force. Command of the Royal Australian Air Force is vested in the Chief of the Air Staff (CAS) assisted by the Deputy Chief of the Air Staff, Chief of Air Force Development, Chief of Air Force Materiel, Chief of Air Force Personnel, Chief of Air Force Technical Services, Director-General Supply—Air Force and Assistant Secretary Resources Planning.

The CAS administers and controls RAAF units through two commands: Operational Command and Support Command. Operational Command is responsible to the CAS for the command of operational units and the conduct of their operations within Australia and overseas. Support Command is responsible to the CAS for training of personnel, and the supply and maintenance of service equipment.

Flying establishment comprises 16 squadrons, of which 2 are equipped with 24 F-111 strike/reconnaissance aircraft. Of the others, 3 are equipped with missile-armed Mirage III-O Mach 2 fighters (replacement with locally-assembled F/A-18A Hornets planned in 1984–89), 2 with Orion maritime reconnaissance aircraft. There are nine transport squadrons, 2 with Hercules turboprop transports, 1 with Boeing 707 jet transports (some equipped as flight refuelling tankers), 1 with Caribou STOL transports, 1 with a mix of fixed-wing Caribou and Iroquois helicopters, 1 with Boeing Vertol CH-47C medium lift helicopters, 2 with Iroquois helicopters, and a special transport squadron equipped with BAC One-Eleven, Mystère 20 and HS 748 aircraft. Training aircraft include piston-engined Airtrainers, built in New Zealand, Aermacchi MB 326H jets and French-built Ecureuil helicopters for pilot training, and HS 748 aircraft for navigator training.

Training for commissioned rank is carried out at the RAAF Academy and Officers' Training School, both located at Point Cook, Victoria. Other major training activities which lead to commissioned rank include basic aircrew training and technical and commercial cadet schemes. Basic ground training to tradesman level is conducted at RAAF technical training schools. Higher command and staff training is, in the main, carried out at the RAAF Staff College, Fairbairn, ACT.

The authorized service manpower ceiling for the Permanent Air Force is 22,677 for 1983–84. There is also an Australian Air Force Reserve.

Long, G. (ed.), *Australia in the War of 1939–45.* 22 vols. Canberra, 1952 ff.
O'Neil, R., and Horner, D. M., *Australian Defence Policy for the 1980s.* Univ. of Queensland Press, 1983

INTERNATIONAL RELATIONS

Membership. Australia is a member of the UN, the Commonwealth, OECD, Colombo Plan, the South Pacific Commission and the South Pacific Bureau for Economic Co-operation.

ECONOMY

Financial relations with the States. Since 1942 the Federal Government alone has levied taxes on incomes. In return for vacating this field of taxation, the States are reimbursed by grants from the Federal Government out of revenue received. Payments to the States represent about one-third of Federal Government outlays, and in turn the payments State Governments receive from the Federal Government account for nearly half of their revenues.

The Financial Agreement of 1927 established the Australian Loan Council which has the task of co-ordinating domestic and overseas borrowings by the Federal and six State Governments including, *inter alia*, and setting of annual borrowing programmes. The Federal Government acts as a central borrowing agency in raising loans to finance the major part of those programmes. The Financial Agreement also sets Sinking Fund contributions in respect of loans. The Loan Council administers a second agreement, known as the Gentlemen's Agreement, which establishes arrangements for the co-ordination of borrowings by semi-government and local authorities.

Budget. In 1929, under a financial agreement between the Federal Government and States, approved by a referendum, the Federal Government took over all State debts existing on 30 June 1927 and agreed to pay $A15·17m. a year for 58 years towards the interest charges thereon, and to make substantial contributions towards a sinking fund on State debt. The sinking fund arrangements were revised under an amendment to the agreement in 1976. The Federal Government arranges all borrowings, with minor exceptions, for both the Federal and States Governments through a Loan Council which consists of representatives of these governments. Since 1942 the Federal Government alone has levied taxes on incomes. The States receive a share of the total tax collected by the Federal Government.

Receipts, Financing Transactions and Outlays of the Federal Government for years ending 30 June (in $A1m.):

Receipts:	1978–79	1979–80	1980–81	1981–82
Income taxes	15,913	18,542	22,343	26,439
Estate duty	82	48	17	4
Gift duty	1	1	—	–
Customs duties	1,457	1,629	1,884	2,157
Excise duties	3,845	4,965	5,834	5,994
Sales tax	1,770	1,865	2,102	2,854
Primary production taxes	216	274	292	234
Stevedoring industry charge	19	20	19	18
Payroll tax	13	12	13	16
Other taxes, fees, fines, etc.	151	193	210	–
Total taxes, fees, fines	23,446	27,548	32,714	37,991
Income from public enterprises	1,010	992	992	1,319
Property income	1,463	1,615	1,859	2,077
Total receipts	25,939	30,155	35,565	41,387
Financing Transactions:	4,194	3,064	2,241	1,808
Total funds available	30,133	33,219	37,807	43,195
Outlay:				
General public services	1,913	2,149	2,479	2,879
Defence	2,606	3,008	3,537	4,135
Education:				
University	810	875	950	1,092
Primary and Secondary	830	818	947	1,160
Other	883	915	1,032	1,096
Total education	2,523	2,608	2,929	3,348
Health				
Hospital and clinical services	1,802	1,972	2,306	2,610
Other	1,095	1,190	1,335	1,462
Total health	2,897	3,162	3,641	4,072
Social security and welfare				
Care of and assistance to				
Aged persons	3,340	3,639	4,072	4,664
Incapacitated and handicapped persons	795	901	1,007	1,125
Unemployed and sick	1,061	1,105	1,241	1,524
Ex-servicemen	896	1,006	1,239	1,388
Families and children	1,038	1,056	1,001	1,100
Other	958	1,088	1,366	1,708
Total social security, etc.	8,092	8,795	9,925	11,508
Housing and community amenities	442	369	400	442
Recreation and culture	274	312	393	463
Economic services				
Agriculture, forestry and fishing	241	381	390	579
Mining, manufacturing and construction	138	367	260	460
Transport and communication	1,801	2,030	2,346	2,498
Other	560	575	784	931
Total economic services	2,740	3,353	3,781	4,468
Other purposes	8,647	9,463	10,723	11,880
Total outlay	30,133	33,219	37,807	43,195

The following table shows Government securities on issue on account of the Commonwealth Government and States, at 30 June 1983:

Currency in which repayable	Australian Government	States	Total
Australian Dollar ($A1,000)	15,953,358	16,255,481	32,208,839
Sterling (£1,000)	107,311	4,373	111,684
United States Dollar (US$1,000)	1,549,710	5,479	1,555,189
Swiss Francs (SW.F.1,000)	2,570,000	—	2,570,000
Netherlands Guilders (fl.1,000)	1,220,000	—	1,220,000
Deutsche Marks (DM 1,000)	2,954,554	—	2,954,554
European Units of Account (EUA1,000)	—	—	—
Japanese Yen (Yen 1m.)	359,000	—	359,000
Total ($A1,000 equivalents) [1]	24,713,933	16,265,333	40,979,266

[1] Converted at rate of exchange ruling at 30 June 1982.

Debt per head of population at 30 June 1983 was $A2,544, while the annual interest charge amounted to $A254 per head.

States: The following table presents a summary of the receipts and outlay of State and local authorities during 1981–82 (in $A1m.).

	NSW	Vic.	Qld	SA	WA	Tas.	NT	All States
Receipts and Financing Transactions								
Taxes, fees, fines, etc.	3,474	2,661	1,204	631	699	210	46	8,925
Income from public enterprises	127	402	249	113	62	94	−45	1,001
Grants from Commonwealth Government	4,037	3,089	2,208	1,331	1,426	551	540	13,181
Advances from Commonwealth Government (net)	282	198	102	76	71	52	80	862
All other	1,780	1,843	1,152	368	483	164	93	5,884
Total funds available	9,700	8,193	4,915	2,519	2,741	1,071	714	29,853
Outlay								
Final consumption expenditure	5,715	4,433	2,350	1,538	1,628	594	431	16,690
Interest paid	1,155	1,138	557	313	264	160	35	3,621
Gross fixed capital expenditure on new assets	3,343	2,557	1,890	606	800	285	182	9,663
All other	−513	65	118	62	49	32	66	−121
Total outlay	9,700	8,193	4,915	2,519	2,741	1,071	714	29,853

Finance (5 parts), Australian Bureau of Statistics, Canberra, 1907–1962/63
Australian National Accounts. Australian Bureau of Statistics. 1953–54 to date
Public Authority Finance, No. 1. Australian Bureau of Statistics, 1972
Public Authority Finance: Commonwealth Government Finance, Australia. Australian Bureau of Statistics, 1962–63 to date
Public Authority Finance: State and Local Government Finance, Australia. Australian Bureau of Statistics, 1971–72 to date
Public Authority Finance: Government Financial Estimates. Australian Bureau of Statistics, 1975–76 to date
National Income and Expenditure. Australian Bureau of Statistics. Canberra, 1946 to date
Treasury Information Bulletin (and Supplements). Canberra Treasury Dept., 1956 to date (quarterly)

Currency. On 14 Feb. 1966 Australia adopted a system of decimal currency. The currency unit, the *dollar* ($) is divided into 100 *cents*. The transition period ended on 31 July 1967. Decimal system notes have been issued in denominations of $1, 2, 5, 10, 20 and 50. Coins have been issued in denominations of 50, 20, 10, 5, 2 and 1 cent.

Australian notes, issued by the note-issue department of the Reserve Bank, are legal tender throughout Australia. The total value of notes in circulation on 30 June 1983 was $A6,362·2m., of which $A5,649·6m. were held by the public. In March 1984, US$1 = 1·06 *dollars*; £1 = 1·56 *dollars*.

Banking. The banking system in Australia comprises:

(a) The Reserve Bank of Australia. This is the central bank which in addition to its central banking business (including the note-issue department) provides special financing facilities through the rural credits department for the processing, manufacture and marketing of primary produce.

(b) Four major trading banks: (i) The Commonwealth Trading Bank of Australia; (ii) 3 private trading banks: The Australia and New Zealand Banking Group Ltd, Westpac Banking Corporation and the National Commercial Banking Corporation of Australia Ltd.

(c) Other trading banks: (i) 3 State Government banks—The State Bank of New South Wales, The State Bank of South Australia, and the Rural and Industries Bank of Western Australia; (ii) one joint stock bank—The Bank of Queensland Ltd, formerly The Brisbane Permanent Building and Banking Co. Ltd, which has specialized business in one district only; (iii) The Australian Bank Ltd; (iv) branches of 2 overseas banks—the Bank of New Zealand and the Banque Nationale de Paris, which are mainly concerned with financing trade, etc., between Australia and overseas countries.

(d) The Commonwealth Development Bank of Australia.

(e) Savings Banks.

(f) The Australian Resources Development Bank Ltd opened on 29 March 1968. Its main objective is to assist Australian enterprises in the development of Australia's natural resources, through direct loans and equity investment or by refinancing loans made by trading banks. The bank is jointly owned by the 4 major Australian trading banks.

(g) The Primary Industry Bank of Australia Ltd commenced operations on 22 Sept. 1978. The equity capital of the bank consists of eight shares. Seven shares are held by the Australian Government and the major trading banks while the eighth share is held equally by the 4 State banks. The main objective of the bank is to facilitate the provision of loans to primary producers on longer terms than are otherwise generally available. The role of the bank is restricted to re-financing loans made by banks and other financial institutions.

The Reserve Bank's functions and responsibilities derive from the Reserve Bank Act 1959 and the Banking Act 1959, which came into effect in 1960. They had their origins, however, in the development of the central banking role of the Commonwealth Bank, which was established in 1911 as a Government savings and trading bank.

Control of the Australian note issue was transferred from the Commonwealth Treasury to a Notes Board in 1920 and, in 1924, to the Bank. The Commonwealth Bank Act 1945 formally constituted the Bank as a central bank, and these powers were carried through into the 1959 Act establishing the Reserve Bank.

The Acts of 1959 provided for: (i) the separation of the central bank from the Commonwealth group of banking institutions and its reconstitution as the Reserve Bank of Australia; (ii) the establishment of an entirely separate Commonwealth Banking Corporation, with responsibilities for the non-central-banking elements that had developed from within the original Commonwealth Bank—namely the Commonwealth Trading Bank, the Commonwealth Savings Bank and the Commonwealth Development Bank, the latter being basically an amalgamation of the Mortgage Bank and Industrial Finance Department of the Commonwealth Bank.

At 30 June 1983 the capital of the Reserve Bank totalled $A49·4m. and reserve funds (including a special reserve for IMF special drawing rights) $A4,695m. The capital was distributed as follows: Central banking business, $A40m.; rural credits department, $A9·4m. Reserve funds held were: Central banking business, $A2,108m.; rural credits department, $A90m.; note issue department, $A2,497m. Profits for the year ended 30 June 1983 (including all departments) amounted to $A676m.

Particulars as at 30 June 1983 for the banks under the control of the Commonwealth Banking Corporation: Commonwealth Trading Bank, capital, $A15m.; reserve fund, $A200m.; profits for the year, $A46m. Commonwealth Development Bank, capital, $A62m.; reserve fund, $A179m.; profits for the year, $A23m.

Commonwealth Savings Bank, reserve fund, $A404m.; profits for the year, $A68m.

At 30 June 1983 the 11 trading banks operating in Australia provided full banking facilities at 5,187 branches and 1,101 agencies all over Australia.

The weekly average of deposits in Australia with all trading banks (under *(b)* and *(c)* above) during June 1983 amounted to $A36,040m.; the average of advances owing to the banks was $A28,646m.; the average of total assets was $A54,892m.

At 30 June 1983, 10 savings banks were operating in Australia. These are the 4 major savings banks being wholly owned subsidiaries of the trading banks; the Bank of New Zealand Saving Bank Ltd; and operating, with certain exceptions, in all States and Territories; the State Bank in Victoria and the State Savings Bank of South Australia; the Rural and Industries Bank of Western Australia, and 2 Trustee Savings Banks in Tasmania. At 30 June 1983 these savings banks provided savings facilities at 5,698 branches and 11,831 agencies throughout Australia. At end of June 1983 they held deposits in Australia amounting to $A30,352m.

In 1983 there were 46 companies registered under the Life Insurance Act, 1945, transacting life insurance business in Australia; in addition there were 3 State government institutions. During 1982–83 premiums received were $A3,007m. and claims, etc., paid were $A2,308m.

The following table is a summary of banking and insurance business (in $A1m.) in the several States of the Commonwealth:

Particulars	NSW	Vic.	Q'ld	SA	WA	Tas.	Australia (including A.C.T. and N.T.)
All trading banks:[1]							
Fixed deposits	10,348	5,343	3,956	1,270	1,866	425	23,616
Current deposits	5,208	3,141	1,927	662	934	218	12,393
Advances	11,905	5,971	4,096	2,562	2,651	443	28,640
Savings bank deposits [2]	8,304	11,307	4,136	2,979	1,911	947	30,352
Life insurance:[3]							
New policies issued (sum insured)							
Ordinary and industrial	3,977	3,737	2,744	1,035	1,202	342	15,917
Superannuation	1,811	5,482	2,523	1,108	1,362	297	22,439
Policies existing [2] (sum insured)							
Ordinary and industrial	17,395	20,849	14,505	6,281	6,760	1,857	83,074
Superannuation	4,744	18,781	7,492	4,236	4,649	1,103	81,603

[1] Weekly averages for June 1983. [2] At June 1983. [3] Year ended 30 June 1983.

Treasury Information Bulletin. Department of the Treasury. Canberra, 1956 to date (quarterly)

Reserve Bank of Australia. *Statistical Bulletin.* Sydney, 1937 to date (monthly)

Weights and Measures. Conversion to the metric system is in progress.

ENERGY AND NATURAL RESOURCES

Electricity. Total production 1982–83, 106,371m. kwh. (of which hydro, 13,319m.).

Minerals. The mineral output was valued ex-mine as follows (in $A1,000):

Mineral	1980–81	1981–82	Mineral	1980–81	1981–82
Copper concentrate	288,768	231,952	Brown coal [3]	107,052	137,138
Gold bullion [1]	184,434	200,408			
Iron ore [2]	1,007,307	1,131,186	Total (value of		
Lead concentrate	375,018	252,136	minerals and		
Tin concentrate	143,343	141,716	construction		
Zinc concentrate	188,075	...	materials)	8,158,251	9,125,172
Black coal	2,392,460	2,926,883			

[1] Includes alluvial gold. [2] Includes iron ore for pellet production.
[3] Excludes value of brown coal used in making briquettes.

Gold production (kg), in 1977–78, 21,047; 1978–79, 19,584; 1979–80, 18,273; 1980–81, 15,991; 1981–82, 22,328.

Black coal (1,000 tonnes) mined in 1976–77, 75,982; 1977–78, 79,338; 1978–79, 81,197; 1979–80, 81,249; 1980–81, 96,074.

Agriculture. In 1983, of a total Australian area of 768m. hectares, 641·5m. hectares (83·5%) were Crown lands; private lands formed the remainder, of which 126·7m. hectares (16·5%) were alienated or in the process of alienation.

Area and production of the principal crops in 1981–82[2]:

Crops	Total area (1,000 hectares)	Total production (1,000 tonnes)
Wheat (grain)	11,546	8,901
Oats (grain)	1,213	829
Barley (grain)	2,454	1,798
Maize (grain)	59	...
Hay (cereal)	404	864
Potatoes (ordinary)	38	...
Sugar-cane (for crushing)	319	24,785
Vineyards	69	...
Wine made	...	...
Fruit	103	...

The following summary shows the production and gross value of the most important items or classes of production, classified by States:

1982–83 [2]	NSW	Vic.	Q'ld	SA	WA	Tas.	Aust.[1]
Area of crops (1,000 hectares)	5,160	2,250	2,681	2,794	6,412	100	19,401
Production of wheat (1,000 tonnes)	1,457	419	801	692	5,531	2	8,901

1982–83 [2]	NSW	Vic.	Q'ld	SA	WA	Tas.	Aust.[1]
Total wool production (1,000m. tons)	233·8	139·3	54·5	101·4	149·3	21·7	700·3

1982–83 [2]	NSW	Vic.	Q'ld	SA	WA	Tas.	Aust.[1]
Factory butter (1,000 kg)	1,956	74,553	3,881	1,260	914	5,768	88,332
All meat (tonnes, carcase weight)							
1980–81	604,177	637,929	507,757	193,125	226,290	59,999	2,278,393
1981–82	538,006	622,455	644,050	194,673	201,490	65,320	2,307,284
1982–83	582,753	607,327	578,409	216,012	203,474	71,057	2,297,001

	NSW	Vic.	Q'ld	SA	WA	Tas.	Aust.[1]
Total Agriculture (value $A1m.) 1982–83[2]	2,922·4	2,352·2	2,210·1	1,188·2	2,125·9	310·8	11,187·0

[1] Includes Northern Territory and Australian Capital Territory. [2] Preliminary, subject to revision.

Livestock (in 1,000) at 31 March 1982 (preliminary):

	NSW	Vic.	Q'ld	SA	WA	Tas.	N. Terr.	ACT	Australia
Cattle	4,940	3,463	9,328	843	1,751	565	1,571	10	22,471
Sheep	48,000	22,734	12,099	15,520	30,249	4,478	—	83	133,186
Pigs	800	406	537	405	300	49	1	—	2,498

Forestry. At 31 March 1981 there were 741,000 hectares of coniferous plantations.

INDUSTRY AND TRADE

Industry. Statistics of the manufacturing industries in Australia in 1981–82: Number of establishments, 28,706; workers employed, 1,154,659; salaries and wages paid, $A17,001m.; value-added, $A31,362m. (excludes small single-establishment enterprises employing less than 4 persons).

Estimated gross value (in $A1,000) of the products of Australia:

Products	1978–79	1979–80	1980–81	1981–82	1982–83 [1]
Crops	4,912·5	5,540·8	5,305·9	6,311·9	4,801·4
Livestock slaughtering and other disposals	3,097·7	3,658·8	3,474·3	3,295·6	3,265·9
Livestock products	2,214·5	2,564·3	2,804·8	3,100·6	3,119·7
Fishing	279·8	317·5	383·8	...	...
Mining and quarrying	5,646·9	7,143·7	8,158·2	9,125·2	...

[1] Preliminary, subject to revision.

Labour. The majority of wage and salary earners in Australia have their minimum wages and conditions of work prescribed in awards of industrial arbitration authorities established under federal and State legislation. However, in some States, some conditions of work (*e.g.*, normal weekly hours of work, long-service leave, annual leave) are set down in State legislation. Practically all employees in Australia have a standard working week of 40 hours or less; paid annual leave of at least 4 weeks; and paid long-service leave (*i.e.*, leave granted to workers who remain with one employer over an extended period of time and in certain other areas) of at least 13 weeks after 15 years' continuous service. For most occupations equal pay for males and females has been granted.

In addition to the minimum rates of pay for a standard working week prescribed in awards of industrial arbitration authorities, many wage-earners are in receipt of over-award pay and payments for overtime. In Nov. 1982 it was estimated that the average weekly earnings of adult males (other than managerial, professional and higher supervisory staff) in full-time private and government employment was $A356·60 and average weekly hours 40.

Employees in all States are covered by workers' compensation legislation and by certain industrial award provisions relating to work injuries.

During 1981 industrial disputes involving stoppages of work of 10 man-days or more accounted for 2,158,000 working days lost. In these disputes 722,900 workers were involved.

The following table shows estimates (in 1,000) of the civilian population, by labour force status. The estimates are derived by the ABS from the population survey which is based on a sample of dwellings, carried out by personal interview, covering about two-thirds of 1% of the population of Australia. Prior to Feb. 1978, when monthly surveys were introduced, the surveys were conducted quarterly. The labour force estimates for Feb. 1978 and subsequent months are based on population estimates derived from the 1976 Population Census, adjusted for under-enumeration and were obtained using a new sample and revised questionnaire. Estimates for earlier periods have been revised to make them comparable with current surveys.

	May 1979	May 1980	May 1981	May 1982	May 1983
In the labour force	6,439·9	6,651·4	6,752·7	6,854·7	6,980·1
Employed	6,043·3	6,237·8	6,377·2	6,404·8	6,261·6
Unemployed	396·6	413·6	375·5	449·9	718·6
Not in the labour force	4,193·6	4,167·7	4,280·5	4,408·7	4,532·5
Civilian population aged 15 years and over	10,633·5	10,819·1	11,033·2	11,263·3	11,512·7

The following table shows population survey estimates (in 1,000) of employed persons in Australia classified by industry:

Industry [1]	May 1980	May 1981	May 1982	May 1983
Agriculture and services to agriculture	382·2	394·6	377·2	388·6
Forestry and logging, fishing and hunting	25·2	30·9	32·7	26·8
Mining	80·3	91·1	96·1	97·2
Manufacturing	1,257·4	1,262·3	1,244·9	1,151·3
Food, beverages and tobacco	190·8	174·9	182·9	190·7
Metal products	200·0	236·1	223·2	198·3
Other manufacturing	866·6	851·3	838·8	762·2
Electricity, gas and water	129·9	129·1	124·9	142·8
Construction	476·3	488·9	469·8	418·7
Wholesale trade	371·7	396·1	389·0	317·5
Retail trade	914·8	869·7	882·2	877·0
Transport and storage	329·4	345·3	366·6	356·1
Communication	121·5	122·7	141·4	133·1
Finance, property and business services	512·1	559·2	573·2	574·3
Public administration and defence	281·3	287·1	286·5	301·0
Community services	968·0	1,005·3	1,020·5	1,030·0
Recreation, personal and other services	387·7	394·7	399·8	393·3
Total employed	6,237·8	5,377·2	6,404·8	6,261·6

[1] Australian Standard Industrial Classification.

The following table shows the number of unemployed persons (from the population survey), job vacancies (from the ABS Job Vacancies survey) and the number of persons in receipt of unemployment benefit:

	May 1979	May 1980	May 1981	May 1982	May 1983
Persons unemployed	396,600	413,600	375,500	449,900	718,600
Job Vacancies	34,300	29,800	35,700	25,300	17,500
Unemployment benefit recipients [1]	312,000	311,200	314,500	390,700	635,000

[1] Data relates to the month of June.

Trade Unions. At the end of 1981 there were 324 trade unions reporting in Australia with an estimated membership of 2,994,100. About 55% of wage and salary earners were estimated to be members of unions. In 1981 there were 36 unions with fewer than 100 members and 7 unions with 80,000 or more members. Many of the larger trade unions are affiliated with central labour organizations, the oldest and by far the largest being the Australian Council of Trade Unions formed in 1927.

Labour Statistics. Australian Bureau of Statistics. Canberra, 1980
Isaac, J. E., and Ford, G. W., *Australian Industrial Relations.* Melbourne, 1971
O'Dea, R., *A Guide to Industrial Relations in Australia.* Sydney, 1967
Portus, J. H., *The Development of Australian Trade Union Law.* Melbourne, 1958
Rawson, D. W., *A Handbook of Australian Trade Unions and Employees' Associations.* Canberra, 1977
Walker, K. F., *Australian Industrial Relations Systems.* Cambridge, Mass., 1970

Commerce. Throughout Australia there are uniform customs duties, and trade between the States is free. For 1980–81[1] the gross revenue collected from customs duties amounted to $A1,826·1m. and from excise $A5,818·4m.

Value of the total imports and exports for years ending 30 June, in $A1,000:

	Imports	Exports (excluding ships' and aircraft stores) Australian produce	Re-exports	Total
1980–81	18,964,266	18,353,692	815,551	19,169,243
1981–82	23,004,930	18,816,343	758,863	19,575,206
1982–83 [1]	21,810,338	22,810,338	1,309,157	20,896,089

[1] Preliminary, subject to revision.

The Australian customs tariff provides for preferences to goods produced in and shipped from certain specified countries such as UK, Canada, New Zealand and Ireland. Preferences occur as a result of reciprocal trade agreements between Australia and these countries.

Australia also has bilateral agreements with a number of other countries guaranteeing reciprocal treatment in matters of trade.

The Australia–New Zealand free-trade agreement came into force on 1 Jan. 1966 in certain scheduled goods.

In addition, Australia is a signatory to the multilateral General Agreement on Tariffs and Trade (GATT).

Principal commodities exported and imported from Australia (in $A1,000) in 1982–83 [1]:

	Exports	Imports		Exports	Imports
Live animals	235,993	27,509	Power generating machinery and equipment	127,712	675,136
Meat	1,577,608	14,741	Machinery specialized for particular industries	179,481	1,076,724
Dairy products	328,919	58,690	Metalworking machinery	28,814	174,261
Fish	356,499	216,395	General industrial machinery and equipment, n.e.s. and machine parts, n.e.s.	157,439	1,155,950
Cereals	1,830,842	38,269			
Fruit and vegetables	239,701	170,082			
Sugar, etc., and honey	581,095	14,710			
Coffee, tea, etc.	36,274	218,616	Office machines and automatic data processing equipment	88,613	819,132
Food for animals	63,973	39.001			
Miscellaneous food	17,517	37.977			
Beverages	52,209	100.514	Telecommunications and sound recording and reproducing apparatus and equipment	71,837	807,467
Tobacco	14,487	83.336			
Hides, skins, etc.	232,755	2,452			
Oil-seeds, nuts, kernels	10,320	15,316	Electrical machinery, apparatus and appliances, n.e.s. and electrical parts thereof (including non-electrical counterparts n.e.s., of electrical household type equipment)	116,737	973,185
Crude rubber	2,471	47,201			
Wood, timber and cork	183,222	164,087			
Pulp and waste paper	3,151	80,991			
Textile fibres and their waste	1,927,209	76,410			
Crude fertilizers and minerals	98,929	196,212			
Metalliferous ores and metal scrap	3,753,540	16,279			
Crude animal & vegetable materials, n.e.s.	55,875	47,914	Road vehicles (including air cushion vehicles)	230,661	1,806,037
Coal, coke & briquettes	3,080,276	5,275	Other transport equipment	132,611	533,465
Petroleum and products	1,303,888	3,085,308	Sanitary, plumbing, heating and lighting fixtures and fittings, n.e.s.	7,064	40,760
Petroleum gases	343,174	678			
Animal oils and fats	78,543	727			
Fixed vegetable oils and fats	1,679	49,647	Furniture and parts thereof	13,158	112,368
Animal and vegetable oils and fats	6,848	31,029	Travel goods, handbags and similar containers	1,840	88,975
Organic chemicals	45,182	466,749	Articles of apparel and clothing accessories	16,766	389,237
Inorganic chemicals	39,071	232,391	Footwear	4,159	144,630
Dyeing, tanning and colouring materials	20,303	77,927	Professional, scientific and controlling instruments and apparatus, n.e.s.	133,699	437,324
Medicinal and pharmaceutical products	115,714	193,427			
Essential oils and perfumes, etc.	33,822	106,074	Photographic apparatus, equipment and supplies and optical goods, n.e.s.; watches and clocks	131,735	373,885
Fertilizers, manufactured	4,324	89,557			
Explosives and pyrotechnic products	8,142	9,299			
Plastic materials	112,879	362,933	Miscellaneous manufactured articles, n.e.s.	167,288	1,144,125
Chemical materials and products, n.e.s.	85,726	234,518	Commodities and transactions of merchandise trade, not elsewhere classified [2]	650,402	456,704
Leather manufactures, n.e.s.	47,665	45,543			
Rubber manufactures, n.e.s.	10,965	245,057			
Wood and cork manufactures (except furniture)	7,907	93,721			
Paper and paperboard	46,760	484,111			
Textile yarn, fabrics, etc.	155,660	1,011,237	Total merchandise trade	21,538,670	21,266,599
Non-metallic mineral manufactures, n.e.s.	110,138	368,613	Commodities and transactions not included in merchandise trade	666,576	543,740
Iron and steel	487,525	549,669			
Non-ferrous metals	1,251,763	93,871			
Manufactures of metal, n.e.s.	178,109	553,126	Total recorded trade	22,205,246	21,810,338

[1] Preliminary.   [2] Industrial petroleum gases.

Total trade in ($A1,000) with the more important countries, according to origin (imports) and consignment (exports):

From or to	1981–82		1982–83 [1]	
	Imports	Exports	Imports	Exports
Belgium–Luxembourg	135,282	129,896	124,563	165,531
Canada	584,925	362,879	434,612	316,569
China–excl. Taiwan Province	284,728	602,528	272,921	611,928
Egypt, Arab Republic of	153	298,431	112	366,608
France	628,031	400,007	454,745	498,833
Germany, Fed. Republic of	1,355,670	465,280	1,300,458	548,913
Hong Kong	500,351	436,932	485,265	349,495
India	118,779	312,129	142,312	208,953
Indonesia	515,885	416,744	561,719	375,423
Iran	58,738	145,076	39,687	213,945
Italy	506,950	393,276	538,172	368,397
Japan	4,527,496	5,351,389	4,504,416	6,007,339
Kuwait	261,066	117,030	354,386	131,869
Malaysia	187,718	438,127	214,683	454,323
Netherlands	357,799	210,288	303,349	292,126
New Zealand	726,178	1,035,856	694,275	1,162,258
Pakistan	48,154	58,019	23,521	55,117
Papua New Guinea	69,909	420,126	69,040	508,516
Saudi Arabia	1,193,137	362,530	978,448	344,544
Singapore, Republic of	652,302	512,885	599,830	729,236
Sri Lanka	12,217	34,426	11,305	22,208
Sweden	321,567	57,406	277,736	33,968
Switzerland	213,619	20,883	197,391	32,890
USSR	8,637	666,213	12,314	506,952
UK	1,649,181	726,376	1,467,787	1,175,706
USA	5,249,370	2,154,515	4,764,367	2,241,850

[1] Preliminary.

Imports and exports for particular State ($A1,000):

States, etc.	1981–82		1982–83 [1]	
	Imports	Exports	Imports	Exports
New South Wales	9,235,864	4,584,912	8,614,832	5,503,634
Victoria	7,167,713	4,177,187	6,987,715	4,362,734
Queensland	2,179,752	4,414,452	1,993,666	4,467,167
South Australia	1,337,311	1,277,098	1,242,902	1,220,720
Western Australia	2,535,112	3,994,562	2,527,669	5,155,238
Tasmania	166,032	647,728	179,728	773,270
Northern Territory	373,895	395,796	215,683	549,763
Aust. Cap. Terr.	9,262	2,710	11,512	47,202
Total	23,004,930	19,575,206	21,810,338	22,205,246

In this table the value of goods sent from one state to another for transhipment abroad has been included in the State from which the goods were finally dispatched.

[1] Preliminary, subject to revision.

Overseas Trade. Australian Bureau of Statistics. Canberra, 1906 to date

Total trade between UK and Australia (British Department of Trade returns, in £1,000 sterling):

	1979	1980	1981	1982	1983
Imports to UK	474,902	484,112	395,387	493,196	552,642
Exports and re-exports from UK	839,871	815,652	863,636	1,043,615	940,279

Tourism. During 1982, 954,674 overseas visitors arrived in Australia intending to stay for less than 12 months, and international tourism receipts were $A1,091m.

Australian Bureau of Statistics, Canberra: *Rural Industries.* 1962–63 to date.—*Manufacturing Establishments: Details of Operations.* 1968–69 to date.—*Non-rural Primary Industries.* 1967–68 and 1968–69.—*Value of Production.* 1964–65 to 1968–69.—*Manufacturing Industry.* 1963–64 to 1967–68.—*Manufacturing Commodities.* 1963–64 and 1964–65.— *Building and Construction.* 1964–65 to date
Quarterly Review of Agricultural Economics. Bureau of Agricultural Economics. Canberra, 1948 to date

Developments in Australian Manufacturing Industry. Department of Trade. Melbourne, 1954–55 to date (annual)

The Australian Mineral Industry Review. Department of National Development—Bureau of Mineral Resources, Geology and Geophysics. Canberra, 1948 to date

Australian Economy. Department of the Treasury. Canberra, 1956 to date

Australasian Institute of Mining and Metallurgy. *Proceedings: New Series.* Melbourne, 1912 to date

COMMUNICATIONS

Roads. The length of roads in Australia for general traffic is about 817,000 km, of which approximately 238,000 is sealed, 211,000 of gravel, crushed stone or other improved surface, and 368,000 of cleared or formed surface only.

At 30 June 1982, 8,346,000 motor vehicles, including 6,293,800 cars and station wagons, 1,028,700 utilities and panel-vans, 632,700 truck type vehicles and buses and 390,800 motor cycles, were registered in Australia. New motor vehicle registration figures for 1982–83 include 453,523 cars and station wagons, 96,046 utilities and panel-vans, 40,454 truck type vehicles and buses and 61,061 motor cycles.

Railways. Government railways for the year ended 30 June 1982:

System	Route-km open [4]	Revenue train-km run, 1,000	Passenger journeys, 1,000	Goods and livestock, carried, 1,000 tonnes	Gross earnings, $A1,000	Working expenses, $A1,000
State:						
New South Wales	9,773	59,960	220,837	40,393	663,216	1,063,725
Victoria	5,812	31,136	76,313	11,623	260,049	496,287
Queensland	9,970	32,696	34,237	43,659	520,265	588,051
South Australia [3]	141	3,921	79,740	...	37,714	100,000
Western Australia	5,609	10.681	219 [5]	19,776	211,385	217,961
Australian National [1] [2]	7,638	12.089	610	11,882	195,267	268,001

[1] The Australian National Railways operates services of the former Commonwealth Railways, the non-metropolitan South Australian Railways and the Tasmanian Railways.

[2] Excludes Adelaide metropolitan rail passenger services and the Tasmanian Region.

[3] The South Australian State Transport Authority operates services in the Adelaide metropolitan area.

[4] Inter system traffic is included in the total for each system over which it passes.

[5] Excludes details of Western Australian suburban rail operations.

The State railway gauges are: New South Wales. 1,435 mm; Victoria, 1,600 mm (325 km 1,435 mm); Queensland, 1,067 mm (111 km 1,435 mm); South Australia, 1,600 mm for 2,533 km, 1,824 km 1,435 mm and the rest 1,067 mm; West Australia, 137 km, 1,435 mm and the rest 1,067 mm, and Tasmania, 1,067 mm. Of the Australian National Railways, the gauge of the Trans-Australian and Australian Capital Territory is 1,435 mm, and for the Central Australia 1,067 mm for 869 km and 1,435 mm for 350 km. Under various Commonwealth–State standardization agreements Brisbane, Sydney and Melbourne are linked by a standard 1,435 mm gauge line and Sydney is linked with Perth, *via* Broken Hill to Port Pirie (South Australia), from Port Pirie to Kalgoorlie (Western Australia) and from Kalgoorlie to Perth. The overall length of the Sydney–Perth railway is 3,961 km. The Central Australia railway extends as far north as Alice Springs (now standard gauge on new alignment from Tarcoola to Alice Springs).

Aviation. All civil flying in Australia and its Territories is subject to legislative control by the Australian Government. In some cases intrastate air services are also subject to legislative control by the relevant State Government. The administration of the Air Navigation Act and Regulations and other Commonwealth aviation legislation is a function of the Commonwealth Department of Aviation under the Minister for Aviation.

All Australian-owned airlines, except Qantas Airways, operate regular internal air services. During 1982 hours flown numbered 259,388; the total distance flown was 134m. km; paying passengers carried numbered 11,005,796; weight of goods carried was 142,516 tonnes, and gross weight of mail was 17,005 tonnes.

During 1982 hours flown by Australian regular overseas services which are operated by or on behalf of Qantas numbered 82,495; km flown, 65m.; paying passengers, 2,169,702; freight, 66,442 tonnes; mail, 4,399 tonnes.

Current expenditure by the Australian Government on air transport for the year 1981–82 was $A396·6m. Capital expenditure for 1981–82 was $A62m.

At 30 June 1983 there were 373 licensed aerodromes and 70 governmental aerodromes in Australia.

Shipping. As at 30 June 1983 the Australian merchant marine (vessels of 150 tons gross and over) consisted of 74 coastal vessels of 1,146,505 tons gross and 30 overseas vessels of 924,037 tons gross.

Entrances and clearances of vessels (with cargo and in ballast) engaged in overseas trade:

	Entrances		Clearances	
	No.	DWT	No.	DWT
1980–81	11,949	360,940,597	12,090	363,543,269
1981–82	11,768	358,910,439	11,685	357,941,627

The following summary shows shipping activity by States, 1981–82:

Particulars	NSW	Vic.	Q'ld	SA	WA	Tas.	N.T.	Unsp.	Aust.
Overseas vessel arrivals									
Calls	2,829	2,347	2,330	916	2,526	401	250	189	11,788
DWT (1,000 tonnes)	78,448	49,405	70,565	19,070	123,394	9,473	6,653	1,905	358,910
Overseas cargo:									
Discharged {1,000 tonnes	6,735	3,605	1,912	2,138	5,408	306	1,059	784	21,947
{1,000 cu. metres	3,195	3,728	1,107	524	602	69	51	198	9,474
Overseas vessel departures									
Calls	2,766	2,260	2,316	915	2,457	412	251	308	11,685
DWT (1,000 tonnes)	77,162	47,066	70,678	19,305	122,632	9,726	6,657	4,714	357,942
Overseas cargo									
Loaded {1,000 tonnes	28,727	7,694	35,841	4,270	88,839	4,629	3,663	1,686	175,350
{1,000 cu. metres	377	813	113	85	112	30	8	90	1,628

Post and Broadcasting. Business, year ended 30 June 1983. Number of post offices, 4,843. Earnings: Postal, $A999·4m. Working expenses: $A990·6m.

At 30 June 1983, there were 5,591,667 telephone services, 70,191 data services, 39,388 telex services and 5,353 telephone exchanges.

Radio broadcasting stations are in operation in all State capitals and in other areas throughout Australia. The National Broadcasting and Television Service is provided by the Australian Broadcasting Corporation, which at 30 June 1983 operated 95 medium-wave, 25 frequency modulation and 6 high-frequency radio stations, and 10 high-frequency radio stations for overseas services. In addition, 130 medium-wave, and 7 frequency modulation, commercial broadcasting stations plus 38 public radio stations (both MW and FM) were operating.

Television services are provided in each State, the Northern Territory and the Australian Capital Territory by the ABC and by commercial television stations. There were 272 national stations (including translators) and 50 commercial television stations in 1983.

The Overseas Telecommunications Commission (OTC), established by the Overseas Telecommunications Act 1946, is responsible for the establishment, maintenance, operation and development of all public telecommunications' services between Australia and other countries, between Australia and its external territories and with ships at sea. In co-operation with Telecom and communications carriers in other countries, OTC provides ISD, other international telephone, telegram, facsimile, phototelegram, telex, leased circuit, audio broadcast and data transmission services to countries throughout the world by means of submarine cables, communications satellites and, in a decreasing number of cases, short wave radio. Television relay is provided to and from countries with access to satellite communications' facilities.

Cinemas (1971). There were 976 cinemas including 241 drive-in cinemas, with a total seating capacity of about 478,000.

Newspapers (1979). There was 1 national newspaper (average daily circulation

126,000) and 14 metropolitan daily newspapers in Australia with a combined daily circulation of 3·6m. Of these, 3 papers published in Melbourne accounted for 1·3m. and 4 published in Sydney for 1·2m.

Australian Transport 1974–75. Annual Report. Department of Transport, Canberra
Australian Transport. Sydney, Institute of Transport, 1937 to date (quarterly)

JUSTICE, RELIGION, EDUCATION AND WELFARE

Justice. The judicial power of the Commonwealth of Australia is vested in the High Court of Australia (the Federal Supreme Court), in the Federal courts created by the Federal Parliament (the Federal Court of Australia and the Family Court of Australia and in the State courts invested by Parliament with Federal jurisdiction.

High Court. The High Court consists of a Chief Justice and 6 other Justices, appointed by the Governor-General in Council. The Constitution confers on the High Court original jurisdiction, *inter alia,* in all matters arising under treaties or affecting consuls or other foreign representatives, matters between the States of the Commonwealth, matters to which the Commonwealth is a party and matters between residents of different States. Federal Parliament may make laws conferring original jurisdiction on the High Court, *inter alia,* in matters arising under the Constitution or under any laws made by the Parliament. It has in fact conferred jurisdiction on the High Court in matters arising under the Constitution and in matters arising under certain laws made by Parliament.

The High Court may hear and determine appeals from its own Justices exercising original jurisdiction, from any other Federal Court, from a Court exercising Federal jurisdiction and from the Supreme Courts of the States. It also has jurisdiction to hear and determine appeals from the Supreme Courts of the Territories. No appeal from the High Court to the Privy Council is permitted on questions as to the limits *inter se* of the constitutional powers of the States or the Commonwealth and the States except on the certificate of the High Court. No appeal to the Privy Council, whether special or otherwise, is permitted from a decision of Federal Courts (not being the High Court) or of the Supreme Court of a Territory. Appeal from the High Court to the Privy Council by special leave of the Privy Council is possible only in a matter in which the decision of the High Court was a decision that *(a)* was given on appeal from a decision of a Supreme Court of a State given otherwise than in the exercise of Federal jurisdiction and *(b)* did not involve the interpretation of the Constitution, a law made by the Federal Parliament or an instrument (including an ordinance, rule, regulation or by-law) made under a law made by the Parliament.

Other Federal Courts. Since 1924, 4 other Federal courts have been created to exercise special Federal jurisdiction, *i.e.* the Federal Court of Australia, the Family Court of Australia, the Australian Industrial Court and the Federal Court of Bankruptcy. The Federal Court of Australia was created by the Federal Court of Australia Act 1976 and commenced to exercise jurisdiction on 1 Feb. 1977. It exercises such original jurisdiction as is invested in it by laws made by the Federal Parliament including jurisdiction formerly exercised by the Australian Industrial Court and the Federal Court of Bankruptcy, and in some matters previously invested in either the High Court or State and Territory Supreme Courts. The Federal Court also acts as a court of appeal from State and Territory courts in relation to Federal matters. Appeal from the Federal Court to the High Court will be by way of special leave only. The State Supreme Courts have also been invested with Federal jurisdiction in bankruptcy.

State Courts. The general Federal jurisdiction of the State courts extends, subject to certain restrictions and exceptions, to all matters in which the High Court has jurisdiction or in which jurisdiction may be conferred upon it. In matters of non-Federal jurisdiction a right of appeal is still possible, depending upon the nature of the matter involved, from the State courts direct to the Privy Council.

Industrial Tribunals. The major Federal industrial tribunal in Australia is the Australian Conciliation and Arbitration Commission, constituted by presidential members (with the status of judges) and commissioners. The Commission's functions include settling industrial disputes, making awards, determining the standard hours of work, wage fixation, etc. Questions of law, the judicial interpretation of awards, imposition of penalties, etc., in relation to industrial matters, are now dealt with by the Federal Court.

Australian Digest of Reported Decisions of the Australian Courts and of Australian Appeals to the Privy Council. 2nd ed. Sydney, Law Book Co. 1963—Supplements 1964 ff.
Baalman, J., *Outline of Law in Australia.* 4th ed. Sydney, 1979
Bates, N., *Introduction to Legal Studies.* 3rd ed. Melbourne, 1980
Benjafield, D. G., and Whitmore, H., *Principles of Australian Administrative Law.* 3rd ed. Sydney, 1966
Cowen, Z., *Federal Jurisdiction in Australia.* 2nd ed. Melbourne, 1978
Fleming, J. G., *The Law of Torts.* 5th ed. Sydney, 1977
Gunn, J. A. L., *Australian Income Tax Law and Practice.* 9th ed. by F. C. Bock and E. F. Mannix, Sydney, 1969, and *Butterworth's Taxation Service* to date
Howard, C., *Criminal Law.* 3rd ed. Sydney, 1975
Joske, P. E., *Matrimonial Causes and Marriage and Practice of in Australia and New Zealand.* 2 vols. 5th ed. Sydney, 1969
Mills, C. P., and Sorrell, G. H., *Federal Industrial Law. (Nolan and Cohen.)* 5th ed. Sydney, 1975
O'Connell, D. P. (ed.), *International Law in Australia.* Sydney, 1966
Paterson, W. E., and Ednie, H. H., *Australian Company Law.* 2nd ed. Sydney, 1976, and *Butterworth's Company Service* to date
Sawer, G., *The Australian and the Law.* Melbourne, 1976
Twyford, J., *The Layman and the Law in Australia.* 2nd ed. Sydney, 1980
Wynes, A., *Legislative, Executive and Judicial Powers in Australia.* 5th ed. Sydney, 1976
Yorston, R. K., and Fortescue, E. E., *Australian Mercantile Law.* 14th ed. Sydney, 1971

Religion. Under the Constitution the Commonwealth cannot make any law to establish any religion, to impose any religious observance or to prohibit the free exercise of any religion, nor can it require a religious test as qualification for office or public trust under the Commonwealth. The figures in the table refer to those religions with the largest number of adherents at the census of 1981. The census question on religion was not obligatory, however.

Religion	Persons	Religion	Persons
Christian		Non-Christian	
Baptist	190,259	Hebrew	62,126
Brethren	21,489	Muslim	76,792
Catholic [1]	3,786,505	Other	23,577
Churches of Christ	89,424		
Church of England	3,810,469	Total Non-Christian	197,568
Congregational	23,017		
Jehovah's Witness	51,815	Indefinite	73,551
Orthodox	421,281	No religion	1,576,718
Lutheran	199,760	No reply	1,595,195
Methodist, inc. Wesley	490,767		
Presbyterian	637,818	Grand Total	14,576,330
Salvation Army	71,570		
Seventh-day Adventist	712,609		
Protestant (undefined)	220,679		
Other (including Christian undefined)	250,188		
Total Christian	11,133,298		

[1] Includes 'Catholic' and 'Roman Catholic'.

Education. The Governments of the Australian States and the Northern Territory have the major responsibility for education, including the administration and substantial funding of primary, secondary and technical and further education. In most States, a single Education Department is responsible for these three levels of education, but in New South Wales and South Australia there is a separate department responsible solely for technical and further education and in Victoria, a Technical and Further Education Board. Furthermore, in New South Wales an

Education Commission advises the Minister on primary, secondary and post-secondary education.

The Australian Government is directly responsible for education services in the Australian Capital Territory, administered through an education authority, and for services to Norfolk Island, Christmas Island and the Cocos (Keeling) Islands. The Australian Government provides supplementary finance to the States and is responsible for the total funding of universities and colleges of advanced education. It also has special responsibilities for student assistance, education programmes for Aboriginal people and children from non-English-speaking backgrounds, and for international relations in education.

The Australian Constitution empowers the Australian Government to make grants to the States and to place conditions upon such grants. This power has been used to provide financial assistance to the States specifically for educational purposes. There are two national Education Commissions which advise the Australian Government on the needs of educational institutions throughout Australia for the purpose of financial assistance. The Commonwealth Schools Commission, established in 1973, advises on the provision of financial assistance to the States for government and non-government schools. The Commonwealth Tertiary Education Commission, which was established in 1977 to replace three former commissions (the Universities Commission, the Commission on Advanced Education and the Technical and Further Education Commission), advises on the provision to the States of total funding for universities and colleges of advanced education and of supplementary financial assistance for their institutions of technical and further education.

In 1983 the national Curriculum Development Centre has been reactivated by the Australian Government and operates under its existing legislation pending its transfer to the Commonwealth Schools Commission as a semi-autonomous body.

School attendance is compulsory throughout Australia between the ages of 6 and 15 years (16 years in Tasmania), at either a government school or a recognized non-government educational institution. Many Australian children attend pre-schools for a year before entering school (usually in sessions of 2-3 hours, for 2-5 days per week). Government schools are usually co-educational and comprehensive. Non-government schools have been traditionally single-sex, particularly in secondary schools, but there is a developing trend towards co-education. Tuition is free at government schools, but fees are normally charged at non-government schools.

The following is a summary at July 1982 of primary and secondary school education:

| | Schools | | Teachers [1] | | Pupils [2] | |
| | Govern-ment | Non-govern-ment | Govern-ment schools | Non-govern-ment schools | Govern-ment schools | Non-govern-ment schools |
States and Territories						
New South Wales	2,242	818	45,762	13,262	782,080	245,010
Victoria	2,140	641	40,775	13,019	584,780	227,200
Queensland	1,259	354	20,470	5,260	367,860	104,490
South Australia	716	169	14,214	2,738	207,940	45,970
Western Australia	711	213	11,840	2,942	208,340	51,540
Tasmania	259	70	4,901	904	69,140	15,330
Northern Territory	132	13	1,566	232	23,800	4,370
Aust. Cap. Terr.	97	34	2,629	938	39,010	17,780
	7,556	2,312	142,157	39,295	2,282,970	711,680

[1] Full-time teachers plus the full-time equivalent of part-time teaching.
[2] Pupil numbers have been rounded to the nearest unit of ten.

Opportunities to pursue post-secondary education are available in universities, colleges of advanced education, technical and further education institutions and some more specialized post-school institutions. Tuition fees were abolished in 1974 and student allowances are provided for full-time students subject to a means test. Universities are autonomous institutions, as are the substantial majority of colleges of advanced education. While both offer degree courses, colleges also offer diploma and associate diploma courses and in general their courses have a more applied emphasis and are more vocationally oriented.

Universities and colleges of advanced education at 30 April 1982:

States and Territory	Universities			Colleges of advanced education		
	Number	Students[1]	Staff[2]	Number	Students[1]	Staff[2]
New South Wales	6	64,150	4,938	17	42,030	2,380
Victoria	4	44,150	3,515	17	57,300	3,521
Queensland	3	22,530	1,750	7	23,880	1,350
South Australia	2	12,890	1,129	3	17,030	1,045
Western Australia	2	12,620	1,027	2	20,940	1,094
Tasmania	1	5,210	416	1	2,180	135
Aust. Cap. Terr.	1	5,850	1,219	1	5,230	304
	19	167,400	13,993	48	168,590	9,828

[1] All student numbers have been rounded to the nearest unit of ten.
[2] Full-time academic staff plus the full-time equivalent of part-time academic staff.

Technical and Further Education institutions offer a wide variety of courses of study which are classified into the following six streams: professional, para-professional, trades, other skilled, preparatory and adult or further education. The majority of TAFE courses are part-time, concurrent with employment, but there is also provision for full-time and external study. A network of over 900 government-run institutions facilitates access to these courses. Enrolments in 1981 numbered 1,014,959 of which 322,945 were classified as Stream 6, Adult Education (*i.e.* courses in home handicrafts, hobbies, self-expression and cultural appreciation). There were 943,786 internal enrolments, 60,801 external and 10,370 multimodal (*i.e.* a mixture of internal and external conditions) enrolments. 63,223 of the enrolled students undertook full-time courses (*i.e.* those involving 540 or more contact hours).

Teacher education usually takes place in colleges of advanced education, though a substantial number of secondary teachers and a few primary teachers receive their pre-service education in a university. Government school teachers are recruited by the State and Northern Territory departments of education, and in the Australian Capital Territory by the ACT Schools Authority and the Public Service Board. Non-government schools recruit their own teachers.

The Australian Government provides a number of schemes of assistance for students to facilitate access to education. The Secondary Allowances Scheme aims to help parents with a limited income to keep their children at school for the final 2 years of secondary education. The Assistance for Isolated Children Scheme provides special support to families whose children are isolated from schooling or are handicapped. The Adult Secondary Education Assistance Scheme provides assistance for mature-age students undertaking full-time a one-year matriculation level programme or a two-year programme if studies beyond the tenth year in the Australian secondary school system have not previously been undertaken. The Tertiary Education Assistance Scheme is a means-tested scheme to assist students enrolled for full-time study in approved courses at post-secondary institutions. Allowances are also available for post-graduate study and overseas study. Aboriginal students are eligible for assistance under the Aboriginal Secondary Grants Scheme and the Aboriginal Study Grants Scheme. The States also offer various schemes of assistance, principally at the primary and secondary levels.

There are a number of bodies at the national level which have an important co-ordinating, planning or funding rôle. These include: the Australian Education Council, comprising the Federal and State Ministers of Education, the Conference of Directors-General of Education and an advisory body, the National Aboriginal Education Committee.

Total expenditure on education in Australia in 1981–82 was estimated at $A8,684m.

Austin, A. G., *Australian Education 1788–1900.* Melbourne, 1961
Australian Education Directory. Canberra, 1983
Directory of Higher Education Courses 1982. Canberra, 1982
Education in Australia. Canberra, 1977
Jones, P. E., *Education in Australia.* Melbourne, 1974
Primary and Secondary Schooling in Australia. Canberra, 1977

Schools Commission, *Triennium 1982–84. Report for 1982*. Canberra, 1981
Tertiary Education Commission, *Report for 1982–84, Triennium Vol. 2: Recommendations for 1982*. Canberra, 1981

Social Security and Welfare. All Commonwealth Government social security pensions, benefits and allowances are financed from the Commonwealth Government's general revenue. In addition, assistance is provided for a wide range of welfare services. Total expenditure during 1982–83 was $A14,112·4m.

The following summarizes the rates and conditions of the major benefits provided at June 1983.

Age and invalid pensions—men 65 years of age or more and women 60 years of age or more may receive an age pension. Persons between 16 years of age and age pension age who are permanently blind or permanently incapacitated for work to the extent of at least 85% may receive an invalid pension. To be paid an age pension, a person must have lived in Australia for a specified period and, unless permanently blind or over 70 years of age, also satisfy an income test. There is no residence qualification for an invalid pension if the permanent incapacity of blindness occurred within Australia or during temporary absence from Australia. An income test must be satisfied for an invalid pension unless permanently blind or over 70 years of age. The maximum rates are $A82.35 a week in the case of the 'standard' rate pension, and in the case of the 'married' rate pension, $A137.30 a week ($A68.65 each). Additional amounts, subject to an income test, are paid to pensioners with dependent children. Supplementary assistance of up to $A10 a week for 'standard' rate pension and $A5 for the 'married' rate pension may be paid to a pensioner paying rent or for lodging. Supplementary assistance and additional pension for children are not taxable.

Wife's pension—payable to the wife of an age or invalid pensioner if she is not eligible for a pension in her own right. The maximum rate and the income test are identical to those for age and invalid pensioners.

Widow's pension—widows, divorcees, certain deserted wives, women who have been the dependant of a man for 3 years immediately prior to his death and women whose husbands have been convicted of an offence and have been imprisoned for not less than 6 months may, if they satisfy a residence requirement and a means test, receive a widow's pension. Such women may be paid a pension of up to $A82.35 a week. If they have any dependent children they also receive a mother's/guardian's allowance of $A6 a week ($A8 if she has an invalid child requiring full-time care or a child under 6 years) plus an additional allowance of $A10 for each child. Persons who pay rent may also receive supplementary assistance of up to $A10 a week. Pensions are subject to income tax, but not mother's allowances, additional pension for children or supplementary assistance.

Supporting parents benefit—sole parents who have custody, care and control of any dependent children may, if they satisfy a residence requirement and a means test, receive supporting parents benefit. It is payable at the same rate as the widow's pension, plus the mother's guardian's allowance and the additional pension for each dependent child, and is subject to the same income test.

Family Allowance—is paid without income test to assist families with children under 16 years or eligible student children aged 16 years to under 25 years. It is not subject to income tax. Monthly rates payable are: first child, $A22.80; second child, $A32.55; third child, $A39; fourth child, $A39 and $A45.55 for each subsequent child. For each child or eligible student in an approved institution, the rate is $A39 per month.

Family income supplement—payable subject to an income test to the main breadwinner of families with one or more children eligible for family allowances so long as they are not in receipt of any Commonwealth pension, benefit or allowance which provides additional payment for dependent children. The maximum rate per child is $A10 a week and this is not taxable.

Handicapped child's allowance—payable to parents or guardians of severely physically or mentally handicapped children in the family home and needing constant care and attention. The allowance is $A85 per month and is free of an income test but is subject to a residence qualification similar to that for family allowance. It may also be paid, subject to an income test, in cases where the child is handicapped but not severely, and requires marginally less care and attention.

Double orphan's pension—the guardian of a child under 16 years of age or of a full-time student under 25, both of whose parents are dead, or one of whose parents is dead and the whereabouts of the other parent unknown, and for refugee children where both parents are outside Australia, may receive double orphan's pension of $A55.70 a month per child. The payment is not subject to an income test nor is it taxable.

Unemployment and sickness benefits—are paid, subject to an income test, to persons between the ages of 16 and age pension age who are unemployed, able and willing to work but lacking reasonable steps to find work, or temporarily unable to work because of sickness or injury. The maximum weekly rates of benefit are for unemployment benefits $A40 (single, under 18 years), $A68.65 (single 18 and over without dependents), $A82.35 (single, 18 and over with dependents), $A137.30 (married); and for sickness benefits $A40 (single, under 18), $A82.35 (single, 18 and over without dependents), $A82.35 (single, 18 and over with dependents), $A137.30 (married). To be granted benefit a person must have resided in Australia for at least 12 months preceding his claim or intend to remain in Australia permanently. For unemployment benefit purposes unemployment must not be due to industrial action by that person or by members of a union to which that person is a member.

Service Pension is a Social-Welfare type payment paid by the Department of Veterans' Affairs, similar to the age and invalid pensions provided by the Department of Social Security. Male Veterans who have reached the age of 60 years or are permanently unemployable, and who served in a theatre of war, are eligible for service pension subject to an income test. Female Veterans who served abroad or embarked for service abroad, and who have reached the age of 55 or are permanently unemployable, are also eligible. Wives of service pensioners are also eligible provided that they do not receive a pension from the Department of Social Security.

Disability pension is a compensatory payment in respect of incapacity attributable to war service. It is paid at a rate commensurate with the degree of incapacity suffered from service-related disabilities and is free of any income test. A separate allowance may be paid to dependents.

In addition to cash benefits, assistance is provided either directly or through State and Local government authorities and voluntary agencies, for a wide range of welfare services for people with special needs. Among the major areas involved were the provision of accommodation and home care for aged or disabled persons, the Commonwealth Rehabilitation Service and other welfare programmes for handicapped persons, assistance to homeless persons and the provision of children's services such as pre-schools, childcare and vacation care and assistance for Aboriginals and migrants.

Health Insurance. The health costs of eligible pensioners (i.e. Pensioner Health Benefits cardholders) and those who qualify under the Commonwealth definition as being in special need, and the dependants of those people, are covered by the Government under the special assistance schemes. These people are entitled to free public hospital accommodation and treatment, and bulk billed medical services. People in special need, as defined, comprise migrants during their first six months in Australia, unemployment and special beneficiaries, and people on low incomes.

All other people must meet their health care costs either through health insurance or by way of personal payments. For those people with basic medical insurance with a registered medical benefits fund, the Commonwealth pays Commonwealth medical benefits at the rate of 30% of the Schedule fee for each medical service.

Basic medical insurance provides benefits, when combined with the 30% Commonwealth medical benefit, at 85% of the Schedule fee or the Schedule fee less $A10, whichever is the greater amount. Other medical benefits tables may provide cover up to 100% of the Schedule fee and/or ancillary services.

Basic hospital insurance provides benefits equal to the standard fees for shared ward accommodation in recognised public hospitals, professional service fees and outpatient charges. Additional insurance may provide benefits to cover private room accommodation charges in recognized hospitals or fees in private hospitals and/or ancillary services.

Hospitals. In respect of recognized public hospitals, cost-sharing arrangements expired on 30 June 1981 for all States other than South Australia and Tasmania. Funds are now provided to non-cost-sharing States through general revenue grants for recognized public hospitals and services previously funded under the Community Health Program and the School Dental Scheme. General revenue grants also provide Commonwealth funds for community and School Dental services in South Australia and Tasmania, while the agreed net operating costs of public hospitals in those States continue to be shared between the Commonwealth and the States under the cost-sharing arrangements. For private hospitals a bed day subsidy of SA28 is paid for patients receiving prescribed surgical procedures in private hospitals. A bed day subsidy of $A16 is payable in respect of all other patients.

Long-term (Nursing Home Type) Patients. In general, long-term patients accommodated in hospitals who no longer require hospital treatment are reclassified as nursing home type patients and are required to contribute towards their care the accommodation in the same way as patients in nursing homes. A 'nursing home type patient' is an inpatient whose hospitalization exceeds sixty days, unless a certificate has been issued by a medical practitioner to certify that a patient is in need of acute care. The arrangements operate in all hospitals except New South Wales and Northern Territory public hospitals.

Nursing Homes. The Commonwealth pays benefits in respect of all qualified patients in nursing homes approved under the National Health Act. As at 5 Nov. 1981 the maximum amount of basic nursing home benefit payable per day in each State was: New South Wales $A23.00; Victoria $A31.65; Queensland $A20.40; South Australia $A27.60; Western Australia $A18.55 and Tasmania $A20.65. For eligible nursing homes approved under the Nursing Homes Assistance Act the Commonwealth meets the approved operating deficit of the home. All nursing home patients are required to make a minimum contribution towards the cost of their care and accommodation. At 5 Nov. 1981 the minimum patient contribution was $A9.30 per day.

Domiciliary Nursing Care Benefit. This benefit of $A42 per fortnight can be paid to any persons who provide nursing care in their own home for eligible patients. A person may not receive benefits for the care of more than two patients at any one time.

Eligible patients must be 16 years of age or more, have a certificate from their doctor that they have a continuing need for nursing care, and be receiving this care by a registered nurse on a regular basis involving at least two visits each week.

This requirement for two visits a week may be relaxed where a registered nurse has certified as to the competence of the caring peson. This benefit is not subject to a means test and is payable under the National Health Act, in addition to any entitlements that persons may have under the Social Services Act or the Repatriation Act for pensions or other supplementary allowances. The benefit cannot be paid in respect of any period prior to the date on which an application is received in the Department of Health. The benefit is not subject to taxation.

Pharmaceutical Benefits. A comprehensive range of drugs and medicinal preparations is available. In general, a fee of $A4 is charged for each prescription.

Department of Territories, *Progress Towards Assimilation.* Canberra, 1958
Bilton, J., *The Royal Flying Doctor Service of Australia.* Sydney, 1961
Henderson, R., *People in Poverty.* Melbourne, 1970

DIPLOMATIC REPRESENTATIVES

Of Australia in Great Britain (Australia House, Strand, London, WC2B 4LA)
High Commissioner: Alfred R. Parsons.

Of Great Britain in Australia (Commonwealth Ave., Canberra)
High Commissioner: Sir John Mason, KCMG.

Of Australia in the USA (1601 Massachusetts Ave., NW, Washington, D.C., 20036)
Ambassador: Sir Robert Cotton.

Of the USA in Australia (Moonah Pl., Canberra)
Ambassador: Robert D. Nesen.

Of Australia to the United Nations
Ambassador: Richard A. Woolcott.

Books of Reference

Statistical Information: The Australian Bureau of Statistics (Cameron Offices, Belconnen, A.C.T., 2616) was established in 1906. All the activities of the Bureau are covered by the Census and Statistics Act, which confers authority to collect information and contains secrecy provisions to ensure that individual particulars obtained are not divulged. Under the provisions of the Statistics (Arrangements with States) Act which became law on 12 May 1956, the statistical services of all the States have been integrated with the Australian Bureau. An outline of the development of statistics in Australia is published in the *Official Year Book*, No. 51, 1965. *Australian Statistician:* Dr R. J. Cameron.

The principal publications of the Bureau are:

Official Year Book of Australia. 1907 to date
Pocket Year Book Australia. 1913 to date
Monthly Summary of Statistics Australia. Oct. 1937 to date
Digest of Current Economic Statistics Australia. Aug. 1959 to date
Catalogue of Publications, 1976 to date

Other Official Publications

Atlas of Australian Resources. Dept. of Resources and Energy, Division of National Mapping
Climatological Atlas of Australia. Bureau of Meteorology. Melbourne, 1940
Norfolk Island—Annual Report. Dept. of Territories and Local Government
Cocos (Keeling) Islands—Annual Report. Dept. of Territories and Local Government
Christmas Island—Annual Report. Dept. of Territories and Local Government
Australian Books: Select List of Works About or Published in Australia. National Library of Australia, Canberra, 1934 to date
Australian National Bibliography. Canberra, 1936 to date
Historical Records of Australia. 34 vols. National Library, Canberra, 1914–25
Australia Handbook. Dept. of Administrative Services. Australian Information Services
Annual Report. Dept. of Foreign Affairs, Canberra, 1932 to date
Australian Foreign Affairs Record. Dept. of Foreign Affairs, Canberra, 1936 to date
Australian Treaty List. Dept. of Foreign Affairs, Canberra, consolidated volume from Federation to 1970 with supplements to date
Coxon, H., *Australian Official Publications.* Oxford, 1981
Documents on Australian Foreign Policy 1937–49. Vol. 1: 1937–38, Vol. 2: 1939, Vol. 3 in preparation. Dept. of Foreign Affairs, Canberra
Diplomatic List. Dept. of Foreign Affairs, Canberra. 1949 to date
Consular and Trade Representatives. Dept. of Foreign Affairs, Canberra. 1936 to date

Non-Official Publications

Australian Quarterly: A Quarterly Review of Australian Affairs. Sydney, 1929 to date
Chipman, E., *Australians in the Frozen South.* Melbourne, 1978
Chisholm, A. H. (ed.), *Australian Encyclopædia.* 10 vols. Sydney, 1962
Clark, C. M. H. (ed.), *Select Documents in Australian History, 1788–1900.* 2 vols. Sydney, 1950–55
Ferguson, Sir John, *Bibliography of Australia, 1784–1850.* 4 vols. Sydney, 1941–55; vol. 5 (1851–1900), Part 1, 1963. Parts 2 and 3 in preparation
Grant, B., *The Crisis of Loyalty: A Study of Australian Foreign Policy.* Sydney, 1972
Hancock, Sir Keith, *Australia.* Brisbane, 1961

Horne, D., *The Australian People*. Sydney, 1972

Kepars, I., *Australia*. [Bibliography] Oxford and Santa Barbara, 1984

Noble, N. S. (ed.), *The Australian Environment*. 3rd ed. Melbourne, 1960

Serle, P., *Dictionary of Australian Biography*. 2 vols. Sydney, 1949

Taylor, T. G., *Australia: A Study of Warm Environments and their Effect on British Settlement*. 7th ed. London, 1959

Who's Who in Australia. Melbourne, 1906 to date

National Library: The National Library, Canberra, A.C.T. *Director-General:* Harrison Bryan.

AUSTRALIAN TERRITORIES

AUSTRALIAN CAPITAL TERRITORY

HISTORY. The area, now the Australian Capital Territory, was first visited by white men in 1820 and settlement commenced in 1824. Until its selection as the seat of government it was a quiet pastoral and agricultural community.

AREA AND POPULATION. The area of the Australian Capital Territory is 2,432 sq. km (including Jervis Bay area). The population (estimate) at 30 June 1982 was 232,000. Previous census population:

	Males	Females	Total		Males	Females	Total
1911	992	722	1,714	1961	30,858	27,970	58,828
1921	1,567	1,005	2,572	1966	49,991	46,041	96,032
1933	4,805	4,142	8,947	1971	73,589	70,474	144,063
1947	9,092	7,813	16,905	1976	100,103	95,519	197,622
1954	16,229	14,086	30,315	1981	110,415	111,194	221,609

(Figures before 1961 exclude particulars of full-blood Aborigines.)

CONSTITUTION AND GOVERNMENT. The Constitution of Australia provided (Sec. 125) that the seat of government should be selected by parliament and that it should be within New South Wales but at least 161 km from Sydney. The present area was surrendered by New South Wales and accepted by the Australian Government from 1 Jan. 1911. In 1915 an additional 73 sq. km at Jervis Bay was transferred from New South Wales to the Commonwealth. In 1911 an international competition was held for the city plan. The plan chosen was that of W. Burley Griffin, of Chicago. Construction was delayed by the First World War, and it was not until 1927 that, with the transfer of parliament and certain departments, Canberra became in fact the seat of government. Most Australian Government departments now have their headquarters in Canberra.

The general administration of the Territory is in the hands of the Minister for the Capital Territory, but certain specific services are undertaken by other Federal Government Departments and Authorities. Since June 1979 the Minister has been advised on matters of local concern by the ACT House of Assembly consisting of 18 elected members. Prior to that date this function was performed by the ACT Legislative Assembly (from 1974), replacing the ACT Advisory Council which had been in existence since 1930 and consisted of both nominated and elected members.

The Australian Capital Territory Representation (House of Representatives) Act, 1973, provided for the representation of residents of the Territory by 2 elected members in the House of Representatives. The Senate (Representation of Territories) Act 1973 provided for the election of 2 Senators from the Territory. Elections took place in Nov. 1980.

FINANCE. The receipts and outlay of the Australian Capital Territory cover the transactions of the Australian Government in the Consolidated Revenue and other funds. They also include details of the ACT public corporations.

Receipts and outlay ($A1,000) for years ended 30 June:

	Receipts	Capital	Current Outlay	Total
1979	98,716	166,360	227,021	393,381
1980	102,297	139,947	260,248	400,195
1981	97,795	78,901	297,206	376,107
1982[1]	114,522	67,489	340,344	407,833

[1] Preliminary.

The chief sources of receipts in 1981–82 were taxes, fees and fines, $A67m.; and interest and rent, $A29m. Capital outlay comprised gross capital formation, $A58m., and net advances to other sectors, $A6m.

PRODUCTION. The Territory is predominantly pastoral. Livestock, 31 March 1983: 10,168 cattle, 82,848 sheep. A considerable amount of reafforestation (mostly pine) has been undertaken, the total area of commercial plantations at 30 June 1981 being 14,119 hectares. There is no secondary industry of any importance.

EDUCATION. In 1974 education in government schools became the direct responsibility of the Commonwealth Government. A Schools Authority was established to administer the Australian Capital Territory government school system. In July 1982 there were 97 government schools comprising 63 primary schools, 25 secondary schools and colleges and 9 special schools. Non-government schools numbered 34 in total of which there were 23 primary schools, 4 secondary schools and 17 schools with both primary and secondary enrolments. Students enrolled full-time in government schools in 1982 numbered 23,760 and 15,250 in primary and secondary school levels respectively. Enrolments at non-government schools comprised 10,090 primary school students and 7,680 secondary school students. Pre-school education is provided at 74 centres with a total enrolment of 4,845 (Nov. 1980). The Canberra, Woden and Bruce College of Technical and Further Education with a total enrolment of about 22,000 in 1982 provide training in commercial and special courses.

The Canberra School of Music, opened in 1965, had 668 students in 1982. The Canberra School of Arts had 1,029 students in 1982. The Canberra College of Advanced Education commenced operation in 1970. Enrolments (1982) 5,230.

The Australian National University is situated in Canberra. Enrolments (1981) 5,955.

Books of Reference

A.C.T. Statistical Summary. Australian Bureau of Statistics. From 1960
Tomorrow's Canberra. National Capital Development Commission, 1970
Wigmore, L., *Canberra: A History of Australia's National Capital.* 2nd ed. Canberra, 1971

NORTHERN TERRITORY

HISTORY. The Northern Territory, after forming part of New South Wales, was annexed on 6 July 1863 to South Australia and in 1901 entered the Commonwealth as a corporate part of South Australia. The Commonwealth Constitution Act of 1900 made provision for the surrender to the Commonwealth of any territory by any state, and under this provision an agreement was entered into on 7 Dec. 1907 for the transfer of the Northern Territory to the Commonwealth, and it formally passed under the control of the Commonwealth Government on 1 Jan. 1911. For details of Constitutional development until 1978 *see* THE STATESMAN'S YEAR-BOOK 1980–81 pp. 123–24. The Commonwealth Government retained responsibility until Self-Government was granted on 1 July 1978.

AREA AND POPULATION. The Northern Territory is bounded by the 26th parallel of S. lat. and 129° and 138° E. long. Its total area is 1,346, 200 sq. km. The coastline is about 6,200 km in length, the principal port being Darwin. The greater part of the interior consists of a tableland rising gradually from the coast to a height of about 700 metres. On this tableland there are large areas of excellent pasturage. The southern part of the Territory is generally sandy and has a small rainfall, but water may be obtained by means of sub-artesian bores.

The capital and seat of Government, Darwin, is situated on the north coast. Darwin had a population of 60,923 in July 1982. The total population of the Territory is about 130,000. Other main centres include Katherine (3,883), 330 km south of Darwin; Alice Springs (19,610), in Central Australia; Tennant Creek (3,050), a rich mining centre 500 km north of Alice Springs; Nhulunbuy (3,864), a bauxite mining centre on the Gove Peninsula in eastern Arnhem Land; and Jabiru, a model town being built to serve the rich Uranium Province in eastern Arnhem Land with a planned population of 6,000. There also are a number of large self-contained Aboriginal communities.

Vital statistics for 1980: Births, 2,843; deaths, 603; marriages, 622; divorces, 289.

CONSTITUTION AND GOVERNMENT. The Northern Territory (Self-Government) Act 1978 established the Northern Territory as a body politic as from 1 July 1978, with Ministers having control over and responsibility for Territory finances and the administration of the functions of government as specified by the Federal Government by regulations made pursuant to the Act. Regulations have been made conferring executive authority for the bulk of administrative functions. Proposed laws passed by the Legislative Assembly in relation to a transferred function require the assent of the Administrator. Proposed laws in all other cases may be assented to by the Administrator or reserved by the Administrator for the Governor-General's pleasure. The Governor-General may disallow any law assented to by the Administrator within 6 months of the Administrator's assent.

The Northern Territory has federal representation, electing 1 member to the House of Representatives and 2 members to the Senate.

FINANCE. Budgets since the introduction of self-government in 1978 in $A1m.:

	1978–79	1979–80	1980–81	1981–82	1982–83
Revenue	349	530	656	744	850
Expenditure	348	529	656	746	852

The revenue available in 1980–81 comprised $A554m. in payments to the Northern Territory from the Commonwealth, as established by agreement at the time of self-government, together with $A102m. raised by the Northern Territory which included $A29m. through state-like taxes.

Expenditure during 1980–81 included $A92.1m. for education; $A72.8m. for lands and housing; $A79.5m. for health; $A49.5m. for community development and $A88m. on the capital works programme.

ENERGY AND NATURAL RESOURCES

Oil and Gas. Significant oil and gas reserves have been discovered in the Amadeus Basin. In 1981 the Territory's first petroleum leases were granted at Mereenie. There are estimated recoverable reserves of 28m. bbls of oil. Estimated gas reserves at Mereenie are 23,000m. cu. metres. A pipeline has been constructed from Palm Valley to carry natural gas 150 km to Alice Springs where it is providing fuel for the local power station. Proven reserves are 1,400m. cu. metres of gas.

Minerals. The Northern Territory's most important natural resources are minerals. In the calendar year 1982 the mining industry, by far the largest commercial industry in the Northern Territory, produced mineral products with a value of $A625m. Projects already committed will boost this amount to more than $A650m. by 1985.

At present there are five major mining organizations extracting bauxite, manganese, uranium, gold and copper; in addition, one firm is producing uranium oxide from stockpiled ore. There are also several smaller mining operations recovering tin, tantalum, gold, lead and silver. Significant amounts of rock, sand and gravel are also being produced for construction materials.

Gove Peninsula bauxite reserves are estimated at 250m. tonnes with an average alumina content of 50%. Over 4m. tonnes of bauxite were mined in 1982. Alumina is exported to Europe, the USA, Africa and Asia. More than half the bauxite goes to Japan.

One of the world's largest high-grade manganese mines is located on Groote Eylandt, which is Australia's largest known manganese deposit. In 1982 there were 1m. tonnes of manganese ore processed, much of which was shipped to Japan.

Copper, gold and bismuth are mined in the Tennant Creek area. Warrego Mine has a proven copper/gold ore resource of 4·8m. tonnes and Gecko Mine has a proven ore resource of 3·3m. tonnes. Nobles Nob has been producing gold since 1938 and currently mills 8,000 tonnes of ore per month. Gold bullion and concentrates with a total value of more than $A32m. were produced in the Territory in 1982.

The Alligator Rivers region is possibly the most prospective area in the world for high-grade uranium deposits. Four world-class deposits have been located to date. Of these, Ranger and Nabarlek are producing uranium oxide. The combined output from these two mines in 1981 was 2,622 tonnes, with a value of about $A175m.

Agriculture. Cattle and buffalo production, valued at $A78m. annually, constitutes the largest primary industry in the Northern Territory. The value of cattle and buffalo exports exceeded $A37m. in 1982.

There are 243 pastoral stations in the Northern Territory which produce cattle for Australian and overseas markets. They vary from small stations of 383 sq. km. to huge properties like Wave Hill Station which runs cattle over 12,380 sq. km.

In 1982, five export abattoirs in the Territory supplied 13,728 tonnes of beef, veal and fancy meats to more than 20 countries. The USA is the largest importer of Territory beef, followed by Japan, Taiwan, Saudi Arabia and Hong Kong. Total value of export beef is more than $A25m.

Live buffaloes and buffalo meat products are part of a growing export industry in the Northern Territory. Current value of these exports is more than $A6·5m. Processed buffalo meat for human consumption overseas is supplied by two export abattoirs in the Territory's Top End. In 1982 their combined exports of buffalo meat products was more than 2,800 tonnes.

General agriculture is conducted on a small scale in the Northern Territory. Small quantities of fruit, vegetables, eggs, dairy produce, poultry and pasture are produced. Properties in the Katherine and Douglas-Daly districts produce the Territory's four main crops – sorghum, maize, mung beans and peanuts.

Forestry. A forest development programme which commenced in 1970 has continued the multiple use management of Northern Territory forested areas; this included a softwood programme of 400 hectares per year, the introduction of additional suitable tree species in both arid and higher rainfall areas, conservation and management of native forests for production and recreational purposes, survey and assessment of resources, fire control activities and the creation of training opportunities for Aboriginals in forestry and allied saw-milling activities.

Local production of sawn timber, mainly Cypress pine, amounted to 870 cu. metres of pine in 1975–76. This was supplemented by 35,500 cu. metres of timber imported from interstate and overseas.

Local production of treated poles and rails amounted to 115 cu. metres. Only 280 hectares of plantation were established during the year because of complications arising from cyclone 'Tracy'.

During 1975–76 the Forestry Section of the Department of the Northern Territory redeveloped parks and open-space areas on behalf of the Darwin Reconstruction Commission.

Fisheries. The fishing industry is second only to beef cattle in Northern Territory primary industries. The total value (*ex*-vessel) of commercial fish products landed in the Northern Territory in 1981–82 was $A18·34m. Of this, prawns contributed $A15·25m. and barramundi $A1·9m. Threadfin salmon, spanish mackerel, mud crabs, reef fish and bay lobsters made up most of the remainder.

Prawns and barramundi provide an employment base for a large number of Territorians – not just in fishing, but in processing, distribution and ancillary services. Almost all products undergo some processing by land-based establishments before reaching the consumer. Some 95% of prawns landed in the Northern Territory are exported to Japan. The value of prawn exports in 1981–82 exceeded $A14·5m., mainly headless uncooked prawns. The bulk of barramundi and threadfin salmon is consigned in frozen packs to southern Australian markets.

INDUSTRY AND TRADE. In 1979–80 value added in the manufacturing industry, from 101 factories (with 4 or more persons employed) was $A77m. 2,512 persons were employed in these factories. In 1980, 70 trade unions had 19,600 members.

Tourism. In 1980–81, there were 363,000 tourists contributing about $A106m. to the economy.

National Parks and Reserves. About 43,000 sq. km have been set aside as wildlife sanctuaries under the Wildlife Conservation and Control Ordinance. They are controlled by the Chief Inspector of Wildlife who is an officer of the Department of the Northern Territory. 236,000 sq. km of Aboriginal reserves are also wild-life protected areas.

The Northern Territory Reserves Board administers some 37 national parks and reserves covering an area of over 249,926 hectares. The Board is responsible under the National Parks and Gardens Ordinance for the care, control and management of these reserves, and its functions include the preservation and protection of natural and historical features and the encouragement of public use and enjoyment of land set aside in such reserves.

COMMUNICATIONS

Roads. There are now 5,460 km of sealed road within the Northern Territory. They include three major interstate links: the Stuart Highway from Darwin to the South Australian border, the Barkly Highway, Tennant Creek to Mt. Isa, 444 km of which is in the Northern Territory, and the Victoria Highway, Katherine to the Western Australian border, a distance of 468 km. In addition to this there are 4,064 km of gravel roads, 4,834 km of formed roads and 6,670 km of unformed roads or tracks, totalling approximately 21,028 km of roads within the Northern Territory. In 1979–80 registrations of new motor vehicles included 1,656 cars, 1,550 utilities etc., 207 trucks, 48 buses and 486 motor cycles.

Railways. Alice Springs is linked to the Trans-continental network by a new standard (1,435 mm) gauge railway to Tarcoola (831 km), opened in 1980. This replaced the largely narrow gauge line to Port Augusta. The standard gauge railway is to be extended to Darwin by 1988, providing Australia with its first north-south rail link.

Aviation. Darwin is the first port of arrival in Australia for some aircraft from Europe and Asia. In 1976–77, 237,411 passengers were carried and 6,389 tonnes of freight. There are regular inland services connecting Darwin with all the State capitals and many inland towns.

Shipping. Regular freight shipping services connect Darwin with Western Australia, the eastern States and overseas. Passenger vessels also call at Darwin at irregular intervals.

The ports of Melville Bay (Gove) and Milner Bay (Groote Eylandt) are connected with Darwin, the eastern States and overseas by regular shipping freight services.

The inland and coastal communities around the coast are provided with regular freight barge services from Darwin. Some of these communities also receive a barge freight-transhipment service out of a Brisbane vessel which calls at Melville and Milner Bays, where the transhipment is effected.

EDUCATION AND WELFARE

Education. In 1982 there were 132 government schools. Teachers totalled 1,566 and pupils 23,800. There were 13 private schools with 232 teachers and 4,370 pupils.

Health. In 1980 there were 6 hospitals with 756 beds. Community health services are provided from 9 urban Health Centres and 62 rural Health Centres including mobile units.

AUSTRALIAN EXTERNAL TERRITORIES

AUSTRALIAN ANTARCTIC TERRITORY. An Imperial Order in Council of 7 Feb. 1933 placed under Australian authority all the islands and territories other than Adélie Land situated south of 60° S. lat. and lying between 160° E. long. and 45° E. long. The Order came into force with a Proclamation issued by the Governor-General on 24 Aug. 1936 after the passage of the Australian Antarctic Territory Acceptance Act 1933. The boundaries of Adélie Land were definitively fixed by a French Decree of 1 April 1938 as the islands and territories south of 60° S. lat. lying between 136° E. long. and 142° E. long. The Australian Antarctic Territory Act 1954 declared that the laws in force in the Australian Capital Territory are, so far as they are applicable and are not inconsistent with any ordinance made under the Act, in force in the Australian Antarctic Territory.

In 1968 responsibility for the administration of this Act was transferred from the Minister for External Affairs to the Minister for Supply; in 1972 responsibility was transferred to the Minister for Science.

On 13 Feb. 1954 the Australian National Antarctic Research Expeditions (ANARE) established a station on Mac. Robertson Land at lat. 67° 37′ S. and long. 62° 52′ E. The station was named Mawson in honour of the late Sir Douglas Mawson. Meteorological and other scientific research is conducted at Mawson, which is the centre for coastal and inland survey expeditions.

A second Australian scientific research station was established on the coast of Princess Elizabeth Land on 13 Jan. 1957 at lat. 68° 34′ S. and long. 77° 58′ E. The station was named Davis in honour of Capt. John King Davis, Mawson's second-in-command on 2 expeditions. The station was temporarily closed down in Jan. 1965 and re-opened in Feb. 1969.

In Feb. 1959 the Australian Government accepted from the US Government custody of Wilkes Station, which was established by the US on 16 Jan. 1957 on the Budd Coast of Wilkes Land, at lat. 66° 15′ S. and long. 110° 32′ E. The station was named in honour of Lieut. Charles Wilkes, who commanded the 1838–40 US expedition to the area, and was closed in Feb. 1969. Operations were then transferred to the new station, Casey. Construction commenced on Casey station in Jan. 1965 and was continued, mainly during summer visits, until Feb. 1969, when it was opened. The station, specially designed to withstand blizzard winds and prevent inundation by snow, is situated 2·4 km south of Wilkes at lat. 66° 17′ S. and long. 110° 32′ E. The Antarctic Division has also operated a station, since March 1948, at Macquarie Island, about 1,370 km south-east of Hobart. Macquarie Island is a dependency of the State of Tasmania.

On 1 Dec. 1959 Australia signed the Antarctic Treaty with Argentina, Belgium, Chile, France, Japan, New Zealand, Norway, South Africa, the USSR, the UK and the USA. Poland, Czechoslovakia, German Democratic Republic, Netherlands, Romania, Brazil, Denmark, Bulgaria, Federal Republic of Germany, Italy, India, People's Republic of China, Spain, Papua New Guinea, Peru and Uruguay have subsequently acceded to the Treaty. Poland became a full member of the Antarctic Treaty in 1977 and the Federal Republic of Germany in 1981 and India and Brazil in 1983. The Treaty reserves the Antarctic area south of 60° S. lat. for peaceful purposes, provides for international co-operation in scientific investigation and research, and preserves, for the duration of the Treaty, the *status quo* with regard to territorial sovereignty, rights and claims. The Treaty entered into force on 23 June 1961. Since then the Antarctic Treaty powers have held 12 consultative meetings. The 13th is scheduled to be held in Belgium in 1985.

COCOS (KEELING) ISLANDS. The Cocos (Keeling) Islands are 2 separate atolls comprising some 27 small coral islands with a total area of about 14·2 sq. km, and are situated in the Indian Ocean at 12ᵉ 05′ S. lat. and 96° 53′ E. long. They lie 2,768 km north-west of Perth and 3,685 km west of Darwin, while Colombo is 2,255 km to the north-west of the group.

The main islands in this Australian Territory are West Island (the largest, about 10 km from north to south) on which is an airport and an animal quarantine station, and most of the European community; Home Islands, occupied by the Cocos Malay community; Direction, South and Horsburgh Islands, and North Keeling Island, 24 km to the north of the group.

Although the islands were discovered in 1609 by Capt. William Keeling of the East India Company, they remained uninhabited until 1826, when the first settlement was established on the main atoll by an Englishman, Alexander Hare. Hare left the islands in 1831, by which time a second settlement had been formed on the main atoll by John Clunies-Ross, a Scottish seaman and adventurer, who landed with several boat-loads of Malay seamen to begin commercial development of the islands' coconut palms.

In 1857 the islands were annexed to the Crown; in 1878 responsibility was transferred from the Colonial Office to the Government of Ceylon, and in 1886 to the Government of the Straits Settlement. By indenture in 1886 Queen Victoria granted all land in the islands to George Clunies-Ross and his heirs in perpetuity (with certain rights reserved to the Crown). The head of the family had semi-official status as resident magistrate and representative of the Government. In 1903 the islands were incorporated in the Settlement of Singapore and in 1942–46 temporarily placed under the Governor of Ceylon. In 1946 a Resident Administrator, responsible to the Governor of Singapore, was appointed.

On 23 Nov. 1955 the Cocos Islands were placed under the authority of the Australian Government as the Territory of Cocos (Keeling) Islands. An Administrator, appointed by the Governor-General, is the Government's representative in the Territory and is responsible to the Minister for Territories and Local Government. The Cocos (Keeling) Islands Council, established as the elected body of the Cocos Malay community in July 1979, advises the Administrator on all issues affecting the Territory.

In 1978 the Australian Government purchased the Clunies-Ross family's entire interests in the islands, except for the family residence. A Cocos Malay co-operative has been established to take over the running of the Clunies-Ross copra plantation (190 tonnes of copra were exported in 1982) and to engage in other business with the Commonwealth in the Territory, including construction projects.

The population of the Territory at 30 June 1983 was 579, distributed between Home Island (363) and West Island (216).

The islands are low-lying, flat and thickly covered by coconut palms, and surround a lagoon in which ships drawing up to 7 metres may be anchored, but which is extremely difficult for navigation.

An equable and pleasant climate, affected for much of the year by the south-east trade winds. Temperatures range over the year from 63° F (20° C) to 88° F (31·1° C) and rainfall averages 80″ (2,000 mm) a year.

The Cocos (Keeling) Islands Act 1955–1975 is the basis of the Territory's administrative, legislative and judicial systems. The laws of the Colony of Singapore which were in force in the islands immediately before the transfer have, with certain exceptions, been continued in force. They can be amended, repealed or substituted by ordinances made by the Governor-General.

The *Singapore Ordinances Application Ordinance* 1979 had the effect of repealing all Singapore Ordinances in force in the Territory and applying the provisions of 95 selected Singapore Ordinances only to be laws of the Territory.

Administrator: E. H. Hanfield.

CHRISTMAS ISLAND is in the Indian Ocean, lat. 10° 25′ 22″ S., long. 105° 39′ 59″ E. It lies 360 km S., 8° E. of Java Head, and 417 km N. 79° E. from Cocos Islands, 1,310 km from Singapore and 2,623 km from Fremantle. Area about 135 sq. km. The climate is pleasant and healthy with temperatures varying little over the year at 74–79° F (23–26° C). The wet season lasts from Nov. to April with an annual total of about 81″ (2,040 mm). The island was formally annexed by the UK on 6 June 1888, placed under the administration of the Governor of the Straits Settlements in 1889, and incorporated with the Settlement of Singapore in 1900. Sovereignty was transferred to the Australian Government on 1 Oct. 1958. The population (estimate, 1983), 3,000 (Europeans, 350; Chinese, 1,820; Malays, 750 and 90 others).

The legislative, judicial and administrative systems are regulated by the Christmas Island Act, 1958–73, which is administered by the Minister for Territories and Local Government with an Administrator, responsible for the local administration. The laws of Singapore which were in force before the transfer have been continued but can be amended, repealed or substituted by ordinances made by the Governor-General.

Extraction and export of rock phosphate and phosphate dust is the island's only industry. In Dec. 1948 Australia and New Zealand bought the lease rights of the Christmas Island Phosphate Co. and set up the Christmas Island Phosphate Commission, for which the Phosphate Mining Co. of Christmas Island (PMG) act as managing agents. The export of phosphate rock during 1982–83 was 1,017,000 tonnes, which is shipped to Australia and New Zealand; in addition, 184,000 tonnes of phosphate was shipped to Singapore and Malaysia.

There is direct radio communication with Australia and Singapore. Regular air charter flights commenced in 1974 to Australia.

At 31 May 1983 there were 621 primary and secondary pupils at the Christmas Island Area School. There is a technical school which provides commercial, apprenticeship and adult education courses, with (1979) some 701 students.

Medical, dental and hospital services are provided free of charge by the Phosphate Mining Co. of Christmas Island.

Administrator: T. F. Paterson.

NORFOLK ISLAND. 29° 04′ S. lat. 167° 57′ E. long., area 3,455 hectares, population, approximately 1,800. The island was formerly part of the colony of New South Wales and then of Van Diemen's Land. It has been a distinct settlement since 1856, under the jurisdiction of the state of New South Wales; and finally by the passage of the Norfolk Island Act 1913, it was accepted as a Territory of the Australian Government. The Norfolk Island Act 1957 is the basis of the Territory's legislative, administrative and judicial systems. An Administrator, appointed by the Governor-General and responsible to the Minister for Territories and Local Government, is the senior government representative in the Territory.

The Norfolk Island Act 1979 equips Norfolk Island with responsible legislative and executive government to enable it to run its own affairs to the greatest practicable extent. Wide powers are exercised by the Norfolk Island Legislative Assembly and by an Executive Council, comprising the executive members of the Legislative Assembly who have ministerial-type responsibilities. The Act preserves the Commonwealth's responsibility for Norfolk Island as a Territory under its authority, with the Minister for Territories and Local Government being the responsible Minister, and indicates the Parliament's intention that consideration will be given to an extension of the powers of the Legislative Assembly and the political and administrative institutions of Norfolk Island within 5 years.

The Executive Council has executive authority over a prescribed range of matters.

The island's Supreme Court sits as required and a Court of Petty Sessions exercises both civil and criminal jurisdiction.

The Territory Administration is financed from local revenue which for 1982–83 totalled $A2,673,723. A further $A286,000 was provided by the Commonwealth during the year for the restoration and maintenance of historic structures.

Public revenue is derived mainly from the sale of postage stamps, customs duties, liquor sales and company registration and licence fees. Residents are not liable for income tax on earnings within the Territory, nor are death and personal stamp duties levied. In 1982–83 imports totalled $A15·1m. and exports $A3·1m.

An estimated 16,220 visitors travelled to Norfolk during 1982–83. Descendants of the *Bounty* mutineer families constitute the 'original' settlers and are known locally as 'Islanders', while later settlers, mostly from Australia, New Zealand and UK, are identified as 'mainlanders'. Over the years the Islanders have preserved their own lifestyle and customs, and their language remains a mixture of West Country English and Tahitian.

The Administration subsidises a public hospital and dispensary, and health services, together with free dental services for children, are provided by qualified government officers.

Norfolk Island's public school is staffed by the New South Wales Department of Education and follows the State's education system. A bursary scheme is available to provide students with secondary education on the mainland.

A radio telephone service between the island and Sydney is maintained by the Overseas Telecommunications Commission, and there is a local automatic telephone service. Number of telephones (1982) 987.

Administrator: Air Vice-Marshal R. E. Trebilico, DFC.

HEARD AND McDONALD ISLANDS. These islands, about 2,500 miles south-west of Fremantle, were transferred from UK to Australian control as from 26 Dec. 1947. Heard Island is about 43 km long and 21 km wide; Shag Island is about 8 km north of Heard. The total area is 412 sq. km (159 sq. miles). The McDonald Islands are 42 km to the west of Heard.

TERRITORY OF ASHMORE AND CARTIER ISLANDS. By Imperial Order in Council of 23 July 1931, Ashmore Islands (known as Middle, East and West Islands) and Cartier Island, situated in the Indian Ocean, some 320 km off the north-west coast of Australia, were placed under the authority of the Commonwealth.

Under the Ashmore and Cartier Islands Acceptance Act, 1933, the islands were accepted by the Commonwealth under the name of the Territory of Ashmore and Cartier Islands, and the effective date was proclaimed by the Governor-General to be 10 May 1934. It was the intention that the Territory should be administered by the State of Western Australia, but owing to administrative difficulties the Territory was annexed to and deemed to form part of the Northern Territory of Australia (by amendment to the Act in 1938) with relevant laws of the Northern Territory, applying to the Territory of Ashmore and Cartier Islands. Responsibility for the administration of Ashmore and Cartier Islands rests with the Minister for Territories and Local Government.

On 16 Aug. 1983 a national nature reserve was declared over Ashmore Reef and the area so declared is now known as Ashmore Reef National Nature Reserve.

The islands are uninhabited but Indonesian fishing boats, which have traditionally plied the area, fish within the Territory and land to collect water in accordance with an agreement between the governments of Australia and Indonesia.

Periodic visits are made to the islands by ships of the Royal Australian Navy, and aircraft of the Royal Australian Air Force make aerial surveys of the islands and neighbouring waters.

TERRITORY OF CORAL SEA ISLANDS. The Coral Sea Islands became a Territory of the Commonwealth of Australia under the Coral Sea Islands Act 1969. It comprises scattered reefs and islands over a sea area of about 1m. sq. km. The Territory is uninhabited apart from a manned meteorological station on Willis Island.

Books of Reference

The Northern Territory: Annual Report. Dept. of Territories, Canberra, from 1911. Dept. of the Interior, Canberra, from 1966–67. Dept. of Northern Territory, from 1972

Australian Territories, Dept. of Territories, Canberra, 1960 to 1973. Dept. of Special Minister of State, Canberra, 1973–75. Department of Administrative Services, 1976
Northern Territory Statistical Summary. Australian Bureau of Statistics, Canberra, from 1960
Prospects of Agriculture in the Northern Territory. Dept. of Territories, Canberra, 1961
Holmes, J. M., *Australia's Open North.* Sydney, 1963
Lockwood, D. W., *Fair Dinkum.* London, 1960

NEW SOUTH WALES

HISTORY. New South Wales became a British possession in 1770; the first settlement was established at Port Jackson in 1788; a partially elective Council was established in 1843, and responsible government in 1856. New South Wales federated with the other Australian states to form the Commonwealth of Australia in 1901.

AREA AND POPULATION. New South Wales is situated between the 28th and 38th parallels of S. lat. and 141st and 154th meridians of E. long., and comprises 309,433 sq. miles (801,428 sq. km), inclusive of Lord Howe Island, 6 sq. miles (17 sq. km), but exclusive of the Australian Capital Territory (911 sq. miles, 2,359 sq. km) at Canberra and 28 sq. miles (73 sq. km), at Jervis Bay.

Lord Howe Island, 31° 33′ 4″ S., 159° 4′ 26″ E., which is part of New South Wales, is situated about 702 km north-east of Sydney; area, 1,656 hectares, of which only about 120 hectares are arable; resident population, estimate (30 June 1982), 300. The Island, which was discovered in 1788, is of volcanic origin. Mount Gower, the highest point, reaches a height of 866 metres.

The Lord Howe Island Board manages the affairs of the Island and supervises the Kentia palm-seed industry.

Census population of New South Wales (including full-blood Aboriginals from 1966):

	Males	Females	Persons	Population per sq. km	Average annual increase % since previous census
1881	410,211	339,614	749,825	1	4·07
1891	609,666	517,471	1,127,137	1	4·16
1901	710,264	645,091	1,355,355	2	1·86
1911	857,698	789,036	1,646,734	2	1·97
1921	1,071,501	1,028,870	2,100,371	3	2·46
1933	1,318,471	1,282,376	2,600,847	3	1·76
1947	1,492,211	1,492,627	2,984,838	4	0·99
1954	1,720,860	1,702,669	3,423,529	4	1·98
1961	1,972,909	1,944,104	3,917,013	5	1·94
1966	2,126,652	2,111,249	4,237,901	5	1·58
1971	2,307,210	2,293,970	4,601,180	6	1·66
1976	2,380,172	2,396,931	4,777,103	6	0·75
1981	2,548,984	2,577,233	5,126,217	6	1·42

At 30 June 1982 the resident population (estimate) of New South Wales was 5,307,900 (1981,5,234,900). Sydney (Statistical Division), 3,310,450 (3,279,500); Newcastle (Statistical District), 410,250 (402,700); Wollongong (Statistical District), 233,650 (231,400). Population of principal country municipalities: Albury, 38,100 (37,350); Armidale, 19,400 (19,350); Bathurst, 23,550 (23,050); Broken Hill, 27,700 (27,850); Casino, 10,400 (10,400); Dubbo, 29,350 (28,900); Goulburn, 22,250 (22,100); Grafton, 17,200 (17,200); Hastings, 37,000 (34,350); Lake Macquarie, 156,950 (153,650); Lismore, 35,500 (34,550); Lithgow, Greater, 20,850 (20,500); Orange, 31,750 (31,350); Queanbeyan, 20,150 (20,050); Shellharbour, 44,350 (43,500); Shoalhaven, 51,750 (48,600); Tamworth, 32,950 (32,400); Greater Taree, 33,100 (32,000); Wagga Wagga, 48,950 (48,700).

Vital statistics for calendar years:

	Live births	Marriages	Divorces	Deaths (excluding still-births)	Infantile mortality per 1,000 live births
1979	77,134	36,906	12,606	38,817	11·4
1980	79,455	38,965	13,449	40,282	10·7
1981	81,530	40,679	14,532	39,959	9·9
1982	83,489	41,955	14,378	42,352	9·9

The annual rates per 1,000 of mean resident population (estimate) in 1982 were: Births, 15·74; deaths, 7·98; marriages, 7·91.

CONSTITUTION AND GOVERNMENT. Within the State there are three levels of government: the Commonwealth Government, with authority derived from a written constitution; the State Government with residual powers; the local government authorities with powers based upon a State Act of Parliament, operating within incorporated areas extending over almost 90% of the State.

The Constitution of New South Wales is drawn from several diverse sources; certain Imperial statutes such as the Colonial Laws Validity Act (1865) and the Commonwealth of Australia Constitution Act (1900); the Australian States Constitution Act (1907); the Letters Patent and the Instructions to the Governor; an element of inherited English law; amendments to the Commonwealth of Australia Constitution Act; the (State) Constitution Act and certain other State Statutes; numerous legal decisions; and a large amount of English and local convention.

The Parliament of New South Wales may legislate for the peace, welfare and good government of the State in all matters not specifically reserved to the Commonwealth Government.

The State Legislature consists of the Sovereign, represented by the Governor, and two Houses of Parliament, the Legislative Council (upper house) and the Legislative Assembly (lower house).

Under legislation passed in 1978, the Legislative Council is to consist of 45 members elected by popular vote for a term of office equivalent to three terms of the Legislative Assembly, with 15 members retiring at the same time as the Legislative Assembly elections. In Oct. 1983, the Council consisted of the following parties: Labor, 24; Liberal, 12; National Party, 16; Australian Democrats, 1; Independent, 1.

Australian citizens, and other British subjects who have resided in Australia for a period of 6 months men and women aged 18 years and over, are entitled to the franchise. Voting is compulsory.

The President of the Legislative Council has an annual salary (1983) of $A50,200; the Leader of the Opposition members, $A43,900; the Chairman of Committees, the Deputy Leader of the Government members (if not a Minister) and the Deputy Leader of the Opposition members (when a leader of a party), $A31,915 each; the Deputy Leader of the Opposition members (when not a leader of a party) and Government and Opposition Whips, $A29,646 each. The President is paid an annual expense allowance of $A7,121; the Leader of the Opposition members, $A4,604; the Chairman of Committees, the Deputy Leader of the Government members (if not a Minister) and the Deputy Leader of the Opposition members (when a leader of a party), $A3,913 each; the Deputy Leader of the Opposition members (when not a leader of a party) and Government and Opposition Whips, $A1,848 each. Other members who are not Ministers receive an annual salary of $A25,200. All members receive an annual electoral allowance of $A8,043. Special expenses allowances ($A4,185 or $A7,000) are paid to members who are not Ministers and reside in outlying electorates.

The Legislative Assembly has 99 members elected by popular vote for a maximum period of 3 years. (Subsequent parliaments maximum period will be 4 years.) The Legislative Assembly, elected on 19 Sept. 1981, consisted in Oct. 1983 of the following parties: Labor, 69; Liberal, 13; National Party, 13; Independents, 4.

The Speaker of the Legislative Assembly and the Leader of the Opposition members receive a salary of (1983) $A59,050 each; the Chairman of Committees, Deputy Leader of the Opposition members and Leader of the National Party, $A43,900 each; Government and Opposition Whips, $A41,230 each. The Speaker and the Leader of the Opposition members also receive an expense allowance of $A8,378 each; the Chairman of Committees, Deputy Leader of the Opposition members and Leader of the National Party, $A4,604 each; Government and Opposition Whips, and Deputy Leader of the National Party, $A2,174 each. Members who are not Ministers receive an annual salary of $A36,000. All members receive an annual electoral allowance ranging from $A11,490 to $A20,684 according to the location of their constituencies. Special expenses allowances ($A4,650–$A7,000) are paid to members who represent outlying electorates.

The executive is in the hands of a Governor, appointed by the Crown, and an Executive Council consisting of members of the Cabinet. Ministers receive the following annual salaries: Premier, $A74,000; Deputy Premier, $A66,620; the Leader of the Government members in the Legislative Council, $A67,370; Deputy Leader of Government members in the Legislative Council, $A64,170; other Ministers, $A62,900. Ministers also receive an expense allowance (Premier, $A17,933; Deputy Premier, $A8,966; other Ministers, $A8,378 each). Ministers also receive an electoral allowance ranging from $A11,490 to $A20,684 to members of the Legislative Assembly, according to the location of their electorate; and $A8,043 to each member of the Legislative Council. A special expenses allowance of $A7,000 is paid to Ministers who represent (in the case of the Legislative Assembly) or reside in (in the case of the Legislative Council), outlying electorates.

Governor: Air Marshal Sir James Anthony Rowland, KBE, DFC, AFC, KStJ (sworn in 20 Jan. 1981).

The Labor Party Cabinet, in Oct. 1983, was as follows:

Premier: The Hon. N. K. Wran, QC, MP.
Deputy Premier, Minister for Public Works and Minister for Ports: The Hon. L. J. Ferguson, MP. *Minister for Transport:* The Hon. P. F. Cox, MP. *Minister for Youth and Community Services, Minister for Aboriginal Affairs and Minister for Housing:* The Hon. F. J. Walker, QC, MP. *Minister for Industrial Relations and Minister for Technology:* The Hon. P. D. Hills, MP. *Attorney-General, Minister of Justice, Minister for Consumer Affairs and Vice-President of the Executive Council:* The Hon. D. P. Landa, MLC. *Treasurer:* The Hon. K. G. Booth, MP. *Minister for Industrial Development and Minister for Decentralization:* The Hon. Donald Day, MP. *Minister for Corrective Services and Minister for Roads:* The Hon. R. F. Jackson, MP. *Minister for Planning and Environment:* The Hon. E. L. Bedford, BA, MP. *Minister for Mineral Resources:* The Hon. K. J. Stewart, MP. *Minister for Education:* The Hon. R. J. Mulock, MP. *Minister for Local Government and Minister for Lands:* The Hon. A. R. L. Gordon, MP. *Minister for Agriculture and Fisheries:* The Hon. J. R. Hallam, MLC. *Minister for Energy and Minister for Finance:* The Hon. T. W. Sheahan, MP. *Minister for Health:* The Hon. L. J. Brereton, MP. *Minister for Police and Emergency Services:* The Hon. P. T. Anderson, MP. *Minister for Leisure, Sport and Tourism:* The Hon. M. A. Cleary, MP. *Minister for Water Resources and Minister for Forests:* The Hon. P. F. P. Whelan, MP.

Agent-General in London: R. F. Watson, CMG (66 Strand, WC2N 5LZ).

Local Government. A system of local government extends over most of the State, including the whole of the Eastern and Central land divisions and almost three-quarters of the sparsely populated Western division. At 1 Jan. 1983 there were 62 municipalities, and 113 corporate bodies called shires. A number of the municipalities and shires have combined to form 43 county councils, which administer electricity or water supply undertakings or render other services of common benefit.

ECONOMY

Budget. State Consolidated Fund: statement of receipts and expenditure (in $A1m.) for financial years ending 30 June:

	1979–80	1980–81	1981–82	1982–83
Receipts: Recurrent	4,000	4,639	5,353	6,119
Capital	524	547	563	619
Total Receipts	4,523	5,186	5,916	6,737
Expenditure: Recurrent	4,004	4,669	5,422	6,301
Capital	522	564	553	477
Total Expenditure	4,527	5,233	5,976	6,777
Surplus/deficit	–3	–46	–60	–40

State Government receipts (in $A1m.) for 1982–83 included receipts from loan raisings, 296; Commonwealth general revenue assistance, 2,362; and state taxation, 2,685. Expenditure included capital works and services, 477; education, 1,971; health, 797; and public debt charges, 585.

Public Debt. In terms of the financial agreement between the Commonwealth and State Governments, the Commonwealth Government has assumed responsibility for debts of the Australian States, and contributes towards the interest thereon and sinking funds established for redemption of the debts. Loans for the States are raised by the Commonwealth Government in accordance with decisions of the Australian Loan Council.

The public debt of New South Wales at 30 June 1983 was $A5,328m. with less than 1% domiciled overseas. Interest liability for 1982–83 amounted to $A559m. Contributions to the sinking fund for New South Wales debt, $A75m., includes $A14m. contributed by the Commonwealth Government. The net cost of securities redeemed in the year was $A76m.

Banking. There were 8 trading banks operating in New South Wales at 30 June 1983, including the Commonwealth Trading Bank and State Bank (Government banks) and 1 New Zealand bank. The trading bank business is transacted chiefly by the Commonwealth Trading Bank, the State Bank and 3 private banks, all of which have their head offices in Australia. At 30 June 1983 the 8 banks operated 1,905 branches and 297 agencies in New South Wales.

The weekly average amount of deposits held in New South Wales by the 8 banks was $A15,556m. in June 1983, consisting of $A11,097·7m. bearing interest and $A4,458·3m. not bearing interest. Bank advances, overdrafts, bills discounted, etc., amounted to $A11,904·5m. A statement of other assets and liabilities of the banks in New South Wales is of little significance, as banking business is conducted on an Australia-wide basis.

Savings bank deposits at the end of June 1983 amounted to $A8,304·2m., representing $A1,557 per head of population.

ENERGY AND NATURAL RESOURCES

Minerals. New South Wales contains extensive mineral deposits. The most important minerals mined are: Coal (which accounts for 72% of the value of the State's mineral production); silver–lead–zinc (11%); construction materials (sand, gravel, stone, etc., 11%); and mineral sands (rutile, zircon, etc., 1%). At 30 June 1982, there were 580 mining establishments with an average employment of 29,723. During 1981–82, wages and salaries paid were $A735m., and value added was $A1,483m. Mine production of coal and metallic minerals (gross content) is shown below:

	1979–80	1980–81	1981–82	1982–83
Antimony (tonnes)	1,435	1,207	1,218	761
Cadmium (tonnes)	1,174	1,156	1,378	1,408
Coal (1,000 tonnes)	48,975	58,549	60,172	66,297
Cobalt (tonnes)	84	74	57	92
Copper (tonnes)	19,043	17,162	22,915	26,525
Gold (kg)	518	572	612	533
Lead (tonnes)	237,189	224,938	253,031	237,967
Silver (kg)	291,017	283,667	307,508	325,231
Sulphur (tonnes)	243,216	236,244	273,956	281,867
Tin (tonnes)	2,424	2,053	1,668	1,464
Titanium dioxide (tonnes)	111,057	111,021	80,454	47,730
Zinc (tonnes)	322,173	309,181	357,185	375,717
Zircon (tonnes)	106,477	113,009	88,479	55,554

The value of output in mining and quarrying in 1981–82 was $A2,196m.

Land settlement. The total area of land alienated, virtually alienated or in process of alienation from the Crown on 30 June 1982 was 30,875,704 hectares; 42,777,144 hectares (including 30,836,838 hectares of the Western Division) were held under lease from the Crown; the total area of land neither alienated nor leased (including roads, reserves for public purposes, etc.) was 6,555,941 hectares.

Agriculture. The area under cultivation in New South Wales during 3 years (ended 31 March) and the principal crops (in tonnes) produced were as follows:

	1980	1981	1982
Area of crops	5,400,333	5,376,115	5,993,393
Value (farm) of all crops	$A1,395m.	$A1,108m.	$A1,517m.

		1980		1981		1982
Principal crops	Hectares	Production	Hectares	Production	Hectares	Production
Wheat { Grain	3,415,027	6,000,000	3,345,000	2,865,000	3,600,000	5,910,000
Wheat { Hay	13,547	40,611	33,081	67,830	22,239	62,796
Barley { Grain	445,195	686,330	455,481	413,325	539,967	766,362
Barley { Hay	1,379	2,600	3,451	6,190	3,207	7,931
Oats { Grain	348,743	460,652	363,250	309,867	555,694	741,275
Oats { Hay	28,128	75,870	42,716	90,151	58,419	171,180
Grain Sorghum	147,858	204,528	127,294	147,828	152,346	325,689
Potatoes	7,443	102,408	6,262	86,526	6,185	107,500
Lucerne (hay)	40,506	191,905	41,858	197,469	58,199	281,358
Rice	110,431	585,980	98,824	703,530	117,607	828,944
Cotton	38,916	149,252	53,743	173,428	63,508	248,665
Oilseeds	130,070	114,122	65,684	47,402	66,430	65,358

In 1981–82, 14,286 hectares of sugar-cane were cut for crushing, the production being 1,505,907 tonnes. The total area under grapes was 13,521 (including 772 not bearing) hectares; the production of table grapes was 5,739 tonnes; of wine, 104,972 tonnes; of dried vine fruits, 13,042 tonnes.

In 1981–82, 5,253 hectares of banana plantations; production from 4,774 hectares, 63,309 tonnes; there were 27,057 hectares of orchard fruit.

At 31 March 1982 the State had 48·7m. sheep and lambs, 5,429,209 cattle and 765,933 pigs. The production of wool in 1981–82 was 216·3m. kg (greasy). In the year ended 30 June 1983 production of butter was 1,956 tonnes; cheese, 11,663 tonnes, and bacon and ham, 22,457 tonnes.

Forestry. The estimated area of Crown and private lands is 16·3m. hectares. The total area of State forests amounts to 3·5m. hectares, and 300,000 hectares have been set apart as timber reserves.

In 1982–83, 2,970 cu. metres of timber (excluding firewood) were produced, including 1,087 cu. metres of forest hardwoood and 1,160 cu. metres of pulpwoods.

INDUSTRY AND TRADE

Industry. Approximately 20% of employed persons in New South Wales are employed in manufacturing industries.

A very wide range of manufacturing activities is undertaken in the Sydney area, and there are large iron and steel works and associated metal fabrication works in operation in proximity to the coalfields at Newcastle and Port Kembla.

The following table shows a summary of manufacturing industries' statistics for 1981–82:

Industry	Establishments [1] No.	Employment [2] Males (No.)	Females (No.)	Wages and salaries [3] ($A1m.)	Value added ($A1m.)
Food, beverages and tobacco	1,010	39,451	16,820	865·2	1,638·5
Textiles	210	5,767	4,550	150·4	289·3
Clothing and footwear	754	5,136	18,981	259·6	420·2
Wood, wood products and furniture	1,435	22,766	4,371	346·2	627·1
Paper, paper products printing and publishing	1,262	26,104	12,493	613·8	1,159·5
Chemical, petroleum and coal products	438	20,244	9,341	526·2	1,332·4
Non-metallic mineral products	591	14,773	1,972	290·1	574·9
Basic metal products	215	50,880	3,998	1,039·9	1,543·6
Fabricated metal products	1,762	34,556	8,353	619·8	1,064·3
Transport equipment	447	31,294	3,396	518·0	833·6
Other machinery and equipment	1,641	52,479	19,403	1,047·8	1,742·5
Miscellaneous manufacturing	860	15,877	8,778	345·8	599·3
Total manufacturing	10,625	319,327	112,456	6,622·7	11,825·3

[1] Operating at 30 June 1982. Excludes single-establishment manufacturing enterprises with less than 4 persons employed.
[2] Persons employed—average over whole year, including working proprietors.
[3] Excludes drawings of working proprietors.

Some of the principal articles manufactured in 1982–83 were:

Article	Quantity	Article	Quantity
Flour (1,000 tonnes)	492	Electric motors (1,000)	1,122
Woven fabric (1,000 sq. metres)	55,252	Clay bricks (1 m.)	645
Ale, beer and stout (1,000 litres)	623,557	Electricity (1 m. kwh.)	38,932
Raw steel (1,000 tonnes)	4,533		

During 1982–83 the value of all building jobs commenced in New South Wales was $A3,048m. (of which jobs valued at $A399m. were being built for government ownership), jobs completed were valued at $A3,484m. ($A564m. for government ownership), and jobs under construction at the end of the period were valued at $A2,680m. ($A577m. for government ownership).

Labour. Two systems of industrial arbitration and conciliation for the adjustment of industrial relations between employers and employees are in operation—the State system which operates within the territorial limits of the State, and the Commonwealth system, which applies to industrial disputes extending beyond State borders.

The industrial tribunals are authorized to fix minimum rates of wages and other conditions of employment. Their awards may be enforced by law, as may be industrial agreements between employers and organizations of employees, when registered.

The principal State tribunal is the Industrial Commission of New South Wales. The Commission is empowered to exercise all the arbitration and conciliation powers conferred on subsidiary tribunals, and has in addition authority to determine any widely defined 'industrial matter', to adjudicate in case of illegal strikes and lockouts, etc., to investigate union ballots when irregularities are alleged and to hear appeals from subsidiary tribunals. Subsidiary tribunals are Conciliation Committees for various industries, each having an equal number representing employers and employees and a Conciliation Commissioner as chairman.

The chief industrial tribunals of the Commonwealth are the Industrial Division of the Federal Court of Australia, composed of judges, and the Australian Conciliation and Arbitration Commission, composed of presidential members, and commissioners.

Most State awards and agreements prescribe a basic wage and, for each industry, margins assessed on skill, etc. Since 1974, the State Industrial Commission has also specified a minimum wage in line with Commonwealth awards. In Sept. 1983, the minimum wage payable in Sydney for a full week's work by an adult male or female was $A146.10 under both State and Commonwealth awards. For the June quarter 1983, average weekly earnings were $A393·00 for full-time adult males and $A290·60 for full-time adult females.

A standard working week of 40 hours is prescribed for employees in most industries. Overtime is permitted under prescribed conditions.

Trade Unions. Registration of trade unions is effected under the New South Wales Trade Union Act, 1881, which follows substantially the Trade Union Acts of 1871 and 1876 of England. Registration confers a quasi-corporate existence with power to hold property, to sue and be sued, etc., and the various classes of employees covered by the union are required to be prescribed by the constitution of the union. For the purpose of bringing an industry under the review of the State industrial tribunals, or participating in proceedings relating to disputes before Commonwealth tribunals, employees and employers must be registered as industrial unions, under State or Commonwealth industrial legislation respectively. At 31 Dec. 1982, there were 187 trade unions with a total membership of 1,127,500. Approximately 60% (estimate) of wage and salary earners were members of trade unions.

Commerce. The external commerce of New South Wales, exclusive of interstate trade, is included in the statement of the commerce of Australia (*see* pp. 110–12). The overseas commerce of New South Wales is given in $A1,000 ending 30 June:

	Imports	Exports		Imports	Exports
1977–78	4,635,018	3,114,401	1980–81	7,951,738	4,103,507
1978–79	5,760,063	3,512,435	1981–82	9,235,864	4,194,663
1979–80	6,704,649	4,103,985	1982–83	8,614,805	5,025,645

The main exports from New South Wales of Australian produce in 1982–83 were coal (29·8%), wool (8·4%), cereals (6·9%), petroleum (6·8%), iron and steel (6·5%), meat (5·9%), metalliferous ores and metal scraps (2·7%). Principal imports were machinery and transport equipment (38%), chemicals (8·7%), petroleum and petroleum products (8·7%), textiles (4·5%), precision instruments and apparatus (2·5%), metal manufactures (2·5%), paper and paperboard (2·3%).

Principal destinations of all exports from New South Wales in 1982–83 were Japan (28·1%), EEC countries (13·5%), ASEAN countries (7·3%), New Zealand (6·3%), USA (5·8%), Republic of Korea (5·3%), China (3·6%). Major sources of supply were USA (23·6%), EEC countries (21·2%), Japan (21·2%), New Zealand (3·8%) and Saudi Arabia (3·7%).

COMMUNICATIONS

Roads. At 30 June 1978 there were 204,571 km of roads and streets in New South Wales, comprising 424 km cement concrete, 7,462 km bituminous concrete, 62,595 km other bitumen surface, 66,413 km gravel, 39,188 km earth formed and 28,490 km natural surface.

The principal bus services in Sydney and Newcastle are operated by the State Government.

The number of registered motor vehicles (excluding tractors and trailers) at 30 June 1983 was 2,821,100, including 1,788,800 cars, 349,400 station wagons, 163,600 utilities, 179,900 panel vans, 188,500 trucks, 16,800 buses and 134,100 motor cycles.

Railways. At 30 June 1982, 9,773 km of government railway were open. The revenue (including supplements) in 1981–82 was $A1,139·4m.; the expenditure from revenue, $A1,139·5m.; the number of passengers carried, 221m. Also open for traffic are 325 km of Victorian Government railways which extend over the border; 68 km of private railways (mainly in mining districts) and 53 km of Commonwealth Government-owned track.

Aviation. Sydney is the major airport in New South Wales and Australia's principal international air terminal. During the year ended 31 Dec. 1981 scheduled air-craft movements at Sydney totalled 99,181. Passengers totalled 5,832,918 on domestic services and 2,395,700 on international services. Freight handled on domestic and international services was 56,353 tonnes and 90,420 tonnes respectively.

Shipping. The number of vessels engaged in overseas trade which entered the ports of New South Wales in 1981–82 was 2,829 and the clearances numbered 2,766. The revenue tonnage of cargo discharged and loaded was 9·9m. and 29·1m. respectively. Sydney Harbour is the principal port of Australia. The number of overseas vessels which entered in 1981–82 was 1,53__.

JUSTICE, RELIGION, EDUCATION AND WELFARE

Justice. Legal processes may be carried on in Lower or Magistrates' Courts, or in the Higher Courts presided over by judges. There is also an appellate jurisdiction. Persons charged with the more serious crimes must be tried before the Higher Courts.

Children's Courts have been established with the object of removing children as far as possible from the atmosphere of a public court. There are also a number of tribunals exercising special jurisdiction, *e.g.*, the Industrial Commission and the Workers' Compensation Commission.

In 1982 there were 3,973 distinct persons convicted at the Higher Criminal Courts. At 30 June 1980 there were 3,299 persons (including 114 females) held under sentence in prison.

Religion. There is no established church in New South Wales, and freedom of worship is accorded to all.

The following table shows the statistics of the religious denominations in New South Wales at the census, and of ministers of religion registered for the celebration of marriages, in 1981:

Denomination	Ministers	Adherents	Denomination	Ministers	Adherents
Church of England	938	1,569,374	Other Christian	1,132	388,887
Roman Catholic	1,693	1,424,499	Muslim	25	25,176
Presbyterian	211	252,725	Hebrew	10	38,527
Uniting Church	563	179,271	Other Non-Christian	13	25,408
Orthodox	77	171,427	Others	...	954,564 [1]
Baptist	342	64,663			
Lutheran	39	31,696	Total	5,043	5,126,217

[1] Comprises 443,159 'no religion' and 511,405 'religion not stated' or 'inadequately described' (this is not a compulsory question in the census schedule).

Education. The State Government maintains a system of primary and secondary education, and attendance at school is compulsory from 6 to 15 years of age. In all government schools education is free. Non-government schools are subject to government inspection.

In July 1982 there were 2,242 government schools, comprising 1,690 primary and infant schools, 74 combined primary and secondary schools, 363 secondary schools and 115 special-purpose schools. In July 1982 the effective enrolment was 782,079 students, comprising 494,966 receiving primary instruction and 287,113 receiving secondary instruction. There were 45,762 teachers (including the full-time equivalent of part-time teachers) in 1982.

In July 1982 there were 818 non-government schools with 13,262 teachers (including the full-time equivalent of part-time teachers) and an effective enrolment of 245,007 students, including 604 Roman Catholic schools, having 10,126 teachers and 199,863 students, and 32 Anglican schools with 1,172 teachers and 17,360 students.

The University of Sydney, founded in 1850, had 17,983 students in 1982. There are 6 colleges providing residential facilities at the university. The University of New England at Armidale, previously affiliated with the University of Sydney, was incorporated in 1954, and in 1982 had 8,899 students.

The University of New South Wales was established in 1949. Enrolments in

1982 numbered 19,016. There are 8 colleges providing residential facilities at the university. The University of Newcastle, previously affiliated with the University of New South Wales, was granted autonomy from 1965, and in 1982 had 4,273 students. The University of Wollongong, also previously associated with the University of New South Wales, became autonomous in 1975, and in 1982 had 3,246 students. Macquarie University in Sydney, established in 1964, had 10,735 students in 1982.

Colleges of Advanced Education were first established in 1971 to provide tertiary training with a vocational emphasis. In 1982 there were 42,026 students (including 23,639 part-time students) enrolled at 17 colleges.

Post-school technical and further education is provided at State technical colleges. Students enrolled in 1982 totalled 332,556 (including 19,119 correspondence students).

State Government expenditure (including loan expenditure) on education in 1981–82 was $A1,900m.

Social Welfare. The Commonwealth Government makes provision for social benefits, such as age and invalid pensions, widows' pensions, supporting parents' benefits, family allowances, and unemployment, sickness and special benefits.

The number of age and invalid pensions (including wives' pensions) current in New South Wales on 30 June 1983 was: Age, 516,723 (males, 166,661; females, 350,062); invalid, 94,265 (males, 52,919; females, 41,346). Expenditure for the year ended 30 June 1983 was $A1,809m. for age pensions and $A378m. for invalid pensions.

Commonwealth Government widows' pensions current in New South Wales at 30 June 1983 numbered 60,024, the expenditure for 1982–83, $A285m. Supporting parents' benefits at 30 June 1983 numbered 52,215; expenditure in 1982–83 was $A284m.

Under the Family Allowance scheme, which commenced in 1976, payments to families and approved institutions for children under 16 years and full-time students under 25 years (1,459,236 such children or students) during 1982–83 amounted to $A491m.

Unemployment, sickness and special benefits commenced in 1945. During the year 1982–83 claims totalling $A1,037m. were paid in New South Wales. At 30 June 1983 unemployment benefit was being paid to an estimated 244,209 persons, and sickness and special benefits to 37,165 persons.

Direct State Government social welfare services are limited, for the most part, to the assistance of persons not eligible for Commonwealth Government benefit and the provision of certain forms of assistance not available from the Commonwealth Government. The State also subsidizes many approved services for needy persons. During 1981–82, expenditure on social amelioration and war obligations was $A238m.

Books of Reference

Statistical Information: The NSW Government Statistician's Office was established in 1886, and in 1957 was integrated with the Commonwealth Bureau of Census and Statistics (now called the Australian Bureau of Statistics). *Deputy Commonwealth Statistician:* T. J. Skinner. Its principal publications are:

New South Wales Year Book (1886/87–1900/01 under the title *Wealth and Progress of NSW):* latest issue, 1983
New South Wales Handbook of Local Statistics: latest issue, 1983
New South Wales Principal Subject Bulletins (previously published under the title *Statistical Register* (since 1858); latest issue of separate bulletins, 1981–82 and 1983
New South Wales Pocket Year Book. Published since 1913; latest issue, 1983
Monthly Summary of Statistics. Published since May 1931
New South Wales in Brief. 1983

New South Wales Dept. of Leisure, Sport and Tourism, *New South Wales–Australia.* Sydney, 1982
New South Wales Dept. of Industrial Development and Decentralisation, *New South Wales Handbook for Industrialists.* 1983
State Planning Authority, *Sydney Region, 1970–2000 A.D.: Outline Plan.* Sydney, 1968

New South Wales Planning and Environment Commission, *Review: Sydney Region Outline Plan*. Sydney, 1980

New South Wales Government Information Service, *The Government of New South Wales: Directory of Administration and Services*. Sydney, 1982

State Library: The State Library of NSW, Macquarie St., Sydney. *State Librarian:* R. F. Doust, BA, M.Lib, FLAA.

QUEENSLAND

AREA AND POPULATION. Queensland comprises the whole north-eastern portion of the Australian continent, including the adjacent islands in the Pacific Ocean and in the Gulf of Carpentaria. Estimated area 1,727,000 sq. km.

The increase in the population as shown by the censuses since 1901 has been as follows:

		Census counts		Intercensal increase	
Year	Males	Females	Total	Numerical	Rate per annum %
1901	277,003	221,126	498,129	—	—
1911	329,506	276,307	605,813	107,684	1·98
1921	398,969	357,003	755,972	150,159	2·24
1933	497,217	450,317	947,534	191,562	1·86
1947	567,471	538,944	1,106,415	158,881	1·11
1954	676,252	642,007	1,318,259	211,844	2·53
1961	774,579	744,249	1,518,828	200,569	2·04
1966	849,390 [1]	824,934 [1]	1,674,324 [1]	144,857	1·84
1971	921,565 [1]	905,400 [1]	1,827,065 [1]	152,741 [1]	1·76 [1]
1976	1,024,611 [1]	1,012,586 [1]	2,037,197 [1]	210,132 [1]	2·20 [1]
1981	1,153,404 [1]	1,141,719 [1]	2,295,123 [1]	257,926 [1]	2·41 [1]

[1] Including Aboriginals.

Since the 1981 census, official population estimates are according to place of usual residence and are referred to as estimated resident population. Estimated resident populations at the census dates of 1971, 1976, and 1981 were 1,851,500; 2,092,400; and 2,345,200; respectively.

Statistics on birthplaces from the 1981 census are as follows: Australia, 1,932,810 (84·2%); UK and Ireland, 147,083 (6·4%); other countries, 183,067 (8%); at sea and not stated, 32,163 (1·4%).

Vital statistics (including Aboriginals) for calendar years:

	Total births	Marriages	Divorces	Deaths
1980	34,972	17,157	6,219	16,497
1981	38,834	18,305	6,470	17,175
1982	40,540	18,928	6,770	18,149

The annual rates per 1,000 population in 1982 were: Marriages, 7·8; births, 16·8; deaths, 7·5. The infant death rate was 10·7 per 1,000 births.

Brisbane, the capital, had on 30 June 1981 a resident population of 1,096,200 (Statistical Division). The resident populations of the other major centres (Statistical Districts) at the same date were: Gold Coast, 143,090; Townsville, 96,310; Sunshine Coast, 65,320; Cairns, 58,270; Rockhampton, 55,260; Mackay, 45,880 and Bundaberg, 40,800. Other cities included Toowoomba, 73,040; Mount Isa, 25,570; Gladstone, 23,850; and Maryborough, 22,250.

CONSTITUTION AND GOVERNMENT. Queensland, formerly a portion of New South Wales, was formed into a separate colony in 1859, and responsible government was conferred. The power of making laws and imposing taxes is vested in a Parliament of one House—the Legislative Assembly, which comprises 82 members, returned from 4 electoral zones for 3 years, elected for single-member constituencies at compulsory ballot. Members are entitled to $A37,695 per annum, with individual electorate allowances for travelling, postage, etc., of from $A9,540 to $A24,620.

At the general election of 29 Nov. 1980 there were 1,341,365 persons registered as qualified to vote under the Elections Act 1915–1976. This Act provides franchise for all males and females, 18 years of age and over, qualified by 6 months' residence in Australia and 3 months in the electoral district.

The Legislative Assembly, following the elections of 29 Nov. 1980, was composed of the following parties: National, 35; Liberal, 22; Australian Labor, 25; total, 82.

Governor of Queensland: Cde Sir James Maxwell Ramsay, KCMG, KCVO,CBE, DSC (assumed office April 1977).

The Executive Council of Ministers, at 19 Aug. 1983, consisted of the following members:

Premier and Treasurer: Johannes Bjelke-Petersen (National). *Commerce and Industry:* William Angus Manson (National). *Local Government, Main Roads and Racing:* Russell James Hinze (National). *Northern Development and Aboriginal and Island Affairs:* Valmond James Bird (National). *Works and Housing:* Claude Alfred Wharton (National). *Mines and Energy:* Ivan James Gibbs (National). *Primary Industries:* Michael John Ahern (National). *Lands, Forestry and Police:* William Hamline Glasson (National). *Tourism, National Parks, Sport and the Arts:* Jannion Anthony Elliott (National). *Education:* Lionel William Powell (National). *Water Resources and Maritime Services:* John Philip Goleby (National). *Health:* Angelo Pietro Dante Bertoni (National). *Transport:* Neil John Turner (National). *Employment and Labour Relations:* Vincent Patrick Lester (National). *Environment, Valuation and Administrative Services:* Martin James Tenni (National). *Justice and Attorney-General:* Neville John Harper (National). *Welfare Services:* Geoffrey Hugh Muntz (National).

Each Minister has a salary of $A61, 963, the Premier receives $A78,725, the Deputy Premier, $A67,513, and the Leader of the Opposition, $A53,471.

Agent-General in London: J. H. Andrews (392–3 Strand, WC2R 0LZ).

Local Government. Provision is made for local government by the subdivision of the State into cities, towns and shires. These are under the management of aldermen or councillors, who are elected by all persons 18 years and over. Local Authorities are charged with the control of all matters of a parochial nature, such as sewerage, cleansing and sanitary services, health services, domestic water supplies, and roads and bridges within their allotted areas. In addition to Government grants and subsidies, Local Authority revenue is derived from general rates, paid by landowners on the unimproved capital value of land, and by charging for some specific services.

For the year ended 30 June 1982, the receipts and expenditure (including loans) for the 134 Local Authorities were $A1,112·4m. and $A1,100·8m. respectively and their rateable values amounted to $A8,139·7m.

ECONOMY

Budget. Revenue and expenditure of the Consolidated Revenue Fund of Queensland during 5 years ending 30 June (in $A1,000):

	1978–79	1979–80	1980–81	1981–82	1982–83
Revenue	1,947,444	2,206,954	2,604,036	3,276,756	3,690,187
Expenditure	1,946,867	2,207,893	2,604,010	3,276,926	3,690,956

Total funds available to the Queensland Government in 1981–82 were $A3,569·1m., of which Taxation and Federal Government grants amounted to $A3,120·8m. Expenditure from these funds included: Education, $A1,105·6m.; economic services (roads, electricity, etc.), $A871·7m.; health, $A561·1m.

Revenue and expenditure of Commonwealth Government departments on account of Queensland are not included.

Debt. The gross public debt of the State at par rates of exchange amounted, on 30 June 1982, to $A2,112·1m. The debt was domiciled as follows (in $A1,000): Australia, 2,110,171; UK, 1,094; USA, 63; European countries, 742. The annual interest charge on the public debt at 30 June 1982 was $A192·8m.

Banking. There were 8 trading banks operating in Queensland at 30 June 1983, including the Commonwealth Trading Bank of Australia, the 4 larger Australian trading banks, the Bank of Queensland Ltd, the Australian Bank Ltd, the Bank of New Zealand and the Banque Nationale de Paris. The Commonwealth Trading Bank had 160 branches and 62 agencies; the other banks had 687 branches and 146 agencies in the State. Queensland deposits of all trading banks, including the Commonwealth Trading Bank of Australia, amounted to $A5,886·5m.; and loans, advances and bills discounted in Queensland were $A4,096·3m. At 30 June 1983 savings bank business was conducted in Queensland by 5 banks, the Commonwealth Savings Bank with 169 branches and 1,197 agencies, and 4 other banks with 667 branches and 1,169 agencies. Depositors' balances amounted to $A4,136m. in 3·39m. accounts.

ENERGY AND NATURAL RESOURCES

Electricity. The State Electricity Commission, established in 1938 and under a single Commissioner since 1948, co-ordinates the electricity industry in Queensland.

Electricity generated by the principal stations in the year ended 30 June 1982 was 13,171m. kwh. Black coal was used to generate over 90% of the power; hydroelectric stations generated about 5% and the balance was generated by gas turbine and diesel power stations using light fuel oil. The Roma diesel power station also uses locally-produced natural gas.

Minerals. Principal minerals produced during 1981–82 were: Copper, 175,000 tonnes; coal, 34,276,000 tonnes; lead, 171,000 tonnes; zinc, 152,000 tonnes; silver, 454,876 kg; tin, 3,147 tonnes; gold, 824 kg; bauxite, 8,705,000 tonnes; mineral sands concentrates, 142,000 tonnes; uranium, 907 tonnes. Value of output, at the mine, was $A2,128m. The chief mines are Mount Isa (copper, silver, lead, zinc), Weipa (bauxite), Mount Morgan (copper, gold), Moreton and Bowen Basin (coal), Greenvale (nickel) and Mary Kathleen (uranium).

Land Settlement. Of the total area of the State, 13·3m. hectares had been alienated at 31 Dec. 1981; in process of alienation, under deferred payment system, were 20·7m. hectares, leaving 138·8m. hectares, still the property of the Crown, or 80·4% of the total area. A large proportion of the area is leased for pastoral purposes (97·1m. hectares at 31 Dec. 1981).

In the western portion of the State water is comparatively easily found by sinking artesian bores. At 30 June 1981, 3,443 such bores had been drilled, of which 2,355 were flowing.

Agriculture. Livestock on farms and stations at 31 March 1982 numbered 9·78m. cattle, 12·34m. sheep and 513,000 pigs. The wool production (greasy) was, in 1981–82, 61m. kg, valued at $A151m. The total area under crops during 1981–82 was 2·76m. hectares.

	Area (hectares)		Yield (tonnes)	
Crop	1980–81	1981–82	1980–81	1981–82
Sugar-cane, crushed	274,259	301,658	22,540,367	23,587,934
Wheat	726,964	941,131	485,255	1,482,331
Maize	42,566	47,568	123,190	150,524
Sorghum	528,394	489,144	1,050,177	982,435
Barley	159,686	206,395	170,339	397,524
Oats	14,268	17,821	5,932	16,378
Potatoes	5,751	6,140	113,339	128,606
Pumpkins	4,102	4,031	32,195	27,673
Tomatoes	3,361	3,314	55,660	58,029
Peanuts	26,773	32,984	42,386	56,429
Tobacco	3,454	3,341	7,592	7,980
Apples [1]	3,423	3,404	23,086	35,957
Grapes [1]	1,411	1,441	5,391	4,212
Citrus [1]	2,041	1,981	44,303	43,723
Bananas [1]	2,414	2,531	53,761	57,146
Pineapples [1]	4,085	4,046	123,220	125,422
Green fodder [2]	399,297	321,082	...	...
Hay (all kinds)	39,157	38,912	196,214	220,664
Cotton (raw)	24,182	28,809	22,548	27,234

[1] Bearing area only.　　　　[2] Excluding lucerne.

Forestry. A considerable area consists of natural forest, eucalyptus, pine and cabinet woods being the timbers mostly in evidence; a large quantity of ornamental woods is utilized by cabinet makers. The amount of native timber processed in 1981–82 was (in cu. metres): Conifers, 556,124; hardwoods, structural timbers and cabinet woods, 785,410.

INDUSTRY AND TRADE

Industry. The 1970s created a milestone in the State's industrial progress when the value added in production by the manufacturing sector exceeded the value of production in the agriculture, forestry, fishing and hunting sector. In 1981–82, there were 3,552 establishments, with four or more workers, employing 99,359 males and 23,266 females, and producing goods and services worth $A10,587m. The value added was $A3,449m. The manufacturing establishments contributing most to the overall production during 1981–82 were those predominantly engaged in the processing of food, beverages and tobacco.

The gross value of Queensland agricultural commodity production (in $A1,000) during 1981–82, amounted to 2,612,728, which included crops, 1,472,311; livestock disposals, 832,322; livestock products, 308,096.

Labour. Of the total population of 2·5m., 969,500 were in employment in Aug. 1983, 133,600 in manufacturing. Industrial wages and conditions are controlled partly by Federal and partly by State authorities. A State Industrial Commission is empowered to determine all industrial matters in relation to employers and employees, to fix minimum wage-rates and other conditions of employment. An Industrial Court hears appeals and decides points of industrial law. The Federal Court of Australia and the Conciliation and Arbitration Commission are superior within their jurisdictions. In Queensland most employees (67%) work under State awards; 25% under Federal awards.

Rates of wages for each occupation are prescribed by these courts. The minimum weighted average award rate of pay for adult male wage and salary earners was $A275·39 and for adult females $A259·64, at 30 June 1983, while for the June quarter 1983, average weekly earnings were $A372·20 for full-time adult males and $A290 for full-time adult females. (Average earnings include award, over-award and overtime payments.) A standard working week of either 38 or 40 hours is prescribed for most awards.

Trade Unions. Unions both of employees and employers must be registered with the State or Australian Commission. There were 71 employees' and 38 employers' unions registered with the State Commission at 31 Dec. 1982, the former comprising 385,211 and the latter 36,617 members.

Commerce. The overseas commerce of Queensland is included in the statement of the commerce of Australia (*see* pp. 110–12).

Total value of the direct overseas imports and exports of Queensland (in $A1,000) f.o.b. port of shipment for both imports and exports:

	1977–78	1978–79	1979–80	1980–81	1981–82	1982–83
Imports	887,179	1,028,010	1,321,214	1,882,815	2,179,752	1,993,666
Exports	2,821,362	3,285,778 ¹	4,265,101 ¹	4,501,290 ¹	4,414,452 ¹	4,467,586 ¹

¹ State of origin.

In 1982–83 interstate exports totalled $A1,848m. and imports $A4,411·8m. The chief exports overseas are minerals including alumina, coal, meat (preserved or frozen), sugar, wool, cereal grains, copper and lead, and manufactured goods. Principal overseas imports are machinery, motor vehicles, mineral fuels (including lubricants, etc.), chemicals and manufactured goods classified by material. Chief sources of imports in 1982–83 were Japan ($A547·8m.), USA ($A485·5m.), Indonesia ($A124·8m.); exports went chiefly to Japan ($A1,764·6m.), USA ($A488·8m.), UK ($A316·2m.), EEC, excluding UK ($A402·9m.).

COMMUNICATIONS

Roads. At 30 June 1982 there were 162,413 km of roads; of these, 141,211 km were formed roads, of which 48,996 km were surfaced with concrete sealed pavement.

At 30 June 1982 motor vehicles registered in Queensland totalled 1,439,457, comprising 997,725 cars and station wagons, 190,325 utilities, 76,533 panel vans, 6,748 buses, 69,715 trucks and 98,410 motor cycles.

Railways. Practically all the railways are owned by the State Government. Total length of line at 30 June 1982 was 9,969 km. In 1981–82, 34·2m. passengers and 43·7m. tonnes of goods and livestock were carried.

Aviation. Queensland is well served with a network of air services, with overseas and interstate connexions. Subsidiary companies provide planes for taxi and charter work, and the Flying Doctor Service operates throughout western Queensland.

Shipping. In 1981–82, cargo discharged was 3m. revenue tonnes and cargo loaded was 36m. revenue tonnes.

Broadcasting. At 30 June 1982, 59 broadcasting and 43 television stations were in operation throughout Queensland.

JUSTICE, RELIGION, EDUCATION AND WELFARE

Justice. Justice is administered by a Supreme Court, District Courts, Magistrates' Courts and Children's Courts. The Supreme Court comprises a Chief Justice, a senior puisne judge, 16 puisne judges and 2 masters; the District Court, 20 district court judges. Stipendiary magistrates preside over the Lower Courts, except in the smaller centres, where justices of the peace officiate. A parole board may recommend prisoners for release.

The total number of persons convicted of serious offences by the superior courts in 1981–82 was 1,344; summary convictions in lower courts numbered 113,922. There were, at 30 June 1982, 5 prisons, 2 gaols for short-term prisoners, 2 prison farms conducted on the honour system and 1 prison for criminally-insane patients, with 1,661 male and 45 female prisoners. The total police force, was 4,543 at 30 June 1982.

Religion. There is no State Church. Membership, census 1981: Anglican, 601,537; Roman Catholic and Catholic (not further defined), 554,912; Uniting Church, 146,898; Presbyterian, 132,525; Methodist, 86,750; Lutheran, 50,401; Baptist, 34,323; other Christian, 166,611; Buddhist, 2,967; Muslim, 2,457; Hebrew, 2,021; all others (including not stated and no religion), 513,721.

Education. Education in Queensland ranges from pre-school level through to tertiary level. In addition, child care, kindergarten and adult education facilities are available. Education is compulsory between the ages of 6 and 15 years and is provided free in government schools. Expenditure on education by government authorities for 1980–81 was $A947m.

At July 1982, pre-school education and child care was provided at 1,119 centres with 3,361 staff and 59,981 children.

Primary and secondary education comprises 12 years of full-time formal schooling and is provided by both the government and non-government sectors. At July 1982, the State administered 1,039 primary, 88 primary/secondary, and 145 secondary schools with 254,330 primary students, 114,022 secondary students and 20,404 teachers. Special education, which is included in the above figures, was provided to 5,230 children at 61 special schools and 50 primary schools with special classes. Non-government enrolments at July 1982 were 58,156 primary students and 46,332 secondary students taught by 5,260 teachers at 222 primary, 56 primary/secondary and 76 secondary schools.

Post-secondary education in Queensland involves technical and further education, advanced education and university education. Tertiary education in 1981 involved 405 full-time and 310 part-time students at technical colleges, 10,515 full-time and 13,306 part-time students at colleges of advanced education and 12,241 full-time and 10,151 part-time students at universities.

Sub-tertiary education in 1981 involved 49,039 students at technical colleges,

846 students at colleges of advanced education and 466 students at rural training schools.

Social Welfare. Public hospitals are maintained by State and Federal Government endowment, supplemented by fees from patients not in standard wards. Welfare institutions providing shelter and social care for the aged, the handicapped, and children, are maintained or assisted by the State. A maternal and child welfare service is provided throughout the State. Age, invalid, widows', disability and war service pensions, family allowances, and unemployment and sickness benefits are paid by the Federal Government. Age pensioners in the State at 30 June 1982 numbered 210,317; invalid pensioners, 33,492; disability pensioners, 127,755 (including dependants).

There were 21,314 widows' pensions current at 30 June 1982, and at the same date family allowances were being paid to 333,822 families in respect of 683,642 children under 16 years or students aged 16 or more but under 25. In addition, family allowances were paid to 2,244 children and students in institutions.

Housing. In 1982–83, 27,143 dwellings valued at $A1,183m. were approved for construction. This total comprised 19,507 houses and 7,636 individual other dwelling units contained in flats, semi-detached units, home units, villa units, town houses, etc. In 1981–82, 35,950 new dwellings were completed and 14,890 were being built at 30 June 1982. The Queensland Housing Commission, financed by Federal and State Government loans, builds dwellings for sale and for rental. Building and co-operative housing societies are assisted by Federal and State Government loans.

Books of Reference

Statistical Information: The Statistical Office (345 Ann St., Brisbane) was set up in 1859.
Deputy Commonwealth Statistician: O. M. May. *A Queensland Official Year Book* was issued in 1901, the annual *ABC of Queensland Statistics* from 1905 to 1936 with exception of 1918 and 1922. Present publications include: *Queensland Year Book.* Annual, from 1937 (omitting 1942, 1943, 1944).—*Queensland Pocket Year Book.* Annual from 1950.—*Monthly Summary of Queensland Statistics.* From Jan. 1961
Australian and New Zealand Association for the Advancement of Science, *Introducing Queensland.* Brisbane, 1961
Queensland Department of Agriculture and Stock, *The Queensland Agricultural and Pastoral Handbook.* 2 vols. Brisbane, 1962
Australian Sugar Year Book. Brisbane, from 1941
Johnston, W. R., *A Bibliography of Queensland History.* Brisbane, 1981
Endean, R., *Australia's Great Barrier Reef.* Brisbane, 1982
Queensland State Public Relations Bureau, *Queensland Resources Atlas,* Brisbane, 1980
Commonwealth Department of National Development and Queensland Department of Industrial Development, *Resources and Industry of Central Queensland,* Canberra, 1969
Australian Department of Northern Development and Queensland Department of Commercial and Industrial Development, *Resources and Industry of the Mackay Region,* Canberra, 1974
School of Business Studies, Darling Downs Institute of Advanced Education, *Resources and Industry of Southern Inland Queensland,* Brisbane, 1975
Queensland Department of Commercial and Industrial Development, *Resources and Industry of Far North Queensland,* Brisbane, 1980

State Library: The State Library of Queensland, William St., Brisbane. *State Librarian:* S. L. Ryan.

SOUTH AUSTRALIA

AREA AND POPULATION. The total area of South Australia is 380,070 sq. miles (984,377 sq. km). The settled part is divided into counties and hundreds. There are 49 counties proclaimed, covering 23m. hectares, of which 19m. hectares are occupied. Outside this area there are extensive pastoral districts, covering 76m. hectares, 46m. of which are under pastoral leases.

Census population (exclusive of full-blood Aboriginals before 1966):

	Males	Females	Total		Males	Females	Total
1901	180,485	177,861	358,346	1961	490,225	479,115	969,340
1911	207,358	201,200	408,558	1966	550,196	544,788	1,094,984
1921	248,267	246,893	495,160	1971	586,051	587,656	1,173,707
1933	290,962	289,987	580,949	1976	620,162	624,594	1,244,756
1947	320,031	326,042	646,073	1981	635,696	649,337	1,285,033

The number of Aboriginals (as reported on Census schedules) in the State at the Census of 30 June 1981 was 9,476.

Vital statistics for calendar years:

	Live Births	Marriages	Divorces	Deaths
1980	18,499	10,064	4,203	9,582
1981	19,351	10,252	4,132	9,706
1982	19,294	10,935	4,526	10,457

The infant mortality rate in 1982 was 11·4 per 1,000 live births.

CONSTITUTION AND GOVERNMENT. South Australia was formed into a British province by letters patent of Feb. 1836, and a partially elective Legislative Council was established in 1851. The present Constitution bears date 24 Oct. 1856. It vests the legislative power in an elected Parliament, consisting of a Legislative Council and a House of Assembly. The former is composed of 22 members. Every 3 years half the members retire, and the resulting vacancies are filled at a general election on the basis of proportional representation with the State as one multi-member electorate. The qualifications of an elector are, to be a natural born or naturalized British subject of at least 18 years of age and to have lived continuously in Australia for at least 6 months, in South Australia for at least 3 months and in the sub-division for which he is enrolled for at least 1 month. War service may substitute for residential qualifications in some cases. By the Constitution Act Amendment Act, 1894, the franchise was extended to women, who voted for the first time at the general election of 25 April 1896. The qualifications for election as a member of both Houses are the same as for an elector. Certain persons are ineligible for election to either House.

The House of Assembly consists of 47 members elected for 3 years, representing single electorates. Election of members of both Houses takes place by preferential secret ballot. Voting is compulsory for those on the Electoral Roll.

The House of Assembly, elected on 6 Nov. 1982, consists of the following members: Liberal Party of Australia, 22; Australian Labor Party, 23; National Party of Australia, 1; Independent, 1. The Legislative Council consists of 11 Liberal Party of Australia, 9 Labor and 2 Australian Democrat members.

Each member of Parliament receives $A31,530 per annum with allowances of $A6,105–22,590 according to location of electorate, a free pass over government railways and superannuation rights. Electors enrolled (June 1982) numbered 858,295.

The executive power is vested in a Governor appointed by the Crown and an Executive Council, consisting of the Governor and the Ministers of the Crown. The Governor has the power to dissolve the House of Assembly but not the Legislative Council unless that Chamber has twice consecutively with an election intervening defeated the same or substantially the same Bill passed in the House of Assembly by an absolute majority.

Governor: Lieut.-Gen. Sir Donald Dunstan, KBE, CB.

The South Australian Labor Ministry, in May 1983 was as follows:

Premier, Treasurer, Minister of State and Development and Minister for the Arts: John Charles Bannon, MP.

Deputy Premier, Minister of Labour and Minister of Public Works: John David Wright, MP. *Attorney-General, Minister of Consumer and Corporate Affairs and Minister of Ethnic Affairs:* Christopher John Sumner, MLC. *Minister for Environment and Planning, Minister of Lands and Minister of Repatriation:* Donald Jack Hopgood, MP. *Minister of Agriculture, Minister of Fisheries and Minister of Forests:* Frank Trevor Blevins, MLC. *Minister of Transport and Minister of*

Marine: Roy Kitto Abbott, MP. *Minister of Health:* John Robert Cornwall, MLC. *Minister of Education and Minister for Technology:* Lynn Maurice Ferguson Arnold, MP. *Chief Secretary and Minister of Tourism:* Gavin Francis Keneally, MP. *Minister of Mines and Energy:* Ronald George Payne, MP. *Minister of Community Welfare and Minister of Aboriginal Affairs:* Gregory John Crafter, MP. *Minister of Water Resources and Minister of Recreation and Sport:* John William Slater, MP. *Minister of Housing and Minister of Local Government:* Terence Henry Hemmings, MP.

Ministers are jointly and individually responsible to the legislature for all their official acts, as in the UK.

Agent-General in London: J. L. Rundle (50 Strand, WC2).

Local Government. The closely settled part of the State (mainly near the sea-coast and the River Murray) is incorporated into local government areas, and sub-divided into district councils (rural areas only), municipal corporations (mainly metropolitan, but including larger country towns) and cities (more densely populated areas with a qualification of 15,000 residents in the Adelaide metropolitan area, and 10,000 in the country). The main functions of councils are the construction and maintenance of roads and bridges, sport and recreational facilities and garbage collection and disposal.

The number and area of the sub-divisions, together with expenditure (in $A1,000) for the year ended 30 June 1982, were:

	No.	Area (1,000 hectares)	Roads and bridges	Recreation and Culture	All other	Total expenditure
Adelaide statistical division	32	229·0	35,698	32,542	107,504	175,744
Other municipal corporations and district councils	96	15,116·7	32,157	9,230	52,985	100,801
Total	128	15,345·7	67,855	41,772	160,489	276,545

ECONOMY

Budget. Revenue and expenditure (in $A1,000) for years ended 30 June:

	1978	1979	1980	1981	1982	1983
Revenue	1,167,196	1,264,705	1,384,589	1,548,299	1,705,499	1,923,808
Expenditure	1,192,063	1,258,252	1,384,589	1,554,884	1,766,772	2,032,765

The public debt of the State amounted, on 30 June 1983, to $A2,035·8m.

Banking. There were 7 trading banks at 30 June 1983, including the Federal and State Government Banks. In June 1983 their average deposits were $A1,933·1m. and average loans and advances $A2,562m.

The 6 savings banks on 30 June 1983 had deposits amounting to $A2,978·6m. or $A2,234 per head of population.

NATURAL RESOURCES

Minerals. The value of minerals produced in 1981–82 was $A259·7m. The principal minerals produced are opals, natural gas, iron ore, copper, gypsum, salt, talc, clays, limestone, dolomite and sub-bituminous coal.

Agriculture. Of the total area of South Australia (984,377 sq. km), 163,210 sq. km were alienated, 547,800 sq. km were held under lease and 273,367 sq. km were unoccupied. Area under cultivation, at 31 March 1981, was 59,596 sq. km.

Soil Conservation. Under the direction of special officers in the Department of Agriculture, determined efforts are made to deal with the problems of erosion and soil conservation. Included in the programme are the planting of cereal rye, perennial rye and other grasses to check sand drifts; contour-furrowing and contour banking; contour planting with vines and fruit trees and several water-diversion schemes.

Irrigation. For the year ended 31 March 1981, 79,474 hectares were under irrigated culture, being used as follows: Vineyards, 20,253; orchards, 12,627; vegetables, 5,676, and other crops and pasture, 40,918. Most of these areas are along the river Murray.

Gross value of agricultural production (in $A1,000), 1981–82: Crops, 759.240; livestock slaughtering, 331,085; livestock products, 338,261. Total gross value, 1.428,587; local value (*i.e.* less marketing costs), 1,288,686.

Chief crops	1980–81		1981–82	
	Hectares	Tonnes	Hectares	Tonnes
Wheat	1,445,287	1,650,390	1,427,481	1,694,733
Barley	988,504	1,158,077	1,031,745	1,227,055
Oats	105,486	96,054	127,279	97,904
Hay	161,312	440,049	194,065	471,447
Vines	...	220,384,000 [1]	...	268,685,000 [1]

[1] Litres of wine.

Fruit culture is extensively carried on, and in 1980–81, 246,832 tonnes of fresh fruit were produced. Other products, in addition to all kinds of root crops and vegetables, are grass seeds and oil seeds. Livestock, March 1982: 1,012,534 cattle, 16,708,863 sheep and 374,378 pigs. In 1981–82, 103,617 tonnes of wool and 305·6m. litres of milk were produced.

INDUSTRY AND TRADE

Industry. The turnover for manufacturing industries for 1981–82 was $A6,651m. The following statistics for 1981–82 are not comparable with factory statistics for years prior to 1968–69.

Industry sub-division	Establish-ments (No.)	Persons employed (No.)	Wages and salaries ($A1m.)	Turnover ($A1m.)	Value added ($A1m.)
Food, beverages and tobacco	374	17,117	223	1,407	486
Textiles, clothing and footwear	126	6,885	77	309	136
Wood, wood products and furniture	312	7,741	93	405	157
Paper, paper products, printing and publishing	202	7,715	104	400	197
Chemical, petroleum and coal products	52	2,846	49	282	107
Non-metallic mineral products	134	3,352	51	292	133
Basic metal products	37	9,091	157	779	243
Fabricated metal products	352	8,481	107	455	189
Transport equipment	118	18,171	268	1,095	446
Other machinery and equipment	327	17,187	232	903	392
Miscellaneous manufacturing	185	6,288	84	324	137
Total	2,219	104,874	1,446	6,651	2,620

Practically all forms of secondary industry are to be found, the most important being, motor vehicle manufacture, saw-milling and the manufacture of household appliances, basic iron and steel, meat and meat products, and wine and brandy.

Labour. Two systems of industrial arbitration and conciliation for the adjustment of industrial relations between employers and employees are in operation—the State system, which operates when industrial disputes are confined to the territorial limits of the State, and the Federal system, which applies when disputes involve other parts of Australia as well as South Australia.

The industrial tribunals are authorized to fix minimum rates of wages and other conditions of employment, and their awards may be enforced by law. Industrial agreements between employers and organizations of employees, when registered, may be enforced in the same manner as awards. The Commission fixed the minimum wage in July 1981 at $A145.70.

Commerce. The commerce of South Australia, exclusive of inter-state trade, is comprised in the statement of the commerce of Australia given under the heading of the Commonwealth, see pp. 110–12.

Overseas imports and exports in $A1,000 (year ending 30 June):

	1976–77	1977–78	1978–79	1979–80	1980–81	1981–82
Imports	629,309	628,568	865,554	882,457	1,072,449	1,337,301
Exports [1]	789,872	661,887	922,754	1,599,199	1,417,811	1,275,938

[1] From 1978–79 exports are recorded by 'State of Origin', whereas details prior to this are by 'State of Lodgment of Documents'.

Principal exports in 1981–82 were (in $A1,000): Wheat, 211,144 (1,291,241 tonnes); barley, 105,280 (637,214 tonnes); wool, 213,237 (77,781 tonnes); lead, 101,669 (168,448 tonnes); meat, 89,710 (55,750 tonnes); live sheep and lambs, 58,630 (2,157,941 head).

Principal imports in 1981–82 were (in $A1,000): Transport equipment, 190,738; petrol and products, 431,823; machinery, 274,785.

In 1981–82 the leading suppliers of imports were (in $A1m.): Saudi Arabia (388·6), Japan (284·1), USA (178·9), Federal Republic of Germany (95·5); main exports went to USSR (152), Japan (140·4), Saudi Arabia (101·9), USA (92·7), New Zealand (74·8), Iraq (63·6), Singapore (49·2).

Tourism. In June 1983 there were 282 hotels and motels with 7,512 rooms; 154 caravan parks had a total of 17,751 sites.

COMMUNICATIONS

Roads. At 30 June 1982, of the roads customarily used by the public, there were 2,594 km of national roads, 10,787 km of arterial roads and 88,758 km of local roads, totalling 102,139 km. Lengths of road classified by surface were as follows: Sealed, 20,777 km; unsealed, 81,362 km. Costs of construction and maintenance are shared by the State and Commonwealth governments and by the councils of the local areas. Motor vehicles registered at 30 June 1983 included 502,896 cars, 90,387 station wagons, 132,618 commercial vehicles and 37,766 cycles.

Railways. At June 1982, there were more than 5,900 km of railway, including the South Australian portion of the Transcontinental Railway from Port Pirie in South Australia to Kalgoorlie in Western Australia, which, in connexion with various State lines, completes a through rail connexion between Brisbane on the north-east coast and Fremantle on the west coast. It also includes the South Australian portion of the Australian National Railways from Tarcoola to the Northern Territory and private railways from Iron Knob to Whyalla and Coffin Bay to Port Lincoln. In June 1982 the State Transport Authority operated 131 km of railway in the metropolitan area of Adelaide.

Aviation. For the year ended 30 June 1982 there were 1,852,906 passengers and 17,267 tonnes of freight handled at Adelaide, South Australia's principal airport. On 30 June 1982 there were 8 government and 24 licensed aerodromes.

Shipping. There are several good harbours, of which Port Adelaide is the principal one. In 1981–82, 855 vessels entered South Australia with 2,854,671 import tonnes of cargo and left with 4,481,598 export tonnes.

Post and Broadcasting. At 30 June 1982, there were 620 post offices. Telephone services connected totalled 507,234 on 30 June 1982. There were 25 radio and 13 television stations at 1 Jan. 1982.

JUSTICE, RELIGION, EDUCATION AND WELFARE

Justice. There is a Supreme Court, which incorporates admiralty, civil, criminal, land and valuation, and testamentary jurisdiction; district criminal courts, which have jurisdiction in many indictable offences; local courts and courts of summary jurisdiction. Circuit courts are held at several places. In the year ended 30 June 1982, 1,541 cases were heard in higher courts and 185,784 cases in courts of summary jurisdiction. During the year ending 30 June 1982 there were 860 sequestrations and schemes under the Bankruptcy Act. There were 810 prisoners in custody on 1 July 1982, of whom 127 were on remand.

Religion. At the Census of 1981 the religious distribution of the population (as reported on Census schedules) was as follows: Church of England, 260,919; Roman Catholic and Catholic (so described), 255,332; Uniting Church, 108,857; Methodist, 85,935; Lutheran, 63,860; Baptist, 22,287; Presbyterian, 21,725; other Christians, 138,350; non-Christian, 7,128; indefinite, 6.529; no religion, 178,136; no reply, 135,970.

Education. Education is secular and is compulsory for children 6–15 years of age. Primary and secondary education at government schools is free. In 1982 there were 716 government schools, comprising 526 primary, 67 primary and secondary, 100 secondary schools and 23 special schools. There were 207,944 full-time students. The Department of Technical and Further Education is responsible for technical, adult and vocational education. In 1982 there were 26 colleges of technical and further education, 1 college of external studies, an adult migrant education service, a centre for performing arts and a school of rural and timber studies. Tertiary education, including teacher education, is provided by the 2 universities and 3 colleges of advanced education. There were 169 non-government schools and colleges, most of which are associated with religious denominations (45,972 students). In 1981 there were 491 day care and pre-school centres with a total enrolment of 29,600 pre-school children.

Social Welfare. Age, invalidity, war, etc., pensions are paid by the Commonwealth Government. The number of pensioners in South Australia at 30 June 1983 was: Disability and service, 70,450; age, 140,036; invalid, 30,238. There are schemes for family allowances, widows, supporting parents, unemployment and sickness and hospital and pharmaceutical benefits.

Books of Reference

Statistical Information. The State branch of the Australian Bureau of Statistics is in City Mutual Centre, 10–20 Pulteney St., Adelaide (GPO Box 2272). *Deputy Commonwealth Statistician:* G. C. Sims. Although the first printed statistical publication was the *Statistics of South Australia, 1854* with the title altered to *Statistical Register* in 1859, there is a written volume for each year back to 1838. These contain simple records of trade, demography, production, etc. and were prepared only for the use of the Colonial Office; one copy was retained in the State.
    The publications of the State branch include the *South Australian Year Book,* the *Pocket Year Book of South Australia* and a *Monthly Summary of Statistics,* a quarterly bulletin of building activity, a quarterly bulletin of tourist accommodation and approximately 40 special bulletins issued each year as particulars of various sections of statistics become available.

South Australia: Development. Dept. of Industry and Commerce, Adelaide, 1977
Best, R. J. (ed.), *Introducing South Australia.* Cambridge, 1959
Crowley, F. K., *South Australian History: A Survey for Research Students.* Adelaide, 1965
Douglas, J., *South Australia from Space.* Adelaide, 1980
Finlayson, H. H., *The Red Centre: Man and Beast in the Heart of Australia.* 2nd ed. Sydney, 1952
Gibbs, R. M., *A History of South Australia.* Adelaide, 1969
Whitelock, D., *Adelaide, 1836–1976: A History of Difference.* Univ. of Queensland Press, 1977

State Library: The State Library of S.A., North Terrace, Adelaide. *State Librarian:* E. M. Miller, MA (Hons), Dip. NZLS, ANZLA, ALAA.

TASMANIA

HISTORY. Abel Janzoon Tasman discovered Van Diemen's Land (Tasmania) on 24 Nov. 1642. The island became a British settlement in 1803 as a dependency of New South Wales; in 1825 its connexion with New South Wales was terminated; in 1851 a partially elective Legislative Council was established, and in 1856 responsible government came into operation. On 1 Jan. 1901 Tasmania was federated with the other Australian states into the Commonwealth of Australia.

AREA AND POPULATION. Tasmania is an island separated from the mainland by the Bass Strait with an area (including islands) of 68,330 sq. km, or 6·83m. hectares, of which 6,441,000 hectares form the area of the main island. The population at 10 consecutive censuses was:

	Population	Increase % per annum		Population	Increase % per annum
1911	191,211	1·04	1961	350,340	1·82
1921	213,780	1·12	1966	371,436	1·18
1933	227,599	0·52	1971	398,100 [1]	0·99
1947	257,078	0·87	1976	412,300 [1]	0·70 [2]
1954	308,752	2·65	1981	427,300 [1]	0·72 [2]

[1] Resident population.   [2] Not comparable with previous censuses.

The resident population (estimate) on 30 June 1981 consisted of 212,400 males and 214,900 females. At the census of 30 June 1981, 2·8% were born in the British Isles, 5·5% in other European countries and 88·7% in Australia. The last full-blooded Tasmanian Aboriginal died in 1876.

Vital statistics for calendar years:

	Marriages	Divorces	Births	Deaths	Natural increase
1979	3,254	1,167	6,757	3,167	3,590
1980	3,433	1,285	6,735	3,392	3,343
1981	3,515	1,139	7,188	3,320	3,868
1982	3,576	1,391	7,002	3,432	3,570

CONSTITUTION AND GOVERNMENT. Parliament consists of the Governor, the Legislative Council and the House of Assembly. The Council has 19 members, elected by adults with 6 months' residence. Members sit for 6 years, 3 retiring annually and 4 every sixth year. There is no power to dissolve the Council. Vacancies are filled by by-elections. The House of Assembly has 35 members; the maximum term for the House of Assembly is 4 years. Members of both Houses are paid a basic salary of $A28,621 (1981–82), plus an electorate allowance, according to the division represented. The annual allowance payable is calculated as a percentage of basic salary. The amounts vary from $A3,148 (11%) to $A10,017 (35%). Women received the right to vote in 1903. Proportional representation was adopted in 1907, the method now being the single transferable vote in 7-member constituencies. Casual vacancies in the House of Assembly are determined by a transfer of the preference of the vacating member's ballot papers to consenting candidates who were unsuccessful at the last general election.

A Minister must have a seat in one of the two Houses; all present Ministers are members of the House of Assembly.

In addition to the salary paid to Ministers as members of either House, the following allowances are payable: Premier, in conjunction with a ministerial office, $A35,776; Deputy Premier, in conjunction with a ministerial office, $A24,328; other Ministers, $A20,034. The Leader of the Opposition in the House of Assembly receives an allowance of $A20,034. The holders of some other offices receive allowances ranging from $A1,717 to $A9,540.

An election, precipitated by the House of Assembly wanting vote of confidence in the minority Labor Government, in May 1982 resulted in the Liberal Party forming a government in its own right. The composition of the new House of Assembly was Liberal, 19 seats, Labor, 14, Australian Democrats, 1 and 1 Independent. On 23 Dec. 1982, the Australian Democrat resigned his seat which was filled on a recount of his quota by Dr R. Brown, an Independent.

The Legislative Council is predominantly independent without formal party allegiance; 1 member is Labor-endorsed.

Governor: Sir James Plimsoll, AC, CBE.

The Liberal Party Cabinet is composed as follows:

Premier, Treasurer, Minister for Energy, Racing and Gaming: R. Gray.
Deputy Premier, Attorney-General, Education, Industrial Relations: M. Bingham. *Tourism, National Parks and Recreational Lands, Environment,*

Licensing, Housing: G. Pearsall. *Industry and Small Business, Inland Fisheries:* N. Robson. *Health, Community Welfare and the Elderly, Ethnic Affairs:* J. Cleary. *Construction, Main Roads, Local Governments, Lands:* I. Braid. *Primary Industry, Forests, Sea Fisheries, Water Resources:* J. Beswick. *Mines, Transport, Administrative Services, Police and Emergency Services:* R. Groom.

Local Government. For the purposes of local government, the State is divided into 49 municipal areas comprising the cities of Hobart, Launceston, Glenorchy and Devonport and 45 municipalities. The cities and municipalities are managed by elected aldermen and councillors, respectively, with reference to local matters such as sanitation and health services, domestic water supplies and roads and bridges within each particular area. The chief source of revenue is rates (based on improved values) levied on owners of property.

Tasmanian Islands. Three inhabited Tasmanian islands (Bruny, King and Flinders) are organized as municipalities. Nearly 1,600 km south-east lies Macquarie Island, part of the State, and used only as an Australian research base and meteorological station.

ECONOMY

Budget. The revenue is derived chiefly from taxation (pay-roll, motor, lottery and land tax, business franchises and stamp duties), and from grants and reimbursements from the Federal Government. Customs, excise, sales and income tax are levied by the Federal Government, which makes grants to Tasmania for both revenue and capital purposes. Federal Government grants to Tasmania in 1982–83 totalled $A637m. These included General Purpose Revenue Funds, $A363m.; Specific Purpose Grants, $A237m.; Capital Grants. $A32m.; and Health Grants, $A5m.

Specific Purpose Grants are mainly used to provide essential services such as hospitals, housing, roads and educational services, while General Purpose Revenue Funds have been paid since 1942 to compensate the State for the loss of income tax to the federal government.

Consolidated Revenue Fund receipts and expenditure, in $A1,000, for financial years ending 30 June:

	1977–78	1978–79	1979–80	1980–81	1981–82	1982–83
Revenue	444,263	495,822	560,192	620,307	683,231	764,990
Expenditure	450,706	492,961	563,917	627,441	717,628	772,735

The public debt at current exchange rates amounted to $A1,114m. at 30 June 1983.

In 1982–83 State taxation revenue amounted to $A160·6m., of which pay-roll tax provided $A55·9m.; motor tax, $A17·1m.; stamp duties, $A31·2m.; business franchises, $A16·1m., and lottery tax, $A10·5m.

Banking. Trading bank activity in Tasmania is divided between 3 private banks and the Commonwealth Trading Bank. For the month of June 1983 liabilities represented by depositors' balances averaged $A643m. and assets represented by advances, $A443m. The 6 savings banks operating in Tasmania are the Commonwealth Savings Bank, 2 trustee savings banks and 3 private savings banks operated by trading banks. At 30 June 1983 total savings bank deposits were $A938m.

ENERGY AND NATURAL RESOURCES

Electricity. Tasmania has good supplies of hydro-electric power because of assured rainfall and high level water storages (natural and artificial). The Hydro-Electric Commission, Tasmania's sole commercial supplier of electricity, has been surveying water power resources of the State for many years and it is estimated that about 3m. kw. can be economically developed. By mid-1982, 1,860,300 kw. of generating plant was in commission. In 1981–82 the peak loading was 1,266,100 kw. One project is currently in progress, the Pieman River Power Development, comprising 3 stations, scheduled for completion in 1986. The Gordon River Power Development Stage 2 (the Gordon-below-Franklin scheme) was halted by a High Court decision.

Minerals. The assayed content of principal metallic minerals contained in locally produced concentrates for 1981–82 was (in tonnes): Zinc, 84,214; iron, 1,387,310; copper, 23,033; lead, 30,820; tin, 7,197; gold, 2,000 kg; silver, 89,821 kg. Coal production, 395,347 tonnes.

Primary Industries. The estimated gross value of recorded production from agriculture in 1981–82 was (in $A1m.): Livestock products, 117·7; livestock slaughterings and other disposals, 90·2; crops, 92·3; total gross value, 300·2. Estimated gross value of fisheries was $A32·9m.

Agriculture. The area occupied by the 5,972 holdings in 1981–82 totalled 2,168,473 hectares, of which 999,888 were devoted to crops and sown pasture. The following table shows the area and production, in tonnes, of the principal crops:

	1979–80		1980–81		1981–82	
	Hectares	Production	Hectares	Production	Hectares	Production
Wheat	1,972	3,727	1,614	2,545	1,293	2,342
Barley	10,558	17,304	10,056	18,307	12,108	23,267
Oats	7,489	7,955	8,781	11,146	9,923	13,381
Green peas	6,997	25,608	7,097	26,547	7,973	30,946
Potatoes	4,115	136,197	4,335	155,965	4,438	160,797
Hay	59,661	249,766	64,088	249,348	63,854	242,593
Hops (bearing) (dry)	620	1,183	672	1,558	811	1,608

Livestock at 31 March 1982: Sheep, 4·5m.; cattle, 628,400; pigs, 47,200.

Wool produced during 1981–82 was 22m. kg, valued at $A57m. In 1981–82 butter production was 3,964 tonnes; cheese, 15,167 tonnes.

Forestry. Indigenous forests cover a considerable part of the State, and the sawmilling and woodchipping industries are very important. Production of sawn timber in 1982–83 was 235,900 cu. metres. 646,600 cu. metres of logs were used for milling in 1982–83 and a further 3·2m. cu. metres were used for chipping, grinding or flaking. Newsprint and paper are produced from native hardwoods, principally eucalypts.

INDUSTRY AND TRADE

Industry. The most important manufactures for export are refined metals, newsprint and other paper manufactures, pigments, woollen goods, fruit pulp, confectionery, butter, cheese, preserved and dried vegetables, sawn timber, and processed fish products. The electrolytic-zinc works at Risdon near Hobart treat large quantities of local and imported ore, and produce zinc, sulphuric acid, superphosphate, sulphate of ammonia, cadmium and other by-products. At George Town, large-scale plants produce refined aluminium and manganese alloys. During 1982–83, 3·2m. tonnes (green weight) of woodchips were produced. In 1981–82 the average employment in manufacturing establishments employing 4 or more persons was 25,809; wages and salaries (excluding proprietors' drawings), $A370·2m.; turnover, $A1,898m.; value added, $A713·1m.; and number operating at 30 June, 555.

Labour. The Commonwealth Industrial Court (judicial powers) and Commonwealth Conciliation and Arbitration Commission (arbitral powers) have jurisdiction over federal unions, *i.e.*, with interstate membership. Most Tasmanian employees are covered by federal awards.

State Industrial Boards, established for the various trades by resolution of Parliament or proclamation of the Governor, cover most of the remaining employees. Each Board consists of a Chairman appointed by the Governor with equal representation of employers and employees. The Boards have authority over minimum rates for wages or piecework, number of working hours for which the wage is payable, conditions of apprenticeship, annual leave and adjustment of wage and piecework rates. Industrial Boards follow to a large extent the wage rates fixed by the Conciliation and Arbitration Commission.

Commerce. Trade by sea and air in $A1m. for years ending 30 June:

	1977–78	1978–79	1979–80	1980–81	1981–82
Imports	750·0	836·8	1,168·8	1,207·1	1,258·5
Exports	1,027·0	1,180·2	1,451·5	1,540·2	1,574·2

In 1981–82 exports by sea and air totalled $A1,574m.; comprising $A927m. to other Australian states and $A647m. to overseas countries. The principal countries of destination (with values in $A1m.) for overseas exports were: Japan, 221; Malaysia, 73; USA, 73; Indonesia, 49; and Hong Kong, 25. Imports totalled $A1,259m.; comprising $A1,093m. from other Australian states and $A166m. from overseas countries. The principal countries of origin (with values in $A1m.) for overseas imports were: Japan, 29; USA, 28; New Zealand, 18; Canada, 17; and UK, 12.

The main commodities by value (with values in $A1m.) exported during 1981–82 were: Ores and concentrates (mainly iron, copper, lead, tin and tungsten), 212; refined zinc, 163; timber, 82; vegetables, 70; and greasy wool, 48. Other main exports, for which details are not available for separate publication were wood-chips, newsprint, printing and writing papers, refined aluminium, ferro-alloys and chocolate confectionery. The main imports (with values in $A1m.) were: Petroleum products, 245; ores and concentrates, 109; new motor vehicles, 89; and machinery, clothing, cocoa beans and wood-pulp.

Tourism. In 1981 (estimate) 306,671 adult visitors spent at least one night in Tasmania.

COMMUNICATIONS

Roads. The total road length at 30 June 1982 was 22.315 km, consisting of a classified road system of 3,902 km maintained by the State Department of Main Roads, and the remainder maintained by local government authorities, the Forestry Commission and the Hydro-Electric Commission. Motor vehicles registered at 30 June 1983 comprised 191,000 cars and station wagons, 52,500 other vehicles and 5,800 motor cycles.

Railways. There is an 864-km network of 1,067-mm gauge lines linking Hobart and Launceston with coastal and country areas, formerly operated by Tasmanian Government Railways, but since 1 July 1975 worked by the Australian National Railways Commission. A private railway of 134 km, operated by the Emu Bay Railway Co. Ltd, connects Burnie with the mining settlements on the west coast.

Aviation. Regular daily passenger and freight air services connect the south, north and north-west of the State with the mainland of Australia. In the year ending 30 June 1982 there was a total of 26,968 scheduled aircraft movements at Tasmanian airports; a total of 1,009,109 passengers and 40,382 tonnes of freight, including mail, was carried.

Shipping. In 1981–82 overseas vessels made a total of 401 calls to Tasmanian ports discharging 374,977 revenue tonnes of cargo; departures numbered 412 with total cargo of 4,658,972 revenue tonnes.

For posts and telegraphs, *see* p. 114.

JUSTICE, RELIGION, EDUCATION AND WELFARE

Justice. The Supreme Court of Tasmania, with civil, criminal, ecclesiastical, admiralty and matrimonial jurisdiction, established by Royal Charter on 13 Oct. 1823, is a superior court of record, with both original and appellate jurisdiction, and consists of a Chief Justice and 5 puisne judges. There are also inferior civil courts with limited jurisdiction, licensing courts, mining courts, courts of petty sessions and coroners courts.

During the year 1980, 35,999 persons were summarily convicted in lower courts (23,973 for traffic offences) and 237 persons were convicted in the Supreme Court.

The total police force on 30 June 1983 was 1,006. There was 1 gaol, with 237 inmates at the end of June 1982.

Religion. There is no State Church. At the census of 1981 the following numbers of adherents of the principal religions were recorded:

Anglican Church	151,207	Other religions	32,213
Roman Catholic	78,143	No religion	36,222
Methodist	19,906	Not stated [1]	64,058
Uniting Church	17,668		
Presbyterian	11,575	Total [1]	418,957
Baptist	7,965		

[1] 'As counted' Census results.

Education. Education is controlled by the State and is free, secular and compulsory between the ages of 6 and 16. At 1 July 1982 government schools had a total enrolment of 69,142 pupils, including 26,891 at secondary level; private schools had a total enrolment of 15,326 pupils, including 6,923 at secondary level.

Technical and further education is conducted at technical and community colleges in the major centres throughout the state. In 1981 there were 1,065 full-time, 15,920 part-time and 1,328 external students. Teaching staff was made up of 490 full-time and 1,506 part-time teachers.

Tertiary education is offered at the University of Tasmania in Hobart and the Tasmanian College of Advanced Education in Launceston. The University (established 1890) had (1982) 3,078 full-time and 2,132 part-time students, and 372 full-time teachers. There were 929 full-time and 1,251 part-time students at the College and a full-time teaching staff of 127.

Social Welfare. Old Age, Invalid, War Service and Widows' Pensions are paid by the Federal Government. The number of pensioners in Tasmania on 30 June 1982 was: Age, 40,413; invalid, 6,615; war (disability), 16,681; widows, 5,153. Benefit payments totalled $A209·3m. (including payments to wives).

Books of Reference

Statistical Information: The State Government Statistical Office (Commonwealth Government Centre, Hobart), established in 1877, became in 1924 the Tasmanian Office of the Australian Bureau of Statistics, but continues to serve State statistical needs as required. *Deputy Commonwealth Statistician and Government Statistician of Tasmania:* D. N. Allen.

Main publications: *Annual Statistical Bulletins (e.g., Demography, Agricultural Industry, Finance, Manufacturing Establishments* etc.).—*Pocket Year Book of Tasmania.* Annual (from 1913).—*Tasmanian Year Book.* Annual (from 1967).—*Monthly Summary of Statistics* (from July 1945).

Department of Planning and Development, *Tasmanian Manufacturers Directory.* Hobart. Annual.

Angus, M., *The World of Olegas Truchanas.* Hobart, 1975
Clark, C. I., *The Parliament of Tasmania.* Hobart, 1947
Davies, J. L. (ed.), *Atlas of Tasmania.* Hobart, 1965
Green, F. C. (ed.), *A Century of Responsible Government.* Hobart, 1956
Mercury-Walch Pty. Ltd, *The Tasmanian Almanac.* Hobart
Townsley, W. A., *The Government of Tasmania.* Univ. of Queensland Press, 1976
Wettenhall, R. L., *A Guide to Tasmanian Government Administration.* Hobart, 1968

State Library: The State Library of Tasmania, Hobart. *Librarian:* W. L. Brown, FLA, ALAA.

VICTORIA

AREA AND POPULATION. The State has an area of 227,600 sq. km, and a resident population (estimate) of 3,994,122 at 30 June 1982.

The resident population (estimate) of the Melbourne Statistical Division at 30 June 1982 was 2,836,800 or 71% of the population of the State. The resident population (estimate) of each statistical district in Victoria was: Ballarat, 73,630; Bendigo, 60,980; Geelong, 142,890; Morwell, 17,230; Shepparton-Mooroopna, 36,760.

The census population (exclusive of full-blood aboriginals prior to 1961) was:

Date of census enumeration	Population Males	Females	Total increase	On previous census Numerical increase	Increase %
5 April 1891	598,222	541,866	1,140,088	278,522	32·33
31 March 1901	603,720	597,350	1,201,070	60,982	5·35
3 April 1911	655,591	659,960	1,315,551	114,481	9·53
4 April 1921	754,724	776,556	1,531,280	215,729	16·40
30 June 1933	903,244	917,017	1,820,261	288,981	18·87
30 June 1947	1,013,867	1,040,834	2,054,701	234,440	12·88
30 June 1954	1,231,099	1,221,242	2,452,341	397,640	19·35
30 June 1961	1,474,536	1,455,830	2,930,366	478,025	19·49
30 June 1966	1,614,240	1,605,977	3,220,217	289,851	9·89
30 June 1971	1,799,486	1,801,866	3,601,352	381,135	11·84
30 June 1976	1,900,488	1,909,938	3,810,426	209,074	5·81
30 June 1981	1,958,717	1,988,200	3,946,917	136,491	3·58

The population of urban Melbourne (capital city) on 30 June 1981 was 2,578,759. The population of urban Geelong was 125,279; urban Ballarat, 62,641; urban Bendigo, 52,741. Other urban centres: Shepparton-Mooroopna, 28,373; Warrnambool, 21,414; Moe-Yallourn, 18,159; Traralgon, 18,057; Morwell, 16,491; Wangaratta, 16,202; Mildura, 15,763; Sale, 12,968; Horsham, 12,034; Colac, 10,587; Hamilton, 9,751; Bairnsdale, 9,459; Portland, 9,353; Swan Hill, 8,398; Ararat, 8,336; Benalla, 8,151; Maryborough, 7,858; Warragul, 7,712; Castlemaine, 7,583.

Vital statistics for calendar years:

	Births	Marriages	Divorces	Deaths
1979	57,767	27,019	9,471	29,078
1980	58,206	27,724	9,207	29,374
1981	59,513	28,648	9,769	29,034
1982	59,983	28,851	11,266	30,611

The annual rates per 1,000 of the mean resident population (estimate) in 1982 were: Marriages, 7·2; births, 15; deaths, 7·7; divorces 2·8.

CONSTITUTION AND GOVERNMENT. Victoria, formerly a portion of New South Wales, was, in 1851, proclaimed a separate colony, with a partially elective Legislative Council. In 1855 responsible government was conferred, the legislative power being vested in a parliament of two Houses, the Legislative Council and the Legislative Assembly. At present the Council consists of 44 members who are elected for 6 years, one-half retiring every third year. The Assembly consists of 81 members, elected for 3 years from the date of its first meeting unless sooner dissolved by the Governor. Members and electors of both Houses must be aged 18 years and natural born or naturalized British subjects. Women are fully enfranchised. No property qualification is required, but judges, members of the Commonwealth Parliament and undischarged bankrupts may not be members of either House. Single voting (one elector one vote) and compulsory preferential voting apply to Council and Assembly elections. Enrolment for Council and Assembly electors is compulsory. The Council may not initiate or amend money bills, but may suggest amendments in such bills other than amendments which would increase any charge. Any Minister, with the consent of the House of which he is not a member, may sit and speak in that House to explain a bill relating to the department administered by him, but may not vote in that House. A bill shall not become law unless passed by both Houses, except that, in the event of a continued disagreement between the two Houses as to a bill passed by the Assembly, other than certain constitutional bills, the Governor having dissolved the Assembly may subsequently dissolve the Council, and if the disagreement still continues he may convene a joint sitting of the members of the Council and the Assembly; if at such joint sitting the bill in dispute is passed by an absolute majority of all members it shall become law.

Private members of both Houses receive salaries of $A38,000 per annum, additional allowances rising from $A11,200 to $A16,240 (outer electorates), and a living-away-from-home allowance of $A57·15 for each day of attendance for each member (not being a responsible Minister or a metropolitan member).

Members holding the following offices receive the salaries and allowances specified: The President of the Council, $A66,500 salary and $A4,180 expense allowance; the Speaker of the Assembly, $A66,500 salary and $A4,180 expense allowance; the Chairman of Committees of the Council, $A50,160 salary and $A1,520 expense allowance; the Chairman of Committees of the Assembly, $A50,160 salary and $A1,520 expense allowance; the Leader of the Opposition in the Assembly, $A66,500 salary and $A6,840 expense allowance; the Deputy Leader of the Opposition in the Assembly, $A50,160 salary and $A2,280 expense allowance; the Leader of the Third Party, $A50,160 salary and $A2,280 expense allowance; a member of either House who is the Parliamentary Secretary of the Cabinet, $A50,160 salary and $A2,280 expense allowance; the Government Whip in the Assembly, $A44,840 salary; the Whip of any recognized Party which consists of at least 12 members of Parliament, of which Party no member is a responsible Minister, $A43,320 salary. All members have free passes over the Victorian Railways; country members are also entitled to certain allowances for air travel.

The Legislative Assembly, elected on 3 April 1982, and following several by-elections is composed as follows: Labor Party, 49; Liberal Party, 23; National Party, 9.

Governor: Rear-Adm. Sir Brian Stewart Murray, KCMG.

In the exercise of the executive power the Governor is advised by a Cabinet of responsible Ministers. Section 50 of the Constitution Act 1975 provides that the number of responsible Ministers shall not at any one time exceed 18, of whom not more than 6 may sit in the Legislative Council. No responsible Minister may hold office for more than 3 months unless he is or becomes a member of the Council or the Assembly.

Responsible Ministers receive the following amounts: The Premier, $A76,000 salary and $A15,960 expense allowance; the Deputy Premier, $A70,300 salary and $A7,980 expense allowance; 16 other responsible Ministers, $A66,500 salary and $A6,840 expense allowance. Each responsible Minister also receives an electorate allowance, an electorate office allowance, a residential allowance (where applicable) and, when travelling on business of the State, a travelling allowance. The President, Speaker, Chairman of Committees in the Assembly and in the Council, Parliamentary Secretary of the Cabinet, Leader and Deputy Leader of the Opposition in the Assembly, Leader of the Opposition in the Council and Leader in the Assembly of the Third Party, also receive a travelling allowance when travelling on official business. Members of Committees receive attendance fees and certain travelling expenses when on Committee duties.

The Labor Party Government (first appointed 8 April 1982) was as follows on 8 Sept. 1983:

Premier: John Cain, MP.
Deputy Premier, Minister of Education and Educational Services: R. C. Fordham, MP. *Planning and Environment and Public Works:* E. H. Walker, MLC. *Minerals and Energy and Water Supply:* D. R. White, MLC. *Housing and Economic Development:* I. R. Cathie, MP. *Transport and Industrial Relations:* S. M. Crabb, MP. *Treasurer:* R. A. Jolly, MP. *Attorney-General:* J. H. Kennan, MLC. *Agriculture:* D. E. Kent, MLC. *Conservation, Forests and Lands:* R. A. Mackenzie, MLC. *Arts, Police and Emergency Services:* C. R. T. Mathews, MP. *Health:* T. W. Roper, MP. *Employment and Training:* J. L. Simmonds, MP. *Labour and Industry and Property and Services:* J. H. Simpson, MP. *Community Welfare Services:* P. T. Toner, MP. *Youth, Sport and Recreation:* N. B. Trezise, MP. *Local Government:* F. N. Wilkes, MP. *Consumer Affairs and Ethnic Affairs:* P. C. Spyker, MP. *Parliamentary Secretary of the Cabinet:* Dr K. A. Coghill, MP.

Agent-General in London: I. M. Haig (Victoria House, Melbourne Place, Strand, London, WC28 4LG).

Local Government. With the exception of Yallourn Works area (26·9 sq. km) and the unincorporated areas—French Island (154 sq. km), Lady Julia Percy Island (1·3 sq. km), the Bass Strait Islands and part of Gippsland Lakes (312·8 sq. km) and Tower Hill Lake Reserve (5 sq. km), the State is divided (at 30 June 1982) into 211 municipal districts, namely 65 cities, 6 towns, 7 boroughs and 133 shires. The constitution of cities, towns, boroughs and shires is based on statutory requirements concerning population, rate revenue and net annual value of rateable property.

ECONOMY

Budget. The receipts and payments (in $A1m.) of the Consolidated Fund in the years shown (ended 30 June) were:

	1979–80	1980–81	1981–82	1982–83	1983–84 [1]
Receipts	3,986	4,482	5,466	7,203	7,859
Payments	3,953	4,502	5,473	7,209	7,859

[1] Estimates.

The principal receipt items (in $A1m.) during 1981–82 were: Taxation, 3,498 (including Federal Government reimbursement, 1,502, but excluding 198 paid to special funds); railways, 264; other Federal Government payments, 669, and mining royalties, 161. The principal heads of expenditure were: Interest and public debt charges (including railways), 404; railways, 495; education, 1,458; health, hospitals and charities, 1,000.

The amount raised by taxation (exclusive of taxes collected by the Federal Government or paid to special funds but inclusive of the Federal Government reimbursements under the uniform taxation scheme), as shown in the above paragraph, was approximately $A875.91 per head of population.

The public debt of Victoria (in $A1m.) on 30 June 1982 was 4,625. During the year ending 30 June 1982, an amount of 453 was expended on capital works. Of this amount, 142 was spent on education, 77 on railways, 32 on water supply, irrigation and drainage, 8 on protection of the environment (including sewerage), 15 on forestry, 58 on health services, 8 on agricultural, pastoral, etc., services, 44 on culture and recreation, 16 on law, order and public safety, 19 on legislature and general administration, 12 on development and decentralization, and 22 on all other purposes. In addition to the public debt noted above, Victoria had other liabilities due to the Federal Government at 30 June 1982. These included 1,136·5 advances for housing, 10·9 special assistance loans for soldier settlement, 72·9 advance for sewerage, 62·7 for rural and dairy reconstruction, 110·5 for growth centres and 38 for land acquisition.

Banking. On 30 June 1983 there were 8m. operative accounts (excluding school bank accounts) in savings banks in Victoria. The total credit due to depositors amounted to $A11,307·5m., made up of State Savings Bank, $A5,383·7m.; Commonwealth Savings Bank, $A2,290·9m.; private savings banks, $A3,632·9m.

The weekly average of deposits and advances of trading banks operating in Victoria during June 1983 were as follows: Deposits, not bearing interest, $A2,572·1m.; deposits, bearing interest, $A5,914·7m.; total deposits, $A8,486·8m.; loans, advances, and bills discounted, $A5,972·8m. The weekly average of debits to customers' accounts (excluding debits to Federal and State Government accounts at City branches in State capitals) for the same period totalled $A13,679·3m.

ENERGY AND NATURAL RESOURCES

Electricity. All electricity in this State for public supply is generated by the largest electricity supply authority in Australia—the State Electricity Commission of Victoria. Its supply network serves over 99% of the entire Victorian population and some New South Wales municipalities as well as irrigation settlements bordering the Murray River.

The major base load generating stations are located in the Latrobe Valley on top of a large brown coal field with estimated geological resources of 107,847m. tonnes. Burning raw brown coal on site and with an installed generating capacity of 2,991,000 kw., these stations produce over 80% of Victoria's electricity. The chief one is Hazelwood, which was completed in 1971 with a capacity of 1·6m. kw. The total installed generating capacity of all thermal stations in Victoria is 4,282,000 kw. including the base load stations in the Latrobe Valley and smaller ones in Melbourne, and some provincial cities.

The total installed capacity of the Commission's system at 30 June 1980 was 5·79m. kw.; it includes Victoria's share of about one-third (1,084,000 kw. at 30 June 1981) of the Snowy Mountains hydro-electric scheme in New South Wales and its half share (25,000 kw.) of the Hume hydro-electric station, shared with New South Wales. Excluding the Snowy and Hume schemes in New South Wales the installed hydro-electric capacity totalled 469,000 kw. at 30 June 1981, with Kiewa (3 stations totalling 184,000 kw.) being the chief undertaking.

Total power generated and purchased in 1980–81 was 23,255 gwh.

Oil and Natural Gas. Crude oil in commercially recoverable quantities was first discovered by the Esso/BHP partnership in 1967 in 2 large fields offshore in East Gippsland in Bass Strait between 65 and 80 km from land. These fields, Halibut and Kingfish, with 10 other fields since discovered—Marlin, Snapper, Barracouta, Mackerel, Tuna, Cobia, Flounder, Fortescue, Bream and Seahorse have been assessed as containing initial recoverable reserves of more than 2,930m. bbls of treated crude oil. Total production since 1969 from the producing fields to the end of Sept. 1980 has amounted to 1,288m. bbls, leaving a balance of recoverable reserves of 1,642m. bbls.

Gippsland crude now supplies approximately 71% of Australia's refinery requirements, and during 1980 a total of 129m. bbls were produced. Depletion of production from the 2 major fields, Kingfish and Halibut and the smaller Barracouta field, is now expected to occur in the late-1980s.

Natural gas was discovered offshore in East Gippsland in 1965. The initial recoverable reserves of treated gas are 7,783,000m. cu. ft. Reserves are sufficient for 30 years. Following an extensive development and distribution programme, natural gas was first connected to homes and industry in Victoria in April 1969. All gas consumers in Melbourne, Geelong, Ballarat, Bendigo, Shepparton, Euroa, Benalla, Wangaratta, Wodonga, Albury and a number of towns near Melbourne, in the Latrobe Valley and in East Gippsland, are now using natural gas. At 30 June 1981 a total of 872,786 consumers were being supplied with it. During the period 1 July 1979 to 30 June 1980 a total volume of 4,262m. cu. metres of gas was consumed in Victoria, including commercial sales and plant usage.

Natural gas and crude oil are conveyed from the producing fields to a large treatment plant at Longford in East Gippsland from where both hydrocarbons are distributed by a network of transmission lines to tank farms and city gate distribution points.

The crude oil is then distributed to refineries in Victoria by pipeline and to other States by seagoing tankers. Natural gas is distributed to residential and industrial consumers through a network of approximately 18,600 km of mains.

Liquefied petroleum gas is now being produced after extraction of the propane and butane fractions from the untreated oil and gas. For the year ended June 1981, approximately 1·8m. tonnes was exported by Esso and BHP, mainly to Japan.

Brown Coal. Major deposits of brown coal are located in the Central Gippsland region and comprise approximately 94% of the total resources in Victoria. In the Latrobe Valley section of this region the thick brown coal seams underlie an area from 10–30 km wide and extend over a length of approximately 70 km from Yallourn in the west to the south of Sale in the east. Small fields have also been found at Stradbroke in the ranges on the southern flank of the Valley and in the Gelliondale–Welshpool area near the coast. On a geological basis the brown coal resources in Central Gippsland are estimated to be in the order of 108,000 megatonnes, of which about 65,000 megatonnes are proven and the remaining 43,000 megatonnes are inferred.

About 54% of the resources occur in areas where the overburden over the uppermost seam is less than 30·5 metres while 95% is in areas with less than 91·4 metres of overburden. The current primary use of these reserves is to fuel the major base load electricity generating stations located at Morwell and Yallourn, and larger cuts have been opened for this purpose at these localities.

Land Settlement. Of the total area of Victoria (22·76m. hectares), 14,063,683 hectares on 30 June 1982 were either alienated or in process of alienation. The remainder (8,696,317) constituted Crown land as follows: Perpetual leases, grazing and other leases and licences, 2,274,043; reservations including forest and timber reserves, water, catchment and drainage purposes, national parks, wildlife reserves, water frontages and other reserves, plus unoccupied and unreserved including areas set aside for roads, 6,422,274. Establishments with agricultural activity at 31 March 1982 numbered 48,608.

Minerals. The recorded production of certain metals and minerals raised in Victoria for the year 1981–82 was: Gold, 92,000 grammes, value $A881,000; coal, brown, 37·6m. tonnes, value $A137·1m.

Agriculture. The following table shows the area under the principal crops and the produce of each for 3 seasons (in 1,000 units):

Season	Total crop area Hectares	Wheat Hectares	Tonnes	Oats Hectares	Tonnes	Barley Hectares	Tonnes	Potatoes Hectares	Tonnes	Hay Hectares	Tonnes
1979–80	2,247	1,457	3,250	256	390	325	494	13	334	412	1,615
1980–81	2,184	1,431	2,538	219	322	303	418	14	349	496	1,893
1981–82	2,184	1,322	2,467	245	306	315	459	14	354	556	1,982

In 1981–82 there were 20,519 hectares of vines, yielding 57,699 tonnes of grapes for wine-making and 80,530 tonnes of grapes for drying or for table use. Green fodder covered 80,898 hectares, and orchards and vegetables, including potatoes and onions, occupied 47,912 hectares.

At March 1982 there were in the State 4·1m. head of cattle, 25,340,923 sheep and 406,253 pigs. In 1981–82, 671,335 tonnes of fresh meat was produced. The wool produced in the season 1981–82 amounted to .48m. kg, valued at $A359m. The quantity of butter produced in 1981–82 was 65·6m. kg.

The gross value of Victorian primary production in (rural and non-rural) 1981–82 was $A2,829m.

INDUSTRY AND TRADE

Industry. From the 1975–76 Census of Manufacturing Establishments onwards only a limited range of data—employment and wages and salaries—has been collected from single-establishment manufacturing enterprises with less than 4 persons employed. This procedure significantly reduces the statistical reporting obligations of small businesses. Data in respect of the larger manufacturers provides reliable information for the evaluation of trends in the manufacturing sector of the economy. From the 1977–78 census, the classification of census units to industry is based on the 1978 edition of the Australian Standard Industrial Classification. The following data relates to manufacturing establishments owned by multi-establishment enterprises, and single-establishment manufacturing enterprises with 4 or more persons employed.

The total number of manufacturing establishments in Victoria in 1981–82 (figures for 1980–81 in brackets) was 8,917 (8,726). Persons employed, including working proprietors, on the last pay day in June were males 279,015 (277,744) and females 113,904 (112,745) and salaries and wages paid were $A5,758m. ($A5,032m.), excluding drawings of working proprietors. The cost of purchases, transfers in, and selected expenses was $A17,044m. ($A14,814m.) and sales, transfers out and other operating revenue were $A27,234m. ($A23,856m.).

The preceding figures exclude gas and electricity producing and distributing establishments. In terms of persons employed the most important manufacturing activities were: Basic and fabricated metal products including transport equipment, other machinery and equipment, 164,042 (160,265); textiles, clothing and footwear, 62,694 (63,325); food, beverages and tobacco, 53,139 (55,349).

Trade Unions. There were 175 trade unions with a total membership of 790,100 operating in Victoria in Dec. 1982.

Commerce. The commerce of Victoria, exclusive of inter-state trade, is included in the statement of the commerce of Australia, *see* pp. 110–12.

The total value of the overseas imports and exports of Victoria, including bullion and specie but excluding inter-state trade, was as follows (in $A1,000):

	1977–78	1978–79	1979–80	1980–81	1981–82	1982–83[1]
Imports	3,855,619	4,694,481	5,506,400	5,929,278	7,167,713	6,987,715
Exports	2,505,768	2,702,452	3,782,993	3,993,482	3,981,601	4,023,680

[1] Preliminary.

The chief exports[1] in 1982–83 were: Cereals and cereal preparations, petroleum products and gases, vegetables and fruit, dairy products, meat, textile fibres and their wastes and road vehicles.

[1] From 1 July 1978 state export figures changed from 'State of Lodgement of documents with the Bureau of Customs' to 'State of Origin'.

COMMUNICATIONS

Roads. At 30 June 1982 there were 157,201 km of road open for general traffic consisting of 63,926 km of bituminous seal, etc., 47,905 km of waterbound macadam, gravel, etc., 23,503 km formed, but not paved, and 21,867 km not formed. The number of registered motor vehicles (other than tractors) at 30 June 1982 was 2,171,800.

Railways. All the railways are the property of the State and are under the management of a 9-member governing board, appointed by, and responsible to, the Victorian Government.

At 30 June 1982, 5,811 km of government railway were open. During the year 1980–81 the gross revenue amounted to $A256,258,700 and the total working expenses to $A448,278,345. 88,538,076 (estimate) passengers, 12,616,183 tonnes of freight and 104,597 tonnes of livestock were carried.

Aviation. During the year ended 31 Dec. 1982 there were 71,812 aircraft movements at Melbourne (Tullamarine) airport. Passengers totalled 4·8m. on domestic flights (international, 968,002). Freight handled, 72,678 tonnes, domestic flights (40,734 international).

JUSTICE, RELIGION, EDUCATION AND WELFARE

Justice. There is a Supreme Court with a Chief Justice and 20 puisne judges. There are magistrates' courts, county courts, a court of licensing, and a bankruptcy court.

Criminal statistics for 1978: 378,054 convictions (in addition approximately for 209,349 driving and traffic offences) in magistrates' courts; 1,210 convicted persons in higher (judges') courts.

There are 11 gaols in Victoria. At 30 June 1982 there were confined in these prisons, 1,809 persons.

Religion. There is no State Church in Victoria, and no State assistance has been given to religion since 1875. At the date of the 1981 census the following were the enumerated numbers of each of the principal religions: Catholic,[1] 524,612; Church of England, 371,873; Uniting, 97,611; Orthodox, 87,119; Presbyterian, 83,223; Protestant (undefined), 46,403; Methodist, 43,030; other Christian, 34,361; Moslem, 15,666; Hebrew, 14,668; no religion, 258,249; no reply, 231,821.

[1] So described on individual census schedules.

Education. Education establishments in Victoria consist of 4 universities, established under special Acts and opened in 1855, 1961, 1967 and 1977; Colleges of Advanced Education; government schools (primary, primary-secondary, high and secondary technical, and further education colleges), and non-government schools.

The University of Melbourne, founded in 1853, had, in 1981, 16,242 students and 1,520 teaching and research staff.

Monash University, founded in 1958 in an eastern suburb of Melbourne, had, in 1981, 14,161 students and 1,177 teaching and research staff.

La Trobe University, founded in 1964 in a northern suburb of Melbourne, had 8,538 students and 603 teaching and research staff in 1981.

Deakin University (1974) near Melbourne had 5,278 students and 250 staff in 1981.

Primary education of children of the ages of 6 to 15 years inclusive is free, secular and compulsory. At 1 July 1981 there were 1,663 government primary schools and 71 special schools with 20,088 teachers and an enrolment of 358,010 pupils; 19 government primary-secondary schools had 549 teachers and an enrolment of 6,346 pupils. There were also 396 government secondary schools, including junior technical schools and high schools with 21,132 teachers and an enrolment of 230,686 pupils. In 1981 there were 164,053 students (excluding adult education programmes) enrolled in technical and further education schools and colleges.

Non-government Schools. There were at 1 July 1981, 632 non-government schools, excluding commercial colleges, with 13,815 teachers and 221,611 pupils enrolled. Of these schools, 488 were Roman Catholic.

Social Services. Victoria was the first State of Australia to make a statutory provision for the payment of Age Pensions. The Act providing for the payment of such pensions came into operation on 18 Jan. 1901, and continued until 1 July 1909, when the Australian Invalid and Old Age Pension Act came into force. The Social Services Consolidation Act, which came into operation on 1 July 1947, repealed the various legislative enactments relating to age (previously old-age) and invalid pensions, maternity allowances, child endowment and unemployment, and sickness benefits and while following in general the Acts repealed, considerably liberalized many of their provisions: it has since been amended. On 30 June 1982 there were 367,345 aged and 72,989 invalid pensioners in Victoria, and the amount paid in pensions, including payments to wives of invalid pensioners, during 1981–82 was $A1,429·9m.

The number of disability pensions (members of the forces and their dependants) payable in Victoria on 30 June 1982 was 101,857, and the number of service pensions was 73,659. The amount paid in war and service pensions by the Federal Government during 1981–82 was $A321m.

Under the Australian Unemployment and Sickness Benefit Act 1944, there were 98,275 persons receiving benefits at June 1982 (excluding migrants in accommodation centres) and the amount paid in benefits totalled $A353·3m. in the year ended 30 June 1982.

The number of widows' pensions in force in Victoria at 30 June 1982 was 45,824, and the total amount paid in allowances during the year was $A195·7m.

The number of family allowances in force in Victoria at 30 June 1982 was 1,142,101 (including students). In addition (in 1982), endowment was being paid in respect of 2,389 children who were being maintained in approved institutions. The total amount paid in endowment in Victoria during the year ended 30 June 1982 was $A283m.

State Housing. The various State housing authorities were consolidated under the control of the Ministry of Housing early in 1973. The authorities include the Housing Commission, the Government Employee Housing Authority and the Co-operative Housing Registry. The Co-operative Housing Registry administers distribution of finance to the co-operative building societies from loan moneys advanced by the Federal Government.

On the coming into operation of amending legislation on 24 Jan. 1979, the Housing Commission, as it was constituted, ceased to exist and was replaced by a Commission consisting of a full-time Chairman and 3 part-time members. The Director of Housing (the Permanent Head of the Ministry of Housing) is, *ex officio*, Chairman of the Commission. The Housing Advisory Council was also created under that legislation, its functions being to advise on and investigate matters affecting housing and to consult with all sections of the housing industry. The Council consists of the Director and 6 part-time members appointed by the Minister of Housing.

Since its inception in 1938, the Housing Commission had built and purchased, to 30 June 1983, 95,356 housing units, of which 50,725 had been sold. Approximately 41% of all construction since 1938 is located outside the Melbourne metropolitan area.

Rental charges for the year ended 30 June 1983 were $A104,290,346, against which $A25,557,061 was allowed in rent rebates to tenants on low incomes, including pensioners.

Books of Reference

Statistical Information: Australian Bureau of Statistics (Commonwealth Banks Building, corner of Elizabeth and Flinders Streets, Melbourne, 3000). *Deputy Commonwealth Statistician:* I. M. Cowie, B.Com.

Victorian Year Book. (Annually since 1873)
Victorian Pocket Year Book. (Annually since 1956)
Victorian Statistical Register. (Annually from 1854 to 1916)
Monthly Summary of Statistics (from Jan. 1960)

Victoria: The First Century. Official History of Victoria. Melbourne, 1934
Victorian Municipal Directory. Melbourne, (From 1866). Melbourne, Arnall and Jackson
Grant, J., and Serle, G., *The Melbourne Scene 1803–1956.* Melbourne Univ. Press, 1956
Pratt, A., *The Centenary History of Victoria.* Melbourne, 1934

State Library: The State Library of Victoria, 328 Swanston St., Melbourne, 3000. *State Librarian:* W. Horton, BA, ALAA.

WESTERN AUSTRALIA

HISTORY. In 1791 Vancouver, in the *Discovery*, took formal possession of the country about King George Sound. In 1826 the Government of New South Wales sent 20 convicts and a detachment of soldiers to King George Sound and formed a settlement then called Frederickstown. In 1827 Captain (afterwards Sir) James Stirling surveyed the coast from King George Sound to the Swan River, and in May 1829 Captain (afterwards Sir) Charles Fremantle took possession of the territory. In June 1829 Captain Stirling, newly appointed Lieut.-Governor, founded the colony now known as the State of Western Australia. On 1 Jan. 1901 Western Australia became one of the 6 federated States within the Commonwealth of Australia.

AREA AND POPULATION. Western Australia lies between 113° 09′ and 129° E. long. and 13° 44′ and 35° 08′ S. lat.; its area is 2,525,500 sq. km.

The population at each census from 1933 was as follows [1]:

	Males	Females	Total		Males	Females	Total
1933	233,937	204,915	438,852	1966	432,569	415,531	848,100
1947	258,076	244,404	502,480	1971	534,100	509,000	1,043,100
1954	330,358	309,413	639,771	1976	596,800	573,100	1,169,800
1961	375,452	361,177	736,629	1981	656,400	642,700	1,299,100

[1] 1961 and earlier exclude full-blood Aboriginals; from 1966 figures refer to total population (*i.e.*, including Aboriginals).

Of the census population in 1981, 910,666 were born in Australia. Married persons numbered 585,465 (285,224 males and 283,241 females); widowers, 10,088; widows, 45,465; divorced, 16,180 males and 19,171 females; never married, 318,273 males and 267,761 females. The number of males under 21 was 240,210 and of females 228,155.

Perth, the capital, had an estimated resident population of 948,850 at June 1982. Of this, the area administered by the City of Perth had a population of 81,950 while the population in the area for which the City of Fremantle is responsible (which includes the chief port of the State) was 23,360.

Principal urban centres outside the metropolitan area, with population at the census of 30 June 1981: Bunbury, 21,749; Geraldton, 20,895; Kalgoorlie–Boulder, 19,848; Albany, 15,222; Port Hedland, 12,948; Mandurah, 10,978; Collie, 7,667; Northam, 6,791; Busselton, 6,463; Esperance, 6,375; Carnarvon, 5,053; Narrogin, 4,965.

Vital statistics for calendar years [1]:

	Births	Ex-nuptial births	Marriages	Divorces	Deaths
1980	20,607	2,833	9,594	3,073	8,166
1981	21,877	3,300	10,111	3,481	7,993
1982	22,236	3,316	10,455	3,842	8,187

[1] Including Aboriginals.

CONSTITUTION AND GOVERNMENT. In 1870 partially representative government was instituted, and in 1890 the administration was vested in the Governor, a Legislative Council and a Legislative Assembly. The Legislative Council was, in the first instance, nominated by the Governor, but it was provided that in the event of the population of the colony reaching 60,000, it should be elective. In 1893 this limit of population being reached, the Colonial Parliament amended the Constitution accordingly.

The Legislative Council consists of 34 members, 2 members representing each of the 17 electoral provinces. Each member is elected for a term of 6 years, one-half of the members retiring every 3 years.

There are 57 members of the Legislative Assembly, each member representing one of the 57 electoral districts of the State. Members are elected for the duration of the Parliament, normally 3 years. The qualifications applying to candidates and electors are identical for the Legislative Council and the Legislative Assembly. A candidate must have resided in Western Australia for a minimum of 12 months, be at least 18 years of age and free from legal incapacity, be a British subject, and be enrolled, or qualified for enrolment, as an elector. A judge of the Supreme Court, the Sheriff of Western Australia, an undischarged bankrupt or a debtor against whose estate there is a subsisting order in bankruptcy may not be elected to Parliament. No person may hold office as a member of the Legislative Assembly and the Legislative Council at the same time. An elector must be at least 18 years of age, be a British subject free from legal incapacity, must have resided in the Commonwealth of Australia for 6 and in Western Australia for 3 months continuously and in the electoral district for which he claims enrolment for a continuous period of 1 month immediately preceding the date of his claim. Enrolment is compulsory for all qualified persons except Aboriginal natives of Australia, who are entitled but not required to enrol. Voting at elections is on the preferential system and is compulsory for all enrolled persons.

Ordinary members of the legislature are paid a salary of $A34,170 a year, with an additional electorate allowance, ranging from $A10,000 to $A22,600 according to location of electorate. Members are entitled to free travel on Western Australian government railways and on the Metropolitan (Perth) Passenger Transport Trust omnibus and ferry services, and, by arrangement, once every year on government railways in other States. All members of Parliament contribute to superannuation benefits.

The Premier receives a salary, including an electorate allowance, of $A81,834, the Deputy Premier $A72,830, the Leader of the Government in the Legislative Council $A70,350, and all other Ministers $A65,458—78,058 according to location of electorate.

The Legislative Assembly, elected on 19 Feb. 1983, is composed as follows: Australian Labor Party, 32; Liberal Party, 20; National Country Party, 3; National Party, 2. The Legislative Council, one-half of which was elected on the same day, is composed of 19 Liberal Party, 13 Australian Labor Party, 1 National Country Party, 1 National Party.

Governor. (Vacant).

The Australian Labor Party Cabinet was, at 30 Sept. 1983:

Premier and Cabinet, Treasurer, Minister Co-ordinating Economic and Social Development, and Minister for Forests, Tourism and Women's Interests: Hon. Brian Thomas Burke, MLA.
Deputy Premier and Minister for Economic Development and Technology: Hon. Malcolm John Bryce, BA, MLA. *Industrial Relations and Leader of the Government in the Legislative Council:* Hon. Desmond Keith Dans, MLC. *Attorney-General, Inter-Governmental Relations and Defence Liaison, Prisons and Minister Assisting the Treasurer:* Hon. Joseph Max Berinson, LLB, MLC. *Water Resources, Consumer Affairs, Parliamentary and Electoral Reform and Leader of the House:* Hon. Arthur Raymond Tonkin, BA, Dip Ed, MLA. *Police and Emergency Services, and Local Government:* Hon. Jeffrey Phillip Carr, BA, MLA. *Environment, Multi-Cultural and Ethnic Affairs, and the Arts:* Hon. Ronald Davies, MLA. *Agriculture, Fisheries and Wildlife and Minister Assisting the Minister for Forests:* Hon. Hywel David Evans, BA, MLA. *Education:* Hon. Robert John Pearce, BA, Dip Ed, MLA. *Health:* Hon. Barry James Hodge, MLA. *Works, and Lands and Surveys:* Hon. Kenneth Finlay McIver, MLA. *Employment and Administrative Services, Planning and Minister Assisting the Minister Co-ordinating Economic and Social Development:* Hon. David Charles Parker, BA, MLA. *Transport, and Regional Development and the North-West with special responsibility for 'Bunbury 2000':* Hon. Julian Fletcher Grill, LLB., MLA. *Housing, Youth and Community Services with special responsibility for Aboriginal Affairs, and Minister for Sport and Recreation:* Hon. Keith James Wilson, MLA. *Mines, and Fuel and Energy:* Hon. Peter M'Callum Dowding, LLB., MLC.

Agent-General in London: R. Douglas (Western Australia House, 115 Strand, WC2R 0AJ).

Local Government. The only unincorporated area in mainland Western Australia is King's Park, a public reserve of about 403 hectares in Perth. Including the lord-mayoralty of Perth there were 12 cities, 12 towns and 115 shires at 30 June 1983. The executive body in each of these districts is normally an elective council, presided over by a mayor (city and town) or a president (shire), but in certain circumstances it may be a commissioner appointed by the Governor. Their functions include road construction and repair, the provision of parks and recreation grounds, the administration of building controls and local services such as health and, in some country districts, traffic. Finance is derived largely from rates levied on property owners as well as charges for services and government grants (mainly for road construction).

ECONOMY

Budget. The revenue and expenditure (in $A) of Western Australia in years ended 30 June, are given as follows:

	1981	1982	1983	1984 [1]
Revenue	1,860,548,032	2,061,893,781	2,324,874,369	2,658,900,000
Expenditure	1,862,006,834	2,061,893,781	2,339,070,164	2,658,900,000

[1] Estimates.

Main items of revenue in 1982–83: Railways ($A210,225,502), taxation ($A475,314,902), lands, timber and mining ($A136,377,880), public utilities other than railways ($A56,484,547), from Federal funds ($A1,141,749,219). Western Australia had a net loan liability of $A1,547,497,840 on 30 June 1983, the charge for the year being $A171,628,379.

Banking. There are 8 trading banks in Western Australia including the Commonwealth Trading Bank and The Rural and Industries Bank of Western Australia. In the June quarter, 1983, the average of customers' balances was $A2,864·5m. and average advances $A2,659m.

At 30 June 1983, the 6 savings banks held deposits of $A1,910·5m., in 1,835,917 accounts.

ENERGY AND NATURAL RESOURCES

Minerals. The mining industry has been for many years of considerable significance in the Western Australian economy. Until the mid-1960s the major mineral produced was gold. However, in recent years gold has been displaced by iron ore and nickel concentrates in terms of value.

The total ex-mine value of minerals from mining and quarrying in the State in 1981–82 was $A2,067·8m Principal minerals produced in 1981–82 were: Iron ore and pellets, 82·5m. tonnes, value $A1,079·8m.; crude oil, 1·24m. cu. metres, value $A122·6m.; gold bullion, 19·3m. grammes, value $A181·9m.; construction materials (excluding sand and gravel), value $A56·3m.; mineral sands, 1·61m. tonnes, value, $A91·2m.; black coal, 3·43m. tonnes, value $A75·1m.; salt, 3·99m. tonnes, value $A42·8m.; t n concentrates, 1,023 tonnes, value $A8·52m.; nickel concentrates, 423,438 tonnes; bauxite, 11·9m. tonnes, and natural gas, 838·2m. cu. metres, value $A30·4m

Land Settlement. Up to 31 Dec. 1981, of the entire area of the State (252·55m. hectares) 17,113,000 hectares had been alienated; on that date 1,959,000 hectares were in process of alienation; the area alienated and in process of alienation thus amounting to 19,072,000 hectares. There were in force leases comprising an area of 97,988,000 hectares, of which 95,118,000 hectares were pastoral, 616,000 hectares were timber, 147,000 hectares mining leases, 12,000 hectares miners' homestead leases and 2,096,000 hectares for reserves, residential lots, special and perpetual leases.

Agriculture.

| | 1980–81 | | 1981–82 | |
Crop	Area 1,000 hectares	Production 1,000 tonnes	Area 1,000 hectares	Production 1,000 tonnes
Wheat	4,333	3,315	4,593	4,803
Oats	382	384	432	442
Barley	535	504	580	576
Hay	240	703	255	711
Potatoes	2	64	2	67
Cauliflower	1	13	1	16

| | 1980–81 | | 1981–82 | |
Crop	No. Trees Bearing (1,000)	Production Tonnes	No. Trees Bearing (1,000)	Production Tonnes
Apples	721	51,157	677	49,577
Pears	71	5,592	77	6,004
Oranges	197	7,303	184	7,676

Irrigation has been established by the Government along the south-western coastal plain and in the north of the State. Reservoirs with an aggregate capacity of 6,137m. cu. metres provided irrigation water for 30,000 hectares in 6 districts during 1981–82.

The livestock at 31 March 1982 consisted of 1,942,000 cattle, 30,268,000 sheep and 263,000 pigs.

The wool clip in 1981–82 was 148,728 tonnes; the overseas exports for 1981–82, greasy wool, 112,471 tonnes; degreased wool, 16,985 tonnes.

Forestry. The area of State forests and timber reserves at 31 Dec. 1981 was 2,231,000 hectares; 1981–82 production of sawn timber was 333,594 cu. metres, principally Jarrah and Karri hardwoods.

Fisheries. The catch of fish, crustaceans and molluscs in Western Australia in 1981–82 totalled 27,634 tonnes for a gross value of $A99·3m. Of this, rock lobsters, with a total catch of 10,509 tonnes accounted for $A74·8m.

Value of Agricultural Commodities Produced. The estimated gross values of Western Australian agricultural commodities during 1981–82 were as follows: Crops and pastures, $A1,067 29m.; livestock slaughterings and other disposals, $A349·49m.; livestock products, $A454·15m.

INDUSTRY AND TRADE

Industry. Up to the early 1950s most of the factories in Western Australia were small and medium sized establishments supplying the local market and carrying out some processing of the State's primary products for export. Development of heavy industry and large-scale operations since the early 1950s has been associated with the establishment of a large oil refinery at Kwinana in 1954 which provided the basis for an integrated industrial complex adjacent to Perth; more recent developments have been associated with the processing of the State's vast deposits of iron ore, nickel, bauxite and mineral sands.

The following table shows manufacturing industry statistics for 1981–82 [1]:

Industry sub-division	Number of establishments operating at 30 June	Persons employed [2]	Wages and salaries $A1,000	Turnover $A1,000	Value added $A1,000
Food, beverages and tobacco	366	12,026	160,235	1,153,018	331,273
Textiles	31	800	10,053	44,966	15,204
Clothing and footwear	64	1,576	14,822	36,031	20,573
Wood, wood products and furniture	468	8,203	90,386	375,422	169,795
Paper, paper products, printing and publishing	207	6,565	94,971	301,173	151,931
Chemical, petroleum and coal products	78	3,246	60,276	451,959	146,690
Non-metallic mineral products	228	5,113	78,157	391,643	173,156
Basic metal products	40	6,175	120,292	1,259,809	412,563
Fabricated metal products	462	10,681	153,061	637,653	258,221
Transport equipment	166	5,343	73,702	202,781	103,272
Other machinery and equipment	311	8,405	124,110	476,675	205,449
Miscellaneous manufacturing	182	2,666	33,332	159,870	64,556
Total	2,603	70,799	1,013,397	5,490,999	2,052,683

[1] Excludes single establishment enterprises with less than 4 persons employed.
[2] Annual average. Includes working proprietors.

Labour. A Court of Arbitration was established in Western Australia in 1901 under the provisions of the 'Industrial Conciliation and Arbitration Act 1900'. The Court of Arbitration was replaced, with effect from 1 Feb. 1964, by the Western Australian Industrial Appeal Court and The Western Australian Industrial Commission, authorities constituted in terms of the *Industrial Arbitration Act 1912–1977*. These authorities continue to operate under the provisions of the *Industrial Arbitration Act 1979–81*.

The Western Australian Industrial Appeal Court consists of 3 Judges, one of whom is the Presiding Judge. The members are nominated by the Chief Justice of Western Australia. An appeal lies to the Court from decisions of the President of the Western Australian Industrial Commission, the Full Bench or the Commission in Court Session but only on the ground that the decision is erroneous in law or is in excess of jurisdiction.

The Western Australian Industrial Commission consists of a President, a Chief Industrial Commissioner, a Senior Commissioner, and 'such number of other Commissioners as may, from time to time, be necessary'. There were 5 'other Commissioners' at 1 March 1983. A person shall not be appointed as President unless he is qualified to be a Judge, and on appointment he is entitled to the status of a Puisne Judge. The President or a Commissioner sitting or acting alone constitutes the Commission and may exercise the appropriate powers of the Commission.

The Commission can inquire into any industrial matter and make an award, order or declaration relating to such matter. 'Industrial matter' means any matter affecting or relating to the work, privileges, rights, or duties of employers or employees in any industry and includes any matter relating to the wages, salaries, allowances, or other remuneration of employees or the prices to be paid in respect of their employment; the hours of employment, sex, age, qualification or status of employees and the mode, terms and conditions of employment including conditions which are to take effect after the termination of employment. The Commission may also make inquiries where industrial action has occurred or is likely to occur.

The Commission in Court Session is constituted by not less than 3 Commissioners sitting or acting together, and may make General Orders, hear matters referred by the Commission, and hear appeals from decisions of Boards of Reference.

The Full Bench is constituted by not less than 3 members of the Commission, 1 of whom is the President, and may hear matters referred by the Commission on questions of law, and appeals from decisions of the Commission and Industrial Magistrates.

The following table shows details of the number of industrial awards, unions and members registered with The Western Australian Industrial Commission.

At 30 June	1979	1980	1981	1982	1983
Awards in force	355	494	459	483	488
Consent agreements in force [1]	135	...[2]	...[2]	...[2]	...[2]
Unions of workers:					
Number	77	74	68	69	66
Membership	192,056	181,409	170,414	171,912	176,065
Unions of employers:					
Number	14	14	14	14	14
Membership	2,102	2,040	2,139	2,142	2,138

[1] Named as 'Industrial agreements' prior to 1980. [2] Included in 'Awards in force'.

Commerce. The external commerce of Western Australia, exclusive of interstate trade, is comprised in the statement of the commerce of Australia, see pp. 110–12.

The total value of imports and exports, including interstate trade, but excluding interstate value of horses, in 5 years (30 June) is, in $A1m., as follows:

	1977–78	1978–79	1979–80	1980–81	1981–82
Imports	2,765·9	3,205·6	3,787·5	4,504·5	5,676·2
Exports[1]	2,944·1	3,266·3	4,489·5	4,604·1	4,796·1

[1] Excluding ships' stores.

Selected overseas exports (in $A) for 1981–82 (excluding ships' stores): Iron ore and concentrates, 1,195,485,520; wheat, 594,991,862; wool, 394,366,899; live sheep and lambs, 94,825,458; petroleum and petroleum products, 89,442,596; beef and veal, 73,672,653; gold bullion, 72,059,924; rock lobster tails, 65,643,223; barley, 48,744,499; salt, 43,217,906; mutton and lamb, 37,057,418; ilmenite and leucoxene, 25,003,154; zirconium, 23,961,055; rutile, 22,288,692; oats, 19,073,692; prawns, 18,090,399; hides and skins, 16,736,014; whole rock lobsters, 12,287,047; fruit and nuts (fresh or dried), 10,953,203; animal oils and fats, 10,502,652; iron and steel, 6,644,623.

Selected overseas imports (in $A) for 1981–82: Petroleum and petroleum products, 817,432,003; transport equipment, 571,304,170; machinery, 415,452,965; iron and steel, 104,985,806; chemicals, 79,405,051; crude fertilizer, 67,059,969; food, 33,115,235; rubber manufactures, 32,995,190; paper and paperboard, 26,009,260.

The chief countries exporting to Western Australia in 1981–82 were (in $A): USA, 433,595,697; Japan, 368,999,021; Indonesia, 225,661,235; Singapore, 207,791,661; UAE, 198,845,644; Saudi Arabia, 141,817,103. Western Australian exports in 1981–82 (in $A) went chiefly to: Japan, 1,540,828,380; USA, 623,655,082; Egypt, 228,760,366; UK, 209,778,024; USSR, 199,601,757; China, People's Republic of, 176,066,386.

Tourism. In 1982, 493,900 (estimate) visitors contributed about $A270m. to the economy; interstate tourists, 4,904,000 (estimate) contributed $A648m. to the economy.

COMMUNICATIONS

Roads. At 30 June 1982 there were 116,026 km of prepared and formed roads in Western Australia, namely, 37,081 km of bituminous surface, 34,168 km other constructed surfaces and 44,777 km formed but not metalled or otherwise prepared. In addition, there are 22,826 km of roads unprepared except for clearing which are used for general traffic.

New motor vehicles registered in Western Australia during the year ended 30 June 1983 were 59,002.

Railways. At 30 June 1982 the State had 5,609 km of State government railway and 731 km of Federal line, the latter being the western portion of the Trans-Australian line (Kalgoorlie–Port Pirie), which links the State railway system to those of the other States of the Commonwealth. At 30 June 1982, mining companies operated 1,181 km of private railways for the transport of ore to ports on the north-west coast.

Aviation. An extensive system of regular air services operates in Western Australia for the transport of passengers, freight and mail. During the year ended 30 June 1982, Perth Airport handled a total of 18,555 aircraft movements, 28,760 tonnes of freight and 1,446,149 passengers on domestic and international services.

Shipping. In 1981–82, the number of overseas direct vessels through the major ports was: Port of Fremantle, 542 entered, 693 cleared; Dampier, 356 entered, 367 cleared; Port Hedland, 375 entered, 325 cleared; Port Walcott, 121 entered, 125 cleared. The gross weight (in tonnes) of overseas cargo through those ports was: Port of Fremantle, 4,706,197 discharged, 4,718,769 loaded; Dampier, 88,058 discharged, 30,523,912 loaded; Port Hedland, 257,256 discharged, 30,025,268 loaded; Port Walcott, 34,500 discharged, 14,803,147 loaded.

Post and Broadcasting. Postal, telephone and telegraph facilities are afforded at 462 offices. An additional 24 offices provide only telephone and telegraph facilities. Telephones connected totalled 652,825 at 30 June 1982.

There were 47 wireless broadcasting and 67 television stations, including translator stations, in operation at 30 June 1982.

JUSTICE, RELIGION, EDUCATION AND WELFARE

Justice. In Western Australia justice is administered by a Supreme Court, consisting of a Chief Justice, puisne judges and a master at 30 June 1983; a District Court comprising a chairman of judges and 8 district court judges and Magistrates' Courts exercising both civil and criminal jurisdiction. The lower courts are presided over by justices of the peace, except in the more important centres, where the court is constituted by a stipendiary magistrate. There are special Magistrates' Courts for juvenile offenders.

Offences against law	1978	1979	1980	1981	1982
Charges	117,408	122,419	126,012	122,176	...
Lower Court convictions [1]	105,136	111,864	115,787	116,541	...
Higher Court convictions	1,204	1,584	...	1,759	1,857

[1] Includes convictions for traffic offences: 50,235 in 1978; 56,310 in 1979; 54,734 in 1980; 55,325 in 1981. In addition, small fines were imposed for minor traffic offences as follows: 1978, 307,396; 1979, 333,545; 1980, 332,754; 1981, 348,452; 1982, 379,444.

Persons in prison at 30 June 1982 numbered 1,291 males and 59 females.

Religion. There is no State Church, and freedom of worship is accorded to all. At the census, 30 June 1981, the principal denominations were: Church of England, 375,848; Roman Catholic and Catholic, 316,337; Methodist, 51,225; Presbyterian, 32,033; Baptist, 15,859; Church of Christ, 14,163; other Christian, 131,637; Hebrew, 3,156; all other, including not stated and no religion, 333,368.

Education. School attendance is compulsory from the age of 6 until the end of the year in which the child attains 15 years. Pre-school education is provided by a kindergarten system partly financed from government subsidy. In 1982 there were 712 government primary and secondary schools providing free education to 208,428 pupils and 213 non-government primary and secondary schools providing education, for which fees are charged, to 51,538 pupils.

Technical education is available at a number of technical colleges, schools and centres, which are staffed and controlled by the Education Department.

In 1982 the full-time teaching and research staff of the University of Western Australia was 748 and the number of students enrolled was 9,660. Murdoch University enrolled 2,958 students in 1982. Full-time teaching and research staff numbered 174.

Tertiary education is also offered by the Western Australian Institute of Technology and the Western Australian College of Advanced Education.

State Government expenditure from consolidated revenue on education, including financial assistance to the Universities, during the year ended 30 June 1982, amounted to $A525,929,240.

Social Welfare. At 30 June 1982 there were 45 general hospitals and 7 nursing homes maintained wholly by public funds and 47 general hospitals and 8 nursing homes partly assisted therefrom. In addition, there are numerous private hospitals. Government mental health services comprise 4 approved hospitals, 39 clinics, 13 rehabilitation units, 59 units concerned with the intellectually handicapped, 1 after-care hostel and 1 in-patient unit for children.

The Department for Community Welfare is responsible for the provision of welfare services throughout the State. There are 28 district offices, 7 country divisional offices, 8 metropolitan divisional offices and 2 metropolitan sub-offices.

The Department runs 9 facilities for the care, assessment, training and support of children who have behavioural problems or are emotionally disturbed. It also provides accommodation at 28 hostels, mainly for Aboriginal children.

There are specialized units working in the areas of child abuse, drug abuse, adoptions and youth activities, and the Department offers help for parents having difficulties looking after their families and supervises all day care centres in the State. There is a homemaker service, a psychological service and a counselling and welfare service attached to the Family Court.

The Department administers the Perth Children's Courts and the Children's (Suspended Proceedings) Panels.

Through the Department, the State Government makes financial assistance available to people in necessitous circumstances.

During the year ended 30 June 1982, 19,436 persons or families received assistance.

Age, invalid, widows' and war and service pensions are paid by the Federal Government. The number of pensioners in Western Australia at 30 June 1982 was: Age, 105,870; invalid, 21,661; widows, 12,654; and disability, service, 60,817.

Housing. In 1981–82, a total of 9,440 new houses and 5,255 new other dwellings were completed in Western Australia. Of these, the State Housing Commission provided 1,024 new dwelling units for sale and for rental.

The value of the total number of dwellings completed during this period was $A563·5m. Additions and alterations valued at $A10,000 or more to dwellings, were valued at $A51·9m.

Books of Reference

Statistical Information: The State Government Statistician's Office was established in 1897 and now functions as the Western Australian Office of the Australian Bureau of Statistics (1–3 St George's Tce, Perth). *Deputy Commonwealth Statistician and Government Statistician:* W. M. Bartlett. Its principal publications are: *Western Australian Year Book* (new series, from 1957). *Western Australian Pocket Year Book* (from 1919). *Monthly Summary of Statistics* (from 1958)

Battye, J. S., *Western Australia: A History from its Discovery to the Inauguration of the Commonwealth.* Oxford, 1924.—*The Cyclopedia of Western Australia.* Adelaide, Vol. 1 (1912), Vol. 2 (1913)

Crowley, F. K., and De Garis, B. K., *A Short History of Western Australia.* Melbourne, 1969

Gentilli, J., *Atlas of Western Australian Agriculture.* Perth, 1941

Kerr, Alex, *The South-West Region of Western Australia.* Perth, 1965.—*Australia's North-West.* Perth, 1967

Kimberley, W. B., *History of Western Australia: A Narrative of Her Past.* Melbourne, 1978

Metropolitan Region Planning Authority, *The Corridor Plan for Perth.* Perth, 1970

Stannage, C. T. (ed.) *A New History of Western Australia.* Perth, 1980

Stephenson, G., and Hepburn, J. A., *Plan for the Metropolitan Region: Perth and Fremantle.* Perth, 1955

State Library: The State Library of Western Australia, Perth. *State Librarian:* R. C. Sharman, BA, FLAA.

AUSTRIA

Republik Österreich

Capital: Vienna
Population: 7·56m. (1981)
GNP per capita: US$10,230 (1980)

HISTORY. On 27 April 1945 a provisional government restored the Republic of Austria and was recognized by the Allied Control Council on 20 Oct. 1945.

AREA AND POPULATION. For the boundaries of Austria according to the Treaty of St Germain, signed in Sept. 1919, see THE STATESMAN'S YEAR-BOOK, 1920, pp. 674–75.

Federal States	Area sq. km	Population (census 12 May 1981)	Percentage of population	Population per sq. km
Vienna (Wien)	415	1,531,346	20·3	3,690
Lower Austria (Niederösterreich)	19,171	1,427,849	18·9	74
Burgenland	3,966	269,771	3·6	68
Upper Austria (Oberösterreich)	11,979	1,269,540	16·8	106
Salzburg	7,154	442,301	5·9	62
Styria (Steiermark)	16,387	1,186,525	15·7	72
Carinthia (Kärnten)	9,533	536,179	7·1	56
Tirol	12,647	586,663	7·8	46
Vorarlberg	2,601	305,164	4·0	117
Total	83,853 [1]	7,555,338	100·0	90

[1] 32,375 sq. miles.

Vital statistics for calendar years:

	Live births	Still births	Deaths [1]	Marriages	Divorces	Emigration Austrians	Others
1979	86,388	561	92,012	45,445	13,042	11	2,597
1980	90,872	602	92,442	46,435	13,327	15	3,818
1981	93,942	511	92,693	47,768	13,369	9	6,909
1982	94,840	469	91,339	47,643	14,298	32	14,317

[1] Excluding still births.

The population of the principal towns (excluding Vienna), according to the census of 12 May 1981 (area, 12 May 1981) was as follows:

Graz	243,405	Steyr	38,967	Feldkirch	23,876	Mödling	19,333
Linz	197,962	Dornbirn	38,663	Klosterneu-		Lustenau	17,404
Salzburg	138,213	Wiener		burg	23,307	Braunau	
Innsbruck	116,100	Neustadt	35,050	Baden	23,235	am Inn	16,192
Klagenfurt	86,303	Leoben	32,006	Krems a.d.D.	23,123	Ternitz	16,154
Villach	52,744	Wolfsberg	28,182	Amstetten	22,015	Hallein	15,404
St Pölten	51,102	Kapfenberg	25,719	Traun	21,524	Bruck an	
Wels	51,024	Bregenz	24,683	Leonding	19,402	der Mur	15,086

CLIMATE. Climate ranges from cool temperate to mountain type according to situation. Winters are cold, with considerable snowfall, but summers are very warm. The wettest months are May to August.

Vienna, Jan. 28°F (–2°C), July 67°F (19·5°C). Annual rainfall 25·6″ (640 mm). Graz, Jan. 28°F (–2°C), July 67°F (19·5°C). Annual rainfall 34″ (849 mm). Innsbruck, Jan. 27°F (–2·7°C), July 66°F (18·8°C). Annual rainfall 34·7″ (868 mm). Salzburg, Jan. 28°F (–2·0°C), July 65°F (18·3°C). Annual rainfall 50·6″ (1,266 mm).

CONSTITUTION AND GOVERNMENT. Austria recovered its sovereignty and independence on 27 July 1955 by the coming into force of the Austrian State Treaty between the UK, the USA, the USSR and France on the one part and the Republic of Austria on the other part (signed on 15 May).

172

On 12 March 1938 Austria was forcibly absorbed in the German Reich until it was liberated by the American, British, French and Soviet armies in spring 1945. Already in the Moscow Declaration of Oct. 1943, UK, the USA and the USSR had resolved upon the re-establishment of a free and independent Austria.

On 27 April 1945 Dr Karl Renner set up a provisional government which restored the Republic of Austria in the spirit of the Constitution of 1920–29, and was recognized by the Four-Power Allied Control Council on 20 Oct. 1945. The last occupation forces left Austria in Oct. 1955.

President of the Republic: Dr Rudolf Kirchschläger, former Minister of Foreign Affairs, elected on 23 June 1974 and re-elected on 18 May 1980.

On 24 April 1983 the elections were held for the National Assembly, which returned 90 Socialists, 81 People's Party, 12 Freedom Party.

The Coalition government between the Socialist Party and the Freedom Party, which was formed in April 1983 is composed as follows:

Chancellor: Fred Sinowatz.

Vice-Chancellor and Trade, Commerce and Industry: Norbert Steger. *Finance:* Herbert Salcher; Elfriede Karl *(Minister of State)*; Holger Bauer *(Minister of State)*. *Social Welfare:* Alfred Dallinger. *Foreign Affairs:* Erwin Lanc. *Interior:* Karl Blecha. *Agriculture and Forestry:* Günther Haiden; Gerulf Murer *(Minister of State)*. *Transport:* Karl Lausecker. *Justice:* Harald Ofner. *Trade, Commerce and Industry:* Erich Schmidt *(Minister of State)*. *Defence:* Friedhelm Frischenschlager. *Construction and Technology:* Karl Sekanina; Beatrix Eypeltauer *(Minister of State)*. *Science and Research:* Heinz Fischer. *Health and Environment:* Kurt Steyrer. *Federal Chancellory:* Ferdinand Lacina *(Minister of State)*. Franz Löschnak *(Minister of State)*. Johanna Dohnal *(Minister of State)*.

The Federal Council *(Bundesrat)* which represents the federal provinces has 63 members and (1983) the Socialist Party had 31 members and the People's Party 32. The *Nationalrat* and *Bundesrat* together form the National Assembly.

National flag: Three horizontal stripes of red, white, red.

National anthem: Land der Berge, Land am Strome (words by Paula Preradovic; tune by W. A. Mozart).

The official language is German.

Local Government. The Republic of Austria comprises 9 Federal States (Vienna, Lower Austria, Upper Austria, Salzburg, Styria, Carinthia, Tirol, Vorarlberg, Burgenland). There is in every province an elected Provincial Assembly.

Every commune has a Council, which chooses one of its number to be head of the Commune (burgomaster) and a committee for the administration and execution of its resolutions.

DEFENCE. Conscription is for a 6-month period, with liability for 60 days reservist refresher training spread over 15 years.

Army. The Army consists of an alert force *(Bereitschaf truppe)*, mainly the 1st Armoured Division organized in 3 armoured infantry brigades; a mobile militia, comprising 8 motorized infantry brigades; and a stationary militia, comprising 26 regiments and security companies. The country is divided into 2 corps areas, I (Graz) and II (Salzburg). Strength was (1984) 45,400 (29,600 conscripts), and 127,000 reserves.

Army Aviation. *(Heeresfliegerkräfte):* The Army Air Division comprises 12 squadrons with about 4,300 personnel and 180 aircraft, organized in three Aviation Regiments each of which including air defence battalions. About 30 SAAB-105 Oe strike/trainer aircraft equip a surveillance wing of two squadrons with responsibility for defence of Austrian airspace and a fighter-bomber wing of two squadrons. Helicopters equip seven squadrons for transport/support, communications, observation, search and rescue duties. Types in service include Alouette III, armed Kiowa, JetRanger and Agusta-Bell 212. Fixed-wing transports comprise two Skyvans and 12 Turbo-Porters.

INTERNATIONAL RELATIONS

Membership. Austria is a member of UN and EFTA.

External debt. The external debt was (1982) 111·9m. schilling.

ECONOMY

Budget. The budget for calendar years provided revenue and expenditure (ordinary and extraordinary) as follows (in 1m. schilling):

	1977	1978	1979	1980	1981	1982	1983 [1]
Revenue	194,782	214,949	237,620	259,028	287,791	309,134	325,811
Expenditure	236,656	266,136	288,134	306,492	339,456	368,349	400,078

[1] Provisional.

Currency. The Austrian unit of currency is the *schilling* of 100 *groschen*. The rate of exchange in March 1984, £1 = 26·43 *schilling*, US$1 = 18·37 *schilling*. Exchange rates since 24 Aug. 1971 have been floating.

Banking. The National Bank of Austria, opened on 2 Jan. 1923, was taken over by the German Reichsbank on 17 March 1938. It was re-established on 3 July 1945. At 31 Aug. 1983 foreign exchange amounted to 77,740m. and note circulation to 87,701m. schilling.

Weights and Measures. The metric system of weights and measures is in use.

ENERGY AND NATURAL RESOURCES

Electricity. Electric energy produced (1m. kwh.): 1981, 42,894; 1982, 42,891.

Oil. The commercial production of petroleum began in the early 1930s. Production of crude oil (in tonnes): 1960, 2,448,391; 1971, 2,798,237; 1982, 1,290,363.

Minerals. The mineral production (in tonnes) was as follows:

	1981	1982		1981	1982
Lignite	3,061,262	3,297,488	Pig-iron	3,477,257	3,114,985
Iron ore	3,050,000	3,330,000	Raw steel	4,655,503	4,258,156
Lead and zinc ore [1]	797,654	841,027	Rolled steel	3,673,022	3,380,743
Raw magnesite [1]	1,158,852	1,031,404			

[1] Including recovery from slag.

Austria is one of the world's largest sources of high-grade graphite. Production, which averaged 20,000 tonnes yearly from 1929 to 1944, dropped to 246 in 1946, but rose to 102,237 in 1964, and fell again to 23,992 in 1970, 40,519 in 1979, 37,199 in 1980, 23,807 in 1981 and 24,451 in 1982.

Agriculture. In 1981 the total area sown amounted to 1,479,869 hectares.

The chief products (area in hectares, yield in tonnes) were as follows:

	1980		1981		1982	
	Area	Yield	Area	Yield	Area	Yield
Wheat	268,753	1,200,599	274,286	1,025,011	289,090	1,236,355
Rye	109,234	382,801	101,109	320,215	100,118	347,834
Barley	373,912	1,514,491	362,202	1,219,816	339,802	1,436,543
Oats	91,989	315,896	91,544	303,898	91,353	324,831
Potatoes	52,569	1,263,922	49,639	1,309,779	45,654	1,120,676

Production of raw sugar in 1949, 66,700; 1955, 219,300; 1960, 308,000; refined sugar: 1970, 298,000; 1979, 377,400; 1980, 419,800; 1981, 446,900 tonnes.

Livestock (1982): Cattle, 2,546,280; pigs, 3,981,151; sheep, 198,971; goats, 31,596; horses, 40,683; poultry, 15,686,537.

Forestry. Felled timber, in cu. metres: 1960, 10,015,925; 1970, 11,122,896; 1980, 12,732,507; 1981, 12,168,535.

INDUSTRY AND TRADE

Industry. On 26 July 1946 the Austrian parliament passed a government bill, nationalizing some 70 industrial concerns. As from 17 Sept. 1946 ownership of the

3 largest commercial banks, most oil-producing and refining companies and the principal firms in the following industries devolved upon the Austrian state: River navigation; coal extraction; non-ferrous mining and refining; iron-ore mining; pig-iron and steel production; manufacture of iron and steel products, including structural material, machinery, railroad equipment and repairs, and shipbuilding; electrical machinery and appliances. Six companies supplying electric power were nationalized in accordance with a law of 26 March 1947.

In 1982, 6,793 industrial establishments employed 576,528 persons, producing a gross output of 546m. schillings.

Commerce. Imports and exports are as follows (excluding coined gold):

	Imports			Exports		
	1980	1981	1982	1980	1981	1982
Quantity (1,000 tonnes)	36,825	35,848	34,248	15,085	15,317	15,299
Value (1m. sch.)	315,846	334,510	332,551	226,169	251,769	266,860

The total trade between Austria and UK (British Department of Trade returns, in £1,000 sterling):

	1979	1980	1981	1982	1983
Imports to UK	345,446	307,267	347,971	404,318	438,445
Exports and re-exports from UK	259,251	279,681	246,877	251,032	273,702

Tourism. Tourism is an important industry. In 1982, 21,800 hotels and boarding-houses had a total of 686,787 beds available; 14,252,624 foreigners visited Austria; of these 679,834 came from the UK and 535,365 from the USA.

COMMUNICATIONS

Roads. On 1 Jan. 1977 federal roads had a total length of 10,140 km, 743·2 km autobahn; provincial roads, 22,996 km. On 31 Dec. 1981 there were registered 3,494,065 motor vehicles, including 2,312,932 passenger cars, 190,296 lorries, 339,506 tractors and 208,332 trailers.

Railways. Austrian railways have been nationalized since before the First World War. Length of track (Dec. 1982), 5,854 km, of which 3,049 km were electrified. Twenty private railways have a total length of 562 km. Passengers in 1981 numbered 170m. and 50m. tonnes of freight.

Aviation. Austria has 6 airports in Vienna (Schwechat), Linz, Salzburg, Graz, Klagenfurt and Innsbruck. In 1981, 79,315 aircraft arrived and departed at Austrian airports on commercial air transport.

Shipping. Austria has no sea frontiers, but the Danube is an important waterway. Goods traffic (in tonnes): 6,583,433 in 1979; 6,587,190 in 1980; 6,108,263 in 1981; 5,531,373 in 1982. Ore and metal, coal and coke and iron ore comprise in bulk more than two-thirds of these cargoes. The Danube Steamship Co. (DDSG) is the main Austrian shipping company.

Post and Broadcasting. All postal, telegraph and telephone services are run by the State. In 1982 there were 2,414,359 telephones.

Österreicher Rundfunk transmits 3 regional and 10 local programmes, including one in English and one in French; there is also a 24 hours overseas service. All broadcasting is financed by licence payments and advertisements. There were 2·5m. registered listeners in Jan. 1983. Television was inaugurated in autumn 1955 and 2 programmes are transmitted, both in colour.

Cinemas (1982). There were 528 cinemas.

Newspapers (1983). There were 30 daily newspapers (6 of them in Vienna) with a combined circulation of 2·65m.

JUSTICE, RELIGION, EDUCATION AND WELFARE

Justice. The Supreme Court of Justice (*Oberster Gerichtshof*) in Vienna is the highest court in the land. Besides there are 4 higher provincial courts (*Oberlandes-gerichte*), 20 provincial and district courts (*Landes- und Kreisgerichte*) and 205 local courts (*Bezirksgerichte*).

Religion. In 1971 there were 6,540,294 Roman Catholics (87·7%), 446,307 Protestants (6%), 111,558 others (1·5%), 320,031 without religious allegiance (4·3%) and 38,213 (0·5%) unknown. The Roman Catholic Church has 2 archbishoprics and 7 bishoprics.

Education (1982–83). There were in Austria 5,189 elementary and special schools with 65,596 teachers and 766,128 pupils. Of all kinds of secondary schools there were 1,522 with 567,481 pupils.

There were also 103 commercial academies with 35,363 students and 4,427 teachers. There were 208 schools of technical and industrial training (including schools of hotel management and catering) with 5,917 teachers and 54,293 pupils; 45 schools of women's professions (secondary level) with 11,904 pupils; 8 training colleges of social workers with 645 pupils. 137 trade schools had 25,757 pupils.

Austria has 12 universities and 6 colleges of arts maintained by the State: Universities at Vienna (2,676 teachers, 47,998 students), Graz (1,055 teachers, 18,222 students), Innsbruck (1,181 teachers, 16,251 students) and Salzburg (464 teachers, 8,587 students). There are also technical universities at Vienna (1,004 teachers, 10,636 students) and Graz (521 teachers, 6,093 students), a mining university at Leoben (174 teachers, 1,353 students), an agricultural university at Vienna (182 teachers, 3,644 students), a veterinary university at Vienna (160 teachers, 1,650 students), a commercial university at Vienna (216 teachers, 9,863 students), a university for social and economic sciences at Linz (297 teachers, 6,178 students) and a university for educational sciences at Klagenfurt (111 teachers, 1,816 students). There is an academy of fine arts at Vienna (144 teachers, 501 students), a college of applied arts at Vienna (176 teachers, 725 students), 3 colleges of music and dramatic art at Vienna (437 teachers, 2,046 students), Salzburg (272 teachers, 1,073 students) and Graz (232 teachers, 948 students); the college for industrial design at Linz (112 teachers, 358 students).

Health. In 1981 there were 19,157 doctors, 327 hospitals and 84,313 hospital beds.

DIPLOMATIC REPRESENTATIVES

Of Austria in Great Britain (18 Belgrave Mews West, London, SW1X 8HU)
Ambassador: Dr Reginald Thomas (accredited 10 March 1982).

Of Great Britain in Austria (Reisnerstrasse 40, 1030 Vienna)
Ambassador: M. O'D. B. Alexander, CMG.

Of Austria in the USA (2343 Massachusetts Ave., NW, Washington, D.C., 20008)
Ambassador: Dr Thomas Klestil.

Of the USA in Austria (IX Boltzmangasse, 16, A-1091 Vienna)
Ambassador: Helene A. von Damm.

Of Austria to the United Nations
Ambassador: Dr Karl Fischer.

Books of Reference

Statistical Information: The Austrian Central Statistical Office was founded in 1863. *Address:* Neue Burg, Heldenplatz, A-1014 Vienna. *President:* Dr Josef Schmidl. Main publications:
    Statistisches Handbuch für die Republik Österreich. New Series from 1950. Annually
    Statistische Nachrichten. Monthly
    Beiträge zur österreichischen Statistik (585 vols.)
    Ergebnisse der Volkszählung vom 12 Mai 1981
    Ergebnisse der Häuser- und Wohnungszählung vom 12 Mai 1981
    HA-Taschenbuch 75. Annually from 1971
    Statistiches Handbuch für die Republik Österreich. Annual.

Bobek, H. (ed.), *Atlas der Republik Österreich.* 3 vols. Vienna, 1961 ff.
Österreich Lexikon. Wien-Munchen, 1966
Scheidl, L. G., and Lechleitner, H., *Österreich—Land, Volk, Wirtschaft.* Vienna, 1967
Sotriffer, K., *Greater Austria: 100 Years of Intellectual and Social Life from 1800 to the Present Time.* Vienna, 1982

National Library: Österreichische Nationalbibliothek, Vienna. *Librarian:* Dr Zessner-Spitzenberg.

THE COMMONWEALTH OF THE BAHAMAS

Capital: Nassau
Population: 209,505 (1981)
GNP per capita: US$3,300 (1980)

HISTORY. The Bahamas were discovered by Colombus in 1492 but the Spanish did not make a permanent settlement. British settlers arrived in the 17th century and it was occupied by Britain, except for a short period in the 18th century, until it gained independence.

AREA AND POPULATION. The Commonwealth of the Bahamas consists of 700 islands and more than 1,000 cays off the south-east coast of Florida. They are the surface protuberances of two oceanic banks, the Little Bahama Bank and the Great Bahama Bank. Land area, 5,353 sq. miles (13,864 sq. km).

Principal islands with census population in 1980: New Providence (135,437, containing capital, Nassau), Abaco (7,324), Andros (8,397), Cat Island (2,143), Eleuthera (10,600), Grand Bahama (33,102), Inagua (939), Long Island (3,358). Total census population, with other islands and cays, 209,505.

Vital statistics, 1977: Births, 4,871; deaths, 1,067 (excluding still-births); marriages, 1,297.

CLIMATE. Winters are mild and summers pleasantly warm. Most rain falls in May, June, Sept. and Oct., and thunderstorms are frequent in summer. Rainfall amounts vary over the islands from 30″ (750 mm) to 60″ (1,500 mm). Nassau. Jan. 71°F (21·7°C), July 81°F (27·2°C). Annual rainfall 47″ (1,179 mm).

CONSTITUTION AND GOVERNMENT. Internal self-government with cabinet responsibility was introduced 7 Jan. 1964.

Qualification for membership of the House of Assembly, under the 1973 Independence Constitution requires that a member shall be a citizen of the Bahamas of the age of 21 years or upwards, and shall have been ordinarily resident in the Bahamas for a period of not less than 1 year immediately before the date of his nomination for election. The Representation of the People's Act provides for adult suffrage. Women are eligible for election to the House of Assembly.

The Constitution of the Commonwealth of the Bahamas (1973) establishes the Bahamas as a free and democratic sovereign state. The constitution is the supreme law of the Bahamas and where any other law is inconsistent with it, the Constitution shall prevail and the other law shall, to the extent of the inconsistency be void.

The Constitution created the office of Governor-General, the holder of which is appointed by Her Majesty. There is a Senate of 16 members, 9 appointed by the Governor-General on the advice of the Prime Minister, 4 appointed by the Governor-General on the advice of the Leader of the Opposition and 3 appointed by the Governor-General on the advice of the Prime Minister after consultation with the Leader of the Opposition. The House of Assembly consists of 43 members. The life of a Parliament is 5 years, but it may be prorogued or dissolved at any time by the Governor-General on the advice of the Prime Minister.

At the elections of 11 June 1982 the Progressive Liberal Party obtained 32 seats and the Free National Movement 11 seats.

Independence from Britain took place on 10 July 1973.

Governor-General: Sir Gerald Cash, GCMG, KCVO, OBE.

The Cabinet in Nov. 1982 was composed as follows:

Prime Minister, Minister of Economic Affairs: Rt. Hon. Sir Lynden O. Pindling. *Deputy Prime Minister and Minister of Finance:* Arthur D. Hanna. *Labour and Home Affairs:* Clement T. Maynard. *Health:* Livingston N. Coakley. *Works and*

Utilities: A. Loftus Roker. *Education:* Darrell E. Rolle. *External Affairs and Attorney-General:* Paul L. Adderley. *Agriculture, Fisheries and Local Government:* George A. Smith. *Economics:* Alfred T. Maycock. *Tourism:* Perry G. Christie. *Transport:* Philip M. Bethel. *Youth, Sports, Culture and Community Affairs:* Kendal W. Nottage. *National Insurance and Housing:* Hubert Ingraham.

National flag: Three horizontal stripes of aquamarine, gold, aquamarine, with a black triangle on the hoist.

INTERNATIONAL RELATIONS

Membership. The Commonwealth of the Bahamas is a member of UN, the Commonwealth and an ACP state of EEC.

ECONOMY

Budget (in B$):

	1979	1980	1981
Revenue	212,405,423	255,257,167	295,923,300
Expenditure	248,227,193	287,408,577	336,339,638

The main sources of revenue were customs duties and receipts from fees, post office and public utilities.

Currency. A decimal system of currency was introduced in 1966. Bahamian $1.47 = £1 sterling (March 1984). Notes: $0.50, 1, 3, 5, 10, 20, 50, 100; coins: 1, 5, 10, 15, 25, 50 cents, $1, 2, 5. Sterling currency has been withdrawn. American currency is generally accepted.

Bank of England and Canadian notes are not accepted, except at the banks from travellers from the UK.

Banking. The Central Bank of the Bahamas was established in June 1974 with assets (Dec. 1980) of B$154·95m. and capital and reserves of B$29·98m. Among these were the Royal Bank of Canada, the Bank of Nova Scotia, the Bank of Montreal, Chase Manhattan Bank, Barclays Bank International, the Canadian Imperial Bank of Commerce and Citibank. While the majority of banks are located in Nassau, there are branches on several of the other islands. The Bahamas Development Bank was established in 1974 and began operations in Jan. 1978; at Dec. 1980 it had total assets of B$7·45m. and paid-up capital of B$6m.

On 31 Dec. 1980 there were 314 institutions licensed to carry on banking and/or trust business under the Banks and Trust Companies Regulations Act. There were 17 designated institutions by the Exchange Control Department as authorized dealers and agents.

The post office savings bank, 31 Dec. 1980, had deposits of B$2·2m.

Weights and Measures. The UK (Imperial) system is in force.

ENERGY AND NATURAL RESOURCES

Electricity. Electricity for lighting and power is available in New Providence, Grand Bahama and the Family Islands. Total units generated in New Providence/ Paradise Island and Family Islands in 1979–80, 390m. kwh.

Agriculture. There were (1978) 4,246 agricultural holdings or parcels of farm land in the Bahamas, totalling 89,565 acres. About 40% of these holdings are cultivated with temporary and permanent crops. Livestock operations within the Bahamas are predominantly sheep and goat enterprises.

Several agricultural programmes exist to further stimulate agricultural production. Some of these programmes are subsidized by government and include land clearing and duty free importation of trucks and other farm implements. Farmers also have access to 2 credit programmes: a) The Agricultural Credit Guarantee Fund; b) The Stores on Credit Programme.

Total agricultural production including fisheries was valued at about B$30m. in 1980.

Livestock (1982): Cattle, 4,000; sheep, 37,000; goats, 18,000; pigs, 18,000; poultry, 810,000.

Forestry. Production of cascarilla bark and pulp-wood in 1976 was B$1·8m., all of which was exported.

Fisheries. Crawfish exports were valued at B$12m. in 1982.

INDUSTRY AND TRADE

Industry. Tourism is the major industry. Several light industries have been established on Grand Bahama and New Providence in response to special encouragement legislation; these include garment manufacturing, ice, furniture, purified water, plastic containers, perfumes, industrial gases, jewellery and others. Larger industrial activities in the Bahamas include oil refining, oil transhipment, manufacture of alcoholic beverages, pharmaceuticals, aragonite mining, solar salt production and cement. Two industrial sites, one in New Providence and the other in Grand Bahama, have been developed as part of the industrialization programme.

Commerce. The principal exports in 1980 were hormones, rum, salt, crawfish, cement, aragonite and plywood.

The principal imports in 1977 were: Food, drink and tobacco, raw materials and articles mainly unmanufactured, articles wholly or mainly manufactured, animals not for food.

Imports and exports (excluding bullion and specie) for 6 calendar years in B$:

	Imports	Exports		Imports	Exports
1977	2,787,943	2,597,352	1980	5,506,577	4,836,366
1978	2,482,235	2,117,938	1981	4,203,000	3,515,000
1979	3,985,034	3,495,043	1982	3,051,000	2,444,000

The Bahamas became affiliated with CARIFTA (now CARICOM) in 1968.

Total trade between Bahamas and UK, in £1,000 sterling (British Department of Trade returns):

	1978	1979	1980	1981	1982	1983
Imports to UK	12,650	21,758	59,123	30,915	18.273	24,013
Exports and re-exports from UK	104,204	79,851	77,366	171,347	26,364	17,815

Tourism. Tourism is the most important industry in the Bahamas. It accounts for approximately 58% of government revenue and 66% of employment. In 1982 there were 1,947,742 foreign arrivals in the Bahamas.

COMMUNICATIONS

Roads. There are 240 miles of paved roads in New Providence, and 426 miles in Grand Bahama. The other major islands have 400 miles of motorable roads. In 1978, 51,290 motor vehicles were registered. There are no railroads.

Aviation. Nassau international airport is located on the island of New Providence, about 10 miles from the city of Nassau. There is another international airport at Freeport. Scheduled flights—Air Canada: 3 times weekly from Toronto and once weekly from Montreal to Nassau; twice weekly from Toronto to Freeport and once weekly from Montreal to Freeport. Delta: twice daily from New York to Nassau; once daily from Boston and Newark. Eastern Airlines: 3 flights daily from New York, 3 times daily from Miami, once daily from Fort Lauderdale, twice weekly from Baltimore, Washington and Philadelphia, once daily from Boston and Newark, once daily from New York via Miami and Fort Lauderdale to Nassau; 3 times daily from Miami, once daily from Baltimore and Philadelphia to Freeport: Lufthansa: 3 times weekly from Frankfurt and Mexico and once weekly from Merida to Nassau. Air Jamaica: once daily from Chicago, Kingston and Montego Bay to Nassau. American Airlines: once daily from New York to Nassau and 4 times weekly from New York to Freeport. British Airways: 4 times weekly from London and Bermuda, twice weekly from Kingston and Panama and once weekly from Mexico City, all to Nassau; once weekly from London, Bermuda, Kingston and Panama to Freeport. There are numerous domestic schedules to the Family Islands and Florida. There are 53 airstrips on the various Family Islands and numerous water alighting areas. During 1977, 494,263 passengers landed at

Nassau and 38,840 aircraft arrivals. At Freeport in 1977, 407,772 passengers landed from 41,799 aircraft arrivals.

Shipping. In 1980, 678 cruise liners cleared Nassau carrying 499,527 passengers; 653 cargo vessels discharged 268,477 tons of cargo at Nassau. There are indirect cargo services with UK and Canada *via* the USA and passenger services with the USA only.

Telecommunications. New Providence and all the major islands have automatic telephone systems of the latest type in operation, together with an extensive system of underground cables. The total number of telephones in use at 1 Jan. 1982 was 75,071; 170 radio-telephone channels provide service *via* the USA to any part of the world. In 1971 direct dialling was introduced to the USA and in 1973 to Canada. All the important islands are connected with Nassau by means of radio-telegraphy, and in most cases radio-telephony is also available. Connexion through Nassau to the UK, the USA, Canada and Central America can be provided. Radio-teletype to Bermuda and Florida and ship-shore radio-telephone services are also available. Radio-teletype service is provided from Nassau to Freeport and West End in Grand Bahama. In 1976 a fully automated Telex exchange came into service. The Bahamas broadcasting station operates on 1,540, 1,240 and 810 kc.

Cinemas (1977). There are 16 cinemas and 3 drive-ins.

Newspapers (1977). There are 2 daily and 1 weekly newspapers in Nassau.

JUSTICE, EDUCATION AND WELFARE

Justice (1977). 9,655 cases (traffic, 3,550; criminal, 3,218; civil, 1,880; domestic, 1,007) were dealt with in the magistrates' court, and civil, 816; divorce, 256 in the Supreme Court. The strength of the police force (1973) was 932 officers and other ranks.

Education. Education is under the jurisdiction of the Ministry of Education and Culture. In 1980–81 there were 227 schools, and of these, 187 are fully maintained by Government and 40 are independent schools. Total school enrolment, 61,160. There are 38 government-owned schools in New Providence and 149 on the Family Islands. 24 independent schools are located on New Providence and 12 on the Family Islands. 181 students attended 4 special schools, 3 on New Providence and 1 on Grand Bahama; total staff, 38. Free education is available in ministry schools in New Providence and the Family Islands. Courses lead to the Bahamas Junior Certificate and the General Certificate of Education (GCE).

Independent schools provide education at primary, secondary and higher levels. Several schools of continuing education offer secretarial and academic courses. The Government-operated Princess Margaret Hospital offers a nursing course at two levels. The College of the Bahamas was established in 1974. It provides a 2- or 3-year programme leading to an associate degree in any of the 7 academic divisions. Several college degree programmes are offered in conjunction with the University of the West Indies and the University of Miami. The Hotel Training College offers a wide range of subjects up to middle management level in aspects of hotel work. Enrolment in this institution includes Bahamian as well as regional and international students.

Health. In 1980 there was a government general hospital in Nassau (460 beds) and 1 in Freeport (50). Grand Bahama has 4 clinics, 3 staffed by district medical officers and 1 by a nurse and the Family Islands have about 50 health centres. There are 2 private hospitals. Dental treatment is provided for smaller islands by a flying dentist service. There are 122 doctors, 387 nurses, 8 midwives and 5 dentists in the government service. There are many private doctors, dentists, nurses and midwives providing health care on a fee basis.

DIPLOMATIC REPRESENTATIVES

Of the Bahamas in Great Britain (39 Pall Mall, London, SW1Y 5JG)
High Commissioner: R. F. Anthony Roberts.

Of Great Britain in the Bahamas (Bitco Bldg., East St., Nassau)
High Commissioner: Peter William Heap.

Of the Bahamas in the USA (600 New Hampshire Ave., NW, Washington, D.C., 20037)
Ambassador: Reginald L. Wood, CBE.

Of the USA in the Bahamas (Queen St., Nassau)
Ambassador: Lev E. Dobriansky.

Of the Bahamas to the United Nations
Ambassador: Dr Davidson L. Hepburn.

Books of Reference

Bahamas Handbook and Businessman's Annual (Annual)
Albury, P., *The Story of the Bahamas.* London, 1975
Barrett, P. J. H., *Grand Bahama.* London, 1982
Craton, M. A., *A History of the Bahamas.* London, 1962
Hughes, C. A., *Race and Politics in the Bahamas.* Univ. of Queensland Press, 1981
Hunte, G., *The Bahamas.* London, 1975

Library: Nassau Public Library.

BAHRAIN

Capital: Manama
Population: 350,798 (1981)
GNP per capita: US$6,000 (1981)

HISTORY. Treaties with Britain of 1882 and 1892 were replaced by a treaty of friendship which was signed on 15 Aug. 1971. Under the earlier treaties Britain had been responsible for Bahrain's defence and foreign relations. On the same day Bahrain declared its independence.

AREA AND POPULATION. The Bahrain islands form an archipelago in the Arabian Gulf, between the Qatar peninsula and the mainland of Saudi Arabia. The total area is about 255 sq. miles. Bahrain ('Two Seas'), largest island, is 30 miles long and 10 miles wide. Muharraq, to the north-east, 4 miles long and 1 mile wide, is connected with Bahrain by a causeway, nearly 1·5 miles long, carrying a motor road. Other islands are Sitra, to the east, 3 miles long and 1 mile wide; Umm An-Nassan, to the west, 3 miles by 2 miles; Jidda, also to the west, 1 mile by 0·5 mile, the Hawar group off Qatar and several islets, some uninhabited. From Sitra oil pipelines and a causeway carrying a road extend out to sea for 3 miles to a deep-water anchorage. The islands are low lying, the highest ground being a hill in the centre of Bahrain, 450 ft high.

The population in 1981 (census) was 350,798. The majority of the people are Moslem Arabs.

Manama, the capital of the state and the commercial centre, is situated at the northern end of the largest island and extends for 1·5 miles along the shore. It has a population of 121,986 (1981 census). Electricity from the government power-station in Manama supplies light and power in Manama, Muharraq (61,853, 1981 census), Hidd (7,111), Rifa'a (28,150) and Isa Town (21,275) and the villages. Water is obtained from artesian wells and desalination plants, and there is a piped supply in Manama, Muharraq, Isa Town, Rifa'a and most villages.

CLIMATE. The climate is pleasantly warm between Nov. and March but from June to Sept. the conditions are very hot and humid. The period June to Nov. is virtually rainless. Bahrain. Jan. 66°F (19°C), July 97°F (36°C). Annual rainfall 5·2" (130 mm).

CONSTITUTION AND GOVERNMENT. A Constitution was ratified in June 1973 providing for a National Assembly of 30 members, popularly elected for a 4-year term, together with all members of the Cabinet (appointed by the Amir). Elections took place in Dec. 1973, but in Aug. 1975 the Amir dissolved the Assembly and has since ruled through the Cabinet alone.

Reigning Amir: The ruling family, the Al Khalifa, an Arab dynasty, who have been in power since 1782. The present Amir, HH Shaikh Isa bin Sulman Al-Khalifa (born 1933) succeeded on 2 Nov. 1961. *Crown Prince and Minister of Defence:* Shaikh Hamed bin Isa Al-Khalifa.

In Nov. 1983 the cabinet was composed as follows:
Prime Minister: Shaikh Khalifa bin Sulman Al-Khalifa.
Defence: Shaikh Hamed bin Isa Al-Khalifa. *Transport:* Ibrahim Mohammed Hassan Homaidan. *Housing:* Shaikh Khalid bin Abdulla Al-Khalifa. *Information:* Tariq Abdulrahman Almoayed. *Education:* Dr Ali Fakhro. *Health:* Jawad Salim Al-Arrayed. *Justice and Islamic Affairs:* Shaikh Abdullah bin Khalid Al-Khalifa. *Labour and Social Affairs:* Shaikh Khalifa bin Salman bin Mohammed Al-Khalifa. *Works, Power and Water:* Majid Jawad Al Jishi. *Interior:* Shaikh Mohammed bin Khalifa Al-Khalifa. *Foreign Affairs:* Shaikh Mohammed bin Mubarak Al-Khalifa. *Finance and National Economy:* Ebrahim Abdul-Karim. *Development and Industry:* Yusuf Ahmed Al-Shirawi. *Commerce and Agriculture:*

Habib Ahmed Qassim. *Acting Minister of State for Cabinet Affairs:* Yusuf Ahmed Al-Shirawi. *Minister of State for Legal Affairs:* Dr Hussain Al Baharna.

Flag: Red, with white serrated vertical strip on hoist.

DEFENCE

Army. The Army consists of 1 infantry battalion, 1 armoured car squadron and 1 artillery battery with a personnel strength of 2,300 (1984). Equipment included 8 Saladin armoured cars and 8 Ferret scout cars.

Navy. The Naval force consists of 2 fast missile craft and 2 fast gunboats; personnel (1983) 300. There is also a Coast Guard with 16 coastal patrol craft.

Air Wing. Formed in 1977, the Air Wing ordered 4 F-5E Tiger IIs and 2 two-seat F-5Fs in May 1982 to equip its first combat unit. Other equipment comprises 2 Bell 412, 3 BO 105 and 2 Hughes 500D light helicopters.

INTERNATIONAL RELATIONS

Membership. Bahrain is a member of UN, the Arab League, the Gulf Co-operation Council and OAPEC.

ECONOMY

Budget. The revenue of the State is derived from oil royalties and from customs duties, which are 10% *ad valorem* for luxury goods and 5% for essential goods. The exceptions are motor vehicles (20%); tobacco (30%); alcoholic beverages (100%); fresh fruit and vegetables (7%). Total revenues in 1977, BD 249m.; 1978, BD 280m.; 1979, BD 311m.; 1980, BD 329m.; 1981, BD 351m.

On 2 Jan. 1958 Manama was declared a free transit port and the former 2% transit duty was abolished, but storage charges are levied.

Currency. The Bahrain *dinar* is divided into 1,000 *fils*. The Bahrain currency board issues notes of 10, 5, 1 and ½ *dinars*, and coins of 100, 50, 25 and 5 *fils*. £1 = BD 0·522 in March 1984; US$1 = BD 0·377.

Banking. The Bahrain Monetary Agency has central banking powers. Other banking facilities are provided by the National Bank of Bahrain, the Bank of Bahrain and Kuwait and branches of the Chartered Bank, the British Bank of the Middle East, the Arab Bank, Habib Bank (Overseas), United Bank, Citibank, Banque du Caire, Chase Manhattan, Grindlays Bank, Bank Melli, Algemene Bank, Bank Saderet, Bank Paribas, National Bank of Abu Dhabi, Rafidain Bank, Barclays International, Al-Ahli Commercial Bank. In Dec. 1982 there were 161 licensed banks and there was (1983) steady progress in offshore banking facilities.

Weights and Measures. The metric system of weights and measures is officially in use.

ENERGY AND NATURAL RESOURCES

Electricity. Production (1980) 1,290m. kwh.

Oil. In 1931 oil was discovered. Operations are being conducted by the Bahrain Petroleum Co., registered in Canada but owned by US interests, under a concession granted by the Shaikh. Production of crude oil in 1982 was 16·1m. bbls. A large oil refinery on Bahrain Island, besides treating crude oil produced locally, also processes oil from Saudi Arabia transported by pipeline.

In 1975 the Bahrain Government assumed a direct 60% interest in the Bahrain oilfield and related crude oil facilities of BAPCO. Bahrain's gas reserves are 100% government-owned.

Under the terms of the agreement signed between Bahrain and Saudi Arabia in 1958, Bahrain will receive 50% of the profits on any oil produced in the Abu Saafa area of sea between Bahrain and Saudi Arabia. Aramco, which is responsible for the development of this field, began production in 1966.

Gas. There is an abundant supply of natural gas with known reserves of 9,000,000m. cu. ft. Production, 1982, 130,507m. cu. ft.

INDUSTRY AND TRADE

Industry. Bahrain is being developed as a major manufacturing state, the first important enterprise being the Aluminium Bahrain Smelter, a company whose original shareholders included the Bahrain Government and British, Swedish, Federal German and US interests. In 1975, the government acquired a majority shareholding in the enterprise. The aluminium operation is the largest non-oil industry in the Gulf. Ancillary industries developed around aluminium smelting include the production of aluminium powder. Other projects at present under consideration include the further development of marine industries. The Arab Shipbuilding and Repair Yard (ASRY), commissioned in 1977, is now in service. The dry dock can handle up to 50 tankers (550,000 DWT each) annually. A US$400m. petrochemical complex will go on stream in 1984. The construction of the Saudi-Bahrain causeway begun in 1982 and which should be completed in 1986, is the largest project in the history of the Gulf. Total cost of the 25 km project is US$800m. and the cost is being borne by Saudi Arabia.

In addition to the traditional minor industries such as boat-building, weaving, pottery, etc., other modern industries have developed, which include the manufacture of building materials, soft drinks, drinking straws, paper bags, woollen garments, plastic and other consumer goods. There is also an important fishing industry and a fairly large farming community. The most important crops are dates and vegetables, and there is also poultry farming.

Livestock (1981): Cattle, 6,000; sheep, 7,000; goats, 15,000; poultry, 790,000.

The pearling industry for which Bahrain used to be famous has considerably declined. Only about 10 boats visit the pearl banks each year, as compared with the 600–1,000 that were employed 30 years ago.

Commerce. In 1982 imports totalled BD 1,402·3m.; exports and re-exports, non-oil, BD 242·7m. Total exports, BD 1,424·8m. Chief imports were manufactured goods, machinery and transport equipment, food and live animals, chemicals.

Import of arms and ammunition and telecommunication equipment is subject to special permission; the sale of alcoholic liquor is restricted and the import of cultured pearls is forbidden.

Total trade between Bahrain and UK (British Department of Trade returns, in £1,000 sterling):

	1979	1980	1981	1982	1983
Imports to UK	23,780	25,063	16,713	35,459	37,488
Exports and re-exports from UK	123,467	115,569	102,337	152,272	150,264

COMMUNICATIONS

Roads. In 1981 there were 70,000 registered vehicles.

Aviation. The airport, situated at Muharraq, can take the largest aircraft. British Airways, Gulf Air, Middle East Airlines, Pakistan International Airways, Qantas, Kuwait Airways, Air India International, Singapore Airlines, UTA, Saudi Arabian Airlines, KLM, Air Lanka, Cathay Pacific Airways, Iraqi Airways, Korean Airways, Philippine Airlines, Thai Airways International, Trans-Mediterranean Airways, Egyptair, Alia, Cyprus Airways, Ethiopia Airlines and Sudan Airways also operate to and from Bahrain. Bahrain International Airport is the Arabian Gulf's main air communication centre.

Shipping. Bahrain's traditional position as the entrepôt of the Southern Gulf has been supplemented by the development of Mina Sulman—the new modern harbour—as a free transit and industrial area. Local and international companies have developed industries in this area, which is also used as a storage centre for firms selling elsewhere in the Gulf. The facilities offered by Mina Sulman include engineering and ship repairing yards; the Basrec slipway is probably the largest between Rotterdam and Hong Kong.

Post and Broadcasting. There were, at Aug. 1982, 84,593 telephones. There is a state-operated radio and television station and in 1978 there were 93,500 radio and 80,000 television receivers.

Newspapers. In 1979 there were 2 Arabic and 2 English daily newspapers published in Manama.

JUSTICE, RELIGION, EDUCATION AND WELFARE

Justice. Criminal law is codified, based on English jurisprudence.

Religion. In 1981 85% of the population were Moslem and 7·3% Christian.

Education. There were, in 1981–82, 125 state schools for boys and girls with 3,405 teachers and 71,177 pupils. Five boys' general and commercial schools had 2,177 pupils; 3 boys' industrial schools at secondary level, had 1,306 pupils. In addition there were 7 private schools. The Men's Teacher Training College (established 1966) and the Women's Teacher Training College (established 1967) give 2-year courses. In 1981–82, 2,619 Bahrainis were in higher education abroad. The Gulf Technical College opened in Bahrain in Sept. 1968 and Bahrain University in 1978. In 1981–82, 35 adult literacy centres were opened throughout Bahrain.

Health. There is a free medical service for all residents of Bahrain. In 1981–82, there were 45 government hospitals and health centres with 1,056 beds, an American mission hospital, an oil company hospital, a military hospital and an international hospital.

Social Security. In Oct. 1976, pensions, sickness and industrial injury benefits, unemployment, maternity and family allowances were established.

DIPLOMATIC REPRESENTATIVES

Of Bahrain in Great Britain (98 Gloucester Rd., London, SW7 4AU)
Ambassador: Shaikh Abdul-Rahman Faris Al-Khalifa (accredited 17 Dec. 1980).

Of Great Britain in Bahrain (21 Government Rd., P.O. Box 114, Manama)
Ambassador: W. R. Tomkys.

Of Bahrain in the USA (3502 International Dr., NW, Washington D.C., 20008)
Chargé d'Affaires: Ahmed Mahdi Al-Haddad.

Of the USA in Bahrain (Shaikh Isa Road, P.O. Box 26431, Manama)
Ambassador: Donald Leidel.

Of Bahrain to the United Nations
Ambassador: Hussain Rashid Al-Sabbagh.

Books of Reference

Bahrain Business Directory. Manama (annual)
Statistical and General Information: Ministry of Information, PO Box 253, Manama
Statistical Abstract. Central Statistics Organisation (annual)

Belgrave, J. H. D., *Welcome to Bahrain.* 9th ed. Manama, 1975
Rumaihi, M. G., *Bahrain: Social and Political Change since the First World War.* New York and London, 1976

BANGLADESH

Capital: Dacca (Dhaka)
Population: 92m. (1982)
GNP per capita: US$120 (1981)

People's Republic
of Bangladesh

HISTORY. The state was formerly the Eastern Province of Pakistan. In Dec. 1970 Sheikh Mujibur Rahman's Awami League Party gained 167 seats out of 300 at the Pakistan general election and immediately made known their wish for greater independence for the then Eastern Province. Martial law was imposed following disturbances in Dacca, and civil war developed in March 1971. The war ended in Dec. 1971 and Bangladesh was proclaimed an independent state.

AREA AND POPULATION. Bangladesh is bounded west and north-west by West Bengal (India), north by Assam and Meghalaya (India), east by Assam, Tripura (India) and Burma, south by the Bay of Bengal. The area is 55,598 sq. miles (144,020 sq. km). The small island of South Talpatty in the estuary of the river Hariabhanga was annexed by India in May 1981. Bangladesh's population (1981 census), 87,052,024. An adjustment for underenumeration produced a revised census figure of 89,940,000. Population estimate, 1982, 92m. Growth rate (1974–82), 2·6%. The capital is Dacca or Dhaka (population, 1981, 3,458,602) and its ports are Chittagong (1,388,475) and Khulna (623,184). Other large cities are Narayanganj (298,400), Rajshahi (171,600) and Barisal (166,680). There are 20 districts:

	Area (sq. km)	Population 1981		Area (sq. km)	Population 1981
Dinajpur	6,757	3,198,000	Kushtia	3,551	2,273,000
Rangpur	9,593	6,490,000	Jessore	6,597	4,016,000
Bogra	3,890	2,718,000	Khulna	12,049	4,353,000
Rajshahi	9,464	5,263,000	Barisal	6,757	4,668,000
Pabna	4,861	3,418,000	Patuakhali	4,224	1,840,000
Rajshahi division	34,565	21,087,000	Khulna division	33,178	17,150,000
Tangail	3,370	2,444,000	Sylhet	12,393	5,650,000
Mymensingh	13,105	6,543,000	Comilla	6,718	6,880,000
Jamalpur	3,405	2,445,000	Noakhali	4,804	3,813,000
Dacca	7,464	10,049,000	Chittagong	7,006	5,476,000
Faridpur	6,977	4,768,000	Chittagong Hill Tracts	13,191	746,000
Dacca division	30,916	26,249,000	Chittagong division	44,112	22,565,000

The official language is Bangla.

CLIMATE. A tropical monsoon climate with heat, extreme humidity and heavy rainfall in the monsoon season, from June to Sept. The short winter season is mild and dry. Rainfall varies between 50″ (1,250 mm) in the west to 100″ (2,500 mm) in the south-east and up to 200″ (5,000 mm) in the north-east. Dacca. Jan. 66°F (19°C), July 84°F (28·9°C). Annual rainfall 81″ (2,025 mm). Chittagong. Jan. 66°F (19°C), July 81°F (27·2°C). Annual rainfall 108″ (2,831 mm).

GOVERNMENT AND CONSTITUTION. Bangladesh is a republic. The Constitution came into force on 16 Dec. 1972 and provided for a parliamentary democracy. On 25 Jan. 1975 Sheikh Mujibur Rahman took on the office of President, with an advisory Parliament. All political parties were abolished, and replaced by the new Bangladesh Krisha Sramik Awami League. On 15 Aug. 1975 Sheikh Mujibur Rahman and his family were killed; martial law was introduced on 20 Aug. and political parties were banned (including the new BKSAL) on 30 Aug.

186

K. M.Ahmed was installed as President on 15 Aug. and replaced on 7 Nov. by former Chief Justice A. M. Sayem. Elections to parliament were promised for Feb. 1977 but postponed indefinitely in 1976. Political parties were made legal once again and requested to apply for registration in Aug. 1976.

On 29 Nov. 1976 Maj.-Gen. Ziaur Rahman became Chief Martial Law Administrator, with the Chiefs of Naval and Air Staff as his deputies. On 21 April 1977 President Sayem resigned and Maj.-Gen. Ziaur Rahman was sworn in as President. On 22 April 1977 the constitution of 1972 was amended to establish 'absolute trust and faith in Allah' as the first fundamental principle of state and to provide for a Supreme Judicial Council which would prescribe a code of conduct for judges and advise the President. Three political parties (JSD, Bangladesh Communist Party (pro-Soviet) and Democratic League) were dissolved in Oct. 1977. The President was confirmed in office by general election. Martial law ended in April 1979. President Ziaur Rahman was murdered by a group of army officers on 30 May 1981. Mr Justice Abdus Sattar was installed as Acting President and elected president in Nov. 1981.

A Presidential election was held on 15 Nov. 1981, resulting in a victory for Mr Justice Abdus Sattar.

On 23 March 1982 there was a bloodless military *coup*, by which Lieut.-Gen. Hossain Mohammad Ershad became chief martial law administrator. President Sattar was deposed. The Constitution was suspended and parliament ceased to function. Lieut.-Gen. Ershad, the commander of the army, said that a temporary military government was necessary to restore economic and social order and democratic civilian government would return as soon as possible. Assanuddin Chowdhury was sworn in as civilian president on 27 March. Lieut-Gen. Ershad assumed the presidency on 11 Dec. 1983.

Parliament has one chamber of 300 members directly elected every 5 years by citizens over 18. There are 30 seats reserved for women members elected by Parliament. It is intended that Parliament will begin to function again in Nov. 1984, following a general election.

The government in autumn 1983 was composed as follows:

President and Prime Minister: Lieut.-Gen. Hossain Mohammad Ershad.

Special Adviser to the Prime Minister: Maj.-Gen. M. I. Karim. *Foreign Affairs:* A. R. Shams-ud Doha. *Home Affairs:* Maj.-Gen. V. M. K. Choudhury. *Finance and Planning:* A. M. A. Muhith. *Industry:* S. M. Shafiul Azam. *Transport and Communications:* Rear-Adml. M. A. Khan. *Flood Control, Energy and Mineral Resources:* Air-Vice-Marshal Sultan Mahmud. *Law, Land Administration, Land Reform, Attorney General:* K. A. Bakr. *Health and Population Control.* Maj.-Gen. M. Shamsul Haq. *Food and Relief:* Air Vice-Marshal A. G. Mahmud. *Public Works and Urban Development:* Maj.-Gen. Abdul Mannan Siddique. *Labour and Manpower:* Air Vice-Marshal Aminul Islam. *Information and Broadcasting:* S. N. Hashim. *Local Government and Rural Development:* M. Rahman. *Agriculture:* A. Z. M. Obaidullah Khan. *Social Welfare and Women's Affairs:* S. Katun. *Education and Religious Affairs:* A. Majid Khan.

National flag: Bottle green with a red disc in the centre.

National anthem: Amar Sonar Bangla, ami tomay bhalobashi (My golden Bengal, I love you). Words by Rabindranath Tagore.

DEFENCE

Army. There are 5 infantry divisional headquarters, with 12 infantry brigades, and 2 armoured and 9 artillery regiments, and 7 engineer battalions. Strength (1984) 73,000, with an additional 80,000 paramilitary volunteers, including an armed police reserve and the Bangladesh Rifles. Equipment includes 30 Soviet T-54 and 20 Chinese Type-59 tanks.

Navy. Naval bases are at Chittagong (handed over by India on 14 Feb. 1972), Kaptai, Khulna and Dacca.

The fleet comprises 3 former British frigates (*Ali Hyder, ex*-HMS *Jaguar*, and

Abu Bakr, *ex*-HMS *Lynx*, each 2,520 tons full load, transferred in July 1978 and March 1982, respectively, and *Umar Farooq*, *ex*-HMS *Llandaff*, 2,408 tons full load, transferred in Dec 1976); 1 new Chinese-built 390-ton fast attack craft, 2 *ex*-Yugoslav 200-ton patrol vessels, 8 *ex*-Chinese 155-ton fast gunboats, 2 *ex*-Indian 150-ton patrol craft, 1 British-built 140-ton patrol craft, 5 indigenously built 70-ton river gunboats, 1 support ship, 1 repair vessel and 1 training ship of 710 tons.

The manpower of the Navy in 1984 was 5,800, comprising 400 officers and 5,400 ratings.

Air Force. Deliveries, from the Soviet Union and China successively, have built up a current strength of about 20 J-6 (MiG-19) fighter-bombers; 3 MiG-21MF fighters; 1 An-24 and 3 An-26 turboprop transports; about 16 Mi-8, Bell 212 and Alouette III helicopters; 12 Chinese CJ-6 piston-engined primary trainers, a few FT-5 (MiG-17) jet advanced trainers, 6 Magister armed jet trainers and some light aircraft. Personnel strength, 3,000.

INTERNATIONAL RELATIONS

Membership. Bangladesh is a member of the UN and all its related agencies, of the Colombo Plan and of the Islamic Conference.

External Debt. Estimated debt, Dec. 1981, US$4,000m. Most of this was in loans from the Western aid group through the World Bank.

Treaties. Bangladesh signed an economic and technical co-operation agreement with China on 4 Jan. 1977. The amended constitution of 1977 states that Bangladesh seeks fraternal relations with Moslem countries based on Islamic solidarity.

ECONOMY

Planning. The development budget for 1982–83 was Tk.27,000m., of which the highest proportion is for agriculture, irrigation, flood control and rural development.

The second 5-year plan was launched in 1980, as part of a 20-year perspective plan; it aims at an annual growth rate of 7·2% (food-grain production, 7%, manufacturing 8·6%). There was a 2-year interim plan 1978–80, with an envisaged investment of Tk.36,700m. mainly for rural development.

Budget. Details were as follows for two financial years (Tk.1m.):

	1980–81	1981–82
Revenue receipts	23,430	25,538
Revenue expenditure	14,816	18,497
Foreign assistance	15,330	20,814

Money supply (June 1979) stood at Tk.15,150·6m. and foreign exchange reserves (Jan. 1981) at about US$100m.

Currency. A new currency, the *Taka*, was floated in 1976 (Tk.36·70 = £1 and Tk.23·75 = US$1 in March 1984).

Banking. The former private banking system, except for foreign banks, has been nationalized. In June 1978 there were 2,756 bank branches (1,594 rural).

Weights and Measures. Imperial measures are in use. Weight is in the *seer* (1 *seer* = 2 lb.); the *maund* (1 *maund* = 40 *seers*) and the ton. The metric system was to be introduced from July 1982.

ENERGY AND NATURAL RESOURCES

Electricity. There is a hydro-electric power station at Kaptai on Karnafulli and other power stations at Siddhirganj (80 mw), Ashuganj (120), Ghorasal (110), Shahjibazar (1,000), Khulna (60) and Bheramara (40). Production of electricity is not significant; its contribution to GDP, together with gas and water, was Tk.470m. in 1980–81.

Water. On 5 Nov. 1977 India and Bangladesh signed an agreement on sharing the water of the river Ganges. The flow will be monitored daily at the Farakka barrage and two other points. By a further agreement of 1982 the waters of the Brahmaputra will be diverted to the Ganges to augment the flow.

Oil. Supplies have been located in the Bay of Bengal. Drilling is in progress.

Gas. Natural gas from Titas is piped to Dacca; drilling is in progress at other sites, and reserves are considered sufficient for 200 years. Production, 1981, 145m. cu. ft. per day.

Minerals. Coal has been found at Jamalpur (about 700m. tons). Other minerals include salt (750,000 tonnes in 1975), limestone, white clay, glass sand. The Rajshahi area has known reserves of deep-lying coal. In 1979 the Saudi fund for Development invested US$30m. for a limestone and cement project at Jaipurhat.

Agriculture. Agriculture contributes about 54% of GDP (Tk. 37,512m. in 1981–82) and employs about 80% of the economically active population; 64% of the total area is under cultivation; 80% of that is under rice and 9% under jute. Cultivable waste is about 1·5m. acres. About 2m. acres (1981–82) is irrigated. Rice is the most important food crop; food grain production (90% rice) in 1981–82, 21m. tons. Other crops (1,000 tons): Sugar-cane, 6,500; wheat, 1,070; tobacco, 47; tea, 90m. lb.; potatoes, 980; sweet potatoes, 690.

Livestock in 1982 (1,000): Poultry, 73,000; cattle, 35,070; goats, 11,800; sheep, 530; buffalo, 512. Livestock products in 1981 (tonnes): beef and veal, 120,900; cow and buffalo milk, 705,000; goats' milk, 507,000; eggs, 1·4m.

Bangladesh produces about 70% of the world production of raw jute which is the principal foreign exchange earner. Production, 1981–82, 4·7m. bales.

Forestry. The total area under forests (1977) is 9,283 sq. miles, of which 5,105 sq. miles are Reserved Forests. The output of roundwood timber in 1980 (1,000 cu. metres): sawlogs, veneer logs and sleepers, 555; pulpwood, 63; fuel wood, 9,754.

Fisheries. Being bounded on the south by the Bay of Bengal and having numerous rivers, streams, khals and bils, the state is pre-eminently a fish-producing area and possesses great possibilities for the manufacture of various oils and fish products. Fish production, 1980–81, 640,000 tons, of which 517,000 was from inland water.

INDUSTRY AND TRADE

Industry. Out of the existing industries, the textile-mills, sugar factories, match factories, glass works, hosiery factories, a paper-mill, jute-mills, aluminium works and a cement factory, with a capacity of 2m. tons per annum, are the most prominent. New government policy in 1982 aimed to restore public-sector jute and textile mills to private ownership and encourage the private sector. Arms and ammunition, atomic energy, forestry, air transport, communications and electrical industries would remain in the public sector.

Refinery distillation capacity, 1·68m. tonnes. There is a steel mill at Chittagong with a capacity of 250,000 ingot-tons per annum. There is also a newsprint factory, 4 fertilizer factories, a shipyard, a dockyard and a liquified natural gas plant. Jute products, 1981–82, 581,000 tons. Industry employs about 7% of the active population and provides 8·8% (1981–82) of the GNP. Industrial output grew by about 5% in 1982. Production, 1980–81: petroleum products, 1·2m. tons; cotton yarn, 102m. lb.; cotton cloth, 86m. yd.; cement, 340,000 tons; steel ingots, 137,000 tons; re-rolled steel products, 194,000 tons, refined sugar, 143,000 tons.

Labour. In 1974–75, 1,417 firms (employing more than 10 people) had 293,200 paid employees earning Tk.1,298·7m.; value added, Tk.3,781m.

Commerce. The main export commodities are jute goods, hide, skins, leather and tea. Bangladesh has resumed trade with Pakistan. In 1981-82 exports were valued at Tk.12,000m., of which Tk.7,720m. was from jute and jute products. Principal imports (Tk.47,780m.) are machinery, transport equipment, food grains, mineral fuels, chemicals, drugs, medicines and consumer goods.

Total trade between Bangladesh and UK (British Department of Trade returns, in £1,000 sterling):

	1980	1981	1982	1983
Imports to UK	73,084	15,063	25,558	25,189
Exports and re-exports from UK	110,408	45,210	58,179	50,979

Tourism. In 1980 there were 64,162 visitors to Bangladesh. They spent TK.238m.

COMMUNICATIONS

Roads. The State is backward in the matter of road communications, but there are some 2,500 miles of paved and 2,000 miles of unpaved road. In 1979 there were 89,000m. motor vehicles.

Railways. In 1980 there were 2,883 km of railways, comprising 973 km of 1,676 mm gauge and 1,910 km of metre gauge. In 1981–82 the railways carried 3·2m. tonnes of freight and 90·4m. passengers.

Aviation. Bangladesh Biman (Bangladesh Airways) has domestic flights from Dacca and international services to Calcutta, Kathmandu, Bombay, Dubai, Abu Dhabi, Jeddah, Bangkok, Singapore, London, Doha, Kuwait, Amsterdam, Rome, Karachi, Kuala Lumpur, Dahrain, Tripoli, Athens and Muscat.

Shipping. Bangladesh possesses important natural advantages in her navigable channels which give valuable service in carrying produce by 5,000 miles of cheap water routes. There are 3 principal waterways, the Padma, Brahmaputra and Meghna. These are freely used by inland steam vessels, which serve areas where railways cannot be economically constructed. The Bangladesh Shipping Corporation owns 24 ships including a 93,000-ton oil tanker *(Banglar Noor)*. The Corporation has the capacity to carry 20% of imports and 12% of exports.

Post and Broadcasting. There were 122,190 telephones in 1982. Dacca and Islamabad were linked by telephone in Oct. 1976 and a second telephone circuit was agreed on 11 April 1977. International communications are by satellite, Chittagong being linked to the Indian Ocean Intelsat IV satellite.

Newspapers. In Nov. 1981 there were 53 daily newspapers, 200 weeklies, 34 fortnightlies, 194 monthlies and 43 quarterly periodicals. Most papers are published in Dacca. The Government has set up a paper *(Dainik Barta-at Rajshahi)* to stimulate a regional press. Most papers are privately owned. There is a Press Institute.

JUSTICE, RELIGION, EDUCATION AND WELFARE

Justice. The amended constitution in 1977 set up a Supreme Judicial Council to establish a code of conduct for Supreme Court and High Court judges, who may be removed from office by the President on the Council's recommendation.

Religion. Islam is the official religion, about 80% of the people being Muslim and the rest Hindus, Buddhists and Christians.

Education. In 1980 (estimate) under 24% of the population was literate. The compulsory primary education scheme has been replaced by model primary education. The Government has dissolved the District School Boards and taken over school administration.

In 1980 there were 43,634 primary schools, 8,946 secondary schools and about 600 intermediate and degree colleges. Primary schools had 8m. students, secondary schools about 2m. and technical colleges about 16,000. There were 6 universities including those at Dacca, Rajshahi, Mymensingh and Chittagong (founded 1964); one university is for engineering and one for agriculture. Universities had about 28,000 students in 1977. There are 14 teacher-training colleges, 47 primary training institutes, 16 polytechnics and 26 vocational institutes.

Health. In 1979 there were 405 hospitals, 1 mental and 5 tuberculosis and chest hospitals, 8 medical colleges and nursing training centres which train about 1,200 nurses annually. In 1979 the number of beds was 17,494.

DIPLOMATIC REPRESENTATIVES

Of Bangladesh in Great Britain (28 Queen's Gate. London, SW7)
High Commissioner: Fakhruddin Ahmed (accredited 11 June 1982)

Of Great Britain in Bangladesh (Abu Bakr Hse., Plot 7, Road 84, Gulshan Dacca, 12)
High Commissioner: T. G. Streeton.

Of Bangladesh in the USA (2201 Wisconsin Ave., NW, Washington, D.C., 20007)
Ambassador: Humayun Rasheed Choudhury.

Of the USA in Bangladesh (Adamjee Court Bldg., Motijheel, Dacca)
Ambassador: Jane A. Coon.

Of Bangladesh to the United Nations
Ambassador: Lieut.-Gen. Khwaja Wasiuddin.

Books of Reference

Bangladesh Planning Commission, *The First Five Year Plan—The Second Five Year Plan.*
Ministry of Finance. *Bangladesh Economic Survey.* 1979–80
Abdullah, T., and Zeidenstein, S., *Village Women of Bangladesh: Prospects for Change.* Oxford, 1981
Chen, L. C. (ed.), *Disaster in Bangladesh, Health Crisis in a Developing Nation.* OUP, 1973
Chowdhury, R., *The Genesis of Bangladesh.* London, 1972
Dutt, K., *Bangladesh Economy: An Analytical Study.* New Delhi, 1973
Franda, M., *Bangladesh. The First Decade.* New Delhi, 1982
Kamal, K. A., *Sheikh Mujibur Rahman.* 2nd ed. Dacca, 1970
Kashyap, S. C. (ed.), *Bangla Desh: Background and Perspectives.* New Delhi, 1971
Khan, A. R., *The Economy of Bangladesh.* London, 1972
de Lucia, R. J., and Jacoby, H. D., *Energy Planning for Developing Countries: A Study of Bangladesh.* John Hopkins Univ. Press, 1982
de Vylder, S., *Agriculture in Chains. Bangladesh: A Case Study in Contradictions and Constraints.* London, 1982
Oliver, T. W., *The United Nations in Bangladesh.* Princeton Univ. Press, 1978
Rahman, M., *Bangladesh Today: An Indictment and a Lament.* London, 1978
Robinson, E. A. G., and Griffin, K. (ed.), *The Economic Development of Bangladesh.* London, 1974

BARBADOS

Capital: Bridgetown
Population: 270,500 (1981)
GNP per capita: US$3,040 (1980)

HISTORY. Barbados was occupied by the British in 1627 and during its colonial history never changed hands. Full internal self-government was attained in 1961. Barbados became an independent sovereign state within the Commonwealth on 30 Nov. 1966.

AREA AND POPULATION. Barbados lies to the east of the Windward Islands. Area 166 sq. miles (430 sq. km). In 1980 the census population was 248,983. Estimate (1981) 270,000. Bridgetown is the principal city: population, 7,552.

CLIMATE. An equable climate in winter, but the wet season, from June to Nov., is more humid. Rainfall varies from 50″ (1,250 mm) on the coast to 75″ (1,875 mm) in the higher interior. Bridgetown. Jan. 76°F (24·4°C), July 80°F (26·7°C). Annual rainfall 51″ (1,275 mm).

CONSTITUTION AND GOVERNMENT. The Legislature consists of the Governor-General, a Senate and a House of Assembly. The Senate comprises 21 members appointed by the Governor-General, 12 being appointed on the advice of the Prime Minister, 2 on the advice of the leader of the opposition and 7 in the Governor-General's discretion. The House of Assembly comprises 27 members elected every 5 years. In 1963 the voting age was reduced to 18.

The Privy Council is appointed by the Governor-General after consultation with the Prime Minister. It consists of 12 members and the Governor-General as chairman. It advises the Governor-General in the exercise of the royal prerogative of mercy and in the exercise of his disciplinary powers over members of the public and police services.

In the general election of June 1981 the Barbados Labour Party held 17 seats and the Democratic Labour Party 10 seats.

Governor-General: Sir Hugh Springer, KCMG, CBE.

The Cabinet, appointed in June 1981, was:

Prime Minister, Finance and Planning: Rt Hon. J. M. G. M. (Tom) Adams, PC. *Deputy Prime Minister, Trade, Industry, Tourism and Caribbean Affairs:* H. Bernard St John. *Foreign Affairs and Attorney-General:* Louis R. Tull. *Parliamentary Affairs:* Lionel S. Craig. *Education:* Miss Billie A. Miller. *Health:* Lloyd B. Braithwaite. *Information and Culture:* Nigel A. Barrow. *Transport and Works:* Dr Donald G. Blackman. *Housing and Lands.* Delisle Bradshaw. *Prime Minister's Office:* O'Brien Trotman. *Labour and Social Security:* Victor L. Johnson. *Agriculture, Food and Consumer Affairs:* Dr R. L. Johnny Cheltenham.

National flag: Three vertical strips of blue, gold, blue, with a black trident in the centre.

INTERNATIONAL RELATIONS

Membership. Barbados is a member of UN, OAS, CARICOM, the Commonwealth and an ACP state of EEC.

ECONOMY

Budget. The budget for 1983–84 envisaged expenditure of BD$638·2m.

Currency. The monetary unit is the *Barbados dollar* (BD$) divided into 100 *cents.* In March 1984, £1 = BD$2.95; US$1 = 2.01.

Banking. Seven main commercial banks operate in Barbados including Barclays

Bank International, the Royal Bank of Canada, Canadian Imperial Bank of Commerce, the Bank of Nova Scotia, Chase Manhattan Bank, First National Bank of Chicago and Citibank, The Barbados National Bank.

Barbados is headquarters for the Caribbean Development Bank. The Barbados Development Bank opened on 15 April 1969 and Barbados became a member of the Inter-American Development Bank on 19 March 1969.

NATURAL RESOURCES

Agriculture. Of the total area of 106,240 acres, about 54,932 acres are arable land. The land is intensely cultivated, and sugar-cane occupies 64,000 acres, 39,178 were reaped in 1977. The agricultural sector accounted for 9·6% of GDP in 1980 (1946, 45%; 1967, 24%). In 1981, 9,500 persons were employed in agriculture. In 1980, 135,000 tons of sugar were produced. There are 12 sugar factories, 1 syrup plant and a rum distillery in production.

Livestock (1982): Cattle, 20,000; sheep, 53,000; goats, 31,000; pigs, 64,000; poultry, 850,000.

Fisheries. There are about 544 powered boats and many men and women are employed during the flying-fish season. Large numbers of these boats are laid up from July to Oct. The fish catch in 1981 was 4,297 tonnes.

INDUSTRY AND TRADE

Industry. Industries operating in Barbados in 1977 numbered 178 and ranged from the manufacture of processed food to small specialized products such as garment manufacturing, furniture and household appliances, electrical components, plastic products and electronic parts.

Commerce. Total trade for calendar years in BD$1,000:

	1977	1978	1979	1980	1981
Imports [1]	545,110	628,221	852,446	1,064,107	1,126,854
Exports [1]	151,055	187,815	234,794	337,592	306,958

[1] Exclusive of bullion and specie.

In 1981 the principal imports (BD$1m.) were: Machinery and transport equipment, 278·3; manufactured goods, 211·8; lubricants, mineral fuels, etc., 193·8; food, 162·3; chemicals, 100·2; crude minerals, 27; animal and vegetable oils, 13·5. In 1981 the principal domestic exports (BD$1m.) were: Sugar, 74·6; clothing, 51·9; electrical parts, 56·2; miscellaneous, 99·8.

Total trade between Barbados and UK (British Department of Trade returns, in £1,000 sterling):

	1979	1980	1981	1982	1983
Imports from UK	8,414	7,630	9,390	14,887	11,899
Exports and re-exports to UK	27,253	29,860	35,409	26,886	31,938

Tourism. In 1981, 352,555 tourists visited Barbados, spending BD$526·9m. The industry employs over 10,000 people.

COMMUNICATIONS

Roads. There are 1,020 miles of road open to traffic, of which 840 miles are all-weather roads. In 1977 there were 22,000 private cars, 2,000 taxis, 266 buses and 4,000 other vehicles.

Aviation. There is an international airport at Seawell, Christ Church, Barbados, served by British Airways, BWIA, Leeward Islands Air Transport, PANAM, Air Canada, SAS, Caribbean Airways and Eastern Airlines, Cubana Airlines, Venezuelan Airlines.

Shipping. A deep-water harbour opened in 1961 at Bridgetown provides 8 berths for ships 500–600 ft in length, including one specially designed for bulk sugar loading. The number of merchant vessels entering in 1972 was 1,381 of 4,067,500 net tons.

Post and Telephone. There is a general post office in Bridgetown and 13 branches on the island. In Jan. 1982 there were 72,850 telephones and stations in service.

Cinemas. There were (1981) 6 cinemas with a seating capacity of 5,040, and 2 drive-in cinemas for 600 cars.

Newspapers. In 1981 there were 2 daily newspapers.

JUSTICE, RELIGION, EDUCATION AND WELFARE

Justice. Justice is administered by the Supreme Court and by magistrates' courts. All have both civil and criminal jurisdiction. There is a Chief Justice and 3 puisne judges of the Supreme Court and 8 magistrates.

Religion. The majority (about 70%) of the population are Anglicans, the remainder mainly Methodists, Moravians and Roman Catholics.

Education. In 1981–82 children in 115 government primary schools numbered 33,395; in 21 secondary schools, 21,457; in 7 vocational centres, 595; in 15 private approved secondary schools, 4,289. There are 25 independent primary schools with 3,101 pupils and a number of independent schools for which no accurate figures are available. Education is free in all government-owned and maintained institutions from primary to university level.

In 1963 Erdiston College became one of the constituent Colleges of the University of the West Indies Institute of Education. The College of Arts and Sciences of the University of the West Indies in Barbados was opened in Sept. 1963 and Cave Hill campus in 1967. In 1979–80, 1,399 students attended the Cave Hill campus. The Barbados Community College for higher education at pre-university level was opened in 1969; in 1979–80, 1,800 students (full- and part-time) were enrolled. In 1980–81, 1,610 students (mainly part-time) attended the Samuel Jackman Prescod Polytechnic which was opened in Nov. 1969 to give training in, among other things, construction, electrical and engineering trades. Government expenditure on education during 1981–82 was estimated at BD$101,261,267.

Health. In 1972 there were 2,220 hospital beds and (1973) 160 doctors.

DIPLOMATIC REPRESENTATIVES

Of Barbados in Great Britain (6 Upper Belgrave St., London, SW1X 8AZ)
Acting High Commissioner: H. G. Brewster, MBE.

Of Great Britain in Barbados (147/9 Roebuck St., Bridgetown)
High Commissioner: G. L. Bullard.

Of Barbados in the USA (2144 Wyoming Ave., NW, Washington, D.C. 20008)
Chargé d'Affaires: Clifton Maynard.

Of the USA in Barbados (PO Box 302, Bridgetown)
Ambassador: Milan Bish.

Of Barbados to the United Nations
Ambassador: Harley S. L. Moseley.

Books of Reference

Statistical Information: The Barbados Statistical Service (NIS Bldg, Fairchild St, St Michael) produces selected monthly statistics and annual abstracts. *Government Statistician:* Selwyn Straughn.
Barbados Development Plan, 1979–83
Chandler, M. J., *A Guide to Records in Barbados.* Univ. of the West Indies, 1965
Hoyos, F. A., *Barbados, Our Island Home.* London, 1970.—*Barbados: A History from the Amerindians to Independence.* London, 1978.—*Barbados: A Visitor's Guide.* London, 1983

Library: The Barbados Public Library, Bridgetown. *Acting Chief Librarian:* Betty Carrillo.

BELGIUM

Royaume de Belgique—
Koninkrijk België

Capital: Brussels
Population: 9·86m. (1982)
GNP per capita: US$12,180 (1980)

HISTORY. The kingdom of Belgium formed itself into an independent state in 1830, having from 1815 been part of the Netherlands. The secession was decreed on 4 Oct. 1830 by a provisional government, established in consequence of a revolution which broke out at Brussels, on 25 Aug. 1830. A National Congress elected Prince Leopold of Saxe-Coburg King of the Belgians on 4 June 1831; he ascended the throne 21 July 1831.

By the Treaty of London, 15 Nov. 1831, the neutrality of Belgium was guaranteed by Austria, Russia, Great Britain and Prussia. It was not until after the signing of the Treaty of London, 19 April 1839, which established peace between King Leopold I and the King of the Netherlands, that all the states of Europe recognized the kingdom of Belgium. In the Treaty of Versailles (28 June 1919) it is stated that as the treaties of 1839 'no longer conform to the requirements of the situation', these are abrogated and will be replaced by other treaties.

AREA AND POPULATION. Belgium is bounded north by the Netherlands, north-west by the North Sea, west and south by France, east by Federal Republic of Germany and Luxembourg. Belgium has an area of 30,519 sq. km (11,778 sq. miles). The Belgium exclave of Baarle-Hertog in the Netherlands has an area of 7 sq. km, and a population (1 Jan. 1983) of 1,099 males and 1,002 females.

By an agreement, 23 Sept. 1956, the frontier with Germany was slightly readjusted.

Census	Population	Increase % per annum	Census	Population	Increase % per annum
1900	6,693,548	1·03	1947	8,512,195	0·36
1910	7,423,784	1·09	1961	9,189,741	0·52
1920	7,465,782	0·06	1970	9,650,944	0·55
1930	8,092,004	0·84			

Provinces	Provincial capitals	Area (hectares)	Estimated population (31 Dec.)			
			1970 [1]	1980	1981	1982
Antwerp (Anvers)	Antwerp	286,725	1,533,249	1,575,530	1,571,092	1,577,246
Brabant	Brussels	335,811	2,176,373	2,221,782	2,222,974	2,221,383
Flanders {West	Bruges	313,439	1,054,429	1,080,400	1,081,913	1,084,350
{East	Ghent	298,167	1,310,117	1,331,043	1,332,547	1,332,265
Hainaut	Mons	378,669	1,317,453	1,305,163	1,296,719	1,291,610
Liège	Liège	386,213	1,008,905	1,004,034	998,007	995,776
Limbourg	Hasselt	242,231	652,547	716,059	720,766	724,032
Luxembourg	Arlon	444,114	217,310	223,396	222,437	222,437
Namur	Namur	366,501	380,561	405,967	408,134	408,741
Total		3,051,871	9,650,944	9,863,374	9,854,589	9,858,017

[1] Census.

In 1983 there were 4,813,139 males and 5,044,878 females.
Foreigners numbered 891,235 on 1 Jan. 1983.
Vital statistics for calendar years:

	Births	Deaths	Marriages	Divorces	Immigration	Emigration
1978	121,983	115,060	67,206	13,645	52,594	58,495
1979	123,658	112,156	65,476	13,499	54,854	59,552
1980	124,794	114,364	66,413	14,538	54,694	58,212
1981	124,827	113,308	65,076	15,704	49,298	60,191
1982	120,382	112,506	62,423	16,159	44,659	61,931

	1980	1981	1982
Of the total births including still-born	124,794	124,827	120,382
Boys	63,917	64,295	61,930
Girls	60,877	60,532	58,452

The most important towns, with estimated population on 1 Jan. 1983:

Brussels and suburbs [1]	989,877	Tournai (Doornik)	67,379
Antwerp (Anvers) [2]	490,524	Hasselt	65,437
Ghent (Gand)	236,540	Seraing	63,001
Charleroi	216,144	Genk	61,808
Liège (Luik)	207,496	Mouscron (Moeskroen)	54,402
Brugge (Bruges)	118,218	Verviers	54,294
Namur (Namen)	101,860	Roeselare (Roulers)	51,649
Mons (Bergen)	91,868	Herstal	38,010
Leuven (Louvain)	85,068	Turnhout	37,461
Aalst (Alost)	78,068	Lokeren	33,741
Mechelen (Malines)	77,010	Vilvoorde (Vilvorde)	32,868
Kortrijk (Courtrai)	75,582	Lier (Lierre)	31,296
Oostende (Ostende)	69,129	Ronse (Renaix)	24,217
St Niklass (St Nicolas)	68,157		

[1] The suburbs comprise 18 distinct communes, viz., Anderlecht, Etterbeek, Forest Ixelles, Jette, Koekelberg, Molenbeek St Jean, St Gilles, St Josse-ten-Noode, Schaerbeek, Uccle, Woluwe-St Lambert, Auderghem, Watermael-Boitsfort, Woluwe-St Pierre, Berchem, Ste Agathe, Evere and Ganshoren.

[2] Including Berchem, Borgerhout, Deurne, Hoboken, Merksem and Wilrijk.

CLIMATE. Cool temperate climate, influenced by the sea. From Dec. to April, conditions are relatively cool (32–43°F, 0–6°C). Warm weather begins in May and continues until Sept. (54–72°F, 12–22°C) and in this period, sunshine averages 200–300 hours per month. Annual rainfall in Brussels, 28·5″ (724 mm); Bruges 34″ (854 mm).

KING. Baudouin, born 7 Sept. 1930, succeeded his father, Leopold III, on 17 July 1951, when he took the oath on the constitution before the two Chambers: married on 15 Dec. 1960 to Fabiola de Mora y Aragón, daughter of the Conde de Mora and Marqués de Casa Riera.

Brother and Sister of the King. (1) Josephine Charlotte, Princess of Belgium, born 11 Oct. 1927; married to Prince Jean of Luxembourg, 9 April 1953; (2) Albert, Prince of Liège, born 6 June 1934; married to Paola Ruffo di Calabria, 2 July 1959; *offspring:* Prince Philippe, born 15 April 1960; Princess Astrid, born 5 June 1962; Prince Laurent, born 19 Oct. 1963. *Half-brother and half-sisters of the King.* Prince Alexandre, born 18 July 1942; Princess Marie Christine, born 6 Feb. 1951; Princess Maria-Esmeralda, born 30 Sept. 1956.

Aunt of the King. Princess Marie-José, born 4 Aug. 1906, married to Prince Umberto (King Umberto II of Italy in 1946) on 8 Jan. 1930.

BELGIAN SOVEREIGNS

Leopold I	1831–65	Leopold III	1934–44, 1950–51
Leopold II	1865–1909	Regency	1944–50
Albert	1909–34	Baudouin	1951–

CONSTITUTION AND GOVERNMENT. According to the constitution of 1831, Belgium is a constitutional, representative and hereditary monarchy. The legislative power is vested in the King, the Senate and the Chamber of Representatives. The royal succession is in direct male line in the order of primogeniture. By marriage without the King's consent, however, the right of succession is forfeited, but may be restored by the King with the consent of the two Chambers. No act of the King can have effect unless countersigned by one of his Ministers, who thus becomes responsible for it. The King convokes, prorogues and dissolves the Chambers. In default of male heirs, the King may nominate his successor with the consent of the Chambers. If the successor be under 18 years of age the two Chambers meet together for the purpose of nominating a regent during the minority.

National flag: Three vertical strips of black, yellow, red.

National anthem: Après des siècles d'esclavage (La Brabançonne; words by Jenneval, 1830; tune by F. van Campenhout, 1930).

French, Dutch and German are official languages.

Those sections of the Belgian Constitution which regulate the organization of the legislative power were revised in Oct. 1921. For both Senate and Chamber all elections are held on the principle of universal suffrage.

The Senate consists of members elected for 4 years, partly directly and partly indirectly. The number elected directly is equal to half the number of members of the Chamber of Representatives. The constituent body is similar to that which elects deputies to the Chamber; the minimum age of electors is 18 years, and the minimum length of residence required is 6 months. Women were given the suffrage at parliamentary elections on 24 March 1948. In the direct elections of members of both the Senate and Chamber of Representatives the principle of proportional representation was introduced by law of 29 Dec. 1899.

Senators are elected indirectly by the provincial councils, on the basis of 1 for 200,000 inhabitants. Every addition of 125,000 inhabitants gives the right to 1 senator more. Each provincial council elects at least 3 senators. There are at present 51 provincial senators. No one, during 2 years preceding the election, must have been a member of the council appointing him. Senators are elected by the Senate itself in the proportion of half the preceding category. The senators belonging to these two latter categories are also elected by the method of proportional representation. All senators must be at least 40 years of age. They receive 900,000 francs per annum. Sons of the King, or failing these, Belgian princes of the reigning branch of the royal family, are by right senators at the age of 18, but have no voice in the deliberations till the age of 25 years; this prerogative is hardly ever used.

The members of the Chamber of Representatives are elected by the electoral body. Their number, at present 212 (law of 3 April 1965), is proportional to the population, and cannot exceed one for every 40,000 inhabitants. They sit for 4 years. Deputies must be not less than 25 years of age, and resident in Belgium.

Each deputy has an annual allowance of 900,000 francs. Senators and deputies have also free railway passes.

The Senate and Chamber meet annually in October and must sit for at least 40 days; but the King has the power of convoking extraordinary sessions and of dissolving them either simultaneously or separately. In the latter case a new election must take place within 40 days and a meeting of the chambers within 2 months.

An adjournment cannot be made for a period exceeding 1 month without the consent of the Chambers.

After the revision of the Constitution by the laws of 24 Dec. 1970 and 28 July 1971 establishing three regions and two cultural councils, legislation on 'preparatory regionalization' was enacted in July 1974. Further revisions of the functions of the Cultural Councils took place on 8 and 9 Aug. 1980. The Cultural Councils became Community Councils with greater authority and the Regional Councils became competent on economic matters.

Parliament was dissolved on 6 Oct. 1981 and general elections were held on 8 Nov. 1981.

Parties in the Senate after the election: *Christelijke Volkspartij,* 22; *Parti social chrétien,* 8; *Socialistische Partij,* 13; *Parti Socialiste Belge,* 18; *Partij voor Vrijheid en Vooruitgang,* 14; *Parti Reformateur Libéral (PRL),* 11; *Other parties,* 20.

Parties in the Chamber of Representatives after the election: *Christelijke Volkspartij,* 43; *Parti social chrétien,* 18; *Parti Socialiste,* 35; *Socialistische Partij,* 26; *Partij voor Vrijheid en Vooruitgang,* 28; *Parti Reformateur Libéral,* 24; *Other parties,* 38.

A 4-party coalition government was formed in Dec. 1981 and in Jan. 1984 was composed as follows:

Prime Minister: Dr Wilfried Martens (CVP).

Deputy Prime Ministers: Jean Gol, PRL *(Justice and Institutional Reform);*

Willy de Clercq, PVV (*Finance and Foreign Trade*); Charles-Ferdinand Nothomb, PSC (*Interior and Civil Service*). *Foreign Affairs:* Léo Tindemans (CVP). *Economic Affairs:* Mark Eyskens (CVP). *Public Works and Middle Classes:* Louis Olivier (PRL). *Posts and Telecommunications:* Herman de Croo (PVV). *Labour and Employment:* Michel Hansenne (PSC). *Education (Flemish):* Daniel Coens (CVP). *Budget, Scientific Policy and Research:* Philippe Maystadt (PSC). *Brussels Regional Affairs:* P. Hatry (PRL). *Defence:* Freddy Vreven (PVV). *Education (French-language):* A. Bertouille (PRL). *Social Affairs and Institutional Reform:* Jean-Luc Dehaene (CVP).

There are ten Secretaries of State.

Local Government. Belgium has 9 provinces and since the so-called 'Amalgamation Law' of 30 Dec. 1975, 589 communes (instead of 2,359). They have a large measure of autonomous government. According to the law of 9 June 1982, all Belgians over 18 years of age, who are recorded in the registers of population of the commune have the right to vote in the communal elections. Proportional representation is applied to the communal elections, and communal councils are to be renewed every 6 years. In each commune there is a college composed of the burgomaster as the president and a certain number of aldermen.

DEFENCE. Belgium is a full member of NATO since 1949 and of the Eurogroup since 1968. The need to extend European armaments co-operation led to the formation of the Independent European Program Group (IEPG) in 1976. Its members include Belgium.

According to the Military Law of 30 April 1962, the Belgian Army is recruited by annual calls to the colours and by voluntary enlistments.

Compulsory service lasts 8 or 10 months for private soldiers, 13 months for voluntary reserve officers and 15 for the paracommando regiment. Duration of military obligation is 8 years for most soldiers called for compulsory service.

Army. The Army comprises as major units 1 armoured and 3 mechanized brigades (2 of which are deployed as the Belgian divisions in the Belgian corps area in the Federal Republic of Germany) and 1 paracommando regiment. There are also 3 reconnaissance battalions. Total strength about 62,500. *Gendarmerie,* 15,750.

Equipment includes nearly 330 LEOPARD Main Battle Tanks, 135 SCORPION Light Tanks, 150 SCIMITAR Armoured Fighting Vehicles, 1,150 Armoured Personnel Carriers and 80 JPK 90mm Self-Propelled Anti-Tank Guns; Artillery Battalions are equipped with 105mm, 155mm and 203mm Self-Propelled Howitzers, LANCE Surface-to-Surface Missiles, HAWK Surface-to-Air Missiles and GEPARD Armoured Vehicles with 35mm Anti-Aircraft Guns.

Other equipment in use: MILAN Anti-Tank Guided Weapon, STRIKER Armoured Fighting Vehicle with SWINGFIRE Anti-Tank Guided Weapon, Islander aircraft, Alouette II helicopters, Epervier Remotely Piloted Vehicle.

Navy. The naval forces include 4 frigates (Navy designed and built) completed in 1978, 7 ocean minehunters, 2 command and logistic support ships, 2 coastal mine-hunters, 4 coastal minesweepers (all in reserve), 14 inshore minesweepers, 1 research ship, 8 river patrol boats, 5 tugs, 1 degaussing ship, 1 ammunition transport and 5 miscellaneous craft. A tripartite minehunter is being built and nine others (with a further 5 option) are projected. Naval personnel in 1984 totalled 4,720 officers and ratings.

The naval air arm comprises 3 Alouette III general utility helicopters.

Air Force. The Air Force has a strength of more than 20,000 personnel and more than 270 aircraft in 14 operational squadrons and support units. There are 5 flying wings. The all-weather fighter wing consists of 2 squadrons of F-16s. One fighter-bomber wing has 2 squadrons of F-16s; 2 others operate Mirage 5s, organized as 3 squadrons of Mirage 5Bs and Mirage 5BD two-seat trainers, and 1 squadron of Mirage 5BR photo-reconnaissance aircraft. The transport wing consists of 1 squadron equipped with 12 C-130H Hercules turboprop transports, and 1 squadron flying 2 Boeing 727s, 3 HS 748 twin-turboprop transports, 5 Swearingen Merlin III light turboprop transports and 2 light twin-jet Falcons. Other types in

BELGIUM

service include Sea King Mk 48 search and rescue helicopters, SIAI-Marchetti SF.260M and Alpha Jet training aircraft. Two surface-to-air missile wings, stationed in Germany, are equipped with Nike Hercules missiles. Aircraft on order include 44 more F-16s.

INTERNATIONAL RELATIONS

Membership. Belgium is a member of UN, EEC, Benelux Economic Union, Council of Europe, NATO, OECD and WEU.

ECONOMY

Budget. Revenue and expenditure for calendar years (in 1 m. francs):

	1977	1978	1979	1980	1981	1982
Receipts						
Current	747,509	877,324	941,484	979,239	1,010,200	1,153,104
Capital	159,515	167,769	175,687	197,867	157,200	253,776
Total	907,024	1,045,093	1,171,171	1,177,106	1,167,400	1,406,880
Expenditure						
Current	865,733	1,012,521	1,092,766	1,107,082	1,300,400	1,434,601
Capital	85,225	113,351	119,212	168,088	186,400	172,107
Total	950,958	1,125,872	1,211,978	1,275,170	1,486,800	1,606,708

On 30 June 1982 the Belgian public debt consisted of (in 1m. francs): Internal debt consolidated, 1,714,200; short and middle terms, 879,700; at sight, 91,700. External debt, 764,800.

Currency. The *franc*, containing 0·01826 gramme of fine gold, is the unit of currency.

No gold has been minted since 1882 (save only 5m. francs struck in 1914). New silver coins of 250 francs have been issued since 16 March 1976. Note circulation 31 Dec. 1982, 382,193m. francs.

The official rate of exchange in March 1984 was US\$1 = 53·34 francs; £1 = 79·55 francs.

Banking. The bank of issue in Belgium is the National Bank, instituted in 1850. It is the cashier of the State, and is authorized to carry on the usual banking operations. The note circulation on 31 Dec. 1982 amounted to 382,193m. francs. The articles of association of the National Bank of Belgium were modified on 13 Sept. 1948 so as to strengthen public control.

The savings banks are mainly operated by the *Caisse Générale d'Epargne et de Retraite* and by the private savings banks. *The Caisse Générale d'Epargne et de Retraite* (CGER), a state institution, consists of 2 parts: *the Caisse d'Epargne* which performs the whole range of banking activities and a further unit which embodies the funds engaged in social security and insurance activities; the CGER operates under the authority of the Minister of Finance. The *Commission bancaire* (bank commission) supervises the financial situation and the activities of the Caisse d'Epargne. It co-operates with the Belgian postal service, thus obviating any need of a postal-savings system. The savings deposits and savings bonds of the Caisse d'Epargne amounted to 583,318m. francs on 31 Dec. 1981. The private savings banks, whose liabilities expressed in savings accounts and bonds amounted to 676,760m. francs on 31 Dec. 1982, are controlled by the 'Commission bancaire'.

Weights and Measures. The metric system is in force.

ENERGY AND NATURAL RESOURCES

Electricity. The production of electricity (1m. kwh.) amounted to 49,648 in 1979; 51,015 in 1980; 48,179 in 1981; 47,936 in 1982.

Gas. Production of gas (in 1m. cu. metres): 730 in 1979; 675 in 1980; 690 in 1981; 594 in 1982.

Minerals. Output (in tonnes) for 5 calendar years:

	1978	1979	1980	1981	1982
Coal	6,590,268	6,124,503	6,324,034	6,136,446	6,538,874
Briquettes	124,496	152,492	81,597	53,981	49,836
Coke	5,747,192	6,450,359	6,047,504	6,003,730	5,216,692
Cast iron	10,127,996	10,775,843	9,844,629	9,786,077	7,831,469
Wrought steel	12,604,240	13,444,799	12,323,519	12,285,083	9,899,850
Finished steel	9,696,177	10,364,011	9,517,357	8,902,482	7,364,139

Agriculture. Of the total area of 3,051,871 hectares, there were, in 1981, 1,408,993 hectares under cultivation, of which 371,731 were under cereals, 22,995 vegetables, 139,469 industrial plants, 118,005 root crops, 697,104 pastures and meadows.

Chief crops	Area in hectares			Produce in tonnes		
	1980	1981	1982	1980	1981	1982
Wheat	179,160	166,092	170,426	852,765	875,426	1,010,009
Barley	152,732	152,403	131,176	807,057	751,885	745,109
Oats	28,284	26,418	33,716	108,892	108,842	153,408
Rye	10,175	8,349	7,101	38,157	31,978	29,752
Potatoes	38,132	34,272	32,626	1,181,470	1,195,291	1,310,043
Beet (sugar)	117,165	130,326	123,816	5,314,597	6,935,934	7,430,205
Beet (fodder)	17,276	16,201	17,249	1,541,871	1,547,953	1,934,621
Tobacco	436	481	477	1,059	1,604	1,701

In 1982 there were 29,910 horses, 2,896,067 cattle, 82,541 sheep, 6,227 goats and 5,113,378 pigs.

Forestry. In 1970 the forest area covered 19·7% of the land surface. In 1970, 2·85 cu. metres of timber were felled.

Fisheries. The total quantity of fish landed amounted to 37,207 tons valued at 2,131m. francs in 1982. The fishing fleet had a total tonnage of 21,847 gross tons at 31 Dec. 1982.

INDUSTRY AND TRADE

Industry. In 1982 there were 14 sugar factories, output 201,740 tonnes of raw sugar; 3 sugar refineries, output 252,598 tonnes; 7 distilleries, output 120,771 hectolitres of potable and industrial alcohol; 134 breweries, output (1981) 13,811,076 hectolitres of beer; margarine factories, output 161,382 tonnes.

Six trusts control the greater part of Belgian industry: the Société Générale (founded in 1822) owns about 40% of coal, 50% of steel, 65% of non-ferrous metals and 35% of electricity; Brufina-Confinindus operates in steel, coal, electricity and heavy engineering; the Groupe Solvay rules the chemical industry; the Groupe Copée has interests in steel and coal; Empain controls tramways and electrical equipment; the Banque Lambert owns petroleum firms and their accessories.

Commerce. By the convention concluded at Brussels on 25 July 1921 between Belgium and Luxembourg and ratified on 5 March 1922 an economic union was formed by the two countries, and the customs frontier between them was abolished on 1 May 1922. Dissolved in Aug. 1940, the union was re-established on 1 May 1945. On 14 March 1947, in execution of an agreement signed in London on 5 Sept. 1944, there was concluded a customs union between Belgium and Luxembourg, on the one hand, and the Netherlands, on the other. The union came into force on 1 Jan. 1948, and is now known as the Benelux Economic Union. A joint tariff has been adopted and import duties are no longer levied at the Netherlands frontier, but import licences may still be required. A full economic union of the three countries came into operation on 1 Nov. 1960.

Benelux information is supplied by the Secrétariat Général de l'Union Douanière Néerlando-Belgo-Luxembourgeoise, Rue de la Régence, 39, 1000 Brussels. It publishes *Benelux. Bulletin Trimestriel de Statistique; Statistisch Kwartaalbericht* (1955 ff.).

Trade by selected countries (in 1,000 Belgian francs):

	Imports from			Exports to		
	1980	1981	1982 [1]	1980	1981	1982 [1]
France	303,328,230	315,952,138	367,320,394	367,103,921	395,582,544	464,276,834
USA	161,130,425	165,939,976	185,807,880	63,336,344	87,152,270	105,375,763
UK	169,453,710	171,442,793	185,957,494	160,281,547	177,660,091	231,274,844
Netherlands	344,508,752	394,397,768	465,072,190	287,019,767	305,357,063	339,604,266
German Dem. Rep.	4,230,277	6,053,009	6,200,191	3,774,302	3,156,944	2,338,707
Germany, Fed. Rep.	413,045,898	435,354,580	528,559,688	401,531,524	414,123,911	489,761,698
Argentina	4,558,478	4,727,455	6,576,131	3,601,825	2,877,342	2,537,641
Italy	75,336,177	77,632,033	95,027,884	104,281,448	104,735,092	120,760,063
Switzerland	57,756,719	80,538,132	61,240,373	72,287,115	64,787,862	76,902,369
Zaïre	36,156,375	35,989,008	26,491,434	7,654,771	7,304,624	8,830,069
Denmark	9,738,732	9,982,649	12,380,236	22,492,972	27,157,142	23,507,666
USSR	32,543,225	36,318,716	67,072,358	18,117,926	21,884,703	24,491,049
India	6,633,042	7,807,996	9,693,691	10,702,620	20,039,004	27,030,652
Rep. of S. Africa	12,967,088	14,535,344	17,647,055	7,421,713	11,159,909	10,393,010
Canada	15,642,112	19,822,425	18,582,030	5,255,669	8,982,712	9,144,449
Brazil	9,066,873	13,168,019	16,737,912	4,333,550	4,557,981	4,982,633
Australia	6,444,824	6,094,337	7,140,122	4,288,391	4,589,326	5,590,162

[1] Provisional.

Imports and exports for 6 calendar years (in 1,000 Belgian francs):

	Imports	Exports		Imports	Exports
1977	1,447,981,180	1,344,704,149	1980	2,100,807,473	1,890,359,149
1978	1,526,044,142	1,410,257,630	1981	2,309,761,017	2,062,315,689
1979	1,784,353,190	1,661,244,397	1982 [1]	2,642,280,047	2,394,463,014

[1] Provisional.

The total trade between Belgium and Luxembourg and UK was as follows (British Department of Trade returns, in £1,000 sterling):

	1979	1980	1981	1982	1983
Imports to UK	2,324,561	2,596,962	2,448,605	2,861,809	3,133,905
Exports and re-exports from UK	2,467,631	2,624,108	2,092,011	2,298,118	2,572,673

Principal Belgian-Luxembourg exports to UK in 1982 [1] (tonnes; francs): Textiles (104,206; 16,852m.); metals (484,636; 17,103m.); chemical and pharmaceutical products (523,031; 19,255m.); precious stones and manufactures thereof (303; 37,841m.).

Principal Belgian-Luxembourg imports from the UK in 1982[1] (tonnes; francs): Machinery and electrical apparatus (42,521; 17,948m.); vehicles, chiefly motor cars, and aircraft (105,657; 19,801m.); textiles (35,584; 6,893m.); precious stones (121; 54,725m.); base metals and manufactures thereof (161,970; 7,740m.).

[1] Provisional.

Tourism. In 1981 receipts totalled 27m. francs, comprising 20m. francs from Belgian tourists and 7m. francs from overseas visitors.

COMMUNICATIONS

Roads. The total length of the roads in Belgium on 31 Dec. 1981 was as follows: State roads (including 1,315 km of motorway), 13,093 km; provincial roads, 1,369 km; communal roads, 110,186 km. The majority of roads are metalled. Number of motor vehicles in Belgium, 1 Aug. 1983, 3,869,822, including 3,262,713 passenger cars, 17,866 buses, 261,126 lorries, 28,284 non-agricultural tractors, 136,868 agricultural tractors, 126,279 motor cycles and 36,686 special vehicles.

Railways. The main Belgian lines were a State enterprise from their inception in 1834. In 1926 the *Société Nationale des Chemins de Fer Belges (SNCB)* was formed to take over the railways. The State is sole holder of the ordinary shares of

SNCB, which carry the majority vote at General Meetings. The length of railway operated on 31 Dec. 1982 was 3,920 km. Revenue (1982), 49,223m. francs; expenditure, 54,960m. francs. In 1981–82, 69·6m. tonnes of freight and 166·8m. passengers were carried.

Aviation. The national Belgian airline SABENA (*Société anonyme belge d'exploitation de la navigation aérienne*) was set up in 1923. Its capital is 750m. francs. In addition to its European network, SABENA operates different routes to North and South America, to North, Central and South Africa and to the Near, the Middle and the Far East. In 1982 its airfleet comprised 26 aircraft. In 1982 SABENA flew 50m. km, carrying 2,007,772 revenue passengers, 479·1m. ton-km of freight and 12·54m. ton-km of mail.

Shipping.[1] On 1 Jan. 1983 the Belgian merchant fleet was composed of 105 vessels of 2,085,601 tons. There were 49 shipping companies, of which the most important were the Compagnie Maritime Belge, with 21 ships, and the Belgian Fruit Lines, SA, with 6 ships.

[1] Belgian shipping returns are given in the official 'Moorsom tons', which may be converted into net tons by deducting 19·85% from the Moorsom total.

The navigation at the port of Antwerp in 1982 was as follows: Number of vessels entered, 16,956; tonnage, 112,188,000. Number of vessels cleared, 16,692; tonnage, 110,904,000.

The total length of navigable waterways (rivers and canals) was 1,559·5 km in 1982.

Post and Broadcasting. On 31 Dec. 1981 there were 2,309 post offices. The gross revenue of the post office in the year 1981 amounted to 20,954m. francs.

A régie of telegraphs and telephones for running the services on business lines was created in 1930. Telegraph offices for dispatching and receiving wires numbered 106; for dispatching only, 26. Receipts for 1981 were 4,549·82m. francs; expenditure, 4,063,125,000 francs.

In 1981 the telephone service comprised 667 exchanges, connecting 7,431 public telephone stations and (1982) 3,818,626 subscribers. Number of telephones, 1 Jan. 1981, 3,818,646. Receipts in 1981, 35,624,476m. francs; expenditure, 36,886,604m. francs.

Radio-Television belge de la Communauté française (RTBF) and *Belgische Radio en Televisie* (BRT) are public institutions broadcasting in French and Dutch respectively.

BRT has 5 radio programmes: BRT 1 is for service and information, documentary programmes, radio drama and light music; BRT 2 is for regional entertainments from each of the Flemish provinces. Both stations broadcast on medium-wave and on FM (stereo). BRT 3, on FM (stereo) is the cultural station; Studio Brussels (medium-wave and FM) gives local information and light music for 6 hours daily to Dutch-speaking residents; the World Broadcasting Station (short- and medium-wave) is for Belgians abroad and to publicise Flemish culture overseas.

RTBF has 5 radio programmes: TRBF 1 (medium-wave) for information; RTBF 2 (FM stereo) for entertainment and local information; RTBF 3 (FM stereo) for classical music; Radio 21 (FM stereo) a young people's popular music and news programme; *La Voix de l'Amitié* (short-wave) which broadcasts to Africa.

Each body has 2 television channels, one general and one mainly for sporting events; broadcasting is by PAL standards. Advertising is not allowed on radio or television, which are financed by the Flemish and French Community Councils. In 1983 the Flemish community had 2·7m. radio receivers and 1·7m. television sets of which 71% were colour sets; the French-speaking community had 1·8m. radio receivers and 1·3m. television sets of which 53% were colour sets; 80% of the Flemish and 89% of the French-speaking households were connected to a television network. Number of receivers (1982), radio, 4,622,649; TV, 2,978,689 (including 1,885,896 colour sets).

Cinemas (1982). There were 479 cinemas, with a seating capacity of 160,607.

Newspapers (1983). There are 38 daily newspapers (some of them only regional or local editions of larger dailies), of which 23 are in French, 14 in Dutch and 1 in German.

JUSTICE, RELIGION, EDUCATION AND WELFARE

Justice. Judges are appointed for life. There is a court of cassation, 5 courts of appeal, and assize courts for political and criminal cases. There are 26 judicial districts, each with a court of first instance. In each of the 222 cantons is a justice and judge of the peace. There are, besides, various special tribunals. There is trial by jury in assize courts.

Religion. Of the inhabitants professing a religion the majority are Roman Catholic, but no inquiry as to the profession of faith is now made at the censuses. There are, however, statistics concerning the clergy, and according to these there were in 1980: Roman Catholic higher clergy, 130; inferior clergy, 6,956; Protestant pastors, 83; Anglican Church, 10 chaplains; Jews (rabbis and ministers), 26. The State does not interfere in any way with the internal affairs of any church. There is full religious liberty, and part of the income of the ministers of all denominations is paid by the State.

There are 8 Roman Catholic dioceses subdivided into 260 deaneries.

Estimated number of Protestants, 24,000; of Jews, 35,000.

The Protestant (Evangelical) Church is under a synod. There is also a Central Jewish Consistory, a Central Committee of the Anglican Church and a Free Protestant Church.

Education. On 8 Nov. 1962/2 Aug. 1963 a linguistic frontier was fixed between the Dutch-speaking, French-speaking and German-speaking parts of Belgium. In the north, Dutch is recognized as the official language, in the south, French, and along the eastern border, German. The city and *arrondissement* of Brussels are bilingual. The percentage of the population in the Flemish, French, German and bilingual regions was 57·1, 32·1, 0·7, 10·1 on 1 Jan. 1981. (*See* map in THE STATESMAN'S YEAR-BOOK, 1967–68.)

Higher Education (1981–82). Higher education is given in state universities: Ghent (12,648 students), Liège (9,384 students), Mons (1,423 students), the Polytechnic Faculty in Mons (508 students), the Antwerp State University Centre (2,033 students), the Gembloux Faculty of Agronomical Sciences (767 students), the Royal Military School in Brussels (759 students) and in the private universities: Catholic University of Louvain (39,363 students), the Free University of Brussels (18,627), University Institution Antwerp (1,443 students), St Ignatius Antwerp (2,874 students), Our Lady of Peace in Namur (2,887 students), Catholic University Faculty in Mons (631 students), St Louis in Brussels (960 students), St Aloysius in Brussels (643 students), the Limbourg University Centre (801 students) and the Protestant Faculty of Theology in Brussels (131 students). The total number of students in university colleges, faculties and institutes was 95,882.

There are 5 royal academies of fine arts and 5 royal conservatoires at Brussels, Liège, Ghent, Antwerp and Mons.

Secondary Education. 1,050 (1977–78) middle schools, 2,353 (1974–75) technical schools and 515 (1974–75) schools of the new system had a total of 199,167 (1980–81) pupils in the general classes and 264,911 in the technical classes in the traditional system and 384,639 pupils in the new system.

Elementary Education. There were 5,648 (1977–78) primary schools, with 857,418 pupils in 1980–81 and 4,607 (1977–78) infant schools, with 384,694 pupils in 1980–81.

Normal Schools. Under the French and German linguistic systems there were 26 (1975–76) schools for training secondary teachers (4,374 students) in 1980–81; 44 (1975–76) for training elementary teachers (3,578 students) in 1980–81, 63 technical normal schools in 1974–75 with (1980–81) 1,212 students and 19 (1975–76) normal infant schools with 1,087 students in 1980–81. The pedagogical education under the Dutch linguistic system is differently organized and totalled 14,306 students in 1980–81.

Health. In 1981 there were 25,629 physicians (including 546 dentists), 4,690 other dentists, 9,942 pharmacists and (1978) 3,593 midwives. Hospital beds numbered 92,436 on 1 Jan. 1981.

Social Security. Social security is based on the law of Dec. 1944. It applies to all workers subject to an employment contract, and is administered by the Central National Office of Social Security (ONSS), which collects from employers and employees all contributions referring to family allowances, health insurance, old age insurance, holidays and unemployment. These sums are distributed by the Central Office to the various institutions concerned with these benefits. Insurance against unemployment is organized through a common fund, which also undertakes to retrain the unemployed for another employment while providing for their families. Since 1944 further laws have increased allowances, made fresh provisions for housing (1945), injuries while working, professional illnesses, etc. (1948).

Apart from private charity, the poor are assisted by the communes through the agency of the *Centre Public d'Aide Sociale* in French-speaking parts of the country and *Openbaar Centrum voor Maatschappelijk Welzijn* in Dutch-speaking areas. Provisions of a national character have been made for looking after war orphans and men disabled in the war. Certain other establishments, either state or provincial, provide for the needs of the deaf-mutes and the blind, and of children who are placed under the control of the courts. Provision is also made for repressing begging and providing shelter for the homeless.

DIPLOMATIC REPRESENTATIVES

Of Belgium in Great Britain (103 Eaton Sq., London, SW1W 9AB)
Ambassador: Jean-Paul Van Bellinghen (accredited 24 Feb. 1984).

Of Great Britain in Belgium (Britannia Hse., rue Joseph II 28, 1040 Brussels)
Ambassador: J. E. Jackson, CMG.

Of Belgium in the USA (3330 Garfield St., NW, Washington, D.C., 20008)
Ambassador: J. Raoul Schoumaker.

Of the USA in Belgium (Blvd. du Régent 27, 1000 Brussels)
Ambassador: Geoffrey Swaebe.

Of Belgium to the United Nations
Ambassador: Edmonde Dever.

Books of Reference

Statistical Information: The Institut National de Statistique (44 rue de Louvain, Brussels) was set up on 24 Jan. 1831, under the designation of Bureau de Statistique Générale; after several changes, it received its present name on 2 May 1946. *Director-General:* E. Rosselle. *Main publications:*

Bulletin du Commerce Extérieur
Bulletin de Statistique. Monthly
Annuaire Statistique de la Belgique (from 1870).—*Annuaire statistique de poche* (from 1965)
Statistiques Agricoles. Monthly
Recensement général de la population au 31 déc. 1970. 13 vols.
Recensement de l'agriculture au 15 mai 1970. 3 vols.
Recensement de l'industrie et du commerce au 31 déc. 1970. 10 vols.

Annuaire administratif et judiciaire de Belgique. Annual. Brussels
L'économie belge. Ministère des Affaires Economiques. Annual (from 1947)
Belgium. Investment Guide. Ministère des Affaires Economique, 1974
Guide des Ministères: Revue de l'Administration Belge. Brussels. Annual
Belgique: Un Panorama. Institut Belge d'Information et de documentation. Brussels, 1969
Molitor, A., *L'Administration de la Belgique.* Brussels, 1974.

BELIZE

Capital: Belmopan
Population: 152,000 (1982)
GNP per capita: US$1,080 (1980)

HISTORY. The early settlement of the territory was probably effected by British woodcutters about 1638; from that date to 1798, in spite of armed opposition from the Spaniards, settlers held their own and prospered. In 1780 the Home Government appointed a superintendent, and in 1862 the settlement was declared a colony, subordinate to Jamaica. It became an independent colony in 1884. Self-government was attained in 1964. Independence was achieved on 21 Sept. 1981.

AREA AND POPULATION. Belize is bounded north by Mexico, west by Guatemala and south and east by the Caribbean sea. Area, 22,963 sq. km. There are 6 districts:

	Sq. km	Population census, 1980		Sq. km	Population census, 1980
Corozal	1,860	22,902	Cayo	5,338	22,837
Belize	4,204	50,801	Stann Creek	2,176	14,181
Orange Walk	4,737	22,870	Toledo	4,649	11,762

Total population (census, 1980) 145,353. Voters on the roll numbered 71,740 in 1980. In 1982 the birth rate per 1,000 was 38·6 and the death rate 4·3; infantile mortality 21·3 per 1,000 births; there were 844 marriages. English is the official language.

Main city, Belize City; population, census 1980, 39,771. Following the severe hurricane which struck the territory on 31 Oct. 1961 the capital Belmopan (population, 1980, 2.932) has been moved to a new site 50 miles inland; construction began in Jan. 1967 and it became the seat of government on 3 Aug. 1970. *See* map in the 1978–79 edition of THE STATESMAN'S YEAR-BOOK.

CONSTITUTION AND GOVERNMENT. Having achieved self-government in Jan. 1964 delays occurred in achieving independence because of the outstanding territorial claim by Guatemala. Attempts to reach agreement on the claim finally failed prior to independence being granted, but guarantees were given by Britain that a military force would remain.

The Constitution, which came into force on 21 Sept. 1981, provided for a National Assembly, with a 5-year term, comprising an 18-member House of Representatives elected by universal adult suffrage, and a Senate consisting of 5 members appointed by the Governor-General on the advice of the Prime Minister and 3 other nominated members.

Governor-General: Elmira Minita Gordon.
Prime Minister and Minister of Foreign Affairs and Finance: Rt. Hon. George Cadle Price PC.
Deputy Prime Minister, Minister of Defence and Home Affairs: Carl L. B. Rogers.
Flag: Blue with red band along the top and bottom edges. In the centre a white disc containing the coat of arms surrounded by a green garland.

CLIMATE. A tropical climate with high rainfall and small annual range of temperature. The driest months are Feb. and March. Belize. Jan. 74°F (23·3°C), July 81°F (27·2°C). Annual rainfall 76″ (1,890 mm).

DEFENCE. The Air Wing of the Belize Defence Force has two twin-engined BN-2B Defenders for maritime patrol and transport duties. RAF aircraft based temporarily in Belize include a detachment of Harrier V/STOL ground attack/reconnaissance aircraft.

ECONOMY

Budget. Revenue and expenditure (in $B1,000) for calendar years:

	1977	1978	1979	1980-81	1981-82
Revenue	54,439	65,359	75,828	88,977	86,687
Expenditure	63,526	66,990	76,850	91,935	71,049

Public debt, 31 March 1980, $B25,739,358; sinking fund, $B961,978.

Currency. There was (29 April 1980) a paper currency of $B17,695,000 in government notes of $B100, 20, 10, 5 and 1, and a subsidiary mixed metal coinage of 1-, 5-, 10-, 25- and 50-cent pieces.

Banking. The Royal Bank of Canada took over the business of the local bank in 1912; it has 8 branches. There are 7 government savings banks.

Barclays Bank International have 7 branches, Bank of Nova Scotia have 5 branches and Atlantic Bank 3 branches.

NATURAL RESOURCES

Agriculture. The main agricultural export is sugar, followed by citrus fruit, chiefly grapefruit and oranges, whole, canned, juice and concentrates. Citrus production, 1982, 1,768,000 boxes. Sugar production in 1981 was 1,059,000 tonnes. Banana production began in 1973, and first shipments began in 1974; exports, 1982, 524,000 boxes. [Ed. note: Box of grapefruit, 80 lb., oranges, 90 lb., bananas, 42 lb.]

Livestock (1982): Cattle, 51,000; sheep, 3,000; pigs, 17,000; poultry, 350,000.

Forestry. 2,964 sq. miles, 49% of the total land area, are under forests which include mahogany, cedar, Santa Maria, pine and rosewood, and many secondary hardwoods of known or probable market value, as well as woods suitable for pulp production. Exports of forest produce in 1982 amounted to $B3·8m.

Fisheries. Food and game fish are plentiful, and domestic consumption is heavy. The total exported in 1982 was valued at $B12·6m. Turtles—Hawksbill, Loggerhead and Green—are plentiful but as yet are not exported.

INDUSTRY AND TRADE

Industry. In 1982 production of the major commodities was: Sugar, 106,000 tons; molasses, 35,100 tons; cigarettes, 56m.; beer, 818,000 gallons; batteries, 4,836; wheat flour, 10·9m. lb.; fertilizer, 3,600 tons; garments, 577,000. The labour market alternates between full employment, often accompanied by local shortages in the citrus and sugar-cane harvesting (Jan.–July), and under-employment during the wet season (Aug.–Dec.), aggravated by the seasonal nature of the major industries.

Trade Unions. There are more than 25 active credit unions with an estimated membership of 30,000.

Commerce. In 1982 total imports amounted to $B262·9m. Total domestic exports, $B119·6m. The principal domestic exports were timber, sugar, fish products, garments, bananas and citrus fruit.

Total trade between Belize and UK (British Department of Trade returns, in £1,000 sterling):

	1978	1979	1980	1981	1982	1983
Imports to UK	13,120	13,515	13,168	15,050	13,326	11,565
Exports and re-exports from UK	10,807	10,347	11,824	9,995	10,455	8,726

COMMUNICATIONS

Roads. There are four major highways and all principal towns and villages are linked by road to Belmopan and Belize City. In 1982, there were 8,127 licensed vehicles.

Aviation. In 1982, 260,200 passengers arrived and departed on international flights.

Shipping (1981). Registered shipping, 55 sailing vessels, 1,348 net tons, and 323 motor vessels, 745,197 net tons.

Post. Number of telephones (1982), 8,645. The Belize Telecommunication Authority has instituted a country-wide fully automatic telephone dialling facility. There are 6 post offices and 45 rural sub-post offices.

Cinemas (1979). There were 13 cinemas with seating capacity of 10,000.

Newspapers. There were 7 weekly newspapers and 2 monthly magazines in 1983.

JUSTICE, RELIGION, EDUCATION AND WELFARE

Justice. There are 3 magistrates' courts in Belize and 1 in each district town. The police force contained (1978) 30 officers and 470 n.c.o.s and constables.

Religion. In 1982 about 62% of the population was Roman Catholic and 28% Protestant, including Anglican, Methodist, Seventh Day Adventist, Mennonite, Nazarene, Jehovah's Witness, Pentecostal and Baptist. There was a small group of Bahai.

Education. In 1982, 196 primary schools had a total enrolment of 35,081 pupils; 22 secondary schools, 6,289 pupils; and 5 other technical schools with 619 students. In Sept. 1979 the Belize College of Arts, Science and Technology was opened for post-sixth form courses. The Teachers' College offers courses for primary school teachers. The 3-year course leads to a teachers' diploma granted by the University of the West Indies.

Health. In 1983 there was 1 general hospital and 6 district hospitals with 75 doctors and 578 hospital beds; one private hospital had 3 doctors and 15 beds.

DIPLOMATIC REPRESENTATIVES

Of Belize in Great Britain (15 Thayer St., London, W1)
High Commissioner: Rudolph Castillo (accredited 20 May 1983).

Of Great Britain in Belize (Belize Hse., Belmopan)
High Commissioner: F. S. E. Trew.

Of the USA in Belize (Gabourel Lane, Belize City)
Ambassador: Malcolm R. Barnebey.

Books of Reference

Abstract of Statistics 1981. Government Printer, Belize City, 1982
Bianchi, W. J., *Belize: The Controversy Between Guatemala and Great Britain.* New York, 1959
Dobson, D., *A History of Belize.* Belize, 1973
Grant, C. H., *The Making of Modern Belize.* CUP, 1976
Setzekorn, W. D., *Formerly British Honduras: A Profile of the New Nation of Belize.* Ohio Univ. Press, 1981
Woodward, R. L., Jr, *Belize.* [Bibliography] Oxford and Santa Barbara, 1980

BENIN

República Populaire du Benin

Capital: Porto Novo
Population: 3·91m. (1983)
GNP per capita: US$300 (1980)

HISTORY. The territory of the present State was occupied by France in 1892 and was constituted a division of French West Africa in 1904 under the name of Dahomey. It became an independent republic within the French Community on 4 Dec. 1958, and acquired full independence on 1 Aug. 1960.

In the sixth *coup* since independence, Maj. Mathieu (now Ahmed) Kerekou came to power on 26 Oct. 1972 and proclaimed a Marxist–Leninist state, whose name was altered from Dahomey to Benin in Dec. 1975.

AREA AND POPULATION. Benin is bounded east by Nigeria, north by Niger and Upper Volta, west by Togo and south by the Gulf of Guinea. The area is 112,622 sq. km, and the population, census 1979, 3,338,240. Estimate (1983) 3,905,000. In 1979, 48% of the inhabitants were male, 14·2% urban and 49% were under 15 years of age. The seat of government is Porto Novo (132,000 inhabitants in 1979); the chief port and business centre is Cotonou (327,600); other important towns are Natitingou (50,800), Abomey (41,000), Kandi (31,000), Ouidah (30,000) and Parakou (23,000).

French is the official language, while 47% of the people speak Fon, 12% Adja, 10% Bariba, 9% Yoruba, 5% Somba and 5% Aizo.

CLIMATE. In coastal parts there is an equatorial climate, with a long rainy season from March to July and a short rainy season in Oct. and Nov. The dry season increases in length from the coast, with inland areas having rain only between May and Sept. Porto Novo. Jan. 82°F (27·8°C), July 78°F (25·6°C). Annual rainfall 52″ (1,300 mm). Cotonou. Jan. 81°F (27·2°C), July 77°F (25°C). Annual rainfall 53″ (1,325 mm).

CONSTITUTION AND GOVERNMENT. Under a *Loi fondamentale* adopted in Aug. 1977, the sole political party is the *Parti de la Revolution Populaire du Bénin;* its Congress held in Nov. 1979 elected a Central Committee of 45 members to direct Party policy and to appoint the 13-member Political Bureau.

There is a unicameral legislature, the National Revolutionary Assembly of 336 People's Commissioners elected on 20 Nov. 1979 from the sole list of the PRPB. On 4 Feb. 1980 this took over the responsibility for state policy from the former National Council of the Revolution.

The Assembly elects the President, who appoints and leads a National Executive Council composed in Jan. 1983 as follows:

President, Minister of National Defence: Lieut.-Col. Ahmed Kerekou.
Foreign Affairs and Co-operation: Tiamiou Ajibade. *Interior and Public Security:* Lieut.-Col. Michel Alladayé. *Finance:* Lieut.-Col. Isidore Amoussou. *Industry, Mines and Energy:* Lieut.-Col. Barthélémy Ohouens. *Transport and Communications:* Lieut.-Col. Bouraima Taofiqui. *Justice:* Lieut.-Col. Francois Dossou. *Labour and Social Affairs:* Maj. Adolphe Biaou. *Information and Propaganda:* Amidou Baba-Moussa. *Youth and Sports:* David Gbaguidi. *Tourism and Crafts:* Grégoire Agbahé. *Public Works and Housing:* Girigissou Gado. *Primary Education:* Ali Moussa Traoré. *Secondary Education and Technical Education:* Maj. Edouard Zodehougan. *Higher Education and Scientific Research:* Armand Monteiro. *Health:* Capt. Philippe Akpo. *Trade:* Manasse Ayayi. *Culture and Literacy:* Gratien Tonakpon Capo-Chichi. *Rural Development and Co-operatives:* Justin Gnindéhou. *Planning and Statistics:* Kifouli Salami. *State Farms and Animal Resources:* Alidou Ba Boukary. *State Corporations:* Alidou Koussé. *Inspectorate of Public and Semi-public Enterprises:* Paul Awhangu.

National flag: Green with a red star in the canton.

Local Government. The 6 provinces, Atakora, Borgou, Zou, Ouémé, Atlantique and Mono, each governed by an appointed Prefect and a Provincial Revolutionary Council, are divided into 84 districts.

DEFENCE. National service is for a period of 18 months.

Army. The Army consists of 3 infantry, 1 para-commando, 1 engineer and 1 service battalion, 1 armoured reconnaissance squadron and 1 artillery battery. Strength (1984) 3,000, with an additional 1,100-strong paramilitary gendarmerie.

Navy. A naval force was formed in 1979 with 4 fast gunboats and 2 fast torpedo boats transferred from the USSR, constituting a somewhat over-ambitious flotilla for such a short coastline. Personnel in 1984 was not expected to exceed 200.

Air Force. The Air Force has a strength of about 100 officers and men, 2 twin-turboprop An-26, 1 F.27, 2 C-47 and 3 An-2 transports, 1 Cessna Skymaster, 1 Aero Commander 500, 2 Broussard communications aircraft, up to 6 L-39 jet trainers, an Agusta-Bell 47G and an Alouette II helicopter. A twin-turbofan Corvette is operated by the Air Force on VIP missions for government agencies.

INTERNATIONAL RELATIONS

Membership. Benin is a member of UN, OAU and is an ACP country of EEC.

ECONOMY

Planning. A 10-year development plan (1980–90) envisages an expenditure of 958,800m. francs CFA.

Budget. The 1982 recurrent budget balanced at 46,863m. francs CFA and the investment budget at 96,730m. francs CFA.

Currency. The monetary unit is the *franc CFA (Communauté financière africaine)*, with a parity value of 50 *francs CFA* to 1 French *franc*. There are coins of 1, 2, 5, 10 and 25 *francs CFA*, and banknotes of 50, 100, 500, 1,000 and 5,000 *francs CFA*.

Banking. The *Banque Centrale des Etats de l'Afrique de l'Ouest* is the bank of issue and the central bank. The *Banque Commerciale du Bénin*, in Cotonou, conducts all government business.

ENERGY AND NATURAL RESOURCES

Electricity. The national electricity and water company, *Société Béninoise d'Electricité et d'Eau*, produced 5m. kwh in 1978 from generating plants at Cotonou, Porto-Novo and Parakou. Major development of hydro-electric resources along the Mono river are being conducted jointly with Togo.

Oil. The Semé oilfield, located 10 miles offshore, was discovered in 1968. Production is expected to commence in 1981–82 and should reach 150,000 bbls a day.

Agriculture. 90% of the population subsist by agriculture. The chief products, 1981 (in 1,000 tonnes) were: Cassava, 975; yams, 800; maize, 349; sorghum, 80; groundnuts, 60; beans, 50; rice,16; and sweet potatoes, 14, while cash crops were palm kernels, 75, and palm oil, 34. Cotton cultivation has been successfully introduced in the north; coffee cultivation has given good results in the south.

Livestock (1982 in 1,000): Cattle (785), sheep (970), goats (940), pigs (475), poultry (4·45m.), horses (6), asses (1).

Fisheries. Total catch in 1980 was 25,000 tonnes (80% from inland and lagoon waters).

Forestry. There are about 16,000 sq. km of classified forest, mainly in the north. Roundwood production in 1978 was 2·53m. cu. metres.

INDUSTRY AND TRADE

Industry. Industrial plants are few, limited mainly to palm-oil processing and brewing. Under the 1977–80 Plan. a sugar complex was built at Savé and a cement plant at Onigbolo. There are textile mills at Cotonou and Parakou.

Labour. In 1973 the small trade unions were amalgamated to form a single body, now named the *Union Nationale des Syndicats des Travaillers du Bénin*.

Commerce. Imports in 1978, 60,210m. francs CFA; exports, 5,776m. francs CFA. The principal imports in 1975 (in 1m. francs CFA): Textiles, 5,744; machinery, 5,415; motor vehicles and parts, 3,852; clothing and footwear, 2,877. The principal exports were: Cotton lint, 1,542; palm-oil, 828; cocoa beans, 642; cement, 556. In 1978, France provided 29% and the UK 13% of imports, while of exports the Netherlands took 28%, Japan 27% and France 24%.

Total trade between Benin and UK (British Department of Trade returns, in £1,000 sterling):

	1979	1980	1981	1982	1983
Imports to UK	2,558	2,856	896	1,227	2,887
Exports and re-exports from UK	12,480	13,119	18,611	14,941	10,577

Tourism. There were 23,033 foreign tourists in 1977.

COMMUNICATIONS

Roads. There were 6,937 km of roads in 1974. There were 17,000 motor cars and 9,500 goods vehicles in 1974.

Railways. There are 579 km of metre-gauge railway. One line connects Cotonou with Parakou (438 km) and is to be extended to Dosso (in Niger); the second runs from Cotonou *via* Porto-Novo Pobé (107 km); and the third from Cotonou *via* Ouidah to Segboroué on the Togo frontier (34 km), continuing to Lomé. In 1979 1·6m. passengers and 322,00 tonnes of freight were carried.

Aviation. In 1980, 75,100 passengers used Cotonou airport. There are other airports at Abomey, Natitingou, Kandi and Parakou.

Shipping. In 1979, 144m. tonnes were unloaded and 1m. tonnes loaded at the port of Cotonou. There were (1979) 8 vessels of 1,074 GRT registered in Benin.

Post and Broadcasting. There were, in 1975, 9,624 telephones. Telegraph lines connect Cotonou with Togo, Niger and Senegal. In 1981 there were 65,000 radios and 12,500 television receivers.

Cinemas. In 1976 there were 4 cinemas with a seating capacity of 4,400.

Newspapers. In 1980 there was 1 daily newspaper with a circulation of 10,000.

JUSTICE, RELIGION, EDUCATION AND WELFARE

Justice. The Supreme Court is at Cotonou. There are Magistrates Courts in Cotonou, Porto-Novo, Natitingou, Abomey, Kandi, Ouidah and Parakou, and a *tribunal de conciliation* in each district. Judges at provincial and district level are appointed by and responsible to the Executive Council.

Religion. 66% of the population follow animist beliefs, chiefly Voodoo, 17% are Christian, mainly Roman Catholic, and 15% Moslem.

Education. There were, in 1979, 357,348 pupils in primary schools, 64,275 in secondary schools and (1977) 3,239 students in technical schools. The University of Benin (Cotonou) had 3,003 students in 1979.

Health. In 1976 there were 361 hospitals and dispensaries with 4,394 beds, 93 doctors, 10 dentists, 34 pharmacists and 243 midwives.

DIPLOMATIC REPRESENTATIVES

Of Benin in Great Britain
Chargé d'Affaires: Alexandre Ladipo (resides in Paris).

Of Great Britain in Benin
Ambassador: W. E. H. Whyte, CMG (resides in Lagos).

Of the USA in Benin (Rue Caporal Anami Bernard, Cotonou)
Chargé d'Affaires: Charles H. Twining.

Of Benin to the United Nations
Ambassador: Simon Ifédé Ogouma.

Book of Reference

Ronen, D., *Dahomey: Between Tradition and Modernity.* Cornell Univ. Press, 1975

BERMUDA

Capital: Hamilton
Population: 54,893 (1980)
GNP per capita: US$11,050 (1980)

HISTORY. The Spaniards visited the islands in 1515, but, according to a 17th-century French cartographer, they were discovered in 1503 by Juan Bermudez, after whom they were named. No settlement was made, and they were uninhabited until a party of colonists under Sir George Somers was wrecked there in 1609. A company was formed for the 'Plantation of the Somers' Islands', as they were called at first, and in 1684 the Crown took over the government.

AREA AND POPULATION. Bermuda consists of a group of some 150 small islands (about 20 inhabited), situated in the western Atlantic (32° 18′ N. lat., 64° 46′ W. long.); the nearest point of the mainland, about 570 miles distant, is Cape Hatteras, N.C., and 690 miles from New York.

The area is 20·59 sq. miles (53·3 sq. km), of which 2·3 sq. miles were leased in 1941 for 99 years to the US Government for naval and air bases. The civil population (*i.e.*, excluding British and American military, naval and air force personnel) in 1980 (Census) was 54,893.

Chief town, Hamilton; population, about 3,000.

In 1981 there were 783 live births, 579 marriages and 452 deaths; infantile mortality rate was 14 per 1,000 live births.

CLIMATE. A pleasantly warm and humid climate, with up to 60″ (1,500 mm) of rain, spread evenly throughout the year. Hamilton. Jan. 63°F (17·2°C), July 79°F (26·1°C). Annual rainfall 59″ (1,463 mm).

CONSTITUTION AND GOVERNMENT. Bermuda is a colony with representative government. Under the constitution of 8 June 1968 the Governor, appointed by the Crown, is normally bound to accept the advice of the Cabinet in matters other than external affairs, defence, internal security and the police, for which he retains special responsibility. The Cabinet is appointed from among members of the bicameral legislature, on the recommendation of the Premier. The Senate, of whom one or two members may serve on Cabinet, consists of 11 members. As a result of a Constitutional Conference held in Feb. 1979, it was decided that 5 Senators would be appointed by the Governor on the recommendation of the Premier, 3 by the Governor on the recommendation of the Opposition Leader and 3 by the Governor in his own discretion. The 40 members of the House of Assembly are elected 2 from each of 20 constituencies under full universal, adult suffrage. The general election on 18 May 1976 resulted in the return of 26 members of the United Bermuda Party and 14 members of the Progressive Labour Party. A by-election was held on 21 Sept. 1976 resulting in a total of 25 members of the United Bermuda Party and 15 members of the Progressive Labour Party. A general election was held on 6 Feb. 1983, which resulted in the United Bermuda Party being returned to power. The United Bermuda Party won 26 seats and the Progressive Labour Party, 14.

Governor: (Vacant).
Premier: John W. D. Swan.
Flag: The British Red Ensign with the badge of the Colony in the fly.

DEFENCE. The Bermuda Regiment had 630 men and women in 1982.

ECONOMY

Budget. Revenue and expenditure in $B for years ending 31 March:

	1978–79	1979–80	1980–81	1981–82[1]	1982–83
Revenue	91,392,263	105,207,166	125,232,000	131,966,000	155,129,150
Expenditure	85,901,549	101,224,172	122,936,000	129,821,000	154,858,550

[1] Estimate.

211

Expenditure in $B1,000 (excluding capital items) was earmarked as follows:

	1978–79	1979–80	1980–81	1981–82 [1]	1982–83
Education	15,862	19,189	24,717	21,928	25,919
Health and Social Services	15,619	18,189	21,353	28,478	30,386
Public Works	11,303	12,011	15,284	14,817	13,333
Police	7,034	8,006	9,244	10,623	12,427
Tourism	6,234	7,136	8,124	8,880	10,851
Marine and Air Services	3,301	4,539	8,028	8,312	3,794
Public Transportation	3,430	4,222	4,707	1,496	4,307
Agriculture and Fisheries	3,112	3,874	4,080	4,452	5,077
Post Office	2,923	2,939	3,429	3,404	4,169
All Other Expenditure	17,084	21,119	23,971	27,341	. . .

[1] Estimate.

Chief sources of revenue in 1981–82 were: Customs duties, $65,650,500; employment tax, $13·65m.; companies tax, $8,107,500; land tax, $7,387,000; hotel occupancy tax, $8·03m.; hospital levy, $14·43m.; vehicle licences, $5·15m.; stamp duties, $4·5m.; passenger taxes, $4,385,000.

Public debt, as at 31 March 1981, was $4·3m.

Currency. Decimal currency based on a *Bermuda dollar* of 100 *cents* was introduced 6 Feb. 1970. In March 1984 £1 = 1.47 Bermuda dollars and US$1 = 1 Bermuda dollar. The Bermuda Monetary Authority issues notes in denominations of $100, $50, $20, $10, $5 and $1, and coins in values of 50c, 25c, 10c, 5c and 1c.

Banking. There are 3 banks, the Bank of Bermuda, Ltd, the Bank of N. T. Butterfield and Son, Ltd, and the Bermuda Provident Bank, Ltd.

Weights and Measures. British, except that US instead of Imperial fluid measures are used.

AGRICULTURE. The chief products are fresh vegetables, bananas and citrus fruit. In 1980–81, 708 acres were under cultivation. In 1980 about 5% of the work force were engaged in agriculture, fishing and horticulture.

In 1980, total value of agricultural products was $B5·2m.

Livestock (1982): Cattle, 1,000; pigs, 2,000; goats, 1,000; poultry, 47,000.

TRADE UNIONS. Legislation providing for trade unions was enacted in Oct. 1946, and there are 9 trade unions with a total membership (1981) of 8,806.

COMMERCE. Imports and exports in $B:

	1978	1979	1980	1981
Imports	211,622,000	234,000,000	311,468,000	322,732,859
Exports	41,177,000	31,290,000	36,489,000	29,383,399

The visible adverse balance of trade is more than compensated for by invisible exports, including tourism and off-shore insurance business.

Imports in 1981 from USA, $171m.; UK, $35m.; Canada, $23m.; Japan, $12m.; West Indies, $5m.; Hong Kong, $5m.; France, $4m.; Federal Republic of Germany, $3m.; Netherlands, $2m.; Italy, $2m.

In 1980 the principal imports were food, drink and tobacco ($65m.), finished manufactures ($62m.), mineral fuels ($54m.), chemicals ($31m.); the principal local exports were beauty preparations ($443,000). The bulk of exports comprise sales of fuel to aircraft and ships, and re-exports of pharmaceuticals.

Total trade between Bermuda and UK, in £1,000 sterling (British Department of Trade returns):

	1978	1979	1980	1981	1982	1983
Imports to UK	11,259	3,794	2,900	5,652	5,128	4,019
Exports and re-exports from UK	22,200	17,209	24,499	17,492	18,222	24,924

TOURISM. In 1982, 544,466 tourists visited Bermuda including those arriving by air and cruise ship. Tourism represents 41% of GDP.

COMMUNICATIONS

Roads. In 1948 the railway service was discontinued and a government-operated bus service introduced.

Between 1908 and Aug. 1946 the use of motor vehicles, with the exception of ambulances, fire engines and other essential services, was prohibited. With the passing of the Motor Car Act in 1946, the use of motor vehicles, subject to certain limitations on size and horse-power, became lawful. In 1981, out of 40,402 registered vehicles 14,442 were private cars.

Aviation. American Airlines, Pan American, Delta Airlines and Eastern Airlines maintain regular services between Bermuda and the USA. British Airways also have regular flights through Bermuda linking London with Mexico and the Caribbean. Air Canada Airlines call at Bermuda on their service between Canada, Barbados, Antigua and Trinidad, they also operate services between Bermuda, Toronto, Montreal and Halifax.

Shipping. At 31 Dec. 1981, 71 commercial vessels of 490,996 gross tons and 213 pleasure yachts of 12,140 gross tons were registered at Hamilton. In 1981 the gross tonnage of 544 vessels entered and cleared was 4,494,572 tons.

Post and Broadcasting (1981). There are 15 post offices. The telephone company is privately owned and operated 48,958 telephones in 1982. Cables connect the islands with the USA, Halifax (N.S.) and Tortola, providing connexion with the world.

Radio and television broadcasting is commercial.

Cinemas. There was (1981) 1 cinema with a seating capacity of 1,054.

JUSTICE, EDUCATION AND WELFARE

Justice. There are 4 magistrates' courts, a Supreme Court and a court of appeal. The police had a strength of 415 men and women in 1982.

Education. Education is compulsory between the ages of 5 and 16, and government assistance is given by the payment of grants, and, where necessary, of school fees. Free elementary education was introduced on 1 May 1949 and free secondary education in Sept. 1965. In 1981, there were 11 government nurseries, 6 special units for the handicapped, 18 government primary schools, 9 government secondary schools, the Bermuda College and 4 private, fee-paying schools. Total enrolment was 11,312 pupils.

Health. In 1982 there were 108 doctors.

Books of Reference

Annual Report, 1971. HMSO, 1972
Bermuda Historical Quarterly. 1944 ff.
Dyer, H. T., *The Next 20 Years: A Report on the Development Plans for Bermuda.* Hamilton, 1963
Hayward, S. J., Holt-Gomez, V., and Sterrer, W., *Bermuda's Delicate Balance: People and the Environment.* Hamilton, 1981
Warwick, J. B., (ed.), *Who's Who in Bermuda 1980–81.* Hamilton, 1982
Wilkinson, H. C., *Bermuda from Sail to Steam.* OUP, 1973
Zuill, W. S., *The Story of Bermuda and Her People.* London, 1973

National Library: The Bermuda Library, Hamilton. *Head Librarian:* Mrs M. Skiffington.

BHUTÁN

Druk-yul

Capital: Thimphu
Population: 1·25m. (1983)
GNP per capita: US$80 (1980)

HISTORY. In 1774 the East India Company concluded a treaty with the ruler of Bhután. Under a treaty signed in Nov. 1865 the Bhután Government was granted an annual subsidy. By an amending treaty concluded in Jan. 1910 the British Government undertook to exercise no interference in the internal affairs of Bhután, and the Bhután Government agreed to be guided by the advice of the British Government in regard to its external relations.

The Government of India concluded a fresh treaty with Bhután on 8 Aug. 1949. Under this treaty the Government of Bhután continues to be guided by the Government of India in regard to its external relations, and the Government of India have undertaken not to interfere in the internal administration of Bhután. The subsidy paid to Bhután has been increased to Rs 500,000, and the Government of India agreed to retrocede to Bhután an area of about 32 sq. miles in the territory known as Dewangiri, which was annexed in 1865.

AREA AND POPULATION. Bhután is situated in the eastern Himalayas, between 26° 45′ and 28° N. lat. and between 89° and 92° E. long., bordered on the north and east by Tibet and India, on the west by Sikkim and on the south by India. Extreme length from east to west 190 miles: extreme breadth 90 miles. Area about 18,000 sq. miles (46,600 sq. km); population estimated at approximately 1·25m. (1983). Life expectancy (1977) was 46 years. The capital is at Thimphu. There are 17 districts.

CLIMATE. The climate is largely controlled by altitude. The mountainous north is cold, with perpetual snow on the summits, but the centre has a more moderate climate, though winters are cold, with rainfall under 40″ (1,000 mm). In the south, the climate is humid sub-tropical and rainfall approaches 200″ (5,000 mm).

KING. Jigme Singye Wangchuck, succeeded his father Jigme Dorji Wangchuck who died 21 July 1972.

GOVERNMENT. In 1907 the Tongsa Penlop (the governor of the province of Tongsa in eastern Bhután), Sir Ugyen Wangchuk, GCIE, KCSI, was elected as the first hereditary Maharaja of Bhután. The Bhutánese title is Druk Gyalpo, but his successor is now addressed as King of Bhután. From Oct. 1969 the absolute monarchy was changed to a form of 'democratic monarchy'. The National Assembly (*Tshogdu*) was reinstituted in 1953. It has approximately 150 members and meets twice a year. Two-thirds are representatives of the people and are elected for a 3-year term. All Bhutánese over 25 years may be candidates. Ten monastic representatives are elected by regional ecclesiastical bodies, while the remaining members are nominated by the King, and include members of the Council of Ministers and the Royal Advisory Council.

The official languages are Dzongkha, Nepali and English.

National flag: Diagonally yellow over orange, over all in the centre a white dragon.

Local government: There are 17 districts, each under a governor *(Dzongda)*.

DEFENCE

Army. There is an Army of about 4,000 men.

INTERNATIONAL RELATIONS

Membership. Bhután is a member of UN.

214

ECONOMY

Planning. The Government of Bhután has drawn up five 5-year development plans (1961–65, 1966–70, 1971–76, 1977–81, 1982–86), with the active co-operation and financial support of the Government of India. Educational facilities are being expanded and medical facilities are being provided. Forest and mineral wealth is to be exploited. About 1,900 km of new roads have been built.

Budget. The budget for 1982–83 envisaged expenditure of N635m. and revenue of N165m.

Currency. Paper currency has been introduced, known as the *Ngultrum*. Silver currency is known as *Tikchung*. Indian currency is also legal tender.

Banking. The Bank of Bhután was established in 1968. The headquarters are at Phuntsholing with 14 branches throughout the country.

ENERGY AND NATURAL RESOURCES

Electricity. In 1974 construction work began on the Chukha hydro-electric project at a cost of US$92m. and in 1979, 15 towns and 97 villages had electricity.

Minerals. Large deposits of limestone, marble, dolomite, graphite, lead, copper, slate, coal, talc, gypsum, beryl, mica, pyrites and tufa have been found.

Agriculture. The area under cultivation in 1978 was 5,534 sq. km. The chief products are rice, millet, wheat, barley, maize, cardomom, potatoes, oranges, apples, handloom cloth, timber and yaks. Extensive and valuable forests abound.

Livestock (1982): Horses, 21,000; asses, 18,000; cattle, 312,000; pigs, 56,000; sheep, 44,000; poultry, 187,000.

INDUSTRY AND TRADE

Industry. In 1980 there were about 40 small-scale industrial units and also a cement plant, a fruit processing factory, a tea-chest ply veneer factory, a resin and turpentine factory and 3 distilleries.

Commerce. Trade with India is considerable but timber, cardomom and liquor are also exported to the Middle East, Singapore and Western Europe. Bhután imported from the UK in 1982 goods valued at £89,000.

Tourism. The country has been opened for tourism since 1974 and it is the largest source of foreign exchange. In 1979–80, 1,500 tourists visited Bhután.

COMMUNICATIONS

Roads. In 1978 there were about 1,775 km of roads. In 1979, there were 2,179 vehicles, of which 1,432 were private cars and 747 buses and trucks.

Post. A modern postal system was introduced in 1962. There are 53 general post offices and 28 branch post offices. In 1979 there were 1,086 km of telephone lines, 15 automatic exchanges and (1978) 1,355 telephones.

Newspapers. There is a government weekly newspaper published in 3 languages (English, Dzongkha and Nepali). Total circulation (1979) about 5,000.

RELIGION, EDUCATION AND WELFARE

Religion. The majority of the people are Mahayana Buddhists of the Drukpa subsect of the Karyud School which was first introduced from Tibet during the 12th century.

Education. In 1980 there were 144 state schools, 1 college and 2 technical schools with 31,892 pupils. There were 1,206 teachers. Many students were receiving training under the Colombo Plan in Australia, New Zealand, Japan, Singapore and UK in 1979.

Health. There were (1980) 12 general hospitals, 39 dispensaries, 43 basic health units, 4 indigenous dispensaries, 3 leprosy hospitals, 1 mobile hospital, 1 health school and 15 malaria eradication centres. In 1979 beds totalled 536 and there were 52 doctors.

DIPLOMATIC REPRESENTATIVE

Of Bhután to the United Nations
Ambassador: Om. Pradhan.

The Government of Bhután is in diplomatic relations with Bangladesh and India at ambassadorial level. Honorary Consuls have also been appointed in Singapore and Hong Kong.

Books of Reference

Bhutan, Himalayan Kingdom. Bhutan Government, Thimphu, 1979
Das, N., *The Dragon Country.* New Delhi, 1973
Labh, K., *India and Bhutan.* New Delhi, 1974
Mehra, G. N., *Bhutan: Land of the Peaceful Dragon.* New Delhi, 1974
Olschak, B. C., *Bhutan: Land of Hidden Treasures.* New Delhi, 1971
Rathore, L. S., *The Changing Bhutan.* New Delhi, 1974
Ronaldshay, the Earl of, *Lands of the Thunderbolt.* 2nd ed. London, 1931
Rose, L. E., *The Politics of Bhutan.* Cornell Univ. Press, 1977
Rustomji, N., *Bhutan: The Dragon Kingdom in Crisis.* OUP, 1978

BOLIVIA

República de Bolivia

Capital: La Paz
Population: 6·08m. (1983)
GNP per capita: US$570 (1980)

HISTORY. Until 1884, when Bolivia was defeated by Chile, she had a strip bordering on the Pacific which contains extensive nitrate beds and at that time the port of Cobija (which no longer exists). She lost this area to Chile; but in Sept. 1953 Chile declared Arica a free port and, although it is no longer a free port for Bolivian imports, Bolivia still has certain privileges.

AREA AND POPULATION. Bolivia is a landlocked state with an area of some 424,160 sq. miles (1,098,580 sq. km). In the series of disastrous wars in the 19th and early 20th centuries its territorial losses to each of 5 neighbouring nations reduced its area from an estimated 1·16m. sq. miles.

The following table shows the area and population of the departments (the capitals of each are given in brackets):

Departments	Area (sq. km)	Census Aug.- Sept. 1950	Census 1976	Per sq. km 1975
La Paz (La Paz)	133,985	948,446	1,456,078	12·50
Cochabamba (Cochabamba)	55,631	490,475	720,952	15·57
Potosí (Potosí)	118,218	534,399	657,743	7·98
Santa Cruz (Santa Cruz)	370,621	286,145	710,724	1·36
Chuquisaca (Sucre)	51,524	282,930	358,516	9·69
Tarija (Tarija)	37,623	126,752	186,704	5·95
Oruro (Oruro)	53,588	210,260	310,409	6·93
Beni (Trinidad)	213,564	119,770	168,367	0·99
Pando (Cobija)	63,827	19,804	34,493	0·55
Total	1,098,581	3,019,031 [1]	4,687,718	4·85

[1] An official estimate allowing for under-enumeration; the total actually recorded was 2,704,165.

Total population (estimate 1983) 6,081,722.

Population (census 1976) of the principal towns: La Paz, 654,713; Santa Cruz, 255,568; Cochabamba, 204,414; Oruro, 124,414; Potosí, 77,233; Sucre, 63,259; Tarija, 38,500.

Crude birth rate, 1968, 42 per 1,000 population; crude death rate (1978), 17·4; crude marriage rate (1958), 4; infantile mortality, 140 (1978) per 1,000 live births.

The language of the educated classes is Spanish, that of the majority of Indians, Aymará (25·2%) or Quechua (34·4%).

CLIMATE. The very varied geography of Bolivia produces several different climates. The two most significant are the low-lying areas in the Amazon Basin, which are very warm and damp throughout the year, with heavy rainfall from Nov. to March, and the alti-plano, which is generally dry between May and Nov. with abundant sunshine, but the nights are cold in June and July, while the months from Dec. to March are the wettest. La Paz. Jan. 53°F (11·7°C), July 47°F (8·3°C). Annual rainfall 23″ (574 mm). Sucre. Jan. 55°F (13°C), July 49°F (9·4°C). Annual rainfall 27″ (675 mm).

CONSTITUTION AND GOVERNMENT. The Republic of Bolivia was proclaimed on 6 Aug. 1825; its first constitution was adopted on 19 Nov. 1826.

La Paz is the actual capital and seat of the Government, but Sucre is the legal capital and the seat of the judiciary.

The following is a list of presidents since 1966 and the date on which they took office:

Gen. René Barrientos Ortuño (Constitutional President killed in air accident), 6 Aug. 1966–27 April 1969.
Dr Luis Adolfo Siles Salinas (deposed), 27 April 1969–26 Sept. 1969.
Gen. Alfredo Ovando Candia, 26 Sept. 1969–6 Oct. 1970.
Gen. Juan José Torres, 7 Oct. 1970–21 Aug. 1971.
Gen. Hugo Banzer Suarez, 21 Aug. 1971–21 July 1978.
Gen. Juan Pereda Asbun, 21 July 1978–24 Nov. 1978.

Gen. David Padilla Arancibia, 24 Nov. 1978–8 Aug. 1979.
Dr Walter Guevara Arze (deposed), 8 Aug. 1979–1 Nov. 1979.
Dr Lydia Gueiler Tejada (deposed), 16 Nov. 1979–17 July 1980.
Maj.-Gen. Luis García Meza Tejada (resigned), 18 July 1980–4 Aug. 1981.
Military Junta, 4 Aug. 1981–4 Sept. 1981.
Gen. Celso Torrelio Villa, (resigned), 4 Sept. 1981–19 July 1982.
Brig.-Gen. Guido Vildoso Calderón, 21 July 1982–10 Oct. 1982.

Following elections in July 1979 which were inconclusive an interim President was chosen with the agreement of the three parties who had polled most votes. For details of political history 1970–78 *see* THE STATESMAN'S YEAR-BOOK, 1980–81 and for the period 1978–1980 *see* THE STATESMAN'S YEAR-BOOK, 1983–84.

The President and Vice-President are elected by universal suffrage for a four year term. The President appoints the members of his Cabinet from candidates nominated by the Senate. There is a bicameral legislature; the Senate comprises 27 members, 3 from each department, and the Chamber of Deputies 117 members, all elected for 4 years. The Congress elected on 29 June 1980 was dissolved following the *coup* on 17 July 1980, but reconvened on 6 Oct. 1982.

The Cabinet consists of the President and 18 Ministers of State.

President: Dr Siles Zuazo (sworn in 10 Oct. 1982).

Foreign Affairs: José Ortíz Mercado. *Interior:* Federico Alvarez Plata. *Defence:* Manuel Cárdenas Mallo. *Aviation:* Gen. Oscar Villa Urioste. *Finance:* Fernando Báptista Gumucio. *Planning:* Roberto Jordán Pando. *Education and Culture:* Alcides Alvara do Daza. *Transport and Communications:* Hernando Poppe Martínez. *Industry, Commerce and Tourism:* Humberto Mur Gutiérrez. *Labour:* Ramiro Barrenechea. *Mining and Metallurgy:* Carlos Carvajal Nava. *Health:* Javier Torrez Goitia. *Agriculture and Peasants Affairs:* Simón Yampara Huarachi. *Energy and Hydrocarbons:* Jorge Medina Pinedo. *Housing:* Jaime Ponce Garcia. *Secretary-General to the Presidency:* Benjamín Miguel Harb. *Secretary-General of Integration:* Jorge Agreda Valderrama. *Secretary-General of Information:* Mario Rueda Péna.

National flag: Three horizontal stripes of red, yellow, green, with the arms of Bolivia in the centre.

National anthem: Bolivianos, el hado propicio (words by I. de Sanjinés; tune by B. Vincenti).

Local Government: The republic is divided into 9 departments, established in Jan. 1826, with 98 provinces administered by sub-prefects, and 1,272 cantons administered by corregidores. The supreme authority in each department is vested in a prefect appointed by the President.

DEFENCE. Bolivia is divided into 8 military districts, with divisional headquarters in Viacha, Oruro, Villa Montes, Camiri, Roboré, Riberalta, Santa Cruz, Cochabamba; regional HQ are located at La Paz, Sucre, Tarija, Potosí, Trinidad and Cobija. There is selective conscription for 12 months at the age of 18 years.

Army. The Army consists of 18 infantry, 6 cavalry, 2 mechanized, 3 artillery, 2 ranger and 1 parachute regiments, and 2 armoured anti-tank and 6 engineer battalions. Equipment includes 24 EE-9 Cascavel armoured cars. Strength is 20,000.

Navy. A small Navy exists for river and lake patrol comprising 36 patrol craft operating in Lake Titicaca and the Bolivia-Paraguay 6,000-mile river systems, 1 transport (a gift from Venezuela for use to and from Bolivian free zones in Argentina and Uruguay) and 2 hospital ships (one a gift from USA).

Personnel in 1984 totalled 4,000 officers and men including marines. Most training of officers and petty officers is carried out in Argentina. The junior ratings are almost entirely converted soldiers.

Air Force. The Air Force, established in 1923, has 3 combat-capable squadrons, equipped with 5 F-86F jet fighters, 12 Canadian-built T-33 armed jet trainers, and 5 T-6G armed piston-engined trainers, for counter-insurgency operations. On order are 12 Mirage 50 fighters. A search and rescue helicopter squadron has 6 Brazilian-assembled Gaviãos (Lamas). Other types in service include Brazilian T-23 Uirapuru and American T-41 primary trainers, Italian SF.260M and Swiss turboprop-powered Pilatus PC-7 basic trainers, 16 PC-6 Turbo Porter utility aircraft, 1 Electra four-turboprop transport, 6 Fokker F.27 and 5 Israeli-built Arava twin-turboprop light transports, 3 Convair 580 twin-turboprop transports, 2 C-130H/L-100-30 Hercules, 8 C-47 and 2 Convair 440 piston-engined transports with which a military airline service is operated, about 30 Cessna single- and twin-engined light aircraft and helicopters. Personnel strength is about 4,000.

INTERNATIONAL RELATIONS

Membership. Bolivia is a member of UN, OAS, LAIA (formerly Lafta), the Andean Group and the Amazon Pact.

External Debt. The contracted external debt was US$3,641m., Dec. 1980.

ECONOMY

Budget. Revenue and expenditures in 1m. *pesos bolivianos* balanced as follows: In 1982 there was a projected budget deficit of $b.110,959m.

Currency. On 1 Jan. 1963 the *peso boliviano* ($b.) was introduced. Exchange rates were $b.500 = US$1 and $b.736 = £1 in March 1984.

Banking. The Banco Central de Bolivia was established in 1911 as Banco de la Nacion Boliviana and re-organized in 1928. The Bank was nationalized in 1939. At 30 Dec. 1982 the Bank's gross gold and foreign exchange reserves amounted to US$214·1m.

Weights and Measures. The metric system of weights and measures is used by the administration and prescribed by law, but the old Spanish system is also employed.

ENERGY AND NATURAL RESOURCES

Electricity. Electric power production is expanding. Installed capacity was estimated at 428,595 kw. at the end of 1978. Estimated production from all sources (1978), 1,340,996 mwh.

Oil and Gas. There are petroleum and natural gas deposits in the Santa Cruz-Camiri areas. A pipeline for crude oil connects Caranda (Santa Cruz) with the Pacific coast at Arica (Chile) and a natural gas pipeline to Argentina was inaugurated in May 1972. All production, refining and internal distribution is now in the hands of *Yacimientos Petroliferos Fiscales Bolivianos* (the State Petroleum Organization). Total production of petroleum and condensates in 1981 was estimated at 8·1m. bbls. Production of natural gas in 1981 was estimated at 175,478m. cu. ft.

Minerals. Mining is the most important industry, accounting for about 69% of the foreign-exchange earnings. About half the mineral mined is tin. Tin mines are at altitudes of from 12,000 to 18,000 ft, where few except native Indians can stand the conditions; transport is costly. Bolivian tin is extracted by shaft-mining, frequently very deep; the ore yields only 0·7% or less of tin and is very refractory; tin is exported in concentrates called *barrilla*, through Pacific ports for refining. Smelting capacity was increased in 1980 and it is planned to smelt all the ores from the State Mining Co. but complex ores still have to be exported for smelting. Tin production in 1981 was 27,562 tonnes.

The state industry is being run by the *Corporación Minera de Bolivia* (COMIBOL) employing about 23,000 in mining and administrative capacities.

Alluvial gold deposits in the Alto Beni region are being exploited. Co-operative mines at Tipuani produced 770 kg in 1978.

Foreign firms are seeking exploration rights for uranium and a small uranium processing plant was opened in Oct. 1980 at Cotaje (Potosí province). Large deposits of salt are found near Lake Poopó and in the south of Bolivia.

Agriculture. The extensive and still largely undeveloped region east of the Andes comprises about three-quarters of the entire area of the country, and since the agrarian reform of 1952 sugar-cane, rice and cotton have been grown in this *Oriente* in increasing abundance, reaching self-sufficiency in all these products. Output in tonnes in 1980 was: Sugar-cane, 2·83m.; rice, 87,700; coffee, 19,600; maize, 327,700; potatoes, 720,000; wheat, 50,000; cotton (lint), 7,500; cocoa, 25,200.

The public lands of the State have an area of about 245,000 sq. miles, of which 104,000 sq. miles are reserved for special colonization.

A colony of Jewish refugees was established in 1940 at Buena Tierra, 60 miles east of La Paz and, more recently, Japanese and Okinawan settlements in the region of Santa Cruz. The Bolivian Development Corporation has a programme for relief of over-population on the barren altiplano and in 1964 resettled 1,217 families in tropical areas.

Livestock: In 1982 there were 4·1m. head of cattle, mostly in the Santa Cruz and Beni departments; some are exported to Peru; horses, 410,000; asses, 790,000; pigs, 1·6m.; sheep, 9·2m.; goats, 3·1m.; poultry, 9·2m.

Forestry. Tropical forests with woods ranging from the 'iron tree' to the light *palo de balsa* are beginning to be exploited. In 1962 the Forestry Service announced proved reserves of 46·3m. hectares, plus a similar amount available for immediate development.

INDUSTRY AND TRADE

Industry. There are few industrial establishments and the country relies on imports for the supply of many consumer goods. However a new investment law passed in 1971 provides incentives and protection for new investment, both foreign and domestic, and for reinvestment in various fields including manufacturing industry, mining, agriculture, construction and tourism.

Labour. The Ministry of Planning estimated economically active population in 1970 at 1·48m., of whom 1m. were employed in agriculture, 118,300 in industrial manufacture, 35,100 in construction, 74,000 in commerce and finance, 65,000 in central and local government, 47,800 in mining and 41,900 in transport. The ban on trade unions, imposed in 1974, was lifted in 1978 but re-imposed in 1980.

Commerce. The value of imports and exports in US$1,000 has been as follows:

	1977	1978	1979	1980	1981	1982
Imports	552,000	848,200	984,000	833,160	917,081	496,084
Exports	556,000	640,300	793,000	942,000	995,298	898,176

Tin ore remains the principal export. Total exports, 1982, of all minerals, in concentrates, ingots or solder, were valued at US$419·4m.

Bolivia having no seaport, imports and exports pass chiefly through the ports of Arica and Antofagasta in Chile, Mollendo-Matarani in Peru, through La Quiaca on the Bolivian-Argentine border and through river-ports on the rivers flowing into the Amazon. The chief imports are lard, flour, cooking oil, iron and steel products, mining machinery, pharmaceuticals, paper products and textiles.

Total trade between Bolivia and UK for 5 years (British Department of Trade returns in £1,000 sterling):

	1979	1980	1981	1982	1983
Imports to UK	37,619	33,179	36,800	20,899	14,834
Exports and re-exports from UK	9,594	8,684	12,676	4,943	4,711

COMMUNICATIONS

Roads. A highway, in poor condition, 497 km long, runs from Cochabamba to the lowland farming region of Santa Cruz. La Paz and Oruro are also connected by a metalled road. Of other main highways (unmetalled) there is one from La Paz through Guaqui into Peru, another from La Paz, *via* Oruro, Potosí, Tarija and Bermejo, into Argentina, with branches to Cochabamba, Sucre and Camiri, passable throughout the year except at the height of the rainy season, and others from Villazón to Villa Montes *via* Tarija, passable during the dry season. The total length of the road system is 37,708 km (1977). Motor vehicles in use in 1980, 134,790, including 65,540 cars, 69,250 heavy goods vehicles and buses and 1,133 agricultural tractors.

Railways. In 1964 Bolivian National Railways (ENFE) was formed by the amalgamation of the Bolivian Government Railways, Bolivian Railway Co. and the Bolivian section of the Antofagasta (Chile) & Bolivia Railway. The Guaqui-La Paz Railway, formerly operated by Peru, became part of ENFE in 1973. Access to the Pacific is by 3 routes: to Antofagasta and Arica in Chile, and to Mollendo in Peru *via* Guaqui, the Lake Titicaca train ferry to Puno (Peru), then rail to the coast. Construction began in 1978 of a 150-km line linking Puno with Desaguadero on the Bolivian border which would by-pass the train ferry, though gauge difference would still prevent through running to Peru. Current network totals 3,538 km of metre gauge, comprising unconnected Eastern (1,386 km) and Western (2,152 km) systems. In 1980 the railways carried 1·7m. passengers and 1·3m. tonnes of freight.

Aviation. The national airline is Lloyd Aéreo Boliviano. The airline runs regular services between La Paz and Lima, São Paulo, Buenos Aires, Miami, Caracas, Salta and Arica as well as many internal services. Eastern Airways runs regular flights between La Paz, Lima, Buenos Aires, Santiago and Asunción linking Bolivia (*via* Lima) to the USA. Lufthansa links Bolivia with Europe. Other airlines serving Bolivia are Aerolineas Argentinas, Cruzeiro, Aero Peru and Lan Chile.

Shipping. Traffic on Lake Titicaca between Guaqui and Puno is carried on by the steamers of the Peruvian Corporation. About 12,000 miles of rivers, in 4 main systems (Beni, Pilcomayo, Titicaca-Desaguadero, Mamoré), are open to navigation by light-draught vessels.

Post and Broadcasting. In Bolivia there were, in 1978, 458 post offices, of these, 205 provided telegraph and telephone services together with a further 245 offices for telegraph and telephone service only. There is telephone service in the cities of La Paz, Cochabamba, Oruro, Sucre, Potosí, Santa Cruz, Tarija, Camiri, Tupiza, Villazon, Riberalta and Trinidad with (1982), 144,300 telephones. There are about 119 broadcasting stations, of which 7 are state-owned. There is a commercial government television service.

Newspapers. There are 6 daily newspapers in La Paz, 2 in Oruro, and 2 in Cochabamba. Several other towns have regular newspapers devoted to local news, but most of them appear only a few times a week. An economic monthly journal *Revista Economica* and 4 daily newspapers are produced in Santa Cruz.

JUSTICE, RELIGION, EDUCATION AND WELFARE

Justice. Justice is administered by the Supreme Court, superior district courts (of 5 or 7 judges) and courts of local justice. The Supreme Court, with headquarters at Sucre, is divided into two sections, civil and criminal, of 5 justices each, with the Chief Justice presiding over both. Members of the Supreme Court are chosen on a two-thirds vote of Congress.

Religion. The Roman Catholic is the recognized religion of the state; the free exercise of other forms of worship is permitted. The Catholic Church is under a cardinal (in Sucre), an archbishop (in La Paz). 6 bishops (Cochabamba, Santa Cruz, Oruro, Potosí, Riberalta and Tarija) and vicars apostolic (titular bishops resident in Cueva, Trinidad, San Ignacio de Velasco, Riberalta and Rurrenabaque).

By a law of 11 Oct. 1911 all marriages must be celebrated by the civil authorities. Divorce is permitted by a law enacted on 15 April 1932.

Education. Primary instruction is free and obligatory between the ages of 6 and 14 years. Estimates for 1974 show that 989,858 children between 6 and 14 years attended school. All illiterates between 15 and 50 years are obliged to attend literacy classes and in 1977 this represented 40% of the population.

At Sucre, Oruro, Potosí, Cochabamba, Santa Cruz, Tarija, Trinidad and La Paz are universities; La Paz is the most important of them while the San Francisco Xavier University at Sucre is one of the oldest in America, founded in 1624.

Health. In 1972 there were 2,143 doctors.

DIPLOMATIC REPRESENTATIVES

Of Bolivia in Great Britain (106 Eaton Sq., London, SW1W 9AD)
Chargé d'Affaires: Carlos Quintanilla.

Of Great Britain in Bolivia (Avenida Arce 2732–2754, La Paz)
Ambassador: S. F. St C. Duncan.

Of Bolivia in the USA (3014 Massachusetts Ave, NW, Washington, D.C. 20008)
Ambassador: Mariano Baptista Gumucio.

Of the USA in Bolivia (Banco Popular Del Peru Bldg, La Paz)
Ambassador: Edwin G. Corr.

Of Bolivia to the United Nations
Ambassador: Jorge Gumucio Granier.

Books of Reference

There is a weekly official gazette.

Anuario Geográfico y Estadístico de la República de Bolivia
Anuario del Comercia Exterior de Bolivia
Boletín Mensual de Información Estadística
Baptista Gumucio, M., *Cultural Policy in Bolivia.* UNESCO, 1978
Fifer, J. V., *Bolivia: Land, Location and Politics Since 1825.* CUP, 1972
Guillermo, L., *A History of the Bolivian Labour Movement 1848–1971.* CUP, 1977
Klein, H., *Bolivia: The Evolution of a Multi-Ethnic Society.* OUP, 1982
Mitchell, C., *The Legacy of Populism in Bolivia.* New York, 1977

BOTSWANA

Capital: Gaborone
Population: 941,027 (1981)
GNP per capita: US$910 (1980)

HISTORY. In 1885 the territory was declared to be within the British sphere; in 1889 it was included in the sphere of the British South Africa Company, but was never administered by the company; in 1890 a Resident Commissioner was appointed, and in 1895, on the annexation of the Crown Colony of British Bechuanaland to the Cape of Good Hope, the British Government was in favour of transferring the Protectorate to the BSA Company, but the three major chiefs of the Bakwena, the Bangwaketse and the Bamangwato went to England to protest against this proposal, and agreement was reached that their country should remain a British Protectorate if they ceded a strip of land on the eastern side of the country for railway construction. This railway was built in 1896–97.

On 30 Sept. 1966 the Bechuanaland Protectorate became an independent and sovereign member of the Commonwealth under the name of the Republic of Botswana.

AREA AND POPULATION. Botswana comprises the territory lying between the Molopo River on the south and the Zambezi on the north, and extending from the Transvaal Province and Zimbabwe on the east to South-West Africa on the west. Area about 222,000 sq. miles (582,000 sq. km); population, census of 1971, was 630,379 (census, 1981, 941,027).

The main business centres (with estimated population, 1980) are Gaborone (1983, 59,657), Francistown (32,000), Selebi-Pikwe (29,000), Kanye (22,000), Lobatse (20,000), Mochudi (20,000), Molepolole (19,000), Mahalapye (19,000), Maun (16,000).

The seat of government is at Gaborone.

The official language is English; the national language is Setswana.

CLIMATE. Most of the country is sub-tropical, but there are arid areas in the south and west. In winter, days are warm and nights cold, with occasional frosts. Summer heat is tempered by prevailing north-east winds. Rainfall comes mainly in summer, from Oct. to April, while the rest of the year is almost completely dry with very high sunshine amounts. Gaborone. Jan. 79°F (26·1°C), July 55°F (12·8°C). Annual rainfall 21" (538 mm).

CONSTITUTION AND GOVERNMENT. The Constitution of the republic is based on the Constitution which came into effect in March 1965, with some minor alterations.

The executive rests with the President of the Republic who is responsible to the National Assembly.

The National Assembly consists of 36 members (32 elected by universal suffrage, 4 nominated by the President, the Attorney-General and the Speaker *ex-officio*). The general election, held in Oct. 1979, returned 33 members of the Botswana Democratic Party, 1 Botswana People's Party and 2 Botswana National Front.

The President is an *ex-officio* member of the Assembly. If the President is already a member of the National Assembly, a by-election will be held in the constituency of that member.

There is also a House of Chiefs to advise the Government. It consists of the Chiefs of the 8 tribes who were autonomous during the days of the British protectorate, and 4 members elected by and from among the sub-chiefs in 4 districts.

The first President of Botswana, who was re-elected 3 times, was Sir Seretse Khama, KBE, who died 13 July 1980.

President of the Republic: Dr Quett Ketumile Joni Masire.

In Sept. 1983 the Cabinet was as follows:

Vice President and Minister of Finance and Development Planning: P. S. Mmusi. *Public Service and Information:* D. K. Kwelagobe. *External Affairs:* A. M. Mogwe. *Health:* L. Makgekgenene. *Agriculture:* W. Meswele. *Local Government and Lands:* M. K. Kgabo. *Works and Communications:* C. Blackbeard. *Commerce and Industry:* M. P. K. Nwako. *Mineral Resources and Water Affairs:* Dr G. K. T. Chiepe. *Education:* K. P. Morake. *Home Affairs:* K. L. Disele. *Assistant for Finance and Development Planning:* O. I. Chilume. *Assistant for Local Government and Lands:* J. L. T. Mothibamele. *Assistant for Agriculture:* G. U. S. Matlhabaphiri. *Attorney-General:* Moleleki Mokama. *Speaker of the National Assembly:* J. G. Haskins.

National flag: Light blue with a horizontal black stripe, edged white, across the centre.

Local Government. Local government is carried out by 9 district councils and 4 town councils. Revenue is obtained mainly from local income tax, levied on all inhabitants in the area; from rates in the towns and from central government subventions in the districts.

DEFENCE

Army. A defence force has been created for border control and comprises 1 infantry battalion; group, strength, total armed forces (1983) 2,850.

Air Force. Equipment includes 5 Britten-Norman Defender armed light transports for border patrol, counter-insurgency and casualty evacuation duties, 6 Bulldog piston-engined basic trainers, 2 Skyvan turboprop passenger/cargo transports and 2 Cessna 152 light aircraft. Personnel total about 150.

INTERNATIONAL RELATIONS

Membership. Botswana is a member of UN, OAU, the Commonwealth and is an ACP state of EEC.

ECONOMY

Planning. The National Development Plan 1979–85 envisages a total capital expenditure of P530m., GDP growth of 10·1% per annum, employment growth of 7% and a strong balance of payments.

Budget. Revenue and expenditure (in 1m. Pula) for financial years ending 31 March:

	1979–80	*1980–81*	*1981–82*
Revenues and grants	220	322	310
Expenditure and net lending	227	334	364

Public debt, on 31 March 1980, amounted to P112·8m.

Currency. The currency was formerly the South African Rand but in Aug. 1976 a new currency, the *pula*, was introduced (P1·674 = £1 sterling in March 1984).

Banking. The Standard Bank Ltd and Barclays Bank International have branches in Francistown, Lobatse, Mahalapye, Maun and Gaborone and about 46 agencies throughout the country. A government-financed National Development Bank was founded in 1964. The Bank of Credit and Commerce (Botswana) Ltd opened in Nov. 1982.

NATURAL RESOURCES

Minerals. An important part of government revenue comes from the diamond mine at Orapa (production started in 1971, 821,914 carats; 1980 (estimate), P223,623,000) and the nickel–copper complex at Selebi-Pikwe (production started in 1974) with production (1980, estimate) valued at P83,258,000. An open-pit coalmine has been developed at Morupule, and produced (1978) 315,000 tonnes valued at P4·3m. A new diamond mine at Jwaneng produced 3m. carats in 1982.

Mineral resources in north-east Botswana are being investigated, including salt and soda ash on the Sua Pan of the Makgadikgadi Salt Pans, nickel–copper at Selkirk and Phoenix, copper south of Maun and close to Ghanzi, and coal at Mmamabula.

Agriculture. Cattle-rearing is the chief industry, but the country is more a pastoral than an agricultural one, crops depending entirely upon the rainfall. Increasing numbers of boreholes are being established where underground supply is adequate. However the rural economy is particularly vulnerable to drought and foot and mouth disease. The abattoir at Lobatse, opened in Oct. 1954, is of great importance to the country's economy. In 1982 the number of cattle was 3m.; goats, 700,000; sheep, 200,000; poultry, 900,000.

LABOUR. In 1977, 68·8% of the labour force were engaged in agriculture, 12% was employed outside Botswana, mainly in the Republic of South Africa in the mining industry and 2·9% was engaged in domestic service. Total labour force was 384,000.

COMMERCE. In 1982 imports totalled P644·4m. and exports P442·3m.

Botswana is a member of the South African customs union with Lesotho, the Republic of South Africa and Swaziland.

Total trade between Botswana and UK (British Department of Trade returns, in £1,000 sterling):

	1979	1980	1981	1982	1983
Imports to UK	26,264	4,044	13,026	19,140	21,713
Exports and re-exports from UK	3,845	2,644	3,397	5,163	3,250

TOURISM. The infrastructure for tourism is being developed and there were 97,260 tourists in 1981.

COMMUNICATIONS

Roads. On 31 Dec. 1981, 1,202 km of road were bitumen-surfaced, 1,626 km gravel and over 5,199 km earth. In 1979 there were 21,800 registered motor vehicles.

Railways. 714 km of the Cape Town to Zimbabwe railway line lie within Botswana. The railway is owned and operated by the National Railways of Zimbabwe but the Government of Botswana is preparing to take over the line of rail in Botswana and has formed the Botswana Railway Corporation.

In addition there are 2 Government-owned branch lines which serve the coalmine at Morupule and the copper and nickel mining complex at Selebi Pikwe.

Aviation. There are 3 airports and many airstrips. Regular international flights are flown by Air Botswana, Air Zimbabwe and SAA into Gaborone.

Post and Broadcasting. The telegraph, telephone and railway lines from Cape Town to Zimbabwe traverse Botswana. Wireless communication has been established between headquarters at Gaborone and various district offices and police stations. There are 39 post offices and 42 agencies. There were 10,833 telephones installed in 1978. A new earth station giving independent access to the international telecommunications system, was completed in 1980.

Newspapers. In 1982 there was 1 daily newspaper.

JUSTICE, EDUCATION AND WELFARE

Justice. The Botswana Court of Appeal succeeded the Court of Appeal for Basutoland, Bechuanaland and Swaziland, which was established in 1954. It has jurisdiction in respect of criminal and civil appeals emanating from the High Court of Botswana. Further appeal lies in certain circumstances to the Judicial Committee of the Privy Council.

The High Court for Botswana succeeded the High Court for Bechuanaland, which was established in 1938. It has jurisdiction in all criminal and civil causes and proceedings. Subordinate courts and African courts are in each of the 12 administrative districts.

Police. The police force consisted of 286 officers and subordinate officers, 234 n.c.o.s and 1,434 other ranks in 1980.

Education (1981). There were 403 primary, 22 secondary, 19 private secondary and continuation, 22 vocational training schools and 3 teacher-training colleges. The great majority of the primary schools and the junior secondary schools are controlled, under the Chief Education Officer, by school committees with district-council and mission representatives. Three secondary schools and the homecraft centre are run by missions with Government support; Moeng College by a governing council; the remaining schools by the Government. District-council schools are financed by district-council treasuries and assisted with grants from the Central Government. Enrolment in primary schools in 1981 was 178,101; government secondary, 14,348; private secondary, 5,800; vocational, 1,794; in teacher-training colleges, 1,020. University students on the Botswana campus of the University of Botswana and Swaziland 928 and university students abroad numbered 197.

In 1981, an estimated 66% of the total population were literate.

Welfare (1981). There were 13 general hospitals, 21 maternity centres, a mental home, 7 health centres, 104 clinics and 533 health posts. Total number of beds, 1,871 (1977). There were 113 registered medical practitioners, 8 dentists, and 1,157 nurses. The health facilities are the concern of central and local government, medical missions, mining companies and voluntary organizations. Government expenditure on medical services was P6·5m. for the year ended 31 March 1977.

DIPLOMATIC REPRESENTATIVES

Of Botswana in Great Britain (162 Buckingham Palace Rd., London, SW1)
High Commissioner: Samuel Akana Mpuchane (accredited 18 Feb. 1982).

Of Great Britain in Botswana (Private Bag 0023, Gaborone)
High Commissioner: W. Jones, CMG.

Of Botswana in the USA (4301 Connecticut Ave., NW, Washington, D.C., 20008)
Ambassador: Mashite K. Motsepe.

Of the USA in Botswana (PO Box 90, Gaborone)
Ambassador: Theodore C. Maino.

Of Botswana to the United Nations
Ambassador: Joseph Legwaila.

Books of Reference

General Information: The Director of Information and Broadcasting, PO Box 0060, Gaborone, Botswana publishes *Facts About Botswana,* the monthly *Kutlwano, The Botswana Daily News* and *Botswana Magazine.*
Statistical Bulletins. Quarterly. Central Statistical Office, Gaborone
Report on the Population Census, 1971. Government Printer, Gaborone, 1972
Campbell, A. C., *The Guide to Botswana.* Gaborone, 1980
Colclough, C. and McCarthy, S., *The Political Economy of Botswana.* OUP, 1980
Harvey, C., (ed.), *Papers on the Economy of Botswana.* London and Nairobi, 1981
Stevens, C., *Food Aid and the Developing World.* London, 1979

BRAZIL

República Federativa do Brasil

Capital: Brasília
Population: 130m. (1983)
GNP per capita: US$2,050 (1980)

HISTORY. Brazil was discovered on 22 April 1500 by the Portuguese Admiral Pedro Alvares Cabral, and thus became a Portuguese settlement; in 1815 the colony was declared 'a kingdom', and on 13 May 1822 Dom Pedro, eldest surviving son of King João VI of Portugal, was chosen 'Perpetual Defender' of Brazil by a National Congress. He proclaimed the independence of the country on 7 Sept. 1822, and was chosen 'Constitutional Emperor and Perpetual Defender' on 12 Oct. 1822. He resigned in 1831 and 9 years later, his 14-year-old son Pedro, became the second Emperor of Brazil.

AREA AND POPULATION. Brazil is bounded east by the Atlantic and on its north-west and southern borders by all the South American countries except Chile and Ecuador. Population as at 1 Sept. 1980 (census) and 1 July 1983 (estimate):

State and Capital	Area (sq. km)	Census 1980	Estimate 1983
North	3,581,180	5,880,300	6,817,000
Rondônia[1] (Porto Velho[2])	243,044	491,100	645,000
Acre (Rio Branco)	152,589	301,300	338,000
Amazonas[3] (Manaus)	1,564,445	1,430,100	1,621,000
Roraima (Boa Vista[2])	230,104	79,100	95,000
Pará (Bélem)[3]	1,250,722	3,403,400	3,918,000
Amapá (Macapá[2])	140,276	175,300	200,000
North-east	1,548,672	34,812,400	37,609,000
Maranhão (São Luis)	328,663	3,996,400	4,411,000
Piauí (Teresina)	250,934	2,139,000	2,326,000
Ceará (Fortaleza)[4]	150,630	5,288,300	5,680,000
Rio Grande do Norte (Natal)	53,015	1,898,200	2,045,000
Paraíba (João Pessoa)	56,372	2,770,200	2,928,000
Pernambuco (Recife)	98,281	6,142,000	6,551,000[10]
Alagoas (Maceió)	27,731	1,982,600	2,154,000
Fernando de Noronha[5]	26	1,300	...
Sergipe (Aracajú)	21,994	1,140,100	1,233,000
Bahia (Salvador)	561,026	9,454,300	10,281,000
South-east:	924,935	51,734,100	56,603,000
Minas Gerais (Belo Horizonte)	587,172	13,378,600	14,166,000
Espírito Santo[6] (Vitória)	45,597	2,023,300	2,192,000
Rio de Janeiro (Rio de Janeiro)[7]	44,268	11,291,500	12,242,000
São Paulo (São Paulo)	247,898	25,040,700	28,003,000
South	577,723	19,031,200	20,077,000
Paraná (Curitiba)	199,554	7,629,400	7,915,000
Santa Catarina (Florianópolis)	95,985	3,627,900	3,929,000
Rio Grande do Sul (Pórto Alegre)	282,184	7,773,900	8,233,000
Central West	1,879,455	7,544,800	8,554,000
Mato Grosso (Cuiabá)[8]	881,001	1,138,700	1,358,000
Mato Grosso do Sul (Campo Grande)[8]	350,548	1,369,600	1,519,000
Goiás (Goiânia)	642,092	3,859,600	4,243,000
Distrito Federal (Brasília)	5,814	1,176,900	1,434,000
Total	8,511,965[9]	119,002,800	129,660,000

For notes *see* p. 228.

Density of census population, 1980, was about 14 per sq. km.

The 1980 census showed 59,123,361 males and 59,879,345 females. The urban and suburban population comprised 45·1% in 1960, 55·9% in 1970 and 67·6% in 1980.

The language is Portuguese.

The new capital, Brasília, was inaugurated 21 April 1960. The federal district (5,814 sq. km) was detached from the west-central state of Goiás, about 1,000 km north-west of Rio de Janeiro.

Population of principal cities (1980 census):

São Paulo	7,032,547	Manaus	611,763
Rio de Janeiro	5,090,700	Campinas	566,627
Salvador	1,491,642	Santo André	549,556
Belo Horizonte	1,441,567	Nova Iguaçu	491,766
Recife	1,183,391	Osasco	474,543
Brasília, DF	1,176,908	Guarulhos	426,693
Porto Alegre	1,114,867	Santos	410,933
Curitiba	842,818	Niterói	382,736
Belém	755,984	São Bernardo do Campo	381,097
Goiânia	702,858	Natal	376,446
Fortaleza	647,917	Maceió	375,771

CLIMATE. Because of its latitude, the climate is predominantly tropical, but factors such as altitude, prevailing winds and distance from the sea cause certain variations, though temperatures are not notably extreme. In tropical parts, winters are dry and summers wet, while in Amazonia conditions are constantly warm and humid. The N.E. sertao is hot and arid, with frequent droughts. In the south and east, spring and autumn are sunny and warm, summers are hot, but winters can be cold when polar air-masses impinge. Brasilia. Jan. 72°F (22·2°C), July 64°F (17·8°C). Annual rainfall 64" (1,600 mm). Bahia. Jan. 80°F (26·7°C), July 74°F (23·3°C). Annual rainfall 76" (1,900 mm). Belem. Jan. 79°F (26°C), July 79°F (26°C). Annual rainfall 97" (2,438 mm). Manaos. Jan. 81°F (27·2°C), July 82°F (27·8°C). Annual rainfall 72" (1,811 mm). Recife. Jan. 81°F (27·2°C), July 75°F (24°C). Annual rainfall 64" (1,610 mm). Rio de Janeiro. Jan. 78°F (25·6°C), July 69°F (20·6°C). Annual rainfall 43" (1,082 mm).

CONSTITUTION AND GOVERNMENT. On 15 Nov. 1889 Dom Pedro II (1825–91) was dethroned by a revolution, and Brazil declared a republic.

Presidents since the establishment of the republic:

Marshal Manuel Deodoro da Fonseca, 15 Nov. 1889–23 Nov. 1891 (resigned).

Marshal Floriano Peixoto (Acting), 23 Nov. 1891–15 Nov. 1894.

Dr Prudente José de Moraes Barros, 15 Nov. 1894–15 Nov. 1898.

Dr Manuel Ferraz de Campos Salles, 15 Nov. 1898–15 Nov. 1902.

Dr Francisco da Paula Rodrigues Alves, 15 Nov. 1902–15 Nov. 1906.

Dr Affonso Augusto Moreira Penna, 15 Nov. 1906–14 June 1909 (died).

---

[1] The name 'Território Federal do Guaporé' was changed to 'Território Federal de Rondônia' on 17 Feb. 1956 and became a state in 1981.

[2] Raised to the status of territorial capitals in 1943; previously, Pôrto Velho and Boa Vista belonged to the state of Amazonas and Macapá to the state of Pará.

[3] Including 2,680 sq. km in dispute with the state of Amazonas.

[4] Includes an area of 2,614 sq. km to be demarcated between states of Piauí and Ceará.

[5] Territory created in 1942 includes 8 sq. km of islets.

[6] Including the islands of Trindade and Martim Vaz.

[7] According to Complementary Law no. 20 1 July 1974, the States of Rio de Janeiro and Guanabara were consolidated, since 15 March 1975, into a single political unit, the State of Rio de Janeiro with the City of Rio de Janeiro as its capital city.

[8] On 1 Jan. 1979, the former state of Mato Grosso was divided into Mato Grosso (capital, Cuiabá) and Mato Grosso do Sul (capital, Campo Grande).

[9] 3,286,000 sq. miles.

[10] Including Fernando de Noronha.

Dr Nilo Peçanha (Acting), 14 June 1909–15 Nov. 1910.
Marshal Hermes Rodrigues da Fonseca, 15 Nov. 1910–15 Nov. 1914.
Dr Wenceslau Braz Pereira Gomes, 15 Nov. 1914–15 Nov. 1918.
Dr Francisco da Paula Rodrigues Alves.[1]
Dr Delphim Moreira da Costa Ribeiro (Acting), 15 Nov. 1918–28 July 1919.
Dr Epitácio da Silva Pessoa, 28 July 1919–15 Nov. 1922.
Dr Arthur Bernardes, 15 Nov. 1922–15 Nov. 1926.
Dr Washington Luiz Pereira de Souza, 15 Nov. 1926–25 Oct. 1930 (deposed).
Dr Getúlio Dornelles Vargas, 26 Oct. 1930–29 Oct. 1945 (resigned).
Dr José Linhares (Provisional President), 30 Oct. 1945–31 Jan. 1946.
Gen. Eurico Gaspar Dutra, 31 Jan. 1946–31 Jan. 1951.
Dr Getúlio Dornelles Vargas, 31 Jan. 1951– died 24 Aug. 1954.

Dr João Café Filho, 24 Aug. 1954–8 Nov. 1955 (resigned).
Carlos Coimbra da Luz (Acting), 8 Nov. 1955–11 Nov. 1955 (deposed).
Nereu de Oliveira Ramos (Acting), 11 Nov. 1955–31 Jan. 1956.
Juscelino Kubitschek de Oliveira, 31 Jan. 1956–31 Jan. 1961.
Jânio da Silva Quadros, 31 Jan. 1961–25 Aug. 1961 (resigned).
João Belchior Marques Goulart, 7 Sept. 1961–31 March 1964 (deposed).
Marshal Humberto de A. Castelo Branco, 15 April 1964–15 March 1967.
Marshal Artur da Costa e Silva, 15 March 1967–31 Aug. 1969 (resigned).
Gen. Emilio Garrastazu Medici, 30 Oct. 1969–15 March 1974.
Gen. Ernesto Geisel, 15 March 1974–15 March 1979.
Gen. João Baptista de Oliveira Figueiredo, 15 March 1979–

[1] Died 10 Jan. 1919 before taking office.

On 24 Jan. 1967 both houses of Congress in joint session approved the new Constitution and press law which came into force on 15 March. An amendment to the Constitution, which came into force on 30 Oct. 1969, was issued on 17 Oct. The present Constitution provides for the indirect election of the President and Vice-President by an electoral college, comprising the members of Congress and delegates from the state legislatures; it grants powers to the President to issue decree-laws on matters connected with the economy and national security; it gives the President authority to intervene in any of the 22 states without consultation with Congress and the right to declare a state of siege and to rule by decree. President and Vice-President are elected for a 6-year term and are not immediately re-eligible.

Under the 1969 Constitution, Congress consists of a 69-member Senate and a 479-member Chamber of Deputies. The Senate is two-thirds directly elected (50% of these elected for 8 years in rotation) and one-third indirectly elected. The Chamber of Deputies is elected by universal franchise (with a literacy qualification) for 4 years.

The name of the country was changed from 'Estados Unidos do Brasil' to 'Brasil' and later to 'República Federativa do Brasil'.

Freedom of speech and press are not absolute: war propaganda, the teaching of 'subversive doctrines' and the dissemination of race or class prejudices are banned, as also are political parties opposed to democracy or to 'fundamental human rights' which include the right to own private property. The Supreme Electoral Court on 7 May 1947 declared the Communist Party illegal and on 20 Dec. 1979 the Political Parties Statute of 1965 was amended to allow for the formation of new political parties.

The Institutional Act No. 5 issued on 13 Dec. 1968 was incorporated into the new Constitution through an amendment on 17 Oct. 1969. It was repealed by the Constitutional Amendment Number 11 of 13 Oct. 1978. The Congress renewed its session on 22 Oct. 1969 and elections were held on 15 Nov. 1970, 1974, 1978 and 1982.

Voting is compulsory for men and women between the ages of 18 and 65 and optional for persons over 65. Enlisted men and illiterates (who comprise about 40% of the adult population) may not vote. Elections were held 15 Nov. 1982.

President of the Republic: Gen. João Baptista de Oliveira Figueiredo, assumed office 15 March 1979.

Vice-President: Antonio Aureliano Chaves de Mendonça.

The cabinet was composed as follows in Jan. 1983:

Foreign Affairs: Ramiro Elysio Saraiva Guerreiro. *Planning and General*

Co-ordination: Prof. Antônio Delfim Netto. *Finance:* Ernane Galvêas. *Justice:* Ibrahim Abi-Ackel. *Interior:* Mário David Andreazza. *Transport:* Cloraldino Severo. *Communications:* Haraldo Corrêa de Mattos. *Agriculture:* Amaury Angelo Stabile. *Labour:* Murilo Macedo. *Education and Culture:* Prof. Esther de Figueiredo Ferraz. *Health:* Dr Waldyr Arcoverde. *Industry and Commerce:* João Camilo Pena. *Mines and Power:* César Cals. *Welfare, Social Security and Debureaucratization:* Hélio Marcos Penna Beltrão. *Land Reform Affairs:* Gen. Danilo Venturini. *Army:* Gen. Walter Pires de Carvalho e Albuquerque. *Navy:* Adm. Maximiliano Eduardo de Silva Fonseca. *Air Force:* Brig. Délio Jardim de Mattos. *Head of President's Military Household:* Gen. Rubem Carlos Ludwig. *Head of President's Civilian Household:* João Leitão de Abreu. *Head of National Information Service* (SNI): Gen. Octávio Aguiar de Medeiros. *Head of General Staff* (EMFA): Gen. Alacyr Frederico Werner.

National flag: Green, with yellow lozenge on which is placed a blue sphere, containing 23 white stars and crossed with a band bearing the motto *Ordem e Progresso.*

National anthem: Ouviram do Ipiranga . . . (words by J. O. Duque Estrada; tune by F. M. da Silva).

Local Government. Brazil consists of 23 states, 3 federal territories (Roraima, Amapá, Fernando de Noronha) and 1 federal district. Each state has its distinct administrative, legislative and judicial authorities, its own constitution and laws, which must, however, agree with the constitutional principles of the Union. The states may unite or split or form new states. Taxes on interstate commerce, levied by individual states, are prohibited. The governors and members of the legislatures are elected, but magistrates are appointed and are not removable from office save by judicial sentence. Rio de Janeiro and Guanabara became one state in 1975.

DEFENCE. Under the constitution military service is compulsory for every Brazilian man from 21 years of age to 45. The terms of service are 9 years (from the 21st to the 30th years of age) in the Army 'first line' (1 in the ranks, the rest in the reserve) and 14 years (from the 30th to the 45th years of age) in the Army 'second line' (7 in the 'second line' and 7 in the reserve of the same). The men in the Territorial Army also have an annual training of 2 to 4 weeks.

Army. The Army is organized in 8 divisions, each with up to 6 armoured, 4 mechanized or motorized infantry brigades; in addition there are 5 light 'jungle' infantry battalions, 2 independent infantry and 1 independent parachute brigades; total strength (1984) 182,750.

Navy. The principal ship of the Brazilian Navy:

Completed	Name	Standard displacement Tons	Aircraft	Guns	Shaft horsepower	Speed Knots
			Aircraft Carrier			
1945	Minas Gerais [1]	15,890	{16 fixed-wing / 4 helicopters}	10 40mm AA	40,000	24·0

[1] Ex-*Vengeance*, purchased from Great Britain in 1956.

There are also 8 diesel-powered submarines (3 modern built in Britain and 5 old *ex*-US), 6 new destroyer leaders (or large frigates), the *Constituição, Defensora, Liberal* and *Niteroi*, built in Britain, and the *Independencia* and *Uniao*, built in Brazil, 12 old *ex*-US destroyers, 10 fleet tug type corvettes, 6 coastal minesweepers, 1 river monitor, 5 river patrol ships, 6 coastal gunboats, 1 submarine rescue ship, 2 tank landing ships, 4 transports, 18 local transports, 4 oilers, 1 repair ship, 6 training ships, 8 survey ships (2 carrying a helicopter), 6 survey launches, 35 minor landing craft, 7 buoy tenders, 20 auxiliaries and 17 tugs. There are also 3 floating docks.

Rather a static navy for such a large country which is apparently suffering from financial stringency. A considerable replacement programme is needed but this has been delayed.

The new construction programme has been revised to replace old *ex*-US submarines and destroyers. A training ship (frigate) and a river support ship were projected.

Among the 50 new units planned are a carrier, submarines, guided missile leaders, frigates and amphibious ships.

Naval bases are at Rio de Janeiro, Aratu (Bahia), Belém, Natal, Recife, Salvador, with a river base at Ladario.

The Fleet Air Arm was formed on 26 Jan. 1965. Aircraft obtained from the USA for service on the carrier include 5 Sikorsky SH-3D helicopters and 8 S-2A/E Tracker anti-submarine aircraft, the latter being operated by the Air Force. Nine Wasp light helicopters were obtained from Britain, and are operated on utility and search and rescue duties with 3 turbine-powered Whirlwind, 8 Bell Jet Ranger and 6 Brazilian-assembled Esquilo (AS 350) helicopters. Nine Westland Lynx helicopters were provided for the destroyer leader/frigates of the 'Niteroi' class. Ten Jet Rangers are used for training.

The active personnel in 1984 totalled 46,000 (4 100 officers and 41,900 men), including 14,500 marines and auxiliary corps.

Air Force. The Air Force, formed in 1918, has been independent of the Army and Navy since 1941. It is organized in 6 zones, centred on Belém, Recife, Rio de Janeiro, São Paulo, Porto Alegre and Brasília. The 1a ALADA (air defence wing) has 13 Mirage IIIE fighters and 2 Mirage IIID trainers, integrated with Roland mobile short-range surface-to-air missile systems deployed by the Army, and a radar/communications/computer network. One fighter group has 2 squadrons of F-5E Tiger II supersonic fighter-bombers and two-seat F-5Bs; 2 others operate AT-26 (Aermacchi MB 326G) Xavante light jet attack/trainers, licence-built by Embraer in Brazil. Counter-insurgency squadrons are equipped with AT-26 Xavantes for reconnaissance and attack, and with Neiva Regente lightplanes, Universal armed piston-engined trainers, and UH-1D/H Iroquois and armed JetRanger helicopters for liaison and observation. There is an ASW group of S-2A/E Trackers for shore-based and carrier-based operations; a maritime patrol group (2 squadrons) with 12 EMB-111 (P-95) twin-turboprop aircraft developed from the Embraer Bandeirante transport; and 3 air-sea rescue units with RC-130E Hercules reconnaissance transports, SC-95B Bandeirantes, SA 330L Puma and SH-1D Iroquois helicopters. Equipment of transport units includes 1 group of C-130E/H Hercules transports and KC-130H Hercules tankers; 1 group made up of a squadron of HS 748 and C-95 Bandeirante turboprop transports and a second squadron of HS 748s with large freight doors; 1 troop-carrier group with DHC-5 Buffaloes; and 6 independent squadrons with Bandeirantes and Buffaloes. Light aircraft for liaison duties include 32 Embraer U-7s (licence-built Piper Senecas). The VIP transport group has 2 Boeing 737s, 8 HS 125 twin-jet light transports, some Bandeirantes, 6 Embraer Xingu (VU-9) twin-turboprop pressurized transports and 6 JetRanger helicopters. Training is performed primarily on locally-built Aerotec T-23 Uirapuru *ab initio* trainers, T-25 Universal and turboprop T-27 Tucano (EMB-312) basic trainers, and AT-26 Xavante armed jet basic trainers. Future equipment will include 79 AM-X jet attack aircraft, produced jointly by Embraer and Aeritalia/Aermacchi of Italy.

Personnel strength (1983) about 45,000, with more than 600 aircraft of all types.

INTERNATIONAL RELATIONS

Membership. Brazil is a member of UN, OAS and LAIA (formerly LAFTA).

ECONOMY

Budget. Receipts and expenditures for the federal government (excluding states, federal district and municipalities) for calendar years have been as follows in 1m. Cr$:

	1978	1979	1980	1981
Revenue	357,705	544,244	1,230,018	2,351,966
Expenditure	356,000	521,136	1,190,994	2,254,896

Chief items of revenue were in 1981 as follows (in Cr$1m.): Taxes, 1,929,554;

government property, 40,792. Principal items of expenditure: Transport, 170,202; education, 172,519; army, 92,188; aviation and navy, 122,888; welfare and security, 97,515; finance, 40,767.

The foreign debt (including states and municipalities) of Brazil on 31 Dec. 1982 amounted to US$69,654m. Internal federal debt, April 1983 was Cr$10,832,934m. Internal states and municipalities (main securities outstanding), April 1983, Cr$1,406,785m.

Currency. The *cruzeiro* (Cr$) is the monetary unit, and is divided into 100 *centavos*. The exchange rate was in March 1984 US$1 = Cr$1,210; £1 = Cr$1,731.

Banking. The Bank of Brazil (founded in 1808 and reorganized in 1906, with an authorized capital of NCr$60m. from 1967) is not a central bank of issue but a closely controlled commercial bank; it had 1,270 branches in 1981 throughout the republic. On 31 Dec. 1981 deposits were Cr$763,407m.

On 31 Dec. 1964 the Banco Central da República do Brasil was founded.

The country's currency held by the public on 31 Dec. 1982 was Cr$1,009,962m. Since Sept. 1939 gold and dollar supply has risen from US$40m. to US$420m., of which the government's gold was US$288m. in May 1961. All banks had on 31 Dec. 1982 deposits of Cr$5,641,867m. and loans of Cr$25,924,139m.

Weights and Measures. The metric system has been in use in all official departments since 1862. It was made compulsory in 1872, but the ancient measures are still partly employed in remote districts. They are: *libra* = 1·012 lb. avoirdupois; *arroba* = 32·98 lb.; *quintal* = 129·54 lb.; *alqueire* (of Roi) = 1 Imperial bushel, or 40 litres; *oitava* = 55·34 grains.

ENERGY AND NATURAL RESOURCES

Electricity. Brazil's hydraulic potential capacity for electric power production was estimated at 106,570 mw. in 1980, one of the largest in the world, of which 34% belongs to the Amazon hydrographic basin. Installed electric power in 1981 was 36,875 mw.; gross production, 141,874 gwh.; consumption, 123,545 gwh.

Oil. There are 13 oil refineries, of which 11 are state owned. Crude oil output was 12,395,760 tonnes in 1981, of which 54% was from the continental shelf. Promising results have been obtained with the exploration of that area which in 1974 represented only 9% of all the national oil production.

The country imported substantial amounts of oil in 1982: 39,766,369 tonnes (value US$9,566m.) representing 49% of total value of all Brazilian imports. Imports come mainly from Iraq and Saudi Arabia.

The government created the National Alcohol Program in 1975 with the aim of a gradual replacement of the consumption of petroleum by combustible alcohol specially produced from sugar-cane and cassava. About US$5,000m. will be invested by 1985. By May 1980, 281 sugar-cane alcohol distillery projects had been approved and their authorized capacity represents 61% of the national aim for 1985 (about 11m. cu. metres). An agreement between the automotive industry and the government was signed in Sept. 1979 and it is hoped that by 1982–83 about 900,000 vehicles utilizing 100% alcohol-combustive will be produced.

Minerals. Brazil is the only source of high-grade quartz crystal in commercial quantities; output, 1981, 144,707 tonnes; exports in 1982, 7,349 tonnes. It is the first largest western producer of chrome ore (reserves of 5m. tonnes; output, 1981, 926,413 tonnes); fifth in the output of mica (10,995 tonnes in 1980); third in zirconium, 6,937 tonnes in 1981; it is the largest producer of beryllium, output, raw beryllium (1981) 158 tonnes; graphite (1981), 464,089 tonnes; titanium ore (1981), 21,800 tonnes, and magnesite (1981), 618,251 tonnes. Along the coasts of the states of Rio de Janeiro, Espírito Santo and Bahia are found monazite sands containing thorium; output, 1981, 2,660 tonnes; reserves are estimated at 27m. tonnes. Manganese ores of high content are important (reserves in the Amapá region alone are estimated at 11m. tonnes); output, 1981, 3,165,744 tonnes. Output of tungsten ore, 1981, totalled 538,354 tonnes, unrough, 2,550 tonnes. Mine production of lead (1981), 334,450 tonnes. Asbestos production, 1981, 1,992,766 tonnes. Coal deposits exist in Rio Grande do Sul, Santa Catarina, Paraná and Minas Gerais. Total reserves are estimated at 398m. tonnes; output (1981), 17,434,051 tonnes.

Iron is found chiefly in Minas Gerais, notably the Cauê Peak at Itabira. The Government is now opening up what is believed to be one of the richest iron-ore deposits in the world, situated in Carajás, in the northern state of Pará, with estimated reserves of 18,000m. tonnes, representing the largest concentration of high-grade (66%) iron ore in the world. Total output of iron ore, 1981, mainly from the Cia. Vale do Rio Doce mine at Itabira, was 122,709,441 tonnes. The National Iron and Steel Co. at Volta Redonda, State of Rio de Janeiro, furnishes a substantial part of Brazil's steel. Brazil's total output, 1982: Pig-iron, 10,827,292 tonnes; crude steel ingots castings, 12,995,241 tonnes.

Production of aluminium was started in Minas Gerais in 1945; output of bauxite, 1981, 6,969,140 tonnes. Production of tin ore (cassiterite, processed) was 14,166 tonnes in 1981. Output of barytes (processed) in 1981, 178,895 tonnes; exports of barytes, 1982, was 19,730 tonnes. Cement output, 1982, was 23,724,638 tonnes. Output of phosphate rock (processed), 1981, was 2,657,986 tonnes.

Gold in large-scale mining was confined to a single mine in Minas Gerais; the production in 1981 (total), 17,726 kg. Large-scale gold deposits have been discovered at Serra Pelada in Pará; production, 1981, 11.174 kg and Minas Gerais, 4,364 kg. Silver output (processed), 1981, 6,726 kg. Salt output (1981), 2,766,319 tonnes. Diamond districts are Minas Gerais, Mato Grosso, Roraima, Bahia and São Paulo; output in 1981 was 135,939 carats (96,935 carats from Minas Gerais, 28,120 carats from Mato Grosso).

Agriculture. 32·41% of Brazil's population is rural. Production (in tonnes):

	1981	1982		1981	1982
Bananas			Cocoa	304,000	349,748
(1,000 bunches)	446,380	459,325	Coffee	3,755,320	2,006,708
Beans	2,338,718	2,907,213	Cotton, raw	1,730,348	1,935,091
Cassava	25,050,215	24,039,008	Jute	38,909	14,222
Castor beans	278,006	192,428	Maize	21,098,300	21,865,439
Oranges	11,429,713	11,583,453	Soya	14,977,972	12,834,624
Potatoes	1,911,289	2,147,918	Sugar-cane	153,858,357	184,219,067
Rice	8,260,547	9,718,074	Tobacco	362,250	421,532
Sisal	243,432	249,236	Wheat	2,206,518	1,819,504
Grapes	661,405	688,589			

The 4 states of São Paulo, Paraná, Espírito Santo and Minas Gerais are the principal districts for coffee-growing. Output, 1982, from 1,857,462 hectares, 2,006,708 tonnes; exports (1982), 888,020 tonnes.

Bahia furnished 90% of the cocoa output in 1982; in 1982 total output was 349,748 tonnes from 529,208 hectares; exports (1982), 143,462 tonnes. Two crops a year are grown. Castor-bean output usually exceeds 250,000 tonnes; output, 1982, 192,428 tonnes from 462,725 hectares.

Tobacco output was 421,532 tonnes in 1982. In 1982, 144,926 tonnes were exported.

Brazil now ranks second only to the US in production of oranges, output 1981, 11,429,713 tonnes; 1982, 11,583,453. Output of bananas (1,000 bunches), 1981, 446,380; 1982, 459,325. Output of cotton, raw, 1981, 1,730,348 tonnes; 1982, 1,935,091. Exports of cotton wool (raw), 1981, 30,266 tonnes; 1982, 56,487. Brazil formerly furnished only 10% of her own requirements in wheat (average output, 1934–38, 144,000 tonnes); output, 1981, 2,206,518 tonnes; 1982, 1,819,504; imports, 4,223,844 tonnes in 1982. Rice is important; output (rough rice), 1981, 8,260,547 tonnes; 1982, 9,718,074.

Rubber is another natural product of the country, chiefly in the states of Acre, Amazonas and Pará. Output, 1982, 260,937 tonnes (natural and synthetic); peak reached in 1912 (when rubber realized US$3 a lb.) was 42.510 gross tons. Output of tyres in local factories has risen from 421,765 units (tyres and tubes) in 1940 to 48,289,248 in 1982. Brazilian consumption of rubber in 1982, was 262,467 tonnes. Brazil is the chief source of carnaúba wax, used for electric insulation and gramophone records, exporting 8,479,738 tonnes in 1982. Caroá fibre is grown as a substitute for Indian jute; production, 1980, 253 tonnes. Jute output, 1981, 38,909 tonnes. Plantations of tung trees established in 1930 (4m. trees in 1946) are beginning to yield tung oils in commercial quantities; output of tung, 1980, 7,981 tonnes.

Livestock (in 1,000): 1982, 93,000 cattle, 33,500 swine, 17,500 sheep, 8,500 goats, 5,100 horses, 1,470 asses and 1,680 mules. In 1982, 12m. cattle, 9m. swine, 900,000 sheep and lambs, 300,000 goats and 789m. poultry were slaughtered for meat.

Fisheries. The fishing industry totalled a fleet of 154,695 vessels in 1968; the catch in 1981 was 833,163 tonnes.

INDUSTRY AND TRADE

Industry. The total number of persons engaged in industry (1980) was 4,734,097 and the value of production Cr$9,528,684m.

A paper-mill, reported to be the largest pulp-and-paper mill in South America, is at Monte Alegre, Paraná. Brazil's output of paper, 1982, was 3,328,566 tonnes.

Commerce. Imports and exports for calendar years in Cr$1,000:

	1978	1979	1980	1981	1982
Imports	264,988,521	500,134,047	1,228,628,361	2,145,425,789	3,340,756,704
Exports	224,114,456	393,531,168	1,038,083,296	2,054,524,562	3,368,796,430

Exports in 1981, 123,994,487 tonnes; 1982, 119,990,263. Imports in 1981, 64,066,069 tonnes; 1982, 60,666,117 tonnes.

Principal imports in 1982 were (in US$1m.): Fuel and lubricants, 10,459; manufactured goods, 3,272; chemical products, 1,446; cereals, 848; steel and cast iron, 431; non-ferrous metals, 422.

Principal exports in 1982 were (in US$1m.): Coffee (green), 1,854; iron ore, 1,769; rolling stock and vehicles, 1,760; soybean bran, 1,600; machinery, 1,210.

Of exports (in US$1m.) in 1982, USA took 4,131; Japan, 1,313; Germany (Fed. Rep.), 1,179; Netherlands, 1,132; Italy, 984; France, 863; UK, 672; Argentina, 650; USSR, 509. Of 1982 imports, Saudi Arabia furnished 3,003; USA, 2,850; Iraq, 2,573; Venezuela, 970; Japan, 877; Germany (Fed. Rep.), 858; Mexico, 789; France, 561; Argentina, 550.

Total trade between Brazil and UK (according to British Department of Trade returns, in £1,000 sterling):

	1978	1979	1980	1981	1982	1983
Imports to UK	282,574	400,378	269,340	389,898	443,956	560,277
Exports and re-exports from UK	221,423	286,481	218,159	174,361	158,837	157,758

Tourism. In 1981, 1,357,879 tourists visited Brazil, 508,508 were Argentinian, 214,919 Uruguayan, 119,147 US citizens, 82,737 Paraguayan, 41,562 German, 56,608 Chilean, 40,321 Italian, 20,967 British and 19,428 Japanese.

COMMUNICATIONS

Roads. There were (1981) 1,548,023 km of highways. In 1981 Brazil had 11,221,151 motor vehicles, including 8,526,984 passenger cars, 1,804,435 commercial vehicles, 126,733 buses and minibuses. 840,305 motor vehicles of all types were produced in 1982.

Railways. Public railways are operated by two administrations, the Federal Railways (RFFSA) formed in 1957 and São Paulo Railways (FEPASA) formed in 1971, which is confined to the state of São Paulo. RFFSA had a route-length of 23,087 km in 1982 and FEPASA 5,066 km. Principal gauges are metre and 1,600 mm. The share of the freight market declined to a low of 15% in 1967, but subsequent heavy government investment in reconstruction and new lines, coupled with a policy of forcing bulk commodities on to rail, had raised the share to over 20% in 1974. Continued investment in new wagons, electrification, gauge-conversion, and 'export corridor' routes to the ports will further improve this figure, and some new lines are planned up to the year 2000. Except in the urban areas of Rio de Janeiro and São Paulo, passenger traffic moving by rail is negligible. Traffic moved by RFFSA in 1981 amounted to 58m. tonnes of freight and 384m. passengers. FEPASA carried 20m. tonnes and 63m. passengers.

There are several important independent freight railways, including the Vitoria à Minas (773 km and 79m. tonnes of freight) and the Amapa (194 km). The city of São Paulo has a rapid metropolitan transit railway, and a similar system opened in Rio de Janeiro city in 1979. Commuter railways are also being developed in Recife, Belo Horizonte, Porto Alegre, Fortaleza and Salvador.

Aviation. There were 34 regular airlines (25 foreign) operating in 1981. The 4 largest Brazilian companies cover the whole territory and in 1981 they carried 13,492,000 passengers (11,611,000 in domestic traffic) and 2,239m. tonne-km of freight. Their commercial fleet consisted of 177 aircraft on 31 Dec. 1981. There were 204 taxiplane companies on 31 Dec. 1983. The chief airline is Viação Aérea Rio Grande do Sul, (VARIG).

Shipping. Inland waterways, mostly rivers, are open to navigation over some 21,944 miles; number of vessels in 1981, 924. Rio de Janeiro and Santos are the 2 leading ports; there are 18 other large ports. Bolivia and Paraguay have been given free ports at Santos. During 1981, 44,917 vessels entered and cleared the Brazilian ports.

The Lloyd Brasileiro is owned and operated by the Government; its fleet comprised (1981), 46 vessels of 656,587 DWT. Brazilian shipping, 1981 (registered with Lloyds) amounted to 1,258 vessels of 8,928,271 DWT. Petrobrás, the government oil monopoly, took over the government tanker fleet of 26 vessels in 1958; total tanker fleet in 1981 was 162 vessels of 4,877,708 DWT (private and government-owned).

Post and Broadcasting. Of the telegraph system of the country, about half, including all interstate lines, is under control of the Government. There were 4,724 post and telegraph offices in 1981. There were 8,536,000 telephones in Jan. 1982 (São Paulo, 1,744,834; Rio de Janeiro, 1,094,691; Brasilia, 184,894). In 1979 there were 1,159 broadcasting and 108 television stations.

Cinemas (1977). Cinemas numbered 2,356 with a seating capacity of 1,505,620.

Newspapers (1979). There were 344 daily newspapers with a total yearly circulation of 1,587,087,000. Foreigners and corporations (except political parties) are not allowed to own or control newspapers or wireless stations. The press law of 1967 prohibits anonymous journalism and the publication of material defamatory to the armed forces and other public institutions.

JUSTICE, RELIGION, EDUCATION AND HEALTH

Justice. There is a Supreme Federal Court of Justice at Brasília. It has 11 judges; all are appointed by the President with the approval of the Senate. There are also federal courts in each state and the federal district and in the Territories, as well as 'electoral courts' to protect the elections, and labour tribunals. Justice is administered in the states in accordance with state law, by state courts, but in Brasília federal justice is administered. Judges are appointed for life. There are also 3,074 magistrates and 5,634 justices of the peace. In Dec. 1977 the Senate approved laws for allowing marriages to be dissolved. Brazilian citizens can apply for one divorce only during their lifetime. In the case of a marriage partner becoming mentally ill, divorce proceedings cannot begin until 5 years after the illness has been proved. The death penalty was re-introduced in Sept. 1969.

Religion. The population is overwhelmingly Roman Catholic (89% at the census, 1980). In 1889 connexion between Church and State was abolished; it was restored by the 1934 constitution, but again abolished in 1946.

In 1980 (census) Catholics numbered 105,861,113; Protestants, 7,885,846, and Spiritualists, 1,538,230.

Education. Elementary education is compulsory. In 1980 (census) there were

69,703,993 persons 5 years of age or over who could read and write; this was 67·95% of that age group; 68·57% of the literates were men.

There were, in 1980, 224,696 first degree school units, with 22,148,809 pupils and 883,029 teachers; 7,224 second degree establishments (not school units), with 2,823,544 pupils and 198,276 teachers; 4,394 third degree units, with 1,377,286 pupils and 116,827 teachers.

There were, in 1980, 65 universities (including 20 private) and 817 faculties not belonging to universities (662 private), including the University of Rio de Janeiro (founded on 7 Sept. 1920), the University of Bahia (founded in 1946), the University of Recife (1946), the University of Paraná (1946), the Rural University (1948, State of Rio de Janeiro), the University of São Paulo (1934), the University of Minas Gerais (1927), the University of Rio Grande do Sul (1934), the University of Brasília (1960) and the University of Mato Grosso (1971). There are also 12 Catholic universities (all private) in Rio de Janeiro (1946), São Paulo (1946), Rio Grande do Sul (1948), Pernambuco (1951), Minas Gerais (1958), Bahia, Paraná, Campinas, Petrópolis and Pelotas. Students in 1980 totalled 1,377,286.

Health. In 1980 there were 18,489 health establishments of which 6,110 were for inpatients; total number of beds, 509,104 (386,382 in private institutions).

DIPLOMATIC REPRESENTATIVES

Of Brazil in Great Britain (32 Green St., London, W1Y 3FD)
Ambassador: Mario Gibson Alves Barboza (accredited 10 Dec. 1982).

Of Great Britain in Brazil (Setor de Embaixadas Sul, Quadra 801, Conjunto K, Brasília, D.F.)
Ambassador: J. B. Ure.

Of Brazil in the USA (3006 Massachusetts Ave., NW, Washington, D.C., 20008)
Ambassador: Dario Castro Alves.

Of the USA in Brazil (Ave das Nações, Lote 3, Brasília, D.F.)
Chargé d'Affaires: Harry Kopp.

Of Brazil to the United Nations
Ambassador: Sérgio Corrêa Da Costa.

Books of Reference

Anuário do Transporte Aéreo. Departamento de Aviação Civil. Rio de Janeiro, 1980
Anuário Estatístico do Brasil. Vol. 43. Fundação Instituto Brasileiro de Geografia e Estatística, Rio de Janeiro, 1982
Anuário Estatístico das Ferrovias do Brasil. Vol. 4. Rede Ferroviária Federal. Rio de Janeiro, 1980
Anuário Estatístico dos Transportes. Vol. 11. Empresa Brasileira de Planejamento de Transportes. Brasília, 1982
Anuário Estatístico Embratur. Vol. 12. Empresa Brasileira de Turismo. Rio de Janeiro, 1982
Anuário Mineral Brasileiro. Departamento Nacional da Produção Mineral. Brasília, 1982
Atlas do Brasil. Instituto Brasileiro de Geografia. 2nd ed. Rio de Janeiro, 1959
Boletim do Banco Central do Brasil. Banco Central do Brasil. Brasília. Monthly
Bulletin of the British Chamber of Commerce in Brazil. Rio de Janeiro. Monthly
Sinopse Estatística do Brasil. Vol. 7. Fundação Instituto Brasileiro de Geografia e Estatística. Rio de Janeiro, 1981
Banco do Brasil, *Boletim Trimestral.* Brasília, D.F. From 1966
Burns, E. B., *A History of Brazil.* 2nd ed. Columbia Univ. Press, 1980
Campbell, G., *Brazil Struggles for Development.* London, 1973
Cowell, A., *The Tribe that Hides from Man.* London, 1973
Dickenson, J. P., *Brazil.* Harlow, 1982
Fiechter, G.-A., *Brazil Since 1964: Modernisation Under a Military Regime.* London, 1975
Hanbury-Tenison, R., *A Question of Survival for the Indians of Brazil.* London, 1973
McDonough, P., *Power and Ideology in Brazil.* Princeton Univ. Press, 1981
Micallef, J., (ed.), *Brazil: Country with a Future.* London, 1982
Moraes, R. Borba de., *Bibliographia Brasiliana (1504–1900).* 2 vols. 1958
Selcher, W. E. (ed.), *Brazil in the International System: The Rise of a Middle Power.* Boulder, 1981
Tyler, W. G., *The Brazilian Industrial Economy.* Aldershot, 1981
Young, J. M., *Brazil: Emerging World Power.* Malabar, 1982
National Library: Biblioteca Nacional Avenida Rio Branco 219–39, Rio de Janeiro, RJ.
Director: Célia Ribeiro Zaher.

BRITISH ANTARCTIC TERRITORY

HISTORY. Formerly part of the Dependencies of the Falklands, this territory was on 3 March 1962 formed from that part of the Antarctic mainland and adjacent islands claimed by the UK lying south of latitude 60°S.

AREA AND POPULATION. The colony consists of the Graham Land peninsula and those parts of the Antarctic mainland between longitudes 20°W. and 80°W., together with adjacent islands and two nearby archipelagoes, the South Shetlands Islands (area, 4,622 sq. km) and South Orkney Islands (area, 620 sq. km), both barren and uninhabited groups used only as bases for Antarctic exploration. The total area is 5·7m. sq. km (2·2m. sq. miles) of which land, excluding ice-shelves, occupies about 388,500 sq. km. The only population comprises scientific staff at research stations (about 100).

High Commissioner: Sir Rex Hunt, CMG (resides in Port Stanley).

BRITISH INDIAN OCEAN TERRITORY

HISTORY. This territory was established by an Order in Council on 8 Nov. 1965, consisting then of the Chagos Archipelago (formerly administered from Mauritius) and the islands of Aldabra, Desroches and Farquhar (all formerly administered from Seychelles). The latter islands being returned to the Seychelles when that country achieved independence on 29 June 1976, the territory now comprises the Chagos Archipelago, lying 1,180 miles (1,899 km) north-west of Mauritius.

AREA AND POPULATION. The group, with a total land area of 20 sq. miles (52 sq. km) comprises 5 coral atolls (Diego Garcia, Peros Banhos, Salomon, Eagle and Egmont) of which the largest and southern-most, Diego Garcia, covers 14 sq. miles (36 sq. km). The British Indian Ocean Territory was established to meet UK and US defence requirements in the Indian Ocean. In accordance with the terms of Exchanges of Notes between the UK and US governments in 1966 and 1976, a US Navy support facility has been established on Diego Garcia. There is no permanent population in the British Indian Ocean Territory.

Commissioner: W. N. Wenban-Smith (non-resident).
Administrator: D. H. Doble.

BRUNEI

Capital: Bandar Seri Begawan
Population: 191,770 (1981)
GNP per capita: US$22,000 (1981)

HISTORY. The Sultanate of Brunei was a powerful state in the early 16th century, with authority over the whole of the island of Borneo and some parts of the Sulu Islands and the Philippines. At the end of the 16th century its power had begun to decline and various cessions were made to Great Britain, the Rajah of Sarawak and the British North Borneo Company in the 19th century to combat piracy and anarchy. By the middle of the 19th century the State had been reduced to its present limits.

In 1847 the Sultan of Brunei entered into a treaty with Great Britain for the furtherance of commercial relations and the suppression of piracy, and in 1888, by a further treaty, the State was placed under the protection of Great Britain. Brunei was the only former British dependency inhabited by a Malay people that did not join the Federation of Malaysia in 1963.

AREA AND POPULATION. Brunei, on the northwest coast of Borneo, is bounded on all sides by Sarawak territory, which splits the State into two separate parts. Area, about 2,226 sq. miles (5,800 sq. km), with a coastline of about 100 miles. Population (1981 census) was 191,770. The 4 districts are Brunei/Muara (114,310), Belait (49,590), Tutong (21,640), Temburong (6,230). The capital is Bandar Seri Begawan, 9 miles from the mouth of Brunei River.

CLIMATE. The climate is tropical marine, hot and moist, but nights are cool. Humidity is high and rainfall heavy, varying from 100″ (2,500 mm) on the coast to 200″ (5,000 mm) inland. There is no dry season. Bandar Seri Begawan. Jan. 80°F (26·7°C), July 82°F (27·8°C). Annual rainfall 131″ (3,275 mm).

CONSTITUTION AND GOVERNMENT. On 29 Sept. 1959 the Sultan promulgated a constitution. There is a Privy Council, an Executive and a Legislative Council. On 6 Jan. 1965 the constitution was amended to provide for general elections to the Legislative Council; at the same time the Executive Council was renamed Council of Ministers. The Legislative Council consists of 20 members and a Speaker appointed by the Sultan. The Council of Ministers is presided over by the Sultan and consists of 6 *ex-officio* members and 4 other members, all of whom except one are members of the Legislative Council. The Mentri Besar, who is one of the *ex-officio* members of the Legislative Council and the Council of Ministers, is responsible to the Sultan for the exercise of executive authority in the State. As a result of negotiations in June 1978, the Sultan and the British Government signed a new treaty on 7 Jan. 1979 under which Brunei became a fully sovereign and independent State on 31 Dec. 1983.

The official language is Malay, but English may be used for other purposes.

Sultan of Brunei: Duli Yang Maha Mulia Paduka Seri Baginda Sultan and Yang di-Pertuan Negeri Brunei Sir Muda Hassanal Bolkiah Mu'izzaddin Waddaulah ibni Duli Yang Teramat Mulia Paduka Seri Begawan Sultan Sir Muda Omar Ali Saifuddin Sa'adul Khairi Waddin, DK, PGGUB, DPKG, DPKT, PSPNB, PSNB, PSLJ, SPMB, PANB, GCMG, DMN, DK (Kelantan), DK (Johore), DK (Negeri Sembilan). The Sultan was crowned on 1 Aug. 1968.

General Adviser to HH The Sultan: The Most Hon., Pehin Orang Kaya Laila Setia Bakti Di-Raja Dato Laila Utama Awang Haji Isa bin Pehin Datu Perdana Mentri Dato Laila Utama Haji Ibrahim, DK, SPMB, DSNB, CVO, OBE, PHBS, PBLI, PJK.

Mentri Besar (Chief Minister, Acting): The Rt Hon. Pehin Orang Kaya Laila

Wijaya Dato Seri Setia Haji Abdul Aziz bin Begawan Pehin Udana Khatib Dato Seri Paduka Haji Umar, PSNB, DPMB, SLJ, PJK

Flag: Yellow, with 2 diagonal strips of white over black with the national arms in red placed over all in the centre.

DEFENCE

Army. The armed forces are known as the Royal Brunei Malay Regiment and contain the naval and air elements. Strength (1984) 3,650. Military units include 2 infantry battalions, 1 armoured reconnaissance squadron, 1 engineer squadron and 1 signals squadron. Equipment includes 16 Scorpion light tanks and 24 Sankey AT-104 armoured personnel carriers.

Navy. The First Flotilla of the Royal Brunei Malay Regiment comprises 3 fast missile-armed attack craft of 200 tons (completed by Vosper, Singapore in 1978–79), 3 coastal patrol boats (built by Vosper-Thornycroft (Singapore)), 2 landing craft and 3 small patrol boats. Special Combat Division (formerly Special Boat Squadron) operates 24 fast assault boats. Personnel in 1984 numbered 450 (42 officers and 408 ratings) in the First Flotilla (for offshore work) and in the Special Combat Division and River Division.

Two coastal patrol craft built by Vosper, Singapore. were supplied in 1979 for the Brunei Police.

Air Wing. The Air Wing of the Royal Brunei Malay Regiment was formed in 1965. Current equipment includes up to 6 MBB BO 105, 2 Bell 206B JetRanger and 10 Bell 212 helicopters, and 2 SF.260M piston-engined trainers. Delivery has begun of 7 Sikorsky S-76 transport helicopters.

Police. Establishment provides over 1,750 officers and men (1980). In addition, there is a small auxiliary force mostly employed on static guard duties.

ECONOMY

Planning. A fourth Five-Year National Development Plan was announced in 1980 to further improve the economic, social and cultural life of the people.

Budget. The budget for 1983 envisaged expenditure of US$1,100m. and revenue of US$2,800m.

Currency. The currency is the *Brunei dollar* with a par value of 0·290 299 gramme of gold.

INTERNATIONAL RELATIONS

Membership. Brunei is a member of ASEAN.

ENERGY AND NATURAL RESOURCES

Oil. The Seria oilfield, discovered in 1929, has passed its peak production. The high level of crude oil production is maintained through the increase of offshore oilfields production, which exceeds onshore oilfields production. Production is about 240,000 bbls a day. The crude oil is exported directly, and only a small amount is refined at Seria for domestic uses.

Gas. Natural gas is also produced at one of the biggest liquefied natural gas plants of its kind in the world and is exported to Japan.

Agriculture. The chief agricultural products in 1981 were rice (10,000 tonnes) and bananas (3,000 tonnes).

Livestock in 1982: Cattle, 4,000; buffaloes, 14,000; pigs, 15,000; chickens, 1·2m.

Forestry. Most of the interior is under forest, containing large potential supplies of serviceable timber. Annual production averages 200,000 cu. metres.

INDUSTRY AND TRADE

Industry. Brunei depends primarily on its oil industry, which employs more than

7% of the entire working population. Crude oil accounts for 62% of the total value of the exports and re-exports. The second main export is liquefied natural gas, which contributes 31% and petroleum products 6%.

Other minor products are rubber, pepper, sawn timber, gravel and animal hides. Local industries include boat-building, cloth weaving and the manufacture of brass-and silverware.

Commerce. In 1982 imports totalled US$875m.; exports, US$3,171m.

Total trade between Brunei and UK (British Department of Trade returns, in £1,000 sterling):

	1978	1979	1980	1981	1982	1983
Imports to UK	408	419	889	2,757	2,434	27,154
Exports and re-exports from UK	16,265	22,763	23,118	24,165	41,804	106,477

COMMUNICATIONS

Roads. The State has about 916 miles of road, of which 451 miles are bituminous surfaced. The main road connects Bandar Seri Begawan with Kuala Belait and Seria. Considerable work is being undertaken for development of secondary roads and a coastal road between Muara and Tutong is being constructed. The number of motor vehicles (1980) was 60,751.

Aviation. Royal Brunei Airlines (RBA) and Singapore Airlines provide daily services linking Brunei and Singapore. RBA also operates services to Bangkok, Manila, Kuala Lumpur, Kuching, Kota Kinabalu and Hong Kong. Cathay Pacific Airways also operates to Brunei and on to Western Australia from Hong Kong. British Airways provides a weekly service between Brunei and UK. Malaysian Airlines System has air connections from neighbouring regions.

Shipping. Regular shipping services operate from Singapore, Hong Kong, and from ports in Sarawak and Sabah to Bandar Seri Begawan. Private companies operate a passenger ferry service between Bandar Seri Begawan and Labuan, Sabah, 7 days a week.

Post and Broadcasting. There were 8 post offices (1980) and a telephone network (21,928 telephones in 1982) linking the main centres. Radio Brunei is operated by the Department of Radio and Television and operates on medium- and short-waves in Malay, Iban, Dusun, English and Chinese. Number of radio receivers, 38,000 and television sets, 32,000.

A satellite communications earth station provides easy and quick long-distance external communication and a feasibility study has been undertaken to establish a second earth satellite station.

RELIGION AND EDUCATION

Religion. The official religion is Islam.

Education (1979). Free education in the Malay language is provided in government primary schools (29,934 pupils) and 4 government secondary Malay schools (1,218 pupils). Free education in English was provided in 30 government preparatory schools (8,546 pupils) and 7 government secondary schools (7,344 pupils) and one 6th form centre (819 pupils). The government also provided one Arabic preparatory school (203 pupils) and 2 Arabic secondary schools (251 pupils). Teacher-training was provided in 2 government teachers' colleges, in both Malay and English for 601 students. Eight non-government Mission schools provided education in English at kindergarten, primary and secondary level for a total of 6,745 pupils; 8 non-government Chinese schools provided education in Chinese at the same levels for a total of 5,813 pupils. One private kindergarten and primary school, administered by the Brunei Shell Petroleum Co., provided education in either English or Dutch for a total of 986 pupils, and there was also 1 private vocational school administered by the Brunei Shell Petroleum Co. (140 artisan-trainees). Two government vocational schools provided full training courses to 274 students in the engineering and building trades.

DIPLOMATIC REPRESENTATIVE

Of Great Britain in Brunei (Jalan Residency, Bandar Seri Begawan)
High Commissioner: R. F. Cornish.

BULGARIA

Narodna Republika Bulgaria

Capital: Sofia
Population: 8·91m. (1982)
GNP per capita: US$4,150 (1980)

HISTORY. The Bulgarian state was founded in 681, but fell under Turkish rule in 1396. By the Treaty of Berlin, which followed the Russo-Turkish war of 1878, the Principality of Bulgaria and the Autonomous Province of Eastern Rumelia, both under Turkish suzerainty, were constituted. In 1885 Rumelia was reunited with Bulgaria. On 5 Oct. 1908 Bulgaria declared her independence of Turkey. *Rulers:* Prince Alexander I of Battenberg, 1879–86; Prince (after 1908, Tsar) Ferdinand, 1887–1918 (abdicated); Tsar Boris III, 1918–43; Tsar Simeon II, lost his throne as a result of a referendum held on 8 Sept. 1946 (3,801,160 votes for a republic, 197,176 for the monarchy, 119,168 invalid).

In 1941 Bulgaria signed the Three Power Pact and the Anti-Comintern Pact. In 1944 Bulgaria asked the UK and the USA for an armistice. The USSR declared war on Bulgaria on 5 Sept. 1944. The Fatherland Front government (established 9 Sept.) asked the USSR for an armistice, which was signed on 28 Oct. 1944 by the USSR, the UK and the USA. The peace treaty was signed in Paris on 10 Feb. 1947.

AREA AND POPULATION. On 8 Sept. 1940 by the treaty of Craiova, Romania ceded to Bulgaria the Southern Dobrudja, fixing the new frontier on the 1912 line.

In April 1941 Bulgaria occupied the Yugoslav part of Macedonia, and the Greek districts of Western Thrace, Eastern Macedonia, Florina and Castoria. The peace treaty of 1947 restored the frontiers as on 1 Jan. 1941.

The area of Bulgaria is 110,911·5 sq. km (42,823 sq. miles) and is bounded in the north by Romania, east by the Black Sea, south by Turkey and Greece and west by Yugoslavia.

The country is divided into 28 provinces (*okrŭg*, plur. *okrŭzi*). Area and population in 1981:

Province	Area (sq. km)	Pop. 1,000	Province	Area (sq. km)	Pop. 1,000	Province	Area (sq. km)	Pop. 1,000
Blagoevgrad	6,464	338	Pleven	4,364	373	Sofia (City)	1,113	1,156
Burgas	7,605	435	Plovdiv	5,512	753	Stara Zagora	5,013	411
Gabrovo	2,068	178	Razgrad	2,646	193	Tolbukhin	4,716	252
Khaskovo	4,008	296	Ruse	2,595	297	Tŭrgovishte	2,754	172
Kŭrdzhali	4,020	286	Shumen	3,374	252	Varna	3,810	467
Kyustendil	3,002	199	Silistra	2,859	174	Veliko Tŭrnovo	4,719	347
Lovech	4,129	211	Sliven	3,618	236	Vidin	3,066	169
Mikhailovgrad	3,628	236	Smolyan	3,518	174	Vratsa	4,006	291
Pazardzhik	4,379	322	Sofia	7,310	309	Yambol	4,162	205
Pernik	2,355	175						

The population at the census of 2 Dec. 1975 was 8,727,771 (males, 4,357,820; urban, 5,061,087). Population on 1 Jan. 1982 was 8,905,581 (4·4m. males; 5·7m. urban). Population density 80 per sq. km.

Ethnic minorities are estimated to total 1·2m. The language estimates are: Bulgarian 88%, Turkish 8·6%. The remainder include Gipsies, Jews, Romanians and Armenians. Some Turks have been repatriated.

Population of principal towns (1981): Sofia, 1,070.358; Plovdiv, 358,176; Varna, 293,950; Ruse, 176,013; Burgas, 173,078; Stara Zagora, 138,902; Pleven, 131,690; Sliven, 99,417; Tolbukhin, 97,310; Shumen, 96,632; Pernik, 93,483; Khaskovo, 86,204; Yambol, 84,528; Gabrovo, 79,523; Pazardzhik, 76,020.

Vital statistics, 1981: Live births, 124,372; deaths, 95,441; marriages, 66,539; divorces, 13,252; crude birth rate, 14 per 1,000 population; crude death rate, 10·7; infant mortality, 18·9 per 1,000; growth rate, 3.3.

Expectation of life in 1980 was: men, 68·7 years, women 73·9.

CLIMATE. The southern parts have a Meditterranean climate, with winters mild and moist and summers hot and dry, but further north the conditions become more continental, with a larger range of temperature and greater amounts of rainfall in summer and early autumn. Sofia, Jan. 28°F(–2·2°C), July 69°F (20·6°C). Annual rainfall 25·4″ (635 mm).

CONSTITUTION AND GOVERNMENT. A People's Republic was proclaimed by the National Assembly on 15 Sept. 1946, and the existing 'Tŭrnovo' Constitution of 1879 was replaced by the 'Dimitrov' Constitution in 1947. This was in turn replaced by a new constitution on 18 May 1971. This provides for a single-chamber National Assembly *(Narodno Sŭbranie)*. The highest permanently operating organ of the state is the Council of State which consists of a chairman, 2 first vice-chairmen, 4 vice-chairmen, a secretary and 17 members; it is elected by the National Assembly from its members. Supreme power is vested in the National Assembly, which consists of 400 deputies elected from areas of equal population by direct, secret and universal suffrage (everybody at age of 18 being eligible to vote and hold office) for a term of 5 years; it is to meet at least three times every year. The National Assembly also elects the Council of State and the ministers who are responsible to it.

A general election was held on 27 Oct. 1946. The Fatherland Front, composed of the Workers (Communist), Agrarian, Socialist and Zveno Parties, and non-party independents, obtained 364 seats (277 of which went to the Communists) and the opposition 101. On 26 Aug. 1947 the oppositional Agrarian Union was dissolved; its leader, Nikola Petkov, was sentenced to death and hanged on 23 Sept. The Socialist Party was merged with the Workers' Party in Aug. 1948, and the Zveno Party dissolved itself.

The Fatherland Front became, in 1948, a unified mass organization with individual memberships. Inside the Fatherland Front, there remain two political parties, the Bulgarian Communist Party and the Bulgarian People's Agrarian Union. Petŭr Tanchev *(1st Vice-Chairman, Council of State)* is Secretary of the Agrarian Union and Pencho Kubadinski Chairman of the Fatherland Front's National Council.

In 1981 the membership of the Communist Party was 825,876; Young Communist League, (1976) 1·3m.; Agrarian Union, 120,000; Fatherland Front, 3,770,080.

At the elections of 7 June 1981, 99·96% of the electorate voted, and 99·93% of the votes were cast for the 400 candidates (87 women) of the Fatherland Front; there were no other candidates. The list comprised 271 Communists, 99 Agrarians and 30 independents. The President of the National Assembly is Stanko Todorov.

There is no constitutional single Head of State, but Todor Zhivkov *(Chairman of the Council of State, Secretary-General of the Communist Party)*, performs some of the functions of a Head of State.

The highest policy-making and executive body of the Bulgarian Communist Party is its Politburo, consisting of 11 full members and 3 candidate members. The Politburo is elected by and from the Central Committee.

The Politburo was in March 1984 composed as follows: FULL MEMBERS: Todor Zhivkov, Grisha Filipov *(Chairman, Council of Ministers, i.e. Prime Minister)*, Todor Bozhinov *(1st Deputy Chairman, Council of Ministers, Minister of Energy and Raw Materials)*, Stanko Todorov, Pencho Kubadinski, Milko Balev, Chudomir Aleksandrov *(1st Deputy Chairman, Council of Ministers)*, Gen. Dobri Dzhurov *(Defence Minister)*, Petŭr Mladenov *(Foreign Minister)*, Ognian Doinov *(Minister of Machine Building)*; Iordan Iotov. CANDIDATE MEMBERS: Petŭr Dyulgerov; Andrei Lukanov *(Deputy Chairman, Council of Ministers)*, Georgi Yordanov *(Deputy Chairman, Council of Ministers, Chairman, Committee for Culture)*. Grigor Stoichkov *(Deputy Chairman, Council of Ministers)*. Stanish Bonev *(Deputy Chairman, Council of Ministers, Chairman, State Planning Committee)*. Georgi Atanasov; Dimitŭr Stoianov *(Minister of Internal Affairs)*.

Ministers not in the Politburo include: Kiril Zarev *(Deputy Chairman, Council of Ministers)*, Georgi Karamanev, *(Deputy Chairman, Council of Ministers, Minister of Internal Trade)*, Khristo Khristov *(Foreign Trade)*, Belcho Belchev *(Finance)*, Svetla Daskalova *(Justice)*.

In May 1967 a second 20-year treaty of friendship, co-operation and mutual assistance with the Soviet Union was signed.

National flag: Three horizontal stripes of white, green, red, with the national emblem in the canton.

National anthem: An arrangement of Mila Rodino (Dear Fatherland), a popular patriotic song, was declared the national anthem in 1964.

Local Government. People's Councils for the 28 provinces, 29 urban areas and 299 other districts are elected for 30 months. In addition to their civic functions they also supervise the management of publicly owned enterprises. The Council's executive organs are Permanent Committees. 4,475 councillors were elected on 4 Dec. 1983.

DEFENCE. There is a compulsory service of 2 years in the Army and Air Force (3 years in the Navy).

Army. In 1984 the Army had a strength of 120,000, including 73,000 conscripts, and is organized in 8 motor rifle divisions and 5 tank brigades. Bulgaria is divided into 3 Military Districts, based on Sofia, Plovdiv and Sliven. Equipment includes 300 T-34, 1,000 T-54/-55 and 60 T-72 tanks. Paramilitary forces, including border guards, security police and People's Territorial Militia, number some 175,000.

Navy. The Navy consists of 2 *ex*-Soviet 'R' class submarines, 2 *ex*-Soviet 'Riga' class frigates, 3 *ex*-Soviet 'Poti' class corvettes, 5 *ex*-Soviet 'Osa' class missile boats, 6 *ex*-Soviet patrol vessels, 10 *ex*-Soviet torpedo boats, 2 fleet minesweepers, 4 coastal minesweepers, 4 inshore minesweepers, 18 minesweeping boats, 28 landing craft, 4 oilers, 3 survey ships, 2 salvage craft, 9 tugs, 2 training ships, 2 degaussing vessels, 2 diving tenders and 28 auxiliaries and service craft. Personnel in 1984 totalled 10,000 officers and ratings of whom 4,000 were afloat.

Air Force. The large tactical Air Force has about 250 Soviet-built combat aircraft and 34,000 personnel. There are 5 squadrons of MiG-21 interceptors; about 8 squadrons of fighter/ground attack MiG-23s and MiG-17s; 2 reconnaissance squadrons of MiG-17s; some Mi-24 helicopter gunships; a total of about 20 Tu-134, Il-14 and An-24/26 transport aircraft; a total of about 70 Mi-4, Mi-2, Ka-26, Mi-6, and Mi-8 helicopters; and L-29 Delfin, MiG-15UTI and MiG-21UTI trainers. Soviet-built 'Guideline', 'Goa' and 'Ganef' surface-to-air missiles have also been supplied to Bulgaria.

INTERNATIONAL RELATIONS

Membership. Bulgaria is a member of UN, Comecon and the Warsaw Pact.

External Debt. Agreements of 1955 and 1963 settled outstanding financial claims by the UK and USA respectively.

ECONOMY

Planning. State economic planning started in 1947. After 1964 there was a limited decentralization in planning, culminating in the economic reform of 1 Jan. 1969. A new economic mechanism was introduced on 1 Jan. 1982. This provides for direct linking of production to the market, a shift from extensive to intensive development, the establishment of profit as the sole criterion of success, the widening of enterprises' powers to make their own plans and the election of managerial staff (except the chief) by the workforce.

For the first seven 5-year plans *see* THE STATESMAN'S YEAR-BOOK for 1980–81 and 1981–82. The eighth 5-year plan (1981–85) envisages a rise in national income of 20%, in industrial production of 28% and in agriculture of 18%.

Budget. The revenue and expenditure of Bulgaria for calendar years were as follows (in 1m. leva):

	1972	1973	1974	1975	1976	1977	1980	1981	1982
Revenue	6,355	7,055	8,060	9,321	8,778	9,498	13,187	15,385	15,824
Expenditure	6,261	7,036	8,044	9,223	8,758	9,477	13,167	15,370	15,809

Of the 1984 revenue 92% came from the national economy. 1980 expenditure was: National economy, 5,777m. leva; social and education, 5,265m.; administration, 291m.

Currency. The unit of currency is the *lev* (pl. *leva*) divided into 100 *stotinki* (sing. *stotinka*). It has been linked to the Soviet rouble since May 1952. A new *lev*, equalling 10 old leva, was introduced on 1 Jan. 1962. The parity (clearing value) is 1 rouble = 1·30 *leva*. Official rate of exchange (March 1984) was £1 = 1·434 *leva*; US$1 = 0·999 *leva*. Rate of exchange for non-commercial transactions: £1 = 2·40 leva; US$1 = 1·65 *leva*.

Banking. The National Bank is the central bank and is responsible for issuing currency. It also plays an important part in the management of the economy: its chairman has ministerial rank. There is also a Foreign Trade Bank, a Mineral Bank and a State Savings Bank. In 1981, 9m. depositors had savings totalling 9,025m. leva. The State Savings Bank has advanced personal loans up to 500 leva at 3·5% interest to some 500,000 users. Interest on deposits is from 1% to 3%.

Weights and Measures. The metric system is in general use. On 1 April 1916 the Gregorian calendar came into force in Bulgaria.

ENERGY AND NATURAL RESOURCES

Energy. Bulgaria has little oil, gas or high-grade coal and energy policy is based on the exploitation of its low-grade coal and limited water resources.

Electricity. In 1981 there were 236 power stations with a potential of 9·06m. kw. (thermal, (149) 5·84m. kw.; hydroelectric, (86) 1·9m. kw.; nuclear, (1) 1·32m. kw.). Output, 1981, 36,971m. kwh.

Oil and Natural Gas. Oil is extracted in the Balchik district on the Black Sea, in an area 100 km north of Varna and at Dolni Dubnik near Pleven. Crude oil production was 129,000 tonnes in 1977. There are refineries at Burgas (annual capacity 5m. tonnes) and Dolni Dubnik (7m. tonnes). 190m. cu. metres of natural gas were produced in 1980.

Minerals. Ore production 1981: Manganese, 13,200 tonnes; iron, 537,000 tonnes. 30·6m. tonnes of coal including 429,000 tonnes of hard coal and 23·3m. tonnes of lignite were mined in 1981. 84 tonnes of salt were extracted in 1981.

Agriculture. In 1979 the National Agro-Industrial Union was formed, replacing the Ministry of Agriculture. It comprises state and collective organizations, and is responsible for agriculture, the food industry and agricultural machine building. In 1981 cultivated agricultural land covered 6,178,700 hectares, of which 4,658,900 hectares are arable.

Size of private plots (maximum, 1 hectare) is based on the number of members of a household. Total area of private plots in 1981 was 584,700 hectares. In 1978 these accounted for 23% of all agricultural production. Collective and state farms have been incorporated into 'agricultural-industrial complexes'. There were 281 of these in 1981 with 4,962,007 hectares. There were 54 machine-tractor stations. 152,377 tractors (in 15-h.p. units) were in use and 20,275 combine harvesters.

In 1981, 26 irrigation systems and 154 dams irrigated 1,169,900 hectares.

Yield in 1981 (in 1,000 tonnes): Wheat, 4,443; rye, 34; maize, 2,401; barley, 1,406; oats, 62; rice, 74; sunflower seed, 457; unginned cotton, 13; tobacco, 130; tomatoes, 917; potatoes, 403; grapes, 1,126. Bulgaria is the world's principal supplier of attar of roses; annual production, 1,200 kg.

Other products (in 1,000 tonnes) in 1981: Meat, 1,144; wool, 35; sugar, 405; 2,431m. eggs were produced and 2,227m. litres of milk.

Livestock (1982): 118,729 horses, 1,806,885 cattle, including 701,334 milch cows, 10,725,518 sheep, 3,843,718 pigs, 40,562,940 poultry and 580,782 bee-hives.

Forestry. The forest area, 1981, was 3,852,000 hectares, of which 1·27m. were con-iferous. 40,211 hectares were afforested in 1981. 7·9m. cu. metres of timber were cut in 1981.

Fisheries. The catch of sea fish was 89,500 tonnes in 1979.

INDUSTRY AND TRADE

Industry. All industry was nationalized in 1947.

Industrial production	1976	1977	1978	1979	1980	1981
Crude steel (1,000 tonnes)	2,460	2,589	2,470	2,482	2,565	2,484
Pig-iron (1,000 tonnes)	1,612	1,664	1,538	1,501	1,583	1,512
Cement (1,000 tonnes)	4,362	4,665	5,149	5,401	5,359	5,433
Sulphuric acid (1,000 tonnes)	857	860	974	998	852	920

In 1981 there were also produced (in 1,000 tonnes): Coke, 1,383; rolled steel, 3,351; artificial fertilizers, 2,681; calcinated soda, 1,469; cotton fabrics, 354m. metres; woollens, 40m. metres.

Labour. There is 42½-hour 5-day working week. The average wage (excluding peasantry) was 207 leva per month in 1983. Population of working age (males 16–60; females 16–55), 1981, 5·07m. (2·7m. males) The labour force (excluding peasantry) in 1981 was 4,047,501 (2.605,691 female), of whom 1,389,871 worked in industry, 346,314 in building and 938,451 in agriculture and forestry.

Commerce. Foreign trade is controlled by the Ministry of Foreign Trade. Bulgarian trade has developed as follows (in 1m. leva):

	1976	1977	1978	1979	1980	1981
Imports	5,436	6,061	6,801	7,363	8,283	9,860
Exports	5,200	6,022	6,650	7,667	8,902	9,958

Structure of imports and exports in 1981: Producers' goods, 87%, 73%; con-sumer goods, 13%, 27%; industrial products, 97%, 77%; agricultural products, 3%, 23%.

Main exports are food products, tobacco, non-ferrous metals, cast iron, leather articles, textiles and (to Communist countries) machinery; main imports are machinery, oil, natural gas, steel, cellulose and timber.

79% of Bulgaria's trade is with the Communist countries. Agreements with USSR envisage the co-ordination of the Soviet and Bulgarian 5-year plans in the spirit of 'socialist internationalism'. In 1979 a 10-year plan of economic specializa-tion and co-operation was signed with the USSR. Greece is Bulgaria's biggest non-Communist export market, Federal Republic of Germany her major non-Communist supplier.

Indebtedness to the West was some US$1,800m. in 1983.

Total trade between Bulgaria and UK (British Department of Trade returns, in £1,000 sterling):

	1979	1980	1981	1982	1983
Imports to UK	12,082	14,425	13,353	21,009	12,355
Exports and re-exports from UK	27,324	35,242	33,838	46,104	44,577

Joint Western-Bulgarian industrial ventures are permitted under laws of June 1974 and March 1980. In 1979 there were 40 in operation. Western share partici-pation may exceed 50%.

On 13 May 1974 Bulgaria and the UK signed a 10-year economic, scientific and technological co-operation agreement.

COMMUNICATIONS

Roads. In 1981 there were 32,354 km of roads, including 108 km of motorways and 2,910 km of main roads. 837m. tonnes of freight and 2,019m. passengers were carried.

Railways. In 1983 Bulgaria had 4,341 km of standard gauge railway, including 1,650 km electrified. 96m. passengers and 81·5m. tons of freight were carried in 1981.

Aviation. BALKAN (Bulgarian Airlines) operates internal flights from Sofia (airport: Vrazhdebna) to Burgas, Khaskovo, Pleven, Plovdiv, Ruse, Silistra, Stara Zagora, Turgovishte, Veliko Turnovo, Varna, Vidin and Yambol and international flights to Algiers, Amsterdam, Athens, Baghdad, Bratislava, Belgrade, Benghazi, Berlin, Brussels, Bucharest, Budapest, Cairo, Casablanca, Copenhagen, Damascus, Dresden, Frankfurt, Istanbul, London, Madrid, Moscow, Nicosia, Paris, Prague, Rome, Stockholm, Syktyvkar, Tunis, Vienna, Warsaw and Zurich. There are also flights from Burgas to Leningrad and Kiev, and from Varna to Leningrad, Kuwait, Athens and Stockholm. In 1981 BALKAN carried 2·3m. passengers and 27,584 tonnes of freight.

Shipping. Ports, shipping and shipbuilding are controlled by the Bulgarian United Shipping and Shipbuilding Corporation. The mercantile marine in 1982 possessed 194 ocean-going vessels and tankers with a total loading capacity of 1·6m. DWT. Burgas is a fishing and oil-port open to tankers of 20,000 tons. Varna is the other important port. In Nov. 1978 a rail ferry, with an initial capacity of 4·5m. tonnes of freight a year, was opened between Varna and Ilitchovsk (USSR). In 1981, 657,000 passengers and 27m. tonnes of cargo were carried.

Post and Broadcasting. In 1981 there were 2,889 post offices, 1,382,076 telephones, 57 broadcasting stations and 26 television stations. Radio Sofia, the government broadcasting station, transmits 2 programmes on medium- and short-waves. There is also a special tourist service, broadcast *via* the Varna II transmitter on 1,124 kHz. Advertisements are broadcast for half an hour a day. Bulgaria participates in the East European TV link 'Intervision'. Colour programmes by SECAM system. Radio receiving sets licensed in 1981, 2,115,059; television, 1,658,688.

Cinemas and Theatres (1981). There were 37 theatres, 17 puppet theatres, 8 opera houses, 1 operetta house and 3,353 cinemas. 486 films were made (42 full-length).

Newspapers and Books. In 1981 there were 14 dailies with a circulation of 2·2m. The Party newspaper is *Rabotnicheskoto Delo* ('The Workers' Cause') with a circulation of 800,000 in 1982. 5,036 book titles were published in 1981.

JUSTICE, RELIGION, EDUCATION AND WELFARE

Justice. A law of Nov. 1982 provides for the election (and recall) of all judges by the National Assembly. The lower courts include lay assessors as well as professional judges. There are a Supreme Court, 28 provincial courts (including Sofia), 105 regional courts and 'Comrades' Courts' for minor offences.

The maximum term of imprisonment is now 20 years except for 'exceptionally dangerous crimes' which carry the death penalty.

The Prosecutor General, elected by the National Assembly for 5 years and subordinate to it alone, exercises supreme control over the correct observance of the law by all government bodies, officials and citizens. He appoints and discharges all Prosecutors of every grade. The powers of this office were extended and redefined by a law of 1980 to put a greater emphasis on crime prevention and the rights of citizens.

Religion. 'The traditional church of the Bulgarian people' (as it is officially described), is that of the Eastern Orthodox Church. It was disestablished under the 1947 Constitution. On 10 May 1953 the Bulgarian Patriarchate was revived and Metropolitan Kiril was elected the first Bulgarian Patriarch since 1393. Upon the death of Kiril Metropolitan Maksim of Lovech was enthroned as the new Patriarch in July 1971. The seat of the Patriarch is at Sofia. There are 11 dioceses, each under a Metropolitan, 10 bishops, 2,600 parishes and 1,500 priests. In 1976 there were 3,720 churches, 500 chapels and some 20 monasteries and nunneries.

The Constitution provides for freedom of conscience and belief but forbids propaganda against the Government. The State provides 17% of Church funds.

Churches may not maintain schools or colleges, except theological seminaries, or organize youth movements.

In 1976 there were some 50,000 Roman Catholics in 3 bishoprics with 40 priests and 30 churches, and 16,000 Protestants with 101 churches and 265 priests. There were 80,000 Moslems under a Grand Mufti and 6 regional mufti boards with 1,180 mosques.

Education. Education is free, and compulsory for children between the ages of 7 and 16. The gradual introduction of unified secondary polytechnical schools offering compulsory education for all children from the ages of 7 to 17 was begun in 1973–74. Complete literacy is claimed. Schools are classified according to which years of schooling they offer: Elementary (1–4), primary (1–8), preparatory (5–8), secondary (9–11), complete secondary (1–11).

Educational statistics for 1981–82: 5,918 kindergartens (407,297 children, 29,092 teachers); 776 elementary schools; 2,288 primary schools; 62 preparatory schools; 105 secondary schools; 319 complete secondary schools. Numbers of teachers and pupils: School years 1 to 4, 22,682 and 415,868; 5 to 8, 35,000 and 614,830; 9 to 11, 7,986 and 103,810. There were also 3 vocational-technical schools (64 teachers, 1,626 students), 232 technical colleges (9,354 teachers, 96,357 students), 24 post-secondary institutions (1,090 teachers, 10,752 students) and 28 institutes of higher education (12,820 teachers, 85,068 students). There are 3 universities: the Kliment Ohrid University in Sofia (founded 1888) had 1,195 teachers and 12,616 students (in 1977–78); the Kirill i Metodii University in Veliko Túrnovo (founded 1971) had 250 teachers and 3,670 students and the Paisi Hilendarski University in Plovdiv (founded 1972) had 274 teachers and 3,500 students in 1980–81.

The Academy of Sciences was founded in 1869.

Social Welfare. Retirement and disablement pensions and temporary sick pay are calculated as a percentage of previous wages (respectively 55–80%, 35–100%, 69–90%) and according to the nature of the employment.

Monthly family allowances for children under 16: 15 leva for 1 child, 25 leva for 2 children and 45 leva for 3 children.

In 1981, 2·09m. persons received pensions totalling 1,800m. leva.

All medical services are free. In 1981 there were 186 hospitals (including 16 mental hospitals and addiction treatment centres) with 74,241 beds. There were 22,088 doctors and 4,984 dentists.

DIPLOMATIC REPRESENTATIVES

Of Bulgaria in Great Britain (186 Queen's Gate, London, SW7 5HL)
Ambassador: Kiril Shterev (accredited 26 Nov. 1980)

Of Great Britain in Bulgaria (Blvd. Marshal Tolbukhin 65–67, Sofia)
Ambassador: J. M. O. Snodgrass, CMG.

Of Bulgaria in the USA (1621–22nd St., NW, Washington, D.C., 20008)
Ambassador: Stoyan I. Zhulev.

Of the USA in Bulgaria (1 Stamboliiski Blvd., Sofia)
Ambassador: Robert L. Barry.

Of Bulgaria to the United Nations
Ambassador: Boris Tsvetkov.

Books of Reference

Kratka Bŭlgarska Entsiklopediia (Short Bulgarian Encyclopaedia), 5 vols. Sofia, 1963–69
Statistecheski Godishnik (Statistical Yearbook). Sofia from 1956
Constitution of the People's Republic of Bulgaria. Sofia, 1971
Modern Bulgaria: History, Politics, Economy, Culture. Sofia, 1981
Atanasova, T., *et al., Bulgarian-English Dictionary.* Sofia, 1975
Brown, J. F., *Bulgaria under Communist Rule.* London, 1970

Dobrin, B., *Bulgarian Economic Development Since World War II.* New York, 1973

Feiwel, G. R., *Growth and Reforms in Centrally Planned Economies: the Lessons of the Bulgarian Experience.* New York, 1977

Markov, M., *System of Social Administration in Bulgaria.* Sofia, 1969

Oren, N., *Communism Administered: Agrarianism and Communism in Bulgaria.* Baltimore, 1973

Pundeff, M. V., *Bulgaria: A Bibliographic Guide.* Library of Congress, 1965

Spasov, B., *La Bulgarie.* Paris, 1973

Todorov, N., and others, *Bulgaria: Historic and Geographical Outline.* Sofia, 1965

Zhivkov, T., *Modern Bulgaria: Problems and Tasks in Building an Advanced Socialist Society.* New York, 1974

BURMA

Capital: Rangoon
Population: 35·31m. (1983)
GNP per capita: US$180 (1981)

Pyidaungsu Socialist Thammada Myanma Naingngandaw

HISTORY. The Union of Burma came formally into existence on 4 Jan. 1948 and became the Socialist Republic of the Union of Burma in 1974. In 1948 Sir Hubert Rance, the last British Governor, handed over authority to Sao Shwe Thaike, the first President of the Burmese Republic, and Parliament ratified the treaty with Great Britain providing for the independence of Burma as a country not within His Britannic Majesty's dominions and not entitled to His Britannic Majesty's protection. This treaty was signed in London on 17 Oct. 1947 and enacted by the British Parliament on 10 Dec. 1947.

For the history of Burma's connexion with Great Britain *see* THE STATESMAN'S YEAR-BOOK, 1950, p. 836.

AREA AND POPULATION. Burma is bounded east by China, Laos and Thailand, west by the Indian ocean, Bangladesh and India. The total area of the Union is 261,789 sq. miles (678,000 sq. km). Some small rectifications of the border with China were agreed upon in 1960 and with Pakistan in 1964. The population in 1983 (census) was 35,313,905. Birth rate (1977 estimate), 29·1; death rate, 10·4 per 1,000 population; infant deaths, 56·3 per 1,000 live births. The leading towns are: Rangoon, the capital (1983), 2,458,712; other towns (1973), Mandalay, 417,266; Bassein, 355,588; Henzada, 283,658; Pegu, 254,761, Myingyan, 220,129; Moulmein, 202,967; Prome, 148,123; Akyab, 143,215; Tavoy, 101,536.

The population of the States and Divisions at the 1983 census (provisional): Kachin State, 903,982; Kayah State, 168,355; Karen State, 1,057,505; Chin State, 368,985; Sagaing Division, 3,855,991; Tenasserim Division, 917,628; Pegu Division, 3,800,240; Magwe Division, 3,241,103; Mandalay Division, 4,580,923; Mon State, 1,682,041; Rakhine State, 2,045,891; Rangoon Division, 3,973,782; Shan State, 3,718,706; Irrawaddy Division, 4,991,057.

The Burmese belong to the Tibeto-Chinese (or Tibeto-Burman) family.

CLIMATE. The climate is equatorial in coastal areas, changing to tropical monsoon over most of the interior, but humid temperate in the extreme north, where there is a more significant range of temperature and a dry season lasting from Nov. to April. In coastal parts, the dry season is shorter. Very heavy rains occur in the monsoon months May to Sept. Rangoon. Jan. 77°F (25°C), July 80°F (26·7°C). Annual rainfall 104″ (2,616 mm). Akyab. Jan. 70°F (21·1°C), July 81°F (27·2°C). Annual rainfall 206″ (5,154 mm). Mandalay. Jan. 68°F (20°C), July 85°F (29·4°C). Annual rainfall 33″ (828 mm).

CONSTITUTION. A new Constitution was approved by referendum in Dec. 1973. On 2 March 1974 military rule ended and Burma became a one-party socialist republic. Elections to the People's Assembly took place in Jan. and Feb. 1974. U Ne Win became President under the new Constitution and in Jan. 1978 his term of office was extended for 4 years. For earlier Constitutions *see* THE STATEMAN'S YEAR-BOOK, 1981–82, p 252.

In Nov. 1981, U San Yu was elected Head of State by the People's Assembly.

The State Council has 27 members with U San Yu as Chairman and U Aye Ko as secretary.

In Jan. 1984 the Council of Ministers consisted of:

Prime Minister: U Maung Maung Kha.

249

Deputy Prime Minister, Planning and Finance: U Tun Tin. *Deputy Prime Minister, Defence:* Gen. Thura Kyaw Htin. *Agriculture and Forests:* U Ye Goung. *Co-operatives:* U Sein Tun. *Transport and Communications:* Thura U Saw Pru. *Foreign Affairs:* U Chit Hlaing. *Industry:* U Tint Swe, U Maung Cho. *Construction:* U Hla Tun. *Mines:* U Than Tin. *Trade:* U Khin Maung Ghi. *Education:* U Kyaw Nyein. *Information and Culture:* U Aung Kyaw Myint. *Home and Religious Affairs:* Maj.-Gen. Min Gaung. *Labour and Social Welfare:* U Ohn Kyaw. *Health:* U Tun Wai. *Livestock and Fisheries:* U Sein Tun.

National flag: Red with a blue canton bearing 2 ears of rice within a cog-wheel and a ring of 14 stars, all in white.

Language: The official language is Burmese; the use of English is permitted.

Local government: Burma is divided into 7 states and 7 administrative divisions; these are sub-divided into townships and thence into villages and wards.

DEFENCE

Army. The strength of the Army (1984) was 163,000. The Army is organized into 9 regional commands comprising 6 light infantry divisions, and 2 armoured, 85 independent infantry and 4 artillery battalions and 1 anti-aircraft battery. Equipment includes 25 Comet tanks, 40 Humber armoured cars and 45 Ferret scout cars. In addition, there are 2 paramilitary units: People's Police Force (38,000) and People's Militia (35,000).

Navy. The fleet includes 2 old escort patrol vessels (*ex*-USA PCE and MSF types), 2 small indigenously built corvettes, 1 support gunboat (*ex*-landing craft), 13 coastal gunboats, 20 river gunboats, 40 small river patrol craft, 1 support ship, 2 survey vessels, 12 fishery protection cutters (3 offshore, 3 coastal, 6 inshore), 10 auxiliaries and 9 landing craft. Personnel in 1984: 10,000 including 800 marines.

Air Force. The Air Force is intended primarily for internal security duties. Its combat force comprises about 6 T-33A jet fighter/trainers supplied under MAP, supplemented by 9 SIAI-Marchetti SF.260W light piston-engined attack/trainers. Other training aircraft include 10 piston-engined SF.260Ms, 16 turboprop Pilatus PC-7s and 10 jet-powered T-37Cs. Transport and second-line units are equipped with small numbers of FH-227, Turbo-Porter and Cessna 180 aircraft, and Japanese-built Bell 47 (H-13) and Vertol KV-107-II, Bell UH-1, and Alouette III helicopters. Personnel about 9,000.

INTERNATIONAL RELATIONS

Membership. Burma is a member of the UN and Colombo Plan.

ECONOMY

Planning. The economy has been controlled since 1972 through a series of 4-year plans. The third plan began in 1978–79 and aims to increase average *per capita* output by 6·6%, and net output value by 5·9%, distributed as follows: Construction, 23·2%; financial institutions, 21·4%; power, 16·8%; mining, 13·4%; processing and manufacturing, 13·4%; transport, 8·6%; communications, 8·5%; agriculture, 5%; livestock and fish, 4·7%; forestry, 4·1%; trade, 3%; social development and administration, 2·3%.

Budget. The budget estimates (in K.1m.) for fiscal year 1 April 1980–31 March 1981 was revenue K.24,968m. and expenditure K.27,104m.

The largest items, in 1980–81, of revenue were commodities and service tax (K.2,360·1m.) and customs (K.590m.); of expenditure, processing and manufacturing (K.8,769m.); trade (K.5,222·3m.); transport and communication (1,736·2m.).

Currency. The currency unit is now the *kyat* divided into 100 *pyas*. There are notes of *kyat* 25, 20, 10, 5 and 1, and coins of *kyat* 1; *pyas* 100, 50, 25, 10, 5 and 1.

Currency in circulation at 31 March 1980 was valued at K.7,172m.

Banking. Banks include the Union of Burma Bank, the Myanma Economic Bank, the Myanma Foreign Trade Bank and the Myanma Agricultural Bank and the corporation is the Myanma Insurance Corporation.

ENERGY AND NATURAL RESOURCES

Electricity. In 1979 the total installed capacity of power plants was 642,230 kw., of which 168,500 was hydro-electricity and 158.850 gas turbine; there were 264 towns and 709 villages with electricity.

Oil. Production (1980–81, provisional) of crude oil was 11·18m. bbls; natural gas (1979–80), 12,846m. cu. ft.

Minerals. Production in 1977–78 (provisional): Silver, 410,000 oz.; zinc, 6,000 tons; copper matte, 90 tons; refined lead, 5,198 tons; nickel speiss, 75 tons; antimony, 1,455 tons; tin, 866 tons; tungsten, 568 tons; tin tungsten-scheelite, 500 tons; coal (1981), 30,000 tons; gypsum, 28,000 tons; limestone, 1m. tons.

Agriculture. Production (1981) in 1,000 tonnes: Paddy, 13,923; sugar-cane, 2,569; groundnuts, 558; jute, 32; cotton, 107.

Livestock (1982): Cattle, 8·7m.; buffaloes, 2m.; pigs, 2·2m.

In 1979–80 the area irrigated by government-controlled irrigation works was 2,417,769 acres.

Forestry. The area of reserved forests in 1977–78 was 23,477,000 acres; other forests, 55,986,000 acres. Teak extracted in 1979–80 (provisional), 400,250 cu. tons; hardwood, 1,049,000 cu. tons. All the teak and about 50% of the hardwood is from the state sector. Other forest produce (1977–78) included 13m. tons of firewood and 680,000 bamboo canes. 2,780 elephants are at work on extraction.

Fisheries. In 1979 sea fishing produced 413,000 tonnes and freshwater fisheries 153,000 tonnes. The contribution of state-owned fishing vessels (32 trawlers and 43 other craft) is about 3%.

INDUSTRY AND TRADE

Industry. Production (1981) in 1,000 metric tonnes: Cement, 372; salt, 242; fertilizers, 132; sugar, 42; paper, 23; cotton, 15.

Labour. In 1977–78 (provisional, 1,000) the workforce numbered 12,640: Agriculture, 8,212 (state sector 73); trade, 1,206 (45); processing and manufacturing, 929 (160); administration, 483 (459); transport and communication, 420 (104); social services, 246 (174); construction, 184 (124); livestock and fisheries, 167 (8); forestry, 152 (73); mining, 67 (65); power, 15 (15).

Trade Unions. Labour disputes are dealt with by the government labour sub-committees.

Commerce. All foreign trade is handled by the government trading organizations. Imports and exports (in K.1m.) for the calendar years.

	1978	1979	1980
Imports	3,638·5	4,189·9	3,965·2
Exports	1,608·4	2,548·8	3,122·6

Total trade between Burma and UK (British Department of Trade returns, in £1,000 sterling):

	1978	1979	1980	1981	1982	1983
Imports to UK	5,773	6,000	5,379	3,613	5,342	4,726
Exports and re-exports from UK	26,439	18,641	20,494	28,036	44,242	21,927

Tourism. There were 23,845 tourists in 1980.

COMMUNICATIONS

Roads. There were 13,948 miles of road in 1977–78, of which 2,452 miles were union highway.

Railways. The Burma Railways were nationalized in 1948 and the present Burma Railways Corporation took over in 1972. In 1980 there were 3,137 km of route on metre gauge. In 1977–78 the railway carried 2·29m. tons of freight and 64·2m. passengers.

Aviation. Burma Airways Corporation, formerly Union of Burma Airways, started its internal service in Sept. 1948 and its external service in Nov. 1950. International services were in 1963 maintained between Rangoon and Bangkok and Calcutta. The routes were extended to Hong Kong in 1969 and to Dacca and Káthmándu in 1970. There were, in 1971, 43 civil aerodromes and landing grounds.

Shipping. Burma has 60 miles of navigable canals. The Irrawaddy is navigable up to Myitkyina, 900 miles from the sea, and its tributary, the Chindwin, is navigable for 390 miles. The Irrawaddy delta has nearly 2,000 miles of navigable water. The Salween, the Attaran and the G'yne provide about 250 miles of navigable waters around Moulmein. The Inland Water Transport Board runs services from Bhamo to Myitkyina.

Post and Broadcasting. There were 1,101 post offices in 1977. Number of telephones was 32,616 in 1978, of which 22,456 are in Rangoon. There is one television broadcasting station in Rangoon.

Cinemas. In 1971 there were about 418 cinemas.

Newspapers. In 1978 there were 7 daily newspapers.

JUSTICE, RELIGION, EDUCATION AND WELFARE

Justice. Since March 1974 the highest judicial authority has been the Council of People's Justices, appointed by the People's Assembly from its own members, which serves as the Supreme Court and Central Criminal Court. At lower levels courts are appointed by the local People's Councils from among their own membership.

Religion. The Revolutionary Government, having repealed the amendment of 1961 which made Buddhism the state religion, recognizes 'the right of everyone freely to profess and practise his religion'.

Education. The medium of instruction in all schools is Burmese; English is taught as a compulsory second language from kindergarten level.

Education is free in the primary, junior secondary and vocational schools; fees are charged in senior secondary schools and universities.

In 1977–78 there were 586 state high schools with 189,146 pupils, 1,262 state middle schools with 825,195 pupils and 21,999 state primary schools with 3,841,687 pupils; the total teaching staff was 111,339, of which 80,343 were in primary schools.

Beside the Arts and Science University, there are independent degree-giving institutes of engineering, education, medicine, agriculture, economics and commerce, and veterinary sciences. The University of Mandalay has been similarly decentralized. A foreign-languages institute in Rangoon has about 800 students learning English, French, German, Russian, Japanese, Chinese and Italian.

There are intermediate colleges at Taunggyi, Magwe, Akyab and Myitkyina, and degree colleges at Moulmein and Bassein, and several technical and agricultural institutes at higher and middle level. 4,656 school teachers were being trained in 15 training colleges in 1977–78. Technical high schools had 2,488 students; agricultural schools, 1,077; other vocational colleges, 1,438, and university colleges, 63,292.

A correspondence course for universities and colleges was introduced in 1975–76.

Health. In 1977 there were 5,787 doctors and 512 hospitals with 22,755 beds. There were 1,459 health centres.

DIPLOMATIC REPRESENTATIVES

Of Burma in Great Britain (19A Charles St., London, W1X 8ER)
Ambassador: U Myo Aung (accredited 16 Dec. 1981).

Of Great Britain in Burma (80 Strand Rd., Rangoon)
Ambassador: N. M. Fenn, CMG.

Of Burma in the USA (2300 S St., NW, Washington, D.C., 20008)
Ambassador: U Kyee Myint.

Of the USA in Burma (581 Merchant St., Rangoon)
Ambassador: Patricia M. Byrne.

Of Burma to the United Nations
Ambassador: Saw Hlaing.

Books of Reference

Burma: Treaty between the Government of the United Kingdom and the Provisional Government of Burma. (Treaty Series No. 16, 1948.) HMSO, 1948
Cornyn, W. S., and Musgrave, J. K., *Burmese Glossary.* New York, 1958
Lehman, F. K., *The Structure of Chin Society.* Univ. of Illincis Press, 1963
Silverstein, J., *Burma: Military Rule and the Politics of Stagnation.* Cornell Univ. Press, 1978.
—*Burmese Politics: The Dilemma of National Unity.* Rutgers Univ. Press, 1980
Steinberg, D. I., *Burma.* Boulder, 1982
Stewart, J. A., and Dunn, C. W., *Burmese–English Dictionary.* London, 1940 ff.

BURUNDI

Capital: Bujumbura
Population: 4·92m. (1983)
GNP per capita: US$200 (1980)

HISTORY. Tradition recounts the establishment of a Tutsi kingdom under successive Mwamis as early as the 16th century. German military occupation in 1890 incorporated the territory into German East Africa. From 1919 Burundi formed part of Ruanda-Urundi administered by the Belgians, first as a League of Nations mandate and then as a United Nations trust territory. Elections supervised by the United Nations in Sept. 1961 resulted in a large majority for the Unité et Progrès National party (UPRONA). Internal self-government was granted on 1 Jan. 1962, followed by independence on 1 July 1962. An agreement, signed with Rwanda under United Nations auspices at Addis Ababa in April 1962, provided for a monetary and customs union. This union and all organizations operated jointly by the two governments were dissolved by 30 Sept. 1964.

On 8 July 1966 Prince Charles Ndizeye deposed his father Mwami Mwambutsa IV, suspended the constitution and made Capt. Michel Micombero Prime Minister. On 1 Sept. Prince Charles was enthroned as Mwami Ntare V. On 28 Nov., while the Mwami was attending a Head of States Conference in Kinshasa (Congo), Micombero declared Burundi a republic with himself as president.

On 31 March 1972 Prince Charles returned to Burundi from Uganda and was placed under house arrest. On 29 April 1972 President Micombero dissolved the Council of Ministers and took full power; that night heavy fighting broke out between rebels from both Burundi and neighbouring countries, and the ruling Tutsi, apparently with the intention of destroying the Tutsi hegemony. Prince Charles was killed during the fighting and it was estimated that up to 120,000 were killed. On 14 July 1972 President Micombero reinstated a Government with a Prime Minister. On 1 Nov. 1976 President Micombero was deposed by the Army. A Supreme Revolutionary Council of the Armed Forces was established which appointed Col. Jean-Baptiste Bagaza president.

AREA AND POPULATION. Burundi extends from lat. 2½° to 4½° S. and long. 29° to 31° E., and has an area of 27,834 sq. km (10,759 sq. miles). It lies astride the main Nile–Congo dividing crest (6,000–7,000 ft) bounded on the west by the narrow plain of the Ruzizi River and Lake Tanganyika (2,534 ft). The interior is a broken plateau at an average height of about 5,000 ft, sloping eastwards down to Tanzania and the valley of the Maragarazi River. The southernmost tributary of the Nile system, the Luvironza, rises in the south of the country.

The population at the census in 1979 was 4,111,310. There are three ethnic groups—Hutu (Bantu, forming the great majority): Tutsi (Nilotic, less than 15%); Twa (pygmoids, less than 1%). There are some 3,500 Europeans and 1,500 Asians. In 1974 some 49,000 Tutsi refugees from Rwanda were living in Burundi.

Bujumbura, the capital, had (1979 census) 141,040 inhabitants. Kitega (15,943 inhabitants) was formerly the royal residence.

CLIMATE. An equatorial climate, modified by altitude. The eastern plateau is generally cool, the easternmost savanna several degrees hotter. The wet seasons are from March to May and Sept. to Dec. Bujumbura. Jan. 73°F (22·8°C), July 73°F (22·8°C). Annual rainfall 33″ (825 mm).

CONSTITUTION AND GOVERNMENT. A new Constitution was promulgated on 21 Nov. 1981 and provides for a one-party state. The 65-member National Assembly elected in Oct. 1982 comprised 52 members elected by universal suffrage from a list of 104 candidates nominated by UPRONA, together with 13 members appointed by the President. President Bagaza became Party Chairman and Head of the Central Committee for a 5-year term in Jan. 1980.

President of the Republic: Col. Jean-Baptiste Bagaza.
Foreign Affairs: Laurent Nzeyimana.

The administrative divisions are: 8 provinces, each under a military governor (Bujumbura, Bubanza, Muramvya, Ngozi, Gitega, Muhinga, Ruyigi and Bururi); 18 arrondissements; and 78 communes.

Flag: White diagonal cross dividing triangles of red and green, in the centre a white disc bearing 3 red green-bordered 6-pointed stars.

DEFENCE. The national armed forces total (1984), 5,200 (there are also about 1,500 in paramilitary units) and include a small naval flotilla and air force flight of 3 SF 260, 2 Cessna 150 and 2 Do 27 liaison aircraft and 4 Alouette III helicopters. The Army comprises 2 infantry battalions, 1 parachute battalion, 1 commando battalion and 1 armoured-car company.

INTERNATIONAL RELATIONS

Membership. Burundi is a member of UN and OAU and is an ACP state of EEC.

ECONOMY

Budget. The 1983 budget envisaged receipts of 14,500m. Burundi francs and expenditure at 21,000m. Burundi francs.

Currency. The currency is administered by the Bank of the Republic of Burundi. The rate was 167·63 *Burundi francs* = £1 and 115·7 *Burundi francs* = US$1 in March 1984.

Weights and Measures. The metric system operates.

ENERGY AND NATURAL RESOURCES

Electricity. Electricity generation capacity was 6 mw in 1976.

Minerals. Mineral ores such as bastnasite and cassenite were formerly mined but output is now insignificant. Deposits of nickel (280m. tonnes) remain to be exploited.

Agriculture. The main economic activity and the main source of employment of the country is subsistence agriculture, which accounts for well over half of the gross national product. Beans, kassava, maize, sweet potatoes, groundnuts, peas, sorghum and bananas are grown according to the climate and the region.

The main cash crop is coffee, of which about 95% is arabica. It accounts for 90% of exports and taxes and levies on coffee constitute a major source of revenue. A coffee board (OCIBU) manages the grading and export of the crop. Production (1981) 41,000 tonnes. Cotton production is falling; 8,000 tonnes 1981. Plantations of good-quality tea are being developed. Production (1981) 1,540 tonnes.

Cattle play an important traditional role, and there were about 890,000 head in 1982. The quality is poor, but efforts are being made to improve it. There were (1982) some 723,000 goats and sheep and 35,000 pigs.

Fisheries. There is a small commercial fishing industry on Lake Tanganyika which produced 7,941 tonnes in 1973 and which dropped to 4,118 tonnes in 1981.

INDUSTRY AND TRADE

Industry. Industrial development is rudimentary. In Bujumbura there are plants for the processing of coffee and by-products of cotton, a brewery, cement works, a textile factory, a soap factory, a shoe factory and small metal workshops.

Commerce. The total value of exports 1981 was 6,260m. Burundi francs, and of imports, 14,559m. Burundi francs. Main exports in 1981 were coffee, (5,352m. Burundi francs); cotton, (188m.); tea, (181m.). Main imports, petrol products, food, vehicles and textiles.

Total trade between Burundi and the UK (British Department of Trade returns, in £1,000 sterling):

	1978	1979	1980	1981	1982	1983
Imports to UK	812	710	1,881	6,329	8,737	3,485
Exports and re-exports from UK	1,710	1,158	583	1,479	1,522	3,155

Tourism. Tourism is developing and there were 13,000 visitors Jan.–June 1976.

COMMUNICATIONS

Roads. There is a road network of 6,400 km connecting with Rwanda, Congo and Tanzania but in 1982 only 310 km were macadamized.

Aviation. Bujumbura has an airport of international standard and there are regular services to Europe, Zaïre and East Africa.

Shipping. There are lake services from Bujumbura to Kigoma (Tanzania). The main route for exports and imports is *via* Kigoma, and thence by rail to Dar es Salaam.

Post and Broadcasting. Number of telephones (1982), 5,601.

JUSTICE, RELIGION, EDUCATION AND WELFARE

Justice. There is a Supreme Court, an appeal court and a *tribunal de première instance* at Bujumbura and provincial tribunals in each arrondissement.

Religion. Over half the population is Roman Catholic; there is a Roman Catholic archbishop and 3 bishops. The Anglican Missions under a bishop fall within the archdiocese of Uganda.

Education. In 1981 the number of children in primary school was 180,290 and 18,000 pupils were receiving secondary education. The university of Bujumbura had (1981) about 1,000 students.

The local language is Kirundi, a Bantu language. French is also an official language. Kiswahili is spoken in the commercial centres.

Health. In 1979 there were about 130 doctors and 21 hospitals.

DIPLOMATIC REPRESENTATIVES

Of Burundi in Great Britain
Ambassador: Cyprien Mbonimpa (resides in Brussels).

Of Great Britain in Burundi
Ambassador: (Vacant).

Of Burundi in the USA (2233 Wisconsin Ave., NW, Washington, D.C., 20007)
Ambassador: Simon Sabimbona.

Of the USA in Burundi (Chaussée Prince Louis Rwagasore, Bujumbura)
Ambassador: James R. Bullington.

Of Burundi to the United Nations
Ambassador: Melchoir Bwakira.

Books of Reference

Lemarchand, R., *Rwanda and Burundi.* London, 1970
Melady, T. P., *Burundi: The Tragic Years.* Maryknoll, New York, 1974
Mpozapara, G., *La République du Burundi.* Paris, 1971
Weinstein, W., *Historical Dictionary of Burundi.* Metuchen, 1976

CAMBODIA

Democratic Kampuchea

Capital: Phnom Penh
Population: 6·7m. (1981)
GNP per capita: No accurate estimate available (1981)

Since April 1975 the situation in Cambodia has been such that it has been impossible to obtain reliable statistical and other information.

HISTORY. The recorded history of Cambodia starts at the beginning of the Christian era with the Kingdom of Fou-Nan, whose territories at one time included parts of Thailand, Malaya, Cochin-China and Laos. The religious, cultural and administrative inspirations of this state came from India. The Kingdom was absorbed at the end of the 6th century by the Khmers, under whose monarchs was built, between the 9th and 13th centuries, the splendid complex of shrines and temples at Angkor. Attacked on either side by the Vietnamese and the Thai from the 15th century on, Cambodia was saved from annihilation by the establishment of a French protectorate in 1863. Thailand eventually recognized the protectorate and renounced all claims to suzerainty in exchange for Cambodia's north-western provinces of Battambang and Siem Reap, which were, however, returned under a Franco-Thai convention of 1907, confirmed in the Franco-Thai treaty of 1937. In 1904 the province of Stung Treng, formerly administered as part of Laos, was attached to Cambodia. For history to 1969 *see* THE STATESMAN'S YEAR-BOOK, 1973–74, p. 1112.

Following a period of increasing economic difficulties and growing indirect involvement in the Vietnamese war Prince Sihanouk was deposed in March 1970 and on 9 Oct. 1970 the Kingdom of Cambodia became the Khmer Republic. From 1970 hostilities extended throughout most of the country involving North and South Vietnamese and US forces as well as Republican and anti-Republican Khmer troops. During 1973 direct American and North Vietnamese participation in the fighting came to an end, leaving a civil war situation which continued during 1974 with large-scale fighting between forces of the Khmer Republic supported by American arms and economic aid and the forces of the United National Cambodian Front including 'Khmer Rouge' communists supported by North Vietnam and China.

After unsuccessful attempts to capture Phnom Penh in 1973 and 1974, the Khmer Rouge ended the 5-year war in April 1975, when the remnants of the republican forces surrendered the city.

From April 1975 the Khmer Rouge instituted a harsh and highly regimented régime. They cut the country off from normal contact with the world and expelled all foreigners. All cities and towns were forcibly evacuated and the population were set to work in the fields.

The régime had difficulties with the Vietnamese from 1975 and this escalated into full-scale fighting in 1977–78. On 7 Jan. 1979, Phnom Penh was captured by the Vietnamese, and the Prime Minister, Pol Pot, fled. In March 1982 Pol Pot still commanded 30,000 guerrillas fighting the Vietnamese in Kampuchea.

In June 1982 the Khmer Rouge (who claim to have abandoned their Communist ideology and to have disbanded their Communist Party) entered into a coalition with Son Sann's Kampuchean People's National Liberation Front and Prince Sihanouk's group. This government is recognized by the UN.

President of the Coalition Government: Prince Norondom Sihanouk. *Deputy President:* Khieu Samphan. *Prime Minister:* Son Sann.

AREA AND POPULATION. Cambodia is bounded north by Laos and Thailand, in the west by Thailand, east by Vietnam and south by the Gulf of

Thailand. It has an area of about 181,000 sq. km (71,000 sq. miles), divided into 17 provinces: Kompong Thom (population, 322,000), Kompong Cham (820,000), Battambang (551,860), Kampot (337,879), Siem Reap (313,000), Kompong Chhang (273,000), Kompong Speu (307,000), Takeo (467,000), Kratié (136,000), Stung Treng (136,000), Svay Rieng (287,000), Prey Veng (492,000), Pursat (180,000), Kandal (population, excluding Phnom Penh, 706,000), Ratanakiri (49,400), Mondolkiri (14,300), Koh Kong (38,700).

The total population of 6,682,000 (1981) included Chinese and Chams. In the uplands and in the north-east live various groups of hillmen, known as Khmer-Loeu.

The chief towns are Phnom Penh, the capital located at the junction of the Mekong and Tonle Sap rivers, and Battambang. Populations of major towns have fluctuated greatly since 1970 by flows of refugees from rural areas and from one town to another. Phnom Penh formerly had a population of at least 2·5m. but a 1983 estimate puts it at 500,000. Khmer is the official language.

CONSTITUTION AND GOVERNMENT. Following the ousting of the Khmer Rouge régime, the Vietnamese-backed Kampuchean National United Front for National Salvation (KNUFNS) on 8 Jan. 1979 proclaimed a People's Republic and established a People's Revolutionary Council to administer the country. A 117-member National Assembly was elected on 1 May 1981 for a 5-year term; in June 1981 it ratified a new Constitution under which it appointed a 7-member Council of State and a 16-member Council of Ministers, replacing the Revolutionary Council.

President of the Council of State: Heng Samrin.
Prime Minister: Chan Si.

National flag: Red with a five-towered silhouette of the temple of Angkor Wat in the centre in yellow.

DEFENCE. Since the end of the war in April 1975 there has been no accurate data on defence and the three sections below should be treated with severe reserve. There is conscription into the armed forces.

Army. Strength (1984) 25,000 including 4 infantry divisions and some 50 supporting units. Equipment reported includes T-54/-55 and PT-76 tanks. There are also paramilitary police and militia units.

Navy. The Marine Royale Khmer was established on 1 March 1954 and became Marine Nationale Khmer on 9 Oct. 1970. It includes 15 coastal patrol craft, 25 river patrol boats, 3 surveying craft, 1 tug, 2 floating docks and 20 small craft, converted junks, etc. Less than a third of this force is operational and the residual navy has little fighting value. Two patrol vessels and 2 support (landing) gunboats escaped from Khmer Rouge, and 2 torpedo boats were believed to have sunk. Units since stricken include 7 amphibious vessels, 8 coastal patrol craft and 55 river patrol boats and service craft.

Naval active personnel in 1984 did not exceed 4,000. In addition there was a battalion of marines numbering some 4,000.

Air Force. In 1974 the Air Force had a strength of about 7,000 officers and men, including 120 pilots, with about 200 aircraft, none of them jets. It is not known how many aircraft remain serviceable.

ECONOMY

Currency. In 1978 money was officially abolished and no wages or salaries were paid, but in 1980 the use of money was restored.

Banking. In 1964 all bank functions were taken over by government banks. In 1972 legislation permitted the re-opening of foreign banks but by the end of Dec. 1973 only a few representational offices had opened. In 1979 there was no longer anything that could be called a normal banking system.

NATURAL RESOURCES

Minerals. A phosphate factory, jointly controlled by the State and private interests, was set up in 1966 near a deposit of an estimated 350,000 tons. Another deposit of about the same size is earmarked for exploitation. High-grade iron-ore deposits (possibly as much as 2·5m. tons) exist in Northern Khmer, but are not exploited commercially because of transportation difficulties. Some small-scale gold panning (6,687 troy oz. in 1963) and gem (mainly zircon) mining is carried out at Pailin where there is potential for considerable expansion.

Agriculture. The overwhelming majority of the population is normally engaged in agriculture, fishing and forestry. Of the country's total area of 44m. acres, about 20m. are cultivable and over 20m. are forest land. In 1980, 1·5m. hectares were cultivated. Before the spread of war the high productivity provided for a low, but well-fed standard of living for the peasant farmers, the majority of whom owned the land they worked. A relatively small proportion of the food production entered the cash economy. The war and unwise pricing policies have led to a disastrous reduction in production to a stage in which the country had become a net importer of rice.

A crop of about 900,000 tonnes of paddy were produced in 1982, 200,000 tonnes short of domestic requirements. Rubber production in 1982 amounted to 12,000 tonnes. Other products are maize, and, in usual order of value, livestock, timber, pepper, haricot beans, soybeans and fish.

Livestock (1982) FAO estimate: Cattle, 1m.; buffaloes, 410,000; sheep, 1,000; pigs, 225,000; horses, 9,000; poultry, 6·8m.

Forestry. Much of Cambodia's surface is covered by potentially valuable forests, 3·8m. hectares of which are reserved by the Government to be awarded to concessionaires, and are not at present worked to an appreciable extent. The remainder is available for exploitation by the local residents, and as a result some areas are over-exploited and conservation is not practised. There are substantial reserves of pitch pine.

Fisheries. Cambodia has the greatest freshwater fish resources in South-East Asia but production in 1970 (30,000 tons) was about a third of that for 1966.

INDUSTRY AND TRADE

Industry. Some development of industry had taken place before the spread of open warfare in 1970. Industry established and in operation in Jan. 1970 included a motor-vehicle assembly plant, 3 cigarette manufacturing concerns, a modern factory, several metal fabricating concerns, a distillery, a saw-mill, textile, fish canning, plywood, paper, cement, sugar sack, tyre, pottery and glassware factories and a cotton-ginnery. In the private sector there are about 3,200 manufacturing enterprises, producing a wide range of goods; most of them are small family concerns. An oil refinery at Kompong Som came into production in 1969 but was put out of action by an attack in early 1971. Since April 1975 a programme for repairing factories has been started and some 70 are back in production.

Commerce. Principal imports by order of value (1972) were petroleum products, metals and machinery (including vehicles), general foodstuffs and chemicals.

The only recorded export in 1972 was 7,328 tonnes of rubber. Much of the country's trade is with Hong Kong and Singapore.

Total trade between Cambodia and UK (British Department of Trade returns, in £1,000 sterling):

	1978	1979	1980	1981	1982	1983
Imports to UK	120	83	73	91	92	184
Exports and re-exports from UK	52	401	825	645	479	826

COMMUNICATIONS

Roads. There were, in 1970, 2,574 km of asphalt roads (including the 'Khmer-American Friendship Highway' from outside Phnom Penh to close to Kompong Som, built under the US aid programme and opened in July 1959), 359 km of macadamized roads, and about 1,213 km of improved dirt roads. Since 1970 many road bridges have been destroyed and long stretches of highway closed to traffic or open only to escorted convoys.

Railways. A line of 385 km (metre gauge) links Phnom Penh to Poipet (Thai frontier). In 1969 traffic amounted to 170m. passenger-km and 76m. ton-km. Work was completed during 1969 on a line Phnom Penh-Kompong Som *via* Takeo and Kampot. Total length, 649 km but by 1973 only a short stretch between Battambang and the Thai border remained in operation, the remainder having been closed by military action. Passenger and freight trains were running over about 80% of the network in 1980.

Aviation. The Pochentong airport is 10 km from Phnom Penh. Air Kampuchea has 2 small aircraft.

Shipping. The port of Phnom Penh can be reached by the Mekong (through Vietnam) by ships of between 3,000 and 4,000 tons. In 1970, 97 ocean-going vessels imported 51,300 tons of cargo at Phnom Penh and exported 86,400 tons.

A new ocean port has been built under the French aid programme at Kompong Som (formerly Sihanoukville) on the Gulf of Siam and is being increasingly used by long-distance shipping.

Post. There were 58 post offices functioning in 1968 but in 1979 it was doubtful if any offices operate. There are telephone exchanges in all the main towns; number of telephones in 1968, 6,325. There is an International Telex network in Phnom Penh and direct telephone and telegraphic links with Singapore.

RELIGION. The majority of the population practised Theravada Buddhism before 1975. The Constitution of 1976 ended Buddhism as the State religion. There are small Roman Catholic and Moslem minorities.

EDUCATION (1970–71). There were 1,490 primary schools (337,290 pupils) compared with 5,699 and 989,464 in 1969-70, 95 secondary schools (81,611 pupils) and 12,453 students in higher education. These figures show the disruption caused by the spread of war in 1970 which led to the concentration of all university education in Phnom Penh and closed many schools in rural areas and provincial towns. In 1980 there were 1·3m. pupils in all types of school.

DIPLOMATIC REPRESENTATIVES

UK and USA Embassies have been closed as have Cambodian Embassies in London and Washington.

Books of Reference

Annuaire Statistique Retrospectif du Cambodge. Vol. I, 1937–57; vol. II, 1958-60. Ministry of Planning, Phnom-Penh
Indo-China: Geographical Appreciation. Department of Mines and Technical Surveys. Ottawa, 1953
Barron, J., and Paul, A., *Murder of a Gentle Land.* New York, 1977.—*Peace with Horror.* London, 1977
Debré, F., *La Révolution de la Forêt.* Paris, 1976
Kirk, D., *Wider War.* London, 1971
McDonald, M., *Angkor.* London, 1958
Ponchaud, F., *Cambodia, Year Zero.* London, 1978
Shawcross, W., *The Sideshow: Nixon, Kissinger and the Destruction of Cambodia.* London, 1979

CAMEROON

République Unie du Cameroun

Capital: Yaoundé
Population: 9·06m. (1983)
GNP per capita: US$670 (1980)

HISTORY. The former German colony of Kamerun was occupied by French and British troops in 1916. The greater portion of the territory (422,673 sq. km) was in 1919 placed under French administration, excluding the territory ceded to Germany in 1911, which reverted to French Equatorial Africa. The portion under French trusteeship was granted full internal autonomy on 1 Jan. 1959 and complete independence was proclaimed on 1 Jan. 1960.

The portion assigned to British trusteeship consisted of 2 parts where separate plebiscites were held in Feb. 1961. The northern part decided in favour of joining Nigeria, while the southern part decided to join the Cameroon Republic. This was implemented on 1 Oct. 1961 with the formation of a Federal Republic of Cameroon. As a result of a national referendum, Cameroon became a unitary republic on 2 June 1972.

AREA AND POPULATION. Cameroon is bounded west by the Gulf of Guinea, north-west by Nigeria and east by Chad, with Lake Chad at its northern tip, and the Central African Republic, and south by Congo, Gabon and Equatorial Guinea. The total area is 465,054 sq. km (179,558 sq. miles). Population (1976 census) 7,663,246 (28·5% urban). Estimate (1983) 9·06m.

The areas, populations and chief towns of the 7 provinces at the 1976 census (now 10 provinces) were:

Province	Sq. km	Census 1976	Chief town	Census 1976
Centre-Sud	116,036	1,491,945	Yaoundé (capital)	313,706
Est	109,011	366,235	Bertoua	18,450
Littoral	20,239	935,166	Douala	458,426
Nord	163,513	2,233,257	Garoua	69,285
Nord-Ouest	17,810	980,531	Bamenda	67,184
Ouest	13,872	1,035,597	Bafoussam	62,239
Sud-Ouest	24,471	620,515	Buea	13,000

Other large towns (1976 census): Nkongsamba (71,298), Maroua (67,187), Foumban (59,701), Kumba (44,175) and Limbe (formerly Victoria) (31,222).

The population is composed of Sudanic-speaking people in the north (Sao, Fulani and Kanuri) and Bantu-speaking groups in the rest of the country. The official languages are French and English.

CLIMATE. An equatorial climate. with high temperatures and plentiful rain, especially from March to June and Sept. to Nov. Further inland, rain occurs at all seasons. Yaoundé. Jan. 76°F (24·4°C), July 73°F (22·8°C). Annual rainfall 62″ (1,555 mm). Douala. Jan. 79°F (26·1°C), July 75°F (23·9°C). Annual rainfall 160″ (4,026 mm).

CONSTITUTION AND GOVERNMENT. The 1972 Constitution, amended 1975, provides for a President as chief of state and commander of the armed forces, who is elected for a 5-year term, and a cabinet whose members must not be members of parliament.

The National Assembly, elected by universal adult suffrage for 5 years, consists of 120 representatives. Elections took place on 28 May 1978. Since 1966 the sole legal party is the *Union National Camerounaise*.

The Economic and Social Council consists of 85 members appointed for 5 years by the President of the Republic to represent various social and economic interests;

261

its chairman, appointed by decree, is assisted by a board appointed for 1 year.

President: Paul Biya (assumed office 6 Nov. 1982).

Prime Minister: Luc Ayang.
Foreign Affairs: Felix Tonye Mbog.

National flag: Three vertical strips of green, red, yellow, with a gold star in the centre.

National anthem: O Cameroun, berceau de nos ancêtres.

Local Government: The provinces are each administered by a governor appointed by the President. They are sub-divided into *départements* (each under a *préfet*) and then into *arrondissements* (each under a *sous-préfet*). In Aug. 1983, 3 additional provinces were created by the division of Centre-Sud and Nord provinces into 2 and 3 new provinces respectively.

DEFENCE. Compulsory military service was introduced in 1975.

Army. The Army consists of 1 armoured car, 1 para-commando, 1 engineer and 4 infantry battalions and 7 artillery batteries. Equipment includes M-8 armoured and Ferret scout cars. Total strength 6,600, there are an additional 5,000 paramilitary troops.

Navy. The Navy operates 2 fast attack craft, 2 patrol vessels (1 new French-built), 3 small patrol craft, 6 coastal patrol launches and 27 auxiliaries. Personnel in 1984 exceeded 350.

Air Force. The Air Force has 3 C-130H Hercules turboprop transports, 4 Buffalo and 1 Caribou STOL transports, 3 C-47s for transport and communications duties, 7 Broussard liaison aircraft, 4 Magister armed jet basic trainers, 6 Alpha Jet close support/trainers, and 2 Alouette II helicopters. Some of 4 Gazelle light helicopters are armed with anti-tank missiles. A small VIP transport fleet, maintained in civil markings, comprises 1 Boeing 727 jet aircraft, 1 Alouette III helicopter and a twin-engined Puma helicopter. Radar-equipped Dornier 128-6 twin-turboprop aircraft were ordered in 1982 for offshore oilfield patrol. Personnel total about 350.

INTERNATIONAL RELATIONS

Membership. Cameroon is a member of UN, OAU and is an ACP state of EEC.

ECONOMY

Planning. The Fourth 5-year Development Plan, 1976–81 envisaged expenditure of 725,232m. francs CFA.

Budget. The budget for 1982–83 balanced at 410,000m. francs CFA.

Currency. The unit of currency is the *franc CFA*, with a parity rate of 50 *francs CFA* to 1 French *franc*.

Banking. The Banque des Etats de l'Afrique Centrale is the sole bank of issue. The main banks are Banque Internationale pour l'Afrique Occidentale, Société Camerounaise de Banque, Société Générale de Banques au Cameroun, Banque International pour le Commerce et l'Industrie du Cameroun and Cameroon Bank. Most of the banks operate in all the large cities and towns throughout the United Republic.

ENERGY AND NATURAL RESOURCES

Electricity. There are 3 hydro-electric power stations at Edéa on the Sanaga river with a capacity of 180,000 kw, and another on the Wouri river near Douala. Total production (1980) 1,340m. kwh.

Oil. Production (estimate, 1981) from Kole oilfield was 4·3m. tonnes.

Minerals. There are considerable deposits of bauxite and kyanite around

Ngaoundéré. Further deposits of bauxite and cassiterite remain to be exploited in the Adamawa plateau.

Agriculture. At the 1976 Census, 80% of the working population were engaged in agriculture. The main food crops (with 1981 production in 1,000 tonnes): Cassava, 1,011; millet, 400; maize, 500; plantains, 1,026; yams, 135; groundnuts, 270; bananas, 97. Cash crops include palm oil, 80; palm kernals, 46; cocoa, 110; coffee, 105; rubber, 18; cotton, 22; raw sugar, 36.

Livestock (1982): 3·3m. cattle, 2·2m. sheep, 2·5m. goats, 1·3m. pigs.

Fisheries. In 1979 the total catch was 69,400 tonnes.

Forestry. Over a third of Cameroon consists of forests, ranging from tropical rain forests in the south (producing hardwoods such as mahogany, ebony and sapele) to semi-deciduous forests in the centre and wooded savannah in the north. Production in 1980 amounted to 10m. cu. metres.

INDUSTRY AND TRADE

Industry. There is a major aluminium smelting complex at Edéa; aluminium production in 1979 amounted to 53,000 tonnes. Production of cement totalled 148,000 tonnes in 1979. There are also factories producing shoes, soap, oil and food products, cigarettes.

Commerce. Imports and exports in 1m. francs CFA were as follows:

	1977	1978	1979	1980	1981
Imports	192,391	237,247	271,160	337,602	386,089
Exports	179,319	196,064	243,699	290,614	299,716

In 1980, 22% (by value) of exports went to France, 19% to the Netherlands and 30% to the USA, while France provided 45% of imports; the main exports were coffee (23%), cocoa (21%), crude oil (31%) and timber (11%).

Total trade between Cameroon and UK (British Department of Trade returns, in £1,000 sterling):

	1979	1980	1981	1982	1983
Imports to UK	16,278	9,798	24,022	9,108	52,481
Exports and re-exports from UK	18,811	17,470	24,014	22,462	26,445

Tourism. There were an estimated 126,337 foreign visitors in 1979. There are 13 National Parks and reserves, with a total area of nearly 20,000 sq. km.

COMMUNICATIONS

Roads. There were (1977) 2,155 km of tarred roads, 9,284 km earth roads and 15,482 km of secondary roads. In 1978 there were 134,900 vehicles in use.

Railways. Cameroon Railways (1,168 km in 1983) link Douala with Nkongsamba and Ngaoundére, with branches M'Banga–Kumba and Makak–M'Balmayo.

Aviation. Douala is the main international airport; other airports are at Yaoundé and Garoua. In 1976, 342,000 passengers and 20,000 tonnes of freight passed through the airports.

Shipping. The merchant-marine consisted (1980) of 44 vessels (over 100 GRT) of 62,080 GRT. The major port of Douala handled (1978) 2·03m. tonnes of imports and 811,000 tonnes of exports. Timber is exported mainly through the south-west ports of Kribi (145,850 tonnes out of 162,496 tonnes of exports in 1975) and Campo (50,000 tonnes). In 1975 ports of Bota and Tiko (at Nimbe) handled 26,305 tonnes and Garoua on the river Benue 21,041 tonnes (comprising 6,022 tonnes fertilizer imports and 15,019 tonnes cotton exports).

Post and Broadcasting. There were (1975) 150 post offices supplemented by a mobile postal service; telephone lines, 2,677 km; main telephones (1978), 14,321; radio stations, 36 with (1980) 760,000 receivers.

Cinemas. There were (1977) 45 cinemas with a capacity of 25,000 seats.

Newspapers. There was (1980) 1 daily newspaper with a circulation of 20,000.

JUSTICE, RELIGION, EDUCATION AND WELFARE

Justice. The Supreme Court sits at Yaoundé, as does the High Court of Justice (consisting of 9 titular judges and 6 surrogates all appointed by the National Assembly). There are magistrates' courts situated in the provinces.

Religion. In 1980, 21% of the population is Roman Catholic, 22% Moslem, 18% Protestant, while 39% follow traditional (animist) religions.

Education (1979–80). There were 1,302,974 pupils in 4,721 primary schools, 153,618 pupils in 317 secondary schools, 51,561 students in 157 vocational schools and (1978–79) 1,677 students and 168 teachers in teacher-training colleges. The University of Yaoundé (established 1962) had (1977–78) 10,001 students and other university centres have been opened at Douala, Buea, Dschang and Ngaoundére.

Health. In 1976 there were 85 hospitals with 16,734 beds, and 347 dispensaries and health centres. In 1977 there were 477 doctors, 19 dentists, 93 pharmacists, 1,805 midwives and 3,533 nursing personnel.

DIPLOMATIC REPRESENTATIVES

Of the United Republic of Cameroon in Great Britain (84 Holland Pk., London, W11 3SB)
Ambassador: Haman Dicko.

Of Great Britain in the United Republic of Cameroon (Ave. Winston Churchill, BP 547, Yaoundé)
Ambassador: B. Sparrow.

Of the United Republic of Cameroon in the USA (2349 Massachusetts Ave., NW, Washington, D.C., 20008)
Ambassador: Vincent Paul-Thomas Pondi.

Of the USA in the United Republic of Cameroon (Rue Nachtigal, BP 817, Yaoundé)
Ambassador: Miles R. Frechette.

Of the United Republic of Cameroon to the United Nations
Ambassador: Simone Mairie.

Books of Reference

Statistical Information: The Service de la Statistique Générale, at Douala, set up in 1945, publishes a monthly bulletin (from Nov. 1950)

Le Vine, V. T., *The Cameroon Federal Republic.* Cornell Univ. Press, 1971
Ndongko, W. A., *Planning for Economic Development in a Federal State: The Case of Cameroon, 1960–71.* New York, 1975
Rubin, N., *Cameroon.* New York, 1972

CANADA

Capital: Ottawa
Population: 24·9m. (1983)
GNP per capita: US$10,130 (1980)

HISTORY. The territories which now constitute Canada came under British power at various times by settlement, conquest or cession. Nova Scotia was occupied in 1628 by settlement at Port Royal, was ceded back to France in 1632 and was finally ceded by France in 1713, by the Treaty of Utrecht; the Hudson's Bay Company's charter, conferring rights over all the territory draining into Hudson Bay, was granted in 1670; Canada, with all its dependencies, including New Brunswick and Prince Edward Island, was formally ceded to Great Britain by France in 1763; Vancouver Island was acknowledged to be British by the Oregon Boundary Treaty of 1846, and British Columbia was established as a separate colony in 1858. As originally constituted, Canada was composed of Upper and Lower Canada (now Ontario and Quebec), Nova Scotia and New Brunswick. They were united under an Act of the Imperial Parliament, 'The British North America Act, 1867', which came into operation on 1 July 1867 by royal proclamation. The Act provided that the constitution of Canada should be 'similar in principle to that of the United Kingdom'; that the executive authority shall be vested in the Sovereign, and carried on in his name by a Governor-General and Privy Council; and that the legislative power shall be exercised by a Parliament of two Houses, called the 'Senate' and the 'House of Commons'.

On 30 June 1931 the British House of Commons approved the enactment of the Statute of Westminster freeing the Provinces as well as the Dominion from the operation of the Colonial Laws Validity Act, and thus removing what legal limitations existed as regards Canada's legislative autonomy. A joint address of the Senate and the House of Commons was sent to the Governor-General for transmission to London on 10 July 1931. The statute received the royal assent on 12 Dec. 1931.

Provision was made in the British North America Act for the admission of British Columbia, Prince Edward Island, Newfoundland, Rupert's Land and Northwest Territory into the Union. In 1869 Rupert's Land, or the Northwest Territories, was purchased from the Hudson's Bay Company. On 15 July 1870, Rupert's Land and the Northwest Territory were annexed to Canada and named the Northwest Territories, Canada having agreed to pay the Hudson's Bay Company in cash and land for its relinquishing of claims to the territory. By the same action the Province of Manitoba was created from a small portion of this territory and they were admitted into the Confederation on 15 July 1870. On 20 July 1871 the province of British Columbia was admitted, and Prince Edward Island on 1 July 1873. The provinces of Alberta and Saskatchewan were formed from the provisional districts of Alberta, Athabaska, Assiniboia and Saskatchewan and originally parts of the Northwest Territories and admitted on 1 Sept. 1905. Newfoundland formally joined Canada as its tenth province on 31 March 1949.

In Feb. 1931 Norway formally recognized the Canadian title to the Sverdrup group of Arctic islands. Canada thus holds sovereignty in the whole Arctic sector north of the Canadian mainland.

In Nov. 1981 the Canadian government agreed on the provisions of an amended constitution, to the end that it should replace the British North America Act and that its future amendment should be the prerogative of Canada. These proposals were adopted by the Parliament of Canada and were enacted by the UK Parliament as the Canada Act of 1982.

The enactment of the Canada Act was the final act of the UK Parliament in Canadian constitutional development. The Act gave to Canada the power to amend the Constitution according to procedures determined by the Constitutional Act 1982, which was proclaimed in force by the Queen on 17 April 1982. The Constitution Act 1982 added to the Canadian Constitution a charter of Rights and Freedoms, and provisions which recognize the nation's multi-cultural heritage, affirm the existing rights of native peoples, confirm the principle of equalization of benefits among the provinces, and strengthen provincial ownership of natural resources.

AREA AND POPULATION. Population of the area now included in Canada:

1851	2,436,297	1901	5,371,315	1951	14,009,429
1861	3,229,633	1911	7,206,643	1961	18,238,247
1871	3,689,257	1921	8,787,949	1971	21,568,311
1881	4,324,810	1931	10,376,786 [1]	1981	24,343,181
1891	4,833,239	1941	11,506,655 [1]		

[1] From 1951 figures include Newfoundland.

Population (estimated), 1 July 1983, was 24,907,100.

Areas of the provinces, etc. (in sq. km) and population at recent censuses:

Province	Land area	Fresh water area	Total land and fresh water area	Popula- tion, 1971	Popula- tion, 1976	Popula- tion, 1981
Newfoundland	371,690	34,030	405,720	522,104	557,725	567,681
Prince Edward Island	5,600	—	5,660	111,641	118,229	122,506
Nova Scotia	52,840	2,650	55,490	788,960	828,571	847,442
New Brunswick	72,090	1,350	73,440	634,557	677,250	696,403
Quebec	1,356,790	183,890	1,540,680	6,027,764	6,234,445	6,438,403
Ontario	891,190	177,390	1,068,580	7,703,106	8,264,465	8,625,107
Manitoba	548,360	101,590	649,950	988,247	1,021,506	1,026,241
Saskatchewan	570,700	81,630	652,330	926,242	921,323	968,313
Alberta	644,390	16,800	661,190	1,627,874	1,838,037	2,237,724
British Columbia	929,730	18,070	947,800	2,184,621	2,466,608	2,744,467
Yukon	478,970	4,480	483,450	18,388	21,836	22,135
Northwest Territories	3,293,020	133,300	3,426,320	34,807	42,609	45,471
Total	9,215,430	755,180	9,970,610	21,568,311	22,992,604	24,343,181

Of the total population in 1981, 20,216,340 were Canadian born, 3,867,160 foreign born, 312,015 of the latter being USA born and 2,586,080 European born.

The population (1981) born outside Canada in the provinces was in the following ratio (%): Newfoundland, 1·7; Prince Edward Island, 3·7; Nova Scotia, 4·9; New Brunswick, 3·9; Quebec, 8·2; Ontario, 23·5; Manitoba, 14·2; Saskatchewan, 8·6; Alberta, 16·3; British Columbia, 23; Yukon, 12·5; Northwest Territories, 6·1.

In 1981, figures for the population, according to origin, were [1]:

Single origins	22,244,885	Polish	254,485
Austrian	40,630	Portuguese	188,105
Belgian and Luxembourg	43,000	Romanian	22,485
British	9,674,245	Russian	48,435
Czech and Slovak	67,695	Scandinavian	282,795
Chinese	289,245	Spanish	53,540
Dutch	408,240	Swiss	29,805
Finnish	52,315	Ukrainian	529,615
French	6,439,100	Other single origins:	1,204,685
German	1,142,365		
Greek	154,365	*Multiple origins:*	1,838,615
Magyar (Hungarian)	116,390	British and French	430,255
Italian	747,970	British and Other	859,800
Japanese	40,995	French and Other	124,940
Native Peoples	413,380	Others	423,620

[1] The 1981 Census was the first to accept more than one ethnic origin for an individual. Therefore, this table includes counts of single and multiple origins.

The native Indian registered population numbered 367,810 in 1981 and the Eskimo population was 25,390 in 1981.

Populations of Census Metropolitan Areas (CMA) and Cities (proper), 1981 census:

	CMA	City proper		CMA	City proper
Toronto	2,998,947	559,217	Winnipeg	584,842	564,473
Montreal	2,828,349	980,354	Quebec	576,075	166,474
Vancouver	1,268,183	414,281	Hamilton	542,095	306,434
Ottawa-Hull	717,978	295,163	St Catharines-		
Edmonton	657,057	532,246	Niagara	304,353	—
Calgary	592,743	592,743	St Catharines	—	124,018

	CMA	City proper		CMA	City proper
Niagara Falls	—	70,960	Saskatoon	154,210	154,210
Kitchener	287,801	139,734	Sudbury	149,923	91,829
London	283,668	254,280	Chicoutimi-		
Halifax	277,727	114,594	Jonquiere	135,172	—
Windsor	246,110	192,083	Chicoutimi	—	60,064
Victoria	233,481	64,379	Jonquiere	—	60,354
Regina	164,313	162,613	Thunder Bay	121,379	112,486
St John's	154,820	83,770	Saint John	114,048	80,521
Oshawa	154,217	117,519	Trois Rivieres	111,453	50,466

The total 'urban' population of Canada in 1981 was 18,435,927, against 17,366,970 in 1976.

While the registration of births, marriages and deaths is under provincial control, the statistics are compiled on a uniform system by Statistics Canada. The following table gives the results for the year 1982, estimate:

Province	Living births Number	Marriages Number	Deaths Number
Newfoundland	10,560	3,420	3,100
Prince Edward Island	1,990	870	990
Nova Scotia	11,890	6,600	6,690
New Brunswick	10,660	4,870	5,280
Quebec	93,620	42,390	43,380
Ontario	123,930	71,770	62,470
Manitoba	17,090	7,830	8,470
Saskatchewan	16,950	7,450	7,520
Alberta	41,240	19,660	12,360
British Columbia	42,400	22,460	20,450
Yukon Territory	560	240	120
N.W. Territories	1,100	260	200
	371,990	187,820	171,030

Immigrant arrivals by country of last permanent residence:

Country	1981	1982
UK	21,154	16,445
France	2,089	2,393
Germany	2,203	4,425
Netherlands	1,797	1,827
Greece	958	885
Italy	2,043	1,506
Portugal	3,290	1,388
Other Europe	12,761	17,281
Asia	48,830	41,617
Australasia	1,317	938
USA	10,559	9,360
West Indies	8,633	8,674
All other	12,984	14,408
Total	128,618	121,147

Dawe, A., *Profiles of a Nation: Canadian Themes and Styles*. Toronto, 1970
Jenness, D., *The Indians of Canada*. 5th ed. Ottawa, 1960
Park, J., *The Culture of Contemporary Canada*. Toronto, 1970
Porter, J., *The Vertical Mosaic*. Toronto, 1965
Rosenberg, S. E., *The Jewish Community in Canada: A History*. Toronto, 1970
Wade, M., *The French Canadians, 1760–1967*. 2 vols. 2nd ed. Toronto and London, 1968

CLIMATE. The climate ranges from polar conditions in the north to cool temperate in the south, but with big differences between east coast, west coast and the interior, affecting temperatures, rainfall amounts and seasonal distribution. Winters are very severe over much of the country, but summers can be very hot inland. Ottawa. Jan. 12°F (−11·1°C), July 69°F (20·6°C). Annual rainfall 35″ (871 mm). Charlottetown. Jan. 19°F (−7·2°C), July 67°F (19·4°C). Annual rainfall 43″ (1,077 mm). Edmonton. Jan. 5°F (−15°C), July 61°F (16·1°C). Annual rainfall 18″ (439 mm). Halifax. Jan. 23°F (−5°C), July 64°F (17·8°C). Annual rainfall 56″

(1,412 mm). Montreal. Jan. 11°F (−11·7°C), July 67°F (19·4°C). Annual rainfall 41″ (1,025 mm). Quebec. Jan. 10°F (−12·2°C), July 66°F (18·9°C). Annual rainfall 40″ (1,008 mm). Saint John. Jan. 19°F (−7·2°C), July 65°F (18·3°C). Annual rainfall 51″ (1,278 mm). Toronto. Jan. 23°F (−5°C), July 69°F (20·6°C). Annual rainfall 33″ (815 mm). Vancouver. Jan. 36°F (2·2°C), July 64°F (17·8°C). Annual rainfall 58″ (1,458 mm). Winnipeg. Jan. −3°F (−19·4°C), July 67°F (19·4°C). Annual rainfall 21″ (539 mm). Yellowknife. Jan. −15°F (−26·1°C), July 61°F (16·1°C). Annual rainfall 10″ (256 mm).

CONSTITUTION AND GOVERNMENT. The members of the Senate are appointed until age 75 by summons of the Governor-General under the Great Seal of Canada. Members appointed before 2 June 1965 may remain in office for life. The Senate consists of 104 senators, namely, 24 from Ontario, 24 from Quebec, 10 from Nova Scotia, 10 from New Brunswick, 4 from Prince Edward Island, 6 from Manitoba, 6 from British Columbia, 6 from Alberta, 6 from Saskatchewan, 6 from Newfoundland, 1 from the Yukon Territory and 1 from the Northwest Territories. Each senator must be at least 30 years of age, a born or naturalized subject of the Queen and must reside in the province for which he is appointed and his total net worth must be at least $4,000. The House of Commons is elected by the people, for 5 years, unless sooner dissolved. Women have the vote and are eligible. From 1867 to the election of 1945 representation was based on Quebec having 65 seats and the other provinces the same proportion of 65 which their population had to the population of Quebec. In the General Election of 1949 readjustments were based on the population of all the provinces taken as a whole. Generally speaking, this format for representation has prevailed in all subsequent elections with readjustments made after each decennial census. However, on 31 Dec. 1974, the law was changed so that it has reverted somewhat to the type of system that had prevailed initially. That is to say, Quebec is to be assigned a fixed number of seats in the House of Commons and the representation of the other provinces calculated by a quotient which reflects this fact.

The thirty-second Parliament, elected on 19 Feb. 1980, comprises 282 members and the provincial and territorial representation are: Ontario, 95; Quebec, 75; Nova Scotia, 11; New Brunswick, 10; Manitoba, 14; British Columbia, 28; Prince Edward Island, 4; Saskatchewan 14; Alberta, 21; Newfoundland, 7; Yukon Territory, 1; Northwest Territories, 2.

State of parties in the Senate (Sept. 1983): Liberals, 58; Progressive Conservatives, 23; Independent, 4; Independent Liberal, 1; Vacant, 18; total 104.

State of the parties in the House of Commons (Dec. 1983): Liberals, 147; Progressive Conservatives, 102; New Democratic Party, 31; Independent, 1; 1 vacant; total, 282. Elections took place on 19 Feb. 1980.

The following is a list of Governors-General of Canada:

Viscount Monck	1867–1868	Viscount Willingdon	1926–1931
Lord Lisgar	1868–1872	Earl of Bessborough	1931–1935
Earl of Dufferin	1872–1878	Lord Tweedsmuir	1935–1940
Marquess of Lorne	1878–1883	Earl of Athlone	1940–1946
Marquess of Lansdowne	1883–1888	Field-Marshal Viscount	
Lord Stanley of Preston	1888–1893	Alexander of Tunis	1946–1952
Earl of Aberdeen	1893–1898	Vincent Massey	1952–1959
Earl of Minto	1898–1904	Georges Philias Vanier	1959–1967
Earl Grey	1904–1911	Roland Michener	1967–1974
HRH the Duke of Connaught	1911–1916	Jules Léger	1974–1979
Duke of Devonshire	1916–1921	Edward Schreyer	1979–1984
Viscount Byng of Vimy	1921–1926		

Governor-General: Jeanne Sauvé.

National flag: Vertically red, white, red with the white of double width and bearing a stylized red maple leaf.

The office and appointment of the Governor-General are regulated by letters patent, signed by the King on 8 Sept. 1947, which came into force on 1 Oct. 1947. In 1977 the Queen approved the transfer to the Governor-General functions discharged by the Sovereign. He is assisted in his functions, under the provisions of the Act of 1867, by a Privy Council composed of Cabinet Ministers.

The following is the list of the Liberal Cabinet in Jan. 1984, in order of precedence, which in Canada attaches generally rather to the person than to the office:

Prime Minister: Rt Hon. Pierre Elliott Trudeau.
External Affairs: Allan MacEachen.
External Relations: Jean-Luc Pépin.
Energy: Jean Chrétien.
Indian Affairs and Northern Development: John Munro.
Government Leader in Senate: Senator H. A. (Bud) Olson.
Treasury Board: Herb Gray.
Agriculture: Eugene Whelan.
Labour: André Ouellet.
Finance: Marc Lalonde.
Public Works and Housing: Roméo LeBlanc.
Employment and Immigration (with responsibility for co-ordination of political events in Toronto): John Roberts.
Health and Welfare: Monique Bégin.
Defence: Jean-Jacques Blais.
Communications: Francis Fox.
Fisheries: Pierre de Bané.
Canadian Wheat Board: Senator Hazen Argue.
International Trade: Gerald Regan.
Justice: Mark MacGuigan.
Solicitor-General: Robert Kaplan.
Mines: William Rompkey.
National Revenue: Pierre Bussières.
Supply and Services: Charles Lapointe.
President of the Privy Council: Yvon Pinard.
Industry: Edward Lumley.
Economic Development, Science and Technology: Donald Johnston.
Transport: Lloyd Axworthy.
Consumer Affairs and Women: Judy Erola.
Social Development: Senator Jack Austin.
Environment: Charles Caccia.
Secretary of State: Serge Joyal.
Veterans' Affairs: Bennett Campbell.
Multiculturalism: David Collenette.
Youth: Celine Hervieux-Payette.
Small Business and Tourism: David Smith.
Minister of State (Finance): Roy MacLaren.
Fitness and Amateur Sport: Jacques Olivier.

The salary of a member of the House of Commons is $50,300 with a tax-free allowance of $16,800. The salary of a senator is $50,300 with a tax-free allowance of $8,200. The salary and allowances of the Prime Minister total $126,600. The salary of the Speaker of the House of Commons is $88,800; the salary of the Speaker of the Senate is $74,700; the salary of the Opposition Leader is $88,800 and that of the National Democratic Party Leader, $73,500; all these also have tax-free allowances of from $12,200–$20,800.

Future increases are to be pegged at 1% less than increases in the consumer price index or industrial composite index, whichever is lower.

An Act to provide retiring allowances, on a contributory basis, to members of the House of Commons was given the Royal Assent on 4 July 1952. This Act was amended in July 1963; a member can now opt for a reduced retiring allowance in favour of an additional allowance for the widow; and provision has been made for retiring allowance for former Prime Ministers and their widows.

The Canadian Parliamentary Guide. Annual. Ottawa

Report of the Royal Commission on Dominion–Provincial Relations, Canada 1867–1939.
3 vols. Ottawa, 1940

Byers, R. B. (ed.), *Canada Challenged: The Viability of the Confederation.* Toronto, 1979

Information Canada, *Organization of the Government of Canada.* Loose-leaf service. Ottawa, 1970

Kennedy, W. F. M., *Statutes, Treaties and Documents of the Canadian Constitution, 1713–1929.* Toronto, 1930

Kernaghan, N. (ed.), *Bureaucracy in Canadian Government, Selected Readings.* Toronto, 1969

Morton, W. L., *The Kingdom of Canada; A General History From Earliest Times.* Toronto, 1969

Olmsted, R. A., *Decisions of the Judicial Committee of the Privy Council Relating to the British North America Act, 1867, and the Canadian Constitution, 1867–1954.* Ottawa, Queens' Printer, 1954

Russell, P. H. (ed.), *Leading Constitutional Decisions; Cases on the British North America Act.* Toronto, 1968

DEFENCE. The Department of National Defence was created by the National Defence Act, 1922, which established one civil Department of Government in place of the previous Departments of Militia and Defence, Naval Service and the Air Board. The Minister of National Defence has the control and management of the Canadian Forces and all matters relating to national defence establishments and works for the defence of Canada. He is the Minister responsible for presenting before the Cabinet, matters of major defence policy for which Cabinet direction is required. Until Oct. 1973, he was responsible for the Canada Emergency Measures Organization which was renamed'Emergency Planning Canada' in 1976, and given wider responsibilities for the co-ordination of civil emergency planning. This organization now reports to the President of the Privy Council, but the Minister of National Defence continues to be responsible for certain civil emergency powers, duties and functions as outlined in Order-in-Council P.C.1. 1965–1041 dated 8 June 1965, as amended.

In Dec. 1976, the Minister of National Defence was named as minister responsible for all aspects of air Search and Rescue in the areas of Canadian SAR responsibility, and for the overall co-ordination of marine search and rescue including provision of air resources for marine SAR within Canadian territorial waters and in designated oceanic areas off the Pacific and Atlantic Coasts in accordance with agreements made with the United States Coast Guard.

Command Structure. The Canadian forces are organized on a functional basis to reflect the major commitments assigned by the Government. All forces devoted to a primary mission are grouped under a single commander who is assigned sufficient resources to discharge his responsibilities. Specifically, the Canadian forces consist of National Defence Headquarters and the following major commands reporting to the Chief of the Defence Staff:

1. *Mobile Command* provides units trained and equipped to support the United Nations or other peacekeeping operations; provides ground forces for the protection of Canadian territory; maintains combat formations in Canada for support of overseas commitments. It is comprised of 3 airportable combat groups in Canada; the United Nations force in Cyprus; the Canadian Airborne Regiment, and 1 combat training centre. The Militia and Air Reserve components are also controlled by Mobile Command. Strength (1983), 13,000.

2. *Maritime Command.* All maritime forces are under the Commander, Maritime Command, with headquarters in Halifax, Nova Scotia. In addition, he also exercises operational control of aircraft assigned to him by the commander Maritime Air Group for Maritime operations. The Commander Maritime Forces (Pacific), who is the Deputy Commander, has his headquarters in Esquimalt, British Columbia. Maritime Command is to defend Canada against attack from the sea; provide anti-submarine defence in support of NATO; provide sea transport in support of Mobile Command. Composition of the maritime forces includes 3 submarines, 4 destroyers, 19 smaller destroyer-escorts (of which 3 are in reserve), 3 supply ships, 1 maintenance ship, 6 patrol craft, 7 small support ships, 6 training

vessels (ex-coastal minesweepers), 3 research ships and 30 auxiliaries and service craft. There are 16 naval reserve personnel units in major Canadian cities which form an essential component of Maritime Command.

Active naval personnel strength in Maritime Command ships and shore establishments in 1983 was about 18% of the Regular Forces, i.e., some 14,000 comprising 2,000 officers and 12,000 ratings (men and women).

3. *Air Command.* On 2 Sept. 1975, the aviation units administered by Mobile Command and Maritime Command were withdrawn and allocated to a newly-formed Air Command, which now controls all Canadian military aviation units through a single senior commander. Air Command responsibilities include maintenance of operationally-ready regular and reserve air forces to meet Canada's sovereignty requirements, participation with the USA in the air defence of North America through NORAD, and support of overseas commitments including NATO responsibilities in Europe and elsewhere. It is organized in 4 operational groups: Air Defence Group, Maritime Air Group, Air Transport Group and Fighter Group; has reinforcement and training responsibilities to 1 Canadian Air Group (1 CAG with 3 squadrons of CF-104s; to be replaced with CF-188 Hornets) in Europe; and exercises command and control over Air Training Schools and the Air Reserve.

Air Defence Group, through NORAD, has entire responsibility for control of Canadian airspace. It comprises 3 squadrons of CF-101 Voodoo all-weather interceptors, armed with nuclear and conventional missiles, with replacement by CF-188 Hornets under way; an electronic warfare squadron with CF-101 Voodov, 9 CC-117 (Falcon) and 16 T-33A aircraft and 1 operational training squadron with CF-188s; eastern and western control centres and a trans-continental radar chain, integrated in NORAD through the semi-automatic ground environment (SAGE) network.

Maritime Air Group's primary responsibilities include coastal and anti-pollution patrol, fishery protection and Arctic surveillance. Its equipment includes 3 operational squadrons of CP-140 Aurora and 1 of CP-121 Tracker maritime patrol aircraft, and 2 ASW helicopter squadrons with CH-124 Sea Kings.

Air Transport Group has 3 squadrons of CC-130E/H turboprop transports; 1 squadron of 5 CC-137 (Boeing 707) jet transports, of which 2 can operate as flight refuelling tankers; a VIP squadron with 2 CC-132 Dash 7 four-turboprop and 7 CC-109 Cosmopolitan twin-turboprop transports and 2 twin-jet CC-144 Challengers; and 4 dual-role transport/search and rescue squadrons with 11 twin-turboprop CC-115 Buffalo and 8 CC-138 Twin Otter aircraft and helicopters. Fighter Group has 2 squadrons of CF-116 (F-5) fighters (to be replaced with CF-188 Hornets) and 6 squadrons of CH-147 Chinook, CH-135 (Bell UH-1N) and CH-136 (Kiowa) helicopters.

Training aircraft include Beech CT-134A Musketeer IIs and CH-139 JetRanger helicopters for basic instruction, CT-114 Tutor advanced trainers, and CC-130E Hercules for navigator training.

4. *Training Command* plans and conducts all recruit and individual trades and classification training that is common to more than one command. The Command is also responsible for the Prairie Region, one of 6 military regions into which Canada is divided. The Command headquarters is in Winnipeg and the 9 bases within the Command are located in 7 provinces. A total of 24,239 students attended one or more of 1,258 courses conducted by the Command during 1973.

5. *Canadian Forces Communications Command (CFCC)* manages, operates and maintains strategic communications for the Canadian Forces and, in the event of emergencies, for the federal and provincial governments. The Command also provides points for interconnecting strategic and tactical networks and CFCC manages, operates and maintains the major DND automatic data processing centres.

6. *The Reserves* are composed of the Naval Reserve, the Militia and the Air Reserve.

Projected National Defence expenditures for 1982–83 were $6,941m. at 31 Oct.

1982. Strength of the Regular Forces in 1983 was about 82,000.

7. *Canadian Forces Europe.* The Canadian Forces allocated to support NATO in Europe are part of Canadian Forces Europe. The land element is No. 4 Canadian Mechanized Brigade Group operationally responsible to the Central Army Group. The air element, No. 1 Canadian Air Group, consisting of 3 CF-104 Starfighter squadrons, is operationally assigned to No. 4 Allied Tactical Air Force. These elements are located in the Baden-Baden area of Federal Republic of Germany and are supported administratively by CFB Europe at Lahr.

Police Forces. The police forces of Canada are organized in three groups: (1) the federal force, which is the Royal Canadian Mounted Police; (2) provincial police forces—the Provinces of Ontario and Quebec have their own provincial police forces, but all other provinces engage the services of the Royal Canadian Mounted Police to perform parallel functions within their borders, and (3) municipal police forces—each urban centre of reasonable size maintains its own police force or engages the services of the provincial police, under contract, to attend to police matters.

In addition, the Canadian National Railways, the Canadian Pacific Railway Company and the National Harbours Board have their own police forces.

Royal Canadian Mounted Police. The Royal Canadian Mounted Police is a civil force maintained by the federal government. It was established in 1873, as the North-West Mounted Police for service in what was then the North-West Territories and, in recognition of its services, was granted the use of the prefix 'Royal' by King Edward VII in 1904. Its sphere of operations was expanded in 1918 to include all of Canada west of Thunder Bay. In 1920 the force absorbed the Dominion Police, and its headquarters was transferred from Regina to Ottawa, and its title was changed to Royal Canadian Mounted Police. The force is responsible to the Solicitor-General of Canada and is controlled and managed by a Commissioner who holds the rank and status of a Deputy Minister. The Commissioner is empowered under the Royal Canadian Mounted Police Act to appoint members to be peace officers in all provinces and territories of Canada.

The responsibilities of the Royal Canadian Mounted Police are national in scope. The administration of justice within the provinces, including the enforcement of the Criminal Code of Canada, is part of the power and duty delegated to the provincial governments.

All provinces except Ontario and Quebec have entered into contracts with the Royal Canadian Mounted Police to enforce criminal and provincial laws under the direction of the respective Attorneys-General. In addition, in these 8 provinces the Force is under agreement to provide police services to 187 municipalities, thereby assuming the enforcement responsibility of municipal as well as criminal and provincial laws within these communities. The Royal Canadian Mounted Police is also responsible for all police work in the Yukon and Northwest territories enforcing federal law and territorial ordinances. The 15 Operational Divisions, alphabetically designated, make up the strength of the Force across Canada; they comprise 48 sub-divisions which include 713 detachments. Headquarters Division, as well as the Office of the Commissioner, is located in Ottawa. The Force maintains liaison officers in 31 countries and represents Canada in the International Criminal Police Organization which has its headquarters in Paris.

Thorough training is emphasized for members of the Force. Recruits receive 6 months of basic training at the Royal Canadian Mounted Police Academy in Regina. This is followed by a further 6 months of supervised on-the-job training. The RCMP also operates the Canadian Police College at which its members and selected representatives of other Canadian and foreign police forces may study the latest advances in the fields of crime prevention and detection.

Many of these advances have been incorporated into the operation of the Force. A teletype system links the widespread divisional headquarters with the administrative centre at Ottawa and a network of fixed and mobile radio units operates within the provinces. The focal point of the criminal investigation work of the Force is the Directorate of Laboratories and Identification; its services, together with those of divisional and sub-divisional units, and of 8 Crime Detection Laboratories, are available to police forces throughout Canada. The Canadian Police Information Centre at RCMP Headquarters, a duplexed computer system, is staffed and operated by the Force. Law Enforcement agencies throughout Canada have access *via* a series of remote terminals to information on stolen vehicles, licences and wanted persons.

In Oct. 1982, the Force had a total strength of 21,642 including regular members, special constables, civilian members and Public Service employees. It maintained 6,071 motor vehicles, 76 police service dogs and 144 horses.

The Force has 13 divisions actively engaged in law enforcement, 1 Headquarters Division and 2 training divisions. In addition it maintains Marine Services and Air Services with headquarters at Ottawa. The Marine Services is comprised of 10 patrol vessels and 360 smaller craft which operate on the east and west coasts, the Great Lakes and the St Lawrence River. The Air Directorate has stations throughout Canada and maintains 36 aircraft.

Eayrs, J., *In Defence of Canada: Growing up Allied.* Univ. of Toronto Press, 1980
Feasby, W. R. (ed.), *Official History of the Canadian Medical Services, 1939–45.* 2 vols. Dept. of National Defence. Ottawa, 1953–56
Swettenham, J., *Canada and the First World War.* Toronto, 1970

INTERNATIONAL RELATIONS

Membership. Canada is a member of UN, the Commonwealth, OECD, NATO and Colombo Plan.

ECONOMY

Budget. Budgetary revenue and expenditure of the Government of Canada for years ended 31 March (in Canadian $1m.):

	1979–80	1980–81	1981–82 [1]	1982–83 [1]	1983–84 [2]
Revenue	40,159	45,200	54,068	54,863	58,618
Expenditure	51,534	59,350	67,674	80,113	89,818

[1] Not comparable to earlier years, adjustment to Canada Post revenues and expenditures.
[2] Estimate.

Budgetary revenue, main items, 1983–84 (estimates in Canadian $1m.):

Income tax, personal	29,000	Non-resident tax	1,040
Income tax, corporation	7,788	Oil export charge	95
Sales	6,410	Natural gas tax	395
Customs duties	2,705	Non-tax revenue	5,855

Details of budget estimates[1], 1983–84 (in Canadian $1m.):

Energy	3,799	External affairs	2,432
Economic development	9,799	Defence	7,900
Social affairs	37,251	Parliament	183
Justice and legal affairs	1,798	Services to government	3,897
Public debt charges	17,950		

[1] The Department of Finance now manages expenditure under a new system of broad categories (listed above) called 'envelopes'.

On 31 March 1983 the net debt (estimate) was $119,208m.

Canadian Tax Foundation. *The National Finances: An Analysis of the Revenues and Expenditures of the Government of Canada.* Toronto. Annual

Currency. The denominations of money in the currency of Canada are dollars and cents. The cent is one-hundredth part of a dollar. Subsidiary coins of the denominations of 1, 5, 10, 25 and 50 cents and $1 are in use. The monetary standard is gold of 900 millesimal fineness (23·22 grains of pure gold equal to 1 gold dollar). The Currency Act provides for gold coins in the denominations of $5, $10 and $20, which are legal tender. The British and US gold coins are also legal tender, at the par rate of exchange. The legal equivalent of the British sovereign is $4.86⅔.

The Bank of Canada has the sole right to issue paper money for circulation in Canada. Restrictions introduced by the 1944 revisions of the Bank Act cancelled the right of chartered banks to issue or re-issue notes after 1 Jan. 1945; and in Jan. 1950 the chartered banks' liability for such of their notes as then remained outstanding was transferred to the Bank of Canada in return for payment of a like sum to the Bank of Canada. On 31 May 1970 the Canadian dollar which was stabilized at 92·50 US cents was allowed to fluctuate. The value of the US$ in Canadian funds was $1·25 and £1 sterling = Canadian $1·85 in March 1984.

The Bank of Canada issues notes, which are legal tender, in denominations of $1, $2, $5, $10, $20, $50, $100, $500 and $1,000. Under the terms of the Bank of Canada Act, the bank is required to sell gold in bars of 400 oz. to any person tendering legal tender. This obligation is at the present time suspended by Order-in-Council. The exportation of gold from Canada is prohibited except by licence issued by the Minister of Finance to the Bank of Canada or a chartered bank.

The Ottawa Mint was established in 1908 as a branch of the Royal Mint, in pursuance of the Ottawa Mint Act, 1901. In Dec. 1931 control of the Mint was passed over to the Canadian Government, and since that time has operated as the Royal Canadian Mint. The Mint issues silver, nickel, bronze and steel coins for circulation in Canada. In 1967, in celebration of Canada's Centennial of Confederation, a $20 gold piece was minted, the first gold coin struck since 1919. In 1935, on the occasion of His Majesty's Silver Jubilee, the Royal Canadian Mint issued the first Canadian silver dollars. Commemorative dollars were also issued in 1939 on the occasion of the visit of King George VI and Queen Elizabeth to Canada; in 1949, when Newfoundland became the tenth Province of Canada; in 1958, the one-hundredth anniversary of the establishment of the Colony of British Columbia; in 1964, the centennial of the Charlottetown and Quebec Conferences which paved the way to confederation. The silver dollar bearing the design of the canoe manned by an Indian and a Voyageur has been issued in the years 1935–38, 1945–48, 1950–57, 1959–63, 1965, 1966 and 1972. For centennial year the Canada goose replaced the usual canoe design on the silver dollar. Because of a world-wide shortage of silver, the Government, in Aug. 1967, authorized the Mint to change the metal content of the 25-cent and 10-cent coins. Commencing in Sept. 1968, the 10-cent, 50-cent and $1 coins were minted in pure nickel. Gold refining is one of the principal activities of the Mint. In 1982, 1,585,467 troy oz. of rough bullion were received for treatment, containing 1,248,421 oz. of fine gold and 189,077 oz. of fine silver. Coin issued: Gold, $59,390,600; silver, $903,888; other metals, $55,668,339.

Banking. Commercial banks in Canada are known as chartered banks and are incorporated under the terms of the Bank Act, which imposes strict conditions as to capital, notes in circulation, returns to the Dominion Government, types of lending operations and other matters. In Oct. 1983 there were 71 chartered banks (13 domestic banks and 58 foreign bank subsidiaries) incorporated under the provisions of the Bank Act; the 13 had 7,300 branches serving 2,000 communities in all provinces in Canada and nearly 300 branches in other countries. There was also one bank incorporated under the Quebec Savings Bank Act. The foreign bank subsidiaries operate 200 offices in Canada including 58 head offices. The Bank Act is subject to revision by Parliament every 10 years. Bank charters expire every 10 years and are renewed at each decennial revision of the Bank Act. The chartered banks make detailed monthly and yearly returns to the Minister of Finance and are subject to periodic inspection by the Inspector-General of Banks, an official appointed by the Government.

The following are some particulars of the 13 chartered banks at 31 Aug. 1983: assets of gold coin and bullion, $674·88m.; Canadian currency, $1,823·74m.; Bank of Canada deposits and notes, $4,032,584; deposits with banks, $41,182,991,000; cheques and other items in transit, $1,404,872; ordinary personal loans, (June 1983) $32,317m.; business and farming loans, (June 1983) $86,448m.; total assets, $348,552,986,000.

The Bank of Canada Act, passed on 3 July 1934, provided for the establishment of a central bank for the Dominion. This bank commenced operations on 11 March 1935 with a paid-up capital of $5m. By reason of certain changes introduced into the composition of stockholders of the bank (for which *see* THE STATESMAN'S YEAR-BOOK, 1944 pp. 322–23), the Minister of Finance on behalf of Canada is the sole registered owner of the capital stock of the bank. The revised Bank Act, which came into force on 1 May 1967, requires the chartered banks, beginning Feb. 1968, to maintain a statutory cash ratio of 12% on demand deposits and 4% on other deposits, in the form of reserves with and notes on the Bank of Canada. A secondary reserve of 7% in treasury bills, government bonds, etc., is also required. All gold held in Canada by the chartered banks was transferred to the Bank of Canada along with the gold held by the Government as reserve against Dominion notes outstanding at the time of the commencement of operations of the Bank of Canada. The liability of the Dominion notes outstanding at the commencement of business of the Bank of Canada was assumed by the bank.

In the year ending 31 March 1983, the Federal Business Development Bank authorized 3,436 loans for a total of $370m.

Weights and Measures. The legal weights and measures are in transition from the Imperial to the International system of units. The Metric Commission, established in June 1971, co-ordinates Canada's conversion to the metric system.

ENERGY AND NATURAL RESOURCES

Electricity. The net generation of electricity in 1981 was 380,131,575 mwh., of which utilities accounted for 340,409,002 mwh. Of the total, 263,394,106 mwh. was from hydro-electricity, 74,908,284 mwh. from conventional steam plants and 37,799,069 mwh. from nuclear plants. Demand (1981) was 346,255,451 mwh.

Oil and Natural Gas. With the discovery of large oilfields in Alberta, the production of petroleum became a major Canadian industry. The Interprovincial Pipeline, Canada's longest oil pipeline, moves crude oil from Edmonton, Alberta, to Montreal, Quebec. The pipeline serves Canadian refineries from Edmonton to Montreal and many in the USA. Another pipeline, Trans-Mountain, extends from Edmonton to Vancouver. Nine refineries, 5 in Canada and 4 in Washington State, are served by the pipeline. At the end of 1981 Canada's oil pipeline system had 36,365·7 km of line in operation. Net oil deliveries in 1981 were 145,616,106 cu. metres. The Trans-Canada natural gas pipeline is the longest in the world (10,389 km). It brings natural gas from the Alberta–Saskatchewan border across the prairies, through northern Ontario to Toronto, then eastward to Montreal. Natural gas pipeline mileage totalled 161,655 km in 1981. Total gas received from fields and processing plants in 1982, 69,289·2m. cu. metres; total gas supplied to gas utilities, 53,942·3m. cu. metres.

Minerals. Alberta, Ontario, British Columbia. Quebec and Saskatchewan are the chief mining provinces. Total value of minerals produced in 1982 (preliminary) was $33,081,908,000. Principal minerals produced in 1982 (preliminary) were as follows:

Metallics	Quantity (1,000)	Value ($1,000)
Copper (kg)	606,202	1,179,767
Nickel (kg)	88,745	581,074
Zinc (kg)	1,032,653	1,108,687
Iron ore (tonnes)	34,496	1,211,657
Gold (grammes)	62,456	929,378
Lead (kg)	290,292	210,203
Silver (kg)	1,204	378,761
Molybdenum (kg)	15,222	327,077
Others	...	1,108,610
Total metallics	...	7,035,214

Non-metallics	Quantity (1,000)	Value ($1,000)
Asbestos (tonnes)	822	402,995
Potash (K₂O) (tonnes)	5,196	625,658
Salt (tonnes)	8,076	161,452
Sulphur, elemental (tonnes)	7,108	600,302
Gypsum (tonnes)	5,726	42,577
Others	...	321,019
Total non-metallics	...	2,154,003

Fuels		
Crude petroleum (cu. metres)	71,095	11,627,923
Natural gas (cu. metres)	73,783	7,081,678
Natural gas by-products (cu. metres)	17,965	2,154,702
Coal (tonnes)	43,200	1,297,800
Total fuels	...	22,162,103

Structural materials		
Cement (tonnes)	8,418	610,387
Sand and gravel (tonnes)	207,227	464,221
Stone (tonnes)	61,929	254,948
Clay products (bricks, tiles, etc.)	...	94,656
Lime (tonnes)	2,191	148,861
Total structural materials	...	1,573,073

Value (in Canadian $1,000) of mineral production by provinces:

Provinces	1981	1982 [1]	Provinces	1981	1982 [1]
Newfoundland	1,030,263	625,913	Saskatchewan	2,292,572	2,190,990
Pr. Ed. Island	1,616	2,054	Alberta	17,559,491	20,155,446
Nova Scotia	268,830	292,086	British Columbia	2,752,185	2,841,709
New Brunswick	530,695	516,744	Yukon Territory	235,575	167,862
Quebec	2,419,946	2,006,051	N.W. Territories	447,436	598,634
Ontario	4,159,827	3,173,065			
Manitoba	642,101	511,355	Total	32,340,807	33,081,908

[1] Preliminary.

Agriculture. Though the manufacturing industries now predominate, agriculture is still very important to the Canadian economy. It contributes about 2·9% of the net value of production and in 1982 accounted for about 12·1% of the value of commodities exported.

According to the census of 1981 the total land area is 2,278·6m. acres of which 162·8m. acres are agricultural land.

Grain growing, dairy farming, fruit farming, ranching and fur farming are all carried on successfully. Total farm receipts (1982) $18,671m.

The following table shows the estimated value of selected agricultural production for 1982, in Canadian $1,000:

Wheat	3,960,278	Tobacco	376,787
Oats and barley	957,276	Cattle and calves	3,586,368
Rapeseed	583,561	Hogs	1,957,341
Potatoes	251,405	Sheep and lambs	27,550
Other vegetables	438,973	Dairy products	2,640,305
Fruit	264,538	Poultry and eggs	1,236,335

Number of occupied farms (census of 1982) was 316,770; average farm size, 540 acres.

Field Crops. In 1983 (estimate), 75,172,300 acres were under principal field crops. The most valuable field crops are wheat, barley, corn for grain, oats, canola-rapeseed-colza, mixed grains, rye, tame hay, soybeans, flaxseed and fodder corn.

The estimated acreage and yield of the principal field crops, by provinces, 1983 were:

	Wheat		Tame hay		Oats	
	1,000	1,000	1,000	1,000	1,000	1,000
Provinces	acres	bu.	acres	bu.	acres	bu.
Prince Edward Island	6	270	126	277	31	1,736
Nova Scotia	5	225	176	475	19	1,045
New Brunswick	9	369	172	335	39	1,872
Quebec	74	3,086	2,445	4,409	420	19,453
Ontario	578	28,010	2,570	7,450	330	15,500
Manitoba	4,600	125,300	1,300	2,400	550	26,000
Saskatchewan	20,600	567,000	1,750	2,900	850	41,000
Alberta	7,700	246,500	3,700	7,200	1,150	68,000
British Columbia	160	5,920	725	1,450	70	4,361
Total, Canada	33,732	976,680	12,964	26,896	3,459	178,967

	Barley		Rye		Corn for Grain	
	1,000	1,000	1,000	1,000	1,000	1,000
Provinces	acres	bu.	acres	bu.	acres	bu.
Prince Edward Island	50	2,500	—	—	—	—
Nova Scotia	11	550	4	168	—	—
New Brunswick	15	705	—	—	—	—
Quebec	340	15,157	8·2	177	450	38,581
Ontario	525	24,200	90	3,060	2,000	168,000
Manitoba	1,750	72,000	210	6,630	180	11,000
Saskatchewan	2,900	120,000	450	13,300	—	—
Alberta	5,200	240,000	270	8,700	11	1,000
British Columbia	180	7,686	21·5	645	—	—
Total, Canada	10,971	482,798	1,053·7	32,680	2,641	218,581

	Flaxseed		Mixed grains		Soybeans	
	1,000	1,000	1,000	1,000	1,000	1,000
Provinces	acres	bu.	acres	bu.	acres	bu.
Prince Edward Island	—	—	83	4,814	—	—
Nova Scotia	—	—	6	324	—	—
New Brunswick	—	—	3	144	—	—
Quebec	—	—	135	6,223	—	—
Ontario	—	—	685	33,600	930	26,000
Manitoba	750	12,000	120	4,800	—	—
Saskatchewan	300	5,500	70	2,800	—	—
Alberta	60	1,200	150	7,800	—	—
British Columbia	—	—	10·6	583	—	—
Total, Canada	1,100	18,700	1,262·6	61,088	930	26,000

	Fodder corn		Canola-Rapeseed-Colza	
	1,000	1,000	1,000	1,000
Provinces	acres	bu.	acres	bu.
Prince Edward Island	5	80	—	—
Nova Scotia	8	116	—	—
New Brunswick	4	60	—	—
Quebec	215	2,646	—	—
Ontario	600	6,600	—	—
Manitoba	75	500	950	18,000
Saskatchewan	—	—	2,100	48,000
Alberta	24	440	2,500	49,000
British Columbia	26	468	200	3,000
Total, Canada	957	10,910	5,750	118,000

Livestock. In parts of Saskatchewan and Alberta stockraising is still carried on as a primary industry, but the livestock industry of the country at large is mainly a subsidiary of mixed farming. The following table shows the numbers of livestock (in 1,000) by provinces in July 1983:

Provinces	Milch cows	Other cattle	Sheep and lambs	Swine
Newfoundland	2·7	4	6·3	19·1
Prince Edward Island	23	76·5	8·2	111
Nova Scotia	35	107	46	148
New Brunswick	27·5	80	11·5	127
Quebec	675	938	128	3,150
Ontario	545	2,181	245	3,450
Manitoba	79	984	39	898
Saskatchewan	85	2,190	68	520
Alberta	157	3,648	197	1,180
British Columbia	88	660	60	254
Total	1,717·2	10,868·5	809	9,857·1

Net production of farm eggs in 1981, 496·2m. doz. ($487·3m.); 1982, 493·6m. doz. ($471·5m.).
Wool production (in tonnes), 1978, 925; 1979, 1,066; 1980, 1,173; 1981, 1,407; 1982, 1,408.

Dairying. The dairy products industry has shown a marked tendency towards centralization; the number of establishments decreased between 1961 and 1981 from 1,710 to 416 (75·7%), whereas the number of employees has decreased only 18%. Production, 1982: Creamery butter, 122,580 tonnes; cheddar cheese, 90,041 tonnes; concentrated whole milk products, 190,154 kl; skim milk powder, 161,606 tonnes.

Fruit Farming. The value of fruit production (excluding apples) in 1982 was (estimated in $1,000): Ontario, 89,479; British Columbia, 73,064 ; Quebec, 27,108; Nova Scotia, 12,903; New Brunswick, 11,509; Prince Edward Island, 1,537. Total apple production in Canada in 1982 was 526,492 tonnes.

Tobacco. Commercial production of tobacco is confined to Ontario and Quebec. Farm cash receipts in 1982 totalled $374m.

Forestry. The total area of land covered by forests is estimated at about 4,364,000 sq. km, of which 2,641,000 sq. km are classed as productive forest land.
Lumber production (in cu. metres) in 1981 was 40,216,790.
The volume of lumber shipments from sawmills and planing mills in 1981 was 16,603,517,000 bd ft valued at $3,623·4m. Pulp production was 20·6m. tonnes in 1981 and 19·9m. tonnes in 1980. In 1981 mill shipments of paper amounted to 13·5m. tonnes valued at $7,065,496,000.

Fur Trade. In 1981–82 (year ended 30 June), 4,423,395 pelts valued at $107,102,323, were taken. In wild-life pelt production beaver led in total value, followed by muskrat, fox, lynx and raccoon. The most important animal raised on fur farms is mink, with 99% of the total production. The value of pelts from fur farms in 1982 was $44,291,029, of which mink accounted for $40,930,523. There were, in 1982, 550 fur farms reporting fox and 704 mink.

Fisheries. During 1982, landings in Canadian commercial fisheries reached 1,394,724 tonnes. The landed value was $889·1m. and the estimated market value was $1,978·5m. The landed value of principal fish in 1982 was (in $1,000): Salmon, 171,210; cod, 203,963; lobster, 112,763; herring, 63,506; scallops, 60,534; freshwater fish, 64,000; halibut, 13,410. Exports of fisheries' products, 1982, were valued at $1,611·7m.

Canadian Mines Handbook. Annual. Toronto, from 1931

INDUSTRY AND TRADE

Industry. Industry groups ranked by value of shipments, survey of 1981:

Industry	Production workers	Wages ($1,000)	Cost of materials ($1,000)	Value of shipments ($1,000)
Food and beverages	159,703	2,745,017	21,958,295	31,841,656
Tobacco products	5,606	119,351	796,597	1,374,802
Rubber and plastics	45,681	746,657	2,415,291	4,513,149
Leather industries	22,577	269,194	624,015	1,218,831
Textile industries	53,252	776,436	2,793,819	5,060,056
Knitting mills	17,851	206,301	541,768	1,012,275
Clothing industries	83,418	954,359	2,019,606	4,090,235
Wood industries	94,328	1,673,887	4,801,675	8,441,830
Furniture and fixtures	44,328	630,847	1,342,288	2,772,278
Paper and allied industries	99,491	2,243,310	7,594,694	15,729,427
Printing, publishing and allied industries	63,964	1,183,575	2,425,960	6,463,077
Primary metal industries	92,337	2,120,019	8,139,081	14,449,480
Metal fabricating industries	120,450	2,205,852	6,445,282	12,375,750
Machinery industries	70,784	1,394,747	4,511,847	8,688,951
Transport equipment	136,102	2,944,002	14,487,903	21,681,301
Electrical products industries	84,282	1,447,376	4,440,910	8,938,284
Non-metallic mineral products	40,145	818,567	1,934,099	4,789,287
Petroleum and coal products	8,457	250,024	18,044,861	20,276,460
Chemical and chemical prods.	46,398	950,434	5,989,954	13,189,537
Miscellaneous manufacturing	48,354	702,615	2,038,382	4,053,714
All industries	1,337,508	24,534,570	114,346,328	190,940,381

Labour. In Aug. 1983 the industrial distribution of the employed was estimated as follows (in 1,000): Service, 3,446; manufacturing, 1,981; trade, 1,886; transport, communication and other utilities, 892; construction, 655; public administration, 829; finance, insurance and real estate, 606; agriculture, 561; other primary industries, 319; total employed, 11,176; unemployed, 1,365.

Union returns filed for 1981 in compliance with the Corporations and Returns Act (1962), show 184 labour organizations reporting on 13,439 local union branches in Canada. Union membership in 1981 was 3·16m. 32·9% of the wage and salary workers in major industry groups were members of reporting labour organizations, with about 73·6% of the organized workers members of unions affiliated with the Canada Labour Congress. Over 1·54m. of the union members were in international unions, which have branches both in Canada and the USA and in most cases belong to central labour organizations in both countries.

It is generally established by legislation, both federal and provincial, that a trade union to which the majority of employees in a unit suitable for collective bargaining belong, is given certain rights and duties. An employer is required to meet and negotiate with such a trade union to determine wage-rates and other working conditions of his employees. The employer, the trade union and the employees affected are bound by the resulting agreement. If an impasse is reached in negotiation conciliation services provided by the appropriate government board are available. Generally, work stoppages may not take place until an established conciliation procedure has been carried out and are prohibited while an agreement is in effect. Almost 28% of the workers affected by collective agreements are in the manufacturing industry.

Freedom of association is a civil right in Canada, and under common law workers are at liberty to join unions and participate in their activities. This right has also been guaranteed by statutes which make it an offence to interfere with freedom of association.

Certain specific minimum standards in regard to working conditions are set by law, for the most part by provincial labour legislation. Minimum wages, maximum hours of work or an overtime rate of pay after a specified number of hours, minimum weekly rest periods and annual vacations with pay are established for the majority of workers.

Workmen injured in the course of employment or disabled by industrial disease are required to receive compensation under workmen's compensation laws which apply to most employees except agricultural workers. Benefits during the period of disability for work are set by law at a proportion (now 75%) of the workman's average earnings, subject to a maximum established in each province. Benefits (which also include monthly allowances to dependants in the case of the death of a workman caused by an accident or disease arising out of his employment) are paid out of an accident fund administered by a government board in each province. The fund is made up of contributions from employers according to an annual assessment rate, varying from a few cents to several dollars per $100 of payroll according to the hazards of the industry.

Dept. of Labour, *Working Conditions in Canadian Industry.* Annual. Ottawa

Commerce. In the past the custom tariff of Canada has been protective, with a preferential tariff in favour of the UK, the Dominions, a number of Crown Colonies, and the Irish and South African Republics. At the Imperial Economic Conference of 1932, held in Ottawa, the UK developed further the policy of preferential tariffs to the Dominions, and on the part of the latter there was a general lowering of the existing tariffs against certain lines of UK manufacturers. Canada is one of the signatories of the General Agreement on Tariffs and Trade (GATT) and of the Kennedy Round agreements.

Imports for home consumption and domestic exports (in Canadian $1,000) for calendar years (merchandise only):

	Imports	Exports		Imports	Exports
1960	5,842,695	5,255,575	1981	79,481,715	81,336,731
1970	13,951,903	16,820,098	1982 [1]	67,926,122	81,828,704
1980	69,273,844	74,445,976			

[1] Estimate

Exports (domestic) by countries in 1982 (in Canadian $1,000):

Australia	650,679	Afghánistán	191
Bahamas	27,471	Albania	59
Bahrain	5,576	Algeria	496,287
Bangladesh	120,704	Angola	979
Barbados	32,088	Argentina	77,809
Belize	2,107	Austria	41,007
Bermuda	34,480	Belgium and Luxembourg	772,578
Britain	2,668,412	Benin	896
British Oceania	1,117	Bolivia	9,112
Cyprus	16,189	Brazil	526,523
Falkland Islands	3	Bulgaria	8,647
Fiji	2,173	Burma	4,663
Gambia	146	Cameroon Republic	28,278
Ghana	10,018	Chile	66,704
Gibraltar	382	China	1,228,754
Guyana	12,470	Colombia	190,901
Hong Kong	242,744	Costa Rica	15,867
India	293,245	Cuba	324,399
Ireland	96,976	Czechoslovakia	31,341
Jamaica	68,479	Denmark	83,312
Kenya	24,438	Dominican Republic	50,389
Leeward and Windward Islands	32,104	Ecuador	58,550
Malawi	1,592	Egypt (UAR)	353,093
Malaysia	118,025	El Salvador	14,186
Malta	2,369	Ethiopia	12,259
Mauritius and Dependencies	592	Finland	110,581
New Zealand	156,936	France	705,284
Nigeria	62,033	French Africa	7,159
Pakistan	104,143	French Guiana	532
Qatar	18,582	French Oceania	1,888
Sierra Leone	350	French West Indies	3,567
Singapore	154,268	Gabon	2,434
South Africa, Republic of	215,156	German Democratic Rep.	21,545
Sri Lanka	16,562	Germany, Fed. Rep. of	1,232,717
Tanzania	20,368	Greece	75,981
Trinidad and Tobago	139,809	Greenland	5,102
Uganda	474	Guatemala	34,021
Zambia	6,395	Guinea	870

Exports *(continued)*

Haiti, Republic of	23,574	Portugal	121,317
Honduras	15,315	Portuguese Africa	1,041
Hungary	13,629	Puerto Rico	98,950
Iceland	6,155	Romania	4,059
Indonesia	201,580	Saudi Arabia	442,348
Iran	181,903	Senegal	11,673
Iraq	190,561	Somalia	3,746
Israel	122,115	Spain	189,731
Italy	692,137	Spanish Africa	13,811
Ivory Coast	4,442	St Pierre and Miquelon	29,743
Japan	4,572,865	Sudan	13,433
Jordan	23,786	Suriname	4,261
Korea, North	41	Sweden	192,537
Korea, South	488,429	Switzerland	218,911
Kuwait	96,506	Syria	3,250
Lebanon	37,017	Taiwan	292,779
Liberia	4,673	Thailand	142,378
Libya	119,030	Togo	1,504
Madagascar	2,336	Tunisia	73,521
Mauritania	1,669	Turkey	109,449
Mexico	446,480	USSR	2,068,651
Morocco	104,683	United Arab Emirates	47,441
Mozambique	28,750	USA	55,839,675
Netherlands	1,041,553	US Oceania	4,249
Netherlands Antilles	34,066	US Virgin Islands	19,752
Nicaragua	15,561	Uruguay	13,638
Norway	254,558	Venezuela	437,572
Panama	36,375	Vietnam (South)	250
Paraguay	690	Yemen	1,603
Peru	105,041	Yugoslavia	71,783
Philippines	102,487	Zaïre	18,395
Poland	358,633	Zimbabwe	6,709

Imports (for consumption) by countries in 1982 (in Canadian $1,000):

Australia	446,096	Tanzania	2,687
Bahamas	66,035	Trinidad and Tobago	18,019
Bahrain	1,113	Uganda	883
Bangladesh	4,875	Zambia	1,927
Barbados	6,753		
Belize	5,841	Afghánistán	458
Bermuda	806	Albania	158
Britain	1,903,683	Algeria	259,614
British Oceania	9	Argentina	58,397
Cyprus	445	Austria	91,860
Fiji	7,866	Belgium and Luxembourg	263,552
Gambia	31	Benin	21
Ghana	4,294	Bolivia	8,017
Gibraltar	2	Brazil	482,573
Guyana	24,318	Bulgaria	4,705
Hong Kong	668,839	Burma	109
India	90,699	Cameroon Republic	208
Ireland	128,787	Chile	119,692
Jamaica	125,249	China	203,654
Kenya	13,680	Colombia	92,257
Leeward and Windward Islands	1,284	Costa Rica	32,266
Malawi	1,020	Cuba	94,483
Malaysia	89,193	Czechoslovakia	60,337
Malta	2,679	Denmark	129,023
Mauritius and Dependencies	2,759	Dominican Republic	18,363
New Zealand	140,455	Ecuador	51,296
Nigeria	64,690	Egypt (UAR)	2,190
Pakistan	16,031	El Salvador	20,873
Qatar	37	Ethiopia	2,440
Singapore	163,562	Finland	96,424
South Africa, Republic of	218,718	France	876,960
Sri Lanka	16,732	French Africa	563

Imports *(continued)*

French Oceania	22	Panama	18,262
French West Indies	69	Paraguay	1,102
Gabon	7,515	Peru	33,201
German Democratic Rep.	9,695	Philippines	82,219
Germany, Fed. Rep. of	1,383,952	Poland	43,562
Greece	30,302	Portugal	43,705
Greenland	2,920	Puerto Rico	126,625
Guatemala	23,088	Romania	30,479
Guinea	23,754	Saudi Arabia	731,331
Haiti, Republic of	8,579	Senegal	366
Honduras	28,462	Somalia	47
Hungary	25,531	Spain	190,078
Iceland	4,931	Spanish Africa	57
Indonesia	30,269	St Pierre and Miquelon	504
Iran	117,183	Sudan	831
Iraq	561	Suriname	7,476
Israel	39,765	Sweden	365,762
Italy	724,852	Switzerland	429,537
Ivory Coast	12,300	Syria	217
Japan	3,536,119	Taiwan	661,268
Jordan	106	Thailand	33,785
Korea, North	11	Togo	96
Korea, South	586,447	Tunisia	392
Kuwait	769	Turkey	11,646
Lebanon	495	USSR	42,849
Liberia	34	United Arab Emirates	34,266
Libya	22,675	USA	47,916,788
Madagascar	242	US Oceania	55
Mauritania	43	US Virgin Islands	486
Mexico	999,410	Uruguay	10,716
Morocco	15,393	Venezuela	1,810,461
Mozambique	967	Vietnam, South	161
Netherlands	267,295	Yemen	134
Netherlands Antilles	6,659	Yugoslavia	24,002
Nicaragua	26,648	Zaïre	14,811
Norway	92,684	Zimbabwe	3,166

Categories of imports in 1982, estimate (in Canadian $1,000):

Live animals	141,696	Fabricated materials, inedible	11,794,381
Food, feed, beverages		End products, inedible	40,932,922
and tobacco	4,797,627	Special transactions	1,015,811
Crude materials, inedible	8,672,904		

Categories of exports (Canadian produce) in 1982, estimate (in Canadian $1,000):

Live animals	325,532	Fabricated materials, inedible	27,886,280
Food, feed, beverages		End products, inedible	28,675,946
and tobacco	9,899,487	Special transactions	263,874
Crude materials, inedible	14,777,586		

Total trade of Canada with UK (British Department of Trade returns, in £1,000 sterling):

	1979	1980	1981	1982	1983
Imports to UK	1,260,057	1,412,156	1,508,756	1,439,619	1,522,187
Exports and re-exports from UK	766,430	758,367	844,978	851,703	968,269

Tourism. The number of visitors to Canada in 1982 was 34,406,501 (1981, 41,953,448). In 1982, 32,431,840 came from USA (1981, 39,808,716).

COMMUNICATIONS

Roads. The total highway mileage in Canada in March 1981 was 928,258 km. Of this total (1976) 442,615 miles (712,319 km) were surfaced and 106,453 miles (171,336 km) improved and other earth roads. Expenditure (1976) on roads, bridges, ferries, etc., reached a total of $4,449m. Federal and provincial governments supplied $2,905m., with the remainder contributed by municipal and other sources. Federal expenditure was chiefly devoted towards the upkeep of national-park roadways and nationally owned bridges and ferries, although for the 'Mackenzie Highway' from Grimshaw, Alberta, to Hay River, Northwest Territories, the federal government paid about 68% of the total cost. In general, however, highways are provincially controlled and maintained, and the responsibility of assisting municipalities and townships falls directly on the provinces.

The Alaska Highway is part of the Canadian highway system. For the Trans-Canada Highway see map in THE STATESMAN'S YEAR-BOOK, 1962.

Registered motor vehicles totalled 14,255,214 in 1982 (preliminary); they included 10,530,355 passenger cars and taxis, 3,293,406 trucks and buses and 431,453 motor cycles.

Urban Transit. In 1981 urban transit systems (motor bus, trolley coach, street car and subway operations) carried 1,368·87m. fare passengers 699,519,361 km for an operating revenue of $1,302,845,000. In 1981, intercity and rural bus operations carried 29,585,000 fare passengers 186,354,034 km, earning revenues of $277,377,000.

Railways. The total length of main track railways in Canada on 31 Dec. 1981 was 66,371·5 km. The total route km, including route duplicate, yardtrack and sidings, was 92,414·6.

Canada has 2 great trans-continental systems: the Canadian National Railway system (CN), a government-owned body which operates 36,151·6 km (1981) of the total first maintrack, and the Canadian Pacific Railway, a joint-stock corporation operating 24,082·9 km (1981). From 1 April 1978, a government funded organization known as Via Rail took over passenger services formerly operated by CP and CN.

Selected statistics of Canadian railways for 1981: Income from passengers carried $569,588,833; freight revenue, $4,635,217,836; total railway operating revenues, $6,144,609,870.

Aviation. Civil aviation in Canada is under the jurisdiction of the federal government. The technical and administrative aspects are supervised by the Administrator of Air Transportation, while the economic functions are assigned to the Canadian Transportation Commission.

In 1981 Canadian airports handled 51,068,585 passengers, 129,918,000 kg of mail and 505·47m. kg of cargo. Operating revenue (1981) was $4,648·8m.; operating expenditure, $4,494·4m.

Shipping. The registered shipping on 31 Dec. 1982, including vessels for inland navigation, totalled 34,832 with a gross tonnage of 5,193,490. A total of 50,599 vessels (international shipping) visited Canadian ports in 1981, loading and unloading 213m. tonnes of cargo.

The major canals in Canada are those of the St Lawrence–Great Lakes waterway with their 7 locks, providing navigation for vessels of 25·75-ft draught from Montreal to Lake Ontario; the Welland Canal by-passing the Niagara River between Lake Ontario and Lake Erie with its 8 locks; and the Sault Ste Marie Canal and lock between Lake Huron and Lake Superior. These 16 locks overcome a drop of 582 ft from the head of the lakes to Montreal. The St Lawrence Seaway was opened to navigation on 1 April 1959 (see map in THE STATESMAN'S YEAR-BOOK, 1957). In 1982, traffic on the Montreal–Lake Ontario Section of the Seaway numbered 4,376 vessels carrying 42·8m. cargo tonnes; on the Welland Canal Section, 5,184 vessels with 49m. gross tonnes. Value of fixed assets was $664,350,443 and investments, $40,506,888 at 31 March 1983.

Coast Guard. The Canadian Coast Guard (formed in 1962) is responsible to the Minister of Transport. In 1983 it comprised 7 heavy icebreakers; a heavy icebreaker/cable repair vessel; 7 medium icebreakers; 3 light icebreakers; 25 aid tenders; 3 special shallow draft vessels; 60 search and rescue vessels (all types and sizes); 4 hovercraft and 34 helicopters.

Post. In Jan. 1983 there were 8,255 postal facilities in operation and 6,400m.

pieces of mail were processed. Gross revenue (estimate 1982–83) was $2,200m.; gross expenditure, $2,600m.

There were 919,143 miles (1,479,216 km) of telegraph wire in Canada in 1979 (including external cable landed in Canada). There were 16,248,428 telephones in July 1983.

Broadcasting. There were 731 originating stations operating in Canada at 31 March 1983, of which 100 were Canadian Broadcasting Corporation stations, 115 were CBC affiliates and 383 were privately owned and operated. Included were 399 AM radio stations, 215 FM radio stations, 117 television stations and 15 shortwave stations. Radio and television licence fees were abolished in 1953.

Wireless 'beam' stations are operated at Montreal for direct communications with Great Britain and Australia, and a station at Louisburg, N.S., provides a long-distance service to ships.

Cinemas (1981). There were 1,036 cinemas with a seating capacity of 628,283 and 286 drive-in theatres with a capacity of 140,559 cars.

Newspapers (1982). There were 120 daily newspapers, of which 108 were in English, 10 in French and 2 others.

JUSTICE, RELIGION, EDUCATION AND WELFARE

Justice. There is a Supreme Court in Ottawa, having general appellate jurisdiction in civil and criminal cases throughout Canada. There is an Exchequer Court, which is also a Court of Admiralty. There is a Superior Court in each province and county courts, with limited jurisdiction, in most of the provinces, all the judges in these courts being appointed by the Governor-General. Police, magistrates and justices of the peace are appointed by the provincial governments.

For the year ended 31 Dec. 1982, 2,203,668 Criminal Code Offences were reported and 386,839 persons were charged.

Canadian Legal and Directory. Toronto. Annual

Religion. Membership of the leading denominations in 1981:

Province	Roman Catholic	United Church of Canada	Anglican Church of Canada	Presbyterian	Lutheran
Newfoundland	204,430	104,835	153,530	2,700	460
Prince Edward Island	56,415	29,645	6,850	12,620	210
Nova Scotia	310,140	169,605	131,130	38,285	12,315
New Brunswick	371,100	87,460	66,260	12,070	1,810
Quebec	5,609,685	126,275	132,115	34,625	17,655
Ontario	2,986,175	1,655,550	1,164,315	517,020	254,175
Manitoba	269,070	240,395	108,220	23,910	58,830
Saskatchewan	279,840	263,375	77,725	16,065	88,785
Alberta	573,495	525,480	202,265	63,890	144,675
British Columbia	526,355	548,360	374,055	89,810	122,395
Yukon	5,470	3,310	4,665	615	915
Northwest Territories	18,215	3,725	15,295	505	665
Total, Canada	11,210,385	3,758,015	2,436,375	812,110	702,905

Other denominations: Baptist, 696,850; Greek Orthodox, 314,870; Jewish, 296,425; Ukrainian (Greek) Catholic, 190,585; Pentecostal, 338,790; Mennonite, 189,370; other, 3,136,815.

Education. Under the Constitution the various provincial legislatures have power over education. These powers are subject to certain qualifications respecting the rights of denominational and minority language schools. Newfoundland and Quebec legislations provide for Roman Catholic and Protestant school boards. School Acts in Ontario, Saskatchewan and Alberta provide tax support for both public and separate schools. School board revenues derive from local taxation on real property and government grants from general provincial revenue.

Except in Quebec the number of private elementary and secondary schools is small; their enrolments in 1982–83 were less than 5% of the total elementary-secondary population. Indian and Northern Affairs Canada finances schools for Indian and Inuit children; the enrolment in 1982–83 was 37,678.

In 1981–82, 402,000 full-time regular students (graduates and under-graduates) were enrolled in universities. In 1981 some 27,200 took first degrees in social sciences, commerce, economics, law, political science and geography; 16,400 in education; 8,500 in humanities; 7,000 in engineering and applied sciences; 5,000 in agriculture; 5,800 in health subjects; 4,300 in mathematics and physical sciences and 2,600 in fine and applied arts. Unclassified, 7,800.

The following statistics give information, for 1982–83, about all elementary and secondary schools, public, federal, private and blind and deaf:

Province	Schools	Teachers	Pupils
Newfoundland	645	7,819	142,886
Prince Edward Island	73	1,365	25,855
Nova Scotia	602	10,825	182,799
New Brunswick	475	7,767	149,633
Quebec	2,818	71,986	1,164,493
Ontario	5,426	95,112	1,876,213
Manitoba	836	12,324	220,488
Saskatchewan	1,072	11,247	210,856
Alberta	1,641	24,649	460,612
British Columbia	1,894	28,824	531,782
Yukon	25	250	4,524
Northwest Territories	71	690	12,760
National Defence (overseas)	10	230	3,066
Total	15,588	273,088	4,985,967

Association of Canadian Universities & Colleges. *Canadian Universities & Colleges*. Ottawa. Annual

Health. Canada achieves national health insurance through a series of interlocking provincial plans which qualify the provinces for federal financial support if they meet the minimum criteria of the federal legislation with respect to comprehensiveness of coverage with regard to services, universality of coverage with regard to people, accessibility to services uninhibited by excessive user charges, portability of benefits and non-profit administration by a public agency. There are also related, unconditional, federal contributions made by yielding points to provinces. The federal contributions to the provinces cover about 50% of the provincial costs for the insured services of the national Hospital Insurance and Medical Care Program. (In the health field the federal government also furnishes the provinces with *per capita* cash contributions towards the cost of extended health care services; *e.g.*, nursing home care, certain home care services; these are unconditional except that the provinces must provide appropriate information.

The Canadian approach to the development of a national health programme has been to progressively provide major segments of personal health care on a publicly financed basis to virtually the whole population, and this is achieved with the co-operation of the provinces, which exercise the primary constitutional prerogative in health matters.

The insurance programmes are designed to ensure that all residents of Canada have reasonable access to needed medical and hospital care on a prepaid basis. The insured services of the Hospital Insurance Programme, which commenced in 1958, include in-patient care (including necessary drugs, diagnostic tests, etc.); out-patient services, although optional under the national programmes, are insured in all provinces. Complementing the protection of the Hospital Insurance Programme is the Medical Care Programme, inaugurated in 1968, which covers all medically required services rendered by medical practitioners no matter where the services are rendered, and certain surgical–dental procedures undertaken by dental surgeons in hospital. All 10 provinces and the 2 northern territories are participating in both programmes, which provide health insurance coverage for over 99% of the population (or over 24m. people).

The approach taken by Canada is one of state-sponsored health insurance. Accordingly, the advent of the programmes produced little change in the ownership of hospitals, almost all of which are owned by non-governmental non-profit corporations, or in the rights and privileges of private medical practice. Patients are free to choose their own general practitioners and/or specialists without losing their insured benefits (there is a minor exception in Quebec involving the non-emergency services of a few physicians). Except for 0·5% of the population whose care is provided for under other legislation (such as serving members of the Canadian Armed Forces), all residents are eligible, regardless of whether they are in the work force. Benefits are available without upper limit so long as they are medically necessary, provided any registration or premium payment obligations are met. Benefits are also portable during any temporary absence from Canada anywhere in the world—subject to any limitation a province may impose upon treatment electively sought outside the particular province without prior approval. Provinces may prescribe limits on benefits payable for out-of-province care.

In addition to the benefits qualifying for federal contributions, provinces are free to provide additional benefits at their own discretion. Most provinces provide such benefits, which cover a variety of services (*e.g.*, optometric care, children's dental programme, drug benefits) depending upon the province. Most provinces fund their portion of health insurance costs out of general provincial revenues. Three provinces levy premiums which meet part of the provincial costs, 2 provinces impose a levy on employers, and 1 province utilizes part of its sales tax revenues for this purpose. Three provinces have nominal co-charges for short-term hospital care. Several provinces have charges for long-term hospital care geared, approximately, to the room and board portion of the OAS–GIS payments mentioned under Social Welfare.

Social Welfare. The Department of National Health and Welfare administers a number of social security programmes. Most notable among them are the Family Allowances programme, introduced in 1945 and amended in 1974; the Old Age Security programme, introduced in 1952 and to which were added the Guaranteed Income Supplement in 1966 and the Spouse's Allowance in 1975; the Canada Pension Plan which came into being in 1966 and the Child Tax Credit implemented in 1979. Social assistance and services programmes which are provided by the provinces and territories and (in some cases) by municipal governments, are cost-shared by the federal government under the Canada Assistance Plan, which was introduced in 1966.

The 1973 federal Family Allowances Act provides for the payment of a monthly Family Allowance ($28.52 in 1983) in respect of a dependent child under the age of 18 who is a resident of Canada, who is wholly or substantially maintained by a parent or guardian. At least one parent must be a Canadian citizen, or admitted to Canada as a permanent resident under the Immigration Act, or admitted to Canada for a period of not less than 1 year, if during that time his or her income is subject to Canadian Income Tax. Benefits are also paid under certain prescribed circumstances to Canadian citizens living abroad. A Special Allowance ($41.87 monthly in 1983) is paid on behalf of a child under the age of 18 who is maintained by a welfare agency, a government department or an institution. In some cases, payment is made directly to a foster parent. The Special Allowance was paid on behalf of over 37,000 children across Canada in March 1983.

Family Allowances are considered as income for income-tax purposes for the parent who claims an exemption for the child. During the month of March 1983, over 3·6m. Canadian families (including 6·7m. eligible children) received Family Allowances from the Federal Government; the total FA bill for the 1982–83 fiscal year was just over $2,200m.

Family Allowance benefits are raised each year in Jan. in accordance with the Consumer Price Index; for 1983 and 1984, however, indexation has been limited to 6% and 5% respectively, in accordance with the federal policy on fiscal restraints announced in late 1982. The Family Allowances Act specifies that a provincial government may request the federal government to vary the allowance rates payable within that province subject to the fulfilment of stipulated conditions. Only the provinces of Alberta and Quebec have exercised this option.

In addition to Family Allowances, parents may receive a Child Tax Credit (CTC), administered through the Income Tax System by Revenue Canada. The

CTC programme is designed to provide additional assistance in meeting the costs of raising children in low to middle income families. The maximum credit payable in 1983 (in respect of the 1982 taxation year) was $343 for each eligible child (*i.e.*, entitled to Family Allowances), where the net annual family income for the 1982 taxation year was less than $26,330; CTC entitlement is reduced by 5% of the amount by which the family's income exceeded this level. The credit and basic income levels are raised each year to reflect changes in the Consumer Price Index. The Child Tax Credit is paid in a single, non-taxable annual lump sum. It is estimated that approximately $1,000m. was paid out to approximately 2·5m. Canadian families in 1982 for the 1981 taxation year.

The Canada Pension Plan (CPP) is designed to provide workers with a basic level of income protection in the event of retirement, disability or death. Benefits are determined by the contributor's earnings and contributions made to the Plan, and are adjusted annually to reflect cost of living increases. Contribution is compulsory for most employed and self-employed Canadians 18 to 65 years of age. The Canada Pension Plan does not operate in Quebec, which has exercised its constitutional prerogative to establish a similar plan, the Quebec Pension Plan (QPP), to operate in lieu of CPP; there is reciprocity between the two to ensure coverage for all adult Canadians in the labour force.

CPP/QPP contributions are deductible for income tax purposes, while benefits are taxable. Benefits are adjusted annually to fully reflect increases in the Consumer Price Index.

Both CPP and QPP are funded by equal contributions of 1·8% of pensionable earnings from the employer and 1·8% from the employee (self-employed persons contribute the full 3·6%), in addition to the interest on the investment of excess funds. In 1983, the range of yearly pensionable earnings was from $1,800 to $18,500; a person who earned and contributed at less than the maximum level receives monthly benefits at rates lower than the maximum allowable under CPP/QPP.

For CPP, an advisory committee representing employers, employees, self-employed persons and the public regularly reviews the operation of the plan, the state of investments and the adequacy of coverage and benefits, and reports to the Minister of National Health and Welfare. CPP authorizes reciprocal agreements with other countries to achieve portability of pensions. Such agreements have been made with Italy, France and Portugal, and agreements with the US, Greece and Jamaica have been signed, but are not yet (1983) in force. In general, parallel provisions apply under QPP. In March 1983, over 1·5m. Canadians received Canada Pension Plan benefits; an additional 477,000 persons received Quebec Pension Plan benefits. Total expenditures during 1982–83 were just over $3,000m. for CPP and $1,000m. for QPP.

The Old Age Security (OAS) pension is payable to persons 65 years of age and over who satisfy the residence requirements stipulated in the Old Age Security Act. The amount payable, whether full or partial, is also governed by stipulated conditions, as is the payment of an OAS pension to a recipient who absents himself from Canada. OAS pensioners with little or no income apart from OAS may, upon application, receive a full or partial supplement known as the Guaranteed Income Supplement (GIS). Entitlement is normally based on the pensioner's income in the preceding year, calculated in accordance with the Income Tax Act. The spouse of an OAS pensioner, aged 60 to 64, meeting the same residence requirements as those stipulated for OAS, may be eligible for a full or partial Spouse's Allowance (SA). SA is payable, on application, the annual combined income of the couple being subject to an income test which does not include the OAS pension, the Guaranteed Income Supplement or the Spouse's Allowance.

The OAS pension is taxable; GIS and SA are not taxable. However, they must be included in computing the net income of a dependant for income-tax purposes. OAS, GIS and SA are subject to an increase every Jan., April, July and Oct. to reflect increases in the Consumer Price Index. For 1983 and 1984 adjustments have been limited to 6% and 5% respectively.

In Oct. 1983, the basic OAS pension was $260.52 monthly; the maximum Guaranteed Income Supplement was $257.68 monthly for a single pensioner or a married pensioner whose spouse was not receiving a pension or a Spouse's Allowance, and $201·65 monthly for each spouse of a married couple where both are pensioners. The maximum Spouse's Allowance for the same quarter was $462.17 monthly (equal to the basic pension plus the maximum GIS married rate). Total OAS expenditure for the 1982–83 financial year was $9,643m.

Under the Canada Assistance Plan, the federal government pays 50% of the cost, to the provinces, of assistance to persons in need; welfare services provided to persons who are in need or likely to become in need if they do not receive such services (welfare services means services having as their object the lessening, removal or prevention of the causes and effects of poverty, child neglect or dependence on public assistance); and work activity projects which are designed to improve the employability of persons who have unusual difficulty in finding or retaining jobs or in undertaking job training.

'Need' is defined by each province and is determined by the 'budget deficit' method, that is, the difference between an applicant's requirements and his income and resources. The rates of assistance payable are also determined by provincial authorities and are non-taxable. Provinces generally adjust social assistance rates once a year in accordance with certain economic indicators.

In addition to persons in need as defined in the Plan, federal contributions may be made towards agency costs of providing welfare services to persons who are likely to become in need, if such services are not provided. The amount of federal subsidy is dependent on the proportion of eligible persons as determined by the use of an income test or a pre-determined income level for different sized families.

In March 1982, close to 1·5m. Canadians (representing 770,000 households) were in receipt of direct financial assistance from provincial programmes shareable under the Canada Assistance Plan. Total payments to the provinces under the Plan (including General Assistance, Homes for Special Care, Child Welfare, Health Care, Welfare Services and Work Activity) for the 1981–82 financial year were over $2,600m.; this amount includes the estimated value of income tax points transferred to the province of Quebec by the Department of Finance under the Interim Arrangements Act.

Unemployment Insurance covers about 95% of workers. To be insurable, workers must be employed by the same employer for at least 15 hours a week or make at least $77.00 a week (1983). Neither the self-employed nor workers over 65 may insure their earnings. Benefit rate is 60% of average weekly insurable earnings. Maximum weekly benefit (1983) $231.

Workers' compensation coverage is compulsory for employees in specified trades and industries. Maximum compensation is 75% of gross earnings except in Quebec, Alberta and New Brunswick where it is 90% of net earnings.

The New Horizons Program, established in 1972 and administered by the Department of National Health and Welfare, is designed to encourage the self-determination and community involvement of retired Canadians. From inception late in 1972 until July 1983, close to $119m. had been approved for over 19,000 projects.

DIPLOMATIC REPRESENTATIVES

Of Canada in Great Britain (Macdonald House., Grosvenor Sq., London, W1X 0AB)
High Commissioner: Donald C. Jamieson.

Of Great Britain in Canada (80 Elgin St., Ottawa, K1P 5K7)
High Commissioner: Lord Moran, KCMG.

Of Canada in USA (1746 Massachusetts Ave., NW, Washington, D.C., 20036)
Ambassador: Allan Gotlieb.

Of the USA in Canada (100 Wellington St., Ottawa)
Ambassador: Paul H. Robinson, Jr.

Of Canada to the United Nations
Ambassador: Gérard Pelletier.

Books of Reference

Statistical Information: Statistics Canada, Ottawa, has been the official central statistical organization for Canada since 1918. The Bureau, which reports to Parliament through the Minister of Industry, Trade and Commerce, serves as the statistical agency for federal government departments; co-ordinates the statistics of the provincial governments along national lines; and channels all Canadian statistical data to internal organizations. *Statistician Chief of Canada:* Dr Peter G. Kirkham.

Publications of Statistics Canada are classified as periodical (issued more frequently than once a year), annual, biennial and occasional publications. The occasional publications frequently supplement the annual reports and usually contain historical information. A complete list is contained in the 1978–79 edition of the Statistics Canada catalogue and supplements, available on request. Official publications include:

The Canada Year Book. Annual, from 1905
Canada, Official Handbook. Annual, from 1930
Canadian Statistical Review. Monthly, with weekly supplements, from 1948
Eleventh Decennial Census of Canada, 1971. Ottawa, 1972
Atlas and Gazetteer of Canada. Dept. of Energy, Mines and Resources. Ottawa, 1969
Cambridge History of the British Empire. Vol. VI. Canada and Newfoundland. Cambridge, 1930
Canadian Almanac and Directory. Toronto. Annual
Canadian Annual Review. Annual, from 1960
Canadian Dictionary: French–English. Toronto, 1970
Canadiana; A List of Publications of Canadian Interest National Library, Ottawa. Monthly, with annual cumulation. 1951 ff.
Cook, R., *French-Canadian Nationalism; An Anthology.* Toronto, 1970.—*The Maple Leaf Forever; Essays on Nationalism and Politics in Canada.* Toronto, 1971
Creighton, Donald G., *Canada's First Century.* Toronto, 1970.—*Towards the Discovery of Canada.* Toronto, 1974
Dictionnaire Bélisle de la langue française au Canada; dictionnaire oxford. 1970
Dictionnaire canadien; français–anglais–français. Toronto, 1962
Encyclopedia Canadiana. 10 vols. Rev. ed. Ottawa, 1967
Hardy, W. G., *From Sea to Sea; Canada, 1850–1920: The Road to Nationhood.* Toronto, 1960
Hockin, T. A., *Government in Canada.* London, 1976
Kerr, D. G. G., *Historical Atlas of Canada.* Toronto, 1960
Lower, A. R. M., *Colony to Nation: A History of Canada.* 4th ed. Toronto, 1964
McCann, L. D., (ed.) *Heartland and Hinterland: A Geography of Canada.* Scarborough, Ontario, 1982
Mallory, J. R., *The Structure of Canadian Government.* Toronto, 1971
Moir, J., and Saunders, R., *Northern Destiny: A History of Canada.* Toronto, 1970

National Library: The National Library of Canada, Ottawa, Ontario. *Librarian:* J. Guy Sylvestre.

CANADIAN PROVINCES

The 10 provinces have each a separate parliament and administration, with a Lieut.-Governor, appointed by the Governor-General in Council at the head of the executive. They have full powers to regulate their own local affairs and dispose of their revenues, provided only they do not interfere with the action and policy of the central administration. Among the subjects assigned exclusively to the provincial legislatures are: the amendment of the provincial constitution, except as regards the office of the Lieut.-Governor; property and civil rights; direct taxation for revenue purposes; borrowing; management and sale of Crown lands; provincial hospitals, reformatories, etc.; shop, saloon, tavern, auctioneer and other licences for local or provincial purposes; local works and undertakings, except lines of ships, railways, canals, telegraphs, etc., extending beyond the province or connecting with other provinces, and excepting also such works as the Dominion Parliament declares are for the general good; marriages, administration of justice within the province; education.

Local Government. Under the terms of the British North America Act the provinces are given full powers over local government. All local government institutions are, therefore, supervised by the provinces, and are incorporated and function under provincial acts.

The acts under which municipalities operate vary from province to province. A municipal corporation is usually administered by an elected council headed by a mayor or reeve, whose powers to administer affairs and to raise funds by taxation and other methods are set forth in provincial laws, as is the scope of its obligations to, and on behalf of, the citizens. Similarly, the types of municipal corporations, their official designations and the requirements for their incorporation vary between provinces. The following table sets out the classifications as at 1 Jan. 1977.

Type and size of group	Nfld.	PEI	NS	NB	Que.	Ont.	Man.
Type:							
Regional municipalities	—	—	—	—	75	39	—
Metropolitan and regional municipalities [1]	—	—	—	—	3	12	—
Counties and regional districts	—	—	—	—	72	27	—
Unitary municipalities	129	36	65	112	1,500	784	185
Cities	2	1	3	6	64	45[2]	5
Towns	127[3]	8	38	21	195	144	35
Villages	—	27	—	85	242	120	40
Rural municipalities [4]	—	—	24	—	999	475	105
Quasi-municipalities [5]	171	—	—	—	—	13	17
Total	300	36	65	112	1,575	836	202
Population size group (1976 census):							
Unitary municipalities—							
Over 100,000	—	—	1	—	4	17	1
50,000 to 99,999	1	—	2	2	14	14	—
10,000 to 49,999	5	1	17	5	72	76	3
Under 10,000	123	35	45	105	1,410	677	181
Total	129	36	65	112	1,500	784	185

Type and size of group	Sask.	Alta.	BC	YT	NWT	Canada
Type:						
Regional municipalities	—	—	28	—	—	142
Metropolitan and regional municipalities [1]	—	—	—	—	—	15
Counties and regional districts	—	—	28	—	—	127
Unitary municipalities	783	327	140	3	7	4,071
Cities	11	10	33	2	1	183
Towns	135	102	10	1	4	820
Villages	344	167	59	—	2	1,086
Rural municipalities [4]	293	48	38	—	—	1,982
Quasi-municipalities [5]	7	22	—	4	10	244
Total	790	349	168	7	17	4,457
Population size group (1976 census):						
Unitary municipalities—						
Over 100,000	2	2	3	—	—	30
50,000 to 99,999	—	—	9	—	—	42
10,000 to 49,999	6	14	26	1	—	227
Under 10,000	775	311	102	2	7	3,772
Total	783	327	140	3	7	4,071

[1] Includes urban communities in Quebec; and Metropolitan Toronto, regional municipalities and the district municipality in Ontario.
[2] Includes the 5 boroughs of Metropolitan Toronto.
[3] Includes 11 rural districts.
[4] Includes municipalities in Nova Scotia; parishes, townships, united townships and municipalities in Quebec; townships in Ontario; rural municipalities in Manitoba and Saskatchewan; municipal districts and counties in Alberta; and districts in British Columbia.
[5] Includes local government communities, local improvement districts and the metropolitan area in Newfoundland; improvement districts in Ontario and Alberta; local government districts in Manitoba; local improvement districts in Saskatchewan and the Yukon Territory; and hamlets in the Northwest Territories.

ALBERTA

HISTORY. The southern half of the province of Alberta was part of Rupert's land which was granted by royal charter in 1670 to the Hudson's Bay Company. The intervention by the North West Company in the fur trade after 1783 led to the establishment of trading posts. In 1869 Rupert's land was transferred from the Hudson's Bay Company (which had absorbed its rival in 1821) to the new Dominion, and in the following year this land was combined with the former Crown land of the North Western Territories to form the Northwest Territories.

In 1882 'Alberta' first appeared as a provisional 'district', consisting of the southern half of the present province. In 1905 the Athabasca district to the north was added when provincial status was granted to Alberta.

Four parties have held office: the Liberals 1905–21; the United Farmers 1921–35; Social Credit 1935–71, and Progressive Conservative since Sept. 1971.

AREA AND POPULATION. The area of the province is 661,188 sq. km; 644,392 sq. km being land area and 16,796 sq. km water area. The population (estimate 1 June 1983) was 2·36m.; the urban population (1982), centres of 1,000 or over, was 1,727,545 and the rural 510,179. Population of the principal cities (1 June 1983): Calgary, 620,692; Edmonton, 560,085; Lethbridge, 58,086; Red Deer, 50,257; Medicine Hat, 41,167; St Albert, 35,032; Fort McMurray, 34,494; Grande Prairie, 24,076; Camrose, 12,809; Leduc, 12,471; Wetaskiwin, 10,022; Lloydminster (Alberta portion), 9,197; Drumheller, 6,671.

Vital statistics, see p. 267.

Religion, see p. 284.

CONSTITUTION AND GOVERNMENT. The constitution of Alberta is contained in the British North America Act of 1867, and amending Acts; also in the Alberta Act of 1905, passed by the Parliament of the Dominion of Canada, which created the province out of the then Northwest Territories. All the provisions of the British North America Act, except those with respect to school lands and the public domain, were made to apply to Alberta as they apply to the older provinces of Canada. On 1 Oct. 1930 the natural resources were transferred from the Dominion to provincial government control. The province is represented by 6 members in the Senate and 21 in the House of Commons of Canada.

The executive is vested nominally in the Lieut.-Governor, who is appointed by the federal government, but actually in the Executive Council or the Cabinet of the legislature. Legislative power is vested in the Assembly in the name of the Queen.

Members of the Legislative Assembly are elected by the universal vote of adults over the age of 18 years.

There are 79 members in the legislature (elected 2 Nov. 1982): 75 Progressive Conservative, 2 New Democratic Party, 2 Independent.

Lieut.-Governor: His Hon. Frank Lynch-Staunton (sworn in 4 Oct. 1979).
Flag: Blue with the shield of the province in the centre.

The members of the Ministry (all Progressive Conservative) are as follows:

Premier, President of Executive Council: Hon. Peter Lougheed.
Provincial Treasurer: Hon. L. D. Hyndman. *Attorney-General and Government House Leader:* Hon. N. Crawford. *Hospitals and Medical Care:* Hon. D. J. Russell. *Transportation:* Hon. M. E. Moore. *Municipal Affairs:* Hon. J. G. J. Koziak. *Federal and Intergovernmental Affairs, Deputy Government House Leader:* Hon. J. D. Horsman. *Economic Development:* Hon. H. Planche. *Advanced Education:* Hon. D. Johnston. *Education:* Hon. D. King. *Labour:* Hon. L. G. Young. *Public Works, Supply and Services:* Hon. T. W. Chambers. *Tourism and Small Business:* Hon. J. A. Adair. *Energy:* Hon. J. B. Zaozirny. *Agriculture:* Hon. E. L. Fjordbotten. *Utilities and Telecommunications:* Hon. R. J. Bogle. *Social Services and Community Health:* Hon. Dr P. N. Webber. *Housing:* Hon. L. R. Shaben. *International Trade:* Hon. H. A. Schmid. *Consumer and Corporate Affairs:* Hon. C. E. Osterman. *Environment:* Hon. F. D. Bradley. *Solicitor-General:* Hon. G. L. Harle.

Culture: Hon. M. J. LeMessurier. *Recreation and Parks:* Hon. P. Trynchy. *Minister responsible for Native Affairs:* Hon. M. G. Pahl. *Manpower:* Hon. E. D. Isley. *Associate Minister of Public Lands and Wildlife:* Hon. D. Sparrow. *Minister responsible for Workers' Health, Safety and Compensation:* Hon. B. W. Diachuk. *Minister responsible for Personnel Administration:* Hon. G. P. Stevens. *Minister without Portfolio:* Hon. W. E. Payne.

Local Government. The local government units are City, Town, New Town, Village, Summer Village, County, Municipal District and Improvement District.

There are 12 cities in Alberta, namely: Calgary, Camrose, Drumheller, Edmonton, Fort McMurray, Grande Prairie, Lethbridge, Lloydminster, Medicine Hat, Red Deer, St Albert and Wetaskiwin. These cities operate under the Municipal Government Act. The governing body consists of a mayor and a council of from 6 to 20 members. A city can be incorporated by order of the Lieut.-Governor-in-Council. A population of 10,000 is required.

There are no limits of area specified in the statutes for any of the different local government units. The population requirement for a Town as specified in the Municipal Government Act is 1,000 people, and the area at incorporation is that of the original village.

A Village must contain 75 separate and occupied dwellings. The Municipal Government Act requires each dwelling to have been occupied continuously for a period of at least 6 months. A Summer Village must contain 50 separate dwellings.

A rural county area is an area incorporated through an order of the Lieut.-Governor-in-Council under the provisions of the County Act. One board of councillors deal with both municipal and school affairs.

A rural Municipal District is an area which has been incorporated under the Municipal Government Act. In Municipal Districts separate boards control municipal and school affairs.

Areas not incorporated as counties or Municipal Districts are termed Improvement Districts or Special Areas. Sparsely populated, such districts are administered and taxed by the Department of Municipal Affairs of the provincial government. There are no requirements as to the minimum number of residents of a County or Municipal District.

FINANCE. The budgetary revenue and expenditure (in Canadian $) for years ending 31 March were as follows:

	1979–80	1980–81	1981–82	1982–83 [1]	1983–84 [1]
Revenue	5,668,000,000 [2]	6,578,000,000 [2]	7,084,710,000 [2]	6,520,000,000 [2]	8,840,000,000 [2]
Expenditure	4,665,000,000	5,561,000,000	7,043,707,000	9,031,029,000	9,685,452,000

[1] Estimates.   [2] Excludes funds allocated to Alberta Heritage Savings Trust Fund.

Personal income *per capita* (1981), $12,459.

ENERGY AND NATURAL RESOURCES

Oil. In 1982, 60,878,000 cu. metres of crude oil and condensate were produced with gross sales value of $10,123,968,000. Alberta produced 85·6% of Canada's oil output in 1982. Production of natural gas by-product was 17·65m. cu. metres, valued at $2,117,663,000.

The 4 major deposits of oil sands are found in areas totalling 106,600 sq. km in northern and eastern Alberta. There are 4 major deposits of oil sands, the Athabasca, Cold Lake, Peace River and Buffalo Head Hills deposits; total area, 105,320 sq. km. A limited part of the deposits along the Athabasca River can be exploited through open-pit mining. The rest of the Athabasca, and all the deposits in the other areas, are deeper reserves which must be developed through in situ techniques. These reserves reach depths of 760 metres.

One recovery plant, situated 25 miles north of Fort McMurray, began production in 1967. The deposit being produced is sufficiently close to the surface to permit strip mining. A second plant, to produce 20,000 cu. metres per day of synthetic crude oil, began production in 1978.

Gas. Natural gas is found in abundance in numerous localities. In 1982, 65,292m. cu. metres valued at $6,659,091,000 were produced.

Minerals. In 1982 the ultimate remaining recoverable coal resources of Alberta were estimated at 16,500m. tonnes; the proved remaining recoverable reserves were estimated at 47,000m. tonnes.

Value of total mineral production increased from $17,559,491,000 in 1981 to $20,155,446,000 in 1982.

Agriculture. Total area of farms (1981) 47·2m. acres; under crops, 20·9m.; improved pasture 3·9m.; summer fallow, 5·4m.; other improved land, 734,716.

For particulars of agricultural production and livestock, *see under* CANADA, pp. 276–78. Farm cash receipts in 1982 totalled $3,813,926,000, of which crops contributed $1,901,012,000; livestock and products, $1,749,258,000, and other sources, $163,656,000.

Forestry. Total woodland (1981) 1·2m acres. Alberta has an estimated net merchantable volume of 1,700m. cu. metres of timber comprised of 700m. cu. metres of hardwood and 1,000m. cu. metres of softwood. In 1981–82, 4,627,783 cu. metres of lumber and plywood were produced.

Fisheries. The lakes of the province contain whitefish, pike and tullibee. Commercial catches are marketed through the Freshwater Fish Marketing Corporation which was inaugurated in May 1969 as the result of an agreement between the federal government and the provinces for the buying and exporting of freshwater fish. Marketed value of commercially caught fish 1982–83 was $3,074,297. This value includes fish not marketed through the corporation.

INDUSTRY. The leading manufacturing industries are food and beverages, petroleum refining, metal fabricating, wood industries, primary metal, chemical and chemical products and non-metallic mineral products industries. There were in 1980 approximately 2,388 manufacturing establishments, in which were employed about 81,206 persons, who earned in salaries and wages $1,543,149,000.

Manufacturing shipments had a total value of $12,528,017,000 in 1982. Chief among these shipments were: Food and beverages, $3,541,324,000; petroleum and coal products, $3,211,968,000; chemicals and chemical products, $1,345,319,000; metal fabricating, $760,687,000; non-metallic mineral products, $631·97m.; primary metals, $575,117,000; machinery, $478.025,000; wood, $342,207,000; other, $1,641·4m.

Total retail sales (1982) $10,941·3m.

Tourism is of increasing importance and in 1982 contributed $1,420m. to the economy.

COMMUNICATIONS

Roads. In 1982 there were 149,691 km of roads and highways, including 99,408 km gravelled and 14,535 km paved.

At 31 March 1983 there were 2,046,863 motor vehicles registered, including 1,245,986 passenger cars, 468,442 public and commercial vehicles, 247,011 trailers and 59,899 motor cycles.

Railways. In 1983 the length of main railway lines was 10,116·4 km. In 1983 there was a rail rapid transit network in Edmonton (10·3 km) and Calgary (12·5 km).

Post and Telecommunications. Alberta's modern telephone system is owned and operated by the provincial government, except in the city of Edmonton (owned and operated by Edmonton) and some rural lines. There were 1,046,040 telephones in service in April 1983.

JUSTICE AND EDUCATION

Justice. The Supreme Judicial authority of the province is the Court of Appeal. Judges of the Court of Appeal and Court of Queen's Bench are appointed by the Dominion Government and hold office until retirement at the age of 75. There are courts of lesser jurisdiction in both civil and criminal matters. The Court of Queen's Bench has full jurisdiction over civil proceedings. A Provincial Court which has jurisdiction in civil matters up to $1,000 is presided over by provincially appointed judges. Juvenile Courts have power to try boys and girls 16 and under for offences against the Juvenile Delinquents Act.

The jurisdiction of all criminal courts in Alberta is enacted in the provisions of the Criminal Code. The system of procedure in civil and criminal cases conforms as nearly as possible to the English system.

Education. Schools of all grades are included under the term of public school (including those in the separate school system which are publicly supported). The same board of trustees controls the schools from kindergarten to university entrance. In 1981–82 there were 419,822 pupils enrolled in elementary, junior high schools and high schools. The University of Alberta (in Edmonton), organized in 1907, had, in 1982–83, 21,045 full-time students. The University of Calgary, formerly part of the University of Alberta and autonomous from April 1966, had in 1982–83, 13,426 full-time students. The University of Lethbridge, organized in 1966, had in 1982–83, 2,208 full-time students. The Athabasca University had in 1982–83, 7,000 full-time students. The full-time enrolment at Alberta's 10 public colleges totalled 12,883 students in 1982–83.

Books of Reference

Statistical Information: The Alberta Bureau of Statistics (Dept. of Treasury, Edmonton), which was established in 1939, collects, compiles and distributes information relative to Alberta. *Director:* Harvey W. Ford. Among its publications are: *Alberta Statistical Review* (Annual).—*Alberta Statistical Review* (Quarterly).—*Alberta Economic Accounts* (Annual).—*Alberta Pay and Benefits* (Annual).—*Retail and Service Trade Statistics, Alberta* (Annual).—*Alberta Facts* (Annual).—*Principal Manufacturing Statistics, Alberta* (Annual).—*Population Projections, Alberta* (Occasional).—*Quarterly Population Growth, Alberta* (Quarterly).—*Place-to-Place Price Comparisons for Selected Alberta Communities* (Annual).

Dept. of Economic Development and Dept. of Federal and Intergovernmental Affairs, *Alberta Profile.* Edmonton, 1980

Hardy, W. G., *Alberta Golden Jubilee Anthology.* Toronto, 1955
Irving, J. A., *The Social Credit Movement in Alberta.* Toronto, 1959
Kroetsch, R., *Alberta.* Toronto, 1968
Macpherson, C. B., *Democracy in Alberta.* 2nd ed. Toronto, 1962
Nesbitt, L. D., *Tides in the West [history of the Alberta Wheat Pool].* Saskatoon, 1962

BRITISH COLUMBIA

HISTORY. Vancouver Island was organized as a colony in 1849; the mainland as far as the watershed of the Rocky Mountains was organized as a colony following a gold rush on the Fraser River in 1858. The two were united as the colony of British Columbia in 1866; this became a Canadian Province in 1871.

AREA AND POPULATION. British Columbia has an area of 948,596 sq. km. The capital is Victoria. The province is bordered westerly by the Pacific ocean and Alaska Panhandle, northerly by the Yukon and Northwest Territories, easterly by the Province of Alberta and southerly by the USA along the 49th parallel. A chain of islands, the largest of which are Vancouver Island and the Queen Charlotte Islands, affords protection to the mainland coast.

The June 1981 census population was 2,744,467; estimate, 1983, 2,823,900.

The principal cities and their populations (1982) are as follows: Greater Vancouver, 1,283,000; Greater Victoria, 236,400; Prince George, 68,867; Kamloops, 64,660; Kelowna, 60,026; Nanaimo, 49,139; Penticton, 23,722; Vernon, 20,484; Port Alberni, 19,794; Prince Rupert, 16,516; Cranbrook, 16,403; Dawson Creek, 11,481.

Vital statistics, *see* p. 267.
Religion, *see* p. 284.

CONSTITUTION AND GOVERNMENT. British Columbia (then known as New Caledonia) originally formed part of the Hudson's Bay Company's concession. In 1849 Vancouver Island and in 1858 British Columbia were constituted Crown Colonies; in 1866 the two colonies amalgamated. The British North America Act of 1867 provided for eventual admission into Canadian Confederation, and on 20 July 1871 British Columbia became the sixth province of the Dominion.

British Columbia has a unicameral legislature of 57 elected members. Government policy is determined by the Executive Council responsible to the Legislature. The Lieut.-Governor is appointed by the Governor-General of Canada, usually for a term of 5 years, and is the head of the executive government of the province.

Lieut.-Governor: The Hon. Robert Gordon Rogers.

Flag: A banner of the arms, *i.e.*, blue and white wavy stripes charged with a setting sun in gold, across the top of a Union Flag with a gold coronet in the centre.

The Legislative Assembly is elected for a maximum term of 5 years. Every male or female Canadian citizen 18 years and over, having resided a minimum of 6 months in the province, duly registered, is entitled to vote. Representation of the parties at 5 May 1983: Social Credit Party, 35; New Democratic Party, 22; total, 57.

The province is represented in the Federal Parliament by 28 members in the House of Commons, and 6 Senators.

The Executive Council was composed as follows, Sept. 1983:

Premier: William Richards Bennett.

Agriculture and Food: Harvey W. Schroeder. *Attorney-General:* Brian R. D. Smith. *Consumer and Corporate Affairs:* James J. Hewitt. *Education:* John H. Heinrich. *Energy, Mines and Petroleum Resources:* Stephen Rogers. *Environment, Lands, Parks and Housing:* A. J. Brummet. *Finance:* Hugh A. Curtis. *Forests:* Thomas M. Waterland. *Health:* James Nielsen. *Industry and Small Business Development:* Donald M. Phillips. *Intergovernmental Relations:* Garde B. Gardom. *Labour:* Robert H. McClelland. *Municipal Affairs:* William S. Ritchie. *Provincial Secretary:* James R. Chabot. *Tourism:* Claude Richmond. *Transportation and Highways:* Alexander V. Fraser. *Universities, Science and Communications:* Patrick L. McGeer.

Agent-General in London: Alexander H. Harte, QC (British Columbia House, 1 Regent St., London, SW1Y 4NS).

Local Government. Vancouver City was incorporated by statute and operates under the provisions of the Vancouver Charter of 1953 and amendments. This is the only incorporated area in British Columbia not operating under the provisions of the Municipal Act. Under this Act municipalities are divided into the following classes: *(a)* a village with a population between 500 and 2,500, governed by a council consisting of a mayor and 4 aldermen; *(b)* a town with a population between 2,500 and 5,000, governed by a council consisting of a mayor and 4 aldermen; *(c)* a city where the population exceeds 5,000 governed by a council consisting of a mayor and 6 or 8 aldermen depending on population; *(d)* a district where the area exceeds 810 hectares and the average density is less than 5 persons per hectare, governed by a council consisting of a mayor and 6 or 8 aldermen depending on population.

There are two other forms of local government: the regional district covering a number of areas both incorporated and unincorporated, governed by a board of directors; and the improvement district governed by a board of 3 trustees.

Revenue for municipal services is derived mainly from real-property taxation, although additional revenue is derived from licence fees, business taxes, fines, public utility projects and grants-in-aid from the provincial government.

ECONOMY

Budget. Current provincial revenue and expenditure, including all capital expenditures, in Canadian $1m. for fiscal years ending 31 March:

	1979–80	1980–81	1981–82	1982–83 [1]
Revenue	5,515·4	5,802·7	6,903·4	6,541·0
Expenditure	5,327·0	6,060·0	7,087·5	7,519·2

[1] Provisional.

The main sources of current revenue are the income taxes, contributions from the federal government, and privileges, licences and natural resources taxes and royalties.

The main items of expenditure in 1982–83 (preliminary) are as follows: Health and social services, $3,434·9m.; education, $1,672·4m.; transport and communication, $517·7m.; natural resources and industry, $459·8m.; protection of persons and property, $350·9m.

Banking. Cheques cashed (in $1m.): 1978, 233,387; 1979, 286,902; 1980, 382,836; 1981, 519,386; 1982, 488,102.

ENERGY AND NATURAL RESOURCES

Electricity. Generation in 1982 totalled 47,919m. kwh. of which a net 4,307m. kwh. were exported. Consumption within the province was 43,612m. kwh.

Minerals. Copper, coal, natural gas, crude oil, molybdenum and silver are the most important minerals produced. The 1982 total of mineral production was estimated at $2,796·6m. Total value of fuels produced in 1981 was estimated at $1,441·9m.

Agriculture. Only 2·4m. hectares or 3% of the total land area is arable or potentially arable. Farm cash receipts, in 1982, reached $918·4m.

Forestry. About 55% of British Columbia's land is forest land, with 47·8m. hectares bearing commercial forest. Over 94% of the forest area is owned or administered by the provincial government. The total cut from forests in 1982 was 56·2m. cu. metres.

Fisheries. In 1982 the wholesale market value of fish products reached $461m.

INDUSTRY AND TRADE

Industry. The selling value of factory shipments from all manufacturing industries reached an estimated $15,446m. in 1982.

Commerce. Exports through British Columbia customs ports during 1982 totalled $15,696m. in value, while imports amounted to $6,256m.

Principal export commodity groups through British Columbia customs ports (1982): Coal, crude petroleum and natural gas, $4,109·1m.; forest products, $3,761·5m.; grain and cereal products, $2,073·2m.; metal ores and ingots, $1,367·5m.; crude non-metallic minerals (excluding fuels), $744·7m.; chemicals and related products, $673m.; fish and marine products, $335m. About 40% of exports through British Columbia customs ports are products from other provinces, primarily grains, potash and fuels from the Prairie Provinces. USA is the largest market for products exported through British Columbia customs ports ($6,306m. in 1982) followed by Japan ($3,739m.) and the EEC ($1,121m.).

COMMUNICATIONS

Roads. At 31 March 1983 there were 43,072 km of provincial roads and rights of way in the province, of which 18,119 km were paved, 19,541 km were gravelled and 5,412 km were dirt.

Railways. The province is served by two transcontinental railways, the Canadian Pacific Railway and the Canadian National Railway. British Columbia is also served by the publicly owned British Columbia Railway, the Railway Freight Service of the B.C. Hydro and Power Authority, the Northern Alberta Railways Company and the Burlington Northern Inc. The combined route-mileage of mainline track operated by the CPR, CNR and BCR totals 7,344 km. The system also includes CPR and CNR railcar barge connections to Vancouver Island, between Prince Rupert and Alaska, and interchanges with American railways at southern border points.

Aviation. International airports are located at Vancouver and Victoria. Daily interprovincial and intraprovincial flights serve all main population centres. Small public and private airstrips are located throughout the province.

Shipping. The major ports are Vancouver, New Westminster, Victoria, Nanaimo and Prince Rupert. The volume of domestic and international cargo handled during 1982 was 67m. tonnes and 47m. tonnes respectively.

The British Columbia Ferries connect Vancouver Island with the mainland and also provide service to other coastal points. Service by other ferry systems is also provided between Vancouver Island and the USA. The Alaska State Ferries connect Prince Rupert with centres in Alaska.

Post and Broadcasting. The British Columbia Telephone Company had (1982) 1·3m. telephones in service. There were 13 television stations and 225 radio stations operating in the province in 1982. Many of these are repeater stations.

EDUCATION AND WELFARE

Education. Education, free up to Grade XII levels, is financed jointly from municipal and provincial government revenues. Attendance is compulsory from the age of 6 to 15. There were 500,336 pupils enrolled in public schools from kindergarten to Grade XII in Sept. 1982.

The universities had a full-time enrolment of 34,403 for 1982–83. They include University of British Columbia, Vancouver; University of Victoria, Victoria; Simon Fraser University, Burnaby, and the David Thompson University Centre, Nelson. The regional colleges are Camosun College, Victoria; Capilano College, North Vancouver; Cariboo College, Kamloops; College of New Caledonia, Prince George; Douglas College, New Westminister; East Kootenay Community College, Cranbrook; Fraser Valley College, Chilliwack/Abbotsford; Kwantlen College, Surrey; Malaspina College, Nanaimo; North Island College, Comox; Northern Lights College, Dawson Creek/Fort St John; Northwest Community College, Terrace/Prince Rupert; Okanagan College, Kelowna with branches at Salmon Arm and Vernon; Selkirk College, Castlegar; Vancouver Community College, Vancouver.

There are also the British Columbia Institute of Technology, Burnaby; Emily Carr College of Art and Design, Vancouver; Justice Institute of British Columbia, Vancouver; Open Learning Institute, Richmond; Pacific Marine Training Institute, North Vancouver; Pacific Vocational Institute, Burnaby/Maple Ridge/Richmond. A televised distance education and special programmes through KNOW, the Knowledge Network of the West is provided.

Health. The Government operates a hospital insurance scheme giving universal coverage after a qualifying period of 3 months' residence in the province. The province has come under a national medicare scheme which is partially subsidized by the provincial government and partially by the federal government.

Books of Reference

Statistical Information: Information Services (Ministry of Industry and Small Business Development, Hon. Don Phillips—Minister, Parliament Buildings, Victoria, B.C. V8V 1 × 4), collects, compiles and distributes information relative to the Province.

Publications include *British Columbia Business Bulletin; Economic Review and Outlook* (Annual); *Manufacturers' Directory; External Trade Report* (Annual); *B.C. Manual of Facts and Statistics* Annual).

Ministry of Finance, *British Columbia Financial and Economic Review.* Victoria, B.C. (Annual)

Fifteenth British Columbia Natural Resources Conference, *Inventory of the Natural Resources of British Columbia,* 1964

MANITOBA

HISTORY. The Hudson's Bay Company formed a colony on the Red River in 1812. This being part of territory annexed to Canada in 1870. The Metis colonists (part-Indian, mostly French-speaking, Catholic) objected to the arrangements for the purchase of the Company territory by Canada and the province of Manitoba was created to accommodate them. It was extended northwards and westwards in 1881 and to Hudson Bay in 1912.

AREA AND POPULATION. The area of the province is 250,946 sq. miles (649,046 sq. km), of which 211,721 sq. miles are land and 39,225 sq. miles water. From north to south it is 793 km and the widest point is 493 km.

The population (June 1981) was 1,017,323. Population of the principal cities (census 1981): Winnipeg (capital), 560,028; Brandon, 35,894; Thompson, 14,102; Portage la Prairie, 12,959; Flin Flon, 7,819.

Vital statistics, see p. 267.

Religion, see p. 284.

CONSTITUTION AND GOVERNMENT. Manitoba was known as the Red River Settlement before its entry into the Dominion in 1870. The provincial government is administered by a Lieut.-Governor and a legislative assembly of 57 members elected for 5 years. Women were enfranchised in 1916. The Electoral Division Act, 1955, created 57 single-member constituencies and abolished the transferable vote. The Electoral Divisions Act, 1979, created 27 rural electoral divisions, and 30 urban electoral divisions. The province is represented by 6 members in the Senate and 14 in the House of Commons of Canada.

Lieut.-Governor: Pearl McGonigal (sworn in 23 Oct. 1981).

Flag: The British Red Ensign with the shield of the province in the fly.

State of parties in the Legislative Assembly (sworn in 30 Nov. 1981): New Democratic Party, 33; Progressive Conservative, 23; Independent, 1.

The members of the New Democratic Party Ministry are as follows (Sept. 1982):

Premier, President of the Council, Minister of Federal Provincial Relations: Howard Russell Pawley.

Health, Recreation and Sport, Minister responsible for the administration of The Lotteries and Gaming Control Act: Laurent Louis Desjardins. *Highways and Transportation:* Samuel Uskiw. *Community Services and Corrections:* Leonard Salusbury Evans. *Agriculture:* Billie Uruski. *Municipal Affairs:* A. R. Adam. *Northern Affairs, Environmental Management, Minister responsible for the administration of The Clean Environment Act, The Workplace Safety and Health Act, The Workers Compensation Act, The Communities Economic Development Fund Act:* Jay Marine Cowan. *Energy and Mines, Crown Investments, Minister responsible for the administration of The Manitoba Hydro Act, Manitoba Forestry Resources Act:* Wilson Dwight Parasiuk. *Finance, Minister responsible for the administration of The Manitoba Data Services Act, Chairman of Treasury Board:* Victor Schroeder. *Education:* Maureen Lucille Hemphill. *Cultural Affairs and Historical Resources, Urban Affairs, Minister responsible for the administration of The Public Printing Act and the Office of the Queen's Printer:* Eugene Michael Kostyra. *Attorney-General, Keeper of the Great Seal, Minister responsible for the administration of The Liquor Control Act:* Roland Penner. *Economic Development and Tourism, Minister responsible for the administration of The Development Corporation Act:* Muriel Ann Smith. *Natural Resources:* Alvin Henry Mackling. *Labour and Manpower, Minister responsible for the administration of The Civil Service Act, The Civil Service Superannuation Act, The Pension Benefits Act, The Public Servants Insurance Act, Minister responsible for the Status of Women:* Mary Elisabeth Dolin. *Housing, Minister responsible for the administration of The Landlord and Tenant Act, The Residential Rent Regulation Act, The Housing and Renewal Corporation Act and The Elderly and Infirm Persons' Housing Act:* Jerry Thomas Storie. *Consumer and Corporate Affairs, Co-operative Development,*

Minister responsible for the administration of The Manitoba Public Insurance Corporation Act: John Bucklaschuk. *Government Services, Minister responsible for the administration of The Manitoba Telephone System Act:* John S. Plohman.

Local Government. Rural Manitoba is organized into rural municipalities which vary widely in size. Some have only 4 townships (a township is 36 sq. miles), while the largest has 22 townships. The province has 105 rural municipalities, as well as 35 incorporated towns, 40 incorporated villages and 5 incorporated cities.

On 1 Jan. 1972, the cities and towns comprising the metropolitan area of Winnipeg were amalgamated to form the City of Winnipeg. A mayor and council are elected to a central government, but councillors also sit on 'community committees' which represent the areas or wards they serve. These committees are advised by non-elected residents of the area on provision of municipal services within the community committee jurisdiction. Taxing powers and overall budgeting rest with the central council. The mayor is elected at the same time as the councillors in a city-wide vote. Revisions to the City of Winnipeg Act came into effect with the municipal elections held in Oct. 1977.

Since Jan. 1945, 17 Local Government Districts have been formed in the less densely populated areas of the province. They are administered by a provincially appointed person, who acts on the advice of locally elected councils.

In the extreme north, many communities have locally elected councils, while others are administered directly by the Department of Northern Affairs. This department provides most of the funding in all these northern settlements.

FINANCE. Provincial revenue and expenditure (current account) for fiscal years ending 31 March (in Canadian $):

	1979–80	1980–81	1981–82	1982–83 [1]	1983–84 [1]
Revenue	1,805,982,583	1,968,405,039	2,180,821,120	2,495,234,300	2,747,819,400
Expenditure	1,850,737,379	2,057,913,309	2,431,863,998	2,838,756,600	3,326,739,600

[1] Estimated.

ENERGY AND NATURAL RESOURCES

Electricity. The total generating capacity of Manitoba's power stations is 4·1m. kw. The Manitoba Hydro system, owned by the province, provides most of this power, while the city-owned Winnipeg Hydro provides about 190,000 kw. The systems have about 397,000 customers and consumption was 14·3m. kwh. in 1982.

Oil. Crude oil production in 1982 was valued at $85·9m. for the 561,000 cu. metres produced.

Minerals. Total value of minerals in 1982 was about $511·4m. Principal minerals mined are nickel, zinc, copper, and small quantities of gold and silver. Manitoba has the world's largest deposits of caesium ore and also produces tantalite concentrates.

Agriculture. Rich farmland is the main primary resource, although the area of Manitoba in farms is only about 14% of the total land area. In 1982 the total value of agricultural production in Manitoba was $1,684·9m., with $1,001·2m. from crops, $671m. from livestock and from the sale of other products including furs, hides and honey.

Forestry. About 43·8% of the land area is wooded, of which 139,000 sq. km is productive forest land. Total sales of wood-using industries (1982, estimate) $431m.

Fur Trade. Value of fur production to the trapper was $5·6m. in 1981–82.

Fisheries. From 22,000 sq. miles of rivers and lakes fisheries production was about $17·1m. in 1981–82. Whitefish, sauger, pickerel, pike, trout and perch are the principle varieties of fish caught.

INDUSTRY AND TRADE

Industry. Manufacturing, the largest industry in the province, encompasses almost every major industrial activity in Canada. Estimated shipments in 1982 totalled $4,847·4m. Manufacturing employed about 59,000 persons. Due to the agricultural base of the province, the food and beverage group of industries is by far the largest, valued at $1,519·8m. in 1982, accounting for about 31·4% of the total value. The next largest segments are machinery, $448·1m. (9·2%), metal fabricating, $327·7m. (6·7%), and transportation equipment, $329·9m. (6·8%).

Trade. Products grown and manufactured in Manitoba find ready markets in other areas of Canada, in the USA, particularly the upper midwest region, and in other countries. Export shipments to foreign countries from Manitoba in 1982 were valued at about $1,358·3m., with $1,010·1m. (74·4%) going to the US. Of these, about 33% are raw materials and about 66% are processed and manufactured products.

Tourism. In 1982, Canadian, US and overseas tourists numbered 2,646,466 contributing $580·3m. to the economy.

COMMUNICATIONS

Roads. Highways and provincial roads totalled 18,874 km in 1982.

Railways. At 31 Dec. 1981 the province had 6,430 km of track, not including industrial track, yards and sidings.

Aviation. A total of 102 licensed commercial air carriers operate from bases in Manitoba, as well as major national and international airlines.

Post. All of the province's 748,170 (1982) telephones are dial-operated.

EDUCATION. Education is controlled through locally elected school divisions. There are 200,619 children enrolled in the province's elementary and secondary schools. The University of Manitoba, founded in 1877, in Winnipeg, had an enrolment of 18,411 (full- and part-time), the University of Winnipeg, 6,419, and Brandon University, 2,457, during the 1981–82 year. Expenditure (estimate) on education in the 1981–82 fiscal year was $644m.

Three community colleges, in Brandon, The Pas and Winnipeg, offer 2-year diploma courses in a number of fields, as well as specialized training in many trades. They also give a large number and variety of shorter courses, both at their campuses and in many communities throughout the province.

Books of Reference

General Information: Inquiries may be addressed to the Information Services Branch, Room 29, Legislative Building, Winnipeg, R3C OV8.

The Department of Agriculture publishes: *Year Book of Manitoba Agriculture*
Information Services Branch publishes: *Manitoba Facts*
Manitoba Statistical Review. Manitoba Bureau of Statistics, Quarterly
Tenth Census of Canada: Manitoba. Statistics Canada, 1971

NEW BRUNSWICK

HISTORY. Touched by Jacques Cartier in 1534, New Brunswick was first explored by Samuel de Champlain in 1604. It was ceded by the French in the Treaty of Utrecht in 1713 and became a permanent British possession in 1763. It was separated from Nova Scotia and became a province in June 1784, as a result of the great influx of United Empire Loyalists. Responsible government came into being in 1848, and consisted of an executive council, a legislative council (later abolished) and a House of Assembly.

AREA AND POPULATION. The area of the province is 28,354 sq. miles (73,000 sq. km), of which 27,633 sq. miles (71,569 sq. km) are land area. The population (census 1976) was 677,250. Of the total population (1971) about 58%

are of British origin, 37% French and the remainder are principally of Netherlands, German and Scandinavian descent, and in 1980 there were about 5,300 Indians. Census population of urban centres: Saint John, 85,956; Moncton, 55,934; Fredericton (capital), 45,248; Bathurst, 16,301; Edmundston, 12,710; Campbellton, 9,282.

Vital statistics, *see* p. 267.

Religion, *see* p. 284.

CONSTITUTION AND GOVERNMENT. The government is vested in a Lieut.-Governor and a Legislative Assembly of 58 members each of whom is individually elected to represent the voters in one constituency or riding. A simultaneous translation system is used in the Assembly. Any Canadian subject of full age and 6 months' residence is entitled to vote. As a result of the provincial election held on 23 Oct. 1978 and subsequent by-elections, the Assembly is composed of 30 Progressive Conservatives and 28 Liberals. The province has 10 members in the Canadian Senate and 10 members in the federal House of Commons.

Lieut.-Governor: George F. S. Stanley (appointed 23 Dec. 1981).

Flag: A banner of the Arms, *i.e.*, yellow charged with a black heraldic ship on wavy lines of blue and white; across the top a red band with a gold lion.

The members of the Progressive Conservative Ministry are as follows (Dec. 1982):

Premier and President of the Executive Council: Richard Hatfield.

Attorney-General and Justice: Fernand Dube, QC. *Finance and Minister Responsible for New Brunswick Housing Corporation:* John B. M. Baxter, QC. *Chairman of the Treasury Board:* Harold N. Fanjoy. *Supply and Services:* Edwin G. Allen. *Transportation:* Wilfred G. Bishop. *Natural Resources and Minister Responsible for Energy Policy:* Gerald Merrithew. *Agriculture and Rural Development:* Malcolm N. MacLeod. *Health:* Charles G. Gallagher. *Social Services:* Nancy E. Clark Teed. *Labour and Manpower:* Joseph W. Mombourquette. *Education:* Mabel M. DeWare. *Municipal Affairs:* Yvon R. Poitras. *Commerce and Development:* Paul W. Dawson. *Fisheries.* Jean Gauvin. *Environment:* C. W. (Bill) Harmer. *Tourism:* Omer Leger. *Youth and Recreation:* Leslie I. Hull. *Cultural and Historical Resources:* Jean-Pierre Ouellet.

Local Government. Under the reforms introduced in 1967 the province has assumed complete administrative and financial responsibility for education, health, welfare and administration of justice. Local government is now restricted to provision of services of a strictly local nature. Under the new municipal structure, units include existing and new cities, towns and villages. Counties have disappeared as municipal units. Areas with limited populations have become local service districts. The former local improvement districts have become towns, villages or local service districts depending on their size.

FINANCE. The ordinary budget (in Canadian $) is shown as follows (financial years ended 31 March):

	1980	1981	1982	1983
Gross revenue	1,449,457,490	1,534,987,829	1,772,232,788	1,945,154,091
Gross expenditure	1,321,661,738	1,505,252,819	1,795,554,444	2,147,955,484

Funded debt and capital loans outstanding (exclusive of Treasury Bills) as of 31 March 1983 was $2,158m. Sinking funds held by the province at 31 March 1983, $573m. The ordinary budget excludes capital spending.

ENERGY AND NATURAL RESOURCES

Electricity. Hydro-electric, thermal and nuclear generating stations of the New Brunswick Electric Power Commission had an installed capacity of 3,136,576 kw. at 31 March 1983, consisting of 14 generating stations. The Mactaquac hydro-electric development near Fredericton, has a nominal capacity of 600,000 kw. The largest thermal generating station, Coleson Cove, near Saint John, has over 1m.

kw. of installed capacity. Atlantic Canada's first nuclear generating station, a 630,000 kw. CANDU plant built on a promontory jutting out in the Bay of Fundy, near Saint John, went into commercial operation in Jan. 1983. New Brunswick is electrically inter-connected with utilities in neighbouring provinces of Quebec, Nova Scotia and Prince Edward Island, as well as the New England States. Electricity export sales accounted for some 35% of revenue in 1982–83; energy purchases, mainly from the large Hydro Quebec system, supplied about 33% of in-province energy requirements.

Minerals. A considerable variety of metals, industrial minerals, fuels and structural materials occur in the province. These include zinc, lead, copper, cadmium, bismuth, nickel, gold, silver, cobalt, tungsten, tin, molybdenum, antimony, potash, salt, glauberite, limestone, dolomite, gypsum, oil, gas, coal, uranium, oil shale, sand, gravel, clay, peat, diatomite and marl. Not all have been explored sufficiently. 51% of the value of minerals produced in 1982, which totalled $517m., was attributed to zinc produced from 2 mines in the Bathurst–Newcastle area: Brunswick Mining and Smelting, Heath Steele Mines Ltd. New Brunswick is the third largest producer of zinc in Canada. A lead smelter, fertilizer plant and port facilities have been constructed at Belledune. Numerous other discoveries have been made in the area and several deposits are now in the final stages of exploration. Canada's only primary antimony producer is located at Lake George, near Fredericton, and a large low-grade tungsten–molybdenum–bismuth deposit at Mount Pleasant commenced production in 1983. Exploration and development is also in process near Sussex (production began in 1983) and Salt Springs, where potash and salt deposits have been found. Limestone and gypsum are quarried at Havelock and Hillsborough and small quantities of oil and natural gas are produced from the Stoney Creek Field south of Moncton. Coal is mined at Grand Lake and exploration is underway for other deposits of this important energy resource.

Agriculture. The total area under crops is estimated at 130,526 hectares, exclusive of improved pasture land (41,479 hectares). Farms numbered 4,063 and averaged 107·8 hectares each (census 1981). Potatoes account for 30% of total farm cash income. Mixed farming is common throughout the province. Dairy farming is centred around the larger urban areas, and is located mainly along the Saint John River Valley and in the south-eastern sections of the province. For particulars of agricultural production and livestock, *see under* CANADA, pp. 276–78. Farm cash receipts in 1982 were approximately $194,524,000.

Forestry. New Brunswick contains some 62,000 sq. km of productive forest lands. The combined value of primary and secondary forest production was about $1,364,000 in 1980, of which wood and paper and allied industries accounted for about $1m. Timber-using plants employ about 14,600 men for all aspects of the forest industry, including harvesting, processing and transportation. Practically all forest products are exported from the province's numerous ports and harbours near which the mills are located or sent by road or rail to the USA.

Fisheries. Commercial fishing is one of the most important basic industries of the province. Nearly 50 commercial species of fish and shellfish are landed, of which lobster, crab, herring and cod are the most valuable. Landings in 1982 (111,027 tonnes) amounted to $67·4m. In 1982 there were 120 fish processing plants employing more than 11,000 people in peak periods. The total market value of fish products in 1981 was approximately $254m.

INDUSTRY. In 1982 there were 1,303 manufacturing and processing establishments, employing about 37,600 persons. New Brunswick's location, with deepwater harbours open throughout the year and container facilities at Saint John, makes it ideal for exporting. Industries include food and beverages, paper and allied industries, timber products. About 20% of the industrial labour force work in Saint John.

TOURISM. Tourism is a major industry. During 1982, more than 4m. tourists spent approximately $330m.

COMMUNICATIONS

Roads. There are about 2,133 km of arterial highways and 2,322 km of collector roads, 95% of which are hard-surfaced. 12,845 km of local roads provide access to most areas in the province. The main highway system, including 616 km of the Trans-Canada Highway, links the province with the principal roads in Quebec and Nova Scotia, as well as the Interstate Highway System in the eastern seaboard states of the USA. Passenger vehicles, 31 March 1979, numbered 250,388; commercial vehicles, 95,010; motor cycles, 10,869.

Railways. New Brunswick is served by main lines of both Canadian Pacific and Canadian National railways.

Post and Broadcasting. In 1980 the New Brunswick Telephone Co. Ltd had 389,466 telephones in service. The province is served by 16 radio stations. Twelve are privately owned and 4 owned by the Canadian Broadcasting Corporation. Three stations broadcast in the French language, 1 is bilingual and the CBC International Service broadcasts in several languages from its station at Sackville. The province is served by 3 television stations, 1 of which broadcasts in French.

Newspapers. New Brunswick had (1983) 5 daily newspapers, and 23 weekly newspapers, 7 in French or bilingual.

EDUCATION. Public education is free and non-sectarian. There are 4 universities. The University of New Brunswick at Fredericton (founded 13 Dec. 1785 by the Loyalists, elevated to university status in 1823, reorganized as the University of New Brunswick in 1859) had 6,121 full-time students at the Fredericton campus and 914 full-time students at the Saint John campus (1982–83); Mount Allison University at Sackville had 1,607 full-time students; the Université de Moncton at Moncton, 2,969 full-time students; St Thomas University at Fredericton, 1,011 full-time students. During the period 1 July 1982 to 30 June 1983, there were 10,780 students enrolled full-time at 10 Community College campuses and at various campus training centres.

There were, in Sept. 1982, 147,277 students and 7,758 full-time (equivalent) teachers in the province's 448 schools. There are 41 school boards.

Books of Reference

Industrial Information: Dept. of Commerce and Development, Fredericton. *Economic Information:* Dept. of Finance, Economics and Statistics Branch. Fredericton. *General Information:* NB Information Service, Fredericton.

New Brunswick and Its People. Fredericton, 1962
Department of Commerce and Development, *Annual Report.* Fredericton, 1973.—*New Brunswick in Profile.* Fredericton

NEWFOUNDLAND AND LABRADOR

HISTORY. Archaeological finds at L'Anse-au-Meadow in northern Newfoundland suggest that the Vikings had established a colony there at about A.D. 1000. Newfoundland was discovered by John Cabot 24 June 1497, and was soon frequented in the summer months by the Portuguese, Spanish and French for its fisheries. It was formally occupied in Aug. 1583 by Sir Humphrey Gilbert on behalf of the English Crown, but various attempts to colonize the island remained unsuccessful. Although British sovereignty was recognized in 1713 by the Treaty of Utrecht, disputes over fishing rights with the French were not finally settled till 1904. By the Anglo-French Convention of 1904, France renounced her exclusive fishing rights along part of the coast, granted under the Treaty of Utrecht, but retained sovereignty of the offshore islands of St Pierre and Miquelon.

AREA AND POPULATION. Area, 156,185 sq. miles (383,300 sq. km). In March 1927 the Privy Council decided the boundary between Canada and Newfoundland in Labrador. This area, now part of the Province of Newfoundland and Labrador, is 112,826 sq. miles. The coastline is extremely irregular. Bays, fiords and inlets are numerous and there are many good harbours with deep water close to shore. The coast is rugged with bold rocky cliffs from 200 to 400 ft high; in the Bay of Islands some of the islands rise 500 ft, with the adjacent shore 1,000 ft above tide level. The interior is a plateau of moderate elevation and the chief relief features trend north-east and south-west. Long Range, the most notable of these, begins at Cape Ray and extends north-east for 200 miles, the highest peak reaching 2,673 ft. Approximately one-third of the area is covered by water. Grand Lake, the largest body of water, has an area of about 200 sq. miles. The principal rivers flow towards the north-east. On the borders of the lakes and water-courses good land is generally found, particularly in the valleys of the Terra Nova River, the Gander River, the Exploits River and the Humber River, which are also heavily timbered.

Census population, 1981, was 567,681.

The capital of Newfoundland is the City of St John's (154,820, metropolitan area). The only other city is Corner Brook (24,339); important towns are Labrador City (11,538), Gander (10,404), Stephenville (8,876), Grand Falls (8,765), Happy Valley–Goose Bay (7,103), Channel-Port aux Basques (5,988) Windsor (5,747), Carbonear (5,335), Bonavista (4,460), Wabana (4,254), Wabush (3,155).

Vital statistics, see p. 267.

Religion, see p. 284.

CONSTITUTION AND GOVERNMENT. Until 1832 Newfoundland was ruled by the Governor under instructions of the Colonial Office. In that year a Legislature was brought into existence, but the Governor and his Executive Council were not responsible to it. Under the constitution of 1855, which lasted until its suspension in 1934, the government was administered by the Governor appointed by the Crown with an Executive Council responsible to the House of Assembly of 27 elected members and a Legislative Council of 24 members nominated for life by the Governor in Council. Women were enfranchised in 1925. At the Imperial Conference of 1917 Newfoundland was constituted as a Dominion.

In 1933 the financial situation had become so critical that the Government of Newfoundland asked the Government of the UK to appoint a Royal Commission to investigate conditions. On the strength of their recommendations, the parliamentary form of government was suspended and Government by Commission was inaugurated on 16 Feb. 1934.

A National Convention, elected in 1946, made, in 1948, recommendations to H.M. Government in Great Britain as to the possible forms of future government to be submitted to the people at a national referendum. Two referenda were held. In the first referendum (June 1948) the three forms of government submitted to the people were: commission of government for 5 years, confederation with Canada and responsible government as it existed in 1933. No one form of government received a clear majority of the votes polled, and commission of government, receiving the fewest votes, was eliminated. In the second referendum (July 1948) confederation with Canada received 78,408 and responsible government 71,464 votes.

In the Canadian Senate on 18 Feb. 1949 Royal assent was given to the terms of union of Newfoundland and Labrador with Canada, and on 23 March 1949, in the House of Lords, London, Royal assent was given to an amendment to the British North America Act made necessary by the inclusion of Newfoundland and Labrador as the tenth Province of Canada.

Under the terms of union of Newfoundland and Labrador with Canada, which was signed at Ottawa on 11 Dec. 1948, the constitution of the Legislature of Newfoundland and Labrador as it existed immediately prior to 16 Feb. 1934 shall, subject to the terms of the British North America Acts, 1867 to 1946, continue as the constitution of the Legislature of the Province of Newfoundland and Labrador until altered under the authority of the said Acts.

The franchise was in 1965 extended to all male and female residents who have attained the age of 19 years and are otherwise qualified as electors.

The House of Assembly (Amendment) Act, 1979, established 52 electoral districts and 52 members of the Legislature.

In Dec. 1983 there were 45 Progressive-Conservatives and 7 Liberals.

The province is represented by 6 members in the Senate and by 7 members in the House of Commons of Canada.

Lieut.-Governor: Hon. Dr W. A. Paddon (assumed office 10 July 1981).

Flag: White, in the hoist 4 solid blue triangles; in the fly 2 red triangles voided white, and between them a yellow tongue bordered in red.

The Progressive-Conservative Executive Council was, at 6 April 1982, composed as follows:

Premier and Intergovernmental Affairs: Brian Peckford.

President of the Executive Council and Minister responsible for Labrador Hydro and the Petroleum Directorate: W. Marshall. *Finance:* J. Collins. *Justice:* G. R. Ottenheimer. *Development:* N. Windsor. *Health:* W. House. *Fisheries:* J. Morgan. *Rural, Agricultural and Northern Development:* J. Goudie. *Labour and Manpower:* J. Dinn. *Social Services:* T. Hickey. *Forest Resources and Lands:* C. Power. *Public Works and Services:* H. Young. *Municipal Affairs:* H. Newhook. *Education:* L. Verge. *Transportation, Mines and Energy:* R. Dawe. *Environment:* H. Andrews. *Culture, Recreation and Youth:* L. Simms. *Minster responsible for Communications:* N.Doyle. *Speaker of the House of Assembly:* J. Russell. *Clerk of the Executive Council:* D. Vardy.

Agent-General in London: H. Watson Jamer (60 Trafalgar Sq., WC2).

FINANCE. Budget [1] in Canadian $1,000 for fiscal years ended 31 March:

	1978–79	1979–80	1980–81	1981–82	1982–83 [2]	1983–84 [3]
Gross revenue	1,084,083	1,215,697	1,359,209	1,511,019	1,657,668	1,834,595
Gross expenditure	1,062,244	1,174,091	1,310,018	1,504,752	1,705,276	1,863,025

[1] Current amount only. [2] Revised estimates. [3] Estimates.

Public debenture debt as at 31 March 1983 (preliminary) was $2,449·2m.; sinking fund, $519·4m.

ENERGY AND NATURAL RESOURCES

Electricity. The electrical energy requirements of the province are met mainly by hydro-electric power, with petroleum fuels being utilized to provide the balance. The total amount of energy generated in the province in 1982 (preliminary) was 44,264,544 mwh., of which approximately 97% was derived from hydro-electric facilities. The greater part of the energy produced in 1982 (preliminary) came from Churchill Falls, of which 35,777.424 mwh. was sold to Hydro-Quebec under the terms of a long-term contract. Energy consumed in the province during 1982 (preliminary) totalled 8,487,117 mwh., with approximately 8,001,641 mwh., or 94%, coming from hydro-electric facilities.

At 31 Dec. 1981 total electrical generating capacity in the province was 6,958,500 kw., with hydro-electric plants accounting for 6,210,256 kw., or 89%. A 75 mw hydro project started in 1978 at Hind's Lake in central Newfoundland and was completed in 1981. It is estimated that potential additional hydro-electric generating capacity of up to 4·5m. kw. can be developed at various sites in the Labrador part of the province.

Oil. In 1981 the province consumed refined petroleum at the rate of 39,000 bbls a day with 30% of this being refined in the province. The refining capacity of the province is 114,000 bbls per day, this refinery was closed in June 1983.

Since 1965, 92 wells have been drilled on the Continental Margin of the Province. In 1983 it is estimated that offshore exploration expenditures would be between $450m. and $500m.

In Oct. 1974, two natural gas finds off the coast of Labrador were announced. Tests of these two wells resulted in rates of flow of 13–20m. cu. ft per day respectively, with some condensate and no water present. Additional natural gas finds with flows of 9·8m. cu. ft per day and 32m. cu. ft per day, with significant condensates and no water present, were announced in 1976 and 1978 respectively.

In 1979, a discovery of oil was made on the Hibernia geological structure located 164 nautical miles east of Cape Spear. The discovery well, Hibernia P–15, tested medium gravity, sweet crude from several intervals with a reported total producing capability in excess of 20,000 bbls of oil per day.

Minerals. The mineral resources are vast but only partially documented. Large deposits of iron ore, with an ore reserve of over 5,000m. tons at Labrador City, Wabush City and in the Knob Lake area are supplying approximately half of Canada's production. Other large deposits of iron ore are known to exist in the Julienne Lake area.

There are a variety of other minerals being produced in the province in more limited amounts.

Uranium deposits in the Kaipokak Bay area near Makkovik in Labrador are presently being studied by Brinex. The Central Mineral Belt, which extends from the Smallwood Reservoir to the Atlantic coast near Makkovik, holds uranium, copper, beryllium and molybdenite potential.

Production in 1982 (preliminary): Iron ore, 25,686,000 tonnes ($886,843,000); copper, 5,154,000 kg ($11·04m.); zinc, 39,971,000 kg ($47,797,000); asbestos, 70,000 tonnes ($51·59m.); lead, 2,749,000 kg ($2·70m.); silver, 7,000 kg ($2,899,000); gold, 209 kg ($3,707,000); cadmium, 16,000 kg ($78,000); gypsum, 512,000 tonnes ($3,824,000); pyrophyllite, soapstone and talc ($1,003,000); cement ($3,580,000); clay products ($921,000); sand and gravel, 2,818,000 tonnes ($9,074,000); stone, 519,000 tonnes ($2·07m.); quartz ($768,000).

Agriculture. The estimated value of agricultural products sold, including livestock, 1982, was $33·9m.

Forestry. The forestry economy in the province is mainly dependent on the operation of 3 newsprint mills. In 1982 the value of newsprint exported from these 3 mills totalled $322·9m. Lumber mills, saw-log operations produced 34m. f.b.m. in 1981–82.

Fisheries. The principal fish landings are cod, flounder, redfish, Queen crabs (in shell), lobster, salmon and herring. In 1982 a yearly average of some 9,100 persons were employed by the fish-processing industry and there were 27,379 licensed full-, part-time and casual fishermen engaged in harvesting operations. Approximately 200 processing operations were licensed in 1982. The production of fresh and frozen fish products was $457·8m. in 1981.

The total catch in 1982 was 414,975 tonnes valued at $142,621,000, which comprised: Cod, 301,619 tonnes ($101,166,000); flounder, 70,292 ($19,251,000); herring, 13,513 tonnes ($2,881,000); redfish, 26,220 ($4,821,000); lobster, 2,011 ($9,811,000); salmon, 1,320 ($4,691,000).

The seal fishery in 1982 had 7 large licensed and 124 small licensed vessels with 733 men who landed 122,024 pelts. The number of pelts landed by landsmen totalled 22,319.

INDUSTRY. The total value of manufacturing shipments in 1982 was $1,365m. This consists largely of first-stage processing of primary resource products with two of the largest components being paper and fish products.

TRADE UNIONS. There were (1981) 400 unions representing 77,026 members of international and national unions, government employee associations as well as 1 local independent union.

COMMUNICATIONS

Roads. In 1982 there were 8,713 km, of which 5,367 were paved.

Railways. In 1981 there were 1,458 km of railway, of which the Canadian National Railways operated 1,130·6 (3 ft 6 in.), the Quebec North Shore and Labrador Railway 324·8 (4 ft 8½ in.) and there were 2·4 km of private line. Car and passenger ferries operate from Port aux Basques and Argentia to North Sydney, Nova Scotia. On the island of Newfoundland, the Canadian National Railways operates a trans-island bus and rail freight service in addition to a coastal service for both passengers and freight. In the months that the Labrador coast is ice-free, usually from June to Nov., the Canadian National Railways operates a scheduled coastal steamer service every week.

Aviation. The province is linked to the rest of Canada by regular air services provided by Air Canada, Eastern Provincial Airways, Quebecair and a number of smaller air carriers.

Shipping. In 1982 there were 1,610 ships registered in Newfoundland.

Post. There were 479 post offices open in 1982, and 2 telegraph offices in the Newfoundland and Labrador postal district. Telephone connexions in the province numbered 265,436 in 1981.

EDUCATION. The number of schools in 1982–83 was 644. The enrolment was 142,775; teachers numbered 7,790. The Memorial University, offering courses in arts, science, engineering, education, nursing and medicine, had approximately 13,247 full- and part-time students. Total expenditure for education by the Government in 1982–83 was $491m.

Books of Reference

Blackburn, R. H. (ed.), *Encyclopaedia of Canada: Newfoundland Supplement.* Toronto, 1949
Bruet, E., *Le Labrador et le Nouveau-Québec.* Paris, 1949
Horwood, H., *Newfoundland.* Toronto, 1969
Loture, R. de, *Histoire de la grande pêche de Terre-Neuve.* Paris, 1949
Mercer, G. A., *The Province of Newfoundland and Labrador: Geographical Aspects.* Ottawa, 1970
Perlin, A. B., *The Story of Newfoundland, 1497–1959.* St John's, 1959
Tanner, V., *Outlines of Geography. Life and Customs of Newfoundland–Labrador.* 2 vols. Helsinki, 1944, and Toronto, 1947
Taylor, T. G., *Newfoundland: A Study of Settlement.* Toronto, 1946

NOVA SCOTIA

HISTORY. The first permanent settlement was made by the French early in the 17th century, and the province was called Acadia until finally ceded to the British by the Treaty of Utrecht in 1713.

AREA AND POPULATION. The area of the province is 21,425 sq. miles (55,000 sq. km), of which 20,401 sq. miles are land area, 1,024 sq. miles water area. The population (census 1981) was 847,442; estimate (1983) 859,300.

Population of the principal cities and towns (census 1981): Halifax, 114,594; Dartmouth 62,277; Sydney, 29,444; Glace Bay, 21,466; Truro, 12,552; New Glasgow, 10,464; Amherst, 9,684; Sydney Mines, 8,501; North Sydney, 7,820; Yarmouth, 7,475.

Vital statistics, see p. 267.
Religion, see p. 284.

CONSTITUTION AND GOVERNMENT. Under the British North America Act of 1867 the legislature of Nova Scotia may exclusively make laws in relation to local matters, including direct taxation within the province, education and the administration of justice. The legislature of Nova Scotia consists of a Lieut.-Governor, appointed and paid by the federal government, and holding office for 5 years, and a House of Assembly of 52 members, chosen by popular vote not more than every 5 years. The province is represented in the Canadian Senate by 9 members, and in the House of Commons by 11.

The franchise and eligibility to the legislature are granted to every person, male or female, if of age (19 years), a British subject or Canadian citizen, and a resident in the province for 1 year and 2 months before the date of the writ of election in the county or electoral district of which the polling district forms part, and if not by law otherwise disqualified. State of parties in Feb. 1984: 36 Progressive Conservatives, 12 Liberals, 1 New Democrat, 1 independent, 2 vacant.

Lieut.-Governor: Alan R. Abraham.

Flag: A banner of the Arms, *i.e.*, white with a blue diagonal cross, bearing in the centre the royal shield of Scotland.

The members of the Progressive Conservative Ministry are as follows:

Premier, President of the Executive Council, Chairman of the Policy Board, Minister of Intergovernmental Affairs: John M. Buchanan, QC.

Finance: Greg Kerr. *Development and Minister in Charge of Administration of the Research Foundation Corporation Act:* Roland J. Thornhill. *Attorney-General, Provincial Secretary and Minister in Charge of Administration of the Regulations Act:* Ronald Griffin. *Education and Minister in Charge of Administration of the Advisory Council on Status of Women Act:* Terence Donahoe. *Lands and Forests:* Kenneth Streatch. *Health, Minister in Charge of Administration of the Drug Dependency Act and Registrar-General:* Gerald Sheehy. *Mines and Energy and Minister in Charge of the Nova Scotia Energy Council:* Joel Matheson. *Agriculture and Marketing:* Roger S. Bacon. *Fisheries:* John Leefe. *Tourism:* Fisher Hudson. *Municipal Affairs:* Thomas McInnis. *Labour and Manpower:* David Nantes. *Chairman of the Management Board, Minister in Charge of Administration of the Civil Service Act and Minister in Charge of Administration of the Liquor Control Act:* Ronald Russell. *Transportation, Minister in Charge of Office of Communication Policy:* John MacIsaac. *Social Services:* Edmund Morris. *Government Services, Minister in Charge of Administration of Communication and Information Act:* Gerald Lawrence. *Environment:* George Moody. *Minister in Charge of Administration of the Nova Scotia Emergency Measures Act and Regulations (EMO) and Chairman of Resource Development Sector Committee Board:* Milne Pickings. *Culture, Recreation and Fitness, Minister in Charge of the Nova Scotia Heritage Property Act and Minister Responsible for Lotteries:* William MacLean. *Consumer Affairs, Minister in Charge of Administration of Human Rights Act, Minister in Charge of Administration of the Residential Tenancies Act and Chairman of Social Development Sector Committee Board:* Laird Stirling. *Minister Without Portfolio:* George Henley.

Agent-General in London: Donald M. Smith (14 Pall Mall, SW1Y 5LU).

Local Government. The main divisions of the province for governmental purposes are the 3 cities, the 39 towns and the 24 rural municipalities, each governed by a council and a mayor or warden. The cities have independent charters, and the various towns take their powers from and are limited by The Towns Act, and the various municipalities take their powers from and are limited by The Municipal Act as revised in 1967. The majority of municipalities comprise 1 county, but 6 counties are divided into 2 municipalities each. In no case do the boundaries of any municipality overlap county lines. The 18 counties as such have no administrative functions.

Any city (of which there are 3) or incorporated town (of which there are 39) that lies within the boundaries of a municipality is excluded from any jurisdiction by the municipal council and has its own government.

FINANCE. Revenue is derived from provincial sources, payments from the federal government under the Federal-Provincial Fiscal Arrangements and Established Programs Financing Act. Recoveries consist generally of amounts received under various federal cost-shared programmes. Main sources of provincial revenues include income and sales taxes.

Revenue, expenditure and debt (in Canadian $1m.) for fiscal years ending 31 March:

	1979	1980	1981	1982	1983 [1]
Budgetary Transactions					
Current Expenditure	1,425·2	1,524·3	1,769·6	2,117·7	2,395·1
Current Revenues and Recoveries	1,393·4	1,565·2	1,750·1	1,937·4	2,265·8
Operating Deficit (Surplus)	31·8	(40·9)	19·5	180·3	129·3
Sinking fund Instalments and Serial Retirements	29·4	30·9	32·2	34·3	45·4
Net Capital Expenditures	124·1	122·7	160·9	249·6	199·5
Net Budgetary Transactions	185·3	112·7	212·6	464·2	374·2
Non-Budgetary Transactions					
Capital Expenditures	9·1	2·5	10·2	3·2	3·2
Net Increase in Advances and Investments	34·3	86·4	108·5	75·6	9·4
Net Other Transactions	27·7	23·8	21·9	25·1	11·2
Non-Budgetary Transactions	71·1	112·7	140·6	103·9	23·8
	256·4	225·4	353·2	568·1	398·0

[1] Estimate.

NATURAL RESOURCES

Minerals. Principal minerals in 1982 were: Coal, 3·1m. tonnes, valued at $170m.; gypsum, 4·3m. tonnes, valued at $28m.; salt, 1·1m. tonnes, valued at $31m.; sand and gravel, 9·5m. tonnes, valued at $24·2m. Total value of mineral production in 1982 was about $292,086,000.

Agriculture. Dairying, poultry and egg production, livestock and fruit growing are the most important branches. Farm cash receipts for 1982 were estimated at $233·1m., with an additional $5·7m. going to persons on farms as income in kind.

Cash receipts from sale of dairy products was $62·9m., with total milk production of 177,159,000 litres.

The production of poultry meat in 1982 was 15,956 tonnes, of which 13,113 tonnes were chickens, 1,160 tonnes were fowls and 1,683 tonnes were turkeys. Egg production was 18·8m. dozen.

The main 1982 fruit crops were apples, 59,058 tonnes; blueberries, 6,558 tonnes; and strawberries, 2,268 tonnes.

Forestry. The estimated forest area of Nova Scotia is 15,555 sq. miles (40,298 sq. km), of which about 25% is owned by the province. The principal trees are spruce, balsam fir, hemlock, pine, larch, birch, oak, maple, poplar and ash. 2,736,324 cu. metres of round forest products were produced in 1982.

Fisheries. The fisheries of the province in 1982 had a landed value of $259·4m. of sea fish including scallop fishery, $55·1m., and lobster fishery, $50m. In 1981 there were about 6,487 employees in the fish processing industry; the value of shipment of goods was $431·8m.

INDUSTRY. The number of manufacturing establishments was 814 in 1981; the number of employees was 38,807; wages and salaries, $691·9m.; value of shipments was $3,822·6m. The value of shipments in 1982, was $3,746·2m., and the leading industries were petroleum and coal products, food and beverages, paper and allied industries and transportation equipment.

TRADE UNIONS. Total union membership during 1983 was 105,511 belonging to 101 unions comprised of 608 individual branches. The largest percentage of the total union membership was in the service sector followed by public administration and defence sector. An estimated 48,550 members in 364 branches were affiliated with the Canadian Labour Congress.

COMMUNICATIONS

Roads. In Feb. 1983 there were 25,531 km of highways; 2,623 km of paved arterial highways; 4,654 km of collector highways (of which 4,384 km are paved); 18,260 km of local highways (of which 4,224 km are paved).

Railways. The province is covered with a network of railways, 1,551 miles in extent.

Aviation. There is a direct air service to major Canadian and USA cities, London, Amsterdam and Bermuda.

Shipping. Ferry services connect Nova Scotia with Newfoundland, Prince Edward Island, New Brunswick and Maine. Direct service by container vessels is provided from the Port of Halifax to ports in Europe, Asia and the Caribbean.

JUSTICE AND EDUCATION

Justice. There is a Supreme Court which is a Court of common law and equity possessing original and appellate jurisdiction in civil and in criminal cases. The Supreme Court consists of an appeal division of 7 judges and a trial division of 9 judges. There are also county courts, family courts, probate courts, magistrates' courts, municipal and justices' courts. Bodies, sometimes referred to as courts, are established for the revision of assessment rolls, voters' lists and like purposes. Juvenile courts under the auspices of the family courts throughout the province have power to try boys and girls under the age of 16 years.

For the year ending 31 Dec. 1981 there were 4,327 admissions to provincial jails, of these, 2,854 were sentenced. The Adult Probation Service handled 6,639 cases during 1981.

Education. Public education in Nova Scotia is free, compulsory and undenominational through elementary and high school. Attendance is compulsory to the age of 16. In addition to over 600 public schools there are the Atlantic Inter-provincial Resource Centres for the Hearing Handicapped and for the Visually Impaired; the Nova Scotia School for Boys and the Nova Scotia School for Girls for delinquent children; and the Nova Scotia Youth Training Centre for mentally handicapped children. The province has 23 universities and colleges of which the largest is Dalhousie University in Halifax. The Nova Scotia Agricultural College and the Nova Scotia Teachers' College are located at Truro. The Technical University of Nova Scotia at Halifax grants degrees in engineering and architecture.

The Adult Education programme of the Nova Scotia Department of Education administers 2 institutes of technology and a nautical institute. It also provides in-school training for the Department of Labour Apprenticeship programme.

The Continuing Education Activity of the Department of Education offers financial support and organizational assistance to local school boards for provision of weekend and evening courses in academic and avocational subjects, and citizenship for new Canadians. It also provides local authorities with specialist support services to assist them in providing community workshops and it operates a correspondence study service for children and adults.

Occupational courses at the high school level are provided by 14 regional vocational schools under the jurisdiction (except in 3 amalgamated school areas) of the Department of Education.

Total estimated expenditure on education for the year 1981–82 was $817·6m., of which 70% was borne by the provincial government. In 1981–82, classrooms operated in 620 school houses, with 10,805 teachers and 184,986 pupils, of whom 85,289 were in elementary school grades and junior auxiliary classes and 86,041 in junior and senior high school grades.

Books of Reference

Atlantic Provinces Economic Council. *The Atlantic Vision, 1990.* Halifax, 1979
Public Archives of Nova Scotia. *Place Names and Places of Nova Scotia.* Halifax, 1967
Beck, Murray, *The Government of Nova Scotia.* Toronto, 1957.—*Joseph Howe. The Voice of Nova Scotia.* 1964.—*The Evolution of Municipal Government in Nova Scotia, 1749–1973.* 1973
Elliott, S. B., *Nova Scotia Book of Days: A Calendar of the Province's History.* Halifax, 1979
Fergusson, C. B., *Nova Scotia in Encyclopedia Canadiana,* Vol. VII. Toronto, 1968
McCreath, P., and Leefe, J., *History of Early Nova Scotia.* Halifax, 1982
Raddall, T. H., *Halifax, Warden of the North.* Toronto, 1972
Vaison, R., *Nova Scotia Past and Present: A Bibliography and Guide.* Halifax, 1976

ONTARIO

HISTORY. The French explorer Samuel de Champlain explored the Ottawa River from 1613. The area was governed by the French, first under a joint stock company and then as a royal province, from 1627 and was ceded to Great Britain in 1763. A constitutional act of 1791 created there the province of Upper Canada, largely to accommodate loyalists of English descent who had immigrated after the United States war of independence. Upper Canada entered the Confederation as Ontario in 1867.

AREA AND POPULATION. The total area is about 412,600 sq. miles (1,068,630 sq. km), of which some 344,100 sq. miles (891,220 sq. km) are land area and some 68,500 sq. miles (177,420 sq. km) are fresh water.

The province extends 1,000 miles from east to west and 1,050 miles from north to south.

Ontario is bounded on the north by the waters of Hudson and James Bay, on the east by Quebec, on the west by Manitoba, and on the south by the states of New York, Pennsylvania, Ohio, Michigan, Wisconsin and Minnesota.

The population of the province (census, 1 June 1981) was 8,625,107. Census population of the principal cities (1981): Toronto (provincial capital), 599,217 (city), 2,998,947 (census metropolitan area); Hamilton, 306,434 (city), 542,095 (census metropolitan area); Ottawa (federal capital), 295,163 (city), 547,399 (census metropolitan area); London, 254,280 (city); Windsor, 192,083 (city), Kitchener, 139,734 (city), 287,801 (census metropolitan area); Sudbury, 89,773 (city), 159,779 (regional municipality).

Vital statistics, *see* p. 267.
Religion, *see* p. 284.

CONSTITUTION AND GOVERNMENT. The provincial government is administered by a Lieut.-Governor, a cabinet and one chamber elected by a general franchise for a period of 5 years. Women have the vote and can be elected to the chamber. The minimum voting age is 18 years.

In Oct. 1981 the provincial legislature was composed as follows: Progressive Conservatives, 70; Liberals, 34; New Democrats, 21; total 125.

Lieut.-Governor: Hon. John B. Aird, QC, BA, LLD (appointed 15 Sept. 1980).
Flag: The British Red Ensign with the shield of Ontario in the fly.

The members of the Executive Council in Oct. 1983 were as follows (all Progressive Conservatives):

Premier and President of the Council: W. G. Davis.
Deputy Premier and Minister Responsible for Women's Issues: R. Welch. *Natural Resources:* A. W. Pope. *Provincial Secretary for Resources Development:* N. Sterling, QC. *Intergovernmental Affairs:* T. L. Wells. *Northern Affairs:* L. Bernier. *Transportation and Communications:* J. W. Snow. *Provincial Secretary for Social Development:* B. McCaffrey. *Municipal Affairs and Housing:* C. Bennett. *Treasury and Economics:* Larry Grossman. *Health:* Keith Norton. *Energy:* P.

Andrewes. *Environment:* Andy Brandt. *Education and Colleges and Universities:* B. M. Stephenson. *Attorney-General:* R. McMurtry. *Agriculture and Food:* Dennis R. Timbrell. *Community and Social Services:* F. Drea. *Consumer and Commercial Relations:* Robert G. Elgie, MD. *Provincial Secretary for Justice:* G. Walker, QC. *Industry and Trade:* F. S. Miller. *Management Board of Cabinet (Chairman):* G. McCague. *Revenue:* B. Gregory. *Solicitor-General:* G. Taylor. *Citizenship and Culture:* S. Fish. *Tourism and Recreation:* R. Baetz. *Government Services:* G. Ashe. *Labour:* Russell Ramsay. *Correctional Services:* N. Leluk. *Without Portfolio and Chief Government Whip:* R. Eaton. *Without Portfolio:* Gordon Dean.

Local Government. Local government in Ontario is divided into two branches, one covering municipal institutions and the other education.

The present municipal system dates from The Municipal Corporations Act enacted by The Province of Canada in 1849. It has been considerably modified in recent years with the creation of the Municipality of Metropolitan Toronto in 1954 and the launching of the Government of Ontario's local government restructuring programme in 1968. Generally, there are two levels of municipal government in Ontario. The upper level consists of 27 counties plus 12 restructured regional municipalities. The local level comprises more than 800 cities, towns and townships. Cities in the traditional county system function independently of the county in which they lie, as do 5 towns which have been separated for municipal purposes. There are no separated municipal units in regional governments.

Ontario's local municipalities are governed by councils elected by popular vote.

A city council usually consists of a mayor, aldermen and, sometimes, an executive committee known as a board of control.

Councils of towns, villages and townships usually consist of a mayor, reeve, deputy reeve, councillors and, in the case of the newer regional municipalities, one or more regional councillors who represent the area municipalities on the regional council.

County and regional government councils are federated assemblies.

A county council consists of the reeves and deputy reeves of the towns, villages and townships. The head of the county council is the warden, who is elected by the council from among its own members.

A regional council consists of the heads of council of the local municipalities, as well as a varying number of regional councillors, who are elected on the basis of representation, either directly or indirectly. The head of the regional council is the chairman who is elected by council but who, unlike a county warden, need not have been a council member.

No municipality in Ontario may incur long-term debts without the sanction of the tribunal created by the Provincial Legislature and known as the Ontario Municipal Board. Debenture obligations incurred by municipalities for utility undertakings (water-works and electric light and power systems) are discharged ordinarily out of revenues derived from the sale of utility services and do not fall upon the ratepayers.

Municipal councils have no jurisdiction for education beyond the collection of taxes for school purposes. Responsibility for providing, operating and maintaining school facilities, and for the supply of teachers, rests with local education authorities known as boards of education or school boards. These boards are now generally organized on a county or regional basis. Apart from some of the larger cities, local municipal school boards no longer exist.

Municipal institutions come under the jurisdiction of the Provincial Ministry of Intergovernmental Affairs. One of the principal functions of the Ministry is to advise and assist municipalities on such matters as accounting, reporting, auditing, budgeting and planning. Educational support and guidance at the provincial level is the responsibility of the Ministry of Education, which deals with the training of teachers and the formulation of curriculum. (At the university and community college level, education support services are provided by the Ministry of Colleges and Universities.)

There are considerable areas in the northernmost parts of Ontario where as yet there is little or no settlement of population. In such areas no municipal organization exists, and control for all purposes over such areas remains in the hands of the Provincial Government.

FINANCE. The gross revenue and expenditure and the net cash requirements (in Canadian $1,000) for years ending 31 March were as follows:

	1979–80	1980–81	1981–82	1982–83	1983–84
Gross revenue	15,246	16,470	18,886	20,395	22,015
Gross expenditure	15,830	17,273	20,389	22,943	24,710
Net cash requirement	584	803	1,503	2,548	2,695

Gross revenue and expenditure figures include all non-budgetary transactions, *i.e.*, the lending and investment activity of the Government to Crown corporations, agencies and municipalities as well as the repayment of these loans or recovery of investments. Transactions on behalf of Ontario Hydro are excluded.

ENERGY AND NATURAL RESOURCES

Electricity (1982). Ontario Hydro recorded for the calendar year a dependable peak capacity of 24·9m. kw. and a net energy output generated and purchased of 112,317m. kwh.

Minerals (1982). The total value of shipments (in $1m.) in the mineral products industry were: Nickel, 413; copper, 336; iron ore, 187; gold, 294. The total value of mineral production was $3,157m. in 1982. The mining industry employed about 50,000 people.

Agriculture. In 1982, 3·5m. hectares were under field crops with total farm receipts of $4,976·5m.

Forestry. According to the most recent inventory (1982) the total area of productive forest is 56·6m. hectares, comprising: Softwoods, 28,626,055; hardwoods, 6,719,105; mixed woods, 17,316,073; reproducing forests, 3,938,749. The growing stock equals 3,638,100m. cu. ft. The estimated value of shipments by the forest products industry (including logging) was (1982) $7,238·8m.

INDUSTRY AND TRADE

Industry (1982). Ontario is Canada's most highly industrialized province. About 73% of value added in commodity-producing industries is accounted for by manufacturing. Construction is next with 13%.

In 1982, the labour force was 4,519,000. Total labour income was $82·75m. The Gross Provincial Product (GPP) was $133,530m.

The leading manufacturing industries are motor vehicles and parts, iron and steel, meat and meat preparations, dairy products, paper and paperboard, chemical products, petroleum and coal products, machinery and equipment, metal stamping and pressing and communications equipment.

Trade. In 1982 Ontario exported 43% ($36,603·4m) of Canada's total foreign trade.

COMMUNICATIONS

Roads. There were, in 1982, 152,173·4 km of roads. Motor licences numbered approximately 5·3m., of which 3·8m. were passenger cars, 1,031,320 trucks and tractors, 23,827 buses, 65,754 trailers, 119,642 motor cycles and 169,385 snow vehicles.

Railways. The provincially-owned Ontario Northland Railway has about 550 miles of track and the Algoma Central Railway 325 miles. The Canadian National and Canadian Pacific Railways operate a total of about 9,500 miles in Ontario.

Post (1982). Telephone service is provided by 120 independent systems and Bell Canada (1982, 6,416,200 telephones).

EDUCATION. There is a complete provincial system of elementary and secondary schools as well as private schools. In 1982 publicly financed elementary and secondary schools had a total enrolment of 1,779,425 pupils.

In 1965 Ontario established Colleges of Applied Arts and Technology (CAATS). There are now 22 of these publicly owned colleges with full-time enrolment (1982) of 88,997 in academic courses.

The University of Toronto, founded in 1827 (full-time enrolment, 1982, 34,730), and 14 other major universities (total full-time enrolment, 1982, 175,840), all receive provincial grants. The net general expenditure of the provincial ministries of education and colleges and universities for the fiscal year ending 31 March 1981 was $4,146m.

Books of Reference

Statistical Information: Annual publications of the Ontario Ministry of Treasury and Economics include: *Ontario Statistics; Ontario Budget; Public Accounts; Financial Report.*

PRINCE EDWARD ISLAND

HISTORY. The earliest discovery of the island is not satisfactorily known, but the first recorded visit was by Jacques Cartier in 1534, who named it Isle St-Jean; it was first settled by the French, but was taken from them in 1758. It was annexed to Nova Scotia in 1763, and constituted a separate colony in 1769. Prince Edward Island entered the Confederation on 1 July 1873.

AREA AND POPULATION. The province, which is the smallest in Canada, lies in the Gulf of St Lawrence, and is separated from the mainland of New Brunswick and Nova Scotia by Northumberland Strait. The area of the island is 2,184 sq. miles (5,656 sq. km). Total population (census, 1981), 124,200. Population of the principal cities (1980): Charlottetown (capital), 17,063; Summerside, 8,532.

Vital statistics, *see* p. 267.
Religion, *see* p. 284.

CONSTITUTION AND GOVERNMENT. The provincial government is administered by a Lieut.-Governor-in-Council (Cabinet) and a Legislative Assembly of 32 members who are elected for up to 5 years. In Oct. 1982, parties in the Legislative Assembly were: Progressive Conservatives, 21; Liberals, 11.

Lieut.-Governor: Joseph Aubin Doiron (sworn in 14 Jan. 1980).

Flag: A banner of the arms, *i.e.*, a white field bearing 3 small trees and a larger tree on a compartment, all green, and at the top a red band with a golden lion; on 3 sides a border of red and white rectangles.

Premier and President of Executive Council: James M. Lee.

Finance and Tourism: Lloyd G. MacPhail. *Justice and Attorney-General and Community and Cultural Affairs:* George R. McMahon, QC. *Industry:* Patrick G. Binns. *Agriculture:* Prowse G. Chappell. *Energy and Forestry:* Frederick L. Driscoll. *Health and Social Services:* Albert Fogarty. *Fisheries and Labour:* R. B. (Roddy) Pratt. *Education:* Leone Bagnall. *Transportation and Public Works:* Gordon Lank.

Local Government. The Village Service Act, 1954, provides for the incorporation of villages. The city of Charlottetown and the town of Summerside have been incorporated under Special Acts. The Town Act, 1951, provides for the incorporation of all towns. The Community Improvement Act, 1968, provides for the establishment of Community Improvement Committees in the unincorporated areas of the province.

FINANCE. Revenue and expenditure (in Canadian $) for 6 financial years ending 31 March:

	1978–79	1979–80	1980–81	1981–82	1982–83	1983–84
Revenue	242,274,000	273,375,400	307,566,300	352,556,900	380,883,900	394,641,400
Expenditure	242,488,500	273,074,300	306,789,900	351,486,200	386,878,700	415,444,500

ENERGY AND NATURAL RESOURCES

Electricity. Electric power is supplied to 98% of the population. The province's net generated and purchased consumption of electricity dropped during 1982 from 514m. kwh. to 510m. kwh. In 1982, peak demand for electricity was 103 mw. In 1977 the province completed the laying of an undersea power cable which links the island with New Brunswick and the Maritime Power Grid. In 1980, 30 miles of additional 138 kv transmission line was added to the PEI system. In 1982, about 94% of power requirements were supplied through this system.

Agriculture. Total area of farms occupies approximately 699,000 acres out of the total land area of 1,399,040 acres. Farm cash receipts in 1982 were $163m. with cash receipts from potatoes accounting for 32% of the total. Cash receipts from dairy products, hogs and cattle followed in importance. The land in natural forest covers 162,000 acres and in 1981 total value of forest products sold was $363,000. For particulars of agricultural production and livestock, *see under* CANADA, pp. 276–77.

Fisheries. The fishery of the province in 1982 had a landed value of $35·4m. Lobsters accounted for 63·7% of the total. Value of groundfish landings accounted for 13·6%; pelagic and estuarial, 7·1%; shellfish, other than lobster, 10·7%; Irish moss, 4·8%.

INDUSTRY AND TRADE

Industry. Value of manufacturing shipments for all industries in 1980 (estimate) was $286·2m.

Commerce. Average personal income rose from $7,829 in 1981 to $8,894 in 1982. The average wage rose from $250.13 per week in 1981 to $278.53 in 1982. The labour force averaged 54,000 in 1982. while employment averaged 47,000.

In 1981, provincial GDP for manufacturing was $63m.; construction, $46·4m.

In 1982, total value of retail trade was $412,417,000.

Tourism. The value of the tourist industry was estimated at $49m. in 1982 with 202,991 tourist parties.

COMMUNICATIONS

Roads. The province has a total of 5,278 km of road, including 3,687 km of paved highway.

Railways. Rail service is provided over 274 miles of track within the province and connects with the national railways system *via* the New Brunswick–Prince Edward Island ferry service.

Aviation. Air service for passengers, mail and cargo is scheduled to provide 8 flights daily in each direction between the province and various points in eastern Canada. A daily bus service operates between various centres in the province as well as to Nova Scotia during the summer months.

Shipping. A ferry service provides rail and highway communication with New Brunswick by means of 4 large ferries, 2 of which are powerful ice-breakers. Another ferry service employing 2 ferries plus an additional 2 for summertime operates between the province and Nova Scotia throughout the season of open navigation. A third ferry service employing 1 ferry operates between the province and Magdalen Islands, Quebec, during the open navigation season.

Post. In 1983 there were approximately 74,594 telephones.

EDUCATION (1982–83). Under the regional school boards there are 72 public schools, 1,425 teachers, 26,600 students. Vocational school enrolment, 845 students. There is one undergraduate university (1,600 full-time students), and a college of applied arts and technology (750 full-time post-secondary students), both in Charlottetown. Total expenditure in education in the year ending 31 March 1984 is forecast to be $99,650,300.

Books of Reference

Clark, A. H., *Three Centuries and the Island.* Toronto, 1959
Hocking, A., *Prince Edward Island.* Toronto, 1978
MacKinnon, F., *The Government of Prince Edward Island.* Toronto, 1951

QUEBEC—QUÉBEC

HISTORY. Quebec was formerly known as New France or Canada from 1534 to 1763; as the province of Quebec from 1763 to 1790; as Lower Canada from 1791 to 1846; as Canada East from 1846 to 1867, and when, by the union of the four original provinces, the Confederation of the Dominion of Canada was formed, it again became known as the province of Quebec (Québec).

The Quebec Act, passed by the British Parliament in 1774, guaranteed to the people of the newly conquered French territory in North America security in their religion and language, their customs and tenures, under their own civil laws.

In the referendum held 20 May 1980, 59·5% voted against and 40·5% for 'separatism'.

AREA AND POPULATION. The area of Quebec (as amended by the Labrador Boundary Award) is 1,540,668 sq. km (594,860 sq. miles), of which 1,315,134 sq. km is land area and 352,792 sq. km water. Of this extent, 351,780 sq. miles represent the Territory of Ungava, annexed in 1912 under the Quebec Boundaries Extension Act. The population (census 1981) was 6,438,403.

Principal cities (1981): Quebec (capital), 166,474; Montreal, 980,354; Laval, 268,335; Sherbrooke, 74,075; Verdun, 61,287; Hull, 56,225; Trois-Rivières, 50,466.

Vital statistics, *see* p. 267.

Religion, *see* p. 284.

CONSTITUTION AND GOVERNMENT. There is a Legislative Assembly consisting of 122 members, elected in 122 electoral districts for 4 years. There were, Sept. 1982, 73 *Parti Québecois*, 46 Liberals, 2 Independent, 1 vacant seat.

Lieut.-Governor: The Hon. Jean Pierre Côté.
Flag: The Fleurdelysé flag, blue with a white cross, and in each quarter a white fleur-de-lis.

The members of the Executive Council as on 10 Sept. 1982, are as follows:

Prime Minister and President of the Council: René Lévesque.
Vice-Prime Minister and Minister of Intergovernmental Affairs: Jacques-Yvan Morin. *Finance:* Jacques Parizeau. *Treasury:* Yves Bérubé. *Education:* Camille Laurin. *Social Affairs:* Pierre-Marc Johnson. *Planning and Regional Development:* François Gendron. *Justice:* Marc-André Bédard. *External Trade:* Bernard Landry. *Manpower:* Pierre Marois. *Energy and Resources:* Yves Duhaime. *Municipal Affairs:* Jacques Léonard. *Agriculture and Fisheries:* Jean Garon. *Transport:* Michel Clair. *Parliamentary Leader and Minister of Communications:* Jean-François Bertrand. *Consumer Affairs:* Guy Tardif. *Industry, Commerce and Tourism:* Rodrigue Biron. *Cultural Affairs:* Clément Richard. *Women's Affairs:* Pauline Marois. *Public Functions:* Denise Leblanc-Bantey. *Social Development:* Denis Lazure. *Revenue and Public Works:* Alain Marcoux. *Immigration:* Gérald Godin. *Works:* Raynald Fréchette. *Recreation and Sport:* Guy Chevrette. *Environment:* Adrien Ouellette. *Science and Technology:* Gilbert Paquette.

General-delegate in London: Patrick Hindman (59 Pall Mall, SW1Y 5SH).
General-delegate in New York: Raymond Gosselin (17 West 50th St., Rockefeller Center, New York 10020).
General-delegate in Paris: Vacant (66 Pergolèse, Paris 75116).

ECONOMY

Budget. Ordinary revenue and expenditure (in Canadian $1,000) for fiscal years ending 31 March:

	1977–78	1978–79	1979–80	1980–81	1981–82
Revenue	10,742,609	11,928,343	13,306,680	14,718,305	17,471,594
Expenditure	11,503,008	13,402,830	15,123,200	17,596,659	20,359,807

The total net debt at 31 March 1982 was $13,836,169,000.

ENERGY AND NATURAL RESOURCES

Electricity. Water power is one of the most important natural resources of the province of Quebec. Its turbine installation represents about 40% of the aggregate of Canada. At the end of 1980 the installed generating capacity was 20,531 mw. Production, 1981, was 102,904 gwh.

Minerals (1982). The estimated value of the mineral production (metal mines only) was $1,203,167,000. Chief minerals: Iron ore, $446,252,000; copper, $176,660,000; gold, $347,278,000; zinc, $70,842,000.

The second major iron-ore development in northern Quebec is, like the one at Knob Lake which gave birth to Schefferville, based on the Quebec–Labrador Trough which extends from Lac Jeannine to the northern tip of Ungava peninsula. The port of Sept-Iles and the railway connecting it with Schefferville allow easy shipment to the furnaces and steel mills of Canada, the USA and Europe. The setting-up of a steel industry is being explored.

Non-metallic minerals produced include: Asbestos ($324,992,000; about 87% of Canadian production), titane-dioxide ($106,006,000), industrial lime, dolomite and brucite, quartz and pyrite. Among the building materials produced were: Stone, $94,760,000; cement, $129,989,000; sand and gravel, $46,479,000; lime, $22,444,000.

Agriculture. In 1982 the total area (estimate) of the principal field crops was 2,073,300 hectares. The yield of the principal crops was (in 1,000 tonnes):

Crops	Yield	Crops	Yield
Tame hay	4,300	Fodder corn	2,600
Oats for grain	360	Maize for grain	910
Potatoes	387	Barley	360
Mixed grains	144	Buckwheat	7

The farm cash receipts from farming operations in 1982 amounted to $2,834,385,000. The principal items being: Livestock and products, $2,322,116,000; crops, $319,766,000; dairy supplements payments, $131,514,000, forest and maple products, $55,465,000.

Forestry. Forests cover an area of 684,480 sq. km. About 490,693 sq. km are classified as productive forests, of which 611,625 sq. km are provincial crown land and 70,912 sq. km are privately owned. Quebec leads the Canadian provinces in pulpwood production, having nearly half of the Canadian estimated total.

In 1980 production of lumber was softwood and hardwood, 8,059,120 cu. metres; woodpulp, 6,356,079 tonnes; paper and paperboard, 5,494,563 tonnes.

Fisheries. The principal fish are cod, herring, red fish, lobster and salmon. Total catch of sea fish, 1982, 79,198 tonnes, valued at $49,944,569.

INDUSTRY AND TRADE

Industry. In 1981 there were 10,915 industrial establishments in the province; employees, 528,269; salaries and wages, $9,845,826,023; cost of materials,

$29,196,369,675; value of shipments, $50,150,142,834. Among the leading industries are petroleum refining, pulp and paper mills, smelting and refining, dairy products, slaughtering and meat processing, motor vehicle manufacturing, women's clothing, saw-mills and planing mills, iron and steel mills, commercial printing.

Commerce. In 1982 the value of Canadian exports through Quebec custom ports was $17,430,942,000; value of imports, $12,766,442,000.

COMMUNICATIONS

Roads. In 1981 there were 59,532 km of roads and (1981) 4,510,982 registered motor vehicles.

Railways. There were (1980) 8,322 km of railway. There is a metro system in Montreal.

Aviation. In 1982 Quebec had 2 international airports, Dorval (Montreal) with landing runway of 8·4 km and Mirabel (Montreal) with 7·3 km.

Post and Broadcasting. Telephones numbered 4,102,671 in 1981 and there were 25 television and 119 radio stations in 1982.·

Newspapers (1982). There were 10 French- and 2 English-language daily newspapers.

EDUCATION.

The province has 7 universities: 3 English-language universities, McGill (Montreal) founded in 1821, Bishop (Lennoxville) founded in 1845 and the Concordia University (Montreal) granted a charter in 1975; 4 French-language universities: Laval (Quebec) founded in 1852, Montreal University, opened in 1876 as a branch of Laval and became independent in 1920, Sherbrooke University founded in 1954 and University of Quebec founded in 1968.

In 1981–82 there were 93,562 full-time university students and 95,166 part-time students.

In 1981–82, in pre-kindergartens, there were 7,228 pupils; in kindergartens, 88,295; primary schools, 551,457; in secondary schools, 530,725; in colleges (post-secondary, non-university), 141,069; and in classes for children with special needs, 93,197. The school boards had a total of 66,830 teachers.

Expenditure of the Department of Education for 1981–82 (Canadian $1,000), 5,914,117 net. This included 859,545 for universities, 3,697,388 for public primary and secondary schools, 163,885 for private primary and secondary schools and 762,146 for colleges.

Books of Reference

Statistical Information: The Quebec Bureau of Statistics was established in 1912. The Bureau, which reports to the Executive council since Sept. 1981, collects, compiles and distributes statistical information relative to Quebec. *Director:* Nicole Gendreau.

A statistical information list is available on request. Among the most important publications are: *Annuaire du Québec* (Quebec Yearbook), *Statistiques* (quarterly), *Comptes économiques du Québec* (annual), *Perspectives démographiques* (annual), *Situation démographique* (annual), *Exportations internationales du Québec* (annual), *Statistiques du travail et de la main-d'oeuvre* (annual), *Investissements privés et publics* (annual), *Eléments de prévisions économiques* (quarterly), *Statistiques manufacturières* (annual).

Atlas du Québec: L'Agriculture. Ministère de l'Industrie et du Commerce, Quebec, 1966
Baudoin, L., *Le Droit civil de la province de Québec.* Montreal, 1953
Blanchard, R., *Le Canada-français.* Paris, 1959
Hamelin, J., *Histoire du Québec.* St-Hyacinthe, 1978
Jacobs, J., *The Question of Separatism: Quebec and the Struggle for Sovereignty.* London, 1981
McWhinney, E., *Quebec and the Constitution.* Univ. of Toronto Press, 1979
Ouellet, F., *Histoire de la Chambre de Commerce de Québec, 1809–1959.* Québec, 1959
Raynauld, A., *Croissance et structure économiques de la province de Québec.* Québec, 1961
Trofimenkoff, S. M., *Action Française.* Univ. of Toronto Press, 1975
Wade, F. M., *The French Canadians, 1760–1967.* Toronto, 1968.—*Canadian Dualism: Studies of French–English Relations.* Quebec–Toronto, 1960

SASKATCHEWAN

HISTORY. Saskatchewan derives its name from its major river system, which the Cree Indians called 'Kis-is-ska-tche-wan', meaning 'swift flowing'. It officially became a province when it joined the Confederation on 1 Sept. 1905.

In 1670 King Charles II granted to Prince Rupert and his friends a charter covering exclusive trading rights in 'all the land drained by streams finding their outlet in the Hudson Bay'. This included what is now Saskatchewan. The trading company was first known as The Governor and Company of Adventurers of England; later as the Hudson's Bay Company. In 1869 the Northwest Territories was formed, and this included Saskatchewan. In 1882 the District of Saskatchewan was formed. By 1885 the North-West Mounted Police had been inaugurated, with headquarters in Regina (now the capital), and the Canadian Pacific Railway's transcontinental line had been completed, bringing a stream of immigrants to southern Saskatchewan. The Hudson's Bay Company surrendered its claim to territory in return for cash and land around the existing trading posts. Legislative government was introduced.

AREA AND POPULATION. Saskatchewan is bounded on the west by Alberta, on the east by Manitoba, to the north by the Northwest Territories; to the south it is bordered by the US states of Montana and North Dakota. The area of the province is 220,121 sq. miles (570,113 sq. km), of which 220,182 sq. miles is land area and 31,518 sq. miles is water. The population, 1981 census, was 968,313 (1983, estimate, 990,700). Population of principal cities, 1981 census (1983 estimate): Regina (capital), 162,613 (167,900); Saskatoon, 154,210 (159,000); Moose Jaw, 33,941; Prince Albert, 31,380; Yorkton, 15,339; Swift Current, 14,747; North Battleford, 14,030; Estevan, 10,359 (9,174); Weyburn, 9,523; Lloydminster, 6,034; Melfort, 6,010; Melville, 5,092.

Vital statistics, *see* p. 267.

Religion, *see* p. 284.

CONSTITUTION AND GOVERNMENT. The provincial government is vested in a Lieut.-Governor, an Executive Council and a Legislative Assembly, elected for 5 years. Women were given the franchise in 1916 and are also eligible for election to the legislature. State of parties in May 1982: Progressive Conservative, 56; New Democratic Party, 8.

Lieut.-Governor: F. W. Johnson.

Flag: Green over gold, with the shield of the province in the canton, and a green and red prairie lily in the fly.

The Progressive Conservative Ministry in Sept. 1983 was composed as follows:

Premier: Grant Devine.

Deputy Premier, Economic Development and Trade, Provincial Secretary: Eric Berntson. *Finance, Potash Corporation of Saskatchewan and Leader of the House:* Bob Andrew. *Energy and Mines:* Paul Schoenals. *Agriculture:* Lorne Hepworth. *Justice and Attorney-General, Saskatchewan Telecommunications:* Gary Lane. *Urban Affairs:* Tim Embury. *Advanced Education and Manpower:* Colin Mazwell. *Culture and Recreation:* Rick Folk. *Education:* Patricia Smith. *Social Services:* Gordon Dirks. *Labour and Saskatchewan Power Corporation:* Lorne McLaren. *Tourism and Small Business:* Jack Klein. *Science and Technology, Telephones:* Gordon Currie. *Health:* Graham Taylor. *Environment:* Neal Hardy. *Highways:* Jim Garner. *Revenue and Financial Services:* Paul Rousseau. *Consumer and Commercial Affairs:* Joan Duncan. *Supply and Services, Northern Saskatchewan, Deputy Leader of the House:* George McLeod. *Parks and Renewable Resources:* Bob Pickering. *Co-operation and Co-operative Development:* Jack Sandberg. *Rural Development:* Louis Domotor. *Ministers without Portfolio:* Sid Dutchak *(Indian and Native Affairs, Saskatchewan Housing Corporation),* Gerald Muirhead *(Saskatchewan Crop Insurance).*

Agent-General in London: R. A. Larter, 21 Pall Mall, SW1Y 5LP.

Local Government. The organization of a city requires a minimum population of 5,000 persons; that of a town, 500; that of a village, 100 people. No requirements as to population exist for the rural municipality and the local improvement district.

Cities, towns, villages and rural municipalities are governed by elected councils, which consist of a mayor and 6–20 aldermen in a city; a mayor and 6 councillors in a town; a mayor and 2 other members in a village; a reeve and a councillor for each division in a rural municipality (usually 6). Local improvement districts are administered by the Department of Municipal Affairs.

FINANCE. Budget and net assets (years ending 31 March) in Canadian $1,000[2]:

	1977–78	1978–79	1979–80[1]	1980–81[12]	1982–83[12]
Budgetary revenue	1,459,979	1,613,470	1,807,160	2,019,345	2,527,308
Budgetary expenditure	1,503,112	1,676,322	1,856,556	2,018,303	2,839,442

[1] Estimate.
[2] Excludes Consolidated Fund, Community Capital Fund, Saskatchewan Heritage Fund, Energy and Resource Development Fund and The Marketing Development Fund.

ENERGY AND NATURAL RESOURCES. Agriculture used to dominate the history and economics of Saskatchewan, but the 'prairie province' is now a rapidly developing mining and manufacturing area. It is a major supplier of oil; has the world's largest deposits of potash; and net value of non-agricultural production account for (1979 estimate) 60% of the provincial economy.

Electricity. The Saskatchewan Power Corporation generated 9,755m. kwh. in 1982.

Minerals. The 1982 mineral production was valued at $2,099,949,000, including (in $1,000): Petroleum 1,066,813; natural gas, 30,858; coal, 75,500; gold, 4,051; silver, 1,405; copper, 8,677; zinc, 4,640; potash, 625,658; salt, 14,363; uranium, 224,000; sodium sulphate, 43,984.

Agriculture. Saskatchewan produces normally about two-thirds of Canada's wheat. Wheat production in 1982 (in 1,000 tonnes), was 17,146 from 19·7m. acres; oats, 1,002 from 1·15m. acres; barley, 3,636 from 3·45m. acres; rye, 203 (1979) from 360,000 acres; rapeseed, 725,700 from 1·4m. acres; flax, 259 (1979) from 800,000 acres. Livestock (1 July 1982): Cattle and calves, 2,365,000; swine, 500,000; sheep and lambs, 75,000. Poultry in 1982: Chickens, 4,793,000; turkeys 459,000. Cash income from the sale of farm products in 1981 was $3,998m. At the June 1981 census there were 67,318 commercial farms in the province, each being a holding having agricultural sales of $2,500 or more.

The South Saskatchewan River irrigation project, whose main feature is the Gardiner Dam, was completed in 1967. It will ultimately provide for an area of 200,000 acres of irrigated cultivation in Central Saskatchewan. In 1981, 38,023 acres were developed. Total irrigated land, 138,164 acres.

Forestry. Half of Saskatchewan's area is forested, but only 115,000 sq. km are of commercial value at present. Forest products valued at $213m. were produced in 1979–80. The province's first pulp-mill, at Prince Albert, went into production in 1968; its daily capacity is 1,000 tons of high-grade kraft pulp.

Fur Production. In 1982–83 wild fur production was estimated at $2,089,568. Ranch-raised fur production amounted to $410,586.

Fisheries. The lakeside value of the 1982–83 commercial fish catch of 3,389,397 kg was $3,075,597.

INDUSTRY. In 1980 Saskatchewan had 771 manufacturing establishments, employing 21,195 persons. The net value of gross domestic production was $14·9m. in 1982. Manufacturing accounted for $885m., construction for $2,757m. in 1980.

TOURISM. An estimated 1·5m. out of province tourists spent $168m. in 1981.

COMMUNICATIONS

Roads. In 1982 there were 21,436 km of provincial highways, 180,647 km of municipal roads (including prairie trails). Motor vehicles registered totalled (1980) 683,955. Bus services are provided by 2 major lines.

Railways. There were (1981) approximately 12,385 km of main railway track in operation.

Aviation. Saskatchewan had 2 major airports, 176 airports and landing strips in 1982.

Post and Broadcasting. There were (1982) 716 post offices (excluding sub-post offices), 68 TV and re-broadcasting stations and 35 AM and FM radio stations. 688,402 telephones were connected to the Saskatchewan Telecommunications system.

EDUCATION. The University of Saskatchewan was established at Saskatoon on 3 April 1907. In 1981–82 it had about 10,818 (day-time) degree students, 1,289 (part-time) and 940 full-time teaching staff; and 4,105 (full-time) and 4,213 (part-time) students and 341 full-time faculty members at the University of Regina which was established 1 July 1974. The Saskatchewan public education system in 1982–83 consisted of 114 school units and districts serving 141,493 elementary pupils, 58,942 high-school students and 3,354 students enrolled in special classes. In addition, 3 provincial technical and vocational schools provided training for approximately 19,762 technical students. There are also 16 Roman Catholic separate school districts and 2 separate high-school districts. In addition there are 15 community colleges with an enrolment of approximately 100,000 registrations per year.

Books of Reference

Tourist and industrial publications, descriptive of the Government's programme, are obtainable from the Department of Industry and Commerce; other government publications from Government Information Services (Legislative Building. Regina).
Saskatchewan Economic Review. Executive Council, Regina. Annual
Archer and Derby, *The Story of a Province.* Toronto, 1955
McCourt, E. A., *Saskatchewan.* Toronto, 1968
Morton, A. S., *Saskatchewan, the Making of a University.* Toronto, 1959
Richards, J. S., and Fung, K. I. (eds.), *Atlas of Saskatchewan.* Univ. of Saskatchewan, 1969
Wright, J. F. C., *Saskatchewan, the History of a Province* Toronto, 1955

THE NORTHWEST TERRITORIES

HISTORY. The Territory was developed by the Hudson's Bay Company and the North West Company (of Montreal) from the 17th century. The Canadian Government bought out the Hudson's Bay Company in 1869 and the Territory was annexed to Canada in 1870. The Arctic Islands lying north of the Canadian mainland were annexed to Canada in 1880 by Queen Victoria.

AREA AND POPULATION. The total area of the Territories is 1,304,903 sq. miles (3,379,700 sq. km), divided into 5 districts, namely, Inuvik, Fort Smith, Keewatin, Baffin and Kitikmeot. The population in June 1981 was 45,741, about 58% of whom were Indians or Inuit (Eskimo). Main centres (census 1980): Inuvik (2,918), Fort Smith (2,265), Hay River (3,322), Frobisher Bay (2,444), Fort Simpson (981). When the transfer of governmental responsibility from Ottawa to the Territorial capital at Yellowknife took place in 1967. the population of Yellowknife increased by the influx of civil servants from 3,741 in 1966 to 9,731 in 1980.

CONSTITUTION AND GOVERNMENT. The Northwest Territories comprises all that portion of Canada lying north of the 60th parallel of N. lat. except those portions within the Yukon Territory and the Provinces of Quebec and

Newfoundland: it also includes the islands in Hudson Bay, James Bay and Ungava Bay except those within the Provinces of Manitoba, Ontario and Quebec.

The Northwest Territories is governed by a Commissioner and a Legislative Assembly. The Assembly is composed of 24 members elected for a 4-year term of office. The seat of government was transferred from Ottawa to Yellowknife when it was named territorial capital on 18 Jan. 1967.

Commissioner: J. H. Parker.

Flag: Vertically, blue, white, blue, with the white of double width and bearing the shield of the Territory.

Legislative powers are exercised by the Commissioner-in-Council on such matters as taxation within the Territories in order to raise revenue, maintenance of justice, licences, solemnization of marriages, education, public health, property, civil rights and generally all matters of a local nature.

The Territorial Government has now assumed responsibility for the administration of the entire Northwest Territories. In a Territories-wide plebiscite in April 1982, a majority of residents favoured dividing the Northwest Territories into two jurisdictions. The Legislative Assembly has asked the Federal Government to agree to division and to establish a Commission to determine a boundary.

ENERGY AND NATURAL RESOURCES

Oil and Gas. As of March 1983, 1,531 permits for oil and gas exploration were held for 40·86m. hectares, of which 107 leases were on the mainland, 1,142 were on the arctic islands and 282 on the marine coast.

Crude oil, discovered in 1920, is produced and refined at Norman Wells on the Mackenzie River. In 1982, oil production was 173,294 cu. metres.

Minerals. Mineral production for the year 1982, from 9 producing mines, was valued at $566·25m., of which zinc accounted for $328·6m.; gold, $84,375,000; lead, $80,625,000; tungsten, $56·4m.; silver, $14·35m.; arsenic trioxide, $1·3m. and cadmium, $600,000.

Yellowknife continues to be the centre of goldmining activity and Canada's Cominco Ltd has completed construction of a lead-zinc mine, the Polaris Project, on Little Cornwallis Island in the central high arctic.

Trapping and Game. Fur produced during the 1981–82 season was valued at $3,738,000, primarily in muskrat, fox, lynx and marten. A herd of some 6,500 buffalo is protected in Wood Buffalo National Park. Barren ground caribou are increasing, due to more effective management techniques.

Forestry. The principal trees are white and black spruce, jack-pine, balsam, poplar and birch. In 1982, 52,498 cu. metres of lumber, 3,307 cu. metres of round timber and 7,526 cu. metres of fuelwood were cut.

Fisheries. Commercial fishing, principally on Great Slave Lake, in 1981–82 produced fish valued at $1·3m., principally trout, char and whitefish.

CO-OPERATIVES. There are 36 active co-operatives in the Northwest Territories. They are active in handicrafts, furs, fisheries, retail stores, print shops, provision of housing, contracting for services, etc. Total sales in 1980–81 were more than $20m.

COMMUNICATIONS

Roads. The Mackenzie Route connects Grimshaw, Alberta, with Hay River, Pine Point, Fort Smith, Fort Providence, Rae-Edzo and Yellowknife. The Mackenzie Highway extension to Fort Simpson and a road between Pine Point and Fort Resolution have both been opened.

Clearing began in 1972 for extending the Mackenzie Highway north of Fort Simpson to the arctic coast. Highway service to Inuvik in the Mackenzie Delta was opened in spring 1980, extending north from Dawson, Yukon as the Dempster Highway. The Liard Highway connecting the communities of the Liard River valley to British Columbia is expected to open in 1984.

Railways. The Great Slave Lake Railway runs from Pine Point and Hay River, on the south shore of Great Slave Lake, 435 miles south to Grimshaw, Alberta, where it connects with the CN Rail's main system.

Aviation (1979). Fourteen licensed and 1 unlicensed airports are operated by the federal Ministry of Transport and there are 17 licensed and 18 unlicensed airports operated by the Government of the Northwest Territories. Two licensed and 10 unlicensed airports are operated by private owners. Regular mail,passenger and express services are maintained throughout the Territories. A seaplane base is operated by the Ministry of Transport and there are 17 private seaplane bases. Scheduled services join major points with centres in scuthern Canada.

Shipping. A direct inland-water transportation route for about 1,700 miles is provided by the Mackenzie River and its tributaries, the Athabasca and Slave rivers. Subsidiary routes on Lake Athabasca, Great Slave Lake and Great Bear River and Lake total more than 800 miles.

Post and Broadcasting (1982). There were 54 post offices. The CBC northern service operated radio stations at Yellowknife, Inuvik, Frobisher Bay and Rankin Inlet. Virtually all communities of 150 or over were receiving television in 1982 *via* satellite. Telephone service is provided by common carriers to nearly all communities in the Northwest Territories. Those few communities without service have high frequency or very high frequency radios for emergency use.

EDUCATION AND WELFARE

Education. In 1982–83 the Government of the Northwest Territories operated 71 schools with 731 teachers. In addition, one public school district operated at Yellowknife, one Roman Catholic separate school district at Yellowknife, and one school society operated a school at Rae-Edzo. The total enrolment was 12,760 in 1983, of whom about 65% were Inuit (Eskimos) and Indians. Three large and 4 small residences accommodate 400 students. Free correspondence courses are available to any pupil in a settlement where appropriate instruction is not available. There is a full range of courses available in the school system: academic, industrial arts, home economics, commercial, technical and occupational training. The continuing and special education programme provides courses and financial assistance to residents who have left the school system or are taking post high school training.

Health. In 1980 there were 7 hospitals in the Territories, 4 operated by the territorial government (Yellowknife, Hay River, Frobisher Bay and Fort Smith) and 3 operated by the federal government. Thirty-nine nursing stations, 6 health stations and 8 health centres were in operation.

Welfare. Welfare services are provided by professional social workers. Facilities included (1978) 5 children's receiving homes, 2 homes for the aged and 1 transient centre.

Books of Reference

Annual Report of the Department of Indian Affairs and Northern Development, 1974–75
Annual Report of the Government of the Northwest Territories, 1980
Boyle, E., and Sprudz, A., *Arctic Cooperatives, Canada 1965–68*
Dawson, C. A., *The New North-West.* Toronto, 1947
MacKay, D., *The Honorable Company.* Toronto, 1949

YUKON TERRITORY

HISTORY. Formerly part of the North-West Territory, Yukon was joined to the Dominion as a separate territory in 1898.

AREA AND POPULATION. The Yukon Territory is situated in the extreme north-western section of Canada and comprises 531,844 sq. km. The census population in 1981 was 23,153; 1982 (estimate), 24,811. Principal centres are Whitehorse (capital), 16,771; Faro, 1,972; Watson Lake, 1,348; Dawson City, 1,251; Mayo-Elsa, 891.

Vital statistics, see p. 267.

Religion, see p. 284.

CONSTITUTION AND GOVERNMENT. The Yukon Territory was constituted a separate territory in June 1898. It is governed by a 5-member Executive Council (Cabinet) appointed from among the 16-member elected Legislative Assembly. The members are elected for a 4-year term. The seat of government is at Whitehorse. A federally appointed Commissioner has the final signing authority for all legislation passed by the Assembly.

Commissioner: Doug Bell.

Flag: Vertically green, white, blue, in the proportions 2 : 3 : 2, charged in the centre with the arms of the Territory.

The legislative authority of the Assembly includes direct taxation, education, property and civil rights, territorial civil service, municipalities and generally all matters of local or private nature. All other major administration including Crown lands, income tax, natural resources and particularly that which requires the spending of large sums of money, is federally controlled.

ECONOMY

Planning. Proposed economic development of the Yukon Territory into the 1980s envisages a total expenditure of about $5,000m. Confirmed development projects include the construction of a natural gas pipeline through the territory to deliver Alaskan natural gas from Prudhoe Bay to the continental 48 states. Another confirmed project is the reconstruction and paving of 482 km of highways through south-western Yukon. Roads subject to this are the Haines Road and the Alaska Highway. In 1981 the opening of 5 new mines in eastern Yukon, the extension of railways from southern Canada and Alaska and a proposed aluminium smelter were under consideration but by 1983 many of these plans were shelved, because of the recession..

Finance. The territorial revenue and expenditure (in Canadian $) for fiscal years ended 31 March was:

	1977–78	1978–79	1979–80	1980–81
Revenue	84,483,715	98,904,000	88,442,000	122,252,300
Expenditure	78,340,311	95,228,000	103,839,000	125,442,200

ENERGY AND NATURAL RESOURCES

Minerals. Mining remains the main industry. Lead, zinc, copper, silver and gold are the chief minerals. Production figures for year ending 31 Dec. 1981 (provisional) in tonnes were: Lead, 51,651 kg; zinc, 86,486 kg; silver, 172 kg; copper, 9,129 kg; gold, 3,046 kg. The value of mining production sales in 1981 was approximately $298m.

There were 209 land use permits issued during the 1979–80 fiscal year including 93 for government projects, 62 private road construction, 20 campsite and staging areas, 17 for quarrying, 13 for woods operations and 4 for research projects.

Forestry. The forests are part of the great Boreal forest region of Canada which stretches from the east coast of Canada into Alaska and north well above the Arctic Circle. Vast areas are covered by coniferous stands in the southern portion of Yukon with white spruce and lodgepole pine forming pure stands on wet sites and in northern aspects. Deciduous species form pure stands or occur mixed with conifers throughout forest areas.

The forest industry is small with approximately 18 active saw-mills and timber operations. Most are portable 'bush' mills although a few semi-permanent mills have been established. There are also 33 commercial cutters of fuelwood the production of which ranges from 10 cords (36 cu. metres) to 200 cords (724·9 cu. metres). Production in 1980–81 was 650,000 cu. ft (3·25m. bd ft) of lumber, 1,095,000 cu. ft (13,695 cords) of cordwood and 131,000 cu. ft of round timber including poles, pilings, building logs, mine timbers and fenceposts.

Game and Furs. The country abounds with big game, such as moose, goat, caribou, mountain sheep and bear (grizzly and black). In 1979–80, 52,800 pelts were taken for a market value of $917,048. Lynx was the most valuable fur and made up 45% of the total harvest bringing in $416,458 in revenues.

TOURISM. In 1982, 365,000 tourists visited Yukon and spent $51m.

COMMUNICATIONS

Roads. The Alaska Highway and its side roads connect Yukon's main communities with Alaska and the provinces and with adjacent mining centres. Interior roads connect the mining communities of Elsa (silver–lead), Faro (lead–zinc–silver). Tungsten (tungsten) and mineral exploration properties (lead–zinc and tungsten) north of Ross River. The Dempster Highway north of Dawson City connects with Inuvik, on the Arctic coast; this highway, the first public road to be built to the Arctic ocean, was opened in Aug. 1979. The Carcross–Skagway road was opened in May 1979, providing a new access to the Pacific ocean. There are 4,230 km of roads in the Territory, of which about 380 km are paved. The rest are all-weather gravel.

Railways. The 176-km White Pass and Yukon Railway connected Whitehorse with year-round ocean shipping at Skagway, Alaska, but was suspended in 1982.

Aviation. Commercial airlines provide regular services between Whitehorse, Watson Lake, Edmonton and Vancouver. Regularly scheduled air services extend from Whitehorse to interior communities of Faro, Mayo, Dawson City, Old Crow, Ross River, Watson Lake, MacMillan Pass, Juneau with connecting service to Anchorage, Seattle, Fairbanks and other points in Alaska. There are several commercial bush plane operations for charter service.

Shipping. Some goods are shipped into the Territory by air or *via* the Alaska Highway, but most are containerized in Vancouver and brought up the coast by ship to Skagway, Alaska. The containers are then taken by train from Skagway to Whitehorse, and then hauled by truck to the outlying communities. Many of these trucks then return to Whitehorse hauling ore to be shipped out. Some goods are transported within the Territory by air. Although navigable, the rivers are no longer used for shipping.

Post and Broadcasting. There are 2 radio stations in Whitehorse and 13 low-power relay radio transmitters operated by CBC. There are also 12 cable-TV channels in Whitehorse, TV channels in Whitehorse and private cable operations in Faro (provided by Canadian Satellite), Dawson City and Watson Lake. Live CBC national television is provided by the Anik satellite to virtually every community in the Territory. All telephone and telecommunications in the Territory are provided by NorthwesTel, a subsidiary of Canadian National Telecommunications. Almost all pole lines have been replaced with microwave transmission.

Newspapers. In 1984 there were 2 newspapers, each 3 days a week, in Whitehorse. Faro has a two-monthly newspaper.

EDUCATION AND WELFARE

Education In Sept. 1982, the Territory had 26 schools with 4,849 pupils. In addition to the courses given in the Yukon Vocational and Technical Centre, the Yukon offers a limited number of post-secondary courses through the University of Alberta, University of Victoria and Red Deer College. A Yukon Teacher Education Programme started in 1977 to train local residents to obtain Bachelor of Education degrees in Education and a Teaching Certificate. The course is conducted by the University of British Columbia. The Government provides financial assistance to students requiring further education elsewhere.

Health. The health care system provides all residents with the care demanded by illness or accident. The federal government operates 1 general hospital at Whitehorse, 3 cottage hospitals, 2 nursing stations, with a total of 150 beds, 11 health centres and 4 health stations. The territorial government also operates a medical evacuation programme to send patients to Edmonton or Vancouver for specialized treatment not available in the Territory.

Books of Reference

Annual Report of the Commissioner.
Yukon Territorial Government, *Statistical Review.*
Berton, P., *Klondike.* Toronto, 1963
McCourt, E., *The Yukon and Northwest Territories.* Toronto, 1969

CAPE VERDE

República de Cabo Verde

Capital: Praia
Population: 296,093 (1980)
GNP per capita: US$300 (1980)

HISTORY. The Cape Verde Islands were discovered in 1460 by Diogo Gomes, the first settlers arriving in 1462. In 1587 its administration was unified under a Portuguese governor. The colony became an Overseas Province in 1951.

On 30 Dec. 1974 Portugal transferred power to a transitional government headed by the Portuguese High Commissioner. Full independence was granted on 5 July 1975.

AREA AND POPULATION. Cape Verde is situated in the Atlantic Ocean 620 km WNW of Senegal and consists of 10 islands and 5 islets. Praia is the capital. The islands are divided into 2 groups, named Barlavento (windward) and Sotavento (leeward). The total area is 4,033 sq. km (1,557 sq. miles). The population (census, 1980) was 296,093.

The areas and populations (1980, census) of the islands are:

	Sq. km	Population		Sq. km	Population
Santo Antão	779	43,198	Maio	269	4,103
São Vicente [1]	227	41,792	São Tiago	991	145,923
São Nicolau	388	13,575	Fogo	476	31,115
Sal	216	6,006	Brava	67	6,984
Boa Vista	620	3,397			
			Sotavento	1,803	188,125
Barlovento	2,230	107,968			
			Total	4,033	296,093

[1] Includes Santa Luzia which is uninhabited.

The main towns are Mindelo on São Vicente (28,797, 1970 census) and Praia on São Tiago, the capital (37,500, 1980 census).

CLIMATE. The climate is arid, with a cool dry season from Dec. to June and warm dry conditions for the rest of the year. Rainfall is sparse, rarely exceeding 5″ (127 mm) in the northern islands or 12″ (304 mm) in the southern ones. There are periodic severe droughts. Praia. Jan. 72°F (22·2°C), July 77°F (25°C). Annual rainfall 10″ (250 mm).

CONSTITUTION AND GOVERNMENT. The Constitution adopted on 12 Feb. 1981 removed all reference to possible future union with Guinea-Bissau, and the *Partido Africano da Independencia de Cabo Verde*, founded 20 Jan. 1981, became the sole legal party. The legislature consists of a unicameral People's National Assembly of 56 members elected for 5 years by universal suffrage; it elects the President, who appoints and leads a Council of Ministers. Elections were held on 7 Dec. 1980.

President: Aristides Maria Pereira (assumed office 5 July 1975; re-elected 1980).
In Jan. 1983 the cabinet comprised:
Prime Minister: Maj. Pedro Verona Rodrigues Pires.
Foreign Affairs: Col. Silvino Manuel da Luz. *Defence:* Col. Honorio Chantre. *Interior:* Col. Julio de Carvalho. *Economy and Finance:* Cmdt Osvaldo Lopez da Silva. *Education and Culture:* José Araújo. *Transport and Telecommunications:* Herculano Vieira. *Health and Social Affairs:* Dr Ireneu Gomes. *Justice:* Dr David Hopffer Cordeiro Almada. *Rural Development:* Cmdt João Pereira Silva. *Housing and Public Works:* Tito Livio Santos de Oliveira Ramos.

National flag: Horizontally yellow over green, with a vertical red strip in the hoist charged slightly above the centre with a black star surrounded by a wreath of maize, and beneath this a yellow clam shell.

Local government: The 2 *distritos* (Barlavento and Sotavento) are sub-divided

327

into 14 *conçelhos* – Ribeira Grande, Paúl, Porto Novo (these 3 covering Santo Antão island), São Vicente (including Santa Luzia), São Nicolau, Sal, Boa Vista, Maio, Praia, Santa Catarina, Tarrafal, Santa Cruz (these 4 covering Sao Tiago island), Fogo and Brava.

DEFENCE

Army. The Popular Revolutionary Armed Forces had a strength of 1,100 in 1983. There is also a paramilitary People's Militia.

Navy. There are 3 fast gunboats and 2 coastal patrol craft.

Air Force. An embryo air force has been formed with two An-26 twin-turboprop transports and about 25 personnel.

INTERNATIONAL RELATIONS

Membership. Cape Verde is a member of UN, OAU and an ACP state of EEC.

ECONOMY

Budget. In 1981, the budget included revenue of 944m. escudos Caboverdianos and expenditure, 1,082m.

Currency. *Escudo Caboverdianos.* In March 1984, 117·45 *Escudo* = £1.

Banking. The Banco de Cabo Verde is the bank of issue and commercial bank, with branches at Praia, Mindelo and Espargos (Sal).

ENERGY AND NATURAL RESOURCES

Electricity. Production in 1972 amounted to 6·8m. kwh; capacity, 6,032 kw.

Minerals. Salt is obtained on the islands of Sal, Boa Vista and Maio. Volcanic rock (pozzolana) is mined for export.

Agriculture. Mostly confined to irrigated inland valleys, the chief crops (production, 1981, in tonnes) are: Sugar-cane, 15,000; bananas, 9,000; cassava, 6,000, sweet potatoes, 5,000; maize, 3,000 and coffee. Bananas and coffee are mainly for export.
Livestock (1982): 70,000 goats, 13,000 cattle, 24,000 pigs and 6,000 asses.

Fisheries. About 8,000 tonnes of tuna and 200 tonnes of lobsters are caught annually.

COMMERCE. Imports in 1980 totalled 2,742·3m. escudos Caboverdianos, of which (1978) 33% came from Portugal; exports in 1980 totalled 170·5m. escudos Caboverdianos, of which (1978) 42% went to Portugal, 18% to Angola and 11% to UK. In 1978 32% by value of exports were fish, 17% salt and 10% bananas.
Total trade of Cape Verde with UK (British Department of Trade returns, in £1,000 sterling):

	1980	1981	1982	1983
Imports to UK	207	22	49	122
Exports and re-exports from UK	1,047	1,260	2,068	1,245

COMMUNICATIONS

Roads. There were 1,287 km of roads in 1976. In 1981, there were 4,000 private cars and 1,343 commercial vehicles.

Aviation. Amilcar Cabral International Airport, on Sal, is a major refuelling point on flights to Africa and South America, with 34,133 passengers in 1980.

Shipping. The main ports are Mindelo and Praia. In 1980 the ports handled 244,856 tonnes of imports and 110,558 tonnes of exports. In 1981, the merchant marine comprised 20 vessels of 10,793 GRT.

Broadcasting. The private broadcasting stations are operating on shortwaves. There were (1982) 42,000 radio receivers and (1981) 1,739 telephones.

Cinemas. In 1972 there were 6 cinemas with 2,800 seats.

JUSTICE, RELIGION, EDUCATION AND WELFARE

Justice. There is a network of People's Tribunals, with a Supreme Court in Praia.

Religion. In 1980, over 96% of the population were Roman Catholic.

Education. In 1980 there were 50,778 pupils and 1,436 teachers at 436 primary schools, 6,500 pupils and 207 teachers at 15 preparatory schools, 2,216 pupils and 141 teachers at 3 secondary schools, and 679 students and 40 teachers at a technical school. In 1978 there were 198 students and 32 teachers in a teacher-training college and about 500 students were at foreign universities.

Health. In 1977 there were 23 hospitals and dispensaries with 640 beds; there were also 43 doctors, 2 dentists, 6 pharmacists and 148 nursing personnel.

DIPLOMATIC REPRESENTATIVES

Of Great Britain in Cape Verde
Ambassador: P. L. O'Keeffe, CVO (resides in Dakar).

Of Cape Verde in the USA (3415 Massachusetts Ave., NW, Washington, D.C., 20007)
Ambassador: José Luis Fernandes Lopes.

Of the USA in Cape Verde (Rua Hoji Ya Yenda 81, Praia)
Ambassador: John M. Yates.

Of Cape Verde to the United Nations
Ambassador: Dr Amaro Alexandre da Luz.

Books of Reference

Annuario Estatistico de Cabo Verde. Praia. Annual
Andrade, E., *The Cape Verde Islands: From Slavery to Modern Times.* Dakar, 1973
Carreira, A., *The People of the Cape Verde Islands.* London, 1982
Lobban, R., *The Cape Verde Islands.* New York, 1974

CAYMAN ISLANDS

Capital: George Town
Population: 18,285 (1982)

HISTORY. The islands were discovered by Columbus on 10 May 1503 and were ceded (with Jamaica) to Britain in 1670. Grand Cayman was settled in 1734 and the other islands in 1833. They became a separate Crown Colony on 4 July 1959, administered by the same governor as Jamaica until the latter's independence on 6 Aug. 1962 when they received their own Administrator.

AREA AND POPULATION. Cayman Islands consist of Grand Cayman, Little Cayman and Cayman Brac. Situated in the Caribbean Sea, about 200 miles NW of Jamaica. Area, 100 sq. miles (260 sq. km). Census population of 1979, 16,677. Grand Cayman (population 15,000), 22 miles long, 4–8 miles broad; capital: George Town (population 7,617). Little Cayman, 10 miles long, 1 mile broad. Cayman Brac, 12 miles long and 1¼ miles wide. Total population of the lesser islands, 1,677. Vital statistics (1982): Births, 339; marriages, 211; deaths, 108.

CLIMATE. The climate is tropical maritime, with a cool season from Nov. to March and temperatures some 10°F warmer for the remaining months. Rainfall averages 56″ (1,400 mm) a year at George Town. Hurricanes may be experienced between July and Nov.

CONSTITUTION AND GOVERNMENT. A new Constitution came into force in Aug. 1972. The Legislative Assembly consists of the Governor, not less than 2 nor more than 3 official members, and 12 elected members.

The Executive Council consists of 3 official members appointed from among the official members of the Legislative Assembly, and 4 elected members elected by the elected members of the Assembly with the Governor as Chairman.

Governor: G. Peter Lloyd, CMG, CVO.
Flag: British Blue Ensign with the arms of the Colony on a white disc in the fly.

ECONOMY

Budget. Revenue 1982, CI$47·92m.; expenditure, CI$45,967,000. Public debt (31 Dec. 1982), CI$8·5m.; total reserves, CI$21·93m.

Banking. Thirty-three commercial banks and trust companies hold category 'A' licences, which permit the holders to offer services to the public. Barclays Bank International has branches at George Town.

INDUSTRY AND TRADE

Industry. Finance and tourism are the main industries.

Commerce. Exports (estimate), 1982 (f.o.b.), totalled CI$2m. and included primary turtle products. Imports, estimate (c.i.f.), CI$110m.; principally foodstuffs, manufactured items, textiles, building materials, automobiles and petroleum products.

Tourism. Tourism is now the chief industry of the islands and in recent years 19 hotels have been completed. There were 279,599 visitors in 1982.

COMMUNICATIONS

Roads. There were (1982) about 110 miles of road and over 8,600 motor vehicles.

Aviation. Cayman Airways provides regular services between Grand Cayman and Miami, Houston, Jamaica and the Turks and Caicos Islands. Republic Airways provide a daily service between Miami and Grand Cayman. CAL provides a regular inter-island service. Air Jamaica also provides services between Grand Cayman and Jamaica.

Shipping. Motor vessels ply regularly between the Cayman Islands, Jamaica and Florida. Shipping registered at George Town, 548 vessels (31 Dec. 1982). An oil transhipment terminal on Little Cayman handled 74·3m. bbls in 1980.

Post and Broadcasting. There were 5,316 telephones in 1982 and there are 2 broadcasting stations in the islands.

Newspapers. The *Caymanian Compass* is published 5 days a week, *The Cayman Islands Sun* twice a week and *The Cayman Pilot* is published weekly.

JUSTICE, RELIGION, EDUCATION AND WELFARE

Justice. There is a Grand Court, sitting 6 times a year at George Town under a Chief Justice. 2 Summary Courts (one civil and one criminal) sit at other times.

Religion. There are Anglican, Roman Catholic, Presbyterian and other Christian communities represented in the islands.

Education. In 1982 there were 9 government primary schools with 1,126 pupils, 6 private elementary schools with 945 pupils and 4 private secondary schools with 222 pupils. Post-primary education at the Government High School and the government Middle School and private schools was attended by 2,147 pupils. There was also a private institution for further education and a government school for special educational needs with 26 pupils.

Health. In 1982 there was a fully-equipped general hospital with 7 doctors, a dental clinic, 6 district clinics and a hospital in Cayman Brac.

Book of Reference

Annual Report, 1982. Cayman Islands Government, 1983

CENTRAL AFRICAN REPUBLIC

Capital: Bangui
Population: 2·52m. (1983)
GNP per capita: US$300 (1980)

République centrafricaine

HISTORY. Central African Republic became independent on 13 Aug. 1960, after having been one of the 4 territories of French Equatorial Africa (under the name of Ubangi Shari) and from 1 Dec. 1958 a member state of the French Community. In Jan. 1959 the 4 republics formed an 'economic, technical and customs union'. A new Constitution was adopted by a special congress of the *Mouvement pour l'évolution sociale de l'Afrique noire* on 4 Dec. 1976. It provided for the country to be a parliamentary democracy and to be known as the Central African Empire. President Bokassa became Emperor Bokassa I. The Emperor was overthrown in a *coup* on 20–21 Sept. 1979 and the empire was abolished. On 15 March 1981 David Dacko was again elected President but was deposed on 1 Sept. 1981 by General André Kolingba.

AREA AND POPULATION. The Central African Republic is bounded north by Chad, east by Sudan, south by Zaïre and Congo, and west by Cameroon. The area covers 624,977 sq. km; its population in 1983 was 2·52m. (35% urban). The capital is Bangui (387,100 inhabitants in 1981): other towns, Berberati (95,000) and Bouar (51,000).

The principal ethno-linguistic groups are the Banda (27·4% of the population), Baya (24·4%), Mandja (21·2%), Ubangi (12·2%), Sara (7%), Mbum (6%) and Fertit (2·4%).

CLIMATE. A tropical climate with little variation in temperature. The wet months are May, June, Oct. and Nov. Bangui. Jan. 80°F (26·5°C), July 77°F (25°C). Annual rainfall 61″ (1,525 mm). Ndele. Jan. 83°F (28·3°C), July 77°F (25°C). Annual rainfall 57″ (1,417 mm).

CONSTITUTION AND GOVERNMENT. Following the bloodless *coup* of 1 Sept. 1981, all legislative and executive power was held by a 23-member Military Committee for National Recovery (CMRN), ruling through an appointed Council of Ministers. The constitution and political parties were suspended.

In June 1983 the Council of Ministers included:

Chairman of CMRN, Head of State and Government, Minister of Defence and Veterans' Affairs: Gen. André Kolingba (assumed office 1 Sept. 1981).

Ministers of State: Lieut.-Col. Jean-Louis Gervil Yambala *(Trade and Industry),* Gen. Sylvestre Bangui *(Economy and Finance),* Lieut.-Col. Alphonse Gombadi *(Agriculture and Stockbreeding),* Lieut.-Col. Thomas Mapouka *(Energy and Water Resources).*

Minister of Foreign Affairs, Planning and International Co-operation: Lieut. Michel Salle.

National flag: Four horizontal stripes of blue, white, green, yellow; over all in the centre a vertical red strip, and in the canton a yellow star.

Local Government: Central African Republic is divided into 14 prefectures, 2 'economic prefectures' and the autonomous commune of Bangui (the capital).

The national language is Sango, used as a *lingua franca* throughout the country; French is the official language.

DEFENCE. Selective national service for a 2-year period is in force.

Army. The Army consists of about 2,000 men, comprising an infantry battalion, with supporting engineer, signals and transport companies. Equipment includes 4 T-55 tanks, 4 BRDM-2 reconnaissance vehicles and 10 Ferret scout cars. There is also a 1,500-strong paramilitary force.

Navy. The naval force has 9 river patrol craft and (1984) 85 personnel.

Air Force. The Air Force has 12 Argentine-built 1A 58 Pucara attack aircraft, 2 Rallye Guerrier armed light aircraft, 1 twin-jet Caravelle, 1 DC-4 and 4 C-47 transports, 2 Reims-Cessna 337, 10 Aermacchi AL.60 and 6 Broussard liaison aircraft, 1 Alouette and 4 H-34 helicopters. It also maintains and operates the Corvette twin-jet VIP aircraft. Personnel strength (1984) about 300.

INTERNATIONAL RELATIONS

Membership. Central African Republic is a member of UN, OAU and an ACP state of EEC.

ECONOMY

Planning. The third 5-year development plan (1976–80) provided for expenditure of 23,623m. francs CFA.

Budget. The budget for 1980 balanced at 25,447m. francs CFA.

Currency. The unit of currency is the *franc CFA* with a parity of 50 *francs CFA* to 1 French *franc*.

Banking. The *Banque des Etats de l'Afrique Centrale* is the bank of issue.

ENERGY AND NATURAL RESOURCES

Electricity. Production in 1980 totalled 64m. kwh (94% hydro-electric).

Minerals. 250,000 carats of gem diamonds were mined in 1980.

Agriculture. Over 90% of the working population is occupied in subsistence agriculture. The main crops (production 1981, in 1,000 tonnes) are cassava, 1,021; groundnuts, 125; bananas, 82; plantains, 62; millet, 50; maize, 40; cotton, 23; coffee, 17; rice, 15.
  Livestock (1982): Cattle, 1·3m.; goats, 988,000; sheep, 87,000; pigs, 140,000.

Forestry. The extensive hardwood forests, particularly in the south-west, provide mahogany, obeche and limba for export. Production (1979) 2·9m. cu. metres.

INDUSTRY AND TRADE

Industry. The small industrial sector includes factories producing cotton fabrics (3m. metres in 1978) and radios.

Commerce. Imports and exports in 1m. francs CFA:

	1978	1979	1980
Imports	12,776	14,816	17,009
Exports	16,182	16,937	24,384

In 1980, France took 52% of exports and provided 61% of imports. Of all exports, coffee comprised 27% (by value), diamonds 25%, timber 29% and cotton 7%.
  Total trade of Central African Republic with UK (British Department of Trade returns, in £1,000 sterling):

	1978	1979	1980	1981	1982	1983
Imports to UK	798	954	1,466	782	878	902
Exports and re-exports from UK	553	808	738	373	576	535

COMMUNICATIONS

Roads. In Dec. 1976 there were 21,950 km of roads and (1974) there were 9,100 passenger cars and 3,900 commercial vehicles in use.

Railways. There are no railways, but a proposal exists (1979) for an 800 km line (1,435 mm gauge) from Bangui through Cameroon and Congo to connect with the Trans-Gabon railway at Belinga.

Aviation. There is an international airport at Mpoko, near Bangui, and Air Centrafrique operates extensive internal services to several airstrips.

Post and Broadcasting. There were (1977) 200 television and 80,000 radio receivers and (1973) 5,000 telephones.

Cinemas. In 1971 there were 8 cinemas.

JUSTICE, RELIGION, EDUCATION AND WELFARE

Justice. The Criminal Court and Supreme Court are situated in Bangui. There are 7 civil courts throughout the country.

Religion. About 57% of the population follow animist beliefs, 20% are Roman Catholic, 15% Protestant and 8% Moslem.

Education. The University of Bangui was founded in 1970 and had 1,489 students in 1980. In 1978 there were 241,201 pupils at primary schools and 46,084 at secondary schools; technical schools held 2,523 students, while (1976) 615 were at the 2 teacher-training establishments.

Health. In 1977 there were 61 hospitals and dispensaries with 2,983 beds and 106 doctors, 3 dentists, 16 pharmacists, 142 midwives and 1,200 nursing personnel.

DIPLOMATIC REPRESENTATIVES

Of Central African Republic in Great Britain
Ambassador: (Vacant).

Of Great Britain in Central African Republic
Ambassador: B. Sparrow (resides in Yaoundé).

Of Central African Republic in the USA (1618 22nd St., NW, Washington, D.C. 20008)
Ambassador: Christian Lingama-Toleque.

Of the USA in Central African Republic (Ave. President Dacko, Bangui)
Chargé d'Affaires: Douglas A. Hartwick.

Of Central African Republic to the United Nations
Ambassador: Simon Pierre Kibanda.

CHAD

République du Tchad

Capital: N'djaména
Population: 4·97m. (1983)
GNP per capita: US$120 (1980)

HISTORY. France proclaimed a protectorate over Chad on 5 Sept. 1900, and in July 1908 the territory was incorporated into French Equatorial Africa. It became a separate colony March 1920, and in 1946 one of the four constituent territories of French Equatorial Africa. On 1 Jan. 1959 Chad became an autonomous republic within the French Community and achieved full independence on 11 Aug. 1960, although the northern prefecture of Borkou-Ennedi-Tibesti remained under French military administration until 1965.

Conflicts between the central government of President François (later Ngarta) Tombalbaye and secessionist groups, particularly in the Moslem north and centre of Chad, began in 1965 and continued despite attempts at reconciliation. President Tombalbaye was assassinated on 13 April 1975 following an Army *coup d'etat.* A Supreme Military Council of 9 members, under the Presidency of Gen. Felix Malloum, ruled until 29 Aug. 1978, when the Council was dissolved and Malloum formed a new government of 'national unity'. After further fighting an accord was finally signed in Lagos on 21 Aug. between representatives of 11 warring factions. A 22-member Transitional Government of National Unity (GUNT) was formed on 10 Nov. under the Presidency of Goukouni Oueddei. The reconciliation agreement broke down on 25 April 1980, and civil war continued until June 1982 when the *Forces Armées du Nord* (FAN) led by Hissène Habré gained control of the country.

AREA AND POPULATION. Chad is bounded west by Cameroon, Nigeria and Niger, north by Libya, east by Sudan and south by Central African Republic. Area, 1,284,000 sq. km; its population in 1983 was estimated at 4·97m. (census 1975, 4,029,917). The capital is N'djaména, formerly Fort Lamy with 303,000 inhabitants in 1979, other large towns being Moundou (66,000), Sarh (65,000) and Abéché (54,000).

Préfecture	sq. km	Population 1979	Capital
Borkou-Ennedi-Tibesti	600,350	88,000	Faya-Largeau
Biltine	46,850	175,000	Biltine
Ouaddaï	76,240	347,000	Abéché
Batha	88,800	354,000	Ati
Kanem	114,520	200,000	Mao
Lac	22,320	139,000	Bol
Chari-Baguirmi	82,910	676,000	N'djaména
Guéra	58,950	207,000	Mongo
Salamat	63,000	107,000	Am Timan
Moyen-Chari	45,180	524,000	Sarh
Logone Oriental	28,035	307,000	Doba
Logone Occidental	8,695	295,000	Moundou
Tandjilé	18,045	302,000	Laï
Mayo-Kabbi	30,105	684,000	Bongor

More than 100 different languages and dialects are spoken. The largest ethnic group is the Sara of southern Chad. Arabic serves as a common language throughout the semi-tropical (Sahelian) centre and the Saharan north.

CLIMATE. A tropical climate, with adequate rainfall in the south, though Nov. to April are virtually rainless months. Further north, desert conditions prevail. N'djaména. Jan. 75°F (23·9°C), July 82°F (27·8°C). Annual rainfall 30″ (744 mm).

CONSTITUTION AND GOVERNMENT. Hissène Habré was sworn in as President on 21 Oct. 1982 and a 31-member government was appointed.

The official language is French.

National flag: Three vertical strips of blue, yellow, red.

Local Government: The 14 *préfectures* are divided into 53 *sous-préfectures.*

DEFENCE

Army. A new national army, the Forces Armées Nationales Tchadiennes (FANT) was formed in Dec. 1982. In 1984 the strength was 4,000 and there was a paramilitary force of 6,000.

Air Force. The Air Force has at least 1 Noratlas, 1 VIP Caravelle, 3 C-54 and 9 C-47 transports, 4 Reims-Cessna F337 light aircraft, 2 Turbo-Porters, 2 Broussard communications aircraft and about 14 Puma and Alouette III helicopters. Personnel about 200.

INTERNATIONAL RELATIONS

Membership. Chad is a member of UN, OAU and is an ACP state of EEC.

ECONOMY

Budget. The budget for 1983 balanced at 36,000m. francs CFA of which defence was 7,000m.

Currency. The unit of currency is the *franc CFA* with a parity value of 50 *francs CFA* to 1 French *franc.*

Banking. The *Banque des Etats de l'Afrique Centrale* is the bank of issue, and the principal commercial banks are the *Banque de Développement du Tchad* and the *Banque Tchadienne de Crédit et de Dépôts.*

ENERGY AND NATURAL RESOURCES

Electricity. Production (1980) amounted to 64m. kwh.

Oil. The oilfield in Kanem préfecture has been linked by pipeline to a new refinery at Laï (in Tandjilé).

Minerals. Salt (about 4,000 tonnes per annum) is mined around Lake Chad, and deposits of uranium, gold and bauxite are to be exploited.

Agriculture. In 1981, 82·7% of the 1,738,000 work force were occupied in agriculture, forestry and fishing. Cotton growing (in the south) and animal husbandry (in the central zone) are the most important industries. Production (1981, in 1,000 tonnes) was: Millet, 580; unginned cotton, 195; groundnuts, 110; cassava, 188; rice, 47.

Livestock (1982): Cattle, 3·8m.; sheep, 2·4m.; goats, 2·4m.; chickens, 3·3m.

Fisheries. Fish production from Lake Chad and the Chari and Logone rivers, was estimated at 115,000 tonnes in 1979.

TRADE (in 1m. francs CFA):

	1974	1975	1976	1977
Imports	20,859	28,325	27,593	11,255
Exports	9,053	10,103	14,861	6,862

Total trade with UK (British Department of Trade returns, in £1,000 sterling):

	1979	1980	1981	1982	1983
Imports to UK	240	279	12	3	8
Exports and re-exports from UK	612	361	375	1,082	2,244

COMMUNICATIONS

Roads. In 1976 there were 30,725 km of roads, of which only 240 km are surfaced. In 1977 there were 7,636 private cars and 9,668 commercial vehicles.

Aviation. There is an international airport at N'djaména, from which UTA and Air

Afrique run 4 flights per week to Paris; there are also flights to Douala, Bangui and Kinshasa. Air Tchad operates internal services to 12 secondary airports.

Post and Broadcasting. In 1978 there were 3,850 telephones and (1981), 70,000 radios in use.

Cinemas. In 1977 there were 13 cinemas with 12,400 seats.

JUSTICE, RELIGION, EDUCATION AND WELFARE

Justice. There are criminal courts and magistrates courts in N'djaména, Moundou, Sarh and Abéché, with a Court of Appeal situated in N'djaména.

Religion. The northern and central parts of the country are predominantly Moslem (52% of the total population) and the southern part is mainly animist (43%) or Christian (5%).

Education. In 1977 there were 229,191 pupils in primary schools, 18,382 in secondary schools, 649 in technical schools and 549 students in teacher-training establishments. The University of Chad (founded 1971) at N'djaména had (1980) 800 students.

Health. There were 33 hospitals with 3,353 beds in 1977; 100 doctors, 4 dentists, 13 pharmacists, 98 midwives and 1,000 nursing personnel.

DIPLOMATIC REPRESENTATIVES

Of Chad in Great Britain
Chargé d'Affaires: Issa Abbas Ali.

Of Great Britain in Chad
Ambassador: M. F. Daly.

Of Chad in the USA (2002 R. St., NW, Washington, D.C., 20009)
Chargé d'Affaires: Mahamat Ali Adoum.

Of the USA in Chad (Ave., Felix Eboue, N'djaména)
Ambassador: J. Peter Moffat.

Of Chad to the United Nations
Ambassador: Ramadane Barma.

Books of Reference

Aperçu sur le Tchad. Publication of the President. 2nd ed. N'djaména, 1973
L'essentiel sur le Tchad. Publication of the President. 2nd ed. N'djaména, 1972
Thompson, V.. and Adloff, R., *Conflict in Chad.* London and Berkeley, 1981
Westebbe, R., *Chad: Development Potential and Constrains.* Washington, D.C., 1974

CHILE

República de Chile

Capital: Santiago
Population: 11·7 (1983)
GNP per capita: US$2,160 (1980)

HISTORY. The Republic of Chile threw off allegiance to the crown of Spain, constituting a national government on 18 Sept. 1810, finally freeing itself from Spanish rule in 1818.

AREA AND POPULATION. Chile is bounded north by Peru, east by Bolivia and Argentina, and south and west by the Pacific ocean.

Many islands to the west and south belong to Chile, including Easter Island (Isla de Pascua; 63·9 sq. miles), discovered in 1722. The coastline is about 2,650 miles in length; the average width of the country, 120 miles. Area, 756,626 sq. km or 292,135 sq. miles.

In 1940 Chile declared, and in each subsequent year has reaffirmed, its ownership of the sector of the Antarctic lying between 53° and 90° W. long.; and asserted that the British claim to the sector between the meridians 20° and 90° W. long. overlapped the Chilean by 27°. Five Chilean bases were established in Antarctica in 1947, 1948, 1951 and 1962. A law promulgated 21 July 1955 put the Intendente of the Province of Magallanes in charge of the 'Chilean Antarctic Territory'.

Three thinly-settled southern provinces of Magallanes, Chiloé and Aysén and the northern provinces of Arica and Iquique are known as 'free zones', which implies that all commodities imported into those areas from abroad are not subject to all national import duties.

The total population at the census in 1970 was 8,884,768. Census (1982) 11,275,440. Estimate (1983) 11,682,260.

The areas of the 13 regions and their populations (census, 1982) were as follows:

Region	Sq. km	Census 1982	Capital	Population 1980
Taracapá	58,073	273,427	Iquique	101,561
Antofagasta	125,306	341,203	Antofagasta	161,226
Atacama	78,268	183,071	Copiapó	39,942[2]
Coquimbo	39,647	419,178	La Serena	61,889[2]
Aconcagua	16,109	1,204,693	Valparaíso	226,280[4]
Metropolitan	13,808	4,294,938	Santiago	3,853,275[3]
Liberador	18,193	584,989	Rancagua	128,733
Maule	30,518	723,224	Talca	128,363
Biobio	36,823	1,516,552	Concepción	198,824[5]
Araucanía	31,760	692,924	Temuco	155,683
Los Lagos	67,090	843,430	Puerto Monti	62,748[2]
Aisén	108,998	65,478	Coihaique	...
Magallanes	132,033	132,333	Punta Arenas	67,600[1]

[1] 1975. [2] 1970. [3] Metropolitan Area 3,992,500.
[4] Metropolitan Area 620,180 including Viña del Mar.
[5] Metropolitan Area 518,950 including Talcahuano.

Vital statistics (1971): Revised birth rate 27·6 per 1,000 population; death rate, 8·4; marriage rate, 8·6; infantile mortality rate, 70·9 per 1,000 live births.

The great majority of the population is mixed or *mestizo*, due to the free inter-marriage between the early Spaniards and women of indigenous tribes; language and culture remain of European origin. The indigenous inhabitants are of 3 branches: The *Fuegians*, mostly nomadic, living in or near Tierra del Fuego; the *Araucanians* in the valleys or on the western slopes of the Andes; the *Changos*, who inhabit the northern coast region and work as labourers and fishermen.

Other large towns (census, 1982) are: Viña del Mar (272,814), Talcahuano (185,744), Arica (116,115), Chillán (115,811), Valdivia (109,484) and Osarno (71,000 in 1975).

CLIMATE. With its enormous range of latitude and the influence of the Andean Cordillera, the climate of Chile is very complex, ranging from extreme aridity in the north, through a Meditarranean climate in Central Chile, where winters are wet and summers dry, to a cool temperate zone in the south, with rain at all seasons. In the extreme south, conditions are very wet and stormy. Santiago. Jan. 67°F (19·5°C), July 46°F (8°C). Annual rainfall 15″ (375 mm). Antofagasta. Jan. 69°F (20·6°C), July 57°F (14°C). Annual rainfall 0·5″ (12·7 mm). Valparaiso. Jan. 64°F (17·8°C), July 53°F (11·7°C). Annual rainfall 20″ (505 mm).

CONSTITUTION AND GOVERNMENT. The Marxist coalition government of President Salvador Allende Gossens was ousted on 11 Sept. 1973 by the 3 Armed Services and the *Carabineros* (para-military police). These forces formed a government headed by a Junta of the 4 Commanders-in-Chief. Gen. Augusto Pinochet Ugarte, Commander-in-Chief of the Army, took over the presidency. President Allende was killed on the day of the *coup*.

Marxist parties were outlawed and all political activities banned. The new Government assumed wide-ranging powers but the 'state of siege' ended in March 1978. A new Constitution was approved by 67·5% of the voters on 11 Sept. 1980 and came into force on 11 March 1981. It provided for a return to democracy after a minimum period of 8 years. Gen. Pinochet would remain in office during this period after which the Junta would nominate a single candidate for President.

For details of the 1925 Constitution and earlier political history *see* THE STATES-MAN'S YEAR-BOOK 1975–76, p. 808.

The capital is Santiago, founded on 12 Feb. 1541.

National flag: Two horizontal bands, white, red, with a white star on blue square in top sixth next to staff.

National anthem: Dulce patria, recibe los votos (words by E. Lillo, 1847; tune by Ramón Carnicer, 1828).

The following is a list of the presidents since 1942:

Juan Antonio Rios, 1 April 1942–27 June 1946 (died).
Alfredo Duhalde (Acting), 27 June–3 Aug. 1946 (resigned).
Vice-Admiral Vicente Merino Bielech (Acting), 3 Aug.–3 Nov. 1946.
Gabriel Gonzalez Videla, 3 Nov. 1946–3 Nov. 1952.
Carlos Ibáñez del Campo, 3 Nov. 1952–3 Nov. 1958.
Jorge Alessandri Rodriguez, 3 Nov. 1958–3 Nov. 1964.
Eduardo Frei Montalva, 3 Nov. 1964–3 Nov. 1970.
Salvador Allende Gossens, 3 Nov. 1970–11 Sept. 1973 (deposed).

President of the Republic: Gen. Augusto Pinochet Ugarte.

Local Government. For the purposes of local government the Military Junta in pursuance of its policy of administrative decentralization, has divided the republic into 13 regions (12 and Greater Santiago). Each Region is presided over by a *Governador,* while the provinces (40) included in it are in charge of an *Intendente* who represents the central government. The provinces are divided into municipalities under an *alcalde* (mayor). All these officials are appointed by the President.

DEFENCE. Military service is for a period of 2 years at the age of 19 (Army and Navy only). Ex-conscripts are liable to 12 years' service in the active reserve and 13 in the second reserve.

Army. The Army is organized in 2 armoured, 8 cavalry and 24 infantry regiments; 10 artillery and 7 engineer battalions; and 1 helicopter-borne ranger unit. Equipment includes 150 M-4A3 and 21 AMX-30 tanks, 75 light tanks and 200 armoured cars. Strength (1984) 53,000 (30,000 conscripts) and 240,000 reserves.

Navy. The principal ships of the Chilean Navy are as follows:

Completed	Name	Standard displacement Tons	Armour Belt In.	Turrets In.	Guns	Shaft horsepower	Speed Knots
			Cruisers				
1947	Latorre [2]	8,200	3–4	3–5	7·6 in.	100,000	33·0
1938	O'Higgins [1]	10,000	4	3–5	15·6 in.;8·5-in.	100,000	32·5

[1] Ex-*Brooklyn,* purchased from USA in 1951 with sister ship *Prat* (ex-*Nashville*) discarded in 1981. *O'Higgins* used as an alongside accommodation ship since she was damaged by grounding in Aug. 1974 was refitted during 1978 and later recommissioned.
[2] Ex-*Göta Lejou,* purchased from Sweden in 1971.

The British guided missile armed destroyer *Norfolk,* 5,440 tons standard, completed in 1970, was purchased in 1982 and re-named *Prat* on transfer.

There are 2 modern diesel powered patrol submarines (British 'Oberon' class), 1 old *ex*-US submarine, 6 destroyers (2 British built and 4 old *ex*-US), 5 frigates (2 modern British 'Leander' class, *Condell* and *Lynch,* and 3 old *ex*-US destroyer escort transports), 2 fast missile craft, 4 torpedo boats, 6 patrol vessels, 12 coastal patrol craft, 1 submarine support vessel, 2 amphibious transports, 2 landing ships, 13 landing craft, 1 survey ship, 5 transports, 1 training ship, 1 antarctic patrol ship, 3 oilers, 2 floating docks and 4 tugs.

Naval personnel in 1984 totalled 28,600 (2,000 officers, 24,000 ratings, 2,600 marines).

Air Force. Approximate current strength is 15,000 personnel, with 85 first-line and 150 second-line aircraft, divided among 12 groups, each comprising 1 squadron, within 4 combat and support wings. Groups 1 and 12 have twin-jet A-37Bs, from a total of 34 acquired for light strike/reconnaissance duties. Group 3 is equipped for general duties with about 12 UH-1H Iroquois and Puma helicopters. Group 4 has 20 Mirage 50 fighters. Group 5 has 14 Twin Otters for light transport and survey duties. Group 6 operates 3 civil-registered Learjet 35 and King Air 100 aircraft on photo survey duties. Group 7 received 15 F-5E Tiger II fighter-bombers and 3 F-5F trainers. Groups 8 and 9 are also fighter-bomber units, with a total of 30 Hunter F.71s, *ex*-RAF FGA.9s, and T.72s. Group 10 is a transport wing, with 2 C-130H Hercules and 5 DC-6Bs. Group 11 has 9 twin-turboprop Beech 99A instrument/navigation trainers. Three *ex*-RAF Canberra PR.9s have been acquired for reconnaissance duties. Training aircraft include piston-engined Piper Dakota and T-35 Pillan basic trainers and T-37 jets. The A-37Bs and T-37s are being replaced by up to 60 Spanish-built CASA C-101BB Aviojets, most of which are being assembled in Chile.

INTERNATIONAL RELATIONS

Membership. Chile is a member of the UN, OAS and LAIA (formerly LAFTA).

ECONOMY

Budget. In 1982 revenue was US$3,309·7m. and expenditure, US$3,603·3m.

Currency. In Jan. 1960 a system came into force based on the *escudo* (equivalent of 1,000 *pesos*), the *centésimo* (10 *pesos*) and the *milésimo (1 peso*). On 29 Sept. 1975 the currency reverted to *pesos* with a value of 1,000 escudos to the new peso.

In March 1984 there were 129·47 *pesos* = £1 and 88·14 *pesos* = US$1.

Banking. Notes in circulation and deposits in currency were 318,134m. pesos at 31 Dec. 1982; total deposits in the commercial banks stood at 237,388m. pesos (1982).

Commercial banks, since Feb. 1983, must maintain cash reserves of 60% of all sight deposits and 20% of time deposits over 30 days.

Inflation has fluctuated as follows: 31·2% (1980), 9·5% (1981), 20·7% (1982).

Weights and Measures. The metric system has been legally established in Chile since 1865, but the old Spanish weights and measures are still in use to some extent.

ENERGY AND NATURAL RESOURCES

Electricity. In 1982 production of electricity was 11,977·8m. kwh.

Oil. Petroleum was discovered in 1945 in the southern area of Magallanes with an output of 2,484,212 bbls of crude oil and 2,505,000 cu. metres of natural gas in 1982.

Minerals. The wealth of the country consists chiefly in its minerals, especially in the northern provinces of Atacama and Tarapacá.

Copper is the most important source of foreign exchange (about 48% of exports) and government revenues (over 30%). The copper industry's output in 1982 was 1,240,700 tonnes. Exports during 1982 were valued at US$1,731m.

Nitrate of soda is found in the Atacama deserts. Exports were US$75m. in 1982. Production was 574,550 tonnes in 1982. Iodine is a by-product: 1982 production totalled 2,609 tonnes. The use of solar evaporation as a means of reducing costs has developed the production of potassium salts as an additional by-product.

Iron ore, of which high-grade deposits estimated at over 1,000m. tons exist in the provinces of Atacama and Coquimbo, has overtaken nitrate as Chile's second mineral. Production in 1982 was 6,469,670 tonnes.

Coal reserves exceed 2,000m. tons, partially low in thermal unit. Net 1982 production was 973,482 tonnes.

In 1982 other minerals include molybdenum (20,043 tonnes, pure), zinc (5,505 tonnes), manganese (16,123 tonnes), lead (1,489 tonnes).

Agriculture. Agriculture and forestry contribute one-twelfth of the national product, although one-third of the population take part in it. Total area of land being exploited (census of 1968) was 52·4m. hectares; 14·9% for agriculture, 26·7% for pasture, 28·8% for forest; 29·6% is desert or unproductive.

Some principal crops were as follows:

Crop	Area sown, 1,000 hectares 1981–82	Production, 1,000 quintals 1981–82	Crop	Area sown, 1,000 hectares 1981–82	Production, 1,000 quintals 1981–82
Wheat	374	6,505	Potatoes	77	8,416
Oats	68	1,176	Beans	122	1,625
Barley	58	1,179	Lentils	39	158
Maize	107	4,841	Peas	10	74
Rice	37	1,312	Sugar-beet	22	9,630

There were in 1955 over 300 large farms, each with more than 12,250 acres, while 500,000 peasants live on less than 4 acres per family. The military government has opted in most cases to increase the number of settlements with access to individual property. The process was completed in early 1979 with some 24,000 property titles issued, a large proportion of which were in co-operative schemes.

Production of animal products in 1982 was (in 1,000 tonnes): Cattle, 194·6; sheep, 14·9; pork, 57·7; poultry, 113. Eggs, 1,100m.; milk, 1,140m. litres.

Livestock (1982): Cattle, 3·8m.; horses, 430,000; asses, 28,000; sheep, 6·3m.; goats, 600,000; pigs, 1·2m.; poultry, 26m.

Forestry. According to the Forestry Institute, by late 1978, there were 277,944 hectares of artificial forests from Maule to Magallanes, the most important species being the pine (*pinus radiata*) which covers 640,000 hectares. Eucalyptus and poplar cover some 72,000 hectares. Native species of importance amounted to 9m. hectares in 1978.

Production during 1982 amounted to about 164m. in. of sawn timber. Exports of forestry products in 1982 were valued at US$122m.

Fisheries. Chile's catch of fish and shellfish in 1982 was 3·8m. tonnes; shellfish, 269,000 tonnes. Exports of seafood in 1982 were US$374m., of which fishmeal accounted for US$256m.

INDUSTRY AND TRADE

Industry. A nationally-owned steel plant operates from Huachipato, near Concepción. Output, 1982, 478,000 tonnes of steel ingots. Cellulose and wood-pulp are two industries which are rapidly developing; in 1982, 542,400 tonnes of cellulose were produced.

Labour. In Sept. 1982 the 'economically active' numbered 3m. Professional and 'white-collar' workers numbered 909,000; agriculture employed 540,000; manufacturing, 404,000; mining, 54,600; construction, 118,600, and transport, 196,100. Trade unions began in the middle 1880s.

Commerce. Imports and exports in US$1m.:

	1977	1978	1979	1980	1981	1982
Imports	2,221	2,917	4,200	5,821	7,368	3,580
Exports	2,171	2,480	3,800	4,818	4,000	3,798

In 1982 imports (in US$1m.) from USA, were valued at 916; Venezuela, 260; Brazil, 258; Japan, 230; Federal Republic of Germany, 214; Argentina, 150; Spain, 150; France, 125; UK, 76; Italy, 73.

In 1982 the principal imports were (in US$1m.): Fuels, 615; chemicals, 434; industrial equipment, 429; transport equipment, 252; spares, 198, and live animals and foodstuffs, 190. The principal exports in 1982 were (in US$1m.): Copper, 1,731; paper and pulp, 230; iron ore, 158; timber, 122; nitrate, 75.

Total trade between Chile and UK for 5 years (British Department of Trade returns, in £1,000 sterling):

	1979	1980	1981	1982	1983
Imports to UK	131,218	126,273	87,939	111,206	107,644
Exports and re-exports from UK	45,640	55,741	62,227	56,897	43,520

Tourism. There were 307,495 foreign visitors in 1982.

COMMUNICATIONS

Roads. In 1978 there were in Chile 75,420 km of highways. There were in 1982 (estimate), 850,000 automobiles, 185,000 goods vehicles and 22,500 buses.

Railways. The total length of state railway lines was (1981) 6,302 km, including 907 km electrified, of broad- and metre-gauge. In 1980 the railways carried 14·7m. tonnes and 9·4m. passengers. Further electrification is in progress between Concepción and Puerto Monti (600 km). An underground railway in Santiago was opened in Sept. 1975.

Aviation. There are 7 international airports, 16 domestic airports and about 300 landing grounds. Chile is served by 19 commercial air companies (2 Chilean). In 1980, 325,800 passengers were carried into and out of Chile on international services; 265,400 passengers were carried on internal routes.

Shipping. The mercantile marine had, in 1982, 60 ships of over 100 tons (825,076 DWT) but most of the fleet operates under flags of convenience. Valparaiso is the chief port. The free ports of Magallanes, Chiloé and Aysén serve the southern provinces. Chilean ports handled 45·6m. tons in 1982. There are 2,185 km of navigable rivers.

Post and Broadcasting. There are 1,486 post offices and agencies. The length of telegraph lines in 1971 was 12,870 km. In 1982 there were 595,108 (Santiago, 364,527) telephones in use.

A chain of wireless stations along the coast for shore-to-ship transmission is operated by the Navy. At the end of 1974 there were some 150 commercial broadcasting stations. Three television stations are operated by the Universities and there is a national television station using NTSC 525 line colour standards. On 9 Aug. 1968 the satellite station at Longovilo, 50 miles south-west of Santiago, was inaugurated to cover transmissions (including colour) from the USA and Europe. In 1977 there were 2m. radio receivers and (1976) 710,000 television receivers.

Cinemas (1975). Cinemas numbered 196; 61 of them are in Santiago.

Newspapers (1975). There were 80 daily newspapers.

JUSTICE, RELIGION, EDUCATION AND WELFARE

Justice. There are a High Court of Justice in the capital, 12 courts of appeal distributed over the republic, tribunals of first instance in the departmental capitals and second-class judges in the sub-delegations. The police force had (1975) about 27,000 officers and men; it is organized and regulated by the Ministry of Defence.

Religion. The Roman Catholic religion was disestablished in 1925; it remains, however, a national Church in a state wherein 89·5% of the population are Catholics. There are 1 cardinal-archbishop, 5 archbishops, 22 bishops and 2 vicars apostolic. Latest estimates show 6·7m. Roman Catholics, 880,500 Protestants and 25,000 Jews.

Education. Education is in 3 stages: Basic (6–14 years), Middle (15–18) and University (19–23). Enrolment (1981): 2,139,319 pupils in the basic schools, 392,940 pupils in the middle schools and 161,809 pupils in technical schools; teachers in 1980 numbered 66,354 in basic, 24,387 in middle and 4,176 in technical schools.

University education is provided in the state university (founded in 1842), the Catholic University at Santiago (1888), the University of Concepción (1919), the Catholic University at Valparaíso (1928), the Universidad Técnica Federico Santa María at Valparaíso (1930), the Universidad Técnica del Estado (1952), Universidad Austral, Valdivia (1954) and Universidad del Norte, Antofagasta (1957) with a total student population of 118,978 in 1981.

Health. In 1982 there were 205 hospitals, 296 health centres and 888 emergency posts. State-owned hospitals had 33,879 beds; private hospitals, 4,088. Total expenditure (1982), US$1,000m.

DIPLOMATIC REPRESENTATIVES

Of Chile in Great Britain (12 Devonshire St., London, W1N 2FS)
Ambassador: Francisco Orrego.

Of Great Britain in Chile (La Concepción 177, Casilla 72-D, Santiago)
Ambassador: J. K. Hickman, CMG.

Of Chile in the USA (1732 Massachusetts Ave., NW, Washington, D.C., 20036)
Ambassador: Enrique Valenzuela.

Of the USA in Chile (Agustinas 1343, Santiago)
Ambassador: James D. Theberge.

Of Chile to the United Nations
Ambassador: Manuel Trucco.

Books of Reference

Statistical Information: The Instituto Nacional de Estadística (Santiago), was founded 17 Sept. 1847. *Director General:* Sergio Chaparro Ruiz. Principal publications: *Anuario Estadística* and the bi-monthly *Estadística Chilena.*
    Other sources are: *Geografía Económica,* by the Corporación de Fomento de la Production, and *Boletín Mensual,* by the Banco Central de Chile.

Allende, S., *Chile's Road to Socialism.* Harmondsworth, 1973
De Vylder, S., *Allende's Chile.* CUP, 1976
Empresa Periodística, *Diccionario biográfico de Chile.* 8th ed. Santiago, 1952
Horne, A., *Small Earthquake in Chile. A Visit to Allende's South America.* London, 1972
Lasaga, M., *The Copper Industry in the Chilean Economy. An Econometric Analysis.* Aldershot, 1981
MacEoin, G., *No Peaceful Way: Chile's Struggle for Dignity.* New York, 1974
Petras, J., and Merino, H. Z., *Peasants in Revolt: A Chilean Case Study.* Univ. of Texas Press, 1972
Pinochet de la Barra, O., *La Antártido Chilena.* Santiago de Chile, 1948
Porteous, J. D., *The Modernization of Easter Island.* Victoria, B.C., 1981

PEOPLE'S REPUBLIC OF CHINA

Capital: Peking (Beijing)
Population: 1,008m. (1982)
GNP per capita: US$290 (1980)

Zhonghua Renmin Gonghe Guo

HISTORY. In the course of 1949 the Communists obtained full control of the mainland of China, and in 1950 also over most islands off the coast, including Hainan.

On 1 Oct. 1949 Mao Zedong (Tse-tung) proclaimed the establishment of the People's Republic of China.

AREA AND POPULATION. China is bounded north by the USSR and Mongolia, east by Korea, the Yellow Sea and the East China Sea, with Hong Kong and Macao as enclaves on the south-east coast; south by Vietnam, Laos, Burma, India, Bhután and Nepál; west by India, Pakistan, Afghánistán and the USSR. China is composed of 22 provinces (this figure includes Taiwan), 5 autonomous regions originally entirely or largely inhabited by national minorities (owing to the immigration of Han Chinese the original nationality is sometimes outnumbered, *e.g.,* by 10 to 1 in Inner Mongolia), namely Inner Mongolia, Xinjiang–Uygur, Guangxi–Zhuang, Ningxia–Hui, Tibet and 3 centrally controlled municipalities (Peking, Shanghai, Tianjin).

The capital is Peking (Beijing).

See map in THE STATESMAN'S YEAR-BOOK, 1968–69.

The total area is estimated at 9,597,000 sq. km (3,704,400 sq. miles).

The latest census took place in July 1982 when the population was 1,008·2m.

Population densities vary from 10 per sq. km in the West to over 100 per sq. km in the East.

Estimates of persons of Chinese race outside China, Taiwan and Hong Kong in 1980 varied from 15m. to 20m. China permits the emigration of a limited number of persons to Hong Kong annually. There were 70,456 in 1979.

A number of widely divergent varieties of Chinese are spoken. The official 'Modern Standard Chinese' is based on the dialect of North China, and the Government is promoting its use generally. The ideographic writing system is uniform throughout the country, and has undergone systematic simplification. In 1958 a phonetic alphabet (*Pinyin*) was devised to transcribe the characters, and on 1 Jan. 1979 this was officially adopted for use in all texts in the Roman alphabet (*see also* Post and Broadcasting, p. 353). The decision of press agencies to use the *Pinyin* transcription led to the supersession of the system previously widely used in English-speaking countries (Wade). Starting with THE STATESMAN'S YEAR-BOOK, 1979–80 new names were introduced in *Pinyin*. In this edition with a few exceptions *Pinyin* forms are used for all names. *Pinyin* forms are not used in Taiwan.

From 1949 to 1955 the country was divided into 6 large administrative regions. This system was terminated in 1955, but in 1961 was revived in the form of 6 regional Party Bureaux. These ceased to function during the Cultural Revolution. The table below shows the Provinces, Autonomous Regions and Government-controlled Municipalities grouped regionally. The cities shown in brackets are the seats of the former regional Party Bureaux.

	Area (in 1,000 sq. km)	Population Census 1953 (in 1,000)	Census 1982 (in 1m.)	Capital
North-Eastern Region (Shenyang)				
Heilongjiang	463·6	11,897	32·67	Harbin
Jilin	187·0	11,290	22·56	Changchun
Liaoning	151·0	18,545	35·72	Shenyang
Northern Region (Peking)				
Hebei	202·7	35,985	53·00	Shijiazhuang
Inner Mongolia (Aut. Region) [1]	450·0	6,100	19·27	Hohhot
Peking (municipality) (Beijing)	17·8	2,768	9·23	—
Shanxi	157·1	14,314	25·30	Taiyuan
Tianjin (municipality)	4·0	2,694	7·76	
Eastern Region (Shanghai)				
Shandong	153·3	48,877	74·42	Jinan
Jiangxi	164·8	16,773	33·18	Nanchang
Jiangsu	102·2	41,252	60·52	Nanking (Nanjing)
Shanghai (municipality)	5·8	6,204	11·89	—
Anhui	139·9	30,344	49·67	Hefei
Zhejiang	101·8	22,866	38·88	Hangzhou
Fujian	123·1	13,143	25·93	Fuzhou
Taiwan	36·0	7,591	18·27	Taibei
Central-Southern Region (Wuhan)				
Henan	167·0	44,215	74·42	Zhengzhou
Hubei	187·5	27,790	47·80	Wuhan
Hunan	210·5	33,227	54·01	Changsha
Guangdong	231·4	34,770	59·30	Canton (Guangzhou)
Guangxi–Zhuang (Aut. Region)	220·4	19,561	36·42	Nanning
South-Western Region (Chongqing)				
Sichuan	569·0	62,304	99·71	Chengdu
Guizhou	174·0	15,037	38·55	Guiyang
Yunnan	436·2	17,473	32·55	Kunming
Tibet (Aut. Region)	1,221·6	1,273	1·83 [2]	Lhasa
North-Western Region (Xian)				
Shaanxi	195·8	15,881	28·90	Xian
Gansu [1]	530·0 }	12,928	{ 19·57	Lanzhou
Ningxia–Hui (Aut. Region) [1]	170·0 }		{ 3·90	Yinchuan
Qinghai	721·0	1,677	3·90	Xining
Xinjiang–Uygur (Aut. Region)	1,646·8	4,874	13·08	Urumqi

[1] Boundaries restored to approximately the pre-1970 position in 1979. [2] Estimate, 1980.

Large towns, with population in 1977: Chongqing, 6m.; Canton (Guangzhou), 5m.; Shenyang, 4·4m.; Wuhan, 3·5m.; Nanjing, 3m.; Harbin, 2·1m.

Manchuria, a term not used by the Chinese, is roughly identical with the 3 provinces of the N.E. Region.

Tibet. For events before the revolt of 1959 *see* THE STATESMAN'S YEAR-BOOK, 1964–65, under TIBET. After the revolt was suppressed the Preparatory Committee for the Autonomous Region of Tibet (set up 1955) took over the functions of local government, led by its Vice-Chairman, the Banqen Lama, in the absence of its Chairman, the Dalai Lama, who had fled to India in 1959. In Dec. 1964 both the Dalai and Banqen Lamas were removed from their posts and on 9 Sept. 1965 Tibet became an Autonomous Region. 301 delegates were elected to the first People's Congress, of whom 226 were Tibetans and in 1968 a Revolutionary Committee was established to administer the Region. This gave way to a People's Government in Aug. 1979. The Banqen Lama was re-elected to the Standing Committee of the Chinese People's Political Consultative Conference in March 1978—he became one of its Vice-Chairmen in July 1979—and has made several appeals to the Dalai Lama to return to China. In 1982 the population was reported to be 1,892,393. 4·25m. Tibetans live outside Tibet, in China, and in India and Nepál. Chinese efforts to modernize Tibet include irrigation, road-building and the establishment of light industry: more than 260 small and medium-sized factories and mines have been set up producing electric power, coal, building materials, lumber, textiles, chemicals and animal products.

In 1979, 1·6m. were engaged in agriculture, including 0·5m. nomadic herdsmen.

Agricultural communes were first introduced in 1965; by 1975 it was announced that 99% of villages had formed them. In 1975 Tibet became self-sufficient in grain for the first time. There are now 21,000 km of highways, and air routes link Lhasa with Chengdu and Xian.

It was officially admitted in Peking in 1980 that the administration of Tibet had been badly conducted hitherto. The borders were opened for trade with neighbouring countries, and agricultural reforms allowing for more individual autonomy within the commune system were announced.

Efforts are being made to revive Tibetan culture as part of China's new liberal policy towards minorities. Buddhist monasteries, closed in the Cultural Revolution, are now re-opening. Circulation of the Tibetan-language *Xizang Daily* now totals 38,000. In 1980 there were 6,000 primary schools, about 100 secondary schools and 4 colleges. There were more than 6,000 medical workers and nearly 500 hospitals, with a total of 4,000 beds.

The Dalai Lama, *My Land and My People* (ed. D. Howarth). London, 1962
Dawa Norbu, *Red Star Over Tibet*. London, 1974
Jäschke, H. A., *A Tibetan–English Dictionary*. London, 1934
Mele, F., *Tibet*. Paris, 1975
Richardson, H. E., *Tibet and its History*. OUP, 1962
Shakabpa, T. W. D., *Tibet: A Political History*. Yale Univ. Press, 1967
Thubten, J. N., and Turnbull, C., *Tibet: Its History, Religion and People*. Harmondsworth, 1972

CLIMATE. Most of China has a temperate climate but, with such a large country, extending far inland and embracing a wide range of latitude as well as containing large areas at high altitude, many parts experience extremes of climate, especially in winter. Most rain falls during the summer, from May to Sept., though amounts decrease inland. Peking (Beijing). Jan. 24°F (–4·4°C), July 79°F (26°C). Annual rainfall 24·9″ (623 mm). Chongging. Jan. 45°F (7·2°C), July 84°F (28·9°C). Annual rainfall 43·7″ (1,092 mm). Shanghai. Jan. 39°F (3·9°C), July 82°F (27·8°C). Annual rainfall 45·4″ (1,135 mm). Tianjin. Jan. 24°F (–4·4°C), July 81°F (27·2°C). Annual rainfall 21·5″ (533·4 mm).

CONSTITUTION AND GOVERNMENT. On 21 Sept. 1949 the 'Chinese People's Political Consultative Conference' met in Peking, convened by the Chinese Communist Party. The Conference adopted a 'Common Programme' of 60 articles and the 'Organic Law of the Central People's Government' (31 articles). Both became the basis of the Constitution adopted on 20 Sept. 1954 by the 1st National People's Congress, the supreme legislative body. The Consultative Conference continued to exist after 1954 as an advisory body. Both bodies stopped functioning in the Cultural Revolution. The People's Congress was revived in 1975 and the Consultative Conference in 1978, when Deng Xiaoping was elected as its head. In 1979 it had 1,734 members.

The 1954 Constitution was both a political and an organizational document. It indicated the steps to be taken to build a 'socialist' society, defined the structure and functions of government organs and the rights and duties of citizens appropriate in the period of transition to 'socialism'.

In Jan. 1975 the 4th National People's Congress approved a constitution, under which China was defined as a 'socialist state of the dictatorship of the proletariat'. The 1975 Constitution was a simpler document than its predecessor emphasizing the role of politics in society, especially the thought of Mao, but giving fewer organizational details. In March 1978 the 5th National People's Congress adopted a new constitution of 60 articles which revives several of the provisions of the 1954 constitution dropped in the 1975 document and eliminates much of the latter's innovatory radicalism. More administrative detail is given. Provisions (Art.45) for freedom of speech and publication were withdrawn in 1980.

A new Constitution was adopted in 1982. It defines 'socialist modernisation' as China's basic task. Its most striking change is the restoration of the post of State President (*i.e.* Head of State).

The National People's Congress is the highest organ of state power. It can amend the Constitution, elects and has power to remove from office the highest State dignitaries, decides on the national economic plan, etc. The Congress elects a *Standing Committee* (which supervises the State Council) and the State President, currently Li Xiannian.

The Constitution provides that the Congress be elected for a 5-year term and should meet once a year. It is composed of deputies elected on a constituency basis by direct secret ballot. Any voter, and certain organizations, may nominate candidates. Nominations may exceed seats by 50–100%. 2,978 deputies were elected to the 6th Congress in June 1983.

Under the streamlining of the government structure which is currently taking place (1983), the number of Ministries, Commissions and other agencies of the State Council has been reduced from 98 to 52. There are now 33 Ministries and 7 Commissions under the State Council. Zhao Ziyang remains Premier. The number of Vice-Premiers was reduced from 13 to 2 (Wanli and Yao Yilin) and two more (Li Peng and Tian Jiyun) were added in 1983. Many of the former Vice-Premiers have taken the newly-created post of State Councillor, of which there are 10. Some of these are also Ministers, *i.e.* Wu Xueqian *(Foreign Affairs)*, Chen Muhua *(Foreign Trade and Economic Relations)*, Zhang Aiping *(Defence)*, Wang Bingqian *(Finance)* and Song Ping heads the Economic Commission and Fang Yi the Scientific and Technological Committee.

Since 1970 when China began to emerge from the isolation of the Cultural Revolution, her diplomatic relations have expanded considerably. On 25 Oct. 1971 the UN voted for the People's Republic to take over the China seat from the Nationalists by 76 votes to 35 with 17 abstentions. US President Nixon visited China in Feb. 1972 and in 1973 'liaison offices' were opened in the capitals of the two countries. On 1 Jan. 1979 the US recognized the Peking government as the sole legal government of China and diplomatic relations were established. In Jan.–Feb. 1979 Deng Xiaoping paid an official visit to USA. On 12 Aug. 1978 China and Japan signed a 10-year treaty of peace and friendship (ratified 22 Oct. 1978). China has announced that it will not renew its treaty of friendship with the USSR which expired in 1980.

State emblem: 5 stars above Peking's Gate of Heavenly Peace, surrounded by a border of ears of grain entwined with drapings, which form a knot in the centre of a cogwheel at the base; the colours are red and gold.

National flag: Red with a large star and 4 smaller stars all in yellow in the canton.

National anthem: 'March of the Volunteers' composed 1935 by Tien Han. (Replacing the 1978 version).

De facto power is in the hands of the Communist Party of China, which had 39·6m. members in 1982. There are 8 other parties, all members of the Chinese People's Political Consultative Conference. Communist Party officials hold key positions in government organs and most social, economic and cultural organizations. In mid-1966 the Party Chairman, Mao Tse-tung, launched the 'Great Proletarian Cultural Revolution' to eradicate 'revisionism' and numerous Party and State officials were dismissed. The Cultural Revolution can be taken to have terminated by April 1969 when the long-delayed 9th Party Congress was convened, although it was not officially declared to have been brought to a 'victorious conclusion' until Aug. 1977. The 9th Congress adopted a new Party Constitution which proclaimed the leading rôle of the Party in the State and designated Lin Biao as Chairman Mao's successor. A factional dispute developed, however, centred on Lin Biao (killed in an air crash in Mongolia in Sept. 1971) and in Aug. 1973 the 10th Party Congress adopted amendments to the Party Constitution, removing references to Lin Biao and the succession to Chairman Mao, and electing a new Central Committee which appointed a new Politburo and Standing Committee. In Jan. 1975 the Central Committee appointed as a vice-chairman of the Politburo Deng Xiaoping, former Party Secretary-General dismissed during the Cultural Revolution. In April 1976 a 'radical' faction in the Politburo engineered a second dismissal of Deng from all his posts, and Hua Guofeng was appointed First Party

Vice-Chairman as well as Premier. On the death of Mao Tse-tung on 9 Sept. 1976 Hua became Party Chairman. In Oct. 1976 the 'radical' faction (now identified and excoriated as the 'Gang of Four': Mao's widow, Jiang Qing, Zhang Chunqiao, Wang Hongwen and Yao Wenyuan) were placed under arrest. At the 11th Party Congress in Aug. 1977 a new Party Constitution was adopted, and a new Central Committee was elected. Changes in the leadership saw the elimination of the 'radical' faction and a second reinstatement of Deng to his Party and government posts. In Feb. 1980 Liu Shaoqi, former head of state denounced by Mao as a traitor, was posthumously reinstated, and 4 Politburo members of Maoist persuasion were dismissed. Hua Guofeng was replaced as Premier by Zhao Ziyang in Sept. 1980. The 'Gang of Four', along with Chen Boda (a former secretary of Mao), were brought to trial only on 20 Nov. 1980. At the same time the trial opened of five generals accused of complicity with Lin Biao in an attempt to seize power. All 10 accused were found guilty on 25 Jan. 1981. Suspended death sentences were passed on Jiang Qing and Zhang Chunqiao. Hua Guofeng was removed from the Party Chairmanship in June 1981 and replaced by Hu Yaobang. At the 12th Party Congress (Sept. 1982), the posts of Chairman and Vice-Chairman of the CPC were abolished, and greater stress laid on the position of General Secretary of the Central Committee. The members of the Standing Committee of the Politiburo elected at the 12th Party Congress are Hu Yaobang *(General Secretary)*, Ye Jianying, Deng Xiaoping *(Chairman of the Military Commission of the Central Committee)*, Zhao Ziyang, Li Xiannian and Chen Yun *(Chairman of the Central Commission for Discipline Inspection)*. Other members of the Politiburo are: Wan Li, Xi Zhongxun, Wang Zhen, Wei Guoqing, Ulanhu, Fang Yi, Deng Yingchao, Li Desheng, Yang Shangkun, Yang Dezhi, Yu Qiuli, Song Renqiong, Zhang Tingfa, Hu Qiaomu, Nie Rongzhen, Ni Zhifu, Xu Xiangqian, Peng Zhen. A new central Party body—the Central Advisory Commission, chaired by Deng Xiaoping— was elected by the Congress.

Local Government. There are 4 administrative levels: (1) Provinces, Autonomous Regions and the municipalities directly administered by the Government; (2) prefectures and autonomous prefectures (*zhou*); (3) counties, autonomous counties and municipalities; (4) towns and rural communes. A policy began in 1982 of replacing rural communes by townships as the basic unit of rural local government. Local government after 1968 was in the hands of Revolutionary Committees. From 1 Jan. 1980 these were replaced by elected People's Congresses and People's Governments. These exist at provincial, county and commune levels and in national minority autonomous prefectures, but not in ordinary prefectures which are just agencies of the provincial government. Up to county level Congresses are elected directly.

DEFENCE. China is divided into 11 military regions. The military commander also commands the air, naval and civilian militia forces assigned to each region.

Conscription is compulsory but for organizational reasons selective: only some 10% of potential recruits are called up. Service is 3 years with the Army, 4 years with the Air Force and 5 years with the Navy.

Marks of rank were abolished in 1965 but uniforms distinguish officers from other ranks.

Army. The Army (PLA: 'People's Liberation Army') is divided into main and local forces. Main forces, administered by the military regions in which they are stationed but commanded by the Ministry of Defence, are available for operation anywhere and are better equipped. Local forces concentrate on the defence of their own regions. The Army consists of 185 divisions including 40 artillery, 11 armoured, 118 infantry, 3 airborne and 85 local divisions. Total strength in 1984 was 3·25m.

The security forces, including the armed police, number some 300,000.

The People's Militia consists of the Armed Militia of up to 6m. strength, the Ordinary Militia of several million, unarmed but with some basic military training, and which includes the Urban Militia, and the Civilian Production and Construction Corps of 4m.

Navy. The steady new construction programme of all classes of warships in modernized yards, many with advanced nuclear and/or missile capability, has been maintained. Chinese naval strength is an important factor in the present and future balance of power in the eastern hemisphere.

Present strength comprises 2 nuclear powered submarines, 1 submarine with ballistic missile tubes, 110 patrol submarines, 18 destroyers, 26 frigates, 20 patrol escorts, 220 missile boats, 21 large patrol boats, 30 fast patrol craft, 380 fast gunboats, 260 fast torpedo boats, 23 ocean minesweepers, 80 mine warfare craft, 120 river patrol craft, 35 coastal patrol craft, 27 survey and research ships, 36 supply ships, 13 support ships, 27 oilers, 6 boom defence vessels, 2 repair ships, 40 landing ships. 470 landing craft, 3 salvage ships, 2 icebreakers, 43 tugs, 375 coast and river defence craft and 525 vessels of the Maritime Militia.

Active personnel in 1984 exceeded 298,000 officers and men, including 30,000 in the naval air force and over 28,000 marines.

Main naval bases: Qingdao (North Sea Fleet); Shanghai (East Sea Fleet); Tsamkong (Zhanjiang) (South Sea Fleet).

The largely land-based naval air force of over 700 aircraft, primarily for defensive and anti-submarine surface, includes MiG-17, MiG-19 and MiG-15 fighters, some 130 Il-28 torpedo bombers, Madge flying boats, Hound Mi4 helicopters and communications and transport aircraft.

Air Force. In 1983 the Air Force was estimated at 5,300 front-line aircraft, organized in over 100 regiments of jet-fighters and about 12 regiments of tactical bombers, plus reconnaissance, transport and helicopter units. Each regiment is made up of 3 or 4 squadrons (each 12 aircraft), and 3 regiments form a division.

Equipment is predominantly Russian in design and includes about 250 J-7 (MiG-21), 3,000 J-6 (MiG-19) and 400 J-5 (MiG-17) interceptors and fighter-bombers, with about 550 H-5 (Il-28) jet-bombers, about 120 H-6 Chinese-built copies of the Soviet Tu-16 twin-jet strategic bomber, and a few piston-engined Tu-4 (Soviet copy of Boeing B-29) strategic bombers, plus several hundred Q-5 twin-jet fighter-bombers (known in the west as 'Fantan'), evolved from the MiG-19. Under development is a new fighter designated J-8 (known in the west as 'Finback'). Transport aircraft include about 300 Y-5 (An-2), Y-8 (An-12), An-24/26, 100 Li-2, 30 Il-14 and a few three-turbofan Trident fixed-wing types, plus 300 Z-5 (Mi-4) and Mi-8 helicopters. The MiG fighters and Antonov transports have been manufactured in China, initially under licence, and other types have been assembled there, including several hundred JJ-5 (2-seat MiG-17) trainers.

Total strength (1983) about 490,000, including 220,000 in air defence organization.

INTERNATIONAL RELATIONS

Membership. The People's Republic of China is a member of UN.

ECONOMY

Planning. For planning history 1953–73 *see* THE STATESMAN'S YEAR-BOOK, 1973–74, p. 817.

The long-term aim of the present leadership is to transform China by the year 2000 into a modern developed economic power by the implementation of 'the 4 modernizations', *i.e.,* of agriculture, industry, defence and science and technology. In 1978, as a first step to the realization of the '4 modernizations', a 10-year plan (1976–85) was introduced. However this proved in practice to be over-ambitious; many of the planned targets were too high and the scale of capital construction was too great. The pursuit of the plan caused serious imbalances in the economy. Since 1979 a policy of 'readjusting, restructuring, consolidating and improving' the economy has been followed.

The more rational approach adopted to China's material and financial limitations embodied in the readjustment programme remains the foundation of Chinese economic policy. Agriculture and light industry receives higher priority in investment compared to heavy industry. The growth rates in 1980 were lower and the 1981 targets were twice revised downwards in an effort to balance the budget. Nevertheless the total value of industrial and agricultural output was 33% higher in 1982 than in 1978.

Budget. 1982 revenue was 112,397m. yuan; expenditure, 115,331m. yuan.

Communes pay an agricultural tax, and this accounts for almost 10% of budgetary revenue. Since 1981 state-owned enterprises have paid a business tax instead of turning over their profits to the state. Income tax was introduced in 1980; it affects mainly foreigners. China will pay off US claims of US$80·5m. before 1 Oct. 1984, and USA will unblock Chinese assets of the same value. Registration of British claims for loss of assets in 1949 was requested by the Foreign Compensation Commission in Jan. 1981. A credit of 450m. SDF was granted by IMF in March 1981.

China's reserves at 31 Dec. 1980 were US$2,361m. of foreign exchange and 12·8m. troy oz. of gold.

Currency. The currency is called Renminbi (RMB, *i.e.*, People's Currency). The unit of currency is the *yuan* which is divided into 10 *jiao*, the *jiao*, into 10 *fen*. The official rate of exchange is £ = 3·01 *yuan*; US$1 = 2·05 *yuan*; Hong Kong $1 = 0·983 *yuan*; 1 rouble = 2·222 *yuan* (non-commercial, 1 rouble = 1·29 *yuan*).

Notes are issued for 1, 2 and 5 *jiao* and 1, 2, 5 and 10 *yuan* and coins for 1, 2 and 5 *fen*.

Banking. A re-organization of the banking system in 1983 resulted in the People's Bank of China assuming the role of a Central Bank. Its former commercial role was taken over by a new specialized bank, The Industrial and Commercial Bank. The Bank of China will continue to be responsible for foreign banking operations.

Weights and Measures. The metric system is in general use. For older units of measurement, *see* THE STATESMAN'S YEAR-BOOK, 1975–76, p. 826 and 1954, pp. 877–88.

ENERGY AND NATURAL RESOURCES

Electricity. In 1979 coal provided over 60% of China's energy, although there is a large hydro-electric potential in the centre and south. Generating is not centralized; local units range between 30 and 60 mw of output. Output in 1981: 309,300m. kwh.

Oil. China has made rapid progress in oil extraction and refining. There are probably about 100 oilfields, of which the largest are at Daqing, Shengli, Dagang and Karamai. Offshore resources in Bohai Bay are also being exploited. Refining capacity is estimated at 80m. tons per annum. Oil reserves may be as much as 10,000m. tonnes. Crude oil production was 101·22m. tonnes in 1981.

Gas. Natural gas is available from fields near Canton and Shanghai and in Sichuan province. Production was 14,890m. cu. metres in 1981, but is only used locally.

Minerals. *Coal.* Most provinces contain coal, and there are 70 major production centres, of which the largest are in Hebei, Shanxi, Shandong, Jilin and Anhui. Coal reserves are estimated at 200,000m. tonnes. Coal production was 643m. tonnes in 1982.

Iron. Iron ores are abundant in the anthracite field of Shanxi, in Hebei, in Shandong and other provinces, and iron (found in conjunction with coal) is worked in Manchuria. 300m. tons of ore are estimated to be in Shanxi; the principal iron-ore reserves total about 44,000m. tons. The Daye iron deposits, near Wuhan, are among the richest in the world. Estimated output of iron ore in 1981, 70m. tonnes. The biggest steel bases are at Anshan (in Manchuria) with a capacity of 6m. tons, Wuhan (capacity 3·5m. tonnes), Baotou and Maanshan (both 2·5m. tonnes).

Tin. Tin ore is plentiful in Yunnan, where the tin-mining industry has long existed. Tin production was 15,000 tonnes in 1981.

Tungsten. China is the world's principal producer of wolfram (tungsten ore), producing 14,000 tonnes in 1981. Mining of wolfram is carried on in Hunan, Guangdong and Yunnan.

Production of other minerals in 1978 (in tonnes): Phosphate rock, 4·5m.; aluminium, 225,000; copper, 200,000; lead, 120,000; zinc, 125,000; antimony, 9,000; manganese, 2m.; (1973) sulphur, 130,000; (1967) bauxite, 350,000; (1973) salt, 18,000; (1969) asbestos, 160,000. Other minerals produced: barite, bismuth, gold, graphite, gypsum, mercury, molybdenum, silver.

Agriculture. China remains essentially an agricultural country. Some 11% of the total land area is under cultivation. Intensive agriculture and horticulture have been practised for millennia. Present-day policy aims to avert the traditional threats from floods and droughts by soil conservancy, afforestation, irrigation and drainage projects, and to increase the 'high stable yields' areas by introducing fertilizers, pesticides and improved crops. Crop priorities: food grains; raw materials for industry (especially cotton); crops for export (especially oil seeds). Among livestock, priority is given to pig production.

Since 1958 modifications have been made in the commune system, including size reductions. There were some 50,000 in 1977. Small private plots account for 20% or more of the peasant income which averaged 83·40 yuan in 1979.

Since 1978 more flexible methods of management have been adopted comprising 'responsibility systems', whereby individual households or other small units are contracted to supply to the commune or government purchasing agency a quantity of crops to be produced from an alloted area of commune land. Any surplus is at the disposal of the household, to be consumed or marketed.

In 1974 there were estimated to be 127m. hectares of arable land. In 1981 there were 53m. tractors (15 h.p. units).

Agricultural production, 1982 (in 1m. tonnes). Total grain, 353; tea, 0·34 (1981); cotton, 3·6; rice, 143·2 (1981); oilseed crops, 10·2 (1981). The gross value of agricultural output in 1982 was 256,600m. yuan.

Livestock, 1982: Horses and cattle, 56m.; sheep and goats, 110m.; pigs, 299m. Meat production in 1980 was 12·06m. tonnes.

Forestry. Forests cover some 12m. hectares. The chief forested areas are in Heilongjiang, Sichuan and Yunnan. Timber output in 1981 was 49·4m. cu. metres.

The most important timber product is teak. It is estimated that some 1·3m. hectares are afforested each year.

INDUSTRY AND TRADE

Industry. 'Cottage' industry is very old in the economy and persists into the 20th century. Modern industrial development began with the manufacture of cotton textiles, and the establishment of silk filatures, steel plants, flour-mills and match factories. Expanding sectors of manufacture are: steel, chemicals, cement, agricultural implements, plastics and lorries.

1981 production (in tonnes): Chemical fertilizer, 12·39m.; chemical fibres, 527,000; pig-iron. 34·2m.; cement, 84m.; cotton cloth, 14,270m. metres; 176,000 motor vehicles were produced, 53,000 tractors and 17·5m. bicycles.

35·6m. tonnes of steel and 5·4m. tonnes of paper re produced in 1981.

The gross value of industrial output in 1982 was 557,900m. yuan.

Labour. Number employed in state and collective urban enterprises in 1981: 109·4m. with an average wage of 772 yuan. Wage increases affecting 40% of the non-agricultural workforce were introduced in Oct. 1977 and in Nov. 1979. There is a 6-day 48-hour working week.

Commerce. Foreign trade, formerly conducted exclusively through national corporations under the Ministry of Foreign Trade, is now being decentralized. Trade authorities are being established in the main cities, to date Beijing (Peking), Shanghai and Tianjin, and in selected provinces, to date Guangdong and Fujian. The quasi-governmental China International Trust and Investment Corporation also handles foreign trade. Special Economic Zones have been set up in the provinces of Guangdong and Fujian, in which concessions are made to foreign businessmen to encourage their investment. In 1978 China reversed its policy of not accepting foreign credit and aid. A law of July 1979 permits the establishment of joint ventures with foreign firms. There is no maximum limit on the foreign share of the holdings; the minimum limit is 25%. Foreign indebtedness was about £1,400m. in 1980.

Imports include grain, raw materials and semi-manufactured products for agriculture (primarily chemical fertilizers), light industry and textiles, advanced equipment, particularly whole plants and consumer goods. Exports include heavy industrial goods including petroleum, chemicals, minerals, machinery and equipment, light industrial goods and agricultural products.

Trade in 1982: Imports, US$17,000m.; exports, US$21,600m.

Some 85% of China's trade is with non-Communist countries. Japan is China's biggest trading partner, and an 8-year trade agreement was signed in Feb. 1978 and extended for 5 years in March 1979. Other major trading partners are Hong Kong, Federal Republic of Germany, USA and Australia. Imports from USA totalled US$1,720m. in 1979; exports to USA were US$551m. Customs duties on imports and exports between Taiwan and the mainland were abolished in April 1980. Trade with USA is increasing rapidly.

Total trade between China and UK (British Department of Trade returns, in £1,000 sterling):

	1979	1980	1981	1982	1983
Imports to UK	137,891	153,433	184,069	193,231	231,417
Exports and re-exports from UK	213,039	169,500	120,048	103,051	159,722

In April 1978 a most-favoured-nation agreement was signed with EEC, and in 1980 the EEC extended preferential tariffs to China.

On 15 Nov. 1978 a science and technology agreement was signed by UK and China and on 4 March 1979 an agreement on economic co-operation. In July 1979 the USA and China signed a 3-year trade agreement which accords China most-favoured-nation status from 1980.

On 17 April 1980 China gained representation in the IMF, and on 15 May 1980 in the IBRD.

COMMUNICATIONS

Roads. The total road length was 897,200 km in 1981. 83% of communes could be reached by road in 1976. Highways are well graded but mostly unmetalled. In 1969 there were some 409,000 lorries, 60,000 cars and 30,000 buses.

In 1978, 27,900m. tonne-km of freight were transported by road.

Railways. Chinese railway history begins in 1876, when the Wusong–Shanghai line was opened. In 1982 there were some 52,000 km of railway including 2,100 km electrified.

The principal railways are:

(1) The great north–south trunk lines: (a) Peking–Canton Railway (over 2,300 km), via Zhengzhou–Wuhan–Zhuzhou–Hengyang.

(b) Tianjin–Shanghai Railway (1,500 km), via Pukow and Nanjing (double-tracked in July 1976).

(c) Baoji–Chongqing Railway, via Chengdu (1,174 km). Chongqing with the east–west route from Hengyang to the Vietnam border, and to Kunming, connecting there with the Yunnan Railway to the Vietnam border. Two further lines connect Baoji.

(2) Great east–west trunk lines: (a) Longhai Railway; Lianyungkang–Xuzhou–Zhengzhou (on the Peking–Canton line) –Xian–Baoji–Tianshui–Lanzhou (1,500 km). The Baoji–Lanzhou section was upgraded in 1978. (b) Lanzhou–Xinjiang Railway: Lanzhou–Yumen–Hami–Turfan–Urumqi (1,800 km); (c) Shanghai–Youyiguan (Vietnam border) via Hangzhou, Nanchang, Hengyang (on the Peking–Canton line), Guilin, Liuzhou and Nanning. (d) Peking–Lanzhou via Xining (from which a branch connects with the lines through Mongolia to the Trans-Siberian

Railway), Dadong (from which a branch serves the province of Shanxi), Baotou and Yinchuan (Ningxia). (e) Zhuzhou–Guiyang (632 km). A new east–west line was opened in 1978 between Xiangfan and Chongqing.

Branches link coastal areas (e.g., Fujian province) and the smaller inland centres with the main parts of the system. Surveys have been made for a new 500-km railway, linking the trunk line with the oilfield of Karamai in Xinjiang.

(3) The Manchurian system: (a) Chinese Eastern (Changchun) Railway (2,370 km), from Manzhouli on the Soviet border through northern Inner Mongolia and Manchuria via Qiqihar, Harbin and Mudanjiang to the Soviet border near Vladivostok. (b) South Manchuria Railway (705 km, 1,120 km with branches), Changchun–Shenyang–Luda. (c) Peking–Shenyang Railway, with branches in Manchuria (854 km, 1,350 km with branches).

Branches give connexions with outlying parts of Manchuria and Inner Mongolia as well as international links with Korean railways. Chinese railways are all constructed to the standard gauge except for some 600 km of metre gauge in Yunnan. Trunk routes are being converted from single to double track. The route between Baoji and Chengdu (676 km) was electrified in 1975 and that between Yangpingguan (on the Baoji–Chengdu route) and Ankang in 1977.

Capacity is being expanded under the 1976–85 development plan: 6 new lines are to be built by 1985. Lines are planned to link Tibet with the Chinese network (opened as far as Golmud in 1979) and to bridge gaps in the system such as Liuzhou–Canton, Kantang–Taiyuan and southern Xinjiang.

In 1981 the railways carried 1,048m. tons of freight and 942m. passengers.

Aviation. The Civil Aviation Administration of China (CAAC) flies routes to Pyongyang, Hanoi, Rangoon, Karachi, Tōkyō, Moscow, Teheran, Addis Ababa, Bucharest, Belgrade, Zürich, Paris, Frankfurt, Manila, New York, San Francisco, London and Hong Kong. It also provides services to Hong Kong. Its inventory includes 3 Boeing 747s, 10 Boeing 707s, 16 Tridents and 5 Il–62s. British Airways have a direct flight London–Beijing. Japan Airlines have a route from Tōkyō to Beijing (via Osaka and Shanghai), Air France Paris to Beijing (via Athens and Karachi), Pakistan Airlines Karachi to Beijing, Aeroflot Moscow to Beijing, Ethiopian Airlines Addis Ababa to Shanghai, Tarom (Romania) Bucharest to Beijing, Swissair Geneva to Peking and Shanghai, Iran Air Paris to Peking and PANAM Peking via Tōkyō.

In 1979 there were 160 internal routes with over 500 weekly flights.

Air services agreements have been signed with Bangladesh, Canada, the Federal Republic of Germany, Greece, Iraq, Italy, Japan, Laos, Nepál, the Netherlands, the Philippines, Spain, Sweden, Thailand, UK and USA.

Shipping. In 1980 the ocean-going merchant fleet consisted of 431 vessels with a total DWT of 7·92m.

The major ports are at Tianjin, Shanghai, Qingdao, Luda and Canton. New ports are under construction at Changchiang, Huangpu, Qinhuangdao, Yantai and Lienyunkang. Ports cannot accommodate vessels over 100,000 GRT and most harbours have a draught limitation of 35 ft. 217m. tonnes of cargo was handled in 1980.

Inland waterways total about 136,000 km. Plans were announced in 1978 for a national transport waterway network.

Pipeline. A pipeline links the Daqing oilfield to the port of Luda and to refineries in Peking. There is a pipeline from Lanzhou to Lhasa.

Post and Broadcasting. Number of post offices of all kinds in 1958 was 67,000. The use of *Pinyin* transcription of place names has been requested for mail to addresses in China (e.g., 'Beijing' *not* 'Peking'; 'Tianjin' *not* 'Tientsin'; 'Guangzhou' *not* 'Canton', etc.).

In 1980 there were 106 radio broadcasting stations. In 1964 there were some 7m. radio receivers. In 1980 there were 38 television stations and 9·02m. TV receivers. Most are communally owned.

Cinemas. Cinemas numbered 1,386 in 1958.

Newspapers. In 1980 newspaper production totalled 14,040m. copies, and journals, 1,120m. copies. The Party newspaper is *Renmin Ribao* (People's Daily). In 1979 it had a daily circulation of 7m.

JUSTICE, RELIGION, EDUCATION AND WELFARE

Justice. Six new codes of law (including criminal and electoral) came into force in Jan. 1980, which, it is claimed, will regularize the legal unorthodoxy of recent years. The new codes specify a process of repentance as a precondition for a possible reduction of sentence. There is no provision for *habeas corpus*. The death penalty is prescribed for murder and treason. Courts will no longer be subject to the intervention of other state bodies, and their decisions will be reversible only by higher courts. 'People's courts' are divided into some 30 higher, 200 intermediate and 2,000 basic-level courts, and headed by the Supreme People's Court. The latter tries cases, hears appeals and supervises the people's courts. The Ministry of Justice, abolished in 1959, was re-established in 1979.

People's courts are composed of a president, vice-presidents, judges and 'people's assessors' who are the equivalent of jurors. 'People's conciliation committees' are charged with settling minor disputes.

There are also special military courts.

Procuratorial powers and functions are exercised by the Supreme People's Procuracy and local procuracies.

Religion. Confucianism, Buddhism and Taoism have long been practised. Confucianism has no ecclesiastical organization and appears rather as a philosophy of ethics and government. Taoism—of Chinese origin—copied Buddhist ceremonial soon after the arrival of Buddhism two millennia ago. Buddhism in return adopted many Taoist beliefs and practices. It is no longer possible to estimate the number of adherents to these faiths. A more tolerant attitude towards religion had emerged by 1979, and the Government's Bureau of Religious Affairs was reactivated.

Ceremonies of reverence to ancestors have been observed by the whole population regardless of philosophical or religious beliefs.

Moslems are found in every province of China, being most numerous in the Ningxia–Hui Autonomous Region, Yunnan, Shaanxi, Gansu, Hebei, Honan, Shandong, Sichuan, Xinjiang and Shanxi. They totalled 10m. in 1980.

Roman Catholicism has had a footing in China for more than 3 centuries. In 1979 there were about 2m. Catholics who are members of the Patriotic Catholic Association, which declared its independence of Rome in 1958, and about 1,000 priests. In 1977 there were 78 bishops and 4 apostolic administrators, not all of whom were permitted to undertake religious activity. This figure included 46 'democratically elected' bishops not recognized by the Vatican. A Catholic bishop of Peking was consecrated in Dec. 1979 without the consent of the Vatican.

Protestants are members of the All-China Conference of Protestant Churches.

Education. During the Cultural Revolution and the 'Gang of Four' period the educational system was in a turmoil of radical reformation involving a reduction in the length of courses at all levels, the substitution of class background for academic achievement as a criterion for entry to higher education, a heavy emphasis on political education, and lengthy periods of manual labour sandwiched between courses. 1977 marked the beginning of a return to a more conventional system, and by 1978 3 out of every 4 children were attending school. University entry now normally follows from secondary schooling and is dependent upon entrance examinations in which political reliability tests are accompanied by tests in academic subjects. Obligatory manual labour has been reduced to 1 month per year. In 1978 a system of 'key' schools for the best-performing pupils was set up, and it was announced that new universities and colleges would be established. It was also announced that several thousand students would be sent to Western universities. In 1982 there were 715 universities and institutes of higher education, with some 1·54m. students. In 1982 there were some 140m. pupils in 880,000 primary schools, and 47m. pupils in 108,000 secondary schools.

The Academy of Sciences had in 1964 some 20 provincial branches and an Academy of Social Sciences was established in 1977.

Among the universities are the following: People's University of China, Peking (founded 1912 by Dr Sun Yat-sen; reorganized 1950; about 3,000 students); Peking University, Peking (1898, enlarged 1945; about 10,000 students); Xiamen University, Fujian (1921 and 1937); Fudan University, Shanghai (1905); Inner Mongolia University, Hohhot; Lanzhou University, Lanzhou (Gansu Prov.); Nankai University, Tianjin (1919); Nanjing University, Nanjing (1888 and 1928); Jilin University, Changchun (Jilin Prov.); North-West University, Xian (Shanxi Prov.); Shandong University, Qingdao (1926); Sun Yat-sen University, Canton (founded 1924 by Dr Sun Yat-sen); Sichuan University, Chengdu (1931); Qinghua University, Peking, Wuhan University, Wuhan (Hubei Prov.; 1905 and 1928); Yunnan University, Kunming. In 1958 a university of science and technology was set up by the Academy of Sciences.

Chen, T. H., *Chinese Education since 1949* Oxford, 1981.

Health. Medical treatment is free only for certain groups of employees, but where costs are incurred they are partly borne by the patient's employing organization. In 1980 there were 891,000 Western-style doctors and 262,000 doctors of Chinese medicine. In rural areas there were also 1·5m. 'bare-foot doctors', who receive 3 months' training and remain in the community treating simple ailments and implementing public health directives.

80% of production brigades have co-operative medical services. There were 1·98m. hospital beds in 1980.

DIPLOMATIC REPRESENTATIVES

Of China in Great Britain (31 Portland Place, London, W1N 3AG)
Ambassador: Chen Zhaoyuan.

Of Great Britain in China (11 Guang Hua Lu, Jian Guo Men Wai, Peking)
Ambassador: Sir Richard Evans.

Of China in the USA (2300 Connecticut Ave., NW, Washington, D.C., 20008)
Ambassador: Zhang Wenuin.

Of the USA in China (Guang Hua Lu 17, Peking)
Ambassador: Arthur W. Hummel, Jr.

Of China to the United Nations
Ambassador: Ling Qing.

Books of Reference

Beijing Review. Peking, weekly
The China Quarterly. London, from 1960
China Reconstructs. Peking, monthly
China's Foreign Trade. Bimonthly. Peking, from 1966
Bartke, W., *Who's Who in the People's Republic of China* New York, 1981
Bennett, G. (ed.), *China's Finance and Trade: a Policy Reader.* London, 1978
Bettelheim, C., and Burton, N. G., *China Since Mao.* New York, 1978
Boardman, R., *Britain and the People's Republic of China, 1949–1974.* London, 1976
Bonavia, D., *The Chinese.* New York, 1980.—*The Chinese: A Portrait.* London, 1981
Boorman, H. L., and Howard, R. C. (eds.), *Biographical Dictionary of Republican China.* 5 vols. Columbia Univ. Press, 1967 ff.
Brugger, B. (ed.), *China since the Gang of Four.* London, 1980
The Cambridge History of China. 14 vols. CUP, 1978 ff.
Cheng, C., *China's Economic Development.* Boulder, 1982
Cheng, P., *China.* [Bibliography] Oxford and Santa Barbara, 1983
China Directory [in Pinyin and Chinese]. Tōkyō, Annual
Fairbank, J. K., *The United States and China.* 4th ed. Cambridge, Mass., 1979
Fung, K. K., (ed.) *Current Economic Problems in China.* Boulder, 1982
Garside, R., *Coming Alive: China after Mao.* New York, 1980
Gittings, J., *The World and China, 1922–1972.* London, 1974

Gray, J., and White, G., *China's New Development Strategy*. London, 1982
Hinton, H. C., (ed), *The People's Republic of China: A Handbook*. Boulder, 1979.—*The Peoples Republic of China 1949–1979*. 5 vols. Wilmington, 1980
Hook, B., (ed.) *The Cambridge Encyclopaedia of China*. CUP, 1982
Houn, F. W., *A Short History of Chinese Communism*. 2nd ed. Englewood Cliffs, N.J., 1973
Hsieh, C. M., *Atlas of China*. New York, 1973
Hsu, R. C., *Ford for One Billion*. Boulder, 1982
Hsüeh, C.-T. (ed.), *Dimensions of China's Foreign Relations*. New York, 1977
Jingrong, W., (ed.), *The Pinyin-Chinese Dictionary*. Beijing and San Francisco, 1979
Kallgren, J., (ed.), *The People's Republic of China after 30 years*. Berkeley, 1979
Kaplan, F. M. (ed.), *Encyclopedia of China Today*. 3rd ed. London, 1982
Kim, S. S., *China, the United Nations and World Order*. Princeton, 1979
Klein, D. W., and Clark, A. B., *Biographic Dictionary of Chinese Communism, 1921–1965*. Harvard U.P., 1971
Lardy, N. R., *Economic Growth and Distribution in China*. CUP, 1978
Mao Tse-tung, Selected works. 5 vols. Peking, 1965–77
Mathews, R. H., *Chinese-English Dictionary*. Cambridge, Mass., 1943–47
Meyer, C., *China Observed*. London, 1981
O'Leary, G., *The Shaping of Chinese Foreign Policy*. London, 1980
Qi Wen, *China: a General Survey*. Peking, 1979
Rodzinski, W., *A History of China*. Vol. 1. Oxford, 1981
Schaller, M., *The United States and China in the Twentieth Century*. OUP, 1979
Scott, G. L., *Chinese Treaties: The Post-revolutionary Restoration of International Law and Order*. New York, 1975
Szuprowicz, B. O. and M. R., *Doing Business with the People's Republic of China*. New York, 1978
The Times Atlas of China. London, 1974
Thornton, R. C., *China: A Political History, 1917–1980*. Boulder, 1982
US Congress Joint Economic Committee. *Chinese Economy, Post-Mao*. Washington, 1978
Wickert, E., *The Middle Kingdom: Inside China Today*. London, 1983
Yahuda, M. B., *China's Role in World Affairs*. London, 1978

TAIWAN

'Republic of China'

Capital: Taipei
Population: 18·7m. (1983)
GNP per capita: US$1,869 (1979)

HISTORY. The island of Taiwan (Formosa) was ceded to Japan by China by the Treaty of Shimonoseki on 8 May 1895. After the Second World War the island was surrendered to Gen. Chiang Kai-shek in Sept. 1945 and was placed under Chinese administration on 25 Oct. 1945. USA broke off diplomatic relations with Taiwan on 1 Jan. 1979 on establishing diplomatic relations with the Peking Government. Relations between the USA and Taiwan are maintained through the American Institute on Taiwan and the Taiwan Co-ordination Council for North American Affairs, set up in 1979 and accorded diplomatic status in Oct. 1980.

AREA AND POPULATION. Taiwan lies between the East and South China Seas about 100 miles from the coast of Fujian province. The total area of Taiwan Island and the Penghu Archipelago is 13,976 sq. miles (36,179 sq. km). Population (1983), 18·7m., of whom some 2m. are mainland Chinese who came with the Nationalist Government. There are also some 300,000 aboriginals. Population density: 503·7 per sq. km.

In 1982, birth rate was 2·2%; death rate, 0·48%; rate of growth, 1·73% per annum.

Taiwan is divided into two special municipalities (Taipei, the capital, population 2·3m. in 1982 and Kaohsiung, population 1·25m. in 1982), 5 municipalities (Keelung, Taichung, Tainan, Chiayi and Hsinchu) and 16 counties (*hsien*):

Changhua, Chiayi, Hsinchu, Hualien, Ilan, Kaohsiung, Miaoli, Nantou, Penghu, Pingtung, Taichung, Tainan, Taipei, Taitung, Taoyuan, Yunlin.

CONSTITUTION AND GOVERNMENT. Taiwan is controlled by the remnants of the Nationalist Government. On 1 March 1950, Chiang Kai-shek resumed the presidency of the 'Republic of China', and was re-elected for his fifth 6-year presidential term in March 1972. He died 5 April 1975 and was succeeded by Dr Yen Chia-kan who was replaced in the presidential elections of 21 March 1978 by Chiang Kai-shek's eldest son Chiang Ching-kuo (nominated for second 6-year term in 1984). There are 3 political parties: the ruling Kuomintang (2m. members in 1982), which has a youth movement (China Youth Corps) of over 1m. members, the Young China Party and the China Democratic Socialist Party.

The National Assembly was elected in 1947. In June 1983 it had 1,105 delegates. The National Assembly operates through 5 *yuan* or councils. The highest administrative organ is the Executive Yuan, headed by the premier, which includes a number of ministers. The highest legislative body is the Legislative Yuan, elected in 1948, which in June 1983 numbered 376 members. The National Assembly, Legislative Yuan and Control Yuan are elected bodies. Their terms of office have been extended indefinitely. As the number of original delegates dwindled, regulations introduced in 1966 and 1972 provided for the election of additional members to the National Assembly and Legislative Yuan, and elections were held in 1969, 1972, 1975 and 1980. There is also a Provincial Assembly of which the current Seventh Assembly with 77 members was elected on 14 Nov. 1981.

A political campaign calling on the Kuomintang to abandon its claim to represent all China and hold representative elections resulted in the sentencing of the prime movers at a court-martial in March 1980.

State emblem: A 12-pointed white sun in a blue sky.
National flag: Red with a blue first quarter bearing the state emblem in white.
National anthem: 'San Min Chu I', words by Dr Sun Yat-sen; tune by Cheng Mao-yun.

Prime Minister: Sun Yun-hsuan.
Vice-Premier: Chiu Chuang-huan. *Secretary-General:* Chu Shao-Lwa. *Foreign Minister:* Chu Fu-sung. *Minister of National Defence:* Adm. Soong Chang-chih. *Minister of the Interior:* Lin Yang-kang. *Minister of Finance:* Hsu Li-teh. *Minister of Education:* Chu Hwei-sen. *Minister of Justice:* Li Yuan-zu. *Minister of Economic Affairs:* Chao Yao-tung. *Minister of Communications:* Lien Chan. *Governor of Taiwan:* Lee Teng-hui.

DEFENCE

Army. The Army, which embodies the remnants of the forces which escaped to Taiwan with Chiang Kai-shek at the end of the civil war in 1949, numbered about 310,000 in 1984. It was reorganized, re-equipped and trained by the USA and now consists of 2 armoured, 12 infantry, 6 light infantry divisions, 2 armoured cavalry regiments and 2 airborne brigades. There is a conscription system for 2 years and reserve liability. US supplies of military equipment were resumed in 1980 after a moratorium in 1979. US forces were withdrawn by 1 May 1979.

Navy. Most of the 235 vessels in naval service are former US Navy ships now well over 30 years old and overdue for replacement. There are 2 diesel powered patrol submarines, 24 destroyers, 10 frigates, 3 escort vessels, 35 fast missile craft, 9 defence boats, 14 coastal minesweepers, 1 coastal minelayer, 9 minesweeping boats, 30 coastal patrol craft, 2 dock landing ships, 1 amphibious flagship, 26 landing ships, 22 utility landing craft, 2 repair ships, 4 surveying ships, 12 support ships, 2 transports, 7 oilers, 1 supply ship, 17 tugs, 5 floating docks and 25 service craft. There are also 260 LCMs and 150 minor landing craft. Customs have 7 coastguard cutters.

Active personnel in 1984 exceeded 7,100 naval officers and 28,000 ratings; 3,000 marine officers and 26,000 men.

The Navy has 12 anti-submarine torpedo helicopters and operational control of 2 squadrons of Air Force anti-submarine warfare Tracker aircraft; and the Marine Corps operates a number of observation aircraft and helicopters.

Air Force. The Nationalist Air Force is equipped mainly with aircraft of US design, including F-5E fighters built in Taiwan. It has 13 squadrons of F-104G Starfighter, F-5A/B/E/F and F-100 Super Sabre fighter-bombers, 1 interceptor squadron of F-104S Starfighters, and 1 tactical reconnaissance squadron of RF-104G Starfighters. The 6 transport squadrons are equipped with a VIP Boeing 720, 4 Boeing 727s, 5 C-54s, 20 C-47s, about 40 C-119Gs and 10 C-123 Providers. There is a naval co-operation squadron with S-2A/E Trackers and an ASW squadron with Hughes 500 MD helicopters. Search and rescue units operate Albatross amphibians and Iroquois helicopters, and there are other helicopter and large training elements, some equipped with AT-3 twin-jet trainers designed and built in Taiwan. Total strength in 1983: 77,000 personnel and 485 combat aircraft.

INTERNATIONAL RELATIONS. By a treaty of 1 Dec. 1954 the USA was pledged to protect Taiwan, but this treaty lapsed 1 year after the USA established diplomatic relations with the People's Republic of China on 1 Jan. 1979. In April 1979 the US Congress approved a law to maintain commercial, cultural and other relations between USA and Taiwan.

The People's Republic took over the China seat in the UN from the Nationalists on 25 Oct. 1971.

ECONOMY

Planning. Government policy is to 'develop industry through agriculture and expand agriculture through industry'. Regional planning was carried out through a series of 4-year plans, of which the sixth (1973–76) was terminated in 1975 because of difficulties arising from the international economic situation. The 6-year programme (1976–81) envisaged a GNP annual growth rate of 8·5% and a 4-year plan (1982–85) envisages a GNP annual growth rate of 8%.

Budget. There are 2 budgets, the national together with a special defence budget (partly secret) and the provincial (*i.e.*, for Taiwan proper). For the fiscal year 1983 (July 1982–June 1983) tax revenue was NT$526,630m.; expenditure, NT$524,520m.

Currency. In 1945 the existing currency was converted into notes of the Bank of Taiwan. Taiwan dollars were linked to Chinese national currency at a fixed rate of exchange. When the Gold Yuan entered upon its last phase in early 1949, the Taiwan currency was detached and linked to the US$. Exchange rates (March 1984): £1 = NT$59; US$1 = NT$40·17.

Banking. The Central Bank of China (reactivated in 1961) regulates the money market, manages foreign exchange and issues currency. The former Bank of China, a foreign exchange bank with branches in New York, Chicago, Tōkyō, Osaka, Panama and Bangkok, was reorganized in 1972 as a private bank for export financing and renamed the International Commercial Bank of China (capital NT$1,000m.).

The Bank of Taiwan is the largest commercial bank and the fiscal agent of the Government. In addition, there are 15 domestic commercial banks and 26 local branches of foreign banks.

Other banking institutions include the China Development Corporation.

ENERGY AND NATURAL RESOURCES

Electricity. Output of electricity in 1982 was 40,899m. kwh.; total generating capacity was 10·2m. kw. One nuclear power-station (capacity 0·7m. kw.) came into use in 1977, two more are under construction and a fourth envisaged.

Minerals. There are reserves of coal (202·9m. tonnes), gold (6·1m. tonnes), copper

(12·5m. tonnes), sulphur (2·4m. tonnes), oil (1·8m. kl.) and natural gas (25,921 cu. metres). In 1976 an offshore gas-field south-west of Taiwan was discovered with an annual capacity of 500m. cu. metres. In 1982, coal production was 2·4m. tonnes; petroleum, 138,986 kl.; natural gas, 1,232·5m. cu. metres.

Agriculture. The cultivated area was 890,830 hectares in 1982, of which 501,644 hectares were paddy fields. Production in 1,000 tonnes, in 1982: Rice, 2,482 (2,375 in 1981); tea, 24; bananas, 203; pineapples, 145; sugar-cane, 8,275; sweet potatoes, 741; wheat, 2·3; soybeans, 12; peanuts, 82·8.

Livestock (1982): Cattle, 129,441; pigs, 5,182,487; goats, 177,120.

Forestry. Forest area, 1982: 1,573,194 hectares; forest reserves, 326,421,000 cu. metres; timber production, 562,719 cu. metres.

Fisheries. The fleet comprised 4,382 vessels over 20 GRT in 1982; the catch was 922,520 tonnes in 1982.

INDUSTRY AND TRADE

Industry. Output (in tonnes) in 1982 (and 1981): Crude steel, 1·7m. (1·6m.); pig-iron, 148,110 (185,578); aluminium, 10,120 (30,532); shipbuilding, 925,323 (776,195); sugar, 662,944 (814,943); cement, 13·4m. (14·3m.); compound fertilizers, 246,626 (329,974); paper, 485,919 (471,369); cotton fabrics, 774m. metres (822m.).

In 1982, 18,936m. litres of crude oil were refined; the main refinery at Kaohsiung has an annual capacity of 17,675m. litres.

Labour. In 1982 the labour force was 7m., of whom 1·3m. worked in agriculture, forestry and fisheries, 2·8m. in industry (including 2·2m. in manufacturing and 0·6m. in building), 1·2m. in commerce, 0·4m. in transport and communications, and 1·3m. in other services. 149,000 were registered unemployed.

Commerce. Foreign trade affairs are handled by the China External Trade Development Council (founded 1970), which operates branches in 28 countries under the name of Far East Trade Service. Principal exports: textiles, electrical machinery, foodstuffs, agricultural products, machinery, plastic products. Principal imports: minerals, oil, agricultural products, metal products, machinery. Total trade, in US$1m.:

	1975	1976	1977	1978	1979	1980	1981	1982
Imports	5,952	7,599	8,511	11,027	14,774	19,733	21,200	18,888
Exports	5,309	8,166	9,361	12,678	16,103	19,811	22,611	22,204

The USA, Japan and Saudi Arabia are Taiwan's major trade partners followed by Hong Kong, Kuwait and the Federal Republic of Germany.

Total trade between Taiwan and UK (British Department of Trade returns, in £1,000 sterling):

	1978	1979	1980	1981	1982	1983
Imports to UK	46,879	217,736	253,915	321,082	335,537	458,307
Exports and re-exports from UK	92,542	103,044	92,386	120,038	125,183	128,467

COMMUNICATIONS

Roads. In 1982 there were 17,572·2 km of roads (12,950 km surfaced). 6,045,268 motor vehicles were registered in 1982 including 592,154 passenger cars, 19,181 buses, 314,555 trucks and 5,100,500 motor cycles. 2,056m. passengers and 180m. tons of freight were transported (excluding urban buses).

Railways. Total route length in 1982 was 28,944 km (1,067 mm to 762 mm gauge), of which a large proportion is owned by the Taiwan Sugar Corporation and other concerns. The state network consists of 1,100·7 km. Taiwan railways have various gauges, ranging from 3 ft 6 in. to 2 ft. Electrification of the west trunk line of the state network from Keelung and Kaohsiung was completed in 1979. Freight traffic in 1982 amounted to 28·3m. tons and passenger traffic to 139·3m.

Aviation. There are 2 international airports: Taoyuan and Kaohsiung. There are 5 domestic airlines, including China Airlines (CAL), which also operates international services to Bangkok, Hong Kong, Kuala Lumpur, Manila, Seoul, Singapore, Amsterdam, Saudi Arabia, Japan and USA.

Shipping. The merchant marine in 1982 comprised 218 vessels over 20 GRT, totalling 2,915,009 GRT; it included 28 passenger ships and 190 freighters. Ocean-going freight-traffic was 28·6m. tonnes.

The 4 international ports, Kaohsiung, Keelung, Hualien and T'aichung, are being extensively redeveloped. The first two are container centres. The lesser port of Suao is also being built up.

Post and Broadcasting. In 1982 there were 12,049 postal establishments. Number of telephones in 1982, 4,356,765. In 1978 there were 8m. radio receivers and 3m. TV receivers. There are 3 TV networks.

Cinemas (1982). Cinemas numbered 621.

Newspapers (1982). There were 31 daily papers and 2,400 periodicals.

RELIGION, EDUCATION AND WELFARE

Religion. The predominant faith is Confucianism, and there were 5,000 temples in 1976. There were 1·15m. Taoists in 1981 with 6,088 temples and 17,973 priests, and 0·8m. Buddhists with 1,157 temples and 3,471 priests. There are some 600,000 Christians, mainly in Hualien, of whom there were 286,088 Catholics and 305,200 Presbyterians in 1981.

Education. Since 1968 there has been free compulsory education for 9 years (6–15). In that year the curriculum was modernized to give more emphasis to science while retaining the traditional basis of Confucian ethics. There were, in 1982–83, 2,457 primary schools with 70,055 teachers and 2,226,699 pupils; 1,038 secondary schools with 73,155 teachers and 1,663,642 students; 105 schools of higher learning, including 28 universities and colleges, with 18,258 full-time teachers and 375,696 students.

Health. In 1982 there were 112,687 registered medical personnel, including 21,526 doctors, 4,716 dentists and 4,690 'herb doctors', and 11,615 health and medical care facilities, including 1,083 public health and medical care facilities and 10,532 private hospitals and clinics.

Books of Reference

Statistical Yearbook of the Republic of China. Taipei, annual
Republic of China: A Reference Book. Taipei, 1983
Taiwan Statistical Data Book. Taipei, annual
Annual Review of Government Administration, Republic of China. Taipei, annual
Chiu, H. (ed.), *China and the Taiwan Issue.* New York, 1979
Clough, R. N., *Island China.* Cambridge, Mass., 1978
Ho, S. P. S., *Economic Development of Taiwan, 1860–1970.* Yale Univ. Press, 1978
Hsiung, J. C., (ed.), *Contemporary Republic of China.* New York, 1981
Simon, D. F. S., *Taiwan, Technology Transfer, and Transnationalism.* Boulder, 1983
Tierney, J. (ed.), *About Face: The China Decision and its Consequences.* New Rochelle, 1979

COLOMBIA

República de Colombia

Capital: Bogotá
Population: 27·5m. (1981)
GNP per capita: US$1,180 (1980)

HISTORY. The Vice-royalty of New Granada gained its independence of Spain in 1819, and was officially constituted 17 Dec. 1819, together with the present territories of Panama, Venezuela and Ecuador, as the state of 'Greater Colombia', which continued for about 12 years. It then split up into Venezuela, Ecuador and the republic of New Granada in 1830. The constitution of 22 May 1858 changed New Granada into a confederation of 8 states, under the name of Confederación Granadina. Under the constitution of 8 May 1863 the country was renamed 'Estados Unidos de Colombia', which were 9 in number. The revolution of 1885 led the National Council of Bogotá, composed of 2 delegates from each state, to promulgate the constitution of 5 Aug. 1886, forming the Republic of Colombia, which abolished the sovereignty of the states, converting them into departments, with governors appointed by the President of the Republic, though they retained some of their old rights, such as the management of their own finances. A decree of May 1928 abolished their right to borrow abroad without the sanction of the central government.

AREA AND POPULATION. Colombia is bounded north by the Caribbean sea, north-west by Panama, west by the Pacific ocean, south-west by Ecuador and Peru, north-east by Venezuela and south-east by Brazil. The estimated area of the republic as given to the United Nations is 1,138,914 sq. km (456,535 sq. miles). It lies between lat. 12° 30′ N. and 4° 30′ S., and between long. 67° and 79° W. of Greenwich. It has a coastline of about 2,900 km, of which 1,600 km are on the Caribbean sea and 1,300 km on the Pacific ocean. The capital is Bogotá with a population (1979, estimate) 4,055,909. The area 1,138,914 sq. km (as estimated by the census bureau) and population 26·5m. according to the estimate of 24 Oct. 1978, were as follows:

Departmentos	Area (sq. km)	Population 1978	Capital	Population 1978
Antioquia	63,612	3,556,058	Medellín	1,506,661 [2]
Atlántico	3,382	1,227,319	Barranquilla	855,195 [2]
Bolívar	25,978	1,049,223	Cartagena	435,361 [2]
Boyacá	23,189	1,179,350	Tunja (M.E.)	125,700 [1]
Caquetá	88,965	88,920 [1]	Florencia	—
Caldas	7,888	754,381	Manizales	246,036
Cauca	29,308	813,937	Popayán	107,800 [1]
César (El)	22,905	492,328	Valledupar	161,500 [1]
Chocó	46,530	253,968	Quibdó	48,800 [1]
Córdoba	25,020	894,279	Montería	173,100 [1]
Cundinamarca	22,623	1,219,406	—	—
Huila	19,890	545,603	Neiva	129,700 [1]
Guajira (La)	20,848	262,056	Riohacha	56,900 [1]
Magdalena	23,188	684,704	Santa Marta	174,200 [1]
Meta	85,635	328,077	Villavicencio	83,700 [1]
Nariño	33,268	993,050	Pasto	140,700 [1]
Norte de Santander	21,658	862,829	Cúcuta	358,240
Quindío	1,845	355,328	Armenia	196,500 [1]
Risaralda	4,140	497,122	Pereira	251,861
Santander	30,537	1,284,035	Bucaramanga	402,379 [2]
Sucre	10,917	475,637	Sincelejo	77,800 [1]
Tolima	23,512	1,024,184	Ibagué	263,669
Valle del Cauca	22,140	2,775,142	Cali	1,316,137 [2]

[1] 1973.   [2] 1979.

361

Intendencias	Area (sq. km)	Population 1978	Capital
Arauca	23,818	27,497 [1]	Arauca
Casanare	44,640	[2]	El Yopal
Putumayo	24,885	29,137 [1]	Mocoa
San Andrés y Providencia	44	22,719 [1]	San Andrés
Comisarías			
Amazonas	109,665	12,962 [1]	Leticia
Guainía	72,238	3,602 [1]	Puerto Inírida
Guaviare	42,327	—	—
Vaupés	65,268	13,403 [1]	Mitú
Vichada	100,242	12,330 [1]	Puerto Carreño
Total	1,141,748	26,500,000	

[1] 1973.   [2] Included in figure for Boyacá.

The bulk of the population lives at altitudes of from 4,000 to 9,000 ft above sea-level. It is divided broadly into: 68% mestizo, 20% white, 7% Indio and 5% Negro. The language spoken is Spanish.

CLIMATE. The climate includes equatorial and tropical conditions, according to situation and altitude. In tropical areas, the wettest months are March to May and Oct. to Nov. Bogotá. Jan. 57°F (13·9°C), July 56°F (13·3°C). Annual rainfall 42″ (1,059 mm).

CONSTITUTION AND GOVERNMENT. The legislative power rests with a Congress of 2 houses, the Senate, of 112 members, and the House of Representatives, of 199 members, both elected for 4 years. In 1968 a congressional committee unanimously approved a constitutional amendment providing for progressive reductions in the membership of Congress to 90 senators and 162 representatives by 1974. Congress meets annually at Bogotá on 20 July. Women were given the vote, which is now open to citizens of either sex, over 18 years of age, on 25 Aug. 1954.

The President is elected by direct vote of the people for a term of 4 years, and is not eligible for re-election until 4 years afterwards. Congress elects, for a term of 2 years, one substitute to occupy the presidency in the event of a vacancy during a presidential term. There are 13 Ministries. The Governors of Departments and the Mayor of Bogotá are nominated by the national government.

A National Economic Council, functioning since May 1935, went through several transformations, becoming in 1954 a Directorate of Planning.

National Flag: Three horizontal stripes of yellow, blue, red with the yellow of double width.

National anthem: Oh! Gloria inmarcesible (words by R. Núñez; tune by O. Síndici).

The following is a list of presidents since 1953:

Gen. Gustavo Rojas Pinilla, 13 June 1953–10 May 1957.
Military Junta, Maj.-Gen. Gabriel París and 4 others, 10 May 1957–7 Aug. 1958.
Dr Alberto Lleras Camargo (Lib.), 7 Aug. 1958–7 Aug. 1962.
Dr Guillermo León Valencia (Cons.), 7 Aug. 1962–7 Aug. 1966.

Dr Carlos Lleras Restrepo (Lib.), 7 Aug. 1966–7 Aug. 1970.
Dr Misael Pastrana Borrero (Cons.), 7 Aug 1970–7 Aug. 1974.
Dr Alfonso López Michelsen (Cons./Lib.), 7 Aug. 1974–7 Aug. 1978.
Dr Julio Cesar Turbay Ayala (Lib.), 7 Aug. 1978–7 Aug. 1982.

President: Dr Belisario Betancur. He was elected on 30 May 1982 and took office on 7 Aug. 1982.

Minister of Foreign Affairs: Dr Rodrigo Lloreda Caicedo.

DEFENCE. Men become liable for 2 years' military service at age 18, although the system is applied selectively. *Ex*-conscripts remain in the reserve, divided into 3 classes, until age 45.

Army. The Army consists of 10 infantry and 1 training brigades, artillery, cavalry, engineer and motorized troops and the usual services. The peace effective is 57,000 men (conscripts, 28,000); reserves 70,000. Number of national police, about 50,000.

Navy. Colombia has 2 Federal German-built 1,200-ton diesel-electric powered patrol submarines completed in 1975, 2 Italian-built midget submarines; 2 destroyers completed in Sweden in 1958; 1 old (1944) ex-US destroyer; 3 new German-built missile-armed frigates; 1 old ex-US frigate (small DE type); 4 old patrol vessels (ex-US fleet tugs); 2 fast patrol gunboats; 4 river gunboats; 5 surveying vessels; 9 coastguard patrol vessels; 10 patrol motor launches; 1 oiler; 4 small transports, 1 training ship, 5 service craft, and 12 tugs. Personnel in 1984 exceeded 700 officers and 6,500 men. The Navy has also a brigade of marines with 2,500 officers and men.

Air Force. Formed in 1922, the Air Force has been independent of the Army and Navy since 1943, when its reorganization began with US assistance. In 1983 it had about 300 aircraft, including a squadron of Mirage 5-COA fighter-bombers, 5-COR reconnaissance aircraft and 5-COD two-seat operational trainers; a squadron of Israeli-built Kfir-C2 fighters, a squadron of A-37B jets for counter-insurgency duties, a transport group equipped with 1 C-130, 17 C-47s, 3 C-54s and a small number of Arava, Beaver and Turbo-Porter light transports; a presidential F-28 Fellowship jet transport; UH-1B/H utility helicopters; and a reconnaissance unit with Hughes OH-6A, 300C and TH-55 helicopters. The Mirage 5s are being converted to Kfir standard. Eleven more C-47s, 1 C-54 and 2 HS.748 transports are flown by the Air Force operated airline SATENA. Thirty Cessna T-41D primary trainer/light transports were delivered in 1968 and were followed by 10 T-37C jet advanced trainers to supplement piston-engined T-34s and T-33A armed jet trainers. Latest deliveries include 6 T-38A jet trainers for operation by the Military Air Academy. Total strength is about 4,000 personnel.

INTERNATIONAL RELATIONS

Membership. Colombia is a member of the UN, OAS, the Andean Group and LAIA (formerly LAFTA).

ECONOMY

Budget. Ordinary revenue and expenditure in 1981 balanced at 196,500 pesos.

Currency. Coins include 50, 20 and 10 *centavos* (90% steel and 10% nickel) and 5, 2 and 1 *centavos* of various combinations of copper–nickel–bronze–steel. There are also notes representing 1, 5, 10, 20, 50, 100 and 500 *gold pesos*. Exchange rate March 1984, 134·82 *pesos* = £1 sterling; 92·25 *pesos* = US$1.

Banking. On 23 July 1923 the Banco de la República was inaugurated as a semi-official central bank, with the exclusive privilege of issuing bank-notes in Colombia; its charter, in 1951, was extended to 1973. Its note issues must be covered by a reserve in gold of foreign exchange of 25% of their value.

There are 25 domestic commercial banks of importance and 5 foreign banks (English, Canadian, American, French and Franco-Italian). External public debt was US$6,000m. in 1982.

Weights and Measures. The metric system was introduced in 1857, but in ordinary commerce Spanish weights and measures are generally used; according to new definitions by the Ministry of Development, *e.g.*, *botella* (750 grammes), *galón* (5 *botellas*), *vara* (70 cm), *arroba* (25 lb., of 500 grammes; 4 *arrobas* = 1 quintal).

ENERGY AND NATURAL RESOURCES

Electricity. Capacity of electric power (1973) is 2,795,000 kw. Electric power produced in 1976, 13,717,170 kwh. There is increasing utilization of natural gas.

Oil. Production in 1982 was 51·8m. bbls (of 42 gallons).

Minerals. Colombia is rich in minerals; gold is found chiefly in Antioquia and moderately in Cauca, Caldas, Tolima, Nariño and Chocó; output in 1981, 516,000 troy oz.

Other minerals are silver (133,300 troy oz. in 1981), copper, lead, mercury, manganese, emeralds and platinum; production of platinum, 1981, 14,800 troy oz. The chief emerald mines are those of Muzo and Chivor.

The Government holds the monopoly, which is leased to the Banco de la República, for extracting salts from the outstanding Zipaquirá mines (several hundred feet in depth and several hundred square miles in area) and for evaporating many sea salt pans; salt production in 1977 was 180,890 tons of land salt from the Zipaquirá mines and 435,542 tons of sea salt from Manaure and Galerazamba on the Caribe coast. Colombia's coal reserves were estimated at 16,500m. tonnes in 1983; production (1982) 5m. tonnes.

Agriculture. Very little of the country is under cultivaton, but much of the soil is fertile and is coming into use as roads improve. The range of climate and crops is extraordinary; the agricultural colleges have different courses for 'cold-climate farming' and 'warm-climate farming'. Some 6m. acres are described as arable, 96m. pasture and 148m. forest.

Coffee covers an area (1980) of 1·01m. hectares. Crops are grown by smallholders, and are picked all the year round. Production (1980, in tonnes): Cotton seed, 300,000; rice, 1,892,000; barley, 72,000; maize, 813,000; potatoes, 2,038,000; soybean, 155,000; wheat, 41,000; bananas, 1·2m.; cacao, 41,000.

The rubber tree grows wild, and its cultivation has begun; output is a few hundred tons. Fibres are being exploited, notably the 'fique' fibre, which furnishes all the country's requirements for sacks and cordage; output about 12,000 tons. Tolú balsam is cultivated, and copaiba trees are tapped but are not cultivated. Tanning is an important industry.

Livestock (1982): 24·49m. cattle, 2·2m. pigs, 2·74m. sheep, 33m. poultry.

Fishery. In Sept. 1963 a *Sección de Caza y Pesca* was set up in the Ministry of Agriculture. It extended territorial waters to 200 nautical miles.

INDUSTRY AND TRADE

Industry. Production (1981): Iron, 410,600 tonnes; cement, 4·47m.; motor cars, 24,732; industrial vehicles, 10,439.

Commerce. For the 'Charter of Quito' trading agreement in 1948 between Colombia, Ecuador, Panama and Venezuela, *see* THE STATESMAN'S YEAR-BOOK, 1956, p. 882. Colombia's entry into the Latin American Free Trade Area (ALALC) was ratified on 29 Sept. 1961. A fresh impulse to this effort was given by the Bases for an Immediate Action Programme under the 'Charter of Bogotá' signed by Colombia, Chile, Equador, Peru and Venezuela on 16 Aug. 1966.

Imports (c.i.f. values) and exports (f.o.b. values) (excluding export tax) for calendar years (in US$1m.):

	1979	1980	1981
Imports	2,996	4,420	4,789
Exports	3,506	4,092	3,127

Important articles of export in 1980 (in US$1m.) were coffee (2,329), cotton (102), sugar (175), fuel oil (239), clothing and textiles (258), bananas (108). The chief imports are machinery, vehicles, tractors, metals and manufactures, rubber, chemical products, wheat, fertilizers and wool.

Total trade between Colombia and UK (British Department of Trade returns, in £1,000 sterling).

	1979	1980	1981	1982	1983
Imports to UK	21,874	34,289	32,951	34,502	56,458
Exports and re-exports from UK	52,258	41,920	45,145	50,328	51,023

Tourism. Foreign visitors totalled 1·3m. in 1981.

COMMUNICATIONS

Roads. Owing to the mountainous character of the country, the construction of arterial roads and railways is costly and difficult. Total length of highways, 51,253 km in 1972. Of the 2,300-mile Simón Bolívar highway, which runs from Caracas in Venezuela to Guayaquil in Ecuador, the Colombian portion is complete. Buena Ventura and Cali are linked by a highway (Carreterra al Mar). Motor vehicles numbered 550,293, of which 258,526 were passenger cars and 54,730 lorries in 1977.

Railways. There are 5 divisions of the State Railway with a total length of 2,822 km in 1981 and a gauge of 914 mm. The Pacific Railway connects Bogotá with the port of Buenaventura. The Atlantic line from Bogotá to Sta. Marta was opened in July 1961. Three connecting links are planned to improve the operating efficiency of the network. Total railway traffic, 1976, was 4m. passengers and in 1981, 1·3m. tonnes of freight.

Aviation. In civil aviation Colombia ranks perhaps second, after Brazil, among South American countries. There are 675 landing grounds of all kinds. In 1977 the national airports moved 8,071,882 passengers and 169,474 tonnes of cargo.

Shipping. Vessels entering Colombian ports in 1977 unloaded 8·07m. tonnes of imports and loaded 1·95m. tonnes of exports. The Colombian merchant fleet in 1966 owned 23 vessels of 187,906 net tons, and leased 20 of 164,360 net tons; in 1965 it carried 1·9m. tonnes.

The Magdelena River is subject to drought, and navigation is always impeded during the dry season, but it is an important artery of passenger and goods traffic. The river is navigable for 900 miles; steamers ascend to La Dorada, 592 miles from Barranquilla.

Post and Broadcasting. The length of telephone lines in service is 705,852 km (Bogotá only); instruments in use, 1 Jan. 1982, 1,747,689, of which 642,000 were in Bogotá. The cable company is government owned. Television was established in 1954 and in 1978 there were 1·75m. sets in use. In 1979 there were 350 radio stations.

Cinemas (1973). There were 352 cinemas.

Newspapers (1973). There were 36 daily newspapers, with daily circulation totalling 1,448,467. There were 388 periodical publications.

JUSTICE, RELIGION, EDUCATION AND WELFARE

Justice. The Supreme Court, at Bogotá, of 20 members, is divided into 3 chambers—civil cassation (6), criminal cassation (8), labour cassation (6). Each of the 61 judicial districts has a superior court with various sub-dependent tribunals of lower juridical grade. Communism was outlawed by government decree on 5 March 1956.

Religion. The religion is Roman Catholic, with the Cardinal Archbishop of Bogotá as Primate of Colombia and 7 other archbishops in Cartagena, Manizales, Medellín, Pamplona, Popayán, Cali and Tunja, 26 bishops, 1,546 parishes and 4,020 priests. Other forms of religion are permitted so long as their exercise is 'not contrary to Christian morals or to the law'.

Education. Primary education is free but not compulsory, and facilities are limited. Schools are both state and privately controlled. In 1974 there were 30,558 primary schools with 3,844,257 pupils and 123,139 teachers. In 4,200 secondary schools there were 1,159,996 pupils with 62,000 teachers. In the 176 industrial schools, there were 27,808 pupils with 2,855 teachers. 178 night schools had 11,504 pupils with 1,668 teachers. 81 agricultural schools catered for 7,930 pupils with 815 teachers. There were 638 commercial schools catering for 69,233 pupils with 7,844 teachers. 110 art schools had 8,681 pupils and 709 teachers. Theological institutes (all private) numbered 22 with 674 students and 180 tutors. In *normalista* schools, of which there were 239, 54,198 pupils had 5,407 teachers.

The National University in Bogotá was founded in 1867 and there are 97 other universities with 171,002 students and 17,963 lecturers.

Health. In 1976 there were 670 hospitals and clinics. There were also 1,499 health centres.

DIPLOMATIC REPRESENTATIVES

Of Colombia in Great Britain (3 Hans Crescent, London, SW1X 0LR)
Ambassador: Dr Augusto Espinosa (accredited 15 Dec. 1982).

Of Great Britain in Colombia (Calle 38, No. 13–35, Bogotá)
Ambassador: J. A. Robson.

Of Colombia in the USA (2118 Leroy Pl., NW, Washington, D.C., 20008)
Ambassador: Alvaro Gomez.

Of the USA in Colombia (Calle 37, 8 40, Bogotá)
Ambassador: Lewis A. Tambs.

Of Colombia to the United Nations
Ambassador: Dr Carlos Sanz de Santamaria.

Books of Reference

Anuario General de Estadística de Colombia. Bogotá. Annual
Anuario de Comercio Exterior de Colombia. Annual
Anuario Estadístico Bogotá D. E. Annual
Boletín Mensual de Estadística. Monthly
Economía y Estadística. Occasional
Informe Financiero del Contralor General. Annual
Informe del Gerente de la Caja de Crédito Agrario, Industrial y Minero. Annual
Memorias (13) de los Ministros al Congreso Nacional. Annual
McGreevey, W. P., *An Economic History of Colombia, 1845–1930.* CUP, 1970
Morairetz, D., *Why the Emperor's New Clothes are not made in Colombia.* OUP, 1982

COMOROS

Capital: Moroni
Population: 385,000 (1983)
GNP per capita: US$300 (1980)

Republique fédérale islamique des Comores

HISTORY. The 3 islands forming the present state became French protectorates at the end of the 19th century, and were proclaimed colonies on 25 July 1912. With neighbouring Mayotte they were administratively attached to Madagascar from 1914 until 1947, when the 4 islands became a French Overseas Territory, achieving internal self-government in Dec. 1961.

In referenda held on each island on 22 Dec. 1974, the 3 western islands voted overwhelmingly for independence, while Mayotte voted to remain French. The Comoran Chamber of Deputies unilaterally declared the islands' independence on 6 July 1975, but Mayotte remained a French dependency.

The first government of Ahmed Abdallah was overthrown on 3 Aug. 1975 by a *coup* led by Ali Soilih (who assumed the Presidency on 2 Jan. 1976), but Ahmed Abdallah regained the Presidency after a second *coup* ousted Ali Soilih in May 1978.

AREA AND POPULATION. The Comoros consists of 3 islands in the Indian ocean between the African mainland and Madagascar. The majority of the population throughout the islands speak Kiswahili, but a small proportion speak French or Arabic. Population (estimate, 1983) 385,000.

	Area sq. km	*Population census 1966*	*Population census 1980*	*Chief town*
Njazidja (Grande Comore)	1,148	126,205	189,000	Moroni
Mwali (Mohéli)	290	10,300	19,000	Fomboni
Nzwami (Anjouan)	424	80,082	148,000	Mutsamudu
	1,862	216,587	356,000	

Population of the capital, Moroni (1978) 16,000; Fomboni, 4,500; Mutsamudu, 10,000.

CLIMATE. There is a tropical climate, affected by Indian monsoon winds from the north, which gives a wet season from Nov. to April. Annual rainfall ranges from 43–217″ (1,100–5,500 mm).

CONSTITUTION AND GOVERNMENT. Under the new Constitution approved by referendum on 1 Oct. 1978 (amended 1983), the Comoros are a Federal Islamic Republic. Mayotte has the right to join when it so chooses.

The President is Head of State, directly elected for a 6-year term (renewable once). He appoints a Prime Minister and up to 9 other Ministers to form the Council of Government, on which each island's Governor has a non-voting seat. There is a 39-member unicameral Federal Assembly, directly elected for 5 years. Each of the 3 islands is administered by a Governor (nominated by the President), up to 4 Commissioners whom he appoints to assist him, and a Legislative Council directly elected for 5 years.

President: Ahmed Abdallah Abderemane.
The Council of Government, as re-organized March 1984, comprised:
Prime Minister: Ali Mroudjae.
Foreign Affairs, Co-operation and External Trade: Saïd Madi Kafe. *Home Affairs:* Omar Tamou. *Equipment, Environment and Town Planning:* Saïd Mohamed Saïd Turqui. *Justice:* Mohamed Moumine. *Agriculture, Industry and*

Handicraft: Mohamed Chaher Ben Saïd Massoundé. *Economy and Finance:* Ali Nassor. *Public Health and Population:* Abdou Moustakin. *National Education:* Ahmed Ali Mohamed. *Secretaries of State:* Antoy Abdou *(Transport and Tourism),* Yahaya Djamadar *(Civil Service),* Abdillah Mbae *(Posts and Telecommunications).*

National flag: Green with a crescent and 4 stars all in white in the centre, tilted towards the lower fly.

DEFENCE

Army. The army had a strength of about 700 in 1983.

Navy. An *ex*-British landing craft built in 1945 was transferred from France in 1976. Two small patrol boats were supplied by Japan in 1982.

Air Arm. Equipment, acquired since 1977–78, comprises 3 SIAI-Marchetti SF.260W Warrior armed trainers built in Italy and a Cessna 402B communications aircraft.

INTERNATIONAL RELATIONS

Membership. Comoros is a member of UN and an ACP state of EEC.

ECONOMY

Budget. In 1982, current revenue amounted to 1,898m. francs CFA and current expenditure to 3,208m. francs CFA; the separate capital budget totalled 667m. francs CFA revenue against 854m. francs CFA expenditure.

Currency. The unit of currency is the *franc CFA,* with a parity value of 50 *francs CFA* to 1 French *franc.*

Banking. The Institut d'émission des Comores was established as the new bank of issue in 1975. The chief commercial banks are the Banque des Comores, established in 1974 by the separation of the former Comoran section of the Banque de Madagascar et des Comores and the Banque de Développement des Comores.

Weights and Measures. The metric system is in force.

NATURAL RESOURCES

Agriculture. The chief product was formerly sugar-cane, but now vanilla, copra, cacao, sisal, coffee, cloves and essential oils (citronella, ylang, lemon-grass) are the most important products. Production (1981 in tonnes): Cassava, 88,000; coconuts, 53,000; bananas, 32,000; sweet potatoes, 16,000 and rice, 14,000.

Livestock (1982): Cattle, 81,000; sheep, 8,000; goats, 88,000; asses, 4,000.

Forestry. Njazídja has a fine forest and produces timber for building.

Fisheries. In 1980 the catch was (estimate) 4,000 tonnes.

COMMERCE. Imports in 1980 amounted to 6,147m. francs CFA, exports to 2,712m. francs CFA. In 1977 France provided 41% of imports and (in 1978) took 71% of exports. The main exports (1978) were vanilla (735m. francs CFA), essential oils (640m.), cloves (460m.) and copra (205m.).

Trade between Comoros and UK (British Department of Trade returns, in £1,000 sterling):

	1980	1981	1982	1983
Imports to UK	40	188	108	278
Exports and re-exports from UK	155	212	258	597

COMMUNICATIONS

Roads. In 1973 there were 750 km of classified roads, of which 262 km were tarmac. There were 3,600 registered vehicles.

Aviation. There is an international airport at Hahaya (on Njazidja). Air Comores have twice-weekly flights to Antanarivo, Dar es Salaam and Mombasa. Air France and Air Madagascar also have twice-weekly flights to Antanarivo. Air Comores has daily internal flights between Moroni and Nzwami, and 5 per week between Moroni and Mwali.

Shipping. In 1973, 279 vessels entered Comoran ports (excluding internal traffic) to discharge 54,391 tonnes and load 8,700 tonnes.

Post and Broadcasting. There were 1,035 telephones in 1977. *Comores-Inter* broadcasts in French and Comorian on short-wave and FM for approximately 8 hours a day. Number of radios (1982): 37,750.

Cinemas. In 1973 there were 2 cinemas with a seating capacity of 800.

JUSTICE, RELIGION, EDUCATION AND WELFARE

Justice. The Supreme Court comprises 7 members, 2 each appointed by the President and the Federal Assembly, and 1 by each island's Legislative Council.

Religion. Islam is the official religion, adhered to by the vast majority of the population.

Education. In 1979, 130 primary classes had 934 teachers and 49,940 pupils, secondary schools had 499 teachers and 8,932 pupils and a teacher-training college had 3 teachers and 45 students.

Health. In 1975 there were 3 hospitals and a number of clinics.

DIPLOMATIC REPRESENTATIVE

Of the Comoros in the USA
Ambassador: Ali Mlahaili (resides in Moroni).

CONGO

République Populaire du Congo

Capital: Brazzaville
Population: 1·66m. (1983)
GNP per capita: US$730 (1980)

HISTORY. First occupied by France in 1882, the Congo became (as 'Middle Congo') a territory of French Equatorial Africa from 1908 until 28 Nov. 1958, when it became a member state of the French Community. It became an independent Republic on 15 Aug. 1960.

The first President, Fulbert Youlou, was deposed on 15 Aug. 1963 by a *coup* led by Alphonse Massemba-Débat, who became President on 19 Dec. Following a second *coup* in Aug. 1968, the Army took power under the leadership of Major Marien Ngouabi, whose colleague, Major Alfred Raoul, was appointed President from 3 Sept. until 1 Jan. 1969, when Ngouabi himself became President.

The country's present name was established on 3 Jan. 1970, when a Marxist-Leninist state was introduced. Ngouabi was assassinated on 18 March 1977, and succeeded by Col. Joachim Yhombi-Opango, who in turn was replaced on 5 Feb. 1979 by Col. Denis Sassou-Nguesso.

AREA AND POPULATION. The Congo is bounded by Cameroon and the Central African Republic in the north, Zaïre to the east and south, the Cabinda province of Angola and the Atlantic to the south-west and Gabon to the west, and covers 342,000 sq. km; census population (1974), 1,300,120. Estimate (1983) 1·66m. The main towns (population in 1980) are Brazzaville, the capital (422,402) and Pointe-Noire, the main port and oil centre (185,105); other large towns (Census 1974) are Loubomo (28,941) and N'Kayi (formerly Jacob) (28,326).

In 1974, 45% spoke Kongo dialects, 15% Téké, 15% Sanga, 12% Ubangi; there are also about 12,000 pygmies and 12,000 Europeans (mainly French). French is the official language.

CLIMATE. An equatorial climate, with moderate rainfall and a small range of temperature. There is a long dry season from May to Oct. in the S.W. plateaux, but the Congo Basin in the N.E. is more humid, with rainfall approaching 100″ (2,500 mm). Brazzaville. Jan. 78°F (25·6°C), July 73°F (22·8°C). Annual rainfall 59″ (1,473 mm).

CONSTITUTION AND GOVERNMENT. In July 1979 a new Constitution was approved by referendum. Executive power was vested in the President, elected for a 5-year term by the National Congress of the *Parti congolais du travail* (the sole legal party since 1969). The President is assisted by a Council of Ministers, appointed and led by him. At its Congress (March 1979), the PCT elected a Central Committee of 60 members and a Political Bureau of 5 to administer it; it nominated all candidates for the 153-member People's National Assembly and for the regional, district and local councils, all of which were elected on 8 July 1979.

President: Col. Denis Sassou-Nguesso.
Prime Minister: Col. Louis-Sylvain Goma.
Foreign Affairs: Pierre Nze.

National flag: Red, in the canton the national emblem of a crossed hoe and mattock, a green wreath and a gold star.

Local Government: The republic is divided into the capital district of Brazzaville and 9 regions (each under an appointed Commissioner and an elected Council), which are sub-divided into 46 districts.

DEFENCE

Army. The Army consists of 5 battalions, 1 armoured, 1 artillery, 1 infantry, 1 engineering, and 1 paracommando. Equipment includes 14 Chinese type-62 and 3 PT-76 light tanks. Total personnel (1984) 8,000.

Navy. The flotilla includes 3 new Spanish-built fast attack craft, 1 *ex*-Soviet torpedo boat, 3 *ex*-Chinese gunboats, 4 *ex*-Chinese river patrol craft, 4 small patrol cutters, 2 French-built new tugs and 12 small river patrol boats. Personnel in 1984 totalled 250 officers and men.

Air Force. The Air Force has about 500 personnel, 20 MiG-17 jet fighters, 1 twin-turbofan F28 Fellowship and 1 Corvette for VIP transport, 1 Frégate and 5 Antonov An-24/26 turboprop transports, 2 C-47 and 5 Il-14 piston-engined transports, 3 Broussard communications aircraft, 6 L-39 jet trainers, 1 Puma and 4 Alouette II and Alouette III light helicopters.

INTERNATIONAL RELATIONS

Membership. Congo is a member of UN, OAU and is an ACP state of EEC.

ECONOMY

Planning. The National Plan runs 1982–86.

Budget. The ordinary budget in 1983 balanced at 388,000m. francs CFA. Oil revenues finance 53% of the operational budget.

Currency. The unit of currency is the *franc CFA* with a parity value of 50 *francs CFA* to 1 French franc.

Banking. The *Banque des États de l'Afrique Centrale* is the bank of issue. There are 4 commercial banks situated in Brazzaville, including the *Banque Commerciale Congolaise* and the *Union Congolaise de Banques*.

ENERGY AND NATURAL RESOURCES

Electricity. Production in 1980 was 120m. kwh from a hydro-electric plant at Djoué near Brazzaville and from about 6 thermal plants.

Oil. Oil reserves are estimated at 500–1,000m. tonnes. Output in 1982 was almost 5m. tonnes from the 26 offshore oil platforms operated by Elf Congo and Agip Congo. A refinery at Pointe-Noire came on stream in Dec. 1982.

Minerals. Lead, copper, zinc and gold (16 kg in 1978) are the main minerals.

Agriculture. Production (1981, in 1,000 tonnes): Cassava, 530; sugar-cane, 225; pineapples, 107; bananas, 31; plantains, 34; yams, 26; groundnuts, 14.

Livestock (1982): Cattle, 78,000; pigs, 56,000; sheep, 72,000; goats, 139,000; poultry, 1·18m.

Forestry. Equatorial forests cover 20m. hectares (60% of the total land area) from which (in 1980) 800,000 cu. metres of timber were produced, mainly okoumé from the south and sapele from the north. Hardwoods (mainly mahogany) are also exported.

Fisheries. In 1977 the catch amounted to 16,400 tonnes.

INDUSTRY AND TRADE

Industry. There is a growing manufacturing sector, located mainly in the 4 major towns, producing processed foods, textiles, cement (55,000 tonnes in 1979), metal industries and chemicals; in 1970 it employed 21·5% of the labour force.

Trade Unions. In 1964 the existing unions merged into one national body, the *Confédération Syndicale Congolaise*.

Commerce. Imports in 1980 totalled 115,200m. francs CFA (mainly machinery) and exports 192,000m. (of which petroleum 79·5%). 50% of imports were from France; 31% of exports were to Italy and 24% to France.

Total trade between the Congo and UK (British Department of Trade returns, in £1,000 sterling):

	1978	1979	1980	1981	1982	1983
Imports to UK	4,520	3,339	3,416	3,670	2,393	4,335
Exports and re-exports from UK	2,072	3,391	2,943	4,434	9,766	9,560

COMMUNICATIONS

Roads. There were (1980) 8,246 km of all-weather roads. In 1976 there were 20,000 cars and 13,000 commercial vehicles.

Railways. A railway (517 km, 1,067 mm gauge) and a telegraph line connect Brazzaville with Pointe-Noire and a 200 km branch railway links Mont-Belo with Mbinda on the Gabon border.

Aviation. The principal airports are at Maya Maya (near Brazzaville) and Pointe-Noire. In addition there are 22 airfields served by the local airline, Lina-Congo.

Shipping. Pointe-Noire handled (1979) 2·4m. tonnes of goods including manganese from Gabon. There were (1979) 16 vessels of 6,942 GNT registered.

Post and Broadcasting. Telephones (1982) numbered 8,899. In 1979 there were 92,000 radios and 3,300 TV sets in use.

Cinemas. In 1973 there were 7 cinemas with a seating capacity of 5,100.

JUSTICE, RELIGION, EDUCATION AND WELFARE

Justice. The Supreme Court, Court of Appeal and a criminal court are situated in Brazzaville, with a network of *tribunaux de grande instance* and *tribunaux d'instance* in the regions.

Religion. In 1977, 50% of the population were Christian (40·5% Roman Catholic and 9·5% Protestant), 47% followed animist beliefs and 3% were Moslem.

Education. In 1980 there were 383,018 pupils and 6,852 teachers in 1,310 primary schools, 148,857 pupils and 3,148 teachers in 122 secondary schools, 8,744 students with (1979) 505 teachers in technical schools and 1,617 students with (1979) 102 teachers in teacher-training establishments. The Université Marien-Ngouabi (founded 1972) in Brazzaville had 4,336 students in 1980.

Health. There were (1976) 121 hospitals with 6,912 beds; and 190 doctors, 4 dentists, 25 pharmacists, 152 midwives and 1,734 nursing personnel.

DIPLOMATIC REPRESENTATIVES

Of the Congo in Great Britain
Ambassador: Jean-Pierre Nonault (resides in Paris).

Of Great Britain in the Congo
Ambassador: (Vacant).

Of the USA in the Congo (PO Box 1015, Brazzaville)
Ambassador: Kenneth L. Brown.

Of Congo to the USA and United Nations
Ambassador: Nicolas Mondjo.

COSTA RICA

República de Costa Rica

Capital: San José
Population: 2·4m. (1983)
GNP per capita: US$1,730 (1980)

HISTORY. The republic of Costa Rica (the 'Rich Coast') has been independent since 1821, although it formed, from 1824 to 1838, part of the Confederation of Central America.

AREA AND POPULATION. Costa Rica is bounded north by Nicaragua, east by the Caribbean, southeast by Panama, and south and west by the Pacific. The area is estimated at 51,100 sq. km (19,344 sq. miles). The population at the census of 14 May 1973 was 1,871,780.

The area and official estimate of population for 1 Jan. 1983 (2,403,781) was as follows:

Province	Population	Area (sq. km)	Capital	Population
San José	890,443	4,959·63	San José	271,873
Alajuela	413,765	9,753·23	Alajuela	42,579
Cartago	259,916	3,124·67	Cartago	27,929
Heredia	171,688	2,656·27	Heredia	29,544
Guanacaste	228,249	10,140·71	Liberia	14,770
Puntarenas	286,082	11,276·97	Puntarenas	34,613
Limón	153,638	9,188·52	Limón	38,916

Vital statistics for calendar years:

	Marriages	Births	Deaths
1980	17,527	69,992	9,273
1981	16,654	72,260	8,990
1982	18,444	73,089	9,136

The population of European descent, many of them of pure Spanish blood, dwell mostly around the capital of the republic, San José, and in the principal towns of the provinces. Limón, on the Caribbean coast, and Puntarenas, on the Pacific coast, are the chief commercial ports. The United Fruit Co., who in 1941 abandoned their banana plantations on the Atlantic coast in favour of large new plantations on the Pacific coast, have constructed ports at Quepos and Golfito. The Standard Fruit Co. and others have cleared land since 1958 in the Atlantic coast area and now have 2,325 acres producing some 4·2m. stems a year. There are some 15,000 West Indians, mostly in Limón province. The indigenous Indian population is dwindling and is now estimated at 1,200.

Spanish is the language of the country.

CLIMATE. The climate is tropical, with a small range of temperature and abundant rains. The dry season is from Dec. to April. San José. Jan. 66°F (18·9°C), July 69°F (20·6°C). Annual rainfall 72″ (1,793 mm).

CONSTITUTION AND GOVERNMENT. The Constitution, promulgated on 7 Dec. 1871, has been modified very frequently, last in 1949. The Constitution forbids the establishment or maintenance of an army. The legislative power is normally vested in a single chamber called the Legislative Assembly, which since 1962 consists of 57 deputies, 1 for every 25,214 inhabitants, elected for 4 years. The President is elected for 4 years; the candidate receiving the largest vote, provided it is over 40% of the total, is declared elected, but a second ballot is required if no candidate gets 40% of the total. By the election law of 18 Jan. 1946 all citizens who are 20 years of age are entitled to vote; married men and teachers, from the age of 18. Women over 21 were enfranchised in 1949. Elections are normally held on the

373

first Sunday in February. Voting for President, Deputies and Municipal Councillors is secret and compulsory for all men under 70 years of age. Independent non-party candidates are barred from the ballot.

President: Luis Alberto Monge, elected 7 Feb. 1982.

Elections for the Legislative Assembly took place on 7 Feb. 1982; preliminary results show that Partido de Liberacíon won 33 and Partido Unidad 19 of the 57 seats.

The administration is carried on by 13 ministers, appointed by the President. The powers of the President are limited by the constitution, which leaves him the power to appoint and remove at will members of his cabinet. All other public appointments are made jointly in the names of the President and of the minister in charge of the department concerned.

National flag: Five unequal stripes of blue, white, red, white, blue, with the national arms on a white disc near the hoist.

National anthem: Noble patria, tu hermosa bandera (words by J. M. Zeledón, 1903; tune by M. M. Gutiérrez, 1851).

DEFENCE

Army. The Army was abolished in 1948, and replaced by a Civil Guard reputed to be 7,000 strong. There has never been compulsory military service or training.

Navy. The flotilla includes 1 fast patrol craft and 1 armed tug on the Atlantic coast and 5 small coastal patrol craft for revenue purposes and 3 smaller craft on the Pacific coast. Personnel (1984) 90 officers and men.

Air Wing. The Civil Guard operates a small air wing equipped with 3 Otter STOL utility transports, plus a few lightplanes and helicopters.

INTERNATIONAL RELATIONS

Membership. Costa Rica is a member of UN and OAS.

ECONOMY

Budget. The budget for 1980 balanced at 8,029m. colones. The income-tax law of 10 March 1972 raised the maximum rate to 50% for personal incomes of 350,000 colones and over, and to 40% for corporate incomes of 1m. colones and over.

External government debt on 31 Dec. 1982 was US$3,500m.

Currency. The unit of currency is the *colone* (₡). The official rate in March 1984 was ₡43·40 = US$1; 63·70 = £1. The official rate is used for all imports on an essential list and by the Government and autonomous institutions and a free rate is used for all other transactions.

The currency is chiefly notes. The Banco Central issue notes for 5, 10, 20, 50, 100, 500 and 1,000 colones. Silver coins of 1 colone, 50 centimos and 25 centimos were in 1935 replaced by coins (2 and 1 colones and 50 and 25 centimos) made up of 3 parts copper and 1 part nickel, and given the same value as the subsidiary silver currency. There are copper coins (and chromium stainless steel coins) of 10 and 5 centimos.

Banking. By a law passed on 28 Jan. 1950 a Central Bank was established for the organization and direction of the national monetary system and of dealings in foreign exchange, the promotion of facilities for credit and the supervision of all banking operations in the country. The bank has a board of 7 directors appointed by the Government, including *ex officio* the Minister of Finance and the Planning Office Director.

The National Insurance Institute *(Instituto Nacional de Seguros)* is a Government organization, created in 1924, which has a monopoly of new insurance business.

Weights and Measures. The metric system is legally established; but in the country districts the following old Spanish weights and measures are found: *libra* = 1·014 lb. avoirdupois; *arroba* = 25·35 lb. avoirdupois; *quintal* = 101·40 lb. avoirdupois, and *fanega* = 11 Imperial bushels.

ENERGY AND NATURAL RESOURCES

Electricity. Electricity, derived from water power in the highlands, is increasingly used as motive power. Output, 1980, was 1,902m. mwh.

Minerals. Gold output is about 3,000 troy oz. per year. Salt production from sea water is about 10,000 tonnes annually. Haematite ore was discovered on the Nicoya Peninsula late in 1960 and sulphur near San Carlos in 1966. The United Nations have offered US$1m. towards a 3-year mining survey.

Agriculture. Agriculture is the principal industry. The cultivated area is about 1m. acres; grass lands cover 1·8m. acres; forests and woodlands, 9,855,000 acres. There are thousands of square miles of public lands that have never been cleared on which can be found quantities of rosewood, cedar, mahogany and other cabinet woods. The principal agricultural products are coffee, bananas, sugar and cattle. Coffee normally accounts for about half the country's foreign-exchange earnings. Cocoa, maize, sugar, tobacco, rice and potatoes are commonly cultivated. The distillation of spirits is a government monopoly.

Coffee production in 1981 was 112,089 tonnes. Sugar production (1981) 2,521,020 tonnes.

Dairy-farming and cattle-raising are substantial pursuits. In 1982 cattle numbered 2·4m. and pigs 243,000.

Costa Rica is the seat of the Inter-American Institute of Agricultural Sciences, with headquarters at Turrialba.

INDUSTRY AND TRADE

Industry. The main manufactured goods are foodstuffs, textiles, fertilizers, pharmaceuticals, furniture, cement, tyres, canning, clothing, plastic goods, plywood and electrical equipment.

Industrial production was valued at 25·1m. colones in 1980, compared with 1·499m. in 1972.

Labour. As Costa Rica is still essentially an agricultural country, the organization of labour has made progress only in the larger centres of population, and even there it is not a strong movement. There are two main trade unions, *Rerum Novarum* (anti-Communist) and *Confederación General de Trabajadores Costarricenses* (Communist).

Commerce. The value of imports into and exports from Costa Rica in 5 years was as follows in US$:

	1978	1979	1980	1981	1982
Imports	1,165,730,038	1,396,812,332	1,523,797,000	1,208,529,000	867,000,000
Exports	864,906,915	934,391,357	1,001,742,230	1,030,203,040	870,800,000

The value (in US$1m.) of the principal imports in 1982 were: Machinery, including transport equipment, 137·2; manufactures, 227·9; chemicals, 200·5; fuel and mineral oils, 188·9; foodstuffs, 72·5.

Chief exports (in US$1m.) in 1982 were: Manufactured goods and other products, 126·4; coffee, 236·9 (mostly to Federal Republic of Germany and USA); bananas, 234·5 (to USA); sugar, 13·2: cocoa, 2·4.

Total trade between Costa Rica and UK (British Department of Trade returns in £1,000 sterling):

	1979	1980	1981	1982	1983
Imports to UK	3,123	5,424	6,433	15,068	22,299
Exports and re-exports from UK	9,752	8,302	4,791	5,455	11,041

Tourism. There was a total of 345,470 visitors in 1980.

COMMUNICATIONS

Roads. In 1981 there were about 28,525 km of all-weather motor roads open. On the Costa Rica section of the Inter-American Highway it is possible to motor to Panama during the dry season. The Pan-American Highway into Nicaragua is metalled for most of the way and there is now a good highway open almost to Puntarenas. Motor vehicles, 1980, numbered 195,105.

Railways. The nationalized railway system *(Ferrocarriles de Costa Rica)*, totalling 700 km (260 km electrified) of 1,067 mm gauge, connect San José with Limón, the Atlantic port, and San José with Puntarenas, the Pacific port.

Aviation. Passenger movement in and out of Costa Rica is almost entirely by air *via* the local company, LACSA, PANAM and TACA. LACSA links San José by daily services with all the more important towns. The international airport at Juan Santamaría was opened in June 1955.

Shipping. In 1981, 1,221 ships entered and cleared the ports of the republic (Puerto Limón, Puntarenas and Golfito); combined cargo, 1,395 tonnes.

Post and Broadcasting. There were 255,898 telephones in 1982.

The commercial wireless telegraph stations are operated by *Cia Radiográfica Internacional de Costa Rica.* The stations are located at Cartago, Limón, Puntarenas, Quepos and Golfito. The Government has 19 wireless telegraph stations in its local network. The principal or central station at San José also maintains international radio-telegraph circuits to Nicaragua, Honduras, San Salvador and Mexico. The Government has 202 telegraph offices and 88 official telephone stations. The official list of broadcasting stations shows 28 long-wave stations and 7 short-wave stations. Television was inaugurated in May 1960; there were 6 stations and (estimate) 277,694 receivers in 1980.

Cinemas (1979). Cinemas numbered 106, with seating capacity of 105,000.

Newspapers (1983). There were 4 daily newspapers all published in San José.

JUSTICE, RELIGION, EDUCATION AND WELFARE

Justice. Justice is administered by the Supreme Court, 4 appeal courts and the Court of Cassation. There are also subordinate courts in the separate provinces and local justices throughout the republic. Capital punishment may not be inflicted.

Religion. Roman Catholicism is the religion of the State, which contributes to its maintenance but controls the Church Patronage and insists on lay instruction in history, economics and similar subjects; there is entire religious liberty under the constitution, but religious appeals are forbidden in current political discussions. The Archbishop of Costa Rica has 4 bishops at Alajuela, Limón, San Isidro el General and Tilarán.

Protestants number about 40,000.

Education. Costa Rica has a very low illiteracy rate. Elementary instruction is compulsory and free; secondary education (since 1949) is also free. Elementary schools are provided and maintained by local school councils, while the national government pays the teachers, besides making subventions in aid of local funds. In 1982 there were 3,509 public primary schools with 11,615 teachers and administrative staff and 377,274 enrolled pupils; there were 242 public and private secondary schools with 165,649 pupils. The University of Costa Rica, founded in San José in 1843, has 2,337 professors in 13 faculties and 38,629 students. A medical school was opened in 1961. The budget for 1971 provides ₡250m. for public education. Since 1944 English has been taught in all secondary schools.

Social Welfare. The labour code of 1943 provides considerable protection for the workers, while a system of social insurance against sickness covering 756,347 workers in 1968, old age and death covering 68,949 is gradually being extended throughout the country.

DIPLOMATIC REPRESENTATIVES

Of Costa Rica in Great Britain (225 Cromwell Rd., London SW5)
Ambassador: Jorge Borbon Zeller (accredited 20 July 1982).

Of Great Britain in Costa Rica (Edificio Centro Color., Apartado 815, San José)
Ambassador and Consul-General: Peter Wayre Summerscale.

Of Costa Rica in the USA (2112 S St., NW, Washington D.C., 20008)
Ambassador: Fernando Soto-Harrison, CBE.

Of the USA in Costa Rica (Avenida 3, Calle 1, San José)
Ambassador: Curtin Winsor, Jr.

Of Costa Rica to the United Nations
Ambassador: Dr Fernando Zumbado Jimenez.

Books of Reference

Statistical Information: Official statistics are issued by the Director General de Estadística (Ministerio de Industria y Comercio, San José) as they become available. The compilation of statistics was started in 1861.

Ameringer, C. D., *Democracy in Costa Rica.* New York, 1982
Biesanz, R., *(et al). The Costa Ricans.* Hemel Hempstead, 1982
Fernandez Guardia, L., *Historia de Costa Rica.* 2nd ed., 2 vols San José, 1941
Seligson, M. A., *Peasants of Costa Rica and the Development of Agrarian Capitalism.* Univ. of Wisconsin Press, 1980
Trejos, Juan, *Geografía ilustrada de Costa Rica.* San José, 1948

CUBA

República de Cuba

Capital: Havana
Population: 9·71m. (1981)
GNP per capita: US$1,410 (1979)

HISTORY. Cuba, except for the brief British occupancy in 1762–63, remained a Spanish possession from its discovery by Columbus in 1492 until 10 Dec. 1898, when the sovereignty was relinquished under the terms of the Treaty of Paris, which ended the struggle of the Cubans against Spanish rule. Cuba thus became an independent republic, but the United States stipulated under the 'Platt Amendment' (abrogated by Roosevelt in 1934) that Cuba must enter into no treaty relations with a foreign power, which might endanger its independence. A convention which assembled on 5 Nov. 1900 adopted the first constitution of the republic on 21 Feb. 1901.

The revolutionary movement against the Batista dictatorship, led by Dr Fidel Castro, started on 26 July 1953 (now a national holiday). It achieved power on 1 Jan. 1959 when Batista fled the country.

An invasion force of émigrés and adventurers landed in Cuba on 17 April 1961; the main body was defeated at the Bay of Pigs (Las Villas province) and mopped up by 20 April.

The US Navy blockaded Cuba from 22 Oct. to 22 Nov. 1962.

AREA AND POPULATION. The island of Cuba forms the largest and most westerly of the Greater Antilles group and lies 135 miles south of the tip of Florida, USA. It has an area of 44,206 sq. miles (114,524 sq. km); the Isle of Youth (formerly Isle of Pines) has 1,180 sq. miles, and other islands about 1,350 sq. miles. Estimated population in 1981 was 9·71m.

The area, population and density of population of the 14 provinces and their capitals were as follows (1981 census):

	Area sq. km	Population	Capital	Population
Pinar del Rió	10,860	640,740	Pinar del Río	312,614
La Habana	5,671	586,029	Güira de Melena	429,090
Ciudad de La Habana	740	1,924,886	La Habana	1,924,886
Isla de la Juventud	2,199	57,879	—	—
Matanzas	11,669	557,628	Matanzas	421,272
Cienfuegos	4,149	326,412	Cienfuegos	235,293
Villa Clara	8,069	764,743	Santa Clara	525,402
Sancti Spíritus	6,737	399,700	Sancti Spíritus	249,092
Ciego de Avila	6,485	320,961	Ciego de Avila	213,913
Camagüey	14,134	664,566	Camagüey	480,620
Las Tunas	6,373	436,341	Victoria de las Tunas	217,177
Holguín	9,105	911,034	Holguín	456,595
Granma	8,452	739,335	Bayamo	375,446
Santiago de Cuba	6,343	909,506	Santiago de Cuba	563,455
Guantánamo	6,366	466,609	Guantánamo	246,739
Total	110,922 [1]	9,706,369		

[1] 42,827 sq. miles, includes outlying islands and cays not within any province.

CLIMATE. Situated in the sub-tropical zone, Cuba has a generally rainy climate, affected by the Gulf Stream and the N.E. Trades, though winters are comparatively dry after the heaviest rains in Sept. and Oct. Hurricanes are liable to occur between June and Nov. Havana. Jan. 72°F (22·2°C), July 82°F (27·8°C). Annual rainfall 48″ (1,224 mm).

CONSTITUTION AND GOVERNMENT. The previous Constitution was

378

suspended in Jan. 1959. The first socialist Constitution came into force on 24 Feb. 1976.

Since the last representative in Cuba of the King of Spain, Gen. Don Adolfo Jiménez Castellanos, handed over the island on 1 Jan. 1899 the following have been at the head of the administration:

	Took office		Took office
US Military Governors		Dr Carlos Manuel de Cés-	
Maj.-Gen. John R. Brooke	1 Jan. 1899	pedes	12 Aug. 1933
Maj.-Gen. Leonard Wood	23 Dec. 1899	Dr Ramón Grau San Martín	10 Sept. 1933
		Col. Carlos Mendieta	Jan. 1934
President of the Republic		Dr José A. Barnet	12 Dec. 1935
Tomas Estrada Palma	20 May 1902	Dr Miguel Mariano Gómez y	
		Arias	20 May 1936
US Provisional Governors		Dr Federico Laredo Bru	24 Dec. 1936
William Howard Taft	29 Sept. 1906	Gen. Fulgencio Batista y	
Charles Edward Magoon	13 Oct. 1906	Zaldívar	10 Oct. 1940
		Dr Ramón Grau San Martín	10 Oct. 1944
Presidents of the Republic		Dr Carlos Frío Socarrás	10 Oct. 1948
Gen. José Miguel Gómez	28 Jan. 1909	Gen. Fulgencio Batista y	
Gen. Mario García Menocal	20 May 1913	Zaldívar	10 March 1952
Dr Alfredo Zayas y Alfonso	20 May 1921	Dr Manuel Urratia Lleo	2 Jan. 1959
Gen. Gerardo Machado y		Osvaldo Dorticos	
Morales	20 May 1925	Torrado	17 July 1959

President: Dr Fidel Castro Ruz became President of the Council of State on 3 Dec. 1976. He is also President of the Council of Ministers, First Secretary of the Cuban Communist Party and C.-in-C. of the Revolutionary Armed Forces. From Jan. 1980 he took overall charge of Defence, Interior, Health and Culture.

Dr Castro on 2 Dec. 1961 proclaimed 'a Marxist–Leninist programme adapted to the precise objective conditions existing in our country'. The provisional *Organizaciones Revolucionarias Integradas* (ORI) were established as an intermediate stage towards a single (communist) party, and gave way to the *Partido Unido de la Revolución Socialista* (PURS). This brought together the *Partido Socialista Popular, Movimiento de 26 Julio* and (Students') *Directorio Revolucionario*. The PURS in turn became (3 Oct. 1965) the *Partido Comunista de Cuba*. The Communist Party had been outlawed by Batista in 1954, but legally reinstated after the revolution.

National flag: 3 blue, 2 white stripes (horizontal); a white 5-pointed star in a red triangle at the hoist.

National anthem: Al combate corred bayameses (words and tune by P. Figueredo, 1868).

Local Government. The country is divided into 14 provinces and 169 municipalities. Local Government is the responsibility of the organizations of Peoples' Power. Elections were held in 1976, 1979 and 1981 for delegates to the provincial and municipal assemblies and to the national assembly.

DEFENCE. On 13 Nov. 1963 conscription was introduced for all men between the ages of 16 and 45, later raised to 50 (3 years); women of the 17–35 age groups may volunteer (for 2 years).

Army. The strength was 125,000 officers and men (75,000 conscripts) in 1984. Reserves are estimated at 190,000.

The Army is organized in 15 infantry brigades, 3 armoured brigades and 8 independent battalions. Equipment includes 350 T-34, 250 T-54/-55 and 60 T-62 tanks. Para-military forces total 15,000 and the new Territorial Militia, more than 500,000.

Navy. The Navy consists of 3 *ex*-Soviet diesel-powered submarines (of which 1 is in static reserve), 1 *ex*-Soviet guided missile-armed frigate, 28 missile boats, 6 hydrofoil attack craft, 13 patrol vessels, 20 torpedo boats, 22 fast gunboats, 12 inshore minesweepers, 12 motor launches, 14 coastguard vessels, 13 survey vessels, 3 landing ships, 7 landing craft and 10 service craft. The large majority of over 160 craft are former units of the Soviet Navy. Personnel in 1984 exceeded 6,000 officers and ratings. One of the 3 old *ex*-US patrol frigates still exists as a harbour hulk. The USA is still in possession of the Guantanámo naval base, but the Cuban Government refuses to accept the nominal rent of US$5,000 per annum.

Air Force. The Air Force has been extensively re-equipped with aircraft supplied by USSR and in 1983 had a strength of some 16,000 officers and men and 250 combat aircraft. About 16 interceptor and 4 ground-attack squadrons fly MiG-23, MiG-21 and MiG-17 jet fighters. There is a squadron of An-26 twin-turboprop transports, some An-24 twin-turboprop transports, piston-engined Il-14s, and about 100 Mi-24 gunship, Mi-8 (some armed) and Mi-4 helicopters, Zlin 326 piston-engined trainers and MiG-15UTI, MiG-21U and MiG-23U jet trainers. Many An-2M biplanes are operated by the Air Force, mainly on agricultural and liaison duties. Soviet-built surface-to-air ('Guideline', 'Goa' and 'Gainful') and coastal defence ('Samlet') missiles are in service.

INTERNATIONAL RELATIONS

Membership. Cuba is a member of the UN and COMECON.

ECONOMY

Planning. The Cuban economy is now centrally planned. Since July 1972 Cuba has been a member of the Council for Mutual Economic Assistance (COMECON) and, since Jan. 1974, of the two COMECON international banks.

Budget. Revenue in 1981 was 11,201·3m. pesos and expenditure, 11,197·4m. pesos.

Currency. The Cuban *peso* has been tied to the French franc since early 1972. In March 1984, the sterling-peso rate was £1 = 1·75 *pesos*. The gold content is 0·888671 gramme of fine gold, thus 1 troy oz. of fine gold = 35 *pesos*. The law of 7 Nov. 1914, established that the monetary unit was a gold *peso* (equal to the US gold dollar) of 1·6718 grammes (1·5046 grammes fine) divided in 100 *centavos*. The old gold *pesos* and all US currency are no longer legal tender.

Copper-nickel coins of 40, 20, 5 and 1 *cent* are issued. Notes are for 100, 50, 20, 10, 5 and 1 *peso*.

Banking. On 23 Dec. 1948 the president signed the law creating a central bank (with capital of US$10m.) and which began operating 27 April 1950.

On 14 Oct. 1960 all banks were nationalized, except the Royal Bank of Canada and the Bank of Nova Scotia, which were bought out later. All banking is now carried out by the National Bank of Cuba through its 250 agencies. In 1964, 1·6m. small savings accounts totalled US$738m.

All insurance business was nationalized in Jan. 1964.

Weights and Measures. The metric system of weights and measures is legally compulsory, but the American and old Spanish systems are much used. The sugar industry uses the Spanish long ton (1·03 tonnes) and short ton (0·92 tonne). Cuba sugar sack = 329·59 lb. or 149·49 kg. Land is measured in *caballerías* (of 13·4 hectares or 33 acres).

ENERGY AND NATURAL RESOURCES

Electricity. Installed capacity 1980 was 2,100 mw. Production in 1982 was 11,016m. kwh.

Minerals. Iron ore abounds, with deposits estimated at 3,500m. tons, of which 90% were held as reserves by American steel interests but are now controlled by the Cuban Mining Institute; output (tonnes), wrought iron (1980), 1,180; steel (1981), 329,835.

Output of copper (1982) was 1,465 tonnes; refractory chrome (1982), 27,300 tonnes. Other minerals are nickel and cobalt (1981, 40,255 tonnes), silica and barytes. Gold and silver are also worked. Cuba has a small output of petroleum (1978: 6·4m. tonnes). Salt output from the solar evaporation of sea water was 130,453 tonnes in 1980.

Agriculture. In May 1959 all land over 30 *caballerías* was nationalized and has since been turned into state farms. In Oct. 1963 private holdings were reduced to a maximum of 5 *caballerías* (approximately 67 hectares). By 1960, 764 co-operative farms had been formed, and by late 1966 almost 65% of farm land was state-owned; the balance being in private hands.

In Sept. 1982 there were 1,402 co-operatives comprising 47,357 *caballerías* of land. The total cultivated land included state-owned, 3,398,200 hectares, and in the private sector, 475,400 hectares.

The staple products are tobacco and sugar, of which latter Cuba is the world's second largest producer; with its by-products it furnishes nearly 80% by value of the national exports. The 1981–82 crop was 8·2m. tonnes. There are 151 mills, including 40 of the largest, which were taken over from US interests, and which represent 39% of total capacity. Coffee, cotton, maize, rice and potatoes are grown.

Production of other important crops in 1982 was (in tonnes): Tobacco, 44,100; rice, 499,700; maize, 15,500; coffee, 26,000.

Tobacco is grown mainly in the Vuelta–Abajo district, near Pinar del Río. Coffee is grown chiefly in the province of Oriente.

Output of henequén fibre in 1964 was 233,919 tons. A fast-growing fibre, *kenaf*, originally from India, soft in texture, is replacing jute for sacking; the tobacco industry uses *majagua*, another local fibre, while a third fibre, *yarey*, from palms is also used. 208,540 tonnes of potatoes were produced in 1980. A nitrate plant has been built at Nuevitas and a large British-built urea plant at Cienfuegos. The principal fruits exported are pineapples, citrus fruit, tomatoes and pimentos. A rice cultivation plan began in 1967 in the south of Havana province. Cultivation is highly mechanized and the area so far sown produces two crops a year.

In 1982 citrus fruit production was 524,600 tonnes.

In 1962, 2,105 *caballerías* were allocated to cotton; cotton produced, 1982, was 3,000 tons against 13,000 tons in 1962.

In 1982 the livestock included 2m. pigs; 841,000 horses; 375,000 sheep; 101,000 goats; 6·2m. head of cattle.

Forestry. Cuba has extensive forest lands. These forests contain valuable cabinet woods, such as mahogany and cedar, besides dye-woods, fibres, gums, resins and oils. Cedar is used locally for cigar-boxes, and mahogany is exported. During the re-forestation campaign of 1959–60, 34,000 eucalyptus saplings were planted over 1,120 *caballerías*. Cedars, mahogany, *majagua*, teca, etc., are also being raised and planted out. In 1980 saplings planted included: Eucalyptus, 2,110; pine, 34,732; majagua, 4,187; mahogany, 1,729; cedar, 1,722; casuarina, 9,671.

INDUSTRY AND TRADE

Industry. Production in 1982 was: Textiles, 152·8m. sq. metres; cement, 3,163,300 tonnes; wheat flour, 376,300 tonnes; fuel oil, 3,298,100 tonnes; diesel oil, 1,126,600 tonnes; 204,900 tyres; 177,500 inner tubes; leather shoes, 13,340,000 pairs; paint, 68,988 hectolitres; soft drinks, 2,051,200 hectolitres; 359m. cigars; 17,043,600m. cigarettes; fertilizers, 1,026,300 tonnes.

Trade Unions. All workers have a right to join a trade union. The Workers' Central Union of Cuba, to which 23 unions are affiliated, had 2m. members in 1978.

Commerce. Imports and exports (including bullion and specie) for calendar years (in 1m. pesos):

	1979	1980	1981	1982
Imports	3,687	4,059	5,081	5,537
Exports	3,500	3,967	4,259	4,939

Cuba's principal exports are sugar, minerals, tobacco and fish, which in 1974 were planned to furnish 86%, 6·4%, 2·7% and 2·3% respectively by value. The main imports from non-Communist countries are chemicals and engineering and electrical machinery and transport equipment.

Sugar accounts for approximately 80% of the exports. In 1980 over 2,207,000 tons were sold in free world markets, the balance going mainly to Eastern Europe under long-term guaranteed price contracts. Tobacco, fish and nickel are the other major exports. Most trade is with Eastern Europe, particularly with the USSR which supplies approximately 50% of total Cuban imports.

Total trade between Cuba and UK (British Department of Trade returns, in £1,000 sterling):

	1978	1979	1980	1981	1982	1983
Imports to UK	7,960	14,970	26,208	16,829	17,688	14,010
Exports and re-exports from UK	27,625	36,112	35,272	27,656	64,835	45,737

COMMUNICATIONS

Roads. There are 31,204 km of highways open to traffic, including the Central Highway, traversing the island for 760 miles from Pinar del Río to Santiago. In 1980 there were 32,662 hire cars (including coaches and buses).

Railways. There were (1980) 5,196 km of public railway (mainly 1,435 mm gauge) of which 199 km is electrified. In 1982 it carried 23m. passengers and 16·6m. tonnes of freight. In addition, the large sugar estates have 9,441 km of lines on 1,435, 914 and 760 mm gauges.

Aviation. The state airline CUBANA operates all internal services, and from Havana to Mexico City, Madrid, Berlin, Montreal, Prague, and also to Lima, Panama, Kingston, Bridgetown, Port of Spain, Georgetown. The other regular foreign services are Mexican, Spanish, Soviet, Czech, East German and Canadian. In Dec. 1977 the first charter flights since 1960 started operating between USA and Cuba.

Shipping. The coastline is over 3,500 miles long and has many fine harbours. The merchant marine, in 1981, consisted of 93 sea-going vessels of 953,700 DWT.

Post and Broadcasting. There are 3,545 miles of public and 8,902 miles of private telegraph wires. Cuba has 103 broadcasting stations and 2 television stations. Radio receiving sets, 1974, numbered 909,000; television sets, 300,000. The national telephone system (1982) had 406,355 instruments.

Cinemas. In 1980 there were 692 cinemas.

Newspapers. In 1980 there were 29 newspapers of which 14 were daily newspapers.

JUSTICE, RELIGION, EDUCATION AND WELFARE

Justice. There is a Supreme Court in Havana and 7 regional courts of appeal. The provinces are divided into judicial districts, with courts for civil and criminal actions, with municipal courts for minor offences. The civil code guarantees aliens the same property and personal rights as are enjoyed by nationals.

The 1959 Agrarian Reform Law and the Urban Reform Law passed on 14 Oct. 1960 have placed certain restrictions on both. Revolutionary Summary Tribunals have wide powers.

Religion. There is no state Church, though Roman Catholics predominate. There is a bishop of the American Episcopal Church in Havana; there are congregations of Methodists in Havana and in the provinces. Protestants numbered 265,000 in 1962; they have been organized as the Cuban Council of Evangelical Churches.

Education. Education is compulsory (between the ages of 6 and 14) and free, and now available everywhere. In 1964 illiteracy was officially declared to have been completely eliminated.

In 1977 the 4 universities had 122,546 students and 9,934 teaching staff. There were (1980–81) 1,468,538 pupils and (1977) 82,250 teachers at primary schools; 1,177,813 pupils at intermediate schools; 151,733 students at higher schools;

277,003 students at adult primary and intermediate schools; and 169,326 students at other schools.

The Camilo Cienfuegos school city in the Sierra Maestra was designed for 12,000 boys and 8,000 girls by 1970 (1965: 4,000, total). In 1974 the V. I. Lenin vocational school opened as a forerunner of 6 such schools.

Health (1981). There were 16,193 posts for doctors and 266 hospitals. The 1982 health and education budget was 2,040·3m. pesos.

Free medical services are provided by the state polyclinics, though some doctors still have private practices. All serious tropical diseases are effectively kept under control, and virtually all children under the age of 15 have been vaccinated against poliomyelitis.

DIPLOMATIC REPRESENTATIVES

Of Cuba in Great Britain (167 High Holborn, London, WC1)
Ambassador: Hermes Herrera (accredited 16 Feb. 1982).

Of Great Britain in Cuba (Edificio Bolivar, Carcel 101–103, Havana)
Ambassador: Patrick Robin Fearn.

Of Cuba to the United Nations
Ambassador: Dr Raúl Roa Kouri.

The USA broke off diplomatic relations with Cuba on 3 Jan. 1961 but both retain residual missions to the Swiss Embassy in Havana and to the Czechoslovak Embassy in Washington respectively.

Books of Reference

Anuario Estadístico de a República de Cuba. Havana, 1914, 1953, 1957, 1972, 1973, 1979
Boletín Oficial, Ministerio de Comercio. Monthly
Estadística General: Commercio Exterior. Quarterly and Annual.—*Movimiento de Población.* Monthly and Annual. Havana
Anuario azucarero de Cuba. Havana, from 1937
Canet, G., and Raisz, E., *Atlas de Cuba.* Cambridge, Mass., 1949
Carpentier, A., *Reasons of State.* London, 1976
Caute, D., ¿*Cuba, Yes?* London, 1974
Dominguez, J. I., *Cuba: Order and Revolution.* Harvard Univ. Press, 1978
Guerra y Sánchez, R., and others, *Historia de la Nación Cubana* 10 vols. Havana, 1952
Gonzalez, E., *Cuba Under Castro: The Limits of Charisma.* Boston, 1974
MacEwan, A., *Revolution and Economic Development in Cuba.* London, 1981
Mesa-Lago, C., *The Economy of Socialist Cuba: A Two-Decade Appraisal.* Univ. of New Mexico Press, 1981
Meyer, K. E., and Szulc, T., *The Cuban Invasion.* New York, 1962
Miller, W., *The Lost Plantation.* London, 1961
Montaner, C. A., *Informe secreto sobre la revolución cubana.* Madrid, 1975
Nelson, L., *Cuba: The Measure of the Revolution.* Univ. of Minnesota Press, 1972
O'Connor, J., *The Origins of Socialism in Cuba.* London, Cornell Univ. Press, 1970
Ritter, A. R. M., *The Economic Development of Revolutionary Cuba: Strategy and Performance.* New York, 1974
Suchlicki, J. (ed.), *Cuba, Castro, and Revolution.* Univ. of Miami Press, 1972.—*Cuba: From Columbus to Castro.* New York, 1974
Vives, J., *Les Maîtres de Cuba.* Paris, 1981

CYPRUS

Capital: Nicosia
Population: 645,500 (1982)
GNP per capita: US$3,193 (1982)

Kypriaki Dimokratia—
Kıbrıs Cumhuriyeti

HISTORY. About the middle of the 2nd millennium B.C. Greek colonies were established in Cyprus and later it formed part of the Persian, Roman and Byzantine empires. In 1193 it became a Frankish kingdom, in 1489 a Venetian dependency and in 1571 was conquered by the Turks. They retained possession of it until its cession to England for administrative purposes under a convention concluded with the Sultan at Constantinople, 4 June 1878. On 5 Nov. 1914 the island was annexed by Great Britain and on 1 May 1925 given the status of a Crown Colony.

For the history of Cyprus from 1931 to 1974 *see* THE STATESMAN'S YEAR-BOOK, 1958, pp. 237–38, 1959, p. 236, and 1983–84, p. 385.

On 15 July 1974 a *coup* was staged in Cyprus by the men of the Greek ruling junta, for the overthrow of President Makarios. The President left the island and the *coup* was short-lived. On 23 July power was handed over to the President of the House of Representatives, Glafcos Clerides, in accordance with the Constitution. He acted as President until the return of President Makarios on Dec. 7.

Turkey invaded the island on 20 July, eventually landing 40,000 troops supported with heavy armament and tanks. In two military operations 20–30 July and 14–16 Aug. the Turkish troops managed to occupy 40% of the northern part of Cyprus. As a result 200,000 Greek Cypriots fled to live as refugees in the south. The Cyprus crisis was raised in the UN and the General Assembly unanimously adopted resolutions calling for the withdrawal of all foreign troops from Cyprus and the return of refugees to their homes, but without result.

On 13 Feb. 1975 at a special meeting of the executive council and legislative assembly of the Autonomous Turkish Cypriot Administration a Turkish Cypriot Federated State was proclaimed. Rauf Denktash was appointed President and he declared that the state would not seek international recognition. The proclamation was denounced by President Makarios and the Greek Prime Minister but welcomed by the Turkish Prime Minister.

AREA AND POPULATION. The island lies in the eastern Mediterranean, about 50 miles off the south coast of Turkey and (at the nearest points) 65 miles off the coast of Syria. Area 3,572 sq. miles (9,251 sq. km); about 150 miles is greatest length from east to west, and about 60 miles is greatest breadth from north to south. Populations by religions:

Religion	1946	1960	1980	1981	1982
Greek Orthodox	361,199	441,656	511,200	514,100	520,900
Turkish Moslem	80,548	104,942	118,800	119,500	121,100
Others	8,367	26,968	3,500	3,500	3,500
Total	450,114	573,566	633,500	637,100	645,500

Population estimate (1982) 645,500, of which 81% are Greek Cypriot (Armenian, Maronite and Latin minorities included) and 19% Turkish Cypriot. Principal towns with populations (1982 estimate): Nicosia (the capital), 161,100 (Greek Cypriots); Limassol, 107,200; Famagusta, 39,500; Larnaca, 48,400.

As a result of the Turkish invasion and the occupation of part of Cyprus, 200,000 Greek Cypriots were displaced and forced to find refuge in the south of the island. The urban centres of Famagusta, Kyrenia and Morphou were completely evacuated.

Vital statistics. The birth rate per 1,000 population in 1982 was 22·1%; death rate, 8·3%; infantile mortality per 1,000 live births, 17·2%.

CLIMATE. The climate is Mediterranean, with very hot, dry summers and variable winters. Maximum temperatures may reach 112°F (44·5°C) in July and Aug., but minimum figures may fall to 22°F (–5·5°C) in the mountains in winter when snow is experienced. Rainfall is generally between 10 and 27" (250 and 675 mm) and occurs mainly in the winter months, but is may be as much as 48" (1,200 mm) in the Troodos mountains. Nicosia. Jan. 50°F (10·0°C), July 83°F (28·3°C). Annual rainfall 15" (371 mm).

CONSTITUTION AND GOVERNMENT. The legislative power is exercised by the House of Representatives of 50 members, of whom 35 were elected by the Greek community and 15 by the Turkish community. As from Dec. 1963 the Turkish members have ceased to attend.

On 13 Dec. 1959 Archbishop Makarios was elected President of the Republic, having received 144,501 votes (against 71,753 cast for the candidate sponsored by the Left). Dr Fazil Kuchuk was elected Vice-President unopposed; he resigned on 4 Jan. 1964. On 13 Feb. 1975, Rauf Denktash the Turkish-Cypriot leader announced the formation of a Turkish-Cypriot state within a federal republic and on 15 Nov. 1983 a unilateral declaration of independence, as the Turkish Republic of Northern Cyprus, was announced.

When President Makarios died in Aug. 1977 Spyros Kyprianou became acting President and was proclaimed President on 31 Aug. 1977 and was elected for a 5-year term on 26 Jan. 1978 and re-elected 13 Feb. 1983.

Flag: White with a copper-coloured outline of the island with 2 green olive-branches beneath.

The elections held on 25 May 1981 returned 8 Democratic Party, 12 Akel Party (Communists), 3 EDEK (Socialist Party), 12 Democratic Rally. The Turks have not participated in the proceedings of the House since Dec. 1963.

The Council of Ministers in Dec. 1983 was as follows:

Foreign Affairs: George Iacovou. *Interior and Defence:* Christodoulos Veniamin. *Finance:* Simos Vasiliou. *Minister to the President:* Dinos Michaelides. *Commerce and Industry:* George Andreou. *Education:* Stelios Katsellis. *Communications and Works:* Christos Mavrellis. *Agriculture and Natural Resources:* Dr Dimitrios Christodoulou. *Labour and Social Insurance:* Pavlos Papageorghiou. *Health:* Dr Christos Pelekanos. *Justice:* Phivos Clerides. *Deputy Minister of the Interior:* Elias Eliades.

DEFENCE

Army. Total strength (1984) 10,000 organized in 1 armoured, 2 reconnaissance/mechanized infantry and 20 infantry battalions, with artillery and support units. The National Guard has a twin-engined Maritime Islander light transport. There is also a para-military force of 3,000 armed police.

The Turkish-Cypriot Security Force consisted of about 4,500 men supported by some T-34 tanks.

INTERNATIONAL RELATIONS

Membership. Cyprus is a member of UN, the Commonwealth, the Council of Europe and the Non-Aligned Movement.

ECONOMY

Planning. A third emergency action plan was launched in 1979 for 3 years; expenditure, 1979, £C34·8m. Agriculture and irrigation have been emphasized (expenditure, 1977–78, £C20·3m.; 1979 (planned) £C15·2m.).

Budget. Revenue and expenditure for calendar years (in £C1m.):

Ordinary	1977	1978	1979	1980	1981	1982
Revenue	87·0	102·4	123·6	151·5	164·6	218·5
Expenditure	81·2	92·7	118·0	168·2	200·8	246·4
Development						
Expenditure	19·1	24·3	32·2	34·8	36·3	41·6

Main sources of ordinary revenue in 1982 (in £C1m.) were: Import duties, 45·7; excise duties, 36·4; income tax, 40·1; rents, royalties and interest, 15·5; sales of goods and services, 12; other duties and taxes, 19·2.

Main divisions of ordinary expenditure in 1982 (in £C1m.): Personal emoluments, 94·5; pensions and gratuities, 8·4; commodity subsidies, 20; subventions and contributions, 26·5; public debt charges, 42; refunds and drawbacks, 9·4.

Development expenditure for 1982 (in £C1m.) included 8·6 for water development, 6·9 for agriculture, forests and fisheries, 2·9 for rural development, 6·5 for roads, 2·7 for airports and 0·6 for tourism. (An independent Ports Authority with its own funds was set up in 1977.)

The outstanding public debt as at 31 Dec. 1982 was £C234·9m., excluding sinking fund reserves, and accumulated sinking funds totalled £C20m. Outstanding loans as at 31 Dec. 1981 totalled £C49·5m.; including £C7·9m. to the Electricity Authority of Cyprus and £C3m. to the Cyprus Telecommunications Authority.

Currency. The *Cyprus £* is divided into 1,000 *cents*. Notes of the following denominations are in circulation: £10, £5, £1, 50 *cents*. Coins in circulation: Cupro-zinc-nickel: 100, 50, 25 *mils*; bronze and aluminium: 5 *mils*. Rate of exchange, March 1984: £1 = £C0·803; US$1 = £C1·833.

Banking. There is a Central and Issuing Bank exercising monetary functions, and the Cyprus Development Corporation created by the Government as a major source of loan funds for industrial development. Commercial banks carrying on business in Cyprus are: Bank of Cyprus Ltd, Turkish Bank Ltd, Cyprus Popular Bank Ltd, Barclays Bank International, The Chartered Bank, National Bank of Greece, Hellenic Bank Ltd, Cyprus Turkish Co-operative Central Bank Ltd, Mortgage Bank of Cyprus Ltd, Turkiye Ish Bankasi, The Co-operative Central Bank, Grindlays Bank and Lombard Banking (Cyprus) Ltd.

The Central Bank of Cyprus, established in 1963, is responsible for the issue of currency, the regulation of money supply and credit, administration of the exchange control law and the foreign-exchange reserves of the republic. The Bank also acts as a banker of the banks operating in Cyprus and of the Government.

At the end of Dec. 1983 total deposits in banks were £C689m. The country's foreign exchange reserves at the end of Dec. 1982 were £C289m.

Weights and Measures. Cyprus weights and measures follow the standard weights and measures of Great Britain. The metric system may also be lawfully used. In internal trade the following special Cyprus weights and measures are in use: 1 *pic* = ⅔ yd; 1 *oke* = 2·8 lb.; 1 *kilé* = 8 Imperial gallons. The Cyprus *donum* is approximately ⅓ acre.

ENERGY AND NATURAL RESOURCES

Water resources. Since 1960, £C85m. has been spent on water dams, water supplies, hydrological research and geophysical surveys. Existing dams have (1982) a capacity of 118m. cu. metres as against 6m. cu. metres before independence.

Minerals. The principal minerals exported during 1982 were (in tonnes): Asbestos, 19,112; clay (bentonite), 17,533; chrome ore, 11,851; umber, 5,221. Mining products provided about 2·5% of all exports in 1982. Total value of minerals exported in 1982 was £C6·7m. No figures for copper cement at the Xeros mines as this is in the Turkish occupied area.

Agriculture. Chief agricultural products in 1982 (1,000 tonnes): Grapes, 201·2; potatoes, 171·7; milk, 83·9; cereals (wheat and barley), 91·5; citrus fruit, 127·8; meat, 38·5; carobs, 12·8; fresh fruit, 25 3; olives, 13·2; other vegetables, 91; eggs, 93m. dozen.

Of the island's 2·3m. acres, approximately 1m. are cultivated. 18·7% of the economically active population are engaged in agriculture.

Livestock in 1982 (in 1,000): Cattle, 31; sheep, 315; goats, 228; pigs, 209; poultry, 2,200.

Forestry. Reforesting the areas burnt during the Turkish invasion is continuing and by Dec. 1981 12,037 hectares of burnt forests were reforested and/or cultivated. Total forest area, 1,734 sq. km.

In 1982 the chief forest products were timber, valued at £C656,024; firewood, £C21,071; figures relate to the area of Cyprus not occupied by Turkey.

INDUSTRY AND TRADE

Industry. Cyprus has no heavy industry, but a wide variety of light manufacturing industries. The establishment of a Development Bank in 1963 has given further impetus to industrial activity. Manufacturing industry in 1982 contributed about 17·2% (C£163·5m.) to the GDP and gave employment to 21·5% of the economically active population.

The highest increases in output in 1981 were production of metal products, chemicals, foodstuffs, furniture, footwear and clothing. Industrial exports rose to £C113m. in 1982 and accounted for 55·9% of total domestic exports.

Trade Unions and Associations. Registration of trade unions and employers' associations is compulsory and freedom of association is constitutionally and statutorily guaranteed. At the end of 1979 the trade unions were distributed as follows: Pancyprian Federation of Labour ('old' trade unions), 55,779 members in 11 unions; Cyprus Workers Confederation ('free' labour syndicates), 36,632 members in 56 unions; Pancyprian Federation of Independent Trade Unions, 909 members in 9 unions; Cyprus Turkish Trade Unions Federation, 5,668 members in 13 unions (1973); Cyprus Democratic Labour Federation, 224 members in 4 unions; Civil Service Trade Union, 11,194 members.

The 'old' trade unions are affiliated to the World Federation of Trade Unions, the 'free' labour syndicates and the Turkish Federation are affiliated to the International Confederation of Free Trade Unions.

In Dec. 1979 the total number of employers' associations was 27 with a total membership of 4,104. Some of the employers' associations are members of the Cyprus Employers' and Industrialists' Federation, an organization with 12 trade associations consisting of 869 members.

Commerce. The commerce and the shipping, exclusive of coasting trade, for calendar years were (in £C1,000):

	1978	1979	1980	1981	1982
Imports [1]	375,972	357,603	424,292	489,536	577,551
Exports [2]	170,732	161,871	188,036	234,773	263,809

[1] Excluding Naafi imports of about £C1·5m. in 1982.
[2] Including re-exports and ships' stores of about £C59m. in 1982.

Chief civil imports, 1982 (in £C1,000):

Petroleum and petroleum products	113,965	Feeding stuff for animals	9,204
Textile yarn and fabrics made up	44,550	Tobacco and manufactures	10,739
Iron and steel	22,427	Meat and meat preparations	5,658
Cereals and cereal preparations	24,870	Vegetable oils and fats	5,738
Transport equipment	130,535	Non metallic mineral manufactures	14,772
Paper, paperboard and pulp and articles thereof	...	Medicinal and pharmaceutical products	8,060
Artificial resins and plastics	12,720	Manufactures of metal, n.e.s.	16,792
		Dairy products and eggs	6,609

Chief domestic exports, 1982 (in £C1,000):

Grapes	3,921	Cigarettes	8,984
Grapefruit	4,985	Paper products	8,965
Lemons	3,498	Cement	13,307
Oranges	4,168	Clothing	31,664
Potatoes	22,530	Footwear	15,841
Wine	6,898		

In 1982 the EEC countries supplied 48% of the imports; Arab countries, 15·1%; Eastern Europe, 5%; others, 31·9%. Of the exports (1982), 48·7% went to Arab countries; 30·9% to EEC countries; 6% to Eastern Europe and 14·4% to other countries.

Total trade between Cyprus and UK (British Department of Trade returns, in £1,000 sterling):

	1978	1979	1980	1981	1982	1983
Imports to UK	112,014	115,636	128,386	80,580	89,908	87,436
Exports and re-exports from UK	111,183	120,101	153,754	115,597	111,882	127,837

Tourism. Foreign tourists (1982), 548,180 and 58,697 excursionists.

COMMUNICATIONS

Roads. In 1982 the total length of roads was 10,943 km, of which 5,277 km were paved and 5,666 km were earth or gravel roads. The main roads which are maintained by the Ministry of Communications and Works (Public Works Department) totalled 2,873 km, of which 2,791 km were paved. The total of urban streets was 1,690 km, of which 1,178 were paved. Village roads and streets totalled 4,037 km, of which 1,308 km were paved, the rest being of earth or gravel surface. There were also 2,343 km of unpaved forest roads.

The area controlled by the Government of the Republic and that occupied by Turkey are now served by separate transport systems, and there are no services linking the two areas.

Aviation. Nicosia airport has been closed since Aug. 1974. During 1982, 1,338,322 persons travelled and 28,576,000 kg of commercial air-freight was handled through Larnaca airport.

Shipping. In 1982, 5,015 ships of 9,577,000 net tons entered Cyprus ports. Ships under Cyprus registry (Sept. 1983) numbered 1,300 of 4·4m. tons. Famagusta has been closed to international traffic since Aug. 1974.

Post and Broadcasting. In 1983 there were 53 post offices and 583 postal agencies. There are 17 post offices and 368 postal agencies in the Turkish occupied area. Telephones (1982) 128,507. Wireless licences issued (1978) were 222,470, including television licences.

Cyprus Broadcasting Corporation broadcasts mainly in Greek, but also in Turkish, English, and Armenian on medium-waves. The corporation also broadcasts one TV programme.

Cinemas (1976). In the Greek part of Cyprus there were 66 winter cinemas (38,500 seats) and 17 open-air cinemas (9,700 seats).

Newspapers (1983). There are 9 Greek, 4 Turkish and 1 English daily newspapers and 10 Greek, 6 Turkish and 1 English weeklies.

JUSTICE, RELIGION, EDUCATION AND WELFARE

Justice. Under the Constitution and other legislation in force the following judicial institutions are established: The Supreme Court of the Republic, the Assize Courts and District Courts.

The Supreme Court is composed of 10, one of whom is the President. The Supreme Court adjudicates exclusively and finally: on all constitutional and administrative law matters, including any recourse that any law or decision of the House of Representatives or the budget is discriminatory against either of the two

Communities; on any conflict of competence between state organs, questions of unconstitutionality of any law or decisions on any question of interpretation of the Constitution in case of ambiguity, as well as recourses for annulment of administrative acts, decisions or omissions. The Supreme Court is the highest appellate court in the republic and has jurisdiction to hear and determine all appeals from any court. It has exclusive jurisdiction to issue orders in the nature of *habeas corpus, mandamus,* prohibition, *quo warranto* and *certiorari* and in admiralty and matrimonial matters.

There are 6 assize courts and 6 district courts, 1 for each district. The assize courts have unlimited criminal jurisdiction and power to order compensation up to £C800. The district courts exercise original civil and criminal jurisdiction, the extent of which varies with the composition of the Bench. In civil matters (other than those within the original jurisdiction of Supreme Court) a District Court composed of not less than 2 and not more than 3 judges has unlimited jurisdiction. A President or a Senior District Judge sitting alone has jurisdiction up to £C3,000, and a District Judge sitting alone up to £C1,000, and is also empowered to deal with any action for the recovery of possession of any immovable property, and certain other specified matters. In criminal matters the jurisdiction of a District Court is exercised by its members sitting singly and is of a summary character. A President, a Senior District Judge or a District Judge sitting alone has power to try any offence punishable with imprisonment up to 3 years, or with a fine up to £C500 or with both, and may order compensation up to £C500.

Religion. *See* Area and Population, p. 384.

Education. Until 31 March 1965 each community in Cyprus managed its own schooling through its respective Communal Chamber. Intercommunal education had been placed under the Minister of the Interior, assisted by a Board of Education for Intercommunal Schools, of which the Minister was the Chairman. In 1965 the Greek Communal Chamber was dissolved and a Ministry of Education was established to take its place. Intercommunal education has been placed under this Ministry.

Greek-Cypriot Education. Elementary education is compulsory and is provided free in 6 grades to children between 5½ and 12 years of age. In some towns and large villages there are separate junior schools consisting of the first three grades. Apart from schools for the deaf and blind and the Lambousa School for juvenile offenders, there are also 7 schools for handicapped children. In 1982–83 the Ministry ran 179 kindergartens for children from low-income families; there were 120 privately run pre-primary schools. There were 430 primary schools with 43,083 pupils and 2,190 teachers in 1982–83.

Secondary education is free for the first 4 years and is fee-paying for the rest, although senior pupils can be wholly or partially exempt from payment. The secondary school is 6 years, 3 years at the gymnasium followed by 3 years at the lykeion. There were 3 types of lykeia: classical, science, economic. There are 5- to 6-year technical schools. In 1982–83 there were 99 secondary schools with 3,059 teachers and 48,527 pupils.

Post-secondary education is provided at the Pedagogical Academy, which organizes 3-year courses for the training of pre-primary and primary school teachers, and at the Higher Technical Institute, which provides 3-year courses for technicians in civil, electrical and mechanical engineering. There is also a 2-year Forestry College (administered by the Ministry of Agriculture), a Hotel and Catering Institute and a 3-year Nurses' School and 1-year School for Health Inspectors (Ministry of Health). Adult education is conducted through youth centres in rural areas, foreign language institutes in the towns and private institutions offering courses in business administration and secretarial work.

In 1982–83, 11,700 students were studying in universities abroad, mainly in Greece and the UK.

Turkish-Cypriot Education. The Office of Education of the Turkish Community of Cyprus caters for some 18% of the island's population and (1976) administered 10 kindergartens, 167 elementary schools (16,014 pupils), 18 secondary schools

(7,190 pupils), 6 technical schools (735 pupils) and 1 teacher-training college (13 students). There were 43 evening institutes for adult education.

Greek is the language of 80% of the population and Turkish of 18%. English is widely spoken. English and French are compulsory subjects in secondary schools. Illiteracy is largely confined to older people.

Social Security. The administration of the social-security services in Cyprus is in the hands of the Ministry of Labour and Social Insurance, with the Ministry of Health providing medical services through public clinics and hospitals on a means test, except medical treatment for employment accidents, which is given free to all insured employees and financed by the Social Insurance Scheme.

DIPLOMATIC REPRESENTATIVES

Of Cyprus in Great Britain (93 Park St., London, W1Y 4ET)
High Commissioner: Tasos Panayides.

Of Great Britain in Cyprus (Alexander Pallis St., Nicosia)
High Commissioner: W. J. A. Wilberforce, CMG.

Of Cyprus in the USA (2211 R. St., NW, Washington, D.C., 20008)
Ambassador: Andrew J. Jacovides.

Of the USA in Cyprus (Therissos St., Nicosia)
Ambassador: Raymond C. Ewing.

Of Cyprus to the United Nations
Ambassador: Constantine Moushoutas.

Books of Reference

Statistical Information: Statistics and Research Department, Nicosia.
Alastos, D., *Cyprus in History.* London, 1955.—*Cyprus Guerilla.* London, 1960
Bitsios, D. S., *Cyprus: The Vulnerable Republic.* Thessaloniki, 1975
Christodoulou, D., *The Evolution of the Rural Land use Pattern in Cyprus.* Bude, 1960
Crawshaw, N., *The Cyprus Revolt: An Account of the Struggle for Union with Greece.* London, 1978
Denktash, R., *The Cyprus Triangle.* London, 1982
Emilianides, A., *Histoire de Chypre.* Paris, 1962—*The Zurich and London Agreements and the Cyprus Republic.* Athens, 1962
Halil, K., *The Rape of Cyprus.* London, 1982
Hill, Sir George F., *A History of Cyprus.* 4 vols. Cambridge, 1940–52
Hunt, D., *Footprints in Cyprus.* London, 1982
Kitromilides, P. M., and Evriviades, M. L., *Cyprus,* [Bibliography]. Oxford and Santa Barbara, 1982
Kosut, H., *Cyprus 1946–68.* New York, 1970
Loizos, P., *The Heart Grows Bitter: A Chronicle of Cypriot War Refugees.* CUP, 1982
Mayes, S., *Makarios.* London, 1981
Oberling, P., *The Road to Bellapais: The Turkish Cypriot Exodus to Northern Cyprus.* Boulder, 1982
Polyviou, P. G., *Cyprus: The Tragedy and the Challenge.* London, 1975.—*Cyprus in Search of a Constitution.* Nicosia, 1976.—*Cyprus: Conflict and Negotiation, 1960–1980.* London, 1980
Salih, H. I., *Cyprus: The Impact of Diverse Nationalism on a State.* Univ. of Alabama Press, 1979
Stavrinides, Z., *The Cyprus Conflict.* Nicosia, 1976
St John-Jones, L. W., *The Population of Cyprus.* London, 1983
Vanezis, P. N., *Makarios: Faith and Power.* New York, 1972

CZECHOSLOVAKIA

Československá Socialistická Republika

Capital: Prague
Population: 15·34m. (1981)
GNP per capita: US$5,820 (1980)

HISTORY. The Czechoslovak State came into existence on 28 Oct. 1918, when the Czech *Národní Výbor* (National Committee) took over the government of the Czech lands upon the dissolution of Austria–Hungary. Two days later the Slovak National Council manifested its desire to unite politically with the Czechs. On 14 Nov. 1918 the first Czechoslovak National Assembly declared the Czechoslovak State to be a republic with T. G. Masaryk as President (1918–35).

The Treaty of St Germain-en-Laye (1919) recognized the Czechoslovak Republic, consisting of the Czech lands (Bohemia, Moravia, part of Silesia) and Slovakia. To these lands were added as a trust the autonomous province of Subcarpathian Ruthenia.

This territory was broken up for the benefit of Germany, Poland and Hungary by the Munich agreement (29 Sept. 1938) between UK, France, Germany and Italy.

In March 1939 the German-sponsored Slovak government proclaimed Slovakia independent, and Germany incorporated the Czech lands into the Reich as the 'Protectorate of Bohemia and Moravia'. A government-in-exile, headed by Dr Beneš, was set up in London in July 1940.

Liberation by the Soviet Army and US Forces was completed by May 1945.

Territories taken by Germans, Poles and Hungarians were restored to Czechoslovak sovereignty. Subcarpathian Ruthenia was transferred to the USSR.

Elections were held in May 1946, at which the Communist Party obtained about 38% of the votes.

A coalition government under a Communist Prime Minister, Klement Gottwald, remained in power until 20 Feb. 1948, when 12 of the non-Communist ministers resigned in protest against infiltration of Communists into the police.

In Feb. a predominantly Communist government was formed by Gottwald. In May elections resulted in an 89% majority for the government and President Beneš resigned.

In the first months of 1968 mounting pressure for liberalization culminated in the overthrow of the Stalinist President and Party Secretary, Antonín Novotný, and his associates. Under a new leadership the Communist Party introduced in April 1968 an 'Action Programme' of far-reaching political and economic reforms. Soviet pressure to abandon this programme was exerted between May and Aug. 1968, and finally, Warsaw Pact forces occupied Czechoslovakia on 21 Aug. The enforced Moscow agreement of 26 Aug. bound the Czechoslovak government to a policy of 'normalization' (*i.e.*, abandonment of most reforms) and to the stationing of Soviet forces on Czechoslovak soil. This situation was confirmed by the Czechoslovak–Soviet 'Status of Forces Agreement' of 16 Oct. In 1969–1970 Soviet pressure led to extensive changes in the Party and Government. In Oct. 1969 Czechoslovakia repudiated its condemnation of the Warsaw Pact invasion.

A Czechoslovak–Soviet 20-year Treaty of Friendship, Co-operation and Mutual Assistance was signed in May 1970. Since 1977 a dissident civil rights movement 'Charter 77' has been active despite official efforts to supress it.

On 11 Dec. 1973 the German Federal Republic and Czechoslovakia signed a treaty normalizing relations and annulling the Munich agreement of 1938. This was ratified by both countries' parliaments in July 1974.

AREA AND POPULATION. At the census of 11 Nov. 1980 the population was 15,276,799 (4,987,853 in Slovakia; 7·8m. females). Population in 1981,

391

15,344,679 (Slovakia, 5,035,840; females 7·9m). There are 12 administrative regions, one of which is the capital, Prague (Praha) and one the capital of Slovakia, Bratislava.

Region	Chief city	Area in sq. km	Population 1981
Czech			
Prague	—	495	1,182,445
Středočeský	Prague (Praha)	11,003	1,149,522
Jihočeský	České Budějovice	11,345	692,094
Západočeský	Plzeň (Pilsen)	10,876	879,442
Severočeský	Ústí nad Labem	7,810	1,170,999
Východočeský	Hradec Králové	11,240	1,248,588
Jihomoravský	Brno	15,028	2,046,416
Severomoravský	Ostrava	11,067	1,939,333
Slovak			
Bratislava	—	368	388,260
Západoslovenský	Bratislava	14,491	1,693,614
Středoslovenský	Banská Bystrica	17,983	1,537,629
Východoslovenský	Košice	16,183	1,416,337

The area of Czechoslovakia is 127,889 sq. km (Slovakia, 49,025 sq. km). Population density in 1981: 120 per sq. km. Growth rate in 1981, 3·8 per 1,000. Expectation of life in 1982 was 67 (males); 74 (females).

Ethnic minorities have equal political and cultural rights. In 1981 there were (in 1,000): Czechs, 9,791; Slovaks, 4,682; Hungarians, 580; Poles, 68; Germans, 61; Ukrainians, 47; Russians, 7. There were 303,000 gipsies in 1983.

Official languages are Czech and Slovak.

The population of the principal towns in 1980 was as follows (in 1,000):

Prague (Praha)	1,182	Hradec Králové	96	Nitra	77
Bratislava	381	Pardubice	92	Prešov	72
Brno	372	České Budějovice	91	Kladno	71
Ostrava	322	Havířov	90	Banská Bystrica	67
Košice	203	Ústí nad Labem	89	Trnava	64
Plzeň	171	Gottwaldov	84	Karlovy Vary	61
Olomouc	102	Žilina	83	Most	60
Liberec	98	Karviná	78	Frýdek-Místek	60

Vital statistics for calendar years:

	Live births	Marriages	Divorces	Deaths
1979	272,352	127,134	32,241	175,786
1980	248,901	117,921	33,863	186,116
1981	237,041	116,581	34,595	179,132

Infant mortality in 1981 (per 1,000 live births), 11·8.

CLIMATE. A humid continental climate, with warm summers and cold winters. Precipitation is generally greater in summer, with thunderstorms. Autumn, with dry, clear weather and spring, which is damp, are each of short duration. Prague, Jan. 29·5°F (–15°C), July 67°F (19·4°C). Annual rainfall 19·3″ (483mm).

CONSTITUTION AND GOVERNMENT. For details of previous constitutions, *see* THE STATESMAN'S YEAR-BOOK, 1968–69, pp. 927–28.

Since 1 Jan. 1969 Czechoslovakia has been a federal socialist republic consisting of two nations of equal rights: the Czech Socialist Republic (the Czech lands, previously Bohemia, Moravia and part of Silesia), and the Slovak Socialist Republic (Slovakia). Each Republic is governed by a National Council (the Czech with 200 deputies, the Slovak with 150), which delegates to an overall Federal Assembly responsibility for constitutional and foreign affairs, defence and important economic decisions. The Federal Assembly consists of the Chamber of Nations, which has 75 Czech and 75 Slovak delegates elected by their respective National Councils, and the Chamber of the People, which has 200 deputies elected by national suffrage.

The previous constitution (1960) remains in force as amended by Constitutional

Acts 143 and 144 of 1968. Since 1971 deputies are elected for a 5-year term so as to coincide with Communist Party congresses. Minimum age of voters is 18, of deputies, 21 years. At the elections of 5–6 June 1981 a single list of National Front candidates was presented. Turnout was 10,736,312 from an electorate of 10,789,574 (99·5%). 99·96% of the votes were cast for the official candidates.

President of the Republic: Gustáv Husák (born 1913), *President of the Federal Assembly:* Alois Indra.

The *de facto* primary source of power is the Communist Party of Czechoslovakia, of which the Communist Party of Slovakia (*First Secretary:* Josef Lenárt) is a constituent part. Communists head the National Front, which incorporates the remaining political parties (Czechoslovak Socialist Party, Czechoslovak People's Party, Slovak Reconstruction Party, Slovak Freedom Party) and the trade unions and youth organizations. The Communist Party had 1,584,011 members and 123,000 candidate members on 1 Oct. 1982. In March 1984 the Presidium consisted of Gustáv Husák *(General Secretary)*; Vasil Bil'ak; Peter Colotka *(Deputy Prime Minister)*; Karel Hoffmann *(Chairman, Central Council of Trade Unions)*; Alois Indra; Miloš Jakeš; Antonín Kapek; Josef Kempný; Josef Korčák *(Deputy Prime Minister)*; Josef Lenárt; Svatopluk Potáč *(Deputy Prime Minister)*; Lubomír Štrougal *(Prime Minister)*. Candidate members: Jan Fojtík, Josef Hamán, Miloslav Hruškovič.

In March 1984 members of the government not mentioned above included: *(Deputy Prime Ministers)* Ladislav Gerle; Karol Laco; Matej Lúčan; Jaromír Obzina *(Chairman, State Planning Commission)*; Rudolf Rohlíček; Josef Šimon; (other ministers) Bohumil Urban *(Foreign Trade)*; Martin Dzúr *(Defence)*; František Ondřich *(Chairman, Czechoslovak Control Committee)*; Bohuslav Chňoupek *(Foreign)*; Leopold Lér *(Finance)*; Michal Štancel' *(Labour)*; Vratislav Vajnar *(Interior)*; Vlastimir Ehrenberger *(Minister of Fuel and Power)*.

The Czech Prime Minister is Josef Korčák; the Slovak, Peter Colotka.

Local government is carried on by National Committees consisting of deputies elected for 5-year terms. There are 10 regional Committees, 2 City Committees with the same status for Prague and Bratislava, 108 district Committees and 7,979 town and community Committees. Elections were held in 1981.

National flag: White and red (horizontal), with a blue triangle of full depth at the hoist, point to the fly.

National anthem: Kde domov můj (words by J. K. Tyl; tune by F. J. Škroup, 1834); combined with, Nad Tatru sa blyska (words by J. Matuška, 1844).

DEFENCE. Defence is the responsibility of the Defence Council set up in Feb. 1969 and headed by the First Secretary of the Party.

The Warsaw Pact invasion of Aug. 1968 brought an estimated 500,000 occupation troops into the country. By early 1970 this number had been reduced to 80,000 Soviet troops, the presence of which is legalized by the Czech–Soviet 'Status of Forces' Agreement of Oct. 1968.

In Feb. 1969 the government announced an increase in defence capacity, and Czechoslovakia resumed participation in Warsaw Pact meetings.

Military service is for 2 years in the Army and 3 years in the Air Force.

Army. The Army had a strength (1984) of 148,000 (100,000 conscripts). It consists of 5 armoured, 5 motor rifle and 1 artillery divisions, 1 airborne brigade, 5 engineer battalions and 5 regiments of Civil Defence Troops. Equipment includes 3,500 T-54/-55/-72 tanks. There are also 2 paramilitary forces: Border Troops (11,000) and People's Militia (120,000).

Air Force. The Air Force is organized as a tactical force, under overall army command, and has a strength of some 56,000 personnel and 475 combat aircraft. Six interceptor regiments (each 3 squadrons of 14 aircraft) are equipped with MiG-23 and MiG-21 jets, and there are 4 regiments of Su-7, Su-20, MiG-23 and MiG-21 ground attack aircraft, as well as Mi-24 gunship helicopters. MiG-21s and adapted L-39 Albatros jet trainers are used for tactical reconnaissance. Transport units have a total of about 50 Let L-410, An-24/26, Il-14, Tu-134, and Tu-154 aircraft and Mil Mi-2 (armed), Mi-4 and Mi-8 helicopters. Training units are equipped with 2-seat MiG-23s and MiG-21s and Czech-built aircraft, including L-39 Albatros jet advanced trainers. Surface-to-air ('Guideline', 'Goa', 'Ganef', 'Gainful' and 'Gaskin') missile units are operational.

INTERNATIONAL RELATIONS

Membership. Czechoslovakia is a member of UN, COMECON and the Warsaw Pact.

ECONOMY

Planning. For the first five 5-year plans see THE STATESMAN'S YEAR-BOOK, 1978–79, p. 385. Economic reforms of the period 1965–68 were abandoned after the Soviet intervention of 1968, and the economy reverted to the traditional communist centrally planned type. In 1980 some rationalizations in the planning system, which have become known as the 'Set of measures', were applied. Food prices were raised in Jan. 1982.

The sixth 5-year plan for 1976–80 saw an increase of 3% in national income, 3·2% in industrial, and 6% in agricultural, production. Targets were not met. The 7th 5-year plan is running from 1981 to 1985. National income is to rise by 2·8%, industrial production by 2·7%, agricultural by 2·6%.

Budget. Budgets for calendar years (in Kčs. 1m.):

	1975	1976	1977	1978	1979	1980	1981
Revenue	278,113	292,165	280,786	286,267	294,638	306,262	311,568
Expenditure	273,774	290,071	278,301	283,912	292,403	304,182	310,928

Main items of the 1981 budget were (in Kčs. 1,000m.): Revenue: from the economy, 256; direct taxes, 42. Expenditure: (1980) national economy, 131; health and social services, 144; defence, 23; administration, 6.

Currency. The monetary unit in the Czechoslovak Republic is the *koruna* (Kčs.) or crown of 100 *haler*. Notes in circulation: Kčs. 10, 20, 50, 100, 500. Coin: 5, 10, 20, 50 *halers*, and Kčs. 1, 2, 5. The *koruna* is based on a gold content of 0·123426 gramme of pure gold and pegged on the rouble at Kčs. 1·80 = R.1. The International Monetary Fund did not approve this change of the par value, and Czechoslovak membership was terminated in 1954, and ceased to be a member of the International Bank. Official rates of exchange (1984): £1 = Kčs. 12·14; US$1 = Kčs. 5·89; 1 Soviet rouble = Kčs. 10. Tourist rate: £1 = Kčs. 16·36.

The return of 18·4 tonnes of gold seized by Nazi Germany and held in London and New York since the nationalization of Western assets in 1948 was agreed in Jan. 1982 by the Czech, British and US governments in exchange for compensation of the asset-holders.

Banking. For previous banking history see THE STATESMAN'S YEAR-BOOK, 1971–72, pp. 858–59. The central bank and bank of issue is the State Bank (Statni Banka), which controls foreign exchange reserves, and is a savings bank and a commercial credit bank to enterprises, except foreign trade enterprises. These are financed by the Commercial Bank (Obchodní Banka) which carries out all foreign trade transactions. The Trade Bank (Živnostenská Banka), provides banking services for private foreign clients, and maintains branches abroad. There is also an Investment Bank (Investiční Banka), one of whose functions is to manage foreign securities. 'Foreign exchange points' (*e.g.*, hotels) have partial foreign exchange authorization.

Weights and Measures. The metric system is in force.

ENERGY AND NATURAL RESOURCES

Energy. There is an oil pipeline from the USSR with branches to Bratislava and Zaluzi and a natural gas pipeline which supplies the German Federal and Democratic Republics, Austria and Italy as well as Czechoslovakia. A second is under construction. Production of electricity in 1982: 74,703m. kwh. In 1982 nuclear plants accounted for 7·8% of electricity production.

Minerals. Czechoslovakia is not rich in minerals. There are hard and soft coal reserves (chief coalfields: Most, Chomutov, Kladno, Ostrava and Sokolov). There is also uranium, glass sand and salt, and small quantities of iron ore, graphite, copper and lead. Production in 1982 (in tonnes): Coal, 27,463,000; lignite and brown coal, 93,655,000.

Agriculture. In 1982 there were 6·9m. hectares of agricultural land (4·8m. hectares arable, 0·8m. meadow, 0·8m. pasture), of which 4·3m. were held by collective farms, 2·1m. by state farms and 95,000 as private plots (maximum size 1 hectare).

In 1981 there were 1,708 collective farms with 984,365 members and 204 state farms with 164,304 employees. Crop production in 1981 (in 1,000 tonnes): Sugarbeet, 6,969; wheat, 4,325; potatoes, 3,743; barley, 3,392; maize, 706; rye, 544.

Livestock. In 1983 the number of livestock was: Cattle, 5·1m. (including 1·9m. milch cows); horses, 44,000; pigs, 7·1m.; sheep, 990,000; poultry, 49·2m. In 1982 production of meat was 1,580,000 tonnes (live weight); milk, 5,753m. litres; 5,030m. eggs. In 1982 there were 132,286 tractors.

Forestry. Czechoslovakia is a richly wooded country, and the timber industry is important. Forest area in 1981 was 4,584,161 hectares (50% spruce, 16% beech and pine, 7% oak). The area reafforested in 1981 was 76,878 hectares. The timber yield was 19·1m. cu. metres in 1981.

INDUSTRY AND TRADE

Industry. Industrialization is well developed and antedates the Communist régime. All industry is nationalized.

Output in 1981 (in 1,000 tonnes): Pig-iron, 9,903; crude steel, 15,270; coke, 10,323; rolled-steel products, 10,795; cement, 10,646; paper, 903; sulphuric acid, 1,317; nitrogenous fertilizers, 539; phosphate fertilizers, 340; plastics, 913; synthetic fibres, 169; sugar, 777; beer, 23·9m. hectolitres; cars, 180,590 (no.).

Textile production (in 1m. metres) in 1981: Cotton, 574; linen, 103; woollen, 60; shoes, 128m. pairs (58·8m. leather).

Labour. There were 8,691,111 persons of employable age in 1981 (*i.e.*, males, 15–59; females 15–54), of whom 7,262,572 were employed (3·3m. women), 5·6m. in production (industry, 2·8m.; agriculture, 958,383; building, 632,655; commerce, 668,192); and 1·8m. in services.

A 5-day 42-hour week with 4 weeks annual holiday is standard. Average monthly wage in 1983: Kčs. 2,630. In 1983 the trade union movement had 7m. members.

Commerce. Total trade (in Kčs. 1m.) for calendar years:

	1977	1978	1979	1980	1981	1982
Imports	63,213	68,074	75,760	81,540	86,276	94,216
Exports	58,246	63,609	70,156	80,163	87,689	95,562

In 1982, trade with Communist countries amounted to 142,809m. Kčs. (79,951m. Kčs. with the USSR, 17,583m. Kčs. with the German Democratic Republic, 11,881m. Kčs. with Poland). The UK is Czechoslovakia's fourth biggest non-Communist trade partner after the Federal German Republic, Austria and Switzerland.

Major exports in 1980 (percentage of total): Machinery, 51·9; industrial consumer goods, 16·7; raw materials and fuel, 27·5. Imports: Machinery, 34·6; raw materials and fuel, 52·7. Oil imports in 1980, 19·3m. tonnes, 98% from USSR.

There are 11 foreign trade agencies (independent legal entities with their own capital run by state-appointed managers). Western firms are permitted to set up their own offices on Czechoslovak soil. Enterprises must obtain agreement from the Ministry of Foreign Trade before trading with foreign firms. Foreign indebtedness was US$3,000m. in 1982; US$3,600m. (1981).

In 1972 an Anglo-Czech Agreement on Co-operation was signed. Under this an Anglo-Czech Joint Commission was established to further the development of trade and industrial and scientific co-operation.

UK-Czechoslovak trade has been conducted since 1 Jan. 1975 on the basis of autonomous EEC measures.

Total trade between Czechoslovakia and UK for calendar years (British Department of Trade returns, in £1,000 sterling):

	1978	1979	1980	1981	1982	1983
Imports to UK	85,439	96,577	87,812	70,503	82,007	101,302
Exports and re-exports from UK	73,167	73,801	81,026	70,686	70,105	69,456

Tourism. In 1981, 10,615,276 tourists visited Czechoslovakia (623,963 from the West) and 8,271,046 Czechoslovak tourists made visits abroad (237,682 to the West).

COMMUNICATIONS

Roads. In 1981 there were 73,640 km of motorways and first-class roads and 2,373,015 passenger cars. In 1981 state road transport carried 2,183m. passengers and 356m. tonnes of freight.

Railways. In 1983 the length of railway track was 13,142 km. Of this, 3,170 km was electrified. In 1981, 404m. passengers and 286m. tonnes of freight were carried.

Aviation. Air transport is run by ČSA (Czechoslovak Airlines). The main airports are: Prague (Ruzyně), Brno (Cernovice), Bratislava (Vajnory), Olomouc (Holice), Košice (Barca). In 1981, 1·2m. passengers and 23,573 tonnes of freight were flown. There are 6 internal and 53 international flights from Prague. British Airways operates air traffic London–Prague, Air France Paris–Prague–Bucharest.

Shipping. In 1983 Czechoslovak Maritime Shipping *(Československá námorní plavba)* (founded 1959) had 14 freighters totalling 264,000 DWT, based on Szczecin. In 1981, 1,464m. tonnes of cargo were carried. Freight transport within Czechoslovakia totalled 11·09m. tonnes. There are fleets on the Danube and Elbe.

Czechoslovak Danube Shipping *(Československá plavba dunajská)* operate 5 ships in the Mediterranean from the port of Bratislava.

Post and Broadcasting. Number of telephones in service in 1982 was 3,225,968. *Československý Rozhlas*, the governmental broadcasting station, broadcasts on 2 networks; 1 from Prague with 3 programmes in Czech and Slovak and 1 from Bratislava with 2 programmes in Slovak and additional broadcasts in Hungarian and Ukrainian. *Československá Televise* broadcast 2 television programmes nation-wide, including colour broadcasts. In 1981, 4·1m. people held wireless and 4·3m. TV licences.

Cinemas and Theatres (1982). There were 2,891 cinemas and 81 theatres. 46 full-length films were made in 1981.

Newspapers (1982). There were 30 daily newspapers, including 12 in Slovak. The party daily *Rudé Právo* ('Red Justice') has a circulation of about 1m.

JUSTICE, RELIGION, EDUCATION AND WELFARE

Justice. The criminal and criminal procedure codes date from 1 Jan. 1962, as amended in April 1973.

Police powers were strengthened in July 1974.

There is a Federal Supreme Court and federal military courts, with judges elected by the Federal Assembly. Both republics have Supreme Courts and a network of regional and district courts whose professional judges are elected by the republican National Councils. Lay judges are elected by regional or district local authorities. Local authorities and social organizations may participate in the decision-making of the courts.

Religion. Churches are under the control of the State Secretariat for Church Affairs and the organization Pacem in Terris. In 1984 there were 18 different faiths with 4,860 clergy and 8,200 churches. The largest single church is the Roman Catholic (10m. members, 5,000 churches, 1983): its main support is in Slovakia. Cardinal František Tomášek was installed as archbishop of Prague in 1978. The archbishoprics of Trnava and of Olomouc are vacant. In 1983 there were 5 bishops (the remaining 8 dioceses are directed by Government-appointed capitulary vicars) and 1 archbishop and 5 bishops working among émigrés. There were 6 seminaries in 1984.

In 1981 there were 600,000 Hussites in 5 dioceses, 270,000 Czech Brethren with 272 parishes, 450,000 Slovak Lutherans with 326 parishes, 46,700 Silesian Lutherans and 180,000 Reformed Christians with 310 parishes. In 1981 there were 15,000 Jews (mainly in Prague, where there is a synagogue). The Uniate Church was suppressed in 1950.

Education. In 1982–83 there were 11,397 kindergartens for children from 3 to 6 years of age, with 49,437 teachers and 714,921 pupils. All children receive free education from the ages of 6 to 15, where possible remaining at a single school for the whole 9 years. In 1982–83 there were 6,516 schools with 1,956,634 pupils and 90,702 teachers.

Subsequent education is of 3 types. First, 3 final years of secondary school (in 1982–83, 336 schools with 9,014 teachers and 150,638 pupils). Secondly, technical, teachers' training and other vocational schools (1982–83, 573 schools with 310,856 students and 17,161 teachers). Thirdly, higher education (1982–83, 154,421 full-time students, and 21,146 teachers). There are 36 institutions of higher education, with 110 faculties. These include 5 universities—the Charles University in Prague (founded 1348); the Purkyně (formerly Masaryk) University in Brno (1919); the Comenius University in Bratislava (1919); the Palacký University in Olomouc (1573); the Šafárik University in Košice (1959); and 12 technical universities or institutes.

Welfare. Medical care is free. In 1981 Kčs. 25,518m. were spent on health insurance benefits. There were, in 1981, 228 hospitals with a total of 120,000 beds, and 50,922 doctors and dentists. Family allowances (Kčs. per month): 1 child, 140; 2 children, 530; 3, 1,030. Old age pensions averaging 67% of salary are paid at the age of 60 (men), 53–57 (women).

DIPLOMATIC REPRESENTATIVES

Of Czechoslovakia in Great Britain (25 Kensington Palace Gdns., London, W8 4QY)
Ambassador: Dr Miroslav Houštecky (accredited 8 Dec. 1983)

Of Great Britain in Czechoslovakia (Thunovská 14, Prague 1)
Ambassador: J. R. Rich, CMG.

Of Czechoslovakia in the USA (3900 Linnean Ave., NW, Washington, D.C., 20008)
Ambassador: Dr Stanislav Suja.

Of the USA in Czechoslovakia (Tržiste 15–12548 Praha, Prague)
Ambassador: J. F. Matlock, Jr.

Of Czechoslovakia to the United Nations
Ambassador: Dr Stanislav Suja.

Books of Reference

The Constitution of the Czechoslovak Socialist Republic [English ed.]. Prague, 1960
Statistická ročenka ČSSR [Statistical Yearbook]. Prague, annual since 1958
Czechoslovak Foreign Trade. Prague, monthly
Facts on Czechoslovak Foreign Trade. Prague, annual since 1965
Bradley, J. F. N. *Politics in Czechoslovakia, 1945–1971.* Lanham, 1981
Czechoslovak Chamber of Commerce and Industry. *Facts on Czechoslovak Foreign Trade.* Prague, annual since 1967.— *Your Trade Partners in Czechoslovakia.* Prague, 1979
Demek, J., and others, *Geography of Czechoslovakia.* Prague, 1971
Eidlin, F. H. *The Logic of 'Normalization': The Soviet Intervention in Czechoslovakia of 21 August 1968 and the Czechoslovak Response.* Columbia Univ. Press, 1980
Hermann, A. H., *A History of the Czechs.* London, 1975
Hejzlar, Z., and Kusin, V. V., *Czechoslovakia, 1968–1969.* New York, 1975
Jičinský, J., and Skála, J. *The Czechoslovak Federation.* Prague, 1969

Kalvoda, J., *Czechoslovakia's Role in Soviet Strategy*. Washington, 1981
Kolafová, V., and Slaba, D. *Czech-English and English-Czech dictionary*. Prague, 1979
Korbel, J., *Twentieth-Century Czechoslovakia: The Meanings of its History*. Columbia Univ. Press, 1977
Krejčí, *Social Change and Stratification in Postwar Czechoslovakia*. London, 1972
Krystufek, Z., *The Soviet Régime in Czechoslovakia*. Columbia Univ. Press, 1981
Kusin, V. V., *From Dubček to Charter 77*. Edinburgh, 1978
Littell, R. (ed.), *The Czech Black Book; prepared by the Institute of History of the Czechoslovak Academy of Sciences*. London, 1969
Mamatey, V. S., and Luža, R. (eds.), *A History of the Czechoslovak Republic 1918–1948*. Princeton Univ. Press, 1973
Mlynař, Z., *Night Frost in Prague: the End of Humane Socialism*. New York, 1980
Procházka, J., *English–Czech and Czech–English Dictionary*. 16th ed. London, 1959
Sejna, J. *We Will Bury You*. London, 1982
Šik, O., *Czechoslovakia: The Bureaucratic Economy*. New York, 1972
Sperling. W., *Tschechoslowakei: Beiträge zur Landeskunde Ostmitteleurapas*. Stuttgart, 1981
Suda, Z. L., *Zealots and Rebels: A History of the Communist Party in Czechoslovakia*. Stanford, 1980
Teplý, J., *Economie Nationale de la Tchécoslovaquie Contemporaine*. Paris, 1977
Wallace, W. V., *Czechoslovakia*. London, 1977

DENMARK

Kongeriget Danmark

Capital: Copenhagen
Population: 5·11m. (1983)
GNP per capita: US$12,950 (1980)

HISTORY. First organized as a unified state in the 10th century, Denmark acquired approximately its present boundaries in 1815, having ceded Norway to Sweden and its north German territory to Prussia. Denmark became a constitutional monarchy in 1849.

AREA AND POPULATION. According to the census held on 9 Nov. 1970 the area of Denmark proper was 43,075 sq. km (16,631 sq. miles) and the population 4,937,579. Population, Jan. 1983: 5,116,464.

Administrative divisions		Area (sq. km) 1983	Population 1970	Population 1983	Population 1983 per sq. km
København (Copenhagen)	(city)	88	622,773	486,593	5,522
Frederiksberg	(borough)	9	101,874	88,409	10,081
Københavns	(county)	522	615,343	619,687	1,186
Frederiksborg	,,	1,347	259,442	331,349	246
Roskilde	,,	891	153,199	205,414	231
Vestsjællands	,,	2,984	259,057	277,914	93
Storstrøms	,,	3,398	252,363	258,670	76
Bornholms	,,	588	47,239	47,313	80
Fyns	,,	3,486	432,699	453,773	130
Sønderjyllands	,,	3,930	238,062	249,970	64
Ribe	,,	3,131	197,843	214,700	69
Vejle	,,	2,997	306,263	327,102	109
Ringkøbing	,,	4,853	241,327	264,103	54
Aarhus	,,	4,561	533,190	578,149	127
Viborg	,,	4,122	220,734	230,909	56
Nordjyllands	,,	6,173	456,171	482,409	78
Total		43,080	4,937,579	5,116,464	119

The population is almost entirely Scandinavian; in July 1976, of the inhabitants of Denmark proper, 97·2% were born in Denmark, including Faroe Islands and Greenland.

On 1 Jan. 1983 the population of the capital, Copenhagen (comprising Copenhagen, Frederiksberg and Gentofte municipalities), was 641,904 (including suburbs, 1,372,019); Aarhus, 248,509; Odense, 170,648; Aalborg, 154,755; Esbjerg, 80,317; Randers, 61,739; Kolding, 56,418; Helsingør, 56,246; Herning, 55,927; Horsens, 54,779.

Vital statistics for calendar years:

	Living births	Still births	Marriages	Divorces	Deaths	Emigration	Immigration
1978	62,036	364	28,763	13,072	52,864	26,735	32,059
1979	59,464	309	27,842	13,044	54,654	27,731	33,183
1980	57,293	253	26,448	13,593	55,939	29,913	30,311
1981	53,089	281	25,411	14,425	56,359	29,719	27,874
1982	52,658	269	24,330	14,621	55,368	28,328	28,223

Illegitimate births: 1979, 30·7%; 1980, 33·2%; 1981, 35·8%; 1982, 38·3%.

CLIMATE. The climate is much modified by marine influences, and the effect of the Gulf Stream, to give winters that are cold and cloudy but warm and sunny summers. In general, the east is drier than the west, though few places have more than 27″ (675 mm) of rain a year. Long periods of calm weather are exceptional and windy conditions are common. Copenhagen. Jan. 33°F (0·5°C), July 63°F

(17°C). Annual rainfall 22·8" (571 mm). Esbjerg. Jan. 33°F (0·5°C), July 59°F (15°C). Annual rainfall 32" (800 mm).

REIGNING QUEEN. Margrethe II, born 16 April 1940; married 10 June 1967 to Prince Henrik, born Count de Monpezat; *offspring:* Crown Prince Frederik, born 26 May 1968; Prince Joachim, born 7 June 1969. She succeeded to the throne on the death of her father, King Frederik IX, on 14 Jan. 1972.

Mother of the Queen: Queen Ingrid, born Princess of Sweden, 28 March 1910.
Sisters of the Queen: Princess Benedikte, born 29 April 1944 (married 3 Feb. 1968 to Prince Richard of Sayn-Wittgenstein-Berleburg); Princess Anne-Marie, born 30 Aug. 1946 (married 18 Sept. 1964 to King Constantine of Greece).

The crown of Denmark was elective from the earliest times. In 1448 after the death of the last male descendant of Swein Estridsen the Danish Diet elected to the throne Christian I, Count of Oldenburg, in whose family the royal dignity remained for more than 4 centuries, although the crown was not rendered hereditary by right till 1660. The direct male line of the house of Oldenburg became extinct with King Frederik VII on 15 Nov. 1863. In view of the death of the king, without direct heirs, the Great Powers signed a treaty at London on 8 May 1852, by the terms of which the succession to the crown of Denmark was made over to Prince Christian of Schleswig-Holstein-Sonderburg-Glücksburg, and to the direct male descendants of his union with the Princess Louise of Hesse-Cassel, niece of King Christian VIII of Denmark. In accordance with this treaty, a law concerning the succession to the Danish crown was adopted by the Diet, and obtained the royal sanction 31 July 1853. Linked to the constitution of 5 June 1953, a new law of succession, dated 27 March 1953, has come into force, which restricts the right of succession to the descendants of King Christian X and Queen Alexandrine, and admits the sovereign's daughters to the line of succession, ranking after the sovereign's sons.

Subjoined is a list of the kings of Denmark, with the dates of their accession, from the time of election of Christian I of Oldenburg:

House of Oldenburg

Christian I	1448	Christian IV	1588	Frederik V	1746
Hans	1481	Frederik III	1648	Christian VII	1766
Christian II	1513	Christian V	1670	Frederik VI	1808
Frederik I	1523	Frederik IV	1699	Christian VIII	1839
Christian III	1534	Christian VI	1730	Frederik VII	1848
Frederik II	1559				

House of Schleswig-Holstein-Sonderburg-Glücksburg

Christian IX	1863	Christian X	1912	Margrethe II	1972
Frederik VIII	1906	Frederik IX	1947		

CONSTITUTION AND GOVERNMENT. The present constitution of Denmark is founded upon the 'Grundlov' (charter) of 5 June 1953.

The legislative power lies with the Queen and the *Folketing* (Diet) jointly. The executive power is vested in the Queen, who exercises her authority through the ministers. The judicial power is with the courts. The Queen must be a member of the Evangelical-Lutheran Church, the official Church of the State. The Queen cannot assume major international obligations without the consent of the *Folketing*. The *Folketing* consists of one chamber. All men and women of Danish nationality of more than 18 years of age and permanently resident in Denmark possess the franchise and are eligible for election to the *Folketing*, which is at present composed of 179 members; 135 members are elected by the method of proportional representation in 17 districts. In order to attain an equal representation of the different parties, 40 *tillægsmandater* (additional seats) are divided among such parties which have not obtained sufficient returns at the district elections. Two members are elected for the Faroe Islands and 2 for Greenland. The term of the legislature is 4 years, but a general election may be called at any time.

The *Folketing* must meet every year on the first Tuesday in October. Besides its legislative functions, it appoints every 6 years judges who, together with the ordinary members of the Supreme Court *(Højesteret),* form the *Rigsret,* a tribunal which can alone try parliamentary impeachments. The ministers have free access to the House, but can vote only if they are members.

Folketing, elected 10 Jan. 1984: 56 Social Democrats, 10 Radical Liberals, 42 Conservatives, 21 Socialist People's Party, 8 Centre Democrats, 5 Christian People's Party, 22 Liberals, 5 Left Socialists, 6 Progress Party, 2 Faroe Islands and 2 Greenland representatives.

The executive (called the State Council *(Statsraadet)* when acting with the Queen presiding) is a minority non-Socialist coalition government, consisting of the Conservatives, the Liberals, the Centre Democrats and the Christian People's Party; it was in March 1984 as follows:

Prime Minister: Poul Schlüter.
Foreign Affairs: Uffe Ellemann-Jensen. *Finance:* Henning Christophersen. *Economy:* Anders Andersen. *Industry:* Ib Stetter. *Greenland:* Tom Høyem. *Social Affairs:* Palle Simonsen. *Agriculture:* Niels Anker Kofoed. *Fisheries:* Henning Grove. *Education:* Bertel Haarder. *Culture:* Mimi Stilling Jakobsen. *Defence:* Hans Engell. *Labour:* Grethe Fenger Møller. *Housing:* Niels Bollman. *Inland Revenue:* Isi Foighel. *Energy:* Knud Enggaard. *Interior:* Britta Schall Holberg. *Justice:* Erik Ninn-Hansen. *Environment and Nordic Affairs:* Christian Christensen. *Public Works:* Arne Melchior. *Ecclesiastical Affairs:* Elsebeth Kock-Petersen.

The ministers are individually and collectively responsible for their acts, and if impeached and found guilty, cannot be pardoned without the consent of the *Folketing.*

In 1948 a separate legislature *(Lagting)* and executive *(Landsstyre)* were established for the Faroe Islands, to deal with specified local matters and in 1979 a separate legislature *(Landsting)* and executive *(Landsstyre)* were established for Greenland, also to deal with specified local matters.

National flag: Red with white Scandinavian cross (Dannebrog).
National anthems: Kong Kristian stod ved højen Mast (words by J. Ewald, 1778; tune by J. E. Hartmann, 1780) and Der er et yndigt land.

Local Government. For administrative purposes Denmark is divided into 275 municipalities *(kommuner);* each of them has a district council of between 5 and 25 members, headed by an elected mayor. The city of Copenhagen forms a district by itself and is governed by a city council of 55 members, elected every 4 years, and an executive *(magistraten),* consisting of the chief burgomaster *(overborgmesteren)* and 6 burgomasters, appointed by the city council for 4 years. There are 14 counties *(amtskommuner),* each of which is administered by a county council *(amtsråd)* of between 13 and 31 members, headed by an elected mayor. All councils are elected directly by universal suffrage and proportional representation for 4-year terms. A third council, the Metropolitan Council, with a constitution similar to the counties was established 1 April 1974. The Metropolitan Council is responsible for overall development within Metropolitan Copenhagen.

The counties and Copenhagen are superintended by a ministry of interior affairs. The municipalities are superintended by 14 local supervision committees, headed by a state county prefect *(statsamtmand)* who is a civil servant appointed by the Queen.

DEFENCE. The Danish military defence is organized in accordance with the Defence Act of May 1982 and the overall organization of the Danish Armed Forces comprises the Defence Command, the Army, the Navy, the Air Force and inter-service authorities and institutions. To this should be added the Home Guard, which is an indispensable part of Danish military defence. The Home Guard is based on the Home Guard Act of May 1982.

In accordance with the Defence Act the Chief of Defence has full command of the three services: the Army, the Navy and the Air Force. The Chief of Defence, and the Defence Staff constitute the Defence Command. The Inspector Generals of the Army, the Navy and the Air Force are members of the Defence Staff.

The Minister of Defence is assisted by a Defence Council consisting of the Chief of Defence, the Chief of Defence Staff, the Chief of Danish Operational Forces, the Inspector Generals of the Army, the Navy and the Air Force and the Chief of the Home Guard.

The Constitution of 1849 declared it the duty of every fit man to contribute to the national defence, and this provision is still in force. According to the Personnel Act of May 1982, the military personnel comprises officers, n.c.o.s and privates. Private personnel are provided by enlistment and by recruiting of volunteers. Selection of conscripts takes place at the age of 18–19 years, and the conscripts are normally called up for 9 months service ½–1½ years later. Afterwards conscripts may be recalled for refresher training or musters.

Army. The peace-time Army strength is about 21,000. The Army comprises field army formations and the local defence forces. The field army formations are organized in an operationally balanced covering force and in reserve units. The covering force numbers about 13,000 men and comprises a standing force, and a supplementary force consisting of men newly released from service. This force is part of the field army reserve which numbers 41,000. The standing force number about 7,000 men organized in standing brigade units, headquarters units and support units. The brigade units are organized in 5 mechanized infantry brigades. The field army is equipped with 200 medium battle tanks and about 650 armoured personnel carriers as well as artillery including 72 self-propelled howitzers. The local defence units consist of about 24,000 men organized in 21 infantry battalions and 7 artillery battalions. The men of the latest annual service groups form the troops of the line, while those of the previous years form the local defence, the reserve and the reserve for the Home Guard. The mobilization units of the field army and the local defence force will total about 59,000 men.

Navy. The Navy comprises the fleet and coast-defence which includes several permanent fortifications. The fleet includes 4 submarines, 2 frigates, 3 new light frigates, 5 ocean escorts (for fishery protection and surveying duties), 10 fast missile craft, 6 fast torpedo boats, 4 ocean minelayers, 3 coastal minelayers, 6 coastal minesweepers, 2 torpedo recovery vessels, 22 patrol vessels, 7 coastal patrol launches, 2 oilers, 20 auxiliary vessels and the royal yacht. The Naval Air Arm comprises 8 helicopters (one is carried in each of the ocean escorts).

Total strength of the Navy is nearly 8,500 officers and men (1,370 officers, 3,220 regular ratings, 1,270 national service, 2,640 civilians) and the mobilization force about 4,000 men.

The Naval Home Guard has 35 vessels and 5,200 officers and men.

Air Force. The operational units of the Air Force comprise 6 surface-to-air missile squadrons and 6 flying squadrons.

The air defence force consists of the 6 Hawk surface-to-air missile squadrons and 2 all-weather air-defence squadrons with a unit establishment of about 16 F-16s and 20 CF-104G/F-104G Starfighters respectively.

The fighter bomber force comprises 2 squadrons with a unit establishment of 16 F-16s, 1 with a unit establishment of 16 F 35 Drakens, and 1 reconnaissance squadron with a unit establishment of 16 RF 35 Drakens.

In addition the Air Force has a number of supplementary units, including 1 transport squadron (C-130 Hercules and Gulfstream III), 1 helicopter rescue squadron (S-61As), and a control and warning system.

Total strength of the Air Force is about 9,800, and the mobilization force about 9,000 men.

Home Guard. The overall Home Guard organization comprises the Home Guard Command, the Army Home Guard, the Navy Home Guard and the Air Force Home Guard.

The personnel of the Home Guard is recruited on a voluntary basis. The personnel establishment of the Home Guard is at present about 77,000 persons (59,300 in the Army Home Guard, 5,300 in the Navy Home Guard and 12,400 in the Air Force Home Guard).

INTERNATIONAL RELATIONS

Membership. Denmark is a member of UN, NATO, OECD and EEC.

ECONOMY

Budget. The budget *(Finanslovforslag)* must be laid before the Parliament *(Folketing)* not later than 4 months before the beginning of a new fiscal year.

The following shows the actual revenue and expenditure as shown in central government accounts for the calendar years 1980, 1981 and 1982, the approved budget figures for 1983 and the budget for 1984 (in 1,000 kroner):

	1980	1981	1982	1983	1984
Revenue	106,707,623	111,997,031	120,561,873	115,810,266	128,328,368
Expenditure	124,602,838	145,863,972	169,981,027	184,267,276	187,653,064

Receipts and expenditures of special government funds and expenditures on public works are included.

The 1982 budget envisages revenue of 62,327m. kroner from income and property taxes and 78,193m. from consumer taxes.

The central government debt on 31 Dec. 1981 amounted to 190,271m. kroner.

Currency. The monetary unit is the *krone* of 100 øre. In 1931 Denmark went off the gold standard, as established in 1873.

Small change: 10-kroner and 5-kroner pieces of copper-nickel, 1-krone pieces of copper-nickel; 25-øre and 10-øre pieces of copper-nickel, and 5-øre pieces of copper–steel–copper clad. In March 1984, £1 = 14·25 *kroner*; US$1 = 9·56 *kroner*.

Banking. On 31 Dec. 1982 the accounts of the National Bank balanced at 122,726m. kroner. The assets included 4,759m. kroner in gold bullion. The liabilities included 14,601m. kroner note issue, 14,484m. kroner general capital fund and reserve fund. On 31 Dec. 1981 there were 157 savings banks, with 6·4m. accounts and deposits of 53,922m. kroner. Their advances amounted to 42,673m. kroner.

On 31 Dec. 1982 there were 73 other banks for commercial, agricultural and industrial purposes; their deposits amounted to 141,684m. kroner; advances were 103,557m. kroner.

Weights and Measures. The use of the metric system of weights and measures has been obligatory in Denmark since 1 April 1912.

ENERGY AND NATURAL RESOURCES

Electricity. Owing to the concentration of power production, the number of generating power stations has declined from 371 in 1949–50 to 23 in 1980, while the net power production (in 1m. kwh.) has risen from 1,689 in 1949–50 to 20,366 in 1982.

Agriculture. Land ownership is widely distributed. In 1982 the total number of farms was 112,397. There were 32,747 small holdings (with less than 10 hectares), 67,031 medium sized holdings (10–50 hectares) and 12,619 holdings with more than 50 hectares.

The number of agricultural workers declined from 120,442 in July 1961 to 26,212 in June 1982, while the index of production was 100 in 1975 and 114 in 1979.

In June 1982 the cultivated area was utilized as follows (in 1,000 hectares): Grain, 1,768; peas and beans, 9; root crops, 243; other crops, 225; green fodder and grass, 640; fallow, 2; total cultivated area, 2,887.

Chief crops	Area (1,000 hectares)			Production (in 1,000 tonnes)		
	1980	1981	1982	1980	1981	1982
Wheat	139	150	181	652	835	1,207
Rye	56	50	55	199	208	235
Barley	1,577	1,541	1,485	6,044	6,044	6,357
Oats	40	42	43	159	176	178
Mixed grain	4	4	4	16	14	16
Potatoes	34	36	35	842	1,053	1,229
Other root crops	207	209	208	9,261	10,277	11,958

Livestock, 1982: Horses, 41,000; cattle, 2,873,000; pigs, 9,319,000; sheep, 58,000; poultry, 15,185,000.

Production (in 1,000 tonnes) in 1982: Milk, 5,217; butter, 121; cheese, 245; beef, 247; pork and bacon, 1,040; eggs, 83.

In June 1982 farm tractors numbered 183,135 and harvester-threshers, 37,578.

Fisheries. The total value of the fish caught was (in 1m. kroner): 1950, 156; 1955, 252; 1960, 376; 1965, 650; 1970, 854; 1975, 1,442; 1979, 2,888. The fishing fleet in 1977 consisted of 7,340 motor boats, 182 sailing boats and 2,761 rowing boats.

INDUSTRY AND TRADE

Industry. The following table sets forth the gross factor income (in 1m. kroner) by industrial origin in 3 calendar years:

	1980		1981		1982	
	Current Prices	1975 Prices	Current Prices	1975 Prices	Current Prices	1975 Prices
Agriculture, fur-farming, forestry, etc.	15,358	10,916	18,021	12,038	23,596	13,568
Fishing	1,575	872	1,778	1,006	2,071	1,024
Total	16,933	11,788	19,799	13,044	25,667	14,592
Mining and quarrying	418	184	1,082	164	2,916	497
Manufacturing	61,135	44,167	66,606	44,404	75,198	45,204
Electricity, gas and water	5,058	4,250	5,784	3,594	7,987	4,241
Construction	21,180	14,633	20,075	12,096	21,209	11,692
Total	87,791	63,234	93,547	60,258	107,310	61,634
Wholesale and retail trade	46,298	32,895	51,449	32,995	55,964	34,507
Restaurants and hotels	4,230	2,419	4,420	2,366	5,061	2,451
Transport and storage	22,073	15,963	25,095	16,456	26,900	15,914
Communication	4,239	3,881	4,665	3,911	5,429	3,938
Financing and insurance	10,558	7,036	11,189	6,925	13,158	7,316
Dwellings	30,027	17,139	33,600	18,118	37,354	18,309
Business services	13,349	8,871	15,320	8,946	18,487	9,543
Market services of education, health	4,614	3,559	5,356	3,610	5,918	3,639
Recreational and cultural services	2,909	2,113	3,171	2,038	3,767	2,042
Household services, incl. auto repair	8,422	5,480	9,722	5,664	10,837	5,555
Total	146,719	99,356	163,987	101,028	182,875	103,214
Other producers, excl. government	2,303	1,379	2,570	1,386	2,989	1,434
Producers of government services	72,828	49,771	83,360	51,572	96,489	53,537
Total	75,132	51,150	85,930	52,958	99,478	54,971
Imputed bank service charges	÷ 9,816	÷ 6,432	÷ 11,048	÷ 6,533	÷ 13,042	÷ 6,969
Gross domestic product at factor cost	316,760	219,094	352,216	220,755	402,289	227,442
Plus indirect taxes	69,827 }	27,729	75,123 }	26,467	82,409 }	27,468
Less subsidies	11,855 }		12,516 }		14,919 }	
Gross domestic product at market prices	374,732	246,824	414,823	247,221	469,779	254,910

According to the registration of business units for VAT settlement there were in 1982 a total of 33,000 manufacturing enterprises. In the following table 'number of wage-earners' refers to 6,400 establishments with 6 employees or more, while 'gross-output' and 'value-added' cover 2,800 kind-of-activity units of enterprises with 20 employees or more.

Branch of industry	Number of wage-earners (1,000)	Gross output in factor values (1m. kroner)	Value added in factor values (1m. kroner)
Mining and quarrying	0·8	406	282
Food products	47·8	68,371	15,844
Beverages	8·0	5,910	3,506
Tobacco	1·8	1,369	686
Textiles	10·8	5,768	2,632
Wearing apparel	8·7	2,720	1,343
Leather and products	0·9	394	188
Footwear	2·3	972	388
Wood products	6·6	3,116	1,381
Furniture and fixtures	9·1	3,590	1,869
Paper and products	6·2	5,031	2,113
Printing, publishing	14·1	8,153	5,394
Industrial chemicals	11·3	16,621	8,340
Other chemical products, petroleum refineries, petroleum coal products and rubber	2·4	10,947	1,325
Plastic products	5·4	2,991	1,506
Pottery, china, glass and products	4·3	1,509	986
Non-metal products	8·4	5,329	3,000
Iron, steel and non-ferrous metals	4·6	3,355	1,366
Metal products	21·4	11,095	5,516
Machinery	35·0	18,432	10,058
Electrical machinery	14·7	8,765	4,880
Transport equipment	22·5	12,325	5,385
Controlling equipment	5·0	3,155	2,059
Other industries	4·0	2,387	1,459
Total manufacturing	256·1	202,305	81,224

Labour. In 1981, 7% of the working population lived on agriculture, forestry and fishery, 25% on industries and handicrafts, 8% on construction, 15% on commerce, etc., 7% on transport and communication, and 38% on administration, professional services, etc.

Commerce. The following table shows the value, in 1,000 kroner, of special trade imports and exports (including trade with the Faroe Islands and Greenland) for calendar years:

	1977	1978	1979	1980	1981	1982 [1]
Imports	79,636,962	81,405,158	96,838,868	109,388,313	124,169,649	140,330,746
Exports	60,436,289	65,307,647	77,361,446	95,670,845	113,796,938	127,623,859

[1] Preliminary.

Imports and exports (in 1,000 kroner) for calendar years:

Leading commodities	1981 Imports	1981 Exports	1982 [1] Imports	1982 [1] Exports
Live animals, meat, etc.	156,869	16,255,082	169,949	18,406,488
Dairy products, eggs	738,513	5,851,165	504,390	7,070,197
Fish and fish preparations	2,109,347	5,442,082	2,441,687	6,355,425
Cereals and cereal preparations	1,218,479	1,756,246	1,134,165	2,459,961
Sugar and sugar preparations	509,258	1,310,582	641,372	1,159,375
Coffee, tea, cocoa, etc.	1,790,434	444,820	2,005,352	425,171
Feeding stuff for animals	4,076,203	1,477,223	4,214,910	1,393,668
Wood, lumber and cork	1,369,434	397,120	1,465,226	657,329
Textiles, fibres, yarns, fabrics, etc.	4,397,121	2,705,253	4,970,422	2,993,037
Fuels, lubricants, etc.	28,669,340	3,239,819	30,565,405	2,780,595
Pharmaceutical products	1,387,161	2,657,699	1,646,175	3,353,830
Fertilizers, etc.	1,600,801	653,655	1,627,565	798,454
Metals, manufactures of metals	10,348,490	5,448,613	13,542,491	6,005,689
Machinery, electric, equipment, etc.	17,197,936	21,815,896	21,594,293	24,492,024
Transport equipment	8,133,820	6,128,395	8,433,818	5,730,699

[1] Preliminary.

Distribution of Danish foreign trade (in 1,000 kroner) according to countries of origin and destination, for calendar years:

		Imports			Exports	
Countries	1980	1981	1982 [1]	1980	1981	1982 [1]
Belgium	3,757,608	4,442,668	3,750,517	1,831,793	1,968,438	2,322,267
Finland	4,151,943	4,603,002	5,793,865	2,034,863	2,353,222	2,792,814
France	4,739,490	5,039,250	5,736,795	4,919,660	5,473,225	7,033,777
Germany (Fed. Rep.)	20,127,384	23,053,477	28,719,578	18,054,729	19,016,954	22,203,326
Norway	4,501,863	5,339,757	5,204,891	5,984,759	7,082,878	8,282,078
Sweden	13,969,307	14,957,255	16,383,385	11,927,330	13,084,262	13,872,415
Switzerland	1,846,237	2,037,630	2,484,832	2,119,119	2,648,222	2,728,931
UK	13,262,568	14,832,377	15,133,554	13,693,651	15,453,691	17,945,543
USA	6,988,269	10,545,243	9,889,510	4,262,046	6,046,825	7,491,263
Allied forces in Fed. Rep. Germany	—	—	—	139,772	146,734	170,755

[1] Preliminary.

Total trade between Denmark (without the Faroe Islands) and UK (British Department of Trade returns, in £1,000 sterling):

	1979	1980	1981	1982	1983
Imports to UK	1,081,247	1,103,590	1,179,065	1,335,640	1,512,620
Exports and re-exports from UK	1,016,403	1,032,525	2,812,957	1,096,642	1,159,184

Tourism. In 1982, foreigners visiting Denmark spent some 10,884m. kroner. In 1982 foreigners spent 4·45m. nights in hotels and 4·42m. nights at camping sites.

Industrial Statistics. Danmarks Statistik. Copenhagen (annually)
Quarterly Statistics for the Industry: Commodity Statistics. Danmarks Statistik, Copenhagen
Statistics on Agriculture, Horticulture and Forestry. Danmarks Statistik. Copenhagen (annually)
Agricultural Statistics 1900–1965. Vol. I: *Agricultural Area and Harvest and Utilization of Fertilizers.*—Vol. II: *Livestock and Livestock Products, and Consumption of Feeding Stuffs.* Danmarks Statistik. Copenhagen, 1968–69
External Trade of Denmark. Danmarks Statistik, Copenhagen
Danish Industry in Facts and Figures. Federation of Danish Industries. Copenhagen (annually)
Energy Supply of Denmark, 1900–58 and *1948–65.* Danmarks Statistik. Copenhagen, 1959, 1967. Annual Supplements 1966–75 have been published in Statistical News
Report on Fisheries. Ministry of Fisheries, Copenhagen (annually)
Nash, E. F., and Attwood, E. A., *The Agricultural Policies of Britain and Denmark.* London, 1961

COMMUNICATIONS

Roads. Denmark proper had (1 Jan. 1983), 516 km of motorways, 4,129 km of other state roads, 6,951 km of provincial roads and 58,065 km of commercial roads. Motor vehicles registered at 31 Dec. 1982 comprised 1,348,088 passenger cars, 235,257 lorries, 10,150 taxicabs (including 3,471 for private hire), 7,785 buses and 36,623 cycles.

Railways. In 1982 there were 2,015 km of State railways (135 km electrified), which carried 4,215m. passenger-km and 1,653m. tonne-km. There were also 526 km of private railways.

Aviation. On 1 Oct. 1950 the 3 Scandinavian airlines, Det Danske Luftfartsselskab, ABA and DNL, combined in Scandinavian Airlines System. In 1982 SAS flew 114·1m. km and carried 8,839,456 passengers.
SAS inaugurated its transpolar routes Copenhagen–Los Angeles on 15 Nov. 1954 and Copenhagen–Tōkyō on 25 Feb. 1957, and its trans-Asian express route Copenhagen–Bangkok–Singapore *via* Tashkent on 4 Nov. 1967.

Shipping. On 31 Dec. 1982 the Danish merchant fleet consisted of 2,886 vessels (above 20 GRT) of 5,244,268 GRT.
In 1982, 35,522 vessels of 31m. NRT entered the Danish ports, unloading 39m. tonnes and loading 15m. tonnes of cargo; traffic by passenger ships and ferries is not included.

Post and Broadcasting. There were, in 1981, 1,315 post offices. On 31 Dec. 1981 the length of telephone circuits of private companies was 11,475,437 km. On 31 Dec. 1981 there were 3,483,323 telephone instruments (including those in the Faroe Islands and Greenland). Postal revenues, 1981, 5,052m. kroner; expenditure, 5,212m. kroner.

Danmarks Radio is the government broadcasting station and is financed by licence fees. Television is broadcast by *Danmarks Radio* with colour programmes by PAL system. Number of receivers: Radio, 1·95m.; television, 2·13m., including 1·59m. colour sets.

Cinemas. In 1982 there were 463 cinema rooms with a seating capacity of 97,545.

Newspapers. In 1982 there were 47 daily newspapers with a combined circulation of 1·82m. on weekdays; 9 of them (881,000) appeared in Copenhagen.

JUSTICE, RELIGION, EDUCATION AND WELFARE

Justice. The lowest courts of justice are organized in 84 tribunals *(byretter)*, where cases are dealt with by a single judge. The tribunals at Copenhagen have 33 judges, Aarhus 12, Odense 9, Aalborg 8, and the other tribunals have 1 to 4. Cases of greater consequence are dealt with by the superior courts *(Landsretterne)*; these courts are also courts of appeal for the above-named cases. Of superior courts there are two: *Østre Landsret* in Copenhagen with 46 judges, *Vestre Landret* in Viborg with 23 judges. From these an appeal lies to the Supreme Court *(Højesteret)* in Copenhagen, composed of 16 judges. Judges under 70 years of age can be removed only by judicial sentence.

In 1978, 10,953 men and 867 women were convicted of crimes and delicts, fines not included. In 1981, the daily average population in penal institutions, local prisons, etc, was 3,352 men and 145 women, of whom 971 men and 67 women were on remand.

Religion. At the Reformation in 1536 the Danish Church ceased to exist as a legally independent unit, a part of the Roman Catholic Church, and became instead a Lutheran Church under the direction of the State. Since that time the State has, in one form or another, continued to exercise supreme authority in the affairs of the Church, and has regulated these by the passing of laws, by royal decree, or other appropriate means. The great majority of Danish citizens (about 90%) belongs to the National Church. Administratively, Denmark is divided into 10 dioceses each with a Bishop who, within the framework of the law, is the supreme diocesan authority in ecclesiastical affairs. The Bishop together with the Chief Administrative Officer of the county make up the diocesan governing body, responsible for all matters of ecclesiastical local finance and general administration. Bishops are appointed by the Crown after an election at which the clergy and parish council members of the diocese have had the opportunity of voting for the candidates nominated. Each diocese is divided into a number of deaneries (about 107 in the whole country) each with its Dean and Deanery Committee, who have certain financial powers. Local government at parish level (there are about 2,200 parishes in all) is in the hands of Parish Councils, who are elected for a 4-year period of office.

Since the Constitution of 1849 complete religious toleration is extended to every sect, and no civil disabilities attach to Dissenters.

Kjær, J. C., *History of the Church of Denmark*. Blair, Nebr., 1945
Roesen, August, *Religion in Denmark*. Copenhagen, 1963

Education. Education has been compulsory since 1814. The *folkeskole* (public primary and lower secondary school) comprises a pre-school class *(børnehaveklassen)*, a 9-year basic school corresponding to the period of compulsory education and 1-year voluntary tenth form. Compulsory education may be fulfilled either through attending the *folkeskole* or private schools or through home-instruction, the only requirement being that the instruction given should be comparable to that offered in the *folkeskole*. *Folkeskolen* are mainly municipal and no fees are paid. In the year 1982–83, 2,278 primary and lower secondary schools had 757,936 pupils and employed 65,563 teachers. Approximately 14% of the total number of schools were private schools and they were attended by 8% of the total number of pupils. The 9-year basic school is in practice not streamed. However, a certain differentiation may take place in the eighth and ninth forms.

After the completion of the eighth and ninth forms the pupils may sit for the leaving examination of the *folkeskole (folkeskolens afgangsprøve)*. After the completion of the tenth form the pupils may sit for either the leaving examination of the *folkeskole (folkeskolens afgangsprøve)* or the advanced leaving examination of the *folkeskole (folkeskolens udvidede afgangsprøve)*.

Under certain conditions the pupils may continue their education either in a 3-year gymnasium ending with *studentereksamen* or in the 2-year higher preparatory school ending with the *højere forberedelseseksamen.* There were (1982–83) 144 of these upper secondary schools with 76,348 pupils and 7,764 teachers.

Youth and leisure-time education: 294 schools (continuation schools, youth residential schools, home economics schools, folk high schools, youth high schools and agricultural schools) with 21,307 pupils.

Vocational education and training consists of Basic Vocational Training in trade and commerce with (1982–83) 23,732 students, and 15,606 received training in technical education. There were 2,818 apprentices commencing training in the field of trade and commerce, and 10,998 trainees in the technical branches. Finally, 10,609 students were admitted to the diploma courses for trade and commerce, and 7,819 students were admitted to the technical diploma courses. In 1982–83, vocational education and training totalled 71,582 students.

There were 30 teacher-training colleges with 9,542 students and 34 colleges for training of teachers for kindergartens and leisure-time activities with 6,481 students.

Degree-courses in engineering: The Technical University of Denmark had 3,866 students. The Engineering Academy had 1,580 students and 8 engineering colleges with 4,419 students.

Universities: The University of Copenhagen (founded 1479) 24,691 students. The University of Aarhus (founded in 1928) 12,272 students. The University of Odense (founded in 1964) 5,015 students. Roskilde University Centre (founded in 1972) 2,326 students. Aalborg University Centre (founded in 1974) 2,668 students.

Other types of post-secondary education: The Royal Veterinary and Agricultural College had 2,216 students. The two dental colleges had 1,198 students. The Danish School of Pharmacy had 745 students. The 11 colleges of economics and business administration had 16,289 students. The 2 schools of architecture had 1,962 students. Five academies of music had 825 students. The Danish School of Librarianship had 873 students. The Royal Danish School of Educational Studies had 2,219 students. The Danish State Institute of Physical Education had 222 students. The 4 schools of social work had 884 students. The Danish School of Journalism had 675 students. Six colleges of physiotherapy had 1,082 students. One School of Midwifery Education had 151 students.

Andresén, A., *The Danish Folk High School To-day.* Copenhagen, 1981
Struve, K., *Schools and Education in Denmark.* Copenhagen, 1981
Thomsen, O. B., *Some Aspects of Education in Denmark.* Toronto, 1976
Thorsen, L., *Public Libraries in Denmark.* English and French eds., Copenhagen, 1972
Trane, E., *Education and Culture in Denmark.* Copenhagen, 1958

Social Security. The main body of Danish social welfare legislation is consolidated in 9 acts concerning (1) public health security, (2) sick-day benefits, (3) disablement pensions, (4) old age pensions, (5) widows pensions, (6) employment injuries insurance, (7) employment services and unemployment insurance, (8) social assistance including assistance to handicapped, rehabilitation, child and juvenile guidance, day-care institutions, care of the aged and sick, and (9) family allowances.

Public health security, covering the entire population, provides free medical care, substantial subsidies for certain essential medicines together with some dental care and a funeral allowance. Hospitals are primarily municipal and the hospital treatment is normally free. Wage-earners are granted daily sickness allowances, others can have limited daily sickness allowances. Daily cash benefits are granted in the case of temporary incapacity for work because of illness, injury or childbirth to all persons who earn an income derived from personal work. The benefit is paid at the rate of 90% of the average weekly earnings. There was a maximum rate of 2,008 kroner a week (Oct. 1983).

Disablement and old-age pensions cover the entire population. Entitlement to benefits at the full rates is subject to the condition that the beneficiary has been ordinarily resident in Denmark for a number of years (40). For a shorter period of residence, the benefits are reduced proportionally. The basic amount of the old-age pension in Oct. 1983 was 61,224 kroner to married couples and 33,324 to single persons. Various supplementary allowances, depending on age and income, may be payable with the basic amount. Persons over 67 years of age are entitled to the basic amount. The pensions to a married couple are calculated and paid to the husband and the wife separately. Invalidity pension is payable, having regard to the degree of disability, at a rate of up to 76,200 kroner to a single person. The rate of the widow's pension corresponds more or less to that of the old-age pension. Invalidity and widow's pensions may be subject to income regulation.

Employment injuries insurance provides for disablement or survivors' pensions and funeral allowances. The scheme covers practically all employees.

Employment services are provided by regional public employment agencies. The insurance against unemployment provides daily allowances. The unemployment insurance funds had at 31 Dec. 1982 a membership of 1,818,096, of which 1,586,651 were full-time insured and 231,445 part-time.

The *Social Assistance Act* applies to the field of social legislation which rules the individually granted benefits in contrast to the other fields of social legislation which apply to fixed benefits.

Total social expenditure, including hospital and health services, statutory pensions, etc, amounted in the financial year 1981 to 119,282m. kroner.

Bibliography of Foreign Language Literature on Industrial Relations and Social Services in Denmark. Ministries of Labour and Social Affairs, Copenhagen, 1975
Social Conditions in Denmark. Vols. 1–8. Ministries of Labour and Social Affairs, Copenhagen
Marcussen, E., *Social Welfare in Denmark* 4th ed. Copenhagen, 1980

THE FAROE ISLANDS
Færøerne

HISTORY. A Norwegian province 1380–1709, the islands secured the restoration of their Parliament in 1852 and since 1948 they have been a self-governing region of the Kingdom of Denmark.

AREA AND POPULATION. Area, 1,399 sq. km (540 sq. miles); population (31 Dec. 1981), 44,070. Capital, Thorshavn. Population (31 Dec. 1981) 13,951.

GOVERNMENT. The parliament *(Lagting)*, elected on 8 Nov. 1980, consists of 32 members: 8 Samband Party, 7 Social Democrats, 6 Folkeflok, 2 Progressive Party, 3 Home Rule Party, 6 Republicans.

Flag: White with a red blue-edged Scandinavian cross.

From 1 Jan. 1972 the Faroe Islands were no longer members of EFTA.

COMMERCE. The main industries are fisheries and crafts. Exports, mainly fresh, frozen, filleted and salted fish, amounted to 1,246m. kroner in 1982; imports to 1,655m. kroner.

Total trade with UK (British Department of Trade returns, in £1,000 sterling):

	1978	1979	1980	1981	1982	1983
Imports to UK	7,342	10,669	10,559	12,530	8,925	15,932
Exports and re-exports from UK	4,357	4,189	2,434	2,568	2,397	2,332

BROADCASTING. *Utvarp Føroya* is the broadcasting station and the number of receivers 16,000.

EDUCATION. In 1980–81 there were 5,879 primary and 2,837 secondary school pupils with 484 teachers.

Books of Reference

Árbog for Færøerne. 1980
Faroes in Figures. Thorshavn, annual, from 1956
Rutherford, G. K., (ed.) *The Physical Environment of the Færoe Islands.* The Hague, 1982
West, J. F., *Faroe.* London, 1973

GREENLAND
Grønland/Kalaallit Nunaat

HISTORY. A Danish possession since 1380, Greenland became on 5 June 1953 an integral part of the Danish kingdom. Following a referendum in Jan. 1979, home rule was introduced from 1 May 1979, and full internal self-government was attained in Jan. 1981 after a transitional period.

AREA AND POPULATION. Area 2,175,600 sq. km (840,000 sq. miles), made up of 1,833,900 sq. km of ice cap and 341,700 sq. km of ice-free land. The population, 1 Jan. 1983, numbered 51,903; West Greenland, 46,516; East Greenland, 3,263; North Greenland (Thule), 795, and 1,329 not belonging to any specific municipality. Of the total, 9,234 were born outside Greenland. Capital, Godthaab (Nuuk) (1983), 9,848.

CONSTITUTION. Greenland has the same rights as other counties in Denmark with a democratically elected council *(landsråd).* A referendum held in Jan. 1979 approved of home rule from 1 May 1979. At the elections held on 12 April 1983 for the new 26-member Parliament, *Landsting,* the *Siumut* gained 12 seats, the *Atassut,* 12 seats and the *Inuit Ataqatigiit,* the remaining 2 seats. The Premier, Jonathan Motzfeldt, formed a 6-member administration, *Landsstyre.*

INDUSTRY. Until the beginning of this century, the hunting of land and sea mammals, especially seals, was the main occupation of the population; now fishing is most important. Fish-processing industries, construction and trade are also important occupations.

Coal production ceased in 1972. A deposit of the valuable mineral cryolite has been mined at Ivigtut. The mine is now worked out, but exports from stock will continue for some years. In 1973 the Danish company Greenex A/S began producing lead and zinc concentrate near Umanak. Annual production of lead and zinc concentrates is about 30,000 tonnes and 160,000 tonnes respectively. In 1975, 6 groups of oil companies were granted 13 oil concessions off the west coast. These concessions were terminated by 31 Dec. 1978.

Public authorities are investigating uranium and coal deposits in Greenland as well as possibilities of hydro-electric power and there are other private prospectors for various minerals.

COMMERCE. Imports (c.i.f. Greenland) (in 1,000 kroner): 1977, 964,579; 1978, 980,292; 1979, 1,447,904; 1980, 1,847,877; 1981 2,096,192; 1982 (provisional), 2,311,205. Exports (f.o.b. Greenland) (in 1,000 kroner): 1977, 555,172; 1978, 559,274; 1979, 866,926; 1980, 1,199,301; 1981 1,324,809; 1982 (provisional), 1,435,622. Trade is mainly with Denmark.

Total trade with UK (British Department of Trade returns, in £1,000 sterling):

	1978	1979	1980	1981	1982	1983
Imports to UK	714	348	282	270	1,095	3,114
Exports and re-exports from UK	3,975	2,283	5,930	2,502	288	140

COMMUNICATIONS

Roads. There were (1970) 150 km of roads, of which 60 km were paved.

Aviation. There is an international airport at Søndre Srømfjord, and about 12 local airports with scheduled services.

Broadcasting. *Grønlands Radio* broadcasts in Greenlandic and Danish. The short wave transmitters are located at Godthaab. Several towns have local television stations.

JUSTICE, RELIGION, EDUCATION AND WELFARE

Justice. The High Court *(Landsret)* in Godthaab comprises one professional judge and 2 lay magistrates, while there are 19 district courts under lay assessors.

Religion. About 88% of the population are Evangelical Lutherans.

Education. There were (1982–83) 10,666 pupils in primary comprehensive schools, of whom 8,045 were in the course of compulsory education (9 years). On 1 Jan. 1982, 1,554 students were enrolled in vocational training.

Health. The medical service is free to all inhabitants. There is a central hospital in Godthaab and 16 smaller district hospitals. In 1968 there were 42 doctors and 672 hospital beds.

Books of Reference

Greenland. R. Danish Ministry of Greenland. Copenhagen. Annual from 1968
Meddelelser om Grønland. Ed. Kommissionen for videnskabelige undersøgelser i Grønland. Copenhagen, 1899 ff. Since 1979 issued in 3 separate series: 'Bioscience', 'Geoscience' and 'Man and Society'
Statistiske Efterretninger (Statistical News), from 1983 special series: *Færøerne og Grønland* (Faroe Islands and Greenland)
Gad, F., *A History of Greenland.* Vol. 1. London, 1970.—Vol. 2. London, 1973
Hertling, K. (ed.), *Greenland Past and Present.* Copenhagen, 1970

DIPLOMATIC REPRESENTATIVES

Of Denmark in Great Britain (55 Sloane St., London, SW1X 9SR)
Ambassador: Tyge Dahlgaard (accredited 28 Feb. 1981).

Of Great Britain in Denmark (36–40 Kastelsvej, DK-2100, Copenhagen)
Ambassador: James Mellon.

Of Denmark in the USA (3200 Whitehaven St., NW, Washington, D.C., 20008)
Ambassador: Eigil Jørgensen.

Of the USA in Denmark (Dag Hammarskjolds Alle 24, Copenhagen)
Ambassador: Terence A. Todman.

Of Denmark to the United Nations
Ambassador: Wilh. Ulrichsen.

Books of Reference

Statistical Information: Danmarks Statistik (Sejrøgade 11, 2100 Copenhagen Ø.) was founded in 1849 and reorganized in 1966 as an incependent institution; it is administratively placed under the Minister of Economic Affairs. *Chief:* N. V. Skak-Nielsen. Its main publications are: *Statistisk Årbog* (Statistical Yearbook). From 1896; *Statistiske Efterretninger* (Statistical News). From 1909; *Statistiske Meddelelser* (Statistical Reports). From 1852; *Handelsstatistiske Meddelelser* (Reports on Foreign Trade). From 1910; *Statistiske Tabelværker* (Statistical Tables). From 1850; *Statistiske Undersøgelser* (Statistical Inquiries).

Ministry of Foreign Affairs, *Danish Foreign Office Journal. Commercial and General Review.—Denmark.* 1961.—*Economic Survey of Denmark* (annual).—*Facts About Denmark.* 1959.—Hæstrup, J., *From Occupied to Ally: the Danish Resistance Movement.* 1963
Atlas over Danmark. R. Danish Geog. Society. Copenhagen, 1963

Bibliografi over Danmarks Offentlige Publikationer. Institut for International Udveksling, Copenhagen. Annual

Dania polyglotta. Annual Bibliography of Books ... in Foreign Languages Printed in Denmark. State Library, Copenhagen. Annual

Kongelig Dansk Hof og Statskalender. Copenhagen. Annual

Brynildsen, F., *A Dictionary of the English and Dano-Norwegian Languages.* 2 vols. Copenhagen, 1902–07

Danstrup, J., *History of Denmark.* 2nd ed. Copenhagen, 1949

Krabbe, L., *Histoire de Danemark.* Copenhagen and Paris, 1950

Nielsen, B. K., *Engelsk–Dansk Ordbog.* Copenhagen, 1964

Trap, J. P., *Kongeriget Danmark.* 5th ed. 11 vols. Copenhagen, 1953 ff.

Vinterberg, H., and Bodelsen, C. A., *Dansk-Engelsk Ordbog.* Copenhagen, 1966

National Library: Det Kongelige Bibliotek, Copenhagen. *Librarian:* P. Birkelund.

DJIBOUTI

Jumhouriyya Djibouti

Capital: Djibouti
Population: 350,000 (1981)
GNP per capita: US$480 (1980)

HISTORY. At a referendum held on 19 March 1967, 60% of the electorate voted for continued association with France rather than independence and the new statute for the territory came into being on 5 July 1967. In Jan. 1976, following discussions between Ali Aref and President Giscard d'Estaing, it was announced that the French Government affirmed that the Territory of the Afars and the Issas was destined for independence but no date was fixed. Legislative elections were held on 8 May and independence as the Republic of Djibouti was achieved on 27 June 1977.

AREA AND POPULATION. Djibouti is bounded north-east by the Gulf of Aden, south-east by Somalia and all other sides by Ethiopia.

Djibouti has an area of 23,000 sq. km (8,880 sq. miles). The population was estimated in 1981 at 350,000, of whom 48% were Somali, 38% Afar, 9% European and 5% Arab. There were (1982) about 40,000 refugees from Ethiopia. Djibouti, the seat of government, had (1981) 150,000 inhabitants; other towns are Tadjoura, Obock and Dikhil and Ali-Sabieh. There are 5 administrative districts.

CLIMATE. Conditions are hot throughout the year, with very little rain. Djibouti. Jan. 78°F (25·6°C), July 96°F (35·6°C). Annual rainfall 5″ (130 mm).

CONSTITUTION AND GOVERNMENT. Under an organic law approved by the Constituent Assembly on 10 Feb. 1981, the President is directly elected for a 6-year term (renewable once) and the Constituent Assembly became a 65-member Chamber of Deputies, with a 5-year term. In Oct. 1981, the Assembly declared Djibouti a one-Party state, the ruling Party being the *Rassemblement Populaire pour le Progrès.* Elections for the Chamber of Deputies were held 21 May 1982, when 26 Somali, 23 Afar and 16 Arab members were elected.

President: Hassan Gouled Aptidon (elected 1977 and re-elected 1981).
Prime Minister and Ports: Barkat Gourad Hamadou.
Foreign Affairs: Moumin Báhdon Farah.

National flag: Horizontally blue over green, with a white triangle based on the hoist charged with a red star.

DEFENCE

Army. The Army comprises 1 infantry regiment, 1 armoured squadron, 1 support battalion, 1 border commando battalion and 1 parachute company. Equipment includes 22 armoured cars. The strength of the Army (of which the Navy and Air Force form part) was (1984) about 2,700 men. There is also a paramilitary force of some 2,000 men.

Navy. The nucleus of a naval force was acquired in 1977 with the commissioning of a coastal patrol craft and in 1984, 3 minor landing craft.

Air Force. As the nucleus of an air force, the French *Armée de l'Air* transferred to the Djibouti Government 2 Noratlas piston-engined tactical transport aircraft. These have since been supplemented by a twin-jet Mystère 20 for VIP duties, 2 light aircraft and an Alouette helicopter. A Boeing 737 has been ordered for VIP use.

INTERNATIONAL RELATIONS

Membership. Djibouti is a member of UN, OAU, the Arab League and an ACP State of the EEC.

ECONOMY

Budget. The ordinary budget for 1983 envisaged an expenditure of 22,269m. Djibouti francs.

Currency. The currency is the *Djibouti franc*. In March 1984, £1 = 250 *Djibouti francs*; US$1 = 168·77 *Djibouti francs*.

Banking. The Banque Nationale de Djibouti is the bank of issue. There are 6 commercial banks.

NATURAL RESOURCES

Minerals. Minerals supposed to exist are gypsum, mica, amethyst and sulphur.

Agriculture. Mainly market gardening at the oasis of Ambouli and near urban areas. Livestock (1982): 43,000 cattle, 380,000 sheep, 550,000 goats, 7,000 donkeys, 54,000 camels.

Fisheries. The catch in 1980 was 2,000 tonnes.

INDUSTRY AND TRADE

Industry. Industry provides employment for 1,500 and the main industry is a bottling plant opened in 1981.

Commerce. The main economic activity is the operation of the port. The chief imports are cotton goods, sugar, cement, flour, fuel oil and vehicles; the chief exports are hides, cattle and coffee (transit from Ethiopia). Trade in 1m. Djibouti francs:

	1979	1980	1981
Imports	28,436	33,782	36,654
Exports	14,147	19,171	20,348

In 1979 France provided 47% of imports and took 87% of exports.

Total trade between Djibouti and UK (British Department of Trade returns, in £1,000 sterling):

	1979	1980	1981	1982	1983
Imports to UK	328	303	227	53	184
Exports and re-exports from UK	6,499	6,682	6,555	6,521	7,712

COMMUNICATIONS

Roads. There were (1978) 1,650 km of roads, of which 75 km were hard-surfaced. In 1977 there were 11,800 passenger cars and 3,300 lorries.

Railway. For the line Djibouti–Addis Ababa *see* p. 448. In 1969–70 the railway carried goods traffic of 411,460 tons and 457,000 passengers.

Aviation. Air Djibouti provides services to Addis Ababa, Nairobi, Jidda and the Gulf. Other airlines serving Djibouti airport are Ethiopian Airlines, Air France, Air Tanzania and Yemen Airways Corporation. In 1981 there were 2,983 inward flights.

Shipping. In 1981 there entered at Djibouti 1,753 vessels, unloading 307,800 tonnes and loading 151,900 tonnes of merchandise. In 1981 the merchant marine comprised 8 vessels of 3,185 GRT.

Post and Broadcasting. Number of telephones (1980), 4,348. *Radiodiffusion-Télévision de Djibouti* broadcasts on medium- and short-waves in French, Somali, Afar and Arabic. There is a television transmitter in Djibouti, broadcasting for 19 hours a week. Number of receivers (1982): radio, 17,200; TV, 10,550.

Cinemas. In 1975 there were 4 cinemas with a seating capacity of 5,800.

JUSTICE, RELIGION, EDUCATION AND WELFARE

Justice. The judicial system is based on Islamic law.

Religion. The vast majority of the population is Moslem, with about 12,000 Roman Catholics.

Education. In 1981 there were 16,841 pupils and 375 teachers at primary schools, 3,812 pupils and 174 teachers at secondary schools, and 1,279 pupils with 88 teachers in technical schools.

Health. There were (1975) 11 hospitals and dispensaries with 1,028 beds; 52 physicians.

DIPLOMATIC REPRESENTATIVES

Of Djibouti in Great Britain
Ambassador: Ahmed Ibrahim Abdi (resides in Paris).

Of Great Britain in Djibouti
Ambassador: J. F. Walker, CMG, MBE (resides in San:a'a).

Of the USA in Djibouti (Villa Plateau du Serpent Blvd., Djibouti)
Chargé d'Affaires: Eugene D. Schmiel.

Of Djibouti to the United Nations and in the USA
Ambassador: Saleh Haji Farah Dirir.

Books of Reference

Poinsot, J.-P., *Djibouti et la Côte française des Somalis.* Paris, 1965
Thompson, V., and Adloff, R., *Djibouti and the Horn of Africa.* Stanford Univ. Press, 1967

COMMONWEALTH OF DOMINICA

Capital: Roseau
Population: 74,859 (1981)
GNP per capita: US$761 (1982)

HISTORY. Dominica was discovered by Columbus. It was a British possession from 1805, a member of the Federation of the West Indies 1958–62, an Associated State of the UK, 1967–78 and became an independent republic as the Commonwealth of Dominica on 3 Nov. 1978.

AREA AND POPULATION. Dominica is an island in the Windward group of the West Indies situated between Martinique and Guadeloupe. It has an area of 751 sq. km (290 sq. miles) and a population at the 1981 Census of 74,859. The chief town, Roseau, had about 20,000 inhabitants in 1981.

The population is mainly of Negro and mixed origins, with small white and Asian minorities. There is a Carib settlement of about 500, almost entirely of mixed blood.

CLIMATE. A tropical climate, with pleasant conditions between Dec. and March, but there is a rainy season from June to Oct., when hurricanes may occur. Rainfall is heavy, with coastal areas having 70″ (1,750 mm) but the mountains may have up to 250″ (6,250 mm). Annual temperatures range from 78°F (25·6°C) to 90°F (32·2°C) in the hottest month.

CONSTITUTION AND GOVERNMENT. The House of Assembly has 21 elected and 9 nominated members. The Speaker is elected from among the members of the House or from outside. The Cabinet is presided over by the Prime Minister and consists of 6 other Ministers including the Attorney-General. Elections were held in July 1980. The Dominica Freedom Party won 17 seats, Dominica Democratic Labour Party, 2 seats and Independents 2 seats.

President: Clarence A. Seignoret.
The Cabinet in Oct. 1983 was composed as follows:

Prime Minister and Minister of Finance, Foreign Affairs, Trade, Tourism, Development and Industry: Mary Eugenia Charles.

Attorney-General and Minister of Legal Affairs: Ronan David. *Home Affairs, Women's Affairs, Industrial Relations and Housing:* Brian G. K. Alleyne. *Agriculture, Lands, Co-operatives and Fisheries:* Heskeith Alexander. *Communications and Works:* Alleyne Carbon. *Education, Health, Youth Affairs, Sports and Culture:* Charles Maynard. *Minister without portfolio in the Prime Minister's Office with special responsibility for Trade and Industry, Tourism and Information:* Charles Savarin.

National flag: Green with a cross over all of yellow, black, and white pieces, and in the centre a red disc charged with a Sisserou parrot in natural colours within a ring of 10 yellow stars.

INTERNATIONAL RELATIONS

Membership. The Commonwealth of Dominica is a member of UN, OAS, CARICOM, the Commonwealth and is an ACP state of EEC.

ECONOMY

Budget. In 1982–83 there was a deficit of EC$11·9m.

Currency. The French *franc,* the £ sterling and the East Caribbean *dollar* are legal tender. In March 1984, EC$2·70 = US$1 and EC$3·98 = £1.

Banking. Savings bank (Dec. 1982), 2,862 depositors, with $593,659 deposits. There are branches of Barclays Bank International, Royal Bank of Canada and

Dominica Cooperative Bank in Roseau, and a branch of Barclays at Portsmouth. The National Commercial and Development Bank was opened in 1977 and Banque Française Commerciale opened in 1979.

NATURAL RESOURCES

Agriculture. Hurricanes in 1979 and 1980 devastated large agricultural areas and damaged infrastructure. Production (1982): Bananas, 34,354 tonnes; coconuts, 11,455,000 nuts; beef, 457,428 lb; pork, 588,993 lb.

Livestock (1982): Cattle, 4,000; pigs, 8,000; sheep, 4,000; goats, 6,000; poultry, 115,000.

INDUSTRY AND TRADE

Industry. The main industries are agriculture and tourism.

Commerce (1982). Imports, EC$128,190,856; exports, EC$61,516,134. Chief products: Bananas, soap, fruit juices, essential oils, coconuts, vegetables, fruit and fruit preparations, and alcoholic drinks.

Total trade between Dominica and UK (British Department of Trade returns, in £1,000 sterling):

	1981	1982	1983
Imports to UK	14,462	11,376	12,251
Exports and re-exports from UK	7,924	7,423	7,653

Tourism. Tourists (1982) totalled 10,419.

COMMUNICATIONS

Roads. In 1976 there were 467 miles of road and 282 miles of track. Vehicles totalled (Sept. 1983) 5,717.

Post and Broadcasting. Telephone lines, 136 route miles; number of telephones, 3,193 (Sept. 1983). Radio receivers (1982) 13,405.

Cinemas. In 1982 there were 2 cinemas with a seating capacity of 1,000.

JUSTICE, RELIGION, EDUCATION AND WELFARE

Justice. There are 4 magistrates' courts. In 1981, 4,891 cases were filed and 4,388 were disposed of. There is also a supreme court which dealt with 38 criminal and 319 civil cases in 1981. The police force consists of 10 officers and 431 other ranks.

Religion. 80% of the population is Roman Catholic.

Education. In 1982 there were 18,780 primary and 6,195 secondary school pupils and 3 colleges of higher education.

Health. In Sept. 1983 there were 3 hospitals with 237 beds, 26 doctors, 7 dentists, 10 pharmacists and 153 nursing personnel.

DIPLOMATIC REPRESENTATIVES

Of Dominica in Great Britain (10 Kensington Ct., London, W8).
High Commissioner: Arden Shillingford, MBE (accredited 13 Dec. 1978).

Of Great Britain in Dominica
High Commissioner: G. L. Bullard, CMG (resides in Bridgetown).

Of Dominica to the USA and the United Nations
Ambassador: Franklyn A. M. Baron.

Book of Reference

Commonwealth of Dominica. HMSO, 1979
Library: Public Library, Roseau. *Librarian:* Miss C. Henry.

DOMINICAN REPUBLIC

Capital: Santo Domingo
Population: 6·3m. (1982)
GNP per capita: US$1,140 (1980)

República Dominicana

HISTORY. On 5 Dec. 1492 Columbus discovered the island of Santo Domingo, which he called La Española; for a time it was called Hispaniola. The city of Santo Domingo, founded by his brother, Bartholomew, in 1496, is the oldest city in the Americas. The western third of the island—now the Republic of Haiti—was later occupied and colonized by the French, to whom the Spanish colony of Santo Domingo was also ceded in 1795. In 1808 the Dominican population, under the command of Gen. Juan Sánchez Ramírez, routed an important French military force commanded by Gen. Ferrand, at the famous battle of Palo Hincado. This battle was the beginning of the end for French rule in Santo Domingo and culminated in the successful siege of the capital. Eventually, with the aid of a British naval squadron, the French were forced to capitulate and the colony returned again to Spanish rule, from which it declared its independence in 1821. It was invaded and held by the Haitians from 1822 to 1844, when they were expelled, and the Dominican Republic was founded and a constitution adopted. Independence day 27 Feb. 1844. Great Britain, in 1850, was the first country to recognize the Dominican Republic. The country was occupied by American Marines from 1916 until 1924. In 1936 the name of the capital city was changed from Santo Domingo to Ciudad Trujillo; and back again in 1961.

AREA AND POPULATION. The Dominican Republic occupies the eastern portion (about two-thirds) of the island of Hispaniola, Quisqueya or Santo Domingo, the western division forming the Republic of Haiti. It consists of the National District (containing the capital, Santo Domingo; population, census 1970, 817,067), and 26 provinces.

Area is 48,442 sq. km (18,700 sq. miles) with 870 miles of coastline, 193 miles of frontier line with Haiti (marked out in 1936).

The populations of the 26 provinces at the 1970 census were:

La Altagracia	88,231	Puerto Plata	186,112
Azua	90,590	La Romana	58,341
Bahoruco	66,398	Salcedo	89,204
Barahona	111,162	Samaná	53,420
Dajabón	51,069	Sánchez Ramírez	106,289
Duarte	200,478	San Cristóbal	324,673
Espaillat	140,508	San Juan	190,624
La Estrelleta	53,598	San Pedro de Macorís	105,463
Independencia	32,632	Santiago	385,625
María Trinidad Sánchez	97,109	Santiago Rodríguez	49,376
Montecristi	69,056	El Seibo	135,156
Pedernales	12,382	Valverde	76,825
Peravia	128,144	La Vega	293,573

Census (1981) 5,647,977. Estimate (1983) 5,982,000.

Population of the principal municipalities (Census 1981): National District (including Santo Domingo) 1,313,172; Santiago de los Caballeros, 278,638; La Romana, 91,571; San Pedro de Macorís, 78,562; San Francisco de Macorís, 64,906; La Vega, 52,432; San Juan de la Managuana, 49,764; Barahona, 49,334; Puerto Plata, 45,348.

The population is partly of Spanish descent, but is mainly composed of a mixed race of European and African blood.

CLIMATE. A tropical maritime climate with most rain falling in the summer months. The rainy season extends from May to Nov. and amounts are greatest in the north and east. Hurricanes may occur from June to Nov. Santo Domingo. Jan. 75°F (23·9°C), July 81°F (27·2°C). Annual rainfall 56" (1,400 mm).

CONSTITUTION AND GOVERNMENT. A new Constitution was promulgated on 28 Nov. 1966.

The President is elected for 4 years, by direct vote. In case of death, resignation or disability, he is succeeded by the Vice-president. There are 12 secretaries of state, a judicial adviser with secretary-of-state rank and 2 ministers without portfolio in charge of departments. Citizens are entitled to vote at the age of 18, or less when married.

Recent Presidents have been: Dr Joaquín Balaguer, 4 Aug. 1960–62; Lic. Rafael Bonnelly, 18 Jan. 1962; Professor Juan Bosch, 27 Feb.–25 Sept. 1963 (deposed); Dr Héctor Gracía Godoy, 3 Sept. 1965–1 July 1966; Joaquín Balaguer, 1 July 1966–15 Aug. 1978; Antonio Guzan, 26 May 1978–4 July 1982.

President: Salvador Jorge Blanc (assumed office 14 Aug. 1982).

The country's first free elections for nearly 40 years were held in Dec. 1962 when Juan Bosch was elected President with a clear majority, after which a new Constitution was approved on 29 April 1963. Bosch was overthrown by a military *coup d'état* in Sept. 1963 and the declared aim of the Constitutionalist side in the Civil War of April–Sept. 1965 was the restoration of Bosch as President and a return to the 1963 Constitution.

On 29 April 1965 USA landed a force of 44,000 Marine and Army, later assisted by Organization of American States contributions. The capital remained divided between these forces and various rival factions of nationals. A provisional government was eventually installed on 3 Sept. 1965.

Until elections on 1 June 1966 there was government by decree.

National flag: Blue, red; quartered by a white cross.
National anthem: Quisqueyanos valientes, alzemos (words by E. Prud'homme; tune by J. Reyes, 1883).

DEFENCE. The armed forces are under the command of the President of the Republic, acting through the Secretary of State for the Armed Forces.

Army. The Army has a strength (1984) of about 14,000. It is organized in 3 infantry brigades, 1 artillery regiment and support battalions, and has some light tanks and armoured cars.

Navy. The Navy, largely comprising former US vessels, consists of 1 very old frigate acting as the operational flagship (former training ship, *ex*-presidential yacht), 2 escort (*ex*-fleet) minesweepers, 3 patrol vessels (*ex*-netlayers), 1 medium landing ship, 2 landing craft, 5 coastguard vessels, 8 patrol cutters, 4 small training craft, 2 oilers, 3 survey craft and 10 tugs. Personnel in 1984 totalled 4,050 officers and men.

Air Force. The Air Force, with HQ at San Isidoro, has 1 squadron of 8 F-51D Mustang piston-engined fighters, supported by 11 T-34B Mentors; 1 squadron with a total of about 16 Bell 205A-1, UH-1, UH-12E, OH-6A, H-19 and Alouette II/III helicopters; 1 transport squadron with 5 C-47s and some smaller communications aircraft; a Presidential Dauphin 2 helicopter; and an assortment of trainers. Personnel strength was (1984) 4,500.

INTERNATIONAL RELATIONS

Membership. The Dominican Republic is a member of UN and OAS.

ECONOMY

Budget. The 1982 budget balanced at RD$1,029·2m.

Currency. In Oct. 1947 the *peso oro*, equal to the US$, was formally made the unit of currency. In March 1984, £1 = RD$1·485; US$1 = RD$1.

There are silver coins for 50, 25 and 10 centavos, a copper-nickel 5-centavo piece and a copper 1-centavo piece.

Banking. There are 4 foreign banks—the Royal Bank of Canada with 12 branches, the Bank of Nova Scotia with 11 branches, the Citibank with 6 branches, the Chase Manhattan Bank with 7 branches and the Bank of America with 4 branches. An agricultural and mortgage bank, with paid-up capital of RD$500,000, was established in 1945; in 1950 its capital was increased to RD$5m. In 1947 the Central Bank of the Dominican Republic was established. A Banco Popular Dominicano, with an authorized capital of RD$5m., opened in Jan. 1964.

Weights and Measures. The metric system was nominally adopted on 1 Aug. 1913, but English and Spanish units have remained in common use in ordinary commercial transactions; on 17 Sept. 1954 a more drastic law requiring the decimal metric system was passed.

ENERGY AND NATURAL RESOURCES

Electricity. Hurricane 'David' (Aug. 1979) damaged 3 of the hydro-electric plants which produce 30% of electricity supply. 2,225·4m. kwh. of electricity was generated in 1982.

Minerals. Bauxite output in 1982 was 152,250 tonnes. Silver and platinum have been found, and near Neiba there are several hills of rock salt (production 1977, 48,592 tonnes). Ferronickel production (1982) 13,817 tonnes. The Rosario Dominicana goldmines were nationalized in Oct. 1979. Exports of Doré, a gold and silver alloy, (1982) RD$163·6m.

Agriculture. Agriculture is the chief source of wealth, sugar cultivation being the principal industry. Of the total area, 27,411 hectares are cultivable.

Livestock in 1982: 2·16m. cattle, 100,000 pigs, 55,000 sheep.

The largest sugar estates are in the south-eastern part of the republic. Sugar production, 1982, was 10·92m. tonnes. Two companies produce four-fifths of the total, but in all there are 16 sugar 'centrals'.

Coffee is exported mainly to USA. Output, 1982, 126,984 tonnes. Production of rice for home consumption and export is fostered; output, 1982, 446,913 tonnes. Cocoa is the second principal crop and covers 2m. *tareas* (340,000 acres); output in 1982, 34,921 tonnes. There are useful crops of yucca (1977: 162,287 tonnes) and beans (1982: 58,075 tonnes) for local consumption. Scientific growing of bananas (1977: 290,837 tonnes) and of leaf tobacco (1982: 33,184 tonnes) is progressing.

Fisheries. The total catch (1981) was 14,500 tonnes.

INDUSTRY AND TRADE

Industry. In 1975, 1,286 industrial establishments employed 130,000 men and women, who earned RD$157·57m. Important manufactures are sugar (114,000 tonnes in 1981), cotton and rayon textiles (17m. metres in 1979), cement (960,000 tonnes in 1981).

Commerce. Total imports and exports in RD$1m. (equal to US$1m.):

	1977	1978	1979	1980	1981	1982
Imports	847·8	860·9	1,080·4	1,498·4	1,450·2	1,255·8
Exports	780·4	675·3	868·6	961·9	1,188·0	767·7

The principal exports in 1980 were (in RD$1m.): Sugar and by-products, 242·9; coffee, 48·5; ferronickel, 92·7; Doré, 184.

Total trade between the Dominican Republic and UK (British Department of Trade returns, in £1,000 sterling):

	1979	1980	1981	1982	1983
Imports to UK	5,174	4,788	7,013	5,752	6,662
Exports and re-exports from UK	9,627	11,514	10,860	10,161	11,594

Tourism. 613,774 tourists visited the Dominican Republic in 1981.

COMMUNICATIONS

Roads. Three main trunk highways, with branches, extend from Santo Domingo eastward to Higuey (106 miles), northward to Santiago and Montecristi and Dajabón (204 miles) and westward to San Juan (128 miles) and Elías Piña on the Haitian border (161 miles). At Elías Piña the road joins the Haitian road to Port-au-Prince. Total highway system in 1977 was 5,224 km first-, 1,538 km second- and 2,505 km third-class roads; there were 647 bridges. Road transport is the chief means of travel. There were 82,001 cars, 40,626 commercial vehicles and 34,967 motor cycles in 1977.

Railways. Some 142 km of the Dominican Government Railway remains in use between La Vega and the port of Sánchez. Other lines, including the Central Romana Railway, exist to serve the sugar industry, totalling 1,600 km.

Aviation. The country is reached from the American continent and the Caribbean islands by 8 international airlines. Two local aviation companies provide interior services and connect Santo Domingo with San Juan in Puerto Rico, Curaçao, Aruba and Miami.

Shipping. Santo Domingo is the leading port; Puerto Plata ranks next. In 1971, vessels of 9,833,000 tons entered the ports to discharge 3,009,000 tonnes of cargo, and vessels of 5,276,000 tons cleared the ports having loaded 1,986,000 tonnes.

Post and Broadcasting. Number of telephone instruments (1982), 175,054, of which 138,169 in Santo Domingo. The telephone system is mainly operated by an American company. The telegraph has a total length of about 500 km, privately owned; they have been leased to All-America Cables, Inc., which also controls submarine cables connecting, in the north, Puerto Plata with Puerto Rico and New York, and in the south, Santo Domingo with Puerto Rico, Cuba and Curaçao.

There are 151 broadcasting stations in Santo Domingo and other towns; this includes the 2 government stations. There are 4 television stations.

Cinemas (1978). Cinemas numbered 72, with seating capacity of about 40,000.

Newspapers (1978). There were 7 daily newspapers with a circulation of 155,000.

JUSTICE, RELIGION, EDUCATION AND WELFARE

Justice. The judicial power resides in the Supreme Court of Justice, the courts of appeal, the courts of first instance, the communal courts and other tribunals created by special laws, such as the land courts. The Supreme Court consists of a president and 8 judges chosen by the Senate, and the procurator-general, appointed by the executive; it supervises the lower courts. Each province forms a judicial district, as does the *Distrito Nacional*, and each has its own procurator fiscal and court of first instance; these districts are subdivided, in all, into 72 municipalities and 18 municipal districts, each with one or more local justices. The death penalty was abolished in 1924.

Religion. The religion of the state is Roman Catholic; other forms of religion are permitted.

Education. Primary instruction (5,245 schools) is free and obligatory for children between 7 and 14 years of age; there are also secondary, normal, vocational and special schools, all of which are either wholly maintained by the State or state-aided; in 1975, primary schools had 15,216 teachers and 833,439 pupils; 997

intermediate and secondary schools had 4,950 teachers and 142,501 pupils.

The University of Santo Domingo (founded 1538) had (1975) 27,675 students; 5 other universities had 14,573 students.

Health. In 1978, 18 towns had complete waterworks. There were, in 1975, 1,310 doctors, 121 hospitals, health centres and polyclinics with 8,389 beds.

DIPLOMATIC REPRESENTATIVES

Of the Dominican Republic in Great Britain (4 Braemar Mansions, London, SW7 4AG)
Ambassador: Alfredo A. Ricart.

Of Great Britain in the Dominican Republic (Ave. Independencia 506, Santo Domingo)
Ambassador: Roy G. Marlow.

Of the Dominican Republic in the USA (1715–22nd St., NW, Washington, D.C., 20008)
Ambassador: Carlos Despradel.

Of the USA in the Dominican Republic (Calle Cesar Nicolas Penson, Santo Domingo)
Ambassador: Robert Anderson.

Of the Dominican Republic to the United Nations
Ambassador: Dr E. Knipping-Victoria.

Books of Reference

Anuario estadístico de la República Dominicana, 1944–45. Ciudad Trujillo. 1949. This has been succeeded by separate annual reports covering foreign trade, vital statistics, banking, insurance, housing and communications.
Dirección General de Estadística. *21 años de estadísticas dominicanas 1936–1956.* Ciudad Trujillo, 1957.—*Republica Dominicana en Cifras 1978.* Ciudad Trujillo, 1979
Official Guide to the Dominican Republic, 79–80. Tourist Information Center, Santo Domingo, 1980
Atkins, G. P., *Arms and Politics in the Dominican Republic.* London, 1981
Bell, I., *The Dominican Republic.* London, 1980
Diederich, B., *Trujillo: The Death of the Goat.* London, 1978
Wiarda, H. J., and Kryzanek, M. J., *The Dominican Republic: A Caribbean Crucible.* Boulder, 1982

ECUADOR

República del Ecuador

Capital: Quito
Population: 9·25m. (1983)
GNP per capita: US$1,430 (1981)

HISTORY. The Spaniards under Francisco Pizarro founded a colony after their victory at Cajamarca (16 Nov. 1532). Their rule was first challenged by the rising of 10 Aug. 1809. Marshal Sucre defeated the Spaniards at Pichincha in 1821, and in 1822 Bolívar persuaded the new republic to join the federation of Gran Colombia. The Presidency of Quito became the Republic of Ecuador by amicable secession 13 May 1830.

AREA AND POPULATION. Ecuador is bounded on the north by Colombia, on the east and south by Peru, on the west by the Pacific ocean. The frontier with Peru has long been a source of dispute between the two countries. The latest delimitation of it was in the treaty of Rio, 29 Jan. 1942, when, after being invaded by Peru, Ecuador lost over half her Amazonian territories. Ecuador unilaterally denounced this treaty in Sept. 1961. *See* map in THE STATESMAN'S YEAR-BOOK, 1942. Fighting between Peru and Ecuador began again in Jan. 1981 over this border issue but a ceasefire was agreed in early Feb.

No definite figure of the area of the country can yet be given, as a portion of the frontier has not been delimited. One estimate of the area of Ecuador is 270,670 sq. km, excluding the litigation zone between Peru and Ecuador, which is 190,807 sq. km.

Ecuador has 3 distinct zones: the *Sierra* or uplands of the Andes, consisting of high mountain ridges with valleys, with 2·57m. of the population and high-priced farming land; the *Costa*, the coastal plain between the Andes and the Pacific, with 2·02m., whose permanent plantations furnish bananas, cacao, coffee, sugar-cane and many other crops; the *Oriente*, the upper Amazon basin on the east, consisting of tropical jungles threaded by large rivers.

The population is predominantly of Amerindians, with small proportions of people of European or African descent.

The official language is Spanish. The Amerindians of the highlands speak mainly the Quechua language; in the Oriental Region various tribes have languages of their own.

Census population in 1974, 6,521,710. Estimate (1983) 9·25m.

The population 28 Nov. 1982 was distributed by provinces (capitals in brackets):

Provinces	Area (sq. km)	Population Census 1982 [1]
Azuay (Cuenca)	7,799	440,571
Bolívar (Guaranda)	3,216	148,161
Cañar (Azogues)	2,677	180,285
Carchi (Tulcán)	3,582	128,113
Chimborazo (Riobamba)	6,161	329,922
Cotopaxi (Latacunga)	4,614	279,622
El Oro (Machala)	7,451	335,630
Esmeraldas (Esmeraldas)	15,866	247,870
Guayas (Guayaquil)	21,259	2,116,819
Imbabura (Ibarra)	4,903	244,421
Loja (Loja)	28,900	358,558
Los Ríos (Babahoyo)	5,937	451,064
Manabí (Portoviejo)	18,963	874,803
Pichincha (Quito)	16,438	1,369,059
Tungurahua (Ambato)	3,204	328,070

[1] Provisional.

423

Provinces	Area (sq. km)	Population Census 1982 [1]
Napo (Tena)		113,042
Pastaza (Puyo)		32,536
Morona-Santiago (Macas)	296,390	67,094
Zamora-Chinchipe (Zamora)		44,841
Colon (Galápagos)	7,844	6,201
Total	455,454	8,053,280

[1] Provisional.

There are 115 cantons, 212 urban parishes and 715 rural parishes. The chief towns (population census, 1974) are the capital, Quito (559,828), Guayaquil (823,219), Cuenca (104,470), Ambato (77,955), Machala (69,170), Esmeraldas (60,364), Portoviejo (59,550), Riobamba (58,087).

Vital statistics for calendar years: Births, (1964) 219,137, (1965) 226,436, (1966) 220,930; deaths, (1964) 58,989, (1965) 60,202, (1966) 59,618.

CLIMATE. The climate varies from equatorial, through warm temperate to mountain conditions, according to altitude. This affects temperatures and rainfall. In coastal areas, the dry season is from May to Dec., but only from June to Sept. in mountainous parts, where temperatures may be 20°F colder than on the coast. Quito Jan. 59°F (15°C), July 58°F (14·4°C). Annual rainfall 44″ (1,115 mm). Guayaquil. Jan. 79°F (26·1°C), July 75°F (23·9°C). Annual rainfall 39″ (986 mm).

CONSTITUTION AND GOVERNMENT. On 22 June 1970 President José Maria Velasco Ibarra assumed dictatorial powers, following months of strife between student and security forces. For details of governments 1963–70, see THE STATESMAN'S YEAR-BOOK, 1974–75, pp. 875–76. On 15 Feb. 1972 President Velasco Ibarra was deposed. A National Military Government under Gen. Guillermo Rodriguez Lara was formed and the 1945 Constitution reintroduced. President Rodriguez Lara resigned in Jan. 1976 and a military Junta assumed power until the 1979 elections. A new Constitution came into force on 10 Aug. 1979. Elections take place in May 1984.

National flag: Three horizontal stripes of yellow, blue, red, with the yellow of double width, and in the centre over all the national arms.

National anthem: Salve, oh patria! (words by J. L. Mera; tune by A. Neumann, 1866).

The following is a list of the presidents and provisional executives since 1940:

Carlos Alberto Arroyo del Rio, elected 12 Jan. 1940; resigned 30 May 1944.

Dr José Maria Velasco Ibarra, elected by Constituent Assembly, Aug. 1944; re-elected 11 Aug. 1946, but deposed 24 Aug. 1947.

Col. Carlos Mancheno, seized power 24 Aug. 1947; deposed 3 Sept. 1947.

Mariano Suárez Veintimilla (Vice-President), 3–15 Sept. 1947.

Carlos Julio Arosemena Tola (provisional), 15 Sept. 1947–31 Aug. 1948.

Galo Plaza Lasso, 1 Sept. 1948–31 Aug. 1952.

Dr José María Velasco Ibarra, 1 Sept. 1952–31 Aug. 1956.

Dr Camilo Ponce Enríquez, 1 Sept. 1956–31 Aug. 1960.

Dr José María Velasco Ibarra, 1 Sept. 1960–8 Nov. 1961 (withdrew).

Dr Carlos Julio Arosemena Monroy, 8 Nov. 1961–11 July 1963 (deposed).

Military Junta, 11 July 1963–31 March 1966.

Clemente Yerovi Indaburu, 31 March–16 Nov. 1966 (interim).

Dr Otto Arosemena Gómez, 17 Nov. 1966–1 Sept. 1968.

Dr José María Velasco Ibarra, 1 Sept. 1968–15 Feb. 1972 (deposed).

Gen. Guillermo Rodriguez Lara, 16 Feb. 1972–11 Jan. 1976 (resigned).

Adm. Alfredo Poveda Burbano, 11 Jan. 1976–10 Aug. 1979.

Jaime Roldós Aguilera, 10 Aug. 1979–24 May 1981.

President: Osvaldo Hurtado Larrea (sworn in on 24 May 1981).

The Cabinet in Sept. 1983 was as follows:

Vice-President and President of the National Development Council: Léon Roldós Aguilera. *Administration:* Vladimiro Alvarez. *Foreign Affairs:* Dr Luis Valencia. *Social Welfare:* Alfredo Mancero. *Public Finance:* Pedro Pinto. *Education and Culture:* Dr Ernesto Albán. *Health:* Dr Luis Sarrazín. *Natural Resources and Energy:* Gustavo Galindo. *Labour:* Dr Jamil Mahauat. *Industry, Trade and Integration:* José Bermeo. *Public Works:* Edwin Ripalda. *Agriculture:* Eduardo Izaguirre. *National Defence:* Jorge Arciniegas. *Secretary-General of Administration:* Andrés Crespo. *Secretary of Administration:* Ramiro Rivera. *President of the Central Bank:* Abelardo Pachano B.

Local Government. The country is divided politically into 20 provinces; 4 of them comprise the 'Región Oriental' and one the Archipelago of Galápagos, officially called 'Colón', situated in the Pacific ocean about 600 miles to the west of Ecuador and comprising 15 islands. The provinces are administered by governors, appointed by the Government; their sub-divisions, or cantons, by political chiefs and elected cantonal councillors; and the parishes by political lieutenants. The Galápagos Archipelago is administered by the Ministry of National Defence.

DEFENCE. Military service is selective, with a 2-year period of conscription. The country is divided into 4 military zones, with headquarters at Quito, Guayaquil, Cuenca and Pastaza.

Army. The Army consists of 7 infantry, 1 armoured and 1 parachute brigade. Strength (1984) 27,500, with about 50,000 reservists. Equipment includes 45 American M-41 and 150 French AMX-13 light tanks.

Navy. The Navy consists of 2 Federal Republic of Germany-built diesel-electric powered patrol submarines; 1 old *ex*-US destroyer; 1 old frigate (*ex*-US destroyer escort transport), 6 Italian-built new corvettes, 6 fast missile boats, 7 coastal patrol craft, 1 landing ship, 2 medium landing ships, 1 supply ship, 1 water carrier, 3 survey vessels, 16 coastguard service craft, 1 repair vessel, 2 training ships, 1 floating dock and 6 tugs. More corvettes are being completed in Italy. Naval personnel in 1984 totalled 3,800 officers and men.

Air Force. The Air Force, formed with Italian assistance in 1920, was reorganized and re-equipped with US aircraft after Ecuador signed the Rio Pact of Mutual Defence in 1947 but latest equipment acquired from Europe and Brazil. Current strength of about 4,800 personnel and 52 combat aircraft includes a strike squadron equipped with 7 single-seat and 2 two-seat Jaguars; an interceptor squadron of 15 single-seat and 2 two-seat Mirage F.1s; a bomber squadron with 3 Canberra B.6s; 2 counter-insurgency units equipped with 7 Cessna A-37B and 6 Strikemaster light jet attack and training aircraft, 1 squadron with 1 piston-engined DC-6 and 2 C-130, 2 Buffalo and 3 HS 748 turboprop transports; Alouette III, SA 330 Puma and SA 315B Lama helicopters; and Cessna 150, T-33, T-34C-1 and T-41A/D trainers; 14 EMB-326 Xavante light jet attack/trainers were acquired from Brazil in 1982. Many other transports are operated by the military airline TAME.

INTERNATIONAL RELATIONS

Membership. Ecuador is a member of UN, OAS and LAIA (formerly LAFTA).

ECONOMY

Budget. Estimated revenue and expenditure for 1982 was 64,770m. sucres.

The division of the budget under main heads was, for 1982: Education and social development, 29·2%; defence, 9·1%; public works, 9·5%; agriculture, 6·4%.

Net international reserves, 31 Dec. 1980, were US$857m.

Currency. The monetary unit is the *sucre,* divided into 100 *centavos.* In circulation are a pure nickel 1-sucre and copper-nickel and copper-zinc 50-, 20-, 10- and 5-centavo pieces. The currency consists mainly of the notes of the Central Bank in denominations of 5, 10, 20, 50, 100, 500 and 1,000 sucres. In March 1984, US$1 = 57·57; £1 = 85·76.

Banking. The Central Bank of Ecuador, at Quito, with a capital of 20m. sucres, is modelled after the Federal Reserve Banks of US: through branches opened in 12 towns it now deals in mortgage bonds. On 31 July 1970 the Central Bank had gold and foreign-exchange reserves worth US$62m. Banks must hold cash equal to 21% of sight, short-term and savings deposits.

All commercial banks must be affiliated to the Central Bank.

The Bank of London and Montreal, Ltd, had branches in Quito and Guayaquil.

Weights and Measures. By a law of 6 Dec. 1856 the metric system was made the legal standard but the Spanish measures are in general use. The quintal is equivalent to 101·4 lb.

The meridian of Quito has been adopted as the official time.

ENERGY AND NATURAL RESOURCES

Electricity. In 1982, total capacity of hydraulic and thermal plants was 990,000 kw. Estimated output was 2,000m. kwh.

Oil. Production of crude petroleum in 1982 was 77·1m. bbls; 1981 77m. New drilling along the coast has had some success, but Ecuador has to import some crude oil. Proven oil reserves (1981, estimate) 1,100m. bbls.

Gas. In 1982, natural gas production was 400,257·9m. cu. ft.

Minerals. Production (1980): Silver, 24,000 troy oz; gold, 3,344 troy oz; copper, 723,000 kg; zinc, 330,000 kg.

The country has some copper, iron and lead. There are coal deposits in the Biblián area, but their exploitation has so far proved uneconomic.

Agriculture. Ecuador is divided into two agricultural zones: the coast and lower river valleys, where tropical farming is carried on in an average temperature of from 18° to 25° C.; and the Andean highlands with a temperate climate, adapted to grazing, dairying and the production of cereals, potatoes, pyrethrum and vegetables suitable to temperate climes. Some wheat has to be imported.

124,000 acres of rich virgin land in the Santo Domingo de los Colorados area has been set aside for settlement of smallholders.

Excepting the two agricultural zones and a few arid spots on the Pacific coast, Ecuador is a vast forest. Roughly estimated, 10,000 sq. miles on the Pacific slope extending from the sea to an altitude of 5,000 ft on the Andes, and the Amazon Basin below the same level containing 80,000 sq. miles, nearly all virgin forest, are rich in valuable timber, but much of it is still not commercially accessible.

The staple export products are bananas, cacao and coffee. Main crops, in 1,000 tonnes, in 1982: Rice, 384; potatoes, 416; maize, 324; coffee, 84; barley, 35; cocoa, 97; bananas, 2,752.

Livestock (1982): Cattle, 3,200,417; sheep, 1,259,000; pigs, 3,520,400; horses, 322,281; poultry, 41,357,000.

Forestry. In 1980, 4·4m. cu. metres of timber were cut.

Fisheries. Fisheries and fish product exports were valued at US$91,823,000 in 1980 (31,717 tonnes).

INDUSTRY AND TRADE

Industry. Production in 1978: Sugar, 178,000 tonnes; beer, 1,560,000 hectolitres; cement 1·06m. tonnes.

Commerce. Imports and exports for calendar years, in US$1m.:

	1978	1979	1980	1981	1982
Imports (c.i.f.)	1,630	1,986	2,250	2,246	1,988
Exports (f.o.b.)	1,494	2,173	2,506	2,541	2,140

Of the total exports (1982); petroleum, US$1,184,218m.; bananas, US$213,297m.; cocoa, US$63,064m.; coffee, US$138,758m.

USA furnished 35% of imports in 1970 and took 43% of the exports.

Total trade between Ecuador and UK (British Department of Trade returns, in £1,000 sterling):

	1979	1980	1981	1982	1983
Imports to UK	6,210	8,344	5,050	9,288	11,022
Exports and re-exports from UK	33,483	30,930	34,149	60,792	35,008

Tourism. There were 239,000 visitors in 1981, mainly from South American countries, spending US$131m.

COMMUNICATIONS

Roads. In 1980, there were 35,000 km of roads of all types in this mountainous country, but most are narrow and subject to landslides. A trunk highway through the coastal plain is under construction which will link Machala in the extreme south-west with Esmeraldas in the north-west and with Quito and the northern section of the Pan-American Highway. In 1974, there were 43,600 cars and 68,400 trucks and buses.

Railways. A 1,067 mm gauge line runs from São Lorenzo through Quito to Guayaquil and Cuenca, total 971 km.

Aviation. There are 2 international airports. The following international lines operate: Air France, Avianca, Eastern, British Caledonian, Ecuatoriana de Aviación, KLM, Lufthansa, Iberia, LAN Chile, and Aerovías Peruanas. They connect Quito with Panama, Bogotá (Colombia), Guayaquil, New York and Europe. All the leading towns are connected by an almost daily service, but landing fields are small.

Shipping. Ecuador has 7 seaports, of which Guayaquil is the chief. The merchant navy comprises 39,964 tons of seagoing and 21.232 tons of river craft. In 1970 ships totalling 8·88m. GRT entered Ecuadorean ports, unloading 1·52m. tons, and loading 1·77m. tons.

There is river communication, improved by dredging, throughout the principal agricultural districts on the low ground to the west of the Cordillera by the rivers Guayas, Daule and Vinces (navigable for 200 miles by river steamers in the rainy season).

Post and Broadcasting. Quito is connected by telegraph with Colombia and Peru, and by cable with the rest of the world. The main towns in the country are connected by radio-telephone. There are over 300 radio stations.

In 1982 there were 290,200 telephones in use, 109,600 in Quito and 109,200 in Guayaquil; most were operated by the Government; 99% were automatic. Television was inaugurated in 1960 in Guayaquil, in 1961 in Quito and in 1967 in Cuenca. In 1980 there were 1·8m. radio receivers and ·3m. television receivers.

Cinemas. (1974). Cinemas numbered about 185 with total seating capacity of 114,600.

Newspapers (1971). There were 22 daily newspapers with an aggregate daily circulation of 283,000; 7 papers in Quito and Guayaquil have the bulk of the circulation.

JUSTICE, RELIGION, EDUCATION AND WELFARE

Justice. The Supreme Court in Quito is the highest tribunal and consists of 5 justices and the Minister Fiscal. Of the 15 superior courts, 4 are composed of 6 judges and 11 of 3 judges each. There are numerous lower courts. The popular jury was abolished in 1928, and criminal cases are heard before a 'special jury' consisting of 1 judge and 3 members of the Ecuadorean bar, appointed annually by the superior courts. Capital punishment and all forms of torture are prohibited under the constitution, as are imprisonment for debt and contracts involving personal servitude or slavery. Substantial amendments expediting judicial procedure were introduced in 1936, and salaries for all judicial officials replaced remuneration by fees.

Religion. The state recognizes no religion and grants freedom of worship to all. Civil registration of births, deaths and marriages is obligatory. Divorce is permitted. Illegitimate children have the same rights as legitimate ones with respect to education and inheritance.

Education. Primary education is free and in principle obligatory. Private schools, both primary and secondary, are under some state supervision. There were (1979–80), primary schools with 1·4m. pupils; secondary schools with 535,000 pupils and universities with 230,637 students.

Social Welfare. From 1 May 1964 social benefits are extended to professional men, artisans and domestic workers; and to agricultural workers from 1 May 1965. The Ministry of Social Welfare and Labour was in 1967 divided into the Ministries of Social Welfare and of Public Health. In 1970 there were 199 hospitals with 14,024 beds.

DIPLOMATIC REPRESENTATIVES

Of Ecuador in Great Britain (3 Hans Crescent, London, SW1X 0LS)
Ambassador: Dr Galo Leoro (accredited 19 July 1983).

Of Great Britain in Ecuador (Calle Gonzalez Suarez 111, Quito)
Ambassador: A. C. Buxton, CMG.

Of Ecuador in the USA (2535–15th St., NW, Washington, D.C., 20009)
Ambassador: Dr Rafael Garcia Velasco.

Of the USA in Ecuador (120 Avenida Patria, Quito)
Ambassador: Samuel F. Hart.

Of Ecuador to the United Nations
Ambassador: Dr Miguel A. Albornoz.

Books of Reference

Anuario de Legislación Ecuatoriana. Quito. Annual
Boletín del Banco Central. Quito
Boletín General de Estadística. Tri-monthly
Boletín Mensual del Ministerio de Obras Públicas. Monthly
Informes Ministeriales. Quito. Annual
Bibliografía Nacional, 1756–1941. Quito, 1942
Invest in Ecuador. Banco Central del Ecuador, Quito, 1980
Buitrón, A., and Collier, Jr, J., *The Awakening Valley: Study of the Otavalo Indians.* New York, 1950
Cueva, A., *The Process of Political Domination in Ecuador.* London, 1982
Holdridge, L. R. and others, *The Forests of Western and Central Ecuador.* Washington, 1947
Martz, J. D., *Ecuador: Conflicting Political Culture and the Quest for Progress.* Boston, 1972
Middleton, A., *Class, Power and the Distribution of Credit in Ecuador.* Glasgow, 1981

EGYPT

Jumhuriyat Misr al-Arabiya

Capital: Cairo
Population: 46m. (1984)
GNP per capita: US$580 (1980)

HISTORY. Part of the Ottoman Empire from 1517 until Dec. 1914 when it became a British protectorate, Egypt became an independent monarchy on 28 Feb. 1922. Following a revolution on 23 July 1952, a Republic was proclaimed on 18 June 1953. Egypt merged with Syria on 22 Feb. 1958 to form the United Arab Republic, retaining that name when Syria broke away from the union on 28 Sept. 1961, finally re-adopting the name of Egypt on 2 Sept. 1971.

AREA AND POPULATION. Egypt is bounded east by Israel, the Gulf of Aqaba and the Red Sea, south by Sudan, west by Libya and north by the Mediterranean. The total area is 1,002,000 sq. km (386,900 sq. miles), but the cultivated and settled area, that is, the Nile valley, delta and oases, covers only about 35,580 sq. km.

The area, population (1976 Census) and capitals of the governerates are:

Governorate	Sq. km	1976 census	Capital
Sinai	60,714	10,104	Al-Arish
Suez	17,840	194,001	Suez
Ismailia	1,442	351,889	Ismailia
Port Said	72	262,620	Port Said
Sharqîya	4,180	2,621,208	Zagazig
Daqahlîya	3,471	2,732,756	Mansûra
Damietta	589	557,115	Damietta
Kafr el Sheikh	3,437	1,403,468	Kafr el-Sheikh
Alexandria	2,679	2,318,655	Alexandria
Behera	4,589	2,517,292	Damanhur
Gharbîya	1,942	2,294,303	Tanta
Menûfîya	1,612	1,710,982	Shibin el-Kom
Qalyûbîya	971	1,674,006	Benha
Cairo	214	5,084,463	Cairo
Gîza	1,010	2,419,247	Gîza
Faiyûm	1,827	1,140,245	Faiyûm
Beni Suef	1,322	1,108,615	Beni-Suef
Minya	2,262	2,055,739	Minya
Asyût	1,530	1,695,378	Asyût
Sohag	1,547	1,924,960	Sohag
Qena	1,851	1,705,594	Qena
Aswân	679	619,932	Aswân
al-Bahr al-Ahmar	203,685	56,191	Al-Ghurdaqah
al-Wadi al-Jadid	376,505	84,645	Al-Kharijah
Mersa Matruh	298,735	112,772	Matruh
Total		36,656,180	

The principal towns, with their census 1976 populations, are:

Cairo	5,074,016	Mansûra	257,866	Minya	146,423
Alexandria	2,317,705	Asyût	213,983	Ismailia	145,978
Gîza	1,246,713	Zagazig	202,637	Aswân	144,377
Shubra el-Khema	393,700	Suez	193,965	Beni-Suef	118,148
Mahalla el-Kubra	292,853	Damanhûr	188,927	Shibin el-Kom	102,840
Tanta	284,636	Faiyûm	167,081	Sohag	101,758
Port Said	262,760	Kafr el-Dwar	160,554		

Population (1984) 46m. and of Greater Cairo (1979) 8·54m. The 1976 census total excluded an estimated 1,572,000 nationals living abroad.

CLIMATE. The climate is mainly dry, but there are winter rains along the

Mediterranean coast. Elsewhere, rainfall is very low and erratic in its distribution. Winter temperatures are everywhere comfortable, but summer temperatures are very high, especially in the south. Cairo. Jan. 56°F (13·3°C), July 83°F (28·3°C). Annual rainfall 1·2" (28 mm). Alexandria. Jan. 58°F (14·4°C), July 79°F (26·1°C). Annual rainfall 7" (178 mm). Aswan. Jan. 62°F (16·7°C), July 92°F (33·3°C). Annual rainfall trace. Gaza. Jan. 55°F (12·8°C), July 78°F (25·6°C). Annual rainfall 16" (389 mm). Luxor. Jan. 59°F (15°C), July 86°F (30°C). Annual rainfall trace. Port Said. Jan. 58°F (14·4°C), July 78°F (27·2°C). Annual rainfall 3" (76 mm). Ismailia. Jan. 56°F (13·3°C), July 84°F (28·9°C). Annual rainfall 1·5" (37 mm).

CONSTITUTION AND GOVERNMENT. The Constitution was approved by referendum on 11 Sept. 1971. It defines Egypt as 'an Arab Republic with a democratic, socialist system' and the Eyptian people as 'part of the Arab nation' with Islam as the state religion and Arabic as the official language.

The President of the Republic is nominated by the People's Assembly and confirmed by plebiscite for a 6-year term. He is the supreme commander of the armed forces and presides over the defence council.

Presidents since the establishment of the Republic have been:

Gen. Mohamed Neguib, 18 June 1953–14 Nov. 1954 (deposed).
Col. Gamal Abdel Nasser, 14 Nov. 1954–28 Sept. 1970 (died).

Col. Mumammad Anwar Sadat, 28 Sept. 1970–6 Oct. 1981 (assassinated).
Lieut.-Gen. Muhammad Hosni Mubarak, 7 Oct. 1981–.

The People's Assembly is a unicameral legislature consisting of 392 members directly elected for a 5-year term; the President of the Republic may appoint up to 10 additional members. At the general elections held in June 1979, the National Democratic Party gained 330 seats, the Socialist Labour Party 29, the Liberal Socialist Party 3, and independents 10. By 1982, 13 of the SLP members had become independent or joined the NDP.

Following the abolition of the Arab Socialist Union in April 1980, a 210-member Consultative Council (*Shura*) was formed in Sept. 1980; all 140 of its elective seats were won by the NDP, and a further 70 members were appointed by the President.

The President may appoint one or more Vice-Presidents, and appoints a Prime Minister and a Council of Ministers, whom he may remove as he wishes.

President of the Republic: Hosni Mubarak.

The Council of Ministers in March 1984 was composed as follows:

Prime Minister and Minister for Al-Azhar Mosque: Dr Fuad Mohieddin.

Deputy Prime Minister and Foreign Minister: Kamal Hassan Ali. *Deputy Prime Minister for Production and Oil Minister:* Ezzedin Hilal. *Deputy Prime Minister and Minister of Defence and Military Production:* Abdelhalim Abu-Ghazala. *Deputy Prime Minister for Services and Education and Minister of Scientific Research:* Mustafa Kamal Helmi. *Finance:* Mahmoud Salahadin Hamed. *Social Insurance and Social Affairs:* Dr Amal Osman. *Construction, Housing and Land Reclamation:* Hassaballah El-Kafrawi. *Foreign Affairs:* Dr Boutros Boutros Ghali. *Manpower and Vocational Training:* Saad Mohamed Ahmed. *Justice:* Ahmed Mamdouh Atai. *Transportation, Communications and Naval Transportation:* Soliman Metwalli Soliman. *Parliament and Shoura Council Affairs:* Mohamed Rashwan Mahmoud. *Culture:* Mohamed Abdul Hamid Radwan. *Irrigation:* Mohamed Abdel-Hadi Samaha. *Electricity and Energy:* Mohamed Maher Abaza. With a further 14 Ministers.

National flag: Three horizontal stripes of red, white, black, with the national emblem in the centre in gold.

Local Government. There are 26 governorates: 16 provinces, 5 cities and 4 frontier districts.

DEFENCE. Conscription is for 3 years, between the ages of 20 and 35.

Army. The Army comprises 3 armoured, 5 mechanized infantry, and 3 infantry divisions; 2 Republican Guard, 2 independent armoured, 9 independent infantry, 2 airmobile, 1 parachute, 12 artillery, 2 heavy mortar, and 6 anti-tank guided weapon brigades; 7 commando groups; and 2 surface-to-surface missile regiments. Strength (1984) 315,000 (180,000 conscripts) and about 300,000 reservists. Equipment includes 860 T-54/-55, 200 M-77, 600 T-62 and 250 AM-60 tanks. There are also paramilitary forces of about 139,000.

Navy. There are 16 elderly diesel-driven *ex*-Soviet submarines (nearing the end of their hull lives of which not more than half can be operational – several having been used for spares), 5 old destroyers, 2 new Spanish-built frigates, 3 very old frigates, 24 missile boats, 30 torpedo boats, 6 new patrol craft, 12 submarine chasers, 10 fleet minesweepers, 2 inshore minesweepers, 15 coastal patrol boats, 4 training ships, 3 medium landing ships, 14 landing craft, 2 survey vessels, 10 service craft, 2 tenders, 3 hovercraft, 7 auxiliaries and 4 tugs.

Naval bases are at Alexandria, Port Said, Mersa Matru, Port Tewfik, Hurghada and Safaqa. The Naval Academy is at Abu Qir.

Naval personnel in 1984 exceeded 20,000 officers and men, including the Coastguard, but not reserves of about 15,000.

Air Force. Until 1979, the Air Force was equipped largely with aircraft of USSR design, but subsequent re-equipment involves aircraft bought in the West, as well as some supplied by China. Current strength is about 27,000 personnel and 500 combat aircraft, of which the interceptors are operated by an independent Air Defence Command, in conjunction with many 'Guideline', 'Goa', 'Gainful', Hawk and Crotale missile batteries. There are about 12 Tu-16 twin-jet strategic bombers, some equipped to carry 'Kelt' air-to-surface missiles. The strike force includes a few Il-28 twin-jet bombers, and about 50 Su-7B and 18 Su-20 supersonic fighter-bombers. Other interceptor/ground attack fighter divisions are equipped with 40 F-16 Fighting Falcons, 75 Mirage 5s, 35 F-4E Phantoms, 50 F-6s (Chinese-built MiG-19s), and more than 120 MiG-21s, with up to 160 F-7s (Chinese-built MiG-21s) being delivered for assembly in Egypt (some for Iraq). Transport units have 21 C-130H Hercules turboprop heavy freighters, 10 twin-turboprop Buffaloes and up to 175 Gazelle, Mi-4, Mi-6. Mi-8, Sea King/Commando and Agusta-built CH-47C helicopters; some Commando helicopters and 2 EC-130H Hercules are equipped for electronic warfare duties. Training units are equipped with Gomhouria piston-engined trainers, Czech-built L-29 Delfin jet trainers, single-seat and two-seat versions of the MiG-15, MiG-17s, two-seat FT-6s, Mirage IIIs, MiG-21Us and Su-7Us, and Gazelle helicopters. Delivery has begun of 45 Alpha Jets, of which 15 are equipped for close air support duties, to replace MiG-17s, MiG-15s and L-29s. On order for mid-80s delivery are at least 40 more F-16s, 40 Mirage 2000 fighters and 2 (of a planned force of 4) E-2C Hawkeye AWACS aircraft. Main aircrew training centre is the EAF Academy at Bilbeis.

INTERNATIONAL RELATIONS

Membership. Egypt is a member of UN, OAU, the Arab League and OAPEC.

ECONOMY

Planning. A 5-year development plan runs 1982/83–1986/87 and provides for investments totalling £E35,000m.

Budget. Ordinary revenue and expenditure for fiscal years ending 30 June, in £E1,000:

	1976 [1]	1977 [1]	1978 [1]	1979 [1]
Revenue	5,976	5,503	6,516	10,249
Expenditure	5,976	5,503	6,516	12,929

[1] Estimates.

Currency. By decree of 18 Oct. 1916 (20 Zi-El-Higga 1934), the monetary unit of Egypt is the gold Egyptian pound of 100 *piastres* of 1,000 *millièmes*. Coins in circulation are 20, 10, 5, 2 piastres (silver); 2, 1 piastre, 5 millièmes, 1 millième (bronze). Gold coins are no longer in circulation. Silver coin is legal tender only up to £E1, and bronze coins up to 10 piastres. The Treasury issues 5- and 10-piastre currency notes. Bank-notes are issued by the National Bank in denominations of 5, 10, 25 and 50 piastres, £E1, 5, 10, 20, and 100.

In March 1984, £1 sterling = £E1·24; US$ = £E1·221.

Banking. On 18 Aug. 1960 a Central Bank of Egypt was established by decree. It manages the note issue, the Government's banking operations and the control of commercial banks. At the same date the National Bank founded in 1898 ceased to be the central bank and became a purely commercial bank.

Weights and Measures. In 1951 the metric system was made official with the exception of the feddân and its subdivisions.

Capacity. Kadah = 1/96th ardeb = 3·36 pints. *Rob* = 4 kadahs = 1·815 gallons. *Keila* = 8 kadahs = 3·63 gallons. *Ardeb* = 96 kadahs = 43·555 gallons, or 5·44439 bu., or 198 cu. decimetres.

Weights. Rotl = 144 dirhems = 0·9905 lb. *Oke* = 400 dirhems = 2·75137 lb. *Qantâr* or 100 rotls or 36 okes = 99·0493 lb. 1 *Qantâr* of unginned cotton = 315 lb. 1 *Qantâr* of ginned cotton = 99·05 lb. The approximate weight of the ardeb is as follows: Wheat, 150 kg; beans, 155 kg; barley, 120 kg; maize, 140 kg; cotton seed, 121 kg.

Surface. Feddân, the unit of measure for land = 4,200·8 sq. metres = 7,468·148 sq. pics = 1·03805 acres. 1 sq. pic = 6·0547 sq. ft = 0·5625 sq. metre.

ENERGY AND NATURAL RESOURCES

Electricity. Electricity generated in 1980 was 18,500m. kwh.

Oil. The first commercial discovery of oil in the Middle East outside Iran was made in Egypt in 1909, but production long remained low and often insufficient to meet Egypt's domestic requirements. In 1979 production was rising again and with the newly-regained Sinai oilfields was 25·5m. tonnes. Policy is controlled by the Egyptian General Petroleum Corporation (EGPC) a wholly state-owned corporation answerable to the Minister of Petroleum. EGPC is whole or part-owner of the various production and refining companies and controls supplies to the domestic marketing companies.

In 1983, 36m. tonnes of crude petroleum.

Minerals. Production (1973 in tonnes): Phosphate rock (1980), 658,000; iron ore, 656,000; marine salt, 454,000.

Agriculture. Rain seldom falls in Upper Egypt, and only at irregular intervals in Cairo, where the average for the year is no more than 1·2 in. At Alexandria the average is 8 in.

The cultivated area of Egypt proper was estimated in 1981 at 6·3m. feddâns (1 feddân = 1·038 acres) and of this (1971), 4,869,000 feddâns were under winter crops, 5,012,000 under summer crops and 613,000 under Nile crops.

The Agricultural Reform Decree of Sept. 1952 limits agricultural ownership to 200 feddâns, reduced to 100 feddâns in July 1961. Foreigners were debarred in 1963 from owning any land. Holdings in excess of this limit will be redistributed; compensation, equivalent to 10 times the rental value of the land, will take the form of 3% (from 1958: 1½%) bonds redeemable within 30 years (from 1958: 40 years). All national *waqfs* are to be dissolved.

Irrigation occupies a predominant place in the economic development of the country. The Aswân reservoir can now hold up to 5,500m. cu. metres of water, and the Gebel Aulia reservoir, completed in 1937, holds 2,000m. cu. metres. Barrages have been erected at Nag' Hammâdi, Asyût and Zifta, and at the bifurcation of the Nile below Cairo. Esna, Nag' Hammâdi barrage, completed in 1930, ensures full basin supplies even in low flood to Girga province, and will facilitate perennial irrigation when basin lands are converted. Asyût barrage, having been remodelled, will meet the greater demands of the area it now commands. The Esna barrage now secures basin irrigation to lands in Qena province. New barrages (Mohamed Ali barrages) have been completed at the bifurcation of the Nile below Cairo to replace the existing structures which, built in 1861, are now unable to meet the conditions following the increase in summer supplies, the reclamation of large areas of waste lands and the earlier watering of food crops.

On 8 Nov. 1959 the United Arab Republic and Sudan concluded agreements on the sharing of the Nile waters (after construction of the Aswân High Dam), and trade, payments and Customs dues. The agreement provides that from the time the High Dam started to store water (15 May 1964) Sudan will be entitled to 18,500m. cu. metres of the total annual flow and Egypt to 55,500m.

In 1982 the area (1,000 hectares) and production (1,000 tonnes) were: Wheat, 577(2,017); barley, 45(122); beans (dry), 7(13); lentils, 5(6); onions, 21(657); maize, 817(2,709); millet, 174(633); sugar-care, 108(8,700).

The rice crop was 2·3m. tonnes in 1977.

Livestock (1982): 2·3m. cattle, 2·4m. buffaloes, 1·7m. sheep, 1·5m. goats, 90,000 camels and 15,000 pigs.

Fisheries. The catch of the Egyptian sea, Nile and lake fisheries in 1957 amounted to 102,600 tonnes. In 1952 there were 48,947 men and 16,347 boys engaged in fishing and 11,739 boats used for fishing.

INDUSTRY AND TRADE

Industry. In 1979 there were 1·5m Egyptians employed in manufacturing. Production in 1981–82 included 690,000 tonnes of crude steel, 4m. tonnes of nitrogenous fertilizers and 4m. tonnes of cement.

Trade Unions. Trade unions were first recognized in 1942. In 1952 the acts concerning trade unions, individual contracts, and conciliation and arbitration were recast. Employment exchanges and unemployment statistics were introduced in 1953. Social insurance was enacted in 1955.

Commerce. Imports and exports for 5 years (in £E1.000):

	1978	1979	1980	1981	1982
Imports	2,632,180	2,686,200	3,092,600	5,588,500	5,776,800
Exports	679,754	1,287,800	2,132,800	2,263,000	2,184,100

In 1979, raw cotton and cotton products represented 34% of total exports, crude oil 31% and petroleum products 11%; 27% of exports went to Italy, 8% to the USSR and 8% to the Netherlands; 18% of imports came from the USA, 11% from Federal Republic of Germany.

Total trade between Egypt and UK (British Department of Trade returns, in £1,000 sterling):

	1979	1980	1981	1982	1983
Imports to UK	252,733	336,595	44,599	412,802	79,826
Exports and re-exports from UK	264,494	346,688	325,141	338,645	370,489

Tourism. In 1983, 1·5m. foreigners visited Egypt.

COMMUNICATIONS

Roads. In 1980, the total length of roads was 21,637 km. of which 16,182 km were paved. Motor vehicles, in 1980, 650,000 private cars, 114,700 commercial vehicles (including buses).

Railways. In 1982 there were 4,321 km of state railways (1,435 mm gauge) which carried 486m. passengers and 7·5m. tonnes of freight.

Aviation. There is an international airport at Cairo. A new airport at Cairo began operations in 1977. The national airline Egyptair has a fleet of 20 aircraft. Egyptair operates scheduled flights connecting Cairo with Athens, Rome, Frankfurt, Zürich, London, Khartoum, Tōkyō, Bombay, Aden, Jeddah, Doha, Dharan, Kuwait, Beirut, Baghdad, Tripoli, Benghazi, Algiers, Entebbe, Nairobi, Dar-es-Salaam, Kano, Lagos, Accra, Abidjan, Damascus, Amman, Manilla, Paris, Munich, Copenhagen, Nicosia, Karach, Aleppo, Bahrain, Abu Dhabi, Dubai, Sharjah, Sanaa and Vienna. In addition, Egyptair operates scheduled flights on a widespread domestic network connecting Cairo with Port Said, Mersa Matruh, Asyût, Luxor, Aswân.

Shipping. The Egyptian merchant navy in 1980 consisted of 75 steamers of 387,460 tons.

In 1977, 3,050 ships of 11,432,000 tons entered the port of Alexandria and 876 ships of 4,583,000 tons entered Port Said.

Suez Canal. The Suez Canal was opened for navigation on 17 Nov. 1869. By the convention of Constantinople of 29 Oct. 1888 the canal is open to vessels of all nations and is free from blockade, except in time of war, but the UAR Government did not allow Israeli ships to use the canal until May 1979, when the embargo was lifted. It is 173 km long (excluding 11 km of approach channels to the harbours), connecting the Mediterranean with the Red Sea. Its minimum width is 197 ft at a depth of 33 ft, and its depth permits the passage of vessels up to 38 ft draught.

In 1976 a 2-stage development project was started. The first stage which was completed in 1980 allowing vessels, of up to 150,000 tons, fully loaded, and up to 370,000 tons in ballast to pass through the canal and give a draught of 53 ft.

During the war with Israel in June 1967 Egypt blocked the Canal. The canal was cleared and re-opened to shipping on 5 June 1975. This is part of a programme to develop and rebuild the whole area of Suez to make it one of the largest tax-free industrial zones. Canal toll fees reached £621·8m. in 1981, and in 1980 21,603 vessels (281·3m. tons) went through the canal.

On 1 Jan. 1981 charges were increased by 30%. The first tunnel below the canal, located 10 miles north of Suez City, was completed on 30 April 1980.

Baxter, R. R., *The Law of International Waterways*. Harvard Univ. Press, 1964
Lauterpacht, E. (ed.), *The Suez Canal Settlement, 1956–59*. London, 1960
Marlow, J., *The Making of the Suez Canal*. London, 1964

Post and Broadcasting. The telephone service was taken over by the Egyptian Government in April 1918. In 1958–59 the state telegraphs had a length of 15,381 km of wire, and telephones, 1,076,159 km. There were, in 1980–81, 1,821 postal agencies, 1,812 mobile offices (1978), 1,747 government and 2,956 private post offices. Number of telephones in 1982, 521,625. Number of wireless licences in 1975, 5·12m. and 620,000 TV licences.

The internal telecommunications system is owned and operated by the Telecommunications Organization. Government landlines connect with those of the Gaza sector and the Sudan.

Cinemas (1971). There were 152 cinemas with a seating capacity of 140,900.

Newspapers. On 23 May 1960 all newspapers were nationalized.

JUSTICE, RELIGION, EDUCATION AND WELFARE

Justice. The National Courts in 1981 were as follows: Court of Cassation with a bench of 5 judges which constitutes the highest court of appeal in both criminal and civil cases; Courts of Appeal with 3 judges situated in Cairo and 4 other cities; Assize Courts with 3 judges which deal with all cases of serious crime; Central Tribunals with 3 judges which deal with ordinary civil and commercial cases; Summary Tribunals presided over by a single judge which hear civil disputes in matters up to the value of £E3,250, and criminal offences punishable by a fine or imprisonment of up to 3 years.

Religion. In 1947 the population (excluding Nomads) consisted of 17,397,946 Moslems (91·46%); 1,186,353 Orthodox Copts; 86,918 Protestant Copts; 72,764 Roman Catholic Copts; 89,062 other Orthodox; 50,200 other Roman Catholics; 16,338 other Protestants; 1,547 Jews, other and unknown.

There are in Egypt large numbers of native Christians connected with the various Oriental Churches; of these, the largest and most influential are the Copts, who adopted Christianity in the 1st century. Their head is the Coptic Patriarch. There are 25 metropolitans and bishops in Egypt; 4 metropolitans for Ethiopia,

Jerusalem, Khartoum and Omdurman, and 12 bishops in Ethiopia. Priests must be married before ordination, but celibacy is imposed on monks and high dignitaries. The Copts use the Diocletian (or Martyrs') calendar, which begins in A.D. 284.

Education. Education was made compulsory for all children between the ages of 6 and 12 in 1933; primary education (6 years) was made free in 1944, secondary and technical education in 1950. Compulsory education is provided in primary schools (6 years).

In 1981–82 there were 4·48m. primary school pupils and (1978–79) 127,021 teachers; 1·56m. secondary school pupils and (1978–79) 67,567 teachers; and 568,000 technical school pupils with (1978–79) 29,353 teachers. Teacher-training colleges had 40,595 students and 3,373 teaching staff in 1978–79.

There are 18 universities in Egypt. Cairo University, founded in 1908 as a private institution and taken over by the Government in 1925; Alexandria University, founded by the Government in 1942; the Ein Shams University, founded by the Government in Cairo in 1950 and universities at Asyût Al-Azhar, Tanta, Mansûra, Zagazig, Helwan, Suez Cana., Minya and Menoufia. The number of students at universities was 476,537 in 1977–78.

Health. In 1983–84 there were about 73,300 doctors and 85,350 hospital beds.

DIPLOMATIC REPRESENTATIVES

Of Egypt in Great Britain (26 South St., London, W1Y 3EL)
Ambassador: Hassan Aly Abou-Seéda (accredited 27 Feb. 1980).

Of Great Britain in Egypt (Ahmed Ragheb St., Garden City, Cairo)
Ambassador: Sir Michael Weir, KCMG.

Of Egypt in the USA (2310 Decatur Pl., NW, Washington, D.C., 20008)
Ambassador: Dr Ashraf A. Ghorbal.

Of the USA in Egypt (5 Sharia Latin America, Cairo)
Ambassador: Nicholas Veliotes.

Of Egypt to the United Nations
Ambassador: A. Khalil.

Books of Reference

Statistical Information: The Department of Statistics and Census (15, Sharia Mansour, Cairo) was formed in 1905. *Chief:* Under-Secretary of State for Statistical Affairs, Dr Hasan M. Husein. Previously, various government departments had their own statistical sections. Estimates of population were made in 1800, 1821 and 1846; the first census took place in 1873. Among the publications of the Department are the following: *Annuaire Statistique* (Arabic and French). *Annual Return of Shipping* (Arabic and English). *Monthly Summary and Annual Statement of Foreign Trade* (Arabic and English). *Monthly Bulletin of Agriculture and Economic Statistics* (Arabic and English). *Vital Statistics* (Arabic and English). *Statistical Pocket Year-Book* (Arabic and English).

The Egyptian Almanac. Annual
Le Mondain Egyptien (Who's Who). Cairo. Annual
Cooper, M. N., *The Transformation of Egypt.* London, 1982
Dawisha, A. I., *Egypt in the Arab World.* London, 1976
Elias, E. A., *Modern Dictionary English–Arabic.* 5th ed. Cairo, 1946
Fedden, R., *Egypt: Land of the Valley.* London, 1977
Hansen, B., and Radwan, S., *Employment Opportunities and Equity in Egypt.* Geneva, 1982
Hirst, D., and Beeson, I., *Sadat.* London, 1981
Hopwood, D., *Egypt: Politics and Society 1945–1981.* London, 1982
Mabro, R., and Radwan, S., *The Industrialization of Egypt 1939–1973.* Oxford, 1976
Springberg, R., *Family, Power and Politics in Egypt.* Univ. of Pennsylvania Press, 1982
Vatikiotis, P. J., *The History of Egypt: From Muhammad Ali to Sadat.* 2nd ed. London, 1980
Waterbury, J., *The Egypt of Nasser and Sadat.* Princeton Univ. Press, 1983

EL SALVADOR

República de El Salvador

Capital: San Salvador
Population: 5m. (1982)
GNP per capita: US$590 (1980)

HISTORY. In 1839 the Central American Federation, which had comprised the states of Guatemala, El Salvador, Honduras, Nicaragua and Costa Rica, was dissolved, and El Salvador declared itself formally an independent republic in 1841.

AREA AND POPULATION. El Salvador is the smallest and most densely populated (222 inhabitants per sq. km) of the Central American states. Its area (including 247 sq. km of inland lakes) is estimated at 21,393 sq. km (8,236 sq. miles) with population (census 1981) of 4,672,900. Estimate (1982) 5m. The capital is San Salvador (1,902,500 inhabitants in 1980).

A Treaty was signed in Peru on 30 Oct. 1980 settling the border dispute between El Salvador and Honduras which caused 4 days of fighting in July 1979.

The republic is divided into 14 departments, each under an appointed governor. Their areas (in sq. km) and populations at census 1971 were:

Department	Area	Population	Department	Area	Population
San Salvador	892	681,656	La Paz	1,155	194,196
Santa Ana	1,829	375,186	Chalatenango	2,507	186,003
San Miguel	2,532	337,325	Ahuachapán	1,281	183,682
Usulután	1,780	304,369	Marazán	1,364	170,706
La Libertad	1,650	293,076	San Vicente	1,175	160,534
Sonsonate	1,133	239,688	Cuscatlán	766	158,458
La Unión	1,738	230,103	Cabañas	1,075	139,312

Important towns (with population census 1978) are: San Salvador, 429,609 (1981); Santa Ana, 114,989; San Miguel, 75,402; Mejicanos, 73,626; Delgado, 55,912; Nueva San Salvador, 45,384; Sonsonate, 41,389.

There has been considerable emigration into nearby states. There are no tribal Indians. The language of the country is Spanish.

CLIMATE. Despite its proximity to the equator, the climate is warm rather than hot and nights are cool inland. Light rains occur in the dry season from Nov. to April while the rest of the year has heavy rains, especially on the coastal plain. San Salvador. Jan. 71°F (21·7°C), July 75°F (23·9°C). Annual rainfall 71″ (1,775 mm). San Miguel. Jan. 77°F (25°C), July 83°F (28·3°C). Annual rainfall 68″ (1,700 mm).

CONSTITUTION AND GOVERNMENT. A new Constitution was enacted in Dec. 1983. The Executive Power is vested in a President elected for a non-renewable term of 5 years, with Ministers and Under-Secretaries appointed by him. The Legislative power is an Assembly of 52 members elected by universal suffrage and proportional representation for a term of 3 years. The judicial power is vested in a Supreme Court, of a President and 9 magistrates elected by the Legislative Assembly for renewable terms of 3 years; and subordinate courts. For governments, 1961–79 *see* STATESMAN'S YEAR-BOOK 1982–83, p. 436.

The Constituent Assembly met on 22 April 1982 following the elections of 28 March. Dr Alvaro Magaña was elected interim President of the Constituent Assembly by 36 votes to 17, with 7 abstentions, on 29 April and was sworn in on 2 May. *See* Addenda.

On 4 May a 14-member cabinet took office including:

Interior: Manuel Isidro López Sermeno. *Foreign Affairs:* Dr Fidel Chávez Mena.

The President announced that general elections would be held in March 1984.

During 1982–3, there was continuing fighting between government forces and guerrillas and it was estimated that 13,000–16,000 people were killed in 1981 as a result of the violence.

The results of Constituent Assembly elections held on 28 March 1982 were: Christian Democratic Party, 24; Arena, 19; National Conciliation Party, 14; Democratic Action, 2; Salvadrean People's Party, 1.

National flag: Blue, white, blue (horizontal): the white stripe charged with the arms of the republic.

National anthem: Saludemos la patria orgullosos (words by J. J. Cañas; tune by J. Aberle).

DEFENCE. There is selective national service for 1 year.

Army. The Army comprises 6 infantry brigades, 1 mechanized cavalry regiment, 1 artillery brigade, 1 engineer, 1 anti-aircraft, 1 parachute and 1 special forces battalion. Equipment includes 12 AMX-13 light tanks and 18 AML-90 armoured cars. Strength is 22,000. There are also National Guard, National Police and Treasury Police, paramilitary units, numbering (1984) about 10,000 and a territorial civil defence force of up to 70,000.

Navy. The Navy includes 4 patrol boats, 1 new French-built tug, 2 cutters, 3 small coastguard craft and 25 service launches. Personnel in 1984 totalled 130 officers and men.

Air Force. The Air Force underwent a major re-equipment programme in 1974–75, with most aircraft coming from Israel and US aid for transport units, but lost 18 aircraft in a guerrilla attack in Jan. 1982. Combat squadron now has 6 A-37 and 4 Ouragan jet fighter-bombers, supported by 7 Israeli-built Magister jets and 15 piston-engined Rallyes for light attack duties, and 4 Cessna O-2s for reconnaissance. Transports include 5 C-47s and 4 Israeli-built light twin-engined Aravas, plus 1 Lama, 1 Alouette III and 14 UH-1H helicopters. Training types include about 15 piston-engined T-41Cs, T-6s and T-34s. Strength totalled about 2,300 personnel in 1983.

INTERNATIONAL RELATIONS

Membership. El Salvador is a member of UN and OAS.

ECONOMY

Budget. Revenue and expenditure for fiscal years ending 31 Dec., in 1,000 cólones:

	1977	1978	1979	1980	1981	1982
Revenue	1,252,000	1,181,185	1,541,017	1,376,337	1,740,424	1,730,899
Expenditure	1,252,000	1,217,409	1,303,707	1,606,335	1,757,600	1,864,699

External debt amounted to US$1,650m. in 1983.

Currency. The monetary unit is the *colón* (₡) of 100 *centavos*. The *colón* (₡) is issued in denominations of 1, 2, 5, 10, 25 and 100 *colónes*; 25 and 50 *centavos* (silver); 1, 2, 3, 5 and 10 *centavos* (copper–nickel and copper–zinc). In March 1984, £1 = ₡3·72; US$1 = ₡2·50.

Banking. There are 10 native commercial banks, including the Banco Salvadoreño (paid-up capital, 6m. colónes). The Bank of London and South America, the Citibank Bank of America and the Bank of Santander and Panama S. A. are the only foreign institutions. The Central Reserve Bank of El Salvador, constructed in 1934 out of the Banco Agricola Comercial, was nationalized on 20 April 1961.

Weights and Measures. On 1 Jan. 1886 the metric system was made obligatory. But other units are still commonly in use, of which the principal are as follows: *Libra* = 1·014 lb. av.; *quintal* = 101·4 lb. av.; *arroba* = 25·35 lb. av.; *fanega* = 1·5745 bushels.

ENERGY AND NATURAL RESOURCES

Electricity. El Salvador's biggest national enterprise, begun in 1950, was the construction of a 200ft high dam across the (unnavigable) Lempa River, 35 miles north-east of San Salvador, with an annual capacity of 344m. kwh. Production in 1981, 1,512m. kwh.; consumption, 1,322m. kwh.

Oil. Production of petroleum derivatives during 1971 totalled ₡422,476,000.

Minerals. The mineral output of the republic is now negligible, but the Ministry of Public Works has recently started to investigate 2 new silver mines in the department of Morazán.

Agriculture. El Salvador is predominantly agricultural; 32·5% of its total area is used for crops and 30·2% for pasture. Area devoted to coffee (1982–83) was about 516,615 acres, entirely owned by nationals. In 1981, 35·5% of the working population was engaged in farming.
Production (1982–83, in 1m. quintales, 46 kg each): Coffee, 3·5 (1981 value ₡1,155·07m.); cotton, 2·8 (1981 value, ₡190,884,000); grain (including maize, beans, rice, sorghum), 14 (1981 value of maize, ₡186,612,000); sugar, 3·3. A little rubber is exported.
Livestock (1982): 1·1m. cattle, 450,000 pigs, 4,000 sheep, 14,000 goats.

Forestry. In the national forests are found dye woods and such woods as mahogany, cedar and walnut. Balsam trees also abound: El Salvador is the world's principal source of this medicinal gum. Production, 1981, ₡36,148,000

Fisheries. In 1981, fish products were valued at ₡57·5m.

INDUSTRY AND TRADE

Industry. Total production was valued at ₡3,148,395m. in 1981, which included: Food, ₡997,902,000; textiles, ₡299,486,000; chemicals, ₡299,449,000; footwear and clothing, ₡290,077,000.

Commerce. The imports (including parcels post) and exports have been as follows in calendar years in 1,000 colónes:

	1977	1978	1979	1980	1981	1982
Imports	2,356,100	2,559,900	2,529,900	2,404,269	2,461,458	2,250,000
Exports	2,431,900	1,577,400	2,579,300	2,683,953	1,991,940	1,845,600

Of total exports (1981), coffee furnished about 31·7% by weight and 57% by value. The coffee is of the 'mild' variety; it is sold in bags of 60 kg, but trade statistics use a bag of 69 kg.
In 1981 US took 515,466,000 colónes of exports and furnished 624,136,000 colónes of the imports. The chief imports in 1981 were manufactured goods (27·6%), chemical and pharmaceutical products (23%), non-edible crude materials, mainly crude oil (19·1%), electric machinery, tools and appliances and transport equipment (12·8%). The other Central American Republics, the Federal Republic of Germany, Japan, Canada, France, the Netherlands and the UK are also important trading partners.
Total trade between El Salvador and UK for 5 years (British Department of Trade returns, in £1,000 sterling):

	1979	1980	1981	1982	1983
Imports to UK	3,517	2,889	1,962	2,017	425
Exports and re-exports from UK	9,354	4,603	3,652	5,244	7,653

Tourism. There were 69,111 visitors in 1981.

COMMUNICATIONS

Roads. In 1981 there were 9,336·1 km of national roads in the republic, including 1,662 km of main paved roads; 3,276 km main asphalted roads; other roads, 4,397·9 km. Motor vehicles registered, 1978, 118,550.

Railways. All railways (602 km) came under the control of National Railways of El Salvador *(Fenadesal)* in 1975. Lines run from Acajutla to San Salvador; Cutuco to San Salvador; between San Salvador and Santa Ana, San Miguel and Sonsonate; there is also a link to the Guatemalan system.

Aviation. International air traffic is expanding and in 1972 there were 80 flights a week. The airport at Ilopango, 8 km from San Salvador, now a military airport, and the new international airport at Cuscatlán, 40 km from San Salvador, opened in 1979.

Shipping. The principal ports are La Unión, La Libertad and Acajutla, all on the Pacific. Passengers (and some freight) use the Guatemalan port of Puerto Barrios on the Atlantic, reaching El Salvador by rail or road.

Post and Broadcasting. The telephone and telegraph systems are government-owned; the radio-telephone systems are partly private, partly government-owned. Telephone instruments, 1982, 86,316. There were (1983) over 50 radio stations. Radio El Salvador is state-owned. There were (1983) 3 commercial television channels and 2 educational channels sponsored by the Ministry of Education.

Cinemas (1976). Cinemas numbered 65.

Newspapers (1983). There are 4 daily newspapers in San Salvador and 1 each in Santa Ana and San Miguel.

JUSTICE, RELIGION, EDUCATION AND WELFARE

Justice. Justice is administered by the Supreme Court of Justice, courts of first and second instance, besides minor tribunals. Magistrates of the Supreme Court and courts of second instance are elected by the Legislative Assembly for a renewable 3-year term.

An anti-Communist law, effective 29 Sept. 1962, has made the propagation of totalitarian or Communist doctrines an offence punishable by imprisonment; supplementary offences, contrary to democratic principles, are punished by prison terms of from 3 to 7 years.

Religion. The dominant religion is Roman Catholicism. Under the 1962 Constitution churches are exempted from the property tax; the Catholic Church is recognized as a legal person, and other churches are entitled to secure similar recognition. There is an archbishop in San Salvador and bishops at Santa Ana, San Miguel, San Vicente, Santiago de María and Usulután.

Education. Education is free and obligatory. In 1929 the State took over control of all schools, public and private, but the provision that the teaching in government schools must be wholly secular was removed in 1945.

In 1982 there were 50,040 pupils in nursery schools, 803,653 in secondary schools, 42,820 students at universities and polytechnics and 42,723 students receiving adult education.

Social Welfare. The Social Security Institute now administers the sickness, old age and death insurance, covering industrial workers and employees earning up to ₡700 a month. Employees in other private institutions with salaries over this amount are included but are excluded from the medical and hospital benefits.

DIPLOMATIC REPRESENTATIVES

Of El Salvador in Great Britain (62 Welbeck St., London. W1)
Ambassador: Dr Alfonso Moisés-Beatriz.

Of Great Britain in El Salvador
Ambassador and Consul-General: C. J. Sharkey, MBE (resides in Tegucigalpa).

Of El Salvador in the USA (2308 California St., NW, Washington, DC., 20008)
Ambassador: Ernesto Rivas-Gallont.

Of the USA in El Salvador (25 Ave. Norte, Colnia Dueñas, San Salvador)
Ambassador: Thomas R. Pickering.

Of El Salvador to the United Nations
Ambassador: Dr Mauricio Rosales-Rivera.

Books of Reference

Statistical Information: The Dirección General de Estadistica y Censos (Villa Fermina, Calle Arce, San Salvador) dates from 1937. *Director General:* Lieut.-Col. José Castro Meléndez. Its publications include *Anuario Estadístico.* Annual from 1911.—*Boletin Estadístico.* Quarterly.—*El Salvador en Gráficas.* Annual.—*Atlas Censal de El Salvador.* 1955 only.— Revista Mensual, Banco Central de Reserva de El Salvador.

Angel Gallardo, M., *Cuatro Constituciones Federales de Centro América y Las Constituciones Políticas de El Salvador.* San Salvador, 1945
Armstrong, R., and Shenk, J., *El Salvador: The Face of Revolution.* London, 1982
Bevan, J., *El Salvador. Education and Repression.* London, 1981
Browning, D., *El Salvador: Landscape and Society.* OUP, 1971
Devire, F. J., *El Salvador: Embassy under Attack.* New York, 1981
Erdozain, P., *Archbishop Romero: Martyr of El Salvador.* Guildford, 1981
Montgomery, T.S., *Revolution in El Salvador: Origins and Evolution.* Boulder, 1982
North, L., *Bitter Grounds: Roots of Revolt in El Salvador.* London, 1981
Schmidt, S. W., *El Salvador: America's Next Vietnam.* Salisbury (N.C.), 1983
Vogt, W., *The Population of El Salvador and Its Natural Resources.* Washington, D.C., 1946
Wallich, H. C. (ed.), *Public Finance in a Developing Country: El Salvador.* Harvard Univ. Press, 1951

EQUATORIAL GUINEA

Capital: Malabo
Population: 380,000 (1982)
GNP per capita: US$330 (1976)

República de Guinea Ecuatorial

HISTORY. The Republic of Equatorial Guinea became independent on 12 Oct. 1968 after having been a Spanish colony (Territorios Españoles del Golfo de Guinea) until 1959. From 1959 to 1963 the territory was made into two Spanish provinces with a status comparable to the metropolitan provinces. From 1964 to 1968 this Equatorial Region became an autonomous entity still retaining the status of two Spanish provinces, but with a certain amount of internal self-government. Serious political disturbances in Rio Muni occurred in March–April 1969. This led to the partial withdrawal of the Spanish community. Agreements for co-operation in education and economic development were signed with Spain in 1971, 1972 and 1979. From 1968–79 the republic depended heavily on the Soviet bloc including Cuba and the People's Republic of China, Spanish economic, technical and social co-operation has become essential since 1979.

AREA AND POPULATION. The total area is 28,051 sq. km (10,831 sq. miles). Total population, 245,989 (1960 census); 1982 estimate, 380,000.

The 6 provinces consist of 2 on the islands of Bioko and Pagalu, and 4 on the mainland, with these separate areas having the following areas (in sq.km) and populations:

	Sq. km	Census 1960	Estimate 1982	Chief town
Bioko	2,034 [1]	62,612 [1]	100,000	Malabo
Rio Muni	26,017 [2]	183,377	280,000	Bata
	28,051	245,989	380,000	

[1] Including 1,415 on the island of Pagalu (17 sq. km).
[2] Including the adjacent islets of Corisco, Elobey Grande and Elobey Chico (17 sq. km).

The majority of the Rio Munian population is Fang (Pámues in Spanish). Along the coast and in the islets are the Combes, the Bengas, the Bujebas, etc.

In Bioko the aborigines are called Bubis. These are now a minority (perhaps 15,000). Other ethnic groups are the Fernandinos (descendants of English-speaking Creoles), the Fangs, coast people from Rio Muni and formerly naturalized migrant workers from Nigeria, Cameroon and São Tomé. A fluctuating mass of plantation workers were about twice as numerous as the Equatorial Guineans. Pagalu is peopled by descendants of slaves brought by the Portuguese; they still speak a Portuguese patois. Pidgin English was the lingua franca in Bioko in spite of the official Spanish. Because of political and economic difficulties about 110,000 citizens are reported to live in neighbouring countries and Spain.

CLIMATE. The climate is equatorial, with alternate wet and dry seasons. In Rio Muni, the wet season lasts from Dec. to Feb.

CONSTITUTION AND GOVERNMENT. A 10-member cabinet was established and the country was placed under military rule and in Aug. 1982, under a new Constitution, the President's mandate was extended for 7 years. A 41-member National Assembly was elected on 28 Aug. 1983.

President: Lieut.-Col. Teodoro Obiang Nguema Mbasogo.

441

National flag: Three horizontal stripes of green, white, red; a blue triangle based on the hoist; in the centre the national arms.

DEFENCE. Under President Macías the *Guardia Nacional* consisted mainly of Fang soldiers with Cuban and Chinese military advisers. Total strength about 1,500. Since the 1979 *coup*, Moroccan troops and Spanish military and police personnel have replaced Soviet bloc advisers.

INTERNATIONAL RELATIONS

Membership. Equatorial Guinea is a member of UN, OAU and is an ACP state of EEC.

ECONOMY

Budget. The 1981 budget envisaged income at 2,732m. Bikuele and expenditure at 2,673m. Bikuele.

Currency. In July 1973 the Guinean *peseta* was redesignated the *Ekuele* (plural, *Bikuele*).

Banking. The Banco Central de Guinea Ecuatorial in Malabo was established in 1969 with Spanish technical and financial assistance.

NATURAL RESOURCES

Agriculture. The chief products are cocoa (71,000 hectares in 1979), coffee (17,000 hectares) and wood; in 1981 production was about 7,000 tonnes of cocoa, most of it high-grade exported to Spain and the US. Production declined by 56%, 1965–76. Coffee, of mediocre quality, is chiefly a Fang product. Production (1981) 1,000–2,000 tonnes and is gradually decreasing. With the departure of Nigerian workers, Fang labourers from Rio Muni were recruited forcibly in 1976 and were still on the island of Bioko in late 1979.

Livestock (1982): Cattle, 4,000; sheep, 34,000; goats, 7,000; poultry, 160,000.

Forestry. Wood was almost entirely exported from Rio Muni to Spain and the Federal Republic of Germany (337,438 tonnes to Spain in 1967). Production: 1980, 25,000 tonnes (1969, 300,000 tonnes). Plantations in the hinterland have been abandoned by their Spanish owners and except for cocoa, commercial agriculture is under serious difficulties.

INDUSTRY AND TRADE

Industry. Bioko has very few industries. Electricity production in 1967: Bioko, 9·47m. kwh.; Rio Muni, 5·7m. kwh. Rio Muni has no industry except lumbering. Post-independence political conditions have not been conducive to private investment. Since 1979 the lumber industry has resumed activity but there was (1981) a shortage of labour.

Trade. In 1965 Equatorial Guinea exported 330,100 tonnes (value, 1,635·6m. pesetas; 1966, 1,817m.), of which 326,000 tonnes to Spain (value, 1,581·6m. pesetas). In 1970 total exports were 1,741m. EG pesetas, of which 91% went to Spain. Imports were 1,472m. EG pesetas, of which 80% came from Spain. In 1975 cocoa exports were US$13·4m. and coffee, US$7m. In 1978, cocoa accounted for 97% of exports.

Total trade between Equatorial Guinea and UK (British Department of Trade returns, in £1,000 sterling):

	1981	1982	1983
Imports to UK	19	156	13
Exports and re-exports from UK	142	633	10

COMMUNICATIONS

Roads. Bioko had a good tarmac road network, but Rio Muni had few surfaced roads; the main artery is Mbini–Bata–Micomeseng–Ebebiyin. Road reconstruction is envisaged.

Aviation. An international airfield exists in Malabo (28,029 passengers in 1967). Bata has more modest facilities (15,031 passengers in 1967). The line Madrid–Malabo–Bata is subsidized by Spain. Links with Douala (from Malabo) and Libreville (Gabon) exist.

Shipping. Malabo is the main port. The other ports are Luba, formerly San Carlos (bananas, cocoa) in Bioko and Bata, Kogo and Mbini (wood) in Rio Muni. A new harbour in Bata has been completed. In 1966 in the 5 ports 141,600 tonnes were unloaded and 429,000 loaded.

Post and Broadcasting. Estimated number of telephones (1969), 1,451. In 1977 there were 80,000 radio and 1,000 TV receivers.

JUSTICE, RELIGION, EDUCATION AND WELFARE

Justice. The Constitution guarantees an independent judiciary. The Supreme Tribunal is the highest court of appeal and is located at Malabo.

Religion. The population of Equatorial Guinea is nominally Roman Catholic (227,517 in 1966) with influential Protestant groups in Malabo and Rio Muni. By order of the President most churches were closed in 1975 and in June 1978 the Roman Catholic Church was banned. Since 1979, religious services have been restored.

Education. There were in 1981 about 45,000 pupils enrolled in primary schools and about 40,000 school-age children among the negroes abroad. In 1976 there were 3,984 pupils and 115 teachers in secondary schools, 370 students and 29 teachers at technical schools and 169 students and 21 teachers at teacher-training establishments.

Health. In 1967 there were 16 hospitals and dispensaries with 1,637 beds. In 1975 there were only 5 doctors, 2 midwives and 248 nursing personnel.

DIPLOMATIC REPRESENTATIVES

Of Equatorial Guinea in Great Britain
Ambassador: (Vacant).

Of Great Britain in Equatorial Guinea
Ambassador: Brian Sparrow (resides at Yaoundé).

Of the USA in Equatorial Guinea
Ambassador: Alan M. Hardy.

Of Equatorial Guinea to the USA and the United Nations
Ambassador: Capt. Florencio Maye Ela.

Books of Reference

Atlas Historico y Geográfico de Africa Española. Madrid, 1955
Plan de Desarrollo Económico de la Guinea Ecuatorial. Pres dencia del Gobierno. Madrid, 1963
Resumén estadistico del Africa española, 1965–66. Madrid, 1967
Berman, S., *Spanish Guinea: An Annotated Bibliography.* Microfilm Service, Catholic University. Washington, D.C. 1961
Liniger-Goumaz, M., *La Guinée équatoriale un pays méconnu.* Paris, 1980
Pélissier, R., *Les Territoires espagnols d'Afrique.* Paris, 1963 —*Los territorios españoles de Africa.* Madrid, 1964.–*Etudes Hispano-Guinéennes.* Orgeval, 1969

ETHIOPIA

Hebretesebawit
Ityopia

Capital: Addis Ababa
Population: 33m. (1983)
GNP per capita: US$140 (1980)

HISTORY. The ancient empire of Ethiopia has its legendary origin in the meeting of King Solomon and the Queen of Sheba. Historically, the empire developed in the centuries before and after the birth of Christ, at Aksum in the north, as a result of Semetic immigration from South Arabia. The immigrants imposed their language and culture on a basic Hamitic stock. Ethiopia's subsequent history is one of sporadic expansion southwards and eastwards, checked from the 16th to early 19th centuries by devastating wars with Moslems and Gallas. Modern Ethiopia dates from the reign of the Emperor Theodore (1855–68).

Menelik II (1889–1913) defeated the Italians in 1896 and thereby safeguarded the empire's independence in the scramble for Africa. By successful campaigns in neighbouring kingdoms within Ethiopia (Jimma, Kaffa, Harar, etc.) he united the country under his rule and created the empire as it is today.

In 1936 Ethiopia was conquered by the Italians, who were in turn defeated by the Allied forces in 1941 when the Emperor returned.

The former Italian colony of Eritrea, from 1941 under British military administration, was in accordance with a resolution of the General Assembly of the UN, dated 2 Dec. 1950, handed over to Ethiopia on 15 Sept. 1952. Eritrea thereby became an autonomous unit within the federation of Ethiopia and Eritrea.

This federation became a unitary state on 14 Nov. 1962 when Eritrea was fully integrated with Ethiopia.

A provisional military government assumed power on 12 Sept. 1974 and deposed the Emperor. On 24 Nov. 1974 the Provisional Military Government announced that on 23 Nov. it had executed 60 former military and civilian leaders including Gen. Aman Andom who was Chairman of the Provisional Military Administrative Council.

On 3 Feb. 1977 it was announced that Brig.-Gen. Teferi Bante, the Chairman of PMAC and 6 other members of the ruling military council were executed.

In early 1978 a reversal of the position in the armed struggle in the Ogaden area of Ethiopia with Somali forces took place. After an offensive mounted with strong USSR and Cuban support the area was recaptured and in March Somalia withdrew all troops from the area. Control was re-established by Ethiopia later in 1978 and nationalist guerrillas were pushed back but sporadic fighting continued in 1982 in the Ogaden and along the border.

AREA AND POPULATION. Ethiopia is bounded north-east by the Red Sea, east by Djibouti and Somalia, south by Kenya and west by Sudan. It has a total area of 1,221,900 sq. km (471,800 sq. miles) and total population (1983) 33,008,000.

The dominant race of Ethiopia, the Amhara, inhabit the central Ethiopian highlands. To the north of them are the Tigréans, akin to the Amhara and belonging to the same Christian church, but speaking a different, though related, language. Both these races are of mixed Hamitic and Semitic origin, and further mixed by intermarriage with Galla and other races. The Gallas, some of whom are Christian, some Moslem and some pagan, comprise about 40% of the entire population, and are a pastoral and agricultural people of Hamitic origin. Somalis, another Hamitic race, inhabit the south-east of Ethiopia, in particular the Ogaden desert region. These like the closely related Afar people, are Moslem. The Afar stretch northwards from Wollo region into Eritrea.

Region	Area (sq. km)	Population July. 1980	Chief town	Population July 1980
Addis Ababa	218	1,277,159	—	—
Arussi	23,500	1,149,400	Assela	34,874
Bale	124,600	879,200	Goba	6,116 [1]
Eritrea	117,600	2,426,200	Asmara	424,532
Gemu Gofa	39,500	1,003,400	Arba Minch	8,914 [1]
Gojjam	61,600	2,037,900	Debre Markos	40,686
Gondar (Begemdir)	74,200	2,053,400	Gondar	76,932
Hararge	259,700	3,125,200	Harar	62,921
Illubabor	47,400	810,800	Mattu	8,115 [1]
Kefa	54,600	1,615,400	Jimma	63,837
Shoa	85,200	5,085,000	—	—
Sidamo	117,300	2,808,300	Awassa	23,038 [1]
Tigre	65,900	2,162,100	Mekele	46,846
Wollega	71,200	2,019,200	Lekemti	21,694 [1]
Wollo	79,400	2,612,600	Dessie	75,616

[1] Jan. 1978.

Other large towns (population, Jan. 1980): Dire Dawa, in Hararge, 82,024; Nazret, in Shoa, 69,865; Bahr Dar, 52,188; Debre Zeit, 49,570.

Local Government. The country is divided into 15 administrative regions, each under a Chief Administrator, and under the administrative control of the Minister of the Interior. The regions are divided into 103 *awraja* (sub-regions), and thence into 505 *woredo* (districts).

CLIMATE. The wide range of latitude produces many climatic variations between the high, temperate plateaus and the hot, humid lowlands. The main rainy season lasts from June to Aug., with light rains from Feb. to April, but the country is very vulnerable to drought. Addis Ababa. Jan. 59°F (15°C), July 59°F (15°C). Annual rainfall 50″ (1,237 mm).

CONSTITUTION AND GOVERNMENT. Pending the promulgation of a new constitution, Ethiopia is controlled by a Provisional Military Administration Council (the *Derg*) to whom the Council of Ministers is responsible. A Commission for Organizing the Party of the Working Peoples of Ethiopia (COPWE) was established in early 1980 and charged with the task of preparing the formation of a civilian party which will ultimately take over from the PMAC. The second congress of COPWE was held in Jan. 1983 and elected a 91-member central committee and a 7-member executive committee, both chaired by Mengistu. A further congress has taken place but the Party itself has not yet been formally created.

Chairman of the Derg, Head of State, Chairman of the Council of Ministers: Lieut.-Col. Mengistu Haile Mariam.

Vice-Chairman of the Council of Ministers: and *Secretary-General of the Derg:* Capt. Fikre Selassie Wogderesse.

Foreign Affairs: Lieut.-Col. Goshu Wolde.

National flag: Three horizontal stripes of green, yellow and red.

National anthem: Ityopya, Ityopia Kidemi (tune by Daniel Yohannes, 1975).

DEFENCE. Ethiopia's military rulers have moved away from US military assistance since they came to power and now rely on USSR for most of their military aid. Large amounts of USSR military equipment have been sent to help her in her conflict with Somalia over the Ogaden desert region.

Selective conscription for a period of 30 months is in force. Some 1,400 Soviet, 11,000 Cuban and 250 East German military advisers and technicians are reported to be serving with the armed forces.

Army. The Army, comprises 24 infantry divisions with some 20 tank battalions, 4 para-commando brigades, 30 artillery battalions and 30 air defence battalions. Equipment includes 700 T-54/-55, 150 T-34 and 40 M-47 tanks. Strength (1984) 244,500 including a People's Militia of about 150,000, with reserves for all 3 services numbering about 200,000.

Navy. The Navy, with headquarters at Addis Ababa, consists of 3 *ex*-Soviet fast missile boats, 2 *ex*-Soviet fast torpedo boats, 1 training ship (1,768 tons; *ex*-US seaplane tender), 1 *ex*-Netherlands coastal minesweeper, 4 patrol craft (*ex*-US coastguard motor gunboats), 4 patrol boats, 1 *ex*-Yugoslav submarine chaser, 2 *ex*-Soviet coastal cutters, 4 harbour defence craft, 1 medium landing ship, 2 landing craft and 4 minor landing craft. The Naval Base and College is at Massawa.

Personnel, in 1984, totalled 1,500 officers and men. It is presumed that Soviet advisers remain embarked in the 6 attack craft recently acquired until Ethiopian naval officers and ratings have sufficient experience to operate independently the missiles and torpedoes.

Air Force. The Air Force, trained originally by Swedish and American personnel, but now operating aircraft of Soviet origin, has its headquarters at Debre Zeit, near Addis Ababa. It includes a training school and a central workshop. Of 6 ground-attack fighter squadrons, 4 have MiG-21s, the others MiG-23s and MiG-17s respectively. There is a squadron of Mi-24 helicopter gunships, and a transport squadron equipped with An-12s, and An-26s. Training aircraft include two-seat MiG-21s and L-39 jet basic trainers. More than 30 Mi-8 helicopters are in service. Personnel, 3,500 officers and men.

INTERNATIONAL RELATIONS

Membership. Ethiopia is a member of UN, OAU and is an ACP state of EEC.

ECONOMY

Planning. In 1978 a new development plan was launched envisaging growth of 6% in 1979–80 and 7% in 1980–81.

Budget. Revenue and expenditure estimates for financial years (ended 7 July) were as follows (in EB1m.):

	1975–76	1976–77	1977–78	1978–79	1979–80
Revenue	1,331	1,466	1,601	2,119	2,365
Expenditure	1,331	1,466	1,601	2,119	2,365

Of the estimated revenue in 1979–80, EB1,327m. is expected to come from taxes and EB417m. from external assistance. Of the 1979–80 expenditure, EB1,655m. is on current account and EB710m. for capital expenditure.

Currency. The Ethiopian *birr*, divided into 100 cents, is the unit of currency; it is based on 5·52 grains of fine gold. It consists of notes of EB1, 2, 10, 50 and 100 denominations, and bronze 1-, 5-, 10-, 25- and 50-cent coins. *Birr* 3·05 = £1 sterling; *Birr* 2·03 = US$1 (in March 1984).

Banking. The State Bank was renamed the National Bank of Ethiopia in Oct. 1963, when its commercial activities were transferred to the newly established Commercial Bank of Ethiopia. At the same time another new bank, the Investment Bank of Ethiopia, was set up with a capital of EB10m., of which the Government held the majority of shares. In Sept. 1965 it became the Ethiopian Investment Corporation, which is a substantial shareholder in a number of industrial and other ventures.

The Investment Corporation has now been merged with the Development Bank of Ethiopia and the two are now known as the Agricultural and Industrial Development Bank, SC.

Two Italian banks have subsidiaries in Asmara, and one has a subsidiary in Addis Ababa. The Addis Ababa Bank Share Co. is connected with National & Grindlays Bank Ltd.

On 1 Jan. 1975 the Government nationalized all banks, mortgage and insurance companies.

Weights and Measures. The metric system of weights and measures is officially in use. Traditional weights and measures vary considerably in the various provinces: the principal ones are: *Frasilla* = approximately 37½ lb.; *gasha*, the principal unit of land measure, which is normally about 100 acres but can vary between 80 and 300 acres, depending on the quality of the land.

ENERGY AND NATURAL RESOURCES

Electricity. Production in 1979 totalled 544m. kwh.

Oil. A Russian built state-owned oil refinery at Assab came on stream in 1967 with a capacity of 600,000 tonnes of crude per annum.

Gas. A natural gas-strike was made offshore near Massawa in Dec. 1969, but it was not exploited. Traces of gas and oil have been found in south-east Ethiopia.

Minerals. Ethiopia has little proved mineral wealth. Salt is produced mainly in Eritrea, while a placer goldmine is worked by the Government of Adola in the south. Gold production, in 1980, was 373 kg. Small quantities of other minerals are produced including platinum.

Agriculture. Coffee is by far the most important source of rural income accounting for 70% of foreign earnings in 1982. Harari coffee (long berry Mocha) is cultivated in the east.

Teff (*Eragrastis abyssinica*) is the principal food grain, followed by barley, wheat, maize and durra. Pulses and oilseeds are imported for local consumption and export. Cane sugar is an important crop.

Production (1982 in 1,000 tons): Maize, 1,000; sorghum, 1,300; barley, 1,150; pulses, 1,002.

Livestock (1982): 26m. cattle, 23·3m. sheep, 17·2m. goats; smaller numbers of donkeys, horses, mules and camels. Hides and skins and butter (ghee) are important for home consumption and export. Sheep, cattle and chickens are the main providers of meat. All agricultural land was nationalized in March 1975, and a radical land reform was carried out. In 1983 85% of the population were engaged in agriculture, producing 40% of GDP.

INDUSTRY AND TRADE

Industry. The most important products of the small but growing industries are cotton yarn (9,600 tons in 1978) and fabrics, cement (100,000 tons), sugar, salt, cigarettes, canned foodstuffs, beer, building materials, footwear, pharmaceuticals, tyres and paint. Most industry is centred around Addis Ababa and Asmara. Industry around Asmara has been severely hit by actions of Eritrean guerrillas.

Commerce. Coffee is by far the most important export, followed by pulses, oilseeds, hides and skins. Imports are textiles, foodstuffs, vehicles, machinery. manufactured goods and petroleum products.

Imports and exports (in US$1m.) for 4 years.

	1978	1979	1980	1981
Imports	440·1	521·3	649·6	629·8
Exports	308·3	429·1	419·3	374·1

Total trade between Ethiopia and UK (British Department of Trade returns, in £1,000 sterling):

	1978	1979	1980	1981	1982	1983
Imports to UK	4,471	12,947	10,281	8,079	10,833	12,071
Exports and re-exports from UK	17,091	16,039	20,962	19,569	27,584	34,092

Tourism. There were 55,000 tourists in 1982.

COMMUNICATIONS

Roads. There were (1984) 30,000 km of roads. Addis Ababa is linked with Nairobi by a highway.

Motor vehicles (1984): Cars, 41,300; lorries and trucks, 8,800; buses, 3,041.

Railways. The former Franco-Ethiopian Railway Co. (782 km, metre-gauge) became the Ethiopian-Djibouti Railway Corp. in 1982, when the remaining France-owned shares were bought out.

Aviation. Ethiopian Air Lines, formed in 1946, carried 242,924 passengers in 1980 and 8,613 tonnes of freight.

Shipping. A state shipping line was established in 1964. In May 1973 it owned 4 cargo vessels and 2 tankers.

Post and Broadcasting. The postal system serves 301 offices, mainly by air-mail. All the main centres are connected with Addis Ababa by telephone or radio telegraph. International telephone services are available at certain hours to most countries in Europe, North America and India. Number of telephones (1982), 100,783.

The Ethiopian Broadcasting Service makes sound broadcasts on the medium and short waves in English, Amharic and in the vernacular languages spoken within the country. Radio Voice of Revolutionary Ethiopia was heard by 250,000 receivers in 1980. There were about 45,000 television sets in 1982

Cinemas (1974). There were 31 cinemas, with seating capacity of about 25,600.

Newspapers. There are 3 government-controlled daily newspapers with a combined circulation of about 45,000.

JUSTICE, RELIGION, EDUCATION AND WELFARE

Justice. The legal system is said to be based on the Justinian Code. A new penal code came into force in 1958 and Special Penal Law in 1974. Codes of criminal procedure, civil, commercial and maritime codes have since been promulgated.

The extra-territorial rights formerly enjoyed by foreigners have been abolished, but any person accused in an Ethiopian court has the right to have his case transferred to the High Court, provided he asks for this before any evidence has been taken in the court of first instance.

Provincial and district courts have been established, and High Court judges visit the provincial courts on circuit. The Supreme Court at Addis Ababa is presided over by the Chief Justice.

Religion. About 45% of the population are Moslem and 40% Christian, mainly belonging to the Ethiopian Orthodox Church.

Education. In the academic year 1980–81 there were more than 2·13m. pupils in primary schools. In secondary schools there were 400,000 students. Higher education is co-ordinated under the National University, chartered in 1961; in 1979–80, there were 14,562 students. The University College, the Engineering, Building and Theological Colleges are in Addis Ababa, the Agricultural College in Harar and the Public Health College in Gondar.

The government claims to have reduced illiteracy from 95% to 54% since 1974.

Health. In 1977 there was one doctor for every 75,000 people and in 1981 it was found that Ethiopia has the shortest life expectancy in the world, at 40 years.

DIPLOMATIC REPRESENTATIVES

Of Ethiopia in Great Britain (17 Prince's Gate, London, SW7 1PZ)
Ambassador: Ato Ayalew Wolde-Giorgis.

Of Great Britain in Ethiopia (Fikre Mariam Abatechan St., Addis Ababa)
Ambassador: B. L. Barder.

Of Ethiopia in the USA (2134 Kalorama Rd., NW, Washington D.C., 20008)
Chargé d'Affaires: Tesfaye Demeke.

Of the USA in Ethiopia (Entoto St., Addis Ababa)
Chargé d'Affaires: David A. Korn.

Of Ethiopia to the United Nations
Ambassador: Mohamed Hamid Ibrahim.

Books of Reference

Gilkes, P., *The Dying Lion: Feudalism and Modernisation in Ethiopia.* London, 1975
Halliday, F. and Molyneaux, M., *The Ethiopian Revolution.* London, 1981
Hess, R. L., *Ethiopia: The Modernization of Autocracy.* Cornell Univ. Press, 1970
Holmberg, J., *Grain Marketing and Land Reform in Ethiopia.* Uppsala, 1977
Mosley, L., *Haile Selassie.* London, 1964
Pool, D., *Eritrea: Africa's Longest War.* London, 1982
Scholler, H. and Brictzke, P., *Ethiopia: Revolution, Law and Politics.* New York, 1976
Thompson, B., *Ethiopia: The Country That Cut Off Its Head.* London, 1975
Ullendorff, E., *The Ethiopians.* New York, 1973
Wolde-Mariam, M., *An Atlas of Ethiopia* Rev. ed. Addis Ababa, 1970

FALKLAND ISLANDS AND DEPENDENCIES

Capital: Stanley
Population: 1,813 (1980)

HISTORY. France established a settlement in 1764 and Britain a second settlement in 1765. In 1770 Spain bought out the French and drove off the British. In 1806 Spanish rule was overthrown in Argentina, and the Argentinians claimed to succeed Spain in the French and British settlements in 1820. The British objected and reclaimed their settlement in 1832 as a Crown Colony.

On 2 April 1982 Argentine forces invaded the Falkland Islands and the Governor was expelled. At a meeting of the UN Security Council, held on 3 April, the voting was 10 to 1 in favour of the resolution calling for Argentina to withdraw. Britain regained possession on 14–15 June after the Argentinians surrendered.

AREA AND POPULATION. The Crown Colony is situated in the South Atlantic Ocean about 480 miles north-east of Cape Horn. The numerous islands cover 4,700 sq. miles. The main East Falkland Island, 2,610 sq. miles; the West Falkland, 2,090 sq. miles, including the adjacent small islands. The Dependency of South Georgia lies 800 miles south-east of the Falklands, has an area of 1,450 sq. miles; the South Sandwich group, 470 miles south-east of South Georgia, has an area of 130 sq. miles.

The population of the Falkland Islands at census 1980 was 1,813. The only town is Stanley, in East Falkland, with a population of just over 1,000. A large garrison of British troops were stationed near Stanley in 1984. The population of South Georgia varies with the season, but the resident population in 1980 was 22 (males). The South Sandwich are uninhabited.

South Georgia, once a base for whaling and sealing operations, is now occupied by members of the British Antarctic Survey at the base at King Edward Point.

The population of the Falkland Islands is nearly all of British descent, with about 80% born in the islands.

CLIMATE. A harsh climate, much affected by strong winds, particularly in spring. Stanley Jan. 49°F (9·4°C), July 35°F (1·7°C). Annual rainfall 27″ (681 mm).

CONSTITUTION AND GOVERNMENT. The present Constitution came into force on 21 Nov. 1977. On 18 June 1982, a Falkland Islands and Dependencies (Interim Administration) Order was introduced which made provision for the interim administration by the establishment of a Civil Commissioner and a Military Commissioner. Under the Order the Military Commissioner has responsibility for the defence and internal security (with the exception of the police). The Civil Commissioner is required to consult the Military Commissioner on any matter which falls within the responsibility of the Military Commissioner and accept any advice on such matters tendered by the Military Commissioner. The Order suspended the office of Governor and Commander-in-Chief and vested the functions of that office in the Civil Commissioner who is assisted by an Executive Council consisting of the Chief Secretary and Financial Secretary, both *ex-officio*; 2 members elected by the Legislature and 2 appointed members; and a Legislative Council composed of the Chief Secretary and Financial Secretary, both *ex-officio*; 3 elected members representing Stanley, 1 elected member from the East Falkland and 1 from the West Falkland and 1 representing the Camp as a whole.

Civil Commissioner: Sir Rex Hunt, CMG.
Chief Secretary: F. E. Baker, OBE.
Flag: British Blue Ensign with arms of Colony on a white disc in the fly.

DEFENCE. Since 1982 the Islands have been defended by a garrison of several thousand troops. The garrison is commanded by a Military Commissioner who is responsible for all military matters in the Islands. He liaises with the Civil Commissioner on civilian and political matters, and advises him on matters of internal security. Apart from their strictly defence role, the military are taking an active part in the rehabilitation and reconstruction of the Islands.

ECONOMY

Budget. Revenue and expenditure (in £ sterling) for fiscal years ending 30 June:

	1976–77	1977–78	1978–79	1979–80	1980–81	1981–82 [1]
Revenue	1,154,204	1,803,151	1,820,561	2,427,934	2,298,325	2,478,311
Expenditure	1,131,045	1,382,744	1,792,780	2,057,928	2,775,697	2,411,004

[1] Estimates.

Currency. The Falkland £ is at parity with the £ sterling.

Banking. On 30 June 1981 the government savings bank held a balance of £2,683,302. Some banking facilities are also offered by Lloyds Bank.

SHEEP FARMING. The whole acreage of the Colony is divided into large sheep runs. Wool is the principal product, but hides are exported. In 1980 there were 663,367 sheep, 8,056 cattle and 2,459 horses in the islands.

DEVELOPMENT. The economy is entirely dependent on the production of wool for export. A comprehensive economic survey, published in 1976, drew attention to the potential for exploitation of fish, kelp and possibly oil, and made recommendations for various areas of development. In 1982 after the repossession of the Islands by British troops, Lord Shackleton's team was asked to update its 1976 survey. The Government announced on 8 Dec. 1982 the provision of £31m. over six years for the development of the Islands' economy. Approximately £21m. are for infrastructure projects (roads, jetty, water and electricity supplies, sewerage, telephone systems and airport buildings). Legislation was passed in the Falkland Islands Legislative Council on 22 April 1983 for the establishment of a Falkland Islands Development Corporation, as proposed by the Shackleton Report.

TRADE. Total imports, 1980, amounted to £2,590,321 and exports to £2,661,731.

COMMUNICATIONS

Roads. There are 13 miles of made-up roads in Stanley. Outside Stanley tracks link all the settlements which are passable in all but the worst weather. Work has continued on an all-weather road from Stanley to Darwin.

Aviation. Air communication was *via* Ascencion Island in early 1984. There are no external civil air links. In June 1983 plans were announced to build a new airfield at Mount Pleasant.

Shipping. A charter vessel calls 4 or 5 times a year to/from the UK. Communication with the Colony, the Dependencies and the British Antarctic Territory is kept up by the Royal research ships *John Biscoe* and *Bransfield* and by the ice-patrol vessel HMS *Endurance*.

Post and Broadcasting. Number of telephones (1980) 500. There is a government-operated broadcasting station at Stanley and the Government also operates a wired broadcasting service to subscribers.

EDUCATION AND WELFARE

Education. Education is compulsory between the ages of 5 and 15 years. In 1980 there were 312 children receiving education in the Colony. This includes Stanley schools, Darwin School and settlement schools, as well as pupils taught by itinerant teachers in rural areas. 9 children were being educated abroad.

Health. The Government Medical Department is responsible for preventative and curative medical services in the territory. A board of health deals with public health problems as they arise. The Senior Medical Officer, who sits on the board is responsible for advising the Falkland Islands Government on health policy. The Military Environmental Health Officer also sits on the board.

There is one hospital in Stanley, shared by civilians and the military. Medical services for the Islands are run from the hospital, including a general practitioner service to Stanley and a routine and emergency flying doctor service for outlying farm settlements.

WILD LIFE. The Falkland Islands and South Georgia are noted for their outstanding wild life, including penguin and seal. Four Nature Reserves have been declared and 18 Wild Animal and Bird Sanctuaries gazetted. The brown trout introduced between 1947 and 1952 can now be found in nearly all the rivers.

Books of Reference

Falkland Islands: The Facts. HMSO, London, 1982
Falkland Islands Journal. Stanley, from 1967
Falkland Islands Review [Franks Report] Cmnd. 8787. HMSO, London, 1983
Falklands/Malvinas, Whose Crisis? Latin American Bureau, London, 1982
Calvert, P., *The Falklands Crisis: The Rights and the Wrongs.* London, 1982
Hanrahan, B., and Fox, R., *'I counted them all out and I counted them all back'.* London, 1982
Hastings, M., and Jenkins, S., *The Battle for the Falklands.* London, 1983
Phipps, C., *What Future for the Falklands?* London, 1977
Shackleton, E., *Falkland Islands Economic Study 1982.* HMSO, London, 1982

FIJI

Capital: Suva
Population: 646,561 (1981)
GNP per capita: US$1,850 (1980)

HISTORY. The Fiji Islands were discovered by Tasman in 1643 and visited by Capt. Cook in 1774, but first recorded in detail by Capt. Bligh after the mutiny of the *Bounty* (1789). In the 19th century the search for sandalwood, in which enormous profits were made, brought many ships. Deserters and shipwrecked men stayed on; firearms salvaged from wrecks were used in native wars, new diseases swept the islands, and rum and muskets became regular articles of trade. Tribal wars became bloody and general until Fiji was ceded to Britain on 10 Oct. 1874, after a previous offer of cession had been refused. British administrators produced order out of chaos, and since then there has been steady political, social and economic progress. Fiji gained independent status on 10 Oct. 1970.

AREA AND POPULATION. Fiji comprises about 332 islands and islets (about 110 inhabited) lying between 15° and 22° S. lat. and 174° E. and 177° W. long. The largest is Viti Levu, area 10,429 sq. km (4,027 sq. miles), next is Vanua Levu, area 5,556 sq. km (2,145 sq. miles). The island of Rotuma (47 sq. km, 18 sq. miles), about 12° 30′ S. lat., 178° E. long., was added to the colony in 1881. Total area, 7,078 sq. miles (18,333 sq. km).

A population census is taken every 10 years. Total population (census, Dec. 1977), 601,485; 1981 (estimate) 646,561. The mid-1981 total population consisted of the following: 287,952 (44·5%) Fijians; 323,707 (50·7%) Indians; 11,145 (1·7%) Part Europeans; 4,048 (0·6%) Europeans; 8,073 (1·2%) Rotumans; 4,603 (0·7%) Chinese; 6,341 (0·9%) other Pacific Islanders; 692 (0·1%) others.

Suva, the capital, is on the south coast of Viti Levu; population (1981), 68,178. Suva was proclaimed a city on 2 Oct. 1953. Lautoka had 24,703 in 1981.

Vital statistics, 1980: Crude birth rate per 1,000 population, Fijian, 26·7, Indian, 32·3; crude death rate per 1,000 population, Fijian, 6·4, Indian, 6·3.

CLIMATE. A tropical climate, but oceanic influences prevent undue extremes of heat or humidity. The S.E. Trades blow from May to Nov., during which time nights are cool and rainfall amounts least. Suva. Jan. 80°F (26·7°C), July 73°F (22·8°C). Annual rainfall 117″ (2,974 mm).

CONSTITUTION AND GOVERNMENT. Fiji became an independent nation within the Commonwealth on 10 Oct. 1970. This had been agreed at a constitutional conference held in London in April 1970. There is a Lower House, the House of Representatives, which consists of 52 elected members and an Upper House, the Senate, of 22 members (8 nominations by the Council of Chiefs, 7 by the Prime Minister, 6 by the Leader of the Opposition and 1 by the Rotuma Council). Elections are held every five years.

At elections held in July 1982 for the 52 seats in the House of Representatives the Alliance Party won 28 seats, the National Federation Party won 22 seats and the Western United Front won 2 seats. In Jan. 1982, the National Federation Party entered into a formal agreement with the Western United Front to form a coalition.

Local Government. The Fijian Administration, established in 1876, had jurisdiction over all Fijians.

Fiji is divided into 13 provinces, each with its own council. Elections to these councils in 90 constituencies were conducted for the first time in 1967 on a full adult franchise amongst Fijians.

The councils have wide powers to make by-laws and draw up their own budget subject to confirmation by the Fijian Affairs Board. Each council has its own treasury and levies rates to raise its revenue. These provincial rates vary from $F6 to $F9 per annum for every male adult, but those maintaining 5 or more children pay lower rates until their children become taxpayers. A start has been made, however, to change over to a system of land rating based upon the unimproved value of Fijian-owned land. This is considered to be more equitable and related to ability to pay.

These newly elected councils held their inaugural and 1968 budget meetings towards the end of 1967, when the chairman for each of these 13 councils was also elected from among its members. Members were elected for 2 years and new elections were held in 1969.

At the apex of the Fijian Administration is the Great Council of Chiefs presided over by the Minister for Fijian Affairs. The Council of Chiefs consists of 22 Fijian members elected to the House of Representatives, 30 representatives, elected by the Provincial Councils and 15 representatives nominated by the Minister for Fijian Affairs.

The Council of Chiefs advises the Government generally on Fijian affairs.

Governor-General: Ratu Sir Penaia Ganilau, GCMG, KCVO, KBE, DSO.

Prime Minister, Minister for Fijian Affairs and Information: Ratu Sir Kamisese Mara, GCMG, KBE.

Employment and Industrial Relations: Mohammed Ramzan, MBE. *Transport and Civil Aviation:* Edward Beddoes. *Communications and Works:* Semesa Sikivou, CBE. *Home Affairs:* Ratu William Toganivalu. *Energy and Mineral Resources:* Peter Stinson. *Attorney-General:* Manikam V. Pillai, MBE. *Agriculture and Fisheries:* Jonati Mavoa. *Economic Planning and Development:* Ratu David Toganivalu. *Finance:* Charles Walker. *Lands, Local Government and Housing:* Militoni Leweniqila. *Foreign Affairs and Tourism:* Mosese Qionibaravi, CMG. *Health and Social Welfare:* Dr Apenisa Kurisaqila. *Education and Youth:* Dr Ahmed Ali.

Flag: Light blue with the Union Flag in the canton and the shield of Fiji in the fly.

DEFENCE. The Fiji Military Forces Ordinance, 1949, provides for the maintenance of a small regular force, with territorial units and trained reserves. This force, comprising 3 infantry battalions, numbers (1984), 2,500.

Navy. A naval squadron was authorized in 1974 to perform fishery protection, surveillance, hydrographic surveying and coastguard duties. Present strength is 3 coastal minesweepers (*ex*-US MSC), 1 utility vessel and 2 survey craft. Naval personnel (trained in Australia) in 1984 numbered 26 officers and 145 ratings. The naval base is HMFS *Viti* in Suva.

INTERNATIONAL RELATIONS

Membership. Fiji is a member of the UN, the Commonwealth, the Colombo Plan and is an ACP state of the EEC.

ECONOMY

Budget. The financial year corresponds with the calendar year. All figures are in $1m. Fijian.

	1978	1979	1980	1981	1982
Revenue	161·6	198·7	232·6	259·4	258·3
Expenditure	170·2	189·0	223·1	239·6	273·2

Currency. The National Bank of Fiji had, at the of 1983, deposits amounting to $F58·2m. due to 242,441 accounts. The headquarters are at Suva, and there are 48 agencies, 8 branches and 3 sub-branches throughout Fiji. Fiji changed to decimal currency on 13 Jan. 1969, with the major unit being $F1. In March 1984, £1 = $F1·52; US$ = $F1·032.

Banking. The Westpac Banking Corporation has 8 branches and 18 agencies; the Bank of New Zealand has 8 branches, and 15 agencies; the Australia and New Zealand Bank has 3 branches and 3 agencies and the Bank of Baroda has 8 branches and 5 agencies in Fiji. Barclays International has 3 branches in Suva and 1 agency.

NATURAL RESOURCES

Agriculture. Some 600,000 acres of land are in agricultural use. Sugar-cane is the principal cash crop (production, 1982, 410,810 tonnes), accounting for more than two-thirds of Fiji's export earnings; one quarter of the population depend on it directly for their livelihood. Copra, Fiji's second major cash crop (output, 1981, 21,000 tons), provides coconut oil and other products for export and employs nearly as many workers as the sugar industry. Ginger is the third major export crop replacing bananas which has declined through disease and hurricane. Other agricultural products include rice, cocoa, maize, tobacco and a variety of fruits and vegetables. There is a small, but fast developing, livestock industry.

Livestock (1982): Cattle, 156,000; horses, 40,000; goats, 55,000; pigs, 28,000; poultry, 920,000.

Forestry. Fiji supplies the bulk of its own timber requirements. A comprehensive pine scheme has been implemented with the aim of planting 186,000 acres by 1988.

INDUSTRY AND TRADE

Industry. Major industries include 4 large sugar-mills, the goldmines (960 kg in 1981) and 3 mills which process copra into coconut oil and coconut meal. There is a great variety of light industries.

Trade Unions. In 1982 there were 45 trade unions operating with about 45,000 members.

Commerce. Exports in 1981, $F268,968,000 (including $F75m. of re-exports). Imports, $F539,907,000. Chief exports: Sugar, gold, molasses and canned fish.

Total trade between Fiji and UK (British Department of Trade returns, in $1,000 sterling):

	1978	1979	1980	1981	1982	1983
Imports to UK	47,521	45,694	36,759	51,144	39,826	46,943
Exports and re-exports from UK	14,717	14,154	12,786	11,401	9,088	12,184

Tourism. In 1982, there were 200,000 visitors.

COMMUNICATIONS

Roads. Total road mileage is 2,019, of which 218 are sealed (paved), 1,663 are gravelled and 138 are unimproved. In 1981, there were 52,338 vehicles including 21,967 private cars, 16,351 goods vehicles, 1,121 buses, 3,386 tractors and (1980) 2,599 motor cycles.

Railway. There is a private 600mm-gauge railway (Fiji Sugar Corporation's Railway) of 644 km from Tavua to Sigatoka serving most of the sugar-cane producing area.

Aviation. Fiji provides an essential staging point for long-haul trunk-route aircraft operating between North America, Australia and New Zealand. Under the South Pacific Air Transport Council, which comprises the UK, Australia, New Zealand and Fiji, the international airport at Nadi has been developed and administered. Fourteen other airports are in use for domestic services.

Shipping. In 1981, 234 vessels of 19,479 net tons were registered. Suva has 4 slipways of 100, 200, 500 and 1,500 tons, and there are 3 shipbuilding and repair firms.

Post. There are 35 post offices and 156 agencies. Overseas telephone and telegram services are available through the Commonwealth cable to most countries except those in the South Pacific, which are served by direct radio circuits. The automatic telex network operates through New Zealand into the international telex system. There are ship-to-shore radio facilities. There were 46,252 telephones in 1983.

Cinemas. In 1979 there were 48 cinemas with a seating capacity of 28,100.

JUSTICE, RELIGION AND EDUCATION

Justice. An independent Judiciary is guaranteed under the Constitution of Fiji.

The Constitution allows for a Supreme Court of Fiji which has unlimited original jurisdiction to hear and determine any civil or criminal proceedings under any law.

The Supreme Court also has jurisdiction to hear and determine constitutional and electoral questions including the membership of members of the House of Representatives and the Senate.

The Chief Justice of Fiji is appointed by the Governor-General acting after consultation with the Prime Minister and the Leader of the Opposition.

Parliament prescribes the number of puisne judges. They are appointed by the Governor-General acting after consultation with the Judicial and Legal Services Commission.

The Constitution provides that a person cannot be qualified to be appointed as a judge of the Supreme Court unless he holds, or has held, high judicial office in some part of the Commonwealth or in any country outside the Commonwealth that may be prescribed by Parliament, or unless he has qualified to practise in the Supreme Court for not less than three years.

The Fiji Court of Appeal of which the Chief Justice is *ex officio* President is formed by four specially appointed Justices of Appeal. The Justices of Appeal are appointed by the Governor-General acting after consultation with the Judicial and Legal Services Commission. Generally any person convicted of any offence has a right of appeal from the Supreme Court to the Fiji Court of Appeal. The final appellant court is the Privy Council. Most matters coming before the Superior Courts originate in Magistrates' Courts.

Police. The Royal Fiji Police Force had (1983) a total strength of 1,404.

Religion. The 1976 census showed: Christians, 299,960; Hindus, 234,520; Moslems, 45,247; Confucians, 731.

Education (1981). School attendance is not compulsory in Fiji. There were 836 schools scattered over 56 islands, staffed by 6,895 teachers, of whom about 88·4% were trained. There were also 140 pre-schools. The primary and secondary schools had 162,034 pupils. The technical and vocational schools had 2,386 students and the teachers' colleges 367. There were 4 teacher-training colleges, 1 medical and 2 agricultural schools.

The University of the South Pacific opened in Feb. 1968 at Laucala Bay in Suva. It had about 1,500 full-time and 1,500 part-time students in 1983. The University has 3 schools, social and economic development, natural resources and education.

Total government expenditure on education in 1980 was over $F55·5m.

Health. In 1981 there were 27 hospitals with 1,716 beds, 318 doctors, 48 dentists and 1,308 nurses.

DIPLOMATIC REPRESENTATIVES

Of Fiji in Great Britain (34 Hyde Park Gate, London, SW7 5DN)
High Commissioner: Ratu Josua Brown Toganivalu, CBE (accredited 19 May 1981).

Of Great Britain in Fiji (Civic Centre, Stinson Parade, Suva)
High Commissioner: R. A. R. Barltrop, CVO.

Of Fiji in the USA (1140 19th St., NW, Washington, D.C., 20036)
Ambassador: Ratu Jone Radrodro.

Of the USA in Fiji (31 Loftus St., Suva)
Ambassador: Fred J. Eckert.

Of Fiji to the United Nations
Ambassador: Ratu Jone Radrodro.

Books of Reference

Statistical Information: A Bureau of Statistics was set up in 1950 (Government Buildings, Suva).
Trade Report. Annual (from 1887 [covering 1883–86]). Bureau of Statistics, Suva.

Journal of the Fiji Legislative Council. Annual (from 1914 [under different title from 1885]).
    Suva
Fiji Today. Suva, Annual
Fiji Fact and Figures. Suva, 1982
Report of Commission of Inquiry Into Natural Resources and Population Trends in Fiji. Suva,
    Government Press, 1960
Capell, A., *New Fijian Dictionary.* 2nd ed. Glasgow, 1957
Nayacakalou, R. R., *Leadership in Fiji.* OUP, 1976
Roth, G. K., *The Fijian Way of Life.* 2nd ed. OUP, 1973

FINLAND

Suomen Tasavalta—
Republiken Finland

Capital: Helsinki
Population: 4·84m. (1982)
GNP per capita: US$10,030 (1981)

HISTORY. Since the Middle Ages Finland was a part of the realm of Sweden. In the 18th century parts of south-eastern Finland were conquered by Russia, and the rest of the country was ceded to Russia by the peace treaty of Hamina in 1809. Finland became an autonomous grand-duchy which retained its previous laws and institutions under its Grand Duke, the Emperor of Russia. After the Russian revolution Finland declared itself independent on 6 Dec. 1917. The Civil War began in Jan. 1918 between the 'whites' and 'reds', the latter being supported by Russian bolshevik troops. The defeat of the red guards in May 1918 consequently meant freeing the country from Russian troops. A peace treaty with Soviet Russia was signed in 1920.

On 30 Nov. 1939 Soviet troops invaded Finland, after Finland had rejected territorial concessions demanded by the USSR. These, however, had to be made in the peace treaty of 12 March 1940, amounting to 32,806 sq. km and including the Carelian Isthmus, Viipuri and the shores of Lake Ladoga.

When the German attack on the USSR was launched in June 1941 Finland again became involved in the war against the USSR. On 19 Sept. 1944 an armistice was signed in Moscow. Finland agreed to cede to Russia the Petsamo area in addition to cessions made in 1940 (total 42,934 sq. km) and to lease to Russia for 50 years the Porkkala headland to be used as a military base. Further, Finland undertook to pay 300m. gold dollars in reparations within 6 years (later extended to 8 years). The peace treaty was signed in Paris on 10 Feb. 1947. The payment of reparations was completed on 19 Sept. 1952. The military base of Porkkala was returned to Finland on 26 Jan. 1956.

AREA AND POPULATION. The area and the population of Finland on 31 Dec. 1982 (Swedish names in brackets):

Province	Area (sq. km) [1]	Population [2]	Population per sq. km [2]
Uusimaa (Nyland)	9,893	1,150,930	116·3
Turku-Pori (Åbo-Björneborg)	22,169	707,401	31·9
Ahvenanmaa (Åland)	1,527	23,196	15·2
Häme (Tavastehus)	17,010	668,839	39·3
Kymi (Kymmene)	10,789	343,055	31·8
Mikkeli (St Michel)	16,343	208,523	12·8
Pohjois-Karjala (Norra Karelen)	17,782	177,242	10·0
Kuopio	16,511	254,056	15·4
Keski-Suomi (Mellersta Finland)	16,230	244,991	15·1
Vaasa (Vasa)	26,447	439,082	16·6
Oulu (Uleåborg)	56,866	426,155	7·5
Lappi (Lappland)	93,057	198,011	2·1
Total	304,623	4,841,481	15·9

[1] Excluding inland water area which totals 33,484 sq. km.   [2] Resident population.

The growth of the population, which was 421,500 in 1750, has been:

End of year	Urban	Rural	Total	Percentage urban
1800	46,600	786,100	832,700	5·6
1900	333,300	2,322,600	2,655,900	12·5
1950	1,302,400	2,727,400	4,029,800	32·3
1960	1,707,000	2,739,200	4,446,200	38·4
1970	2,340,308	2,258,028	4,598,336	50·9
1980	2,865,063	1,922,715	4,787,778	59·8
1982	2,897,678	1,943,678	4,841,481	59·9

The population on 31 Dec. 1981 by language primarily spoken: Finnish, 4,500,986 (93·5%); Swedish, 300,150 (6·2%); other languages, 9,629; Lappish, 1,385.

The principal towns with resident census population, 31 Dec. 1982, are (Swedish names in brackets):

Helsinki (Helsingfors)—capital	484,399	Imatra	35,749
(metropolitan area)	921,596	Kajaani	35,328
Tampere (Tammerfors)	167,335	Kokkola (Gamlakarleby)	34,236
(metropolitan area)	247,756	Kouvola	31,458
Turku (Åbo)	163,655	Rovaniemi	31,272
(metropolitan area)	244,000	Rauma (Raumo)	30,941
Espoo (Esbo)	145,154	Mikkeli (St Michel)	28,923
Vantaa (Vanda)	135,880	Savonlinna (Nyslott)	28,487
Lahti	96,557	Kemi	26,709
Oulu (Uleåborg)	95,933	Seinäjoki	25,636
Pori (Björneborg)	79,086	Kerava	24,871
Kuopio	76,106	Varkaus	24,755
Jyväskylä	64,546	Järvenpää	24,214
Kotka	60,411	Riihimäki	24,094
Vaasa (Vasa)	54,134	Nokia	23,903
Lappeenranta (Villmanstrand)	53,828	Iisalmi	23,087
Joensuu	45,650	Valkeakoski	22,624
Hämeenlinna (Tavastehus)	42,138	Kuusankoski	22,347
Hyvinkää (Hyvinge)	37,827		

Vital statistics in calendar years:

	Living births	Of which illegitimate	Still-born	Marriages	Deaths (exclusive of still-born)	Emigration
1978	63,983	7,263	314	29,760	43,692	16,327
1979	63,428	7,603	269	29,277	43,737	16,661
1980	63,064	8,247	266	29,388	44,398	14,824
1981	63,586	8,431	260	30,100	44,404	10,042
1982	66,245	...	...	30,564	43,427	7,669

In 1982 the rate per 1,000 was: Births, 13·7; marriages, 6·3; deaths, 9, and infantile deaths (1981, per 1,000 live births), 6·5.

Population and Housing Census 1980. 19 vols. Helsinki, 1981–83
Population. Annual. Helsinki

CLIMATE. The climate is severe in winter, which lasts about 6 months, but mean temperatures in south and south-west are less harsh, 21°F (–6°C). In the north, mean temperatures may fall to 8·5°F (–13°C). Snow covers the ground for three months in the south and for over six months in the far north. Summers are short but quite warm, with occasional very hot days. Precipitation is light throughout the country, with one third falling as snow, the remainder mainly as convectional rain in summer and autumn. Helsinki (Helsingfors), Jan. 21°F (–6°C), July 62°F (16·5°C). Annual rainfall 24·7″ (618 mm).

CONSTITUTION AND GOVERNMENT. Finland is a republic according to the Constitution of 17 July 1919.

Parliament consists of one chamber of 200 members chosen by direct and proportional election in which all Finnish citizens (men or women) who are 18 years have the vote (since 1969). The country is divided into 15 electoral districts with a representation proportional to their population. Every citizen over the age of 20 is eligible for Parliament, which is elected for 4 years, but can be dissolved sooner by the President.

The President is elected for 6 years by a college of 301 electors, elected by the votes of the citizens in the same way as the members of Parliament.

President of Finland: Dr Mauno Koivisto (elected 27 Jan. 1982).

State of Parties for Parliament elected on 20–21 March 1983: Conservative 44; Swedish Party, 11 (including 1 for Coalition of Åland); Centre, 38; Rural, 17; Social Democratic Party, 57; Communists, 27; Christian League, 3; Constitutional Party, 1. In addition there were 2 representatives of the Greens.

The Council of State (Cabinet), appointed by the President in May 1983 was composed as follows:

Prime Minister: Kalevi Sorsa.
Agriculture and Forestry: Toivo Yläjärvi. *Foreign Affairs:* Paavo Väyrynen.
Justice: Christoffer Taxell. *Environment:* Matti Ahde. *Interior:* Matti Luttinen.
Defence: Veikko Pihlajamäki. *Deputy Prime Minister and Finance:* Ahti Pekkala.
Finance (Deputy): Pekka Vennamo. *Education:* Kaarina Suonio. *Education (Deputy):* Gustav Björkstrand. *Communication:* Matti Puhakka. *Trade and Industry:* Seppo Lindblom. *Social Affairs and Health:* Vappu Taipale. *Social Affairs and Health (Deputy):* Eeva Kuuskoski-Vikatmaa. *Labour:* Urpo Leppänen. *Foreign Trade:* Jermu Laine.

National flag: White with a blue Scandinavian cross.
National anthem: Maamme; Swedish: Vårt land (words by J. L. Runeberg, 1843; tune by F. Pacius, 1948).

Finnish and Swedish are the official languages of Finland.

Local Government. For administrative purposes Finland is divided into 12 provinces (*lääni*, Sw.: *län*). The administration of each province is entrusted to a governor (*maaherra*, Sw.: *landshövding*) appointed by the President. He directs the activities of the provincial office (*lääninhallitus*, Sw.: *länsstyrelse*) and of local sheriffs (*nimismies*, Sw.: *länsman*). In 1983 the number of sheriff districts was 225.

The unit of local government is the commune. Main fields of communal activities are local planning, roads and harbours, sanitary services, education, health services and social aid. The communes raise taxes independent from state taxation. Two different kinds of communes are distinguished: Urban communes (*kaupunki*, Sw.: *stad*) and rural communes. In 1983 there were altogether 461 communes of which 84 were urban and 377 rural. In all communes communal councils are elected for terms of 4 years; all inhabitants (men and women) of the commune who have reached their 18th year are entitled to vote and eligible. The executive power is in each commune vested in a board which consists of members elected by the council and one or a few chief officials of the commune. Several communes often form an association for the administration of some common institution, *e.g.*, a hospital or a vocational school.

The autonomous county (*landskap*) of Åland has a county council (*landsting*) of one chamber, elected according to rule corresponding to those for parliamentary elections. In addition to its provincial governor it has a county board with executive power in matters within the field of the autonomy of the county.

Constitution Act and Parliament Act of Finland. Helsinki, 1978
The Finnish Parliament. Porvoo, 1969
Local Self-Government in Finland and the Finnish Municipal Law. Helsinki, 1960
Report of the Second Parliamentary Defence Committee. Helsinki, 1976

DEFENCE. The period of military training is 240 to 330 days and refresher training 40 to 100 days. Total strength of trained and equipped reserves is about 700,000.

Army. The country is divided into 7 military regions. The Army consists of 1 armoured brigade, 7 infantry brigades, 7 independent infantry battalions, 3 field-artillery regiments, 2 independent field-artillery battalions, 2 coastal artillery regiments, 3 independent coastal artillery battalions, 1 anti-aircraft regiment, 1 surface-to-air missile battalion, 4 independent anti-aircraft battalions, 2 engineering battalions, 1 signals regiment and 1 signals battalion, making a total strength in 1984, of about 34,500.

Navy. The Fleet comprises 2 corvettes, 2 minelayers (including a modified *ex*-Soviet frigate), 1 coastal minelayer, 6 missile craft, 12 fast patrol boats, 6 inshore minesweepers, 5 patrol boats capable of minelaying, 6 support ships, 1 headquarters ship, 10 transport craft, 14 landing craft, 3 tugs, 1 supply ship and a cable ship. There is a naval academy. Personnel in 1983 totalled 2,500 (200 officers and 2,300 ratings).

The Frontier Guard comprises 5 large patrol vessels,9 coastal patrol craft and 34 coastal patrol boats.

Air Force. The Air Force has 2 fighter squadrons, 1 transport squadron, 1 training squadron, a military school of aviation, a technical school, a signal school and a depot. The fighter squadrons have MiG-21bis and Saab J35 Draken aircraft (1 additional J35 squadron to be formed). Other equipment includes 30 Valmet Vinka piston-engined primary trainers of Finnish design, Magister jet basic trainers (being replaced by 50 Hawk trainers), MiG-21U and Saab J35C jet advanced trainers, C-47 and Fokker F.27 transport aircraft, Cessna 402 liaison aircraft, Learjet 35A target tugs, Piper Chieftain utility transports, and Mi-8 and Hughes 500 helicopters. Personnel total 3,000 officers and men.

INTERNATIONAL RELATIONS

Membership. Finland is a member of UN, the Nordic Council, OECD and an associate member of EFTA.

Treaties. A Treaty of friendship, co-operation and mutual assistance between Finland and the USSR was concluded in Moscow on 6 April 1948 for 10 years, extended on 19 Sept. 1955 to cover a period of 20 years, extended on 19 July 1970 for a further period of 20 years and extended again on 6 June 1983 for a further period of 20 years.

Treaty of Peace with Finland (10 Feb. 1947). Cmd. 7484

ECONOMY

Budget. Actual revenue and expenditure for the calendar years 1976–82, the ordinary budget for 1983 and the proposed budget for 1984 in 1m. marks:

	1977	1978	1979	1980	1981	1982	1983	1984
Revenue	35,168	40,393	43,319	48,916	58,795	63,043	74,259	84,484
Expenditure	35,064	38,938	45,036	50,812	57,797	68,008	74,220	84,484

Of the total revenue, 1982, 23% derived from sales tax, 25% from income and property tax, 18% from excise duties, 11% from other taxes and similar revenue, 12% from loans and 11% from miscellaneous sources. Of the total expenditure, 1982, 17% went to education and culture, 14% to social security, 9% to transport, 13% to agriculture and forestry, 10% to general administration, public order and safety, 9% to health, 5% to communities and housing policy, 6% to defence, 4% to promotion of industry and 12% to other expenditures.

At the end of Dec. 1982 the foreign loans totalled 18,807m. marks, of which 18,401m. were long-term loans, 406m. promissory notes to international organizations. The internal loans amounted to 11,441m. marks, of which, 11,378m. were consolidated debt. The cash surplus was 256m. marks. The total public debt was 30,248m. marks.

Currency. The unit of currency, starting 1 Jan. 1963, is the new *mark* of 100 *pennis*, equalling 100 old *marks*. The gold standard was suspended on 12 Oct. 1931. Aluminium bronze coins are 50, 20 and 10 *pennis*; copper coins, 5 and 1 *pennis*; aluminium coins, 5 and 1 *pennis*; silver, 1 *mark* pieces. Exchange rate in March 1984: 8·27 marks = £1; 5·63 marks = US$1.

Banking. The Bank of Finland (founded in 1811) is owned by the State and under the guarantee and supervision of Parliament. It is the only bank of issue, and the limit of its right to issue notes is fixed equal to the value of its assets of gold and foreign holdings plus 500m. marks. Notes of 500, 100, 50, 10, 5 and 1 marks are in circulation, and their total value at the end of 1981 was 5,571·7m. marks.

At the end of 1982 the deposits in banking institutions totalled 97,779m. marks and the loans granted by them 112,908m. marks. The most important groups of banking institutions were:

	Number of institutions	Number of offices	Deposits (1m. marks)	Loans (1m. marks)
Commercial banks	7	1,324	34.353	38,542
Savings banks	273	1,388	27.950	25,698
Post office savings bank	1	36 [1]	11,593	11,746
Co-operative banks	370	1,253	22,809	23,603

[1] In addition: 3,267 post offices.

Bank of Finland Monthly Bulletin. Helsinki, from 1926
Unitas. Quarterly Review, issued by Union Bank of Finland. Helsinki, from 1929
Economic Review (issued quarterly by Kansallis–Osake–Pankki). Helsinki, from 1948

Weights and Measures. The metric system of weights and measures was introduced in 1887 and is officially and universally employed.

Economic Survey of Finland. Annual

ENERGY AND NATURAL RESOURCES

Electricity. Electricity production was (in 1m. kwh.) 8,605 in 1960; 22,562 in 1970; 38,710 in 1980, 39,115 in 1981 and 39,354 in 1982, of which 33% was hydro-electric.

Minerals. The most important mines are Outokumpu (copper, discovered in 1910) and Otanmäki (iron, discovered in 1953). In 1981 the metal content (in tonnes) of the output of copper concentrates was 38,100, of zinc concentrates 54,665, of nickel concentrates 6,335, of iron concentrates and pellets 890,000 and of lead concentrates 1,882.

Agriculture. The cultivated area covers only 9% of the land and of the economically active population 12·6% were employed in agriculture and forestry in 1975. The arable area was divided in 1981 into 218,904 farms, and the distribution of this area by the size of the farms was: Less than 5 hectares cultivated, 66,948 farms; 5–20 hectares, 122,037 farms; 20–50 hectares, 26,871 farms; 50–100 hectares, 2,664 farms; over 100 hectares, 384 farms.

The principal crops (area in 1,000 hectares, yield in tonnes) were in 1981:

Crop	Area	Yield	Crop	Area	Yield
Rye	16	35,000	Oats	459	1,319,900
Barley	540	1,598,500	Potatoes	39	601,100
Wheat	143	435,400	Hay	445	1,689,400

The total area under cultivation in 1982 was 2,516,600 hectares. Production of dairy butter in 1982 was 69,887 tonnes, and of cheese, 74,123 tonnes.

Livestock (1983): Horses, 32,900; cattle, 1,662,100; pigs, 1,440,700; poultry, 7,609,300; reindeer, 316,000.

Forestry. The total forest land amounts to 30–31m. hectares. The productive forest land covers 17·35m. hectares. The growing stock was valued at 1,520m. cu. metres in 1971–76 and the annual growth at 57·4m. cu. metres.

In 1982 there were exported: Round timber, 1,101,440 cu. metres; sawn wood, 4,600,187 cu. metres; plywood and veneers, 760,201 cu. metres.

Monthly Review of Agriculture. Board of Agriculture
Agriculture 1981: Annual Statistics of Agriculture. Helsinki

INDUSTRY AND TRADE

Industry. The following data cover establishments with a total personnel of 5 or more in 1981 [1]:

Industry	Establish-ments	Person-nel [2]	Gross (1m. marks)	Value added (1m. marks)
Mining and quarrying	110	7,535	1,762	983
Metal ore mining	13	4,751	842	456
Other mining	97	2,964	957	559
Manufacturing	7,082	517,713	179,491	63,161
Manufacture of food, beverages and tobacco	1,096	60,456	33,839	8,335
Textile, wearing apparel and leather industries	930	54,026	10,200	4,994
Manufacture of textiles	286	20,879	3,920	1,826
Manufacture of wearing apparel, except footwear	461	32,097	4,463	2,374
Manufacture of wood and wood products, incl. furniture	1,120	53,556	12,161	4,381
Manufacture of paper and paper prod., printing, publishing	925	83,756	38,227	12,581
Manufacture of paper and paper products	196	47,474	29,124	7,486
Printing, publishing, etc.	729	36,674	9,229	5,228
Manufacture of chemicals and chemical, petroleum, coal, rubber and plastic products	457	39,302	27,420	7,127
Manufacture of industrial chemicals	150	13,822	7,995	2,110
Manufacture of other chemical products	115	10,423	3,280	1,705
Petroleum refineries	2	2,608	13,048	1,806
Manufacture of non-metallic mineral products	422	20,810	5,689	2,983
Basic metal industries	88	19,123	12,075	2,610
Iron and steel basic industries	58	13,988	8,402	2,133
Non-ferrous metal basic industries	30	5,135	3,682	483

[1] Preliminary.   [2] Working proprietors, salaried employees and wage earners.

Industry	Establish-ments	Person-nel [1]	Value of production Gross (1m. marks)	Value added (1m. marks)
Manufacture of fabricated metal products, machinery, etc.	1,927	172,250	39,324	19,742
Manufacture of fabricated metal products, excl. machinery	648	31,696	7,309	3,771
Manufacture of machinery, except electrical	718	65,214	14,649	7,677
Manufacture of electrical machinery, apparatus, etc.	206	29,029	6,150	3,372
Manufacture of transport equipment	283	41,595	10,255	4,248
Other manufacturing industries	117	4,843	851	498
Electricity, gas and water	535	27,620	22,658	8,081
All industry	7,727	552,868	203,911	72,225

[1] Working proprietors, salaried employees and wage earners.

GDP (at market prices) *per capita* (1982) 49,048 marks.

Industrial Statistics of Finland. Annual

Commerce. Imports and exports for calendar years, in 1m. marks:

	1978	1979	1980	1981	1982
Imports	32,338	44,222	58,250	61,269	64,751
Exports	35,206	43,430	52,795	60,308	63,026

The trade with some principal import and export countries was (in 1,000 marks):

	Imports		Exports	
Country	1981	1982	1981	1982
Australia	52,342	145,343	558,509	527,617
Austria	717,527	806,389	369,846	422,100
Belgium–Luxembourg	1,050,913	1,148,099	910,487	869,615
Brazil	370,615	468,401	182,027	178,879
Canada	430,416	573,188	408,189	440,951
China	122,747	147,686	182,231	193,110
Colombia	293,465	327,534	83,585	79,638
Czechoslovakia	360,432	338,757	171,454	268,887
Denmark	1,335,918	1,501,357	1,999,591	2,282,487
France	1,931,561	2,023,280	2,379,890	2,486,551
German Dem. Rep.	378,672	387,220	404,945	337,314
Germany (Fed. Rep.)	7,442,233	8,585,831	5,510,085	5,699,772
Greece	66,732	48,995	443,251	341,983
Hungary	264,311	276,920	261,332	363,290
Iran	632,189	323,597	486,065	476,113
Iraq	1,499	1,150	561,082	728,401
Ireland	162,042	205,296	347,994	402,787
Israel	176,013	164,932	225,607	203,844
Italy	1,379,750	1,707,913	1,169,195	1,134,317
Japan	2,213,150	2,723,217	510,808	677,793
Netherlands	1,606,873	1,714,545	2,050,399	1,928,125
Norway	1,528,619	1,456,549	2,839,682	3,084,494
Poland	761,548	938,492	78,805	86,328
Portugal	279,502	365,211	181,029	143,250
Saudi Arabia	2,643,382	1,362,691	434,132	538,842
Spain	1,335,918	453,791	464,104	530,082
Sweden	6,920,340	7,869,684	8,058,531	7,547,167
Switzerland	1,024,476	1,059,441	816,175	838,689
USSR	14,378,000	14,909,962	14,923,625	16,805,316
UK	4,934,117	4,641,997	6,424,072	6,827,279
USA	4,577,509	3,947,018	2,229,888	2,007,538

Principal imports 1982 (in 1m. marks): Machinery, apparatus and appliances, 18,327; mineral fuels, lubricants, etc., 17,754; chemicals, 5,653; food and live animals, 4,247; road vehicles, 4,056; crude materials, inedible, except fuels, 3,900; textile yarn, fabrics, etc., 2,501; iron and steel, 2,087.

Principal exports in 1982 (in 1m. marks): Paper and paper-board, 14,019;

machinery and transport equipment, 15,889; wood shaped or simply worked, 3,152; wood pulp, 3,064; ships, 4,866; clothing, 3,127; veneers, plywood, etc., and other wood manufactures, 1,473; food and live animals, 1,877; road vehicles, 1,229.

Total trade between Finland and UK (British Department of Trade returns, in £1,000 sterling):

	1979	1980	1981	1982	1983
Imports to UK	794,485	793,218	844,379	849,933	995,017
Exports and re-exports from UK	410,537	525,488	524,973	513,558	539,721

Foreign Trade. Annual.

Tourism. In 1982 tourism contributed 2,789m. marks to the economy.

COMMUNICATIONS

Roads. In Jan. 1982 there were 75,203 km of public roads, of which 36,581 km were paved. At the end of 1982 there were 1,352,055 registered cars, 52,996 lorries, 108,684 vans and 9,066 buses.

Railways. On 31 Dec. 1982 the total length of the line operated was 6,090 km (1,056 km electrified), of which all except 6 km was owned by the State. The gauge was 1,524 mm. In 1982 the number of passengers carried was 41m. and the amount of goods carried was 28·7m. tonnes. The total revenue in 1982 was 2,261m. marks and the total expenditure 3,060m. marks.

Aviation. The scheduled traffic of Finnish airlines covered 37m. km in 1982. The number of passengers was 2,815,200 and the number of passenger-km 2,589m. The air transport of freight and mail amounted to 67m. tonne-km.

Shipping. The total registered mercantile marine on 31 Dec. 1982 was 483 vessels of 2·21m. gross tons. In 1982 the total number of vessels arriving in Finland from abroad was 15,486 and the goods discharged amounted to 30·3m. tonnes. The goods loaded for export from Finland ports amounted to 16m. tonnes.

The lakes, rivers and canals are navigable for about 6,600 km. Timber floating is important, and there are about 41,500 km of floatable inland waterways. In 1982 bundle floating was about 5·3m. tonnes and river floating 1·6m. tonnes. In 1981, timber floated by vessels, 412,319 tonnes (rafts, 6·83m.).

On 27 Aug. 1963 the USSR leased to Finland the Russian part of the canal connecting Lake Saimaa with the Gulf of Finland. After extensive rebuilding the canal was opened for traffic in 1968. The Saimaa Canal and deepwater channels on Lake Saimaa (520 km) can be used by vessels with dimensions not larger than as follows: length 82 metres, width 11·8 metres, draught 4·4 metres and height of mast 24·5 metres.

Post and Broadcasting. In 1982 there were 3,720 post offices and 963 telegraph offices. The total length of telegraph wires was 571,087 km and that of domestic trunk and net group telephone wires 6·3m. km. The number of telephones was (1982), 2,643,574. All post and telegraph systems are administered by the State jointly with a large part of the telephone services. The total revenues from postal services were 2,139m. marks and from (wire and radio) telegraph services 1,264m. marks.

On 31 Dec. 1982 the number of television licences, 1,678,249, of which licences for colour television, 1,064,447. Oy Yleisradio AB broadcasts 2 programmes in Finnish and 1 in Swedish on long-, medium- and short-waves, and on FM. Two TV programmes (1 commercial) are broadcast.

Cinemas. In Dec. 1982 there were 357 cinemas with a seating capacity of 87,977.

Newspapers. In 1982 the number of newspapers published more often than once a week was 146, of which 134 in Finnish and 12 in Swedish.

JUSTICE, RELIGION, EDUCATION AND WELFARE

Justice. The lowest courts of justice are the municipal courts in towns and district courts in the country. Municipal courts are held by the burgomaster and at least 2 members of court, district court by judge and 5 jurors, the judge alone deciding, unless the jurors unanimously differ from him, when their decision prevails. From these courts an appeal lies to the courts of appeal *(Hovioikeus)* in Turku, Vaasa, Kuopio, Kouvola and Helsinki. The Supreme Court *(Korkein oikeus)* sits in Helsinki. Appeals from the decisions of administrative authorities are in the final instance decided by the Supreme Administration Court *(Korkein hallinto-oikeus)*, also in Helsinki. Judges can be removed only by judicial sentence.

Two functionaries, the *Oikeuskansleri* or Chancellor of Justice, and the *Oikeusasiamies*, or Solicitor-General, exercise control over the administration of justice. The former acts also as counsel and public prosecutor for the Government; while the latter, who is appointed by the Parliament, exerts a general control over all courts of law and public administration.

At the end of 1982 the prison population numbered 4,614 men and 157 women; the number of convictions in 1981 was 324,770, of which 300,471 were for minor offences with maximum penalty of fines and 24,270 with penalty of imprisonment.

Religion. Liberty of conscience is guaranteed to members of all religions. National churches are the Lutheran National Church and the Greek Orthodox Church of Finland. The Lutheran Church is divided into 8 bishoprics (Turku being the archiepiscopal see), 78 provostships and 594 parishes. The Greek Orthodox Church is divided into 3 bishoprics (Kuopio being the archiepiscopal see) and 25 parishes, in addition to which there are a monastery and a convent.

Percentage of the total population at the end of 1981: Lutherans, 90·1; Greek Orthodox, 1·1; others, 0·9; not members of any religion, 7·9.

Education (1981–82). *Primary and Secondary Education:*

	Number of institutions	Teachers	Students
First-level Education	4,234	26,664	365,418
(Lower sections of the comprehensive schools, grades I–VI)			
Second-level Education	1,601	34,247	441,232
General education	1,066	19,862	336,605
(Upper sections of the comprehensive schools, grades VII–IX, and senior secondary schools)			
Vocational education	535	14,385	104,627

Higher Education. Education at the third level (including universities and third level education at vocational institutes) was provided for 124,831 students. Education at universities was provided at 21 institutions with 6,471 teachers and 86,026 students.

University Education. Universities and similar types of institutions and the number of teachers and students are:

	Founded	Teachers	Students Total	Students Women
Universities				
Helsinki	1640	662	23,916	13,454
Turku (Swedish)	1919	281	3,902	2,099
Turku (Finnish)	1922	750	8,951	5,213
Jyväskylä	1958	472	6,043	3,813
Oulu	1958	699	7,142	3,273
Tampere	1966	465	8,577	5,311
Joensuu	1969	276	3,315	2,182
Kuopio	1972	212	1,590	954
Lappi	1979	46	482	223
Vaasa	1968	69	1,314	684
Polytechnic, Lappeenranta	1969	98	1,164	168
Polytechnic, Helsinki	1849	545	7,855	1,300
Polytechnic, Tampere	1972	164	2,908	300
College of Veterinary Medicine, Helsinki	1946	50	249	180
Schools for Economics				
Helsinki (Finnish)	1911	148	3,625	1,555
Helsinki (Swedish)	1927	82	1,559	642
Turku (Finnish)	1950	56	1,335	602
Swedish school of social sciences and local administration	1964 [1]	21	365	265

[1] Previously Swedish Civic College since 1943.

	Founded	Teachers	Students Total	Women
Universities of Art				
Sibelius Academy	1939	184	779	395
University of Industrial Arts	1949	134	862	520
Theatre Academy	1979	57	93	38
Teachers' training colleges [2]				

[2] Included in data for the universities above.

General adult education (at civic institutes, folk high schools and study centres) had 210,992 students.

General Education. Central Statistical Office, Helsinki (annual), *Higher Education.* Central Statistical Office, Helsinki (annual), *Vocational Education.* Helsinki (annual)

Health. In 1980 there were 9,538 physicians, 4,068 dentists and 74,441 hospital beds.

Social Security. The Social Insurance Institution administers general systems of old age pensions (to all persons over 65 years of age and disabled younger persons) and of health insurance. An additional system of compulsory old age pensions paid for by the employers is in force and works through the Central Pension Security Institute. Systems for child welfare, care of vagrants, alcoholics and drug addicts and other public aid are administered by the communes and supervised by the National Social Board and the Ministry of Social Affairs and Health.

The total cost of social security amounted to 49,379·6m. marks in 1981. Out of this 14,420m. (29·2%) was spent for health, 1,065m. (2·2%) for industrial accidents, 3,080m. (6·2%) for unemployment, 20,156m. (40·8%) old age and disability, 7,864m. (15·9%) for family allowances and child welfare, 601m. (1·2%) for general welfare purposes, 1,336m. (2·7%) for war-disabled, etc., 858m. (1·7%) as tax reductions for children. Out of the total expenditure 29% was financed by the State, 14% by local authorities, 46% by employers, 7% by the beneficiaries and 4% by users.

Labour Protection and Legislation. Helsinki, 1977
Social Welfare and Social Allowances. Helsinki, 1976
Social Security in the Nordic Countries 1978. Statistical Reports of the Nordic Countries, vol. 38. Stockholm, 1981
Arajarvi, E., *Social Expenditure in 1980 and Preliminary Data for 1981.* Official Statistics of Finland, Helsinki, 1982
Ellala, Esa, Suominen Risto, and Kotiranta, Maija-Liisa, *The Development of Social Security in Finland from 1950 to 1974.* Official statistics of Finland, special social studies XXXII : 48. Helsinki, 1976

DIPLOMATIC REPRESENTATIVES

Of Finland in Great Britain (38 Chesham Place, London, SW1X 8HW)
Ambassador: Ilkka Olavi Pastinen, KCMG (accredited 24 Feb. 1983).

Of Great Britain in Finland (16–20 Uudenmaankatu, Helsinki 12)
Ambassador: Alan Brooke Turner, CMG.

Of Finland in the USA (3216 New Mexico Ave., NW, Washington, D.C., 20016)
Ambassador: Richard Müller.

Of the USA in Finland (Itäinen Puistotie 14A, Helsinki 14)
Ambassador: Keith F. Nyborg.

Of Finland to the United Nations
Ambassador: Dr Keijo Korhonen.

Books of Reference

Statistical Information: The Central Statistical Office (Tilastokeskus, Swedish: Statistikcentralen; address: PO Box 504, SF-00101 Helsinki 10) was founded in 1865 to replace earlier official statistical services dating from 1749 (in united Sweden–Finland). Statistics on foreign trade, agriculture, forestry, navigation, health and social welfare are produced by other state authorities. Its publications include: *Statistical Yearbook of Finland* (from 1879) and *Bulletin of Statistics* (monthly, from 1924). A bibliography of all official statistics of Finland was published in Finnish, Swedish and English in *Statistical publications 1856–1979.* Helsinki, 1980.

Constitution Act and Parliament Act of Finland. Helsinki, 1978

Suomen valtiokalenteri (*State Calendar of Finland;* a Swedish version *Finlands statskalender* is published separately). Helsinki. Annual

Facts About Finland. Helsinki. Annual (Union Bank of Finland)

Finland Facts and Figures. Helsinki, 1979

Finland in Figures. Helsinki, Annual

Finland in Maps. Helsinki, 1979

Finnish Press Laws. Helsinki, 1976

Making and Applying Law in Finland. Ministry of Justice, 1973

Statistical Yearbook of Finland. Helsinki, Annual

Yearbook of Finnish Foreign Policy. Helsinki, Annual

The Finnish Banking System. Helsinki, 1983

Finnish Industry. Helsinki, 1981

Finnish Local Government. Helsinki, 1982

Health Services in Finland. Helsinki, 1980

Alanne, V. S., *Finnish-English General Dictionary.* Helsinki, 1982

Hurme-Pesonen, *English–Finnish General Dictionary.* Helsinki, 1982

Jutikkala, E., and Pirinen, K., *A History of Finland.* 3rd ed. New York, 1979

Kekkonen, U., *Neutrality: The Finnish Position.* 2nd ed. London, 1973.—*President's View.* London, 1982

Kirby, D. G., *Finland in the Twentieth Century.* London, 1979

Klinge, M., *A Brief History of Finland.* Helsinki, 1981

Korhonen, K., *Urho Kekkonen: A Statesman for Peace.* Helsinki, 1975

Layton, R., *Sibelius: The Master Musician.* London, 1978

Nousiainen, J., *The Finnish Political System.* Harvard Univ. Press, 1971

Paasivirta, J., *Finland and Europe. The Period of Autonomy and the International Crises 1808–1914.* London, 1981

Pearson, P., *Alvar Aalto and the International Style.* New York, 1978

Puntila, L. A., *The Political History of Finland, 1809–1966.* Helsinki, 1974

Uotila, J., *The Finnish Legal System.* Helsinki, 1966

FRANCE

République Française

Capital: Paris
Population: 54·45m. (1983)
GNP per capita: US$11,730 (1980)

HISTORY. The republic proclaimed on the fall of the Bourbon monarchy in 1792 lasted until the First Empire, under Napoleon I, was established in 1804. The Bourbon monarchy was restored in 1814 and (with an interval during 1815) lasted until the abdication of Louis Philippe in 1848. The Second Republic was established on 12 March 1848, the Second Empire (under Louis Napoleon) on 2 Dec. 1852. The Third Republic was established on 4 Sept. 1870 following the capture and imprisonment of Louis Napoleon in the Franco-Prussian war, and lasted until the German occupation of 1940. The Fourth Republic was established on 24 Dec. 1946 and lasted until 4 Oct. 1958.

AREA AND POPULATION. France is bounded north by the English Channel *(La Manche)*, north-east by Belgium and Luxembourg, east by Federal Republic of Germany, Switzerland and Italy, south by the Mediterranean (with Monaco as a coastal enclave), south-west by Spain and Andorra, and west by the Atlantic Ocean The total area is 543,965 sq. km (210,033 sq. miles).

The population (present in actual boundaries) at successive censuses has been:

1801	27,349,003	1881	37,672,048	Mar. 1946	40,506,639
1821	30,461,875	1891	38,342,948	May 1954	42,777,174
1841	34,230,178	1901	38,961,945	Mar. 1962	46,519,997
1861	37,386,313	1911	39,604,992	Mar. 1968	49,778,540
1866	38,067,064	1921	39,209,518	Feb. 1975	52,655,802
1872	36,102,921	1931	41,834,923	Mar. 1982	54,334,871

The 1975 total included 3,442,415 foreigners, of whom 758,925 were Portuguese, 710,690 Algerian, 497,480 Spanish and 462,940 Italian.

The latest population estimate (at 30 June 1983) is 54,453,000.

Vital statistics for calendar years:

	Marriages	Divorces	Live births	Stillborn	Deaths
1976	374,003	59,200	720,395	7,522	557,114
1977	368,000	72,000	745,830	8,600	535,900
1978	354,628	73,200	737,062	7,852	546,916
1979	340,405	86,900	757,354	7,570	541,805
1980	334,377	...	800,376	7,900	547,107
1981	314,600	...	805,680	7,735	555,360

Live birth rate in 1980 was 15 per 1,000 inhabitants; death rate, 10·3; marriage rate, 5·8; divorce rate, 1·6; infant mortality, 9·6 per 1,000 live births. Life expectation at birth; men, 70·2; women, 78·5. Population growth rate, 4·5 per 1,000.

The areas, populations and chief towns of the 22 Metropolitan regions were as follows:

Regions	Area (sq. km)	Census April 1975	Census March 1982	Chief town
Alsace	8,280	1,517,330	1,566,048	Strasbourg
Aquitaine	41,308	2,550,340	2,656,544	Bordeaux
Auvergne	26,013	1,330,479	1,332,678	Clermont-Ferrand
Basse-Normandie	17,589	1,306,152	1,350,979	Caen
Bourgogne (Burgundy)	31,582	1,570,943	1,596,054	Dijon
Bretagne (Brittany)	27,208	2,595,431	2,707,886	Rennes
Centre	39,151	2,152,500	2,264,164	Orléans
Champagne-Ardenne	25,606	1,336,832	1,345,935	Reims
Corse (Corsica)	8,680	289,842	240,178	Ajaccio
Franche-Comté	16,202	1,060,317	1,084,049	Besançon
Haute-Normandie	12,317	1,595,695	1,655,362	Rouen

Regions	Area (sq. km)	Census April 1975	Census March 1982	Chief town
Île-de-France	12,012	9,878,524	10,073,059	Paris
Languedoc-Roussillon	27,376	1,789,474	1,926,514	Montpellier
Limousin	16,942	738,726	737,153	Limoges
Lorraine	23,547	2,330,821	2,319,905	Nancy
Midi-Pyrénées	45,348	2,268,245	2,325,319	Toulouse
Nord-Pas-de-Calais	12,414	3,913,773	3,932,939	Lille
Pays de la Loire	32,082	2,767,163	2,930,398	Nantes
Picardie	19,399	1,678,644	1,740,321	Amiens
Poitou-Charentes	25,810	1,528,118	1,568,230	Poitiers
Provence-Côte d'Azur	31,400	3,675,730	3,965,209	Marseille
Rhône-Alpes	43,698	4,780,723	5,015,947	Lyon

Populations of the principal conurbations and towns at Census 1975:

	Conurbation	Town		Conurbation	Town
Paris	8,549,898	2,317,227	Limoges	167,664	147,406
Lyon	1,170,660	462,841	Avignon	162,562	93,024
Marseille	1,070,912	914,356	Mantes-la-Jolie	154,988	42,564
Lille	935,882	177,218	Amiens	152,997	135,992
Bordeaux	612,456	226,281	Béthune	145,155	28,279
Toulouse	509,939	383,176	Thionville	141,881	44,191
Nantes	453,500	263,689	Briey	133,853	—
Nice	437,566	346,620	Montbéliard	132,343	31,591
Grenoble	389,088	169,740	Nîmes	131,638	133,942
Rouen	388,711	118,332	Pau	126,859	85,860
Toulon	378,430	185,050	Troyes	126,611	75,500
Strasbourg	365,323	257,303	Besançon	126,349	126,187
Valenciennes	350,599	43,202	Bayonne	121,474	44,706
St-Étienne	334,846	221,775	Saint-Nazaire	119,418	69,769
Lens	328,741	40,281	Perpignan	117,689	107,971
Nancy	280,569	111,493	Bruay-en-Artois	116,340	25,951
Le Havre	264,422	219,583	Trappes	112,353	—
Cannes	258,479	71,080	Aix-en-Provence	110,659	114,014
Clermont-Ferrand	253,244	161,203	Lorient	105,797	71,923
Tours	245,631	145,441	Valence	104,330	70,307
Rennes	229,310	205,733	Annecy	103,543	54,954
Mulhouse	218,743	119,326	La Rochelle	100,649	77,494
Montpellier	211,430	195,603	Boulogne-sur-Mer	100,581	49,284
Douai	210,508	47,570	Angoulême	100,528	50,500
Orléans	209,234	109,956	Calais	100,327	79,369
Dijon	208,432	156,787	Poitiers	98,554	85,466
Reims	197,021	183,610	Forbach	97,970	25,385
Le Mans	192,057	155,245	Maubeuge	97,494	35,474
Brest	190,812	172,176	Béziers	88,619	85,677
Angers	188,695	142,966	Chambéry	88,081	56,788
Dunkerque	186,314	83,759	Bourges	86,041	80,379
Caen	181,390	122,794	Roanne	83,561	56,498
Metz	181,191	117,199	Colmar	83,435	67,410

Recensement de la population de 1982. Paris, Institut National de la Statistique et des Etudes Economiques, 1983

CLIMATE. The north-west has a moderate maritime climate, with small temperature range and abundant rainfall, but inland, rainfall becomes more seasonal, with a summer maximum, and the annual range of temperature increases. Southern France has a Mediterranean climate, with mild moist winters and hot dry summers. Eastern France has a continental climate and a rainfall maximum in summer, with thunderstorms prevalent.

Paris. Jan. 37°F (3°C), July 64°F (18°C). Annual rainfall 22·9″ (573 mm). Bordeaux. Jan. 41°F (5°C), July 68°F (20°C). Annual rainfall 31·4″ (786 mm). Lyon. Jan. 37°F (3°C), July 68°F (20°C). Annual rainfall 31·8″ (794 mm).

CONSTITUTION AND GOVERNMENT. The Constitution of the Fifth

Republic, superseding that of 1946, came into force on 4 Oct. 1958. It consists of a preamble, dealing with the Rights of Man, and 92 articles.

France is a Republic, indivisible, secular, democratic and social; all citizens are equal before the law (Art. 2). National sovereignty resides with the people, who exercise it through their representatives and by referenda (Art. 3). Political parties carry out their activities freely, but must respect the principles of national sovereignty and democracy (Art. 4).

The President of the Republic sees that the Constitution is respected; he ensures the regular functioning of the public authorities, as well as the continuity of the state. He is the protector of national independence and territorial integrity (Art. 5). He is elected for 7 years by direct universal suffrage (Art. 6). He appoints a Prime Minister and, on the latter's advice, appoints and dismisses the other members of the Government (Art. 8). He presides over the Council of Ministers (Art. 9). He can dissolve the National Assembly, after consultation with the Prime Minister and the Presidents of the two Houses (Art. 12). He appoints to the civil and military offices of the state (Art. 13). In times of crisis, he may take such emergency powers as the circumstances demand; the National Assembly cannot be dissolved during such a period (Art. 16).

Previous Presidents of the Fifth Republic:
General Charles André Joseph de Gaulle, 8 Jan. 1959–28 April 1969 (resigned); Alain Poher (interim), 28 April 1969–20 June 1969; Georges Jean Raymond Pompidou, 20 June 1969–2 April 1974 (died); Alain Poher (interim), 2 April 1974–27 May 1974; Valéry Giscard d'Estaing, 27 May 1974–21 May 1981.

President of the Republic: François Mitterrand (elected 10 May 1981; took office 21 May 1981).

The government determines and conducts the policy of the nation (Art. 20). The Prime Minister directs the operation of the Government, is responsible for national defence and ensures the execution of laws (Art. 21). Members of the Government must not be members of Parliament (Art. 23).

The Council of Ministers was composed as follows in Jan. 1984:

Prime Minister: Pierre Mauroy (Soc.)
Finance and Budget: Jacques Delors (Soc.)
Social Affairs: Pierre Bérégovoy (Soc.)
Interior and Decentralization: Gaston Defferre (Soc.)
Transport: Charles Fiterman (Comm.)
Justice: Robert Badinter (Soc.)
Foreign Affairs: Claude Cheysson (Soc.)
Defence: Charles Hernu (Soc.)
Agriculture: Michel Rocard (Soc.)
Industry and Research: Laurent Fabius (Soc.)
Education: Alain Savary (Soc.)
Foreign Trade and Tourism: Mme Edith Cresson (Soc.)
Urbanism and Housing: Paul Quilés (Soc.)
Commerce and Small Businesses: Michel Crépeau (MRG)
Professional Training: Marcel Rigout (Comm.)

The Government also includes 8 Ministers–Delegate and 20 Secretaries of State.

Parliament consists of the National Assembly and the Senate; the National Assembly is elected by direct suffrage and the Senate by indirect suffrage (Art. 24). It convenes as of right in two ordinary sessions per year, the first on 2 Oct. for 80 days and the second on 2 April for not more than 90 days (Art. 28).

The National Assembly comprises 491 Deputies, elected for a 5-year term from single-member constituencies – 474 in Metropolitan France, 11 in Overseas Departments, 1 for Mayotte (a 'special collectivity'), and 5 in Overseas Territories. The latest General Elections, held in June 1981, resulted in a new composition of 269 *Parti Socialiste,* 44 *Parti Communiste Français,* 14 *Mouvement des Radicaux de Gauche* and 6 others supporting the Government, together with 88 *Rassemblement Pour la République* (Gaullists), 63 *Union de la Démocratie Française* (Giscardians and Centrist Union), and 7 others forming the opposition.

The Senate comprises 318 Senators elected for 9-year terms (one-third every 3 years) by an electoral college in each Department or Overseas Territory, made up of all members of the Departmental Council or Territorial Assembly together with all members of Municipal Councils within that area; 298 Senators represent Metropolitan France, 8 Overseas Departments, 1 Mayotte, 3 Overseas Territories and 8 Frenchmen residing outside France. Following the partial elections in Sept. 1980, the Senate was composed of 69 *Parti Socialiste*, 67 *Union Centriste*, 52 *Parti Républicain* (Giscardians), 41 RPR (Gaullists), 26 *Gauche Démocratique*, 23 *Parti Communiste Français*, 13 MRG and 13 *non-inscrits* (unaffiliated).

The Constitutional Council is composed of 9 members whose term of office is 9 years (non-renewable), one-third every 3 years; 3 are appointed by the President of the Republic, 3 by the President of the National Assembly, and 3 by the President of the Senate; in addition, former Presidents of the Republic are, by right, life members of the Constitutional Council (Art. 56). It oversees the fairness of the elections of the President (Art. 58) and Parliament (Art. 59) and of referenda (Art. 60), and acts as a guardian of the Constitution (Art. 61).

The Economic and Social Council advises on Government and Private Members' Bills (Art. 69). It comprises representatives of employers', workers' and farmers' organizations in each Department and Overseas Territory.

National flag: The Tricolour of three vertical stripes of blue, white, red.

National anthem: La Marseillaise (words and music by C. Rouget de Lisle, 1792).

Local Government. France is divided into 22 regions for national development work, for planning and for budgetary policy. Under far-reaching legislation on decentralisation promulgated in March 1982, state-appointed Regional Prefects were abolished and their executive powers transferred to the Presidents of the Regional Councils, which are to be directly elected.

There are 96 *départements* within the 22 regions each governed by a directly-elected *Conseil Général.* From 1982 their Presidents' powers are greatly extended to take over local administration and expenditure from the former Departmental prefects, now called 'Commissioners of the Republic' with responsibility for public order. The *arrondissement* (324 in 1975) and the *canton* (3,509 in 1975), have little administrative significance.

The unit of local government is the *commune,* the size and population of which vary very much. There were, in 1975, in the 96 metropolitan departments, 36,394 communes. Most of them (31,593) had less than 1,500 inhabitants, and 16,550 had less than 300, while 229 communes had more than 30,000 inhabitants. The local affairs of the commune are under a Municipal Council, composed of from 9 to 36 members, elected by universal suffrage for 6 years by French citizens of 21 years or over after 6 months' residence. Each Municipal Council elects a mayor, who is both the representative of the commune and the agent of the central government.

In Paris the *Conseil de Paris* is composed of 109 members elected from the 20 *arrondissements.* It combines the functions of departmental *Conseil Général* and Municipal Council.

d'Estaing, V. G., *French Democracy.* New York, 1977
Suleiman, E. N., *Politics, Power, and Bureaucracy in France.* Princeton Univ. Press, 1974
Wright, V., *The Government and Politics of France.* London, 1978

DEFENCE. The President of the Republic exercises command over the Armed Forces. He is assisted by the research organization of the High Council of Defence (*Conseil Supérieur de la Défense Nationale*) and two Committees (*Comité de Défense* and *Comité de Défense restreint*) which formulate directives. The Prime Minister is responsible for the national defence; he exercises his military responsibilities through the General Secretariat of National Defence (SGDN). Under the Prime Minister's authority, the *Comité d'Action Scientifique de Défense* co-ordinates research.

On 5 July 1969 the Army Ministry was replaced by the Ministry of State for National Defence which is responsible for the Army, Air Force and Navy. In addition to the powers of the Army Ministry, the Ministry of State prepares general directives for negotiations relating to defence. It is assisted by the Departmental Assistant for Weapons, the Secretary-General for Administration, the Chief of Staff of the Armed Forces and the Chiefs of Staff of the 3 Armed Forces—Army, Navy and Air.

In 1962 the Armed Forces were reorganized in 3 groups: (1) nuclear strategic force; (2) operational forces; (3) home defence forces. Total strength (1983) 721,123 including 98,536 not included in totals for individual services.

French forces are not formally committed to NATO.

Army. The Army consists of regular officers and n.c.o.s, long-term n.c.o.s and soldiers, and conscripts serving 12 months.

The peace-time units comprise infantry, armoured troops and cavalry, artillery, engineering, signals, transport, matériel, naval infantry and artillery. In addition, there are the Foreign Legion, mountain and airborne troops and other specialized units.

In 1983 the effective strength of the Army was 353,932 all ranks (excluding *Gendarmerie*).

Higher military instruction is provided in 3 stages: the staff school (*École d'État-major*) for officers of formation staffs; the *École Supérieure de Guerre* for officers earmarked for the higher command; the *Institut des Hautes Études de Défense Nationale* where high-ranking officers and civilians study together the problems of national defence.

Light Army Aircraft. Formed in 1952, the *Aviation Légère de l'Armée de Terre* (ALAT) is a well-equipped force, with 75 light aeroplanes and more than 560 helicopters for observation, reconnaissance, combat area transport, liaison and supply duties. Effective strength, 1981, 6,450.

The *Gendarmerie* is an integral part of the Armed Forces but also co-operates with the civil administration in maintaining public order. Effective strength, 1983, 36,164.

Navy. The Navy is under the supreme direction of the Minister of Defence, being administered by the Chief and Deputy Chiefs of Naval Staff.

All naval aircraft and coastal defences are under the control of the Navy, and have been reorganized in 3 coast 'naval frontier' districts (with headquarters in Cherbourg, Brest and Toulon), in relation to the aircraft attached to the active fleet.

The French Navy is manned partly by conscription but mainly by voluntary enlistment. In 1984 the active personnel was 68,290 officers and men, including 9,150 in the Naval Air Arm.

The following is a summary of the strength of the fleet at the periods shown:

	1975	*1976*	*1977*	*1978*	*1979*	*1980*	*1981*	*1982*	*1983*
					Completed at end of				
Aircraft carriers	3[1]	3[1]	3[1]	3[1]	3[1]	3[1]	3[1]	3[1]	3[1]
Submarines	24[2]	24[2]	26[2]	27[2]	29[3]	28[3]	27[3]	28[3]	24[4]
Cruisers	1	1	1	1	1	1	1	1	1
Destroyers	21	20	21	22	20	19	20	20	18
Frigates	28	27	29	27	24	22	22	25	26

[1] Including 1 helicopter-carrier.
[2] Including 4 nuclear-powered ballistic missile submarines.
[3] Including 5 nuclear-powered ballistic missile submarines.
[4] Including 6 nuclear-powered ballistic missile submarines.

The principal ships of the French Navy are as follows:

Com-pleted	Name	Standard displace-ment Tons	Aircraft	Principal armament	Shaft horse-power	Speed Knots

Aircraft Carriers

| 1963 | Foch ⎱ | 27,300 | ⎰30 fixed wing, | 8 3·9 in. | 126,000 | 32·0 |
| 1961 | Clemenceau ⎰ | (normal) | ⎱ 4 helicopters | | | |

Helicopter Carrier

| 1964 | Jeanne d'Arc[1] | 10,000 | 8 helicopters | 4 3·9 in. | 40,000 | 26·5 |

[1] Cruiser type forward, flat-topped midships to aft.

Cruiser

| 1959 | Colbert | 8,500 | — | 4 'Exocet' (singles) 1 twin 'Masurca' 2 3·9 in. AA | 86,000 | 32·0 |

Capital (Strategic) Submarines

Class	No.	Displacement (submerged) tons	Missile Tubes (vertical)	Nuclear Reactors	Shaft horse-power	Speed Knots
'611'	6	8,940	16 M 20	1	16,000	25 dived 20 surface

In order of completion: Le Redoutable (1971)   L'Indomptable (1976)
                         Le Terrible (1973)   Le Tonnant (1980)
                         Le Foudroyant (1974)   L'Inflexible (1984)

The latter, completing, will be of intermediate type between her predecessors and a new class. One more is reportedly planned and two or three more of an improved class envisaged.

All the named vessels above are also armed with four 21-inch torpedo tubes.

The sixth vessel will have M 4 missiles.

There are also 2 nuclear-powered fleet submarines of 2,670 tons (submerged), 17 diesel-powered submarines, 2 guided-missile destroyer leaders of 5,090 tons, 3 guided-missile leaders of 4,580 tons, 4 missile leaders of 3,830 tons, 1 missile leader of 3,500 tons, 8 old conventional destroyers of 2,750 tons, 26 escorts (frigates), of 950 to 1,750 tons, 5 fast attack missile craft, 2 offshore patrol vessels, 10 large minehunters (ex-ocean minesweepers), 8 coastal minehunters, 20 coastal mine-sweepers (4 used as patrol vessels and 4 as diving ships), 8 inshore minesweepers (used as diving craft), 7 surveying vessels, 1 coastal patrol craft, 2 dock landing ships, 8 tank landing ships, 14 landing craft, 40 minor landing craft, 7 mainten-ance, repair and depot ships, 9 oilers, 11 boom defence vessels, 6 support ships, 14 transports, 16 training vessels, 40 auxiliary ships and 100 tugs.

One more nuclear-powered ballistic missile submarine, 3 nuclear-powered fleet (torpedo-armed) submarines, 4 guided missile destroyers and 8 avisos (escorts) are under construction. One nuclear-powered aircraft carrier, 4 more nuclear-powered fleet, torpedo-armed (hunter-killer) submarines, 6 fast missile craft and 12 mine-hunters are projected.

The naval air arm, known usually as Aéronavale, has 2 squadrons of nationally designed Etendard transonic fighter-bombers, 1 squadron of Etendard reconnaissance fighters, 2 squadrons of US-built Crusader all-weather fighters, 3 squadrons of Alizé turboprop anti-submarine aircraft, 5 maritime reconnaissance squadrons with Atlantic and Neptune aircraft and 3 anti-submarine and assault squadrons with Super Frelon and HSS-1 helicopters. Strength is 323 air-craft comprising 235 fixed-wing and 88 helicopters.

Air Force. Formed as the Service Aéronautique in April 1910, the Armeé de l'Air is organized in 7 major commands. Its bases and installations were regrouped and modernized in 1967. The Commandement des Forces Aériennes Stratégiques (CFAS) commands the nuclear deterrent force. The Commandement de la Force Aérienne Tactique (FATAC) directs the tactical air forces, commands the air force reserve and is responsible for support of the ground forces. Under FATAC the 1st *Commandement Aérien Tactique* (1° CATAC) controls tactical air units based in eastern France; the 2nd *Commandement Aérien Tactique* (2° CATAC) controls the reserve forces and the air component of the *Force d'Intervention.* The *Commandement du Transport Aérien Militaire* (COTAM) is responsible for air transport operations and for the training and transport of airborne forces. The *Commandement Air des Forces de Défense Aérienne* (CAFDA) controls air defence forces. The *Commandement des Écoles de l'Armée de l'Air* (CEAA) is responsible for training the personnel for all branches of the Air Force. The *Commandement des Transmissions* has responsibility for communications and electronic warfare. Finally, the *Commandement du Génie de l'Air,* made up mainly of Army personnel, undertakes airbase construction and maintenance under Air Force control.

The home-based French Air Force is divided territorially among 4 metropolitan air regions (Metz, Villacoublay, Bordeaux, Aix-en-Provence); overseas, small air units are integrated into the local joint-service commands. There are about 40 combat squadrons plus about 30 transport, helicopter and support squadrons, and the Air Force uses a total of 66 bases.

The strategic, tactical and air defence forces are equipped entirely with jet aircraft. The CFAS has 34 first-line Mirage IV supersonic nuclear bombers, and 10 reserves, deployed in 2 wings (each 3 squadrons) supported by 11 C-135F refuelling tanker transports. The 1° CATAC deploys 7 wings (20 squadrons), with about 180 Mirage III-E and 5F ground-attack fighters, and 135 Jaguar strike aircraft, plus 2 OCUs equipped with Mirage III-Bs and Jaguars. Five of these squadrons can deliver AN 52 nuclear weapons. The 3 reconnaissance squadrons re-equipped with Mirage F1-CRs in 1983–84. The air defence forces have 4 wings, with 8 squadrons of Mirage F1 multi-mission fighters and 1 squadron of Mirage III-Cs (to be replaced by Mirage 2000s). The COTAM is organized into 4 wings, equipped with 45 Transall C.160 turboprop transports, 50 Nord 250ls, 4 DC-8s and 92 helicopters. Training aircraft include CAP-10 piston-engined primary trainers, Epsilon piston-engined and Magister jet basic trainers, Alpha Jet and Mirage III-B advanced trainers, and two-seat Jaguars; 25 EMB-121 Xingus bought from Brazil and dual-purpose training/liaison aircraft.

Total officers and other ranks (1983) 100,225; 495 combat aircraft.

INTERNATIONAL RELATIONS

Membership. France is a member of UN, the Council of Europe, NATO and EEC.

ECONOMY

Planning. For the history of planning in France from 1947 to 1980, *see* THE STATESMAN'S YEAR-BOOK, 1982–83, p. 474. The eighth plan, covering the 1981–85 period, was set aside after the change of government in May 1981 and replaced by an interim plan for 1982–83, followed by a new ninth plan for 1984–88.

Budget. Receipts and expenditure (in 1m. francs) for calendar years:

Receipts	1982	%	1983	%
Direct taxation				
Income tax	177,280	21·1	200,592	21·4
Corporation tax	71,020	8·5	90,800	9·7
Wealth and other taxes	63,202	7·5	65,092	6·9
Indirect taxation				
Value-added tax	348,395	41·5	385,685	41·2
Petrol tax	54,395	6·5	58,010	6·2
Stamp duty and other taxes	83,327	9·9	90,869	9·7
Non-fiscal receipts	41,284	4·9	45,770	4·9
Gross total	838,903		936,818	
Net budget receipts (gross total taxes minus various deductions)	704,599		772,234	

Expenditure	1982	%	1983	%
Public authorities and general administration	83,724	10·3	92,980	10·3
Education and culture	188,655	23·1	208,757	23·1
Social affairs, health, employment	176,517	21·6	199,911	22·1
Agriculture and countryside	21,946	2·7	22,886	2·5
Housing and town planning	41,904	5·1	48,211	5·4
Transport and communications	36,342	4·5	41,592	4·6
Industry and services	43,408	5·3	46,313	5·1
External affairs	21,921	2·7	25,639	2·9
Defence	131,452	16·1	141,505	15·7
Miscellaneous expenditure	70,408	8·6	75,317	8·3
Total expenditure	816,277		903,111	

The accounts of revenue and expenditure are examined by a special administrative tribunal (Cour des Comptes), instituted in 1807.

Currency. The unit of currency is the franc. Coins are issued for 5, 10, 20 and 50 centimes, 1, 2, 5 and 10 francs; and bank-notes for 10, 50, 100 and 500 francs. In March 1984, £1 sterling = 11·78 francs; US$1 = 8·02 francs.

Banking. The Banque de France, founded in 1800, and placed under the authority of a state-appointed Governor in 1806, has the monopoly (since 1848) of issuing bank-notes throughout France. Note circulation at 31 Dec. 1981 was 151,900m. francs.

On 2 Dec. 1945 a law was passed to nationalize the Banque de France and the principal deposit banks. It also established a new body, the National Credit Council, formed to regulate banking activity and consulted in all political decisions on monetary policy. This new body comprises 45 members nominated by the Government; its president is the Minister for the Economy, its vice-president is the Governor of the Banque de France which as a Central Bank puts monetary policy into effect and supervises its application. On 11 Feb. 1982, a law was passed to nationalize the remaining deposit banks, the principal ones being: (i) those nationalized in 1945: Crédit Lyonnais (founded 1863), Banque Nationale de Paris (founded by amalgamation 1966) and the Société Générale (founded 1864), and (ii) among those nationalized in 1982: Crédit Industriel et Commercial, Crédit Commercial de France, the Banque de Paris et des Pays-Bas and the Crédit du Nord. Total deposits and short- and medium-term held bills by the banks at 31 Dec. 1981 was 1,302,800m. francs. The rest of the banking system comprises the popular banks, the Crédit agricole, the Crédit mutuel, the Banque française du commerce exterieur and the various financial establishments.

The state savings organization (Caisse nationale d'epargne) is administered by the post office on a giro system. On 31 Dec. 1981 the private savings banks (Caisses d'epargne et de prévoyance), numbering about 500 had 434,000m. francs in deposits; the state savings banks had 206,300m. francs in deposits. Deposited funds are centralized by a non-banking body, the Caisse de Dépôts et Consignations, which finances a large number of local authorities and state aided housing projects, and carries an important portfolio of transferable securities.

Weights and Measures. The metric system is in general use.

ENERGY AND NATURAL RESOURCES

Electricity. Production of electrical power (in 1m. kwh.): 1979, 230,700; 1980, 243,282; 1981, 260,759. In 1978, 37% was hydro-electric and 9% nuclear.

Oil. In 1981 2·42m. tonnes of crude oil were produced. The greater part came from the Parentis oilfield in the Landes. France has an important oil-refining industry, utilizing imported crude oil. Total yearly capacity at the end of 1979 was about 166·84m. tonnes. The principal plants are situated in Basse Seine (capacity in tonnes, 1979), 56·1m.; Mediterranean, 45·5m.; Atlantic, 15·9m.; Nord, 14·8m.; Alsace, 13·9m.; Paris region, 11·6m.; Lyonnais, 9m.

There has been considerable development of the production of natural gas and sulphur in the region of Lacq in the foothills of the Pyrenees. Production of natural gas was 7,757m. cu. metres in 1979, 7,529 in 1980, 7,080 in 1981.

Minerals. Principal minerals and metals produced, in 1,000 tonnes:

	1976	1977	1978	1979		1976	1977	1978	1979
Coal	21,879	21,293	19,690	18,612	Potash salts	1,738	1,719	1,928	2,075
Lignite	3,189	3,080	2,732	2,454	Pig-iron	19,024	18,257	18,497	19,415
Iron ore	45,181	36,630	33,454	31,627	Crude Steel	23,221	22,094	22,841	23,360
Bauxite	2,330	2,059	1,978	1,969	Aluminium	385	400	391	395

Agriculture. Of the total area of France (54·9m. hectares) 17·3m. were under cultivation, 12·9m. were pasture, 1·2m. were under vines, 14·3m. were forests and 8·3m. were uncultivated land in 1980.

The following table shows the area under the leading crops and the production for 4 years:

	Area (1,000 hectares)				Produce (1,000 tonnes)			
Crop	1977	1978	1979	1980	1977	1978	1979	1980
Wheat	4,126	4,167	4,063	4,580	17,546	21,057	19,411	23,668
Rye	129	138	116	128	389	432	353	405
Barley	2,909	2,814	2,816	2,648	10,319	11,414	11,238	11,758
Oats	625	611	539	534	1,938	2,194	1,865	1,927
Potatoes	279	269	252	227	8,190	7,459	6,698	6,722
Sugar-beet	585	556	547	541	24,500	24,488	26,444	26,206
Maize	1,639	1,802	2,003	1,754	8,316	9,473	10,293	9,254

Other crops in 1980 (figures for 1979 in brackets) include (in 1,000 tonnes): Rice, 27 (29); tobacco, 48 (53); flax, 293 (307).

France is the world's second largest producer of wine (after Italy); production in 1978 amounted to 5,882,000 tonnes.

The annual production of wine (in 1,000 hectolitres) appears as follows:

	Vineyards (1,000 hectares)	Wine produced		Vineyards (1,000 hectares)	Wine produced
1938	1,513	60,332	1977	1,180	53,137
1948	1,433	47,437	1978	1,141	58,599
1958	1,315	47,735	1979	1,219	80,319
1968	1,228	66,460	1980	1,174	71,546

The production of fruits (other than for cider making) for 4 years was (in 1,000 tonnes) as follows:

	1977	1978	1979	1980		1977	1978	1979	1980
Apples	1,243	1,867	1,716	1,810	Cherries	53	99	112	106
Pears	273	366	418	422	Nuts	18	37	30	30
Plums	73	165	158	136	Grapes	211	234	213	192
Peaches	319	406	386	397	Strawberries	77	68	82	85
Apricots	72	81	59	71					

In 1981 the numbers of farm animals (in 1,000) were (figures for 1980 in brackets): Horses, 317 (364); cattle, 23,553 (23,919); sheep, 12,980 (11,911); goats, 1,241 (1,125); pigs, 11,629 (11,446); poultry, 185,965 (176,290).

Forestry. The total area of forested land (1980) was 148,633 sq. km. Timber sold (1981), 30,341m. cu. metres valued at 7,985m. francs.

Fisheries. (1982). There were 75,060 fishermen, and 10,780 sailing-boats, steamers and motor-boats. Catch (in 1,000 tonnes): Fish, total, 640; crustaceans, 29; shell fish, 191.

INDUSTRY AND TRADE

Industry. Industrial production (in 1,000 tonnes) for 3 years was as follows:

	1980	1981	1982
Sulphuric acid	4,952	4,412	4,143
Caustic acid	1,333	1,314	1,380
Sulphur	1,839	1,700	1,839
Polystyrene	254	262	445
Polyvinyl	725	710	789
Polyethylene	1,074	883	912
Wool	64	63	49
Cotton	172	158	161
Linen	2·3	2	1·8
Silk	51	46	48
Man-made fibres, yarns	68	55	46
Jute	8	7	5
Cheese	1,067	1,098	1,125
Chocolate	116	118	115
Biscuits	368	379	380
Sugar	3,921	5,130	4,436
Fish preparations	85	87	92
Jams and jellies	116	120	125
Cement	29,104	28,229	26,136

Engineering production (in 1,000 units) for 3 years:

	1980	1981	1982
Motor vehicles	3,378	3,019	3,148
Television sets	1,928	1,960	2,148
Radio sets	2,141	2,266	2,724
Tyres	50,601	43,196	37,296

See map in THE STATESMAN'S YEAR-BOOK, 1968–69, Industrial Redeployment.

Employment (1975). Out of an economically active population of 21,061,215 persons, there are 2·01m. engaged in agriculture; 1,841,083 in building and public works; 6,327,818 in other manufacturing industries; 829,289 in transport; 3,632,478 in business, banking and insurance; 3,543,881 in services; 2,522,544 in commerce. In 1981, there were 23,044,900 employed (40·9% female), of whom 1,427,000 were foreign workers; in April 1982, there were 1,928,200 unemployed.

Trade Unions. The main confederations recognized as nationally representative are: the CGT (Confédération Générale du Travail), founded in 1895; the CGT-FO (Confédération Générale du Travail–Force Ouvrière) which broke away from the CGT in 1948 as a protest against Communist influence therein; the CFTC (Confédération Française des Travailleurs Chrétiens), which was founded in 1919 and divided in 1964, with a breakaway group retaining the old name and the main body continuing under the new name of CFDT (Confédération Française Démocratique du Travail); and the CGC (Confédération Générale des Cadres) formed in 1944 which only represents managerial and supervisory staff.

Membership is estimated because unions are not required to publish figures; but at elections held on 8 Dec. 1982 for labour tribunals, the CGT was supported by 2·8m. members, the CGT-FO by 1·4m., the CFDT by 1·8m., the CFTC by 650,000 and the CGC by 740,000. Except for the CGC unions operate within the framework of industries and not of trades.

Commerce. Imports (c.i.f.) and exports (f.o.b.) in 1m. francs for 5 calendar years were (including gold):

	1978	1979	1980	1981	1982
Imports	368,401	457,100	569,900	653,100	758,339
Exports	344,594	414,700	470,400	548,700	606,967

The chief imports for home use and exports of home goods are to and from the following countries, in 1m. francs (including gold):

	Imports (c.i.f)			*Exports (f.o.b.)*		
Countries	1980	1981	1982	1980	1981	1982
Algeria	7,431	12,994	25,914	11,078	12,815	14,022
Belgium-Luxembourg	47,547	48,779	58,496	43,941	45,566	52,427
Germany (Fed. Rep.)	93,160	104,036	127,661	75,350	81,373	89,564
Italy	53,408	58,616	72,777	58,628	62,440	68,445
Netherlands	30,897	37,665	42,021	22,898	24,316	27,953
Saudi Arabia	37,053	65,783	48,105	6,167	10,193	12,896
Spain (excluding Canary Is.)	16,474	17,876	23,105	13,084	15,758	18,759
Sweden	8,739	9,476	11,175	6,116	5,953	6,949
Switzerland (and Liechtenstein)	12,810	13,841	15,262	22,088	23,651	24,168
USSR	15,062	18,406	18,782	10,352	9,991	10,225
UK	30,775	35,718	46,064	32,743	39,120	43,920
USA	45,350	53,305	59,733	20,783	30,372	34,333

Total trade between France and UK (British Department of Trade returns, in £1,000 sterling):

	1979	1980	1981	1982	1983
Imports to UK	4,064,233	3,899,174	3,978,646	4,269,103	5,043,118
Exports and re-exports from UK	3,070,498	3,651,470	3,625,923	4,486,458	5,651,521

Tourism. In 1982 foreign visitors contributed about 40,320m. francs to the French economy.

COMMUNICATIONS

Roads. At the end of 1978 the French road system consisted of 4,248 km of motorway, 29,068 km of national roads, 345,990 km of departmental roads and 424,950 km of local roads. Total, 804,256 km. In 1980, there were 19·13m. passenger cars and 2·46m. commercial vehicles in use.

Railways. As from 1 Jan. 1938 all the independent railway companies were merged with the existing state railway system in a Société Nationale des Chemins de Fer Français, which became a public industrial and commercial establishment in 1983.

In 1982, the State railway totalled 34,599 km (10,600 km electrified) of 1,435 mm gauge, and carried 184m. tonnes of freight and 713m. passengers. A new railway for high-speed trains was completed in 1983 between Paris and Lyon.

The Paris transport network consisted in 1982 of 466 km of underground railway (métro) and regional express railways and 2,115 km of bus routes. In 1982 it carried 1,376m. passengers on the métro and 724m. by bus.

Aviation. Air France, UTA and Air Inter, the national airlines, had (31 Dec. 1979) a fleet of 166 aircraft, servicing Europe, North America, Central and South America, West and East Africa, Madagascar, the Near, Middle and Far East. There are local networks in the West Indies and Central America.

In 1980 Air France, UTA and Air Inter flew 2,093m. tonne-km (excluding mail, 120m. tonne-km) and 34,130m. passenger-km (18m. passengers).

Shipping. French merchant ships of more than 100 tons, on 1 Oct. 1981, numbered 399 vessels of 10·58m. GRT.

Shipping (excluding fishing vessels) in foreign trade in 1979: Entered, 85,026 vessels and disembarked 259·2m. tonnes of imports and loaded 71·6m. tonnes of exports. Total cargo traffic 330·8m. tonnes.

In 1981 there were 8,623 km of navigable rivers, waterways and canals (of which 1,617 km accessible to vessels over 3,000 tons), with a total traffic of 83·6m. tonnes.

Post and Broadcasting. In 1977 the receipts on account of posts, telegraphs and telephones amounted to 56,275m. francs.

On 31 Dec. 1982 the telephone system (government-owned) had 26,940,296 subscribers; the Paris region (including the Paris and Seine-et-Marne, Yvelines, Essonne, Hauts-de-Seine, Seine-Saint-Denis, Val-de-Marne and Val-d'Oise departments) accounted for 4,153,586 in 1978.

Radio and television broadcasting was reorganized under the Act of 7 Aug. 1974 which replaced the Office de Radiodiffusion Télévision Française with 4 broadcasting companies, a production company and an audio-visual institute. Organization, development, operation and the maintenance of networks and installations became the responsibility of the Public Broadcasting Establishment. Radio programmes are broadcast from 298 transmitters (including 260 VHF) by 3 stations: *France Inter, France Musique* and *France Culture.* Television programmes are broadcast from 325 transmitters and 4,661 relay stations on 3 channels. There were about 19m. sets in use in 1981 (of which 8·9m. in colour).

Cinemas (1981). There were 4,532 cinemas with a seating capacity (1979) of 1,472,400; attendances totalled 187·6m.

Newspapers (1977). There were 69 daily papers published in the provinces with a circulation of 7·48m. copies, and 10 published in Paris with a national circulation of 3·05m. Among Paris dailies *France-Soir* sells 671,000; *Le Monde* 546,000; *Le Parisien Libéré* 474,000; *Le Figaro* 407,000, and *L'Aurore* 347,000. Among provincial dailies *Ouest-France* (Rennes) sells 749,000; *Le Progrès* (Lyon) 436,000; *La Voix du Nord* (Lille) 389,000; *Sud-Ouest* (Bordeaux) 383,000; *La Dauphine Libérée* (Grenoble) 362,000 and *Le Provençal* (Marseilles) 345,000.

JUSTICE, RELIGION, EDUCATION AND WELFARE

Justice. Since 1958, 470 *tribunaux d'instance* (11 in overseas departments), under a single judge each and with increased material and territorial jurisdiction, have replaced the former *juges de paix* (1 in each canton); and 181 *tribunaux de grande instance* (6 in overseas departments) have taken the place of the 357 *tribunaux de première instance* (1 in each *arrondissement*).

The *tribunaux de grande instance* usually have a collegiate composition, however a law dated 10 July 1970 has allowed them to administer justice under a single judge in some civil cases.

All petty offences (*contraventions*) are disposed of in the Police Courts (*Tribunaux de Police*) presided over by a Judge on duty in the *tribunal d'instance.* The Correctional Courts pronounce upon all graver offences (*délits*), including cases involving imprisonment up to 5 years. They have no jury, and consist of 3 judges who administer both criminal and civil justice. An Act of 29 Dec. 1972 established that there is only 1 judge; in some cases, the correctional courts may consist of a single judge each. In all cases of a *délit* or a *crime* the preliminary inquiry is made in secrecy by an examining magistrate (*juge d'instruction*), who either dismisses the case or sends it for trial before a court where a public prosecutor (*Procureur*) endeavours to prove the charge.

The Conciliation Boards (*Conseils des Prud'hommes*) composed of an equal number of employers and employees deal with labour disputes. Commercial litigation goes to the Commercial Courts (*Tribunaux de Commerce*) composed of tradesmen and manufacturers elected for 2 years. The judges hold office for 2 years and they can be re-elected; 3 years for the President.

When the decisions of any of these Tribunals are susceptible of appeal, the case goes to one of the 35 Courts of Appeal (*Cours d'Appel*), (including 3 in overseas departments and 2 in overseas territories), composed each of a president and a variable number of members.

The Courts of Assizes (*Cours d'Assises*), composed each of a president, assisted by 2 other magistrates who are members of the Courts of Appeal, and by a jury of 9 people, sit in every *département*, when called upon to try very important criminal cases. The decisions of the Courts of Appeal and the Courts of Assizes are final; however, the Court of Cassation (*Cour de Cassation*) has discretion to verify if the law has been correctly interpreted and if the rules of procedure have been followed exactly. The Court of Cassation may annul any judgment, and the cases have to be tried again by a Court of Appeal or a Court of Assizes.

The State Security Court, established in 1963, was abolished by law on 4 Aug. 1981. Capital punishment was abolished in the same month.

On 24 Jan. 1973 the first Ombudsman (*médiateur*) was appointed for a 6-year period.

The French penal institutions consist of: (1) *maisons d'arrêt* and *de correction*, where persons awaiting trial as well as those condemned to short periods of imprisonment are kept; (2) central prisons (*maisons centrales*) for those sentenced to long imprisonment; (3) special establishments, namely (*a*) schools for young adults, (*b*) hostels for old and disabled offenders, (*c*) hospitals for the sick and psychopaths, (*d*) institutions for recidivists. Special attention is being paid to classified treatment and the rehabilitation and vocational re-education of prisoners including work in open-air and semi-free establishments. There are 2 penal institutions for women.

Juvenile delinquents go before special judges and courts; they are sent to public or private institutions of supervision and re-education.

The population at 1 April 1983 of all penal establishments was 37,203 men and women.

Religion. No religion is officially recognized by the State. Under the law promulgated on 9 Dec. 1905, which separated Church and State, the adherents of all creeds are authorized to form associations for public worship (*associations culturelles*). The law of 2 Jan. 1907 provided that, failing *associations culturelles*, the buildings for public worship, together with their furniture, would continue at the disposition of the ministers of religion and the worshippers for the exercise of their religion; but in each case there was required an administrative act drawn up by the *préfet* as regards buildings belonging to the State or the departments and by the *maire* as regards buildings belonging to the communes.

There are 18 archbishops and 92 bishops of the Roman Catholic Church, with (1974) 43,557 clergy of various grades and 45·3m. church members. The Protestants of the Augsburg confession are, in their religious affairs, governed by a General Consistory, while the Reformed Church is under a Council of Administration, the seat of which is in Paris. In 1975 communicant Protestants numbered 750,000. There were (1978) about 2m. Moslems.

Education. The primary, secondary and higher state schools constitute the 'Université de France'. The Supreme Council of 84 members has deliberative, administrative and judiciary functions, and as a consultative committee advises respecting the working of the school system, the inspectors-general are in direct communication with the Minister. For local education administration France is divided into 25 academic areas, each of which has an Academic Council whose members include a certain number elected by the professors or teachers. The Academic Council deals with all grades of education. Each is under a Rector, and each is provided with academy inspectors, 1 for each department.

By decree of 6 Jan. 1959 the whole system of public instruction was reorganized and the structure of the Ministry of National Education has consequently been modified. A further Education Act was passed on 11 July 1975. Compulsory education is now provided for children of 6–16. The educational stages are as follows:

1. Non-compulsory pre-school instruction for children aged 2–5, to be given in infant schools or infant classes attached to primary schools.

2. Compulsory elementary instruction for children aged 6–11, to be given in primary schools and certain classes of the *lycées*. It consists of 3 courses: preparatory (1 year), elementary (2 years), intermediary (2 years). Physically or mentally handicapped children are cared for in special institutions or special classes of primary schools.

3. Lower secondary education (*Enseignement du premier cycle du Second Degré*) for pupils aged 11–15, consists of 4 years of study in the *lycées* (grammar schools), *Collèges d'Enseignement Secondaire* or *Collèges d'Enseignement Général*.

4. Upper secondary education (*Enseignement du second cycle du Second Degré*) for pupils aged 15–18:

    Long, *général* or *professionel* provided by the *lycées* and leading to the *baccalauréat* or to the *baccalauréat de technicien* after 3 years.

    Court, professional courses of 3, 2 and 1 year are taught in the *lycées d'enseignement professionel*, or the specialized sections of the *lycées*, CES or CEG.

The following table shows the various types of schools in 1981 and the numbers of enrolled pupils:

Description	State	Private	Total
Pre-primary	2,070,060	313,386	2,383,446
Primary	3,940,782	668,660	4,609,442
Secondary:			
First and second cycle	3,983,623	1,030,043	5,013,666
Specialized	233,296	8,728	242,024
Total	10,227,761	2,020,817	12,248,578

The state schools in 1978 had 64,676 nursery, 172,969 primary, 18,908 special school, 143,572 secondary and 44,624 secondary technical school and 65,797 grammar school (*lycée*) teachers.

Higher Instruction is supplied by the State in the universities and in special schools, and by private individuals in the free faculties and schools. The law of 12 July 1875 provided for higher education free of charge. This law was modified by that of 18 March 1880, which granted the state faculties the exclusive right to confer degrees. A decree of 28 Dec. 1885 created a general council of the faculties, and the creation of universities, each consisting of several faculties, was accomplished in 1897, in virtue of the law of 10 July 1896.

The law of 12 Nov. 1968 laying down future guidelines for higher education redefined the activities and working of universities. Bringing several disciplines together, 780 units for teaching and research (UER–Unités d'Enseignement et de Récherche) were formed which decided their own teaching activities, research programmes and procedures for checking the level of knowledge gained. They and the other parts of each university must respect the rules designed to maintain the national standard of qualifications.

The UERs form the basic units of the 62 Universities, 6 Universities Centres and 3 National Polytechnic Institutes, all of which have university status. They are grouped geographically into 25 *académies* with student populations in 1978–79 as follows:

Academie	1978–79	Academie	1978–79	Academie	1978–79
Aix-Marseille	47,292	Lille	39,375	Paris	224,655
Amiens	10,661	Limoges	7,668	Poitiers	13,026
Besançon	11,149	Lyon	50,720	Reims	12,528
Bordeaux	42,985	Montpellier	36,604	Rennes	33,262
Caen	12,490	Nancy-Metz	28,223	Rouen	12,775
Clermont	15,191	Nantes	26,219	Strasbourg	27,495
Créteil	24,599	Nice	19,030	Toulouse	45,211
Dijon	13,297	Orléans-Tours	18,746	Versailles	44,901
Grenoble	31,896				
				Total	849,998

The following table shows the number of students by faculties, for 5 years:

Students of	1974–75	1975–76	1976–77	1977–78	1978–79
Law and economics	178,215	183,566	182,533	184,361	183,592
Medicine and dentistry	146,912	154,660	159,874	160,900	160,917
Science	117,389	121,028	122,205	125,945	129,441
Letters	233,954	251,421	252,134	253,364	260,090
Pharmacy	31,599	33,510	33,474	34,821	36,014
Technology	41,949	43,526	44,243	47,398	50,237
Multi-discipline courses	4,843	18,527	21,818	25,329	29,707
Total	754,861	806,238	816,281	838,118	849,998

In 1978–79 there were also 99,000 students in preparatory classes leading to the Grandes Écoles, the Sections de Techniciens Supérieurs and other bodies; there were also 21,000 students in Écoles normales d'instituteurs.

The other higher institutions under the Ministry of Public Instruction are the Collège de France (founded by Francis I in 1530), which has courses of study bearing on various subjects (literature and language, archaeology, mathematical, natural science, psychology and social science, political economy, etc.); the

Museum of Natural History, giving instruction in science and natural history; the École Pratique de Hautes Études (history and philology, mathematical and physicochemical sciences, natural science, theology, economics and social science), having its seat at the Sorbonne; the École Normale Supérieure, which prepares teachers for secondary education and, since 1904, follows the curricula of the Sorbonne without special teachers of its own; the École des Chartes, which trains archivists and palaeographers; the École des Langues Orientales vivantes; the École du Louvre, devoted to art and archaeology; the Bureau des Longitudes, the central meteorological bureau; the Observatoire de Paris; and the French Schools at Athens, Rome, Cairo and South-East Asia.

Outside Paris there are 12 observatories (Meudon, Besançon, Bordeaux, etc.). The observatory at Nice belongs to the University of Paris.

There are free faculties in Paris (the Catholic Institute of Paris comprising theology and literary studies), Angers, Lille, Lyon and Toulouse.

Professional and Technical Instruction. The principal institutions of higher or technical instruction are: (*i*) The *Grandes Écoles* with 96,726 students in 1981, the Conservatoire des Arts et Métiers at Paris (with 20 evening courses on the applied sciences and social economy), the École Central des Arts et Manufactures (953 students in 1971–72), the École des Hautes Études Commerciales (803 students in 1972–73), 17 higher schools of commerce (4,461 pupils in 1969–70), under the Ministry of Public Instruction; (*ii*) the National Agronomic Institute at Paris, the veterinary school at Maisons-Alfort, Lyon and Toulouse, a school of forestry at Nancy, Écoles Nationales Supérieures Agronomiques at Grignon, Rennes, Montpellier, Nancy and Toulouse, 98 schools of agriculture, etc., under the Ministry of Agriculture; (*iii*) the École Supérieure de Guerre, the École Polytechnique, the military school at Coëtquidan (formerly St Cyr), the École d'Artillerie at Fontainebleau, the École de Cavalerie at Saumur and other schools under the Ministry of Defence; the Naval School at Brest under the Ministry of Marine; (*iv*) the School of Mines at Paris, the School of Civil Engineering at Paris, the School of Mines at St Etienne and the Schools of Miners at Alès and Douai with other schools under the Ministry of Public Works; (*v*) the École Nationale Supérieure des Beaux Arts, the École Nationale Supérieure des Arts Décoratifs and the Conservatoire de Musique et de Déclamation under the Department of Fine Arts, which is attached to the Ministry of Cultural Affairs. In the provinces there are national schools of fine arts, and schools of music, and several municipal schools, as well as free subventional schools, etc.

Health. On 1 Jan. 1981 there were 108,054 physicians, 37,820 pharmacists, 31,872 dentists, 249,450 nursing personnel and 8,479 midwives practising. On 1 Jan. 1982 there were 934 public hospitals (446,901 beds) excluding mental hospitals and 2,420 private hospitals (180,769 beds) including private mental homes.

Social Welfare. An order of 4 Oct. 1945 laid down the framework of a comprehensive plan of Social Security and created a single organization which superseded the various laws relating to social insurance, workmen's compensation, health insurance, family allowances, etc. All previous matters relating to Social Security are dealt with in the Social Security Code, 1956; this has been revised several times, and finally by orders laid down on 21 Aug. 1967, which were ratified on 31 July 1968. The Social Security general scheme covers all wage-earning workers in industry and commerce that are not covered by a special scheme of their own.

Contributions. All wage-earning workers or those of equivalent status are insured regardless of the amount or the nature of the salary or earnings. The funds for the general scheme are raised mainly from professional contributions, these being fixed within the limits of a ceiling (assessed at 68,760 francs per annum on 1 Jan. 1981) and calculated as a percentage of the salaries. The calculation of contributions payable for family allowances, old age and industrial injuries relates only to this amount; on the other hand, the amount payable for sickness, maternity expenses, disability and death is calculated partly within the limit of the 'ceiling' and partly on the whole salary. These contributions are the responsibility of both employer and employee, except in the case of family allowances or industrial injuries, where they are the sole responsibility of the employer.

Contributions and benefits paid in 1982 (in 1 m. francs) were:

	Contributions	Benefits
Health service	260,300	254,900
Old age pensions	123,900	125,000
Family benefits	103,000	114,900

Self-employed Workers. From 17 Jan. 1948 allowances and old-age pensions were paid to self-employed workers by independent insurance funds set up within their own profession, trade or business. Schemes of compulsory insurance for sickness were instituted in 1961 for farmers and in 1966, with modifications in 1970, for other non-wage-earning workers.

Social Insurance. The orders laid down in Aug. 1967 ensure that the whole population can benefit from the Social Security Scheme; at present all elderly persons who have been engaged in the professions, as well as the surviving spouse, are entitled to claim an old-age benefit; 98% of the population, both working and retired, are covered by a compulsory scheme of insurance for sickness, the remaining 2% who are not covered by a compulsory insurance scheme have been able to participate in a voluntary scheme since 1967; the whole population benefit from the legislation regarding family allowances.

Sickness Insurance refunds the costs of treatment required by the insured, of the needs of his wife, of children under 16 and a half who are in his care and not earning, under 18 who are apprenticed, under 20 who are still studying or who cannot work on account of some chronic illness or infirmity, as well as relations older or younger or of similar age living under the same roof who are engaged exclusively in domestic duties and in the education of at least 2 children under 14. A decree of 12 Oct. 1976 laid down conditions on which students of 20 or over at public or private educational institutions, who do not benefit from a social security scheme in their own right, are guaranteed insurance benefits for sickness or maternity, holding their parents entitlement until the end of the academic year in which they attain their 21st birthday, provided they have proof that their studies have been interrupted by illness. The general principles relating to medical care consist of: a free choice by the patient of his doctor, his pharmaceutical chemist, his place of treatment, etc.; the medical practitioner is granted freedom of prescription. Reimbursement is not as a rule made in full; the insured person usually pays between 10% and 30% of the legal rate except in cases of exemption. The insured who is recognized as medically unfit for work receives daily allowances equal to half of the wage which has been used to calculate the contributions, or to two-thirds of this if the person has 3 or more children. These allowances may be paid for 3 years, plus 1 additional year if the insured undergoes re-adaptation treatment or takes up fresh vocational training.

Maternity Insurance covers the costs of medical treatment relating to the pregnancy, confinement and lying-in period; the beneficiaries being the insured person or the spouse. The daily allowances are equal to 90% of the salary on which contributions were calculated.

Insurance for Invalids is divided into 3 categories: (1) those who are capable of working; (2) those who cannot work; (3) those who, in addition, are in need of the help of another person. According to the category, the pension rate varies from 30 to 50% of the average salary for the last 10 years, with additional allowance for home help for the third category.

Old-age Pensions for workers were introduced in 1910 and are now fixed by the Social Security Code of 28 Jan. 1972. Since 1975 people who have paid insurance for at least 37½ years (150 quarters) receive at 60 a pension equal to 25% of basic annual salary, to be increased by 1·25% of the basic salary for every quarter that realization is deferred; thus at 65 the pension rate is equal to 50% of basic salary. People who have paid insurance for less than 37½ years but no less than 15 years can expect a pension equal to as many 1/150ths of the full pension as their quarterly payments justify. In the event of death of the insured person, the husband or wife of the deceased person receives half the pension received by the latter. Compulsory supplementary schemes ensure benefits additional to the old-age pensions.

Family Allowances. The system comprises: (*a*) Family allowances proper, equivalent to 25·5% of the basic monthly salary (1,246 francs) for 2 dependent children, 46% for the third child, 41% for the fourth child, and 39% for the fifth and each subsequent child; a supplement equivalent to 9% of the basic monthly salary for the second and each subsequent dependent child more than 10 years old and 16% for each dependent child over 15 years. (*b*) Family supplement (519 francs) for persons with at least 3 children or one child aged less than 3 years. (*c*) Antenatal grants. (*d*) Maternity grant equal to 260% of basic salary; increase for multiple births or adoptions, 198%; increase for birth or adoption of third or subsequent child, 457%. (*e*) Allowance for specialized education of handicapped children. (*f*) Allowance for orphans. (*g*) Single parent allowance. (*h*) Allowance for opening of school term. (*i*) Allowance for accommodation, under certain circumstances. (*j*) Minimum family income for those with at least 3 children. Allowances (*b*), (*g*), (*h*) and (*j*) only apply to those whose annual income falls below a specified level.

Workmen's Compensation. The law passed by the National Assembly on 30 Oct. 1946 forms part of the Social Security Code and is administered by the Social Security Organization. Employers are invited to take preventive measures. The application of these measures is supervised by consulting engineers (assessors) of the local funds dealing with sickness insurance, who may compel employers who do not respect these measures to make additional contributions; they may, in like manner, grant rebates to employers who have in operation suitable preventive measures. The injured person receives free treatment, the insurance fund reimburses the practitioners, hospitals and suppliers chosen freely by the injured. In cases of temporary disablement the daily payments are equal to half the total daily wage received by the injured. In case of permanent disablement the injured person receives a pension, the amount of which varies according to the degree of disablement and the salary received during the past 12 months.

A law promulgated on 11 Oct. 1946 has created a medical labour service of doctors who hold a diploma of 'industrial health specialists'. These doctors are entrusted with the control of hygiene and health matters in all industrial undertakings or groups of undertakings. In addition, it is the duty of this medical service to examine wage-earners when they are engaged, to carry out periodical medical examinations and to ensure the application of the existing rules relating to safety in work.

Unemployment Benefits vary according to circumstances (full or partial unemployment) which are means-tested. Since 1926 unemployment benefits have been paid from public funds. Full unemployment benefit amounts to 13·50 francs per day for the head of the family and 5·40 francs for the spouse or a dependent person. After 3 months the payment is reduced to 12·40 francs.

A collective agreement signed on 31 Dec. 1958 between the national council of employers and certain trade unions has established a system of special allowances for totally unemployed workers in industry and trade. The costs are shared by employers (2·76% of wages) and employees (0·84%) and the benefits vary according to circumstances. The system is now governed by the law of 16 Jan. 1979. A similar agreement of 21 Feb. 1968 extends the system to partial unemployment.

Social Security in France. I.N.S.E.E., 1970
Questions de Sécurité Sociale. Paris, 1970

DIPLOMATIC REPRESENTATIVES

Of France in Great Britain (58 Knightsbridge, London, SW1X 7JT)
Ambassador: Emmanuel de Margerie (accredited 27 March 1981).

Of Great Britain in France (35 rue du Faubourg St Honoré, Paris)
Ambassador: Sir John Fretwell, KCMG.

Of France in the USA (2535 Belmont Rd., NW, Washington, D.C., 20008)
Ambassador: Bernard Vernier-Palliez.

Of the USA in France (2 Ave. Gabriel, Paris)
Ambassador: Evan G. Galbraith.

Of France to the United Nations
Ambassador: Luc de la Barre de Nanteuil.

Books of Reference

Statistical Information: The Institut national de la Statistique et des Études économiques (18, Boulevard Adolphe Pinard, 75014 Paris) is the central office of statistics. It was established by a law of 27 April 1946, which amalgamated the Service National des Statistiques (created in 1941 by merging the Direction de la Statistique générale de la France and the Service de la Démographie) with the Institut de Conjoncture (set up in 1938) and some statistical services of the Ministry of National Economy. The Institut comprises the following departments: Metropolitan statistics, Overseas statistics, Market research and economic studies, Documentation, Research statistics and economics, Informatics, Foreign Economic Studies.

The main publications of the Institut include:

Annuaire statistique de la France (from 1878)
Annuaire statistique des Territoires d'Outre-Mer (from 1959)
Bulletin mensuel de statistique (monthly)
Documentation économique (bi-monthly)
Données statistiques africaines et Malgaches (quarterly)
Economie et Statistique (monthly)
Tableaux de l'Economie Française (biennially, from 1956)
Tendances de la Conjoncture (monthly)

Bonnefous, E., Duroselle, J. B., and Gerbet, P., *L'année politique, économique, sociale et diplomatique en France.* Paris, 1970
Caron, F., *An Economic History of Modern France.* London, 1979
Coffey, P., *The Social Economy of France.* London, 1973
Crozier, M., *A Strategy for Change: The Future of French Society.* MIT Press, 1982
Dyer, C., *Population and Society in Twentieth Century France.* London, 1978
Hoffman, S., *Decline or Renewal? France Since the 1930's.* New York, 1973
Ouston, P. A., *France in the Twentieth Century.* London, 1972
Peyrefitte, A., *The Trouble with France,* New York, 1981
Tuppen, J. N., *France.* Folkestone, 1981

OVERSEAS DEPARTMENTS

GUADELOUPE

HISTORY. Discovered by Columbus in Nov. 1493, the two main islands were then known as *Karukera* (Isle of Beautiful Waters) to the Carib inhabitants, who resisted Spanish attempts to colonize. A French colony was established on 28 June 1635, and apart from short periods of occupancy by British forces, Guadeloupe has since remained a French possession. On 19 March 1946 the status of Guadeloupe was changed to that of an Overseas Department; in 1973 it additionally became an administrative region.

AREA AND POPULATION. Guadeloupe consists of a group of islands in the Lesser Antilles. The two main islands, Basse-Terre to the west and Grande-Terre to the east, are separated by a narrow channel, called Rivière Salée. Adjacent to these are the islands of Marie Galante *(Ceyre* to the Caribs) to the south-east, La Désirade to the east, and the Îles des Saintes to the south. The islands of St Martin and St Barthélemy lie 250 km to the north-west.

	Area in sq. km	Census 1974	Census 1982	Chief town
St Martin[1]	54	6,191	8,072	Marigot
St Barthélemy	21	2,491	3,059	Gustavia
Basse-Terre	848	135,746	141,313	Basse-Terre
Grande-Terre	585	159,424	157,696	Pointe-à-Pitre
Îles des Saintes	14	3,084	2,901	Terre-de-Bas
La Désirade	22	1,682	1,602	Grande Anse
Marie-Galante	158	15,912	13,757	Grand-Bourg
	1,702	324,530	328,400	

[1] Northern part only; the southern third belongs to the Netherlands.

Population (estimate, 1982) 328,400. The vast majority are black or mulatto, but the populations of St Barthélemy and Les Saintes are still mainly descended from 17th-century Breton and Norman settlers. French is the official language, but a Creole dialect is also widely used.

The seat of government is Basse-Terre (13,656 inhabitants) at the south-west end of that island but the largest towns are Pointe-à-Pitre (25,310 inhabitants), the economic centre with a large commercial harbour, and its suburb Abymes (53,165).

Vital statistics (1982): Births, 6,657; deaths, 2,115.

GOVERNMENT. Guadeloupe is under an appointed Commissioner, an elected *Conseil Général* of 36 members (assisted by an Economic and Social Committee of 40 members) and an elected regional council of 41 members. It is represented in the National Assembly by 3 deputies, in the Senate by 2 senators and on the Economic and Social Council by 2 councillors. There are 3 *arrondissements,* sub-divided into 34 communes, each administered by an elected municipal council.

Commissioner: Robert Miguet.
President of the Conseil Général: Lucette Michaux-Chevry.

ECONOMY

Budget. The budget for 1982 balanced at 1,196,207,767 francs.

Banking. The Banque des Antilles Françaises (founded 1853), with a capital of 32,583,000 francs and reserve funds amounting to 1·44m. francs, advances loans chiefly for agricultural purposes; it has 6 branches in the department. The Banque Populaire de la Guadeloupe has a capital of 5m. francs and 6 branches in the department. The Banque Nationale de Paris has 12 branches in the department, the Crédit Agricole 25, the Banque Française Commerciale 7, and the Société Generale de Banque aux Antilles and the Chase Manhattan Bank 1 each. The Caisse Centrale de Coopération économique is the official banking institution of the department, enjoying the privilege of issuing bank-notes. Silver coin has disappeared from circulation.

ENERGY AND NATURAL RESOURCES

Electricity. Production in 1982 totalled 394,972,000 kwh.

Agriculture. Chief products (1982) are bananas (165,000 tonnes), sugar (868,357 tonnes), rum (92,172 hectolitres of pure alcohol), vegetables (46,586 tonnes), fruit (3,115 tonnes), flowers (no.) 8,505,000.
Livestock (1982): Cattle, 82,113; goats, 28,918; sheep, 3,768; pigs, 36,300.

Forestry. In 1982, 421 cu. metres of wood were produced.

Fisheries. The catch in 1982 was 8,362 tonnes; crustacea (120 tonnes), shell fish (300 tonnes), turtles (20 tonnes).

COMMERCE. Trade for 1982 (in 1m. francs) was imports 4,117 and exports 548·4. In 1982, 62·5% of imports were from France, while 67·8% of exports went to France and 18% to Martinique; bananas formed 50·69% of the exports and sugar 17·47%. St Martin and St Barthélemy are free ports.

There are Chambers of Commerce and Industry at Basse-Terre and Pointe-à-Pitre. There is a British consular agent at Pointe-à-Pitre.

Tourism. In 1982 there were 337,500 tourists.

COMMUNICATIONS

Roads. In 1982 there were 2,059 km of roads of which 330 km were national roads. There were 87,785 passenger cars and 33,350 commercial vehicles in 1981.

Aviation. Air France and 7 other airlines call at Guadeloupe. In 1982 there were 48,480 arrivals and departures of aircraft and 1,177,489 passengers at Raizet (Pointe-à-Pitre) airport making it the sixth most frequented French airport.

Shipping. Guadeloupe is in direct communication with France by means of 12 steam navigation companies. In 1982, 1,159 vessels arrived to disembark 31,078 passengers and 1,074,660 tonnes of freight and to embark 30,646 passengers and 426,535 tonnes of freight.

Post and Broadcasting. In 1982 there were 47 post offices and 47,247 telephones. ORTF broadcasts for 17 hours a day in French and television broadcasts for 6 hours a day. There were (1977) 13,979 radio and (1981) 32,886 TV receivers.

Newspapers. There was (1982) 1 daily newspaper *(France-Antilles)* with a circulation of 25,000.

JUSTICE, RELIGION, EDUCATION AND WELFARE

Justice. There are 4 *tribunaux d'instance* and 2 *tribunaux de grande instance* at Basse-Terre and Pointe-à-Pitre; there is also a court of appeal and a court of assizes at Basse-Terre.

Religion. The majority of the population are Roman Catholic.

Education. In 1982 there were 61,511 pupils at pre-primary schools and primary schools and 45,876 at secondary schools. The *University Antilles-Guyane* had 4,600 students in 1982–83, of which Guadeloupe itself had 1,719.

Health. The medical services in 1983 included 12 public hospitals (2,974 beds), 15 private clinics (1,261 beds) and 42 dispensaries. There were 418 physicians, 80 dentists, 127 pharmacists, 76 midwives and 1,196 nursing personnel.

Books of Reference

Information: Office du Tourisme du départemente, Point-à-Pitre. *Director:* Eric W. Rotin.
Lasserre, G., *La Guadeloupe, étude géographique.* 2 vols. Bordeaux, 1961

GUIANA

Guyane Française

HISTORY. A French settlement on the island of Cayenne was established in 1604 and the territory between the Maroni and Oyapock rivers finally became a French possession in 1817. Convicts settlements were established from 1852, that on off-shore Devil's Island being most notorious; all were closed by 1945. On 19 March 1946 the status of Guiana was changed to that of an Overseas Department.

AREA AND POPULATION. French Guiana is situated on the north-east coast of South America, and has an area of about 83,533 sq. km (32,252 sq. miles) and a population at the 1982 Census of 73,022, of whom 4,500 are tribal Indians. Cayenne, the chief town, has a population of (1982) 38,135. These figures are exclusive of the floating population of miners, officials and troops.

Vital statistics (1981): Live births, 2,081; deaths, 417.

GOVERNMENT. French Guiana is administered by an appointed Commissioner and an elected *Conseil Général* of 16 members and a Regional Council of 31 members. It is represented in the National Assembly by 1 deputy and in the Senate by 1 senator. There are 2 *arrondissements* (Cayenne and Saint-Laurent-du-Maroni) sub-divided into 20 communes.

Commissioner: Claude Silberzahn.
President of the Conseil Général: Emmanuel Bellony.
President of the Conseil Régional: Georges Othily.

ECONOMY

Budget. The budget for 1982 balanced at 578m. francs, excluding duplicated items and national expenditure.

Banking. The Bank of Guiana has a capital of 10m. francs and reserve fund of 2·39m. francs. Loans totalled 206m. francs in 1981. Other banks include Bank National of Paris-Guyane and Banc Française Commerciale.

ENERGY AND NATURAL RESOURCES

Electricity. Production in 1981 totalled 97m. kwh.

Agriculture. The country has immense forests (about 80,000 sq. km) rich in many kinds of timber. Only 10,436 hectares are under cultivation. The crops (1981, in tonnes) consist of rice (983, 1983), maize (280), manioc (7,650), bananas (680) and sugar-cane (7,900, 1983) as well as a large variety of other fruits, vegetables and spices (3,000 tonnes, 1983).

Livestock (1982): 9,290 cattle, 9,000 swine and 100,000 poultry.

Fisheries. The fishing fleet for shrimps comprises 59 US, 22 Japanese and 11 French boats. The catch in 1982 totalled 4,503 tonnes, of which shrimps comprised 3,000 tonnes, exports 2,750 tonnes. Production of *Macrobrachium Rosenbergii* (an edible river shrimp) is now established.

COMMERCE. Trade in 1,000 tonnes and 1m. francs:

	1980		1981		1982	
	Quantity	Value	Quantity	Value	Quantity	Value
Imports	859·7	1,087	222·6	1,355	261·1	1,643
Exports	54·0	108	32·7	192	30·3	212

In 1981, 15% of imports came from Trinidad and Tobago, 53% from France and 10% from the USA, while 54% of exports went to the USA, 17% to Japan and 15% to France. In 1980, shrimps formed 36% of exports.

Total trade between Guiana and UK (British Department of Trade returns, in £1,000 sterling):

	1979	1980	1981	1982	1983
Imports to UK	24	117	844	1,956	853
Exports and re-exports from UK	1,213	1,264	7,117	6,840	897

COMMUNICATIONS

Roads. Three chief and some secondary roads connect the capital with most of the coastal area by motor-car services. There are (1981) 321 km of national and 269 km of departmental roads. Connexions with the interior are made by waterways which, despite rapids, are navigable by local craft.

Aviation. Air France calls at Cayenne (Rochambeau Airport) 4 times a week, Air Suriname Airways and Cruseiro do Sul once a week; Air Guyane services interior connexions. In 1981, about 150,000 passengers and 3,600 tonnes of freight passed through the airport.

Shipping. The chief ports are: Cayenne, St-Laurent-du-Maroni and Kourou. Dégrad des Cannes, the port of Cayenne is visited regularly by ships of the Compagnie Général Maritime, the Compagnie Maritime des Chargeurs Réunis and Marseille Fret. In 1981, 594 arrivals and departures of vessels were registered in French Guiana (113,219 tonnes of petroleum products arrived and 165,140 tonnes of other freight arrived and departed).

Post and Broadcasting. An automatic telephone system connects Cayenne with 10 other communes as well as with Europe and most parts of North and South America. Number of telephones (1983), 13,755. There are wireless stations at Cayenne, Oyapoc, Régina, St-Laurent-du-Maroni and numerous other locations.

RFO-Guyane (Guiana Radio) broadcasts for 116 hours each week on medium- and short-waves and FM in French. Television is broadcast for 43 hours each week on 7 transmitters. In 1980 there were 35,000 radio and 9,063 TV receivers.

Newspapers. There was (1983) 1 daily newspaper *'Presse de la Guyane)* with a circulation of 1,000, a bi-weekly paper *(France-Guyane)* with a circulation of 3,200 and a weekly *(Debout Guyane)*.

JUSTICE, RELIGION, EDUCATION AND WELFARE

Justice. At Cayenne there is a *tribunal d'instance* and a *tribunal de grande instance*, from which appeal is to the regional *cour d'appel* in Martinique.

Religion. The majority of the population is Roman Catholic.

Education. Primary education has been free since 1889 in lay schools for the two sexes in the communes and many villages. In 1981 public primary schools had 580 teachers and 11,953 pupils, the *lycées* and *collèges d'enseignement secondaire*, 510 teachers and 7,277 pupils. Private schools had 119 teachers and 2,528 pupils. The *Institut Henri Visioz* forms part of the *Université des Antilles-Guyane*.

Health. There were (1981) 80 physicians, 14 dentists, 18 pharmacists, 16 midwives and 309 nursing personnel. In 1980 there were 5 hospitals with 907 beds and 3 private clinics.

Books of Reference

Abonnec, A., Hurrault, J., Saban, R., *Bibliographie de la Guyane Française.* 2 vols. Paris, 1957
Henry, *Guyane Française, son histoire 1604–1946.* Cayenne
Hurrault, J., *Guide du voyageur en Guyane.* Paris, 1949
Masse, D., *La Guyane Française: Histoire, Géographie, Possibilités.* Abbeville, 1978

MARTINIQUE

HISTORY. Discovered by Columbus in 1493, the island was known to its inhabitants as *Madinina*, from which its present name was corrupted. A French colony was established in 1635 and, apart from brief periods of British occupation, has since remained under French control. On 19 March 1946 its status was altered to that of an Overseas Department.

AREA AND POPULATION. The island, situated in the Lesser Antilles between Dominica and St Lucia, occupies an area of 1,079 sq. km (417 sq. miles). The total population, 1982 Census was 328,566, of whom 99,844 lived in Fort-de-France, the capital and chief commercial town, which has a landlocked harbour nearly 40 sq. km in extent.

French is the official language, but the majority of the population use a Creole dialect.

Vital statistics (1981): Live births 5,397; deaths 2,040.

GOVERNMENT. The department is administered by an appointed Commissioner and an elected *Conseil Général* of 36 members. The region is administered by a regional general council of 41 members. There are 3 *arrondissements*, sub-divided into 34 communes, each administered by an elected municipal council. Martinique is represented in the National Assembly by 3 deputies, in the Senate by 2 senators and on the Economic and Social Council by 2 councillors.

Commissioner: Jean Chevance.
President of the Conseil Général: Émile Maurice.

ECONOMY

Budget. The budget, 1981, included revenue of 906m. francs and expenditure of 3,816m. francs.

Banking. The Institut d'Émission des Départements d'Outre-mer is the official bank of the department. The Caisse Centrale de Coopération économique is used by the Government in assisting the economic development of the department.

The Banque des Antilles Françaises (with a capital of 10·8m. francs), the Crédit Martiniquais (11·4m. francs), branches of the Banque Nationale de Paris (22·6m. francs), Crédit Agricole, The Chase Manhattan Bank, Société Générale de Banque and Banque Française Commerciale are operating at Fort-de-France.

ENERGY AND NATURAL RESOURCES

Electricity. Production in 1981 totalled 315m. kwh.

Agriculture. Bananas, sugar and rum are the chief products, followed by pineapples, food and vegetables. In 1981 there were 4,546 hectares under sugar-cane, 7,215 hectares under bananas and 625 hectares under pineapples. Production (1982): Sugar, 2,002 tonnes; industrial rum, 16,569 hectolitres; agricultural rum, 79,967 hectolitres; cane for sugar, 59,047 tonnes; cane for rum, 124,986 tonnes.

Livestock (1982): 57,000 cattle, 54,000 sheep, 40,000 pigs, 24,000 goats and 2,000 horses.

COMMERCE. Trade in 1m. francs:

	1979	1980	1981	1982
Imports	2,870	3,523	4,142	4,943
Exports	567	554	977	1,016

In 1980 the main items of import were foodstuffs; main items of export were petroleum products (45%), bananas (21%) and rum (11%); 63% of imports came from France and 52% of exports went to France and 39% to Guadeloupe.

Total trade of the French West Indian Islands with UK (British Department of Trade returns, in £1,000 sterling):

	1979	1980	1981	1982	1983
Imports to UK	21	578	295	34	35
Exports and re-exports from UK	2,539	2,588	2,268	2,400	3,029

The Chamber of Commerce and Industry administers the port, airport and industrial zones.

Tourism. In 1981 there were 141,000 tourists.

COMMUNICATIONS

Roads. In 1983 there were 7 km of motorway, 260 km of national roads, 618 km of district roads and 980 km of local roads. In 1982 there were 8,734 passenger cars and 1,915 commercial vehicles registered.

Aviation. In 1982, 763,960 passengers arrived and departed by air.

Shipping. The island is visited regularly by French and American steamers. In 1982, 1,650 vessels called at Martinique.

Post and Broadcasting. There were, in 1978, 44 post offices and, 1982, 41,121 telephones. Radio-telephone service to Europe is available. In 1981 there were 45,000 radio and 39,570 TV receivers.

Newspapers. In 1981 there was 1 daily newspaper with a circulation of 30,000.

JUSTICE, RELIGION, EDUCATION AND WELFARE

Justice. Justice is administered by 2 *tribunaux d'instance*, a *tribunal de grande instance*, a regional court of appeal, a commercial court, a court of assizes and an administrative court.

Religion. The majority of the population is Roman Catholic.

Education. Education is compulsory between the ages of 6 and 16 years. In 1982–83, there were 57,132 pupils in primary schools, and 45,603 pupils in secondary and technical schools. The *Institut Henri Visioz*, which forms part of the *Centre Universitaire Antilles-Guyane*, had (1978) 2,100 students of law, politics and economics.

Health. There were (1982) 18 hospitals with 3,973 beds and in 1980 there were 364 physicians, 138 pharmacists, 120 midwives and 101 dentists.

Books of Reference

Annuaire statistique I.N.S.E.E. 1977–80. Martinique, 1982
La Martinique en quelques chiffres. Martinique, 1982
Guide Economique des D.O.M.-T.O.M., Paris, 1982

MAYOTTE

HISTORY. Mayotte was a French colony from 1843 until 1914, when it was attached, with the other Comoro islands, to the government-general of Madagascar. The Comoro group was granted administrative autonomy within the French Republic and became an Overseas Territory.

When the other 3 islands voted to become independent (as the Comoro state) in 1974, Mayotte voted against this and remained a French dependency. In 1976, it became (following a further referendum) a *collectivité territoriale*, being an intermediate status between Overseas Territory and Overseas Department.

AREA AND POPULATION. Mayotte, east of the Comoro Islands, has an area of 374 sq. km (144 sq. miles) and a 1978 Census population of 47,246 (1982, estimate, 53,000). The main towns are Mamoundzou (7,800) and the capital, Dzaoudzi (4,147 inhabitants) situated on a tiny offshore islet. The main languages are Mahorian (a Swahili dialect) and French.

GOVERNMENT. The island is administered by an appointed Commissioner and an elected *Conseil Général* of 17 members. Mayotte is represented by 1 deputy in the National Assembly and by 1 member in the Senate.

Commissioner: Christian Pellerin.
President of the Conseil Général: Younoussa Bamana.

ECONOMY

Budget. The budget for 1982 balanced at 144·3m. French francs.

Currency. In Feb. 1976 the currency was changed from the *franc CFA* to the (metropolitan) *French franc.*

NATURAL RESOURCES

Agriculture. The main products are vanilla, ylang-ylang, coffee and copra.

Fisheries. A lobster and shrimp industry has recently been created. Annual catch is about 2,000 tonnes.

COMMERCE. In 1982, exports totalled 5·1m. francs (81% to France) and imports 121·7m. francs (57% from France). Total trade between Mayotte and UK (1982): Imports to UK, £26,000 and exports and re-exports from UK, £771,000.

COMMUNICATIONS

Roads. In 1982 there were 96 km of main roads (72 km bitumenized) and 120 km of local roads, with about 1,300 motor vehicles.

Aviation. In 1981, 7,458 passengers and 739 tonnes of freight arrived by air and 9,100 passengers (314 tonnes) departed.

JUSTICE, RELIGION AND EDUCATION

Justice. There is a *tribunal d'instance* and a *tribunal supérieur d'appel.*

Religion. The population is 99% Moslem, with a small Christian (mainly Roman Catholic) minority.

Education. In 1982 there were 11,338 pupils and 317 teachers in primary schools and 794 pupils and 40 teachers in secondary and technical schools.

RÉUNION

HISTORY. Réunion became a French possession in 1638 and remained so until 19 March 1946, when its status was altered to that of an Overseas Department; in 1972 it additionally became part of an administrative region.

AREA AND POPULATION. Réunion (or Bourbon), about 569 miles east of Madagascar, has an area of 2,511·6 sq. km (968·5 sq. miles) and population of 515,814 (March 1982 census). The capital is Saint-Denis (1982 census) 109,072, (1983 estimate) 110,000.

Vital statistics (1982): Live births, 11,927; deaths, 3,120.

The small islands of Juan de Nova, Europa, Bassas da India, Îles Glorieuses and Tromelin, with a combined area of about 60 sq. km, are all uninhabited and lie at various points in the Indian Ocean adjacent to Madagascar. They remained integral parts of the French Republic after Madagascar's independence in 1960, and are now administered by Réunion. Both Mauritius and the Seychelles have laid claim to Tromelin (which had been transferred by the UK from the Seychelles to France in 1954), and Madagascar to all 5 islands.

GOVERNMENT. The region is under a Commissioner, an elected *Conseil Général* of 36 members and an elected Regional Council of 45 members. Réunion is represented in the National Assembly by 3 deputies, in the Senate by 2 senators, and in the Economic and Social Council by 1 councillor. There are 4 *arrondissements*, sub-divided into 24 communes each administered by an elected municipal council.

Commissioner: Michel Levallois.
President of the Conseil Général: Auguste Legros.

ECONOMY

Budget. The budget for 1982 balanced at 6,366·3m. French francs.

Banking. The Institut d'émission des Départements d'Outre-mer has the right to issue bank-notes. Banks operating in Réunion are the Banque de la Réunion (Crédit Lyonnais), the Banque Nationale de Paris Internationale, the Caisse Régionale de Crédit Agricole Mutuel de la Réunion, the Banque Française Commerciale (BFC) and the Banque Populaire Fédérale de Développement.

NATURAL RESOURCES

Agriculture (1982). The chief produce is sugar (258,279 tonnes), rum (62,843 hectolitres), maize (12,180 tonnes), potatoes (4,280 tonnes), onions (141,000 tonnes), vanilla, essences and tobacco. The forests occupy about 88,430 hectares.

Livestock (1982): 18,910 cattle, 71,400 swine, 2,900 sheep, 42,900 goats and 2,809,000 poultry.

Fisheries. In 1982 the catch was 2,792 tonnes.

INDUSTRY AND TRADE

Industry (1982). Total number of workers (in 418 firms employing 10 or more) 19,242. The sugar industry employed 1,339.

Commerce. Trade in 1m. French francs:

	1977	1978	1979	1980	1981	1982
Imports	2,412	2,659	3,230	3,749	4,282	5,304
Exports	561	519	594	554	573	668

The chief export is sugar, forming (1982) 77·7% by value. In 1982 (by value) 62·1% of imports were from, and 76% (1981) of exports to, France.

Total trade between Réunion and UK (British Department of Trade returns, in £1,000 sterling):

	1979	1980	1981	1982	1983
Imports to UK	7,855	60	290	74	73
Exports and re-exports from UK	2,296	3,022	3,117	2,889	3,684

COMMUNICATIONS

Roads. There were, in 1982, 2,680 km of roads. There were 108,725 passenger cars and 50,000 other vehicles in 1982.

Aviation. Air France maintains an air service 6 times a week. In 1982, 185,064 passengers and 6,224 tonnes of freight arrived and 186,302 passengers and 2,430 tonnes of freight departed at Saint-Denis-Gillot airport.

Shipping. Four shipping lines serve the island. In 1982, 383 vessels visited the island to discharge 978,000 tonnes of freight and 386 passengers, and load 319,000 tonnes of freight and 324 passengers at Pointe-des-Galets.

Post and Broadcasting. There are telephone and telegraph connexions with Mauritius, Madagascar and metropolitan France. There are 38 post offices and a central telephone office; number of telephones (1983), 55,000.

France Régions 3 broadcast in French on medium- and short-waves for more than 18 hours a day. There is 1 television programme *via* 14 transmitters for 21 hours a week. In 1983 there were about 100,000 radio and 87,000 TV receivers.

Newspapers. There were (1982) 3 daily newspapers with a combined circulation of 57,500.

JUSTICE, RELIGION, EDUCATION AND WELFARE

Justice. There are 3 *tribunaux d'instance*, 2 *tribunaux de grande instance*, 1 *Cour d'Appel*, 1 *tribunal administratif* and 2 *conseils de prud'homme*.

Religion. The vast majority of the population is Roman Catholic.

Education. Réunion had (1983) 6 *lycées*, 50 *collèges*, and 9 *lycées d'enseignement technique* with 66,653 pupils and 13 private secondary schools with 3,407 pupils. Primary education is given in 333 public schools with 4,630 teachers and 106,437 pupils; and in 28 private schools, with 333 teachers, and 8,827 pupils. The *Université Française de l'Océan Indien* (founded 1971) had 2,420 students in 1982.

Health. In 1982 there were 21 hospitals with 4,183 beds; in 1982 there were 608 physicians, 160 dentists, 156 pharmacists, 82 midwives and 1,609 nursing personnel.

Books of Reference

Bulletin de l'Académie de la Réunion. Biennial
Bulletin de la Chambre d'Agriculture de la Réunion
Panorama de l'Economie de la Reunion. 1983
Statistiques et Indicateurs Economiques. 1983

ST PIERRE AND MIQUELON

HISTORY. The tiny remaining fragment of the once extensive French possessions in North America, the archipelago was settled from France in the 17th century and finally became a French territory from 1816 until July 1976, when its status was altered to that of an Overseas Department.

AREA AND POPULATION. The department consists of 8 small islands off the south coast of Newfoundland, with a total area of 242 sq. km, comprising the Saint-Pierre group (26 sq. km) and the Miquelon-Langlade group (216 sq. km). The population (census, 1982) was 6,041 of whom 5,415 were on Saint-Pierre and 626 on Miquelon. The chief town is St Pierre.

Vital statistics (1982): Births, 127; marriages, 33; deaths, 44.

GOVERNMENT. The department is administered by an appointed Commissioner and an elected *Conseil Général* of 14 members, directly elected for a 6-year term; it is represented in the National Assembly by 1 deputy, in the Senate by 1 senator and in the Economic and Social Council by 1 councillor.

Commissioner: Gerard Lefebvre.
President of the Conseil Général: Marc Plantegenest.

BUDGET. The ordinary budget for 1982 balanced at 51·4m. francs.

INDUSTRY AND TRADE

Industry. The islands, being mostly barren rock, are unsuited for agriculture. The chief industry is fishing.

Commerce. Trade in 1,000 tonnes and 1,000 francs:

	1980		1981		1982	
	Quantity	*Value*	*Quantity*	*Value*	*Quantity*	*Value*
Imports	47·7	177,203	58·6	220,910	58·6	275,390
Exports	4·3	24,213	4·9	38,658	3·6	41,045

The imports comprise textiles, salt, wines, coal, petrol, foodstuffs, meat; and the exports (in 1982), dried and salted fish (213 tonnes); frozen and smoked fish (2,588 tonnes); fish meal (877 tonnes). In 1981, 66% of imports came from Canada and 28% from France, while 58% of exports were to USA, 17% to France and 11% to UK.

Total trade between St Pierre and Miquelon and UK (British Department of Trade returns in £1,000 sterling):

	1979	1980	1981	1982	1983
Imports to UK	224	3	1,352	254	578
Exports and re-exports from UK	435	884	481	363	250

Tourism. There were (1982) 11,293 visitors.

COMMUNICATIONS

Roads. In 1982 there were 108 km of roads, of which 43 km were paved. In 1981 there were about 1,637 passenger cars and 531 commercial vehicles.

Aviation. Air Saint-Pierre connects the department with Halifax and Sydney (Nova Scotia), and there are occasional flights to and from St John's (Newfoundland), Gander and New York.

Shipping. St Pierre is in regular motor-vessel communication with North Sydney, Fortune (Newfoundland) and Halifax. In 1980, about 47,600 tonnes of freight were unloaded and 4,250 tonnes loaded. 1,033 ships (615,176 gross tonnage) entered the harbour in 1981.

Post and Broadcasting. There were 2,907 telephones in 1982. *France Régions 3* broadcasts in French on medium-waves. St Pierre is connected by radio-telecommunication with most countries of the world. Radio licences totalled 4,300 and TV 1,950 in 1980.

Cinemas. There were (1983) 2 cinemas with a seating capacity of 760.

JUSTICE, RELIGION, EDUCATION AND WELFARE

Justice. There is a *tribunal de premier instance* and a *tribunal supérieur d'appel* at St Pierre.

Religion. The population is chiefly Roman Catholic.

Education. Primary instruction is free. There were, in 1982–83, 7 nursery and primary schools with 1,023 pupils and 3 secondary schools (including 1 technical school) with 693 pupils.

Health. There was (1983) 1 hospital on St Pierre with 100 beds; 11 doctors and 2 dentists.

Books of Reference

De Curton, E., *Saint-Pierre et Miquelon*. Paris, 1944
De La Rüe, E. A., *Saint-Pierre et Miquelon*. Paris, 1963
Ribault, J. Y., *Histoire de Saint-Pierre et Miquelon: Des Origines à 1814*. St Pierre, 1962

OVERSEAS TERRITORIES

SOUTHERN AND ANTARCTIC TERRITORIES

Terres Australes et Antarctiques Françaises

The Territory of the TAAF was created on 6 Aug. 1955. It comprises the islands of Saint Paul and Amsterdam (formerly Nouvelle Amsterdam), all in the southern Indian ocean, the Kerguelen and Crozet archipelagoes, and Terre Adélie.

The Administrator is assisted by a 7-member consultative council which meets twice yearly in Paris; its members are nominated by the Government for 5 years. The 12 members of the Scientific Council are appointed by the Senior Administrator after approval by the Minister in charge of scientific research. A 15-member Consultative Committee on the Environment, created in Nov. 1982, meets at least once a month to discuss all problems relating to the preservation of the environment. The administration has its seat in Paris.

Administrateur supérieur: Vice-Adm. Claude Piéri.

There are 4 postal agencies; the TAAF has its own postage stamps.

The scientific stations of the TAAF which took an important part in the International Geophysical Year, 1956–58, have been made permanent; the staff of the French bases (168 in 1983) is renewed annually and forms the only population.

Kerguelen islands, situated 48–50° S. lat., 68–70° E. long., consists of 1 large and 85 smaller islands and over 200 islets and rocks with a total area of 7,215 sq. km (2,786 sq. miles), of which Grande Terre occupies 6,675 sq. km (2,577 sq. miles). It was discovered in 1772 by Yves de Kerguelen, but was effectively occupied by France only in 1949. Port-aux-Français has several scientific research stations (76 members). Reindeer, trout and sheep have been acclimatized.

Crozet islands, situated 46° S. lat., 50–52° E. long., consists of 5 larger and 15 tiny islands, with a total area of 300 sq. km (116 sq. miles); the western group includes Apostles, Pigs and Penguins islands; the eastern group, Possession and Eastern islands. The archipelago was discovered in 1772 by Marion Dufresne, whose mate, Crozet, annexed it for Louis XV. A meteorological and scientific station (33 members) at Base Alfred-Faure on Possession Island was built in 1964.

Amsterdam Island and **Saint-Paul Island,** situated 38–39° S. lat., 77° E. long. Amsterdam, with an area of 54 sq. km (21 sq. miles) was discovered in 1522 by Magellan's companions; Saint-Paul, lying about 100 km to the south, with an area of 7 sq. km (2·7 sq. miles), was probably discovered in 1559 by Portuguese sailors. Both were first visited in 1633 by the Dutch explorer, Van Diemen, and were annexed by France in 1843. They are both extinct volcanoes, barren and uninhabited;

but in 1949 an administrative office, research stations (33 members) and a hospital were established at Base Martin de Vivies on Amsterdam.

Terre Adélie comprises that section of the Antarctic continent between 136° and 142° E. long., south of 60° S. lat. The ice-covered plateau has an area of about 432,000 sq. km (166,800 sq. miles), and was discovered in 1840 by Dumont d'Urville. A research station (26 members) is situated at Base Dumont d'Urville, which is maintained by the French Polar Expeditions.

Books of Reference

T.A.A.F. Revue trimestrielle. Paris, 1957 ff.
Expéditions Polaires Françaises. Études et Rapports. Paris, 1948–59

NEW CALEDONIA
Nouvelle Calédonie

HISTORY. New Caledonia was annexed by France in 1853 and, together with most of its former dependencies, became an Overseas Territory in 1958.

AREA AND POPULATION. The territory comprises the island of New Caledonia and various outlying islands, all situated in the south-west Pacific with a total land area of 19,103 sq. km (7,374 sq. miles). In 1976 the population (census) was 133,233, including 50,757 Europeans (majority French), 55,598 Melanesians, 7,054 Vietnamese and Indonesians, 6,391 Polynesians, 9,571 Wallisians, 3,862 others; 1983 (estimate) 146,600. The capital, Noumea had (1976) 74,335 inhabitants.

Vital statistics (1981): Live births, 3,861; deaths, 866.

The main islands are:

1. The island of New Caledonia with an area of 16,627 sq. km, has a total length of about 400 km, and an average breadth of 50 km, and a population (census, 1976) of 116,996.

2. The Loyalty Islands, 100 km (60 miles) east of New Caledonia, consisting of 3 large islands, Maré, Lifou and Uvéa, and many small islands with a total area of about 2,353 sq. km and a population (census, 1976) of 14,518, nearly all Melanesians except on Uvéa, which is partly Polynesian. The chief culture in the islands is that of coconuts: the chief export, copra.

3. The Isle of Pines, 50 km (30 miles) to the south-east of Nouméa, with an area of 153 sq. km and a population of 1,095 (census 1976), is a tourist and fishing centre.

4. The Bélep Archipelago, about 50 km north-west of New Caledonia, with an area of 70 sq. km and a population of 624 (census 1976).

The remaining islands are all very small and none have permanent inhabitants, although many were formerly exploited for their guano deposits. The largest are the Chesterfield Islands, a group of 11 well-wooded coral islets with a combined area of 10 sq. km, about 550 km west of the Bélep Archipelago. The Huon Islands, a group of 4 barren coral islets with a combined area of just 65 hectares, are 225 km north of the Bélep Archipelago. Walpole, a limestone coral island of 1 sq. km, lies 150 km east of the Isle of Pines; Matthew Island and Hunter Island, respectively 250 km and 330 km east of Walpole, are spasmodically active volcanic islands of similar size.

CONSTITUTION AND GOVERNMENT. From Jan. 1976 State affairs are administrated by the High Commissioner and Territorial affairs by a Council of Government of 7 elected members (until 1976 the Council was advisory). A Territorial Assembly of 36 elected members decides the more important territorial affairs including local revenue.

New Caledonia is represented in the National Assembly by 2 deputies, in the Senate by 1 senator and in the Economic and Social Council by 1 councillor.

At territorial elections held 1 July 1979, the *Rassemblement Pour la Calédonie dans la République* (Gaullists) gained 15 seats, *Front Indépendantiste* 14 seats, *Fédération pour une Nouvelle Société Cáledonienne* 7 seats.

The Territory is divided into 4 *circonscriptions* (of which the Loyalty Islands form one), and sub-divided into 32 communes which are administered by locally elected councils and mayors.

High Commissioner: Jacques Roynette.
President of the Territorial Assembly: Jean Pierre Aïfa.

ECONOMY

Budget. The budget for 1982 balanced at 22,860m. francs CFP. Revenues included special grants by France totalling 6,290m. francs CFP.

Currency. The unit of currency is the *franc* CFP, with a parity of CFP *francs* 18·18 to the French *franc*.

Banking. There are branches of the Banque de Indosuez, the Banque Nationale de Paris, the Banque de Paris et des Pays-Bas, and the Société Générale, in addition to the Banque de la Nouvelle-Calédonie (Crédit Lyonnais).

ENERGY AND NATURAL RESOURCES

Electricity. In 1981, production totalled 1,164m. kwh.

Minerals. The mineral resources are very great; nickel, chrome and iron abound; silver, gold, cobalt, lead, manganese, iron and copper have been mined at different times. The nickel deposits are of special value, being without arsenic. Production of nickel ore in 1981, 3·9m. tonnes. About 467,000 hectares of mining land are owned, and 97,000 hectares have been granted for exploitation. In 1981 the furnaces produced 15,330 tonnes of matte nickel and 27,989 tonnes of ferro-nickel.

Agriculture. Of the total area only about 6% is cultivable; about 416,000 hectares are pasture land; about 6,000 hectares are commercially cultivated and about 250,000 hectares contain forest; forest produce, 1976, 19,849 cu. metres. There are 4 forms of landownership: native reserves belonging to the local tribes, private estates, public land belonging to the New Caledonian territory and public land belonging to the metropolitan government. The chief agricultural products are beef, pork, poultry, coffee, maize, fruit and vegetables.

Livestock (1982): Cattle, 110,000; pigs, 19,000; goats, 8,000; poultry, 220,000.

Fisheries. The catch in 1980 totalled 705 tonnes.

INDUSTRY AND TRADE

Industry. Local industries include chlorine and oxygen plants, cement, soft drinks, barbed wire, nails, pleasure and fishing boats, clothing, pasta, household cleaners and confectionery.

Commerce. Imports and exports in 1m. francs CFP for 5 years:

	1977	1978	1979	1980	1981
Imports	26,032	23,926	27,791	35,041	40,434
Exports	27,809	17,484	28,549	29,652	33,435

In 1981, 32·5% of the imports came from, and 67% of the exports went to France.

Chief imports in 1981 were (in 1m. francs CFP): Food, 8,406; fuels and minerals, 11,777; machines and electrical equipment, 4,015. Chief exports: Nickel metal, 25,946; nickel ore, 5,037.

COMMUNICATIONS

Roads. There were, in 1980, 5,496 km of roads, excluding 470 km on minor islands.

Aviation. New Caledonia is connected by air routes with France (by UTA),

Australia (UTA, Air Pacific and Qantas), New Zealand (UTA and Air New Zealand), Fiji (by UTA and Air Pacific), Vanuatu, Wallis archipelago and Tahiti (by UTA), and Nauru (by Air Nauru). In 1981, 112,147 passengers arrived and 111,846 departed *via* La Tontouta airport, near Nouméa.

Shipping. In 1981, 363 vessels entered Nouméa unloading 876,000 tonnes of goods and loading 1,763,000 tonnes. A new harbour for deep-water alongside discharge was completed in 1974.

Post and Broadcasting. There were 52 post offices and telex, telephone, radio and television services. There were (1981) 27,953 telephones. *Radio Nouméa* belongs to *Société Nationale des Programmes* and broadcasts in French on medium- and short-waves. *Télé Nouméa* broadcasts 1 television programme 28 hours a week. Number of receivers (1978): radio, 65,000; TV, 28,000.

Cinemas. In 1979 there were 10 cinemas.

Newspapers. In 1982 there was 1 daily newspaper with a circulation of 12,000 and 16 other periodicals.

JUSTICE, RELIGION, EDUCATION AND WELFARE

Justice. There is a *tribunal de grande instance* and a *cour d'appel* in Nouméa.

Religion. Over 60% of the population are Roman Catholic and 30% Protestant.

Education. In 1981, there were 34,281 pupils and 1,516 teachers in primary schools, 9,366 pupils and 545 teachers in secondary schools, 3,961 students and 315 teachers in technical and vocational schools and 421 students in higher education.

Health. In 1979 there were 158 physicians, 42 dentists, 42 pharmacists, 15 midwives and 436 nursing personnel. In 1978, 66 hospitals had a total of 1,541 beds.

Books of Reference

Journal Officiel de la Nouvelle Calédonie et Dépendances
Annuaire Statistique de la Nouvelle Calédonie et Dépendances

FRENCH POLYNESIA

Polynésie Française

HISTORY. French protectorates since 1843, these islands were annexed to France 1880–82 to form 'French Settlements in Oceania', which opted in Nov. 1958 for the status of an Overseas Territory within the French Community.

AREA AND POPULATION. The total area of these 5 archipelagoes, scattered over a wide area in the Eastern Pacific is 3,941 sq. km (1,522 sq. miles). The population, Census, 1977, was 137,382; 1983 estimate, 148,000. The islands are administratively divided into 5 *circonscriptions:*

1. The **Windward Islands** (Îles du Vent) (101,392 inhabitants in 1977) comprise Tahiti with an area of 1,042 sq. km and (1977) 95,604 inhabitants; Moorea with an area of 132 sq. km and 5,788 inhabitants; and the smaller Mehetia, Tetiaoro and Tubuai Manu. The capital is Papeete (62,735 inhabitants including suburbs).

2. The **Leeward Islands** (Îles sous le Vent) (16,311 inhabitants), comprising the volcanic islands of Huahine (3,140), Raiatéa (6,376), Tahaa (3,513), Bora-Bora (2,572), Maupiti (710) together with 4 small (uninhabited) atolls, the group having a total area of 507 sq. km. The chief town is Uturoa (2,517 inhabitants) on Raiatéa.

The Windward and Leeward Islands together are called the Society Archipelago (Archipel de la Société). Tahitian, a Polynesian language, is spoken throughout the archipelago.

3. The **Tuamotu Archipelago**, consisting of two parallel ranges of 78 atolls lying between 135° and 143° W. long. and 14° and 23° S. lat., east of the Society Archipelago, have a total area of 774 sq. km and a population of 8,537; its major islands are Rangiroa, Hao and Turéia. The *circonscription* (total 9,052 inhabitants) also includes the **Gambier Islands** further east (of which Mangareva is the principal), an atoll having an area of 36 sq. km and a population of 515; the chief centre is Rikitea.

4. The **Austral or Tubuai Islands**, lying south of the Society Archipelago, comprise a 1,300 km chain of volcanic islands and reefs. They include Rimatara, Rurutu, Tubuai, Raivaevae and, 500 km to the south, Rapa-Iti, with a combined area of 174 sq. km and 5,208 inhabitants; the chief centre is Mataura on Tubuai.

5. The **Marquesas Islands**, lying north of the Tuamotu Archipelago, with a total area of 1,274 sq. km and 5,419 inhabitants, comprise Nuku-Hiva, Ua Pu, Ua Huka, Hiva-Oa, Tahuata, Fatu-Hiva and 5 smaller (uninhabited) islands; the chief centre is Taiohae on Hiva-Oa.

CONSTITUTION AND GOVERNMENT. Under the 1977 Constitution, the Territory is administered by a High Commissioner, a Council of Government (over which the High Commissioner presides) of 8 members, a Territorial Assembly of 30 members elected every 5 years by universal suffrage, and an advisory Economic and Social Committee. French Polynesia is represented in the National Assembly by 2 deputies, in the Senate by 1 senator, and in the Economic and Social Council by 1 councillor.

At the territorial elections held in May 1982, the *Tahoeraa Huiratira* (Gaullists) won 13 seats, the *Pupu Here Ai'a* (moderate autonomists), 6 seats and others, 11 seats.

High Commissioner: Alain Ohrel.

ECONOMY

Budget. The ordinary budget for 1981 balanced at 23,100m. francs CFP.

Currency. The unit of currency is the *franc* CFP, with a parity of CFP *francs* 18·18 to the French *franc*.

ENERGY AND NATURAL RESOURCES

Electricity. Production in 1981 (Tahiti only) amounted to 151·7m. kwh.

Agriculture. An important product is copra (coconut trees covering the coastal plains of the mountainous islands and the greater part of the low-lying islands), production (1982) 17,000 tonnes. Tropical fruits, such as bananas, pineapples, oranges, etc.. are grown only for local consumption.

Livestock (1982): Cattle, 10,000; horses, 2,000; pigs, 34,000; sheep, 2,000; goats, 3,000; poultry, 600,000.

Fisheries. The catch in 1979 amounted to 4,217 tonnes of fish.

COMMERCE. Trade in 1,000 tonnes and 1m. francs CFP:

	1977		1978		1979	
	Quantity	*Value*	*Quantity*	*Value*	*Quantity*	*Value*
Imports	396	29,187	407	33,070	450	36,645
Exports	11	1,464	9	2,973	12	2,252

Total trade between the French possessions in the Pacific and UK (British Department of Trade returns, in £1,000 sterling):

	1979	1980	1981	1982	1983
Imports to UK	6	32	8	2	93
Exports and re-exports from UK	2,285	2,154	1,421	1,962	2,601

Chief imports (by value) include metalwork, textiles. petrol, sugar and flour.

Chief exports are coconut oil, cultured pearls, vanilla and citrus fruits. Tourism is very important, earning almost half as much as the visible exports. There were 96,826 tourists in 1981.

COMMUNICATIONS

Roads. In 1981 there were 741 km of roads.

Aviation. Five international airlines connect Tahiti with Paris, Honolulu, USA, Mexico and New Zealand. There is also a regular air service between Faaa airport (on Tahiti) and the Leeward Isles with occasional connexions to the other groups. In 1981, 351,489 passengers arrived and 338,006 departed *via* Faaa airport and (1976) 210,300 *via* Moorea airport.

Shipping. Several shipping companies connect France, San Francisco, New Zealand and Australia with Papeete.

Post and Broadcasting. Number of telephones (1982), 24,818. *Radio Tahiti* belongs to *Office de Radiodiffusion-Télévision Française* and broadcasts in French, Tahitian and English on medium- and short-waves and also broadcasts 1 television programme *via* 5 transmitters. Number of receivers (1980): radio, 80,000; TV, 25,000.

Cinemas. In 1975 there were 6 cinemas with a seating capacity of 3,200.

Newspapers. In 1975 there were 4 daily newspapers with a combined circulation of 11,000 and 2 other periodicals with 2,000.

JUSTICE, RELIGION, EDUCATION AND WELFARE

Justice. There is a *tribunal de grande instance* and a *cour d'appel* at Papeete.

Religion. In 1975 it was estimated that 50% of the inhabitants were Protestants, 34% Roman Catholic and 6% Mormon.

Education. Education at primary level was reorganized in 1974 and secondary education in 1975. There were, in 1979-80, 38,964 pupils and 1,687 teachers in primary schools, 9,613 pupils and 610 teachers in secondary schools, 2,757 pupils and 214 teachers in technical schools, and 225 students and 20 lecturers at teacher-training colleges.

Health. There were (1977) 117 physicians, 23 dentists, 10 pharmacists, 24 midwives and 286 nursing personnel. There was a main hospital at Mamao (on Tahiti), 6 secondary hospitals, 41 dispensaries and medical centres and 45 first aid posts.

DEPENDENCY. The uninhabited Clipperton Islands, 1,000 km off the coast of Mexico, are administered by the High Commissioner for French Polynesia but do not form part of the Territory; they comprise an atoll whose 2 islands cover 7 sq. km.

Books of Reference

Journal Officiel des Etablissements Françaises de l'Océanie, and *Supplement Containing Statistics of Commerce and Navigation.* Papeete
Andrews, E., *Comparative Dictionary of the Tahitian Language.* Chicago, 1944
Luke, Sir Harry, *The Islands of the South Pacific.* London, 1961
O'Reilly, P., and Reitman, E., *Bibliographie de Tahiti et de la Polynésie française.* Paris, 1967
O'Reilly, P., and Teissier, R., *Tahitiens. Répertoire bio-bibliographique de la Polynésie française.* Paris, 1963

WALLIS AND FUTUNA

HISTORY. French dependencies since 1842, the inhabitants of these islands voted on 22 Dec. 1959 by an overwhelming majority in favour of exchanging their status to that of an Overseas Territory, which took effect from 29 July 1961.

AREA AND POPULATION. The Territory comprises two groups of islands (total area 274 sq. km) in the central Pacific, north-east of Fiji; the Wallis Archipelago (area 159 sq. km) and the Îles de Hooru (115 sq. km). The capital is Mata-Utu on Uvea, the main island of the Wallis Archipelago.

The resident population (census March 1982) was 11,943, comprising 7,843 on Uvea and 4,100 on Futuna in the Îles de Hooru (whose other main island, Alofi, is uninhabited). About 11,000 Wallisians and Futunians live abroad, mainly in New Caledonia and Vanuatu. Uvean and Futunan are distinct Polynesian languages.

CONSTITUTION AND GOVERNMENT. The Senior Administrator carries out the duties of Head of the Territory, assisted by an elected 20-member Territorial Assembly. The territory is represented by 1 deputy in the National Assembly, by 1 senator in the Senate, and by 1 member on the Economic and Social Council.

Administrateur supérieur: Robert Thil.
President of the Territorial Assembly: Manuele Lisiahi.

ECONOMY

Budget. The 1982 budget provided for expenditure of 303·8m. francs CFP.

Currency. The unit of currency is the *franc* CFP, with a parity of CFP *francs* 18·18 to the French *franc*.

AGRICULTURE. The chief products are copra, yams, taro roots and bananas.
Livestock: Cattle, 100 (1976); pigs, 17,000 (1982); horses, 400 (1978); goats, 7,000 (1980).

COMMERCE. Imports (1981) amounted to 667m. francs CFP.

COMMUNICATIONS

Roads. In 1977 there were 100 km of roads on Uvea.

Aviation. In 1980 there were 581 aircraft arrivals and departures at Hihifo airport, on Uvea. There is a weekly flight *via* Vila (Vanuatu) to Noumea (New Caledonia) and three flights each week to Futuna.

Post and Broadcasting. In 1979 a radio station was established on Uvea. In 1982 there were 151 telephones.

RELIGION, EDUCATION AND WELFARE

Religion. The majority of the population is Roman Catholic.

Education. In 1983, there were 3,962 pupils in 13 primary and lower secondary schools.

Health. In 1974 there were 3 physicians and 26 nursing personnel (including 10 midwives). There were (1972) 5 small hospitals and dispensaries with 108 beds.

GABON

République Gabonaise

Capital: Libreville
Population: 1·29m. (1983)
GNP per capita: US$3,680 (1980)

HISTORY. First colonized by France in the mid-19th century, Gabon was annexed to French Congo in 1888 and became a separate colony in 1910 as one of the 4 territories of French Equatorial Africa. It became an autonomous republic within the French Community in 1958 and achieved independence on 17 Aug. 1960. The first President, Leon M'ba, died on 30 Nov. 1967 and was succeeded on 2 Dec. by his Vice-President, Albert-Bernard (now Omar) Bongo.

AREA AND POPULATION. Gabon is bounded west by the Atlantic ocean, north by Equatorial Guinea and Cameroon and east and south by Congo. The area covers 267,667 sq. km; its population at the 1970 census was 950,007; estimate (1983) is 1,292,000. The capital is Libreville (251,400 inhabitants, 1974), other large towns being Port-Gentil (77,611) and Lambaréné (22,682).

Vital statistics (1975): Birth rate, 3·22%; death rate, 2·22%.

Provincial areas, populations (census 1970, in 1,000) and capitals are as follows:

Province	sq. km	1970	Capital	Province	sq. km	1970	Capital
Estuaire	20,740	195	Libreville	Nyanga	21,285	67	Tchibanga
Woleu-Ntem	38,465	148	Oyem	Ngounié	37,750	130	Mouila
Ogooué-Ivindo	46,075	60	Makokou	Ogooué-Lolo	25,380	52	Koulamoutou
Moyen-Ogooué	18,535	52	Lambaréné	Haut-Ogooué	36,547	127	Franceville
Ogooué-Maritime	22,890	120	Port-Gentil				

The largest ethnic groups are the Fang (30%) in the north, Eshira (25%) in the south-west, and the Adouma (17%) in the south-east. French is the official language.

CLIMATE. The climate is equatorial, with high temperatures and considerable rainfall. Mid-May to mid-Sept. is the long dry season, followed by a short rainy season, then a dry season again from mid-Dec. to mid-Feb., and finally a long rainy season once more. Libreville. Jan. 80°F (26·7°C), July 75°F (23·9°C). Annual rainfall 99″ (2,510 mm).

CONSTITUTION AND GOVERNMENT. The 1967 Constitution (as subsequently revised) provides for an Executive President directly elected for a 7-year term, who appoints a Council of Ministers to assist him. The unicameral National Assembly consists of 84 members, directly elected for a 5-year term (latest elections, Feb. 1980) and a further 9 members nominated by the President.

The sole legal political party is the *Parti democratique gabonais* founded in 1968.

President: Omar Bongo (re-elected on 25 Feb. 1973 and 30 Dec. 1979).
Prime Minister: Léon Mébiame.
Foreign Minister: Martin Bongo.
Flag: Three horizontal stripes of green, yellow, blue.
Local government: The 9 provinces, each administered by a governor appointed by the President, are divided into 37 *départements*, each under a prefect.

DEFENCE

Army. The Army consists of 1 all-arms battalion with support units, totalling (1984), 1,500 men.

Navy. The small naval flotilla in 1984 comprised 4 fast attack craft, 2 patrol craft and 3 landing craft with a base at Port-Gentil. Personnel, 170 officers and men. The Coastguard has 9 small patrol craft and 1 service tender.

Air Force. The Air Force has 5 single-seat and 2 two-seat Mirage 5 ground-attack aircraft, and 1 EMB-111 maritime patrol aircraft. Transport duties are performed primarily by 3 Hercules and 4 EMB-110 Bandeirante turboprop aircraft, supported by 3 C-47s and 3 Nord 262s. Single Gulfstream III, Mystère 20, YS-11 and DC-8 aircraft are used for VIP duties; 4 Broussards and a Cessna Skymaster for liaison. Four T-34C-1 armed turboprop aircraft are operated for *La Présidentiale Garde.* Also in service are 4 Puma and 3 Alouette III helicopters. Personnel number 500.

INTERNATIONAL RELATIONS

Membership. Gabon is a member of UN, OAU and OPEC; it is an ACP state of the EEC.

ECONOMY.

Planning. The 1982–84 Interim Development Plan proposed public expenditure of 362,512m. francs CFA, of which 188,202m. were to develop the transport infrastructure.

Budget. The provisional budget for 1983 balanced at 562,000m. francs CFA.

Currency. The unit of currency is the franc CFA, divided into 100 centimes, with a parity value of 50 francs CFA to 1 French franc.

Banking. The *Banque des États de l'Afrique Centrale* is the bank of issue. There are 6 commercial banks situated in Gabon. The *Banque Gabonaise de Développement* and the *Union Gabonaise de Banque* are Gabonese controlled.

ENERGY AND NATURAL RESOURCES

Electricity. The semi-public *Société d'energie et d'eau du Gabon* produced 567m. kwh. in 1980, mainly from thermal plants but increasingly from hydro-electric schemes at Kinguélé (near Libreville), Tchimbélé and Poubara (near Franceville).

Oil. Extraction from offshore fields totalled 7·56m. tonnes in 1981. Gabon operates 2 refineries, at Port-Gentil and at nearby Pointe Clairette.

Gas. Natural gas production (1979) was 206m. cu. metres.

Minerals. Production (1981) of manganese ore (from deposits around Moanda in the south-east) amounted to 1·5m. tonnes. Uranium is mined nearby (1,062 tonnes in 1981). An estimated 850m. tonnes of iron ore deposits, discovered 1971 at Mékambo (near Bélinga in the north-east) await completion of the branch railway line to be exploited. Gold (50 kg in 1978), zinc and phosphates also occur.

Agriculture. Agriculture, forestry and fisheries occupy 85% of the working population. The major crops (production, 1981, in 1,000 tonnes) are: Sugar-cane, 140; cassava, 100; plantains, 63; maize, 10; bananas, 8; palm products, cocoa, coffee and rice.

Livestock (1982): 6,000 cattle, 77,000 sheep, 59,000 goats, 140,000 pigs.

Forestry. Gabon's equatorial forests covering 78% of the land area produced 1,224,924 cu. metres of *okoumé* in 1978. Hardwoods (mahogany, ebony and walnut) are also exported.

Fisheries. The total catch (1980) amounted to 26,400 tonnes in the Atlantic and 400 tonnes in inland waters.

TRADE. In 1980 imports totalled 154,210m. francs CFA and exports 477,760m. francs CFA. France and USA are Gabon's principal trading partners. In 1978 petroleum made up 72% of exports; metals, 18% and timber, 6%.

Total trade between Gabon and the UK (British Department of Trade returns, in £1,000 sterling):

	1978	1979	1980	1981	1982	1983
Imports to UK	4,401	12,893	10,657	36,726	27,634	66,135
Exports and re-exports from UK	7,725	8,507	9,155	12,099	14,179	18,798

COMMUNICATIONS

Roads. There were (1981) 7,276 km of roads and (1976) there were 30,100 (12,700 goods) vehicles.

Railways. A 1,435-mm gauge (Transgabonais) railway runs 325 km from Owendo *via* N'Djole to Booué, and will be extended to Moanda and Franceville with a projected branch from Booué to Bélinga.

Aviation. There are 3 international airports at Port-Gentil, Franceville, and Libreville; internal services link these to 65 domestic airfields.

Shipping. Owendo (near Libreville), Mayumba and Port-Gentil are the main ports. In 1980, 10·1m. tonnes were loaded and 617,000 tonnes unloaded at the ports. In 1978 there were 15 merchant vessels of 98,645 gross tons.

Post and Broadcasting. Telephones (1982), 11,133. In 1982 there were 10,000 television and 98,000 radio licences.

Cinemas. In 1974 there were 6 cinemas with a seating capacity of 4,100.

Newspapers. There are 2 newspapers published in Libreville; *Gabon-Matin* (daily) has a circulation of 18,000 and *L'Union* (weekly) 15,000.

JUSTICE, RELIGION, EDUCATION AND WELFARE

Justice. There are *tribunaux de grande instance* at Libreville, Port-Gentil, Lambaréné, Mouila, Oyem, Franceville and Koulamoutou, from which cases move progressively to a central Criminal Court, Court of Appeal and Supreme Court, all 3 located in Libreville.

Civil police number about 900.

Religion. It is estimated that 50% of the population is Christian (mainly Roman Catholic), the majority of the balance following animist beliefs. There are about 2,000 Moslems.

Education. Education is compulsory between 6–16 years. In 1981 there were 155,081 pupils with 3,281 teachers in primary schools; 22,005 pupils with 1,088 teachers in secondary schools; 3,465 students with 266 teachers in 9 technical schools; and 2,119 students with 120 teaching staff at 13 teacher-training schools.

The Université Omar Bongo, founded in 1970 in Libreville, had (1978) 1,284 students; about 750 Gabonese students study abroad.

Health (1977). There were 207 doctors, 20 dentists, 28 pharmacists (1971), 99 midwives and 823 nursing personnel. In 1981 there were 16 hospitals and 87 medical centres, with a total of 4,815 beds, as well as 258 local dispensaries.

DIPLOMATIC REPRESENTATIVES

Of Gabon in Great Britain (48 Kensington Ct., London, W8)
Ambassador: Léon N'Dong.

Of Great Britain in Gabon (Bâtiment Sogame, Blvd de l'Indépendance, Libreville)
Ambassador: Alan Grey.

Of Gabon in the USA (2034 20th St., NW, Washington, D.C., 20009)
Ambassador: Etienne Mezui Mendo.

Of the USA in Gabon (Blvd de la Mer, Libreville)
Ambassador: Francis McNamara.

Of Gabon to the United Nations
Ambassador: Jean Davin.

Books of Reference

Bory, P., *The New Gabon.* Monaco, 1978
Remy, M., *Gabon Today.* Paris, 1977

THE GAMBIA

Capital: Banjul
Population: 695,886 (1983)
GNP per capita: US$344 (1983)

HISTORY. The Gambia was discovered by the early Portuguese navigators, but they made no settlement. During the 17th century various companies of merchants obtained trading charters and established a settlement on the river, which, from 1807, was controlled from Sierra Leone; in 1843 it was made an independent Crown Colony; in 1866 it formed part of the West African Settlements, but in Dec. 1888 it again became a separate Crown Colony. The boundaries were delimited only after 1890. The Gambia achieved full internal self-government on 4 Oct. 1963 and became an independent member of the Commonwealth on 18 Feb. 1965. The Gambia became a republic within the Commonwealth on 24 April 1970.

AREA AND POPULATION. The Gambia is bounded west by the Atlantic ocean and on all other sides by Senegal. Area of Banjul (formerly Bathurst) and environs, 87·8 sq. km. In the provinces (area, 10,601·5 sq. km) the settled population (1971) was 275,469, not including temporary immigrants. Total population (census, April 1983), 695,886. The largest tribe is the Mandingo (1973) (186,241), followed by the Fulas (79,994), Woloffs (69,291), Jolas (41,988) and Sarahulis (38,478). The capital is Banjul, 1983 census (44,536), and the surrounding urban area, Kombo St Mary (102,858). There were 1,159 non-Africans in 1973.

CONSTITUTION AND GOVERNMENT. Parliament consists of the House of Representatives which consists of a Speaker, Deputy Speaker and 35 elected members; in addition, 4 Chiefs are elected by the Chiefs in Assembly; 3 nominated members are without votes and the Attorney-General is nominated and has a vote. *See* Senegal for details about Senegambia.

A general election was held on 4–5 May 1982. State of parties (Jan. 1984): The People's Progressive Party 29, the National Convention Party 3, and Independents 3 seats.

The Government was in Jan. 1984 composed as follows:

President: Sir Dawda Kairaba Jawara.
Vice-President (Information and Tourism): Bakary B. Darbo. *External Affairs:* Alhaji Lamine Kiti Jabang. *Finance and Trade:* Sherif Sisay. *Agriculture (Finance and Trade):* Saikou Sabally. *Education, Youth, Sport and Culture:* Alhaji Abdoulie K. N'Jie. *Health, Labour and Social Welfare:* Momodou Cherno Jallow. *Works and Communications:* Lamine Bora M'Boge. *Economic Planning and Industrial Development:* Dr Momodou S. K. Manneh. *Justice and Attorney-General:* Fafa M'Bye. *Water Resources and Environment:* Omar A. Jallow. *Information and Tourism (Local Government):* Landing Jallow Sonko. *Interior:* A. E. W. F. Badji. *Local Government and Lands:* Amulai Janneh.

National flag: Three horizontal stripes of red, blue, green, with the blue edged in white.

Local Administration. The Gambia is divided into 35 districts, each traditionally under a Chief, assisted by Village Heads and advisers. These districts are grouped into 6 Area Councils containing a majority of elected members, with the Chiefs of the district as *ex-officio* members. The city of Banjul is administered by a City Council.

CLIMATE. The climate is characterized by two very different seasons. The dry season lasts from Nov. to May, when precipitation is very light and humidity moderate. Days are warm but nights quite cool. The SW monsoon is likely to set in

with spectacular storms and produces considerable rainfall from July to Oct., with
increased humidity. Banjul. Jan. 73°F (22·8°C), July 80°F (26·7°C). Annual rainfall 52" (1,295 mm).

INTERNATIONAL RELATIONS

Membership. The Gambia is a member of UN, OAU, the Commonwealth and is
an ACP state of EEC.

ECONOMY

Budget. Revenue and expenditure for years ending 30 June are (in dalasi):

	1979–80	1980–81	1981–82	1982–83
Revenue	88,045,000	85,001,700	134,286,323	104,947,970
Expenditure	81,190,000	96,792,176	137,268,189	144,220,280

Currency. The currency is the *dalasi* and is divided into 100 *butut*. 4 *dalasi* = £1
sterling; 3·35 *dalasi* = US$1 (March 1984).

Banking. There are 4 banks in the Gambia, the Standard Bank of Gambia Ltd,
Central Bank of the Gambia, Commercial and Development Bank and la Banque
Internationale pour le Commerce et l'Industrie (BICI). On 30 Nov. 1978 the
government savings bank had about 36,000 depositors holding approximately
992,496 dalasi.

NATURAL RESOURCES

Minerals. Heavy minerals, including ilmenite, zircon and rutile, have been discovered (1m. tons up to 31 Dec. 1980) in Sanyang, Batakunku and Kartong areas.

Agriculture. Almost all commercial activity centres upon the marketing of groundnuts, which is the only export crop of financial significance; in 1982–83, 128,000
tonnes were produced. Cotton is also exported on a limited scale. Rice is of increasing importance for local consumption.
   Livestock (1982): 350,000 cattle, 185,000 goats, 175,000 sheep, 11,000 pigs and
300,000 poultry.

Fisheries. Total catch (1975) 10,800 tonnes, of which 800 tonnes were from inland
waters.

LABOUR. There are 4 large and 10 small trade unions.

TRADE. Chief items of imports are textiles and clothing, vehicles and machinery,
metal goods and petroleum products.
   Imports and exports, in 1,000 dalasi:

	1978–79	1979–80	1980–81	1981–82	1982–83
Imports	221,014	500,000	275,800	220,600	218,900
Exports	94,913	417,000	...	82,900	86,000

   Chief items of exports are groundnuts, palm kernels, dried and smoked fish,
hides and skins and groundnut oil.
   Total trade between the Gambia and UK (British Department of Trade returns,
in £1,000 sterling):

	1978	1979	1980	1981	1982	1983
Imports to UK	5,721	2,357	2,417	2,335	2,031	3,781
Exports and re-exports from UK	17,332	13,953	17,792	11,889	10,087	13,251

TOURISM. In 1982–83, 24,800 tourists visited the Gambia.

COMMUNICATIONS

Roads. There are 2,990 km of motorable roads, of which 1,718 km rank as all-
weather roads including 306 km of bituminous surface and 531 km of laterite
gravel. Number of licensed motor vehicles (1974–75): 11,765 private cars, 5,777
commercial vehicles, 240 buses and coaches, 410 tractors and 143 trailers.

Aviation. The Gambia is served by Air Guinea, Air Mali, British Caledonian Airways, Ghana Airways and Nigeria Airways. Air movements at Yundum Airport in 1975 numbered 2,756, including scheduled services.

Shipping. The chief port, Banjul, handled 303 ships of 686,300 DWT in 1975–76. The first phase of development of the port was completed in 1974; a new 400 ft berth will take one large vessel of up to 36 ft draught. Internal communication is maintained by steamers and launches.

The Gambia River Development Organization was founded in 1978 as a joint project with Senegal to develop the river and its basin.

Post and Broadcasting. There are several post offices and agencies; postal facilities are also afforded to all river towns by means of a travelling post office on the government river mail-steamers. Banjul is connected with St Vincent (Cape Verde islands) and with Sierra Leone by cable. Banjul is in wireless communication with London and the main centres up river. A trans-Gambia telephone system provides direct communications with Dakar and Ziguinchor. Telephones numbered 3,476 in Jan. 1980. A telex service was introduced in 1968.

Radio Gambia, a government station, broadcasts for about 12 hours a day; Radio Syd, a commercial station, broadcasts for 15 hours. Number of radio receivers (1983, estimate), 66,000.

Cinemas. In 1979 there were 10 cinemas.

Newspapers. There is an official (three times weekly) and several newssheets.

JUSTICE, RELIGION, EDUCATION AND WELFARE

Justice. Justice is administered by a Supreme Court consisting of a chief justice and puisne judges. It has unlimited jurisdiction but there is a Court of Appeal. Two magistrates' courts and divisional courts are supplemented by a system of travelling magistrates. There are also Moslem courts, group tribunals dealing with cases concerned with customs and traditions, and one juvenile court.

Religion. About 70% of the population is Moslem. Banjul is the seat of an Anglican and a Roman Catholic bishop. There are some Methodist missions. Some sections of the population retain their original animist beliefs.

Education (1979–80). There were 133 primary schools (1,371 teachers, 37,644 pupils), 17 secondary technical schools (260 teachers, 5,274 pupils), 7 senior secondary schools (179 teachers, 3,040 pupils) and 1 post-secondary school; total number of teachers, 1,810. Gambia College, which is to replace Yundum College as a teacher-training and vocational centre, opened for agricultural students in 1979

Health. In 1980 there were 43 government doctors, 23 private doctors and about 635 hospital beds.

DIPLOMATIC REPRESENTATIVES

Of the Gambia in Great Britain (57 Kensington Ct., London, W8 5DG)
High Commissioner: Samuel J. O. Sarr, MBE.

Of Great Britain in the Gambia (48 Atlantic Rd., Fajara, Banjul)
High Commissioner: D. F. B. Le Breton, CBE.

Of the Gambia in the USA and to UN (1785 Massachusetts Ave., NW, Washington, D.C., 20036)
Ambassador: Dr Lamin A. Mbye.

Of the USA in the Gambia (Pipeline Road, Kombo St. Mary, Banjul)
Ambassador: Francis R. C. Blain.

Books of Reference

The Gambia in Brief. Gambia Information Services, Banjul, 1979
The Gambia Independence Act, 1964
The Gambia Independence Order, 1965
The Gambia since Independence 1965–1980. Banjul, 1980
Tomkinson, M., *The Gambia: A Holiday Guide.* London, 1983

GERMANY

POST-WAR HISTORY. Since the unconditional surrender of the German armed forces on 8 May 1945 there has been no central authority whose writ runs in the whole of Germany. Consequently no peace treaty has been signed with a government representing the whole of Germany, and the country is virtually partitioned between the Federal Republic of Germany and the German Democratic Republic.

By the Berlin Declaration of 5 June 1945 the governments of the USA, the UK, the USSR and France assumed supreme authority over Germany. Each of the 4 signatories was given a zone of occupation, in which the supreme power was to be exercised by the C.-in-C. in that zone (*see* map in THE STATESMAN'S YEAR-BOOK, 1947). Jointly these 4 Cs.-in-C. constituted the Allied Control Council in Berlin, which was to be competent in all 'matters affecting Germany as a whole'. The territory of Greater Berlin, divided into 4 sectors, was to be governed as an entity by the 4 occupying powers.

At the Potsdam Conference (17 July–2 Aug. 1945) the northern part of the Province of East Prussia, including its capital Königsberg (renamed Kaliningrad), was transferred to the Soviet Union, pending final ratification by a peace treaty; and it was agreed that, pending the final peace settlement, Poland should administer those parts of Germany lying east of a line running from the Baltic Sea immediately west of Swinemünde along the river Oder to its confluence with the Western Neisse and thence along the Western Neisse to the Czechoslovak frontier.

The agreements between the war-time allies concerning the occupation zones (12 Sept. 1944) and control of Germany (1 May 1945) were repudiated by the USSR on 27 Nov. 1958.

A Treaty was signed in East Berlin between the German Democratic Republic and the Federal Republic of Germany on 21 Dec. 1972 agreeing the basis of relations between the two countries.

GERMAN DEMOCRATIC REPUBLIC

Capital: Berlin (East)
Population: 16·7m. (1982)
GNP per capita: US$7,180 (1980)

Deutsche Demokratische Republik

HISTORY. For the immediate post-war history *see* p. 508.

AREA AND POPULATION. Area and population, 30 June 1982 (in 1,000):

Districts	Area in sq. km	Population Male	Female	Total	Per sq. km
Berlin (East)	403	541·1	625·5	1,166·6	2,895
Cottbus	8,262	423·3	461·2	884·5	107
Dresden	6,738	835·8	966·1	1,801·9	267
Erfurt	7,349	584·2	652·9	1,237·1	168
Frankfurt	7,186	338·0	356·6	704·5	98
Gera	4,004	348·6	392·7	741·2	185
Halle	8,771	857·2	961·9	1,819·0	207
Karl-Marx-Stadt	6,009	884·8	1,028·6	1,913·5	318
Leipzig	4,966	646·6	752·0	1,398·6	282
Magdeburg	11,526	593·6	667·3	1,260·9	109
Neubrandenburg	10,948	299·8	321·2	621·0	57
Potsdam	12,568	530·2	588·4	1,118·5	89
Rostock	7,074	427·3	463·4	890·6	126
Schwerin	8,672	281·2	309·0	590·2	68
Suhl	3,856	260·2	289·0	549·1	142
German Democratic Republic	*108,333*	*7,851·8*	*8,845·5*	*16,697·4*	*154*

An agreement proclaiming the Oder–Neisse line the permanent frontier between Germany and Poland was concluded between the German Democratic Republic and Poland on 6 July 1950. A protocol on the delimitation of the frontier was signed on 27 Jan. 1951.

Resident population of the principal towns as at 30 June 1982:

Berlin (East), capital	1,166,641	Rostock	237,413	Schwerin	122,700
Leipzig	558,414	Halle	233,437	Zwickau	120,852
Dresden	521,011	Erfurt	212,449	Cottbus	117,217
Karl-Marx-Stadt	319,055	Potsdam	133,225	Jena	105,287
Magdeburg	287,579	Gera	127,347	Dessau	103,380

Vital statistics:

	Live births	Marriages	Divorces	Deaths
1979	235,233	136,884	44,735	232,805
1980	245,132	134,195	44,794	238,254
1981	237,543	128,174	48,567	232,244
1982	240,102	124,890	49,874	227,989

Crude birth rate per 1,000 population was 13·3 in 1977; 13·9 in 1978; 14 in 1979; 14·6 in 1980; 14·2 in 1981; 14·4 in 1983; marriage rate, 8·8 in 1977; 8·4 in 1978; 8·2 in 1979; 8 in 1980; 7·7 in 1982; death rate, 13·5 in 1977; 13·9 in 1978; 13·9 in 1979; 14·2 in 1980; 13·9 in 1981; 13·7 in 1982; infantile mortality per 100 live births, 1·3 in 1977, 1978 and 1979; 1·2 in 1980 and 1981; 1·1 in 1982.

CLIMATE. The continental-type climate makes winters crisp and clear, but with cold easterly winds bringing very low temperatures and appreciable snowfall. Summers are hot, but with much convectional rainfall. Berlin, Jan. 31°F (−0·5°C), July 66°F (19°C). Annual rainfall 22·5″ (563 mm). Dresden, Jan. 30°F (−1°C), July 65°F (18·5°C). Annual rainfall 27·2″ (680 mm).

CONSTITUTION AND GOVERNMENT. Upon the establishment of the Federal Republic of Germany, the People's Council of the Soviet-occupied zone, appointed in 1948, was converted into a provisional People's Chamber.

On 7 Oct. 1949 the provisional People's Chamber enacted a constitution of the 'German Democratic Republic'.

In July 1952 the 5 Länder of Mecklenburg, Saxony-Anhalt, Brandenburg, Saxony and Thuringia were replaced by 14 districts *(Bezirke)*.

A new 'socialist constitution' was approved by a referendum on 6 April 1968 (revised in 1974), when 94·54% of the electorate voted for the constitution; it came into force on 8 April 1968. The People's Chamber, of 500 deputies, is 'the supreme organ of state power'; it elects the Council of State, the Council of Ministers, the National Defence Council and the judges of the Supreme Court.

Council of State. After the death of President Wilhelm Pieck (7 Sept. 1960), the People's Chamber on 12 Sept. 1960 abolished the office of president and elected instead a council of state. This consists of a chairman, 6 deputy chairmen, 18 members and a secretary. The Council is authorized to issue decisions and to interpret existing laws. The Chairman of the Council of State represents the GDR in international law. *Chairman:* Erich Honecker.

On 13 Oct. 1978 the People's Chamber passed a 'law for the defence of the GDR'; the People's Chamber is authorized to declare a 'state of defence'.

At the elections held on 16 Oct. 1976, the list of the National Front parties and democratic organizations of the GDR received 99·86% of the valid votes.

The cabinet was, in Oct. 1983, composed as follows:

Chairman: Willi Stoph.

First Deputy Chairmen: Alfred Neumann, Werner Krolikowski.

Deputy Chairmen: Günther Kleiber, Wolfgang Rauchfuss, Gerhard Schürer, Dr Gerhard Weiss, Dr Herbert Weiz, Manfred Flegel, Hans-Joachin Heusinger, Dr Hans Reichelt, Rudolph Schulze.

Members of the Presidium of the Council of Ministers: All members of the cabinet and Bruno Lietz, Walter Halbritter, Horst Sölle.

Considerable political power is exercised by the Politburo of the Socialist Unity Party (SUP).

National flag: Black, red, golden (horizontal); in the centre, on both sides, the coat of arms showing a hammer and compass with a wreath of grain entwined with a black, red and golden ribbon.

National hymn: Auferstanden aus Ruinen (tune by Hanns Eisler).

East Berlin ('Democratic Berlin') is the capital of the German Democratic Republic. *Head of the Administration (Magistrat):* Erhard Krack.

DEFENCE. On 18 Jan. 1956 the Diet passed laws for the establishment of a 'national people's army' and a defence ministry. A 12-member defence council, under the chairmanship of E. Honecker, General Secretary of the Central Committee, was set up on 10 Feb. 1960.

The 'law for the defence of the GDR', of 20 Sept. 1960, makes military service (in case of emergency) and civil defence compulsory for all citizens.

Conscription for men between 18 and 25 years was introduced on 24 Jan. 1962 (18 months' service in the army, 2 years in the navy and air force).

Twenty Soviet divisions of about 258,000 men with about 1,000 heavy tanks and 6,000 armoured vehicles are stationed in the German Democratic Republic, chiefly along the Polish border.

Army. The Army, set up on 1 March 1956, is organized in 2 army corps, including 2 armoured divisions and 4 motorized infantry divisions. Operationally these divisions are subordinate to the Soviet formations of the Warsaw Pact forces.

They are armed with about 3,100 tanks (mostly Soviet T-54, T-55 and T-72), 216 self-propelled guns and ground-to-air 'Guideline' missiles. The Border Police was incorporated in the Army in Sept. 1961. Total army strength was (1984) 116,000 (69,000 conscripts) with a reserve of 580,000 men.

Police. The Police force *(Volkspolizei)* numbered 25,000 security and 46,500 border troops. There are also 450,000 militiamen organized in combat groups. The militia receive military instruction from the People's Police.

Navy. The 'People's Navy' includes 2 frigates, 9 corvettes, 15 missile boats, 50 torpedo boats, 9 patrol vessels, 50 coastal minesweepers, 3 intelligence ships, 16 coastguard boats, 12 tank landing ships, 10 oilers, 2 training ships, 4 supply ships, 4 survey vessels, 9 small survey craft, 13 buoy tenders, 3 diving vessels, 1 cable layer, 2 torpedo recovery craft, 2 icebreakers, 30 auxiliary ships and service craft and 13 tugs. Personnel in 1984 totalled 16,000 officers and men, including the GBK Coastal Frontier Guards *(Grenz Brigade Küste)*.

Air Force. The *ex*-'air-police', set up in Nov. 1950, had in 1983 a strength of about 37,000 officers and men and 375 combat aircraft. Two air defence divisions consist respectively of 2 and 4 regiments (each with 3 squadrons of 12 aircraft), plus a fighter training division, equipped with MiG-21 and a small number of MiG-23 supersonic day and all-weather interceptors. There is 1 squadron of MiG-21 reconnaissance fighters. Four ground attack squadrons have begun replacing MiG-17s with MiG-27s, and Mi-24 gunship helicopters have been delivered to the German Democratic Republic. Other units include a regiment of Mi-2, Mi-4 and Mi-8 helicopters, a regiment of An-2, Let L.410, Il-14, An-26 and Tu-134 transports and a Flight Training Division with Yak-18, Trener, L-29 Delfin, L-39 Albatros, MiG-15UTI and MiG-21U training aircraft. 'Guideline' and 'Goa' surface-to-air missile units are operational.

INTERNATIONAL RELATIONS

Membership. The German Democratic Republic is a member of UN and Comecon.

ECONOMY

Budget. The budget of the German Democratic Republic was as follows (in M 1m.) for calendar years:

	1977	1978	1979	1980	1981	1982
Revenue	124,543	132,612	140,633	160,652	167,466	177,913
Expenditure	124,103	132,103	140,223	160,283	167,159	177,838

Of the 1982 expenditures, 54,875m. was earmarked for health and social services, education and *Kultur*.

Currency. The circulating Reichsmark notes were in June 1948 exchanged for 'Deutsche Mark' (East), renamed 'Mark of the German Bank of Issue' (MDN) from 1 Aug. 1964 and further renamed 'the Mark of the GDR' (M) from 1967. The circulation of notes and coins at 31 Dec. 1980 was M 12,250m. In March 1984, £1 = 3·83 M; US$1 = 2·60 M.

Banking. The most important banking institutions of the GDR are the Staatsbank der DDR Berlin, which is the bank of issue, and the Industrie- und Handelsbank der DDR. Savings, as at 31 Dec. 1982, totalled M 107,573m.

Weights and Measures. The metric system is in force.

ENERGY AND NATURAL RESOURCES

Electricity. Generation of electric power (in 1m. kwh.): 1950, 19,466; 1960, 40,305; 1970, 67,650; 1976, 89,150; 1977, 91,996; 1978, 95,963; 1979, 96,845; 1980, 98,808; 1981, 100,720; 1982, 102,906.

Minerals. In the production of lignite, the German Democratic Republic takes first place in world output. Rare metals, such as uranium, cobalt, bismuth, arsenic and antimony, are being exploited in the western Erzgebirge and eastern Thuringia.

The principal minerals are as follows (in 1,000 tonnes):

	1979	1980	1981	1982		1979	1980	1981	1982
Coal	256	258	267	276	Potash	3,395	3,422	3,460	3,434
Lignite	256,000	258,097	266,734	...					

Agriculture. In 1982 the arable land was 4·73m. hectares; meadows and pastures, 1,256,800 hectares; forests, 2,959,200 hectares. Since 1945, the estates of Junkers, war criminals and leading Nazis have been sequestrated; 3·1m. hectares have been distributed among farmers. In 1982 there were 3,949 collective farms of 5m. hectares of land independently cultivated and 86,842 hectares of land given for co-operative cultivation and 478 state farms of 435,104 hectares.

The yield of the main crops in 1982 was as follows (in 1,000 tonnes): Potatoes, 8,883; sugar-beet, 7,193; barley, 4,055; wheat, 2,739; rye, 2,119; oats, 848.

Livestock (in 1,000) in 1982: Cattle, 5,690 (including 2,124 milch cows); pigs, 12,107; sheep, 2,198; goats, 24; horses, 70; poultry, 51,611.

Forestry. In 1982 there were 2,959,200 hectares of forest and woodland. Production (1982) 10,348,100 cu. metres. The industry employed 45,877 people in 1982.

Fisheries. Total catch (1982) 269,867 tonnes. Inland catch (1982) was 19,971 tonnes, of which 10,022 tonnes was carp.

INDUSTRY AND TRADE

Industry. Industry produced about 69% of the national income in 1982; the nationally owned and co-operative undertakings were responsible for 96·5% of the net product. The percentage of privately owned enterprises was 32·8 in 1950 and 2·9 in 1982.

There were, at 31 Dec. 1982, 4,029 industrial establishments with 3,190,361 employees.

Production of iron and steel (in 1,000 tonnes):

	1977	1978	1979	1980	1981	1982
Crude steel	6,850	6,976	7,023	7,308	7,467	7,168
Pig-iron	2,628	2,560	...	...	...	...
Rolled steel	4,802	5,002	5,100	5,128	5,061	4,959

Leading chemical products in 1982 were (in 1,000 tonnes): Sulphuric acid, 920; nitrogen fertilizers, 948; calcined soda, 882; caustic soda, 695; other industrial products: cement, 11,721; passenger cars (no.), 183,000; television receivers (no.), 652,000; shoes, 82m. pairs; plastics and synthetic resins, 990.

The 340-km pipeline from Schwedt on the Oder to Leuna near Halle was completed in Jan. 1967; it carried Soviet oil direct to the industrial centre of the GDR. Total pipeline length within GDR (1980) 1,301 km.

Commerce. Total trade was as follows (in 1m. Valuta-Mark):

	Total Imports	Exports		Total Imports	Exports
1970	39,597	15,485	1981	132,927	49,888
1979	108,845	39,271	1982	145,109	55,164
1980	120,101	42,609			

Total trade between the German Democratic Republic and UK (British Department of Trade returns, in £1,000 sterling):

	1978	1979	1980	1981	1982	1983
Imports to UK	88,392	111,705	88,127	93,507	133,921	157,625
Exports and re-exports from UK	47,466	58,162	94,124	82,975	63,665	60,997

COMMUNICATIONS

Roads. There were, in 1982, 47,461 km of classified roads. Road traffic amounted to 16,236m. ton-km of goods and 27,408km. passenger-km. Motor vehicles included, 2,921,574 passenger cars, 228,368 lorries and 1·3m. motor cycles.

Railways. There were, in 1982, 28,222 km of railway line, of which 1,788 km were electrified. Traffic amounted to 54,016m. ton-km of goods and 24,785m. passenger-km.

Aviation. Interflug operates services between Berlin and Prague, Warsaw, Budapest, Bucharest, Moscow, Sofia, Belgrade, Tirana, Cairo, Baghdad, Beirut and other capitals. Passengers carried (1982), 1,286,700; freight, 27,975 tonnes.

Shipping. The port of Rostock is being reconstructed and enlarged so as to absorb the sea-going traffic of the German Democratic Republic and the Czechoslovak hinterland. In 1982 navigable inland waterways had a length of 2,319 km; they handled 2,290m. ton-km of goods. The state-owned merchant fleet had, in 1982, 173 vessels of 1,171,468 BRT.

Post and Broadcasting. In 1978 there were 11,999 post offices and agencies and (1982) 3,251,950 telephone subscribers. *Staatliches Kommittee für Rundfunk*, the governmental broadcasting station, broadcasts 4 programmes on long-, medium- and short-waves, and on FM. The foreign service is broadcast in 11 languages on medium-and short-waves, using the name Radio Berlin International. The transmitters are located at Königswusterhausen, Leipzig and Nauen. Radio Volga transmits on long-waves from Burg and broadcasts in Russian for the Soviet Armed Forces in Germany. More than 80% of the programmes are relays from Radio Moscow. Radio Moscow is using relay transmitters on medium-waves at Leipzig for programmes in German. *Deutsche Freiheitssender 904* and *Deutsche Soldatensender* are clandestine stations claiming to be operating from the Federal Republic although they are located not far from Burg. *Fernsehen der DDR* broadcasts 2 TV programmes in colour, using SECAM-system. Number of wireless licences (1982), 6·44m.; TV licences, 5·85m.

Cinemas (1982). There were 832 cinemas with a seating capacity of 260,285.

Newspapers (1978). There were 39 daily newspapers with a combined circulation of 7·1m.

RELIGION, EDUCATION AND WELFARE

Religion. According to the census of 1950, 80·5% of the population were Protestants and 11% were Roman Catholics.

Education. There are 2 types of schools: *(a)* the General polytechnical secondary schools, with 10 grades (the former elementary and middle schools), numbering (1982) 5,156 with 2,024,220 pupils; *(b)* the Extended polytechnical secondary schools, with the 11th and 12th grades, numbering (1982) 220 with 45,334 pupils.

In addition there were (1982), 973 vocational schools *(Berufsschulen)* with 16,640 teachers and 431,000 pupils and 240 technical schools with 172,058 pupils. There were also 54 universities and other high schools with 130,442 students, including 64,248 women.

Health. In 1978, 559 hospitals had 171,280 beds. There were (1982) 577 polyclinics each with at least 6 special branches. There were 35,377 physicians and 10,512 dentists.

DIPLOMATIC REPRESENTATIVES

Of the German Democratic Republic in Great Britain (124 The Broadway, London, NW9 7BS)
Ambassador: Martin Bierbach.

Of Great Britain in the German Democratic Republic (108 Berlin, Unter den Linden 32/34)
Ambassador: P. M. Maxey, CMG.

Of the German Democratic Republic in the USA (1717 Massachusetts Ave., NW, Washington, D.C. 20036)
Ambassador: Dr Gerhard Herder.

Of the USA in the German Democratic Republic (108 Berlin, Neustädtische Kirchstrasse 4-5)
Ambassador: Rozanne L. Ridgway.

Of the German Democratic Republic to the United Nations
Ambassador: Harry Ott.

Books of Reference

Statistical Information: The central statistical agency is the Staatliche Zentralverwaltung für Statistik (Hans-Beimler-Str. 70–72, 102, Berlin).

The Zentralverwaltung publishes: *Statistisches Jahrbuch der Deutschen Demokratischen Republik* (from 1956).—*Statistisches Taschenbuch der DDR* (annual, from 1959; also Arabic, English, French, Russian, Spanish editions).—*Statistische Praxis* (from 1946).

Deutsche Demokratische Republik, Handbuch. Leipzig, 1979

Jahrbuch der Deutschen Demokratischen Republik, ed. Institut für Zeitgeschichte (latest issue, 1961).

Biermann, W., *Demokratiserung in der DDR?* Cologne, 1978
Childs, D., *East Germany.* London, 1969.—*The GDR: Moscow's German Ally.* London, 1983
Heitzer, H., *GDR: An Historical Outline.* Dresden, 1981
Jacobsen, H.-A., *Drei Jahrzehnte Aussenpolitik der DDR.* Munich, 1979
Krisch, H., *German Politics under Soviet Occupation.* New York and London, 1974
Legters, L. H., *The German Democratic Republic: A Developed Socialist Society.* Boulder, 1978

National Library: Deutsche Bücherei, Leipzig C.1. *Director:* Helmut Rötzsch.—Deutsche Staatsbibliothek, Berlin. *Director:* Professor H. Kunze.

FEDERAL REPUBLIC OF GERMANY

Capital: Bonn
Population: 61·6m. (1982)
GNP per capita: US$13,590 (1980)

Bundesrepublik Deutschland

HISTORY. The Federal Republic of Germany became a sovereign independent country on 5 May 1955 and is a member of EEC, the Council of Europe, Western European Union, NATO, the European Coal and Steel Community, Euratom, the European Monetary Agreement and the Agencies of the UN.

In June 1948 USA, UK and France agreed on a central government for the 3 western zones. An Occupation Statute, which came into force on 30 Sept. 1949, reduced the responsibilities of the occupation authorities. Formally, the Federal Republic of Germany came into existence on 21 Sept. 1949. The Petersberg Agreement of 22 Nov. 1949 freed the Federal Republic of numerous restrictions of the Occupation Statute. In 1951 USA, UK and France as well as other states terminated the state of war with Germany; the Soviet Union followed on 25 Jan. 1955. On 5 May 1955 the High Commissioners of USA, UK and France signed a proclamation revoking the Occupation Statute. On the same day, the Paris and London treaties, signed in Oct. 1954, came into force and established the sovereignty of the Federal Republic of Germany.

AREA AND POPULATION. In April 1949 some minor frontier rectifications were carried out in favour of the Netherlands (68 sq. km), Belgium (18 sq. km), Luxembourg (6 sq. km) and France (7 sq. km), subject to a final peace settlement. Belgium (1956) and the Netherlands (1963) returned most of this territory to Germany.

Area and estimated population as at 30 June 1982:

Länder	Area in sq. km	Population Male	Female	Total	Per sq. km
Schleswig-Holstein	15,720	1,263,200	1,356,200	2,619,400	167
Hamburg	755	762,700	867,700	1,630,400	2,160
Lower Saxony	47,431	3,485,000	3,776,600	7,261,600	153
Bremen	404	324,500	364,500	689,000	1,704
North Rhine-Westphalia	34,066	8,134,800	8,875,600	17,010,400	499
Hessen	21,114	2,696,300	2,910,000	5,606,300	266
Rhineland-Palatinate	19,848	1,740,000	1,898,900	3,639,000	183
Baden-Württemberg	35,752	4,472,200	4,808,900	9,281,100	269
Bavaria	70,546	5,246,900	5,714,400	10,961,300	155
Saarland	2,571	503,000	557,400	1,060,400	412
Berlin (West)	480	854,800	1,024,300	1,879,100	3,914
Federal Republic	248,687 [1]	*29,483,300*	*32,154,600*	*61,637,900*	*248*

[1] 96,018 sq. miles.

Vital statistics for calendar years:

	Marriages	Live births	Of these illegitimate	Deaths
1979	344,823	581,984	41,504	711,732
1980	362,408	620,657	46,923	714,117
1981	359,658	624,557	49,363	722,192
1982	...	621,173	52,750	715,857

The annual rate of the population increase or decrease (including migration) was −0·2% in 1974; −0·6% in 1975; −0·3% in 1976; −0·2% in 1977; −0·1% in 1978; +0·2% in 1979.

Crude birth rate in 1981 was 10·1 per 1,000 population; marriage rate, 5·8; death rate, 11·7; infantile mortality (1979), 1·5 per 100 live births.

Migrants from Eastern Germany to the Federal Republic, including West Berlin, totalled about 2,022,000 between 1955 and 1961. The East German Government tried to stop the outflow by erecting a concrete wall which later became a heavily fortified barrier along the border in Berlin on 13 Aug. 1961; despite the Berlin wall, the figures registered for persons moving from Eastern Germany and East Berlin into the Federal Republic were 20,700 in 1970, 19,900 in 1971, 19,700 in 1972, 17,300 in 1973, 16,200 in 1974, 20,300 in 1975, 17,100 in 1976, 13,900 in 1977, 14,400 in 1978 and 15,400 in 1979; most of them are older people with permission to emigrate. Migrants from the Federal Republic to Eastern Germany totalled about 279,000 between 1955 and 1961, 2,500 in 1969, 2,100 in 1970, 1,900 in 1971, 1,800 in 1972, 1,700 in 1973, 1,500 in 1974, 1,400 in 1975, 1,300 in 1976, 1,200 in 1977, 1,200 in 1978 and 1,300 in 1979.

The resident population of the principal towns was estimated as follows on 30 June 1982:

Town	Land	Population	Town	Land	Population
Berlin (West)	Berlin (West)	1,879,100	Herne	N. Rhine-Westph.	180,100
Hamburg	Hamburg	1,630,400	Mülheim a.d.		
München	Bavaria	1,288,200	Ruhr	N. Rhine-Westph.	178,800
Köln	N. Rhine-Westph.	967,700	Freiburg im		
Essen	N. Rhine-Westph.	641,500	Breisgau	Baden-Württ.	177,700
Frankfurt am			Hamm	N. Rhine-Westph.	171,000
Main	Hessen	622,500	Solingen	N. Rhine-Westph.	163,500
Dortmund	N. Rhine-Westph.	603,000	Leverkusen	N. Rhine-Westph.	159,500
Düsseldorf	N. Rhine-Westph.	585,900	Ludwigshafen		
Stuttgart	Baden-Württ.	575,200	am Rhein	Rhinel.-Pal.	158,700
Duisburg	N. Rhine-Westph.	551,700	Osnabrück	Lower Saxony	156,800
Bremen	Bremen	551,000	Neuss	N. Rhine-Westph.	148,100
Hanover	Lower Saxony	527,500	Darmstadt	Hessen	138,400
Nürnberg	Bavaria	481,000	Bremerhaven	Bremen	138,000
Bochum	N. Rhine-Westph.	396,000	Oldenburg	Lower Saxony	137,900
Wuppertal	N. Rhine-Westph.	390,000	Heidelberg	Baden-Württ.	134,100
Bielefeld	N. Rhine-Westph.	·311,100	Regensburg	Bavaria	132,300
Mannheim	Baden-Württ.	303,800	Göttingen	Lower Saxony	131,500
Gelsenkirchen	N. Rhine-Westph.	299,700	Würzburg	Bavaria	129,300
Bonn	N. Rhine-Westph.	292,200	Remscheid	N. Rhine-Westph.	127,500
Wiesbaden	Hessen	274,100	Wolfsburg	Lower Saxony	125,300
Münster			Recklinghausen	N. Rhine-Westph.	119,500
(Westf.)	N. Rhine-Westph.	271,600	Bottrop	N. Rhine-Westph.	114,000
Karlsruhe	Baden-Württ.	271,300	Koblenz	Rhinel.-Pal.	113,300
Braunschweig	Lower Saxony	258,800	Salzgitter	Lower Saxony	112,500
Mönchenglad-			Heilbronn	Baden-Württ.	111,500
bach	N. Rhine-Westph.	258,600	Siegen	N. Rhine-Westph.	111,000
Kiel	Schleswig-Holstein	249,400	Paderborn	N. Rhine-Westph.	110,100
Augsburg	Bavaria	247,500	Offenbach am		
Aachen	N. Rhine-Westph.	244,000	Main	Hessen	110,000
Oberhausen	N. Rhine-Westph.	228,200	Pforzheim	Baden-Württ.	105,400
Krefeld	N. Rhine-Westph.	223,800	Witten	N. Rhine-Westph.	105,200
Lübeck	Schleswig-Holstein	218,500	Erlangen	Bavaria	102,700
Hagen	N. Rhine-Westph.	215,600	Hildesheim	Lower Saxony	102,400
Kassel	Hessen	193,300	Bergisch		
Saarbrücken	Saarland	191,500	Gladbach	N. Rhine-Westph.	101,500
Mainz	Rhinel.-Pal.	186,600	Ulm	Baden-Württ.	100,100

CLIMATE. Oceanic influences are only found in the north-west where winters are quite mild but stormy. Elsewhere a continental climate is general. To the east and south, winter temperatures are lower, with bright frosty weather and considerable snowfall. Summer temperatures are fairly uniform throughout. Rainfall is well distributed over the year, varying from 20″ (500 mm) on low ground to 80″ (2,000 mm) in Alpine parts.

CONSTITUTION. The Constituent Assembly (known as the 'Parliamentary Council') met in Bonn on 1 Sept. 1948, and worked out a Basic Law which was approved by a two-thirds majority of the parliaments of the participating Länder and came into force on 23 May 1949.

The Basic Law *(Grundgesetz)* consists of a preamble and 146 articles. The first section deals with the basic rights which are legally binding for legislation, administration and jurisdiction.

The Federal Republic of Germany is a democratic and social federal state. For the time being the Basic Law applies to the Länder Baden-Württemberg, Bavaria, Bremen, Greater Berlin (temporarily suspended), Hamburg, Hessen, Lower Saxony, North Rhine-Westphalia, Rhineland-Palatinate, Saarland and Schleswig-Holstein. The Basic Law decrees that the general rules of international law form part of the federal law. The constitutions of the Länder must conform to the principles of a republican, democratic and social state based on the rule of law. Executive power is vested in the Länder, unless the Basic Law prescribes or permits otherwise. Federal law supersedes Land law.

The organs of the Federal Republic are:

The Federal Diet *(Bundestag)*, elected in universal, direct, free, equal and secret elections, for a term of 4 years.

The Federal Council *(Bundesrat)*, consisting of members of the governments of the Länder. Each Land has at least 3 votes. Länder with more than 2m. inhabitants have 4, Länder with more than 6m. inhabitants have 5 votes.

The Federal President *(Bundespräsident)* is elected by the Federal Assembly for a term of 5 years and represents the Federal Republic in international relations. Re-election is admissible only once. The Federal Assembly (which meets only for the election of the Federal President) consists of the members of the Federal Diet and an equal number of members elected by the popular representative bodies of the Länder according to a particular system of semi-proportional representation.

The Federal Government consists of the Federal Chancellor, elected by the Federal Diet on the proposal of the Federal President, and the Federal Ministers, who are appointed and dismissed by the Federal President upon the proposal of the Federal Chancellor.

The Federal Republic has exclusive legislation on: (1) foreign affairs (2) federal citizenship; (3) freedom of movement, passports, immigration and emigration, and extradition; (4) currency, money and coinage, weights and measures, and regulation of time and calendar; (5) customs, commercial and navigation agreements, traffic in goods and payments with foreign countries, including customs and frontier protection; (6) federal railways and air traffic; (7) post and telecommunications; (8) the legal status of persons in the employment of the Federation and of public law corporations under direct supervision of the Federal Government; (9) trade marks, copyright and publishing rights; (10) co-operation of the Federal Republic and the Länder in the criminal police and in matters concerning the protection of the constitution, the establishment of a Federal Office of Criminal Police, as well as the combating of international crime; (11) federal statistics.

For concurrent legislation in which the Länder have legislative rights if and as far as the Federal Republic does not exercise its legislative powers, *see* THE STATESMAN'S YEAR-BOOK, 1956, p. 1038.

Federal laws are passed by the Federal Diet and after their adoption submitted to the Federal Council, which has a limited veto. The Basic Law may be amended only upon the approval of two-thirds of the members of the Federal Diet and two-thirds of the votes of the Federal Council.

The foreign service, federal finance, railways, postal services, waterways and shipping are under direct federal administration.

In the field of finance the Federal Republic has exclusive legislation on customs and financial monopolies and concurrent legislation on: (1) excise taxes and taxes on transactions, in particular, taxes on real-estate acquisition, incremented value and on fire protection; (2) taxes on income, property, inheritance and donations; (3) real estate, industrial and trade taxes, with the exception of the determining of the tax rates.

Customs, the yield of monopolies, excise taxes with the exception of the beer tax, the transportation tax, the turnover tax and property dues serving non-recurrent purposes accrue to the Federal Republic. The Federal Republic can, by federal law, claim part of the income and corporation taxes to cover its expenditures not covered by other revenues. Financial jurisdiction is uniformly regulated by federal legislation.

National flag: Three horizontal stripes of black, red, gold.

National anthem: Einigkeit und Recht und Freiheit (words by H. Hoffmann, 1841; tune by J. Haydn, 1797).

GOVERNMENT. The *Federal Diet*, elected in March 1983 was composed of 498 members. In addition, there are 22 members for Berlin who, however, have no vote.

State of the parties: Social Democrats (SPD), 193 (1980: 218); Christian Democrats (CDU), 191 (174); Free Democrats (FDP), 34 (53); Christian Socialists (CSU), 53 (52); *Die Grünen* 27 (–).

Bonn on the Rhine is the capital of the Federal Republic.

Federal President: Karl Castens (elected 1 July 1979).

The Cabinet, a coalition of Christian Democrats, Christian Socialists and Free Democrats, in March 1984, was as follows:

Chancellor: Dr Helmut Kohl (CDU).
Deputy Chancellor, Minister of Foreign Affairs: Hans-Dietrich Genscher (FDP).
Interior: Dr Friedrich Zimmermann (CSU).
Justice: Hans A. Engelhard (FDP).
Finance: Dr Gerhard Stoltenberg (CDU).
Economics: Dr Otto Count Lambsdorff (FDP).
Food, Agriculture and Forestry: Ignaz Kiechle (CSU).
Intra-German Relations: Heinrich Windelen (CDU).
Labour and Social Affairs: Dr Norbert Blüm (CDU).
Defence: Dr Manfred Wörner (CDU).
Youth, Family Affairs and Health: Dr Heiner Geissler (CDU).
Transport: Dr Werner Dollinger (CSU).
Posts and Telecommunications: Dr Christian Schwarz-Schilling (CDU).
Regional Planning, Building and Urban Development: Dr Oscar Schneider (CSU).
Research and Technology: Dr Heinz Riesenhuber (CDU).
Education and Science: Dr Dorothee Wilms (CDU).
Economic Co-operation: Dr Jürgen Warnke (CSU).

DEFENCE. The Paris Treaties, which entered into force in May 1955, stipulated a contribution of the Federal Republic to western defence within the framework of NATO and the Western European Union. The Federal Armed Forces *(Bundeswehr)* had a total strength (1984) of 495,000 all ranks (236,000 conscripts) and a further 750,000 reserves.

Army. The Army is divided into the Field Army, containing the units assigned to NATO in event of war, and the Territorial Army. The Field Army is organized in 3 corps, comprising 17 armoured, 15 armoured infantry, 1 mountain and 3 airborne brigades. Equipment includes 1,232 M-48, 2,437 Leopard I and 585 Leopard II tanks. The Territorial Army is organized into 6 Military Districts, under 3 Territorial Commands. Its main task is to defend rear areas and remains under national control even in wartime. Total strength was (1984) 335,500 (conscripts 185,000; Territorial Army 38,000).

Navy. The Federal Navy comprises 24 diesel-powered coastal submarines, 7 destroyers, 10 frigates, 6 corvettes, 40 fast missile boats (Exocet armed), 10 fast torpedo boats, a light cruiser type training ship, 10 frigate-type support ships, 18 coastal minesweepers and minehunters, 21 fast minesweepers, 20 inshore minesweepers, 22 landing craft, 13 supply and support ships, 2 fleet replenishment ships, 7 oilers, 6 coast patrol boats, 12 torpedo recovery vessels, 9 coastguard cutters, 3 repair ships, 24 tugs and 70 auxiliaries and service craft.

The construction programme includes submarines and mine countermeasures vessels. Two more guided missile frigates and 10 minehunters are projected under the new development programme.

The Naval Air Arm has 2 wings (each 2 squadrons of 18 aircraft) of F-104G Starfighters and 1 wing of Breguet Atlantic maritime patrol bombers, supplemented by an anti-submarine helicopter wing (Lynx for new frigates). The air-sea rescue wing has re-equipped with Sea King helicopters.

Navy personnel in 1984 totalled 5,640 officers and 32,860 men, including the Naval Air Arm.

Air Force. Since Oct. 1970, the *Luftwaffe* has comprised the following commands: German Air Force Tactical Command, German Air Force Support Command (including two German Air Force Regional Support Commands—North and South) and General Air Force Office. Its strength in 1983 was approximately 105,900 officers and other ranks and about 500 first-line combat aircraft. Combat units, including 12 heavy fighter-bomber squadrons, 7 light ground attack/reconnaissance squadrons, 4 reconnaissance squadrons, 8 surface-to-surface missile squadrons, and an air defence force of 4 interceptor squadrons, 24 batteries of *Nike-Hercules* and 36 batteries of *Improved Hawk* surface-to-air missiles, are assigned to NATO. There are 4 F-4F Phantom interceptor squadrons, 3 Tornado attack squadrons, 5 F-104G fighter-bomber squadrons (re-equipping with Tornados), 4 attack squadrons of F-4Fs, 4 RF-4E Phantom reconnaissance squadrons, and 7 light attack/reconnaissance squadrons of Alpha Jets. Four transport squadrons (each 15 aircraft) with turboprop Transall C-160 aircraft and 1 wing of 5 helicopter squadrons with UH-1D Iroquois add to the air mobility of the *Bundeswehr*. There are also VIP, support and light transport aircraft, and Piaggio P.149D initial training aircraft. Guided weapons in service include 8 squadrons of *Pershing* surface-to-surface missiles and 6 battalions of *Nike-Hercules* and 9 battalions of *Improved Hawk* surface-to-air missiles.

Pilots undergo basic and advanced training in USA.

INTERNATIONAL RELATIONS

Membership. The Federal Republic of Germany is a member of UN, OECD, EEC, NATO and the Council of Europe.

ECONOMY

Budget. The budget of the Federal Government shows the following figures (in DM 1m.) for calendar years:

	1976	1977	1978	1979
Revenues				
Federal taxes and customs duties	35,647	37,130	39,343	40,656
Share of Federal Government in joint taxes and trade tax levy	95,253	106,874	114,744	125,480
Tax-like charges	0	4	2	0
Others	5,727	9,063	5,746	11,380
Total revenue	136,627	149,755	163,152	177,515

	1976	1977	1978	1979
Expenditures				
Defence	33,300	34,206	36,675	38,594
Social security	59,085	62,119	67,102	69,509
Agriculture and food	1,919	1,923	2,071	2,167
Transport and communications	11,491	11,853	12,932	14,511
Electricity, gas, water supply, industries and services	3,148	3,765	5,428	5,519
Education and science	8,450	8,569	9,632	10,934
Housing and settlements	2,046	2,077	1,779	2,265
All other expenditure	43,075	47,872	53,457	59,859
Total expenditure	162,514	171,952	189,508	203,358
Balance of transitory means	+ 31	− 10	+ 43	− 210
Net financing balance	−25,856	−22,206	−26,313	−26,053
Financed from:				
Loans	−46,316	−36,755	−46,505	−54,542
Coinage	− 74	− 494	− 373	− 443
Less:				
Redemption payments	+20,533	+15,043	+20,565	+28,931
Withdrawals from reserves	—	—	—	—

The total debt of the Federal Government, the Equalization of Burdens Fund, ERP-Special Fund and the Länder was DM 322,344m., as at 31 Dec. 1979 (excluding debt of communities/local authorities).

Currency. On 31 Aug. 1980 the circulation of coins in the Federal Republic amounted to DM 7,225m.; that of notes and coins to DM 87,981m. In March 1984, £1=3·83 DM; US$1=2·60.

Banking. On 14 Feb. 1948 the Bank of German Länder (Bank deutscher Länder) was established in Frankfurt as the central bank of issue for the Federal Republic and designated the exclusive agency for issuing notes and coins.

The Land Central Banks and the Berlin Central Bank were merged with the Bank deutscher Länder as from 1 Aug. 1957. The Bank deutscher Länder became the Deutsche Bundesbank.

The most important items of the balance sheets of the Deutsche Bundesbank in Frankfurt on 31 Aug. 1980 were as follows (in DM 1m.):

Assets	
Gold	13,688·0
Balances at foreign banks and money market investments abroad	42,886·3
Foreign notes, coins, bills and cheques	3,657·1
Loans to international institutions and consolidation loans	4,035·0
Domestic bills of exchange and advances against securities	37,233·1
Equalization claims [1]	8,136·4
Liabilities	
Bank-notes in circulation	80,755·4
Deposits	61,964·7

[1] From the monetary reform.

Weights and Measures. The metric system is in force.

ENERGY AND NATURAL RESOURCES

Electricity. In 1981, 368,810m. kwh. were produced.

Oil. In 1979, 67,445 tonnes of petroleum and 12,097,009 tonnes of diesel oil were produced.

Minerals. The great bulk of the minerals in Germany is produced in North Rhine-Westphalia (for coal, iron and metal smelting-works), Central Germany (for brown coal), Lower Saxony (Salzgitter for iron ore; the Harz for metal ore). The chief oil-fields are in Lower Saxony (Emsland).

The quantities of the principal minerals raised in the Federal Republic were as follows (in 1,000 tonnes):

Minerals	1977	1978	1979	1980	1981	1982
Coal	84,513	83,936	86,319	87,146	88,460	89,014
Lignite	122,920	123,559	130,579	129,833	130,619	127,307
Iron ore	2,868	1,608	1,655	1,945	1,572	1,304
Metal ore	1,031	762	...	...	...	...
Potash	23,799	25,260	27,674	29,317	28,192	22,536
Crude oil	5,401	5,059	4,774	4,631	4,459	4,256

The production of iron and steel in the Federal Republic was (in 1,000 tonnes):

	1977	1978	1979	1980	1981	1982
Pig-iron	28,959	30,148	35,167	33,873	31,876	27,621
Steel ingots and castings	38,985	41,253	46,040	43,838	41,610	35,880
Rolled products finished	29,411	31,102	33,616	...	...	...

Agriculture. In 1979 the agricultural holdings with a farm area of 1 hectare or more in the Federal Republic of Germany cultivated an agricultural area of 12·3m. hectares, of which the arable land was 7,290,400 hectares; meadows and pastures 4,796,700 hectares; vineyards, orchards, nurseries 226,400.

The total number of agricultural holdings in the Federal Republic, and their classification by size, according to the agricultural area, were as follows (1982):

	Total	1–5 hectares	5–20 hectares	20–100 hectares	Over 100 hectares
Schleswig-Holstein	32,106	6,319	6,142	18,496	1,149
Hamburg	1,463	908	324	222	9
Lower Saxony	119,699	32,873	35,233	49,886	1,707
Bremen	484	163	122	197	2
North Rhine-Westphalia	96,926	30,199	35,315	30,833	579
Hessen	60,385	23,608	23,634	12,934	209
Rhineland-Palatinate	59,367	24,429	22,868	11,957	113
Baden-Württemberg	131,855	54,326	54,196	23,003	330
Bavaria	257,093	68,627	133,327	54,544	595
Saarland	4,606	2,049	1,393	1,140	24
Berlin (West)	139	83	32	24	—
Federal Republic	764,123	243,584	312,586	203,236	4,717

Area (in 1,000 hectares) and yield (in 1,000 tonnes) of the main crops in the Federal Republic, were as follows:

	Area				Yield			
	1979	1980	1981	1982	1979	1980	1981	1982
Wheat	1,627	1,668	1,631	1,578	8,061	8,156	8,313	8,632
Rye	564	546	484	407	2,114	2,098	1,729	1,639
Barley	1,989	2,001	2,044	2,021	8,184	8,826	8,687	9,460
Oats	728	691	682	723	2,994	2,658	2,678	3,113
Potatoes	276	258	246	238	8,716	6,694	7,585	7,049
Sugar-beet	393	395	444	418	18,340	19,122	24,380	22,732

Wine must production (in 1m. hectolitres): 7·4 in 1960; 9·9 in 1970; 6·8 in 1974; 9·2 in 1975; 8·7 in 1976; 10·4 in 1977; 7·3 in 1978; 8·2 in 1979; 4·6 in 1980; 7·2 in 1981; 15·4 in 1982.

Livestock on 3 Dec. 1982 were as follows: Cattle, 15,098,400 (including 5,530,300 milch cows); horses, 369,100; sheep, 1,172,200; pigs, 22,477,800; goats, 36,000 (1981); poultry, 79,697,800.

Forestry. Forestry is an industry of great importance, conducted under the care of the State on scientific methods. The forest area is 7·2m. hectares. In 1979 cuttings amounted to 27·3m. cu. metres in the Federal Republic.

Fisheries. In 1982 the yield of sea and coastal fishing in the Federal Republic was 276,349 tonnes live weight, valued at DM 359·73m.

At the end of 1981 the number of vessels of the fishing fleet was 32 trawlers (70,490 gross tons), 2 luggers and 646 cutters.

INDUSTRY AND TRADE

Industry. In 1979, 49,176 establishments (with 20 and more employees; production industries including handicrafts) in the Federal Republic employed 7,607,239 persons; of these 1,011,981 were employed in machine construction; 310,571 in textile industry; 969,444 in electrical engineering; 228,954 in mining; 559,729 in chemical industry (average of 12 months).

The production of important industrial products in the Federal Republic was as follows:

Products	1978	1979	1980	1981	1982
Aluminium (1,000 tonnes)	740	742	731	729	723
Potassium fertilizers, K_2O (1,000 tonnes)	2,470	2,616	2,737	2,592	2,057
Sulphuric acid, SO_3 (1,000 tonnes) [1]	3,813	4,136	3,900	3,945	3,092
Soda, Na_2CO_3 (1,000 tonnes) [1]	1,230	1,401	1,411	1,189	1,106
Cement (1,000 tonnes) [1]	34,000	35,659	34,551	31,498	30,079
Rayon:					
Staple fibre (1,000 tonnes)	73	76	73⎫	149	134
Continuous rayon filament (1,000 tonnes) [1]	62	62	70⎭		
Cotton yarn (1,000 tonnes) [1]	164	161	170	148	168
Woollen yarn (1,000 tonnes) [1]	53	56	60	52	47
Passenger cars (1,000) [2]	3,901	3,943	3,530	3,590	3,771
Commercial cars and buses (1,000)	282	297	...	...	...
Bicycles (1,000)	2,923	3,099	3,643	3,441	3,089

[1] Including the quantities processed in the same factories. [2] Including dual-purpose vehicles.

Labour. The economically active persons (excluding the armed forces) totalled 25·81m. at the 1%-sample survey of the microcensus of April 1979. Of the total, 2,339,000 were self-employed, 943,000 unpaid family workers and 22·53m. dependently employed persons. 1,441,000 were engaged in agriculture and forestry; 11,872,000 in production industries; 4,682,000 in commerce and transport; 7,817,000 in other industries; 852,000 were unemployed.

In June 1979 foreign workers numbered 1,933,651, including 540,471 Turks, 367,301 Yugoslavs, 300,442 Italians, 140,139 Greeks, 89,992 Spaniards and 495,306 others.

Trade Unions. The main trade union organization is the German Trade Union Federation *(Deutscher Gewerkschaftsbund)* with 7,751,523 members at 31 Dec. 1978 in 17 unions, the largest being *I.G.Metall* (with 2,680,798 members), *Gewerkschaft Öffentliche Dienste, Transport und Verkehr* (1,099,396 members), *I.G.Chemie-Papier-Keramik* (650,675 members), *I.G.Bau-Steine-Erden* (517,842 members), *Deutsche Postgewerkschaft* (428,878 members) and *Gewerkschaft der Eisenbahner Deutschlands* (414,195 members); they are organized in industrial branches such that only one union operates within each enterprise. Outside the DGB lie several smaller unions, the principal being the *Deutscher Beamtenbund* (DBB) or civil servants union with about 800,000 members and the *Deutsche Angestellten-Gewerkschaft* (DAG) or union of salaried staff with about 480,000 members. There is also a smaller Christian Trade Union movement with about 250,000 members.

Commerce. The distribution of the imports and exports of the Federal Republic according to principal countries was as follows (in DM 1m.):

Country	Imports			Exports		
	1980	1981	1982	1980	1981	1982
Argentina	1,289·5	1,125·8	1,399·5	2,285·3	2,360·6	1,495·7
Australia	1,298·1	1,405·6	1,487·9	2,092·5	2,703·9	3,193·5
Austria	9,825·4	10,279·3	11,115·1	19,257·4	20,009·7	20,620·4
Belgium–Luxembourg	24,461·6	24,674·8	25,480·2	27,481·7	28,907·0	31,081·6
Brazil	2,908·7	3,449·4	4,191·7	2,798·6	2,277·1	2,162·6
Canada	3,603·4	3,278·3	3,360·9	2,178·3	2,740·6	2,528·1
Denmark	5,735·2	5,926·9	6,547·1	6,668·4	7,525·8	8,451·6
Finland	2,953·9	3,363·8	3,201·2	3,309·4	3,697·1	4,220·1
France	36,591·0	40,123·8	42,878·0	46,614·8	51,909·9	60,128·7
Greece	2,754·2	2,946·5	2,747·7	3,774·2	4,653·0	4,686·2
India	1,134·8	1,278·6	1,267·9	1,372·2	2,249·4	2,102·1
Iran	3,381·9	1,527·0	1,738·5	2,734·4	3,639·5	3,402·9
Italy	27,083·4	27,562·0	28,710·0	29,935·9	31,306·5	32,374·8
Japan	10,434·3	12,910·0	12,646·6	3,960·0	4,758·7	5,165·8
Libya	7,865·8	7,417·1	7,232·0	2,282·5	3,379·9	2,835·0
Netherlands	39,147·5	44,322·9	45,946·3	33,273·3	33,884·0	36,144·1
Norway	7,737·8	9,418·1	9,901·4	4,016·4	4,950·3	5,536·6
Rep. of South Africa	3,262·5	3,184·0	3,075·5	4,595·0	6,160·5	6,128·9
Spain	4,410·8	4,662·4	5,036·6	5,068·2	6,283·9	7,462·8
Sweden	7,223·9	7,681·5	7,496·2	10,127·4	10,426·7	11,350·0
Switzerland	12,139·2	12,615·2	12,927·6	20,007·2	20,727·8	21,691·2
USSR	7,517·4	9,224·8	11,357·7	7,943·2	7,621·4	9,395·0
UK	22,859·7	27,502·2	27,001·9	22,917·3	26,162·9	31,316·7
USA	25,689·9	28,387·5	28,212·6	21,477·6	25,975·9	28,120·1

The main items of imports in 1979 were finished manufactures (US$61,963m.) and raw materials (US$23,383m.); exports, finished manufactures (US$112,875m.) and semi-finished manufactures (US$32,059m.).

Total trade between the Federal Republic of Germany and UK (British Department of Trade returns, in £1,000 sterling):

	1979	1980	1981	1982	1983
Imports to UK	5,799,403	5,700,861	5,941,130	7,414,073	9,667,444
Exports and re-exports from UK	4,243,975	5,113,032	5,515,965	5,414,733	6,063,989

Tourism. In 1979, 10·3m. arrivals and 24·7m. 'overnights' of foreign visitors were registered. Foreign exchange receipts from international tourism amounted to DM 10,524m.

COMMUNICATIONS

Roads. On 1 Jan. 1981 the total length of classified roads in the Federal Republic was 172,392 km, including 7,538 km autobahn, 32,558 km federal highways, 65,637 km first-class and 66,659 km second-class country roads. Motor vehicles licensed in the Federal Republic on 1 July 1979 numbered 26,109,079 (including 479,100 motor cycles, 22,535,469 passenger cars, 1,236,120 trucks, 68,360 buses and 1,624,713 tractors; not including 186,814 motor cycles and motor vehicles up to 50 cm³ cylinder capacity and 2,014,129 mopeds).

Road casualties in 1979 totalled 486,441 injured and 13,222 killed.

Railways. Length of Federal Railway in 1982 was 28,238 km (1,435 mm gauge) of which 11,180 km was electrified. In 1982 it carried 61,667m. tonne-km and 46,651m. passenger-km. There are also some 3,000 km of privately-owned and other minor railways.

Aviation. The Deutsche Lufthansa AG (set up on 6 Jan. 1953, as AG für Luftverkehrsbedarf and renamed on 6 Aug. 1954), with headquarters at Cologne, has capital of DM 900m. The Federal Republic owns 74·3%, Land North Rhine-Westphalia 2·2%, the Federal Railways, 0·9%, Federal Post 1·8%, Kreditanstalt für Wiederaufbau 3% and private industry 17·8%.

Lufthansa operate internal, European, African, North and South Atlantic, Near and Far East routes. In 1979 the Lufthansa carried 13·7m. passengers, 399,327 tonnes of cargo and 47,730 tonnes of mail.

Shipping. On 31 Dec. 1979 the Federal German mercantile marine comprised 1,732 ocean-going vessels of 7,877,100 BRT.

The inland-waterways fleet in the Federal Republic on 31 Dec. 1979 comprised 3·79m. tons. The length of the navigable rivers and canals in use was 4,329 km.

Sea-going ships (foreign trade only) in 1979 loaded 36m. tonnes clearing and unloaded 121m. tonnes entering in the ports of the Federal Republic. Inland waterways carried 246m. tonnes in 1979.

Post and Broadcasting. The Federal Republic had, on 31 Dec. 1980, 18,688 post and telecommunications offices. Number of telephones (1982) 30,122,023.

The postal bus services covered, in 1979, 187m. km and carried 331m. passengers.

The post office savings banks had, on 31 Dec. 1980, 18,966,000 depositors with DM 28,359m. to their credit.

In the financial year 1978 the postal revenues amounted to DM 35,501m. and the expenditure to DM 33,406m.

Arbeitsgemeinschaft der öffentlich-rechtlichen Rundfunkanstalten der Bundesrepublik Deutschland (ARD) is an organization for co-operation between the German broadcasting stations. ARD also broadcast a common TV programme under the name *Deutsches Fernsehen* throughout the Federal Republic. In addition regional programmes are broadcast. Number of wireless licences, 21,151,540; of television licences, 19,421,539 (1979).

Cinemas (31 Dec. 1977). There were 2,698 cinemas with a seating capacity of 800,000 and 12 drive-in cinemas for 9,978 cars.

Newspapers (1977). There were 372 daily newspapers with a combined circulation of 24m.

JUSTICE, RELIGION, EDUCATION AND WELFARE

Justice. Justice is administered by the federal courts and by the courts of the Länder. In criminal procedures, civil cases and procedures of non-contentious jurisdiction the courts on the Land level are the local courts *(Amtsgerichte)*, the regional courts *(Landgerichte)* and the courts of appeal *(Oberlandesgerichte)*. On the federal level decisions regarding these matters are taken by the Federal Court *(Bundesgerichtshof)* at Karlsruhe. In labour law disputes the courts of the first and second instance are the labour courts and the Land labour courts and in the third instance, the Federal Labour Court *(Bundesarbeitsgericht)* at Kassel. Disputes about public law in matters of social security, unemployment insurance, maintenance of war victims and similar cases are dealt with in the first and second instances by the social courts and the Land social courts and in the third instance by the Federal Social Court *(Bundessozialgericht)* at Kassel. In most tax matters the finance courts of the Länder are competent and in the second instance, the Federal Finance Court *(Bundesfinanzhof)* at Munich. Other controversies of public law in non-constitutional matters are decided in the first and second instance by the administrative and the higher administrative courts *(Observerwaltungsgerichte)* of the Länder, and in the third instance by the Federal Administrative Court *(Bundesverwaltungsgericht)* at Berlin.

For the inquiry into maritime accidents the admiralty courts *(Seeämter)* are competent on the Land level and in the second instance the Federal Admiralty Court *(Bundesoberseeamt)* at Hamburg.

The constitutional courts of the Länder decide on constitutional questions. The Federal Constitutional Court *(Bundesverfassungsgericht)* as the supreme German court decides such questions as loss of basic rights, unconstitutional character of political parties, validity of laws, charges against judges and complaints regarding violations of basic rights by the public force.

The death sentence is abolished.

Religion. Of the population 49% are Protestants, 44·6% Roman Catholics and 0·1% Jews (census, 1970).

The Evangelical Church in Germany consists of 18 member-churches in the Federal Republic of Germany and West Berlin (7 Lutheran Churches, 8 United-Lutheran-Reformed-Churches, 2 Reformed Churches and 1 Confederation of United member Churches: 'Church of the Union'). Its organs are the Synod, the Church Conference and the Council under the chairmanship of Bishop Dr Eduard Lohse (Hanover). The Protestants numbered about 26·5m. in 1978. There are also some 12 Evangelical Free Churches. The 8 territorial churches in German Democratic Republic established the Federation of Evangelical Churches in 1969.

There are 5 Catholic archbishops and 17 bishoprics. Chairman of the German Bishops' Conference is Cardinal Höffner, Archbishop of Cologne. A concordat between Germany and the Holy See was signed on 20 July and ratified on 10 Sept. 1933.

The 'Old Catholics', who are in full communion with the Anglican Churches, numbered about 30,000 in 1977; they have a bishop at Bonn.

Evangelische Kirche in Deutschland. Hanover, 1979
Taschenbuch der evangelischen Kirche in Deutschland. Frankfurt, 1980
Kirchliches Handbuch. Amtliches statistisches Jahrbuch der Katholischen Kirche Deutschlands. Vol. 28. Cologne, 1976
Pastoral der Kirche fremden—Eroffnungsreferat der Deutschen Bischofskonferenz 1979 in Fulda—von Kardinal Joseph Höffner. Bonn, 1979
Alt-Katholisches Jahrbuch. Bonn, 1978
Katholiken und ihre Kirche, Protestanten und ihre Kirche. Munich, 1977

Education. Schools providing general education are primary and post-primary schools *(Grund- und Hauptschulen)*, special schools *(Sonderschulen)*, secondary modern schools *(Realschulen)*, grammar schools *(Gymnasien)* and comprehensive schools. Primary schools: Attendance is compulsory for all children having completed their 6th year of age. Compulsory education extends 9 years. After the first 4 (or 6) years at primary school children may attend post-primary schools, secondary modern schools, grammar schools and other schools of general secondary education. The secondary modern school comprises 6, the grammar school 9 years. The final Grammar School Certificate (Abitur-Higher School Certificate) entitles the holder to enter any institution of higher education. There are also special schools for retarded, physically or mentally handicapped and socially maladjusted children.

In 1981 there were in the Federal Republic 18,541 primary and post-primary schools with 4,775,189 pupils; 2,827 special schools with 336,980 pupils, 2,633 secondary modern schools with 1,323,467 pupils; 2,480 grammar schools with 2,106,430 pupils; 262 comprehensive schools (primary and secondary stage) with 225,562 pupils.

Vocational education is provided in part-time, full-time and advanced vocational schools (*Berufs-, Berufsaufbau-, Berufsfach-* and *Fachschulen*, including *Fachschulen für Technik* and *Schulen des Gesundheitswesens*). Running parallel to the occupation, part-time vocational schools offer 6 to 12 hours per week of additional compulsory schooling. All young people who are apprentices, in some other employment or even unemployed have to attend them in general up to the age of 18 years or until the completion of the practical vocational training. Full-time vocational schools comprise courses of at least one year. They prepare for commercial and domestic occupations as well as specialized occupations in the field of handicrafts. Advanced full-time vocational schools are attended by pupils having completed their 18th year of age; courses vary from 6 months to 3 or more years.

In 1981 there were 7,140 full- and part-time vocational schools with 72,604 teachers and 2,490,732 pupils (1,082,174 female); 2,954 advanced vocational schools with 8,979 teachers and 203,745 pupils (130,604 female).

Higher Education. Universities and equivalent institutions; teacher-training colleges and equivalent institutions which train teachers for primary schools, special schools, intermediate schools and schools providing vocational education; colleges of music, fine arts and the college for physical education in Cologne.

Higher technical colleges offer highly qualified full-time vocational instruction. There were, in the winter term 1979–80, 111 higher technical colleges with 180,651 students (50,609 female).

During the winter term 1979–80 there were 228 academic institutions of higher education with 981,808 students (353,432 female; 56,601 foreigners); they comprise 64 universities with 728,334 students (258,422 female); 6 Roman Catholic theological colleges and 4 Protestant theological colleges with together 2,182 students (591 female).

In the winter term 1979–80 there were 17 teacher-training colleges and equivalent institutions with 53,665 students (36,133 female); 15 colleges of music, 10 colleges of fine arts and the college of film and television with together 16,976 students (7,677 female).

Health. There were in 1980, 3,234 hospitals with 707,710 beds in the Federal Republic. In 1978 public assistance (including aid to tuberculars) and aid to war victims amounted to DM 12,274m. or DM 200.14 per head of population.[1]

[1] All subsequent statistics relate to the end of 1978 or the calendar year 1978.

Social Welfare. *Social Health Insurance* (originally introduced in 1883). Compulsory insurants are in particular wage-earners and apprentices, salaried employees with an income below the limit of compulsory insurance and the social-insurance pensioners. Voluntary insurance is possible; insurants may voluntarily continue to insure when no longer liable to do so.

Benefits: Medical treatment, medicaments, hospital and nursing care, maternity benefits, death benefits for the insured and their families, sickness payments and out-patients' allowances.

Number of insurants, 34·4m., including compulsory insurants (19·8m.) and pensioners (10·2m.). Number of the cases of incapacity for work 23·4m. Total expenditure, DM 74,991m.

Accident Insurance (originally introduced in 1884). Insured are all persons in employment or service, apprentices and the greater part of the self-employed and the unpaid family workers.

Benefits in the case of industrial injuries and occupational diseases: Medical treatment and nursing care, sickness payments, pensions and other payments in cash and in kind, surviving dependants' pensions.

Number of insurants, 27m.; number of current pensions, 1m.; total expenditure, DM 8,916m.

Workers' and Employees' Old-age Insurance Funds (originally introduced in 1889). Compulsory insurants are all wage-earners and salaried employees, the members of certain liberal professions and—subject to certain conditions—self-employed craftsmen. Insurants may voluntarily continue to insure when no longer liable to do so or increase the insurance.

Benefits: Measures designed to maintain, improve and restore the earning capacity; pensions paid to persons incapable for work, old age and surviving dependants' pensions.

Number of pensions paid, 12m., of which pensions to insurants, 7·8m.; pensions to widows and widowers, 3·6m.; pensions to orphans, 0·5m. Total expenditure, DM 130,763m.

Miners' Pension Insurance Funds. Compulsory insurants are all persons employed in mining, excluding salaried employees functioning as employers. Insurants may voluntarily continue to insure when no longer liable to do so or increase the insurance.

Benefits: Measures designed to maintain, improve and restore the earning capacity; pensions paid to underground workers because of partial disability to work in mines, miners' pensions in the case of complete disability, miners' retirement benefits, surviving dependants' pensions.

Number of pensions paid, 0·7m., of which pensions to insurants, 0·4m.; pensions to widows and widowers, 0·3m.; pensions to orphans, 0·03m. Total expenditure, DM 12,401m.

Farmers' Old-age Pension Funds: Unemployment Insurance and *Unemployment Relief* granted to unemployed persons who are not entitled to unemployment pay. Number of insured, 0·7m.; number of current pensions, 0·3m. Total expenditure, DM 2,505m.

Assistance for War Victims (war-disabled and surviving dependants of war victims).

Benefits: Medical treatment and nursing care, aid to war victims, disablement pensions, basic and equalization pensions paid to widows and orphans, parents' pensions, allowances for nursing care, compensation for occupational detriment, funeral allowances, lump-sum indemnification and indemnification paid upon marriage.

Persons (including those with permanent residence abroad) qualifying for pensions, 2·1m., of which disabled persons, 1m.; widows and widowers, 1m.; orphans, 0·03m.; parents, 0·1m. Total expenditure, DM 12,693m.

Equalization of Burdens (public relief and compensation payments). Eligible are expellees and persons who suffered damage because of the war or in connexion with the currency reform.

Benefits: Basic compensation, war-damage pensions, compensation for household equipment, accommodation assistance, currency-conversion compensation, compensation for holders of 'old savings', training grants, loans and other promotive measures.

Number of recipients of war damage pensions, 0·3m.; payments made (1 Sept. 1952–31 Dec. 1978), DM 99,253m., including basic compensation, DM 24,235m.; war damage pension, DM 38,842m.; accommodation assistance, DM 5,611m.; compensation for household equipment, DM 9,127m.

Family Assistance. From 1 Jan. 1975, children's allowances are being paid, beginning with the first child, to all persons living in the area of application of the law, the income limit being abolished. The monthly allowance is for the first child DM 50. As from 1 Jan. 1978, the allowance has been raised for the second child from DM 70 to DM 80 and for the third and any further child from DM 120 to DM 150. Beginning with 1 Jan. 1979, the beneficiaries have been receiving for the third and any further child DM 200 each per month and as from 1 July 1979 for the second child DM 100. Before, the Federal Law on Children's Allowances *(Bundeskindergeldgesetz)* had provided that all persons living in the area of application of the law were to be paid children's allowances for the third and any further child, unless the beneficiaries were public service employees or recipients of social benefits and as such already entitled to children's allowances. For the second child allowances were paid only to persons who together with their husband/wife had a yearly income not exceeding DM 15,000 (as of 1 Jan. 1973 = DM 16,800, as of 1 Jan. 1974 = DM 18,360); this limitation did not apply in the case of persons with 3 or more children.

Accommodation Allowances for tenants, owners of a homestead, a freehold flat or a small-holder's cottage.

Public Welfare. Public assistance or welfare (the latter from 1 June 1962) for needy persons, namely livelihood aid and aid in special situations (including aid to tuberculars) provided outside and inside institutions, homes and similar establishments.

Aid provided outside institutions, DM 4,376m.; aid provided inside institutions, DM 6,973m.

Aid to War Victims. Benefits for disabled persons and members of their families as well as for surviving dependants, namely vocational assistance, education allowances, supplementary livelihood aid; recovery, accommodation and special assistance. Total expenditure, DM 925m.

Public Youth Welfare. In particular, supervision of foster children, official guardianship, assistance with adoptions and affiliations, social assistance in juvenile courts, educational assistance and correctional education under a court order. Total expenditure, DM 4,427m.

Übersicht über die soziale Sicherung. Bundesministerium für Arbeit und Sozialordnung. 9th ed. Bonn, 1977
Tietz, G., *Zahlenwerk zur Sozialversicherung in der Bundesrepublik Deutschland* (and supplements). Berlin, 1963
Arbeits- und Sozialstatistik. Bundesminister für Arbeit und Sozialordnung, Bonn (from 1950)
Fachserie 13 Sozialleistungen. Statistisches Bundesamt (from 1951)
Fachserie 12 Gesundheitswesen. Statistisches Bundesamt (from 1946)

DIPLOMATIC REPRESENTATIVES

Of the Federal Republic of Germany in Great Britain (21–23 Belgrave Sq., London, SW1X 8PZ)
Ambassador: Baron Rüdiger von Wechmar (accredited 7 Feb. 1984).

Of Great Britain in the Federal Republic of Germany (Friedrich-Ebert-Allee 77, 5300, Bonn)
Ambassador: Sir Jock Taylor, KCMG.

Of the Federal Republic of Germany in the USA (4645 Reservoir Rd, NW, Washington, D.C. 20007)
Ambassador: Peter Hermes.

Of the USA in the Federal Republic of Germany (Delchmannsaue, 5300, Bonn)
Ambassador: Arthur F. Burns.

Of the Federal Republic of Germany to the United Nations
Ambassador: Günther van Well.

Books of Reference

Statistical Information: The central statistical agency is the Statistisches Bundesamt, 62 Wiesbaden, Gustav Stresemann Ring 11. *President:* Franz Kroppenstedt. Its publications include:

Statistisches Jahrbuch für die Bundesrepublik Deutschland (latest issue, 1980); *Wirtschaft und Statistik* (monthly, from 1949); *Das Arbeitsgebiet der Bundesstatistik* (latest issue 1976; also in English: *Survey of German Federal Statistics*).

Documents on Germany under Occupation, 1945–54. Ed. B. Ruhm von Oppen. R. Inst. of Int. Affairs, 1955
Bluhm, G., *Die Oder-Neisse-Linie in der Deutschen Aussenpolitik.* Freiburg, 1963
Dickinson, R. E., *The Regions of Germany.* London, 1945
Grosser, A., *Germany in our Time: A Political History of the Postwar Years.* New York, 1971
Kohl, W. L., and Basevi, G., *West Germany: A European and Global Power.* London, 1982
Pounds, N. J. G., *The Economic Pattern of Modern Germany.* 2nd ed. London, 1966
Roberts, G. K., *West German Politics.* London, 1972
Ryder, A. J., *Twentieth-Century Germany: From Bismarck to Brandt.* London, 1973
Trene, W., *Germany Since 1884.* Bad Godesberg, 1969
Wiskemann, E., *Germany's Eastern Neighbours.* R. Inst. of Int. Affairs, 1956

National Library: Deutsche Bibliothek, Zeppelinallee 4–8; Frankfurt (Main). *Director:* Professor Dr Kurt Köster.

THE LÄNDER

BADEN–WÜRTTEMBERG

AREA AND POPULATION. Baden-Württemberg comprises 35,752 sq. km, with a population (at 31 March 1983) of 9,262,479 (4,459,486 males, 4,802,993 females).

The Land is administratively divided into 4 areas, 9 urban and 35 rural districts, and numbers 1,111 communes. The capital is Stuttgart.

Vital statistics for calendar years:

	Live births	Marriages	Divorces	Deaths
1980	99,721	52,646	12,899	92,418
1981	100,673	52,521	14,006	93,979
1982	100,268	53,768	14,736	93,197

CONSTITUTION. The Land Baden-Württemberg is a merger of the 3 Länder, Baden, Württemberg-Baden and Württemberg-Hohenzollern, which were formed in 1945. The merger was approved by a plebiscite held on 9 Dec. 1951, when 70% of the population voted in its favour.

The Diet, elected on 16 March 1980, consists of 68 Christian Democrats, 40 Social Democrats, 10 Free Democrats, 6 Ecologists.

The Government is formed by Christian Democrats, with Lothar Späth (CDU) as Prime Minister.

AGRICULTURE. Area and yield of the most important crops:

	Area (in 1,000 hectares)			Yield (in 1,000 tonnes)		
	1981	1982	1983[1]	1981	1982	1983[1]
Rye	17·9	14·0	14·1	65·4	54·8	53·5
Wheat	224·3	215·9	223·1	1,114·0	1,071·1	1,046·0
Barley	193·8	202·2	198·8	802·7	901·3	821·4
Oats	93·7	93·2	87·0	385·2	370·1	337·1
Potatoes	23·0	20·4	19·0	693·4	584·7	422·6
Sugar-beet	24·4	22·6	22·3	1,298·8	1,233·8	901·7

[1] Preliminary.

Livestock (3 Dec. 1982): Cattle, 1,832,799 (including 683,422 milch cows); horses, 48,985; pigs, 2,210,520; sheep, 199,374; poultry, 6,054,972.

INDUSTRY. In June 1983 9,709 establishments (with 20 and more employees) employed 1,356,505 persons; of these, 241,153 were employed in machine construction (excluding office machines, data processing equipment and facilities); 80,915 in textile industry; 220,981 in electrical engineering; 205,120 in car building.

LABOUR. The economically active persons totalled 4,280,100 at the 1%-sample survey of the microcensus of April 1982. Of the total 361,400 were self-employed, 125,100 unpaid family workers, 3,773,600 employees; 270,000 were engaged in agriculture and forestry; 2,143,700 in power supply, mining, manufacturing and building, 614,400 in commerce and transport, 1,312,000 in other industries and services.

ROADS. On 1 Jan. 1983 there were 27,797 km of 'classified' roads, including 922 km of autobahn, 4,868 km of federal roads, 12,704 km of first-class and 9,303 km of second-class highways. Motor vehicles, at 1 July 1983, numbered 4,559,262, including, 3,860,609 passenger cars, 8,744 buses, 190,672 lorries, 300,223 tractors and 157,953 motor cycles.

JUSTICE. There are a constitutional court *(Staatsgerichtshof)*, 2 courts of appeal, 17 regional courts, 108 local courts, a Land labour court, 9 labour courts, a Land social court, 8 social courts, a finance court, a higher administrative court *(Verwaltungsgerichtshof)*, 4 administrative courts.

RELIGION. On 1 Jan. 1983, 44% of the population were Protestants and 47·1% Roman Catholics.

EDUCATION. In 1983 there were 2,555 primary schools with 25,595 teachers and 640,143 pupils; 542 special schools with 6,846 teachers and 52,779 pupils; 435 intermediate schools with 10,007 teachers and 243,380 pupils; 412 high schools with 16,207 teachers and 324,303 pupils; 25 *Freie Waldorf* schools with 775 teachers and 12,687 pupils; 15 *Integrierte Gesamtschulen* (comprehensive schools) including stage of orientation, with 693 teachers and 12,859 pupils; 168 *Berufliche Gymnasien* (technical secondary schools) with 34,175 pupils; 391 part-time vocational schools with 276,231 pupils; 1,073 full-time vocational schools with 92,722 pupils; 207 advanced vocational schools with 10,659 pupils; 234 schools for public health occupations with 14,493 students; there were also 64 (full- and part-time) institutions for the training of technicians with 5,024 participants and 35 *Fachhochschulen* (colleges of engineering and others) with 39,087 students; in all vocational schools there were 15,199 teachers.

In the winter term 1982–83 there were 9 universities (Freiburg, 20,982 students; Heidelberg, 24,328; Konstanz, 4,836; Tübingen, 21,082; Karlsruhe, 13,995; Stuttgart, 14,881; Hohenheim, 4,404; Mannheim, 8,169; Ulm, 3,727): 10 teacher-training colleges with 12,242 students; 5 colleges of music and 2 colleges of fine arts, comprising together 3,600 students.

Statistical Information: Statistisches Landesamt Baden-Württemberg (P.O.B. 898, D7000 Stuttgart 1) (*President:* Prof. Max Wingen), publishes: Monatsschrift *Baden-Württemberg in Wort und Zahl*; *Jahrbücher für Statistik und Landeskunde von Baden-Württemberg; Statistik von Baden-Württemberg* (series); *Statistischer und prognostischer Jahres-bericht* (latest issue 1980–81); *Statistisches Taschenbuch* (latest issue 1981).

State Library: Württembergische Landesbibliothek, Konrad-Adenauer-Str. 8, 7000 Stuttgart 1. *Director:* Dr Hans-Peter Geh.

BAVARIA
Bayern

AREA AND POPULATION. Bavaria has an area of 70,553 sq. km. The capital is Munich. There are 7 areas, 96 urban and rural districts and 2,052 communes. The population (30 June 1983) numbered 10,964,228 (5,248,323 males, 5,715,905 females).

Vital statistics for calendar years:

	Live births	Marriages	Divorces	Deaths
1980	114,451	66,368	13,408	122,859
1981	117,063	65,409	15,456	123,736
1982	116,576	65,764	16,538	123,033

CONSTITUTION. The Constituent Assembly, elected on 30 June 1946, passed a constitution on the lines of the democratic constitution of 1919, but with greater emphasis on state rights; this was agreed upon by the Christian Social Union and the Social Democrats.

The elections for the Diet, held on 10 Oct. 1982, had the following results: 133 Christian Social Union, 71 Social Democrats. The cabinet of the Christian Social Union is headed by Minister President Dr Franz Josef Strauss (CSU).

AGRICULTURE. Area and yield of the most important products:

	Area (1,000 hectares)			Yield (1,000 tonnes)		
	1981	1982	1983[1]	1981	1982	1983[1]
Wheat	489·6	443·5	491·1	2,047·5	2,142·1	2,651·0
Rye	69·2	56·2	60·6	239·3	189·9	222·2
Barley	510·6	558·3	533·7	2,073·2	2,395·6	2,232·0
Oats	148·5	150·6	132·0	540·8	589·3	499·3
Potatoes	99·0	94·4	87·7	2,951·1	2,747·8	2,264·0
Sugar-beet	92·5	84·7	77·6	5,580·2	4,911·4	3,869·4

[1] Preliminary results.

Livestock (3 Dec. 1982): 4,966,700 cattle (including 1,992,700 milch cows); 56,700 horses; 287,200 sheep; 3,982,900 pigs; 15,275,900 poultry.

INDUSTRY. In July 1983, 9,573 establishments (with 20 and more employees) employed 1,265,743 persons; of these, 217,399 were employed in electrical engineering; 176,650 in mechanical engineering; 129,315 in clothing industry.

LABOUR. The economically active persons totalled 5,148,400 at the 1% sample survey of the microcensus of April 1982. Of the total, 530,200 were self-employed, 313,400 unpaid family workers, 4,304,800 employees; 2,274,500 in power supply, mining, manufacturing and building; 843,400 in commerce and transport; 1,555,700 in other industries and services.

ROADS. There were, on 1 Jan. 1983, 40,157·5 km of 'classified' roads, including 1,736·3 km of autobahn, 7,158 km of federal roads, 13,752·3 km of first-class and 17,510·8 km of second-class highways. Number of motor vehicles, at 1 July 1983, was 5,339,482, including 4,283,881 passenger cars, 221,043 lorries, 12,503 buses, 542,832 tractors, 231,041 motor cycles.

JUSTICE. There are a constitutional court *(Verfassungsgerichtshof)*, a supreme Land court *(Oberstes Landesgericht)*, 3 courts of appeal, 21 regional courts, 72 local courts, 2 Land labour courts, 11 labour courts, a Land social court, 7 social courts, 2 finance courts, a higher administrative court *(Verwaltungsgerichtshof)*, 6 administrative courts.

RELIGION. At the census of 27 May 1970 there were 69·9% Roman Catholics and 25·7% Protestants.

EDUCATION. In 1982–83 there were 2,828 primary schools with 44,681 teachers and 842,790 pupils; 400 special schools with 4,946 teachers and 43,299 pupils; 333 intermediate schools with 8,754 teachers and 174,712 pupils; 400 high schools with 19,181 teachers and 322,658 pupils; 247 part-time vocational schools with 6,958 teachers and 376,055 pupils, including 61 special part-time vocational schools with 328 teachers and 5,965 pupils; 555 full-time vocational schools with 3,386 teachers and 65,742 pupils including 220 schools for public health occupations with 660 teachers and 15,173 pupils; 275 advanced full-time vocational schools with 1,861 teachers and 25,652 pupils; 79 vocational high schools *(Berufsoberschulen, Fachoberschulen)* with 1,732 teachers and 35,245 pupils.

In the winter term 1982–83 there were 10 universities with 134,909 students (Augsburg, 5,643; Bamberg, 3,575; Bayreuth, 3,191; Eichstätt, 1,990; Erlangen–Nürnberg, 22,145; München, 48,125; Passau, 2,562; Regensburg, 12,055; Würzburg, 16,215; the Technical University of München, 19,408); 2 *Gesamthochschulen* with 2,715 students and the college of philosophy, München, 419. There were also 2 colleges of music, 2 colleges of fine arts and 1 college of television and film, with together 2,283 students; 13 vocational colleges *(Fachhochschulen)* with 43,195 students.

Statistical Information: Bayerisches Landesamt für Statistikund Daten, 51 Neuhauser Str. 8000 Munich, was founded in 1833. *President:* Dr Hans Helmut Schiedermaier. It publishes: *Statistisches Jahrbuch für Bayern.* 1894 ff—*Bayern in Zahlen.* Monthly (from Jan. 1947).—*Zeitschrift des Bayerischen Statistischen Landesamts.* July 1869–1943; 1948 ff.— *Beiträge zur Statistik Bayerns.* 1850 ff.—*Statistische Berichte.* 1951 ff.—*Schaubilderhefte.* 1951 ff.—*Kreisdaten.* 1972 ff.—*Gemeindedaten.* 1973 ff.

Nawiasky, H., and Luesser, C., *Die Verfassung des Freistaates Bayern vom 2. Dez. 1946.* Munich, 1948; supplement, by H. Nawiasky and H. Lechner. Munich, 1953

State Library: Bayerische Staatsbibliothek, Munich 22. *Director:* Dr Franz G. Kaltwasser.

BERLIN

GOVERNMENT. Greater Berlin was under quadripartite Allied government (Kommandatura) until 1 July 1948, when the Soviet element withdrew. On 30 Nov. 1948, a separate Municipal Government was set up in the Soviet Sector (*see* p. 508).

AREA. The total area of Berlin is 883 sq. km, of which Western Berlin covers 480 sq. km and the Soviet Sector 403 sq. km. The *British Sector* includes the administrative districts of Tiergarten, Charlottenburg, Wilmersdorf and Spandau; the *American Sector* those of Kreuzberg, Neukölln, Tempelhof, Schöneberg, Zehlendorf and Steglitz; the *French Sector* covers the administrative districts of Wedding and Reinickendorf, and the *Soviet Sector,* those of Mitte, Friedrichshain, Prenzlauer Berg, Pankow, Weissensee, Lichtenberg, Treptow and Köpenick. The British, American and French sectors form an administrative unit, called Berlin (West).

On 13 Aug. 1961 the East German Government completely severed all communications between West and East Berlin.

BERLIN (WEST)

POPULATION. Population, 31 Dec. 1980, 1,896,230 (855,594 males, 1,040,636 females). According to the census of 27 May 1970, 70·2% were Protestants and 12·5% Roman Catholics.

Vital statistics for calendar years:

	Live births	Marriages	Divorces	Deaths
1978	16,678	10,804	5,600	36,060
1979	17,259	10,754	3,700	35,008
1980	19,000	12,000	5,600	35,000

CONSTITUTION AND GOVERNMENT. According to the constitution of 1 Sept. 1950, Berlin is simultaneously a Land of the Federal Republic (though not yet formally incorporated) and a city. It is governed by a House of Representatives (at least 200 members); the executive power is vested in a Senate, consisting of the Ruling Burgomaster, the deputy Burgomaster and not more than 16 senators.

In the municipal elections, held on 10 May 1981, the Christian Democrats obtained 65 seats; the Social Democrats, 51 seats; the Free Democrats, 7 seats.

Governing Mayor: Dr Richard v. Weizäcker (Christian Democrat).

ECONOMY

Currency. The legal tender of Berlin (West) is the German Mark (DM).

Banking. On 20 March 1949 when the DM (West) became the only legal tender of the Western Sectors, the Zentralbank of Berlin was established. Its functions were similar to those of the Zentralbanks of the Länder of the Federal Republic. The Berlin Central Bank was merged with the Bank deutscher Länder as from 1 Aug. 1957, when the latter became the Deutsche Bundesbank. The legal tender for the Western Sectors of Berlin is being issued by the Deutsche Bundesbank (formerly Bank deutscher Länder).

AGRICULTURE. Agricultural area (May 1980), 3,615 hectares, including 1,100 hectares arable land and 150 hectares gardens, orchards, nurseries.

Livestock (3 Dec. 1980): Cattle, 837; pigs, 4,469; horses, 3,086; sheep, 991.

INDUSTRY. In 1980 (monthly averages), 1,188 establishments (with 20 or more employees) employed 180,000 persons; of these, 64,000 were employed in electrical engineering, 19,000 in machine construction, 4,000 in cloth manufacture, 4,118 in steel construction.

LABOUR. The economically active persons totalled 841,900 at the 1%-sample survey of the microcensus of April 1979. Of the total, 71,900 were self-employed including unpaid family workers, 770,000 employees; 5,300 were engaged in agriculture and forestry; 274,400 in power supply, manufacturing and building; 167,600 in commerce and transport; 394,600 in other industries and services.

ROADS. There were, on 1 Jan. 1976, 117 km of 'classified' roads, including 25 km of autobahn and 92 km of federal roads. On 1 July 1981, 657,041 motor vehicles were registered, including 581,605 passenger cars, 38,050 lorries, 23,578 motor cycles, 2,220 buses and 3,031 tractors.

JUSTICE. There are a court of appeal *(Oberlandesgericht)*, a regional court, 7 local courts, a Land Labour court, a labour court, a Land social court, a social court, a higher administrative court, an administrative court and a finance court.

EDUCATION. In 1980 (preliminary figures) there were 448 schools providing general education (excluding special schools) with 14,784 teachers and 231,000 pupils; 64 special schools with 1,277 teachers and 10,300 pupils. There were a further 45 vocational schools with 1,068 teachers and 38,000 pupils; 24 full-time vocational schools with 432 teachers and 4,805 pupils; 13 *Fachoberschulen* (full-time vocational schools leading up to vocational colleges) with 125 teachers and 1,529 pupils; 34 advanced full-time vocational schools with 250 teachers and 4,754 pupils; 68 schools for public-health occupations with 340 teachers and 4,599 pupils. Moreover, there were 2 schools for technicians with 38 teachers and 543 participants.

In the winter term 1980–81 there was 1 university (142,929 students); 1 technical university (23,592); 1 theological (evangelical) college (354); 1 teacher-training college with 4,768 students; 1 college of fine arts with 3,194 students; 1 vocational college (for economics) (787); 2 colleges for social work (1,483); 1 technical college

(2,702), 1 college of the Federal postal administration (355) and 1 college for public administration (1,307).

Statistical Information: The Statistisches Landesamt Berlin, formerly Statistisches Amt der Stadt Berlin, was founded in 1862 (Fehrbelliner Platz 1, 1000 Berlin 31). *Director:* Günter Appel. It publishes: *Statistisches Jahrbuch* (from 1867): *Berliner Statistik* (monthly, from 1947).—*100 Jahre Berliner Statistik* (1962).

Childs, D. and Johnson, J., *West Berlin: Politics and Society.* London, 1981
Hillenbrand, M. J., *The Future of Berlin.* Monclair, 1981

State Library: Amerika-Gedenkbibliothek-Berliner Zentra bibliothek-, Blücherplatz 1, D1000 Berlin 61. *Director:* Dr Peter K. Liebenow.

BREMEN
Freie Hansestadt Bremen

AREA AND POPULATION. The area of the Land, consisting of the towns and ports of Bremen and Bremerhaven, is 404 sq. km. Population, 31 Dec. 1982, 685,388 (322,650 males, 362,738 females).

Vital statistics for calendar years:

	Live births	Marriages	Divorces	Deaths
1980	5,945	3,778	1,451	8,762
1981	5,966	3,854	1,835	9,246
1982	5,892	3,726	1,951	8,824

CONSTITUTION. Political power is vested in the House of Burgesses *(Bürgerschaft)* which appoints the executive, called the Senate.

The elections of 25 Sept. 1983 had the following result: 58 Social Democratic Party, 37 Christian Democrats, 5 Die Grünen. The Senate is only formed by Social Democrats; its president is Hans Koschnick (Social Democrat).

AGRICULTURE. Agricultural area comprised (1979), 14,440 hectares: yield of grain crops (1982), 8,942 tonnes; potatoes, 429 tonnes.

Livestock (3 Dec. 1982): 16,807 cattle (including 4,802 milch cows); 4,939 pigs; 357 sheep; 1,153 horses; 17,820 poultry.

INDUSTRY. In 1982, 384 establishments (20 and more employees) employed 84,919 persons; of these, 14,066 were employed in shipbuilding (except naval engineering); 7,239 in machine construction; 10,466 in electrical engineering; 4,136 in coffee and tea processing.

LABOUR. The economically active persons totalled 282,400 at the 1%-sample survey of the microcensus of April 1982. Of the total, 19,300 were self-employed, 261,000 employees; 93,100 in power supply, mining, manufacturing and building, 79,800 in commerce and transport, 106,800 in other industries and services.

ROADS. On 1 Jan. 1976 there were 139 km of 'classified' roads, including 45 km of autobahn, 82 km of federal roads, 7 km of first-class and 5 km of second-class highways. Registered motor vehicles on 1 July 1982 numbered 268,298, including 239,585 passenger cars, 15,323 trucks, 2,249 tractors, 688 buses and 7,790 motor cycles.

SHIPPING. Vessels entered in 1982, 9,831 of 45,073,699 net tons; cleared, 9,826 of 45,162,711 net tons. Sea traffic, 1982, incoming 15,302,620 tonnes; outgoing, 10,919,247 tonnes.

JUSTICE. There are a constitutional court *(Staatsgerichtshof)*, a court of appeal, a regional court, 3 local courts, a Land labour court, 2 labour courts, a Land social court, a social court, a finance court, a higher administrative court, an administrative court.

RELIGION. On 27 May 1970 (census) there were 82·4% Protestants and 10·2% Roman Catholics.

EDUCATION. In 1982 there were 332 new system schools with 6,025 teachers and 90,390 pupils; 27 special schools with 574 teachers and 3,900 pupils; 24 part-time vocational schools with 25,870 pupils; 24 full-time vocational schools with 2,160 pupils; 11 advanced vocational schools (including institutions for the training of technicians) with 1,139 pupils; 12 schools for public health occupations with 1,022 pupils.

In the winter term 1982–83 about 7,977 students were enrolled at the university. In addition to the university there were 4 other colleges in 1982–83 with about 5,422 students.

Statistical Information: Statistisches Landesamt Bremen (An der Weide 14–16 (P.B. 101309), D2800 Bremen 1), founded in 1850. *Director:* Ltd Reg. Dir. Volker Hannemann. Its current publications include: *Statistische Mitteilungen Freie Hansestadt Bremen* (from 1948).—*Monatliche Zwischenberichte* (1949–53); *Statistische Monatsberichte* (from 1954).—*Statistische Berichte* (from 1956).—*Statistisches Handbuch für das Land Freie Hansestadt Bremen (1950–60,* 1961; *1960–64,* 1967; *1965–69,* 1971; *1970–74,* 1975; *1975–80,* 1982).—*Bremen im statistischen Zeitvergleich 1950–1976.* 1977.—*Bremen in Zahlen.* 1983.

Beutin, L., *Bremen und Amerika.* Bremen, 1953

University Library: Universitats Str., D2800 Bremen 33. *Director:* Dr Koch.

HAMBURG
Freie und Hansestadt Hamburg

AREA AND POPULATION. In 1938 the territory of the town was reorganized by the amalgamation of the city and its 18 rural districts with 3 urban and 27 rural districts ceded by Prussia. Total area, 754·7 sq. km (1982), including the islands Neuwerk and Scharhörn (7 sq. km). Population (31 Dec. 1982), 1,623,848 (759,758 males, 864,090 females).

Vital statistics for calendar years:

	Live births	Marriages	Divorces	Deaths
1980	13,580	8,930	4,494	23,726
1981	13,494	9,042	5,037	23,746
1982	13,262	8,991	4,762	23,761

CONSTITUTION. The constitution of 6 June 1952 vests the supreme power in the House of Burgesses *(Bürgerschaft)* of 120 members. The executive is in the hands of the Senate, whose members are elected by the Bürgerschaft.

The elections of 19 Dec. 1982 had the following results: Social Democrats, 64; Christian Democrats, 48; Green Alternatives, 8. The First Burgomaster is Dr Klaus von Dohnanyi (Social Democrat).

The territory has been divided into 7 administrative districts.

AGRICULTURE. The agricultural area comprised 16,500 hectares in 1981. Yield, in tonnes, of cereals, 23,000; potatoes, 1,500.

Livestock (3 Dec. 1982): Cattle, 13,288 (including 3,404 milch cows); pigs, 9,651; horses, 2,877; sheep, 2,323; poultry, 66,543.

FISHERIES. In 1982 the yield of sea and coastal fishing was 17,830 tonnes valued at DM 24m.

INDUSTRY. In June 1983, 895 establishments (with 20 and more employees) employed 150,953 persons; of these, 19,575 were employed in electrical engineering; 17,344 in machine construction: 12,978 in shipbuilding (except naval engineering); 14,309 in chemical industry.

LABOUR. The economically active persons totalled 745,700 at the 1%-sample survey of the microcensus of May 1982. Of the total, 64,200 were self-employed, 6,700 unpaid family workers, 674,800 employees; 7,500 were engaged in agriculture and forestry, 221,000 in power supply, mining, manufacturing and building, 205,600 in commerce and transport, 311,600 in other industries and services.

ROADS. On 1 Jan. 1981 there were 3,628 km of roads, including 60 km of autobahn, 157 km of federal roads. Number of motor vehicles (1 July 1982), 639,804, including 570,286 passenger cars, 35,964 lorries, 1,832 buses, 4,727 tractors, 19.697 motor cycles and 7,298 other motor vehicles.

SHIPPING. Hamburg is the largest port in the Federal Republic.

Vessels		1938	1958	1978	1981	1982
Entered:	Number	18,149	19.033	16,636	15,721	15,619
	Tonnage	20,567,311	27,454,640	61,785,643	63,634,740	65,345,047
Cleared:	Number	19,316	20,363	17,414	16,201	16,116
	Tonnage	20,547,148	27,579,914	62,028,141	62,929,364	65,281,211

JUSTICE. There is a constitutional court *(Verfassungsgericht)*, a court of appeal *(Oberlandesgericht)*, a regional court *(Landgericht)*, 6 local courts *(Amtsgerichte)*, a Land labour court, a labour court, a Land social court, a social court, a finance court, a higher administrative court, an administrative court.

RELIGION. On 27 May 1970 (census) Evangelical Church and Free Churches 73·6%, Roman Catholic Church 8·1%.

EDUCATION. In 1982 there were 392 schools of general education (not including *Internationale Schule*) with 8,589 teachers and 190,546 pupils; 60 special schools with 961 teachers and 8,361 pupils; 46 part-time vocational schools with 50,644 pupils; 23 schools with 2,615 pupils in their vocational preparatory year; 23 schools with 1,663 pupils in manual instruction classes; 50 full-time vocational schools with 10,639 pupils; 9 economic secondary schools with 2,258 pupils; 27 advanced vocational schools with 3,793 pupils; 38 schools for public health occupations with 2,670 pupils; 11 vocational introducing schools with 428 pupils and 21 technical superior schools with 2,871 pupils; all these vocational and technical schools have a total number of 2,882 teachers.

In the winter term 1982–83 there was 1 university with 37,693 students; 1 college of music and 1 college of fine arts with together 1,916 students; 1 high school of the *Bundeswehr* with 1,837 students; 1 professional high school *(Fachhochschule)* with 10,097 students; 1 high school for economics and politics with 1,582 students; 1 high school of public administration with 907 students, as well as 1 private professional high school with 155 students.

Statistical Information: The Statistisches Landesamt der Freien und Hansestadt Hamburg (Steckelhörn 12, D2000 Hamburg 11) publishes: *Hamburg in Zahlen, Statistische Berichte, Statistisches Taschenbuch, Statistik des Hamburgischen Staates.*

Klessmann, E., *Geschichte der Stadt Hamburg.* Hamburg, 1981
Meyer-Marwitz, B., *Großer Hamburg Spiegel.* Hamburg, 1978
Studt, B., and Olsen, H., *Hamburg—eine kurzgefaßte Geschichte der Stadt.* Hamburg, 1964

State Library: Staats- und Universitätsbibliothek, Carl von Ossietzky, Von-Melle-Park 3, D2000 Hamburg 13. *Director:* Prof. Dr Horst Gronemeyer.

HESSEN

AREA AND POPULATION. The state of Hessen comprehends the areas of the former Prussian provinces Kurhessen and Nassau (excluding the exclaves belonging to Hessen and the rural counties of Westerwaldkreis and Rhine-Lahn) and of the former Volksstaat Hessen, the provinces Starkenburg (including the parts of Rheinhessen east of the river Rhine) and Oberhessen. Hessen has an area of 21,114 sq. km. Its capital is Wiesbaden. Since 1 Jan. 1981 there have been 3 areas with 5 urban and 21 rural districts and 421 communes. Population, 31 March 1983, was 5,591,794 (2,687,047 males, 2,904,747 females).

Vital statistics for calendar years:

	Live births	Marriages	Divorces	Deaths
1980	54,535	30,199	8,396	63,625
1981	54,132	30,306	9,388	64,570
1982	54,015	30,596	10,546	63,603

CONSTITUTION. The constitution was put into force by popular referendum on 1 Dec. 1946. The Diet, elected on 25 Sept. 1983, consists of 51 Social Democrats, 44 Christian Democrats, 8 Free Democrats, 7 *Die Grünen*.

The Social Democrat cabinet is headed by Minister President Holger Börner (SPD).

AGRICULTURE. Area and yield of the most important crops:

	Area (in 1,000 hectares)			Yield (in 1,000 tonnes)		
	1980	1981	1982	1980	1981	1982
Wheat	140·7	142·0	135·2	675·5	664·0	773·2
Rye	37·8	35·2	31·4	155·2	131·4	124·0
Barley	135·0	139·0	143·0	666·5	565·6	728·4
Oats	73·9	73·6	75·2	284·6	280·7	308·3
Potatoes	13·9	12·6	12·1	309·2	308·1	325·4
Sugar-beet	21·7	24·2	22·4	982·0	1,216·0	1,118·5

Livestock, 3 Dec. 1982: Cattle, 853,500 (including 287,200 milch cows); horses, 32,200; pigs, 1·27m.; sheep, 115,200; poultry, 4,223,800.

INDUSTRY. In Sept. 1982, 3,977 establishments (with 20 and more employees) employed 632,734 persons; of these, 94,765 were employed in chemical industry; 81,731 in electrical engineering; 83,824 in car building; 83,821 in machine construction; 30,819 in food industry.

LABOUR. The economically active persons totalled 2·45m. at the 1%-sample survey of the microcensus of April 1982. Of the total, 205,800 were self-employed, 56,800 unpaid family workers, 2,186,900 employees; 88,900 were engaged in agriculture and forestry, 1,048,900 in power supply, mining, manufacturing and building, 454,000 in commerce and transport, 857,700 in other services.

ROADS. On 1 Jan. 1983 there were 16,624 km of 'classified' roads, including 912 km of autobahn, 3,592 km of federal highways, 7,125 km of first-class highways and 4,994 km of second-class highways. Motor vehicles licensed on 1 July 1983 totalled 2,727,535, including 2,359,170 passenger cars, 5,692 buses, 114,981 trucks, 137,585 tractors and 86,799 motor cycles.

JUSTICE. There are a constitutional court *(Staatsgerichtshof)*, a court of appeal, 9 regional courts, 58 local courts, a Land labour court, 12 labour courts, a Land social court, 7 social courts, a finance court, a higher administrative court *(Verwaltungsgerichtshof)*, 4 administrative courts.

RELIGION. On 27 May 1970 (census) there were 60·5% Protestants and 32·8% Roman Catholics.

EDUCATION. In 1982 there were 1,264 primary schools with 14,137 teachers and 294,288 pupils; 241 special schools with 2,784 teachers and 23,893 pupils; 155 intermediate schools with 2,776 teachers and 61,392 pupils; 152 high schools with 8,794 teachers and 149,886 pupils; 185 *Gesamtschulen* (comprehensive schools) with 11,089 teachers and 200,804 pupils; 117 part-time vocational schools with 3,908 teachers and 165,985 pupils; 257 full-time vocational schools with 2,452 teachers and 40,140 pupils; 56 advanced vocational schools with 356 teachers and 5,320 pupils; 157 schools for public health occupations with 9,214 pupils; there were a further 37 full- and part-time institutions for the training of technicians with 3,272 participants.

In the winter term 1982–83 there were 3 universities (Frankfurt/Main, 27,077 students; Giessen, 15,822; Marburg, 14,618); 1 technical university in Darmstadt (13,354); 1 *Gesamthochschule* (8,510); 15 *Fachhochschulen* (26,519); 2 Roman Catholic theological colleges and 1 Protestant theological college with together 463 students; 1 college of music and 2 colleges of fine arts with together 1,099 students.

Statistical Information: The Hessisches Statistisches Landesamt (Rheinstr. 35–37, D6200 Wiesbaden). *President:* Götz Steppuhn. Main publications: *Statistisches Handbuch für das Land Hessen* (1978–79).—*Statistisches Taschenbuch für das Land Hessen* (1982–83).—*Staat und Wirtschaft in Hessen* (monthly).—*Beiträge zur Statistik Hessens.—Statistische Berichte. —Hessische Gemeindestatistik 1960–61* (5 vols., 1963 ff.).—*Hessische Gemeindestatistik 1970* (5 vols., 1972 ff.).—*Hessische Gemeindestatistik* (annual, 1980 ff.).

State Library: Hessische Landesbibliothek, Rheinstr. 55–57. D6200 Wiesbaden. *Director:* Dr Helmut Schwitzgebel.

LOWER SAXONY
Niedersachsen

AREA AND POPULATION. Lower Saxony (excluding the town of Bremerhaven, and the districts on the right bank of the Elbe in the Soviet Zone) comprises 47,426 sq. km, and is divided into 4 administrative districts, 38 rural districts, 9 towns and 1,019 communes; capital, Hanover.

Estimated population, on 31 Dec. 1982, was 7,256,769 (3,482,680 males, 3,774,089 females).

Vital statistics for calendar years:

	Live births	Marriages	Divorces	Deaths
1980	71,752	40,742	9,792	84,869
1981	72,022	40,282	11,383	86,364
1982	71,407	40,938	12,779	85,867

GOVERNMENT. The Land Niedersachsen was formed on 1 Nov. 1946 by merging the former Prussian province of Hanover and the *Länder* Brunswick, Oldenburg and Schaumburg-Lippe. The Diet, elected on 21 March 1982, consists of 87 Christian Democrats, 63 Social Democrats; Free Democrats, 10 and *Die Grünen*, 11.

The cabinet of the Christian Democratic Union is headed by Minister President Dr Ernst Albrecht (CDU).

AGRICULTURE. Area and yield of the most important crops:

	Area (in 1,000 hectares)			Yield (in 1,000 tonnes)		
	1980	1981	1982	1980	1981	1982
Wheat	293	279	301	1,475	1,449	1,694
Rye	217	198	164	841	675	668
Barley	498	513	464	2,226	2,203	2,077
Oats	175	163	185	691	634	871
Potatoes	72	72	72	2,210	2,436	2,239
Sugar-beet	148	169	160	6,334	7,509	7,712

Livestock, 3 Dec. 1982: Cattle, 3,165,725 (including 1,125,063 milch cows); horses, 80,200; pigs, 6,848,913; sheep, 155,725; poultry, 35,146,159.

FISHERIES. In 1981 the yield of sea and coastal fishing was 110,218 tonnes valued at DM 127m.

INDUSTRY. In Sept. 1982, 4,679 establishments (with 20 and more employees) employed 678,797 persons; of these 62,926 were employed in machine construction; 144,642 in car building; 60,529 in electrical engineering.

LABOUR. The economically active persons totalled 3,066,600 at the 1%-sample survey of the microcensus of April 1982. Of the total 270,700 were self-employed, 129,300 unpaid family workers, 2,666,600 employees; 224,200 were engaged in agriculture and forestry, 1,222,500 in power supply, mining, manufacturing and building, 572,600 in commerce and transport, 1,047,300 in other industries and services.

ROADS. At 1 Jan. 1982 there were 27,886 km of 'classified' roads, including 1,009 km of autobahn, 5,194 km of federal roads, 8,684 km of first-class and 12,999 km of second-class highways.

Number of motor vehicles, 1 Jan. 1982, was 3,265,826 including 2,759,124 passenger cars, 150,794 lorries, 8,785 buses, 241,820 tractors, 92,481 motor cycles.

JUSTICE. There are a constitutional court *(Staatsgerichtshof)*, 3 courts of appeal, 11 regional courts, 79 local courts, a Land labour court, 15 labour courts, a Land social court, 8 social courts, a finance court, a higher administrative court (together with Schleswig-Holstein), 3 administrative courts.

RELIGION. On 27 May 1970 (census) there were 74·6% Protestants and 19·6% Roman Catholics.

EDUCATION. In 1980 there were 2,307 primary schools with 28,092 teachers and 502,497 pupils; 293 special schools with 4,743 teachers and 43,450 pupils; 320 stages of orientation with 179,811 pupils; 270 intermediate schools with 7,157 teachers and 165,699 pupils; 241 grammar schools with 12,623 teachers and 207,542 pupils; 9 evening high schools with 138 teachers and 1,514 pupils; 20 integrated comprehensive schools with 1,684 teachers and 24,492 pupils; 17 co-operative comprehensive schools with 1,490 teachers and 26,186 pupils; 142 part-time vocational schools with 211,447 pupils; 114 year of basic vocational training with 21,071 pupils; 538 full-time vocational schools with 38,008 pupils; 89 *Fachgymnasien* with 8,696 pupils; 126 *Fachoberschulen* with 7,557 pupils (full-time vocational schools leading up to vocational colleges); 56 vocational extension schools with 1,544 pupils; 151 advanced full-time vocational schools (including schools for technicians) with 9,662 pupils; 219 public health schools with 11,527 pupils.

In the winter term 1982–83 there were 4 universities (Göttingen, 27,706 students; Hanover, 22,698; Oldenburg, 7,305; Osnabrück, 5,899); 2 technical universities (Braunschweig, 12,733; Clausthal, 3,241); the medical college of Hanover (3,460), the veterinary college in Hanover (1,726) and the colleges of Hildesheim (1,679) and Lüneburg (1,282).

Statistical Information: The Niedersächsisches Landesverwaltungsamt—Statistik' (Geibelstr. 65, D3000 Hanover 1) fulfils the function of the 'Statistisches Landesamt für Niedersachsen'.
Head of Division: Abteilungsdirektor Dr Günter Koop. Main publications are: *Statistisches Jahrbuch Niedersachsen* (from 1950).—*Statistische Monatshefte Niedersachsen* (from 1947).—*Statistik Niedersachsen.*
State Library: Niedersächsische Staats- und Universitätsbibliothek, Prinzenstr. 1, 3400, Göttingen. *Director:* Helmut Vogt; Niedersächsische Landesbibliothek, Waterloostr. 8, D3000 Hannover 1. *Director:* Dr Wilhelm Totok.

NORTH RHINE-WESTPHALIA

Nordrhein-Westfalen

AREA AND POPULATION. The Land comprises 34,067 sq. km. It is divided into 5 areas, 23 urban and 31 rural districts. Capital Düsseldorf. Population, 31 Dec. 1982, 16,961,183 (8,104,749 males, 8,856,434 females).

Vital statistics for calendar years:

	Live births	Marriages	Divorces	Deaths
1980	169,828	103,547	28,397	195,205
1981	169,704	101,603	32,709	196,773
1982	169,191	102,049	35,331	195,044

GOVERNMENT. The Land Nordrhein-Westfalen is governed by Social Democrats; Minister President, Johannes Rau (SPD). The Diet, elected on 11 May 1980, consists of 106 Social Democrats and 95 Christian Democrats.

AGRICULTURE. Area and yield of the most important crops:

	Area (in 1,000 hectares)			Yield (in 1,000 tonnes)		
	1980	1981	1982	1980	1981	1982
Wheat	221·1	214·1	215·9	1,158·2	1,164·4	1,293·0
Rye	83·3	72·1	56·4	336·1	272·7	241·5
Barley	372·9	382·5	343·8	1,791·1	1,682·8	1,731·7
Oats	109·9	104·4	121·2	436·2	422·4	555·2
Potatoes	22·0	20·4	19·8	648·4	681·0	644·7
Sugar-beet	82·3	89·0	85·5	4,074·9	4,927·6	4,649·4

Livestock, 3 Dec. 1982: Cattle, 1,974,086 (including 637,933 milch cows); pigs, 5,713,050; sheep, 170,836; horses, 85,994; poultry, 14,016,448.

INDUSTRY. In June 1982, 11,200 establishments (with 20 and more employees) employed 2,069,730 persons; of these, 179,347 were employed in mining; 289,010 in machine construction; 181,876 in iron and steel production; 199,708 in chemical industry; 176,819 in electrical engineering; 69,404 in textile industry.

Output and/or production in 1,000 tonnes, 1981: Hard coal, 77,086; lignite, 119,471; pig-iron, 20,432; raw steel ingots, 25,391; rolled steel, 18,217; castings (iron, steel and malleable castings), 1,561; cement, 11,483; fireproof products, 1,123; sulphuric acid (including production of cokeries), 2,185; staple fibres and rayon, 295; metalworking machines, 134; equipment for smelting works and rolling mills, 163; machines for mining industry, 239; cranes and hoisting machinery, 67; installation implements, 77; cables and electric lines, 223; springs of all kinds, 221; chains of all kinds, 79; locks and fittings, 310; spun yarns, 207; electric power, 171,663m. kwh. Of the total population, 12% were engaged in industry.

LABOUR. The economically active persons totalled 6,883,600 at the 1%-sample survey of the microcensus of April 1982. Of the total, 535,000 were self-employed, 90,500 unpaid family workers, 6,258,100 employees; 157,600 were engaged in agriculture and forestry, 3,191,300 in power supply, mining, manufacturing and building, 1·26m. in commerce and transport, 2,279,400 in other industries and services.

ROADS. There were (1 Jan. 1983) 29,588 km of 'classified' roads, including 1,860 km of autobahn, 5,521 km of federal roads, 12,274 km of first-class and 9,933 km of second-class highways. Number of motor vehicles, 1 July 1983, 7,558,582, including 6,144,017 passenger cars, 511,792 lorries, 322,630 motor lorries/trucks, 17,078 buses, 206,572 tractors and 297,559 motor cycles.

JUSTICE. There are a constitutional court *(Verfassungsgerichtshof)*, 3 courts of appeal, 19 regional courts, 131 local courts, 3 Land labour courts, 30 labour courts, a Land social court, 8 social courts, 3 finance courts, a higher administrative court, 7 administrative courts.

RELIGION. On 27 May 1970 (census) there were 41·9% Protestants and 52·5% Roman Catholics.

EDUCATION. In 1982 there were 4,730 primary schools with 70,717 teachers and 1,279,656 pupils; 749 special schools with 12,502 teachers and 102,058 pupils; 556 intermediate schools with 16,784 teachers and 343,010 pupils; 65

Gesamtschulen (comprehensive schools) with 4,288 teachers and 59,588 pupils; 646 high schools with 38,857 teachers and 632,122 pupils; in 1982 there were 296 part-time vocational schools with 443,859 pupils; vocational preparatory year 250 with 31,994 pupils; 326 full-time vocational schools with 112,905 pupils; 117 *Berufsaufbauschulen* with 4,341 pupils; 241 full-time vocational schools leading up to vocational colleges with 30,664 pupils; 148 advanced full-time vocational schools with 15,916 pupils; 562 schools for public health occupations with 9,134 teachers and 30,531 pupils; 19 schools within the scope of a pilot system of courses with 40,556 pupils and 1,508 teachers.

In the winter term 1982–83 there were 7 universities (Bielefeld, 12,524 students; Bochum, 27,012; Bonn, 37,543; Dortmund, 16,456; Düsseldorf, 13,660; Cologne, 39,995; Münster, 42,188); the Technical University of Aachen (33,214); 1 Roman Catholic and 2 Protestant theological colleges with together 961 students. There were also 3 colleges of music, 1 college of fine arts and the college for physical education in Cologne with together 9,737 students; 19 *Fachhochschulen* (vocational colleges) with 73,476 students, and 6 *Gesamthochschulen* with together 67,121 students.

Statistical Information: The Landesamt für Datenverarbeitung und Statistik Nordrhein-Westfalen (Mauerstr. 51, D4000 Düsseldorf 1) was founded in 1946, by amalgamating the provincial statistical offices of Rhineland and Westphalia. *President:* A. Benker. The Landesamt publishes: *Statistisches Jahrbuch Nordrhein-Westfalen.* From 1949.—*Statistisches Taschenbuch Nordrhein-Westfalen.* From 1955 to 1971.

Müller-Wille, W., *Westfalen.* Münster, 1981.

Land Library: Universitätsbibliothek, Universitätsstr. 1, D4000 Düsseldorf. *Director:* Dr G. Gattermann.

RHINELAND-PALATINATE

Rheinland-Pfalz

AREA AND POPULATION. Rhineland-Pfalz comprises 19,845 sq. km. Capital Mainz. Population (at 31 Dec. 1982), 3,636,506 (1,738,284 males, 1,898,222 females).

Vital statistics for calendar years:

	Live births	Marriages	Divorces	Deaths
1980	37,253	23,268	5,579	43,576
1981	37,402	22,710	6,172	44,269
1982	37,132	23,002	6,965	43,567

CONSTITUTION. The constitution of the Land Rheinland-Pfalz was approved by the Consultative Assembly on 25 April 1947 and by referendum on 18 May 1947, when 579,002 voted for and 514,338 against its acceptance.

The elections of 6 March 1983 returned 57 Christian Democrats, 43 Social Democrats.

The cabinet is headed by Bernhard Vogel (Christian Democrat).

AGRICULTURE. Area and yield of the most important products:

	Area (1,000 hectares)			Yield (1,000 tonnes)		
	1980	1981	1982	1980	1981	1982
Wheat	115·7	119·1	112·7	506·0	554·8	574·9
Rye	35·2	31·5	27·2	129·8	119·5	103·8
Barley	138·3	137·1	140·5	546·0	531·7	622·1
Oats	49·2	50·8	51·4	189·5	203·3	193·0
Potatoes	15·4	13·2	13·4	318·4	345·6	349·3
Sugar-beet	22·8	24·1	22·5	1,168·1	1,374·9	1,209·6
Wine (1,000 hectolitres)	59·0	57·9	58·0	3,390·2	5,305·3	10,560·7
Tobacco	1·1	1·1	1·0	...	...	...

Livestock (3 Dec. 1982): Cattle, 638,400 (including 228,000 milch cows); horses, 20,900; sheep, 95,000; pigs, 658,400; poultry, 3,315,500.

INDUSTRY. In Sept. 1983, 2,728 establishments (with 20 and more employees) employed 364,939 persons; of these 69,870 were employed in chemical industry; 21,120 in production of leather goods and footwear; 46,779 in machine construction; 15,746 in processing stones and earthenware.

LABOUR. The economically active persons totalled 1,585,700 at the census of April 1982. Of the total, 141,800 were self-employed, 55,100 unpaid family workers, 1,389,000 employees; 95,100 were engaged in agriculture and forestry, 675,200 in power supply, mining, manufacturing and building, 279,000 in commerce and transport, 536,400 in other industries and services.

ROADS. There were (1 Jan. 1983) 18,503 km of 'classified' roads, including 717 km of autobahn, 3,225 km of federal roads, 6,947 km of first-class and 7,613 km of second-class highways. Number of motor vehicles, 1 July 1983, was 1,859,108, including 1,533,596 passenger cars, 78,184 lorries, 4,937 buses, 145,150 tractors and 82,940 motor cycles.

JUSTICE. There are a constitutional court *(Verfassungsgerichtshof)*, 2 courts of appeal, 8 regional courts, 47 local courts, a Land labour court, 5 labour courts, a Land social court, 4 social courts, a finance court, a higher administrative court, 4 administrative courts.

RELIGION. On 27 May 1970 (census) there were 40·7% Protestants and 55·7% Roman Catholics.

EDUCATION. In 1982 there were 1,192 primary schools with 15,577 teachers and 269,189 pupils; 156 special schools with 2,695 teachers and 16,031 pupils; 106 intermediate schools with 3,198 teachers and 65,758 pupils; 138 high schools with 6,871 teachers and 121,691 pupils; 102 vocational schools with 123,674 pupils; 129 advanced vocational schools and institutions for the training of technicians (full-and part-time) with 7,090 pupils; 116 schools for public health occupations with 342 teachers and 7,202 pupils.

In the summer term 1983 there were the University of Mainz (24,358 students), the University of Kaiserslautern (4,790 students), the University of Trier (5,327 students), the *Hochschule für Verwaltungswissenschaften* in Speyer (400 students), the Roman Catholic Theological College in Trier (376 students) and the Roman Catholic College in Vallendar (44 students). There were also the Teacher-Training College of the Land Rheinland-Pfalz *(Erziehungswissenschaftliche Hochschule)* with 2,654 students and the *Fachhochschule des Landes Rheinland-Pfalz* (college of engineering) with 10,226 students; also 2 private colleges for social-pedagogy (765 students).

Statistical Information: The Statistisches Landesamt Rheinland-Pfalz (Mainzer Str., 15–16, D5427 Bad Ems) was established in 1948. *President:* Dr Weis. Its publications include: *Statistisches Jahrbuch für Rheinland-Pfalz* (from 1948); *Statistische Monatshefte Rheinland-Pfalz* (from 1958); *Statistik von Rheinland-Pfalz* (from 1949) 309 vols. to date; *Rheinland-Pfalz im Spiegel der Statistik* (1968); *Die kreisfreien Städte und Landkreise in Rheinland-Pfalz* (1977); *Rheinland-Pfalz heute* (from 1973); *Benutzerhandbuch des Landesinformationssystems* (1976); *Rheinland-Pfalz heute und morgen* (Mainz, 1981); *Raumordnungsbericht 1981 der Landesregierung Rheinland-Pfalz* (Mainz, 1981). *Landesentwicklungsprogramm 1980* (Mainz, 1980).

Klöpper, R., and Korber, J., *Rheinland-Pfalz in seiner Gliederung nach zentralörtlichen Bereichen.* Remagen, 1957
Süsterhenn, A., and Schäfer, H., *Verfassung von Rheinland-Pfalz: Kommentar.* Koblenz, 1950

SAARLAND

HISTORY. In 1919 the Saar territory was placed under the control of the League of Nations. Following a plebiscite, the territory reverted to Germany in 1935. In

1945 the territory became part of the French Zone of occupation, and was in 1947 accorded an international status inside an economic union with France. In pursuance of the German–French agreement signed in Luxembourg on 27 Oct. 1956 the territory returned to Germany on 1 Jan. 1957. Its re-integration with Germany was completed by 5 July 1959.

AREA AND POPULATION. Saarland has an area of 2,570 sq. km. Estimated population, 31 Dec. 1981, 1,063,033 (504,248 males, 558,785 females). The capital is Saarbrücken.

Vital statistics for calendar years:

	Live births	Marriages	Divorces	Deaths
1979	9,787	7,331	2,259	13,106
1980	10,511	7,587	1,628	13,061
1981	10,496	7,400	2,012	13,097

CONSTITUTION. Saarland now ranks as a *Land* of the Federal German Republic and is represented in the Federal Diet by 8 members. The constitution passed on 15 Dec. 1947 is being revised.

The Saar Diet, elected on 27 April 1980, is composed as follows: 24 Social Democrats, 23 Christian Democrats, 4 Free Democrats.

Saarland is governed by Christian Democrats and Free Democrats in spite of deadlock in Parliament. Minister President: Werner Zeyer (Christian Democrat).

AGRICULTURE AND FORESTRY. The cultivated area occupies 126,500 hectares or slightly more than half the total area; the forest area comprises nearly 32% of the total.

Area and yield of the most important crops:

	Area (1,000 hectares)			Yield (1,000 tonnes)		
	1979	1980	1981	1979	1980	1981
Wheat	7·7	8·0	7·3	36·9	30·7	28·6
Rye	7·7	7·8	6·4	29·8	26·9	21·6
Barley	11·8	12·5	11·7	49·3	47·4	44·3
Oats	7·2	7·1	7·1	26·8	24·4	28·1
Potatoes	1·1	0·9	0·7	31·1	14·7	15·0
Sugar-beet	...	...	...	1·0	0·7	...

Livestock, 3 Dec. 1980: Cattle, 71,667 (including 25,305 milch cows); pigs, 48,817; sheep, 10,472; horses, 3,669; poultry, 408,275.

INDUSTRY. In June 1981, 590 establishments (with 20 and more employees) employed 154,060 persons; of these 25,757 were engaged in coalmining, 30,203 in iron and steel production, 12,153 in machine construction, 10,306 in steel construction. In 1981 the coalmines produced 10·8m. tonnes of coal. Four iron foundries had 13 blast furnaces working and produced 4·2m. tonnes of pig-iron and 4·7m. tonnes of crude steel.

LABOUR. The economically active persons totalled 402,200 at the 1%-sample survey of the microcensus of April 1981. Of the total, 25,900 were self-employed, 6,900 unpaid family workers, 369,400 employees; 5,400 were engaged in agriculture and forestry, 199,500 in power supply, mining, manufacturing and building, 69,000 in commerce and transport, 128,300 in other industries and services.

ROADS. At 1 Jan. 1981 there were 2,139 km of 'classified' roads, including 163 km of autobahn, 443 km of federal roads, 765 km of first-class and 767 km of second-class highways. Number of motor vehicles, 1 July 1981, 473,086, including 419,686 passenger cars, 21,286 lorries, 1,527 buses, 12,018 tractors and 15,041 motor cycles.

JUSTICE. There are a constitutional court *(Verfassungsgerichtshof)*, a court of appeal, a regional court, 11 local courts, a Land labour court, 3 labour courts, a Land social court, a social court, a finance court, a higher administrative court, an administrative court.

RELIGION. On 27 May 1970 (census) 73·8% of the population were Roman Catholics and 24·1% were Protestants.

EDUCATION. In 1982–83 there were 333 primary schools with 4,013 teachers and 71,558 pupils; 53 special schools with 661 teachers and 4,647 pupils; 38 intermediate schools with 1,133 teachers and 18,165 pupils; 37 high schools with 1,985 teachers and 30,491 pupils; 2 *Gesamtschule* (comprehensive high schools) with 125 teachers and 2,096 pupils; 2 *Freie Waldorfschulen* with 38 teachers and 494 pupils; 42 part-time vocational schools with 33.259 pupils; year of commercial basic training: 85 institutions with 241 classes and 5,332 pupils; 20 advanced full-time vocational schools and schools for technicians with 2,297 pupils; 58 full-time vocational schools with 7,234 students; 20 vocational extension schools with 1,477 pupils; 23 *Fachoberschulen* (full-time vocational schools leading up to vocational colleges) with 3,521 students; 39 schools for public health occupations with 2,234 pupils; 2 evening high schools and 1 *Saarland-Kolleg* with together 403 pupils. The number of pupils visiting the vocational schools amounts to 55,757. They are instructed by 1,751 teachers.

In the winter term 1982–83 there was the University of the Saarland with 15,346 students; 1 conservatory with 272 students; 1 vocational college (economics, engineering and design) with 2,082 students; 1 vocational college for social affairs with 155 students; 1 vocational college for public administration with 196 students.

Statistical Information: The Statistisches Amt des Saarlandes (Hardenbergstrasse 3, D6600 Saarbrücken 1) was established on 1 April 1938. As from 1 June 1935, it was an independent agency; its predecessor, 1920–35, was the Statistical Office of the Government Commission of the Saar. *Chief:* Direktor Dr Kunkel. The most important publications are: *Statistisches Handbuch für das Saarland,* from 1950.—*Statistisches Taschenbuch für das Saarland,* from 1959.—*Saarländische Bevölkerungsund Wirtschaftszahlen.* Quarterly, from 1949. —*Saarland in Zahlen* (special issues).—*Einzelschriften zur Statistik des Saarlandes,* from 1950.

Fischer, P., *Die Saar zwischen Deutschland und Frankreich.* Frankfurt, 1959
Freymond, J., *Le Conflit sarrois, 1945–55.* Brussels, 1959. [*The Saar Conflict.* New York, 1960]
Schmidt, R. H., *Saarpolitik 1945–57.* 3 vols. Berlin, 1959–62

SCHLESWIG-HOLSTEIN

AREA AND POPULATION. The area of Schleswig-Holstein is 15,721 sq. km; it is divided into 4 urban and 11 rural districts and 1,131 communes. The capital is Kiel. The population (estimate, 31 Dec. 1982) numbered 2,618,156 (1,262,718 males, 1,355,438 females).

Vital statistics for calendar years:

	Live births	Marriages	Divorces	Deaths
1980	24,545	13,460	4,609	31,278
1981	24,650	13,873	5,030	31,927
1982	24,481	14,416	5,676	31,601

GOVERNMENT. The elections of 13 March 1983 gave the Christian Democrats 39, the Social Democratic Party 34 and the South Schleswig Association 1 seat. Minister President, Dr Uwe Barschel (Christian Democrat).

AGRICULTURE. Area and yield of the most important crops:

	Area (1,000 hectares)			Yield (1,000 tonnes)		
	1980	1981	1982	1980	1981	1982
Wheat	166·8	154·4	144·8	906·0	918·6	1,040·4
Rye	67·6	52·7	51·5	263·1	198·3	233·0
Barley	136·1	153·7	154·5	730·0	773·3	939·8
Oats	41·7	39·4	38·4	166·8	179·4	193·9
Potatoes	5·3	4·8	5·0	142·0	152·8	142·5
Sugar-beet	18·7	21·0	19·4	719·9	888·7	686·2

Livestock, 3 Dec. 1982: 33,200 horses, 1,565,400 cattle (including 541,300 milch cows), 1·74m. pigs, 133,200 sheep, 3,932,900 poultry.

FISHERIES. In 1981 the yield of small-scale deep-sea and inshore fisheries was 48,300 tonnes valued at DM58m.

INDUSTRY. In 1982 (average), 1,654 establishments (with 20 and more employees) employed 174,251 persons; of these, 15,487 were employed in shipbuilding (except naval engineering); 29,470 in machine construction; 23,856 in food and kindred industry; 18,329 in electrical engineering.

LABOUR. The economically active persons totalled 1·12m. at the 1%-sample survey of the microcensus of April 1982. Of the total, 105,000 were self-employed, 31,000 unpaid family workers, 987,000 employees; 69,000 were engaged in agriculture and forestry, 368,000 in power supply, mining, manufacturing and building, 227,000 in commerce and transport, 459,000 in other industries and services.

ROADS. There were (1 Jan. 1983) 9,741 km of 'classified' roads, including 383 km of autobahn, 1,983 km of federal roads, 3,500 km of first-class and 3,875 km of second-class highways. Number of motor vehicles, 1 Jan. 1983, was 1,166,272, including 996,508 passenger cars, 54,170 lorries, 2,784 buses, 72,423 tractors, 29,132 motor cycles.

SHIPPING. The Kiel Canal, 98·7 km (51 miles) long, is on Schleswig-Holstein territory. In 1938, 53,530 vessels of 22·6m. net tons passed through it; in 1980, 56,677 vessels of 53·9m. net tons; in 1981, 52,641 vessels of 53·3m. net tons; in 1982, 49,100 vessels of 52·7m. net tons.

JUSTICE. There are a court of appeal, 4 regional courts, 34 local courts, a Land labour court, 6 labour courts, a Land social court, 4 social courts, a finance court, an administrative court.

RELIGION. On 27 May 1970 (census) there were 86·5% Protestants and 6% Roman Catholics.

EDUCATION. In 1982–83 there were 696 primary schools with 6,504 teachers and 177,104 pupils; 167 special schools with 1,650 teachers and 17,531 pupils; 173 intermediate schools with 3,373 teachers and 80,548 pupils; 96 high schools with 4,495 teachers and 84,574 pupils; 7 *Integrierte Gesamtschulen* (comprehensive schools) with 219 teachers and 3,889 pupils; 39 part-time vocational schools with 1,526 teachers and 88,940 pupils; 140 full-time vocational schools with 485 teachers and 12,503 pupils; 56 advanced vocational schools with 298 teachers and 5,534 pupils; 54 schools for public health occupations with 3,279 pupils; 46 vocational grammar schools with 379 teachers and 6,590 pupils; 5 *Fachhochschulen* (vocational colleges) with 7,307 pupils in the summer term 1983.

In the summer term 1983 the University of Kiel had 15,735 students, 2 teacher-training colleges had 3,189 students, 1 music college had 345 students and 1 *Medizinische Hochschule* in Lübeck had 607 students.

Statistical Information: Statistisches Landesamt Schleswig-Holstein (Fröbel Str. 15–17, D2300 Kiel 1). *Director:* Dr Mohr. Publications: *Statistisches Taschenbuch Schleswig-Holstein,* since 1954.—*Statistisches Jahrbuch Schleswig-Holstein,* since 1951.—*Statistische Monatshefte Schleswig-Holstein,* since 1949.—*Statistische Berichte,* since 1947.—*Beiträge zur historischen Statistik Schleswig-Holstein,* since 1967.—*Lange Reihen,* since 1977.

Baxter, R. R., *The Law of International Waterways.* Harvard Univ. Press, 1964
Brandt, O., *Grundriss der Geschichte Schleswig-Holsteins.* 5th ed. Kiel, 1957
Handbuch für Schleswig-Holstein. 21st ed. Kiel, 1982

State Library: Schleswig-Holsteinische Landesbibliothek, Kiel, Schloss. *Director:* Prof. Dr Klaus Friedland.

GHANA

Capital: Accra
Population: 12·83m. (1983)
GNP per capita: US$420 (1980)

HISTORY. The State of Ghana came into existence on 6 March 1957 when the former Colony of the Gold Coast and the Trusteeship Territory of Togoland attained Dominion status. The name of the country recalls a powerful monarchy which from the 4th to the 13th century A.D. ruled the region of the middle Niger.

The Ghana Independence Act received the royal assent on 7 Feb. 1957. The General Assembly of the United Nations in Dec. 1956 approved the termination of British administration in Togoland and the union of Togoland with the Gold Coast on the latter's attainment of independence.

The country was declared a Republic within the Commonwealth on 1 July 1960 with Dr Kwame Nkrumah as the first President. On 24 Feb. 1966 the Nkrumah regime was overthrown in a military *coup* and ruled by the National Liberation Council until 1 Oct. 1969 when the military regime handed over power to a civilian regime under a new constitution. Dr K. A. Busia was the Prime Minister of the Second Republic. In Aug. 1975 the Government announced that they would commemorate the late Dr Nkrumah as 'a great Ghanaian responsible for taking the country to independence'.

On 13 Jan. 1972 the armed forces and police took over power again from the civilian regime in a *coup.*

In Oct. 1975 the National Redemption Council was subordinated to a Supreme Military Council (SMC). In 1979 the SMC was toppled in a *coup* led by Flight-Lieut. J. Rawlings. The new government permitted elections already scheduled and these resulted in a victory for Dr Hilla Limann and his People's National Party.

AREA AND POPULATION. The area of Ghana is 92,010 sq. miles (238,305 sq. km); census population 1970, 8,559,313. Estimate (1983) 12,827,000.

The capital is Accra (population, 1970, 636,067).

Ghana is divided into 9 regions:

Regions	Area (sq. km)	Population census 1970	Capital	Population census 1970
Eastern	19,833	1,262,882	Koforidua	69,804
Western	24,214	770,089	Sekondi-Takoradi	254,543
Central	9,469	890,135	Cape Coast	71,594
Ashanti	25,123	1,505,049	Kumasi	351,629
Brong-Ahafo	39,709	766,509	Sunyani	61,772
Northern	70,338	728,572	Tamale	120,000
Volta	20,651	947,012	Ho	46,348
Upper	16,877	862,723	Bolgatanga	18,896
Greater Accra	2,023	903,445	Accra	636,067

Other chief towns (population, census, 1970); Asamankese, 101,144; Nsawam, 57,350; Oda, 40,740; Obuasi, 40,001; Winneba, 36,104; Keta, 27,461; Swedru (Agona), 23,843.

Estimated birth rate, between 47 and 52 per 1,000; death rate, about 23 per 1,000.

CLIMATE. The climate ranges from the equatorial type on the coast to savannah in the interior and is typified by the existence of well-marked dry and wet seasons. Temperatures are relatively high throughout the year. The amount, duration and seasonal distribution of rain is very marked, from the south, with over 80″ (2,000 mm) to the north, with under 50″ (1,250 mm). In the extreme north, the wet season is from March to Aug.; but further south it lasts until Oct. Near Kumasi, two wet seasons occur, in May and June and again in Oct. and this is repeated, with greater amounts, along the coast of Ghana. Accra. Jan. 80°F (26·7°C), July 77°F (25°C).

545

Annual rainfall 29" (724 mm). Kumasi. Jan. 77°F (25°C), July 76°F (24·4°C). Annual rainfall 58" (1,402 mm). Sekondi-Takoradi. Jan. 79°F (25°C), July 76°F (24·4°C). Annual rainfall 47" (1,181 mm).

CONSTITUTION AND GOVERNMENT. Dr Hilla Limann became President of the Third Republic, but on 31 Dec. 1981 Rawlings led a second *coup* which dismissed the government and Parliament, suspended the Constitution, and established a Provisional National Defence Council to exercise all government powers.

For earlier political history of Ghana *see* THE STATESMAN'S YEAR-BOOK, 1971–72.

Chairman of the Provisional National Defence Council: Flight-Lieut. J. J. Rawlings.

National flag: Red, gold, green (horizontal); a black star in the centre.

National anthem: Hail the name of Ghana.

DEFENCE. The Ministry of Defence is responsible for the armed services, the military academy and the border guards. The Military Academy provides a 2-year course for army officers, a 1-year course for later entrants in the flying-training school and a preliminary 6-month course for navy cadets.

Army. The Ghana Army consists of 6 infantry battalions, 1 reconnaissance battalion, 1 field engineer battalion, 1 mortar battalion, 5 with armoured cars,: and ancillary units. Total strength, (1984) 10,000. There are also 3 border battalions and a paramilitary militia of 5,000.

Navy. The Ghana Navy was formed in 1959. It comprises 2 British-built 500-ton corvettes, 4 fast attack craft, 2 patrol craft, 2 old seaward defence boats, 4 coastal patrol boats and 2 service craft. Naval personnel in 1984 numbered 1,340 officers and ratings.

Air Force. The Ghana Air Force was formed in 1959, when an Air Force Training School was established at Accra. Its first combat unit has 6 Italian-built Aermacchi M.B.326K light ground attack jets ordered in 1976. It has, for training, transport, search and rescue, and air survey operations, 5 Fokker Friendship twin-turboprop transports, and a twin-turbofan Fokker Fellowship for Presidential use, all built in the Netherlands; 6 Shorts Skyvan twin-turboprop STOL transports, some Islanders, and 11 Bulldog primary trainers, all built in the UK; 2 Bell 212 helicopters built in the US; 2 French-built Alouette III helicopters, 8 Italian-built SF.260TP turbo-prop trainers, and 6 Aermacchi M.B.326F armed jet trainers. There are air bases at Takoradi and Tamale. Personnel strength (1983) about 1,400.

INTERNATIONAL RELATIONS

Membership. Ghana is a member of UN, the Commonwealth, OAU, ECOWAS and is an ACP state of EEC.

ECONOMY

Planning. In Jan. 1983 a 4-year economic reconstruction and development programme was announced and aims at increasing state involvement in economic activity.

Budget. In 1983 revenue was envisaged at ₡ 18,200m.

Currency. The monetary unit is the *cedi* (₡), divided into 100 *pesewas* (P) and equivalent to £0·51 or US$0·87. Notes are issued of 1, 2, 5, 10 and 50 ₡; copper coins of ½ and 1 P, and cupro-nickel coins of 2½, 5, 10 and 20 P. In March 1984, £1 = ₡ 44·58; US$1 = 30.

Banking. The Bank of Ghana was established in Feb. 1957 as the central bank of the country. The Ghana Commercial Bank, also established in Feb. 1957, is the former Bank of the Gold Coast. It is a purely commercial institution and has 120 branches in the country, 1 in London and 1 in Lomé (Togo). Barclays Bank

(Ghana) Ltd has 54 branches and agencies and the Standard Bank (Ghana) Ltd has 27 branches.

The Ghana National Investment Bank, opened in June 1963, is a finance-cum-development agency. The former post office savings bank has been transformed into the Ghana Savings Bank. The Bank for Housing and Construction opened in 1973.

ENERGY AND NATURAL RESOURCES

Oil. The Government announced in Jan. 1978 that oil had been found in commercial quantities with known reserves (1980) 7m. bbls and in Oct. 1983 formed the Ghanaian National Petroleum Corporation with exploration rights in all areas not covered by existing agreements.

Minerals. In 1981 gold production was 310,600 kg; diamonds, 836,000 carats; manganese, 223,000 tons; bauxite, 181,000 tons.

Agriculture. Cocoa is by far the most important crop and covers about 2m. acres. Production (1982) 190,000 tons. There has been considerable increase in cocoa yields as a result of the Capsid control and the introduction of improved varieties. A Cocoa Affairs Ministry has been established to formulate policy and provide technical supervision for developing cocoa, coffee, shea-nuts, copra and bananas. Coffee, improved types of oil-palm and coconut are being planted on an increased scale and production from these crops is increasing. Progress has been made in the planting of Clonal rubber in south-west Ghana. In the south-east coastal belt irrigation works have been constructed and black-clay farming is being successfully undertaken in the Accra plains.

Of the main foodstuffs in south and central Ghana, maize, rice, cassava, plantain, groundnuts, yam and cocoyam predominate. Tobacco is proving an attractive and very important cash crop in food-crop producing areas.

In northern Ghana the chief food crops are groundnuts, rice, maize, guinea corn, millet and yams, with tobacco and cotton as important cash crops.

Agricultural cash crops, e.g., pepper, ginger, pineapple, avocado and citrus, etc., are being extensively cultivated for export. Active steps have also been taken to provide within the next few years industrial raw materials, e.g., kenaf, cotton, tobacco, palm-oil, mango, pineapple, sugar-cane, etc., to feed the local factories. The trend is towards diversification of agriculture.

Production of main food crops (1982) was: Cassava, 1·9m. tons; plantain, 950,000 tons; coconut, 160,000; maize, 420,000; plantains, 950,000; millet, 90,000; sugar-cane, 220,000.

Livestock, 1982: Cattle, 950,000; sheep, 1·75m.; goats, 2·2m.; horses, 4,000; pigs, 435,000; poultry, 13m. The Central Veterinary Laboratory is located at Pong-Tamale under the Veterinary Research Officer. The efficient control of rinderpest and bovine pleuro-pneumonia, the two main killing diseases of cattle, has made it possible to quadruple the cattle in the past 20 years. The control of imported livestock is effected by 8 quarantine stations along the frontier, and new veterinary centres are being established.

Forestry. Area of closed forest is 82,576 sq. km, (16,852·2 sq. km are reserved).

Fisheries. Catch (1980) 224,100 tonnes (40,000 from inland waters).

COMMERCE. In 1981 exports were US$ 766·4m.; imports, US$ 748·7m. Principal exports: cocoa, timber and gold; imports were raw materials, capital equipment, petroleum and food.

Total trade between Ghana and UK (British Department of Trade returns, in £1,000 sterling):

	1979	1980	1981	1982	1983
Imports to UK	89,808	104,545	61,167	74,438	58,192
Exports and re-exports from UK	88,058	88,511	87,849	66,709	82,234

Tourism. In 1979 there were 48,000 tourists.

COMMUNICATIONS

Roads. The total mileage of roads maintained by the Public Works Department in 1980 was 33,000.

The number of vehicles in use (1977) was 121,700, of which private cars, 49,300.

Railways. Total length of railways open in 1980 was 953 km of 1,067 mm gauge. In 1976–77 railway income was ₵ 13·8m. from 6m. passenger-journeys and 1m. tonnes of freight carried.

Aviation. There are 4 major airports in Ghana, situated at Accra, Takoradi, Kumasi and Tamale; and 3 airstrips for domestic services. Accra airport is an international airport. The following airlines operate scheduled services: Ghana Airways, Air France, Nigerian Airways, Air Mali, United Arab Airlines, KLM, Swissair, PANAM, British Caledonian and several other companies. Total aircraft freight in 1975 was 3m. ton-km.

Shipping. The chief ports are Takoradi and Tema; the 'surf' ports at Accra, Winneba, Cape Coast and Keta ceased to operate when Tema harbour was opened in 1962, 18 miles east of Accra. In 1970, 4,164,329 tons of cargo were imported and 2,154,759 tons were exported by 3,116 ships.

Post and Broadcasting. There were 431 telephone exchanges and 742 call offices with (1982) 70,653 telephones in use. There are internal wireless stations at Accra, Kumasi, Bawku, Lawra, Kete-Krachi, Tamale, Yendi, Kpandu, Tumu and Sekondi-Takoradi. In 1982 there were 1·88m. radio and 60,000 television receivers.

Cinemas. In 1977 there were 8 cinemas with a seating capacity of 13,200.

Newspapers. There are 5 daily and 7 weekly papers, 8 fortnightly and 5 monthly magazines.

JUSTICE, RELIGION, EDUCATION AND WELFARE

Justice. In June 1983 the legal system was being re-organized. The Courts were constituted as follows:

Supreme Court. The Supreme Court consists of the Chief Justice who is also the President and not less than 6 other Justices of the Supreme Court. The Chief Justice presides at the sittings of the Supreme Court and in his absence the most senior of the Justices of the Supreme Court as constituted presides. The Supreme Court is the final court of appeal in Ghana. The final interpretation of the provisions of the constitution has been entrusted to the Supreme Court.

Court of Appeal. The Court of Appeal consists of the Chief Justice together with not less than 5 other Justices of the Appeal court and such other Justices of Superior Courts as the Chief Justice may nominate. The Court of Appeal is duly constituted by 3 Justices. The Court of Appeal is bound by its own previous decisions and all courts inferior to the Court of Appeal are bound to follow the decisions of the Court of Appeal on questions of law. Divisions of the Appeal Court may be created, subject to the discretion of the Chief Justice.

High Court of Justice. The Court has jurisdiction in civil and criminal matters as well as those relating to industrial and labour disputes including administrative complaints. The High Court of Justice has supervisory jurisdiction over all inferior Courts and any adjudicating authority and in exercise of its supervisory jurisdiction has power to issue such directions, orders or writs including writs or orders in the nature of habeas corpus, certiorari, mandamus, prohibition and quo warrantto. The High Court of Justice has no power in a trial for the offence of treason to convict any person for any offence other than treason. The High Court consists of the Chief Justice and not less than twelve other judges and such other Justices of the Superior Court as the Chief Justice may appoint.

Religion. Christians represent 43% of the population (Protestant, 29%; Roman Catholic, 14%), Moslem, 12%, animist, 38%.

Education. A complete re-organization of the system took place in 1974. There are kindergartens for the age-groups 4–6 years. Primary schools are free and attendance is compulsory. In 1978–79 there were 11,422 primary schools with 1,784,834 pupils. In 1979 there were 300 secondary schools with 1m. pupils. At the beginning of the 1979 academic year there were 41 training colleges with 12,350 students. In 1978–79 there were 8,455 students at the 3 universities (University of Ghana, the University of Science and Technology and the University of the Cape Coast). University education is free.

Health. Medical facilities include 50 government hospitals, 116 health centres and posts, 4 university hospitals, 3 mental hospitals, 4 leprosaria, 7 military hospitals, 1 prison hospital, 40 mission hospitals and 16 private hospitals. In addition, there are 30 nurses and midwives training schools.

There were 1,224 doctors, 7,608 nurses and 4,168 midwives at work in 1976.

DIPLOMATIC REPRESENTATIVES

Of Ghana in Great Britain (13 Belgrave Sq., London, SW1X 8PR)
High Commissioner: Kenneth Kweku Sinaman Dadzie (accredited 13 Oct. 1982).

Of Great Britain in Ghana (Barclays Bank Bldg., High St., Accra)
High Commissioner: K. F. X. Burns, CMG.

Of Ghana in the USA (2460 16th St., NW, Washington, D.C. 20009)
Ambassador: Eric K. Atoo.

Of the USA in Ghana (Ring Rd., East, Accra)
Ambassador: Robert E. Fritts.

Of Ghana to the United Nations
Ambassador: James Victor Gbeho.

Books of Reference

Digest of Statistics. Accra. Quarterly (from May 1953)
Ghana. Official Handbook. Annual
The Volta River Project. 3 vols. HMSO, 1956
Davidson, B., *Black Star.* London, 1973
James, C. L. R., *Nkrumah and the Ghana Revolution.* London, 1977
Jones, T., *Ghana's First Republic 1960–1966.* London, 1975
Killick, T., *Development Economics in Action: A Study of Economic Policies in Ghana.* London, 1978

GIBRALTAR

Population: 31,183 (1982)
GNP per capita: US$5,040 (1980)

HISTORY. The Rock of Gibraltar was settled by Moors in 711; they named it after their chief Jebel Tariq, 'the Mountain of Tarik'. In 1462 it was taken by the Spaniards, from Granada. It was captured by Admiral Sir George Rooke on 24 July 1704, and ceded to Great Britain by the Treaty of Utrecht, 1713. The cession was confirmed by the treaties of Paris (1763) and Versailles (1783).

On 10 Sept. 1967, in pursuance of a United Nations resolution on the de-colonization of Gibraltar, a referendum was held in Gibraltar in order to ascertain whether the people of Gibraltar believed that their interests lay in retaining their link with Britain or in passing under Spanish sovereignty. Out of a total electorate of 12,762, 12,138 voted to retain the British connexion, while 44 voted for Spain.

On 15 Dec. 1982 the border between Gibraltar and Spain was re-opened for Spaniards and Gibraltarian pedestrians who are residents of Gibraltar. The border was closed by Spain in June 1969.

AREA AND POPULATION. Area, 2½ sq. miles (6·5 sq. km). Total population, including port and harbour (census, 1981), 28,719. Estimate (1982) 31,183. The population is mostly of Genoese, Portuguese and Maltese as well as Spanish descent.

Vital statistics (1982): Births, 566; marriages, 429; deaths, 223.

CLIMATE. The climate is warm temperate, with westerly winds in winter bringing rain. Summers are pleasantly warm and rainfall is low. Frost or snow is very rare. Jan. 55°F (12·8°C), July 75°F (23·9°C). Annual rainfall 29″ (772 mm).

CONSTITUTION AND GOVERNMENT. Following a Constitutional Conference held in July 1968, a new Constitution was introduced in 1969. The Legislative and City Councils were merged to produce an enlarged legislature known as the Gibraltar House of Assembly. Executive authority is exercised by the Governor, who is also Commander-in-Chief. The Governor, while retaining certain reserved powers, is normally required to act in accordance with the advice of the Gibraltar Council, which consists of 4 *ex-officio* members (the Deputy Governor, the Deputy Fortress Commander, the Attorney-General and the Financial and Development Secretary) together with 5 elected members of the House of Assembly appointed by the Governor after consultation with the Chief Minister. Matters of primarily domestic concern are devolved to elected Ministers, with Britain responsible for other matters, including external affairs, defence and internal security. There is a Council of Ministers presided over by the Chief Minister.

The House of Assembly consists of a Speaker appointed by the Governor, 15 elected and 2 *ex-officio* members (the Attorney-General and the Financial and Development Secretary).

A Mayor of Gibraltar is elected from among the members of the Assembly by the elected members of the Assembly.

Governor and C.-in-C.: Admiral Sir David Williams, GCB.
Chief Minister: Sir Joshua Hassan, CBE, MVO, QC.
Flag: White with a red strip along the bottom, a red triple-towered castle with a gold key depending from the gateway.

DEFENCE. The Gibraltar Regiment is a part-time infantry battalion with a small regular cadre. There is also a resident battalion from the British Army.

ECONOMY

Budget. Revenue and expenditure (in £ sterling):

	1978–79	1979–80	1980–81	1981–82	1982–83
Revenue	26,408,993	32,338,140	...	44,265,500	47,789,100
Expenditure	25,704,366	26,368,784	...	42,594,000	51,980,283

Currency. The legal currency consists of Gibraltar government notes and UK coins. The amount of local currency notes in circulation at 31 March 1979 was £5,651,410.

Banking. There are 5 banks, including a branch of Barclays Bank International. Government savings banks had 5,927 depositors and £1,890,333 savings at 31 March 1983.

INDUSTRY AND TRADE

Industry. There are a number of relatively small industrial concerns engaged in the bottling of beer and mineral waters, etc., mainly for consumption. There is a small but important commercial ship-repair yard.

Labour. The full-time labour force at 31 Dec. 1982, was 12,445. The labour supply from the local population is insufficient to meet the demand and since the withdrawal of the Spanish frontier workers in June 1969, a substantial part of the labour has had to come from other places. A quota system is in existence which takes into account the demand from the various industries and seasonal variations and the issue of employment permits is based on this. Approximately 60% of the local labour force is employed by the UK departments or the Gibraltar government.

A considerable proportion of the workers are organized in one or other of the 13 registered employees' trade unions, of which the Transport and General Workers Union has the largest membership; 7 of these are local branches of parent associations in the UK.

Commerce. Imports and exports (in £ sterling):

	1979	1980	1981	1982
Imports	55,519,064	63,141,753	65,826,282	68,393,000
Exports [1]	4,695,339	4,182,217	5,701,416	5,673,215

[1] Exclusive of petroleum and petroleum products.

Britain and the Commonwealth provide the bulk of the imports, but fresh vegetables, fruit and fish come mainly from Morocco, Portugal and the Netherlands. Exports of local produce are negligible. Gibraltar depends largely on tourism, the entrepôt trade and the provision of supplies to visiting ships.

Tourism. The number of tourists in 1982 was 173.838. 46,595 were Spanish nationals who crossed through the land frontier.

COMMUNICATIONS

Roads. There are 30 miles of roads including 4 miles of pedestrian way.

Aviation. There are 5 weekly flights between London and Gibraltar (3 operated by Gibraltar Airways and 2 by British Airways) during the winter; these are increased to daily flights during the summer.

Shipping. Gibraltar is a naval and air base of strategic importance. There is a deep Admiralty harbour of 440 acres. A total of 2,704 merchant ships, 15,155,818 NRT, entered the port during 1982. An additional 6,706 calls were made by yachts, 57,580 NRT.

Post and Broadcasting. An automatic telephone system exists in the town; number of telephones (1982), 9,870. There is also world-wide communication *via* the cable and/or wireless circuits of Cable & Wireless Ltd and international direct dialling facilities. Air-mails arrive by British Airways daily. A direct air-mail service between Gibraltar and Tangier is run by Gibraltar Airways, Ltd. Surface mails arrive direct and through France, Spain and Tangier. Radio Gibraltar broadcasts for 17 hours daily, in English and Spanish, and there are about 40 hours of television per week. Number of receivers (1982), radio, 83; TV, 6,600.

Cinemas. In 1981 there were 3 cinemas with a seating capacity of 2,400.

Newspapers. There were (1982) 1 daily and 5 weeklies.

JUSTICE, RELIGION, EDUCATION AND WELFARE

Justice. The judicial system is based on the English system. There is a Court of Appeal, a Supreme Court, presided over by the Chief Justice, a court of first instance and a magistrates' court.

Religion. Religion of civil population mostly Roman Catholic; 1 Anglican and 1 Roman Catholic cathedral and 2 Anglican and 6 Roman Catholic churches; 1 Presbyterian and 1 Methodist church and 4 synagogues; annual subsidy to each communion, £500.

Education. Free compulsory education is provided for children between ages 5 and 15 years. Scholarships are made available for universities, teacher-training and other higher education in Britain. The comprehensive system was introduced in Sept. 1972. There were (1981) 7 first, 4 middle, 1 primary school and 2 comprehensive schools. All first and middle schools are mixed but the comprehensives are single-sex. In addition, there are 2 Services primary schools and 1 private primary school. A new purpose-built Special School for Handicapped Children was opened in 1977. Technical education is available at the Gibraltar and Dockyard Technical College managed by the UK Ministry of Defence for which Government pays 50% of all recurrent costs and scholarships are made available in Britain for university, teacher-training and other forms of higher education. In Sept. 1982, there were 3,014 pupils at government primary schools, 185 at private and 162 at services schools; 28 at the special school; 850 at the boys' comprehensive school and 914 at the girls' comprehensive. In addition there were 47 full-time and 246 part-time students in the Technical College. In 1981–82, government expenditure on education was £3,749,372.

Health. In 1982 there was 1 hospital with 241 beds and 15 doctors. Total expenditure on medical and health services during year ended 31 March 1982 was £4,572,722.

Books of Reference.

Annual Report on Gibraltar, 1972. London, 1974
Gibraltar Year Book. Gibraltar, (Annual)
Dennis, P., *Gibraltar.* Newton Abbot, 1977
Ellicott, D., *Our Gibraltar.* Gibraltar, 1975
Garcia, S., *Gibraltar: An Analysis of How the Economy was Affected by the Spanish Restrictions 1963–72* (unpublished). Garrison Library, 1974
Green, M. M., *A Gibraltar Bibliography.* London, 1980.—*Supplement.* London, 1982
Hills, G., *Rock of Contention: A History of Gibraltar.* London, 1974
Howes, H. W., *The Story of Gibraltar.* London, 1946

GREECE

Elliniki Dimokratia

Capital: Athens
Population: 9·7m. (1981)
GNP per capita: US$4,520 (1980)

HISTORY. Greece gained her independence from Turkey in 1821–29, and by the Protocol of London, of 3 Feb. 1830, was declared a kingdom, under the guarantee of Great Britain, France and Russia. For details of the subsequent history to 1947 *see* THE STATESMAN'S YEAR-BOOK, 1957, pp. 1069–70 and for details of the monarchy *see* THE STATESMAN'S YEAR-BOOK, 1973–74, p. 1000.

AREA AND POPULATION. Greece is bounded north by Albania, Yugoslavia and Bulgaria, east by Turkey and the Aegean Sea, south by the Mediterranean and west by the Ionian Sea. The total area is 131,986 sq. km (50,960 sq. miles), of which the islands account for 24,761 sq. km (9,560 sq. miles).

The population was 9,706,687 according to the census of 5 April 1981.

Athens is the capital; population of Greater Athens, in 1981, 3,016,457.

The following table shows the prefectures *(Nomoi)* and their population:

Nomoi	Area in sq. km	Population 1981	Capital	Population 1981
Greater Athens [1]	433	3,027,331		
Central Greece and Euboea [2]	24,475	1,099,841		
Aetolia and Acarnania	5,447	219,764	Missolonghi	11,275
Attica [2]	2,496	342,093	Athens	885,136
Boeotia	3,211	117,175	Levadeia	17,697
Euboea	3,908	188,410	Chalcis	44,774
Evrytania	2,045	26,182	Karpenissi	5,243
Phthiotis	4,368	161,995	Lamia	42,019
Phokis	2,121	44,222	Amphissa	7,233
Piraeus (1971) [2]	879	55,660	Piraeus (1971)	187,458
Peloponnessos	21,439	1,012,528		
Argolis	2,214	93,020	Nauplion	10,554
Arcadia	4,419	107,932	Tripolis	21,140
Akhaïa	3,209	275,193	Patras	140,878
Elia	2,681	160,305	Pyrgos	21,992
Korinthia	2,289	123,042	Korinthos	22,495
Lakonia	3,636	93,218	Sparte	15,915
Messenia	2,991	159,818	Calamata	41,998
Ionian Islands	2,307	182,651		
Zakynthos	406	30,014	Zante	9,742
Kerkyra	641	99,477	Kerkyra	35,787
Kefallenia	935	31,297	Argostolion	7,294
Lefkas	325	21,863	Levkas	6,631
Epirus	9,203	324,541		
Arta	1,612	80,044	Arta	20,077
Thesprotia	1,515	41,278	Hegoumenitsa	6,190
Yannina	4,990	147,304	Yannina	44,362
Preveza	1,086	55,915	Preveza	13,555
Thessaly	13,904	695,654		
Karditsa	2,576	124,930	Karditsa	27,670
Larissa	5,354	254,295	Larisa	103,263
Magnessia	2,636	182,222	Volos	70,967
Trikkala	3,338	134,207	Trikkala	45,138

[1] Comprising parts of Attica and Piraeus prefectures.
[2] Excluding figures for the parts of Attica and Piraeus prefectures within Greater Athens.

Nomoi	Area in sq. km	Population 1981	Capital	Population 1981
Macedonia	*34,203*	*2,121,953*		
Grevena	2,338	36,421	Grevena	7,725
Drama	3,468	94,772	Drama	36,963
Imathia	1,699	133,750	Verria	37,528
Thessaloniki	3,560	871,580	Thessaloniki	402,443
Kavalla	2,109	135,218	Kavala	56,260
Kastoria	1,685	53,169	Kastoria	20,532
Kilkis	2,597	81,562	Kilkis	11,694
Kozani	3,562	147,051	Kozani	31,247
Pella	2,506	132,386	Edessa	15,980
Pieria	1,548	106,859	Katerini	38,488
Serres	3,987	196,247	Serres	46,168
Florina	1,863	52,430	Florina	12,708
Khalkidiki	2,945	79,036	Polyghyros	5,228
Mount Athos	336	1,472	Karyai (1971)	301
Thrace	*8,578*	*345,220*		
Evros	4,242	148,486	Alexandroupolis	35,856
Xanthi	1,793	88,777	Xanthi	33,713
Rodopi	2,543	107,957	Komotini	37,633
Aegean Islands	*9,071*	*428,533*		
Cyclades	2,572	88,458	Hermoupolis	14,115
Lesvos	2,154	104,620	Mitylini	24,937
Samos	778	40,519	Limin Vatheos	5,892
Khios	904	49,865	Khios	24,115
Dodecanese	2,663	145,071	Rhodes	40,656
Crete	*8,331*	*502,165*		
Iraklion	2,641	243,622	Heraklion	101,668
Lassithi	1,818	70,053	Aghios Nikolaos	8,194
Rethymnon	1,496	62,634	Rethymnon	17,940
Canea	2,376	125,856	Canea	47,804

In 1971 cities (*i.e.*, communes of more than 10,000 inhabitants, including Greater Athens) had 4,667,489 inhabitants (53·2%), towns (*i.e.*, communes with between 2,000 and 9,999 inhabitants), 1,028,769 (11·7%), villages and rural communities (under 2,000 inhabitants), 3,072,383 (35·1%).

Mount Athos, the easternmost of the three prongs of the peninsula of Chalcidice, is a self-governing community composed of 20 monasteries. (*See* THE STATESMAN'S YEAR-BOOK, 1945, p. 983.) For centuries the peninsula has been administered by a Council of 4 members and an Assembly of 20 members, 1 deputy from each monastery. The Greek Government on 10 Sept. 1926 recognized this autonomous form of government; Articles 109–112 of the Constitution of 1927 gave legal sanction to the Charter of Mount Athos, drawn up by representatives of the 20 monasteries on 20 May 1924. Article 103 of the 1952 Constitution and Article 105 of the 1975 Constitution confirmed the special status of Mount Athos.

Vital statistics (1981): 140,953 live births; 1,323 still births; 2,234 illegitimate births; 71,178 marriages; 86,261 deaths; 16,510 emigrants (Jan.–Sept. 1977); 12,572 immigrants (Jan.–Sept. 1977).

CLIMATE. Coastal regions and the islands have typical Mediterranean conditions, with mild, rainy winters and hot, dry, sunny summers. Rainfall comes almost entirely in the winter months, though amounts vary widely according to position and relief. Continental conditions affect the northern mountainous areas, with severe winters, deep snow cover and heavy precipitation, but summers are hot. Athens. Jan. 48°F (8·6°C), July 82·5°F (28·2°C). Annual rainfall 16·6″ (414·3 mm).

CONSTITUTION AND GOVERNMENT. A *coup d'état* took place on 21 April 1967, 'to avert the danger of a communist threat against the nation'. A Military Government was formed, which suspended the 1952 Constitution. Following the unsuccessful counter-*coup* in 1967, King Constantine went abroad. Voting took place on 29 July 1973 in the referendum to change Greece from a

Monarchy to a Republic and to elect a President. 77·2% of the valid votes were cast for a republican régime.

On 25 Nov. 1973, in a bloodless *coup*, President Papadopoulos was overthrown and Lieut.-Gen. Phaedon Ghizikis was sworn in. The military dictatorship collapsed on 23 July 1974 and the 1952 Constitution was reintroduced in a modified form. A new Constitution was introduced in June 1975. Parliamentary elections took place on 12 Nov. 1974.

A further referendum on the Monarchy took place on 8 Dec. 1974 and 69·2% of the valid votes were cast for an 'uncrowned democracy'.

Elections were again held on 18 Oct. 1981. The results were New Democracy, 115; Pan-Hellenic Socialist Movement, 172; Communists, 12.

President: Konstantinos Karamanlis (elected President in May 1980).

The Cabinet in March 1984:

Prime Minister and Minister of Defence: Andreas Papandreou.
Agriculture: Constantine Simitis. *Commerce:* Vassilios Kedikoglou. *Communications:* Nicolaos Akritidis. *Culture and Sciences:* Melina Mercouri. *Education and Religion:* Apostolos Kaklamanis. *Energy and National Resources:* Evangelos Kouloumbis. *Finance:* Ioannis Pottakis. *Foreign Affairs:* Ioannis Haralambopoulos. *Health and Welfare:* George Yennimatas. *Interior:* Agamemnon Koutsogiorgas. *Justice:* George Alex Mangakis. *Labour:* Evangelos Yannopoulos. *Merchant Marine:* George Katsifaras. *National Economy:* Gerassimos Arsenis. *Northern Greece:* Vassilis Intzes. *Physical Planning, Housing and Environment:* Antonios Tritsis. *Minister to the Presidency:* Apostolos Lazaris. *Public Order:* Ioannis Skoularikis. *Public Works:* Apostolos Tsohatzopoulos. *Research and Technology:* George Lianis. *Social Security:* Eleftherios Verivakis. *Without Portfolio:* Anastasios Peponis *(TV and Radio);* Paraskevas Avgerinos *(Social Policies).*

National flag: Nine horizontal stripes of blue and white, with a canton of blue with a white cross.

National anthem: Hymn to Freedom, Imnos eis tin Eleftherian (words by Dionysios Solomos, 1824; tune by N. Mantzaros, 1828).

DEFENCE. In Aug. 1950 the Ministries of War, Marine and Military Aviation were fused into a single Ministry of National Defence. The General Staff of National Defence is directly responsible to the Minister on general defence questions, besides the special staffs for Army, Navy and Air Force. Defence expenditure in 1982 was 134,694,000m. drachmai. Military service in the Armed Forces is compulsory and universal. Liability begins in the 21st year and lasts up to the 50th. The normal terms of service are Army 22 months, Navy 26 months, Air Force 24 months, followed by 19 years in the First Reserve and 10 years in the Second Reserve.

Army. The Army is organized into 3 Military Regions, comprising 1 armoured, 1 mechanized, 1 para-commando and 11 infantry divisions; 3 armoured brigades; 13 field artillery, 7 anti-aircraft, 2 surface-to-surface missile, 2 surface-to-air missile, and 2 army aviation battalions; and 4 independent aviation companies. Equipment includes 350 M-47, 818 M-48, 285 AMX-30 and 10 Leopard I main battle tanks. Strength (1984) 142,000 (110,000 conscripts), with a further 350,000 reserves. There is also a paramiltary gendarmerie of 25,000 men.

Navy. The Hellenic Navy includes 2 new Netherlands-built leader-size guided missile frigates, 10 submarines (8 modern German (Fed. Rep.)-built small and 2 old *ex*-US large), 14 old *ex*-US destroyers, 1 *ex*-German support frigate, 1 new armed training ship carrying a helicopter, 4 old *ex*-US frigates (small DE type), 2 coastal minelayers, 14 fast missile boats, 11 fast torpedo boats, 14 coastal minesweepers, 11 coastal patrol boats, 1 dock landing ship, 8 tank landing ships, 5 medium landing ships, 10 landing craft, 68 minor landing craft, 1 ammunition ship, 6 oilers, 2 transports, 1 depot ship, 4 surveying craft, 2 light-house tenders, 6 water carriers, 1 netlayer and 14 fleet tugs.

Personnel in 1984 exceeded 2,500 officers and 17,000 ratings.

Air Force. The Hellenic Air Force has a strength of about 24,500 officers and men and 275 combat aircraft, consisting of 3 squadrons of F-4E Phantom air-superiority fighters, 2 squadrons of F-104G Starfighters, 2 squadrons of Mirage F.1 fighters, 3 squadrons of A-7H Corsair II attack aircraft, 2 squadrons of F-5 fighters, 1 squadron of RF-4E and RF-5A reconnaissance fighters and 1 squadron of HU-16B Albatross ASW amphibians. There are also transport squadrons equipped with C-130H Hercules (12), Noratlas, NAMC YS-11 and C-47 aircraft, 7 Canadair CL-215 twin-engined amphibians, 36 T-2E Buckeye training/attack air-craft, other training and helicopter units, and anti-aircraft units equipped with Nike-Hercules and Hawk surface-to-air missiles.

The HAF is organized into Tactical, Training and Air Materiel Commands.

INTERNATIONAL RELATIONS

Membership. Greece is a member of UN, EEC, the Council of Europe and the military and political wings of NATO.

ECONOMY

Budget. The estimated revenue and expenditure for calendar years were as follows (in 1m. drachmai):

	1974	1975	1976	1977	1978	1980	1981
Revenue	129,380	138,320	174,362	210,234	249,202	359,100	438,900
Expenditure	129,380	170,496	210,231	252,094	300,950	460,500	650,500

Currency. On 11 Nov. 1944 the Greek currency was stabilized at 1 new *drachma* equalling 50,000m. old *drachmai*. Further readjustments took place in 1946, 1949 and 1953. A 'new issue' of notes and coins was put into circulation on 1 May 1954, 1 new drachma equalling 1,000 old drachmai (72 drachmai = £1; 30 drachmai = US$1). The 'new issue' comprises notes of 50, 100, 500 and 1,000 drachmai and metal coins of 1, 2, 5, 10 and 20 drachmai and 10, 20 and 50 *lepta*. Rate of ex-change, March 1984, £1 = 149·55 drachmai; US$1 = 101·05.

Banking. The Bank of Greece *(Trapeza Tis Ellados)* is the bank of issue.

The National Investment Bank for industrial development was set up in Dec. 1963; of its capital of 180m. drachmai, the National Bank provided 60%.

Other important banks are the Ionian and Popular Bank of Greece, the Commercial Bank of Greece, the National Mortgage Bank, the Hellenic Industrial Development Bank, the Investment Bank, the Commercial Credit Bank and the General Bank of Greece.

Weights and Measures. The metric system was made obligatory in 1959; the use of other systems is prohibited. The Gregorian calendar was adopted in Feb. 1923.

ENERGY AND NATURAL RESOURCES

Electricity. Total installed capacity of the Public Power Corporation was 5,410m. mw as at 31 Dec. 1980. Total net production in 1981 was 21,657m. kwh.

Minerals. Greece produces a variety of ores and minerals, including iron-pyrites (145,443 tonnes in 1980), bauxite (3·01m. tonnes, 1980), nickel (1·46m. tonnes, 1980), magnesite (1·2m. tonnes, 1980), dead burnt magnesite (392,666 tonnes, 1980), mixed sulphur ores (752,000 tonnes, 1976), barytes, chromite, marble (white and coloured) and various other earths, chiefly from the Laurium district, Thessaly, Euboea and the Aegean islands. There is little coal, and lignite of indifferent quality (23·2m. tonnes, 1980). Oil was struck in 1963 by British Petro-leum at Kleisoura in west central Greece. Salt production (1970) 68,471 tonnes.

Agriculture. Of the total area only 33% is cultivable, but it supports about 45%

of the whole population. The total area under cultivation in 1971 was 3,586,232 hectares, forest area (1965) was 2,512,418 hectares (445,715 of which were privately owned). The average holding was 3·42 hectares in 1975.

Yield (1.000 tonnes) of the chief crops (1982):

Wheat	2,983	Table grapes	267
Tobacco	130	Wine	470
Cotton	290	Citrus fruit	863
Sugar-beet	2,426	Other fruit	911
Currants and raisins	132	Milk	1,700
Olive oil	321	Meat and poultry	524

About 496,260 hectares of olives are under cultivation.

Rice is cultivated in Macedonia, the Peloponnese, Epirus and Central Greece. Successful experiments have been made in growing rice on alkaline land previously regarded as unfit for cultivation. The main kinds of cheese produced are sliced cheese in brine (commercially known as Fetta) and hard cheese, such as Kefalotyri.

Livestock (1982): 836,000 cattle, 2,000 buffaloes. 1·38m. pigs, 8·32m. sheep, 4·6m. goats, 97,000 horses, 107,000 mules, 223,000 asses, 36·3m. poultry.

Fisheries. In 1980, 10,116 fishermen were active and landed 94,900 tonnes of fish. 37,182 kg of sponges were produced in 1981.

INDUSTRY AND TRADE

Industry. The main products are canned vegetables and fruit, fruit juice, beer, wine, alcoholic beverages, cigarettes, textiles, yarn, leather, shoes, synthetic timber, paper, plastics, rubber products, chemical acids, pigments, pharmaceutical products, cosmetics, soap, disinfectants, fertilizers, glassware, porcelain sanitary items, wire and power coils and household instruments.

Production, 1976 (1,000 tonnes): Textile yarns, 137; cement, 8,714; fertilizers, 1,554; ammonia, 287; iron (concrete-reinforcing bars), 589; iron-nickel, 16; alumina, 450; aluminium, 133; electrical domestic goods (1,000 pieces), 325.

Labour. Of the economically active population in 1971, 1·92m. were engaged in agriculture. 677,451 in industry and 1,000,684 in other employment.

Pepelasis, A. A., and Yotopoulos, P. A., *Surplus Labor in Greek Agriculture, 1953–60.* Athens, 1962

Trade Unions. The status of trade unions in Greece is regulated by the Associations Act 1914. Trade-union liberties are guaranteed under the Constitution, and a law of June 1982 altered the unions' right to strike.

The national body of trade unions in Greece is the Greek General Confederation of Labour.

Commerce. Foreign trade (in US$1m.) for 4 calendar years was:

	1979	1980	1981	1982
Imports	10,110	10,903	11,468	10,079
Exports	3,932	4,094	4,772	4,139

Total trade between Greece and UK (British Department of Trade returns, in £1,000 sterling):

	1978	1979	1980	1981	1982	1983
Imports to UK	107,600	151,880	142,456	167,655	151,688	164,917
Exports and re-exports from UK	214,178	273,026	224,619	254,154	255,281	280,204

Tourism. Tourists visiting Greece in 1981 numbered 5,094,300. They spent the equivalent of US$1,878m.

COMMUNICATIONS

Roads. There were, in 1980, 37,000 km of roads, of which 8,680 were national and 27,253 provincial roads.

Number of motor vehicles in Dec. 1981: 1,517,737, of which 911,240 were passenger cars, 458,006 goods vehicles, 18,493 buses.

Railways. In 1981 the State network, Hellenic Railways (CH), totalled 2,479 km comprising 1,565 km of 1,435 mm gauge, 872 km of 1,000 mm gauge, and 22 km of 750 mm gauge, and carried 814m. tonne-km and 1,933m. passenger-km.

Aviation. Olympic Airways connects Athens with all important cities of the country, Europe, the Middle East and USA. Thirty-four foreign companies connect Athens with the principal cities of the world.

The principal airport is at Athens. In 1980, 88,618 aircraft arrived, carrying 8·2m. passengers.

Shipping. In March 1980 the merchant navy comprised 3,970 vessels of 39,327,594 GRT. Greek-owned ships under foreign flags totalled more than 11,192,683 GRT.

There is a canal (opened 9 Nov. 1893) across the Isthmus of Corinth (about 4 miles).

Post and Broadcasting. In 1981 there were 2,686 telephone exchanges, handling 8,000m. calls. There were (1982) 2,956,663 telephones.

Elliniki Radiophonia Tileorasis (ERT), the Hellenic National Radio and Television Institute, is the government broadcasting station. ERT broadcasts 1 TV programme. AFRTS broadcasts 1 TV programme in Iraklion (Crete). Number of receivers: radio, 5m.; television, 1·4m.

Cinemas (1981). There were 1,150 cinemas.

Newspapers (1980). There were 14 daily newspapers published in Athens.

JUSTICE, RELIGION, EDUCATION AND WELFARE

Justice. There are administrative, civil and criminal courts and they are organized by special laws.

Religion. The Christian Eastern Orthodox faith is the established religion to which 98% of the population belong.

The Greek Orthodox Church is under an archbishop and 67 metropolitans, 1 archbishop and 7 metropolitans in Crete, and 4 metropolitans in the Dodecanese. The Roman Catholics have 3 archbishops (in Naxos and Corfu and, not recognized by the State, in Athens) and 1 bishop (for Syra and Santorini). The Exarchs of the Greek Catholics and the Armenians are not recognized by the State.

Complete religious freedom is recognized by the Constitution of 1968, but proselytizing from, and interference with, the Greek Orthodox Church is forbidden.

Education. Public education is provided in nursery, primary and secondary schools, starting at 6 years of age and since 1963 free at all levels.

In 1980–81 there were 4,752 nursery schools with 6,146 staff and 142,520 pupils; 9,541 public day primary schools with 36,168 staff and 902,558 pupils. There were 2,253 secondary schools with 31,057 staff and 648,742 pupils. There were 1,212 public and 644 private technical and vocational schools with a total of 155,750 students.

In 1980–81 there were 6 universities at Athens, Crete, Thessaloniki, Thrace, Patras and Ioannina with 119,000 students and 6,148 lecturers.

Illiteracy in the age groups of 10 years and over was 18% in 1961 (8% among men). 1972 estimate 12%.

The Greek language consists of 2 branches, *katharevousa*, a conscious revival of classical Greek, used for official purposes and in newspapers, and *demotiki*, the spoken language.

Health (1982). There were 688 hospitals and sanatoria with a total of 59,914 beds.

There were 24,724 doctors and 7,727 dentists.

DIPLOMATIC REPRESENTATIVES

Of Greece in Great Britain (1A Holland Park, London, W11 3TP)
Ambassador: Nikolaos Kyriazides.

Of Great Britain in Greece (1 Ploutarchou St., Athens 139)
Ambassador: Peregrine Rhodes, CMG.

Of Greece in the USA (2221 Massachusetts Ave.. NW, Washington, D.C. 20008)
Ambassador: George D. Papoulias.

Of the USA in Greece (91 Vasilissis Sophia Blvd., Athens)
Ambassador: Monteagle Stearns.

Of Greece to the United Nations
Ambassador: Mihalis Dountas.

Books of Reference

Clogg, R. and M. J., *Greece.* [Bibliography] Oxford and Santa Barbara, 1980
Holden, D., *Greece Without Columns: The Making of the Modern Greeks.* London, 1972
Katris, J. A., *Eyewitness in Greece: The Colonels Come to Power.* St Louis, 1971
Kayser, B., *Géographie humaine de la Grèce.* Paris, Presses Universitaires, 1964
Kolodny, E. Y., *La Population des Îles de la Grèce.* Aix-en-Provence, 1973
Kousoulas, D. G., *Revolution and Defeat: The Story of the Greek Communist Party.* OUP, 1965
Kykkotis, I., *English–Modern Greek and Modern Greek–English Dictionary.* 3rd ed. London, 1957
Mouzelis, N. P., *Modern Greece.* London, 1978
Munkman, C. A., *American Aid to Greece.* New York, 1958
Phillipson, A., *Die griechischen Landschaften: eine Landeskunde.* 4 vols. Frankfurt, 1951–59
Pring, J. T., *The Oxford Dictionary of Modern Greek, Greek-English, English-Greek.* OUP, 1965–82
Tsoukalis, L., *Greece and the European Community.* Farnborough, 1979
Woodhouse, C. M., *The Struggle for Greece, 1941–1949.* London, 1976.—*Karamanlis: The Restorer of Greek Democracy.* OUP, 1982
Xydis, S. G., *Greece and the Great Powers, 1944–47.* Thessaloniki, 1963
Young, K., *The Greek Passion.* London, 1967

GRENADA

Capital: St George's
Population: 115,000 (1981)
GNP per capita: US$850 (1981)

HISTORY. Grenada became an independent nation within the Commonwealth on 7 Feb. 1974. Grenada was formerly an Associated State under the West Indies Act, 1967.

AREA AND POPULATION. Grenada is the most southerly island of the Windward Islands with an area of 133 sq. miles (344 sq. km); population, census 1970, 92,775; estimated population 1981, 115,000. The borough of St George's, the capital, had population (1978) 30,813. The largest of the Grenadines attached to Grenada is Carriacou, area 32 sq. km; population 1970, 5,950 (including Petit Martinique).

Vital statistics (1978): Births, 2,521; deaths, 765; infant deaths, 73; marriages, 360.

CLIMATE. The tropical climate is very agreeable in the dry season, from Jan. to May, when days are warm and nights quite cool, but in the wet season there is very little difference between day and night temperatures. On the coast, annual rainfall is about 60″ (1,500 mm) but it is as high as 150–200″ (3,750–5,000 mm) in the mountains.

CONSTITUTION AND GOVERNMENT. The 1973 Constitution was suspended in 1979 following a revolution. On 19 Oct. 1983 the army took control after a power struggle led to the killing of Maurice Bishop the Prime Minister. At the request of a group of Caribbean countries, Grenada was invaded by US-led forces on 24–28 Oct. On 1 Nov. a State of Emergency was imposed which ended on 15 Nov. when an interim government was installed. Elections are due in Nov. 1984.

Governor-General: Sir Paul Scoon, GCMG.
Head of Interim Government: Nicholas Braithwaite.
National flag: Divided into 4 triangles of yellow, top and bottom, and green, hoist and fly; in the centre a red disc bearing a gold star; along the top and bottom edged red stripes each bearing 3 gold stars; on the green triangle near the hoist a pod of nutmeg.

DEFENCE

Army. A People's Revolutionary Army was created in 1979. Personnel about 6,500 organized into 3 infantry battalions and an artillery battery.

INTERNATIONAL RELATIONS

Membership. Grenada is a member of the UN, OAS, Caricom, the Commonwealth and is an ACP state of EEC.

ECONOMY

Budget. The 1981 estimates balanced at EC$169m. Public debt at 31 Dec. 1970 was EC$15,168,705.

Currency. The currency is the *Eastern Caribbean dollar.* In March 1984, £1 = EC$4·01; US$ = EC$2·70.

Banking. In 1981 there were 5 commercial banks in Grenada: The National Commercial Bank, Barclays Bank International, Royal Bank of Canada, Bank of Nova Scotia and the Grenada Co-operative Bank. The Grenada Agricultural Bank was established in 1965 to encourage agricultural development. In 1981, bank deposits were EC$164·7m.

AGRICULTURE (1981). The principal crops (production in lb.) are: Cocoa (6,409,227), nutmegs (6,767,199), bananas (25,609,408), and mace (506,950); coconuts, corn and pigeon peas, citrus, sugar-cane, root-crops and vegetables are also grown, in addition to small scattered cultivations of cotton, cloves, cinnamon, pimento, coffee and fruit trees The fish catch was about 3m. lb.

Livestock (1982): Cattle, 9,000; sheep, 16,000; goats, 13,000; pigs, 10,000; poultry, 260,000.

COMMERCE (1981). Total value of imports, EC$146,709,830; exports, EC$50,275,362. The main exports are cocoa, nutmegs and bananas.

Of exports in 1981, UK took 35·6%; Netherlands, 15·8%; Trinidad, 15·6%; Federal Republic of Germany, 9%; Canada, 2·8%; USA, 2·5%. Of 1981 imports, Trinidad furnished 19·2%; USA, 18·6%; UK, 16·6%; Canada, 5·5%; Netherlands, 1·6%; Federal Republic of Germany, 1·3%.

Total trade between Grenada and UK (British Department of Trade returns, in £1,000 sterling):

	1980	1981	1982	1983
Imports to UK	5,225	4,890	4,704	5,387
Exports and re-exports to UK	3,371	3,839	3,687	7,293

TOURISM. In 1981, there were 102,668 visitors; 131 cruise ships and 1,376 yachts visited the island.

COMMUNICATIONS

Roads. The scheduled road mileage is 577, of which 377 have an oiled surface and 210 are graded as third- and fourth-class roads. Vehicles registered (1979) 6,676.

Aviation. A new international airport is being constructed at Point Salines. Pearls Airport has daily connexions to London, New York and South America *via* nearby islands. There is a small airstrip on Carriacou.

Shipping. Total shipping for 1978 was 927 motor and steamships and 166 sailing and auxiliary vessels, with a total net tonnage of 2,210,532 and 7,479 respectively.

Post and Broadcasting. The telephone system is owned and operated by the Grenada Telephone Co. Ltd. The Government of Grenada is a shareholder. The system is completely automatic, and in 1981 served 5,648 subscribers. Cable & Wireless (W.I.) Ltd operates a VHF radio system (telephone and telegraph) to Trinidad and Barbados, from where connexion is made to all other parts of the world. There were (1978) 63,500 radios.

JUSTICE, RELIGION AND EDUCATION

Justice. The Grenada Supreme Court, situated in St George's, comprises a High Court of Justice, a Court of Magisterial Appeal (which hears appeals from the lower Magistrates' Courts exercising summary jurisdiction) and an Itinerant Court of Appeal (to hear appeals from the High Court).

Religion. The majority of the population are Roman Catholic; the Anglican and Methodist churches are also well represented.

Education. There are 20 primary schools, 4 junior schools and 16 secondary schools, as well as 46 schools taking the full age range. There is a Technical Centre in each district and a Technical Institute in St George's, where there is also a Teacher Training College and a branch of the University of the West Indies. There were 28,745 primary and 4,773 secondary school pupils in 1973.

DIPLOMATIC REPRESENTATIVES

Of Grenada in Great Britain (1 Collingham Gdns., London, SW5)
High Commissioner: O. M. Gibbs (accredited 15 March 1984).

Of Great Britain in Grenada
High Commissioner: G. L. Bullard, CMG (resides at Bridgetown).

Of Grenada in the USA (1701 New Hampshire Ave., NW, Washington, DC., 20009)
Ambassador: Bernard K. Radix.

Of the USA in Grenada
Ambassador: (Vacant).

Of Grenada to the United Nations
Ambassador: Caldwell Taylor.

Books of Reference

Hodge, M. and Searle, C. (eds), *Is Freedom We Making.* Govt. Information Service, 1981
Searle, C., *Grenada: The Struggle against Destabilization.* London, 1983
Searle, C. and Rojas, D. (eds), *To Construct from Morning.* Grenada, 1982
Wheaton, P. and Sunshine, C. (eds), *Grenada: The Peaceful Revolution.* Washington, 1982

GUATEMALA

República de Guatemala

Capital: Guatemala City
Population: 6·04m. (1983)
GNP per capita: US$1,110 (1980)

HISTORY. From 1524 to 1821 Guatemala was a Spanish captaincy-general, comprising the whole of Central America. It became independent in 1821 and formed part of the Confederation of Central America from 1823 to 1839, when Rafael Carrera dissolved the Confederation.

AREA AND POPULATION. Guatemala is bounded on the north and west by Mexico, south by the Pacific ocean and east by El Salvador, Honduras and Belize, and the area is 108,889 sq. km (42,042 sq. miles). In March 1936 Guatemala, El Salvador and Honduras agreed to accept the peak of Mount Montecristo as the common boundary point.

The population was 6,043,559 in 1983. About 45% are pure Indians, of 21 different groups descended from the Maya; most of the remainder are mixed Indian and Spanish and these supply the ruling classes. Density of population, 1978, 63 per sq. km.

Vital statistics, 1980: Births, 303,643; deaths, 51,769.

Guatemala is administratively divided into 22 departments, each with a governor appointed by the President. Population, 1982:

Departments	Area (sq. km)	Population	Departments	Area (sq. km)	Population
Alta Verapaz	8,686	383,178	Petén	35,854	102,803
Baja Verapaz	3,124	152,374	Quezaltenango	1,951	447,428
Chimaltenango	1,979	267,182	Quiché	8,378	430,003
Chiquimula	2,376	215,409	Retalhuleu	1,858	206,543
El Progreso	1,922	101,203	Sacatepéquez	465	137,815
Escuintla	4,384	496,522	San Marcos	3,791	552,094
Guatemala	2,126	1,785,665	Santa Rosa	2,955	249,930
Huehuetenango	7,403	524,829	Sololá	1,061	173,401
Izabal	9,038	290,203	Suchitepéquez	2,510	304,826
Jalapa	2,063	162,907	Totonicapán	1,061	236,033
Jutiapa	3,219	329,185	Zacapa	2,690	149,267

The capital is Guatemala City with about 1·3m. inhabitants (1983). Other towns are Quezaltenango (65,733), Puerto Barrios (38,956), Mazatenango (38,319), Antigua (26,631), Zacapa (35,769) and Cobán (43,538). An earthquake in central Guatemala in Feb. 1976 killed 24,103 people and destroyed 200,000 dwellings.

CLIMATE. A tropical climate, with little variation in temperature and a well marked wet season from May to Oct. Guatemala City. Jan. 63°F (17·2°C), July 69°F (20·6°C). Annual rainfall 53″ (1,316 mm).

CONSTITUTION AND GOVERNMENT. On 23 March 1982 a junta, consisting of Brig.-Gen. Efrain Ríos Montt, Gen. Horacio Maldonado and Col. Francisco Gordillo, took power in a bloodless *coup*. Gen. Ríos Montt later became President. The Constitution and political activity was suspended, Congress abolished and government was to be by decree. A further *coup* on 8 Aug. 1983 removed Brig.-Gen. Montt from the presidency. Brig.-Gen. Oscar Humberto Mejia Victores became President. On 1 Oct. he announced that there would be elections to a National Constituent Assembly on 1 July 1984 and a return to civilian rule in 1985.

National flag: Three vertical strips of blue, white, blue, with the national arms in the centre.

National anthem: ¡Guatemala! feliz (words by J. J. Palma; tune by R. Alvarez).

DEFENCE. There is conscription into the armed forces for 24–30 months.

Army. The Army numbers 20,000, organized in 17 infantry, 1 armoured, 2 para-chute and 1 engineer battalions, 1 field artillery group, 1 anti-aircraft artillery group and 4 reconnaissance squadrons. Equipment includes light tanks and armoured cars.

Navy. A Naval force was formed in 1959. It comprises 12 small patrol craft, 1 landing craft, 2 small troop carriers, 6 motor launches, 2 utility cutters, 30 river patrol craft and 1 tug. Since 1973 the base at Santo Tomas has had a 230-ton marine elevator (synchrolift), greatly improving naval repair facilities. Personnel in 1984 numbered 600 officers and men (including 210 marines).

Air Force. There is a small Air Force with 10 A-37B light attack aircraft, 1 DC-6, 10 C-47 and 8 Israeli-built Arava transports, 12 Pilatus PC-7 turboprop trainers, and a number of light aircraft and helicopters, including a few armed UH-1 Iroquois. Total strength is about 550 personnel and 70 aircraft.

INTERNATIONAL RELATIONS

Membership. Guatemala is a member of UN, OAS and Caricom.

External Debt. In 1978 the external debt was Q.220m.

ECONOMY

Planning. The 1979–82 National Economic Development Plan involved government investment of Q.1,937·5m.

Budget. The estimates of ordinary revenue and expenditure balanced as follows, in quetzales (1 quetzal = US$): 1980, 1,280m.; 1981, 1,467m.

Currency. The gold *quetzal* was established 7 May 1925 equal to 60 old Guatemala paper pesos, with a gold content equal to that of the US$. Coins of 25, 10, 5 and 1 *centavos* were issued by the Banco de Guatemala on 16 Sept. 1965; they are of a lower content value than the previous ones. There are also paper notes of 100, 50, 20, 10, 5, 1 and ½ *quetzales* (50 *centavos*). In March 1984, £1 = Q.1·49; US$1 = Q.1.

Banking. By an Act effective 4 Feb. 1946 the Central Bank of Guatemala (founded in 1926 as a mixed central and commercial bank) was superseded by a new institution, the Banco de Guatemala, to operate solely as a central bank. Savings and term deposits at commercial banks were Q.979·7m. at the end of 1980. Total currency circulation (backed by a gold reserve fixed by law at a minimum of 40%) on 31 Dec. 1980 was Q.923·9m.; total net international reserves amounted to Q.396·7m. on 31 Dec. 1980. In July 1965 the country's quota with the IMF was increased from US$15m. to 25m.

There are 17 banks, including the Banco de Guatemala, Banco Nacional de Desarollo, set up in 1971 to promote agricultural development, its counterpart for small industries (Banco de los Trabajadores) set up in Jan. 1966 with initial capital of US$1·3m., a branch of Lloyds Bank International Ltd and a branch of the Bank of America.

Weights and Measures. The metric system has been officially adopted, but is little used in local commerce.

Libra of 16 oz.	= 1·014 lb.	*League*	= 3 miles
Arroba of 25 libras	= 25·35 lb.	*Vara*	= 32 in.
Quintal of 4 arrobas	= 101·40 lb.	*Manzana*	= 100 varas sq.
Tonelada of 20 quintals	= 18·10 cwt	*Caballeria* of 64 man-	
Fanega	= 1½ Imp. bushels	zanas	= 110 acres

ENERGY AND NATURAL RESOURCES

Electricity. 1,045m. kwh. of electricity were generated in 1976. A large-scale hydro-electric development is now underway and others are planned.

Oil. Guatemala began exporting crude oil in 1980; exports, 1980, were valued at Q.23·7m. Production is from wells in Alta Verapaz department from where the oil is piped to Santo Tomas de Castilla. Further exploration is proceeding in the Petén.

Minerals. Mineral production includes zinc and lead concentrates, some antimony and tungsten, a small amount of cadmium and silver; some copper is also being mined. Exports (1980) Q.5·5m. In 1965 a subsidiary of International Nickel Company of Canada was granted a 40-year concession to extract and process nickel ore in northern Guatemala. Production and exports started in 1977 but production had ceased temporarily in 1982.

Agriculture. The Cordilleras divide Guatemala into two unequal drainage areas, of which the Atlantic is much the greater. The Pacific slope, though comparatively narrow, is exceptionally well watered and fertile between the altitudes of 1,000 and 5,000 ft, and is the most densely settled part of the republic. The Atlantic slope is sparsely populated, and has little of commercial importance beyond the chicle and timber-cutting of the Petén, coffee cultivation of Cobán region and banana-raising of the Motagua Valley and Lake Izabal district. Soil erosion is serious and a single week of heavy rains suffices to cause flooding of fields and much crop destruction.

The principal crop is coffee; there are about 12,000 coffee plantations with 138m. coffee trees on about 338,000 acres, but 80% of the crop comes from 1,500 large coffee farms employing 426,000 workers. Coffee exports in 1980 were valued at Q.463·9m. mainly to USA and Federal Republic of Germany.

Bananas are still an important export crop, but exports have at times been seriously reduced, partly by labour troubles and by hurricanes. Exports 1980 were worth Q.45·4m.

Cotton exports in 1980 were valued at Q.166·1m. Other important exports (1980) were sugar, Q.69·3m.; beef, Q.29·1m. Guatemala is, after Mexico, the largest producer of chicle gum (used for chewing-gum manufacture in USA). Rubber development schemes are under way, assisted by US funds. Guatemala is one of the largest sources of essential oils (citronella and lemon grass); exports in 1980 were valued at Q.2·7m. Cardamom, exported mainly to the Arab countries, was valued at Q.55·6m. in 1980.

Livestock (1980): Cattle, 1·88m.; pigs, 835,000; sheep, 500,000; horses, 100,000; poultry, 14·5m.

Forestry. The forest area has an extent of 17,784,000 acres. The department of Petén is rich in mahogany and other woods. Production (1980) 11·23m. cu. metres.

Fisheries. Exports were about Q.8m. in 1980.

INDUSTRY AND TRADE

Industry. The principal industries are food and beverages, tobacco, chemicals, hides and skins, textiles, garments and non-metallic minerals. New industries include electrical goods, plastic sheet and metal furniture.

Trade Unions. Trade unions are small. In 1954 the trade unions were ordered to reorganize and there are now two main federations.

Commerce. Values in Q.1,000 (1 quetzal = US$1) were:

	1976	1977	1978	1979	1980	1981
Imports (c.i.f.)	981,600	1,052,507	1,285,640	1,503,900	1,615,000	1,773,600
Exports (f.o.b.)	782,400	1,160,115	1,089,457	1,241,400	1,522,000	1,281,200

Total trade between Guatemala and UK for 6 years (British Department of Trade returns, in £1,000 sterling):

	1978	1979	1980	1981	1982	1983
Imports to UK	5,726	7,596	23,657	8,197	13,476	9,764
Exports and re-exports from UK	14,529	13,371	13,835	11,280	8,127	7,440

Tourism. There were 466,041 foreign visitors in 1980.

COMMUNICATIONS

Roads. In 1979 there were 17,278 km of roads, of which 2,850 are paved. There is a trunk highway from coast to coast *via* Guatemala City. There are 2 trunk highways from the Mexican to the Salvadorean frontier: the Pacific Highway serving the fertile coastal plain and the Pan-American Highway running through the highlands and Guatemala City. Motor vehicles number about 200,000.

Railways. The principal railway system is the government-owned (since 1968) *Ferrocarriles de Guatemala.* All railways are of 914 mm gauge. Total length of all lines is 820 km. Passengers carried, 1976, numbered 386,000, and freight carried (1976), 703,600 short tons. The bridge across the Suchiate River between Mexico and Guatemala in 1942 linked the railways of North and Central America, though differences in gauge make it necessary to change trains at Ayutla.

Aviation. The government-owned airline, Aviateca, furnishes both domestic and international services; 6 other airlines handle international traffic.

Shipping. The chief ports on the Atlantic coast are Puerto Barrios and Santo Tomás de Castilla: on the Pacific coast, San José and Champerico. Total tonnage handled was, 1980, 4·57m. tons.

Post and Broadcasting. The Government own and operate the telegraph and telephone services; there were (1982) 97,670 telephone instruments. There are some 70 broadcasting stations. Radio receiving sets in use, 1976, numbered about 1m. There are 4 commercial TV stations, 1 government station and about 192,000 TV receivers.

Cinemas (1979). Cinemas numbered approximately 100.

Newspapers (1980). There are 8 daily newspapers.

JUSTICE, RELIGION, EDUCATION AND WELFARE

Justice. Justice is administered in a Supreme Court, 6 appeal courts and 28 courts of first instance. Supreme Court and appeal court judges are elected by Congress. Judges of first instance are appointed by the Supreme Court.

All holders of public office have to show on entering office, and again on leaving, a full account of their private property and income.

Religion. Roman Catholicism is the prevailing faith; but all other creeds have complete liberty of worship. Guatemala has an archbishopric.

Education. In 1980 there were 7,708 primary schools with 24,242 teachers and an attendance of 826,613 pupils; these figures include private schools. There are 753 secondary and other schools having 9,613 teachers and an attendance of 171,903 pupils; the autonomous University of San Carlos de Borromeo, founded in 1678, was reopened in 1910 with 7 faculties and schools and there are 4 new universities. Students at state university (1977) approximately 25,925. All education is in theory free, but owing to a grave shortage of state schools private schools flourish. The 1964 census showed that 63% of those 10 years of age and older were illiterate.

Social Welfare. A comprehensive system of social security was outlined in a law of 30 Oct. 1946. Medical personnel include about 1,250 doctors and 275 dentists for the whole republic. There are about 60 public hospitals and about 100 dispensaries.

DIPLOMATIC REPRESENTATIVES

Of Guatemala in the USA (2220 R St., NW, Washington, D.C. 20008)
Chargé d'Affaires: Norma J. Vasquez.

Of the USA in Guatemala (7–01 Avenida de la Reforma, Zone 10, Guatemala City)
Ambassador: Frederic L. Chapin.

Of Guatemala to the United Nations
Ambassador: Mario Rafael Quiñones Amezquita.

Guatemala broke off diplomatic relations with UK on 31 July 1963 and consular relations were broken on 7 Sept. 1981.

Books of Reference

The official gazette is called *Diario de Centro America.*

Banco de Guatemala, *Memoria annual, Estudio económico* and *Boletín Estadístico*
Bloomfield, L. M., *The British Honduras–Guatemala Dispute.* Toronto, 1953
Franklin, W. B., *Guatemala.* [Bibliography] Oxford and Santa Barbara, 1981
Glassman, P., *Guatemala Guide.* Dallas, 1977
Humphreys, R. A., *The Diplomatic History of British Honduras 1638–1901.* London, 1961
Immerman, R. H., *The CIA in Guatemala. The Foreign Policy of Intervention.* Univ. of Texas Press, 1982
Mendoza, J. L., *Britain and Her Treaties on Belize.* Guatemala, 1946
Morton, F., *Xeláhuh.* London, 1959
Plant, R., *Guatemala: Unnatural Disaster.* London, 1978
Schlesinger, S., and Kinzer, S., *Bitter Front: The Untold Story of the American Coup in Guatemala.* London and New York, 1982

National Library: Biblioteca Nacional, 5a Avenida y 8a Calle, Zona 1, Guatemala City.

GUINEA

République populaire et révolutionnaire de Guinée

Capital: Conakry
Population: 5·41m. (1983)
GNP per capita: US$290 (1980)

HISTORY. Guinea was proclaimed a French protectorate in 1888 and a colony in 1893. It became a constituent territory of French West Africa in 1904. The independent republic of Guinea was proclaimed on 2 Oct. 1958, after the territory of French Guinea had decided at the referendum of 28 Sept. to leave the French Community.

AREA AND POPULATION. Guinea, a coastal state of West Africa, is bounded north-west by Guinea-Bissau and Senegal, north-east by Mali, south-east by the Ivory Coast, south by Liberia and Sierra Leone, and west by the Atlantic Ocean.

The area is 245,857 sq. km (94,926 sq. miles), and the population, census, 1972, was 5,143,284, including an estimated 1·5m. living abroad (estimate, 1983, 5,412,000.). The capital, Conakry, had 763,000 inhabitants in 1980; other large towns (1972) were Kankan (85,310), Kindia, (79,861), Labé (79,670), and N'Zérékoré (about 23,000).

The ethnic composition is Fulani (40·3%, predominant in Moyenne-Guinée), Malinké (or Mandingo, 25·8%, prominent in Haute-Guinée), Susu (11%, prominent in Guinée-Maritime), Kissi (6·5%) and Kpelle (4·8%) in Guinée-Forestière, and Dialonka, Loma and others (11·6%).

CLIMATE. A tropical climate, with high rainfall near the coast and constant heat, but conditions are a little cooler on the plateau. The wet season on the coast lasts from May to Nov., but only to Oct. inland. Conakry. Jan. 80°F (26·7°C), July 77°F (25°C). Annual rainfall 172″ (4,293 mm).

CONSTITUTION AND GOVERNMENT. The provisional Constitution of 12 Nov. 1958 declared Guinea 'a democratic, secular and social republic'. The unicameral National Assembly consists of 210 deputies, elected by universal suffrage on a national list for a 7-year term (elections were held 27 Jan. 1980). The President is also directly elected for a 7-year term and can be re-elected; he is head of the Executive, and appoints a Council of Ministers to assist him.

All candidates are nominated by the National Council of the *Parti démocratique de Guinée*, the sole legal party. At the PDG's latest Congress in Nov. 1978 it elected a 25-member Central Committee (for 5 years; membership to be raised to 75) and a 15-member Political Bureau to administer the party until the election of a new National Council.

President: Col. Lansana Konté (assumed power, 2 April 1984, confirmed in office 5 April 1984).
Prime Minister: Col. Diarra Traore.
Foreign Affairs: Capt. Massini Touré.

The administrative division comprises 33 regions, grouped into 4 'supra-regions' which correspond to the 4 major geographical and ethnic areas: Guinée-Maritime (Lower Guinea, headquarters at Kindia); Moyenne-Guinée (Fouta Djallon, headquarters at Labé); Haute-Guinée (Upper Guinea, headquarters at Kankan) and Guinée-Forestière (Forest-Guinea, headquarters at N'Zérékoré).

The regional governor and PDG Party chief in each region are now popularly elected. The regions are divided into 175 *arrondissements,* each under a commandant.

National flag: Three vertical strips of red, gold, green.

Besides French, there are 8 official languages taught in schools: Fulani, Malinké, Susu, Kissi, Kpelle, Loma, Basari and Koniagi.

DEFENCE

Army. The Army of 8,500 men (1984), which comprises 1 armoured, 5 infantry, 1 commando and 1 engineer, 1 artillery and 1 special force battalions. Equipment includes 30 T-34 and 20 PT-76 tanks. There are also 3 paramilitary forces: People's Militia (7,000), Gendarmerie (1,000) and Republican Guard (1,000).

Navy. The Navy comprises an ocean minesweeper, 12 fast attack craft, 5 coastal patrol craft, and 2 small landing craft. There are bases at Conakry and Kakanda. Personnel (1984) 600.

Air Force. The Air Force, formed with Soviet assistance, is reported to be equipped with 6 MiG-17 jet-fighters and 2 MiG-15UTI trainers, 2 Il-18 turboprop transports, 4 An-14 and 4 Il-14 piston-engined transports and a Yak-40 jet aircraft for VIP duties, all Russian built, plus a few helicopters, piston-engined Yak-18 and L-29 jet trainers. Personnel about 800.

INTERNATIONAL RELATIONS

Membership. Guinea is a member of UN, OAU and is an ACP state of EEC.

ECONOMY

Planning. The Development Plan, 1981–85 envisaged expenditure of 38,000m. sylis.

Budget. The budget for 1979 balanced at 11,250m. sylis.

Currency. The monetary unit is the *syli*, divided into 100 *cauris*, introduced in 1972. The issue consists of notes of 100, 50, 25 and 10 *sylis*, and coins of 50 *cauris*, 5, 2 and 1 *sylis*. In March 1984, £1 = 34·60 *sylis*; US$1 = 23·28 *sylis*.

Banking. In 1980 the Central Bank was replaced by a National Currency Institute, through which a governor with ministerial rank controls all banking and insurance, state monopolies since Jan. 1962.

ENERGY AND NATURAL RESOURCES

Electricity. Production of electrical energy was 495m. kwh. in 1979. The development of 2 new dams (1981) on the Konkouré river will expand capacity, primarily for the aluminium industry.

Minerals. Bauxite is mined at Fria, Boké and elsewhere in Guinée-Maritime; output 12,034,000 tonnes in 1980. Reserves (estimate,1982) 8,000m. tonnes. Production of iron ore from the Nimba and Simandou mountains commenced in 1981, following exhaustion of the Kaloum peninsula deposits. Diamond mining was suspended in 1978 but resumed in 1981.

Agriculture. There are experimental fruit gardens at Camayenne near Conakry, Kindia and Dalaba, 2 stations for rice selection (Kankan, Koba) and an experimental quinine station at Seredou. Coffee is grown in forest districts. Fouta Djallon contains cattle in abundance.

The chief crops (production, 1981, in 1,000 tonnes) are: Cassava, 600; rice, 330; plantains, 227; sugar-cane, 220; bananas, 100; groundnuts, 83; sweet potatoes, 75; maize, 63; palm-oil, 42; palm kernels, 35; pineapples, 17; coffee, 15; coconuts, 15.

Livestock (1982): Cattle, 1.85m.; sheep, 445,000; goats, 425,000; pigs, 42,000.

Forestry: There were 5,756 sq. km of classified forests in 1977. Round-wood production amounted to 3·37m. cu. metres in 1978.

Fisheries: Catch (1980) 18,500 tonnes, 90% in coastal waters.

COMMERCE. In 1979 imports totalled 5,700m. sylis; exports, 7,000m. sylis. Alumina forms about 30% and bauxite 58% of the exports.

Total trade between Guinea and the UK (British Department of Trade returns, in £1,000 sterling):

	1979	1980	1981	1982	1983
Imports to UK	489	10,777	844	1,956	668
Exports and re-exports from UK	5,057	26,596	7,117	6,840	7,190

COMMUNICATIONS

Roads. There are 28,400 km of roads and tracks, of which 520 km are bitumenized. In 1978 there were 9,948 cars and 9,992 commercial vehicles.

Railways. A railway connects Conakry with Kankan (662 km) and may be extended to Bamako in Mali. A line 134 km long linking bauxite deposits at Sangaredi with Port Kamsar was opened in 1973 and a third line links Conakry and Fria (144 km).

Aviation. There are airports at Conakry and Kankan; in 1977, 66,000 passengers disembarked and embarked.

Shipping. There are ports at Conakry (facilities expanded 1976–80) and for bauxite exports at Kamsar (opened 1973). There were (1980) 15 vessels of 16,412 GRT registered in Guinea.

Post and Broadcasting. The territory is connected by cable with France and Pernambuco; also with Freetown, Monrovia and other places. There is a wireless station at Conakry affording communication with all territories of West Africa. Telephones, 1972, numbered about 7,488. There were 121,000 radio receivers in 1979; television broadcasting commenced 1977.

JUSTICE, RELIGION, EDUCATION AND WELFARE

Justice. There are *tribunaux du premier degré* at Conakry and Kankan, and a *juge de paix* at N'Zérékoré. The High Court, Court of Appeal and Superior Tribunal of Cassation are at Conakry, while the National Assembly serves as the 'supreme revolutionary tribunal'.

Religion. About 62% of the population is Moslem, 15% Christian and 35% follow tribal religions.

Education. There were, in 1977, 324,165 pupils in primary schools, 124,455 in secondary schools, 6,000 in technical schools and teacher-training colleges and 5,850 in higher education.

Health. In 1976 there were 314 hospitals and dispensaries with 7,650 beds; there were also 277 doctors, 21 dentists, 159 pharmacists, 394 midwives and 1,533 nursing personnel.

DIPLOMATIC REPRESENTATIVES

Of Guinea in Great Britain
Ambassador: Aboubacar Somparé (resides in Paris).

Of Great Britain in Guinea
Ambassador: P. L. O'Keeffe, CMG, CVO (resides in Dakar).

Of Guinea in the USA (2112 Leroy Pl., NW, Washington, D.C., 20008)
Ambassador: Thierno Habib Diallo.

Of the USA in Guinea (2nd Blvd. and 9th Ave., Conakry)
Ambassador: James D. Rosenthal.

Of Guinea to the United Nations
Ambassador: Djebel Coumbassa.

Books of Reference

Bulletin Statistique et Economique de la Guinée. Monthly. Conakry
Adamolekun, L., *Sékou Touré's Guinea.* London, 1976
Camara, S. S., *La Guinée sans la France.* Paris, 1976
Rivière, C., *Guinea: The Mobilization of a People.* Cornell Univ. Press, 1977
Taylor, F. W., *A Fulani-English Dictionary.* Oxford, 1932

GUINEA-BISSAU

Capital: Bissau
Population: 826,000 (1983)
GNP per capita: US$160 (1980)

HISTORY. Guinea-Bissau, formerly Portuguese Guinea, on the coast of Guinea, was discovered in 1446 by Nuno Tristão. It became a separate colony in 1879. It is bounded by the limits fixed by the convention of 12 May 1886 with France. In 1951 Guinea-Bissau became an overseas province of Portugal. The struggle against colonial rule began in 1963. Independence was declared on 24 Sept. 1973. In 1974 Portugal formally recognized the independence of Guinea-Bissau.

AREA AND POPULATION. Guinea-Bissau is bounded by Senegal in the north, the Atlantic ocean in the west and by Guinea in the east and south. It includes the adjacent archipelago of Bijagoz, with the island of Bolama. The capital and chief port is Bissau, estimated population (census 1979), 109,486. Other ports are Bolama and Cacheu. Area is 36,125 sq. km (13,948 sq. miles); population (census, 1979), 767,739 (estimate, 1983) 826,000.

The regional populations at the 1979 Census were as follows:

Bissau City	109,214	Bolama-Bijagos	25,473	Gabú	104,227
Bafatá	116,032	Buba	35,532	Oio	135,114
Biombo	56,463	Cacheu	130,227	Tombali	55,099

The main ethnic groups are the Balante (32%), Malinké (13%), Fulani (22%), Mandjako (14%) and Pepel (7%).

CLIMATE. The tropical climate has a wet season from June to Nov., when rains are abundant, but the hot, dry Harmattan wind blows from Dec. to May. Bissau. Jan. 76°F (24·4°C), July 80°F (26·7°C). Annual rainfall 78″ (1,950 mm).

CONSTITUTION AND GOVERNMENT. A new Constitution was adopted on 10 Nov. 1980, 4 days before the *coup* which ousted President Luis Cabral. It retains the 150-member National People's Assembly as the legislature, and the *Partido Africano da Independencia da Guiné e Cabo Verde* (PAIGC) as the sole permitted Party, but provides for the President to become Head of government. Following the *coup*, the new Constitution remains in force, but the Assembly was suspended and a new 13-member Revolutionary Council proclaimed as the prime political institution, overseeing the work of the appointed Council of Ministers, which from 16 Sept. 1983 was composed of the following:

President, Minister of Defence and the Interior: Maj. João Bernardo Vieira.
Prime Minister: Vítor Saúde Maria.
Foreign Affairs: Dr Fidelis Cabral d'Almada. *Justice:* Filinto de Barros. *Economy and Finance:* Dr Vítor Freire Monteiro. *Education:* Avito José da Silva. *Natural Resources:* Joseph Turpin. *Commerce and Fisheries:* Carlos Correia. *Rural Development:* Col. Paulo Correia. *Transport and Tourism:* Maj. Manuel dos Santos. *Information and Culture:* Adelino Nunes Correia. *Health and Social Affairs:* Carmen Pereira. *Administration and Labour:* Dr João Cruz Pinto. *Energy and Industry:* Albertino Lima Gomez. *Governor of Central Bank:* Pedro Godinho Gomes. *Secretaries of State:* Maj. Brahima Bangura *(Veterans' Affairs),* Musa Djassi *(Posts and Telecommunications),* Luis Oliveira Samca *(Fisheries),* Bartolomeu Simoes Pereira *(Planning and International Co-operation).*

National flag: Horizontally yellow over green with red vertical strip in the hoist bearing a black star.

Local government: The administrative division is in 8 regions (each under an elected regional council), in turn subdivided into 37 sectors; and the city of Bissau, treated as a separate region.

DEFENCE

Army. The Army consisted in 1984 of 4 infantry battalions, 1 engineer unit and 1 tank squadron. Equipment includes 10 T-34 tanks. Personnel, 6,000 men.

Navy. The naval flotilla includes 3 fast attack craft, 10 coastal patrol craft, 2 small landing craft and 1 survey ship. Based at Bissau. Personnel (1984) 250.

Air Force. Formation of a small Air Force began in 1978 with the delivery of a French-built Cessna FTB-337 twin-engined counter-insurgency and general-purpose light transport. It has been followed by about 12 Czechoslovak-built L-39 jet trainers, an Mi-8 and 2 Alouette III helicopters, an An-26 twin-turboprop transport and 2 Dornier Do 27 utility aircraft.

INTERNATIONAL RELATIONS

Membership. Guinea-Bissau is a member of UN, OAU and is an ACP state of EEC.

ECONOMY

Budget. The revenue in 1979 was 890m. pesos; the expenditure, 1,474m. pesos.

Currency. The monetary unit is the *peso* divided into 100 *centavos*. In March 1984, £1 = 117·85 *pesos*; US$1 = 79·27 *pesos*.

Banking. The Banco Nacional da Guiné-Bissau, founded 1976, is the bank of issue and also the commercial bank. There are also state-owned savings institutions.

NATURAL RESOURCES

Minerals. Mining is very little developed although bauxite (200m. tonnes) has been located in the Boé area. Exploration for oil is taking place but no reports of finds have been reported.

Agriculture. Chief crops (production, 1981, in 1,000 tonnes) are: Groundnuts, 30; sugar-cane, 25; plantains, 25; coconuts, 25; rice, 23; rubber, 23; palm kernels, 10; millet, 6; palm-oil, 5; sorghum, 5; maize, 4; timber, hides, seeds and wax.

Livestock (1982): Cattle, 220,000; sheep, 60,000; goats, 140,000; pigs, 125,000; chickens, 420,000.

Fishing. Total catch (1978) 2,000 tonnes.

COMMERCE. Imports in 1980, 1,826m. pesos; exports, 368m. of which 27% went to Portugal and 21% to Spain.

Total trade between Guinea-Bissau and UK (British Department of Trade returns, in £1,000 sterling):

	1980	1981	1982	1983
Imports to UK	1	–	–	94
Exports and re-exports from UK	483	595	431	477

COMMUNICATIONS

Roads. There were (1979) 3,570 km of roads.

Aviation. There is an international airport at Bissalanca (for Bissau).

Shipping. In 1974, 169 vessels entered the ports unloading 134,000 tonnes.

Post. In 1973 there were 2,723 telephones and (1979) 6,000 radio receivers.

Cinemas. There were 7 cinemas (1972) with a seating capacity of 3,000.

Newspapers (1978). There was one daily newspaper, with a circulation of 3,000.

JUSTICE, RELIGION, EDUCATION AND WELFARE

Justice. Following the 1980 *coup*, the judicial system has been subject to the authority of the Council of the Revolution.

Religion. About 40% of the population are Moslem and about 4% Christian.

Education. There were, in 1978, 93,256 pupils in primary schools with 2,620 teachers; 4,612 pupils in secondary schools and 284 students in teacher-training establishments.

Health. In 1976 there were 9 hospitals with 1,056 beds and 74 doctors, 2 dentists, 2 pharmacists, 70 midwives and 292 nursing personnel.

DIPLOMATIC REPRESENTATIVES

Of Great Britain in Guinea-Bissau
Ambassador: P. L. O'Keeffe, CMG, CVO (resides in Dakar).

Of Guinea-Bissau in the USA
Ambassador: Inacio Semedo, Jr.

Of the USA in Guinea-Bissau (Ave. Domingos Ramos, Bissau)
Ambassador: Wesley W. Eagan, Jr.

Of Guinea-Bissau to the United Nations
Ambassador: Dr Inacio Semedo, Jr.

Books of Reference

Relatório e Mapas do Movimento Comercial e Maritimo da Guiné. Bolama, Annual
Cabral, A., *Revolution in Guinea.* London, 1969.—*Return to the Source.* New York, 1973
Davidson, B., *Growing from the Grass Roots.* London, 1974
Gjerstad, O., and Sarrazin, C., *Sowing the First Harvest: National Reconstruction in Guinea-Bissau.* Oakland, 1978
Rudebeck, L., *Guinea-Bissau: A Study of Political Mobilization.* Uppsala, 1974

GUYANA

Capital: Georgetown
Population: 900,000 (1983)
GNP per capita: US$715 (1980)

HISTORY. The territory, including the counties of Demerara, Essequibo and Berbice, named from the 3 rivers, was first partially settled by the Dutch West Indian Company about 1620. The Dutch retained their hold until 1796, when it was captured by the English. It was finally ceded to Great Britain in 1814 and named British Guiana. On 26 May 1966 British Guiana became an independent member of the Commonwealth under the name of Guyana and the world's first Co-operative Republic on 23 Feb. 1970.

AREA AND POPULATION. Guyana is situated on the north-east coast of South America on the Atlantic ocean, with Suriname on the east, Venezuela on the west and Brazil on the south and west. Area, 83,000 sq. miles (216,000 sq. km). Estimated population (1983), 900,000. Births (1972), 25,065; deaths (1974), 3,418. In 1976, the population comprised 362,700 Indians, 218,400 Africans, 2,100 Europeans, 3,400 Chinese, 800 others. The Greater Georgetown area had in 1983 an estimated population of 188,000.

Venezuela demanded the return of the Essequibo region in 1963. It was finally agreed in March 1983 that the UN Secretary-General should mediate. There was also an unresolved claim (1984) by Suriname for the return of an area between the New river and the Courantyne river.

CLIMATE. A tropical climate, with rainy seasons from April to July and Nov. to Jan. Humidity is high all the year but temperatures are moderated by sea-breezes. Rainfall increases from 90" (2,280 mm) on the coast to 140" (3,560 mm) in the forest zone. Georgetown. Jan. 79°F (26·1°C), July 81°F (27·2°C). Annual rainfall 87" (2,175 mm).

CONSTITUTION AND GOVERNMENT. A new Constitution was promulgated in Oct. 1980. The National Assembly consists of 65 elected members. Elections are held under the single-list system of proportional representation, with the whole of the country forming one electoral area and each voter casting his vote for a party list of candidates. The legislature is elected for 5 years unless earlier dissolved.

The elections held on 15 Dec. 1980 gave the People's National Congress 41 seats, the People's Progressive Party 10 seats, the Liberator Party 2 seats. The PNC with an overall majority formed a 25-member cabinet.

The Cabinet was in Nov. 1983 composed as follows:

President: L. F. S. Burnham.

Prime Minister and First Vice-President: Dr P. A. Reid.
Vice-President and Production: H. D. Hoyte. *Vice-President and Social Infrastructure:* H. Green. *Vice-President, Party and State Matters:* B. Ramsaroop. *Vice-President and Attorney-General:* Dr M. Shahabuddeen. *Education, Social Development and Culture:* R. Chandisingh. *National Mobilisation:* R. H. O. Corbin. *Foreign Affairs:* R. E. Jackson. *Home Affairs:* J. R. Thomas. *Energy and Mines:* H. Rashid. *Finance and Economic Planning:* C. B. Greenidge. *Information and Public Service:* Y. V. Harewood-Benn. *Manpower and Co-operatives:* K. W. E. Denny. *Office of the Prime Minister:* U. E. Johnson. *Agriculture:* Sallahuddin. *Youth and Sport:* R. C. Fredericks. *Transport:* S. Prashad. *Health and Public Welfare:* Dr R. A. VanWest Charles.

There are 2 Ministers of State.

National flag: Green with a yellow triangle based on the hoist, edged in white, charged with a red triangle edged in black.

DEFENCE

Army. The Guyana Army has a strength of 7,000 (which includes all armed services), including a women's army corps. It comprises 3 infantry battalions and 1 artillery battery.

Air Force. The Air Command is equipped with light aircraft and helicopters, including 2 Skyvan and 1 Super King Air 200 twin-turboprop transports, 6 Islander twin-engined STOL transports, a Cessna U206- utility lightplane, and 4 Bell 206/212 light helicopters.

INTERNATIONAL RELATIONS

Membership. Guyana is a member of UN, the Commonwealth, Caricom and is an ACP state of EEC.

ECONOMY

Budget. Revenue and expenditure for calendar years (in G$1,000):

	1976 [1]	1977	1978	1979	1980	1981
Revenue	500,942	442,475	539,591	693,921	803,460	1,009,936
Expenditure	746,329	567,322	632,749	868,654	1,049,836	1,176,678

[1] Revised estimates.

Currency. The Bank of Guyana, established in 1965, issued Guyana dollar notes of $1, 5, 10 and 20 and coins of 1-, 5-, 10-, 25- and 50-cent pieces. In March 1984: £1 = 5·57 G$; US$1 = 3·75 G$.

Banking. Barclays Bank International and the Royal Bank of Canada maintain branches in Berbice, Demerara and Essequibo while the Bank of Baroda (India) has branches in Demerara and Berbice. The Chase Manhattan Bank (USA) and the Bank of Nova Scotia each have a branch in Georgetown. The Guyana National Co-operative Bank opened in Feb. 1970 with headquarters in Georgetown and 12 branches throughout the country. In 1973 the Guyana Agricultural and Industrial Development Bank (Gaibank) and the Guyana Co-operative Mortgage Finance Bank were established.

NATURAL RESOURCES

Minerals. Placer gold mining commenced in 1884, and was followed by diamond mining in 1887. From 1884 to 1973 the output of gold was 431,413 bullion oz. (11,000 oz. in 1980). From 1901 to 1973 the production of diamonds was 4,008,211 metric carats (10,200 in 1980). There are large deposits of bauxite; 2,717,000 tons, 2,111,000 tons of alumina and 318,000 tonnes of alumina hydrate were produced in 1980. Full-scale production of manganese began in 1960 and other minerals include uranium, oil, copper and molybdenum.

Agriculture. Production, 1982: Sugar-cane, 292,000 tonnes; rice, 182,000 tonnes. Other important products are coconuts, ground provisions and citrus fruit. Other tropical fruits and vegetables are grown mostly in scattered plantings; they include mangoes, papaws, avocado pears, melons, bananas and gooseberries. Other important crops are tomatoes, cabbages, black-eye peas, peanuts, carrots, onions, turmeric, ginger, pineapples, red kidney beans, soybeans, eschallot and tobacco. Large areas of unimproved land in the coastal region, which vary in width up to about 30 miles from the sea, are still available for agricultural and cattle-grazing projects.

Livestock estimate (1982): Cattle, 305,000; pigs, 140,000; sheep, 116,000; goats, 74,000; poultry, 13·5m.

Forestry. Guyana can be divided roughly into 3 regions: (1) A low coastal region varying in width up to about 30 miles and constituting the agricultural area; (2) an intermediate area about 100 miles wide, of slightly higher undulating land containing the chief mineral and forest resources of the country; and (3) a hinterland of several mountain ranges and extensive savannahs. 19,844,170 hectares of the land area is forested out of 21,497,000 hectares.

COMMERCE. Imports and exports (in G$) for calendar years:

	1978	1979	1980	1981	1982
Imports	711,056,000	811,000,000	1,009,664,425	1,236,488,611	840,442,362
Exports	739,589,440	732,900,000	992,608,557	974,327,562	775,544,161

Chief imports (1981): Wheat flour, 555,000 kg, $999,000; unmilled wheat, 42,569,000 kg, $30,311,000; milk, 4,748,000 gallons, $31,617,000; textile fabrics, 18,195,000 sq. metres, $25,221,000.

Chief domestic exports (1981): Sugar, 267,000 tonnes, $327·81m.; rice, 78,000 tonnes, $110m.; bauxite, dried, 1,011,000 tonnes, $78,123,000; bauxite, calcined, 496,000 tonnes, $259,464,000; alumina and alumina hydrate, 152,000 tonnes, $91,915,000; rum, 3,204,000 proof gallons, $24,046,000; timber, 36,000 cu. metres, $15,582,000; molasses, 85,344,000 kg, $12,902,000; shrimps, 477 kg, $7,849,000.

Imports (exclusive of transhipments), 1981, from CARICOM Territories, 35%; from USA, 25%; from UK, 16%; from Canada, 4%; exports (exclusive of transhipments) to UK, 26%; to CARICOM Territories, 17%; to Canada, 5%.

Total trade between Guyana and UK (British Department of Trade returns, in £1,000 sterling):

	1979	1980	1981	1982	1983
Imports to UK	43,009	47,143	50,841	50,495	42,810
Exports and re-exports from UK	27,607	30,191	28,969	13,145	13,585

COMMUNICATIONS

Roads. Roads and vehicular trails in the national, provincial and urban systems amount to 8,870 km. Motor vehicles, as of 31 Dec. 1976, totalled 64,272, including 26,599 passenger cars, 6,979 lorries and vans, 9,072 tractors and trailers, and 19,109 motor cycles. The main road on the Atlantic Coast, some 290 km (180 miles) long extends from Charity on the Pomeroon River to Crabwood Creek on the Corentyne, there are two unbridged gaps made by the Berbice and Essequibo Rivers, and the banks of the Demerara River are linked by a 1,853 metre (6,074 ft) floating bridge.

Railways. There is a government-owned railway in the North West District, while the Guyana Mining Enterprise operates a standard gauge railway of 133 km from Linden on the Demerara River to Ituni and Coomacka.

Aviation. Guyana Airways Corporation operates scheduled services within the state and also to Trinidad, Barbados, Paramaribo, New York, Miami and Brazil. In 1982, Guyana Airways Corporation carried 108,402 passengers and 1·6m. kg of freight on its international service and 46,373 passengers and 1·5m. kg freight locally. Other services in operation: British Airways 4 times weekly to the Caribbean, Europe and North America: PANAM 3 times weekly to North, Central and South America: Air France, to and from Guadeloupe, Paramaribo and Cayenne 4 times a week; British West Indian Airways, Ltd, to and from Trinidad 3 times a week, providing direct connexion with New York and London; Cubana Airlines once weekly; Suriname Airways. The International Airport at Timehri serves Arrow Air Airlines, BWIA, Cubana Airways, and Suriname Airways.

Shipping. In 1975, 1,273 vessels of 2,823,912 NRT entered and 1,225 of 2,266,220 NRT cleared the port of Georgetown. There are 217 nautical miles of river navigation. There are ferry services across the mouths of the Demerara, Berbice and Essequibo rivers, the last providing a link between the islands of Leguan and Wakenaam and the mainland at Adventure, and a number of coastal and river-boat services carrying both passengers and cargo. A number of launch services are operated in the more remote areas by private concerns.

Georgetown harbour, about ½ mile wide and 2½ miles long, has a minimum depth of 24 ft. New Amsterdam harbour is situated at the mouth of the Berbice River; there are wharves for coastal vessels only. Bauxite is loaded on ocean-going freighters at Mackenzie, 67 miles up the Demerara River, and at Everton on the Berbice River, about 10 miles from the mouth of the waterway. The Essequibo River has several timber-loading berths ranging from 20 to 40 ft. Springlands on the Corentyne River is the point of entry and departure of passengers travelling by launch services to and from Suriname. It is also a shipping point for rice and other produce from the Corentyne to Georgetown.

Post and Broadcasting. The inland public telegraph and radio communication services are operated and maintained by the Telecommunication Corporation, established on 1 March 1967. On 31 Dec. 1976 there were 57 post offices and 94 agencies (including travelling post offices and agencies).

The telephone exchanges had at the end of 1979 a total of 17,464 direct exchange lines with (1982), 28,468 telephone instruments. The number of route miles in the coastal and inland areas was 2,982 km. 39 land-line stations were maintained at post offices in the coastal area, and 8 telegraph stations in the interior provide communication with the coastal area through a central telegraph office in Georgetown.

The Guyana Broadcasting Corporation, which came into operation on 1 July 1980, has 2 channels.

Cinemas (1981). There are 52 cinemas.

Newspapers (1982). There is 1 daily newspaper with a circulation of 42,000 and 4 weekly papers with a combined circulation of about 100,000.

JUSTICE, EDUCATION AND WELFARE

Justice. The law, both civil and criminal, is based on the common and statute law of England, save that the principles of the Roman–Dutch law have been retained in respect of the registration, conveyance and mortgaging of land.

The Supreme Court of Judicature consists of a Court of Appeal and a High Court.

Education. In Sept. 1976 the Government assumed total responsibility for education from nursery school to university. Private education was abolished. In Sept. 1983, the total number of schools was 879: Nursery, 368; primary, 423; secondary and community high, 30; general secondary, 58.

There are now 5 technical and vocational schools and 2 schools for the teaching of home economics and domestic crafts. Training in co-operatives is provided by the Kuru-Kuru Co-operative College and agriculture by the Guyana School of Agriculture and the Burnham Agricultural Institute. Art training is provided by the Burrowes School of Art. The training of primary and secondary school teachers is undertaken by 3 institutions. Higher education is also provided by the University of Guyana which was established in 1963 with faculties of natural science, social science, art, technology and education as well as first year students in law. There were 2,004 students in July 1983. The total number of pupils in all schools was 233,723 in 1983.

Health. In 1981 there were 29 hospitals, 149 health centres and stations, 4 dispensaries and 11 medical outposts. There were (1982) 270 doctors and 24 dentists.

DIPLOMATIC REPRESENTATIVES

Of Guyana in Great Britain (3 Palace Court, London, W2 4LP)
High Commissioner: Cedric Joseph (accredited 17 Feb. 1982).

Of Great Britain in Guyana (44 Main St., Georgetown)
High Commissioner: W. K. Slatcher, CMG, CVO.

Of Guyana in the USA (2490 Tracy Place, NW, Washington, D.C., 20008)
Ambassador: Dr Cedric H. Grant.

Of the USA in Guyana (31 Main St., Georgetown)
Ambassador: (Vacant).

Of Guyana to the United Nations
Ambassador: Noel G. Sinclair.

Books of Reference

Daly, P. H., *From Revolution to Republic.* Georgetown, 1970
Daly, Vere T., *A Short History of the Guyanese People.* Rev. ed. London, 1975
Hope, K. R., *Development Policy in Guyana: Planning, Finance and Administration.* London, 1979

HAITI

République d'Haiti

Capital: Port-au-Prince
Population: 6m. (1982)
GNP per capita: US$270 (1980)

HISTORY. Haiti occupies the western third of the large island of Hispaniola which was discovered by Christopher Columbus in 1492. The Spanish colony was ceded to France in 1697 and became her most prosperous colony. After the extirpation of the Indians by the Spaniards (by 1533) large numbers of African slaves were imported whose descendants now populate the country. The slaves obtained their liberation following the French Revolution, but subsequently Napoleon sent his brother-in-law, Gen. Leclerc, to restore French authority and re-impose slavery. Toussaint Louverture, the leader of the slaves who had been appointed a French general and governor, was kidnapped and sent to France, where he died in gaol. However, the reckless courage of the Negro troops and the ravages of yellow fever forced the French to evacuate the island and surrender to the blockading British squadron.

The country declared its independence on 1 Jan. 1804, and its successful leader, Gen. Jean-Jacques Dessalines, proclaimed himself Emperor of the newly-named Haiti. After the assassination of Dessalines (1806) a separate régime was set up in the north under Henri Christophe, a Negro general who in 1811 had himself proclaimed King Henry. In the south and west a republic was constituted, with the mulatto Alexander Pétion as its first President. Pétion died in 1818 and was succeeded by Jean-Pierre Boyer, under whom the country became re-united after Henry had committed suicide in 1820. From 1822 to 1844 Haiti and the eastern part of the island (later the Dominican Republic) were united. After one more monarchical interlude, under the Emperor Faustin (1847–59), Haiti has been a republic. From 1915 to 1934 Haiti was under United States occupation.

Following a military *coup* in 1950, and subsequent uprisings, Dr François Duvalier was elected President on 22 Oct. 1957 and subsequently became President for Life in 1964. He died on 21 April 1971 and was succeeded as president for life by his son, Jean-Claude Duvalier.

AREA AND POPULATION. The area is 27,750 sq. km (10,700 sq. miles), of which about three-quarters is mountainous. The population at the census in 1975 was 4,583,785, of which 85% are living in rural areas.

The areas and populations of the 5 *départements* are as follows:

Département	Sq. km	1977	Chief town	1975
Nord-Ouest	2,750	247,326	Port-de-Paix	21,733
Nord	4,100	747,360	Cap Haïtien	54,691
Artibonite	6,800	748,357	Gonaïves	36,736
Ouest	7,900	1,983,826	Port-au-Prince	458,675
Sud	6,200	1,041,232	Les Cayes	27,222
Totals	27,750	4,768,101		

The Île de la Gonave, some 40 miles long, lies in the gulf of the same name. Among other islands is La Tortue, off the north peninsula. The majority of the population are Negroes, with an important minority of mulattoes and only about 5,000 white residents, almost all foreign.

Haiti is the only French-speaking republic in the Americas. The standard French of government, parliament and the press is spoken by the small literate minority, but the great majority of the people habitually speak the dialect known as Créole.

579

CLIMATE. A tropical maritime climate with a small range of temperature. The wet season extends from May to Sept. Port-au-Prince. Jan. 76°F (24·4°C), July 82°F (27·8°C). Annual rainfall 54″ (1,350 mm).

CONSTITUTION AND GOVERNMENT. The 1957 Constitution, as subsequently amended, provides for an Executive President who is elected for life and may nominate his successor. He nominates a Cabinet to assist him and, in cases of national emergency, may dismiss both the Cabinet and the National Assembly and govern by decree.

The unicameral National Assembly comprises 58 deputies elected for 6-year terms (renewable) by universal suffrage at age 18. Of the deputies elected on 11 Feb. 1979, all but one belonged to the Parti de l'Unité Nationale of President Duvalier.

The Cabinet in Oct. 1982 was composed as follows:

President: Jean-Claude Duvalier.

Foreign Affairs and Worship: Jean-Robert Estimé. *Interior and Defence:* Dr R. Lafoutant. *Labour and Social Affairs:* Theodore Achille. *Co-ordination, Presidency and Information:* Jean-Marie Chanoine. *Agriculture and Natural Resources:* R. Leveillé. *Public Works, Transport and Communications:* Alix Cinéas. *Finance and National Economy:* Franz Merceron. *Public Health and Population:* Y. R. Joseph. *Commerce and Industry:* J. B. Siméon. *Justice:* B. Edouard. *Planning:* Claude Weil. *Mines and Energy:* Jean E. Pierre. *Education:* F. St Victor. *Youth and Sports:* H. Rémy.

National flag: Vertically black and red, with a small white panel in the centre bearing the national arms.

National anthem: 'La Dessalinienne': Pour le pays, pour les ancêtres (words by J. Lhérisson; tune by N. Geffrard, 1903).

DEFENCE. The Haitian Defence Force (*Forces Armées d'Haiti*) totalling about 7,500 men, is divided into Army, Navy, and Air Force. The President is Commander-in-Chief and appoints the officers.

Army. Total strength, about 7,000, organized into 9 Military Departments and the 'Leopards'. Three of the Departments are in Port-au-Prince and consist of the Presidential Guard (4 Companies); the Dessalines Barracks (7 Companies including the Dessalines Battalion and Headquarters troops); and the Port-au-Prince Police (6 Companies in blue uniforms). The other 6 Military Departments are located outside Port-au-Prince; their troops (21 Companies) operate as District Police. The Fire Brigade and the Prison Guard Company are also part of the Armed Forces. Only the Presidential Guard, the Dessalines Battalion and the Leopards (2 companies of 'Commandos' or Special Forces) with a third company of about 200 recruits, now in training, have any potential for tactical military operations. They are armed mainly with light infantry weapons but have a few elderly pieces of light artillery, 9 light tanks and 6 V-150 commando vehicles.

Navy. The Navy/coastguard of 40 officers and 260 men has 1 *ex*-US armed tug, and 12 coastal patrol boats. The base is at Port-au-Prince.

Air Force. Personnel strength is about 200, with about 28 aircraft of some 12 varieties. They include 8 Summit/Cessna O2-337 Sentry twin piston-engined counter-insurgency aircraft, 3 DC-3s, 5 light transports, 5 training/liaison aircraft, and 7 Hughes and Sikorsky helicopters.

Militia. There is in addition a volunteer civilian force, the *Volontaires de la Sécurité Nationale*, total strength is now estimated at about 14,900, about half of whom have access to antiquated rifles. This force, formerly of some importance as Dr François Duvalier's 'private army' of tough, devoted followers (sometimes called Tontons Macoute or Bogeymen) is much less prominent since his death, having been reduced in strength and reorganized under Defence Force Headquarters on lines roughly parallel to the regional Military Departments.

INTERNATIONAL RELATIONS

Membership. Haiti is a member of UN and OAS.

ECONOMY

Budget. Revenue and expenditure (fiscal year ending 30 Sept.) in US$1m. (5 gourdes = US$1), balanced as follows: 1971–72, 29·6; 1972–73, 31·3; 1973–74, 33·2; 1974–75, 38·9; 1975–76, 43·3.

Currency. The unit of currency is the *gourde* and its value fixed at 5 *gourdes* = US$1. In March 1984, £1 = 7·43 *gourdes*. There are copper–nickel coins for 50, 20, 10 and 5 *centimes* and copper–zinc–nickel coins of 10 and 5 centimes.

Banking. The Banque Nationale de la République d'Haïti, owned by the State, was established 21 Oct. 1910 with a capital of US$5m., and has a monopoly of the note issue. US dollars may be included in the minimum required reserves. The Royal Bank of Canada, the Citibank, the Bank of Nova Scotia, the Bank of Boston, the Banque de l'Union Haitienne (mainly local capital with participation from American, Canadian and Dominican Republic Banks), Banque Nationale de Paris and First National Bank of Chicago all have branches in Port-au-Prince.

Weights and Measures. The metric system is officially accepted.

ENERGY AND NATURAL RESOURCES

Electricity. The hydro-electric plant at Péligre, which was inaugurated in July 1971, provides some 45m. kw. to the capital. The thermal plant in Port-au-Prince, formerly US and now state-owned, is now on standby for emergencies. Generating capacity at Cap Haitien is 3·1m. kw.

Minerals. A US company is engaged in mining bauxite (609,000 tonnes in 1979). Copper exists but is at present uneconomic to exploit. Haiti may possess undeveloped mineral resources of oil, gold, silver, antimony, sulphur, coal and lignite, nickel, gypsum and porphyry.

Agriculture. Only one-third of the country is arable and most people own the tiny plots they farm; the resulting pressure of population is the main cause of rural poverty. Number of farms is estimated at over 500,000.

The occupations of Haiti are nine-tenths agricultural, carried on in 7 large plains, from 200,000 to 25,000 acres, and in 15 smaller plains down to 2,000 acres. Irrigation is used in some areas. Haiti's most important product is coffee of good quality, classified as 'mild', and grown by peasants. Production in 1981 totalled about 33,000 tonnes. Second most important crop is sugar. Sisal is grown extensively. Much of the fibre is exported as or for cordage. New types of cotton are being tried with success. New varieties of rice should significantly boost future production, especially in the Artibonite Valley. Output of main crops in 1981 (in 1,000 tonnes) was: Sugar, 3,000; mangoes, 330; plantains; 300; sweet potatoes, 270; cassava, 255; bananas, 210; maize, 180; sorghum, 110; rice, 90; sisal, 10; cotton, 5; cocoa, 3.

Rum and other spirits are distilled. Essential oils from vetiver, neroli and amyris are important. Cattle and horse breeding are encouraged.

Livestock (1982); Cattle, 1·2m.; sheep, 91,000; pigs, 600,000; goats, 1m.; horses, 420,000; poultry, 5m.

INDUSTRY AND TRADE

Industry. Light manufacturing industries assembling or finishing goods for re-export constitute the fastest growing sector. There are 2 textile mills producing cheap denim with a total of 550 looms and 14,000 spindles. Soap factories produce laundry soap, toilet soap and detergent. A cement factory located near the capital produced 140,000 tons in 1973–74 and is extending to 300,000 tons per year. A steel plant making rods, beams and angles was opened in 1974. There are also a pharmaceutical plant, a tannery, a plastics plant, 2 paint works, 2 shoe factories, a large factory producing enamel cookingware, 2 pasta-making factories, a tomato cannery and a flour-mill, all located in or near Port-au-Prince.

Labour. Trade unions were recognized in Feb. 1946. Strong government influence is exercised over the insignificant portion of the labour force that is unionized and organized labour has virtually no strength in Haiti.

Commerce. In 1982 exports were US$150m. and imports, US$330m.

The leading imports are foodstuffs, textiles, machinery, mineral oils, raw materials for transformation industries and vehicles.

Total trade between Haiti and UK (British Department of Trade returns, in £1,000 sterling):

	1977	1978	1979	1980	1981	1982	1983
Imports to UK	1,063	635	1,118	915	1,439	2,615	1,646
Exports and re-exports from UK	3,394	4,155	3,162	2,818	2,541	3,704	4,171

Tourism. In 1978, 112,000 tourists visited Haiti.

COMMUNICATIONS

Roads. Total length of roads is some 4,000 km, little of which is practicable in ordinary motors in the rainy season. There were (1980) about 35,000 vehicles in Haiti.

Railways. The only railway is owned by the Haitian American Sugar Company.

Aviation. An airport capable of handling jets was opened at Port-au-Prince in 1965. US and French carriers provide daily direct services to New York, Miami, Jamaica, Puerto Rico and the French Antilles. There are also services to the Dominican Republic and the Netherlands Antilles. A Haitian company provides a cargo service to the US and Puerto Rico. Air services connecting Port-au-Prince with other Haitian towns are operated by Haiti Air Inter.

Shipping. US, French, Federal Republic of Germany, Dutch, British, Canadian and Japanese lines connect Haiti with the US, Latin America (except Cuba), Canada, Jamaica, Europe and the Far East.

Post and Broadcasting. Most principal towns are connected by the government telegraph system, telephones and wireless.

The telephone company, of which the Haitian Government is now the majority stockholder, is in process of being modernized. Telephone subscribers totalled 22,000 in 1980.

In 1982 there were 105,000 radio and 65,000 television receivers.

Cinemas (1980). There were 15 cinemas in Port-au-Prince.

Newspapers (1982). There were 6 daily newspapers in Port-au-Prince, also a monthly in English and 1 weekly newspaper in Cap Haitien.

JUSTICE, RELIGION, EDUCATION AND WELFARE

Justice. Judges, both of the lower courts and the court of appeal, are appointed by the President. The legal system is basically French. The divorce law has recently been amended to permit parties to obtain 'quick and painless' divorces at a moderate cost, in the hope of attracting the US trade, now that the Mexican 'divorce mills' have closed down. This has developed a useful flow of dollar revenue.

Police. The Police number about 750 in Port-au-Prince and are part of the armed forces.

Religion. Since the Concordat of 1860, the official religion is Roman Catholicism, under an archbishop with 5 suffragan bishops. There are still quite a number of foreigners, French and French Canadians mainly, among the clergy but the first Haitian archbishop took office in 1966. The Episcopal Church now has its first Haitian bishop who was consecrated in 1971. Other Christian churches number perhaps 10% of the population. The folk religion is Voodoo.

Education. Education is divided into primary (first 6 years), secondary (the next 7 years) and finally superior or university. The school system is modelled on that of

France. The law calls for free and compulsory elementary education in the French language.

For the 1973–74 academic year, urban primary schools numbered 360 (221 lay and 139 religious) attended by 127,330 pupils with 3,532 teachers. There were, for the same period, at the secondary level, 21 public secondary *lycées* with 15,760 students (4,163 of them girls), 563 teachers (39 of them women). In the private secondary sector, 129 schools were reported with 35,414 students (16,398 girls), 1,172 teachers (107 women). Professional education is divided into 3 categories: (*a*) 41 pre-vocational schools; (*b*) 18 vocational schools which prepare trained workers, and (*c*) 5 vocational schools preparing technicians. There are also 10 licensed private commercial schools. The total number of students was 13,000, 2,000 of whom were in the private sector.

Higher education is offered at the University of Haiti.

Health. There were, in 1972, 332 doctors and 104 dentists in practice, 44 hospitals, and 196 health centres and rural clinics. The hospitals had 3,329 beds, of which 776 were in private and charitable establishments.

DIPLOMATIC REPRESENTATIVES

Of Haiti in Great Britain (33 Abbots Hse., St Mary Abbots Terr., London, W14)
Chargé d'Affaires: Théo Duval.

Of Great Britain in Haiti
Ambassador: B. G. Smallman, CMG, CVO (resides in Kingston).

Of Haiti in the USA (2311 Massachusetts Ave., NW, Washington, D.C., 20008)
Ambassador: Fritz N. Cineas.

Of the USA in Haiti (Harry Truman Blvd., Port-au-Prince)
Ambassador: (Vacant).

Of Haiti to the United Nations
Ambassador: Fritz N. Cineas.

Books of Reference

The official gazette is *Le Moniteur.*

Revue Agricole d'Haïti. From 1946. Quarterly
Bellegarde, D., *Histoire du Peuple Haïtien.* Port-au-Prince, 1953
Chambers, F. J., *Haiti.* [Bibliography] Oxford and Santa Barbara, 1983
Diedrich, B., and Burt, D., *Papa Doc.* London, 1969
Laguerre, M. S., *The Complete Haitiana.* [Bibliography] London and New York, 1982
Nicholls, D., *From Dessalines to Duvalier: Race, Colour and National Independence in Haiti.* CUP, 1979

National Library: Bibliothèque Nationale, Rue du Centre, Port-au-Prince.

HONDURAS

República de Honduras

Capital: Tegucigalpa
Population: 4·09m. (1983)
GNP per capita: US$520 (1980)

HISTORY. On 5 Nov. 1838 Honduras declared itself an independent sovereign state, free from the Federation of Central America, of which it had formed a part.

EVENTS. A Treaty was signed in Peru on 30 Oct. 1980 settling the border dispute between El Salvador and Honduras.

AREA AND POPULATION. Honduras is bounded north by the Caribbean, east and south-east by Nicaragua, west by Guatemala, south-west by El Salvador and south by the Pacific ocean. Area is 112,088 sq. km (43,277 sq. miles), with a population, census (1974) of 2,656,948. Estimate (1983) 4,092,175.

The capital of Honduras is Tegucigalpa with (1983, estimate) a population of 532,519. The next most important town is San Pedro Sula, 344,497; other towns are: Choluteca, 53,033; El Progreso, 53,835; Comayagua, 28,121; Siguatepeque, 23,235; Copán, 19,055; Danlí, 17,986; Juticalpa, 14,121. The main ports are Henecan on the Pacific, and, on the Atlantic coast, La Ceiba (61,248), Puerto Cortés (40,249) and Tela (27,343). The port of entry for the Bay Islands is Roatán. A new port at Puerta Castilla, on the Atlantic coast, is under construction.

The republic is divided into 18 departments with their populations (1983, estimate): Atlántida (242,235); Choluteca (289,637); Colón (128,370); Comayagua (211,465); Copán (217,258); Cortés (624,090); El Paraíso (206,601); Francisco Morazán (736,272); Gracias a Dios (35,471); Intibucá (111,412); Islas de La Bahía (18,744); La Paz (86,627); Lempira (174,916); Ocotepeque (64,151); Olancho (228,122); Santa Barbara (286,854); Valle (125,640); and Yoro (304,310).

Aboriginal tribes number over 35,000, principally Miskito, Payas and Xicaques Indians and Sambos (the latter a mixture of Miskito and Negro), each speaking a different dialect. The Spanish-speaking inhabitants are chiefly *mestizos*, Indians with an admixture of Spanish blood. Gracias a Dios is still largely unexplored and is inhabited by pure native races who speak little or no Spanish.

In 1980 the birth rate was 49·3 per 1,000; death rate, 12·4 per 1,000 and infant mortality rate, 11·8 per 1,000 live births.

CLIMATE. The climate is tropical, with a small annual range of temperature but with high rainfall. Upland areas have two wet seasons, from May to July and in Sept. and Oct. The Caribbean Coast has most rain in Dec. and Jan. and temperatures are generally higher than inland. Tegucigalpa. Jan. 66°F (19°C), July 74°F (23·3°C). Annual rainfall 64″ (1,621 mm).

CONSTITUTION AND GOVERNMENT. In 1972 Congress was suspended and a military junta was established until 1981.

Elections were held on 29 Nov. 1981 for deputies to a Congress. The election results were Liberals, 44 deputies; Nationalists, 34 and Party of Innovation and Unity, 3; Christian Democratic Party, 1.

At the elections for President held on 29 Nov. 1981 Dr Roberto Suazo Córdova (Liberal) was elected for a 4-year term, with 53% of the votes.

A new Constitution was promulgated on 20 Jan. 1982.

President: Dr Roberto Suazo Córdova (sworn in 27 Jan. 1982).

National flag: Three horizontal stripes of blue, white, blue, with 5 blue stars in the centre.

National anthem: Tu bandera es un lampo de cielo (words by A. C. Coello; tune by C. Hartling).

Local government: Honduras comprises a Federal District (containing the cities of Tegucigalpa and Comayaguela) and 18 departments (each administered by an appointed Governor), sub-divided into 282 municipalities (each under an elected Council).

DEFENCE. Conscription into the Armed Forces is for approximately 12 months. Although there is no actual reserves programme, those men who have served on active duty for 1 year or more, are eligible for recall.

Army. The Army consists of 11 infantry, 3 artillery, 1 engineer and 1 special forces battalions and 1 armoured car regiment. Equipment includes 16 Scorpion light tanks. Strength (1984) 13,500 (10,000 conscripts). There is also a paramilitary Public Security Force of 4,500 men.

Air Force. Equipment includes 12 J52-engined Super Mystère fighters acquired from Israel, 6 A-37B jet light attack aircraft, about 10 F-86E/F/K jet fighters, 4 Spanish-built CASA C-101BB armed jet trainers, 3 RT-33A reconnaissance aircraft, some Summit/Cessna O2-337 Sentry twin piston-engined COIN aircraft, 8 T-28S Fennec and 4 T-28E armed piston-engined trainers, 5 C-47, 3 Israeli-built Arava and 1 Westwind transports, some helicopters, and T-28 and T-41A trainers. Total strength is about 1,200 personnel, of whom many are civilian maintenance staff.

INTERNATIONAL RELATIONS

Membership. Honduras is a member of UN and OAS.

ECONOMY

Budget. In 1982 revenue (in 1m. lempiras) was 837 (1983, 984); expenditure, 1,267 (1983, 1,370).

The largest sources of income (1982) were (in 1m. lempiras): Income tax, 198·7; production (and domestic transactions) taxes, 237·1; import taxes, 178·2; export taxes, 93·3.

Total external debt (1981) was (in 1m. lempiras), 2,621·8 and net reserves of foreign currency, 34.

Currency. The unit of the monetary system is the *lempira* also known as a *peso*, comprising 100 *centavos*. Notes are issued by the Banco Central de Honduras which has the sole right to issue, in denominations of 100, 50, 20, 10, 5, 2 and 1 *lempiras*. Coins in circulation are 50 and 20 *centavos* in silver, 10 and 5 *centavos* in cupro-nickel and 2 and 1 *centavos* in copper.

Rate of exchange, March 1984: £1 = 2·99 *lempiras;* US$1 = 2 *lempiras.*

Banking. The central bank of issue is the Banco Central de Honduras. The Banco Atlántida has branches in Tegucigalpa, San Pedro Sula, Comayaguela, Puerto Cortés, La Ceiba, Tela, El Progreso, Choluteca and other towns. The Banco de Honduras which operates in many parts of the country is controlled by the Citibank. The Bank of America has branches in Tegucigalpa and San Pedro Sula. The Bank of London and Montreal has branches in Tegucigalpa, San Pedro Sula, Comayaguela and La Ceiba. The Central American Bank for Economic Integration has its head office in Tegucigalpa.

Weights and Measures. The metric system has been legal since 1 April 1897, but English pounds and yards and the old Spanish system are still in use: 1 *vara* = 32 in.; 1 *manzana* (10,000 sq. *varas*) = 700 sq. metres; 1 *arroba* = 25 lb.; 1 *quintal* = 100 lb.; 1 *tonelada* = 2,000 lb.

NATURAL RESOURCES

Minerals. Mineral resources include gold, silver, lead, tin, zinc and mercury, which are exported. There are probably reserves of other minerals which have not yet been exploited. The Rosario Resources Company, which owned and operated the famous Rosario mines near Tegucigalpa from 1882 to 1954, developed and now operates a mine at El Mochito (Department of Santa Barbara) while the Compañía Minera Los Angeles SA has a mine currently extracting lead, zinc and silver at Valle de Angeles (Department of Francisco Morazán).

Agriculture. Although Honduras is essentially an agricultural country, less than a quarter of the total land area is cultivated and by far the larger portion of this is on the Caribbean and Pacific coastal plains. Agriculture employs 58·9% of the working population and provides 80% of the exports. The main agricultural crops are: Bananas, coffee, sugar and tobacco. Exports of meat amounted to 92·6m. lempiras in 1982.

Livestock (1982): Cattle, 2·4m.; sheep, 5,000; pigs, 590,000; goats, 22,000; horses, 151,000; poultry, 5·1m.

Forestry. Forests cover nearly 45% of the total land area. Honduras has an abundance of hard- and soft-woods. Large stands of mahogany and other hardwoods—granadino, guayacán, walnut and rosewood—grow in the north-eastern part of the country, in the interior valleys, and near the southern coast. Stands of pine occur almost everywhere in the interior, but are severely damaged by bark beetle and fires. In 1982, total wood exports amounted to 86·3m. lempiras. The Olancho Forest Development Programme involving the construction of saw- and pulp-mills is in progress.

Fisheries. Commercial fishing in territorial waters is restricted to Honduran nationals and Honduran companies in which the controlling share of the capital is owned by a Honduran national. Shrimps and lobsters are important catches.

INDUSTRY AND TRADE

Industry. Small-scale local industries include beer and mineral waters, cement, flour, vegetable lard, coconut oil, sweets, cigarettes, cigars, textiles and clothing, panama hats, plastics, nails, matches, plywood, furniture, paper bags, soap, candles, fruit juices and household chemicals. An important hydro-electric scheme has been built at Rio Lindo to serve the Central and North Coast regions. The El Cajon hydro-electric project is now under construction and will come on stream in 1985 (290 mw). A small integrated steel-mill may be erected in Agalteca (Department of Francisco Morazán). The manufacturing industry employed 13% of the working population in 1979.

Labour. The organization of trade unions was begun in 1954 with the assistance of ORIT (Inter-American Regional Organization) sponsored by the USA trade unions. In 1972 there were 166 trade unions, of which only 119 were active, with about 67,956 members. A 'Charter of Labour' was granted in Feb. 1955 and an advanced Labour Code and Social Security Bill passed into law in May 1959. A Ministry of 'Labour, Social Assistance and the Middle Class' was created in 1955; the last four words of its title were expunged in 1957.

Commerce. Imports in 1982 were valued at 1,436·8m. lempiras and exports at 1,308·2 lempiras.

Imports (1982) in 1m. lempiras: Mineral fuel and lubricants, 340·1; machinery and transport equipment, 273·6; chemicals, 256·3; food products, 116·8.

Exports (1982) in 1m. lempiras: bananas, 436·6; coffee, 306·2; timber, 89·3; refrigerated meats, 67·4; shrimps and lobster, 55·9; lead and zinc, 39·2; silver, 22; tobacco, 21·5; cotton, 20·8.

Trade with main countries in 1m. lempiras (1981) was: USA, 1,604·5; Japan, 234·2; Federal Republic of Germany, 214·7; Venezuela, 99·9; Guatemala, 181·4; Netherlands, 102.

Total trade between Honduras and UK (British Department of Trade returns, in £1,000 sterling):

	1979	1980	1981	1982	1983
Imports to UK	4,000	3,687	4,065	4,695	7,082
Exports and re-exports from UK	9,013	11,835	8,617	4,659	9,539

Tourism. There were 188,177 tourists in 1981, of which 1,589 were from UK.

COMMUNICATIONS

Roads. Honduras is connected with Guatemala, El Salvador and Nicaragua by the Pan-American Highway. Out of a total of 14,001 km of road (1981), 1,756 are paved. There are good asphalted highways between Puerto Cortés in the north and Choluteca in the south passing through San Pedro Sula and Tegucigalpa with branches to Guatemala and El Salvador. In 1981 there were 95,997 motor vehicles.

Railways. Only 4 railways exist; they are confined to the north coastal region and are used mainly for transportation of bananas. Tegucigalpa, the capital, is not served by any railway, and there are no international railway connexions. The total railways operating in 1981 were 981 km of 1,067 mm and 914 mm gauge.

Aviation. Over a large part of the country the aeroplane is the normal means of transport for both passengers and freight. There are international airports at Tegucigalpa, San Pedro Sula, La Ceiba and over 30 smaller airstrips in various parts of the country.

Shipping. Sailings to the Atlantic coast port of Puerto Cortés from Europe are frequent, mainly operated by the Harrison Line, Cia Generale Transatlantique, the Royal Netherlands Steamships Co., Hapag Lloyd and vessels owned or chartered by the Tela Railroad Co., a subsidiary of United Brands, and the Standard Fruit Co.

Post and Broadcasting. The Government in April 1972 operated 18,845 km of telephone lines and 12,526 km of telegraph lines. Number of telephones in use, 1982, 33,667; telephone exchanges, 58; number of telegraph offices, 250; combined telephone and telegraph offices, 140. In 1981 there were 509 post offices and agencies, 148 commercial broadcasting stations. There were (1979) 3 commercial channels and about 27,000 receivers in use. Transmission in colour commenced mid-1973.

Cinemas (1982). Cinemas numbered about 60 with seating capacity of some 60,000.

Newspapers (1982). The 4 most important daily papers are *El Heraldo* and *La Tribuna* in Tegucigalpa, *La Prensa* and *El Tiempo* in San Pedro Sula. Several others exist but their circulation is low and their influence is very limited.

JUSTICE, RELIGION, EDUCATION AND WELFARE

Justice. The judicial power resides in the Supreme Court, with 7 judges elected by the National Constituent Assembly in 1980 for 6 years; it appoints the judges of the courts of appeal, labour tribunals and the district attorneys who, in turn, name the justices of the peace.

Religion. Roman Catholicism is the prevailing religion, but the constitution guarantees freedom to all creeds, and the State does not contribute to the support of any.

Education. Instruction is free, compulsory (from 7 to 15 years of age) and secular. In 1982 the 6,056 primary schools had 672,918 children (18,598 teachers); the 340 secondary, normal and technical schools had 129,606 pupils (5,916 teachers); the teachers' college had 2,604 students in 1981 (168 teachers). In 1982, the three universities had a total of 28,266 students and 1,623 teachers.
The illiteracy rate was 40% of those 10 years of age and older in 1978.

Health. In 1981 there were about 1,370 doctors, 530 health centres and 5,230 hospital beds.

DIPLOMATIC REPRESENTATIVES

Of Honduras in Great Britain (47 Manchester St., London, W1M 5PB)
Ambassador: Edgardo Dumas-Rodriguez (accredited 29 July 1982).

Of Great Britain in Honduras (Ave. República de Chile, Tegucigalpa)
Ambassador: C. J. Sharkey, MBE.

Of Honduras in the USA (4301 Connecticut Ave., NW, Washington, D.C., 20008)
Ambassador: Juan Agurcia Ewing.

Of the USA in Honduras (Ave. La Paz, Tegucigalpa)
Ambassador: J. D. Negroponte.

Of Honduras to the United Nations
Ambassador: Dr Enrique Ortez Colindres.

Books of Reference

The *Anuario Estadístico* (latest issue, *Comercio Exterior de Honduras*, 1980) is published by the Dirección de Estadísticas y Censos, Tegucigalpa. *Director:* Elizabeth Zavala de Turcios.

Monthly Bulletin.—Honduras en Cifras. Banco Central de Honduras, 1980
Checchi, V. (and others), *Honduras, a Problem in Economic Development.* New York, 1959
Rubio Melhado, A., *Geografía General de la República de Honduras.* Tegucigalpa, 1953
Stokes, W. S., *Honduras: An Area Study in Government.* Madison, Wisc., 1950

HONG KONG

Population: 5·31m. (1983)
GDP per capita: US$4,300 (1980)

HISTORY. The Dependent Territory of Hong Kong was ceded by China to Great Britain in Jan. 1841; the cession was confirmed by the Treaty of Nanking in Aug. 1842, and the charter bears the date 5 April 1843. Since then Hong Kong has been under British administration, with the exception of the period from 25 Dec. 1941 to 30 Aug. 1945, when it was occupied by the Japanese.

AREA AND POPULATION. Hong Kong island is 32 km east of the mouth of the Pearl River and 130 km south-east of Canton. The area of the island is 78·12 sq. km. It is separated from the mainland by a fine natural harbour. On the opposite side is the peninsula of Kowloon (10·48 sq. km), which, with Stonecutters Island (0·75 sq. km), was added to the Territory by the Convention of Peking, 1860. By a further convention, signed at Peking on 9 June 1898, about 950 sq. km, consisting of all the immediately adjacent mainland and numerous islands in the vicinity, were leased to Great Britain by China for 99 years. This area is known as the New Territories. Total area of the territory is 1,065·02 sq. km (including recent reclamations), a large part of it being steep and unproductive hillside. Some 40% of the territory is conserved as country parks. Shortage of land suitable for development for housing and industry, is a serious problem. Since 1945, the Government has reclaimed about 1,790 hectares from the sea, principally from the seafronts of Hong Kong and Kowloon, facing the harbour. In the New Territories, the new town of Tsuen Wan, incorporating Tsuen Wan, Kwai Chung and Tsing Yi, already houses 680,000 of its planned ultimate population of 918,000. The construction of 5 further new towns at Sha Tin, Tuen Mun, Tai Po, Fanling and Yuen Long is now well underway, with designed population capacities of 756,000, 547,000, 220,000, 170,000 and 128,000 respectively. Planning has started for a new town at Junk Bay to house 300,000 people.

The population was 5,021,066 at 1981 census. Estimate (mid-1983) 5,313,000. During the war years the population of Hong Kong fluctuated sharply. In Sept. 1945, at the end of the Japanese occupation, it was about 600,000. In mid-1950 it was estimated at 2·24m. Since 1971 the average annual growth rate has been 2·3%. Of the present population about 33% are under 20 years of age. About 57% of the population was born in Hong Kong.

CLIMATE. The climate is sub-tropical, the winter being cool and dry and the summer hot and humid. The average annual rainfall is 2,225 mm. May to Sept. being the wettest months. Jan. 60°F (15·6°C), July 83°F (28·3°C). Annual rainfall 85″ (2,162 mm).

CONSTITUTION AND GOVERNMENT. The administration is in the hands of a Governor, aided by an Executive Council, composed of the Commander, British Forces, the Chief Secretary, the Financial Secretary, the Attorney-General (who are members *ex officio*) and such other members, both official and unofficial, as may be appointed by the Queen upon the Governor's nomination. In 1983 there were, in addition to the 4 *ex-officio* members, 2 nominated officials and 11 appointed unofficial members. There is also a Legislative Council, presided over by the Governor. In 1983 it consisted of 3 *ex-officio* members, namely the Chief Secretary, the Financial Secretary, the Attorney-General, and 29 appointed unofficial members and 15 nominated official members. Chinese and English are the official languages.

Governor and C.-in-C.: Sir Edward Youde, GCMG, MBE.
Commander British Forces: Maj.-Gen. Derek Boorman, CB.
Chief Secretary: Sir Philip Haddon-Cave, KBE, CMG.
Flag: British Blue Ensign with the arms of the Territory on a white disc in the fly.

DEFENCE. The Hong Kong Garrison, under the Commander British Forces, comprises units of all three services. Its principal rôle is to assist the Hong Kong Government in maintaining security and stability.

Army. The Army constitutes the bulk of the garrison. It comprises a UK battalion, based at Stanley Fort, and 4 Gurkha infantry battalions, one based at Lyemun, the other 3 in the New Territories; supporting units include the Queen's Gurkha Engineers, the Queen's Gurkha Signals, the Gurkha Transport Regiment, and 660 Squadron Army Air Corps.

Navy. The Naval Base is at HMS *Tamar*. The Hong Kong Squadron comprises five patrol craft, converted Ton-class old wooden minesweepers which are being replaced in 1984 and 1985 by five new larger, faster and better-armed patrol vessels of the 'Bird' class (HMS *Peacock* is the first, followed by *Plover*, to be joined by *Starling, Swallow* and *Swift*) all built by Hall Russell, Aberdeen, Scotland.

(Thirty armed patrol craft are operated by the Marine Division of the Royal Hong Kong Police–*see* p. 594.)

Air Force. The Royal Air Force is based at Shek Kong. No. 28 (Army Co-operation) Squadron operates 8 Wessex helicopters. In addition to its operational rôle in support of the army and navy, the RAF carries out search and rescue and medical evacuation tasks. It is also responsible for air traffic control services at Shek Kong, and provides a territory-wide air traffic advisory service.

Auxiliary Defence Units. The local Auxiliary Defence Units, consisting of the Royal Hong Kong Regiment and the Royal Hong Kong Auxiliary Air Force, are administered by the Hong Kong Government, but, if called out, would come under the command of the Commander British Forces. The Royal Hong Kong Regiment (The Volunteers) has a strength of about 870. It is fully mobile and its rôle is to operate in support of regular army battalions stationed in Hong Kong. The Royal Hong Kong Auxiliary Air Force is intended mainly for internal security and air-sea rescue duties. It has a strength of about 136, operating a fleet of seven aircraft – a twin-engined Britten-Norman Islander, a twin-engined Cessna 404 Titan Courier, two Scottish Aviation Bulldog Trainers and three Aérospatiale Dauphin 365C1 helicopters.

ECONOMY

Budget. The public revenue and expenditure for financial years ending 31 March were as follows (in HK$):

	1979–80	1980–81	1981–82	1982–83
Revenue	16,796,000,000	30,290,300,000	32,887,700,000	31,098,000,000
Expenditure	13,872,000,000	23,593,500,000	25,061,800,000	34,598,000,000

The revenue is derived chiefly from rates, licences, duties on liquor, tobacco and hydrocarbon oils, a tax on earnings and profits, land sales and stamp duties.

Currency. The unit of currency is the Hong Kong *dollar*. Banknotes (of denominations of $10 upwards) are issued by the Hongkong and Shanghai Banking Corporation, and the Chartered Bank. Their combined note and coin issue was, at 31 July 1983, HK$12,996m. Subsidiary currency consisting of HK$5, HK$2, HK$1, 50-cent, 20-cent, 10-cent, 5-cent copper-nickel-alloy coins and 1-cent notes is issued by the Hong Kong Government and at 31 July 1983 totalled HK$1,226m.

Since 1975, the Hong Kong Government has issued annually a limited quantity of HK$1,000 gold coins. The first in the series was issued to commemorate the Queen's visit to Hong Kong in 1975. Gold coins have since been minted to mark the Chinese Lunar Years of the Dragon, the Snake, the Horse, the Goat, the Monkey, the Cockerel, the Dog and the Pig.

Banking. There are 132 licensed banks and 115 foreign banks maintaining representative offices in Hong Kong. Deposits in the first 7 months of 1983 totalled HK$220,053m.

Weights and Measures. Metric, British Imperial, Chinese and US units are all in current use in Hong Kong. However Government Departments have now effectively adopted metric units; all new legislation uses metric terminology and existing legislation is being progressively metricated. Metrication is also proceeding in the private sector.

The Chinese units in the table below are those which have statutory equivalents under Hong Kong's Weights and Measures Ordinance.

The statutory equivalent for the *chek* is 14 5/8 inches. The variation of the size of the *chek* with usage still persists in Hong Kong but the *chek* and derived units are now used much less than in the past. For the retail sale of cloth, a 'yard' of 24 Chinese inches (35.1 inches) is frequently used.

AGRICULTURE. In 1982, 155,000 tonnes of vegetables were produced. Livestock (1982): Cattle, 1,104; pigs, 388,420; poultry, 37m.

WATER. The provision of sufficient capacity to store the summer rainfall to meet water requirements, particularly during the dry winter months, has always been a serious problem. However, this has been alleviated to some extent by the raising of the Plover Cove Dams in 1973, giving the reservoir a capacity of 230m. cu. metres, and the completion in 1978 of the 273m. cu. metre High Island Reservoir which involved the conversion of another sea inlet to a fresh water lake, as was the case with Plover Cove.

Total available storage capacity now stands at 586m. cu. metres distributed in 17 impounding reservoirs. This is supplemented by water purchased from China for which the agreement is a supply of 255m. cu. metres during the financial year 1983–84 with provision for staged increases thereafter. These resources can be further supplemented when necessary by up to 181,000 cu. metres of fresh water a day from a desalting plant completed in 1976 and now considered as a 'reserve resource'.

INDUSTRY AND TRADE

Industry. An economic policy based on free enterprise and free trade; an industrious work force; an efficient and aggressive commercial infrastructure; modern and efficient sea-port (including container shipping terminals) and airport facilities: its geographical position relative to markets in North America and its traditional trading links with Britain have all contributed to Hong Kong's success as a modern industrial complex.

In March 1983, there were 47,081 factories employing 848,703 people out of a total population of approximately 5·3m. The type of factory involved ranges from the small cottage type to large highly complex modern establishments. Given the scarcity of land it is most common for light industry to operate in multi-storey buildings specially designed for this purpose. The main industry is textiles and clothing, which employed 43% of the total industrial workforce and accounted for 41% of total domestic exports in 1982. Other major light manufacturing industries include electronic products, clocks and watches, toys, plastic products, metalware, footwear, cameras and travel goods. Heavy industry includes ship-building, ship-repairing, aircraft engineering and iron and steel rolling. Agriculture, fishing and some mining are the main primary industries.

Commerce. Hong Kong's industries are mainly export oriented. The total value of domestic exports in 1982 was HK$83,032m. The major markets were USA (38%), UK (9%), Federal Republic of Germany (8%), Japan (4%), Australia (3%), and Singapore (2%). There is also a sizeable and flourishing entrepôt trade which accounted for another HK$44,353m. in 1982.

The total value of imports in 1982 was HK$142,893m., mainly from Japan (22%), China (21%), USA (11%), Taiwan (7%), Singapore (7%) and UK (5%).

The chief import items were machinery and transport equipment (22%), textiles (13%), foodstuffs (12%), chemicals and related products (7%), petroleum products and related materials (7%), crude materials, inedible, except fuel (4%).

Imports from the Commonwealth countries (HK$23,345m. in 1982) amounted to 16% of total imports, and exports to the Commonwealth countries (HK$17,386m.) accounted for 21% of Hong Kong's domestic exports.

Duties are levied only on tobacco, hydrocarbon oils, methyl alcohol and alcoholic liquors (including toilet preparations containing more than 1·2% of ethyl alcohol but excluding registered pharmaceutical products), whether imported into or manufactured in Hong Kong for local consumption.

All imports (apart from foodstuffs, which are subject to a flat charge of HK50 cents for every $1,000 worth of goods shipped) and exports are subject to a varying *ad valorem* charge.

The adverse balance on visible trade is offset by a favourable balance from exchange, shipping and insurance transactions, an inflow of capital, ship-repairing, a flourishing tourist industry, remittances from overseas Chinese, etc.

Hong Kong has a free exchange market. Foreign merchants may remit profits or repatriate capital. Import and export controls are kept to the minimum, consistent with strategic requirements.

Total trade between Hong Kong and UK (British Department of Trade returns, in £1,000 sterling) is given as follows:

	1978	1979	1980	1981	1982	1983
Imports to UK	531,368	689,252	850,340	898,634	872,545	1,178,343
Exports and re-exports from UK	362,444	442,452	559,420	618,525	732,489	726,711

Tourism. 1·28m. tourists spent an estimated HK$5,102m. in Hong Kong during the first half of 1983.

COMMUNICATIONS

Roads. At 31 Dec. 1982 there were 1,206 km of roads, distributed as follows: Hong Kong Island, 358; Kowloon and New Kowloon, 334, and New Territories, 514. A cross-harbour tunnel, 1·6 km in length, opened to traffic in Aug. 1972, now links Hong Kong Island with the Kowloon peninsula. The 1·4 km twin-tube Lion Rock Tunnel, which links Kowloon with Sha Tin New Town and other areas of the north-eastern New Territories, became fully operational in Oct. 1978. The 1·8 km twin-tube Aberdeen Tunnel, which connects Aberdeen and Wanchai, became operational in March 1983.

Railways. There is an electric tramway 13·2 km, and a cable tramway connecting the Peak district with the lower levels in Victoria. The Kowloon-Canton Railway runs for 34 km from the terminus at Hung Hom in Kowloon to the border point at Lo Wu. On 4 April 1979 a direct 'through' passenger train to Guangzhou (Canton) was re-introduced after a lapse of nearly 30 years. A second express train came into operation on 11 Feb. 1980. Both trains are invariably full and cater mainly for the business and tourist communities as well as Hong Kong residents visiting friends and relatives in China. There are also other passenger services to Lo Wu to allow for connexions to be made for onward trains at the Shenzhen border point (Chinese section). Mail and freight are conveyed across the border without transhipment.

The railway has undergone a massive modernization and electrification programme. Stage 1 of the electrified inner suburban service between Kowloon and Sha Tin was opened on 6 May 1982. The remaining sections of the line were electrified in two stages—the first to Tai Po Market in May 1983 and the second to Lo Wu in July 1983. The entire line is electrified and fully double-tracked under the HK$3,500m. electrification and modernization programme. All existing stations were rebuilt and three new stations were constructed for Tai Wai, Fo Tan and Kowloon Tong (already opened in May to cope with the electrified service). The Kowloon Tong Station is designed as an interchange with the underground Mass Transit Railway.

The status of the Kowloon-Canton Railway changed from a government department to a public corporation on 1 Jan. 1983. The decision was taken in view of the major development of the KCR into a much expanded and more sophisticated railway.

An underground Mass Transit Railway system, comprising 25 stations, is now in operation. The system consists of two lines, one linking the Central District of Hong Kong Island with Tsuen Wan in the west of Kowloon, and the other linking Kwun Tong in East Kowloon with Waterloo in Nathan Road. Cross platform interchange facilities are provided at Prince Edward and Argyle stations for passengers travelling between the two lines. The system is about 26 km in length.

Work began at the end of 1981 on the Island Line, which will serve the northern foreshore of Hong Kong Island. Scheduled to be fully operational in mid-1986, the new line will run for 12·5 km and incorporate 14 stations.

Aviation. Hong Kong International Airport is situated on the north shore of Kowloon Bay. It is regularly used by 31 airlines and many charter airlines which provide frequent services throughout the Far East to Europe, North America, Africa, the Middle East, Australia and New Zealand. British Airways operates 12 passenger and cargo services per week, to UK, Africa and many Asian countries. Cathay Pacific Airways, the Hong Kong-based airline, operates 119 passenger and cargo services to the UK, the Far and Middle East and Australia weekly. During 1981, British Caledonian Airways also commenced scheduled services on the Hong Kong to London route. About 1,000 scheduled services are operated weekly to and from Hong Kong by various airlines. In 1982, 54,635 aircraft arrived and departed on international flights, carrying 8·6m. passengers and 306,000 tonnes of freight.

Shipping. The total vessels entering and clearing Hong Kong and engaged in foreign trade in the first 7 months of 1983 amounted to 13,173 ocean-going vessels of 77,503,273 net tons. Launches and junks engaging in local trade, totalled 37,767 vessels of 6,712,898 net tons. 741 vessels (4·4m. gross tons) were registered in Hong Kong as British ships.

Telecommunications, Post and Broadcasting. There were 94 post offices in 1983; postal revenue totalled HK$571·3m.; expenditure, HK$420·3m. Telephone services are provided by the Hong Kong Telephone Co. Ltd. It operates through a network of 64 fully automatic main exchanges and served (1983) 2m. subscribers. Cable & Wireless Ltd is responsible for all external telecommunications and also provides for marine, meteorological and aeronautical communications. Telecommunication systems employed in Hong Kong include satellite, tropospheric scatter, HF, VHF, UHF, submarine and land coaxial cables. Services provided to the community include international telephone, telegram, telex, leased circuits, data transmission, facsimile and ship-shore communications.

There is a government broadcasting station, Radio Television Hong Kong, with daily transmissions in English and Chinese. Wireless licences were abolished as from 1 March 1967. A commercial station, the Commercial Broadcasting Co. Ltd, transmits daily in English and Cantonese. Two radio stations operate 8 channels.

Television Broadcasts Ltd and Asia Television Ltd transmit commercial television in English and Chinese on 4 channels, mainly in colour.

Cinemas. In 1983 there were 89 cinemas with a seating capacity of over 101,435. Attendance 62m. during the financial year 1982–83.

Newspapers. In Sept. 1983 there were 68 daily or weekly newspapers, registered and in circulation, including 13 daily English-language papers; the remainder are almost all in Chinese.

JUSTICE, EDUCATION AND WELFARE

Justice. There is a Supreme Court, having original, bankruptcy and companies winding-up, criminal, probate, divorce, admiralty and prize jurisdiction, and a court of appeal. There is also a District Court which, for administrative purposes, is divided into 3 geographical areas. It sits in several different buildings. There are 57 Magistrates sitting in 8 separate Magistracies. The District Court, apart from hearing civil cases where the claim does not amount to more than HK$40,000, also has jurisdiction over criminal matters. The labour tribunal provides speedy settlements to individual money claims arising from contracts of employment. The lands tribunal adjudicates on all statutory claims for compensation over land and certain landlord and tenant matters. The small claims tribunal deals with monetary claims involving amounts not exceeding HK$5,000.

Police. The Royal Hong Kong Police Force in Sept. 1983 totalled 28,612, composed of 392 gazetted, 1,934 inspectorate officers, 21,311 junior officers and 4,975 civilians. These figures include 2,007 women police officers, who are completely integrated throughout the force. There are also 5,314 auxiliary officers.

The maritime force operated by the Marine Division of the Royal Hong Kong Police comprises 70 sea-going patrol launches. Personnel in 1983 numbered 2,459 (138 officers, 475 n.c.o.s and 1,768 constables).

Education. The majority of schools have to be registered with the Education Department under the Education Ordinance. They are required to comply with regulations as to staff, building, fire and health requirements. From Sept. 1971, free and compulsory primary education was introduced in government and the majority of government-aided schools. Free junior secondary education of 3 years' duration was achieved in 1978 and it was made compulsory in stages beginning in Sept. 1979.

In March 1983 there were 217,937 pupils in kindergartens (all private), another 540,023 in primary schools and 451,428 in secondary schools.

There are 5 technical institutes with a total full-time and part-time enrolment of 35,134, 1 technical teachers' college and 3 colleges of education with a total enrolment of 3,893.

The University of Hong Kong had 6,723 undergraduates in 1983 and the Chinese University of Hong Kong, inaugurated in Oct. 1963, had 5,250 undergraduates. The Hong Kong Polytechnic, 1983, had a total of 25,858 students.

Health. In 1983 there were 3,880 doctors and about 22,690 hospital beds.

Social Security. The Government co-ordinates and implements expanding programmes in social welfare, which include social security, family services, child care, services for the elderly, youth and community work, probation and corrections and rehabilitation. More than 128 voluntary welfare agencies are subsidised by public funds.

The Government gives non-contributory cash assistance to needy families, unemployed able-bodied adults, the severely disabled and the elderly. Caseload at 31 Aug. 1983 totalled 281,658. Victims of natural disasters, crimes of violence and traffic accidents are financially assisted.

Books of Reference

Statistical Information: The Census and Statistics Department is responsible for the preparation and collation of Government statistics. These statistics are published mainly in the *Hong Kong Monthly Digest of Statistics* which is also available in a collected annual edition. The Department also publishes monthly trade statistics, economic indicators, annual review of overseas trade, etc. Statistical information is also published in the annual reports of Government departments. *Hong Kong 1982,* and other government publications are available from the Hong Kong Government Publications Centre, GPO Building, Connaught Place, Hong Kong, and the Hong Kong Government Office in London, 6 Grafton Street, London, W1X 3LB.

The Hong Kong Trade Development Council, Connaught Centre, Connaught Place, Hong Kong, issues a monthly *Hong Kong Enterprise* and other publications.

Hong Kong 1982. Hong Kong Government Press, 1982
Beazer, W. F., *The Commercial Future of Hong Kong.* New York, 1978
Bonavia, D., *Hong Kong 1997.* London, 1984
Endacott, G. B., *A History of Hong Kong.* 2nd ed. OUP, 1973.–*Government and People in Hong Kong, 1841–1962. A Constitutional History.* OUP, 1965
Hopkins, K., *Hong Kong: The Industrial Colony.* OUP, 1971
Rabushka, A., *The Changing Face of Hong Kong: New Departures in Public Policy.* Washington, 1973
Tregear, E. R., *Land Use in Hong Kong.* Hong Kong Univ. Press, 1958.—*Hong Kong Gazetteer.* Hong Kong Univ. Press, 1958.—*The Development of Hong Kong as Told in Maps.* Hong Kong Univ. Press, 1959
Youngson, A. J., *Hong Kong: Economic Growth and Policy.* OUP, 1982

HUNGARY

Magyar Népköztársaság

Capital: Budapest
Population: 10·7m. (1983)
GNP per capita: US$4,180 (1980)

HISTORY. Hungary first became an independent kingdom in 1001. For events in Hungary since 1918 *see* THE STATESMAN'S YEAR-BOOK, 1945, pp. 1006–7, and 1957, p. 1096.

On 23 Oct. 1956 an anti-Stalinist revolution broke out, and the newly formed coalition government of Imre Nagy on 1 Nov. withdrew from the Warsaw Pact and asked the UN for protection. János Kádár, formed a counter-government on 3 Nov. and asked the USSR for support.

Russian troops suppressed the revolution and abducted Nagy and his Ministers, who were later secretly executed.

On 7 Sept. 1967 the Soviet-Hungarian treaty of friendship was renewed for 20 years.

In 1978 the crown of St Stephen, the symbol of Hungarian nationhood, which had been in US hands since 1945, was returned to Hungary.

AREA AND POPULATION. Hungary is bounded north by Czechoslovakia, north-east by the USSR, east by Romania, south by Yugoslavia and west by Austria. The peace treaty of 10 Feb. 1947 restored the frontiers as of 1 Jan. 1938. The area of Hungary is 93,032 sq. km (35,911 sq. miles).

The official language is Hungarian (Magyar), which is a member of the Finno-Ugrian group.

At the census of 1 Jan. 1980 the population was 10,709,550 (5,195,300 males). Population in 1983: 10·7m. (males, 5·18m.).

54% of the population is urban (20% in Budapest). Population density, 115 per sq. km. Birth rate, 1982, 12·5 per 1,000; growth rate, –1% per annum; expectation of life (1981): males, 66; females, 73. In 1970 there were some 1·25m. Hungarian émigrés. There are Hungarian minorities in Romania, Yugoslavia and Czechoslovakia.

Vital statistics, 1982: Births, 133,579; marriages. 75,557; divorces, 28,500; deaths, 144.112; abortions, 78,000; infant mortality, 19·7 per 1,000 live births.

Area (in sq. km) and population (in 1,000) of counties, county boroughs and county towns:

Counties (1983)	Area	Population	Chief town (1983)	Population
Baranya	4,487	433	Pécs	173
Bács-Kiskun	8,363	566	Kecskemét	96
Békés	5,632	431	Békéscsaba	68
Borsod-Abaúj-Zemplén	7,248	803	Miskolc	210
Csongrád	4,263	454	Hódmezővásárhely	54
Fejér	4,374	423	Székesfehérvár	108
Győr-Sopron	4,012	430	Győr	127
Hajdú-Bihar	6,212	553	Debrecen	198
Heves	3,638	348	Eger	63
Komárom	2,250	323	Tatabánya	78
Nógrád	2,543	238	Salgótarján	50
Pest	6,394	983	Budapest	2,067
Somogy	6,035	358	Kaposvár	74
Szabolcs-Szatmár	5,938	588	Nyíregyháza	113
Szolnok	5,608	443	Szolnok	79
Tolna	3,702	269	Szekszárd	37
Vas	3,337	285	Szombathely	86
Veszprém	4,689	389	Veszprém	59
Zala	3,786	316	Zalaegerszeg	58

County boroughs (1983)	Area	Population	County boroughs (1983)	Area	Population
Budapest (capital)	525	2,067	Szeged	145	174
Miskolc	224	210	Pécs	113	173
Debrecen	446	198	Győr	175	127

Ethnic minorities in 1980 (in 1,000): Germans, 200; Slovaks, 100; Croats and Serbs, 100; Romanians, 20–25. There were 500,000 gipsies in 1984.

CLIMATE. A humid continental climate, with warm summers and cold winters. Precipitation is generally greater in summer, with thunderstorms. Dry, clear weather is likely in autumn, but spring is damp and both seasons are of short duration. Budapest. Jan. 32°F (0°C), July 71°F (21·5°C). Annual rainfall 25" (625 mm). Pécs. Jan. 30°F (–0·7°C), July 71°F (21·5°C). Annual rainfall 26·4" (661 mm).

CONSTITUTION AND GOVERNMENT. On 1 Feb. 1946 the National Assembly proclaimed a republic.

The present People's Republic was established by a constitution adopted on 18 Aug. 1949. Supreme power was vested in Parliament. Parliament elects a Presidential Council, which exercises the functions of Parliament between sessions. It can dissolve government bodies and annul legislation. The 1949 Constitution was amended in 1972. The distinction between 'working people' and 'citizens' disappears. Citizens are stated to have both indirect (through elected representatives) and direct (through local and enterprise councils) democratic rights. State and co-operative property are recognized as co-existing with equal status. Personal property is 'recognized and protected' up to the limit set by law (this includes for private artisans and, since 1 Jan. 1982, for various classes of small companies and 'economic working groups', places of business and machinery).

Ethnic minorities have equal rights and education in their own tongue.

National flag: Three horizontal stripes of red, white, green.

National anthem: God bless the Hungarians–Isten áldd meg a magyart (words by Ferenc Kölcsey, tune by Ferenc Erkel).

Chairman of the Presidential Council (Head of State): Pál Losonczi, appointed on 14 April 1967. *Deputy Chairmen:* Sándor Gáspar and Rezső Trautmann.

In 1949 the Hungarian Working People's Party (Communists), the Smallholders' Party, the National Peasant Party, the Trade Union Federation, the Association of Working Peasants, the Democratic Women's Association and the Federation of Working Youth were merged in the Hungarian People's Independence Front. In 1954 a new comprehensive organization was formed, the People's Patriotic Front. The Communist Youth Association (Kisz) had 870,000 members in 1981.

The Communist Party was reorganized after the 1956 revolution and changed its name to 'Hungarian Socialist Workers' Party'. It had 812,000 members in 1980 (32% women; 46% manual workers and peasants). Supreme *de facto* power is in the hands of the Party's Politburo, composed in March 1984 of: János Kádár, *First Secretary of the Central Committee*; György Aczél *(Secretary of the Central Committee)*; Valéria Benke; Sándor Gáspár; Ferenc Havasi; Mihály Korom; György Lázár; Pál Losonczi; László Márothy; Lajos Méhes; Károly Németh; Miklos Óvári; István Sárlos.

The Government was in March 1984 composed as follows:

Prime Minister: György Lázár.
Deputy Prime Ministers: János Borbándi, Lájos Faluvégi *(Chairman, State Planning Committee)*, Jozsef Marjai, István Sárlos. *Finance:* Dr István Hetényi. *Foreign Affairs:* Péter Varkonyi. *Speaker, National Assembly:* Antal Apró. *Interior:* Dr István Horváth. *Culture and Education:* Dr Béla Köpeczi. *Defence:* Gen. Lájos Czinege. *Foreign Trade:* Péter Veress. *Justice:* Imre Markója.

Parliament consists of 352 deputies (106 women), elected for a 5-year term by all citizens over 18 years.

The right to select candidates is vested solely in pre-election nomination meetings open to all voters. More than one candidate is permitted to stand in each constituency. Such 'alternative' candidates must receive 30% of the votes at nomination meetings. All candidates must support the Patriotic People's Front (PPF). To be elected candidates must gain at least 50% of the votes cast. Proposals are under discussion to make multiple candidatures compulsory in the next elections in 1985. Candidates coming second with more than 25% of the votes will become deputy members. 10% of deputies are to be elected on a national list voted upon by all citizens.

Elections were held on 8 June 1980. Electorate, 7,661,361; votes cast, 7,577,401; votes for PPF candidates, 7,462,953; against, 54,070. Alternative candidates stood in 15 constituencies.

Local Government. Hungary is divided into the capital, Budapest, 19 counties *(megyék)* and 5 county boroughs (large towns with county status), which are subdivided into districts, towns and boroughs. All of these are administered by a hierarchy of local councils which in turn elect Executive Committees to carry on day-to-day administration. Members of county councils are elected by the lower councils. Elections are held every 5 years. The last local elections were held in June 1980. There are 59,270 councillors (18,240 women).

DEFENCE. The 1947 Treaty authorized Hungary to have an army up to a strength of 65,000 personnel, and an air force of 90 aircraft, of which not more than 70 may be combat types with a personnel strength of 5,000.

By a law of 1976 the Presidential Council may establish a National Defence Council which in times of war would exercise supreme control over defence.

Men between the ages of 18 and 23 are liable for 18 months' conscription in the Army, 24 months in the Air Force. Compulsory military service age-limits are 18 to 55 (18 to 45 women).

The security police (BKH) is controlled by the Ministry of the Interior.

The Workers' Militia is a para-military organization armed with automatic weapons. Strength (1983), 60,000.

Four Soviet divisions are stationed in Hungary.

Army. Hungary is divided into 4 army districts: Budapest, Debrecen, Kiskunfélegyháza, Pécs. The strength of the Army was (1984) 84,000 (including 50,000 conscripts). It is organized in 1 tank division, 5 motor rifle divisions, 1 artillery and 1 surface-to-surface missile brigade, 1 anti-aircraft regiment, 3 surface-to-air missile regiments and 1 airborne battalion. Equipment includes 1,200 T-54/-55, 60 T-72 and 100 PT-76 tanks.

Navy. The maritime wing of the Army in 1984 deployed 500 officers and men operating 45 vessels, including 10 patrol craft of 100 tons, 5 utility landing craft and 30 other craft including river mine-warfare vessels, troop transports of up to 1,000 tons, river monitors, icebreakers and tugs, constituting the River Guard, and Army amphibious logistic and bridging vessels are active along the Danube.

Air Force. The Air Force is an integral part of the Army, with a strength of about 21,000 officers and men and 150 combat aircraft. The interceptor division has 2 regiments of MiG-23 and MiG-21 fighters. Other combat aircraft include about 20 Mi-24 helicopter gunships. Transport units are equipped with An-2, An-24, An-26 and Il-14 aircraft. Other types in service include Ka-26, Mi-2 and Mi-8 helicopters and L-29 Delfin and MiG-15UTI trainers. 'Guideline' and 'Goa' surface-to-air missiles are also operational.

INTERNATIONAL RELATIONS

Membership. Hungary is a member of UN, the Warsaw Pact and Comecon and, since 1982, IMF and IBRD.

External Debt. Hungary settled its debt to the UK in 1967. By an agreement of 6 March 1973 Hungary is to meet US claims of US$189m. arising from war damage and nationalization in 20 yearly instalments.

ECONOMY

Planning. For details of past plans *see* THE STATESMAN'S YEAR-BOOK, 1975–76. A

'New Economic Mechanism' (NEM) came into effect on 1 Jan. 1968. It restricted central direction to overall policies, replaced direct by financial control and gave local managers more initiative. Reforms aimed ultimately at adapting the economy to world prices by reducing costs, bringing salaries into line with productivity, re-deploying labour, cutting import subsidies and encouraging exports were set in train in 1980. Since 1976, enterprises have been required to repay state investment credits in full, usually over 10 years, and to cover unscheduled increases in costs. Regulations introduced in 1982 allow the creation of various types of small private enterprizes. Targets for the sixth 5-year plan (1976–80) were not met. The seventh 5-year plan (1981–85) is one of consolidation and envisages rises of only 6% in real incomes and 15% in the national income. There were large price increases in 1983. Inflation was officially quoted at 6·9% in 1983.

Budget. The budget for calendar years was as follows (in 1,000 forints):

	1975	1976	1977	1978	1979	1980	1981
Revenue	313,264	320,384	361,272	382,900	411,600	423,500	472,600
Expenditure	316,224	322,874	364,808	386,400	415,200	428,000	482,400

1981 revenue included (in 1,000m. forints): 257·1 from enterprises, 10·3 from collective farms, 10·3 from personal taxation and 64·2 turnover tax. Expenditure included: subsidies to enterprises, 81·4; investment, 60·4; welfare, 23·5; social security 90·4; culture, 44·1.

Currency. A decree of 26 July 1946 instituted a new monetary unit, the *forint* sub-divided into 100 *fillér*. The rate of exchange (March 1984) 67·16 forints to the £1 sterling, 46·48 forints = US$1. A uniform exchange rate was established in Oct. 1981 as a final step before the introduction of external, central-bank convertibility for foreign trade. There was a 3% devaluation in April 1983.

Banking. All banking activities are controlled by the National Bank, including the National Savings Bank, which handles local government, as well as personal, accounts. (Deposits in 1982: 175,700m. forints.) The National Bank finances investment to individual enterprises and is the main authority over foreign-exchange transactions. There is also a Foreign Trade Bank for Hungarian enter-prises trading abroad. The State Development Bank (formerly Investment Bank) finances large-scale investment projects and oversees national investment trends.

The National Credit Institute of Co-operatives handles all credit transactions for farmers, artisans and co-operatives. The Hungarian International Trade Bank opened in London in 1973. In 1980 the Central European International Bank was set up in Budapest with 7 Western banks holding 66% of the shares.

Weights and Measures. The metric system of weights and measures is in use. For land measure a cadastral yoke (1 acre = 0·7033 cadastral yoke) is used.

ENERGY AND NATURAL RESOURCES

Electricity. An 880-mw nuclear power station has been built with Soviet help at Paks. A 750 kv power line links Albertirsa with the Soviet grid at Vinnitsa (USSR).

Oil. Oil and natural gas have been found in the Szeged basin and in Zala county. There are pipelines for crude oil ('Friendship' I and II from USSR) and natural gas totalling 4,752 km in 1982. Imports in 1982 (in 1,000 tonnes): Oil, 8,776; gas, 3,934. The Hungarian section of the Adria oil pipeline (from Rijeka to Czechoslovakia) came on stream 1978.

Minerals. Coal and bauxite are mined, and there is some iron ore.

Agriculture. Agricultural land was collectivised in 1950. A law of 1968 permits collectives to own land, and guarantees individuals' rights to private plots. Collectives meet in a National Council of Agricultural Co-operatives.

In 1982 the agricultural area was (in 1,000 hectares) 6,582, of which 4,679 were arable, 1,283 meadows and pastures, and 280 orchards and vineyards.

In 1982 there were 1,302 collective farms with 5·6m. hectares of land (including 326,000 hectares of household plots) and 129 state farms with 927,200 hectares of land. The irrigated area was 157,000 hectares; 55,000 tractors were in use.

Production statistics (in 1,000 tonnes):

Crops	1980	1981	1982	Crops	1980	1981	1982
Wheat	6,048	4,602	5,747	Maize	6,575	6,813	7,730
Rye	138	115	116	Potatoes	949	1,112	975
Barley	926	899	865	Sugar-beet	3,873	4,719	5,363
Oats	104	159	123	Sunflowers	453	624	577

Livestock in 1982 was (in 1,000 head) as follows: Cattle, 1,922; pigs, 9,035; poultry, 45,397; sheep, 3,183; horses, 111,000.

Livestock products (1982): Eggs, 4.440m.; milk, 2,639m. litres; wool, 12,220 tonnes; animals for slaughter, 2,178,000 tonnes.

The north shore of Lake Balaton and the Tokaj area are important wine-producing districts. Wine production in 1982 was 601m. litres.

Forestry. The area under forest in 1982 was 1·63m. hectares. 26,000 hectares were afforested and 8m. cu. metres of timber were cut.

Fisheries. There are fisheries in the rivers Danube and Tisza and Lake Balaton, and in 1977 there were 24,000 hectares of commercial fishponds. Catch in 1982: 41,900 tonnes.

INDUSTRY AND TRADE

Industry. Production (in 1,000 tonnes):

	1978	1979	1980	1981	1982
Coal	25,700	25,700	25,700	25,942	26,079 [1]
Iron ore	534	532	426	422	467
Pig-iron	2,330	2,369	2,214	2,193	2,183
Crude steel	3,877	3,907	3,763	3,643	3,703
Rolled steel	3,188	3,240	3,046	2,816	2,856
Bauxite	2,899	2,976	2,950	2,914	2,627
Aluminium	71	72	73	74	74
Alumina	785	793	811	792	745
Crude oil	2,200	2,027	2,031	2,024	2,027
Natural gas (1m. cu. metres)	7,333	6,506	6,127	6,011	6,027
Electricity (1m. kwh.)	25,542	24,519	23,876	24,300	24,523
Cement	4,764	4,857	4,660	4,635	4,369
Artificial fertilizers	887	1,043	1,045	647	726
Synthetic materials (PVC, etc.)	213	294	328	314	326
Sulphuric acid	644	588	590	573	569
Sugar	496	497	468	490	459
Cotton cloth (1m. sq. metres)	365	349	335	320	310
Woollen (1m. sq. metres)	43	41	43	45	41
Silk and rayon (1m. sq. metres)	62	57	56	59	57
Leather footwear (1m. pairs)	46	45	43	44	44

[1] Including lignite (8,286) and brown coal (14,754).

Labour. In 1981 there were 5,001,900 wage-earners (2,247,600 female) in the following categories: working-class, 2,847,200; white-collar, 1,286,200; co-operative peasantry, 691,900; self-employed tradesmen, 176,600. 4,822,800 worked in the socialist sector. Percentage distributions of the workforce: industry, 32·4; agriculture, 21·1; social and cultural services, 11; trade, 9·8; transport and communications, 7·9; building, 7·7. In 1981 to simplify administration the Ministry of Labour was abolished and replaced by a National Office for Wages and Labour. A 42-hour 5-day week was introduced in 1982. Average monthly wages of employed persons in 1982: 4,950 forints. Retirement age: Men, 60; women, 55.

Trade Unions. Trade union membership was 4·3m. in 1980.

Commerce. Hungary is heavily dependent on foreign trade, which even under the 'New Economic Mechanism' remains basically under state control. Trade for calendar years (in 1m. forints):

	1976	1977	1978	1979	1980	1981	1982
Imports	230,056	267,300	300,900	308,900	299,900	314,300	324,800
Exports	204,834	238,600	240,700	282,100	281,000	299,400	324,500

In 1982 Hungary's trade with communist countries totalled 358·3m. forints. In 1982 USSR was Hungary's major trading partner (33% of turnover), ahead of West Germany (9·5%) and East Germany (6·8%). Major exports to communist countries: Machinery, industrial consumer goods, raw materials; elsewhere, raw materials and industrial consumer goods.

All exports and imports require licensing by the Ministry of Foreign Trade, and may be handled by 29 specialized foreign-trade agencies. Enterprises may handle their own foreign trade relations, set up companies abroad and participate in foreign companies. Hard currency is available through the National Bank. Tax-free zones for foreign companies exporting their own products were established in 1983. The Marketexpo branch of the Hungarian National Market Research Institute will conduct research for foreign firms. The agency Interag acts for Western firms in Hungary. Main imports from the West are machinery, fuel and consumer goods. Hungarian indebtedness to the West was US$8,300m. in 1983. A US$400m. loan was granted by IBRD in 1983.

Joint ventures with Western firms holding up to 49% of the capital are permitted, and foreign companies may set up offices in Hungary. In Nov. 1978 the US and Hungary signed a most-favoured-nation trade agreement. In May 1982 Hungary was granted membership of the IMF.

Total trade between Hungary and UK (British Department of Trade returns, in £1,000 sterling):

	1978	1979	1980	1981	1982	1983
Imports to UK	42,476	51,748	43,327	40,684	44,051	53,834
Exports and re-exports from UK	64,510	60,917	68,977	84,181	77,446	91,845

Tourism. In 1982, 9·83m. foreigners visited Hungary (2·7m. from the West), of whom 6·47m. were tourists (1·47m. from the West); and 3·89m. Hungarians travelled abroad (0·48m. to the West).

COMMUNICATIONS

Roads. In 1982 there were 29,666 km of roads. In 1982 passenger cars numbered 1,181,655 (1,146,539 private). 238m. tonnes of freight and 709m. passengers were transported by road in 1982 (excluding urban traffic).

Railways. Route length of public lines in 1982, 7,758 km, of which 1,516 km are electrified. 127m. tonnes of freight and 266m. passengers were carried.

Aviation. Hungarian Air Lines (Malév) operate from Ferihegy airport, 16 km from Budapest. 1982 arrivals, 810,864; departures, 830,526. Malév has 22 aircraft and flies 42 routes (including one to UK), and in 1982 carried 1·07m. passengers. British Airways, PANAM, Air France, SABENA, Swissair, OS, Lufthansa and KLM have services to Budapest.

Shipping. Permanently navigable waterways have a length of 1,302 km; 4·2m. tonnes of cargo were carried in 1982 and 4·6m. passengers.

Post and Broadcasting. Number of post offices (1982), 2,520; number of telephones, 1,296,682 (1982). Radio licences were abolished in 1980; television licences, (1982) 2,838,000. *Magyar Rádió és Televízió* broadcasts 3 programmes on medium-waves and FM and also regional programmes, including transmissions in German and Serbo-Croat. Two TV programmes are broadcast. Colour broadcasts are only transmitted in Budapest, using the SECAM system.

Cinemas and Theatres (1982). There were 3,556 cinemas; attendance 70m. 28 full-length feature films were made. There were 40 theatres; attendance 6·1m.

Newspapers and Books. In 1981 there were 29 dailies and 978 other periodicals. The Party daily is *Népszabadság* ('People's Freedom') (average daily circulation, 800,000). 7,845 book titles were published in 1982 in 95·4m. copies.

JUSTICE, RELIGION, EDUCATION AND WELFARE

Justice. The administration of justice is the responsibility of the Procurator-General, who is elected by Parliament for a term of 6 years. Civil and criminal cases fall under the jurisdiction of the district courts, county courts and the Supreme

Court in Budapest. Criminal proceedings are dealt with by district courts through 3-member councils and by county court and the Supreme Court in 5-member councils. A new Civil Code was adopted in 1978 and a new Criminal Code in 1979.

District Courts act only as courts of first instance; county courts as either courts of first instance or of appeal. The Supreme Court acts normally as an appeal court, but may act as a court of first instance in cases submitted to it by the Public Prosecutor. All courts, when acting as courts of first instance, consist of 1 professional judge and 2 lay assessors, and, as courts of appeal, of 3 professional judges. Local government Executive Committees may try petty offences.

District or county judges and assessors are elected by the district or county councils, all members of the Supreme Court by Parliament.

There are also military courts of the first instance. Military cases of the second instance go before the Supreme Court.

Judges are elected by the Presidential Council.

Religion. There are 20 authorized religious denominations which share proportionally an annual state subsidy of 70m. forints. 8·5m. of the population professed a religious faith in 1976; the number of active church members was put between 1m. and 1·5m.

Senior church appointments require the consent of the Presidential Council. Lower ones are ratified by the State Office for Church Affairs. Certain appointments become valid if the Office makes no comment within 15 days, and for the most minor church appointments neither state consent nor prior notification is required. Ecclesiastics are required to take an oath of allegiance to the state.

In 1976 there were 5·25m. Roman Catholics with 11 dioceses, 4,000 priests and 4,400 churches, and 500,000 uniates. In 1979 there were 3 seminaries and 1 uniate seminery, a theological academy, and 8 secondary schools. The Primate of Hungary is the Archbishop of Esztergom, Laszló Lekai, appointed Feb. 1976. There are also 2 archbishops, 8 bishops and an apostolic administrator. There is one Uniate bishopric.

In 1976 there were 2m. Calvinists with 4 dioceses, 1,300 ministers and 1,567 churches. There were 2 theological colleges (20% of students female) with 16 teachers, and 1 secondary school. There were 500,000 Lutherans with 16 dioceses, 374 ministers and 673 churches. There is a theological college with 6 teachers. The 10 denominations in the Association of Free Churches had 37,000 members, 230 ministers and 675 churches. There are 4 Orthodox denominations with 40,000 members in 1979. The Unitarian Church has 10,000 members, 11 ministers and 6 churches. In 1979 there were 80,000–100,000 Jews (825,000 in 1939) with 130 synagogues, 26 rabbis, a rabbinical college with 6 teachers and a secondary school.

Education. Education is free and compulsory from 6 to 14. Primary schooling ends at 14; thereafter education may be continued at secondary, secondary technical or secondary vocational schools, which offer diplomas entitling students to apply for higher education, or at vocational training schools which offer tradesmen's diplomas. Students at the latter may also take the secondary school diploma examinations after 2 years of evening or correspondence study.

In 1982–83 there were 4,826 kindergartens with 31,972 teachers and 408,153 pupils; 3,567 general schools with 80,798 teachers and 1,244,100 pupils; 539 secondary schools with 6,357 teachers and 218,000 pupils. There are 4 universities proper (Budapest, Pécs, Szeged, Debrecen), and 14 specialized universities (6 technical, 4 medical, 3 arts, 1 economics). At these and at 37 other institutions of higher education there were, in 1982–83, 63,300 students and 14,011 teachers.

Libraries and Museums. In 1982 there were 4,899 public and 5,591 trade union libraries. Major national libraries (1982): National Széchenyi, 6m. volumes; Budapest University, 3·2m.; Academy of Sciences, 1·6m.; National Technical Library and Documentation Centre, 1·2m. In 1982 there were 532 museums with 17·73m. visitors.

Health. In 1982 there were 32,476 doctors and dentists and 98,535 hospital beds.

Social Security. Medical treatment is free. Patients bear 15% of the cost of medicines. Sickness benefit is 75% of wages, old age pensions (at 60 for men, 55 for women) 60–70%. In 1982, 103m. forints were paid out in social insurance benefits. Pensions and family allowances were raised in July 1983.

DIPLOMATIC REPRESENTATIVES

Of Hungary in Great Britain (35 Eaton Place, London, SW1X 8BY)
Ambassador: Dr Rezső Bányász (accredited 21 July 1981).

Of Great Britain in Hungary (Harmincad Utca 6, Budapest V)
Ambassador: P. W. Unwin, CMG.

Of Hungary in the USA (3910 Shoemaker St., NW, Washington, D.C., 20008)
Ambassador: Dr Vencel Hazi.

Of the USA in Hungary (Szabadság Tér 12, Budapest V)
Ambassador: (Vacant).

Of Hungary to the United Nations
Ambassador: Pál Rácz.

Books of Reference

Report of the Hungarian Statistical Office on the Economic Development and Plan Fulfilment. Budapest, annual from 1973
Statisztikai Évkönyv. Budapest, annual; since 1871, abridged English version, *Statistical Year-Book*
Statistical Year-Book. (in English and Russian). Budapest, annual from 1982
Statistical Pocket Book of Hungary (in English). Budapest, annual from 1959
Hungarian Digest. Budapest, 6 a year from 1980
The Hungarian Economy: a Quarterly Economic and Business Review. Budapest, since 1972
Hungary 66 (67 etc.). Budapest, annual from 1966
Marketing in Hungary. Budapest, quarterly
Information Hungary. Budapest, 1980
The Constitution of the Hungarian People's Republic. Budapest, 1972
Bako, E., *Guide to Hungarian Studies.* 2 vols. Stanford Univ. Press, 1973
Berend, I. T., and Ranki, G., *Hungary: A Century of Economic Development.* New York and Newton Abbot, 1974; *Underdevelopment and Economic Growth: Studies in Hungarian Social and Economic History.* Budapest, 1979
Cave, M., *Alternative Approaches to Economic Planning.* London, 1981
Donath, F., *Reform and Revolution: Transformation of Hungary's Agriculture, 1945–1970.* Budapest, 1980
Enyedi, G., *Hungary: An Economic Geography.* Boulder, Colorado, 1976
Fekete, J., *Back to the Realities: Reflections of a Hungarian Banker.* Budapest, 1982
Gadó, O., *The Economic Mechanism of Hungary.* Leiden and Budapest, 1976
Halász, Z., *Hungary: A Guide with a Difference.* 2nd ed. Budapest, 1979
Hare, P. G., and others (eds.), *Hungary: a Decade of Economic Reform.* London, 1981
Hegedüs, A., *The Structure of Socialist Society.* London, 1977
Ignotus, P., *Hungary.* London, 1972
Kabdebo, T., *Hungary.* [Bibliography] Oxford and Santa Barbara, 1980
Kádár, J., *For a Socialist Hungary.* Budapest, 1974
Kornai, J., *Economics of Shortage.* Oxford, 1980
Kourig, B., *Communism in Hungary.* Stanford, 1979
Kozma, F., *Economic Integration and Economic Strategy.* The Hague, 1982
Macartney, C. A., *Hungary: A Short History.* London, 1962
Németh, G. (ed.), *Hungary: A Comprehensive Guide.* Budapest, 1980
Országh, L., *Hungarian-English Dictionary.* Budapest, 1977.—*English-Hungarian Dictionary.* Budapest, 1970
Pamlényi, E. (ed.), *A History of Hungary.* Budapest, 1975
Pécsi, M. and Sárfalvi, B., *Physical and Economic Geography of Hungary.* 2nd ed. Budapest, 1979
Toma, P. A., and Volgyes, I., *Politics in Hungary.* San Francisco, 1977

ICELAND

Lýðveldið Ísland

Capital: Reykjavík
Population: 235,453 (1982)
GNP per capita: US$11,330 (1980)

HISTORY. The first settlers came to Iceland in 874. Between 930 and 1264 Iceland was an independent republic, but by the 'Old Treaty' of 1263 the country recognized the rule of the King of Norway. In 1381 Iceland, together with Norway, came under the rule of the Danish kings, but when Norway was separated from Denmark in 1814, Iceland remained under the rule of Denmark. Since 1 Dec. 1918 it has been acknowledged as a sovereign state. It was united with Denmark only through the common sovereign until it was proclaimed an independent republic on 17 June 1944.

AREA AND POPULATION. Iceland is a large island in the North Atlantic, close to the Arctic Circle, and comprises an area of about 103,000 sq. km (39,758 sq. miles), with its extreme northern point (the Rifstangi) lying in 66° 32′ N. lat., and its most southerly point (Dyrhólaey, Portland) in 63° 24′ N. lat., not including the islands north and south of the land; if these are included, the country extends from 67° 10′ N. (the Kolbeinsey) to 63° 19′ N. (Geirfuglasker, one of the Westman Islands). It stretches from 13° 30′ (the Gerpir) to 24° 32′ W. long. (Látrabjarg). The skerry *Hvalbakur* (The Whaleback) lies 13° 16′ W. long.

The 25 constituencies of the country are now grouped in 7 districts.

District	Inhabited land (sq. km)	Mountain pasture (sq. km)	Waste-land (sq. km)	Total area (sq. km)	Popula-tion (1 Dec. 1982)
Reykjanes area	1,266	716	—	1,982	140,143
West	5,011	3.415	275	8,711	15,109
Western Peninsula	4,130	3.698	1,652	9,470	10,452
Northland West	4,867	5.278	2,948	13,093	10,770
Northland East	9,890	6.727	5,751	22,368	26,087
East	16,921	17.929	12,555	{ 21,991	13,068
South				{ 25,214	19,824
Iceland	42,085	37.553	23,181	102,819	235,453

In 1982, 26,784 were domiciled in rural districts and 208,669 in towns and villages (of over 200 inhabitants.) The population is almost entirely Icelandic.

In 1982 foreigners numbered 3,465; of these 1,020 were Danish, 682 US, 326 British, 277 Norwegian and 245 German (Fed. Rep.) nationals.

The capital, Reykjavík, had on 1 Dec. 1982, a population of 86,092; other towns were Akranes, 5,344; Akureyri, 13,758; Bolungarvík, 1,287; Dalvík, 1,341; Eskifjörður, 1,103; Garðabaer, 5,451; Grindavík, 2,012; Hafnarfjörður, 12,460; Húsavík, 2,487; Ísafjörður, 3,427; Keflavík, 6,747; Kópavogur, 14,279; Neskaupstaður, 1,689; Njarðvík, 2,149; Ólafsfjörður, 1,189; Sauðárkrókur, 2,295; Selfoss, 3,557; Seltjarnarnes, 3,512; Seyðisfjörður, 1,001; Siglufjörður, 1,945; Vestmannaeyjar, 4,657.

Vital statistics for calendar years:

	Living births	Still-born	Marriages	Divorces	Deaths	Infant deaths
1980	4,528	21	1.306	441	1,538	35
1981	4,345	21	1,357	463	1,655	26
1982	4,337	17	1.303	421	1,583	31

CLIMATE. The climate is cool temperate oceanic and rather changeable, but mild for its latitude because of the Gulf Stream and prevailing S.W. winds. Precipitation is high in upland areas, mainly in the form of snow. Reykjavik. Jan. 34°F (1°C), July 52°F (11°C). Annual rainfall 34″ (860 mm).

CONSTITUTION AND GOVERNMENT. On 24 May 1944 the people of Iceland decided in a referendum to sever all ties with the Danish Crown. The voters were asked whether they were in favour of the abrogation of the Union Act, and whether they approved of the bill for a republican constitution: 70,725 voters were for severance of all political ties with Denmark and only 370 against it; 69,048 were in favour of the republican constitution, 1,042 against it and 2,505 votes were invalid. On 17 June 1944 the republic was formally proclaimed, and as the republic's first president the Alþingi elected Sveinn Björnsson for a 1-year term (re-elected 1945 and 1949; died 25 Jan. 1952). The President is now elected for a 4-year term.

President of the Republic of Iceland: Vigdís Finnbogadóttir (elected 29 June 1980, with 43,611 out of 129,049 valid votes, inaugurated 1 Aug. 1980).

National flag: Blue with a red white-bordered Scandinavian cross.

National anthem: Ó Guð vors lands (words by M. Jochumsson, 1874; tune by S. Sveinbjørnsson).

The official language is Icelandic (*íslenzka*).

The *Alþingi* (Parliament) is divided into two Houses, the Upper House and the Lower House. The former is composed of one-third of the members elected by the whole Alþingi in common sitting. The remaining two-thirds of the members form the Lower House. The members of the Alþingi receive payment for their services.

The budget bills must be laid before the two Houses in joint session, but all other bills can be introduced in either of the Houses. If the Houses do not agree, they assemble in a common sitting and the final decision is given by a majority of two-thirds of the voters, with the exception of budget bills, where a simple majority is sufficient. The ministers have free access to both Houses, but can vote only in the House of which they are members.

The electoral law enacted in 1959 provides for an Alþingi of 60 members. Of these, 49 are elected in 8 constituencies by proportional representation; the remaining 11 are apportioned to the parties according to their total vote.

At the elections held on 23 April 1983 the following parties were returned: Independence Party, 23; Progressives, 14; People's Alliance, 10; Social Democrats, 6; Social Democratic Alliance, 4; Women's Alliance, 3.

The executive power is exercised under the President by the Cabinet. The coalition Cabinet, as constituted in May 1983, was as follows:

Prime Minister: Steingrímur Hermannsson (Progress).

Foreign Affairs: Geir Hallgrímsson (Ind.). *Finance:* Albert Guðmundsson (Ind.). *Social Affairs:* Alexander Stefánsson (Progress). *Fisheries:* Halldór Ásgrimsson (Progress). *Agriculture, Justice and Church:* Jón Helgason (Progress). *Health and Social Security, Communications:* Matthías Bjarnason (Ind.). *Commerce:* Matthías A. Mathiesen (Ind.). *Education:* Ragnhildur Helgadóttir (Ind.). *Energy and Industry:* Sverrir Hermannsson (Ind.).

The ministers take responsibility for their acts. They can be impeached by the Alþingi, and in that case their cause will be decided by the *Landsdómur*, a special tribunal for parliamentary impeachments.

Local Administration. Iceland is divided into 224 communes, of which 23 have the status of towns, while the 201 remaining communes make up 23 counties *(sýslur)*. The commune and county councils are elected by universal suffrage (men and women 20 years of age and over), in town and other urban communes by proportional representation, but in rural communes by simple majority. The county councils consist of one representative for each of the constituent communes, their purpose being the superintendence of local government within the county. Town councils and county councils come under the supervision of the Ministry of Social Affairs. For national government there are 27 divisions, consisting of towns and counties, single or combined, with the exception of Keflavik Airport. In the capital the different branches of national government are independent (courts, police, customs), while in other national government divisions they are the charge of one official, who, in the case of counties, presides over the county council as well.

DEFENCE. Iceland possesses neither an army nor a navy. Under the North Atlantic Treaty, US forces are stationed in Iceland as the Iceland Defence Force.

Four armed fishery protection vessels are maintained by the Coastguard, with 1 patrol aircraft and 2 helicopters. Coastguard Service personnel in 1982 totalled about 130 officers and men.

INTERNATIONAL RELATIONS

Membership. Iceland is a member of UN, EFTA, OECD, the Council of Europe, NATO and the Nordic Council.

ECONOMY

Budget. Current revenue and expenditure for calendar years (in 1,000 new kr.):

	1978	1979	1980	1981	1982	1983
Revenue	1,394,960	2,089,508	3,461,773	5,514,780	7,967,266	13,007,315
Expenditure	1,384,730	2,022,864	3,432,401	5,457,475	7,909,270	12,972,958

Main items of the Treasury accounts for 1982 (in 1,000 new kr.):

Revenue		Expenditure	
Direct taxes	1,799,607	Presidency	7,281
Indirect taxes	8,230,231	Alþingi	63,220
Profit from government enter-		Cabinet	11,023
prises	39,796	Justice and ecclesiastical affairs	573,155
		Culture and education	1,538,876
		Social affairs	246,508
		Commerce	849,076
		Foreign affairs	123,422
		Fisheries and agriculture	533,985
		Finance	423,873
		Communications	957,985

The public debt of Iceland was on 31 Dec. 1981, 2,540m. new kr., of which the foreign debt amounted to 370m. new kr. and the internal debt to 2,170m. new kr.

Currency. The Icelandic monetary units are the *króna*, pl. *krónur* and the *eyrir*, pl. *aurar*. There are 100 *aurar* to the *króna*. On 1 Jan. 1981 a currency reform took place and 100 old krónur equal 1 new króna. In March 1984, US$1 = kr. 28·91; £1 = kr. 42·91. Note and coin circulation, 31 Dec. 1982, was 567·6m. new kr.

Banking. By Act of 29 March 1961 the Central Bank of Iceland was established, which took over the central bank function up to that date exercised by the *Landsbanki Íslands* (The National Bank of Iceland, owned entirely by the State). Other banks are: *Búnaðarbanki Íslands* (the Agricultural Bank of Iceland), a state bank, founded in 1930; *Útvegsbanki Íslands* (the Fisheries Bank of Iceland), founded in 1930 as a joint-stock bank, which in 1957 became a state bank; *Iðnaðarbanki Íslands* (Industrial Bank of Iceland Ltd), a joint-stock bank, established 1953, part of the shares being owned by the Government; *Verzlunarbanki Íslands* (Iceland Bank of Commerce Ltd), established in 1961; *Samvinnubanki Íslands* (The Icelandic Co-operative Bank), established in 1963; *Alþýðubankinn* (The People's Bank Ltd) established 1971. On 30 Sept. 1983 the accounts of the Central Bank balanced at 13,945·8m. new kr.

At the end of 1982 there were 40 savings banks with deposits amounting to 1,711m. new kr.

Weights and Measures. The metric system of weights and measures is obligatory.

ENERGY AND NATURAL RESOURCES

Electricity. The installed capacity of public power plants at the end of 1982 totalled 904,000 kw., of which 752,000 kw. comprised hydro-electric plants. Total energy production in public-owned plants in 1982 amounted to 3,575m. kwh.; in privately-owned plants, 14m. kwh.

Agriculture. Of the total area of Iceland, about six-sevenths is unproductive, but only about 0·5% is under cultivation, mostly confined to hay, potatoes and turnips. In 1982 the total hay crop was 3,413,000 cu. metres; the crop of potatoes, 14,300 tonnes, and of turnips 643 tonnes. At the end of 1982 the livestock was as follows: Horses, 53,650; cattle, 64,435 (including 32,845 milch cows); sheep, 747,701; pigs, 16,055; poultry, 292,621.

Fisheries. Fishing vessels in Dec. 1982 numbered 841 with a gross tonnage of 111,848. Total catch in 1982, 766,000 tonnes; 1981, 1,431,550 tonnes.

The Icelandic Government announced that the fishery limits off Iceland were extended from 12 to 50 nautical miles from Sept. 1972. An interim agreement for 2 years signed by the UK and Iceland in Nov. 1973 expired in Nov. 1975.

On 15 July 1975 the Icelandic Government issued a decree that from 15 Oct. 1975 the fishery limits of Iceland were extended from 50 to 200 nautical miles. The Icelandic Government maintain that this extension is necessary to protect the fish stocks in Icelandic waters because the fishing industry is of vital importance to the national economy.

COMMERCE. Total value of imports and exports in 1,000 new kr.:

	1978	1979	1980	1981	1982
Imports	1,843,206	2,913,072	4,801,616	7,484,684	11,647,000
Exports	1,762,857	2,784,515	4,459,529	6,536,214	8,479,000

Leading exports (in 1,000 kg and 1,000 new kr.):

	1981		1982	
	Quantity	Value	Quantity	Value
Fish and whale products	493,449,900	5,115,457	365,219,200	6,354,366
Agricultural products	7,254,300	88,555	6,051,000	107,088

Leading imports (in 1,000 tonnes and 1,000 new kr.):

	1981		1982	
	Quantity	Value	Quantity	Value
Ships (number)	13	266,072	15	302,026
Fuel oil	434,309·4	845,571	349,824·5	1,208,479
Cereals	12,935·3	45,465	15,365,·5	79,291
Animal feed	60,401·5	114,255	65,113·7	175,550
Gasoline	93,587·2	234,751	94,222·7	346,257
Motor vehicles (number)	10,525	405,686	10,565	616,149
Fishing nets and other gear	1,910	87,165	1,843·1	128,483

Value of trade with principal countries for 3 years (in 1,000 new kr.):

	1980		1981		1982	
	Imports (c.i.f.)	Exports (f.o.b.)	Imports (c.i.f.)	Exports (f.o.b.)	Imports (c.i.f.)	Exports (f.o.b.)
Austria	23,299	4,141	45,612	4,486	81,093	6,099
Belgium	96,837	28,401	200,980	82,664	305,040	117,630
Brazil	56,429	6,753	66,218	6,905	70,100	12,821
Canada	67,785	26,657	83,724	44,028	66,677	44,581
Czechoslovakia	27,448	39,157	39,698	49,379	44,249	21,854
Denmark	391,991	94,427	777,025	111,851	1,133,722	148,238
Faroe Islands	900	23,170	33,103	55,919	1,280	65,988
Finland	131,794	136,314	168,599	92,481	289,005	130,242
France	118,778	111,290	169,693	124,716	304,956	243,790
German Dem. Rep.	11,772	2,221	20,660	1,118	41,471	2,570
Germany, Fed. Rep. of	478,784	438,257	858,270	420,803	1,422,183	600,492
Greece	427	57,759	989	73,317	1,265	115,127
Hungary	2,705	5,112	5,617	6,596	8,020	4,961
India	7,726	—	12,430	—	20,145	1
Ireland	8,747	3,385	12,865	12,338	25,447	10,788
Israel	4,924	355	8,285	832	8,890	4,868
Italy	117,264	212,864	174,253	209,161	289,555	321,938
Japan	193,376	65,235	336,811	108,870	545,186	273,719
Netherlands	437,687	45,415	555,424	75,638	852,213	80,103
Nigeria	42	317,927	188	858,368	226	325,335
Norway	359,982	75,087	734,028	78,697	871,681	62,935
Poland	23,207	108,462	27,510	56,463	39,192	41,390
Portugal	118,713	211,776	135,171	702,137	268,449	999,498
Spain	45,791	151,706	76,038	243,620	120,130	345,865
Sweden	343,019	94,461	623,416	110,218	963,472	118,377
Switzerland	44,429	154,008	85,002	165,371	106,463	300,017
USSR	467,723	238,822	600,045	403,040	1,063,158	639,827
UK	454,890	734,886	573,204	933,349	1,015,647	1,118,684
USA	450,466	962,137	581,709	1,361,079	982,751	2,188,650

Total trade between Iceland and UK (British Department of Trade returns, in £1,000 sterling):

	1979	1980	1981	1982	1983
Imports to UK	83,269	82,042	75,729	72,721	66,505
Exports and re-exports from UK	48,520	47,223	50,558	102,714	65,176

TOURISM. There were 72,600 visitors to Iceland in 1982.

COMMUNICATIONS

Roads. There are no railways in Iceland. Iceland possesses between 11,000–12,000 km of high roads and country roads. Motor vehicles registered at the end of 1982 numbered 106,459, of which 95,984 were passenger cars and 10,475 trucks; there were also 279 motor cycles. On 26 May 1968 Iceland changed from left-hand to right-hand traffic.

Aviation. One large and some small companies maintain regular services between Reykjavík and various places in Iceland (the large one 1981: 221,296 passengers; 854 tonnes of mail; 2,346 tonnes of freight). The large company maintains regular services between Iceland and the UK, the Scandinavian countries, some other European countries and USA. In 1982 the company carried in scheduled foreign flights 324,874 passengers, 1,515 tonnes of mail and 5,228 tonnes of freight.

Shipping. The mercantile marine of Iceland consisted in Dec. 1982 of 4 steam vessels (1,953 gross tons) and 943 motor vessels (191,353 gross tons).

Post and Broadcasting. At the end of 1982 the number of post offices was 157 and telephone and telegraph offices 118; number of telephones, 116,856. The government station, *Rikisútvarpid*, broadcasts 1 programme on long and medium-waves and on FM. *Rikisútvarpid-Sjónvarp* uses 150 transmitters and broadcasts 1 TV programme. Number of licenced receivers: radio, 70,059; television, 62,623.

Cinemas (1978). There were 29 cinemas with a seating capacity of 10,450.

Newspapers (1981). There are 5 daily newspapers, all in Reykjavík, with a combined circulation of about 125,000.

JUSTICE, RELIGION, EDUCATION AND WELFARE

Justice. The lower courts of justice are those of the provincial magistrates (*sýslumenn*) and town judges (*bæjarfógetar*). From these there is an appeal to the Supreme Court (*hæstiréttur*) in Reykjavík, which has 6 judges.

Religion. The national church, and the only one endowed by the State, is Evangelical Lutheran. But there is complete religious liberty, and no civil disabilities are attached to those not of the national religion. The affairs of the national church are under the superintendence of a bishop. In 1982, 4,379 persons (1·9%) were Dissenters and 2,845 persons (1·2%) did not belong to any religious community.

Education. Compulsory education for children began in 1907, and a university was founded in Reykjavík in 1911. There is in Reykjavík a teachers' training college and a technical high school; various specialized institutions of learning and a number of second-level schools are scattered throughout the country. There are many part-time schools of cultural activities, including music.

Compulsory education comprises 8 classes, 7-14 years of age. After completion of a facultative 9th class, attended by 92%-94% of the relevant age group, there is access to further schooling free of charge. Some 60% of the age groups 15-19 years old attend schools. Around 15%-20% of each age group go into handicraft apprenticeship. 25%-30% pass matriculation examination, generally at the age of 20. Approximately one third-level student out of every four goes abroad for studies, two-thirds of them to Scandinavia, the rest mainly to English- and German-speaking countries.

Immatriculation in Iceland in autumn 1980: Preceding the first level, 4,041. First-level (1st-6th class) 24,736. Second-level first stage (7th-9th class) 13,074.

Second-level second stage general programmes (4-year courses) 5,766. Second-level second stage vocational programmes (3 or 4 year courses) 7,428. Third-level first stage non-university 778. Third-level first and second stage university and equivalent 3,618.

Social Welfare. The main body of the Icelandic social welfare legislation is consolidated in six main acts:

(i) The social security legislation (a) health insurance, including sickness benefits; *(b)* social security pensions, mainly consisting of old age pension, disablement pension and widows' pension, and also children's pension; *(c)* employment injuries insurance.

(ii) The unemployment insurance legislation, where daily allowances are paid to those who have met certain conditions.

(iii) The subsistence legislation. This is controlled by municipal government, and social assistance is granted under special circumstances, when payments from other sources are not sufficient.

(iv) The tax legislation. In 1975 family allowances were abolished and children's support included in the tax legislation, according to which a certain amount is subtracted from levied taxes for each child in a family.

(v) The rehabilitation legislation.

(vi) Child and juvenile guidance.

Health insurance covers the entire population. Citizenship is not demanded and there is no waiting period. Most hospitals are both municipally and state run, a few solely state run and all offer free medical help. Medical treatment out of hospitals is partly paid by the patient, the same applies to medicines, except medicines of lifelong necessary use, which are paid in full by the health insurance. Dental care is free for the age groups 6-15, but is paid 75% for those five years or younger and the age group 16 but 50% for old age and disabled pensioners. Sickness benefits are paid to those who lose income because of periodical illness. The daily amount is fixed and paid from the 11th day of illness. On 1 Oct. 1983 it was 135 new kr. a day.

Entitlement to old age and disablement pensions at the full rates is subject to the condition that the beneficiary has been resident in Iceland for 40 years at the age period of 16–67. For shorter period of residence, the benefits are reduced proportionally. Entitled to old age pension are all those who are 67 years old, and have been residents in Iceland for 3 years of the age period of 16–67. Entitled to disablement pension are those who have lost 75% of their working capacity and have been residents in Iceland for 3 years before application or have had full working capacity at the time when they became residents. Old age and disablement pension are of equally high amount, in the year 1983 the total sum was 34,939 new kr. for an individual. Married pensioners are paid 90% of two individuals' pensions. In addition to the basic amount, supplementary allowances are paid according to social circumstances and income possibilities. Widows' pensions are the same amount as old age and disablement pension, provided the applicant is over 60 when she becomes widowed. Women at the age 50–60 get reduced pension. Women under 50 are not entitled to widows' pensions.

The employment injuries insurance covers medical care, daily allowances, disablement pension and survivors' pension and is applicable to practically all employees.

All benefits within the above-mentioned laws shall go up in step with general wages within 6 months from their increase.

Social assistance is primarily municipal and granted in cases outside the social security legislation. Domestic assistance to old people and disabled is granted within this legislation, besides other services.

Child and juvenile guidance is performed by chosen committees according to special laws, such as home guidance and family assistance. In cases of parents' disablement the committees take over the guidance of the children involved.

DIPLOMATIC REPRESENTATIVES

Of Iceland in Great Britain (1 Eaton Terrace, London, SW1W 8EY)
Ambassador: Einar Benediktsson (accredited 11 Nov. 1982).

Of Great Britain in Iceland (Laufásvegur 49, 101 Reykjavík)
Ambassador and Consul-General: Richard Thomas.

Of Iceland in the USA (2022 Connecticut Ave., NW, Washington, D.C., 20008)
Ambassador: Hans G. Andersen.

Of the USA in Iceland (Laufasvegur 21, 101 Reykjavík)
Ambassador: Marshall Brement.

Of Iceland to the United Nations
Ambassador: Hörður Helgason.

Books of Reference

Statistical Information: The Icelandic Statistical Office, Hagstofa Íslands (Reykjavík) was founded in 1914. *Director:* Klemens Tryggvason. Its main publications are:

Hagskýrslur Íslands. Statistics of Iceland (from 1912)
Hagtíðindi (Statistical Journal) (from 1916)
Statistical Bulletin. Issued quarterly by the Statistical Bureau of Iceland and the Central Bank of Iceland (from 1931 to 1962, monthly). Ceased publication May 1980
Economic Statistics. Central Bank of Iceland (quarterly from 1980)
Icelandic Currency Reform January 1st 1981. Central Bank of Iceland, 1980
Heilbrigðisskýrslur. Public Health in Iceland (latest issue for 1977; published 1980)
Cleasby, R., *An Icelandic-English Dictionary.* 2nd ed. Oxford, 1957
Foss, H. (ed.), *Directory of Iceland.* Annual. Reykjavik, 1907–40, 1948 ff.
Hermannsson, Halldór, *Islandica.* An annual relating to Iceland and the Fiske Icelandic Collection in Cornell University Library. Ithaca (from 1908)
Hood, J. C. F., *Icelandic Church Saga.* London, 1946
Horton, J. J., *Iceland.* [Bibliography] Oxford and Santa Barbara, 1983
Leaf, H., *Iceland Yesterday and Today.* London, 1949
Magnússon, S. A., *Northern Sphinx: Iceland and the Icelanders from the Settlement to the Present.* London, 1977
Nordal, J., and Kristinsson, V. (eds), *Iceland 874–1974.* Central Board of Iceland, Reykjavik, 1975
Þórðarson, Matthias, *The Althing, Iceland's Thousand-Year-Old Parliament, 930–1930.* Reykjavik, 1930
Þorsteinsson, Þorsteinn, *Iceland, 1946: A Handbook Published on the 60th Anniversary of the National Bank of Iceland.* 4th ed. Reykjavik, 1946
Zoëga, G. T., *Íslensk-ensk (and Ensk-íslensk) orðabók.* 3rd ed. 2 vols. Reykjavík, 1932–51

National Library: Landsbókasafnið, Reykjavík, *Librarian:* Dr Finnbogi Guðomundsson.

INDIA

Bharat

Capital: New Delhi
Population: 684m. (1981)
GDP per capita: US$240 (1980)

HISTORY. The Indus civilization was fully developed by *c.* 2500 B.C., and collapsed *c.* 1750 B.C. An Aryan civilization spread from the west as far as the Ganges valley by 500 B.C.; separate kingdoms were established and many of these were united under the Mauryan dynasty established by Chandragupta in *c.* 320 B.C. The Mauryan Empire was succeeded by numerous small kingdoms. The Gupta dynasty (A.D. 320–600) was followed by the first Arabic invasions of the north-west. Moslem, Hindu and Buddhist states developed together with frequent conflict until the establishment of the Mogul dynasty in 1526. The first settlements by the East India Company were made after 1600 and the company established a formal system of government for Bengal in 1700. During the decline of the Moguls frequent wars between the Company, the French and the native princes led to the Company's being brought under British Government control in 1784; the first Governor-General of India was appointed in 1786. The powers of the Company were abolished by the India Act, 1858, and its functions and forces transferred to the British Crown. Representative government was introduced in 1909, and the first parliament in 1919. The separate dominions of India and Pakistan became independent within the Commonwealth in 1947 and India became a republic in 1950.

AREA AND POPULATION. India is bounded north-west by Pakistan, north by China, Tibet, Nepál and Bhután, east by Burma, south-east, south and south west by the Indian ocean. The far eastern states and territories are almost separated from the rest by Bangladesh as it extends northwards from the Bay of Bengal. The area of the Indian Union (excluding the Pakistan and China-occupied parts of Jammu and Kashmir) is 3,166,829 sq. km. Its population according to the 1981 census (preliminary figures) was 683,810,051 (excluding the occupied area of Jammu and Kashmir); this represents an increase of 24·8% since 1971. Sex ratio was 940 females per 1,000 males (929 in 1971); density of population, 221 per sq. km. About 23·7% of the population was urban in 1981 (in Maharashtra, 35%; in Himachal Pradesh, 7·7%).

Many births and deaths go unregistered. Data from certain areas of better registration and field studies suggest that the average annual birth rate for the decade 1971–80 was about 36 per 1,000 population, the death rate 14·8 per 1,000. In 1980 (estimate) the age-group 0–14 years represented 39·7% of the population and only 5·5% were over 60. In 1981 expectation of life for men was 52 years, for women 50.

Marriages and divorces are not registered. The minimum age for a civil marriage is 18 for women and 21 for men; for a sacramental marriage, 14 for girls and 18 for youths.

The main details of the census of 1 March 1971 and of 1 March 1981 are:

Name of State	Land area in sq. km (1981)	Population 1971	1981
States			
Andhra Pradesh	276,814	43,502,708	53,403,619
Assam	78,523	14,625,152	19,902,826
Bihar	173,876	56,353,369	69,823,154
Gujarat	195,984	26,697,475	33,960,905
Haryana	44,222	10,036,808	12,850,902
Himachal Pradesh	55,673	3,460,434	4,237,569
Jammu and Kashmir[1]	101,283	4,617,000	5,981,600

[1] Excludes the Pakistan-occupied area.

610

Name of State	Land area in sq. km (1981)	Population 1971	Population 1981
Karnataka	191,773	29,299,014	37,043,451
Kerala	38,864	21,347,375	25,403,217
Madhya Pradesh	442,841	41,654,119	52,131,717
Maharashtra	307,762	50,412,235	62,693,898
Manipur	22,356	1,072,753	1,433,691
Meghalaya	22,489	1,011,699	1,327,824
Nagaland	16,527	516,449	773,281
Orissa	155,782	21,944,615	26,272,054
Punjab	50,362	13,551,060	16,669,755
Rajasthan	342,214	25,765,806	34,102,912
Sikkim	7,299	...	315,682
Tamil Nadu	130,069	41,199,168	48,297,456
Tripura	10,477	1,556,342	2,060,189
Uttar Pradesh	294,413	88,341,144	110,858,019
West Bengal	87,853	44,312,011	54,485,560
Union Territories			
Andaman and Nicobar Islands	8,293	115,133	188,254
Arunachal Pradesh	83,578	467,511	628,050
Chandigarh	114	257,251	450,061
Dadra and Nagar Haveli	491	74,170	103,677
Delhi	1,485	4,065,698	6,196,414
Goa, Daman and Diu	3,813	857,771	1,082,117
Lakshadweep	32	31,810	40,237
Mizoram	21,087	332,390	487,774
Pondicherry	480	471,707	604,136
Grand total	3,166,829	547,949,809	683,810,051

Greatest density occurs in Delhi (4,178 per sq. km), Chandigarh (3,948), Lakshadweep (1,257) and Pondicherry (1,228). The lowest occurs in Arunachal Pradesh (7).

There were (1981) 353,347,249 males and 330,462,802 females.

In 1981, 502m. were rural (c. 76%) and 156m. were urban.

Cities and Urban Agglomerations (with states in brackets) having more than 250,000 population at the 1981 census were (1,000):

Agra (U.P.)	770	Erode (T.N.)	275	Patna (Bih.)	916
Ahmedabad (Guj.)	2,515	Faridabad		Pondicherry	251
Ajmer (Raj.)	374	agglomeration	327	Pune (Mah.)	1,685
Aligarh (U.P.)	320	Ghaziabad (U.P.)	292	Raipur (M.P.)	339
Allahabad (U.P.)	642	Gorakhpur (U.P.)	306	Rajahmundry	
Amravati (Mah.)	261	Guntur (A.P.)	367	(A.P.)	268
Amritsar (Pun.)	589	Gwalior (M.P.)	560	Rajkot (Guj.)	444
Asansol (W.B.)	365	Hubli-Dharwar (Kar.)	526	Ranchi (Bih.)	501
Aurangabad		Hyderabad (A.P.)	2,528	Rourkela (Ori.)	321
(Mah.)	316	Indore (M.P.)	827	Saharanpur (U.P.)	294
Bangalore (Kar.)	2,914	Jabalpur (M.P.)	758	Salem (T.N.)	515
Bareilly (U.P.)	438	Jaipur (Raj.)	1,005	Sangli (Mah.)	269
Belgaum (Kar.)	300	Jalandhar (Pun.)	406	Sholapur (Mah.)	514
Bhavnagar (Guj.)	308	Jamnagar (Guj.)	317	Srinagar (J. & K.)	520[1]
Bhopal (M.P.)	672	Jamshedpur (Bih.)	670	Surat (Guj.)	913
Bikaner (Raj.)	280	Jhansi (U.P.)	281	Thana (Mah.)	389
Bokaro Steel City		Jodhpur (Raj.)	494	Tiruchirapalli	
(Bih.)	261	Kanpur (U.P.)	1,688	(T.N.)	608
Bombay (Mah.)	8,227	Kolhapur (Mah.)	351	Tirunelveli (T.N.)	324
Calcutta (W.B.)	9,166	Kotah (Raj.)	347	Trivandrum (Ker.)	520
Calicut (Ker.)	546	Lucknow (U.P.)	1,007	Tuticorin (T.N.)	251
Chandigarh (Ch.)	421	Ludhiana (Pun.)	606	Ujjain (M.P.)	282
Cochin (Ker.)	686	Madras (T.N.)	4,277	Ulhasnagar (Mah.)	648
Coimbatore (T.N.)	917	Madurai (T.N.)	904	Vadodara (Guj.)	744
Cuttack (Ori.)	326	Mangalore (Kar.)	306	Varanasi (U.P.)	794
Dehra Dun (U.P.)	294	Meerut (U.P.)	538	Vijayawada (A.P.)	545
Delhi	5,714	Moradabad (U.P.)	348	Visakhapatnam	
Dhanbad (Bih.)	677	Mysore (Kar.)	476	(A.P.)	594
Durgapur (W.B.)	306	Nagpur (Mah.)	1,298	Warangal (A.P.)	336
Durg-Bhilainagar (M.P.)	490	Nasik (Mah.)	916		

[1] Estimate.

Report of the Officials of the Government of India and the People's Republic of China on the Boundary Question. New Delhi, Ministry of External Affairs, 1961
Census of India: Reports and Papers, Decennial Series. (Government of India.)
Annual Report on the Working of Indian Migration. Government of India, from 1956
Report of the Commissioner for Scheduled Castes and Scheduled Tribes. Government of India. Annual
Public Health. Report of the Public Health Commission with the Government of India. Annual
Agarwala, S. N., *India's Population Problems.* New York, 1973

CLIMATE. India has a variety of climatic sub-divisions. In general, there are four seasons. The cool one lasts from Dec. to March, the hot season is in April and May, the rainy season is June to Sept., followed by a further dry season till Nov. Rainfall, however, varies considerably, from 4" (100 mm) in the N.W. desert to over 400" (10,000 mm) in parts of Assam.

Range of temperature and rainfall: New Delhi. Jan. 57°F (13·9°C), July 88°F (31·1°C). Annual rainfall 26" (640 mm). Bombay. Jan. 75°F (23·9°C), July 81°F (27·2°C). Annual rainfall 72" (1,809 mm). Calcutta. Jan. 67°F (19·4°C), July 84°F (28·9°C). Annual rainfall 64" (1,600 mm). Cherrapunji. Jan. 53°F (11·7°C), July 68°F (20°C). Annual rainfall 432" (10,798 mm). Cochin. Jan. 80°F (26·7°C), July 79°F (26·1°C). Annual rainfall 117" (2,929 mm). Darjeeling. Jan. 41°F (5°C), July 62°F (16·7°C). Annual rainfall 121" (3,035 mm). Hyderabad. Jan. 72°F (22·2°C), July 80°F (26·7°C). Annual rainfall 30" (752 mm). Madras. Jan. 76°F (24·4°C), July 87°F (30·6°C). Annual rainfall 51" (1,270 mm). Patna. Jan. 63°F (17·2°C), July 90°F (32·2°C). Annual rainfall 46" (1,150 mm).

CONSTITUTION AND GOVERNMENT. On 26 Jan. 1950 India became a sovereign democratic republic. India's relations with the British Commonwealth of Nations were defined at the London conference of Prime Ministers on 27 April 1949.

Unanimous agreement was reached to the effect that the Republic of India remains a full member of the Commonwealth and accepts the Queen as 'the symbol of the free association of its independent member nations and, as such, the head of the Commonwealth'. This agreement was ratified by the Constituent Assembly of India on 17 May 1949.

The constitution was passed by the Constituent Assembly on 26 Nov. 1949 and came into force on 26 Jan. 1950. It has since been amended 44 times.

India is a Union of States and comprises 22 States and 9 Union territories. Each State is administered by a Governor appointed by the President for a term of 5 years while each Union territory is administered by the President through an administrator appointed by him.

The capital is New Delhi.

Presidency. The head of the Union is the President in whom all executive power is vested, to be exercised on the advice of ministers responsible to Parliament. He is elected by an electoral college consisting of all the elected members of Parliament and of the various state legislative assemblies. He holds office for 5 years and is eligible for re-election. He must be an Indian citizen at least 35 years old and eligible for election to the Lower House. He can be removed from office by impeachment for violation of the constitution.

There is also a Vice-President who is *ex-officio* chairman of the Upper House of Parliament.

Central Legislature. The Parliament for the Union consists of the President, the Council of States *(Rajya Sabha)* and the House of the People *(Lok Sabha).* The Council of States, or the Upper House, consists of not more than 250 members; in 1980 there were 232 elected members and 12 members nominated by the President. The election to this house is indirect; the representatives of each State are elected by the elected members of the Legislative Assembly of that State. The Council of States is a permanent body not liable to dissolution, but one-third of the members retire every second year. The House of the People, or the Lower House, consists of 544 members, 525 directly elected on the basis of adult suffrage from territorial constituencies in the States, and 17 members to represent the Union territories, chosen in such manner as the Parliament may by law provide; in March 1982 there were 542 elected members and 2 members nominated by the President. The House of the People unless sooner dissolved continues for a period of 5 years from the date appointed for its first meeting; in emergency, Parliament can extend the term by 1 year.

State Legislatures. For every State there is a legislature which consists of the Governor, and *(a)* 2 Houses, a Legislative Assembly and a Legislative Council, in the States of Andhra Pradesh, Jammu and Kashmir, Karnataka, Madhya Pradesh, Maharashtra, Tamil Nadu and Uttar Pradesh, and *(b)* 1 House, a Legislative Assembly, in the other States. Every Legislative Assembly, unless sooner dissolved, continues for 5 years from the date appointed for its first meeting. In emergency the term can be extended by 1 year. Every State Legislative Council is a permanent body and is not subject to dissolution, but one-third of the members retire every year. Parliament can, however, abolish an existing Legislative Council or create a new one, if the proposal is supported by a resolution of the Legislative Assembly concerned.

Legislative Councils have one-third of the total membership of the Assemblies but not less than 40 members, of whom one-third are elected by local authorities, one-third by members of the Assembly, one-twelfth by state university graduates and one-twelfth by teachers of secondary school upwards; the rest are named by the Governor. Legislative Assemblies have between 60 and 500 directly elected members.

Legislation. The various subjects of legislation are enumerated in three lists in the seventh schedule to the constitution. List I, the Union List, consists of 97 subjects (including defence, foreign affairs, communications, currency and coinage, banking and customs) with respect to which the Union Parliament has exclusive power to make laws. The State legislature has exclusive power to make laws with respect to the 66 subjects in list II, the State List; these include police and public order, agriculture and irrigation, education, public health and local government. The powers to make laws with respect to the 47 subjects (including economic and social planning, legal questions and labour and price control) in list III, the Concurrent List, are held by both Union and State governments, though the former prevails. But Parliament may legislate with respect to any subject in the State List in circumstances when the subject assumes national importance or during emergencies.

Other provisions deal with the administrative relations between the Union and the States, interstate trade and commerce, distribution of revenues between the States and the Union, official language, etc.

Fundamental Rights. Two chapters of the constitution deal with fundamental rights and 'Directive Principles of State Policy'. 'Untouchability' is abolished, and its practice in any form is punishable. The fundamental rights can be enforced through the ordinary courts of law and through the Supreme Court of the Union. The directive principles cannot be enforced through the courts of law; they are nevertheless fundamental in the governance of the country.

Citizenship. Under the Constitution, every person who was on the 26 Jan. 1950, domiciled in India and *(a)* was born in India or *(b)* either of whose parents was born in India or *(c)* who has been ordinarily resident in the territory of India for not less than 5 years immediately preceding that date became a citizen of India. Special provision is made for migrants from Pakistan and for Indians resident abroad. Under the Citizenship Act, 1955, which supplemented the provisions of the Constitution, Indian citizenship is acquired by birth, by descent, by registration and by naturalization. The Act also provides for loss of citizenship by renunciation, termination and deprivation. The right to vote is granted to every person who is a citizen of India and who is not less than 21 years of age on a fixed date and is not otherwise disqualified.

Parliament. Parliament and the state legislatures are organized according to the following schedule (figures show distribution of seats in March 1982):

| | Parliament | | State Legislatures | |
	House of the People (Lok Sabha)	Council of States (Rajya Sabha)	Legislative Assemblies (Vidhan Sabhas)	Legislative Councils (Vidhan Parishads)
States:				
Andhra Pradesh	42	18	294	90
Assam	14	7	126	–
Bihar	54	22	324	–
Gujarat	26	11	182	–
Haryana	10	5	90	–
Himachal Pradesh	4	3	68	–
Karnataka	28	12	224	63
Kerala	20	9	140	–
Madhya Pradesh	40	16	320	90
Maharashtra	48	19	288	78
Manipur	2	1	60	–
Meghalaya	2	1	60	–
Nagaland	1	1	60	–
Orissa	21	10	147	–
Punjab	13	7	117	–
Rajasthan	25	10	200	–
Sikkim	1	1	32	–
Tamil Nadu	39	18	234	63
Tripura	2	1	60	–
Uttar Pradesh	85	34	425	108
West Bengal	42	16	294	–
Jammu and Kashmir	6	4	76[2]	36[4]
Union Territories:				
Andaman and Nicobar Islands	1	–	–	–
Arunachal Pradesh	2	1[3]	30	–
Chandigarh	1	–	–	–
Dadra and Nagar Haveli	1	–	–	–
Delhi	7	3	61	–
Goa, Daman and Diu	2	–	30	–
Lakshadweep	1	–	–	–
Mizoram	1	1	30	–
Pondicherry	1	1	30	–
Nominated by the President under Article 80 (1) (a) of the Constitution	–	12	–	–
Total	544[1]	244	4,034	528

[1] Includes 2 nominated members to represent Anglo-Indians.
[2] Excludes 25 seats for Pakistan-occupied areas of the State which are in abeyance.
[3] Nominated by the President.   [4] Excludes seats for the Pakistan-occupied areas.

The number of seats allotted to scheduled castes and scheduled tribes in the House of the People is 77 and 42 respectively. Out of the 3,864 seats allotted to the Legislative Assemblies, 521 are reserved for scheduled castes and 329 for scheduled tribes.

Following the general election of Jan. 1980 the composition of the House of the People was: Indira Congress 352, Janata 31, Lok Dal 41, Communist Party (Marxist) 36, Dravida Munnetra Kazhagam 16, Congress 13, Communist Party of India 11; others 17; vacant, 16.

The Council of States (July 1980) was composed as follows: Indira Congress 121, Congress 21, Janata 17, Bhartiya Janata 14, Lok Dal 14, CPI (Marxist) 9, CPI 7, All-India Anna DMK 6, DMK 6, Akali Dal 3, National Conference 2, Muslim League 1, Kerala Congress 1, Forward Bloc 1, NNDP 1, RSP 1, RPI (Khobragade) 1, Socialist 1, Independent 6, Nominated 8, Vacant 3.

On 2 Jan. 1978 the Congress Party split into two: Congress and Indira Congress.

National flag: Three horizontal stripes of saffron (orange), white and green, with the wheel of Asoka in the centre in blue.
National anthem: Jana-gana-mana (words by Rabindranath Tagore).

Indian Independence Act, 1947. (Ch. 30.) London, 1947
The Constitution of India (Modified up to 15 April 1967). Delhi, 1967
Appadorai, A., *Indian Political Thinking in the Twentieth Century: From Naoroji to Nehru.*
  OUP, 1971.—*Documents on Political Thought in Modern India.* OUP, 1974
Austin, G., *The Indian Constitution.* OUP, 1972
Gandhi, I., *The Speeches and Reminiscences of Indira Gandhi.* London, 1975
Mansergh, N., ed. *The Transfer of Power 1942–47.* 5 vols. HMSO, 1970–75
Menon, V. P., *Transfer of Power in India.* Bombay, 1957
Pylee, M. V., *Constitutional Government in India.* 2nd ed. Bombay, 1965
Rao, K. V., *Parliamentary Democracy of India.* 2nd ed. Calcutta, 1965
Seervali, H. M., *Constitutional Law of India.* Bombay, 1967

Language. The Constitution provides that the official language of the Union shall be Hindi in the Devanagari script. It was originally provided that English should continue to be used for all official purposes until 1965. But the Official Languages Act 1963 provides that, after the expiry of this period of 15 years from the coming into force of the Constitution, English might continue to be used, in addition to Hindi, for all official purposes of the Union for which it was being used immediately before that day, and for the transaction of business in Parliament. According to the Official Languages (Use for official purposes of the Union) Rules 1976, an employee may record in Hindi or in English without being required to furnish a translation thereof in the other language and no employee possessing a working knowledge of Hindi may ask for an English translation of any document in Hindi except in the case of legal or technical documents.

The following 15 languages are included in the Eighth Schedule to the Constitution: Assamese, Bengali, Gujarati, Hindi, Kannada, Kashmiri, Malayalam, Marathi, Oriya, Punjabi, Sanskrit, Sindhi, Tamil, Telugu, Urdu.

There are numerous mother tongues grouped under each language. Hindi, Bengali, Telugu and Marathi languages (including mother tongues grouped under each) are spoken by 162·6m., 44.8m., 44·8m. and 42·3m. of the population respectively.

Ferozsons English–Urdu, Urdu–English Dictionary. 2 vols. 4th ed. Lahore, 1961
Fallon, S. W., *A New English–Hindustani Dictionary.* Lahore, 1941
Grierson, Sir G. A., *Linguistic Survey of India.* 11 vols. (in 19 parts). Delhi, 1903-28
Mitra, S. C., *Student's Bengali–English Dictionary.* 2nd ed. Calcutta, 1923
Scholberg, H. C., *Concise Grammar of the Hindi Language.* 3rd ed. London, 1955
University of Madras, *Tamil Lexicon.* 7 vols. Madras, 1924-39
Vyas, V. G., and Patel, S. G., *Standard English–Gujarati Dictionary.* 2 vols. Bombay, 1923

Government. *President of the Republic:* Zail Singh (sworn in July 1982).
Vice-President: Mohammad Hidayatullah.

There is a Council of Ministers to aid and advise the President of the Republic in the exercise of his functions; this comprises Ministers who are members of the Cabinet, Ministers of State who are not members of the Cabinet and Deputy Ministers. A Minister who for any period of 6 consecutive months is not a member of either House of Parliament ceases to be a Minister at the expiration of that period. The Prime Minister is appointed by the President; other Ministers are appointed by the President on the Prime Minister's advice.

The salary of each Minister is Rs 27,000 per annum, and that of each Deputy Minister is Rs 21,000 per annum. Each Minister is entitled to the free use of a furnished residence throughout his term of office. At the administrative head of each Ministry is a Secretary of the Government.

Following was the composition of the Cabinet in March 1983:

Prime Minister: Indira Gandhi.
Defence: R. Venkataraman.
Finance: P. Mukherjee
Home Affairs: P. C. Sethi
Industry, Steel and Mines: N. D. Tiwari
Agriculture and Rural Reconstruction: R. B. Singh.
Law and Justice, Company Affairs: J. Kaushal.
Health and Family Welfare: B. Shankaranand.

External Affairs: P. V. Narasimha Rao.
Parliamentary Affairs, Sports, Works and Housing: B. Narain Singh.
Energy, Petroleum and Coal: P. S. Shankar.
Shipping and Transport: V. B. Reddy.
Planning: S. B. Chavan.
Irrigation: K. Pandey.
Railways: A. B. A. Ghani Khan Chaudhury.
Chemicals and Fertilizers: V. Sathe.
Labour and Rehabilitation: V. Patil.
Commerce: V. P. Singh.

Local Government. There were in 1980, 40 municipal corporations, 1,274 municipalities, 815 town area and notified area committees and 62 cantonment boards. The municipal bodies have the care of the roads, water supply, drainage, sanitation, medical relief, vaccination and education. Their main sources of revenue are taxes on the annual rental value of land and buildings, octroi and terminal, vehicle and other taxes. The municipal councils enact their own bye-laws and frame their budgets, which in the case of municipal bodies other than corporations generally require the sanction of the State government. All municipal councils are elected on the principle of adult franchise.

For rural areas there is a 3-tier system of *panchayati raj* at village, block and district level, although the 3-tier structure may undergo some changes in State legislation to suit local conditions. All *panchayati raj* bodies are organically linked, and representation is given to special interests. Elected directly by and from among villagers, the *panchayats* are responsible for agricultural production, rural industries, medical relief, maternity and child welfare, common grazing grounds, village roads, tanks and wells, and maintenance of sanitation. In some places they also look after primary education, maintenance of village records and collection of land revenue. They have their own powers of taxation. There are some judicial *panchayats* or village courts.

Panchayati raj now cover all the States with the exception of Nagaland and Meghalaya, although Nagaland has area, range and tribal councils. They exist in all the Union Territories except Mizoram and Lakshadweep. In Pondicherry they have been created by declaring existing Municipal Communes to be Commune Panchayat Councils; this is a transition arrangement. In Arunachal Pradesh and Chandigarh the 3-tier system of *panchayati raj* has been introduced. With most of the country covered by *panchayati raj*, the emphasis now is on consolidation and clarifying their role in rural development.

The powers and responsibilities of *panchayati raj* institutions are derived not only from State Legislatures, but also from the executive orders of State governments.

NAGARLOK (Municipal Affairs Quarterly). Quarterly. Institute of Public Administration. Delhi
Proceedings of the 13th Meeting of the Central Council of Local Self Government. Delhi, 1970
Report of the Committee on Budgetary Reforms in Municipal Administration. Delhi, 1974
State Machinery for Municipal Supervision. Institute of Public Administration. Delhi, 1970
Statistical Abstract of India. Annual. Delhi.

DEFENCE. The Supreme Command of the Armed Forces vests in the President of the Indian Republic. Policy is decided at different levels by a number of committees, including the Political Affairs Committee presided over by the Prime Minister and the Defence Minister's Committee. Administrative and operational control rests in the respective Service Headquarters, under the control of the Ministry of Defence.

The Ministry of Defence is the central agency for formulating defence policy and for co-ordinating the work of the three services. Among the organizations directly administered by the Ministry are the Research and Development Organization, the Production Organization, the National Defence College, the National Cadet Corps and the Directorate-General of Armed Forces Medical Services.

The Research and Development Organization (headed by the Scientific Adviser to the Minister) has under it about 30 research establishments. The Production Organization controls 8 public-sector undertakings and 28 ordnance and 2 departmental factories.

The National Defence College, New Delhi, was established in 1960 on the pattern of the Imperial Defence College (UK): the 1-year course is for officers of the rank of brigadier or equivalent and for senior civil servants. The Defence Services Staff College, Wellington, trains officers of the three Services for higher command for staff appointments. There is an Armed Forces Medical College at Pune.

The National Defence Academy, Khadakvasla, gives a 3-year basic training course to officer cadets of the three Services prior to advanced training at the respective Service establishments.

Army. The Army Headquarters functioning directly under the Chief of the Army Staff is divided into the following main branches: General Staff Branch; Adjutant General's Branch; Quartermaster-General's Branch; Master-General of Ordnance Branch; Engineer-in-Chief's Branch; Military Secretary's Branch.

The Army is organized into 4 commands—eastern, central, western and southern—each divided into areas, which in turn are subdivided into sub-areas.

Recruitment of permanent commissioned officers is through the Indian Military Academy, Dehra Dun. It conducts courses for ex-National Defence Academy, National Cadet Corps and direct-entry cadets, and for serving personnel and technical graduates.

The Territorial Army came into being in Sept. 1949, its role being to: (1) relieve the regular Army of static duties and, if required, support civil power; (2) provide anti-aircraft units, and (3) if and when called upon, provide units for the regular Army. The Territorial Army is composed of practically all arms of the Services.

The authorized strength of the Army is 944,000, that of the Territorial Army, 40,000. There are 2 armoured, 17 infantry and 10 mountain divisions, 5 independent armoured brigades, 1 independent infantry, 14 independent artillery brigades, 1 commando and 2 parachute brigades.

Navy. Since 26 Jan. 1950 the former Royal Indian Navy, which traced its history in an unbroken line from the foundation in 1613 of the East India Company's Marine, has been known as 'Indian Navy', and the ships referred to as 'INS' instead of 'HMIS'. There are 3 commands: Eastern, Western and Southern.

Principal ships of the Indian Navy:

Com-pleted	Name	Standard displace-ment Tons	Armour Belts in.	Turrets in.	Principal armament	Shaft horse-power	Speed Knots
		Aircraft Carrier					
1961	Vikrant (ex-Hercules)	16,000	–	–	7 40 mm. AA (22 aircraft)	40,000	24·5
		Cruisers [1]					
1940	Mysore (ex-Nigeria)	8,700	3-4½	2	9 6-in.; 8 4-in.	72,500	31·5

[1] The cruiser *Delhi* (ex-*Achilles*) completed in 1933, was scrapped in 1979.

The fleet also includes 8 ex-Soviet submarines, 3 new Soviet-built guided missile armed destroyers, 2 new 'stretched', or improved 'Leander' type missile frigates and 6 broad-beamed 'Leander' class general purpose frigates (all eight built in India), 2 anti-submarine frigates and 3 anti-aircraft frigates (all five built in Great Britain), 1 old ex-British frigate, 12 Soviet-built escorts, 3 ex-Soviet corvettes, 6 ex-Soviet ocean minesweepers, 4 ex-British coastal minesweepers, 4 inshore minesweepers 16 missile boats, 4 patrol craft, 7 landing ships, 4 landing craft, 6 survey ships, 1 repair ship, 1 submarine parent ship, 1 submarine rescue ship, 7 oilers, 20 service craft and 3 tugs.

New construction projected includes 2 Federal German-built patrol submarines. Two indigenously built similar submarines, 3 more frigates and 4 corvettes are envisaged. Plans are reported for the purchase of a second carrier or a sea control ship.

The major training establishments of the Navy include INS *Venduruthy* at Cochin (Basic and Divisional, Gunnery, Torpedo and Anti-Submarine, Navigation and Direction, Communication), INS *Vaisura* at Jamnagar (Electrical), INS *Shivaji* at Lonavla (Engineering), INS *Hansa* at Goa (Aviation), INS *Hamla* at Bombay (Supply and Secretariat) and INS *Satyavahana* (Submarine) and INS *Circars* (Boys') at Vishakhapatnam.

The Fleet Requirement Unit of the Naval Aviation Station, INAS *Garuda*, is at Cochin. Over 110 aircraft include Sea Harriers, Sea Hawk fighters, Alize anti-submarine aircraft and Sea King anti-submarine helicopters acquired for the aircraft carrier.

Naval personnel in 1984 comprised 47,000 officers and ratings, including the Naval Air Arm.

The Coast Guard was constituted as an independent para-military service by 1978 Act of Parliament. It comprised the frigates *Kirpan* and *Kuthar* and five patrol craft all transferred from the Indian Navy and 2 larger patrol vessels custombuilt. It has recently been augmented by new specifically built ships and aircraft, including three 1,040-ton offshore patrol vessels, three 205-ton inshore protection craft, 5 *ex*-Soviet cutters, 6 South Korean-built launches and 5 Defender aircraft. It is administered by a Director-General (Vice-Admiral) and a Deputy Director-General (Commodore). It functions under the Defence Ministry but is funded by the Revenue Department.

Air Force. The Indian Air Force Act was passed in 1932, and the first flight was formed in 1933.

The Air Headquarters, under the Chief of Air Staff, consists of 4 main branches, viz., Air Staff, Administration, Policy and Plans, and Maintenance. Units of the IAF are organized into 4 operational commands–Western at Delhi, Central at Allahabad, Eastern at Shillong and South-Western at Jodhpur. Training Command HQ is at Bangalore, Maintenance Command at Nagpur. Nominal strength in 1983 was more than 100,000 personnel and 1,400 aircraft of all types, in 45 squadrons of fixed-wing aircraft, 14 helicopter squadrons and about 30 squadrons of 'Guideline' and 'Goa' surface-to-air missiles, and close-range missiles such as 'Gainful' and Tigercat.

Air defence units include 2 squadrons of MiG-23 variable-geometry interceptors, and 19 squadrons of MiG-21s. Initial delivery of MiG-21s from the Soviet Union was followed by large-scale licence production in India. There are 2 squadrons of Sukhoi Su-7s, 1 of Indian-designed Maruts, 3 of Ajeet (Gust Mk 2) fighters, 3 of Canberras, 2 of Jaguars, 2 of Hunter F56s, 3 of MiG-23 supersonic fighter-bombers and one of MiG-25 reconnaissance aircraft plus a MiG-25U two seat trainer. Canberra and Hunter squadrons are being re-equipped with at least 76 Jaguars, assembled in India, to create a force of 5 Jaguar squadrons. Some of those flying MiG-21s and SU-7s will re-equip with MiG-27s licence-built in India; also on order are 40 Mirage 2000s from France.

The large transport force includes An-12s, jet-boosted C-119Gs, C-47s, HS 748s, Caribou, 2 Boeing 737s, and smaller aircraft and helicopters for VIP and other duties. Replacement of the C-119Gs and Caribou with An-32s is under way. C-47s, Otters and Devons will be replaced with Dornier 228s. Helicopter units have Mi-8s (6 squadrons), Chetaks (Aero spatiale Alouette IIIs) and licence-built Cheetahs (Aerospatiale Lamas); main training types are the Hindustan HT-2 and Kiran, Polish built TS-11 Iskra, Hunter T.66 (to be replaced with 2-seat Ajeets), MiG-21UT1, MiG-23U and Su-7U. Replacement of the HT-2s with HPT-32s is expected to begin in 1985-86.

Primary flying training is provided at the Elementary Flying School, Bidar, and advanced flying training at the Air Force Academy, Dundigal, Hyderabad. There is a Navigation and Signals School at Begumpet. The IAF Technical College, Jalahalli, imparts technical training, while the IAF Administrative College, Coimbatore, trains officers of the ground duty branch. There are also land-air warfare, flying instructors' and medical schools.

INTERNATIONAL RELATIONS

Membership. India is a member of the UN, the Commonwealth and the Colombo Plan.

External Debt. At the end of Dec. 1982 India's external public debt was Rs 205,330m.

Treaties. India pursues a general policy of non-alignment; the exception is a Treaty of Peace, Friendship and Cooperation with the USSR, 1971; the parties agreed to mutual support short of force in the event of either being attacked by a third party.

ECONOMY

Planning. The sixth plan (1980–85) envisages total investment of Rs 1,587,100m., of which Rs 975,000m. is for the public sector. The amount of this financed from abroad would be Rs 90,630m. The aim is an annual 5·2% growth rate and the prime objective is to alleviate rural poverty. Intended investment in energy, Rs 265,350m.; in social services, Rs 140,350m.; transport and industry both get Rs 124,110m.

Ministry of Agriculture. *Serving the Small Farmer. Policy Choices in Indian Agricultural Development.* 1975
Dutt, A. K. (ed.), *India: Resources, Potentialities and Planning.* Rev. ed. Dubuque, India, 1973
Singh, T., *India's Development Experience.* London, 1975

Budget. Revenue and expenditure (on revenue account) of the central government[1] for years ending 31 March, in crores of rupees:

	1981–82	1982–83[2]	1983–84[3]
Revenue	15,373	18,117	20,625
Expenditure	15,948	19,415	22,419

[1] Excluding states' share of excise duties and other taxes.
[2] Revised.   [3] Budget estimates.

Important items of revenue and expenditure on the revenue account of the central government for 1982-83 (estimates), in Rs 1m.:

Revenue		Expenditure	
Net tax revenue	133,680	General Services	56,060
Non-tax revenue	42,330	Defence	45,990
		Grants in aid to States, etc.	33,640

Total capital account receipts (1983–84), Rs 126,560m.; capital account disbursements, Rs 124,170m. Total (revenue and capital) receipts, Rs 332,810m.; disbursements, Rs 348,360m.

Under the Constitution (Part XII and 7th Schedule), the power to raise funds has been divided between the central government and the states. Generally, the sources of revenue are mutually exclusive. Certain taxes are levied by the Union for the sake of uniformity and distributed to the states. The Finance Commission (Art. 280 of the Constitution) advises the President on the distribution of the taxes which are distributable between the centre and the states, and on the principles on which grants should be made out of Union revenues to the states. The main sources of central revenue are: customs duties; those excise duties levied by the central government; corporation, income and wealth taxes; estate and succession duties on non-agricultural assets and property, and revenues from the railways and posts and telegraphs. The main heads of revenue in the states are: taxes and duties levied by the state governments (including land revenues and agricultural income tax); civil administration and civil works; state undertakings; taxes shared with the centre; and grants received from the centre.

Currency. A decimal system of coinage was introduced in 1957. The Indian *rupee* is divided into 100 *paise* (until 1964 officially described as *naye paise*), the decimal coins being 1, 2, 3, 5, 10, 20, 25 and 50 *paise*.

The rupee is valued in relation to a package of main currencies. The £ is the currency of intervention. In March 1984 Rs 15.88 = £1; Rs 10.68 = US$1.

The paper currency consists of: (1) Reserve Bank notes in denominations of Rs 2, 5, 10, 20, 50 and 100; and (2) Government of India currency notes of denominations of Re 1 deemed to be included in the expression 'rupee coin' for the purposes of the Reserve Bank of India Act, 1934.

According to the Reserve Bank of India, the total money supply with the public on the last Friday of June 1982 was Rs 26,423 crores.

100,000 rupees are called 1 lakh; 100 lakhs are called 1 crore.

Banking. The Reserve Bank, the central bank for India, was established in 1934 and started functioning on 1 April 1935 as a shareholder's bank; it became a nationalized institution on 1 Jan. 1949. It has the sole right of issuing currency-notes. The Bank acts as adviser to the Government on financial problems and is the banker for central and state governments, commercial banks and some other financial institutions. The Bank manages the rupee public debt of central and state governments. It is the custodian of the country's exchange reserve and supervises repatriation of export proceeds and payments for imports. The Bank gives short-term loans to state governments and scheduled banks and short and medium-term loans to state co-operative banks and industrial finance institutions. The Bank has extensive powers of regulation of the banking system, directly under the Banking Regulation Act, 1949, and indirectly by the use of variations in Bank rate, variation in reserve ratios, selective credit controls and open market operations. Bank rate was raised to 10% in July 1981. The statutory cash reserves were at 7% of net demand and time liabilities on 11 June 1982.

The statutory liquidity ratio was 35% in Oct. 1981. Except refinance for food credit and export credit, the Reserve Bank's refinance facility to commercial banks has been placed on a discretionary basis. The net profit of the Reserve Bank of India for the year ended June 1982, after making the usual or necessary provisions, amounted to Rs 210 crores.

The commercial banking system consisted of 201 scheduled banks (*i.e.*, banks which are included in the 2nd schedule to the Reserve Bank Act) and 4 non-scheduled banks on 30 June 1982; scheduled banks included 121 Regional Rural Banks. Total deposits in commercial banks, June 1982, stood at Rs 45,831 crores. The business of non-scheduled banks forms less than 0.1% of commercial bank business. Of the 201 scheduled banks, 18 are foreign banks which specialize in financing foreign trade but also compete for domestic business. The largest scheduled bank is the State Bank of India, constituted by nationalizing the Imperial Bank of India in 1955. The State Bank acts as the agent of the Reserve Bank and the subsidiaries of the State Bank act as the agents of the State Bank for transacting government business as well as undertaking commercial functions. Fourteen banks with aggregate deposits of not less than Rs 50 crores were nationalized on 19 July 1969. Six banks were nationalized in April 1980. The 28 public sector banks (which comprise the State Bank of India and its seven associate banks and 20 nationalised banks) account for over 90% of deposits and bank credit of all scheduled commercial banks.

Reserve Bank of India: Report on Currency and Finance.—Report on the Trend and Progress of Banking in India.—Report of the Central Board of Directors. Annual. Bombay

Weights and Measures. Uniform standards of weights and measures, based on the metric system, were established for the first time by the Standards of Weights and Measures Act, 1956, which provided for a transition period of 10 years. So far the system has been fully adopted in trade transactions but there are a few fields such as engineering, survey and land records and the building and construction industry where it has not; efforts are being made to complete the change as early as possible.

In order to align this legislation with the latest international trends an expert committee (Weights and Measures (Law Revision) Committee) was set up by the central government to suggest a revised Bill which was passed by Parliament in April 1976. The new Standards of Weights and Measures Act, 1976, has recognized the International System of Units and other units recommended by the General Conference on Weights and Measures and is in line with the recommendations of the International Organisation of Legal Metrology (OIML). The new Act also covers the system of numeration, the approval of models of weights and measures, regulation and control of inter-state trade in relation to weights and measures. The Act also protects consumers through proper indication of weight, quantity, identity, source, date and price on packaged goods. A draft Standards of Weights and Measures (Enforcement) Bill has also been prepared by the committee for adoption either by Parliament or State legislatures, as enforcement is now in the 'concurrent' list of legislation.

The provisions of the 1976 Act came into force in Sept. 1977, as did the accompanying Standards of Weights and Measures (Packaged Commodities) Rules, 1977.

While the Standards of Weights and Measures are laid down in the Central Act, enforcement of weights and measures laws is entrusted to the state governments; the central Directorate of Weights and Measures is responsible for co-ordinating activities so as to ensure national uniformity.

An Indian Institute of Legal Metrology trains officials of the Weights and Measures departments of India and different developing countries. The Institute is being modernized with technical assistance from the Federal Republic of Germany.

There are 2 Regional Reference Standards laboratories at Ahmedabad and Bhubaneswar which (besides calibrating secondary standards of physical measurements) also provide testing facilities in metrological and industrial measurements. These laboratories are equipped with Standards next in line to the National Standards of physical measurements which are maintained at the National Physical Laboratory in New Delhi.

For weights previously in legal use under the Standards of Weight Act, 1956, *see* THE STATESMAN'S YEAR-BOOK, 1961, p. 171.

Calendar. The dates of the Saka era (named after the north Indian dynasty of the first century A.D.) are being used alongside Gregorian dates in issues of the *Gazette of India*, news broadcasts by All-India Radio and government-issued calendars, from 22 March 1957, a date which corresponds with the first day of the year 1879 in the Saka era.

ENERGY AND NATURAL RESOURCES

Electricity. In March 1983 about 55% of all villages had electricity. Total installed capacity (1981, provisional) was 33m. kw. Production of electricity in 1981–82 was 122,000m. kwh., of which 72,400m. kwh. came from thermal and nuclear stations and 49,600m. kwh from hydro-electric stations.

Oil and Gas. The Oil and Natural Gas Commission, Oil India Ltd and the Assam Oil Co. are the only producers of crude oil. Total production, 1983, about 26m. tonnes; consumption, about 35m. tonnes. The main fields are in Assam and offshore in the Gulf of Cambay (the Bombay High field). Natural gas production, 1981–82, 1,655m. cu. metres.

Water. The net area of 57m. hectares (1982) under irrigation exceeds that of any other country except China, and equals about 38% of the total area under cultivation. Irrigation projects have formed an important part of all three Five-Year Plans. The possibilities of diverting rivers into canals being nearly exhausted, the emphasis is now on damming the monsoon surplus flow and diverting that. Usable surface and groundwater resources were assessed (1972) at 870,000m. cu. metres. Utilization (1974) 337,000m. cu. metres. Irrigation plant in operation in 1976 could make use of 67m. hectare-metres of surface water and 26·5m. hectare-metres of ground water. Ultimate potential of irrigation is assessed at 107m. hectares, total cultivated land being 142m. hectares. In 1977 India and Bangladesh reached an agreement to share the water of the Ganges at the Farakka barrage: India needs this supply to supplement the Hooghly River in flushing silt from Calcutta port. A further agreement (1982) also includes the waters of the Brahmaputra.

Minerals. Bihar, West Bengal and Madhya Pradesh produce 42%, 25% and 19% of all coal, respectively. The coal industry was nationalized in 1973; planned state investment during sixth five-year plan (1980-85), Rs 2,573 crores. Production, 1981–82, 125m. tonnes; reserves (including lignite) are estimated at 114,000m. tonnes. (Coal in seams at least 1·2 metres thick and down to a depth of 600 metres, 86,428m. tonnes; lignite, 2,100m. tonnes). Sixth-plan investment in the Neyveli

Lignite Corporation, Rs 647 crores. Production of other minerals, 1982 (in 1,000 tonnes): Iron ore, 40,824; bauxite, 1,860; chromite 336; copper ore, 2,016; manganese ore, 1,452; gold, 2,204 kg. Other important minerals are lead, zinc, limestone, apatite and phosphorite, dolomite, magnesite and silver. Value of mineral production, 1982 (provisional), Rs 53,912m. of which mineral fuels produced Rs 48,140m., metallic minerals Rs 2,671m. and non-metallic Rs 3,102m.

Agriculture. The chief industry of India has always been agriculture. About 70% of the people are dependent on the land for their living. In 1981-82 it provided 35·4% of GDP; growth rate, 1981–82, 5·5%.

Agricultural commodities account for about 26% by value of Indian exports, while agricultural commodities, machinery and fertilizers account for about 20% of imports. Tea accounted for about 19% of agricultural exports in 1982–83; exports have since been limited.

An increase in food production of at least 2% per annum is necessary to keep pace with the rising population. Foodgrain production, 78·4m. tons in 1962–63, was 133m. tonnes in 1981–82.

The Indian Council of Agricultural Research works through 37 institutes and research centres, and 70 national research projects. It supports the establishment of at least 1 agricultural university in each of the states.

The farming year runs from July to June through three crop seasons: kharif (monsoon); rabi (winter) and summer.

Agricultural production, 1981-82 (in 1,000 tonnes): rice, 53,593; wheat, 37,833; total foodgrains, 133,061; coffee, of which the main cash varieties are Arabica and Robusta (main growing areas Karnataka, Kerala and Tamil Nadu), 150; sugarcane 183,647; cotton, 7·8m. bales (of 170 kg); jute is grown in West Bengal (half total yield), Bihar and Assam, total yield, 6·8m. bales; oilseeds, 12,073; maize, 6,761; pulses, 11,351; milk, 33,000.

The tea industry is important, with production concentrated in Assam, West Bengal, Tamil Nadu, Kerala and Karnataka. Total crop in 1981–82, about 556,000 tonnes from 370,000 hectares.

Livestock (1982). Cattle, 182m.; sheep, 42m.; pigs, 10·5m.; horses, 750,000; asses, 1m.; goats, 72m; buffaloes, 62m.

Fertilizer consumption in 1981–82 was 6·4m. tonnes.

Land Tenure. There are three main traditional systems of land tenure: *ryotwari* tenure, where the individual holders, usually peasant proprietors, are responsible for the payment of land revenues; *zamindari* tenure, where one or more persons own large estates and are responsible for payment (in this system there may be a number of intermediary holders); and *mahalwari* tenure, where village communities jointly hold an estate and are jointly and severally responsible for payment.

Agrarian reform, initiated in the first Five-Year Plan, being undertaken by the state governments includes: (1) The abolition of intermediaries under *zamindari* tenure. (2) Tenancy legislation designed to scale down rents to ¼ – ⅕ of the value of the produce, to give permanent rights to tenants (subject to the landlord's right to resume a minimum holding for his personal cultivation), and to enable tenants to acquire ownership of their holdings (subject to the landlord's right of resumption for personal cultivation) on payment of compensation over a number of years. (3) Fixing of ceilings on existing holdings and on future acquisition; the holding of a family is between 4·05 and 7·28 hectares if it has assured irrigation to produce two crops a year; 10·93 hectares for land with irrigation facilities for only one crop a year; and 21·85 hectares for all other categories of land. Tea, coffee, cocoa and cardamom plantations have been exempted. (4) The consolidation of holdings in community project areas and the prevention of fragmentation of holdings by reform of inheritance laws. (5) Promotion of farming by co-operative village management (*see* p. 624).

The average size of holding for the whole of India is 2·63 hectares. Andhra Pradesh, 2·87; Assam, 1·46; Bihar, 1·53; Gujarat, 4·49; Jammu and Kashmir, 1·43; Karnataka, 4·11; Kerala, 0·75; Madhya Pradesh, 3·99; Maharashtra, 4·65; Orissa, 1·98; Punjab, 3·85; Rajasthan, 5·5; Tamil Nadu, 1·49; Uttar Pradesh, 1·78; West Bengal, 1·56.

Of the total 71m. rural households possessing operational holdings, 34% hold on the average less than 0·20 hectare of land each.

Opium. By international agreement the poppy is cultivated under licence, and all raw opium is sold to the central government. Opium, other than for wholly medical use, is available only to registered addicts.

Fisheries. Total catch (1981–82) was 2·4m. tonnes, of which Kerala, Tamil Nadu, and Maharashtra produced about half. Of the total catch, 1,441,000 tonnes were marine fish. There were 102 commercial deep-sea fishing boats, including trawlers, operating in 1982–83 and about 20,000 small craft. Fishermen's co-operatives had 552,000 members in 1981; their total sales were worth Rs 177m.

Forestry. The lands under the control of the state forest departments are classified as 'reserved forests' (forests intended to be permanently maintained for the supply of timber, etc., or for the protection of water supply, etc.), 'protected forests' and 'unclassed' forest land.

In 1982–83 the total forest area was 75m. hectares. Main types are teak and sal. Production, 1983, 39m. tonnes. About 16% of the area is inaccessible, of which about 45% is potentially productive. Forest revenue, 1981–82 (provisional), Rs. 5,239·3m. There are about 3,000 sawmills. In 1981–82 1·3m. saplings were planted; this is considered insufficient to meet future demands for fuel and industrial wood. Fuel wood consumption, 1983, 133m. tonnes. Some states have encouraged planting small areas around villages.

INDUSTRY AND TRADE

Industries. Railways, air transport, armaments and atomic energy are government monopolies. In a number of industries (including the manufacture of iron and steel and mineral oils, shipbuilding and the mining of coal, iron and manganese ores, gypsum, gold and diamonds) new units are set up only by the state. In a further group of industries (road transport, manufacture of chemicals such as drugs, dye-stuffs, plastics and fertilizers) the state established new undertakings, but private enterprise may develop either on its own or with state backing, which may take the form of loans or purchase of equity capital. Nationalized industries employed 4m. in 1981. Under the Industries (Development and Regulation) Act, 1951, as amended, industrial undertakings are required to be licensed; 162 industries are within the scope of the Act. The Government are authorized to examine the working of any undertaking, to issue directions to it and to take over its control if this be deemed necessary. A Central Advisory Council has been set up consisting of representatives of industry, labour, consumers and primary producers. There are Development Councils for individual industries and (1981) 4 national development banks.

Foreign investment is encouraged by a tax holiday on income up to 6% of capital employed for 5 years. There are special depreciation allowances, and customs and excise concessions for export industries.

Oil refinery installed capacity, 1983, was 37·8m. tonnes; production of refined oils (1980–81), 24·1m. tonnes. The Indian Oil Corporation was established in 1964 and had (1981) most of the market.

Industry, particularly steel, has suffered from a shortage of power and coal. There is expansion in petrochemicals, based on the oil and associated gas of the Bombay High field, and gas from Bassein field. Small industries (initial outlay on capital equipment of less than Rs 2m.) are important; they employ about 7m. and produced (1980) goods worth Rs 209,000m. The industrial growth rate, 1982–83 was 4%.

Industrial production, 1981–82 (in 1,000 tonnes): Pig-iron and ferro-alloys, 9,832 (1982); steel ingots, 10,940; finished steel, 7,240; aluminium, 207; motor cycles (nos.), 315,900. commercial vehicles (nos.), 91,000; petroleum products, 28,200; sulphuric acid, 2,137; cement, 20,900; board and paper, 1,237; nitrogen fertilizer, 3,144; phosphate fertilizer, 949; jute goods, 1,337; cotton yarn, 989; cotton cloth. 7,983m. metres; man-made fibre and yarn, 242·7; diesel engines, 172,000 engines; electric motors, 4·4m. h.p.; refractories, 875 (estimate); sugar, 8,434.

Labour. At the 1981 census there were 220·1m. workers, of whom 91·4m. were cultivators, 55·4m. agricultural labourers; in 1982 there were 6·2m. in manufacturing, 8·8m. in social, community and personal services, 1·2m. in construction and 2·8m. in transport, communications and storage. There were in 1983 over 30,000 unions. The bond labour system was abolished in 1975. Man-days lost by industrial disputes, 1982, 43·37m., of which 2·33m. were in the public sector (this excludes the Bombay textile strike with 62·07m. man-days lost). An ordnance of July 1981 gave the government power to ban strikes in essential services; the ordnance was to remain in force for six months and would then be renewable.

Dasgupta, A. K., *A Theory of Wage Policy.* OUP, 1976

Companies. The total number of companies limited by shares at work in India, 31 March 1981, was 62,001; aggregate paid-up capital was Rs 14,676·5 crores. There were 9,101 public limited companies with an aggregate paid-up capital of Rs 3,952·1 crores, and 52,900 private limited companies (Rs 10,724·4 crores). There were also 176 companies with unlimited liability.

During 1980–81, 6,616 new limited companies were registered in the Indian Union under the Companies Act 1956 with a total authorized capital of Rs 968·3 crores; 594 were public limited companies (Rs 269·2 crores) and 6,022 were private limited companies (Rs 699·1 crores). There were 98 private companies with unlimited liability also registered in 1980–81, authorized capital Rs 0·27 crores. Of the new limited companies, 109 had an authorized capital of Rs 1 crore and above, and 149 of between Rs 50 lakhs and Rs 1 crore; 38 were government companies (i.e., companies in which Government owns at least 51% of share capital). During 1980–81, 167 companies with an aggregate paid-up capital of Rs 9,70 lakhs went into liquidation and 224 companies (Rs 60 lakhs) were struck off the register.

On 31 March 1981 there were 851 government companies at work with a total paid-up capital of Rs 10,853·1 crores; 352 were public limited companies and 499 were private limited companies.

On 31 March 1981, 300 companies incorporated elsewhere were reported to have a place of business in India; of these 133 were of UK and 57 of USA origin.

Department of Company Affairs, Govt. of India. *Joint Stock Companies in India.* New Delhi

Co-operative Movement. Agricultural primary credit societies (which constitute the base of the co-operative credit structure of the country) derive their funds from state co-operative banks which work with the central co-operative banks and the land development banks. The societies have been reorganised to ensure that each is big enough to be efficient. In 1981 there were about 110,000; short-term loans advanced had reached Rs 14,000m. in 1979, medium-term Rs, 1,130m. and long-term Rs 3,070m. To ensure that a fair proportion of this credit went to small farmers and labourers, Small and Marginal Farmers Development Agencies have been set up.

Following the recommendations (1954) of a committee appointed by the Reserve Bank of India, the co-operation movement was extended from its chief function of providing credit to include marketing, processing, warehousing, etc. In 1978 there were 156,817 non-credit societies including 3,592 primary marketing societies, 186 sugar factories, 848 other agricultural processing societies, 4,947 farming societies, 14,251 primary weavers' societies, 24,804 other industrial societies; there were 15,827 primary consumers' stores.

In 1978 non-credit societies marketed agricultural produce, agricultural requisites and consumer goods worth Rs 969 crores. Co-operative sugar factories crushed 29·7m. tonnes of cane and produced sugar worth Rs 6,018m.

Indian Labour Guide. Monthly. Delhi
Co-operative Movement in India, Statistical Statements Relating to. Annual. Reserve Bank of India, Bombay

Commerce. The external trade of India (excluding land-borne trade with Tibet and Bhután) was as follows (in 1,000 rupees):

	Imports		Exports and Re-exports	
	Merchandise	Treasure	Merchandise	Treasure
1975–76	5,264,77,87	7,40	4,036,25,87	4,32
1976–77	5,073,79,13	9,04	5,142,24,84	3,88
1977–78	6,020,22,62	20,03	5,407,87,19	6,07
1978–79	6,810,63,93	65,82	5,726,07,00	7,82
1979–80	9,142,58,48	29,18	6,418,43,25	6,05
1980–81	12,560,28,75	8,36	6,710,70,55	2,53

The distribution of commerce by countries and areas was as follows in the year ended 31 March 1981 (in 1,000 rupees):

Countries	Exports to	Imports from	Countries	Exports to	Imports from
Afghánistán	19,22,96	8,47,16	Japan	596,88,55	748,78,15
Argentina	5,28,28	18,02,14	Kenya	33,30,08	12,42,08
Australia	91,60,91	170,07,65	Malaysia	52,24,86	266,07,45
Belgium	144,45,49	295,86,25	Nepál	77,97,96	23,61,02
Burma	3,3 ,08	7,47,86	Netherlands	150,62,03	214,50,07
Canada	62,20,72	332,34,10	New Zealand	18,57,05	12,80,49
Czechoslovakia	55,30,35	39,00,97	Poland	68,96,52	34,40,65
Denmark	26,38,40	20,50,45	Saudi Arabia	164,87,63	540,04,85
Egypt	85,81,32	29,60,35	Singapore	108,56,91	427,88,00
Federal Rep.			Sri Lanka	80,53,22	29,55,11
of Germany	383,09,64	693,76,79	Sudan	38,62,56	1,53,01
France	146,64,47	280,30,44	Switzerland	110,52,54	120,62,64
German Dem.			USSR	1,225,71,75	1,013,70,88
Republic	48,88,84	44,26,84	UK	393,47,36	730,98,72
Hungary	15,81,37	31,37,04	USA	739,39,99	1,518,61,04
Iran	123,18,34	1,338,90,29	Yemen	26,22,23	23,91
Italy	151,54,99	242,47,65	Yugoslavia	33,90,00	44,91,01

The value (in 1,000 rupees) of the leading articles of merchandise was as follows in the year ended 31 March 1981:

Exports	Value
Fish	212,88,83
Edible nuts and fresh fruits	161,27,25
Coffee	214,23,55
Tea and mate	425,50,39
Spices	111,35,78
Oilseed, oilnuts and oil kernels	60,49,14
Tobacco	140,67,92
Hides and skins, undressed	58,47
Wood (unworked)	2,96,66
Wool and other animal hair	97,76
Cotton, raw	177,10,29
Cottonwaste; shoddy	2,08,00
Stone, sand and gravel	29,45,13
Iron ore and concentrates	303,33,08
Iron and steel scrap	87,75
Ore and concentrates, non-ferrous base metals	41,02,50
Coal, coke and briquettes	2,93,21
Fixed vegetable oils	14,69,65
Leather	277,14,72
Textile yarn and thread	50,14,14
Textile fabrics (woven) except cotton and man-made fibre	203,71,00
Cotton fabrics, woven	276,48,73
Man-made fibre fabrics, woven	31,63,72
Floor coverings, tapestries, except cotton and jute	185,82,37
Manufactures of leather or artificial leather	59,14,08

Imports	
Milk and cream	41,09,70
Wheat, spelt and meslin	76,58,70
Rice	3,69,11
Edible nuts and fresh fruit	33,57,90
Pulp and waste paper	18,30,21
Wool and other animal hair	50,79,32

Imports	Value
Cotton, raw	1,69
Jute	2,01,99
Vegetable fibres except cotton and jute	2,27,85
Crude fertilizers	79,05,59
Sulphur and unroasted iron pyrites	86,40,29
Petroleum, crude and partly refined	3,348,97,10
Petroleum products	1,914,50,10
Animal oils and fats	21,80,56
Fixed vegetable oils	682,89,72
Organic chemicals	201,78,66
Medical and pharmaceutical products	84,58,11
Manufactured fertilizers	652,29,90
Plastic materials	121,37,21
Chemical materials and products, n.e.s.	72,10,53
Paper, paperboard and manufactures	186,51,31
Pearls, precious and semiprecious stones	416,74,88
Iron and steel bars, angles, shapes, sections	148,55,95
Iron and steel universals, plates and sheets	479,86,91
Iron and steel tubes, pipes, fittings	123,54,99
Copper	128,28,40
Zinc	44,51,09
Tin	30,99,16
Machinery other than electrical	1,038,61,73
Electrical machinery	259,70,88
Transport equipment	471,94,81

Total trade between India and UK (British Department of Trade returns, in £1,000 sterling):

	1979	1980	1981	1982	1983
Imports to UK	365,843	315,858	294,323	379,169	366,928
Exports and re-exports from UK	455,606	529,007	638,867	805,321	804,779

Annual Statement of the Foreign Trade of India. 2 vols. Calcutta
Monthly Statistics of the Foreign Trade of India. Calcutta
Review of the Trade of India. Annual. Delhi
India–Handbook of Commercial Information. 3 vols. Calcutta
Guide to Official Statistics of Trade, Shipping, Customs and Excise Revenue of India. Rev. ed. Calcutta

Tourism. There were 1·3m. visitors in 1983 bringing Rs 8,250m. in foreign exchange.

COMMUNICATIONS

Roads. In 1980 there were about 1,534,000 km of roads, of which 658,000 km were metalled. Roads are divided into 5 main administrative classes, namely, national highways, state highways, major district roads, district roads and village roads. The national highways (31,358 km in 1982) connect capitals of states, major ports and foreign highways. The national highway system is linked with the ESCAP (Economic and Social Commission for Asia and the Pacific) international highway system. The state highways are the main trunk roads of the states, while the major district roads connect subsidiary areas of production and markets with distribution centres, and form the main link between headquarters and neighbouring districts.

There were (31 March 1980) about 4,106,000 motor vehicles in India, comprising 884,000 private cars and jeeps, 1,888,000 motor cycles, scooters and autorickshaws, 92,000 taxis, 133,000 buses and 436,000 goods vehicles.

Railways. The Indian railway system is government-owned and (under the control of the Railway Board) is divided into 9 zones, with route-km as follows at 31 March 1980:

Zone	Headquarters	Route-km
Central	Bombay	5,892
Eastern	Calcutta	4,202
Northern	Delhi	10,688
North Eastern	Gorakhpur	5,113
North East Frontier	Gauhati	3,627
Southern	Madras	6,330
South Central	Secunderabad	6,479
South Eastern	Calcutta	6,990
Western	Bombay	10,337

Passengers carried in 1979–80 were approximately 3,505m. Revenue-earning-goods traffic, 1982–83, 227m. tonnes.

Indian Railways pay to the central government a fixed dividend of 4·5% on capital-at-charge.

Financial years	Gross traffic receipts (Rs crores)	Working ex-penses (Rs crores)	Net revenues (Rs crores)	Net surplus or deficit (Rs crores)
1979–80	2,337·84	2,142·38	227·29	–66·24
1980–81[1]	2,707·22	2,468·61	272·09	–52·34
1981–82[2]	3,276·75	2,913·14	399·80	+49·89

[1] Revised estimate.   [2] Budget.

Aviation. The air transport industry in India was nationalized in 1953 with the formation of two Air Corporations: Air India for operating long-distance interna-tional air services, and Indian Airlines for operating air services within India and to adjacent countries. A third airline, Vayudoot, was formed in 1981 as an internal feeder airline. Air India has 10 Boeing 747s and 5 707s, and 3 Airbus A-300B4s; it operates from Bombay, Delhi, Madras, Trivandrum and Amritsar to Africa (Addis Ababa, Nairobi, Accra, Lagos, Seychelles, Mauritius, Dar es Salaam, Lusaka and Harare); to Europe (London, Birmingham, Paris, Amsterdam, Frankfurt, Geneva, Zurich, Brussels, Moscow and Rome); to western Asia (Doha, Abu Dhabi, Dharan, Dubai, Bahrain, Kuwait, Aden, Muscat, Jeddah, Ras al Khaymah, Sharjah, Bagh-dad and Sanna); to east Asia (Dakha, Bangkok, Hong Kong, Tōkyō, Osaka, Kuala Lumpur, Singapore, Perth and Sydney).

Indian Airlines has a fleet of 55 aircraft consisting of Airbus A-300B2, Boeing 737, F-27 and HS-748 aircraft (Sept. 1983). During 1982–83 they flew an average of 260 flights daily, carried 6·9m. passengers and made a net profit of about Rs.18 crores. Vagudoot serves remote areas of India with 5 aircraft; it has 4 regular routes in the north-east, 3 in the north and 1 in the west.

The Civil Aviation Department maintains and operates 87 aerodromes. The management of the 4 international airports at Bombay (Santa Cruz), Calcutta (Dum Dum), Delhi (Palam) and Madras is vested in the International Airports Authority of India.

Shipping. In March 1981, 389 ships totalling 5,740,000 GRT were on the Indian Register; of these, 58 ships of 250,000 GRT were engaged in coastal trade, and 331 ships of 5,490,000 GRT in overseas trade. Traffic of major ports, 1981–82, was as follows:

Port	Ships entered	Imports (1m. tonnes)	Exports (1m. tonnes)
Calcutta	811	5·02	2·0
Bombay	2,530	9·5	3·8
Madras	962	5·1	3·6
Cochin	671	3·1	1·1
Marmagoa	339	0·8	8·1
Vishakhapatnam	401	2·9	4·8
Kandla	427	6·5	4·9
Paradip	80	0·2	1·2
New Mangalore	186	0·5	0·7
Tuticorin	276	1·7	0·2

The shipyard at Vishakhapatnam is capable of building vessels of a maximum of 21,500 DWT. Present capacity is about 64,500 DWT per year. The Cochin Ship-yard can build Panamax type bulk carriers of 85,000 DWT each. On full develop-ment the capacity of the shipyard will be 2 such ships a year. Garden Reach Ship-builders and Engineers are building bulk carriers of 26,000 DWT, ferry ships (6,000 DWT), hydrographic research ships, tugs and fast patrol craft. There are about 14,544 km navigable inland waterways, of which 10,241 km are rivers and 4,303 km canals.

Post and Broadcasting. On 31 March 1980 there were 137,000 post offices and 28,300 telegraph offices (including (1979) 2,570 licensed offices, 23,867 combined offices and 346 DTOs). Of the post offices, 117,260 were rural and 13,728 urban in 1979.

The telephone system is in the hands of the Indian Posts and Telegraphs Department. In 1982 there were 2,981,609 telephones. There were (1979) 117 telex exchanges and 16,449 subscribers.

There were (1978) 82 radio stations and 2 auxiliary centres; on 31 Dec. 1976, 17,359,710 receiver licences were in force and programmes were sent out from 155 transmitters. A communications satellite ('APPLE') went into operation in July 1981. 'Home Service' broadcasts reach 87·75% of the population. The television service was started at Delhi, 15 Sept. 1959. There were (1974) 275,424 television receiver licences. There were 7 television centres and a relay station at Pune. Entertainment films occupy 29·3% of broadcasting time, news and current affairs, 21·3%.

Cinemas. In 1976 there were 9,017 cinemas, including about 2,660 touring cinemas: about 500 feature films were produced.

Newspapers. In Jan. 1981 the total number of newspapers and periodicals was 18,140; about 30% were published in Delhi, Bombay, Calcutta and Madras. There were 1,173 daily and 5,280 weekly papers. Circulation of dailies, 13·2m., of weeklies, 12·9m. Hindi papers have the highest number and circulation, followed by English. Circulation of dailies per 1,000 of the literate population in other languages was highest in Gujarati, followed by Malayalam, Marathi and Urdu.

Annual Report of the Register of Newspapers for India. New Delhi

JUSTICE, RELIGION, EDUCATION AND WELFARE

Justice. All courts form a single hierarchy, with the Supreme Court at the head, which constitutes the highest court of appeal. Immediately below it are the high courts and subordinate courts in each state. Every court in this chain, subject to the usual pecuniary and local limits, administers the whole law of the country, whether made by Parliament or by the state legislatures.

The states of Andhra Pradesh, Assam (in common with Nagaland, Meghalaya, Manipur and Tripura and the Union territories of Arunachal Pradesh and Mizoram), Bihar, Gujarat, Himachal Pradesh, Jammu and Kashmir, Karnataka, Kerala, Madhya Pradesh, Maharashtra, Orissa, Punjab (in common with the state of Haryana and the Union Territory of Chandigarh), Rajasthan, Tamil Nadu, Uttar Pradesh, West Bengal and Sikkim have each a High Court. The jurisdiction of Bombay High Court extends to the Territory of Goa. There is a separate High Court for Delhi. For the Andaman and Nicobar Islands the Calcutta High Court, for Pondicherry the High Court of Madras, and for Lakshadweep the High Court of Kerala are the highest judicial authorities; in Dadra and Nagar Haveli the High Court of Bombay is the relevant high court. The Allahabad High Court has a Bench at Lucknow, the Bombay High Court has a Bench at Nagpur, the Madhya Pradesh High Court has Benches at Gwalior and Indore, the Patna High Court has a Bench at Ranchi and the Rajasthan High Court has a Bench at Jaipur. Judges and Division Courts of the Gauhati High Court also sit in Meghalaya, Manipur, Nagaland and Tripura. Below the High Court each state is divided into a number of districts under the jurisdiction of district judges who preside over civil courts and courts of sessions. There are a number of judicial authorities subordinate to the district civil courts. On the criminal side magistrates of various classes act under the overall supervision of the High Court.

The Code of Criminal Procedure, 1898, has been replaced by the Code of Criminal Procedure, 1973 (2 of 1974), which came into force with effect from 1 April 1974. The new Code provides for complete separation of the Judiciary from the Executive throughout India.

Police. The states control their own police force through the state Home Ministers. The Home Minister of the central government co-ordinates the work of the states and controls the Central Detective Training School, the Central Forensic Laboratory, the Central Fingerprint Laboratory as well as the National Police Academy at Mount Abu (Rajasthan) where the Indian Police Service is trained. This service is recruited by competitive examination of university graduates and provides all senior officers for the state police forces. The Central Bureau of Investigation functions under the control of the Cabinet Secretariat.

The cities of Pune, Ahmedabad, Nagpur, Bangalore, Calcutta, Madras, Bombay and Hyderabad have separate police commissionerates.

Sarkar, P. C., *Civil Laws of India and Pakistan.* 2 vols. Calcutta, 1953.—*Criminal Laws of India and Pakistan.* 2nd ed. 2 vols. Calcutta, 1956
Setalvad, M. C., *The Common Law of India.* London, 1960
Sharma, S. R., *Supreme Court in the Indian Constitution.* Delhi, 1959

Religion. The principal religions in 1971 (census) were: Hindus, 453·2m. (82·7%); Moslems, 61·4m. (11·21%); Christians, 14·2m. (2·6%); Sikhs, 10·3m. (1·89%); Buddhists, 3·8m. (0·7%); Jains, 2·6m. (0·47%).

In 1971 the Christian population consisted of 8·2m. Roman Catholics, 2·69m. Anglicans of the Church of South India, 1·37m. Anglicans of the Church of North India and about 2m. nonconformists.

Sundkler, B., *Church of South India.* London, 1954

Education. Literacy. According to the 1981 census the literacy percentage in the country (excluding age-group, 0-4) was 36 (34·45 in 1971): 46·74% among males, 24·88% among females. Of the states and territories, Chandigarh and Kerala have the highest rates.

Educational Organization. With some exceptions, education is the concurrent responsibility of state and Union governments. In the union territories it is the responsibility of the central government. The Union Government is directly responsible for the central universities and all institutions declared by parliament to be of national importance; the promotion of Hindi as the federal language; coordinating and maintaining standards in higher education, research, science and technology. Professional education rests with the Ministry or Department concerned, e.g., medical education, the Ministry or Department of Health. The Union Minister of Education is in overall charge of the separate Departments of Education and Culture, assisted by a Minister of State. There are several autonomous organizations attached to the Department of Education. The Central Advisory Board of Education meets to recommend directions for educational policy. The University Grants Commission is a statutory body and is responsible for the funding of the central universities and some institutions deemed to be universities, besides providing developmental assistance to the state universities as well. The Commission also influences the policies and the course curricula of the universities. The National Council of Educational Research and Training provides advisory and consultancy services in respect of school education, and also produces standard school textbooks which can be used all over the country. The Union Ministry of Education is also concerned with non-formal education, youth activities, promotion of regional languages, sports, the institution of scholarships, the award of foreign scholarships, liaison with Unesco and its organizations and promoting book production.

School Education. The school system in India can be divided into four stages: primary, middle, secondary and senior secondary.

Primary education is imparted either at independent primary (or junior basic) schools or primary classes attached to middle or secondary schools. The period of instruction in this stage varies from 4 to 5 years and the medium of instruction is in most cases the mother tongue of the child or the regional language. Free primary education is available for all children. Legislation for compulsory education has been passed by 16 state governments and 3 Union Territories but it is not practicable to enforce compulsion when the reasons for non-attendance are socioeconomic.

The period for the middle stage varies from 2 to 3 years.

Under the new system, general education has been recommended up to Class X, with compulsory study of languages, sciences, mathematics and social sciences, health, physical education, fine arts and socially useful productive work.

After that there are diversified courses both academic and vocational.

Most states and territories have adopted this system.

There are, in addition, schools for professional subjects such as agriculture, commerce, fine arts, forestry, medicine, veterinary science, physical education, social service, teachers' training, technical, industrial and crafts subjects. There are also special schools for the physically and mentally handicapped and reformatory pupils. There are schools of oriental studies and adult education centres.

Higher Education. Higher education is given in arts, science or professional colleges, universities and all-India educational or research institutions. In Aug. 1982 there were 118 universities, 10 institutions of national importance and 13 institutions deemed as universities. Of the 118 universities, 7 are central: Aligarh Muslim University; Banaras Hindu University; University of Delhi; University of Hyderabad; Jawaharlal Nehru University; North Eastern Hill University; Visva Bharati. The rest are state universities. Total enrolment at universities, 1981–82, 2·95m., of which 2·59m. were undergraduates. Women students, 817,000.

Grants are paid through the University Grants Commission to the central universities and institutions deemed to be universities for their maintenance and development and to state universities for their development projects only; their maintenance is the concern of state governments. During 1981–82 the University Grants Commission sanctioned grants of Rs 93·14 crores.

Technical Education. The number of institutions awarding degrees in engineering and technology in 1979–80 was 149 (in 1947: 38), and those awarding diplomas in engineering and technology numbered 306 (in 1947: 53); the former admitted about 28,000, the latter about 47,500 students; enrolment in some has been less than capacity, following a period of unemployment in engineering. There were also 7 rural institutes and 30 Girls' Polytechnics with about 455 and 4,090 students respectively. For training high-level engineers and technologists 5 Institutes of Technology, the Indian Institute of Science, Bangalore, and 89 other institutions conduct postgraduate and research courses.

Adult Education. In spite of the improvement in the literacy rate, the number of adult illiterates over 14 was over 423m. in 1981. Adult education is, therefore, being accorded a high priority; it forms part of the Minimum Needs Programme under the sixth Five-Year Plan (1980–85), in which it is proposed to cover all illiterate persons in the age-group 15–35 by 1990. A National Board of Adult Education has been established for this purpose; effort is concentrated on backward areas, women, scheduled castes, scheduled tribes and migrant labourers. The Rural Functional Literacy Project and the programme for urban workers still operate. The Directorate of Adult Education, established in 1971, is the national resource centre responsible for producing teaching/learning materials, training and orientation, monitoring and evaluating the programme.

There were about 108,000 adult education centres in March 1982.

Educational statistics for the year 1980–81:

Type of recognized institution	No. of institutions	No. of students on rolls	No. of teachers
Primary/junior basic schools	485,538	51,330,138	1,345,376
Middle/senior basic schools	116,447	27,493,826	830,649
High/higher secondary schools	51,594	24,633,848	901,329
Training schools and colleges	1,397	173,838[1]	–
Arts, Science and Commerce colleges	2,425	2,177,769[2]	–

[1] Enrolment by stages of teachers' training courses at school and college level.
[2] Enrolment by stages of all post-graduate and graduate courses.

Primary pupils represent 83·1% of the age-group 6–11; middle school pupils, 40% of 11s–14s.

Expenditure (on recognized institutions) during the Sixth Plan (1980–85) is estimated at Rs 1,986 crores.

Health. Health programmes are primarily the responsibility of the state governments. The Union Government has sponsored and supported major schemes for disease prevention and control which are implemented nationally. These include the prevention and control of malaria, filaria, tuberculosis, leprosy, venereal diseases, smallpox, trachoma and cancer. There are also Union Government schemes in connexion with water supply and sanitation, and with nutrition. The Nutrition Advisory Committee of the Indian Council of Medical Research sponsors schemes for research and advises the Government. The National Nutrition Advisory Committee is to formulate a national nutrition policy and recommend measures for improving national standards.

Medical relief and service is primarily the responsibility of the states. In 1977 there were 5,372 primary health centres and 37,745 sub-centres. In 1975 there was 1 doctor to every 4,200 people. Medical education is also a state responsibility, but there is a co-ordinating Central Health Educational Bureau. In 1977 there were 106 medical colleges and 74 colleges for homeopathic medicine. There were 601 nursing schools. In 1977 there were 38 mental hospitals and 51 institutions for the mentally handicapped and retarded; there were 600 TB clinics.

Family planning is centrally sponsored and locally implemented. The goal is to reduce the birth-rate by means of education in family planning methods.

Health expenditure under the fifth development plan was Rs 681·66 crores, of which the greatest single item was the control of communicable diseases.

Social Security. Annual plan expenditure (estimate) 1977-78, Rs 1,286·65 lakhs: services for children in need of care, Rs 210 lakhs; assistance to voluntary organizations, Rs 375 lakhs; integrated child development services, Rs 107 lakhs; hostels for working women, Rs 161·5 lakhs; education for employment and vocational training for adult women, Rs 80 lakhs; national institute for the handicapped, Rs 65 lakhs; functional literacy, Rs 57·5 lakhs.

DIPLOMATIC REPRESENTATIVES

Of India in Great Britain (India House, Aldwych, London, WC2 4NA)
High Commissioner: Prakash Mehrotra.

Of Great Britain in India (Chanakyapuri, New Delhi 21, 1100-21)
High Commissioner: Sir Robert Wade-Gery, KCMG.

Of India in the USA (2107 Massachusetts Ave., NW, Washington, D.C., 20008)
Ambassador: K. R. Narayanan.

Of the USA in India (Shanti Path, Chanakyapuri, New Delhi 21)
Chargé d'Affairs: Harry G. Barnes, Jr.

Of India to the United Nations
Ambassador: Natarajan Krishnan.

Books of Reference

Special works relating to States are shown under their separate headings.

The Gazetteer of India Central Gazetteers Unit. Delhi, 1965
India: A Reference Annual. Delhi Govt. Printer. Annual
Cambridge History of India. 6 vols. CUP, 1922-47. Supp., 1953
The Times of India Directory and Yearbook. Bombay and London. Annual
Bhatia, K., *Indira: A Biography of Prime Minister Gandhi.* New York, 1974
Cassen, R. H., *India: Population, Economy and Society.* London, 1978
Chatterjee, S. P., *Indian Climatology.* Calcutta, 1956.(ed.), *National Atlas of India (Preliminary* (Hindi) *edition).* Calcutta, 1957
Fishlock, T., *India File: Inside the Subcontinent.* London, 1983
von Fürer-Haimendorf, C., *Tribes of India: the Struggle for Survival.* Univ. of California Press, 1983
Kesavan, B. S., and Kulkarni, V. Y. (eds), *The National Bibliography of Indian Literature, 1901–53,* New Delhi, 1963 ff.
Hall, A., *The Emergence of Modern India.* Columbia Univ. Press, 1981
Hart, D., *Nuclear Power in India: a Comparative Analysis.* London, 1983
Majumdar, R. C., Raychandhuri, H. C., and Datta, K., *An Advanced History of India.* 2nd ed. London, 1950
Mitra, H. N., *The Indian Annual Register.* Calcutta, from 1953
Moraes, D., *Mrs. Gandhi.* London, 1980

Nanda, B. R. (ed.), *Socialism in India*. Delhi, Bombay, Bangalore, Kanpur, London, 1972
Pachauri, R. K., *Energy and Economic Development in India*. New York, 1977
Philips, C. H. (ed.), *The Evolution of India and Pakistan: Select Documents*. OUP, 1962 ff.–
Politics and Society in India. London, 1963
Poplai, S. L. (ed.), *India, 1947–50* (select documents). 2 vols. Bombay and London, 1959
Smith, V. E., *Oxford History of India*. 3rd ed. OUP, 1958
Spear, P., *India: A Modern History*. 2nd ed. Univ. of Michigan Press, 1972
Sutton, S. C., *Guide to the India Office Library (founded in 1801)*. HMSO, 1952
Thomas, R., *India's Emergence as an Industrial Power*. Royal Institute of International Affairs, London, 1982
Yasdani, C. (ed.), *Early History of the Deccan*. 2 vols. London, 1960

STATES AND TERRITORIES

The Republic of India is composed of the following 22 States and 9 centrally administered Union Territories:

States	Capital	States	Capital
Andhra Pradesh	Hyderabad	Manipur	Imphal
Assam	Dispur	Meghalaya	Shillong
Bihar	Patna	Nagaland	Kohima
Gujarat	Ahmedabad	Orissa	Bhubaneswar
Haryana	Chandigarh	Punjab	Chandigarh
Himachal Pradesh	Simla	Rajasthan	Jaipur
Jammu and Kashmir	Srinagar	Sikkim	Gangtok
Karnataka	Bangalore	Tamil Nadu	Madras
Kerala	Trivandrum	Tripura	Agartala
Madhya Pradesh	Bhopal	Uttar Pradesh	Lucknow
Maharashtra	Bombay	West Bengal	Calcutta

Union Territories

Andaman and Nicobar Islands; Arunachal Pradesh; Chandigarh; Dadra and Nagar Haveli; Delhi; Goa, Daman and Diu; Lakshadweep; Mizoram; Pondicherry.

States Reorganization. The Constitution, which came into force on 26 Jan. 1950, provided for 9 Part A States (Assam, Bihar, Bombay, Madhya Pradesh, Madras, Orissa, Punjab, Uttar Pradesh and West Bengal) which corresponded to the previous governors' provinces; 8 Part B States (Hyderabad, Jammu and Kashmir, Madhya Bharat, Mysore, Patalia-East Punjab (PEPSU), Rajasthan, Saurashtra and Travancore-Cochin) which corresponded to Indian states or unions of states; 10 Part C States (Ajmer, Bhopal, Bilaspur, Coorg, Delhi, Himachal Pradesh, Kutch, Manipur, Tripura and Vindhya Pradesh) which corresponded to the chief commissioners' provinces; and Part D Territories and other areas (*e.g.*, Andaman and Nicobar Islands). Part A States (under governors) and Part B States (under rajpramukhs) had provincial autonomy with a ministry and elected assembly. Part C States (under chief commissioners) were the direct responsibility of the Union Government, although Kutch, Manipur and Tripura had legislatures with limited powers. Andhra was formed as a Part A State on its separation from Madras in 1953. Bilaspur was merged with Himachal Pradesh in 1954.

The States Reorganization Act, 1956, abolished the distinction between Parts A, B and C States and established two categories for the units of the Indian Union to be called States and Territories. The following were the main territorial changes: the Telugu districts of Hyderabad were merged with Andhra; Mysore absorbed the whole Kannada-speaking area (including Coorg, the greater part of 4 districts of Bombay, 3 districts of Hyderabad and 1 district of Madras); Bhopal, Vindhya Pradesh and Madhya Bharat were merged with Madhya Pradesh, which ceded 8 Marathi-speaking districts to Bombay; the new state of Kerala, comprising the majority of Malayalam-speaking peoples, was formed from Travancore-Cochin with a small area from Madras; Patalia-East Punjab was included in Punjab; Kutch and Saurashtra in Bombay; and Ajmer in Rajasthan; Hyderabad ceased to exist.

On 1 May 1960 Bombay State was divided into two parts: 17 districts (including Saurashtra and Kutch) in the north and west became the new state of Gujarat; the remainder was renamed the state of Maharashtra.

In Aug. 1961 the former Portuguese territories of Dadra and Nagar Haveli became a Union territory. The Portuguese territory of Goa and the smaller territories of Daman and Diu, occupied by India in Dec. 1961, were constituted a Union territory in March 1962. In Aug. 1962 the former French territories of Pondicherry, Karikal, Mahé and Yanaon were formally transferred to India and became a Union territory. In Sept. 1962 the Naga Hills Tuensang Area was constituted a separate state under the name of Nagaland. On 1 Nov. 1966, under the Punjab Reorganization Act 1966, a new state of Haryana and a new Union Territory of Chandigarh were created from parts of Punjab (India); for details, *see* pp. 640 and 672. On 26 Jan. 1971 Himachal Pradesh became a state. In 1972 the North East Frontier Agency and Mizo hill district were made Union territories (as Arunachal Pradesh and Mizoram) and Manipur, Meghalaya and Tripura full states. Sikkim became a state in 1975.

Report of the States Reorganization Commission. Government of India. Delhi, 1956

ANDHRA PRADESH

HISTORY. Andhra was constituted a separate state on 1 Oct. 1953, on its partition from Madras, and consisted of the undisputed Telugu-speaking area of that state. To this region was added, on 1 Nov. 1956, the Telangana area of the former Hyderabad State, comprising the districts of Hyderabad, Medak, Nizamabad, Karimnaga, Warangal, Khammam, Nalgonda and Mahbubnaga, parts of the Adilabad district and some taluks of the Raichur, Gulbarga and Bidar districts, and some revenue circles of the Nanded district. On 1 April 1960, 221·4 sq. miles in the Chingleput and Salem districts of Madras were transferred to Andhra Pradesh in exchange for 410 sq. miles from Chittoor district. The district of Prakasam was formed on 2 Feb. 1970. Hyderabad was split into 2 districts on 15 Aug. 1978. A new district, Vizianagaram, was formed in 1979.

AREA AND POPULATION. Andhra Pradesh is in south India and is bounded south by Tamil Nadu, west by Karnataka, north and northwest by Maharashtra, northeast by Madhya Pradesh and Orissa, east by the Bay of Bengal. The state has an area of 275,068 sq. km and a population (1981 census) of 53·5m. Density, 195 per sq. km. Growth rate 1971–81, 23·19%. The principal language is Telugu. Cities with over 250,000 population (1981 census), see p. 611. Other large cities (1981): Nellore (236,879); Kakinada (226,600); Kurnool (206,700); Nizamabad (183,135); Eluru (168,074); Machilipatnam (138,525); Anantapur (119,536); Tenali (119,200); Tirupati (115,200); Vizianagaram (115,200); Adoni (108,900); Proddatur (107,100); Cuddapah (103,006); Bheemavaram (101,940).

CONSTITUTION AND GOVERNMENT. Andhra Pradesh has a bicameral legislature. There are 295 seats in the Legislative Assembly and 90 in the Legislative Council. At the election of Jan. 1983, the Telegu Dasam party gained a two-thirds majority.

For administrative purposes there are 23 districts in the state. The capital is Hyderabad.

Governor: Ram Lal.
Chief Minister: N. T. Rama Rao.

BUDGET. The budget (estimate) for 1983–84 showed total receipts on revenue account of Rs 2,145·04 crores, and expenditure of Rs 2,105·29 crores.

ENERGY AND NATURAL RESOURCES

Gas. Natural gas was found at Reyzole in 1983.

Electricity. There are hydro-electric plants at Machkund, Upper Sileru, Nizam Sagar, Nellore and Kothagudam. Installed capacity, 1982, 2,298 mw., power generated 8,874m. kwh. In 1983 there were 20,159 electrified towns and villages and 532,000 electric pump sets.

Water. The irrigation potential of the state in 1982 was 10,300,000 hectares; actual area under irrigation, 3,693,000 hectares. A joint project with Tamil Nadu, agreed in 1983, will irrigate about 230,000 hectares.

Minerals (1981). Production of principal minerals (in 1,000 tonnes): Coal, 9,800; limestone, 3,142; barytes, 340·7; iron ore (1980), 390. The state also has bauxite, asbestos, steatite, mica and chromite.

Agriculture. There were (1981–82) about 13·04m. hectares of cropped land, of which 35·9% is irrigated. Yield per hectare, in kg: Sugar-cane, 9,142; rice, 2,102; ground-nuts, 990; tobacco, 1,053; jowar, 602; cotton, 239; castor, 208.

Livestock (1979 census): Cattle, 12·03m.; buffaloes, 7·16m.; goats, 4·4m.; sheep, 7·07m.

Forests. In 1982 it was estimated that forests occupy 23·3% of the total area of the state or 64,154 sq. km; main forest products are teak, eucalyuptus, cashew, casuarina, softwoods and bamboo.

Fisheries. Production 1981–82, 118,300 tonnes of marine fish and 124,170 tonnes of inland water fish. The state has a coastline of 974 km.

INDUSTRY. The main industries are textile manufacture, sugar-milling machine tools, pharmaceuticals, cement, chemicals, glass, fertilizers, electronic equipment, heavy electrical machinery, aircraft parts and paper-making. There is an oil refinery at Vishakhapatnam, where India's only major shipbuilding yards are situated. In 1983 a steel plant was under construction at Vishakhapatnam and a railway repair shop at Tirupathi.

Cottage industry includes the manufacture of carpets, wooden and lacquer toys, brocades, bidriware, filigree and lace-work. The wooden toys of Nirmal and Kondapalli are particularly well known. Sericulture is developing rapidly. District Industries Centres have been set up to promote small-scale industry.

Tourism is growing; the main centres are Hyderabad, Nagarjunasagar, Warangal, Araku Valley, Horsley Hills and Tirupathi.

COMMUNICATIONS

Roads. In 1981–82 there were 2,437 km of national highways, 8,387 km of state highways, 18,072 km of major district roads, 74,930 km of other roads. Number of vehicles, 1981–82: 170,040 motor cycles and scooters, 41,224 cars and jeeps, 36,605 goods vehicles and 10,156 buses.

Railways. In 1981–82 there were approximately 4,813 route-km of railway, of which 3,079 km were broad gauge.

Aviation. There are airports at Hyderabad, Tirupathi, Vijayawada and Vishakapatnam, with regular scheduled services to Bombay, Delhi, Calcutta, Bangalore and Madras.

Shipping. The chief port is Vishakhapatnam. There are minor ports at Kakinada, Machilipatnam, Bheemunipatnam, Narsapur, Krishnapatnam, Vadarevu and Calingapatnam.

JUSTICE, RELIGION AND EDUCATION

Justice. The high court of Judicature at Hyderabad has a Chief Justice and 19 puisne judges.

Religion. At the 1971 census Hindus numbered 38,119,279; Moslems, 3,520,166; Christians, 1,823,436; Jains 16,103; Sikhs, 12,591; Buddhists, 10,035.

Education. In 1981, 29·94% of the population were literate (39·13% of men and 20·52% of women). There were, in 1980–81 40,408 primary schools (5,368,000 students); 4,577 upper primary (882,000); 3,706 secondary (811,000). Education is free for children up to 14.

There were in 1981–82 387 degree colleges, 468 junior colleges, 53 oriental colleges and 10 universities: Osmania University, Hyderabad; Andhra University, Waltair; Sri Venkateswara University, Tirupathi; Kakatiya University, Warangal; Nagarjuna University, Guntur; Sri Jawaharlal Nehru Technological University, Hyderabad; Central University, Hyderabad; A.P. Agricultural University, Hyderabad; Sri Krishnadevaraya University, Anantapur; Smt. Padmarathi Mahila Vishwaridyalayam (University for Women), Tirupathi. An Open University was inaugurated at Nagarjunasagar in 1982.

ASSAM

HISTORY. Assam first became a British Protectorate at the close of the first Burmese War in 1826. In 1832 Cachar was annexed; in 1835 the Jaintia Hills were included in the East India Company's dominions, and in 1839 Assam was annexed to Bengal. In 1874 Assam was detached from Bengal and made a separate chief commissionership. On the partition of Bengal in 1905, it was united to the Eastern Districts of Bengal under a Lieut.-Governor. From 1912 the chief commissionership of Assam was revived, and in 1921 a governorship was created. On the partition of India almost the whole of the predominantly Moslem district of Sylhet was merged with East Bengal (Pakistan). Dewangiri in North Kamrup was ceded to Bhután in 1951. The Naga Hill district, administered by the Union Government since 1957, became part of Nagaland in 1962. The autonomous state of Meghalaya within Assam, comprising the districts of Garo Hills and Khasi and Jaintia Hills, came into existence on 2 April 1970, and achieved full independent statehood in Jan. 1972, when it was also decided to form a Union Territory, Mizoram, from the Mizo Hills district.

EVENTS. The issue of immigration from Bangladesh has continued to inspire violent incidents and unrest.

AREA AND POPULATION. Assam is in eastern India, almost separated from central India by Bangladesh. It is bounded west by West Bengal, north by Bhután and the Territory of Arunachal Pradesh, east by Nagaland, Manipur and Burma, south by Meghalaya, Bangladesh and Tripura. The area of the state is now approximately 78,523 sq km. Its population (1981 census) 19·9m. Density, 254 per sq. km. Growth rate since 1971, 36·09%. Principal towns with population (1971) are; Gauhati, 122,981; Dibrugarh, 80,344; Tinsukia, 55,392; Nowgong, 52,892; Silchar, 52,612. The principal language is Assamese.

CONSTITUTION AND GOVERNMENT. Assam has a unicameral legislature of 126 members. In Feb. 1983 elections were held despite unrest and an outbreak of communal violence against Bangladeshi immigrants. A congress (I) government was returned. The capital is Gauhati.

Governor: P. Mehrotra.
Chief Minister: H. Saikia.

BUDGET. The budget estimates for 1983–84 showed total receipts of Rs 1,753·8 crores and expenditure of Rs 1,778·19 crores. Provision for relief and rehabilitation following communal disturbances, Rs 60 crores.

ENERGY AND NATURAL RESOURCES

Electricity. In 1978 there was an installed capacity of 141·5 mw and 2,260 villages (out of 21,995) with electricity. A further 583 mw capacity is to be installed by 1984. New power stations are under construction at Bongaigaon and Lakwa.

Oil. Assam contains important oilfields and produces about 50% of India's crude oil. There is also natural gas.

Water. In 1978, 88,300 hectares were irrigated and 228 projects were in hand. Intended Sixth Plan outlay, Rs 300 crores.

Minerals. Coal production (1973), 436,000 tonnes. The state also has limestone, refractory clay, dolomite, and corundum.

Agriculture. There are 756 tea plantations, and growing tea is the principal industry. Production in 1976, 276m. kg, over 50% of Indian tea. Over 72% of the cultivated area is under food crops, of which the most important is rice. Total food-grains, 1976–77, 21·47m. tonnes. Main cash crops: jute, tea, cotton, oilseeds, sugar-cane, fruit and potatoes. Wheat has been introduced recently and yielded 71,045 tonnes in 1976–77. Cattle are important; milk production, 1976–77, 343m. litres.

Forestry. There are 1·62m. hectares of reserved forests under the administration of the Forest Department and 1,229,000 hectares of unclassed forests, altogether about 30% of the total area of the state. Revenue from forests, 1978–79, Rs 821 lakhs.

INDUSTRY. Sericulture and hand-loom weaving, both silk and cotton, are important home industries together with the manufacture of brass, cane and bamboo articles. Hand-loom weaving of silk is stimulated by state and central development schemes; outlay, Rs 18,34·5 lakhs. There is a silk-spinning mill and 2 cotton-mills. The main heavy industry is petro-chemicals; there are 3 oil refineries. Other industries include manufacturing paper, fertilizers, sugar, jute and plywood products, rice and oil milling.

COMMUNICATIONS

Roads. In 1972 there were 17,839 km of road maintained by the Public Works Department in Assam, including national highway. There were 63,616 motor vehicles in the state in 1976.

Railways. The open length of railways in 1974 was 2,193·65 km, of which 105·22 km are broad gauge.

Aviation. Daily scheduled flights connect the principal towns with the rest of India. There are airports at Gauhati, Tezpur, Jorhat, Dimapur, Silchar and Dibrugarh.

Shipping. Water transport is important in Lower Assam; the main waterway is the Brahmaputra River.

JUSTICE, RELIGION AND EDUCATION

Justice. The seat of the High Court is Gauhati. It has a Chief Justice and 6 puisne judges.

Religion. At the 1971 census Hindus numbered 10,604,618; Moslems, 3,592,124; Christians, 381,010; Buddhists, 22,565; Jains, 12,914; Sikhs, 11,920.

Education. The 1971 census showed 28·74% of the population to be literate.

In 1976 there were 26,000 primary schools; 2,504 middle schools; 1,657 high schools; 70 higher secondary schools; in 1977 there were 25,768 schools altogether, 126 general colleges and institutions for professional education, 507 vocational and technical schools, 31 teacher-training colleges and 3 universities.

Goswami, P. C., *Economic Development of Assam*. London, 1963
Reid, Sir Robert, *History of the Frontier Areas Bordering on Assam*. Shillong, 1942

BIHAR

The state contains the ethnic areas of North Bihar, Santhalpargana and Chota Nagpur. In 1956 certain areas of Purnea and Manbhum districts were transferred to West Bengal.

AREA AND POPULATION. Bihar is in north India and is bounded north by Nepál, east by West Bengal, south by Orissa, south-west by Madhya Pradesh and west by Uttar Pradesh. The area of Bihar is 173,876 sq. km and its population (1981 census), 69,823,154, a density of 402 per sq. km. Growth rate since 1971, 23·9%. Population of principal towns, *see* p. 611. Other large towns (1981): Muzaffarpur, 189,765; Darbhanga, 175,879; Biharsharif, 151,305; Munghyr, 129.187; Arrah, 124,614; Katihar, 121,693; Dhanbad, 119,807; Chapra, 111,407; Purnea, 109,649; Bermo, 101,502.

The official language is Hindi and the second language Urdu.

CONSTITUTION AND GOVERNMENT. Bihar has a unicameral legislature. The Legislative Assembly consists of 325 elected members. In autumn 1983 Congress (I) held 194 seats; Janata, 40; CPI, 21; Bhartiya Janata, 23; B.L.D., 12; others, 35. For the purposes of administration the state is divided into 10 divisions covering 37 districts. The capital is Patna; the hot-weather seat is Ranchi.

Governor: Dr A. R. Kidwai.
Chief Minister: Chandra Shekhar Singh.

BUDGET. The budget estimates for 1981–82 show total receipts of Rs 15,221·3m and expenditure of Rs 14,443·5m. Per capita income (1983) Rs 870.

ENERGY AND NATURAL RESOURCES

Electricity. Installed capacity (1982) 939·68 mw. Power generated (1982–83), 2,753m. kw. In March 1983 there were 29,187 villages with electricity.

Minerals. Bihar is the foremost state for mineral deposits. Value of production, 1976, Rs 3,628·2m. Coal is the principal mineral; the Jharia and Bokaro fields are (with Raniganj across the West Bengal border) the most important in India. Jharia produces coking coal. Copper, of which Bihar is the only Indian producer, iron ore, ruby mica (61% of national output), chromite, manganese, kyanite and bauxite are important. The recently discovered large deposits of pyrites in the Shahabad district are being exploited.

Agriculture. About 26% of the cultivable area is irrigated. Total cropped area, 8·5m. hectares. Main crops are rice, jute, sugar-cane, oilseeds, tobacco, wheat, jowar, bajra and maize. A three-year drought was broken in 1983.

Forests in 1982 covered 29,220 hectares.

INDUSTRY. Main plants are the Tata Iron and Steel Co., the Tata Engineering and Locomotive Co., the steel plant at Bokaro, oil refinery at Barauni and aluminium plant at Muri. Other important industries are machine tools, fertilizers, electrical engineering, sugar-milling, paper-milling, silk-spinning, manufacturing explosives and cement. There is a copper smelter at Ghatsila and a lead refining plant at Tundo. Industrial disputes lost 1·18m. man-days in 1979.

COMMUNICATIONS

Roads. In 1972 the state had 116,575 km of highway (including 88,040 km of unmetalled roads). Passenger transport has been nationalized in 7 districts. There were 181,694 motor vehicles in 1980–81.

Railways. The North Eastern and Eastern railways traverse the state.

Aviation. There are airports at Patna and Ranchi with regular scheduled services to Calcutta and Delhi.

Shipping. The length of waterways open for navigation is 900 miles.

JUSTICE, RELIGION AND EDUCATION

Justice. There is a High Court (constituted in 1916) at Patna, and a bench at Ranchi, with a Chief Justice, 32 puisne judges and 4 additional judges.

Police. The police force is under a Director General of Police; in 1983 there were 957 police stations (and 56 for railway police).

Religion. At the 1961 census Hindus numbered 39,347,050; Moslems, 5,785,631; Christians, 502,195; Sikhs, 44,413; Jains, 17,598; Buddhists, 2,885.

Education. At the census of 1981 the number of literates was 18·16m. (26%: males 37·78%; females, 13·58%). There were, 1971, 2,581 high and higher secondary schools with 601,000 pupils, 8,025 middle schools with 965,000 pupils, 46,582 primary schools with 5,009,000 pupils. Primary schools had 144,559 teachers, higher secondary and high schools 25,740. Education is free for children aged 6-11.

There were 7 universities in academic year 1972–73; Patna University (founded 1917) with 12,577 full-time students (1970); Bihar University, Muzaffarpur (1952) with 4 constituent colleges, 35 affiliated colleges and 41,640 students (1970); Bhagalpur University (1960) with 40,746 students (1970); Ranchi University (1960) with 36,892 students (1968–69); Darbhanga Sanskrit University (1961); Magadha University, Gaya (1962) and Mithila University (1972), Darbhanga.

Health. In 1983 there were 259 hospitals with 19,583 beds, and 861 dispensaries with 4,166 beds.

Das, A. N., *Agrarian Movements in India: Studies in 20th Century Bihar.* London, 1982

GUJARAT

HISTORY. On 1 May 1960, as a result of the Bombay Reorganization Act, 1960, the state of Gujarat was formed from the north and west (predominantly Gujarati-speaking) portion of Bombay State, the remainder being renamed the state of Maharashtra. Gujarat consists of the following districts of the former state of Bombay: Banas Kantha, Mehsana, Sabar Kantha, Ahmedabad, Kaira, Panch Mahals, Vadodara, Bharuch, Surat, Dangs, Amreli, Surendranagar, Rajkot, Jamnagar, Junagadh, Bhavnagar, Kutch, Gandhinagar and Bulsar.

EVENTS. Floods in Saurashtra region in June 1983 caused over 600 deaths and extensive damage; monsoon rains caused Fodana dam to burst.

AREA AND POPULATION. Gujarat is in western India and is bounded north by Pakistan and Rajasthan, east by Madhya Pradesh, south-east by Maharashtra, south and west by the Indian ocean and Arabian sea. The area of the state is 195,984 sq. km and the population at the 1981 census was 33,960,905; a density of 173 per sq. km. Growth rate 1971–81, 27·2%. The chief cities, *see* p. 611. Gujarati and Hindi in the Devanagari script are the official languages.

CONSTITUTION AND GOVERNMENT. Gujarat has a unicameral legislature, the Legislative Assembly, which has 182 elected members. In Oct. 1983, Congress (I) held 141 seats; Janata, 16; Bhartiya Janata, 12; other parties, 7; independents, 6.

The capital is Gandhinagar. There are 19 districts.

Governor: Prof. K. M. Chandy
Chief Minister: M. Solanki

BUDGET. The budget estimates for 1983–84 showed a surplus on revenue account of Rs 176·64 crores and an overall deficit of Rs 29·07 crores.

ENERGY AND NATURAL RESOURCES

Electricity. In 1983 the total generating capacity was 2,770 mw of electricity, serving 14,150 towns and villages and 264,392 wells and tube-wells. A thermal power station of 1,260 mw eventual capacity was commissioned at Vanakbori in 1981.

Oil and Gas. There were crude oil and gas reserves in 23 fields in 1982–83. Production: Crude oil, 3·2m. tonnes; gas, 658·5m. cu. metres.

Minerals. Chief minerals produced in 1982 (in tonnes) included chalk (90,897), lime stone (2·8m.), agate stone (1,317), calcite (323), quartz (51,775), bauxite (492,241), china clay (49,320), other clays (11,131), dolomite (260,042), crude fluorite (115,586), silica-glass sand (156,333) and lignite (510,230). Enormous reserves of coal were found under the Kalol and Mehsana oil and gas fields in May 1980. The deposit, mixed with crude petroleum, is estimated at 100,000m. tonnes, extending over 500 km.

Agriculture. Cropped area, 1979–80, was 10·6m. hectares. Area and production of principal crops, 1979–80 (in 1,000 hectares and 1,000 tonnes): Rice, 550,516; groundnuts, 2,108, 1,856; cotton, 1,717, 1,797,000 bales of 170 kg. Estimates, 1982–83: Rice, 476, 489; groundnuts, 2,057, 133; cotton, 1,496, 1,558,000 bales.

Livestock (1982): Buffaloes, 4·43m.; other cattle, 6·93m.; sheep, 2·33m.; goats, 3·26m.; horses and ponies, 24,000.

Fisheries. There were (1982) about 81,000 active fishermen and 187 fishing co-operatives. There were (1983) 11,014 fishing vessels (4,016 motor vessels). The catch for 1982–83 (estimate) was 212,419 tonnes.

INDUSTRY. Gujarat is one of the 4 most industrialized states. In 1981 there were over 10,000 registered factories including over 2,000 textile factories. There were about 77 industrial estates. There were also about 35,000 small units. Principal industries are textiles, general and electrical engineering, petrochemicals, machine tools, heavy chemicals, pharmaceuticals, dyes, sugar, soda ash and cement. Large fertilizer plants have been set up and there is an oil refinery at Koyali near Vadodara, with a developing petro-chemical complex.

State production of soda-ash is about 85% of national output, and of salt, about 60%. The capacity of state cement plants (1983) was 3·5m. tonnes a year.

COMMUNICATIONS

Roads. In 1983 there were 52,621 km of roads. Gujarat State Transport Corporation operated 11,932 routes.

Railways. In 1982 the state had 3,057 km metre gauge railway, 1,099 km narrow gauge and 1,422 km broad gauge.

Aviation. Ahmedabad is the main airport. There are 5 services daily between Ahmedabad and Bombay, Jaipur and Delhi. There are 8 other airports: Baroda, Bhavnagar, Bhuj, Jamnagar, Kandla, Keshod, Porbandar and Rajkot.

Shipping. The largest port is Kandla. There are 45 other ports, including Okha, Bedi, Bhavnagar, Verawal, Sikka and Porbandar.

Post. There were (March 1983) 8,522 post offices, 1,647 telegraph offices. Ahmedabad has direct dialling telephone connexion (or night S.T.D.) with 26 cities and telex connexions with 19 cities.

JUSTICE, RELIGION, EDUCATION AND WELFARE

Justice. The High Court of Judicature at Ahmedabad has a Chief Justice and 10 puisne judges.

Religion. At the 1971 census Hindus numbered 23,835,471; Moslems, 2,249,055; Jains, 451,578; Christians, 109,341; Sikhs, 18,233; Buddhists, 5,469.

Education. In 1981 the number of literates was 14·85m. (43·7%). Primary and secondary education are free. In 1982–83 there were 26,908 primary schools; nearly all villages with more than 200 people have one within 1·5 km. In 1980–81 there were 2,186 secondary schools and 967 higher secondary schools with 1,027,000 pupils.

There are 6 universities in the state. Gujarat University, Ahmedabad, founded in

1949, is teaching and affiliating; it has 149 affiliated colleges. The Maharaja Sayajirao University of Vadodara (1949) is residential and teaching. The Sardar Patel University, Vallabh-Vidyanagar, (1955) has 16 constituent and affiliated colleges. The 2 newer universities (1967) are Saurashtra University at Rajkot with 54 affiliated colleges, and South Gujarat at Surat with 37. Bhavnagar University (1978) is residential and teaching with 7 affiliated colleges. In 1980–81 the total number of students was 180,303. Gujarat Vidyapith at Ahmedabad is deemed a university under the University Grants Commission Act. There were also 1 agricultural and 1 Ayurvedic university.

There are 9 technical institutions for degree courses (student capacity 2,226) and 27 for full-time diploma courses (4,491).

Health. In 1983 there were 251 primary health centres and 13,000 hospital beds. The annual intake at 5 medical colleges was 675.

Rushbrook Williams, L. F., *The Black Hills: Kutch in History and Legend*. London, 1958
Desai, I. F., *Untouchability in Rural Gujarat*. Bombay, 1977

HARYANA

HISTORY. The state of Haryana, created on 1 Nov. 1966 under the Punjab Reorganization Act, 1966, was formed from the Hindi-speaking parts of the state of Punjab (India). It comprises the districts of Hissar, Mohindergarh, Gurgaon, Rohtak and Karnal; parts of Sangrur and Ambala districts; and part of Kharar tehsil.

AREA AND POPULATION. Haryana is in north India and is bounded north by Himachal Pradesh, east by Uttar Pradesh, south and west by Rajasthan and north-west by Punjab. Delhi forms an enclave on its eastern boundary. The state has an area of 44,222 sq. km and a population (1981) of 12,850,902; density, 291 per sq. km. Growth rate, 1971–81, 28·04%. The principal language is Hindi.

CONSTITUTION AND GOVERNMENT. The state has a unicameral legislature with 90 members. After the elections of May 1982 when 89 seats were contested, Congress (I) held 36 seats; Lok Dal, 31; independents, 12 and others, 10. The state shares with Punjab (India) a High Court, a university and certain public services. The capital (shared with Punjab) is Chandigarh (*see* p. 672). There are 12 districts.

Governor: G. D. Tapase.
Chief Minister: Bhajan Lal.

BUDGET. Budget estimates for 1981–82 show income of Rs 872 crores and expenditure of Rs 921 crores.

ENERGY AND NATURAL RESOURCES

Electricity. Approximately 1,000 mw are supplied to Haryana, mainly from the Bhakra Nangar system. In 1976 installed capacity was 612 mw and all the 3,302 villages had electric power.

Minerals. Minerals include iron ore, limestone, china clay and marble. Value of production, 1976, Rs 8·6m.

Agriculture. Haryana has sandy soil and erratic rainfall, but the state shares the benefit of the Sutlej-Beas scheme. Agriculture employs over 82% of the working population; in 1981 there were about 900,000 holdings (average 3·7 hectares), and the gross irrigated area was 1·97m. hectares. Area under high-yielding varieties of foodgrains, 2·2m. hectares. During 1980–81 foodgrain production was 6·2m. tonnes; sugar (gur), oilseeds, and cotton, are important.

Forests cover 3·3% of the state.

INDUSTRY. Haryana has a large market for consumer goods in neighbouring Delhi. In 1981 there were 233 large and medium scale industries employing 100,000 and producing goods worth Rs 8,000m. There were 25,000 small units. The main industries are cotton textiles (11 mills in 1976), agricultural machinery, woollen textiles, scientific instruments, glass, cement, paper and sugar milling.

COMMUNICATIONS

Roads. There were (1971) about 13,259 km of metalled roads and 262 km unsurfaced. Road transport was nationalized by 1971; Haryana Roadways has a fleet of 725 vehicles running on 335 routes and daily carrying 125,255 passengers over 149,630 km.

Railways. The state is crossed by lines from Delhi to Agra, Ajmer, Ferozepur and Chandigarh. The main stations are at Ambala and Kurukshetra.

Aviation. There is no airport within the state but Delhi is on its eastern boundary.

JUSTICE AND EDUCATION

Justice. Haryana shares the High Court of Punjab and Haryana at Chandigarh which had (1968) a Chief Justice and 16 puisne judges.

Education. In 1981 the number of literates was 4·6m. In 1969-70 there were 5,967 schools and colleges with 1.250,590 attending. This includes 4,362 primary schools, 776 high and higher secondary schools, 777 middle schools and 47 colleges.

HIMACHAL PRADESH

HISTORY. The territory came into being on 15 April 1948 and comprised 30 former Hill States. The state of Bilaspur was merged with Himachal Pradesh in 1954. The 6 original districts were: Mahasu, Sirmur, Mandi, Chamba, Bilaspur and Kinnaur. On 1 Nov. 1966, under the Punjab Reorganization Act, 1966, certain parts of the state of Punjab (India) were transferred to Himachal Pradesh. These comprise the districts of Simla, Kulu, Kangra, and Lahaul and Spiti; and parts of Hoshiarpur and Ambala districts, with an estimated population (1967) of 1·5m.

AREA AND POPULATION. Himachal Pradesh is in north India and is bounded north by Kashmir, east by Tibet, south-east by Uttar Pradesh, south by Haryana, south-west and west by Punjab. The area of the state is 55,673 sq. km and it had a population at the 1981 census of 4.237,569. Density, 76 per sq. km. Growth rate, 1971–81, 22·46%. Principal language is Pahari.

CONSTITUTION AND GOVERNMENT. Full statehood was attained, as the 18th state of the Union, on 25 Jan. 1971.

On 1 Sept. 1972 districts were reorganized and 2 new districts created, Hamirpur and Una, making a total of 12. The capital is Simla.

There is a unicameral legislature. After the elections of May 1982 Congress (I) held 31 seats; Bhartiya Janata, 29; independents 6; Janata, 2.

Governor: A. N. Banerjee.
Chief Minister: V Bhadra Singh.

BUDGET. Budget estimates for 1980–81 showed revenue receipts of Rs 193 crores and expenditure on revenue account of Rs 161 crores. The capital account showed a deficit of Rs 73·57 crores.

ENERGY AND NATURAL RESOURCES

Electricity. In 1977 7,245 villages (out of 16,916) had electricity.

Water. An artificial confluence of the Sutlej and Beas rivers has been made, directing their united flow into Govind Sagar Lake.

Minerals. The state has rock salt, slate, gypsum, limestone, barytes, dolomite and pyrites.

Agriculture. Farming employs 76% of the people. Irrigated area is 16·7% of the area sown. Main crops are seed potatoes, wheat, maize, rice and fruits such as apples, peaches, apricots, nuts, pomegranates.

Production of foodgrains (1976) 1·13m. tonnes.

Livestock (1966 census): Buffaloes, 415,356; other cattle, 1,048,917; goats, 813,041.

Forestry. Himachal Pradesh forests cover 38·3% of the state and supply the largest quantities of coniferous timber in northern India. They are the main source of revenue of Pradesh. The forests also ensure the safety of the catchment areas of the Jumna, Sutlej, Beas, Ravi and Chenab rivers.

INDUSTRY. The main sources of employment are the forests and their related industries; there are factories making turpentine and rosin, fertilizers, cement and TV sets. There is a foundry and a brewery. Other industries include salt production and handicrafts, including weaving.

COMMUNICATIONS

Roads. The national highway from Chandigarh runs through Simla; other main highways from Simla serve Kulu, Manali, Kangra, Chemba and Pathankot. The rest are minor roads. Pathankot is also on national highways from Punjab to Kashmir. There were 9,400 motor vehicles in 1976.

Railways. There is a line from Chandigarh to Simla, and the Jammu-Delhi line runs through Pathankot.

Aviation. The state has no airport, but Chandigarh is on its southern boundary.

JUSTICE. The state has its own High Court at Simla.

EDUCATION. The number of literates in 1981 was 1·7m.

JAMMU AND KASHMIR

HISTORY. The state of Jammu and Kashmir, which had earlier been under Hindu rulers and Moslem sultans, became part of the Mogul Empire under Akbar from 1586. After a period of Afghan rule from 1756, it was annexed to the Sikh kingdom of the Punjab in 1819. In 1820 Ranjit Singh made over the territory of Jammu to Gulab Singh. After the decisive battle of Sobraon in 1846 Kashmir also was made over to Gulab Singh under the Treaty of Amritsar. British supremacy was recognized until the Indian Independence Act, 1947, when all states decided on accession to India or Pakistan. Kashmir asked for standstill agreements with both. Pakistan agreed, but India desired further discussion with the Government of Jammu and Kashmir State. In the meantime the state became subject to armed attack from the territory of Pakistan and the Maharajah acceded to India on 26 Oct. 1947, by signing the Instrument of Accession. India approached the UN in Jan. 1948; India-Pakistan conflict ended by ceasefire in Jan. 1949. Further conflict in 1965 was followed by the Tashkent Declaration on Jan. 1966. Following further hostilities between India and Pakistan a ceasefire came into effect on 17 Dec. 1971, followed by the Simla Agreement in July 1972, whereby a new line of control was delineated bilaterally through negotiations between India and Pakistan and came into force on 17 Dec. 1972.

AREA AND POPULATION. The state is in the extreme north and is bounded north by China, east by Tibet, south by Himachal Pradesh and Punjab and west by Pakistan. The area is 222,236 sq. km, of which about 78,932 sq. km is occupied by Pakistan and 42,735 sq. km by China; the population of the territory on the Indian side of the line, 1981 census, was 5,981,600. Growth rate, 1971–81, 29·57%. For the population of Srinagar, see p. 611. The official language is Urdu; other commonly spoken languages are Kashmiri, Dogri, Balti, Ladakhi and Punjabi.

CONSTITUTION AND GOVERNMENT. The Maharajah's son, Yuvraj Karan Singh, took over as Regent in 1950 and, on the ending of hereditary rule (17 Oct. 1952), was sworn in as Sadar-i-Riyasat. On his father's death (26 April 1961) Yuvraj Karan Singh was recognized as Maharajah by the Indian Government; he decided not to use the title while he was elected head of state.

The permanent Constitution of the state came into force in part on 17 Nov. 1956 and fully on 26 Jan. 1957. There is a bicameral legislature; the Legislative Council has 36 members and the Legislative Assembly has 76. The state of the parties in the Legislative Assembly in autumn 1983 was: Congress (I) 26; National Conference, 47; Panthers Party, 1; Peoples' Conference, 1; Independent, 1. Since the 1967 elections the 6 representatives of Jammu and Kashmir in the central House of the People are directly elected; there are 4 representatives in the Council of States. The Council of Ministers consists of 7 Ministers and 4 Junior Ministers.

Kashmir Province has 8 districts and Jammu Province has 6 districts. Srinagar is the summer and Jammu the winter capital.

Governor: B. K. Nehru
Chief Minister: Farooq Abdullah.

BUDGET. Budget estimates for 1980–81 show revenue of Rs 576·62 crores, and expenditure of Rs 578·37 crores.

Total planning expenditure for 1980–81 was Rs 147·48 crores., of which agriculture and allied sectors received Rs 26·38 crores; power Rs 21·25 crores; water supply Rs 16·50 crores and irrigation and flood control Rs 16·00 crores.

ENERGY AND NATURAL RESOURCES

Electricity. Installed capacity (1980) 208·78 mw.; 4,631 villages had electricity.

Minerals. Value of production, 1976, Rs 5·46m. Minerals include coal, bauxite and gypsum.

Agriculture. About 80% of the population are supported by agriculture. Rice, wheat and maize are the major cereals. The total area under food crops (1978-79) was estimated at 1,847,000 acres. Total foodgrains produced, 1980, 1·4m. quintals. Fruit is important; exports (1980–81 estimate), 360,000 tonnes.

The Agrarian Reforms Act came into force in July 1978; the Debtors Relief Act and the Restriction of Mortgage Properties Act also alleviate rural distress. The redistribution of land to cultivators is continuing.

Livestock (1977 census): Cattle, 2,138,000; buffaloes, 501,000; goats, 1,216,000; horses, 629,000, and poultry, 2,039,000.

Forestry. Forests cover about 21,080 sq. km., forming an important source of revenue, besides providing employment to a large section of the population. About 7,480 sq. km of forests yield valuable timber; state income in 1978–79 was Rs 231·1m.

INDUSTRY. The largest industrial complex is the Bari Brahmara estate in Jammu which covers 320 acres and accommodates diverse manufacturing, as does the Khanmuh estate. The Sopore industrial area in Kashmir Division is intended for industries based on horticulture. There are 6,386 small units (1980) with production valued at Rs 661·3m., employing 34,000. The main traditional handicraft industries are silk spinning and carpet-weaving.

COMMUNICATIONS

Roads. Kashmir is linked with the rest of India by the motorable Jammu-Pathankot road. The Jawahar Tunnel, through the Banihal mountain, connects Srinagar and Jammu, and maintains road communication with the Kashmir Valley during the winter months. In 1981 there were 7,866 km of roads; work on the Batote–Kishtwar road was in progress, up-grading to National Highway standard. There were 33,361 motor vehicles in 1979–80.

Railways. Kashmir was linked with the Indian railway system on 3 Dec. 1972 when the line between Jammu and Pathankot was opened.

Aviation. Major airports, with daily service from Delhi, are at Srinagar and Jammu. Srinagar airport is being developed as an international airport.

Post. There were 1,290 post offices in 1980, 82 telephone exchanges and approximately 12,120 private telephones.

JUSTICE, RELIGION, EDUCATION AND WELFARE

Justice. The High Court, at Srinagar and Jammu, has a Chief Justice and 4 puisne judges.

Religion. The majority of the population, except in Jammu, are Moslems. At the 1971 census Moslems numbered 3,040,129; Hindus, 1,404,292; Sikhs, 105,873; Buddhists, 57,956; Christians, 7,182; Jains, 1,150.

Education. The proportion of literates was 18·59% in 1980. Education is free. There are (1981) 9,715 schools and about 953,000 children attend. Jammu and Srinagar Universities (founded 1948) have 37 teaching departments and 42 affiliated colleges. There are 2 medical colleges, an engineering college, 1 agricultural college, 2 polytechnics, 12 professional colleges, 8 oriental colleges and an Ayurvedic college.

Health. In 1979–80 there were 43 hospitals, 279 primary health units, 279 sub-centres, about 530 clinics and dispensaries, and 50 other units. There were 800 doctors. Expenditure on health was Rs 27·15 in 1980–81. There is a National Institute of Medical Sciences under construction.

Bamzai, P. N. K., *A History of Kashmir.* Delhi, 1962
Gupta, S., Kashmir: *A Study in IndiaPakistan Relations.* London, 1967

KARNATAKA

HISTORY. The state of Karnataka, constituted as Mysore under the States Reorganization Act, 1956, brought together the Kannada-speaking people distributed in 5 states, and consisted of the territories of the old states of Mysore and Coorg, the Bijapur, Kanara and Dharwar districts and the Belgaum district (except one taluk) in former Bombay, the major portions of the Gulbarga, Raichur and Bidar districts in former Hyderabad, and South Kanara district (apart from the Kasaragod taluk) and the Kollegal taluk of the Coimbatore district in Madras. The state was renamed Karnataka in 1973.

AREA AND POPULATION. The state is in south India and is bounded north by Maharashtra, east by Andhra Pradesh, south by Tamil Nadu and Kerala, west by the Indian ocean and north-east by Goa. The area of the state is 191,773 sq. km, and its population (1981 census), 37,043,451, an increase of 26·43% since 1971. Density, 193 per sq. km. Kannada is the language of administration and is spoken by about 60% of the people. Other languages include Telugu (8·7%), Urdu (8·6%), Marathi (4·5%), Tamil (3·6%), Tulu and Konkani. Principal cities, *see* p. 611.

CONSTITUTION AND GOVERNMENT. Karnataka has a bicameral legislature. The Legislative Council has 63 members. The Legislative Assembly consists of 223 elected members and 1 nominated member. After elections in Jan. 1983 the Janata party formed a government supported by Bharatiya Janata.

The state has 19 districts (of which Coorg is one) in 4 divisions: Bangalore, Mysore, Belgaum and Gulbarga. The capital is Bangalore.

Governor: Govind Narain.
Chief Minister: Ramakrishna Hegde.

BUDGET. Budget estimates for 1981–82 showed a deficit of Rs 461·1m.

ENERGY AND NATURAL RESOURCES

Electricity. In 1980 the state's installed capacity was to be revised (by the Kalinadi project) to 2,000 mw.

Water. About 2m. hectares were irrigated in 1980.

Minerals. Karnataka has India's only sources of gold and silver. The estimated reserves of high grade iron ore are 5,000m. tonnes. These reserves are found mainly in the Chitradurga belt. The National Mineral Development Corporation of India has indicated total reserves of nearly 1,000m. tonnes of magnesite and iron ore (with an iron content ranging from 25 to 40) which have been found in Kudremukh Ganga-Mula region in Chickmagalur District. The estimated reserves of manganese are over 100m. tonnes.

Limestone is found in many regions; deposits are about 1,500m. tonnes.

Karnataka is the largest producer of chromite. It is one of the only two states of India producing magnesite. The other minerals of industrial importance are corundum and garnet.

Agriculture. Agriculture forms the main occupation of more than three-quarters of the population. Physically, Karnataka divides itself into four regions–the coastal region, the southern and northern 'maidan' or plain country, comprising roughly the districts of Bangalore, Tumkur, Chitaldrug, Kolar, Bellary, Mandya and Mysore, and the 'malnad' or hill country, comprising the districts of Chickmagalur, Hassan and Shimoga. Rainfall is heavy in the 'malnad' tracts, and in this area there is dense forest. The greater part of the 'maidan' country is cultivated. Coorg district is essentially agricultural.

The main food crops are rice and jowar, and ragi which is also about 30% of the national crop. Sugar, groundnut, castor-seed, safflower, mulberry silk and cotton are important cash crops. The state grows about 70% of the national coffee crop.

In 1975–76, 7·48m. hectares were under foodgrains (production, 5·53m. tonnes); other crops included oilseeds (950,000 tonnes), cotton (700,000 bales of 180 kg), arecanut (66,100 tonnes), chillies, tobacco, sugar-cane and rubber. Yield of raw rubber from 1,120 hectares, 2 tonnes per day. There were, in 1977, 730,241 hectares under cotton, 730,240 under groundnuts, 963,017 under rice, 1·8m. under jowar, 9·14m. under ragi and 362,713 under wheat.

Livestock (1977): Buffaloes, 3,215,873; other cattle, 10,018,714; sheep, 662,420; goats, 726,016.

Forestry. Total forest in the state (1979) is 18% of the land area, producing sandal wood, bamboo and other timbers, and ivory.

INDUSTRY. The Visvesvaraya Iron and Steel Works is situated at Bhadravati, while at Bangalore are national undertakings for the manufacture of aircraft, machine tools, light engineering and electronics goods. Other industries include textiles, vehicle manufacture, cement, chemicals, sugar, paper, porcelain and soap. In addition, much of the world's sandalwood is processed, the oil being one of the most valuable productions of the state. Sericulture is a more important cottage industry giving employment, directly or indirectly, to about 2·4m. persons; production is about 3,000 tonnes, over two-thirds of national production. Industrial production, 1972 (tonnes): Iron, 180,637; steel, 290,307; paper, 71,618; cement, 1·2m. and sugar, 254,000.

COMMUNICATIONS

Roads. In 1977 the state had 89,496 km of roads. There were 195,483 motor vehicles in 1976.

Railways. In 1976 there were 2,803 km of railway (including 154 km of narrow gauge) in the state.

Aviation. There are airports at Bangalore, Mangalore and Belgaum, with regular scheduled services to Bombay, Calcutta, Delhi and Madras.

Shipping. Mangalore is a deep-water port for the export of mineral ores. Karwar is being developed as an intermediate port.

JUSTICE, RELIGION AND EDUCATION

Justice. The seat of the High Court is at Bangalore. It has a Chief Justice and 11 puisne judges.

Religion. At the 1971 census Hindus numbered 25,332,388; Moslems, 3,113,298; Christians, 613,026; Jains, 218,862; Buddhists, 114,139; Sikhs, 6,830.

Education. The number of literates, according to the 1981 census, was 14·2m. In 1977 the state had 33,137 primary schools, 2,326 high schools, 314 schools for professional and technical education and 30 polytechnic and engineering schools. Education is free up to pre-university level.

The University of Mysore (founded in 1916) at Mysore has 3 university colleges at Mysore and 134 affiliated colleges. Karnatak University (1950) at Dharwar has 4 constituent colleges and 95 affiliated colleges. Bangalore University (1964) has 46 constituent colleges, the University of Agricultural Sciences, Hebbal, Bangalore, (1964) has 3 constituent colleges.

The Indian Institute of Science. Bangalore, is unaffiliated; it conducts diploma courses in engineering, metallurgy and technology. There are 415 other colleges, including medical, law and commercial.

Learmouth, A. T. A., and Bhat, L. T., *Mysore State.* 2 vols. London, 1961–62

KERALA

HISTORY. The state of Kerala, created under the States Reorganization Act, 1956, consists of the previous state of Travancore-Cochin, except for 4 taluks of the Trivandrum district and a part of the Shencottah taluk of Quilon district. It took over the Malabar district (apart from the Laccadive and Minicoy Islands) and the Kasaragod taluk of South Kanara (apart from the Amindivi Islands) from Madras State.

AREA AND POPULATION. Kerala is in south India and is bounded north by Karnataka, east and south-east by Tamil Nadu, south-west and west by the Indian ocean. The state has an area of 38,855 sq. km. The 1981 census showed a population of 25,403,217; density of population was 654 per sq. km (highest of any state). Growth rate, 1971–81, 19%. Population of principal cities, *see* p. 611.

Languages spoken in the state are Malayalam, Tamil and Kannada.

The physical features of the land fall into three well-marked divisions: (1) the hilly tracts undulating from the Western Ghats in the east and marked by long spurs, extensive ravines and dense forests; (2) the cultivated plains intersected by numerous rivers and streams; and (3) the coastal belt with dense coconut plantations and rice fields.

CONSTITUTION AND GOVERNMENT. The state has a unicameral legislature of 140 members including the Speaker. After the elections of May 1982 the Indira Congress Party held 77 seats, the Democratic Front (CPI, CPI (M) and allies), 63.

The state has 12 districts. The capital is Trivandrum.

Governor: J. Vencatachellum.
Chief Minister: K. Karunakaran.

BUDGET. Budget estimates for 1980–81 showed revenue account receipts of Rs 591 crores, expenditure Rs 575 crores. Total receipts, Rs 1,491·79 crores; total expenditure, Rs 1,523·54 crores. Annual Plan expenditure, Rs 206·60 crores. The estimated budget deficit, 1981–82, was Rs 85m.

ENERGY AND NATURAL RESOURCES

Electricity. Installed capacity (1979), 1,011·5 mw.; energy generated in 1978–79 was 4,730·4m. kw. Stage I of the Idukki hydro-electric plant has a capacity of 390 mw, the Sabarigiri scheme 300mw. Hydro-electricity has been severely limited by drought during 1980–83.

Minerals. Next to Bihar, Kerala possesses the widest variety of economic mineral resources among the Indian States. The beach sands of Kerala contain monazite, ilmenite, rutile, zircon, sillimanite, etc. There are extensive whiteclay deposits; other minerals of commercial importance include mica, graphite, limestone, quartz sand and lignite. Iron ore has been found at Kozhikode (Calicut). Value of mineral production, 1976, Rs 11·5m.

Agriculture. The state suffered three successive monsoon failures up to 1983, with severe effects on crops. The chief agricultural products are rice, tapioca, coconut, arecanut, cashewnut, oilseeds, pepper, sugar-cane, rubber, tea, coffee and cardamom. About 98% of Indian black pepper and about 95% of Indian rubber is produced in Kerala. Area and production of principal crops, 1978–79 (in 1,000 hectares and 1,000 tonnes): Rice, 799·2, 1,270; black pepper, 108·3, 25·1; ginger (dry), 11, 28; arecanut, 62·8, 10,576 (million nuts); bananas and other plantains, 50·9, 615·9; cashewnuts, 135·5, 89·7; coconuts, 678·6, 3,075 (million nuts); tea, 36·1, 47·2; coffee, 51·7, 21·7; rubber, 214·4, 123·6; tapioca, 289·8, 4,226; cardamom, 51·9, 2·9.

Livestock (1972, provisional); Buffaloes, 469,515; other cattle, 2,855,856; sheep, 10,390; goats, 1,450,587.

Forestry. About a third of the area is comprised of forests, including teak, sandal wood, ebony and blackwood and varieties of softwood. Forest revenue, 1978–79, Rs 26·2 crores, from timber, bamboos, reeds and ivory.

Fisheries. Fishing is a flourishing industry; the catch in 1979 was about 398,000 tonnes.

INDUSTRIES. Most of the major industrial concerns are either owned or sponsored by the Government. The Government owns 11 industrial concerns and has substantial shares in more than 40. Among the privately owned factories are the numerous cashew and coir factories. Other important factory industries are rubber, tea, tiles, oil, textiles, ceramics, fertilizers and chemicals, zinc-smelting, sugar, cement, rayon, glass, matches, pencils, monazite, ilmenite, titanium oxide, rare earths, aluminium, electrical goods, paper, shark-liver oil, etc.

The number of factories registered under the Factories Act 1948 on 31 Dec. 1978 was 7,784, with daily average employment of 272,392. Man-days lost by industrial disputes in 1979, 3·51m.

Among the cottage industries, coir-spinning and handloom-weaving are the most important, forming the means of livelihood of a large section of the people. Other industries are the village oil industry, ivory carving, furniture-making, bell metal, brass and copper ware, leather goods, screw-pines, mat-making, rattan work, bee-keeping, pottery, etc. These have been organized on a co-operative basis.

COMMUNICATIONS

Roads. In 1979 there were 90,440 km of roads in the state; national highways, 838 km. There were 154,595 motor vehicles in 1979.

Railways. There is a coastal line from Mangalore (Karnataka) which serves Mahe, Kozhikode (Calicut), Ernakulam (for Cochin) and Quilon, and connects them with main towns in Tamil Nadu. In 1980 there were 806 km broad gauge and 113 km metre gauge lines.

Aviation. There are airports at Cochin and Trivandrum with regular scheduled services to Bombay and Madras.

Shipping. Port Cochin, administered by the central government, is one of India's 6 major ports; in 1983 it became the out-port for the Inland Container Depot at Coimbatore (Tamil Nadu). There are 10 other ports and harbours.

JUSTICE, RELIGION AND EDUCATION

Justice. The High Court at Ernakulam has a Chief Justice and 11 puisne judges and 4 additional judges.

Religion. At the 1971 census Hindus numbered 12,683,277; Christians, 4,494,089; Moslems, 4,162,718; Jains, 3,336.

Education. Kerala is the most literate Indian State with 17m. literates at the 1981 census. Education is free up to the age of 14.

In 1979–80 there was a total school enrolment of 5·59m. students. There were 7,013 lower primary schools 2,739 upper primary schools and 1,680 high schools. About 62% of schools are privately run.

Kerala University (established 1937) at Trivandrum, is affiliating and teaching; in 1979 it had 79 affiliated arts and science colleges and 25 affiliated professional colleges. The University of Cochin is federal, and for post-graduate studies only. The University of Calicut (established 1968) is teaching and affiliating and has 65 affiliated colleges. Kerala Agricultural University (established 1971) has 3 constituent colleges.

MADHYA PRADESH

HISTORY. Under the provisions of the States Reorganization Act, 1956, the State of Madhya Pradesh was formed on 1 Nov. 1956. It consists of the 17 Hindi districts of the previous state of that name, the former state of Madhya Bharat (except the Sunel enclave of Mandsaur district), the former state of Bhopal and Vindhya Pradesh and the Sironj subdivision of Kotah district, which was an enclave of Rajasthan in Madhya Pradesh.

For information on the former states, *see* THE STATESMAN'S YEAR-BOOK, 1958, pp. 180–84.

AREA AND POPULATION. The state is in central India and is bounded north by Rajasthan and Uttar Pradesh, east by Bihar and Orissa, south by Andhra Pradesh and Maharashtra, west by Gujarat. Madhya Pradesh is the largest Indian state in size, with an area of 442,841 sq. km. In respect of population it ranks sixth. Population (1981 census), 52,138,467, an increase of 25·15% since 1971. Density, 118 per sq. km.

Cities with over 250,000 population, *see* p. 611. Other large cities (1981): Sagar, 207,401; Bilaspur, 186,885; Ratlam, 156,490; Burhanpur, 141,142; Mudwari-Katni, 125,096; Khandwa, 114,463; Rewa, 100,519.

The number of persons speaking each of the more prevalent languages (1971 census) were: Hindi, 32,873,079; Urdu, 988,275; Marathi, 1,385,952; Gujarati, 155,723.

CONSTITUTION AND GOVERNMENT. Madhya Pradesh is one of the 9 states for which the Constitution provides a bicameral legislature, but the Vidhan Parishad or Upper House (to consist of 90 members) has yet to be formed. The Vidhan Sabha or Lower House has 320 elected members. Following the election of

May 1980 (318 seats contested), Congress (I) held 245; Bhartiya Janata, 59; others, 14.

For administrative purposes the state has been split into 11 divisions with a Commissioner at the head of each; the headquarters of these are located at Bhopal, Bilaspur, Gwalior (2), Hoshangabad, Indore, Jabalpur, Raipur, Rewa, Sagar and Ujjain. There are 45 districts.

The seat of government is at Bhopal.

Governor: B. D. Sharma.
Chief Minister: A. Singh.

BUDGET. Budget estimates for 1982–83 showed total revenue of Rs 14,26,51·83 lakhs, and expenditure of Rs 12,68,30 lakhs. Receipts included: Contributions and adjustments between central and state governments, Rs 4,84,55·97 lakhs; taxes on income, Rs 81,92 lakhs; state excise, Rs 68,63·70 lakhs; stamps and registration, Rs 26,45 lakhs; forests, Rs 1,95,00 lakhs; sales tax, Rs 2,40,96 lakhs; vehicles taxes, Rs 26,11 lakhs; debt services, Rs 77,49·27 lakhs; civil administration, Rs 22,39·68 lakhs; land revenue, Rs 12,98·00 lakhs. Expenditure included: Education, Rs 2,11,24·16 lakhs; public works and improvements, Rs 55,26·89 lakhs; irrigation, embankment, etc., Rs 40,24·01 lakhs; medical, and public health, Rs 1,34,46·65 lakhs; police, Rs 83,32·72 lakhs; agriculture, Rs 40,94·18 lakhs; general administration, Rs 20,13·25 lakhs; debt services, Rs 1,19,05·35 lakhs; community projects and local development, Rs 65,80·76 lakhs; industries, Rs 16,41·25 lakhs; forests, Rs 1,05,66·69 lakhs; social security and welfare, Rs 71,88·49 lakhs.

ENERGY AND NATURAL RESOURCES

Electricity. Madhya Pradesh is rich in low-grade coal suitable for power generation, and also has immense potential hydro-electric energy. The present installed capacity is 1,630·5 mw; of this 193 mw from hydro-electric power stations. The thermal power stations are at Korba in Bilaspur district, Amarkantak in Shahdol district and Satpura in Betul district, new stations are being built. The only hydro-electric power station is at Gandhi Sagar lake in Mandsaur district; this, with a maximum water surface of 165 sq. miles, is the biggest man-made lake in Asia.

Water. Major irrigation projects include the Chambal Valley scheme (started in 1952 with Rajasthan), the Tawa project in Hoshangabad district, the Barna and Hasdeo schemes, the Mahanadi canal system and schemes in the Narmada valley at Bargi and Narmadasagar. Total irrigation potential in 1983, 10m. hectares, of which 3 m. had been achieved.

Minerals. The state has extensive mineral deposits including coal (35% of national deposits), iron ore (30%) and manganese (50%), bauxite (44%), ochre, sillimanite, limestone, dolomite, rock phosphate, copper, lead, tin, fluorite, barytes, china clay and fireclay, corundum, gold, diamonds, pyrophyllite and diaspore, lepidolite, asbestos, vermiculite, mica, glass sand, quartz, felspars, bentonite and building stone.

In 1980 the output of major minerals was (in tonnes): Coal, 25·1m.; limestone, 6·53m.; dolomite, 770,000; diamonds, 14,432 carats; bauxite, 470,000; iron ore, 9·7m.; manganese ore, 270,000. Value of production, 1980, Rs 3,626m.

Agriculture. Agriculture is the mainstay of the state's economy and 80% of the people are rural. Over 42% of the land area is cultivable, of which 13% is irrigated. The Malwa region abounds in rich black cotton soil, the low-lying areas of Gwalior, Bundelkhand and Baghelkhand and the Chhatisgarh plains have a lighter sandy soil, while the Narmada valley is formed of deep rich alluvial deposits. Production of principal crops, 1980–81 (in tonnes): Foodgrains, 12·4m.; sugar-cane (gur), 107,000; oilseeds, 608,000; and cotton, 268,000 bales (of 170 kg).

Livestock (1977 census): Buffaloes, 5,852,549; other cattle, 34,256,725; sheep, 968,595; goats, 6,573,467; horses and ponies, 121,908.

Forestry. In 1982 155,411 sq. km, or about 35% of the state's area was covered by forests. The forests are chiefly of sal, saja, bija, bamboo and teak. They are the chief source in India of best-quality teak; they also provide firewood for about 60% of domestic fuel needs, and form valuable watershed protection.

INDUSTRY. The major industries are the steel plant at Bhilai, Bharat Heavy Electricals at Bhopal, the aluminium plant at Korba, the security paper mills at Hoshangabad, the Bank Note Press at Dewas, the newsprint mill at Nepanagar and alkaloid factory at Neemuch, cement factories, vehicle factory, ordnance factory, and gun carriage factory. There are also 23 textile mills, 7 of them nationalized.

The Bhilai steel plant near Durg is one of the 6 major steel mills. A power station at Korba (Bilaspur) with a capacity of 420 mw serves Bhilai, the aluminium plant and the Korba coalfield.

The heavy electricals factory was set up by the Government of India at Bhopal during the second-plan period. This is India's first heavy electrical equipment factory and also one of the largest of its type in Asia. It makes a variety of highly complicated equipment required for generation, transmission, distribution and utilization of electric power.

Other industries include cement, sugar, straw board, paper, vegetable oil, refractories, potteries, textile machinery, steel casting and rerolling, industrial gases, synthetic fibres, drugs, biscuit manufacturing, engineering, tools, rayon and art silk. The number of heavy and medium industries in the state is 193, with 181 ancillary industries; the number of small-scale industries in production is 77,360. Thirty-nine out of 45 districts in the state are categorized as industrially backward districts.

The main industrial development agencies are Madhya Pradesh Financial Corporation, Madhya Pradesh Audyogik Vikas Nigam Ltd, Madhya Pradesh State Industries Corporation, Madhya Pradesh Laghu Udyog Nigam, Madhya Pradesh State Textile Corporation, Madhya Pradesh Handicrafts Board, Khadi and Village Industries Board and Madhya Pradesh State Mining Corporation.

The state is known for its traditional village and home crafts such as handloom weaving, best developed at Chanderi and Maheshwar, toys, pottery, lacework, woodwork, zari work, leather work and metal utensils. The ancillary industries of dyeing, calico printing and bleaching are centred in areas of textile production.

COMMUNICATIONS

Roads. Total length of roads in 1982 was 65,889 km, of which 50,934 km were surfaced. In 1977–78 there were 225,278 motor vehicles.

Railways. Bhopal, Bilaspur, Katni, Khandwar and Ratlam are important junctions for the central and northern networks.

Aviation. There are airports at Bhopal, Indore, Jabalpur, Khajuraho and Raipur with regular scheduled services to Bombay, Calcutta and Delhi.

JUSTICE, RELIGION AND EDUCATION

Justice. The High Court of Judicature at Jabalpur has a Chief Justice and 21 puisne judges.

Religion. At the 1971 census Hindus numbered 39,024,162; Moslems, 1,815,685; Christians, 286,072; Buddhists, 81,823; Sikhs, 98,973.

Education. The 1981 census showed 14·5m. people to be literate. Education is free for children aged up to 14.

In 1975–76 there were 355 higher educational institutions. Primary schools (1974–75) had 3·5m. pupils and higher secondary schools, 620,897 pupils.

There are 10 universities in Madhya Pradesh: the University of Sagar (established 1946), at Sagar, had 53 affiliated colleges and 26,516 students in 1975; Jabalpur University (1957) had 30 affiliated colleges and 12,962 students; Vikram University (1957), at Ujjain, had 46 affiliated colleges and 38,011 students; Indira Kala Sangeet Vishwavidyalaya (1956), at Khairagarh, had 9 affiliated colleges and

1,164 students on roll (this university teaches music and fine arts); Indore University (1964) had 21 affiliated colleges and 22,915 students; Jivagi University (1963), at Gwalior, had 43 affiliated colleges and 31,462 students; Jawaharlal Nehru Krishi University (1964), at Jabalpur, had 9 affiliated colleges and 2,274 students in 1964; Ravishankar University (1964), at Raipur, had 63 affiliated colleges and 41,607 students. In 1975–76 there were 256 degree-granting colleges, 19 teacher-training colleges, and 71 professional colleges including polytechnics.

MAHARASHTRA

HISTORY. Under the States Reorganization Act, 1956, Bombay State was formed by merging the states of Kutch and Saurashtra and the Marathi-speaking areas of Hyderabad (commonly known as Marathwada) and Madhya Pradesh (also called Vidarbha) in the old state of Bombay, after the transfer from that state of the Kannada-speaking areas of the Belgaum, Bijapur, Kanara and Dharwar districts which were added to the state of Mysore, and the Abu Road taluka of Banaskantha district, which went to the state of Rajasthan.

By the Bombay Reorganization Act, 1960, which came into force 1 May 1960, 17 districts (predominantly Gujarati-speaking) in the north and west of Bombay State became the new state of Gujarat, and the remainder was renamed Maharashtra.

The state of Maharashtra consists of the following districts of the former Bombay State: Ahmednagar, Akola, Amravati, Aurangabad, Bhandara, Bhir, Buldana, Chanda, Dhulia (West Khandesh), Greater Bombay, Jalgaon (East Khandesh), Kolaba, Kolhapur, Nagpur, Nanded, Nasik, Osmanabad, Parbhani, Pune, Ratnagiri, Sangli, Satara, Sholapur, Thana, Wardha, Yeotmal; certain portions of Thana and Dhulia districts have become part of Gujarat.

AREA AND POPULATION. Maharashtra is in central India and is bounded north and east by Madhya Pradesh, south by Andhra Pradesh, Karnataka and Goa, west by the Indian ocean and north-west by Daman and Gujarat. The state has an area of 307,762 sq. km. The population at the 1981 census was 62,693,898 (an increase of 24·36% since 1971), of whom about 30m. were Marathi-speaking. Density, 204 per sq. km. The area of Greater Bombay was 603 sq. km. and its population 8,227,000. For other principal cities, see p. 611.

CONSTITUTION AND GOVERNMENT. Maharashtra has a bicameral legislature. The Legislative Council has 78 members. The Legislative Assembly has 287 elected members and 1 member nominated by the Governor to represent the Anglo-Indian community. Following the election of May 1980 Congress (I) held 186 seats; Congress (U), 47; Janata, 17; Bhartiya Janata, 14; others, 24.

The Council of Ministers consists of the Chief Minister, 13 other Ministers, 12 Ministers of State and 5 Deputy Ministers.

The capital is Bombay.

Governor: Sadiq Ali.
Chief Minister: Vasantrao Patil.

BUDGET. Budget estimates, 1980–81, show revenue receipts of Rs 1,921·97 crores, revenue account expenditure Rs 1,857·39 crores. Capital account receipts, Rs 799·03 crores; expenditure, Rs 873·33 crores. The estimates for 1981–82 showed a deficit of Rs 291m.

ENERGY AND NATURAL RESOURCES

Electricity. Installed capacity, 1984, 4,358 mw. (2,351 mw. thermal, 1,897 mw. hydro-electricity and 210 mw. nuclear).

Minerals. Value of production, 1976, Rs 26·7m. The state has coal, chromite, limestone, iron ore, manganese, bauxite.

Agriculture. About 10% of the cropped area is irrigated. Area (in 1,000 hectares) and production (in 1,000 tonnes) of principal crops in 1973–74: Rice, 1,351, 1,637; wheat, 965, 547; jowar, 6,088, 2,819; bajri, 2,215, 850; total cereals, 11,091, 6,177; total pulses, 2,762, 868; total foodgrains, 13,853, 7,045; sugar-cane, 215 (of gur, 1,544); groundnuts, 758, 566; cotton, 2,348 (1,058 bales of 180 kg). Total food-grains, 1976, 9,119,000 tonnes. Cash crops, 1976: Sugar-cane, 2m. tonnes; cotton, 781,000 bales (of 180 kg); groundnuts, 671,000 tonnes.

Livestock (1972 census): Buffaloes, 3,300,746; other cattle, 14,705,147; sheep, 2,128,036; goats, 5,910,554; horses and ponies, 58,287; poultry, 12,216,567.

Forestry. Forests occupy 17·4% of the state.

INDUSTRY. Industry is concentrated mainly in Bombay, Pune and Thana. The main groups are chemicals and products, textiles, electrical and non-electrical machinery, petroleum and products, and food products. The state industrial development corporation had invested Rs 840m. in 57 industrial estates by 1980.

COMMUNICATIONS

Roads. On 31 March 1975 there were 89,007 km of roads, of which 41,484 km were surfaced. There were 432,901 motor vehicles in 1976. Passenger and freight transport has been nationalized.

Railways. The total length of railway is about 5,162 km. The main junctions and termini are Bombay, Manmad, Akola, Nagpur, Pune and Sholapur.

Aviation. The main airport is Bombay, which has national and international flights. Nagpur airport is on the route from Bombay to Calcutta and there are also airports at Pune and Aurangabad.

Shipping. Maharashtra has a coastline of 720 km. Bombay is the major port, and there are 42 minor ports.

JUSTICE, RELIGION AND EDUCATION

Justice. The High Court has a Chief Justice and 27 judges. There are 8 additional judges. The seat of the High Court is Bombay, but it has a bench at Nagpur.

Religion. At the 1961 census Hindus numbered 32,530,901; Moslems, 3,034,332; Buddhists, 2,789,501; Christians, 560,594; Jains, 485,672; Sikhs, 57,617.

Education. The number of literates, according to the 1981 census, was 29·6m.

The total number of recognized institutions in 1975 was 56,656, with 10,528,258 students. Higher and secondary schools numbered 6,579 with 2,986,636 pupils; primary schools, 48,018, with 7,367,045 pupils; pre-primary schools, 827 with 62,781.

Bombay University, founded in 1857, is mainly an affiliating university. It has 99 constituent colleges and 21 post-graduate departments in Bombay with a total (1975–76) of 137,922 students. Colleges in Goa can affiliate to Bombay University. Nagpur University (1923) is both teaching and affiliating. In addition to the 26 post-graduate departments there were (1975–76) 140 affiliated colleges and constituent colleges with 87,153 students. Pune University, founded in 1948, is teaching and affiliating; in 1975–76 it had 103 affiliated colleges and constituent colleges, 26 post-graduate departments and a total of 88,232 students. The SNDT Women's University had, in 1975–76, 16 constituent colleges and affiliated colleges with a total of 9,911 students. Marathwada University, Aurangabad, was founded in 1958 as a teaching and affiliating body to control colleges in the Marathwada or Marathi-speaking area, previously under Osmania University; in 1975–76 there were 82 affiliated and constituent colleges and 6 post-graduate departments and 71,419 students. Shiwaji University, Kolhapur, was established in 1963 to control affiliated colleges previously under Pune University. In 1975–76 it had 84 affiliated and constituent colleges and 14 post-graduate departments and 65,526 students. There are 4 agricultural universities with 16 affiliated colleges and 6,114 students in 1975–76. There were altogether 682 institutions for higher education in 1975–76, with 474,067 students.

Statistical Information: The Director of Publicity, Sachivalaya, Bombay.
Annual Statistical Abstract (from 1951)
Tindall, G., *City of Gold*, London, 1982

MANIPUR

HISTORY. Formerly a state under the political control of the Government of India, Manipur, on 15 Aug. 1947, entered into interim arrangements with the Indian Union and the political agency was abolished. The administration was taken over by the Government of India on 15 Oct. 1949 under a merger agreement, and it is centrally administered by the Government of India through a Chief Commissioner. In 1950–51 an Advisory form of Government was introduced. In 1957 this was replaced by a Territorial Council of 30 elected and 2 nominated members. Later in 1963 a Legislative Assembly of 30 elected and 3 nominated members was established under the Government of Union Territories Act 1963. Because of the unstable party position in the Assembly, it had to be dissolved on 16 Oct. 1969 and President's Rule introduced. The status of the administrator was raised from Chief Commissioner to Lieut.-Governor with effect from 19 Dec. 1969. On the 21 Jan. 1972 Manipur became a state and the status of the administrator was changed from Lieut.-Governor to Governor.

AREA AND POPULATION. The state is in north-east India and is bounded north by Nagaland, east by Burma, south by Burma and Mizoram, and west by Assam. Manipur has an area of 22,356 sq. km and a population (1981) of 1,433,691. Density, 64 per sq. km. Growth rate, 1971–81, 33·65%. The valley, which is about 1,813 sq. km, is 2,600 ft above sea-level. The hills rise in places to nearly 10,000 ft, but are mostly about 5,000–6.000 ft. The average annual rainfall is 65 in. The hill areas are inhabited by various hill tribes who constitute about one-third of the total population of the state. There are about 40 tribes and sub-tribes falling into two main groups of Nagas and Kukis. Manipuri and English are the official languages. A large number of dialects are spoken, while Hindi is gradually becoming prevalent.

CONSTITUTION AND GOVERNMENT. With the attainment of statehood, Manipur has a Legislative Assembly of 60 members, of which 19 are from reserved tribal constituencies. There are 6 districts. Capital, Imphal (population, 1981, 155,639). Presidential rule was imposed in Feb. 1981.

Governor: L. P. Singh.

BUDGET. Revised estimates for 1977–78 show revenue of Rs 4,247·82 lakhs and expenditure on revenue account of Rs 4,774·24 lakhs.

ENERGY AND NATURAL RESOURCES

Electricity. Installed capacity (1983) is 22 mw. from diesel generators. This has been augmented since 1981 by the North Eastern Regional Grid. In 1983 there were 488 villages with electricity.

Water. The main power, irrigation and flood-control schemes are the Loktak Lift Irrigation scheme (irrigation potential, 40,000 hectares of which (1983) 19,000 have been achieved); the Singda scheme (potential 4,000 hectares, and improved water supply for Imphal); the Thoubal scheme (potential 34,000 hectares, 7·5 mw. of electricity and 10 MGD of water supply), and four other large projects.

Agriculture. Rice is the principal crop, with wheat, maize and pulses. Total food-grains, 1982–83, 358,000 tonnes.

Agricultural work force, about 348,000. Only 210,000 hectares are cultivable, of which 186,000 are under paddy. Fruit and vegetables are important in the valley, including pineapple, oranges, bananas, mangoes, pears, peaches and plums. Soil erosion, produced by shifting cultivation, is being halted by terracing.

Forests. Forests occupy about 15,154 sq km. The main products are teak, jurjan, pine; there are also large areas of bamboo and cane, especially in the Jiri and Barak river drainage areas, yielding about 300,000 tonnes annually. Total revenue from forests, 1981–82, Rs 3·9m.

Fisheries. Landings in 1981–82, 3,450 tonnes.

INDUSTRY. Handloom weaving is a popular industry. Larger-scale industries include sugar, cement, starch and glucose. Sericulture produces about 45 tonnes of raw silk annually. Estimated non-agricultural work force, 240,000.

COMMUNICATIONS. A national highway from Kazirangar (Assam) runs through Imphal to the Burmese frontier. There are no railways, but the highway runs through Dimapur which has a rail-head, 215 km. from Imphal. There is an airport at Imphal with regular scheduled services to Gauhati and Calcutta.

EDUCATION AND HEALTH

Education. The 1981 census gave the number of literates as 600,000. In 1982–83 there were 2,821 primary schools, 459 middle schools, 301 high and higher schools and 23 colleges, as well as Manipur University.

Health. In 1977–78 there were 33 hospitals (including primary health centres) and 125 dispensaries (including primary health centres).

MEGHALAYA

HISTORY. The state was created under the Assam Reorganization (Meghalaya) Act 1969 and inaugurated on 2 April 1970. Its status was that of a state within the State of Assam until 21 Jan. 1972 when it became a fully independent state of the Union. It consists of the former Garo Hills district and United Khasi and Jaintia Hills district of Assam.

AREA AND POPULATION. Meghalaya is bounded north and east by Assam, south and west by Bangladesh. In 1981 (census figure) the area was 22,489 sq. km and the population 1,327,824. Density 59 per sq. km. Growth rate, 1971–81, 31·25%. The people are mainly of the Khasi, Jaintia and Garo tribes.

CONSTITUTION AND GOVERNMENT. Meghalaya has a unicameral legislature. The Legislative Assembly has 60 seats.
There are 2 districts. The capital is Shillong.

Governor: L. P. Singh.
Chief Minister: D. D. Dohpugh.

BUDGET. Budget estimates for 1981–82 showed a deficit of Rs 6·6m. Annual Plan expenditure, Rs 464·5m.

ENERGY AND NATURAL RESOURCES

Electricity. Total installed capacity (1977) was 65·2 mw. 388 villages had electricity.

Minerals. The United Khasi and Jaintia Hills district produces coal, sillimanite (95% of India's total output), limestone, white clay and corundum. The state also has deposits of coal (estimated reserves 1,200m. tonnes), limestone (2,100m.), fire clay (100,000) and sandstone which are virtually untapped because of transport difficulties. Value of production, 1976, Rs 3·26m.

Agriculture. About 80% of the people depend on agriculture, and 27% of the cultivable area is irrigated. Principal crops are potatoes, fresh fruit and cotton. Production 1978 (in 1,000 tonnes): Foodgrains, 130; potatoes, 71; tapioca, 5; jute, 50,000 bales (of 180 kg). Annual production (in 1,000 tonnes, estimated) of pine-apples, 70; oranges, 80; bananas, 35.

Forest products are the state's chief resources.

INDUSTRY. Apart from agriculture the main source of employment is the extraction and processing of minerals; there are also important timber processing mills.

COMMUNICATIONS. A national highway from Gauhati (Assam) runs through Dispur and Shillong. The state has no railways. There is no airport but Gauhati airport is on the northern boundary.

JUSTICE. There is a High Court at Shillong which is common to Assam, Meghalaya, Nagaland, Manipur, Tripura and the Union Territories of Mizoram and Arunachal Pradesh.

NAGALAND

HISTORY. The territory was constituted by the Union Government in Sept. 1962. It comprises the former Naga Hills district of Assam and the former Tuensang Frontier division of the North-East Frontier Agency; these had been made a Centrally Administered Area in 1957, administered by the President through the Governor of Assam. In Jan. 1961 the area was renamed and given the status of a state of the Indian Union, which was officially inaugurated on 1 Dec. 1963.

For some years a section of the Naga leaders sought independence. Military operations from 1960 and the prospect of self-government within the Indian Union led to a general reconciliation, but rebel activity continued. A 2-month amnesty in mid 1963 had little effect. A 'ceasefire' in Sept. 1964 was followed by talks between a Government of India delegation and rebel leaders. The peace period was extended and the 'Revolutionary Government of Nagaland' (a breakaway group from the Naga Federal Government) was dissolved in 1973. Further talks with the Naga underground movement resulted in the Shillong Peace Agreement of Nov. 1975.

AREA AND POPULATION. The state is in the extreme north-east and is bounded west and north by Assam, east by Burma and south by Manipur. Nagaland has an area of 16,527 sq. km and a population (1981) census of 773,281. Density 47 per sq. km. Growth rate, 1971–81, 49·73%. Towns include Kohima, Mokokchung, Tuensang and Dimapur. The chief tribes in numerical order are: Angami, Ao, Sema, Konyak, Chakhesang, Lotha, Phom, Khiamngan, Chang, Yimchunger, Zeliarg-Kuki, Rengma and Sangtam.

CONSTITUTION AND GOVERNMENT. An Interim Body (Legislative Assembly) of 42 members elected by the Naga people and an Executive Council (Council of Ministers) of 5 members were formed in 1961, and continued until the State Assembly was elected in Jan. 1964. The initial strength of this Assembly was 46, with 8 cabinet ministers. Since 1974 there have been 60 members. The Governor has extraordinary powers, which include special responsibility for law and order. On 5 June 1980 a Naga National Democratic Party government took office.

The state has 7 districts (Kohima, Mon, Zunheboto, Wokha, Phek, Mokokchung and Tuensang). The capital is Kohima.

Governor: S. M. H. Burney.
Chief Minister: S. C. Jamir.

BUDGET. Budget estimates for 1974–75 show total revenue of Rs 47,43·32 lakhs and expenditure of Rs 47,53·19 lakhs. Receipts included: Statutory grant under the Finance Commission award, Rs 23,77 lakhs; share of central taxes and duties, Rs 1,17·18 lakhs; grants-in-aid for plan expenditure, Rs 6,40·80 lakhs; loans from the Government of India, Rs 71·20 lakhs; grant for roads, Rs 3,64·94 lakhs.

ENERGY AND NATURAL RESOURCES

Electricity. Installed capacity (1976) 2,126 kw; 273 towns and villages (out of 814) had electricity in 1981.

Agriculture. More than 80% of the people derive their livelihood from agriculture. The Angamis, in Kohima district, practise a fixed agriculture in the shape of terraced slopes, and wet paddy cultivation in the lowlands. In the other two districts there is a traditional form of shifting cultivation (*jhumming*). About 1,223,000 hectares were under cultivation in 1977. Production of rice (1977) was 94,530 tonnes.

Forests cover 17·56% of the state.

INDUSTRY. There is a forest products factory at Tijit; a paper-mill (100 tonnes daily capacity) and a distillery unit. There is also a sugar-mill (1,200 tonnes daily capacity). There are also over 600 small units.

COMMUNICATIONS. There is a national highway from Kaziranga (Assam) to Kohima and on to Manipur. There were 3,502 motor vehicles in 1976. There are no railways, and no airports.

RELIGION AND EDUCATION

Religion. At the 1971 census Christians numbered 344,798; Hindus, 59,031; Moslems, 2,966; others, 108. The Naga Baptist Christian Convention had, 1969, 632 churches and a total church membership of 73,500.

Education. The 1981 census records 300,000 literates, or 41·9%: 49·16% of men and 33·72% of women. In 1980 there were 3 government and 3 private colleges, 50 government and 47 private high schools, 201 government and 84 private middle schools and 1,109 primary schools, 1 polytechnic, 1 agricultural college, 2 law colleges. The North Eastern Hill University opened in 1978.

Aram, M., *Peace in Nagaland,* New Delhi, 1974

ORISSA

HISTORY. Orissa, ceded to the Mahrattas by Alivardi Khan in 1751, was conquered by the British in 1803. In 1803 a board of 2 commissioners was appointed to administer the province, but in 1805 it was designated the district of Cuttack and was placed in charge of a collector, judge and magistrate. In 1829 it was split up into 3 regulation districts of Cuttack, Balasore and Puri, and the non-regulation tributary states which were administered by their own chiefs under the ægis of the British Government. Angul, one of these tributary states, was annexed in 1847, and with the Khondmals, ceded in 1835 by the tributary chief of the Boudh state, constituted a separate non-regulation district. Sambalpur was transferred from the Central Provinces to Orissa in 1905. These districts formed an outlying tract of the Bengal Presidency till 1912, when they were transferred to Bihar, constituting one of its divisions under a commissioner. Orissa was constituted a separate province on 1 April 1936, some portions of the Central Provinces and Madras being transferred to the old Orissa division.

The rulers of 25 Orissa states surrendered all jurisdiction and authority to the Government of India on 1 Jan. 1948, on which date the Provincial Government took over the administration. The administration of 2 states, viz., Saraikella and Kharswan, was transferred to the Government of Bihar in May 1948. By an agreement with the Dominion Government, Mayurbhanj State was finally merged with the province on 1 Jan. 1949. By the States Merger (Governors' Provinces) Order, 1949, the states were completely merged with the state of Orissa on 19 Aug. 1949.

EVENTS. Serious flooding in Aug. 1982 caused the deaths of about 1,000 people.

AREA AND POPULATION. Orissa is in eastern India and is bounded north by Bihar, north-east by West Bengal, east by the Bay of Bengal, south by Andhra Pradesh and west by Madhya Pradesh. The area of the state is 155,707 sq. km, and its population (1981 census), 26,370,271, density 169 per sq. km. Growth rate, 1971–81, 20.17%. The second-largest city next to Cuttack (327,412) is Rourkela (322,610). The principal language is Oriya, which will be the official language from 1 April 1985.

CONSTITUTION AND GOVERNMENT. The Legislative Assembly has 147 members. State of the parties in Sept. 1982: Congress (I), 118; Janata (Charan Singh), 13; others, 16.

The state consists of 13 districts.

The capital is Bhubaneswar (18 miles south of Cuttack).

Governor: B. N. Pandey.
Chief Minister: J. B. Patnaik.

BUDGET. Budget estimates, 1980–81 showed total revenue of Rs 1,257.3 crores and expenditure of Rs 1,235.6 crores (capital and revenue accounts).

ENERGY AND NATURAL RESOURCES

Electricity. The Hirakud Dam Project on the river Mahanadi (started 1949) irrigates 628,000 acres and has a scheduled capacity of 270,000 kw. The dam (the largest earth dam in the world) was completed in 1957. Hydro-electric power totalling 85,000 kw. is now serving a large part of the state. The installed capacity of the Machkund hydro-electric project (financed jointly with Andhra Pradesh) is 114,750 kw. Total installed capacity, 1979, 923 mw.; there were 20,953 electrified villages in 1981.

Minerals. Orissa is India's leading producer of chromite (95% of national output), dolomite (50%), manganese ore (25%), graphite (80%), iron ore (16%), fire-clay (34%), limestone (20%), and quartz-quartzite (18%). Production in 1980 (1,000 tonnes): iron ore, 7,019; manganese ore, 568; chromite, 261; coal, 3,042; limestone, 2,591; dolomite, 761; fire-clay, 100; china clay, 31; graphite, 32; quartz and quartzite, 53; lead ore, 40. About 56,000 workers are employed in the mines. Value of mineral production annually is about Rs 900m.

Agriculture. The cultivation of rice is the principal occupation of nearly 80% of the population. Production amounted to 4.44m. tonnes in 1978–79; only a very small amount of other cereals is grown. Production of foodgrains (1978–79) totalled 5.7m. tonnes from 6.7m. hectares. Jute (439,000 tonnes), wheat (110,000 tonnes), oilseeds (426,950 tonnes) and sugar-cane (281,000 tonnes) are also grown. Turmeric is cultivated in the uplands of the districts of Ganjam, Phulbani and Koraput, and is exported.

Livestock (1977 census): Buffaloes, 1,358,451; other cattle, 12·1m.; sheep, 1·5m.; goats, 3·4m.; horses and ponies, 3,675.

Forests. Forests occupy about 43% of the area of the state, the most important species being sal, teak, kendu, sandal, sisu, bija, kuruma, kongada and bamboo.

Fisheries. There were, in 1981, 484 fishery co-operative societies.

INDUSTRY. Fifty-five large industries have been set up (1978–79), mostly based on minerals, including the steel plant of Hindustan Steel Ltd at Rourkela, a pig-iron plant at Barbil, a ferrochrome plant, 2 ferromanganese plants at Joda and Rayagada, 1 ferrosilicon plant at Theruvelli and an aluminium smelter plant at Hirakud, 4 refractory plants and 2 cement plants. There are 3 large paper mills at Rayagada, Chowdwar and Brajrajnagar, two fertilizer plants, a caustic soda plant, a salt manufacturing unit and an industrial explosives plant. An aluminium-alumina plant at Damanjodi was begun in 1981.

Other industries of importance are sugar, glass, aluminium, heavy machine tools, a re-rolling mill and textile mills.

There are cottage and small-scale industries in the state, e.g., handloom weaving and the manufacture of baskets, wooden articles, hats and nets; silver filigree work and hand-woven fabrics are specially well known.

TOURISM. Tourist traffic is concentrated mainly on the 'Golden Triangle', Konark, Puri and Bhubaneswar, and its temples. Tourists also visit Gopalpur, the Similipal Forest and Chilka Lake.

COMMUNICATIONS

Roads. On 31 March 1980 length of roads was: State highway, 2,821 km; national highway, 1,631 km; major district roads, 4,974 km; other district roads, 2,748 km; village roads, about 5,796 km. There were 94,156 motor vehicles in 1979. A 144-km expressway, part national highway, connects the Daitari mining area with Paradip Port.

Railways. The total length of railway in 1979 was 1,948 km, of which 1,310 km was single line.

Aviation. There is an airport at Bhubaneswar with regular scheduled services to New Delhi, Calcutta, Vizag and Hyderabad.

Shipping. Paradip was declared a 'major' port in 1966 and has been developed to handle 4m. tons of traffic. Other minor ports at Chandbali and Gopalpur.

JUSTICE, RELIGION AND EDUCATION

Justice. The High Court of Judicature at Cuttack has a Chief Justice and 6 puisne judges.

Religion. There were in 1971: Hindus (including scheduled castes and scheduled tribes), 21,121,056; Christians, 378,888; Moslems, 326,507; Sikhs, 10,204; Buddhists, 8,462; Jains, 6,521.

Education. The percentage of literates in the population is 34·12% (males, 46·9%, females, 21·11%).

In 1981–82 there were 32,797 primary, 7,413 middle English and 2,466 high schools.

Utkal University was established in 1943 at Cuttack and moved to Bhubaneswar in 1962; it is both teaching and affiliating. It has 2 university colleges (law) and 113 affiliated colleges. Berhampur University has 20 affiliated colleges and Orissa University of Agriculture and Technology 4 constituent colleges. Sambalpur University has 42 affiliated colleges. Sri Jagannath Sanskrit Viswavidyalaya University was established in 1981 for oriental studies.

PUNJAB (INDIA)

HISTORY. The Punjab was constituted an autonomous province of India in 1937. In 1947, the province was partitioned between India and Pakistan into East and West Punjab respectively, under the Indian Independence Act, 1947, the boundaries being determined under the Radcliffe Award. The name of East Punjab was changed to Punjab (India) under the Constitution of India. On 1 Nov. 1956 the erstwhile states of Punjab and Patiala and East Punjab States Union (PEPSU) were integrated to form the state of Punjab. On 1 Nov. 1966, under the Punjab Reorganization Act, 1966, the state was reconstituted as a Punjabi-speaking state comprising the districts of Gurdaspur (excluding Dalhousie), Amritsar, Kapurthala, Jullundur, Ferozepore, Bhatinda, Patiala and Ludhiana; parts of Sangrur, Hoshiarpur and Ambala districts; and part of Kharar tehsil. The remaining area comprising an area of 18,000 sq. miles and an estimated (1967) population of 8·5m. was shared between the new state of Haryana and the Union Territory of Himachal Pradesh. The existing capital of Chandigarh was made the joint capital of Punjab and Haryana.

EVENTS. The Akali Dal party has continued its campaign for Sikh autonomy; violent incidents precipitated the imposition of President's rule.

AREA AND POPULATION. The Punjab is in north India and is bounded at its northernmost point by Kashmir, north-east by Himachal Pradesh, south-east by Haryana, south by Rajasthan, west and north-west by Pakistan. The area of the state is 50,376 sq. km, with census (1981) population of 16,669,755. Density 331 per sq. km. Growth rate, 1971–81, 23·01%. The largest cities, *see* p. 611. The official language is Punjabi.

CONSTITUTION AND GOVERNMENT. Punjab (India) has a unicameral legislature of 117 members. The Legislative Council was abolished in Jan. 1970. The Legislative Assembly was composed as follows after the election of May 1980: Congress (I), 64; Akali Dal, 36; others, 17. President's rule was imposed in Oct. 1983.

There are 12 districts. The capital is Chandigarh (*see* p. 673). There are 104 municipalities, 118 community development blocks and 9,331 elected village *panchayats*.

Governor: B. D. Pande.

BUDGET. Budget estimates, 1980–81, showed a deficit of Rs 70 crores. Annual Plan outlay, 1981–82, Rs 113·52 crores.

ENERGY AND NATURAL RESOURCES

Electricity. Installed capacity, 1979, was 1,541 mw; all villages had electricity.

Agriculture. About 75% of the population depends on agriculture. Agricultural prosperity is mainly due to irrigation. The irrigated area rose from 2·21m. hectares in 1950-51 to 5·5m. hectares in 1978–79: total production of foodgrains rose from 1·99m. tonnes to 11·9m. tonnes in 1980–81. Production in 1,000 tonnes (area in 1,000 hectares) in 1980–81: Wheat, 7,677 (2,812); maize, 605 (378); rice, 3,223 (1,178); oil-seeds, 167 (220); sugar-cane (gur), 397 (72); cotton, 605,000 bales (of 180 kg) from 1,178 hectares.

Livestock (1972 census): Buffaloes, 3,839,200; other cattle, 3·41m.; sheep and goats, 1,205,400; horses and ponies, 54,700; poultry, 3m.

Forestry. In 1981 there were 260,235 hectares of forest land, of which 130,008 hectares belonged to the Forest Department.

INDUSTRY. In Jan. 1981 the number of registered factories in the Punjab (India) was 7,397; 7,053 operational factories employed about 210,735 people. The chief manufactures are textiles (especially woollen hosiery), sewing machines, sports goods, sugar, starch, fertilizers, bicycles, scientific instruments, electrical goods, machine tools and pine oil. In 1981 there were 61,667 important small manufacturing units.

COMMUNICATIONS

Roads. The total length of metalled roads on 31 March 1980 was 33,288 km. State transport services cover 671,000 route km daily with a fleet of 2,776 buses carrying a daily average of 1m passengers. Coverage by private operators is estimated as 40%. In 1978 there were 276,748 motor vehicles.

Railways. The Punjab possesses an extensive system of railway communications, served by the Northern Railway. Total length, (1980) 3,511·4 km.

Aviation. There is an airport at Amritsar, and Chandigarh airport is on the north-eastern boundary; both have regular scheduled services to Delhi.

JUSTICE, RELIGION, EDUCATION AND WELFARE

Justice. The Punjab and Haryana High Court exercises jurisdiction over the states of Punjab and Haryana and the territory of Chandigarh. It is located in Chandigarh. It consists (1981) of a Chief Justice and 19 puisne judges.

Religion. At the 1971 census Hindus numbered 5,037,235; Sikhs, 8,159,172; Moslems, 114,447; Christians, 162,202; Jains, 21,383; Buddhists, 1,374.

Education. Compulsory education was introduced in April 1961; at the same time free education was introduced up to 8th class for boys and 9th class for girls as well as fee concessions. The aim is education for all children of 6-11.

In 1980 there were 17,784 primary schools, 1,432 middle schools and 2,313 higher secondary schools.

Punjab University was established in 1947 at Chandigarh as an examining, teaching and affiliating body. It is shared with Haryana and Himachal Pradesh. In 1962 Punjabi University was established at Patiala and an agricultural university at Ludhiana. Guru Nanak University has been established at Amritsar to mark the 500th anniversary celebrations for Guru Nanak Dev, first Guru of the Sikhs. Altogether there are 202 affiliated colleges, 160 for arts and science, 18 for teacher training, 8 medical, 2 dental, 2 engineering and 12 for other studies.

Health. Punjab claims the longest life expectancy (57·9 years for women, 58·5 for men) and lowest death rate (8·9 per 1,000). There were (1980) 254 hospitals, 467 Ayurvedic and Unani hospitals and dispensaries, 129 primary health centres and 1,485 dispensaries.

Singh, Khushwant, *A History of the Sikhs.* 2 vols. Princeton and OUP, 1964–67

RAJASTHAN

HISTORY. As a result of the implementation of the States Reorganization Act, 1956, the erstwhile state of Ajmer, Abu Taluka of Bombay State and the Sunel Tappa enclave of the former state of Madhya Bharat were transferred to the state of Rajasthan on 1 Nov. 1956, whereas the Sironj subdivision of Rajasthan was transferred to the state of Madhya Pradesh.

AREA AND POPULATION. Rajasthan is in north-west India and is bounded north by Punjab, north-east by Haryana and Uttar Pradesh, east by Madhya Pradesh, south by Gujarat and west by Pakistan. The area of the state is 342,239 sq. km and its population (census 1981, revised), 34,261,862, density 100 per sq. km. Growth rate, 1971–81, 32·36%. The chief cities, see p. 611.

CONSTITUTION AND GOVERNMENT. There is a unicameral legislature, the Legislative Assembly, having 200 members. The state of the parties in the Assembly in Feb. 1984, was: Congress (I), 149; Congress (S), 3; Bhartiya Janata, 30; Janata, 8; Lok Dal, 7; others, 3.

The capital is Jaipur. There are 27 districts.

Governor: Air Chief-Marshal O. P. Mehra.
Chief Minister: S. Charan Mathur.

BUDGET. Budget estimates for 1983–84 show total revenue receipts of Rs 1,088·29 crores, and expenditure of Rs 1,074·21 crores. Receipts included: share in Central taxes, Rs 242·31 crores; state excise, Rs 57 crores, sales tax, Rs 245 crores; vehicles taxes, Rs 54 crores; non-tax revenue, Rs 412·77 crores. Expenditure included: Education, Rs 261·56 crores; water and power, Rs 184·43 crores; medical and public health, Rs 179·69 crores; agriculture, Rs 144·77 crores. Gross Plan expenditure, Rs 428·97 crores (of which Rs 216·38 crores were for irrigation and power).

ENERGY AND NATURAL RESOURCES

Electricity. Installed capacity in Oct. 1983, 1,673 mw.; 17,900 villages and 246,375 wells had electric power.

Water. The main canal of an extensive irrigation system was still under construction in 1983; by Aug. 355 km had been built and 90 km remained. Rs 8,200m. has been allocated to the whole project.

Minerals. The state is rich in minerals. In 1982, 888,700m. tonnes of gypsum and (1976) 581,000 tonnes of rock phosphate were produced. Other minerals include silver, asbestos, felspar, copper, limestone and salt. Total value of mineral production in 1982 was about Rs 67·23 crores. Lead-zinc reserves have been found near Rampura-Agucha, estimated at 45m. tonnes.

Agriculture. The state has suffered drought for 5 years. The cultivable area is (1983) about 26·6m. hectares, of which 3·9m. is irrigated. Production of principal crops (in 1,000 tonnes), 1982–83: pulses, 1,574; sugar-cane (gur), 1,429; total oilseeds, 629; cotton, 551,000 bales (of 180 kg). Total foodgrains, 8,306 from 12·8m. hectares.

Livestock (1983): Buffaloes, 6,034,743; other cattle, 13,466,474; sheep, 15,389,100; goats, 15,397,993; horses and ponies, 45,381; camels, 7,528,287.

INDUSTRY. In 1983 there were 7,000 registered factories and 9,000 small industrial units. There were 148 industrial estates. Total capital investment, Rs 13,000m., of which small units, Rs 3,250m. Chief manufactures are cotton textiles, cement, glass and sugar.

COMMUNICATIONS

Roads. In 1983 there were 45,291 km of roads including 10,867 km of unsurfaced roads in Rajasthan; there were 2,533 km of national highway. Motor vehicles numbered 377,121 in 1982.

Railways. Jodhpur, Marwar, Udaipur, Ajmer, Jaipur and Sawai Madhopur are important junctions of the north-western network.

Aviation. There are airports at Jaipur, Jodhpur, Khota and Udaipur with regular scheduled services by Indian Airlines.

JUSTICE, RELIGION, EDUCATION AND WELFARE

Justice. The seat of the High Court is at Jodhpur. There is a Chief Justice and 11 puisne judges. There is also a bench of 5 judges at Jaipur.

Religion. At the 1971 census Hindus numbered 23,093,895; Moslems, 1,778,275; Jains, 513,548; Sikhs, 341,182; Christians, 30,202.

Education. The proportion of literates to the total population was 19·07% at the 1971 census.

In 1977–78 enrolment in 27,141 schools was 3,545,000; primary schools had 1·59m. students, 5,031 middle schools had 1m. students and 1,814 secondary and higher schools had 673,466. Elementary education is free but not compulsory. The percentage in 1977–78 of children attending schools in the age-group 6-11 was 57·29 (40·9 in 1961), in the 11-14 age-group 27·22 (14·4).

In 1980–81 there were 120 colleges. Enrolment at these and at the 3 universities was 135,543. Rajasthan University, established at Jaipur in 1947, is teaching and affiliating; Jodhpur University and Udaipur University were founded in 1962. There are also 2 agricultural colleges, 1 veterinary and animal science college, 2 engineering colleges, 3 Ayurvedic colleges and 7 polytechnics. There is 1 music college.

Health. In 1980 there were 1,169 hospitals and dispensaries, 232 primary health centres, 59 Unani, 63 homoepathic and 2 naturopathy hospitals. There were 104 maternity centres, and 2,425 Ayurvedic hospitals and dispensaries. There were 5 medical colleges and a nursing college.

SIKKIM

HISTORY. Sikkim became the twenty-second state of the Indian Union in May 1975. It is inhabited chiefly by the Lepchas, who are a tribe indigenous to Sikkim with their own dress and language, the Bhutias, who originally came from Tibet, and the Nepalis, who entered from Nepál in large numbers in the late 19th and early 20th century. The main languages spoken are Bhutia, Lepcha and Nepáli. Being a small country Sikkim had frequently been involved in struggles over her territory, and as a result her boundaries have been very much reduced over the centuries. In particular the Darjeeling district was acquired from Sikkim by the British East India Company in 1839. The Namgyal dynasty had been ruling Sikkim since the 14th century; the first consecrated ruler was Phuntsog Namgya I who was consecrated in 1642 and given the title of 'Chogyal', meaning 'King ruling in accordance with religious laws', derived from Cho–religion and Gyalpo–king. The last Chogyal was deposed in 1975 and died in America in 1982.

Sikkim is a land of wide variation in altitude, climate and vegetation, and is known for the great number and variety of birds, butterflies, wild flowers and orchids to be found in the different regions. It is a fertile land and to the Sikkimese is known as Denjong, The Valley of Rice.

AREA AND POPULATION. Sikkim is in the Eastern Himalayas and is bounded north by Tibet, east by Tibet and Bhután, south by West Bengal and west by Nepál. Area, 7,298 sq. km. Census population (1981), 314,999, of whom 36,768 lived in the capital, Gangtok. Density 43 per sq km. Growth rate, 1971–81, 50·01%.

CONSTITUTION AND GOVERNMENT. Sikkim was joined to the British Empire by a treaty in 1886 until 1947, but that relationship ceased when Britain withdrew from India in 1947. Thereafter there was a standstill agreement between India and Sikkim until a treaty was signed on 5 Dec. 1950 between India and Sikkim by which Sikkim became a protectorate of India and India undertook to be responsible for Sikkim's defence, external relations and strategic communications. The Chogyal had governed Sikkim with the help of the Sikkim Council, consisting of 18 elected members and 6 members nominated by the Chogyal. Sikkim parties represented were: National Party, Sikkim National Congress and, later, Sikkim Janta Congress.

Political reforms were demanded by the National Congress and the Janta Congress in March-April 1973 and Indian police took over control of law and order at the request of the Chogyal. On 13 April it was announced that the Chogyal had agreed to meet most of the political demands. Elections were held in April 1974 to a popularly-elected assembly. By the Government of Sikkim Act, June 1974, the Chogyal became a constitutional monarch with power of assent to the Assembly's legislation. By the Constitution (Thirty-Sixth Amendment) Act 1974 Sikkim became a state associated with the Indian Union. The office of Chogyal was abolished in April 1975. By the Constitution (Thirty-Eighth Amendment) Act 1975 Sikkim became the twenty-second state of the Indian Union. The Assembly has 32 members with a cabinet of 10 ministers including the Chief Minister. The Janata Parishad party, which merged with the Congress (I) party in July 1981, holds (in autumn 1983) 26 seats, the Sikkim Revolutionary Congress party holds 2, Sikkim Prajatantra Congress holds 1, Sikkim United Congress, 2 and Sikkim Himalayan Congress, 1.

Governor: J. H. Taleyarkhan.
Chief Minister. N. Bahadur Bhandari.

The official language of the Government is English. Lepcha, Bhutia, Nepali and Limboo have also been declared official languages.

Sikkim is divided into 4 districts for administration purposes, Gangtok, Mangan, Namchi and Gyalshing being the headquarters for the Eastern, Northern, Southern and Western districts respectively. Each district is administered by a District Collector. Within this framework are the Panchayats or Village Councils, representing the villages.

ECONOMY

Planning. The sixth Five-Year Plan began in 1980.

Budget. The annual budget for 1983–84 is Rs 30·50 crores.

ENERGY AND NATURAL RESOURCES

Electricity. There are 4 operational hydro-electric power stations; the Lagyap project is also being implemented by the Government of India as aid to meet the growing demand for electrical power for new industries. The first of its two 6 mv generators was commissioned 1 Sept. 1979.

Agriculture. The economy is mainly agricultural; main crops are rice, maize, millet, cardamom (a spice), mandarin oranges, apples, potatoes, ginger and soybean. A tea plantation has recently been started. Forests occupy about 1,000 sq. km. of the land area (excluding hill pastures) and the potential for a timber and wood-pulp industry is being explored. Some medicinal herbs are exported.

INDUSTRY AND TRADE

Industry. There is a state Industrial Development Investment Corporation and an Industrial Training Institute offering 7 trades. There are two cigarette factories (at Gangtok and Rangpo), two distilleries and a tannery at Rangpo and a fruit preserving factory at Singtam. Copper, zinc and lead are mined by the Sikkim Mining Corporation. A recent survey by the Geological Survey of India and the Indian Bureau of Mines has confirmed further deposits of copper, zinc, silver and gold in Dikchu, North Sikkim. There is a jewel-bearing factory for the production of industrial jewels. A watch factory has been set up in collaboration with Hindustan Machine Tools (India). A number of small manufacturing units for leather, wire nails, storage cells batteries, candles, safety matches and carpets, are already producing in the private sector. Local crafts include carpet weaving, making handmade paper, wood carving and silverwork. To encourage trading in indigenous products, particularly agricultural produce, the State Trading Corporation of Sikkim has been established.

Tourism. There is great potential for the tourist industry; a 78-bed lodge at

Gangtok and a 50-bed tourist lodge in West Sikkim have been opened. Tourism has been stimulated by the opening of new roads from Pemayangtse to Yuksam in West Sikkim and from Yuksam to the Dzongri Glacier.

COMMUNICATIONS

Roads. There are 1,201 km. of metalled roads, all on mountainous terrain, and 18 major bridges under the Public Works Department. Public transport and road haulage is nationalized.

Railways. The nearest railhead is at Siliguri (72 miles from Gangtok).

Aviation. The nearest airport is at Bagdogra (80 miles from Gangtok).

Post and Broadcasting. There are 1,118 telephones (1983) and 32 wireless stations. A radio broadcasting station, Akashvani Gangtok, was built in 1982, and a permanent station was under construction in 1983.

RELIGION, EDUCATION AND WELFARE

Religion. The state religion is Mahayana Buddhism, but a large proportion of the population is Hindu. There are some Christians, Moslems and members of other religions.

Education. At the 1981 census there were 100,000 literates. Sikkim has (1983) 100 pre-primary schools, 438 primary schools, 99 junior high schools and high schools, and 11 higher secondary schools. Education is free up to class XII; text books are free up to class V. There are 500 adult education centres. There is also a training institute for primary teachers, a law college and a degree college. Estimated spending on education, 1980–81, Rs 29·78m.

Health. There are (1983) 4 district hospitals at Singtam, Gyalshing, Namchi and Mangan, and one central referral hospital at Gangtok, besides 16 primary health centres, 62 sub-centres and 8 dispensaries, a maternity ward, chest clinic and 2 blocks for tuberculosis patients. There is a blood bank at Gangtok. There are 81 doctors. Medical and hospital treatment is free; there is a health centre for every 20,000 of the population. Small-pox and Kala-azar have been completely eliminated and many schemes for the provision of safe drinking water to villages and bazaars have been implemented.

Coelho, V. H., *Sikkim and Bhutan.* New Delhi, 1970
Mele, F., *Sikkim.* Paris, 1974

TAMIL NADU

HISTORY. The first trading establishment made by the British in the Madras State was at Peddapali (now Nizampatnam) in 1611 and then at Masulipatnam. In 1639 the English were permitted to make a settlement at the place which is now Madras, and Fort St George was founded. By 1801 the whole of the country from the Northern Circars to Cape Comorin (with the exception of certain French and Danish settlements) had been brought under British rule.

Under the provisions of the States Reorganization Act, 1956, the Malabar district (excluding the islands of Laccadive and Minicoy) and the Kasaragod district taluk of South Kanara were transferred to the new state of Kerala; the South Kanara district (excluding Kasaragod taluk and the Amindivi Islands) and the Kollegal taluk of the Coimbatore district were transferred to the new state of Mysore; and the Laccadive, Amindivi and Minicoy Islands were constituted a separate Territory. Four taluks of the Trivandrum district and the Shencottah taluk of Quilon district were transferred from Travancore-Cochin to the new Madras State. On 1 April 1960, 405 sq. miles from the Chittoor district of Andhra Pradesh were transferred to Madras in exchange for 326 sq. miles from the Chingleput and Salem districts. In Aug. 1968 the state was renamed Tamil Nadu.

AREA AND POPULATION. Tamil Nadu is in south India and is bounded north by Karnataka and Andhra Pradesh, east and south by the Indian ocean and west by Kerala. Area, 130,357 sq. km. Population (1981 census), 48,297,456, density of 371 per sq. km. Growth rate, 1971–81, 17·23%. Tamil is the principal language and has been adopted as the state language with effect from 14 Jan. 1958. The principal towns, *see* p. 611.

CONSTITUTION AND GOVERNMENT. The Governor is aided by a Council of 16 ministers. There is a bicameral legislature; the Legislative Council has 63 members and the Legislative Assembly has 234 members. The Legislative Assembly was composed as follows after the election of May 1980: All-India Anna DMK, 129; DMK, 38; Congress (I), 30; CPM, 11; CPI, 10; others, 16.

There are 14 districts. The capital is Madras.

Governor: S. L. Khurana.
Chief Minister: M. G. Ramachandran.

BUDGET. Budget estimates for 1981-82, revenue receipts, Rs 1,128·3 crores, revenue account expenditure, Rs 1,137·8 crores. Capital outlay, Rs 434·4 crores; capital account receipts, Rs 289·9.

ENERGY AND NATURAL RESOURCES

Electricity. Installed capacity 1977 amounted to 2,634 mw; 63,289 towns, hamlets and villages were supplied with electricity. The Kalpakkam nuclear power plant became operational in 1983; initial capacity, 235 mw.

Water. A joint project with Andhra Pradesh was agreed in 1983, to supply Madras with water from the Krishna river, also providing irrigation, *en route,* for Andhra Pradesh.

Minerals. Value of production, 1976, Rs 306·37m. The state has coal, chromite, bauxite, limestone, manganese, mica, quartz, salt, gypsum and feldspar.

Agriculture. Agriculture engages 29% of the population. The land is a fertile plain watered by rivers flowing east from the Western Ghats, particularly the Cauvery and the Tambaraparani. Temperature ranges between 18°C. and 43°C., rainfall between 25 in. and 75 in. Of the total land area (13·01m. hectares), 7,698,000 hectares were cultivable and 3m. hectares were irrigated in 1977. The staple food crops grown are paddy, maize, jawar, bajra, pulses and millets. Important commercial crops are sugar-cane, oilseeds, cashewnuts, cotton, tobacco, coffee, tea, rubber and pepper. The production of foodgrains was 7·39m. tonnes; sugar-cane and oilseeds, 1·35m., and 1,343,000 tonnes respectively.

Livestock (1966 census): Buffaloes, 2,753,049; other cattle, 11,009,368; sheep, 6,641,843; goats, 3,796,736; swine, 874,880; horses, ponies, mules, camels, etc., 185,336; poultry, 10,898,862.

Forestry. The revenue from forests in 1973-74 was Rs 7,35·40 lakhs: sandalwood, Rs 2,82·19 lakhs; timber, Rs 1,08·24 lakhs; firewood, Rs 1,07·91 lakhs. Area of forest land, 1977, 20,910 sq. km.

Fisheries. Landings, 1976, 510,000 tonnes.

INDUSTRY AND TRADE

Industry. The contribution of the industrial sector to the state income was Rs 373 crores in 1972-73. The number of registered factories was 6,713 in 1973. The consumption of power in the industrial sector was 49·5% of total state consumption in 1974. The biggest central sector project is Salem steel plant. Man-days lost in industrial disputes, 1979, 8·38m.

Cotton textiles is one of the major industries. There are nearly 180 cotton textile mills and most of the spinning mills supplying yarn to the decentralized handloom industry. Other important industries are tanning, manufacture of textile machinery, power-driven pumps, bicycles, electrical machinery, tractors, rubber tyres and tubes, bricks and tiles and silk. Tamil Nadu is the second largest producer of cement, while its sugar industry has been expanding rapidly.

Public sector undertakings include the Neyveli lignite complex, integral coach factory, high-pressure boiler plant, photographic film factory, surgical instruments factory, teleprinter factory, oil refinery, continuous casting plant and defence vehicles manufacture. Main exports: tanned hides and skins, leather and cotton goods, tea, coffee, spices, engineering goods, motor-car ancillaries.

Tourism. In 1973, 50,074 tourists visited the state, 35,929 of whom came by air and 14,145 by sea.

COMMUNICATIONS

Roads. At the end of 1973 the state had approximately 78,463 km of roads (about 50,000 km metalled). In 1976 there were 184,475 registered motor vehicles.

Railways. In 1970 there were 6,038 km of railway. Madras and Madurai are the main centres.

Aviation. There are airports at Madras, Tiruchirapalli and Madurai, with regular scheduled services to Bombay, Calcutta and Delhi. Madras is the main centre of airline routes in South India.

Shipping. Madras is the chief port. Important minor ports are Cuddalore and Nagapattinam. There are 9 intermediate ports. A harbour is under construction at Tuticorin. The Inland Container Depot at Coimbatore has a capacity of 50,000 tonnes of export traffic; it is linked to Cochin (Kerala).

JUSTICE, RELIGION AND EDUCATION

Justice. There is a High Court at Madras with a Chief Justice and 18 judges. *Police.* Strength of armed police battalions, 1973, 4,420; strength of the armed reserve (1972) in the state and in Madras, 356,461.

Religion. At the 1971 census Hindus numbered 36,674,150 (89·2%), Christians, 5·75%; Moslems, 5·11%.

Education. At the 1981 census 22·1m. people were literate.

Education is free up to pre-university level. In 1973-74 there were 2,823 high schools with a total enrolment of 1,627,030 students. The number of primary schools was 26,726, and their enrolment, 3,759,140; 5,773 upper primary schools had 2,113,981 pupils. Allotment of expenditure for education for 1974-75, Rs 1,08·52 crores.

There are 3 universities. Madras University (founded in 1857) is affiliating and teaching. It had (1968) 119 colleges for arts and sciences with 106,571 students. Annamalai University, Annamalainagar (founded 1928) is residential; Madurai University (founded 1966) is an affiliating and teaching university.

Statistical Information: The Department of Statistics (Fort St George, Madras) was established in 1948 and reorganized in 1953. *Director:* D. S. Rajabushanam, MA. Main publications: *Annual Statistical Abstract; Decennial Statistical Atlas; Season and Crop Report; Quinquennial Wages Census; Quarterly Abstract of Statistics.*

TRIPURA

HISTORY. A Hindu state of great antiquity having been ruled by the Maharajahs for 1,300 years before its accession to the Indian Union on 15 Oct. 1949. With the reorganization of states on 1 Sept. 1956 Tripura became a Union Territory. The Territory was made a State on 21 Jan. 1972.

AREA AND POPULATION. Tripura is bounded on the north, west and south by Bangladesh, and on the east by Mizoram. The major portion of the state is hilly and mainly jungle. It has an area of 10,477 sq. km and a population of

2,060,189 (1981 census); Density, 196 per sq. km. Growth rate, 1971-81, 32·37%. The predominant language is Bengali.

GOVERNMENT. There is a Legislative Assembly of 60 members. The election of Jan. 1983 was won by the Communist Party of India (Marxist). The territory has 1 district, divided into 10 administrative sub-divisions, namely, Sadar, Khowai, Kailasahar, Dharmanagar, Sonamura, Udaipur, Belonia, Kamalpur, Sabroom and Amarpur.

The capital is Agartala.

Governor: L. P. Singh.
Chief Minister: N. Chakravarty.

BUDGET. Budget estimates 1980-81 show revenue receipts of Rs 107·1 crores, and expenditure on revenue account of Rs 108·8 crores. Annual plan expenditure, Rs 35 crores.

ENERGY AND NATURAL RESOURCES

Electricity. Installed capacity (1980), 14·72 mw; there were (1976) 245 electrified villages.

Agriculture. About 23% of the land area is cultivable. The tribes practise shifting cultivation, but this is being slowly replaced by modern methods. The main crops are rice, wheat, jute, mesta, potatoes, oilseeds and sugar-cane. Foodgrain production (1979-80), 310,000 tonnes. There are 56 registered tea gardens producing 4,500,000 kg. per year, and employing about 10,000.

Forestry. Forests cover about 65% of the land area. They have been much depleted by clearance for shifting cultivation and, recently, for refugee settlements of Bangladeshis. About 8% of the forest area still consists of dense natural forest; losses elsewhere are being replaced by plantation. Commercial rubber plantation has also been encouraged and covers over 65,000 hectares.

INDUSTRY. There is a jute mill, a steel re-rolling mill and a flour mill at Agartala; a second flour mill at Dharmanagar. Small scale industries produce diverse manufacture. The main village industries are hand-loom weaving, sericulture and cane-work. The Tripura Handloom and Handicrafts Development Corporation marketed goods worth Rs 6m. in 1979-80.

COMMUNICATIONS

Roads. Total length of motorable roads (1974) 3,692 km, of which 1,123 km were surfaced. Vehicles registered, 31 March 1980, 7,889.

Railways. There is a railway between Dharmanagar and Kalkalighat (Assam).

Aviation. There is 1 airport and 3 airstrips. The airport (Agartala) has regular scheduled services to Calcutta.

EDUCATION AND WELFARE

Education. In autumn 1978 there were 1,885 primary schools (209,836 pupils); 436 middle schools (51,418); 144 high schools (21,238), and 52 higher grade schools (6,202). There were 6 colleges of general education (7,772). 9 colleges of professional and technical education (1,346) and 859 social education centres.

Health. There were (1980) 12 hospitals, with 1,357 beds, 128 dispensaries, 297 doctors and 459 nurses. There were 26 primary health centres and about 35 other medical units.

UTTAR PRADESH

HISTORY. In 1833 the then Bengal Presidency was divided into two parts, one of which became the Presidency of Agra. In 1836 the Agra area was styled the North-

West Province and placed under a Lieut.-Governor. The two provinces of Agra and Oudh were placed, in 1877, under one administrator, styled Lieut.-Governor of the North-West Province and Chief Commissioner of Oudh. In 1902 the name was changed to 'United Provinces of Agra and Oudh', under a Lieut.-Governor, and the Lieut.-Governorship was altered to a Governorship in 1921. In 1935 the name was shortened to 'United Provinces'. On Independence, the states of Rampur, Banaras and Tehri-Garwhal were merged with United Provinces. In 1950 the name of the United Provinces was changed to Uttar Pradesh.

AREA AND POPULATION. Uttar Pradesh is in north India and is bounded north by Himachal Pradesh, Tibet and Nepál, east by Bihar, south by Madhya Pradesh and west by Rajasthan, Haryana and Delhi. The area of the state is 294,413 sq. km. Population (1981 census), 110,885,874, a density of 377 per sq. km. Growth rate, 1971–81, 25·49%. Cities with more than 250,000 population, *see* p. 611. The official language is Hindi.

CONSTITUTION AND GOVERNMENT. Uttar Pradesh has had an autonomous system of government since 1937. There is a bicameral legislature. The Legislative Council has 108 members; the Legislative Assembly has 426, of which 424 are elected. Party strength in the Assembly, Oct. 1982: Congress (I) 320; Lok Dal, 54; Democratic Socialists, 11; Bhartiya Janata, 8; others, 29; vacant, 2.

There are 11 administrative divisions, each under a Commissioner, and 57 districts.

The capital is Lucknow.

Governor: C. P. N. Singh.
Chief Minister: Shripati Misra.

BUDGET. Budget estimates 1982–83 show revenue and capital receipts of Rs 3,088·00 crores; revenue and capital account expenditure, Rs 3,336·87 crores. An outlay of Rs 1,202 crores was approved for the 1982–83 annual plan.

ENERGY AND NATURAL RESOURCES

Electricity. The State Electricity Board had, 31 March 1982, an installed capacity of 3,494 mw. There were (Sept. 1983) 53,630 villages with electricity.

Minerals. The state has magnesite, fire-clay, coal, copper, dolomite, limestone, soapstone, gypsum, bauxite, diaspore, ochre, phosphorite, pyrophyllite, silica sand and steatite among others.

Agriculture. Agriculture occupies 78% of the work force. About 9·5m. hectares are irrigated. The state is India's largest producer of foodgrains; production (1980–81), 24·9m. tonnes; sugar-cane 64·2m.; oilseeds, 1·56m. The state is one of India's main producers of sugar. There were (1981) 1,199 veterinary centres for cattle.

Forests cover (1980) about 5·1m. sq. km.

INDUSTRY. Sugar production is important; other industries include edible oils, textiles, distilleries, brewing, leather working, agricultural engineering, paper and chemicals. There is an aluminium smelter at Renukoot. An oil refinery at Mathura has capacity of 6m. tonnes per annum. Large public-sector enterprises have been set up in electrical engineering, pharmaceuticals, locomotive building, general engineering, electronics and aeronautics. Village and small-scale industries are important; there were 68,426 small units in 1982. About one-third of cloth output is from hand-looms. Total working population (1981) 30·8m., of whom 6·8m. were non-agricultural. Man days lost by industrial disputes, 1981, 2·39m

COMMUNICATIONS

Roads. There were, 31 March 1978, 184,263 km of motorable roads, of which 36,350 km were metalled. (This excludes forest roads.) In 1981 there were 533,836 motor vehicles of which 300,311 were motorcycles.

Railways. Lucknow is the main junction of the northern network; other important junctions are Agra, Kanpur, Allahabad and Varanasi.

Aviation. There are airports at Lucknow, Kanpur, Varanasi, Allahabad, Agra, Jhansi, Lalitpur and Gorakhpur.

JUSTICE, RELIGION AND EDUCATION

Justice. The High Court of Judicature at Allahabad (with a bench at Lucknow) has a Chief Justice and 59 puisne judges including additional judges. There are 56 sessions divisions in the state.

Religion. At the 1971 census Hindus numbered 73,997,597; Moslems, 13,676,533; Sikhs, 369,672; Christians, 131,810; Jains, 124,728; Buddhists, 39,639.

Education. At the 1981 census 27·4m. people were literate. In 1981–82 there were 88 nursery schools, 72,733 junior basic schools, 14,221 senior basic schools and 5,629 higher secondary schools.

Uttar Pradesh has 19 universities: Allahabad University (founded 1887); Agra University (1927); the Banaras Hindu University, Varanasi (1916); Lucknow University (1921); Aligarh Muslim University (1920); Roorkee University (1948), formerly Thomason College of Civil Engineering (established in 1847); Gorakhpur University (1957); Varanasaya Sanskrit Vishwavidyalaya, Varanasi (1958); Kashi Vidyapith, Varanasi (1963). Kanpur University and Meerut University were founded in 1966. Govind Ballabh Pant University, Pantnagar (1969); Garhwal University, Srinagar, (1973). Two universities of agriculture were founded in 1974–75 and Avadh, Kumaon, Rohilkhand and Jhansi Universities in 1975.

There are also two institutions with university status: Gurukul Kangri and Dayal Bagh Educational Institute. There are 9 medical colleges.

HEALTH. In 1982 there were 3,188 allopathic and 1,842 ayurvedic and unani hospitals. There were 8,569 doctors and 19,181 nurses and midwives in state service. There were TB hospitals and clinics with 3,437 beds.

WEST BENGAL

HISTORY. For the history of Bengal under British rule, from 1633 to 1947, *see* THE STATESMAN'S YEAR-BOOK, 1952, p. 183.

Under the terms of the Indian Independence Act, 1947, the Province of Bengal ceased to exist. The Moslem majority districts of East Bengal, consisting of the Chittagong and Dacca Divisions and portions of the Presidency and Rajshahi Divisions, became what was then East Pakistan (now Bangladesh).

AREA AND POPULATION. West Bengal is in north-east India and is bounded north by Sikkim and Bhután, east by Assam and Bangladesh, south by the Bay of Bengal and Orissa, west by Bihar and north-west by Nepál. The total area of West Bengal is 87,853 sq. km. At the 1981 census its population was 54,485,560, an increase of 23% since 1971, the density of population 614 per sq. km. Population of chief cities, *see* p. 611. The principal language is Bengali.

CONSTITUTION AND GOVERNMENT. The state of West Bengal came into existence as a result of the Indian Independence Act, 1947. The territory of Cooch-Behar State was merged with West Bengal on 1 Jan. 1950, and the former French possession of Chandernagore became part of the state on 2 Oct. 1954. Under the States Reorganization Act, 1956, certain portions of Bihar State (an area of 3,157 sq. miles with a population of 1,446,385) were transferred to West Bengal.

The Legislative Assembly has 294 seats. Distribution Sept. 1982: Communist Party of India (Marxist), 174; Forward Bloc, 28; Revolutionary Socialist Party, 19;

Communist Party of India, 7; Revolutionary Communist Party of India, 2; Forward Bloc (Marxist), 2; Democratic Socialist Party, 3; Socialist Party, 3. Total "Left Front", 238. Opposition: Indian National Congress, 49; others, 7.

The capital is Calcutta.

For administrative purposes there are 3 divisions (Jalpaiguri, Burdwan and Presidency), under which there are 16 districts, including Calcutta. The Calcutta Metropolitan Development Authority has been set up to co-ordinate development in the metropolitan area (1,250 sq. km). For the purposes of local self-government there are 15 *zilla parishads* (district boards), 339 *panchayat samities* (regional boards), and 3,305 *gram* (village) *panchayats*. There are 99 municipalities, 2 Corporations, 3 Town Committees and 10 Notified Areas. The Calcutta Corporation was reconstituted in 1969 with a mayor and deputy mayor, a commissioner, aldermen and standing committees.

Governor: A. P. Sharma.
Chief Minister: J. Basu.

BUDGET. Budget estimates for 1982–83 showed a deficit of Rs 10m.

ENERGY AND NATURAL RESOURCES

Electricity. Installed capacity, 1980–81, 1,945 mw; 16,512 villages had electricity.

Water. The major irrigation and power scheme at present under construction is (1983) the Teesta barrage. Major irrigation schemes are the Mayurakshi, Kansabati and Damodar Valley. During 1981–82 government canals irrigated 1m. hectares. At March 1982 there were 5,701 tubewells and 2,789 riverlift irrigation schemes.

Minerals. Value of production, 1981, Rs 3,131·9m. The state has coal (the Raniganj field is one of the 3 biggest in India) including coking coal. Coal production (1981) 20·9m. tonnes.

Agriculture. About 74% of the cultivated area is rice-paddy, one-third of it irrigated. Total foodgrain production, 1981–82, 6·3m. tonnes; oilseeds (provisional), 175,800 tonnes; jute and other fibres, 4·7m. tonnes; wheat, 389,300 tonnes. The state produces 57·4% of the national output of jute.

Livestock (1971 census): 11,878,083 cattle, 824,161 buffaloes; 1981 census, 758,000 sheep and goats, and 15,052,000 poultry.

Forests cover 13·4% of the state.

Fisheries. Landings, 1981–82, about 378,000 tonnes. During 1981–82 Rs 26·96m. was invested in fishery schemes.

INDUSTRY. The total number of registered factories, 1981, was 6,548; average daily employment in 12 major industries, 1·3m. The coalmining industry had 109 units with average daily employment of 127,000. Man-days lost by industrial disputes, 1982, 16·6m.

There is a large automobile factory at Uttarpara, and there are aluminium rolling-mills at Belur and Asansol. At Durgapur a major steel plant was completed in 1962. Durgapur has other industries under the state sector—a thermal power plant, coke oven plant, fertilizer factory, alloy steel plant and ophthalmic glass plant. There are a locomotive factory and cable factory at Chittaranjan and Rupnarayanpur. A refinery and fertilizer factory are operating at Haldia.

Small industries are important. The state government set up 4,519 units in 1981–82, (17,628 jobs); 5,677 units in 1982–83 (38,170).

COMMUNICATIONS

Roads. In 1980 the length of national highway was 1,471 km, of state highway 3,147 km and of other motorable roads 138,666 km. In 1982 the state had 321,291 motor vehicles.

Railways. The length of railways within the state (1981–82) is 6,085 km. The main centres are Howrah, Sealdah, Kharagpur, Asansol and New Jalpaiguri.

Aviation. The main airport is Calcutta which has national and international flights. The second airport is at Bagdogra in the extreme north, which has regular scheduled services to Calcutta.

Shipping. Calcutta is the chief port: a barrage is being built at Farakka to control the flow of the Ganges and to provide a rail and road link between North and South Bengal. A second port is being developed at Haldia, halfway between the present port and the sea, which is intended mainly for bulk cargoes. West Bengal possesses 779 km of navigable canals.

JUSTICE, RELIGION AND EDUCATION

Justice. The High Court of Judicature at Calcutta has a Chief Justice and 38 puisne judges. The Andaman and Nicobar Islands *(see below)* come under its jurisdiction.

Police. In 1983 the police force numbered 52,772, under a director-general and an inspector-general. Calcutta has a separate force under a commissioner directly responsible to the Government; its strength was 20,777 in 1982.

Religion. At the 1971 census Hindus numbered 34,611,864; Moslems, 9,064,338; Christians, 251,752; Buddhists, 121,504; Sikhs, 35,084; Jains, 32,203.

Education. At the 1981 census 22·2m. people were literate. In 1981–82 there were 47,626 primary and junior basic schools, with about 6·8m. pupils and 8,307 high and secondary schools with about 2·3m. pupils. Primary education is free.

The University of Calcutta (founded 1857) is affiliating and teaching; in 1976–77 it had 234,661 students. Visva Bharati, Santiniketan, was originally established in 1951 and is residential and teaching; it had 2,911 students in 1977–78. The University of Jadavpur, Calcutta (1955), had 4,222 students in 1977–78. Burdwan University was established 15 June 1960 with 31 affiliated colleges previously under the supervision of the University of Calcutta; in 1977–78 there were 48,550 students. Kalyani University was established in 1960 (1,839 students in 1977). The University of North Bengal (1962) had 17,728 students in 1977–78. Rabindra Bharati University had 2,783 students in 1977–78. Bidhan Chandra Krishi Viswavidyalaya (1974) had 1,047 students in 1977–78.

UNION TERRITORIES

ANDAMAN AND NICOBAR ISLANDS. The Andaman and Nicobar Islands are administered by the President of the Republic of India acting through a Lieut.-Governor. There is a Pradesh Council, 5 members of which are selected by the Chief Commissioner as advisory counsellors. The seat of administration is at Port Blair, which is connected with Calcutta (1,255 km away) and Madras (1,190 km) by steamer service which calls about every 10 days: there is a bi-weekly air service from Calcutta and a weekly service from Madras. There are 2 districts.

The population (1981 census) was 188,254; density 23 per sq. km.; growth rate 1971–81, 63·5%.

Revised estimates for 1981–82 show total revenue receipts of Rs 6,61·19 lakhs, and total expenditure on revenue account of Rs 35,85·51 lakhs, and total capital expenditure of Rs 30,02·59 lakhs. Estimates for 1983–84 show plan expenditure of Rs 25·15 crores, out of a total Sixth Plan allocation of Rs 96·6 crores.

Lieut.-Governor: M. L. Kampani.

The **Andaman Islands** lie in the Bay of Bengal, 193 km from Cape Negrais in Burma, 1,255 from Calcutta and 1,190 from Madras. Five large islands grouped together are called the Great Andamans, and to the south is the island of Little Andaman. There are some 204 islets, the two principal groups being the Ritchie Archipelago and the Labyrinth Islands. The total area is about 6,475 sq. km. The Great Andaman group is about 467 km long and, at the widest, 51 km broad.

The original inhabitants live in the forests by hunting and fishing; they are of a small Negrito type and their civilization is about that of the Stone Age. Their exact numbers are not known, as they avoid all contact with civilization. The total population of the Andaman Islands (excluding the aboriginals) was in 1951, 18,962 (12,734 males and 6,228 females). Under a central government scheme started in 1953, some 4,000 displaced families, mostly from East Pakistan, had been settled in the islands by May 1967.

Japanese forces occupied the Andaman Islands on 23 March 1942. Civil administration of the islands was resumed on 8 Oct. 1945.

From 1857 to March 1942 the islands were used by the Government of India as a penal settlement for life and long-term convicts, but the penal settlement was abolished on re-occupation in Oct. 1945.

The Great Andaman group, densely wooded, contains many valuable trees, both hardwood and softwood. The best known of the hardwoods is the *padauk* or Andaman redwood; *gurjan* is in great demand for the manufacture of plywood. Large quantities of softwood are supplied to match factories. Annually the Forest Department export about 25,000 tons of timber to the mainland. Coconut, coffee and rubber are cultivated. The islands are slowly being made self-sufficient in paddy and rice, and now grow approximately half their annual requirements. The average yield of rice in 1966–67 was 1·24 tonnes per hectare. Total livestock (1961 census) was 38,617. There is a sawmill at Port Blair and a coconut-oil mill at Dunbar Point. There are about 338 km of black top road in the entire territory.

The islands possess a number of harbours and safe anchorages, notably Port Blair in the south, Port Cornwallis in the north and Elphinstone and Mayabandar in the middle.

The **Nicobar Islands** are situated to the south of the Andamans, 121 km from Little Andaman. The British formally took possession in 1869. There are 19 islands, 7 uninhabited; total area, 1,645 sq. km. The islands are usually divided into 3 subgroups (southern, central and northern), the chief islands in each being respectively, Great Nicobar, Camotra with Nancowrie and Car Nicobar. There is a fine landlocked harbour between the islands of Camotra and Nancowrie, known as Nancowrie Harbour.

The population numbered, in 1961, 14,563. The coconut and arecanut are the main items of trade, and coconuts are a major item in the people's diet.

The Nicobar Islands were occupied by the Japanese in July 1942; and Car Nicobar was developed as a big supply base. The Japanese built some roads in Car Nicobar and small jetties at Malacca in Car Nicobar, and in the harbour at Nancowrie. The Allies reoccupied the islands on 9 Oct. 1945.

ARUNACHAL PRADESH. On 21 Jan. 1972 the former North East Frontier Agency of Assam was created a Union Territory. The territory includes the Kameng, Tirap, Subansiri, Siang and Lohit frontier divisions and has an area of 81,426 sq. km and a population (1981 census) of 628,050; density, 7 per sq. km.; growth rate, 1971–81, 34·34%.

There is a Legislative Assembly of 30 members and a Council of Ministers. The election of 1978 was won by the Janata party.

There are 5 districts. The centre of administration is at Itanagar.

Chief Commissioner: S. M. Krishnatry.
Chief Minister: Prem Khandu Thungon.

About 60% of the land area is forest. Agriculture employs 18·5% of the people. In 1970 there were 200,000 acres under cultivation, 32,600 acres of it irrigated. Crops include rice (13,000 tonnes, 1976), rubber, coffee, coconut, arecanut, fruits and spices. There were about 100 co-operatives. The budget estimates for 1980–81 provided Rs 81·7 crores, of which Rs 1·16 crores was allotted to agriculture.

CHANDIGARH. On 1 Nov. 1966 the city of Chandigarh and the area surrounding it was constituted a Union Territory. Population (1981), 450,061; density, 3,948 per sq. km.; growth rate, 1971–81, 74·9%. Area, 114 sq. km. It serves as the joint capital of both Punjab (India) and the state of Haryana, and is the seat of a

High Court and of a university serving both states. The city will ultimately be the capital of just the Punjab; joint status is to last while a new capital is built for Haryana.

There is some cultivated land (foodgrain production, 1977, 8,000 tonnes) and some forest (27·5% of the territory).

Evenson, N., *Chandigarh.* Berkeley, Cal., 1966

DADRA AND NAGAR HAVELI. Formely Portuguese, the territories of Dadra and Nagar Haveli were occupied in July 1954 by nationalists, and a pro-India administration was formed; this body made a request for incorporation into the Union, 1 June 1961. By the 10th amendment to the constitution the territories became a centrally administered Union Territory with effect from 11 Aug. 1961, forming an enclave at the southernmost point of the border between Gujarat and Maharashtra. Area 491 sq. km.; population (1981), 103,676 (males 52,515, females 51,161); density 211 per sq. km; growth rate, 1971–81, 39·78%. There is an Administrator appointed by the Government of India. The day-to-day business is done by various departments, co-ordinated by the Administrator's secretary and headed by a Collector. Headquarters are at Silvassa. The territory is tribal and organised in 72 villages. Languages used are Bhilli, Gujarat, Bhilodi (83%), Marathi and Hindi.

Administrator: K. T. Satarawala
Collector: H. Haukhum

Electricity. Electricity is supplied by Gujarat, and 62 villages had been electrified by 1983.

Water. A joint project with the governments of Gujarat, Goa, Daman and Diu has been set up; a reservoir at Damanganga is being built with irrigation potential of 8,280 hectares.

Agriculture. Farming is the chief occupation, and about 21,400 hectares were under crops in 1982–83. Much of the land is terraced and there is a 75% subsidy for soil conservation. The major food crops are rice and ragi; wheat, small millets and pulses are also grown. There is little irrigation (915 hectares). There are veterinary centres, an agricultural research centre and breeding centres to improve strains of cattle and poultry. During 1982–83 the Administration distributed 256 tonnes of high yielding paddy seed, and high yielding wheat seed, and 302 tonnes of fertilizer.

Forests. About 20,200 hectares or 41·2% of the total area is forest, mainly of teak, sadad and khair. Timber production provides the largest simple contribution to the territory's revenue.

Industry. Industrial estates have been set up at Piparia, Masat and Khadoli. There are 133 small units, and 3 medium scale, employing about 3,000. Concessions are available for small industries, and the whole Territory is aided as a backward area.

Communications. There are (1978) 167 km of motorable road. The railway line from Bombay to Ahmedabad runs through Silvassa. The nearest airport is Bombay.

Justice. The territory is under the jurisdiction of the Bombay (Maharashtra) High Court. There is a District and Sessions Court and one junior Division Civil Court at Silvassa.

Education. Literacy was 14·86% of the population at the 1971 census. In 1982–83 there were 70 adult education centres (2,225 students); there were 141 government primary schools, 12 government-aided mission schools and one unaided; there were 2 higher secondary schools and 5 high schools. Total primary enrolment was 16,962; high-school and higher secondary, 1,893.

Health. The territory has 1 cottage hospital, 3 primary health centres and 7 dispensaries; there is also a mobile dispensary.

DELHI. Delhi became a Union Territory on 1 Nov. 1956.

Area and Population. The territory forms an enclave inside the eastern frontier of Haryana in north India. Delhi has an area of 1,485 sq. km. At the 1981 census its population was 6,220,406 (density per sq. km, 4,189). Growth rate, 1971–81, 53%. In the rural area of Delhi there are 241 inhabited and 17 deserted villages in 5 community development blocks.

Government. The Lieut-Governor is the Administrator, assisted by 4 Executive Councillors (1 Chief Executive Councillor and 3 Executive Councillors) appointed by the President of India on the recommendation of the Union Home Ministry. There is a Metropolitan Council of 61 members including 5 nominated by the President of India. The Territory is covered by 3 local bodies: Delhi Municipal Corporation, New Delhi Municipal Committee and Delhi Cantonment Board.

Lieut.-Governor: Shri Jagmohan.

Budget. Revised estimates 1982–83 show total revenue of Rs 4,605m. and expenditure of Rs 5,204m. Plan expenditure: Rs 2,500m.; power, Rs 374·4m.; transport and communication, Rs 364m.; water and sewerage, Rs 337·5m.; general education, Rs 327m.; urban development, Rs 295m.; medical services, Rs 213·6m.

Agriculture. The contribution to the economy is not significant. About 84,450 hectares are cultivated. Animal husbandry is increasing and mixed farms are common. Chief crops in 1981–82, (production in 1,000 tonnes) were: Wheat, 106; jowar and bajra, 15; gram, 1; sugar-cane (gur), 0·2; fruit, vegetables and flowers.

Industry. The modern city of Delhi and New Delhi is not only the largest commercial centre in northern India but is also an important industrial centre. Since 1947 a large number of industrial concerns have been established; these include factories for the manufacture of razor blades, sports goods, radios and television and parts, bicycles and parts, plastic and PVC goods including footwear, textiles, chemicals, fertilizers, medicines, hosiery, leather goods, soft drinks, hand and machine tools. There is also metal forging, casting, galvanising and electro-plating, printing and warehousing. The number of industrial units functioning was about 50,000 in 1981–82; average number of workers employed was 480,000. Production was worth Rs 2,350 crores and investment was about Rs 965 crores.

Some traditional handicrafts, for which Delhi was formerly famous, still flourish; among them are ivory carving, miniature painting, gold and silver jewellery and papier mâché work. The handwoven textiles of Delhi were particularly fine; this craft is being successfully revived.

Delhi publishes 13 major daily newspapers, including the *Times of India, Hindustan Times, Indian Express, Statesman, Nav Bharat Times* and *Hindustan.*

Roads. Five national highways pass through the city. There were (1982) 648,531 registered motor vehicles in Delhi including 7,744 taxis. The Transport Corporation had 4,845 buses in 1982–83.

Railways. Delhi is an important rail junction with three main stations: Delhi, New Delhi, Hazart Nizamuddin. There is an electric ring railway for commuters.

Aviation. Palam airport operates internal and international flights.

Religion. At the 1971 census Hindus numbered 3,407,835; Sikhs, 291,123; Moslems, 263,019; Jains, 50,513; Christians, 43,720; Buddhists, 8,720.

Education. The proportion of literates to the total population was 61·54% at the 1981 census (68·4% of males and 53·07% of females).

The total number of educational institutions in 1981–82 was 3,994, with an enrolment of 1,484,092 students.

The University of Delhi was founded in 1922; it had 65 constituent colleges and institutions in 1981–82, with a total of 74,890 students. There are also Jawaharlal Nehru university and Jamia Millia Islamia; the Indian Institute of Technology at Haus Khaz; the Indian Agricultural Research Institute at Pusa; the All India Institute of Medical Science at Ansari Nagar and the Indian Institute of Public Administration.

GOA, DAMAN AND DIU. The coast was captured for Portugal by Alfonso de Albuquerque in 1510 and the inland area was added in the 18th century. Daman (Damão) on the Gujarat coast, 70 miles north of Bombay, was seized by the Portuguese in 1531 and ceded to them (1539) by the Shar of Gujarat. The island of Diu, captured in 1534, lies off the south-east coast of Kathiawar (Gujarat); there is a small coastal area. In Dec. 1961 the territories were occupied by India and incorporated into the Indian Union.

Area and Population. Goa, bounded on the north by Maharashtra and on the east and south by Karnataka, has a coastline of 105 km. The area of the territory is 3,813 sq. km, that of Goa itself being about 3,701 sq. km. Daman, 72 sq. km; Diu, 40 sq. km. Population (1981) 1,082,117. Density, 284 per sq. km. Growth rate, 1971–81, 26·15%. Estimated population, 1982, 1,086,730. Panaji is the largest town, population (urban agglomeration, 1981) 76,839. The languages spoken are Gujarati, Marathi and Konkani.

Government. The Indian Parliament passed legislation in March 1962 by which Goa, Daman and Diu became a Union Territory with retrospective effect from 20 Dec. 1961. Goa is represented by 2 elected members in the Indian House of the People. For judicial purposes there is a Panaji bench of the High Court of Bombay. The capital is Panaji. There are 198 village *panchayats*.

There is a Legislative Assembly of 30 members.

Administrator: K. T. Satarawala.
Chief Minister: P. R. Rane.

Budget. Annual Plan expenditure, 1983–84, Rs 566m.

Electricity. Units sold, 251·9m. kwh. in 1981–82. Seventeen towns and 382 villages were supplied with electric power by March 1982. Power is generated in neighbouring states.

Minerals. Resources include manganese ore and iron ore, both of which are exported. There are also reserves of bauxite, limestone and clay.

Agriculture. Agriculture is the main occupation; important crops are rice, wheat, ragi, pulses, groundnuts, fruit and coconuts. The net area sown is 139,178 hectares. Area irrigated, 11,277 hectares. Area under paddy (1982–83), 35,325 hectares of high-yielding strain (producing 177,863 tonnes). Area under pulses, 9,312; ragi, 8,166. Government poultry and dairy farming schemes yielded 180m. eggs and 28,000 litres of milk in 1982–83.

Fisheries. The fishing industry is important; fish is the territory's staple food. In 1982 the catch of seafish was 31,500 tonnes (value Rs 1,025·75 lakhs). The whole territory has a coastline of about 140 km. There are about 4,950 active fishing vessels.

Industry. In 1983 there were 36 large and medium industrial projects and 2,689 small units registered. There were 9 government industrial estates. Small units were mainly occupied in making nylon fishing-nets, ready made clothing, pesticides, pharmaceuticals and footwear.

Employment. In 1980 there were 86 unions with 42,300 members.

Roads. In 1983 there were 4,500 km of motorable road (national highway, 223 km). In 1983 there were 47,434 registered vehicles.

Railways. There is a metre gauge line from the Pune–Bangalore line into Goa. There are no railways on Diu or in Daman.

Aviation. There are regular services to Bombay and Bangalore.

Shipping. The main port is Marmagoa, which handled 11·18m. tonnes of cargo, mainly iron ore, in 1982–83. There is a daily steamer service between Panaji and Bombay.

Post and Telegraphs. There are (1982) 249 post offices and 34 telephone exchanges providing links to 60 countries. There are 3 telex exchanges.

Justice. The territory comes under the High Court of Bombay.

Religion. About 62% of the population is Hindu, 36% Christian, 2% Muslim and other communities.

Education. The 1981 census recorded 57% literacy. Education is free up to grade VIII. In 1982–83 primary schools numbered 1,272 with 138,815 pupils, middle schools 421 with 75,059 pupils and secondary schools 271 with 51,501 pupils. There were 21 higher secondary schools, with 8,381 pupils, and 18 arts, commercial and science colleges with 7,063 students.

Health. There were (1983) 102 hospitals (3,580 beds) including 3 tuberculosis hospitals; also mobile and specialist clinics. There were also 133 health centres and about 1,081 doctors. There is 1 medical college and 1 dental college.

Richards, J. M., *Goa*. London, 1982
Soeiro de Brito, R., *Goa e as Praças do Norte*. Lisbon, 1966

LAKSHADWEEP. The territory consists of a group of 27 islands (10 inhabited), about 300 km off the west coat of Kerala. It was constituted a Union Territory in 1956 as the Laccadive, Minicoy and Amindivi Islands, and renamed in Nov. 1973. The total area of the islands is 32 sq. km. The northern portion is called the Amindivis. The remaining islands are called the Laccadives (including Minicoy Island). Androth is the largest island, 4·8 sq. km, and is nearest to Kerala. An Advisory Committee associated with the Union Home Minister and an Advisory Council to the Administrator assist in the administration of the islands; these are constituted annually. Population (1981 census), 40,237, nearly all Moslems. Density, 1,257 per sq. km.; growth rate, 1971–81, 26·49%. The language is Malayalam, but the language in Minicoy is Mahl. There were, in 1980, 8 high schools and 9 nursery schools, 18 junior basic schools, 4 senior basic schools and 1 junior college. There are 2 hospitals and 7 primary health centres. The staple products are coconut-husk fibre (coir), coconuts and fish. There is a tourist resort at Bangarem, an uninhabited island with an extensive lagoon. Headquarters of administration, Kavaratti Island.

Administrator: O. Saigal.

MIZORAM. On 21 Jan. 1972 the former Mizo Hills District of Assam was created a Union Territory. The area is approximately 21,090 sq. km and the population (1981 census), 487,774, of whom about 55% are literate and 90% are Christian. Density, 23 per sq. km.; growth rate, 1971–81, 46·75%.

There is a Council of Ministers responsible to a Legislative Assembly with 30 seats. The present ministry took office in June 1978. The nationalist Mizo National Front was banned in 1982. The main town is Aizawl, which is connected by a main road (not a national highway) to Silchar, Assam; Silchar is also the nearest airport. There are no railways.

The budget for 1980–81 estimated receipts of Rs 52·28 crores on revenue account and Rs 24·50 crores on capital account. Outlay for the sixth Five-Year Plan is Rs 24·50 crores.

Agriculture employs 46% of the people and 17% of cultivated land is irrigated; there are some terraced holdings, elsewhere shifting cultivation is practised in forest clearings. Industry is based on the forests. Total installed power capacity, 1975, 3·4 mw supplying 61 villages.

Lieut.-Governor: K. A. A. Raja.
Chief Minister: Brig. Sailo.

PONDICHERRY. Formerly the chief French settlement in India, Pondicherry was founded by the French in 1674, taken by the Dutch in 1693 and restored to the French in 1699. The English took it in 1761, restored it in 1765, re-took it in 1778, restored it a second time in 1785, retook it a third time in 1793 and finally restored it to the French in 1814. Administration was transferred to India on 1 Nov. 1954. A Treaty of Cession (together with Karikal, Mahé and Yanam) was signed on 28 May

1956; instruments of ratification were signed on 16 Aug. 1962 from which date (by the 14th amendment to the Indian Constitution) Pondicherry, comprising the 4 territories, became a Union Territory.

Area and Population. The territory forms an enclave on the Coromandel Coast of Tamil Nadu, with Karikal forming a separate enclave further south. The total area of Pondicherry is 492 sq. km, divided into 4 Districts: Pondicherry, Karikal, Mahe and Yanam. Population (1981 census), 604,471; density, 1,229 per sq. km.; growth rate, 1971–81, 28·15%. Pondicherry Municipality had (1981) 162,639 inhabitants. The principal languages spoken are French, English, Tamil, Telegu and Malayalam.

Government. By the Government of Union Territories Act 1963 Pondicherry is governed by a Lieut.-Governor, appointed by the President, and a Council of Ministers responsible to a Legislative Assembly. President's rule was imposed on 24 June 1983.

Lieut.-Governor: K. Prabhakara Rao.

Planning. Outlay for 1983–84 was Rs 205m. Of this, Rs 32·3m. was for agriculture, Rs 93·6m. for social and community services, Rs 28·4m. for irrigation, flood control and power development, Rs 20·4m. for transport and communications and Rs 14·9m. for industry.

Budget. Budget estimates for 1982–83 show revenue receipts of Rs 399·3m.

Electricity. Power is bought from neighbouring states. All main villages have electricity and there is a programme under the Sixth Plan to bring power to hut-dwellers. Consumption, 1982–83, 183·96m. units: 51·5% in industry, 28% in agriculture. Peak demand, 46·69 mw.

Agriculture. Nearly 45% of the population is engaged in agriculture and allied pursuits; 89% of the cultivated area is irrigated. The main food crop is rice. Estimated foodgrain production, 120,000 tonnes from 39,915 hectares in 1981–82, of which 99,000 tonnes was paddy; cash crops include groundnuts (11,700 tonnes), cotton (9,350 bales of 180 kg) and sugar-cane (200,000 tonnes).

Industry. There are 12 large and medium-scale industries manufacturing consumer goods such as textiles, sugar, cotton yarn, paper, spirits and beer, and employing 14,143 people in 1983. There were 11,766 people employed in 1,738 small industrial units engaged in varied manufacturing.

Railways. Pondicherry is on a branch from the main Madurai–Madras line.

Aviation. The nearest airport is Madras.

Education. There were, in July 1983, 97 pre-primary schools (4,399 pupils and 124 teachers), 324 primary schools (42,195 and 1,357), 103 middle schools (44,137 and 1,388), 61 high schools (33,658 and 1,253) and 18 higher secondary schools (16,783 and 582). There were 9 general education colleges, a medical college, a law college, a technical higher secondary school and a polytechnic; these had a total of 6,077 students; there were also professional and vocational colleges.

Health. In 1983 there were 10 hospitals and 40 health centres, one doctor to each 1,100 population, and one hospital bed to each 250.

INDONESIA

Republik Indonesia

Capital: Jakarta
Population: 158m. (1983)
GNP per capita: US$520 (1982)

HISTORY. In the 16th century Portuguese traders in quest of spices settled in some of the islands, but were ejected by the British, who in turn were ousted by the Dutch (1595). From 1602 the Netherlands East India Company conquered the Netherlands East Indies, and ruled them until the dissolution of the company in 1798. Thereafter the Netherlands Government ruled the colony from 1816 to 1941, when it was occupied by the Japanese until 1945. An independent republic was proclaimed by Dr Sukarno and Dr Hatta on 17 Aug. 1945.

Complete and unconditional sovereignty was transferred to the Republic of the United States of Indonesia on 27 Dec. 1949, except for the western part of New Guinea, the status of which was to be determined through negotiations between Indonesia and the Netherlands within one year after the transfer of sovereignty. A union was created to regulate the relationship between the two countries. A settlement of the New Guinea (Irian Jaya) question was, however, delayed until 15 Aug. 1962, when, through the good offices of the United Nations, an agreement was concluded for the transfer of the territory to Indonesia on 1 May 1963. In Feb. 1956 Indonesia abrogated the union and in Aug. 1956 repudiated Indonesia's debt to the Netherlands.

During 1950 the federal system which had sprung up in 1946–48 (*see* THE STATESMAN'S YEAR-BOOK, 1950, p. 1233) was abolished, and Indonesia was again made a unitary state. The provisional constitution was passed by the Provisional House of Representatives on 14 and came into force on 17 Aug. 1950. On 5 July 1959 by Presidential decree, the Constitution of 1945 was reinstated and the Constituent Assembly dissolved. For history 1960–66 *see* THE STATESMAN'S YEAR-BOOK, 1982–83, p. 678.

On 11–12 March 1966 the military commanders under the leadership of Lieut.-Gen. Suharto took over the executive power while leaving President Sukarno as the head of State. The Communist Party was at once outlawed and the National Front was dissolved in Oct. 1966. On 22 Feb. 1967 Sukarno handed over all his powers to Gen. Suharto.

AREA AND POPULATION. Indonesia, covering a total land area of 485,427 sq. miles (2,034,255 sq. km), consists of the islands of Sumatra, Java and Madura, Sulawesi (Celebes), Kalimantan (Borneo), Nusa Tenggara (Lesser Sundas), Maluku (Moluccas), Irian Jaya (the western half of New Guinea) and some 3,000 smaller islands and islets. It extends about 3,200 miles east to west through three time-zones (East, Central and West Standard time) of 1 hour's difference.

The total population in 1980 (census) was 147,490,298, distributed as follows:

Province	Sq. km	Census 1980	Chief town	Census 1971
Aceh (D.I.)	59,904	2,611,271	Banda Aceh	53,668
Sumatera Utara	71,104	8,360,894	Medan	635,562
Sumatera Barat	49,333	3,406,816	Padang	196,339
Riau	124,084	2,168,535	Pakanbaru	145,030
Jambi	62,150	1,445,994	Telanaipura	158,559
Sumatera Selatan	104,363	4,629,801	Palembang	582,961
Bengkulu	20,760	768,064	Bengkulu	31,866
Lampung	33,866	4,624,785	Tanjungkarang	198,986
Sumatra	524,097	28,016,160		

Province	Sq. km	Census 1980	Chief town	Census 1971
Jakarta Raya (D.C.I.)	592	6,503,449	Jakarta	4,576,009
Jawa Barat	49,144	27,453,525	Bandung	1,201,730
Jawa Tengah	34,353	25,372,889	Semarang	646,590
Yogyakarta (D.I.)	3,090	2,750,813	Yogyakarta	342,267
Jawa Timur	46,865	29,188,852	Surabaya	1,556,255
Jawa and Madura	134,044	91,269,528		
Kalimantan Barat	157,066	2,486,068	Pontianak	217,555
Kalimantan Tengah	156,552	954,353	Palangkaraya	27,132
Kalimantan Selatan	33,966	2,064,649	Banjarmasin	281,673
Kalimantan Timur	202,619	1,218,016	Samarinda	137,521
Kalimantan	550,203	6,723,086		
Sulawesi Utara	24,200	2,115,384	Menado	169,684
Sulawesi Tengah	88,655	1,289,635	Palu	...
Sulawesi Selatan	83,799	6,062,212	Ujung Padang	434,766
Sulawesi Tenggara	32,454	942,302	Kendari	...
Sulawesi	229,108	10,409,533		
Bali	5,623	2,469,930	Denpasar	88,142
Nusu Tenggara Barat	21,740	2,724,664	Mataram	...
Nusu Tenggara Timur	48,889	2,737,166	Kupang	52,698
Loro Sae [1]	14,925	555,350	Dili	65,451
Maluku	83,675	1,411,006	Amboina	79,636
Irian Jaya	421,981	1,173,875	Jajapura	45,786
Palau–Palau Lain	596,833	11,071,991		
Totals	2,034,255	147,490,298		

[1] Formerly Portuguese East Timor.

Other major cities (1971): Malang, 422,428; Surakarta, 414,285; Bogor, 195,882; Kediri, 178,865; all on Java. Estimate (1983) 158m.

The principal ethnic groups are the Aceh, Bataks and Minangkabaus in Sumatra, the Javanese and Sundanese in Java, the Madurese in Madura, the Balinese in Bali, the Sasaks in Lombok, the Menadonese, Minahas, Torajas and Buginese in Sulawesi, the Dayaks in Kalimantan, Irianese in Irian Jaya, the Ambonese in the Moluccas and Timorese in Timor Timur.

Bahasa Indonesia is the official language of the Republic.

CLIMATE. Conditions vary greatly over this spread of islands, but generally the climate is tropical monsoon, with a dry season from June to Sept. and a wet one from Oct. to April. Temperatures are high all the year and rainfall varies according to situation on lee or windward shores. Jakarta. Jan. 78°F (25·6°C), July 78°F (25·6°C). Annual rainfall 71″ (1,775 mm). Padang. Jan. 79°F (26·7°C), July 79°F (26·7°C). Annual rainfall 177″ (4,427 mm). Surabaya. Jan. 79°F (27·2°C), July 78°F (25·6°C). Annual rainfall 51″ (1,285 mm).

CONSTITUTION AND GOVERNMENT. Indonesia is a sovereign, independent republic.

The People's Consultative Assembly is the supreme power. It has 920 members and it sits at least once every 5 years. The House of People's Representatives has 460 members, 360 of them elected and 100 nominated by the President upon recommendation and sits for a 5-year term.

General elections to the 360 elected seats in the House of Representatives were held on 4 May 1982 and 242 seats were won by the Golkar Party

President, Prime Minister and Minister of Defence: Gen. Suharto, elected by the People's Consultative Assembly in 1968 and re-elected in 1973, 1978 and 1983.

Vice-President: H. Adam Malik. *Minister and Secretary of State:* Lieut.-Gen. S. H. Soedharmono. *Economics, Finance and Industry, and Chairman of the National Planning Board:* Dr Widjojo Nitisastro. *Public Welfare:* Gen. Surono. *Politics, Security and Defence:* Gen. Maraden Panggabean. *Development and Environment:* Dr Emil Salim. *Research and Technology:* Dr B. J. Habibie. *Administration Reform and Deputy Chairman of the National Planning Board:* Dr J. B. Soemarlin. *Agriculture:* Soedarsono Hadisapoetro. *Communications:* Roesmin Nurjadin. *Defence, Security and Commander of the Armed Forces:* Gen. M. Yusuf. *Education and Culture:* Dr Daoed Joesoef. *Foreign Affairs:* Dr Mochtar Kusumaatmadja. *Health:* Dr Suwardjono Suryaningrat. *Home Affairs:* Amir Machmud. *Industry:* A. R. Soehoed. *Information:* Gen. Ali Moertopo. *Justice:* Ali Said. *Manpower and Transmigration:* Dr Harun Alrasjid Zain. *Mining and Energy:* Professor Dr Soebroto. *Public Works and Electric Power:* Dr Pernomosidi Hadjisaroso. *Religion:* Alamsjah Ratu Prawiranegara. *Social Affairs:* Sapardjo. *Trade and Co-operatives:* Dr Radius Prawiro.

There are 6 junior ministers.

National flag: Horizontally red over white.

National anthem: Indonesia Raya (tune by Wage Rudolf Supratman, 1928).

DEFENCE. The Indonesian Armed Forces were formally set up on 5 Oct. 1945. On 11 Oct. 1967 the Army, Navy, Air Force and Police were integrated under the Department of Defence and Security. Their commanders no longer hold cabinet rank. There is selective military service.

Army. There is 1 armoured cavalry brigade, 13 infantry brigades, 2 airborne infantry brigades, 1 artillery regiment, 1 engineer and 2 air defence regiments, 15 artillery battalions. Equipment includes 93 AMX-13 and 41 PT-46 light tanks. Total strength in 1984 was 210,000.

Navy. The fleet comprises 5 diesel powered patrol submarines (3 new Fed. German built and 2 *ex*-Soviet), 10 small frigates, 8 fast missile boats, 2 fast torpedo boats, 12 patrol vessels, 4 fleet minesweepers, 8 small patrol craft, 15 landing ships, 2 landing craft, 2 training ships, 4 surveying vessels, 5 oilers, 2 command and support ships, 1 destroyer depot ship, 1 repair ship, 1 cable ship, 10 auxiliaries, 62 minor landing craft, 20 service craft and 9 tugs. Of the 100 ships acquired from the USSR very few now remain. The naval air arm has 70 aircraft, including 20 helicopters. There are 70 customs patrol cutters, 6 maritime security agency boats and 30 armed marine police craft.

Naval personnel in 1984 numbered 36,000 officers and men, including 5,000 of the Marine Commando Corps and 1,000 in the Naval Air Arm.

Air Force. Operational combat units comprise two squadrons of A-4E Skyhawk attack aircraft, and single squadrons of F-5E Tiger II fighters and OV-10F Bronco twin-turboprop counter-insurgency aircraft. There are 3 transport squadrons, equipped with turboprop C-130 Hercules, Nurtanio/CASA NC-212 Aviocar and F27 Friendship aircraft, and piston-engined C-47s, plus 3 specially-equipped Boeing 737 dual-purpose maritime surveillance/transports; and an assortment of other aircraft in transport, helicopter and training units including 16 Hawk attack/trainers, 25 T-34C-1 armed turboprop trainers, and 20 Swiss-built AS 202 Bravo piston-engined primary trainers. On order are 32 CN-235 twin-turboprop transports and a large number of MBB NBO 105, Super Puma and Bell 412 helicopters, all from Nurtanio of Indonesia. Personnel (1983) approximately 29,000.

INTERNATIONAL RELATIONS

Membership. Indonesia is a member of UN and ASEAN.

ECONOMY

Planning. The third Five-Year Development Plan (1979–84) provides funds from central government for food production and other programmes implemented by village, region, province and municipal authority. Village projects include building and credits to farmers; regions and municipalities implement schemes to create employment, often in road-making; provinces receive sums for specific projects. Aid is also provided for school building, health centres, irrigation and fertilizer plant. The largest single programme is that for increased production of paddy, secondary and horticultural crops (7·6% of plan budget). Other important programmes are those for stimulating fisheries and stock-farming, and for generally lessening dependence on rice by encouraging other food crops.

Budget. The ordinary budget, excluding the development budget, was as follows in 1983–84 (in Rp. 1m.): Gross revenue, 16,565,000m.; gross expenditure, 16,565,000m.

Currency. The monetary unit is the *rupiah* (abbreviated Rp.), divided into 100 *sen*. There are banknotes of 1, 2½, 5, 10, 25, 50 and 100 rupiahs and aluminium coins of 1, 5, 10, 25 and cupro-nickel coins of 50 sen.

In March 1984 there were 1,477 rupiahs = £1 sterling; 993 rupiahs = US$1.

Banking. The Bank Indonesia, formerly the Java Bank, established in 1828, was made the central bank of Indonesia on 1 July 1953. It had an original capital of Rp. 25m.; a reserve fund of Rp. 18m. and a special reserve of Rp. 84m.

Bank Negara Indonesia is a state bank and is designed to act as a source of credit for reconstruction purposes. The Bank Pembangunan Indonesia accords long-term credits for agricultural, industrial and mining projects. The Bank Koperasi Tani & Nelayan extends credits to co-operative societies and smaller business men.

There are 7 major commercial banks and 14 foreign banks; the latter include the Chartered Bank, the Hongkong and Shanghai Banking Corporation, the Bank of America, the Citibank, the Bank of Tōkyō, Chase Manhattan and the American Express International Banking Corporation.

Weights and Measures. The metric system of weights and measures was officially introduced in Feb. 1923, and came into full operation on 1 Jan. 1938.

The following are the old weights and measures: *Pikol* = 136·16 lb. avoirdupois; *Katti* = 1·36 lb. avoirdupois; *Bau* = 1·7536 acres; *Square Pal* = 227 hectares = 561·16 acres; *Jengkal* = 4 yd; *Pal* (Java) = 1,506 metres; *Pal* (Sumatra) = 1,852 metres.

ENERGY AND NATURAL RESOURCES

Electricity. All gas and electricity undertakings were nationalized by presidential decree of 3 Oct. 1953, retroactive from 23 Dec. 1952. Three large-scale hydro-electric plants are operating on the Jatiluhur and Brantas rivers in Java and on the Asahan River in Sumatra. Electricity capacity, 1984, 4,631m. mw.

Oil. Indonesia is the principal producer of petroleum in the Far East, production coming from Sumatra, Kalimantan (Indonesian Borneo) and Java, where Anglo-Dutch and US interests operate. Indonesia is the tenth largest OPEC producer. The 1982 (preliminary) output of crude oil was 488m. bbls.

Gas. Pertamina, the state oil company, started to pump natural gas to Jakarta in 1979.

Minerals. The high cost of extraction means that little of the large mineral resources outside Java is exploited; however, there is copper mining in Irian Jaya, nickel mining and processing on Sulawesi, aluminium smelting in northern Sumatra. The tin mines of Bangka, Billiton and Riouw are worked by the Government. In 1981 their total yield was 33,600 tonnes. Output (in 1000 tonnes, 1981) of bauxite was 1,270; iron sand, 1,339; coal 329; copper, 180; silver, 2·4 (tons); gold, 233·9 kg.

Agriculture. Rice production (1982), 34·1m. tonnes. In 1982 production was (in

1,000 tonnes): Copra, 1,260; sugar-cane, 21·8m.; rubber, 990; palm oil, 874; tea, 92.

Livestock (1982): Cattle, 6,435,000; buffaloes, 2,506,000; horses, 616,000; sheep, 4,196,000; goats, 7,985,000; pigs, 3,296,000.

Forestry. The forest area is 122m. hectares. Production (1981): All timber, 27·38m. cu. metres.

Fisheries. In 1978 (provisional) the catch of sea fisheries was 1,655,000 tons.

INDUSTRY AND TRADE

Industry. There are shipyards at Jakarta Raya, Surabaya, Semarang and Amboina. There are many textile factories (total production in 1978–79, 1,400m. metres), large paper factories (83,496 tonnes, 1977–78), match factories, automobile and bicycle assembly works, large construction works, tyre factories, glass factories, a caustic soda and other chemical factories. Production (1977–78): Cement, 2,878,500 tonnes; fertilizers, 1·55m. tonnes; glass, 43,571,720 tons; 7·4m. cycle tyres; 6,806,000 cu. metres of oxygen; 305,000 cu. metres of acetylene.

For details of nationalization *see* THE STATESMAN'S YEAR-BOOK, 1981–82, p. 677.

Trade Unions. The largest group of trade unions in Indonesia is the Serekat Organasasi Karyawan Seluruh Indonesia (SOKSI), the Central Council of All Indonesia Trade Unions, with a membership of 2·6m., to which 28 national unions and 832 local unions are affiliated. The second largest is the Kongres Buruh Seluruh Indonesia (KBSI), the All Indonesia Trades Union Congress, with a membership of nearly 400,000. To the KBSI 25 national unions and 54 local unions are affiliated. There are also the HISSBI (Federation of Indonesian Trade Unions) with a membership of 180,203, and the KBKI (Indonesian Democratic Labour Organization), with a membership of 94,477. In addition, there are also trade-union centres which are closely connected with the Islamic Parties.

Commerce. Imports and exports (including oil) in US$1m. for year April–March:

	1977	1978	1979	1980	1981
Imports	6,230·3	6,690·4	7,202·3	10,834·4	13,272·0
Exports	10,625·6	11,643·2	15,590·1	21,908·9	23,120·0

The main export items (in US$1m.) in 1979 were: Oil, 15,590·1; coffee, 614·5; rubber, 936·8; palm-oil and kernels, 186·9 (1977); tin ore, 404·4; tea, 834; tobacco, 56·6; copra, 36·2 (1977); wood, 1,796·7.

The main import items are non-crude oil, rice, consumer goods, fertilizer, chemicals, weaving yarn, iron and steel, industrial and business machinery.

Total trade between Indonesia and UK (British Department of Trade returns, in £1,000 sterling):

	1978	1979	1980	1981	1982	1983
Imports to UK	33,384	55,950	56,971	73,756	91,704	169,454
Exports and re-exports from UK	83,632	76,704	112,170	139,236	212,066	193,642

Tourism. In 1980 about 561,000 tourists visited Indonesia mainly from USA, Australia, Japan, Netherlands, Germany, France, UK and Singapore.

COMMUNICATIONS

Roads. The projected Trans-Sumatra trunk road will connect Aceh (north) and Lampung (south). The feeder-road between West Sumatra and Riau provinces was completed with the building of the bridge over the Kampar River at Pekanbaru in 1974. Motor vehicles, at 31 Dec. 1979, totalled 577,345 passenger cars, 383,648 vans and trucks, 69,545 buses and about 2,266,183 motor cycles.

Railways. In 1980 the State Railways totalled 6,877 km, comprising 4,922 km of 1,067 mm gauge on Java, and 1,458 km of 1,067 mm gauge and 497 km of 750 mm gauge on Sumatra. In 1980–81, railways carried 6,030m. passenger-km and 976m. tonne-km.

Aviation. The Government and KLM in 1949 set up 'Garuda Indonesian Airways' as a mixed enterprise on a 50–50 capital basis under KLM management. The agreement was to last until 1960. In 1954, however, the Government bought up the shares held by KLM for 15m. guilders and nationalized GIA; and in Jan. 1958, the Government unilaterally terminated the contracts with the technical assistants provided by KLM. GIA maintains a direct service between Jakarta and Manila, Bangkok, Hong Kong, Tōkyō and Amsterdam.

Shipping. The national shipping company Pelajaran Nasional Indonesia (PELNI) maintains interinsular communications. The Jakarta Lloyd maintains regular services between Jakarta, Amsterdam, Hamburg and London.

Post and Broadcasting. In 1979 the postal and telegraph services of Indonesia included 2,796 post offices. There were 660 telegraph offices which handled 3·9m. domestic and 488,000 international cables. Post offices handled 176m. letters and Rp. 250,000m. in money orders, Giro and postal cheques. Deposits with post office savings accounts, Rp. 31,210m. Number of telephones (1982), 600,643.

Radio Republik Indonesia, under the Department of Information, operates 26 stations. Television broadcasting covers 82m. people in an area of 72,100 sq. km. There were, in 1979, 82 transmission stations and 11 relay stations.

Newspapers (1973). There were 117 daily newspaper publishers with estimated daily circulation of 1·6m. There were 270 publishers of weekly papers and magazines with a circulation of 3·3m.

JUSTICE, RELIGION, EDUCATION AND WELFARE

Justice. There are courts of first instance, high courts of appeal in every provincial capital and a Supreme Court of Justice for the whole of Indonesia in Jakarta. Administrative matters on judicial organization are under the direction of the Department of Justice.

In civil law the population is divided into three main groups: Indonesians, Europeans and foreign Orientals, to whom different law systems are applicable. When, however, people from different groups are involved, a system of so-called 'inter-gentile' law is applied.

The present criminal law, which has been in force since 1918, is codified and is based on European penal law. This law is equally applicable to all groups of the population. For private and commercial law, however, there are various systems applicable for the various groups of the population. For the Indonesians, a system of private and agrarian law is applicable; this is called Adat Law, and is mainly uncodified. For the other groups the prevailing private and commercial law system is codified in the Private Law Act (1847) and the Commercial Law Act (1847). These Acts have their origins in the French *Code Civile* and *Code du Commerce* through the similar Dutch codifications. These Acts are entirely applicable to Indonesian citizens and to Europeans, whereas to foreign Orientals they are applicable with some exceptions, mainly in the fields of family law and inheritance. Penal law was in the process of being codified in 1981.

Religion. Religious liberty is granted to all denominations. The majority of the Indonesians are Moslems. There are nearly 6m. Christians; their main strength is in Central and East Java, North Sulawesi, East Nusa Tenggara, the Moluccas and Irian Jaya. There are also about 1m. Buddhists, probably for the greater part Chinese. Hinduism has 6m. members, of whom 2·5m. are on Bali.

In 1978–79 there were 423,570 Islamic houses of worship, 24,215 Christian (7,052 of them Catholic), 4,365 Hindu and 1,762 Buddhist.

Education. The following table shows the number of school and college students in 1978 (1,000):

Total population aged 7–13	23,000
Pupils in public and private elementary schools	97,948 [1]
Pupils in Islamic schools	3,032 [1]
Total population aged 13–18	16,196 [1]
Junior high school pupils	2,800 [1]
Senior high school pupils	1,472 [1]
Academy and university students	195,994

[1] 1979–80.

English is the first foreign language taught in schools.

There are 51 universities (23 are private).

In 1961 a separate Department of Higher Education and Science was set up. Five training centres for technical education were opened in May 1975 and these continue to expand.

Health. In 1978–79 there were 4,573 public health centres, 2,412 mother-and-child clinics, 4,180 polyclinics, 10,456 doctors and 31,061 nurses and midwives.

DIPLOMATIC REPRESENTATIVES

Of Indonesia in Great Britain (38 Grosvenor Sq., London W1X 9AD)
Ambassador: Sjahabuddin Arifin (accredited on 12 Nov. 1981).

Of Great Britain in Indonesia (Jalan, M.H. Thamrin, 75, Jakarta)
Ambassador: Alan Donald.

Of Indonesia in the USA (2020 Massachusetts Ave., NW, Washington, D.C., 20036)
Ambassador: A. Hasnan Habib.

Of the USA in Indonesia (Medan Merdeka Selatan 5, Jakarta)
Ambassador: John H. Holdridge.

Of Indonesia to the United Nations
Ambassador: Ali Alatas.

Books of Reference

Bee, O. J., *The Petroleum Resources of Indonesia.* OUP, 1982

Bemmelen, R. W. van, *Geology of Indonesia.* 2 vols. The Hague, 1949

Echols, J. M., and Shadily, H., *An Indonesian–English Dictionary.* 3rd ed. Cornell Univ. Press, 1975

Leifer, M., *Indonesia's Foreign Policy.* London, 1983

McDonald, H., *Suharto's Indonesia.* Univ. Press of Hawaii, 1981

Neill, W. T., *Twentieth-Century Indonesia.* Columbia Univ. Press, 1973

Papenek, G., *The Indonesian Economy.* Eastbourne, 1980

Polomka, P., *Indonesia Since Sukarno.* London, 1971

Taylor, A. M., *Indonesian Independence and the United Nations.* Cornell Univ. Press, 1960

Weinstein, F. B., *Indonesian Foreign Policy and the Dilemma of Dependence.* Cornell Univ. Press, 1977

IRAN

Jomhori-e-Islami-e-Irân

Capital: Tehrán
Population: 40·55m. (1982)
GNP per capita: US$2,160 (1977)

HISTORY. Persia was ruled by the Shahs as an absolute monarchy until 30 Dec. 1906 when the first Constitution was granted. Reza Khan took control after a *coup d'état* on 31 Oct. 1925 deposed the last Shah of the Qajar Dynasty, and became Reza Shah Pahlavi on 12 Dec. 1925. The country's name was changed to Iran on 21 March 1935. Reza Shah abdicated on 16 Sept. 1941 (and died 25 July 1944) in favour of his son, Mohammad Reza Pahlavi (born 26 Oct. 1919).

Following widespread civil unrest, the Shah left Iran with his family on 17 Jan. 1979 (and died in Egypt 27 July 1980). The Ayatollah Ruhollah Khomeini, spiritual leader of the Shi'a Moslem community, returned from 15 years exile on 1 Feb. 1979 and appointed a provisional government on 5 Feb. The Shah's government resigned and Parliament dissolved itself on 11 Feb. Following a referendum in March, an Islamic Republic was proclaimed on 1 Apr. 1979. In 1980 Iraq invaded Iran and the war was continuing in early 1984.

AREA AND POPULATION. Iran is bounded north by the USSR and the Caspian Sea, east by Afghánistán and Pakistan, south by the Gulf of Oman and the Persian Gulf, and west by Iraq and Turkey. It has an area of about 1,648,000 sq. km (636,000 sq. miles), but a vast portion is desert, and the average density is only (1982) 25 inhabitants to the sq. km.

The population at recent censuses was as follows: (1956) 18,944,821; (1966) 25,781,090; (1976) 33,591,875. Estimate (1982) 40,550,000.

The populations (census 1976) and capitals of the provinces *(ostán)* were:

Province	Population	Capital	Province	Population	Capital
Azarbáiján Bákhtari	1,407,970	Rezáyeh	Hamadán	1,093,079	Hamadán
			Ilam	242,812	Abdanan
Azarbáiján Khavari	3,204,761	Tabriz	Kermán	1,085,097	Kermán
			Kermánsháhán	1,025,257	Kermánsháh
Bakhtiári va Chahár Mahál	398,807	Shahr Kord	Khorásán	3,250,085	Mashhad
			Khuzestán	2,187,198	Ahváz
Balúchestán va Sistán	662,677	Záhedán	Kordestán	783,740	Sánándáj
			Lorestan	932,297	Khorramábád
Boyer ahmadi va Kohkiluyeh	242,207	Yasoof	Markazi	6,954,729	Tehrán
			Mázándárán	2,386,956	Sári
Bushehr	347,703	Bushehr	Semnán	487,531	Semnán
Esfáhán	1,971,745	Esfáhán	Yazd	358,082	Yazd
Fárs	2,020,942	Shiráz	Zanjan	577,286	Zanjan
Gilán	1,579,317	Rasht			

The principal cities at census 1976 were:

City	Pop.	City	Pop.	City	Pop.
Tehrán	4,496,159	Qom	246,831	Karaj	138,774
Esfáhán	671,825	Rasht	187,203	Qazvin	138,527
Mashhad	670,180	Rezáyeh	163,991	Yazd	135,978
Tabriz	598,576	Hamadán	155,846	Arak	114,507
Shiráz	416,408	Ardabil	147,404	Desful	110,287
Ahváz	329,006	Khorramshahr	146,709	Khorramábád	104,928
Abadán	296,081	Kermán	140,309	Borujerd	100,103

The national language is Farsi or Persian, spoken by 45% of the population. 23% spoke related languages, including Kurdish and Luri in the west and Baluchi in the south-east, while 26% spoke Turkic languages, primarily the Azarbáijáni-speaking peoples of the north-west and the Turkomen of Khorásan in the north-east.

CLIMATE. Mainly a desert climate, but with more temperate conditions on the shores of the Caspian Sea. Seasonal range of temperature is considerable. Tehrán. Jan. 36°F (2·2°C), July 85°F (29·4°C). Annual rainfall 10″ (246 mm).

CONSTITUTION AND GOVERNMENT. The Constitution of the Islamic Republic was approved by a national referendum in Dec. 1979. It gives supreme authority to a religious leader (*wali faqih*), which position will be held by Ayatollah Khomeini for the rest of his natural life, and thereafter be elected by the Moslem clergy.

The President of the Republic is popularly-elected for a 4-year term and is head of the executive; he appoints a Prime Minister and other Ministers, subject to approval by the *Majlis*.

Presidents since the establishment of the Islamic Republic:

Abolhassan Bani-Sadr, 4 Feb. 1980–22   Mohammad Ali Raja'i, 24 July 1981–
June 1981 (deposed)   30 Aug. 1981 (assassinated).

In Sept. 1980 war began with Iraq with destruction of some Iranian towns and damage to the oil installations at Abadán. The war was still in progress in early 1984.

The Cabinet was composed as follows in Jan. 1984.

President: Hojatolislam Sayed Ali Khamenei (from 12 Oct. 1981).

Prime Minister: Mir Hussein Moussavi.

Foreign Affairs: Dr Ali Akbar Vellayati. *Interior:* Hojatolislam Ali Akbar Nateq Nouri. *Defence:* Col. Mohammed Salimi. *Labour and Social Affairs:* Abdul Ghasem Sar Hadizadeh. *Education and Training:* Ali Akbar Parvaresh. *Islamic Guidance:* (Vacant). *Commerce:* Hassen Abedi Jafari. *Health:* Dr Hadi Manafi. *Posts and Telecommunications:* Morteza Nabavi. *Justice:* Sayyed Mohammed Asghari. *Roads and Transport:* Hadinezhad Hoseyniyan. *Industry:* Sayyed Mostafa Hashemi. *Higher Education and Culture:* Dr Mohammad Ali Najafi. *Mines and Metals:* Hussain Nili Ahmad Abadi. *Agriculture:* Abbas Ali Zali. *Housing and Urban Development:* (Vacant). *Energy:* Dr Hassan Ghafuri-Fard. *Oil:* Sayyed Mohammed Gharazi. *Heavy Industry:* Behzad Nabavi. *Economic Affairs and Finance:* Dr Hussein Namazi. *Ministers of State:* Dr Mohammad Taqi Banki (*Planning and Budget*), Gholamreza Agazadeh (*Executive Affairs*).

Legislative power is held by a 270-member Islamic Consultative Assembly (*Majlis*), directly elected for a 4-year term on 9 May 1980; but all legislation is subject to approval by a 12-member Council of Guardians who ensure it is in accordance with the Islamic code and with the Constitution. Six members of this constitutional Council are appointed by the *wali faqih* and six by the judiciary.

National flag: Three horizontal stripes of green, white and red; on the borders of the green and red stripes the legend *Allah Akbar* in white Kufi script repeated 22 times in all; in the centre of the white stripe the national emblem in red.

Local Government. The country is divided into 21 provinces *(ostán)* and 2 governor-generalships; these are sub-divided into 172 *shahrestán* (counties), each under a *farmándár* (governor) and thence into 499 *bakhsh* (districts), each under a *bakhshdár.* The districts are sub-divided into *dehistán* (groups of villages) each under a *dehdár,* each village having its elected *kadkhodá* (headman).

DEFENCE. Two years' military service is compulsory.

Army. The Army consisted (1984) of 150,000 men (100,000 conscripts), with some 400,000 reservists. It is organized in 3 armoured, 4 infantry and 1 airborne divisions, and auxiliary units. Equipment includes 190 T-54/-55/-62, 300 Chieftain, 300 M-47/-48 and 150 M-60A1 main battle tanks. There is also a 150,000-strong Revolutionary Guard Corps.

Navy. The fleet, declining since the revolution, before the war comprised 3 very old destroyers, 4 frigates, 4 old corvettes, 3 old coastal minesweepers, 2 inshore minesweepers, 7 patrol boats, 14 hovercraft, 2 landing ships, 1 landing craft, 2 supply ships, 1 repair ship, 2 oilers, 4 survey vessels, 1 water carrier and 3 tugs. There were also 30 coastguard cutters and 2 customs craft.

The construction of 12 fast missile craft in France was to have been completed by mid-1979, but later boats did not receive their missiles and the last 3 boats were embargoed in France. They eventually sailed on 2 Aug. 1981 but one was seized by a Royalist group off Cadiz and after she surrended to the French all three were sent to Iran in a merchant ship to obviate further trouble.

The naval air arm comprised 14 assorted aircraft and 20 helicopters.

Naval personnel nominally totalled 20,000 officers and ratings including cadets, apprentices and marines, but not more than 10.000 were reported active in 1984.

With war following revolution and withdrawal of UK and US maintenance teams the fleet is suffering from lack of spares and the navy has run down, several ships being laid up. The situation is worsened by cessation of foreign help in training semi-illiterate conscripts and with poor morale following general instability and casualties the above ships do not represent an efficient maritime force.

Claims of sinkings during the Iran-Iraq war have not been officially confirmed. Figures for ship and personnel strengths should be interpreted with caution.

Air Force. In Aug. 1955 the Air Force became a separate and independent arm, and had a strength of about 23 first-line squadrons (each 15 aircraft, plus reserves), with 100,000 personnel before the 1979 revolution. Current strength is uncertain, but has been estimated at 35,000 personnel and 75 serviceable combat aircraft. The latter include some MiG-19/Chinese-built F-6 fighter-bombers, supplied via North Korea, and surviving US fighters that might total 5 F-14A Tomcat interceptors, 50 F-5E Tiger II and 10 F-4D/E Phantom II fighter-bombers, plus a few RF-4E reconnaissance-fighters. Transport aircraft include about 25 C-130E/H Hercules, F27s and Boeing 707s and 747s, some equipped as flight refuelling tankers. The status of the large fleet of CH-47C Chinook, Bell Model 214 and other helicopters is not known; but two P-3F Orion maritime patrol aircraft remain operational. Training aircraft include Bonanza basic trainers and 6 turboprop PC-7 Turbo-Trainers.

INTERNATIONAL RELATIONS

Membership. Iran is a member of UN, OPEC and the Colombo Plan.

ECONOMY

Planning. The sixth 5-year development plan, 1978–83 was abandoned following the revolution.

Budget. Budget estimate for year commencing 21 March 1981: Revenue 2,025,000m. *rials*; expenditure 3,300,000m. *rials*.

Currency. The Iranian unit of currency is the *rial* sub-divided into 100 *dinars*.

Notes in circulation are of denominations of 5–10,000 *rials*. Coins in circulation are bronze–aluminium and copper, 50 *dinar*; silver alloy, 1, 2, 5, 10 and 20 *rials*. In March 1984, US$1 = 87·05 *rials*; £1 = 128 *rials*.

Banking. The *Bank Markazi Iran* was established in 1960 as the note-issuing authority and government bank of Iran. All other banks were nationalized in June 1979, and re-organized into 8 new state banking corporations.

All insurance companies were nationalized in June 1979.

Weights and Measures. By a law passed on 8 Jan. 1933, the official weights and measures are those of the metric system.

The Iranian year is a solar year running from 21 March to 20 March; the Hejira year 1362 corresponds to the Christian year 21 March 1983–20 March 1984.

ENERGY AND NATURAL RESOURCES

Electricity. Electric energy installed capacity, 1980, was 5·3m. kw., and 17,150m. kwh. was generated.

Oil. For a history of Iran's oil industry 1951–79, *see* STATESMAN'S YEAR-BOOK, 1982–83.

The petroleum industry was seriously disrupted by the 1979 revolution, and many facilities, including the vast refinery at Abadan, the new refinery at Bandar

Khomeini and the tanker terminal at Kharg Island, have been destroyed or put out of action during the Gulf war with Iraq. All operating companies were nationalised in 1979 and operations are now run by the National Petrochemical Company. Total production of petroleum, 73·7m. tonnes, 1980 (113·2m. tonnes, 1979).

Gas. Natural gas production (1979) was 44,300m. cu. metres.

Minerals. Iran has substantial mineral deposits relatively underdeveloped. Production figures for 1977 (in 1,000 tonnes): Iron ore, 670; coal, 900; zinc, 62; lead, 40; manganese, 15; chromite, 80; salt (1973), 500.

Agriculture. Reliable statistics of production are not available. It is estimated, however, that out of 164·8m. hectares of land area only 16,857,000 are crop land (including 10,300 hectares fallow), 27·8m. hectares are forests and ranges and 32·7m. hectares are potentially cultivable waste.

Crop returns for 1982 (in 1,000 tonnes): Wheat, 6,500; barley, 1,200; rice, 1,400; sugar-beet, 2,100; sugar-cane, 1,300; tobacco, 24.

Wool comes principally from Khorásán, Kermánsháh, Mázandarán and Azerbáiján. Production, 1972, 20,000 tonnes.

Rice is grown largely on the Caspian shores.

Tobacco is grown along the shores of the Caspian. It is purchased by the Tobacco Monopoly and manufactured in the government factory at Tehrán.

Opium, until 1955, was an important export commodity in Iran. On 7 Oct. 1955 an Act was approved by Parliament to prohibit the cultivation and usage of opium.

Livestock (1982): 34·8m. sheep, 13·8m. goats, 8·6m. cattle, 350,000 horses, 27,000 camels, 58,000 pigs, 220,000 buffaloes, and 1·8m. donkeys.

Fisheries. The Caspian Fisheries Co. (Shilát) is a government monopoly. Exports of caviar (1975) were valued at US$72m.

INDUSTRY AND TRADE

Industry. Iran's chief natural products are oil, wool, cotton, silk, fruit, nuts, cereals, vegetables, gum, timber, oil seeds, copper and other metalliferous ores, coal, cattle, sheep and goats. Its principal manufactured or processed products are textiles, carpets, skins, casings, vegetable oil, soap, metal products, plastic products, furniture, beet sugar, tea, tobacco and cigarettes, wine, vodka, soft drinks, caviar, footwear, petroleum products, glass products, tiles, bricks, cement, leather and leather goods, dairy products and manufactured foodstuffs, and printed matter.

Apart from the oil industry, the industries employing most workers are textiles, sugar refining, flour-milling, fruit processing, tea, furniture, printing, leather, matches, glass, building materials and light metal goods. The most popular carpets are manufactured in the environs of Tabriz, Kermán, Arák, Káshán, Esfahán, Shiráz and Hamadán. Esfahán is the traditional textile manufacturing centre, but in recent years important textile mills, particularly cotton, have been built in other towns, including Tehrán. A number of automobile assembly plants have been set up in recent years employing several thousand workers. A steel-mill, a machine-tool factory, a tractor plant and a huge petrochemical complex are also going into production.

Commerce. Imports totalled 863,300m. rials and exports 963,500m. rials in 1980. Crude oil amounted to 73% of exports and refined products to 21%; 27% of exports went to Japan and 12% to Federal Republic of Germany while these two countries each provided 14% of imports.

Total trade between Iran and UK (British Department of Trade returns, in £1,000 sterling):

	1979	1980	1981	1982	1983
Imports to UK	243,589	107,176	154,385	225,971	100,545
Exports and re-exports from UK	231,798	393,335	402,753	333,715	629,980

COMMUNICATIONS

Roads. In 1980 there were 24,806 km of first-class roads and 26,484 km of second-class (graded, all weather) roads, and 11,825 km of third class (earth) roads.

In 1974 passenger cars and taxis numbered 119,851; commercial vehicles, 13,193; buses, 2,611, and motor cycles, 19,785.

Railways. The State Railways total 4,567 km, comprising 4,473 km of 1,435 mm gauge of which 145 km electrified and 94 km of 1,676 mm gauge. Revenue in 1978–79 was 9,119m. rials, and expenditure 13,513m. rials. In 1980–81 the railways ran 6,030m. passenger-km and 976m. tonne-km. Construction started in 1983 of a link from Kermán to Zahedán to connect with the network in Pakistan.

Aviation. The principal airlines which link Tehrán with Europe and the Middle East are Air France, British Airways, Ariana, Alitalia, Swissair, LIA, KLM, PIA, SAS, Qantas, SABENA, Lufthansa, Aeroflot and Middle East Air Lines. British Airways, Qantas, Lufthansa, PANAM and Air France also connect Tehrán with the Far East. Aryana (Afghánistán) Airline connects Tehrán with Lebanon, Syria and Afghánistán. British Airways, KLM and SAS operate services to Tehrán and Iran National Airlines Corporation, registered on 29 March 1962, has monopoly rights on all internal flights and also operates in the Persian Gulf; in 1965 it inaugurated European services. The Iranian Government owns 51% of its shares.

Shipping. In 1979, 80·22m. tonnes of goods were loaded at Iranian ports and 15m. tonnes were unloaded.

Navigation on the Lake of Rezáyeh, from Sharaf-Khaneh to Kolmankháneh, is served by some 5 tugs and 9 barges for the transport of goods and passengers. The service runs twice a week. On the river Karun likewise, from Khorramshahr to Ahwáz, an irregular service for cargo only both ways is run by the Iran Transport Co. and the Karun Navigation Co., and some local firms run daily trips by motor boat, for passengers and merchandise. By changing into lighter-draught boats at Ahwáz both can be taken up to Shallili near Shushtar.

Post and Broadcasting. Postal, telegraph and telephone services are administered by the Iranian Ministry of Posts, Telegraphs and Telephones.

There is wireless-telegraph communication between Tehrán and Tabriz, Meshed, Kermánshah, Kermán, Khorramshahr, Bushehr, Yezd, Shiráz and Lingeh and a wireless-telephone link between Tehrán and Tabriz. Tehrán is also in wireless communication with Europe and is linked by wireless telephone with Baghdad, London, Berne and New York. In 1982 the number of telephones was 1,041,939, of which some 423,861 were in Tehrán. Wireless sets numbered 10m. in 1980, and television sets 2·1m.

Cinemas (1975). There were 430 cinemas with 299,191 seats.

Newspapers. There were in 1982, 17 daily papers in Tehrán and other cities. Their circulation is relatively small, *Ettela'át* and *Kayhán* leading with about 220,000 and 350,000 respectively. Two English-language and a French-language daily ceased publication in March 1979.

JUSTICE, RELIGION, EDUCATION AND WELFARE

Justice. A new legal system based on Islamic law was introduced by the new constitution in 1979. The President of the Supreme Court and the public Prosecutor-General are appointed by the *wali faqih* (Ayatollah Khomeini). The Supreme Court has 16 branches and 109 offences carry the death penalty.

Religion. The official religion is the Shia branch of Islam, known as the *Ithna-Ashariyya*, which recognizes 12 Imáms or spiritual successors of the Prophet Mohammad. Of the total population, 96% are *Shiá*, 3% are *Sunni* and 1% non-Moslem (mainly Armenian Christians).

The Gregorian National Armenians form 3 dioceses. There are also a few thousand Roman Catholic Armenians, who have a bishop of their own rite at Esfahán, the bishop of the Latin rite residing at Rezayeh (Urmia). There is an Anglican bishop residing at Esfahán.

Education. The great majority of primary and secondary schools are state schools. Grants are made to private schools. Elementary education in state schools and university education are free; small fees are charged for state-run secondary schools. Text-books are issued free of charge to pupils in the first 4 grades of elementary schools.

In 1978–79 there were 4,403,106 pupils in primary schools and 2,370,341 in secondary schools; there were 256,303 students in technical schools and 57,832 in teacher-training establishments. There were 17 universities and almost 200 other institutes of higher education, with 175,675 students in 1978–79. The Free Islamic University was established after the revolution and in 1983 the International University of Islamic Studies was being organized.

Health. The Ministry of Health controls the health of the country through the Department of Public Health, which has achieved some remarkable results in the fight against malaria; large areas along the Caspian and the Persian Gulf and in Azerbáiján are now free from malaria. Opium addiction has been greatly reduced, and the cultivation of the poppy has been practically eradicated. Programmes to combat tuberculosis, smallpox, trachoma, venereal diseases, etc., have been introduced.

In 1981 about 62,056 hospital beds (33% of them in Tehrán) were available in 579 hospitals. Medical personnel included 10,054 physicians and surgeons and 1,462 dentists.

Social Security. A system of social security benefits covering accident, sickness, retirement, death, marriage, maternity and childbirth and free medical attention and hospitalization for insured contributors and their families is embodied in the Workers' Social Insurance Law, 1960. This law provides for the insurance under the scheme of all workers in receipt of wages or salaries, but is at present being applied to some 683,496 workers employed mainly in industrial and mining establishments employing 10 or more workers. It also provides for the compulsory payment by employers of family allowances to workers with 2 or more children.

DIPLOMATIC REPRESENTATIVES

Of Iran in Great Britain (27 Prince's Gate, London, SW7 1PX)
Chargé d'Affaires: Seyed Jalal Sadatian.

Of Great Britain in Iran (Ave. Ferdowsi, Tehrán)
Head of Interests Section: M. K. O. Simpson-Orlebar, CMG (at Swedish Embassy).

Of Iran in the USA (3005 Massachusetts Ave., NW, Washington, D.C., 20008)
Ambassador: (Vacant).

Of the USA in Iran (260 Takhte Jamshid Ave., Tehrán)
Ambassador: (Vacant).

Of Iran to the United Nations
Ambassador: Dr Said Rajaie-Khorassani.

Books of Reference

Statistical Information: The principal statistical agencies of the Government are: (1) Department of Census, Civil Registration, and Statistics (Ministry of the Interior). *Director-General:* Sayyed Mehdi Hesabi; Publications on demographical statistics, in Persian. (2) Publicity and Information Department of the Seven-year Plan Organization. *Director:* Dr Mohammed Ali Rashti; Publications on industry, labour, agriculture, in English and Persian. (3) Statistical and Economic Research Department of the Bank Melli Iran; Publishes *Monthly Bulletin*, in English and Persian. (4) Customs Department (Ministry of Finance), publishes monthly and annual reports, in French and Persian. (5) and (6) Ministry of Labour and Ministry of Industry and Mines, publish statistical year-books.

Adli, Abolfazi, *Aussenhandel und Aussenwirtschaftspolitik des Iran.* Berlin, 1960
Arberry, A. J. (ed.), *The Cambridge History of Iran.* 8 vols. CUP, 1968ff.
Bharier, J., *Economic Development in Iran, 1900–1970.* OUP, 1971
Forbis, W. H., *Fall of the Peacock Throne.* New York, 1979
Haim, S., *Shorter Persian–English Dictionary.* Tehran, 1958
Heikal, M., *Iran: The Untold Story.* New York, 1982

Katouzian, H., *The Political Economy of Iran*. London, 1981

Keddie, N., *Roots of Revolution*. Yale Univ. Press, 1981

Lambton, A. K. S., *Landlord and Peasant in Persia*. OUP, 1953.—*Persian Vocabulary*. CUP, 1954

Looney, R. E., *The Economic Development of Iran: A Recent Survey with Projections to 1981*. New York, 1973

Nashat, G., *Women and Revolution in Iran*. Boulder, 1983

Rubin, B., *Paved with Good Intentions: The American Experience in Iran*. OUP, 1981

Steinglass, F. J., *A Comprehensive Persian–English Dictionary*. 2nd ed. London, 1930

Stempel, J. D., *Inside the Iranian Revolution*. Indiana Univ. Press, 1981

Sullivan, W. H., *Mission to Iran*. New York, 1981

Zabih, S., *Iran's Revolutionary Upheaval: An Interpretive Essay*. San Francisco, 1979.—*The Mosadegh Era: Roots of the Iranian Revolution*. Chicago, 1982.—*Iran since the Revolution*. London, 1982

Zakhoder, B. N. (ed.), *Sovremennyi Iran*. Moscow, 1957

IRAQ

al Jumhouriya al 'Iraqia

Capital: Baghdad
Population: 14m. (1982)
GNP per capita: US$3,020 (1980)

HISTORY. Part of the Ottoman Empire from the 16th century, Iraq was captured by British forces in 1916 and became in 1921 a Kingdom under a League of Nations mandate, administered by Britain. It became independent on 3 Oct. 1932 under the Hashemite Dynasty, which was overthrown on 14 July 1958 by a military *coup* which established a Republic, controlled by a military-led Council of Sovereignty under Gen. Qassim. The republican régime terminated the adherence of Iraq to the Arab Federation (*see* THE STATESMAN'S YEAR-BOOK, 1958, p. 806). In 1963 Qassim was overthrown and Gen. Abdul Salam Aref became President, to be succeeded in 1966 by his brother Abdul Rahman Aref. In 1968 a successful *coup* was mounted by the Ba'th Party, which brought Gen. Ahmed Al Bakr to the Presidency. His Vice-President, from 1969, Saddam Hussein, became President in a peaceful transfer of power in 1979.

An attempt at succession by the Kurdish minority in the north-east of Iraq flared up in 1962, and fighting continued until the acceptance of a peace plan in June 1966. The Revolutionary Command Council formed after the 17 July 1968 *coup* announced in March 1970 a complete and constitutional settlement of the Kurdish issue. This was not, however, fully accepted by the Kurdish opposition leader.

In Sept. 1980 Iraq invaded Iran in a dispute over territorial rights in the Shatt-al-Arab waterway. Fighting was continuing in early 1984.

AREA AND POPULATION. Iraq is bounded north by Turkey, east by Iran, south-east by the Gulf, south by Kuwait and Saudi Arabia, and west by Jordan and Syria. The country has an area of 434,924 sq. km (167,925 sq. miles) and its population census (1977) was 12,029,700 and (estimate) 1982, 14m.

The areas, populations (1976 estimate) and capitals of the governorates were:

Governorate	sq. km	1976	Capital	1970
Al-Anbar	89,540	405,000	Ar-Ramadi	79,488
Al-Basrah	19,702	897,000	Al-Basrah	333,684
Al-Muthanna	49,206	184,000	As-Samawah	33,473 [2]
Al-Qadisayah	8,569	395,000	Ad-Diwaniyah	60,553 [2]
An-Najaf	26,834	354,000	An-Najaf	179,160
As-Sulaymaniyah [1]	16,482	656,000	As-Sulaymaniyah	98,063
Babil (Babylon)	5,503	565,000	Al-Hillah	128,811
Baghdad	5,023	3,036,000	Baghdad	2,183,760
Dahuk [1]	6,374	217,000	Dahuk	19,736
Dhi Qar	13,668	617,000	As-Nasiriyah	62,368
Diyala	19,047	663,000	Ba'qubah	39,186
Irbil [1]	14,428	492,000	Irbil	107,355
Karbala	52,856	243,000	Karbala	107,496
Maysan	16,774	419,000	Al-Amarah	80,078
Ninawa (Nineveh)	41,320	1,158,000	Mosul	293,079
Salah ad-Din	21,326	356,000	Samarra	62,008
Ta'min	9,426	439,000	Kirkuk	207,852
Wasit	17,922	386,000	Al-Kut	58,647

[1] Forming Kurdish Autonomous Region   [2] Census 1965

The national language is Arabic, spoken by 81% of the population. There is a major minority group of Kurdish-speakers in the north-east (15·5%) and smaller groups speaking Turkic, Aramaic and Iranian languages.

CLIMATE. The climate is mainly arid, with small and unreliable rainfall and a large annual range of temperature. Summers are very hot and winters cold. Baghdad. Jan. 50°F (10°C), July 95°F (35°C). Annual rainfall 6″ (140 mm).

CONSTITUTION AND GOVERNMENT. The Provisional Constitution was published on 22 Sept. 1968 and promulgated on 16 July 1970. The highest state authority remains the 9-member Revolutionary Command Council (RCC) but some legislative power has now been given to the 250-member National Assembly, elected 20 June 1980 for a 4-year term.

The only legal political grouping is the National Progressive Front (founded July 1973) comprising the Arab Socialist Renaissance (Ba'th) Party and various Kurdish parties; the Iraqi Communist Party left the Front in March 1979.

The President and Vice-President are elected by the RCC; the President appoints and leads a Council of Ministers responsible for administration.

President: Saddam Hussein at-Takriti (assumed office 17 July 1979).
Vice-President: Taha Moheddin Marouf.

The RCC was composed as follows in Oct. 1983:
Saddam Hussein at-Takriti *(Chairman)*, Taha Moheddin Marouf, Izzat Ibrahim *(Vice-Chairman)*, Na'im Hamid Haddad *(Secretary-General of the National Progressive Front)*, Taha Yasin Ramadan *(First Deputy Prime Minister)*, Gen. Adnan Khairallah *(Deputy Prime Minister, Defence)*, Tariq Aziz Isa *(Deputy Prime Minister, Foreign Affairs)*, Sa'doun Shakir Mahmud *(Interior)*, Hasan Ali Nasar al-Amiri *(Trade)*.

Besides those named above, the Council of Ministers comprises 5 Ministers of State, 21 other Ministers and 6 Presidential advisors with ministerial status.

National flag: Three horizontal stripes of red, white, black, with 3 green stars on the white stripe.

Local Government. Iraq is divided into 18 governorates *(liwa),* each administered by an appointed Governor; three of the governorates form a (Kurdish) Autonomous Region, with an elected 20-member Kurdish Legislative Council. Each governorate is divided into *qadhas* (under Qaimaqams) and *nahiyahs* (under Mudirs).

DEFENCE. Military training is compulsory for all men when they reach the age of 18. This consists of 2 years' service with the colours and 18 years on the reserve. However, a man may volunteer for service in the army or change his conscript service into voluntary service. In such circumstances voluntary service is for 2 years, and he may extend it by periods of 2 years until he reaches the age of 45. The 2-year compulsory service can be extended in a national emergency as in the present war with Iran. Many technicians and technically qualified officers serve up to 4 or 5 years.

Army. The Army is organized into 6 armoured, 4 mechanized, and 6 infantry divisions; 2 Republican Guard armoured, 3 special forces, 9 Reserve and 15 People's Army brigades. Equipment includes Soviet T-54/-55/-62/-72 and Chinese Type-69 main battle tanks. Strength (1984) 475,000, with an additional 75,000 reserves and the paramilitary People's Army of 450,000.

Navy. The Navy comprises 1 new frigate/training ship, 12 *ex*-Soviet missile boats, 12 *ex*-Soviet torpedo boats, 4 *ex*-Soviet but Polish-built medium landing ships, 3 Danish-built landing craft, 3 *ex*-Soviet submarine chasers, 2 fleet minesweepers, 3 inshore minesweepers, 1 training ship, 10 gunboats, 8 coastal patrol craft, 10 harbour patrol boats, 3 mine warfare boats, 1 presidential yacht, 1 harbour authority craft (former presidential yacht), 5 diving craft and 10 service tenders.

In 1984 naval personnel totalled over 3,000 officers and ratings, to be increased on the acquisition of 4 frigates and 6 missile corvettes being built in Italy with a replenishment tanker, if this 1981 contract is fulfilled.

Air Force. Except for a few Hunter jet fighter-bombers bought from Britain and 89 Mirage F.1E/B fighters, 5 Exocet missile-armed Super Etendard attack aircraft, about 40 Alouette III, 10 Super Frelon, 20 Puma and 59 Gazelle helicopters acquired from France, the combat and transport squadrons are equipped primarily with aircraft of Soviet design, including 9 Tu-22 supersonic medium bombers, 20 Su-7 and 80 Su-20 fighter-bombers, 70 MiG-23 interceptors and fighter-bombers, and 150 Chinese-built F-7 and MiG-21 interceptors, 40 Chinese-built F-6 (MiG-19) fighters, 18 MiG-25 interceptors and reconnaissance aircraft, 13 Mi-24 gunship helicopters, 10 Mi-8 helicopters, and four-turbofan Il-76, turbo-prop An-12 and An-24/26 transports. A few Il-14s and smaller types are used in a transport/communications role. Hunter, L-29 Delfin and L-39 Albatros aircraft are employed for training, with Swiss-built Bravo piston-engined primary trainers and Pilatus PC-7 turboprop basic trainers, Soviet MiG-15UTI trainers and other types in the Air Force College and operational conversion unit. Total strength is about 45,000 personnel and 400 combat aircraft. Soviet 'Guideline', 'Goa', 'Gain-ful', 'Gaskin' and Roland surface-to-air missiles are operational.

INTERNATIONAL RELATIONS

Membership. Iraq is a member of UN, Arab League and the Non-Aligned Movement.

ECONOMY

Planning. A new plan for 1981–85 was introduced but has been affected, to some extent, by the hostilities with Iran.

Budget. Revenue and expenditure (in 1,000 Iraqi dinars) for 1981 balanced at I.D. 19,250m.

Oil revenues account for nearly 50%, customs and excise for about 26% of the total revenue.

Currency. The monetary unit is the *Iraqi dinar* (I.D.) = 1,000 *fils* = 10 *riyals* = 20 *dirhams*. Silver alloy coins for 100 and 50 fils (*dirham*) and 25 fils are in circula-tion, and other coins for 10, 5 and 1 fils. Notes are for ¼, ½ and 1 dinar, and for 5 and 10 dinars. In March 1984, £1 = 0·46 *dinar*; US$1 = 0·311 *dinar*.

Banking. All banks were nationalized on 14 July 1964. The Central Bank of Iraq is the sole bank of issue. In 1941 the Rafidain Bank, financed by the Iraqi Govern-ment, was instituted to carry out normal banking transactions with head office in Baghdad and branches in the chief towns and abroad, including London. In addi-tion, there are 4 government banks which are authorized to issue loans to compan-ies and individuals: the Industrial Bank, the Agricultural Bank, the Estate Bank, and the Mortgage Bank.

Weights and Measures. The metric system is in general use.

ENERGY AND NATURAL RESOURCES

Electricity. Production in 1978 amounted to 6,950m. Kwh.

Oil. Following the nationalization of the Iraqi oil industry in June 1972, the Iraqi National Oil Company (INOC) is responsible for the exploration, production, transport and marketing of Iraqi crude oil and oil products.

The total crude petroleum production was (1980) 130·2m. tonnes and of natural gas (1980) 1,760m. cu. ft. Oil exports are essential for the economy but oil termin-als in the Gulf were destroyed in 1980 and the trans-Syria pipeline closed in 1982. Iraq is now wholly reliant on the 625 mile pipeline from Kirkuk to the Mediterra-nean *via* Turkey.

Water. Iraq is a land of great potentialities. The soil of the country is rich, but there are vast areas which can be cultivated only if irrigated by canals or pumps. The Irrigation Ministry operates several canal systems, new dams have been com-pleted and other irrigation works are under construction.

Agriculture. The chief winter crops (1980) are wheat, 1·3m. tonnes and barley, 575,000 tonnes. The chief summer crop is rice, 220,000 tonnes. The date crop is important (395,000 tonnes), the country furnishing about 80% of the world's trade in dates (exports, 1975, I.D.11,493,000); the chief producing area is the total-ly irrigated riverain belt of the Shatt-el-Arab. Wool is also an important export (1975: I.D.1,013,000). In 1975, I.D.20,000 of cotton were exported.

Livestock (1980): Cattle, 3·1m.; buffaloes, 240,000; sheep, 11·9m.; goats, 3·8m.; horses, 350,000; camels, 27,000; chickens, 20m.

Forestry. Up to 1969, 614,953 *dunums* have been demarcated and surveyed in Arbil, Mosul and Sulaimaniya Governorates.

INDUSTRY AND TRADE

Industry. Industrial and constructional establishments in 1974 numbered 26,332. Constructional establishments employed the largest number of workers. Other large employers were the brick industry, water and electricity services, date packing, the textile industry, cigarette factories, oil refining and the cement industry. Iraq is still relatively under-developed industrially but work has begun on 13 new industrial plants which are being established with Soviet equipment and technical assistance.

Commerce. Imports and exports for 4 calendar years were (in 1m. Iraqi dinars):

	1977	1978	1979	1980
Imports	1,151	1,244	2,225	4,440
Exports	2,854	3,251	6,350	7,782

In 1980, crude oil formed 99% of all exports, of which 18% went to France, 15% to Brazil and 14% to Japan. 18% of imports came from Japan, 15% from Federal Republic of Germany and 9% from France.

Total trade between Iraq and UK for 5 years (British Department of Trade returns, in £1,000 sterling):

	1979	1980	1981	1982	1983
Imports to UK	393,738	532,483	72,644	79,764	30,334
Exports and re-exports from UK	201,176	321,883	623,889	875,179	400,259

Tourism. About 600,000 tourists visited Iraq in 1977.

COMMUNICATIONS

Roads. About 9,291 km of roads and tracks had been developed for vehicular traffic. The main surfaced roads are: (1) the road north from Baghdad *via* Kirkuk, Arbil and Nineveh to a point near the Turkish frontier at Zakho, with branches from Kirkuk to the northern province of Sulaimaniya, from Arbil to the Iranian frontier, and from Nineveh to Sinjar; (2) about 350 miles of the main road west from Baghdad to the Jordan frontier; (3) the road east of Baghdad, which connects the road system of Iran near Khanaqin; and (4) the road south from Baghdad to Hilla and the holy city of Kerbela.

Vehicles registered in 1979 totalled 120,600 passenger cars and 129,400 commercial vehicles.

Railways. The Iraqi Republic Railways were originally largely metre gauge but now comprise a 1,435 mm gauge main line from Um Qasr through Basra to Baghdad, Mosul and Tel-Kotchek on the Syrian frontier, and the remaining metre gauge route from Baghdad to Khanaqin, Kirkuk and Erbil. A 1,435 mm gauge line is under construction from Baghdad to Husaiba (404 km) on the Syrian frontier, which will form part of a through route to the Mediterranean port of Latakia. A branch of 155 km has opened to serve phosphates deposits at Akashat. In 1981 the railways carried 5m. tonnes of freight and 3·8m. passengers.

Aviation. Baghdad airport is served by British Airways, Lufthansa, Alitalia, SAS, Swissair, KLM, Middle East Air Lines, PIA, Iraqi Airways, Air Liban, United Arab Airlines and Aeroflot. In 1977 there were 728,266 passengers using Iraqi airports and 10,000 tons of cargo handled.

Shipping. The merchant fleet in 1980 comprised 142 vessels (over 100 gross tons) with a total tonnage of 1,465,949. The ports of Basra and Um Qasr have been closed since Sept. 1980.

Post and Broadcasting. In 1973 there were 352 post and telegraph offices. Wireless telegraph services exist with UK, USA, UAR, Lebanon and Saudi Arabia, and wireless telephone services with UK, USA, Italy, UAR and USSR. Telephones, 1978, 319,591. In 1978 there were 2·1m. radio and 623,000 television receivers.

Cinemas (1979). There were 87 cinemas.

Newspapers (1983). In Baghdad there are 4 main daily newspapers (one of which is in English with a circulation of 200,000).

JUSTICE, RELIGION, EDUCATION AND WELFARE

Justice. The courts are established throughout the country as follows: For civil matters: the court of cassation in Baghdad; 6 courts of appeal at Baghdad (2), Basra, Babylon, Mosul and Kirkuk; 18 courts of first instance with unlimited powers and 150 courts of first instance with limited powers, all being courts of single judges. In addition, 6 peace courts have peace court jurisdiction only. Tribal law was abolished in Aug. 1958.

For *Shara'* (religious) matters: the Shara' courts at all places where there are civil courts, constituted in some places of specially appointed Qadhis (religious judges) and in other places of the judges of the civil courts. For criminal matters: the court of cassation; 6 sessions courts (2 being presided over by the judge of the local court of first instance and 4 being identical with the courts of appeal). Magistrates' courts at all places where there are civil courts, constituted of civil judges exercising magisterial powers of the first and second class. There are also a number of third-class magistrates courts, powers for this purpose being granted to municipal councils and a number of administrative officials. Some administrative officials are granted the powers of a peace judge to deal with cases of debts due from cultivators.

Religion. In 1965 there were 7,711,712 Moslems, 232,406 Christians (1979), 2,500 Jews, 69,653 Yazidis and 14,262 Sabians.

Education. Primary and secondary education is free and primary education became compulsory in Sept. 1976. Primary school age is 6–12. Secondary education is for 6 years, of which the first 3 are termed intermediate. The medium of instruction is Arabic; Kurdish is used in primary schools in northern districts.

There were, in 1976–77, 8,156 primary schools with 1,947,182 pupils, and 1,320 secondary schools with 555,184 pupils. Eighty-two vocational schools had 28,365 students and 43 teacher-training colleges had 21,186 students.

There are 6 universities with (1977) 71,536 students and 15 other higher educational establishments with 9,962 students.

Health. In 1974 there were 4,734 doctors (including dentists); 162 hospitals with 21,582 beds.

DIPLOMATIC REPRESENTATIVES

Of Iraq in Great Britain (21–22 Queen's Gate, London, SW7 5JG)
Ambassador: Dr Wahbi Abdul-Razzaq Al Qaraghuli (accredited 19 Nov. 1982).

Of Great Britain in Iraq (Sharia Salah Ud-Din, Karkh, Baghdad)
Ambassador: John Moberly, CMG.

Of Iraq to the United Nations
Ambassador: Dr Riyadh Mahmoud Al Qaisi.

Iraq broke off diplomatic relations with USA on 7 June 1967.

Books of Reference

Statistical Information: The Central Statistical Organization, Ministry of Planning, Baghdad (*President:* Dr Salah Al-Shaikhly) publishes an annual *Statistical Abstract* (latest issue 1973). Foreign Trade statistics are published annually by the Ministry of Planning.

Abdulrahman, A. J., *Iraq.* Oxford and Santa Barbara, 1984
Arfa, H., *The Kurds.* OUP, 1966
Ghareeb, E., *The Kurdish Question in Iraq.* Syracuse Univ. Press, 1981
Khadduri, M., *Independent Iraq.* OUP, 1960.—*Republican Iraq.* OUP, 1970.—*Socialist Iraq: A Study of Iraqi Politics since 1968.* OUP, 1978
Postgate, E., *Iraq: International Relations and National Development.* London, 1983

IRELAND

Éire

Capital: Dublin
Population: 3·44m. (1981)
GNP per capita: US$4,880 (1980)

HISTORY. In April 1916 an insurrection against British rule took place and a republic was proclaimed. The armed struggle was renewed in 1919 and continued until 1921. The independence of Ireland was reaffirmed in Jan. 1919 by the National Parliament (*Dáil Éireann*), elected in Dec. 1918.

In 1920 an Act was passed by the British Parliament, under which separate Parliaments were set up for 'Southern Ireland' (26 counties) and 'Northern Ireland' (6 counties). The Unionists of the 6 counties accepted this scheme, and a Northern Parliament was duly elected on 24 May 1921. The rest of Ireland, however, ignored the Act.

On 6 Dec. 1921 a treaty was signed between Great Britain and Ireland by which Ireland accepted dominion status subject to the right of Northern Ireland to opt out. This right was exercised, and the border between *Saorstát Éireann* (26 counties) and Northern Ireland (6 counties) was fixed in Dec. 1925 as the outcome of an agreement between Great Britain, the Irish Free State and Northern Ireland. The agreement was ratified by the three parliaments.

Subsequently the constitutional links between *Saorstát Éireann* and the UK were gradually removed by the *Dáil*. The remaining formal association with the British Commonwealth by virtue of the External Relations Act, 1936, was severed when the Republic of Ireland Act, 1948, came into operation on 18 April 1949.

AREA AND POPULATION. The Republic of Ireland lies in the Atlantic ocean, separated from Great Britain by the Irish Sea to the east, and bounded north-east by Northern Ireland.

Counties and county boroughs	Area in hectares [1]	Population, 1981		
		Males	Females	Total
Province of Leinster				
Carlow	89,635	20,195	19,625	39,820
Dublin County Borough	11,499	248,016	277,866	525,882
Dublin [2]	78,937	209,533	213,253	422,786
Dun Laoghaire Borough	1,720	24,793	29,703	54,496
Kildare	169,425	53,967	50,155	104,122
Kilkenny	206,167	36,395	34,411	70,806
Laoighis	171,954	26,774	24,397	51,171
Longford	104,387	16,234	14,906	31,140
Louth	82,334	44,125	44,389	88,514
Meath	233,587	48,957	46,462	95,419
Offaly	199,774	30,290	28,022	58,312
Westmeath	176,290	31,388	30,135	61,523
Wexford	235,143	50,336	48,745	99,081
Wicklow	202,483	43,663	43,786	87,449
Total of Leinster	1,963,335	884,666	905,855	1,790,521
Province of Munster				
Clare	318,784	45,366	42,201	87,567
Cork County Borough	3,731	66,177	70,167	136,344
Cork	742,257	136,211	129,910	266,121
Kerry	470,142	63,492	59,278	122,770
Limerick County Borough	1,904	29,723	31,013	60,736
Limerick	266,676	51,872	49,053	100,925
Tipperary, N. R.	199,622	30,247	28,737	58,984
Tipperary, S. R.	225,836	39,256	37,021	76,277

[1] Exclusive of certain rivers, lakes and tideways.
[2] Excludes Dun Laoghaire borough.

Counties and county boroughs	Area in hectares [1]	Males	Population, 1981 Females	Total
Province of Munster—contd.				
Waterford County Borough	3,809	18,751	19,722	38,473
Waterford	179,977	25,762	24,356	50,118
Total of Munster	2,412,738	506,857	491,458	998,315
Province of Connacht				
Galway	593,966	88,330	83,688	172,018
Leitrim	152,476	14,699	12,910	27,609
Mayo	539,846	58,987	55,779	114,766
Roscommon	246,276	28,653	25,890	54,543
Sligo	179,608	28,183	27,291	55,474
Total of Connacht	1,712,172	218,852	205,558	424,410
Province of Ulster (part of)				
Cavan	189,060	28,338	25,517	53,855
Donegal	483,058	63,962	61,150	125,112
Monaghan	129,093	26,679	24,513	51,192
Total of Ulster (part of)	801,211	118,979	111,180	230,159
Total	6,889,456	1,729,354	1,714,051	3,443,405

[1] Exclusive of certain rivers, lakes and tideways.

The population has declined since 1841, when the 26 counties had 6,528,799 inhabitants; there were 3,221,823 in 1901; 3,139,688 in 1911; 2,971,992 in 1926; 2,968,420 in 1936; 2,955,107 in 1946; 2,898,264 in 1956; 2,884,002 in 1966; 2,978,248 in 1971, and 3,443,405 in 1981.

Vital statistics for 4 calendar years:

	Births	Marriages	Deaths		Births	Marriages	Deaths
1977	68,892	20,016	33,632	1980	74,064	21,792	33,472
1978	70,299	20,724	33,794	1981	72,355	20,550	32,410
1979	72,539	20,806	33,771	1982	70,933	20,441	32,876

CLIMATE. Influenced by the Gulf Stream, there is an equable climate with mild south-west winds, making temperatures almost uniform over the whole country. The coldest months are Jan. and Feb. (39–45°F, 4–7°C) and the warmest July and Aug. (57–61°F, 14–16°C). May and June are the sunniest months, averaging 5·5 to 6·5 hours each day, but over 7 hours in the extreme S.E. Rainfall is lowest along the eastern coastal strip. Dublin has 30″ (750 mm). The central parts vary between 30–44″ (750–1,125 mm), and up to 60″ (1,500 mm) may be experienced in low-lying areas in the west.

CONSTITUTION AND GOVERNMENT. Ireland is a sovereign independent, democratic republic. Its parliament exercises jurisdiction in 26 of the 32 counties of Ireland.

The first Constitution of the Irish Free State came into operation on 6 Dec. 1922. Certain provisions which were regarded as contrary to the national sentiments were gradually removed by successive amendments, with the result that at the end of 1936 the text differed considerably from the original document. On 14 June 1937 a new Constitution was approved by Parliament (*Dáil Éireann*) and enacted by a plebiscite on 1 July 1937. This Constitution came into operation on 29 Dec. 1937. Under it the name Ireland (*Éire*) was restored.

The Constitution provides that, pending the reintegration of the national territory, the laws enacted by the Parliament established by the constitution shall have the same area and extent of application as those of the Irish Free State.

The *Oireachtas* or National Parliament consists of the President and two Houses, viz., a House of Representatives, called *Dáil Éireann*, and a Senate, called *Seanad Éireann*, consisting of 60 members. The *Dáil*, consisting of 166 members, is elected by adult suffrage. Of the 60 members of the Senate, 11 are nominated by the *Taoiseach* (Prime Minister), 6 are elected by the universities and the remaining 43 are elected from 5 panels of candidates established on a vocational basis, representing the following public services and interests: (1) national language and culture, literature, art, education and such professional interests as may be defined by law for the purpose of this panel; (2) agricultural and allied interests, and fisheries; (3) labour, whether organized or unorganized; (4) industry and commerce, including banking, finance, accountancy, engineering and architecture; (5) public administration and social services, including voluntary social activities. The electing body is a college of about 900 members, comprising members of the *Dáil*, Senate, county boroughs and county councils.

A maximum period of 90 days is afforded to the Senate for the consideration or amendment of Bills sent to that House by the *Dáil*, but the Senate has no power to veto legislative proposals.

No amendment of the Constitution can be effected except with the approval of the people given at a referendum.

Agreement on the establishment of a Council of Ireland was reached at a meeting held at Sunningdale on 6–9 Dec. 1973. Members of the Irish and UK governments attended together with the Northern Ireland Executive-designate.

Irish is the first official language; English is recognized as a second official language. For further details of the Constitution *see* THE STATESMAN'S YEAR-BOOK, 1952, pp. 1123–34.

President: Pádraig Óhlrighile (Patrick Hillery), installed on 3 Dec. 1976 and re-elected for a second 7-year term in 1983.

Former Presidents: Dr Douglas Hyde (1938–45); Seán T. O. Ceallaigh (1945–59; 2 terms); Éamon de Valéra (1959–73; 2 terms); Erskine Childers (1973–74; died in office); Cearbhall Ó Dálaigh (1974–76; resigned).

A general election was held on 24 Nov. 1982: Fianna Fáil, 75 (Feb. 1982 election, 81); Fine Gael, 70 (66); Labour Party, 16 (15); Workers' Party, 2 (3); Independents, 3 (4).

There are no formal party divisions in the Senate.

The National Coalition Government consisted of the following members in Feb. 1983 (Fine Gael and Labour Parties):

Taoiseach (Prime Minister): Dr Garret Fitzgerald.
Tanaiste (Deputy Prime Minister) and Minister for Environment: Dick Spring. *Finance:* Alan Dukes. *Agriculture:* Austin Deasy. *Trade, Commerce and Tourism:* Frank Cluskey. *Foreign Affairs:* Peter Barry. *Industry and Energy:* John Bruton. *Education:* Gemma Hussey. *Justice:* Michael Noonan. *Transport, Posts and Telegraphs:* Jim Mitchell. *Gaeltacht, Fisheries and Forestry:* Paddy O'Toole. *Health and Social Welfare:* Barry Desmond. *Labour:* Liam Kavanagh. *Defence:* Paddy Cooney. *Public Service:* John Boland.

There were 15 Ministers of State.

National flag: Three vertical strips of green, white, orange.
National anthem: The Soldier's Song (words by P. Kearney; music by P. Heaney).

Local Government. The elected local authorities comprise 27 county councils, 4 county borough corporations, 7 borough corporations, 49 urban district councils and 24 Boards of Town Commissions. All the members of these authorities are elected under a system of proportional representation, normally every 5 years. All residents of an area who have reached the age of 18 are entitled to vote in the local election for their area. Women are eligible for election as members of local authorities in the same manner and on the same conditions as men. Elected members are not paid, but provision is made for the payment of travelling expenses and subsistence allowances.

The range of services for which local authorities are responsible is broken down into 8 main programme groups as follows: Housing and Building; Road Transportation and Safety; Water Supply and Sewerage; Development Incentives and

Controls; Environmental Protection; Recreation and Amenity; Agriculture, Education, Health and Welfare and Miscellaneous Services. Because of the small size of their administrative areas the functions carried out by town commissioners and some of the smaller urban district councils have tended to become increasingly limited, and the more important tasks of local government have tended to become the responsibility of the county councils.

The local authorities have a system of government which combines an elected council and a whole-time manager. The elected members have specific functions reserved to them which include the striking of rates (local tax), the borrowing of money, the adoption of development plans, the making, amending or revoking of bye-laws and the nomination of persons to other bodies. The managers, who are paid officers of their authorities, are responsible for the performance of all functions which are not reserved to the elected members, including the employment of staff, making of contracts, management of local authority property, collection of rates and rents and the day-to-day administration of local authority affairs. The manager for a county council is manager also for every borough corporation, urban district council and board of town commissioners whose functional area is wholly within the county. A central body called the Local Appointments Commission is charged with the duty of selecting suitable persons to be appointed by local authorities to chief executive offices, professional offices and other prescribed offices. Where a prescribed office becomes vacant, the local authority must request the Commissioners to recommend to them a suitable person. The Commissioners normally select persons for appointment by the machinery of selection boards.

The revenue expenditure of local authorities is financed by a local tax, called rates, on the occupation of immovable property, grants and subsidies from the central government and payments for certain services which they provide.

Since 1978 full rates relief has applied to houses, the domestic element of mixed property, *i.e.* property embodying a domestic as well as a non-domestic use, secondary schools, community halls and farm buildings not previously de-rated. A grant not exceeding the aggregate of these allowances is made to the local authorities by central government. Since 1983 such relief also applies in relation to all land.

DEFENCE. Under the direction of the President, and subject to the provisions of the Defence Act, 1954, the military command of the Defence Forces is exercisable by the Government through the Minister for Defence. To aid and counsel the Minister for Defence on all matters in relation to the business of the Department of Defence on which he may consult it, there is a Council of Defence consisting of the Minister for State at the Department of Defence, the Secretary of the Department of Defence, the Chief of Staff, the Adjutant-General and the Quartermaster-General. Establishments provide at present for a Permanent Defence Force of approximately 18,000 all ranks including the Air Corps and the Naval Service. The Reserve Defence Force caters for 23,000 all ranks. Recruitment is on a voluntary basis. Minimum term of enlistment is 4 years in the Permanent Defence Force and 6 years in the Reserve.

The Defence Estimates for the year ending 31 Dec. 1983 provide for an expenditure of £200,638,000.

Since May 1978 an Irish contingent has formed part of the United Nations force in Lebanon. The contingent now comprises 732 men (all ranks). Irish officers are at present serving with the UN Truce Supervision Organization and the UN Disengagement Observer Force in the Middle East. There is a small detachment with UN.

Army. The Army has 4 brigades each having two infantry battalions (one brigade has three battalions), a field artillery regiment and a squadron/coy size unit from each Corps. There is in addition a special Infantry force consisting of two battalions. The establishment strength of the Army is 15,787 all ranks.

Navy. The Naval Service comprises 4 offshore patrol vessels built in Cork between 1972 and 1980, three coastal minesweepers purchased from Great Britain in 1971 for fishery protection purposes, one supply and service ship and seven other craft. A heli carrying patrol vessel is on order and will be in service in 1984. The Naval

Base is at Haulbowline Island in Cork Harbour. The establishment strength of the Naval Service is 1,105.

Air Force. The Air Corps has an establishment of 1,172 all ranks, and 37 aircraft. There are 8 Cessna Fr 172H, 6 Fouga – Magister armed jet trainers, 9 SIAI – Marchetti, SF 260W armed piston-engined trainers, 8 Alouette III and 2 Gazelle helicopters, 3 twin-turbo prop Super Beech King 200 for coastal fishery patrol and a BAe 125/700 twin turbofan aircraft.

INTERNATIONAL RELATIONS

Membership. Ireland is a member of UN, OECD, the Council of Europe and EEC.

ECONOMY

Budget. Current revenue and expenditure (in IR£1m.):

Current revenue	1982	1983 [1]
Customs duties	62·9	67·0
Excise duties	1,131·8	1,216·3
Estate, etc, duties	1·7	1·0
Capital taxes	20·5	24·3
Stamp duties	85·9	104·2
Income tax	1,459·1	1,739·0
Income levy	—	47·0
Corporation tax	231·8	206·0
Value-added tax	946·1	1,131·7
Agricultural levies (EEC)	8·3	11·0
Motor vehicle duties	70·8	92·5
Youth employment levy	34·2	80·0
Post Office	350·0	431·0
Total (including other items)	4,908·2	5,757·9

Current expenditure		
Debt service	1,249·3	1,731·5
Agriculture, etc.	237·7	278·6
Education	678·8	755·3
Tourism and Transport	137·5	142·8
Post Office	240·3	236·5
Defence	204·6	197·1
Justice (including Police)	224·3	250·5
Social Welfare	923·8	1,026·9
Health	824·5	911·4
Superannuation	142·6	161·3
Industry and Energy	124·6	169·9
Total (including other items)	5,896·5	6,654·6

[1] Estimate.

Capital expenditure amounted to £1,309m. in 1980, and £1,887m. in 1981.

On 31 Dec. 1980 the liabilities totalled £7,896m. The assets were: Electricity scheme, £42·6m.: local loans fund, £1,313·2m.; national transport organization, £33·3m.; industrial credit, £59·8m.; turf development, £29·6m.; reconstruction finance, £33m.; shares in companies established under state auspices, £240·7m.; exchequer balance, £613,000; other assets, £150·2m.; total, £1,903m.

Currency. The unit of currency is the Irish *pound* or *an punt Eirennach*. From 10 Sept. 1928 when the first Irish legal-tender notes were issued, the Irish currency was linked to Sterling on a one-for-one basis. This relationship was discontinued on 30 March 1979 when, following Ireland's adherence to the European Monetary System, market forces pushed sterling exchange rates beyond the upper intervention limit established for the Irish pound against the Belgian franc.

The Central Bank has the sole right of issuing legal tender notes; token coinage is issued by the Minister for Finance through the Bank. In March 1984, £1 = IR£1·12; US$ = IR£1·18.

The volume of legal-tender notes outstanding in June 1983 was £822·66m. Total notes and coins outstanding amounted to £870·04m.

Banking. The Central Bank, which was established as from 1 Feb. 1943, in accordance with the Central Bank Act, 1942, replaced the Currency Commission, which was set up under the Currency Act, 1927, and had been responsible *inter alia* for the regulation of the note issue. In addition to the powers and functions of the Currency Commission the Central Bank has the power of receiving deposits from banks and public authorities, of rediscounting Exchequer bills and bills of exchange, of making advances to banks against such bills or against Government securities, of fixing and publishing rates of interest for rediscounting bills, or buying and selling certain Government securities and securities of any international bank or financial institution formed wholly or mainly by governments. The Bank also collects and publishes information relating to monetary and credit matters. The Central Bank Act, 1971, gives further powers to the Central Bank in the regulation of banking including licensing of banks, the supervision of their operations and control of liquidity and reserve ratios. The capital of the Bank is £40,000, of which £24,000 has been paid up and is held by the Minister for Finance.

The Board of Directors of the Central Bank consists of a Governor, appointed by the President on the advice of the Government, and 8 directors, all appointed by the Minister for Finance, 6 direct and 2 from among directors of the Associated Banks (the term applied to the 4 shareholding banks associated with the former Currency Commission).

There are 4 commercial banks associated with the Central Bank: The Bank of Ireland, Allied Irish Banks Ltd, the Ulster Bank and the Northern Bank.

At 16 Feb. 1983 the Associated Banks had liabilities, within the State, of £6,089·5m. including current and deposit accounts amounting to £4,967·5m.; assets, within the State, amounted to £6,338m., of which the main components were liquid assets of £735·2m. and lending of £5,147·6m. At the same date liabilities, outside the State, stood at £5,569·9m. and assets at £5,320·9m., giving a net external liability of £249m. Total liabilities and assets balanced at £11,659·4m. The commercial banking system also includes 40 licensed banks not 'associated' with the Central Bank. At 16 Feb. 1983 these non-associated banks had total liabilities and assets, within the State and elsewhere, balancing at £6,410·6m.

The post office savings bank has approximately 2·7m. (including 1·2m. dormant) accounts and the amount due at 31 Aug. 1983 was IR£322m. The trustee savings banks had deposits of IR£285m. at 31 Aug. 1983.

Weights and Measures. The Imperial system is in use but conversion to metric is in progress.

ENERGY AND NATURAL RESOURCES

Electricity. The generating and supplying of electricity and the construction and maintenance of the nationwide electricity distribution system is the function of the Electricity Supply Board, a State-sponsored body established in 1927. The total generating capacity is 2,975 mw. In the year ending 31 March 1983 the total sales of electricity amounted to 8,508m. units supplied to 1,124,461 consumers. Electricity generated by fuel source (1982–83): Oil, 26%; natural gas, 49%; peat, 16%; hydro, 9%.

Oil. About 551,000 sq. km of the continental shelf has been made an exploration area; at its furthest point the limit of jurisdiction is 520 nautical miles from the coast. An exploration well drilled by Gulf Oil on block 49/9 in 1983 flowed oil on test from three different levels at an aggregate 9,901 bbls per day. A fourth level flowed gas at 2·1m. cu. ft per day. Further appraisal work must be carried out on the block to determine the commerciality or otherwise of this discovery. Since 1970, 76 exploratory offshore oil wells have been drilled.

Gas. There has been one commercial discovery of natural gas, off the south-west coast at Kinsale Head. The total reserves of the field are 1·35m. cu. ft. Gas Transmission is controlled by the Irish Gas Board (BGE), who sell the gas into electricity generation, fertilizer production, and distribution systems for domestic and industrial use.

Peat. The country has very little indigenous coal, but possesses large reserves of peat, the development of which is handled by Bord na Mona (Peat Board). To date, the Board has acquired over 70,000 hectares of bog and has established 23 locations around the country. In the year ending 31 March, 1983, production totalled 5m. tonnes, of which 2·8m. tonnes went to generate electricity and 0·9m. tonnes for the domestic market. In addition moss peat production for the year was 1·3m. cu. metres.

Minerals. Lead and zinc concentrates are important. Metal content of production, 1982: zinc, 167,200 tonnes; lead, 38,800 tonnes. Barytes and gypsum are also important, and there is some dolomite, limestone, aggregates, coal, green and black marble. About 35 companies are prospecting.

Agriculture. General distribution of surface (in hectares) in 1980: Crops and pasture, 4,695,751; other land, including grazed mountain, 2,193,646; total, 6,889,195.

Estimated area (hectares) under certain crops calculated from sample returns:

Crops	1980	1981	1982	1983
		Area[1]		
Wheat	52,988	48,100	57,000	59,300
Oats	24,513	22,500	22,600	22,000
Barley	366,316	354,200	334,200	304,300
Potatoes	41,583	35,000	36,900	32,300
Sugar-beet	32,979	34,900	34,300	...

[1] Provisional.

Gross agricultural output (excluding value changes in livestock) for the year 1982 was valued at £2,148·46m.

Livestock (1983): Cattle, 6·77m.; sheep, 3·66m.; pigs, 1·14m.; horses (1980), 68,500; poultry (1982), 9·9m.

Forestry. The total area of state forests at 31 Dec. 1982 was 386,622·3 hectares.

Fisheries. The number of vessels engaged in fishing in 1982 were 1,449 boats propelled by outboard engines, sails and oars and 1,551 other fishing boats; men 8,506. The quantities and values of fish landed during 1982 were: Demersal fish, 35,000 tonnes, value £13,908,000; pelagic fish, 144,000 tonnes, value £17,992,000; shellfish, 16,000 tonnes, value £11,909,000. Total quantity: 195,000 tonnes; total value, £43,809,000.

INDUSTRY AND TRADE

Industry. The census of industrial production for 1979 gives the following details of the values (in £1,000) of gross and net output for the principal manufacturing industries. The figures for net output are those of gross output minus cost of materials, including fuel, light and power, repairs to plant and machinery and amounts paid to others in connexion with products made.

	Gross output	Net output
Slaughtering, preparing and preserving meat	861·5	111·5
Dairy products	833·4	112·4
Bread, biscuit and flour confectionery	136·5	54·9
Sugar, cocoa, chocolate and sugar confectionery	232·6	69·3
Grain milling, animal and poultry foods	388·1	68·8
Brewing and malting	142·0	87·8
Tobacco products	70·4	37·9
Paper and paper products	126·9	50·8
Printing and publishing	171·2	114·2
Production and preliminary processing of metals	74·1	24·1
Manufacture of metal articles	301·6	135·9
Manufacture of non-metallic mineral products	418·4	192·9
Chemicals, including fertilizers and manmade fibres	784·0	345·9
Mechanical engineering	166·8	71·0
Manufacture of office machinery and data-processing machinery	205·3	90·0
Electrical engineering	248·1	115·3
Manufacture of motor vehicles, parts and accessories	165·4	40·5
Manufacture of other means of transport	88·4	39·2
Textiles (including knitting industry)	344·9	124·4
Footwear and clothing	206·5	96·2
Timber and wooden furniture	146·3	61·5
Processing rubber and plastics	191·0	74·2
Gas, water and electricity	395·1	177·4
All other industries [1]	799·6	446·5
Total (all industries)	7,498·1	2,742·6

[1] Including mining, fuel production, instrument engineering, various food and drink industries, etc.

Labour. The total labour force at mid-April 1982 was about 1,283,000, of which about 137,000 persons were out of work.

The number of trade unions holding negotiation licences in Sept. 1983 was 79, of which 63 were workers' trade unions and the remainder employers' trade unions. The total membership of these unions is estimated at 500,796, of whom 10,480 were in the employers' trade unions. Approximately 314,767 were organized in 6 general unions catering for both white-collar and manual workers.

Commerce. Value of imports and exports of merchandise for calendar years (in £):

	1978	1979	1980	1981	1982
Imports	3,713,098,432	4,827,922,798	5,420,704,523	6,578,406,480	6,812,274,532
Exports	2,963,180,624	3,477,738,139	4,082,496,312	4,777,570,799	5,687,924,840

The values of the chief imports and total exports are shown in the following table (in £):

	Imports		Exports	
	1981	1982	1981	1982
Live animals and food	762,681,879	753,339,159	1,408,535,859	1,535,021,627
Raw materials	204,780,425	186,649,609	181,814,186	230,958,961
Mineral fuels and lubricants	966,278,264	1,009,401,858	31,637,412	36,016,177
Chemicals	690,997,710	737,228,774	642,555,102	805,419,687
Manufactured goods	1,126,611,047	1,153,558,478	592,385,419	638,956,446
Machinery and transport equipment	1,805,912,092	1,872,370,864	1,049,493,433	1,394,273,332
Manufactured articles [1]	767,347,619	832,806,112	539,377,435	645,997,991

[1] Not elsewhere specified.

Distribution of trade, by principal countries of origin in the case of imports and destination in the case of exports (in £):

	Imports		Total exports	
Country	1981	1982	1981	1982
Belgium and Luxembourg	135,733,710	148,049,872	199,026,006	254,397,556
Canada	95,387,299	83,241,254	87,029,804	69,189,693
Denmark	50,832,691	55,340,257	35,736,723	38,612,027
Finland	60,403,687	57,643,391	20,672,557	29,960,406
France	338,982,589	315,310,073	341,135,872	494,899,678
Germany, Fed. Rep. of	495,030,003	522,305,981	453,910,533	531,477,855
Hong Kong	25,286,779	30,347,340	7,314,323	8,466,986
India	19,696,536	16,120,398	8,536,599	6,922,027
Iran	217,372	162,824	6,036,583	4,342,971
Iraq	12,728	186,189	21,364,764	58,960,538
Israel	16,448,229	18,254,429	6,020,262	6,498,439
Italy	168,858,364	179,499,099	139,816,225	166,238,515
Japan	203,127,509	200,564,167	40,756,451	72,408,144
Kuwait	18,849,263	124,301	6,333,976	11,663,977
Malaysia	13,419,057	17,133,919	4,893,631	5,930,000
Netherlands	202,985,651	258,175,419	274,445,445	295,949,829
New Zealand	9,862,711	9,404,985	4,146,471	7,458,413
Norway	27,140,198	22,391,249	24,093,685	32,305,009
Poland	17,382,007	33,211,208	6,049,556	1,936,137
Portugal	18,099,588	22,157,736	17,988,058	17,213,484
Saudi Arabia	68,381,398	54,495,655	26,960,425	48,533,865
South Africa, Rep. of, and Namibia	10,881,369	13,421,520	21,766,846	23,774,488
Spain	64,592,074	68,390,531	47,885,639	69,769,021
Sweden	104,145,368	105,317,611	61,453,985	79,962,608
Switzerland	44,414,991	72,334,704	39,983,634	55,207,676
USSR	31,635,784	37,811,091	24,649,698	29,993,248
UK	3,267,394,497	3,274,129,529	1,919,450,856	2,205,174,894
USA	767,930,440	876,232,897	303,993,181	406,225,721

An Anglo-Irish free-trade agreement to remove progressively all duties between July 1966 and July 1975 was signed in London on 14 Dec. 1965.

Total trade between Ireland and UK (British Department of Trade returns, in £1,000 sterling):

	1979	1980	1981	1982	1983
Imports to UK	1,689,206	1,784,329	1,787,065	2,000,033	2,290,067
Exports and re-exports from UK	2,554,839	2,660,024	2,812,957	2,890,497	3,055,275

Tourism. Estimated number of visits by foreigners (including cross-border movement) in 1982 was 9,794,000; they spent £487m.

COMMUNICATIONS

Roads. At 31 Dec. 1982 there were 92,294 km of public roads, consisting of 5,365 km of national roads, 10,616 km of main (trunk and link) roads other than national roads, 73,975 km of county roads and 2,338 km of county borough and urban roads; of the total length 87,679 km (95%) was paved. Five miles of motorway were opened in 1983.

Number of licensed motor vehicles at 30 Sept. 1982: Private cars, 709,000; public-service vehicles, 6,408; goods vehicles, 68,087; agricultural tractors, 617,333; motor cycles, 25,676; other vehicles, 11,236.

The total number of km run by road motor passenger vehicles of the omnibus type during 1982 was 96,209,000. Passengers carried numbered 230,735,000 and the gross receipts from passengers were £84,686.

Railways. The total length of railway open for traffic at 31 Dec. 1983 was 1,876 km, all 1,600 mm gauge. Córas Iompair Éireann, the national transport undertaking, operates all rail services in the State.

Railway statistics for years ending 31 Dec.	1981	1982
Passengers (no.)	15,374,000	12,813,000
Miles run by coaching trains	5,300,000	5,025,000
Merchandise and mineral traffic conveyed (tons)	3,664,000	3,680,000
Miles run by freight trains	3,281,000	2,843,000
Receipts (£)	45,445,595	49,943,000
Expenditure (£)	105,663,970	121,607,000

Aviation. During the year ended 31 March 1983 Aer Lingus-Irish International Airlines carried 2,036,179 passengers, 37,508 short tons of cargo and 1,318 short tons of mail on its European services and 322,516 passengers, 14,339 short tons of cargo and 789 short tons of mail on its trans-Atlantic services.

Shipping. The Irish merchant fleet, of vessels of 100 gross tonnes or over, consisted of 69 vessels totalling 180,176 GRT at 31 Dec. 1982. Total cargo traffic passing through the country's ports amounted to 15·3m. tonnes in 1982.

Inland Waterways. The principal inland waterways open to navigation are the Shannon Navigation (130 miles) and the Grand Canal and Barrow Navigation (156 miles). Merchandise traffic is not now transported on them and navigation is confined to pleasure craft operated either privately or commercially.

Post and Broadcasting (31 Dec. 1982). Number of post offices, 2,096; telegraph offices, 1,340; telephones, 580,000; public telephones, 3,939; telephone exchanges, 1,097.

Radio and television broadcasting is operated by Radio Telefís Éireann, a statutory public body appointed by the Minister for Posts and Telegraphs under the Broadcasting Authority Acts. On 31 Dec. 1982 there were 695,500 holders of current television licences.

Cinemas. There are 124 cinemas and 169 screens.

Newspapers (1983). There are 7 daily newspapers (all in English) with a combined circulation of 711,319; 5 of them are published in Dublin (circulation, 609,858).

JUSTICE, RELIGION, EDUCATION AND WELFARE

Justice. The Constitution provides that justice shall be administered in public in Courts established by law by Judges appointed by the President on the advice of the Government. The jurisdiction and organization of the Courts are dealt with in the Courts (Establishment and Constitution) Act, 1961, the Courts (Supplemental Provisions) Acts, 1961–81. These Courts consist of Courts of First Instance and a Court of Final Appeal, called the Supreme Court. The Courts of First Instance are the High Court with full original jurisdiction and the Circuit and the District Courts with local and limited jurisdiction. A judge may not be removed from office except for stated misbehaviour or incapacity and then only on resolutions passed by both Houses of the *Oireachtas*. Judges of the Supreme, High and Circuit Courts are appointed from among practising barristers. Judges of the District Court (called District Justices) may be appointed from among practising barristers or practising solicitors.

The Supreme Court, which consists of the Chief Justice (who is *ex officio* an additional judge of the High Court) and 5 ordinary judges, has appellate jurisdiction from all decisions of the High Court. The President may, after consultation with the Council of State, refer a Bill, which has been passed by both Houses of the *Oireachtas* (other than a money bill and certain other bills), to the Supreme Court for a decision on the question as to whether such Bill or any provision thereof is repugnant to the Constitution.

The High Court, which consists of a President (who is *ex officio* an additional Judge of the Supreme Court) and 14 ordinary judges, has full original jurisdiction in and power to determine all matters and questions, whether of law or fact, civil or criminal. In all cases in which questions arise concerning the validity of any law having regard to the provisions of the Constitution, the High Court alone exercises original jurisdiction. The High Court on Circuit acts as an appeal court from the Circuit Court.

The Court of Criminal Appeal consists of the Chief Justice or an ordinary Judge of the Supreme Court, together with either 2 ordinary judges of the High Court or the President and one ordinary judge of the High Court. It deals with appeals by persons convicted on indictment where the appellant obtains a certificate from the trial judge that the case is a fit one for appeal, or, in case such certificate is refused, where the court itself, on appeal from such refusal, grants leave to appeal. The decision of the Court of Criminal Appeal is final, unless that court or the Director of Public Prosecutions certifies that the decision involves a point of law of exceptional public importance, in which case an appeal is taken to the Supreme Court.

The High Court exercising criminal jurisdiction is known as the Central Criminal Court. It consists of a judge or judges of the High Court, nominated by the President of the High Court. The Court sits in Dublin and tries criminal cases which are outside the jurisdiction of the Circuit Court or which may be sent forward for trial from the Circuit Court on the application of the Director of Public Prosecution.

The country is divided into a number of circuits for the purposes of the Circuit Court. The President of the Circuit Court is *ex officio* an additional judge of the High Court. The jurisdiction of the court in civil proceedings is limited to £15,000 in contract and tort, £15,000 in actions founded on hire-purchase and credit-sale agreements, £5,000 in equity and £5,000 in probate and administration, save by consent of the parties, in which event the jurisdiction is unlimited. In criminal matters it has jurisdiction in all cases except murder, treason, piracy and allied offences. The Circuit Court acts as an appeal court from the District Court.

The District Court has summary jurisdiction in a large number of criminal cases where the offence is not of a serious nature. In civil matters the Court has jurisdiction in contract and tort (except slander, libel, seduction, slander of title and false imprisonment) where the claim does not exceed £2,500; in proceedings founded on hire-purchase and credit-sale agreements, the jurisdiction is £2,500.

All criminal cases, except those of a minor nature, are tried by a judge and a jury of 12. Juries are also used in many civil cases in the High Court. In a criminal case the jury must be unanimous in reaching a verdict, but in a civil case the agreement of 9 members is sufficient.

Religion. According to the census of population taken in 1971 the principal religious professions were as follows:

	Leinster	Munster	Connacht	Ulster (part of)	Total
Roman Catholics	1,387,644	849,382	378,613	180,027	2,795,666
Church of Ireland	60,115	17,807	6,084	13,733	97,739
Presbyterians	5,172	627	347	9,906	16,052
Methodists	3,187	1,321	248	890	5,646
Other religious denominations	6,914	1,269	272	426	8,881
Not stated or no religion	35,108	11,596	5,338	2,222	54,264

Education. *Elementary.* Elementary education is free and was given in about 3,405 national schools (including 113 special schools) in 1981. The average daily enrolment of pupils in 1981 was 555,656; the number of teachers of all classes (1981) about 19,932, including remedial teachers and teachers of special classes. Average daily pupil attendance is about 91%. There are 6 Colleges of Education for the training of primary school teachers, all co-educational. The estimated state expenditure on elementary education for 1982 (1 Jan.–31 Dec.) is £285,528,000, excluding the cost of administration.

Special provision is made for handicapped and deprived children in special schools which are recognized on the same basis as primary schools, in special classes attached to ordinary schools and in certain voluntary centres where educational services appropriate to the needs of the children are provided. Categories of handicapped children catered for include visually handicapped, hearing impaired, physically handicapped, mentally handicapped, emotionally disturbed, travelling children and other socially disadvantaged children. Provision is also being made on an increasing scale for children with dual or multiple handicaps. In each case a programme suited to the needs of the particular kind of handicap is provided. The number of children in each class in such schools is very much smaller than in ordinary classes in a primary school and because of the size of the catchment areas involved an extensive system of school transport has been developed. Many handicapped children who have spent some years in a special school or class are integrated into normal schools for part of their school career, if necessary with special additional facilities such as nursing services, special equipment, etc. For others who cannot progress within the ordinary school system the special schools or classes provide both the primary and secondary level of education. In addition to the services being provided on a full-time basis many children are being catered for by the provision of part-time teaching facilities in hospitals, child guidance clinics, rehabilitation workshops, special 'Saturday-morning' centres and home teaching schemes.

Special schools (1980–81) were numbered 113 with 8,324 pupils. There were 226 special classes attached to ordinary schools with 2,630 pupils. 574 remedial teachers were employed for backward pupils in ordinary schools. 30 peripatetic teachers were employed for children with hearing or visual impairments.

Secondary. Voluntary secondary schools are under private control and are conducted in most cases by religious orders; all schools receive grants from the State and are open to inspection by the Department of Education. The number of recognized secondary schools during the school year 1981–82 was 520, and the number of pupils in attendance was 204,392. Total estimated state expenditure for 1982 (1 Jan.–31 Dec.) is £167·64m.

Grants for the provision of a wide range of audio visual teaching aids are available to secondary schools. The schools television service, *Telefís Scoile*, provides programmes in Irish, English, history, geography, mathematics and science subjects for senior and junior pupils. The vast majority of secondary schools now have at least one television receiving set which was purchased with the aid of a state grant.

Vocational Education Committee schools provide courses of general and technical education. The number of vocational schools during the school year 1981–82 was 241, full-time students, 66,419. These schools are controlled by the local Vocational Education Committees, and are maintained partly from the rates and partly by state grants. The estimated state expenditure for 1982 (1 Jan.–31 Dec.) is £117m., and the estimated expenditure from the local rates, £2,301,000.

Comprehensive Schools which are financed by the State combine academic and technical subjects in one broad curriculum so that each pupil may be offered a range of educational options structured to his needs, abilities and interests. Pupils are prepared for the State examinations and for entrance to universities and institutes of further education. The number of comprehensive schools during the school year 1981–82 was 15 with 8,515 students.

Community Schools continue to be established through the amalgamation of existing voluntary secondary and Vocational Education Committee schools where this is found feasible and desirable and in new areas where a single larger school is considered preferable to 2 smaller schools under separate managements. These schools cater for all aspects of second-level education and provide adult education facilities in the areas in which they are situated. They also make facilities available to voluntary organizations and to the adult community generally. The number of community schools during the school year 1981–82 was 38 with 21,028 students. The estimated State expenditure on running costs for 1982 (1 Jan.–31 Dec.) is £27,175,000 for community and comprehensive schools.

Regional Technical Colleges and Colleges of Technology. Apprentice, technician and professional courses are provided in the colleges of technology of the City of Dublin Vocational Education Committee, the Limerick College of Technology and 9 regional technical colleges at Athlone, Carlow, Cork, Dundalk, Galway, Letterkenny, Sligo, Tralee and Waterford. Students (full-time) 1981–82, 12,393.

University Education is provided by the National University of Ireland, founded in Dublin in 1908, and by the University of Dublin (Trinity College), founded in 1592. The National University comprises 3 constituent colleges–University College, Dublin, University College, Cork, and University College, Galway. St Patrick's College, Maynooth, Co. Kildare, is a national seminary for Catholic priests and a pontifical university with the power to confer degrees up to doctoral level in philosophy, theology and canon law. It also admits lay students (men and women) to the courses in arts, celtic studies, science and education which it provides as a recognized college of the National University. Besides the University medical schools, the Royal College of Surgeons in Ireland, provides medical qualifications which are internationally recognized. There are six Colleges of Education for the training of primary school teachers. For degree awarding purposes, three of these colleges are associated with Trinity College, two with University College, Dublin and one with University College, Cork. Third-level courses with a technological bias, leading to degree, diploma and certificate qualifications are also provided by the National Institutes for Higher Education, Limerick and Dublin. The Thomond College of Education, Limerick, is a specialist teacher-training institution concerned with the training of post-primary teachers in the areas of physical education, rural and general science, metalwork and engineering science, woodwork and building science and commercial and secretarial subjects.

The National Council for Educational Awards, established on a statutory basis in 1979, is the validating and awarding authority for degree, diploma and certificate courses in the third-level non-university sector.

Agricultural. An Chomhairle Óiliuna Talmhaíochta (ACOT) is the agency responsible for providing agricultural advisory and training services. Full-time instruction in agriculture is provided for all sections of the farming community. There are 4 agricultural colleges for young people, administered by ACOT, and 7 private ACOT- aided agricultural colleges, at each of which a 1-year course in agriculture is given. Second-year courses in farm machinery and dairying are provided at a number of the colleges. Advanced courses in pig and poultry husbandry and management are also provided. Scholarships tenable at these colleges, all of which are residential, are awarded by ACOT which also provides a comprehensive agricultural advisory service and conducts winter classes in agriculture and horticulture at local centres. A more comprehensive course is provided in winter farm schools, which are intended, in general, for persons of not less than 17 years of age who are engaged in farming. A comprehensive 3-year training programme leading to a 'Certificate in Farming' involving both formal instruction and a period of supervised on-farm work experience, was introduced by ACOT in 1982.

Horticultural. A 2-year course in commercial horticulture is provided at 3 residential colleges. There is also a 2-year course in amenity horticulture at the National Botanic Gardens in Dublin.

A scheme of farm apprenticeship and a trainee farmer scheme are operated by the Farm Apprenticeship Board, which represents various agricultural interests. The scheme provides for practical training on well-managed commercial farms.

Higher Education in Agriculture, Horticulture, Dairy Science and Veterinary Science. Higher education in general agriculture and horticulture is provided by University College, Dublin, and in dairy science by University College, Cork. Training in veterinary medicine and surgery is provided at the Veterinary College, Ballsbridge, Dublin.

Health Services. Persons in the lower income group (those who are unable to afford general practitioner services for themselves and their dependants) are entitled to a free comprehensive health service (family doctor, hospital and specialist services, maternity and infant-welfare services, dental, ophthalmic and aural services). Persons and dependants in the middle-income groups (less than £11,000 per annum income) are entitled to in-patient and out-patient hospital services including specialist services, free maternity care and help towards the cost of drugs and medicines. Such persons must pay a contribution of 1% of income, subject to a maximum of £95 per year, towards the cost of these services. All persons, irrespective of income, qualify for the benefit of assistance towards the cost of prescriptions, which limits the total outlay of a family to £23 per month. Hospital treatment for tuberculosis and certain other infectious diseases as well as for children suffering from certain long-term diseases and disabilities is provided free of charge to all classes of the community. Persons suffering from diabetes and other specified long-term conditions are eligible for a free supply of drugs and other necessary medicines, etc.

Pupils of national (elementary) schools are provided with a free school health-examination service and are also eligible for free dental, ophthalmic and aural services for defects discovered at school health examinations.

A free child-welfare clinic service for children under 6 years of age is available in many urban areas. A disabled persons maintenance allowance is payable in cases of need to chronically disabled persons over 16 who are not living in institutions. The disabled are also entitled to free travel and in certain circumstances to a free electricity allowance, a free television licence, free telephone rental and fuel vouchers. There is a mobility allowance of £280 per year for those unable to walk. The mother of a severely handicapped child maintained at home may qualify for a constant care allowance. There are also schemes which provide for the education of the blind, and for the training and placement in suitable employment of the blind and the disabled. Welfare services include day care services for children, families in stress and the old. Home helps, meals-on-wheels, home nursing etc, are provided where neccessary. All these services are provided by regional health boards under the direction and control of the Minister for Health.

Social Security. Social-welfare services concerned primarily with income maintenance are under the general control of the Minister for Social Welfare. The services administered by the Department of Social Welfare are divided into Insurance and Assistance schemes.

Insurance Services. All employees irrespective of their level of earnings are compulsorily insured from age 16 to 66 years and are liable for pay-related social insurance contributions. The majority of employees pay a contribution of 8·5% of their earnings prescribed up to a ceiling of £11,000 while a contribution of 7·5% of their earnings continues to be deducted up to a ceiling of £13,000. Their employers pay a further 11·61% up to a prescribed ceiling of £13,000. (The insured population is approximately 1m.) Subject to appropriate statutory conditions (but without regard to the recipients' means) the following flat-rate insurance benefits are available: Disability benefit, invalidity pension, unemployment benefit, maternity benefit, widow's pension, deserted wife's benefit, orphan's allowance, treatment benefit, retirement pension payable at 65, old-age pension payable at 66 and a death grant. Pay-related benefit is payable with disability benefit, unemployment benefit, maternity allowance and injury benefit to persons whose employment is insurable at certain class rates of pay-related social insurance contribution. The cost of the flat-rate and pay-related benefits is met by pay-related social insurance contributions from employers and employees and by a state grant.

The insurance services also provide for payment of benefits in respect of injury, disablement or death, as well as medical care resulting from an occupational accident or disease. These benefits are available to employees, irrespective of age, and are paid from an Occupational Injuries Fund which is financed by employers' contributions and income from investments.

Assistance Services. Children's allowances are payable without a means test in respect of each child under 16 years of age and children between 16 and 18 who are at school or incapacitated for a prolonged period. The following Assistance services are subject to a means test: Non-contributory widows' and orphans' pensions to the survivors of persons whose lack of insurance (or inadequate insurance record) precludes payment of contributory pensions; deserted wife's allowance to women who have been deserted by their husbands and for whom the deserted wife's benefit is similarly precluded; allowances for unmarried mothers, prisoners' wives and single women between the ages of 58 and 66 years; old age pensions payable at age 66 to persons not entitled to insurance pensions; blind pensions (under the same general conditions as apply to old age pensions) payable at age 18; unemployment assistance payable during unemployment to persons not entitled to receive unemployment benefit; supplementary welfare allowance, payable when a person has no other resources or when such resources are insufficient to meet his needs.

DIPLOMATIC REPRESENTATIVES

Of Ireland in Great Britain (17 Grosvenor Place, London, SW1X 7HR)
Ambassador: Noel Dorr (accredited 19 Oct. 1983).

Of Great Britain in Ireland (33 Merrion Rd., Dublin, 4)
Ambassador: A. C. Goodison, CMG, CVO.

Of Ireland in the USA (2234 Massachusetts Ave., NW, Washington, D.C. 20008)
Ambassador: Tadhg F. O' Sullivan.

Of the USA in Ireland (42 Elgin Rd., Ballsbridge, Dublin)
Ambassador: Peter H. Dailey.

Of Ireland to the United Nations
Ambassador: Robert McDonagh.

Books of Reference

Statistical Information: The Central Statistics Office (Earlsfort Terrace, Dublin, 2) was established in June 1949, and is attached to the Department of the Taoiseach. *Director:* T. P. Linehan, B.E., B.Sc.

The Central Statistics Office took over the work carried out since 1922 by the Statistics Branch, Department of Industry and Commerce, which in turn had continued the statistical work carried out by the Department of Agriculture and Technical Instruction (since 1900) and by the Irish Department of the Ministry of Labour, London (since 1919). Vital statistics from 1864, annual agricultural statistics prior to 1900 and decennial census of population were compiled by the Registrar-General for Ireland. The population censuses were carried out in 1926, 1936 and 1946 by the Statistics Branch of the Department of Industry and Commerce and are now the responsibility of the Central Statistics Office, which has also, as from July 1950, taken over from the Registrar-General the compilation of Vital Statistics. The Statistics Act 1926 confers wide powers for the collection, compilation and publication of statistics. Other Acts under which statistics are collected are Workmen's Compensation Act, Merchant Shipping Act, Customs Consolidation Act and Road Transport Act.

Principal publications of the Central Statistics Office are *National Income and Expenditure* (annually), *Statistical Abstract* (annually), *Census of Population Reports, Census of Industrial Production Reports, Trade and Shipping Statistics* (annually and monthly), *Trend of Employment and Unemployment* (annually), *Reports on Vital Statistics* (annually), *Irish Statistical Bulletin* (quarterly).

Aspects of Ireland. (Series). Dublin Department of Foreign Affairs.
Atlas of Ireland. Royal Irish Academy, Dublin, 1979
Facts About Ireland. Dublin Department of Foreign Affairs, 5th ed. 1981
The Gill History of Ireland. 11 vols. Dublin
Bartholomew, P. C., *The Irish Judiciary.* Dublin, Institute of Public Administration, 1974
Brown, T., *Ireland: A Social and Cultural History, 1922–1979.* London, 1981
Chubb, B., *The Constitution and Constitutional Change in Ireland.* Dublin, 1978
Delaney, V. T. H., *The Administration of Justice in Ireland.* 4th ed. Dublin, Institute of Public Administration, 1975

Eager, A. R., *A Guide to Irish Bibliographical Material.* 2nd ed. London, 1980

Encyclopaedia of Ireland. Dublin, 1968

Freeman, T. W., *Ireland: A General and Regional Geography.* 4th ed. London, 1972

Harbison, P., *Guide to the National Monuments of Ireland.* Dublin, 1975

Hickey, D. J. and Doherty, J. E., *A Dictionary of Irish History since 1800.* Dublin, 1980

Johnston. T. J., and others, *A History of the Church of Ireland.* Dublin, 1953

Keatinge, P., *Formulation of Irish Foreign Policy.* Dublin, 1973.—*A Place Among the Nations: Issues of Irish Foreign Policy.* Dublin, 1978

Kee, R., *The Green Flag.* London, 1972

Kelly, J. M., *Fundamental Rights in the Irish Law and Constitution.* 2nd ed. Dublin, 1967

Lehane, B., *The Companion Guide to Ireland.* London, 1973

Lyons, F. S. L., *Ireland Since the Famine.* London, 1971

McDunphy, Michael, *The President of Ireland: His Powers, Functions and Duties.* Dublin, 1945

Meenan, J., *The Irish Economy Since 1922.* Liverpool, 1970

Nevill, W. E., *Geology and Ireland.* Dublin, 1963

Thom's Directory of Ireland. 2 vols. (Dublin, Street Directory, Commercial). Dublin, 1979–80

ISRAEL

Medinat Israel—State of Israel

Capital: Jerusalem
Population: 4·06m. (1983)
GNP per capita: US$5,160 (1981)

HISTORY. In 1967, following some years of uneasy peace, local clashes on the Israeli-Syrian border were followed by Egyptian mass concentration of forces on the borders of Israel. The UN emergency force was expelled and a blockade of shipping to and from Israel was imposed by Egypt in the Red Sea. Israel struck out at Egypt on land and in the air on 5–9 June 1967. Jordan joined in the conflict which spread to the Syrian borders. By 11 June the Israelis had occupied the Gaza Strip and the Sinai peninsula as far as the Suez Canal in Egypt, West Jordan as far as the Jordan valley and the heights east of the Sea of Galilee, including Quneitra in Syria.

A further war broke out on 6 Oct. 1973 when an Egyptian offensive was launched across the Suez Canal and Syrian forces struck on the Golan Heights. Following UN Security Council resolutions a ceasefire finally came into being on 24 Oct. In Dec. agreement was reached by Egypt and Israel on disengagement and a disengagement agreement was signed with Syria on 31 May 1974. A further disengagement agreement was signed between Israel and Egypt in Sept. 1975.

Developments in 1977 included President Sadat of Egypt's visit to Israel and peace inititative and in March 1978 Israeli troops entered southern Lebanon but later withdrew after the arrival of a UN peace-keeping force.

In Sept. 1978 President Carter convened the Camp David conference at which Egypt and Israel agreed on frameworks for peace in the Middle East with treaties to be negotiated between Israel and her neighbours. Negotiations began in USA between Egypt and Israel in Oct. 1978 and a peace treaty was signed in Washington 26 March 1979.

Under the Israel-Egypt peace treaty signed in Washington on 26 March 1979, Israel withdrew from the Sinai Desert in two phases, part was achieved on 26 Jan. 1980 and the final withdrawal by 26 April 1982.

AREA AND POPULATION. The area of Israel, within the boundaries defined by the 1949 armistice agreements with Egypt, Jordan, the Lebanon and Syria, is 20,770 sq. km (8,017 sq. miles), with a population (May 1972 census) of 3·2m. (estimated, Jan. 1983, 4·06m.). Population of areas under Israeli administration as a result of the 6-day war was: Judaea and Samaria (West Bank), 747,500, Gaza Strip, 476,300, and the Golan Heights, 18,900.

Crude birth rate per 1,000 population of Jewish population (1982), 21·8; non-Jewish, 34·9; crude death rate, Jewish, 7·5; non-Jewish, 4·1; infant mortality rate per 1,000 live births, Jewish, 11·6; non-Jewish, 21.

Israel is administratively divided into 6 districts:

District	Area (sq. km)	Population [1]	Chief town
Northern	4,946	661,000	Nazareth
Haifa	854	576,400	Haifa
Central	1,242	829,800	Ramla
Tel Aviv	170	1,008,800	Tel Aviv
Jerusalem [2]	627	468,200	Jerusalem
Southern	14,107	497,700	Beersheba

[1] 1983.   [2] Includes East Jerusalem, annexed from Jordan after 1967 War.

On 23 Jan. 1950 the Knesset proclaimed Jerusalem the capital of the State and on 14 Dec. 1981 extended Israeli law into the Golan Heights. Population of the main towns (31 Dec. 1982): Tel-Aviv/Jaffa, 325,700; Jerusalem, 424,400; Haifa, 226,100; Ramat Gan, 118,300; Bat-Yam, 134,500; Holon, 134,600; Petach Tikva, 124,000; Beersheba, 112,600.

The official languages are Hebrew and Arabic.

Immigration. The following table shows the numbers of Jewish immigrants entering Palestine (Israel), including persons entering as travellers who subsequently registered as immigrants. For a year-by-year breakdown, *see* THE STATESMAN'S YEAR-BOOK, 1951, p. 1167.

1919–32	129,349	1940–47	101,173	1969–79	384,066
1933–39	235,170	1948–68	1,290,610	1980–82	46,750

During the period 1948–68, 45·5% of the immigrants came from Europe and America and 54·5% from Asia and Africa; during the period 1969–79, 79·5% came from Europe and America and 20·5% from Asia and Africa.

The Jewish Agency, which, in accordance with Article IV of the Palestine Mandate, played a leading role in laying the political, economic and social foundations on which the State of Israel was established, continues to be instrumental in organizing immigration.

CLIMATE. From April to Oct., the summers are long and hot, and almost rainless. From Nov. to March, the weather is generally mild, though colder in hilly areas, and this is the wet season. Jerusalem. Jan. 48°F (9°C), July 73°F (23°C). Annual rainfall 21″ (528 mm). Tel Aviv. Jan. 57°F (14°C), July 81°F (27°C). Annual rainfall 22″ (550 mm).

CONSTITUTION AND GOVERNMENT. Israel is an independent sovereign republic, established by proclamation on 14 May 1948. For the history of the British Mandate, *see* THE STATESMAN'S YEAR-BOOK, 1920–49, under PALESTINE.

In 1950 the Knesset (*Parliament*), which in 1949 had passed the Transition Law dealing in general terms with the powers of the Knesset, President and Cabinet, resolved to enact from time to time fundamental laws, which eventually, taken together, would form the Constitution. The first of these fundamental laws, dealing with the Knesset, Israel Lands and the President, were passed in 1958, 1960 and 1964 respectively and with the Government in 1968.

National flag: White with 2 horizontal blue stripes, the blue Shield of David in the centre.

National anthem: Hatikvah (The Hope). Words by N. N. Imber (1878); adopted as the Jewish National Anthem by the first Zionist Congress (1897).

The Knesset, a one-chamber Parliament, consists of 120 members. It is elected for a 4-year term by secret ballot and universal direct suffrage. The system of election is by proportional representation. In June 1981 the Knesset was composed as follows: Likud, 48; Labour Party-Mapam Alignment, 47; National Religious Party, 6; Democratic Front for Peace and Equality, 4; Agudat Israel, 4; Citizens Rights Movement, 1. The President is elected by the Knesset by secret ballot by a simple majority; his term of office is 5 years. He may be re-elected once.

Former Presidents of the State: Chaim Weizmann (1949–52); Izhak Ben-Zvi (1952–63); Zalman Shazar (1963–68); Ephraim Katzir (1968–78); Yitzhak Navon (1978–83).

President: Chaim Herzog, elected 22 March 1983 by 61 votes to 56 against with 3 abstentions.

The Cabinet in March 1984 was composed as follows:

Prime Minister and Minister of Foreign Affairs: Yitzchak Shamir.
Deputy Prime Minister and Minister of Construction and Housing: David Levy.
Defence: Moshe Arens. *Labour and Social Affairs and Emigrants Absorption:* Aharon Uzan. *Finance:* Yigal Cohen-Orgad. *Interior and Religious Affairs:* Yossef Burg. *Agriculture:* Pesach Grupper. *Without Portfolio:* Sarah Doron. *Education and Culture:* Zvulun Hammer. *Energy and Infrastructure:* Yitzchak Moday. *Econ-

omy and Inter-Ministerial Co-ordination: Ya'akov Meridor. *Science and Development:* Yuval Ne'eman. *Justice:* Moshe Nissim. *Industry and Trade:* Gideon Patt. *Communications:* Mordechai Zipori. *Transport:* Chaim Corfu. *Health:* Eliezer Shostak. *Without Portfolio:* Ariel Sharon. *Tourism:* Avraham Sharir.

Local Government. Local authorities are of three kinds, namely, municipal corporations, local councils and regional councils. Their status, powers and duties are prescribed by statute. Regional councils are local authorities set up in agricultural areas and include all the agricultural settlements in the area under their jurisdiction. All local authorities exercise their authority mainly by means of bye-laws approved by the Minister of the Interior. Their revenue is derived from rates and a surcharge on income tax. Local authorities are elected for a 4-year term of office concurrently with general elections.

There are 36 municipalities (2 Arab), 115 local councils (46 Arab and 6 Druze) and 49 regional councils (1 Arab) comprising 700 villages.

DEFENCE. The Defence Service Law, provides a compulsory 39-month conscription for men between the ages of 18 and 26 and a 30-month conscription for men in the age-group of 27–29 years. Unmarried women aged 18–26 serve 24 months. After their term of military service, men are on the reserves until the age of 55 years. Until they are 40, men usually report for 31 days training annually and from then until they are 55, for 14 days. Commissioned and n.c.o.s usually serve 7 extra days a year.

The Israel Defence Force is a unified force, in which army, navy and air force are subordinate to a single chief-of-staff. The Minister of Defence is *de facto* commander-in-chief but from Oct. 1973 the cabinet formed a defence committee with authority to make decisions on military operations.

Army. The Army is organized in 11 armoured divisions, 33 armoured brigades, 10 mechanized infantry brigades, 12 territorial/border infantry brigades and 15 artillery brigades. Equipment includes some 3,600 main battle tanks and 4,000 other armoured fighting vehicles. Strength (1984) 135,000 (conscripts 110,000), rising to 450,000 on mobilization.

Navy. The Navy includes 3 diesel-electric patrol submarines (built in Britain), 28 missile vessels (6 of 500 tons with helicopter and hangar, 8 of 415 tons, 12 of 220 tons and 2 of 47 tons, the smallest missile boats yet built), 2 missile-armed hydrofoils of 105 tons, 40 coastal patrol craft, 2 transports, 3 medium landing ships, 6 landing craft, 1 'firefish', 1 support ship, 1 training ship, 4 coastguard cutters, 2 hovercraft and 3 minor landing craft.

New construction includes 2 missile armed corvettes of 850 tons, and 10 improved guided-missile hydrofoils of 105 tons, all being built in Israel.

The former Nautical School in Haifa has been reorganized as a Naval Officers' School in Acre. Naval personnel in 1984 totalled 800 officers and 5,800 men, of whom 3,500 are conscripts, including a Naval Commando. There are also 5,000 naval reservists.

Air Force. The Air Force has a personnel strength of about 30,000, with about 580 first-line aircraft, all jets, of Israeli, US and French manufacture. There are 2 squadrons with about 40 F-15s, 3 squadrons with about 95 Israeli-built Kfirs, and 3 squadrons with the first 72 of a planned 145 F-16s in an interceptor role; 5 squadrons with 130 F-4E Phantoms, 2 squadrons with 65 Kfirs, and 4 squadrons with A-4E/H/N Skyhawks in the fighter-bomber/attack role; and 12 RF-4E reconnaissance fighters; supported by 4 E-2C Hawkeye airborne early warning and control aircraft and a few OV-1 Mohawk and RU-21 elint aircraft. There are transport squadrons of turboprop C-130/KC-130 Hercules, C-47, Arava, Islander, and Boeing 707 (some equipped for tanker or ECM duties) aircraft, helicopter squadrons of CH-53, Super Frelon, AH-1G/S HueyCobra, Hughes 500MD/TOW Defender, JetRanger, Agusta-Bell 205 and 212 aircraft, and training units with locally-built Magister jet trainers, which can be used also in a light ground attack role. Missiles in service include surface-to-air Hawks and surface-to-surface Lances.

INTERNATIONAL RELATIONS

Membership. Israel is a member of UN.

ECONOMY

Budget. The budget year runs from 1 April to 31 March (in shekel 1m.):

	1980–81	1981–82
Revenue	101,423	228,506
Revenue for development budget	20,156	44,804
Business enterprises	11,323	22,506
Expenditure	101,423	228,506

In 1981–82 the main items of expenditure (in shekel 1m.) were: Defence, 63,816; education and culture, 15,202; health, 3,722; labour and social welfare, 8,070.

Currency. The unit of currency is the *shekel* and was introduced in Feb. 1980. Currency in circulation on 31 Dec. 1978 was I£6,860m. (bank-notes and coins). In March 1984, £1 = 207·5 *shekel*; US$ = 133·85 *shekel*.

Banking. The Bank of Israel was established by law in 1954 as Israel's central bank. Its Governor is appointed by the President on the recommendation of the Cabinet for a 5-year term. He acts as economic adviser to the Government and has ministerial status.

There are 21 commercial banks headed by Bank Leumi Le Israel, Bank Hapoalim and Israel Discount Bank.

Weights and Measures. The metric system is in general use. The (metrical) *dunam* = 1,000 sq. metres (about 0·25 acre).

Jewish Year. The Jewish year 5744 corresponds to 8 Sept. 1983–26 Sept. 1984; 5745 to 27 Sept. 1984–15 Sept. 1985; 5746 to 16 Sept. 1985–3 Oct. 1986.

ENERGY AND NATURAL RESOURCES

Electricity. Electric-power consumption amounted during 1982 to 11,790m. kwh.

Oil and Gas. Oil was first discovered in Sept. 1955 at Heletz in the Negev. Crude oil production in 1982 was 15m. litres and natural gas 73m. cu. metres.

Minerals. The most valuable natural resources of the country are the potash, bromine and other salt deposits of the Dead Sea, which are exploited by the Dead Sea Works, Ltd. Geological research and exploration of the natural resources in the Negev are undertaken by the Israel Mining Corporation. Potash production in 1982 was 1,694,000 tons.

Agriculture. In the coastal plain (Sharon, Emek Hefer and the Shephelah) mixed farming, poultry raising, citriculture and vineyards are the main agricultural activities. The Emek (the Valley of Jezreel) is the main agricultural centre of Israel. Mixed farming is to be found throughout the valleys; the sub-tropical Beisan and Jordan plainlands are also centres of banana plantations and fish breeding. In Galilee mixed farming, olive and tobacco plantations prevail. The Hills of Ephraim are a vineyard centre; many parts of the hill country are under afforestation. In the northern Negev farming has been aided by the Yarkon–Negev water pipeline. This has become part of the overall project of the 'National Water Carrier', which is to take water from the Sea of Galilee (Lake Kinnereth) to the south. The plan includes a number of regional projects such as the Lake Kinnereth –Negev pipeline which came into operation in 1964; it has an annual capacity of 320m. cu. metres.

The area under cultivation (in 1,000 dunams) in 1981–82 was 4,100, of which 2,030 were under irrigation. Of the total cultivated area 2,595 dunams were under field crops, 334 under vegetables, potatoes, pumpkins and melons, 941 under citrus and orchards, 40 under fish ponds and 190 under miscellaneous crops, including auxiliary farms, nurseries, flowers, etc.

Industrial crops, such as cotton and sugar-beet, have successfully been introduced. In 1981–82 the area under cotton totalled 557,800 dunams and under sugar-beet (1976–77), 54,000.

Livestock (1982) included 273,000 cattle, 270,000 sheep,119,000 goats, 103,000 pigs, 4,000 horses, 26·2m. chickens.

Characteristic types of rural settlement are, among others, the following: (1) The *Kibbutz* and *Kvutza* (communal collective settlement), where all property and earnings are collectively owned and work is collectively organized. (2) The *Moshav Ovdim* (workers' co-operative smallholders' settlement) which is founded on the principles of mutual aid and equality of opportunity between the members, all farms being equal in size; hired labour is prohibited. (3) The *Moshav Shitufi* (co-operative settlement), which is based on collective ownership and economy as in the *Kibbutz*, but with each family having its own house and being responsible for its own domestic services. (4) The *Moshav* (smallholders' settlement), which resembles the *moshav ovdim* but lacks the latter's rigid ideological basis; hired labour, for instance, is permitted. (5) The *Moshava* (village), in which land and property are privately owned and every resident is responsible for his own well-being.

INDUSTRY AND TRADE

Industry. A wide range of products is manufactured, processed or finished in the country, including chemicals, metal products, textiles, tyres, diamonds, paper, plastics, leather goods, glass and ceramics, building materials, precision instruments, tobacco, foodstuffs, electrical and electronic equipment.

Labour. The General Federation of Labour (Histadrut) founded in 1920, had, in 1973, 1,259,200 members (including 89,000 Arab and Druze members); including workers' families, this membership represents 56·1% of the population covering 85% of all wage-earners. Several trades unions of lesser importance also exist.

Histadrut participates in over 70% of Israeli agriculture and 23% of industrial production; it runs the Kuput Holim (workers' health service) and has large interests in banking, insurance, retail business, construction and building.

Commerce. External trade, in US$1,000, for calendar years:

	1976	1977	1978	1979	1980	1982
Imports	4,140	4,844	5,843	7,511	8,024	7,960
Exports	2,414	3,082	3,921	4,546	5,540	5,017

The main exportable commodities are citrus fruit and by-products, fruit-juices, wines and liquor, sweets, polished diamonds, chemicals, tyres, textiles, metal products, machinery, electronic and transportation equipment, flowers. The main exports were, in 1982 (US$1m.): Diamonds, 1,157·7; chemical and oil products, 580·1; food, beverages and tobacco, 332·4; citrus fruit, 185·6.

Total trade between Israel and UK (British Department of Trade returns, in £1,000 sterling):

	1979	1980	1981	1982	1983
Imports to UK	227,600	236,599	256,000	275,139	314,148
Exports and re-exports from UK	270,733	231,658	212,000	224,362	354,860

Tourism. In 1982 there were about 1m. tourists. There are over 300 recommended hotels with over 27,000 rooms.

COMMUNICATIONS

Roads. There were 12,360 km of paved roads in 1982. Registered motor vehicles in 1982 totalled 661,671, including 7,707 buses, 104,116 trucks and 512,716 private cars.

Railways. Internal communications (1982) are provided by 536 km of standard gauge line. Construction is in progress (1982) of 215 km of new line linking Eilat on the Gulf of Aqaba with Sedom and the existing rail network by means of the 34 km line opened between Oron and Nahal Zin in Nov. 1977. In 1982–83, 2·9m. passengers and 5·5m. tonnes of freight were carried.

Aviation. Air communications are centred in the airport of Ben Gurion, near Tel-Aviv. In 1982, 9,806 planes landed at Israeli airports on international flights;

2·74m. passengers arrived, 1,381,000 departed. In 1981, 59,359 tons of freight were loaded and 52,183 tons unloaded. The Israeli airline El Al maintains regular flights to London, Paris, Rome, Amsterdam, Brussels, Athens, Vienna, New York, Zurich, Munich, Nicosia, Istanbul, Johannesburg, Nairobi, Frankfurt and Copenhagen. In 1980–81 El Al carried 1·25m. passengers.

Shipping. Israel has 3 commercial ports, Haifa, Ashdod and Eilat. In 1982, 3,108 ships anchored in Israeli ports; 12·6m. tons. of freight were handled. The merchant fleet consisted in 1982 of 102 vessels, totalling 2,119,000 GRT.

Post and Broadcasting. The Ministry of Posts controls the postal, telegraph and telephone service. In 1982 there were 603 post offices and postal agencies, 47 mobile post offices and 1,302,000 telephones.

The broadcasting station in Jerusalem, *Kol Israel*, is controlled by the Broadcasting Authority, established in 1965. Wireless licences in 1974 numbered approximately 460,000 and television licences 385,000.

Cinemas (1979). There were 214 cinemas with a seating capacity of approximately 152,300.

Newspapers (1981). There were 36 daily newspapers, including 17 in Hebrew.

JUSTICE, RELIGION, EDUCATION AND WELFARE

Justice. *Law.* Under the Law and Administration Ordinance, 5708/1948, the first law passed by the Provisional Council of State, the law of Israel is the law which was obtaining in Palestine on 14 May 1948 in so far as it is not in conflict with that Ordinance or any other law passed by the Israel legislature and with such modifications as result from the establishment of the State and its authorities.

Capital punishment was abolished in 1954, except for support given to the Nazis and for high treason.

The law of Palestine was derived from three main sources, namely, Ottoman law, English law (Common Law and Equity) and the law enacted by the Palestine legislature, which to a great extent was modelled on English law. The Ottoman law in its turn was derived from three main sources, namely, Moslem law which had survived in the Ottoman Empire, French law adapted by the Ottomans and the personal law of the non-Moslem communities.

Civil Courts. Municipal courts, established in certain municipal areas, have criminal jurisdiction over offences against municipal regulations and bye-laws and certain specified offences committed within a municipal area.

Magistrates courts, established in each district and sub-district, have limited jurisdiction in both civil and criminal matters.

District courts, sitting at Jerusalem, Tel-Aviv and Haifa, have jurisdiction, as courts of first instance, in all civil matters not within the jurisdiction of magistrates courts, and in all criminal matters, and as appellate courts from magistrates courts and municipal courts.

The Supreme Court has jurisdiction as a court of first instance (sitting as a High Court of Justice dealing mainly with administrative matters) and as an appellate court from the district courts (sitting as a Court of Civil or of Criminal Appeal).

In addition, there are various tribunals for special classes of cases, such as the Rents Tribunals and the Tribunals for the Prevention of Profiteering and Speculation. Settlement Officers deal with disputes with regard to the ownership or possession of land in settlement areas constituted under the Land (Settlement of Title) Ordinance.

Religious Courts. The rabbinical courts of the Jewish community have exclusive jurisdiction in matters of marriage and divorce, alimony and confirmation of wills of members of their community other than foreigners, concurrent jurisdiction with the civil courts in such matters of members of their community who are foreigners if they consent to the jurisdiction, and concurrent jurisdiction with the civil courts in all other matters of personal status of all members of their community, whether foreigners or not, with the consent of all parties to the action, save that such courts may not grant a decree of dissolution of marriage to a foreign subject.

The courts of the several recognized Christian communities have a similar jurisdiction over members of their respective communities.

The Moslem religious courts have exclusive jurisdiction in all matters of personal status over Moslems who are not foreigners, and over Moslems who are foreigners, if under the law of their nationality they are subject in such matters to the jurisdiction of Moslem religious courts.

Where any action of personal status involves persons of different religious communities, the President of the Supreme Court will decide which court shall have jurisdiction, and whenever a question arises as to whether or not a case is one of personal status within the exclusive jurisdiction of a religious court, the matter must be referred to a special tribunal composed of 2 judges of the Supreme Court and the president of the highest court of the religious community concerned in Israel.

Religion. Religious affairs are under the supervision of a special Ministry, with departments for the Christian and Moslem communities. The religious affairs of each community remain under the full control of the ecclesiastical authorities concerned: in the case of the Jews, the Sephardi and Ashkenazi Chief Rabbis, in the case of the Christians, the heads of the various communities, and in the case of the Moslems, the Qadis. The Druze were officially recognized in 1957 as an autonomous religious community.

In 1983 there were: Moslems, 530,800; Christians, 94,000; Druze and others, 65,600.

The Jewish Sabbath and Holy Days are observed as days of rest in the public services. Full provision is, however, made for the free exercise of other faiths, and for the observance by their adherents of their respective days of rest and Holy Days.

Education. Laws passed by the Knesset in 1949 and 1978 provide for free and compulsory education from 5 to 16 years of age. There is free education until 18 years of age.

The State Education Law of 12 Aug. 1953 established a unified state-controlled elementary school system with a provision for special religious schools. The standard curriculum for all elementary schools is issued by the Ministry with a possibility of adding supplementary subjects comprising not more than 25% of the total syllabus. Many schools in towns are private, a number are maintained by municipalities and some are administered by teachers' co-operatives or trustees.

Statistics relating to schools under government supervision, 1983:

Type of School	Schools	Teachers	Pupils
Hebrew Education—Total	2,570	74,300	795,060
Primary schools	1,277	35,897	458,734
Schools for handicapped children	214	2,989	12,463
Schools of intermediate division	253	10,824	87,873
Secondary schools	499		159,354
Vocational schools	301	19,620	76,636
Agricultural schools	26		4,970
Arab Education—Total	491	9,519	186,381
Primary schools	315	6,498	134,499
Schools for handicapped children	15	104	818
Schools of intermediate division	50	1,267	18,091
Secondary schools	73		28,236
Vocational schools	36	1,650	3,953
Agricultural schools	2		694

There are also a number of private schools maintained by religious foundations—Jewish, Christian and Moslem—and also by private societies.

The Hebrew University of Jerusalem, founded in 1925, comprises faculties of the humanities, social sciences, law, science, medicine and agriculture. In 1978–79 it had a teaching staff of 2,184 and 14,000 students.

The Technion in Haifa had, in 1978–79, 21 faculties and departments with 1,500 teachers and 7,800 students. The Weizmann Institute of Science in Rehovoth is engaged in research in chemistry, mathematics, physics and biology; founded in 1949, it had a staff of 400 and 486 students in 1978–79.

In 1978–79 the Tel Aviv University had 16 faculties, some 2,388 teachers and 19,000 students. The religious Bar-Ilan University at Ramat Gan, opened in 1965 had, in 1978–79, 5 faculties (Jewish studies, humanities, natural sciences, social sciences, philology), 900 teachers and 7,600 students. The Haifa University had, in 1978–79, 29 faculties with 568 teachers and 7,522 students. The Ben Gurion University had, in 1978–79, 28 departments with 628 teachers and 4,300 students.

Social Welfare. In 1982 Israel had 145 hospitals with 27,072 beds. The 'Malben' organization cares for the aged. The Women's International Zionist Organization has a number of children's homes, crèches and kindergartens as well as vocational schools and training institutions for nurses. In addition, there are several other voluntary bodies providing specific services to the community.

The National Insurance Law, which took effect in April 1954, provides for old-age pensions, survivors' insurance, work-injury insurance, maternity insurance, family allowances and unemployment benefits.

DIPLOMATIC REPRESENTATIVES

Of Israel in Great Britain (2 Palace Green, London, W8 4QB)
Ambassador: Yehuda Avner (accredited 3 Aug. 1983).

Of Great Britain in Israel (192 Rehov Hayarkon, Tel Aviv 63405)
Ambassador: P. H. Moberly, CMG.

Of Israel in the USA (3514 International Drive, NW, Washington, D.C., 20008)
Ambassador: Meir Rosenne.

Of the USA in Israel (71 Hayarkon St., Tel Aviv)
Ambassador: Samuel W. Lewis.

Of Israel to the United Nations
Ambassador: Dr Yehuda Z. Blum.

Books of Reference

Statistical Information: There is a Central Bureau of Statistics and Economic Research at the Prime Minister's Office, Jerusalem. It publishes monthly bulletins of economic statistics, social statistics, foreign trade statistics and an English summary.
Government Yearbook. Government Printer, Jerusalem. 1951 ff. (latest issue, 1971/72)
Facts about Israel. Government Printer, Jerusalem, 1979
Statistical Abstract of Israel. Government Printer, Jerusalem (from 1949/50)
Israel Yearbook. Tel-Aviv, 1948–49 ff.
Statistical Bulletin of Israel. 1949 ff.
Reshumoth (Official Gazette)
Middle East Record, ed. Y. Oron. London, 1960 ff.
Laws of the State of Israel. Authorized translation. Government Printer, Jerusalem, 1958 ff.
Alkalay, R., *The Complete English–Hebrew Dictionary.* 4 vols. Tel-Aviv, 1959–61
Atlas of Israel. Amsterdam, Jerusalem and London, 1970
Ben-Gurion, D., *Ben-Gurion Looks Back.* London, 1965.—*The Jews in Their Land.* London, 1966.—*Israel: A Personal History.* New York, 1971
Churchill, R. S. and W. S., *The Six-Day War.* London, 1967
Dayan, M., *Breakthrough.* New York, 1981
Efrat, E. and Orni, E., *Geography of Israel.* Jerusalem, 1976
Frankel, W., *Israel Observed.* London, 1980
Gilbert, M., *The Arab-Israeli Conflict: Its History in Maps.* 3rd ed. London, 1981
Goldman, N., *The Jewish Paradox.* New York, 1978
Harris, W., *Taking Root: Israeli Settlement in the West Bank, The Golan and Gaza Sinai 1967–1980.* Chichester, 1981
Hyamson, A. M., *Palestine under Mandate, 1920–48.* London, 1951
Jiryis, S., *The Arabs in Israel.* New York, 1976
Kieval, G. R., *Party Politics in Israel and the Occupied Territories.* Westport, 1983
Laquer, W. (ed.), *The Israel–Arab Reader.* London, 1970.—*A History of Zionism.* New York, 1972

Likhovski, E. S., *Israel's Parliament: The Law of the Knesset.* Oxford, 1971
Lucas, N., *A Modern History of Israel.* London and New York, 1975
Luttwak, E., and Horowitz, D., *The Israeli Army.* London, 1975
Meir, G., *My Life.* New York, 1975
Peretz, D., *The Government and Politics of Israel.* Folkestone, 1979
Pryce-Jones, D., *The Face of Defeat: Palestinian Refugees and Guerrillas.* New York, 1973
Sachar, H., *A History of Israel.* London and New York, 1976
Safran, N., *Israel: The Embattled Ally.* Harvard Univ. Press, 1978
Segal, R., *Whose Jerusalem? The Conflicts of Israel.* London, 1973
Shimshoni, D., *Israeli Democracy: The Middle of the Journey.* New York, 1982
Who's Who in Israel. Tel-Aviv, 1978
Wolffsohn, M., *Politik in Israel.* Opladen, 1983

National Library: The Jewish National and University Library, Jerusalem.

ITALY

Repubblica Italiana

Capital: Rome
Population: 56m. (1982)
GNP per capita: US$6,480 (1980)

HISTORY. On 10 June 1946 Italy became a republic on the announcement by the Court of Cassation that a majority of the voters at the referendum held on 2 June had voted for a republic. The final figures, announced on 18 June, showed: For a republic, 12,718,641 (54·3% of the valid votes cast, which numbered 23,437,143); for the retention of the monarchy, 10,718,502 (45·7%); invalid and contested, 1,509,735. Total 24,946,878, or 89·1% of the registered electors, who numbered 28,005,449. For the results of the polling in the 13 leading cities, *see* THE STATESMAN'S YEAR-BOOK, 1951, p. 1175. Voting was compulsory, open to both men and women 21 years of age or older, including members of the Civil Service and the Armed Forces; former active Fascists and a few other categories were excluded.

On 18 June the then Provisional Government without specifically proclaiming the republic, issued an 'Order of the Day' decreeing that all court verdicts should in future be handed down 'in the name of the Italian people', that the *Gazzetta Ufficiale del Regno d'Italia* should be re-named *Gazzetta Ufficiale della Repubblica Italiana*, that all references to the monarchy should be deleted from legal and government statements and that the shield of the House of Savoy should be removed from the Italian flag.

Thus ended the reign of the House of Savoy, whose kings had ruled over Piedmont for 9 centuries and as Kings of Italy since 18 Feb. 1861. (For fuller account of the House of Savoy, *see* THE STATESMAN'S YEAR-BOOK, 1946, p. 1021.) The Crown Prince Umberto, son of King Victor Emmanuel III, became Lieut.-Gen. (*i.e.*, Regent) of the kingdom on 5 June 1944. Following the abdication and retirement to Egypt of his father on 9 May 1946, Umberto was declared King Umberto II; his reign lasted to 13 June, when he left the country. King Victor Emmanuel III died in Alexandria on 28 Dec. 1947.

AREA AND POPULATION. The population (present in actual boundaries) at successive censuses were as follows:

31 Dec. 1881	29,277,927	21 April 1936	42,302,680
10 Feb. 1901	33,370,138	4 Nov. 1951	47,158,738
10 June 1911	35,694,582	15 Oct. 1961	49,903,878
1 Dec. 1921	37,403,956	24 Oct. 1971	53,744,737
21 April 1931	40,582,043	25 Oct. 1981	56,243,935

The following table gives area and population of the Regions (census 1981 and estimate, 1982):

Regions	Area in sq. km (1981)	Resident pop. census, 1981	Resident pop. estimate, 1982	Density per sq. km (1981)
Piemonte	25,399	4,479,031	4,454,150	176
Valle d'Aosta	3,262	112,353	112,962	34
Lombardia	23,834	8,891,652	8,894,236	373
Trentino-Alto Adige	13,613	873,413	874,534	64
Bolzano-Bozen	7,400	430,568	431,565	58
Trento	6,213	442,845	442,969	71
Veneto	18,368	4,345,047	4,355,049	237
Friuli-Venezia Giulia	7,846	1,233,984	1,231,169	157
Liguria	5,413	1,807,893	1,796,381	336
Emilia Romagna	22,123	3,957,513	3,957,346	179
Toscana	22,992	3,581,051	3,581,742	156
Umbria	8,456	807,552	810,227	96
Marche	9,692	1,412,404	1,417,806	146
Lazio	17,203	5,001,684	5,025,158	291

Regions	Area in sq. km (1981)	Resident pop. census, 1981	Resident pop. estimate, 1982	Density per sq. km (1981)
Abruzzi	10,794	1,217,791	1,225,827	113
Molise	4,438	328,371	329,745	74
Campania	13,595	5,463,134	5,513,462	402
Puglia	19,347	3,871,617	3,908,484	200
Basilicata	9,992	610,186	612,785	61
Calabria	15,080	2,061,182	2,078,391	137
Sicilia	25,708	4,906,878	4,957,510	191
Sardegna	24,090	1,594,175	1,605,410	66
Total	301,245	56,556,911	56,742,374	188

Vital statistics for calendar years:

	Marriages	Legitimate	Living births Illegiti- mate	Total	Still-born	Deaths excl. of still-born
1976	354,202	757,187	24,451	781,638	8,345	550,565
1977	347,928	715,414	25,689	741,103	7,219	545,694
1978	331,416	681,350	27,693	709,043	6,564	540,671
1979	323,930	643,835	26,386	670,221	5,748	534,563
1980 [1]	323,362	617,878	26,123	644,001	5,193	551,408
1981 [1]	313,736	595,195	26,610	621,805	4,950	542,204
1982 [1]	310,938	589,342	28,165	617,507	4,739	531,632

[1] Provisional.

Emigrants to non-European countries, by sea and air: 1977, 22,508; 1978, 23,589; 1979, 21,302; 1980, 20,360; 1981, 20,628. Since 1960 nearly nine-tenths of these emigrants have gone to Canada, USA and Australia.

Communes of more than 100,000 inhabitants, with population resident on 25 Oct. 1981 (census):

Roma (Rome)	2,840,259	Brescia	206,661	Sassari	119,596
Milano (Milan)	1,604,773	Modena	180,312	Siracusa (Syracuse)	117,615
Napoli (Naples)	1,212,387	Parma	179,019	La Spezia	115,392
Torino (Turin)	1,117,154	Livorno (Leghorn)	175,741	Vicenza	114,598
Genova (Genoa)	762,895	Reggio di C.	173,486	Terni	111,564
Palermo	701,782	Prato	160,220	Forli	110,806
Bologna	459,080	Salerno	157,385	Piacenza	109,039
Firenze (Florence)	448,331	Foggia	156,467	Cosenza	106,801
Catania	380,328	Ferrara	149,453	Ancona	106,498
Bari	371,022	Perugia	142,348	Bolzano	105,180
Venezia (Venice)	346,146	Ravenna	138,034	Pisa	104,509
Verona	265,932	Pescara	131,330	Torre del Greco	103,605
Messina	260,233	Reggio nell'E.	130,376	Novara	102,086
Trieste	252,369	Rimini	127,813	Udine	102,021
Taranto	244,101	Monza	123,145	Catanzaro	100,832
Padova (Padua)	234,678	Bergamo	122,142	Alessandria	100,523
Cagliari	233,848				

CLIMATE. The climate varies considerably with latitude. In the south, it is warm temperate, with little rain in the summer months, but the north is cool temperate with rainfall more evenly distributed over the year.

Rome, Jan. 44·5°F (7°C), July 77°F (25°C). Annual rainfall 32·5″ (812 mm). Milan, Jan. 35°F (2°C), July 75°F (24°C). Annual rainfall 39″ (972 mm).

CONSTITUTION AND GOVERNMENT. The new Constitution was passed by the constituent assembly by 453 votes to 62 on 22 Dec. 1947; it came into force on 1 Jan. 1948. The Constitution consists of 139 articles and 18 transitional clauses. Its main dispositions are as follows:

Italy is described as 'a democratic republic founded on work'. Parliament consists of the Chamber of Deputies and the Senate. The Chamber is elected for 5 years by universal and direct suffrage and it consists of 630 deputies. The Senate is elected for 5 years on a regional basis; each Region having at least 7 senators, consisting of 315 elected senators; the Valle d'Aosta is represented by 1 senator only. The President of the Republic can nominate 5 senators for life from eminent men in the social, scientific, artistic and literary spheres. On the expiry of his term of office, the President of the Republic becomes a senator by right and for life, unless he declines.

The President of the Republic is elected in a joint session of Chamber and Senate, to which are added 3 delegates from each Regional Council (1 from the Valle d'Aosta). A two-thirds majority is required for the election, but after a third indecisive scrutiny the absolute majority of votes is sufficient. The President must be 50 years or over: his term lasts for 7 years. The President of the Senate acts as his deputy.

The President can dissolve the chambers of parliament, except during the last 6 months of his term of office.

The Cabinet can be forced to resign only on a motivated motion of censure; the defeat of a government bill does not involve the resignation of the Government.

A Constitutional Court, consisting of 15 judges who are appointed, 5 each, by the President of the Republic, Parliament (in joint session) and the highest law and administrative courts, has rights similar to those of the Supreme Court of the USA. It can decide on the constitutionality of laws and decrees, define the powers of the State and Regions, judge conflicts between the State and Regions and between the Regions, and try the President of the Republic and the Ministers. The court was set up in Dec. 1955.

The reorganization of the Fascist Party is forbidden. Direct male descendants of King Victor Emmanuel are excluded from all public offices, have no right to vote or to be elected, and are banned from Italian territory; their estates are forfeit to the State. Titles of nobility are no longer recognized, but those existing before 28 Oct. 1922 are retained as part of the name.

National flag: Three vertical strips of green, white, red.

National anthem: Fratelli d'Italia (words by G. Mameli; tune by M. Novaro, 1847).

The peace treaty was signed in Paris on 10 Feb. 1947, and ratified on 15 Sept. 1947. Italy ceded to France 4 frontier districts on the Little St Bernard Pass, the Mont-Cenis Plateau, the Mont-Thabor and Chaberton areas, and the upper valleys of the Tinée, Vésubie and Roya (*see* map in THE STATESMAN'S YEAR-Book, 1948); to Yugoslavia, nearly the whole of the provinces of Venezia Giulia, the commune of Zara and the island of Pelagosa; to Greece, the Dodecanese; to Albania, the island of Saseno; to China the Italian concession at Tientsin. Italy also gave up her former colonies.

Under the peace treaty Italy was to pay reparations to the following states: Greece, US$105m.; Yugoslavia, US$125m.; USSR, US$100m.; Ethiopia, US$25m.; Albania, US$5m. By 30 Nov. 1967 the whole debt had been paid.

Head of State: On 8 July 1978 Chamber and Senate in joint session elected by an absolute majority (832 votes out of 1,008 votes cast) Alessandro Pertini (Socialist; born 1896), President of the Republic.

Former Presidents of the Republic: Luigi Einaudi (1948–55); Giovanni Gronchi (1955–62); Antonio Segni (1962–64); Giuseppe Saragat (1964–71); Giovanni Leone (1971–78).

General elections for the Senate and Chamber of Deputies took place on 26 June 1983.

Senate. Christian Democrats, 120; Communists, 107; Socialists, 38; Italian Social Movement, 18; Social Democrats, 8; Republicans, 10; Liberals, 6; other groups, 8. Total: 315.

Chamber. Christian Democrats, 225; Communists, 198; Socialists, 73; Italian Social Movement, 42; Republicans, 29; Social Democrats, 23; Liberals, 16; Radical Party, 11; other groups, 13. Total: 630.

The coalition government was composed as follows in Dec. 1983.

Prime Minister: Benedetto Craxi (PSI).
Vice Prime Minister: Arnaldo Forlani (DC).
Foreign Affairs: Giulio Andreotti (DC).
Interior: Oscar Scalfaro (DC).
Justice: Fermo Martinazzoli (DC).
Budget: Pietro Longo (PSDI).
Finance. Bruno Visentini (PRI).
Treasury: Giovanni Goria (DC).
Defence: Giovanni Spadolini (PRI).

Education: Franca Falcucci (DC).
Public Works: Franco Nicolazzi (PSDI).
Agriculture: Filippo Pandolfi (DC).
Transport: Claudio Signorile (PSI).
Post: Antonio Gava (DC).
Industry: Renato Altissimo (PLI).
Labour: Gianni De Michelis (PSI).
Foreign Trade: Nicola Capria (PSI).
Merchant Navy: Gianuario Carta (DC).
State Industry: Clelio Darida (DC).
Health: Costante Degan (DC).
Tourism: Lelio Lagorio (PSI).
Culture: Antonino Gullotti (DC).
EEC Affairs: Francesco Forte (PSI).
Public Administration: Remo Gaspari (DC).
Scientific Research: Luigi Granelli (DC).
Southern Affairs: Salverino De Vito (DC).
Regional Affairs: Pier Luigi Romita (PSDI).
Relations with Parliament: Oscar Mammi (PRI).
Civil Protection: Vincenzo Scotti (DC).
Ecology: Alfredo Biondi (PLI).

Allum, P. A., *Italy: Republic Without Government.* New York, 1974
Cross, E. (ed.), *La Constitution Italienne de 1948.* Paris, 1950
Ruini, M., and others, *La Nuova Costituzione Italiana.* Rome, 1947

Regional Administration. Italy is administratively divided into regions (*regioni*), provinces (*province*) and municipalities (*comuni*).

Art. 116 of the 1948 constitution provided for the establishment of 5 autonomous regions with special statute (*regioni autonome con statuto speciale*) and 15 autonomous regions with ordinary statute (*regioni autonome con statuto normale*). The regions have their own parliaments (*consiglio regionale*) and governments (*giunta regionale e presidente*) with certain legislative and administrative functions adapted to the circumstances of each region.

A government commissioner co-ordinates regional and national activities. The results of the last regional elections were as follows:

Regions	Election date	Christ-ian Demo-crats	Com-mun-ists	Social-ists	Social Move-ment	Social Demo-crats	Repub-licans	Lib-erals	Others	Total
Piemonte	8 June 1980	20	20	9	2	3	2	3	1	60
Valle d'Aosta [1]	26 June 1983	7	6	3	1	1	1	1	15[2]	35
Lombardia	8 June 1980	34	23	11	3	3	2	2	2	80
Trentino-Alto Adige [1]	19 Nov. 1978	22	7	4	2	2	1	1	31[3]	70
Veneto	8 June 1980	32	13	7	2	2	1	1	2	60
Friuli-Venezia Giulia [1]	26 June 1983	23	14	7	3	3	3	1	8[4]	62
Liguria	8 June 1980	13	15	5	2	2	1	2	–	40
Emilia-Romagna	8 June 1980	13	26	4	1	2	2	1	1	50
Toscana	8 June 1980	15	25	5	1	1	1	1	1	50
Umbria	8 June 1980	9	14	4	1	1	1	–	–	30
Marche	8 June 1980	16	15	4	1	1	1	1	1	40
Lazio	8 June 1980	22	19	6	6	3	2	1	1	60
Abruzzi	8 June 1980	20	12	4	2	1	1	–	–	40
Molise	8 June 1980	17	5	3	1	2	1	1	–	30
Campania	8 June 1980	25	15	7	7	3	1	1	1	60
Puglia	8 June 1980	22	13	6	4	2	1	1	1	50
Basilicata	8 June 1980	14	8	4	2	2	–	–	–	30
Calabria	8 June 1980	18	10	7	2	2	1	–	–	40
Sicilia [1]	21 June 1981	38	20	14	6	2	5	3	2	90
Sardegna [1]	17 June 1979	32	22	9	4	4	3	1	5[5]	80

[1] Autonomous regions with special statute.
[2] Including 4 Democrates Populaires – Union Valdôtaine Progressiste, 9 Union Valdôtaine.
[3] Including 21 Südtiroler Volkspartie.
[4] Including 1 Slovenian Union, 2 Movimento Friuli, 4 Liste per Trieste.
[5] Including 3 Sardinian Action Party.

DEFENCE. Most of the restrictions imposed upon Italy in Part IV of the peace treaty signed on 10 Feb. 1947 were repudiated by the signatories on 21 Dec. 1951, only the USSR objecting.

Head of the armed forces is the Defence Chief of Staff. In 1947 the ministries of war, navy and air were merged into the ministry of defence. The technical and scientific council for defence directs all research activities.

National service lasts 12 months in the Army and Air Force, and 18 months in the Navy.

Army. The Army is divided into the expeditionary force and the national defence force. It is composed of 1 armoured division, 3 mechanized divisions, 2 independent mechanized and 4 independent motorized brigades, 5 Alpine brigades, 1 airborne brigade, 2 amphibious battalions and 1 missile brigade. Equipment includes 550 M-47, 300 M-60A1 and 920 Leopard I main battle tanks. The Army air corps operates light aircraft and helicopters. Strength (1984) 258,000 (187,000 conscripts), with 545,000 reserves. There is also the paramilitary Carabinieri of 90,000 men.

Navy. Particulars of the principal surface ships in the Italian Navy:

Com-pleted	Name	Standard displace-ment Tons	Aircraft	Principal armament	Tor-pedo tubes	Shaft horse-power	Speed Knots
			Cruisers				
1969	Vittorio Veneto	7,500	9 helicopters	8 3-in.; twin 'Terrier';	6	73,000	32
1964 1964	Andrea Doria [1] Caio Duilio [1]	6,000	4 helicopters	8 3-in.; twin 'Terrier';	6	60,000	31

[1] Rated as guided-missile escort cruisers.

There are also 10 diesel-powered submarines, 4 guided-missile destroyers, 15 frigates, 8 corvettes, 4 ocean minesweepers, 12 minehunters, 14 coastal minesweepers, 5 inshore minesweepers, 7 hydrofoil missile boats, 4 fast torpedo-boats, 2 fast gunboats, 2 landing ships, 3 surveying vessels, 2 salvage ships, 1 transport, 1 support ship, 4 training ships, 2 replenishment oilers, 14 water carriers, 1 netlayer, 7 repair craft, 18 auxiliaries, 8 coastal transports (landing craft), 7 motor transports (minor landing craft), and 46 tugs.

Giuseppe Garibaldi of 10,000 tons standard displacement, a flat-topped ship designed as an improved helicopter cruiser with 18 helicopters, but latterly regarded as a light aircraft carrier is being completed (1985). Two frigates and 2 minehunters are under construction. Two submarines, 12 corvettes and 4 minehunters are projected.

The coastline of the peninsula is divided into zones, with headquarters at Spezia, Naples, Taranto and Ancona; all are under the jurisdiction of flag officers with the status of C.-in-C. The admirals commanding on the coasts of Sardinia and Sicily do not rank as C.-in-C.

Other localities of strategic importance under naval administration are Brindisi, where there is an admiral commanding, and Genoa, Leghorn, Augusta and Venice, each of which is under a senior naval officer.

The personnel of the Navy in 1984 numbered 42,000 officers and ratings, including the naval air arm and the marine battalion.

Air Force. Control is exercised through 2 regional HQ near Taranto and Milan. Units assigned to NATO comprise the 1st air brigade of Nike-Hercules surface-to-air missiles, 6 fighter-bomber, 3 light attack, 6 interceptor and 2 tactical reconnaissance squadrons, with supporting transport, search and rescue, and training units. Two of the fighter-bomber squadrons have Tornados, others have F-104S Starfighters and Aeritalia G91Ys. (One more F-104S squadron is re-equipping with Tornados). The light attack squadrons operate G91Rs. F-104S Starfighters have been standardized throughout the interceptor squadrons. The reconnaissance force operates RF-104G Starfighters. A total of 187 AM-X jet aircraft, built jointly by

Aeritalia, Aermacchi and Embraer of Brazil, will replace G91R, G91Y and F-104G/S aircraft in eight squadrons in 1986–90.

One transport squadron has turboprop C-130H Hercules aircraft; 2 others have turboprop Aeritalia G222s. There is a VIP and personnel transport squadron, equipped with DC-9, PD-808 and P.166M aircraft. Electronic warfare duties are performed by specially equipped G222s, PD-808s and MB 339s. Two land-based anti-submarine squadrons operate Breguet Atlantics. ASW helicopters, including Italian-built SH-3D Sea Kings, operate from ships of the Italian Navy. Search and rescue are performed by 12 Agusta-Sikorsky HH-3F helicopters and smaller types. There are also strong support and training elements; some MB 339 jet trainers have armament provisions for secondary close air support and anti-helicopter roles.

Air Force strength in mid-1983 was about 70,600 officers and men, about 300 combat aircraft, 500 fixed-wing second-line aircraft and over 100 helicopters.

INTERNATIONAL RELATIONS

Membership. Italy is a member of UN, NATO and EEC.

ECONOMY

Budget. Total revenue and expenditure for fiscal years, in 1m. lire:

	Revenue	Expenditure		Revenue	Expenditure
1975	32,312,962	40,201,458	1979	62,431,447	92,127,557
1976	37,882,716	50,036,796	1980	88,303,000	128,994,000
1977	43,666,361	59,548,331	1981	105,343,000	149,246,000
1978	51,696,512	78,844,114	1982	150,842,000	206,444,000

In the revenue for 1982 turnover and other business taxes accounted for 36,085,500m. lire, customs duties and indirect taxes for 12,669,700m. lire.

The public debt at 31 Dec. 1982 totalled 282,424,100m. lire, including consolidated debt of 42,200m. lire and the floating debt 190,239,000m. lire.

Currency. The standard coin is the *lira*. From 30 March 1960 the gold standard was formally established as equal to 0·00142187 gramme of gold per lira.

State metal coins are of 5, 10, 20, 50, 100, 200, and 500 lire. There are also in circulation State notes of 500 and bank-notes of 1,000, 2,000, 5,000, 10,000, 20,000, 50,000 and 100,000 lire; they are neither convertible into gold as foreign moneys nor exportable abroad, nor importable from abroad into Italy (except for certain specified small amounts).

Circulation of money at 31 Jan. 1983: State coins and notes, 831,900m. lire; bank-notes, 31,703,200m. lire.

In March 1984 the rate of exchange was 1,620 lire per US$1 and 2,382 lire per £1 sterling.

Banking. According to the law of 6 May 1926 there is only one bank of issue, the Banca d'Italia. Its gold reserve amounted to 32,449,000m. lire in Dec. 1982; the foreign credit reserves of the Exchange Bureau (*Ufficio Italiano Cambi*) amounted to 11,082,900m. lire at the same date.

Since 1936, all credit institutions have been under the control of a State organ, named 'Inspectorate of Credit'; the Bank of Italy has been converted into a 'public institution', whose capital is held exclusively by corporate bodies of a public nature. Other credit institutions, totalling 1,085, are classified as: (1) 6 chartered banks (Banco di Napoli, Banco di Sicilia, Banca Nazionale del Lavoro, Monte dei Paschi di Siena, Istituto di S. Paolo di Torino, Banca di Sardegna); (2) 3 banks of national interest (Banca Commerciale Italiana in Milan, Credito Italiano in Genoa and Banco di Roma); (3) banks and credit concerns in general, including 159 joint-stock banks and 153 co-operative banks; (4) 87 savings banks and Monti di pegno (institutions granting loans against personal chattels as security); (5) 672 *Casse rurali e agrarie* (agricultural banks, established as co-operative institutions with unlimited liability of associates); (6) 5 Istituti di Categoria.

At 31 Dec. 1982 there were 300 credit institutes handling 95% of all deposits and current accounts, with capital and reserves of 21,340,821m. lire.

On 31 March 1983 the post office savings banks had deposits and current accounts of 50,673,000m. lire; credit institutions, 316,749,000m. lire.

Insurance. By a decree of 29 April 1923 life-assurance business is carried on only by the National Insurance Institute and by other institutions, national and foreign, authorized by the Government. At 31 Dec. 1981 the insurances vested in the *Istituto Nazionale delle Assicurazioni* amounted to 6,623,000m. lire, including the decuple of life annuities.

Weights and Measures. The metric system is in general use.

ENERGY AND NATURAL RESOURCES

Electricity. Italy has greatly developed her water-power resources. In 1981 the total power generated was 181,656m. kwh., of which 45,736m. kwh. were generated by hydro-electric plants.

Oil. Production in 1981 amounted to 1,465,093 tonnes, of which 817,197 came from Sicily.

Minerals. The Italian mining industry is most developed in Sicily (Caltanissetta), in Tuscany (Arezzo, Florence and Grosseto), in Sardinia (Cagliari, Sassari and Iglesias), in Lombardy (particularly near Bergamo and Brescia) and in Piedmont.

Italy's fuel and mineral resources are wholly inadequate. Only sulphur and mercury outputs yield a substantial surplus for exports. In 1981 outputs, in tonnes, of raw steel were 24,777,415; rolled iron, 20,823,638; cast-iron ingots, 12,259,190; solid fuels, 1,957,958.

Production of metals and minerals (in tonnes) was as follows:

	1976	1977	1978	1979	1980	1981
Iron pyrites	854,477	863,785	786,666	804,469	858,992	680,988
Iron ore	514,172	478,198	352,611	218,762	184,624	123,407
Manganese	4,461	9,314	9,741	9,782	9,165	8,756
Zinc	274,725	169,717	120,492	100,825	79,190	43,785
Crude sulphur	349,132	627,690	523,355	108,309	100,852	96,172
Bauxite	24,200	34,525	24,410	26,095	23,260	19,000
Mercury	757	14	5	–	–	20,017
Lead	42,601	33,152	31,110	27,237	40,477	37,191
Aluminium	205,723	255,397	270,770	266,814	265,803	243,959

Agriculture. The area of Italy in 1982 comprised 301,268 sq. km, of which 269,451 sq. km was agricultural and forest land and 31,817 sq. km was unproductive; the former was mainly distributed as follows (in 1,000 hectares): Forage and pasture, 8,985; woods, 6,365; cereals, 5,121; vines, 1,283; olive trees, 1,047; olive trees grown among other crops, 1,074; garden produce, 537; vines grown among other crops, 383; leguminous plants, 314.

At the second general census of agriculture (25 Oct. 1970) agricultural holdings numbered 3,620,799 and covered 25,091,267 hectares. 3,142,608 owners (86·8%) farmed directly 14,706,204 hectares (58·6%); 278,157 owners (7·7%) worked with hired labour on 8,523,107 hectares (34%); 130,648 share-croppers (3·6%) tilled 1,271,485 hectares (5·1%); the remaining 69,408 holdings (1·9%) of 590,471 hectares (2·3%) were operated in other ways.

According to the labour force survey in July 1978 persons engaged in agriculture numbered 3·17m. (2·02m. males and 1·15m. females).

In 1976, 909,580 farm tractors were being used.

The production of the principal crops (in 1,000 metric quintals) in 1982: Sugar beet, 114,322; wheat, 90,570; maize, 69,397; tomatoes, 44,765; potatoes, 26,574; oranges, 16,350; rice, 9,795; barley, 10,808; lemons, 6,760; oats, 3,649; olive oil, 4,300; tangerines, 3,009; other citrus fruit, 479; rye, 329.

Production of wine, 1982, 72,648,000 hectolitres; of tobacco, 140,230 tonnes.

In 1982 consumption of chemical fertilizers in Italy was as follows (in 1,000 tons): Perphosphate, 687; nitrate of ammonia, 756·1; sulphate of ammonium, 394·6; potash salts, 164·6; nitrate of calcium$^{15/16}$, 71·6; deposed slags, 41·8.

Livestock estimated in 1982: Cattle, 9,127,000; pigs, 9,132,000; sheep and goats, 10,316,000; horses, 256,000; donkeys, 105,000; mules, 61,000.

Fisheries. The Italian fishing fleet comprised in 1981, 22,981 motor boats (316,788 gross tons) and 12,276 sailing vessels (15,109 gross tons). The catch in 1981 was 392,261 tonnes.

INDUSTRY AND TRADE

Industry. The main branches of industry are: (% of industrial value added at factor cost in 1982) Textiles, clothing, leather and footwear (17·7%), food, beverages and tobacco (10·4%), energy products (7·9%), agricultural and industrial machines (7·7%), metal products except machines and means of transport (7%), mineral and non-metallic mineral products (7%), timber and wooden furniture (6·6%), electric plants and equipment (6·3%), chemicals and pharmaceuticals (6·2%), means of transport (6·1%).

Production, 1981: Methane, 13,961m. cu. metres; steel, 24,566,572; motor vehicles, 1,436,243; cement, 41,553,166 tonnes; artificial and synthetic fibres (including staple fibre and waste), 575,681 tonnes; ethylene, 914,171 tonnes; polyethylene resins, 555,765 tonnes.

Labour. As at April 1982, 20·1m. persons were employed, 1·9m. unemployed (figures from a new series of statistics on the labour force, 1977, which is not comparable with previous series).

Trade Unions. Membership of the 4 main groups: Confederazione Generale Italiana del Lavoro (Communist-dominated), 4,485,930 (1977); Confederazione Italiana Sindacati Lavoratori (Catholic), 3,059,800 (1980); Unione Italiana del Lavoro, 1,151,370 (1977); Confederazione Italiana Sindacati Nazionali Lavoratori, 1,015,988 (1961).

Commerce. The territory covered by foreign trade statistics includes Italy, the Republic of San Marino, but excludes the municipalities of Livigno and Campione. The following table shows the value of Italy's foreign trade (in 1m. lire):

	1977	1978	1979	1980	1981	1982
Imports	42,429,110	47,867,899	64,597,204	85,564,303	103,674,405	116,212,033
Exports	39,967,593	47,505,301	59,926,272	66,719,410	86,039,719	99,246,476

The following table shows trade by countries in 1m. lire:

Countries	Imports into Italy from			Exports from Italy to		
	1980	1981	1982	1980	1981	1982
Argentina	426,463	476,796	515,890	543,517	491,201	298,295
Australia	493,688	580,140	616,175	392,551	575,103	689,534
Austria	1,614,537	1,878,070	1,954,004	1,788,047	1,914,230	2,140,799
Belgium-Luxembourg	3,042,358	3,205,365	3,746,390	2,219,349	2,370,425	2,879,716
France	11,857,740	12,938,148	14,530,632	10,094,105	11,686,202	15,104,170
Germany, Fed. Rep. of	14,180,383	16,190,684	18,656,421	12,210,666	13,351,362	15,489,283
Japan	1,110,781	1,435,861	1,477,152	605,763	762,691	1,068,768
Netherlands	3,632,428	4,287,907	5,023,621	2,461,582	2,615,611	3,049,045
Switzerland	2,175,340	3,300,745	3,984,454	2,951,636	3,454,960	3,961,150
USSR	2,695,919	3,536,935	4,788,595	1,090,618	1,467,690	2,042,458
UK	3,783,634	4,011,549	4,601,252	4,064,060	4,998,901	6,220,520
USA	5,920,974	7,032,025	7,862,571	3,554,502	5,841,374	6,999,094
Yugoslavia	773,152	840,963	1,137,668	1,045,999	1,235,970	1,333,898

In 1982 the main imports were maize, wood, greasy wool, metal scrap, pit-coal, petroleum, raw oils, meat, paper, rolled iron and steel, copper and alloys, mechanical and electric equipment, motor vehicles. The main exports were fruit and vegetables, fabrics, footwear and other clothing articles, rolled iron and steel, machinery, motor vehicles, plastic materials and petroleum by-products. Italy's balance of trade (in 1,000m. lire) has been estimated as follows:

	Goods and services			Income from investments and work, balance	Net balance
	Export	Import	Balance		
1977	49,412	47,277	+2,135	−142	+1,993
1978	58,866	53,465	+5,401	+184	+5,585
1979	74,377	71,123	+3,254	+702	+3,956
1980	83,710	93,967	−10,257	+927	−9,330
1981	105,630	113,721	−8,091	−1,995	−10,086
1982	123,793	128,912	−5,119	−3,429	−8,548

Remittances from Italians abroad (in US$1m. until 1969 and then 1,000m. lire): 1950, 72; 1960, 214; 1970, 289; 1974, 351; 1975, 338; 1976, 385; 1977, 626; 1978, 785; 1979, 956; 1980, 1,059; 1981, 1,325; 1982, 1,607.

Total trade between Italy and UK (British Department of Trade returns, in £1,000 sterling):

	1979	1980	1981	1982	1983
Imports to UK	2,491,013	2,311,071	2,330,349	2,745,094	3,188,219
Exports and re-exports from UK	1,469,048	1,899,181	1,742,514	2,022,711	2,292,788

Tourism. In 1982, 48·3m. foreigners visited Italy; they included 10·5m. German, 8·9m. Swiss, 7·4m. French, 4·4m. Austrian, 3·2m. Yugoslav, 2m. British, 1·8m. Dutch and 1·7m. US citizens. They spent about 11,277,000m. lire.

COMMUNICATIONS

Roads. Italy's roads totalled (31 Dec. 1982) 296,986 km, of which 45,147 km were state roads, 104,272 km provincial roads, 141,666 km communal roads. Motor vehicles, Dec. 1981: Cars, 18·6m.; buses, 62,168; lorries, 1,485,193; motor cycles, light vans, etc., 4,525,373.

The Mont Blanc tunnel road (11·6 km) from Entreves to Les Pelerins (France) was opened on 16 July 1965.

Railways. Railway history in Italy begins in 1839, with a line between Naples and Portici (8 km). Length of railways (31 Dec. 1982), 19,817 km, including 16,146 km of state railways, of which 7,386 had not yet been electrified. The first section of a new high-speed direct railway linking Rome and Florence opened in Feb. 1977. In 1982 the state railways carried 396m. passengers and 51m. tonnes of goods. The Rome Underground opened in Feb. 1980.

Aviation. The Italian airline Alitalia (with a capital of 210,600m. lire, of which 98·7% is owned by the State) operates flights to every part of the world. Airports include 21 international, 32 national and 75 club airports. Domestic and international traffic in 1982 registered 14,239,074 passengers arrived and 14,194,504 departed, while freight and mail (excluding luggage) amounted to 153,358 tonnes unloaded and 202,670 tonnes loaded.

Shipping. The mercantile marine at 31 Dec. 1982 consisted of 2,177 vessels of 10,341,417 gross tons, not including pleasure boats (yachts, etc.), sailing and motor vessels. There were 1,422 motor vessels of 100 gross tons and over.

In 1982, 252,344,973 tonnes of cargo were unloaded, and 86,915,911 tonnes of cargo were loaded in Italian ports.

In 1972 navigable waterways had a length of 2,237 km (849 km of which were canals).

Post and Broadcasting. On 31 Dec. 1982 there were 14,107 post offices and 13,503 telegraph offices. The maritime radio-telegraph service had 20 coast stations. On 1 Jan. 1982 the telephone service had 20,452,749 apparatus. *Radiotelevisione Italiana* broadcasts 3 programmes and additional regional programmes, including transmissions in English, French, German and Slovenian on medium- and short-waves and on FM. It also broadcasts 2 TV programmes. Radio licences numbered 532,800; television and radio licences, 13,400,609.

Cinemas. There were 7,475 cinemas in 1980.

Newspapers. There were 74 daily newspapers with a combined circulation of 6·71m. copies; of the papers 15 are published in Rome and 8 in Milan. One daily each is published in German and Slovene, and 2 in English.

JUSTICE, RELIGION, EDUCATION AND WELFARE

Justice. Italy has 1 court of cassation, in Rome, and is divided for the administration of justice into 23 appeal court districts (and 3 detached sections), subdivided into 159 tribunal districts, and these again into *mandamenti* each with its own magistracy (*Pretura*), 899 in all. There are also 89 first degree assize courts and 26 assize courts of appeal. For civil business, besides the magistracy above mentioned, *Conciliatori* have jurisdiction in petty plaints.

On 31 Dec. 1980 there were 21,988 male and 1,364 female prisoners in establishments for preventive custody, 6,215 males and 115 females in penal establishments and 1,991 males and 92 females in establishments for the execution of safety measures.

Religion. The treaty between the Holy See and Italy, of 11 Feb. 1929, confirmed by article 7 of the Constitution of the republic, lays down that the Catholic Apostolic Roman Religion is the only religion of the State. Other creeds are permitted, provided they do not profess principles, or follow rites, contrary to public order or moral behaviour.

The appointment of archbishops and of bishops is made by the Holy See; but the Holy See submits to the Italian Government the name of the person to be appointed in order to obtain an assurance that the latter will not raise objections of a political nature.

Catholic religious teaching is given in elementary and intermediate schools. Marriages celebrated before a Catholic priest are automatically transferred to the civil register. Marriages celebrated by clergy of other denominations must be made valid before a registrar. In 1972 there were 279 dioceses with 28,154 parishes and 43,714 priests. There were 187,153 members (154,796 women) of about 20,000 religious houses.

In 1962 there were about 100,000 Protestants and about 50,000 Jews.

Annuario Cattolico d'Italia, a cura del CNEC. 14th ed. 1969–70, Rome, 1970
Annuario di Pastorale. Rome, 1970
Burgalassi, S., *La Sociologia della Religione in Italia dalle originiai 1967.* Rome, 1967

Education. Education is compulsory from 6 to 14 years of age. An optional preschool education is given to the children between 3 and 5 years in the preparatory schools (kindergarten schools). Illiteracy of males over 6 years was 4% in 1971, of females 6·3%.

Compulsory education can be classified as primary education (5-year course) and junior secondary education (3-year course).

Senior secondary education is subdivided in classical (*ginnasio* and classical *liceo*), scientific (scientific *liceo*), language lyceum, professional institutes and technical education: agricultural, industrial, commercial, technical, nautical institutes, institutes for surveyors, institutes for girls (5-year course) and teacher-training institutes (4-year course).

University education is given in Universities and in University Higher Institutes (4, 5, 6 years, according to degree course).

Statistics for the academic year 1982–83:

Elementary schools	No.	Pupils
Kindergarten	29,495	1,759,892
Public elementary schools	26,841	3,885,366
Private elementary schools	} 2,456	330,475
Private elementary recognized schools (*parificate*)		

Government secondary schools		Total students
Junior secondary schools	10,074	2,862,639
Classical lyceum	752	206,248
Lyceum for science	971	343,336
Language lyceum	280	47,927
Teachers' schools	207	31,849
Teachers' institutes	672	205,808
Professional institutes	1,671	472,252
Technical institutes, of which:		
Industrial institutes	632	276,804
Commercial institutes	1,154	543,188
Surveyors' institutes	502	144,602
Agricultural institutes	} 384	133,327
Nautical institutes		
Technical institutes for tourism		
Managerial institutes		
Girls technical schools		
Artistic studies	247	60,562

Universities and higher institutes	Date of foundation	Students 1982–83	Teachers 1981–82	Universities and higher institutes	Date of foundation	Students 1982–83	Teachers 1981–82
Ancona	1965	6,497	308	Padova	1222	40,769	2,359
Arezzo	1971	1,120	74	Palermo	1805	42,550	2,144
Bari	1924	48,795	1,812	Parma	1502	16,044	975
Bergamo	1970	2,596	122	Pavia	1390	17,947	1,225
Bologna	1200	57,392	2,912	Perugia	1276	18,634	1,092
Brescia	1970	5,374	69	Pescara	1965	8,186	157
Cagliari	1626	16,392	1,095	Piacenza	1924	616	71
Camerino	1727	2,685	239	Pisa	1338	27,479	1,786
Cassino	1968	1,665	43	Reggio di C.	1968	8,101	98
Catania	1434	31,320	1,496	Roma	1303	155,945	5,989
Chieti	1965	5,144	142	Salerno	1944	20,508	599
Cosenza	1972	5,362	452	Sassari	1677	8,512	506
Feltre (Belluno)	1969	386	22	Siena	1300	9,897	754
Ferrara	1391	5,620	596	Teramo	1965	3,991	83
Firenze	1924	42,607	2,251	Torino	1404	55,033	2,444
Genova	1243	30,910	1,946	Trento	1965	2,627	216
L'Aquila	1956	6,064	700	Trieste	1924	12,724	979
Lecce	1959	6,430	377	Udine	1969	2,193	192
Macerata	1290	4,167	213	Urbino	1564	11,250	394
Messina	1549	24,754	1,188	Venezia	1868	19,639	676
Milano	1924	112,329	3,708	Verona	1969	7,472	145
Modena	1678	8,025	631	Viterbo	1980	661	...
Napoli	1224	112,367	4,356				

Health. In 1976 there were 130,846 doctors and 588,103 hospital beds.

Social Security. Social expenditure is made up of transfers which the central public departments, local departments and social security departments, make to families. Payment is principally for pensions, family allowances and health services. Expenditure on subsidies, public assistance to various classes of people and people injured by political events or national disasters are also included.

In 1975 government expenditure on social welfare amounted to 27,291,000m. lire.

DIPLOMATIC REPRESENTATIVES

Of Italy in Great Britain (14 Three Kings Yard, London, W1Y 2EH)
Ambassador: Andrea Cagiati, GCVO (accredited 20 Feb. 1980).

Of Great Britain in Italy (Via XX Settembre 80A, 00187, Rome)
Ambassador: The Lord Bridges, KCMG.

Of Italy in the USA (1601 Fuller St., NW, Washington, D.C., 20009)
Ambassador: Rinaldo Petrignani.

Of the USA in Italy (Via Veneto 119/A, Rome)
Ambassador: Maxwell M. Rabb.

Of Italy to the United Nations
Ambassador: Umberto La Rocca.

Books of Reference

Statistical Information: The Istituto Centrale di Statistica (16 Via Cesare Balbo 00100 Rome) was set up by law of 9 July 1926 as the central institute in charge of census and all statistical information. *President:* Prof. Guido Mario Rey. *Director-General:* Dr Luigi Pinto. Its publications include:

Annuario statistico italiano. 1983
Compendio statistico italiano. 1983
Bollettino mensile di statistica. Monthly, from 1950
Annuario di statistiche industriali. 1981
Annuario di statistiche demografiche. 1981
Popolazione e movimento anagrafico dei Comuni. Vol. XXIV, 1981

Annuario di statistica agraria. 1981
Annuario statistico della navigazione marittima. 1982
Annuario statistico del commercio interno e del turismo. 1980–81
Statistica annuale del commercio con l'estero. 1981
Statistica mensile del commercio con l'estero. Monthly
Annuario di statistiche del lavoro. 1982
Censimento generale dell'agricoltura. 1982
Censimento generale della popolazione, 1981. 1 vol.
Censimento generale dell'industria e del commercio. 1981
Sintesi Statistica di un Ventennio di Vita Economica Italiana, 1952–71
Cinquanta anni di attivita, 1926–1976. 1978

Italy. Documents and Notes. Servizi delle Informazioni, Rome. 1952 ff.
Italian Books and Periodicals. Bimonthly from 1958
Banco di Roma, *Review of the Economic Condition in Italy* (in English). Bimonthly, 1947 ff.
Credito Italiano, *The Italian Economic Situation.* Bimonthly. Milan, from June 1961 (in Italian), from June 1962 (in English)
Compendio Economico Italiano. Rome, Unione Italiana delle Camere di Commercio. Annually from 1954
Allum, P. A., *Italy: Republic Without Government.* London, 1973
Carone, G., *Il Turismo nell'economia internazionale.* Milan, 1959
Clough, S. B., *The Economic History of Modern Italy.* Columbia Univ. Press, 1964
Di Vittorio, G. (ed.), *I sindacati in Italia.* Bari, 1955
Grindrod, M., *The Rebuilding of Italy, 1945–55.* R. Inst. of Int. Affairs, 1955
Large, P. and Tarrow, S. (eds.), *Italy in Transition – Conflict and Consensus.* London, 1980
Nichols, P., *Italia, Italia.* London, 1974
Wiskemann, E., *Italy Since 1945.* London, 1971
Woolfe, S. J. (ed.), *The Rebirth of Italy, 1943–50.* New York, 1972

National Library: Biblioteca Nazionale Centrale Vittorio Emanuele II Viale Castro Pretorio, Rome. *Director:* Dr L. M. Crisari.

IVORY COAST

République de la Côte d'Ivoire

Capital: Abidjan
Population: 9·27m. (1983)
GNP per capita: US$1,150 (1980)

HISTORY. France obtained rights on the coast in 1842, but did not actively and continuously occupy the territory till 1882. On 10 Jan. 1889 Ivory Coast was declared a French protectorate, and it became a colony on 10 March 1893; in 1904 it became a territory of French West Africa. On 1 Jan. 1933 most of the territory of Upper Volta was added to the Ivory Coast, but on 1 Jan. 1948 this area was returned to the re-constituted Upper Volta. The Ivory Coast became an autonomous republic within the French Community on 4 Dec. 1958 and achieved full independence on 7 Aug. 1960.

AREA AND POPULATION. Ivory Coast is bounded west by Liberia and Guinea, north by Mali and Upper Volta, east by Ghana, and south by the Gulf of Guinea. It has an area of 322,463 sq km and a population at the 1975 census of 6,702,866 (of whom 31·8% were urban). Estimate (1983) 9,273,167.
The areas and populations of the 26 departments at the 1975 census were:

Department	Sq. km	Population	Department	Sq. km	Population
Abengourou	6,713	175,891	Danané	4,650	169,589
Abidjan	14,819	1,388,321	Dimbokro	13,822	478,054
Aboisso	6,135	146,876	Divo	9,869	275,171
Adzopé	5,151	159,502	Ferkéssédougou	19,292	90,901
Agboville	3,900	140,250	Gagnoa	6,873	256,006
Biankouma	2,897	74,408	Guiglo	14,232	135,252
Bondoukou	16,465	293,838	Katiola	8,469	75,909
Bouaflé	8,362	265,875	Korhogo	12,164	276,846
Bouaké	23,405	805,359	Man	7,004	277,648
Bouna	21,470	77,232	Odienné	21,336	124,196
Boundiali	10,273	132,160	Sassandra	26,263	195,620
Dabakala	8,694	55,356	Séguéla	22,861	157,644
Daloa	13,918	367,414	Touba	8,767	77,696

The principal cities (populations, census 1975) are the capital, Abidjan (685,828; estimate 1980, 1·69m.), Bouaké (173,248), Daloa (59,500), Man (48,521), Korhogo (45,146) and Gagnoa (42,000). The new capital will be at Yamoussoukro (70,000 in 1983).
The principal ethnical groups are the Agnis-Ashantis, Kroumen, Mandé, Baoulé, Dan-Gouro and Koua.

CLIMATE. A tropical climate, affected by distance from the sea. In coastal areas, there are wet seasons from May to July and in Oct. and Nov., but in central areas the periods are March to May and July to Nov. In the north, there is one wet season from June to Oct. Abidjan. Jan. 81°F (27·2°C), July 75°F (23·9°C). Annual rainfall 84″ (2,100 mm). Bouake. Jan. 81°F (27·2°C), July 77°F (25°C). Annual rainfall 48″ (1,200 mm).

CONSTITUTION AND GOVERNMENT. The 1960 Constitution was amended in 1971, 1975 and 1980. Under it, the sole legal Party is the *Parti Démocratique de la Côte d'Ivoire*. There is a 147-member National Assembly elected by universal suffrage (latest elections, Nov. 1980) for a 5-year term. The President is also directly elected for a 5-year term (renewable).

The Government was in Sept. 1983 composed as follows:
President: Félix Houphouët-Boigny. (Re-elected for a fifth 5-year term in 1980).

Minister of State: Auguste Denise. *Minister of State responsible for Reform of State-owned Companies:* Mathieu Ekra. *Public Health and Population:* Lazeni N. P. Coulibaly. *Minister of State:* Alexis Thierry-Lebbé. *Justice:* Camille Alliali. *Defence and Civic Service:* Jean Konan Banny. *Interior:* Leon Konan Koffi. *Foreign Affairs:* Siméon Ake. *Economy and Finance:* Abdoulaye Koné. *Planning and Industry:* Maurice Seri Gnoleba. *Agriculture:* Denis Bra Kanon. *Scientific Research and National Education:* Balla Keita. *Technical Education and Vocational Training:* Ange Francois Barry-Battesti. *Social Affairs:* Yaya Ouattara. *Cultural Affairs:* Bernard Dadié. *Commerce:* Amoakon Edjampan Thiemelé. *Public Works and Transport:* Désiré Boni. *Construction and Town Planning:* Eugene Niagne Lasmé. *Animal Production:* Dicoh Garba. *Labour and 'Ivorization' of Personnel:* Albert Vanié-Bi-Tra. *Youth, Popular Education and Sport:* Laurent Dona-Fologo. *Information:* Amadou Thiam. *Mines:* Paul Gui Dibo. *Water and Forests:* Christian Lohourignon Zagote. *Internal Security:* Gaston Ouassenan Koné. *Posts and Telecommunications:* Kouassi Apete. *Navy:* Lamine Fadiga. *Public Service:* Emile Kei Boguinard. *Women's Affairs:* Jeanne Gervais. *Tourism:* Duon Sadia. *Relations with the National Assembly:* Emile Brou. *Environment:* Antoine Brou Tanch.

National flag: Three vertical strips of orange, white, green.

Local government: Since the 1975 census, 8 further *départements* have been created (Bongouanou, Issia, Lakota, Mankono, Oumé, Soubré, Tengréla and Zuénoula) bringing the total to 34 *départements*, sub-divided into 163 sub-prefectures.

DEFENCE

Army. The Army consisted of 3 infantry battalions and support units in 1984. Equipment includes 5 AMX-13 light tanks and 7 ERC-90 armoured cars. Total strength, 4,000.

Navy. Offshore, riverine and coastal patrol squadrons include 2 fast missile craft, 2 patrol vessels, 3 river defence craft, 1 training vessel, 1 light transport, 10 fast assault boats, 6 small protection launches and 2 minor landing craft. Personnel in 1984 totalled 50 officers and 500 ratings.

Air Force. The Air Force, formed in 1962, has 5 Alpha Jet advanced trainers, with combat potential, 2 turboprop C-130H Hercules, 2 turbofan F-28 Fellowship and 1 turbofan Gulfstream II transports, 1 Falcon light jet transport, 2 Reims-Cessna 150s, 6 Beech F-33Cs and 2 Reims-Cessna 337s for liaison and training, and 3 SA330 Puma, 4 Dauphin 2 and 3 Alouette II/III helicopters. Other transport aircraft are leased to the national airline. Personnel total 570.

INTERNATIONAL RELATIONS

Membership. Ivory Coast is a member of UN, OAU and is an ACP state of EEC.

ECONOMY

Budget. The budget for 1982 balanced at 712,200m. francs CFA.

Currency. The currency is the *franc CFA* with a parity rate of 50 *francs CFA* to 1 French *franc*. In March 1984, £ sterling = 588·75 francs CFA; US$1 = 401 francs CFA.

Banking. The *Banque Centrale des Etats de l'Afrique de l'Ouest* is the bank of issue. Numerous foreign and domestic banks have offices in Abidjan, and *Societè Ivoirienne de Banque, Banque Internationale pour le Commerce et l'Industrie de la Côte d'Ivoire* and *Banque Internationale pour l'Afrique Occidentale* main wide branch network throughout the country.

ENERGY AND NATURAL RESOURCES

Electricity. Production in 1980 amounted to 1,830m. kwh mostly from new hydroelectric projects at Kassou and Taabo on the Bandama river, Buyo on the Sassandra river, and from 2 older dams on the Bia river.

Oil. Petroleum has been produced (offshore) since Oct. 1977. Production (1979) 1·57m. tonnes.

Minerals. Annual diamond extraction had dwindled to 25,000 carats by 1979, and manganese mining ceased. Exploitation of iron ore deposits at Bangolo in the west await completion of hydro-electric projects.

Agriculture. The main export crops (production 1981 in 1,000 tonnes) are coffee (350), cocoa (430), bananas (160), pineapples (350), palm oil (190), palm kernels (30), cotton (55) and rubber (23); food crops include yams (1,800), cassava (780), plantains (830), rice (550), maize (300), millet (48) and groundnuts (54). Sugarcane (800,000 tonnes in 1979) is grown on new plantations in the north at Ferkessedougou and elsewhere.

Several factories produce palm-oil, fruit preserves and fruit juice.

Livestock, 1982: 750,000 cattle, 1·32m. sheep, 1·3m. goats, 385,000 pigs, 1,000 horses and 1,000 donkeys.

Fisheries. The catch in 1980 amounted to 77,000 tonnes.

Forestry. Production in 1980 was 11·94m. cu. metres.

INDUSTRY AND TRADE

Industry. Industrialization has developed rapidly since independance, particularly food processing, textiles and sawmills.

Commerce. Trade for calendar years in 1m. francs CFA:

	1977	1978	1979	1980	1981
Imports	429,566	522,515	528,850	539,600	653,320
Exports	529,212	524,380	534,847	628,000	689,800

In 1981 exports of coffee furnished 18% of exports, cocoa 34%, timber 14% and petroleum products, 8%. 19% went to France, 13% to the Netherlands, 11% to the USA, 8% to Italy and 7% to Federal Republic of Germany. Of the imports, France supplied 31%, Venezuela 8%, the USA 5% and Japan 5%.

Total trade between the Ivory Coast and UK (British Department of Trade returns, in £1,000 sterling):

	1979	1980	1981	1982	1983
Imports to UK	73,622	53,563	63,055	56,097	79,255
Exports and re-exports from UK	24,001	27,916	30,128	28,238	25,591

Tourism. In 1980 there were 137,750 foreign tourists.

COMMUNICATIONS

Roads. In 1980 roads totalled 45,350 km. In 1980 there were 138,079 vehicles.

Railways. From Abidjan a metre-gauge railway runs to Léraba and thence through Upper Volta to Ouagadougou (1,140 km). An extension to Tambao is proposed and a new network for the export of iron ore from the port of San Pedro is under study. In 1982 the railways carried 910m. passenger-km and 622m. tonne-km of freight.

Aviation. The main airport is at Abidjan-Port-Buet. In 1978 it handled 564,830 passengers and 25,396 tonnes of freight and 1,216 tonnes of mail. Air Ivoire provides domestic services to 10 regional airports and landing strips.

Shipping. The main ports are Abidjan and San Pedro. In 1979 Abidjan port handled 8·7m. tonnes and San Pedro 1·5m. tonnes.

Post and Broadcasting. There were 78,370 telephones in 1980 and (1978), 939 telex machines. In 1980 there were 300,000 television and 900,000 radio receivers.

Cinemas. There were 60 cinemas in 1977 with a seating capacity of 41,000.

Newspapers. In 1980 there were 3 daily newspapers.

JUSTICE, RELIGION, EDUCATION AND WELFARE

Justice. There are 28 courts of first instance, 3 assize courts and a court of appeal.

Religion. Of the total population, 23·5% are Moslems, 12·5% Christians and 65% animists.

Education. There were, in 1979, 954,656 pupils and 21,640 teachers in 2,697 primary schools, 172,280 pupils and 4,026 teachers in secondary schools and (1979) 22,437 in technical schools. The *Université Nationale de Côte d'Ivoire,* at Abidjan (founded 1964), had 12,765 students in 1980.

Health. In 1978 there were 9,962 hospital beds, 429 doctors, 36 dentists, 615 midwives, 3,052 nurses and 76 pharmacists.

DIPLOMATIC REPRESENTATIVES

Of the Ivory Coast in Great Britain (2 Upper Belgrave St., London, SW1X 8BJ)
Ambassador: Saydou Diarra (accredited 9 Dec. 1983).

Of Great Britain in the Ivory Coast (Immeuble 'Les Harmonies', Blvd. Corde, Abidjan)
Ambassador: John M. Wilson.

Of the Ivory Coast in the USA (2424 Massachusetts Ave., NW, Washington, D.C., 20008)
Ambassador: Amani Rene.

Of the USA in the Ivory Coast (5 Rue Jesse Owens, Abidjan)
Ambassador: Nancy V. Rawls.

Of the Ivory Coast to the United Nations
Ambassador: Amara Essy.

Books of Reference

Statistical Information: Service de la Statistique, Abidjan. It publishes *Bulletin Statistique Mensuel* and *Inventoire Économique de la Côte d'Ivoire.*

La Côte d'Ivoire en Chiffee. Abidjan, 1979
Panorama de la Côte d'Ivoire, 1978, ed. Direction de l'Information, Abidjan
Holas, B., *Industries et cultures en Côte d'Ivoire.* Abidjan, 1979
Zolberg, A. R., *One-Party Government in the Ivory Coast.* Rev. ed. Princeton Univ. Press, 1974

JAMAICA

Capital: Kingston
Population: 2·23m. (1982)
GNP per capita: US$1,030 (1980)

HISTORY. Jamaica was discovered by Columbus in 1494, and was occupied by the Spaniards between 1509 and 1655, when the island was captured by the English; their possession was confirmed by the Treaty of Madrid, 1670. Self-government was introduced in 1944 and gradually extended until Jamaica achieved complete independence within the Commonwealth on 6 Aug. 1962.

AREA AND POPULATION. The area of Jamaica is 4,411 sq. miles (11,425 sq. km). The population at the census of 7 April 1970 was 1,861,300, distributed on the basis of the 14 parishes of the island as follows: Kingston and St Andrew, 550,100 (estimate 1977, 643,800); St Thomas, 71,400 (78.800); Portland, 68,500 (74,300); St Mary, 100,000 (108,900); St Ann, 121,300 (134,300); Trelawny, 61,300 (67,600); St James, 103,700 (122,800); Hanover, 59,000 (64,200); Westmoreland, 113,200 (121,600); St Elizabeth, 126,000 (139,000); Manchester, 123,500 (142,600); St Catherine, 186,000 (217,900); Clarendon, 176,600 (193,900).

Estimated population, in 1982, was 2·23m.

Vital statistics (1979): Births, 58,257; deaths, 13,311; infant deaths, (1978) 869; emigrants (1978) to USA, 19,265; to Canada, 3,858, and to UK, 599.

CLIMATE. A tropical climate but with considerable variation. High temperatures on the coast are usually mitigated by sea breezes, while upland areas enjoy cooler and less humid conditions. Rainfall is plentiful over most of Jamaica, being heaviest in May and from Aug. to Nov. The island lies in the hurricane zone. Kingston. Jan. 76°F (24·4°C), July 81°F (27·2°C). Annual rainfall 32″ (800 mm).

CONSTITUTION AND GOVERNMENT. A new Constitution was enacted with independence in Aug. 1962. The Crown is represented by a Governor-General appointed by the Crown on the advice of the Prime Minister. The Governor-General is assisted by a Privy Council.

The Legislature comprises two chambers, an elected House and a nominated Senate. The executive is chosen from both chambers.

The Executive comprises the Prime Minister, who is the leader of the majority party, and Ministers appointed by the Prime Minister. Together they form the Cabinet, which is the highest executive power. An Attorney-General is a member of the House and is legal adviser to the Cabinet.

The Senate consists of 20 senators appointed by the Governor-General, 12 on the advice of the Prime Minister, 8 on the advice of the Leader of the Opposition. The House of Representatives (60 members, Dec. 1976) is elected by universal adult suffrage for a 5-year period. Electors and elected must be Jamaican or Commonwealth citizens resident in Jamaica for at least 12 months before registration. The powers and procedure of Parliament correspond to those of the British Parliament.

The Privy Council consists of 6 members appointed by the Governor-General in consultation with the Prime Minister.

Governor-General: Florizel Augustus Glasspole.
National flag: A yellow diagonal cross dividing triangles of green, top and bottom, and black, hoist and fly.

The elections to House of Representatives, held on 30 Oct. 1980, returned 51 members of the Jamaica Labour Party and 9 members of the People's National Party.

The Cabinet in March 1984 was comprised as follows:

Prime Minister and Minister of Finance and Planning: Edward Seaga. *Deputy Prime Minister, Minister of Foreign Affairs and Foreign Trade:* Hugh Shearer. *Environment, Science and Technology:* Dr Ronald Irvine. *Construction:* Bruce Golding. *Public Utilities and Transport:* Pearnel Charles. *Agriculture:* Percival Broderick. *National Security and Justice:* Winston Spaulding. *Labour and Leader of the House:* J. A. G. Smith. *Public Service and Social Security:* Errol Anderson. *Education:* Dr Mavis Gilmour. *Industry and Commerce:* Douglas Vaz. *Health:* Dr Kenneth Baugh. *Local Government:* Neville Lewis. *Tourism:* Eric Anthony Abrahams. *Youth and Community Development:* Edmund Bartlett. *Mining and Energy:* Hugh Hart.

DEFENCE

Army. The Jamaica Defence Force consists of a Regular and a Reserve Force. The Regular Force is comprised of the 1st battalion, Jamaica Regiment and Support Services which include the Air Wing and Coast Guard. The Reserve Force consists of the 3rd battalion, Jamaica Regiment. Total strength (all services, 1984), 3,000; there is also a paramilitary force of 6,000.

Air Force. The Air Wing of the Jamaica Defence Force was formed in July 1963 and has since been expanded and trained successively by the British Army Air Corps and Canadian air force personnel. Equipment for army liaison, search and rescue, police co-operation, survey and transport duties includes 2 Defender armed STOL transports; 1 Beech King Air, 1 Cessna 210 and 1 Cessna 337 light transports; 4 JetRanger and 3 Bell 212 light helicopters.

INTERNATIONAL RELATIONS

Membership. Jamaica is a member of UN, the Commonwealth, OAS, CARICOM and is an ACP state of EEC.

ECONOMY

Budget. Revenue and expenditure for fiscal years ending 31 March (in J\$1m.):

	1979–80	1980–81	1981–82	1982–83
Revenue	1,112	1,233	1,555	1,739
Expenditure	1,860	1,547	1,655	1,897

The chief heads of recurrent revenue are customs and excise duties, income tax, motor vehicle licences and post office receipts. Capital revenue is derived mainly from royalties.

Official foreign debt at 31 March 1982, US\$2,434m.

Currency. The currency, is the *dollar*, divided into 100 cents. Currency circulation in Dec. 1980 was J\$302·1m., comprising notes of J\$283·6m. and J\$18·5m. coin. In March 1984, £1 = J\$5·05; US\$1 = J\$3·17.

Banking. On 1 May 1961 the Bank of Jamaica opened as Jamaica's Central Bank. It has the sole right to issue notes and coins in Jamaica, acts as Banker to the Government and to the commercial banks, and administers the island's external reserves and exchange control.

There are 8 commercial banks with about 170 branches and agencies in operation, with main offices in Kingston. Six of these banks are subsidiaries of major British and North American banks, of which 4 are incorporated locally. The Workers' Savings and Loan Bank is owned by the Government, Trade Unions and the private sector. The National Commercial Bank (Jamaica) Ltd, formally Barclays Bank Jamaica Ltd, is 100% government-owned. The other 6 banks which operate are: The Bank of Nova Scotia (Jamaica) Ltd, City Bank of North America, Royal Bank (Jamaica) Ltd, Bank of Commerce, Jamaica Citizens Bank Ltd and First National Bank of Chicago (Jamaica) Ltd.

ENERGY AND NATURAL RESOURCES

Electricity. The Jamaica Public Service Co. is the public supplier of electricity. The bauxite companies, sugar estates and the Caribbean Cement Co. generate their own electricity.

Minerals. Bauxite, ceramic clays, marble, silica and gypsum are commercially valuable. Jamaica has become the world's third largest producer of bauxite and alumina. The bauxite deposits are worked by a Canadian and 4 American companies. Three companies process bauxite into alumina. In 1980, 6,135m. tons of bauxite ore was mined and 2,478m. tons of alumina were produced.

Agriculture (1980). Production: Sugar-cane, 2,736,000 tons; sugar (commercial), 247,000 tons; rum, 5,532,000 proof gallons; molasses, 101 tons; bananas, 33,000 tons; citrus fruit, 1,112,000 boxes: pimento, 928 tons; cocoa, 1,368 tons; coffee, 250,000 boxes; ginger, 438 short tons; copra, 1,738 short tons; meat, 109m. lb.; fish, 36m. lb.; eggs, 102m.; root crops, 481m. lb; vegetables, 290m. lb.

In 1980 a hurricane destroyed about 90% of the banana farms. A replanting programme is in progress.

Livestock (1982): Cattle, 310,000; goats, 400,000; pigs, 265,000; poultry, 4·4m.

INDUSTRY AND TRADE

Industry. In 1976 there were 1,280 registered factories employing 52,633. In 1983 the government decided to close its 7 sugar mills. From processing only a few agricultural products—sugar, rum, condensed milk, oils and fats, cigars and cigarettes—the island is now producing a wide range of manufactures using both local and imported raw materials. Among the manufactured goods are clothing, footwear, textiles, paints, building materials, including cement, agricultural machinery and toilet articles. An oil refinery in Kingston meets local fuel demand. In 1980 manufacturing contributed J$721·2m. to the total GDP at current prices.

Commerce. Value of imports and domestic exports for calendar years (in J$1m.):

	1976	1977	1978	1979	1980
Imports	829·8	781·6	1,260·0	1,002·0	1,173·0
Domestic exports	575·0	686·4	1,057·1	814·7	959·3

Principal imports in 1978 (in J$1,000): Raw materials, 537·1; capital goods, 171·6; consumer goods, 184·8.

Principal exports, 1978 (in J$1m.): Alumina, 554·9; bauxite, 202·2; sugar, 92·5.

Total trade between Jamaica and UK (British Department of Trade returns, in £1,000 sterling):

	1979	1980	1981	1982	1983
Imports to UK	82,145	95,578	114,219	92,760	95,036
Exports and re-exports from UK	44,554	33,122	42,650	56,025	116,188

Tourism. In 1982, 530,000 tourists arrived in Jamaica, spending about J$340m.

COMMUNICATIONS

Roads (1978). The island has 2,944 miles of main roads, and over 7,264 miles of parochial and subsidiary roads. Main roads in the corporate area of Kingston and St Andrew are constructed and maintained by that corporation, those elsewhere by the Public Works Department of the Ministry of Public Utilities. Parochial or subsidiary roads are constructed and maintained by parish councils.

Railways. There are 294 km of railway open of 1,435 mm gauge, operated by the Jamaica Railway Corporation, which also operates 31 km (Alcoa Mineral Railway) on behalf of one of the bauxite companies. In 1982 the railway carried 154 tonne-km and 421,760 passengers.

Aviation. In 1978, 11 scheduled commercial international airlines served Jamaica, operating through the Norman Manley and Sangster international airports at Palisadoes and Montego Bay. Trans-Jamaica Airlines Ltd operates internal flights. Air Jamaica, originally set up in conjunction with BOAC and BWIA in 1966, became a new company, Air Jamaica (1968) Ltd, and is affiliated to Air Canada. In 1969 it began operations as Jamaica's national airline. In 1978 Air Jamaica had a revenue of J$131,628,000 and operating expenses of J$122,033,000.

Shipping. Jamaica has 19 specified ports. In 1980 the port of Kingston unloaded 1·1m. tons of cargo.

Post and Broadcasting. In the financial year 1980 there were 318 post offices and 471 postal agencies.

The Jamaica Telephone Co. operates the telephone system. In Jan. 1982 there were 124,258 telephones in use. All telephone exchanges are automatic. Jamaica is linked to USA by a submarine telephone cable. Jamaica International Telecommunications Ltd (JAMINTEL) established in 1971, provides a wide range of international telecommunications services for Jamaica. There are 1 commercial and 1 publicly owned broadcasting stations; the latter also operates a television service.

Cinemas. In 1981 there were 25 cinemas and 3 drive-in cinemas.

JUSTICE, RELIGION, EDUCATION AND WELFARE

Justice. The Judicature comprises a Supreme Court, a court of appeal, a revenue court, resident magistrates' courts, petty sessional courts, coroners' courts, a traffic court and a family court which was instituted in 1975. The Chief Justice is head of the judiciary. All prosecutions are initiated by the Director of Public Prosecutions.

Police. The Constabulary Force in 1980 stood at approximately 6,000 officers, sub-officers and constables (men and women). There are, in addition, district constables and special constables.

Religion. Freedom of worship is guaranteed under the Constitution. The main Christian denominations are Anglican, Baptist, Roman Catholic, Methodist, Church of God, United Church of Jamaica, and Grand Cayman (Presbyterian–Congregational) Moravian, Seventh-day Adventists, Pentecostal, Salvation Army, Quaker, and Disciples of Christ. Pocomania is a mixture of Christianity and African survivals. Non-Christians include Hindus, Jews, Moslems and Bahai followers. There is also a growing number of Rastafarians who believe in the deity of the late Emperor, Hailé Selassié of Ethiopia.

Education. In Sept. 1973 education became free for all government grant-aided schools (the majority of all schools) and for all Jamaicans entering the University of the West Indies, the College of Arts, Science and Technology and the Jamaica School of Agriculture. In 1979–80 there were 283 primary schools (2,168,103 pupils); 504 all-age schools (256,411 pupils).

In 1980 there were 2 vocational schools, 7 technical high schools, 11 teacher-training colleges, 4 special education schools, 4 community colleges, the College of Arts, Science and Technology, C. G. Foster Sports College, the Cultural Training Centre and the Mona campus of the University of the West Indies.

Health. In 1980 there were about 700 doctors and 29 government hospitals with 6,229 beds. There are several private hospitals and nursing homes.

DIPLOMATIC REPRESENTATIVES

Of Jamaica in Great Britain (50 St James's St., London, SW1A 1JS)
High Commissioner: H. S. Walker.

Of Great Britain in Jamaica (Trafalgar Rd., Kingston 10)
High Commissioner: H. M. S. Reid, CMG.

Of Jamaica in the USA (1850 K. St., NW, Washington, D.C., 20006)
Ambassador: Keith Johnson.

Of the USA in Jamaica (2 Oxford Rd., Kingston)
Ambassador: William Hewitt.

Of Jamaica to the United Nations
Ambassador: Sir Egerton Richardson, CMG.

Books of Reference

Statistical Information: The Department of Statistics (93 Hanover St., Kingston) was set up in 1945—the nucleus being the Census Office, which undertook the operations of the 1943 Census of Jamaica and its Dependencies. *Director:* Mrs C. P. McFarlane. Publications of the Bureau include the *Bulletin of Statistics on External Trade* and the *Annual Abstract of Statistics.*

Economic and Social Survey, Jamaica 1976. National Planning Agency. Yearly

Social and Economic Studies. Institute of Social and Economic Research, Univ. of the West Indies. Quarterly

Beckford, G. and Witter, M., *Small Garden ... Bitter Weed. The Political Struggle and Change in Jamaica.* 2nd ed. London, 1982

Black, C. V., *History of Jamaica.* London, 1965

Cassidy, F. G., and Le Page, R. B., *Dictionary of Jamaican English.* CUP, 1966

Delattre, R., *A Guide to Jamaica Reference Material.* Kingston, 1965

Floyd, B., *Jamaica. An Island Microcosm.* London, 1979

Hurwitz, S. J. and E. F., *Jamaica: A Historical Portrait.* New York, 1971 and London, 1972

Ingram, K. E., *Jamaica.* [Bibliography] Oxford and Santa Barbara, 1984

Jefferson, O., *The Post-War Economic Development of Jamaica.* Kingston, 1972

Kuper, A., *Changing Jamaica.* London and Boston, 1976

Lacey, T., *Violence and Politics in Jamaica, 1960–70.* Manchester Univ. Press, 1977

Manley, M., *A Voice at the Work Place.* London, 1975.—*Jamaica: Struggle in the Periphery.* London, 1983

Post, K., *Strike the Iron. A Colony at War: Jamaica 1939–1945.* 2 vols. Atlantic Highlands, N.J., 1981

Stone, C., *Class, Race and Political Behaviour in Urban Jamaica.* Kingston, 1973. —*Democracy and Clientalism in Jamaica.* London and New Brunswick, N.J., 1981

Bibliography of Jamaica, 1900–1963. Jamaica Library Service, 1963

Libraries: Institute of Jamaica, Kingston. Jamaica Library Service, Kingston.

JAPAN

Nippon (or Nihon)

Capital: Tōkyō
Population: 118·69m. (1982)
GNP per capita: US$9,890 (1980)

HISTORY. The house of Yamato, from about 500 B.C. the rulers of one of several kingdoms, in about A.D. 200 united the nation; the present imperial family are their direct descendants. From 1186 until 1867 successive families of Shoguns exercised the temporal power. In 1867 the Emperor Meiji recovered the imperial power after the abdication on 14 Oct. 1867 of the fifteenth and last Tokugawa Shogun Keiki (in different pronunciation: Yoshinobu). In 1871 the feudal system (Hōken Seido) was abolished; this was the beginning of the rapid westernization.

At San Francisco on 8 Sept. 1951 a Treaty of Peace was signed by Japan and representatives of 48 countries. For details *see* THE STATESMAN'S YEAR-BOOK, 1953, p. 1169. On 26 Oct. 1951 the Japanese Diet ratified the Treaty by 307 votes to 47 votes with 112 abstentions. On the same day the Diet ratified a Security Treaty with the US by 289 votes to 71 votes with 106 abstentions. The treaty provided for the stationing of American troops in Japan until she was able to undertake her own defence. The peace treaty came into force on 28 April 1952, when Japan regained her sovereignty. In 1960 Japan signed the Japan–US Mutual Security Treaty, valid for 10 years, which was renewed in 1970. In June 1971 the Okinawa Reversion Agreement providing for the return from the US to Japan of Okinawa on 15 May 1972 was signed.

AREA AND POPULATION. Census population, 1 Oct. 1982, was 118,693,000 and consists of 4 major islands, Honshu, Hokkaido, Kyushu and Shikoku with an area of 377,709 sq. km. Males 58,402,000, females 60,291,000. Foreigners registered 31 Dec. 1982 were 802,477, of whom 669,854 were Koreans, 59,122 Chinese, 24,825 Americans, 6,563 Philippines, 5,642 British, 3,132 Vietnamese, 2,960 West Germans, 2,232 Indians, 2,026 French, 1,974 Thais, 1,847 Canadians, 2,078 stateless persons.

Japanese overseas, Oct. 1982, 463,680; of these 131,143 lived in Brazil, 128,205 in USA, 15,953 in Argentina, 14,379 in Federal Republic of Germany, 14,251 in Canada, 13,400 in UK, 9,497 in Singapore, 8,724 in France, 8,287 in Peru.

The leading cities, with census population, 31 March 1982 (in 1,000), are:

Akita	287	Kitakyushu	1,055	Otaru	181
Amagasaki	510	Kōbe	1,361	Sagamihara	448
Aomori	288	Kōchi	302	Sakai	805
Asahikawa	356	Koriyama	287	Sapporo	1,419
Chiba	749	Kumamoto	514	Sasebo	254
Fujisawa	309	Kurashiki	409	Sendai	650
Fukuoka	1,065	Kure	234	Shimonoseki	262
Fukushima	262	Kyōto	1,458	Shizuoka	459
Fukuyama	351	Machida	298	Suita	328
Funabashi	482	Maebashi	268	Takamatsu	317
Gifu	408	Matsudo	406	Takatsuki	339
Hachioji	388	Matsuyama	408	Tokushima	249
Hakodate	319	Miyazaki	263	Tōkyō	8,139
Hamamatsu	495	Nagano	325	Toyama	306
Higashiosaka	499	Nagasaki	446	Toyohashi	308
Himeji	446	Nagoya	2,053	Toyonaka	393
Hirakata	362	Naha	301	Toyota	283
Hiroshima	891	Nara	305	Urawa	362
Ichinomiya	253	Neyagawa	252	Utsunomiya	384
Ichikawa	369	Niigata	454	Wakayama	403
Iwaki	350	Nishinomiya	397	Yao	265
Kagoshima	507	Oita	362	Yokkaichi	257
Kanazawa	409	Okayama	546	Yokohama	2,823
Kawaguchi	388	Omiya	357	Yokosuka	426
Kawasaki	1,027	Osaka	2,542		

Vital statistics (in 1,000) for calendar years:

	1974	1975	1976	1977	1978	1979	1980	1981	1982
Births	2,030	1,901	1,833	1,755	1,709	1,643	1,616	1,546	1,515
Deaths	710	702	703	690	696	690	722	725	712

Crude birth rate of Japanese nationals in present area, 1982, was 12·8 per 1,000 population (1947: 3·43); crude death rate, 6; crude marriage rate, 6·6; infant mortality rate per 1,000 live births, 6·6.

CLIMATE. The islands of Japan lie in the temperate zone, north-east of the main monsoon region of S.E. Asia. The climate is generally mild except for the more mountainous areas. Summers are warm and humid, following a month's rainy season in June-July, but the best seasons are spring and autumn, though Sept. may bring typhoons. There is a summer rainfall maximum. Tōkyō. Jan. 37°F (3°C), July 76°F (24·4°C). Annual rainfall 63″ (1,565 mm). Hiroshima. Jan. 37°F (3°C), July 78°F (25·6°C). Annual rainfall 61″ (1,527 mm). Nagasaki. Jan. 42°F (5·6°C), July 79°F (26°C). Annual rainfall 77″ (1,917 mm). Osaka. Jan. 39°F (3·9°C), July 80°F (26·7°C). Annual rainfall 53″ (1,336 mm). Sapporo. Jan. 23°F (−5°C), July 68·4°F (20°C). Annual rainfall 47″ (1,167 mm).

EMPEROR. The Emperor bears the title of Nihon-koku Tennō ('Emperor of Japan'). **Hirohito,** born in Tōkyō, 29 April 1901; succeeded his father, Yoshihito, 25 Dec. 1926; married 26 Jan. 1924, to Princess Nagako, born 6 March 1903. Living sons: (1) Prince Akihito (Tsugunomiya), born 23 Dec. 1933; formally installed as Crown Prince on 10 Nov. 1952; married to Michiko Shoda (born 20 Oct. 1934), 10 April 1959. *Offspring:* Prince Naruhito (Hironomiya), born 23 Feb. 1960; Prince Fumihito (Ayanomiya), born 30 Nov. 1965; Princess Sayako (Norinomiya), born 18 April 1969. (2) Prince Masahito (Hitachinomiya), born 28 Nov. 1935; married to Hanako Tsugaru, 30 Sept. 1964.

By the Imperial House Law of 11 Feb. 1889, revised on 16 Jan. 1947, the succession to the throne was fixed upon the male descendants.

CONSTITUTION AND GOVERNMENT. Japan's Government is based upon the Constitution of 1947 which superseded the Meiji Constitution of 1889. In it the Japanese people pledge themselves to uphold the ideas of democracy and peace. The Emperor is the symbol of the States and of the unity of the people. Sovereign power rests with the people. The Emperor has no powers related to government. Japan renounces war as a sovereign right and the threat or the use of force as a means of settling disputes with other nations. Fundamental human rights are guaranteed.

National flag: White, with a red disc.

National anthem: Kimi ga yo wa (words 9th century, tune by Hiromori Hayashi, 1881).

Legislative power rests with the Diet, which consists of the House of Representatives (of 511 members), elected by men and women over 20 years of age for a 4-year term, and the House of Councillors of 252 members (100 elected by party list system with proportional representation according to the d'Hondt method and 152 from prefectural districts), one-half of its members being elected every 3 years. The Lower House controls the budget and approves treaties with foreign powers.

The former House of Peers is replaced by the House of Councillors, whose members, like those of the House of Representatives, are elected as representatives of all the people. The House of Representatives has pre-eminence over the House of Councillors.

On 26 Dec. 1983 the House of Representatives consisted of 267 Liberal-Democrats-New Liberal Club National Union, 113 Socialists, 59 Komeito, 39 Democratic Socialists, 27 Japan Communist Party, 3 Social Democratic Federation and 3 Independents.

The Cabinet, as constituted in Jan. 1984, was as follows:

Prime Minister: Yasuhiro Nakasone.

Justice: Eisaku Sumi.
Foreign Affairs: Shintaro Abe.
Finance: Noboru Takeshita.
Education: Yoshiro Mori.
Health and Welfare: Kozo Watanabe.
Agriculture, Forestry and Fishery: Shinjiro Yamamura.
Trade and Industry: Hikosaburo Okonogi.
Transport: Kichizo Hosoda.
Postal Service: Keiwa Okuda.
Labour: Misoji Sakamoto.
Construction: Kiyoshi Mizuno.
Home Affairs: Seiichi Tagawa.

Local Government. The country is divided into 47 prefectures (*Todōfuken*), including Tōkyō-to (the capital), Ōsaka-fu and Kyōto-fu, Hokkai-dō, and 43 *Ken*. Each *Todōfuken* has its governor (*Chiji*) elected by the voters in the area. The prefectural government of Tōkyō-to is also responsible for the urban part (formerly Tōkyō-shi) of the prefecture. Each prefecture, city, town and village has a representative assembly elected by the same franchise as in parliamentary elections.

New legislation, which came into effect on 1 July 1954, has given the central government complete control of the police throughout the country.

DEFENCE

Army. The 'Ground Self-Defence Force' had in 1983 an authorized strength of 180,000 uniformed personnel, plus a reserve of 43,000 men. The Army is organized in 12 infantry divisions, 1 armoured division, 1 airborne brigade, 2 air defence brigades, 1 artillery, 5 engineer, 1 signal, 2 composite and 1 helicopter brigades in addition to 4 anti-aircraft artillery groups. Equipment includes 1,040 tanks.

The Northern Army, stationed in Hokkaido, consists of 4 divisions (1 of which is armoured), an artillery brigade, an anti-aircraft artillery brigade, a tank group and an engineering brigade. The Western Army, stationed in Kyushu, consists of 2 divisions and 1 composite brigade. The North-Eastern Army (2 divisions), the Eastern Army (2 divisions) and 1 airborne brigade, the Middle Army (3 divisions and 1 composite brigade). The infantry division establishment is approximately 9,000 with 4 infantry regiments or 7,000 (lower establishment) with 3 infantry regiments. Each infantry division has an artillery unit, an anti-tank unit, a tank battalion and an engineering battalion in addition to administrative units.

Navy. The 'Maritime Self-Defence Force' comprises 14 submarines, 2 large destroyers of 5,200 tons each and 2 destroyers of 4,700 tons each carrying 3 helicopters, 8 guided-missile destroyers, 26 other destroyers, 18 frigates, 1 minelayer/support ship, 5 large patrol vessels, 2 modern purpose-built training ships (destroyer and frigate types, with hangars), 37 coastal minesweepers, 2 minesweeper support ships, 2 submarine rescue vessels, 6 minesweeping boats, 5 fast torpedo-boats, 9 patrol boats, 8 landing ships, 1 new fleet support ship, 2 experimental ships, 7 surveying vessels, 2 icebreakers (including the antarctic support ship), 1 cable layer (ocean survey), 1 cable layer (*ex*-minelayer), 2 oilers, 26 harbour tankers, 38 tugs, 15 tenders, 20 auxiliaries and 37 minor landing craft.

The Fleet Air Arm, numbering 21 squadrons, includes 90 patrol aircraft and 19 flying boats for anti-submarine patrol, 85 trainers and 104 helicopters plus transports and mine countermeasures units.

Personnel in 1984 numbered 46,400 officers and ratings including the Naval Air Arm. There are also 4,300 in civil maritime defence.

In addition to the 300 naval ships and 300 naval aircraft of the Maritime Self-Defence Force there are some 525 vessels (including over 100 armed patrol vessels of destroyer, frigate and corvette size and potentiality) and 55 aircraft of the Maritime Safety Agency or Coastguard (q.v.) which would undoubtedly be deployed as naval craft in war emergency.

Air Force. An 'Air Self-Defence Force' was inaugurated on 1 July 1954. In 1983 its equipment included 2 interceptor squadrons of F-15J/DJ Eagles (total of 100 aircraft to be acquired by 1987); 3 squadrons of F-104J Starfighters, and 6 of F-4EJ

Phantoms; 3 squadrons of Mitsubishi F-1 close-support fighters; 1 squadron of RF-4E reconnaissance fighters; the first 4 of 8 E-2C Hawkeye AWACS aircraft; ECM flight with 2 YS-11Es; 3 squadrons of turbofan Kawasaki C-1 and turboprop C-130H Hercules and NAMC YS-11 transports. About 35 helicopters, mostly KV-107s (to be replaced with CH-47 Chinooks), and MU-2 twin-turboprop aircraft perform search, rescue and general duties. Training units use piston-engined Fuji T-3 basic trainers, Fuji T-1 jet intermediate trainers, T-33 jet trainers and supersonic Mitsubishi T-2 jet advanced trainers. The T-1s and T-33s will be replaced with Kawasaki T-4s in the late '80s. Six surface-to-air missile groups (19 squadrons) are in service. Total strength is about 300 combat aircraft and 43,000 officers and men.

INTERNATIONAL RELATIONS

Membership. Japan is a member of UN, the Colombo Plan and OECD.

ECONOMY

Planning. The 1981–85 Plan envisages an onward growth rate of 5·5%. The real growth rate for 1984 is envisaged at 4·1% and the nominal 5·9%.

Budget. Ordinary revenue and expenditure for fiscal year ending 31 March 1984 balanced at 50,379,600m. yen.

Of the proposed revenue in 1983, 32,315,000m. was to come from taxes and stamps, 13,345,000m. from public bonds. Main items of expenditure: Social security, 9,139,754m.; public works, 6,655,448m.; local government, 7,315,145m.; education, 4,818,631m.; defence, 2,754,234m.

The outstanding national debt incurred by public bonds was estimated in March 1983 to be 97,862,580m. yen, including 11,290m. yen of Japan's foreign currency bonds.

The estimated 1983 budgets of the prefectures and other local authorities forecast a total revenue of 47,486,000m. yen, to be made up partly by local taxes and partly by government grants and local loans.

Currency. Coins of 1, 5, 10, 50, 100 and 500 yen are in circulation as well as notes of the Bank of Japan, of 100, 500, 1,000, 5,000 and 10,000 yen. Bank-notes for 100 yen are still in circulation in country districts but are gradually being replaced by coins. In March 1984, £1 = 333 yen; US$1 = 233 yen.

In Dec. 1982 the currency in circulation consisted of 21,426,000m. yen Bank of Japan notes and 1,154,600m. yen subsidiary coins.

Banking. The modern banking system dates from 1972. The Nippon Ginko (Bank of Japan) was founded in 1882. The Bank of Japan has undertaken to finance the Government and the banks; its function is similar to that of a Central Bank in other countries. The Bank undertakes the actual management of Treasury funds and foreign exchange control.

Gold bullion and cash holdings of the Bank of Japan at 31 Dec. 1982 stood at 283,000m. yen.

The Yokohama Specie Bank (specializing in foreign exchange) became the Bank of Tōkyō in Aug. 1954. Total assets of all banks at 31 Dec. 1982 was 272,412,600m. yen.

The post office savings bank is modelled upon the British; deposits amounted to 82,505,650m. yen in Nov. 1983.

Many foreign banks operate branches in Japan including: Bank of Indo-China, Hongkong & Shanghai Banking Corporation, Chartered Bank of India, Australia and China, Bank of India, Mercantile Bank of India, Bank of Korea, Bank of China, Algemene Bank Nederland NV, National Handelsbank NV, Bank of America, National City Bank of New York, Chase Manhattan Bank, Bangkok Bank and American Express Co.

Weights and Measures. The metric system was made obligatory by a law passed in March 1921, and the period of grace for its compulsory use ended on 1 April 1966.

ENERGY AND NATURAL RESOURCES

Electricity. In 1981 generating facilities were capable of an output of 150,041,000 kw.; electricity produced was 583,245m. kwh.

Oil and Gas. Output of crude petroleum, 1981, was 456,000 kl, almost entirely from oilfields on the island of Honshu, but 230,239,000 kl crude oil had to be imported. Output of natural gas, 1981, 20,661,189m. kilocalories.

Minerals. Ore production in tonnes, 1981, of chromite, 10,959; coal, 17,687,000; iron, 441,844; zinc, 242,042,000; molybdenum (1980), 100; manganese, 86,696; copper, 51,513; lead, 46,922; tungsten, 1,901; silver, 280,228 kg.; gold, 3,087 kg.

Agriculture. Agricultural workers in 1982 were 6,600,980, including 836,760 subsidiary and seasonal workers; 9% of the labour force as opposed to 24·7% in 1962. The arable land area in 1982 was 5,426,000 hectares (5,796,000 in 1970). Division of ordinary fields to non-agricultural use accounted largely for this decrease. Rice cultivation accounted for 2,257,000 hectares in 1982. The area planted with industrial crops such as rapeseed, tobacco, tea, rush, etc., was 269,000 hectares in 1981.

In 1982 there were 4,314,000 power cultivators and tractors in use together with 3·61m. power sprayers and power dusters and 1,986,000 rice power planters.

Output of rice was 12m. tonnes in 1979, 9·6m. in 1980, 10,259,000 in 1981 and 10·27m. in 1982.

Production in 1981 (in 1,000 tonnes) of barley was 330·3; wheat, 587·4; soybeans, 211·7. Sweet potatoes, which in the past mitigated the effects of rice famines, have, in view of rice over-production, decreased from 4,955,000 tons in 1965 to 1,458,000 tons in 1981. Domestic sugar-beet and sugar-cane production accounted for only 32·3% of requirement in 1981. In 1981, 1,591,000 tonnes were imported, 37·4% of this being imported from Australia, 23% from South Africa, 15·4% from Cuba, 8·6% from Philippines, 6·2% from Formosa, 6% from Thailand.

Fruit production, 1981 (in 1,000 tonnes): Mandarins, 2,821; apples, 845·7; pears, 486·5; grapes, 309·9; peaches, 238·8; and persimmons, 260·5.

Livestock (1982): 4,485,000 cattle (including about 2·1m. milch cows), 23,000 horses, 10·04m. pigs, 19,000 sheep, 60,000 goats, 299m. chickens. Milk (1981), 6·61m. tonnes.

Forestry. Forests and grasslands cover about 25m. hectares (nearly 70% of the whole land area), with an estimated timber stand of 2,484m. cu. metres in 1981. In 1981, 39,498,000 cu. metres were felled.

Fisheries. Before the War, Japanese catch represented one-half to two-thirds of the world's total fishing, in 1980 it was 14·4%. The catch in 1981 was 11·3m. tonnes, excluding whaling. Japan now ranks first in whaling.

INDUSTRY AND TRADE

Industry. Japan's industrial equipment, 1980, numbered 734,600 plants of all sizes, employing 10,932,000 production workers.

Since 1920 there has been a shift from light to heavy industries. The production of electrical appliances and electronic machinery has made great strides: television sets (1981: 14,578,000), radio sets (1981: 15,196,000), cameras (1981: 15,174,000), computing machines and automation equipment are produced in increasing quantities. The chemical industry ranks third in production value after machinery and metals (1981). Production, 1981, included (in tonnes): Sulphuric acid, 6,572,000; caustic soda, 2,786,000; ammonium sulphate, 1·62m.; calcium superphosphate, 512,000.

Output (1981), in 1,000 tonnes, of pig iron was 80,048; crude steel, 101,676; ordinary rolled steel, 79,797.

In 1981 paper production was 9·94m. tonnes; paperboard, 7·04m. tonnes.

Japan's textile industry before the War had 13m. cotton-yarn spindles. After the War she resumed with 2·78m. spindles; in 1964, 8·42m. spindles were operating.

Output of cotton yarn, 1981, 456,000 tonnes, and of cotton cloth, 2,067m. sq. metres.

In wool, Japan aims at wool exports sufficient to pay for the imports of raw wool. Output, 1981, 114,000 tonnes of woollen yarns and 291m. sq. metres of woollen fabrics.

Output, 1981, of rayon woven fabrics, 775m. sq. metres; synthetic woven fabrics, 3,121m. sq. metres; silk fabrics, 129m. sq. metres.

Shipbuilding has been decreasing and in 1981, 8·3m. gross tons were launched, of which 3,373,000 GRT were tankers.

Labour. Total labour force, Oct. 1981, was 55·8m., of which 5·1m. were in agriculture and forestry, 470,000 in fishing, 100,000 in mining, 5·4m. in construction, 13·9m. in manufacturing, 14·7m. in commerce and finance, 3·76m. in transport and other public utilities, 10·3m. in services (including the professions) and 1·94m. in government work.

In 1982 there were 12,526,000 workers organized in 74,091 unions. The largest federation is the 'General Council of Japanese Trade Unions' (Sōhyō) with 4·55m. members. The 'Japanese Confederation of Labour' (Dōmei Kaigi) had 2,197,000 members. The 'Federation of Independent Unions' (Chūritsu Rōren) founded in 1956 had 1,439,000 members.

In Nov. 1982, 1·34m. (2·3%) were unemployed. In 1982, 538,143 working days were lost in industrial stoppages.

Commerce. Trade (in US$1m.)

	1976	1977	1978	1979	1980	1981	1982
Imports	64,799	70,808	79,343	110,672	140,528	152,030	138,831
Exports	67,225	80,494	97,543	103,031	129,807	143,289	131,931

Distribution of trade by countries (customs clearance basis) (US$1m.):

	Exports		Imports	
	1981	1982	1981	1982
Africa	5,760	4,167	2,397	1,610
Australia	4,779	4,581	7,419	6,961
Canada	3,399	2,861	4,464	4,441
China	5,095	3,511	5,292	5,352
Fed. Rep. of Germany	5,968	5,018	2,429	2,355
Hong Kong	5,311	4,718	669	622
Latin America	10,487	9,086	6,649	6,268
Philippines	1,928	1,803	1,731	1,576
South-east Asia	34,321	31,873	31,784	29,985
Thailand	2,251	1,907	1,061	1,041
USSR	3,259	3,899	2,021	1,682
UK	4,789	4,813	2,694	1,874
USA	38,609	36,330	25,297	24,179

Principal items in 1982, with value in 1m. yen were:

Imports, c.i.f.		Exports, f.o.b.	
Mineral fuels	16,235,889	Machinery and transport equip-	
Foodstuffs	3,616,794	ment	22,441,834
Metal ores and scrap	1,674,352	Metals and metal products	5,255,820
Machinery and transport equip-		Textile products	1,549,066
ment	2,262,979	Chemicals	1,580,370
Textile fibres	573,157		

Total trade between Japan and UK (British Department of Trade returns, in £1,000 sterling):

	1979	1980	1981	1982	1983
Imports to UK	1,490,288	1,712,108	2,236,170	2,657,977	3,355,450
Exports and re-exports from UK	606,011	597,147	620,273	681,483	797,848

Tourism. In 1981, 1,583,000 foreigners visited Japan, 353,200 of whom came from USA, 121,500 from UK. Japanese travelling abroad totalled 4,006,388 in 1981.

COMMUNICATIONS

Roads. The total length of roads (including urban and other local roads) was

1,118,008 km at 1 April 1981; the 'national' roads extended 40,381 km, of which 38,752 km were paved. Motor vehicles, at 31 Dec. 1982, numbered 40,486,000, including 25,539,000 passenger cars and 14,717,000 commercial vehicles.

Railways. The first railway was completed in 1872, between Tōkyō and Yokohama (29 km). Total length of railways, in March 1981, was 26,914 km, of which the national railways had 21,419 km (8,435 km electrified) and private railways, 5,594 km (4,923 km electrified). In 1981 the national railways carried 6,793m. passengers (private, 11,425m.) and 111m. tons of freight (private, 41m.).

Aviation. The principal airlines are Japan Airlines and All Nippon Airways. Japan Airlines, founded in 1953, operate international services from Tōkyō to the USA, Europe, the Middle East and Southeast Asia, including flights to London over the North Pole and to Moscow by way of Siberia. In 1980 Japanese companies carried 40,424,000 passengers in domestic services and 4,927,000 passengers in international services.

Shipping. On 30 June 1982 the merchant fleet consisted of 8,744 vessels (over 100 gross tons); there were 713 ships for passenger transport (1,131,000 gross tons), 2,893 cargo ships (3,083,000 gross tons) and 1,613 oil tankers (16,795,000 gross tons).

Coastguard. The 'Maritime Safety Agency' (Coastguard) consists of 11 regional MS headquarters, 65 MS offices, 51 MS bases, 14 air bases, 7 Control Communications Centres, 1 Traffic Advisory Service Centre, 4 hydrographic observatories and 136 navigation aids offices (with 4,907 navigation aids facilities) and controls 43 large patrol vessels, 47 medium patrol vessels, 19 small patrol vessels, 231 patrol craft, 22 hydrographic service vessels, 5 firefighting vessels, 10 firefighting boats, 63 guard and rescue boats and 81 navigation aids service supply vessels. Personnel in 1983 numbered 12,027 officers and men.

The Coastguard aviation service includes 22 fixed-wing aircraft and 33 helicopters.

Post and Broadcasting. The telephone services, operated by a public corporation, at 31 March 1982 had 58,678,000 instruments.

On 31 March 1982, 98·9% of all households owned colour television sets, 17·4% black and white television sets.

Cinemas (1981). Cinemas numbered 2,298 with an annual attendance of 149m. (1960: 1,014m.).

Newspapers (1981). Daily newspapers numbered 125 with aggregate circulation of 67,292,563, including 4 major English-language newspapers.

JUSTICE, RELIGION, EDUCATION AND WELFARE

Justice. The Supreme Court is composed of the Chief Justice and 14 other judges. The Chief Justice is appointed by the Emperor, the other judges by the Cabinet. Every 10 years a justice must submit himself to the electorate. All justices and judges of the lower courts serve until they are 70 years of age.

Below the Supreme Court are 8 regional higher courts, district courts (*Chihōsaibansho*) in each prefecture (4 in Hokkaidō) and the local courts.

The Supreme Court is authorized to declare unconstitutional any act of the Legislature or the Executive which violates the Constitution.

Religion. There has normally been religious freedom, but Shintō (literally, The Way of the Gods) was given the status of *quasi*-state-religion in the 1930s; in 1945 the Allied Supreme Command ordered the Government to discontinue state support of Shintō. State subsidies have ceased for all religions, and all religious teachings are forbidden in public schools.

In Dec. 1981 Shintoism claimed 104,583,537 adherents, Buddhism 87,128,333; these figures obviously overlap. Christians numbered 1,434,408, of whom 1,053,269 are Protestants and 381,139 Catholics.

Education. Education is compulsory and free between the ages of 6 and 15. Almost all national and municipal institutions are co-educational. On 1 May 1982 there were 15,152 kindergartens with 99,600 teachers and 2,227,600 pupils; 25,043 elementary schools with 475,000 teachers and 11,901,500 pupils; 10,879 junior high schools with 269,600 teachers and 5,624,000 pupils; 5,213 senior high schools with 243,100 teachers and 4,600,600 pupils; 526 junior colleges with 16,900 teachers and 374,300 pupils.

There were also 882 special schools for handicapped children (36,400 teachers, 94,900 pupils).

Japan has 7 main state universities, formerly known as the Imperial Universities: Tōkyō University (1877); Kyōto University (1897); Tōhoku University, Sendai (1907); Kyūshū University, Fukuoka (1910); Hokkaidō University, Sapporo (1918); Osaka University (1931), and Nagoya University (1939). In addition, there are various other state and municipal as well as private universities of high standing, such as Keio (founded in 1859), Waseda, Rikkyō, Hōsei, Maiji universities, and several women's universities, among which Tōkyō and Ochanomizu are most notable. There are 455 colleges and universities with (1 May 1982) 1,817,600 students and 107,400 teachers.

Social Welfare. Hospitals at the end of 1980 numbered 9,055 with 1,319,406 beds. Physicians at the end of 1981 numbered 162,882; dentists, 56,841.

There are in force various types of social security schemes, such as health insurance, unemployment insurance and old-age pensions. The total population come under one or more of these schemes.

In 1981 11,270,712 persons and 9,080,712 households received some form of regular public assistance.

DIPLOMATIC REPRESENTATIVES

Of Japan in Great Britain (43 Grosvenor St., London, W1X 0BA)
Ambassador: Tsuyoshi Hirahara (accredited 24 Feb. 1982.)

Of Great Britain in Japan (1 Ichiban-cho, Chiyoda-ku, Tōkyō 102)
Ambassador: Sir Sydney Giffard, KCMG.

Of Japan in the USA (2520 Massachusetts Ave., NW, Washington, D.C. 20008)
Ambassador: Yoshio Ōkawara.

Of the USA in Japan (10–5, Akasaka 1-chome, Minato-Ku, Tōkyō)
Ambassador: Michael J. Mansfield.

Of Japan to the United Nations
Ambassadors: Mizuo Kuroda and Tomohiko Kobayashi.

Books of Reference

Statistics Bureau of the Prime Minister's Office: *Statistical Year-Book* (from 1949).—*Statistical Abstract* (from 1950)).—*Statistical Handbook of Japan 1977.—Monthly Bulletin* (from April 1950)
Economic Planning Agency: *Economic Survey* (annual), *Economic Statistics* (monthly), *Economic Indicators* (monthly)
Ministry of International Trade: *Foreign Trade of Japan* (annual)
The Bank of Japan Research Department. *Money and Banking in Japan.* London, 1973
Kodansha Encyclopedia of Japan. 9 vols. Tōkyō, 1983
Japan Times Year Book. (I. Year Book of Japan. II. Who's Who in Japan. III. Business Directory of Japan.) Tōkyō, first issue 1933
Treaty of Peace with Japan. (Cmd. 8392). HMSO, 1951; (Cmd. 8601). HMSO, 1952
Ackerman, E. A., *Japan's National Resources.* Univ. of Chicago Press, 1953
Allen, G. C., *Short Economic History of Modern Japan.* London, 1946.—*The Japanese Economy.* London, 1981
Baerwald, H. H., *Japan's Parliament.* CUP, 1974
Boltho, A., *Japan: An Economic Survey, 1953–1973.* OUP, 1976
Burks, A. W., *Japan: Profile of an Industrial Power.* Boulder, 1981
Kahn, H., and Pepper. T., *The Japanese Challenge.* New York, 1979
Kenkyusha's *New Japanese–English [and English–Japanese] Dictionary.* 2 vols. New ed. Cambridge, Mass., and Berkeley, Cal., 1960

Kennedy, M. D., *A History of Japan*, London, 1963
Kitamura, H., *Choices for the Japanese Economy*. London, 1976
Langdon, F. C., *Japan's Foreign Policy*. Univ. of British Columbia Press, 1973
McNelly, T., *Politics and Government in Japan*. 2nd ed. London, 1972
Miyazaki, S., *The Japanese Dictionary Explained in English*. Tōkyō, 1950
Morishima, U. *Why has Japan 'Succeeded'?*. CUP, 1984
Murata, K., *An Industrial Geography of Japan*. London, 1980
Nippon: A Chartered Survey of Japan. Tsuneta Yano Memorial Society. Tōkyō, annual
Ohkawa, K., and Rosovsky, H., *Japanese Economic Growth: Trend Acceleration in the Twentieth Century*. Stanford Univ. Press, 1973
Prindl, A., *Japanese Finance: Guide to Banking in Japan*. Chichester, 1981
Sansom, G. B., *The Western World and Japan*. New York, 1950.—*A History of Japan*. 3 vols. London, 1958–64
Simonis, H. and U. E. (ed.), *Japan: Economic and Social Studies in Development*. Wiesbaden, 1974
Tanaka, K., *Building a New Japan: A Plan for Remodelling the Japanese Archipelago*. Tōkyō, 1973
Tsoukalis, L., (ed.), *Japan and Western Europe*. London, 1982
Vogel, E. F., *Japan as Number One*. Harvard Univ. Press, 1979
Yabuki, K. (ed.), *Japan Bibliographic Annual*. 2 vols. Tōkyō, annual

THE HASHEMITE KINGDOM OF JORDAN

Capital: Amman
Population: 2·25m. (1982) E. Bank
1·25m. (1982) W. Bank
GNP per capita: US$1,420 (1980)

Al Mamlaka al Urduniya al Hashemiyah

HISTORY. By a Treaty, signed in London on 22 March 1946, Britain recognized Transjordan as a sovereign independent state. A new Anglo-Transjordan treaty was signed in Amman on 15 March 1948. The treaty was to remain in force for 20 years, but by mutual consent was terminated on 13 March 1957.

The Arab Federation between the Kingdoms of Iraq and Jordan, which was concluded on 14 Feb. 1958, lapsed after the revolution in Iraq of 14 July 1958, and was officially terminated by royal decree on 1 Aug. 1958.

On 25 May 1946 the Amir Abdullah assumed the title of King, and when the treaty was ratified on 17 June 1946 the name of the territory was changed to that of 'The Hashemite Kingdom of Jordan'. The legislature consists of a lower house of 60 members elected by universal suffrage (30 from East Jordan and 30 from West Jordan), and a senate of 30 members nominated by the King.

AREA AND POPULATION. The part of Palestine remaining to the Arabs under the armistice with Israel 3 April 1949, with the exception of the Gaza strip, was in Dec. 1949 placed under Jordan rule and formally incorporated in Jordan on 24 April 1950. For the frontier lines *see* map in THE STATESMAN'S YEAR-BOOK, 1951. On 10 Aug. 1965 a treaty with Saudi Arabia provided for an exchange of about 6,000–7,000 sq. km in order to facilitate the development of the port of Aqaba.

Total East Bank area, 91,000 sq. km. West Bank enclaves 5,000 sq. km: census population (18 Nov. 1961), 1,706,226; estimate, 1982, 3·5m. (2·25m. in East Bank, 1·25m. in West Bank).

The country is divided into 8 districts (*muhafaza*), viz., Amman, Irbid, Balqa, Karak, Ma'an, Jerusalem, Hebron and Nablus. The last 3 named districts are known collectively as the West Bank, which, since the hostilities of June 1967, has been occupied by Israel.

The largest towns, with estimated population, 1980: Amman, the capital, 1,232,600; Zarka, 269,780 (1977); Irbid, 140,000.

In 1979 registered births numbered 91,622; deaths, 6,547; marriages, 15,491; divorces. 3,295.

CLIMATE. Predominantly a Mediterranean climate, with hot dry summers and cool wet winters, but in hilly parts summers are cooler and winters colder. Those areas below sea-level are very hot in summer and warm in winter. Eastern parts have a desert climate. Amman. Jan. 46°F (7·5°C), July 77°F (24·9°C). Annual rainfall 12″ (290 mm) Aqaba. Jan. 61°F (16°C), July 89°F (31·5°C). Annual rainfall 1·5″ (35 mm).

KING. The Kingdom is a constitutional monarchy headed by HM King **Hussein**, GCVO, eldest son of King Talal, who, being incapacitated by mental illness, was deposed by Parliament on 11 Aug. 1952 and died 8 July 1972. The King was born 14 Nov. 1935, and married Princess Dina Abdul Hamid on 19 April 1955 (divorced 1957), Toni Avril Gardiner (Muna al Hussein) on 25 May 1961 (divorced 1972), A.ia Toukan on 26 Dec. 1972 (died in air crash 1977) and Elizabeth Halaby on 15 June 1978. *Offspring:* Princess Alia, born 13 Feb. 1956; Prince Abdulla, born 30 Jan. 1962; Prince Faisal, born 11 Oct. 1963; Princesses Zein and Aisha, born 23 April 1968; Princess Haya, born 3 May 1974; Prince Ali, born 23 Dec. 1975; Prince Hamzah, born 1 April 1980; Prince Hashem, born 10 June 1981; Princess Iman, born 4 April 1983. *Crown Prince* (appointed 1 April 1965): Prince Hassan, younger brother of the King.

CONSTITUTION AND GOVERNMENT. The Constitution passed on 7 Nov. 1951 provides that the Cabinet is responsible to Parliament.

On 5 Feb. 1976 both Houses of Parliament approved amendments to the Constitution by which the King was empowered to postpone calling elections until further notice. The lower house was dissolved. This step was taken because no elections could be held in the West Bank which has been under Israeli occupation since June 1967.

Parliament was reconvened on 9 Jan. 1984. By-elections for 8 vacant East Bank seats were called and 6 members will be nominated for the West Bank bringing Parliament to 60 members.

The Cabinet, in Jan. 1984, was composed as follows:
Prime Minister and Defence: Ahmed Obaidat.
Deputy Prime Minister and Interior: Sulaiman Arar. *Minister of State for the Prime Ministry and Minister of Justice:* Ahmed Abdelkareem Al Tarawneh. *Foreign Affairs:* Taher Al Masri. *Communication:* Dr Mahammad Adoub Al Zaben. *Supplies:* Ibrahim Ayoub. *Education:* Hekmat Al Saket. *Industry and Trade and Tourism:* Dr Jawad Alanani. *Transport:* Taher Hekmat. *Finance:* Dr Hanna Owdeh. *Information:* Lyla Sharaf. *Municipal and Rural Affairs:* Hamadallah Al Nabulsi. *Awqaf and Religious Affairs:* Ebed Khala Dawoudeyeh. *Agriculture:* Mohammed Basheer. *Labour:* Dr Tayseer Abdel Jaber. *Occupied Territories Affairs:* Shawkat Mahmoud. *Health:* Dr Kamal Alajlouni. *Public Works:* Raef Najm. *Culture, Youth and Antiquities:* Dr Abdellah Awaydat. *Social Development:* Abdelsalam Kenaan.

National flag: Three horizontal stripes of black, white, green, with a red triangle based on the hoist, bearing a white 7-pointed star.

The official language of the country is Arabic.

DEFENCE

Army. The Army is organized in 5 armoured, 2 infantry and 6 mechanized brigades, 1 independant Royal Guards brigade and 16 artillery battalions. In addition there are 3 special forces battalions. Total strength (1984) 65,000 men.

Navy. The Coastal Guard or Jordan Sea Force has 14 patrol launches and 1 support craft based at Aqaba. Personnel (1984) totalled 300 officers and ratings.

Air Force. The Air Force has 2 interceptor and 3 ground attack squadrons equipped respectively with Mirage F1 and F-5E Tiger II fighters, and 2-seat F-5Fs, plus an OCU equipped with F-5A fighters and 2-seat F-5Bs. There are 6 C-130B/H Hercules and 3 CASA Aviocar turboprop transports, S-76, Alouette III and Hughes 500D helicopters, piston-engined Bulldog and AS 202 Bravo basic trainers and T-37B jet trainers. Aircraft on order include 24 AH-1S HueyCobra anti-tank helicopters for 1985 delivery. Hawk surface-to-air missiles equip 14 batteries. Strength is about 7,500 officers and men.

INTERNATIONAL RELATIONS

Membership. Jordan is a member of the UN and the Arab League.

ECONOMY

Planning. A 5-year plan (1981–85) aims at achieving a growth rate of 10·4% per annum.

Budget. The budget estimates for the year 1981 provide for revenue of JD.656,900,000 and expenditure of JD.654,100,000.

Currency. The Jordan *dinar,* divided into 1,000 *fils.* The following bank-notes and coins are in circulation: 10, 5 dinars, 1 dinar, 500 fils (notes), 250, 100, 50, 25, 20 fils (cupronickel), 10, 5, 1 fils (bronze). In March 1984, £1 = JD.0·547; US$ = JD.0·366.

Banking. The Central Bank of Jordan started operations on 1 Oct. 1964, taking over the sterling assets and the commitments of the Jordan Currency Board.

NATURAL RESOURCES

Oil. Oil was discovered in 1982 at Azraq, 70 km east of Amman.

Minerals. Phosphates production in 1981 was 4,243,000 tons. Potash is found in the Dead Sea. Reserves, over 800m. tonnes. A potash plant is being built on the southeast shore to extract compounds by solar evaporation. Cement production (1982), 964,000 tons.

Agriculture. The country east of the Hejaz Railway line is largely desert; northwestern Jordan is potentially of agricultural value and an integrated Jordan Valley project began in 1973; 21,000 hectares had been irrigated by 1980. The main crops are tomatoes and other vegetables, fruit, wheat.

Production in 1981 included (in tonnes): Tomatoes, 204,500; citrus fruit, 53,800; wheat, 90,000.

Livestock (1982): 1m. sheep; 500,000 goats; 39,000 cattle; 14,000 camels.

INDUSTRY AND TRADE

Industry. The most important activity is processing potash and other minerals. There is a large chemical fertilizer plant at Aqaba, an oil refinery at Zarka and a cement plant at Fuhers. Production (1981): Iron, 134,000 tons; textiles, 1·3m. yards; cigarettes, 4,711m.

Commerce. Imports in 1981 were valued at JD.935,250,000 and exports and re-exports at JD.269,740,000.

Total trade between Jordan and UK (British Department of Trade returns, in £1,000 sterling):

	1979	1980	1981	1982	1983
Imports to UK	7,855	8,152	10,300	17,487	28,680
Exports and re-exports from UK	86,894	100,318	203,651	295,274	262,503

Tourism. In 1981, 2·22m. foreigners visited Jordan.

COMMUNICATIONS

Roads. Asphalt roads connect Amman with all the chief towns in the country. Unmetalled roads have been constructed, making motor traffic possible from Amman to most other areas. The road from Amman to Ma'an and Aqaba (394 km) has branches to Karak, Tafileh, Shobak and Wadi Musa (Petra). The town of Jerash is joined by a good road to Amman. The normal asphalted route from Amman to Deraa (in Syria) and thence to Damascus is through Jerash. The oasis of Azraq may be reached by motor car from Mafraq, Zarka or Amman. Total length of public highways, 4,095 km. Motor vehicles in 1980 included 73,078 private passenger cars, 11,207 taxis, 1,415 buses, 29,517 goods vehicles, 4,888 motor cycles.

Railways. The 1,050 mm gauge Hejaz Jordan and Aqaba Railway runs from the Syrian border at Nassib to Ma'an and Naqb Ishtar and Aqaba Port (total, 618 km). In 1981 the railways carried 57,753 passengers and 10,000 tons of freight.

Aviation. The Queen Alia International airport, at Zizya, 30 km south of Amman was inaugurated in 1983. There are other international airports at Amman and Aqaba.

Shipping (1980). The port of Aqaba handled 6,598,591 tons of cargo.

Post. In 1982 there were 791 post offices and 60,533 telephones in 1980.

Cinemas (1975). Cinemas numbered 40 with a total attendance of 4,341,900.

Newspapers (1980). There were 4 daily (including 1 in English) and 5 weekly papers.

RELIGION, EDUCATION AND WELFARE

Religion. About 80% of the population are Sunni Moslems.

Education (1980, East Bank only). There were 189 pre-primary schools with 639 teachers and 17,160 pupils; 1,095 primary schools with 13,898 teachers and 448,411 pupils; 341 secondary schools had 3,648 teachers and 80,173 pupils and 16 teacher-training institutes had 362 teachers and 8,621 students. The University of Jordan, inaugurated on 15 Dec. 1962 had in 1980-81, 10,767 students and 431 teachers. The Yarmouk University (Irbid) was inaugurated in 1976 with (1980-81) 5,677 students and 225 teachers.

Health (1980). There were 1,715 physicians, 351 dentists and 35 hospitals with 2,743 beds.

DIPLOMATIC REPRESENTATIVES

Of Jordan in Great Britain (6 Upper Phillimore Gdns., London, W8 7HB)
Ambassador: (Vacant).

Of Great Britain in Jordan (Third Circle, Jebel Amman)
Ambassador: A. B. Urwick, CMG.

Of Jordan in the USA (2319 Wyoming Ave., NW, Washington, D.C., 20008)
Ambassador: Ibrahim Izziddin.

Of the USA in Jordan (Jebel Amman, Amman)
Ambassador: Richard N. Viets.

Of Jordan to the United Nations
Ambassador: Abdullah Salah.

Books of Reference

The Department of Statistics, Ministry of National Economy, publishes a *Statistical Yearbook* (in Arabic and English), latest issue 1968, and a *Statistical Guide,* latest issue 1965.–*External Trade Statistics,* 1968.–*National Accounts and Input-Output Analysis, 1959–65,* 1967

The Constitution of the Hashemite Kingdom of Jordan. Amman, 1952

Glubb, J. B., *The Story of the Arab Legion.* London, 1948.–*A Soldier with the Arabs.* London, 1957

Gubser, P., *Jordan.* Boulder, 1982

Haas, J., *Husseins Königreich: Jordaniens Stellung in Nahen Osten.* Munich, 1975

Morris, J., *The Hashemite Kings.* London, 1959

Seton, C. R. W., *Legislation of Transjordan, 1918-30.* London, 1931. [Continued by the Government of Jordan as an annual publication: *Jordan Legislation.* Amman, 1932 ff.]

Toni, Y. T., and Mousa, S., *Jordan: Land and People.* Amman, 1973

KENYA

Jamhuri ya Kenya

Capital: Nairobi
Population: 18·75m. (1983)
GNP per capita: US$420 (1980)

HISTORY. Until Kenya became independent on 12 Dec. 1963, it consisted of the colony and the protectorate. The protectorate comprised the mainland dominions of the Sultan of Zanzibar, viz., a coastal strip of territory 10 miles wide, to the northern branch of the Tana River; also Mau, Kipini and the Island of Lamu, and all adjacent islands between the rivers Umba and Tana. The Sultan on 8 Oct. 1963 ceded the coastal strip to Kenya with effect from 12 Dec. 1963.

The colony and protectorate, formerly known as the East African Protectorate were, on 1 April 1905, transferred from the Foreign Office to the Colonial Office and in Nov. 1906 the protectorate was placed under the control of a governor and C.-in-C. and (except the Sultan of Zanzibar's dominions) was annexed to the Crown as from 23 July 1920 under the name of the Colony of Kenya, thus becoming a Crown Colony.

The territories on the coast became the Kenya Protectorate.

A Treaty was signed (15 July 1924) with Italy under which Great Britain ceded to Italy the Juba River and a strip from 50 to 100 miles wide on the British side of the river. Cession took place on 29 June 1925. The northern boundary is defined by an agreement with Ethiopia in 1947.

AREA AND POPULATION. Kenya is bounded by Ethiopia in the north, Uganda in the west. Tanzania in the south and the Somali Republic and the Indian ocean in the east. The total area is 224,960 sq. miles (582,600 sq. km), of which 219,790 sq. miles is land area. In the 1969 census, the population was 10,942,708, of which 10,735,192 were Africans, 139,037 Asians, 40,593 Europeans, 27,886 Arabs. Census (1979) 15,322,000; estimate (1983) 18·75m.

On the coast the Arabs and Swahili predominate, farther inland the races speaking Bantu languages, and non-Bantu tribes, such as the Luo, the Nandi and Kipsigis, the Masai, the Somali and the Gallas. There are more than forty tribes.

Population of the provinces (1979): Rift Valley, 3·24m.; Eastern, 2,717,000; Nyanza, 2,634,000; Central, 2,348,000; Coast, 1,339,000; Western, 1,033,000; Nairobi district, 835,000; North-Eastern, 373,000.

Nairobi, the capital, was given a Royal charter on 30 March 1950; the 1969 census showed a population of 509,286, including 19,195 Europeans and 67,189 Asians. Estimate (1983) 827,800.

Population of the largest towns: Mombasa, 341,000; Kisumu, 153,000; Nakuru, 93,000; Machakos, 84,000; Meru, 70,000; Eldoret, 51,000; Thika, 41,000. A new town is being developed (in 1981) at Bura, which will be the centre of a production area using irrigated water from the Tana river.

CLIMATE. The climate is tropical, with wet and dry seasons, but considerable differences in altitude make for varied conditions between the hot, coastal lowlands and the plateau, where temperatures are very much cooler. Heaviest rains occur in April and May, but in some parts there is a second wet season in Nov. and Dec. Nairobi. Jan. 65°F (18·3°C), July 60°F (15·6°C). Annual rainfall 39″ (958 mm). Mombasa. Jan. 81°F (27·2°C), July 76°F (24·4°C). Annual rainfall 47″ (1,201 mm).

CONSTITUTION AND GOVERNMENT. A Constitution conferring internal self-government was brought into force on 1 June 1963, and full independence was achieved on 12 Dec. 1963. On 12 Dec. 1964 Kenya became a republic.

President of the Republic: Daniel Arap Moi (elected 1979, re-elected 1983).
Vice-President and Home Affairs: Mwai Kibaki.

Foreign Affairs: Robert Ouko.

The House of Representatives and the Senate were in Dec. 1966 amalgamated into one National Assembly consisting of 158 elected Members, 12 nominated members, together with the Speaker and the Attorney-General.

On 10 Nov. 1964 Kenya became a one-party state of the Kenya African National Union (KANU) when the voluntary dissolution of the Kenya African Democratic Union (KADU) was declared. Later a second party, the Kenya People's Union (KPU) was formed but on 30 Oct. 1969 was proscribed.

At general elections held in Sept. 1983 there were over 740 candidates for 153 seats. The turnout was low, ranging from 27% to 40%.

National flag: Three horizontal stripes of black, red, green, with the red edged in white; bearing in the centre an African shield in black and white with 2 crossed spears behind.

Administration. The country is divided into the Nairobi Area and 7 provinces over which there are local councils with administrative functions. The provinces are: Coast, Central, Eastern, Rift Valley, Western, Nyanza and North Eastern.

Swahili became the official language in 1974 but English is in general use.

DEFENCE

Army. The Army consists of 2 armoured, 1 armoured reconnaissance, 5 infantry, 2 artillery, 1 parachute, 1 independent air cavalry and 2 engineer battalions. Equipment includes 72 Vickers Mk 3 main battle tanks. 32 Hughes Defender helicopters, of which 15 are armed with TOW missiles. Total strength (1984) 13,000, and there is also a paramilitary police force of 1,800.

Navy. The Navy in 1984 consists of 7 British built patrol craft and 350 officers and ratings. The base is at Mombasa which has a dry dock with a capacity of 18,000 tons.

Air Force. An air force, formed 1 June 1964, was built up with RAF assistance and is under Army command. Equipment includes 11 F-5E/F-5F supersonic combat aircraft/trainers, 12 Hawk and 5 BAC 167 Strikemaster light jet attack/trainers, 6 twin-turboprop Buffaloes and 5 twin-engined Caribou for transport, air ambulance, anti-locust spraying and security duties, 6 Skyservant and 1 VIP Navajo Chieftain light twin, 14 Bulldog piston-engined primary trainers and Puma, Gazelle and Bell 47 helicopters. Personnel about 2,300 in 1983.

INTERNATIONAL RELATIONS

Membership. Kenya is a member of UN, the Commonwealth, OAU and is an ACP state of EEC.

ECONOMY

Budget. Ordinary revenue and expenditure (in K£1,000) for 1982–83: Revenue, 801,000; expenditure, 948,000.

Currency. The monetary unit is the Kenya *Shilling* divided into 100 *cents*; 20 shillings = K£1. In March 1984, £1 = 20·02 *Shilling*; US$1 = 13·60 *Shilling*.

Banking. Banks operating in Kenya: the National & Grindlays Bank International, Ltd; the Standard Bank, Ltd; Barclays Bank International; Algemene Bank Nederland NV; Bank of India, Ltd; Bank of Baroda, Ltd; Habib Bank (Overseas), Ltd; Commercial Bank of Africa, Ltd; Citibank; The Co-operative Bank of Kenya, Ltd; National Bank of Kenya, Ltd; The Kenya Commercial Bank; The Central Bank of Kenya.

NATURAL RESOURCES

Minerals. By mid-1970 over 75% of the area of Kenya had been geologically mapped. A special and 2 ordinary oil-prospecting licences were extant at the end of 1969, together covering 22,250 sq. miles. A joint UN–Kenya Government project is investigating the mineral resources in western Kenya and the exploration and development of mineral deposits is proceeding.

Mineral production in 1975 (provisional) was: Soda ash, 91,733 tons; gold (refined), 3,062 grammes; limestone and products, 197,414 tons; diatomite, 1,799 tons; salt, 5,553 tons. Other minerals comprised barytes, magnesite, felspar, sapphires, fluorspar ore, garnets, sand and raw soda.

Agriculture. As agriculture is possible from sea-level to altitudes of over 9,000 ft, tropical, sub-tropical and temperate crops can be grown and mixed farming can be advocated. Four-fifths of the country is range-land which produces mainly livestock products and wild game which constitutes the major attraction of the country's tourist industry.

The main areas of crop production are the Central, Rift Valley, Western and Nyanza Provinces and parts of Eastern and Coastal Provinces. Coffee, tea, sisal, pyrethrum, maize and wheat are crops of major importance in the Highlands, while coconuts, cashew nuts, cotton, sugar, sisal and maize are the principal crops grown at the lower altitudes. Principal crops with production for sale (in 1,000 tonnes, 1981): Wheat, 192; maize, 388·6; rice paddy (1980), 23; pyrethrum extract, 25; sugar-cane, 4,582; clean coffee, 90·4; sisal, 39; tea, 88.

Livestock (1982): Cattle, 12m.; sheep, 5·5m.; goats, 5·5m.; pigs, 90,000; poultry, 18m.

Forestry. The total area of gazetted forest reserves in Kenya amounts to 16,800 sq. km, of which the greater part is situated between 6,000 and 11,000 ft above sealevel, mostly on Mount Kenya, the Aberdares, Mount Elgon, Tinderet, Londiani, Mau watershed, Elgeyo and Charangani ranges. These forests may be divided into coniferous, broad-leaved or hardwood and bamboo forests. The upper parts of these forests are mainly bamboo, which occurs mostly between altitudes of 8,000 and 10,000 ft and occupies some 10% of the high-altitude forests. Production (1979): Coniferous, 97,000 cu. metres; broad leaved, 97,000.

INDUSTRY AND TRADE

Industry. Processing of agricultural products is one of the major industries, followed by beer brewing, cement, chemicals, footwear and textiles. Heavy industries include manufacture of tyres and assembly of trucks and pick-ups. Production, 1981 (in tonnes): Maize meal, 290,200; wheat flour, 216,600; cement, 1·28m.; cigarettes (no.), 4·8m.; mineral water (litres), 172m.

Commerce. Total domestic exports (1981) K£532·4m.; imports K£955·9m.

Chief imports (1980): Mineral fuels, K£325m.; machinery and transport equipment, K£274m. Chief exports (1980): Petroleum products, K£163m.; unroasted coffee, K£108m.; tea, K£58m.

Total trade between Kenya and UK (British Department of Trade returns, in £1,000 sterling):

	1978	1979	1980	1981	1982	1983
Imports to UK	114,604	115,624	105,443	95,238	104,312	128,464
Exports and re-exports from UK	195,679	170,278	259,103	173,663	153,858	111,249

Tourism. In 1981, about 352,300 overseas visitors travelled to Kenya spending K£90m.

COMMUNICATIONS

Roads. In 1976 there were 4,045 km of bitumen surfaced roads and 46,046 km of gravel-surfaced roads.

Railways. On 11 Feb. 1977 the independent Kenya Railways Corporation was formed following break-up of the East African Railways administration. The network totals 2,654 km of metre-gauge and extensive upgrading and re-equipment was in progress in 1984. In 1982, the railways carried 2·3m. passengers and 4·2m. tonnes of freight.

Aviation. Total number of passengers handled at the 4 airports (1976) was

2,188,000. Jomo Kenyatta Airport, Nairobi, handles nearly 30 international airlines as well as Kenya Airways.

Shipping. A national shipping service is planned (1981) to be based in Mombasa, the Kenyan main port at Kilindini on the Indian Ocean. The port handles cargo freight both for Kenya as well as for the neighbouring East African states. The Port Authority also runs a modern harbour college.

Post and Broadcasting. The Voice of Kenya operates 2 national services (Swahili–English) from Nairobi and regional services in Kisumu, Nairobi and Mombasa. The television service provides programmes mainly in English and Swahili. A new television station opened in Mombasa in 1970. Telephones (1982) 216,674.

Cinemas (1971). Cinemas numbered 32, with seating capacity of 18,800.

JUSTICE, RELIGION, EDUCATION AND WELFARE

Justice. The courts of justice comprise the High Court, established in 1921, with full jurisdiction both civil and criminal over all persons and all matters in Kenya, including Admiralty jurisdiction arising on the high seas and elsewhere, and Subordinate Courts. The High Court has its headquarters at Nairobi and consists of the Chief Justice and 11 puisne judges; it sits continuously at Nairobi, Mombasa, Nakuru and Kisumu; civil and criminal sessions are held regularly at Eldoret, Nyeri, Meru, Kitale, Kisii and Kericho.

The Subordinate Courts are presided over by Senior Resident, Resident or District Magistrates and are established in the main centres of all districts. They sit throughout the year. There are also Moslem Subordinate Courts established in areas where the local population is predominantly Moslem; they are presided over by Kadhis and exercise limited jurisdiction in matters governed by Moslem law.

Religion. The indigenous African background is largely influenced by belief in God in Judaic forms, but Christianity is making an important contribution to the life of the whole territory, not only through the educational and medical services of Christian missions, but by the growth of churches under African leadership, and by its impact on the thought and policy of the country. The Roman Catholic Church (about 4m. adherents) has been developed mainly by Irish, British, Dutch and Italian missionary bodies and is now organized in 12 dioceses under the archbishop of Nairobi.

The Protestant Churches (about 2·5m. adherents) were started mainly by British and American mission societies; most of them are now linked together by the National Christian Council of Kenya. The Church of the Province of Kenya, formerly the Anglican Church Province of East Africa, was inaugurated on 3 Aug. 1970; at the same time the first Archbishop of Kenya was enthroned. The East African Yearly Meeting of Friends (Religious Society of Friends) has 90,000 adherents.

The Arabs on the coast are Moslems, and Islam has spread among some of the African coastal tribes and the cities. The Asians are Hindus and Moslems, with the exception of the Goans, who are Roman Catholics.

Education. *Primary* (1982). 11,500 primary schools with 4·2m. pupils and 71,000 teachers.

Secondary (1982). There were 2,131 secondary schools with a total enrolment of 465,000 and 8,611 teachers.

Technical (1982). 17 technical colleges with 9,200 pupils and 343 teachers.

Teacher training (1982). 14,000 students were training as teachers in 20 colleges with 900 lecturers.

Higher Education. The University of Nairobi was inaugurated on 10 Dec. 1970 and is now wholly supported by Kenya Government, and provides courses in arts, science, education, agriculture, medicine, art, architecture, engineering, veterinary, law and domestic science. In 1982 there were 8,772 students and 900 lecturers at the University of Nairobi (including Kenyatta University College).

Health. In 1974 beds in hospitals (including mission hospitals) totalled 16,934. 603 health centres, including sub-centres and dispensaries, were in operation. Free medical service for all children and adult out-patients was launched in 1965.

DIPLOMATIC REPRESENTATIVES

Of Kenya in Great Britain (45 Portland Pl., London, W1N 4AS)
High Commissioner: Bethuel A. Kiplagat (accredited 31 July 1981).

Of Great Britain in Kenya (Bruce Hse., Standard St., Nairobi)
High Commissioner: Sir Leonard Allinson, KCVO, CMG.

Of Kenya in the USA (2249 R. St., NW, Washington, D.C., 20008)
Chargé d'Affaires: Gideon W. Uku.

Of the USA in Kenya (Moi/Haile Selassie Ave., Nairobi)
Ambassador: (Vacant).

Of Kenya to the United Nations
Ambassador: Wafula Wabuge.

Books of Reference

Kenya Economic Survey, 1981. Nairobi, 1982
Statistical Abstract. Government Printer, Nairobi, 1969
Standard English–Swahili Dictionary. Ed. Inter-territorial Language Committee of East Africa. 2 vols. London, 1939
Who's Who in Kenya 1982–1983. London, 1983
Arnold, G., *Kenyatta and the Politics of Kenya.* London, 1974.—*Modern Kenya.* London, 1982
Bienen, H., *Kenya: The Politics of Participation and Control.* Princeton Univ. Press, 1974
Bolton, K., *Harambee Country: A Guide to Kenya.* London, 1970
Collison, R. L., *Kenya.* [Bibliography] London and Santa Barbara, 1982
Harbeson, J. W., *Nation-Building in Kenya: The Role of Land Reform.* Northwestern Univ. Press, 1973
Hazlewood, A., *The Economy of Kenya: The Kenyatta Era.* OUP, 1980
Huxley, E., and Perham, M., *Race and Politics in Kenya.* Rev. ed. London, 1956
Langdon, S. W., *Multinational Corporations in the Political Economy of Kenya.* London, 1981
Mutalik-Desai, P., *Economic and Political Development in Kenya.* Bombay, 1979
Tomkinson, M., *Kenya: A Holiday Guide.* 5th ed. London and Hammamet, 1981

KIRIBATI

Capital: Tarawa
Population: 58,518 (1980)
GNP per capita: US$770 (1980)

HISTORY. The Gilbert and Ellice Islands were proclaimed a protectorate in 1892 and annexed (at the request of the native governments) as the Gilbert and Ellice Islands Colony on 10 Nov. 1915 (effective on 12 Jan. 1916). On 1 Oct. 1975 the former Ellice Islands severed its constitutional links with the Gilbert Islands and took a new name Tuvalu.

Internal self-government was obtained on 1 Nov. 1976 and independence achieved on 12 July 1979 as the Republic of Kiribati.

AREA AND POPULATION. Kiribati consists of 3 groups of coral atolls and one isolated volcanic island, spread over a large expanse of the Central Pacific with a total land area of 684 sq. km (264 sq. miles). It comprises Banaba or Ocean Island (5 sq. km), the 16 Gilbert Islands (295 sq. km), the 8 Phœnix Islands (55 sq. km), and 8 of the 11 Line Islands (329 sq.km), the other 3 Line Islands (Jarvis, Palmyra and Kingman Reef) being uninhabited dependencies of the US. Banaba, all 16 Gilbert Islands, and 3 atolls in the Line Islands (Teraina, Tabuaeran and Kiritimati—formerly Washington, Fanning and Christmas Islands respectively) are inhabited; their populations in 1980 were as follows:

Banaba (Ocean Is.)	300	Kuria	803	Arorae	1,527
Makin	1,419	Aranuki	850	Teraina	416
Butaritari	3,149	Nonouti	2,284	Tabuaeran	434
Marakei	2,335	Tabiteuea	4,157	Kiritimati	1,265
Abaiang	3,447	Beru	2,212	Aboard ships	255
Tarawa	22,148	Nikunau	1,829	In Nauru and	
Maiana	1,688	Onotoa	2,034	Overseas	2,299
Abemama	411	Tamana	1,349		
				Total	58,518

The remaining 13 atolls have no permanent population; the 8 Phœnix Islands comprise Birnie, Rawaki (formerly Phœnix), Enderbury, Kanton (or Abariringa), Manra (formerly Sydney), Orona (formerly Hull), McKean and Nikumaroro (formerly Gardner), while the others are Malden and Starbuck in the Central Line Islands and Caroline, Flint and Vostok in the Southern Line Islands. The population is almost entirely Micronesian.

CLIMATE. The Phœnix Islands and Banaba have a maritime equatorial climate, but the islands further north and south are tropical. Annual and daily ranges of temperature are small and mean annual rainfall ranges from 50″ (1,250 mm) near the equator to 120″ (3,000 mm) in the north.

CONSTITUTION AND GOVERNMENT. Under the independence Constitution the republic has a uni-cameral legislature, comprising 36 members elected from 20 constituencies for a 4-year term. The *Beretitenti* (President) is both Head of State and of Government.

In May 1983 the government was composed as follows:

President and Foreign Affairs: Ieremia Tabai, GCMG.
Vice-President, Home Affairs and Decentralization: Teatao Teannaki. *Trade, Industry and Labour:* Teewe Arobati. *Finance:* Boanareke Boanareke. *Health and Family Planning:* Baitika Toum. *Natural Resource Development:* Babera Kirata, OBE. *Education:* Baitika Toum. *Communications:* Taomati Iuta, OBE. *Minister for the Line and Phœnix Group of Islands:* Uera Rabaua. *Works and Energy:* Tiwau Awira. *Attorney-General:* Michael Takabwebwe.

Flag: Red, with blue and white wavy lines in base, and in the centre a gold rising sun and a flying frigate bird.

INTERNATIONAL RELATIONS

Membership. Kiribati is a member of the Commonwealth and is an ACP state of the EEC.

ECONOMY

Budget. Revenue for the calendar year 1980 amounted to $A13,099,320; principal items: customs duties, $A2·9m.; direct taxation, $A700,000; taxation on phosphate, $A6,642,000. Expenditure in 1975 amounted to $A30,405,012.

Currency. The currency in use is the Australian *dollar.*

AGRICULTURE. The land is basically coral reefs upon which coral sand has built up, and then been enriched by humus from rotting vegetation and flotsam which has drifted ashore. The principal tree is the coconut, which grows prolifically on all the islands except some of the Phœnix Islands. Other food-bearing trees are the pandanus palm and the breadfruit. As the amount of soil is negligible, the only vegetable which grows in any quantity is a coarse calladium (alocasia) with the local name 'babai', which is cultivated most laboriously in deep pits. Pigs and fowls are kept throughout the Colony, and there is an abundance of fish.

Copra production is mainly in the hands of the individual landowner, who collects the coconut products from the trees on his own land.

Livestock (1982): Pigs, 10,000; poultry, 163,000.

TRADE. The principal imports are rice, flour, cotton piece-goods, tobacco and manufactured articles such as bicycles. The value of imports for 1977 amounted to $A11,565,685; exports, $A18,211,996. Exports are almost exclusively copra. The British Phosphate Commissioners withdrew from Banaba in Dec. 1979 and the Cooperative Federation is responsible for the export of copra.

Total trade between Kiribati and UK (British Department of Trade returns, in £1,000 sterling):

	1981	1982	1983
Imports to UK	8	79	42
Exports and re-exports from UK	573	321	371

COMMUNICATIONS

Shipping. The main ports are at Banaba and at Betio (Tarawa). In 1977, 256 vessels were handled at Betio.

Aviation. Air Tungaru is the national carrier. It operates services from Tarawa to the other 15 outer Islands in the Gilbertese Group, services varying between one and four flights each week. It also operates a weekly service to Christmas Island, in the Line Islands, which continues to Honolulu. A weekly service operates externally to Apia, Funafuti, Majuro, Nandi and Pago Pago. There are five flights per week to Nauru, while Air Nauru also has five flights from Nauru to Tarawa. There are air fields at Maiana and Christmas Island from which local services link to Tarawa.

Post and Broadcasting. There were 821 telephones in 1982. Radio Tarawa transmits daily in English and I-Kiribati. A telephone line to Australia was installed in 1981.

Cinemas. In 1974 there were 5 cinemas with a seating capacity of 2,000.

Newspapers. There was (1980) 1 weekly newspaper and 1 monthly.

JUSTICE, RELIGION, EDUCATION AND WELFARE

Justice. In 1978 Kiribati had a police force of 188 under the command of a Commissioner of Police. The Commissioner of Police is also responsible for prisons, immigration, fire service (both domestic and airport) and firearms licensing.

Religion. The majority of the population belong to the Roman Catholic or Protestant (Congregational) church; there are small numbers of Seventh-day Adventist and Baha'i.

Education (1979). The Government maintains a co-educational boarding school, the King George V and Elaine Bernacchi School at Tarawa, with (1977) 211 boys and 178 girls, 87 primary schools, with a total of 13,092 pupils, 1 government secondary school with 385 pupils, and 4 community high schools with 562 pupils attending the first year of a new rurally oriented 3-year post-primary course. The Government also maintains a teachers' training college with 100 students and a marine training school with 180 full-time students. The Tarawa Technical Institute at Betio offers a variety of part-time and evening technical and commercial courses to about 500 students each year in addition to providing full-time courses for 34 students. The Marine Training School, also at Betio, offers training for 150 merchant seamen every year. There are in addition 4 Mission secondary schools with a total enrolment of 213 boys and 230 girls.

In 1978, 120 islanders were in overseas countries for secondary and further education or training.

Welfare. Government maintains free medical and other services. There are few towns, and the people are almost without exception landed proprietors, thus eliminating child vagrancy and housing problems to a large extent, except in the Tarawa urban area. Destitution is almost unknown.

DIPLOMATIC REPRESENTATIVES

Of Kiribati to Great Britain and to the USA
High Commissioner: Atenroi Ba'teke, OBE (resides in Tarawa).

Of Great Britain in Kiribati (Tarawa)
High Commissioner: Charles Thompson.

Books of Reference

Kiribati, Aspects of History. Univ. of South Pacific, 1979
Bailey, E., *The Christmas Island Story.* London, 1977
Cowell, R., *Structure of Gilbertese.* Suva, 1950
Grimble, Sir Arthur, *A Pattern of Islands.* London, 1953.—*Return to the Islands.* London, 1957
Maude, H. E., *Of Islands and Men.* London, 1968.—*Evolution of the Gilbertese Boti.* Suva, 1977
Sabatier, E., *Astride the Equator.* Melbourne, 1978
Whincup, T., *Nareau's Nation.* London, 1979

KOREA

Han Kook

Capital: Seoul
Population: 39·3m. (1982)
GNP per capita: US$1,506 (1980)

HISTORY. Korea was united in a single kingdom under the Silla dynasty from 668. China, which claimed a vague suzerainty over Korea, recognized Korea's independence in 1895. Korea concluded trade agreements with the USA (1882), Great Britain, Germany (1883). After the Russo-Japanese war of 1904–5 Korea was virtually a Japanese protectorate until it was formally annexed by Japan on 29 Aug. 1910 thus ending the rule of the Yi dynasty which had begun in 1392.

Following the collapse of Japan in 1945, American and Russian forces entered Korea to enforce the surrender of the Japanese troops there, dividing the country for mutual military convenience into two portions separated by the 38th parallel of latitude. Negotiations between the Americans and Russians regarding the future of Korea broke down in May 1946.

On 25 June 1950 the North Korean forces crossed the 38th parallel and invaded South Korea. The same day, the Security Council of the United Nations asked all member states to render assistance to the Republic of Korea. When the UN forces had reached the Manchurian border Chinese troops entered the war on the side of the North Koreans on 26 Nov. 1950 and penetrated deep into the south. By the beginning of April 1951, however, the UN forces had regained the 38th parallel. On 23 June 1951 Y. A. Malik, President of the Security Council, suggested a cease-fire, and on 10 July representatives of Gen. Ridgway met representatives of the North Koreans and of the Chinese Volunteer Army. An agreement was signed on 27 July 1953.

For the contributions of member-nations of the United Nations to the war, *see* THE STATESMAN'S YEAR-BOOK, 1954, p. 1195, and 1956, p. 1180.

On 16 Aug. 1953 the USA and Korea signed a mutual defence pact and on 28 Nov. 1956 a treaty of friendship, commerce and navigation.

On 4 July 1972 it was announced in Seoul and Pyongyang (North Korea) that talks had taken place aimed at 'the peaceful unification of the fatherland as early as possible'. By late 1975 no progress had been made.

A North Korean–UN agreement of 6 Sept. 1976 established a joint security area 850 metres in diameter, divided into 2 equal parts to ensure the separation of the two sides.

AREA AND POPULATION. South Korea is bounded north by the de-militarized zone (separating it from North Korea), east by the Sea of Japan, south by the Korea Strait (separating it from Japan) and west by the Yellow Sea. After a transfer of some frontier districts by the United Nations command on 12 Aug. 1954, the area of South Korea is now 98,992 sq. km (38,221 sq. miles). The population (census, 1 Nov. 1980) was 37,449,000 (male, 18,764,000); estimate (1982), 39,331,000 (male, 19,847,000).

The areas (in sq. km) and 1980 census populations of the provinces are as follows:

Province	sq. km	1980	Province	sq. km	1980
Seoul (city)	613	8,367,000	Chollapuk	8,051	2,288,000
Kyonggi	10,958	4,935,000	Chollanam	12,060	3,779,000
Kangwon	16,712	1,792,000	Kyongsangpuk	19,798	4,962,000
Chungchongpuk	7,437	1,424,000	Kyongsangnam	11,948	3,323,000
Chungchongnam	8,699	2,956,000	Pusan (city)	373	3,160,000
Cheju	1,830	463,000			

The chief cities (populations in 1980) are:

Seoul	8,366,756	Kwangchu	727,627	Seongnam	376,447
Pusan	3,160,276	Taejon	651,642	Chonchu	366,997
Taegu	1,607,458	Ulsan	418,415	Suweon	310,757
Inchon	1,084,730	Masan	386,773		

CLIMATE. The extreme south has a humid warm temperate climate while the rest of the country experiences continental temperate conditions. Rainfall is concentrated in the period April to Sept. and ranges from 40″ (1,020 mm) to 60″ (1,520 mm). Seoul. Jan. 23°F (–5°C), July 77°F (25°C). Annual rainfall 50″ (1,250 mm).

CONSTITUTION AND GOVERNMENT. A new constitution was approved by national referendum on 22 Oct. 1980 and came into force on 27 Oct. It provides for a President with reduced executive powers, to be indirectly elected for a single 7-year term (by an electoral college of 5,271 directly-elected members), a State Council of ministers whom he appoints and leads, and a National Assembly (276 members) directly elected for 4 years (184 from 2-member constituencies and 92 by proportional representation).

The National Assembly elected on 25 March 1981 comprised 151 members of the Democratic Justice Party, 81 Democratic Korea Party, 25 Korean National Party, 8 from other parties and 11 independents.

President of the Republic: Gen. Chun Doo-Hwan (inaugurated March 1981).

The Cabinet at Jan. 1984 was composed as follows:

Prime Minister: Chin Jee Chung.

Deputy Prime Minister and Minister of Economic Planning: Shin Byung Hyun. *Foreign Affairs:* Lee Won Kyong. *Home Affairs:* Chod Young Bok. *Finance:* Kim Man Jae. *National Defence:* Yoon Sug Min. *Education:* Kwow Hee Hyuk. *Commerce and Industry:* Kum Jin Ho. *Energy and Resources:* Choi Dong Kyu. *Agriculture and Fisheries:* Park Chung Moon. *Justice:* Bae Myong In. *Construction:* Kim Sung Bae. *Transportation:* Sun Soo Ik. *Health and Social Affairs:* Kim Chum Rae. *Information and Culture:* Lee Jin Hie. *Labour:* Chung Han Joo. *National Unification:* Sohn Jae Sik. *Government Administration:* Park Chan Gung. *Communications:* Kim Sung Jin. *Science and Technology:* Lee Tae Sup. *Secondary Political Affairs:* Ahn Ung Mo.

National flag: White charged in the centre with the *yang-um* in red and blue and with 4 black *pal-kwar* trigrams.

Local government: South Korea is divided into 9 provinces (Do) and 4 cities with provincial status (Seoul, Pusan, Taegu and Inchon); the provinces are sub-divided into 138 districts (Gun) and 46 cities (Si).

DEFENCE. Military service is compulsory for 30 months in the Army and Marines and 3 years in the Navy and Air Force.

Army. The Army is organized in 20 infantry divisions, 2 mechanized infantry divisions, 11 independent special forces brigades, 2 anti-aircraft artillery brigades, 2 surface-to-air missile brigades, 1 army aviation brigade and 2 surface-to-surface battalions. Equipment includes 1,200 M-47/-48 main battle tanks. Strength (1984) 540,000, with a Regular Army Reserve of 1·4m. and a Homeland Reserve Defence Force of 3·3m.

Navy. The Fleet comprises 1 indigenously built modern frigate, 11 aged (1943–46) *ex*-US destroyers, 7 equally old *ex*-US frigates (1 of destroyer-escort type and 6 former fast transports, *ex*-destroyer escorts), 9 fast missile patrol craft, 4 new corvettes, 6 fast attack craft, 10 patrol vessels, 22 coastal patrol boats, 8 coastal minesweepers, 1 minesweeping boat, 8 landing ships, 9 medium landing craft, 20 utility landing craft, 1 repair ship, 6 surveying vessels, 2 salvage ships, 4 supply ships, 6 oilers, 13 auxiliary ships, 35 service craft, and 2 tugs. Nearly all South Korea's naval vessels are *ex*-US ships.

It was reported that the first submarine built in South Korea entered service in 1983. Probably the first of a class of four or five, she displaces only 175 tons.

The South Korean Coastguard operates 30 vessels including rescue craft and tugs.

Personnel in 1984 totalled 27,000 in the Navy; plus 20,000 in the Marine Corps.

Air Force. With a 1983 strength of about 32,600 men, the Air Force is undergoing rapid expansion with US assistance. Its combat aircraft include about 55 F-4D/E Phantoms, 65 F-5A/B tactical fighters, more than 200 F-5E/F tactical fighters (being delivered from local production), 10 RF-5A reconnaissance fighters, 12 O-2A forward air control aircraft, 20 Tracker anti-submarine aircraft and 10 Hughes 500-D Defender ASW helicopters. There are also 6 C-130H turboprop transports, 15 C-123 piston-engined transports, 2 VIP HS 748s; UH-1D and Bell 212 helicopters, and T-41, T-28, T-33 and T-37C trainers. Aircraft on order include 36 F-16 Fighting Falcons for delivery from 1986.

ECONOMY

Planning. The fifth 5-year social and economic plan (1982–86) aims at an annual growth rate of 7–8%.

Budget. The 1983 budget balanced at 10,416,700m. won.

Currency. Notes are issued by the Bank of Korea in denominations of 10,000, 5,000 and 500 won and coin in denominations of 500, 100, 50, 10, 5 and 1 won. The exchange rate is determined daily by the Bank of Korea. In March 1984, 793 won = US$1; 1,179 won = £1 sterling.

Banking. State-run banks include the Bank of Korea, the Korean Development Bank, the Medium & Small Industry Bank, the Citizen's National Bank, the Korea Exchange Bank, the National Agricultural Co-operatives Federation, the Federation of Fisheries Co-operatives serving as banking and credit institutions for farmers and fishermen, the Korea Housing Bank, the Export and Import Bank of Korea.

There are 5 commercial banks: the Bank of Seoul & Trust Co. Ltd, the Cho Heung Bank Ltd, the Commercial Bank of Korea, the Korea First Bank, the Hanil Bank, Ltd, the Taegu Bank Ltd. The Bank of Korea is the central bank and the only note-issuing bank, the authorized purchaser of domestically produced gold.

In addition, there are non-bank financial institutions consisting of 19 insurance companies, the Land Bank of Korea, the Credit Guarantee Fund, 10 short-term financial companies, 211 mutual credit companies, and the Merchant Banking Corporation.

ENERGY AND NATURAL RESOURCES

Electricity. Electricity generated (1982) was 43,122m. kwh.

Minerals. In 1979, 1,779 mining companies employed 79,229 people. Mineral deposits are mostly small, with the exception of tungsten; the Sangdong mine is one of the world's largest deposits of tungsten. Korea's output, 1982, included (in 1,000 tonnes): Anthracite coal, 20,116; iron ore, 620; tungsten concentrate, 4,361 short tons; kaolin, 225 (1981); copper ore, 7·6 (1981); lead ore, 24; gold refined, 247 kg; silver refined, 76,623 kg.

Agriculture. The arable land in South Korea comprises 24·4m. acres, of which over 5·5m. acres are cultivated.

The chief crops are rice (1982: 6·8m. tonnes), barley, wheat, beans, grain of all kinds and tobacco.

Output of tobacco manufactures, a government monopoly, was 92,506 tonnes in 1982.

Raising of livestock has recently become a flourishing industry. In 1982 cattle numbered 1,526,000; pigs, 2,183,000; poultry, 46m.

Fisheries. Deep-sea fishing fleets increased from 5 ships (600 gross tons) in 1962 to 833 ships (316,000 gross tons) in 1975. In 1976, 849 Korean deep-sea fishing vessels were engaged based on 25 overseas fishing bases, 345 in the Atlantic, 143 in the Indian and 361 in the Pacific oceans. In 1981, there was a total of 80,500 boats (781,582 gross tons) and the fish catch (inland and marine) was 2,811,914 tonnes.

INDUSTRY AND TRADE

Industry. Manufacturing industry, which (Dec. 1982) employed 3·1m. persons, was concentrated primarily in the production of light consumer goods for domestic consumption and export. This is now shifting towards heavy and petro-chemical industries rapidly.

Output of principal products in 1982 (in tonnes): Cotton yarn, 271,862; Portland cement, 17·8m.; urea fertilizers, 780,000.

Trade Unions. Membership of trade unions at 31 Dec. 1977 was 954,682.

Commerce. In 1982 the total exports were equal to US$21,853m., while imports (including 'aid goods') were US$24,251m. USA provided 24·6% and Japan 21·9% of imports; USA received 28·6% of exports, Japan 15·5%.

Total trade between Korea and UK (British Department of Trade returns, in £1,000 sterling):

	1979	1980	1981	1982	1983
Imports to UK	269,706	244,583	325,650	321,691	440,354
Exports and re-exports from UK	145,319	101,103	158,811	167,752	168,942

Tourism. In 1982 there were 1,145,044 tourists. They spent the equivalent of US$502,318,000.

COMMUNICATIONS

Roads. In 1982 there were 50,336 km of roads. Motor vehicles totalled 1,057,279 including 263,936 trucks, 66,326 buses, 305,811 passenger cars.

Railways. In 1982, 3,121 km of railways existed, including 411 km electrified, and carried 444m. passengers and 47m. tonnes.

Shipping. In 1982, there were registered 90,520 vessels of 6,457,098 GRT, excluding state-owned fishing vessels and lease-purchased vessels.

Aviation. There are regular international services by Korean Air Lines, Japan Air Lines, Northwest Airlines, China Air Lines, Cathay Pacific Airways, Thai International, Singapore Airlines and Malaysian Airlines. In 1980, 3·56m. passengers and nearly 198·11m. tons of cargo were carried.

Post. Post offices total 2,130 (1982); telephones (all government-owned) were 4,268,270 in 1980; a direct distance dialling telephone system was completed in 1976.

Cinemas. In 1982 there were 404 with a seating capacity of 300,000.

Newspapers (1982). There were 25 daily papers, including 6 national dailies and 2 in English appearing in Seoul.

RELIGION, EDUCATION AND WELFARE

Religion. Basically the religions of Korea have been Animism, Buddhism (introduced A.D. 372) and Confucianism, which was the official faith from 1392 to 1910. Catholic converts from China introduced Christianity in the 18th century, but the ban on Roman Catholics was not lifted until 1882. Christian population in 1981 was 9,076,788 (1,439,778 Catholics, 7,637,010 Protestants).

Education. In 1982 Korea had 5,465,248 pupils enrolled in 6,501 elementary schools, 2,603,433 pupils in 2,213 middle schools and 1,922,221 pupils in 1,436 high schools (including 626 vocational schools).

For higher education, 947,334 students who attended 424 universities, colleges and junior colleges. There are 121 graduate schools granting master's degrees in 2 years and doctor's degrees in 4 years, where 33,939 students attended in 1980. An Open University was inaugurated in March 1982.

The Korean language belongs to the Ural–Altaic group, is polysyllabic, agglutinative and highly developed syntactically. The modern Korean alphabet of 10 vowels and 14 consonants forms a script known as Hangul.

Health. In Dec. 1982 there were 28,365 physicians (including herb doctors), 4,266 dentists, 4,222 midwives (1980), 101,445 nurses (including assistant nurses, 1980), 4,712 technicians (1980) and 27,000 pharmacists. There were 11,181 hospitals and clinics in 1980.

DIPLOMATIC REPRESENTATIVES

Of Korea in Great Britain (4 Palace Gate, London, W8 5NF)
Ambassador: Dr Young Hoon Kang (accredited 25 Feb. 1981).

Of Great Britain in Korea (4 Chung-Dong, Chung-Ku, Seoul)
Ambassador and Consul-General: J. N. T. Spreckley, CMG.

Of Korea in the USA (2370 Massachusetts Ave., NW, Washington, D.C., 20008)
Ambassador: Byong Hion Lew.

Of the USA in Korea (Sejong-Ro, Seoul)
Ambassador: Richard L. Walker.

Books of Reference

A Handbook of Korea. 4th ed. Seoul, 1982
Economic Planning Board. *Guide to Investment in Korea.* Seoul, 1980
Korea Annual 1983. 20th ed. Seoul, 1983
Korea Statistical Year Book. Seoul, 1981
Guide to Geographical Names in Korea (Chosen). United States Board of Geographical Names. Washington, 1945
Major Economic Indicators, 1979–80. Seoul, 1980
Monthly Statistics of Korea. Seoul, 1980
Lew, H. J., *New Life Korean–English, English–Korean Dictionary.* 2 vols. Seoul, 1947–50
Martin, S. F. (ed.), *A Korean–English Dictionary.* Yale Univ. Press, 1968
Srivastava, M.P., *The Korean Conflict: Search for Unification.* New Delhi, 1982
Wright, E. R., *Korean Politics in Transition.* Univ. of Washington Press, 1976

NORTH KOREA

Chosun Minchu-chui Inmin Konghwa-guk

Capital: Pyongyang
Population: 18·49m. (1983)
GNP per capita: US$736 (1982)

HISTORY. In northern Korea the Russians, arriving on 8 Aug. 1945, one month ahead of the Americans, established a Communist-led 'Provisional Government'. The newly created Korean Communist Party merged in 1946 with the New National Party into the Korean Workers' Party. In July 1946 the KWP, with the remaining pro-Communist groups and non-party people, formed the United Democratic Patriotic Front. On 25 Aug. 1948 the Communists organized elections for a Supreme People's Assembly, both in Soviet-occupied North Korea (212 deputies) and in US-occupied South Korea (360 deputies, of whom a certain number went to the North and took their seats). A People's Democratic Republic was proclaimed on 9 Sept. 1948. In 1973 North Korea was admitted to WHO, and granted observer status at the UN. Talks between North and South Korea on reunification began in 1980, but were broken off by the North. In 1981 North Korea announced a new reunification plan, but plans put forward by South Korea were rejected.

AREA AND POPULATION. North Korea is bounded north by China, east by the sea of Japan, west by the Yellow Sea and south by South Korea, from which it is separated by a demilitarized zone of 1,262 sq km. Its area is 122,098 sq. km. Population estimate in 1983, 18·49m. Rate of population increase, 2·2% per annum. Death rate, 1979: 4·4 per mille. Marriage is discouraged before the age of 32 for men and 29 for women. Expectation of life in 1982 was 74 years. The capital is Pyongyang, with 1·28m. inhabitants in 1981. Other large towns (with 1972 population): Hamhung (420,000); Chongjin (265,000); Kimchaek (formerly Songjin) (265,000).

The country is divided into 13 administrative units: 4 cities (Pyongyang, Chongjin, Hamhung and Kaesong) and 9 provinces (capitals in brackets): South Pyongan (Nampo), North Pyongan (Sinuiji), Jagang (Kanggye), South Hwanghai (Haeju), North Hwanghai (Sariwon), North Kangwon (Wonsan), South Hamgyong (Hamheung), North Hamgyong (Chongjin), Yanggang (Hyesan).

CLIMATE. There is a warm temperate climate, though winters can be very cold in the north. Rainfall is concentrated in the summer months. Pyongyang. Jan. 18°F (−7·8°C), July 75°F (23·9°C). Annual rainfall 37″ (916 mm).

CONSTITUTION AND GOVERNMENT. The political structure is based upon the Constitution of 27 Dec. 1972. The Constitution provides for a Supreme People's Assembly elected every 4 years by universal suffrage. Citizens of 17 years and over can vote and be elected. Elections were held in 1948, 1957, 1962, 1972, 1977 and 1 March 1982. At the latter it was claimed that 100% of the electorate voted for the candidates presented. There are 615 deputies. The government consists of the Administration Council directed by the Central People's Committee (*Secretary,* Kim I Hun).

In practice the country is ruled by the Korean Workers' (*i.e.,* Communist) Party which elects a Central Committee which in turn appoints a Politburo, the first 4 members of which constitute its Standing Committee. In March 1984 this was composed of: Marshal Kim Il Sung, *(General Secretary of the Party, President of the Republic, Chairman of the Central People's Committee, Supreme Commander of the Armed Forces)*; Kim Il *(Vice-President of the Republic)*; O Jin U *(Defence Minister)*; Kim Jong Il (Kim Il Sung's son and designated successor); Li Jong Ok *(Vice-President of the Republic)*; Pak Sung Chul *(Vice-President of the Republic)*;

768

Rim Chun Chu *(Vice-President of the Republic)*; So Chol; O Baek Ryong; Kim Jung Rin; Kim Yong Nam *(Deputy Prime Minister, Foreign Minister)*; Chon Mun Sop; Kim Hwan; Yon Hyong Muk; O Guk Ryol; Kang Song San *(Prime Minister)*; Paek Hak Rim; Choe Yong Rim; So Yun Sok, Ho Dam.

Ministers not full members of the Politburo include Ho Dam *(Deputy Prime Minister, Foreign Minister)*; Kye Ung Tae *(Deputy Prime Minister)*; Yun Gi Jong *(Finance)*; Choe Jong Gun *(Trade)*; Chong Song Nam *(Foreign Economic Affairs)*; Hong Song Ryong *(Deputy Prime Minister, Chairman, State Planning Commission)*; Lee Jin Su *(Public Security)*.

In 1981 the Party had some 2m. members.

There are also the puppet religious Chongu and Korean Social Democratic Parties and various organizations combined in a Fatherland Front.

National flag: Blue, red and blue horizontal stripes separated by narrow white bands. The red stripe bears a white circle within which is a red 5-pointed star.

National anthem: 'A chi mun bin na ra i gang san' (Shine bright, o dawn, on this land so fair'). Words by Pak Se Yong; music by Kim Won Gyun.

Local government is administered by People's Assemblies at city (or province), county (or district) and *ri* (town, workers' or rural commune) level. The latest elections were on 6 March 1983. There are 24,562 local deputies.

DEFENCE. Military service is compulsory at the age of 17 for periods of 5 years in the Army and Navy and 3–4 years in the Air Force.

Army. The Army is organized in 2 armoured, 3 motorized infantry and 35 infantry divisions; 5 armoured, 4 infantry and 26 special forces brigades; 2 independent tank, 5 independent infantry and 5 river-crossing regiments; 250 artillery, 82 multiple-rocket-launcher and 5 surface-to-surface missile battalions. Equipment includes 2,500 T-34/-55/-62 and 175 Type-59 main battle tanks. Strength (1984) 784,500, with 230,000 reserves. There is also a paramilitary militia of some 1·8m. men and a ranger commando force of 100,000.

Navy. The Navy comprises 19 diesel-powered patrol submarines (15 *ex*-Chinese and 4 *ex*-Soviet), 4 small frigates, 26 fast missile boats, 155 fast torpedo boats, 155 fast gunboats, 40 patrol vessels, 30 coastal patrol craft, 20 light gunboats, 10 utility landing craft, 100 minor landing craft, 30 trawlers and auxiliaries and 100 service craft. Up to 5 small submarines are reported as built locally with a dozen X-craft in commission. Personnel in 1984 totalled 33,500 officers and men, plus 40,000 reservists.

Air Force. The Air Force has a total of about 930 aircraft and 51,000 personnel. Equipment is believed to include about 160 supersonic MiG-21 interceptors, more than 120 F-6s (Chinese-built MiG-19s), 250 MiG-17s for ground attack and reconnaissance, 20 Su-7 fighter-bombers, 70 Il-28 twin-jet light bombers, and a variety of transport and training aircraft and helicopters.

ECONOMY

Planning. For previous plans *see* THE STATESMAN'S YEAR-BOOK, 1983–84. A 7-year plan for 1978–84 gives priority to the fuel and mining industries, foreign trade development and transport, and expects an annual industrial growth rate of 12·1%.

Budget (in 1m. won) for calendar years:

	1979	1980	1981	1982	1983	1984
Revenue	17,478	19,139	20,479	22,680	24,384	26,237
Expenditure	16,972	18,837	20,479	22,204	24,018	26,237

In 1983, 3,602m. won were spent on defence (3,242m. in 1982). South Korean estimates of 1983 expenditure (in 1m. won): economy, 15,196; social welfare, 4,919; administration. 618. Personal taxation was abolished in 1974.

Currency. The monetary unit is the *won*, divided into 100 *jun*. In March 1984, US$1 = 0·94 *won*; £1 = 1·66 *won*.

Weights and Measures. While the metric system is in force traditional measures are in frequent use. The *jungbo* = 1 hectare; the *ri* = 3,927 metres.

ENERGY AND NATURAL RESOURCES

Oil. An oil pipeline from China came on stream in 1976. Crude oil refining capacity was 80,000 barrels a year in 1981.

Electricity. There are thermal power stations at Pyongyang, Unggi and Chongchongang. There are hydro-electric plants at Kanggye, Unbong and Sodusu, and another is under construction at Taedonggang. Output in 1981, was 22,150m. kwh. Installed capacity was 5·1m. kw in 1981. Hydroelectric potential exceeds 8m. kw.

Minerals. North Korea is rich in minerals (coal, iron, lead, zinc, copper, tungsten, nickel, manganese and graphite) and has important metallurgical works. Oilwells went into production in 1957. Coalmines are being enlarged and modernized. There are large opencast workings at Yonghung. 50m. tonnes of coal were mined in 1975. 7·4m. tonnes of iron ore and 12,000 tonnes of copper ore were extracted in 1969.

Agriculture. In 1981 there were 2·1m. hectares of arable land, including 635,000 hectares of paddy fields. In 1982, 38% of the population made a living from agriculture.

Collectivization took place between 1954 and 1958, when there were 13,309 'co-operatives' averaging 130 *jungbo*. In 1958 these were merged into 3,843 larger units *(ri)*, averaging 500 *jungbo*. 90% of the cultivated land is farmed by co-operatives, of which there were 3,700 in 1970. A law of 1977 proclaims that there is no private property in land; land belongs either to the State or to co-operatives, and it is intended gradually to transform the latter into the former. Livestock farming is mainly carried on by large state farms. There were 200 state farms in 1970.

There were 37,600 km of irrigation canals in 1976. The 6-year plan (1971–76) extended irrigation so as to make possible 2 rice harvests a year. In 1981 there were 114,000 tractors (15 h.p. units). The technical revolution in agriculture (nearly 95% of ploughing, etc., is mechanized) considerably increased the yield of grain (sown on 2·3m. *jungbo* of land); this was 9·5m. tonnes in 1982 (mainly rice). 268,000 tonnes of potatoes were produced in 1981.

Livestock (FAO estimates for 1982): 970,000 cattle, 2·3m. pigs.

Forestry. Between 1961 and 1970, 800,000 hectares were afforested, 500,000 hectares of oil-bearing trees are scheduled for planting.

Fishery. The annual catch is about 1·6m. tonnes. There is a fishing fleet of about 3,400 modern motor and sailing fishing craft, equipped with factory and refrigerator ships.

INDUSTRY AND TRADE

Industry. Industries were intensively developed by the Japanese, notably cotton spinning, hydro-electric power, cotton, silk and rayon weaving, and chemical fertilizers. Production (in tonnes) in 1981: Pig-iron, 3,540; copper, 60; cement, 810; textiles, 600m. metres, and in 1975: Chemical fertilizers, 3m.; steel, 4m. Industrial workers make up some 40% of the total work force. 10 ships were built between 1978 and 1982. There is a steel complex at Kangson with an annual productive capacity of 4m. tonnes.

Commerce. Exports in 1981: US$1,260m.; imports, US$1,610m. 51·5% of trade was with Communist countries (85% in 1971). In 1981 manufactured goods formed 59% of exports. In 1978 North Korea's indebtedness was estimated at US$2,000m. An agreement regulating the repayment of North Korea's US$390m. debt to Japan over 10 years was signed in Sept. 1979. The chief exports are metal ores and products, the chief imports machinery and petroleum products.

Exports to the USSR in 1980 (and 1981) were worth 284·2m. (250·3m.) roubles; imports from the USSR, 287·9m. (278·9m.) roubles.

Total trade between North Korea and UK (British Department of Trade returns, in £1,000 sterling):

	1978	1979	1980	1981	1982	1983
Imports to UK	1,494	961	391	701	235	362
Exports and re-exports from UK	851	808	981	727	3,857	2,527

COMMUNICATIONS

Roads. There were 20,800 km of road in 1981, including 240 km of motorways.

Railways. Extensive railway construction was carried out under the Japanese occupation. Because these lines served strategic purposes, however, and because of the separation of North and South Korea, not all of them were suitable for inclusion in the present railway network. The two trunk-lines Pyongyang–Sinuiji and Pyongyang–Myongchon are both electrified, and the Pyongyang–Sariwon trunk is in course of electrification. The 'Wonra' line runs from Wonsan to Rajin and is electrified from Myongchon to Rajin. The Namdokchon–Toknam line was opened in 1983. Lines are under construction from Pukchong to Toksong, from Palwon to Kujang and Kanggye *via* Hyesan to Musan. The Hyesan–Samsok section of the latter opened to traffic in 1971. In 1981 there were 4,380 km of track, of which 2,706 km were electrified. In 1980, 87% of trains were hauled by electricity and 30·6m. tonnes were transported in 1969. A weekly service from Pyongyang to Beijing opened in 1983.

Aviation. There are weekly flights to Moscow and Peking. Domestic lines: Pyongyang–Hamhung–Chongjin.

Shipping. The leading ports are Chongjin and Hungnam (near Hamhung). Nampo, the port of Pyongyang, has been dredged and expanded. Pyongyang is connected to Nampo by railway and river. In 1983 the ocean-going merchant fleet numbered 56 vessels totalling 651,180 tonnes.

The biggest navigable river is the Yalu, 698 km up to the Hyesan district.

Broadcasting. In 1982 there were some 200,000 television receivers. The Pyongyang central broadcasting station was rebuilt about 1955.

Newspapers. The party newspaper is *Nodong* (or *Rodong*) *Sinmun* (Labour Party News). Circulation about 1m.

JUSTICE, RELIGION, EDUCATION AND WELFARE

Justice. The judiciary consists of the Supreme Court, whose judges are elected by the Assembly for 3 years; provincial courts; and city or county people's courts. The procurator-general, appointed by the Assembly, has supervisory powers over the judiciary and the administration; the Supreme Court controls the judicial administration.

Religion. According to the 1972 Constitution 'The people shall enjoy the freedom of religion as well as the freedom of anti-religious propaganda'. There are 3 religious organizations: The Buddhist League, the Chondoist Society and the Christians' League.

Education. In 1975–76 the 10-year system of free compulsory universal technical education was extended to 11 years (1 pre-school year, 4 years primary education starting at the age of 6, followed by 6 years secondary).

In 1970–71, 9,260 schools of all grades were attended by 3·2m. pupils, including 214,000 students in institutes of higher education, two-thirds of whom were studying technical and engineering subjects. There were some 100,000 teachers. In 1975–76 there were 5–6m. children in the 11-year system and nearly 1m. students in higher education. In 1980 there were 170 institutes of higher education, including 3 universities—Kim Il Sung University (founded 1946), Kim Chaek Technical University, Pyongyang Medical School—and an Academy of Sciences (founded 1952).

In 1977–78 Kim Il Sung University had some 17,000 students.

Health. Medical treatment is free. In 1982 there were 24 doctors and 130 hospital beds per 10,000 population.

Books of Reference

An, T. S., *North Korea in Transition.* Westport, 1983

Baik Bong, *Kim Il Sung: Biography.* 3 vols. New York, 1969–70

Brun, E., and Hersh, J., *Socialist Korea: A Case Study in the Strategy of Economic Development.* New York, 1976

Chung, C.-S., (ed.), *North Korean Communism: A Comparative Analysis.* Seoul, 1980

Kim Han Gil, *Modern History of Korea.* Pyongyang, 1979

Kim Il Sung, *Works.* Pyongyang, 1980–83

Kim, Y. S., (ed.), *The Economy of the Korean Democratic People's Republic, 1945–1977.* Kiel, 1979

Lee, C.-S., *The Korean Workers' Party: A Short History.* Stanford, 1978

McCormack, G., and Selden, M. (eds.), *Korea North and South: The Deepening Crisis.* New York, 1978

Park, J. K., and Kim, J.-G., *The Politics of North Korea.* Boulder, 1979

Scalapino, R. A., and Lee, C.-S., *Communism in Korea. Part I: The Movement. Part II: The Society.* Univ. of Calif. Press, 1972

Yang, S. C., *Korea and Two Regimes: Kim Il Sung and Park Chung Hee.* Cambridge, Mass., 1981

KUWAIT

Dowlat al Kuwait

Capital: Kuwait
Population: 1·47m. (1981)
GNP per capita: US$22,840 (1980)

HISTORY. The ruling dynasty was founded by Shaikh Sabah al-Owel, who ruled from 1756 to 1772. In 1899 the then ruler Shaikh Mubarak concluded a treaty with Great Britain wherein, in return for the assurance of British protection, he undertook not to alienate any of his territory without the agreement of Her Majesty's Government. In 1914 the British Government recognized Kuwait as an independent government under British protection. On 19 June 1961 an agreement reaffirmed the independence and sovereignty of Kuwait and recognized the Government of Kuwait's responsibility for the conduct of internal and external affairs; the agreement of 1899 was terminated and Her Majesty's Government expressed their readiness to assist the Government of Kuwait should they request such assistance.

AREA AND POPULATION. The independent and sovereign State of Kuwait is situated on the north-western coast of the Arabian Gulf. Area, about 7,000 sq. miles (17,818 sq. km); the total population at the census of 1981 was 1,466,431, of which about 59% were non-Kuwaitis.

The country is divided into 3 governorates, Kuwait (the capital, 80,405 population 1970 (1981, 276,356); metropolitan area, 217,749 (141,256)), Ahmadi and Hawali (106,542) (576,589).

The Neutral Zone (3,560 sq. miles, 5,700 sq. km), jointly owned and administered by Kuwait and Saudi Arabia from 1922 to 1966, was partitioned between the two countries in May 1966, but the exploitation of the oil and other natural resources will continue to be shared.

CLIMATE. Kuwait has a dry, desert climate which is cool in winter but very hot and humid in summer. Rainfall is extremely light. Kuwait. Jan. 56°F (13·5°C), July 99°F (36·6°C). Annual rainfall 5″ (125 mm).

RULER. HH Shaikh Jabir al-Ahmad al-Jabir al-Sabah the 13th Amir of Kuwait, succeeded on 31 Dec. 1977.

CONSTITUTION AND GOVERNMENT. Elections for a National Assembly of 50 members were held on 27 Jan. 1975 but in Aug. 1976 the Amir dissolved the Assembly and at the same time parts of the Constitution were suspended. Elections were held on 24 Feb. 1981 for the National Assembly.

The official language is Arabic; English is used as the second language.

The Cabinet in Nov. 1983 was composed as follows:

Prime Minister: Shaikh Saad al-Abdullah al-Salem al-Sabah.
Deputy Prime Minister, Foreign Affairs and Information: Shaikh Sabah al-Ahmad al-Jaber al-Sabah. *Interior:* Shaikh Nawwaf al-Ahmad al-Jaber al-Sabah. *Defence:* Shaikh Salem al-Sabah al-Salem al-Sabah. *Oil, Finance and Planning:* Shaikh Ali al-Khalifah al-Sabah. *Public Health:* Abdel-Rahman Abdullah al-Awadi. *Social Affairs, Labour and Housing:* Hamad Isa al-Rajib. *Public Works:* Abdullah al-Rashid. *Electricity and Water:* Khalaf Ahmad al-Khalaf. *Justice, Legal Affairs and Administrative Affairs:* Shaikh Salman al-Duaij al-Sabah. *Education:* Yacoub Yousef al-Ghunaim. *Commerce and Industry:* Jassem al-Marzouk. *Communications:* Isa al-Mazidi. *Awqaf and Islamic Affairs:* Ahmad Saad al-Jasser. *Minister of State (Cabinet Affairs):* Abdel-Aziz Hussain.

Flag: Three horizontal stripes of green, white, red, with a black trapezium based on the hoist.

DEFENCE. Military service is compulsory for 18 months.

Army. Kuwait maintains a small, well-equipped and mobile army of 1 armoured and 2 mechanized infantry brigades and 1 surface-to-surface missile battalion. Equipment includes 70 Vickers Mk I, 10 Centurion and 160 Chieftain main battle tanks. Strength (1984) about 10,000 men.

Air Force. From a small initial combat force the Air Force has grown rapidly. It has 1 squadron with 14 Mirage F1-C fighters and 2 Mirage F1-B 2-seat trainers; and 2 squadrons with 31 A-4KU/TA-4KU Skyhawk attack aircraft; 24 more Mirage F1s have been ordered. Other equipment includes 2 DC-9 jet transports, 1 L-100-20 and 4 L-100-30 Hercules turboprop transports, 9 BAC 167 Strikemaster armed jet trainers (to be replaced with 12 Hawks), 10 Puma, 6 Exocet missile-armed Super Puma and 23 missile-armed Gazelle helicopters. Hawk surface-to-air missiles are in service. Personnel strength (1983) about 1,900.

INTERNATIONAL RELATIONS

Membership. Kuwait is a member of UN, the Arab League, OPEC and OAPEC.

ECONOMY

Budget. The financial year runs 1 April–31 March. In 1983–84 revenue, KD 3,037m.; expenditure, KD 3,605m.

Currency. The Kuwait *dinar* of 1,000 *fils* replaced the Indian external rupee on 1 April 1961. In March 1984, £1 sterling = KD 0·433; US$1 = KD 0·292. Coins in circulation are, 1, 5, 10, 20, 50 and 100 fils and notes of KD, 10, 5, 1, ½ and ¼.

Banking. Ten banks operate in Kuwait: the Bank of Kuwait and Middle East, the Kuwait National Bank, the Commercial Bank of Kuwait Ltd, the Gulf Bank of Kuwait, the Alahli Bank, The Burgan Bank, Savings and Credit Bank, the Industrial Bank of Kuwait, Real Estate Bank of Kuwait, the Bank of Kuwait and Bahrain.

Weights and Measures. The metric system was adopted in 1962.

ENERGY AND NATURAL RESOURCES

Electricity. 8,835m. kw. were produced in 1981.

Oil. Kuwait oil comes mainly from the Burgan oilfields, the residential and administrative centre for oil operations being at Ahmadi. Oil reserves in Kuwait and its share of the Neutral Zone was estimated at 77,000m. bbls in 1975. The Kuwait Petroleum Gas and Energy Co. (KPGEC) formed in 1974 as a result of the Government's take-over of 60% of oil production, is controlling all oil exploration and the processing and marketing of oil and gas. Production of crude oil (in 1,000 bbls); 1980, 607,268; 1981, 411,174.

Gas. Production (1981) 223,525m. cu. ft.

Agriculture. Major crops (production, 1981, in tonnes) are melons (5,000), tomatoes (12,000), onions (3,000), dates (1,000), radishes, clover.
Livestock (1982): Cattle, 17,000; sheep, 500,000; goats, 300,000; poultry, 7·2m.

Fisheries. Shrimp fishing is becoming one of the important non-oil industries.

INDUSTRY AND TRADE

Industry. Industries, apart from oil, include boat building, fishing, food production, petrochemicals, gases and construction. The manufacture or import of alcoholic drinks is prohibited.

Labour. Of the working population 75% are foreigners.

Commerce. The port of Kuwait formerly served mainly as an entrepôt for goods for the interior, for the export of skins and wool, and for pearl fishing. Entrepôt trade continues but, with the development of the oil industry, is declining in importance.

Pearl fishing is now on a small scale. Dhows and launches of traditional construction are still built.

In 1981 total imports were KD1,875m.; exports, KD4,363m. Oil accounted for more than 80% of exports.

Total trade between Kuwait and UK (British Department of Trade returns, in £1,000 sterling):

	1979	1980	1981	1982	1983
Imports to UK [1]	743,149	655,024	477,262	104,793	67,281
Exports and re-exports from UK	233,438	258,696	281,203	333,247	333,273

[1] Including oil.

COMMUNICATIONS

Roads. Number of private cars (1977) 379,100.

Aviation. Kuwait Airways flew over 9,000 flights in 1980, carrying 1·76m. passengers and 25,000 tonnes of freight. British Airways, Kuwait Airways, Iraqi Airways, Iranian Airways, United Arab Airlines, Middle East Airlines, Saudi Arabian Airways, Lebanese International Airways, Air Liban, Air India, Lufthansa, Japanese Airlines, TWA, PIA, Aden Air Lines, Air France, Alitalia, SAS, Swiss Air, SABENA, KLM and Gulf Aviation operate scheduled air services.

Shipping. Ships of 27 lines make regular calls at Kuwait.

Post and Broadcasting. There were (1982), 231,643 telephones and there is a broadcasting and a television station.

Cinemas. In 1976 there were 10 cinemas with a seating capacity of 13,000.

EDUCATION AND WELFARE

Education. In 1981 there were 302,510 pupils at 481 government schools. In 1980–81 there were 4,143 students at teacher-training institutes (608 teachers) and teacher-training colleges had 1,584 students (289 teachers). A technical college was opened in 1954 and in 1970 had 931 students (212 teachers). The University of Kuwait had 10,082 students in 1982.

Health. Medical services are free to all residents. There were (1981) 23 hospitals with over 5,563 beds in the State and 232 clinics and health centres. The Ministry of Health employs 2,348 physicians and 708 dentists.

DIPLOMATIC REPRESENTATIVES

Of Kuwait in Great Britain (45 Queen's Gate, London, SW7)
Ambassador: Ghazi Mohammed Amin Al-Rayes (accredited 12 Feb. 1981).

Of Great Britain in Kuwait (Arabian Gulf St., Kuwait)
Ambassador: M. R. Melhuish, CMG.

Of Kuwait in the USA (2940 Tilden St., NW, Washington, D.C., 20008)
Ambassador: Shaikh Saud Naser Al-Sabah.

Of the USA in Kuwait (PO Box 77, Kuwait)
Ambassador: (Vacant).

Of Kuwait to the United Nations
Ambassador: Mohammad A. Abulhasan.

Books of Reference

Arabian Year Book. Kuwait, 1978
Annual Statistical Abstract of Kuwait. Kuwait
The Oil of Kuwait: Facts and Figures. 3rd ed. Kuwait Government Press, 1970
Khouja, M. W., and Sadler, P. G., *The Economy of Kuwait.* London, 1979
Sabah, Y. S. F., *The Oil Economy of Kuwait.* London, 1980

LAOS

Capital: Vientiane
Population: 3·52m. (1979)
GNP per capita: US$90 (1978)

HISTORY. The Lao People's Democratic Republic was founded on 2 Dec. 1975. Until that date Laos was a Kingdom, once called Lanxang (the land of a million elephants).

In 1893 Laos became a French protectorate and in 1907 acquired its present frontiers. In 1941 French authority was suppressed by the Japanese. When the Japanese withdrew in 1945 an independence movement known as Lao Issara (Free Laos) set up a government under Prince Phetsarath, the Viceroy of Luang Prabang. This government collapsed with the return of the French in 1946 and the leaders of the movement fled to Thailand.

Under a new Constitution of 1947 Laos became a constitutional monarchy under the Luang Prabang dynasty, and in 1949 became an independent sovereign state within the French Union. Most of the Lao Issara leaders returned to Laos but a few remained in dissidence under Prince Souphanouvong, who allied himself with the Vietminh and subsequently formed the 'Pathet Lao' (Lao State) rebel movement.

The war in Laos from 1953 to 1973 between the Royal Lao Government (supported by American bombing and Thai mercenaries) and the Patriotic Front *Pathet Lao* (supported by large numbers of North Vietnamese troops) ended in 1973 when an agreement and a protocol were signed. A provisional coalition government was formed by the two sides in 1974. However, after the communist victories in neighbouring Vietnam and Cambodia in April 1975, the *Pathet Lao* took over the running of the whole country, although maintaining the façade of a coalition. On 29 Nov. 1975 HM King Savang Vatthana signed a letter of abdication and the People's Congress proclaimed a People's Democratic Republic of Laos. For the history of *Pathet Lao* and the military intervention of the Vietminh, *see* THE STATESMAN'S YEAR-BOOK, 1971–72, pp. 1126–28 and 1975–76 ed., pp. 1115–16.

AREA AND POPULATION. Laos is a landlocked country of about 91,400 sq. miles (236,800 sq. km) bordered on the north by China, the east by Vietnam, the south by the People's Republic of Democratic Kampuchea (Cambodia) and the west by Thailand and Burma. Apart from the Mekong River plains along the border of Thailand, the country is mountainous, particularly in the north, and in places densely forested. The climate is of a tropical monsoon type with a wet season from May to Oct. and a dry one from Nov. to April. Most of northern Laos receives about 40–80 in. of rainfall annually, while parts of the Bolovens Plateau in southern Laos have over 150 in.

There has been no complete census in Laos, but estimates place the population at about 3·5m. The most heavily populated areas are the Mekong River plains by the Thailand border. Otherwise, the population is sparse and scattered, particularly in the northern provinces, and the eastern part of the country has been depopulated by war. The majority of the population is officially divided into 4 groups: about 56% Lao-Lum (Valley-Lao), 34% Lao-Theung (Lao of the mountain sides); and 9% Lao-Soung (Lao of the mountain tops), who comprise the Meo and Yaoe. Other minorities include Vietnamese, Chinese, Europeans, Indians and Pakistanis.

The Lao-Lum and Lao-Tai belong to the Lao branch of the Tai peoples, who migrated into South-East Asia at the time of the Mongol invasion of South China. The valley Lao are Buddhists, following the Hinayana (Theravada) form. The majority of the Lao-Theungma diverse group consisting of many tribes but mostly belonging to the Mon-Khmer group—are animists.

The Meo and Yaoe live in northern Laos. Far greater numbers live in both North Vietnam and China, having migrated over the last century. Their religions have strong Confucian and animistic features but some are Christians.

There are 13 provinces. Compared with other parts of Asia, Laos has few towns. The administrative capital and largest town is Vientiane, with a population of (census, 1973) 176,637; estimate (1979) 90,000. Other important towns are Luang Prabang, 44,244; Pakse, 44,860, in the extreme south, and Savannakhet, 50,690.

Language: Lao is the official language of the country. The liturgical language of Theravada Buddhism is Pali.

CLIMATE. A tropical monsoon climate, with high temperatures throughout the year and very heavy rains from May to Oct. Vientiane. Jan. 70°F (21·1°C), July 81°F (27·2°C). Annual rainfall 69″ (1,715 mm).

CONSTITUTION AND GOVERNMENT. On 1–2 Dec. 1975 a national congress of 264 people's representatives met and declared Laos a People's Democratic Republic. A People's Supreme Council was appointed to draw up a new Constitution.

President: Prince Souphanouvong.
Prime Minister Secretary General of the Central Committee of the Lao People's Revolutionary Party: Kaysone Phomvihane.

There are 4 deputy prime ministers.

National flag: Three horizontal stripes of red, blue, red, with blue of double width with in the centre a large white disc.
National anthem: Peng Sat Lao (Hymn of the Lao People).

Provincial Administration: All provincial administration is in the hands of the Lao People's Revolutionary Party. Orders come from the Central Committee through a series of 'People's Revolutionary Committees' at the province, town and village level.

DEFENCE. Military service is compulsory for 18 months.

Army. The Army is organized in 4 infantry and 1 artillery divisions; 7 independent infantry regiments and 65 independent infantry companies; and 5 artillery and 9 anti-aircraft battalions. Equipment includes 25 PT-76 light tanks. Strength (1984) about 50,000.

Navy. In 1984 there were nominally 4 river squadrons comprising 42 small craft of 6 different types, of which 14 were in commission and 28 in reserve. Naval personnel totalled 550 officers and ratings.

Air Force. Since 1975, the Air Force has received aircraft from the USSR, including about 20 MiG-21 fighters, 6 An-24 and 3 An-26 turboprop transports and 10 Mi-8 helicopters. They may be supplemented by a few of the C-47 transports, T-41D trainers and UH-34 helicopters supplied by the USA to the former régime. Personnel strength, about 2,000.

INTERNATIONAL RELATIONS

Membership. Laos is a member of UN.

Aid. Foreign aid in 1981 (estimate), was US$72·1m.; 1980, 78·2m.; 1979, 75m.

ECONOMY

Planning. Following the completion of the original 3-year Development Plan 1978–80, a 5-year plan (1981–85), which is basically a list of investment projects, was drawn up by the government with Soviet assistance.

Budget. Total revenue 1981, K.1,190m.; total expenditure, K.2,152m.

Currency. The currency is the *kip*. 1 *kip* = 100 *att*. Coinage, 1, 2 and 5 *att*; banknotes, 1, 5, 10, 20 and 50 *kip*. The official rate of exchange was (March 1984) K.35 = US$1; £1 = K51·98, but in June 1983 a new 'non-commercial' rate of K.108 = US$1 was established.

ENERGY AND NATURAL RESOURCES

Electricity. Only a few towns in Laos have an electricity service. A power plant with a capacity of 8,000 kw. is installed at Vientiane, but there are only small thermo-electric plants in other towns. The Nam Ngum Dam situated about 45 miles north of Vientiane was inaugurated in Dec. 1971 with an initial installed capacity of 30,000 kw. and a planned ultimate capacity of 130,000 kw. The generators of Phase II of the scheme were brought into operation in 1978, giving an installed capacity of 110,000 kw. Transmission lines to Vientiane and to Thailand have been constructed. Other sources of electric power are the dams on the Sedone River about 20 miles north of Pakse and on the Nam Dong about 5 miles south of Luang Prabang, with installed capacities of 2,400 and 1,200 kw. respectively. Production (1979) 840m. kwh.

Minerals. Various minerals are found, but only tin is mined to any significant extent at present, and only at 2 mines (Tin exports (1980) US$500,000). There are extremely rich deposits of high-quality iron in Xieng Khouang province and potash near Vientiane.

Agriculture. The chief products are rice (production in 1980, 1m. tonnes; 1978, estimate, 420,000 tonnes), maize (production 27,200 tonnes), tobacco (4,200 tonnes), cotton (2,100 tonnes), citrus fruits, sticklack, benjohn tea and in the Boloven plateau coffee (2,070 tonnes), potatoes, cardamom and cinchara. Opium is produced but its manufacture is controlled by the state.

Livestock (1982): Cattle, 473,000; buffaloes, 877,000; horses, 36,000; pigs, 1,223,000; goats, 56,000; poultry, 5·9m.

Forestry. The forests, which cover over 50% of the country, produce valuable woods such as teak. Their potential is being exploited with Swedisn and Soviet aid.

INDUSTRY AND TRADE

Industry. Industry is limited to beer, rubber sandals, cigarettes, matches, soft drinks, plastic bags, saw-mills, rice-mills, weaving, pottery, distilleries, ice, plywood, bricks, etc. but most factories have been working at limited capacity in recent years. Plans for increased production are limited by lack of funds and skilled machine operators.

Commerce. In 1981 imports (estimate) amounted to US$121m. and exports to US$48m. The main imports were food and beverages, petroleum products and agricultural and other machinery. The chief supplying countries were Thailand and Japan. The main exports were timber, coffee and electricity.

Total trade between Laos and UK (British Department of Trade returns, in £1,000 sterling):

	1978	1979	1980	1981	1982	1983
Imports to UK	17	49	32	65	355	56
Exports and re-exports from UK	1,527	264	720	542	880	626

COMMUNICATIONS

Roads. In 1981 the national road network, which was nearing completion, consisted of 1,300 km paved, 5,300 km gravel and 3,600 km earth roads.

Railways. There is no railway in Laos, but the Thai railway system extends to Nongkhai, on the Thai bank of the Mekong, which is connected by ferry with Thadeua about 12 miles east of Vientiane.

Aviation. Lao Aviation provides scheduled domestic air services linking major towns in Laos and international services to Bangkok, Phnom Penh and Hanoi. Thai Airways, Aeroflot and Air Vietnam provide flights from Bangkok, Hanoi, Rangoon, Ho Chi Min City and Moscow.

Shipping. The river Mekong and its tributaries are an important means of transport, but rapids, waterfalls and narrow channels often impede navigation and make trans-shipments neccessary.

Telecommunications. There is a radio network in Laos as well as an experimental TV service with the main station at Vientiane. A ground station constructed near Vientiane under the Soviet aid programme enables USSR television programmes to be received in the capital. It also provides a telephone service to Hanoi and Eastern Europe.

In 1974 there were 5,506 telephones in Laos

RELIGION, EDUCATION AND WELFARE

Religion. The majority of the population is Buddhist (Hinayana).

Education. In 1978–79 school year there were 5,900 elementary schools (451,000 pupils); 260 secondary schools (60,400 pupils); 86 senior high schools (7,800 pupils); 72 nursery schools (3,400 pupils); 24 teacher training schools (8,300 students) and 7 technical schools (2,000 students).

Literacy has improved from 40% in 1975, 65% in 1978 to 85% in 1981 according to official reports.

There is 1 teachers' training college, 1 college of education, 1 school of medicine, 1 agricultural college and an advanced school of Pali.

Health. In 1981 there were about 30 qualified doctors and 8,729 hospital beds.

DIPLOMATIC REPRESENTATIVES

Of Laos in Great Britain (5 Palace Green, London, W8 4QA)
Chargé a'Affaires: Ouan Phommachack.

Of Great Britain in Laos (Rue Pandit J. Nehru, Vientiane)
Ambassador: W. B. J. Dobbs.

Of Laos in USA (2222 S St., NW, Washington, D.C., 20008)
Chargé d'Affaires: Bounkeut Sangsomsak.

Of USA in Laos (Rue Bartholonie, Vientiane)
Chargé d'Affaires: Theresa Tull.

Of Laos to the United Nations
Ambassador: Soubanh Srithirath.

Books of Reference

La Constitution du Laos. Notes et Etudes. 1957
International Conference on the Settlement of the Laotian Question. Geneva, 12th May 1961– 23rd July 1962 (Cmnd. 1828). HMSO, 1962
Declaration and Protocol on the Neutrality of Laos. Geneva, 23rd July 1962 (Cmnd. 2025). HMSO, 1963
White Book on the Violations of the Geneva Accords of 1962 by the Government of North Vietnam. Ministry of Foreign Affairs, Vientiane, 1968
Halpern, Joel M., *Economy and Society of Laos: Brief Survey.* Yale Univ. Press, 1964.— *Government, Politics and Social Structure in Laos.* Yale Univ. Press, 1964
Stuart-Cox, M., *Contemporary Laos.* Univ. of Queensland Press, 1983
Zasloff, J. J., *The Pathet Lao: Leadership and Organization.* Lexington, Toronto and London, 1973

LEBANON

al-Jumhouriya
al-Lubnaniya

Capital: Beirut
Population: 2·6m. (1980)
GNP per capita: US$1,070(1974)

HISTORY. After 20 years' French mandatory regime, Lebanon was proclaimed independent at Beirut on 26 Nov. 1941. On 27 Dec. 1943 an agreement was signed between representatives of the French National Committee of Liberation and of Lebanon, by which most of the powers and capacities exercised hitherto by France were transferred as from 1 Jan. 1944 to the Lebanese Government. The evacuation of foreign troops was completed in Dec. 1946.

In early May 1958 the opposition to President Chamoun, consisting principally (though not entirely) of Moslem pro-Nasserist elements, rose in insurrection; and for 5 months the Moslem quarters of Beirut, Tripoli, Sidon and the northern Bekaa were in insurgent hands. On 15 July the US Government acceded to President Chamoun's request and landed a considerable force of army and marines who re-established the authority of the Government.

Israeli attacks on Lebanon resulted from the presence and activities of armed Palestinian resistance units. Internal problems, which had long been latent in Lebanese society, were exacerbated by the politically active Palestinian population and by the deeply divisive question of the Palestine problem itself. An attempt to regulate the activities of Palestinian fighters through the secret Cairo agreement of 1969 was frustrated both by the inability of the Government to enforce its provisions and by an influx of battle-hardened fighters expelled from Jordan in Sept. 1970. A further attempt to control the guerrillas in 1973 also failed. From March 1975, Lebanon was beset by civil disorder causing considerable loss of life and economic life was brought to a virtual standstill.

By Nov. 1976 it was estimated that 40,000 people has been killed and up to 100,000 injured. By the end of the year, however, large scale fighting had been brought to an end by the intervention of the Syrian-dominated Arab Deterrent Force which ensured sufficient security to permit Lebanon to establish quasi-normal conditions under President Sarkis. Large areas of the country, however, remained outside Governmental control, including West Beirut which was the scene of frequent conflict between opposing militia groups. The South, where the Arab Deterrent Force could not deploy, remained unsettled and subject to frequent Israeli attacks. In March 1978 there was an Israeli invasion following a Palestinian attack inside Israel. Israeli troops eventually withdrew in June, but instead of handing over all their positions to UN Peacekeeping Forces they installed Israeli-controlled Lebanese militia forces under Maj. Sa'ad Haddad in border areas. Severe disruption continued in the South. In June 1982, following on the attempted assassination of the Israeli ambassador in London, Israeli forces once again invaded, this time in massive strength, and swept through the country, eventually laying siege to and devastatingly bombing Beirut. In Sept. Palestinian forces, together with the PLO leadership, evacuated Beirut. On 23 Aug. Bashir Gemayel was elected President of Lebanon in succession to Sarkis. On 14 Sept. he was assassinated. His brother, Amin Gemayel, was elected in his place on 21 Sept.

AREA AND POPULATION. Lebanon is a mountainous country about 135 miles long and varying between 20 and 35 miles wide, bounded on the north and east by Syria, on the west by the Mediterranean and on the south by Israel. Between the two parellel mountain ranges of Lebanon and Anti-Lebanon lies the fertile Bekaa Valley. About one-half of the country lies at an altitude of over 3,000 ft.

The area of Lebanon is estimated at 10,400 sq. km (3,400 sq. miles) and the population at 2·6m. (1980, estimate). The principal towns, with estimated population, are: Beirut (the capital), 702,000; Tripoli 175,000; Zahlé, 46,800; Saida (Sidon), 24,740; Tyre, 14,000.

Vital statistics. 1971: Births. 76,099; deaths, 12,799; marriages, 16,516; divorces, 1,382.

The official language is Arabic. French and, increasingly, English are widely spoken in official and commercial circles.

CLIMATE. A Mediterranean climate with short, warm winters and long, hot and rainless summers, with high humidity in coastal areas. Rainfall is largely confined to the winter months and can be torrential, with snow on high ground. Beirut. Jan. 55°F (13°C), July 81°F (27°C). Annual rainfall 35·7″ (893 mm).

CONSTITUTION AND GOVERNMENT. Lebanon is an independent republic. The first Constitution was established under the French Mandate on 23 May 1926. It has since been amended in 1927, 1929, 1943 (twice) and 1947. It is a written constitution based on the classical separation of powers, with a President, a single chamber elected by universal adult suffrage, and an independent judiciary. The Executive consists of the President and a Prime Minister and Cabinet appointed by him. The system is, however, adapted to the peculiar communal balance on which Lebanese political life depends. This is done by the electoral law which allocates deputies according to the confessional distribution of the population, and by a series of constitutional conventions whereby, *e.g.*, the President is always a Maronite Christian, the Prime Minister a Sunni Moslem and the Speaker of the Chamber a Shia Moslem. There is no highly developed party system other than on religious confessional lines. The Constitution was amended on 11 April 1976 to allow a new President to be elected up to 6 months before the end of the incumbent's term.

Former Presidents of the Republic:

Bishara al-Khuri, 1 Jan. 1944–23 Sept. 1952
Camille Chamoun, 23 Sept. 1952–23 Sept. 1958
Gen. Fouad Chehab, 23 Sept. 1958–23 Sept. 1964
Charles Hélou, 23 Sept. 1964–17 June 1970
Suleiman Frangié, 17 June 1970–13 Sept. 1976
Elias Sarkis, 13 Sept. 1976–23 Sept. 1982

President of the Republic: Amin Gemayel (elected on 21 Sept. and took office on 23 Sept. 1982).

On 5 Feb. 1984 the government resigned and the following day Moslem militiamen took over West Beirut from the Lebanese army. Fighting between the various factions became intense. On 5 March, President Gemayel issued a statement that the unratified military withdrawal agreement of 17 May 1982 with Israel was null and void. Later in March the re-convened Conference of National Reconciliation met in Lausanne but this achieved no positive results.

'Caretaker' Prime Minister: Chafiq al-Wazzan.

National flag: Three horizontal stripes of red, white, red, with the white of double width and bearing in the centre a green cedar of Lebanon.

National anthem: Kulluna lil watan lil 'ula lil' alam (words by Rashid Nachleh, tune by Mitri El-Murr).

DEFENCE. Compulsory military service was made law in 1975, but enjoys limited application.

Army. The strength of the Army was about 25,000 in 1983 but it is in a state of flux and most of its units are well below strength. Its equipment includes M-48 and AMX-13 tanks and Saladin armoured cars. In addition, there are numerous private militias under arms in Lebanon, divided between the Maronite-Christian factions, notably the Phalange of some 10,000 men, and the Muslim-Leftist groups, such as the Druze Free Lebanese Militia led by Walid Jumblat.

Navy. The small flotilla consisted in 1984 of 4 patrol boats and 8 coastal patrol craft. Personnel totalled 400 officers and men.

Air Force. The Air Force has about 1,250 men and 50 aircraft. In addition to a single combat squadron of Hunter jet fighter-bombers, it has (in storage) 9 Mirage III supersonic fighters and 1 Mirage 2-seat trainer. Other aircraft include 1 Dove light transport, 11 Alouette II and III and 10 Agusta-Bell 212 helicopters, and Fouga Magister jet and piston-engined Bulldog trainers.

INTERNATIONAL RELATIONS

Membership. Lebanon is a member of UN and the Arab League.

ECONOMY

Planning. Since the civil war a Development and Reconstruction Council has been responsible for co-ordinating all efforts.

Budget. The budget for 1979 provides for a total expenditure of £Leb.3,103·91m. (2,583·66m. in 1978). A draft budget for 1980 envisages a total expenditure of £Leb4,109·5m.

Currency. The Lebanese *pound*, divided into 100 *piastres*, is issued by the Banque du Liban, which commenced operations on 1 April 1964. There is a fluctuating official rate of exchange, fixed monthly (March 1984: £Leb.8·08 = £1 sterling; £Leb.5·86 = US$1), this in practice is used only for the calculation of *ad-valorem* customs duties on Lebanese imports and for import statistics. For other purposes the free market is used.

Banking. Beirut was an important international financial centre, and there were about 80 banks registered with the central bank in 1979, including 2 British banks, the British Bank of the Middle East and the Chartered Bank. As a result of the civil war in 1975–76, Beirut lost much of its status as an international and regional banking centre; in general only local offices for banks remain.

Weights and Measures. The use of the metric system is legal and obligatory throughout the whole of the country. In outlying districts the former weights and measures may still be in use. They are: 1 *okiya* = 0·47 lb.; 6 *okiyas* = 1 *oke* = 2·82 lb.; 2 *okes* = 1 *rottol* = 5·64 lb.; 200 *okes* = 1 *kantar*.

ENERGY AND NATURAL RESOURCES

Oil. There are 2 oil refineries in Lebanon, one at Tripoli, which refines oil brought by ship from Iraq, and the other at Sidon, which refines oil brought from Saudi Arabia by a pipeline owned by the Trans-Arabian Pipeline Co. These refineries received 2m. tonnes of crude oil in 1977 and their production is normally sufficient to meet the country's requirements of refined fuel.

Minerals. Iron ore exists but is difficult to work. Other minerals known to exist are iron pyrites, copper, bituminous shales, asphalt, phosphates, ceramic clays and glass sand; but the available information is of doubtful value.

Agriculture. Lebanon is essentially an agricultural country, although owing to its physical character only about 38% of the total area of the country is at present cultivated. The forests of the past have been denuded by exploitation and the unrestricted grazing of goats, and only about 80,000 hectares of indifferent timber remain, and soil erosion is considerable.

The estimated yield (in 1,000 tonnes) of the main crops in 1982 was as follows: Citrus fruits, 315; apples, 130; grapes, 161; potatoes, 126; sugar-beet, 61; wheat, 23; bananas, 15; olives, 75.

Livestock (estimated, 1982): Goats, 440,000; sheep, 145,000; cattle, 54,000; pigs, 19,000; horses, 2,000; donkeys, 10,000; mules, 4,000.

INDUSTRY AND TRADE

Industry. Industry suffered badly during the civil war. The manufacturing industry was small but had doubled in size in the 10 years before the war. As a result of the war some industrial concerns have closed but a few light industries have since been established.

Commerce. Foreign as well as local wholesale and retail trade is the principal source of income in Lebanon and provides about 31% of the total. Because of the protectionist policies followed in some neighbouring countries, this sector has been declining, the sectors to gain being those of banking, real estate, government and services.

In 1978 imports were estimated at £Leb.5,220m.; exports were valued at £Leb.1,639m. Imports came mainly from USA, Federal Republic of Germany, France, Italy and UK. Exports went mainly to Saudi Arabia, Kuwait, Syria, Libya and Iraq.

Total trade between Lebanon and UK (British Department of Trade returns, in £1,000 sterling):

	1979	1980	1981	1982	1983
Imports to UK	9,892	9,076	7,470	24,237	11,521
Exports and re-exports from UK	65,793	70,692	61,945	67,640	81,435

Customs duties are usually imposed on an *ad-valorem* basis: the receipts are the Lebanese Government's main source of income; actual yield in 1978, £Leb.509m. The considerable adverse balance of trade is offset by invisible receipts, including foreign capital investment in Lebanese real estate, remittances from émigrés and receipts from tourism and international arbitrage operations.

Tourism. Receipts from tourism were £Leb.573m. in 1973; since 1975 they have been negligible, this sector having suffered badly as a result of the war.

COMMUNICATIONS

Roads. The main roads in Lebanon are good. The surface is normally of asphalt and they are well maintained in normal times. In Dec. 1971 there were 570 km of international roads, 1,420 km of main roads and 4,310 km of secondary and local roads, all asphalted. The main arterial routes are the north–south coastal road and the west–east trunk road (Beirut to Damascus).

At 31 Dec. 1978 there were 282,404 cars and taxis, 2,592 buses and 28,553 commercial vehicles.

Railways. There are 3 railway lines in Lebanon, all operated by the *Office des Chemins de Fer de l'Etat Libanais* (CFL): (1) Nakoura–Beirut–Tripoli (standard gauge); the Nakoura–Sidon section has been idle since the establishment of Israel: (2) a narrow-gauge line running from Beirut to Riyak in the Bekaa Valley (now closed) and thence to Damascus, Syria; (3) a standard-gauge line from Tripoli to Homs and Aleppo in Syria, providing access to Ankara and Istanbul. From Homs a branch of the CFL line extends south and re-enters Lebanon, terminating at Riyak. Total length 417 km.

Aviation. Beirut International Airport is used by many international airlines which connect Lebanon with most countries in the world. Extensive local services cover the Middle East, Persian Gulf and Europe. There are 2 national airlines, Middle East Airlines/Air Liban and Trans-Mediterranean Airways. In 1978, 24,500 flights passed through Beirut international airport (1974: 44,406), carrying a total of 1,405,600 passengers (1974: 2,806,632).

Shipping. Beirut is by far the largest and busiest port. In 1978, 1,786 vessels and 1,753,000 tonnes of goods were handled. Activity in the port of Tripoli is growing due to increased movements in goods and petroleum. The small port of Sidon in the south, near to the closed Lebanese-Israeli frontier, is at present of little importance. General activity since the civil war has been reduced to about 60%, but was increasing in late 1977. However, sporadic fighting in Beirut closed the port at times in 1978 and 1979.

Post and Broadcasting. There is an automatic telephone system in Beirut, Tripoli, Sidon, Zahlé and several other towns and villages, which is being extended to all parts of the country. There are no telegraph, postal or telephone communications with Israel. Number of telephones (1978), 231,000.

The state radio transmits in Arabic, French, English and Armenian. Before 1978 there were 2 commercial television stations, transmitting in Arabic, French and English. In 1978 they were amalgamated into a new company in which the Government has a 50% shareholding. There were 325,000 sets in 1975.

Cinemas (1973). There were 161 cinemas with a seating capacity of about 77,400.

Newspapers (1977). There were about 30 daily newspapers in Arabic, 2 in French, 1 in English and 4 in Armenian, with a total circulation of 215,000.

RELIGION, EDUCATION AND WELFARE

Religion. Probably less than half the population are Christians, some of whom have been indigenous since the earliest time of Christianity. There were in 1958, 792,000 Christians, of whom 424,000 were Maronites, 150,000 Greek Orthodox, 69,000 Armenians, 91,000 Greek and Roman Catholics, 14,500 Armenian Catholics, 14,000 Protestants. Moslems numbered 536,000, of whom 286,000 were Sunnis and 250,000 Shiites. There were also 88,000 Druzes and 6,600 Jews.

Education. Government schools in 1970 comprised 1,290 primary and secondary schools. There were also 1,484 private primary and secondary schools. There are also 5 teachers' training colleges and 5 universities, namely the Lebanese (State) University, the American University of Beirut, the French University of St Joseph (founded in 1875), the Arab University, a branch of Alexandria University and Beirut University College. The French Government runs the École Supérieure de Lettres and the Centre d'Études Mathématiques. The Maronite monks run the University of the Holy Spirit at Kaslik.

The Lebanese Academy of Fine Arts includes schools of architecture, art, music, political and social science.

Health. In 1973 there were 2,300 physicians and 8,000 hospital beds.

DIPLOMATIC REPRESENTATIVES

Of Lebanon in Great Britain (21 Kensington Palace Gdns., London, W8 4QM)
Ambassador: Gen. Ahmad al-Hajj (accredited 25 May 1983).

Of Great Britain in Lebanon (Ave. de Paris, Ras Beirut)
Ambassador: H. D. A. C. Miers, CMG.

Of Lebanon in the USA (2560–28th St., Washington, D.C., 20008)
Ambassador: Dr Abdallah Bouhabib.

Of the USA in Lebanon (Ave. de Paris, Beirut)
Ambassador: Robert S. Dillon.

Of Lebanon to the United Nations
Ambassador: Kesrouan Lebaki.

Books of Reference

Statistical Information: Import and export figures are produced by the Conseil Supérieur des Douanes. The Service de Statistique Générale (M. A. G. Ayad, *Chef du Service*) publishes a quarterly bulletin (in French and Arabic) covering a wide range of subjects, including foreign trade, production statistics and estimates of the national income.

Cowan, J. M., *Dictionary of Modern Arabic.* Wiesbaden, 1961
Deeb, M., *The Lebanese Civil War.* New York, 1980
Gilmour, D., *Lebanon: The Fractured Country.* Oxford, 1983
Gordon, D. C., *The Republic of Lebanon: Nation in Jeopardy.* London, 1983
Khairallah, S., *Lebanon.* [Bibliography] Oxford and Santa Barbara, 1979
Murray, G., *Lebanon: The New Future.* London, 1974
Randal, J., *The Tragedy of Lebanan.* London, 1983
Salem, E. A., *Modernization Without Revolution: Lebanon's Experience.* Indiana Univ. Press, 1973
Salibi, K. S., *Modern History of Lebanon.* London, 1965.—*Crossroads to Civil War: Lebanon 1958-76.* New York, 1976

National Library: Dar el Kutub, Parliament Sq., Beirut.

LESOTHO

Capital: Maseru
Population: 1·7m. (1983)
GNP per capita: US$390 (1980)

HISTORY. Basutoland first received the protection of Britain in 1868 at the request of Moshesh. the first paramount chief. In 1871 the territory was annexed to the Cape Colony, but in 1884 it was restored to the direct control of the British Government through the High Commissioner for South Africa.

On 4 Oct. 1966 Basutoland became an independent and sovereign member of the Commonwealth under the name of the Kingdom of Lesotho.

AREA AND POPULATION. Lesotho is bounded on the west by the Orange Free State, on the north by the Orange Free State and Natal, on the east by Natal and East Griqualand, and on the south by the Cape Province. The altitude varies from 5,000 to 11,000 ft. The area is 11,716 sq. miles (30,340 sq. km). Lesotho is a purely African territory, and the few European residents are government officials, traders, missionaries and artisans.

The census taken on 12 April 1976 showed a total population of 1,246,815 persons. Estimate (1983) 1·7m.

The capital is Maseru (population, 1976, 45,000).

The official languages are Sesotho and English.

CLIMATE. A healthy and pleasant climate, with variable rainfall, but averaging 29″ (725 mm) a year over most of the country. The rain falls mainly in the summer months of Oct. to April, while the winters are dry and may produce heavy frosts in lowland areas and frequent snow in the highlands. Temperatures in the lowlands range from a maximum of 90°F (32·2°C) in summer to a minimum of 20°F (–6·7°C) in winter.

CONSTITUTION AND GOVERNMENT. On 4 Oct. 1966 the country became the Kingdom of Lesotho, with the Paramount Chief as King.

Parliament consists of the National Assembly (60 members elected by adult suffrage) and a Senate (22 principal chiefs and 11 members nominated by the King). The general election held on 30 April 1965 returned 31 members of the National Party, 25 members of the Congress Party and 4 members of the Marematlou Freedom Party. The elections of 27 Jan. 1970 were declared invalid on 31 Jan. Parliamentary rule, with a National Assembly of nominated members, was reintroduced in April 1973. Elections are planned for 1984.

A Constitution is being drafted.

King of Lesotho: Moshoeshoe II.

Prime Minister: Chief Leabua Jonathan. *Minister of the Interior:* Chief Sekhonyana 'Maseribane.

The College of Chiefs settles the recognition and succession of Chiefs and adjudicates cases of inefficiency, criminality and absenteeism among them.

National flag: Blue with a white Basuto hat; in the hoist 2 vertical strips of green and red.

Local Government. The country is divided into 10 districts as follows: Maseru, Qacha's Nek, Mokhotlong, Leribe, Butha–Buthe, Teyateyaneng, Mafeteng, Mohale's Hoek, Quthing, Thaba–Tseka. Each district is subdivided into wards, most of which are presided over by hereditary chiefs allied to the Moshoeshoe family.

DEFENCE

Police Mobile Unit. Formed in 1978, to facilitate deployment of men and equipment to less accessible regions, this small air wing has 2 Skyvan twin-turboprop transports, 1 Do 27 and 1 Do 28 liaison aircraft, and a total of 5 Bell 412, BO 105 and Bell 47 helicopters. The Skyvans are available also as ambulance aircraft.

INTERNATIONAL RELATIONS

Membership. Lesotho is a member of UN, OAU, the Commonwealth and is an ACP state of the EEC.

ECONOMY

Planning. A third 5-year plan (1981–84), to exploit natural resources and promote investment was published in 1983.

Budget. Expenditure (1982–83) M269m.; revenue, M216m.

The major items of expenditure in 1983–84 were education (M25·8m.), agriculture (M10·1m.) and health (M8·4m.). The revenue situation was greatly improved by the re-negotiation of the Republic of South Africa's customs agreement in 1970.

Currency. The currency is the *Loti* (plural *Maloti*) divided into 100 *Lisente* which is at par with the South African *Rand*. In March 1984, £1 = 1·77 *Maloti*; US$1 = 1·20 *Maloti*.

Banking. The Standard Bank of South Africa and Barclays Bank International have branches at Maseru, Mohale's Hoek and Leribe. The Lesotho Bank has branches throughout the country.

ENERGY AND NATURAL RESOURCES

Electricity. A feasibility study was announced (1982) to be undertaken by the Republic of South Africa and Lesotho to divert river waters from Lesotho to South Africa and to provide hydro-electricity for Lesotho.

Agriculture. The chief crops are wheat, maize and sorghum; barley, oats, beans, peas and other vegetables are also grown. The land is held in trust for the nation by the King and may not be alienated.

Soil conservation and the improvement of crops and pasture are matters of vital importance. A total area of 1,006,817 acres has been protected against soil erosion by means of terracing, training banks, tree planting and grass strips. Efforts are being made to secure the general introduction of rotational grazing in the mountain area.

Livestock (1982): Cattle, 562,000; horses, 103,000; donkeys, 97,000; pigs, 62,000; sheep, 1,337,000; goats, 930,000; mules, 1,000; poultry, 115,000.

INDUSTRY AND TRADE

Industry. Industrial development is progressing under the National Development Corporation. Diamond production (1981) 52,000 carats.

Commerce. Lesotho, Botswana and Swaziland are members of the South African customs union, by agreement dated 29 June 1910.

Total values of imports and exports into and from Lesotho (in Mm.):

	1979	1980	1981	1982
Imports	312	372	453	541
Exports	38	45	43	38

Principal imports were food, livestock, drink and tobacco, machinery and transport equipment, mineral fuels and lubricants; principal exports were wool and mohair and diamonds.

The majority of international trade is with the Republic of South Africa.

Total trade between Lesotho and UK (British Department of Trade returns, in £1,000 sterling):

	1980	1981	1982	1983
Imports to UK	340	489	682	216
Exports and re-exports from UK	394	1,483	1,260	2,080

Tourism. In 1980 there were 150,000 visitors.

COMMUNICATIONS

Roads. There were (1983) 311 km of tarred roads and 1,500 km of gravel-surfaced roads. In addition to the main roads there were (1983) 931 km of food aid tracks leading to trading stations and missions. Communications into the mountainous interior are by means of bridlepaths suitable only for riding and pack animals, but a mountain road of 80 miles has been constructed, and some parts are accessible by air transport, which is being used increasingly. In 1977 there were 11,509 motor vehicles.

Railways. A railway built by the South African Railways, 1 mile long, connects Maseru with the Bloemfontein–Natal line at Marseilles.

Aviation. There is a scheduled passenger service between Maseru and Jan Smuts Airport, Johannesburg, operated jointly by Lesotho National Airways and SAA. There are also 30 airstrips for light aircraft.

Post and Broadcasting. There were 5,409 telephones in 1983. Radio Lesotho transmits daily in English and Sesotho. Radio receivers (1983), 37,786.

Cinemas. In 1971 there were 2 cinemas with a seating capacity of 800.

JUSTICE, RELIGION, EDUCATION AND WELFARE

Justice. An appeal court for Lesotho was established at Maseru on 4 Oct. 1966.
    The police force on 31 Dec. 1982 had an establishment of 348 officers and subordinate officers and 1,530 other ranks.

Religion. About 70% of the population are Christians, 40% being Roman Catholics.

Education. Education is largely in the hands of the 3 main missions (Paris Evangelical, Roman Catholic and English Church), under the direction of the Ministry of Education. In 1982 the total enrolment in 1,103 primary schools was 277,945; in 108 secondary schools, 27,799; in the National Teacher-Training College enrolment was 1,136. University education was provided at the University of Botswana, Lesotho, Swaziland, which now has a campus in each of the 3 countries. Total enrolment in 1974–75 was 538, of which 322 were Basotho students. In 1975 a National University was established; enrolment in 1982–83, 1,139. Recurrent government expenditure on education was estimated at R3,948,700 in 1973–74. Bursaries are provided at all stages for secondary, teacher-training and university work. In 1972, 106 Basotho were studying at universities and places of higher education, outside Lesotho.

Health. The government medical staff of the territory consists of 1 Permanent Secretary for Health, 1 Director of Health Services, 1 medical superintendent, 8 district medical officers and a total of 102 doctors including 20 specialists.
    There are 11 government hospitals staffed by 308 matrons, sisters and nurses. There is accommodation for 2,175 patients in government hospitals. The 360-bed Queen Elizabeth II hospital in Maseru was completed in 1957. There are 9 mission hospitals subsidized by the Government with 153 staff and 729 beds. 116 health centres (319 beds) and mountain dispensaries provide outpatient medical facilities and maternity services to people living in remote areas. The leper settlement 5 miles out of Maseru had 67 patients in 1983.
    Typhus and plague occur.

DIPLOMATIC REPRESENTATIVES

Of Lesotho in Great Britain (10 Collingham Rd., London, SW5)
High Commissioner: Odilon Tlali Sefako (accredited 25 Oct. 1983).

Of Great Britain in Lesotho
High Commissioner: P. E. Rosling.

Of Lesotho in the USA (1601 Connecticut Ave., NW, Washington, D.C., 20009)
Ambassador: 'M'alineo N. Tau.

Of the USA in Lesotho (P.O. Box MS 333, Maseru, 100)
Ambassador: Keith L. Brown.

Of Lesotho to the United Nations
Ambassador: Thabo Makeka.

Books of Reference

Statistical Information: Bureau of Statistics, PO Box 455, Maseru, Lesotho.
Ambrose, A., *The Guide to Lesotho.* Johannesburg and Maseru, 1976
Ashton, H., *The Basuto.* 2nd ed. OUP, 1967
Hailey, Lord, *The Republic of South Africa and the High Commission Territories.* OUP, 1963
Jones, D., *Aid and Development in Southern Africa.* London, 1977
Murray, C., *Families Divided: The Impact of Migrant Labour in Lesotho.* OUP, 1981
Spence, J. E., *Lesotho.* OUP, 1968
Stevens, C., *Food, Aid and the Developing World.* London, 1979

LIBERIA

Capital: Monrovia
Population: 1·9m. (1981)
GNP per capita: US$520 (1980)

HISTORY. The Republic of Liberia had its origin in the efforts of several American philanthropic societies to establish freed American slaves in a colony on the West African coast. In 1822 a settlement was formed near the spot where Monrovia now stands. On 26 July 1847 the State was constituted as the Free and Independent Republic of Liberia. The new State was first recognized by Great Britain and France, and ultimately by other powers.

AREA AND POPULATION. Liberia has about 350 miles of coastline, extending from Sierra Leone, on the west, to the Ivory Coast, on the east, and it stretches inland to a distance, in some places, of about 250 miles. The boundaries were determined by the Anglo-Liberian agreement of 1885 and the Franco-Liberian agreements of 1882 and 1907–10. In 1911 the territory of Kailahun was transferred to Sierra Leone in exchange for a strip on the south side of Mano River, which now is the boundary.

The total area is about 43,000 sq. miles (112,600 sq. km). A census taken in 1978 gave the total population as 1,715,973 (872,105 males). Estimate (1981) 1·9m. The indigenous natives belong in the main to 4 principal stocks: Mendetan, West Atlantic, Mande-fu, and Kru. These are in turn subdivided into 16 major tribes, namely: Bassa, Belle, Gbandi, Mende, Gio, Dey, Mano, Gola, Kpelle, Kissi, Krahn, Kru, Loma, Mandingo, Vai and Grebo.

Monrovia, the capital, had (1981) a population of 306,460. It is one of the 4 ports of entry along the 350 miles of coast, the others being Buchanan (Grand Bassa), River Cess, Greenville (Sinoe), Harper (Maryland). Other towns are Kolba City, Voinjama, Tubmanburg, Bensonville, Zorzor, Kakata, Suakoko, Gbarnga, Ganta, Sanniquellie, Saclape, Tappita, Robertsport, Bendja, Yekepa and Zwedru.

The country is divided into 9 counties and 6 territories and the district of Monrovia.

CLIMATE. An equatorial climate, with constant high temperatures and plentiful rainfall, though Jan. to March is drier than the rest of the year. Monrovia. Jan. 79°F (26·1°C), July 76°F (24·4°C). Annual rainfall 206″ (5,138 mm).

CONSTITUTION AND GOVERNMENT. The Constitution of the Republic is modelled on that of the US. The executive power is vested in a President and the legislative power in a legislature of 2 Houses, the Senate (27 members) and the House of Representatives (71 members). The President is elected for 8 years in the first instance, the House of Representatives for 4 and the Senate for 6 years. A Legislative Act was approved on 22 July 1974, setting up a National Commission to give consideration to possible changes in the Constitution in preparation for a return to civilian rule in 1985.

On 12 April 1980, President Tolbert was assassinated; his government was overthrown and the Constitution suspended. President Tolbert's party, the True Whig Party, was formed in 1860 and had been in power since 1870. Recent economic decline and pressure for change had undermined the Government. In March 1980, the newly formed People's Progressive Party was banned and its leaders arrested. The *coup* was led by Master-Sergeant Doe who was later installed as Head of State and Commander-in-Chief of the army.

Executive power is vested in the Head of State and a Cabinet of 17 which is supervised by a People's Redemption Council. A draft Constitution was published in 1983 and a return to civilian rule is envisaged for 1985.

Head of State and Commander-in-Chief: Samuel Kanyon Doe.
Foreign Minister: T. Ernest Eastman.

The official language is English.

National flag: Six red and 5 white horizontal stripes alternating. In the upper corner, nearest the staff, is a square of blue covering a depth of 5 stripes. In the centre of this blue field is a 5-pointed white star.

National anthem: All hail, Liberia, hail! (words by President Warner; tune by O. Lucas, 1860).

DEFENCE

Army. The establishment organized on a militia basis numbers 4,900 (1983), divided into 5 infantry battalions with support units. There is in addition an enlisted frontier force, the Liberian National Guard, of 93 officers and 2,200 men. Equipment includes 12 M-3A1 scout cars.

Navy. The small naval service or coastguard comprises 3 small patrol boats and 3 new coastguard cutters. Personnel in 1984 totalled 445 officers and men.

Air Force. The nucleus of an Air Force has been formed, as the Air Reconnaissance Unit, to support the Liberian Army. Equipment includes 2 C-47 transports, an Israeli-built Arava twin-turboprop light transport and a small number of Cessna 172, 185, 207 and 337G light aircraft. HAL Chetak (licence-built Alouette III) helicopters are expected to follow from India. Personnel about 250.

INTERNATIONAL RELATIONS

Membership. Liberia is a member of UN, OAU, ECOWAS and is an ACP state of EEC.

ECONOMY

Budget. The budgets for calendar years were as follows (in US$1,000):

	1977	1978	1979	1980	1981
Revenue	166,500	185,500	204,100	222,400	223,000
Expenditure	194,000	227,600	286,300	279,300	303,000

Currency. The legal currency of Liberia is the *dollar* which is equivalent to US$1 which itself has been in circulation since 1 Nov. 1942, but there is a Liberian coinage in silver and copper. Official accounts are kept in dollars and cents. The Liberian coins are as follows: Silver,$5, $1, 50-, 25-, 10- and 5-cent pieces; alloy, 2-and 1-cent pieces. The Government has not yet issued paper money. In March 1984, £1 = 1·49 Liberian $; US$1 = 1 Liberian $. ·

Banking. The First National City Bank (Liberia) was founded in 1935. An Italian bank, Tradevco, started business in 1955. The International Trust Co. of Liberia opened a commercial banking department at the end of 1960. A branch of the Chase Manhattan Bank opened in 1961. The Liberian Bank for Development and Investment (LBDI) was founded in 1964 and began operations in 1965. The National Bank of Liberia opened on 22 July 1974, to act as a central bank. The National Housing and Savings Bank opened on 20 Jan. 1972. The Liberian Finance & Trust Corporation was incorporated Oct. 1976 and began operations in May 1977. The Liberian Agricultural and Co-operative Development Bank started operations in 1978. The Bank of Credit & Commerce International opened in Sept. 1978.

Weights and Measures. Weights and measures are the same as in UK and USA.

NATURAL RESOURCES

Minerals. The National Iron Ore Co. near the Mano River, the Liberian Swedish Mineral Co. in the Nimba Mountains and the Bong Mining Co. (DELIMCO) at Bong Mountain Range are exploiting their iron-ore concession areas. Iron ore production amounted to 20·6m. tonnes in 1981. Total employment in iron ore mining was 8,815 in 1981. Gold and diamonds are found on a small scale.

Agriculture. The soil is productive, but due to excessive rainfall (from 160 to 180 in. per year), there are large swamp areas. Rice, cassava, coffee, citrus and sugar-cane are cultivated. The Government is negotiating the financing of large-scale investment in rice production aimed at making the country self-sufficient in rice production. Coffee, cocoa and palm-kernels are produced mainly by the traditional agricultural sector. In 1981, the total volume of coffee and cocoa exports alone were 18·3m. lb. (US$19·4m.), and 14·8m. lb. (US$13·8m.), respectively.

The Liberia Produce Marketing Corporation (LPMC) operates an oil-mill in Monrovia, processing most of the palm-kernels. There were 2 large commercial oil-palm plantations in the country. The Liberia Industrial Co-operative (LBINC) has 6,000 acres of oil-palm (of which 5,000 acres are in production) in Grand Bassa County,and West Africa Agricultural Co. (WAAC) has 4,020 acres in production in Grand Cape Mount County.

Livestock (1982): Cattle, 41,000; pigs, 112,000; sheep, 220,000; poultry, 2·8m.

Forestry. The Firestone Plantation Co. have large rubber plantations, employing over 40,000 men. Their concession comprises about 1m. acres and expires in the year 2025. About 100,000 acres have been planted. Independent producers have a further 65,000 acres planted. In 1976 the total area under rubber cultivation was 294,400 acres, of which 195,800 acres were under actual production.

Other rubber producing companies include Goodrich Rubber Plantation, Allen L. Grant, L. A. C and Salala Rubber Co. Together, the foreign concessions produced 131·6m. lb. in 1981 while independent Liberian farmers produced 148·7m. lb. in 1981. The production of logs in 1981 was 451m. cu. metres; 1980, 745m.

INDUSTRY AND TRADE

Industry. There are a number of small factories (brick and tile, soap, nails, mattresses, shoes, plastics, paint, oxygen, acetylene, tyre retreading, a brewery, soft drinks, cement, matches, candy and biscuits).

Commerce. Foreign trade for 6 calendar years was as follows (in US$1m.):

	1976	1977	1978	1979	1980	1981
Imports	399·2	463·5	486	537	533·8	477·4
Exports	457·0	447·4	481	505	600·4	529·2

The principal exports in 1981 were: Iron cre, and concentrates, US$325·4m.; rubber, US$86·7m.; logs and lumber, US$36·8m. The principal imports in 1981 were machinery and transport equipment (US$118·9m.) and manufactured goods (US$61·3m.). Main suppliers in 1981 were: Asia and European countries (US$200m.), USA (US$142·1m.), other countries (US$136·3m.).

Total trade between Liberia and UK (British Department of Trade returns, in £1,000 sterling):

	1979	1980	1981	1982	1983
Imports to UK	14,359	8,671	6,014	8,213	7,181
Exports and re-exports from UK	78,408	45,412	24,262	14,069	13,877

The figures for exports from the UK include the value of shipping transferred to the Liberian flag; the genuine exports are considerably lower.

Tourism. The National Bureau of Culture and Tourism was created in July 1981.

COMMUNICATIONS

Roads. In 1981, there were 4,794 miles of public roads (1,165 primary, 366 paved, 799 all-weather, 3,629 secondary and feeder) and 1,474 miles of private roads (93 paved, 1,381 laterite and earth). The principal highway connects Monrovia with the road system of Guinea, with branches leading into the Eastern and Western areas of Liberia. The latter branch reaches the Sierra Leone border and joins the Sierra Leone road system. A bridge over the St Paul River carries road and rail traffic to the iron-ore mines at Bomi Hills.

Railway. A railway (for freight only) was built in 1951, connecting Monrovia with the Bomi Hills iron-ore mines about 69 km distant; this has been extended to the National Iron Ore Co. area by 79 km. A line from Nimba to Lower Buchanan (267 km) was completed in 1963 and another line from Bong to Monrovia (78 km) was completed in 1965.

Aviation. The airport for Liberia is Roberts Airport (30 miles from Monrovia). The James Spriggs Payne Airfield, 5 miles from Monrovia, can be used by light aircraft and mini jumbo jets. Air services are maintained by PANAM, Ghana Airways, Nigeria Airways, UTA, Middle East Airlines, Air Mali, Air Afrique, SAS, KLM, Swissair, British Caledonian, Air Guinée, SABENA, Iberia Airlines, Romanian Airlines and Air Liberia.

Shipping. In 1981, 2,277 vessels entered Monrovia.

The Liberian merchant navy, in 1976, consisted of 2,666 ships of 76,412,842 GRT. The Liberian Government requires only a modest registration fee and an almost nominal annual charge and maintains no control over the operation of ships flying the Liberian flag.

Post and Broadcasting. There is cable communication (French) with Europe and America *via* Dakar, and a wireless station is maintained by the Government at Monrovia. There is a telephone service (7,079 telephones, 1980), in Monrovia, which is gradually being extended over the whole country. An earth station constructed by Itacable in 1976 is equipped for 24 telephone type channels and its traffic can be increased to 60 telephone type channels. With the aid of the satellite, automatic telephone and telegraph services to and from many countries are transmitted on a 24-hour basis.

There are wireless stations at Monrovia, Bassa, Harper, Kolahun, Cape Mount and Sinoe. There were (1982) 320,000 radio and 21,000 television receivers.

JUSTICE, RELIGION, EDUCATION AND WELFARE

Justice. Justice is administered by a Supreme Court of 5 judges, circuit courts and lower courts. A new Liberian code of laws has been published (5 vols. to 1956).

Religion. The main denominations represented in Liberia are Methodist, Baptist, Episcopalian, African Methodist, Pentecostal, Seventh-day Adventist, Lutheran and Roman Catholic, working through missionaries and mission schools. There are about 670,000 Moslems.

Education. Schools are classified as: (1) Public schools, maintained and run by the Government; (2) Mission schools, supported by foreign Missions and subsidized by the Government, and operated by qualified Missionaries and Liberian teachers; (3) Private schools, maintained by endowments and sometimes subsidized by the Government.

By the end of 1981 there were estimated to be 1,651 schools with 8,804 teachers and 303,268 pupils.

Health. There were 236 doctors in 1981 and about 3,000 hospital beds.

DIPLOMATIC REPRESENTATIVES

Of Liberia in Great Britain (21 Prince's Gate, London, SW7 1QB)
Ambassador: Dr Harry Moniba (accredited 13 May 1981).

Of Great Britain in Liberia (Mamba Point, Monrovia)
Ambassador and Consul-General: D. G. Reid, CMG.

Of Liberia in the USA (5201–16th St., NW, Washington, D.C., 20011)
Chargé d'Affaires: W. Elwood Greaves.

Of the USA in Liberia (United Nations Drive, Monrovia)
Ambassador: William L. Swing.

Of Liberia to the United Nations
Ambassador: Dr Abeodu B. Jones.

Books of Reference

Economic Survey of Liberia, 1981. Ministry of Planning and Economic Affairs
Dunn, D. E., *The Foreign Policy of Liberia during the Tubman Era, 1944–71.* London, 1979
Fraenkel, M., *Tribe and Class in Monrovia.* OUP, 1964
Wilson, C. M., *Liberia: Black Africa in Microcosm.* New York, 1971

LIBYA

Al-Jamahiriyah Al-Arabiya
Al-Libya Al-Shabiya
Al-Ishtirakiya

Capital: Tripoli
Population: 3·5m. (1982)
GNP per capita: US$8,640 (1980)

HISTORY. Tripoli fell under Turkish domination in the 16th century, and though in 1711 the Arab population secured some measure of independence, the country was in 1835 proclaimed a Turkish vilayet. In Sept. 1911 Italy occupied Tripoli and on 19 Oct. 1912, by the Treaty of Ouchy, Turkey recognized the sovereignty of Italy in Tripoli.

After the expulsion of the Germans and Italians in 1942 and 1943, Tripolitania and Cyrenaica were placed under British, and the Fezzan under French, military administration. Britain recognized the Amir Mohammed Idris Al-Senussi as Amir of Cyrenaica in June 1949.

Libya became an independent, sovereign, federal kingdom under the Amir of Cyrenaica, Mohammed Idris Al-Senussi, as King of the United Kingdom of Libya, on 24 Dec. 1951, when the British Residents in Tripolitania and Cyrenaica and the French Resident in the Fezzan transferred their remaining powers to the federal government of Libya, in pursuance of decisions passed by the United Nations in 1949 and 1950.

On 1 Sept. 1969 King Idris was deposed by a group of army officers. Twelve of the group of officers formed the Revolutionary Command Council chaired by Col. Muammar Qadhafi and proclaimed a republic. The RCC ruled the country through an appointed Council of Ministers until 2 March 1977, when both were abolished as constitutional government was resumed.

AREA AND POPULATION. The area is estimated at 1,759,540 sq. km (679,358 sq. miles). The population, according to the census of 1973, was 2,249,237. Estimate (1982) 3·5m.

The country is divided administratively in 25 municipalities with the following main population centres: Tripoli, 980,000; Benghazi, 650,000; Misurata, 285,000; Zavia, 247,000; Sebha (the main town in the southern province) 113,000.

CLIMATE. The coastal region has a warm temperate climate, with mild wet winters and hot dry summers, though most of the country suffers from aridity. Tripoli. Jan. 52°F (11·1°C), July 81°F (27·2°C). Annual rainfall 16″ (400 mm). Benghazi. Jan. 56°F (13·3°C), July 77°F (25°C). Annual rainfall 11″ (267 mm).

CONSTITUTION AND GOVERNMENT. Under the new 1977 Constitution, Libya is now divided into 25 municipalities and 126 'Basic People's Congresses', which form the primary level of government. The General People's Congress, created in Jan. 1976 as the national legislature, comprises 3 delegates from each of the 186 Basic People's Congresses. The General People's Committee, which replaced the Council of Ministers, is assisted by the 5-member General People's Secretariat, which replaced the Revolutionary Command Council. It was ruled by the Revolutionary Command Council (RCC) under the leadership of Col. Muammar Qadhafi.

In March 1977 a new form of direct democracy, the 'Jamahiriya' (state of the masses) was promulgated and the official name of the country was changed to Socialist Peoples Libyan Arab Jamahiriya. At local level authority is now vested in 186 Basic and 25 Municipal People's Congresses which appoint Popular Committees to execute policy. Officials of these Congresses and Committees form at national level the General People's Congress, a body of some 1,000 delegates which normally meets for about a week twice a year. This is the highest policy-making body in the country. The General People's Congress appoints its own General Secretariat and the General People's Committee, whose members head the 20 government departments which execute policy at national level. The Secretary of the General People's Committee has functions similar to those of a Prime Minister.

Following the re-organization of March 1979 Col. Qadhafi retained his position as leader of the Revolution. But neither he nor his former RCC colleagues have any formal posts in the new administration.

Arabic is the official language. Tripoli is the capital.

Secretary-General of the General Secretariat of the General People's Congress: Muhamed Áz-Zaruq Rajab.

National flag: Plain green.

DEFENCE. Libyans are liable for 18 months' service at the age of 18. Enrolment in the reserves, numbering about 40,000, continues until aged 49.

Army. The Army is organized into 20 tank battalions, 30 mechanized infantry, 1 National Guard, 10 artillery, 2 anti-aircraft and 2 surface-to-surface missile battalions. Equipment includes 2,600 T-54/-55/-62, 200 T-72 and 100 OF-40 main battle tanks. Strength (1984) 58,000. The paramilitary Pan-African Legion numbers about 10,000.

Navy. The fleet comprises 6 *ex*-Soviet diesel-driven submarines, 1 missile-armed frigate, 6 missile-armed corvettes, 1 gun corvette, 4 ocean minesweepers, 25 fast missile craft, 2 fast gunboats, 8 patrol boats, 1 medium (dock type) logistic support ship, 2 landing ships, 3 medium landing ships, 20 landing craft, 1 maintenance repair craft, 1 diving ship, 1 transport and 7 tugs. Under construction or projection are 2 missile-armed corvettes, 10 fast attack craft and 30 landing craft.

Libya has procured naval equipment and weapons from both the East (particularly the USSR) and the West; and the increasing and up-to-date fleet constitutes a force of crucial importance in the Mediterranean.

Personnel in 1984 was upwards of 4,000 officers and ratings, including coastguard. A large proportion of naval personnel have been trained in the Soviet Union since 1975.

Air Force. The creation of an Air Force began in 1959. In 1974, delivery was completed of a total of 110 Mirage 5 combat aircraft and trainers, of which about 50 remain. They have been followed by 7 Tu-22 supersonic reconnaissance bombers, 50 MiG-25 interceptors and reconnaissance aircraft, 102 Su-22 ground attack fighters, 94 MiG-21s, and about 160 MiG-23 variable-geometry fighters and fighter-bombers from the USSR. Other equipment includes 50 Mirage F1 fighters from France, 6 Mirage F1-B two-seat trainers, 25 Mi-24 gunship helicopters, Mi-14 anti-submarine helicopters, up to 15 Il-76, 7 C-130H Hercules and 20 Aeritalia G222T transports, 7 Super Frelon and 20 Agusta-built CH-47C Chinook heavy-lift helicopters, and a total of about 23 Bell 212, Bell 47, Alouette III and Mi-8 helicopters. Training is performed on piston-engined SF.260Ms (some of which are armed for light attack duties) from Italy; L-39 Albatros, Galeb and Magister jet aircraft; and twin-engined Xingus built in Brazil. Personnel total about 8,500, with many of the combat aircraft operated by foreign aircrew. Aircraft on order include more Mirage F1 fighters from France and MiG-23s from the USSR.

INTERNATIONAL RELATIONS

Membership. Libya is a member of UN, OAU and the Arab League.

ECONOMY

Planning. Declining oil revenues (50% down on 1980 levels) has meant postponing of most projects envisaged in the 5-year development plan (1981–85).

Budget. A development budget of LD2,370m. was announced for 1983 but is likely to be under-spent by 50%.

Currency. The currency is the Libyan *dinar* which is divided into 1,000 *millemes*. Rate of exchange, March 1984: LD0·44 = £1; LD0·30 = US$1.

Banking. A National Bank of Libya was established in 1955; it was renamed the Central Bank of Libya in 1972. All foreign banks were nationalized by Dec. 1970. In 1972 the Libyan Government set up the Libyan Arab Foreign Bank whose function is overseas investment and to participate in multinational banking corporations. The National Agricultural Bank, which has been set up to give loans and subsidies to farmers to develop their land and to assist them in marketing their crops, has offices in Tripoli, Benghazi, Sebha and other agricultural centres. The National Industrial and Real Estate Bank has been divided to form a Real Estate Bank to provide loans for house-buyers and the Development Bank to finance industrial projects.

Weights and Measures. Although the metric system has been officially adopted and is obligatory for all contracts, the following weights and measures are still used: *oke* = 1·282 kg; *kantar* = 51·28 kg; *draa* = 46 cm; *handaza* = 68 cm.

ENERGY AND NATURAL RESOURCES

Electricity. Electricity output capacity in 1980 was 1,950 mw and under the development plan was scheduled to rise to 3,878 mw by 1985.

Oil. Production (1981) 420m. bbls. Reserves (1981) 21,000m. bbls. The Libyan National Oil Corporation (NOC) was established in March 1970 to be the state's organization for the exploitation of Libya's oil resources. NOC does not participate in the production of oil but has a majority share in all the operating companies with the exception of two small producers Aquitaine-Libya and Wintershall Libya.

The largest producers are Oasis (59·2% NOC, Marathon and Conoco, 16·3% and Amerada Hess 8·2%) and AGOCO (100% NOC) who together produce more than 50% of total production. The other significant producers are Occidental Libya (51% NOC, 49% Occidental US) AGIP N.A.M.E. (50% NOC, 50% AGIP Italy) SIRTE Oil Co. (formerly ESSO Libya until EXXON withdrew in Oct. 1981) and Mobil Oil Libya Ltd. (82·8% NOC, 17·2% Veba-Gelsenberg) who continue to use the Mobil name despite the fact that Mobil Inc. followed EXXON's example and withdrew in July 1982.

Gas. Reserves (1982) 670,000m. cu. metres. Production (1982) 29,000m. cu. metres. In 1983 a gas pipeline was under construction which will take gas from Brega, along the coast to Misurata.

Minerals. There were (1984) 5 cement factories with a capacity of 4·75m. tonnes per annum. Two new plants were under construction in 1984 with a capacity of 2·5m. tonnes. Gypsum output (1975) 15,000 tonnes. Iron ore deposits have been found in the south.

Agriculture. Tripolitania has 3 zones from the coast inland—the Mediterranean, the sub-desert and the desert. The first, which covers an area of about 17,231 sq. miles, is the only one properly suited for agriculture, and may be further subdivided into: (1) the oases along the coast, the richest in North Africa, in which thrive the date palm, the olive, the orange, the peanut and the potato; (2) the steppe district, suitable for cereals (barley and wheat) and pasture; it has olive, almond, vine, orange and mulberry trees and ricinus plants; (3) the dunes, which are being gradually afforested with acacia, robinia, poplar and pine; (4) the Jebel (the mountain district, Tarhuna, Garian, Nalut-Yefren), in which thrive the olive, the fig, the vine and other fruit trees, and which on the east slopes down to the sea with the fertile hills of Msellata. Of some 25m. acres of productive land in Tripolitania, nearly 20m. are used for grazing and about 1m. for static farming. The sub-desert zone produces the alfa plant. The desert zone and the Fezzan contain some fertile oases, such as those of Ghadames, Ghat, Socna, Sebha, Brak.

Cyrenaica has about 10m. acres of potentially productive land, most of which, however, is suitable only for grazing. Certain areas, chief of which is the plateau known as the Barce Plain (about 1,000 ft above sea-level), are suitable for dry farming; in addition, grapes, olives and dates are grown. With improved irrigation, production, particularly of vegetables, could be increased, but stock raising and dry farming will remain of primary importance. About 143,000 acres are used for settled farming; about 272,000 acres are covered by natural forests. The Agricultural Development Authority plans to reclaim 6,000 hectares each year for agriculture.

In the Fezzan there are about 6,700 acres of irrigated gardens and about 297,000 acres are planted with date palms.

Production (1980, in tonnes): Wheat, 141,000; barley, 71,000; milk, 85,000; meat, 119,000. Olive trees number about 3·4m. and productive date-palm trees about 3m.

Livestock (1982): 5·6m. sheep, 1·5m. goats, 194,000 cattle, 7m. poultry.

INDUSTRY AND TRADE

Industry. Among the traditional industries of Tripolitania and Cyrenaica are sponge fishing, tunny fishing, tobacco growing and processing, dyeing and weaving of local wool and imported cotton yarn, and olive oil. Tripolitania also produces bricks, salt, leather and esparto grass for paper-making. Home industries of both territories include the making of matting, carpets, leather articles and fabrics embroidered with gold and silver. The Government has embarked on an ambitious programme of industrial development aimed at the local manufacture of building materials (steel and aluminium pipes and fittings, electric cables, cement, bricks, glass, etc.), foodstuffs (dairy products, flour, tinned fruits and vegetables, dates, fish processing and canning, etc.), textiles and footwear (ready-made clothing, woollen and cotton cloth, blankets, leather footwear, etc.) and development of mineral deposits (iron ore, phosphates, mineral salts). Small scale private sector industrialization is encouraged by government loans and subsidies.

On 21 Sept. 1969 a decree laid down that all business concerns should be 100% Libyan-owned, but oil companies and banks were excluded.

Commerce. Total imports in 1981 were valued at US$8,390 (f.o.b.) and exports of US$15,466 (f.o.b.), mostly crude oil.

Total trade between Libya and UK (British Department of Trade returns, in £1,000 sterling):

	1979	1980	1981	1982	1983
Imports to UK	62,167	46,528	74,810	342,476	224,050
Exports and re-exports from UK	253,153	288,358	520,416	260,937	274,169

COMMUNICATIONS

Roads. Good motor roads connect Tripoli through Zuara with Tunis, and through Homs and Misurata with Benghazi and thence with Tobruk and Alexandria, although the border with Egypt has been closed for some years. Other roads go south and south-west from Tripoli to Tiagura, Garian, Yefren, Nalut and Ghadames. A road connects Sebha in the south with the main coastal road. An ambitious road building programme is being implemented and a road will eventually link Libya with Chad and Niger through Sebha. A further main road is being built to link Kufra, a major agricultural centre in the south-eastern part of Libya with the coastal road.

Surface communication between Benghazi and Tripoli is by frequent bus service, and there are also bus services between Benghazi and Alexandria, and between Tripoli, Tunis and Algiers.

Railways. There were in 1982 no railways, but a major railway project has been planned to run along the coast from the Tunisian to the Egyptian border.

Aviation. Benghazi and Tripoli are both served by international airlines, linking them with each other and Athens, Rome, Malta, Tunis, Frankfurt, Paris, Amsterdam, Algiers, Lagos and London. British Caledonian has 5 flights weekly between Tripoli and London.

A national airline, the Libyan Arab Airlines (LAA), was inaugurated on 30 Sept.

1965. Apart from internal flights LAA operate to Athens, London, Rome, Beirut, Paris, Malta, Algiers, Moscow, Cotonou and Tunis.

Post and Broadcasting. Tripoli is connected by telegraph cable with Malta and by microwave link with Bengardane (Tunis). There are overseas wireless-telegraph stations at Benghazi and Tripoli, and radio-telephone services connect Libya with most countries of western Europe. In 1971 some 41,495 telephones were in use and in 1982 there were 150,000 radio sets and 160,000 television receivers.

Newspapers. There is one daily in Tripoli with a circulation of about 40,000.

JUSTICE, RELIGION, EDUCATION AND WELFARE

Justice. The Civil, Commercial and Criminal codes are based mainly on the Egyptian model. Matters of personal status of family or succession matters affecting Moslems are dealt with in special courts according to the Moslem law. All other matters, civil, commercial and criminal, are tried in the ordinary courts, which have jurisdiction over everyone.

There are civil and penal courts in Tripoli and Benghazi, with subsidiary courts at Misurata and Derna; courts of assize in Tripoli and Benghazi, and courts of appeal in Tripoli and Benghazi.

Religion. Islam is declared the State religion, but the right of others to practise their religions is provided for.

Education. There were (1980–81) 675,000 pupils in primary schools, 223,000 in preparatory schools and 40,000 in secondary schools. There are 2 universities of Al Fatah (in Tripoli) and Garyounes (in Benghazi).

Social Welfare. In 1980 there were 14,472 hospital beds and 4,300 physicians and dentists.

DIPLOMATIC REPRESENTATIVES

Of Libya in Great Britain (5 St James's Sq., London, SW1)
Secretary-General of the People's Committee: Adem Saleh Kuwiri.

Of Great Britain in Libya (30 Sharia Gamal Abdul Nasser, Tripoli)
Ambassador: R. O. Miles, CMG.

USA suspended all embassy activities in Tripoli on 2 May 1980.

Of Libya to the United Nations
Ambassador: Dr Ali A. Treiki.

Books of Reference

Allen, J. A., *Libya: The Experience of Oil.* London and Boulder, 1981
Ansell, M. O., and al-Arif, I. M., *The Libyan Revolution.* London, 1972
Bianco, M., *Gadafi: Voice from the Desert.* London, 1975
Cooley, J. K., *Libyan Sandstorm.* London, 1983
Waddhams, F. C., *The Libyan Oil Industry.* London, 1980
Wright, J., *Libya: A Modern History.* London, 1982

LIECHTENSTEIN

Capital: Vaduz
Population: 26,380 (1982)
GNP per capita: US$16,440 (1980)

HISTORY. The Principality of Liechtenstein, situated between the Austrian province of Vorarlberg and the Swiss cantons of St Gallen and Graubünden, is a sovereign state whose history dates back to 3 May 1342, when Count Hartmann III became ruler of the county of Vaduz. Additions were later made to the count's domains, and by 1434 the territory reached its present boundaries. It consists of the two former counties of Schellenberg and Vaduz (until 1806 immediate fiefs of the Roman Empire). The former in 1699 and the latter in 1712 came into the possession of the house of Liechtenstein and, by diploma of 23 Jan. 1719, granted by the Emperor Charles VI, the two counties were constituted as the Principality of Liechtenstein.

AREA AND POPULATION. Liechtenstein is bounded on the east by Austria and the west by Switzerland. Area, 160 sq. km (61·8 sq. miles); population, of Alemannic race (census 1980), 25,215; estimate, 1982, 26,380. In 1982 there were 379 births and 170 deaths. Population of Vaduz (census 1980), 4,606; estimate, 1982, 4,904.

REIGNING PRINCE. Francis Joseph II, born 16 Aug. 1906; succeeded his great uncle, 26 July 1938; married on 7 March 1943 to Countess Gina von Wilczek; there are 4 sons, Princes Hans Adam (*heir apparent*, born 14 Feb. 1945; married on 30 July 1967 to Countess Marie Aglaë Kinsky), Philipp Erasmus (married on 11 Sept. 1971 to Isabelle de l'Arbre de Malander), Nikolaus Ferdinand (married on 20 March 1982 to Princess Margaretha of Luxembourg) and Franz Josef Wenzel, and one daughter, Princess Nora Elisabeth. The monarchy is hereditary in the male line.

National flag: Horizontally blue over red, with a gold coronet in the first quarter.
National anthem: Oben am jungen Rhein (words by H. H. Jauch, 1850; tune, 'God save the Queen').

CONSTITUTION AND GOVERNMENT. Liechtenstein is a constitutional monarchy ruled by the hereditary princes of the House of Liechtenstein. The present constitution of 5 Oct. 1921 provides for a unicameral parliament (Diet) of 15 members elected for 4 years. Election is by universal adult male suffrage and is on the basis of proportional representation. In 2 communes (Vaduz and Gamprin) women are allowed to vote and hold office on communal basis. The prince can call and dismiss the parliament. On parliamentary recommendation, he appoints the prime minister and the 4 councillors for a 4-year term. Any group of 600 persons or any 3 communes may propose legislation (initiative). Bills passed by the parliament may be submitted to popular referendum. A law is valid when it receives a majority approval by the parliament and the prince's signed concurrence. The capital and seat of government is Vaduz and there are 10 more communes all connected by modern roads. The 11 communes are fully independent administrative bodies within the laws of the principality. They levy additional taxes to the state taxes. Since Feb. 1921 Liechtenstein has had the Swiss currency, and since 29 March 1923 has been united with Switzerland in a customs union. Switzerland has also since 1919 represented the Principality diplomatically.

At the elections for the Diet, on 7 Feb. 1982, the Fatherland Union obtained 8 seats, the opposition Progressive Citizens' Party, 7 seats.

Head of Government: Hans Brunhart.

INTERNATIONAL RELATIONS

Membership. Liechtenstein is a member of EFTA, the Council of Europe and the International Court of Justice.

ECONOMY

Budget. Budget estimates for 1983: Revenue, 263,346,000 Swiss francs; expenditure, 259,563,000 Swiss francs. There is no public debt.

Currency. The Swiss *franc*.

Banking. There were (1983) 3 banks: Liechtensteinische Landesbank, Bank in Liechtenstein Ltd, Verwaltungs-und Privatbank Ltd.

Weights and Measures. The metric system is in force.

ENERGY AND NATURAL RESOURCES

Electricity. Electricity produced in 1982 was 53·35m. kwh.

Agriculture. The rearing of cattle, for which the fine alpine pastures are well suited, is highly developed. In July 1983 there were 6,052 cattle (including 2,578 milch cows), 131 horses, 2,218 sheep, 144 goats, 3,048 pigs. Total production of dairy produce, 1982, 9,840,526 kg.

INDUSTRY AND TRADE

Industry. The country has a great variety of light industries (textiles, ceramics, steel screws, precision instruments, canned food, pharmaceutical products, heating appliances, etc.).

Since 1945 Liechtenstein has changed from a predominantly agricultural country to a highly industrialized country. The farming population has gone down from 70% in 1930 to only 3% in 1982. The rapid change-over has led to the immigration of foreign workers (Austrians, Germans, Italians, Spaniards). Industrial undertakings in 1982 employed 6,130 workers earning 264m. Swiss francs.

Commerce. Exports of home produce in 1982 amounted to 894m. Swiss francs. 31·9% went to EFTA countries, of which Switzerland took 231·8m. (23·9%) and 39·2% went to EEC countries.

Total trade with UK is included with Switzerland from 1968.

Tourism. In 1982, 79,757 foreign visitors stayed in Liechtenstein.

COMMUNICATIONS

Roads. There are 250 km of roads. Postal buses are the chief means of public transportation within the country and to Austria and Switzerland.

Railways. The 18·5 km of main railway passing through the country is operated by Austrian Federal Railways.

Post and Broadcasting. In 1982 there were 10,986 telephones, 409 telex, 8,068 wireless sets and 7,608 television sets. The post and telegraphs are administered by Switzerland.

Cinemas. There were 3 cinemas in 1983.

Newspapers. In 1982 there were 2 daily newspapers with a total circulation of 15,200.

JUSTICE, RELIGION, EDUCATION AND WELFARE

Justice. The principality has its own civil and penal codes. The lowest court is the county court, *Landgericht*, presided over by one judge, which decides minor civil cases and summary criminal offences. The criminal court, *Kriminalgericht*, with a bench of 5 judges is for major crimes. Another court of mixed jurisdiction is the court of assizes (with 3 judges) for misdemeanours. The superior court, *Obergericht*, and Supreme Court, *Oberster Gerichtshof*, are courts of appeal for civil and criminal cases (both with benches of 5 judges). An administrative court of appeal from government actions and the State Court determines the constitutionality of laws.

Police. The principality has no army. Police force, 40; auxiliary police, 22 (1983).

Religion. In 1982, 85·2% of the population was Roman Catholic and 8·7% was Protestant.

Education (1983). In 14 primary, 3 upper, 4 secondary, 1 grammar and 3 (for backward children) schools there were 3,723 pupils and 290 teachers. There is also an evening technical school, a music school and a children's pedagogic-welfare day school.

Health. In 1983 there was 1 hospital, but Liechtenstein has an agreement with the Swiss cantons of St Gallen and Graubünden that her citizens may use certain hospitals.

DIPLOMATIC REPRESENTATIVES

British Consul-General: G. N. Smith (resident in Zürich).
USA Consul-General: Dr Alfred P. Brainard (resident in Zürich).

Books of Reference

Statistical Information: Amt für Volkswirtschaft, Vaduz.

Rechenschaftsbericht der Fürstlichen Regierung. Vaduz. Annual, from 1922
Jahrbuch des Historischen Vereins. Vaduz. Annual since 1901
Kranz, W., *The Principality of Liechtenstein.* Press and Information Office. 5th ed, Vaduz, 1981
The Liechtenstein Economy. Press and Information Office, Vaduz, 1982
Batliner, E. H., *Das Geld- und Kreditwesen des Fürstentums Liechtenstein in Vergangenheit und Gegenwart.* 1959
Green, B., *Valley of Peace.* Vaduz, 1967
Larke, T. A. T., *Index and Thesaurus of Liechtenstein.* 2nd ed. Berkeley, 1984
Malin, G., *Kunstführer Fürstentum Liechtenstein.* Berne, 1977
Raton, P., *Liechtenstein: History and Institutions of the Principality.* Vaduz, 1970
Seger, O., *A Survey of Liechtenstein History.* 2nd English ed. Vaduz, 1970
Steger, G., *Fürst und Landtag nach Liechtensteinischem Recht.* Vaduz, 1950

LUXEMBOURG

Grand-Duché de Luxembourg

Capital: Luxembourg
Population: 365,500 (1983)
GNP per capita: US$14,510 (1980)

HISTORY. The country formed part of the Holy Roman Empire until it was conquered by the French in 1795. In 1815 the Grand Duchy of Luxembourg was formed under the house of Orange-Nassau, also sovereigns of the Netherlands. In 1839 the Walloon-speaking area was joined to Belgium. In 1890 the personal union with the Netherlands ended with the accession of a member of another branch of the house of Nassau, Grand Duke Adolphe of Nassau-Weilburg.

AREA AND POPULATION. Luxembourg has an area of 2,586 sq. km (998 sq. miles) and is bounded on the west by Belgium, south by France, east by the Federal Republic of Germany. The population (1983) was 365,500. The capital, Luxembourg, had 79,000 inhabitants; Esch-Alzette, the centre of the mining district, 25,142; Differdange, 8,588; Dudelange, 14,074, and Petange, 6,416. In 1982 the foreign population was about 95,900.

Vital statistics (1982): 4,300 births, 4,133 deaths, 2,089 marriages.

CLIMATE. Cold, raw winters with snow covering the ground for up to a month are features of the upland areas. The remainder resembles Belgium in its climate, with rain evenly distributed throughout the year. Jan. 31°F (0·5°C), July 63°F (17·5°C). Annual rainfall 29·6″ (740 mm).

REIGNING GRAND DUKE. Jean, born 5 Jan. 1921, son of Grand Duchess Charlotte and the late Prince Felix of Bourbon-Parma; succeeded 12 Nov. 1964 on the abdication of his mother; married to Princess Joséphine-Charlotte of Belgium, 9 April 1953. *Offspring:* Princess Marie Astrid, born 17 Feb. 1954, married Christian of Habsbourg-Lorraine 6 Feb. 1982; Prince Henri, *heir apparent,* born 16 April 1955, married Maria Teresa Mestre 14 Feb. 1981; *Offspring:* Prince Guillaume Jean Joseph Marie, born 11 Nov. 1981; Prince Jean and Princess Margaretha (married Prince Nikolaus of Liechtenstein 20 March 1982), born 15 May 1957; Prince Guillaume, born 1 May 1963.

The civil list is fixed at 300,000 gold francs per annum, to be reconsidered at the beginning of each reign.

On 28 Sept. 1919 a referendum was taken in Luxembourg to decide on the political and economic future of the country. The voting resulted as follows: For the reigning Grand Duchess, 66,811; for the continuance of the Nassau-Braganza dynasty under another Grand Duchess, 1,286; for another dynasty, 889; for a republic, 16,885; for an economic union with France, 60,133; for an economic union with Belgium, 22,242. But France refused in favour of Belgium, and on 22 Dec. 1921 the Chamber of the Grand Duchy passed a Bill for the economic union between Belgium and Luxembourg. The agreement, which is for 60 years, provides for the disappearance of the customs barrier between the two countries and the use of Belgian, in addition to Luxembourg, currency as legal tender in the Grand Duchy. It came into force on 1 May 1922.

The Grand Duchy was under German occupation from 10 May 1940 to 10 Sept. 1944. The Grand Duchess Charlotte and the Government carried on an independent administration in London. Civil government was restored in Oct. 1944.

National flag: Three horizontal stripes of red, white, blue.
National anthem: Ons Hemecht (words by M. Lentz, 1859; tune by J. A. Zinnen).

CONSTITUTION AND GOVERNMENT. The Grand Duchy of Luxembourg is a constitutional monarchy, the hereditary sovereignty being in the Nassau family. The constitution of 17 Oct. 1868 was revised in 1919, 1948, 1956 and 1972. The revision of 1948 has abolished the 'perpetually neutral' status of the country and introduced the concepts of right to work, social security, health services, freedom of trade and industry, and recognition of trade unions. The revision of 1956 provides for the devolution of executive, legislative and judicial powers to international institutions.

The national language is Luxemburgish; French, German and English are widely used.

The country forms 4 electoral districts. An elector must be a citizen (male or female) of Luxembourg and have completed 18 years of age; to be eligible for election the citizen must have completed 21 years of age.

The Chamber of Deputies consists of 24 Christian Social, 14 Socialists, 15 Democrats, 2 Social Democrats, 2 Communists, 1 Independent Socialist and 1 co-opted deputy (elections of 10 June 1979). Members are elected for 5 years; they receive a salary and a travelling allowance.

The head of the state takes part in the legislative power, exercises the executive power and has a certain part in the judicial power. The constitution leaves to the sovereign the right to organize the Government, which consists of a Minister of State, who is President of the Government, and of at least 3 Ministers.

The Cabinet was, in Feb. 1983, composed as follows:

President of the Government, Minister of State, Treasury, Culture, General Affairs, National Protection, Information and Press: Pierre Werner.

Vice-President, Foreign Affairs, External Commerce and Co-operation, Economy and Middle Classes, Justice: Colette Flesch. *Health, Public Forces, Physical Education and Sport:* Emile Krieps. *Agriculture, Viticulture, Water and Forests:* Ernest Mühlen. *Environment, Transport, Communications and Information, Energy:* Josy Barthel. *Finance:* Jacques Santer. *Public Works and Functions:* René Konen. *Interior, Family, Social Living and Social Solidarity:* Jean Spautz. *National Education and Tourism:* Fernand Boden. *Secretary of State for Foreign Affairs, External Commerce and Co-operation, Economy and Middle Classes, Justice:* Paul Helminger. *Labour and Social Security:* Jean-Claude Juncker.

Besides the Cabinet there is a Council of State. It deliberates on proposed laws and Bills, and on amendments; it also gives administrative decisions and expresses its opinion regarding any other question referred to it by the Grand Duke or the Government. The Council of State is composed of 21 members chosen for life by the sovereign, who also chooses a president from among them each year.

DEFENCE. A law passed by Parliament on 29 June 1967 abolished compulsory service and instituted a battalion-size army of volunteers enlisted for 3 years. Strength (1983) 500. The defence estimates for 1984 amounted to 1,659m. francs. Luxembourg is an original member of NATO and the battalion is committed to NATO ACE mobile force.

INTERNATIONAL RELATIONS

Membership. Luxembourg is a member of the UN, Benelux, the EEC, OECD, the Council of Europe, NATO and WEU.

ECONOMY

Budget. Revenue and expenditure (including extraordinary) for years ending 30 April (in 1m. francs):

	1979	1980	1981	1982 [1]	1983 [1]	1984 [2]
Revenue	42,579·0	48,244·0	53,411·2	59,897·5	62,537·5	68,107·2
Expenditure	43,665·2	48,918·4	54,968·9	61,761·6	68,262·5	67,381·8

[1] Provisional.   [2] Budget.

Consolidated debt at 31 Dec. 1982 amounted to 31,719·8m. francs (long-term) and 2,250·4m. francs (short-term).

Currency. On 14 Oct. 1944 the Luxembourg *franc* was fixed at par value with the Belgian franc. Notes of the Belgian National Bank are legal tender in Luxembourg.

Banking. On 31 Dec. 1982 there were 299,991 depositors in the State Savings Bank with a total of 30,584m. francs to their credit. There are 115 banks established in Luxembourg which has become an international financial centre.

Weights and Measures. The metric system is in force.

ENERGY AND NATURAL RESOURCES

Electricity. Power production was 902m. kwh. in 1982.

Minerals. The mining and metallurgical industries are the most important. In 1982 production (in tonnes) of pig-iron, 2,586,820; of steel, 3,509,850.

Agriculture. Agriculture is carried on by about 8,900 of the population; 127,015 hectares were under cultivation in 1982. The principal crops are potatoes, barley, beet, oats and wheat.

Livestock (1982): 1,386 horses, 222,061 cattle, 67,867 pigs, 3,459 sheep.

INDUSTRY AND TRADE

Commerce. By treaty of 5 Sept. 1944, signed in London, and the treaty of 14 March 1947, signed in The Hague, the Grand Duchy, together with Belgium and the Netherlands, became a party to the Benelux Customs Union, which came into force on 1 Jan. 1948. For further particulars *see* p. 200.

Total trade between Luxembourg and UK included with Belgium from 1974.

Tourism. In 1982 there were 449,600 tourists.

COMMUNICATIONS

Roads. In 1982 the network had a total of 5,108 km. Motor vehicles registered in Luxembourg on 1 Jan. 1983 included 141,100 passenger cars, 9,009 trucks, 687 buses, 17,264 tractors and special vehicles.

Railways. In 1982 there were 270 km of railway (standard gauge).

Aviation. Findel is the airport for Luxembourg.

Post and Broadcasting. In 1982 the telephone system had more than 5,200 km of telegraph and telephone line, 228,000 telephones (1982), 104 post offices and 393 telegraph offices. *Compagnie Luxembourgeoise de Télédiffusion* broadcasts 1 programme in Luxembourgian on FM. Powerful transmitters on long-, medium- and short-waves are used for commercial and religious programmes in French, Dutch, German, English and Italian. Five TV programmes are broadcast. Colour transmission by SECAM system.

Cinemas (1977). There were 20 cinemas.

Newspapers (1982). There were 6 daily newspapers with an aggregate circulation of 130,000.

RELIGION, EDUCATION AND WELFARE

Religion. The population is Catholic, save (31 Dec. 1970) 3,900 Protestants, 700 Jews, 2,100 belonging to other denominations and 3,700 without religion (or having given no indication on this subject). The Protestant Church is organized on an interdenominational basis.

Education (1982–83). Education is compulsory for all children between the ages of 6 and 15. The nursery schools had 7,551 pupils; primary schools had 27,927 pupils; technical secondary schools, 15,734 pupils; secondary schools, 9,145 pupils; the Superior Institute of Technology, 468 pupils; pedagogic education, 146 pupils; university studies, 332 pupils.

Health. In 1982 there were 580 doctors and 4,816 hospital beds.

DIPLOMATIC REPRESENTATIVES

Of Luxembourg in Great Britain (27 Wilton Crescent, London, SWIX 8SD)
Ambassador: Roger Hastert, CMG.

Of Great Britain in Luxembourg (28 Boulevard Royal, Luxembourg)
Ambassador and Consul-General: The Hon. Humphrey Maud, CMG.

Of Luxembourg in the USA (2200 Massachusetts Ave. NW, Washington, D.C., 20008)
Ambassador: Paul Peters.

Of the USA in Luxembourg (22 Blvd. Emmanuel Servais, Luxembourg)
Ambassador: John E. Dolibois.

Of Luxembourg to the United Nations
Ambassador: Joseph Weyland.

Books of Reference

Statistical Information: The Service Central de la Statistique et des Études Économiques was founded in 1900 and reorganized in 1962 (19–21 boulevard Royal, C.P. 304 Luxembourg-City). *Director:* Georges Als. Main publications: *Bulletin du Statec.—Annuaire statistique.—Cahiers économiques.*

Bulletin de Documentation. Government Information Service. From 1945 (monthly)
The Institutions of the Grand Duchy of Luxembourg. Press and Information Service, Luxembourg, 1976
Als, G., *Le Luxembourg, situation politique, économique et sociale.* Luxembourg, 1982
Calmes, C., *Au Fil de l'Histoire.* Luxembourg, 1977
Cooper-Pritchard, A. H., *History of the Grand-Duchy of Luxembourg.* Luxembourg, 1950
Heiderscheid, A., *Aspects de Sociologie Religieuse du Diocèse de Luxembourg.* 2 vols. Luxembourg, 1961
Hury, C. and Christophory, J., *Luxembourg.* [Bibliography] Oxford and Santa Barbara, 1981
Majerus, P., *Le Luxembourg independant.* Luxembourg, 1948.—*L'État Luxembourgeois.* Luxembourg, 1948
Trausch, G., *Le Luxembourg à l'Époque Contemporaine.* Luxembourg, 1975

Archives of the State: Luxembourg-City. *Director:* Paul Spang.
National Library: Luxembourg-City, 14a Boulevard Royal. *Director:* Gilbert Trausch.

MADAGASCAR

Repoblika Demokratika n'i Madagaskar

Capital: Antananarivo
Population: 9·47m. (1983)
GNP per capita: US$350 (1980)

HISTORY. Madagascar was discovered by the Portuguese, Diego Diaz, in 1500. The island was unified under the Imérina monarchy between 1797 and 1861, but French claims to a protectorate led to hostilities culminating in the establishment of a protectorate on 30 Sept. 1895. The monarchy was abolished and Madagascar became a French Colony on 6 Aug. 1896.

Madagascar became an Overseas Territory in 1946, and on 14 Oct. 1958, following a referendum, was proclaimed the autonomous Malagasy Republic within the French Community, achieving full independence on 26 June 1960.

The government of Philibert Tsiranana, President from independence, resigned on 18 May 1972 and executive powers were given to Maj.-Gen. Gabriel Ramanantsoa, who replaced Tsiranana as President on 11 Oct. 1972. On 5 Feb. 1975, Col. Richard Ratsimandrava became Head of State, but was assassinated 6 days later. A National Military Directorate under Brig.-Gen. Gilles Andriamahazo was established on 12 Feb. On 15 June it handed over power to a Supreme Revolutionary Council (SRC) under Didier Ratsiraka.

AREA AND POPULATION. Madagascar is situated off the south-east coast of Africa, from which it is separated by the Mozambique channel, the least distance between island and continent being 250 miles; its length is 980 miles; greatest breadth, 360 miles.

The area is 587,041 sq. km (226,658 sq. miles). In 1975 (census) the population was 7,603,790 (more than 50% under 18 years). Estimate (1983) 9,472,000.

Province	Area in sq. km	Population 1978	Chief town	Population 1978
Antseranana	42,725	620,228	Antseranana	48,000
Mahajanga	152,165	857,610	Mahajanga	57,500
Toamasina	72,212	1,254,639	Toamasina	59,100
Antananarivo	57,775	2,322,019	Antananarivo	400,000
Fianarantsoa	100,326	1,908,465	Fianarantsoa	55,500
Toliary	162,283	1,084,083	Toliary	34,000

Vital statistics, 1972: Births, 280,131; deaths, 81,760.

The indigenous population are of Malayo-Polynesian stock, divided into 18 linguistic groups of which the principal are Merina (30%) of the central plateau, the Betsimisaraka (15%) of the east coast, and the Betsileo (14%) of the southern plateau. Foreign communities include Europeans, mainly French (40,000), Indians (16,000), Chinese (9,000), Comorians and Arabs.

CLIMATE. A tropical climate, but the mountains cause big variations in rainfall, which is very heavy in the east and very light in the west. Antananarivo. Jan. 70°F (21·1°C), July 59°F (15°C). Annual rainfall 54″ (1,350 mm). Toamasina. Jan. 80°F (26·7°C), July 70°F (21·1°C). Annual rainfall 128″ (3,256 mm).

CONSTITUTION AND GOVERNMENT. The new Constitution of the Democratic Republic of Madagascar was approved by referendum on 21 Dec. 1975 and came into force on 30 Dec. It provides for a bicameral Parliament, comprising a Senate of 50 members and a National People's Assembly of 137 members elected by universal suffrage for a 5-year term from the single list of the *Front National pour la Défense de la Révolution Malgache;* following the general elections held on 28 Aug. 1983, this comprised 117 members of the *Avant-garde de* *la Révolution Malgache,* 9 of the *Parti du Congrès de l'Indépendence* and 11 others. Executive power is vested in the President, elected for 7 years, who appoints a Council of Ministers to assist him, with the guidance of the 20-member Supreme Revolutionary Council.

President: Lieut.-Cdr. Didier Ratsiraka (re-elected 7 Nov. 1982). The Council of Ministers in Oct. 1983 was composed as follows:

Prime Minister: Lieut.-Col. Désiré Rakotoarijaona. *Foreign Affairs:* Jean Bemanjara. *Defence:* Capt de Vaisseau Guy Sibon. *Interior:* Ampy Portos. *Civil Service and Labour:* Georges Ruphin. *Finance:* Pascal Rakotomavo. *Health:* Jean-Jacques Séraphin. *Commerce:* Georges Solofoson. *Industry:* Tantely René Andrianarivo. *Animal Production:* Joseph Randrianasolo. *Agricultural Production:* Yves Léone Ramélison. *Posts and Telecommunications:* Rakotovao Andriantiana. *Secondary and Basic Education:* Charles Zany. *Higher Education:* Ignace Rakoto. *Scientific Research:* Antoine Zafera. *Information and Ideological Guidance:* Bruno Rakotomavo. *Revolutionary Art and Culture:* Gisêle Rabesahala. *Transport, Supply and Tourism:* Joseph Bedo. *Public Works:* Lieut.-Col. Victor Ramahatra. *Population and Social Welfare:* Dr Rémi Tiandraza. *Justice:* Gilbert Sambson.

National flag: Horizontally red over green, in the hoist a vertical white strip.
National anthem: Ry tanindrazanay malala ô!

Malagasy, which is a language of Malayo-Polynesian origin, is the official language. French and English are understood and taught in Malagasy schools.

Local Government: The six provinces are sub-divided into 18 prefectures, which in turn are divided in 92 sub-prefectures and finally into 11,000 *fokontany* (the traditional communal divisions). Each level is governed by an elected council.

DEFENCE

Army. The Army is organized in 2 battalion groups, and 1 engineer, 1 signals, 1 service and 7 construction regiments. Equipment includes PT-76 light tanks and M-8 armoured cars. Strength (1984) 20,000.

Navy. The small maritime guard in 1984 had a strength of 600 (including a company of marines), equipped with 1 large patrol craft, 5 patrol boats, 1 landing ship, 7 small landing craft and a training ship.

Air Force. Created in 1961, the Malagasy Air Force received its first combat equipment in 1978, with the arrival of 8 MiG-21 and 4 MiG-17 fighters, plus flying and ground staff instructors, from North Korea. Other equipment includes An-12 and 4 An-26 turboprop transports, 6 L-39 jet trainers, 1 Britten-Norman Defender armed transport, 5 C-47s, 1 HS. 748 and 2 Yak-40s for VIP use, 1 Aztec, 3 Cessna Skymasters, 4 Cessna 172Ms and 6 helicopters, comprising 2 Mi-8s, 1 Bell 47, 1 Alouette II and 2 Alouette IIIs. Personnel about 500.

INTERNATIONAL RELATIONS

Membership. Madagascar is a member of UN, OAU and is an ACP state of EEC.

ECONOMY

Planning. A development plan, 1978–80, envisaged an annual growth rate of 5%.

Budget. The general budget 1982, envisaged expenditure of 274,530m. FMG.

Currency. The Malagasy *franc* is divided into 100 *centimes.* In March 1984, £1 = 672 FMG; US$1 = 484 FMG.

Banking. A Central Bank was formed in July 1973, replacing the former *Institut d'Emission Malgache* as the central bank of issue. All commercial banking and insurance was nationalised in June 1975. Industrial development is financed through the *Bankin'ny Indostria,* and other commercial banking undertaken by the *Bankin'ny Tantsaha Mpamokatra* and the *Banky Fampandrosoana ny Varotra.*

Weights and Measures. The metric system is in use.

ENERGY AND NATURAL RESOURCES

Electricity. Production (1980) 336m. kwh.

Oil. The oil refinery at Toamasina has a capacity of 12,000 bbls a day.

Minerals. Mining production (in tonnes) included: Mica (1977), 1,498; graphite (1977), 15,726; chrome (1979), 200,000; ilmenite, 1,857; zircon, 209; beryl, 1971 (industrial), 52; gold (1971), 17 kg; garnet, 1971 (industrial), 40.

Agriculture. In 1978, 83% of the working population was employed in agriculture. The principal agricultural products in 1982 were (in 1,000 tonnes): Rice, 2,000; cassava, 1,807; mangoes, 175; bananas, 280; potatoes, 271; sugar-cane, 1,525; maize, 127; sweet potatoes, 422; coffee, 80; oranges, 88; pineapples, 58; groundnuts, 38; sisal, 20; cotton, 31; tobacco, 5.

Cattle breeding and agriculture are the chief occupations. There were, in 1982, 10·15m. cattle, 721,000 pigs, 633,000 sheep, 1·5m. goats and 15m. poultry.

Forestry. The forests contain many valuable woods, while gum, resins and plants for tanning, dyeing and medicinal purposes abound.

Fisheries. The fish catch in 1980 was 54,000 tonnes.

INDUSTRY AND TRADE

Industry. Industry, hitherto confined mainly to the processing of agricultural products, is now extending to cover other fields.

Commerce. Trade in 1m. FMG:

	1977	1978	1979	1980
Imports (c.i.f)	85,217	99,632	135,319	126,775
Exports (f.o.b)	82,634	87,214	83,826	84,781

The chief exports in 1980 were coffee (53%) and cloves (8%); France took 20% of exports, the USA 20% and Japan 10%, while France provided 41% of imports, Federal Republic of Germany 10% and Japan 5%.

Total trade between Madagascar and UK (British Department of Trade returns, in £1,000 sterling):

	1979	1980	1981	1982	1983
Imports to UK	2,963	4,148	2,937	3,355	3,731
Exports and re-exports from UK	4,152	11,817	5,322	3,548	4,907

COMMUNICATIONS

Roads. In 1979 there were 27,556 km of roads of which 4,526 km bitumenized, with 57,000 passenger cars and 50,000 commercial vehicles (including buses).

Railways. In 1981 there were 883 km of railways, all metre gauge. In 1980, 3·1m. passengers and 586,570m. tonnes of cargo were transported.

Aviation. Air France and Air Madagascar connect Antananarivo with Paris, Alitalia connects with Rome. Several weekly services operated by Air Madagascar connect the capital with the ports and the chief inland towns. The main airfields are at Ivato, Toamasina, Toliary and Mahajanga. In 1979, 326,275 passengers arrived and 8,684 tonnes of cargo arrived and departed on international flights.

Shipping. Toamasina, Mahajanga, Antseranana, Toliary, Nossi-Bé and Manakara are the principal ports. In 1980, registered merchant marine was 56 vessels (of more than 100 GRT) with a total of 91,211 GRT.

Post and Broadcasting. There were in 1971, 547 post offices and agencies and 55 wireless telegraph stations. The telegraph line has a length of 17,400 km. There were 66,000 km of telephone line and, in 1978, 28,686 telephone subscribers. In Dec. 1979, there were 1·15m. radio receivers and (1980) 9,000 television receivers.

Cinemas. There were, in 1974, 31 cinemas with a seating capacity of 12,500.

JUSTICE, RELIGION, EDUCATION AND WELFARE

Justice. The Supreme Court and the Court of Appeal are in Antananarivo. In each provincial capital there is a Court of First Instance (for civil and commercial cases) and a *juge de paix* (for criminal cases).

Religion. 50% of the population follow animist religions; 25% are Roman Catholic, 20% Protestant (mainly belonging to the Fiangonan'i Jesosy Kristy eto Madagaskar) and 5% Moslem.

Education. Education is compulsory from 6 to 14 years of age in the primary schools. In 1978 there were 1,311,000 pupils and 23,937 teachers in public primary schools, while in 1976 there were 114,468 pupils in secondary schools and about 7,000 in technical schools. The University of Madagascar has a main campus at Antananarivo and 5 university centres in the other provincial capitals, with 22,857 students in 1979. There are also 4 agricultural schools at Nanisana, Ambatondrazaka, Marovoay and Ivoloina.

Health. In 1976 there were 886 hospitals and dispensaries with 19,781 beds; there were also 767 doctors, 93 dentists, 141 pharmacists, 1,010 midwives and 2,252 nursing personnel.

DIPLOMATIC REPRESENTATIVES

Of Madagascar in Great Britain
Ambassador: Henri Raharijaona (resides in Paris).

Of Great Britain in Madagascar (Immeuble Ny Havana, Cite de 67 Ha, Antananarivo)
Ambassador: R. J. Langridge.

Of Madagascar in the USA (2374 Massachusetts Ave., NW, Washington, D.C., 20008)
Chargé d'Affairs: Jean Rene Tsiangalara.

Of USA in Madagascar (14 rue Rainitovo, Antsohavola, Antananarivo)
Ambassador: Robert B. Keating.

Of Madagascar to the United Nations
Ambassador: Blaise Rabetafika.

Books of Reference

Statistical Information: The Service de Statistique Générale in Antananarivo published the *Bulletin mensuel de Madagascar* (from 1971); continuation of the trimestrial *Bulletin de statistique générale* (1949–71), the *Revue de Madagascar,* the *Madagascar à travers ses provinces* (latest issue, 1953), the *Annuaire Statistique de Madagascar* (vol. 1, 1938–51, published 1953, the *Situation Economique au Janvier 1968, Population de Madagascar au 1er Jan. 1971,* and the *Statistiques du Commerce Extérieur de Madagascar).*
Bulletin de l'Académie Malgache (from 1902)
Brown, M., *Madagascar Rediscovered.* London, 1978
Deschamps, H., *Histoire de Madagascar.* Paris, 4th ed. 1972
Heseltine, N., *Madagascar.* London and New York, 1971

MALAWI

Capital: Lilongwe
Population: 6·1m. (1981)
GNP per capita: US$230 (1980)

HISTORY. Malawi was formerly the Nyasaland (until 1907 British Central Africa) Protectorate, constituted on 15 May 1891.

Nyasaland became a self-governing country on 1 Feb. 1963, and on 6 July 1964 an independent member of the Commonwealth under the name of Malawi. It became a republic on 6 July 1966.

AREA AND POPULATION. Malawi lies along the southern and western shores of Lake Malawi (the third largest lake in Africa), and is otherwise bounded north by Tanzania, south by Mozambique and west by Zambia. Land area (excluding inland water of Lakes Palombe, Chilwa and Chiuta) 36,325 sq. miles, divided into 3 regions and 24 districts, each administered by a District Commissioner.

Lake Malawi waters belonging to Malawi are 9,250 sq. miles and the whole Lake Malawi (including the waters under Mozambique by an agreement made between the two countries in 1950) is 11,650 sq. miles.

The results of the census held in Aug. 1966: 4,020,724 Africans, 11,299 Asians, 7,395 Europeans, 165 undetermined; total 4,039,583 (1,913,262 males, 2,126,321 females). Estimate (1981), 6·1m. Over 90% of the population live in rural areas.

Population of main towns (census 1977) was as follows: Blantyre, 219,011; Lilongwe, 98,718; Zomba, 24,234; Mzuzu, 16,108. The capital was Zomba, and on 1 Jan. 1975 Lilongwe, in the Central Region, was officially declared the capital. All ministries were to be located there by 1977–78. A new Constitution was introduced in 1966.

Population of the regions, 1966 (and census 1977): Northern, 497,491 (648,853); Central, 1,474,952 (2,143,716); Southern, 2,067,140 (2,754,891).

CLIMATE. The tropical climate is marked by a dry season from May to Oct. and a wet season for the remaining months. Rainfall amounts are variable, within the range of 29–100″ (725–2,500 mm), and maximum temperatures average 75–89°F (24–32°C), and minimum temperatures 58–67°F (14·4–19·4°C). Lilongwe. Jan. 73°F (22·8°C), July 60°F (15·6°C). Annual rainfall 36″ (900 mm). Blantyre. Jan. 75°F (23·9°C), July 63°F (17·2°C). Annual rainfall 45″ (1,125 mm). Zomba. Jan. 73°F (22·8°C), July 63°F (17·2°C). Annual rainfall 54″ (1,344 mm).

CONSTITUTION AND GOVERNMENT. The President of the republic is also head of Government and of the Malawi Congress Party. Malawi is a one-party state. Parliament is composed of 101 elected members elected for up to 5 years, and any number of nominated members. Elections were held in June 1983.

Life President, External Affairs, Agriculture, Justice, Works and Supplies: Ngwazi Dr H. Kamuzu Banda. (Took office 6 July 1966 and became Life President on 6 July 1971).

Finance: L. Chakakala Chaziya. *Transport and Communications:* Edward Chitsulo Isaac Bwanali. *Education and Culture:* Louis J. Chimango. *Local Government:* B. L. Kapichira Banda. *Trade, Industry and Tourism:* E. C. Katola Phiri. *Health:* Dalton S. Katopola. *Youth:* S. Chimwemwe Hara. *Labour:* Wadson Bini Deleza. *Without Portfolio, Administrative Secretary of Malawi Congress Party:* Robson Watayacharga Chirwa.

National flag: Three equal horizontal stripes of black, red, green, with a red rising sun on the centre of the black stripe.

DEFENCE. All services form part of the Army and have a strength (1984) 4,650.

Army. The army is organized into 3 infantry battalions and 1 support battalion. Equipment includes scout cars.

Navy. There are 3 small lake patrol boats and 1 gunboat. Uniformed personnel in 1984 totalled 30.

Air wing. To support the infantry battalion, the Air Wing has 4 C-47 Transport aircraft, 1 Defender armed light transport, 12 Do 28D Skyservant light transports, 6 Do 27 training aircraft, and 6 Puma and 1 Alouette III helicopters. An HS 125 jet is used for VIP transport.

INTERNATIONAL RELATIONS

Membership. Malawi is a member of UN, the Commonwealth, OAU, and is an ACP state of EEC.

ECONOMY

Planning. The Government of Malawi operates a 3-year 'rolling' public-sector investment programme, revised annually to take into account changing needs and the expected level of resources available. The greatest part of the development programme is annually financed from external aid, and priority in the use of resources has always been given to providing the counterpart contributions to funds received from external sources. The balance of these local resources is used for financing projects commanding high national priority for which no external funds can be secured.

Budget. Revenue Account receipts and expenditure (in K.1,000) for years ending 31 March:

	1979–80	1980–81	1981–82	1982–83
Revenue	282,969	282,962	344,484	340,723
Expenditure	173,048	199,793	257,282	259,507

Currency. In 1971 a new decimalized currency was introduced, the *kwacha* (dawn), which is subdivided into 100 *tambala* (cockerels). From 9 June 1975 the kwacha has been pegged to Special Drawing Rights. In March 1984: £1 sterling = K.1·95, US$1 = K.1·333.

Banking. In July 1964 the Reserve Bank of Malawi was set up with a capital of K.1m. to be responsible for the issue of currency and the holding of external reserves and to issue treasury bills and local registered stock on behalf of the Government. Since then, the Reserve Bank has fully assumed the responsibilities of a Central Bank.

The National Bank of Malawi has a total of 10 branches in major urban areas and 19 static and 35 mobile agencies in rural areas. The Commercial Bank of Malawi Ltd opened in 1970 and has branches at Limbe, Lilongwe and Zomba and an agency in Dedza and headquarters at Blantyre.

In 1972 The Investment Development Bank of Malawi was established in Blantyre. Its resources are derived from domestic and foreign official sources and its objective is to provide medium and long-term credits to private entities considered of importance to the economy.

The post office savings bank has 223 offices conducting savings business throughout the country, and the New Building Society has agencies in Limbe, Zomba and Lilongwe with its head office in Blantyre. Two finance houses now operate in Malawi, providing longer-term industrial and consumer finance.

Weights and Measures. The metric system became fully operational in 1982.

ENERGY AND NATURAL RESOURCES

Electricity. The first stage of the Tedzani Project, two 8 mw sets, was commissioned in July 1973 which, together with the 24 mw Nkula hydro-electric station, will meet the power demands of the interconnected systems of the Southern Region and

Lilongwe. With the completion of a barrage at Tedzani these machines will be up-rated to 10 mw each and, with the addition of thermal plant to the system suffi-cient power will be available to meet forecast demands prior to the commissioning in 1977 of the second stage of the Tedzani Project, a further two 10 mw sets. The Electricity Supply Commission also operates stations at Mangochi, Mzuzu, Kasungu, Liwonde, Chikwawa and Salima. A total of 252·96m. kwh. were sold by the Electricity Supply Commission in 1976.

Minerals. The main product in 1976 was marble (149,254 tonnes) for the manu-facture of cement.

Agriculture. Malawi is predominantly an agricultural country. Up to March 1977 519,300 of the rural population had been reached by self-help piped water projects, of which 427,700 were in the Southern region. In 1983 agriculture contributed about 43% to the GDP, and agricultural produce accounted for 90% of total exports. Of the total area of 23·3m. acres, 13·1m. could be cultivated and, in 1969, 3·36m. were being cultivated, of which 2·64m. were under maize. Maize is the main subsistence crop and is grown by over 95% of all smallholders. Tea cultiva-tion is of growing importance; in 1982, 38m. kg were produced. Almost all the sur-plus crops produced by smallholders are sold to the Agricultural Development and Marketing Corporation. In 1982 the corporation purchased crops valued at K.41·2m., including maize (K.27·3m.), cotton, tobacco, groundnuts and rice.

Livestock in 1982: Cattle, 888,000; sheep, 78,000; goats, 656,000; pigs, 186,000.

Forestry. In 1976 (estimate) 535,510 cu. ft of sawn timber were produced, valued at K.1·3m. The value of other forest products was K.536,986.

Fisheries. Landings in 1977 (provisional) were 66,000 short tons valued at K.6·6m.

INDUSTRY AND TRADE

Industry. Index of manufacturing output (1970 = 100): manufacturing for domestic consumption 177·7 (229·5 in 1980); of this consumer goods were at 191·9 (252·5) and intermediate goods mainly for building and construction were at 128·6 (150·4). Manufacturing for export, 172·3 (201·6).

Labour:

	1978		
	Private	*Government*	*Total*
Agriculture, forestry, fishing	147,962	21,371	169,333
Mining and quarrying	564	–	564
Manufacturing	34,862	1,093	35,955
Electricity and water	2,459	463	2,922
Building and construction	27,418	4,052	31,470
Trade, hotels, restaurants	26,829	382	27,211
Transport storage, communications	13,809	3,808	17,617
Financial services	6,194	623	6,817
Community, social, personal services	10,794	36,601	47,395
Total	270,891	68,393	339,284

Commerce. The main items of export in 1979 were (in K.1m.): Tobacco, 98·6; tea, 30·6; sugar, 16·1; groundnuts, 8·7. Malawi's imports in the same year (in K.1m.) included capital equipment, 44·6; means of transport, 46·1; con-sumer goods, 46·7; building materials, 25·2.

Trade statistics for calendar years are (in K.1m.):

	1979	*1980*	*1981*	*1982*
Imports	324·8	356·2	321·9	322·1
Exports	181·7	238·2	257·5	269·8

Total trade between Malawi and UK (British Department of Trade returns, in £1,000 sterling):

	1980	*1981*	*1982*	*1983*
Imports to UK	45,651	34,744	42,478	42,060
Exports and re-exports from UK	25,749	21,503	20,893	18,183

Tourism. There were 47,220 visitors to Malawi in 1980.

COMMUNICATIONS

Roads. In 1976 there were 1,877 miles of main road, of which 772 were bitumen-surfaced and 206 gravel; 1,520 miles of secondary roads, of which 215 were surfaced; 3,426 miles of district and other roads, of which 148 were surfaced. Motor vehicles licensed, 29,085, of which 10,222 were cars and 10,642 goods vehicles.

Railways. Malawi Railways (789 km–1,067 mm gauge) operates a main line from Salima to the Mozambique border near Nsanje, from which running powers over the Trans-Zambesia Railway allow access to the port of Beira; a branch opened in 1970 runs eastwards from a point 16 km south of Balaka to the Mozambique border to give a direct route to the deep-water port of Nacala. The 26-km section from Nsanje to the border is operated by the Central Africa Railway Co. Ltd. An extension of 111 km from Salima to the new state capital of Lilongwe was opened in Feb. 1979, and a further extension to Mchinji on the Zambian border (120 km) was completed in 1981. In 1981, 1·2m. tonnes hauled, 77·9m. passenger-km run.

Aviation. In 1980 Chileka airport handled 188,514 passengers and 12,472 tonnes of freight. Lilongwe airport handled 50,223 and 538 tonnes.

Shipping. In 1976 lake ships carried 131,000 passengers and 33,000 short tons of freight.

Post. Number of telephones (1981) 15,130.

Newspapers (1980). *The Daily Times* (English, Monday to Friday); 5,700–6,300 copies daily (1977). *Malawi News* (English and Chichewa, Saturdays); 16,000 copies weekly. *The Odini* (English and Chichewa, fortnightly).

JUSTICE, RELIGION, EDUCATION AND WELFARE

Justice. Justice is administered in the High Court, the magistrates' courts and traditional courts. There are 23 magistrates' courts, 176 traditional courts and 23 local appeal courts.

Appeals from traditional courts are dealt with in the traditional appeal courts and in the national traditional appeal court. Appeals from magistrates' courts lie to the High Court, and appeals from the High Court to Malawi's Supreme Court of Appeal.

Religion. In 1972 the Roman Catholic Church claimed 1,073,000 members; the Presbyterian Church of Central Africa, 846,000; the Diocese of Malawi (part of the Province of Central Africa of the Anglican Communion), 79,000; Seventh-day Adventist Church, 93,000; Zambezi Evangelical Church (formerly Nyasa Mission), 36,000; Assemblies of God, 7,000; Seventh-day Baptists (Central Africa conference), 11,000; Churches of Christ, 21,000; African Evangelical Church, 7,000; Evangelical Church of Malawi, 18,000. Moslems are estimated to number between 500,000 and 1m.

Education (1981–82). The Ministry of Education and Culture controls all aspects of education.

The number of pupils in the 2,250 primary schools was 882,903; in the 62 secondary schools, 19,329. There were 11,425 teachers in primary schools and 739 in secondary schools. The primary school course is of 8 years duration, followed by a 4-year secondary course. English is taught from the 1st year and becomes the general medium of instruction from the 4th year.

Teacher-training is undertaken in 5 residential colleges, 2 of which are directly controlled by the Ministry; the others receive grants in aid as assisted institutions. Courses last 3 years. Enrolment 8,303. Technical and trade courses are offered in commerce, building, woodwork and mechanical engineering, as well as home craft for girls; 1,904 trainees undertook courses at government and voluntary schools in 1966.

The University of Malawi was inaugurated on 6 Oct. 1965. In 1981–82 there were 1,718 students taking degree and diploma courses.

Health. In 1979 there were 482 medical institutions and 8,991 hospital beds.

DIPLOMATIC REPRESENTATIVES

Of Malawi in Great Britain (33 Grosvenor St., London, W1)
High Commissioner: C. Mkona.

Of Great Britain in Malawi (Lingadzi Hse., Lilongwe, 3)
High Commissioner: A. H. Brind, CMG.

Of Malawi in the USA (1400 20th St., NW, Washington, D.C., 20036)
Ambassador: N. T. Mizere.

Of the USA in Malawi (PO Box 30016, Lilongwe)
Ambassador: John A. Burroughs, Jr.

Of Malawi to the United Nations
Ambassador: N. T. Mizere.

Books of Reference

General Information. The Chief Information Officer, PO Box 494, Blantyre.
Boeder, R. B. *Malawi* [Bibliography] Oxford and Santa Barbara, 1981
McMaster, C., *Malawi: Foreign Policy and Development.* London, 1974
Read, F. E., *Malawi, Land of Promise.* Govt. Dept. of Information, 1967.—*Malawi, Land of Progress.* Govt. Dept. of Information, 1969
Williams, T. D., *Malawi: The Politics of Despair.* Cornell Univ. Press, 1979

MALAYSIA

Capital: Kuala Lumpur
Population: 14·42m. (1982)
GNP per capita: US$1,670 (1980)

HISTORY. On 16 Sept. 1963 Malaysia came into being, consisting of the Federation of Malaya, the State of Singapore and the colonies of North Borneo (renamed Sabah) and Sarawak. The agreement between the UK and the 4 territories was signed on 9 July (Cmnd. 2094); by it, the UK relinquished sovereignty over Singapore, North Borneo and Sarawak from independence day and extended the 1957 defence agreement with Malaya to apply to Malaysia. Malaysia became automatically a member of the Commonwealth of Nations. *See* map in THE STATESMAN'S YEAR-BOOK, 1964–65.

On 9 Aug. 1965, by a mutual agreement dated 7 Aug. 1965 between Malaysia and Singapore, Singapore seceded from Malaysia to become an independent Sovereign nation.

POPULATION. 1980 census gave 11,800,000 in Peninsular Malaysia, 1,034,000 in Sabah, and 1,323,000 in Sarawak. Estimate (1982) 14·42m.

CLIMATE. Malaysia is affected by the monsoon climate. The N.E. monsoon prevails from Oct. to Feb., bringing rain to the east coast of the peninsula. The S.W. monsoon lasts from mid-May to Sept. and affects the opposite coastline the most. Temperatures are uniform throughout the year. Kuala Lumpur. Jan. 81°F (27·2°C), July 81°F (27·2°C). Annual rainfall 97·6" (2,441 mm). Penang. Jan. 82°F (27·8°C), July 82°F (27·8°C). Annual rainfall 109·4" (2,736 mm).

CONSTITUTION AND GOVERNMENT. The Constitution of Malaysia is based on the Constitution of the former Federation of Malaya, but includes safeguards for the special interests of Sabah and Sarawak. It was amended in 1983.

The federal capital is Kuala Lumpur, established on 1 Feb. 1974 with an area of approximately 94 sq. miles. The official language is Bahasa Malaysia.

The Constitution provides for one of the 9 Rulers of the Malay States to be elected from among themselves to be the *Yang di-Pertuan Agong* (Supreme Head of the Federation). He holds office for a period of 5 years. The Rulers also elect from among themselves a Deputy Supreme Head of State, also for a period of 5 years.

Supreme Head of State (Yang di-Pertuan Agong): HM Sultan Mahmood Iskandar ibni Al-Marhum Sultan Ismail DK, SPMJ, SPDK, DK (Brunei) SSIJ, PIS, BSI, elected as 8th *Yang di-Pertuan Agong* from 26 April 1984.

Raja of Perlis: HRH Tuanku Syed Putra ibni Al-Marhum Syed Hassan Jamalullail, DK, DKM, DMN, SMN, SPMP, SPDK, acceded 12 March 1949.

Sultan of Kedah: HRH Tuanku Haji Abdul Halim Mu'adzam Shah ibni Al-Marhum Sultan Badlishah, DK, DKH, DKM, DMN, DUK, SPMK, SSDK, acceded 20 Feb. 1959.

Regent of Johore: HRH Tengku Ibrahim Ismail ibni Sultan Mahmood Iskandar Al-Haj, DK, SPMJ, appointed from 26 April 1984.

Sultan of Selangor: HRH Sultan Salahuddin Abdul Aziz Shah ibni Al-Marhum Sultan Hisamuddin 'Alam Shah Al-Haj, DK, DMN, SPMS, SPDK, acceded 3 Sept. 1960.

Rajah of Perak: HRH Rajah Tun Azlan Shah, DK, DMN, PMN, SPCM, SPMP, acceded 3 Feb. 1984.

Yang di-Pertuan Besar of Negeri Sembilan: HRH Tuanku Ja'afar ibni Al-Marhum Tuanku Abdul Rahman, DMN, DK, acceded 8 April 1968.

Sultan of Kelantan: HRH Sultan Ismail Petra ibni Al-Marhum Sultan Yahya Petra, DK, SPMK, SJMK, SPSM, appointed 29 March 1979.

Sultan of Trengganu: HRH Sultan Mahmud Al Marhum ibni Al-Marhum Tuanku Al-Sultan Ismail Nasiruddin Shah, DK, SPMT, SPCM, appointed 2 Sept. 1979.

Sultan of Pahang: Sultan Haji Ahmad Shah Al-Musta'in Billah Ibni Al-Marhum Sultan Abu Bakar Ri'Ayatuddin Al-Mu'Adzam Shah, DKM, DKP, DK, SSAP, SPCM, SPMJ.

Yang di-Pertua Negeri Pulau Pinang: HE Dato' Dr Awang bin Hassan, DUPN, SPMJ, appointed 1 May 1981.

Governor of Malacca: HE Tun Haji Syed Zahiruddin bin Syed Hassan, SMN, PSM, DUNM, SPMP, JMN, PJK, appointed 23 May 1975; re-appointed 23 May 1979.

Yang di-Pertua Negeri Sarawak: HE Tan Sri Dr Haji Abdul Rahman bin Ya'kub, DP, PMN, SPMJ, SIMP, SPMK, SSDK, SPMP, SPMS, SPDK, appointed 2 April 1981.

Yang di-Pertua Sabah: HE Datuk Mohamad Adnan Roberts, SMN, SPDK, SPMP, DUPN, DP, appointed 26 June 1978.

Parliament consists of the *Yang di-Pertuan Agong* and two *Majlis* (Houses of Parliament) known as the *Dewan Negara* (Senate) of 68 members and *Dewan Rakyat* (House of Representatives) of 154 members. There are 149 members from the states in Malaysia and 5 from the Federal Territory. Appointment to the Senate is for 3 years. The maximum life of the House of Representatives is 5 years, subject to its dissolution at any time by the *Yang di-Pertuan Agong* on the advice of his Ministers.

National flag: Fourteen horizontal stripes of red and white, with a blue quarter bearing a crescent and a star of 14 points, all in gold.

The elections to the House of Representatives held on 22 April 1982, returned the following members: National Front, 139; Democratic Action Party, 9; PAS, 5; Independent, 8.

The Cabinet was in June 1983 composed as follows:

Prime Minister and Minister of Defence: Datuk Seri Dr Mahathir bin Mohamad, SSDK, SPMJ, SPMS, SSAP, DP.

Deputy Prime Minister and Home Affairs: Dato Musa Hitam. *Housing and Local Government:* Dato Dr Neo Yee Pan. *Works:* Dato S. Samy Vellu. *Foreign Affairs:* Tan Sri Haji Muhammad Ghazali bin Shafie. *Welfare Services:* Datin Paduka Hajjah Aishah Binti Haji Abdul Ghani. *Trade and Industry:* Tengku Dato Ahmad Rithauddeen Al-Haj bin Tengku Ismail. *Finance:* Tengku Razaleigh Hamzah. *Transport.* Tan Sri Chong Hon Nyan. *Primary Industries:* Dato Paul Leong Khee Seong. *Agriculture:* Dato Abdul Manan bin Othman. *Energy, Telecommunications and Posts:* Datuk Leo Moggie Anak Irok. *Public Enterprises:* Datin Paduka Rafidah Aziz. *Education:* Datuk Dr Sulaiman bin Haji Daud. *National and Rural Development:* Dato Sanusi bin Junid. *Land and Regional Development:* Dato Rais Yatim. *Labour:* Dato Mak Hon Kam. *Information:* Datuk Seri Mohd Adib bin Haji Mohd Adam. *Science, Technology and Environment:* Datuk Amar Stephen Yong Kuet Tze. *Minister-cum-Ambassador to Indonesia:* Dato Mohamed bin Rahmat. *Health:* Dato Chin Hon Ngian. *Federal Territory:* Dato Shahrir bin Abdul Samad. *Culture, Youth and Sports:* Anwar bin Ibrahim. *Prime Minister's Department:* Datuk Abdullah bin Haji Ahmad Badawi; Datuk Dr James P. Ongkili.

DEFENCE. The Malaysian Armed Forces are made up of the Malaysian Army, the Royal Malaysian Navy and the Royal Malaysian Air Force. Each Service has its own component of reserves.

The Malaysian Constitution provides for the *Yang di-Pertuan Agong* (Supreme Head of State) to be the Supreme Commander of the Armed Forces who exercises his powers and authority in accordance with the advice of the Cabinet. Under the general authority of the Yang di-Pertuan Agong and the Cabinet, there is the Armed Forces Council which is responsible for the command, discipline and administration of all other matters relating to the Armed Forces, other than those relating to its operational use.

The Armed Forces Council is chaired by the Minister of Defence and its membership consists of the chief of the Defence Forces, the 3 Service Chiefs and 2 other senior military officers, the Secretary-General of the Ministry of Defence, a representative of State Rulers and an appointed member.

The chief of the Armed Forces Staff is the professional head of the Armed Forces and the senior military member in the Armed Forces Council. He is the principal adviser to the Minister of Defence on the military aspects of all defence matters. The chief of the Armed Forces Staff's committee, established under the authority of the Armed Forces Council, is the highest level at which joint planning and co-ordination with the Armed Forces are carried out. The Committee is chaired by the chief of the Armed Forces Staff and its membership consists of the chief of the Army, Navy and Air Force, the chief of Personnel Staff, the chief of logistic Staff and the chief of Staff of the Ministry of Defence.

Army. The Army is organized into 4 divisions, comprising 9 infantry brigades made up of 36 infantry battalions; 3 cavalry, 4 field artillery, 1 armoured personnel carrier, 1 special service, 5 engineer and 5 signals regiments and 2 anti-aircraft batteries. Equipment includes 140 AML armoured and 60 Ferret scout cars. Strength (1984) about 80,000, with as reserves the Malaysian Territorial Army (45,000), the Local Defence Corps (15,000) and the regular reservists who have completed their full-time service.

Navy. The Royal Malaysian Navy is commanded by the Chief of the Naval Staff from the integrated Ministry of Defence in Kuala Lumpur. The main naval bases are KD Malaya situated on Singapore Island, KD Sri Labuan on Labuan Island and KD Pelandok in Lumut, Perak. These establishments are responsible for the operation and administration of the ships, and KD Pelandok for the training of personnel.

The ships include 2 British (Yarrow)-built frigates (including the former HMS *Mermaid*), 2 logistic support ships, 8 fast missile craft, 6 fast gunboats, 22 patrol craft, 2 landing ships, 1 diving tender, 1 survey vessel and 6 tugs. The peace-time tasks include fishery protection and anti-piracy patrols. There are also 48 armed patrol launches, 46 operated by the Royal Malaysian Police and 2 by the Government of Sabah (North Borneo) which also operates 3 patrol boats, 1 landing craft and a yacht.

New construction includes 4 corvettes or light frigates, 4 minehunters, 6 coastguard patrol craft and 12 marine police patrol boats.

Naval personnel in 1984 totalled 11,000 officers and ratings, including 1,000 reservists and 800 volunteer reserve.

Air Force. Formed on 1 June 1958, the Royal Malaysian Air Force is equipped primarily to provide air defence and air support for the Army, Navy and Police. Its secondary rôle is to render assistance to Government departments and civilian organizations, especially during periods of national disasters. There were in early 1983 11 squadrons, of which 6 operated transport aircraft and helicopters. Up to 68 *ex*-US Navy A-4L/C Skyhawks are being refurbished progressively as the primary attack force. Other equipment includes 13 F-5E Tiger II jet fighter-bombers, 2 RF-5E reconnaissance-fighters, and 4 F-5F trainers, 11 Canadair CL-41G Tebuan dual-purpose light jet strike and training aircraft (being supplemented with Aermacchi MB 339s), 9 C-130H/H-MP Hercules four-turboprop heavy transports and maritime reconnaissance aircraft, 2 F.28 Fellowship VIP transports, 15 Caribou twin-engined STOL transports, 35 Sikorsky S-61A-4 Nuri heavy troop and cargo transport helicopters, 20 Alouette III, 3 Agusta-Bell 212, 9 Bell 47 and 5 Bell 206B JetRanger helicopters, 12 Cessna 402Bs for twin-engine training and liaison, 44 PC-7 Turbo-Trainers and 2 H.S. 125 Merpati twin-jet executive transports. Personnel (1982) totalled about 11,000.

Volunteer Forces. The Army Volunteer Force (Territorial Army) consists of first-line infantry, signals, engineer and logistics units able to take the field with the active army, and a second-line organization to provide local defence. There is also a small Naval Volunteer Reserve with Headquarters in Penang and Kuala Lumpur. The Royal Malaysian Air Force Volunteer Reserve has both air and ground elements.

INTERNATIONAL RELATIONS

Membership. Malaysia is a member of UN, the Commonwealth, Non-Aligned countries, the Colombo Plan and ASEAN.

ECONOMY

Planning. The fourth 5-year plan, 1981–85 envisages an expenditure of M$42,830m. and aims at national unity through the two-pronged objectives of eradicating poverty irrespective of race and of restructuring society to eliminate the identification of race with economic functions.

Budget. Revenue and expenditure for calendar years, in M$1m.:

	1979	1980	1981	1982[1]	1983[2]
Revenue	10,505	13,926	15,806	16,434	17,266
Operating expenditure[3]	10,040	13,617	15,686	16,185	17,079
Development expenditure	4,282	7,463	11,358	10,434	11,270

[1] Latest Estimate.   [2] Budget Estimate.
[3] Including contribution to sinking fund from 1975.

Currency. Bank Negara Malaysia (Central Bank of Malaysia) assumed sole currency issuing authority in Malaysia on 12 June 1967. The unit of currency issued by Bank Negara Malaysia is the Malaysian *ringgit* ($) which is divided into 100 *sen.* Currency notes are of denominations of $1, 5, 10, 50, 100 and $1,000. Coins are of denominations of 1 *sen*, 5, 10, 20, 50 *sen* and $1, $5, $10, $15, $25, $100, $200, $250 and $500. The circulation of currency on 31 Dec. 1981 was M$5,493m.
Rate of exchange, March 1984: 2·33 *ringgit* = US$1; 3·39 *ringgit* = £1.

Banking. Thirty-eight banks were operating in Dec. 1981; of these 21 were domestic banks with a total of 573 banking offices. Five were banks incorporated in Singapore with 63 banking offices and the remaining 12 banks were foreign incorporated with 85 banking offices. Total deposits amounted to M$23,326·3m. on 31 Dec. 1981 and loans and advances amounted to M$25,521·4m.
The National Savings Bank (formerly known as the post office savings bank) held M$973·8m. due to 3,600,948 depositors at 31 Dec. 1978.

TRADE. Total trade of Malaysia with UK (British Department of Trade returns, in £1,000 sterling):

	1980	1981	1982	1983
Imports to UK	187,050	188,327	185,239	222,673
Exports and re-exports from UK	223,516	196,213	210,805	248,239

COMMUNICATIONS

Post. The Postal Services in Malaysia are under the Ministry of Energy, Telecommunications and Post and are headed by the Director-General of Post, Malaysia.

Cinemas. In 1974 there were 500 cinemas with a seating capacity of 345,400.

JUSTICE. By virtue of Art. 121(1) of the Federal Constitution judicial power in the Federation is vested on 2 High Courts of co-ordinate jurisdiction and status namely the High Court of Malaya and the High Court of Borneo, and the inferior courts. The Federal Court with its principal registry in Kuala Lumpur is the Supreme Court in the country.
The Lord President as the supreme head of the Judiciary, the 2 Chief Justices of

the High Courts and 6 other Judges form the constitution of the Federal Court. Apart from having exclusive jurisdiction to determine appeals from the High Court the Federal Court is also conferred with such original and consultative jurisdiction as is laid out in Articles 128 and 130 of the Constitution.

A panel of 3 Judges or such greater uneven number as may be determined by the Lord President preside in every proceeding in the Federal Court.

The right of appeal to the Yang di-Pertuan Agong (who in turn refers the appeal to the Judicial Committee of the British Privy Council) from a decision of the Federal Court in respect of criminal and constitutional matters was abolished on 1 July 1978.

DIPLOMATIC REPRESENTATIVES

Of Malaysia in Great Britain (45 Belgrave Sq., London, SW1X 8QT)
High Commissioner: M. H. Kassim (accredited 16 March 1983).

Of Great Britain in Malaysia (Wisma Damansara, Jalan Semantan, Kuala Lumpur)
High Commissioner: D. H. Gillmore, CMG.

Of Malaysia in the USA (2401 Massachusetts Ave., NW, Washington, D.C., 20008)
Ambassador: Datuk Zain Azraai bin Zainal Abidin.

Of the USA in Malaysia (A.I.A. Bldg., Jalan Ampang, Kuala Lumpur)
Ambassador: Ronald D. Palmer.

Of Malaysia to the United Nations
Ambassador: Tan Sri Zainal Abidin bin Sulong.

Books of Reference

Statistical Information: The Department of Statistics, Malaysia, Kuala Lumpur, was set up in 1963, taking over from the Department of Statistics, States of Malaya. *Chief Statistician:* Khoo Teik Huat. Main publications: *Peninsular Malaysia Monthly* and *Annual Statistics of External Trade; Malaysia External Trade* (quarterly); *Peninsular Malaysia Statistical Bulletin* (monthly); *Rubber Statistics* (monthly); *Rubber Statistics Handbook* (annual); *Oil Palm Statistics* (monthly); *Oil Palm, Coconut and Tea Statistics* (annual); *Survey of Manufacturing Industries, 1974; National Accounts Statistics, 1973–1977; Malaysia Industrial Classification, 1972; Monthly Industrial Statistics, Malaysia; Census of Selected Service Trades, 1973.*

Gullick, J., *Malaysia: Economic Expansion and National Unity.* Boulder and London, 1982
Huk Tee, L., and Sook Jean, W., *Malaysia.* [Bibliography] Oxford and Santa Barbara, 1983
Snodgrass, D. R., *Inequality and Economic Development in Malaysia.* OUP, 1982

PENINSULAR MALAYSIA

AREA AND POPULATION. The total area of Peninsular Malaysia is about 50,806 sq. miles (131,587 sq. km). The federal capital is Kuala Lumpur (244 sq. km).

State	Area (sq. miles)	Population (1980 Census)	Capital	Population (1980 Census)
Johore	7,330	1,601,504	Johore Bharu	249,880
Kedah	3,639	1,102,200	Alor Star	71,682
Kelantan	5,765	877,575	Kota Bharu	170,559
Malacca	637	453,153	Malacca	88,073
Negeri Sembilan	2,565	563,955	Seremban	136,252
Pahang	13,886	770,644	Kuantan	136,625
Penang	399	911,586	Georgetown	250,578
Perak	8,110	1,762,288	Ipoh	300,727
Perlis	307	147,726	Kangar	12,956
Selangor	3,074	1,467,441	Shah Alam	24,138
Trengganu	5,002	542,280	Kuala Trengganu	186,608
Federal Territory	94	937,875	Kuala Lumpur	937,875
Peninsular Malaysia	50,806	11,128,227		

Population by races (1981 Census): 11,428,000 Malays; 6,168,000 Chinese; 3,995,000 Indians; 1,183,000 others. In 1974 Kuala Lumpur became a Federal District. Shah Alam became capital of Selangor. Vital statistics (1979): Births, 336,848; deaths, 64,345.

CONSTITUTION AND GOVERNMENT. The States of the Federation of Malaya, now known as Peninsular Malaysia, comprises the 11 States of Johore, Pahang, Negeri Sembilan, Selangor, Perak, Kedah, Perlis, Kelantan, Trengganu, Penang and Malacca. On 31 Aug. 1957 the Federation became the 11th sovereign member-state of the Commonwealth of Nations.

For earlier history of the States and Settlements see THE STATESMAN'S YEAR-BOOK, 1957, p. 241.

The Constitution is based on the agreements reached at the London conference of Jan.-Feb. 1956, between HM Government in the UK, the Rulers of the Malay states and the Alliance Party (which at the first federal elections on 27 July 1955 obtained 51 of the 52 elected members), and subsequently worked out by the Constitutional Commission appointed after that conference.

ECONOMY

Budget. See p. 817.

Weights and Measures. The standard measures are the imperial yard, pound and gallon. The Weights and Measures Act of 1972 provides for a 10-year transition to the metric system, and was completed by 31 Dec. 1981.

ENERGY AND NATURAL RESOURCES

Electricity. In 1980, 8,974·1m. kwh. were generated; commerce and industry are the main consumers.

Minerals. Production (in tonnes): Tin-in-concentrates: 1980, 61,404; 1979, 62,995. Iron ore: 1980, 371,186; 1979, 350,498. Bauxite: 1980, 920,356; 1979, 386,520. Ilmenite (exports): 1980, 189,121; 1979, 199,819. Gold: 1980, 4,621 troy oz.; 1979, 5,273.

Agriculture. Total area under agricultural crops, 1978, 8m. acres. This included 254,830 acres of second season rice crops. Rice: Production in 1982, 1,365,900 tons from 771,080 hectares. Rubber: Production in 1982, 1·41m. tonnes; Oil-palms: Production in 1982 (estimate), 3·2m. tonnes of palm oil; 50,500 tonnes of cocoa; 257,000 tonnes of coconut oil.

Tea: Production in 1980, 3,202,000 kg.

Livestock: (1982) Cattle, 555,000; buffaloes, 295,000; sheep, 66,000; pigs, 1,785,000; goats, 385,000.

Forestry (1982). Reserved forests, 4·9m. hectares. Production of logs (estimate), 6·4m.cu. metres; sawn timber, 5,488,000 cu. metres; plywood, 88,168,000 sq. metres (5mm thickness). Exports of veneer, 31·9m. sq. metres (5mm thickness).

Fisheries. Landings in 1982 (estimate), 861,000 tons; 1981, 827,700 tons. Number of vessels in 1979, 21,439 powered, 5,955 non-powered.

INDUSTRY AND TRADE

Trade Unions. There were, on 31 Dec. 1981, 292 registered trade unions with 549,000 members in Peninsular Malaysia.

Commerce. Imports and exports for calendar years in M$1m.:

	1975	1976	1977	1978	1979	1980
Imports	7,516·1	8,513·5	9,880·7	12,156·7	17,161	23,539
Exports	7,595·8	10,042·7	11,230·9	13,680·3	24,219	28,201

Chief imports (1982); Machinery and transport equipment, M$5,666m.; manufactured goods, M$2,893m.; food, M$1,491m.

Chief exports (1982): Rubber, 704,000 tonnes (M$1,373m.); crude petroleum (M$3,702m.); sawn timber, 8,649,000 cu. metres (M$1,554m.); other exports (1981) palm oil, 2·35m. tonnes (M$2,710m.); palm oil, crude, 2,822,000 tonnes (M$1,177m.); saw logs, 15,816,000 cu. metres (M$2,473m.); bauxite (1980), 718,300 tonnes (M$20·8m.).

In 1982 imports came chiefly from Japan (M$3,023m.), USA (M$2,299m.), Australia (M$699m.), Thailand (M$686m.), UK (M$464m.), Saudi Arabia (M$454m.), China (M$238m.), Singapore (M$211m.). Exports went mainly to Singapore (M$2,663m.), Japan (M$2,332m.), Netherlands (M$439m.), USA (M$406m.), Thailand (M$318m.), Korea (M$293m.), Taiwan (M$213m.), UK (M$134m.), India (M$131m.).

Tourism. In 1978, 3,017,864 foreigners visited Peninsular Malaysia.

COMMUNICATIONS

Roads. In 1982 the Public Works Department maintained 29,934 km of public roads, of which 15,983·44 km was of bituminous metalled surface, 81·44 km waterbound metalled surface, 1,799 km hard surface bitumen sealed, 2,931·99 km hard surface waterbound and 1,038·67 km earth surface.

In 1980, 374,939 motor vehicles were registered, including 124,428 private cars, 854 buses, 23,436 lorries and vans, 210,682 motor cycles.

Railways. The Malayan Railway main line runs from Singapore to Butterworth opposite Penang Island. From Bukit Mertajam 8 miles south of Butterworth a branch line connects Peninsular Malaysia with the State Railways of Thailand at the frontier station of Padang Besar. Other branch lines connect the main line with Port of Klang, Teluk Anson, Port Dickson and Ampang. The east-coast line, branching off the main line at Gemas, runs for over 300 miles to Tumpat, Kelantan's northernmost coastal town; a 13-mile branch line linking Pasir Mas with Sungei Golok makes a second connexion with Thailand.

In 1982 there were 1,639 km (metre gauge) which carried 7·4m. passengers and 3·4m. tonnes of freight.

Aviation (1980). There are 9 airports used by scheduled air services and international air services are operated into Kuala Lumpur and Penang airports. The national carrier, Malaysian Airlines System (MAS), began operation on 1 Oct. 1972 to provide both domestic and international services. The Malaysian Airlines System (MAS) operate international services to Amsterdam, Bandar Seri Begawan, Bangkok, Dubai, Frankfurt, Haadyai, Hong Kong, Jakarta, Jeddah, Kuwait, London, Madras, Manila, Medan, Melbourne, Paris, Perth, Seoul, Singapore, Sydney, Taipei and Tōkyō. The number of domestic points served by the airline is 37. Charter services are provided within Peninsular Malaysia by Malaysia Air Charter Co., Pan Malaysia Air Charter, Wira Kris, Genting Helicopter Service and Kris Udara Malaysia. The following airlines operate scheduled services through Kuala Lumpur besides MAS: Air Lanka, Cargoluse Airways, Bangladesh Beiman, Iraqi Airways, Philippine Airlines, PIA, Aeroflot Soviet Airlines, Air India, British Airways, Cathay Pacific Airways, Czechoslovakia Airlines, Garuda Indonesian Airways, Japan Airlines, KLM, PANAM, SAS, SABENA, Singapore Airlines, Thai International Airways and Trans Mediterranean Airways.The airlines operating scheduled services through Penang besides MAS are Garuda Indonesian Airways, Cathay Pacific Airways, Thai Airways Co. and Thai Airways International.

Civil aviation statistics for airports in Peninsular Malaysia (1980): Aircraft movements, 90,530; terminal passengers, 3,940,078; freight, 37,511 tonnes; mail, 3,473 tonnes.

Shipping. The major ports of Peninsular Malaysia are Penang, Malacca, Port Klang, Pasir Gudang, Port Dickson and Kuantan. The volume of shipping (vessels of over 75 NRT only) handled at these ports, exclusive of coasting trade, was as follows (in 1,000 NRT):

Ports		Arrivals		Departures	
		Number	Tonnage	Number	Tonnage
Penang	1979	1,711	7,236	1,720	7,244
	1980	1,805	7,627	1,796	7,610
Port Klang	1979	2,794	16,463	2,799	16,434
	1980	2,785	15,891	2,796	15,996
Total (all ports)	1979	5,399	34,103	5,408	34,090
	1980	5,611	34,132	5,558	34,072

The total cargo handled in all ports during 1979 was 25·37m. tonnes; 1980, 27·25m. tonnes.

Post and Broadcasting. As at 31 Dec. 1979, 445 post offices, 1,381 postal agencies, 177 mobile post offices and 1 riverine postal office were operating in Malaysia, and the cash turnover for the year amounted to M$4,688,113,241.

There were 825,289 telephones on 1 Jan. 1982. In 1979, 208,731 wireless licences and 911,749 television licences were issued.

JUSTICE, RELIGION, EDUCATION AND WELFARE

Justice. Unlike the Federal Court and the High Court which were established under the Constitution, the subordinate courts in Peninsular Malaysia comprising the sessions court, the Magistrate's court and the Penghulu's court were established under a Federal Law (the subordinate Courts Act, 1948 (Revised 1972)).

All offences other than those punishable with death are tried before a Sessions Court President who is empowered to pass any sentence allowed by law other than the sentence of death. In civil matters, the sessions court has jurisdiction to hear all actions and suits where the amount in dispute does not exceed M$25,000.

A First Class Magistrate's criminal jurisdiction is limited to offences for which the maximum term provided by law does not exceed 10 years' imprisonment and to certain specified offences where the term of imprisonment provided for may be extended to 14 years' imprisonment or which are punishable with fine only.

Juvenile courts established under the Juvenile Courts Act, 1947 for juvenile offenders below the age of 18 are presided over by a First Class Magistrate assisted by 2 advisers.

There are 30 penal institutions, including Borstal establishments and an open prison camp. The average prison population (1979) was 9,254.

Religion. More than half the population are Muslims, and Islam is the official religion. In 1970 there were 4,673,670 Muslims, 765,250 Hindus, 220,897 Christians and 2,495,739 Buddhists.

Education. In 1981 there were 4,357 state assisted primary schools with 2,003,803 pupils and 4,357 teachers and in 1980, 208 private primary schools with 5,130 pupils and 224 teachers.

In 1981 there were 2,855 secondary schools with 1,160,967 pupils and 46,960 teachers.

There were (1980): 10 special schools with 1,312 pupils and 104 teachers; 401 classes for further education with 10,281 students and 997 teachers; 25 teacher training colleges with over 12,000 students.

In the academic year 1980–81 there were 10 institutions of higher learning:

	1981–82	
	Staff	Students
Ungku Omar Polytechnic, Ipoh	112	2,449
Kuantan Polytechnic, Kuantan	49	575
MARA Institute of Technology, Shah Alam	665	11,108
Tunku Ab. Rahman College, Kuala Lumpur	156	6,285
University of Malaya, Kuala Lumpur	1,085	9,310
University of Kebangsaan, Bangi	864	7,514
University of Science, Penang	417	4,387
University of Agriculture, Serdang	502	4,136
University of Technology, Kuala Lumpur	431	4,862

The International Islamic University opened in 1983.

Health. In 1981 Government maintained 65 general, district hospitals with 29,712 beds, 2 institutions with 2,688 beds for the treatment of Hensens' disease, 2 mental institutions with 6,577 beds and 1 institution (293 beds) for tuberculosis treatment. For the care of the rural population there were 3,131 medical and health facilities comprising 65 main health centres, 254 health sub-centres, 1,375 midwives' clinics, 414 static, 284 travelling dispensaries, 739 dental clinics, 41 maternal and child health clinics. The Government also maintains an Institute for Medical Research with 2 branch laboratories at Ipoh and Penang.

Books of Reference

Morris, M. W., *Local Government in Peninsular Malaysia.* London, 1980
Wilkinson, R. J., *Malay-English Dictionary.* 2 vols. New ed. London, 1956
Winstedt, Sir R., *Malaya and Its History.* 3rd ed. London, 1953.—*An English–Malay Dictionary.* 3rd ed. Singapore, 1949.—*The Malays: A Cultural History.* London, 1959

SABAH

HISTORY. The territory now named Sabah, but until Sept. 1963 known as North Borneo, was in 1877-78 ceded by the Sultans of Brunei and Sulu and various other rulers to a British syndicate, which in 1881 was chartered as the British North Borneo (Chartered) Company. The Company's sovereign rights and assets were transferred to the Crown with effect from 15 July 1946. On that date, the island of Labuan (ceded to Britain in 1846 by the Sultan of Brunei) became part of the new Colony of North Borneo. On 16 Sept. 1963 North Borneo joined the new Federation of Malaysia and became the State of Sabah.

AREA AND POPULATION. Area, about 29,388 sq. miles (80,520 sq. km), with a coastline of about 900 miles. The interior is mountainous, Mount Kinabalu being 13,455 ft (4,175 metres) high. Population, 1970 census 655,295, (1978 estimate, 981,544), of whom, 421,962 (613,150) were natives, 140,969 (178,469) Chinese, 2,489 Europeans 97,717 (189,925) others. The native population comprises Kadazans (largest and mainly agricultural), Bajaus and Bruneis (agriculture and fishing), Muruts (hill tribes), Suluks (mainly seafaring) and several smaller tribes.

The island of Labuan, 35 sq. miles (75 sq. km) in area, lying 6 miles off the north-west coast of Borneo is a free port. It has a fine port, Victoria Harbour.

The principal towns are situated on or near the coast. They include Kota Kinabalu, the capital (formerly Jesselton), 1980 census population (preliminary), 59,500, Sandakan (73,815), Tawau (45,249), Kudat (10,938); and Keningau in the hinterland (4,279).

CLIMATE. The climate is tropical monsoon, but on the whole is equable, with temperatures around 80°F (26·5°C) throughout the year. Annual rainfall varies, according to locality, from 10″ (250 mm) to 148″ (3,700 mm). The north-east monsoon lasts from Dec. to April and chiefly affects the east coast, while the south-west monsoon from May to Aug. gives the west coast its wet season.

CONSTITUTION AND GOVERNMENT. The Constitution of the State of Sabah provides for a Head of State, called the *Yang Dipertua Negeri Sabah.* Executive authority is vested in the State Cabinet headed by the Chief Minister.

Head of State: Tun Mohamed Adam Robert, SMN, SPDK.

Flag: Four horizontal stripes of red, white, yellow and blue, with a green quarter bearing an outline of Mount Kinabalu in brown.

The Cabinet was composed as follows in March 1982:

Chief Minister and Minister of Natural Resources: Datuk Harris bin Mohd. Salleh, SPDK.

Deputy Chief Minister and Industrial Development: Datuk James Peter Ongkili, DIMP. *Financial Planning and Development:* Datuk Hj. Mohd. Noor Mansoor, PGDK. *Agriculture and Fisheries:* Datuk Lim Guan Sing, DPMK. *Work and Utilities:* Datuk Suffian Koroh, PGDK. *Community Services:* Toh Puan Hajjah Rahimah Stephens, PGDK. *Local Government and Housing:* Datuk Joseph Pairin Kitingan, PGDK. *Manpower and Environmental Development:* Datuk Yap Pak Leong, PGDK. *Culture, Youth and Sports:* Datu Abdul Hamid bin Tun Datu Haji Mustapha.

The Legislative Assembly consists of the Speaker, 48 elected members and not more than 6 nominated members.

The official language was English for a period of 10 years from Sept. 1963 but in Aug. 1973 Bahasa Malaysia was introduced and in 1974 was declared the official language.

ECONOMY

Budget. Budgets for calendar years, in M$:

Ordinary Budget	1976	1977	1978	1979	1980
Revenue	557,496,990	716,291,841	777,282,219	1,439,748,354	1,538,251,203
Expenditure	342,008,618	556,660,409	637,510,015	926,035,864	1,383,481,653

Development Budget					
Revenue	122,458,589	184,895,412	198,347,347	201,937,626	331,753,502
Expenditure	120,620,884	165,749,561	186,816,759	264,620,018	396,634,910

Banking. There are branches of The Chartered Bank at Kota Kinabalu, Sandakan, Tawau, Labuan, Kudat, Tenom and Lahad Datu. The Hongkong and Shanghai Bank has branches at Kota Kinabalu, Sandakan, Labuan, Beaufort, Papar and Tawau. The Hock Hua Bank (S) has branches at Kota Kinabalu, Sandakan and Tawau. The Chung Khiaw Bank has branches at Kota Kinabalu, Tuaran and Sandakan. Malayan Banking Ltd has branches at Kota Kinabalu, Tawau, Semporna and Sandakan. United Overseas Bank and the Overseas Chinese Banking Corporation have each a branch at Kota Kinabalu. Bank Bumiputra Malaysia has branches at Kota Kinabalu. Lahad Datu, Sandakan and Keningau. Overseas Union Bank and the Development and Commercial Bank have each a branch at Sandakan. The Sabah Bank Berhad and Sabah Development Bank were established in Kota Kinabalu in 1979.

The National Savings Bank has taken over the functions of the post office savings bank as from 1 Dec. 1974 and had (1981) M$29·4m. due to 118,436 depositors. It also provides additional services to depositors including the granting of loans for housing.

COMMERCE. The main imports are machinery, tobacco, provisions, petroleum products, metals, rice, textiles and apparel, vehicles, sugar, building material. Statistics for calendar years, in M$:

	1978	1979	1980	1981	1982
Imports	1,527,640,000	2,035,061,720	3,060,819,153	3,644,281,463	3,217,971,724
Exports	2,709,779,873	4,132,247,959	4,455,982,812	4,357,069,182	5,726,240,301

The main imports and exports were (in M$1m.):

Imports	1960	1970	1979	1980	1981	1982 [1]
Rice	8·4	15·4	57·8	47·9	86·7	75·0
Provisions	22·3	45·7	158·1	218·8	261·7	261·8
Textiles and apparel	9·2	20·5	77·3	87·9	109·0	99·8
Tobacco, cigars and cigarettes	12·8	32·9	76·4	92·2	96·0	79·2
Sugar	3·5	6·7	21·9	34·0	38·6	32·3
Vehicles	8·1	47·6	217·9	389·1	394·9	279·2

[1] Provisional

Imports	1960	1970	1979	1980	1981	1982[1]
Machinery	30·0	109·0	86·0	138·3	168·4	160·2
Petroleum products	16·1	28·6	180·2	332·9	437·9	332·3
Metals	12·1	36·8	202·7	296·8	407·5	416·4
Building materials	2·8	13·0	57·6	89·7	128·7	120·4

Exports						
Rubber	49·5	36·5	79·8	82·3	56·2	36·5
Timber	90·7	396·8	2,077·0	1,855·1	1,777·6	1,319·1
Hemp	5·2	0·3	–	–	–	–
Fish, fresh, dried and salted	0·9	8·0	44·4	34·3	40·7	44·7
Copra (including re-exports)	40·2	6·8	34·5	33·3	22·5	17·0
Cocoa beans	15·8	4·4	64·8	67·6	83·1	104·6
Veneer sheets	0·5	2·5	10·0	10·4	18·1	19·0
Palm oil	–	18·1	183·4	159·6	159·6	182·7
Copper concentrates	–	–	134·3	177·3	167·3	152·3

[1] Provisional.

Tourism. In 1982 some 127,777 tourists visited Sabah.

COMMUNICATIONS

Roads (1982). There were 6,586 km of roads, of which 1,962 km were bitumen surfaced, 4,434 km gravel surfaced and 190 km of earth road. Work is in progress on a network of roads, notably the Kota Kinabalu-Sandakan and Sandakan-Lahad Datu road links.

Railways. A metre-gauge railway, 140 km, runs from Kota Kinabalu on Gaya Bay to Tenom in the interior. It carried 689,213 passengers in 1981.

Aviation. External communications are provided from the international airport at Kota Kinabalu by Cathay Pacific Airways Ltd to Hong Kong; Malaysian Airways to Hong Kong, Manila, Brunei, Kuching, Singapore and Kuala Lumpur; Brunei Airways to Brunei and Kuching and Philippine Airlines to Manila.

The total air traffic handled at Sabah airports during 1982 was 2,188,914 passengers, 15,296,902 kg freight and 2,985,677 kg mail.

Shipping (1982). Merchant shipping totalling 15,777,329 NRT used the ports, handling 15,954,193 tonnes of cargo.

Post. As at 31 Dec. 1976 there were 32 post offices, 13 mobile post offices and 84 postal agencies. There were 56,768 telephones on 31 Dec. 1982. As at 31 Dec. 1982, there were 63,125 wireless and 75,894 television licences issued.

JUSTICE, EDUCATION AND WELFARE

Justice. Pursuant to the Subordinate Courts Ordinance (Cap. 20) (1951) Courts of a Magistrate of the First Class, Second Class and Third Class were established to adjudicate upon the administration of civil and criminal law. The civil jurisdiction of a First Class Magistrate is limited to cases where the amount in dispute does not exceed M$1,000. but provision is made for the Chief Justice to enlarge that jurisdiction to M$3,000. This has been established so as to confer this jurisdiction on all stipendiary magistrates. A Second Class Magistrate can only try suits where the amount involved does not exceed M$500 and a Third Class Magistrate where it does not exceed M$100.

The criminal jurisdiction of these Magistrates' Courts is limited to offences of a less serious nature although stipendiary magistrates have enhanced jurisdiction. There are no Juvenile Courts.

There are also Native Courts with jurisdiction to try cases arising from breach of native law and custom (including Moslem Law and custom) where all parties are natives or one of the party is a native (if the matter is a religious, matrimonial or sexual one). Appeals from Native Courts lie to a District Judge or a Native Court of Appeal presided over by a Judge.

In 1982, 3,336 convictions were obtained in 918 cases taken to court.

Education. In 1982, there were 159,545 primary and 71,211 secondary pupils.

There are 834 primary schools (654 government, 169 grant-aided and 11 private), and 105 general secondary schools (54 government, 37 grant-aided and 14 private) throughout the State. There are 3 teacher-training colleges, with (1982) 987 students.

The Government also runs 4 vocational schools in Kota Kinabalu and Sandakan offering carpentry, motor mechanics, electrical installation, fitting/turning, radio and television and heavy plant fitting.

The Department of Education also runs further education classes in most towns and districts. The main medium of instruction in primary schools is Bahasa Malaysia although there are some Chinese medium primary schools. Secondary education is principally English but this is progressively being replaced by Bahasa Malaysia.

Health. The principal diseases are malaria, pulmonary tuberculosis and intestinal infestations. Specific control programmes for malaria and tuberculosis have drastically reduced the incidence of these two diseases.

As at 31 Dec. 1982 there were 16 hospitals (2,665 beds).Seventy-six fixed dispensaries in outlying districts providing in-patient and out-patient care are staffed by hospital assistants under the supervision of district medical officers. There are mental hospitals at Sandakan and Kota Kinabalu. There are 17 district health centres and 45 travelling clinics throughout the State providing maternal and child health care.

Book of Reference

Statistical Information: Director, Federal Department of Information, Kota Kinabalu.

Tregonning, K. G., *North Borneo.* HMSO, 1960

SARAWAK

HISTORY. The Government of part of the present territory was obtained on 24 Sept. 1841 by Sir James Brooke from the Sultan of Brunei. Various accessions were made between 1861 and 1905. In 1888 Sarawak was placed under British protection. On 16 Dec. 1941 Sarawak was occupied by the Japanese. After the liberation the Rajah took over his administration from the British military authorities on 15 April 1946. The Council Negri, on 17 May 1946, authorized the Act of Cession to the British Crown by 19 to 16 votes, and the Rajah ceded Sarawak to the British Crown on 1 July 1946.

On 16 Sept. 1963 Sarawak joined the Federation of Malaysia.

AREA AND POPULATION. The area is about 48,250 sq. miles (121,449 sq. km), with a coastline of 450 miles and many navigable rivers.

The population at 1980 census was 1,294,753 (1978 estimate, 1,173,906, including 386,260 Dayaks; 182,700 Malays; 103,194 other natives; 294,020 Chinese; 9,735 others). The annual rate of increase is 2·4% (estimate). Working population (1980), 710,000.

The chief towns are the capital, Kuching, about 21 miles inland, on the Sarawak River (1980 population: 120,000), Sibu, 80 miles up the Rejang River, which is navigable by large steamers (1980 population: 86,000), and Miri, the headquarters of the Sarawak Shell Ltd (1980 population: 66,000).

CONSTITUTION AND GOVERNMENT. On 24 Sept. 1941 the Rajah began to rule through a constitution. Since 1855 two bodies, known as Majlis Mesyuarat Kerajaan Negeri (Supreme Council) and the Dewan Undangan Negeri (State Legislature), had been in existence. By the constitution of 1941 they were given, by the Rajah, powers roughly corresponding to those of a colonial executive council and legislative council respectively. Sarawak has retained a considerable measure of local autonomy in state affairs. The State or Legislature consists of 48 elected members and sits for 5 years unless sooner dissolved.

A ministerial system of government was introduced in 1963. The Chief Minister presides over the Supreme Council, which contains no more than 8 other Council Negri members, all of whom are Ministers.

Elections to the State Legislature on 22 Sept. 1979 returned 3 Independents and 45 members of the Sarawak Barisan Nasional comprising the Party Pesaka Bumiputra Bersatu, the Sarawak United Peoples' Party, and Sarawak National Party.

Sarawak has 24 seats in the Malaysia House of Representatives (154 members) and 5 seats in the Senate (58 members).

Sarawak has 7 divisions each under a Resident.

Head of State: Tun Datuk Patinggi Tan Sri Haji Abdul Rahman Ya'kub, SMN, DP, PMN, SPMJ, SPMK, SIMP, SPMS, SSDK, SPMP, SPDK, PNBS.

Chief Minister: Datuk Patinggi Haji Abdul Taib Mahmud, DP, SPMJ, PGDK.

Deputy Chief Ministers: Tan Sri Datuk Amar Sim Kheng Hong, PSM, DA, PGDK (*Finance and Development*), Datuk Daniel Tajem anak Miri, JMN (*Agriculture and Community Development*), Datuk Alfred Jabu anak Numpang, PNBS, KMN (*Housing*). *Communications and Works:* Datuk Dr Wong Soon Kai, PNBS. *Local Government:* Joseph Balan Seling. *Forestry:* Datuk Haji Noor Tahir, PNBS, AMN. *Culture, Youth and Sports:* Hafsah Harun, JMN.

State Secretary: Datuk Amar Abang Haji Yusuf Puteh, DA, PNBS, PGDK, JSM. *State Attorney-General:* Datuk Jemuri Serjan, PNBS, JBS. *State Financial Secretary:* Datuk Haji Bujang mohd Nor, PNBS, JBS, JSM.

The official languages are Malay and English. The continuing use of English as official language in Sarawak will be reviewed in 1985.

Flag: Horizontally red over white with a blue triangle on the hoist.

ECONOMY

Budget. In 1981 State revenue was M$516·8m.; expenditure, M$413·5m. The revenue is mainly derived from royalties on oil and timber.

The fourth Malaysian 5-year development plan (1981-85) provides for Sarawak an expenditure of M$2,608m.; of this sum M$2,491m. is to be spent on roads and bridges, land development, port development, education, electricity and water supply and agriculture.

Currency. The Malaysian *dollar* is on a par of £0·24 or US$0·42.

Banking. The National savings bank had 86,157 depositors at the beginning of 1981; the amount to their credit was M$38·8m. There is a branch of Bank Negara Malaysia in Kuching, and branches of the Chartered Bank, the Hongkong & Shanghai Bank, Bank Bumiputra Malaysia, the Overseas Chinese Banking Corporation, the Malayan Bank and 9 other banks.

PRODUCTION. The State produces rubber (exports, 1982, 15,919 net tons, M$24·2m.; 1981, 28,158 net tons, M$57·6m.), timber logs (exports, 1982, 9·2m. tons, M$1,261m.; 1981, 6·9m. tons, M$812m.), sawn timber (exports, 1982, 183,759m. tons, M$100m.; 1981, 162,963m. tons, M$84·8m.), palm oil (exports, 1982, 31,919 tons, M$23·8m.; 1981, 18,660 tons, M$21·9m.), pepper (exports, 1982, 25,010 tons, M$65·7m.; 1981, 28,606 tons, M$81·3m.), and other jungle produce. There are also gold (1981, 2,108 grammes), antimony ore (1981, 318 tons) and silica sand (1981, 141,048 tons).

COMMERCE. Export of crude oil in 1982 was 4·41m. tons (M$2,725m.), about 60% of total exports. The bulk of crude production was exported to Japan, USA, Philippines and Thailand.

Total import value, 1982, M$3,313m.; 1981, M$3,001m. Export, 1982, M$4,967m.; 1981, M$4,514m.

COMMUNICATIONS

Roads. There are no railways. In 1981 there were 3,069 miles of roads, consisting of 793 miles of bitumen surfaced, 2,169 miles of gravel or stone surfaced and 108 miles of earth roads.

Aviation. There are daily Malaysian Airline System (MAS) B737 flights between Kuching and Kuala Lumpur *via* Singapore, and also scheduled flights between Kuching, Brunei and Hong Kong. Major towns in Sarawak are linked up by internal air routes.

Shipping. In 1981 Sarawak ports loaded 12,164,000 tons (1980: 10·58m. tons) and discharged 1·38m. tons (1980: 900,000 tons). New Kuching wharf, operational since Dec. 1974, can accommodate vessels up to 15,000 tons.

Post and Broadcasting. There are 53 post offices, 19 mobile offices, wireless-telegraph stations and 53 agencies. A telephone system with 57 exchanges (64,310 telephones) covers the country. There is communication by wireless with Singapore and other Commonwealth countries. The government radio and television service had, at the end of 1981, 33,202 registered receivers.

Newspapers (1982). There are 1 Malay, 2 English and 7 Chinese daily; 1 English weekly; 1 Malay and 1 Iban (Sea Dayak) monthly newspapers as well as a weekly news review in Malay and Iban published by Government.

JUSTICE, RELIGION, EDUCATION AND WELFARE

Justice (1980). In Sarawak subordinate courts were established pursuant to the Subordinate Courts Ordinance (Cap. 42) (1952). The limits of civil and criminal jurisdiction of a First Class, Second Class and Third Class Magistrate are the same as in Sabah. As in Sabah, here too there is provision for the Chief Justice to enhance the jurisdiction of a First Class Magistrate in civil and criminal matters, the reason being that there are no Sessions Courts in both Sabah and Sarawak.

Native Courts were set up under the Native Courts Ordinance (Cap. 43) (1955) with the same limited jurisdiction as Native Courts in Sabah. In addition these courts have jurisdiction to try civil cases where the amount in dispute does not exceed M$50. Appeals from Native Courts lie to a Resident's Native Court and, subject to some limitations, to the Native Court of Appeal which is presided over by a High Court Judge. There are no Juvenile Courts. There are 5 prisons. There were 1,866 admissions, of whom 1,028 were sentenced to penal imprisonment and 723 committed on remand or awaiting trial, and 75 paid fines. Daily average prison population was 409.

Police. There is a Royal Malaysia Police, Sarawak Component, with a total establishment of about 8,000 regular officers and men.

Religion. There are Church of England, Roman Catholic, American Methodist, Seventh-day Adventist and Borneo Evangelical missions. There is a large Moslem population and many Buddhists. Islam is the national religion.

Education (1981). All schools (government, missions, private) numbered about 1,500 with 310,841 pupils, of whom about 100,319 were in secondary classes. There are 3 teacher-training centres and an agricultural university campus conducting pre-university courses.

Health. At the end of 1981 there were 15 government and private hospitals (2,829 beds), 140 static and 94 travelling dispensaries, 121 public dental and school dental clinics and 158 maternal and child health centres. There were 179 registered doctors.

Books of Reference

Population and Housing Census of Malaysia, 1980. Dept. of Statistics, Kuala Lumpur
Sarawak Annual of Statistics. Dept. of Statistics, Kuching, 1981
Sarawak Annual External Trade Statistics Dept. of Statistics, Kuching, 1982
1983 Sarawak Budget. Information Dept., Sarawak
Milne, R. S., and Ratnam, K. J., *Malaysia, New States in a New Nation: Political Development of Sarawak and Sabah in Malaysia.* London, 1974
Runciman, S., *The White Rajahs.* CUP, 1960
Scott, N. C., *Sea Dyak Dictionary.* Govt. Printing Office, Kuching, 1956
National Library: The Sarawak Central Library, Kuching.

MALDIVES

Divehi Jumhuriya

Capital: Malé
Population: 158,500 (1983)
GNP per capita: US$260 (1980)

HISTORY. The islands were under British protection from 1887 to mid–1965. They now enjoy complete independence under the agreement signed in Colombo on 26 July 1965. Maldives became a republic on 11 Nov. 1968.

AREA AND POPULATION. The Republic of Maldives, 400 miles to the south-west of Sri Lanka, consists of some 2,000 low-lying coral islands (only 220 inhabited), grouped into 12 clearly defined clusters of atolls but divided into 19 districts for administrative purposes. Area 115 sq. miles (298 sq. km). Population (census 1978), 143,046. Estimate (1983) 158,500. Capital Malé (29,555 inhabitants).

CONSTITUTION AND GOVERNMENT. The President is elected every 5 years by universal adult suffrage. He is assisted by the Ministers' *Majlis*, a cabinet of ministers of his own choice whom he may dismiss at will. There is also a Citizens' *Majlis* (House of Representatives) which consists of 48 members, 8 nominated by the President, 2 elected from Malé and 2 elected from each of the 19 atolls. The life of the Citizens' *Majlis* is 5 years. There are no political parties.

President and Prime Minister: Maumoon Abdul Gayoom.

External Affairs: Fathulla Jameel. *Justice:* Ibrahim Fareed Didi. *Home Affairs:* Umar Zahir. *Provincial Affairs:* Abdulla Homeed. *Education:* Mohamed Zahir Hussain. *Health:* Mohamed Mustapha Hussain. *Fisheries:* Abdul Sattar Moosa Didi. *Agriculture:* Ahamed Hilmy Didi. *Transport:* Ahamed Shareef.

The official language is Divehi, which is akin to Elu or old Sinhalese.

National flag: Red with a green panel bearing a white crescent.

INTERNATIONAL RELATIONS.
Membership. The Republic of the Maldives is a member of UN and a special member of the Commonwealth.

ECONOMY
Budget. There is no direct taxation.
Currency. The *rufiyaa* (Maldivian rupee) is divided into 100 *laaris*; there are notes of 1, 2, 5, 10, 50 and 100 rufiyaa.

NATURAL RESOURCES
Agriculture. The islands are covered with coconut palms and yield millet and fruit as well as coconut produce.
Production in 1981 included (in 1,000 tonnes): Coconuts, 9; copra, 2.
Fisheries. The Maldivian economy is based on the fishing industry.

INDUSTRY AND TRADE
Commerce. Bonito ('Maldive fish') is the main export commodity and Japan the main buyer. Exports (1978) US$4·1m.: imports, US$13·1m.
Total trade between the Republic of Maldives and UK (British Department of Trade returns, in £1,000 sterling):

	1980	1981	1982	1983
Imports to UK	294	254	57	44
Exports and re-exports from UK	1,121	2,403	615	840

Tourism. Tourism, introduced in 1972, is expanding and there were 35,000 visitors in 1978–79.

COMMUNICATIONS

Aviation. The Maldives' national airline, Maldives International Airline, was established in 1977, and is a joint venture between the Maldives' government and Indian Airlines. It replaced an earlier airline, Air Maldives which was wound up in 1977. The airline operates one Boeing 737, leased from Indian Airlines, from Hulule airport on Malé atoll. Hulule airport is being extended. The Maldives' government hopes to reactivate the former RAF staging post on Gan in order to attract additional tourist traffic.

Shipping. The merchant fleet consists of about 50 vessels of 200,000 GRT.

Post and Broadcasting. There were (1982) 1,540 telephones. An external telephone service links Tortola with Bermuda and the rest of the world, and cable communications also exist to all parts of the world. Radio ZBVI transmits 10,000 watts and has stand-by transmitting facilities of 1,000 watts. Cable and Wireless operate a commercial cable television service to provide subscribers with good quality reception of approximately 7 television channels plus a number of FM stereo broadcasting stations.

JUSTICE, RELIGION EDUCATION AND WELFARE

Justice. Justice is based on the Islamic Shari'ah.

Religion. The State religion is Moslem of the Sunni sect.

Education. In 1978 there were 8,749 pupils in primary and 3,652 in secondary schools.

Health. In 1977 there was a 40-bed hospital in Malé, and 9 doctors, 1 dentist, 177 midwives and 34 nursing personnel.

DIPLOMATIC REPRESENTATIVES

Of Great Britain in the Republic of Maldives
High Commissioner: Sir John Nicholas, KCVO, CMG (resides in Colombo).

Of the Republic of Maldives to the United Nations
Ambassador: (Vacant).

Books of Reference

Bell, H. C. P., *History, Archaeology and Epigraphy of the Maldive Islands.* Ceylon Govt. Press, Colombo, 1940
Bernini, F. and Corbin, G., *Maldive.* Turin, 1973

MALI

République du Mali

Capital: Bamako
Population: 7·49m. (1983)
GNP per capita: US$190 (1980)

HISTORY. Annexed by France between 1881 and 1895, the region became the territory of French Sudan as a part of French West Africa. It became an autonomous state within the French Community on 24 Nov. 1958, and on 4 April 1959 joined with Sénégal to form the Federation of Mali. The Federation achieved independence on 20 June 1960, but Sénégal seceded on 22 Aug. and Mali proclaimed itself an independent republic on 22 Sept. The National Assembly was dissolved on 17 Jan. 1968 by President Modibo Keita, whose government was then overthrown by an Army *coup* on 19 Nov. 1968; power was assumed by a Military Committee for National Liberation led by Lieut. (now General) Moussa Traoré, who became President on 19 Sept. 1969.

AREA AND POPULATION. Mali is a landlocked state, consisting of the Middle and Upper Niger basin in the south, the Upper Sénégal basin in the south-west, and the Sahara in the north. It is bounded west by Sénégal, north-west by Mauritania, north-east by Algeria, east by Niger and south by Upper Volta, the Ivory Coast and Guinea. The republic covers an area of 1,240,142 sq. km (478,832 sq. miles) and had a population of 6,398,914 at the 1976 Census; the latest estimate (1983) is 7,492,000. The chief cities (with populations in 1976) are Bamako, the capital (404,022), Ségou (64,890), Mopti (53,885), Sikasso (47,030), Kayes (44,736), Gao (30,714), Tombouctou (20,483) and Koulikora (16,876).

The population of the regions (census 1976): Kayes, 871,871; Koulikoro, 916,148; Capital district, 404,022; Sikasso, 1,044,664; Ségou, 1,111,810; Mopti, 1,104,708; Tombouctou, 487,278; Gao, 367,819.

The various indigenous languages belong chiefly to the Mande group; of these the principal are Bambara (spoken by 60% of the population), Soninké, Malinké and Dogon; non-Mande languages include Fulani, Songhai, Senufo and Minianka. The official language is French.

CLIMATE. A tropical climate, with adequate rain in the south and west, but conditions become increasingly arid towards the north and east. Bamako. Jan. 76°F (24·4°C), July 80°F (26·7°C). Annual rainfall 45″ (1,120 mm). Kayes. Jan. 76°F (24·4°C), July 93°F (33·9°C). Annual rainfall 29″ (725 mm). Tombouctou. Jan. 71°F (21·7°C), July 90°F (32·2°C). Annual rainfall 9″ (231 mm).

CONSTITUTION AND GOVERNMENT. A new constitution was announced on 26 April 1974 and approved by a national referendum on 2 June; it was amended by the National Assembly on 2 Sept. 1981. The sole legal party is the *Union démocratique du peuple malien* (UDPM), formally constituted on 30 March 1979 and governed by a 19-member Central Executive Bureau responsible to a 137-member National Council who nominate all candidates for election.

The President is directly elected and his term of office is now 6 years; Gen. Moussa Traoré was elected unopposed on 19 June 1979. The 82-member National Assembly is also directly elected (latest elections, 13 June 1982); its term of office is now 3 years.

The Council of Ministers in June 1983 comprised:

President, Head of Government, Defence and Security: Gen. Moussa Traoré.
Ministers of State: Brig.-Gen. Amadou Baba Diarra *(Equipment)*, Oumar Coulibaly *(Economy and Plan)*.
Foreign Affairs and Co-operation: Alioune Blondin N'guéye. *Planning:* Ahmed

Mohamed Ag Hamani. *Agriculture:* Nfagnanama Kone. *Education:* Lieut.-Col. Sékou Ly. *Labour and Civil Service:* Modibo Keita. *Rural Development:* Mady Diallo. *Justice:* Lieut.-Col. Issa Ongoiba. *Public Works and Transport:* Mamadou Haidara. *Health and Social Affairs:* Dr Ngolo Traoré. *Finance and Commerce:* Ydrissa Keita. *State Enterprises:* Bandiougou Bidia Doucoure. *Interior:* Lieut.-Col. Abdourahmane Maiga. *Information and Telecommunications:* Gakou Nee Fatou Niang. *Sports, Arts and Culture:* N'tji Idrissa Mariko.

National flag: Three vertical stripes of green, yellow, red.

Local Government: Mali is divided into the Capital District of Bamako and 7 regions, sub-divided into 46 *cercles* and then into 279 *arrondissements*.

DEFENCE. There is a selective system of 2 years' military service.

Army. The Army consists of 4 infantry battalions, 1 tank company, 1 artillery battalion and support units. Equipment includes 37 T-34 tanks. Strength (1984) 4,600. There is also a paramilitary force of 5,000 men.

Air Force. The Air Force has 5 MiG-17 jet fighters, 1 MiG-15UTI jet trainer, some Yak-18 piston-engined trainers, 2 An-24, 1 An-26 and 3 An-2 transports, and 3 Mi-8 and Mi-4 helicopters from USSR. A twin-turbofan Corvette is used for VIP transport. Personnel total about 300.

INTERNATIONAL RELATIONS

Membership. Mali is a member of UN, OAU and is an ACP state of EEC.

ECONOMY

Planning. The 1981–85 Four Year Plan provides for expenditure of MF 937,000m., comprising 30·1% for the rural sector, 26·9% for town planning, housing and communications, 30·4% for the industrial, water supply, energy and mining sectors.

Budget. The budget for 1982 balanced at MF 88,800m.

Currency. The unit of currency is the *Mali franc* (MF), introduced in July 1962. It has a parity value of MF 100 to 1 French franc. In March 1984, £1 = MF 1,178; US$1 = MF 802·15.

Banking. The *Banque Centrale du Mali* (founded in 1968) is the bank of issue. There are 4 domestic and 2 French-owned banks.

ENERGY AND NATURAL RESOURCES

Electricity. Production (1980) totalled 110m. kwh. Hydro-electric dams have been built at Selingué (near Bamako) on the Upper Niger and at Manantali (near Kayes) on the Sénégal river.

Minerals. Mineral resources are limited, but marble (at Bafoulabé) and limestone (at Diamou) are being extracted in the Upper Sénégal valley; iron ore deposits in this area await development. Salt is mined at Taoudenni in the far north (5,000 tonnes in 1979).

Agriculture. Production in 1981 included (in 1,000 tonnes): Millet, 930; sugarcane, 225; groundnuts, 190; rice, 142; maize, 80; cottonseed, 70; cotton lint, 40; cassava, 56; sweet potatoes, 50.

Livestock, 1982: Cattle, 5,134,000; horses, 139,000; asses, 420,000; sheep, 6·35m.; goats, 7m.; camels, 173,000; chickens, 12·5m.

Important irrigation schemes have been carried out in the Ségou and Mopti districts on the Niger River, of which the Sansanding Barrage and the Sahel Canal are the most important; 50,000 hectares of cotton and rice lands are being irrigated.

Fisheries. About 100,000 tonnes of fish per annum are caught in the rivers.

TRADE. Imports in 1981 totalled MF 200,900m., exports, 83,830m. Chief imports are foodstuffs, automobiles, petrol, building material, sugar, salt, beer and cotton formed 39% of exports.

Total trade between Mali and UK (British Department of Trade returns, in £1,000 sterling):

	1979	1980	1981	1982	1983
Imports to UK	12,108	11,318	4,534	3,385	3,833
Exports and re-exports from UK	6,120	7,878	2,761	4,403	15,856

Tourism. There were 19,583 foreign tourists in 1976.

COMMUNICATIONS

Roads. There were (1980) 13,360 km of roads, of which 6,869 km are usable in all seasons; they include 2,606 km of metalled road Dakar–Niger (of which 1,693 km are in Mali). There were 19,500 road vehicles in 1974.

Railways. Mali has a railway from Kayes to Koulikoro by way of Bamako, a continuation of the Dakar–Kayes line in Sénégal. Total length 645 km and in 1979 the railways ran 129m. passenger-km and 149m. tonne-km.

Aviation. Air services connect the republic with Paris, Dakar and Abidjan. There are international airports at Bamako and Mopti, and Air Mali operates domestic services to 10 other airports.

Shipping. For about 7 months in the year small steamboats perform the service from Koulikoro to Tombouctou and Gao, and from Bamako to Kouroussa.

Post and Broadcasting. There were, in 1982, 8,485 telephones and 95,000 radio receivers.

JUSTICE, RELIGION, EDUCATION AND WELFARE

Justice. The Supreme Court was established at Bamako in 1969 with both judicial and administrative powers. The Court of Appeal is also at Bamako, at the apex of a system of regional tribunals and local *juges de paix*.

Religion. In 1979, 65% of the population were Sunni Moslems, 30% animists and 5% Christians.

Education. In 1979 there were 293,227 pupils and 6,877 teachers in primary schools, 64,491 pupils (1978) in secondary schools, (1977) 2,609 in technical schools, 2,261 in teacher-training colleges and 4,216 students in higher educational establishments. A further 30,000 students were at 1,321 adult literacy centres.

Health. In 1980 there were 12 hospitals, 327 health centres and 445 dispensaries, with a total of 3,200 beds; there were 319 doctors, 18 surgeons, 12 dentists (1976), 18 pharmacists (1976), 250 midwives and 1,312 nursing personnel.

DIPLOMATIC REPRESENTATIVES

Of Mali in Great Britain
Ambassador: Yaya Diarra (resides in Brussels).

Of Great Britain in Mali
Ambassador: P. L. O'Keeffe, CMG, CVO (resides in Dakar).

Of Mali in the USA (2130 R. St., NW, Washington, D.C., 20008)
Ambassador: Lassana Keita.

Of the USA in Mali (Rue Testard and Rue Mohamed V, Bamako)
Ambassador: Parker W. Borg.

Of Mali to the United Nations
Ambassador: Seydou Traoré.

Books of Reference

Hopkins, N. S., *Popular Government in an African Town.* Univ. of Chicago Press, 1972
Jones, W., *Planning and Economic Policy: Socialist Mali and Her Neighbors.* New York, 1974

MALTA

Repubblika Ta' Malta

Capital: Valletta
Population: 326,178 (1982)
GNP per capita: US$3,470 (1980)

HISTORY. Malta was held in turn by Phoenicians, Carthaginians and Romans, and was conquered by Arabs in 870. From 1090 it was joined to Sicily until 1530, when it was handed over to the Knights of St John, who ruled until dispersed by Napoleon in 1798. The Maltese rose in rebellion against the French and the island was subsequently blockaded by the British aided by the Maltese from 1798 to 1800. The Maltese people freely requested the protection of the British Crown in 1802 on condition that their rights and privileges be preserved. The islands were finally annexed to the British Crown by the Treaty of Paris in 1814.

On 15 April 1942, in recognition of the steadfastness and fortitude of the people of Malta during the Second World War, King George VI awarded the George Cross to the island.

AREA AND POPULATION. The area of Malta is 246 sq. km (94·9 sq. miles); Gozo, 67 sq. km (25·9 sq. miles); Comino, 3 sq. km (1·1 sq. miles); total area, 316 sq. km (121·9 sq. miles). Population, census 27 Nov. 1967, 314,216; estimate (31 Dec. 1982) 326,178. Malta, 302,314; Gozo and Comino, 23,864. Chief town and port, Valletta, population 14,527 (1982).

Vital statistics, 1982, estimate: Births, 5,912; deaths, 3,050; marriages, 2,788; emigrants, 938; returned emigrants, 1,193.

CLIMATE. The climate is Mediterranean, with hot, dry and sunny conditions in summer and very little rain from May to Aug. Rainfall is not excessive and falls mainly between Oct. and March. Average daily sunshine in winter is 6 hours and in summer over 10 hours. Valetta. Jan. 55°F (12·8°C), July 78°F (25·6°C). Annual rainfall 20″ (516 mm).

CONSTITUTION AND GOVERNMENT. Malta became independent on 21 Sept. 1964 and became a republic within the Commonwealth on 13 Dec. 1974. For earlier constitutional and government history *see* THE STATESMAN'S YEAR-BOOK, 1980–81, p. 837.

In 1971 Malta began to follow a policy of strict non-alignment and closed the NATO base. In March 1972 agreement was reached on the phasing out of the British Military base which was closed down completely on 31 March 1979.

Malta is a democratic republic and the Constitution, which has been amended 7 times, the last in 1977, provides for a Parliament consisting of a President of the Republic, a House of Representatives of elected members and a Cabinet consisting of the Prime Minister and such number of Ministers as may be appointed. The Constitution which is founded on work, makes provision for the protection of fundamental rights and freedom of the individual, and ensures that all persons in Malta shall have full freedom of conscience and religious worship.

Maltese and English, and such other language as may be prescribed by Parliament, are the official languages.

Elections were held on 12 Dec. 1981. State of parties in Feb. 1983: Malta Labour Party, 34; Nationalist Party, 31.

President: A. Barbara.

The Cabinet (Malta Labour Party) was as at Sept. 1983:

Prime Minister: Dom Mintoff.
Senior Deputy Prime Minister and Minister of Education: Dr Karmenu Mifsud Bonnici. *Senior Deputy Prime Minister and Minister of Justice and Parliamentary*

Affairs: Dr Joseph Cassar. *Deputy Prime Minister and Minister of Finance and Customs:* Wistin Abela. *Works and Housing:* Lorry Sant. *Labour and Social Services:* Freddie Micallef. *Health:* Dr Vincent Moran. *Parastatal and People's Investments:* Dr Philip Muscat. *Tourism:* Joseph Grima. *Industry:* Karmenu Vella. *Foreign Affairs:* Dr Alex Sceberras Trigona. *Economic Planning and Trade:* Lino Spiteri. *Agriculture and Fisheries:* Joseph Debono Grech.

National flag: Vertically white and red, with a representation of the George Cross medal in the canton.

DEFENCE. The Maltese armed forces include 800 personnel, organized into 1 infantry battalion, and supported by a Helicopter Flight equipped with 4 Bell 47G-2 and 1 JetRanger light helicopters received in 1972–73, and 1 Agusta-Bell 204 received subsequently. Duties of the Flight include patrol, search and rescue. There is also a para-military force of 1,100.

A coastal patrol force of small craft was formed in 1973. It is manned by the Maltese Regiment and primarily employed as a coastguard. In 1984 it comprised 15 patrol craft and customs launches manned by 150 officers and men.

All UK forces were withdrawn in March 1979.

INTERNATIONAL RELATIONS

Membership. Malta is a member of UN, the Commonwealth and the Council of Europe.

ECONOMY

Planning. The Development Plan (1981–85) aims at continued economic growth as a means towards improving living standards and towards enhancing the quality of life of the community. Given the lack of national resources and the small size of the home market, the development strategy is based on export-led growth in the production of goods and services and, in particular, in manufacturing industry as the mainstay of the economy; ship repair and shipbuilding; food production and the service sector including tourism and transhipment. This should enable the further diversification of the productive base of the economy and generate new employment opportunities.

Budget. Revenue and expenditure (in Lm) for financial years ending 31 March:

	1978–79	1979 [1]	1980 [2]	1981 [2]	1982 [2]
Revenue	110,268,917	98,708,773	170,152,444	204,661,944	210,724,438
Expenditure	107,780,619	105,603,164	161,490,920	192,435,435	216,494,068

[1] Nine months. April–Dec.   [2] Calendar year.

The most important sources of revenue are customs duties, income tax, National Insurance contributions, receipts from the Central Bank of Malta and until 1979, rent from defence facilities.

Currency. The Maltese currency is (Lm) *Lira Maltija* (Maltese £). Central Bank of Malta notes of Lm1, Lm5 and Lm10 denominations are in circulation. Malta coins are issued in the following denominations: 50, 25, 10, 5, 2 and 1 cents; 5, 3 and 2 *mils*. Total notes in circulation on 31 Dec. 1982 was Lm260·1m.; coins, Lm5·1m. In March 1984, £1 sterling=Lm0·641; US$1 =Lm2·29.

Banking. The Central Bank of Malta was founded in 1968. Commercial banking facilities are provided by Bank of Valletta Ltd, Lombard Bank (Malta) Ltd and Mid-Med Bank Ltd. The other domestic banking institutions are the Government Savings Bank, the Investment Finance Bank (long-term industrial loans), the Apostleship of Prayer Savings Bank Ltd, Lohombus Corporation Ltd (house mortgage) and Melita Bank International Ltd (Offshore Bank).

ENERGY AND NATURAL RESOURCES

Electricity. All towns and villages in Malta and Gozo are provided with electric current. Up to Sept. 1978 the islands obtained their electricity power supplies from

2 interconnected power stations located at Marsa (Malta) having a total installed capacity of 115 mw. The bigger power station with a generating capacity of 85 mw is also equipped with distillation plant capable of also producing fresh water for public consumption at the rate of 4m. gallons per day. An expansion programme is currently under way for the erection of two 30 mw turbo-generating sets and boiler plant which will increase the installed capacity to 175 mw.

In Oct. 1978 another power station, which was formerly used to supply foreign military installations on the Island, was handed over to the Government of Malta and has been integrated in the national electricity supply system. The station has a generating capacity of 12 mw.

The gross electricity generated in 1981 was 557·9m. kwh.

Agriculture. In 1982 agriculture contributed Lm16·1m. to the Gross Domestic Product as against Lm15·3m. in 1981. (The 1982 figure represents a share of 3·8% in the GDP.) In 1982 there was a slight increase in the cultivable area, which totalled 11,639 hectares as against 11,617 hectares in 1981. In 1982 agriculture employed 4,332 full-time farmers, 346 full-time wage earners and 11,026 part-time farmers against, 4,352, 422 and 10,923 respectively in 1981.

In 1982 the value of Malta's main agricultural exports reached Lm1·34m. The 1982 exports consisted mainly of: Potatoes, Lm338,500; seeds, cut-flowers and plants, Lm583,013; wine, Lm105,628; onions, Lm76,702; hides and skins, Lm91,160; live animals, Lm520; capers, Lm148,020.

Livestock (1982): Cattle, 12,087; pigs, 27,889; sheep, 4,037; goats 5,064; poultry, 1m.

Fisheries. In 1980 the fishing industry occupied 964 power propelled and 105 other fishing boats, engaging 360 full-time and 582 part-time fishermen. The catch in 1982 was 1,197 tonnes valued at Lm1,093,000 at first sale.

INDUSTRY AND TRADE

Industry. Investors in industry in Malta are offered the following advantages: political stability, excellent industrial relations, a strategic geographic location, a special association agreement with the EEC, a fully developed and highly functional infrastructure, free repatriation of profits and capital, easily trainable and highly adaptable labour force, financing facilities at favourable rates of interest, ready-built factories at attractive rents. About 260 aided firms are in operation in various industrial sectors, of which the majority are foreign-owned or have foreign interests. The Malta Development Corporation is the Government agency responsible for promoting and implementing new industrial projects, including joint ventures. The Corporation may also participate by way of equity capital, in certain projects jointly with Maltese or foreign industrialists.

Labour. The total work force in Dec. 1982 was 122,296; males, 91,956; females, 30,340, distributed as follows: Agriculture and fisheries, 6,578; manufacturing, 29,640; building, construction and quarrying, 6,022; services, 36,372; electricity, gas and drydocks, 5,983; government, 24,303; armed forces, 766; Dejma and auxiliary workers, 1,430. The number of registered unemployed under Part I of the Employment Register was 10,356, and under Part II, 846.

There were 14 trade unions registered as at 30 June 1983, with a total membership of 48,609 and 20 employers' associations with a total membership of 4,836.

Commerce. Imports and exports including bullion and specie (in Lm1,000):

	1976	1977	1978	1979	1980	1981	1982
Imports	179,923	217,681	221,505	271,960	323,737	332,269	325,073
Exports	97,409	121,791	131,949	152,169	166,722	173,725	169,036

In 1982 the principal items of imports were: Semi-manufactures, Lm98·1m.; machinery and transport, Lm66·9m.; food, Lm47·9m.; fuels, Lm47·2m.; manufactures, Lm23·3m.; chemicals, Lm21m.; others, Lm20·7m. Of domestic exports: Manufactures, Lm102·4m.; machinery and transport, Lm19·4m.; semi-manufactures, Lm17·5m.; beverages and tobacco, Lm5·7m.; food, Lm2·8m.; others, Lm2·3m.

In 1982, Lm93·7m. of the imports came from Italy, Lm56·1m. from UK, Lm48·8m. from Federal Republic of Germany, Lm25·3m. from USA, Lm18·6m. from Asia, Lm10·2m. from the EFTA, Lm4m. from Africa, Lm3·2m. from Oceania, Lm19m. from other European countries; of domestic exports, Lm48·2m. to Federal Republic of Germany, Lm31·3m. to UK, Lm14·8m. to Italy, Lm9·2m. to Africa, Lm7·4m. to Asia, Lm5·7m. to USA, Lm5m. to EFTA and Lm26·3m. to other European countries.

Total trade between Malta and UK (British Department of Trade returns, in £1,000 sterling):

	1980	1981	1982	1983
Imports to UK	46,609	40,713	42,792	40,852
Exports and re-exports from UK	87,527	78,286	71,823	71,895

Tourism. In 1981, 705,710 tourists visited Malta, 514,062 from UK, 29,953 from Italy, 25,290 from Scandinavia, 20,035 from Federal Republic of Germany, 14,538 from Libya, 13,500 from France and 7,084 from USA. In 1980, gross tourist expenditure was Lm111·9m. (estimate).

COMMUNICATIONS

Roads. Every town and village is served by motor omnibuses. There are ferry services running between Malta and Gozo; cars can be transported on the ferries. Motor vehicles registered at 31 Dec. 1982 totalled 110,502, of which 76,409 were private cars, 3,421 hire cars, 17,665 commercial vehicles, 57 buses, 11,880 motor cycles and 1,070 other motor vehicles.

Aviation. In 1982 the principal airlines, Air Malta, Alitalia, British Airways, Libyan Arab Airlines, Union de Transports Aeriens, Yugoslav Air Transport, Austrian Airlines, Balkan Airlines and Tunisavia, operated scheduled services between Malta and UK, Austria, Belgium, Bulgaria, Egypt, Federal Republic of Germany, France, Italy, Libya, Netherlands, Nigeria, Switzerland, Tunisia and Yugoslavia. In 1982 there were 13,750 civil aircraft movements at Luqa Airport. 1,110,257 passengers, 5,281 tonnes of freight and 632 tonnes of mail were handled.

Shipping. The number of ships registered in Malta on 31 Dec. 1981 was 343; 320,190 GRT. Ships entering harbour during 1982, 3,020.

Post and Telecommunications. Telegraph and telephone services are administered by Telemalta Corporation with exchanges at Malta and Gozo. On 31 Dec. 1982 there were 98,125 telephones. A world-wide cable and telex service is also operated.

Cinemas (1981). There were 29 cinemas with a seating capacity of 20,179.

Newspapers. There were (1982) 1 English, 3 Maltese daily newspapers and 5 weekly papers.

JUSTICE, RELIGION, EDUCATION AND WELFARE

Justice. The number of persons convicted of crimes in 1982 was 1,755; those convicted for contraventions against various laws and regulations numbered 8,311. Seventy-three were committed to prison and 6,580 were awarded fines.

Police. On 31 Dec. 1982 police numbered 40 officers and 1,212 other ranks, including 79 women police.

Religion. The majority of the population belong to the Roman Catholic Church.

Education. Education in Malta is compulsory between the ages of 6 and 16 and free in government schools. In 1982 there were 188 kindergarten groups, with nearly 3,612 children in 62 centres throughout Malta and Gozo. The primary level enrols children between 5 and 11 years in a 6-year course. There were 24,643 children (12,842 boys and 11,801 girls) in 80 government schools. Four new Junior Lyceums (2 on Malta and 2 on Gozo) were opened in Sept. 1981 with a total of 3,074 students (1,178 boys, 1,896 girls). There were 31 other government secondary schools with a total of 11,512 (4,936 boys, 6,576 girls). Secondary schools run 5-year courses leading to GCE 'O' level. Two-year courses leading to GCE 'A' level on a worker/pupil system which alternates work with study periods are provided for in the New Lyceum, *i.e.*, upper secondary schools (1,124 students). Enrolment in craft and technician courses in 3 technical institutes amounted to 1,117, while 4,108 (3,015 boys and 1,093 girls) were enrolled in the 12 trade schools for boys and 6 trade schools for girls. Another 171 students are enrolled in specialized vocational schools. Trade schools offer 2- to 4-year courses in specialized trades and are open to students who finish their third year of secondary education. The number of children in special education amounted to 876.

There were 80 private schools with a population of 4,385 at the nursery level, 9,290 at the primary level and 6,813 at the secondary level.

3,982 students attended evening courses in academic, commercial, technical and practical subjects established in 82 centres. The School of Art had an enrolment of 276 students while another 1,450 students enrolled in courses organized by the School of Music.

The University of Malta consists of 6 faculties: Law, Medicine and Surgery, Engineering and Architecture, Dental Surgery, Education and Management Studies (1,004 students in 1982–83). Degrees in Law, Mechanical Engineering, Electrical Engineering, Architecture and Civil Engineering, Accountancy, Business Management, Public Administration, Education, Medicine and Surgery, Pharmacy and Dental Surgery are conferred by the University.

Welfare. The National Insurance Act, 1956, provides cash benefits for marriage, sickness, unemployment, widowhood, orphanhood, invalidity, old age, children's allowances and industrial injury. An agreement, signed on 26 Oct. 1956, established reciprocity in matters of social insurance between Malta and the UK.

The total number of persons in receipt of benefits on 31 Dec. 1982 was 82,083, viz., 902 in receipt of sickness benefit, 1,244 unemployment benefit, 371 injury benefit, 216 disablement benefit, 88 death benefit, 19,750 retirement pensions, 7,509 widows' pensions, 12 widows' special allowance, 18 guardian's allowance, 4,942 invalidity pensions, 46,651 children's allowances and 380 maternity benefit.

The National Assistance Act, 1956, provides for the payment of social assistance and medical assistance, while the Old Age Pensions Act of 1948 provides for the payment of non-contributory old-age pensions to persons over 60 years of age and to blind persons over the age of 14 years.

The number of households in receipt of social assistance and of medical assistance on 31 Dec. 1982 was 5,120 and 5,645 respectively, and the number of old-age pensioners under the Old Age Pensions Act, 1948, was 7,961.

DIPLOMATIC REPRESENTATIVES

Of Malta in Great Britain (16 Kensington Sq., London, W8 5HH)
Deputy High Commissioner: Francis Cassar.

Of Great Britain in Malta (7 St Anne St., Floriana)
High Commissioner: Charles L. Booth, CMG, MVO.

Of Malta in the USA (2017 Connecticut Ave., NW, Washington, D.C., 20008)
Ambassador: Leslie Agius.

Of the USA in Malta (Development Hse., St Anne St., Floriana)
Ambassador: James Malone Rentschler.

Of Malta to the United Nations
Ambassador: Victor J. Gauci.

Books of Reference

Statistical Information: The Central Office of Statistics (Auberge de Castille, Valletta) was set up in 1947. It publishes *Statistical Abstracts of the Maltese Islands*, a quarterly digest of statistics, quarterly and annual trade returns, annual vital statistics and annual publications on shipping and aviation, education, agriculture and industry and National Accounts and Balance of Payments.

Government publications: Information Division (Kastilja, Malta), set up in 1955, publishes

The *Malta Government Gazette* (twice weekly), *Il-Gzejjer* (monthly), *Malta Review* (bi-monthly), *Malta Handbook, Economic Survey, Malta: Guidelines for Progress, Development Plan for Malta 1981–85* and *Supplement Paper Currency in Malta, Heritage of an Island, Reports on the Working of Government Departments.* Malta, 1982.

Malta Independence Constitution (Cmnd 2406). HMSO, 1964
Constitution of the Republic of Malta. Information Division, 1975
Malta Manufacturers and Exporters. Department of Industry, 1981
Malta Who's Who. Malta, 1969–70
Economic Survey 1983. Malta, 1983
Malta Handbook 1982. Information Division
Blouet, Brian, *The Story of Malta.* London, 1967
Busuttil, E. D., *Kalepin Dizzjunarju Malti-Ingliz.* Valletta, 1971.—*Kalepin Dizzjunarju Ingliz-Malti.* 1976
Cassar, P., *Medical History of Malta.* London, 1966
Cremona, J. J., *The Malta Constitution of 1835 and its Historical Background.* Malta, 1959.—*The Constitutional Developments of Malta under British Rule.* Malta Univ. Press, 1963.—*Human Rights Documentation in Malta.* Malta Univ. Press, 1966
Dobie, E., *Malta's Road to Independence.* Univ. of Oklahoma, Norman, USA, 1967
Gerada, E. and Zuber, C., *Malta: An Island Republic.* Paris, 1979
Luke, Sir Harry, *Malta.* 2nd ed. London, 1962
Price, G. A., *Malta and the Maltese: A Study in 19th-century Migration.* Melbourne, 1954
Smith, Harrison, *Britain in Malta.* 2 vols. Malta, 1954

MAURITANIA

République Islamique de Mauritanie

Capital: Nouakchott
Population: 1·78m. (1983)
GNP per capita: US$320 (1980)

HISTORY. Mauritania became a French protectorate in 1903 and a colony in 1920. It became an autonomous republic within the French Community on 28 Nov. 1958 and achieved full independence on 28 Nov. 1960. Under its first President, Moktar Ould Daddah, Mauritania became a one-party state in 1964, but following his deposition by a military *coup* on 10 July 1978, the ruling *Parti du peuple mauritanien* was dissolved.

Following the Spanish withdrawal from Western Sahara on 28 Feb. 1976, Mauritania occupied the southern part (88,667 sq. km) of this territory and incorporated it under the name of Tiris el Gharbia; on 8 Aug. seven additional members of the National Assembly were nominated to represent this territory. However in Aug. 1979 Mauritania renounced sovereignty and withdrew from Tiris el Gharbia.

Following the *coup* of 10 July 1978, power was placed in the hands of a Military Committee for National Recovery (CMRN); the constitution was suspended and the 70-member National Assembly dissolved. Col. Mustafa Ould Salek, Head of the CMRN, assumed the Presidency on 20 March 1979, and on 6 April the CMRN was renamed the Military Committee for National Salvation (CMSN). On 3 June Col. Salek was replaced as President by Lieut.-Col. Mohamed Mahmoud Ould Ahmed Louly, who was in turn replaced on 4 Jan. 1980 by his Prime Minister, Lieut.-Col. Mohamed Khouna Ould Haydalla.

AREA AND POPULATION. Mauritania is bounded west by the Atlantic ocean, north by Western Sahara, north-east by Algeria, east and south-east by Mali, and south by Sénégal. The total area is 1,030,700 sq. km (398,000 sq. miles), and the population at the Census of 1976 was 1,419,939 including 12,897 in Tiris el Gharbia; latest estimate (1983) 1,781,000. The main towns (with 1976 populations) are the capital Nouakchott (134,986), Nouâdhibou (21,961), Kaédi (20,848), Zouérate (17,474), Rosso (16,466) and Atâr (16,326).

In 1976, 22% of the population were urban and 36% were nomadic. 68% of the inhabitants are Moorish, speaking the Hassaniyah dialect of Arabic, while the other 32% consist of Negro peoples, speaking mainly Tukulor (20%), Sarakole (10%), and Wolof, all inhabiting the Sénégal valley in the extreme south.

The official languages are French and Arabic.

CLIMATE. A tropical climate, but conditions are generally arid, even near the coast, where the only appreciable rains come in July to Sept. Nouakchott. Jan. 71°F (21·7°C), July 82°F (27·8°C). Annual rainfall 6″ (158 mm).

CONSTITUTION AND GOVERNMENT. A draft Constitution was published on 19 Dec. 1980, but not promulgated. Pending a return to constitutional rule, the 24-member CMSN wields all executive and legislative powers, working through an appointed Council of Ministers composed as follows in Jan. 1984:

President: Lieut.-Col. Mohamed Khouna Ould Haydalla.
Prime Minister, Minister of Defence: Lieut.-Col. Maaouya Ould Sidi Mohamed Taya.
Foreign Affairs and Co-operation: Cdr Ahmed Ould Minneh. *Interior:* Lieut.-Col. Ahmedou Ould Abdallah. *Justice and Islamic Affairs:* Abdel Aziz Ould Ahmed. *Planning and Territories:* Ahmed Ould Zein.. *Finance:* Sidi Ould Ahmed Deya. *Minerals and Industry:* Lieut.-Col. Aane Amadou Baraly. *Fisheries:*

Mohamed Ould Sidi Aly. *Energy and Water:* Mohamed Fadel Ould Dah. *Rural Development:* Mohamed Ould Amar. *Equipment and Transport:* Cdr Gabriel Cimper. *Housing and Water:* Mahjoub Ould Bayyeh. *National Education:* Hassiny Ould Didi. *Higher Education, Cadre Training and Civil Service:* Maj. Athie Hamath. *Health and Employment:* Maj. Mohamed Mahmoud Ould Deh. *Culture, Youth and Sports:* Dr Youssouf Dia Jana. *Telecommunications and Information:* Dr Mohamed Salem Ould Zein. Secretary-General of the Government: Mahmoud Ba.

National flag: Green, with a crescent beneath a star in yellow in the centre.

Local government: Mauritania is divided into the District of Nouakchott and 12 regions—Hodh ech Chargui, Hodh el Gharbi, Assaba, Gorgol, Brakna, Trarza, Adrar, Dakhlet Nouâdhibou, Tagent, Guidimaka, Tiris Zemmour and Inchiri. The regions are sub-divided into 44 *départements*.

DEFENCE

Army. The Army consists of 1 infantry and 1 artillery battalion, 3 armoured car squadrons and support units; total strength, 8,000 in 1984.

Navy. The Navy consists of 4 patrol vessels and 5 small patrol craft. Personnel (1984) 320.

Air Force. The Air Force has 7 Britten-Norman Defender armed light transports, 2 Maritime Surveillance Cheyennes for coastal patrol, 2 DC-4, 1 Buffalo and 2 Skyvan transports, 2 Islander and 1 Broussard liaison aircraft, and 4 Reims-Cessna 337 Milirole twin-engined counter-insurgency, forward air control and training aircraft. Personnel 150.

INTERNATIONAL RELATIONS

Membership. Mauritania is a member of UN, OAU, the Arab League and is an ACP state of EEC.

ECONOMY

Planning. The 1981–85 development plan stresses the development of agriculture and light industry.

Budget. The ordinary budget for 1981 balanced at 10,300m. ouguiyas.

Currency. The monetary unit is *ouguiya* which is divided into 5 *khoums*. Banknotes of 1,000, 200 and 100 *ouguiya* and coins of 20, 10, 5 and 1 *ouguiya* and 1 *khoum* are in circulation. In March 1984, £1 = 84·80 *ouguiya*; US$1 = 57·03 *ouguiya*.

Banking. *The Banque Centrale de Mauritanie* (created 1973) is the bank of issue, and there are 5 commercial banks situated in Nouakchott.

ENERGY AND NATURAL RESOURCES

Electricity. Production (1979) 100m. kwh.

Minerals. Iron ore deposits of (estimate) 200m. tonnes are found at Zouérate. Production (1981) 8·9m. tonnes. Copper mining, suspended in 1978, resumed in 1983.

Agriculture. Agriculture is mainly confined to the south, in the Sénégal river valley. Production (tonnes) (1981) of millet, 67,000; dates, 14,000; potatoes, 4,000; maize, 6,000; sweet potatoes, 2,000; rice, 6,000; groundnuts, 4,000.

In 1982 there were 800,000 camels, 1·2m. cattle, 142,000 asses, 14,000 horses, 4·9m. sheep, 2·65m. goats.

Fisheries. About 300,000 tonnes of fish are caught in Mauritanian coastal waters each year, but only 34,200 tonnes (1978) are landed in the country (mainly at Nouâdhibou).

Forestry. There are 151,340 sq. km of forests, chiefly in the southern regions, where wild acacias yield the main product, gum arabic.

TRADE. In 1981 imports totalled 12,793m. ouguiya, and exports, 12,505 ouguiya.

In 1981, iron ore comprised 65% of exports and salted and dried fish 35%; 25% of all exports went to Spain, 19·6% to France, and 14% to Japan, while France provided 17% of imports and Spain 12%.

Total trade between Mauritania and UK (British Department of Trade returns, in £1,000 sterling):

	1979	1980	1981	1982	1983
Imports to UK	7,450	9,438	9,679	5,462	6,044
Exports and re-exports from UK	2,845	5,647	3,517	1,943	1,719

Tourism. In 1975 there were 20,700 tourists.

COMMUNICATIONS

Roads. There were 8,900 km of roads in 1978. In 1976 there were 6,600 passenger cars and 4,250 commercial vehicles.

Railways. A 652-km railway links Zouérate with the port of Point-Central, 10 km south of Nouâdhibou, and is used primarily for iron ore exports.

Aviation. There are international airports at Nouakchott, Nouâdhibou and Néma.

Shipping. The major ports are at Point-Central (for mineral exports), Nouakchott and Nouâdhibou.

Post and Broadcasting. There were, in 1977, over 2,000 telephones and 82,000 radio receivers.

Cinemas. In 1977 there were 12 cinemas with a seating capacity of 8,800.

JUSTICE, RELIGION, EDUCATION AND WELFARE

Justice. There are *tribunaux de première instance* at Nouakchott, Atar, Kaédi, Aïoun el Atrouss and Kiffa. The Appeal Court and Supreme Court are situated in Nouakchott. Islamic jurisprudence was adopted in Feb. 1980.

Religion. Over 99% of Mauritanians are Moslem, mainly of the Qadiriyah sect.

Education. In 1979 there were 82,408 pupils in primary schools, 11,957 in secondary schools, and (in 1975) 1,591 in technical schools.

Health. In 1976 there were 9 hospitals with 567 beds; there were 71 doctors, 4 dentists, 5 pharmacists, 20 midwives and 560 nursing personnel.

DIPLOMATIC REPRESENTATIVES

Of Mauritania in Great Britain
Ambassador: Ely Ould Allaf (accredited 15 Dec. 1983).

Of Great Britain in Mauritania
Ambassador: P. L. O'Keeffe, CMG, CVO. (resides in Dakar).

Of Mauritania in the USA (2129 Leroy Pl., NW, Washington, D.C., 20008)
Ambassador: Abdellah Ould Daddah.

Of the USA in Mauritania (PO Box 222, Nouakchott)
Ambassador: Edward L. Peck.

Of Mauritania to the United Nations
Ambassador: Mohamed Said Ould Hamody.

Books of Reference

Stewart, C. C., and Stewart, E. K., *Islam and Social Order in Mauritania.* New York, 1970
Westebbe, R. M., *The Economy of Mauritania.* New York, 1971

MAURITIUS

Capital: Port Louis
Population: 994,000 (1982)
GNP per capita: US$1,060 (1980)

HISTORY. Mauritius was known to Arab navigators probably not later than the 10th century. It was probably visited by Malays in the 15th century, and was discovered by the Portuguese between 1507 and 1512, but the Dutch were the first settlers (1598). In 1710 they abandoned the island, which was occupied by the French under the name of Ile de France (1715). The British occupied the island in 1810, and it was formally ceded to Great Britain by the Treaty of Paris, 1814. Mauritius attained independence on 12 March 1968.

AREA AND POPULATION. Mauritius has an area of about 720 sq. miles (1,865 sq. km). According to the census of 30 June 1972, the population of the island was 826,199 (413,580 males, 412,619 females); that of the dependencies was 25,135 (30 June 1972). Estimated population of the island at the end of 1982 was 994,000, and the population of Port Louis, the capital with its suburbs, numbered 149,000. Port Louis was granted city status on 25 Aug. 1966. Other towns: Beau Bassin-Rose Hill, 87,682; Curepipe, 57,505; Quatre Bornes, 56,491; Vascoas-Phoenix, 55,512.

Rodrigues (formerly a dependency but now a part of Mauritius) is about 350 miles east of Mauritius, 9½ miles long, 4½ miles broad. Area, 40 sq. miles (103·6 sq. km). Population (31 Dec. 1981, estimate), 32,977. Imports, 1980, Rs 75·11m.; 1978, Rs 54,605,564. Exports, 1980, Rs 1·9m.; 1978, Rs 2,872,012. There are 5 government, 5 aided primary, 1 private and 1 state secondary school.

Vital statistics, June 1980: Births, 24,983 (27 per 1,000); marriages, 8,629; deaths, 6,685 (7·2 per 1,000).

The official language is English.

Dependencies. Agalega and St Brandon Group. St Brandon is 250 miles from Mauritius. Area, 71 sq. km. Total population of the dependencies, census 1972, 366; estimated population on 31 Dec. 1981, 350. The main exports (to Mauritius) in 1974 were 227 tonnes of salted fish. In 1965 the Chagos Archipelago was transferred to the British Indian Ocean Territory.

CLIMATE. The sub-tropical climate produces quite a difference between summer and winter, though conditions are generally humid. Most rain falls in the summer so that the pleasantest months are Sept. to Nov. Rainfall amounts vary between 40″ (1,000 mm) on the coast to 200″ (5,000 mm) on the central plateau, though the west coast only has 35″ (875 mm). Mauritius lies in the cyclone belt, whose season runs from Nov. to April, but is seldom affected by intense storms. Port Louis. Jan. 73°F (22·8°C), July 81°F (27·2°C). Annual rainfall 40″ (1,000 mm).

CONSTITUTION AND GOVERNMENT. Mauritius became an independent state and a monarchial member of the British Commonwealth on 12 March 1968 after 7 months of internal self-government. The Governor-General is the local representative of HM the Queen, who remains the Head of the State.

The Cabinet is presided over by the Prime Minister. Each of the other 18 members of the Cabinet is responsible for the administration of specified departments or subjects and is bound by the rule of collective responsibility. 10 Parliamentary Secretaries may also be appointed by the Governor-General on the advice of the Prime Minister but in 1981 there were only 8.

The Legislative Assembly consists of a Speaker, elected from its own members, and 62 elected members (3 each for the 20 constituencies of Mauritius and 2 for Rodrigues) and 8 additional seats in order to ensure a fair and adequate representation of each community within the Assembly. General Elections are held every 5 years on the basis of universal adult suffrage.

The Constitution also provides for the Public Service Commission and the Judicial and Legal Service Commission, which have both assumed executive powers for appointments to the Public Service. An Ombudsman assumed office on 2 March 1970. Adequate provision is also made for the protection of fundamental rights and freedoms of the individual.

Elections were held in Aug. 1983.

Governor-General: The Rt Hon. Sir Seewoosagur Ramgoolam, GCMG.

The Cabinet was composed as follows in Aug. 1983:

Prime Minister and Defence: Aneerood Jugnauth.
Deputy Prime Minister: Gaetan Duval. *Foreign:* Anil Kumarsingh Gayan. *Women's Rights:* Sheilabai Bappoo. *Works:* Rohit Niemo Beedassy. *Commerce:* Kadar Bhayat. *Economic Planning:* Sit Satcam Boolell. *Employment:* Diwakur Bundhun. *Industry:* Ramsamy Chedumbarum Pillay. *Agriculture:* Nunkeswarsingh Deerpalsingh. *Labour:* Joseph Hervé Duval. *Rodrigues and Outlying Islands:* France Félicité. *Health:* Beergoonath Ghurburrun. *Youth and Sport:* Michael Glover. *Housing, Environment:* Dwarkanath Gungah. *Finance:* Seetanah Lutchmeenaraldoc. *Local Government:* Louis Sylvio Michel. *Education:* Armoognum Parsuraman. *Energy:* Mahyendrah Utchanah.

National flag: Horizontally 4 stripes of red, blue, yellow and green.

DEFENCE. The Mauritius Police, which is responsible for defence, is equipped with arms; its strength at 30 June 1982 was 4,082 officers and men.

INTERNATIONAL RELATIONS

Membership. Mauritius is a member of UN, the Commonwealth, OAU and is an ACP state of EEC.

ECONOMY

Budget. Revenue and expenditure (in Rs) for years ending 30 June:

	1978–79	1979–80	1980–81	1981–82	1982–83[1]
Revenue	1,486,394,583	1,863,872,536	2,163,055,708	2,398,000,000	2,846,000,000
Expenditure	1,769,964,582	2,016,144,439	2,525,190,433	3,075,000,000	3,716,048,000

[1] Estimate.

Principal sources of revenue, 1982–83 (estimate): Direct taxes, Rs 499·3m.; indirect taxes, Rs 1,822·4m.; receipts from public utilities, Rs 125·1m.; receipts from public services Rs 111·2m.; interest and royalties, Rs 207·9m., reimbursement, RS 71·2m. Capital expenditure, June 1982, was Rs 1,275. Capital revenue, Rs 853·9m. On 30 June 1981 the public debt of Mauritius was Rs 4,232,068,803 after deducting the value of accumulated sinking funds.

Currency. The unit of currency is the Mauritius *Rupee*, divided into 100 *cents*.

The currency consists of: (i) Bank of Mauritius notes of Rs 50, 25, 10 and 5; (ii) Cupro-nickel coins of 1 rupee, ½ rupee, ¼ rupee and 10 cents; (iii) Bronze coins of 5 cents, 2 cents and 1 cent. In March 1984, £1 = 18·47 *rupees*; US$1 = 12·02.

Banking. The Bank of Mauritius was established in 1966, with an authorized capital of Rs 10m., to exercise the function of a central bank. There are 12 commercial banks, the Mauritius Commercial Bank Ltd (established 1838), Barclays Bank International. the Bank of Baroda Ltd, The Mercantile Bank Ltd, the Mauritius Co-operative Central Bank Ltd, Banque Nationale de Paris (Intercontinentale), the Habib Bank (Overseas) Ltd, Citibank, the State Commercial Bank, the Bank of Credit and Commerce International SA, Indian Ocean International Bank Ltd and Habib Bank (Zurich). Other financial institutions include the Mauritius Housing Corporation, the Development Bank of Mauritius and the post office savings bank.

On 30 June 1982 the post office savings bank held deposits amounting to Rs 113·5m., belonging to 187,098 depositors.

NATURAL RESOURCES

Agriculture (1981). The area planted with sugar-cane was 209,010 acres. There were 21 factories in operation and the amount of sugar produced was: Raw sugar (1983), 630,000 tonnes; white sugar, 38,000 tonnes; molasses, 159,000 tonnes.

The main secondary crops are tea (9,370 acres, yielding 4,900 tonnes of tea), tobacco (1,759 acres, yielding 950 tonnes of tobacco), potatoes (16,000 tonnes) and onions (2,295 tonnes).

Livestock (1982): Cattle, 57,000; goats, 70,000; poultry, 1·7m.

Forestry. The total forest area is estimated at 21,027 hectares including some 11,600 hectares of plantations; if scrub and grazing are included the total area is approximately 56,110 hectares.

In 1981 sales of forest produce from Crown land totalled 29,806 cu. metres, round wood.

INDUSTRY AND TRADE

Industry. Manufactures include: Knitwear, clothing, diamond cutting, watch straps, fertilizers.

Labour. There were on 31 Dec. 1981, 330 registered trade unions with a total membership of 68,666 (on roll).

Commerce. Total trade (in Rs) for calendar years:

	1978	1979	1980	1981	1982
Imports [1]	3,076,400,000	3,634,400,000	4,721,400,000	4,976,800,000	5,048,200,000
Exports [2]	1,987,100,000	2,432,700,000	3,341,300,000	2,999,200,000	3,988,700,000

[1] Excluding bullion and specie.
[2] Including value of sugar quota certificates.

In 1981, Rs 535·2m. of the imports came from France, Rs 480·5m. from South Africa, Rs 423·5m. from UK and Rs 275·8m. from Australia; 1,651·4m. of the exports went to UK, Rs 587·3m. to France, Rs 161·1m. to Federal Republic of Germany and Rs 150·1m. to USA.

Sugar exports in 1980, 617,400 tonnes (Rs 2,168·3m.); 1981, 432,800 tonnes (Rs 1,625m.).

Total trade between Mauritius and UK (British Department of Trade returns, in £1,000 sterling):

	1978	1979	1980	1981	1982	1983
Imports to UK	122,892	116,004	145,227	97,435	119,450	128,437
Exports and re-exports from UK	31,705	30,370	24,688	21,612	20,857	22,499

Tourism. In 1982, 118,300 tourists visited Mauritius spending Rs 40·5m.

COMMUNICATIONS

Roads. There are 25·5 miles of motorway, 523 miles of main roads, 361 miles of urban roads and 216 miles of rural roads. All the main urban and rural roads have a bitumen surface. At 31 Dec. 1981 there were 25,180 cars, including 3,151 for public hire, 1,469 buses, 8,087 motor cycles and 17,703 auto cycles. Commercial vehicles comprised 12,762 lorries and vans.

Aviation. Mauritius is linked by air with Europe, Africa, Asia and Australia by the following airlines: Air France, Air India, Air Malawi, Air Mauritius, Alitalia, British Airways, Lufthansa, South African Airways and Zambia Airways. In addition to passenger services a weekly cargo flight is operated by Air France on the Mauritius–Paris route.

Air Mauritius operates a Boeing 707 service to London *via* Nairobi and Rome and to Bombay *via* the Seychelles, and Twin Otter services to Réunion and Rodrigues. The company has commercial arrangements with Air France, Lufthansa, Alitalia, Zambia Airways and Air Malawi for the operation of services to Paris, Frankfurt, Rome, Lusaka and Blantyre.

Shipping. In 1981 1,075 vessels entered Port Louis; total tonnage of cargo, about 1·7m. tonnes.

Post and Broadcasting. In Dec. 1981 there were 31 telephone exchanges and 37,812 individual telephone installations in Mauritius and Rodrigues. Communication with other parts of the world is established *via* radio links. A radio-telephone service operates with countries all over the world.

Television was introduced in Feb. 1965. At 31 Dec. 1981 there were 84,184 television sets and 114,580 radio sets.

Cinemas (1981). There were 46 cinemas, with a seating capacity of about 45,000.

Newspapers. There are 5 French daily papers (with occasional articles in English) and 2 Chinese daily papers with a combined circulation of about 75,000.

RELIGION, EDUCATION AND WELFARE

Religion. At the 1972 census there were 245,570 Roman Catholics, 7,050 Protestants (Church of England and Church of Scotland). The Hindus numbered 421,707 and the Moslems. 136,997. State aid is granted to the churches and Rs 4·9m. is budgeted for 1982–83.

Education. Primary education is free but not compulsory, though under the Education Ordinance of 1957 compulsion may be introduced as circumstances permit. In 1981 there were 222 government and 50 state-aided primary schools, 2 Hindu and 48 Roman Catholic. Enrolment at government schools was 99,762 and at state-aided primary schools 27,680. There were 8 special schools (blind, deaf, educationally sub-normal and industrial).

For secondary education there were in 1981, 5 government boys' schools (one of which has technical and commercial streams), 16 junior secondary schools (including one in Rodrigues) and 3 government girls' schools and 125 private secondary schools (including Mahatma Gandhi Institute) with 78,332 pupils.

There is also a teachers' training college, known as the Mauritius College of Education, and 9 private vocational and technical training centres, 1,040 on roll including students following part-time courses.

Health. In 1981 there were 562 doctors, including 114 specialists, and 2,776 hospital beds.

DIPLOMATIC REPRESENTATIVES

Of Mauritius in Great Britain (32–33 Elvaston Pl., London, SW7)
High Commissioner: D. Gian Nath (accredited 13 Dec. 1983).

Of Great Britain in Mauritius (Cerné Hse., Chausée, Port Louis)
High Commissioner: James Nicholas Allan, CBE.

Of Mauritius in the USA (4301 Connecticut Ave., NW, Washington, D.C., 20008)
Ambassador: Chitmansing Jesseramsing.

Of the USA in Mauritius (Rogers Bldg., John Kennedy St., Port Louis)
Ambassador: Roger C. F. Gordon.

Of Mauritius to the United Nations
Ambassador: Armand Maudave.

Books of Reference

Statistical Information: The Central Statistical Information Office (Rose Hill, Mauritius) was founded in July 1945. Its main publication is the *Bi-annual Digest of Statistics.*

Brouard, N. R., *A History of Woods and Forests in Mauritius.* Government Printer, 1964
Buckory, S., *Our Constitution.* Port Louis, 1971.—*An Outline of Local Government.* Port Louis, 1970
Chelin, A., *Une île et son passé (1507–1947).* Mauritius Printing, 1973
Ministry of Information and Broadcasting, *Fruits of Political and Social Democracy.—Mauritius Facts and Figures 1980*
Napal, D., *Les constitutions de l'île Maurice.* Port Louis, 1962
Simmons, A. S., *Modern Mauritius: The Politics of Decolonization.* Indiana Univ. Press, 1982
Société de l'Histoire de 'Ile Maurice. *Dictionnaire de biographie mauricienne.* Port Louis, 1967
Toussaint A., *History of Mauritius.* London, 1978
Library: The Mauritius Institute Public Library, Port Louis.

MEXICO

Estados Unidos Mexicanos

Capital: Mexico City
Population: 75·39m. (1983)
GNP per capita: US$3,008 (1981)

HISTORY. Mexico's history falls into four epochs: the era of the Indian empires (before 1521), the Spanish colonial phase (1521–1810), the period of national formation (1810–1910), which includes the war of independence (1810–21) and the long presidency of Porfirio Díaz (1876–80, 1884–1911), and the present period which began with the social revolution of 1910–21 and is regarded by Mexicans as the period of social and national consolidation.

AREA AND POPULATION. Mexico is at the southern extremity of North America and is bounded in the north by USA, west and south-west by the Pacific, south by Guatemala and Belize and east by the Gulf of Mexico and comprises 1,958,201 sq. km (756,198 sq. miles), including uninhabited islands (5,073 sq. km) offshore.

The population at recent censuses has been as follows:

| 1900 | 13,545,462 | 1960 | 34,923,129 | 1980 | 67,382,581 |
| 1930 | 16,552,722 | 1970 | 48,225,238 | | |

The areas (in sq. km), populations and capitals of the states are:

States	Sq. km	Census 1980	Capital
Aguascalientes	5,471	503,410	Aguascalientes
Baja California	69,921	1,225,436	Mexicali
Baja California Sur	73,475	221,389	La Paz
Campeche	50,812	372,277	Campeche
Chiapas	74,211	2,096,812	Tuxtla Gutiérrez
Chihuahua	244,938	1,933,856	Chihuahua
Coahuila	149,982	1,558,401	Saltillo
Colima	5,191	339,202	Colima
Distrito Federal	1,479	9,373,353	México City
Durango	123,181	1,160,196	Victoria de Durango
Guanajuato	30,491	3,044,402	Guanajuato
Guerrero	64,281	2,174,162	Chilpancingo
Hidalgo	20,813	1,516,511	Pachuca de Soto
Jalisco	80,836	4,293,549	Guadalajara
México	21,355	7,545,692	Toluca de Lerdo
Michoacán	59,928	3,048,704	Morelia
Morelos	4,950	931,675	Cuernavaca
Nayarit	26,979	730,024	Tepic
Nuevo León	64,924	2,463,298	Monterrey
Oaxaca	93,952	2,518,157	Oaxaca de Juárez
Puebla	33,902	3,279,960	Puebla de Zaragoza
Querétaro	11,449	726,054	Querétaro
Quintana Roo	50,212	209,858	Chetumal
San Luis Potosí	63,068	1,670,637	San Luis Potosí
Sinaloa	58,328	1,830,098	Culiacán Rosales
Sonora	182,052	1,498,931	Hermosillo
Tabasco	25,267	1,149,756	Villahermosa
Tamaulipas	79,304	1,924,934	Ciudad Victoria
Tlaxcala	4,016	547,261	Tlaxcala
Veracruz	71,699	5,264,611	Jalapa Enríquez
Yucatán	38,402	1,034,648	Mérida
Zacatecas	73,252	1,145,327	Zacatecas

At the 1980 census 33,295,260 were males, 34,087,321 females. Urban population, 1978, was 65·2% and rural population was 34·8%. Estimate (1983)

75,391,000. The official language is Spanish, the mother tongue of over 90% of the population, but there are 5 indigenous language groups (Náhuatl, Maya, Zapotec, Otomi and Mixtec) from which are derived a total of 59 dialects spoken by 3,111,415 inhabitants (1970 census). In 1980, about 16% of the population were of European ethnic origin, 55% mestizo and 29% Amerindian.

Estimates (1979) of the largest cities (proper) were:

Mexico [1]	9,191,295	Saltillo	258,492	Uruapan	147,030
Netzahuacóyotl [2]	2,331,351	Aguascalientes	257,179	Ciudad Madero	141,571
Guadalajara [3]	1,906,145	Tampico	248,369	Tepic	139,881
Monterrey [4]	1,064,629	Morelia	251,011	Ensenada	139,317
Puebla de Zaragoza	710,833	Toluca de Lerdo	241,920	Monclova	139,257
Ciudad Juárez	625,040	Cuernavaca	241,337	Oaxaca de Juárez	135,601
Léon de los Aldamas	624,816	Reynosa	231,082	Coatzacoalcos	128,115
Tijuana	566,344	Victoria de Durango	228,686	Ciudad Victoria	126,817
Acapulco de Juárez	462,144	Nuevo Laredo	223,606	Cordoba	121,723
Chihuahua	385,953	Jalapa Enríquez	201,473	Orizaba	121,053
Mexicali	348,528	Poza Rica de Hidalgo	198,003	Minatitlán	119,432
San Luis Potosí	327,333	Matamoros	193,305	Celaya	118,665
Culiacán Rosales	324,292	Mazatlán	186,290	Los Mochis	118,631
Hermosillo	319,257	Queretaro	185,821	Campeche	108,680
Veracruz Llave	306,843	Ciudad Obregón	181,733	Pachuca	108,119
Torreón	274,717	Villa Hermosa	175,845	Tuxtla Gutiérrez	106,894
Mérida	269,582	Irapuato	161,047	Salamanca	105,543

[1] Greater Mexico City, 14,750,182.   [2] Suburb of Mexico City.
[3] Greater Guadalajara, 2,467,657.   [4] Greater Monterrey, 2,018,625.

Vital statistics for calendar years:

	Marriages	Births	Deaths
1976	427,335	2,156,430	406,033
1977	419,047	2,278,233	404,880
1978	444,700	2,277,708	402,322

Crude birth rate in 1980 was 34 per 1,000 population; crude death rate, 6; marriage rate 6·9.

CLIMATE. Latitude and relief produce a variety of climates. Arid and semi-arid conditions are found in the north, with extreme temperatures, whereas in the south there is a humid tropical climate, with temperatures varying with altitude. Conditions on the shores of the Gulf of Mexico are very warm and humid. In general, the rainy season lasts from May to Nov. Mexico City. Jan. 55°F (12·6°C), July 61°F (16·1°C). Annual rainfall 30″ (747 mm). Guadalajara. Jan. 59°F (15·2°C), July 69°F (20·5°C). Annual rainfall 36″ (902 mm). Puebla de Zaragoza. Jan. 54°F (12·2°C), July 63°F (17·2°C). Annual rainfall 34″ (850 mm).

CONSTITUTION AND GOVERNMENT. A new Constitution was promulgated on 5 Feb. 1917 and has been amended from time to time. Mexico is a representative, democratic and federal republic, comprising 31 states and a federal district, each state being free and sovereign in all internal affairs, but united in a federation established according to the principals of the Fundamental Law. Citizenship, including the right of suffrage, is vested in all nationals of 18 years of age and older who have 'an honourable means of livelihood'.

There is complete separation of legislative, executive and judicial powers (Art. 49). Legislative power is vested in a General Congress of 2 chambers, a Chamber of Deputies and a Senate (Art.50). The Chamber of Deputies consists of 400 members directly elected for 3 years, 300 of them from single-member constituencies and 100 chosen under a system of proportional representation (Arts.51–55). At the general elections held on 4 July 1982, 299 of the single-member seats were won by the *Partido Revolucionario Institucional* (PRI) and 1 by the *Partido de Acción Nacional* (PAN); of the extra 100 seats, 54 were won by PAN, 17 by the *Partido Socialista Unido Mexicana*, 11 by the *Partido Popular Socialista*, 10 by the *Partido Socialista de los Trabajadores* and 8 by the *Partido Demócrata Mexicano*. The Senate comprises 64 members, 2 from each state and 2 from the federal district, directly elected for 6 years (Arts.56–58). At the elections of 4 July 1982, the PRI won all 64 seats. Members of both chambers are not immediately re-eligible for election (Art.59). Congress sits from 1 Sept. to 31 Dec. each year; during the recess there is a permanent committee of 15 deputies and 14 senators appointed by the respective chambers.

The President is the supreme executive authority. He appoints the members of the Council of Ministers and the senior military and civilian officers of the state. He is directly elected for a single 6-year term.

The names of the presidents from 1934 are as follows:

Gen. Lázaro Cárdenas, 1 Dec. 1934–30 Nov. 1940.

Gen. Manuel Avila Camacho, 1 Dec. 1940–30 Nov. 1946.

Miguel Alemán Valdés, 1 Dec. 1946–30 Nov. 1952.

Adolfo Ruiz Cortines, 1 Dec 1952–30 Nov. 1958.

Adolfo López Mateos, 1 Dec. 1958–30 Nov. 1964.

Gustavo Diaz Ordaz, 1 Dec. 1964–30 Nov. 1970.

Luis Echeverría Alvarez, 1 Dec. 1970–30 Nov. 1976.

José López Portillo y Pacheco, 1 Dec. 1976–30 Nov. 1982.

President: Miguel de la Madrid Hurtado (born in 1934), formerly Minister of Planning, elected 4 July 1982. He assumed office on 1 Dec. 1982.

In June 1983 the Council of Ministers was composed as follows:

Agrarian Reform: Luis Martínez Villicaña. *Agriculture and Water Resources:* Horacio García Aguilar. *Commerce:* Héctor Hernández Cervantes. *Communication and Transport:* Rodolfo Félix Valdés. *Finance and Public Credit:* Jesús Silva Herzog Flores. *Foreign Relations:* Bernardo Sepúlveda Amor. *Interior:* Manuel Bartlett Díaz. *Health and Assistance:* Dr Guillermo Soberón Acevedo. *Human Settlements and Public Works:* Marcelo Javelly Girard. *Labour and Social Welfare:* Asenio Farell Cubillas. *National Defence:* Gen. Juan José Arrévalo Gardoqui. *Navy:* Adm. Miguel Angel Gómez Ortega. *Patrimony and Industrial Development:* Francisco Labastida Ochoa. *Planning and Budget:* Carlos Salinas de Gortari. *Public Education:* Jesús Reyes Heroles. *Tourism:* Antonio Enríquez Savignac. *Fisheries:* Pedro Ojeda Paullada. *Comptroller-General:* Francisco Rojas. *Attorney-General:* Sergio García Ramírez. *Governor of the Federal District:* Román Aguirre Velázquez. *Attorney-General of the Federal District:* Sra. Victoria Adato de Ibarra. *Head of Petróleos Mexicanos (PEMEX):* Mario Ramón Beteta. *Governor of the Bank of Mexico:* Miguel Mancera Aguayo.

National flag: Three vertical strips of green, white, red, with the national arms in the centre.

National anthem: Mexicanos, al grito de guerra (words by F. González Bocanegra; tune by Jaime Nunó, 1854).

Local Government. Mexico is divided into 31 states and a Federal District. The latter is co-extensive with Mexico City and is administered by a Governor appointed by the President. Each state has its own constitution, with the right to legislate and to levy taxes (but not inter-state customs duties); its Governor is directly elected for 6 years and its unicameral legislature for 3 years; judicial officers are appointed by the Federal government.

DEFENCE. Supreme command is vested in the President, exercised through the Ministries of Defence (for Army and Air Force) and Marine.

Army. Enlistment into the regular army is voluntary, but there is conscription into a part-time militia, which numbers some 250,000. The regular army consists of 1 mechanized brigade group, 2 infantry brigade groups, 1 parachute brigade, 1 reconnaissance regiment, 1 armoured regiment, a garrison for each of the country's 35 military zones, and support units. Equipment includes 40 M-3A1 and 20 M-5A1 light tanks and some 140 armoured cars. Strength of the regular army (1984) 95,000.

Navy. The fleet comprises 3 old *ex*-US destroyers, 5 old *ex*-US frigates (including 4 former destroyer escort transports), 6 new corvette-type and 1 frigate-size listed as patrol ships, 1 armed transport and 4 old *ex*-US armed tugs used as patrol ships, 18 old *ex*-US fleet minesweepers, 16 old *ex*-US escort minesweepers, 21 fishery protection cutters of 130 tons built in Britain in 1974–76 and 10 built in Mexico in 1978–80, 18 patrol boats, 7 survey ships, 1 transport, 3 armed landing ships (2 used for rescue and 1 (with helicopter landing deck) for light forces repair), 2 oilers, 1 training ship, 21 auxiliary vessels and 8 tugs. There are 5 naval zones on the Gulf and 11 on the Pacific coast and 6 naval air bases holding 54 aircraft. Naval personnel in 1984 totalled 23,630 officers and men including naval air force and 3,810 marines.

Air Force. The Air Force has a strength of about 5,500 officers and men, and has nine operational groups, each with one or two squadrons. No. 1 Group comprises No. 208 Squadron with 10 IAI Aravas for transport, search and rescue and counter-insurgency duties; and No. 209 Squadron with Bell 205A, 206B Jet-Ranger, 212, Alouette III and Puma helicopters. No. 2 Group has two Squadrons (Nos. 206 and 207) of Swiss-built Pilatus PC-7 Turbo-Trainers for light attack duty. No. 3 Group (203 and 204 Squadrons) also operates PC-7s; No. 4 Group (201 and 205 Squadrons) is in process of conversion to PC-7s. No. 5 Group consists of No. 101 communications Squadron and a photo-reconnaissance unit, both equipped with Aero Commander 500S piston-engined light twins. Nos. 301 and 302 Squadrons, in No. 6 Group, operate a total of 5 C-54, 2 C-118A and 1 DC-7 piston-engined transports. The main combat Group, No. 7, comprises No. 401 Squadron with 12 F-5E Tiger II and F-5F 2-seat fighters; and No. 202 Squadron with AT-33A jet trainer/fighter-bombers. No. 8 Group has 7 C-47s in a VIP transport squadron. No. 9 Group operates the Air Force's remaining 12 or more C-47s in Nos. 311 and 312 transport Squadrons. There is a Presidential Squadron with 9 Boeing 727s, 1 737-247, 1 HS.125, 1 JetStar, 1 Islander and 1 Bell 212. The Military Academy continues to fly 14 veteran Stearman PT-17 biplanes. Other training aircraft include 20 Mudry CAP-10Bs, 20 Beech Musketeers, 20 Bonanzas, and PC-7 Turbo-Trainers.

INTERNATIONAL RELATIONS

Membership. Mexico is a member of UN, OAS and ALIDE (formerly LAFTA).

External Debt. The public sector external debt (June 1980) was US$27,939m.

ECONOMY

Budget. The 1982 budget provides for expenditure of 3,286,000m. pesos.

Currency. The monetary unit is the *peso* divided into 100 *centavos*.

There are coins for 1, 5 and 10 pesos and 50, 20, 10 and 5 centavos; notes for 10,000, 5,000, 500, 100, 50, 20, 10 and 5 pesos.

Rate of exchange, March 1984: 170 pesos = US$1; 251 pesos = £1.

Banking. The Bank of Mexico, established 1 Sept. 1925, is the central bank of issue; it is modelled on the Federal Reserve system, with large powers to 'manage' the currency. The Government holds 51% of the capital stock.

On 1 Sept. 1982 the private banking sector was nationalized.

In 1983 the total outstanding public external debt was US$80,000m.

Weights and Measures. The metric system was introduced in 1896, and its sole use is enjoined by law of 14 Dec. 1928.

ENERGY AND NATURAL RESOURCES

Electricity. In 1979 the 3,928 electric generating plants had installed capacity of 16·9m. kw. Production, 1981, 73,071m. kwh.

Oil. The chief Mexican oilfields had proven reserves of oil and gas, in 1981, of 67,800m. bbls (potential, 250,000m. bbls). In 1980 the oil industry generated 6% of the GDP and supplied about 85% of the energy consumed in the country. Since the nationalization of the industry in 1938, Petróleos Mexicanos, a government-owned enterprise, has exclusive rights to the exploitation, refining and sale of oil and its by-products. PEMEX is exploiting mainly the rich Poza Rica and Faja de Oro fields in the state of Veracruz (discovered in 1938), which extend into the Gulf of Mexico shelf and the nearby fields in Escolín and Mecatepec. New discoveries in Reforma, state of Chiapas, and Samaria, state of Tabasco, however, increased oil production in 1974 over the previous year by 25%. 43% of the current national yield is obtained from these two states. Exploration has been intensified in various states throughout Mexico leading to important discoveries in Cotaxtla, state of Veracruz, and Chac, state of Campeche. Crude petroleum output was 148m. tonnes in 1982. Mexico exports crude oil but still imports petrol, gasoil (diesel), fuel oil and some petroleum gas.

Gas. Natural gas production came to 30,840m. cu. metres in 1981.

Minerals. Mining is an important industry and, of the 48 principal non-metallic minerals in the world, Mexico produces at least 23. However, in view of the international price of mineral-metallurgical products, mining production, lacking incentives, has been both sluggish and fluctuating. Mining policy is aimed at the rational exploitation and increased industrialization of its mineral resources, procuring, at the same time, to completely Mexicanize the firms dedicated to this activity. In addition to the uranium deposits discovered in the states of Chihuahua, Durango, Sonora and Queretaro announced in 1959, rich deposits have been located in Nuevo León. Total reserves (proven 1982) 15,000 tonnes of uranium 308; potential reserves, 150,000 tonnes.

Silver output (in tonnes) was 1,473 in 1980; 1,655 in 1981. About half the production is minted, including a 'token' coin (1949) weighing 1 troy oz. Gold output: 1981, 6,319 kg.

Mexico has large coal resources, calculated at 5,448m. tonnes, including high-grade coking coal at Sabinas in Coahuila. There are large underdeveloped reserves of iron ore with known reserves of 300m. tonnes; the new Peña Colorado field in Colima State seems to be promising. Output, 1981 (in tonnes): Iron ore, 5,292,609; lead, 157,384; copper, 230,466; zinc, 211,629; fluorite, 924,854; crude steel, 7,449,000; cement, 17,842,000; pig iron, 5,512,000; sulphur, 2,077,117.

Agriculture. About 80% of Mexico's territory is made up of arid and semi-arid lands. Irrigation is needed, 43% of the land having less than 500 mm of rain a year. In 1980 Mexico had 21·8m. hectares of arable land, 74·5m. hectares of meadows and pastures, 48·5m. hectares of forests, 1·5m. hectares of permanent crops and 46m. hectares of other land. In 1980, the government launched the *Sistema Alimentario Mexicano* to raise food production and rationalize land tenure, with the aim of achieving self-sufficiency in basic crops. Grains occupy 68% of the cultivated land, with about 53% given to maize and about 9% to wheat. In the 1970 census there were 91,354 tractors. It is estimated that Mexico should be self-supporting with at least 17m. hectares of land under irrigation and 20·3m. hectares under cultivation. Government agricultural programmes are being carried out by the National Basic Commodities Company (CONASUPO) and the National Deposit Warehouses (ANDSA) which regulate the market, intervening in the marketing process and protecting the low-income producers as well as the low-income consumer by assuring him access to basic commodities. ANDSA has undertaken the construction of silos, warehouses, storage, machinery and equipment.

Livestock (1982): Cattle, 36·2m.; sheep, 7·99m.; pigs, 13·12m.; horses, 6·7m.; goats, 7·2m.; mules, 3·13m.; donkeys, 3·2m.; poultry, 164m.

Production of hides reached 9·5m. in 1976; production of meat, 909,733 tonnes.

Mexico's basic food crop is maize, and a rapid expansion of this crop is one of the chief aims of Mexican agricultural policy, balanced by the demand for 'cash crops' for export, such as cotton, sugar, garbanzos (chick peas), bananas, winter vegetables and coffee.

Production of crops for 1981 was as follows (in 1,000 tonnes):

Crop	1981	Crop	1981	Crop	1981
Maize	14 766	Sugar-cane	35,975	Oranges	1,894
Sorghum	6 296	Tomatoes	1,093	Bananas	1,163
Wheat	3 189	Potatoes	868	Lemons	562
Barley	559	Dry beans	1,469	Pineapples	655
Rice	644	Soybeans	712	Apples	296
Cottonseed	530	Coconuts	113	Grapes	578
Cotton lint	344	Coffee	217	Mangoes	914

Sugar-cane is linked closely with the export markets, although not to the same degree as coffee, in view of the fact that despite the large crop, the national consumption of sugar, at approximately 35 kg a year per person, is one of the highest in the world. Exports have however remained more or less stable: 1972 exports represented 25% of total output.

Forestry. Timber lands represent 22% of the Mexican territory and are estimated to extend over 43m. hectares (about 43% of commercial importance), containing pine, spruce, cedar, mahogany, logwood and rosewood. Despite the existence of forests that would support a higher production, output for 20 years up to 1973, averaged an annual growth of only 1·1%. In 1973 only 15·7% of the productive capacity of the country's forests was being exploited. Reckless lumbering had destroyed the timber stands on many watersheds, resulting in spring floods and lowered water supplies in summer. In 1951 federal edicts had halted all timber-cutting in 22 states, regardless of concessions; but they have been resumed under strict supervision. There are 14 forest reserves (nearly 800,000 hectares) and 47 national park forests of 750,000 hectares. In 1980 total roundwood production amounted to 12·2m. cu. metres.

Fisheries. Fishing is important because of Mexico's 9,903 km of coastline. Catch (1979, tonnes): Anchoveta, 200,430; pilchards, 164,436; shrimp and prawns, 44,979; oysters, 29,395; tuna, 26,261; sea perch *(mojarras)*, 19,371; sea bass, 10,216. Total catch in 1979 was 850,525 tonnes.

INDUSTRY AND TRADE

Industry. In 1980, the primary sector (agriculture, mining etc.) provided 9·3% of GDP, the oil and petrochemical industry 7%, manufacturing and construction 29·1% and the service sector (commerce, transport and communications, power supply and other services) 54·6%.

Labour. In 1980, the economically active population was 23·7m., of whom 35% were engaged in agriculture and 18% in manufacturing. Approximately 5m. people belong to trade unions, of whom 85% are affiliated to the *Congreso del Trabajo*.

Commerce. Trade for calendar years in 1m. pesos:

	1978	1979	1980	1981
Imports	177,278	273,775	448,290	590,140
Exports	131,403	199,973	351,324	474,340

Export figures for metals and for certain foreign-owned agricultural products are heavily undervalued to reduce export taxes.

Of total imports in 1980, 66% came from USA, 5% from Japan, 5% from Federal Republic of Germany and 3% from France. Leading imports were machinery, transport equipment, iron and steel, chemicals, machine tools, parts and spares.

Of total exports in 1980, 63% went to USA, 7% to Spain, 4% to Japan and 3% to Israel. The main visible exports (1980) were crude oil (60%), machinery and industrial goods, coffee, chemicals and cotton.

Total trade between Mexico and UK (British Department of Trade returns, in £1,000 sterling):

	1979	1980	1981	1982	1983
Imports to UK	36,336	111,636	108,749	106,067	160,978
Exports and re-exports from UK	134,816	188,133	209,596	162,946	95,674

Tourism. Tourism is the largest single source of dollar income. In 1980, there were 4,144,600 tourists; gross revenue, including border visitors, amounted to US$1,670m.

COMMUNICATIONS

Roads. Total length, (1980) 213,192 km, of which 978 km were motorways. Motor vehicles registered in 1980 comprised 4,031,970 passenger cars, and 1,534,100 commercial vehicles.

Railways. In 1937 the main railway lines were nationalized. The principal group is the *Ferrocarriles Nacionales de México*, with 20,288 km of track. Three lines (215 km) remain privately owned. In 1979, FNM carried 55m. tonnes of freight and 18·6m. passengers. In Mexico City an urban railway system opened in 1969 had 78 km of track and 5 lines in 1982.

Aviation. Mexico has an excellent air service. There are 28 international and 20 national airports. Each of the larger states has a local airline which links them with main airports, which, in turn, furnish services to US, Central and South America and Europe. Thirty companies in 1976 maintained international services, of these 2 were Mexican. Domestic flights are handled by 77 companies. In 1979 commercial aircraft carried 13·1m. national and international passengers and some 109,000 tonnes of mail and freight.

Shipping. Mexico has 49 ocean ports, of which, on the Gulf coast, the most important include Tampico, Veracruz, Coatzacoalcos, Progreso and Yucalpletón. On the Pacific are Ensenada, La Paz, Santa Rosalía, Guaymas, Mazatlán, Manzanillo, Acapulco and Salina Cruz.

Merchant shipping loaded 36·9m. tonnes and unloaded 11·9m. tonnes in 1979. Passengers (1976), embarked, 375,042; landed, 373,320. In 1980, the merchant marine comprised 361 vessels (of over 100 GRT) with a total tonnage of 1,006,417 GRT.

Post and Broadcasting. On 31 Dec. 1975 the federal, state and private telegraph and telephone system had 5,938 offices and 220,442 km of telegraph lines and 16·2m. km of telephone line. *Teléfonos de México*, a state-controlled company, controls about 98% of all the telephone service. Telephones in use, Jan. 1982, 5,411,108; 96·4% were automatic.

In 1982 there were 816 commercial radio stations and 47 cultural government radio stations while 10,338,024 homes had receiving sets. In 1982 commercial television stations numbered 191 and cultural stations 8; there were 4,589,170 homes with receiving sets.

Cinemas (1980). Cinemas numbered 1,832 with annual attendance of 264m.

Newspapers (1974). There were 178 dailies and 21 weeklies, with an aggregate circulation in excess of 5m.; 23 in México City have about half of the total circulation.

JUSTICE, RELIGION, EDUCATION AND WELFARE

Justice. Magistrates of the Supreme Court are appointed for 6 years by the President and confirmed by the Senate; they can be removed only on impeachment. The courts include the Supreme Court with 21 magistrates, 12 collegiate circuit courts with 3 judges each and 9 unitary circuit courts with 1 judge each, and 68 district courts with 1 judge each.

The penal code of 1 Jan. 1930 abolished the death penalty, except for the Army, and set up a commission of alienists and other specialists, in place of courts, to deal with criminal cases (for federal offences); each state also appoints its own local magistrates.

The Mexican Constitution provides a guarantee of individual rights by means of a judicial procedure known as *amparo*, which gives any injured person whose constitutional rights have, in his opinion, been infringed, right to immediate access to the courts and full remedy, combining the swiftness of the Anglo-Saxon writ of *habeas corpus* and the breadth of remedy available through the injunction.

Religion. The prevailing religion is the Roman Catholic (89·4% of the population in 1980); with (1976) 2 cardinals, 9 archbishops and 84 bishops, but by the constitution of 1857, the Church was separated from the State, and the constitution of 1917 provided strict regulation of this and all other religions. No ecclesiastical body may acquire landed property, and since 1917 the property of the Church has been held to belong to the State. In the 1920s the Government suppressed the political influence of the priesthood and temporarily (1929–31) closed the churches. An understanding between State and Church was, however, reached, and all churches eschewing public affairs flourish freely. At the 1980 census there were also 3·6% Protestants, and 7% members of other religions.

Education. Primary and secondary education is free and compulsory, and secular. Clergy are forbidden to establish primary schools. All private schools must conform to government standards. Military drill is compulsory for boys of 18 years. In the Federal District education is controlled by the national government; elsewhere by the state authorities.

In 1981–82 there were:

	Establishments	Teachers	Students
Nursery	17,937	43,531	1,411,316
Primary	76,860	400,417	14,981,028
Secondary	14,343	252,487	4,512,582
Preparatory/Vocational	3,576	36,325	615,992
Teacher-training	558	18,885	329,417
Higher education:			
Universities	84	59,301	681,032
Institutes	115	14,282	130,336
Other higher education	75	3,626	29,000

The most important university is the Universidad Nacional Autónoma de México (UNAM) in México City which, with its associated institutions, had, in 1980, 252,971 students (excluding post-graduates). UNAM was founded in 1551, re-organized in 1910, and granted full autonomy in 1920. Other universities of particular importance in México City are the Instituto Politécnico Nacional, specializing in technology and applied science, with over 110,000 students, and the Universidad Autónoma Metropolitana with 22,703 students, opened in 1973. Outside México City the principal universities are, in Monterrey, the Universidad de Nuevo León with 89,000 students and the Instituto Tecnólogico y de Estudios Superiores de Monterrey with 22,880 students; in Guadalajara, the Universidad de Guadalajara (184,167 students) and the Universidad Autónoma de Guadalajara (19,002 students); in Xalapa, the Universidad Veracruzana (40,414 students); and at Morelia, the Universidad Michoacana (29,167 students).

Health. In 1974 Mexico had 45,322 physicians; there were 5,469 state and private hospitals and clinics with 76,413 beds.

Social Welfare. The social welfare system administered by the Mexican Social Security Institute covered 38m. on 31 Dec. 1979.

DIPLOMATIC REPRESENTATIVES

Of Mexico in Great Britain (8 Halkin St., London, SW1X 7DW)
Ambassador: Francisco Cuevas-Cancino (accredited 11 Feb. 1983).

Of Great Britain in Mexico (Lerma 71, Col. Cuauhtémoc, México City 06500, D.F.)
Ambassador: C. M. James, CMG.

Of Mexico in the USA (2829–16th St., NW, Washington, D.C., 20009)
Ambassador: Jorge Espinosa de los Reyes.

Of the USA in Mexico (Paseo de la Reforma 305, México City 5, D.F.)
Ambassador: John A. Gavin.

Of Mexico to the United Nations
Ambassador: Porfirio Muñoz Ledo.

Books of Reference

Anuario Estadístico de los Estados Unidos Mexicanos. Annual

México A Vuelo de Pajaro. Secretaria de la Presidencia, 1976
México Statistical Data. Banco National de México, 1975
Petroleos Mexicanos: Anuario Estadistico, 1975. Mexico City
Revista de Estadística (Monthly); *Revista de Economia* (Monthly)
Alba, V., *A Concise History of Mexico.* London, 1973
Banco de México S.A., Annual report
Banco Nacional de Comercio Exterior. *Comercio Exterior,* monthly.—*Mexico.* Annual (in Spanish or English)
Bazant, J., *A Concise History of Mexico.* CUP, 1977
Calvert, P., *Mexico.* London, 1973
Carrada-Bravo, F., *Oil, Money, and the Mexican Economy.* Boulder, 1982
Cheetham, N., *New Spain, the Birth of Modern Mexico.* London, 1974
Davies, N., *The Aztecs.* London, 1973
Dominguez, J. I., (ed.) *Mexico's Political Economy: Challenges at Home and Abroad.* London, 1982
Johnson, K. F., *Mexican Democracy: A Critical View.* Rev. ed. New York, 1978
Kaufman, S., (ed.) *The Politics of Mexican Oil.* Univ. of Pittsburgh Press, 1981
Ker, A. M., *Mexican Government Publications: A Guide, 1821–1936.* Washington, 1940
López-Portillo, J., *Mexico in Facts and Figures.* México City, 1976
Millor, M. R., *Mexico's Oil.* Boulder, 1982
Parkes, H. B., *A History of Mexico.* Rev. ed. Boston, 1950
Peña, M. T. de la, *El Pueblo y su Tierra.* México City, 1964
Robbins, N., *Mexico.* [Bibliography] Oxford and Santa Barbara, 1984
Ross, J. B., *The Economic System of Mexico.* Stanford, 1971

MONACO

HISTORY. Monaco is a small Principality on the Mediterranean, surrounded by the French Department of Alpes Maritimes except on the side towards the sea. From 1297 it belonged to the house of Grimaldi. In 1731 it passed into the female line, Louise Hippolyte, daughter of Antoine I, heiress of Monaco, marrying Jacques de Goyon Matignon, Count of Torigni, who took the name and arms of Grimaldi. The Principality was placed under the protection of the Kingdom of Sardinia by the Treaty of Vienna, 1815, and under that of France in 1861. Prince Albert I (reigned 1889–1922) acquired fame as an oceanographer; and his son Louis II (1922–49) was instrumental in establishing the International Hydrographic Bureau.

AREA AND POPULATION. The area is 190 hectares or 467 acres. The Principality is divided into 4 districts: Monaco-Ville, la Condamine, Monte-Carlo and Fontvieille. Population (1980), 28,000. The official language is French.

REIGNING PRINCE. Rainier III, born 31 May 1923, son of Princess Charlotte, Duchess of Valentinois, daughter of Prince Louis II, 1898–1977 (married 19 March 1920 to Prince Pierre, Comte de Polignac, who had taken the name Grimaldi, from whom she was divorced 18 Feb. 1933). Prince Rainier succeeded his grandfather Louis II, who died on 9 May 1949. He married on 19 April 1956 Miss Grace Kelly, a citizen of the USA (died 14 Sept. 1982). *Issue:* Princess Caroline Louise Marguerite, born 23 Jan. 1957; married Philippe Junot on 28 June 1978, divorced, 9 Oct. 1980, married Stefano Casiraghi on 29 Dec. 1983. Prince Albert Alexandre Louis Pierre, born 14 March 1958 *(heir apparent)*; Princess Stephanie Marie Elisabeth, born 1 Feb. 1965.

CONSTITUTION AND GOVERNMENT. Prince Rainier III on 28 Jan. 1959 suspended the Constitution of 5 Jan. 1911, thereby dissolving the National Council and the Communal Council. On 28 March 1962 the National Council (18 members elected every 5 years, last elections 1978) and the Communal Council (16 members elected every 4 years, last elections 1979) were re-established as elected bodies.

On 17 Dec. 1962 a new constitution was promulgated. It maintains the hereditary monarchy, though Prince Rainier renounces the principle of divine right. The supreme tribunal becomes the custodian of fundamental liberties, and guarantees are given for the right of association, trade union freedom and the right to strike. It provides for votes for women and the abolition of the death penalty.

The constitution can be modified only with the approval of the elected National Council. Women were given the vote in 1945.

Monegasque relations with France were based on a convention of neighbourhood and administrative assistance of 1951. This was terminated by France on 11 Oct. 1962, but has been replaced by several new conventions signed on 18 May 1963.

National flag: Horizontally red over white.

ECONOMY

Planning. A 55-acre site has been reclaimed from the sea at Fontvieille. This land has been earmarked for office and residential development. The present industrial zone is to be reorganized and developed with a view to attracting new light industry to the Principality.

Budget. The budget (in 1,000 francs) was as follows:

	1976	*1977*	*1978*	*1979*	*1980*
Revenue	528,246	595,874	671,035	784,319	987,158
Expenditure	464,421	515,207	518,129	551,632	629,449

Currency. The monetary unit is the French *franc* divided into 100 *centimes*.

Weights and Measures. The metric system is in use.

INDUSTRY AND TRADE

Tourism. There were 214,000 tourists in 1980.

Trade Unions. Membership of trade unions is estimated at 2,500 out of a work force of 22,822 (1980).

Commerce. International trade is included with France.

COMMUNICATIONS

Roads. There were 46 km of roads in 1982.

Railways. The 1·6m. km of main line passing through the country is operated by the French National Railways (SNCF).

Aviation. The nearest airport is at Nice, France.

Shipping. The harbour has an area of 47 acres, depth at the entrance 90 ft, and alongside the quay 24 ft at least. In 1980 there was 1 registered ship of 12,573 GRT.

Post and Broadcasting. Telephone subscribers numbered about 17,000 in 1982 and telex subscribers, 446. Monaco issues its own postage stamps.

Radio Monte Carlo broadcasts 2 commercial programmes in French (long- and medium-waves). Radio Monte Carlo owns 55% of Radio Monte Carlo Relay Station on Cyprus. The foreign service is dedicated exclusively to religious broadcasts and is maintained by free-will contributions. It operates in 36 languages under the name 'Trans World Radio' and has relay facilities on Bonaire, West Indies, and is planning to build relay facilities in the southern parts of Africa. *Télé Monte-Carlo* broadcasts TV programmes in French, Italian and English.

Cinemas. In 1981 there were 3 cinemas (one open air) with seating capacity of 800.

JUSTICE, RELIGION, EDUCATION AND WELFARE

Justice. The Code Louis, adopted in 1919, is based upon the French codes. There is a Court of First Instance as well as a Juge de Paix's Court. A semi-military police force has taken the place of the 'guard of honour' and troops formerly maintained.

Religion. There has been since 1887 a Roman Catholic bishop, directly dependent on the Holy See.

Education. In 1980 there were 3,412 pupils with over 400 teachers.

Health. In 1980 there were 357 hospital beds and 61 physicians.

DIPLOMATIC REPRESENTATIVES

British Consul-General (resident in Marseille): D. A. S. Gladstone.
British Honorary Consul (resident in Nice): Lieut.-Col. R. W. Challoner, OBE.
Consul-General for Monaco in London: I. S. Ivanovic.

Books of Reference

Journal de Monaco. Bulletin Officiel. 1858 ff.
Handley-Taylor, G., *Bibliography of Monaco.* London, 1968
La Gorce, P. M. de, *Monaco.* Lausanne, 1969

MONGOLIAN PEOPLE'S REPUBLIC

Capital: Ulan Bator
Population: 1·76m. (1982)
GNP per capita: US$940 (1978)

Bügd Nayramdakh Mongol Ard Uls

HISTORY. Outer Mongolia was a Chinese province from 1691 to 1911, an autonomous state under Russian protection from 1912 to 1919 and again a Chinese province from 1919 to 1921. On 13 March 1921 a Provisional People's Government was established which declared the independence of Mongolia and on 5 Nov. 1921 signed a treaty with Soviet Russia annulling all previous unequal treaties and establishing friendly relations. On 26 Nov. 1924 the Government proclaimed the country the Mongolian People's Republic.

On 5 Jan. 1946 China recognized the independence of Outer Mongolia after a plebiscite in Mongolia (20 Oct. 1945) had resulted in an overwhelming vote for independence. A Sino-Soviet treaty of 14 Feb. 1950 guaranteed this independence.

AREA AND POPULATION. Mongolia is bounded north by the USSR, east and south and west by China. Area, 1,565,000 sq. km (604,250 sq. miles); population (1982) 1,760,000 (in 1977 719,000 urban; 51% male). Density, 1·07 per sq. km. Birth rate (1981), 37·9 per 1,000; death rate, 10·4 per 1,000. Rate of increase, 1982, 3%. The population is predominantly made up of Mongolian peoples (75% Khalkha). There is a Turkic Kazakh minority (5·2% of the population) and 8 Mongol minorities. The official language is Mongol. Expectation of life in 1983 was 65 years. 50% of the population is under 16.

The republic is administratively divided into 3 cities (Ulan Bator, the capital, population 400,000 (1978), Darkhan, 52,000 (1981) and Erdenet 35,000 (1978)), and 18 provinces *(aimag)*. Local government is administered by People's Deputies' Khurals. The provinces are sub-divided into districts *(somon)*.

CLIMATE. A very extreme climate, with six months of mean temperatures below freezing, but much higher temperatures occur for a month or two in summer. Rainfall is very low and limited to the months mid-May to mid-Sept. Ulan Bator. Jan. −14°F (−25·6°C), July 61°F (16·1°C). Annual rainfall 8″ (208 mm).

CONSTITUTION AND GOVERNMENT. According to the fourth Constitution (1960) power is vested in the *Great People's Khural* of deputies elected for 5 years by universal suffrage of voters over 18 years of age on a basis of 1 deputy per 2,500 inhabitants. It elects from its number 9 members of the Presidium, which carries on current state affairs. *De facto* power is in the hands of the only political party, the Mongolian People's Revolutionary (*i.e.*, Communist) Party, which had 76,240 members and candidates in 1981 (workers 33%; peasants, 18%; women, 27%). The youth organization had over 180,000 members in 1982.

The last general election took place on 21 June 1981; 99·99% of an electorate of 792,896 were said to have voted for the 370 deputies (344 Party members; 100 industrial workers; 90 women).

The Chairman of the Presidium of the Khural and head of state is Yumjagiin Tsedenbal, who is also *Secretary-General of the People's Revolutionary Party*. The

857

Prime Minister is Dr Jambyn Batmunkh. The other members of the Politburo of the Party are: D. Maydar, *First Deputy Prime Minister and Chairman, State Committee for Science and Technology*; T. Ragchaa, *First Deputy Prime Minister*; D. Molomjamts. D. Gombojav, B.-O. Altangerel. *Candidate members:* B. Dejid, N. Jagvaral. Ministers not in the Politburo include: *Chairman, State Planning Commission:* D. Sodnom; *Minister of Defence:* Col.-Gen. J. Yondon; *Minister of Public Security:* O. Choijilsuren; *Foreign Minister:* Mangalyn Dügesüren; *Minister of Foreign Trade:* Yë Ochir. *Minister of Agriculture:* S. Sodnomdorj.

National flag: Red–sky-blue–red (vertical), with a golden 5-pointed star and under it the golden *soyonbo* emblem on the red stripe nearest to the flagpole.

DEFENCE. Military service is 3 years.

Army. The Army comprises 2 infantry divisions and 1 infantry brigade. Equipment includes T-54/-55/-62 main battle tanks. Strength is 25,000, with reserves of 40,000. There is a paramilitary Ministry of Public Security force of about 15,000 men. A civil defence force was set up in 1970.There were (1984) some 25,000 Soviet service personnel.

Air Force. The Air Force has about 100 pilots and more than 60 aircraft, including 12 MiG-21 fighters; a total of about 40 An-2, An-24 and An-26 transports used mainly on civil air services; 3 Wilga utility aircraft; 10 Mi-4 and 3 Mi-8 helicopters; and Yakovlev trainers.

INTERNATIONAL RELATIONS

Membership. Mongolia is a member of UN and Comecon.

Aid. Mongolia receives economic aid from the USSR and other communist countries. There is also a UN development aid programme running at US$2m. per annum.

Treaties. Relations with the USSR were based on treaties of friendship and mutual aid (27 Feb. 1946), trade (17 Dec. 1957), economic and technical assistance (9 Sept. 1960), now replaced by a 20-year treaty of friendship, co-operation and mutual assistance (15 Jan. 1966).

Sino-Mongolian relations have deteriorated since the estrangement between China and USSR.

On 28 Oct. 1961 Mongolia was admitted to the United Nations.

ECONOMY

Planning. Mongolia has had for centuries a traditional nomadic pastoral economy, which the Government aims to transform into an 'agricultural–industrial economy'. For earlier plans *see* THE STATESMAN'S YEAR-BOOK, 1976–77, p. 1156. The 5-year plan (1976–80) increased national income by 30·9%, industrial production by 50% and agricultural production by 6·3% (Targets were 42%, 63% and 30%). The seventh 5-year plan is running from 1981 to 1985. Industrial output is scheduled to rise by 58%, agricultural by 25%. There is also a long-term plan to 1990 which emphasizes energy production, mining, metallurgy, chemicals, food processing and building.

Budget (in 1m. tugriks):

	1973	1974	1975	1976	1977	1978	1980
Revenue	2,678	2,716	2,696	2,988	3,312	3,660	4,070
Expenditure	2,530	2,670	2,686	2,973	3,300	3,650	4,058

In the 1971–75 planning period 7,010m. tugriks were invested in the national economy. During the 1976–80 plan period overall investment was doubled.

Currency. 100 *möngö* = 1 *tugrik*. Official exchange rates: £1 = 5·10 *tugriks*; 1 rouble = 4·44 *tugriks*; US$1 = 3·36 *tugriks*.

Weights and Measures. The metric system is in use.

ENERGY AND NATURAL RESOURCES

Electricity. There are 6 thermal electric power stations. Production of electricity, 1980, 1,400m. kwh.

Minerals. There are large deposits of copper, nickel, zinc, molybdenum, phosphorites, tin, wolfram and fluorspar; annual production of the latter is 300,000 tonnes, entirely exported to the USSR. The ore-dressing plant at Erdenet was completed in 1981. Coal reserves are 17,000m. tonnes. Coal accounted for 74·6% of energy production in 1980. There are major coalmines near Ulan Bator and Darkhan. Coal (mainly lignite) production in 1981 was 4·1m. tonnes.

Agriculture. The economy remains predominantly agricultural (70% of agricultural production derives from cattle-raising). In 1981 there were 1,991,000 horses, 2·4m. cattle, 14·7m. sheep, 580,000 camels and 4·6m. goats. Pastures occupy 84% of the total area, forests 10·5%. In 1983 there were 719,000 hectares of arable land. In 1981 there were 255 collective farms, 30 inter-farm associations and 57 state farms. All cultivated land and 75% of livestock belong to collective or state farms. Farms cover vast areas. In 1978 collective farms averaged 64,000 head of cattle and state farms about 36,000.

The sown area 1978 was some 680,000 hectares, 500,000 hectares of which were sown to grain. The 1980 crop was 207,000 tonnes of wheat; 1,700 tonnes of rye; 31,800 tonnes of barley. Production of hay fodder was 10·4m tonnes in 1977. In 1981 there were 7,500 tractors (15 h.p. units) and 2,000 combine harvesters.

Forestry. Forests, chiefly larch, cedar, fir and birch, occupy 150,000 sq. km. Production, 1976: 1,067,000 cu. metres of timber.

INDUSTRY AND TRADE

Industry. Industry though still small in scale and local in character, is being vigorously developed and now accounts for a greater share of GNP than agriculture. The food industry accounts for 20% of industrial production. The main industrial centre is Ulan Bator; others Erdenet and Baga-Nuur, and another is under construction at Khutul. Production figures (1980): textiles, 1·4m. cu metres; leather, 1·4m. tonnes; cement, 178,000 tonnes; leather footwear, 2·1m. pairs; meat, 56,700 tonnes; animal fat 3,800 tonnes; beer 98,000 hectolitres.

Employment. The labour force was 370,000 in 1980, including 130,000 shepherds. Average wage was 500 tugriks per month in 1981. Trade union membership was 400,000 in 1982.

There is a serious labour shortage necessitating the employment of military personnel, and workers from the USSR and Eastern Europe.

Commerce. Foreign trade is a state monopoly. Trade figures for 1976 (in 1m. tugriks): exports, 775; imports, 1,007. Mongolia has been a member of Comecon since 1962. The main exports are live cattle and horses, wool and hair, meat, grain, hides, furs, ores, and butter. 96% of foreign trade is with communist countries (80% with USSR). There is a chronic trade deficit. Just over 25% of imports are consumer goods and the remainder are machinery and industrial raw materials. In 1976 trade with China was 28m. tugriks. Trade with Japan, previously valued at US$1m. per annum, increased slightly after the establishment of diplomatic relations in 1972.

Mongolia exported goods to the UK valued at £1,350,000 in 1983 and imported from the UK goods valued at £242,000 (British Department of Trade and Industry returns). Exports to USSR in 1981: 248·6m. roubles; imports: 787·3m. roubles.

COMMUNICATIONS

Roads. There are surfaced roads in and around Ulan Bator, from Ulan Bator to Darkhan and at points on the frontier with USSR. Truck services run throughout the country where there are no surfaced roads. 120m. passengers were carried in 1981.

Railways. The Trans-Mongolian Railway (1,423 km in 1983) connects Ulan Bator with the Soviet Union and China. The Moscow–Ulan Bator–Peking express runs each way once a week. There are spur lines to Erdenet and to the coalmines at Nalaykha and Sharin Gol. A separate line connects Choybalsan in the east with Borzya on the Trans-Siberian railway. 1·1m. passengers and 8·1m. tonnes of freight were carried in 1976.

Aviation. Mongolair operates internal services and a flight to Irkutsk which links with the Moscow service. 7,000 tons of freight were carried in 1976 and 370,000 passengers. Soviet airlines (Aeroflot) and Mongolair jointly operate a daily service to Moscow.

Shipping. There is a steamer service on the Selenge River and a tug and barge service on Hobsgol Lake. 3,000 tonnes of freight were carried in 1976.

Post and Broadcasting. There were, in 1976, 382 post offices and 218 telephone exchanges. Number of telephones (1977), 37,792.

There are wireless stations at Ulan Bator, Gobi Altai and Olgiy. In 1978 there were 128,000 radio and 3,800 television receivers. Television services began in 1967. A Mongolian television station opened in 1970.

Cinemas. In 1976 there were 23 cinemas, 439 mobile cinemas and, in 1981, 10 theatres.

Newspapers and books. In 1982, 13 newspapers and 32 journals were published. The Party daily paper *Ünen* ('Truth') had a circulation of 112,000 in 1978. 400 book titles were published in 1982 in 70m. copies

JUSTICE, RELIGION, EDUCATION AND WELFARE

Justice. The Procurator-General is appointed, and the Supreme Court elected, by the *Khural* for 4 years. There are also courts at province, town and district level. Lay assessors sit with professional judges.

Religion. Tibetan Buddhist Lamaism was the prevalent form of religion. The Church was suppressed in the 1930s, and only one functioning monastery exists today, at Ulan Bator.

Education. In 1983 there were 620 nurseries with 52,000 children. Schooling begins at the age of 8. There are 8- and 10-year schools. In 1983-84 there were 579 'general' schools with 394,000 pupils, and 40 technical schools with 22,000 pupils. There is a state university (founded 1942) at Ulan Bator (40 professors, 240 lecturers and 10,000 students in 1982) and 9 other institutes of higher learning (teacher training, medicine, agriculture, economics, etc.) with 14,000 students in 1982 under the supervision of an Academy of Sciences (founded 1953) which has 15 institutes and 190 research workers. In 1977 there were 23,550 students in institutes of higher learning, and some 6,000 students a year are sent to study abroad, principally in the USSR. In 1982–83 there were 885 'general' schools with 385,000 pupils and 37 technical schools with 21,100 pupils.

In 1946 the Mongolian alphabet was replaced by a modern Cyrillic alphabet.

Health. In 1983 there were 22 doctors and 107 hospital beds per 10,000 inhabitants.

DIPLOMATIC REPRESENTATIVES

Of Mongolia in Great Britain (7 Kensington Ct., London, W8 5DL)
Ambassador: Oyuny Hosbayar.

Of Great Britain in Mongolia (30 Enkh Taivny Gudamzh, Ulan Bator)
Ambassador: J. R. Paterson.

Of Mongolia to the United Nations
Ambassador: Tsogtyn Narkhuu.

Books of Reference

The Central Statistical Office: *Economic Statistics of the MPR for 40 Years.* 1961.—*40 Years of the MPR Revolution.* 1961.—*National Economy MPR 1973.* 1974

Bawden, C. R., *The Modern History of Mongolia.* London, 1968

Boberg, F., *Mongolian–English, English–Mongolian Dictionary.* 3 vols. Stockholm, 1954–55

Haltod, M. (ed.), *Mongolian–English Dictionary.* Berkeley, Cal., 1961

Jagchid, S., and Hyer, P. *Mongolia's Culture and Society.* Folkestone, 1979

Lattimore, O., *Nationalism and Revolution in Mongolia.* Leiden, 1955.—*Nomads and Commissars.* OUP, 1963

News from Mongolia Ulan Bator, fortnightly, Jan. 1980

Petrov. V. P., *Mongolia: A Profile.* London, 1971

Rupen, R. A., *How Mongolia is Really Ruled: A Political History of the Mongolian People's Republic, 1900–1978.* Stanford, 1979

Sanders, A. J. K., *The People's Republic of Mongolia: A General Reference Guide.* OUP, 1968

Shirendev, B., and Sanjdorj, M. (eds.), *History of the Mongolian People's Republic.* Vol. 3 (vols. 1 and 2 not translated). Harvard Univ. Press, 1976

Socialist Mongolia. Ulan Bator, 1981

MONTSERRAT

Capital: Plymouth
Population: 12,073 (1980)
GNP per capita: US$1,370 (1980)

HISTORY. Montserrat was discovered by Columbus in 1493 and colonized by Irish settlers in 1632.

AREA AND POPULATION. Montserrat is situated in the Caribbean Sea 25 miles south-west of Antigua. The area is 39·5 sq. miles (106 sq. km). Population, 1980, 12,073. Chief town, Plymouth, 3,200 inhabitants.

CLIMATE. A tropical climate but with no well-defined rainy season, though July to Dec. shows slightly more rainfall, with the average for the year being about 60″ (1,500 mm). Dec. to March is the cooler season while June to Nov. is the hotter season, when hurricanes may occur.

CONSTITUTION AND GOVERNMENT. Montserrat is a crown colony. The Executive Council is composed of 4 unofficial members (the Chief Minister and 3 other Ministers) and 2 official members (Attorney-General and Financial Secretary). The Legislative Council consists of 7 elected and 2 official members (the Attorney-General and Financial Secretary) and 2 nominated members. The Executive Council is presided over by the Governor and the Legislative Council by the Speaker.

Governor: D. K. H. Dale, CBE.
Chief Minister: Dr J. A. Osborne.
Flag: The British Blue Ensign with the shield of Montserrat in the fly.

FINANCE. In 1982 the budget estimates balanced at EC$660,000 (US$240,000). In 1981 the territorial budget ceased to be grant-aided by the British Government.

AGRICULTURE. Agriculture has been in decline for several years, but is likely to recover with the progress of the Integrated Sea Island Cotton Project and revised land tenure and settlement arrangements associated with the government's acquisition of a number of estates.

Livestock (1981); Cattle, 4,000; pigs, 400; sheep, 4,500; goats, 4,500; poultry, 60,000.

INDUSTRY AND TRADE

Industry. Considerable light industry was attracted to the territory from abroad during 1979–81 and there is 83,000 sq. ft of modern factory space available.

Commerce. Imports in 1982 totalled EC$55m. (US$20·4m.); domestic exports, EC$7m. Chief imports were manufactured goods, food and beverages, machinery and transport equipment and fuel. Chief exports in 1981 were hot peppers, live plants, cattle and manufactured articles. Balance of payments (1982) remained favorable at EC$4m.

Total trade between Montserrat and UK (British Department of Trade returns, in £1,000 sterling):

	1980	1981	1982	1983
Imports to UK	125	397	193	164
Exports and re-exports from UK	1,351	935	1,786	2,159

Tourism. In 1982, 24,900 tourists arrived in Montserrat.

COMMUNICATIONS

Aviation. At the modernized Blackburne airport 3,685 aircraft landed in 1982, disembarking 30,115 passengers and (1981) 2,000 tons of cargo.

Shipping. In 1982, 311 vessels arrived, landing 34,698 and loading 789 tons of cargo.

Post. Number of telephones (1982), 2,600; telex, 27.

JUSTICE, RELIGION, EDUCATION AND WELFARE

Justice. There are 2 magistrates' courts, at Plymouth and Cudjoe Head. Strength of the police force (1982), 2 gazetted officers, 4 inspectors and 100 other ranks.

Religion. In 1981 there were 1,329 Roman Catholics, 4,332 Anglicans, 3,249 Methodists, 804 Seventh Day Adventists, 1,091 Pentecostals and 254 members of the Church of God. There is also a Christian Council of Churches.

Education. There are 12 government elementary, 1 government secondary, 2 grant-aided denominational elementary schools, 2 junior secondary schools, 2 preparatory private schools for children between the ages of 5 and 12 and 11 nursery schools. In 1982, 1,943 children were enrolled in the primary schools, with 84 teachers; 872 in the secondary schools, with 61 teachers. There was 1 technical college with 50 students and 9 teachers.

Health. In 1982 there were 8 doctors and 67 hospital beds.

Books of Reference

Overseas Trade 1982. Montserrat Government
Preliminary National Account Statistics, 1975–1982. 1982
Vital Statistics Report. Montserrat Government, 1982
Statistical Digest 1979. Montserrat Government
Fergus, H.A., *Montserrat: Emerald Isle of the Caribbean.* London, 1983

Library. Public Library, Plymouth. *Librarian:* Miss J. Grell.

MOROCCO

al-Mamlaka al-Maghrebia

Capital: Rabat
Population: 21m. (1983)
GNP per capita: US$860 (1980)

HISTORY. From 1912 to 1956 Morocco was divided into a French protectorate (established by the treaty of Fez concluded between France and the Sultan on 30 March 1912), a Spanish protectorate (established by the Franco-Spanish convention of 27 Nov. 1912) and the international zone of Tangier (set up by France, Spain and Great Britain on 18 Dec. 1923).

On 2 March 1956 France and the Sultan terminated the treaty of Fez; on 7 April 1956 Spain relinquished her protectorate, and on 29 Oct. 1956 France, Spain, Great Britain, Italy, USA, Belgium, the Netherlands, Sweden and Portugal abolished the international status of the Tangier Zone. The northern strip of Spanish Sahara was ceded by Spain on 10 April 1958, and on 30 June 1969 the former Spanish province of Ifni was returned to Morocco.

A tripartite agreement was announced on 14 Nov. 1975 providing for the transfer of power from Spanish Sahara (Western Sahara) to the Moroccan and Mauritanean governments on 28 Feb. 1976. Spanish troops left El Aaiún on 20 Dec. 1975. On 14 April 1976 a Convention was signed by Mauritania and Morocco in which the 2 countries agreed to partition the former Spanish territory, but on 14 Aug. 1979 Mauritania renounced its claim to its share of the territory (Tiris El-Gharbiya) which was added by Morocco to its area.

AREA AND POPULATION. Morocco is bounded by Algeria to the east and south-east, Western Sahara to the south-west, the Atlantic ocean to the north-west and the Mediterranean to the north. Excluding the Western Saharan territory claimed and occupied since 1976 by Morocco, the total area is 458,730 sq. km and its total population at the Sept. 1982 census was 20,255,687; the latest estimate (1983) is 21m.

The areas (in sq. km) and populations (census 1982) of the provinces are:

Province	Sq. km	1982	Province	Sq. km	1982
Agadir	} 17,460 [2] {	579,741	Nador	6,130	593,255
Taroudant		558,501	Ouarzazate	46,460	533,892
Al-Hoceima	3,550	311,298	Oujda	20,700	780,762
Azilal	10,050	387,115	Rabat-Salé [1]	1,275	1,020,001
Beni Mellal	7,075	668,703	Safi	7,285	706,618
Ben Slimane	2,760	174,464	Settat	9,750	692,359
Boulemane	14,395	131,470	Tangier	1,195	436,227
Casablanca-Anfa [1]	} 1,615 [2] {	923,630	Tan-Tan	17,295	47,040
Aïn Chok-Hay Hassani [1]		298,376	Taounate	5,585	535,972
Ben Msik-Sidi Othmane [1]		639,558	Tata	25,925	99,950
Hay Mohamed-Aïn Sebâa [1]		421,272	Taza	15,020	613,485
Mohamedia-Znata [1]		153,828	Tétouan	6,025	704,205
Chechaouèn	4,350	309,024	Tiznit	6,960	313,140
El Jadida	6,000	763,351			
El Kelâa-Srarhna	10,070	577,595	Morocco	458,730	20,255,687
Er Rachidia	59,585	421,207			
Es Saouira	6,335	393,683			
Fez	5,400	805,464	Boujdour		
Figuig	55,990	101,359	(Bojador)		8,481
Guelmim	28,750	128,676	Es Semara		
Kénitra	} 8,805 [2] {	715,967	(Smara)		20,480
Sidi Kacem		514,127	Laâyoune		
Khémisset	8,305	405,836	(Al Aaiún)		113,411
Khénifra	11,115	363,716	Oued Ed		
Khouribga	4,250	437,002	Dahab		21,496
Marrakesh	14,755	1,266,695			
Meknès	} 8,510 [2] {	626,868	Sahara	252,120	163,868
Ifrane		100,255			

[1] Urban prefectures   [2] Area before division in 1981.

The population of the largest municipalities (census) June 1971: Casablanca, 1,506,373; Rabat (capital), 367,620; Marrakesh, 332,741; Fez, 325,327; Meknès, 248,369; Tangier, 187,894; Oujda, 175,532; Salè, 155,557; Kenitra, 139,206; Tétouan, 139,105; Safi, 129,113; Khouribga, 73,667; Mohammedia, 70,392; Agadir, 61,192; El Jadida, 55,501.

The official language is Arabic, spoken by 75% of the population; the remainder speak Berber. French and Spanish are considered subsidiary languages.

CLIMATE. The climate ranges from semi-arid in the south to warm temperate Mediterranean conditions in the north, but cooler temperatures occur in the mountains. Rabat. Jan. 55°F (12·9°C), July 72°F (22·2°C). Annual rainfall 23" (564 mm). Agadir. Jan. 57°F (13·9°C), July 72°F (22·2°C). Annual rainfall 9" (224 mm). Casablanca. Jan. 54°F (12·2°C), July 72°F (22·2°C). Annual rainfall 16" (404 mm). Marrakesh. Jan. 52°F (11·1°C), July 84°F (28·9°C). Annual rainfall 10" (239 mm). Tangier. Jan. 53°F (11·7°C), July 72°F (22·2°C). Annual rainfall 36" (897 mm).

REIGNING KING. Hassan II, born on 9 July 1929, succeeded on 3 March 1961, on the death of his father Mohammed V, who reigned 1927–61. The royal style was changed from 'His Sherifian Majesty the Sultan' to 'His Majesty the King' on 18 Aug. 1957. *Heir apparent:* Crown Prince Sidi Mohammed, born 21 Aug. 1963.

The King holds supreme civil and religious authority; the latter in his capacity of Emir-el-Muminin or Commander of the Faithful. He resides usually at Rabat, but occasionally in one of the other traditional capitals, Fez (founded in 808), Marrakesh (founded in 1062), or at Skhirat.

CONSTITUTION AND GOVERNMENT. A new Constitution was approved by referendum in March 1972 and amendments were approved by referendum in May 1980. The Kingdom of Morocco is a constitutional monarchy with a legislature of a single chamber composed of 267 deputies. Deputies for 89 seats are elected by indirect vote through an electoral college representing the town councils, the regional assemblies, the chambers of commerce, industry and agriculture, and the trade unions. Deputies for the remaining 178 seats are by general election. The King, as sovereign head of State, appoints the Prime Minister and other Ministers, has the right to dissolve Parliament and approves legislation.

National flag: Red, with a green pentacle star in the centre.

Cabinet in Nov. 1983:

Prime Minister: Mohamed Karim Lamrani.

Justice: Moulay Mustapha Belarbi Alaoui. *Interior:* Driss Basri. *Foreign Affairs:* Abdelouahed Belakziz. *Information:* Abdellatif Filali. *Waqfs and Islamic Affairs:* Hachemi Filali. *Planning, Executive and Professional Training:* Mhamed Douiri. *National Education:* Azzeddine Laraki. *Economic Affairs:* Taib Bencheikh. *Finance:* Abdellatif Jouahri. *Trade, Industry and Tourism:* Azzeddine Guessous. *Handicrafts and Social Affairs:* Abbas el Fassi. *Transport:* Mansouri Ben Ali. *Energy and Mining:* Moussa Saadi. *Health:* Rahhali Rahal. *Maritime Fishing and Merchant Navy:* Bensalem Smili. *Secretary-General of the Government:* Abbas Kaissi. *Cultural Affairs:* Said Bel Bachir. *Housing, Urban Affairs and Protection of the Environment:* Mfadel Lahlou. *Equipment:* Mohamed Kabbaj. *Minister at the Prime Minister's Office:* Abdelkrim Ghallab. *Posts and Telecommunications:* Mohand Laensar. *Agriculture and Land Reform:* Otman Demnati. *Relations with Parliament:* Ahmed Belhadj. *Youth and Sports:* Abdellatif Semlali. *Minister in charge of Co-operation:* Abdelouahed Radi. *Labour:* Moulay Zine Zahidi. There are 8 Ministers of State, 4 Secretaries and 1 Under Secretary of State.

Local Government: The country is administratively divided into 39 provinces and 6 urban prefectures.

DEFENCE. Military service is compulsory for 18 months.

Army. The Army comprises 4 mechanized infantry, 1 light security, 1 parachute and 1 anti-aircraft brigades; 10 mechanized infantry regiments; 9 artillery groups; 7 armoured, 1 Royal Guard, 5 camel corps, 2 desert cavalry, 1 mountain, 3 commando and 4 engineer battalions; and 4 armoured car squadrons. Equipment includes 120 M-48 and 15 T-54 main battle tanks, 80 light tanks and 1,000 armoured cars. Strength (1984) 125,000 men. There are also 30,000 paramilitary troops.

Navy. Navy includes 1 new missile-armed light frigate (completing), 4 new missile armed large patrol vessels or small corvettes, 2 modern fast attack (corvette size) gunboats, 1 coastal minesweeper, 1 patrol vessel, 1 gunboat, 1 seaward patrol craft, 9 coastal patrol boats, 4 landing craft acquired from France, 2 logistic support vessels and 1 yacht training vessel. The construction of 5 corvettes of new design is under discussion. Personnel in 1984 totalled 1,800 officers and ratings including 500 marines. There are also 12 small customs cutters and a coastguard picket.

Air Force. The Air Force was formed in Nov. 1956. Equipment in current use is mainly of US and West European origin. It includes 41 Mirage F1s, a total of 26 F-5A/B/E/F fighter-bombers and RF-5A reconnaissance-fighters, 4 OV-10 Bronco counter-insurgency aircraft, a Falcon 20 for electronic warfare, and 24 Hughes 500MD Scout Defender armed helicopters, 24 Alpha Jet advanced trainers, 22 Magister armed jet basic trainers, 12 T-34C-1 turboprop armed basic trainers, 10 Swiss-built Bravo primary trainers, 2 Mudry CAP 10B aerobatic trainers, 4 Broussard liaison aircraft, 75 Agusta-Bell 205 and 212, Puma and JetRanger helicopters, 10 Do 28D Skyservants for coastal patrol, 9 CH-47C heavy-lift helicopters, 19 C-130H turboprop transport aircraft, 3 KC-130H tanker/transports, a Falcon 50 VIP transport and 6 turboprop King Air light transports. The T-34C-1s are intended to be replaced in the mid-80s by locally designed Gepal Mk IV 550 turboprop trainers. Personnel strength is about 10,000.

INTERNATIONAL RELATIONS

Membership. Morocco is a member of UN, OAU, the Non-Aligned Movement, the Islamic Conference and the Arab League.

ECONOMY

Planning. A 5-year plan (1973–77) envisaged a total investment of 11,751,874m. DH. A new 3-year plan (1978–80) was approved in Dec. 1978. The 5-year plan (1981–85) was approved in June 1981.

Budget. The budget for 1982 envisaged revenue of 39,900m. DH and expenditure of 46,800m. DH.

Currency. In Oct. 1959, a national currency was introduced. Its unit is the *dirham* (abbreviated DH), equalling 100 *centimes*. Notes: 5, 10, 50, 100 DH; coins: 0·02, 0·05, 0·10, 0·20, 0·50, 1 DH. The exchange rate in March 1984 was £1 sterling = 11·40 DH; US$1 = 7·95 DH.

Banking. The bank of issue is the Banque du Maroc in Rabat. Other important institutions are the Banque Marocaine du Commerce Extérieur (Casablanca), the Banque Nationale pour le Développement Economique (Rabat), Crédit Populaire and the Crédit Immobilier et Hotelier (Casablanca). There are 23 other banks in Casablanca, 3 in Tangier and 1 each in Tétouan, Fez, Kenitra, Meknès, Oujda and Rabat.

Weights and Measures. The metric system of weights and measures is the sole legal system.

ENERGY AND NATURAL RESOURCES

Electricity. Electric power-plants produced 4,785·3m. kwh. in 1981.

Oil. Crude oil production, 48,000 tonnes 1980.

Minerals. The principal mineral exploited is phosphate, the output of which (under a state monopoly) was 18·56m. tonnes in 1981. Other important minerals (in 1,000 tonnes) are: Iron ore (49·9), lead (168·4), cobalt (6), zinc (14·7), manganese (109·6), silver (21·2). Production of minerals (1978) 2,829,284m. dirhams.

Agriculture. Agriculture is by far the most important industry, on which 70% of the population exists. The principal crops are cereals, especially wheat and barley; beans, chickpeas, fenugreek and other legumens; canary seed; cumin and coriander; linseed; olives; almonds and other fruits, especially citrus. The almost universal wild palmetto is put to various uses, including the manufacture of *crin végétal*. The trees include cork, cedar, arar, argon, oak and various conifers. Wine production, 1975, 830,000 hectolitres. Tizra wood is exported for tanning purposes. Stockraising is an important industry.

Production in 1982: Barley, 19·1m.; wheat, 18·2m.; maize, 315,000; sugar-cane, 630,000; citrus fruit, 1m.

Livestock (in 1,000 heads), 1982: Camels, 230; horses, 310; cattle, 2,900; pigs, 11; sheep, 14,900; goats, 6,250; poultry, 24m.

Fishing. The chief fishing centres are Agadir, Safi, Essaouira and Casablanca. There are over 5,000 fishing vessels and about 100 freezing and processing plants. The industry employs 50,000 workers. Total catch in 1980 was 300,000 tons.

COMMERCE. Imports and exports were (in 1m. DH):

	1977	1978	1979	1980	1981
Imports	14,401	12,361	14,327	16,792	22,455
Exports	5,860	6,262	7,622	9,645	12,002

Main imports, 1981, consumer goods and industrial products. Main exports, (1980), phosphates (31%), fruit and vegetables (21%), phosphoric acid (8%) and metal ores (6%).

Main trading partners (1981): Exports, France (22%), Federal Republic of Germany (7%), Spain (7%). Imports, France (25%), Saudi Arabia (15%) Spain (7%), USA (7%).

A royal proclamation of 30 Aug. 1959 abrogated the former economic status of Tangier and integrated the zone in the Kingdom. However, Tangier was declared a free port from 1 Jan. 1962; and commercial transactions within the free zone were further liberalized by decree of 8 Nov. 1965.

Total trade between Morocco and UK (British Department of Trade returns, in £1,000 sterling):

	1978	1979	1980	1981	1982	1983
Imports to UK	44,079	50,392	62,582	67,697	60,219	75,602
Exports and re-exports from UK	76,535	67,604	69,223	55,939	95,487	99,727

TOURISM. In 1982, 1·9m. foreign visitors came to Morocco.

COMMUNICATIONS

Roads. In 1980 there were 57,634 km of classified roads, of which (1978) 27,671 km were surfaced. At the end of 1980 there were in use 200,559 lorries, 447,992 private cars and (1978) 17,820 motor cycles.

Railways. In 1982 there were 1,779 km of railways, of which 709 km were electrified. The principal standard-gauge lines are from Casablanca eastward to the Algerian border, forming part of the continuous rail line to Tunis; Casablanca to Marrakesh with 2 important branches, one eastward to Oued Zem tapping the Khouribga phosphate mines, the other westward to the port of Safi. Another branch serves the manganese mines at Bou Arfa. Two new double-track electrified lines are to serve a new deep-water port at Jorf Lasfar, and a 650 km south-east extension from Marrakesh to Laayoun in the south Sahara is planned.

In 1982 the railways ran 1,374m. passenger-km and 3,851m. tonne-km of goods.

Aviation. There are 19 airfields, of which Casablanca–Arfa and Casablanca–Nouaceur are the most important. Total international air services in 1981 comprised 3,205,314 passengers arrived and departed and 32,893 tonnes of freight including mail.

Shipping. In 1980, 17,752 vessels of 46m. net tons entered and cleared the ports of Morocco. In 1980 the merchant marine consisted of 145 vessels (of over 100 gross tons) with a total tonnage of 359,552 GRT.

Post and Broadcasting. Communication with Europe is maintained by cables between Casablanca and Brest, Tangier–Casablanca–Le Havre, Tangier–Gibraltar, Tangier–Cádiz, Larache–Cádiz via Algeciras.

Telephone subscribers totalled 241,000 in 1982.

Broadcasting is done in Arabic, Berber, French, Spanish and English from Rabat and Tangier; television in Arabic and French began in 1962. In 1977 there were 1·6m. radio and 597,000 television receivers.

Cinemas. There were about 235 cinemas in 1971.

JUSTICE, RELIGION, EDUCATION AND WELFARE

Justice. A uniform legal system is being organized, based mainly on French and Islamic law codes and French legal procedure. The judiciary consists of a Supreme Court, courts of appeal, regional tribunals and magistrates' courts.

Religion. Islam is the established state religion. 98% are Sunni Moslems of the Malekite school and 2% are Christians, mainly Roman Catholic.

Education. In 1959 a standardization of the various school systems (French, Spanish, Israeli, Moslem, etc.) was begun. Education has been made compulsory from the age of 7 to 13.

In 1981 there were 2,331,000 pupils and 55,303 teachers in state primary schools; 826,500 pupils and (1980) 31,794 teachers in secondary schools; 10,020 students in technical schools and 16,148 students in teacher-training establishments.

The language of instruction in primary schools is Arabic during the first 2 years, and half-Arabic and half-French during the following 3 years; in secondary schools lessons are in French and Arabic. A third language of the choice of the student is learnt during the last 3 years of secondary education.

There are six universities, Mohamed V at Rabat, Hassan II at Casablanca, Mohamed Ben Abdallah at Fez, Quaraouyine at Fez, Oujda and Marrakesh with a total enrolment of 80,345 students and 2,558 teaching staff in 1981.

Health. In 1981 there were 1,153 doctors and (1979) 24,453 hospital beds.

DIPLOMATIC REPRESENTATIVES

Of Morocco in Great Britain (49 Queen's Gate Gdns., London, SW7 5NE)
Ambassador: Medhi Benabdeljalil (accredited 11 Feb. 1982).

Of Great Britain in Morocco (17 Blvd de la Tour Hassan, Rabat)
Ambassador: S. J. G. Cambridge, CMG, CVO.

Of Morocco in the USA (1601 21st St., NW, Washington, D.C., 20009)
Ambassador: Ali Benjelloun.

Of the USA in Morocco (2 Ave. de Marrakech, Rabat)
Ambassador: Joseph V. Reed, Jr.

Of Morocco to the United Nations
Ambassador: Mehdi Mrani Zentar.

Books of Reference

Statistical Information: The Service Central des Statistiques (BP 178, Rabat) was set up in 1942. Its publications include: *Annuaire de Statistique Générale.—La Conjoncture Économique Marocaine* (monthly; with annual synthesis).—*Résultats du Recensement général de la population de 1971.—Bulletin économique et social du Maroc* (trimestral).—*La situation Economique du Maroc, 1975*

Bulletin Official (in Arabic and French). Rabat. Weekly

Findlay, A. M. and A. M., and Lawless, R. I., *Morocco.* [Bibliography] Oxford and Santa Barbara, 1984

Kinross, Lord, and Hales-Gary, D., *Morocco.* London, 1971

Rivière, P. L., *Précis de Législation marocaine.* New ed. in collaboration with G. Catteriz. 2 vols. Caen, 1942–46

National Library: Bibliothèque Générale et Archives, Rabat.

MOZAMBIQUE

República Popular de Moçambique

Capital: Maputo
Population: 13·14m. (1983)
GNP per capita: US$270 (1980)

HISTORY. Trading settlements were established by Arab merchants at Sofala (Beira), Quelimane, Angoche and Mozambique Island in the fifteenth century. Mozambique Island was visited by Vasco da Gamba's fleet on 2 March 1498, and Sofala was occupied by Portuguese in 1506. At first ruled as part of Portuguese India, a separate administration was created in 1752, and on 11 June 1951 Mozambique became an Overseas Province of Portugal. Following a decade of guerrilla activity, Portugal and the nationalists jointly established a transitional government on 20 Sept. 1974. Independence was achieved on 25 June 1975. In March 1984 the Republic of South Africa and Mozambique signed a non-agression pact.

AREA AND POPULATION. Mozambique is bounded east by the Indian ocean, south by South Africa, south-west by Swaziland, west by South Africa and Zimbabwe and north by Zambia, Malawi and Tanzania. It has an area of 799,380 sq. km (308,642 sq. miles) and a population, according to the census of 1980, of 12·13m. Estimate (1983) 13·14m. of whom (1982) 850,000 lived in the capital, Maputo. The areas, populations and capitals of the 10 provinces are:

Province	Sq. km	Census 1970	Capital
Cabo Delgado	78,374	546,113	Pemba
Niassa	120,135	285,329	Lichinga
Nampula	78,265	1,716,486	Nampula
Zambézia	102,880	1,747,888	Quelimane
Tete	100,714	488,668	Tete
Manica ⎱ Sofala ⎰	129,854	1,079,718	⎧ Chimoio ⎨ Beira ⎩
Inhambane	68,470	748,575	Inhambane
Gaza	82,534	756,654	Xaixai
Maputo	16,783	799,502	Maputo

At the 1970 census, Maputo had 354,684 inhabitants; other large towns are Nampula (126,126) and Beira (113,770). The main ethnolinguistic groups are the Makua/Lomwe (37% of the population), mainly in Nampula and Zambézia provinces in the north, the Shona (10%) in Manica and Sofala, and the Thonga (23%) in the south. Portuguese remains the official language, but Swahili serves as a lingua franca, particularly north of the Zambézi.

CLIMATE. A humid tropical climate, with a dry season from June to Sept. In general, temperatures and rainfall decrease from north to south. Maputo. Jan. 78°F (25·6°C), July 65°F (18·3°C). Annual rainfall 30" (760 mm). Beira. Jan. 82°F (27·8°C), July 69°F (20·6°C). Annual rainfall 60" (1,522 mm).

CONSTITUTION AND GOVERNMENT. Under the Constitution adopted at independence on 25 June 1975, the directing power of the state is vested in the *Frente de Libertação de Moçambique* (FRELIMO), the liberation movement, which in Feb. 1977 was reconstituted as sole political Party. The legislative organ is the People's Assembly of 210 members, elected in Dec. 1977.

The Council of Ministers in Dec. 1983 consisted of:

President, and Commander-in-Chief of the Armed Forces, with overall responsibility for the Ministry of Defence: Samora Moises Machel.
Foreign Affairs: Joaquim Alberto Chissano. *Defence:* Lieut.-Gen. Alberto Joaquim Chipande. *Interior:* Armando Emílio Guebuza. *Security:* Mariano de Araújo Matsinhe. *Deputy Minister of Defence and Chief of Staff of the Armed*

Forces: Sebastião Marcos Mabote. *Minister in the Presidency for Economic Affairs:* Jacinto Soares Veloso. *Planning:* Mário da Graça Machungo. *Justice:* Dr José Oscar Monteiro. *Finance:* Dr Rui Baltazar dos Santos Alves. *Education and Culture:* Graça Simbine Machel. *Information:* José Luís Cabaço. *Public Works:* Júlio Zamith Carrilho. *Foreign Trade:* Joaquim Ribeiro de Carvalho. *Agriculture:* João dos Santos Ferreira. *Mineral Resources:* José Carlos Lobo. *Industry and Energy:* António José Lima Rodigues Branco. *Health:* Pascual Manuel Mocumbi. *Ports, Railways and Shipping:* Luis Maria Alcântara Santos. *Posts and Telecommunications:* Rui Jorge Gomes de Lousã. *Domestic Trade:* Manuel Jorge Aranda da Silva. *Governor of the Bank of Mozambique:* Prakash Ratilal.

There are 8 Deputy Ministers and 9 Secretaries of State.

National flag: Horizontally green, black, yellow with the black fimbriated in white; a red triangle based on the hoist, charged with a yellow star surmounted by an open white book and a crossed rifle and hoe in black.

DEFENCE. Selective conscription for 2 years is in force.

Army. The Army consists of 1 tank brigade and 7 infantry brigades. Equipment includes T-34/-54/-55 main battle tanks. Strength (1984) 11,000. There are also 4,000 Border Guards and various militias.

Navy. The small flotilla comprises 6 former Portuguese coastal patrol boats, 6 *ex*-Soviet gunboats, 4 *ex*-Netherlands patrol craft, 1 *ex*-Portuguese survey ship (former British fleet minesweeper), 1 *ex*-Portuguese landing craft (used as a transport) and 2 *ex*-Portuguese minor landing craft. Naval personnel in 1984 totalled 700 officers and men.

Air Force. The Air Force is reported to have about 35 MiG-17 and 20 MiG-21 fighters, probably flown by Cuban pilots, An-26 turboprop transports, a Tu-134A for VIP use, Mi-8 helicopters, about 28 L-39 jet trainers, Zlin 326 primary trainers and a few *ex*-Portuguese Air Force transport/liaison aircraft.

INTERNATIONAL RELATIONS

Membership. Mozambique is a member of UN, OAU and SADCC.

ECONOMY

Budget. In 1982 the revenue was 18,500m. meticais; expenditure, 21,370m. meticais.

Currency. In June 1980 the currency became the *metical* (pl. *meticais*) divided into 100 *centavos*. The *metical* was established at par with the former *escudo*. In March 1984, £1 = 63·30 *meticais*; US$1 = 32·59 *meticais*.

Banking. Most banks had been nationalized by 1979. The *Banco de Moçambique* (bank of issue) and the *Banco Popular de Desenvolvimento* (state investment bank) each have a capital of 1,000m. meticais.

Weights and Measures. The metric system is in force.

ENERGY AND NATURAL RESOURCES

Electricity. Production (1980) 14,000 kwh. Capacity (1977) 1,213 mw. The hydro-electric dam at Cabora Bassa on the Zambezi is the largest producer in Africa.

Minerals. Coal mining is the main mineral being exploited. Output reached 565,000 tonnes in 1975 but has since fallen. Coal reserves (estimate) 400m. tonnes. Small quantities of bauxite, gold, titanium, fluorite and colombo-tantalite are produced. Iron ore deposits and natural gas are known to exist.

Agriculture. Production in tonnes (1981): Cereals, 495,000; tea, 18,000; maize, 270,000; bananas, 65,000; sisal, 12,000; rice, 162,000; groundnuts, 80,000; copra, 70,000.

Livestock 1982: 1·43m. cattle, 345,000 goats, 110,000 sheep, 130,000 pigs, 20,000 asses.

Forestry. Production (1978) 10·84m. cu. metres.

Fisheries. In 1981 the catch was 30,000 tonnes.

INDUSTRY AND TRADE

Industry. Although the country is overwhelmingly rural, there is some substantial industry in and around Maputo (steel, engineering, textiles, processing, docks and railways).

Commerce. Imports in 1979 totalled 23,000m. meticais and exports 12,700m. meticais. 15·3% of imports came from the Republic of South Africa and 12·7% from the Federal Republic of Germany. Exports (1976 in tonnes): Coal, 204,843 while 27% of exports went to USA and 16% to Portugal. In 1977 cashew nuts formed 30%, textiles, 9% and tea, 8% of all exports.

Total trade between Mozambique and UK (British Department of Trade returns, in £1,000 sterling):

	1980	1981	1982	1983
Imports to UK	11,416	5,716	10,611	9,176
Exports and re-exports from UK	11,345	21,763	14,473	28,618

COMMUNICATIONS

Roads. There were, in 1982, 26,000 km of roads, of which 4,600 km were tarred. Motor vehicles, in 1980, included 99,400 passenger cars and 24,700 lorries and buses. The Government is devoting effort to constructing a new North/South road link, and to improving provincial rural feeder road systems.

Railways. The Mozambique State Railways consist of 5 independent networks known as the Maputo, Mozambique, Sofala (Beira), Inhambane and Gaza, and Quelimane systems. The Maputo system has links with the Republic of South Africa, Swaziland and Zimbabwe railways; the Sofala system links with Zimbabwe at Machipanda and by way of the Trans–Zambesia Railway with Malawi at Dona Ana; and the Mozambique system links with Malawi at Entre Lagos. The Inhambane and Quelimane systems have no international connections. Total route-km (1980), 3,696 km (1,067 mm gauge), and 147 km (762 mm gauge). Trans–Zambesia Railway, 318 km (1,067 mm gauge). In 1981, 12m. passengers and 5,166m. tonne-km of goods were carried. Rail links with Zimbabwe reopened in 1979.

Aviation. There are international airports at Maputo, Beira and Nampula with regular services to European and Southern African destination by several foreign airlines and by *Linhas Aéreas de Moçambique*, who also serve 13 domestic airports.

Shipping. The total tonnage handled by Mozambique ports (1977) was 10,554,660. The principal ports are Maputo, Beira, Naçala and Quelimane.

Post and Broadcasting. Maputo is connected by telegraph with the Transvaal system. Quelimane has telegraphic communication with Chiromo. Number of telephones (1982), 56,305.

Radio Moçambique broadcasts 5 programmes in Portuguese, English, Afrikaans, Ronga and Shangane as well as 4 regional programmes in 8 languages. Number of receivers (1979): radio, 255,000; TV, 1,500.

Cinemas. There were, in 1971, 31 cinemas with a seating capacity of 20,195.

Newspapers. There are 2 daily newspapers in Mozambique: *Noticias,* published in Maputo, and *Diario de Mozambique*. There is also a weekly magazine, *Tempo.*

RELIGION, EDUCATION AND WELFARE

Religion. About 60% of the population follow traditional animist religions, while some 18% are Christian (mainly Roman Catholic) and 16% Moslem.

Education. In 1981 there were 1,376,865 pupils in primary schools and 135,956 in secondary schools. The *Universidade Eduardo Mondlane* had 746 students in 1979. About 500,000 attend adult literacy classes.

Health. There were (1980) 321 hospitals and medical centres and 13,180 hospital beds; there were 823 doctors, 96 dentists, 8 pharmacists, 457 midwives and 2,156 nursing personnel.

DIPLOMATIC REPRESENTATIVES

Of Great Britain in Mozambique (Ave. Vladimir 1 Lenine, 310, Maputo)
Ambassador: J. A. B. Stewart, CMG, OBE.

Of USA in Mozambique (35 Rua Da Mesquita, Maputo)
Ambassador: Peter John de Vos.

Of Mozambique to the United Nations
Ambassador: Manuel dos Santos.

Books of Reference

Henriksen, T. H., *Mozambique: A History.* London and Cape Town, 1978
Houser, G., and Shore, H., *Mozambique: Dream the Size of Freedom.* New York, 1975
Isaacman, A., *A Luta Continua: Building a New Society in Mozambique.* New York, 1978
Mondlane, E., *The Struggle for Mozambique.* London, 1983
Munslow, B., *Mozambique: The Revolution and its Origins.* London, 1983

NAURU

HISTORY. The island was discovered by Capt. Fearn in 1798, annexed by Germany in Oct. 1888, and surrendered to the Australian forces in 1914. It was administered under a mandate, effective from 17 Dec. 1920, conferred on the British Empire and approved by the League of Nations until 1 Nov. 1947, when the United Nations General Assembly approved a trusteeship agreement with the governments of Australia, New Zealand and UK as joint administering authority. Independence was gained in 1968.

AREA AND POPULATION. The island is situated 0° 32′ S. lat. and 166° 56′ E. long. Area, 5,263 acres (2,130 hectares). It is an oval-shaped upheaval coral island of approximately 12 miles in circumference, surrounded by a reef which is exposed at low tide. There is no deep water harbour but offshore moorings, reputedly the deepest in the world, are capable of holding medium-sized vessels, including 30,000 tonne capacity bulk carriers. On the seaward side the reef dips abruptly into the deep waters of the Pacific at an angle of 45°. On the landward side of the reef there is a sandy beach interspersed with coral pinnacles. From the sandy beach the ground rises gradually, forming a fertile section ranging in width from 150 to 300 yd and completely encircling the island. On the inner side of the fertile section there is a coral cliff which rises to a height of 200 ft. Above the cliff there is an extensive plateau bearing phosphate of a high grade, the mining rights of which were vested in the British Phosphate Commissioners until 1 July 1970, subject to the rights of the Nauruan landowners. In July 1970 the Nauru Phosphate Corporation assumed control and management of the enterprise. It is chiefly on the fertile section of land between the sandy beach and the plateau that the Nauruans have established themselves. With the exception of a small fringe round a shallow lagoon, about 1 mile inland, the plateau, which contains the phosphate deposits, has few foodbearing trees and is not settled by the Nauruans.

At the census held on 22 Jan. 1977 the population totalled 7,254, of whom 4,174 were Nauruans. Estimate (1983) 8,421.

Vital statistics, 1982: Births, 286 (224 Nauruan); deaths, 77 (42 Nauruan).

CLIMATE. A tropical climate, tempered by sea breezes, but with a high and irregular rainfall, averaging 82″ (2,060 mm).

CONSTITUTION AND GOVERNMENT. A Legislative Council was established by the Nauru Act, passed by the Australian Parliament in Dec. 1965 and was inaugurated on 31 Jan. 1966. The trusteeship agreement terminated on 31 Jan. 1968, on which day Nauru became an independent republic but having special relationship with the Commonwealth. An 18-member Parliament is elected on a 3-yearly basis.

President and Minister for Foreign Affairs: Hammer DeRoburt, OBE.

National flag: Blue with a narrow horizontal gold stripe across the centre, beneath this near the hoist a white star of 12 points.

FINANCE. Revenue and expenditure (in $A) for financial year ending 30 June 1983 (estimate): revenue, 97,279,300; expenditure, 111,284,800 (health, 1,602,200; education, 2,004,200).

The interests in the phosphate deposits were purchased in 1919 from the Pacific Phosphate Company by the governments of the UK, the Commonwealth of Australia and New Zealand at a cost of £Stg3·5m., and a Board of Commissioners representing the 3 governments was appointed to manage and control the working of the deposits. In May 1967, in Canberra, the British Phosphate Corporation agreed to hand over the phosphate industry to Nauru and on 15 June 1967 agreement was reached that the Nauruans could buy the assets of the B.P.C. for approximately $20m. over 3 years. Final payment was made on 23 April 1969 and control was handed over on 1 July 1970.

It is estimated that the deposits will be exhausted by 1993.

COMMERCE. The export trade consists almost entirely of phosphate shipped to Australia, New Zealand and Japan. Phosphate exported, 1976–77, 1m. tonnes. The imports consist almost entirely of food supplies, building construction materials and machinery for the phosphate industry. Value of imports, 1973–74, $A10m.

Total trade between Nauru and UK (British Department of Trade returns, in £1,000 sterling):

	1979	1980	1981	1982	1983
Imports to UK	160	70	83	32	1,421
Exports from UK	619	821	326	1,843	1,715

COMMUNICATIONS

Aviation. There is an airfield on the island capable of accepting medium size jet aircraft. Air Nauru, a wholly owned government subsidiary, operates services with Boeing 727 and 737 aircraft to Melbourne, Sydney, Apia, Honiara, Guam, Tarawa, Majuro, Kagoshima, Okinawa, Noumea, Port Vila, Suva, Nadi, Ponape, Manila, Taipei, Truk, Saipan, Korer (Pelan), Honolulu, Singapore, Auckland, Pago Pago and Niue.

Shipping. The Nauru Local Government Council, through its agency the Nauru Pacific Shipping Line, owns 6 ships and 2 fishing boats. These ships ply between Australia, Pacific Islands, west coast of USA, New Zealand, Japan, Singapore etc. Other shipping coming to the island consists of those under charter to the phosphate industry.

Telecommunications. An earth satellite station became operational in 1976, offering 24 hour telephone, telegram and telex services world-wide. Number of telephones (1978) 1,500. Direct daily high frequency service is maintained with Tarawa and both long- and short-wave transmissions with merchant shipping. A separate tele-radio service exists between Nauru and Ocean Island.

Cinemas. In 1978 there were 7 cinemas with seating capacity of 1,500.

JUSTICE, RELIGION AND EDUCATION

Justice. The highest Court is the Supreme Court of Nauru. It is the Superior Court of record and has the jurisdiction to deal with constitutional matters in addition to its other jurisdiction. There is also a District Court which is presided over by the Resident Magistrate who is also the Chairman of the Family Court and the Registrar of Supreme Court. The laws applicable in Nauru are its own Acts of Parliament and a large number of British statutes and the common law have been adopted for Nauru.

Religion. The population is mainly Roman Catholic or Protestant.

Education. Attendance at school is compulsory for all children between the ages of 6 and 16. In June 1983 there were 8 infant and primary schools and 2 secondary schools. There were 44 teachers and 2,164 pupils in infant, primary and secondary schools. In addition, there is a trade school with 4 instructors and an enrolment of 74 trainees. Scholarships are available for Nauruan children to receive secondary and higher education and vocational training in Australia and New Zealand. In June 1983, 77 Nauruans were receiving secondary education abroad in Australia and New Zealand and 10 were enrolled in university and vocational training courses in Australia, New Zealand and Fiji.

DIPLOMATIC REPRESENTATIVE

Of Great Britain in Nauru
High Commisioner: R. A. R. Barltrop, CVO. (resides in Suva).

Books of Reference

Text of Trusteeship Agreement. (Cmd. 7290; Treaty Series No. 89, 1947)
Packett, C. N., *Guide to the Republic of Nauru.* Bradford, 1970
Pittman, G. A., *Nauru, the Phosphate Island.* London, 1959
Viviani, N., *Phosphate and Political Progress.* Canberra, 1970

NEPÁL

Sri Nepala Sarkar

Capital: Káthmándu
Population: 16·10m. (1982)
GNP per capita: US$140 (1980)

HISTORY. From 1846 to 1951 Nepál was virtually ruled by the Ráná family, a member of which always held the office of prime minister, the succession being determined by special rules. The last Ráná prime minister (and, until 18 Feb. 1951, Supreme C.-in-C.) was HH Máhárája Mohan Shumsher Jung Bahádur Ráná, who resigned in Nov. 1951.

AREA AND POPULATION. Nepál, situated between 26° 20′ and 30° 10′ N. lat. and between 80° 15′ and 88° 15′ E. long., is bounded on the north by Tibet, on the east by Sikkim and West Bengal, on the south and west by Bihar and Uttar Pradesh. On 5 Oct. 1961 a treaty was signed in Peking, according to which the Chinese–Nepalese boundary line 'runs generally south-eastwards along the mountain ridge, passing through Cho Oyu mountain, Pumoli mountain, Mount Chomo Lungma (the Chinese name for Everest) and Lhotse Too Makalu mountain'. Nepál gained about 300 sq. miles of territory. Area 56,136 sq. miles (145,391 sq. km); population (estimate, 1982), 16·10m.; (census, 1981) 15,020,451 of whom 52·5% were Nepali-speaking and 18·5% Bihari-speaking.

Capital, Káthmándu, 75 miles from the Indian frontier; population about 195,260. Other towns (1971) include Pátan (also called Lalitpur), 48,577; Moráng (Biratnagar), 44,938; Bhádgáon (Bhaktapur), 40,112.

The aboriginal stock is Mongolian with a considerable admixture of Hindu blood from India. They were originally divided into numerous hill clans and petty principalities, one of which, Gorkha or Gurkha, became predominant in 1559 and has since given its name to men from all parts of Nepál. The 15 feudal chieftainships were integrated into the kingdom on 10 April 1961.

The country is administratively divided into 14 zones and 75 development districts.

CLIMATE. The rainfall is high, with maximum amounts from May to Sept., but conditions are very dry from Nov. to Jan. The range of temperature is moderate. Káthmándu. Jan. 50°F (10°C), July 76°F (24·4°C). Annual rainfall 57″ (1,428 mm).

RULING KING. The sovereign is HM Mahárájádhirája **Birendra Bir Bikram Sháh Dev**, who succeeded his father Mahendra Bir Bikram Sháh Dev on 31 Jan. 1972.

CONSTITUTION AND GOVERNMENT. On 18 Feb. 1951 the King proclaimed a constitutional monarchy, and on 16 Dec. 1962 a new Constitution of the 'Constitutional Monarchical Hindu State'. The village and town *panchayat*, recognized as the basic units of democracy, elect the district *panchayat*, these elect the zonal *panchayat*, and these finally the 112 members of the national *panchayat*. The Constitution was amended in 1975. In addition, 28 representatives of professional organizations and royal nominees not exceeding 15% of the elected members, will be included in the national *panchayat*. The executive power is vested in the King, who appoints a council of ministers from the national *panchayat*. A state council will advise the King and proclaim the successor or, if the heir is a minor, a regency council. Art. 81 empowers the King to declare a state of emergency and to suspend the Constitution.

The Cabinet appointed in July 1983 was as follows:

Prime Minister: Lokendra Bahadur Chand.
Parliament and Local Development: Jog Mehar Shrestha. *Home Affairs:* Padma Sunder Lawati. *Water Resources and Supply:* Pashupati Shumsher Rana. *Agricul-*

ture and Land Reform: Hem Bahadur Malla. *Commerce, Industry and Health:* Narayan Dutta Bhatta. *Law and Justice:* Bakhan Singh Gurung. *Foreign Affairs:* Padma Bahadur Khatri. *Public Works and Transport:* Damber Narayan Yadau. *Finance and Communications:* Prakash Chandra Lohani.
There were also 4 Ministers of State and 7 Assistant Ministers.

National flag: Two triangular parts of red, with a blue border all round, bearing symbols of the moon and the sun in white.
National anthem: 'May glory crown our illustrious sovereign' (1952).

DEFENCE

Army. The Army consists of 6 infantry brigades, and single artillery, engineer, signals, parachute and transport battalions, and 1 air squadron. Equipment includes AMX-13 light tanks. Strength (1984) about 25,000, and there is also a 15,000-strong paramilitary police force.

Air Force. Independent of the army since 1979, the Air Force has 2 Skyvan transport aircraft, 1 Puma helicopter and 2 Alouette III helicopters. An H.S. 748 turboprop transport and a Puma helicopter are operated by the Royal Flight.

INTERNATIONAL RELATIONS

Membership. Nepál is a member of UN and the Colombo Plan.

ECONOMY

Planning. The fifth plan ran from 1975 to 1980. Its cost was estimated at NRs 10,110m. Priority was given to transport, communications, power, agriculture, irrigation, training of technicians and schools.

Budget. The general budget for the fiscal year 1982–83 envisages total expenditure of NRs 9,200m. Revenues are estimated at NRs 4,000m.

Currency. The Nepalese *rupee* is 171 grains in weight, as compared with the Indian rupee, which weighs 180 grains. The rate of exchange is 135 Nepalese rupees for 100 Indian rupees. 100 Nepalese *pice* = 1 Nepalese rupee. Coins of all denominations are minted. The Rástra Bank also issues notes of 1, 5, 10, 100 and 1,000 rupees. In March 1984, US$1 = 15·75 *rupees;* £1 = 23·40 *rupees.*

ENERGY AND NATURAL RESOURCES

Electricity. Production (1981) 232 kwh. A hydro-electric power scheme costing US$120m. was inaugurated in Dec. 1982.

Agriculture. Nepál has valuable forests in the southern part of the country. In the northern part, on the slopes of the Himálayas, there grow large quantities of medicinal herbs which find a world-wide market. Of the total area, nearly one-third (11·2m. acres) is under forest; 5·4m. acres is covered by perpetual snow; 9·6m. acres is under paddy, 2·9m. maize and millet, 800,000 wheat. Production (1982 in 1,000 tonnes): Rice, 2,560; maize, 752; wheat, 526; sugar-cane, 590; potatoes, 320; millet, 122.
Livestock (1982): Cattle, 6·95m., including about 435,000 cows; 4·25m. buffaloes; sheep, 2·37m.; goats, 2·52m.; pigs, 360,000; poultry, 22·5m.

INDUSTRY AND TRADE

Industry. Industries, such as jute- and sugar-mills, match, leather, cigarette, and shoe factories, and chemical works have been established, including two industrial estates at Pátan and Balaju. Production (1982 in 1,000 tonnes): Jute goods, 15·7; sugar, 21·1; cement, 30; iron goods, 7·4.

Commerce. The principal articles of export are food grains, jute, timber, oilseeds. ghee (clarified butter), potatoes, medicinal herbs, hides and skins, cattle. The chief imports are textiles, cigarettes, salt, petrol and kerosene, sugar, machinery, medicines, boots and shoes, paper, cement, iron and steel, tea.

Imports and exports in NRs 1,000:

	1979	1980	1981	1982
Imports	3,509,600	3,911,700	4,332,400	4,930,000
Exports	1,136,900	964,200	1,797,500	1,492,000

Total trade between Nepál and UK (British Department of Trade returns, in £1,000 sterling):

	1978	1979	1980	1981	1982	1983
Imports to UK	642	1,591	2,253	2,324	3,844	6,115
Exports and re-exports from UK	1,572	5,096	2,956	2,980	4,650	5,011

Tourism. There were 148,789 tourists in 1980.

COMMUNICATIONS

Roads. With the co-operation of India and the USA 900 miles of motorable roads are being constructed, including the East-West Highway through southern Nepál. A road from the Tibetan border to Káthmándu was recently completed with Chinese aid.

There are about 1,300 miles motorable roads. A ropeway for the carriage of goods covers the 14 miles from Dhursing above Bhimphedi into the Káthmándu valley.

A road connects Káthmándu with Birgung.

Railways. Railways (762 mm gauge) connect Jayanagar on the North Eastern Indian Railway with Janakpur and thence with Bijulpura (54 km).

Aviation. The Royal Nepál Airline Corporation has linked Káthmándu, the capital, with 11 districts of Nepál; and 23 more airfields are under construction. The Royal Nepalese Airline Corporation has services between Káthmándu and Calcutta, Patna, New Delhi, Bangkok, Rangoon and Dacca, employing Boeing 727 jet aircraft.

Post and Broadcasting. Káthmándu is connected by telephone with Birganj and Raxaul (North Eastern Indian Railway) on the southern frontier with Bihar; and with the eastern part of the Terai foothills; an extension to the western districts is being completed. Number of telephones (1978) 9,425, of which 5,431 were in Káthmándu. Under an agreement with India and the USA, a network of 91 wireless stations exists in Nepál, with further stations in Calcutta and New Delhi. Radio Nepál at Káthmándu broadcasts in Nepáli and English. Wireless telecommunication was inaugurated on 1 Oct. 1964.

All post, telephone and telegraph services have been taken over from India. The Indian, originally English, post office, established 1816, closed on 13 April 1965.

JUSTICE, RELIGION, EDUCATION AND WELFARE

Justice. The Supreme Court Act, established a uniform judicial system, culminating in a supreme court of a Chief Justice and no more than 6 judges. Special courts to deal with minor offences may be established at the discretion of the Government.

Religion. Sánáton of Pauranic, *i.e.*, traditional or ancient Hinduism, and Buddhism are the religions of the bulk of the people. Christian missions are admitted, but conversion is forbidden.

The royal family is Hindu.

Education. In 1979 there were 9,886 primary schools, 3,705 secondary schools, 98 colleges and the Tribhuvan University (founded 1960).

About 20% of the population are literate. The national language is Nepáli.

Health. There were about 420 doctors and 2,586 hospital beds in 1979.

DIPLOMATIC REPRESENTATIVES

Of Nepál in Great Britain (12a Kensington Palace Gdns., London, W8 4QU) *Ambassador:* Ishwari Raj Pandey (accredited 4 Aug. 1983).

Of Great Britain in Nepál (Láincháur, Káthmándu)
Ambassador: A. G. Hurrell.

Of Nepál in the USA (2131 Leroy Pl. NW, Washington, D.C., 20008)
Ambassador: Bhekh Bahadar Thapa.

Of the USA in Nepál (PaniPokhari, Káthmándu)
Ambassador: Carleton S. Coon.

Of Nepál to the United Nations
*Ambassador:*Uddhav Deo Bhatt.

Books of Reference

Statistical Information: A Department of Statistics was set up in Káthmándu in 1950.

Baral, L. S., *Political Development in Nepal.* London,1980
Bezruchka, S., *A Guide to Trekking in Nepal.* Leicester, 1981
Turner, R. L., *Nepali Dictionary.* 1980.
Wadhwa, D. N., *Nepal.* [Bibliography] Oxford and Santa Barbara, 1983

THE NETHERLANDS

Capital: Amsterdam
Seat of Government: The Hague
Population: 14·31m. (1982)
GNP per capita: US$11,470 (1980)

Koninkrijk der Nederlanden

HISTORY. William of Orange (1533–84), as the German count of Nassau, inherited vast possessions in the Netherlands and the Princedom of Orange in France. He was the initiator of the struggle for independence from Spain (1568–1648); in the Republic of the United Netherlands he and his successors became the 'first servants of the Republic' with the title of 'Stadhouder' (governor). In 1689 William III acceded to the throne of England, becoming joint sovereign with Mary II, his wife. William III died in 1702 without issue, and after a stadhouderless period a member of the Frisian branch of Orange–Nassau was nominated hereditary stadhouder in 1747; but his successor, Willem V, had to take refuge in England, in 1795, at the invasion of the French Army. In Nov. 1813 the United Provinces were freed from French domination.

The Congress of Vienna joined the Belgian provinces, the 'Austrian Netherlands' before the French Revolution, to the Northern Netherlands. The son of the former stadhouder Willem V was proclaimed King of the Netherlands at The Hague on 16 March 1815 as Willem I. The union was dissolved by the Belgian revolution of 1830, and the treaty of London, 19 April 1839, constituted Belgium an independent kingdom.

Netherlands Sovereigns

Willem I	1815–1840 (died 1843)	Wilhelmina	1890–1948 (died 1962)
Willem II	1840–1849	Juliana	1948–1980
Willem III	1849–1890	Beatrix	1980–

AREA AND POPULATION. The Netherlands is bounded north and west by the North Sea, south by Belgium and east by the Federal Republic of Germany. Growth of census population:

1829	2,613,298	1909	5,858,175	1960	11,461,964
1849	3,056,879	1920	6,865,314	1971	13,060,115
1869	3,579,529	1930	7,935,565		
1889	4,511,415	1947	9,625,499		

Area, density and estimated population on 1 Jan. 1973 and 1983:

Province	Land area (in sq. km) 1983	Population 1973	Population 1983	Density per sq. km 1983
Groningen	2,334·47	530,361	560,708	240
Friesland	3,352·43	539,222	595,248	178
Drenthe	2,653·54	386,400	424,720	160
Overijssel	3,811·28	956,343	1,038,369	272
Gelderland	5,008·62	1,580,041	1,727,487	345
Utrecht	1,331·39	838,435	923,182	693
Noord-Holland	2,667·40	2,283,414	2,308,047	865
Zuid-Holland	2,907·47	3,018,905	3,129,913	1,076
Zeeland	1,786·70	319,392	354,863	199
Noord-Brabant	4,963·76	1,879,848	2,093,969	422
Limburg	2,171·50	1,030,235	1,080,516	498
Dronten [1]	332·56	13,651	21,519	65
Lelystad [1]	229·30	—	52,251	228

[1] Dronten and Lelystad are municipalities and have not been incorporated into any province.

879

Province	Land area (in sq. km) 1983	Population 1973	1983	Density per sq. km 1983
Zuideijke				
Ijsselmeerpolders [1]	386·90	8,447	27,483	71
Central Register of				
population [2]	—	2,929	1,276	—
Total	33,938·57 [3]	13,387,623	14,339,551	423

[1] The Zuidelijke Ijsselmeerpolders (drained in 1957) are part of the former Zuiderzee, now called Ijsselmeer; they have not been incorporated into any province.

[2] The Central population register includes persons who are residents of the Netherlands but who have no fixed residence in any particular municipality (living in caravans and houseboats, population on inland vessels, etc.).

[3] Including 1·25 sq. km not municipally classified.

Of the total population on 1 Jan. 1982, 7,081,566 were males, 7,204,263 females.

The total area of the Netherlands is 41,548 sq. km (16,042 sq. miles), of which 33,930 sq. km (13,100 sq. miles) is land area.

On 14 June 1918 a law was passed concerning the reclamation of the Zuiderzee. The work was begun in 1920; the following sections have been completed: 1. The Noordholland–Wieringen Barrage (2·5 km), 1924; 2. The Wieringermeer Polder (210 sq. km), 1930 (inundated by the Germans in 1945, but drained again in the same year); 3. The Wieringen–Friesland Barrage (30 km), 1932; 4. The Noordoost Polder (501 sq. km), 1942; 5. Oost Flevoland (604 sq. km), 1957; 6. Zuidelijk Flevoland (499 sq. km), 1967.

The polder Markerwaard (400 sq. km) is being reclaimed. A portion of what used to be the Zuiderzee behind the barrage will remain a fresh-water lake: Ijsselmeer (1,400 sq. km). The 'Delta-project', scheduled to be completed in the 1980s, comprises the building of (semi) enclosure dams in the estuaries between the islands in the south-western part of the country, excluding the sea-entrances to the ports of Rotterdam and Antwerp; it will also create fresh-water reservoirs. *See* map in THE STATESMAN'S YEAR-BOOK, 1959.

Vital statistics for calendar years:

	Live births Total	Illegitimate	Still births	Marriages	Divorces	Deaths	Net migration
1980	181,294	7,454	1,205	90,182	25,735	114,279	+ 53,034
1981	178,569	8,609	1,122	85,574	28,509	115,515	+ 16,988
1982	172,071	10,080	1,010	83,516	30,877	117,264	+ 3,233

Population of principal municipalities on 1 Jan. 1983:

Achtkarspelen	26,989	Dordrecht	107,612	Den Helder	63,660
Alkmaar	80,992	Ede (Gld.)	85,894	Hellendoorn	33,363
Almelo	63,080	Eindhoven	194,552	Hellevoetsluis	29,428
Alphen a/d Rijn	53,561	Emmen	90,828	Helmond	59,354
Amersfoort	87,461	Enschede	144,897	Hengelo (O.)	76,532
Amstelveen	68,894	Epe	33,386	's-Hertogenbosch	89,470
Amsterdam	687,397	Etten-Leur	30,174	Hilversum	89,518
Apeldoorn	143,178	Geldrop	26,600	Hoogeveen	44,774
Arnhem	128,598	Geleen	35,319	Hoogezand-	
Assen	45,906	Goes	30,852	Sappemeer	35,253
Barneveld	37,971	Gorinchem	28,021	Hoorn	46,824
Bergen op Zoom	45,178	Gouda	59,179	Huizen	33,614
Beverwijk	35,238	's-Gravenhage	449,338	Kampen	31,581
de Bilt	31,976	Groningen	166,942	Katwijk	38,604
Breda	118,819	Haarlem	154,347	Kerkrade	53,353
Brunssum	29,735	Haarlemmermeer	82,261	Krimpen a/d Ijssel	28,142
Bussum	33,941	Hardenberg	31,677	Landgraaf	39,513
Capelle a/d Ijssel	51,401	Harderwijk	32,284	Leeuwarden	85,055
Delft	86,278	Heemskerk	31,753	Leiden	103,819
Delfzijl	25,055	Heemstede	25,785	Leidschendam	30,239
Deurne	28,352	Heerenveen	37,390	Lelystad	52,251
Deventer	64,455	Heerhugowaard	33,932	Maarssen	32,225
Doetinchem	38,585	Heerlen	92,162	Maassluis	33,291

Maastricht	112,605	Schiedam	71,280	Venlo	62,567
Middelburg	38,709	Sittard	43,764	Venray	33,833
Naaldwijk	25,869	Smallingerland	50,402	Vlaardingen	77,072
Nieuwegein	52,282	Sneek	28,545	Vlissingen	46,382
Noordoostpolder	37,885	Soest	40,463	Voorburg	42,577
Nijmegen	147,139	Spijkenisse	51,437	Waalwijk	28,961
Oldenzaal	28,747	Stadskanaal	34,262	Wageningen	31,638
Oosterhout	45,446	Stein	26,379	Wassenaar	27,025
Opsterland	26,145	Terneuzen	35,440	Weert	39,293
Oss	49,392	Tiel	29,742	Winterswijk	27,674
Papendrecht	25,665	Tietjerksteradeel	29,677	Woerden	25,060
Purmerend	41,711	Tilburg	153,893	Wychen	25,983
Raalte	25,311	Uden	33,500	Zaanstad	129,341
Renkum	33,828	Utrecht	231,769	Zeist	61,329
Rheden	48,506	Valkenswaard	27,936	Zevenaar	26,812
Ridderkerk	47,108	Veendam	28,486	Zoetermeer	74,853
Roermond	38,126	Veenendaal	42,320	Zutphen	31,495
Roosendaal	55,968	Veghel	25,107	Zwolle	86,388
Rotterdam	558,832	Veldhoven	35,190	Zwijndrecht	39,795
Rijswijk (Z.-H.)	50,514	Velsen	59,118		

Urban agglomerations as at 1 Jan. 1983: Rotterdam, 1,024,702; Amsterdam, 936,410; The Hague, 674,546; Utrecht, 498,877; Eindhoven, 373,877; Arnhem, 290,746; Heerlen-Kerkrade, 264,988; Enschede-Hengelo, 247,759; Nijmegen, 229,408; Tilburg, 220,852; Haarlem, 219,350; Groningen, 205,659; Dordrecht-Zwijndrecht, 198,600; 's-Hertogenbosch, 186,628; Geleen-Sittard, 177,504; Leiden, 175,457; Maastricht, 156,478; Breda, 153,484; Zaanstad, 141,351; Velsen-Beverwijk, 126,109; Hilversum, 106,779.

CLIMATE. A cool temperate maritime climate, marked by mild winters and cool summers, but with occasional continental influences. Coastal temperatures vary from 37°F (3°C) in winter to 61°F (16°C) in summer, but inland the winters are slightly colder and the summers slightly warmer, Rainfall is least in the months Feb. to May, but inland there is a well-defined summer maximum in July and Aug.

The Hague, Jan. 37°F (2·7°C), July 61°F (16·3°C). Annual rainfall 32·8" (820 mm). Amsterdam, Jan. 36°F (2·3°C), July 62°F (16·5°C). Annual rainfall 34" (850 mm). Rotterdam, Jan. 36·5°F (2·6°C), July 62°F (16·6°C). Annual rainfall 32" (800 mm).

REIGNING QUEEN. Beatrix Wilhelmina Armgard, born 31 Jan. 1938 daughter of Queen Juliana and Prince Bernhard; married to Claus von Amsberg on 10 March 1966; succeeded to the crown on 1 May 1980, on the abdication of her mother. *Offspring:* Prince Willem-Alexander, born 27 April 1967; Prince Johan Friso, born 25 Sept. 1968; Prince Constantijn, born 11 Oct. 1969.

Mother of the Queen: Queen Juliana Louise Emma Marie Wilhelmina, born 30 April 1909, daughter of Queen Wilhelmina (born 31 Aug. 1880, died 28 Nov. 1962) and Prince Henry of Mecklenburg-Schwerin (born 19 April 1876, died 3 July 1934); married to Prince Bernhard Leopold Frederick Everhard Julius Coert Karel Godfried Pieter of Lippe-Biesterfeld (born 29 June 1911) on 7 Jan. 1937. Abdicated in favour of her daughter, the Reigning Queen, on 30 April 1980.

Sisters of the Queen: Princess Irene Emma Elisabeth, born 5 Aug. 1939, married to Prince Charles Hugues de Bourbon-Parma on 29 April 1964, divorced 1981 (*sons:* Prince Carlos Javier Bernardo, born 27 Jan. 1970; Prince Jaime Bernardo, born 13 Oct. 1972; *daughters:* Princess Margarita Maria Beatriz, born 13 Oct. 1972; Princess Maria Carolina Christina, born 23 June 1974); Princess Margriet Francisca, born in Ottawa, 19 Jan. 1943, married to Pieter van Vollenhoven on 10 Jan. 1967 (*sons:* Prince Maurits, born 17 April 1968; Prince Bernhard, born 25 Dec. 1969; Prince Pieter-Christiaan, born 22 March 1972; Prince Floris, born 10 April 1975); Princess Maria Christina, born 18 Feb. 1947, married to Jorge Guillermo on 28 June 1975 (*sons:* Bernardo, born 17 June 1977; Nicolas Daniel Mauricio, born 6 July 1979; *daughter:* Juliana, born 8 Oct. 1981).

CONSTITUTION AND GOVERNMENT. According to the Constitution of the Kingdom of the Netherlands, the Kingdom consists of the Netherlands and the Netherlands Antilles. Their relations are regulated by the 'Statute' for the Kingdom, which came into force on 29 Dec. 1954. Each part enjoys full autonomy; they are united, on a footing of equality, for mutual assistance and the protection of their common interests.

The first Constitution of the Netherlands after its restoration as a Sovereign State was promulgated in 1814. It was revised in 1815 (after the addition of the Belgian provinces, and the assumption by the Sovereign of the title of King), 1840 (after the secession of the Belgian provinces), 1848, 1884, 1887, 1917, 1922, 1938, 1946, 1948, 1953, 1956, 1963, 1972 and 1983.

The Netherlands is a constitutional and hereditary monarchy. The royal succession is in the direct male or female line in the order of primogeniture. The Sovereign comes of age on reaching his 18th year. During his minority the royal power is vested in a Regent—designated by law—and in some cases in the Council of State.

The central executive power of the State rests with the Crown, while the central legislative power is vested in the Crown and Parliament (the *Staten-Generaal*), consisting of 2 Chambers. After the 1956 revision of the Constitution the Upper or First Chamber is composed of 75 members, elected by the members of the Provincial States, and the Second Chamber consists of 150 deputies, who are elected directly from all Netherlands nationals who are aged 18 or over on polling day. Members of the States-General must be Netherlanders or recognized as Netherlands subjects and 21 years of age or over; they may be men or women. They receive an allowance.

First Chamber (as constituted in 1983): Labour Party, 17; Christian Democratic Appeal, 26; People's Party for Freedom and Democracy, 17; Democrats '66, 6; Party of Political Radicals, 1; Communist Party, 2; Pacifist Socialist Party, 2; Calvinist Party, 2; Reformed Political Federation, 1; Calvinist Political Union, 1.

Second Chamber (elected on 8 Sept. 1982): Labour Party, 47; Christian Democratic Appeal, 45; People's Party for Freedom and Democracy, 36; Democrats '66, 6; Communist Party, 3; Party of Political Radicals, 2; Pacifist Socialist Party, 3; Calvinist Party, 3; Reformed Political Federation, 2; Calvinist Political Union, 1; Evangelical People's Party, 1; Conservative Nationalist Party, 1.

The revised Constitution of 1917 has introduced an electoral system based on universal suffrage and proportional representation. Under its provisions, members of the Second Chamber are directly elected by citizens of both sexes who are Netherlands subjects not under 18 years (since 1972).

The members of the First Chamber and of the Second Chamber are elected for 4 years, and retire in a body. The Sovereign has the power to dissolve both Chambers of Parliament, or one of them, subject to the condition that new elections take place within 40 days, and the new House or Houses be convoked within 3 months.

Both the Government and the Second Chamber may propose Bills; the First Chamber can only approve or reject them without inserting amendments. The meetings of both Chambers are public, though each of them may by a majority vote decide on a secret session. It is a fixed custom, that Ministers and Secretaries of State, on their own initiative or upon invitation of the Parliament, attend the sessions to defend their policy, their budget, their proposals of Bills, etc., when these are in discussion. A Minister or Secretary of State, however, cannot be a member of Parliament at the same time.

The Constitution can be revised only by a Bill declaring that there is reason for introducing such revision and containing the proposed alterations. The passing of this Bill is followed by a dissolution of both Chambers and a second confirmation by the new States-General by two-thirds of the votes. Unless it is expressly stated, all laws concern only the realm in Europe, and not the oversea part of the kingdom, the Netherlands Antilles.

Every act of the Sovereign has to be covered by a responsible Minister.

The Ministry, a coalition of Christian Democrats and Liberals, was composed as follows in Nov. 1982:

Prime Minister: Ruud Lubbers (CDA).

Deputy Prime Minister and Economic Affairs: Gijs van Aardenne (VVD). *Foreign Affairs:* Hans van den Broek (CDA). *Finance:* Dr Herman Ruding (CDA). *Defence:* Jacob de Ruiter (CDA). *Development Aid Co-operation:* Eegje Schoo (VVD). *Social Affairs and Employment:* Jan de Koning (CDA). *Home Affairs:* Koos Rietkerk (VVD). *Justice:* Frits Korthals Altes (VVD). *Agriculture and Fisheries:* Gerrit Braks (CDA). *Welfare, Public Health and Culture:* Elco Brinkman (CDA). *Education and Science:* Wim Deetman (CDA). *Transport and Public Works:* Neelie Smit-Kroes (VVD). *Housing, Physical Planning and Environment:* Pieter Winsemius (VVD).

There are also 16 state secretaries.

The Council of State *(Raad van State)*, appointed and presided over by the Sovereign, is composed of a vice-president and not more than 28 members. It can be consulted on all legislative matters. Decisions of the Crown in administrative disputes are prepared by a special section of the Council.

The Hague is the seat of the Court, Government and Parliament; Amsterdam is the capital.

National flag: Three horizontal stripes of red, white, blue.

National anthem: Wilhelmus van Nassoue (words by Philip Marnix van St Aldegonde, c. 1570).

Local Government. The kingdom is divided in 11 provinces and about 770 municipalities. The creation of more provinces by splitting up the most densely populated provinces and creation of a new province in the Zuiderzee area is in preparation. Each province has its own representative body, the Provincial States. The members must be 21 years of age or over; they are elected for 4 years, directly from the Netherlands inhabitants of the province who are 18 years of age or over. The electoral register is the same as for the Second Chamber. The members retire in a body and are subject to re-election. The number of members varies according to the population of the province, from 83 for Zuid-Holland to 43 for Zeeland. The Provincial States are entitled to issue ordinances concerning the welfare of the province, and to raise taxes pursuant to legal provisions. The provincial budgets and the provincial ordinances and resolutions relating to provincial property, loans, taxes, etc., must be approved by the Crown. The members of the Provincial States elect the First Chamber of the States-General. They meet twice a year, as a rule in public. A permanent commission composed of 6 of their members, called the 'Deputy States', is charged with the executive power and, if required, with the enforcement of the law in the province. Deputy as well as Provincial States are presided over by a Commissioner of the Queen, appointed by the Crown, who in the former assembly has a deciding vote, but attends the latter in only a deliberative capacity. He is the chief magistrate in the province. The Commissioner and the members of the Deputy States receive an allowance.

Each municipality forms a Corporation with its own interests and rights, subject to the general law, and is governed by a Municipal Council, directly elected from the Netherlands inhabitants of the municipality who are 18 years of age or over, for 4 years. All Netherlands inhabitants aged 21 or over are eligible, the number of members varying from 7 to 45, according to the population. The Municipal Council has the right to issue bye-laws concerning the communal welfare. The Council may levy taxes pursuant to legal provisions; these ordinances must be approved by the Crown. All bye-laws may be vetoed by the Crown. The Municipal Budget and resolutions to alienate municipal property require the approbation of the Deputy States of the province. The Council meets in public as often as may be necessary, and is presided over by a Burgomaster, appointed by the Crown. The day-to-day administration is carried out by the Burgomaster and 2–7 Aldermen *(wethouders)*, elected by and from the Council; this body is also charged with the enforcement of the law. The Burgomaster may suspend the execution of a resolution of the council for 30 days, but is bound to notify the Deputy States of the province. In maintaining public order, the Burgomaster acts as the chief of police. The Burgomaster and Aldermen receive allowances.

DEFENCE. The Netherlands are bordered on the south by Belgium, on the east by the Federal Republic of Germany. On both sides the country is quite level and has no natural defences, except the barriers of some large rivers, running east to west and south to north. The country has an excellent roadnet and a vast railway system, enabling rapid movement. The west part of the country is densely populated.

Army. Service is partly voluntary and partly compulsory; the voluntary enlistments bear a small proportion to the compulsory. The total peacetime strength amounts to 72,000, including Military Police. The number of regulars is 24,000. The Army also employs 13,000 civilians. The legal period of active service for national servicemen is 22–24 months; the actual service period is 14 months for other ranks and 16 months for reserve-officers and n.c.o.s. The balance may be spent at will as 'short leave'. After their period of actual service or short leave, conscript personnel are granted long leave. However, they will be liable to being called up for refresher training or in case of mobilization until they have reached the age of 35 (n.c.o.s 40, reserve officers 45).

The 1st Netherlands Army Corps is assigned to NATO. It consists of 10 brigades and Corps troops. The active part of the Corps comprises 2 armoured brigades and 4 armoured infantry brigades, grouped in two divisions and 40% of the Corps troops. Part of this force is stationed in the Federal Republic of Germany. The peacetime strength of the active brigades is 80% of the war-authorized strength.

The mobilizable part of the Corps comprises 1 armoured brigade, 2 armoured infantry brigades, 1 infantry brigade and the remaining Corps troops.

The mechanized brigades comprise tank battalions (Centurion and Leopard I), armoured infantry battalions (YP-408 and YPR-765), medium artillery battalions (155 mm self-propelled), armoured engineer units, armoured reconnaissance units and armoured anti armour units. The Corps troops comprise headquarters units, combat-support units, including Engineer and Corps artillery (203 mm, 155 mm and Lance) and service-support units. Helicopter squadrons are also available.

The National Territorial Command forces consist of territorial brigades, security forces, some logistical units and staffs. The major part of these units is mobilizable. Some units in the Netherlands are earmarked for assignment to the United Nations as peace-keeping forces. Since early 1979 an armoured infantry battalion, composed of regulars and conscripts, has been involved in the UN peace-keeping operations in Lebanon. For civil defence purposes there are a number of mobilizable fire-fighting, rescue and medical battalions. The army is responsible for the training of these units which in time of war are placed under the command of the National Commander of the Civil Defence.

Navy. The Royal Netherlands Navy has its main base in the Netherlands at Den Helder and minor bases at Flushing and Curaçao (Netherlands Antilles). The Ministry of Defence is located in The Hague.

Principal surface ships of the Royal Netherlands Navy:

Completed	Name	Normal displacement (tons)	Guided Missile launchers	Guns	Shaft horsepower	Max. speed (knots)
1975	Tromp		8 single Harpoon	2 4·7 in.		
1976	De Ruyter	4,500	1 single Tartar	(1 twin)	50,000	30
			1 octuple Sea Sparrow			

There are also 6 diesel-electric patrol submarines, 10 standard frigates, 6 general-purpose frigates, 2 fast combat support ships, 4 corvettes, 1 mine countermeasures support ship (ex-ocean minesweeper), 11 coastal minesweepers, 8 coastal mine-hunters, 3 diving vessels, 1 torpedo maintenance vessel (ex-ocean minesweeper), 5 patrol vessels, 3 hydrographic survey ships, 10 minor landing craft, 2 training ships, 12 tugs and 30 small auxiliary ships.

Two diesel-electric patrol submarines, 2 large frigates, 5 medium frigates, 5 coastal minehunters and 12 minor landing craft are under construction. The future construction programme includes two more diesel-electric patrol submarines.

In 1984 naval personnel provided for totalled 16,800 officers and other ranks, including the Naval Air Service, over 400 female ratings, and the Royal Netherlands Marine Corps.

The naval air service (1,700 personnel) maintains 13 Orion P3C, 5 Breguet

Atlantics (SP-13A), 17 Westland Lynx SH14B/C embarked and 5 Lynx UH 14A for SAR, utility and transport.

Naval estimates (in 1m. guilders): 1981, 2,218; 1982, 2,352; 1983, 2,446; 1984, 2,418.

Air Force. The Royal Netherlands Air Force was established 1 July 1913. Its current strength is approximately 17,500 personnel and it has a first-line combat force of 9 squadrons of aircraft and 14 squadrons of surface-to-air missiles. All squadrons are operated by Tactical Air Command. Aircraft operated are F-16 (4 squadrons for air defence and ground attack, 1 for tactical reconnaissance), and NF-5A/B fighter-bombers (4 squadrons, to re-equip with F-16s in 1985–89). Also under control of Tactical Air Command is 1 squadron of the USAF, flying F-15C Eagles in the air defence role. 3 squadrons of Alouette III and Bölkow BO 105C helicopters are under control of the Royal Netherlands Army, but flown and maintained by the RNethAF for use in the communications and observation roles. Also operated is 1 squadron of F.27 Friendship/Troopship transport aircraft, and another (based in Curaçao) with 2 F.27 maritime patrol aircraft.

Training of RNethAF pilots is undertaken in Canada and the USA. The surface-to-air missile force consists of 3 squadrons of Nike Hercules (high altitude) and 11 squadrons of Hawk (low and medium altitude).

INTERNATIONAL RELATIONS

Membership. The Netherlands is a member of UN, EEC, OECD, the Council of Europe and NATO.

ECONOMY

Budget. The revenue and expenditure of the central government (ordinary and extraordinary) were, in 1m. guilders, for calendar years:

	1977 [2]	1978 [2]	1979 [2]	1980 [3]	1981 [3]	1982 [4]	1983 [6]
Revenue [1]	83,902	92,262	98,810	107,162	110,809	113,892	115,498
Expenditure [5]	90,324	101,067	110,776	121,163	130,444	143,066	147,157

[1] Without the revenue of loans. [2] Accounts. [3] Preliminary accounts. [4] Revised budget figures. [5] Without redemption of loans. [6] Budget figures.

The revenue and expenditure of the Agriculture Equalization Fund, the Fund for Central Government roads, the Property Acquisition Fund (established in 1971), the Fund for the Development of a fast Breeder Reactor (established in 1972 but discontinued in 1978) and of the Investment Account Fund (established in 1978) have been incorporated in the general budget.

The national debt, in 1m. guilders, was on 31 Dec.:

	1978	1979	1980	1981	1982
Internal funded debt	55,180	64,086	78,090	96,830	122,777
,, floating ,,	17,356	20,314	21,433	21,629	21,878
Total	72,537	84,400	99,523	118,459	144,655

Currency. The monetary unit is the *gulden* (guilder, florin) of 100 *cents*. In March 1984 the rate of exchange was US\$1 = 2·94 guilders; £1 = 4·32 guilders.

Legal tender are bank-notes, silver 10-guilder pieces, nickel 2½- and 1-guilder pieces, 25-cent, 10-cent pieces, bronze 5-cent and 1-cent pieces. Note circulation, 31 Dec. 1980, 21,709m. guilders and 31 Dec. 1981, 21,895m.

Banking. The Netherlands Bank, founded as a private institution, was nationalized on 1 Aug. 1948, the shareholders receiving, for a share of 1,000 guilders, a security of 2,000 guilders on the 2½% National Debt. Since 1863 the bank has the sole right of issuing bank-notes. The bank does the same business as other banks, but with more guarantees. The capital amounts to 20m. guilders.

In the year 1981 the state post office savings bank had deposits of 5,935m. guilders and withdrawals of 5,919m. guilders. Private savings banks: Deposits, 17,777m. guilders; withdrawals, 17,322m. guilders.

Weights and Measures. The metric system of weights and measures was adopted in the Netherlands in 1820.

ENERGY AND NATURAL RESOURCES

Electricity. The total production of electrical energy (in 1m. kwh.) amounted in 1938 to 3,688; 1958, 13,854; 1970, 40,859; 1979, 64,464; 1980, 64,806; 1981, 64,053; 1982, 60,313.

Gas. Production of manufactured gas (milliard k joule): 1978, 181,033; 1979, 233,553; 1980, 210,011; 1981, 197,586. Production of natural gas in 1950, 8m. cu. metres; 1955, 139; 1960, 384; 1970, 31,688; 1979, 96,488; 1980, 91,153; 1981, 84,617; 1982, 72,035.

Minerals. On 1 Jan. 1975 all coalmines were closed.

The production of crude petroleum (in 1,000 tonnes) amounted in 1943 (first year) to 0·2; 1953, 820; 1970, 1,919; 1977, 1,382; 1978, 1,402; 1979, 1,316; 1980, 1,280; 1981, 1,348; 1982, 1,637.

There are saltmines at Hengelo and Delfzijl; production (in 1,000 tonnes), 1950, 412·6; 1960, 1,096; 1970, 2,871; 1977, 3,111; 1978, 2,939; 1979, 3,951; 1980, 3,464; 1981, 3,578; 1982, 3,191.

Agriculture. The net area of all holdings was divided as follows (in hectares):

	1979 [1]	1980 [1]	1981	1982 [1]	1983 [1]
Field crops	700,126	704,710	702,510	702,287	706,120
Grass	1,212,634	1,197,592	1,187,719	1,178,098	1,181,297
Market gardening	89,706	87,121	89,600	94,210	89,371
Land for flower bulbs	13,949	14,307	14,390	14,189	14,165
Flower cultivation	4,829	5,180	5,267	5,472	5,615
Nurseries	6,049	6,228	6,413	6,386	6,431
Fallow land	6,190	5,099	4,769	4,577	5,713
Total	2,033,483	2,020,237	2,010,668	2,005,219	2,008,712

[1] Excluding holdings of less than 10 SFU (SFU = standard farm unit). 10 SFU is equal to a computed net value added at factor cost of about 4,000 guilders, in 1975.

The net areas [1] under special crops were as follows (in hectares):

Products	1982	1983	Products	1982	1983
Autumn wheat	112,760	141,724	Colza	10,753	13,211
Spring wheat	18,123	6,535	Flax	3,178	3,193
Rye	5,938	6,660	Agricultural seeds	17,734	17,675
Autumn barley	6,590	10,199	Potatoes, edible [2]	100,856	100,998
Spring barley	37,088	27,275	Potatoes, industrial [3]	65,089	62,458
Oats	23,685	13,527	Sugar-beet	133,973	122,820
Peas	6,006	7,636	Fodder-beet	2,314	2,119

[1] Excluding non-agrarian holdings of less than 10 SFU.
[2] Including early and seed potatoes.
[3] Including seed potatoes.

The yield of the more important products, in tonnes, was as follows:

Crop	Average 1940–49	Average 1950–58	1981 [1]	1982 [1]	1983 [1]
Wheat	322,003	348,464	882,055	967,263	1,045,445
Rye	439,055	454,992	28,616	26,492	26,173
Barley	145,892	258,049	248,531	247,416	179,394
Oats	315,642	464,041	114,655	136,122	61,393
Field beans	15,799	5,693	1,184	2,418	...
Peas	65,460	93,664	15,297	28,153	30,781
Colza	24,763	18,358	37,205	33,336	36,687
Flax, unrippled	82,906	138,165	23,771	25,062	23,373
Potatoes, edible [2]	2,861,793	2,745,505	3,913,288	4,145,765	3,338,190
Potatoes, industrial	1,242,326	1,003,994	2,531,435	2,072,857	...
Sugar-beet	1,667,711	2,935,881	7,060,677	7,945,554	...
Fodder-beet	...	...	166,451	213,457	...

[1] Excluding holdings of less than 10 SFU.   [2] Including early potatoes.

Livestock, May 1983: 5,410,889 cattle, 10,656,113 pigs; 43,536 horses, 3 years old and over, 772,342 sheep, 82·2m. poultry.

In 1982 the production of butter, under state control, amounted to 217,539 tonnes; that of cheese, under state control, to 474,657 tonnes. Export value (processed and unprocessed) of arable crops amounted to 15,255m. guilders; animal produce, 17,942m. guilders and horticultural produce, 8,025m. guilders.

Fisheries. The total produce of fish landed from the sea and inshore fisheries in 1981 was valued at 595m. guilders; the total weight amounted to 399,438 tonnes. In 1981 the herring fishery had a value of 26m. guilders and a weight of 16,710 tonnes. The quantity of oysters produced in 1981 amounted to 573 tonnes (10m. guilders).

INDUSTRY AND TRADE

Industry. Numbers employed (in 1,000) and turnover (in 1m. guilders) in manufacturing enterprises with 10 employees and more, excluding building:

	Numbers employed		Turnover	
Class in industry	1980	1981[1]	1980	1981[1]
Mining and quarrying	7·5	7·8	21,870	29,500
Manufacturing industry	893·0	856·3	204,200	223,600
Foodstuffs and tobacco products	144·7	141·0	54,700	60,900
Textile industry	32·5	28·9	4,420	4,300
Clothing	17·4	14·0	1,810	1,600
Leather and footwear	7·9	7·1	810	800
Wood and furniture industry	34·5	30·7	4,320	4,000
Paper industry	25·9	23·9	4,910	5,300
Graphic industry, publishers	64·0	62·5	9,460	9,600
Petroleum industry	10·4	10·8	27,240	32,600
Chemical industry, artificial yarns and fibre industry	85·2	84·9	28,680	33,700
Rubber and synthetic materials processing industry	24·7	23·9	4,000	4,100
Building materials, earthenware and glass	37·6	35·0	5,660	5,500
Basic metal industry	36·5	35·9	7,850	8,600
Metals products (excl. machinery and means of transport)	83·8	79·1	10,560	10,400
Machinery	84·4	80·3	10,690	11,300
Electrical industry	117·1	112·8	17,410	17,900
Means of transport	72·0	71·7	10,180	11,400
Instrument making and optical industry	8·9	8·9	910	1,100
Other industries	5·6	5·3	610	600
Public utilities	46·4	47·0	15,780	19,200

[1] Preliminary.

Commerce. On 5 Sept. 1944 and 14 March 1947 the Netherlands signed agreements with Belgium and Luxembourg for the establishment of a customs union. On 1 Jan. 1948 this union came into force and the existing customs tariffs of the Belgium–Luxembourg Economic Union and of the Netherlands were superseded by the joint Benelux Customs Union Tariff. It applies to imports into the 3 countries from outside sources, and exempts from customs duties all imports into each of the 3 countries from the other two. The Benelux tariff has 991 items and 2,400 separate specifications.

Returns of special imports and special exports (including parcel post and diamond trade, excluding unrefined and partly-worked gold, gold coins and coins in current circulation made of other metal) for calendar years (in 1,000 guilders):

	Imports	Exports		Imports	Exports
1949	5,331,569	3,851,126	1979[1]	134,885,386	127,689,416
1959	14,968,454	13,702,927	1980[1]	152,279,265	146,967,410
1969	39,955,406	36,205,110	1981[1]	163,998,929	170,772,393
1978[1]	114,371,926	108,205,427	1982[1]	167,116,253	176,851,097

[1] Including unrefined and partly-worked gold and gold coins.

Value of the trade (including parcel post and diamond trade, excluding unrefined and partly-worked gold, gold coins and coins in current circulation made of other metal) with leading countries (in 1,000 guilders):

Country	Imports 1980	1981	1982	Exports 1980	1981	1982
Belgium–Luxembourg	17,736,654	18,627,846	18,312,904	22,078,294	24,486,748	25,092,899
France	10,232,238	10,535,248	10,865,041	15,508,812	17,860,028	18,404,759
Germany (Fed. Rep.)	33,943,703	35,202,710	37,022,529	44,004,257	50,272,569	52,188,052
Indonesia	544,226	582,710	419,327	929,156	678,251	601,520
Italy	4,819,585	4,892,484	5,087,217	8,477,334	9,543,802	9,766,040
Kuwait	2,785,330	2,506,535	1,131,699	204,449	344,519	318,363
Sweden	2,824,146	2,956,972	3,217,048	2,579,750	2,541,386	3,172,025
UK	12,465,829	14,003,953	15,723,378	11,575,763	14,112,136	16,359,875
USA	13,433,621	15,567,121	15,323,775	3,685,728	5,495,426	5,741,457
Venezuela	346,677	424,431	402,348	268,149	352,819	479,623

Total trade between the Netherlands and UK (British Department of Trade returns, in £1,000 sterling):

	1979	1980	1981	1982	1983
Imports to UK	3,446,271	3,406,928	3,895,486	4,474,663	5,097,673
Exports and re-exports from UK	3,062,642	3,845,412	4,019,435	4,653,416	5,440,701

Tourism. There were 3,080,200 foreign visitors in 1982 (hotels and boarding houses only). 604,600 came from the Federal Republic of Germany, 590,200 from UK and 427,900 from USA. Total income from tourism (1980) US$1,640m.

COMMUNICATIONS

Roads. In 1981 the length of the Netherlands network of surfaced inter-urban roads was 53,222 km, of which 1,749 km were motor highways. Number of private cars (1982), 4·6m.

Railways. All railways are run by the mixed company 'N.V. Nederlandsche Spoorwegen'. Length of line in 1982 was 2,956 km, of which 1,799 km were electrified. Passengers carried (1982), 209m.; goods transported, 18·2m. tonnes.

Aviation. The Royal Dutch Airlines (KLM) was founded on 7 Oct. 1919. The company has a paid-up capital of 704m. guilders (1982–83). Revenue traffic, 1982–83: Passengers, 4·6m.; freight, 240m. kg; mail, 12m. kg.

Sea-going Shipping. Survey of the Netherlands mercantile marine as at 1 Jan. (capacity in 1,000 GRT):

Ships under Netherlands flag (including Netherlands Antilles)	1982 Number	Capacity	1983 Number	Capacity
Passenger ships [1]	9	144	9	122
Freighters (500 GRT and over)	457	2,524	474	2,641
Freighters (under 500 GRT)	64	27	62	26
Tankers	87	2,331	84	2,008
	617	5,026	629	4,796

[1] With accommodation for 13 or more cabin passengers.

In 1982, 44,169 sea-going ships of 337·4m. gross tons entered Netherlands ports (1981, 42,132 ships of 330m. gross tons).

Total goods traffic by sea-going ships in 1982 (with 1981 figures in brackets), in 1m. tonnes, amounted to 241·7 (245·3) unloaded, of which 118·4 (116·7) tankshipping, and 75·7 (74·9) loaded, of which 31·7 (28·9) tankshipping. The total seaborne freight traffic at Rotterdam was 246m. (250·3m.) and at Amsterdam 23·7m. (21·3m.) tonnes.

The number of containers at Rotterdam in 1982 was: unloaded from ships, 738,596, of which 193,607 from North America, and 753,618 loaded into ships, of which 111,776 to North America.

Inland Shipping. The total length of navigable rivers and canals is 4,387 km, of which about 1,974 km is for ships with a capacity of 1,000 and more tonnes. On 1

Jan. 1983 the Netherlands inland fleet actually used for transport (with carrying capacity in 1,000 tonnes) was composed as follows:

	Number	Capacity
Self-propelled barges	5,534	3,817
Dumb barges	486	469
Pushed barges	441	941
	6,461	5,227

In 1982, 241m. (1981: 254m.) tonnes of goods were transported on rivers and canals, of which 173m. (172m.) was international traffic. Goods transport on the Rhine across the Dutch–German frontier near Lobith amounted to 124m. (123m.) tonnes.

Post and Broadcasting. On 1 Jan. 1983 there were 5·3m. telephone connexions (37 per 100 inhabitants). Number of telex lines, 36,000; teleprinters, 38,000. *Nederlandse Omroep Stichting* (NOS) provides 4 programmes on medium-waves and FM in co-operation with broadcasting organizations. Regional programmes are also broadcast.

Advertisements are transmitted. NOS broadcasts 2 TV programmes. Advertisements, in the last quarter of 1980, were restricted to 4% of the transmission time in the evening. Television sets (1 Jan. 1983) totalled 4·4m.; holders of television licences may, in addition, have wireless receiving sets.

Cinemas (end 1982). There were 557 cinemas with a seating capacity of 152,000.

Newspapers (31 Dec. 1982). There were 83 daily newspapers with a total circulation of over 4·5m.

JUSTICE, RELIGION, EDUCATION AND WELFARE

Justice. Justice is administered by the High Court of the Netherlands (Court of Cassation), by 5 courts of justice (Courts of Appeal), by 19 district courts and by 62 cantonal courts; trial by jury is unknown. The Cantonal Court, which deals with minor offences, is formed by a single judge; the more serious cases are tried by the district courts, formed as a rule by 3 judges (in some cases one judge is sufficient); the courts of appeal are constituted of 3 and the High Court of 5 judges. All judges are appointed for life by the Sovereign (the judges of the High Court from a list prepared by the Second Chamber of the States-General). They can be removed only by a decision of the High Court.

At the district court the juvenile judge is specially appointed to try children's civil cases and at the same time charged with administration of justice for criminal actions committed by young persons between 12 and 18 years old, unless imprisonment of 6 months or more ought to be inflicted; such cases are tried by 3 judges.

Number of persons convicted including those who paid a fine to the public prosecutor to evade prosecution (tax offenders excluded):

Major offences	1979	1980	1981	Minor offences	1979	1980	1981
Males	58,299	62,750	63,248	Males	1,298,410	1,295,067	1,246,192
Females	4,345	4,809	5,449	Females	201,720	216,811	228,875

In addition, prosecution was evaded by paying a fine to the police in 1,045,000 cases in 1981.

Police. There are both State and Municipal Police. The State Police, about 8,600 men strong, serves 630, and the Municipal Police, about 19,600 men strong, serves 140 municipalities. The State Police includes ordinary as well as water, mounted and motor police. The State Police Corps is under the jurisdiction of the Police Department of the Ministry of Justice, which also includes the Central Criminal Investigation Office, which deals with serious crimes throughout the country, and the International Criminal Investigation Office, which informs foreign countries of international crimes.

Religion. Entire liberty of conscience is granted to the members of all denominations. The royal family belong to the Dutch Reformed Church.

The number of adherents of the Churches according to the census of 1971 was: Dutch Reformed Church, 3,075,565; Reformed Churches (excluding other reformed denominations), 937,840; Roman Catholics, 5,273,665; other creeds (including other reformed denominations), 694,405; no religion, 3,078,640; total, 13,060,115.

The government of the Reformed Church is Presbyterian. On 1 July 1972 the Dutch Reformed Church had 1 synod, 11 provincial districts, 54 classes, 147 districts and 1,905 parishes.

Their clergy numbered 2,000. The Roman Catholic Church had, Jan. 1973, 1 archbishop (of Utrecht), 6 bishops and 1,815 parishes and rectorships. The Old Catholics had (1 July 1972) 1 archbishop (Utrecht), 2 bishops and 29 parishes. The Jews had, in 1970, 46 communities.

Education. Statistics for the scholastic year 1981–82:

	Full-time			Part-time [1]		
		Pupils			Pupils	
	Schools	Total	Female	Schools	Total	Female
Nursery schools	8,108	399,769	194,069	—	—	—
Primary Schools	8,727	1,269,868	627,180	—	—	—
Special schools	983	94,308	29,601	—	—	—
Secondary general schools	1,503	828,731	434,883	78	114,709	84,176
Secondary vocational schools:						
Junior—						
Technical, nautical	389	208,328	11,245	515	135,752	42,103
Agricultural	128	29,163	7,311	168	4,314	1,099
Domestic science	562	118,305	114,699	...	489	481
Other	223	48,593	28,365	14	877	25
Senior—						
Technical, nautical	124	62,569	4,017	48	5,623	202
Agricultural	48	13,927	2,124	27	2,206	71
Domestic science	192	38,693	37,068	17	2,944	2,892
Teachers' training (nursery schools)	49	7,490	7,394	49	3,029	3,018
Other	197	62,621	31,981	81	25,593	14,200
Third level non-university training:						
Technical, nautical	61	33,888	3,632	41	5,016	448
Agricultural	11	4,894	791	1	19	11
Arts	37	11,890	5,879	20	3,686	1,383
Teachers' training:						
Primary schools	91	12,703	8,065	127	21,009	19,359
Secondary general schools	29	22,039	10,845	102	32,072	17,208
Secondary vocational schools	3	91	20	21	5,396	163
Other	121	48,480	27,190	61	18,191	8,995

[1] Including apprenticeship schemes, young workers' educational institutes.

Full-time: 1982–83 [1]

		Pupils	
	Schools	Total	Female
University education:			
Humanities		27,311	14,292
Social sciences		67,884	24,846
Natural sciences	14	14,933	3,052
Technical sciences		18,958	1,128
Medical sciences		18,030	5,882
Agricultural sciences		5,774	1,653

[1] Provisional figures.

Health. On 1 Jan. 1983 there were 28,807 doctors and about 69,617 licensed hospital beds.

DIPLOMATIC REPRESENTATIVES

Of the Netherlands in Great Britain (38 Hyde Park Gate, London, SW7 5DP)
Ambassador: Jan Louis Reinier Huydecoper van Nigtevecht, GCVO (accredited 3 March 1982).

Of Great Britain in the Netherlands (Lange Voorhout, 10, The Hague)
Ambassador: Philip Robert Aked Mansfield, CMG.

Of the Netherlands in the USA (4200 Linnean Ave., NW, Washington, D.C., 20008)
Ambassador: Dr J. H. Lubbers.

Of the USA in the Netherlands (Lange Voorhout, 102, The Hague)
Ambassador: Paul Bremer, III.

Of the Netherlands to the United Nations
Ambassador: Max van der Stoel.

Books of Reference

Statistical Information: The 'Centraal Bureau voor de Statistiek' at Voorburg and Heerlen, is the official Netherlands statistical service. *Director-General of Statistics:* Prof. Dr W. Begeer.

The Bureau was founded in 1899. Prior to that year, statistical publications were compiled by the 'Centrale commissie voor de statistiek', the 'Vereniging voor staathuishoudkunde en statistiek' and various government departments. These activities have gradually been taken over and co-ordinated by the Central Bureau, which now compiles practically all government statistics.

Its current publications include:

Statistical Yearbook of the Netherlands. From 1923/24 (preceded by *Jaarcijfers voor het Koninkrijk der Nederlanden, 1898–1922);* latest issue, 1982
Statistisch zakboek (Pocket Year Book). From 1899/1924 (1 vol.); latest issue, 1983
CBS Select 1 (Statistical Essays), 1980.–*CBS Select 2 (Statistical Essays),* 1983
Maandstatistiek var. de buitenlandse handel (monthly statistical bulletin of foreign trade). From 1917
Monografieën Volkstelling 1971. Nr. 1–18. From 1978
Nationale Rekeningen (National Accounts). From 1948–50; latest issue, 1982
Statistisch Magazine. From 1981
Statistische onderzoekingen. From 1977
Statistical Studies. From 1953

Other Official Publications

Central Economic Plan. Centraal Plan bureau, The Hague (Dutch text), annually, from 1946
Netherlands. Organization for Economic Co-operation and Development. Paris, annual from 1964
Staatsalmanak voor het Koninkrijk der Nederlanden. Annual. The Hague, from 1814
Staatsblad van het Koninkrijk der Nederlanden. The Hague, from 1814
Staatscourant (State Gazette). The Hague, from 1813
Atlas van Nederland Government Printing Office, The Hague, 1970 and supplements up to and including 1973
Memoranda on the Condition of the Netherlands State Finances. Ministry of Finance, The Hague, from 1906
Basic Guide to the Establishing of Industrial Operations in the Netherlands 1976. Ministry of Economic Affairs, The Hague, 1976
The Kingdom of the Netherlands. Ministry of Foreign Affairs, The Hague, Occasional
Huggett, F. E., *The Dutch Today.* Ministry of Foreign Affairs, The Hague, 1973.–*The Dutch Connection.* Ministry of Foreign Affairs, The Hague, 1982
Aspects of Dutch Agriculture. Ministry of Agriculture and Fisheries, The Hague, 1976

Non-Official Publications

Jansonius. H., *Nieuw Groot Nederlands—Engels Woordenboek Voor Studie en Praktijk.* 3 vols. Leiden, 1973 (Vols. 1–3)
Newton, G., *The Netherlands: An Historical and Cultural Survey, 1795–1977.* Boulder, 1978
Pinder, D., *The Netherlands.* Folkestone, 1976
Veldman, J., *Agriculture in the Netherlands.* Utrecht, 1974
Pyttersen's Nederlandse Almanak. Zaltbommel, annual, from 1899
Commerce and Industry in the Netherlands. Amsterdam–Rotterdam Bank. Amsterdam, 1977
Foreign Investment in the Netherlands. The Hague, 1975
The Information You Need When Planning a Business in the Netherlands. Algemene Bank Nederland. Amsterdam, 1975
A Compact Geography of the Netherlands. Utrecht, 1980

National Library: De Koninklijke Bibliotheek, Prinz Willem Alexanderhof 5, The Hague.
Director: Dr C. Reedijk.

THE NETHERLANDS ANTILLES
De Nederlandse Antillen

AREA AND POPULATION. The Netherlands Antilles are an integral part of the Netherlands and comprise two groups of islands, viz., the Leeward Islands, Curaçao, Aruba and Bonaire, and the Windward Islands, St Maarten, St Eustatius and Saba. The Leeward Islands are situated 40–70 miles north of the Venezuelan coast between 12° and 13° N. lat. and 68° and 71° W. long. The Windward group lies east of Puerto Rico. For the constitutional position of the Netherlands Antilles *see* p. 882. The total area is 993 sq. km (383 sq. miles) and the population was 260,000 in 1981.

Leeward group	Sq. km	Population	Windward group	Sq. km	Population
Curaçao	444	170,000	St Maarten (St Martin)[1]	34	17,000
Aruba	193	65,000	St Eustatius	21	1,500
Bonaire	288	9,500	Saba	13	1,000

[1] The southern part belongs to the Netherlands Antilles, the northern to France.

The capital is Willemstad on Curaçao, population (1983) 50,000.
In 1975, 4,258 births, 1,193 deaths and 1,536 marriages were registered.

CLIMATE. All the islands have a tropical marine climate, with very little difference in temperatures over the year. There is a short rainy season from Oct. to Jan. Willemstad. Jan. 79°F (26·1°C), July 82°F (27·8°C). Annual rainfall 23″ (582 mm).

GOVERNMENT. Since Dec. 1954, the Netherlands Antilles have been fully autonomous in internal affairs, and constitutionally equal with the Netherlands and Suriname. The Sovereign of the Kingdom of the Netherlands is Head of the Government of the Netherlands Antilles and is represented by a Governor.

The executive power in internal affairs rests with the Governor and the Council of Ministers, who together form the Government. The Ministers are responsible to the unicameral legislature (*Staten*). This consists of 22 members (12 from Curaçao, 8 from Aruba, 1 from Bonaire, 1 from the Windward Islands) and is elected by general suffrage. It was agreed in 1977 that the 2 smallest islands, Saba and St Eustatius would each have a representative (non-voting) in the *Staten*.

The executive power in external affairs is vested in the Council of Ministers of the Kingdom, in which the Antilles is represented by a Minister Plenipotentiary with full voting powers.

In 1951 the Netherlands Antilles Islands Regulation provided for self-government of each of the 4 insular communities Aruba, Bonaire, Curaçao and the Windward Islands. The autonomous powers of the insular communities are divided between the Island Council (elected by general suffrage), the Executive Council and the Lieut.-Governor (*Gezaghebber*), who is responsible for maintaining public peace and order.

At the general election held on 25 June 1982, 6 of the 12 *Staten* seats in Curaçao were won by the *Movimiento Antijas Nobo*, 3 by the Democratic Party and 3 by the *Nationale Volkspartij-Unie;* of the 8 seats in Aruba, 5 were won by the *Movimiento Electoral di Puebla,* 2 by the *Arubaanse Volkspartij* and 1 by the *Partido Patriotico Arubano;* the 1 seat in Bonaire was won by the *Unión Patriotico Bonairiano* and the 1 seat in the Windward Islands by the Democratic Party. Following an earlier referendum, the government of the Netherlands announced on 28 Oct. 1981 that it had agreed that Aruba should at an early date proceed to independence separately from the other islands.

Governor: Dr B. M. Leito.

Prime Minister: Dominico F. Martina.
Deputy Prime Minister: Gualberto Hernández.

Flag: White, with a red vertical strip crossed by a blue horizontal strip bearing 6 white stars.

Dutch is the official language. Spanish and English are also spoken. In addition a 'lingua franca', *Papiamento* has evolved out of Spanish, Dutch and some other languages.

FINANCE. The central budget for 1979 envisaged 213m. guilders revenue and 256m. guilders expenditure.

The official rate of exchange was £1 = 2·67 *Antillian guilder*; US$1 = 1·50 *Antillian guilder* in March 1984.

ENERGY AND NATURAL RESOURCES

Oil. The economy of the Netherlands Antilles is almost entirely based on the refining of oil imported from Venezuela to Curaçao and Aruba. About 25% (Curaçao) and 30% (Aruba) of the gainfully occupied are working at the refineries or their shipping establishments. On account of the activities of the oil companies (affiliated to the Royal Dutch/Shell and the Standard Oil of New Jersey), the prosperity on Curaçao and Aruba is good in comparison with the other islands.

Minerals. About 100,000 tons of calcium phosphate are annually mined in Curaçao.

Agriculture. Livestock (1981): Cattle, 9,000; goats, 21,000; poultry, 122,000.

INDUSTRY AND TRADE

Industry. In Aruba there are some petrochemical factories; Curaçao has a paint factory, 2 cigarette factories, a textile factory, a brewery and some smaller industries. The Texas Instruments Co. and Electronic Fabriek have established electronic factories. Almost all products needed for consumption and production are imported, as the rocky soil permits little agriculture and local fishing is insufficient for home consumption. Bonaire has a textile factory and a modern-equipped salt plant. St Maarten has a rum factory and fishing is important. St Eustatius and Saba are of less economic importance.

Trade (1980). Total imports amounted to US$5,944m., total exports to US$6,054m.

Total trade between the Netherlands Antilles and UK (British Department of Trade returns, in £1,000 sterling):

	1979	1980	1981	1982	1983
Imports to UK	44,841	36,243	29,761	62,946	25,871
Exports and re-exports from UK	59,070	33,375	135,017	47,396	78,879

The Free-Zones Ordinance of 1956 has established free zones in the ports of Curaçao and Aruba.

Tourism. In 1981, 764,000 foreign tourists visited the Netherlands Antilles.

COMMUNICATIONS

Roads. In 1984, the Netherlands Antilles had 1,200 km of surfaced highway distributed as follows: Curaçao, 550; Aruba, 380; Bonaire, 210; St Maarten, 3. Number of motor vehicles (31 Dec. 1975): 41,955 in Curaçao, 15,393 in Aruba.

Shipping (1977). There entered the port of Curaçao, 11,432 vessels of 95m. gross tons; Aruba, 2,798 vessels of 52m. gross tons. Curaçao has a dry dock of 120,000 tons.

Post and Broadcasting. Number of telephones, 1 Jan. 1982, 72,168. Eight radio stations are operating on medium-waves from Curaçao, Aruba, Bonaire, and St Maarten. These stations broadcast in *Papiamento*, Dutch, English and Spanish and are mainly financed by income from advertisements. In addition, Radio Nederland and Trans World Radio have powerful relay stations operating on medium- and short-waves from Bonaire. There were (1975) 132,000 radio and 35,000 TV receivers.

Cinemas (1973). Curaçao and Aruba had 13 cinemas with a seating capacity of 11,000. There is a drive-in for 500 cars in Curaçao, for 200 cars in St Maarten and for 350 cars in Aruba.

JUSTICE, RELIGION, EDUCATION AND WELFARE

Justice. There is a Court of First Instance, which sits in each island, and a Court of Appeal in Willemstad.

Religion. In 1980, 82% of the population were Roman Catholics, 8% were Protestants.

Education (1974). Schools numbered 186, with 51,989 pupils and 2,296 teachers.

Health. In June 1973 there were 155 physicians, 55 specialists, 33 dentists and 18 pharmacists. In 1973, 11 hospitals had 2,037 beds.

DIPLOMATIC REPRESENTATIVE

USA Consul-General: Alta F. Fowler.

The British consulate closed on 1 Sept. 1976.

Books of Reference

Statistical Information: Statistical publications (on population, trade, cost of living, etc., are obtainable on request from the Statistical Office, Willemstad, Curaçao. *Statistical Jaarboek 1970* (text in Dutch, English and Spanish).

De West Indische Gids. The Hague. Monthly from 1919
Braam, H. L., *Hoe ons land geregeerd wordt.* Willemstad, 4th ed. 1972
Hartog, J., *Aruba.* Oranjestad, 1953.—*Bonaire.* Oranjestad, 1958.—*Curaçao.* Oranjestad, 1961
Nordlohne, E., *De Economisch-geographische Structuur der Benedenwindse Eilanden.* Rotterdam, 1951
Poll, W. van de, *De Nederlandse Antillen.* The Hague, 1950
Walle, J. van de, *De Nederlandse Antillen.* Willemstad, 1954
Westerman, J. H., *Overzicht van de geologische en mijnbouwkundige kennis der Nederlandse Antillen.* Amsterdam, 1949

NEW ZEALAND

Capital: Wellington
Population: 3·2m. (1983)
GNP per capita: US$7,090 (1980)

HISTORY. The first European to discover New Zealand was Tasman in 1642. The coast was explored by Capt. Cook in 1769. From about 1800 onwards, New Zealand became a resort for whalers and traders, chiefly from Australia. By the Treaty of Waitangi, in 1840, between Governor William Hobson and the representatives of the Maori race, the Maori chiefs ceded the sovereignty to the British Crown and the islands became a British colony. Then followed a steady stream of British settlers.

The Maoris are a branch of the Polynesian race, having emigrated from the eastern Pacific before and during the 14th century. Between 1845 and 1848, and between 1860 and 1870, misunderstandings over land led to war, but peace was permanently established in 1871, and the development of New Zealand has been marked by racial harmony and integration.

AREA AND POPULATION. New Zealand lies south-east of Australia in the south Pacific, Wellington being 1,233 miles from Sydney by sea. There are two principal islands, the North and South Islands, besides Stewart Island, Chatham Islands and small outlying islands, as well as the territories overseas (*see* pp. 910–12).

New Zealand (*i.e.*, North, South and Stewart Islands) extends over 1,750 km from north to south. Area, excluding territories overseas, 268,704 sq. km.; North Island, 11,469,000 hectares; South Island, 15,046,000 hectares; Stewart Island, 174,000 hectares; Chatham Islands, 96,000 hectares; minor islands, 82,900 hectares. Census population, exclusive of territories overseas:

	Total population	Average annual increase %		Total population	Average annual increase %
1858	115,462	—	1921	1,271,644	2·27
1874	344,984	—	1926	1,408,139	2·06
1878	458,007	7·33	1936	1,573,810	1·13
1881	534,030	5·10	1945[1]	1,702,298	0·83
1886	620,451	3·05	1951[1]	1,939,472	2·37
1891	668,632	1·50	1956[1]	2,174,062	2·31
1896	743,207	2·13	1961[1]	2,414,984	2·12
1901[1]	815,853	1·89	1966[1]	2,676,919	2·10
1906	936,304	2·75	1971[1]	2,862,631	1·34
1911	1,058,308	2·52	1976[1]	3,129,383	1·71
1916[1]	1,149,225	1·50	1981[1]	3,175,737	0·20

The census of New Zealand is quinquennial, but the census falling in 1931 was abandoned as an act of national economy, and owing to war conditions the census due in 1941 was not taken until 25 Sept. 1945.

[1] Excluding members of the Armed Forces overseas.

The areas and populations of statistical areas (with principal centres) as at 31 March 1982 were as follows [1]:

Statistical area [2]	Sq. km	Total population
Northland (Whangarei)	12,653	115,800
Central Auckland (Auckland)	5,581	839,500
South Auckland—Bay of Plenty (Hamilton)	36,882	496,000
East Coast (Gisborne)	10,885	48,700
Hawke's Bay (Napier, Hastings)	11,289	148,400
Taranaki (New Plymouth)	9,729	105,300
Wellington (Wellington)	27,766	586,000
Total, North Island	*114,785*	*2,339,700*

[1] For statistical purposes, the 9 provincial districts have now been replaced by 13 statistical areas.
[2] Listed from north to south.

Statistical area [1]	Sq. km	Total population
Marlborough (Blenheim)	10,210	36,200
Nelson (Nelson)	18,948	77,600
Westland (Greymouth)	15,477	23,300
Canterbury (Christchurch) [2]	43,346	422,800
Otago (Dunedin)	36,873	182,400
Southland (Invercargill) [3]	28,464	108,100
Total, South Island	153,318	850,400
Total, New Zealand	268,103	3,190,100

[1] Listed from north to south.   [2] Includes Chatham Islands County.
[3] Includes Stewart Island County.

New Zealand-born residents made up 85·4% of the population at the 1981 census. Foreign-born (provisional): UK, 253,810; Australia, 44,500; Netherlands, 21,630; Samoa, 26,180; Cook Islands, 14,370; USA, 5,430; Ireland, 6,970; others, 97,070.

Maori population: 1896, 42,113; 1936, 82,326; 1945, 98,744; 1951, 115,676; 1961, 171,553; 1971, 227,414; 1976, 270,035; 1981 (provisional), 280,380.

Populations of statistical divisions and main urban areas as at 31 March 1982 were as follows:

Auckland	839,500	Invercargill	53,900
Christchurch	322,100	Nelson	43,400
Dunedin	112,800	New Plymouth	44,300
Hamilton	161,500	Rotorua	48,900
Napier–Hastings	112,700	Tauranga	54,300
Palmerston North	92,700	Timaru	29,100
Wellington	343,200	Wanganui	39,600
Urban areas:		Whangarei	40,600
Gisborne	32,100		

Vital statistics for calendar years:

	Total live births	Ex-nuptial births	Deaths	Marriages	Divorces (decrees absolute)
1980	50,542	10,857	26,676	22,981	6,493
1981	50,794	11,441	25,150	23,660	8,590
1982	49,938	11,386	25,532	25,537	12,395

Birth rate, 1982, 15·69 per 1,000; death rate, 8·02 per 1,000; marriage rate, 8·02 per 1,000; infant mortality, 11·75 per 1,000 live births.

External migration (exclusive of crews and through passengers) for years ended 31 March:

	Arrivals	Departures		Arrivals	Departures
1978	715,780	737,936	1981	970,427	986,636
1979	805,876	832,420	1982	946,287	951,030
1980	925,939	947,253	1983	915,463	900,021

Population and Migration: Part B—External Migration. Dept. of Statistics, Wellington, Annually

CLIMATE. Lying in the cool temperate zone, New Zealand enjoys very mild winters for its latitude owing to its oceanic situation, and only the extreme south has cold winters. The situation of the mountain chain produces much sharper climatic contrasts between east and west than in a north-south direction. Auckland. Jan. 66°F (19°C), July 51°F (10·6°C). Annual rainfall 50″ (1,247 mm). Christchurch. Jan. 61°F (16°C), July 42°F (5·6°C). Annual rainfall 25″ (638 mm). Dunedin. Jan. 58°F (14·5°C), July 42°F (5·6°C). Annual rainfall 38″ (940 mm). Hokitika. Jan. 59°F (15°C), July 45°F (7·2°C). Annual rainfall 116″ (2,900 mm). Rotorua. Jan. 64°F (17·8°C), July 45°F (7·2°C). Annual rainfall 56″ (1,397 mm). Wellington. Jan. 62°F (16·7°C), July 47°F (8·3°C). Annual rainfall 48″ (1,204 mm).

CONSTITUTION AND GOVERNMENT. Definition was given the status of New Zealand by the (Imperial) Statute of Westminster of Dec. 1931, which had received the antecedent approval of the New Zealand Parliament in July 1931. The Governor-General's assent was given to the Statute of Westminster Adoption Bill on 25 Nov. 1947.

The powers, duties and responsibilities of the Governor-General and the Executive Council under the present system of responsible government are set out in Royal Letters Patent and Instructions thereunder of 11 May 1917, published in the *New Zealand Gazette* of 24 April 1919. In the execution of the powers vested in him the Governor-General must be guided by the advice of the Executive Council.

The following is a list of Governors-General, the title prior to June 1917 being Governor:

Earl of Liverpool	1917–20	Lord Norrie	1952–57
Viscount Jellicoe	1920–24	Viscount Cobham	1957–62
Sir Charles Fergusson, Bt	1924–30	Sir Bernard Fergusson	1962–67
Lord Bledisloe	1930–35	Sir Arthur Porrit, Bt	1967–72
Viscount Galway	1935–41	Sir Denis Blundell	1972–77
Sir Cyril Newall	1941–46	Sir Keith Holyoake	1977–80
Lord Freyberg, VC	1946–52	Sir David Beattie	1980–

National flag: The British Blue Ensign with 4 stars of the Southern Cross in red, edged in white, in the fly.

National anthems: God Save the Queen; God Defend New Zealand (words by Thomas Bracken, music by John J. Woods).

Since Nov. 1977 both 'God Save the Queen' and 'God Defend New Zealand' have equal status as national anthems.

Parliament consists of the House of Representatives, the former Legislative Council having been abolished since 1 Jan. 1951.

The statute law on elections and the life of Parliament is contained in the Electoral Act, 1956. In 1974 the voting age was reduced from 20 to 18 years.

The House of Representatives from Nov. 1978 consists of 92 members, including 4 members representing Maori electorates, elected by the people for 3 years. The 4 Maori electoral districts cover the whole country and adult Maoris of half or more Maori descent are the electors. From 1976 a descendant of a Maori is entitled to register either for a general or a Maori electoral district. Women's suffrage was instituted in 1893: women became eligible as members of the House of Representatives in 1919. The House in 1983 included 8 women members.

During Parliamentary sittings the proceedings of the House are broadcast regularly on sound radio.

House of Representatives as composed following the General Election in Nov. 1981: National Party, 47; Labour, 43; Social Credit, 2.

The Executive Council was composed as follows in Jan. 1983:

Governor-General and C.-in-C.: The Hon. Sir David Beattie, GCMG, GCVO (from Oct. 1980).

Prime Minister, Finance, Legislative Department, Audit Department, Security Intelligence Service: Sir Robert Muldoon, GCMG.

Deputy Prime Minister, Agriculture and Fisheries, Rural Bank: Duncan MacIntyre.

Minister of State, Leader of the House of Representatives, Defence, State Services, War Pensions, Rehabilitation: David Thomson.

Energy, National Development, Regional Development: William Birch.

Labour: James Bolger.

Transport, Railways, Civil Aviation and Meteorological Services: George Gair.

Trade and Industry: Hugh Templeton.

Foreign Affairs, Overseas Trade: Warren Cooper.

Attorney-General and Justice: James McLay.

Housing, Works and Development: Anthony Friedlander.

Social Welfare, Public Trust Office, Government Printing Office: Venn Young.

Internal Affairs, Local Government, Arts, Recreation and Sport, Civil Defence: Allan Highet.

Education: Mervyn Wellington.

Maori Affairs and Police: Benjamin Couch.

Health and Immigration: Anthony Malcolm.

Environment, Science and Technology, Broadcasting: Dr Ian Shearer.

Postmaster-General, Tourism and Publicity: Rob Talbot.

Lands, Forests, Valuation: Jonathan Elworthy.

Inland Revenue, Friendly Societies, Statistics, Associate Minister of Finance: John Falloon.

Customs, Government Life Insurance, State Insurance Office, Earthquake and War Damage Commission, Associate Minister of Trade and Industry: Kenneth Allen.

The Prime Minister (provided with residence) had in 1983 a salary of NZ$79,717 plus a tax-free expense allowance of $14,000 per annum; Ministers with portfolio, $55,115 plus a tax-free expense allowance of $5,750 (Minister of Foreign Affairs $10,750) per annum; Minister without portfolio, $44,572 plus a tax-free expense allowance of $4,500 per annum; Parliamentary Under-Secretaries, $42,814 plus an expense allowance of $4,500 per annum. In addition, Ministers and Parliamentary Under-Secretaries not provided with residence at the seat of Government receive $600 per annum house allowance. An allowance of $58 per day while travelling within New Zealand on public service is payable to Ministers.

The Speaker of the House of Representatives receives $51,161 plus an expense allowance of $7,100 per annum in addition to his electorate allowance, and residential quarters in Parliament House, and the Leader of the Opposition $55,115 plus expense allowance of $5,750 per annum, and allowances for travelling and housing.

Members were paid $32,271 per annum, plus an expense allowance varying from $4,500 to $9,250 according to the area of electorate represented.

There is a compulsory contributory superannuation scheme for members; retiring allowances are payable to a member after 9 years' service and the attainment of 50 years of age.

Dollimore, H. N., *The Parliament of New Zealand and Parliament House.* 3rd ed. Wellington, 1973

Scott, K. J., *The New Zealand Constitution.* OUP, 1962

Local Government. For purposes of local government New Zealand is divided into counties, district councils, boroughs and town districts. Some counties are subdivided into ridings. There are also numerous other local authorities created for specific functions, such as electric-power districts, river (*i.e.*, river protection) districts, pest destruction districts, etc.

DEFENCE. The control and co-ordination of defence activities is obtained through the Ministry of Defence. This is a unitary department combining not only all joint-Service functions but also the former Departments of Army, Navy and Air.

Army. The Chief of the General Staff commands the Army, assisted by the General Staff and the staffs of Defence Headquarters. A regular force battalion is stationed in Singapore.

Regular personnel, in 1983, totalled 5,675 all ranks; territorial personnel totalled 5,934; the cadet corps totalled (1981) 3,399 Army School cadets.

Navy. The Royal New Zealand Navy is administered by the Chief of Naval Staff and the Deputy Chief of Naval Staff at Defence Headquarters.

The RNZN ships include 5 frigates (including *Wellington* (ex-*Bacchante*) and *Southland* (ex-*Dido*) transferred from the Royal Navy in 1982 and 1983 respectively), 1 surveying vessel, 4 patrol craft, 5 old harbour defence motor launches, 2 survey boats, 1 oceanographic research ship, 1 tug and 1 tender.

Personnel, in 1984, totalled 2,760 officers and ratings and 440 in the naval reserve.

Air Force. The Chief of Air Staff and Air Officer Commanding the RNZAF exercises command and administration of the RNZAF. Operational units of the

RNZAF comprise a utility helicopter support unit (UH-1H Iroquois) based in Singapore as part of the NZ force, South-east Asia; maritime (P-3B Orion), long and medium-range transport (Boeing 727, C-130H Hercules, Andover, F.27 Friendship) and helicopter (Sioux, Iroquois, Wasp) squadrons based at RNZAF Base Auckland; and offensive support (A-4K Skyhawk) and medium-range transport/communications squadrons (Andover, F.27 Friendship, Cessna 421) at RNZAF Base Ohakea. Flying training units (Airtrainer, Strikemaster, TA-4K Skyhawks, Sioux) are located at RNZAF Bases Wigram and Ohakea; ground training is carried out at RNZAF Bases Auckland, Woodbourne and Wigram.

The strength as at 31 March 1983 was 4,409 regular personnel, 1,377 reserves.

INTERNATIONAL RELATIONS

Membership. New Zealand is a member of UN, the Commonwealth, OECD and the Colombo Plan.

ECONOMY

Budget. The following tables of revenue and expenditure relate to the Consolidated Account, which covers the ordinary revenue and expenditure of the general government—i.e., apart from capital items, commercial and special undertakings, advances, etc. Revenue in the Account (in NZ$1m.) was as follows:

Year ended 31 March	Customs and excise	Sales tax	Income tax	Other taxes	Trading profits and departmental receipts	Interest	Total
1980	389·8	624·1	4,465·6	401·0	418·8	539·0	6,838·3
1981	413·6	775·6	5,298·9	373·4	493·1	597·8	7,952·4
1982	549·4	1,084·1	6,514·7	439·3	592·5	664·4	9,843·4
1983	660·9	1,211·7	7,455·5	536·3	709·7	719·5	11,293·6

Expenditure from Consolidated Account, year ended 31 March, was as follows (in NZ$1m.):

	Debt services	Social services [1]	Industrial development	Defence	Total (including other)
1980	825·6	4,353·8	814·2	346·1	7,529·1
1981	999·9	5,296·7	999·7	455·9	8,992·5
1982	1,327·2	6,205·9	1,337·4	593·6	11,123·8
1983	1,636·4	7,227·5	1,641·6	652·1	12,992·3

[1] Includes education, health and social welfare.

Taxation receipts in 1982–83 for all purposes amounted to $10,097m., giving an average of $3,175 per head of mean population. Included in the total taxation is $232·9m. National Roads Fund taxation. The estimate for 1983–84 is $10,355m., the total being inclusive of an estimated $240m. of National Roads Fund taxation.

The gross public debt at 31 March 1983 was $18,733m., of which $10,968m. was held in New Zealand, $5,837m. in London, Europe and Asia, $1,862m. in USA and $13m. with the World Bank. The gross annual interest charge on the public debt at 31 March 1983 was $1,475,792,000.

New Zealand System of National Accounts. This replaces the National Income and Expenditure Accounts which have been produced since 1948. National Accounts aggregates for 4 years are given in the following table (in NZ$1m.):

Year ended 31 March	Gross domestic product	Gross national product	National income
1979	17,541	17,121	15,791
1980	20,966	20,513	19,034
1981	24,127	23,615	21,965
1982	28,598	27,969	26,099

Currency. The monetary unit is the New Zealand *dollar*, divided into 100 *cents*. In March 1984, £1 = 2·208NZ$; US$1 = 1·501NZ$.

Banking. The Reserve Bank is the sole note-issuing authority. Six denominations of Reserve Bank notes are issued: NZ$1, 2, 5, 10, 20, 100.

The New Zealand banking system comprises a central bank, the Reserve Bank of New Zealand, and 4 commercial or trading banks. There are also 12 trustee savings banks and the Post Office Savings Bank, while each trading bank has a private savings bank subsidiary. In addition, a number of trading companies, investment societies, etc., perform quasi-banking functions, accepting deposits and granting credits to clients.

The primary functions of the Reserve Bank are to act as the central bank, to advise the Government on matters relating to monetary policy, banking and overseas exchange, and to give effect to the monetary policy of the Government.

Of the 4 trading banks 2 are primarily Australian concerns, 1 until recently had its head office in London and the Bank of New Zealand has been state owned since 1 Nov. 1945.

At the end of March 1983 the amount on deposit at trading banks was NZ$8,460·7m., while advances amounted to NZ$5,888·1m. The weekly average of bank debits for 1982 was $4,912m. excluding government.

The number of accounts with the post office savings bank at 31 March 1983 was 3·23m.; amount deposited during year ended March 1983, $4,932m.; withdrawn, $4,879m., total amount to credit of depositors at end of year, $2,102m. At 31 March 1983, $2,589m. was on deposit in Trustee Savings Banks to the credit of 3·1m. depositors. The amount to the credit of depositors with savings accounts in the trading banks was $887,189,000 at 31 March 1983.

Weights and Measures. Conversion to the metric system of weights and measures has been completed.

ENERGY AND NATURAL RESOURCES

Electricity. The general policy of the Government in regard to electric power is to supply power in bulk, leaving the reticulation and retail supply in the hands of local authorities; some of these are cities and boroughs but most are electric power boards. During the year ending 31 March 1982 hydro energy provided 85% of the national electricity supply, the balance coming from coal, oil, natural gas and geothermal energy. The last is obtained from Wairakei in the thermal region; natural steam is used to drive the turbines.

The transmission systems of the North and South Islands are linked by a high-voltage direct-current transmission and 40 km of submarine cable in Cook Strait.

Principal statistics for 4 years ended 31 March are:

	1980	1981	1982	1983
Number of establishments	79	81	82	82
Generators (capacity) AC (1,000 kw.)	5,860	6,018	5,827	5,820
Units generated (1 m. kwh.)	21,607	22,111	22,963	24,301
Revenue ($1,000)	1,154,206	1,276,853	1,440,235	1,720,058
Expenditure:				
Operating ($1,000)	580,000	666,419	773,764	947,179
Management, etc. ($1,000)	96,933	118,898	142,714	163,403
Capital charges ($1,000)	266,611	299,756	329,162	359,989
Capital outlay:				
During year ($1,000)	350,500	370,700	459,200	491,286
To date ($1,000)	3,414,200	3,359,100	3,744,100	4,235,386

Natural Gas. Resources discovered in the Taranaki area of the North Island in 1961 are now supplying gas for household use to North Island cities including Auckland and Wellington. The much larger Maui offshore gasfield was discovered in 1969 and is at present being developed.

Minerals. New Zealand's production of minerals in 1981 included 189 kg of gold, 2,000 tonnes of bentonite, 132,200 tonnes of clay for bricks, tiles, etc., 49,300 tonnes of potters' clays, 3,025,900 tonnes of iron sand, 1,829,400 tonnes of limestone for agriculture and 187,900 tonnes of limestone for industry, 1,457,600 tonnes of limestone, marl, etc., for cement, 33,800 tonnes of pumice, 65,700 tonnes of serpentine, 129,100 tonnes of silica sand. Mineral fuel production amounted to 2,196,900 tonnes of coal, 521,900 cu. metres of petroleum condensate and 1,378·79m. cu. metres of natural gas. Salt produced by the solar evaporation of sea water amounted to 55,500 tonnes. Mineral production for the year was valued at $193·7m.

Agriculture. Two-thirds of the surface of New Zealand is suitable for agriculture and grazing. The total area under cultivation at 30 June 1981 was 11,129,000 hectares (including residential area and domestic orchards). There were 10,176,000 hectares of grassland, lucerne, and land in or prepared for fruit, grain, crops and vegetables, and 953,000 hectares of exotic timber plantations. The area of Crown lands (other than reserves) leased under various tenures at 31 March 1983 was 5,575,799 hectares.

The largest freehold estates are held in the South Island. The extent of occupied holdings as at 30 June 1981 (exclusive of holdings within borough boundaries) was as follows:

Size of holdings (hectares)	Number	Aggregate area (hectares)	Size of holdings (hectares)	Number	Aggregate area (hectares)
Under 5	7,711	23,368	400–799	4,361	2,379,252
5–19	11,569	115,548	800–999	829	736,246
20–39	6,966	199,240	1,000–1,199	483	529,874
40–79	12,384	737,351	1,200–1,999	959	1,469,018
80–99	4,391	388,174	2,000–3,999	583	1,596,973
100–149	6,943	849,167	4,000 and over	589	8,765,043
150–199	4,736	820,768			
200–299	6,296	1,531,592	Total	72,515	21,249,584
300–399	3,215	1,107,970			

The area and yield for each of the principal crops are given as follows (area and yield for threshing only, not including that grown for chaff, hay, silage, etc.):

	Wheat		Maize		Barley	
Crop years	Area (1,000 hectares)	Yield (1,000 tonnes)	Area (1,000 hectares)	Yield (1,000 tonnes)	Area (1,000 hectares)	Yield (1,000 tonnes)
1981	81·2	325·7	17·2	152·1	67·4	271·4
1982	71·5	292·1	18·8	170·1	88·5	355·8

Private air companies are carrying out such aerial work as top-dressing, spraying and crop-dusting, seed-sowing, rabbit poisoning, aerial photography and surveying, and dropping supplies to deer cullers and dropping fencing materials in remote areas. In 1980 a total area of 6,485,500 hectares was top-dressed with fertilizer and lime; 2,336,400 tonnes by ground spread and 1,260,200 by air.

Livestock at 30 June 1982: 7,912,000 cattle, 70m. sheep and 406,000 pigs. Total meat produced in the year ended 30 Sept. 1982 was estimated at 1·3m. tonnes (including 519,400 tonnes of beef and 454,700 tonnes of lamb). Total liquid milk produced in the year ended 31 May 1982 was 6,446m. litres.

Production of wool for 1980–81, 381,000 tonnes (greasy basis).

Agricultural Statistics. Dept. of Statistics, Wellington. Annual.
New Zealand Agriculture. Ministry of Agriculture and Fisheries, Wellington, 1974
Allsop, F., *The First Fifty Years of New Zealand's Forest Service.* Wellington, 1973
Evans, B. L., *A History of Agricultural Production and Marketing.* Palmerston North, 1969
Levy, E. B., *Grasslands of New Zealand.* Wellington, 1970

Forestry. Of the 6·2m. hectares of indigenous forest only about 1m. hectares are merchantable; they are being depleted at the rate of 5,000 hectares a year (although the rate of cutting is diminishing) and mainly for sawn timber. There are about 939,000 hectares of productive exotic forest, and this produces far more timber than the indigenous forests. Introduced conifer pines form the bulk of the large exotic forest estate and among these radiata pine is the best multi-purpose tree, reaching saw-log size in 25–30 years. Other major species are Douglas fir, Corsican pine and ponderosa pine. The table below shows production of rough sawn timber in cu. metres for years ending 31 March:

	Indigenous			Exotic			All Species
	Rimu and			Exotic	Douglas		
	Miro	Beech	Total	Pines	Fir	Total	Total
1979–80	137,036	23,061	195,073	1,608,894	163,454	1,815,420	2,010,493
1980–81	121,971	19,280	175,101	1,798,060	168,025	2,007,245	2,182,346
1981–82	111,614	18,208	164,442	1,885,761	173,377	2,105,991	2,270,433

Forest industries consist of 387 saw-mills, 9 plywood and veneer plants, 4 particle board mills, 7 pulp and paper mills and 2 fibreboard mills.

The basic products of the pulp and paper mills are mechanical and chemical pulp which are converted into newsprint, kraft and other papers, paperboard and fibreboard. Production of woodpulp, 31 March 1982, amounted to 1m. tonnes and of paper (including newsprint paper and paperboard) to 702,600 tonnes.

Fisheries. The total value of New Zealand Fisheries exports during the year ended 30 June 1982 was $230·1m., an increase of $61·9m. (26·1%) over the previous year.

	Exports, 1981		Exports, 1982	
	Quantity	Value	Quantity	Value
	kg (1,000)	$ (1,000)	kg (1,000)	$ (1,000)
Finfish or wetfish	86,590	101,552	80,164	112,574
Rock lobster	2,527	31,879	2,375	41,386
Shellfish (squid, mussels, oysters, etc)	30,858	34,683	42,980	64,161
Total	119,974	168,113	125,519	218,121

INDUSTRY AND TRADE

Industry. Major industrial developments in recent years have included the establishment of an oil refinery, an iron and steel industry using New Zealand iron sands and an aluminium smelter using hydro-electric power.

Statistics of manufacturing industries for 3 years:

Production year	Persons engaged	Salaries and wages paid (NZ$1,000)	Cost of materials (NZ$1,000)	Value of production (NZ$1,000)	Net output (net value added) (NZ$1,000)
1976–77	306,177	1,801,717	6,381,347	8,987,242	2,865,278
1978–79	298,331	2,293,756	7,595,457	10,925,685	3,478,002

The following is a statement of the provisional value of the products (including repairs) of the principal industries for the year 1978–79 (in NZ$1,000):

Industry group	Value of production	Industry group	Value of production
Food manufacturing	2,824,089	Pottery, china and earthenware	19,081
Beverages	245,551	Glass and products	82,656
Tobacco manufactures	76,502	Other non-metallic mineral	
Textiles	525,556	products	317,028
Wearing apparel	353,714	Iron and steel	252,026
Leather products	124,188	Non-ferrous metal	206,467
Footwear (except rubber, plastic		Metal products (except machinery	
or wooden)	98,551	and equipment)	829,707
Wood and cork products	522,114	Machinery (except electrical)	472,098
Furniture	163,709	Electrical machinery, apparatus,	
Paper and paper products	720,224	appliances and supplies	514,963
Printing and publishing	419,193	Transport equipment	743,276
Industrial chemicals	360,935	Measuring and controlling	
Other chemical products	365,340	equipment, etc.	31,312
Petroleum products	55,664	Other manufacturing industries	222,776
Petroleum and coal products	18,341		
Rubber products	166,254	Total	10,925,685
Plastic products not elsewhere			
specified	194,372		

Census of Manufacturing. Dept. of Statistics, Wellington. Annual

Labour. In Dec. 1981 there were 258 industrial unions of workers with a total of 519,705 members.

The industrial distribution of the labour force as estimated in Sept. 1981 was: Primary industries, 146,700; manufacturing, 303,800; construction, 87,300; commerce, 320,000; transport and communication, 109,900; services, 297,600; armed forces, 10,700; unemployed, 49,400; total labour force, 1,325,400.

By the Accident Compensation Act 1972 immediate compensation without proof of fault is provided for every injured person and wherever the accident occurred. Compensation is paid both for permanent physical disability and also—in the case cf earners—for income losses on an income related basis. Regular adjustment in the level of payment is provided for in accordance with variations in the value of money. Non-earners such as tourists, housewives, children, students, retired people do not normally qualify for earnings related compensation but are eligible for all other benefits. These are not taxable. Housewives—including visiting women from overseas—who are non-earners are eligible for the benefits available to non-earners and home help can be paid for or the husband compensated for loss of earnings while he is looking after the home until the injured wife can resume her duties.

After the first week's incapacity and for the ensuing 4 weeks the earner can be paid 80% of his average earnings for the 28 days preceding the accident; after that the 80% is related to average earnings over the 12 preceding months. In addition—for earners—lump sums are payable for impairment, pain and disfigurement and for funeral expenses and weekly sums and lump payments to their widows and dependent children. All employees are covered by the Accident Compensation Act 1972.

Commerce. Trade (excluding specie and bullion) in NZ$1m. for 12 months ended 30 June:

	Total merchandise imported (v.f.d.)[1]	Exports of domestic produce	Re-exports	Total merchandise exported (f.o.b.)
1978–79	3,574·1	3,946·0	121·4	4,067·4
1979–80	4,809·6	5,012·5	139·8	5,152·2
1980–81	5,587·3	5,830·0	235·2	6,065·3
1981–82	7,044·8	6,527·8	206·0	6,733·8

[1] Value for duty.

The principal imports for the 12 months ended 30 June 1982 (provisional):

Commodity	Value (NZ$1,000) (c.i.f.)
Cereals and cereal preparations	27,232
Fruit and vegetables	100,558
Sugar and sugar preparations	63,285
Coffee. tea, cocoa, spices, etc.	56,028
Beverages	48,649
Tobacco and manufactures	24,694
Crude rubber	35,791
Textile fibres	25,529
Crude fertilizers and minerals other than coal	152,214
Petroleum and petroleum products	1,356,329
Organic chemicals	148,944
Inorganic chemicals	108,716
Dyeing, tanning, etc. materials	45,322
Medicinal and pharmaceutical products	121,665
Fertilizers, manufactured	80,939
Plastic materials, etc.	241,425
Miscellaneous chemical materials and products	80,069
Rubber manufactures [1]	55,972
Paper and paperboard manufactures	100,819
Textile yarn and fabrics, etc.	460,943
Non-metallic mineral manufactures [1]	101,837
Iron and steel	426,676
Non-ferrous metals	125,984
Manufactures of metals	180,848
General industrial machinery	321,711
Electric machinery	261,778
Road vehicles	746,874
Professional scientific instruments	122,600
Miscellaneous manufactured articles [1]	266,196
Total merchandise imported [2]	7,463,243

[1] Not elsewhere specified.   [2] Including commodities not listed.

The principal exports of New Zealand produce for the 12 months ended 30 June 1982 (provisional) were:

Commodity	Value (NZ$1,000)	Commodity	Value (NZ$1,000)
Meat		Pulp and waste paper	155,274
Beef and veal	619,067	Wool	918,832
Lamb	707,104	Sausage casings (hanks)	48,574
Mutton	146,363	Tallow	52,989
Edible offals	65,221	Casein	176,172
Dairy products		Newsprint	110,642
Fresh milk and cream	12,659	Textile yarn	46,315
Butter	557,068	Carpets	53,377
Cheese	175,707	Aluminium	205,825
Fish	229,957	Metal manufactures	89,994
Cereals and cereal preparations	18,447	General industrial machinery	54,392
Apples	50,741	Electric machinery, etc.	83,280
Animal feeding stuff	57,923		
Wood and cork	107,546	Total produce exported	6,594,275

The following table shows the trade with different countries for the year ended 30 June (in NZ$1,000):

Countries	Imports v.f.d. from 1981[1]	1982[1]	Exports and re-exports f.o.b. to 1981[1]	1982[1]
Australia	1,043,634	1,365,584	798,687	1,028,962
Bahrain	61,787	92,781	8,093	9,753
Belgium	22,559	40,562	45,369	53,452
Canada	125,386	149,099	132,209	128,204
China	34,981	47,930	172,804	122,704
Fiji	22,009	22,539	86,533	91,763
France	48,380	72,771	94,756	106,960
Germany (Fed. Rep. of)	160,522	280,640	133,826	122,268
Greece	1,248	2,551	50,099	49,378
Hong Kong	59,902	90,149	80,492	94,963
India	24,870	33,853	29,673	60,781
Iran	136	166	243,073	103,506
Italy	60,462	86,799	83,270	112,130
Japan	827,839	1,199,587	784,336	873,340
Korea, Republic of	37,084	52,974	57,488	102,217
Kuwait	69,451	31,437	6,581	13,464
Malaysia	24,580	36,510	85,106	101,818
Netherlands	57,916	76,739	94,171	89,616
Philippines	4,859	8,351	80,506	98,938
Saudi Arabia	286,710	273,622	49,157	50,754
Singapore	311,580	278,809	98,478	97,277
Sweden	41,782	58,857	4,450	5,495
UK	585,087	634,464	760,028	960,608
USSR	11,595	9,018	222,416	347,651
USA	979,271	1,094,153	767,061	850,049

[1] Provisional.

Total trade between New Zealand and UK was as follows (British Department of Trade returns, in £1,000 sterling):

	1980	1981	1982	1983
Imports to UK	414,630	427,174	539,137	486,305
Exports and re-exports from UK	250,413	253,373	323,201	266,054

Tourism. The country has a growing tourist industry. In the year ended 31 March 1983, 487,658 travellers visited New Zealand (including 372,669 tourists), compared with 472,581 (including 357,138 tourists) in 1982.

COMMUNICATIONS

Roads. Total length of formed roads and streets in New Zealand at 31 March 1982 was 93,133 km. There were 14,260 bridges of over 3 metres in length and over with a total length of 321,456 metres at 31 March 1982. The network of state highways comprised, at 31 March 1982, 11,556 km, including the principal arterial traffic routes.

Total expenditure on roads, streets and bridges by the central government and local authorities combined for the financial year 1982–83 amounted to $273·08m.

In the main, roads are financed from the National Roads Fund which is administered by the National Roads Board. This fund which is derived largely from petrol tax is used for the maintenance and improvement of existing roads. The board's income is currently of the order of $272m. per annum. Funds are apportioned on the following basis: 39% or more of motor revenue to local authorities, 47% or more to state highways and the remaining 14% is allocated at the discretion of the board.

At 31 March 1983 motor vehicles licensed numbered 2,325,386, of which 1,408,982 were cars and 3,780 omnibuses and service vehicles. Included in the remaining numbers were 144,188 motor cycles, 1,479 power cycles, 288,028 trucks, 386,510 trailers and caravans, 874 contract vehicles and 80,193 farm tractors and other farm equipment.

Railways. On 31 March 1983 there were 4,332 km of 1,067 mm gauge railway open for traffic (99 km electrified). Operating earnings from government railways, 1982–83, $534,447,000; operating expenses, $512,671,000. In 1982–83 the tonnage of goods (including livestock) carried was 11·09m. tonnes, and passengers numbered 13,698,000. In addition, the railways road motor services carried 17·6m. passengers. Four rail/road ferries maintain a regular service between the North and South Islands.

The total revenue (including road motor and other subsidiary services) amounted to $661·5m., and total expenditure $637·3m. in 1982–83.

Aviation. International services are operated to and from New Zealand by a state-owned company, Air New Zealand Ltd, and by a number of overseas companies. Air New Zealand Ltd also operates most domestic scheduled passenger services. Non-scheduled services are run by the main companies and also by a number of small operators and aero clubs.

Domestic scheduled services during the 12 months ended Dec. 1982: Passengers carried, 2,248,000. International services: Passengers carried, 1,664,000; mail, 3,099 tonnes; freight, 70,484 tonnes.

Shipping. Container ships operate from Auckland, Wellington, Lyttelton and Port Chalmers to the UK, Europe, North America and Japan. The government-owned New Zealand Shipping Corporation has begun to increase its activity into New Zealand—UK and Pacific trades.

Entrances and clearances of vessels from overseas:

	Entrances		Clearances	
	No.	Tons	No.	Tons
1980	2,894	13,014,000	2,710	13,079,000
1981	2,671	12,738,000	2,704	12,868,000
1982	2,855	13,083,000	2,846	13,071,000

Post and Broadcasting. Receipts of the Post Office for year ended 31 March 1983 were $1,240·2m.; total expenditure was $1,042·5m. The average staff for 1982–3 was 37,979.

The telegraph and telephone systems are operated by the Post Office. At 31 March 1983 there were 1,939,488 telephones. The telecommunications receipts for the year 1982–83 were $789·9m.

An earth satellite station has been built north of Auckland to link with the Pacific satellite Intelsat III to augment the Compac and Seacon telecommunications systems which link New Zealand with overseas countries.

There are 2 TV channels both operated by the state-owned New Zealand Broadcasting Corporation, which also operates most of the broadcasting stations. Over 85% of New Zealand households have TV sets. There are 65 medium-wave broadcasting stations and 2 short-wave transmitters. Some commercial material is broadcast by both sound and TV services. Number of TV receiving licences at 31 March 1983 was 921,724.

Cinemas. There were in 1981, 154 cinemas with a seating capacity of 89,364.

Newspapers. There were (1982), 31 daily newspapers (8 morning and 23 evening) with a combined circulation of 1,035,009. Seven of these newspapers (2 each in Auckland, Wellington and Christchurch and 1 in Dunedin) had a circulation of 703,034.

JUSTICE, RELIGION, EDUCATION AND WELFARE

Justice. The judiciary consists of the Court of Appeal, the High Court and District Courts. All exercise both civil and criminal jurisdiction. Other special courts include the Maori Land Court, Family Courts and Young Persons' Courts. At the end of Dec. 1982 the gaols and Borstal institutions contained 2,643 prisoners, 2,513 males and 130 females. The death penalty for murder was replaced by life imprisonment in 1961.

The Criminal Injuries Act, 1963, which came into force on 1 Jan. 1964, provided for compensation of persons injured by certain criminal acts and the dependants of persons killed by such acts. However, this has now been phased out in favour of the Accident Compensation Act, 1972, except in the residual area of property damage caused by escapers. Since 1970 legal aid in civil proceedings (except divorce) has been available for persons of small or moderate means. For the year ended 31 March 1983 expenditure amounted to $3,469,075 and 8,561 applications for aid were granted.

Police. The police in New Zealand are a national body maintained wholly by the central government. The total strength at 31 March 1983 was 5,014, the proportion of police to population being 1 to 636. The total cost of police services for the year 1982–83 was NZ$181m., equivalent to $57 per head of population. In New Zealand the police do not control traffic.

Ombudsmen. The office of Ombudsman was created in 1962. From 1975 additional Ombudsmen have been authorized. There are currently three. Ombudsmen's functions are to investigate complaints from members of the public relating to administrative decisions of government departments, local authorities and statutory organizations.

During the year ended 31 March 1983, 1,972 complaints were received, 71 of which were sustained.

Religion. No direct state aid is given to any form of religion. For the Church of England the country is divided into 7 dioceses, with a separate bishopric (Aotearoa) for the Maoris. The Presbyterian Church is divided into 23 presbyteries and the Maori Synod. The Moderator is elected annually. The Methodist Church is divided into 10 districts; the President is elected annually. The Roman Catholic Church is divided into 4 dioceses, with the Archbishop of Wellington as Metropolitan Archbishop.

Religious denomination	Number of clergy (April 1977)	Number of adherents 1976 census	Number of adherents 1981 census
Church of England	780	915,202	814,740
Presbyterian	686	566,569	523,221
Roman Catholic (including 'Catholic' undefined)	931	478,530	456,858
Methodist	349	173,526	148,512
Baptist	254	49,442	50,043
Brethren	187	24,414	24,324
Ratana	142	35,082	35,781
Protestant (undefined)	—	33,309	16,986
Salvation Army	241	22,019	20,490
Latter-day Saints (Mormon)	162	36,130	37,686
Congregationalist	10	6,600	3,825
Seventh-day Adventist	55	11,958	11,523
Ringatu	88	6,230	6,114
Christian (undefined)	—	52,478	101,901
Jehovah's Witnesses	125	13,392	13,737
Hebrew	7	3,921	3,360
All other religious professions	—	194,271	279,768
Agnostic	—	14,136	24,201
Atheist	—	14,283	21,528
Not specified	—	39,380	108,015
Object to state	—	438,511	473,115
Total	4,712	3,129,383	3,175,737

¹ Provisional.

Education. New Zealand has 6 universities, the University of Auckland, University of Waikato (at Hamilton), Victoria University of Wellington, Massey University (at Palmerston North), the University of Canterbury (at Christchurch) and the University of Otago (at Dunedin). There is, in addition, Lincoln College near Christchurch, a university college of agriculture, which is a constituent college of the University of Canterbury. The number of students in 1982 was 54,149. There were 8 teachers' training colleges with 4,503 students in 1982.

At 1 July 1982 there were 273 state secondary schools with 12,693 full-time teachers and 199,845 pupils. There were also 34 district high schools with 2,718 scholars in the secondary division. At 1 July 1982, 100,407 part-time pupils attended technical classes, and 29,837 received part-time instruction from the technical correspondence institute. At 1 July 1982, 937 pupils received tuition from the secondary department of the correspondence school. There were 45 registered private secondary schools with 1,161 teachers and 19,376 pupils.

At 1 July 1982, there were 2,341 state primary schools (including intermediate schools and departments), with 448,064 pupils; the number of teachers was 18,652. A correspondence school for children in remote areas and those otherwise unable to attend school had 1,451 primary pupils. There were 185 registered private primary schools with 1,095 teachers and 27,199 pupils.

Education is compulsory between the ages of 6 and 15. Children aged 3 and 4 years may enrol at the 535 free kindergartens maintained by Free Kindergarten Associations, which receive government assistance. There are also 682 play centres which also receive government subsidy. In July 1982 there were 40,009 and 16,395 children on the rolls respectively.

Total expenditure out of government funds in 1981–82 upon education was NZ$1,639m.

The universities and the affiliated agricultural colleges are autonomous bodies. Most secondary schools are controlled by their own boards. Virtually all state primary schools are controlled by the district education boards: there are 10 education districts. The Department of Education exercises certain defined functions in connexion with the general supervision of the education provided in state primary and secondary schools and disburses the government grants payable to controlling authorities for the running of those schools. Education in state schools is free for children under 19 years of age. Private schools are regularly visited by state school inspectors.

Report of the Minister of Education ('E.1. Report'). Annually. Wellington, Government Printer

NZ Committee on Secondary Education. *Towards Partnership.* Dept. of Education, 1976

Social Welfare. New Zealand's record for progressive legislation reaches back to 1898, when it was second only to Denmark in introducing non-contributory old-age pensions.

The present system came into operation from 1 April 1972. It provides for retirement, unemployment, widowhood, invalidity and sickness, as well as hospital and other medical care. Since 1 April 1969 the scheme has been financed from general taxation. Previously there was a special social security tax on virtually all income of individuals and companies in excess of $4 a week which met approximately three-quarters of the cost of the scheme, the balance being met from general taxation.

At 31 March 1983 the current weekly rates of widows', invalids', sickness, domestic purposes, unemployment and miners' benefits were $146·76 for a married couple, $88·06 for an unmarried person aged 20 years or over, and $66·99 for those under 20 years.

There are additional payments for dependent children.

All benefits except superannuation and family allowances are subject to an income test.

Family Benefit. A family benefit of $6 a week is payable for each dependent child.

Unemployment Benefit. The payment is subject to the condition that the applicant is capable and willing to undertake suitable employment.

Sickness Benefit. Payment is subject to medical evidence of incapacity of a person who has suffered a loss of weekly earnings as a result.

Other benefits include emergency benefits and additional benefits for those in need but who either do not qualify for one of the standard benefits or who have special needs or commitments for which a benefit at the standard rate is insufficient.

Medical, Hospital and Related Benefits. Medical, hospital and other related benefits are also provided under the Social Welfare scheme. These consist mainly of the payment of certain fees for medical attention by private practitioners, free treatment in public and mental hospitals, certain fees for treatment in private hospitals, maternity benefits (including ante-natal and post-natal treatment and services of doctors and nurses at confinements), pharmaceutical benefits (medicines, drugs, etc., prescribed by medical practitioners), etc. There are also benefits in connexion with dental services up to the age of 16, X-ray diagnosis, massage, home-nursing, artificial aids, etc.

Pensions. Provision is made for the payment of pensions and allowances to members or dependants of disabled, deceased or missing members, of the New Zealand Forces who served in the South African War, the two World Wars, the Korean War and the Vietnam War, to members of the New Zealand Mercantile Marine during the Second World War, or in connexion with any emergency whether arising out of the obligations undertaken by New Zealand in the Charter of the United Nations or otherwise. Principal rates are: War pensions are payable to widows at a rate of $43·54 a week, together with a mother's allowance of $52·70 a week, increased by $6 a week for each additional child, in addition to the normal child allowances of $6 per week for each child. These rates may be increased by an amount not exceeding $35·42 per week if the pensioner is suffering from total blindness, two or more serious disabilities or one extremely severe disability.

An 'economic pension' is defined as a supplementary pension granted on economic grounds and is additional to any pension payable as of right in respect of death or disablement. The maximum weekly rates are $73·38 to a married person (if unmarried, $88·06); to the widow or dependent widowed mother of a member, $88·06.

War veterans' allowances are $88·06 weekly for a single person and $73·38 for a married person, plus an equal amount to a wife, increased by $1.50 a week each at age 65, subject to income qualifications.

Domestic Purposes Benefit. A domestic purposes benefit is payable to unsupported male and female solo parents including divorced, separated and unmarried persons, prisoners' spouses and also to those who are required to give full-time care to a person (other than their spouse) who would otherwise have to be admitted to hospital.

Death Benefit. A death benefit of $1,000 is payable to a widow or widower if totally dependent on the deceased plus $500 for each dependent child but not exceeding $1,500.

Social Welfare Benefits and War Pensions:

Benefits	Number in force at 31 March 1983	Total payments 1982–83 (NZ$1,000)
SOCIAL WELFARE:		
Monetary—		
Superannuation	441,789	2,418,930
Widows	14,125	73,954
Orphans	362	1,114
Family	486,603	293,044
Invalids	18,757	79,073
Miners	16	94
Unemployment	50,744	195,217
Sickness	7,669	52,354
Domestic purposes	48,121	333,616
Total	1,068,186	3,447,399

		Total payments 1981–82 (NZ$1,000)
Benefits		
SOCIAL WELFARE (*contd.*):		
Health, etc.—		
Medical		52,081
Hospital		39,604
Maternity		9,951
Pharmaceutical		174,068
Supplementary		37,937
Total		313,641

WAR PENSIONS as at 31 March 1983:

Type of Person	Number in Force	Dependent Wives Included	Annual Value NZ$ (1,000)
War disablement	22,246	–	23,996
Dependants of disabled	113	–	429
Widows	4,540		
Other dependants of deceased	66	–	10,394
Economic	2,067	113	9,318
War service	3,137	2,081	20,736
War veteran's allowance	1,911	918	12,279
Police	35	–	41
Total	34,115	3,112	77,193

Reciprocity with Other Countries. There are reciprocal arrangements between New Zealand and Australia in respect of age, invalids', widows', family, unemployment and sickness benefits, and between New Zealand and the UK in respect of family, age, superannuation, widows', orphans', invalids', sickness and unemployment benefits.

Superannuation. Following the change of Government in Dec. 1975 the earnings-related superannuation scheme described in THE STATESMAN'S YEAR-BOOK, 1977–78, was abolished. Under the new system (operative from Feb. 1977) super-annuation is payable to all New Zealanders on reaching the age of 60. It is taxable but not subject to an income test. The rates are based on the national average wage, of which married couples now receive 80% and single persons 60% of the married rate.

Health. At 30 June 1982 there were 8,565 doctors on the medical register. At 31 March 1982 there were 25,524 public hospital beds, of which 2,352 were for maternity cases.

MINOR ISLANDS

The minor islands (total area, 320 sq. miles, 775 sq. km) included within the geographical boundaries of New Zealand are the following: Kermadec Islands, Three Kings Islands, Auckland Islands, Campbell Island, Antipodes Islands, Bounty Islands, Snares Islands, Solander Island. With the exception of Raoul Island in the Kermadec Group (population, 5, 1981 census) and Campbell Island (population, 10, 1981 census) none of these islands is inhabited.

The **Kermadec Islands,** which were annexed to New Zealand in 1887, have no separate administration and all New Zealand laws apply to them. Situation, 29° 10′ to 131° 30′ S. lat., 177° 45′ to 179° W. long., 600 miles NNE of New Zealand. Area, 13 sq. miles (33·5 sq. km). The largest of the group is Raoul or Sunday Island, 20 miles in circuit, while Macauley Island is 3 miles in circuit.

A meteorological station and an aeradio station have been established on Raoul Island, the official staff being the only inhabitants.

TERRITORIES OVERSEAS

Territories Overseas coming within the jurisdiction of New Zealand consist of Tokelau and the Ross Dependency.

Tokelau. Situated some 480 km to the north of Western Samoa between 8° and 10° S. lat., and between 171° and 173° W. long., are the 3 atoll islands of Atafu, Nukunonu and Fakaofo of the Tokelau (Union) group. Formerly part of the Gilbert and Ellice Islands Colony, the group was transferred to the jurisdiction of New Zealand on 11 Feb. 1926. By legislation enacted in 1948, the Tokelau Islands were declared part of New Zealand as from 1 Jan. 1949. The area of the group is 1,011 hectares; the population at census 25 Oct. 1976 was 1,575; estimate, 31 Dec. 1981, 1,572.

By the Tokelau Islands Act 1948 the Tokelau Group was included within the territorial boundaries of New Zealand; legislative powers are now invested in the Governor-General in Council. The inhabitants are British subjects and New Zealand citizens. In Dec. 1976 the territory was officially renamed 'Tokelau', the name by which it has customarily been known to its inhabitants.

From 8 Nov. 1974 the office of Administrator was invested in the Secretary of Foreign Affairs. Certain powers are delegated to the district officer in Apia, Western Samoa.

Because of the very restricted economic and social future in the atolls, the islanders agreed to a proposal put to them by the Minister of Island Territories in 1965 that over a period of years most of the population be resettled in New Zealand. Up to March 1975, 528 migrants entered New Zealand as permanent residents under Government sponsorship. At the request of the people the scheme has now been suspended.

New Zealand Government aid to Tokelau totalled $1·9m. for the year ended 31 March 1983.

Ross Dependency. By Imperial Order in Council, dated 30 July 1923, the territories between 160° E. long. and 150° W. long. and south of 60° S. lat. were brought within the jurisdiction of the New Zealand Government. The region was named the Ross Dependency. From time to time laws for the Dependency have been made by regulations promulgated by the Governor-General of New Zealand.

The mainland area is estimated at 400,000–450,000 sq. km and is mostly ice-covered. In Jan. 1957 a New Zealand expedition under Sir Edmund Hillary established a base in the Dependency. In Jan. 1958 Sir Edmund Hillary and 4 other New Zealanders reached the South Pole.

The main base—Scott Base—at Pram Point, Ross Island—is manned throughout the year, about 12 people being present during winter. Vanda Station in the dry ice-free Wright Valley is manned every summer.

Quartermain, L. B., *New Zealand and the Antarctic.* Wellington, 1971

SELF-GOVERNING TERRITORIES OVERSEAS
THE COOK ISLANDS

HISTORY. The Cook Islands, which lie between 8° and 23° S. lat., and 156° and 167° W. long., were proclaimed a British protectorate in 1888, and on 11 June 1901 were annexed and proclaimed part of New Zealand.

AREA AND POPULATION. The islands within the territory fall roughly into two groups—the scattered islands towards the north (Northern group) and the islands towards the south known as the Lower group. The names of the islands with their populations as at the census of 1 Dec. 1981 were as follows:

Lower Group—	Area sq. km	Population	Northern Group—	Area sq. km	Population
Rarotonga	67·2	9,530	Nassau	1·2	134
Mangaia	51·8	1,364	Palmerston (Avarau)	2·0	51
Atiu	26·9	1,225	Penrhyn (Tongareva)	9·8	608
Aitutaki	18·0	2,335	Manihiki (Humphrey)	5·4	405
Mauke (Parry Is.)	18·4	681	Rakahanga (Reirson)	4·1	272
Mitiaro	22·3	256	Pukapuka (Danger)	5·1	796
Manuae and Te au-o-tu	6·2	12	Suwarrow (Anchorage)	0·4	—
			Total	293	17,754

In 1982, 439 live births and 130 deaths were registered. In 1982 there were 24,000 Cook Islanders living abroad, mainly in New Zealand.

CONSTITUTION AND GOVERNMENT. The Cook Islands Constitution Act 1964, which provides for the establishment of internal self-government in the Cook Islands, came into force on 4 Aug. 1965.

The Act establishes the Cook Islands as fully self-governing but linked to New Zealand by a common Head of State, the Queen, and a common citizenship, that of New Zealand. It provides for a ministerial system of government with a Cabinet consisting of a Premier and 6 other Ministers. The New Zealand Government is represented by a New Zealand Representative and the position of a Queen's Representative has recently been created by changes in the Constitution. New Zealand continues to be responsible for the external affairs and defence of the Cook Islands, subject to consultation between the New Zealand Prime Minister and the Prime Minister. The changed status of the Islands does not affect the consideration of subsidies or the right of free entry into New Zealand for exports from the group.

Prime Minister Geoffery Arama Henry.

ECONOMY AND TRADE

Budget. Revenue is derived chiefly from customs duties which follow the New Zealand customs tariff, income tax and stamp sales.

Grants from New Zealand, mainly for medical, educational and general administrative purposes totalled $5·8m. in 1981–82.

Currency. The Cook Island *dollar* is at par with the New Zealand *dollar*.

Agriculture. Livestock (1980): Pigs, 17,000; goats, 3,000; poultry, 66,000.

Commerce. Exports, mainly to New Zealand, were valued at $5m. in 1982. Main items of export were fresh fruit and vegetables, fruit juice, canned pineapple, copra and clothing. Imports totalled $26·6m. in 1980; approximately 60% of the total were imports (including re-exports from New Zealand). The main items were foodstuffs, manufactured goods (including transport equipment), petrol and oil.

COMMUNICATIONS

Aviation. New Zealand has financed the construction of an international airport at Rarotonga which became operational for jet services in Sept. 1973.

Shipping. A fortnightly cargo shipping service is provided between New Zealand, Niue and Rarotonga.

Telecommunications. Wireless stations are maintained at all the permanently inhabited islands. In 1982 there were 1,583 telephones.

EDUCATION AND HEALTH

Education. Twenty-eight primary schools are established in the various islands. Of these, two are Roman Catholic missionary schools and two are Seventh-Day Adventist missionary schools. Five primary schools have secondary school attachments, and there are also ten secondary schools. Two of these secondary schools are run by missions; one by the Roman Catholic Mission and the other by the Seventh-

Day Adventist Mission. The number of students enrolled at school on 31 March 1982, was 6,424.

The instruction given at school is based on the New Zealand School syllabus and students can sit for the New Zealand School Certificate and University Entrance examinations. Most schools teach in both the English and Cook Island Maori languages, but the use of Cook Islands Maori is restricted to the primary school level.

There were 102 Government-funded students studying at overseas tertiary or technical institutes in 1983.

Health. All Cook Islanders receive free medical and surgical treatment in their villages, the hospital and the tuberculosis sanatorium. Cook Island Maori patients in the hospital and the sanatorium and all schoolchildren receive free dental treatment.

NIUE

History. Niue achieved internal self-government in Oct. 1974.

Area and Population. Distance from Auckland, New Zealand, 1,343 miles; from Rarotonga, 580 miles. Area, 100 sq. miles; circumference, 40 miles; height above sea-level, 220 ft. Population at 28 Sept. 1981 was 3,296; 1983, estimate, 3,032. During 1982 births registered numbered 100, deaths 21. Migration to New Zealand is the main factor in population change.

Constitution and Government. There is a Legislative Assembly of 20 members, and legislative measures apply as in the case of the Cook Islands.
Premier: Robert R. Rex, CMG, OBE.

Budget. Financial aid from New Zealand, 1982–83, totalled $5,906,000.

Agriculture. The most important products of the island are coconuts, passion fruit, honey, limes and root crops.

Trade. Exports, 1982, $642,175 (main export, canned coconut cream); imports, $3,431,367.

Communications. There is a wireless station at Alofi, the port of the island. Two weekly commercial air services link Niue with Western Samoa, Cook Islands, American Samoa and New Zealand. Telephones (1982) 205.

Education. There were 8 government schools with 938 pupils in 1982.

Health. There is a 30-bed hospital in Alofi and clinics in some villages.

DIPLOMATIC REPRESENTATIVES

Of New Zealand in Great Britain (New Zealand Hse, Haymarket, London, SW1Y 4TQ)
High Commissioner: William Young (accredited 5 Nov. 1982).

Of Great Britain in New Zealand (Reserve Bank of New Zealand Bldg., 2 The Terrace, Wellington, 1)
High Commissioner: Sir Richard Stratton, KCMG.

Of New Zealand in the USA (37 Observatory Cir., NW, Washington, D.C., 20008)
Ambassador: L. R. Adams-Schneider.

Of the USA in New Zealand (29 Fitzherbert Terrace, Wellington)
Ambassador: H. Monroe Brown.

Of New Zealand to the United Nations
Ambassador: Bryce Harland.

Books of Reference

Statistical Information: The central statistical office for New Zealand is the Department of Statistics (Wellington, 1).

The beginning of a statistical service may be seen in the early 'Blue books' prepared annually from 1840 onwards under the direction of the Colonial Secretary, and designed primarily for the information of the Colonial Office in England. A permanent statistical authority was created in 1858. The Department of Statistics functions under the Statistics Act 1975 and reports to Parliament through the Minister of Statistics. A comprehensive statistical service has been developed to meet national requirements, and close contact is maintained with the United Nations Statistical Office and other international statistical organizations; through the Conference of Asian Statisticians assistance is being given with the development of statistics in the region.

The oldest publications consist of *(a)* census results from 1858 onwards and *(b)* annual volumes of statistics (first published 1858 but covering years back to 1853). Main current publications:

New Zealand Official Yearbook. Annual, from 1893
Catalogue of New Zealand Statistics. 1972
Statistical Reports of New Zealand. Annual
Monthly Abstract of Statistics. From 1914
Pocket Digest of Statistics. Annual, 1927–31, 1938 ff.

Parliamentary Reports of Government Departments. Annual
Pacific Islands Yearbook. Sydney, 1977
Dictionary of New Zealand Biography. 2 vols. Wellington, 1940
Encyclopaedia of New Zealand. 3 vols. Wellington, 1966
National Bibliography. Wellington, 1968
Alley, R., *New Zealand and the Pacific.* Boulder, 1983
Bedggood, D., *Rich and Poor in New Zealand.* Sydney, 1980
Bush, G., *Local Government and Politics in New Zealand.* Sydney, 1980
Easton, B., *Social Policy and the Welfare State in New Zealand.* Auckland, 1980
Grover, R. F., *New Zealand.* [Bibliography] Oxford and Santa Barbara, 1981
Holcroft, M. H., *The Shaping of New Zealand.* Auckland, 1975
Kennaway, R., Jackson, K., Henderson, J. (eds.) *Beyond New Zealand: The Foreign Policy of a Small State.* Auckland, 1980
Levine, S. (ed.), *Politics in New Zealand.* London, 1978.—*The New Zealand Political System.* London, 1979
Morrell, W. P., and Hall, D. O. W., *A History of New Zealand Life.* Christchurch and London, 1957
Oliver, W. H. (ed.), *The Oxford History of New Zealand.* OUP, 1981
Robson, J. L. (ed.), *New Zealand: The Development of its Laws and Constitution.* 2nd ed. London, 1967
Shadbolt, M. F. R., *The Shell Guide to New Zealand.* Christchurch, 1976
Sinclair, K., *A History of New Zealand.* Rev. ed. London, 1980
Traue, J. E., *Who's Who in New Zealand.* 11th ed. Wellington, 1978
Wards, I., *A Descriptive Atlas of New Zealand.* Wellington, Government Printer, 1976
Wise's New Zealand Guide. 7th ed. Auckland, 1979

NICARAGUA

República de Nicaragua

Capital: Managua
Population: 2·82m. (1981)
GNP per capita: US$720 (1980)

HISTORY. Active colonization of the Pacific coast was undertaken by Spaniards from Panama, beginning in 1523. After links with other Central American territories, and Mexico, Nicaragua became completely independent in 1838, but subject to a prolonged feud between the 'Liberals' of León and the 'Conservatives' of Granada. Mosquitia remained an autonomous kingdom on the Atlantic coast, under British protection until 1860.

On 5 Aug. 1914 the Bryan–Chamarro treaty between Nicaragua and the US was signed, under which the US in return for US$3m. acquired a permanent option for a canal route through Nicaragua and a 99-year option for a naval base in the Bay of Fonseca on the Pacific coast and Corn Island on the Atlantic coast. It was ratified by Nicaragua on 7 April 1916 and by the US on 22 June 1916. US Marines finally left in 1933. The Bryan–Chamarro treaty was abrogated on 14 July 1970.

In 1962 the Sandinist National Liberation Front was established. A left-wing organization formed to overthrow the existing government by revolutionary means. In 1979 a 'provincial government' was formed and after heavy fighting the President (Gen. Somoza) resigned.

AREA AND POPULATION. Area estimated at 148,000 sq. km (57,143 sq. miles) or 139,000 sq. km (54,296 sq. miles) if the lakes are excluded. The coastline runs 336 miles on the Atlantic and 219 miles on the Pacific. Population at the census of April 1971 was 1,911,543 (922,433 males, 989,110 females). Estimate (1981) 2,823,979.

Nicaragua is the largest in area and most thinly populated of the Central American republics. In 1981, births, 104,000; marriages, 16,000; deaths, 10,000.

The people of the western half of the republic are principally of mixed Spanish and Indian extraction, some of pure Spanish descent and many Indians. The population of the eastern half is composed mainly of Mosquito and other Indians and Zambos, and Negroes from Jamaica and other islands of the Caribbean. The main ethnic groups in 1974 were: Mestizo, 69%; white, 19%; Negro, 9%; Indio, 5%.

Nicaragua is administratively divided into the following 16 departments with population as in 1981:

Boaco	88,862	Jinotega	127,159	Matagalpa	220,548
Carazo	109,450	Léon	248,704	Nueva Segovia	97,765
Chinandega	228,573	Madriz	72,408	Río San Juan	29,001
Chontales	98,462	Managua	819,679	Rivas	108,913
Esteli	110,076	Masaya	149,015	Zelaya	202,462
Granada	113,102				

Of the 134 *municipios*, 98 have from 2,000 to 50,000 inhabitants. The capital is Managua, situated on the lake of the same name, 180 ft above sea level, with (1981) 819,679 inhabitants. Other cities (1978): León, 81,647; Granada, 56,232; Masaya, 47,276; Chinandega, 44,435; Matagalpa, 26,986; Estelí, 26,892; Bluefields, 18,252; Jinotega, 14,088; Juigalpa, 13,468; Boaco, 8,684.

CLIMATE. The climate is tropical, with a wet season from May to Jan. Temperatures vary with altitude. Managua. Jan. 79°F (26°C), July 86°F (30°C). Annual rainfall 45″ (1,140 mm).

CONSTITUTION AND GOVERNMENT. Following the fall of Gen. Somoza, a Government of National Reconstruction abrogated the 1974 Constitution and in Aug. 1979 issued a manifesto guaranteeing the basic freedoms and a fundamental statute confirmed these in 1980. Elections for a President and Vice-President and for a 90-member National Assembly will be held in Nov. 1984. Elections for the President and Vice-President will be by direct vote and for the National Assembly by proportional representation. The minimum voting age would be 16 years.

Members of the Junta were in 1984: Cdr Daniel Ortega Saavedra, Dr Sergio Ramírez Mercado, Dr Rafael Córdova Rivas. There is a cabinet of 22 ministers.

The republic is divided into 16 departments, each of which is under a political head (appointed by the President), who has supervision of finance, education and other matters. The departments have 134 *municipios*, headed by a mayor (*alcalde*). The Mosquito Reserve now forms part of the departments of Zelaya and Río San Juan.

National flag: Three horizontal stripes of blue, white, blue, with the national arms in the centre.

National anthem: Salve a ti Nicaragua (words by S. Ibarra Mayorga, 1937).

DEFENCE. Conscription was introduced in 1983 for men between 17 and 22 years.

Army. The Army is organized into 3 armoured, 10 infantry, 3 artillery and 1 engineer battalions and 1 anti-aircraft artillery group. Equipment includes 45 T-54/-55 and 3 M-4A3 main battle tanks. Strength (1984) 22,000 with an additional 25,000 regular reservists. The Civilian Militia numbers about 30,000.

Navy. Four coastguard cutters, 11 coastal patrol craft and 2 minor landing craft operated by the marine section of the National Guard picket the east and west coasts. Personnel in 1984 totalled 200 officers and men.

Air Force. Formed in June 1938 as the Nicaraguan Army Air Force, the Air Force has been semi-independent since 1947. Its combat units are reported to have more than 80 L-39 Albatross light jet attack/trainers, 4 Summit O2-337 Sentry counter-insurgency aircraft, 4 T-33 armed jet trainers, and 4 T-28 armed piston-engined trainers. Other equipment includes some C-47s, 5 Spanish-built Aviocar and 2 Israeli-built Arava STOL transports and smaller communications aircraft and helicopters, including 6 Mi-8s.

INTERNATIONAL RELATIONS

Membership. Nicaragua is a member of the UN, OAS and the C00

Membership. Nicaragua is a member of the UN, OAS and the Central American Common Market.

ECONOMY

Planning. The objects of the National Reconstruction Plan 1975–79 included the reconstruction of Managua which took one-third of the US$6,000m. envisaged for the plan.

Budget. Revenue and expenditure for fiscal years, ending 31 Dec., in 1m. córdobas:

	1975	1976	1977	1978	1979	1980
Revenue	1,820·3	2,052·3	2,774·3	3,255·3	3,760·1	5,972·0
Expenditure	1,881·9	2,223·1	2,427·6	3,433·8	3,409·0	5,972·0

Currency. The monetary unit is the *córdoba* (C$), divided into 100 *centavos.* On 31 Dec. 1978 total money supply was 1,887·8m. córdobas. Bills form the greater part of the currency, in denominations from 1,000 córdobas to 1 córdoba. Silver coins struck, but now out of circulation, are 50, 25 and 10 centavos; copper–nickel and copper–zinc coins, 1 córdoba, 50, 25, 10 and 5 centavos. March 1984, US$1 = 10 *córdobas*; £1 = 14·87 *córdobas.*

Banking. The National Bank of Nicaragua at Managua founded in 1912, owned by the Government since 1924 was reorganized in July 1979, becoming the National

Development Bank and including the National Development Institute (INFONAC) and Special Fund for Development (FED). This new law gave it increased responsibilities as a development bank. The Central Bank of Nicaragua came into operation on 1 Jan. 1961 as an autonomous bank of issue, absorbing the issue department of the National Bank.

In July 1979 private financial banking was nationalized and branches of foreign banks were prohibited from receiving deposits.

Weights and Measures. Since 1893 the metric system of weights and measures has been recommended.

ENERGY AND NATURAL RESOURCES

Electricity. Installed capacity for electric energy was 357,700 kw. in 1977 and 1,180·3 kwh. was produced.

Minerals. Production of gold in 1980 was 67,000 troy oz.; of silver, 167,000 troy oz.; of copper, 3,000 tonnes. There is no iron or coalmining. Large deposits of tungsten in Nueva Segovia were announced in 1961. Exploration for petroleum began off the Pacific and Atlantic coasts in 1965. A petroleum refinery of 650,000 tonnes capacity is functioning at Managua.

Agriculture. Agriculture is the principal source of national wealth, finding work for 65% of the labour force, and furnishing, 1975, 22% of the GNP.

Of the total land area (about 36·5m. acres), about 17·5m. acres are under timber 0·9m. acres are used for grazing and 2·1m. acres are arable. The unit of area used locally is the *manzana* (= 1·73 acres). Of the arable only 1·2m. acres are actively cultivated, 780,000 in annual crops such as cotton and rice and the remainder in perennial crops such as coffee and sugar-cane, or in two harvests a year in the cases of maize, sorghum and beans.

The products of the western half are varied, the most important being cotton, coffee, now under the aegis of the new *Instituto del Café*, sugar-cane, cocoa, maize, sesame and beans. Production (1982): Coffee, 57,000 tonnes; sugar, 3m. tonnes; cotton, 190,000 tonnes.

There were about 2·19m. head of cattle in 1982. There were 520,000 pigs (1982).

Forestry. Timber production has been declining, though the forests, which cover 10m. acres and 4 distinct zones, contain mahogany and cedar, which were formerly largely exported, three varieties of rosewoods, guayacán (*lignum vitae*) and dyewoods. Production of sawn wood in 1978, 270,000 tonnes.

Fishery. On the Atlantic coast fisheries are an important subsistence activity. Over 6·4m. lb. of shrimps were exported in 1978 and were processed in 3 plants at Schooner Cay, El Bluff and Corn Island. Catch (1980) 19,900 tonnes.

INDUSTRY AND TRADE

Industry. Chief local industries are cane sugar, cooking oil, cigarettes, beer, leather products, plastics, textiles, chemical products, metal products, cement (181,000 tonnes in 1979), strong and soft drinks, soluble coffee, dairy products, meat, plywood. Production of oil products, in 1978, was valued at 526m. córdobas; food products, 3,338·4m.; beverages, 565·8m.; textiles, 328·7m.; chemical substances and products, 1,054m.

Labour. In 1980 there were some 813,000 persons gainfully employed.

Commerce. The foreign trade of Nicaragua, in US$1m., was as follows in calendar years:

	1977	1978	1979	1980	1981
Imports	761·9	553·0	388·0	870·0	807·6
Exports	636·8	645·9	598·0	469·7	520·0

Total trade between Nicaragua and UK (British Department of Trade returns, in £1,000 sterling):

	1979	1980	1981	1982	1983
Imports to UK	895	1,510	1,030	3,282	1,810
Exports and re-exports from UK	3,229	2,478	4,269	4,940	2,367

COMMUNICATIONS

Roads. In 1980, 4,000 km were paved, out of a total of 25,000 km. The whole 368·5 km of the Nicaraguan section of the Pan-American Highway is now paved. The all-weather Roosevelt Highway linking Managua with the river port Rama was completed in 1968, to provide the first overland link with the Atlantic coast. There are paved roads to San Juan del Sur, Puerto Somoza and Corinto. In 1981 there were 66,000 vehicles in use including 23,000 cars.

Railways. The Pacific Railroad of Nicaragua, owned and operated by the Government, has a total length of 373 km, all single-track, and connects Corinto, Chinandega, León, Managua, Masaya and Granada. Passengers carried (1981) 640,000.

Aviation. LANICA, the Nicaraguan airline has daily flights to Miami and 6 flights a week to Guatemala and to the inner cities of Bluefields, Puerto Cabezas and the mining towns of Siuna and Bonanza. PANAM and TACA (Transportes Aéreos Centroamericanos), COPA (Compañía Panameña de Aviacíon), have daily services to Panama. Mexico, the other Central American countries and USA. SAM (Servicio Aéreo de Medellín) has 3 flights a week to Nicaragua and Colombia. In 1977, 223,420 passengers and 24·2m. tonnes of cargo were carried.

Shipping. The Pacific ports are Corinto (the largest), San Juan del Sur and Puerto Saudino through which pass most of the external trade. The chief eastern ports are El Bluff (for Bluefields) and Puerto Cabezas. The merchant marine consists solely of the Mamenic Line with 8 vessels. In 1980, 471,000 tonnes of goods were loaded and 1·14m. tonnes unloaded at Nicaraguan ports.

Post and Broadcasting. In 1982 there were 51,237 telephones.

The Tropical Radio Telegraph Company maintains a powerful station at Managua, and branch stations at Bluefields and Puerto Cabezas. The Government operates the National Radio with 47 broadcasting stations: there are 31 commercial stations and some 70 others. Number of wireless sets in 1981 was 140,000 and television sets 180,000. There are 2 television stations at Managua.

Cinemas. Cinemas numbered over 100 in 1977 and seated over 60,000.

Newspapers. There are 3 daily newspapers (2 in Managua and 1 in León), with a total circulation of about 105,000.

JUSTICE, RELIGION, EDUCATION AND WELFARE

Justice. The judicial power is vested in a Supreme Court of Justice at Managua, 5 chambers of second instance (León, Masaya, Granada, Matagalpa and Bluefields) and 153 judges of inferior tribunals.

Religion. The prevailing form of religion is Roman Catholic, but religious liberty is guaranteed by the Constitution. The republic constitutes 1 archbishopric (seat at Managua) and 7 bishoprics (León, Granada, Estelí, Matagalpa, Juigalpa, Masaya and Puerto Cabezas). Protestants, established principally on the Atlantic coast, numbered 54,100 in 1966.

Education. There were, in 1981, 4,577 primary schools, with a total of 503,497 pupils and 14,113 teachers; and 377 secondary schools, with 139,743 pupils and 4,221 teachers. It was claimed that the illiteracy rate was 13% in 1980. In 1977 there were 6 universities and technical colleges with 1,204 professors and 23,171 students.

Social Welfare. In 1980 there were 1,600 physicians and 50 hospitals with 4,573 beds.

DIPLOMATIC REPRESENTATIVES

Of Nicaragua in Great Britain (8 Gloucester Rd., London, SW7 4PP)
Ambassador: Francisco d'Escoto.

Of Great Britain in Nicaragua
Ambassador and Consul-General: P. W. Summerscale (resides in San José).

Of Nicaragua in the USA (1627 New Hampshire Ave., NW, Washington, D.C., 20009)
Ambassador: Antonio Jarquin.

Of the USA in Nicaragua (Km. 4½ Carretera Sur., Managua)
Ambassador: Anthony C. Quainton.

Of Nicaragua to the United Nations
Ambassador: Javier Chamorro Mora.

Books of Reference

Dirección General Estadística y Censos, *Boletín de Estadística* (irregular intervals); and *Indicadores Economicos.*
Black, G., *Triumph of the People: The Sandinista Revolution in Nicaragua.* London, 1981
Boletín de la Superintendencia de Bancos. Banco Central, Managua
Walker, T. W., *Nicaragua: The Land of Sandino.* Boulder, 1982
Weber, H., *Nicaragua: The Sandinista Revolution.* London and New York, 1981

National Library: Biblioteca Nacional, Managua, D.N.

NIGER

République du Niger

Capital: Niamey
Population: 6·04m. (1983)
GNP per capita: US$330 (1980)

HISTORY. Niger was occupied by France between 1883 and 1899, and became a territory of French West Africa in 1904. It became an autonomous republic within the French Community on 18 Dec. 1958 and achieved full independence on 3 Aug. 1960.

On 15 April 1974 the first President, Hamani Diori, was overthrown in a military *coup* led by Lieut.-Col. Seyni Kountché, who suspended the constitution, dissolved the National Assembly and banned political groups.

AREA AND POPULATION. Niger is bounded north by Algeria and Libya, east by Chad, south by Nigeria, south-west by Benin and Upper Volta and west by Mali. Area, 1,186,408 sq. km (458,075 sq. miles), with a population at the 1977 census of 5,098,657. Estimate (1983) 6,040,000. The major towns (populations 1977) are: Niamey, the capital (225,314 inhabitants), Zinder (58,436), Maradi (45,852), Tahoua (31,265), Agadez (20,475). The population is composed chiefly of Hausa (54%), Songhai and Djerma (23%), Fulani (10%), Beriberi-Manga (9%) and Tuareg (3%). The official language is French.

CLIMATE. Precipitation determines the geographical division into a southern zone of agriculture, a central zone of pasturage and a desert-like northern zone. The country lacks water, with the exception of the south-western districts, which are watered by the Niger and its tributaries, and the southern zone, where there are a number of wells. Niamey, 95°F (35°C). Annual rainfall varies from 22" (560 mm) in the south to 7" (180 mm) in the Sahara zone.

CONSTITUTION AND GOVERNMENT. The country is administered by a Supreme Military Council of 12 officers led by the President, who appoints a Council of Ministers to assist him.

The Council of Ministers, in Nov. 1983, comprised:

Head of State, President of SMC, Defence and Interior: Maj.-Gen. Seyni Kountché.

Prime Minister: Habid Algabid.

Ministers: Idé Oumarou *(Foreign Affairs and Co-operation)*, Boukari Adji *(Finance)*, Daouda Diallo *(Information)*, Issoufou Mayaki *(National Education)*, Annou Mahamane *(Planning)*, Amadou Nouhou *(Commerce and Transport)*, Salaou Barmou *(Posts and Telecommunications)*, Yahaya Tounkara *(Hydrology and Environment)*, Hadji Nadji *(Civil Service and Labour)* Sani Koutoubi *(Mines and Industry)*, Dr Ari Toubo Ibrahim *(Rural Development)*, Illa Maikassoua *(Higher Education and Research)*, Amadou Djibo *(Youth, Sports and Culture)*, Moumouni Yacouba *(Public Works and Town Planning)*, Dr Abdou Moudi *(Public Health and Social Affairs)*, al-Haji Allele Habibou *(Justice)*.

Minister-Delegate: Amadou Fity Maiga *(Interior)*.

Secretaries of State: Amadou Modieli *(National Education)*, al-Housseini Mouloul *(Planning)*, al-Moustapha Soumeila *(Commerce and Transport)*.

National flag: Three horizontal strips of orange, white and green, with an orange disc in the middle of the white strip.

Local government: Niger is divided into 7 *départements* (Agadez, Diffa, Dosso, Maradi, Niamey, Tahoua and Zinder), each under a prefect; they are sub-divided into 38 *arrondissements*, each under a sub-prefect.

DEFENCE. Selective military service for 2 years operates.

Army. The Army consists of 2 armoured reconnaissance squadrons, 4 infantry, 1 engineer, 1 parachute and 1 support company. Equipment includes 10 M-8 and 30 ERC-60-20 armoured cars. Strength (1984) 2,150. There are additional paramilitary forces of some 2,500 men.

Air Force. The Air Force has 70 officers and men, 2 C-130H and 3 C-47 transports, 1 Boeing 737 VIP transport, 2 Cessna Skymasters, 3 Do 28D Skyservants and 1 Aero Commander 500 for communications duties.

INTERNATIONAL RELATIONS

Membership. Niger is a member of UN, OAU and is an ACP state of the EEC.

ECONOMY

Planning. An economic development plan, covering the period 1965–68 was followed by a 3-year preparatory plan and was part of a 10-year economic programme (1965–74). This was followed by a further 10-year plan (1973–82).

Budget. The ordinary budget for 1983 balanced at 81,250m. francs CFA.

Currency. The unit of currency is the *franc CFA*, with a parity rate of 50 francs CFA to 1 French franc.

Banking. The *Banque Centrale des États de l'Afrique de l'Ouest* is the bank of issue, and there are 7 commercial banks in Niamey.

ENERGY AND NATURAL RESOURCES

Electricity. Production (1980) amounted to 52,000 kwh.

Oil. Deposits in the Lake Chad area, located in 1978, are to be exploited.

Minerals. Large uranium deposits are mined at Arlit and Akouta, in the Aïr mountains of northern Niger, with French and Japanese assistance. Concentrate production (1981) 4,585 tonnes. Phosphates are mined in the Niger valley, and coal reserves are being exploited by open-cast mining. Salt and natron are produced at Manga and Agadez, tin ore in Aïr.

Agriculture. The chief agricultural products in 1981 (in 1,000 tonnes) were: Millet, 1,117; pulses, 280; sorghum, 273; cassava, 225; sugar-cane, 190; in the river districts, cotton and rice (38,000 tonnes). Gum arabic is produced at Gouré, nearly all of which is exported to Nigeria.

Livestock (1982): Cattle, 3·3m.; horses, 270,000; asses, 460,000; sheep, 2·9m.; goats, 7·3m.; camels, 410,000; chickens, 11m.

INDUSTRY AND TRADE

Industry. Some small manufacturing industries, mainly in Niamey, produce textiles, food products, furniture and chemicals.

Trade Unions. The sole national body is the *Union Nationale des Travailleurs du Niger,* which has 15,000 members in 31 unions.

Commerce. Imports in 1980 were valued at 111,000m. francs CFA and exports at 97,000m. francs CFA.

Total trade between Niger and UK (British Department of Trade returns, in £1,000 sterling):

	1979	1980	1981	1982	1983
Imports to UK	297	184	5,762	574	6,854
Exports and re-exports from UK	16,576	7,885	5,201	17,346	9,650

In 1980, France provided 45% of imports and took 74% of the exports. Main exports were uranium (76%), livestock and peanut oil.

COMMUNICATIONS

Roads. In 1981 there were 8,547 km of roads. Niamey and Zinder are the termini of two trans-Sahara motor routes; the Hoggar–Aïr–Zinder road extends to Kano and the Tanezrouft-Gao-Niamey road to Benin. A 648-km 'uranium road' runs from Arlit to Niamey. There were (1980), 25,800 private cars and 4,400 commercial vehicles.

Aviation. There are international airports at Niamey, Zinder and Maradi. Air Niger operates domestic services to over 20 other public airports.

Post and Broadcasting. There were (1977) 8,147 telephones. In Dec. 1979 there were 200,000 radio and 500 television receivers.

Cinemas. In 1970 there were 4 cinemas with a seating capacity of 3,800.

Newspapers. In 1982 there was 1 daily newspaper with a circulation of 3,000.

JUSTICE, RELIGION, EDUCATION AND WELFARE

Justice. There are Magistrates' and Assize Courts at Niamey, Zinder and Maradi, and justices of the peace in smaller centres. The Court of Appeal is at Niamey.

Religion. In 1979, 85% of the population was Moslem and the remainder mainly followed animist beliefs. There were about 20,000 Christians.

Education. There were, in 1979, 187,151 pupils and 4,762 teachers in primary schools, 25,491 and 866 teachers in secondary schools, 1,259 and 64 teachers in 4 teacher-training colleges, 354 students and 31 teachers in the technical school in Maradi and 939 students and 185 teaching staff at the University of Niamey.

Health. In 1982 there were 2 hospitals, 36 medical centres and 116 dispensaries. In 1976 there were 110 doctors, 6 dentists, 8 pharmacists, 70 midwives and 575 nursing personnel.

DIPLOMATIC REPRESENTATIVES

Of Niger in Great Britain
Ambassador: (Vacant).

Of Great Britain in Niger
Ambassador and Consul-General: J. M. Willson (resides in Abidjan).

Of Niger in the USA (2204 R. St., NW, Washington, D.C. 20008)
Ambassador: Joseph Diatta.

Of the USA in Niger (PO Box 11201, Niamey)
Ambassador: William R. Casey, Jr.

Of Niger to the United Nations
Ambassador: (Vacant).

Books of Reference

Bonardi, P.. *La République du Niger.* Paris, 1960
Fugelstad, F., *A History of Niger, 1850–1960.* OUP, 1984
Séré de Rivières, E., *Histoire du Niger.* Paris, 1965

NIGERIA

Federal Republic of Nigeria

Capital: Lagos
Population: 82·39m. (1983)
GNP per capita: US$1,010 (1980)

HISTORY. The Federal Republic comprises a number of areas formerly under separate administrations. Lagos, ceded in Aug. 1861 by King Dosunmu, was placed under the Governor of Sierra Leone in 1866. In 1874 it was detached, together with Gold Coast Colony, and formed part of the latter until Jan. 1886, when a separate 'colony and protectorate of Lagos' was constituted. Meanwhile the United African Company had established British interests in the Niger valley, and in July 1886 the company obtained a charter under the name of the Royal Niger Company. This company surrendered its charter to the Crown on 31 Dec. 1899, and on 1 Jan. 1900 the greater part of its territories was formed into the protectorate of Northern Nigeria. Along the coast the Oil Rivers protectorate had been declared in June 1885. This was enlarged and renamed the Niger Coast protectorate in 1893; and on 1 Jan. 1900, on its absorbing the remainder of the territories of the Royal Niger Company, it became the protectorate of Southern Nigeria. In Feb. 1906 Lagos and Southern Nigeria were united into the 'colony and protectorate of Southern Nigeria', and on 1 Jan. 1914 the latter was amalgamated with the protectorate of Northern Nigeria to form the 'colony and protectorate of Nigeria', under a Governor. On 1 Oct. 1954 Nigeria became a federation under a Governor-General.

On 1 Oct. 1960 Nigeria became sovereign and independent and a member of the Commonwealth and on 1 Oct. 1963 Nigeria became a republic.

For the history of Nigeria from 1961 to 1978, see THE STATESMAN'S YEAR-BOOK, 1979–80, pp. 923-924.

AREA AND POPULATION. Area approximately 356,669 sq. miles (923,773 sq. km). Census population, Nov. 1963, 55,670,052.

There are 19 states:

States	Area (in sq. km)	Population	States	Area (in sq. km)	Population
Anambra	17,675	3,596,618	Kwara	66,869	1,714,485
Bauchi	64,605	2,431,296	Lagos	3,345	1,443,568
Bendel	35,500	2,460,962	Niger	65,037	1,194,508
Benue	45,174	2,427,017	Ogun	16,762	1,550,966
Borno	116,400	2,997,498	Ondo	20,959	2,729,690
Cross River	27,237	3,478,131	Oyo	37,705	5,208,884
Gongola	91,390	2,605,263	Plateau	58,030	2,026,657
Imo	11,850	3,672,654	Rivers	21,850	1,719,925
Kaduna	70,245	4,098,306	Sokoto	102,535	4,538,787
Kano	43,285	5,774,840			

See map in THE STATESMAN'S YEAR-BOOK, 1977–78.

The results of the 1973 census were abandoned in Aug. 1975 because they 'will not command general acceptance throughout the country'. There is considerable uncertainty over the total population, but one estimate based on electoral registration in 1978 is 95m. Estimate (1983) 82·39m.

The populations of the largest towns were (1975 estimate) as follows: Lagos, 1,060,848; and (in 1,000) Ibadan, 847; Ogbomosho, 432; Kano, 399; Oshogbo, 282; Ilorin, 282; Abeokuta, 253; Port Harcourt, 242; Zaria, 224; Ilesha, 224; Onitsha, 220; Iwo, 214; Ado-Ekiti, 213; Kaduna, 202; Mushin, 197; Maiduguri, 189; Enugu, 187; Ede, 182; Aba, 177; Ife, 176; Ila, 155; Oyo, 152; Ikere-Ekiti, 145; Benin, 136; Iseyin, 129.

It was announced in Feb. 1976 that the federal capital would be moved inland from Lagos to Abuja area (federal district, 8,094 sq. km) north of river Niger, and in Sept. 1982, Abuja was established as the future capital.

CLIMATE. Lying wholly within the tropics, temperatures everywhere are high. Rainfall varies very much, but decreases from the coast to the interior. The main rains occur from April to Oct. Lagos. Jan. 81°F (27·2°C), July 78°F (25·6°C). Annual rainfall 72″ (1,836 mm). Ibadan. Jan. 80°F (26·7°C), July 76°F (24·4°C). Annual rainfall 45″ (1,120 mm). Kano. Jan. 70°F (21·1°C), July 79°F (26·1°C). Annual rainfall 35″ (869 mm). Port Harcourt. Jan. 79°F (26·1°C), July 77°F (25°C). Annual rainfall 100″ (2,497 mm). Victoria. Jan. 80°F (26·7°C), July 78°F (25·6°C). Annual rainfall 95″ (2,375 mm).

CONSTITUTION AND GOVERNMENT. Under the Constitution drafted and ratified in 1977–78, Nigeria is a sovereign, federal republic comprising 19 states and a federal capital district. Elections were held in Aug. 1983 and President Shagari was returned with 48% of the vote but in Dec. 1983 the military again took over control in a *coup* and on 3 Jan. 1984 a 18-member Supreme Military Council was sworn in.

Head of Government and C.-in-C. of Armed Forces: Maj.-Gen. Mohammed Buhari.

Chief of Staff: Brig. Tunde Idiagbon. *Defence:* Maj.-Gen. B. Y. Bali. *Army Chief of Staff:* Maj.-Gen. Ibrahim Babangida. *Navy Chief of Staff:* Cmdre. Augustine Aikomo. *Air Force Chief of Staff:* Air Vice-Marshal Ibrahim Alfa.

Other Members of the Council: Maj.-Gen. Mamman Vatsa, Brig. Mohammed Magoro, Brig. Sanni Abacha, Brig. Ola Oni, Brig. M. J. Nasco, Brig. Y. Y. Kure. Brig. Paul Omu, Capt. Ebelo Okiwe. Air Cmdre. L. Koynian.

Insp.-Gen. of Police: Col. Salihu Ibrahim James Etim Nyang. *Director-Gen. of Nigeria Security Organization:* Mohammed Rafindadi. *Attorney-General and Minister of Justice:* Chibe Offodice.

The official language is English but Hausa, Igbo and Yoruba languages are also used in the National Assembly, *i.e.* the Senate and the House of Representatives as well as in each of the State Houses of Assembly.

National flag: Three vertical strips of green, white, green.

Local Government: Elections were held in Aug. 1983 for the House of Assembly in each State. Beneath the State is a third tier of government.

DEFENCE

Army. The Army consists of 1 armoured division, 2 mechanized divisions and 1 airborne and amphibious forces division, each with supporting artillery, engineer and reconnaissance units, and 1 Guards brigade. Equipment includes 65 T-55 and Vickers Mk 3 main battle tanks. Strength (1984) 120,000 men.

Navy. The Nigerian Navy was established in 1958. It includes the new large guided missile frigate *Aradu* (completed in the Federal Republic of Germany in 1982) and the frigate *Obuma* (*ex*-Nigeria) acting as a training ship (completed in the Netherlands in 1965), 4 corvettes built in Britain in 1970–72 (*Dorina* and *Otobo*), and 1975–80 (*Erinmi* and *Enyimiri*), 6 fast missile-armed attack vedettes (3 built in France and 3 in FR Germany), 10 patrol craft, 50 coastal patrol boats, 2 tank landing ships, 2 utility landing craft, 1 survey ship, 1 training ship, 60 launches and 5 tugs. There are also 40 small patrol launches operated by the Nigerian Police. Naval personnel in 1984 totalled 550 officers and 3,550 ratings.

Air Force. The Nigerian Air Force was established in Jan. 1964. Pilots were trained initially in Canada, India and Ethiopia. The Air Force was built up subsequently with the aid of a Federal Republic of Germany mission; much first-line equipment has since been received from the Soviet Union. It has 18 MiG-21 supersonic jet-fighters, 18 Jaguar attack aircraft, a few MiG-15UTI and MiG-21U fighter-trainers, and 24 Alpha Jet light attack/trainers. Two F27 Maritime twin-turboprop aircraft are used for maritime patrol. About 20 BO 105 twin-turbine helicopters have been acquired from the Federal Republic of Germany for search and rescue. Transport units operate 9 C-130H-30 and C-130H Hercules 4-turboprop heavy transports, 5 twin-turboprop Aeritalia G222s and 5 F.27s, a Boeing 727, a Gulfstream II and a Fokker F.28 Fellowship twin-turbofan airliner for VIP use, 18 Dornier 128-6 twin-turboprop utility aircraft, 2 Navajos and a Navajo Chieftain. Training types include 30 Bulldog primary trainers and about 12 MB 339 jets, plus 20 Dornier Skyservants for instrument training, transport and ambulance duties. Five heavy-lift CH-47C Chinooks, 13 medium-lift Aérospatiale Pumas and a few light helicopters are also in service. Personnel (1983) total about 9,000.

INTERNATIONAL RELATIONS

Membership. Nigeria is a member of UN, the Commonwealth, ECOWAS, OAU, OPEC and is an ACP state of EEC.

ECONOMY

Planning. The fourth plan (1981–85) was launched in 1981 but was rescheduled because of lower oil prices.

Budget. Capital expenditure in 1983 was envisaged at ₦7,200m.; recurrent expenditure, ₦3,440m. and revenue at ₦9,307m.

Currency. Since 1 Jan. 1973 a decimal currency has been issued by the Central Bank of Nigeria, consisting of *Naira* (₦) and divided into 100 *kobo* (k). Notes in circulation ₦20, ₦10, ₦5, ₦1, 50k. Coins, 25k, 10k, 5k, 1k, ½k.
    In March 1984, £1 = ₦1·08; US$1 = ₦0·69.

Banking. There are 20 commercial banks including the First Bank of Nigeria (formerly Standard), Union Bank of Nigeria (formerly Barclays) and the United Bank of Africa. Eleven of the banks are indigenous. There are 3 merchant banks and 3 government-owned development banks in addition to the Post Office Savings Bank. In 1976 the Government took a 60% shareholding in all foreign banks.

Weights and Measures. The metric system is in force.

ENERGY AND NATURAL RESOURCES

Electricity. The National Electric Power Authority generated 4,712m. kwh. in 1977–78. The Niger dams at Kainji were completed in early 1969 (investment of £87m.) and provide cheap hydro-electricity for rapid industrialization.

Oil. There are refineries at Port Harcourt, Warri and at Kaduna. Oil represents 95% of exports. Production, 1983, 1·24m. bbls. per day.

Gas. Natural gas is being used at electric power stations at Afam and Ughelli. Production, 1972, 601,237,000 cu. ft. Reserves: 1,422,000m. cu.metres.

Minerals. Production: Tin, 1979, 2,750 tonnes; columbite, 1977 (the world's largest producer), 800 tonnes; coal (1981) 114,875 tonnes. There are large deposits of iron ore, coal (reserves estimate 245m. tonnes), lead and zinc. There are small quantities of gold and uranium.

Agriculture. Groundnuts, cotton and soybean come mainly or wholly from the north, palm produce, cocoa, timber and rubber from the south. Tobacco is grown in commercial quantities. Production (estimates) 1981 were (in tonnes): Groundnuts (unshelled), 580,000; cocoa, 160,000; cereals, 9·9m. In 1981, the National Rice Production Scheme was launched; production (1981), about 75,000 tons from 66,000 hectares.
    Livestock (1982). There were 12·6m. cattle, 12·4m. sheep, 25·6m. goats, 1·22m. pigs and 140m. poultry.

Forestries. There are plywood factories at Epe, Sapele and Calabar, and numerous saw-mills. The most important timber species include mahogany, iroko, obeche, abwa, ebony and camwood.

Fisheries. The total catch (1980) was 480,000 tonnes.

INDUSTRY AND TRADE

Industry. There were more than 2,000 industrial establishments in 1982. Timber and hides and skins are major export commodities. Industrial products include soap, cigarettes, beer, margarine, groundnut oil, meat and cake, concentrated fruit juices, soft drinks, canned food, metal containers, ply-wood, textiles, ceramic products and cement. Of growing importance is the local assembly of motor vehicles, bicycles, radio equipment, electrical goods and sewing machines. In 1982, the Delta Steel Plant opened at Ovwian—Aladja in Bendel State.

Under a decree on indigenization Nigerians must have a minimum of 40% shareholding in all foreign enterprises.

Trade Unions. All trade unions were dissolved in 1976 and 42 new unions, each organized around a particular occupation, have since been created.

Commerce. There is a great deal of internal commerce in local foodstuffs and imported goods moving by rail, lorry and pack animals overland, and by launches, rafts and canoes along an extensive and complex network of inland waterways. Kano is still, as it has been for centuries, the focus of caravan routes linking a territory which stretches from the Sudan in the east to Senegal in the west, with branches northwards across the Sahara.

Total trade in ₦m. for 4 years:

	1979	1980	1981	1982
Imports (c.i.f.)	7,139·4	8,716·4	11,876·5	7,800·0
Exports and re-exports (f.o.b.)	10,106·8	12,800·9	10,529·6	7,215·9

Total trade between Nigeria and UK (according to British Department of Trade returns, in £1,000 sterling):

	1979	1980	1981	1982	1983
Imports to UK	186,046	151,563	95,069	356,802	387,975
Exports and re-exports from UK	638,239	1,204,358	1,428,018	1,225,164	798,276

Tourism. There were 114,000 foreign visitors in 1976.

COMMUNICATIONS

Roads (1980). There were 108,000 km of maintained roads.

In 1980, 633,268 vehicles were registered. Bus services, by private owners, operate in the larger towns and between the main towns in southern Nigeria, but the bulk of passenger and goods traffic by road is carried in lorries (mammy wagons).

Railways. There are 3,505 route-km of line 1,067 mm gauge, which in 1979 carried 988,000 tonnes of freight and 6·7m. passengers.

Aviation. There is an extensive system of internal and international air routes, serving Europe, USA, Middle East and South and West Africa. Regular services are operated by Nigerian Airways (WAAC), British Caledonian, UTA, KLM, SABENA, Swissair, PANAM and other lines. In 1981, 2·3m. passengers were carried on domestic and international routes.

Shipping. The principal ports are Lagos, Port Harcourt, Warri and Calabar.

Post and Broadcasting. Postal facilities are provided at 1,667 offices and agencies; telegraph, money order and savings bank services are provided at 280 of these. Most internal letter mail is carried by air at normal postage rates. External telegraph services are owned and operated by Nigerian External Telecommunications, Ltd, at Lagos, from which telegraphic communication is maintained with all parts of the world. There were 708,390 telephones in use in 1982, of which 249,150 were in Lagos and 33,138 in Ibadan. There is also a telex service.

Federal and some state governments have established commercial corporations for sound and television broadcasting, which are widely used in schools. In 1980 there were 5·6m. radio and 450,000 television receivers.

Cinemas (1974). There were 120 cinemas, with a seating capacity of 60,000. Mobile cinemas are used by the Federal and States Information Services.

Newspapers. There are over 119 newspapers, magazines and periodicals; the highest circulation of a daily is about 125,000. Most of the papers are published in English but some in the vernaculars.

JUSTICE, RELIGION, EDUCATION AND WELFARE

Justice. The highest court is the Federal Supreme Court, which consists of the Chief Justice of the Republic, not less than 2 Federal Judges and the Chief Justice of each State. It has original jurisdiction in any dispute between the Federal Republic and any State or between States; and to hear and determine appeals from any of the High Courts and from any court or tribunal established by Parliament. It may be given powers of advisory jurisdiction by Parliament in respect of the exercise of the prerogative of mercy by the Heads of State of the Republic or the States.

High Courts, presided over by a Chief Justice, are established in most of the states. Magistrates' courts are established throughout the Republic, and customary law courts in southern Nigeria. In northern States of Nigeria there are the Sharia Court of Appeal and the Court of Resolution. Moslem Law has been codified in a Penal Code and is applied through Alkali courts.

The Advisory Judicial committee has powers of appointment and discipline.

Religion. The 1963 census figures were: Moslems, 26·2m.; Christians, 19·2m.; others, 10·1m. Northern Nigeria is mainly Moslem; Southern Nigeria is predominantly Christian. The Protestant and Roman Catholic Churches have 2·5m. each.

Education. In 1976 primary education became free throughout the country. Literacy rate (1973) 25%.

In 1979 there were 12·6m. primary school pupils, and 1·9m. secondary school pupils.

Teacher-training institutions totalled 157 in 1973. There were also 67 trade centres and vocational training institutes for sub-professional technicians and tradesmen.

There are 24 universities in Nigeria, providing 3–5-year courses leading to the award of a first degree in various disciplines; these include 7 Federal Universities of Technology. There are also opportunities for taking higher degrees. Free tuition was provided from 1977. The total number of students (1982–83) was 88,636 in universities and 53,766 in polytechnics.

Health. Most tropical diseases are endemic to Nigeria. Blindness, yaws, leprosy, sleeping sickness, worm infections, malaria are major health problems which, however, are yielding to remedial and preventative measures. In co-operation with the World Health Organization river blindness and malaria are being tackled on a large scale, while annual campaigns are undertaken against the danger of smallpox epidemics. Dispensaries and travelling dispensaries are found in most parts of the country.

The teaching hospital at Lagos University has 350 beds; there is also a nursing school and a teaching hospital at Ibadan University. There are medical courses at Ahmadu Bello University, University of Ife, Benin University and at Nsukka.

DIPLOMATIC REPRESENTATIVES

Of Nigeria in Great Britain (9 Northumberland Ave., London, WC2N 5BX)
High Commissioner: (Vacant).

Of Great Britain in Nigeria (11 Eleke Cres., Victoria Island, Lagos)
High Commissioner: W. E. H. Whyte, CMG.

Of Nigeria in the USA (2201 M. St., NW, Washington, D.C., 20037)
Ambassador: Chief Abundu Yesufu Eke.

Of the USA in Nigeria (2 Eleke Cres., Lagos)
Ambassador: (Vacant).

Of Nigeria to the United Nations
Ambassador: Alhaji Yusuff Maitama-Sule.

Books of Reference

Nigeria Digest of Statistics. Lagos, 1951 ff. (quarterly)

Annual Abstract of Statistics. Federal Office of Statistics. Lagos, 1960 ff.

Nigeria Trade Journal. Federal Ministry of Commerce and Industries (quarterly)

Nigeria Handbook 1975–76. Ministry of Information, Lagos, 1975

Arnold, G., *Modern Nigeria.* London, 1977

Barbour, K. M. (ed.), *Nigeria in Maps.* London, 1982

Blitz, F. (ed.), *The Politics and Administration of Nigerian Government.* Lagos and London, 1965

Burns, Sir Alan, *History of Nigeria.* 8th ed. London, 1972

Comhaire, J., *Le Nigeria et ses populations.* Brussels, 1981.

Kirk-Greene, A., and Rimmer, D., *Nigeria since 1970.* London, 1981

Luckham, R., *The Nigerian Military: A Sociological Analysis of Authority and Revolt, 1960–67.* CUP, 1971

Nnoli, O., *Path to Nigerian Development.* Dakar, 1981

Nwabueze, B. O., *The Presidential Constitution of Nigeria.* Lagos and London, 1982

Olaloku, F. A., (ed.) *Structure of the Nigerian Economy.* London, 1980

Oyediran, O., *Nigerian Government and Politics under Military Rule, 1966–1979.* New York, 1980

Panter-Brick, S. K., *Nigerian Politics and Military Rule: Prelude to Civil War.* London, 1970.—*Soldiers and Oil.* London, 1978

Peil, M., *Nigerian Politics: The People's View.* London, 1976

Simmons, M., and Obe, O. A., *Nigerian Handbook 1982–83.* London, 1982

Tijjani, A. and Williams, D., (eds.) *Shehu Shagari: My Vision of Nigeria.* London, 1981

Van Apeldoorn, G. J., *Perspectives on Drought and Famine in Nigeria.* London, 1981

Williams, D., *President and Power in Nigeria.* London, 1982

Williams, G., *Nigeria: Economy and Society.* London, 1977

Zartman, I. W., *The Political Economy of Nigeria.* New York, 1983

NORWAY

Kongeriket Norge

Capital: Oslo
Population: 4·1m. (1982)
GNP per capita: US$13,497 (1981)

HISTORY. By the Treaty of 14 Jan. 1814 Norway was ceded to the King of Sweden by the King of Denmark, but the Norwegian people declared themselves independent and elected Prince Christian Frederik of Denmark as their king. The foreign Powers refused to recognize this election, and on 14 Aug. a convention proclaimed the independence of Norway in a personal union with Sweden. This was followed on 4 Nov. by the election of Karl XIII (II) as King of Norway. Norway declared this union dissolved, 7 June 1905, and Sweden agreed to the repeal of the union on 26 Oct. 1905. The throne was offered to a prince of the reigning house of Sweden, who declined. After a plebiscite, Prince Carl of Denmark was formally elected King on 18 Nov. 1905, and took the name of Haakon VII.

Norwegian Sovereigns

Inge Baardssøn	1204	Erik of Pomerania	1389
Haakon Haakonssøn	1217	Kristofer af Bavaria	1442
Magnus Lagabøter	1263	Karl Knutssøn	1449
Eirik Magnussøn	1280	Same Sovereigns as in Denmark	1450–1814
Haakon V Magnussøn	1299	Christian Frederik	1814
Magnus Erikssøn	1319	Same Sovereigns as in Sweden	1814–1905
Haakon VI Magnussøn	1355	Haakon VII	1905
Olav Haakonssøn	1381	Olav V	1957
Margreta	1388		

AREA AND POPULATION. Norway is bounded north by the Arctic ocean, east by the USSR, Finland and Sweden, south by the Skagerrak Straits and west by the North Sea.

Fylker (counties)	Area (sq. km)	Census population 1 Nov. 1970	Population 1 Jan. 1983	Pop. per sq. km (total area) 1983
Oslo (City)	450·0	477,898	448,775	988·5
Akershus	4,916·4	322,321	376,202	76·5
Østfold	4,183·4	220,892	234,726	56·1
Hedmark	27,388·3	178,923	187,779	6·9
Oppland	25,259·6	172,163	182,126	7·2
Buskerud	14,933·2	198,225	217,348	14·6
Vestfold	2,215·8	174,640	188,664	85·1
Telemark	15,315·3	156,405	161,939	10·6
Aust-Agder	9,211·8	80,575	92,738	10·1
Vest-Agder	7,280·3	124,013	138,739	19·1
Rogaland	9,140·6	268,171	312,550	34·2
Hordaland	15,633·7	372,172	394,568	25·2
Sogn og Fjordane	18,633·5	100,761	106,140	5·7
Møre og Romsdal	15,104·2	223,360	237,268	15·7
Sør-Trøndelag	18,831·4	233,420	246,206	13·0
Nord-Trøndelag	22,463·3	117,718	126,696	5·6
Nordland	38,327·1	240,461	244,974	6·4
Troms	25,953·9	136,224	147,690	5·7
Finnmark	48,649·0	75,791	77,383	1·6
Total	323,894·8 [1]	3,874,133	4,122,511	12·7

[1] 125,056 sq. miles.

On 1 Nov. 1980, 2,893,193 persons lived in densely populated areas and 1,197,939 in sparsely populated areas.

928

Population of the principal towns at 1 Jan. 1983:

Oslo	448,775	Sandnes	38,085	Halden	26,219
Bergen	207,292	Sandefjord	35,151	Gjøvik	26,070
Trondheim	134,665	Ålesund	34,895	Moss	24,975
Stavanger	91,964	Bodø	33,642	Lillehammer	21,981
Kristiansand	61,824	Porsgrunn	31,251	Harstad	21,773
Drammen	50,581	Fredrikstad	27,578	Molde	21,047
Tromsø	47,316	Haugesund	27,030	Steinkjer	20,692
Skien	46,730	Ringerike	26,828	Kongsberg	20,621

Vital statistics for calendar years:

	Marriages	Divorces	Births	Still-born	Illegitimate [2]	Deaths
1980	22,230	6,634	51,039	363	7,392	41,340
1981	22,271	7,136	50,708	299	8,169	41,893
1982	21,706	7,165	51,245	324	9,041	41,381 [1]

[1] Provisional figures. [2] Excluding still-born.

CLIMATE. There is considerable variation in the climate because of the extent of latitude, the topography and the varying effectiveness of prevailing westerly winds and the Gulf Stream. Winters along the whole west coast are exceptionally mild but precipitation is considerable. Oslo. Jan. 41°F (5°C), July 63°F (17°C). Annual rainfall 29·6″ (740 mm). Bergen. Jan. 35°F (1·5°C), July 59°F (15°C). Annual rainfall 78·3″ (1,958 mm). Trondheim. Jan. 26°F (–3·5°C), July 57°F (14°C). Annual rainfall 32·1″ (870 mm).

REIGNING KING. Olav V, born 2 July 1903, married on 21 March 1929 to Princess Märtha of Sweden (born 28 March 1901, died 5 April 1954), daughter of the late Prince Carl (son of King Oscar II). He succeeded on the death of his father, King Haakon VII, on 21 Sept. 1957. *Offspring:* Princess Ragnhild Alexandra, born 9 June 1930 (married, 1953, Hr. Erling Lorentzen); Princess Astrid Maud Ingeborg, born 12 Feb. 1932 (married, 12 Jan. 1961, Hr. Johan Martin Ferner); Crown Prince Harald, born 21 Feb. 1937, married, 29 Aug. 1968, Sonja Haraldsen. *Offspring:* Princess Märtha Louise, born 22 Sept. 1971; Prince Haakon Magnus, born 20 July 1973.

CONSTITUTION AND GOVERNMENT. Norway is a constitutional and hereditary monarchy. The royal succession is in direct male line in the order of primogeniture. In default of male heirs the King may propose a successor to the Storting, but this assembly has the right to nominate another, if it does not agree with the proposal.

The Constitution, voted by the constituent assembly at Eidsvoll on 17 May 1814 and modified at various times, vests the legislative power of the realm in the Storting (Parliament). The royal veto may be exercised twice; but if the same Bill passes three Stortings formed by separate and subsequent elections it becomes the law of the land without the assent of the sovereign. The King has the command of the land, sea and air forces, and makes all appointments.

Since June 1938 all branches of the Government service, including the state church, are open to women.

National flag: Red with a blue white-bordered Scandinavian cross.

National anthem: Ja, vi elsker dette landet (words by B. Bjørnson, 1865; tune by R. Nordraak, 1865).

The Storting assembles every year. The meetings take place *suo jure*, and not by any writ from the King or the executive. They begin on the first weekday in Oct. each year, until June the following year. Every Norwegian subject of 18 years of age is entitled to vote, unless he is disqualified for a special cause. Women are, since 1913, entitled to vote under the same conditions as men. The mode of election is direct and the method of election is proportional. The country is divided into 19 districts, each electing from 4 to 15 representatives.

At the elections for the Storting held in 1981 the following parties were elected: Labour, 66; Conservative, 53; Centre Party, 11; Christian Democratic Party, 15; Socialist Left Party, 4; Party of Progress, 4, and Liberal, 2.

The Storting, when assembled, divides itself by election into the *Lagting* and the *Odelsting*. The former is composed of one-fourth of the members of the Storting, and the other of the remaining three-fourths. Each Ting (the Storting, the Odelsting and the Lagting) nominates its own president. Most questions are decided by the Storting, but questions relating to legislation must be considered and decided by the Odelsting and the Lagting separately. Only when the Odelsting and the Lagting disagree, the Bill has to be considered by the Storting in plenary sitting, and a new law can then only be decided by a majority of two-thirds of the voters. The same majority is required for alterations of the Constitution, which can only be decided by the Storting in plenary sitting. The Storting elects 5 delegates, whose duty it is to revise the public accounts. The Lagting and the ordinary members of the Supreme Court of Justice (the *Høyesterett*) form a High Court of the Realm (the *Riksrett*) for the trial of ministers, members of the *Høyesterett* and members of the Storting. The impeachment before the *Riksrett* can only be decided by the Odelsting.

The executive is represented by the King, who exercises his authority through the Cabinet or Council of State *(Statsråd)*, composed of a Prime Minister (*Statsminster*) and (at present) 17 ministers *(Statsråder)*. The ministers are entitled to be present in the Storting and to take part in the discussions, but without a vote.

A Conservative Government was formed and took office on 14 Oct. 1981; the members of the Government were:

Prime Minister: Kåre Willoch.
Foreign Affairs: Svenn Stray. *Finance:* Rolf Presthus. *Defence:* Anders C. Sjaastad. *Agriculture:* Finn T. Isaksen. *Commerce and Shipping:* Asbjørn Haugstvedt. *Justice:* Mona Røkke. *Ecclesiastical Affairs and Education:* Kjell Magne Bondevik. *Culture:* Lars Roar Langslet. *Local Government and Labour:* Arne Rettedal. *Industry:* Jan P. Syse. *Communications:* Johan J. Jakobsen. *Environment:* Rakel S. Surlien. *Social Affairs:* Leif Arne Heløe. *Consumer Affairs and Government Administration:* Astrid Gjertsen. *Fisheries:* Thor Listau. *Oil and Energy:* Kåre Kristiansen. *Development Co-operation:* Reidun Brusletten.

The official languages are Bokmål (or Riksmål) and Nynorsk (or Landsmål).

Local Government. For the purposes of administration the country is divided into 19 counties *(fylker)*, in each of which the central government is represented by a county governor *(fylkesmannen)*. In addition, there are 47 urban districts *(bykommuner)* and 407 rural districts *(herredskommuner)*, each of which usually corresponds in size to a parish *(prestegjeld)*. The districts are administered by district councils *(kommunestyrer)*, whose membership may vary between 13 and 85 councillors, and by a committee *(formannskap)* which is elected by and from the members of the council. The council is four times the size of the committee. The council elects a chairman and a vice-chairman from among its members.

Each of the 18 counties forms a county district *(fylkeskommune)*, while the remaining one, Oslo, comprises an urban district. The supreme authority in a county district is the county council *(fylkesting)*. Every district council has until now elected its district representatives in the proportion of one to every 6,000 inhabitants, though no one district may elect more than one-third of the total number of representatives in the county council. From 1 Jan. 1976, members of the county council are elected directly by the electors of the county and the number of representatives varies between 25 and 85. In a county district the county committee *(fylkesutvalg)* occupies a position corresponding to that of the committee *(formannskap)* in the primary districts. The county committee is elected by and from among the members of the county council. The number of county committee members is one-fourth of the membership of the county council, but must be not more than 15. The county council elects from among the members of the county committee a county sheriff *(fylkesordfører)* and a deputy sheriff.

DEFENCE. Service is universal and compulsory, liability in peace-time commencing at the age of 19 and continuing till the age of 44. The training period in the Army is 12 months, in the Navy and Air Force, 15 months. The Norwegian Defence forces are organized into 2 integrated regional commands.

Army. The largest standing element is Brigade North (in Northern Command), which comprises 2 infantry battalions, 1 tank company and 1 self-propelled field artillery and 1 anti-aircraft artillery batteries. Brigade North would come under NATO command in event of war, while other forces remained under national control. Southern Command comprises 1 infantry battalion, 1 tank company and 1 self-propelled field artillery and 1 anti-aircraft artillery batteries. Equipment includes 78 Leopard I and 38 M-48A5 main battle tanks. Strength (1984) 24,200 (including 18,300 conscripts). Reserves number 122,000.

Navy. The Navy consists of the coastal batteries and other static defence systems and the following naval units: 14 coastal submarines, 5 small frigates, 2 minelayers, 2 corvettes, 39 fast missile craft, 8 fast torpedo boats, 1 patrol vessel, 9 coastal minesweepers, 1 minehunter, 1 coastal minehunter, 1 controlled minelayer, 2 coastal patrol boats, 1 research ship, 2 diving tenders, 7 coastal transports, 1 torpedo recovery vessel, 2 training craft, 7 landing craft, 1 depot ship, 2 tugs and the royal yacht.

Personnel in 1984 totalled 8,500 officers and ratings including 1,600 in the Coast Artillery.

Coastguard. The Coastguard was established in 1977 within the framework of the Armed Forces. Main tasks are Fishery Protection and Economic Zone Patrol. The Coastguard assists other government agencies in rescue service, environment, surveillance and police duties. It comprises 3 frigate-size monitors each equipped with a Lynx helicopter, 3 corvette type cutters, 7 armed trawlers (chartered until completion of new construction patrol vessels), 20 survey and inspection vessels.

Air Force. The Royal Norwegian Air Force consists of 4 squadrons of F-16 Fighting Falcons, 1 squadron of F-5 fighter-bombers, 1 maritime patrol squadron of P-3B Orions, 1 squadron of C-130H Hercules transports and Mystère 20s equipped for EW/VIP duties, 1 squadron with Twin Otter light transports and UH-1B Iroquois helicopters. Ground based air defence forces deploy 4 Nike surface-to-air missile batteries and several light anti-aircraft artillery units. Hawk missiles are being procured to improve area and airfield defence. Ten Westland Sea King helicopters are used for search and rescue duties; 6 Lynx helicopters are operated for the Coast Guard.

Total strength is more than 8,000 personnel.

Home Guard. The Home Guard is organized in small units equipped and trained for special tasks in their home area. Service after basic training is 50 hours a year. The total strength is approximately 90,000.

INTERNATIONAL RELATIONS

Membership. Norway is a member of UN, NATO, EFTA, OECD, the Council of Europe and the Nordic Council.

ECONOMY

Budget. Current revenue and expenditure for years ending 31 Dec. (in 1,000 kroner):

	1978	1979	1980	1981	1982	1983 [1]
Revenue	54,299,000	61,112,000	82,938,000	100,924,000	110,539,000	118,577,000
Expenditure	62,956,000	67,373,000	80,054,000	91,629,000	100,898,000	111,948,000

[1] Voted budget.

National debt [1] for years ending 31 Dec. (in 1,000 kroner):

1974	33,943,000	1977	66,786,000	1980	106,908,000
1975	41,082,800	1978	86,556,000	1981	107,662,000
1976	50,290,300	1979	103,605,000	1982	103,799,400

[1] At the rate of par on foreign loans: including treasury bills (in 1m. kroner) which amounted to 8,690 in 1977; 6,000 in 1978; 9,600 in 1979; 14,600 in 1980, 17,200 in 1981 and 13,880 in 1982.

Currency. The Norwegian *krone*, of 100 øre, is of the value of about 11 *kroner* to £1 sterling. National bank-notes of 10, 50, 100, 500 and 1,000 *kroner* are legal means of payment. March 1984, US$1 = 7·513 *kroner*; £1 = 11·045 *kroner*.

On 31 Aug. 1983 the nominal value of the coin in circulation was 950m. kroner; notes in circulation, 19,919m. kroner.

Banking. The Bank of Norway is a joint-stock bank; in 1949 the state acquired all the shares hitherto privately owned. The bank is governed by laws enacted by the State, and its directors are elected by the Storting, except the president and vice-president of the head office, who are nominated by the King. It is the only bank of issue.

At the end of 1982 there were 22 private joint-stock banks. Their total amount of capital and funds was 5,201m. kroner (capital 2,773m., funds 2,428m.). Deposits amounted to 113,749m. kroner, of which 26,106m. kroner were at call and notice, and 87,643m. kroner on time.

The number of savings banks at the end of 1982 was 270. The total amount of funds of the savings banks amounted to 5,085m. kroner, and total deposits 79,524m. kroner, of which 14,295m. kroner were at call and notice and 65,229m. kroner on time.

Weights and Measures. The metric system of weights and measures has been obligatory since 1875.

ENERGY AND NATURAL RESOURCES

Electricity. Norway is a large producer of hydro-electric energy. The potential total hydro-electric power, for a whole year at regulated minimum water flow and by 82% efficiency, is estimated at 15m. kw. or about 131,000m. kwh. annually. About 60% of the water power suitable for development consists of waterfalls with a height of at least 900 ft.

By the end of 1981 the capacity of the installations for production of thermo-electric energy amounted to only 254 mw. On 31 Dec. 1981, the total capacity of generators (of hydro-electric plants) was 25·11m. kva.

In 1981 the total production of electricity amounted to 93,397m. kwh. of which 99·8% was produced by hydro-electric plants.

Most of the electricity is used for industrial purposes, especially by the chemical and basic metal industries for production of nitrate of calcium and other nitrogen products, carbide, ferrosilicon and other ferro-alloys, aluminium and zinc. The paper and pulp industries are also big consumers of electricity.

Bjerve, P. J., *Planning in Norway 1947–1956.* Amsterdam, 1959
Bourneuf, A., *Norway, the Planned Revival.* Cambridge, Mass., 1958
Galenson, W., *Labor in Norway.* Cambridge, Mass., and London, 1949
Leiserson, M. W., *Wages and Economic Control in Norway, 1945–57.* Harvard Univ. Press, 1959

Minerals. Production and value of the chief concentrates, metals and alloys were:

	1980		1981	
Concentrates and minerals	Tonnes	1,000 kroner	Tonnes	1,000 kroner
Copper concentrates	113,857	211,993	110,550	180,490
Pyrites	421,367	...	435,493	36,684
Iron ore and titaniferous concentrates	4,711,427	...	...	...
Zinc and lead concentrates	56,422	62,427	61,610	97,286
Metals and alloys				
Copper	33,690	...	31,951	...
Nickel	37,123	...	36,954	...
Aluminium	653,377	5,240,115	633,585	4,749,804
Ferro-alloys	814,703	2,204,338	778,612	2,119,754
Pig-iron	611,660	...	586,584	...
Zinc	79,416	...	80,279	...
Lead and tin	328	...	189	...

Agriculture. Norway, including Svalbard and Jan Mayen, is a barren and mountainous country. The arable soil is found in comparatively narrow strips, gathered in deep and narrow valleys and around fiords and lakes. Large, continuous tracts fit for cultivation do not exist. Of the total area, 79·3% is unproductive, 18% productive forest and 2·6% under cultivation.

Principal crops	Area [1] (hectares)			Produce [1] (tonnes)		
	1980	1981	1982	1980	1981	1982
Wheat	15,560	12,850	16,690	65,000	57,600	75,500
Rye	1,410	880	700	4,700	2,900	2,200
Barley	186,910	176,130	16,953	651,000	607,400	623,300
Oats	112,690	126,060	133,550	427,800	464,000	495,100
Mixed corn	630	480	510	2,400	2,000	1,800
Potatoes	20,500	20,680	21,140	488,900	454,000	476,000
Hay	405,470	411,250	417,370	2,852,600	2,859,700	2,808,000

Livestock, 1982 [1]: 15,400 horses, 1,009,000 cattle (384,500 milch cows), 2,227,100 sheep, 71,100 goats, 686,100 pigs, 3,552,600 hens.

Fur production in 1982–83 was as follows (1981–82 in brackets): Silver fox, 32,000 (31,000); blue fox, 395,000 (360,000); mink, 737,000 (811,000).

[1] Holdings with at least 5 decares agricultural area in use.

Forestry. The area covered with productive forests is 66,600 sq. km. 81% of the productive forest area consists of conifers and 19% of broadleaves. Forests in public ownership cover 8,470 sq. km of productive forests. Besides the home consumption of timber and fuel wood, the essential part of the cut is consumed as raw material in sawmills and the pulp and paper industry. The annual increment (estimate, 1979) is about 16m. cu. metres. In 1981–82, 8·4m. cu. metres were cut for production of pulp, sawn timber and other industrial wood products.

Fisheries. The total number of registered fishermen in 1981 was 35,311, of whom 10,022 had another chief occupation. In 1982, the number of fishing vessels (all with motor) was 26,733, and of these, 17,828 were open boats.

The value of sea fisheries in 1m. kroner in 1982 was: Cod, 1,283; capelin, 629; mackerel, 122; coal-fish (saithe), 527; deep-water prawn, 416; haddock, 146; herring, 79; dogfish, 11. The catch totalled in 1982, 2·5m. tons, valued at 3,877m. kroner.

From 1 Jan. 1977 Norway established an economic zone of 200 nautical miles, and from 3 June 1977 a fishery protection zone of 200 nautical miles around Svalbard.

INDUSTRY AND TRADE

Industry. Industry is chiefly based on raw materials produced within the country (wood, fish, etc.) and on water power, of which the country possesses a large amount. Crude petroleum and natural gas production, the manufacture of paper and paper products, industrial chemicals and basic metals are the most important export manufactures. In the following table are given figures for industrial establishments in 1981, excluding one-man units. Electrical plants, construction and building industry are not included. The values are given in 1m. kroner.

Industries	Establishments	Number of Salaried staff	Wage earners	Gross value of production	Value added
Coalmining	1	178	573	198	66
Crude petroleum and natural gas	6	5,699	2,162	56,729	50,700
Metal-mining	14	767	3,130	1,395	478
Other-mining	549	530	2,633	1,286	614
Food manufacturing	2,448	9,165	40,733	34,047	2,761
Beverages	68	1,458	3,678	2,581	1,584
Tobacco	6	494	589	1,361	1,100
Textiles	478	1,997	9,209	2,942	1,084
Clothing, etc.	360	955	5,323	1,312	532
Footwear	46	155	1,104	256	109
Leather	76	162	928	264	98
Wood	1,614	4,787	17,982	9,972	3,033
Furniture and fixtures	559	1,645	7,424	2,867	1,086
Pulp and paper	165	3,813	12,440	10,434	2,487
Printing and publishing	1,655	12,843	22,107	9,480	3,911
Chemical, industrial	60	4,048	5,548	8,677	2,093
Chemical, other	169	3,255	4,322	3,567	1,242

Industries	Establish-ments	Salaried staff	Number of Wage earners	Gross value of produc-tion	Value added
Petroleum, refined	3	325	537	12,041	146
Petroleum and coal	58	572	1,327	1,484	305
Rubber	85	413	1,577	617	244
Plastics	313	1,583	5,186	2,639	863
Ceramics	41	233	931	239	142
Glass	63	618	1,853	817	301
Other mineral products	503	1,876	6,284	4,313	1,540
Iron, steel and ferro-alloys	53	3,082	10,006	5,825	1,803
Non-ferrous metals	69	3,829	10,287	10,613	2,586
Metal products, except machinery	1,592	5,555	20,821	7,817	3,386
Machinery and equipment	1,140	10,838	23,711	19,164	5,727
Electrical apparatus and supplies	413	8,176	13,055	7,483	3,353
Transport equipment	1,015	8,307	35,174	15,231	5,358
Professional and scientific instruments, photographic and optical goods	50	330	913	370	180
Other manufacturing industries	324	620	2,385	743	299
Total (all included)	13,996	98,308	273,932	236,765	98,920

The following table sets forth the estimated value of net production, at factor cost by industries, in 1m. kroner:

	1977	1978	1979	1980	1981	1982 [1]
Agriculture	6,703	7,283	7,273	7,972	8,722	9,343
Forestry	1,349	1,410	1,535	1,716	2,279	2,061
Fishing	1,381	1,043	1,162	1,404	2,042	1,827
Mining and quarrying	779	767	809	836	1,175	1,156
Manufacturing	34,008	35,309	41,484	42,978	45,813	48,169
Crude petroleum and gas production	4,116	8,458	15,346	32,007	37,893	42,203
Electricity, gas and water	2,912	3,975	4,020	4,181	5,775	7,080
Construction [2]	11,927	13,476	13,326	14,753	18,242	19,450
Wholesale and retail trade	16,489	18,256	18,336	23,101	26,927	30,125
Restaurants and hotels	2,190	2,490	2,682	3,049	3,586	4,547
Water transport	2,230	3,235	4,708	6,747	7,151	5,358
Other transport [3]	7,303	8,386	9,192	10,464	12,794	15,284
Financial institutions	5,977	7,217	8,164	10,015	12,326	16,450
Real estate	6,113	6,731	7,407	8,321	9,962	11,250
Business services	3,843	4,278	5,665	6,380	7,684	8,747
Government services, social and personal services	36,567	40,825	43,596	49,423	56,863	64,761
Imputed bank service charge	−5,629	−6,158	−7,278	−8,724	−11,349	−14,753
Net production at factor cost	138,258	156,981	177,427	214,623	247,885	273,058
+ Indirect taxes	36,327	37,946	41,106	49,024	55,484	60,911
− Subsidies	14,111	16,446	16,743	19,960	21,768	23,273
Net domestic product (market price)	160,474	178,481	201,790	243,687	281,601	310,696

[1] Provisional figures.
[2] Including drilling of crude oil and natural gas wells.
[3] Including pipeline transport of oil and gas.

Labour. The distribution of the population according to professions in 1980, showed 142,025 (7%) economically active[1] in agriculture, forestry and gardening; 598,567 (29·6%) in mining, manufacturing, building, etc.; 308,408 (15·3%) in commerce; 176,605 (8·7%) in transport; 21,694 (1·1%) in fishery, sealing and whaling; 773,772 (38·3%) in public administration, liberal professions and services; total, 2,021,071.

[1] Persons aged 16 or more with at least 100 hours paid work in one year.

Commerce. Total imports and exports in calendar years (in 1,000 kroner):

	1977	1978	1979	1980	1981	1982
Imports	68,579,245	60,168,613	69,338,924	83,601,605	89,687,802	99,747,271
Exports	46,438,663	57,083,799	68,527,167	91,672,433	104,265,370	113,236,296

Trading according to countries was as follows (in 1,000 kroner):

| Countries | 1981 | | 1982 | |
	Imports	Exports	Imports	Exports
Argentina	97,472	124,707	103,205	53,139
Australia and New Zealand	789,888	260,620	495,595	258,667
Belgium and Luxembourg	2,482,085	1,037,904	2,320,466	1,207,635
Brazil	825,975	386,017	830,260	461,411
Canada	1,747,167	389,810	1,353,791	456,574
Czechoslovakia	213,957	139,546	231,509	120,708
Denmark	5,451,703	4,156,264	6,174,176	4,269,930
Fed. Republic of Germany	13,179,236	18,698,078	15,494,658	22,914,654
Finland	3,914,027	1,883,965	4,514,625	1,812,090
France	3,135,168	2,221,306	3,365,032	2,501,412
India	113,948	284,214	109,239	515,537
Italy	1,890,708	1,287,315	2,336,569	1,581,639
Netherlands	2,870,960	3,833,542	3,411,649	6,586,928
Poland	378,711	307,670	624,149	305,602
Portugal	519,537	354,894	533,508	324,805
Spain	738,602	490,603	706,612	550,927
Sweden	14,737,658	9,377,609	17,053,968	10,434,765
Switzerland	1,344,503	790,756	1,517,745	887,846
UK	12,195,035	41,658,718	11,822,301	41,291,127
USA	8,271,973	3,872,343	9,147,880	3,173,182
USSR	1,019,231	715,252	1,455,688	624,692

Principal items of import in 1982 (in 1,000 kroner): Machinery, transport equipment, etc., 36,673,454; fuel oil, etc., 13,149,144; base metals and manufactures thereof, 10,416,298; chemicals and related products, 6,043,656; textiles, 2,537,508.

Principal items of export in 1982 (in 1,000 kroner): Machinery and transport equipment, 16,826,367; base metals and manufactures thereof, 12,248,521; crude oil, 31,878,574; edible animal products, 5,370,141; pulp and paper, 4,622,186.

Total trade between Norway and UK (British Department of Trade returns, in £1,000 sterling):

	1979	1980	1981	1982	1983
Imports to UK	1,327,212	1,441,418	1,943,206	2,023,441	2,820,760
Exports and re-exports from UK	768,815	791,530	876,937	924,651	828,612

COMMUNICATIONS

Roads. On 31 Dec. 1982 the length of the public roads (including roads in towns) was 83,377 km. Of these, 57,136 km were main roads; 50,473 km had some kind of paving, mostly bituminous and oil-gravel treatment, the rest being gravel-surfaced.

Number of registered motor vehicles (31 Dec. 1982) was 1,842,356, including 1,337,884 passenger cars (including taxis), 166,456 lorries and vans, 14,152 buses, 164,113 motor cycles and mopeds. The scheduled bus and lorry services in 1981 drove 4,297m. passenger-km and 612m. net ton-km.

Railways. The length of state railways on 31 Dec. 1982 was 4,242 km; of private companies, 16 km. On 2,443 km of state and 16 km of private railways electric traction is installed. Total receipts of the state railways and road traffic in 1982 were 2,368m. kroner; total expenses (excluding depreciation and interest on capital), 3,193m. kroner. The state railways carried 20·4m. tonnes of freight (of which 10·4m. was iron ore on the Ofoten railway) and 37·4m. passengers.

Aviation. Det Norske Luftfartselskap (DNL) started its post-war activities on 1 April 1946. On 1 Aug. 1946 DNL, together with DDL (Danish Airlines) and ABA/SILA (Swedish Airlines), formed the 'Scandinavian Airlines System'—SAS. The 3 companies remained independent units, but all services were co-ordinated. In 1951 a new agreement was signed (retroactive from 1 Oct. 1950) according to which the 3 national companies became holding partners in a new organization which took over the entire operational system. Denmark and Norway hold each two-sevenths and Sweden three-sevenths of the capital, but they have joint responsibility towards third parties.

In the autumn of 1982 SAS had a fleet of 86 jet planes. Length of route network, about 252,000 km. Scheduled air services are run by SAS, Braathens South-American and Far East Air transport service (SAFE) and Wideroes Flyveselskap service. The Norwegian share of the scheduled air service run by SAS is two-sevenths of the SAS service on international routes and the total SAS service in Norway.

	1,000 km flown	Passengers carried	1,000 passenger-km	Post, luggage, freight and passengers (1,000 ton-km) Total	Of which post
1979	58,950	4,866,926	4,070,000	497,000	16,000
1980	57,885	4,809,612	4,068,000	493,000	18,000
1981	55,091	4,967,880	4,062,000	498,000	19,000
1982	56,040	5,210,452	4,118,000	498,000	19,000

Shipping. The total registered mercantile marine on 1 Jan. 1983 was 1,656 vessels, 20m. gross tons (steam and motor vessels above 100 gross tons). These figures do not include fishing and catching boats, tugs, salvage vessels, icebreakers and similar special types of vessels, totalling 803 vessels of 352,000 gross tons.

Vessels entering Norway from foreign countries 1980	No.	Total Net tons
Norwegian	7,720	13,635
Foreign	8,545	23,635
Total entered	16,265	37,270

Goods (in 1,000 tonnes) in 1982 discharged, 18,097; loaded, 33,379, of which 11,297 was Swedish iron ore shipped from Narvik.

Post and Broadcasting. Number of telephones on 31 Dec. 1982 was 2,203,649 (53·4 per 100 of population). Receipts, 6,593·8m. kroner; expenses, 5,949·9m. kroner (interest on capital included) for State Telecommunications. *Norsk Rikskringkasting* is a non-commercial enterprise operated by an independent state organization and broadcasts 1 programme (P1) on long-, medium-, and short-waves and on FM and 1 programme (P2) on FM. Local programmes are also broadcast. It broadcasts 1 TV programme from 1,543 transmitters. Colour programmes are broadcast by PAL system. Number of television licences, 1,295,267.

Cinemas. There were 456 cinemas with a seating capacity of 134,394 in 1981.

Newspapers. There were 69 daily newspapers with a combined circulation of 1,802,000 in 1982.

JUSTICE, RELIGION, EDUCATION AND WELFARE

Justice. The judicature is common to civil and criminal cases. The same professional judges, who are legally educated, preside over both kinds of cases. These judges are as such state officials. The participation of lay judges and jurors, both summoned for the individual case, varies according to the kind of court and kind of case.

The ordinary Court of First Instance *(Herredsrett* and *Byrett)* is in criminal cases composed of one professional judge and 2 lay judges, chosen by ballot from a panel elected by the district council. In civil cases 2 lay judges may participate. The ordinary Court of First Instance is in general competent in all kinds of cases with the exception of criminal cases where the maximum penalty prescribed in the Criminal Code for the offence in question exceeds five years imprisonment. Altogether there are 98 ordinary courts of first instance.

In every community there is a Conciliation Council *(Forliksråd)* composed of 3 lay persons elected by the district council. A civil lawsuit usually begins with mediation in the council which also has judicial authority in minor civil cases.

The ordinary Courts of Second Instance *(Lagmannsrett)*, of which there are 5, are composed of 3 professional judges. Additionally, in civil cases 2 or 4 lay judges may be summoned. In criminal cases a jury of 10 lay persons is summoned to determine whether the defendant is guilty according to the charge. In civil cases, the Court of Second Instance is an ordinary court of appeal. In criminal cases in which the lower court does not have judicial authority, it is itself the court of first instance. In other criminal cases it is an appeal court as far as the appeal is based on an attack against the lower court's assessment of the facts when determining the guilt of the defendant. An appeal based on any other alleged mistakes is brought directly before the Supreme Court.

The Supreme Court *Høyesterett)* is the court of last resort. There are 18 Supreme Court judges. Each individual case is heard by 5 judges. Some major cases are determined in plenary session. The Supreme Court may in general examine every aspect of the case and the handling of it by the lower courts. However, in criminal cases the Court may not overrule the lower court's assessment of the facts as far as the guilt of the defendant is concerned.

The Court of Impeachment *(Riksretten)* is composed of 5 judges of the Supreme Court and 10 members of Parliament.

All serious offences are prosecuted by the State. The Public Prosecution Authority *(Påtalemyndigheten)* consists of the Attorney-General *(Riksadvokaten)*, 18 district attorneys *(statsadvokater)* and legally qualified officers of the ordinary police force. Counsel for the defence is in general provided for by the State.

There are 3 central prisons in which were detained (6 Sept. 1983) 313 persons. There are also 35 local prisons in which were detained (6 Sept. 1983) 1,558 persons.

Religion. There is complete freedom of religion, the Evangelical Lutheran Church, however, being the national church, endowed by the State. Its clergy are nominated by the King. Ecclesiastically Norway is divided into 10 *Bispedømmer* (bishoprics), 89 *Prostier* (provostships or archdeaconries) and 616 *Prestegjeld* (clerical districts). There were 134,349 members of registered religious communities outside the Evangelical Lutheran Church, subsidized by central government and local authorities in 1982. The Roman Catholics are under a Bishop at Oslo, a Vicar Apostolic at Trondheim and a Vicar Apostolic at Tromsø.

Education. In Norway the children normally start their school attendance the year they complete 7 and finish compulsory school the year they complete 16.

On 1 Oct. 1982 the number of primary schools and pupils were as follows: 3,539 primary schools, 576,910 pupils; 89 special schools for the handicapped, 3,178 pupils.

On 1 Oct. 1981 the number of pupils in upper secondary schools, *i.e.*, folk high schools, secondary general schools and vocational schools, was 184,334.

There are in Norway 4 universities and 8 institutions equivalent to universities. In autumn 1981 the total number of students was 39,827. The University of Oslo, founded in 1811, had 18,332 students. The University of Bergen, founded in 1948, had 7,502 students. The University of Trondheim consists of the Norwegian Institute of Technology, founded in 1910, and the College of Arts and Science, founded in 1925. At each of them the number of students was in autumn 1981, 4,851 and 3,330 respectively. The University of Tromsø was established in 1968; 1,657 students were registered in autumn 1981. The other university institutions had 4,035 students.

In addition there were at other schools of higher education, 41,779 students. These included 13,982 at colleges for teachers, 6,637 at colleges for engineers and 6,118 at district colleges.

In 1981 there were 4,717 Norwegian students and pupils attending foreign universities and schools.

Health. In 1981 there were 9,329 doctors and 67,384 hospital beds.

Social Security. In 1982, 56,000m. kroner were paid under different social insurance schemes, amounting to 18% of the net national income.

The National Insurance Act of 17 June 1966, which came into force on 1 Jan. 1967, replaced the schemes relating to old age pensions, disability benefits, widows' and mothers' pensions, benefits to unmarried women, 'survivors' benefit for children and rehabilitation aid. Schemes relating to health insurance, unemployment insurance and occupational injury insurance were revised and incorporated in National Insurance Scheme on 1 Jan. 1971. As from 1 Jan. 1981, benefits to divorced and separated supporters also are covered by the National Insurance Scheme.

The following conspectus gives a survey of schemes established by law. Many municipalities grant additional benefits to old-age, disablement and survivor's pensions.

938   NORWAY

Type of scheme	Intro- duced [1]	Scope	Principal benefits as from 1 May 1983
National insurance	1967 (1983)		
Sickness benefits [2]	1911	All residents	Medical benefits: hospital expenses; about one-half of a doctor's fee for the first and second consultation, all the fee for additional consultations; important medicines, etc., daily sickness allowances: kr. 38 to 695 per day cash (5 days a week). The new sickness allowance scheme (1 July 1978) entitles employees to a daily allowance equal to 100% of their gross earned income (within certain limits) from and including the first day of absence; self-employed persons, ordinarily 65% of gross earned income as from the 15th day. Supplementary insurance available. The allowances are taxable
Unemployment benefits [2]	1939	Nearly all wage-earners	Daily allowance during unemployment kr. 34 to 422 per day, excluding supplement for supported child(ren) (six days a week), taxable as from 1 Jan. 1980. Contributions to training and retraining, removal expenses, wage subsidies in the case of relief work
Rehabilitation benefits [3]	1961	Persons unfit for work because of disablement and persons who have a substantially limited general functional capacity	Training; treatment; rehabilitation allowance grants and loans Full rehabilitation allowance equals old age pension
Disability benefits [3]	1961	All residents	A basic grant (ordinary rate kr. 3,192 per annum) and an assistance grant (ordinary rate kr. 5,316 per annum) to persons with special needs. In certain cases the benefits may be increased. The rates are fixed by the Storting, independent of the basic amount
		All residents between 16 and 67 years of age	Disability pension to persons between 16 and 67 years of age, occupationally disabled by at least 50%, unfit for rehabilitation Full disability pension equals old age pension
Occupational injury benefits [2] (industrial workers 1895; fishermen 1909; seamen 1913; military personnel 1953, combined in the act of occupational injury insurance 1960)	1960	All employed persons, school children and students; self-employed on a voluntary basis	The ordinary benefits of the National Insurance, e.g., sickness and rehabilitation benefits, basic grants, assistance grants, disability pensions, and benefits to survivors granted according to special rules which in almost all cases are more favourable for the insured person —or his survivors than the ordinary rules An occupational injury compensation, alone or in addition to a disability pension
Old age pensions [3]	1937	All persons above 67 years of age	Basic pensions: Single, kr. 22,600; couples, kr. 33,900 per annum; supplementary pensions based on previous pensionable income; basic grant; assistance grant; various allowances
Death grants	1967	All residents	A certain amount fixed by the Storting, for the time being kr. 4,000

For notes see bottom of p. 939.

Type of scheme	Intro-duced[1]	Scope	Principal benefits as from 1 May 1983
Survivors' benefits[3]	1965	All residents	Full pension = kr. 22,600 per annum + 55% of the supplementary pension due to the deceased, *transitional benefits,* child care allowance and educational allowances
Children's pension[3]	1958	Under 18 (20) years of age, after loss of one or both parents	40% of basic amount (kr. 9,040) for first child, 25% (kr. 5,650) for each additional child. If both parents are dead, full survivors' pension for first, 40% of basic amount for second, 25% third, etc., child
Benefits to un-married supporters[3]	1965	Unmarried mothers or fathers	Maternity grant kr. 7,020, transitional benefit, full amount kr. 22,600 per annum, child care allowance and educational allowances
Benefits to divorced and separated supporters[4]	1972	Divorced and separated supporters	Same kind of benefits as unmarried supporters above
Benefits to un-married persons forced to live at home[3]	1965	Unmarried persons under 67 years of age having stayed at home for at least 5 years to give necessary care and attention to parents or other near relatives	Transitional benefit or a pension that equals the basic amount, educational allowances
Special supplement to National Insurance pensions or transitional benefits	1969 (1983)	Pensioners and persons with transitional allowance on basic rates	Full special supplement, 51·5% of basic amount, *i.e.* kr.11,639. For a married pensioner full supplement is lower when spouse has her own pension (47·5%)
Compensation supplement to National Insurance pensions or transitional benefits	1970 (1972)	Pensioners, persons with transitional benefits (except unmarried, divorced and separated supporters) or rehabilitation allowances	Full compensation supplement kr. 500 for single persons and kr. 750 for married couples
Family allowances	1946 (1983)	All families with children under 16 years of age	Kr. 3,816, for the first child, kr. 4,644 for the second, kr. 5,772 for the third, kr. 6,204 for the fourth and kr. 6,516 for the fifth and each additional child. Single supporters receive benefit for one more child than the actual number of children
War pensions	1946 (1981)	War victims, 1939–45	Pensions up to kr. 94,356 per annum (excluding supplement for supported child(ren); widows' and children's pensions
Special pension schemes:		Persons with at least:[5]	Maximum old-age pension for couples:
Seamen	1948 (1983)	150 months service (360 ,, ,,)	Kr. 74,063[6] per annum (officers) Kr. 52,902[6] ,, ,, (others)
Forestry workers	1952 (1980)	750 premium weeks (1,500 ,, ,,)	Kr. 18,000 per annum (excluding supplement for supported child(ren)
Fishermen	1958 (1983)	750 premium weeks (1,500 ,, ,,)	Kr. 31,500 ,, ,,

[1] Date of latest revision in brackets.
[2] Transferred to national insurance scheme and revised in 1971.
[3] Transferred to national insurance scheme and revised in 1967.
[4] Transferred to national insurance scheme and revised in 1981.
[5] Requirements for maximum pensions in brackets.
[6] Supplements for service during war not included.

Provisions have been laid down for the integration of more than one benefit, pension, etc., so as to limit the total amount.

SVALBARD

An archipelago situated between 10° and 35° E. long. and between 74° and 81° N. lat. Total area, 62,000 sq. km (24,000 sq. miles).

The main islands of the archipelago are Spitsbergen (formerly called Vestspitsbergen), Nordaustlandet, Edgeøya, Barentsøya, Prins Karls Forland, Bjørnøya, Hopen, Kong Karls Land, Kvitøya, and many small islands. The arctic climate is tempered by mild winds from the Atlantic.

The archipelago was probably discovered by Norsemen in 1194 and rediscovered by the Dutch navigator Barents in 1596. In the 17th century the very lucrative whale-hunting caused rival Dutch, British and Danish–Norwegian claims to sovereignty and quarrels about the hunting-places. But when in the 18th century the whale-hunting ended, the question of the sovereignty of Svalbard lost its significance; it was again raised in the 20th century, owing to the discovery and exploitation of coalfields. By a treaty, signed on 9 Feb. 1920 in Paris, Norway's sovereignty over the archipelago was recognized. On 14 Aug. 1925 the archipelago was officially incorporated in Norway.

Coal is the principal product. Of the 3 Norwegian and 3 Soviet mining camps, 2 Norwegian and 2 Soviet camps are operating. Total population on 31 Dec. 1982 was 4,012, of which 1,450 Norwegians, 2,550 Soviet citizens, and 12 Poles. In 1982, 359,003 tonnes of coal were exported from the Norwegian and 475,403 tonnes from the Soviet mines.

Norwegian and foreign companies have been prospecting for oil. So far 5 deep drillings have been made, but oil and gas finds have not been reported.

There are Norwegian meteorological and/or radio stations at the following places: Bjørnøya (since 1920), Hopen (1945), Isfjord Radio (1934), Longyearbyen (1930), Svalbard Lufthavn (1975) and Ny-Ålesund (1961). A research station, administered by Norsk Polarinstitutt, was erected at Ny-Ålesund in 1968 for various observations and investigations. An airport near Longyearbyen (Svalbard Lufthavn) opened in 1975.

Norsk Polarinstitutt, Skrifter, Oslo, from 1948 (under different titles from 1922)
Greve, T., *Svalbard: Norway in the Arctic.* Oslo, 1975
Hisdal, V., *Geography of Svalbard.* Norsk Polarinstitutt, Oslo, 1976
Orvin. A. K., 'Twenty-five Years of Norwegian Sovereignty in Svalbard 1925–1950' (in *The Polar Record,* 1951)

JAN MAYEN

This bleak, desolate and mountainous island of volcanic origin and partly covered by glaciers, is situated 71° N. lat. and 8° 30′ W. long., 300 miles NNE of Iceland. The total area is 380 sq. km (147 sq. miles). Beerenberg, its highest peak, reaches a height of 2,277 metres. Volcanic activity, which had been dormant, was reactivated in Sept. 1970.

The island was possibly discovered by Henry Hudson in 1608, and it was first named Hudson's Tutches (Touches). It was again and again rediscovered and renamed. Its present name derives from the Dutch whaling captain Jan Jacobsz May, who indisputably discovered the island in 1614. It was uninhabited, but occasionally visited by seal hunters and trappers, until 1921 when Norway established a radio and meteorological station. On 8 May 1929 Jan Mayen was officially proclaimed as incorporated in the Kingdom of Norway. Its relation to Norway was finally settled by law of 27 Feb. 1930. A LORAN station (1959) and a CONSOL station (1968) have been established.

BOUVET ISLAND
Bouvetøya

This uninhabited volcanic island, mostly covered by glaciers and situated 54° 25′ S. lat. and 3° 21′ E. long., was discovered in 1739 by a French naval officer, Jean Baptiste Loziert Bouvet, but no flag was hoisted till, in 1825, Capt. Norris raised the Union Jack. In 1928 Great Britain waived its claim to the island in favour of Norway, which in Dec. 1927 had occupied it. A law of 27 Feb. 1930 declared Bouvetøya a Norwegian dependency. The area is 50 sq. km (19 sq. miles). From 1977 Norway has had an automatic meteorological station on the island, and 5 men operated a meteorological station there during the 1978–79 season.

PETER I ISLAND
Peter I Øy

This uninhabited island, situated 68° 48′ S. lat. and 90° 35′ W. long., was sighted in 1821 by the Russian explorer, Admiral von Bellingshausen. The first landing was made in 1929 by a Norwegian expedition which hoisted the Norwegian flag. On 1 May 1931 Peter I Island was placed under Norwegian sovereignty, and on 24 March 1933 it was incorporated in Norway as a dependency. The area is 180 sq. km (69 sq. miles).

QUEEN MAUD LAND
Dronning Maud Land

On 14 Jan. 1939 the Norwegian Cabinet placed that part of the Antarctic Continent from the border of Falkland Islands dependencies in the west to the border of the Australian Antarctic Dependency in the east (between 20° W. and 45° E.) under Norwegian sovereignty. The territory had been explored only by Norwegians and hitherto been ownerless. Since 1949 expeditions from various countries have explored the area. In 1957 Dronning Maud Land was given the status of a Norwegian dependency.

DIPLOMATIC REPRESENTATIVES

Of Norway in Great Britain (25 Belgrave Sq., London, SW1X 8QD)
Ambassador: Rolf Busch.

Of Great Britain in Norway (Thomas Heftyesgate 8, Oslo, 2)
Ambassador: William Bentley, CMG.

Of Norway in the USA (2720 34th Street, NW, Washington, D.C., 20008)
Ambassador: Knut Hedemann.

Of the USA in Norway (Drammensveien 18, Oslo, 2)
Ambassador: Mark E. Austad.

Of Norway to the United Nations
Ambassador: Tom Eric Vraalsen.

Books of Reference

Statistical Information: The Central Bureau of Statistics, Statistisk Sentralbyrå (Dronningensgate 16, Oslo 1), was founded in 1876 as an independent state institution. *Director:* Arne Øien. The earliest census of population was taken in 1769. The Sentralbyrå publishes the series *Norges Offisielle Statistikk,* Norway's official statistics (from 1828), and *Social Economic Studies* (from 1954). The main publications are:

Statistisk Årbok for Norge (annual, from 1880; from 1952 bilingual Norwegian–English)
Økonomisk Utsyn (annual, from 1935; with English summary from 1952)
Historisk Statistikk 1978 (historical statistics; bilingual Norwegian–English)
Statistisk Månedshefte (monthly, from 1880; with English index)
Sosialt Utsyn 1983 (social survey). Irregular

Norges Statskalender. From 1816; annual from 1877
Facts about Norway. Ed. by Aftenposten. 17th ed. Oslo, 1982
Derry, T. K., *A History of Modern Norway, 1814–1972.* OUP, 1973.—*A History of Scandinavia.* London, 1979
Glässer, E., *Norwegen* [bibliography] Darmstadt, 1978
Gleditsch, Th., *Engelsk–norsk ordbok,* 2nd ed. Oslo, 1948

Greve, T., *Haakon VI of Norway, Founder of a New Monarchy.* London, 1983
Grønland, E., *Norway in English. Books on Norway . . . 1742–1959.* Oslo, 1961
Haugen, E., *Norwegian–English Dictionary.* Oslo, 1965
Helvig, M., *Norway: Land, People, Industries, a Brief Geography.* 3rd ed. Oslo, 1970
Holtedahl, O. (ed.), *Geology of Norway.* Oslo, 1960
Hove, O., *The System of Education.* Oslo, 1968
Imber, W., *Norway.* Oslo, 1980
Knudsen, O., *Norway at Work.* Oslo, 1972
Larsen, K., *A History of Norway.* New York, 1948
Midgaard, J., *A Brief History of Norway.* Oslo, 1969
Nielsen, K., and Nesheim, A., *Lapp Dictionary: Lapp–English–Norwegian.* 5 vols., Oslo 1963
Orvik, N. (ed.), *Fears and Expectations: Norwegian Attitudes Toward European Integration.* Oslo, 1972
Paine, R., *Coast Lapp Society.* 2 vols. Tromsø, 1957–65
Popperwell, R. G., *Norway.* London, 1972
Udgaard, N. M., *Great Power Politics and Norwegian Foreign Policy.* Oslo, 1973
Vorren, Ø. (ed.), *Norway North of 65.* Oslo, 1960

National Library: The University Library, Drammensvein 42b, Oslo. *Director:* Ben Rugaas.

OMAN

Sultanate of Oman

Capital: Muscat
Population: 1·5m. (1982)
GNP per capita: US$4,380 (1980)

AREA AND POPULATION. The Sultanate of Oman, known as the Sultanate of Muscat and Oman until 1970, is an independent sovereign state, situated in south-east Arabia. Its coastline is over 1,000 miles long and extends from the Ras al Khaimah Shaikdom near Bukha on the west side of the Musandum Peninsula to Ras Dharbat Ali, which marks the boundary between Oman and the territory of the People's Democratic Republic of Yemen. The Sultanate extends inland to the borders of the Rub' al Khali ('Empty Quarter') across three geographical divisions—a coastal plain, a range of hills and a plateau. The coastal plain varies in width from 10 miles near Suwaiq to practically nothing in the vicinity of Mutrah and Muscat towns, where the hills descend abruptly into the sea. These hills are for the most part barren except at the highest part of the mountainous region of the Jebel Akhdar (summit 9,998 ft) where there is some cultivation. The plateau has an average height of 1,000 ft. With the exception of oases there is little or no cultivation. North-west of Muscat the coastal plain, known as the Batinah, is fertile and prosperous. The date gardens extend for over 150 miles. Whereas the coastline between the capital, Muscat, and the southern province of Dhofar is barren, Dhofar itself is highly fertile. Its principal town is Salalah on the coast which is served by the port of Rasut.

In the valleys of the interior, as well as on the Batinah, date cultivation has reached a high level and there are possibilities of agricultural development subject to present water resources and soil surveys. The average annual crop of dates is estimated at 50,000 tons, most of which is exported to India. Camels are bred in large numbers by the inland tribes. There are no industries of any importance, although a copper industry was being established in 1980, and fishing, water resources, soil and agricultural surveys are being undertaken.

The area has been estimated at about 105,000 sq. miles and the population at 1·5m., chiefly Arabs; of these, some 40,000 live in Dhofar. The town of Muscat is the capital which, while formerly of some commercial importance, has now lost most of its trade to the adjacent port of Mutrah (combined populations, 80,000), the starting point for the trade routes into the interior. The population of both towns consists of pure Arabs, Indians, Pakistanis and Negroes; numerous merchants are Khojas (from Sind and Kutch) and Hindus (mostly from Gujarat and Bombay). Other ports are Sohar, Khaburah and Sur, Rasut in the south; none, however, affords shelter from bad weather.

The port of Gwadur and a small tract of country on the Baluchistán coast of the Gulf of Oman were handed over to Pakistan on 8 Sept. 1958.

The **Kuria Muria** islands were ceded to the UK in 1854 by the Sultan of Muscat and Oman for the purpose of a cable station. On 30 Nov. 1967 the islands were retroceded to the Sultan of Muscat and Oman, in accordance with the wishes of the population.

CLIMATE. Oman has a desert climate, with exceptionally hot and humid months from April to Oct., when temperatures may reach 117°F (47°C). From Dec. to the end of March, the climate is more pleasant. Light monsoon rains fall in the south from June to Sept., with highest amounts in the western highland region. Muscat. Jan. 72°F (22·2°C), July 91°F (33·3°C). Annual rainfall 4·0″ (99·1 mm). Salalah. Jan. 72°F (22·2°C), July 78°F (25·6°C). Annual rainfall 3·3″ (81·3 mm).

RULER. The present Sultan is Qaboos bin Said (born Nov. 1940). He took over from his father Said bin Taimur, on 23 July 1970 in a Palace *coup*.

In Oct. 1981 the Sultan issued three decrees establishing a 45-member State advisory council.

CONSTITUTION AND GOVERNMENT. Oman is an absolute monarchy and there is no formal constitution. The Sultan legislates by decree and appoints a Cabinet to assist him; he holds the posts of Prime Minister and Minister of Foreign Affairs, Defence and Finance. Besides 17 departmental Ministers, the Cabinet also includes:

Deputy Prime Minister for Security and Defence: Sayyid Fahar Bin-Taimur al-Said.
Deputy Prime Minister for Legal Affairs: Sayyid Fahad Bin-Mahmoud al-Said.
Special Advisor to Sultan, Governor of Muscat: Sayyid Thuwaini Bin-Shihab al-Said.
Special Advisor to Sultan on Religious and Historical Affairs: Mohammad Bin-Ahmad.
Minister of State for Foreign Affairs: Yusuf Alawi.
Minister of State, Governor of Dhofar: Hilal Bin-Saud Bin-Hareb al-Busaidi.

National flag: Red, with a white panel in the upper fly and a green one in the lower fly, and in the canton the national emblem in white.

Local government: Oman is divided into 10 provinces *(liwas)* and sub-divided into 41 governates *(wilayats)* each under a governor *(wali).*

DEFENCE

Army. The Army consists of 1 Royal Guard brigade; 1 armoured, 1 reconnaissance and 3 artillery regiments; 8 infantry battalions; 1 special force, 1 signals regiment, 1 engineer squadron and 1 parachute squadron. Equipment includes 6 M-60A1 and 12 Chieftain main battle tanks. Strength (1984) about 20,000.

Navy. The Navy comprises 3 new very fast missile-armed corvettes, 2 fast missile-armed patrol boats, 4 fast gunboats, 4 inshore patrol craft, 1 training ship/offshore patrol vessel, a logistic support ship, 1 supply ship, 6 landing craft, 1 survey craft and 1 training ship. Under construction is 1 logistic landing ship. All the warships are British-built. The marine police operate 10 coastal patrol boats, 7 launches, 2 logistics support craft and 2 inshore patrol boats. Naval personnel in 1984 totalled 2,000 officers and ratings.

Air Force. The Air Force, formed in 1959, had in 1984 two strike/interceptor squadrons of Jaguars, a ground attack/interceptor squadron of Hunters, a squadron of Strikemaster light jet training/attack aircraft, 1 DC-8, 3 BAC One-Eleven and 1 Falcon VIP transports, 3 C-130H Hercules, 1 twin-turboprop Buffalo, 7 Defender and 15 Skyvan light transports, 26 Agusta-Bell 205, 212, 214B and JetRanger helicopters for security duties, 2 Super Puma VIP helicopters and 2 Bravo piston-engined trainers. Air defence force has batteries of Rapier low-level surface-to-air missiles. Personnel (1983) about 2,100.

INTERNATIONAL RELATIONS

Membership. Oman is a member of UN, the Arab League, the Islamic Conference Organisation and the Gulf Co-operation Council.

Treaties. The Treaty of Friendship, Commerce and Navigation between Britain and the Sultan signed on 20 Dec. 1951, reaffirmed the close ties which have existed between the British Government and the Sultanate of Oman for over a century and a half. A Memorandum of Understanding signed in June 1982 provided for regular consultations on international and bilateral issues.

ECONOMY

Planning. The 5-year development plan (1976–80) had an expenditure of R.O. 2,556m. Expenditure for the second 5-year plan (1981–85) is (estimate) R.O.

7,368m. and a primary aim is to develop new sources of national income to augment and eventually to replace oil revenues.

Budget. Revenue (1982) R.O. 3,483m. (3,062. from oil); expenditure, 4,039m. (defence, 723m.).

Currency. The *Rial Omani* was introduced in Nov. 1972 replacing the *Rial Saidi*. It is divided into 1,000 *baiza*. There are notes of 100, 250 and 500 *baiza* and 1, 5 and 10 *Rial Omani* and coins of 2, 5, 10, 20, 50 and 100 *baiza*. The exchange rate in March 1984 was £1 = 514 *baiza*; US$1 = 346 *baiza*.

Banking. In 1983 there were 25 banks operating in Oman apart from the Central Bank of Oman.

Weights and Measures. The metric system of measurement is in operation. Transactions in the former measurements are now illegal.

ENERGY AND NATURAL RESOURCES

Oil. The economy of Oman is dominated by the oil industry, which provides nearly all Government revenue. In 1937 Petroleum Concessions (Oman) Ltd, a subsidiary of the Iraq Petroleum Co., was granted a 75-year oil concession extending over the whole of Oman, although it relinquished Dhofar in 1950. In 1951 the company's name was changed to Petroleum Development (Oman) Ltd. The company (PDO) regained the Dhofar concession area in 1969. When some of the IPC partners withdrew from Oman in 1960, Shell took over the management of PDO with an 85% interest (minority interests were held by Compagnie Française des Pétroles, 10% and Gulbenkian, 5%). At the beginning of 1974 the Oman Government bought a 25% share in PDO, increasing this retroactively to 60% in July. A Joint Management Committee was established. Other companies active in exploration activities in Oman, with mixed success, include Amoco, Elf-Acquitaine and a consortium of Deminex, Agip and Hispanoil with BP as operator.

Oil in commercial quantities was discovered in 1964 and production began at a rate of 200,000 bbls per day in 1967. Production has fluctuated from year to year, peaking in 1976 at 366,000 bbls per day. Due to conditions on the international oil market, production fell to a low of 282,000 bbls per day in 1980 but was restored to about 330,000 bbls per day in 1981. Production in 1982 was 120·9m. bbls. Total reserves were estimated in 1982 to be 2,900m. bbls, or sufficient for 23 years at the current rate of production.

Oman is nt a member of OPEC or OAPEC but tends to follow OPEC pricing policy.

Gas. Production (1981) 215m. cu. ft per day.

Minerals. Production of refined copper at the smelter at Sohar was about 6,700 tonnes in 1983. Copper mines produce about 11m. tonnes annually.

COMMERCE. The total imports for 1981 were valued at US$2,722m., including machinery and transport equipment (1,078m.), manufactured goods (504m.), food and drink (359m.), petroleum products (357m.) and chemicals (95m.). The total exports for 1981 were valued at US$4,696m. Crude oil accounted for US$4,419m., other exports including fish, dry limes and wheat flour.

In 1981, 22·5% of imports came from Japan, 18·6% from UK, 13·5% from United Arab Emirates, 8·9% from USA and 4·8% from the Federal Republic of Germany; 50·2% of exports went to Japan, 11·1% to the Netherlands, 10·8% to the Federal Republic of Germany, 8·6% to Singapore and 7·7% to USA.

Total trade between Oman and UK (British Department of Trade returns, in £1,000 sterling):

	1978	1979	1980	1981	1982	1983
Imports to UK	41,942	31,844	28,728	40,460	46,425	91,216
Exports and re-exports from UK	125,721	129,729	131,094	170,835	265,283	448,900

COMMUNICATIONS

Roads. A network of adequate graded roads links all the main sectors of population, and only a few mountain villages are not accessible by Land-Rover. A rapid road construction programme began in 1976, and by the end of the year there were 1,272 km of paved roads and 8,500 km of graded roads. There are good waterproof roads in the north of Oman, between Muscat and Sohar, Sohar and Buraimi, Nizwa and Buraimi and Nizwa and Seeb. In Dhofar tarmac roads have been completed from Raysut through Salalah to Taqa and also Bid Bid to Sur.

Aviation. Gulf Air run regional services in and out of Seeb international airport (20 miles from Muscat) to Bahrain, Doha, Abu Dhabi, Dubai, Karachi and Bombay. They and British Airways each operate daily flights to and from London. Other airlines serving Muscat are MEA, Kuwait Airlines, PIA, Air India, Iran Air, TMA (cargo) and Trade Winds (cargo).

Shipping. In Mutrah a deep-water port (named Mina Qaboos) was completed in 1974 at a cost of R.O. 18·2m. It provides 12 berths, 9 of which are deep-water berths, warehousing facilities and a harbour for dhows and coastal vessels. The annual handling capacity has been raised to 1·5m. tons.

Post and Broadcasting. There are Sultanate post offices in Muscat and Mutrah, relying solely upon a Post Office Box system for delivery. Omantel maintain a telegraph office at Muscat and an automatic telephone exchange (13,068 lines, 1978) which includes Mutrah, Bait-al-Falaj and Mina al-Fahal, the oil company terminal. A high-frequency radio link with Bahrain was opened in Aug. 1972 providing communications with other parts of the world. Internally, there are radio telephone, telex and telegraph services direct between Salalah and Muscat, and a VHF radio link between Seeb international airport and Muscat. The airport is also served by a SITA telex system. Radio Oman broadcasts daily for 17 hours in Arabic and 2 hours in English.

A colour television service covering Muscat and the surrounding area started transmission in Nov. 1974. A television service for Dhofar opened in 1975.

Newspapers. There were (1984) 3 daily newspapers.

EDUCATION AND WELFARE

Education. Until 1970 there were only 3 schools in Oman, and it has been estimated that as many as 80% of Omanis are still illiterate. All Omanis desiring further education must obtain it abroad, but plans are being implemented for the development of technical and agricultural training and craft training at intermediate and secondary level. Oman's first university, in Nizwa, was under construction in 1981. There are also programmes to combat adult illiteracy.

Health. Health services in 1982 were widely spread with 14 hospitals in use and 2 more planned, 12 health centres and 60 clinics. There are also Save the Children Fund Welfare Clinics at Sohar and Sur.

DIPLOMATIC REPRESENTATIVES

Of Oman in Great Britain (44A Montpelier Sq., London, SW7 1JJ)
Ambassador: Ahmed Mohamed Nasser Al-Lamki (accredited 29 Oct. 1982).

Of Great Britain in Oman (PO Box 300, Muscat)
Ambassador: Duncan Slater, CMG.

Of Oman in the USA (2342 Massachusetts Ave., NW, Washington, DC., 20008)
Ambassador: Ali Salim Bader Al-Hinai.

Of the USA in Oman (PO Box 966, Muscat)
Ambassador: John R. Countryman.

Of Oman to the United Nations
Ambassador: Mahmoud Aboul-Nasr.

Books of Reference

Achievements. Ministry of Health. Oman, 1975
Hints to Exporters: UAE and the Sultanate of Oman 1981–82. British Overseas Board

Oman in 10 years. Ministry of Information. Oman, 1980

Oman: A MEED Practical Guide. London, 1981

Clements, F. A., *Oman: The Reborn Land.* London and New York, 1980.—*Oman.* [Bibliography] Oxford and Santa Barbara, 1981

Graz, L., *The Omani's: Sentinals of the Gulf.* London, 1982

Hawley, D., *Oman and its Rennaissance.* London, 1977

Peterson, J. E., *Oman in the Twentieth Century.* London and New York, 1978

Shannon, M. O., *Oman and South-eastern Arabia: A Bibliographic Survey.* Boston, 1978

Skeet, I., *Muscat and Oman: The End of an Era.* London and New York, 1974

Thesiger, W., *Arabian Sands.* London, 1959

Wikan, U., *Behind the Veil in Arabia: Women in Oman.* John Hopkins Univ. Press, 1982

PAKISTAN

Islamic Republic of Pakistan

Capital: Islamabad
Population: 88m. (1983)
GNP per capita: US$300 (1980)

HISTORY. Pakistan was constituted as a Dominion on 14 Aug. 1947, under the provisions of the Indian Independence Act, 1947, which received the royal assent on 18 July 1947. The Dominion consisted of the following former territories of British India: Balúchistán, East Bengal (including almost the whole of Sylhet, a former district of Assam), North-West Frontier, West Punjab and Sind; and those States which had acceded to Pakistan.

On 23 March 1956 an Islamic republic was proclaimed after the Constituent Assembly had adopted the draft constitution on 29 Feb.

On 7 Oct. 1958 President Mirza declared martial law in Pakistan, dismissed the central and provincial Governments, abolished all political parties and abrogated the constitution of 23 March 1956. Field Marshal Mohammad Ayub Khan, the Army Commander-in-Chief, was appointed as chief martial law administrator and assumed office on 28 Oct. 1958, after Maj.-Gen. Iskander Mirza had handed all powers to him. His authority was confirmed by a ballot in Feb. 1960. He proclaimed a new constitution on 1 March 1962.

On 25 March 1969 President Ayub Khan resigned and handed over power to the army under the leadership of Maj.-Gen. Agha Muhammad Yahya Khan who immediately proclaimed martial law throughout the country, appointing himself chief martial law administrator on the same day. On 29 March 1970 the Legal Framework Order was published, defining a new constitution: Pakistan to be a federal republic with a Moslem Head of State; the National Assembly and Provincial Assemblies to be elected in free and periodical elections, the first of which was held on 7 Dec. 1970.

At the general election the Awami League based in East Pakistan and led by Sheikh Mujibur Rahman gained 167 seats and the Peoples' Party 90. Martial law continued pending the settlement of differences between East and West, which developed into civil war in March 1971. The war ended in Dec. 1971 and the Eastern province declared itself an independent state, Bangladesh. On 20 Dec. 1971 President Yahya Khan resigned and Mr Z. A. Bhutto became President and chief martial law administrator. On 30 Jan. 1972, Pakistan withdrew from the Commonwealth.

A new Constitution was adopted by the National Assembly on 10 April 1973 and enforced on 14 Aug. 1973. It provided for a federal parliamentary system with the President as constitutional head and the Prime Minister as chief executive. President Bhutto stepped down to become Prime Minister and Fazal Elahi Chaudhry was elected President.

The Chief of the Army Staff, Gen. M. Zia-ul-Haq, proclaimed martial law on 5 July 1977 and the armed forces took control of the administration; scheduled elections were postponed. Mr Bhutto was hanged (for conspiracy to murder) on 4 April 1979. Gen. M. Zia-ul-Haq succeeded Fazal Elahi Chaudhry as President in Sept. 1978.

Governors-General of Pakistan: Quaid-I-Azam Mohammed Ali Jinnah (14 Aug. 1947–11 Sept. 1948); Khawaja Nazimuddin (14 Sept. 1948–18 Oct. 1951; took over the premiership after the assassination of Liaquat Ali Khan); Ghulam Mohammad (19 Oct. 1951–6 Aug. 1955); Maj.-Gen. Iskander Mirza (assumed office of President on 6 Oct. 1955, elected President on 5 March 1956).

Presidents of Pakistan: Maj.-Gen. Iskander Mirza (23 March 1956–28 Oct. 1958); Field Marshal Mohammad Ayub Khan (28 Oct. 1958–25 March 1969); Maj.-Gen. Agha Muhammad Yahya Khan (31 March 1969–20 Dec. 1971);

Zulfiqar Ali Bhutto (20 Dec.1971–14 Aug. 1973); Fazal Elahi Chaudhri (14 Aug. 1973–16 Sept. 1978); Gen. Mohammad Zia ul-Haq (16 Sept. 1978–).

AREA AND POPULATION. Pakistan is bounded north-west by Afghánistán, north by the USSR and China, east by India and south by the Arabian Sea. The total area of Pakistan is 307,293 sq. miles (796,095 sq. km); population (1981 census), 83·78m.; male to female ratio, 111 to 100. Density, 105 per sq. km. Estimate (1983) 88m. Urban population, 28·3%. Annual average growth rate, 1982–83, 2·8%. The crude birth rate was 41 (per 1,000 population); infant mortality 90 (per 1,000 live births); life expectancy, 55 years.

The population of the principal cities is:

Census of 1981

Islamabad	201,000	Multan	730,000
Karachi	5,103,000	Gujranwala	597,000
Lahore	2,922,000	Peshawar	555,000
Faisalabad	1,092,000	Sialkot	296,000
Rawalpindi	928,000	Sargodha	294,000
Hyderabad	795,000	Quetta	285,000

Population of the provinces (census of 1981) was:

	Area (sq. km)	Total population (1,000)	Male and Female ratio	Density per sq. km
North-west Frontier Province	74,521	10,885	108	146
Federally administered Tribal Areas	27,219	2,175	108	80
Federal Capital Territory Islamabad	907	335	119	369
Punjab	205,344	47,116	111	229
Sind	140,914	18,966	110	134
Balúchistán	347,190	4,305	112	12

Language. The commonest languages are Urdu and Punjabi. Urdu is the national language while English is used in business and in central government. Provincial languages are Punjabi, Sindhi, Pushtu (North-West Frontier Province), Baluchi and Brahvi.

CLIMATE. A weak form of tropical monsoon climate occurs over much of the country, with arid conditions in the north and west, where the wet season is only from Dec. to March. Elsewhere, rain comes mainly in the summer. Summer temperatures are high everywhere, but winters can be cold in the mountainous north. Islamabad. Jan. 50°F (10°C), July 90°F (32·2°C). Annual rainfall 36″ (900 mm). Karachi. Jan. 61°F (16·1°C), July 86°F (30°C). Annual rainfall 8″ (196 mm). Lahore. Jan. 53°F (11·7°C), July 89°F (31·7°C). Annual rainfall 18″ (452 mm). Multan. Jan. 51°F (10·6°C), July 93°F (33·9°C). Annual rainfall 7″ (170 mm). Quetta. Jan. 38°F (3·3°C), July 80°F (26·7°C). Annual rainfall 10″ (239 mm).

CONSTITUTION AND GOVERNMENT. Under the Constitution of 1973 Parliament is bi-cameral, comprising the National Assembly and the Senate. The strength of the National Assembly is 210 including 10 women. The Senate consists of 63 members, 14 from each province, 5 from Federally Administered Tribal Areas and 2 from the federal capital area, elected by the members of the Provincial Assemblies. A constitutional amendment of 29 March 1976 provided 6 National Assembly seats reserved for non-Moslem minority representatives.

With the proclamation of martial law the Constitution has been kept in abeyance, but not abrogated: The Provisional Constitution Order, 1981, promulgated on 24 March 1981, retains 119 Articles in whole or in part. Articles not included in the Order are 34 comprising Part II of the Constitution, a further 56 relating to the President's office, Parliament and Legislative procedure, articles relating to the Judiciary, the six Schedules and Part XI.

The Constitution obliges the Government to use such ways and means as may enable the people to order their lives collectively and individually in accordance with the principles of Islam. The Council of Islamic Ideology was set up to this end under article 228 of the Constitution.

An Ombudsman was appointed in Jan. 1983.

In Jan. 1982 a Federal Council of 288 members was inaugurated, under the chairmanship of K. M. Safdar. The Council, which may have up to 350 members, is to act as an interim body until an elected Parliament can be set up. Members are nominated by the President. Members of the Cabinet and Ministers of State are *ex-officio* members. The Council's role is advisory.

In Aug. 1983 the President announced that national elections would be held by 23 March 1985 on the basis of the 1973 Constitution, amended to provide wider presidential powers.

President and Chief Martial Law Administrator, Chairman of the Planning Commission, Science and Technology, States and Frontier Regions, Establishment: Gen. M. Zia-ul-Haq.

Federal Cabinet in March 1984:

Finance and Economic Affairs: G. Ishaq Khan. *Foreign Affairs:* S. Y. Khan. *Attorney-General:* S. Pirzada. *Interior:* M. A. Haroon. *Defence:* A. A. Talpur. *Planning and Development:* Mahboobul Haq. *Housing and Works:* Air Marshal I. Haq Khan. *Water and Power:* R. Sikandar Zaman. *Industry:* E. Bux Soomro. *Culture, Sports and Tourism:* A. Niaz Mohammad Arbab. *Local Government and Rural Development:* F. Imam. *Labour, Manpower and Overseas Pakistanis:* G. Dastegir Khan. *Kashmir and Northern Affairs:* Lieut.-Gen. J. Said Mian. *Education:* M. Afzal. *Food, Agriculture and Co-operatives:* Vice-Adm. M. F. Janjua. *Communications:* M. Baluch. *Railways:* N. A. Ghafoor Khan Hoti. *Information and Broadcasting:* Raja M. Zafarul Haq. *Without portfolio;* A. M. A. Khan Abbas.

National flag: Green, charged at the centre, with a white crescent and white 5-pointed star, a white vertical stripe at the mast to one-quarter of the flag.

Local Government. Pakistan comprises the provinces of the Punjab, the North-West Frontier, Sind and Balúchistán, the states of Bahawalpur and Khairpur, the Balúchistán States Union, the frontier states and the tribal areas of Balúchistán and the north-west. These were merged into a single unit on 14 Oct. 1955. In July 1970 the single unit was dissolved into the original 4 provinces. The provincial capitals are Peshawar (NW Frontier Province), Lahore (Punjab), Karachi (Sind) and Quetta (Balúchistán). Provincial governors are appointed by the President and are assisted by provincial councils.

Within the provinces there are divisions administered by Commissioners appointed by the President; the divisions are divided into districts and agencies administered by Deputy Commissioners or Political Agents who are responsible to the Provincial Governments.

Kashmir. Between one-third and one-half of Kashmir is controlled by Pakistan. This area is the northern and western portion of the country. It has an area of 83,806 sq. km. and a population of about 1·3m. Under a United Nations resolution of 1949 its future was to be decided by plebiscite; it is still a disputed territory.

The people of Azad Kashmir have their own Assembly (42 members including 2 women), their own Council (of 14 members), High Court and Supreme Court. There is a Parliamentary form of Government with a Prime Minister as the executive head and the President as the Constitutional head. Elections to the Legislative's 40 general seats are to be held within 10 days of the general elections in Pakistan, according to a presidential proclamation of 8 Oct. 1977. The seat of government is Muzaffarabad.

The Pakistan Government is directly responsible for Gilgit and Baltistan.

DEFENCE

Army. The Army consists of 2 armoured and 16 infantry divisions; 4 independent armoured, 5 independent infantry, 7 artillery and 2 anti-aircraft brigades; 6 armoured reconnaissance regiments, 6 surface-to-air missile batteries and 1 Special Services Group. Equipment includes 370 M-47/-48, 51 T-54/-55 and 900 Type-59 main battle tanks. Strength (1984) 450,000, with a further 500,000 reservists. There are also 100.000 men in paramilitary units: National Guard, Frontier Corps, Pakistan Rangers, Coast Guard and Frontier Constabulary.

Navy. The fleet comprises 6 diesel-powered patrol submarines (completed in France in 1969–80), 5 midget submarines, 1 "County" class destroyer, *Babur* (*ex*-HMS *London*) transferred from the Royal Navy in 1982, the ex-British very old light cruiser (cadet training ship) ex-HMS *Diadem*, re-named *Jahangir*, 6 old destroyers (5 *ex*-US and 1 *ex*-British), 4 corvette-type patrol vessels, 4 fast missile craft, 12 fast gunboats, 4 fast (hydrofoil) torpedo boats, 1 seaward defence boat, 1 survey ship (*ex*-frigate), 6 coastal minesweepers, 1 destroyer parent ship, 1 fleet replenishment ship, 1 degaussing vessel, 1 rescue ship, 2 landing craft, 2 oilers, 1 water carrier and 4 tugs.

The principal naval base and dockyard are at Karachi. Naval personnel in 1984 totalled 1,250 officers and 14,550 ratings.

The naval air arm comprises 4 fixed-wing aircraft and 10 helicopters.

Air Force. The Pakistan Air Force came into being on 14 Aug. 1947.It has its headquarters at Peshawar and is organized within 3 air defence sectors, in the northern, central and southern areas of the country. Tactical units include 1 squadron of B-57B (Canberra) bombers, at least 4 squadrons of Mirage III-EP/5 supersonic fighters, 7 squadrons of MiG-19 (F-6) supersonic fighter-bombers and 3 squadrons of A-5 (Q-5) attack aircraft acquired from China, 1 squadron equipped with Mirage III-RP reconnaissance aircraft, and C-130 Hercules turboprop transports. Delivery of 32 F-16A and 8 F-16B Fighting Falcons began in late 1982, for operational service with 3 interceptor squadrons (replacing F-6s) from 1984. Flying training schools are equipped with Masshaq (Saab Supporter) armed piston-engined primary trainers, T-37B/C jet trainers supplied by the USA, Mirage III-DPs and Chinese-built FT-5s (two-seat MiG-17s). Three Breguet Atlantics and 4 Super Frelon helicopters, plus a small number of Alouette III helicopters, are available to perform maritime reconnaissance, search and rescue duties in co-operation with Sea King helicopters of the Pakistan Navy Air Arm. A VIP transport squadron operates the Presidential F27 turboprop aircraft, a twin-jet Falcon 20 and smaller types. There is a flying college at Risalpur and an aeronautical engineering college at Korangi Creek. Total strength in 1983 was about 250 combat aircraft and 18,000 all ranks.

INTERNATIONAL RELATIONS

External Debt (June 1983), about US$9,865m.

Membership. Pakistan is a member of the UN, the Colombo Plan, and Regional Co-operation for Development.

Treaties. A mutual defence assistance agreement between Pakistan and the USA was signed in Karachi on 19 May 1954.

ECONOMY

Planning. The sixth 5-year plan (1983–88) envisages a total fixed investment of Rs 495,000m. including Rs 77,000m. for industry, of which Rs 62,000m. would be spent in the private sector. Real growth in GDP is planned at 6·5% annually (agriculture 5%; industry 9%). Expenditure will be met mainly (75%) from internal resources. Allocations for energy (Rs 116,000m.), agriculture and irrigation (Rs 88,000m.), special development programmes (Rs 22,000m.) and family planning (Rs 1,800m.) have been made.

Budget. The following table shows the budget for the years 1982–83 and 1983–84 in Rs 1m.:

	1982–83 Revised	1983–84 Budget
Internal revenue	58,040·2	63,212·3
External revenue	14,973·9	16,775·3
Current expenditure	50,949·6	57,289·6
Development expenditure	28,255·0	31,000·0

Currency. The monetary unit is the Pakistan *rupee*. In March 1984 Rs 19·46 = £1; Rs 13·41 = US$1. Decimal coinage was introduced on 1 Jan. 1961. The rupee, which previously consisted of 64 *pice*, now consists of 100 *paisas*. The notes are of Rs 100, 50, 10 and 5 denominations issued by the State Bank in the name of the Government, and Rs 1 issued by the State Bank incurring no liability; the coinage in the decimal series is 0·5, 0·25, 0·1, 0·05 and 0·01 rupee.

Total monetary assets (including currency in circulation and deposits) in March 1980 amounted to Rs 93,087m. Currency in circulation, Oct. 1980, Rs 30,812·4m.

Banking. The State Bank of Pakistan is the central bank; it came into operation as the Central Bank on 1 July 1948 with an authorized capital of Rs 30m. and was nationalized in Jan. 1974. As on 27 Oct. 1983 total assets or liabilities of the issue department amounted to Rs 46,464m. and those of the banking department Rs 59,254m.; reserve fund, Rs 1,300m. and total deposits, Rs 36,745m. It is the sole bank of issue for Pakistan, custodian of foreign exchange reserves (US$1,670m. in Oct. 1983) and banker for the federal and provincial governments and for scheduled banks. It also manages the rupee public debt of federal and provincial governments. It provides short-term loans to the Government and commercial banks and short- and medium-term loans to specialized banks. The State Bank raised the bank rate from 9 to 10% with effect from 7 June 1977, but it provides finance for export sales of locally manufactured machinery at 2% per annum and for other export sales at 3% per annum. The Bank's subsidiary Federal Bank for Co-operatives makes loans to provincial co-operative banks. Loans made 1979–80, Rs 601·2m.

There were 24 scheduled banks (banks with capital and reserves of an aggregate value of not less than Rs 500,000) in Pakistan on 30 June 1979. Of these 9 were Pakistani including 5 commercial banks (National Bank of Pakistan, Habib Bank Ltd, United Bank Ltd, Muslim Commercial Bank Ltd and Allied Bank Ltd), 2 specialized banks (Agricultural Development Bank of Pakistan and Industrial Development Bank of Pakistan) and 2 co-operative banks (Punjab Provincial Co-operative Bank and Federal Bank for Co-operatives). Pakistani scheduled banks were nationalized in Jan. 1974. In addition, there were 15 foreign banks operating in Pakistan on 30 June 1979. In 1980 foreign banks were given the option of meeting part or all of their reserve requirements with the State Bank in specified foreign currencies. The total number of offices of scheduled banks in 1982 was 7,000, of foreign banks 58. Total deposits of all the scheduled banks stood at Rs 110,139m. on 27 Jan. 1983. The National Bank of Pakistan acts as an agent of the State Bank for transacting Government business and managing currency chests at places where the State Bank has no offices of its own.

Weights and Measures. The metric system is in general use.

ENERGY AND NATURAL RESOURCES

Electricity. Installed capacity (1981) by type of generation: Thermal 1,648,830 kw.; hydro-electric, 1,767,200 kw.; nuclear, 137,000 kw. Total generated electrical energy in 1980, 13,000m. kwh; 60% of this was hydro-electricity, the main source being the Tarbela Dam. By 1983 30% of the population had access to electric power.

Oil. Oil comes mainly from the Potowar Plain, from fields at Meyal, Tut, Balkassar, Joya Mair and Dhullian. Production in 1982–83 was 4,082,000 bbls. Oil reserves were also found at Dhodak in Dec. 1976. Exploitation is mainly through government incentives and concessions to foreign private sector companies. The Pak-Arab refinery pipeline runs 865 km. from Karachi to Multan; capacity, 4·5m. tonnes of oil annually.

Gas. Gas pipelines from Sui to Karachi (345 miles) and Multan (200) supply natural gas to industry and domestic consumers. A pipeline between Quetta and Shikarpur was constructed in 1982. There are 4 other productive fields. Reserves (1983), 500,000m. cu. metres; production in 1982–83 was 323,000m. cu. ft., or about 42% of energy needs.

Water. The Indus water treaty of 1960, concluded between India and Pakistan, has created the basis for a large-scale development programme. The Indus Basin Development Fund Agreement has been subscribed by Australia, Canada, Federal Republic of Germany, New Zealand, UK and USA and is administered by the International Bank; the works to be constructed call for expenditure of US$1,000m. The main purpose of the treaty is the division of the water power of the Indus and its 5 tributaries between India and Pakistan. After the construction of some 460 miles of canals, the Indus and the 2 western tributaries will serve Pakistan and the entire flow of the 3 eastern tributaries will be released for use in India.

The largest project is the construction of the Tarbela Dam, an earth-and-rock filled dam on the river Indus, 485 ft high, which has a gross storage capacity of 11·1m. acre feet of water for irrigation.

The Lloyd Barrage and Canal Construction Scheme, consists of a barrage across the river Indus at Sukkur and 7 canals—4 on the left and 3 on the right bank. Another barrage across the Indus, 4½ miles north of Kotri, called the Ghulam Muhammad Barrage, was completed in 1955. The Taunsa barrage on the Indus, 80 miles downstream of Kalabagh, was completed in 1958. The Gudu barrage, 10 miles from Kashmore, was completed in 1962.

The province of the Punjab set up in 1949 the Thal Development Authority to colonize the Thal desert between the Indus and Jhelum rivers.

The Chashma canal will carry water 172 miles across Dera Ismail Khan from the Chashma barrage on the Indus. The Mangla Dam on the Jhelum was inaugurated in Nov. 1967.

Minerals. The main agencies are the Pakistan Mineral Development Corporation, the Resource Development Corporation and the Gemstone Corporation of Pakistan. Coal is mined at Sharigh and Harnai on the Sind–Pishin railway and in the Bolan pass, also in Sor Range and Degari in the Quetta–Pishin district and in the Punjab; total recoverable reserves, about 480m. tonnes, mainly low-grade. A further 55m. tonnes was found at Lakhra in 1980 and reserves of over 500m. tonnes were found in the 300 sq. mile Thatta Sadha field in 1981. Chromite is extracted in and near Muslimbagh. Limestone is quarried generally. Gypsum is mined in the Sibi district and elsewhere; reserves (1983), about 370m. tonnes. Iron ore is being worked in Kalabagh and elsewhere; reserves, about 400m. tonnes, low-grade. A further 18m. tonnes, high-grade, has been found in Balúchistán. Uranium has been found in Dera Ghazi Khan. Production (tonnes, 1983): Coal, 1·54m.; chromite, 3,225; limestone, 4·2m.; gypsum, 215,000; rock salt, 526,000; china clay, 72,705. Other minerals of which useful deposits have been found are magnesite, sulphur, barites, marble, bauxite, antimony ore, bentonite, celestite, dolomite, fireclay, fluorite, fuller's earth, phosphate rock, silica sand and soapstone.

Agriculture. The entire area in the north and west is covered by great mountain ranges. The rest of the country consists of a fertile plain watered by 5 big rivers and their tributaries. Agriculture is dependent almost entirely on the irrigation system based on these rivers. It employs (1983) 55% of labour and provides about 30% of GNP and 35% of foreign exchange earnings. Growth rate, 1982–83, 4·8%. The main crops are wheat, cotton, maize, sugar-cane and rice, while the Quetta and Kalat divisions (Balúchistán) are known for their fruits and dates.

By 31 March 1977, 3·34m. acres of land had been taken away from landlords, and 1·48m. acres had been distributed to 137,005 tenants. An ordinance of Jan. 1977 reduced the upper limit of land holding to 100 irrigated or 200 non-irrigated acres; it also replaced the former land revenue system with a new agricultural income tax, from which holders of up to 25 irrigated or 50 unirrigated acres are exempt. Of about 4m. farms, 89% are of less than 25 acres. Of the surveyed area of 156m. acres, cultivated land accounts for 63m. acres, of which 11m. acres consist of fallow land, so that the net area sown is 52m. acres.

Pakistan is self-sufficient in wheat, rice and sugar.

Production, 1982–83 (in 1,000 tonnes): Rice (cleaned), 3,272; wheat, 12,300; sugar-cane (gur), 31,604; cotton (lint, 1,000 bales), 4,800.

Livestock (FAO estimate, 1982): Cattle, 15m.; buffaloes, 12·05m.; sheep, 30·89m.; goats, 35·6m.; poultry, 76·2m.

Forestry. There were (1976) 7·3m. acres of reserved and protected forests and 10·6m. acres managed as pasture ranges by the Forest Department. Of the forests 1·5m. acres are in Punjab, 1·66m. in Balúchistán, 1·46m. in Sind and 2·65m. in the North-West Frontier Province. Forests produce an annual average of over 20m. cu. ft of timber and 16m. cu. ft of fuel. Annual value of this and other produce, about Rs. 60m. Forest lands are also used as national parks, wildlife and game reserves.

Fisheries. Landings of inland water and marine fish, about 200,000 tonnes annually.

INDUSTRY AND TRADE

Industry. Industry employs about 10% of the population, contributing (1982–83) about 17·5% of GDP. The growth rate in manufacturing, 1982–83, was 8·3%. In 1972 public sector companies were re-organized under a Board of Industrial Management. Government policy since 1977 has been to encourage private industry, particularly small industry. The public sector, however, is still dominant in large industries; in 1981–82 its gross value added was Rs. 4,291·8m., number of employees 81,689, investment Rs. 45,886·98m., of which 60% was for Pakistan Steel. Pakistan is self-sufficient in cotton cloth and sugar. A public sector steel-mill (Pakistan Steel) has been built at Port Qasim near Karachi, capacity 1·1m. tonnes; production of coke and pig-iron began in autumn 1981 and of steel in 1983. Also recently completed are a heavy mechanical complex and a heavy forge and foundry plant at Taxila. There are plants processing barites and china clay. A private sector ferrous alloys plant has been approved near Peshawar, capacity 40 tonnes of ferrous silicon and manganese per day. There is an Export Processing Zone at Karachi, covering 500 acres; at 30 June 1981 investment here stood at US$58·8m. The largest project (approved Aug. 1981) is a Pakistan-Saudi aluminium extrusion plant. At Machi Goth there is a fertilizer plant, capacity 1,800 tonnes per day.

Production 1982–83 (tonnes): Refined sugar, 1·1m.; vegetable ghee, 522,000; jute textiles, 62,461; soda ash, 93,638; sulphuric acid, 61,659; caustic soda, 41,195; chip board and paper board, 58,690; cycle tyres and tubes, 9·2m. units; cotton cloth, 305m. sq. metres; cotton yarn, 399m. kg.; cement, 3·9m.

Labour. The Labour Force Survey of 1974–75 gave the total work force as 20·42m., of whom 54·8% (11·22m.) were engaged in agriculture, forestry and fishing, 13·6% (2·8m.) in manufacturing; the textile industry was the largest single manufacturing employer. Estimates (1979–80) gave a labour force of 22·97m., 5·6m. of them urban.

Commerce. Total value of exports during 1982–83 amounted to Rs 34,442m., and the total value of imports to Rs 68,151m. The value of the chief articles imported into and exported from Pakistan in 1982–83 was (in Rs 1m.):

Imports		Exports	
Minerals, fuels,		Raw cotton	3,896·6
lubricants etc.	20,909·5	Cotton cloth	3,579·0
Machinery and		Cotton yarns	3,308·2
transport equipment	16,814·5	Rice	3,682·6
Manufactured goods	8,896·3	Woollen carpets	1,885·5
Chemicals	7,508·2	Leather	1,195·0

Total trade between Pakistan and UK (British Department of Trade returns, in £1,000 sterling):

	1978	1979	1980	1981	1982	1983
Imports to UK	54,387	68,021	58,289	63,249	81,531	80,277
Exports and re-exports from UK	92,723	139,759	139,692	149,370	199,178	191,647

Tourism. Earnings in 1980, US$154m. There were 292,000 tourists.

COMMUNICATIONS

Roads. At the end of financial year 1975–76 Pakistan had 31,029 miles of roads, of which 16,875 miles were all-weather roads. The Karakoram highway to the Chinese border, through Kohistan and the Hunza valley, was opened in 1978. An all-weather road linking Skardu and the remote NE Indus valley to the highway was built in 1980.

In 1979 there were about 1m. vehicles registered, including 421,000 motor-cycles and 279,000 cars.

Railways. Pakistan Railways had (1982) a route of 8,822 km mainly on 1,676 mm. gauge, with some metre gauge and narrow gauge line. In 1981–82: ran 16,502 passenger-km and 7,067m. tonne-km..

Aviation. Karachi is served by British Airways, KLM, PANAM, Lufthansa, Swissair, SAS, Iran National Airlines, Air France, Garuda, Gulf Air and by Philippine, Japanese, Chinese, East African, Syrian, Iraqui, Kuwait, Jordanian, Saudi Arabian, Romanian, Egyptian and Russian airlines.

Pakistan International Airlines (founded 1955; the majority of shares is held by the Government) had 4 DC-10s, 7 Boeing 707Cs, 5 720Bs, 2 747Bs and 8 Fokker F27s in 1977; 2 other Boeing 720Bs were on lease to Air Malta. Services operate to 20 home airports, New York, Paris, Amsterdam, Copenhagen, Istanbul, Athens, Rome, Cairo, Tripoli, Nairobi, Dhahran, Damascus, Amman, Baghdad, Persian Gulf points, Tōkyō, Peking (Beijing), Zahedan, Singapore, Manila, Kuala Lumpur, Bangkok, Colombo, London, Frankfurt, Bombay, Delhi, Dacca, Kábul, Tehrán and Jeddah.

Shipping. There is a seaport at Karachi. A second port is being built at Phitti Creek on the Makram coast, 26 miles east of Karachi, to be called Port Muhammad Bin Qasim; this port will have iron and coal berths for Pakistan Steel Mills, multi-purpose berths, bulk-cargo handling, oil and container-traffic terminals; the first phase (handling bulk and bagged cargo) will be operational it is hoped in 1983. The Pakistan National Shipping Corporation had 51 vessels in 1982, of 700,000 DWT, carrying 38% of dry cargo handled. National flag carriers now operate between Pakistan and UK; USA and Canada; the Far East; the (Persian) Gulf, Arabian Gulf, Red Sea, Black Sea and Mekran Coast; Continental Europe and the Middle East. The Karachi Shipyard and Engineering Works Ltd construct all types of vessels up to 27,000 DWT and repairs all types; dry-dock and under-water repairs can be done on vessels up to 29,000 DWT, above-water repairs on vessels and drilling rigs of all sizes.

Post and Broadcasting. The telegraph and telephone system is government-owned. Telephones, on 1 Jan. 1982, numbered 393,010; a nationwide dialling system is in operation between 46 cities. In 1979 there were 10,488 post offices (8,193 rural) and 93 main telegraph offices; emphasis was laid on improving rural communications and 28 public call offices and 47 small exchanges were opened. Pakistan has international telephone connections by 102 satellite, 7 HF, 4 microwave and 10 carrier circuits. An international direct-dialling exchange with 25,000 connections was opened in July 1980. The Pakistan Broadcasting Corporation had 16 radio stations in Dec. 1983. Television stations operate in Lahore, Karachi, Peshawar, Quetta and Rawalpindi–Islamabad.

Cinemas (1983). There are about 600 cinemas.

Newspapers. Dailies and periodicals numbered 1,156 in 1983: 763 were in Urdu, 272 in English and 70 in Sindhi; 121 were dailies, 315 weeklies, 562 monthlies and 158 quarterlies. Top circulation 300,000 for an Urdu daily paper.

JUSTICE, RELIGION, EDUCATION AND WELFARE

Justice. The Central Judiciary consists of the Supreme Court of Pakistan, which is a court of record and has three-fold jurisdiction, namely, original, appellate and advisory. There are 4 High Courts in Lahore, Peshawar, Quetta and Karachi. Under the Constitution, each has power to issue directions of writs of *Habeas Corpus, Mandamus, Certiorari* and others. Under them are district and sessions courts of first instance in each division; they have also some appellate jurisdiction. Criminal cases not being sessions cases are tried by district magistrates and subordinate magistrates. There are subordinate civil courts also.

The Constitution provides for an independent judiciary, as the greatest safeguard of citizens' rights. The Laws (Continuance in Force) (Eleventh Amendment) Order, 1980, prescribed the date of 14 Aug. 1981 by which the judiciary shall be separated from the executive. There is an Attorney-General, appointed by the President, who has right of audience in all courts.

A Federal Shariat Court at the Supreme Court level has been established to decide whether any law is wholly or partially un-Islamic. Islamic law is to be enforced as the law of the state; penalties for offences involving intoxicating liquor, offences against property and sexual offences have been specified. Imprisonment remains as a penalty in general use, but some offences in all the above categories are liable to whipping and some property offences, to amputation.

Religion. Religious groups (1972 census): Moslems, 63·28m.; Christians, 907,861; Scheduled Castes, 603,369; Caste Hindus, 296,837; Parsees, 9,589; Buddhists, 4,318; others, 205,250. There is a Ministry to safeguard the constitutional rights of religious minorities.

Education. At the census of 1981, 23·3% of the population were able to read and write. Adult literacy programmes have been established.

The principle of free and compulsory primary education has been accepted as the responsibility of the state; duration has been fixed provisionally at 5 years. In 1982–83 there were 61,354 elementary schools with 7·1m. pupils; 5,686 middle schools with 1·6m.; 3,773 high schools with 600,000; 257 secondary vocational schools with 41,000. Present policy stresses vocational and technical education, disseminating a common culture based on Islamic ideology.

Sixth plan (1983–88) expenditure: Rs. 11,000m. on primary and secondary schools; Rs. 1,300m. on colleges and Rs. 2,100m. on universities.

There were 1983, 442 general colleges, 102 professional colleges. In 1983 there were 20 universities, including the open university at Islamabad and the privately-funded Aga Khan University. University and other college students, 1982–83, 379,000.

Health. In 1980 there were 536 hospitals (42,469 beds) and about 23,000 doctors. Sixth plan (1983–88) expenditure: Rs. 15,750m.

Social Security. In 1981–82 expenditure on cash benefits under the employees' social security scheme was Rs15·3m., on medical care, Rs.93·2m.

DIPLOMATIC REPRESENTATIVES

Of Pakistan in Great Britain (35–36 Lowndes Sq., London, SW1X 9JN)
Ambassador: Ali Arshad (accredited 13 Feb. 1981).

Of Great Britain in Pakistan (Diplomatic Enclave, Ramna 5, Islamabad)
Ambassador: Sir Oliver Forster, KCMG, MVO.

Of Pakistan in the USA (2315 Massachusetts Ave., NW, Washington, D.C., 20008)
Ambassador: Ajaz Azim.

Of the USA in Pakistan (AID/UN Bldg., Islamabad)
Ambassador: Ronald I. Spiers.

Of Pakistan to the United Nations
Ambassador: S. Shah Nawaz.

Books of Reference

Pakistan Year-Book, Annual
Burke, S. M., *Pakistan's Foreign Policy.* OUP, 1973
Burki, S. J., *Pakistan Under Bhutto.* London, 1980
Griffin, K., and Khan, A. R. (ed.), *Growth and Inequality in Pakistan.* London and New York 1972
Hasan, M., (ed.) *Pakistan in a Changing World.* Karachi, 1978
Jennings, Sir Ivor, *Constitutional Problems in Pakistan.* CUP, 1957
Siddiqui, K., *Conflict, Crisis and War in Pakistan.* London, 1972

PANAMA

República de Panamá

Capital: Panama City
Population: 1·97m. (1983)
GNP per capita: US$1,730 (1980)

HISTORY. A revolution, inspired by the USA, led to the separation of Panama from the United States of Colombia and the declaration of its independence on 3 Nov. 1903. The *de facto* Government was on 13 Nov. recognized by the USA, and soon afterwards by the other Powers. In 1914 Colombia agreed to recognize the independence of Panama. This treaty was ratified by the USA and Colombia in 1921, and on 8 May 1924 diplomatic relations between Colombia and Panama were established. On 10 Oct. 1979 Panama assumed sovereignty over what was previously known as the Panama Canal Zone and now called the Canal Area.

For the treaties regulating the relations between Panama and the USA *see* pp. 961–62.

AREA AND POPULATION. Panama is bounded north by the Caribbean, east by Colombia, south by the Pacific and west by Costa Rica. Extreme length is about 480 miles (772 km); breadth between 37 (60) and 110 miles (177 km); coastline, 426 miles (685 km) on the Atlantic and 767 (1,234 km) on the Pacific; total area (excluding the Canal Zone) is 29,761 sq. miles (77,082 sq. km); population according to the census of 11 May 1980 was 1,830,175. Over 75% are of mixed blood and the remainder Indians, negroid, white and Asiatic.

The capital is Panama City, on the Pacific coast; estimated population, 1980, 467,000. There are 9 provinces (with populations, 1980) as follows (the capitals in brackets): Bocas del Toro (Bocas del Toro), 53,579; Chiriquí (David), 287,801; Coclé (Penonomé), 140,320; Colón (Colón), 166,439; Los Santos (Las Tablas), 70,200; Herrera (Chitré), 81,866; Darién (La Palma), 26,497 ; Panamá (Panama City), 830,278; Veraguas (Santiago), 173,195. The port of Colón on the Atlantic coast had 95,300 (78,000). Smaller ports on the Pacific are Aguadulce, Pedregal, Montijo, Puerto Mutis and Puerto Armuelles; in the Atlantic, Bocas del Toro, Almirante, Portobello, Mandinga and Permé. A new fishing port came into operation at Vacamonte in Aug. 1979.

Birth rate, 1981, was 29 per 1,000 population.

CLIMATE. A tropical climate, unvaryingly with high temperatures and only a short dry season from Jan. to April. Rainfall amounts are much higher on the north side of the isthmus. Panama City. Jan. 79°F (26·1°C), July 81°F (27·2°C). Annual rainfall 70″ (1,770 mm). Colón. Jan. 80°F (26·7°C), July 80°F (26·7°C). Annual rainfall 127″ (3,175 mm).

CONSTITUTION AND GOVERNMENT. The 1972 Constitution, as amended in 1978 and 1983, provides for an Assembly of 505 representatives of municipal districts elected on a community rather than a party basis, a Legislative Council of 57 members and a directly-elected President and Vice-President; The formation of political parties is now permitted, subject to statutory regulations, and 5 such parties had achieved full legal recognition by Sept. 1981.

Elections, the first to be held in Panama for 12 years, for the National Legislative Council were held in Sept. 1980. The Democratic Revolutionary Party (PRD) gained 10 of the 19 seats; Liberals, 5; Christian Democrats, 2; Independents, 2.

President, ad interim: Dr Jorge Illuera.
The Cabinet appointed in Sept. 1983 was composed as follows:
Foreign Affairs: Oyden Ortega. *Interior and Justice:* Dr Carlos Ozores Typaldos. *Treasury and Finance:* Dr Gabriel Castro. *Agriculutral Development:* Frank Pérez.

Public Works: Carlos Clement. *Commerce and Industry:* Dr Carlos Hoffman. *Labour and Social Welfare:* Arturo Melo. *Health:* Dr Guillermo Gaspar García de Paredes. *Housing:* Raúl Rolando Rodríguez. *Education:* Sra. Susana Richa de Torrijos. *Planning and Economic Policy:* Menalco Solis. *Presidency:* Mario de Diago.

The official language is Spanish.

National flag: Quarterly: first a white panel with a blue star, second red, third blue, fourth white with a red star.

National anthem: Alcanzamos por fin la victoria (words by J. de la Ossa; tune by Santos Jorge, 1903).

Local government: The 9 provinces and a Special Territory (another is envisaged) are sub-divided into 64 municipal districts and 2 *comarcas* (special districts) and are further sub-divided into 505 *corregimientos* (electoral districts).

DEFENCE

Army. The Army numbered (1984) 1,500 men organized in 7 light infantry companies, equipped with 16 V-150 armoured cars. There is also a paramilitary force of about 7,500 men.

Navy. Divided between both coasts, the flotilla comprises 4 patrol craft, 2 coast-guard cutters, 3 medium landing ships, 3 utility landing craft and 3 logistic support vessels. In 1984 personnel totalled 500 officers and men.

Air Force. The air force has 1 Lockheed Electra, 4 C-47, 3 CASA 212, 2 Islander and 3 Twin Otter transports, 3 Cessna and 2 DHC-3 Otter liaison aircraft, a Shorts Skyvan, a Falcon VIP jet transport, and 21 UH-1B/D/H Iroquois and twin-engined UH-1N helicopters.

INTERNATIONAL RELATIONS

Membership. Panama is a member of UN and OAS.

ECONOMY

Budget. The 1981 budget provided for expenditure of 966,686,670 balboas and revenue of 752·9m. balboas.
Public sector debt was 2,333m. balboas in Dec. 1981.

Currency. The monetary unit is the *balboa*, which is of the same size and fineness as the US silver dollar but is maintained equivalent to the gold dollar. Other coins whose metallic content is required by law to correspond exactly to that of similar US coins are the half-balboa (equal to 50 cents US); the quarter and tenth of a balboa piece; a cupro-nickel coin of 5 cents, and a copper coin of 1 cent. US coinage is also legal tender. Volume of the currency has not been disclosed since 31 Dec. 1950, when it stood at 1·5m. balboas. The only paper currency used is that of the USA. In March 1984, US$1 = 1 *balboa*; £1 = 1·49 *balboas*.

Banking. There is no statutory central bank. The Government accounts are handled through the *Banco Nacional de Panama.* The number of commercial banks rose from 9 in 1964 to 116 by Sept. 1981; 62 have a general licence, 42 an international licence and 12 a representational licence. Leading banks are the Citibank, Lloyds Bank International (Bahamas) Ltd., and the Chase Manhattan Bank of New York. Other foreign-owned banks include the Bank of America, as well as Canadian, Columbian, Swiss, Federal German, French, Spanish, Dutch, Taiwan, Japanese and Brazilian banks.

Weights and Measures. English weights and measures are in general use; those of the metric system are also used.

ENERGY AND NATURAL RESOURCES

Electricity. Production of electric energy, 1981, amounted to 1,792·38m. kwh.

Minerals. There are known to be copper deposits in the provinces of Chiriquí, Colón and Darien. The most important, containing possibly the largest undeveloped reserves in the world, is Cerro Colorado (Chiriquí) on which a feasibility study is being undertaken by the Rio Tinto Zinc Coporation Ltd. If it is eventually decided to develop the mine, it is expected that the annual production of copper will reach 260,000 to 280,000 tonnes within a few years. The cost of construction is estimated at about US$1,800m. The deposit has estimated reserves of 1,300m. tonnes, with an average grade of 0·76% copper.

Agriculture. Of the whole area (1975) 18·5% is cultivated, 57·1% is natural or artificial pasture land and 9·5% is fallow. Of the remainder only a small part is cultivated, though the land is rich in resources. About 60% of the country's food requirements are imported. The Ministry of Agricultural Development (MIDA) buys leading crops at field prices. Of the land under cultivation, 26·4% is owned and 44·7% is usufructuary. The most important export products are bananas, grown by an affiliate of the United Brands Company and sugar from 4 state-owned and 2 private mills. Value of exports of these commodities in 1980 was 24·7m. balboas and 31·6m. balboas respectively. Most important food crop, for home consumption, is rice, grown on 80% of the farms; Panama's *per capita* consumption is very high. Output of rough rice was 150,000 tonnes in 1982. Other products are maize (63,000 tonnes in 1982), cocoa (1,000 tonnes), coffee (8,000 tonnes) and coconuts (25,000 tonnes). Beer, whisky, rum, 'seco', anise and gin are produced. Coffee is mainly grown in the province of Chiriquí, near the Costa Rican frontier; total production in 1982 was 8,000 tonnes, and small amounts were exported. The country has great timber resources, notably mahogany. Livestock (1982): 1·68m. cattle, 200,000 pigs and 5·3m. poultry.

INDUSTRY AND TRADE

Industry. Local industries include cigarettes, clothing, food processing, shoes, soap, cement factories; foreign firms are being encouraged to establish industries, and a petrol refinery is operating in Colón.

Commerce. The imports and exports (including re-exports) for the Republic of Panama, for 6 calendar years are as follows (in 1,000 balboas; 1 balboa = US$1):

	Imports	Exports		Imports	Exports
1975	789,700	262,000	1978	862,000	381,700
1976	783,500	378,200	1979	1,185,000	291,506
1977	777,761	243,051	1980	1,277,000	407,000

Chief exports (48·2% to the USA) in 1980 were: Petroleum products, bananas, sugar, shrimps.

Chief imports, 1979, were valued (in 1m. balboas f.o.b.): Machinery and transport material, 214·7; manufactured goods, 308·9; fuel, minerals and similar, 319·4; chemicals, 116·7; food, 77·1. USA provided 32% of imports in 1979.

Total trade between Panama (including Colón Free Zone) and UK (British Department of Trade returns, in £1,000 sterling):

	1979	1980	1981	1982	1983
Imports to UK	4,131	3,941	7,815	9,521	5,341
Exports and re-exports from UK [1]	26,384	24,032	35,855	83,250	42,276

[1] Including new ships built for foreign owners and registered in Panama.

Tourism. In 1980, 392,062 people visited Panama.

COMMUNICATIONS

Roads. Panama had on 1 Jan. 1980, 8,606 km of roads. The road from Panama City westward to the cities of David and Concepción and to the Costa Rican frontier, with several branches, is part of the Pan-American Highway. A concrete highway connects Panama City and Colón.

On 1 Jan. 1980 registered motor vehicles, private and commercial, numbered 111,052, this excludes vehicles owned by government departments.

Railways. The *Ferrocarril de Panama* (Panama Railroad) (1,524 mm gauge) (through the Canal area), which connects Ancón on the Pacific with Cristóbal on the Atlantic, is the principal railway. It is 76 km long and runs along the banks of the Canal. As most vessels unload their cargo at Cristóbal (Colón), on the Atlantic side, the greater portion of the merchandise destined for Panama City is brought overland by the *Ferrocarril de Panama*. The United Brands Company runs 376 km of railway, and the Chiriqui National Railroad 126 km.

Aviation. Commercial aviation has developed rapidly. PANAM, Braniff Airways, British Airways, KLM, Iberia Airlines and other international companies operate at Tocumen Airport, 17 miles from Panama City. Air Panama provides services between Panama City and New York, Los Angeles, Miami, Central America and some countries in South America. The *Compañia Panameña de Aviación* (COPA) and *Aerolineas Las Perlas* provide a local service between Panama City and the provincial towns. COPA also provides an international service to Central America.

Shipping. Ships under Panamanian registry on 25 Sept. 1981 numbered 10,859 of 27·2m. gross tons; most of these ships elect Panamanian registry because fees are low and labour laws lenient. All the international maritime traffic for Colón and Panama runs through the Canal ports of Cristóbal, Balboa and Bahia Las Minas (Colón); Almirante is used for both the provincial and international trade. There is an oil transfer terminal at Puerto Armuelles on the Pacific coast.

Panama Canal. On 18 Nov. 1903 a treaty between the USA and the Republic of Panama was signed making it possible for the US to build and operate a canal connecting the Atlantic and Pacific oceans through the Isthmus of Panama. The treaty granted the US in perpetuity the use, occupation and control of a Canal Zone, approximately 10 miles wide, in which the US would possess full sovereign rights 'to the entire exclusion of the exercise by the Republic of Panama of any such sovereign rights, power or authority'. In return the US guaranteed the independence of the republic and agreed to pay the republic $10m. and an annuity of $250,000. The US purchased the French rights and properties—the French had been labouring from 1879 to 1899 in an effort to build the Canal—for $40m. and in addition, paid private landholders within what would be the Canal Zone a mutually agreeable price for their properites.

Two new treaties between Panama and USA were agreed on 10 Aug. and signed on 7 Sept. 1977. One deals with the operation and defence of the canal until the end of 1999 and the other guarantees permanent neutrality.

The USA maintains operational control over all lands, waters and installations, including military bases, necessary to manage, operate and defend the canal until 31 Dec. 1999. A new agency of the US Government, the Panama Canal Commission, operates the canal, replacing the Panama Canal Co. A policy-making board of 5 US citizens and 4 Panamanians serves on the Commission's board of directors. Until 1990 the canal administrator will be a US citizen and the deputy will be Panamanian. After that date the position will be reversed.

Six months after the exchange of instruments of ratification Panama assumed general territorial jurisdiction over the former Canal Zone and became able to use portions of the area not needed for the operation and defence of the canal. Panamanian penal and civil codes became applicable. At the same time Panama assumed responsibility for commercial ship repairs and supplies, railway and pier operations, passengers, police and courts, all of which were among other areas formerly administered by the Canal Co. and the Canal Zone Government.

66% of the electorate of Panama agreed to the ratification of the treaties when a referendum was held on 23 Oct. 1977 and on 18 April 1978 the treaty was ratified by the US Congress. The treaty went into effect on 1 Oct. 1979.

The treaty of 1936 increased the annuity to US$430,000 and, as desired by Panama, withdrew the guarantee of independence. In 1955 the annuity was increased to US$1·93m., and the Panama Canal Co. turned over to the Republic the Panama City railroad yards and other properties valued at US$22m. At the end of 1962 the US completed the construction of a high-level bridge over the Pacific entrance to the Canal, and the flags of Panama and the US were flown jointly over areas of the Canal Zone under civilian authority. Following the devaluation of the dollar in 1972 and 1973, the annuity was adjusted proportionally to US$2·1m. and US$2·33m. respectively.

The Panama Canal Commission, a US Government Agency, is concerned primarily with the actual operation of the Canal. On 8 July 1974, 18 Nov. 1976 and 10 Oct. 1979 tolls were increased. These were the first increases of toll rates in the history of the Canal. Tolls were raised again on 12 March 1983. The new rates are US$1.83 a Panama Canal ton for vessels carrying passengers or cargo. A Panama Canal ton is equivalent to 100 cu. ft of actual earning capacity. The new toll rate for warships, hospital ships and supply ships, which pay on a displacement basis, is US$1·02 a ton.

The changes were designed to continue the approximately break-even financial operating results after paying its own expenses and paying interest on the net direct investment of the US in the Canal.

Administrator of the Panama Canal Commission: Dennis P. McAuliffe.
Deputy Administrator: Fernando Manfredo (Panama).

The total civilian and military population of the Canal area is 34,700 (estimate), of whom about 30,750 are US citizens. The total force employed by the Panama Canal Commission is 8,399, comprising 1,701 US citizens, 6,460 Panamanians and 238 others.

The Canal was opened to commerce on 15 Aug. 1914. It is 85 ft above sea-level. It is 51·2 statute miles in length from deep water in the Caribbean Sea to deep water in the Pacific ocean, and 36 statute miles from shore to shore. The channel ranges in bottom-width from 500 to 1,000 ft; the widening of Gaillard Cut to a minimum width of 500 ft was completed in 1969. Normally, the average time of a vessel in Canal waters is less than 24 hours, 8–10 of which are in transit through the Canal proper. A map showing the Panama, Suez and Kiel canals on the same scale will be found in THE STATESMAN'S YEAR-BOOK, 1959 and a new map in the 1978–79 edition.

Particulars of the ocean-going commercial traffic through the canal are given as follows (vessels of 300 tons Panama Canal net and 500 displacement tons and over; cargo in long tons):

Fiscal year ending 30 Sept.	North-bound (Pacific to Atlantic)		South-bound (Atlantic to Pacific)		Total		Tolls levied (in US$)
	Vessels	Cargo	Vessels	Cargo	Vessels	Cargo	
1980	6,390	82,473,041	7,117	84,741,894	13,507	167,214,935	291,838,590
1981	6,623	81,902,966	7,261	89,318,796	13,884	171,221,762	301,762,600
1982	6,618	88,895,265	7,391	96,557,067	14,009	185,452,332	323,958,366
1983	5,540	57,762,250	6,167	87,828,509	11,707	145,590,759	285,985,719

In the fiscal year ending 30 Sept. 1983, of the 11,707 ships which passed through the Canal, 1,697 were Panamanian; 1,555 Liberian; 1,165 Japanese; 1,023 US; 888 Greek; 623 British; 458 Russian; 413 Norwegian; 358 Ecuadorian; 272 Peruvian; 254 Danish.

Statistical Information: The Panama Canal Commission Office of Public Affairs.

Annual Reports on the Panama Canal, by the Administrator of the Panama Canal Commission.
Rules and Regulations Governing Navigation of the Panama Canal. The Panama Canal Commission, Miami, Florida *or* Washington, DC
Cameron, I., *The Impossible Dream.* London, 1972
Le Feber, W., *The Panama Canal: The Crisis in Historical Perspective.* OUP, 1978
McCullough, D., *The Path Between the Seas.* New York and London, 1978

Post and Broadcasting. There are telegraph cables from Panama to North America and Central and South American ports, and from Colón to the USA and Europe. There is also inter-continental communication by satellite. There are 93 licensed commercial broadcasting stations, nearly all operated by private companies, one of which functions in the canal. There are 5 television stations, one of them run by the US Army at Fort Clayton. On 1 Jan. 1982 there were 212,992 telephones.

Cinemas. In 1977 there were 52 cinemas in the district of Panama. All films must have Spanish subtitles.

Newspapers. There are 1 English language and 4 Spanish language daily morning newspapers and 1 English/Spanish evening newspaper.

JUSTICE, RELIGION, EDUCATION AND WELFARE

Justice. The Supreme Court consists of 9 justices appointed by the executive. There is no death penalty.

Religion. 95% of the population is Roman Catholic and 5% Protestant. There is freedom of religious worship and separation of Church and State. Clergymen may teach in the schools but may not hold public office.

Education. Elementary education is compulsory for all children from 7 to 15 years of age, with an estimated 545,800 students in schools in 1977. The University of Panama at Panama City, inaugurated on 7 Oct. 1935, had a total enrolment (1978) of 32,868 students. The Catholic university Sta. Maria La Antigua, inaugurated on 27 May 1965, had 1,916 students in Sept. 1978.

DIPLOMATIC REPRESENTATIVES

Of Panama in Great Britain (109 Jermyn St., London, SW1)
Ambassador: Dr Calixto Arias (accredited 21 Feb. 1983).

Of Great Britain in Panama (Apartado 889, Panama City 1)
Ambassador: T. H Steggle.

Of Panama in the USA (2862 McGill Terr., NW, Washington, D.C., 20008)
Ambassador: Aquilino E. Boyd.

Of the USA in Panama (Ave. Balboa y Calle 38, Panama City)
Ambassador: Everett E. Briggs.

Of Panama to the United Nations
Ambassador: Dr Carlos Ozores Typaldos.

Books of Reference

Statistical Information: The Comptroller-General of the Republic (Contraloria General de la República, Calle 35 y Avenida 6, Panama City) publishes an annual report and other statistical publications.

Langstaff, E. DeS., *Panama.* [Bibliography] Oxford and Santa Barbara 1982
Larsen, H. and M., *The Forests of Panama.* London, 1964
Ropp, S. C., *Panamanian Politics.* New York, 1982

National Library: Biblioteca Nacional, Departamento de Información. Calle 22, Panama.

PAPUA
NEW GUINEA

Capital: Port Moresby
Population: 3·19m. (1983)
GNP per capita: US$780 (1980)

HISTORY. To prevent that portion of the island of New Guinea not claimed by the Netherlands or Germany from passing into the hands of a foreign power, the Government of Queensland annexed Papua in 1883. This step was not sanctioned by the Imperial Government, but on 6 Nov. 1884 a British Protectorate was proclaimed over the southern portion of the eastern half of New Guinea, and in 1887 Queensland, New South Wales and Victoria undertook to defray the cost of administration, and the territory was annexed to the Crown the following year. The federal government took over the control in 1901; the political transfer was completed by the Papua Act of the federal parliament in Nov. 1905, and on 1 Sept. 1906 a proclamation was issued by the Governor-General of Australia declaring that British New Guinea was to be known henceforth as the Territory of Papua. The northern portion of New Guinea was a German colony until the First World War. It became a League of Nations mandated territory in 1921, administered by Australia, and later a UN Trust Territory (of New Guinea).

The Papua New Guinea Act 1949–1972 provides for the administration of the UN Australian Trust Territory of New Guinea in an administrative union with the Territory of Papua, in accordance with Art. 5 of the New Guinea Trusteeship Agreement, under the title of Papua New Guinea.

Australia granted Papua New Guinea self-government on 1 Dec. 1973 and, on 16 Sept. 1975, Papua New Guinea became a fully independent state.

AREA AND POPULATION. Papua New Guinea extends from the equator to Cape Baganowa in the Louisiade Archipelago to 11° 40′ S. lat. and from the border of West Irian to 160° E. long. with a total area of 462,840 sq. km. According to the census the 1980 population was 3,010,727. Port Moresby, (1980) 123,624; Lae, 61,617; Rabaul, 14,954; Madang, 21,335; Mount Hagen, 13,441. Area and population of the provinces:

Provinces	Sq.km	Census 1971	Census 1980	Capital
Milne Bay	14,000	109,460	127,975	Alotau
Northern	22,800	66,514	77,442	Popondetta
Central	29,500	117,330	116,964	Port Moresby
National Capital District	240	76,507	123,624	—
Gulf	34,500	58,564	64,120	Kerema
Western	99,300	70,898	78,575	Daru
Southern Highlands	23,800	192,854	236,052	Mendi
Enga	12,800 }	346,032	{ 164,534	Wabag
Western Highlands	8,500 }		{ 265,656	Mount Hagen
Chimbu	6,100	160,245	178,290	Kundiawa
Eastern Highlands	11,200	239,640	276,726	Goroka
Morobe	34,500	249,032	310,622	Lae
Madang	29,000	170,953	211,206	Madang
East Sepik	42,800	181,893	221,069	Wewak
West Sepik	36,300	93,978	114,192	Vanimo
Manus	2,100	24,866	26,036	Lorengau
West New Britain	21,000	61,515	88,941	Kimbe
East New Britain	15,500	113,750	133,197	Rabaul
New Ireland	9,600	59,543	66,028	Kavieng
North Solomons	9,300	96,363	128,794	Arawa

Vital statistics (1983, estimate): Crude birth rate, 39 per 1,000; crude death rate, 17.

CLIMATE. There is a monsoon climate, with high temperatures and humidity

964

the year round. Port Moresby. Jan. 82°F (27·8°C), July 78°F (25·6°C). Annual rainfall 40" (1,011 mm).

CONSTITUTION AND GOVERNMENT. Papua New Guinea has a Westminster type of government. A single legislative house, known as the National Parliament, is made up of 109 members from all parts of the country. The members are elected under universal suffrage and general elections are held every 5 years. All persons over the age of 18 who are Papua New Guinea citizens are eligible to vote and stand for election. Voting is by secret ballot and follows the preferential system.

The first Legislative Council was established in 1951. It was abolished in 1964 and replaced with the House of Assembly. In 1950 the first village council was formed which established the basis of the now extensive local government system. A system of provincial government was introduced in 1976.

In the national elections of 1982 a Pangu government, supported by the United Party, came to power with 67 members of Parliament.

The administrative centre and capital is located at Port Moresby. National administration is carried out by a public service under the direction of 28 ministries. The country is divided into the National Capital District and 19 provinces: Western, Gulf, Central, Milne Bay, Northern, Southern Highlands, Enga, Western Highlands, Chimbu, Eastern Highlands, Morobe, Madang, East Sepik, West Sepik, Manus, New Ireland, East New Britain, West New Britain, and North Solomons. Each of the provincial governments has a secretariat headed by an Administrative Secretary. In many provinces the system of local governments still operates, although the provinces may make changes to this if they wish.

Governor-General: Sir Kingsford Dibela, GCMG.

The Cabinet in Nov. 1983 was as follows:

Prime Minister: Michael Thomas Somare.

Deputy Prime Minister: Paias Wingti. *Finance:* Philip Bouraga, OBE. *Foreign Affairs and Trade:* Rabbie Namaliu. *Public Service:* Anthony Siaguru. *Education:* Barry Holloway. *Defence:* Boyamo Sali. *Provincial Affairs:* John Nilkare. *Primary Industry:* Dennis Young. *Commerce and Industry:* Karl Stack. *Health:* Martin Tovadek. *Works and Supply:* Pato Kakarya. *Justice:* Anthony Bais. *Labour and Employment:* Caspar Anggua. *Lands:* Bebes Korowaro. *Planning and Physical Services:* Kala Swokim. *Environment and Conservation:* Halalu Mai. *Posts and Telecommunications:* Roy Evara. *Transport:* Mathew Bendumb. *Information and Broadcasting:* Epel Tito. *Minerals and Energy:* Francis Pusal. *Police:* John Giheno. *Civil Aviation:* Tom Pais. *Religion, Youth, Women and Recreation:* Tom Awasa. *Forestry:* Lukas Waka. *Administrative Services:* Sir Pita Lus. *Correctional Services and Liquor Licensing:* Pundia Kange. *Culture and Tourism:* McKenzie Javopa.

The seat of the Government is at Port Moresby.

National flag: Diagonally ochre-red over black, on the red a bird of paradise in gold, and on the black 5 stars of the Southern Cross in white.

DEFENCE. The Papua New Guinea Defence Force has a total strength of 3,800 (1984) consisting of land, maritime and air elements. The Army is organized in 2 infantry battalions, 1 engineer and 1 signals battalion with logistic units. The Navy has 4 large patrol craft and 2 landing craft. The nucleus of an Air Force was formed by 4 DC-3 piston-engined transports delivered from Australia in 1975; two more were delivered later. They have been followed by 7 Australian-built Missionmaster twin-turboprop support transports. A Gulfstream II and a Super King Air are available for VIP use. Personnel total 75.

INTERNATIONAL RELATIONS

Membership. Papua New Guinea is a member of UN, the Commonwealth, the Colombo Plan and is an ACP state of EEC.

ECONOMY

Budget. Revenue (in K1,000) for calendar years was:

Source	1980	1981	1982
Customs, excise and export tax	108,950	115,534	131,252
Other taxes	130,701	144,270	163,872
Foreign government grants [1]	174,599	184,348	186,684
Loans	60,590	57,178	81,736
Other revenue	104,162	127,545	84,867
Total	579,002	628,875	648,411

[1] Mainly from Australia.

Expenditure (in K1,000) for the same periods:

Source	1980	1981	1982
Consumption	281,155	302,997	303,460
Capital	85,588	75,952	55,803
Other expenditure [1]	223,679	280,094	307,479
Total	590,422	659,043	666,760

[1] Includes transfers to provincial governments.

Currency. The unit of currency is the *kina* divided into 100 *toea* and is the sole legal tender. In March 1984, £1 = K1·26; US$1 = K0·86.

Banking. The Bank of Papua New Guinea assumed the central banking functions formerly undertaken by the Reserve Bank of Australia on 1 Nov. 1973.

A national banking institution which has been named the Papua New Guinea Banking Corporation, has been established. This bank has assumed the Papua New Guinea business of the Commonwealth Trading Bank of Australia except where certain accounts give rise to special financial or contractual problems.

The subsidiaries of 3 Australian commercial banks also operate in Papua New Guinea. These are the Australia and New Zealand Banking Group (PNG) Ltd, the Bank of New South Wales (PNG) Ltd, and the Bank of South Pacific Ltd, all of which offer trading and savings facilities. As from 1 Nov. 1973 these banks operated under Papua New Guinea banking legislation.

In 1983, two additional commercial banks Indosuez Niugini Bank Ltd and Niugini Lloyds International Bank Ltd began operating, each with 51% national ownership, and the remaining 49% held by the affiliate of a major international bank.

In addition to these five commercial banks, the Papua New Guinea Development Bank has provided long-term development finance with a particular attention to the needs of small-scale enterprises since 1967. The country's first merchant bank, Resources and Investment Finance Ltd (RIFL), specializing in large-scale financial services began business in late 1979. Its shares are owned by the Hong Kong and Shanghai Banking Corporation, the Commonwealth Trading Bank of Australia and the Papua New Guinea Banking Corporation.

Weights and Measures. The metric system is in force.

ENERGY AND NATURAL RESOURCES

Electricity. In 1982 installed capacity was 341,900 mw, production 1,274·5m. kwh.

Minerals. Copper is the main mineral product. Oil companies have been searching for oil, but by 1983 no commercial deposits had been found. Gold, copper and silver are the only minerals produced in quantity. Major copper deposits in the Kieta district of Bougainville have proved reserves of about 800m. tonnes and are worked by Bougainville Copper Ltd and production of copper concentrates for export began in 1972 from this source. Copper and gold deposits which were found in the Star Mountains of the Western Province are being developed by Ok Tedi Mining Ltd at the Mt. Fubilan mine and production is expected to commence in 1984. In 1982, B.C.L. produced 598,600 tonnes of copper concentrate containing approximately 170,000 tonnes of copper. 17·54 tonnes of gold and 43·16 tonnes of silver were exported.

Agriculture. At 31 Dec. 1981, the total area of larger holdings was 393,000 hectares, of which 233,000 hectares were for agricultural purposes, the principal crops being coffee, copra and cocoa. Production of palm oil is of growing importance. Minor commercial crops include pyrethrum, tea, peanuts and spices. Locally consumed food crops include sweet potatoes, taro, bananas, rice and sago. Tropical fruits grow abundantly. There is extensive grassland. A newly-established sugar industry has made the country self-sufficient in this commodity while a beef-cattle industry is being developed.

Livestock (1982): Cattle, 133,000; pigs, 1·43m.; goats, 16,000; poultry, 1·27m.

Forestry. Timber production is of growing importance for both local consumption and export. In 1981, about 1,307,000 cu. metres of logs were harvested; logs exported, 742,800 cu. metres.

Production of sawn timber, 1981, 124,300 cu. metres, exports, 23,800 cu. metres; exports of woodchips, 102,700 tonnes.

Fisheries. Tuna, both skipjack and yellowfin species, is the major fisheries resource; in 1980 the catch was 33,000 tonnes. Exports of various crustacea, 1981, 1,281 tonnes, value K6·85m.

INDUSTRY AND TRADE

Industry. Secondary and service industries are expanding for the local market. Industries include the manufacture of paint, gases, concrete, twist tobacco and cigarettes, matches, soap, brewing, boat-building, furniture and the assembly of electrical appliances. In 1980 there were 776 factories employing 25,901 persons. Value of output K558m.

Labour. In 1980 about 733,000 were gainfully employed.

Trade. Imports (in K1,000) for calender years:

	1980	1981	1982
Food and live animals	133,176	136,339	138,692
Beverages and tobacco	8,690	8,362	8,388
Crude materials, inedible, except fuels	2,117	3,569	3,566
Mineral fuels, lubricants and related materials	117,863	158,369	146,093
Oils and fats (animal and vegetable)	1,870	1,877	2,212
Chemicals	36,584	45,055	39,319
Manufactured goods, chiefly by material	91,607	108,510	118,928
Machinery and transport equipment	206,329	224,595	230,393
Miscellaneous manufactured articles	52,891	54,593	53,873
Commodities and transactions of merchandise trade, not elsewhere specified	33,044	10,149	10,203
Total imports	684,172	751,419	751,667

Exports (in K1,000) for calendar years:

	1980	1981	1982
Coconut and copra products—			
Copra	24,594	19,476	12,878
Copra (coconut) oil	16,610	12,508	12,110
Copra cake and pellets	1,484	689	745
Total	42,688	32,673	25,733
Coffee beans	118,643	74,218	77,780
Cocoa beans	46,493	34,135	31,822
Crude rubber	3,751	3,403	1,406
Tea	8,507	7,131	6,682
Pyrethrum extract	19	890	498

	1980	1981	1982
Forest and timber products			
Logs	29,979	31,517	49,312
Sawn timber	6,155	3,897	3,508
Veneers	281	272	–
Plywood	2,520	3,000	2,151
Other	7,748	6,982	4,424
Total	46,684	45,667	59,395
Crocodile skins	1,620	1,320	2,341
Crayfish and prawns	6,560	6,851	6,463
Gold	7,811	7,132	6,242
Copper concentrate	...	...	298,034
Other domestic produce	354,972 [1]	332,170 [2]	28,412
Total domestic produce	637,748	545,589	545,396
Re-exports	53,972	19,334	24,351
Total exports	691,720	564,923	570,247

[1] Includes K313,264,000 for copper ore and concentrate.
[2] Includes K292,336,000 for copper ore and concentrate.

Of exports in 1981, Japan took 38%, Federal Republic of Germany, 22% and Australia, 12%; of imports, Australia furnished about 38%, Singapore, 19% and Japan, 16%.

Total trade between Papua New Guinea and UK (British Department of Trade returns, in £1,000 sterling):

	1979	1980	1981	1982	1983
Imports to UK	30,148	22,861	18,506	28,031	28,142
Exports and re-exports from UK	10,409	10,978	11,316	15,911	18,236

Tourism. In 1982, there were 16,445 visitors.

COMMUNICATIONS

Roads. In Sept. 1976 there were approximately 19,538 km of roads including approximately 1,016 km of urban roads. Motor vehicles numbered (1979) 47,436 including 12,980 cars.

Aviation. Frequent air services operate to and from Australia (Sydney, Brisbane and Cairns), and there are regular flights to Djayapura (Indonesia), Manila, Hong Kong, Singapore and Auckland. A service is also maintained to Honiara in the Solomon Islands. In addition to Air Niugini, the national flag carrier, Qantas, Philippine Airlines, Air New Zealand and Cathay Pacific operate in and out of Papua New Guinea.

Shipping. There are regular shipping services between Australia and Papua New Guinea ports, and also services to New Zealand, Japan, Hong Kong, US west coast, Singapore, Solomon Islands, Taiwan, Philippines and Europe. Small coastal vessels run between the various ports. In 1979 cargo discharged from overseas was 1·7m. tonnes; cargo loaded for overseas was 1·8m. tonnes.

Post and Broadcasting. Telephones numbered 50,050 on 1 Jan. 1982. The National Broadcasting Commission broadcasts on short-wave and medium-wave from Port Moresby, Rabaul, Wewak, Goroka, Lae, Daru, Alotau, Vanimo and Madang. There are 11 other stations broadcasting on short-wave only, at a number of centres, broadcasting programmes in several local languages.

JUSTICE, EDUCATION AND WELFARE

Justice. In 1978, 893 cases were heard in the National Court and (1977) 45,289 cases in the district courts.

Police. Total strength (1979) 4,268.

Education. At 30 June 1982 about 319,174 children attended 2,197 primary schools and 49,567 enrolled in 210 secondary, technical and vocational schools. The University of Papua New Guinea and the Papua New Guinea University of Technology had 3,245 students enrolled in full-time courses in 1982.

Health. In 1978, there were 20 hospitals, 384 health centres and 235 doctors.

DIPLOMATIC REPRESENTATIVES

Of Papua New Guinea in Great Britain (14 Waterloo Pl., London, SW1R 4AR)
High Commissioner: Ilinome Frank Tarua, OBE (accredited 25 Oct. 1983).

Of Great Britain in Papua New Guinea (Douglas St., Port Moresby)
High Commissioner: A. J. Collins, OBE.

Of Papua New Guinea in the USA (1140, 19th St., NW, Washington D.C., 20036)
Chargé d'Affaires. John Balagetuna.

Of the USA in Papua New Guinea (Armit St., Port Moresby)
Ambassador: M. Virginia Schafer.

Of Papua New Guinea to the United Nations
Ambassador: Renagi Lohia.

Books of Reference

The Territory of Papua. Annual Report. Commonwealth of Australia. 1906–1940–41 and from 1945–46
The Territory of New Guinea. Annual Report. Commonwealth of Australia. 1914–1940–41 and from 1946–47
Papua New Guinea, Annual Report. From 1970–71
Report on New Guinea. UN visiting missions to . . . Nauru and New Guinea. New York, 1962
Bettison, D. G., and others, *Independence of Papua–New Guinea.* Sydney, 1962.—*The Papua–New Guinea Elections 1964.* Canberra, 1966
Hasluck, P., *A Time for Building.* Melbourne Univ. Press, 1976
Hastings, P. (ed.), *Papua New Guinea: Prospero's Other Island.* London, 1971
Ross, A. C., and Langmore, J., *Alternative Strategies for Papua New Guinea.* OUP, 1974
Ryan, J., *The Hot Land.* London, 1970
Ryan, P. (ed.), *Encyclopaedia of Papua and New Guinea.* Melbourne Univ. Press, 1972
Skeldon, R., (ed.) *The Demography of Papua New Guinea.* Institute of Applied Social and Economic Research, 1979

PARAGUAY

República del Paraguay

Capital: Asunción
Population: 3·02m. (1982)
GNP per capita: US$1,389 (1981)

HISTORY. The Republic of Paraguay gained its independence from Spain on 14 May 1811. In 1814 Dr José Gaspar Rodríguez de Francia was elected dictator, and in 1816 perpetual dictator by the National Assembly. He died 20 Sept. 1840. In 1844 a new constitution was adopted, under which Carlos Antonio López (first elected in 1842, died 10 Sept. 1862) and his son, Francisco Solano López, ruled until 1870. During the devastating war against Brazil, Argentina and Uruguay (1865–70) Paraguay's population was reduced from about 600,000 to 232,000. Argentina, in Aug. 1942, and Brazil, in May 1943, voided the reparations which Paraguay had never paid. Further severe losses were incurred during the war with Bolivia (1932–35) over territorial claims in the Chaco. A peace treaty by which Paraguay obtained most of the area her troops had conquered was signed in July 1938.

AREA AND POPULATION. The area of the Oriental province is officially estimated at 159,827 sq. km (61,705 sq. miles) and the Occidental province at 246,925 sq. km (95,337 sq. miles), making the total area of the republic 406,752 sq. km (157,042 sq. miles).

The population according to the official census in 1982 was 3,023,092. The capital, Asunción, had 455,517 inhabitants; other towns: San Lorenzo (74,632), Fernando de la Mora (66,810), Lambaré (61,722), Presidente Stroessner (39,676), Pedro Juan Caballero (37,331), Encarnación (27,632), Concepcíon (22,866), Coronel Oviedo (21,782) and Villarrica (21,203).

The capital district and 19 departments had the following populations in 1982:

Asunción	455,517	Misiones	79,278
Central	494,575	Neembucu	70,689
Caaguazú	299,227	Amambay	68,422
Itapua	263,021	Canendiyú	65,807
Paraguari	202,152	Oriente	2,959,568
Cordillera	194,826	Presidente Hayes	43,787
San Pedro	189,751	Boquerón	14,685
Alto Paraná	188,351	Alto Paraguay	4,535
Guairá	143,374	Chaco	286
Concepción	135,068	Nueva Asunción	231
Caazapá	109,510	Occidente	63,524

Number of births, 1976, was 88,371; deaths, 13,754.

The population is overwhelmingly *mestizo* (mixed Spanish and Guaraní Indian) forming a homogeneous stock. There are some 46,700 unassimilated Indians of other tribal origin, in the Chaco and the forests of eastern Paraguay. There are some small traces of Negro descent. About half the population speak only Guaraní; some 4% speak only Spanish; the rest are bilingual.

Mennonites who arrived in 3 groups (1927, 1930 and 1947) are settled in the Chaco and Oriental Paraguay and were estimated in 1969 to number 13,000, of whom 2,000 came from Canada and 11,000 from Germany. The Japanese colonists in the Oriental section, who first came in 1935, were reckoned to number 7,000 in 1969. Under an agreement signed with Japan in 1959 up to 85,000 Japanese were to be admitted over 30 years. An agreement with Korea was signed in 1966 and there were (1978) about 3,000 Korean families living in Paraguay.

CLIMATE. A tropical climate, with abundant rainfall and only a short dry season from July to Sept., when temperatures are lowest. Asunción. Jan. 81°F (27·2°C), July 64°F (17·8°C). Annual rainfall 53″ (1,316 mm).

970

CONSTITUTION AND GOVERNMENT. A new constitution replacing that of 1940 was drawn up by a Constituent Convention in which all legally recognized political parties were represented and was signed into law on 25 Aug. 1967. It provides for a two-chamber parliament consisting of a 30-seat Senate and a 60-seat Chamber of Deputies, each elected for a 5-year term. Two-thirds of the seats in each Chamber are allocated to the majority party and the remaining one-third shared among the minority parties in proportion to the votes cast. Voting is compulsory for all citizens over 18. The President is directly elected for a 5-year (renewable) term; he appoints the Cabinet and during parliamentary recess can govern by decree through the Council of State, the members of which are representatives of the Government, the armed forces and other bodies.

On 6 Feb. 1977 elections were held for a 60-member Constitutional Assembly to revise the 1967 Constitution.

President: Gen. Alfredo Stroessner, Commander-in-Chief, elected 11 July 1954 to complete the presidential period of his predecessor. He was re-elected as 'Colorado' candidate in 1958, 1963, 1968, 1973, 1978 and 1983.

The following is a list of past presidents since 1940, with the date on which each took office:

Gen. Higinio Morínigo, 7 Sept. 1940 (re-signed).
Dr Juan Manuel Frutos, 3 June 1948.[1]
Dr J. Natalicio González, 15 Aug. 1948 (deposed).
Gen. Raimundo Rolón, 30 Jan. 1949.

Dr Felipe Molas López, 26 Feb. 1949[1] (re-signed).
Dr Federico Chávez, 16 July 1950 (resigned).
Tomás Romero Pereira, 4 May 1954.

[1] Provisional, *i.e.,* following a *coup d'état.*

The President has a cabinet of 11 ministers.

Interior: Dr Sabino A. Montanaro. *Foreign Affairs:* Dr Alberto Nogués. *Finance:* César Barrientos. *Education and Worship:* Dr Raúl Peña. *Public Works and Communications:* Juan A. Cáceres. *Agriculture and Livestock:* Hernando Bertoni. *National Defence:* Marcial Samaniego. *Public Health and Social Welfare:* Dr Adan Godoy Giménez. *Justice and Labour:* Dr Saúl González. *Industry and Commerce:* Dr Delfín Ugarte Centurión. *Without Portfolio:* Vacant.

National flag: Red, white, blue (horizontal); the white stripe charged with the arms of the republic on the obverse, and, on the reverse, with a lion and the inscription *Paz y Justicia*—the only flag in the world with different obverse and reverse.

National anthem: ¡ Paraguayos, república o muerte! (words by F. Acuña de Figueroa; tune by F. Dupey).

The country is divided into 2 provinces: the 'Oriental', east of Paraguay River, and the 'Occidental', west of the same river. The Oriental section is divided into 14 departments and the capital. The more important departments are supervised by a *Delegado* appointed by and directly responsible to the central government. The Occidental province, or Chaco, is divided into 5 departments.

DEFENCE. The army, navy and air forces are separate services under a single command. The President of the Republic is the active Commander-in-Chief. The armed forces total about 15,500 officers and men.

Army. The Army consists of 1 cavalry division, 8 infantry divisions, 1 independent infantry battalion, 1 Presidential Escort Regiment and supporting artillery, engineer and signals units. Equipment includes 6 M-4A3 main battle and 15 M-3A1 light tanks. Strength (1984) 12,500 (including 9,000 conscripts), and there are 25,000 reserves.

Navy. The flotilla comprises 5 armoured river defence gunboats (2 ancient monitors of 636 tons built in Italy and 3 old *ex*-Argentinian minesweepers of 620 tons), 1 helicopter lighter, 1 river patrol boat, 2 patrol launches, 6 coastal patrol craft, 2 landing craft, 1 survey craft, 1 transport training ship, 12 service craft and 2 tugs. There are 12 naval aircraft. Personnel in 1984 totalled 2,000 officers and men including coastguard and 500 marines.

Air Force. The Air Force came into being in the early thirties. After operating only transport and training aircraft for a number of years, it received 6 A-37B light jet attack aircraft from USA in 1978, followed by 9 Xavante light jet strike/training aircraft from Brazil. Other types in service include 3 DC-6B and 2 C-54 four-engined transports more than 20 C-47 and 4 Bandeirante twin-engined transports, 1 Convair C-131A, a Twin Otter, an Otter, 8 Brazilian-built Uirapuru primary trainers, 22 T-6 Texan armed basic trainers, 12 T-37C jet basic trainers and a number of light aircraft and helicopters. HQ and flying school are at Campo Grande, Asunción. Personnel total about 1,000.

INTERNATIONAL RELATIONS

Membership. Paraguay is a member of UN, OAS and LAIA (formerly LAFTA).

ECONOMY

Budget. In 1981 revenue was Gs.64,626m. and expenditure Gs.70,908m.

The 1982 budget provided Gs.13,307m. for national defence, Gs.13,412m. for education and worship and Gs.6,002m. for public health and social welfare. Total external debt outstanding at the end of Dec. 1981 was US$948·6m.

Currency. The *guarani* was established on 5 Oct. 1943 equal to 100 old paper pesos. Total monetary circulation was Gs.71,871m. in Dec. 1981.

Rate of exchange, March 1984: 160 *guaranies* = US$1; 187 *guaranies* = £1.

Banking. The Banco Central del Paraguay opened 1 July 1952 to take over the central banking functions previously assigned to the National Bank of Paraguay, which had opened in March 1943 and been reorganized as the Banco del Paraguay in Sept. 1944 with a monetary, a banking and a mortgage department. The Banco del Paraguay closed in Nov. 1961 and has been replaced, with the aid of a US loan of US$3m., by the Banco Nacional de Fomento; the latter's assets in Jan. 1979 were Gs.27,546m.

The Banco Central in Dec. 1981 had gold and exchange reserves amounting to US$733·5m.; contribution to the IMF was Gs.47·7m.

The Banco Nacional de Fomento, Bank of London and South America, Ltd, Banco Exterior do Brasil, Citibank, Banco de Asunción, Banco Exterior SA, Banco Unión SA, Banco Paraguayo de Comercio, Banco Real del Paraguay SA, Banco Aleman Transatlantico, Banco Holandés Unido, Banco Nacional del Estado de São Paulo, Yegros y Azara, Bank of America, Chase Manhattan Bank, Bank of Boston and Interbanco all have agencies in Asunción and branches in some main towns.

Weights and Measures. The metric system was officially adopted on 1 Jan. 1901.

ENERGY AND NATURAL RESOURCES

Electricity. Electricity from a 90,000 kw. hydro-electric plant at Acaray, with an output of 180,000 kw. (1979), supplies Asunción and 70 small towns and villages. Electricity is exported to Argentina and Brazil. Paraguay has signed agreements with Brazil to build jointly a 10m. kw. scheme on the river Paraná which will be in operation in 1982, and with Argentina another which will yield approximately 3m. kw.

Oil. The oil refinery at Villa Elisa, which has been in operation since 1966, has a production of about 3,500 bbls a day. Exploration for petroleum in the Chaco yielded negative results but prospecting was continuing in 1979.

Minerals. Iron, manganese and other minerals have been reported but have not been shown to be commercially exploitable. There are large deposits of limestone, and also salt, kaolin and apatite. *Pennzoil Paraguay* and other national and international firms have acquired licences to prospect for oil and natural gas in the Chaco. A uranium survey was being carried out in 1978 in the Oriental region.

Agriculture. In 1981 it was estimated that agriculture absorbs some 51·4m. hectares. Area (in hectares) and yield (in tonnes per hectare) of the main agricultural products in 1981:

	Area	Yield		Area	Yield
Cotton	243,782	265,000	Soybeans	393,890	850,000
Maize [1]	420,000	680,000	Mandioca [1]	135,000	2,049,807
Tobacco	7,597	10,332	Rice (Paddy) [1]	38,300	72,779
Wheat	49,032	80,000			

[1] 1979–80 figures.

Wheat, soybean (850,000 tons, 1981), cotton, sugar, tobacco, coffee are increasing in importance, as are also essential oils and oilseeds. *Yerba maté*, or strongly flavoured Paraguayan tea, continues to be produced but is declining in importance; 712 tons were exported in 1981.

Livestock (1982). Paraguay had about 5·5m. cattle, 330,000 horses, 1·35m. pigs, 430,000 sheep.

Forestry. In the Oriental section there are huge reserves of hardwoods and cedars that have scarcely been exploited. Palms, tung and other trees are exploited for their oils. The Japanese are experimenting with mulberries for silk growing. Pines and firs have been introduced under a United Nations project. In the Chaco the accessible Quebracho forests have nearly been worked out but plans are being made to open up new areas. In 1979, 5,206 tons of timber were exported and 393 tons of quebracho.

INDUSTRY AND TRADE

Industry. Production, 1981 (tons): Hides, 9,519; preserved meat, 257; frozen meat, 311; cotton fibre, 105,869 (1,000 metres); tannin, 17 (1978); petit grain, 220; tung oil, 12 (1978); cement, 161,419; sugar, 76,518; cigarettes (1,000 packets), 37,826; matches (1,000 boxes), 14,901. There are 3 meat-packing plants and other factories producing vegetable oils. A textile industry in Pilar and Asunción meets a large part of local needs.

Labour. Trade unionists number about 30,000 (*Confederación Paraguaya de Trabajadores* and *Confederación Cristiana de Trabajadores*).

Commerce. Imports and exports (in US$1m.):

	1975	1976	1977	1978	1979	1980	1981
Imports	212·7	180·2	250·4	375	402	517·1	506
Exports	176·2	181·8	278·9	285	276	310·2	295

Chief exports in 1981 included (in US$1m.): Fruit, 152; cotton, 129·2; sugar, 72; soybeans, 47·5; timber, 36·9; yerba maté, 34·9; palm shoots, 30; vegetable oils, 22·4; tung oil, 11·6; tobacco, 6·4.

Chief imports 1981 in (US$1m.): Machinery and apparatus, 107·7; fuels and lubricants, 94·5; foodstuffs, 89·2; vehicles and accessories, 65·4; iron and manufactures, 22·6; drinks and tobacco, 12·7.

Imports and exports (in US$), by country, 1981:

Country	Imports	Exports
Algeria	27,458	...
Argentina	100,090	68,542
Belgium	2,392	3,027
Brazil	131,257	54,156
Federal Republic of Germany	41,038	32,902
France	9,098	4,603
Italy	6,005	...
Japan	41,990	24,940
Netherlands	2,599	13,257
Spain	6,014	3,791
Sweden	4,283	...
Switzerland	3,078	14,651
UK	24,898	2,894
Uruguay	15,475	9,124
USA	49,156	15,308

Total trade between Paraguay and UK (British Department of Trade returns, in £1,000 sterling):

	1979	1980	1981	1982	1983
Imports to UK	2,107	1,279	2,241	2,790	3,129
Exports and re-exports from UK	12,746	13,384	13,105	16,915	15,263

Tourism. Visitors numbered 178,454 in 1982.

COMMUNICATIONS

Roads. In 1980 there were 15,500 km of roads, of which 1,500 were paved. The principal paved roads are Route No. 2/7 running from Asunción to the bridge over the Paraná at Puerto Presidente Stroessner, and thence down to the ocean at Paranaguá; and Route No. 1 to Encarnación in the south. The other main arteries are Coronel Oviedo-Pedro Juan Caballero road (unpaved from Coronel Oviedo) in the north and the Trans-Chaco road which starts from the bridge across the river Paraguay north of Asunción and ends at Nueva Asunción on the Bolivian border. Unpaved roads are closed when it rains. In the Argentine, a paved road starts from Pilcomayo, opposite Asunción, and provides good communication with Buenos Aires. Motor cars, 1976, numbered 17,600; commercial vehicles, 15,200, and passenger vehicles, 7,580.

Railways. The President Carlos Antonio López (formerly Paraguay Central) Railway runs from Asunción to Encarnación, on the Río Alto Paraná, with a length of 441 km (1,435 mm gauge). In 1980, traffic amounted to 191,724 tonnes and 287,318 passengers.

Aviation. International services are operated by 9 airlines (domestic and foreign) and internal routes by military airlines and some small private lines.

Shipping. In flood the Paraguay River, which divides the country into two distinct parts, is navigable for 12ft-draught vessels as far as Concepción, 180 miles north of Asunción, and for smaller vessels for a further distance of 600 miles northward. Drought conditions often restrict navigation to lighter traffic. The Paraná River is navigable by large boats from Corrientes up to Puerto Aguirre, at the mouth of the Yguazú River. Boats of a few hundred tons capacity navigate the tributary rivers.

Asunción, the chief port, is 950 miles from the sea. The cargo fleet includes 25 vessels of 300–1,000 tons, 3 tankers of 1,100–1,700 tons, 2 passenger river boats and 1 ocean-going freighter of 713 tons.

Post and Broadcasting. The national telegraph (137 offices) connects Asunción with Corrientes and Posadas in the Argentine Republic, and thus with the outside world; new direct links have been opened with the Federal Republic of Germany, USA, Bolivia and Chile. In addition, 34 stations are operated by the President Carlos Antonio López Railway; total, 2,070 miles. Three companies (12 stations) offer radio-telegraph and telex services to several countries. Telephones, 1981, 58,713, of which 45,818 were in Asunción and were automatic. There are 1 state and 9 commercial radio stations in Asunción, 22 in provincial towns, 2 commercial television stations in Asunción and 1 in Encarnación in the south.

Cinemas (1974). Cinemas numbered 65 in Asunción. The larger country towns usually have an outdoor cinema.

Newspapers (1980). There are 5 daily newspapers in Asunción with an aggregate circulation of about 200,000.

JUSTICE, RELIGION AND EDUCATION

Justice. The highest court is the Supreme Court with 5 members. There are special Chambers of Appeal for civil and commercial cases, and criminal cases. Judges of first instance deal with civil, commercial and criminal cases in 6 departments. Minor cases are dealt with by Justices of the Peace.

The Attorney-General represents the State in all jurisdictions, with representatives in each judicial department and in every jurisdiction. In matters of revenue, taxes, etc., the State is represented by the *Abogado del Tesoro*.

Religion. Religious liberty is guaranteed by the 1967 constitution. Article 6 thereof recognizes Roman Catholicism as the official religion of the country. The same article disposes that relations between Paraguay and the Holy See shall be regulated by concordats or other bilateral agreements, but no such agreements have yet been negotiated.

The Roman Catholic Church is organized into the Archdiocese of Asunción, 3 other dioceses (San Juan Bautista de las Misiones, Concepción and Villarrica); 4 Prelatures (Coronel Oviedo, Encarnación, Alto Paraná and Caacupé); and 2 Vicariates Apostolic (Chaco and Pilcomayo). The bishops meet in a Conference of Paraguayan Bishops. Only civil marriages are legally valid. There are numerous non-catholic communities, the largest of whom are the Mennonites. There is a small Anglican church in Asunción, with missions in the Chaco, which comes under the jurisdiction of an Anglican Bishop resident in Asunción.

Education. Education is free and nominally compulsory, but schools are not everywhere available, and the system has been extensively revised to provide, *inter alia,* primary education for adults. Illiteracy is estimated at 22% (urban) and 30% (rural). In 1973 there were 2,288 government primary schools and 421 private schools, with 459,393 pupils and 15,871 teachers; 652 secondary schools had 66,746 students and 6,729 teachers. In 1978 there was an intensive school building programme in progress. The National University in Asunción had, in 1973, 7,919 students and 1,209 professors. In 1973 the Catholic University and associated colleges had 4,546 students and 355 professors.

DIPLOMATIC REPRESENTATIVES

Of Paraguay in Great Britain (51 Cornwall Gdns, London, SW7 4AQ)
Ambassador: Antonio R. Zuccolillo.

Of Great Britain in Paraguay (Calle Presidente Franco, 706, Asunción)
Ambassador and Consul-General: Derrick Mellor.

Of Paraguay in the USA (2400 Massachusetts Ave., NW, Washington, D.C., 20008)
Chargé d'Affaires: Juan Carlos A. Hrase von Bargen.

Of the USA in Paraguay (1776 Mariscal López Ave., Asunción)
Ambassador: Arthur H. Davis, Jnr.

Of Paraguay to the United Nations
Ambassador: Dr Luis Gonzalez Arias.

Books of Reference

Gaceta Official, published by Imprenta Nacional, Estrella y Estero Bellaco, Asunción
Anuario Daumas. Asunción
Anuario Estadístico de la República del Paraguay. Asunción. Annual
Lewis, P. H., *Paraguay under Stroessner.* Univ. of North Carolina Press, 1980
Maybury-Lewis, D. and Howe, J., *The Indian Peoples of Paraguay: Their Plight and Their Prospects.* Cambridge, Mass., 1980

National Library: Biblioteca Nacional, De la Rosidenta, Asunción.

PERU

República del Perú

Capital: Lima
Population: 18·3m. (1982)
GNP per capita: US$987 (1981)

HISTORY. The Republic of Peru, formerly the most important of the Spanish vice-royalties in South America, declared its independence on 28 July 1821; but it was not till after a war, protracted till 1824, that the country gained its actual freedom.

AREA AND POPULATION. The total area of Peru is estimated to be 1,285,215 sq. km (496,093 sq. miles).

The long-standing dispute with Chile over the provinces of Tacna and Arica (*see* THE STATESMAN'S YEAR-Book, 1928, p. 1198) reached an amicable settlement on 3 June 1929 at Lima, Tacna going to Peru and Arica to Chile. In response to demands by Bolivia for permanent access to the Pacific Coast, proposals for a Bolivian corridor to the sea and a new Bolivian port to be built in the disputed area have been put forward by Chile and Peru. To date, little progress has been made. One result has been increased tension along the Chilean–Peruvian border, there is no sign of a settlement of the border dispute, and the armed forces of both countries remain on the alert in the disputed border area. Fighting broke out between Peruvian and Ecuadorean Forces, in early 1981, along part of the disputed border (the Cordillera del Condor) which has to date not been adequately mapped. A number of proposals for settling the issue permanently have been put forward but a final settlement is unlikely to be reached in the near future. For an account of the settlement of other boundary disputes, *see* THE STATESMAN'S YEAR-Book, 1948, p. 1173.

A map of the boundary with Ecuador is to be found in THE STATESMAN'S YEAR-BOOK, 1942.

The census taken in 1981 gave the population as 17,762,231. Children under 15 years, 7·2m. (41% of total population). Birth rate, 4·2%; death rate, 1·3%. Lima, the capital, had 4,164,597 population. Other major cities (with census population 1981), are Callao (296,220, 1972), Arequipa (447,431), Trujillo (354,557), Chiclayo (280,244), Chimbote (216,406), Piura (186,354), Cuzco (181,604), Huancayo (115,693, 1972), Iquitos (173,629). The language is Spanish, but the Indian population speak either Quechua (the second official language) or Aymará.

The area of the 24 departments and the constitutional province of Callao are given below with the population, according to the official census of 1981 and 1972. The area of the department of Puno includes the Peruvian zone of Lake Titicaca, 4,996·28 sq. km. The chief towns are shown in brackets:

	Area (sq. km) 1959	Population 12 July 1981 (census)	2 June 1972 (census)	Pop. per sq. km 1961
Departments				
Amazonas (Chachapoyas)	41,297·1	254,560	196,469	2·85
Ancash (Huaraz)	36,308·3	818,289	726,665	16·20
Apurímac (Abancay)	20,654·6	323,346	307,805	16·36
Arequipa (Arequipa)	63,527·6	706,580	530,528	6·47
Ayacucho (Ayacucho)[1]	45,503·1	430,289	459,747	9·85
Cajamarca (Cajamarca)	35,417·8	1,045,569	916,331	21·15
Callao (Callao)[2]	73·8	443,413	315,605	2,901·46
Cuzco (Cuzco)	84,140·9	832,504	708,719	7·30
Huancavelica (Huancavelica)	22,870·9	346,797	331,155	13·07
Huánuco (Huánuco)	35,314·6	484,780	420,764	10·24
Ica (Ica)	21,251·4	433,897	357,973	11·48
Junín (Huancayo)	32,354·4	852,238	691,216	15·64
La Libertad (Trujillo)	23,241·3	962,949	806,368	25·29
Lambayeque (Chiclayo)	16,585·9	674,442	515,363	20·93
Lima (Lima)	33,894·9	4,745,877	3,485,411	68·42
Loreto (Iquitos)	478,336·2	445,368	494,895	0·69

[1] 1961. [2] With province.

	Area (sq. km.) 1959	Population 12 July 1981 (census)	2 June 1972 (census)	Pop. per sq. km 1961
Departments				
Madre de Dios (Maldonado)	78,402·7	33,007	21,968	0·19
Moquegua (Moquegua)	16,174·7	101,610	74,573	3·60
Pasco (Cerro de Pasco)	21,854·1	213,125	176,750	5·79
Piura (Piura)	33,067·1	1,125,865	854,668	21·68
Puno (Puno)	72,382·4	890,258	799,594	10·20
San Martín (Moyobamba)	53,063·6	319,751	224,310	3·06
Tacna (Tacna)	14,766·6	143,085	95,623	4·68
Tumbes (Tumbes)	4,731·5	103,839	75,399	21·10
Total	1,285,215·6	17,762,231	13,567,939	8·06

A new department of Ucayali is to be created in the central Amazon area, to include the provinces of Coronel Portillo and Ucayali, which were previously part of the department of Loreto. Pucallpa will be the capital of the new department.

CLIMATE. There is a very wide variety of climate, ranging from equatorial to desert, (or perpetual snow on the high mountains). In coastal areas, temperatures vary very little, either daily or annually, though humidity and cloudiness show considerable variation, with highest humidity from May to Sept. Little rain is experienced in that period. In the Sierra, temperatures remain fairly constant over the year, but the daily range is considerable. There the dry season is from April to Nov. Desert conditions occur in the extreme south, where the climate is uniformly dry, with a few heavy showers falling between Jan. and March. Lima. Jan. 74°F (23·3°C), July 62°F (16·7°C). Annual rainfall 2″ (48 mm). Cuzco. Jan. 56°F (13·3°C), July 50°F (10°C). Annual rainfall 32″ (804 mm).

CONSTITUTION AND GOVERNMENT. On 3 Oct. 1968 a military junta overthrew the government of President Fernando Belaúnde Terry and installed Gen. Juan Velasco Alvarado as President of a 'Revolutionary Government' with a cabinet composed entirely of officers of the armed services. Gen. Velasco was ousted in bloodless *coup* in Aug. 1975 and was replaced by Gen. Francisco Morales Bermudez. The new democratic government, under President Fernando Belaúnde Terry, took office on 28 July 1980.

The new Constitution, which became effective when a civilian government was installed in July 1980, provides for a Legislature consisting of a Senate (60 members) and a Chamber of Deputies (180 members) and an Executive formed of the President of the Republic and a Council of Ministers appointed by him. Elections were held in May 1980. They will be held every 5 years with the President and Congress elected at the same time, by separate ballots. All Peruvians over the age of 18 are eligible to vote; in May 1980 the number of registered voters was over 6m., including 1m. in Lima province. Voting is compulsory; women were fully enfranchised in 1955.

Presidents since 1948 were:

Gen. Manuel A. Odría (Acting), 27 Oct. 1948-1 June 1950.[1]
Gen. Zenón Noriega, 1 June 1950-28 July 1950.
Gen. Manuel A. Odría, 28 July 1950-28 July 1956.
Dr Manuel Prado y Ugarteche, 28 July 1956-July 1962.
Gen. Ricardo Pérez Godoy, 18 July 1962-3 March 1963.[2]
Gen. Nicolás Lindley López, 3 March-28 July 1963.
Fernando Belaúnde Terry, 28 July 1963-3 Oct. 1968.[2]
Gen. Juan Velasco Alvarado, 3 Oct. 1968-29 Aug. 1975.[2]
Gen. Francisco Morales Bermudez, 29 Aug. 1975-28 July 1980.

[1] Resigned.   [2] Deposed.

President: Fernando Belaúnde Terry.

The Cabinet was in March 1984 composed as follows:
Prime Minister and Minister of Foreign Affairs: Dr Fernando Schwalb López Aldana.

Economy, Finance and Commerce: (Vacant). *Interior:* Dr Joaquín Leguía Galvez. *Energy and Mines:* José Benavides Muñoz. *Education:* Dr Patricio Ricketts Rey de Castro. *Transport and Communications:* Carlos Pestana Zevallos. *Industry, Tourism and Integration:* Ivan Rivera Flores. *Housing:* Javier Velarde Aspillaga. *Health:* Dr Juan Franco Ponce. *Agriculture:* Juan Hurtado Miller. *Fisheries:* Ismael Benavides Ferreyros. *Justice:* Dr Ernesto Alayza Grundy. *Defence:* Oscar Brush Noel; Jorge Du Bois Gervasi; José Zlatar Stambuk.

In 1984 the 24 departments were divided into 158 provinces (plus the constitutional province of Callao) and 1,690 districts; the province of Callao has some of the functions of a department.

National flag: Three vertical strips of red, white, red, with the national arms in the centre.

National anthem: Somos Libres, seámoslo siempre (words by J. de la Torre Ugarte; tune by J. B. Alcedo, 1821).

DEFENCE.

Army. While military service is compulsory youths are only conscripted to fill the annual quota. The term of service is 2 years and all males of 20–25 years of age are liable. The country is divided into 5 military regions.

The Army comprises (1984) approximately 75,000 men (including 51,000 conscripts). There are 8 infantry and mechanized brigades, 1 paracommando and 2 armoured brigades, 1 jungle brigade, 3 armoured reconaissance squadrons and 10 artillery and 4 engineer battalions. There is an air element of 4 Helio Courier 395 communications aircraft. Equipment consists of approximately 420 tanks (T-54/-55, M-4 and AMX-13), over 100 light armoured fighting vehicles and 105-mm./155-mm. field artillery.

The section of the national police force with a para-military role is known as the *Guardia Civil* and comprises approximately 25,000 personnel.

Navy. The principal surface ships of the Peruvian Navy are the cruisers:–

Completed	Name	Standard Displacement (tons)	Main Guns	Aircraft	Shaft horsepower	Max. Speed (knots)
1953	*Aguirre* (ex-*De Zeven Provincien*)	9,850	4 6in.	3	85,000	32
1953	*Almirante Grau* [1] (ex-*De Ruyter*)	9,530	8 6in.	–	85,000	32

[1] When the Dutch cruiser *De Ruyter* was purchased in 1973 she was re-named *Almirante Grau* after Peru's principal naval hero. In consequence the cruiser whose name had been changed from *Newfoundland* to *Almirante Grau* when she was purchased from Britain in 1959 was again re-named *Capitan Quinones*, after an air force hero; but this ship has since been retired (latterly used as harbour training ship); and her sister ship *Colonel Bolognesi* (ex- HMS *Ceylon*) was laid up in 1983. *Aquirre* was bought from the Netherlands in 1976.

There are also 12 submarines comprising 6 completed in Federal Republic of Germany in 1974–82, 4 completed in USA in 1954–57 and 2 old *ex*-USN; 2 reconstructed 'Daring' class destroyers delivered from Britain during 1973; 8 old destroyers purchased from the Netherlands in 1978–82, 2 new Italian-built frigates, 6 new French-built fast missile-armed corvettes, 1 training ship and 1 submarine accommodation ship (both old *ex*-US destroyer escorts); 3 landing ships; 2 medium landing ships; 5 river gunboats; 3 river patrol boats; 2 transports; 3 hospital craft; 1 research craft; 7 oilers; 4 survey vessels; 1 repair ship; 1 torpedo recovery vessel; 4 floating docks; 4 water carriers, and 5 tugs.

The new construction programme includes 2 frigates being built in Peru (sister ships of 2 completed in Italy in 1978–80)

All naval training takes place in the Callao area at various schools. The main naval base and dockyard are also in Callao. Smaller bases are at Iquitos on the Amazon, and at San Lorenzo.

Naval personnel in 1984 totalled 2,000 officers and 18,500 men including the Naval Air Arm.

The Coast Guard includes 6 new patrol vessels built in Peru, 5 fast patrol craft built in Britain in 1964–65, 2 former US gunboats, 3 coastal patrol boats and 7 minor patrol craft.

Air Force. The Air Force is under the direction of the Air Minister, who is also C.-inC.

The operational force consists of 3 combat groups. No 13 Group has 2 squadrons of Mirage 5 jet fighters and 1 squadron of A-37B light attack aircraft; No. 21 Group has 2 squadrons of Canberra light jet bombers and 1 squadron of A-37Bs; No. 12 Group has about 50 Soviet-built Su-22 variable-geometry fighter bombers in 3 operational squadrons. Other aircraft in service include medium transports (1 F.28 Fellowship, 16 An-26, 6 L-100-20 Hercules), light transports (9 Twin Otter, 15 Buffalo, 1 twin-jet Falcon and 12 Turbo-Porter), helicopters (6 Mi-6 and a total of 54 Mi-8, Bell 212 and 214ST, BO 105, Alouette III and Bell 47G), 70 training aircraft (including Aermacchi MB 339, T-37 and T-41D) and a small number of miscellaneous types for photographic and communications duties. The T-37 trainers, and A-37B attack aircraft, will be replaced from 1985 by further MB 339s, built in Peru. Two DC-9s and some of the C-54 and C-130 aircraft are used by the Air Force to run a commercial airline network (SATCO). There are military airfields at Talara, Chiclayo, Piura, Pisco, Lima (2), Iquitos and La Joya, and a seaplane base at Iquitos. All officers and pilots are trained at the Air Academy at Lima (Las Palmas). The approximate strength of the Peruvian Air Force is 40,000 personnel and 120 combat aircraft.

INTERNATIONAL RELATIONS

Membership. Peru is a member of UN, OAS, Andean Group and LAIA (formerly LAFTA).

ECONOMY

Planning. A Public Investment Programme for 1981–85 envisages expenditure of US$11,500m.

Budget. The authorized budget for 1984 envisaged expenditure of S/.10,729,000m. The external debt was US$11,644m. in Dec. 1982.

Currency. The monetary unit is the *sol.* A new currency the *Sol Nuevo* is to be introduced in 1985. In March 1984, £1=3,661·7; US$1=2,475·02.

Coins include 50,000 soles (gold) and 10,000 soles (silver) coins as well as 10- and 5-sole pieces (copper 75%; nickel 25%), the sol and half sol (copper 30%; zinc 70%); the 20, 10 and 5 centavos (copper–zinc) and the 2- and 1-centavo pieces (zinc) have been discontinued. Peru has a paper currency issued by the Banco Central de la Reserva in denominations of 5,000, 1,000, 500, 200, 100 and 50. The 10 and 5 soles notes have been discontinued.

Banking. The government bank of issue is the Banco Central de la Reserva del Perú, which was established in 1922. A new charter for the bank was promulgated in Aug. 1968; this. *inter alia,* extended the bank's authority with regard to the organization of the commercial banking system.

The Government's fiscal agent is the Banco de la Nación which, since May 1970, has control of the 'giro' market through which most non-trade foreign currency transactions are channelled.

There were in 1983, 7 commercial banks (of which 3 state-owned), 4 foreign commercial banks, 9 development banks (5 state-owned), 6 regional commercial banks and a savings bank.

Weights and Measures. The metric system of weights and measures was established by law in 1869, and since 1916 has come into general use.

ENERGY AND NATURAL RESOURCES

Electricity. In 1972 control of electricity production and distribution passed to ELECTROPERU, a state company. In 1981 the production of electric energy was

3,200 mw (60% hydro-electric). An electrification programme to construct a series of large hydro-electric power stations, was started in 1980.

Oil. Proven oil reserves in the jungle region amount to about 900m. bbls. A further 75m. tonnes have been found in the north-west, some of it offshore. The new 850 km pipeline, linking the new jungle oilfields to coastal terminals, was opened in 1977. Output amounted to 174,000 bbls per day by 1983 and Peru became an oil exporter in that same year. The total value of exports in 1982 of petroleum and derivative was US$715m.

Minerals. Peru's mining industry produces 13 metals and 25 non-metallic minerals. Lead, copper, iron, silver, zinc and petroleum are the chief minerals exploited. Mineral exports in 1980: Copper, US$752m.; lead, US$383m.; zinc, US$210m.; silver, US$312m.; iron ore, US$95m.; gold, US$40m. Mineral production (in tonnes, 1982) of iron, 3,767,000; zinc, 556,000; copper, 370,000; lead, 212,000.

Agriculture. There are 4 natural zones: the coast strip, with an average width of 80 km; the Sierra or Uplands, formed by the coast range of mountains and the Andes proper; the Montaña or high wooded region which lies on the eastern slopes of the Andes, and the jungle in the Amazon Basin, known as the Selva. Land under cultivation, 1967, was about 2·75m. hectares. There are 4 fertilizer factories, near Callao and in Cuzco.

Nearly half of the population is dependent on agriculture, which accounted for 13% of the GDP in 1981–82. Peru's third land reform law, that of June 1969, is one of the most comprehensive. It provides for the large sugar estates in the north of Peru to be turned into co-operatives. Maximum permitted sizes for other types of land holding are stipulated for the various regions of the country. These range from 150 hectares for irrigated land on the coast to an area capable of supporting 5,000 sheep for pasture land in the Sierra. These sizes may be increased if certain efficiency criteria are met. Holdings too small to be economically viable are to be consolidated into co-operative units. The chief agricultural productions of Peru are, in the order named: Sugar, cotton, coffee and wool.

Production in 1981 (in 1,000 tonnes): Sugar-cane, 4,160; sugar, 493; cotton, 87; coffee, 95; wool, 13.

Output of cattle and buffalo hides (in tonnes), 1981, 13,220; sheepskins, 7,350; goatskins, 2,100. Output of sheep wool in 1976 was 9,000 tonnes. Exports, 1970, were sheep wool, unwashed, 606 tonnes; llama, alpaca and vicuña wool, 1,537 tonnes.

Livestock (1982): 653,000 horses, 3·6m. cattle, 1·9m. goats, 14·5m. sheep, 2m. swine, 39m. poultry.

Fisheries. Until the early 1970s Peru was the world's foremost fishing nation in terms of value of catch, due mainly to anchoveta which was converted into fishmeal for export as animal feed. Peru produced almost 45% of the world's fishmeal supplies, or nearly 2m. tonnes a year. However, abnormal marine conditions and over-fishing combined had, by 1983 considerably reduced the anchoveta catch.

Since then the industry has been partly denationalized and the number of fishing vessels reduced by approximately 50%, to some 700. Increased attention has been paid to fishing for human consumption.

Fish production 1980 (1,000 tonnes): Anchoveta, 720; other species, 1,006. Fresh, 155·7; frozen, 219·8; dried salted, 28·3; conserves, 567. Fish caught include (1980, tonnes): Anchoveta, 720,100; sardine, 1,480,400; hake, 159,400; black mackerel, 123,400; mackerel, 59,100; seafish, 6,800.

INDUSTRY AND TRADE

Industry. About 70% of Peru's manufacturing industries are located in or around the Lima/Callao metropolitan area.

Peru's first iron and steel mill came into production at Chimbote in April 1958. Products include pig-iron, blooms, billets, largets, round and round-deformed bars, wire rod, black and galvanized sheets and galvanized roofing sheets. Refractories are manufactured at Lima.

The Government has a monopoly of the import and/or local manufacture and sale of guano, salt, alcohol and explosives. The monopoly of matches was abandoned in 1954 and that of tobacco in June 1955.

Peru's manufacturing industry stagnated since 1972 but by 1980 had recovered substantially, mainly due to exports of non-traditional goods. In 1977 production in the following industries was (in tonnes):

Cement	1,964,000	Refined lead	169,000
Tyres (units)	700,000	TV receivers (units)	100,000
Refined zinc	389,000	Sulphuric acid	60,000
Refined copper	350,000	Vehicle assembly	11,300
Crude steel	347,000		

Labour. In 1976 the total labour was considered to number 5m. persons, of which 40% was either under-employed or unemployed. This was 52% of the urban population of the country or about 30% of the country's population. The population was distributed roughly as follows in 1972: Agriculture, stock-raising and fishing, 2m.; manufacturing industry, 611,000; construction, 183,000; mining, 98,000; government, 317,000; commerce, 475,000; services, 477,000.

Trade Unions. Trade unions have about 2m. members (approximately 1·5m. in peasant organizations and 500,000 in industrial). The major trade union organization is the *Confederación de Trabajadores del Perú*, which was reconstituted in 1959 after being in abeyance for some years. The other labour organizations recognized by the Government are the *Confederación General de Trabajadores del Perú*, the *Confederación Nacional de Trabajadores* and the *Central de Trabajadores de la Revolución Peruana*.

Commerce. The value of trade has been as follows (in US$1m.):

	1976	1977	1978	1979	1980	1981	1982
Imports	1,360	1,726	1,601	2,090	3,062	3,803	3,502
Exports	2,100	2,095	1,941	3,474	3,898	3,255	3,212

In 1982 the principal imports were: Machinery and appliances, chemicals, foodstuffs; fuel, lubricants and other non-metallic minerals.

Total trade between Peru and UK (British Department of Trade returns, in £1,000 sterling):

	1979	1980	1981	1982	1983
Imports to UK	61,518	77,487	66,726	92,120	118,414
Exports and re-exports from UK	23,949	46,541	50,280	39,370	32,947

Tourism. There were 336,000 visitors in 1981.

COMMUNICATIONS

Roads. In 1980 there were, 58,685 km, of which 6,455 km were paved and 12,323 km gravel.

In 1981 there were 529,000 registered motor vehicles.

Railways. Since 1972 all public railways have been nationalized and run by Peruvian National Railways (ENAFER). Total length (1981), 1,628 km on 1,435- and 914-mm gauges. In 1981 railways carried 1·9m. short tons and 3·2m. passengers.

Aviation. There are 3 international and 61 other airports.

Shipping. In 1966, 6,900 vessels of 26,602,270 tons entered, and 6,871 of 26,610,772 tons cleared the ports. Since 1928 the coasting trade has been largely reserved for Peruvian-owned vessels with Peruvian crews; in 1960 it handled 2,246,000 tonnes, valued at S/.1,665m.

Post and Broadcasting. An earth satellite ground communication station at Lurin connects Peru through Intelsat. III to the US and Europe. In 1981 there were 629,742 telephones, 371,673 in Lima. Radio-telephone circuits connect Lima with distant towns. Three submarine telegraph cables connect Peru and Chile, and one connects Peru and the republics to the north. There are 153 broadcasting stations, of which 29 are in Lima. Wireless receiving sets, about 2m. There are 7 television stations in Lima, 16 in the provinces and 45 relay stations. All radio and television stations are supervised by the Government.

Cinemas. In 1972 there were 276 cinemas.

Newspapers. The main Lima newspapers are *La Prensa, El Comercio, Expreso, Correo* and *La Crónica*.

JUSTICE, RELIGION, EDUCATION AND WELFARE

Justice. The Peruvian judicial system is a pyramid at the base of which are the justices of the peace who decide minor criminal cases and civil cases involving small sums of money. The apex is the Supreme Court with 17 members; in between are the judges of first instance, who usually sit in the provincial capitals, and the superior courts of which there are 18.

The Revolutionary Government decreed in Dec. 1969 that all judges, except justices of the peace, would in future be elected by the National Council of Justice, composed of representatives of the Executive, the Legislature, the Judiciary, the National Federation of the College of Lawyers and 2 of the university law faculties. Justices of the peace are appointed, by the superior courts.

Religion. Religious liberty exists, but the Roman Catholic religion is protected by the State, and since 1929 only Roman Catholic religious instruction is permitted in schools, state or private. In 1972 there were 1 Roman Catholic cardinal, 7 archbishops, 14 bishops, 3 vicars-general, 8 vicars apostolic, 2,672 priests, 506 cloistered monks and 4,558 members of religious orders.

Protestants numbered 128,000 in 1966.

All marriages must be civil, regardless of religion and preceded by medical examination; there are liberal divorce regulations, including divorce for 'absence without just cause for more than 2 years', and by mutual consent. Divorcees may remarry immediately. A law of 1936 emphasizes that the religious obligations of marriage are fully recognized.

Education. A new law for education was promulgated in March 1972. Elementary education is compulsory and free for both sexes between the ages of 7 and 16; secondary education is also free. But schools, despite substantial increases, are still too few. The system is highly centralized; all teaching appointments are made by the Minister of Education for the public schools; for the private schools he supervises plant and equipment and limits fees but does not appoint teachers.

In 1970 there were 20,034 public, private and primary schools, with 64,004 teachers and 2·75m. pupils; 1,452 secondary schools, with 21,863 teachers and 674,000 students. Training in 414 public technical schools is also free; in 1970 they had 6,333 teachers and 223,300 pupils. The 90 teacher-training schools had 1,075 teachers and 18,000 pupils. Total literacy (1975) was 68% of total population. Because of the increase in the number of pupils state schools have divided their teaching timetable into three divisions, morning, afternoon and evening. Those pupils in the last shift have to spend an extra year at school to make up for the difference in the length of the daily timetable.

In 1970 the total number of university students was 105,600.

Social Welfare. Contributory social security schemes exist for employees and workers. These are administered by the Ministry of Labour. There were in 1975, 182 hospitals (33,350 beds). In addition in 1969 there were 63 health centres, 307 medical posts and 842 sanitary posts, all administered by the authorities. In 1975 there were 9,445 doctors, 2,119 obstetricians, 115 chemists and 8,920 trained nurses.

DIPLOMATIC REPRESENTATIVES

Of Peru in Great Britain (52 Sloane St., London, SW1X 9SP)
Ambassador: Dr Andres A. Aramburú-Menchaca (accredited 10 May 1983).

Of Great Britain in Peru (Edificio El Pacifico Washington, Ave. Arequipa, Lima)
Ambassador: John W. R. Shakespeare, MVO.

Of Peru in the USA (1700 Massachusetts Ave., NW, Washington, D.C., 20036)
Ambassador: (Vacant).

Of the USA in Peru (PO Box 1995, Lima)
Ambassador: Frank V. Ortiz, Jr.

Of Peru to the United Nations
Ambassador: Dr Javier Arias Stella.

Books of Reference

The official gazette is *El Peruano,* Lima.

Anario Estadistico del Perú. Annual.—*Boletin de Estadistica Peruana.* Quarterly.—
Demarcación Política del Perú. (Dirección Nacional de Estadística), Lima
Censo Nacional Población, 4 June 1972. Lima, 1972
Estadistica del Comercio Exterior (Superintendencia de Aduanas). Lima
Banco Central de Reserva. Monthly Bulletin.—*Renta Nacional del Perú.* Annual, Lima

Ministerio de Fomento Lima publishes separate annual statistics on the mining and petroleum industries and on general industry; the wool textile and cotton textile industries, the Peruvian Chamber of Commerce furnish annual studies.

Alba, V., *Peru.* Boulder, 1977
Figueroa, A., *Capitalist Development and the Peasant Economy of Peru.* CUP, 1984
Fitzgerald, E. V. K., *The Political Economy of Peru 1958–78.* CUP, 1979
Hemming, J., *The Conquest of the Incas.* London, 1970
Lowenthal, A. F., *The Peruvian Experiment.* Princeton Univ. Press, 1975
McClintock, C., and Lowental, A. F., (eds.) *The Peruvian Experiment Reconsidered.* Princeton Univ. Press, 1983
Mejia Baca, J., and Tauro, A., *Diccionário Enciclopédico del Perú.* 3 vols. 1966
Philip, G. D. E., *The Rise and Fall of the Peruvian Military Radicals, 1968–1976.* London, 1978
Sharp, D. A. (ed.), *US Foreign Policy and Peru.* Univ. of Texas Press, 1972
Stepan, A., *The State and Society. Peru in Comparative Perspective.* Princeton Univ. Press, 1978
Thorp, R., and Bertram, G., *Peru 1890–1977.* London, 1978
Vargas, Padre, *Historia General del Perú.* Lima, 1967
Webb, R. C., *Government Policy and the Distribution of Income in Peru, 1963–1973.* Harvard Univ. Press, 1977

National Library: Avenida Abancay, Lima.

REPUBLIC OF THE PHILIPPINES

Capital: Manila
Population: 51·95m. (1983)
GNP per capita: US$720 (1980)

República de Filipinas—
Republika ng Pilipinas

HISTORY. Before the Spanish discovery of the Philippines, the native Filipinos came in contact with India, China and Arabia. According to the early records of China, 'some Filipinos from the country of Ma-i arrived in Canton and sold their merchandise' as early as 982. The Philippine islands were discovered by Magellan in 1521 and conquered by Spain in 1565. Following the Spanish–American war, the islands were ceded to the USA on 10 Dec. 1898, after the Filipinos had tried in vain to establish an independent republic in 1896.

The Republic of the Philippines came into existence on 4 July 1946, by agreement with the US Government embodied in an Act of Congress signed by President Roosevelt on 24 March 1934, accepted by the Philippine Legislature on 1 May 1934 and ratified at a plebiscite on 14 May 1935. This Act established a 10-year transitional period, designated as that of the Philippine Commonwealth, at the end of which complete independence was automatically effective.

AREA AND POPULATION. The Philippines is situated between 21° 25′ and 4° 23′ N. lat. and between 116° and 127° E. long. It is composed of 7,100 islands and islets, 2,773 of which are named. Approximate land area, 115,830 sq. miles (300,000 sq. km). The 16 most important islands with their areas (in sq. miles) are: Luzon, 40,420; Mindanao, 36,537; Samar, 5,050; Negros, 4,906; Palawan, 4,550; Panay, 4,446; Mindoro, 3,759; Leyte, 2,786; Cebu, 1,707; Bohol, 1,492; Masbate, 1,262; Sulu group, 379; Tawi-tawi, 229; Romblon, 32; Marinduque, 347, and Siquijor, 129.

Census population 1980 was 48,098,460. Estimate (1983) 51·95m.

The population of Manila, the present capital, in 1980 was 1,630,485 (metropolitan Manila, 5,925,884). The old capital, Quezon City, just north-east of Manila, had a population of 1,165,865. Other cities, with their population in May 1980 are: Iloilo on Panay, 244,827; Cebu on Cebu, 490,281; Zamboanga on Mindanao, 343,722; Davao on Mindanao, 610,375; Bacolod on Negros, 262,415; San Carlos on Negros Occidental, 91,627; San Carlos on Pangasinan, 101,243; Pasay on Rizal, 287,770.

On 7 June 1946 the President of the Philippines approved a law, effective 4 July 1946, making a new language (Pilipino) based on Tagalog (a Malayan dialect) the official national language of the republic. In 1970 about 16,409,133 people spoke English and about 1,335,945 Spanish; for government and commercial purposes these two languages are commonly used. Some 77 native languages are spoken in the Philippines, of which 9 are of major importance; they belong to the Malayo-Polynesian family.

CLIMATE. Some areas have an equatorial climate while others experience tropical monsoon conditions, with a wet season extending from May to Nov. Mean temperatures are high all year, with very little variation. Manila. Jan. 77°F (25°C), July 82°F (27·8°C). Annual rainfall 82″ (2,083 mm).

CONSTITUTION AND GOVERNMENT. The republic was governed by a constitution adopted on 14 May 1935 and amended in 1939, 1940 and 1947. On 17 Jan. 1973 a new constitution was ratified naming President Marcos President and Prime Minister without a fixed term of office. The President is assisted by 26 ministers in charge of Foreign Affairs, Finance, Justice, Agriculture, Public Works and Highways, Transportation and Communications, Education and Culture, Labour and Employment, National Defence, Energy, Trade and Industry, Health, Social Services and Development, Agrarian Reform, Media Affairs, Local Government, Tourism, Natural Resources, Human Settlements, National Economic and Development Authority, Budget and Management, National Science and Technology Authority, the Presidential Executive Assistant, Muslim Affairs, Presidential Assistant on National Minorities and the Solicitor-General.

President: Ferdinand E. Marcos (re-elected for a third 6-year term in June 1981).
Prime Minister and Minister of Finance: Cesar Virata.

Martial law was introduced on 21 Sept. 1972. A referendum held in Dec. 1977 decreed that President Marcos should remain in power. On 12 June 1978 a limited experiment in parliamentary democracy began and the President also became Prime Minister. Limited power to legislate was given to the new Assembly but the right to legislate by decree was retained by the President and no date was given for lifting the martial law. On 17 Jan. 1981 martial law was lifted but the President retained wide powers under a National Security Code and Public Safety Act.

The 1973 Constitution provides that all male and female citizens 15 years of age or older who can read or write Spanish, English or a native dialect and who meet certain residential qualifications are entitled to vote.

The constitution vests in the republic all ownership of the country's natural resources, which, apart from public agricultural land, may not be alienated.

National flag: Horizontally blue over red, with a white triangle based on the hoist bearing a gold sun of 8 rays and 3 gold stars.

National hymn: 'Tierra Adorada', 'Land of the morning', lyric in English by M. A. Sane and C. Osias, in Spanish by José Palma (1899), tune by Julian Felipe (1898); 'Pambansang Awit ng Pilipinas', Tagalog lyric by the Institute of National Language, music by Julian Felipe.

Local Government. The country is administratively divided into 13 regions, 73 provinces, 60 cities, 1,493 municipalities, 21 municipal districts, 40,207 *barangays* with 241,242 councilmen. On 14 Nov. 1975 the name of provincial boards and city or municipal boards or councils was changed into *Sangguniang Bayan.* The latter assumes all the powers and responsibilities on matters of legislation of the defunct provincial, city or municipal boards.

The *Sangguniang Pambayan* is the direct successor of the old municipal council; *Sangguniang Panglunsod* for the old city council; *Sangguniang Panlalawigan* for the old provincial council and *Batasang Pambansa* for the defunct Congress.

DEFENCE. On 14 March 1947 the Philippine and US Governments signed a 99-year military-base arrangement since reduced to 25 years and will end in 1991. The USA was granted the use of a series of army, navy and air bases, with the right to use a number of others on mutual agreement. On 21 March a second agreement provided for a US Military Advisory Group as well as military assistance. A treaty of mutual assistance was signed in Washington on 30 Aug. 1951; the instruments of ratification were exchanged in Manila on 27 Aug. 1952. The Philippines is also a signatory of the S.E. Asia Collective Defence Treaty.

The Chief of Staff of the Armed Forces has overall command over the Army, Air Force, Navy and Constabulary.

Army. The Army comprises 5 infantry divisions, 1 special warfare brigade, 2 engineer brigades, 1 light armoured regiment and 4 artillery regiments. Equipment includes 28 Scorpion light tanks. Strength (1984) 60,000, with reserves totalling 90,000. There are also paramilitary forces; the Philippine Constabulary (44,000) and the Civil Home Defence Force (65,000).

Navy. The fleet includes 7 old frigates (3 former US destroyer escorts and 4 *ex*-USCG cutters, *ex*-USN seaplane tenders); 3 new fast missile craft; 10 corvettes (3 *ex*-US fleet minesweepers and 7 *ex*-US escorts), 2 *ex*-US PC-type patrol vessels, 6 other patrol craft, 5 gunboats, 59 coastal patrol craft, 1 training ship, 24 landing ships, 4 medium landing ships, 6 landing craft (3 LSSL and 3 LCU), 3 repair ships, 2 oilers, 3 water carriers, 1 supply ship, 4 survey ships, 5 tenders, 68 minor landing craft, 2 yachts (command ships), 6 tugs and 16 auxiliaries. There are some 30 patrol craft, cutters and tenders in the coast guard.

The Philippine Navy was considerably increased in 1976 by taking over many vessels (nearly all former US warships) from the Vietnamese Navy which escaped from Indo-China when the Saigon government collapsed in 1975. But some 60 of the larger ships are aged (40 years).

Naval personnel in 1984 totalled 1,600 officers and 13,070 men. There are also 330 officers and 6,500 enlisted men in the marine corps, and 300 officers and 1,700 men in the coast guard.

Air Force. The Air Force has a strength of 16,800 officers and men, with 390 aircraft, and was built up with US assistance. Its fighter-bomber wing is equipped with 1 squadron of F-5A/Bs and 1 squadron of F-8H Crusaders. There are transport, observation, air/sea rescue, helicopter and training units, for which recently acquired equipment has included 3 Fokker F27 Maritime patrol aircraft, a squadron of OV-1 Mohawk observation aircraft, 12 Australian-built Mission-master twin-turboprop STOL light transports, 8 HU-16 Albatross amphibians and a total of 48 Italian-built SF.260WP (armed) and SF.260MP piston-engined trainers. Many of the Air Force's other trainers are armed for counter-insurgency duties. No. 16 and 18 squadrons of the 15th Strike Wing each operate 16 T-28Ds. No. 17 has 16 SF.260WPs. Aircraft on order include 2 Sikorsky S-70A-5 assault helicopters and 17 S-76 utility helicopters.

Police. Public order is maintained partly through the Philippine constabulary and partly through the local police forces. The constabulary now forms part of the Armed Forces and has 27,000 personnel.

INTERNATIONAL RELATIONS

Membership. The Republic of the Philippines is a member of UN and the Colombo Plan.

External Debt. At 31 March 1983 the external debt amounted to US$13,520·4m.

ECONOMY

Budget. The revenues and expenditures of the central government for calendar years were, in 1m. Philippine pesos, as follows:

	1980	1981	1982¹	1983¹
Revenue	34,716	35,152	38,634	44,300
Expenditure	41,955	52,945	59,749	65,000

¹ Estimate.

Expenditure (1982) included (in 1m. pesos): National defence, 6,771; education, health and social services, 20,928; economic development, 17,155; public debt, 8,382.

At 30 June 1982 the total internal public debt outstanding of the national and local governments, including those of the government corporations, stood at P.53,868m.

Currency. Total money supply, Sept. 1983, was P.23,503·2m., of which P.12,369·6m. was currency in circulation and P.11,133·6m. were demand deposits. The coins used are: 5 *peso*, 1 *peso*, one-half *peso*, quarter *peso*, media *peseta* (10 *centavos*), all contain 70 grammes copper, 18 grammes zinc and 12 grammes nickel; 5 *centavo* in copper and zinc, and 1 *centavo* in aluminium and magnesium zinc. Central Bank notes are issued in 2, 5, 10, 20, 50, 100 *pesos* denominations.

In March 1984, £1 = 20·15 *pesos*; US$1 = 14·02 *pesos*.

Banking. On 31 July 1982 there were 1,815 branches of commercial banks operating under 34 head offices, with 4 overseas, 1 each in New York, Hong Kong, Taipei and London. Agencies exist in Honolulu, San Francisco and Los Angeles. Total deposits of the commercial banks in July 1982 were P.82,288·2m.

Under the law passed 15 June 1948 the Central Bank of the Philippines was created to have sole control of the credit and monetary supply, independent of the Treasury. It has a capital of P.10m. furnished solely by the Government. Its total assets, at 31 Dec. 1982 were P.91,691·8m.

Weights and Measures. The metric system of weights and measures was established by law in 1869, and since 1916 has come into general use.

ENERGY AND NATURAL RESOURCES

Electricity. Government and private electric systems furnish the Philippines with electric power, with total generating capacity of 5,002,800 mw (1983). The Manila Electric Co., was bought by the Government in July 1978. MECO plants generated a total of 2,207,964 mwh. in 1979 while the Government's National Power Corporation produced 10,282,411 mwh.; others, 303,073 mwh.

Minerals. Mineral production in 1981 (in tonnes): Lead concentrate, 1,992; nickel metal, 21,485; nickel direct shipping ore, 345,310; zinc concentrate, 100,479; copper concentrate, 1,120,382; cobalt metal, 997; coal, 318,170; salt, 355,289; gold, 23,435 kg; silver, 62,565 kg. Other minerals include cement, rock asphalt, sand and gravel.

Agriculture. Of the total area of 30m. hectares, 7·04m. hectares are commercial forests; 5·4m. hectares non-commercial forests; 794,000 hectares open grassland; 115,000 hectares mangrove and marshes; 14,794,000 hectares cultivated.

About 98·4% of the total cultivated area is owned by Filipinos; the average size of the farm was 2·63 hectares in 1980. The principal products are unhusked rice (palay), Manila hemp (abaca), copra, sugar-cane, maize and tobacco. During the first quarter of 1983 9,139,000 persons were employed in agriculture (50·17% of the working population).

The products (in tonnes) are (1982, provisional): Rough rice, 8·1m.; copra, 3·3m.; coconut, 3·8m.; sugar (centrifugal muscovado and molasses), 3·4m.; shelled corn, 3·3m.; tobacco, 46,400; abaca fibre, 119,700.

Minor crops are fruits, nuts, root crops, vegetables, onions, beans, coffee, cacao, peanuts, ramie, rubber, maguey and kapok.

Livestock, estimated in 1982: 2·8m. carabaos (water buffaloes), 1·9m. cattle, 7·8m. pigs, 1·6m. goats and 58m. poultry.

Forestry. The forests covered some 11,862,000 hectares in 1982. Log production, 4,514,000 cu. metres, of which 752,000 cu. metres were exported in 1982.

Fisheries. Fish production from all sources was 1,772,897 tonnes and was valued at P.13,953,798 in 1981.

INDUSTRY AND TRADE

Industry. Manufacturing is a major source of economic development contributing 24·9% to GNP in 1981. Leading growth sectors were textile, footwear and wearing apparel, chemical and chemical products, beverage industries and food manufacture. In 1980 (annual survey), there were 85,236 manufacturing establishments, of which 29,282 were engaged in food; 28,200 wearing apparel; 1,370 footwear; 4,472 textile; 1,076 beverages; 4 petroleum refineries; 3,465 furniture and fixtures; 4,743 fabricated metal products and 890 transport equipment. The non-agricultural labour force during the first quarter of 1983 was 9,115,000 out of a total of 19,408,000 employed.

Commerce. The values of imports and exports (f.o.b.) for calendar years are stated as follows in US$1m.:

	1979	1980	1981	1982
Imports	6,142	7,727	7,946	7,667
Exports	4,601	5,788	5,722	5,021

The principal exports in 1982 were (in US$1m.): Electronics, 961·9; garments, 541·3; sugar, 416; coconut oil (crude), 401; copper concentrates, 312·4; gold, 168·7; fresh bananas, 146·1; lumber, 123·7; iron ore agglomerates, 105·6; pineapple in syrup, 87·6.

Main imports in 1982 (in US$1m.): Mineral fuels, lubricants and related materials, 2,105; machinery other than electric, 988; base metals, 528; transport equipment, 295; electric machinery apparatus and appliances, 289; chemical elements and components, 259; cereals and cereal preparations, 242; explosives and miscellaneous chemical materials and products, 216; metal manufactures, 172; unmanufactured textile fibres, 99.

For over a half-century the foreign trade has been chiefly with the USA. The trade relationship of the two countries is governed by the Philippine Trade Act of 1946 as amended.

Total trade between the Philippines and UK (British Department of Trade returns, in £1,000 sterling):

	1978	1979	1980	1981	1982	1983
Imports to UK	63,447	81,122	99,018	105,535	127,061	160,701
Exports and re-exports from UK	115,038	105,709	88,998	85,650	97,908	102,949

Tourism. In 1982, 890,807 tourists visited the Philippines spending US$450m.

COMMUNICATIONS

Roads. In 1982 highways totalled 154,473·3 km; of this, 10,649·52 km were concrete; 17,598·54, asphalt; 54,759·46, earth; 71,465·78, macadam. In 1982 there were registered 1,087,180 motor vehicles of all types.

Railways. The National Railways totals 1,027 km of 1,067 mm gauge on Luzon, and Phividec Railways operates 116 km on Panay Island. In 1982, 5,657,091 passengers and 76,694 tonnes of freight were carried by rail.

Aviation. The Philippine Air Lines, Inc., with a working capital of P.292m., in 1981 carried 3,523,000 passengers, 55,234,396 kg of cargo and 928,676 kg of mail.

Shipping. In 1981, 71,787 vessels of 24,608,624 net tons entered and 71,796 vessels of 23,834,150 net tons cleared all ports.

Post and Broadcasting. In 1982 there were in operation 2,108 post offices and 1,438 telegraph stations. The Philippine Long Distance Telephone Co. had 732,742 telephones in service in 1982 while other major operators had 61,827 connexions.

Licensed radio stations in 1982 numbered 33,138, including 2,934 ship stations and 702 aircraft stations.

Newspapers (1979). There were 300 registered publications (210 published in Manila), 15 of which were dailies.

JUSTICE, RELIGION, EDUCATION AND WELFARE

Justice. There is a Supreme Court which is composed of a chief justice and 14 associate justices; it can declare a law or treaty unconstitutional by the concurrent votes of the majority sitting. There is an intermediate appellate court, which consists of a presiding appellate justice and 49 associate appellate justices. There are 13 regional trial courts, one for each judicial region, with a presiding regional trial judge in its 720 branches. There is a metropolitan trial court in each metropolitan area established by law, a municipal trial court in each of the other cities or municipalities and a municipal circuit trial court in each area defined as a municipal circuit comprising one or more cities and/or one or more municipalities.

The Supreme Court may designate certain branches of the regional trial courts to handle exclusively criminal cases, juvenile and domestic relations cases, agrarian cases, urban land reform cases which do not fall under the jurisdiction of quasijudicial bodies and agencies and/or such other special cases as the Supreme Court may determine.

Religion. In 1970 there were 31,169,488 Roman Catholics, 1,434,688 Aglipayans, 1,584,963 Moslems, 1,122,999 Protestants, 475,407 members of the Iglesia ni Kristo, 33,639 Buddhists and 863,302 others.

The Roman Catholics are organized in 12 archbishoprics, 30 bishoprics, 12 prelatures nullius, 4 apostolic vicariates, 4 apostolic prefectures and some 1,633 parishes. The Philippine Independent Church, founded in 1902, and comprising about 3·9% of the population, denies the spiritual authority of the Roman Pontiff. It is divided into two groups, one of which has accepted ordinations by the Episcopalian Church.

Education. Formal education consists of 3 levels: elementary, secondary and further education Public elementary education is free and public elementary schools are established in almost every *barangay* or *barrio*. The majority of the secondary and post-secondary schools are private, sectarian or non-sectarian. The number of years required to complete the elementary and secondary levels are 6 and 4 years respectively, while the tertiary level requires at least 4 years for an academic degree. Pre-school education is also offered mostly in private schools to children from ages 3–6.

Non-formal education consists of adult literacy classes, agricultural and farming training programmes, occupation skills training, youth clubs, and community programmes of instructions in health, nutrition, family planning and co-operatives.

Public and private schools in 1981–82 enrolled 8·5m. pupils in primary schools, 2·9m. in secondary schools and 1·3m. students in further education. The University of the Philippines (founded in 1908) had 34,531 students in 1982–83.

Health. In 1981 there were 43,736 registered physicians and (1982) 80,465 hospital beds.

Social Welfare. The Government programme includes the construction of urban and rural housing units for lease or sale to middle and low-income families to ease the housing problem, the settlement of landless families, the opening of rural farm-to-market roads, the setting up of rural schools and rural health units, the granting of loans to farmers, fishermen and small cottage industries, self-employment assistance to the most disadvantaged persons and practical skills development and job placement services to out-of-school youths, jobless family heads and disabled persons, and the extension of emergency services like rescue and relief operations in times of typhoons, earthquakes, fires and other calamities.

DIPLOMATIC REPRESENTATIVES

Of the Philippines in Great Britain (9 A Palace Green, London, W8 4QE)
Ambassador: José V. Cruz (accredited 17 Dec. 1982).

Of Great Britain in the Philippines (115 Esteban St., Manila)
Ambassador: M. H. Morgan, CMG.

Of the Philippines in the USA (1617 Massachusetts Ave., NW, Washington, D.C., 20036)
Ambassador: Benjamin T. Romualdez.

Of the USA in the Philippines (1201 Roxas Blvd., Manila)
Ambassador: Michael H. Armacost.

Of the Philippines to the United Nations
Ambassador: Luis Moreno-Salcedo.

Books of Reference

Philippine Yearbook 1983. National Census and Statistics Office, Manila, 1983
Gazetteer of the Philippine Islands. United States Department of Commerce. Washington, 1945
Foreign Trade Statistics of the Philippines, 1982. National Census and Statistics Office, Manila, 1982
Burley, T. M., *The Philippines. An Economic and Social Geography.* London, 1973
Chapman. A., *Philippine Nationalism.* New York, 1950
Golay, F. H., *The Philippines: Public Policy and National Economic Development.* Cornell Univ. Press, 1961
Hainsworth, R. G., and Moyser, R. T., *Agricultural Geography of the Philippine Islands.* Washington, 1945
Lightfort, K., *The Philippines.* London, 1973

PITCAIRN
ISLAND

HISTORY. It was discovered by Carteret in 1767, but remained uninhabited until 1790, when it was occupied by 9 mutineers of HMS *Bounty*, with 12 women and 6 men from Tahiti. Nothing was known of their existence until the island was visited in 1808. In 1856 the population having become too large for the island's resources, the inhabitants (194 in number) were, at their own request, removed to Norfolk Island; but 43 of them returned in 1859–64.

AREA AND POPULATION. Pitcairn Island (1·75 sq. miles; 4·6 sq. km) is situated in the Pacific Ocean, nearly equidistant from New Zealand and Panama (25° 04′S. lat., 130° 06′ W. long). The population has been declining and on 30 June 1983 it was 61.

The uninhabited islands of Henderson (12 sq. miles), Ducie (1½ sq. miles) and Oeno (2 sq. miles) were annexed in 1902 and are included in the Pitcairn group.

CLIMATE. An equable climate, with average annual rainfall of 80″ (2,000 mm), spread evenly throughout the year. Mean monthly temperatures range from 75°F (24°C) in Jan. to 66°F (19°C) in July.

CONSTITUTION. Pitcairn was brought within the jurisdiction of the High Commissioner for the Western Pacific in 1898 and transferred to the Governor of Fiji in 1952. When Fiji became independent in Oct. 1970, the British High Commissioner in New Zealand was appointed Governor.

The Local Government Ordinance of 1964 constitutes a Council of 10 members, of whom 4 are elected, 5 are nominated (3 by the 4 elected members and 2 by the Governor) and the Island Secretary is an *ex-officio* member. The Island Magistrate, who is elected triennially, presides over the Council; other members hold office for only 1 year. Liaison between Governor and Council is through a Commissioner in the Auckland, New Zealand, office of the British Consulate-General.

TRADE. Fruit, vegetables and curios are sold to passing ships; fuel oil, machinery, building materials, flour, sugar and other foodstuffs are imported.

Governor: Sir Richard Stratton, KCMG (resides in Wellington).
Island Magistrate: Ivan Christian (re-elected Dec. 1981).

Books of Reference

A Guide to Pitcairn. Pitcairn Island Administration, Auckland, revised ed. 1982
Ball, I., *Pitcairn: Children of the Bounty.* London, 1973
Ross, A. S. C., and Moverly, A. W., *The Pitcairnese Language.* London, 1964

POLAND

Polska Rzeczpospolita Ludowa

Capital: Warsaw
Population: 36·4m. (1983)
GNP per capita: US$3,900 (1980)

HISTORY. In 1966 Poland celebrated its millennium, but modern Polish history begins with the partitions of the once-powerful kingdom between Russia, Austria and Prussia in 1772, 1793 and 1795. For 19th century events *see* THE STATESMAN'S YEAR-BOOK 1980–81.

On 10 Nov. 1918 independence was proclaimed by Józef Piłsudski, the founder of the Polish Legions during the war. On 28 June 1919 the Treaty of Versailles recognized the independence of Poland.

On 1 Sept. 1939 Germany invaded Poland, on 17 Sept. 1939 Russian troops entered eastern Poland, and on 29 Sept. 1939 the fourth partition of Poland took place. After the German attack on Russia, the Germans occupied the whole of Poland. By March 1945 the country had been liberated by the Russians.

In July 1944 the USSR recognized the Polish Committee of National Liberation *(Polski Komitet Wyzwolenia Narodowego)* established in Lublin as an executive organ of the National Council of the Homeland *(Krajowa Rada Narodowa)*. The Committee was transformed into the Provisional Government in Dec. 1944, and on 28 June 1945, supplemented by members of the Polish Government in London (which had been recognized by the UK and USA), it was re-established—in Moscow—as the Polish Provisional Government of National Unity and on 6 July recognized as such by the UK and USA.

Elections were held on 19 Jan. 1947. Of the 12·7m. votes cast, 11·24m. were recognized as valid and 9m. were given for the Communist-dominated 'Democratic Bloc'. After riots in Poznań in June 1956 nationalist anti-Stalinist elements gained control of the Communist Party, under the leadership of Wladyslaw Gomułka.

In 1970 the Federal Republic of Germany recognized Poland's western boundary as laid down by the Potsdam Conference of 1945 (the 'Oder–Neisse line').

In Dec. 1970 strikes and riots in Gdańsk, Szczecin and Gdynia led to the resignation of a number of leaders including Gomułka. He was replaced by Edward Gierek.

The introduction of price rises in June 1976 was again followed by strikes and riots. The rises were withdrawn and some demonstrators were imprisoned. In the campaign of protest which followed a Committee for the Defence of the Workers (KOR) was formed.

The raising of meat prices on 1 July 1980 resulted in a wave of strikes which broadened into generalized wage demands and eventually by mid-Aug. acquired a political character. Workers in Gdańsk, Gdynia and Sopot elected a joint strike committee, led by Lech Wałęsa demanding the right to strike and form independent Trade Unions, the abolition of censorship, access to the media and the release of political prisoners.

Gierek offered pay rises, but no political concessions at first.

However, on 24 Aug. Gierek reshuffled the Party and Government leadership, and Józef Pińkowski replaced Edward Babiuch as Prime Minister. On 31 Aug. the Government and Wałęsa signed the 'Gdańsk Agreements' permitting the formation of independent Trade Unions.

On 5 Sept. Gierek suffered a heart attack and was replaced as First Secretary by Stanislaw Kania (Gierek was expelled from the Party in July 1981). On 17 Sept. various Trade Unions decided to form a national confederation ('Solidarity') and applied for legal status, which was granted on 24 Oct. after some Government resistance. A reference inserted into its charter to the supremacy of the party was removed by the Supreme Court on 10 Nov.

On 9 Feb. Pińkowski was replaced as Prime Minister by the Defence Minister, Gen. Wojciech Jaruzelski who proposed a reconstruction of the Government to tackle the economic crisis. At an extraordinary Communist Party congress in July a new leadership was elected. At Solidarity's first national congress (4–10 Sept. and 2–8 Oct. 1981) Wałęsa was re-elected chairman and a radical programme of action was adopted. On 18 Oct. Kania resigned from the Party leadership and was replaced by Jaruzelski. On 13 Dec. 1981 the Government imposed martial law (*stan wojenny*), banning a wide range of civil liberties, and establishing the rule of a 20-member Military Council of National Salvation (WRON). Solidarity was proscribed and its leaders detained. Government control was consolidated only after mass arrests and some bloodshed. The proclamation of martial law was retro-actively approved by the Sejm on 26 Jan. 1982 with only one dissident vote and 5 abstentions. The Party Central Committee similarly approved the measure on 25 Feb. Wałęsa was released in Nov. 1982. On 8 Oct. the Sejm voted (with 12 dissident votes and 9 abstentions) a law dissolving all registered trade unions including Solidarity. These have been replaced by workplace unions which are required to pledge support for the Communist Party and the Constitution. No alternative unions are permitted. In Dec. 1982 martial law was suspended. Internment was ended and the Army withdrawn from many sectors of public life. Martial law was finally lifted in July 1983, although certain special legislation remains in force. An amnesty was granted which covers the majority of those sentenced by martial law courts.

AREA AND POPULATION. Poland is bounded north by the Baltic and the RSFSR, east by Lithuania, White Russia and the Ukraine, south by Czecho-slovakia and west by the German Democratic Republic. Poland comprises an area of 312,683 sq. km (120,628 sq. miles). The country is divided into 49 voivodships (*wojewodztwo*) (including 3 urban: Warsaw, Kraków and Łódź) and these in turn are divided into 803 towns and 2,070 wards (*gmina*). The capital is Warsaw (Warszawa).

Area (in sq. km) and population (in 1,000, with urban in brackets) in 1981.

Voivodship	Area	Population	Voivodship	Area	Population
Biała Podlaska	5,348	288 (87)	Opole	8,535	979 (491)
Białystok	10,055	647 (358)	Ostrołęka	6,498	373 (109)
Bielsko–Biała	3,703	840 (408)	Piła	8,205	442 (234)
Bydgoszcz	10,349	1,043 (649)	Piotrków	6,266	613 (264)
Chełm	3,865	233 (89)	Płock	5,117	497 (215)
Ciechanów	6,362	407 (127)	Poznań	8,151	1,249 (866)
Częstochowa	6,182	751 (374)	Przemyśl	4,436	382 (132)
Elbląg	6,103	446 (257)	Radom	7,295	706 (296)
Gdańsk	7,394	1,345 (1,027)	Rzeszów	4,398	656 (236)
Gorzów	8,484	462 (276)	Siedlce	8,499	621 (166)
Jelenia Góra	4,378	495 (317)	Sieradz	4,869	392 (122)
Kalisz	6,512	673 (295)	Skierniewice	3,959	399 (162)
Katowice	6,650	3,806 (3,336)	Słupsk	7,453	374 (198)
Kielce	9,211	1,075 (461)	Suwałki	10,490	426 (202)
Konin	5,139	444 (165)	Szczecin	9,981	907 (670)
Koszalin	8,470	465 (282)	Tarnobrzeg	6,283	560 (185)
Kraków (Cracow)	3,255	1,177 (812)	Tarnów	4,151	613 (203)
Krosno	5,702	453 (143)	Toruń	5,348	616 (372)
Legnica	4,037	466 (298)	Wałbrzych	4,168	718 (522)
Leszno	4,154	361 (161)	Warsaw	3,788	2,342 (2,069)
Łódź	1,525	1,136 (1,038)	Włocławek	4,402	415 (181)
Łomża	6,684	328 (108)	Wrocław	6,287	1,083 (782)
Lublin	6,793	944 (508)	Zamość	6,980	476 (111)
Nowy Sącz	5,577	634 (224)	Zielona Góra	8,868	615 (385)
Olsztyn	12,320	690 (382)			

Population (in 1,000) of the largest towns (1982):

Warsaw	1,628	Bydgoszcz	356	Radom	198
Łódź	845	Lublin	314	Zabrze	196
Kraków (Cracow)	723	Sosnowiec	255	Kielce	192
Wrocław (Breslau)	627	Częstochowa	238	Toruń	183
Poznań	563	Bytom	238	Tychy	177
Gdańsk (Danzig)	462	Gdynia	237	Bielsko-Biala	170
Szczecin (Stettin)	390	Białystok	230	Ruda Śląska	162
Katowice	366	Gliwice	202	Chorzów	158

At the census of 7 Dec. 1978 the population was 35,032,000 (17m. males; 58% urban). Population on 1 Jan. 1983, 36,399,000 (18·7m. females; 21·7m. urban), density, 116 per sq. km. Vital statistics, 1982 (per 1,000): Marriages, 8·7; divorces, 1·3; live births, 19·4; deaths, 9·2; infant mortality (per 1,000 live births), 20·4.

The rate of natural growth, 1982, 10·2 per 1,000. Expectation of life in 1981 was 66·9 years for males, 75·4 years for females. In 1981, 50% of the population was under 30.

In 1969, 10·33m. Poles lived abroad (6·5m. in USA, 1·4m. in USSR, 150,000 (1976) in UK). In 1982 there were 900 immigrants and 32,100 emigrants.

CLIMATE. Climate is continental, marked by long and severe winters. Rainfall amounts are moderate, with a marked summer maximum. Warsaw. Jan. 26°F (–3·5°C), July 66°F (19°C). Annual rainfall 22·1'' (553 mm).

CONSTITUTION AND GOVERNMENT. The present Constitution was adopted on 22 July 1952. Amendments were adopted in 1976 and 1983.

The titular head of state is the Chairman of the Council of State, Henryk Jabłoński.

Since 1983 the Constitution has defined the position of political parties as follows: 'The alliance and cooperation of the Polish United Workers' (*i.e.* Communist) Party with the United Peasant Party and the Democratic Party in the construction of socialism and their cooperation with those social organizations and associations that are grounded in the principles of the system of the Polish People's Republic form the basis of the Patriotic Movement of National Renaissance.' The latter was set up on 24 Nov. 1982 to replace the National Unity Front.

At the 9th, extraordinary, congress of the Communist Party on 19 July 1981 a new Politburo was elected by democratic vote. Only four of the 16 former members were re-elected. Changes were made in the Party and Government leadership in July and Oct. 1982. In March 1984 the Politburo consisted of: Wojciech Jaruzelski *(First Secretary and Prime Minister)*; Kazimerz Barcikowski; Tadeusz Czechowicz; Józef Czyrek; Zofia Grzyb; Stanisław Kalkus; Hieronim Kubiak; Zbigniew Messner *(Deputy Prime Minister responsible for coordination)*; Mirosław Milewski; Stefan Olszowski *(Foreign Minister)*; Stanisław Opalko; Tadeusz Porebski; Jerzy Romanik; Albin Siwak; Marian Wozniak. Candidate members: Stanisław Bejger; Jan Główczyk; Czesław Kiszczak *(Minister of the Interior)*; Włodzimierz Mokrzyszczak; Marian Orzechowski; Gen. Florian Siwicki *(Defence)*. Ministers not in the Politburo include: Zenon Komender *(Catholic representative)*, Edward Kowalczyk; Zbigniew Madej; Roman Malinowski; Janusz Obodowski; Mieczysław Rakowski; Zbigniew Szalajda *(Deputy Prime Ministers)*; Gen. Tadeusz Hupałowski *(Chairman, Supreme Chamber of Control)*; Zdzisław Krasiński *(Minister responsible for prices)*; Władysław Baka *(Plenipotentiary for the economic reform)*; Włodzimierz Oliwa *(Administration and Environment)*; Stanisław Zieba *(Agriculture and Food)*; Stanisław Niekarz *(Finance)*; Tadeusz Nesterowicz *(Foreign Trade)*; Zygmunt Łakomiec *(Home Trade)*; Sylwester Zawadzki *(Justice)*; Stefan Ciosek *(Labour)*; Manfred Gorywoda *(Chairman, State Planning Commission)*.

In 1983 the Polish United Workers' Party had 2,340,900 (3,091,900 in 1980) members (40% workers), and in 1981 the United Peasants' Party had 463,100, and the Democratic Party, 112,000 members.

The authority of the republic is vested in the Sejm, elected for 4 years by all citizens over 18. The Sejm elects a Council of State, composed of a Chairman, the Secretary and 14 members, including 4 vice-chairmen; and a Council of Ministers. Local government is carried out by People's Councils elected every 4 years at voivodship and community level. Alongside these are the offices of state administration. The chairman of the People's Council is the Secretary of the regional organization for the area.

The last local elections were held on 23 March 1980.

The last elections for the Sejm were held on 23 March 1980. 646 candidates stood on the single list of the National Unity Front and obtained 99·52% of the vote. 98·87% of the electorate voted. The 460 seats are distributed as follows: 261

United Workers' Party, 113 United Peasants' Party, 37 Democratic Party, 49 independents, including 5 Catholic representatives nominated by the Government but repudiated by the Church. There are 106 women deputies.

National flag: Horizontally white over red.

National anthem: Jeszcze Polska nie zginęla (words by J. Wybicki, 1797; tune by M. Ogiński, 1796).

DEFENCE. A National Defence Committee was set up in Nov. 1983 with Gen. Jaruzelski at its head. Poland is divided into 3 military districts: Warsaw (the eastern part of Poland); Pomerania (Baltic coast, part of central Poland; headquarters at Bydgoszcz); Silesia (Silesia and southern Poland; headquarters at Wrocław).

Armed forces are on Soviet lines and divided into army and air force (2 years' conscription), navy (3 years), anti-aircraft, rocket and radio-technological units (3 years) and internal security forces (2 years). In 1965 the security forces were taken away from the Ministry of Internal Affairs and placed under the Defence Ministry. The military age extends from the 19th to the 50th year. The strength of the armed forces was (1983) 317,500, plus 85,000 security and frontier forces. Security forces include armoured brigades.

Army. The Army consists of 5 armoured, 8 mechanized, 1 airborne and 1 amphibious assault divisions; 3 artillery brigades and 1 regiment; 3 anti-tank regiments; 4 surface-to-surface missile brigades; 1 air defence brigade and 5 regiments. Equipment includes 3,400 T-54/-55 and 50 T-72 main battle tanks. Strength (1984) 230,000 (including 158,000 conscripts).

Navy. The fleet comprises 4 submarines, 1 destroyer, 24 fleet minesweepers, 13 missile craft, 23 patrol boats, 10 torpedo boats, 45 coastal patrol boats, 3 inshore minesweepers, 23 medium landing ships, 3 intelligence vessels, 8 training ships, 3 degaussing vessels, 2 salvage ships, 2 torpedo recovery vessels, 20 minor landing craft, 23 minesweeping boats, 3 surveying vessels, 7 oilers, 20 tugs and 40 auxiliaries and tenders. The Fleet Air Arm has 50 fixed-wing aircraft (MiG-17) and 20 helicopters. Personnel in 1984 totalled 22,500 comprising 7,500 afloat, 2,000 under training, 5,000 of coastal defence, 2,000 in naval aviation and 6,000 on shore support.

Air Force. The Air Force has a strength of some 88,000 officers and men and 700 first-line jet aircraft of Soviet design, forming 4 air divisions. There are 11 air defence regiments (33 squadrons) with about 400 MiG-21 supersonic interceptors, and 6 regiments (18 squadrons) operating variable-geometry MiG-23BM and Su-20, Su-7B and MiG-17 close-support fighters. Another fighter division supports the Navy. There are also reconnaissance, ECM, transport, helicopter (including Mi-24 gunship) and training units. Soviet 'Guideline' 'Goa', 'Ganef', 'Gainful' and 'Gaskin' surface-to-air missiles are operational.

Two Soviet armoured divisions are stationed on Polish territory.

INTERNATIONAL RELATIONS

Membership. Poland is a member of UN, Comecon and the Warsaw Pact.

Planning. For planning history until 1980 *see* THE STATESMAN'S YEAR-BOOK 1981–82, p.1002. Industrialization without sufficient expenditure on infrastructure; neglect of agriculture and the inefficiency of the planning mechanism, exacerbated by higher prices and declining Western demand for exports, and the social unrest since 1980, have brought the economy to a state of paralysis. Some foodstuffs are rationed, and price increases were introduced in Feb. 1982. and Jan. 1984. In Apr. 1982 a Consultative Economic Council was set up as an advisory body to the Government. A socio-economic plan for 1983–85 has the task of overcoming the economic crisis.

Budget. Budget in 1m. złotys, for calendar years:

	1977	1978	1979	1980	1981	1982
Revenue	993.948	1,103,457	1,154,800	1,215,200	1,334,600	2,346,100
Expenditure	887,599	994,158	1,107,700	1,246,200	1,465,600	2,433,600

Main items of 1982 revenue (in 1m. złotys): Sales tax and profits tax from state enterprises, 1,865,900; finance and insurance, 376,300; income tax, 20,900.
Main items of 1982 expenditure (in 1m. złotys): State enterprises, 1,095,900; welfare, 213,600; defence, 174,000; administration, 105,000; education, 192,900.

Currency. The currency unit is the *złoty*, divided into 100 *groszy*. The currency consists of notes of 10, 20, 50, 100, 500, 1,000, 2,000 and 5,000 złotys; and of coins of 10, 20 and 50 groszy and 1, 2, 5, 10, 20 and 50 złotys. In Jan. 1982 the złoty was substantially devalued against Western currencies. In March 1984, £1 sterling = 162 złotys, US$1 = 95 złotys.

Banking. The National Bank of Poland (established 1945) is the central bank, has exclusive authority to issue currency, is charged with control of money and credit, and has responsibility for financial implementation of the national economic plan. Since its merger with the former Investment Bank on 1 Jan. 1970 it exercises centralized control over investment financing. The Food Economics Bank (Bank Gospodarki Żywnościowej) has exclusive responsibility for direct financing of rural areas through both short-term and investment loans. It operates banks. The General Savings Bank (Powszechna Kasa Oszczedności) exercises central control over savings activities, transfers and checking transactions, including activities of workers' co-operative banks.

In addition to the National Bank of Poland other authorized foreign-exchange banks are, the Polish Welfare Bank (Bank Polska Kasa Opieki SA) and the Commercial Bank of Warsaw (Bank Handlowy w Warszawie SA).

Deposits in savings institutions amounted to 866,900m. złotys on 31 Dec. 1982.

Weights and Measures. The metric system is in general use.

ENERGY AND NATURAL RESOURCES

Energy. Power sources in 1979: Coal, 76%; lignite, 22%; hydroelectric, 2%. A nuclear power station is being built at Zarnowiec.

Minerals. Poland is a major producer of coal (reserves of some 71,000m. tonnes) and sulphur. Copper reserves are estimated at 10m. tonnes. There is also iron ore, lead and zinc. Production in 1982 (in 1,000 tonnes): Coal, 189,000; brown coal, 37,600; copper ore, 27,030; zinc-lead ores, 5,341; iron ore, 49.

Agriculture. In 1982 there were 18·9m. hectares of agricultural land, of which 14·3m. hectares were in private hands, 3·58m. in state farms, 0·74m. in co-operatives and 0·12m. in agricultural circles. There were 2·9m. private farms in 1982. Private holdings average 5·3 hectares, and may not exceed 100 hectares. 11m. hectares were arable, 233,000 orchards, 1·9m. meadows, 1m. pasture lands.

Collectivization has been largely abandoned but remains a long-term aim. There were 2,248 co-operatives in 1982. A new agricultural policy of 1981 gave more autonomy to co-operatives, linked wages to productivity and equalized resources between the state and private sectors. The peasants' trade union 'Rural Solidarity' won recognition in 1981 but was dissolved in Oct. 1982. A compulsory contributory pension scheme was introduced in 1978 for farmers who turn over their farms to their successors or the State. 250,000 such pensions had been paid by June 1980. 'Agricultural circles' numbered 26,000 with 2·2m. members in 1982. In 1981 there were 4,233 state agricultural holdings.

Crops	Area (1,000 hectares)			Yield (1,000 tonnes)		
	1980	1981	1982	1980	1981	1982
Wheat	1,609	1,418	1,456	4,175	4,203	4,476
Rye	3,039	3,002	3,273	6,566	6,731	7,792
Barley	1,322	1,294	1,236	3,420	3,540	3,647
Oats	997	1,156	1,086	2,245	2,730	2,608
Potatoes	2,344	2,258	2,178	26,391	42,562	31,951
Sugar-beet	460	470	493	10,139	15,867	15,085

Livestock (1982): 11·9m. cattle (5·8m. cows), 19·5m. pigs, 3·9m. sheep, 1·7m. horses, 61m. poultry. Milk production in 1982 was 14,749m. litres.
Tractors in use in 1982: 694,000 (in 15-h.p. units).

Forestry. In 1982, 8·4m. hectares were forests (predominantly coniferous). 61,000 hectares were afforested in 1982, and 23·3m. cu. metres of timber gained.

Fisheries. In 1981 the fishing fleet had 103 deep-sea vessels totalling 315,900 GRT. In 1982 the catch was 582,400 tonnes.

INDUSTRY AND TRADE

Industry. Production in 1981 (and 1982) (in 1,000 tonnes): Coke, 17,900 (17,300); pig-iron, 9,351 (8,524); crude steel, 15,719 (14,795); rolled steel, 11,064 (10,478); cement, 14,200 (16,035); sulphuric acid (100%), 2,776 (2,682); fertilizers, 2,242 (2,281); aluminium, 66 (43); electrolytic copper, 327 (348); lead, 69 (79); zinc, 167 (165); crude oil, 315 (240); salt, 4,271 (4,328); sugar, 1,685 (1,777); electricity, 115,000m. kwh. (118,000m.); natural gas, 6,172m. cu. metres (5,533m.). In 1982, 34 ships over 100 DWT were built (358,000 DWT), 229,000 cars, 37,800 lorries and 9,500 buses were built in 1982.

Output of light industry in 1981 (and 1982): Cotton fabrics, 738m. metres (693); woollen fabrics, 106m. metres (91); silk and synthetic fibres, 142m. metres (128); shoes, 145m. pairs (143); household glass, 71,500 tonnes (67,400); paper, 909,000 tonnes (966,000); washing machines 625,000 (712,000), refrigerators 553,000, and TV sets 764,400 (576,400).

Labour. In 1982 the total number in employment was 16·8m. (including 7·7m. women), of whom 12·2m. worked in the state-controlled sector and 4·6m. in the private sector, and including in agriculture 5m., industry 5m., building 1·2m., trade 1·3m. and transport and communications 1·1m. Founded in Aug. 1980 the 'independent self-governing union' organization Solidarity (Chairman Lech Wałęsa) was proscribed in Dec. 1981 and dissolved in Oct. 1982 along with all other trade unions. Some 2,500 new unions began operating in Jan. 1983 at workplace level and in national federations after Jan. 1984. Membership of Solidarity had been 9,447,000 in Sept. 1981. Average wage in 1982, 11,138 złotys per month. A law of Oct. 1982 makes voluntary unemployment an offence; offenders are liable for compulsory labour for the state.

Commerce. Trade statistics for calendar years (in 1m. złotys):

	1977	1978	1979	1980	1981 [1]	1982
Imports	48,600	50,938	54,015	58,299	963,447 (52,013)	862,040
Exports	40,800	44,685	50,141	51,908	846,209 (44,529)	947,384

[1] 'Official statistics for 1980 and before were expressed in exchange rate złotys, but thereafter in convertible złotys. The dramatic increase for 1981 is therefore only apparent. To facilitate comparison, the exchange rate złotys figure is also given (in brackets) for 1981.

Main imports in 1982 (in tonnes): Petroleum, 13·2m.; iron ore, 13·5m.; fertilizers, 5·7m.; wheat, 3·6m.; coal, 1m.; passenger cars, 46,759 units.

Main exports in 1982 (in tonnes): Coal, 28·5m.; coke, 1·7m.; sawn softwood, 616,000 cu. m.; ships, 334,000 DWT.

54% of Poland's trade is with Comecon countries.

Foreign trade deals should be made directly with the appropriate foreign trade enterprise. Information may be obtained from the Polish Chamber of Foreign Trade, Trebacka 4, 00–950 Warsaw. Joint ventures with Western firms are encouraged both at home and abroad. The Western partner may own up to 49% of the shares of ventures on Polish soil, and is guaranteed a share of profits and interest.

An over-ambitious programme of imports coinciding with the world recession and rise in oil prices was followed by a decline in output caused by the social and economic unrest of 1980–82. In 1982 Poland officially acknowledged debts to the West of 2,147,400m. złotys and to Comecon countries of 254,800m. złotys. Total hard currency debt to the West was US$27,000m. Western economic sanctions imposed in Dec. 1981 as a mark of disapproval of martial law were relaxed in Nov. 1983 and Jan. 1984, and talks began on rescheduling Poland's debts. Poland does not accept liability for the £495,000 debts of pre-war Danzig (Gdańsk). 1982 saw a 27% drop in Western imports and a trade surplus of £250m.

Soviet exports include plant and equipment and raw materials; Polish exports, machinery, ships, coal, chemicals and consumer goods.

Total trade between Poland and UK for 5 years (British Department of Trade returns £1,000 sterling):

	1979	1980	1981	1982	1983
Imports to UK	229,318	194,523	133,605	151,737	177,057
Exports and re-exports from UK	260,606	296,254	175,728	133,340	151,721

An Anglo-Polish 10-year agreement on the development of economic, industrial, scientific and technical co-operation was signed on 20 March 1973, and a 10-year programme implementing this was signed on 4 Sept. 1975. Some Polish imports are subject to quota restrictions.

In Oct. 1982 the US suspended Poland's most-favoured-nation status in retaliation to the proscription of Solidarity.

Tourism. In 1982, 1,404,000 tourists visited Poland (388,000 from the West) and 995,000 Polish citizens made visits abroad (317,000 to the West).

COMMUNICATIONS

Roads. In 1982 Poland had 150,177 km of hard-surfaced roads. A road-improvement programme is bringing 75% of all roads up to suitability for heavy traffic. Number of motor vehicles: Passenger cars, 2,634,000 (of which, 2,587,000 private); lorries, 641,000 (180,000 private); motor cycles, 1,751,000.

In 1982 road transport carried 2,320m. passengers and 1,379m. tonnes of freight.

Railways. The length of the standard gauge railway system was (1982) 24,347 km (7,410 km electrified). In 1981 the railways carried 402m. tons of freight and 1,114m. passengers.

Aviation. In 1984 the state airline 'Lot' had 37 aircraft including 5 Il-62s, operated 10 internal routes and flew services to 30 countries. 907,000 passengers were flown and 9,000 tonnes of freight in 1982. There are British Airways, SABENA, KLM, PANAM, Alitalia, Swissair, Air France, Austrian Airlines and Lufthansa services to Okęcie (Warsaw) airport.

Shipping. The principal ports are Gdynia, Gdańsk (Danzig) and Szczecin (Stettin). The merchant marine is grouped into Polish Ocean Lines (179 vessels totalling 1·04m. DWT in 1975) based on Gdynia and operating regular liner services, and the Polish Shipping Company based on Szczecin and operating cargo services. Poland also has a share in the Gdynia America Line. There are 4,040 km of inland navigable waterways. 13·7m. tonnes of freight were carried in 1982.

In 1982 the merchant marine had 317 vessels totalling 3,005,000 GRT (including 19 vessels over 30,000 tons). There are regular lines to London, Hull, China, Indonesia, Australia, Vietnam and some African and Latin-American countries.

Total shipping entering Polish ports in 1982 was 7,242 vessels of 19·7m. NRT. Freight traffic in 1982 was 39·2m.

Pipeline. In 1982 there were 1,975 km of oil pipeline.

Post and Broadcasting. In 1982 there were 8,155 post offices and 3,648,000 telephones.

Polskie Radio i Telewizja broadcasts 3 programmes in Polish on long-, medium- and short-waves and on FM. There are 2 TV programmes. Colour programmes are transmitted by SECAM system. Wireless licences in 1982 numbered 8·87m.; television licences, 8·34m.

Cinemas and Theatres. In 1982 there were 2,089 cinemas, 96 theatres and 46 concert halls. Cinema attendance was 89·5m.; theatres, 7·4m.

Newspapers (1982). There were 90 papers with an overall circulation (in 1981) of 2,437m. 1,870 periodicals were published. The Party newspaper is *Trybuna Ludu* (People's Tribune), weekend circulation 1·1m.

JUSTICE, RELIGION, EDUCATION AND WELFARE

Justice. The penal code was adopted in 1969. Espionage and treason carry the severest penalties For minor crimes there is provision for probation sentences and fines. A more liberal law of censorship came into force on 1 Oct. 1981. Trade union publications are freed from censorship, but restrictions remain on matters concerning national security, foreign policy, foreign allies and morals. The Censor's office has been placed under the Council of State, and its rulings are subject to appeal.

There exist the following courts: The Supreme Court; voivodship, district and special courts. Judges and lay assessors are elected. The State Council elects the judges of the Supreme Court for a term of 5 years, and appoints the Prosecutor-General. The office of the Prosecutor-General is separate from the judiciary.

Family courts were established (1977) for cases involving divorce and domestic relations.

Religion. In 1978, 93% of the population was baptized into the Catholic Church, and 78% of the population attended church regularly. Church–State relations are regulated by agreements of 1950, 1956 and 1972. A joint government-episcopal commission was reactivated in Sept. 1980, and religious broadcasting began. The Church has a university (Lublin), an Academy of Catholic Theology and a seminary in every diocese. Religious education of children is conducted in 'catechism centres' of which there were 18,254 in 1973–74.

The archbishop of Warsaw and Gniezno is the primate of Poland (since 1981, Cardinal Józef Glemp). The Vatican considers the archbishoprics of Lwów and Vilnius (incorporated in the USSR in 1940) as still being under Polish jurisdiction. In 1977 there were 5 archbishoprics, 27 dioceses and 6,716 parishes, 75 bishops, 30,162 monks and nuns and 14,162 churches and chapels. In 1983 there were 2 cardinals and 21,643 priests. 100 churches were built. In 1975 some 4,000 students were studying for the priesthood. In Oct. 1978 Cardinal Karol Wojtyla, archbishop of Cracow, was elected Pope as John Paul II.

On 28 June 1972 the Vatican adjusted the Church boundaries, to coincide with the State's western frontier ('Oder–Neisse line') and the 4 apostolic administrators in the former German territories became bishops.

Figures for other churches in 1977: Polish Autocephalous Orthodox, 4 dioceses, 233 parishes, 301 churches, 221 priests, 2 monasteries (460,000 adherents in 1975). Lutheran, 6 dioceses, 122 parishes, 310 churches, 100 parsons (100,000 adherents in 1975). Uniate, 3 dioceses, 84 parishes, 89 churches, 90 priests (200,000 adherents in 1975). Old-Catholic Mariavite, 3 dioceses, 42 parishes, 56 churches, 33 priests (30,000 adherents in 1975). Methodist, 5 districts, 66 parishes, 65 chapels, 39 parsons (4,133 adherents in 1975). United Evangelical, 222 congregations, 68 chapels, 215 parsons. Seventh-day Adventist, 124 communities, 122 churches, 66 parsons. Baptist, 127 congregations, 53 chapels, 60 parsons (2,300 adherents in 1975). Moslems, 6 communities, 2 mosques, 6 imams. Jews, 16 congregations, 24 synagogues (12,000 adherents in 1978). Epiphany World Mission, 80 communities, 157 churches, 427 priests.

Education. Basic education from 7 to 15 is free and compulsory. Free secondary education is then optional in general or vocational schools. Primary schools are organized in complexes based on wards under one director ('gmina collective schools'). In 1982–83 there were: Kindergartens, 26,273 with 1·23m. pupils and 79,000 teachers; primary schools, 14,341 (of which 1,760 gmina collective schools) with 4,465,000 pupils and 245,000 teachers; secondary schools, 1,171 with 381,000 pupils and 23,000 teachers; vocational schools, 9,973 with 1,556,000 pupils and 85,000 teachers, and 91 institutions of higher education (including 10 universities, 18 polytechnics, 9 agricultural schools, 6 schools of economics, 11 teachers' training colleges and 10 medical schools) with 423,500 students and 55,450 teaching staff.

Beginning in 1978–79 the 8-year primary school is being progressively replaced by a 10-year general secondary school.

Health. In 1982 there were 686 hospitals (including 41 mental hospitals) with 240,000 beds, 5,893 dispensaries and 3,246 health centres. There were 66,848 doctors and 17,176 dentists.

Social Security. In 1982, 121,563m. złotys were paid out in 5·25m. retirement pensions, 32·51m. zlotys in family allowances and 49·82m. złotys in sick pay.

DIPLOMATIC REPRESENTATIVES

Of Poland in Great Britain (47 Portland Place, London, W1N 3AG)
Ambassador: Stefan Staniszewski (accredited 12 Feb. 1982).

Of Great Britain in Poland (Aleje Roz No. 1, Warsaw)
Ambassador: J. A. L. Morgan, CMG.

Of Poland in the USA (2640–16th St., NW, Washington, D.C., 20009)
Chargé d'Affaires: Zdzislaw Ludwiczak.

Of the USA in Poland (Aleje Ujazdowskie 29/31, Warsaw)
Chargé d'Affaires: John Davis.

Of Poland to the United Nations
Ambassador: Włodzimierz Natorf.

Books of Reference

Statistical Information: The Central Statistical Office, Warsaw (Wawelska 1–3), publishes *Rocznik statystyczny* (annual, 1930–39; 1947–); *Concise Statistical Yearbook of Poland* (1959–); *Statystyka Polski* (irreg., 1947–); *Biuletyn statystyczny* (monthly, 1957–).

Constitution of the Polish People's Republic. Warsaw, 1964
Ascherson, N., *The Polish August: The Self-Limiting Revolution.* London, 1981
Beneš, V. L., and Pounds, N. G. J., *Poland.* London, 1970
Brumberg, A., *Poland: Genesis of a Revolution.* New York, 1983
Budrewicz, O., *Poland for Beginners.* 3rd ed. Warsaw, 1980
Bulas, K., and others, *English–Polish and Polish–English Dictionary.* 2 vols. The Hague, 1959
Burda, A., *Parliament of the Polish People's Republic.* Wrocław, 1978
Davies, N., *Poland, Past and Present: A Select Bibliography of Works in English.* Newtonville, 1977.—*God's Playground: A History of Poland.* OUP, 1981
De Weydentuat, J. B., et al. *The Polish Drama, 1980–1982.* Lexington, 1983
Dobbs, M., *Poland, Solidarity, Wałęsa.* New York, 1981
Dziewanowski, M. K., *Poland in the Twentieth Century.* Columbia Univ. Press, 1977
Eringer, R., *Strike for Freedom: The Story of Lech Wałesa and Polish Solidarity.* New York, 1982
Gieysztory, A., and others, *History of Poland. 2nd ed.* Warsaw, 1979
Halecki, O., *A History of Poland.* 4th ed. London, 1983
Kieniewicz, S. (ed.) *History of Poland.* 2nd ed. Warsaw, 1979
Lane, D., and Kolankiewicz, G. (ed.) *Social Groups in Polish Society.* London, 1973
Leslie, R. F., (ed.) *The History of Poland since 1863.* CUP, 1980
Lewanski, R. C., *Poland.* [Bibliography] Oxford and Santa Barbara, 1984
MacShane, D., *Solidarity: Poland's Independent Trade Union.* Nottingham, 1981
Polonsky, A. and Drukier, B., *The Beginnings of Communist Rule in Poland.* London, 1980
Pomian-Srzednicki, M. *Religious Change in Contemporary Poland: Secularization and Politics.* London, 1982
Portes, R., *The Polish Crisis: Western Economic Policy Options.* London, 1981
Potel, J.-I., *The Summer Before the Frost: Solidarity in Poland.* London, 1982
Preibisz, J. M., (ed.) *Polish Dissident Publications: an Annotated Bibliography.* New York, 1982
Raina P., *Political Opposition in Poland, 1954–1977.* London, 1978.—*Independent Social Movements in Poland.* London, 1981
Robinson, W.F. (ed.) *August 1980: the Strikes in Poland.* Munich, 1980
Roos, H., *A History of Modern Poland.* London, 1966
Ruane, K., *The Polish Challenge.* London, 1982
Sanford, G., *Polish Communism in Crisis.* London, 1983
Simon, M. D. and Kanet, R. E. (eds.) *Background to Crisis: Policy and Politics in Gierek's Poland.* Boulder, 1980
Singer, D., *The Road to Gdańsk: Poland and the USSR.* New York and London, 1981
Szczypiorski, A., *The Polish Ordeal: The View from Within.* London, 1982
Who's Who in Poland. New York, 1983
Wielka Encyklopedia Powszechna. 13 vols. Warsaw, 1962–70
Woodall, J., (ed.) *Policy and Politics in Contemporary Poland: Reform, Failure and Crisis.* London, 1982

National Library: Biblioteka Narodowa, Rakowiecka 6, Warsaw.

PORTUGAL

República Portuguesa

Capital: Lisbon
Population: 9·93m. (1983)
GNP per capita: US$2,237 (1982)

HISTORY. Portugal has been an independent state since the 12th century, apart from one period of Spanish rule (1580–1640). The monarchy was deposed on 5 Oct. 1910 and a republic established.

A *coup* on 28 May 1926 established a military provisional government from 1 June. A corporatist constitution was adopted on 19 March 1933 under which a civil dictatorship governed until a fresh *coup* on 25 April 1974 established a Junta of National Salvation.

Following an attempted revolt on 11 March 1975, the Junta was dissolved and a Supreme Revolutionary Council formed which ruled until 25 April 1976 when constitutional government was resumed; the SRC was renamed the Council of the Revolution, becoming a consultative body until its abolition in 1982.

AREA AND POPULATION. Mainland Portugal is bounded north and east by Spain and south and west by the Atlantic ocean. The Atlantic archipelagoes of the Azores and of Madeira form autonomous but integral parts of the republic, which has a total area of 92,072 sq. km (35,549 sq. miles) and census populations:

1940	7,755,423	1960	8,889,392	1981	9,806,333
1950	8,510,240	1970	8,648,369		

The areas and populations of the districts and Autonomous Regions are:

Districts:	sq. km	census 1981		sq. km	census 1981
Aveiro	2,708	623,762	Portalegre	5,882	140,609
Beja	10,240	186,340	Porto	2,282	1,550,806
Braga	2,730	700,728	Santarém	6,689	460,591
Bragança	6,545	181,386	Setúbal	5,152	649,053
Castelo Branco	6,704	232,419	Viano de Castelo	2,108	253,525
Coimbra	3,956	442,885	Vila Real	4,239	262,630
Evora	7,393	179,242	Viseu	5,019	420,766
Faro	5,072	322,866	Total mainland	88,941	9,297,159
Guarda	5,496	205,103	*Autonomous Regions:*		
Leiria	3,516	422,821	Azores	2,335	251,352
Lisboa	2,762	2,061,627	Madeira	796	257,822

At the 1970 census, 37·2% of the population was urban and 47·4% were male. The chief cities (census, 1981) are Lisbon, the capital (812,385) and Porto (329,104); other towns (1970) are Amadora (66,189), Coimbra (56,568), Barreiro (53,200), Setúbal (50,730), Vila Nova de Gaia (50,219), Braga (49,693), Funchal (40,057), Almada (38,714), Covilhã (27,018), Guimarães (25,113), Evora (24,003), Matosinhos (22,475), Moscavide (21,647), Ponta Delgada (21,347), Faro (20,687) and Santarém (20,030).

The Azores islands lie in the mid-Atlantic ocean, between 1,200 and 1,600 km west of Lisbon. They are divided into 3 widely separated groups with clear channels between, São Miguel (747 sq. km) together with Santa Maria (97 sq. km) being the most easterly; about 100 miles north-west of them lies the central cluster of Terceira (397 sq. km), Graciosa (61 sq. km), São Jorge (238 sq. km), Pico (433 sq. km) and Faial (172 sq. km); still another 150 miles to the north-west are Flores (143 sq. km) and Corvo (17 sq. km), the latter being the most isolated and primitive of the islands. São Miguel contains over half the total population of the archipelago, including the regional capital, Ponta Delgada.

Madeira comprises the island of Madeira (740 sq. km), containing the capital, Funchal; the smaller island of Porto Santo (42 sq. km), lying 46 km. to the north-east of Madeira; and two groups of uninhabited islets, Ilhas Desertas being 20 km. south-east of Funchal and Ilhas Selvagens near the Canaries.

Vital statistics for calendar years:

	Births	Still-births	Marriages	Divorces	Deaths	Emigrants
1980 [1]	160,957	2,196	73,290	5,874	97,698	25,207
1981 [1]	153,529	1,935	75,351	6,827	97,448	23,147
1982 [1]	153,783	1,862	74,806	6,769	94,583	...

[1] Provisional.

In 1979 the births included 82,726 boys and 77,585 girls; deaths, 47,896 males and 44,836 females. In 1981, 4,951 emigrants went to France, 4,295 to USA, 2,484 to Venezuela and 2,196 to Canada.

CLIMATE. Because of westerly winds and the effect of the Gulf Stream, the climate ranges from the cool, damp Atlantic type in the north to a warmer and drier Mediterranean type in the south. July and Aug. are virtually rainless everywhere. Inland areas in the north have greater temperature variation, with continental winds blowing from the interior. Lisbon. Jan. 52°F (11°C), July 72°F (22°C). Annual rainfall 27·4″ (686 mm).

CONSTITUTION AND GOVERNMENT. A new Constitution, replacing that of 1976, was approved by the Assembly of the Republic (by 197 votes to 40) on 12 Aug. 1982 and promulgated in Sept. It abolished the (military) Council of the Revolution and reduced the role of the President of the Republic.

Portugal is a sovereign, unitary republic with all citizens possessing fundamental rights and duties before the law. Executive power is vested in the President of the Republic. directly elected for a 5-year term (for a maximum of 2 consecutive terms). Presidents since 1926:

Marshal António Oscar de Fragoso Carmona, 29 Nov. 1926–18 April 1951 (died).
Dr Antonio de Oliveira Salazar (acting), 18 April 1951–22 July 1951.
Marshal Francisco Higino Craveiro Lopez, 22 July 1951–9 Aug. 1958.

Rear-Adm. Américo de Deus Rodrigues Tomás, 9 Aug. 1958–25 April 1974. (deposed).
Gen. Antonio Sebastião Ribeiro de Spinola, 25 April 1974–30 Sept. 1974 (resigned).
Gen. Francisco da Costa Gomes, 30 Sept. 1974–14 July 1976.

President of the Republic: Gen. Antonio Ramalho Eanes, elected 27 June 1976 (took office 14 July 1976) and re-elected 7 Dec. 1980.

The President appoints a Prime Minister and, upon the latter's nomination, other members of the Council of Ministers, as well as Secretaries and Under-Secretaries of State, who are outside the Council.

The coalition government formed on 9 June 1983 was composed as follows:

Prime Minister: Dr Mário Alberto Nobre Lopes Soares (PS).

Deputy Prime Minister and Defence: Prof. Carlos Mota Pinto (PSD). *Minister of State:* Antonio Almeida Santos (PS). *Interior:* Eduardo Pereira (PS). *Foreign Affairs:* Jaime Gama (PS). *Justice:* Rui Manchete (PSD). *Culture:* Antonio Coimbra Martins (PS). *Social Affairs:* Jose Rosado Correia (PS). *Industry:* Jose Veiga Simão (PS). *Labour:* Amandio de Azevedo (PSD). *Education:* Jose Augusto Seagra (PSD). *Quality of Life:* Antonio Capucho (PSD). *Finance:* Ernani Lopes (Ind.). *Trade:* Alvaro Barreto (PSD). *Agriculture:* Soares Costa (PSD). *Sea:* Carlos Melancia (PS). *Health:* Maldonado Gonelha (PS).

There is a unicameral legislature, the Assembly of the Republic, comprising 250 deputies elected for 4 years by universal adult suffrage under a system of proportional representation. At the General Election of 25 April 1983, there were 99 seats won by the *Partido Socialista* (PS), 72 by the *Partido Social Democrata* (PSD), 44 by the *Partido Comunista Português* (PCP) and 29 by the *Partido do Centro Democrático Social* (CDS).

National flag: Vertical green and red, with the red of double width, and over all on the dividing line the national arms.

National anthem: A Portuguesa (words by Lopes de Mendonça, 1890; tune by Alfredo Keil).

Local government: Since 1976, the archipelagoes of the Azores and of Madeira are Autonomous Regions with their own legislatures and governments. Pending the formation of other regional governments, Continental Portugal is divided into 18 districts. Regions and districts are divided into municipal authorities *(concelhos)* and sub-divided into parishes. Each level is governed by an assembly elected by direct universal suffrage under a system of proportional representation, with an executive body responsible to the assembly.

DEFENCE. Military service is compulsory for 16 months in the Army, 24 months in the Navy and 21–24 months in the Air Force. Reserves for all services number about 90,000.

Army. The Army consists of 1 mixed brigade, 2 cavalry regiments, 12 infantry regiments, 3 independent infantry battalions, 1 commando regiment, 2 field, 1 anti-aircraft and 1 coast artillery regiments and 2 engineer regiments. Equipment includes 32 M-47 and 23 48A5 main battle tanks. Strength (1984) 41,000 (including 30,000 conscripts). Paramilitary forces are National Republic Guard (14,600, Public Security Police (15,291) and Fiscal Guard (7,385).

Navy. The fleet comprises 3 small French-built diesel-powered patrol submarines, 17 frigates, 10 patrol vessels, 4 coastal minesweepers, 20 patrol launches, 1 sail training ship, 3 surveying vessels, 1 fleet oiler, 2 landing craft, 11 minor landing craft, 3 tugs and 1 harbour tanker. The navy personnel in 1984 totalled 14,000 officers and men including 2,000 marines.

Air Force. Formed in 1912, the Air Force has been independent since 1952, when it was combined with the naval air service and given equal status with the Army and Navy. In 1983, it had a strength of about 9,500 officers and men, excluding paratroops (3,766).

Equipment comprises a strike squadron of 20 A-7P Corsair IIs (30 more ordered); 2 squadrons of G.91Rs for dual attack and air defence (with Sidewinder missiles); 1 squadron of 5 C-130H Hercules for transport and secondary maritime surveillance duties; 2 transport squadrons, a survey squadron, a search and rescue unit and an OCU equipped with 22 Spanish-built CASA 212 Aviocars, of which 4 are equipped for photographic duties; 32 Cessna 337 Skymasters for counter-insurgency and liaison duties; and a force of Puma and Alouette III helicopters. Other aircraft in service include Chipmunk piston-engined trainers, T-37C jet basic trainers, T-33, T-38A Talon and G.91T jet advanced trainers.

INTERNATIONAL RELATIONS

Membership. Portugal is a member of UN, EFTA, OECD, NATO and the Council of Europe.

ECONOMY

Planning. The aim of the 1981–84 plan is to modernize existing industry and pave the way for entry into the European Community.

Budget. Revenue and expenditure (in 1m. escudos) have balanced as follows: 1979, 280,659; 1980, 374,780; 1981, 490,017.

Currency. The unit of currency is the *escudo* of 100 *centavos*, which contains 0·06651 gramme of fine gold. It was stabilized on 9 June 1931, and the paper currency re-linked to gold when the notes of the Bank of Portugal became payable in gold or its equivalent in foreign currency. 1,000 escudos is called a *conto*.

At present there are bank notes of 5,000, 1,000, 500, 100, 50 and 20 escudos; cupro-nickel coins of 25, 10, 5 and 2½ escudos; nickel-brass coins of 1 escudo; alpaca coins of 1 and ½ escudo (50 centavos), bronze coins of 1 and ½ escudo and 20 and 10 centavos and aluminium coins of 10 centavos. In March 1984, £1 = 193 *escudos*; US$1 = 131 *escudos*.

Banking. Since 1931, the central bank for Portugal and the only bank of issue for the country (including the Azores and Madeira) has been the Banco de Portugal, founded 19 Nov. 1846 and nationalized on 13 Sept. 1974. Its capital is fixed at 200m. escudos. All other Portuguese banks and insurance companies were nationalized on 14 March 1975.

The National Development Bank began operations on 4 Jan. 1960. Its total capital is 1,500m. escudos.

There are 11 commercial banks registered on the mainland and 1 in the Azores, with cash in hand on 31 Dec. 1981, 12,916m. escudos; bills, loans and other credits, 810,357m. escudos; deposits, 1,215,516m. escudos. The deposits in the savings banks including the general deposit bank (state) amounted to 440,829m. escudos.

There are also 3 foreign banks, the Bank of Brazil, Bank of London and South America and Crédit Franco-Portugais.

Weights and Measures. The metric system is the legal standard. The arroba (of 14·69 kg) is sometimes used locally.

ENERGY AND NATURAL RESOURCES

Electricity. Total production of electrical power in 1981 was 13,900m. kwh.; the installed capacity totalled 5,569,221 kva. of which 50·24% was hydro-electric.

Minerals. Portugal possesses considerable mineral wealth. Production in tonnes:

	1980	1981	1982		1980	1981	1982
Coal	177,451	183,760	178,540	Gold (refined)	0·240	0·244	0·211
Cupriferous pyrites	387,171	286,622	262.142	Uranium	89	119	134
Tin ores	421	506	585	Wolframite	2,670	2,365	2,300
Kaolin	83,145	107,978	63.021	Magnetite	14,773	...	...

Uranium mining commenced in Aug. 1979. Annual production, 115 tonnes; reserves, 7,000 tonnes.

Agriculture. The following figures show the area (in 1,000 hectares) and yield (in 1,000 tonnes) of the chief crops:

	1979		1980		1981	
Crop	Area	Yield	Area	Yield	Area	Yield
Wheat	281·3	247·8	350·8	429·5	339·8	315·2
Maize	375·6	461·4	376·6	489·2	347·7	376·7
Oats	159·1	69·5	174·7	95·6	160·3	71·8
Barley	72·0	41·2	79·2	53·7	74·1	40·7
Rye	208·8	120·2	205·8	138·4	199·4	125·7
Rice	34·7	145·3	34·7	154·8	25·2	111·9
Dried beans	260·0	38·4	272·7	41·7	241·6	30·4
Potatoes	108·0	1,020·6	113·8	1,117·9	107·6	892·2

Wine production (in hectolitres), 1980, 10,290,400; olive oil (hectolitres), 1980, 348,200. In 1978, 51,937 tonnes of port wine were exported.

Livestock (1982). 29,000 horses, 91,000 mules, 181,000 asses, 1m. cattle, 750,000 goats, 5·2m. sheep and 3·5m. pigs.

Forestry. Forest area covers 3m. hectares, of which 1·33m. are pine, 652,580 cork oak, 576,070 other oak, 213,960 eucalyptus, 29,730 chestnut and 366,660 other species.

Portugal surpasses the rest of the world in the production of cork; 81,787 tonnes in 1981. Most of it is exported crude. Production of resin was 123,627 tonnes in 1981; more than two-thirds are exported.

Fisheries. The fishing industry for the continent and adjacent isles is of importance. At 31 July 1979 there were 37,422 men and boys employed, with 10,936 boats. The sardine catch, 1980, was 106,537 tonnes valued at 1,173,566 contos; The most important centres of the sardine industry are at Matosinhos, Peniche, Setúbal, Portimão and Olhão.

TRADE

Commerce. Imports for consumption and exports (exclusive of coin and bullion and re-exports) for calendar years, in 1m. escudos:

	1977	1978	1979	1980	1981
Imports	190,684	230,128	331,927	475,486	608,871
Exports	77,685	106,451	176,051	231,623	256,663

The principal exports in 1981 were clothing (14% by value), textile yarns and fabrics (13%), machinery (9%), petroleum products (7%), chemicals (6%), cork and cork products (6%) and wine (5%).

The distribution of the imports and exports (in 1m. escudos):

	Imports (c.i.f.)			Exports (f.o.b.)		
From or to	1980	1981	1982	1980	1981	1982
Angola	769	940	1,794	8,904	13,890	6,773
Belgium	14,645	14,677	18,291	7,201	6,798	10,255
France	34,534	47,252	64,782	24,531	32,268	43,616
Germany, Fed.						
Rep. of	55,811	66,880	88,348	31,373	32,002	43,013
Italy	24,936	32,811	41,345	13,234	10,941	15,961
Mozambique	1,101	1,131	1,123	1,860	2,066	5,389
Netherlands	13,562	17,815	4,240	10,945	12,068	5,898
Spain	26,145	40,032	44,635	8,349	7,280	11,834
UK	41,617	48,718	58,077	34,325	37,068	49,168
USA	52,325	72,919	80,966	13,220	13,402	20,463

Total trade between Portugal (excluding the Azores and Madeira) and UK (British Department of Trade returns, in £1,000 sterling):

	1979	1980	1981	1982	1983
Imports to UK	338,337	335,112	333,355	379,949	475,902
Exports and re-exports from UK	307,670	389,849	368,080	430,684	396,988

Trade Unions. 331 unions had in 1976 a membership of 1,436,142.

Tourism. Tourism is of increasing importance for the invisible balance of payments. In 1982 there were 7,299,000 visitors and income from tourism represented 5–6% of GNP.

COMMUNICATIONS

Roads (1981). There were 33,961 km of road. There were registered in continental Portugal in 1981, 1,753,661 motor vehicles (excluding 95,755 motor cycles, 119,734 tractors and vehicles used by the armed forces).

Railways. In 1981 total railway length was 3,611 km (1,668 mm and metre gauges), of which 430 km of broad-gauge was electrified. In 1981, 5,867m. passenger-km were carried and 1,060m. tonne-km of merchandise transported.

Aviation. There are international airports at Portela (Lisbon), Pedras Rubras (Porto), Faro (Algarve), Santa Maria (Azores) and Funchal (Madeira). Regular services connect Lisbon with most major centres in North and South America, Western Europe and Africa. Airlines in 1981 carried 2·01m. passengers and 33,271 tonnes of freight. The national airline changed its name to Air Portugal in 1979.

Shipping. In 1981, 14,309 vessels of 63·75m. tons entered the ports (continental and islands), of which 5,793 (13·69m. tons) were Portuguese, 629 (4·33m. tons) British and 539 (2·78m. tons) Spanish. In 1981 the merchant marine consisted of 351 transport vessels of 1,376,529 gross tons.

Post and Broadcasting (1981). The number of telegraph offices was 1,581. The State owned 6,193,377 km of telephone line through the *Telefones de Lisboa e Porto* (nationalized in 1977). Number of telephones was 1,455,804 (1982).

Radio Difusão Portuguesa broadcasts 3 programmes on medium-waves and on FM as well as 3 regional services. *Radiotelevisão Portuguesa* broadcasts 2 commercial TV programmes. *Radio Renascença* is a commercial, nationwide network. In addition there are 6 local, commercial stations, operating on medium-waves. Radio Trans Europe is a high-powered short-wave station, retransmitting programmes of different broadcasting organizations, *e.g.*, IBRA, Radio Canada and

Deutsche Welle. Radio Free Europe also has relay facilities on short-waves in Portugal. Number of receivers: Radio (1979), 1,575,000; TV (1981), 1,460,902.

Cinemas (1979). There were 435 cinemas with a seating capacity of 240,874.

Newspapers (1982). There were 32 daily newspapers with a combined circulation of 188,836m.; 16 of these, with a combined circulation of 130,988m., appeared in Lisbon.

JUSTICE, RELIGION, EDUCATION AND WELFARE

Justice. Portuguese law distinguishes civil (including commercial) and penal, labour, administrative and fiscal law, each branch having its lower courts, courts of appeal and the Supreme Court.

The republic is divided for civil and penal cases into 216 *comarcas*; in every comarca there is a lower court. In the comarca of Lisbon there are 39 lower courts (22 for criminal procedure and 17 for civil or commercial cases); in the comarca of Oporto there are 21 lower courts (12 for criminal and 9 for civil or commercial cases); at Coimbra, Setúbal, Sintra and Vila Nova de Gaia there are 4 courts; at Almada, Braga, Cascais, Funchal, Guimarães, Leiria, Loures, Matosinhos, Oeiras, Santarém and Viseu there are 3 courts; 19 comarcas have 2 courts each. There are 4 courts of appeal *(Tribunal de Relação)* at Lisbon, Coimbra, Evora and Oporto, and a Supreme Court in Lisbon *(Supremo Tribunal de Justiça)*.

Capital punishment was abolished completely after the new constitution of 1976.

The prison population as at 31 Dec. 1981 was 5,797.

Religion. In 1976, 83% of the population were Roman Catholic, but there is freedom of worship, both in public and private, with the exception of creeds incompatible with morals and the life and physical integrity of the people.

Education. According to the latest statistics, 70% of the population over 7 years could read and write. Compulsory education has been in force since 1911. In 1980–81 there were 9,727 public primary schools with 886,046 pupils and 38,815 teachers. In 1977–78 private elementary schools numbered 627 with 57,635 pupils and 2,366 teachers. Basic preparatory schools numbered 1,765 with (1979–80) 304,519 pupils and 1,649 teachers. Secondary instruction is supplied in two types of schools: in the *liceus* and other grammar schools, and in schools of technical instruction. In 1977–78 there were 422 *liceus* and 185 institutions of *liceu* standard, with 146,634 pupils, and 164 professional and technical secondary schools, with 77,335 pupils. There were also (1980–81) 20 schools which taught art activities (cinema, music and theatre) with 7,838 students. There are 11 universities, of which 5 are in Lisbon: the University of Lisbon (founded 1911), the Technical University (1930), the private Catholic University (1968), the New University (1973) and the Free University (1977); the other six are Coimbra (founded 1290), Porto (1911), Aveiro (1973), Minho, at Braga (1974), Evora (1979) and Azores, at Ponta Delgado (1980). Including other colleges, there were 85,111 students in higher education in 1980–81.

Health. In 1977 there were 495 hospitals with 51,449 beds; there were 13,816 doctors, 489 dentists, 3,781 pharmacists, 1,214 midwives and 19,440 nursing personnel.

DIPLOMATIC REPRESENTATIVES

Of Portugal in Great Britain (11 Belgrave Sq., London, SW1X 8PP)
Ambassador: (Vacant).

Of Great Britain in Portugal (35-37 Rua S. Domingos à Lapa, Lisbon)
Ambassador: H. C. Byatt, CMG.

Of Portugal in the USA (2125 Kalorama Rd., NW, Washington, D.C., 20008)
Ambassador: Leonardo Charles de Zaffiri Mathias.

Of the USA in Portugal (Ave. das Forcas Armadas, 1600)
Ambassador: H. Allen Holmes.

Of Portugal to the United Nations
Ambassador: Rui E. Barbosa de Medina.

Books of Reference

Statistical Information: The Instituto Nacional de Estatistica (Avenida Dr António José de Almeida, Lisbon) was set up in 1935 in succession to the Direcção-Geral de Estatistica. The Centro de Estudos Económicos and the Centro de Estudos Demográficos were affiliated to the Instituto in 1944. The main publications are:

Anuário Estatistico. Annuaire statistique. Annual, from 1875
Estatísticas do Comércio Externo. 2 vols. Annual from 1967 (replacing *Comércio Externo,* 1936–66, and *Estatística Comercial,* 1865–1935)
Censo da População de Portugal. 1864 ff. Decennial (latest ed. 1972)
Estatística da Organização Corporativa. 1938–49. Estatísticas da Organização Corporativa e Previdência Social. 1950 ff.
Estatísticas das Finanças, Publicas and *Estatísticas Nometárias.* 1969 ff. (replacing *Estatísticas Financeiras.* 1947–68 and *Situação Bancária,* 1919–46)
Estatísticas Agrícolas. Statistique Agricole. 1943–64; replaced by *Estatísticas Agrícolas e Alimentares.* From 1965. Annual
Estatísticas Industrials. 1967 ff. (replacing *Estatística Industrial. Statistique Industrielle.* 1943–66)
Estatísticas Demográficas. From 1967 (replacing *Anuário Demográfico,* 1929–66)
Boletim Mensal do Instituto Nacional de Estatística. Monthly since 1929
Centro de Estudos Económicos. Revista. 1945 ff.
Centro de Estudos Demográficos. Revista. 1945 ff.
Estatísticas das Contribuições e Impostos. Annual from 1967 (replacing *Anuário Estatístico das Contribuições e Impostos,* 1936–66)
Estatísticas da Educação. 1940 ff.
Estatísticas da Justica. 1968 ff. (replacing *Estatísticas Judiciária.* 1936–66)
Estatísticas das Sociedades. 1939 ff.
Estatísticas do Turismo. 1969 ff.
Estatísticas do Energia. 1969 ff.

Azevedo, Gonzaga de, *Historia de Portugal.* 6 vols. Lisbon, 1935–44
Ferreira, J. A., *Dictionario inglês-portugês.* 2 vols. Porto, 1948
Gallagher, T., *Portugal: A Twentieth Century Interpretation.* Manchester Univ. Press, 1983
Graham, L. S., and Wheeler, D. L., *In Search of Modern Portugal: The Revolution and its Consequences.* Univ. of Wisconsin Press, 1983
Harvey R., *Portugal: Birth of a Democracy.* London, 1978
Robertson, I., *Blue Guide: Portugal.* London, 1982
Robinson, R., *Contemporary Portugal.* London, 1979
Rogers, F. M., *Atlantic Islanders of the Azores and Madeiras.* North Quincy, 1979
Soares, M., *Le Portugal Bâillonné: Une Témoignage.* Paris, 1972
Sobel, L. A. (ed.), *Portuguese Revolution 1974–76.* New York, 1976
Spinola, A. de, *Portugal e o Futoro.* Lisbon, 1974
Taylor, J. L., *Portuguese-English Dictionary.* London, 1959

National Library: Biblioteca Nacional, Campo Grande, Lisbon. *Director:* A. H. C. Marques.

MACAO

HISTORY. Macao was visited by Portuguese traders from 1513 and became a Portuguese colony in 1557; it remains a Portuguese-administered territory by virtue of a Sino-Portuguese treaty of 1 Dec. 1887. It was an Overseas Province of Portugal, 1961–74.

AREA AND POPULATION. The territory, which lies at the mouth of the Canton (Pearl) River, comprises a peninsula (5 sq. km) on which is built the city of Nome de Deus de Macao, and the islands of Taipa (4 sq. km), linked to Macao by a 2-km bridge, and Colôane (7 sq. km) linked to Taipa by a 2-km causeway (total area, 16 sq. km (6 sq. miles). The population (Census, 1981) is 261,680, of which 91·5% live in the city of Macao. The official language is Portuguese, but Cantonese is used by virtually the entire population.

Vital statistics (1981): Births, 4,207; marriages, 988; deaths, 1,465.

CONSTITUTION AND GOVERNMENT. By agreement with Beijing in 1974, Macao is a Chinese territory under Portuguese administration. An 'organic statute' was published on 17 Feb. 1976. It defined the territory as a collective entity, *pessoa colectiva,* with internal legislative authority which, while remaining subject to Portuguese constitutional laws, would otherwise enjoy administrative, economic and financial autonomy. The Governor is appointed by the Portuguese President, who also appoints up to 5 Secretaries-Adjunct on the Governor's nomination. The Legislative Assembly of 17 deputies, chosen for a 3-year term, comprises 6 members elected by universal suffrage, 6 elected by the business community and 5 appointed by the Governor.

Governor: Cdr Vasco Almeida e Costa.

ECONOMY

Budget. In 1982, revenue was 852,780,199 *patacas* and expenditure 757,221,494 *patacas.*

Currency. The unit of currency is the *pataca,* of 100 *avos,* which is tied to the Hong Kong dollar at a rate of 104 *patacas*=HK$100.

Banking. The bank of issue is the Instituto Emissor de Macau. Commercial business is handled by 7 local and 6 foreign banks with branches in Macao.

INDUSTRY AND TRADE

Industry. Textile manufacturing forms the basis of local industry. In 1981, 23,477 tonnes of clothing and 11,977 tonnes of knitwear were produced.

Commerce. The trade, mostly transit, is handled by Chinese merchants. Imports, in 1982, were 4,475m. patacas and exports, 4,506m. patacas.

In 1981, 36% of imports came from Hong Kong, 33% from China and 10% from Japan; 22% of exports went to Hong Kong, 21% to USA, 13% to Federal Republic of Germany, 11% to France and 7% to UK; clothing and knitwear accounted for 62% of exports.

Tourism. There were 4,719,612 visitors in 1981.

COMMUNICATIONS.

Roads. In 1981 there were 90 km of roads, 14,300 passenger cars and 3,670 commercial vehicles.

Shipping. Macau is served by Portuguese, British and Dutch steamship lines. In 1981, 28,751 vessels of 9·77m. gross tons entered the port. Regular services connect Macao with Hong Kong, 65 km to the north-east.

Post and Broadcasting. The territory has 1,577 km of telephone line (15,955 instruments in 1982). One government and 1 private commercial radio station are in operation on medium-waves broadcasting in Portuguese and Chinese. Number of receivers (1977), 70,000. Macau receives television broadcasts from Hong Kong and had (1979) 50,000 receivers.

Newspapers. In 1979, there were 5 daily newspapers with a circulation of 59,000.

JUSTICE, RELIGION, EDUCATION AND WELFARE

Justice. There is a court of First Instance, from which there is appeal to the Court of Appeal and then the Supreme Court, both in Lisbon.

Religion. The majority of the Chinese population are Buddhists. About 6% are Roman Catholic.

Education. In 1981–82 education was provided at 25 secondary schools (10,996 pupils), 61 elementary schools, 3 secondary preparatory schools (28,236 pupils), 13 technical schools (2,762 pupils) and 2 art schools (180 pupils). The University of East Asia, established in 1981 on Taipa, had 860 students in 1982.

Health. In 1977 there were 4 hospitals with 1,708 beds; there were 231 doctors, 54 dentists, 20 pharmacists, 21 midwives and 342 nursing personnel.

Books of Reference

Anuário Estatístico de Macau. Macao
Brazão, E., *Macau.* Lisbon, 1957

QATAR

Dawlat al-Qatar

Capital: Doha
Population: over 260,000 (1982)
GNP per capita: US$26,080 (1980)

HISTORY. The State of Qatar declared its independence from Britain on 3 Sept. 1971, ending the Treaty of 3 Nov. 1916 which was replaced by a Treaty of friendship between the 2 countries.

AREA AND POPULATION. The State of Qatar, which includes the whole of the Qatar peninsula, extends on the landward side from Khor al Odeid to the boundaries of the Saudi Arabian province of Hasa. Area, 11,437 sq. km; population estimate in 1982 over 260,000, including a number of migrant labourers from neighbouring states.

The capital is Doha (population, 190,000), which is the main port. Other towns are Dukhan, the centre of oil production, Umm Said, oil-terminal of Qatar and Ruwais, Wakra, Al-Khour and Umm-Bab.

RULER. *The Amir:* HH Shaikh Khalifa bin Hamad Al-Thani, assumed power on 22 Feb. 1972. On 31 May 1977, HH Shaikh Hamed bin Khalifa Al-Thani, was appointed Heir Apparent of the State of Qatar, the portfolio of Minister of Defence was added to his existing responsibility of Commander-in-Chief of the Armed Forces.

Foreign Minister: Shaikh Suhaim bin Ahmed Al-Thani.

There is no Parliament, but the Ministers are assisted by a 30-member nominated Consultative Council.

Flag: Maroon, with white serrated border on hoist.

DEFENCE

Army. The Army consists of 1 Royal Guard regiment, 1 tank, 5 infantry battalions and 1 artillery battery. Equipment includes 24 AMX-30 tanks. Personnel (1984) 5,000.

Navy. The Navy has 3 new French-built fast gunboats, 6 British-built large patrol craft and 36 coastal patrol craft. Personnel (1983) 400.

Air Force. The Air Force has 12 Mirage F1 fighters, 2 Hunter jet fighter-bombers, 1 Hunter 2-seat trainer, 2 Boeing 707, 1 Boeing 727 (VIP) and 1 Islander transport aircraft, 4 Commando, 2 Whirlwind, 3 Lynx and some Puma helicopters, 6 Alpha Jet armed trainers and Tigercat surface-to-air missile systems. Personnel (1983) 300.

INTERNATIONAL RELATIONS

Membership. Qatar is a member of UN and the Arab League.

ECONOMY

Budget. Revenue (1982) 16,432m. riyals; expenditure 15,165m. riyals.

Currency. On 13 May 1973 the Qata *Riyal* (of 100 *dirhams*) was introduced. In March 1984, £1 = 5·41 *riyals*, US$1 = 3·64 *riyals*.

Banking. Banks operating in Qatar include: Qatar National Bank, the Commercial Bank of Qatar (also Qatari-owned), the Arab Bank, Bank Al Mashrek, Bank Saderat Iran, Doha Bank, Banque de Paris et des Pays Bas, British Bank of the Middle East, the Chartered Bank, the First National City Bank, Grindlays Bank, the Bank of Oman and United Bank.

ENERGY AND NATURAL RESOURCES

Electricity. Production (1980) 1,450m. kwh.

Oil. On 9 Feb. 1977 Qatar gained national control over its 2 natural resources, oil and gas, with the signing of an agreement with Shell Qatar over the procedure for the transfer to the State of the company's remaining 40% share. A similar agreement had been reached with the Qatar Petroleum Co. on 16 Sept. 1976.

The Qatar General Petroleum Corporation (QGPC) had been established by decree in July 1974 to assume overall responsibility for the State's domestic and foreign oil interests and operations. On 16 Oct. 1976 the Qatar Petroleum Producing Authority (QPPA) was established to serve as the executive arm of the QGPC—but in 1980 it was merged into the QGPC, which now directly oversees oil production through two operational divisions, Onshore and Offshore. A new 50,000 bbls a day refinery has been constructed at Umm Said to supplement the existing 10,000 bbls a day refinery.

Production, 1982, 119,700,000m. bbls. Proven reserves (1982) 3,434,000m. bbls.

Gas. The North West Dome oilfield is being developed which contains 12% of the known world gas reserves. Production (1981) 220,000m. cu. feet (47,000 offshore).

Agriculture. 10% of the working population is engaged in agriculture and between Jan.–May Qatar is self-sufficient in fruit and vegetables.

Livestock (1982): Cattle, 10,000; camels, 10,000; sheep, 51,000; goats, 57,000; poultry, 380,000.

INDUSTRY AND TRADE

Industry. Several major projects have been established including the production of ammonia, urea and cement. The Qatar Iron and Steel Co. factory was opened in April 1978 and the Qator Petro-chemical Company polyethylene plant in Feb. 1981, both in the Umm Said industrial zone.

Commerce. In 1981 exports totalled 21,272m. riyals, and imports, 5,224m. riyals. Japan provided 18% of imports, the UK 18% and the USA 11%, while 12% of exports went to the Netherlands, 11% to Japan and 11% to France; crude oil was 95% of exports.

Total trade between Qatar and UK (British Department of Trade returns, in £1,000 sterling):

	1979	1980	1981	1982	1983
Imports to UK	40,503	44,654	10,675	33,984	10,063
Exports and re-exports from UK	101,486	101,898	135,722	245,390	216,385

Tourism. Tourism was being developed in 1978.

COMMUNICATIONS

Roads. In 1981 there were about 800 miles of road.

Aviation. The Gulf Aviation Co., Ltd (owned equally by Qatar, Bahrain, Oman and the UAE), operates daily services from Bahrain; British Airways, Middle East and about 15 other airlines operate regular international flights from Doha airport.

Shipping. Ships of several lines used to call at Umm Said; with the completion in 1969 of the new Doha port, it has become the main port of Qatar.

Post and Telecommunications. Telephone and radio-telephone services connect Qatar with Europe and America; there were 67,500 telephones in Jan. 1982. An earth satellite station was inaugurated in March 1976.

Cinemas. In 1981 there were 5 cinemas with a seating capacity of 7,000.

RELIGION, EDUCATION AND WELFARE

Religion. The population is almost entirely Moslem.

Education. There were, in 1979–80, 24,248 pupils (12,452 boys, 11,796 girls) at 85 elementary schools with 1,072 teachers in boys' and 1,836 teachers in girls' schools. In addition, 6,902 boys and 6,498 girls were attending 54 secondary schools. In 1980–81 the total number of pupils was 39,944. Students in higher institutions and universities numbered 2,700 in 1980, many of whom attended the 2 colleges of education in Doha, the nucleus of the University of the Lower Gulf. 941 university students graduated from 1976–80. Post-graduate students abroad numbered 1,305. In 1980, 7,458 men and 2,541 women attended evening classes.

Health. There are 5 hospitals (including 1 for women and 1 for gynaecology and obstetrics) with a total of 682 beds. The 660-bed hospital at Doha is nearing completion and clinics are being built throughout the State. In 1974 there were 96 doctors, 7 dentists, 3 pharmacists and 247 midwives and nursing personnel.

DIPLOMATIC REPRESENTATIVES

Of Qatar in Great Britain (27 Chesham Pl., London, SWIX 8HG)
Ambassador: Sharida Sa'ad Jubran Al Ka'abi (accredited 26 March 1981).

Of Great Britain in Qatar (Doha, Qatar)
Ambassador: S. P. Day.

Of Qatar in the USA (600 New Hampshire Ave., NW, Washington, D.C., 20037)
Ambassador: Abdelkader Braik Al-Ameri.

Of the USA in Qatar (Farig Bin Omran, Doha, Qatar)
Ambassador: (Vacant).

Of Qatar to the United Nations
Ambassador: Jasim Yousif Jamal.

Books of Reference

Qatar into the Seventies. Information Ministry, Doha, 1973
El Mallakh, R., *Qatar: The Development of an Oil Economy.* New York, 1979
Unwin, P. T. H., *Qatar.* [Bibliography] Oxford and Santa Barbara, 1982

ROMANIA

Republica Socialistă România

Capital: Bucharest
Population: 22·6m. (1984)
GNP per capita: US$2,340 (1980)

HISTORY. 1918 is celebrated as the year of foundation of the 'unitary national Romanian state'. For the history and constitution of Romania from 1859 to 1947, see THE STATESMAN'S YEAR-BOOK, 1947, pp. 1187–89. On 30 Dec. 1947 King Michael abdicated under Communist pressure and parliament proclaimed the 'People's Republic'.

AREA AND POPULATION. The area of Romania is 237,500 sq. km (91,699 sq. miles). Pre-war Romania had an area of 113,918 sq. miles. Population at censuses: 1930, 18,057,208 (14,280,729 within present-day Romania); 1948, 15,872,624 (48·3% male); 1966, 19,103,163 (49% male, 38·2% urban); 1977, 21,559,910 (49·3% male, 47·5% urban).

On 1 Jan. 1983 the population was 22·5m., density per sq. km, 93·5. Vital statistics, 1982 (per 1,000 population): Live births, 15·3; deaths, 10; marriages, 7·8; divorces, 1·48; stillborn (per 1,000 live births), 8·4; infant mortality (per 1,000 live births), 28; population growth rate, 5·3 per 1,000. Expectation of life in 1982: men, 67·4 years; women, 72·4.

Administratively, Romania is divided into 40 counties (*judeţ*), 236 towns (*oraş*) (of which 56 are municipalities) and 2,705 local authorities (*comune*). The capital is Bucharest (Bucureşti) a municipality with county status.

District	Area in sq. km	Population 1982	Capital	Population 1980
Alba	6,231	419,080	Alba Iulia	50,943
Arad	7,652	509,168	Arad	178,248
Argeş	6,801	659,289	Piteşti	139,029
Bacău	6,606	695,693	Bacău	149,033
Bihor	7,535	649,009	Oradea	184,871
Bistriţa-Năsăud	5,305	306,936	Bistriţa	55,505
Botoşani	4,965	459,774	Botoşani	78,636
Braşov	5,351	668,415	Braşov	304,670
Brăila	4,724	393,467	Brăila	214,940
Buzău	6,072	517,434	Buzău	112,760
Caraş-Severin	8,503	400,761	Reşiţa	94,040
Călăraşi	5,075	339,942	Călăraşi	60,200
Cluj	6,650	741,580	Cluj-Napoca	283,647
Constanţa	7,055	680,472	Constanţa	283,629
Covasna	3,705	221,851	Sf. Gheorghe	55,162
Dîmboviţa	4,035	584,877	Tirgovişte	75,550
Dolj	7,413	767,127	Craiova	227,444
Galaţi	4,425	619,587	Galaţi	260,898
Giurgiu	3,810	375,750	Giurgiu	55,987
Gorj	5,641	363,707	Tirgu Jiu	72,743
Harghita	6,610	349,416	Miercurea-Ciuc	39,521
Hunedoara	7,016	543,643	Deva	70,349
Ialomiţa	4,449	299,717	Slobozia	37,043
Iaşi	5,469	765,791	Iaşi	271,441
Maramureş	6,215	526,556	Baia Mare	117,763
Mehedinţi	4,900	327,522	Drobeta-Turnu Severin	83,170
Mureş	6,696	612,618	Tirgu Mureş	134,287
Neamţ	5,890	555,018	Piatra-Neamţ	88,145
Olt	5,507	528,661	Slatina	60,041
Prahova	4,694	852,785	Ploieşti	211,505
Satu Mare	4,405	405,739	Satu Mare	111,358
Sălaj	3,850	265,848	Zalău	40,296
Sibiu	5,422	502,851	Sibiu	161,049
Suceava	8,555	660,500	Suceava	74,513

District	Area in sq. km	Population 1982	Capital	Population 1980
Teleorman	5,760	510,523	Alexandria	40,778
Timiş	8,692	711,022	Timişoara	287,543
Tulcea	8,430	263,054	Tulcea	70,660
Vaslui	5,297	448,430	Vaslui	46,181
Vîlcea	5,705	419,398	Rîmnicu Vîlcea	78,097
Vrancea	4,863	379,232	Focşani	65,341
Bucharest [1]	1,521	2,211,460	Bucharest [2]	1,861,007

[1] Total conurbation.　　　　[2] Central area.

Ethnic groups: In 1978 there were 1·7m. Hungarians, mainly in Transylvania, and some 400,000 Germans. The official language is Romanian.

An 'education tax' was imposed on emigrants in Nov. 1982, but withdrawn in May 1983 after the USA had threatened to withdraw Romania's most-favoured-nation status.

CLIMATE. A continental climate with a large annual range of temperature and rainfall showing a slight summer maximum.

Bucharest. Jan. 27°F (−2·7°C), July 74°F (23·5°C). Annual rainfall 23·1″ (579 mm).

CONSTITUTION AND GOVERNMENT. The present Constitution was adopted on 21 Aug. 1965 and supersedes those of 13 April 1948 and 24 Sept. 1952. Under it Romania becomes a 'Socialist' (as opposed to 'People's') Republic. The leading role of the Communist Party is reaffirmed. The Grand National Assembly of 369 is elected for 5 years (before 1972 for 4 years). It holds short sessions twice a year, and between sessions delegates its legislative rights to the State Council (the President, head of state; 3 Vice-presidents, 1 secretary and 20 members).

All citizens of 18 and over have the right to vote and electoral law provides for the nomination of 'one or more' candidates in each constituency.

Local government is carried out by people's councils at all admistrative levels. In the municipal elections of Nov. 1982 117,316 candidates stood for 45,893 seats.

The National Council of the Socialist Democracy and Unity Front functions as a consultative body on home and foreign affairs. It has central and local councils in which workers, peasants, professional bodies, ethnic minorities and the Communist Party are represented. It replaced the Popular Democratic Front (*see* STATESMAN'S YEAR-BOOK, 1979–80).

Elections were held on 30 Nov. 1952, 3 Feb. 1957, 5 March 1961, 7 March 1965, 2 March 1969, 9 March 1975 and 9 March 1980.

At the 1980 elections 99·9% of the 15·6m. electorate voted, 98·52% of these for the Socialist Democracy and Unity Front. 2 candidates stood in 151, and 3 in 39, constituencies.

In 1965 the Romanian Workers' Party was renamed the Romanian Communist Party. The Party Congress elects the General Secretary, and its Central Committee elects the Executive Political Committee with its Permanent Bureau and the Secretariat (General Secretary and 7 secretaries). The Party had 2,960,917 members in 1980 (of whom 53% workers, 28% women). During 1982 extensive purges of Government and Party leaders took place, including the then Prime Minister, Ilie Verdeţ, and other members of President Ceauşescu's family.

President of the Republic and Chairman of the State Council: Nicolae Ceauşescu, succeeded Chivu Stoica in Dec. 1967. *Vice-Chairmen:* Stefan Voitec, Gheorghe Rădulescu, Iosif Kovacs, Maria Ciocan, Petru Enache, Mănea Mănescu.

In April 1984 the Permanent Bureau of the Party consisted of: Nicolae Ceauşescu (*General Secretary*); Ştefan Andrei; Iosif Banc; Emil Bobu; Virgil Cazacu; Elena Ceauşescu; Nicolae Constantin; Constantin Dăscălescu; Petru Enache; Gheorghe Oprea; Ion Păţan; Gheorghe Rădulescu; Ilie Verdeţ.

Council of Ministers (April 1984). *Chairman (Prime Minister):* Constantin Dăscălescu. *First Deputy Prime Ministers:* Elena Ceauşescu, Gheorghe Oprea, Ion

Dinca; *Deputy Prime Ministers:* Alexandra Găinuşe; Gheorghe Petrescu; Ludovic Fazekaş; Marin Enache; Ion Totu. Other ministers include: Ştefan Bîrlea *(Chairman, State Planning Committee)* Ion Tesu *(Agriculture and Food)*; Petre Gigea *(Finance)*; Ştefan Andrei *(Foreign)*; Maj.-Gen. Constantin Olteanu *(Defence)*; Gheorghe Homoştean *(Interior)*; Maxim Berghianu *(Labour)*; Vasile Pungan *(Foreign Trade)*; Gheorghe Chivulescu *(Justice)*.

In July 1970 Romania signed a treaty of friendship, co-operation and mutual assistance with the USSR. A previous such treaty had expired in 1968. Since the mid-1960s Romania has been taking a relatively independent stand in foreign affairs generally, and within Comecon and the Warsaw Pact.
financial contributions.

National flag: Three vertical strips of blue, yellow, red, with the national arms in the centre.

National anthem: Trei culori (Three colours). Introduced, 1977. Music by Ciprian Porumbescu.

DEFENCE. Defence is the responsibility of the Defence Council, which is controlled by the Council of State and headed by President Ceauşescu. Military service is compulsory for 16 months in the Army and Air Force and 30 months in the Navy.

Army. The 4 Army Areas consist of 2 tank and 8 motor rifle divisions; 3 mountain, 2 artillery, 2 anti-aircraft and 2 surface-to-surface missile brigades; and 3 artillery, 1 anti-aircraft, 5 anti-tank and 1 airborne regiments. Equipment includes 200 T-34, 1,000 T-54/-55, 30 T-72 and 150 M-77 main battle tanks. Strength (1984) 150,000 (including 95,500 conscripts), and 500,000 reservists. There are a further 37,000 men in paramilitary border guard and internal security forces.

Navy. The fleet comprises 3 small escorts, 5 fast missile boats, 25 fast torpedo boats, 20 fast gunboats, 3 old patrol vessels, 4 old minesweepers (refitted recently), 20 inshore minesweepers, 1 logistic support ship, 1 oceanographic ship, 1 headquarters ship, 2 training ships, 8 minesweeping boats, 42 river patrol craft, 8 landing craft, 2 survey vessels, 10 transports, 3 oilers and 4 tugs. Headquarters of the Navy is at Mangalia, and of the Danube flotilla at the main river port of Brăila. The naval school is in Constanţa. Personnel in 1984 totalled 10,500 officers and ratings including 2,000 Coastal Defence and 3,000 shore support.

Air Force. The Air Force numbers some 32,000 men, with 300 combat aircraft in 2 air divisions (4 regiments). These are organized into 12 interceptor squadrons with MiG-21 and MiG-23 fighters, 6 ground-attack and close-support squadrons with MiG-17 fighters, and 1 reconnaissance squadron of Il-28s. There are also more than 300 training aircraft, An-24/26/30 transports and helicopters. Under delivery are 185 IAR-93 close-support/interceptors, and Puma helicopters. 'Guideline' and 'Gainful' surface-to-air missiles are operational, and short-range surface-to-surface missiles have been displayed.

INTERNATIONAL RELATIONS

Membership. Romania is a member of UN, IMF, Comecon and the Warsaw Pact.

ECONOMY

Planning. In Oct. 1982 the Supreme Council of Economic and Social Development, presided over by Nicolae Ceauşescu, was raised to the level of an economic legislative chamber. Annual growth targets of the sixth 5-year plan (1981–85): GNP, 9%; national income, 10%; industrial production, 10%; agricultural production, 24·5–27·5%. Romania is committed to intensive industrialization and President Ceauşescu admitted in Feb. 1981 that agriculture had been neglected. Bread rationing was introduced in Oct. 1981 and food prices were raised by 35% in Feb. 1982. Virtual rationing was introduced in 1982 in the form of limitations of calorie intake. Industries scheduled for particular development: machine-building, iron and steel, non-ferrous metals, chemicals and electric power. A 10-year programme introduced in 1980 is designed to make Romania self-sufficient in energy. For previous plans see THE STATESMAN'S YEAR-BOOK, 1976–77.)

There is no move towards any fundamental decentralization of planning authority but limited devolutions of reponsibility in an attempt to improve efficiency were introduced in 1967, 1979 and 1983. There are 102 economic units intermediate between ministries and enterprises.

Budget. Revenue and expenditure (in 1 m. lei) for calendar years:

	1977	1978	1979	1980	1981	1982	1983
Revenue	281,980	300,836	339,309	298,004	262,227	288,511	301,908
Expenditure	280,423	299,314	337,629	296,787	262,227	288,511	301,908

In 1983 sources of revenue (in 1 m. lei) included: Profit payments of state enterprises and turnover tax, 194,832; personal taxes, 4,101; insurance contributions, 39,303; taxes on enterprise wage funds, 42,170. Expenditure: National economy, 139,466; social and cultural, 83,184; defence, 11,725.

Revenue and expenditure of local councils was 53,286m. lei in 1983.

In 1974 a Court of Preventive Financial control was set up to oversee most official transactions and combat waste and corruption.

By an agreement signed 12 Jan. 1976 Romania paid £3·5m. as 'full and final settlement' of defaulted Romanian bonds held by UK citizens in 4 annual instalments of £875,000 starting at the end of 1976. Payments of £1·25m. in settlement of UK claims arising out of the peace treaty were completed by 31 Jan. 1967.

Currency. The monetary unit is the *leu*, pl.*lei* (of 100 *bani*). On 1 Feb. 1954 the gold content of the leu was to 0·148112 gramme of fine gold. Exchange rates (March 1984): £1 = 6·67 lei; US$1 = 4·47 lei; 1 rouble = 6·67 lei. Tourist rates: £1 = 20·40 lei; US$1 = 11 lei; 1 rouble = 8·30 lei.

Bank-notes of 1, 5, 10, 25, 50 and 100 *lei* are issued by the National Bank, and there are coins of 5, 10, 15 and 25 *bani* and 1, 3 and 5 *lei*.

Banking. The National Bank of Romania (founded 1880, nationalized 1946) is the State Bank under the Minister of Finance. Half its profits are allotted to the State budget. There are also a Bank of Investments, a Foreign Trade Bank, an Agriculture and Food Industry Bank and a Savings Bank. In 1972 Romania joined IMF. The US Export-Import Bank has granted Romania borrowing rights. In 1974 the American bank Manufactures Hanover Trust Co. opened a branch in Bucharest, the first Western bank to do so in a Communist country.

Weights and measures. The Gregorian calendar was adopted in 1919. The metric system is in use. Tubes and pipes are measured in *tol* (= 1 inch).

ENERGY AND NATURAL RESOURCES

Electricity. Installed electric power 1980: 16,109,000 kw.; output (1982), 68,923m. kwh. There are two joint Romanian–Yugoslav hydro-electric power plants on the Danube at the 'Iron Gates' with a combined yearly output of 22,250m. kwh. A nuclear power programme has been subject to cut-backs and delays. A nuclear power station (capacity 660,000 kw.) is due to open in 1985.

Oil. The oilfields are in the Prahova, Bǎcǎu, Gorj, Crişana and Argeş districts. Petrol prices were raised by 60% and restrictions placed on official and private car use in 1979. Oil imports are approximately equivalent to domestic production. Oil reserves are expected to be exhausted by the mid-1990s.

Minerals. The principal minerals are oil and natural gas, salt, brown coal, lignite, iron and copper ores, bauxite, chromium, manganese and uranium. Salt is mined in the lower Carpathians and in Transylvania; production in 1982 was 4·8m. tonnes.

Output, 1980 (and 1982) (in 1,000 tonnes): Iron ore, 2,333 (2,146); crude oil, 11,511 (11,742); coal, 37,814 (41,433); methane gas (cu. metres), 28,156m. (28,620m.). The share of coal in the overall production of energy rose from 28% in 1975 to 40% in 1980 and is expected to reach 60% by 1990.

Agriculture. There were 14·96m. hectares of agricultural land in 1982, including (in 1,000 hectares): Arable, 9,870; meadows and pasture, 4,440; vineyards and fruit trees, 663.

Production in 1982 (in 1,000 tonnes): Wheat and rye, 6,505; barley, 3,052; maize, 12,620; potatoes, 5,006; sunflower seeds, 847; sugar-beet, 6,647.

Livestock (1982): 6·1m. cattle, 12·5m. pigs, 17·3m. sheep and 99m. poultry.

In 1980 there were 4,643 collective farms, with 9m. hectares of land (7·3m. arable; 921,200 in private plots). State farms numbered 407, with 2m. hectares of land, of which 1·64m. hectares were arable. A further 2·4m. hectares of land were in the hands of other state agricultural organizations. There were 714 agriculture mechanization stations with 140,074 tractors. Individual holdings totalled 1·41m. hectares. Since 1984 production quotas on private plots must be met on pain of confiscation. The National Union of Agricultural Co-operatives promotes self-management in collective farms, and gives guidance on planning and marketing. A minimum income is guaranteed to peasants. In 1984 there were 3·3m. hectares of irrigated land.

Forestry. Total forest area was 6·34m. hectares in 1982. In 1982, 52,183 hectares were afforested.

INDUSTRY AND TRADE

Industry. Output of main products in 1980 (and 1982) (in tonnes): Pig-iron, 9,012 (8,637); steel, 13,175 (13,055); steel tubes, 1,464 (1,422); blast furnace coke, 3,033 (3,513); rolled steel, 9,319 (9,346); chemical fertilizers, 2,451 (2,692); washing soda, 937 (870); caustic soda, 723 (760); paper, 822 (801); cement, 15,611 (14,995); sugar, 509 (596); edible oils, 369 (352); butter, 35 (20). Fabrics (in 1m. sq. metres): Cotton, 738 (707); woollens, 128 (142); man-made fibres, 205,753 (222,379). In 1,000 units: Radio sets, 863 (599); TV sets, 541 (412); bicycles, 214 (261); washing machines, 344 (372); refrigerators, 376 (431); motor cars, 88,232 (103,725); footwear, 113m. pairs (1980).

Labour. The employed population in 1982 was 10·43m., of whom 2·99m. worked in agriculture and 4·61m. industry and building. Wage differentials (at a ratio of 5·25:1) are in accordance with the 'social evaluation' of the work and a range of incentives for productivity. The average monthly wage was 2,256 lei in 1980. Minimum monthly wage was 1,500 lei in 1983. The working week is of 44 hours with alternate Saturdays free. Men retire at 62, women at 57.

Commerce. Some 60% of external trade is with Communist countries (15% with the USSR).

In 1982 exports totalled 151,837m. lei and imports 124,850m. lei.

Principal exports in 1980 were (in 1,000 tonnes): Petroleum products, 9,175; cement, 2,791; cereals, 1,720; tractors, 52,744 units; oilfield equipment, 1,852m. lei; equipment for cement mills, 80m. lei; equipment for chemical factories, 483m lei; shipbuilding, 852m. lei. Principal imports (in 1,000 tonnes): Iron ore, 15,984; industrial coke, 3,133; rolled ferrous metals, 1,040; electrical equipment, 1,239m. lei; motor cars, 19,329 units, and industrial and agricultural equipment.

In 1980 Romania's main trading partners (trade in 1m. lei) were: USSR (48,794), Federal Republic of Germany (18,137), Iran, 17,838; Iraq, 16,961, German Democratic Republic (14,518), China, 11,579; Poland, 10,217.

Total trade between Romania and UK for calendar years (British Department of Trade returns, in £1,000 sterling):

	1979	1980	1981	1982	1983
Imports to UK	65,914	64,795	46,518	51,515	58,865
Exports and re-exports from UK	70,372	98,914	150,256	115,244	82,160

On 18 Sept. 1975 Romania and the UK signed a 10-year economic co-operation agreement. In Nov. 1976 Romania and the USA signed a 10-year commercial agreement. Both the UK and the USA have joint economic commissions with Romania.

Romania owed some US$10,000m. to Western banks in 1982, and unilaterally suspended principal payments in Jan. 1973 pending a rescheduling of the loans.

The IMF suspended credit from Nov. 1981 until certain economic conditions were accepted by Romania in June 1982.

Joint companies with Western firms have been set up; at least 51% of the capital must be in Romanian hands. The 'Romconsult' and 'Publicom' agencies will carry out respectively market research and publicity campaigns on behalf of foreign firms.

Romania has a trade link with EEC under the generalized preference system.

Agreements with the EEC on industrial products and establishing a joint economic commission were reached in March 1980.

On 1 Jan. 1975 a 2-tier tariff system was introduced, graded according to the grant of most favoured nation status to Romania.

COMMUNICATIONS

Roads. There were in 1982, 14,675 km of national roads of which 11,673 km were modernized. Freight carried, 479m. tons; passengers, 1,000m.

Railways. Length of route (1,435 mm gauge) in 1980 was 11,125 km and (narrow-gauge), 521 km. A total of 2,772 km is electrified. Freight carried, 271m. tons; passengers, 375m.

Aviation. TAROM (*Transporturi Aeriene Române*), the state airline, operates all internal services, and also services to Amsterdam, Athens, Beirut, Belgrade, Berlin, Brussels, Budapest, Cairo, Cologne, Copenhagen, Düsseldorf, Frankfurt, Istanbul, London, Moscow, Paris, Prague, Rome, Sofia, Tel-Aviv, Vienna, Warsaw and Zürich. Bucharest is also served by British Airways, PANAM, SABENA, Aeroflot, Air France, Interflug, ČSA, MALEV, Austrian Air Lines, SAS, Lot, TABSO, El Al, Alitalia, Lufthansa and Swissair. An air agreement with China was signed in 1973.

Bucharest's airports are at Băneasa (internal flights) and Otopeni (international flights; 12 miles from Bucharest). Air transport in 1982 carried 1,304,000 passengers and 14,000 tons of freight.

Shipping. The main ports are Constanţa on the Black Sea and Galaţi and Brăila on the Danube. A new port has been constructed at Agigea on the Black Sea and the 64 km canal between the Danube and the Black Sea was nearing completion in 1983. The largest shipyard is at Galaţi.

In 1975 the mercantile marine (NAVROM) had 94 ships totalling 1,365,000 DWT. In 1982 sea-going transport carried 17·79m. tons of freight; river transport, 14·2m. tons.

Post and Broadcasting. *Radio-televiziunea Româna* broadcasts 3 programmes on medium-waves and FM. There are also 6 regional programmes, including transmission in Hungarian, German and Serbo-Croat. Two TV programmes are broadcast. Number of telephone subscribers, in 1982, 1,748,000. Radio receiving sets, in 1982 3·2m.; TV sets, 3·86m.

Cinemas and Theatres. There were, in 1982, 5,665 cinemas and 149 theatres and concert halls. 30 full-length feature films were made in 1982.

Newspapers. There were, in 1982, 60 newspapers and 425 periodicals. These figures include 52 in minority languages. The party newspaper is *Scînteia* ('The Spark').

JUSTICE, RELIGION, EDUCATION AND WELFARE

Justice. Justice is administered by the Supreme Court, the 40 district courts, and lower courts. Lay assessors (elected for 4 years) participate in most court trials, collaborating with the judges. The Procurator-General exercises 'supreme supervisory power to ensure the observance of the law' by all authorities, central and local, and all citizens. The Procurator's Office and its organs are independent of any organs of justice or administration, and only responsible to the Grand National Assembly (which appoints the Procurator-General for 4 years) and between its sessions, to the State Council. The Ministry of the Interior is responsible for ordinary police work. State security is the responsibility of the State Security Council. A new penal code came into force on 1 Jan. 1969. It is based on 'the rule of law' and is aimed at preventing illegal trials. The death penalty is retained for 'specially serious offences' (treason, some classes of murder, theft of property having serious consequences).

Religion. Churches are organized and function in accordance with art. 30 of the Constitution. Churches administer their own affairs and run seminaries for the training of priests. Expenses and salaries are paid by the State. There are 14 Churches, all under the control of the 'Department of Cults'. The largest is the Romanian Orthodox Church, which claimed 13·67m. members in 1950. It is autocephalous, but retains dogmatic unity with the Eastern Orthodox Church. It is administered by the consultative Holy Synod and National Ecclesiastical Assembly and the executive National Ecclesiastical Council and Patriarchal Administration. It is organized into 12 dioceses grouped into 5 metropolitan bishoprics (Hungaro-Wallachia; Moldavia-Suceava; Transylvania; Olt; Banat), and headed by Patriarch Justin Moisescu (since May 1948). There are some 11,800 churches, 2 theological colleges and 6 'schools of cantors', as well as seminaries.

The Uniate (Greek Catholic) Church (which severed its connexion with the Vatican in 1698) was suppressed in 1948. It had 1·6m. adherents and 1,818 priests. Estimates for 1973: 700,000 adherents and 600 priests.

Other churches: Serbs have a Serbian Orthodox Vicariate at Timişoara. In 1982 there were 1·2m. Roman Catholics, mainly among the Hungarian and German minorities. There is an Archbishop of Bucharest-Iaşi and a bishop of Alba Iulia. There were 734 priests in 1982. The Church has not secured approval for a Statute and has no hierarchical ties with the Vatican.

Calvinists (600,000; mainly Hungarian) have bishoprics at Cluj and Oradea; Lutherans (150,000; mainly Germans) a bishopric at Sibiu and Unitarians (60,000, Hungarians) a bishopric at Cluj. These sects share a seminary at Cluj.

In 1983 there were 32,000 Jews under a Chief Rabbi (Moses Rosen). There were 130 synagogues in 1973.

There were 40,000 moslems in 1983 and they have a Muftiate at Constanţa.

Education. Education is free and compulsory for 10 years (6 to 16), consisting of 8 years of primary school and 2 years of secondary (gymnasium). Further secondary education is available at *lycées*, professional schools or advanced technical schools.

In 1980–81[1] there were 13,467 kindergartens with 38,512 teachers and 935,711 children; 14,381 primary and secondary schools with 156,817 teachers and 3,308,462 pupils; 971 *lycées* with 46,500 teachers and 979,741 pupils; 603 professional schools with 1,954 teachers and 139,758 pupils; and 300 advanced technical schools with 257 teachers and 28,380 pupils. There are general and secondary schools for minorities, with over 250,000 pupils.

There are universities at Iaşi (founded 1860), Bucharest (1864), Cluj (1919), Timişoara (1962), Craiova (1965) and Braşov (1971). In 1980–81 there were in all 134 faculties of higher education, with a student population of 192,769.

The Academy, with seat at Bucharest, has 2 branches at Iaşi and Cluj. The National Council for Scientific Research co-ordinates research.

[1] Figures include evening classes.

Health. In 1982 there were 210,088 hospital beds and 44,030 doctors. Some hospitals began to charge fees in 1983.

DIPLOMATIC REPRESENTATIVES

Of Romania in Great Britain (4 Palace Green, London, W8 4QD)
Ambassador: Vasile Gliga.

Of Great Britain in Romania (24 Strada Jules Michelet, Bucharest)
Ambassador: P. McKearney, CMG.

Of Romania in the USA (1607–23rd St., NW, Washington, D.C., 20008)
Ambassador: Mircea Malitza.

Of the USA in Romania (7–9 Strada Tudor Arghezi, Bucharest)
Ambassador: David B. Funderburk.

Of Romania to the United Nations
Ambassador: Teodor Marinescu.

Books of Reference

Anuarul Statistic al R.S.R. Bucharest, annual
Atlas Geografic Republica Socialistă Romania. Bucharest, 1965
Dicționar Enciclopedic Român. Bucharest, 1962–66
Economic and Commercial Guide to Romania. Bucharest, annual since 1969
Mic Dicționar Enciclopedic. Bucharest, 1973
Revista de Statistică. Bucharest, monthly
Romania: An Encyclopaedic Survey. Bucharest, 1980
Romania Facts and Figures. Bucharest, 1980
Romania, the Industrialization of an Agrarian Economy under Socialist Planning: Report of a Mission sent to Romania by the World Bank. Washington, 1979
Academia Republicii Socialiste România. *Dicționar Englez-Român.* Bucharest, 1974
Ceaușescu, N., *Romania on the Way of Completing Socialist Construction.* 3 vols. Bucharest, 1968–69.—*Romania on the Way of Completing the Many-sided Developed Socialist Society.* Bucharest, 1970 ff.
Fischer-Galati, S. A., *Rumania: A Bibliographical Guide.* Library of Congress, 1963.—*The New Rumania.* Mass. Inst. of Technology, 1968.—*The Socialist Republic of Rumania.* Baltimore, 1969.—*Twentieth Century Rumania.* New York, 1970
Gilberg, T., *Modernization in Romania Since World War II.* New York, 1975
Giurescu, C. C. (ed.), *Chronological History of Romania.* 2nd ed. Bucharest, 1974
Graham, L. S., *Romania, a Developing Socialist State.* Boulder, 1982
Hemy, G. W., *Romania: Business Opportunities.* London, 1977
Ionescu, A. (ed.), *The Grand National Assembly of the Socialist Republic of Romania: A Brief Outline.* Bucharest, 1974
King, R. R., *History of the Romanian Communist Party.* Stanford, 1980
Levițchi, L., *Dicționar Român-Englez.* 2nd ed. Bucharest, 1965
Morariu, T., and others, *The Geography of Rumania.* 2nd ed. Bucharest, 1969
Nelson, D. N. (ed.), *Romania in the 1980's.* Boulder, 1981
Turnock, D., *An Economic Geography of Romania.* London, 1974

RWANDA

Republika y'u Rwanda

Capital: Kigali
Population: 5·58m. (1983)
GNP per capita: US$200 (1980)

HISTORY. From the 16th century to 1959 the Tutsi kingdom of Rwanda shared the history of Burundi (*see* p. 254). In 1959 an uprising of the Hutu destroyed the Tutsi feudal hierarchy and led to the departure of the Mwami Kigeri V. Elections and a referendum under the auspices of the United Nations in Sept. 1961 resulted in an overwhelming majority for the republican party, the Parmehutu (*Parti du Mouvement de l'Emancipation du Bahutu*), and the rejection of the institution of the Mwami. The republic proclaimed by the Parmehutu on 28 Jan. 1961 was recognized by the Belgian administration (but not by the United Nations) in Oct. 1961. Internal self-government was granted on 1 Jan. 1962, and by decision of the General Assembly of the UN the Republic of Rwanda became independent on 1 July 1962. An agreement, signed with Burundi under United Nations auspices at Addis Ababa in April 1962, provided for a monetary and customs union. These and other common organizations came to an end by 1 Oct. 1964. The first President, Gregoire Kayibanda, was deposed in a *coup* on 5 July 1973.

AREA AND POPULATION. Rwanda is bounded south by Burundi, west by Zaïre, north by Uganda and east by Tanzania. A mountainous state of 26,338 sq. km (10,169 sq. miles), its western third drains to Lake Kivu on the border with Zaïre and thence to the Congo river, while the rest is drained by the Kagera river into the Nile system.

The population was 4,819,317 at the 1978 Census, of whom over 90% were Hutu, 9% Tutsi and 1% Twa (pygmy); latest estimate (1983) 5,576,000.

The areas and populations (1978 Census) of the 10 prefectures are:

Prefecture	Census 1978	Prefecture	Census 1978
Cyangugu	331,380	Kigali	698,063
Kibuye	337,729	Kibungo	360,934
Gisenyi	468,786	Gitarama	602,752
Ruhengeri	528,649	Gikongoro	369,891
Byumba	519,968	Butare	601,165

Kigali, the capital, had 117,749 inhabitants in 1978; other towns being Butare (21,691), Runhengeri (16,025) and Gisenyi (12,436). Kinyarwanda, the language of the entire population, and French are official languages, and Kiswahili is spoken in the commercial centres, where most of the 1,200 Europeans and 750 Asians reside.

Vital statistics (1975): Live births, 113,154; deaths, 41,385; marriages, 13,899.

CLIMATE. Despite the equatorial situation, there is a highland tropical climate. The wet seasons are from Oct. to Dec. and March to May. Highest rainfall occurs in the west, at around 70″ (1,770 mm), decreasing to 40–55″ (1,020–1,400 mm) in the central uplands and to 30″ (760 mm) in the north and east. Kigali. Jan. 67°F (19·4°C), July 70°F (21·1°C). Annual rainfall 40″ (1,000 mm).

CONSTITUTION AND GOVERNMENT. A new Constitution was approved by referendum on 17 Dec. 1978; under it, the *Mouvement revolutionnaire national pour le développement* (MRND) founded 5 July 1975 becomes the sole political organisation. Executive power is vested in a President, elected by universal suffrage for a (renewable) 5-year term. He presides over a Council of Ministers, whom he appoints and dismisses; on 1 Jan. 1983 this was comprised as follows:

President: Maj.-Gen. Junéval Habyarimana (took office 5 July 1975; elected 24 Dec. 1978 and re-elected Dec. 1983).

Foreign Affairs and Co-operation: François Ngarukiyintwari.

Legislative power rests with a National Development Council of 70 deputies, elected for a 5-year term; elections were held on 26 Dec. 1983.

National flag: Three equal vertical panels of red, yellow and green (left to right), the letter 'R' in black superimposed on the centre panel.

Local government: The 10 prefectures, each under an appointed Prefect, are divided into 144 communes, each with an appointed Burgomaster and an elected Council.

DEFENCE

Army. The Army consists of 1 commando battalion, 1 reconnaissance, 8 infantry and 1 engineer companies. Equipment includes 12 AML-60/-90 armoured cars. Strength (1984) about 5,000.

Air Force. Initial equipment ordered for the Air Force in 1972 comprised 3 Italian-built Aeritalia/Aermacchi AM.3C liaison aircraft, now supplemented by 2 Guerrier armed light aircraft, 3 armed Magister jet trainers, 1 twin-engined Defender, 2 C-47s, 1 Islander light transport, 6 Gazelle and 2 Alouette III helicopters. A Caravelle is operated on VIP duties. Personnel, about 150.

INTERNATIONAL RELATIONS

Membership. Rwanda is a member of UN, OAU and is an ACP state of EEC. With Burundi and Zaïre it forms part of the Economic Community of Countries of the Great Lakes.

ECONOMY

Planning. The 1981–90 Development Plan gave priority to rural development.

Budget. The budget for 1982 envisaged expenditure of US$174·5m.

Currency. The currency is the *Rwanda franc.* The official rate of Rwanda francs 140·80 = £1; 96·86 = US$1 (March 1984).

Banking. On 5 April 1967 the Development Bank of Rwanda *(Banque Rwandaise de Développement—BRD)* was created with a capital of 50m. Rwanda francs, in 1983, 1,000m. Rwanda francs. Other banks are the Central Bank *(Banque Nationale du Rwanda)*; 2 commercial banks which are majority foreign owned—the *Banque Commerciale du Rwanda* and the *Banque de Kigali*; the People's Bank, the Savings Association and the *Caisse Hypothécaire.*

ENERGY AND NATURAL RESOURCES

Electricity. 4 hydro-electric installations and 1 thermal plant produced 30·5m. kwh in 1979, but over half of the country's needs come from Zaïre.

Minerals. Cassiterite and wolframite are mined east of Lake Kivu, from which (in 1979) 1,300 tons of tin and 505 tons of tungsten were respectively extracted. About 1m. cu. metres of natural gas are obtained from under the lake each year.

Agriculture. Subsistence agriculture accounts for most of the gross national product. Staple food crops are beans, cassava, maize, sweet potatoes, peas, groundnuts and sorghum.

The main cash crop is *aravica* coffee; the 1980 crop was about 430,000 sacks (60 kg). Tea and pyrethrum are also produced. There is a pilot rice-growing project.

Long-horned Ankole cattle, 639,000 head in 1980, play an important traditional role. Efforts are being made to improve their present negligible economic value. There were (1982) 653,000 cattle, 947,000 goats, 312,000 sheep and 144,000 pigs.

INDUSTRY AND TRADE

Industry. There are about 100 small-sized modern manufacturing enterprises in the country. Food manufacturing is the dominant industrial activity (64%) followed by construction (15·3%) and mining (9%). There are 4 hydro-electric installations and a large modern brewery. The industrial sector's contribution to GDP in 1976 was 23%.

Commerce. In 1980 imports amounted to 22,568m. Rwanda francs and exports to 7,025m. of which coffee comprised 55%, tea 18% and tin 8%; Belgium provided 16% of imports, Japan 12% and Kenya 11%, while Tanzania took 63% of exports and Kenya 13%.

Total trade between Rwanda and UK (British Department of Trade returns, in £1,000 sterling):

	1979	1980	1981	1982	1983
Imports to UK	4,145	4,666	2,058	510	2,919
Exports and re-exports from UK	1,508	1,245	1,446	2,079	2,326

COMMUNICATIONS

Roads. There were (1979) 6,579 km of roads. There are road links with Burundi, Uganda, Tanzania and Zaire. There were in 1976 3,352 cars and 4,456 trucks. Most imports and exports travel to and from Mombasa *via* Uganda.

Aviation. There are international airports at Kanombe for Kigali, and at Kamembe, with services to Bujumbura, Bukavu, Entebbe, Goma, Lubumbashi, Athens and Brussels.

Post and Broadcasting. Telephones (1978) 4,543. In 1979 there were 2 radio stations and 152,000 receivers.

Cinemas. In 1975 there were 3 cinemas with a seating capacity of 1,000.

JUSTICE, RELIGION, EDUCATION AND WELFARE

Justice. A system of Courts of First Instance and provincial courts refer appeals to Courts of Appeal and a Court of Cassation situated in Kigali.

Religion. The population is predominantly Roman Catholic (45%); there is an archbishop (Kigali) and 3 bishops. 45% of the population follow traditional religions, 9% are Protestants and 1% Moslems. The Ruanda Mission of the Church Missionary Society have 4 stations.

Education. In 1980 there were 607,480 pupils attending 1,573 primary schools with 10,002 teachers. There were 56 secondary schools with a total of 12,000. The National University, opened at Butare in 1963, had 975 students in 1979.

Health. In 1980 there were 248 hospitals and health centres with 7,889 beds; there were also 164 doctors, 1 dentist, 10 pharmacists, 464 midwives and 525 nursing personnel.

DIPLOMATIC REPRESENTATIVES

Of Rwanda in Great Britain
Ambassador: Callixte Hatungimana (resides in Brussels).

Of Great Britain in Rwanda
Ambassador: (Vacant).

Of Rwanda in the USA (1714 New Hampshire Ave, NW, Washington, D.C., 20009)
Ambassador: Simon Insonere.

Of the USA in Rwanda (Blvd. de la Revolution, Kigali)
Ambassador: John Blane.

Of Rwanda to the United Nations
Ambassador: Jean-Marie Sibomana.

Books of Reference

Hance, W. A., *African Economic Development*. London, 1967
Lacroix, B., *Le Rwanda*. Montreal, 1966
Northumb, D., *Un Humanisme Africain*. Brussels, 1965

ST CHRISTOPHER
(ST KITTS)—NEVIS

Capital: Basseterre
Population: 44,404 (1980)
GNP capita: US$ 920 (1980)

HISTORY. St Christopher (known to its Carib inhabitants as *Liamuiga*) and Nevis were discovered and named by Columbus in 1493. They were settled by Britain in 1623 and 1628 respectively, but ownership was disputed with France until 1713. Forming part of the Leeward Islands Federation from 1871 to 1956, and part of the Federation of the West Indies from 1958 to 1962, the colony achieved self-government as an Associated State of the UK on 27 Feb. 1967. In Feb. 1967 the colonial status was replaced by an 'association' with Britain, giving the islands full internal self-government, while Britain remained responsible for defence and foreign affairs. St Christopher–Nevis became fully independent on 19 Sept. 1983.

AREA AND POPULATION. The islands form part of the Lesser Antilles in Eastern Caribbean. The area is 261 sq. km: St Kitts, 168; Nevis, 93. Population, 1980: St Kitts, 35,104; Nevis, 9,300. Chief town of St Kitts, Basseterre (14,725); of Nevis, Charlestown (1,771).

CLIMATE. A pleasantly healthy climate, with a cool breeze throughout the year, low humidity and no recognised rainy season. Average annual rainfall is about 55″ (1,375 mm).

CONSTITUTION AND GOVERNMENT. The 1983 Constitution described the country as 'a sovereign democratic federal state'. It allowed for a uni-cameral Parliament consisting of 9 elected Members (6 from St Kitts and 3 from Nevis) and 3 appointed Senators. Nevis was given its own Island Assembly and gave Nevis the right to secession from St Kitts.

Governor-General: Sir Clement Athelston Arrindell.
Prime Minister: Dr Kennedy Alphonse Simmonds.
Flag: Diagonally green, black, red, with the black fimbriated in yellow and charged with two white stars.

ECONOMY
Budget. The 1982 budget envisaged revenue of EC$105,044,598 and expenditure of EC$104,591,599.

Banking. The National Bank operates 4 branches in St. Kitts and Nevis. The main office is located in Basseterre. Other banks include Barclay's Bank International, with a sub-branch in Nevis, Royal Bank of Canada, Bank of Commerce, and the Nevis Co-operative Bank in Charlestown. A branch of the Bank of Nova Scotia is located in Basseterre.

AGRICULTURE. The main crops are sugar and cotton. There are 30 sugar estates and 202 acres of cotton. Sugar occupies 50% of the cultivable land. Most of the farms are small-holdings and there are a number of coconut estates amounting to some 1,000 acres under private ownership. Sugar production (1983) 28,000 tons and 48 bales of cotton were produced in 1980.

Livestock (1982): Cattle, 8,000; pigs, 20,000; sheep, 24,000; goats, 15,000; poultry, 82,000.

INDUSTRY AND TRADE
Industry. The main employer of labour is the sugar industry. Other industries are: Clothing, footwear and assembly of electronic equipment.

Commerce. Imports, (1982) EC$120·4m.; exports, EC$50·9m. Chief exports (1981) were sugar (29,131 tons) and molasses (1·3m. gallons).

Tourism. In 1982, there were 34,575 tourists.

COMMUNICATIONS

Roads. There are about 200 km of roads.

Railways. There are 36 miles of railway operated by the sugar industry.

Aviation. There is an airport at Golden Rock (St Kitts) which is served by BWIA, PANAM, LIAT, WINAIR, PRINAIR, AIR BVI, CARICARGO. 35,296 passengers arrived by air in 1981.

Shipping. A deep water port was opened in 1981 at Bird Rock with accommodation for cargo, tourist, roll-on-roll-off ships and bulk sugar and molasses loading.

Post and Telecommunications. There is a general post office in Basseterre. Five branches are on the island. Charlestown has a general post office, and there are two branches in Nevis. There were 3,259 telephones at 30 June 1983.

JUSTICE AND EDUCATION

Justice. Justice is administered by the Supreme Court and by Magistrates' Courts. They have both civil and criminal jurisdiction.

Education. There were (1983) 34 government, 14 private and 6 denominational schools in St Kitts and Nevis. Primary education is compulsory for all children between the ages of 5 and 14, but no pupil is required to leave school before the age of 16 years. There is an Extra-Mural Department of the University of the West Indies, a Technical College and a Teachers' Training College which prepares approximately 30 teachers annually in a two-year course.

Library: Public Library, Basseterre. *Librarian:*Miss V. Archibald.

DIPLOMATIC REPRESENTATIVES

Of St Christopher and Nevis in Great Britain (10 Kensington Ct., London W8)
High Commissioner: Dr Claudius C. Thomas, CMG.

Of Great Britain in St Christopher and Nevis
High Commissioner: G. L. Bullard, CMG.

ST HELENA

HISTORY. The island was administered by the East India Company from 1659 and became a British colony in 1834.

AREA AND POPULATION. St Helena, of volcanic origin, is 1,200 miles from the west coast of Africa. Area, 47 sq. miles (121·7 sq. km), with a cultivable area of about 600 acres (243 hectares). The port of the island is Jamestown, population (1976) 1,516.

Population (1982), 5,499. Births, 123; deaths, 52; marriages, 26.

CLIMATE. A mild climate, with little variation. Temperatures range from 75–85°F (24–29°C) in summer to 65–75°F (18–24°C) in winter. Rainfall varies between 13″ (325 mm) and 37″ (925 mm) according to altitude and situation.

GOVERNMENT. The Government of St Helena is administered by a Governor, with the aid of a Legislative Council consisting of the Governor, 2 *ex-officio* members (the Government Secretary and the Treasurer) and 12 elected members. Committees of the Legislative Council are responsible for the general oversight of the activities of government departments and have, in addition, statutory and administrative functions.

The Governor is also assisted by an Executive Council consisting of the 2 *ex-officio* members and the chairmen of the five Council committees.

Governor and C.-in-C.: J. D. Massingham.
Government Secretary: P. Dale, OBE.
Flag: The British Blue Ensign with the shield of the colony in the fly.

FINANCE AND TRADE, for years from 1 April–31 March, in £ sterling:

	1977–78	1978–79	1979–80	1980–81	1981–82	1982 [3]
Revenue [1]	2,244,550	2,683,681	4,226,899	4,488,257	5,656,518	4,126,548
Expenditure [1]	2,200,299	2,764,150	4,325,910	4,551,657	5,681,934	3,988,900
Imports [2]	1,758,337	1,164,437	1,835,000	2,117,126	2,485,819	2,381,632

[1] Including imperial grants (1977–78, £1,657,231; 1978–79, £1,771,618; 1979–80, £3,347,631; 1980–81, £3,232,093· 1981–82, £3,296,933; 1982, £2,819,256).
[2] Including government stores.
[3] April–Dec.

The revenue from customs was, in 1977–78, £150,438; 1978–79, £193,576; 1979–80, £215,995; 1980–81, £283,068; 1981–82, £272,602; 1982, £305,635.

The colony's liabilities at 31 March 1982 exceeded the assets by £177,060; 31 Dec. 1982, £39,412.

Total trade between Ascension and St Helena and UK (British Department of Trade returns, in £1,000 sterling):

	1979	1980	1981	1982	1983
Imports to UK	207	476	224	754	457
Exports and re-exports from UK	2,570	3,016	3,471	7,049	10,343

BANKING. Savings-bank deposits on 31 Dec. 1982, £1,467,079, belonging to 3,800 depositors.

COMMUNICATIONS

Roads. There were 87 km of all-weather motor roads.

Shipping. The number of merchant vessels that called in 1982 (April–Dec.) was 30; total tonnage entered and cleared was 218,257.

Post and Broadcasting. The Cable & Wireless Ltd cable connects St Helena with Cape Town and Ascension Island. There is a telephone service with 85 miles of wire and (1982), 310 telephones.

St Helena Government Broadcasting Station broadcasts in English on medium-waves. Number of radio receivers (1982), 1,500.

JUSTICE, RELIGION, EDUCATION AND WELFARE

Justice. Police force, 32; cases dealt with by police magistrate, 205 in 1981.

Religion. There are 10 Anglican churches, 4 Baptist chapels, 3 Salvation Army halls, 1 Seventh Day Adventist church and 1 Roman Catholic church.

Education. Three pre-school playgroups, 8 primary, 3 senior and 1 secondary schools controlled by the Government had 980 pupils in Sept. 1982.

Health. There were 3 doctors, 1 dentist and 54 hospital beds in 1982.

Ascension is a small island of volcanic origin, of 34 sq. miles (88 sq. km), 700 miles north-west of St Helena. In Nov. 1922 the administration was transferred from the Admiralty to the Colonial Office and annexed to the colony of St Helena. There are 120 hectares providing fresh meat, vegetables and fruit. Population, 31 March 1982, was 1,625; St Helenians 759, others 866.

The island is the resort of sea turtles, which come to lay their eggs in the sand annually between Jan. and May. Rabbits, wild goats and partridges are more or less numerous on the island, which is, besides, the breeding ground of the sooty tern or 'wideawake', these birds coming in vast numbers to lay their eggs every eighth month.

Cable & Wireless Ltd own and operate a cable station, connecting the island with St Helena, Sierra Leone, St Vincent, Rio de Janeiro and Buenos Aires. There is an airstrip (Miracle Mile) near the settlement of Georgetown.

Administrator: I. G. Thow.

Tristan da Cunha, a small group of islands in the Atlantic, halfway between the Cape and South America, in 37° 6′ S. lat., 12° 1′ W. long. Besides Tristan da Cunha and Gough Island, there are Inaccessible and Nightingale Islands, the former 2 and the latter 1 mile long, and a number of rocks. As from 12 Jan. 1938 the 4 islands have become dependencies of St Helena.

Tristan consists of a volcano rising to a height of 6,760 ft, with a circumference at its base of 21 miles. The volcano, believed to be extinct, erupted unexpectedly early in Oct. 1961. The whole population was evacuated without loss and settled temporarily in the UK. In 1963 they returned to Tristan where they all dwell in the settlement of Edinburgh.

Before the disaster occurred the habitable area was a small plateau on the north west side of about 12 sq. miles, 100 ft above sea-level. Only about 30 acres was under cultivation, three-quarters of it for potatoes. There were apple and peach trees. Potatoes remain the chief crop, cattle, sheep and pigs are now reared, and fish are plentiful.

The island is extremely lonely, but the community is growing. In 1880 it numbered 109, in 1982, 325. The original inhabitants were shipwrecked sailors and soldiers who remained behind when the garrison from St Helena was withdrawn in 1817.

At the end of April 1942 Tristan da Cunha was commissioned as HMS *Atlantic Isle*, and became an important meteorological and radio station. In Jan. 1949 a South African company commenced crawfishing operations. An Administrator was appointed at the end of 1948 and a body of basic law brought into operation. The Island Council, which was set up in 1932, in 1982 consisted of a Chief Islander, 3 nominated and 7 elected members under the chairmanship of the Administrator. Women's affairs are discussed by the Island Women's Council, which presents them for consideration to the general council.

Administrator: C. F. Redston.

Books of Reference

Booy, D. M., *Rock of Exile: A Narrative of Tristan da Cunha.* London, 1957
Crawford, A., *Tristan da Cunha and the Roaring Forties.* Edinburgh, 1982
Cross, A., *Saint Helena.* Newton Abbot, 1980
Holdgate, M., *Mountains in the Sea.* London, 1958
Munch, P. A., *Sociology of Tristan da Cunha.* Oslo, 1945.—*Crisis in Utopia.* New York, 1971
Stonehouse, B., *Wideawake Island* (Ascension). London, 1960

ST LUCIA

Capital: Castries
Population: 120,300 (1980)
GNP per capita: US$970 (1981)

HISTORY. St Lucia was discovered about 1500 A.D. Attempts to colonize the island by the English took place in 1605 and 1638. The French settled in 1650 and St Lucia was ceded to Britain in 1814. Self-government was achieved in 1967 and independence on 22 Feb. 1979.

AREA AND POPULATION. St Lucia is a small island of the Lesser Antilles situated in the Eastern Caribbean, 238 sq. miles (616 sq. km); population (1980) 120,300. The capital is Castries (population, 45,000). Life expectancy (1983) was 65 (men) and 71 (women).

CLIMATE. The climate is tropical, with a dry season lasting from Jan. to April, a wet season from May to Aug., followed by an Indian summer for two months, but most rain falls in Nov. and Dec. Amounts vary over the year, according to altitude, from 60″ (1,500 mm) to 138″ (3,450 mm). Temperatures are uniform at about 80°F (26·7°C).

CONSTITUTION AND GOVERNMENT. There is a 17-seat House of Assembly elected for 5 years; an 11-seat Senate appointed by the Governor-General, 6 on the advice of the Prime Minister, 3 on the advice of the Leader of the Opposition, and 2 'after consultation with appropriate religious, economic or social bodies or associations'.

At the elections in May 1982, the United Workers' Party gained 14 seats, the St Lucia Labour Party, 2 and the Progressive Labour Party, 1.

Governor-General: Sir Allen Lewis.
Prime Minister: John George Melvin Compton.
Flag: Blue with a design of a black triangle edged in white, bearing a smaller yellow triangle, in the centre.

INTERNATIONAL RELATIONS

Membership. St Lucia is a member of UN, OAS, Caricom, the Commonwealth and is an ACP state of the EEC.

ECONOMY

Budget. The budget in 1983–84 amounted to EC$185·7m. expenditure.

Banking. There are Barclays Bank International with 2 branches and 4 agencies, the Royal Bank of Canada, the Bank of Nova Scotia and the Canadian Imperial Bank of Commerce (all of which have 1 branch each), the Chase Manhattan Bank, the St Lucia Co-operative bank, the National Development Bank with 1 branch and the Government Savings Bank. The Government Savings Bank (end of 1974), 8,400 depositors, $359,086 deposits.

INDUSTRY AND TRADE

Agriculture. Bananas, cocoa, copra and coconut oil are the chief products.
Livestock (1982): Cattle, 11,000; pigs, 10,000; sheep, 14,000; goats, 10,000; poultry, 200,000.

Commerce. Value of imports (1980), EC$123·8m.; of exports, EC$40·4m., including coconut oil, cocoa beans, copra and bananas. Main items of imports were artificial silk and cotton piece-goods, cement, plastic goods, iron and steel products, hardware, motor vehicles, agricultural machinery, fertilizers, wheat flour, codfish and rice, meat and meat preparations.

Tourism. The total number of visitors during 1982 was 98,181.

COMMUNICATIONS

Roads. The island has 500 miles of main and secondary roads.

Aviation. The island is served on a scheduled basis by Leeward Islands Air Transport, British West Indian Airways and Eastern Airline. There are 2 airfields—Hewanorra International Airport, with 9,000 ft runway, and Vigie.

Shipping. Registered fleet (31 Dec. 1974): 3 motor vessels (94 gross tons). In 1974, 2,798 vessels of 3·5m. gross tons entered Castries and Vieux Fort.

Post and Broadcasting. There are 104 miles of telephone trunk lines, plus 300 miles of local lines. There were (1982) 9,500 telephone instruments coupled to some (1982) 4,881 exchange lines. They operate through 10 automatic exchanges. There were 1,700 TV and 82,000 radio receivers in 1975.

Cinemas. There were 9 cinemas in 1970 with a seating capacity of 9,500.

JUSTICE, EDUCATION AND WELFARE

Justice. The island is divided into 2 judicial districts, and there are 9 magistrates' courts. Appeals lie with the Court of Appeal of the Windward and Leeward Islands, subject to exceptions and conditions as may be enacted by the St Lucia legislature.

Police establishment in 1974 was 11 officers, 11 inspectors and 267 others.

Education (1983–84). 81 primary schools (39 Roman Catholic, 3 Anglican, 3 Methodist, 35 government, 1 other), with 31,888 pupils on roll; government expenditure, 1982–83, $19,338,834. Primary education is free and compulsory by law, but the legislation is not enforced. There are 12 secondary schools (2 Roman Catholic, 1 Seventh-day Adventist, 9 government) with 4,984 pupils; government expenditure, 1982–83, $15,745,832. There is 1 technical college with (1982–83) 199 students and 1 teachers' college with (1982–83) 131 students.

Health. Victoria Hospital (in Castries) has 213 beds; there is also a 162-bed mental hospital, 3 other hospitals (150 beds) and 29 health centres. In 1983 there were 36 doctors, 5 dentists, 16 pharmacists and 246 nursing personnel.

Library: The Central Library, Castries. *Acting Librarian:* Frances Niles.

DIPLOMATIC REPRESENTATIVES

Of St Lucia in Great Britain (10 Kensington Ct., London, W8)
High Commissioner: Dr Claudius C. Thomas, CMG.

Of Great Britain in St Lucia (Colombus Sq., Castries)
High Commissioner: G. L. Bullard, CMG.

Of St Lucia in USA and to the United Nations
Ambassador: Donatus St Aimee.

ST VINCENT AND THE GRENADINES

Capital: Kingstown
Population: 123,000 (1984)
GNP per capita: US$630 (1981)

HISTORY. The date of discovery of St Vincent is not known. In 1969 St Vincent became a self-governing Associated State of UK and acquired full independence on 27 Oct. 1979.

AREA AND POPULATION. The total area of 389 sq. km (150·3 sq. miles) comprises the island of St Vincent itself (345 sq. km) and the Northern Grenadines (44 sq. km) of which the largest are Bequia, Mustique, Canouan, Mayreau and Union. Population, estimate, 1984, 123,000. Capital, Kingstown, population (1978), 22,782. Vital statistics (1981): Live births, 3,327; still births, 10; deaths, 772; marriages, 403.

CLIMATE. The climate is tropical marine, with north-east Trades predominating and rainfall ranging from 150″ (3,750 mm) a year in the mountains to 60″ (1,500 mm) on the south-east coast. The rainy season is from June to Dec., and temperatures are equable throughout the year.

CONSTITUTION AND GOVERNMENT. Independence from the UK was achieved on 27 Oct. 1979. The House of Assembly consists of 13 elected members, directly elected for a 5-year term from single-member constituencies, the Attorney-General (elected) and 6 Senators appointed by the Governor-General (4 on the advice of the Prime Minister and 2 on the advice of the Leader of the Opposition).

Governor-General: Sir Sydney Gun-Munro, GCMG, MBE.
Prime Minister: Robert Milton Cato, PC.

National Flag: Three vertical stripes of blue, yellow, green, with white fimbriations, charged in the centre with a green leaf of bread-fruit bearing the arms of St Vincent.

INTERNATIONAL RELATIONS

Membership. St Vincent and the Grenadines is a member of UN, OAS, Caricom, the Commonwealth and is an ACP state of the EEC.

ECONOMY

Budget. Revenue (estimate), 1983–84, $90,247,930; development aid, $3,778,025, and other sources, $49,223,330; expenditure, $86,060,065; $3,778,025 on British development projects and $49,223,330 on other projects. Public debt at the end of the financial year 1982–83 was $10,119,900.

Currency. The currency is the Eastern Caribbean *dollar.* In March 1984, £1 = EC$4·01; US$1 =EC$2·70.

Banking. There are branches of Barclays Bank International, the Royal Bank of Canada, the Canadian Imperial Bank of Commerce, the National Commercial Bank, the Bank of Nova Scotia, St Vincent Co-operative Bank and the St Vincent Agricultural Credit and Loan Bank at Kingstown.

ENERGY AND NATURAL RESOURCES

Electricity. The electricity system is owned jointly by the Government (49%) and the Commonwealth Development Corporation (51%) and operated by the St Vincent Electricity Services (VINLEC). The system consists of 4 power stations: South

Rivers Hydro (870 kw.); Cane Hall Diesel (3,640 kw.); Kingstown Diesel (2,075 kw.) and Richmond Hydro (1,100 kw.), which are linked by 11,000-volt transmission lines covering the island from Richmond through Kingstown to Georgetown. In Bequia there is one diesel station (800 kw.) with transmission at 11,000, 3,300 and 400 volts to Hamilton and Port Elizabeth. Current is supplied at 400 volts 3-phase, 50 cycles for industrial purposes and 230 volts single phase for domestic purposes. At 31 Dec. 1982 there were 11,384 consumers in St Vincent, 837 in Bequia and 266 in Union Island.

Agriculture. The estimated alienated area is about 47,000 of the total acreage of 85,120. 34,000 acres are under forest and woodland; of these about 5,000 acres are used for grazing; 3,000 are considered potentially productive for agriculture and 5,000 for forestry. About 14,000 acres are considered unsuitable for either agriculture or forestry. Of the total alienated area, 34,000 acres are considered arable land, of which 20,000 acres are under temporary crops, 4,000 acres under temporary meadows, 300 acres devoted to market-garden crops with temporary fallow and all other arable land making up a further 9,700 acres. About 11,000 acres are devoted to permanent crops, of which approximately 6,000 acres are under coconuts; the remainder produce cocoa, nutmegs, mangoes, avocado pears, guavas and miscellaneous crops. About 2,000 acres are under permanent meadow, of which 750 are cultivated.

Land ownership: Crown, 38,000 acres; planters, 17,000 acres; small farmers, 25,500 acres; settlements, 6,000 acres.

Livestock (1982): Cattle, 6,690; pigs, 5,757; sheep, 14,010; goats, 4,917; chickens (1981), 50,000.

INDUSTRY AND TRADE

Trade (1982). Imports, EC$164,395,560; exports, EC$87,371,301. Value of imports from the UK (1982), £10,891,000; of exports to the UK (1982), £3,265,000.

Principal exports, 1982:

		ECS			ECS
Arrowroot starch	293,735 lb.	577,745	Coconut oil,		
Eddoes	8,038,719 lb.	5,627,862	crude	112,905 gals.	1,237,439
Bananas	58,865,459 lb.	23,503,964	Coconut oil,		
Sweet potatoes [1]	869,906 lb.	301,912	refined	1,350 gals.	19,413
Coconuts	1,022,051 nuts	423,361	Tannias	4,127,331 lb.	2,879,085

[1] July–Dec.

Labour (1983). The Department of Labour serves both worker's and employers' organizations as a conciliatory body in case of dispute. Conciliatory meetings are held on dispute matters such as delay in the recognition of a union as collective bargaining agent for the workers, dismissals, overtime pay, delay in finalizing collective agreements and other conditions of work. There are 5 active trade unions: the St Vincent Union of Teachers, the Public Service Union, the Commercial, Technical and Allied Workers' Union, the National Workers' Movement and the National Farmers' Union.

Tourism. There were 82,196 visitors in 1982.

COMMUNICATIONS

Roads. There are 313 km of all-weather roads, 160 km of rough motorable roads and 161 km of tracks.

Aviation. Scheduled services are operated daily by LIAT, Air Martinique and WINLINK. Non-scheduled services are operated by Mustique Airways, Tropical Air Services, Aero-Services and St Lucia Airways. Passengers are able to travel daily through the chain of islands stretching as far north as San Juan, Puerto Rico and south to Trinidad. Connexions to the USA, Canada, South America and Europe are possible *via* Barbados, Antigua, Trinidad and St Lucia.

Shipping (1982): (a) 51 auxiliary sailing vessels of 1,597 NRT entered and cleared.

(b) 19 steamships of 142,030 NRT entered and cleared. (c) 649 motor vessels of 226,826 NRT entered and cleared. (d) 60 tankers of 49,612 NRT bringing 16,169 tons of fuel entered. A deep-water harbour at Kingstown was completed in 1964.

Post and Broadcasting. There is a General Post Office at Kingstown and 47 district post offices. There is a telephone system with 2,000 miles of line and (1982), 6,047 subscribers; 5,745 stations and a radio telephone service to Bequia, Mustique, Union Island, Petit St Vincent and Palm Island. In 1974 there were 600 TV and 30,000 radio receivers.

Cinemas. There were 3 cinemas in 1979 with a seating capacity of 2,400.

JUSTICE, EDUCATION AND WELFARE

Justice (1981). There were 3,552 criminal matters disposed of in the 3 magisterial districts which comprise 11 courts. Strength of police force (1982), 525 (including 12 officers).

Education (1982). Sixty-two primary schools; pupils on roll, 24,569, average attendance, 20,389. Expenditure on primary education, $7,688,803. There is also a secondary school for girls (655 pupils), a co-educational school (492 pupils), as well as 11 assisted secondary schools (2,630 pupils) and 6 junior secondary schools with 1,346 pupils. Expenditure on secondary education, $2,277,990.

Health. There is a General Hospital in Kingstown (204 beds), 4 rural hospitals at Chateaubelair, Georgetown, Union Island and Bequia, 2 specialist hospitals and 34 medical clinics. In 1982 there were 29 doctors, 3 dentists, 5 midwives, 260 nursing personnel and 36 community health aides.

Library: St Vincent Public Library, Kingstown. *Librarian:* Mrs Lorna Small.

DIPLOMATIC REPRESENTATIVES

Of St Vincent and the Grenadines in Great Britain (10 Kensington Ct, London, W8)
High Commissioner: Dr Claudius C. Thomas, CMG.

Of Great Britain in St Vincent and the Grenadines
High Commissioner: G. L. Bullard, CMG (resides in Bridgetown).

Of St Vincent and the Grenadines in the USA and to the United Nations
Ambassador: Hudson Kemul Tannis.

SAN MARINO

Capital: San Marino
Population: 21,622 (1981)

Repubblica di San Marino

HISTORY. On 22 March 1862 San Marino concluded a treaty of friendship and co-operation, including a *de facto* customs union with the kingdom of Italy, preserving the independence of the ancient republic, although completely surrounded by Italian territory. The treaty was renewed on 27 March 1872, 28 June 1897 and 31 March 1939, with 7 amendments in 1942–71.

The republic has extradition treaties with Belgium, France, the Netherlands, UK and USA.

AREA AND POPULATION. San Marino is a land-locked state in central Italy, 20 km from the Adriatic. The frontier line is 38·6 km in length, area is 61·19 sq. km (24·1 sq. miles) and the population (30 June 1981), 21,622; some 20,000 citizens live abroad.

CONSTITUTION AND GOVERNMENT. The legislative power is vested in the Great and General Council of 60 members elected every 5 years by popular vote, 2 of whom are appointed every 6 months to act as regents *(Capitani reggenti).*

The elections held on 29 May 1983 gave 26 seats to the Christian Democrats, 15 to the Communists, 17 to Socialist parties, 2 to others.

The regents exercise executive power together with the Congress of State *(Congresso di Stato),* which comprises 11 departments, and through Commissions on social welfare, public works, etc.

National flag: Horizontally white over light blue, with the national arms over all in the centre.

DEFENCE. The militia consists, in case of necessity, of all able-bodied citizens between the ages of 16 and 55, with certain exceptions (teachers and students, etc.).

ECONOMY. The budget (ordinary and extraordinary) for the financial year ending 31 Dec. 1981 balanced at 144,103,052,187 lire.

The chief exports are wood machinery, chemicals, wine, textiles, tiles, varnishes and ceramics.

Italian and Vatican City currency is in general use, but the republic issues its own postage stamps and coins.

In 1980, 3·5m. tourists visited San Marino.

COMMUNICATIONS

Roads. A bus service connects San Marino with Rimini.

Aviation. There is a helicopter service to Rimini in summer.

Post. In 1982 there were 8,712 telephones.

Cinemas. In 1974 there were 8 cinemas with a seating capacity of 2,300.

JUSTICE AND EDUCATION

Justice. Law is administered by a Commissioner for civil and commercial cases and a Commissioner for criminal cases (acting with a penal judge), from whom appeals can be made to a civil appeals judge and a criminal appeals judge respectively. The highest legal authority is, in certain cases, the *Consiglio dei XII.*

Education. There are 19 infant schools, 16 elementary schools, a secondary school and a grammar school, the diplomas of which are recognized by Italian universities. Civil marriage was instituted in Sept. 1953.

DIPLOMATIC REPRESENTATIVES

British Consul-General (resides at Florence): R. A. Eilbeck.
USA Consul-General (resides at Florence): Donald A. Johnston.
Consul-General in London: Charles Forte.

Books of Reference

Information: Segreteria di Stato per gli Affari Esteri; Ente Governativo per il Turismo.

Garbeletto, A., *Evoluzione storica della costituzione di S. Marino.* Milan, 1956
Packett, C. N., *Guide to the Republic of San Marino.* Bradford, 1970
Rossi, G., *San Marino.* San Marino, 1954

SÃO TOMÉ E PRINCIPE

Capital: São Tomé
Population: 100,000 (1983)
GNP per capita: US$490 (1980)

HISTORY. The islands of São Tomé and Príncipe, were discovered in 1471 by Pedro Escobar and João Gomes, and from 1522 until independence had constituted a province of Portugal.

On 26 Nov. 1974 the Government of Portugal and the liberation movement of São Tomé e Príncipe signed an agreement granting independence to the archipelago on 12 July 1975 to become the Democratic Republic of São Tomé e Príncipe.

AREA AND POPULATION. The republic, which lies about 200 km off the west coast of Gabon, in the Gulf of Guinea, comprises the main islands of São Tomé (845 sq. km) and Príncipe and several smaller islets including Pedras Tinhosas and Rolas. It has a total area of 964 sq. km (372 sq. miles). Total population (census, 1970) 73,631 (São Tomé, 69,032; Príncipe, 4,599). Estimate (1983) 100,000. Capital, São Tomé (25,000).

Vital statistics (1978): Births, 3,479; deaths, 800.

CLIMATE. The tropical climate is modified by altitude and the effect of the cool Benguela current. The wet season is generally from Oct. to May, but rainfall varies very much, from 40" (1,000 mm) in the hot and humid north-east to 150–200" (3,800–5,000 mm) on the plateau.

CONSTITUTION AND GOVERNMENT. A new constitution was approved by the Constitutional Assembly (elected 6 July 1975) on 12 Dec. 1975. Under it, the sole legal party is the *Movimento de Libertação de São Tomé e Príncipe,* who nominate candidates for the Presidency and People's Assembly. The President is elected by the People's Assembly for a 4-year term; he is also head of government and appoints a Cabinet of Ministers to assist him. The 40-member People's Assembly is also elected for 4 years.

The Cabinet was composed as follows in June 1983:

President, Prime Minister, National Security and Defence: Dr Manuel Pinto da Costa.

Foreign Affairs: Maria do Nascimento da Graça Amorim. *Education and Culture:* Joaquim Rafael Branco. *Information:* Maria de Rosário Lima Barros. *Health and Sports:* Carlos Alberto Peres Tini. *Planning:* Henrique Pinto da Costa. *Labour and Social Security:* Dionisio Tomé Dias. *Industry, Works and Housing:* Lieut. Oscar Aguiar Sacramento e Sousa. *Commerce:* Fausto Soares de Vera Cruz. *Justice:* Celestino Rocha da Costa. *Agriculture and Fishing:* Arlindo Braganca Gomes. *Secretaries of State:* Fernando José Paquete da Costa *(Transport and Communications),* Aurélio do Espírito Santo *(Fishing).*

Flag: Three horizontal stripes of green, yellow, green, with the yellow of double width and bearing 2 black stars; in the hoist a red triangle over all.

INTERNATIONAL RELATIONS

Membership. São Tomé e Príncipe is a member of UN, OAU and is an ACP state of EEC.

DEFENCE. Initial equipment of the air force comprises a few L-39 jet trainers from Czechoslovakia and Soviet-built An-32 twin-turboprop transports. Armed forces strength (estimate, 1976) 160.

ECONOMY

Budget. In 1977 the budget envisaged revenue of 179·6m. dobra and expenditure of 454·2m. dobra.

Currency. The currency is the *dobra*, introduced in 1977, divided into 100 *centavos*. In March 1984, £1 = 63·55 *dobra*; US$1 = 42·67 *dobra*.

Banking. *Banco Nacional de São Tomé e Príncipe* (established, 1975) is the central bank.

AGRICULTURE. The chief commercial products are cacao, copra, coconut, coffee, palm-oil and cinchona. In 1982 there were 4,000 goats, 2,000 sheep, 3,000 pigs and 3,000 cattle.

COMMERCE. Imports in 1975 amounted to 288,469,000 dobras and exports to 180,432,000 dobras, the main exports being cocoa (87%), copra (8%), coffee, bananas and palm-oil. In 1975 Portugal provided 61% of imports and Angola 13%, while the Netherlands took 52% of exports and Portugal 33%.

Total trade between São Tomé e Príncipe and UK (British Department of Trade returns, in £1,000 sterling):

	1980	1981	1982	1983
Imports to UK	99	207	494	218
Exports and re-exports from UK	2,103	625	1,510	597

COMMUNICATIONS

Roads. There were 288 km of roads in 1973.

Shipping. In 1975, 70 vessels entered the port of São Tomé to unload 26,693 tonnes and load 9,880 tonnes.

Aviation. São Tomé airport is linked by regular services to Douala, Lisbon, Luanda and Malabo, as well as to Príncipe. In 1975, 10,050 passengers arrived and 9,240 departed.

Post. There were, in 1973, 3 wireless stations with (1977) 21,000 radio receivers, 352 km of telephone lines and a telephone exchange (with 850 instruments in 1980).

Cinemas. In 1972 there was 1 cinema with a seating capacity of 1,000.

JUSTICE, RELIGION, EDUCATION AND WELFARE.

Justice. The members of the Supreme Court are appointed by the People's Assembly.

Religion. The vast majority of the population are Roman Catholic.

Education. In 1977 there were 14,162 pupils and 527 teachers in primary schools, 3,145 pupils and 81 teachers in 3 secondary schools, and 155 students and 30 teachers in technical schools.

Health. In 1976 there were 11 hospitals and dispensaries with 530 beds. In 1973 there were 12 doctors, 6 midwives and 63 nursing personnel.

DIPLOMATIC REPRESENTATIVES

Of Great Britain in São Tomé and Príncipe
Ambassador: M. I. Goulding, CMG (resides in Luanda).

Of São Tomé and Príncipe to the United Nations
Ambassador: (Vacant).

Book of Reference

S. Tomé e Príncipe. Agência-Geral do Ultramar, 1964

SAUDI ARABIA

al-Mamlaka al-'Arabiya as-Sa'udiya

Capital: Riyadh
Population: 9·32m. (1981)
GNP per capita: US$11,260 (1980)

HISTORY. Saudi Arabia was founded by Abdul-Aziz ibn Abdur-Rahman al-Faisal Al Sa'ud, GCB, GCIE (born about 1880; died 9 Nov. 1953), who had been proclaimed King of the Hejaz on 8 Jan. 1926 and had in 1927 changed his title of Sultan of Nejd and its dependencies to that of king, thus becoming 'King of the Hejaz and of Nejd and its Dependencies'. On 20 May 1927 a treaty was signed at Jiddah between Great Britain and Ibn Sa'ud, by which the former recognized the complete independence of the dominions of the latter. The name of the State was changed to 'The Saudi Arabian Kingdom' by decree of 23 Sept. 1932.

In Nov. 1937 a general agreement between Saudi Arabia and the Yemen concerning the settlement of disputes was ratified, and an agreement regarding the delimitation of the frontiers was negotiated.

In March 1953 the treaty of Taif, first signed with the Yemen in May 1934, was extended for 20 lunar years.

In 1942 Saudi Arabia and the British Government, acting on behalf of the Shaikh of Kuwait, signed agreements for friendship and neighbourly relations, for the extradition of offenders and for the regulation of trade between Saudi Arabia and Kuwait.

In Aug. 1962 Saudi Arabia and Jordan agreed on measures of co-operation in the military, political and economic fields.

King Faisal ibn Abdul-Aziz was assassinated on 25 March 1975 by his nephew. There appeared to be no political motive.

AREA AND POPULATION. The total area of Saudi Arabia is estimated to be 927,000 sq. miles (2·4m. sq. km).

The principal cities of the Western Province (formerly *Hejaz*) are Jiddah (561,104 inhabitants at the 1974 Census), Mecca (366,801), Taif (204, 857) and Medina (198,196); of the Central Province (formerly *Nejd*) are Riyadh, the national capital (666,840), Buraidah (69,940), Ha'il (40,502), Anaiza and Al-Kharj; of the Northern Province are Tabouk (74,825), Al-Jawf and Sakaka; of the Eastern Province (formerly *Al-Hasa*) are Dammam (127,844), Hofuf (101,271), Haradh (100,000), Al-Mobarraz (54,325), Al-Khabar (48,817) and Qatif; and of the Southern Province (formerly *Asir*) are Khamis-Mushait (49,581), Najran (47,501), Qizan (32,814) and Abha (30,150). New industrial cities are being built at Jubail (future pop. 300,000) and Yanbu (150,000).

Taif, about 3,800ft above sea-level and some 50 miles from Mecca, is a summer resort.

The total population was (1974 census) 7,012,642, of which 5,128,655 were categorized as settled and 1,883,987 as nomadic. Estimate (1981) 9·32m.

CLIMATE. A desert climate, with very little rain and none at all from June to Dec. The months May to Sept. are very hot and humid, but winter temperatures are quite pleasant. Riyadh. Jan. 58°F (14·4°C), July 92°F (33·3°C). Annual rainfall 4″ (100 mm). Jiddah. Jan. 73°F (22·8°C), July 87°F (30·6°C). Annual rainfall 3″ (81 mm).

KING. Fahd bin Abdulaziz; succeeded in May 1982, after King Khalid's death. *Crown Prince:* Prince Abdullah ibn Abdul-Aziz, First Deputy Prime Minister, brother of the King.

National flag: Green, with the text 'There is no God but Allah and Mohammed is his prophet' in white Arabic script, and beneath this a white sabre.

GOVERNMENT AND CONSTITUTION. The Kingdom has been welded together from Hejaz, Nejd, Asir and Al-Hasa. Riyadh is the political capital and Mecca the religious capital. There is no formal Constitution.

In May 1958 a 'Cabinet system' was instituted under which, from 1962, effective power devolved upon the President of the Council of Ministers.

The King has the post of Prime Minister.

First Deputy Prime Minister and Commander of the National Guards: Prince Abdullah ibn Abdulaziz.

Second Deputy Prime Minister and Defence and Aviation: Prince Sultan ibn Abdul-Aziz.

Foreign Minister: Prince Saud al Faisal. *Interior:* Prince Nayef ibn Abdul-Aziz. *Petroleum and Natural Resources:* Sheikh Ahmed Zaki Yamani. *Finance and Economy:* Sheikh Muhammad Ali Aba al Khail. *Health:* Dr Ghazi Algosaibi. *Industry and Electricity:* Abdul-Aziz Zamil.

There are provisions for the setting up of certain advisory councils, comprising a consultative Legislative Assembly in Mecca, municipal councils in each of the towns of Mecca, Medina and Jidda, and village and tribal councils throughout the provinces. The country is divided for administrative purposes into 6 major and 12 minor provinces.

DEFENCE. In 1937 a Ministry of Defence and a training school for officers were established. British Military and Civil Air Missions helped in training the Army and civil aviation from 1947 to 1951. The US now maintains a Military Mission (with an Air Force element) as do France and Pakistan. UK provides small army and air force teams. Personnel are trained in Saudi Arabia, France, Pakistan, UK and the USA. Military service is compulsory for men aged 18–35 years.

Army. The Army comprises 2 armoured brigades (1 manned by Pakistan troops), 3 mechanized brigades and 1 infantry brigade. Equipment is mainly US or French (M114, M101, M109 and M198 artillery, M113 APCs, M60 tanks; AMX10 APC, AMX30 tanks, CGT155mm Howitzer, HOT on AMX30 chassis. Ground-to-air defence provided by Shahine (with armoured brigades), 20mm Vulcan gun. There are two airborne battalions. Total strength of Army (1984) approximately 27,000. There are para-military forces with the Ministry of Interior; Frontier Force (approximately 9,000) and Special Security Force (1,800) of which the latter is equipped with anti-riot and internal security equipment (mostly West German).

National Guard. The National Guard comprises 1 mechanized brigade (trained by the US), 1 Special Security Unit. An additional mechanized brigade is planned. Additionally there are a number of regular and irregular units, the total strength of the National Guard amounting to approximately 30,000. National Guard's primary role is the protection of the Royal Family and vital points in the Kingdom. It does not come under command of the Ministry of Defence and Aviation.

Navy. The Royal Saudi Naval Forces, with recent modernisation programme impetus under the aegis of USA and France, comprise 1 new French-built guided missile frigate of 2,600 tons, 4 new US-built missile-armed fast corvettes of 800 tons, 9 fast missile craft of 380 tons (all completed in 1980–82 in USA), 3 *ex*-German torpedo boats, 4 US-built MSC-type coastal minesweepers, 1 *ex*-US coastguard cutter, 8 new French-built patrol craft, 30 coastal patrol boats, 6 custom launches, 16 hovercraft, 2 air-sea rescue launches, 1 training ship, 4 landing craft, 12 minor landing craft, 1 salvage vessel, 2 tugs and the royal yacht. New construction includes 3 more guided missile frigates in France and 2 fleet replenishment tankers of 10,500 tons. There are 24 helicopters. An intensive training programme is under-way in USA and Saudi Arabia. $70m. is being spent on three naval bases. The main port facilities are at Jubail and Jedda.

Naval personnel in 1984 totalled 400 officers and 4,000 other ranks plus instructors and trainees. RSNF rely on considerable US and Pakistan support.

The Coast Guard operates 130 coastal patrol craft, 4 hovercraft, 300 inshore patrol cutters, 3 small oilers and 12 service craft.

Air Force. Formed as a small army support unit in 1932, the Air Force has been built up considerably with British and US assistance since 1946. Complete re-equipment began in 1966 and delivery of 62 F-15 Eagles to equip 3 air superiority squadrons began in 1982; they will operate in conjunction with 5 E-3A Sentry AWACS aircraft and 6 KC-707 flight refuelling tankers. Current combat units include 1 squadron of Lightning F.53 supersonic interceptors, supported by 2-seat fighter-trainers. There are 3 squadrons of F-5E Tiger II supersonic fighter-bombers, supported by a conversion unit with F-5B/F combat trainers. Two squadrons of Strikemaster light jet attack/trainers are based at the King Faisal Air Academy, Riyadh, together with 12 Reims/Cessna FR172 piston-engined primary trainers. Other types in current service include 34 C-130E/H and 8 KC-130H Hercules transports and tankers, 2 C-130H hospital aircraft, 1 Boeing 747 SP, 1 Boeing 707, and 2 JetStar VIP jet transports, more than 70 Agusta-Bell 205, 212 and JetRanger helicopters, 2 Agusta AS-61A-4 VIP transport helicopters, 16 Kawasaki-Boeing Vertol KV-107 helicopters, and communications aircraft. On order are 10 RF-5E Tiger Eye reconnaissance-fighters and 40 Indonesian-built CASA Aviocar twin-turboprop transports. Personnel, about 14,500.

Air Defence Command. This separate Command was formerly part of the Army, which retains a point air defence capability. It is heavily reliant on Pakistan assistance. particularly manpower. Equipment comprises approximately 18 Crotale missile systems, 15 batteries of Improved Hawk surface-to-air missiles, 30 mm Oerlikon and 20 mm Vulcan guns. Personnel strength about 3,000.

INTERNATIONAL RELATIONS

Membership. Saudi Arabia is a member of UN, the Arab League and OPEC.

ECONOMY

Planning. The third development plan runs 1980–85, and emphasizes industrial development and the training of an indigenous work force. GDP is expected to grow at 6·2% in the non-oil economy: industrial growth will be much higher than this, but an anticipated decline in the construction sector depresses the figure. Government expenditure during the third plan is expected to total 783,000m. rials, of which 262,000m. for the development of economic resources, 130,000m. for education and training, 61,000m. for social welfare and 249,000m. for physical infrastructure.

Budget. The fiscal year runs from 1 Rajab to 30 Jumad II in the lunar calendar, and consequently starts approximately 10 days earlier each year. The 1983–84 budget envisaged expenditure of 260,000m. rials and revenue of 225,000m. rials.

Currency. The paper *rial* is divided into 100 *halalas*. In March 1984, £1 = 5·21 *rials*; US$1 = 3·51 *rials*.

Banking. There are 2 commercial banks of Saudi Arabian origin: the National Commercial Bank and the Riyadh Bank. It is government policy to encourage foreign banks operating in the kingdom to become Saudized. By 1982 there were 7 banks in which foreign capital represents only 40%: al Jazira Bank (National Bank of Pakistan), Saudi Dutch Bank (Algemene Bank Nederland), Saudi French Bank (Banque de l'Indochine et de Suez), Saudi British Bank (British Bank of the Middle East), Saudi Cairo Bank (Banque du Caire), the Saudi-American Bank (Citibank) and the Arab National Bank (Arab Bank of Jordan). All these banks are entitled to open branches nationwide.

In addition the Banque du Liban et d'Outremer and the Bank Melli in Jiddah and the United Bank (of Pakistan) in Dammam have invited subscription to an eighth bank that will operate by 1983.

ENERGY AND NATURAL RESOURCES

Electricity. 7,010m. kwh. was generated by the main electricity companies in 1977, 9,435m. kwh. in 1978 and 17,597m. kwh in 1980.

Oil. The first general geologic–geographical survey of Saudi Arabia was completed in 1961 under the joint sponsorship of the Saudi Arabian and US governments but surveying continues.

The original oil concession agreement was signed in 1933 with Standard Oil Co. of California. The name Aramco appeared in 1944, and by 1948 Exxon, Texaco and Mobil held shares in the company. In 1973 the Saudi Arabian Government acquired a 25% interest in Aramco: this became 60% in 1974, and in 1979 it was announced that the Government had taken full control of Aramco equity retroactively from Jan. 1976. By 1979 Aramco retained only 189,000 sq. km or 15·4% of the original concession areas.

Two other companies have concessions of Saudi Arabia's oil rights in the Kuwait/Saudi Arabian Neutral Zone. Getty Oil's concession dates from 1953 and that of the Arabian Oil Co. (Japanese) from 1958.

Crude oil production in 1981 was 3,586m. bbls. Crude oil exports in 1980 were 3,374m. bbls, of which Aramco provided 97·4%, Arabian Oil 1·94% and Getty Oil 0·6%. 1980 oil exports earned US$101,421m. (95m. for crude) and Aramco earned 98% of this total.

The agency responsible for co-ordination of national oil policy is Petromin (General Petroleum and Minerals Organization). Petromin manages exploration and concession agreements, oil refineries (except that of Aramco at Ras Tanura) and the distribution and marketing of oil and oil products.

In 1982, when Aramco produced 2,300m. bbls of crude oil, 55m. (2·38%) were sent by pipeline to Bahrain, and 1,500m. bbls (67·78%) were shipped out *via* Gulf terminals. The volume of crude exported will decline as the national refining capacity increases. In 1982 total refining capacity was 725,000 bbls per day including Ras Tanura (Aramco) 470,000 bbls per day, 120,000 bbls per day at Riyadh and 105,000 bbls per day at Jiddah (both Petromin). In 1982, 834,900 bbls per day of refined products were produced by Saudi Arabian refineries, of which fuel oil accounted for 382,700, gasoline, 194,000, Kerozene, 33,400.

About 3,000m. cu. ft per day of associated gas produced with crude oil is collected at gas-oil separator plants and piped to gas plants in the Eastern Province. There, impurities such as hydrogen sulfide are removed and a sweet, dry gas is extracted for use as an industrial fuel. From gas-processing centres at Shedgum and Uthmaniyah, the remaining natural gas liquids and ethane are piped to plants at Yanbu and Juaymah for fractionation. In 1981 Aramco produced 156m. bbls of natural gas liquids, obtained in association with crude production.

Water Resources. Intensive efforts are underway to provide adequate supplies of water for urban, industrial, rural and agricultural use. There is an important programme to tap non-renewable (3,450m. cu. metres per annum) and renewable (1,145m. cu. metres) water reserves by wells and small dams, and there are plans to reclaim urban waste water. Most investment however has gone into seawater desalination. By early 1982 14 plants in 10 towns had the capacity to produce 373,000 cu. metres per day and 5 more, totalling 1,143,000 cu. metres per day were under construction. Another 12, amounting to 554,000 cu. metres per day, were at various stages of planning.

Minerals. Surveys were launched during the second development plan to investigate potential mineral wealth other than oil. Deposits of several minerals including viable quantities of iron and gold have been found. There are also reports of uranium deposits.

Agriculture. Since 1970 the Government has devoted huge resources to raise the Kingdom's agricultural potential, and spent substantially on desert reclamation, irrigation schemes, drainage and control of surface water and control of moving sands. Undeveloped land has been distributed to farmers and there are research and extension programmes. Large scale private investment has concentrated on meat, poultry and dairy production. Support finance from the Saudi Arabian Agricultural Bank in 1980 totalled 1,129m. rials, chiefly for equipment 223m., well drilling 196m. and purchases of poultry stock 121m.

Production, 1982 (in 1,000 tonnes) were: Alfalfa, 605; dates, 400; tomatoes, 19; sorghum, 110; water melons, 340; wheat, 400; dry onions, 60; grapes, 60. The use of greenhouses and hydroponics is increasing.

Livestock estimates for 1982 include 450,000 cattle, 110,000 asses, 160,000 camels, 3·5m. sheep and 2·3m. goats.

Fisheries. Total catch (1980) 24,000 tonnes.

INDUSTRY AND TRADE

Industry. The Government actively encourages the establishment of manufacturing industries in the country. The policy includes the provision of industrial estates and loans covering 50% of capital investment. By the end of 1980, 1,170 private industrial plants were in operation, with authorized capital investment of 17,000m. rials. The Government has also established two industrial poles at Jubail and Yanbu, to be the focus of heavy industrial development. Linked by gas and oil pipelines both are to have petrochemical complexes producing, initially, ethylene and methanol, for which agreements have been signed with American and Japanese companies. Six plants are under construction, to come on stream in 1985. In addition an integrated steel complex (German partners) and a urea fertilizer factory (Taiwanese), both in Jubail started production in 1983.

Commerce. Exports amounted to 405,481m. rials in 1981 and imports 119,298m. rials. In 1981 the USA was the main supplier, accounting for 21·4% of the total. Other major supplying countries were Japan (18·3%), Federal Republic of Germany (9·5%), Italy (6·2%) and the UK (6·2%). The main imports were machinery and electrical equipment (25·4%), metal articles (14·6%), transport equipment (14·4%) and foodstuffs (14·4%).

Total trade between Saudi Arabia and UK (British Department of Trade returns, in £1,000 sterling):

	1979	1980	1981	1982	1983
Imports to UK	1,108,644	1,927,583	1,892,605	1,447,775	897,702
Exports and re-exports from UK	893,600	1,050,145	1,133,921	1,361,665	1,478,587

Tourism. In 1982 there were nearly 2m. pilgrims to Mecca from abroad.

COMMUNICATIONS

Roads. All the main regions and population centres of the Kingdom are linked by asphalted roads, of which there were 22,501 km in 1981 and 28,586 km of graded, unpaved agricultural roads. An additional 12,492 km of roads were under construction including the Trans-Peninsula Expressway. There are road links with Yemen, Jordan, Kuwait and Qatar, and a causeway link to Bahrain is being built. In 1980 there were nearly 200,000 cars, over 142,000 commercial vehicles and about 4,500 buses.

Railways. A railway from Riyadh to Dammam on the Gulf (571 km, 1,435 mm gauge) via Dhahran and the oilfields Abqaiq, Ithmaniya (near Hofuf) and Haradh was completed in Oct. 1951. A 'dry port' at Riyadh station opened in 1981, and a new 465 km Dammam-Riyadh direct line was partially opened in 1984. There are plans to extend the line via Medina to Jiddah. That section of the Hejaz Railway which is in Saudi Arabian territory is not now in working order, but studies have been initiated to restore the whole line from Damascus to Medina. In 1981–82 railways carried 100m. passenger-km and 509m. tonne-km.

Aviation. Saudi Arabian Air Lines, a government-owned company operates regular internal air services, and international routes to Africa, the Middle East, Europe and the Far East, as well as special flights for pilgrims. There are 3 major international airports at Jiddah, Dhahran and Riyadh and 19 domestic airports. In 1981, 9·4m. passengers and 100,000 tonnes of cargo were carried.

Shipping. The ports of Dammam and Jubail on the Gulf and Jiddah, Yanbu and Jizan on the Red Sea had 101 deep-water piers at 31 Dec. 1981 and discharged 53·3m. freight tonnes.

Post and Broadcasting. Jiddah, Mecca, Taif, Riyadh and Dammam are linked by telephone, Jiddah and Cairo by radio-telephone. An international radio-telephone station at Riyadh was opened in 1956. Number of telephones (1982), 788,576. Number of post offices (1981) 437. In 1982 there were (estimate) 2·7m. radio receivers and 1·7m. television receivers.

Newspapers. There are 8 daily newspapers in Arabic and 2 in English and 9 weekly or monthly magazines.

JUSTICE, RELIGION, EDUCATION AND WELFARE

Justice. The religious law of Islam is the common law of the land, and is administered by religious courts, at the head of which is a chief judge, who is responsible for the Department of Sharia (legal) Affairs.

Religion. About 85% are Sunni Moslems and 15% Shiites.

Education. Administration is in educational districts. Schooling is in three stages, primary, intermediate and secondary which is to prepare older pupils for university; pre-primary schools are being introduced. Education is free in all these stages; monthly scholarships are paid to students in higher education. Girls' education is separate. In 1981 there were 184 pre-primary schools with 27,843 pupils, 5,744 primary schools with 930,436 pupils and 50,010 teachers, and 2,181 intermediate/secondary schools with 377,681 students and 24,866 teachers. There were also adult literacy classes (136,103 students, 35% women), and special schools for 1,971 handicapped children. There were 107 teacher-training schools in 1980.

In 1981 there were 18 vocational centres, where 3,684 primary school graduates were instructed in basic trades. There were also 5 technical and 8 commercial secondary schools, taking 5,418 intermediate school graduates, and 4 industrial, one agricultural and 2 commercial higher institutes (1,466 students).

University courses concentrating on science, engineering, agriculture and medicine, but also covering education, commerce and arts, are available at the Riyadh University, King Abdulaziz University, Jiddah, and King Faisal University, Dammam and Hofuf. New general universities are to be created in Abha and Mecca. Specialized engineering studies are available at the University of Petroleum and Minerals, Dhahran, and Arabic and Sharia law studies at the Islamic University, Medina and the Imam Muhammad bin Saud University, Riyadh. There were 54,397 university students (about 19% women) in 1981.

Welfare. The Ministry of Health is responsible for medical services, serving both Saudi citizens, foreign residents and pilgrims. In 1979 there were 65 hospitals with 10,978 beds, 824 clinics and health centres, 2,883 doctors, 5,159 nurses and midwives, 1,247 pharmacists and assistants and 1,161 X-ray and laboratory technicians. There were also 25 private hospitals (2,019 beds) and 22 private clinics employing 666 doctors. Five new hospitals with 2,275 beds opened in 1980 and a further five with 900 beds in 1981. In 1982 33 hospitals (7,112 beds) were under construction and another 11 (4,150 beds) were projected. The Jiddah Quarantine Centre, designed by WHO and primarily for pilgrims, can take 2,400 patients. In 1980 there were 7 schools for female nurses and 4 institutes for male trainees. There is a strict system of health controls for visiting pilgrims and strict supervision of sanitation and water supply.

DIPLOMATIC REPRESENTATIVES

Of Saudi Arabia in Great Britain (30 Belgrave Sq., London, SW1X 8QB)
Ambassador; Sheikh Nasser H. Almanaour, GCVO.

Of Great Britain in Saudi Arabia (PO Box 393, Jiddah)
Ambassador: Sir James Craig, GCMG.

Of Saudi Arabia in the USA (1520–18th Street, NW, Washington, D.C. 20036)
Ambassador: HRH Prince Bandar bin Sultan.

Of the USA in Saudi Arabia (Palestine Rd., Ruwais, Jiddah)
Ambassador: Richard W. Murphy.

Of Saudi Arabia to the United Nations
Ambassador: (Vacant).

Books of Reference

The Gulf Handbook. Bath (annual)
Anderson, N., *The Kingdom of Saudi Arabia.* (Rev. ed.). London, 1982
Clements, F. A., *Saudi Arabia.* [Bibliography] Oxford and Santa Barbara, 1979
Helms, C. M., *The Cohesion of Saudi Arabia.* Baltimore, 1981
Hobday, P., *Saudi Arabia Today: An Introduction to the Richest Oil Power.* London, 1978
Holden, D. and Johns, R., *The House of Saud.* London and New York, 1981
Looney, R. E., *Saudi Arabia's Development Potential.* Lexington, 1982
McMaster, B., *The Definitive Guide to Living in Saudi Arabia.* London, 1980
Niblock, T., *State, Society and Economy in Saudi Arabia.* New York, 1981
Pesce, A., *Jiddah: Portrait of an Arabian City.* 3rd ed. Cambridge, 1978
Quandt, W. B., *Saudi Arabia in the 1980's: Foreign Policy, Security and Oil.* Washington, 1981
Stacey International (ed.) *The Kingdom of Saudi Arabia.* (4th ed.) London, 1979

SENEGAL

République du Sénégal

Capital: Dakar
Population: 6·18m. (1983)
GNP per capita: US$450 (1980)

HISTORY. France established a fort at Saint-Louis in 1659 and later acquired other coastal settlements from the Dutch; the interior was occupied in 1854–65. Senegal became a territory of French West Africa in 1902 and an autonomous state within the French Community on 25 Nov. 1958. On 4 April 1959 Senegal joined with French Sudan to form the Federation of Mali, which achieved independence on 20 June 1960, but on 22 Aug. Senegal withdrew from the Federation and became a separate independent republic. Senegal was a one-Party state from 1966 until 1974, when a pluralist system was re-established. Léopold Sédar Senghor, President since independence, resigned on 31 Dec. 1980 and was succeeded by his Prime Minister, Abdou Diouf. From 1 Feb. 1982 Senegal joined with Gambia to form a Confederation of Senegambia.

AREA AND POPULATION. Senegal is bounded by Mauritania to the north and north-east, Mali to the east, Guinea and Guinea-Bissau to the south and the Atlantic to the west with The Gambia forming an enclave along that shore. The republic has a total area of 196,192 sq. km; the population (census, 1976) 5,085,388 (estimate, 1983) 6,177,000.

The areas (in sq. km), Census populations and capitals of the 8 regions are:

Region	sq. km	1976 Census	Capital	1979 Estimate
Cap-Vert	550	984,660	Dakar	978,553
Casamance	28,350	736,527	Ziguinchor	79,464
Diourbel	33,547	425,113	Diourbel	55,307
Louga		417,137	Louga	...
Fleuve	44,127	528,473	Saint-Louis	96,594
Sénégal-Oriental	57,602	286,148	Tambacounda	...
Sine-Saloum	23,945	1,007,736	Kaolack	115,679
Thiès	6,601	698,994	Thiès	126,886

The principal ethnic groups are the Wolof (29% of the population), Serer (17%), Fulani (17%), Tukulor (10%), Diola (8%), Malinké (6%), Bambara (6%) and Sarakole (2%).

CLIMATE. A tropical climate with wet and dry seasons. The rains fall almost exclusively in the hot season, from June to Oct., with high humidity. Dakar. Jan. 72°F (22·2°C), July 82°F (27·8°C). Annual rainfall 22″ (541 mm).

CONSTITUTION AND GOVERNMENT. Under the Constitution promulgated on 7 Mar. 1963 (as subsequently amended) there are simultaneous elections by universal adult suffrage for 5-year terms for both the Presidency and for the unicameral 120-member National Assembly; for the latter 60 members are elected in single-member constituencies and 60 by a form of proportional representation.

In the general election of Feb. 1983 the *Parti socialiste* gained 111 seats, the *Parti démocratique sénégalais* 8 seats and the *Rassemblement national democratique* 1 seat.

On 14 Nov. 1981, President Diouf of Senegal and President Jawara of The Gambia issued a joint communiqué proposing the establishment of a confederation, to be known as Senegambia. Both parliaments ratified the agreement at the end of the year. The instruments of ratification were exchanged in Banjul on 11 Jan. 1982 and the Confederation formally came into existence on 1 Feb.

The agreement stated that each confederal state shall maintain its independence and sovereignty and calls for the integration of the armed security forces, economic and monetary union, co-operation in the fields of communications and external relations, and the establishment of joint institutions (*i.e.* President, Vice President, Council of Ministers, Confederal Parliament). The President of the Confederation would be President Diouf, and the Vice President President Jawara, The Confederal Parliament would have one third Gambian representation and two thirds Senegalese.

President Jawara said in Nov. 1981 that 'the Confederation would not compromise any of the agreements which link The Gambia direct to Britain and the rest of the Commonwealth'.

President of the Republic: Abdou Diouf (took office in Jan. 1981, re-elected Feb. 1983).

The Council of Ministers appointed 3 Apr. 1983 was composed as follows:
Foreign Affairs: Moustapha Niasse. *Defence:* Medoune Fall. *Interior:* Ibrahima Wone. *Finance and Economic Affairs:* Mamadou Touré. *Supply:* Robert Sagna. *Culture:* Abdel Kader Fall. *Higher Education:* Ibrahima Fall. *Education:* Iba der Thiam. *Rural Development:* Bator Diop. *Industrial Development and Handicrafts:* Serigne Lamine Diop. *Scientific and Technical Research:* Moussa Daffe. *Housing and Urban Affairs:* Hamidou Sakho. *Commerce:* Abdourahmane Touré. *Planning and Co-operation:* Cheikh Amidou Kané. *Information and Telecommunications:* Djibo Ka. *Justice and Keeper of the Seals:* Doudou Ndoye. *Civil Service, Employment and Labour:* André Sonko. *Public Health:* Mamadou Diop. *Social Affairs:* Mme. Maïmouna Kané. *Water Resources:* Samba Yella Diop. *Youth and Sports:* Français Bob. *Environment:* Cheikh Cissokho. *Emmigration:* Mme. Fambaye Fall Diop. *Tourism:* Momar Talla Cisse. *Secretaries of State:* Landing Sané *(Decentralisation),* Mme. Marie Sarr Mbodj *(Technical and Professional Training),* Bocar Diallo *(Rural Development and Fisheries),* Thierno Bâ *(Employment).*

National flag: Three vertical strips of green, yellow, red, with a green star in the centre.

The official language is French.

Local Government. Senegal is divided into 8 *régions,* each with an appointed governor and an elected regional assembly. They are divided into 28 *départements,* each under an appointed *Préfet,* and thence into 99 *arrondissements.*

DEFENCE. There is selective conscription.

Army. The Army had a strength of 8,500 (1984), organized in 5 infantry battalions, 1 engineer battalion, 1 reconnaissance squadron and minor units. Equipment includes about 50 armoured cars. There is also a paramilitary force of some 7,000 men.

Navy. The flotilla includes 1 patrol vessel, 3 patrol craft, 3 fast gunboats, 14 small patrol craft, 1 fishery protection trawler, 4 coastal patrol launches, 1 landing craft, 2 minor amphibious craft, 12 service craft and 1 training tender. Personnel (1984) 380.

Air Force. The Senegal Air Force, formed with French assistance, has 1 Summit O2-337 Sentry counter-insurgency aircraft, 4 Rallye Guerrier armed trainers, 2 Magister jet trainers, 1 Boeing 727 and 1 Caravelle VIP transports, 5 DC-3/C-47 transports, 6 F.27 and 1 Twin Otter twin-turboprop transports, 2 Broussard liaison aircraft, 3 Puma, 1 Gazelle and 2 Alouette II helicopters. Personnel total about 500.

INTERNATIONAL RELATIONS

Membership. Senegal is a member of UN, OAU and is an ACP state of EEC.

ECONOMY

Planning. The sixth 4-year Development Plan (1981–85) provides 463,847m. francs CFA for investment in mineral exploration, tourism, cotton, fishing, livestock, seed selection, rice growing and fertilizers.

Budget. The budget for 1983–84 balanced at 273,984m. francs CFA.

Currency. The currency is the *franc* CFA, with a parity value of 50 *francs* CFA to 1 French *franc.*

Banking. The bank of issue is the *Banque Centrale des États de l'Afrique de l'Ouest.* The principal commercial bank is the *Union Sénégalaise de la Banque pour le Commerce et l'Industrie* (established 1961 with assistance from Crédit Lyonnais) in which the Senegalese government has the majority share-holding; also state controlled is the *Banque Nationale de Développement du Sénégal.* There are 3 private banks.

At 31 Dec. 1981 the savings banks had deposits of 85,120m. francs CFA.

ENERGY AND NATURAL RESOURCES

Electricity. Production (1979) was 636m. kwh.

Minerals. Extraction of phosphate rock in 1980 amounted to 1,756,100 tonnes. Titanium ores and zirconium are extracted from coastal (sand) deposits. Iron ore deposits amounting to an estimated 980m. tonnes have been located at La Faleme.

Agriculture. 80% of the labour force is engaged in agriculture. The main food crops (1981 production in 1,000 tonnes) are millet (750), sugar-cane (600), rice (120), maize (55), cassava and sorghum, while the primary cash crop is groundnuts (1,980).

Livestock (1982): 3·15m. sheep and goats, 2·3m. cattle, 150,000 pigs, 240,000 asses, 6,000 camels and 220,000 horses.

Fisheries. The 1980 catch totalled 359,100 tonnes.

INDUSTRY AND TRADE

Industry. Dakar has numerous industrial works. A major ship-repairing complex has been constructed there for vessels of up to 28,000 tonnes. Cement production (1980) 371,300 tonnes; petroleum products, 726,400; groundnut oil, 125,200.

Trade Unions. There are two major unions, the *Union Nationale des Travailleurs Sénégalais* (government-controlled) and the *Conféderation Nationale des Travailleurs Sénégalais* (independent) which broke away from the former in 1969.

Commerce. In 1980 imports totalled 222,256m. francs CFA (of which 37% came from France) and exports 100,767m. francs CFA (of which 34% went to France); fisheries provided 24% of exports, petroleum products 18%, phosphates 16% and peanut oil 12%.

Total trade between Senegal and UK (British Department of Trade returns, in £1,000 sterling):

	1979	1980	1981	1982	1983
Imports to UK	18,088	15,440	17,430	14,196	22,333
Exports and re-exports from UK	11,000	16,030	26,276	22,349	13,212

Tourism. In 1979, 198,433 tourists visited Senegal.

COMMUNICATIONS

Roads. The length of roads (1981) was 14,500 km of which 3,400 km was bitumenized. In 1978 there were 65,507 passenger cars and 9,558 commercial vehicles.

Railways. There are 5 railway lines: Dakar-Kidira (continuing in Mali), Thiès-Saint-Louis (193 km), Guinguinéo-Kaolack (22 km), Louga-Linguère (129 km), and Diourbel-Touba (46 km). Total length (1979), 1,186 km (metre gauge). In 1979–80 railways carried 732,000 passengers and 1·7m. tonnes of freight.

Aviation. In 1979 aircraft disembarked 297,170 and embarked 322,921 passengers and disembarked 7,676 tonnes and embarked 5,605 tonnes of freight at Yoff (Dakar).

Shipping. In 1978, 4,870 vessels entered the port of Dakar. There is a river service on the Senegal from Saint-Louis to Podor (363 km) open throughout the year, and to Kayes (924 km) open from July to Oct. The Senegal River is closed to foreign flags. The Saloum River is navigable as far as Kaolack, the Casamance River as far as Ziguinchor.

Post and Broadcasting. There were, in 1972, 74 post offices. Telephones in 1978 numbered 42,105, of which 33,863 were in Dakar. In 1981 there were 2 radio networks with 300,000 radio receivers and 2 television stations with 4,000 receivers.

Cinemas. In 1975 there were 77 with a seating capacity of 33,500.

JUSTICE, RELIGION, EDUCATION AND WELFARE

Justice. There are *juges de paix* in each *département* and a court of first instance in each region. Assize courts are situated in Dakar, Kaolack, Saint-Louis and Ziguinchor, while the Court of Appeal resides in Dakar.

Religion. The population (1980) was 91% Moslem, 6% Christian (mainly Roman Catholic) and 3% animist.

Education. Secondary education is provided at 11 *lycées,* 66 *collèges d'enseignement secondaire, 2 lycées techniques, 2 écoles normales* and 3 *cours normaux.* Total pupils in the elementary schools in 1979 was 370,412, including 44,262 attending private schools; in the secondary schools, 82,631 (of whom 15,969 attend private colleges). The University in Dakar established on 24 Feb. 1957, had 11,852 students in 1980.

Health. In 1976 there were 43 hospitals with 6,025 beds; also 311 doctors, 37 dentists, 90 pharmacists, 380 midwives and 3,080 nursing personnel.

DIPLOMATIC REPRESENTATIVES

Of Senegal in Great Britain (11 Phillimore Gdns., London, W8 7QG)
Ambassador: Ousmane Camara (accredited 20 May 1981)

Of Great Britain in Senegal (20 Rue du Docteur Guillet, Dakar)
Ambassador: P. L. O'Keeffe, CMG, CVO.

Of Senegal in the USA (2112 Wyoming Ave., NW, Washington, D.C., 20008)
Ambassador: Abdourahmane Dia.

Of the USA in Senegal (Ave. Jean XXIII, Dakar)
Ambassador: Charles W. Bray, III.

Of Senegal to the United Nations
Ambassador: Massamba Sarré

Books of Reference

Crowder, M., *Senegal: A Study in French Assimilation.* OUP, 1962
Gellar, S., *Senegal.* Boulder, 1982
Samb, M. (ed.), *Spotlight on Senegal.* Dakar, 1972

SEYCHELLES

Capital: Victoria
Population: 69,000 (1983)
GNP per capita: US$1,770 (1980)

HISTORY. The islands were first colonized by the French in 1768, in order to establish plantations of spices to compete with the Dutch monopoly. They were captured by the English in 1794 and incorporated as a dependency of Mauritius in 1814. In Nov. 1903 the Seychelles archipelago became a separate colony. Internal self-government was achieved on 1 Oct. 1975 and independence as a republic within the Commonwealth on 29 June 1976. The first President, James Mancham, was deposed in a *coup* on 5 June 1977 and replaced by his Prime Minister.

AREA AND POPULATION. The Seychelles consists of 112 islands and islets in the Indian ocean, north of Madagascar, with a combined area of 156 sq. miles (444 sq. km) within two distinct groups. The Mahé or Granitic group of 40 islands cover 87 sq. miles (234 sq. km); the principal island is Mahé, with 56 sq. miles (144 sq. km) and 45,204 inhabitants at the 1971 census, the other inhabited islands of the group being Praslin, La Digue, Silhouette, Frigate and North, which together have 6,660 inhabitants.

The Outer or Coralline group comprises 60 islands spread over a wide area of ocean between the Mahé group and Madagascar, with a total land area of 69 sq. miles and a population of less than 1,000. The main islands are the Amirante Isles (including Desroches, Poivre, Daros and Alphonse), Coetivy Island and Platte Island, all lying south of the Mahé group; the Farquhar, St Pierre and Providence Islands, north of Madagascar; and Aldabra, Astove, Assumption and the Cosmoledo Islands, about 1,000 km south-west of the Mahé group. Aldabra (whose lagoon covers 55 sq. miles), Farquhar and Desroches were transferred to the new British Indian Ocean Territory in 1965, but were returned by Britain to the Seychelles on the latter's independence in 1976. Population (1983, estimate) 69,000.

Vital statistics (1982): Births, 1,544; deaths, 482.

CLIMATE. Though close to the equator, the climate is tropical. The hot, wet season is from Dec. to May, when conditions are humid, but south-east trades bring cooler conditions from June to Nov. Temperatures are high throughout the year, but the islands lie outside the cyclone belt. Victoria. Jan. 80°F (26·7°C), July 78°F (25·6°C). Annual rainfall 95″ (2,375 mm).

CONSTITUTION AND GOVERNMENT. A new Constitution came into force on 5 June 1979, under which the Seychelles People's Progressive Front is the sole legal Party and nominates all candidates for election. There is a unicameral People's Assembly comprising 23 members elected for 4 years with 2 further nominated members. There is an Executive President directly elected for a 5-year term, who nominates and leads a Council of Ministers.

The official languages are Creole, English and French but 95% of the population speak Creole.

President, Minister of Administration, Finance, Industry and Transport: Hon. France Albert René.

Foreign Affairs and Economic Planning: Dr Maxime Ferrari. *Development:* Jacques Hodoul. *Health:* Esmé Jumeau. *Labour and Social Security:* Joseph Belmont. *Education and Information:* Maj. James Michel. *Youth and Defence:* Ogilvy Berlouis.

National flag: Divided horizontally red over green by a wavy white stripe, with red of double width.

DEFENCE. A People's Liberation Army was created in 1977. Personnel (1984) 750 organized in 1 infantry battalion and 1 artillery troop.

INTERNATIONAL RELATIONS

Membership. Seychelles is a member of UN, the Commonwealth, OAU and is an ACP state of EEC.

ECONOMY

Budget, in 1m. rupees, for calender years:

	1979	1980 [1]	1981 [1]	1982 [1]
Recurrent revenue	315·5	394·7	383·9	408·6
Recurrent expenditure	327·4	395·7	380·9	408·6

[1] Provisional.

Currency. The currency is the Seychelles *rupee*. In March 1984, £1 = 10 *rupees;* US$1 = 6·82 *rupees.*

Banking. Barclays Bank International, Standard Bank, Bank of Credit and Commerce, Banque Francaise Commerçiale, Habib Bank, Bank of Baroda and Seychelles Development Bank, have branches in Victoria, Mahé.

ENERGY AND NATURAL RESOURCES

Electricity. Production (1982) 52·7m. kwh.

Agriculture. Chief crops (production 1982, in tonnes) are copra (2,176), cinnamon bark (810) and tea (146). Food crop production is being increased for home consumption and fishing is actively pursued mainly for home consumption but also for export as frozen fish.

Livestock (1982): Cattle, 2,000; pigs, 11,000; goats, 4,000; poultry, 134,000.

INDUSTRY AND TRADE

Industry. Local industry is expanding, the largest development in recent years being the brewery, (output, 1982, 4,438,000 litres), but steel fabricated goods, furniture, plastics, soap manufacturing form a growing element. In 1982, 3,182,000 litres of soft drinks and 51·6m. cigarettes were produced.

Commerce. Total trade, in rupees, for calendar years:

	1979	1980	1981	1982
Imports (less re-exports)	534,800,000	631,400,000	589,000,000	641,300,000
Domestic exports	30,900,000	32,900,000	27,500,000	20,400,000

Principal imports (1982): Manufactured goods, Rs 175·9m.; food, Rs 130·9m.; petroleum products, Rs 127·9m., machinery and transport equipment, Rs 142·5m. Principal exports (1982): Copra, Rs 8·8m.; frozen fish, Rs 7·4m.; cinnamon bark, Rs 3m., guano (1981), Rs 0·4m.

Imports (1977) from: UK, Rs 94·59m.; Kenya, Rs 40·79m.; Republic of South Africa, Rs 31·85m.; Singapore, Rs 21·22m.; Australia, Rs 18·44m.

Exports (1977) to: Pakistan, Rs 14·04m.; Mauritius, Rs 2·6m.; USA, Rs 671,292.

Tourism. Tourism has now established itself as an important sector of the economy. The number of visitors has grown very rapidly since the opening of the international airport in 1978 and in 1979 there were 78,852, but the rapid growth has been reversed in 1981 (60,425) and 1982 (47,280).

COMMUNICATIONS

Roads. There is a good system of tarmac (84 miles) and earth roads (21 miles) in Mahé; Praslin and La Digue have 28 miles (9 miles tarmac); extensive roadmaking is being undertaken. At 31 Dec. 1982, there was a total of 148 km surfaced, and 106 km unsurfaced.

Aviation. British Airways operates 1 service a week between London and Seychelles, and once a week from Johannesburg. Air France and Seychelles International Safari Airline operate 2 services a week. British Caledonian and Air

Tanzania operate a weekly service. Kenya Airways operates a service 3 times a week. In 1982 aircraft movements were 1,722; passenger movements, 206,000 (including domestic flights); freight loaded, 195 tonnes, unloaded, 775 tonnes.

Shipping. Shipping (1982), goods unloaded, 173,900 tonnes, goods loaded, 6,200 tonnes. There are regular cargo vessels from Australia and the Far East, South Africa and Europe. The vessel *Cinq Juin* travels to and from Mauritius and visits the outlying islands.

Post and Broadcasting. Services operated by Cable & Wireless Ltd provide telegraphic communications with all parts of the world by satellite, the company's radiotelephone service also extends to all principal countries in the world. In 1978, an automatic dialling telex system was introduced. Telephones in Jan. 1981 numbered 4,008. There are 2 radio stations and (1979) 18,000 receivers.

Cinemas. In 1983 there were 3 cinemas with seating capacity of 1,038.

JUSTICE, RELIGION, EDUCATION AND WELFARE

Justice. In 1977, 6,337 criminal and other cases were recorded by the police. The police force numbered 492 all ranks and 69 special constabulary.

Religion. 90% of the inhabitants are Roman Catholic and 8% Anglican.

Education. Equality of educational opportunity exists for all children for a minimum of 9 years. In Jan. 1983 there were 25 primary schools, 2 secondary schools and 1 Polytechnic school with 10 departments.

In Jan. 1983 there were 14,456 pupils in primary schools, 2,603 pupils in junior secondary and secondary grammar schools and 974 students in the Polytechnic. In 1983, a total of 239 students were undergoing training overseas, mainly in the UK; 153 were in university, 39 teacher-training and 6 nursing.

Health. In 1983 there were 41 doctors and dental officers in government service, 374 nurses and 326 hospital beds.

DIPLOMATIC REPRESENTATIVES

Of Seychelles in Great Britain (50 Conduit St., London, W1A 4PE)
High Commissioner: Danielle de St Jorre (accredited 27 July 1983).

Of Great Britain in Seychelles (Victoria Hse., Victoria)
High Commissioner: C. G. Mays.

Of Seychelles in USA
Ambassador: Giovinella Gonthier.

Of the USA in Seychelles (Victoria Hse., Victoria)
Ambassador: David J. Fischer.

Books of Reference

Statistical Information: Information Office, 52 Kingsgate House, Victoria, Mahé.
Report of Seychelles Constitutional Conference. HMSO, 1970
Population Census 1977.–Agricultural Survey 1980. Government Printer
Benedict, B., *People of the Seychelles.* HMSO, 1966
Benedict, M., and Benedict, B., *Men, Women and Money in Seychelles.* Univ. of California Press, 1983
Franda, M., *The Seychelles: Unquiet Islands.* Boulder, 1982
Lionnet, G., *The Seychelles.* Newton Abbot, 1972

SIERRA LEONE

Capital: Freetown
Population: 3·47m. (1980)
GNP per capita: US$270 (1980)

HISTORY. The Colony of Sierra Leone originated in the sale and cession, in 1787, by native chiefs to English settlers, of a piece of land intended as a home for natives of Africa who were waifs in London, and later it was used as a settlement for Africans rescued from slave-ships. The hinterland was declared a British protectorate on 21 Aug. 1896. Sierra Leone became independent as a member state of the Commonwealth on 27 April 1961, and a republic on 19 April 1971.

AREA AND POPULATION. Sierra Leone is bounded on the north-west, north and north-east by the Republic of Guinea, on the south-east by Liberia and on the south-west by the Atlantic ocean. The coastline extends from the boundary of the Republic of Guinea to the north of the mouth of the Great Scarcies River to the boundary of Liberia at the mouth of the Mano River, a distance of about 212 miles (341 km). The area of Sierra Leone is 27,925 sq. miles (73,326 sq. km). Population (census Dec. 1974, provisional), 2,735,159, of whom about 2,000 are Europeans, 3,500 Asiatics and 30,000 non-native Africans. Estimate (1980) 3·47m. The capital is Freetown, with 316,312 inhabitants.

Vital statistics (1981); Live births, 49,553; deaths, 20,842.

Sierra Leone is divided into 3 regions and the Western Area:

	Sq. km	Estimate 1976	Capital	Census 1974
Western Area	663	400,000	Freetown	316,312
Southern region	20,378	744,000	Bo	597,000
Eastern region	15,219	970,000	Kenema	773,500
Northern region	36,066	1,126,000	Makeni	1,046,000

The principal peoples are the Temnes, Limbas, Lokos and Korankos in the north, the Temnes in the centre, the Mendis in the south, and the Kissis and Konos in the east.

CLIMATE. A tropical climate, with marked wet and dry seasons and high temperatures throughout the year. The rainy season lasts from about April to Nov., when humidity can be very high. Thunderstorms are common from April to June and in Sept. and Oct. Freetown. Jan. 80°F (26·7°C), July 78°F (25·6°C). Annual rainfall 135″ (3,434 mm).

CONSTITUTION AND GOVERNMENT. For earlier Constitutional history *see* THE STATESMAN'S YEAR-BOOK 1978–79, p. 1046. Following a referendum in June 1978, a new Constitution was instituted under which the ruling All People's Congress (APC) became the sole legal Party. The 100-member Parliament elected in May–June 1982 comprised 85 members all belonging to the APC.

President: Dr Siaka Probyn Stevens.
Vice-Presidents: Sorie Ibrahim Koroma, Christian Alusine Kamara-Taylor.
Finance: Salia Jusu Sheriff.
Foreign Affairs: Dr Abdulai Conteh.

National flag: Three horizontal stripes of green, white, blue.

Local Government. The regions are administered through the Ministry of Internal Affairs and divided into 148 Chiefdoms, each under the control of a Paramount Chief and Council of Elders known as the Tribal Authorities, who are responsible for the maintenance of law and order and for the administration of justice (except for serious crimes). All of these Chiefdoms have been organized into local government units, empowered to raise and disburse funds for the development of the Chiefdom concerned.

DEFENCE

Army. The Army consists of 2 infantry battalions, 2 artillery batteries and 1 engineer squadron. Strength (1984), 3,000 officers and men.

Navy. There are 1 fast attack craft (in reserve), 1 coastal patrol craft and 3 landing craft. Personnel (1984), 150.

Air Force. The nucleus of an air arm for the defence forces came into existence in 1973. It operates currently a single MBB BO 105 helicopter. Personnel, about 30.

INTERNATIONAL RELATIONS

Membership. Sierra Leone is a member of UN, OAU, ECOWAS, the Commonwealth, the Mano River Union and is an ACP state of EEC.

ECONOMY

Planning. A 5-year plan (1974–79) was launched to develop industry and plantation agriculture but failed its main objectives.

Budget. Revenue and expenditure (in 1,000 leone) for years ending 30 June:

	1973–74	1974–75	1978–79	1979–80	1980–81	1981–82
Revenue	82,500	86,700	173,875	195,946	216,736	182,644
Expenditure	82,500	86,700	168,151	205,964	236,045	312,462

Currency. The Bank of Sierra Leone, which was established on 4 Aug. 1964, is responsible for providing the currency in the country. It introduced on 4 Aug. 1964 a decimal currency, the *leone* and the *cent*. The paper currency consists of 1, 2, 5, 10 and 20 *leone* and 50-*cent* notes; the coinage of 1, 5, 10, 20 and 50 *cents*.

At 30 June 1976 total Sierra Leone notes and coins in circulation was Le. 39·19m. In March 1984, £1 = 3·70 *leone*; US$1 = 2·51 *leone*.

Banking. The Standard Bank Sierra Leone, the National Commercial Bank, International Bank of Credit and Commerce, International Bank of Trade and Industry and Barclays Bank Sierra Leone have their headquarters at Freetown; the Standard Bank has 14, Barclays Bank 12 and the National Commercial Bank, 8 branches and agencies.

The Post Office Savings Bank has 94,910 depositors with total credit balance of nearly Le. 3,455,469 in 1983.

NATURAL RESOURCES

Minerals. The chief minerals mined are diamonds (303,000 carats, 1983), bauxite (631,000 tonnes, 1982), gold (6,997 oz., 1982 and rutile (35,000 tons, 1982). Molybdenite is being prospected. Rutile production started in 1979 with expected production of 54,000 tonnes per annum and a potential of 100,000 tonnes per annum. Iron ore production was resumed in Feb. 1983 at Marampa by a new company, Austro Minerals, with a production of 64,000 tonnes.

Agriculture. In the western area farming is largely confined to the production of cassava and garden crops, such as maize, vegetables and mangoes, for local consumption. In the provincial areas the principal products include rice, which is the staple food of the country, cassava, groundnuts and export crops such as palm-kernels, cocoa beans, coffee, ginger and piassava. Cattle production is important in the northern part of the country, and most of the poultry, eggs and pork are produced in the Western Area.

Livestock (1982): Cattle, 350,000; goats, 158,000; sheep, 275,000; chickens, 4m.

Fisheries. The estimated tonnage of catch of all species of fish during 1982 was 121,909 tonnes. The FAO has carried out a 5-year survey of pelagic fish resources along the coastline and continental shelf.

Total catch of fish is still below the demand of the country. In 1980, 247 tonnes of fish value Le. 483,488 were imported.

INDUSTRY AND TRADE

Industry. Four pioneer oil-mills for the expressing of palm-oil are operated by the Sierra Leone Produce Marketing Board. Government also operates 4 rice-mills, and there are a number of privately owned mills. At Kenema the Government Corporation Forest Industries produces sawn timber, joinery products (including prefabricated buildings) and high-class furniture. In addition, there is a smaller privately owned saw-mill at Panguma and several small furniture workshops are used internally. Village industries include fishing, fish curing and smoking, weaving and hand methods of expressing palm-oil and cracking palm kernels.

Labour. A large proportion of the population is engaged in agriculture and about 125,000 workers are in wage-earning employment. The number of workers in establishments employing 6 or more persons was 64,092 in 1982, distributed as follows: Services, 24,142; mining and quarrying, 6,170; transport, storage and communications, 4,814; construction, 9,721; commerce, 6,870; manufacturing, 9,407; agriculture, forestry and fishing, 5,834; electricity and water services, 24,142.

Commerce. Total trade (in 1,000 leone) for calendar years:

	1977	1978	1979	1980	1981	1982
Imports	206,228	290,844	333,920	447,476	360,440	368,473
Exports	156,734	194,000	201,251	220,797	168,576	133,245

Of the imports (1971) 28·8% came from UK,10·2% from Japan, 7·1% from Federal Republic of Germany. Of the exports (1971) 62·8% went to UK, 9·4% to Netherlands, 6·8% to Japan and 6·5% to the USA.

Total trade between Sierra Leone and UK (British Department of Trade returns, in £1,000 sterling):

	1978	1979	1980	1981	1982	1983
Imports to UK	39,093	75,744	65,697	43,303	14,438	17,710
Exports and re-exports from UK	31,702	32,753	36,785	24,591	19,110	13,735

Tourism. Tourism is being developed and was a major growth industry in 1983.

COMMUNICATIONS

Roads. There were (1977) about 4,406 miles of main roads, of which 665 miles are surfaced with bitumen.

Motor vehicles licensed in 1982 totalled 47,796; passenger cars, 27,925; buses and trucks, 3,801, and motor cycles, 9,018.

Railways (1983). The government railway closed in 1974, and an 84-km mineral line of 1,067-mm gauge connecting Marampa with the port of Pepel is being rehabilitated.

Aviation. Freetown Airport (Lungi), situated north of Freetown in the Port Loko District, is the only international airport in Sierra Leone.

The airport is served by Sierra Leone Airlines, Ghana/Nigeria Airways, British Caledonian, Union de Transport Aériens, KLM, Air Afrique and Aeroflot. A once weekly non-stop flight from London (Gatwick) to Freetown and *vice versa* is also provided.

Sierra Leone Airlines provide domestic flights daily (except Sundays) from Hastings (14 miles from Freetown) to Gbangbatoke, Bo, Kenema, Yengema, twice weekly to Bonthe and occasional flights to Marampa and Port Loko on charter basis.

Shipping. During 1981 the total imports handled by the port of Freetown amounted to 423,447 freight-tons and exports 166,994 freight-tons; a total of 576 vessels called at Freetown; 564 were cargo vessels and 12 were tourist ships with a total of 718 passengers.

Bonthe-Sherbro, 80 miles south of Freetown, is used for the shipment of pias-sava, palm kernels, rutile and bauxite. Pepel lies some 12 miles from Freetown and (1983) was exporting iron ore.

Post and Broadcasting. The Posts and Telecommunications Department main-tains a trunk network of radio and overhead telephone and telegraph routes of approximately 3,000 miles linking the Western Area with the other regions. Auto-matic telephone exchanges have been introduced at the provincial centres of Bo, Kenema and Makeni; microwave radio relay link now replaces overhead open wire on main trunk routes. An extension programme to link important mining areas at Koidu and Mokanji to the national network by microwave links is well on the way.

The wired broadcasting relay service was replaced in Jan. 1964 by a transistor radio service. Approximately 20,000 transistor radios purchased under this scheme are now in service.

Number of telephones (1981) 220,000. Telegraphic facilities are provided at 58 offices.

There were (1983) 37 post offices and 76 postal agencies.

The number of private wireless-licence holders (1981, estimate) was 500,000 and 20,000 television sets were in operation.

JUSTICE, RELIGION, EDUCATION AND WELFARE

Justice. The High Court has jurisdiction in civil and criminal matters. Subordinate courts are held by magistrates in the various districts. Native Courts, headed by court Chairmen, apply native law and custom under a criminal and civil jurisdic-tion. Appeals from the decisions of magistrates' courts are heard by the High Court. Appeals from the decisions of the High Court are heard by the Sierra Leone Court of Appeal. Appeal lies from the Sierra Leone Court of Appeal to the Supreme Court which is the highest court.

Police. The police force at 31 Dec. 1982 had an authorized strength of 136 superior police officers, 485 junior police officers and 4,934 other ranks including 415 women. In the provinces each Chiefdom keeps an additional force known as Chief-dom Police.

A non-pensionable force, known as the Auxiliary Force and consisting of 3 Junior police officers and 260 other ranks, are helping the regular force in main-taining law and order in the diamond protected area in the Eastern region.

Religion. The majority of the population follow traditional tribal religions. Islam was brought to the region by the nomadic cattle-rearing Fula people from the north around 1600. The Temne people in the north-west form the main part of the Moslem community who were estimated in 1977 to comprise about 20% of the population.

Christianity came to West Africa in the 16th century from Portugal and Spain. The Roman Catholics have 2 dioceses in Sierra Leone and number about 25,000 (1977).

The Evangelical group who led the anti-slavery movement in England founded the Sierra Leone Company in 1791 to settle freed slaves in and around Freetown. In 1966 there were 16 Protestant denominations with a total community of 77,000. Members of the Sierra Leone Church (Anglican) were 25,000 in 1977.

Education (1982). There were over 1,182 registered primary schools with a total enrolment of over 276,911. Primary education is partially free but not compulsory though parents and guardians are urged to send their children and wards to school. School attendance varies considerably in different parts of the country. There were 165 secondary schools with a total enrolment of 66,464 pupils; 71 of these schools are fully assisted by the Government. Technical education was provided in 4 tech-nical institutes, 2 trade centres and in the technical training establishments of the mining companies. There is also a rural institute.

Fourah Bay College and Njala University College (1,863 students) are the 2 con-stituent colleges of the University of Sierra Leone. The Institute of Education, which is part of the University, is now responsible for teacher education, educa-tional research and curriculum development in the country.

Health (1977). In the Western Area there are 12 government hospitals (1,108 beds and 217 cots), including a maternity hospital, a children's hospital and an infectious diseases hospital near Freetown. There are 6 government health centres in the Western Area. Three private hospitals are located in Freetown with 108 beds. A mental hospital at Kissy has accommodation for 224 patients. In the provinces there are 14 government hospitals, 4 hospitals associated with mining companies and 7 mission hospitals. There is a school of nursing in Freetown. There are 156 government dispensaries and health treatment centres and two military hospitals with 124 beds.

DIPLOMATIC REPRESENTATIVES

Of Sierra Leone in Great Britain (33 Portland Pl., London,W1N 3AG)
High Commissioner: Victor E. Sumner.

Of Great Britain in Sierra Leone (Standard Bank of Sierra Leone Ltd Bldg., Lightfoot Boston St., Freetown)
High Commissioner: T. D. O'Leary, CMG.

Of Sierra Leone in the USA (1701 19th St., NW, Washington, D.C., 20009)
Ambassador: Dauda S. Kamara.

Of the USA in Sierra Leone (Corner Walpole and Siaka Stevens St., Freetown)
Ambassador: Arthur Winston Lewis.

Of Sierra Leone to the United Nations
Ambassador: Abdul G. Koroma.

Books of Reference

Atlas of Sierra Leone. Ed. Survey and Lands Dept. Freetown, 1953
Sierra Leone Studies. Ed. J. D. Hargreaves, Freetown, 1953 ff.
Fyfe, C., *A History of Sierra Leone.* OUP, 1962.—Fyfe, C., and Jones, E. (ed.), *Freetown.* Sierra Leone Univ. Press and OUP, 1968
Fyfe, C. N. and Jones, E. D., *A Krio–English Dictionary.* OUP and Sierra Leone Univ. Press, 1980
Kup, A. P., *Sierra Leone.* Newton Abbot, 1975
Porter, A. T., *Creoledom: A Study in the Development of Freetown Society.* OUP, 1963

REPUBLIC OF SINGAPORE

Population: 2·5m. (1983)
GNP per capita: US$6,515 (1980)

HISTORY. For the early history of the settlement (1819) and colony (1867) *see* THE STATESMAN'S YEAR-BOOK, 1959, pp. 246 f.

By an agreement entered into between the Governments of Malaysia and of the State of Singapore on 7 Aug. 1965, effective on 9 Aug. 1965, Singapore ceased to be one of the 14 states of the Federation of Malaysia and became an independent sovereign state. The separation was ratified by the Constitution and Malaysia (Singapore Amendment) Act of the Malaysian Parliament on 9 Aug. The 2 governments agreed to enter into a treaty on external defence and mutual assistance. The Singapore Government retains its executive authority and legislative powers under its State Constitution and took over the powers of the Malaysian Government under the Malaysian Constitution in Singapore. The sovereignty and jurisdiction of the head of the Malaysian State was transferred to the Singapore Government. Civil servants working in Singapore for the Federal Departments became Singapore civil servants. Singapore citizens ceased to be Malaysian citizens.

Singapore accepted responsibility for international agreements entered into by the Malaysian Government on its behalf.

AREA AND POPULATION. The Republic of Singapore consists of Singapore Island itself, and some 54 islets.

Singapore Island is situated off the southern extremity of the Malay peninsula, to which it is joined by a causeway carrying a road, railway and water pipeline. The Straits of Johore between the island and the mainland are about three-quarters of a mile wide. The island is some 26 miles (41·8 km) in length and 14 miles (22·9 km) in breadth, and about 241·4 sq. miles (617·9 sq. km) in area, including the adjacent islets.

Census of population (1980): 1,856,237 Chinese, 351,508 Malays, 154,632 Indians and 51,568 others; total 2,413,945. Estimate (mid-1983), 2,502,000.

Report on the Census of Population 1980. Dept. of Statistics, Singapore, 1980

CLIMATE. The climate is equatorial, with uniformly high temperatures and no defined wet or dry season, rain being copious throughout the year. Singapore. Jan. 80°F (26·7°C), July 81°F (27·2°C). Annual rainfall 95·1″ (2,413 mm).

CONSTITUTION AND GOVERNMENT. By a constitutional amendment the name of the state was changed to 'Republic of Singapore', the head of state was named 'President of Singapore' and the legislative assembly was renamed 'Parliament'.

Malay, Chinese, Tamil and English are the official languages; English is the language of administration.

Parliament consists of 75 members, elected by secret ballot from single-member constituencies, and is presided over by a Speaker, chosen by Parliament from its own members or from outside Parliament. In the latter case, the Speaker has no vote. With the customary exception of those serving criminal sentences, all citizens over 21 are eligible to vote irrespective of sex, race, education or property qualification. There is a common roll without communal electorates. Citizenship is automatic by birth; it can also be acquired by registration or by naturalization.

A Presidential Council was established under Part IVA of the Constitution enacted on 9 Jan. 1970. The general function of the Council is to consider and report on matters affecting persons of any racial or religious community in Singapore as referred to it by Parliament or the Government. The Council will draw attention to any bill or subsidiary legislation which in the opinion of the Council is a differentiating measure.

Parliament, as from Nov. 1981, is composed of 74 People's Action Party members and one member from the Workers' Party.

President of Singapore: Devan Nair (sworn in 24 Oct. 1981).

The People's Action Party Cabinet at Oct. 1983 was composed as follows:
Prime Minister: Lee Kuan Yew.

First Deputy Prime Minister and Education: Dr Goh Keng Swee. *Second Deputy Prime Minister and Foreign Affairs:* S. Rajaratnam. *Labour:* Prof. S. Jayakumar *(acting).* *Communications:* Dr Yeo Ning Hong *(acting).* *Culture and Foreign Affairs:* S. Dhanabalan. *National Development:* Teh Cheang Wan. *Law and Leader of the House:* E. W. Barker. *Defence and Second Minister for Health:* Goh Chok Tong. *Home Affairs:* Chua Sian Chin. *Social Affairs:* Dr Ahmad Mattar. *Health:* Howe Yoon Chong. *Environment:* Ong Pang Boon. *Trade and Industry and Finance:* Tony Tan Keng Yam. *Without Portfolio:* Ong Teng Cheong.

National flag: Horizontally red over white, charged in the canton with a crescent and a circle of 5 stars, all in white.

DEFENCE. The Ministry of Defence exercises command and control over all armed forces in the republic. It comprises 5 major divisions, *i.e.*, the general staff, manpower, logistic, security and intelligence and finance divisions. Compulsory military service in peace-time was introduced in 1967. Periods of service are officers/n.c.o.s. 30 months, other ranks 24 months. Reserve liability is to 40 for men, 50 for officers.

The governments of Australia, Britain, Malaysia, New Zealand and Singapore continue to co-operate closely in defence arrangements and have agreed on a new 5-nation defence set-up in SE Asia designed to protect Malaysia and Singapore against outside attack. The new defence arrangement came into force on 1 Nov. 1971.

Army. The Army consists of 1 armoured and 3 infantry brigades, 6 artillery, 1 commando. 6 engineer and 3 signals battalions. Equipment includes 273 AMX-13 light tanks. Strength (1984) 45,000 (including 30,000 conscripts) and 150,000 reserves. Paramilitary forces number some 40,000.

Navy. Naval vessels comprise 3 new fast attack craft and 6 fast missile craft, all 9 of German design, 6 fast patrol craft built by Vosper Thornycroft (2 at Portsmouth, Britain, and 4 in Singapore), 2 *ex*-US coastal minesweepers, 12 coastal patrol boats, 1 seaward defence boat, 1 training vessel, 6 landing ships (*ex*-USN LST) and 6 small landing craft (2 *ex*-Australian). Personnel in 1984 numbered 3,000 officers and men. There are 40 coastal patrol craft deployed by the marine police and 3 small survey craft operated by the Singapore Port Authority.

Air Defence Command. The formation of an Air Defence Command began in 1968. The Republic of Singapore Air Force now has 1 squadron of F-5E supersonic fighters supported by 2-seat F-5Fs; 2 fighter-bomber squadrons equipped with A-4S Skyhawks, supported by TA-4S two-seat trainers; 2 squadrons of Hunter jet fighters and reconnaissance-fighters, supported by Hunter 2-seat trainers, a radar unit and Bloodhound, Rapier and Hawk surface-to-air missile squadrons; a transport squadron of C-130s (including 4 equipped as flight refuelling tankers) and Skyvans equipped for search and rescue; a squadron of Bell UH-1H Iroquois and Bell 212 helicopters; and training units equipped with SF.260MS piston-engined basic trainers, T-33A jets (to be replaced with SIAI-Marchetti S.211s), and AS 350 Ecureuil helicopters. Four E-2C Hawkeye AWACS aircraft are on order. Personnel strength about 6,000.

INTERNATIONAL RELATIONS

Membership. Singapore is a member of UN, the Commonwealth, the Colombo Plan and ASEAN.

ECONOMY

Planning. The GDP in 1982, at current factor cost was $28,900m., an increase of 10·3% over 1981.

Budget. Public revenue and expenditure for financial years (in S$1m.):

	1978	1979	1980	1981	1982 [1]
Revenue	3,739	4,603	5,904	7,862	7,639
Expenditure	5,879	6,839	9,363	10,175	11,692

[1] Estimate.

Currency. The *Singapore dollar* (S$) is divided in 100 *cents*. Gross circulation on 31 Dec. 1982 was S$4,339·1m. In March 1984, £1 = 3·08 *dollars*; US$1 = 2·12 dollars.

Banking. The functions of the Commissioner of Banking have been assumed by the Monetary Authority of Singapore from 1 Jan. 1971.

The Development Bank of Singapore was established in 1968, primarily to provide long-term financing of manufacturing and other industries. In Dec. 1982 it had a paid up capital of S$228·6m. and shareholders' funds amounted to S$1,216·6m.

There were 118 commercial banks with 357 banking offices operating in Singapore as at 31 Dec. 1982. The total assets/liabilities amounted to S$50,917·9m. as at June 1983. Total deposits of non-bank customers amounted to S$24,236·5m. while loans and advances including bills financing, totalled S$31,061m.

In July 1983, the total balance of the Singapore Post Office Savings Bank was S$5,525m.

Weights and Measures. The metric system or the International System of Units (SI) was introduced in 1971 in Singapore.

ENERGY AND NATURAL RESOURCES

Electricity. The Public Utilities Board is responsible for the provision of electricity, gas and water. Electrical power is generated by 5 power stations, with a total generating capacity of 7,860 mw at the end of 1982.

Fisheries. As the prospect of increasing fish production from inshore waters is poor, in 1967 various projects were introduced, with the aim of making Singapore self-sufficient in fish as well as a major fishing base in the region.

The Jurong fishing port and fish market began operating 26 Feb. 1969. A Fishery Training Institute was established at Changi with the assistance of the United Nations Development Programme (Special Fund) to train youths and fishermen in modern fishing techniques. At Changi, too, a Marine Fisheries Research Department was set up under the sponsorship of the South-East Asian Fisheries Development Centre. Research on fish culture and ornamental fish was carried out at the Freshwater Fisheries Laboratory at Sembawang. Ornamental fish industry is fast becoming a valuable foreign exchange earner. Export of aquarium fish in 1982, S$31m. The local catch of fresh fish in 1982 was 18,830 tonnes.

INDUSTRY AND TRADE

Industry. The largest industrial area is the Jurong Industrial Estate with 1,363 factories employing 112,000 workers as at March 1982.

Industries in Jurong include shipbuilding and those manufacturing steel rods, steel pipes, tyres, chemicals, pharmaceuticals, plywood and veneer, plastics, cement, bricks, cables, textiles and wiremesh. Smaller industrial estates have light industry factories producing food, paper and miscellaneous consumer goods.

Labour. In June 1982, 1,142,374 persons were employed, of whom 967,556 were employees, 49,889 were employers, 98,134 were self-employed and 26,792 were unpaid family workers. The majority were working in manufacturing, 336,741; commerce, 253,500; transport and communications, 129,837.

There were 135 registered trade unions comprising 89 employee unions, 45 employer unions and 1 federation of trade unions in 1982. The total membership of employee unions numbered 214,337, of whom 205,152 of the unionized workers belonged to 66 employee unions affiliated to the National Trades Union Congress. Members of employer unions numbered 7,008.

The Employment Act and the Industrial Relations Act provide principal terms and conditions of employment such as hours of work, sick leave and other fringe benefits. A new labour legislation was introduced allowing youths of 14-16 years to work in industrial establishments, and also children from 12-14 years to be employed in approved apprenticeship schemes. A trade dispute may be referred to the Industrial Arbitration Court which was established in 1960.

The Ministry of Labour operates 3 employment exchanges to assist job seekers to obtain suitable employment and employers to recruit suitable workers. The Central Provident Fund was established in 1955 to make provision for employees in their old age. In 1982 there were 1,725,293 members with S$15,655·5m. standing to their credit in the fund. The total number of active employers registered with the board in 1982 was 80,253 comprising 63,391 business employers and 16,862 domestic employers.

Commerce. The major trading countries for 1982 were Malaysia (18%), Japan (15%), US (13%), Saudi Arabia (11·5%) and the EEC (10%). In 1982, imports (S$60,245m.) rose by 3%. Exports rose from S$44,291m. in 1981 to S$44,473m. in 1982.

In the following table (British Department of Trade returns, in £1,000 sterling) the imports include produce from Borneo, Sarawak and other eastern places, transhipped at Singapore, which is thus entered as the place of export:

	1979	1980	1981	1982	1983
Imports to UK	185,290	535,915	245,209	245,453	404,122
Exports and re-exports from UK	270,718	328,112	406,791	406,172	469,565

Tourism. There were 2,956,690 visitors in 1982.

COMMUNICATIONS

Roads. Singapore has 2,480 km of public roads, of which 2,185 km are asphalt-paved. In July 1983 motor vehicles registered in Singapore numbered 464,156, of which 193,815 were private cars, 7,950 buses, 140,716 motor cycles and scooters, 15,073 public cars including taxis, school taxis and private hire cars.

Railways. A 16-mile (25·8-km) main line runs through Singapore, connecting with the States of Malaysia and as far as Bangkok. Branch lines serve the port of Singapore and the industrial estate at Jurong. A metro was under construction in 1983.

Aviation. The new international airport at Changi was completed and operational from 1 July 1981. Thirty-six international airlines operated 514 scheduled services a week, totalling 62,000 aircraft movements at Singapore International Airport in Changi in 1982. Freight handled (1982) 217,000 tonnes and there were 8·5m. passengers.

Shipping. A total of 60,973 vessels of 554m. NRT entered into and cleared from Singapore during 1982.

Post. In Sept. 1982, 72 post offices and 63 postal agencies were in operation. Telephones numbered 795,737 in 1982.

Cinemas (1982). There were 72 cinemas with a total seating capacity of 71,000.

Newspapers (1983). There were 9 daily newspapers, in 4 languages, with a total daily circulation of 631,593.

JUSTICE, EDUCATION AND WELFARE

Justice. There is a Supreme Court in Singapore which consists of the High Court, the Court of Appeal and the Court of Criminal Appeal. The Supreme Court is composed of a Chief Justice and 6 Judges. An appeal from the High Court lies to the Court of Appeal in civil matters and to the Court of Criminal Appeal in criminal matters. Further appeal can in certain cases be made to the Judicial Committee of the Privy Council. The High Court has original civil and criminal jurisdiction as well as appellate civil and criminal jurisdiction in respect of appeals from the Subordinate Courts. There are 9 district courts, 11 magistrates' courts, 1 juvenile and 1 coroner's court.

Education. Statistics of schools in 1982:

	Schools	Pupils	Teachers
Primary			
Government schools	212	220,197	8,532
Government-aided schools	107	68,734	2,147
Private schools	2	161	8
Secondary			
Government schools	94	128,854 [1]	6,823
Government-aided schools	52	46,198 [1]	2,851
Private schools	4	1,793 [1]	69

[1] Includes pre-university classes.

The National University of Singapore was established on 8 Aug. 1980 following the merger of the University of Singapore and the Nanyang University. The National University of Singapore has 8 faculties: Arts and social sciences, law, science, medicine, dentistry, engineering, architecture and building, accountancy and business administration and 3 schools, post-graduate medical studies, post-graduate dental studies, and school of management.

The Department of Extramural Studies and the English Language Proficiency Unit are non-faculty departments. Total student enrolment for 1982 was 11,748. The Nanyang Technological Institute, situated in the former Nanyang University, was established on 8 Aug. 1981. The institute admitted about 650 second-year students of the University's Faculty of Engineering in July 1982. It will be developed into a University of Technology by 1992. The Singapore Polytechnic had 9,746 students and the Ngee Ann Technical College, re-named Ngee Ann Polytechnic on 16 April 1982, had 3,660 students in 1982. The Institute of Education, established on 1 April 1973, is now the only institution responsible for teacher education in Singapore and for promoting research in education. There were 1,000 students in 1982.

The Adult Education Board and the Industrial Training Board were merged to form the Vocational and Industrial Training Board, on 1 April 1979. The VITB has taken over all the functions and responsibilities in vocational training and continuing education. The VITB runs 17 training institutes and centres offering full-time and part-time courses. The total student enrolment for 1982 was 15,680.

Health. There were 13 government hospitals with a total of 8,246 beds in 1982. There were 2,225 doctors registered.

DIPLOMATIC REPRESENTATIVES

Of Singapore in Great Britain (2 Wilton Cres., London, SW1X 8RW)
High Commissioner: Jek Yeun Thong (accredited 1 Dec. 1977).

Of Great Britain in Singapore (Tanglin Rd, Singapore, 1024)
High Commissioner: Sir Peter Moon, KCVO, CMG.

Of Singapore in the USA (1824 R St., NW, Washington, D.C., 20009)
Ambassador: P. Coomaraswamy.

Of the USA in Singapore (30 Hill St., Singapore, 0617)
Ambassador: Harry E. T. Thayer.

Of Singapore to the United Nations
Ambassador: T. T. B. Koh.

Books of Reference

Statistical Information: The Department of Statistics (PO Box 3010, Singapore) was established 1 Jan. 1922 Its publications include: *Singapore External Trade Statistics* (quarterly), *Monthly Digest of Statistics, Yearbook of Statistics, Population Estimates of Singapore* (bi-annual). *Census of Population 1980. Singapore Yearbook of Labour Statistics. Chief Statistician:* Khoo Chian Kim.

National Library. *Books About Singapore.* Singapore. Biennial
National Trades Union Congress, *Singapore. Towards Tomorrow.* Singapore, 1973
Singapore. Constitution. The Constitution of Singapore. Singapore, 1966
The Budget for the Financial Year 1983–84.
Singapore. Singapore, Publicity Division, Ministry of Culture (formerly *Annual Report*)
Singapore. Government Gazette (published weekly with supplement)
Economic Survey of Singapore, 1982. Ministry of Trade and Industry, Singapore, 1983
Singapore. Facts and Pictures. Singapore, Publicity Division, Ministry of Culture (annual)
Singapore Government Directory. Singapore, Publicity Division, Ministry of Culture
The Statutes of the Republic of Singapore. 8 vols., 1970 (with annual supplements). Singapore, Law Revision Commission, 1970—.
Practice of Economic Growth. Singapore, Federal Publications, 1977
Josey, A., *Lee Kuan Yew, The Struggle for Singapore.* London, 1980.—*Singapore: Its Past, Present and Future.* Singapore, 1979
Lee, S. Y., *Public Finance and Public Investment in Singapore.* Singapore, 1978
Saw, S.-H., *Population Control for Zero Growth in Singapore.* Singapore, 1980
Tan, C. H., *Financial Institutions in Singapore.* Singapore, 1978
Turnbull, C. M., *A History of Singapore, 1819–1975.* OUP, 1977
Wee, T.B. (ed.), *The Future of Singapore: The Global City.* Singapore, 1977
Wilson, R., *The Future Role of Singapore.* OUP, 1972
Yeo, K. W., *Political Development in Singapore, 1945–1955.* Singapore Univ. Press, 1973

National Library: National Library, Stamford Rd, Singapore. *Director:* Mrs Hedwig Anuar.

SOLOMON ISLANDS

Capital: Honiara
Population: 234,000 (1981)
GNP per capita: US$430 (1981)

HISTORY. The Solomon Islands were discovered in 1568 by Alvaro de Mendana, on a voyage of discovery from Peru; 200 years passed before European contact was again made with the Solomons. The Solomon Islands lie within the area 5° to 12° 30′ S. lat. and 155° 30′ to 169° 45′ E. long. The group includes the main islands of Guadalcanal, Malaita, San Cristobal, New Georgia, Santa Isabel and Choiseul; the smaller Florida and Russell groups; the Shortland, Mono (or Treasury), Vella La Vella, Kolombangara, Ranongga, Gizo and Rendova Islands; to the east, Santa Cruz, Tikopia, the Reef and Duff groups; Rennell and Bellona in the south; Ontong Java or Lord Howe to the north; and innumerable smaller islands. The 4 first-named were placed under British protection in 1893; the other islands were added in 1898 and 1899.

AREA AND POPULATION. The land area of the Solomons is estimated at 11,500 sq. miles (29,785 sq. km). The larger islands are mountainous and forest clad, with flood-prone rivers of considerable energy potential. Guadalcanal has the largest land area and the greatest amount of flat coastal plain.

The population of Guadalcanal (including Honiara the main town) was 46,619 at census date (Feb. 1976); Malaita (58,721).

Population of the Solomon Islands was (1978) 215,000. Census (1976) 196,823, over 50% being under 20 years (183,665 Melanesians, 7,821 Polynesians, 452 Chinese, 1,359 Europeans, 2,753 Gilbertese and 773 others).

The islands are administratively divided into 5 provinces replacing the former districts. These provinces are (with 1976 Census population): Western Province (40,329), Guadalcanal (46,619), Central Islands and Santa Isabel (23,996), Malaita (60,043) and Makula and Temotu (formerly Eastern District, 25,836). The government has announced plans to create a federal system.

The capital, Honiara, on Guadalcanal, is the largest urban area, with census population in 1979 of 18,346.

CLIMATE. An equatorial climate with only small seasonal variations. Southeast winds cause cooler conditions from April to Nov., but north-west winds for the rest of the year bring higher temperatures and greater rainfall, with annual totals ranging between 80″ (2,000 mm) and 120″ (3,000 mm).

CONSTITUTION AND GOVERNMENT. A Constitutional Conference was held in London during Sept. 1977, where it was agreed that there should be full independence for the Solomon Islands and this was granted on 7 July 1978.

The main provisions of the 1978 Constitution are that Solomon Islands is a constitutional monarchy with the British Sovereign (represented locally by a Governor-General, who must be a Solomon Island citizen) as Head of State, while legislative power is vested in the unicameral National Parliament composed of 38 members, elected by universal adult suffrage for four years (subject to dissolution), and executive authority is effectively held by the Cabinet, led by the Prime Minister.

The Governor-General is appointed for up to five years, on the advice of Parliament, and acts in almost all matters on the advice of the Cabinet. The Prime Minister is elected by and from members of Parliament. Other Ministers are appointed by the Governor-General on the Prime Minister's recommendation, from members of Parliament. The Cabinet is responsible to Parliament. Emphasis is laid on the devolution of power to provincial governments, and traditional chiefs and leaders have a special role within the arrangement.

The Constitution contains comprehensive guarantees of fundamental human rights and freedom, and provides for the introduction of a leadership code and the appointment of an Ombudsman and a Public Solicitor. It also provides for the establishment of the underlying law, based on customary law and concepts of the Solomon Islands people.

Solomon Islands citizenship was automatically conferred on the indigenous people of the islands and on other residents with close ties with the islands upon independence. The acquisition of land is reserved for indigenous inhabitants or their descendants.

Governor General: Sir Baddeley Devisi, GCMG.
Prime Minister. Solomon Mamaloni.
National flag: Divided blue over green by a diagonal yellow band, and in the canton 5 white stars.

INTERNATIONAL RELATIONS

Membership. The Solomon Islands is a member of UN and is an ACP state of EEC.

ECONOMY

Planning. The 1980–84 Development Plan envisages improvement in education and agricultural development.

Budget. The budget for 1981 envisaged revenue of SI\$34·8m. and expenditure SI\$61·3m.

Currency. The *Solomon Island dollar* (SI\$) was introduced in 1977. In March 1984, US\$1 = 1·21 *dollars*; £1 = 1·77 *dollars.*

NATURAL RESOURCES

Agriculture. Coconuts, cocoa, rice and other minor crops are grown. Oil-palm is being developed successfully with a total of 3,355 hectares having been planted by Dec. 1979. Production of copra (1980), 29,169 tonnes.

An oil-mill became operational in 1976. 3,500 tons of palm-oil out of 300 tons of palm-kernels were exported in 1976.

Rice-cropping in 1980 yielded 5,670 tonnes of milled rice.

Livestock (1982): Cattle, 24,000; pigs, 40,000; poultry, 149,000.

Forestry. Timber extraction is an important development in the Solomons. Timber (logs, sawn timber and veneer sheets) exports for 1980 were 258,000 cu. metres (\$A149m.).

Fisheries. A total catch of 20,700 tonnes of skipjack was made in 1978. Exports of fish totalled 21,578 tonnes (\$A19·8m.) in 1980.

INDUSTRY AND TRADE

Commerce. The main imports (1980) were food, fuels and capital goods and totalled \$A61·5m. Exports comprised copra (316,821 tonnes, \$A10·5m.), frozen fish (21,578 tonnes, \$A19·8m.), rough timber (258,000 cu. metres, \$A149m.), palm-oil (15,619 tonnes), marine shell, cocoa and manufactured tobacco; total exports, \$A60·8m.

Tourism. In 1980, there were 7,100 tourists.

COMMUNICATIONS

Roads. There were 455 km of main roads in 1976.

Aviation. Regular flights from Fiji and Australia (*via* Papua New Guinea) provide the main communication link. Solair, the internal airline, and innumerable small ships, provide inter-island transport.

Shipping. Shipping services are maintained with Australia, New Zealand, UK and the Far East.

Post and Broadcasting. Number of telephones (Jan. 1982), 2,708. A VHF radio telephone service operates internally as well as overseas. In 1982 there were about 25,000 radio receivers.

Newspapers. There are 4 weekly newspapers, 1 with a circulation of 4,000 and the other 3 with 3,000.

RELIGION, EDUCATION AND WELFARE

Religion. At the 1976 census, 34% of the population were Anglican, 19% Roman Catholic, 17% South Sea Evangelical and 25% other Protestant.

Education. In 1981 there were 28,831 primary school pupils. There were five aided national secondary schools, one private national secondary school and eight new secondary schools. Total enrolment secondary schools, 3,547 (1980).

Training of teachers is carried out at Solomon Islands Teachers' College and trade and vocational training is carried out at Honiara Technical Institute. There were 160 students on pre-service scholarships overseas and 73 students on overseas professional course.

Health. In 1980 there were 8 hospitals, 183 clinics and health centres and 30 doctors.

DIPLOMATIC REPRESENTATIVES

Of the Solomon Islands in Great Britain
High Commissioner: (Vacant).

Of Great Britain in the Solomon Islands (Soltel House, Mendana Ave., Honiara)
High Commissioner: George Stansfield, OBE.

Books of Reference

B.S.I.P. Annual Report, 1969. Honiara, 1970
Building the Nation. Honiara, 1975
Amhurst, Lord, and Thompson, B., *The Discovery of the Solomon Islands in 1568.* London, 1967
Kent, J., *The Solomon Islands.* Newton Abbot, 1972
Miller, J., *Guadalcanal: The First Offensive.* Washington, 1949

SOMALIA

Jamhuriyadda Dimugradiga Somaliya

Capital: Mogadiscio
Population: 3·86m. (1982)
GNP per capita: US$130 (1978)

HISTORY. The Somali Republic came into being on 1 July 1960 as a result of the merger of the British Somaliland Protectorate, which became independent on 26 June 1960, and the Italian Trusteeship Territory of Somalia.

For the previous history of these territories *see* THE STATESMAN'S YEAR-BOOK, 1960, pp. 337 and 1367.

On 21 Oct. 1969 the Somali armed forces led by Maj.-Gen. Mohammed Siyad Barre took power in a *coup,* suspended the Constitution and formed a Supreme Revolutionary Council to administer the country, which was renamed the Somali Democratic Republic. Constitutional government was re-established on 23 Sept. 1979.

AREA AND POPULATION. Somalia is bounded north by the Gulf of Aden, east and south by the Indian ocean, and west by Kenya, Ethiopia and Djibouti. Total area of 637,657 sq. km (246,201 sq. miles). Census population (1975) 3,253,024 of whom 15% urban. Estimate (1982) 3,862,000 excluding an estimated 700,000 Somali-speaking refugees from the disputed Ogaden area of Ethiopia, were (1983) living in camps in Somalia.

The capital is Mogadiscio (377,000), other large towns being Hargeisa (70,000), Kisimayu (70,000), Merca (60,000) and Berbera (55,000).

There are long-standing territorial disputes with Kenya and Ethiopia.

CLIMATE. Much of the country is arid, though rainfall is more adequate towards the south. Temperatures are very high on the northern coasts. Mogadiscio. Jan. 79°F (26·1°C), July 78°F (25·6°C). Annual rainfall 17″ (429 mm). Berbera. Jan. 76°F (24·4°C), July 97°F (36·1°C). Annual rainfall 2″ (51 mm).

CONSTITUTION AND GOVERNMENT. A new Constitution was approved by referendum on 25 Aug. 1979 and came into force on 23 Sept. The sole legal Party (since 1 July 1976) is the Somali Revolutionary Socialist Party, administered by a 51-member Central Committee. There is an Executive President nominated by the Central Committee and elected for a 6-year term by the People's Assembly; the latter consists of 121 members elected by universal suffrage for a 5-year term and a further 6 members appointed by the President.

President: Maj.-Gen. Mohammed Siyad Barre.

The Council of Ministers, appointed and led by the President, also includes:

Vice-President, Presidential Advisor on Government Affairs: Maj.-Gen. Hussein Kulmia Afrah. *Vice-President, Minister of Defence:* Lieut.-Gen. Mohamed Ali Samater. *Foreign Affairs:* Dr. Abderrahman Jama Barreh.

National flag: Light blue with a white star in the centre.

The national language is Somali. Arabic is also an official language and English and Italian are extensively spoken.

Local Government. There were (1982) 17 regions, sub-divided into 78 districts.

DEFENCE

Army. The Army consists of 3 tank, 20 infantry, 1 commando and 1 surface-to-air missile brigades. Equipment includes 100 T-34/-54/-55 and 40 Centurion main battle tanks. Strength (1984) 60,000. There are additional paramilitary forces: Police (8,000), Border Guards (1,500) and People's Militia (20,000).

Navy. The flotilla includes 4 submarine chasers (fast attack/torpedo/patrol craft), 2 fast missile craft, 4 fast torpedo boats, 5 patrol craft, 1 medium landing ship and 4 minor landing craft. All are former Soviet naval units which could deteriorate with the withdrawal of the Soviet element. Personnel increased to 600 officers and men by 1984.

Air Force. Formed with a nucleus of aircraft taken over from the former Italian Air Corps of Somalia, in 1960, the Air Corps was built up with Soviet aid. Current equipment includes a squadron of Hunter fighters and two-seat trainers, 7 MiG-21 and 30 J-6 (Chinese-built MiG-19) supersonic fighters, about 9 MiG-17 jet-fighters and 2 MiG-15UTI two-seat advanced trainers, and small transport, helicopter and training units. Latest equipment includes 2 Aeritalia G222 and 2 An-26 twin-turboprop transports, 16 SIAI-Marchetti SF.260W armed trainers and 4 Agusta-Bell 212 helicopters from Italy. Personnel total about 2,000.

INTERNATIONAL RELATIONS

Membership. Somalia is a member of UN, OAU, the Arab League and is an ACP state of EEC.

ECONOMY

Planning. The 1979-81 development plan envisages expenditure of Som.Sh. 7,104m., of which 37% is allocated to livestock, agriculture and mineral development, 9% to health and education and 21% to transport and communications.

Budget. The budget for 1982 envisaged Som.Sh.3,130m. expenditure.

Currency. The currency is the *Somali shilling,* divided into 100 cents. The money is issued in notes of 1, 5, 10, 20 and 100 shillings and coins of 1, 5, 10, 50 cents and 1 shilling. Currency in circulation (1979) Som.Sh.1,152·6m. In March 1984 £1 = 26·07 Som.Sh.; US$1 = 15·56 Som.Sh.

Banking. The bank of issue is the Central Bank of Somalia (founded in 1960 as the Somali National Bank). All foreign banks were nationalised in May 1970, and the Commercial and Savings Bank of Somalia and the Somali Development Bank, both state-owned, are the only other banks.

Weights and Measures. The metric system is in use.

ENERGY AND NATURAL RESOURCES

Electricity. Electricity production (1981) was 69·1m. kwh.

Minerals. Deposits of iron ore in the south and gypsum in the north are known to exist. Beryl and columbite are also found in the north. None are commercially exploited. Several firms hold exploration and drilling licences for oil. Uranium is found in the Juba area.

Agriculture. Somalia is essentially a pastoral country, and about 80% of the inhabitants depend on livestock-rearing (cattle, sheep, goats and camels). In Southern Somalia, especially along the Shebeli and Juba rivers, there are banana and sugar-cane plantations with a cultivated area of some 90,000 hectares. Estimated production, 1982 (in 1,000 tons): Sugar, 460; bananas, 70; maize, 150; sorghum, 235; grapefruit, 6; cotton, 5. Fresh fruit and oil seeds are grown in increasing quantities.

Livestock (1982): 16·7m. goats; 10·3m. sheep; 5·6m. camels; 4m. cattle; 1,000 horses, 24,000 asses and 22,000 mules.

Fisheries. 21 co-operatives, including 4,000 full-time and 10,000 part-time fishermen, caught some 10,000 tonnes in 1981.

INDUSTRY AND TRADE

Industry. Production (1981): Textiles, 10·1m. yards; sugar, 26,800 tonnes; flour and pasta, 5,900 tonnes.

Trade. In 1981 imports were Som.Sh.1,199m. and exports Som.Sh.1,104m. The chief exports are fresh fruit, livestock, hides and skins.

In 1978, 30% of imports came from Italy, 11% from Federal Republic of Germany and 10% from the UK, while 86% of exports went to Saudi Arabia.

Total trade between the Somali Republic and UK (British Department of Trade returns, in £1,000 sterling):

	1979	1980	1981	1982	1983
Imports to UK	96	303	856	883	581
Exports and re-exports from UK	20,959	6,682	12,606	12,095	18,987

COMMUNICATIONS

Roads. Somalia has no developed transport system. Internal freight and passenger transport is almost entirely by means of road haulage. In 1978 there were 19,380 km of roads (2,153 km were paved). In 1977 there were 4,200 passenger cars and 5,700 commercial vehicles, including buses.

Aviation. There is a commercial national airline, Somali Airlines. Mogadiscio airport is used by Alitalia, Alyemda, Air Tanzania, PIA and Kenya Airways.

Shipping. There are 3 deep-water harbours at Kisimayu, Berbera and Mogadiscio. Because of the shape of the country, coastal shipping is an important form of internal transport. The merchant fleet (1980) amounted to 22 vessels of 45·55m. gross tons.

Post and Broadcasting. There is a manual telephone system in several towns, but Mogadiscio has an automatic system; number of telephones (1971), about 4,740. The state radio stations transmit in Somali, Arabic, English and Italian from Mogadiscio, Hargeisa, Anhazic, Koti. Receivers (1981) 87,000. A television service was under consideration in 1983.

Cinemas. In 1970 there were 26 cinemas with a seating capacity of 23,000.

JUSTICE, RELIGION, EDUCATION AND WELFARE

Justice. There are 84 district courts, each with a civil and a criminal section. There are 8 regional courts and 2 Courts of Appeal (at Mogadiscio and Hargeisa), each with a general section and an assize section. The Supreme Court is in Mogadiscio.

Religion. The population is almost entirely Sunni Moslems. There are very few Roman Catholics, mainly in the capital.

Education. The nomadic life of a large percentage of the population inhibits education progress. In 1981 there were 418,935 pupils and 12,007 teachers in primary schools, and 23,810 students and 2,380 pupils in technical schools; in 1979 there were 17,020 pupils and 925 students in secondary schools, and 2,156 students with 540 teachers at 2 teacher-training establishments.

The National University of Somalia in Mogadiscio (founded 1959) had 3,607 students in 1978.

Health. In 1976 there were 179 doctors, 21 pharmacists (1972), 586 medical assistants, 480 nurses (1972), 193 midwives (1972), 75 hospitals and 187 dispensaries (1972). There was a total of 5,691 beds.

DIPLOMATIC REPRESENTATIVES

Of Somalia in Great Britain (60 Portland Place, London, W1N 3DG)
Ambassador: Mohamed Jama Elmi.

Of Great Britain in Somalia (Waddada Xasan Geeddi Abtoow 7/8, Mogadiscio)
Ambassador: Wiliam Fullerton.

Of Somalia in USA (600 New Hampshire Ave., NW, Washington, D.C., 20037)
Ambassador: Mohamud Haji Nur.

Of USA in Somalia (Corso Primo Luglio, Mogadiscio)
Ambassador: Robert B. Oakley.

Of Somalia to the United Nations
Ambassador: Ahmed Mohamed Adan.

Books of Reference

Background to the Liberation Struggle of the Western Somalis. Ministry of Foreign Affairs, Mogadiscio, 1978

The Agricultural Economy of Somalia. US Dept. of Agriculture, Washington, 1971

Legum, C. and Lee, B., *Conflict in the Horn of Africa.* London, 1977

Lewis, I. M., *A Pastoral Democracy.* London, 1962—*The Modern History of Somaliland.* London, 1965

Touval, S., *Somali Nationalism.* Harvard Univ. Press and OUP, 1963

REPUBLIC OF SOUTH AFRICA

Capital: Pretoria
Population: 26·12m. (1983)
GNP per capita: US$2,290 (1980)

Republiek van Suid-Afrika

HISTORY. The Union of South Africa was formed in 1910 and comprised the former self-governing British colonies of the Cape of Good Hope, Natal, the Transvaal and the Orange Free State.

The Union remained a member of the British Commonwealth until it became a republic on 31 May 1961.

AREA AND POPULATION. South Africa is bounded north by South West Africa, Botswana and Zimbabwe, north-east by Mozambique and Swaziland, east by the Indian ocean. south and west by the South Atlantic. Lesotho forms an enclave between the Orange Free State and Natal. The total area of the republic was (1983) 433,678[1] sq. miles (1,123,226 sq. km), divided between the provinces as follows: Cape Province, 249,331 (645,767); Natal, 33,578 (86,967); Transvaal, 101.351 (262,499); Orange Free State, 49,418 (127,993).

On 25 Dec. 1947 the Union formally took possession of Prince Edward Island and, on 30 Dec., of Marion Island, about 1,200 miles south-east of Cape Town.

[1] Excludes Walvis Bay (434 sq. miles), which is an integral part of the Cape Province but is administered under Act No. 24 of 1922 by South West Africa, Transkei, Ciskei, Bophuthatswana and Venda.

The census taken in 1904 in each of the 4 colonies was the first simultaneous census taken in South Africa. In 1911 the first Union census was taken.

		All races		*Whites*		*Non-whites*[1]	
	Total	*Whites*	*Non-Whites*	*Males*	*Females*	*Males*	*Females*
1904	5,174,827	1,117,234	4,057,593	635,317	481,917	2,046,370	2,011,223
1911	5,972,757	1,276,319	4,696,438	685,206	591,113	2,383,879	2,312,559
1921	6,927,403	1,521,343	5,406,060	783,006	738,337	2,753,188	2,652,872
1936	9,587,863	2,003,334	7,584,529	1,017,557	985,777	3,818,211	3,766,318
1946	11,415,925	2,372,044	9,043,881	1,194,201	1,177,843	4,610,862	4,433,019
1951	12,671,452	2,641,689	10,029,763	1,322,754	1,318,935	5,109,331	4,920,432
1960	15,994,181	3,080,159	12,914,022	1,534,923	1,545,236	6,504,317	6,409,705
1970	21,402,470	3,726,540	17,675,930	1,856,180	1,870,360	8,689,920	8,986,010
1980[1]	24,885,960	4,523,100	20,357,860	2,265,400	2,262,700	10,393,780	9,964,080

[1] Excludes Transkei, Bophuthatswana and Venda, but includes Ciskei (678,000).

Of the non-White population in 1980, 16,923,760 were Black, 2,612,780 Coloured and 821,320 Asiatic. The numerically leading Black nations are the Zulu (5,682,520), Xhosa (2,987,340), Sepedi (North Sotho) (2,347,600), Seshoeshoe (South Sotho) (1,742,060), Tswana (1,357,360). Population, (1980) of the Black national areas: Kwa Zulu, 3,422,000 (of which 3,409,000 are Black); Gazankulu, 514,000 (512,000); Lebowa, 1,747,000 (1,739,000); Qwaqwa, 158,000 (156,000); Ka Ngwane, 161,000 (161,000); Kwa Ndebele, 156,000 (156,000). These places are included in the land area figures for the provinces where they lie, but their inhabitants are not included in the provincial population figures. Population of the Republic. 1983, 26,124,000 (4,748,000 White, 2,765,000 Coloured, 870,000 Asian). Growth rate 1970–80, 2·6% (Black, 2·7%; Coloured, 2%; Asian, 2·4%; White, 1·5%).

In 1980 (estimate) Afrikaans was the home language of 2,360,000 Whites, English of 1,652,000 Whites. Of the 15,970,019 Black about 50% could read and write, and 3·5m. (75%) of Black children of school-going age were attending school in 1981.

Vital statistics for calendar years:

		Whites				Asians and Coloureds		
	Births	Deaths	Marriages	Immi-grants	Emigrants	Births	Deaths	Marriages
1979	73,090	35,814	41,813	18,680	15,694	91,360	28,618	26,746
1980	74,777	37,664	45,165	29,365	11,363	92,741	28,850	28,511
1981	79,061	39,376	46,653	41,542	8,791	98,163	30,707	29,502

Of the 41,542 immigrants in 1981, 41,429 were white; of the 8,791 emigrants 7,700 were white.

The registration of Black essential data was introduced on a compulsory basis many years ago. However, despite serious efforts on the part of the registering authorities, the Blacks are still largely reluctant to have their essential data registered. Consequently no complete vital statistics are available for this population group.

Principal cities (excluding suburbs) according to the latest statistics (1980) are:

Town	Whites	Africans	Coloureds	Asians	Total
Alberton (Trans.)	45,902	177,123	7,410	232	230,667
Benoni (Trans.)	56,508	135,752	997	13,553	206,810
Bloemfontein (O.F.S.)	90,625	124,768	15,295	...	230,688
Boksburg (Trans.)	61,337	73,385	15,408	157	150,287
Brakpan (Trans.)	31,902	46,135	1,674	21	79,732
Cape Town (C. Prov.)	124,876	5,608	80,748	2,598	213,830
Durban (Natal)	232,616	73,701	44,020	155,626	505,963
East London (C. Prov.)	62,735	77,372	18,150	2,325	160,582
Germiston (Trans.)	117,492	33,740	1,616	2,587	155,435
Johannesburg (Trans.)	435,586	947,290	101,769	51,812	1,536,457
Kempton Park (Trans.)	71,505	217,998	295	17	289,815
Kimberley (C. Prov.)	33,440	66,162	44,125	1,196	144,923
Krugersdorp (Trans.)	46,280	53,752	277	2,631	102,940
Pietermaritzburg (Natal)	53,780	62,330	11,424	51,438	178,972
Port Elizabeth (C. Prov.)	128,605	241,844	115,383	6,308	492,140
Pretoria (Trans.)	351,590	146,766	14,746	15,305	528,407
Roodepoort Maraisburg (Trans.)	83,217	77,511	3,620	967	165,315
Springs (Trans.)	49,752	101,691	1,254	1,277	153,974
Vereeniging (Trans.)	65,500	72,432	7,930	3,548	149,410
Welkom (O.F.S.)	38,027	133,679	4,902	...	176,608

CLIMATE. The climate is healthy and invigorating, with abundant sunshine and relatively low rainfall. The factors controlling this include the latitudinal position, the oceanic location of much of the country, and the existence of high plateaus. The south-west has a Mediterranean climate, with rain mainly in winter, but most of the country has a summer maximum, though quantities show a clear decrease from east to west. Temperatures are remarkably uniform over the whole country. Pretoria. Jan. 70°F (21·1°C), July 52°F (11·1°C). Annual rainfall 31″ (785 mm). Bloemfontein. Jan. 73°F (22·8°C), July 47°F (8·3°C). Annual rainfall 23″ (564 mm). Cape Town. Jan. 69°F (20·6°C), July 54°F (12·2°C). Annual rainfall 20″ (508 mm). Durban. Jan. 75°F (23·9°C), July 62°F (16·7°C). Annual rainfall 40″ (1,008 mm). Johannesburg. Jan. 68°F (20°C), July 51°F (10·6°C). Annual rainfall 28″ (709 mm).

CONSTITUTION AND GOVERNMENT. The Republic of South Africa Constitution Act 1961 established with effect from 31 May 1961, the republic, consisting of the 4 provinces–the Cape of Good Hope, Natal, the Transvaal and the Orange Free State–which until then comprised the Union of South Africa.

On 5 Oct. 1960 a referendum was held among the white voters (1,800,426 on roll) to decide whether the Union should become a republic. Of the 1,634,240 votes polled, 850,458 were in favour of a republican constitution, 775,878 against it; 7,904 votes were invalid. The voting was as follows: Transvaal, 406,632 for, 325,041 against; Cape Province, 271,418 for, 269,784 against; Orange Free State,

110,171 for, 33,438 against; Natal, 42,299 for, 135,598 against; South West Africa, 19,938 for, 12,017 against.

The head of the republic is the State President; he is elected for a 7-year term (at a meeting specially convened for the purpose) by an electoral college consisting of members of the houses of Parliament and presided over by the Chief Justice or a judge of appeal designated by him.

On 29 May 1980 the Republic of South Africa Constitution Fifth Amendment Bill was passed and became operative on 1 Jan. 1981. The Senate was abolished from 1 Jan. 1981 and a 60-member President's Council was formed.

On 2 Nov. 1983 a referendum among white voters approved the South Africa Constitution Bill which had previously been passed in the House of Assembly by 119 votes to 35. Turnout for the referendum was 2,062,469 (76·02%), of whom 1,360,223 voted in favour.

The new constitution is expected to become effective during the second half of 1984. It provides for a tri-cameral parliament: the House of Assembly with 178 members elected by White voters; the House of Representatives with 85 members elected by Coloured voters; the House of Delegates with 45 members elected by Indian voters.

These houses choose respectively 50 White, 25 Coloured and 13 Indian members of an electoral college which elects the President. The President initiates legislation and resolves disputes between houses. He is helped by a 60-member President's Council, of which 35 members are elected by the houses, 15 are MPs nominated by himself and 10 are MPs nominated by Opposition parties.

The President appoints a Ministerial Council for each house, choosing members from the majority party; he appoints a central executive cabinet from the three Councils.

Each house discusses separately legislation on the affairs of its own community (education, housing, health and welfare, local government). Corporate discussion on national issues takes place through joint standing committee.

To hold an office of profit under the State (with certain exceptions) is a disqualification for membership of either House, as are also insolvency, crime and insanity. Pretoria is the seat of government, and Cape Town is the seat of legislature.

The state of the parties in the present House of Assembly after the general election of April 1981 was as follows: National Party, 131; Progressive Federal Party, 26; New Republic Party, 8; South African Party, 3. In March 1982 a group of MPs was expelled from the National Party after their refusal to support party policy on power-sharing with Coloureds and Asians. They formed the Conservative Party of South Africa (17 members in June 1982) led by Dr A. P. Treurnicht.

State President: Marais Viljoen.

The Executive Council (National Party) was, March 1984, composed as follows:

Prime Minister, Minister of National Security: P. W. Botha.
Manpower: P. T. C. Du Plessis. *Co-operation and Development:* Dr P. G. J. Koornhof. *Transport:* H. Schoeman. *Industrial Affairs and Trade and Tourism:* D. J. de Villiers. *Finance:* O. P. F. Horwood. *Internal Affairs:* F. W. de Klerk. *Justice:* H. J. Coetzee. *Health and Welfare:* Dr C. V. van der Merwe. *Posts and Telecommunications:* L. A. P. A. Munnik. *Foreign Affairs and Information:* R. F. Botha. *Mines and Energy:* D. Steyn. *Law and Order:* L. le Grange. *National Education:* Dr G. V. N. Viljoen. *Education and Training:* B. Du Plessis. *Constitutional Development:* J. C. Hennis. *Defence:* Gen. M. Malan. *Community Development and State Auxiliary Services:* S. F. Kotzé. *Agriculture:* J. J. G. Wentzel.

The Prime Minister receives an annual salary of R43,000 and a reimbursive allowance of R20,000; a member of the Cabinet an annual salary of R23,500 and a reimbursive allowance of R6,500; and a Deputy Minister an annual salary of R19,000 and a reimbursive allowance of R6,500.

The English and Afrikaans languages are both official, subject to amendments carried by a two-thirds majority in joint session of both Houses of Parliament.

National flag: Three horizontal stripes of orange, white, blue, with the flags of the Orange Free State and the Transvaal, and the Union Jack side by side in the centre.

National anthem: The Call of South Africa/Die Stem van Suid-Afrika (words by C. J. Langenhoven, 1918; tune by M. L. de Villiers, 1921).

Provincial Administration. In each province there is an Administrator appointed by the State President-in-Council for 5 years, and a provincial council elected for 5 years, each council electing an executive committee of 4 (either members or not of the council), the Administrator acting as chairman. Members of the provincial council are elected on the same system as members of Parliament. The provincial committees and councils have authority to deal with local matters, of which provincial finance, education (primary and secondary, other than higher education and technical education), hospitals, roads and bridges, townships, horse and other racing, and game and fish preservation are the most important. In 1953 the administration and control of Black education was transferred from the provincial councils to the central government. All ordinances passed by a provincial council are subject to the veto of the State President-in-Council.

Black Administration. In 1951 the Bantu Authorities Act was enacted to provide a system of Black tribal, regional and territorial authorities. These were given limited administrative, executive and judicial functions and limited legislative powers. In 1959 the main ethnic groups received legislative recognition by the passing of the Promotion of Bantu Self-Government Act, which provided *inter alia* for the various ethnic groups to develop into self-governing national units, each with a Commissioner-General representing the Government of the Republic.

As the territorial authorities became experienced an executive body in the form of a government service was set up for each authority to increase their administrative power.

As the Act envisages eventual political autonomy for each of the various national units and as representation in the highest White governing bodies is regarded as a retarding factor, the representation of Blacks by Whites in Parliament and the Cape Provincial Administration was abolished with effect from 30 June 1960.

In 1968 the Ciskei (whose people are also Xhosa-speaking) and the Tswana Territorial Authorities were established, followed by the Lebowa (North Sotho), Machangana (Tsonga-Shangaan), Venda and South Sotho Territorial Authorities in 1969 and the Zulu Territorial Authority in 1970.

During 1971 these authorities, with the exception of the Zulu, were granted increased powers in terms of the Bantu Homelands Constitution Act 1971. In terms of the provisions of part I of this Act, 6 of the existing 7 territorial authorities in the Republic of South Africa (the Transkei became a self-governing territory in 1963 by virtue of the provisions of the Transkei Constitution Act of 1963) have been converted to Legislative Assemblies with extended legislative and administrative powers.

Part II of the Bantu Homelands Constitution Act makes provision for the areas of these legislative assemblies to be proclaimed self-governing territories with *inter alia* the power to repeal or amend, with minor exceptions, acts of the Republican Parliament. Executive power is vested in an Executive Council. These Councils, each headed by a Chief Councillor, consist of 6 members, except in the case of the South Sotho, where there are only 4. Each of these Councillors is responsible for the administration of a Department. A civil service has been established in each instance, staffed by citizens of the respective homelands. White officials will serve the homeland governments on secondment, until trained Black citizens are able to take over all duties.

In 1971 the Zulus established a Legislative Assembly. Their seat of government is Ulundi.

The Transkei, territory of the Xhosa nation, became independent on 25 Oct. 1976 (*see* p. 1092), Bophuthatswana on 6 Dec. 1977 (*see* p. 1090), Venda on 13 Sept. 1979 (*see* p. 1093) and Ciskei on 4 Dec. 1981 (*see* p. 1095).

There were (1984) 6 territories with a degree of self-government but still forming part of the Republic, Kwa Zulu, Gazankulu (Machangana-Tsonga people), Lebowa (North Soto), Qwaqwa (South Soto), Ka Ngwane (Swazi) and Kwa Ndebele (Southern Ndebele).

Rhoodie, N. J., and Venter, H. J., *Apartheid: A Socio-Historical Exposition of the Origin and Development of the Apartheid Idea.* Cape Town, 1959

DEFENCE. The South African Defence Force comprises a Permanent Force, a Citizen Force and a Commando organization. The Permanent Force consists of professional soldiers, airmen and seamen who are responsible for the administration and training of the whole Defence Force in peace-time, but who are gradually absorbed into the Citizen Force in time of war. The Permanent Force and the Citizen Force consist of Army, Air Force and Naval components; the Commando organization is an army and air organization.

Every white male citizen between 18 and 65 is liable to undergo training and to render personal service in time of war. Those between the ages of 16 and 25 are liable to undergo a compulsory course of peace training. Peace-time training in Commando organizations extends over a period of 16 years' intermittent training. Training in the Citizen Force takes the form of 2 years of continuous training, followed by 9 years during which training takes place at regular intervals.

Aliens have become liable for military service after 5 years' residence by Act of Parliament, 1967.

The S.A. Defence Force is administered by the Chief of the Defence Force, his advisers being the Chief of the Army, Chief of the Air Force and Chief of the Navy, Chief of Staff Operations, Chief of Staff Personnel, the Chief of Staff Management Services and the Surgeon-General.

Army. South Africa is divided into 9 territorial Commands: Western Province, Eastern Province, Natal, Orange Free State, North Western, Northern Transvaal, Witwatersrand, South West Africa and Southern Cape Commands. Within the various Commands are training units, of which members of the Permanent Force form the permanent staff. Courses of various types are held also at the S.A. Military College. The Army includes 1 armoured, 1 mechanized, 4 motorized and 1 parachute brigade; 1 special reconnaissance regiment and supporting artillery, engineer and signals units. Equipment includes some 250 Centurion/Olifant main battle tanks. Strength (1984) 67,400 (including 50,000 conscripts) with an Active Reserve of 130,000. Paramilitary forces are Commandos (90,000), South African Police (35,500) and Police Reserves (20,000).

Navy. The South African Navy has its headquarters at Pretoria.

A custom-built submarine complex incorporating an operations centre alongside a Syncholift marine elevator capable of docking all South African warships except the large tanker, was opened at Simonstown in July 1972. A new maritime headquarters was opened at Silvermine in March 1973.

The Navy includes 3 French-built diesel-powered patrol submarines, 2 British-built anti-submarine frigates, 9 fast missile armed patrol vessels (6 built in Durban and 3 in Israel), 10 coastal minesweepers (2 converted to minehunters and 2 employed for patrol), 5 seaward defence boats (1 used for surveying), 1 motor gun-boat, 1 modern British-built survey ship, 1 fleet replenishment ship, 1 boom defence vessel, 1 small training vessel, 1 torpedo recovery vessel, 4 rescue launches, 30 harbour patrol boats and 7 tugs.

New construction includes three more missile-armed fast attack craft being built in South Africa.

Naval personnel in 1984 totalled 700 officers and 4,500 ratings, plus some 1,600 national service men.

Air Force. There is 1 light bomber squadron with 6 Canberra B.12 and 3 Canberra T.4; 1 light bomber squadron with 6 Buccaneer Mk.50; 1 coastal patrol squadron with 18 Piaggio P.166S; 1 fighter-bomber squadron with 32 Mirage F1-AZ ground attack aircraft; 1 general-purpose fighter squadron with Mirage IIICZ interceptors and Mirage IIIRZ reconnaissance fighters; and 1 squadron with Mirage F1-CZ interceptors. Transport squadrons have 9 Transall C-160s, 7 C-130B/E Hercules, more than 40 C-47s, 7 C-54s, 1 Viscount, 4 twin-jet HS.125s and 5 twin-turboprop Merlin IVA light transports. Four helicopter squadrons and No. 22 Flight have more than 50 Alouette IIIs, 10 Wasps, 50 Pumas and 12 Super Frelons. T-6Gs are used for primary training, followed by advanced training on Impalas and Mirage IIIEZ/DZ, weapons training on Impalas, and multi-engine/crew training on C-47s. Built under licence in the Republic of South Africa, about 150 two-seat Impala Mk. 1s have been followed by 75 single-seat Impala Mk. 2s, based on the Aermacchi MB.326M and 326K respectively. Three squadrons operate C4M Kudu and AM.3C Bosbok liaison aircraft.

The Citizen Force has 5 squadrons of Impalas for counter-insurgency duties and 1 squadron of C4M Kudu and AM.3C Bosbok liaison aircraft. CF personnel have additional functions in regular SAAF squadrons, notably those equipped with C-47 transports and P.166 light transport/coastal patrol aircraft. Total strength (1983) was about 10,000 regular officers and men and 4,000 Citizen Force.

INTERNATIONAL RELATIONS

Membership. The Republic of South Africa is a member of UN.

ECONOMY

Budget. A new basis of subsidy has, with effect from the 1971–72 financial year, been brought into operation by the Government following the investigation of the commission of enquiry into the financial relations between the central government and the provinces. The formula on which this subsidy is based is mainly derived from the calculation of: (1) The needs of the various provinces in respect of the services which they have to provide in the fields of education, health, roads and miscellaneous services; (2) the capacity to pay of the various provinces in respect of the different sources from which their 'own' revenue has to be derived; (3) the deficit which arises when the available revenue of each province, as reflected in its capacity to pay, is subtracted from its expenditure, as adjusted in accordance with its needs.

Total revenue and expenditure of the central government's State Revenue Account in R1m.:

	1979–80	1980–81	1981–82	1982–83 [1]
Revenue	9,787·5	13,310·3	14,290·3	15,417·4
Expenditure	11,441·0	13,595·4	16,350·0	18,042·1

[1] Estimate.

Details of total revenue and expenditure (1981-82) of the State Revenue Account for years ended 31 March (in R1m.):

Revenue		Expenditure	
Direct taxes	8,346·5	Foreign affairs	397·8
Indirect taxes	4,885·4	Defence	3,017·5
Miscellaneous	1,532·5	Education	1,614·3
		Social welfare and pensions	857·2
		Public health	295·9
		Police	715·1
		Transfers and loans to provinces, national states and Development Trust Fund	4,101·8

Public debt on 31 March 1981, R19,986m., of which R606m. was foreign debt; internal debt, R19,380m.

Currency. Decimal coinage was introduced in 1959, the units being the *rand* (abbreviated as R) and the *cent* (abbreviated as c). The rand/cent coinage system came into operation on 14 Feb. 1961. The decimal coins are: *Gold coins.* 2 rand; 1 rand. *Silver coins.* 50 cents; 20 cents; 10 cents; 5 cents. *Bronze coins.* 2 cents; 1 cent. In March 1984, £1 = R1·77; US$1 = R1·20.

Banking. In Dec. 1920, under the South African Currency and Banking Act, 1920, a Central Reserve Bank was established at Pretoria. It commenced operations in

June 1921, and began to issue notes in April 1922. The bank has branches in Pretoria (Head Office), Johannesburg, Cape Town, Durban, Port Elizabeth, East London, Bloemfontein, Pietermaritzburg and Windhoek. Total deposits, 31 Dec. 1982, R2,666m.; assets, R7,900m. The powers of the South African Reserve Bank to control banking and credit were extended by the Banks Act, 1965.

In Jan. 1983 there were 9 commercial banks and 25 general banks (total liabilities, 31 Dec. 1982, R26,092m.), 10 merchant banks (R1,452m.) and 3 discount houses. The Post Office Savings Bank had 2,447,197 current accounts on 31 March 1982; deposits, R236m.

Weights and Measures. Prior to 1969 the imperial system of weights and measures was generally used in the country. However, during 1969 the Weights and Measures Act was amended to provide for the gradual change-over to the metric system of weights and measures.

ENERGY AND NATURAL RESOURCES

Oil. Small amounts of oil and gas were found off-shore (south west of Mossel Bay) in Oct. 1982.

Electricity. The total capacity of the power plants controlled by the Electricity Supply Commission was 18,000 mw at the end of 1980. There were 20 coal-fired stations, 2 hydro-electric stations (540 mw) and 2 gas-turbine stations (342 mw).

Water. The government activities in respect of the control and utilization of water are governed by the Water Act, 1956 (as amended), which is administered by the Directorate of Water Affairs. A Water Research Commission was established in 1971 to co-ordinate and promote research; it is responsible for hydrological research, major water resource development, water pollution control. The combined average flow of South Africa's rivers is about 52,000m. cu. metres annually, most of it lost by evaporation and spillage. About 3,100m. cu. metres annually is available from storage dams, and 1,100m. cu. metres from ground water. Water demand (now mainly urban-industrial) grows at 7% annually.

The Orange River Project, launched in 1966, is near completion of its first phase. The estimated cost (at April 1981) was R490m. It is to embrace 3 major dams on the Orange River, 9 smaller dams or weirs, a 51½-mile tunnel, 20 hydro-electric power stations and a system of canals. The first of the major dams—the Hendrik Verwoerd Dam—was built 5 miles upstream from Norvalspont.

Minerals. Value of the main mineral production sales (in R1,000):

	1979	1980	1981	1982
Asbestos	106,421	102,148	117,335	107,420
Chrome ore	88,752	90,276	86,304	55,774
Coal	1,145,878	1,495,016	2,112,532	2,572,435
Copper	270,989	299,605	277,604	298,574
Diamonds	524,678	553,043	339,915	341,551
Fluorspar	30,131	36,673	48,042	29,467
Gold	5,844,041	10,369,611	8,556,613	8,779,328
Iron ore	293,829	296,141	361,162	366,320
Lime and limestone	92,508	119,052	142,222	154,092
Manganese	175,522	145,486	165,645	191,714
Nickel	...	65,295	...	49,680
Phosphate	62,714	69,135	64,153	75,513
Silver	29,608	81,693	70,143	51,712
Tin	29,362	38,424	30,575	38,048
Vermiculite	6,458	7,998	12,816	13,013
Zinc	...	17,304	...	20,141

Total value of all minerals sold (1982), R14,447·6m.

Mineral production 1982: Coal, 140·1m. tonnes; iron ore, 24·5m. tonnes; phosphates, 2·8m. tonnes; manganese ore, 5·22m. tonnes; chrome, 2·16m. tonnes; asbestos, 211,860 tonnes; copper, 188,709 tonnes; vermiculite, 182,641 tonnes; zinc concentrates, 91,516 tonnes; gold, 662,516 kg; silver, 215,958 kg; diamonds, 9,153,990 carats.

In 1981 the number of persons engaged in mining was 728,506. Of these, about 450,000 were engaged in goldmining.

The Mineral Resources of the Union of South Africa, With a Summary of the Mineral Resources of South West Africa. Geological Survey, Department of Mines. 5th ed. Pretoria, 1976

Minerals. A Quarterly Report of Production and Sales. Department of Mines. Pretoria, from 1936

Agriculture. Much of the land suitable for mechanical farming has unreliable rainfall. Of the total area natural pasture occupies 58% (71·3m. hectares); about 14m. hectares are suitable for dry-land farming, of which 10·6m. are actually cultivated.

South African farmers produced mainly the following crops for the years indicated:

Product (1,000 tonnes)	1978–79	1979–80	1980–81
Maize	8,271	10,782	14,198
Sorghum	366	695	557
Wheat	1,690	2,086	1,470
Groundnuts	132	250	273
Sunflower seed	321	338	495
Sugar-cane	18,821	18,412	14,073
Citrus fruit	733	702	701
Deciduous fruit	798	897	821
Potatoes	696	686	814
Vegetables	1,459	1,445	1,561

Livestock, in 1,000 (1982): 12,200 cattle, 31,700 sheep, 5,340 goats, 1,330 pigs. The 1981 production of butter was 16,584 tonnes; condensed milk, 41,367 tonnes; milk powder, 12,873 tonnes; cheese, 32,309 tonnes.

Wool sold in 1981 was 101,764 tonnes.

Cotton-growing is now undertaken by many farmers, the plant being found a better drought resistant than either tobacco or maize. Gross value of production (1980–81), R84m.

Viticulture produced grapes and products valued at R131m. (1980–81).

In 1980-81 the gross value of agricultural production was R6,642m. (field crops, R3,160m.; livestock products, R2,464m.; horticultural products, R1,018m.).

Forestry. The commercial forests occupy about 1·62m. hectares, of which 148,000 hectares are indigenous trees and the rest exotic trees (pine, gum, wattle). The annual output of forest products is about 85m. cu. metres. Production now meets about 90% of domestic need. Capital invested is about R1,100m., and the number of employees about 100,000.

Fisheries. South Africa is no longer engaged in whaling.

In 1981 sea fisheries caught 379,176 tonnes of pelagic shoal fish, mainly anchovy, and trawl fisheries (hake and sole) landed 135,000 tonnes. The fishing fleet consists of about 6,300 vessels, including 144 purse-seiners and 140 trawlers.

INDUSTRY AND TRADE

Industry. Net value of production of the principal groups of industries (in R1m.) in 1980: Processed food, 4,848; beverages and tobacco, 2,169; motor vehicles, 2,508; basic metals, 4,446; chemicals and products, 7,561; non-electrical machinery, 1,701; non-metallic mineral products, 1,367; electrical machinery, 1,693; clothing, 860; paper and products, 1,274; textiles, 1,701; total net value including other groups, 36,064. Manufacturing industry contributed 24·5% to gross domestic product in 1981 (preliminary).

Industrial employment (except mining) in 1981: Manufacturing employed 1,468,400 workers (earning R8,348,978,000); construction, 440,600 (R1,868,346,000); transport, communications, 349,317 (R2,395,787,000); trade and accommodation services, 764,722 (R3,590,420,000); government and services, 976,135 (R5,283,077,000).

Of the above figures the following proportion of jobs and salaries were held by white South Africans: Total jobs in manufacturing, 322,500 (earning

R4,386,540,000); construction, 57,800 (R758,721,000); transport, communications, 160,895 (R1,832,601,000); trade and accommodation services, 278,909 (R2,378,377,000); government and services, 342,725 (R3,373,738,000).

In 1981 in private manufacturing 174,600 workers were employed in the food industry (earning R696,092,000); textiles employed 118,400 (R437,742,000); clothing, 115,900 (R307,998,000); transport equipment, 115,800 (R831,572,000); non-metallic mineral products, 94,300 (R449,853,000).

Communications comprises the Department of Posts and Telegraphs. Transport comprises South African Railways and Harbours.

Trade Unions. In 1980 there were 188 trade unions with an estimated total membership of 808,053. There were 80 White unions, 54 Coloured and Asian, and 12 Black. Two unions had members from all population groups.

The Industrial Conciliation Amendment Act (1979) provides for freedom of association to all workers irrespective of race; it is now possible for a Black trade union (as opposed to a union with some Black members) to register. Unions are barred from political activity.

Commerce. South Africa, Botswana, Lesotho, Swaziland and Transkei are members of a customs union and the foreign trade statistics shown below represent the combined imports and exports of these countries. The total value of the imports and exports, exclusive of specie and gold bullion, was as follows (in R1m.):

Imports		*Exports*	
1978	6,253	1978	7,333
1979	9,904	1979	14,811
1980	14,381	1980	19,915
1981	18,511	1981	18,014
1982	18,391	1982	19,082

The principal commodity groups of imports and exports (in R1m.) in 1981 (preliminary) were:

Imports		*Exports*	
Chemicals	1,284	Food, beverages and tobacco	573
Base metals and metal manufactures	875	Pearls, precious stones and	
Machinery and parts	4,901	precious metals	2,184
Textiles	789	Base metals and metal	
Artificial resins, plastics and		manufactures	1,571
products	579	Mineral products	1,951
Vehicles, aircraft and other		Vegetables and products	948
transport equipment	2,668		

The geographical origin of South Africa's imports and the direction of its export trade were mainly as follows (in R1m.) in 1981 (preliminary):

	Imports	*Exports*
Africa	317·4	1,037·5
Europe	7,551·4	4,881·0
America	3,095·3	1,977·7
Asia	2,763·0	2,161·2
Oceania	167·1	103·6

Total trade between South Africa and UK (British Department of Trade returns, in £1,000 sterling):

	1979	1980	1981	1982	1983
Imports to UK	533,659	756,397	649,166	745,803	764,909
Exports and re-exports from UK	713,466	1,002,073	1,219,949	1,192,891	1,109,039

Tourism. In 1980, 702,794 tourists visited the Republic of South Africa, spending approximately R476m.

COMMUNICATIONS

Roads. The railway administration operates the long-distance road motor services, together with private operators.

There were at 31 March 1981, 181,389 km of roads, of which some 1,742 km of national roads and 45,589 km of provincial roads were tarred.

South African Transport Services carried 17·9m. passengers and 3·7m. tonnes of goods by road in the year ended 31 March 1982; private operators carried 1m. passengers and 251·2m. tonnes of goods.

Motor vehicles in operation in 1980 included 2,333,172 passenger cars, 870,894 commercial vehicles, 95,430 buses and mini-buses and 192,134 motor cycles. Motor vehicles licensed in 1980, 3,793,481.

Railways. Railway history in South Africa begins in 1860 with the line Durban–Point. With the formation of the Union in 1910, the state-owned lines in the 4 provinces (12,194 km) were amalgamated into one state undertaking, which also took over the control of the harbours–the South African Railways and Harbours Administration.

Government-owned lines operated by the administration (1983) totalled 22,876 km, of which 7,128 km were electrified. Passenger journeys, 1981–82, 753m.; goods traffic, 188m. tonnes.

Aviation. Civil aviation in South Africa is controlled by the Department of Transport, which administers the following state-owned airports: Jan Smuts Airport, Johannesburg; D. F. Malan Airport, Cape Town; Louis Botha Airport, Durban; J. B. M. Hertzog Airport, Bloemfontein; Ben Schoeman Airport, East London; H. F. Verwoerd Airport, Port Elizabeth; B. J. Vorster Airport, Kimberley; P. W. Botha Airport, George; Upington Airport. At 13 other airports the Department provides air navigation services.

South African Airways, as the national air carrier, operate scheduled international air services within Africa and to Europe, South America, the USA, the Far East and Australia. Twenty-three other lines also operate scheduled international air services; they include British Airways, PANAM, KLM, SAS, TAP, Swissair, Olympic Air, El-Al, Alitalia, SABENA, Lufthansa, DETA, Air Zimbabwe, Iberia, DJA, UTA, LUXAIR, Lesotho Airways, Swazi Air, Air Malawi, Air Madagascar. Luxavia operate international non-scheduled flights.

Eighteen independent operators provide internal flights.

During 1982 South African Airways carried 3,937,217 passengers (3,142,956 on internal flights) and 77,548 tonnes of freight and mail (46,871).

Shipping. The main ports are Durban, Cape Town, Saldanha, Richards Bay, Port Elizabeth and East London. Smaller ports are Mossel Bay, Port Nolloth, Walvis Bay and Lüderitz. During 1981–82 these ports handled 78·0m. tons of cargo, of which Richards Bay handled 31·0m. tons and Durban handled 18·5m. tons.

Post and Broadcasting. On 31 March 1982 there were in South Africa 1,641 money-order post offices and 555 postal agencies.

On 30 Sept. 1982 the international telex switchboard served 26,323 telex subscribers in South Africa. Line capacity of automatic telephone exchanges, 2·1m.; there were 3,356,833 telephones.

The South African Broadcasting Corporation had, in Sept. 1980, 2·3m. listeners' licences.

On 5 Jan. 1976 the South African Television Service began official transmissions. There were 1·45m. licences in 1980.

Cinemas (1980). There were 620 including 140 drive-ins.

Newspapers (1981). There are 8 Afrikaans and 14 English daily newspapers.

JUSTICE, RELIGION, EDUCATION AND WELFARE

Justice. The common law of the republic is the Roman–Dutch law–that is, the uncodified law of Holland as it was at the date of the cession of the Cape in 1806. The law of England as such is not recognized as authoritative, though by statute the principles of English law relating to evidence and to mercantile matters, *e.g.*, companies, patents, trademarks, insolvency and the like, have been introduced. In shipping and insurance, English law is followed in the Cape Province, and it has also largely influenced civil and criminal procedure throughout the republic. In all other matters, family relations, property, succession, contract, etc., Roman–Dutch law rules, English decisions being valued only so far as they agree therewith.

The Supreme Court of South Africa is constituted as follows: (i) The Appellate Division, consisting of the Chief Justice and as many Judges of Appeal as the State President may stipulate, is the highest court and its decisions are binding on all courts. It has no original jurisdiction, but is purely a Court of Appeal. (ii) The Provincial Divisions: In each province there is a provincial division of the Supreme Court, while in the Cape there are three such divisions possessing both original and appellate jurisdiction. (iii) The Local Divisions: There is a local division each in the Transvaal and Natal exercising the same original jurisdiction within limited areas as the provincial divisions. The judges hold office till they attain the age of 70 years. No judge can be removed from office except by the State President upon an address from both Houses of Parliament on the ground of misbehaviour or incapacity. The circuit system is fully developed.

The Black appeal courts and 3 Black divorce courts have jurisdiction to some extent concurrent with and in certain respects exclusive of that of the Supreme Court in cases in which the parties are Black.

Each province is further divided into districts with a magistrate's court having a prescribed civil and criminal jurisdiction. From this court there is an appeal to the provincial divisions of the Supreme Court, and thence to the appellate division. Magistrates' convictions carrying sentences above a prescribed limit are subject to automatic review by a judge. In addition, several regional divisions consisting of a number of districts have been constituted. Convictions of such courts are not subject to automatic review by a judge.

Courts of Black affairs commissioners have been constituted in defined areas to hear all civil cases and matters between Black and Black only. An appeal lies to the Black appeal court, whose decision is final, unless the court consents to an appeal to the appellate division of the Supreme Court on a point stated by the court itself. Black affairs commissioners have concurrent criminal jurisdiction with magistrates' courts in respect of certain offences committed by Black, while a limited civil and criminal jurisdiction is conferred upon the Black chief or headman over his own tribe.

Police. In 1980 the staff of the Police department numbered 34,271 (18,370 White). There were 46 police stations manned exclusively by Blacks, 16 by Coloureds and 1 by Indians.

In 1983 there were 242 prisons with (Sept. 1983) a monthly average of 106,000 prisoners.

Religion. A sample tabulation of the 1980 census results as regards religious denominations shows the following: *Whites:* Nederduits Gereformeerd Kerk, 1,693,640; Anglicans, 456,020; Methodists, 414,080; Roman Catholics, 393,640; Nederduits Hervormde Kerk, 246,340; Presbyterians, 128,920; Gereformeerd Kerk, 128,360; Apostolics, 125,920; other Christians, 566,640; Jews, 119,220; others, 255,320. *Blacks:* Methodists, 11,554,280; Black independent churches, 4,954,000; Nederduits Gereformeerd kerk, 1,103,560; Roman Catholics, 1,676,680; Anglican, 797,040; Lutheran, 698,400; other Christian churches, 1,760,860; non-Christian churches, 101,700; others, 4,277,240. *Coloureds and Asians:* Nederduits Gereformeerd kerk, 678,380; Hindus, 512,360; Anglican, 360,380; Roman Catholic, 285,980; Islam 318,000; others, 1,279,020.

Education. *Higher Education.* There are 17 universities in the republic: (1) The University of Cape Town. (2) The University of Natal, Durban and Pietermaritzburg. (3) The University of the Orange Free State at Bloemfontein. (4) Potchefstroom University for Christian Higher Education, Potchefstroom. (5) The University of Pretoria. (6) Rhodes University, Grahamstown, C.P. (7) The University of Stellenbosch. (8) The University of the Witwatersrand, Johannesburg. (9) The University of South Africa, with its seat in Pretoria, which conducts a Division of External Studies by means of correspondence and vacation courses; it is also an examining body. (10) The University of Port Elizabeth. (11) Rand Afrikaans University, Johannesburg.

The University of Fort Hare (12), the University of the North (13) near Pietersburg and the University of Zululand (14) near Empangeni, Natal, are operated by the Department of Education and Training and provide education at university level for Blacks, the University of the Western Cape (15), Bellville (Cape), offers university facilities to the Coloured population and is administered by the Department of Coloured Affairs; while the University for Indians (16), the University of Durban-Westville, at Durban falls under the Department of Indian Affairs. The Medical University of South Africa (17) is for Black students.

The following statistics refer to 1981:

University	Students	University	Students
Cape Town	10,488	Pretoria	16,238
Durban-Westville	4,961	Rand Afrikaans	5,325
Fort Hare	2,410	Rhodes	3,009
Medunsa	510	South Africa	56,572
Natal	8,249	Stellenbosch	11,396
North	2,859	West Cape	3,923
Orange Free State	8,368	Witwatersrand	13,457
Port Elizabeth	2,954	Zululand	2,196
Potchefstroom	6,764		

Technical and Vocational Education. Technical, vocational and special education for persons other than those for whom specific provision is made (*e.g.,* Black): The Department of National Education is responsible for the maintenance, management and control of or the payment of subsidies to colleges for advanced technical education, technical colleges, technical institutes, special schools, schools of industries and reform schools. Colleges for advanced technical education provide education on an advanced level for a variety of technical, commercial and general courses of study as well as secondary education on a part-time basis. Technical colleges and technical institutes are mainly responsible for the training of apprentices and the education, on a part-time basis, of persons not subject to compulsory school attendance. Special schools for handicapped children cater for the educational needs of those who are blind, partially sighted, deaf, hard of hearing, epileptic, cerebral palsied and physically handicapped. Children found to be in need of care by a children's court, are admitted to schools of industries and reform schools.

The Department of Coloured Affairs has taken over all schools of this nature for Coloureds.

In 1982, 77 technical and training colleges for Whites had 95,184 students; 12 for Coloureds had about 9,160 students; 1 for Asians had 3,911 students. Provision is made for technical education for Black students at 4 institutions for advanced technical education and 33 industrial or trade schools; total enrolment at these institutions was 15,519 in 1982.

State and State-aided Education other than Higher Education. Primary and secondary public education, other than that specifically provided elsewhere, falls under the Provincial Administration. In terms of the National Education Policy Act, 1967, the Minister of Education, Arts and Science may, after consultation with the Provincial Administrators and the National Advisory Education Council, determine general educational policy within the framework of the Act. Black education is the responsibility of the Department of Black Education and Training, while education for Coloureds and Indians is controlled by the Departments of Coloured Affairs and Indian Affairs respectively.

Public schools in 1982: 2,373 for Whites with 50,387 teachers and 931,429 pupils; 1,990 for Coloureds with 27,924 teachers and 764,804 pupils; 410 for Asians with 9,186 teachers and 224,229 pupils; 12,014 for Blacks (in the republic) with 91,994 teachers and 3,603,039 pupils.

Private Schools. To a certain extent the activities of private schools are controlled by government regulations. Their pupils generally sit for the state schools' examinations. These schools make provision for kindergarten, elementary and preparatory, general primary, secondary and commercial education.

In 1982, 134 private or aided schools for Whites had 3,024 teachers and 43,985 students. In 1982, 13 schools for Coloureds had 160 teachers and 2,536 students; 1 for Asians had 13 teachers and 93 students; in 1975 416 for Bantu had 1,878 teachers and 80,904 students.

Teacher-training colleges in 1982: 20 for Whites had 1,248 teachers and 13,196 students;16 for Coloureds and Asians had 234 teachers and 2,909 students; 35 for Bantu had 12,900 students.

Health. At 1 Jan. 1982 there were 16,787 medical practitioners, 3,904 specialists, 2,286 hospital interns, 2,923 dental specialists and dentists; in 1980 there were 595 hospitals. More tuberculosis patients were treated as outpatients than in hospital.

Social Welfare. *Social Security.* Pensions paid in 1981:

	Beneficiaries	Amount (R1,000)
Old age	457,987	335,519
War veterans	22,389	25,868
Blind	7,232	3,907
Disability grants	185,209	117,025
Maintenance	95,271	114,320

Welfare Services. South Africa is not a welfare state, yet provides many services for the community. Welfare work on behalf of the Government is done by the Departments of Social Welfare and Pensions, Coloured Affairs, Indian Affairs, and Plural Relations and Development.

There are also a great number of voluntary welfare societies which undertake a variety of welfare services. Social assistance is not based on compulsory insurance but is financed from taxation.

The Department of Social Welfare and Pensions formulates the broad policy and takes care of the co-ordination of the various welfare services. The National Council for Welfare, a statutory body set up under the National Welfare Act of 1965, among others, is used by the Government for the execution of this policy. Four specialized commissions serve under the National Council. These are: the Social Work Commission, the Commission for Family Life, the Commission for Welfare Planning and the Commission for Welfare Organizations. The Department also provides such personal services as pensions and allowances, and practical assistance to individuals or families who may have social problems, neglected and uncared-for children, juvenile delinquents, adults needing special guidance and alcoholics. There is assistance for mental or physical disability, death or absence of the breadwinner. There are professional field services and institutions available as well as financial help.

Voluntary Welfare Societies. These organizations supply supplementary services to those provided by the Government. Voluntary welfare organizations must register at the Department of Social Welfare and Pensions under the National Welfare Act of 1965. There are more than 2,000 registered welfare organizations; they have organized themselves into national and provincial councils so as to co-ordinate their activities.

Funds for these voluntary services are raised from Government subsidies and by public subscription.

In the past the State, with the assistance of local authorities, voluntary welfare agencies and church organizations, provided welfare services for the Blacks, the voluntary agencies being controlled by White committees. However, this situation is gradually changing as more Blacks are taking an interest in welfare work. The various Black nations are being encouraged and assisted to form their own voluntary agencies and so to provide, as far as possible, welfare services for their own people. As far as is practicable, the institutions required for the care of the aged and the disabled and for needy children are sited in the homelands, and are staffed by Blacks.

Child and Family Welfare. Welfare or professional officers employed by the State are responsible for the implementation and administration of the Children's Act (amended and consolidated in 1960). This Act makes provision for the prevention and treatment of neglected and maladjusted children, with the full integration of the services of voluntary child and family welfare organizations. Children's institutions, mainly established and controlled by private organizations, are subsidized by the State, as are crèches, community centres and other projects in aid of child and family welfare.

DIPLOMATIC REPRESENTATIVES

Of South Africa in Great Britain (South Africa Hse., Trafalgar Sq., London, WC2N 5DP)
Ambassador: Dr Dennis Worral.

Of Great Britain in South Africa (6 Hill St., Arcadia, Pretoria, 0002)
Ambassador: Ewen Fergusson.

Of South Africa in the USA (3051 Massachusetts Ave., NW, Washington, D.C., 20008)
Ambassador: Bernardus G. Fourie.

Of the USA in South Africa (225 Pretorius St., Pretoria)
Ambassador: Herman W. Nickel.

Of South Africa to The United Nations
Ambassador: Kurt Robert Samuel von Schirnding.

Books of Reference

Statistical Information: The Bureau (formerly Office) of Census and Statistics (Schoeman St., Pretoria), established on 1 April 1917 as a division of the Department of the Interior and now directly under the Minister of Economic Affairs, is based mainly on the Consolidated Census Act, No. 76, of 1957, and the Consolidated Statistics Act, No. 73, of 1957. Main publications:

> *Official Year Book of the Union of South Africa and of Basutoland, Bechuanaland Protectorate and Swaziland.* From 1918 (preceded by the *Statistical Year Book, 1913–17)*
> *Union Statistics for 50 Years: Jubilee Issue, 1910–1960* (1960)
> *Statistical Year Book.* From 1964
> *Statistics of Production: Industrial.* Annual, from 1915/16 (but suspended from 1929/30 to 1931/32 and from 1938 to 1942)
> *Statistics of Production: Agricultural.* Annual, from 1917/18 (but suspended from 1920/30 to 1931/32 and from 1939 to 1946)
> *Monthly Bulletin of Statistics* (from 1922)
> *Population Census, 1970.* (Various special reports in course of publication)
> South African Reserve Bank, *Quarterly Bulletin of Statistics*
> *Homelands: The Role of the Corporations in the Republic of South Africa,* Johannesburg, 1976

The Customs and Excise Office, Pretoria, publishes *Monthly Abstract of Trade Statistics* (from 1946) and *Trade and Shipping of the Union of South Africa* (annually, 1910–55); *Foreign Trade Statistics* (annually, from 1956)

Bissell, R. E., and Crocker, C. A., *South Africa in the 1980s.* Boulder, 1979
Böhning, W. R., *Black Migration to South Africa.* Geneva, 1981
Bosman, D. B., *Tweetalige Woordeboek.* 2 vols. Cape Town, 1946–49
Branford, J., *A Dictionary of South African English.* Rev. ed. OUP, 1980
de Villiers, L., *South Africa: A Skunk Among Nations.* London, 1975
Friedman, B., *Smuts: A Reappraisal.* London, 1975
Gann, L. H. and Duignan, P., *Why South Africa will Survive.* London, 1981
Hellmann, E. and Lever, H., *Race Relations in Africa, 1929–1979.* London, 1980
Kruger, D. W., *The Making of a Nation.* Johannesburg, 1969
Lacour-Gayet, R., *A History of South Africa.* London, 1977
Metrowich, F. R., *Africa in the Sixties.* Pretoria, 1970
Muller, C. F. J., *500 Years of South African History.* Pretoria, 1969
Musiker, R., *South Africa,* [Bibliography] Oxford and Santa Barbara, 1980
Talbot, A. M. and W. J., *Atlas of South African History.* Pretoria, 1969
Troup, F., *South Africa: An Historical Introduction.* London, 1972
Walker, E. A., *History of Southern Africa.* London, 1957
The Oxford History of South Africa. OUP, Vol. 1, 1969; Vol. 2, 1971

PROVINCE OF THE CAPE OF GOOD HOPE

Kaapprovinsie

HISTORY. The colony of the Cape of Good Hope was founded by the Dutch in the year 1652. Britain took possession of it from 1795 to 1803 and again in 1806, and it was formally ceded to Great Britain by the Convention of London, 13 Aug. 1814. Letters patent issued in 1850 declared that in the colony there should be a Parliament which should consist of the Governor, a Legislative Council and a House of Assembly. On 31 May 1910 the colony was merged in the Union of South Africa, thereafter forming an original province of the Union.

AREA AND POPULATION. The following table gives the population of the Cape of Good Hope[1] (area (1980) 646,332 sq. km) at the last census:

	All races			Whites		Non-Whites	
	Total	Males	Females	Males	Females	Males	Females
1936	3,527,865	1,663,169	1,864,796	396,058	394,993	1,267,011	1,469,803
1946	4,051,424	1,924,334	2,127,090	433,849	436,300	1,490,485	1,690,790
1951	4,426,726	2,110,674	2,316,052	463,917	471,168	1,646,757	1,844,884
1960	5,360,234	2,553,245	2,806,989	493,370	507,398	2,059,875	2,299,591
1970[2]	4,293,726	2,151,629	2,142,097	546,761	567,448	1,604,868	1,579,649
1980[2]	5,091,360	2,575,460	2,515,900	624,680	639,360	1,950,780	1,876,540

[1] Including Walvis Bay (699 sq. km). [2] Excluding Republic of Transkei.

Present area (excluding Griqualand East, Mafikeng and the Republic of Bophuthatswana), 645,767 sq. km (249,331 sq. miles).

Of the non-White population in 1980, 32,120 were Asians, 1,569,040 were Blacks and 2,226,160 Coloureds.

Vital statistics for calendar years:

	Whites			Asians and Coloureds		
	Births	Deaths	Marriages	Births	Deaths	Marriages
1966	21,818	10,290	10,055	72,771	24,110	9,758
1978	17,993	11,859	11,129	58,421	19,274	16,711
1979	17,755	11,594	11,081	63,145	20,591	16,488

ADMINISTRATION. The division of parties in the Provincial Council (Sept. 1983) was: National Party, 45; Progressive Federal Party, 10; New Republic Party, 1.

Cape Town is the seat of the provincial administration.

Administrator: Eugene Louw.

The province is divided into 128 magisterial districts and 38 divisional council divisions. Each division has a council of at least 6 members (15 in the Cape Division) elected quinquennially by the owners or occupiers of immovable property. The duties devolving upon divisional councils include the construction and maintenance of roads and bridges, local rating, vehicle taxation (except motor vehicle taxation) and preservation of public health. There are 219 municipalities, each governed by a mayor and councillors. Municipal elections are held biennially.

FINANCE. In 1983–84 revenue amounted to R1,535,241,000 and expenditure to R1,519,178,000.

MINING. For mineral production, see pp. 1073–74.

AGRICULTURE. Viticulture in the republic is almost exclusively confined to the Cape Province, but practically all other forms of agricultural and pastoral activity are pursued.

INDUSTRY. The province has brick, tile and pottery works, saw-mills, engineering works, foundries, grain-mills, distilleries and wineries, clothing factories, furniture, boot and shoe factories, etc.

RELIGION. Sample tabulation, 1970 census. *Whites:* Nederduits Gereformeerd Kerk, 553,548; Gereformeerd Kerk, 11,771; Nederduits Hervormde Kerk, 7,102; Anglicans, 141,858; Presbyterians, 34,243; Congregationalists, 11,590; Methodists, 98,717; Lutherans, 12,433; Roman Catholics, 77,608; Apostolics, 33,044; other Christians, 67,149; Jews, 32,076; others, 28,070. *Non-Whites:* Afrikaans Churches, 585,570; Anglicans, 397,668; Presbyterians, 50,863; Congregationalists, 189,823; Methodists, 393,843; Lutherans, 101,881; Roman Catholics, 198,692; Apostolics, 149,801; Black Christian Churches, 253,055; other Christians, 185,096; Islam, 127,523; Hindus, 5,722; others, 551,422.

EDUCATION. *Training.* Higher education is under the control of the Department of National Education, Pretoria. Primary and secondary education (including vocational education and the training of primary teachers) are controlled by the Provincial Administration in respect of White pupils, by the Department of Education and Training in respect of Black pupils and by the Department of Internal Affairs in respect of Coloured pupils. Education is compulsory for all White children. Primary and secondary education is free to the end of the calendar year in which the age of 19 years is attained.

Whites (1983). There were 829 government and aided schools with 14,210 teachers and 239,463 pupils; 8 teacher-training colleges with 296 lecturers and 1,984 students; 53 private schools with 12,904 pupils.

Coloureds (1982). There were 1,810 state and aided schools with 24,499 teachers and 664,286 pupils; 12 teacher-training colleges with 3,748 students; 14 private schools with 2,687 pupils (1981).

Black (1981). There were 1,137 state schools with 5,703 teachers and 248,553 pupils and 17 private schools with 118 teachers and 5,063 pupils.

Asians (1982). There were 7 state schools with 191 teachers and 4,068 pupils.

PROVINCE OF NATAL

HISTORY. Natal was annexed to Cape Colony in 1844, placed under separate government in 1845, and on 15 July 1856 established as a separate colony. By this charter partially representative institutions were established, and in 1893 the colony obtained responsible government. The province of Zululand was annexed to Natal on 30 Dec. 1897. The districts of Vryheid, Utrecht and part of Wakkerstroom, formerly belonging to the Transvaal, were annexed in Jan. 1903. On 31 May 1910 the colony was merged in the Union of South Africa as an original province of the Union.

AREA AND POPULATION. The province (including Kwa Zulu, 10,375 sq. miles) has an area of 86,976 sq. km (33,578 sq. miles), with a seaboard of about 360 miles. The climate is sub-tropical on the coast and somewhat colder inland. The province is divided into 45 magisterial districts.

The returns of the total population (excluding Kwa Zulu) at the census were:

	All races			Whites		Non-Whites	
	Total	Males	Females	Males	Females	Males	Females
1960	2,979,034	1,443,561	1,535,473	166,404	222,750	1,227,157	1,362,468
1970	4,236,770	2,009,410	2,227,360	171,005	214,960	1,794,430	2,004,610
1980	2,676,340	1,360,600	1,315,740	276,240	285,620	1,084,360	1,030,120

Of the non-White population in 1980, 665,340 were Asians, 91,020 Coloureds and 1,358,120 Blacks. Population of Kwa Zulu, see p. 1067.

ADMINISTRATION. At the provincial council elections in 1981 there were returned: New Republic Party, 14; National Party, 2; Progressive Federal Party, 5.

The seat of provincial government in Natal is Pietermaritzburg. In April 1978 the area of East Griqualand was transferred to Natal from Cape Province.

Administrator: The Hon. Jan Christoffel Greyling Botha.

FINANCE. In 1982–83 revenue amounted to R613·14m. and expenditure to R621·02m.

MINING. The province is rich in mineral wealth, particularly coal. For figures of mineral production, *see* pp. 1073–74.

AGRICULTURE. Sugar and citrus growing are of major importance. On the coast and in Zululand there are vast plantations of sugar-cane (about 800,000 acres), producing, in 1967, 15,547,000 tons. Cereals of all kinds (especially maize), fruits, vegetables, the *Acacia molissima* (the bark of which is much used for tanning purposes) and other crops are produced. Large areas are being afforested.

INDUSTRY. Natal is highly industrialized. There are metallurgical, chemical, paper, rayon and food-processing plants, iron and steel foundries, petrol refineries, pulp-mills, explosives and fertilizer plants, milk- and meat-canning factories.

EDUCATION. The Natal Provincial Administration controls primary and secondary technical and vocational education for Whites. Higher technical and vocational education for all races is provided by the central government. *See also* pp. 1077–79.

Whites (1983). There were 309 government and aided schools with 116,346 pupils; 3 teacher-training colleges with 1,151 students; 11 private schools with 1,037 pupils.

Coloureds (1983). There were 63 government and aided schools with 1,185 teachers and 29,072 pupils; 11 pre-primary schools with 30 teachers and 628 pupils (1982); 1 teacher-training college with 223 students and 25 lecturers; 1 technical college with 367 students and 36 lecturers (1982).

Blacks (1982). There were 1,000 schools with 4,584 teachers and 184,911 pupils. These schools are situated in the white area of Natal and the south-eastern Transvaal.

Asians (1983). There were 349 state and state-aided schools with 8,275 teachers and 194,216 pupils.

PROVINCE OF THE TRANSVAAL

HISTORY. The Transvaal was one of the territories colonized by the Boers who left the Cape Colony during the Great Trek in 1831 and following years. In 1852, by the Sand River Treaty, Great Britain recognized the independence of the Transvaal, which, in 1853, took the name of the South African Republic. In 1877 the republic was annexed by Great Britain, but the Boers took up arms towards the end of 1880. In 1881 peace was made and self-government, subject to British suzerainty and certain stipulated restrictions, was restored to the Boers. The London Convention of 1884 removed the suzerainty and a number of these restrictions but reserved to Great Britain the right of approval of the Transvaal's foreign relations, excepting with regard to the Orange Free State. In 1886 gold was discovered on the Witwatersrand, and this discovery, together with the great influx of foreigners which it occasioned, gave rise to many grave problems. Eventually, in 1899, war broke out between Great Britain and the Transvaal. Peace was concluded on 31

May 1902, the Transvaal and the Orange Free State both losing their independence. The Transvaal was governed as a crown colony until 12 Jan. 1907, when responsible government came into force. On 31 May 1910 the Transvaal became one of the four provinces of the Union.

AREA AND POPULATION. The area of the province is 262,499 sq. km or 101,351 sq. miles, including Gazankulu, Lebowa, Ka Ngwane and Kwa Ndebele. The province is divided into 53 districts. The following table shows the population, excluding Gazankulu, Lebowa, Ka Ngwane and Kwa Ndebele, at each of the last censuses:

	All races Total	Males	Females	*Whites* Males	Females	*Non-Whites* Males	Females
1936	3,341,470	1,846,576	1,494,894	424,470	396,286	1,422,108	1,098,608
1946	4,283,038	2,374,323	1,908,715	541,053	522,068	1,833,270	1,386,647
1951	4,812,838	2,619,314	2,193,524	737,194	731,111	2,575,119	2,230,053
1960	6,270,711	3,310,948	2,959,763	735,845	729,730	2,575,103	2,230,034
1970	8,717,530	4,460,130	4,257,400	946,430	938,210	3,513,700	3,319,190
1980	8,350,500	4,567,500	3,783,000	1,190,740	1,171,320	3,376,760	2,611,680

Of the non-White population in 1980, 5,644,660 were Black, 115,560 Asians and 228,220 Coloureds. Population of Gazankulu, Lebowa, Ka Ngwane and Kwa Ndebele, *see* pp. 1067.

Important towns of the province are listed on p. 1068.

ADMINISTRATION. At the provincial council election in 1981 there were returned: National Party, 67; Progressive Federal Party, 9.

The seat of provincial government is at Pretoria, which is also the administrative capital of the Republic of South Africa.

Administrator: Willem Cruywagen.

FINANCE. In 1976–77 revenue amounted to R560,953,000 and expenditure to R667,523,000.

MINING. For mineral production, *see* p. 1073. Gold output in 1967 was 19,591,000 oz. worth R492,978,000.

AGRICULTURE. The province is in the main a stock-raising country, though there are considerable areas well adapted for agriculture, including the growing of tropical crops.

INDUSTRY. The province has iron and brass foundries and engineering works, grain-mills, breweries, brick, tile and pottery works, tobacco, soap, and candle factories, coach and wagon works, clothing factories, etc.

RELIGION. Sample tabulation, 1960 census. *Whites:* Nederduits Gereformeerde Kerk, 539,491; Gereformeerde Kerk, 72,404; Nederduits Hervormde Kerk, 167,693; Anglicans, 137,207; Presbyterians, 50,196; Congregationalists, 3,071; Methodists, 123,218; Lutherans, 13,880; Roman Catholics, 91,235; Apostolics, 67,550; other Christians, 90,504; Jews, 74,221; others, 37,635. *Non-Whites:* Afrikaans Churches, 278,006; Anglicans, 309,047; Presbyterians, 50,924; Congregationalists, 29,839; Methodists, 318,424; Lutherans, 365,836; Roman Catholics, 270,493; Apostolics, 179,739; Black Churches, 1,030,853; other Christians, 310,162; Mohammedans, 42,707; Hindus, 23,190; others, 1,595,952.

EDUCATION. All education for Whites except that of universities is under the provincial authority. The province has been divided for the purposes of local control and management into 21 school districts. Instruction in government schools, both primary and secondary, is free. The medium of instruction is the home language of the pupil. The teaching of the other language begins at the earliest stage at which it is appropriate on educational grounds. Both languages are taught as examination subjects to every pupil.

Whites (1982). There were 1,153 public schools with 27,797 teachers and 547,452 pupils; 5 teacher-training colleges with 5,904 students; 84 private schools with 2,009 teachers and 31,597 pupils.

Coloureds (1982). There were 92 state and state-aided schools with 1,898 teachers and 59,547 pupils; 1 teacher-training college with 272 students.

Asians (1982). There were 71 public schools with 1,259 teachers and 28,958 pupils; 1 teacher-training college with 30 teachers and 377 students.

Blacks (1977). There were 2,170 public and private school sections with 15,450 teachers and 735,325 pupils (Homelands excluded).

PROVINCE OF THE ORANGE FREE STATE

Oranje-Vrystaat

HISTORY. The Orange River was first crossed by Europeans in the middle of the 18th century. Between 1810 and 1820, settlements were made in the southern parts of the Orange Free State, and the Great Trek greatly increased the number of settlers during and after 1836. In 1848, Sir Harry Smith proclaimed the whole territory between the Orange and Vaal rivers as a British possession called the 'Orange River sovereignty'. However, in 1854, by the Convention of Bloemfontein, British sovereignty was withdrawn and the independence of the country was recognized.

During the first 5 years of its existence the Orange Free State was much harassed by incessant raids by the Basutos. These were at length conquered, but, owing to the intervention of the British Government, the treaty of Aliwal North incorporated only part of the territory of the Basutos in the Orange Free State.

On account of the treaty with the South African Republic, the Orange Free State took a prominent part in the South African War (1899–1902) and was annexed on 28 May 1900 as the Orange River Colony. Crown colony government continued until 1907, when responsible government was introduced. On 31 March 1910 the Orange River Colony was merged in the Union of South Africa as the province of the Orange Free State.

AREA AND POPULATION. The area of the province is 127,993 sq. km or 49,418 sq. miles, including Qwaqwa. The province is divided into 34 administrative and 57 magisterial districts. The census population (excluding Qwaqwa) has varied as follows:

		All races		Whites		Non-Whites	
	Total	Males	Females	Males	Females	Males	Females
1936	772,060	381,903	390,157	101,872	99,106	280,031	291,051
1946	879,071	432,896	446,175	101,874	100,203	331,022	345,972
1951	1,016,570	519,166	497,404	115,637	112,015	403,529	385,389
1960	1,386,202	731,486	654,716	139,304	137,103	601,182	553,613
1970	1,716,350	899,140	817,210	148,110	148,030	751,030	669,180
1980	1,931,860	1,039,220	892,640	166,380	159,840	872,840	732,800

Of the non-White population in 1980, 1,549,600 were Black and 56,040 Coloureds. Population of Qwaqwa, *see* p. 1067.

ADMINISTRATION. At the provincial council election in 1981 there were returned 28 National Party.

The seat of provincial government is at Bloemfontein. There are 68 municipalities and 8 village management boards.

Administrator: A. C. van Wyk.

FINANCE. In 1976–77 revenue amounted to R134,288,000 and expenditure to R159,883,000.

MINING. For mineral statistics, *see* p. 1073. The production of the gold-fields in the province has increased tremendously since 1951, when the output was 18,545 oz. valued at R230,186. The output in 1961 was 7,235,647 oz. valued at R181,320,401.

AGRICULTURE. The province consists of undulating plains, affording excellent grazing and wide tracts for agricultural purposes. The rainfall is moderate. The country was mainly devoted to stock-farming, but now a rapidly increasing quantity of grain is being raised, especially in the eastern districts.

INDUSTRY. The more important manufacturing industries in the province are the oil-from-coal factory (as well as industries based on its by-products) at Sasolburg; fertilizer, agricultural implements, blanket and woollen products, clothing, hosiery, cement and pharmaceutical factories, grain-mills and brick, tile and pottery works.

EDUCATION. *Whites.* Primary, secondary and vocational education and the training of primary teachers are controlled and financed by the Provincial Administration. The province is divided into 11 school board areas.

Education is free in all public schools up to the university matriculation standard. Attendance is compulsory between the ages of 7 and 16, but exemption may be granted in special cases. The home language of the pupil is the medium of instruction.

Whites (1982). There were 208 government and aided schools with 4,232 teachers and 73,355 pupils.

Coloureds (1982). There were 40 government and aided schools with 452 teachers and 12,918 pupils.

Blacks (1977). There were 2,026 school sections with 5,880 teachers and 302,286 pupils (Homelands excluded).

SOUTH WEST AFRICA

Suidwes-Afrika—Namibia

HISTORY. The territory (excluding Walvis Bay and certain islands) was proclaimed a German protectorate in 1884, but was surrendered to the Forces of the Union of South Africa on 9 July 1915 at Khorab. The administration was vested in the Government of the Union of South Africa by mandate of the League of Nations dated 17 Dec. 1920. In 1921 the Governor-General delegated certain of his functions to the Administrator of the Territory, who was assisted by an Advisory Council and, from 1925, by an Executive Committee and the Legislative Assembly. On 18 July 1966 the International Court of Justice decided, by the President's casting vote, that Ethiopia and Liberia had no legal right in applying for a decision on the international status of South West Africa. In 1971 the International Court of Justice ruled in an advisory opinion that the Republic of South Africa's presence in South West Africa was illegal. In Dec. 1973 the UN appointed Sean McBride as UN Commissioner for Namibia. The Republic of South Africa was given until May 1975 to declare its intentions on the future of Namibia, by the UN.

Independence was envisaged for 31 Dec. 1978. However in Dec. 1978 an election for a Constituent Assembly was held without UN supervision. The Democratic Turnhalle Alliance Party gained 41 of the 50 seats. The South West Africa People's Organisation (SWAPO) boycotted the election. The Constituent Assembly was not recognized by the UN, the Western Powers or SWAPO. UN plans for a ceasefire and UN-supervised elections were rejected by the Constituent Assembly on 20 April 1979. Discussions continued during 1980 aiming at solutions to the Namibia problem and in Jan. 1981 a UN Conference was held in Geneva but this also ended in failure as did various discussions held in 1982.

AREA AND POPULATION. The total area of the Territory, including the Caprivi-Zipfel, is 318,261 sq. miles (824,269 sq. km); this figure includes that of Walvis Bay, administered by South West Africa, 434 sq. miles (1,124 sq. km).

The country is bounded on the north by Angola and Zambia, on the west by the Atlantic ocean, on the south and southern portion of the eastern boundary by the Cape Province, and on the remainder of the eastern boundary by Botswana and Zambia. There are 3 main regions: the Namib, an extremely arid and desolate region stretching along the entire coastline to a width of between 80 to 130 km. The major portion of the Namib receives an annual rainfall of less than 50 mm. The Central Plateau is the region lying to the east of the Namib. It varies in altitude between 1,000 and 2,000 metres and offers a diversified landscape of rugged mountains, rocky outcrops, sand-filled valleys and plains. It covers approximately 50% of the total area; the Kalahari covers the eastern, north-eastern and northern areas of South West Africa.

The rainfall increases steadily from less than 50 mm. in the west and south-west up to 600 mm. in the Caprivi Strip.

The Kunene River and the Okavango, which form portions of the northern border of the country, the Zambesi, which forms the eastern boundary of the Caprivi-Zipfel, the Kwando or Mashi, which flows through the Caprivi-Zipfel from the north between the Okavango and the Zambesi, and the Orange River in the south, are the only permanently running streams. But there is a system of great, sandy, dry river-beds throughout the country, in which water can generally be obtained by sinking shallow wells. In the Grootfontein area there are large supplies of underground water, but except for a few springs, mostly hot, there is no surface water in the country.

On 13 Oct. 1964 and 29 Jan. 1969 the Republic of South Africa and Portugal signed agreements on the common use of the Kunene River.

Owing to the difficulty of satisfactorily controlling that part of the Caprivi-Zipfel, east of the line running due south from Beacon 22, situated west of the Kwando (or Mashi) River, the control of this area was in Aug. 1939 transferred to the Union Department of Native Affairs.

The population at the census 1960 and 1970 and estimate 1982 was:

	1960	1970	1982
Ovambos	239,363	342,455	516,600
Whites	73,464	90,658	75,600
Damaras	44,353	64,973	76,800
Hereros	44,588	55,670	77,600
Namas	34,806	32,853	49,700
Kavangos	27,871	49,577	98,000
Caprivians	15,840	25,009	39,500
Coloureds	12,708	28,275	43,500
Basters	11,257	16,474	23,800
Bushmen	11,762	21,909	29,900
Tswana	...	4,407	6,800
	516,012	732,260	1,039,800

The population grew at a rate of 3·7% per annum between 1960 and 1970.

The Ovambos are a Bantu race and are both agriculturists and owners of stock. They still possess tribal organization to its full extent.

The Hereros are a pastoral people who formerly owned enormous herds of cattle. Wars with Namas and Germans destroyed their tribal organization. Under the Union and Republic administration, reserves have been set apart and they have considerably increased in numbers and in animal wealth.

The ethnic origin of the Bergdamaras or Damara is still not certain. They were alternatively the slaves of the Hereros and the Namas, whose language they now speak, in pre-European days.

The Namas consist of 2 distinct sections: one, the Hamitic, whose remnants are found in the central portions of the country, being of pure native extraction, is thought to have migrated from the region of the Central African lakes in prehistoric times; the other, the Khoisan, is composed of tribes whose members are descended from persons born in the Cape a couple of centuries ago with an admixture of European and Nama blood.

The Bushmen are among the oldest inhabitants of southern Africa.

In the centre of the country just south of the Windhoek district is the Rehoboth Gebiet, occupied by a race known as the Basters, who are of mixed Nama–European descent and whose ordinary language is Afrikaans.

ADMINISTRATION. The South West Africa Affairs Amendment Act, 1949, abolished the Advisory Council and the nominated members of the Legislative Assembly. All 18 members of the Assembly are now elected by the registered voters of the Territory.

The election held on 24 April 1974 returned 18 Nationalists.

Until 1977 the Territory was represented in the South African House of Assembly by 6 members elected by the registered voters of the Territory, and in the Senate by 4 Senators, of which number 2 were elected by the members of the Legislative Assembly and the representatives of the Territory in the House of Assembly, and 2 nominated by the President of the Republic. Under the South West Africa Constitution Amendment Act 1977 this representation was abolished.

A commission of inquiry, appointed by the South African Government, in 1964 recommended the establishment of 'homeland areas' for the non-White groups. All these areas should be governed by legislative councils, headed by executive committees; franchise should be granted to males and females over 18 years who qualify for citizenship in their respective homelands.

On 17 Oct. 1968, 22 Oct. 1970 and 15 March 1973 respectively the first sessions of the Legislative Councils of Ovambo (77 members), Kavango (30 members) and Eastern Caprivi (28 members) were opened.

On 1 May 1973 and 9 May 1973 respectively Ovambo and Kavango obtained self-government.

On 13 Oct. 1966 the security and apartheid laws of the Republic of South Africa were extended to South West Africa, retrospective to 1950. The Legislative Assembly adopted a resolution on 22 Nov. 1974 inviting the representatives of the various population groups to deliberate with the representatives of the Whites on the manner in which they should exercise their right of self-determination in view of the South African government's desire that the inhabitants of South West Africa should themselves decide upon their future.

The seat of the administration is Windhoek. The country is divided into 22 districts controlled by magistrates and commissioners.

Administrator-General: Dr Willem van Niekerk.

ECONOMY

Budget. The revenue and expenditure (in R1,000) were:

	1978–79	1979–80	1980–81	1982–83	1983–84
Revenue	293,800	460,600	888,267	839,591	975,186
Expenditure	320,100	519,900	837,442	840,111	1,035,884

Banking. Barclays Bank International, Standard Bank, Bank Windhoek, Netherlands Bank, Trust Bank, South African Reserve Bank and Boland Bank have branches in the Territory. The only indigenous bank, The Bank of South West Africa, was established in 1973.

NATURAL RESOURCES

Minerals. Mineral export/sales amounted to R545·05m. in 1979. Diamonds, which constitute the principal production, are mainly recovered from alluvial terraces on a 60-mile stretch along the coastline from the Orange River mouth northward.

Agriculture. South West Africa is essentially a stock-raising country, the scarcity of water and poor rainfall rendering agriculture, except in the northern and north-eastern portions, almost impossible. Generally speaking, the southern half is suited for the raising of small stock, while the central and northern portions are better fitted for cattle.

Livestock (1982): 2m. cattle, 2·8m. sheep, 1·2m. goats. In 1981, 330,642 head of cattle and 48,889 beef carcasses and 583,182 head of small stock were exported.

In 1977–78, 188,402 kg of butter and 115,197 kg of factory cheese were manufactured. Other products produced are maize, 9,239 tons (1978); millet, 25,000 tons (1978); sunflower, 2,000 tons (1977); peanuts, 500 tons (1977).

The production of karakul pelts is of increasing importance. In 1983, 850,000 pelts, worth R9m. were produced.

Fisheries. The total catch in 1982 was 207,000 tonnes. The sales value of fish products (1977) was R67m.

COMMERCE. The statistics concerning the external trade of South West Africa are included in those of the Republic of South Africa (*see* p. 1075).

The bulk of the direct imports into the country is landed at Walvis Bay.

Total trade between South West Africa and UK (British Department of Trade returns, in £1,000 sterling):

	1979	1980	1981	1982	1983
Imports to UK	20,446	18,898	45,301	45,413	62,437
Exports and re-exports from UK	1,593	2,726	2,028	3,973	3,425

COMMUNICATIONS

Roads. In 1983 there were 4,361 km of trunk roads, 37,000 km of main and district roads, of which 4,133 km are bitumen surfaced. In 1983 there were 120,000 registered motor vehicles.

Railways. The South West Africa system connects with the main system of the South African Railways at De Aar. The total length of the line inside South West Africa is 2,340 km of 1,065 mm gauge.

Aviation. In 1977 the Territory's 4 major airports handled 177,901 passengers.

Shipping. In 1979–80 Walvis Bay harbour handled 1,899 vessels, of which 570 were freighters, and Luderitz, 233 vessels.

Post and Broadcasting. At 31 March 1983 there were 82 post offices and postal agencies, and 656 private bag services distributed by rail or road transport.

There were 26,361 circuit km of trunk lines, 447,146 circuit km of microwave channels, 447,733 km of carrier circuits, 354,194 km of telegraph circuits and 50,100 km of farm telephone lines; 81 telegraph offices, 149 telephone exchanges, and 60,737 telephones. There were 9,297 licensed radio stations in operation.

In 1982–83, 45,296 wireless licences and 14,717 television licences were issued. There were 18,886 km of broadcast circuits.

A post office savings bank was established in 1916. The number of accounts opened in 1982–83 was 3,398. The balance due to holders as at 31 March 1983 amounted to R1,726,169.

EDUCATION AND WELFARE

Education (1983). There were 1,100 schools for all races, 272,615 pupils and 8,984 teachers. This included 36 academic high schools, 3 centres for handicapped children, 3 technical schools and 4 agricultural colleges.

Health (1983). There were 75 hospitals and 135 clinics. The ratio of beds per population was 7 per 1,000. There were 180 general practitioners, 19 specialists and 40 dentists. Nursing staff numbered 3,293.

Books of Reference

The Territory of South West Africa. (In *Official Year Book of the Republic of South Africa*)
Department of Mines: *Quarterly Information Circulars: Industrial Minerals*
Green, R. H., Kiljunen, K. and Kiljunen, M.-L. (eds.) *Namibia: The Last Colony.* London, 1982
Rotberg, R. I., *Namibia: Political and Economic Prospects.* Lexington, 1983
Schoeman, E. R., and H. S., *Namibia.* [Bibliography] Oxford and Santa Barbara, 1984
Thomas, W. H., *Economic Development in Namibia.* Munich, 1978
Tötemeyer, G. *Namibia Old and New.* New York, 1979
Vigne, R., *A Dwelling Place of Our Own: The Story of the Namibian Nation.* London, 1973

BOPHUTHATSWANA

HISTORY. Bophuthatswana was first to obtain self-government under the Bantu Homelands Constitution Act of 1971 and was the second black homeland to ask the Republic of South Africa for full independence, which was granted on 6 Dec. 1977.

AREA AND POPULATION. The total area is 44,000 sq. km.

In 1980 Bophuthatswana had a *de jure* population of 2·6m., of which 67% lived in the White areas. The remaining 35% (736,000) lived in the homeland. In addition, the homeland has a further population of about 300,000 non-Tswanas, giving the homeland a *de facto* population of about 1,036,000.

CONSTITUTION AND GOVERNMENT. The Bophuthatswana Government is a compromise between the traditional chief-in-council system and a democratic electoral system. There are 72 nominated and 24 elected members in the Legislative Assembly. Self-government was granted in 1972. Each regional authority (coinciding with the 12 districts of the homeland) nominates 2 members, and each district elects six members to the Legislative Assembly.

Executive power vests in the President, who is elected by the Assembly, and he elects his Cabinet.

The first general election was held in Oct. 1972, 2 political parties taking part. Kgosi Lucas Mangope's Bophuthatswana National Party (BNP) won 20 of the 24 contested seats, but in 1974 he formed the Bophuthatswana Democratic Party which in 1979 held two-thirds of the seats in the Assembly and in the 1983 elections gained all the seats.

Members of regional authorities are elected from among the tribal and community authorities in their area.

The Cabinet in Nov. 1983 consisted of:

President, Minister of Economic Affairs and National Assembly: Kgosi L. M. Mangope.
Foreign Affairs: T. M. Molatlhwa. *Law and Order:* Kgosi B. L. M. Motsatsi. *Agriculture:* Kgosi E. M. Mokgoko. *Works and Water Affairs:* M. A. Kgomongwe. *Lands and Rural Development:* D. C. Mokale. *Defence:* Brig. H. F. Riekert. *Health and Social Welfare:* Dr K. P. Mokhobo. *Transport:* G. J. Makodi. *Finance:* L. G. Young. *Post and Telecommunications:* C. M. A. V. Sehume. *Internal Affairs:* Rev. S. M. Seodi. *Manpower Utilization:* R. Cronje. *Local Government and Housing:* S. L. L. Rathebe. *Education:* G. L. Holele. *Speaker:* M. S. E. Motshumi.

There were 5 Deputy Ministers.

Flag: Blue, crossed by a diagonal orange stripe, and in the canton a white disc charged with a leopard's face in black and white.

INTERNATIONAL RELATIONS

Aid. The Republic of South Africa granted aid of R22m. in 1980–81.

ECONOMY

Budget. The 1983–84 budget balanced at R618m.

Currency. South African Rand.

NATURAL RESOURCES

Water. The Department of Agriculture inherited the following improvements from South Africa: 2,833 reservoirs; 6,845 boreholes, of which more than 4,000 have been equipped; 648 earth dams.

Minerals. The territory is particularly rich in minerals. In 1976 there were 34 mines employing 53,000 people. Minerals include platinum, asbestos, iron ore, manganese, chrome, vanadium, limestone, diamonds and fluorspar.

Exploration for more platinum, chrome and coal is currently being carried out both by the private sector and by the Mining and Geological Survey Division of the Department of Economic Affairs. The platinum mines around Rustenburg produce about 66% of the free world's total production. The major chrome mines are near Rustenburg and Marico, while vanadium is mined in the Odi district near Brits.

The Rustenburg, Western and Impala Platinum mines which Bophuthatswana shares with the Republic of South Africa produce about 1·9m. oz. a year.

AGRICULTURE. Bophuthatswana is a semi-arid area of bushveld and grass veld suitable for stock farming. The annual rainfall is 300 mm in the west and 700 mm in the east and there are 3 river catchment areas—those of the Molopo, Limpopo and Vaal rivers.

Although the land tenure system militates against establishing large farms, some land which is unsuitable for building on is leased by the Government to successful farmers.

Livestock (1980): Cattle, 601,711.

Only 6·6% of the territory is suited to dryland cropping, but crop yields have shown a steady improvement in recent years. In Ditsobotla district, 3,500 hectares of fertile land has been developed by 3 primary co-operatives comprising 190 Tswana farmers. Silkworm farming was being tried in 1983. By 1981 the country was self sufficient in maize and exported the surplus. Three rice projects were under trial in 1983.

INDUSTRY. The first industries were started on an agency basis at Babelegi; the fastest growing industrial area in the homeland, in 1977 it covered 183 hectares and by March 1976 more than R56m. had been invested in the project. Other industries include 2 breweries at Tlhabane and Garankuwa. There is also a furniture factory near Heystekrand, and a tannery at Montshiwa. Border industries are also promoted by the central government, notably Rosslyn where 128 industries had been established by Dec. 1975.

COMMUNICATIONS

Roads. Total length (1977) 6,300 km, of which 63 km are tarred. 1976–77, 32 km were covered by bus, and 116m. passengers transported.

Post and Broadcasting. There were 12,979 telephones in 1982.

EDUCATION AND WELFARE

Education. In 1982 the territory's total school attendance was 485,680 at 1,115 educational institutions which include special schools and technical schools. Primary school attendance in 1983 was 353,721; middle schools, 97,293; high schools, 44,599; teacher training college, 2,382; technical and vocational schools, 1,381; university, 1,100. There were (1983) 13,708 teachers and lecturers.

Education is free apart from a nominal contribution to school funds, and hostel fees at post-primary schools.

Instruction from Grade I to Standard 2 is in Setswana, while Standard 4 to senior standards are taught in English. The education is controlled by the Department of Education.

Health. In 1982 there were 9 hospitals, 138 clinics, 4,496 hospital beds, 91 doctors and 3,342 nurses. The health budget in 1983–84 was R48·4m.

Book of Reference

Five Years of Independence: Republic of Bophuthatswana. Mafikeng, 1983

TRANSKEI

HISTORY. Transkei is the homeland of the Xhosa nation and was granted self-government by the Republic of South Africa in 1963. Over 1·5m. Transkeians live permanently in the Republic of South Africa but were deprived of their South African citizenship on independence.

AREA AND POPULATION. The total area is 16,910 sq. miles (43,798 sq. km). Population (1983 estimate) 2·5m., of which (1976) Coloured 7,650 and Whites 10,000. The capital is Umtata (population (1976) 24,805; 20,196 Blacks, 1,067 Coloured and 3,542 Whites). Other towns include Gcuwa, Kwabhaca, Umzimvubu and Lusikisiki.

CONSTITUTION AND GOVERNMENT. The Status of Transkei Bill passed its third reading in the South African House of Assembly on 11 June 1976 and received its second reading in the Senate on 17 June. The Bill gave Transkei a unicameral National Assembly instead of the then existing Legislative Assembly.

General elections were held on 29 Sept. 1976 and the Transkei National Independence Party gained 69 of the 75 elective seats in the National Assembly. Members were elected for a 5-year period. In addition there are 75 traditional (co-opted) members (70 chiefs and 5 paramount chiefs).

President: Paramount Chief Dr K. D. Matanzima.

Prime Minister: Chief George Matanzima.
Defence, Police, Foreign Affairs and Information: G. T. Vika. *Finance and Auditor-General:* R. Madikizela. *Local Government and Local Tenure:* G. S. Ndabankulu. *Interior:* S. N. Sigcau. *Education:* H. H. Bubu. *Works and Energy, Commerce and Industry:* W. S. Mbanga. *Posts, Telecommunications and Transport:* A. N. Jonas. *Health:* D. D. P. Ndamase. *Prisons and Justice:* T. T. Letlaka. *Agriculture and Forestry:* E. Z. Booi.

Flag: Three horizontal stripes of ochre, white, green.

FINANCE. The budget (1982–83) balanced at R627m.

AGRICULTURE. Notable examples of successful commercial enterprises in agriculture are the Magwa tea estate and various fibre plantations. 70,000 hectares of land are under indigenous forests and 61,000 hectares have been put under exotic plantations. There are 28 sawmills in the country.

Livestock (1976): Cattle, 1·3m.; sheep, 2·5m.; goats, 1·25m.

COMMUNICATIONS

Roads. There are above 8,800 km of roads.

Railways. There is a 209 km railway line linking Umtata with the port of East London in the Republic of South Africa.

Aviation. An international airport exists at Umtata.

Shipping. A start was made in 1978 on a 'free port' at Mnganzana. It will be completed in 5–6 years at a cost of R125m. by a French consortium.

Post. There were 11,498 telephones in 1978.

EDUCATION AND WELFARE

Education. In 1976 there were more than 500,000 pupils in nearly 2,000 schools with 10,000 teachers. The national university was inaugurated in Umtata in 1977.

Health. There are 31 hospitals with a total of 7,561 beds.

DIPLOMATIC REPRESENTATIVES

No country, other than the Republic of South Africa, has recognized Transkei as an independent state.

VENDA

HISTORY. Traditionally the territory of the Vhavenda, the country was granted self-government in 1973, and became the third black homeland to be granted independence by the Republic of South Africa on 13 Sept. 1979.

AREA AND POPULATION. The total area is 6,500 sq. km. Of the 381,000 Vhavenda living in the Republic of South Africa in 1970, nearly 70% lived in Venda. In 1980 the *de jure* population of Venda was estimated at 513,890, the *de facto* population at 343,480.

Vital statistics, 1981: Births, 13,568; deaths, 1,069; marriages, 228.

CONSTITUTION AND GOVERNMENT. Executive power is vested in the President, who is elected for the duration of each Parliament, which consists of the President and the National Assembly; legislative power is vested in Parliament. In addition to the National Assembly there is an Executive Council, or Cabinet, and a judiciary independent of the Executive. The National Assembly comprises the 28 chiefs, 15 members designated by 4 regional councils, 42 members elected by popular vote and 3 members nominated by the President. A new Assembly must be elected after every 5 years, but it may be dissolved at any time by the President. All existing tribal, community and regional councils were retained with their status and powers unchanged, like those of the tribal leaders.

The first general election was held in Aug. 1973; the sole political party, the Venda Independence People's Party (VIPP) won 10 of the 18 contested seats. Shortly after, the Chief Minister, Chief Mphephu, formed the Venda National Party (VNP); in the second general election of July 1978 the VIPP won 31 of the 42 contested seats, VNP the remaining 11. Chief Mphephu was re-elected Chief Minister.

President: Paramount Chief P. R. Mphephu.

Foreign Affairs: Chief A. M. Madzivhandila. *Economic Affairs:* Headman F. N. Ravele. *Education:* Headman E. R. B. Nesengani. *Urban Affairs and Land Tenure:* Chief C. A. Nelwamondo. *Justice:* Chief J. R. Rambuda. *Health and Welfare:* Chief C. N. Makuya. *Agriculture and Forestry:* G. M. Ramabulana. *Internal Affairs:* Chief M. M. Mphaphuli. *Transport, Works and Communications:* A. A. Tshivhase. *Deputy for Posts and Telecommunications:* Headman B. R. Nemulodi. *Deputy for Information and Broadcasting and of Public Service Commission:* W. R. Rabuma.

Flag: Three horizontal stripes of green, yellow, and brown, with a brown V on the yellow stripe, and a blue vertical strip in the hoist.

INTERNATIONAL RELATIONS

Aid. The Republic of South Africa granted aid of R45m. in 1981–82.

ECONOMY

Budget. The 1982–83 budget balanced at R115·07m.

Currency. South African Rand.

NATURAL RESOURCES

Water. In Oct. 1982 there were 118 hectares of canals, 250 dams and 520 bore-holes.

Minerals. Venda is relatively poor in mineral resources, although there are large supplies of stone for construction. Coal is the most important mineral; there are large deposits in the west near Makhado and in the north-east, bordering on the Kruger National Park, which it is hoped will soon be exploited. In addition there are deposits of graphite, copper sulphides, phosphates and magnesite; in 1978 the 2 graphite mines and 2 magnesite mines provided employment for 233 people, and the value of their output was R963,900.

Agriculture. About 85% of Venda is suitable only for the raising of livestock because of insufficient rainfall and poor soils, while some 10% is suited to dry-land crop production. Over 10,965 hectares have been given over to forest, mainly pine and eucalyptus. Eighteen irrigation schemes are being developed and there is extensive reclamation and conservation of eroded or overgrazed land; nearly R2m. were spent on these projects in 1980–81. Only maize is grown on a comparatively large scale, but tea, sisal, groundnuts, coffee and sub-tropical fruits are increasing in importance. A fish-breeding project produced 3 tonnes in 1980–81.

Over 80% of the working population are engaged in agriculture. The Venda Agricultural Corporation (Agriven) was established on 1 April 1982 to promote agricultural development.

INDUSTRY. Industrial development is still in its early stages, and since Venda's location is unfavourable, the Government is concentrating on the promotion of agro-industries utilizing local produce, and small-scale industries. A chutney factory has recently been established, in addition to a tea processing plant, a furniture factory and several saw-mills. A copper-chrome arsenate preservation plant has been established at Phiphidi. At Shayandima a 20-hectare industrial area has been prepared. The construction industry is particularly important owing to the substantial increase in the demand for buildings caused by the recent expansion of government, educational and health services.

In Dec. 1982 total investment in industry was estimated at R18·9m. The Venda Development Corporation was established in 1975 to promote and finance economic developments.

COMMUNICATIONS

Roads. There were (1982) 1,226 km of roads, of which 50 km had a permanent surface.

Aviation. An airline, inaugurated in 1981, operates between Nwangundu in Thohoyandu and Johannesburg *via* Pietersburg and Pretoria.

Post and Broadcasting. In 1982 there were 28 post offices and postal agencies. Telephones (1982) numbered, 1,547. In 1982 the government-owned Radio Thohoyandu broadcast 15 hours daily.

EDUCATION AND WELFARE

Education. The Department of Education assumed responsibility for education on independence. Education is free up to Standard 2, and pupils are taught in the native tongue, Luvenda, for the first 4 years (up to Standard 2), after which English is gradually introduced. Secondary education comprises Standards 6 to 10.

The number of primary schools increased from 233 (1970) to 472 (1982), the number of pupils from 65,500 (1970) to 157,014 (1982) and the number of teachers from 956 (1970) to 4,586 (1982).

In 1970 there were 12 secondary schools, which had increased to 112 by 1982. Pupils numbered 2,465 in 1970, 33,432 in 1982, while the number of teachers increased from 100 (1970) to 1,062 (1982).

In addition there is a technical school at Sibasa with about 320 pupils, an agricultural school at Dimani with 476 pupils, and a school for the handicapped at Shayandima. There are 2 teacher-training colleges; enrolment was 270 in 1970, and 704 in 1982. The University of Venda was established in 1981.

Health. In 1982 there were 5 hospitals/homes with 1,506 beds and 43 clinics. White doctors numbered 10 and coloured, 3; there were 712 nurses.

Welfare. In 1981–82 the Government spent R7·3m. on grants and pensions to 22,249 recipients. There is one welfare home.

CISKEI

HISTORY. On 4 Dec. 1981 the Republic of South Africa gave independence to Ciskei the fourth of the tribal homelands.

AREA AND POPULATION. Ciskei lies between latitudes 32° and 33°35′ and longitudes 26°20′ and 27°48′, and has a coastal boundary between East London and Port Alfred. The total area is about 7,700 sq. km. The population was (1981) 2·1m. but only 660,000 live in Ciskei. The remainder work in the Republic of South Africa and as a result can be deported as aliens.

Populations of towns (1980): Mdantsane, 158,864; Zwelitsha, 30,773; Sada, 28,966; Dimbaza, 18,715.

CONSTITUTION AND GOVERNMENT. In 1981 Ciskei became an independent democratic republic with an Executive Council consisting of the President, Vice-President and 11 ministers appointed by the President. The legislature is a National Assembly consisting of about 87 members of which a maximum of 37 are traditional leaders, the others being elected on the basis of adult suffrage every five years.

President: Dr Lennox Sebe.

Flag: Blue, a broad diagonal band from lower hoist to upper fly, charged with a black crane.

National Anthem: Nkosi Sikelel' i Afrika, composed by Enoch Sontonga.

ECONOMY

Budget. In 1980–81, revenue was R119·09m. and expenditure R137·71m.

Currency. South African Rand.

ENERGY AND NATURAL RESOURCES

Electricity. Ciskei is totally dependent on power supply lines maintained by the Republic of South Africa.

Minerals. Mineral resources are mainly undeveloped and in 1981 no mines existed in Ciskei.

Agriculture. In 1977–78, total agricultural production was valued at R8·26m.

In 1979–80, the dryland products included (in tons): Maize, 4,458; wheat, 481; dry beans, 148; dry peas, 141; grain sorghum, 69. The main crops produced under irrigation were (in tons): Potatoes, 385; lucerne, 364; maize, 333; beans, 77; wheat, 64.

Livestock (1980): 187,000 cattle, 215,000 sheep, 187,000 goats, 15,525 pigs.

Forestry. In 1976–77, 1,434 hectares were planted with conifers. The indigenous forest covered some 18,700 hectares. In 1977–78, production of timber was valued at R960,000.

INDUSTRY AND TRADE

Industry. In 1977 industry was valued at R5·6m. and construction at R11·2m. The chief manufactures include wood and leather goods, metal products, crafts and light industrial articles.

Commerce. International trade is mainly with the Republic of South Africa and no separate figures are available. The main exports are pineapples, timber and manufactured goods.

Tourism. Tourism is an important and developing industry.

COMMUNICATIONS

Roads. In 1980 there were 407 km of tarred roads and 1,397 km of gravel roads.

Railways. There are two main railway lines serving the southern part of Ciskei only.

Aviation. Ciskei depends mainly on East London's airport though there is a small airfield at King William's Town and minor landing strips elsewhere.

Shipping. Ciskei has no harbour of its own but has full access to the facilities of East London in the Republic of South Africa.

Post and Broadcasting. All major centres have post offices and manual telephone exchanges; automatic exchanges and telex are gradually being provided. There were (1982) 5,441 telephones. Radio Xhosa broadcasts daily.

Newspapers (1981). There were two Ciskeian newspapers, one of which, *Imvo,* was first published in 1884.

JUSTICE, RELIGION, EDUCATION AND WELFARE

Justice. The Supreme Court acts as Court of Appeal for the seven Magistrates' Courts, which in turn act as Courts of Appeal for the chiefs' courts. Appeals from the Supreme Court are heard by the Appellate Division of the Republic of South Africa's Supreme Court in Bloemfontein.

Religion. In 1980 (estimate) the population was 24% Methodists, 21% Independent, 8% Presbyterian Congregationalists, 7% Anglicans, 6% Roman Catholics, 2% Dutch Reformed Church, 2% other Christians, 28% ancestor worship and 2% other religions.

Education. In 1981 there were 498 primary schools with 180,214 pupils and 4,058 teachers; 123 secondary and teacher-training schools with 46,913 pupils and 1,463 teachers; and 2 vocational schools with 304 pupils and 32 teachers. The University of Fort Hare had a total of 2,304 students in 1981.

Health. In 1979–80, there were 5 hospitals with 1,491 beds, and a total of 2,643 nursing staff.

Social Welfare. Pensions paid in 1980:

	Beneficiaries	Amount (R1,000)
Old age	32,319	9,365
Blind	598	188
Disability	4,773	1,474
War veterans	49	13

Books of Reference

Charlton, N., *Ciskei: Economics and Politics of Dependence in a South African Homeland.* London, 1980
Pauw, B. A., *Christianity and the Xhosa Tradition.* OUP, 1975
Van der Kooy, R, (ed.) *The Republic of Ciskei: A Nation in Transition.* Pretoria, 1981

SPAIN

España

Capital: Madrid
Population: 38·22m. (1983)
GNP per capita: US$4,880 (1982)

HISTORY. Although Spain has traditionally been a monarchy there have been two Republics, the first in 1873, which lasted for 11 months, and the second 1931–39; both were democratically and peacefully proclaimed. Part of the army rebelled against the republican government on 18 July 1936, thus beginning the Spanish Civil War, *see* THE STATESMAN'S YEAR-BOOK, 1939, pp. 1325–26. The new regime was led by Gen. Franco, who had been proclaimed Head of State and Government in 1936, and its institutions were based on single party rule, with the *Falange* as the only legal political organization.

In July 1969, Prince Don Juan Carlos de Borbón y Borbón, grandson of Alfonso XIII, was sworn in as successor to the Head of State and he had the title of HRH Prince of Spain until he became King.

Gen. Francisco Franco y Bahamonde died on 20 Nov. 1975 and on 22 Nov. Prince Juan Carlos de Borbón y Borbón took the oath as Juan Carlos I, King of Spain.

On 23 Feb. 1981 there was an attempted military *coup*. During 18 hours the deputies of the lower house of Parliament and the Cabinet were held hostage. The King, the only high authority who kept his liberty, obtained the surrender of the rebels without bloodshed.

AREA AND POPULATION. Spain is bounded north by the Bay of Biscay and the Pyrenees (which form the frontier with France and Andorra), east and south by the Mediterranean and the Straits of Gibraltar, south-west by the Atlantic and west by Portugal and the Atlantic. Continental Spain has an area of 492,592 sq. km, and including the Balearic and Canary Islands and the towns of Ceuta and Melilla 504,750 sq. km (194,884 sq. miles). Population (estimate, 1983), 38,219,534.

The growth of the population has been as follows:

Census year	Population	Rate of annual increase	Census year	Population	Rate of annual increase
1860	15,655,467	0·34	1950	27,976,755	0·81
1910	19,927,150	0·72	1960	30,903,137	0·88
1920	21,303,162	0·69	1970	33,823,918	0·94
1930	23,563,867	1·06	1981	37,746,260	1·15
1940	25,877,971	0·98			

Area and population of the autonomous communities and provinces, census of 1 March 1981:

Autonomous community Province	Area (sq. km)	Population	Per sq. km	Autonomous community Province	Area (sq. km)	Population	Per sq. km
Andalusia	87,268	6,441,755	73	Zaragoza	17,194	842,386	48
Almería	8,774	405,513	47	*Asturias*	10,565	1,127,007	106
Cádiz	7,385	1,001,716	135	*Baleares*	5,014	685,088	136
Córdoba	13,718	717,213	52	*Basque*			
Granada	12,531	761,734	60	Country, The	7,261	2,134,967	296
Huelva	10,085	414,492	41	Álava	3,047	260,580	85
Jaén	13,498	627,598	46	Guipúzcoa	1,997	692,986	347
Málaga	7,276	1,036,261	142	Vizcaya	2,217	1,181,401	532
Sevilla	14,001	1,477,428	105	*Canary Islands*	7,273	1,444,626	200
Aragón	47,669	1,213,099	25	Palmas, Las	4,065	756,353	185
Huesca	15,671	219,813	14	Santa Cruz			
Teruel	14,804	150,900	10	de Tenerife	3,208	688,273	217

Autonomous community Province	Area (sq. km)	Population	Per sq. km	Autonomous community Province	Area (sq. km)	Population	Per sq. km
Cantabria	5,289	510,816	96	Tarragona	6,283	516,078	82
Castilla-La				Extremadura	41,602	1,050,119	25
Mancha	79,226	1,628,005	20	Badajoz	21,657	635,375	29
Albacete	14,858	334,468	22	Cáceres	19,945	414,744	20
Ciudad Real	19,749	468,327	23	Galicia	29,434	2,753,836	93
Cuenca	17,061	210,280	12	Coruña, La	7,876	1,083,415	137
Guadalajara	12,190	143,124	11	Lugo	9,803	399,185	40
Toledo	15,368	471,806	30	Orense	7,278	411,339	56
Castilla-León	94,147	2,577,105	27	Pontevedra	4,477	859,897	192
Ávila	8,048	178,997	22	Madrid	7,995	4,726,986	591
Burgos	14,269	363,474	25	Murcia	11,317	957,903	84
León	15,468	517,973	33	Navarra	10,421	507,367	48
Palencia	8,029	186,512	23	Rioja, La	5,034	253,295	50
Salamanca	12,336	368,055	29	Valencian			
Segovia	6,949	149,286	21	Community	23,305	3,646,765	156
Soria	10,287	98,803	9	Alicante	5,863	1,148,597	195
Valladolid	8,202	489,636	59	Castellón	6,679	431,755	64
Zamora	10,559	224,369	21	Valencia	10,763	2,066,413	192
Catalonia	31,930	5,958,208	186	Ceuta [1]	18	70,864	...
Barcelona	7,773	4,618,734	598	Melilla [1]	14	58,449	...
Gerona	5,886	467,945	80				
Lérida	12,028	355,451	29	Total	504,750	37,746,260	74

[1] Ceuta and Melilla are municipalities located in the northern coast of Morocco.

The capitals of the autonomous communities are as follows: Andalusia, cap. Sevilla (Seville); Aragón, cap. Zaragoza (Saragossa); Asturias, cap. Oviedo; Baleares (Balearic Islands), cap. Palma de Mallorca; The Basque Country, cap. Vitoria; Canary Islands, dual and alternative capital, Las Palmas and Santa Cruz de Tenerife; Cantabria, cap. Santander; Catalonia, cap. Barcelona; Galicia, cap. Santiago de Compostela; Madrid, cap. Madrid; Murcia, cap. Murcia (but regional parliament in Cartagena); Navarra, cap. Pamplona; La Rioja, cap. Logroño; Valencian Community, cap. Valencia. Castilla-La Mancha, Castilla-León and Extremadura had not chosen (1983) a capital town.

The capitals of the provinces are in the towns from which they take the name, except in Álava (capital Vitoria), Asturias (Oviedo), Baleares (Palma de Mallorca), Cantabria (Santander), Guipúzcoa (San Sebastián), La Rioja (Logroño), Navarra (Pamplona) and Vizcaya (Bilbao).

In 1981 there were 19,216,496 females and 18,529,764 males.

By decree of 21 Sept. 1927 the islands which form the Canary Archipelago were divided into 2 provinces, under the name of their respective capitals: Santa Cruz de Tenerife and Las Palmas de Gran Canaria. The province of Santa Cruz de Tenerife is constituted by the islands of Tenerife, La Palma, Gomera and Hierro, and that of Las Palmas by Gran Canaria, Lanzarote and Fuerteventura, with the small barren islands of Alegranza, Roque del Este, Roque del Oeste, Graciosa, Montaña Clara and Lobos. The area of the islands is 7,273 sq. km; population (census 1981), 1,444,626. Places under Spanish sovereignty in Morocco are: Alhucemas, Ceuta, Chafarinas, Melilla and Peñón de Vélez.

The following were the registered populations of principal towns at census 1981:

Town	Population	Town	Population	Town	Population
Albacete	117,126	Burgos	156,449	Getafe	127,060
Alcalá de Henares	142,862	Cáceres	71,852	Gijón	255,969
Alcorcón	140,657	Cádiz	157,766	Granada	262,182
Algeciras	86,042	Cartagena	172,751	Hospitalet	294,033
Alicante	251,387	Castellón	126,464	Huelva	127,806
Almería	140,946	Córdoba	284,737	Jerez de la Frontera	176,238
Ávila	86,584	Cornellá	90,956	Jaén	96,424
Badajoz	114,361	Coruña, La	232,356	Laguna, La	112,635
Badalona	227,744	Elche	162,873	Leganés	163,426
Baracaldo	117,422	Ferrol, El	91,764	León	131,134
Barcelona	1,754,900	Fuenlabrada	77,626	Lérida	109,573
Bilbao	433,030	Gerona	87,648	Logroño	110,980

Town	Population	Town	Population	Town	Population
Lugo	73,986	Reus	80,710	Santiago de	
Madrid	3,188,297	Sabadell	184,943	Compostela	93,695
Málaga	503,251	Salamanca	167,131	Sevilla	653,833
Mataró	96,467	San Baudilio del		Tarragona	111,689
Móstoles	149,649	Llobregat	74,550	Tarrasa	155,360
Murcia	288,631	San Fernando	71,846	Torrejón de Ardoz	75,398
Orense	96,085	San Sebastián	175,576	Valencia	751,734
Oviedo	190,123	Santa Coloma de		Valladolid	330,242
Palencia	74,080	Gramanet	140,588	Vigo	258,724
Palma de Mallorca	304,422	Santa Cruz de		Vitoria	192,773
Palmas, Las	366,454	Tenerife	190,784	Zaragoza	590,750
Pamplona	183,126	Santander	180,328		

Vital statistics for calendar years:

	Marriages	Births	Deaths
1977	262,015	656,357	294,324
1978[1]	258,070	636,892	296,781
1979[1]	245,856	597,252	289,864
1980[1]	213,363	565,401	287,621
1981[1]	199,057	532,255	286,400
1982[1]	188,597	509,685	282,266

[1] Provisional figures.

Languages. The Constitution states that 'Castilian is the Spanish official language of the State', but also that 'All other Spanish languages will also be official in the corresponding Autonomous Communities'.

Catalan is spoken by a majority of people in Catalonia and Baleares, and by a large minority in Valencian Community (where it is frequently called Valencian language); in Aragón, a narrow strip close to Catalonia and Valencian Community boundaries, speaks Catalan.

Galician, a language very close to Portuguese, is spoken by a majority of people in Galicia. Basque, by a significative minority in the Basque Country. About 50% of population in Guipúzcoa province, about 25% in Vizcaya province and about 10% in Álava province, and by a small minority in north-west Navarra.

In bilingual communities, both Spanish and the regional language are taught in the schools.

CLIMATE. Most of Spain has a form of Mediterranean climate with mild, moist winters and hot, dry summers, but the northern coastal region has a moist, equable climate, with rainfall well-distributed throughout the year, mild winters and warm summers, though having less sunshine than the rest of Spain.

Madrid. Jan. 41°F (5°C), July 77°F (25°C). Annual rainfall 16·8" (419 mm). Barcelona. Jan. 46°F (8°C), July 74°F (23·5°C). Annual rainfall 21" (525 mm). Cartagena. Jan. 51°F (10·5°C), July 75°F (24°C). Annual rainfall 14·9" (373 mm). La Coruña. Jan. 51°F (10·5°C), July 66°F (19°C). Annual rainfall 32" (800 mm). Sevilla. Jan. 51°F (10·5°C), July 85°F (29·5°C). Annual rainfall 19·5" (486 mm). Palma de Mallorca (Balearic Islands). Jan. 51°F (11°C), July 77°F (25°C). Annual rainfall 13·6" (347 mm). Santa Cruz de Tenerife (Canary Islands). Jan. 64°F (17·9°C), July 76°F (24·4°C). Annual rainfall 7·72" (196 mm).

KING. Juan Carlos I, born 5 Jan. 1938. The eldest son of Don Juan, Conde de Barcelona. Juan Carlos was given precedence over his father as pretender to the Spanish throne in an agreement in 1954 between Don Juan and Gen. Franco. Don Juan resigned his claims to the throne in May 1977. King (then Prince) Juan Carlos married, in 1962, Princess Sophia of Greece, daughter of the late King Paul of the Hellenes and Queen Frederika. *Offspring:* Elena, born 20 Dec. 1963; Cristina, 13 June 1965; Felipe, Prince of Asturias, Heir to the throne, 30 Jan. 1968.

CONSTITUTION AND GOVERNMENT. The *Cortes* (Parliament) was freely elected on 15 June 1977. The text of the new Constitution was approved by referendum on 6 Dec. 1978, and came into force 29 Dec. 1978. It established a parliamentary monarchy, with King Juan Carlos I as head of state. Legislative power is vested in the *Cortes,* a bicameral parliament composed of the Congress of Deputies (lower house) and the Senate (upper house). The Congress of Deputies has not less than 300 nor more than 400 members (350 in the general elections of 1977, 1979 and 1982), all elected in a proportional system regarding the population of every province. The members of the Senate are elected in a majority system: the 47 peninsular provinces elect 4 senators each, regardless of population; the insular provinces electing 5 (Baleares, Las Palmas) or 6 (Santa Cruz de Tenerife); and Ceuta and Melilla, 2 senators each. There are 208 senators, to whom are added some other members of the upper house elected by the parliaments of the autonomous communities. Deputies and senators are elected in universal (but not compulsory), direct, free, equal and secret suffrage, for a term of 4 years, liable to dissolution. Executive power is vested in the President of the Government (prime minister), with his Cabinet; he is elected by the Congress of Deputies.

A general election took place on 28 Oct. 1982.

Congress of Deputies (350 members): Spanish Workers Socialist Party (PSOE), 202; Popular Alliance (AP, conservative), 106; Centre Democratic Union (UCD), 12; Convergence and Union (CiU, Catalan nationalists), 12; Basque Nationalist Party (PNV), 8; Spanish Communist Party (PCE), 4; Social and Democratic Centre (CDS), 2; Herri Batasuna (Basque independentists), 2; Euskadido Eskerra (nonradical Basque independentists), 1; Esquerra Republicana de Catalunya (Catalan republican nationalists), 1.

Senate (208 members, excluding those elected by regional parliaments): PSOE, 134; AP, 54; CiU, 7; PNV , 7; UCD, 4; Asamblea Majorera (from Canary island of Fuerteventura). 1; independent from Soria province, 1.

The *Council of Ministers* appointed 2 Dec. 1982 was composed as follows in Jan. 1984:

President of the Government (Prime Minister): Felipe González Márquez (Secretary-General of PSOE).

Vice-President of the Government (Deputy Premier): Alfonso Guerra González. *Foreign Affairs:* Fernando Morán López. *Economy, Finance and Commerce:* Miguel Boyer Salvador. *Industry and Energy:* Carlos Solchaga Catalán. *Interior:* José Barrionuevo. *Defence:* Narcís Serra i Serra. *Public Administration:* Javier Moscoso del Prado. *Education and Science:* José María Maravall. *Public Works:* Julián Campo. *Justice:* Fernando Ledesma Bartret. *Culture:* Javier Solana Madariaga. *Territorial Administration (relations with Autonomous Communities):* Tomás de la Quadra Salcedo. *Agriculture, Fisheries and Food:* Carlos Romero Herrero. *Health and Consumers Affairs:* Ernest Lluch i Martín. *Labour and Social Security:* Joaquín Almunia Amann. *Transport, Tourism and Communications:* Enrique Barón Crespo.

All ministers are members of PSOE, excepting the Minister of Justice, who is a non-party magistrate.

National flag: Three horizontal stripes of red, yellow, red, with the yellow of double width, and charged near the hoist with the national arms.

National anthem: Marcha real.

Regional and local government. The Constitution of 1978 establishes a semifederal system of regional administration, with the autonomous community *(Comunidad Autónoma)* as its basic element. There are 17 autonomous communities, each of them having a Parliament, elected by universal vote, and a regional government; all possess exclusive legislative and executive power in many matters, as listed in the national Constitution and in their own fundamental law *(estatuto de autonomía).* The Basque Country and Catalonia elected their parliaments in March 1980, Galicia in Oct. 1981 and Andalusia in May 1982. All others in May 1983.

There are 7 autonomous communities composed of one only province, i.e., Asturias (*ex*-Oviedo province), Cantabria (*ex*-Santander province), La Rioja (*ex*-Logroño province), Navarra, Baleares, Murcia and Madrid. The other 10 are formed by 2 or more provinces. In all, there are in Spain 50 provinces, since the administrative division established in 1833; Ceuta and Melilla, municipalities in the northern coast of Morocco, are not part of any province. The provincial council *(Diputación Provincial)* is the administrative organ of the province, except in the 7 autonomous communities composed of one only province, where there are only the regional legislative and executive powers. The provincial council is indirectly elected. Each of the 7 main islands of the Canaries (provinces of Las Palmas and Santa Cruz de Tenerife) has a directly elected corporation, the *Cabildo Insular,* to rule its special interests.

The provinces are constituted by the association of municipalities (8,022 in 1981 census). Municipalities are autonomous in their own sphere. At their head stands the municipal council *(Ayuntamiento),* members of which are elected in a universal ballot every 4 years, and they, in turn, elect one of them as Mayor *(Alcalde).*

DEFENCE. On 26 Sept. 1953 the US and Spain signed three agreements covering the construction and use of military facilities in Spain by the US, economic assistance, and military end-item assistance. These agreements were renewed several times, the last in July 1982. The American naval and air base at Rota (near Cádiz) is connected by pipelines with the American bomber bases at Morón de la Frontera (near Seville), Torrejón (near Madrid) and Zaragoza.

Length of service is 16 months in the army, 24 months in the navy and 18 months in the air force.

Army. The Army is divided into 2 principal parts: the Immediate Intervention Forces and Territorial Defence Forces. The former consist of 1 armoured, 1 mechanized and 1 motorized divisions; 1 armoured cavalry, 1 parachute and 1 airportable brigades; and supporting artillery, engineer and signals units. The Territorial Defence Forces are divided between 9 Military Regions, and include 3 mountain and 10 infantry brigades. There are also other reserve and independent units, and the Army Aviation forces. Equipment includes 300 AMX-30, 350 M-47E and 110 M-48 tanks. Strength (1984) 260,000 (including 190,000 conscripts). Of these 5,800 are stationed on the Balearic Islands, 16,000 on the Canary Islands and 19,000 in Ceuta/Melilla. The paramilitary National Police number 40,000 men and the Civil Guard 65,000.

Navy. Particulars of the principal ship:

Completed	Name	Standard displacement Tons	Guns	Aircraft	Shaft horsepower	Speed Knots
			Helicopter Carrier			
1943	Dédalo[1]	13.000	22 40-mm. A.A.	7 VSTOL aircraft and 20 helicopters	100,000	32 (original) now 24

[1] The former US fixed-wing aircraft carrier *Cabot,* converted in 1966 and transferred to Spain on loan in 1967 and purchased in 1973.

There are also 9 diesel-powered patrol submarines (3 new French-built, 4 modern French-built and 2 old *ex*-US), 12 destroyers, 11 frigates, 4 old corvettes, 12 new fast attack craft, 10 new patrol vessels, 4 ocean minesweepers, 8 coastal minesweepers, 3 patrol ships (*ex*-coastal minesweepers), 40 coastal patrol craft, 30 inshore patrol launches, 1 dock landing ship, 6 survey ships, 3 landing ships, 9 landing craft, 120 minor landing craft, 1 replenishment ship, 15 oilers, 2 attack vehicle and troop transports, 2 tenders, 2 training ships, 1 boom defence vessel, 30 tugs, 1 royal yacht, 10 water carriers, 40 auxiliary craft and 40 service barges.

The Spanish Navy is being renewed and modernized. Ships under construction include 1 small aircraft carrier scheduled to be completed in 1986 and 1 more patrol submarine of French design. Ships projected include 3 missile armed frigates and 6 corvettes, although a modified new construction programme is being considered including 2 large destroyers, 5 frigates and 4 minehunters.

Shipbuilding is mainly carried on at the dockyards at El Ferrol and Cartagena,

Cádiz having a smaller share in it. Barcelona, Bilbao, Seville and Cádiz are the chief naval yards.

There are naval radio telegraphic stations at Cádiz, Barcelona, Mahón, Pontevedra, Cartagena and El Ferrol.

In 1984 naval personnel totalled 63,250, comprising 4,200 naval officers, 37,900 ratings, 8,950 civil branch, 700 marine officers and 11,500 marine other ranks.

The Naval Air Service operates 40 fixed-wing aircraft and 30 helicopters.

Air Force. The Air Force is organized as an independent service, dating from 1939. It is administered through 4 operational commands. These comprise Air Combat Command which controls interceptor squadrons (including USAF elements) and the control and warning radar network, Tactical and Transport Commands, and Air Command of the Canaries. Strength is about 33,000 and 215 combat aircraft.

The Tactical Air Command has 1 fighter-bomber squadron of Spanish-built Northrop SF-5s, 1 squadron of HA-220 Super Saeta light attack jet aircraft of Spanish design and manufacture, 1 reconnaissance squadron of HA-220s, 1 aeronaval co-operation squadron with 6 P-3A Orion anti-submarine aircraft, and a liaison flight at Tablada with CASA 127s and Bird Dogs. Air Combat Command has 2 squadrons of Mirage III-Es, 2 squadrons of F-4C/RF-4C Phantom IIs and 2 squadrons of Mirage F1-Cs, plus a flight of CASA 127 liaison aircraft. Four KC-130H tankers support the F-4C squadrons. Three wings of Air Transport Command operate C-130 Hercules, Caribou and Spanish-built CASA Aviocars. Air Command of the Canaries has 3 squadrons, equipped with Aviocar transports; Mirage F1 fighter-bombers; F27 Maritime aircraft and Super Puma helicopters for search and rescue. Other equipment includes 2 DC-8s, 4 Falcons and helicopters for VIP transport; and aircraft for photographic, firefighting, target towing and research duties. Air-sea rescue units have Aviocars and Super Puma helicopters. Replacement of F-4s and SF-5s with a total of 72 F-18 Hornets will begin in 1986.

American-built F33 Bonanza, T-34A and T-6 piston-engined aircraft are used for basic training, after which pupil pilots progress to CASA C-101 and T-33A jet aircraft. Two-seat versions of operational types are used as advanced trainers. Other training types include Beechcraft King Air C90s for instrument flying and liaison duties.

INTERNATIONAL RELATIONS

Membership. Spain is a member of UN, the Council of Europe, NATO and OECD.

ECONOMY

Budget. Revenue and expenditure in 1m. pesetas:

	1978	1979	1980	1981	1982	1983
Revenue	1,433,000	1,747,500	2,284,456	2,823,000	3,533,820	4,513,305
Expenditure	1,433,000	1,747,500	2,284,456	2,823,000	3,533,820	4,513,305

The budget is made up as follows (in 1m. pesetas):

Revenue (1982)		*Expenditure (1983) continued*	
Direct taxes	1,195,912	Ministry of Finance	75,170
Indirect taxes	1,100,022	,, Interior	197,842
Levies and taxes	209,910	,, Public Works and Housing	186,030
Current transactions	158,204	,, Education and Science	497,259
Investment income	169,846	,, Labour and Social	
Expenditure (1982)		Security	109,605
H.M. House	300	,, Industry and Energy	164,584
Cortes (Parliament)	6,588	,, Agriculture and Food	175,678
Court of Accounts	1,010	,, Transport, Tourism and	
Constitutional Court	522	Communications	320,014
Council of State	246	,, Culture	34,711
Public Debt	336,455	,, Territorial Administration	1,431
Civil Service Pensions	306,331	,, Health and Consumer	
General Council of the Judicial		Affairs	32,986
Power	524	Regional governments	374,520
Presidency of the Government	63,219	Regional Compensation Fund	204,000
Ministry of Foreign Affairs	23,809	Social Security and unemployment	
,, Justice	70,890	funds	749,579
,, Defence	478,332	Expenses in several ministries	101,659

Currency. The *peseta* is divided into 100 *céntimos*.

Bank-notes of 5,000, 1,000, 500 and 100 *pesetas* and coins of 1 *peseta* (copper and aluminium), 5, 25, 50, 100 *pesetas* (nickel and copper) are in circulation. In Jan. 1982 the circulation of bank-notes was 1,371,192m. *pesetas* and of coins, 53,095m. *pesetas.*

In March 1984, £1 = 220 *pesetas*; US$1 = 150.

Banking. On 1 Jan. 1922 the Bank of Spain came under the Bank Ordinance Law, according to which the Government participate in its net profits.

The 10 largest banks are: Banco Central; Banco Español de Crédito; Banco Hispano Americano; Banco de Bilbao; Banco de Vizcaya; Banco de Santander; Banco Exterior de España; Banco Popular Español; Banco Urquijo; Banco Pastor. All are privately owned except the Banco Exterior de España.

Savings bank deposits (Popular Savings Banks) in Spain, 31 Dec. 1980, amounted to 3,298,412m. pesetas. The Post office savings bank opened on 12 March 1916. Deposits, 31 Dec. 1980, amounted to 160,304m. pesetas; private banks saving deposits, 7,468,000m. pesetas.

Weights and Measures. On 1 Jan. 1859 the metric system of weights and measures was introduced.

ENERGY AND NATURAL RESOURCES

Electricity. Electric power-stations in 1980 had a total installed capacity of 30·8m. kw., of which 13·3m. was hydro-electric. The total output 1982, amounted to 111,706m. kwh of which 26,060m. hydro-electric and 8,771m. nuclear.

Natural Gas. Production in 1981 was 317,821 tonnes.

Oil. Crude oil production (1981) 1,226,049 tonnes.

Minerals. Spain is relatively rich in minerals. The production of the more important minerals in 1980 were as follows (in 1,000 tonnes):

Anthracite	4,047	Iron ore	9,227	Tin ore	0·7
Coal	9,070	Lead ore	134	Zinc ore	329·4
Lignite	15,390	Copper	199	Wolfram ore	0·7
Uranium ore	501	Mercury	95·2		

Agriculture. Spain is mainly an agricultural country. In 1982 the total value of agricultural produce was 959·1m. pesetas; of livestock, 770·3m.; of forestry, 53·6m. Land under cultivation in 1982 (in 1,000 hectares) included: Cereals, 7,308; vegetables, 385; potatoes, 332. In 1982, 580,053 tractors and 47,174 harvesters were in use.

Principal crops	Area (in 1,000 hectares)				Yield (in 1,000 tonnes)			
	1978[1]	1979[1]	1980	1981	1978[1]	1979[1]	1980	1981
Wheat	2,752	2,551	2,698	2,635	4,806	4,082	6,039	3,408
Barley	3,519	3,477	3,575	3,506	8,068	6,251	8,705	4,758
Oats	442	436	458	464	553	456	680	445
Rye	228	220	217	220	251	221	283	212
Rice	58	69	68	69	401	427	433	444
Maize	443	467	454	429	1,969	2,212	2,313	2,157
Potatoes	371	355	355	343	5,364	5,637	5,737	5,470
Sugar-beet	235	166	183	218	8,292	5,124	6,908	7,941
Tomatoes	72	64	61	60	2,223	2,204	2,147	2,159

[1]Provisional.

In 1981, 1,721,000 hectares were under vines; production of wine was 33·6m. hectolitres. The area of onions was 34,000 hectares, yielding 1,053,000 tons. Production of oranges and mandarines was 2,175,000 tons, lemons, 443,000. Other products are esparto, flax, hemp and pulse. Spain has important industries connected with the preparation of wine and fruits. Silk culture is carried on in Murcia, Alicante and other South-eastern provinces; 3,000 tons were produced in 1978. Spain produced in 1980, 12,513 tonnes of honey and 680 tonnes of beeswax. Alcoholic beverages produced totalled 102·2m. litres in 1977.

Industrial crops (1981 in 1,000 tonnes): Sunflower, 1,233; cotton, 205; olives, 1,512; olive oil, 207; tobacco (1980), 36.

Livestock (1982): Horses, 252,000; mules, 174,000; cattle, 5,069,000; sheep, 11,072,000; goats, 2,504,000; pigs, 11,627,000; poultry, 46,158,000.

Forestry. Total forests (1980) 26m. hectares; production, 1981, 11,297,000 cu. metres of wood.

Fisheries. The most important catches are those of sardines, whiting, anchovy and hake. The total catch amounted in 1982 to 1·24m. tons. In the tinned fish industry there were, in 1978, 405 factories, producing 129,265 tons. The Spanish fishing fleet in 1981 consisted of 17,555 vessels of 749,411 tonnes, with a total crew of 108,414.

INDUSTRY AND TRADE

Industry. The manufacture of cotton and woollen goods is important, principally in Catalonia. In 1978 there were 3,756 textile factories in operation. Production, in 1,000 tonnes (1978): Wool yarn, 29; cotton (yarn, 61; fabrics, 62); rayon fabrics, 6. 245 paper-mills produced in 1977, 2m. tonnes of writing, printing, packing and other paper. The production of cement reached 29,488,000 tonnes in 1982. Steel production (1982) 13·1m. tonnes; the three great blast-furnaces concentrations are in Bilbao area, Avilés (Asturias) and Sagunto (Valencia). The chemical industry is located in the areas of Madrid, Barcelona and Bilbao; sulphuric acid production (1982), 2m. tonnes; nitrogenous fertilizers, 822,000 tonnes. The 9 oil refineries refined 47,583,000 tonnes of crude oil. In 1982 900,000 TV sets (550,000 colour sets), 1m. refrigerators, 918,000 washing machines and 880,000 bicycles were manufactured. Spain has important toys and shoe industries, toys especially in Alicante and Barcelona provinces and shoe in Alicante province and the Balearic islands.

Spanish shipyards launched 747,600 BRT in 1982. In 1982, 1,045,000 vehicles were built, including 910,000 passenger cars.

Labour. The daily minimum wage for workers is 1,072 pesetas (Jan. 1983).

The economically active population numbered 13,212,400 in Jan. 1983. Of these, 2,114,500 were occupied in agriculture and fishing, 3,176,400 in manufactures, 1,258,700 in construction industry, 5,746,700 in trade and other public and personal services and 916,300 in unspecified jobs. 16·53% of the active population was unemployed at the beginning of 1983 (2,150,947 persons).

Trade Unions. The Constitution guarantees the establishment and activities of trade unions provided they have a democratic structure. The two most important trade unions are *Unión General de Trabajadores* (UGT), founded in 1888 by Pablo Iglesias (who had founded in 1879 the Spanish Workers Socialist Party, PSOE), and *Comisiones Obreras*, which was gradually established 1958–63, then as a clandestine labour organization.

Commerce. Foreign trade of Spain (Peninsula, Baleares, Canaries, Ceuta, Melilla) (in 1m. pesetas):

	1977	1978	1979	1980	1981	1982
Imports	1,350,352	1,431,538	1,704,022	2,450,652	2,970,435	3,473,208
Exports	775,150	1,001,599	1,221,441	1,493,187	1,888,422	2,260,198

In 1982 the most important items of import were (in 1m. pesetas): Crude petroleum and other energetic sources, 1,376,425; boilers, machinery and mechanical hardware, 324,421; iron, steel and castings, 149,707; electric and electronic machinery and hardware, 138,244; vehicles, 119,734; organic chemical products, 109,712; cereals, 108,901; oleaginous seeds and fruits, 92,230; optical and photographic products, 80,816.

The most important exports in 1982 (in 1m. pesetas) were: Iron and steel castings, 272,159; vehicles, 245,828; boilers, machinery and mechanical hardware, 216,602; refined petroleum and related products, 159,896; citrus and other fruits, 105,145; electric and electronic machinery and hardware, 76,130; footwear,

66,661; cement. salt, sulphur, limestone, 64,729; organic chemical products, 53,022; vegetables and pulses, 52,097.

Distribution of Spanish foreign trade (in 1m. pesetas) according to origin and destination, for calendar years:

	Imports		Exports	
	1981	1982	1981	1982
Europe	1,073,877	1,366,122	1,038,865	1,260,853
EEC	861,869	1,087,705	812,346	1,036,930
France	237,576	277,516	270,578	370,217
Germany, Federal Republic	241,524	328,861	163,343	185,590
UK	132,890	171,112	130,646	161,022
Italy	118,446	155,634	108,002	127,284
EFTA	126,664	164,757	121,396	144,093
Comecon	79,562	98,867	81,233	52,320
USA	412,372	482,025	126,912	145,532
LAIA (ex LAFTA)	330,456	346,158	162,382	180,611
Mexico	183,930	206,584	49,665	56,970
Venezuela	60,662	40,779	30,416	38,515
Saudi Arabia	324,163	...	47,193	60,653
Iran	123,770	119,563	31,482	37,781
Japan	79,427	110,552	29,994	28,306
Libya	122,256	120,701	40,032	29,248
Oceania	18,237	19,109	8,855	8,862

Total trade between Spain and UK (British Department of Trade returns, in £1.000 sterling):

	1978	1979	1980	1981	1982	1983
Imports to UK	505,894	710,901	804,232	804,781	956,935	1,110,029
Exports and re-exports from UK	472,035	573,015	708,998	707,767	870,416	1,128,439

Total trade of the Spanish territories and UK (British Department of Trade returns, in £1,000 sterling):

	Imports to UK			Exports from UK		
	1981	1982	1983	1981	1982	1983
Canary Islands	61,450	44,574	55,305	42,124	83,508	93,600
North Africa	6	...	24	6,859	4,679	8,190

Tourism. In 1982, 42,011,141 tourists visited Spain (from France, 10·87m.; Portugal, 9·23m.; Federal Germany, 4·77m.; UK, 4·85m.). Receipts of foreign currency (1981) US$6·71m.

COMMUNICATIONS

Roads. In 1981 the total length of highways and roads in Spain was 148,766 km, of which 123,809 km were macadamized or had other good surface. Motorways, 1,959 km. Number of cars was 8,354,050, lorries, 1,461,946, buses, 42,996 and motorcycles, 1,282,945 in 1982.

Railways. The total length of the state railways in 1982 was 13,572 km, mostly 1,676-mm gauge. There are 6,162 km of lines electrified. On 1 Feb. 1941 the Spanish railways, of broad gauge only, passed into state ownership; they are under a board known as the *Red Nacional de Ferrocarriles Españoles* (RENFE). The gauge of the principal Spanish railways has, for strategic reasons, been kept different from that of France; passengers therefore must change trains at the French frontier stations except by certain trains having variable gauge axles. In 1981 freight carried was 10,503m. tonne-km and 14,703m. passenger-km.

Aviation. The most important Spanish airline is 'Iberia': it maintains a regular service with Europe, America, Africa and the Middle East. 'Aviaco' operates mainly internal flights. There are 43 airports open to civil traffic; those of Madrid, Palma de Mallorca and Barcelona are the most active. A small airport in Seo de Urgel, in the Pyrenees, used especially for the air service of Andorra was opened in 1982.

Aircraft movements in 1982 (provisional), 291,732 internal and 243,024 international, carrying 48·7m. passengers and 354,940 tonnes of merchandise.

Shipping. The merchant navy in 1982 contained 1,109 vessels of a gross tonnage of 7,299,000.

In 1982 (provisional), 99,548 ships entered Spanish ports, carrying 6,459,000 passengers and discharging 432·58m. tonnes of cargo.

Post and Broadcasting. The receipts of the post office in 1982 were 55,093m. pesetas; expenses, 66,651m. pesetas. There were in 1982, 13,369 post offices and 12,350,058 telephones, these all privately operated.

Radio Nacional de España broadcasts 4 programmes on medium-waves and FM, as well as many regional programmes; it does not broadcast advertising. There is another state broadcasting network, *Radio-Cadena Española,* this self-financing with advertising. The greatest radio audience is that of a private network, *Sociedad Española de Radiodifusión* (SER); *Cadena de Ondas Populares Españolas* (COPE) belongs to the Roman Catholic church. Two private broadcasting networks were established in 1982 covering the whole of Spain, *Antena 3* and *Radio 80. Televisión Española* broadcasts 2 programmes. Colour transmissions are carried by PAL system. Number of receivers (1979): radio, 9·6m.; television, 9·4m. (about 50% colour sets).

Cinemas (1981). There were 3,970 cinemas with an estimated seating capacity of 4m.

Newspapers (1981). There were about 100 daily newspapers with a total daily circulation of about 5m. copies.

JUSTICE, RELIGION, EDUCATION AND WELFARE

Justice. Justice is administered by *Tribunales* and *Juzgados* (Tribunals and Courts), which conjointly form the *Poder Judicial* (Judicial Power). Judges and magistrates cannot be removed, suspended or transferred except as set forth by law. The Constitution of 1978 has established a new organ, the *Consejo General del Poder Judicial* (General Council of the Judicial Power), formed by magistrates, judges, attorneys and lawyers, governing the Judicial Power in full independence from the other two powers of the State, the Legislative (Cortes) and the Executive (President of the Government and his Cabinet). The territorial organization of justice is being gradually changed, adapting it to the new map of the country in Autonomous Communities.

The Judicature is composed of the *Tribunal Supremo* (Supreme High Court); 16 *Audiencias Territoriales* (Division High Courts); 50 *Audiencias Provinciales* (Provincial High Courts); 518 *Juzgados de Primera Instancia* (Courts of First Instance), 742 *Juzgados de Distrito* (District Courts) and 7,532 *Juzgados Municipales y de paz* (Municipal and Peace Courts, Court of Lowest Jurisdiction held by Justices of the Peace).

The *Tribunal Supremo* consists of a President (appointed by the King, on proposal from the *Consejo General del Poder Judicial*) and various judges distributed among 6 chambers: 1 for trying civil matters, 3 for administrative purposes, 1 for criminal trials and 1 for social matters. The *Tribunal Supremo* has disciplinary faculties; is court of cassation in all criminal trials; for administrative purposes decides in first and second instance disputes arising between private individuals and the State, and in social matters resolves in the last instance all cases involving over 100,000 pesetas.

The *Audiencias Territoriales* have power to try in second instance sentences passed by judges in civil matters.

The *Audiencias Provinciales* try and pass sentence in first instance on all cases filed for delinquency. The jury system, re-established by the art. 125 of the Constitution, had not been applied by Jan. 1984, pending its parliamentary regulation.

The *Juzgados Municipales* try small civil cases and petty offences. The *Juzgados Comarcales* deal with the same charges, but their jurisdiction embraces larger districts.

Military cases are tried by the *Tribunal Supremo de Justicia Militar* but its sentences can now pass to the (civil) *Tribunal Supremo,* as final cassation instance.

The *Tribunal Constitucional* (Constitutional Court) has power to solve conflicts between the State and the Autonomous Communities, to determine if legislation passed by the Cortes is contrary to the Constitution and to protect constitutional rights of the individuals violated by any authority. Its 12 members are appointed by the King in the following way: 4, on proposal of the Congress of Deputies; 4, on proposal of the Senate; 2 on proposal of the *Consejo General del Poder Judicial;* and 2 on proposal of the Cabinet.

The death penalty was abolished in 1978 by the Constitution (art. 15). Divorce is again in force since July 1981.

The prison population was, on 31 Dec. 1982, 21,942.

Religion. Roman Catholicism is the religion of the majority. There are 11 metropolitan sees and 52 suffragan sees, the chief being Toledo, where the Primate resides.

The archdioceses of Madrid-Alcalá and Barcelona depend directly from the Vatican.

The Constitution guarantees full religious freedom and states that no religion has an established legal condition (art. 16); so, since 29 Dec. 1978 there has been no official religion in Spain. A report issued in 1982 by the Episcopal Conference of the Roman Catholic Church claims that 82·76% of all children born in 1981 were baptized in that church.

There are about 150,000 other Christians, including several Protestant denominations, Jehovah Witnesses (about 60,000) and Mormons. The British and Foreign Bible Society was, on 10 March 1963, allowed to resume its activities.

The first synagogue since the expulsion of the Jews in 1492 was opened in Madrid on 2 Oct. 1959. The number of Jews is estimated at about 13,000.

Education. Primary education is compulsory and free between 6 and 14 years of age.

In 1980–81 pre-primary education (under 6 years) was conducted by 35,610 schools, with 35,588 teachers and 1,182,425 pupils. Primary or basic education (6 to 14 years): 176,424 schools, 211,074 teachers and 5,606,452 pupils. Secondary education (14-17 years) is conducted on two branches: 2,445 middle schools *(Institutos),* with 66,160 teachers and 1,091,197 pupils, and 2,142 vocational and technical centres *(Formación Profesional),* with 36,556 teachers and 558,808 pupils. For higher education there were (in 1979–80) 559 centres, with 20,445 teachers and 544,834 pupils.

In 1982 there were in all 33 universities: 22 State Universities, in Madrid, Barcelona, Valencia, Granada, Sevilla, Santiago de Compostela, Zaragoza, Bilbao (University of the Basque Country), Oviedo, Valladolid, Salamanca (founded in 1215), La Laguna (Canaries), Murcia, Málaga, Córdoba, Badajoz-Cáceres (University of Extremadura), Cádiz, León, Santander, Alicante, Palma de Mallorca and Alcalá de Henares; 4 Polytechnic Universities, in Madrid, Barcelona, Valencia and Las Palmas (Canaries); 2 Autonomous Universities, in Madrid and Barcelona; 4 private (catholic) universities, in Deusto (Bilbao), Pamplona, Salamanca and Madrid (University of Comillas); and the *Universidad Nacional de Educación a Distancia* (National University for Education at Home), which teaches by mail, radio and TV, with its central seat at Madrid. The number of university students was 470,058 (1980–81), and teachers 29,287.

DIPLOMATIC REPRESENTATIVES

Of Spain in Great Britain (24 Belgrave Sq., London SW1X 8QA)
Ambassador: José Joaquín Puig de la Bellacasa.

Of Great Britain in Spain (Calle de Fernando el Santo, 16, Madrid, 4)
Ambassador: Sir Richard Parsons, KCMG.

Of Spain in the USA (2700–15th St., NW, Washington, D.C., 20009)
Ambassador: Gabriel Mañueco de Lecea.

Of the USA in Spain (Serrano 75, Madrid)
Ambassador: Thomas O. Enders.

Of Spain to the United Nations
Ambassador: Jaime de Piniés.

Books of Reference

Statistical Information: The Instituto Nacional de Estadistica (Paseo de la Castellana, 183, Madrid) combines the administrative work of a government department attached to the Presidency of the Government with a centre of statistical studies. *Director-General:* José Montes. Its publications include: *Anuario Estadístico de España.* Annual. *Edición manual* (latest vol., 1983).—*Reseñas estadísticas provinciales.—Nomenclátor de las ciudades, villas lugares, aldeas, y demás entidades de población de España.* 52 vols. Madrid, 1973.—*Poblaciones de Derecho y de Hecho de los Municipios Españoles: Censo de Poblacion de 1981.* Madrid, 1982.—*Diccionario Corográfico de España.* 4 vols. Madrid, 1948.—*Boletin de Estadística.* Madrid. (No. 1, Jan.–March 1939: monthly from 1948).—*Estadística española. Revista trimestral* (from 1959).
Spain at a Glance, 1972. Servicio Informativo Español, Madrid, 1972

Aguilar (ed.), *Nuevo Atlas de España.* Madrid, 1961
Altamira y Crevea, R., *A History of Spain.* New York and London, 1950
Anuario del Mercado Español. Madrid, 1965
Bell, D., (ed.), *Democratic Politics in Spain: Spanish Politics after Franco.* London, 1983
Carr, R., *Modern Spain, 1875–1980.* OUP, 1980
Enciclopedia Universal Ilustrada. 70 vols., 10 appendices, 10 supplements. Madrid
Garcia Venero, M., *Historia del Nacionalismo Vasco, 1793–1936.* Madrid, 1945
Lafuente, M., and Valera, J., *Historia General de España.* New ed. 25 vols. Barcelona, 1925
Lieberman, S., *The Contemporary Spanish Economy: A Historical Perspective.* London, 1982
López Oliván, J., *Repertorio Diplomático Español. [Collection of treaties, 1125–1935.]* Madrid, 1944
Maravall, J., *The Transition to Democracy in Spain.* London, 1982
Morris, J., *Spain.* London, 1979
Russell, P. E. (ed.), *Spain: A Companion to Spanish Studies.* 6th ed. London, 1973
Vicens Vives, J., *Historia Económica de España.* 5 vols. Barcelona, 1959
Wright, A., *The Spanish Economy 1959–1976.* London, 1977

National Library: Biblioteca Nacional, Madrid. *Director:* Guillermo Cuastavino Callent.

FORMER PROVINCE IN AFRICA (WESTERN SAHARA)

It was announced in Madrid on 14 Nov. 1975 that Spain, Morocco and Mauritania had reached agreement on the transfer of power over Western Sahara to Morocco and Mauritania on 28 Feb. 1976. Morocco occupied El Aiaún in late Nov. and on 12 Jan. 1976 the Spanish army withdrew from Western Sahara which had ceased to be a Spanish province on 31 Dec. 1975. The country was partitioned by Morocco and Mauritania. In Aug. 1979 Mauritania withdrew from the territory it took over in 1976. The area was taken over by Morocco and reorganized into provinces.

Algeria stated that the former province should be handed over to the people of the territory, objected to the partition and is (1982) backing the claims of *Frente Polisario* for an independent state. In spite of occupation of all western centres by Moroccan troops, Saharan guerrillas based in Algeria continue to attempt to liberate their country. They have renamed it the Democratic Saharan Arab Republic and hold most of the desert beyond a defensive line built by Moroccan troops encompassing Smara, Bu Craa and Laayoune.

In 1982 the Democratic Saharwi Arab Republic became a member of the Organization of African Unity (OAU).

The area was 266,769 sq. km (102,680 sq. miles). The population at the census (1970) was 76,425; Saharans, 59,777 and 16,648 Europeans. The capital was El Aaiún (Laayoune) (population, 24,048).

Rich phosphate deposits were discovered in 1963 at Bu Craa. Morocco holds 65% of the shares of the former Spanish state-controlled company. While production reached 5·6m. tonnes in 1975, exploitation has been severely reduced by guerrilla activity in 1976 and 1977. After a nearly complete collapse, production and transportation of phosphate resumed in 1978, ceased again, and then resumed in 1982.

Books of Reference

Atlas Histórico y Geográfico de Africa Española. Madrid, 1955

Damis, J., *Conflict in Northwest Africa: The Western Sahara Dispute.* Stanford, 1983

Hernández-Pacheco, E., and others, *El Sahara español.* Madrid, 1949

Hodges, T., *Historical Dictionary of Western Sahara.* London, 1982

Mercer, J., *Spanish Sahara.* London, 1976

Pélissier, R., *Les Territoires Espagnols d'Afrique.* Paris, 1963.—*Los Territorios Españoles de Africa.* Madrid, 1964

Rumeu de Armas, A., *España en el Africa Atlántica.* 2 vols. Madrid, 1956–57

Thompson, V. and Adloff, R., *The Western Saharans· Background to Conflict.* London, 1980

SRI LANKA

Ceylon

Capital: Colombo
Population: 14·9m. (1981)
GNP per capita: US$270 (1980)

HISTORY. According to the Mahawansa chronicle, an Indian prince from the valley of the Ganges, named Vijaya, arrived in the 6th century B.C. and became the first king of the Sinhalese. The monarchical form of government continued until the beginning of the 19th century when the British subjugated the Kandyan Kingdom in the central highlands.

In 1505 the Portuguese formed settlements on the west and south, which were taken from them about the middle of the next century by the Dutch. In 1796 the British Government annexed the foreign settlements to the presidency of Madras. In 1802 Ceylon was constituted a separate colony.

Ceylon reached fully responsible status within the British Commonwealth when the Ceylon Independence Act, 1947, came into force on 4 Feb. 1948. Sri Lanka became a republic in 1972.

EVENTS. In July 1983 a serious outburst of violence between Tamils and other groups led to the imposition of a State of Emergency; 14 Tamil MPs boycotted Parliament, and pressed for a separate Tamil state. They lost their seats in Oct. 1983 when the separatist campaign became illegal.

AREA AND POPULATION. Sri Lanka lies off the south-east coast of the Indian State of Tamil Nadu, separated from it by the Indian ocean but almost joined to it by the chain of islands called Adam's Bridge. On 28 June 1974 the frontier between India and Sri Lanka in the Palk Strait was re-defined, giving to Sri Lanka the island of Kachchativu. Area (in sq. km.) and census population on 17 March 1981.

Provinces	Area	Population	Provinces	Area	Population
Western	3,708·87	3,915,001	North-Central	10,723·21	850,575
Central	5,590·17	2,005,956	Uva	8,481·90	922,636
Southern	5,558·77	1,882,912	Sabaragamuwa	4,901·56	1,478,879
Northern	8,882·05	1,111,468			
Eastern	9,951·34	976,475	Total	65,609·63	14,850,001
North-Western	7,811·73	1,706,099			

Population (1981 census), 14,850,001, an increase of 17·1% since 1971. Population (in 1,000) according to race and nationality at the 1981 census: 10,986 Sinhalese, 1,872 Ceylon Tamils, 1,057 Ceylon Moors, 38 Burghers, 43 Malays, 825 Indian Tamils, 29 others. Non- nationals of Sri Lanka totalled 1,202,000. By agreement with the Government of India in 1964 and 1974, Indian nationals who have not been granted Sri Lanka citizenship were to be repatriated. The 1964 agreement covered 525,000 people; the 1974 agreement, 75,000.

Vital statistics, 1981: birth-rate (per 1,000 population), 28·0; death-rate, 6·0; infant death-rate (per 1,000 live births), 43·7 in 1980.

The urban population was 21·5% of the total in 1981. The principal towns and their population according to the census of 1981 are: Colombo, 585,776; Dehiwela-Mt. Lavinia, 174,385; Moratuwa, 135,610; Jaffna, 118,215; Kotte, 101,563; Kandy, 101,281; Galle, 77,183; Negombo, 61,376; Trincomalee, 44,913; Batticaloa, 42,934; Matara, 39,162; Ratnapura, 37,354; Anuradhapura, 36,248; Badulla, 32,954; Kalutara, 31,495. Population of the Greater Colombo area, 1980, about 1m.

The national languages are Sinhala, English and Tamil; Sinhala is the official language and Tamil is used in the northern and eastern provinces.

CLIMATE. Sri Lanka has an equatorial climate with low annual temperature variations, but it is affected by the north-east Monsoon (Nov. to March) and the south-west Monsoon (May to Sept.). Rainfall is generally heavy but never lasts long; it is heaviest in the south-west and central highlands while the north and east are relatively dry. Colombo. Jan. 79°F (26°C), July 81°F (27°C). Annual rainfall 96″ (2,400 mm). Trincomalee. Jan. 77°F (25°C), July 85°F (29·4°C). Annual rainfall 66″ (1,648 mm).

CONSTITUTION AND GOVERNMENT. A new constitution for the Democratic Socialist Republic of Sri Lanka was promulgated in Sept. 1978.

The Executive President is directly elected by the people and has to receive more than one-half of the valid votes cast. His term of office is six years and he shall not hold the office for more than two consecutive terms. He is the Head of the State, the Head of the Executive and of the Government and the Commander-in-chief of the Armed Forces. He does not have any veto power over legislation; even in a time of public emergency, he must act with Parliamentary control and approval.

Parliament consists of one chamber, composed of 168 members elected by universal suffrage, and proportional representation. The Senate was abolished by constitutional amendment in Sept. 1971.

The term of Parliament is six years. In Nov. 1982 Parliament voted to extend its present term (expiring Aug. 1983) for a further six years. The vote was subject to national referendum on 20 Dec. 1982; 71% of the electorate voted and 55% approved the extension.

The Prime Minister and other Ministers, who must be members of Parliament, are appointed by the President. The President is head of the Cabinet.

The electorate consists of all who are 18 years of age and over.

National flag: A yellow field bearing 2 panels: in the hoist 2 vertical strips of green and orange; in the fly, dark red with a gold lion holding a sword and in each corner a gold 'bo' leaf.

The Cabinet was in March 1984 as follows:

President, Defence, Higher Education, Janata States Development, State Plantations, Power and Energy, and Plan Implementation: J. R. Jayawardene.

Prime Minister, Leader of the House, Local Government, Highways, Housing and Construction: Ranasinghe Premadasa.

Land, Land Development and Mahaweli Development: Gamini Dissanayake. *Foreign Affairs:* A. C. S. Hameed. *Home Affairs:* K. W. Devanayagam. *Trade and Shipping:* Lalith W. A. Mudali. *Rural Development:* Wimala Kannangara. *Justice:* N. P. Wijeyeratne. *Finance and Planning:* Ronnie de Mel. *Labour:* C. P. J. Seneviratne. *Industries and Scientific Affairs:* Cyril Mathew. *Cultural Affairs:* E. L. B. Hurulle. *Fisheries:* M. F. W. Perera. *Health:* R. Atapattu. *Post and Telecommunications:* D. B. Wijetunge. *Parliamentary Affairs and Sports:* M. Vincent Perera. *Transport:* H. M. Mohamed. *Agricultural Development and Research:* G. Jayasuriya. *Public Administration and Plantation Industries:* M. Jayawickreme. *Textile Industry:* W. Mendis. *Social Services:* Asoka Karunaratne. *Rural Industrial Development:* R. S. Thondaman. *Youth Affairs, Education and Employment:* R. Wickremasinghe. *State:* A. de Alwis. *Regional Development:* C. Rajadurai. *Women's Affairs and Teaching Hospitals:* S. Ranasinghe. *Without Portfolio:* M. A. Bakeer Markar.

For purposes of general administration, the island is divided into 24 districts, administered by government agents. There are 12 Municipal Councils and 24 District Councils.

The capital is Colombo.

DEFENCE

Army. The Army was constituted on 10 Oct. 1949. It consists of 5 infantry brigades, 1 reconnaissance, 1 field artillery, 1 anti-aircraft and 1 engineer regiments and 1 signals battalion. Equipment includes 18 Saladin armoured cars and 15 Ferret scout cars. Strength (1984) 11,000, with 14,000 reserves. There are also paramilitary forces: Police Force (14,500), Volunteer Force (5,000) and Home Guard.

Navy. The Navy was constituted on 9 Dec. 1950. It comprises 8 (1 *ex*-Soviet and 7 *ex*-Chinese) fast gunboats, 30 small patrol boats and 1 service craft. *Gemunu* and *Rangalla* are commissioned as shore establishments. The naval base is established at Trincomalee. Personnel in 1984 numbered 220 officers and 2,740 ratings. Naval personnel are sent to the UK for training. There is also a Volunteer Naval Reserve of 43 officers and 540 ratings, and a Naval Reserve of 130.

Air Force. The Air Force was formed on 10 Oct. 1950. Its flying bases are at Katunayake and China Bay, Trincomalee. Equipment of 4 squadrons comprises 7 Chipmunk and 4 Cessna 150/152 trainers, 4 Herons, 1 HS748, 2 DC-3s, 3 Cessna Skymasters, 1 Cessna 421 and a Cessna Cardinal for general transport and utility purposes; 3 Doves for navigation training; and 2 Dauphin and 7 JetRanger helicopters for internal security operations. In storage are 5 MiG-17F jet fighter-bombers, 1 MiG-15UTI jet trainer, 5 Jet Provosts (armed), six Bell 47G-2 and 2 Ka-26 helicopters. Total strength about 2,500 officers and airmen. There is also an Air Force Reserve.

INTERNATIONAL RELATIONS

Membership. Sri Lanka is a member of UN, the Commonwealth, the Non-Aligned Movement and the Colombo Plan.

External debt. External debt in Dec. 1982 was Rs34,726·9m.

ECONOMY

Planning. The 1983–87 plan aims at 6% annual growth rate. Investment allocated is mainly for agriculture, including the Mahaweli energy and irrigation scheme. Total investment, about Rs 125,006m.

Budget. Revenue and expenditure of central government in Rs 1m. for financial years ending 31 Dec.:

Year	Revenue	Expenditure Recurrent	Capital	Total
1980–81	16,228	17,721	11,765	29,486
1981–82	17,809	19,231	16,056	35,287
1982–83 [1]	25,734	25,988	17,948	43,936

[1] Estimate.

The principal sources of revenue in 1982–83 were (in Rs 1m.): Income tax, 3,624; import duties, 4,896; export duties, 2,604; other indirect taxes, 10,688.

The principal items of recurrent expenditure in 1982–83 (in Rs 1m.): Administration including defence, 4,168; food subsidies, 100; education, social services and health, 3,824; interest on public debt, 7,369. Capital expenditure on agriculture, 1,132; communications, 1,333.

Currency. The Monetary Law Act provides that the standard monetary unit is the Ceylon *rupee*.

The Central Bank is the sole authority for the issue of currency and all currency notes and coins issued by the Central Bank are legal tender for the payment of any amount, except notes of Rs 50 and Rs 100 dated before 25 Oct. 1970. Currency notes are issued in the denominations of Rs 2, 5, 10, 20, 50, 100, 500 and 1,000. Coins are issued in the denominations of 1, 2, 5, 10, 25 and 50 cents; Rs 1, 2 and 5. The total circulation was Rs 7,590·8m. on 30 June 1983. In March 1984, £1 = Rs 37·28; US$1 = Rs 25·19.

Banking. The narrow money supply (M1) at 30 June 1983 stood at Rs 12,589·2m.

The main commercial banks in Sri Lanka are: The Bank of Ceylon and the People's Bank (state-managed), the State Bank of India, Grindlays Bank, the Hongkong and Shanghai Banking Corporation, the Chartered Bank, the Commercial Bank of Ceylon, the Hatton National Bank, the Habib Bank (Overseas) Ltd., Indo-Suez Bank, American Express and the Indian Overseas Bank Ltd. Total assets of 25 commercial banks at 30 June 1983, Rs 45,387·3m.

The state-owned Ceylon Insurance Corporation and the National Insurance Corporation have a monopoly of all insurance business.

Sri Lanka National Savings Bank at 30 June 1983 had a balance to depositors' credit of Rs 8,641·2m. Sri Lanka State Mortgage and Investment Bank, National Development Bank, Development Finance Corporation and the National Housing Department are the main long-term credit institutions.

Weights and Measures. The metric system has been established by the Weights and Measures (Amendment) Law No. 24 of 1974.

ENERGY AND NATURAL RESOURCES

Electricity. Installed capacity of electric energy (1982), 561,000 kw. Energy produced, 2,066m. kwh; the main source is hydro-electricity. The Mahaweli power scheme is planned to begin production in 1984; installed capacity, 507mw.

Water. The Mahaweli Ganga irrigation scheme has entered phase 2 and will benefit 896,000 acres. Two major river diversions, at Polgolla near Kandy and at Bowatenna on the Amban Ganga River, will benefit 120,000 acres of land already cultivated and irrigate an extra 104,000 acres of new land. There is a Water Resources Board (set up in 1966) and a National Water Supply and Drainage Board (1974). Water supply to the city and area of Colombo comes from the Labugama and Kalatuwawa reservoirs. Consumption within Colombo city limits is estimated at 10,000m. gallons a year.

All domestic consumers receive a free water allowance; commercial consumers do not.

Minerals. Gems are among the chief minerals mined and exported. Precious and semi-precious stones are found among the layers of older alluvium and river gravels of quaternary age in the valleys of the Ratnapura district in the south-west. The most important are sapphire, ruby, crysoberyl, beryl, topaz, spinel, garnet, ziran and tourmaline. Value of gemstones exported in 1982, Rs 685m.

Graphite is also important. The State Graphite Corporation was set up in 1971. There were 3 large mines (Bogala, Kahatagaha and Kalangaha), and several smaller mines working at the end of 1976. Graphite produced (tonnes), 1981, 7,453; 1982 8,803.

The Ceylon Mineral Sands Corporation was established in 1957, mainly to extract ilmenite. Production of ilmenite, 1982, 68,282 tonnes. Some rutile is also produced (7,212 tonnes in 1982).

Salt extraction is the oldest industry in Sri Lanka and is now controlled by the National Salt Corporation. The method is solar evaporation of sea-water. Production, 1982, 176,437 tonnes.

Agriculture. The area of the island is approximately 6,560,963 hectares, of which 2,164,325 hectares are under cultivation. Agriculture engages about 46% of the labour force. The main crops in 1982 were as follows: Paddy (2·2m. tons from 746,000 hectares), rubber (125,230 tons), tea (187,816 tons) and coconuts (2,521m. nuts).

In March 1976 the Sri Lanka State Plantation Corporation took over management of all private tea and rubber estates. Compensation was paid on condition that it be re-invested in Sri Lanka. The Sri Lanka Tea Corporation was formed in March 1972.

Livestock in 1982 (estimate): 1·7m. cattle, 879,200 buffaloes, 75,100 swine, 511,600 goats, 28,000 sheep, 6·2m. poultry.

Fisheries. The Government is implementing a programme (1979–83) for the development of fisheries. Production for 1982 was 207,120m. tons including 173,000m. tons of coastal water fish, 30,400m. tons of fresh water fish and 3,720m. tons from deep-sea fisheries. In 1982 (provisional) there were 26,970 fishing craft, of which 13,947 were not motorized.

INDUSTRY AND TRADE

Industry. The Business Undertakings (Acquisition) Act was passed in May 1971 empowering the Government to acquire any business for the state. The British Ceylon Corporation Ltd and its subsidiaries were nationalized in Feb. 1972. The nationalization of the oil industry was completed in Dec. 1971. The first objective was the development of heavy industry through state investment in small companies and the setting up of public corporations. Three such corporations have been established for the mining and processing of graphite; the importing, manufacture and distribution of pharmaceuticals; the importing and distribution of materials for textile manufacture. Other important manufactures are ceramics, vegetable oils, fertilizers, cement, wood and paper products, leather, rubber products and sugar. The government has set up Investment Promotion Zones; by Aug. 1980 these had 119 projects employing over 7,600; the main industry was clothing manufacture. Foreign investment is encouraged by a tax holiday of up to 10 years for approved industries. Export profits may have a 3-year tax holiday.

Trade unions. The registration and control of trade unions are regulated by the Trade Unions Ordinance (Ch. 138 of the Legislative Enactments). In 1982 there were 1,241 registered trade unions with a membership of 1,220,110.

Commerce. The values of total imports and exports (imports excluding bullion, specie and postal articles; exports, including re-exports and ship's stores) for calendar years (in Rs 1,000):

	1979	1980	1981	1982 [1]
Imports	22,560,000	33,637,000	35,530,235	36,875,519
Exports	15,273,000	17,273,000	19,657,851	20,728,491

[1] Provisional

Principal exports (domestic) in 1982 (in Rs 1m.): Tea, 6,342; rubber, 2,323; copra, coconut oil and desiccated coconut, 1,003; other crops, 1,645; textiles and garments, 3,502; precious and semi-precious stones, 685.

Principal imports (Rs 1m.) in 1982 were petroleum, 10,175m.; machinery and equipment, 5,834m.; vehicles and transport equipment, 2,873; food and beverages, 3,546.

In 1982 the principal sources of imports were (in Rs 1m.): Saudi Arabia, 4,568; Japan, 5,600; UK, 2,425; USA, 2,322; India, 1,520; Iran, 4,289; Singapore, 2,211; FRG, 1,589; South Korea, 742.

Principal export destinations 1982 were (in Rs 1m.): UK, 1,369; USA, 2,980; Japan, 1,041; Pakistan, 797; FRG, 1,159; Saudi Arabia, 563.

Total trade between Sri Lanka and UK (British Department of Trade returns, in £1,000 sterling):

	1979	1980	1981	1982	1983
Imports to UK	40,826	53,681	36,569	42,000	39,784
Exports and re-exports from UK	55,260	76,831	59,236	60,211	70,136

Tourism. About 407,230 tourists visited the country in 1982.

COMMUNICATIONS

Roads. There are about 25,466 km. of motorable roads, of which 75% are black-topped. Number of motor vehicles, 31 Dec. 1982, 403,014, including 131,657 private cars and cabs, 74,770 lorries, 43,539 tractors, 107,545 motor cycles, 26,172 buses.

Railways. In 1982 there were about 1,453 km of railway open, of which 1,394 km were broad gauge and 59 narrow gauge. In 1982 railways ran 3,121m. passenger-km and 216m. tonne-km.

Aviation. Air Lanka operates international services. Foreign airlines which operate scheduled services to Sri Lanka are British Airways, UTA, India Airlines Corporation, Swissair, Aeroflot, KLM, Singapore Airlines, Thai Airways International, Pakistan International Airlines, Korean Airlines, Gulf Air, Royal Nepal Airlines,

Balkan Bulgarian Airlines, Kuwait Airlines, UTA French Airlines and Maldivian International Airlines; various others operate charter services.

Shipping. In 1981, merchant vessels totalling 14·1 GRT entered the ports of Sri Lanka. The Sri Lanka Shipping Corporation began functioning as ship-owners, charterers, brokers and shipping agents in 1979. The Sri Lanka Port Authority was also established in 1979.

Post and Broadcasting. In 1982 there were 438 post offices, 3,145 sub-post offices and 1,900 telegraph offices. There were (1982) 109,900 telephones. Throughout the Greater Colombo Area inter-dialling facilities are now available between 52 stations.

The Overseas Telecommunication Service operates telegraph and telephone services to most parts of the world. Broadcasting is provided by the Sri Lanka Broadcasting Corporation, which assumed the functions of Radio Ceylon on 5 Jan. 1967.

Cinemas. In 1982 there were 363 cinemas with a seating capacity of 191,561. The National Film Corporation established in 1971 has exclusive rights to import films and arranges distribution of foreign and local films. Films released, 1982, 169.

Newspapers. There are 4 main newspaper groups: Associated Newspapers of Ceylon Ltd (5 daily and 3 weekly papers and other periodicals); Times of Ceylon Ltd (2 daily, 2 weekly and other periodicals); Express Newspapers (Ceylon) Ltd (2 daily and 2 weekly papers); Independent Newspapers Ltd. (3 daily and 3 weekly papers and other periodicals).

There are 5 daily and 4 weekly papers in Sinhala; 4 daily and 4 weekly in Tamil; 5 daily and 4 weekly in English.

JUSTICE, RELIGION, EDUCATION AND WELFARE

Justice. The systems of law which obtain in Sri Lanka are the Roman-Dutch law, the English law, the Tesawalamai, the Moslem law and the Kandyan law.

The Kandyan law applies to the Kandyan Sinhalese in the Central, North-Central, Uva and Sabaragamuwa provinces in respect of all matters relating to inheritance, matrimonial rights and donations. The law of England is observed in most commercial matters. The law of Tesawalamai is applied to all Tamil inhabitants of Jaffna, in all matters relating to inheritance, marriages, gifts, donations, purchases and sales of land. The Moslem law is applied to all Moslems in respect of succession, donations not involving Fidei Commissa, marriage, divorce and maintenance. These customary and religious laws have been modified in many respects by local enactments.

The courts of original jurisdiction are the High Courts, district courts, magistrates' courts and primary courts. The High Courts try major crimes and also exercise admiralty jurisdiction. The district court has unlimited civil jurisdiction in civil, revenue, trust, insolvency and testamentary matters, over persons and estates of persons of unsound mind, and wards. Family Courts were established in 1978; District Courts can act as Family Courts. The magistrates' courts exercise criminal jurisdiction carrying the power to impose terms of imprisonment not exceeding 2 years and fines not exceeding Rs 1,500. The Primary Courts which were established in 1978 exercise civil jurisdiction where the value of the subject matter does not exceed Rs 1,500 and also have jurisdiction in respect of by-laws of local authorities and matters relating to the recovery of revenue of such local authorities. Primary Courts exercise exclusive criminal jurisdiction in respect of offences which may be prescribed by regulation by the Minister. A Judge of a Primary Court has a duty to make every effort to settle such matter whether civil or criminal, by conciliation. The Primary Courts have the power to impose sentences of imprisonment not exceeding three months and fines not exceeding Rs 250.

The Constitution of 1978 provided for the establishment of two superior courts, the Supreme Court and the Court of Appeal.

The Supreme Court is the highest and final superior court of record and exercises jurisdiction in respect of constitutional matters, jurisdiction for the protection of fundamental rights, final appellate jurisdiction, consultative jurisdiction, jurisdiction in election petitions, jurisdiction in respect of any breach of the privileges of Parliament. The Court of Appeal exercises appellate jurisdiction for the correction of all errors in fact or in law committed by any court, tribunal or institution, the power to grant and issue orders in the nature of writs of certiorari, prohibition, procedendo, mandamus, quo warrants and Habeas corpus, the power to grant injunctions and jurisdiction to try election petitions in respect of election of Members of Parliament.

Police. The strength of the police service as on 31 Aug. 1983 was 15,881.

Religion. Buddhism was introduced from India in the 3rd century B.C. and is the religion of 69·3% of the inhabitants. There were (1981) 10,292,586 Buddhists, 2,295,858 Hindus, 1,111,736 Christians, 1,134,556 Moslems and 15,265 others.

Education. Education is free from the kindergarten to the university and is imparted in the medium of the mother tongue. In 1981 about 86% of the population (10 years old and older) was literate.

In 1982 there were 9,901 schools including 9,544 government schools; the rest were private and estate schools. The government schools had 137,340 teachers and 3·4m. students from grades L.K.G. to XII. Department of Education expenditure (1982), Rs 2,203·5m. Education is now administered under 31 regional directors.

The overall control of the education regions is vested in the Ministry of Education.

There are 6 Universities: Peradeniya, Colombo, Jaffna, Sri Jayawardenepura, Moratuwa and Kelaniya, an Open University and two University Colleges: Ruhuna and Batticaloa. Dumbara Campus comes under Peradeniya University.

In 1982 there were 19,694 students and 2,013 teachers in the 6 Universities and 2 University Colleges. The Open University had 10,263 students. There were 22 institutions for technical education, 7 of which were polytechnics; total enrolment (1982), 19,733.

Health. In 1982 there were 493 hospitals, including 102 maternity homes, and 340 central dispensaries. Hospitals had 43,389 beds and there were 2,035 Department of Health doctors. Total state budget expenditure on health, 1981, Rs 931·4m.

Social Security. The activities of the Department of Social Services fall into five main divisions:

Public assistance (monthly allowances); casual relief; relief to leprosy and tuberculosis patients and their dependants.

Relief of widespread distress due to failure of crops, floods, storms, etc., including relief to individual cases of distress among fishermen due to acts of God such as fire, storms and accidents; rehabilitation and resettlement of flood victims.

Provision of custodial care and welfare services to the elderly and infirm.

Provision of vocational training facilities, rehabilitation measures and aids and appliances for the physically handicapped.

Provision of custodial care, vocational training and rehabilitation for socially handicapped persons.

Financial assistance to voluntary institutions that provide welfare services.

Special study of social problems affecting the community.

The payment of compensation to workmen meeting with accidents in the course of their work is provided for under the Workmen's Compensation Ordinance No. 19 of 1934, as amended in 1957, 1959 and 1966. It was brought into operation in 1935, and has been administered by the Ministry of Justice since 1980.

DIPLOMATIC REPRESENTATIVES

Of Sri Lanka in Great Britain (13 Hyde Park Gdns., London, W2 2LX)
High Commissioner: (Vacant).

Of Great Britain in Sri Lanka (Galle Rd., Kollupitiya, Colombo 3)
High Commissioner: Sir John Nicholas, KCVO, CMG.

Of Sri Lanka in the USA (2148 Wyoming Ave., NW, Washington, D.C., 20008)
Ambassador: Ernest Corea

Of the USA in Sri Lanka (44 Galle Rd., Kollupitiya, Colombo 3)
Ambassador: John H. Reed.

Of Sri Lanka to the United Nations
Ambassador: Ignatius Benedict Fonseka

Books of Reference

The Sri Lanka Year Book. Department of Census and Statistics. Colombo, Annual
Census Publications from 1871
Economic Atlas. Department of Census and Statistics. Colombo, 1980
Performance 1980. Ministry of Plan Implementation, Colombo. 1981
Review of the Economy. Central Bank of Ceylon. Annual
Statistical Pocket-Book. Department of Census and Statistics. Colombo, 1983

de Silva, K. M. (ed.), *Sri Lanka: A Survey.* London, 1977.–*A History of Sri Lanka.* 1980
Ferguson's *Ceylon Directory.* Annual (from 1858)
Johnson, B. L. C., and Scrivenor, M. le M., *Sri Lanka: Land, People and Economy.* London, 1981.
Kearney, R. N., *The Politics of Ceylon (Sri Lanka).* Cornell Univ. Press, 1973
Ponnambalam, S., *Dependent Capitalism in Crisis: The Sri Lankan Economy 1948–80.* London, 1980.
Pyatt, G. and Roe, A., *Social Accounting for Development Planning with Special Reference to Sri Lanka.* CUP, 1977
Ratnasuriya, M. D., and Wijeratne, P. B. F., *Shorter Sinhalese-English Dictionary.* Colombo, 1949
Richards, P., and Gooneratne, W., *Basic Needs, Poverty and Government Policies in Sri Lanka.* Geneva, 1981.
Robinson, M. S., *Political Structure in a Changing Sinhalese Village.* CUP, 1975
Wilson, A. J., *Politics in Sri Lanka 1947-73.* London, 1974.—*The Gaullist System in Asia: the Constitution of Sri Lanka.* London, 1980

THE DEMOCRATIC REPUBLIC OF THE SUDAN

Capital: Khartoum
Population: 18·9m. (1981)
GNP per capita: US$470 (1980)

Jamhuryat es-Sudan
Al Democratia

HISTORY. Sudan was proclaimed a sovereign independent republic on 1 Jan. 1956. On 19 Dec. 1955 the Sudanese parliament passed unanimously a declaration that a fully independent state should be set up forthwith, and that a Council of State of 5 should temporarily assume the duties of Head of State. The Codomini, the UK and Egypt, gave their assent on 31 Dec. 1955.

For the history of the Condominium and the steps leading to independence, *see* THE STATESMAN'S YEAR-BOOK, 1955, pp. 340–341.

On 8 July 1965 the Constituent Assembly elected Ismail El-Azhari as President of the Supreme Council. Following a crisis in the coalition Cabinet the Prime Minister, Mohammed Ahmed Mahgoub resigned on 23 April 1969. For political history *see* THE STATESMAN'S YEAR-BOOK, 1973–74, p. 1333. The Government was taken over by a 10-man Revolutionary Council on 25 May 1969 under the Chairmanship of Col. Jaafar M. al Nemery. This Council was dissolved in 1972.

AREA AND POPULATION. Sudan is bounded north by Egypt, north-east by the Red Sea, east by Eritrea and Ethiopia, south by Kenya, Uganda and Zaïre, west by the Central African Republic and Chad, north-west by Libya. Sudan covers an area of 967,500 sq. miles (2·5m. sq. km). The Eritrea-Sudan frontier and the frontier with the Chad and Central African Republic have been delimited and demarcated, as also has the greater part of the frontier with Ethiopia.

The population according to the 1973 census was 14,171,732 (estimate (1981) 18·9m.), and consists mainly (two-thirds to four-fifths) of Moslem Arabs, and Nubians in the north and Nilotic and Negro tribes in the south. In 1983 there were 665,000 refugees in Sudan (460,000 from Ethiopia).

The capital is Khartoum (census, 1973, 333,921; estimate, 1980, 1m.). Other important cities are: Omdurman (299,401), Khartoum North (150,991), Port Sudan (132,631), Wadi Medani (106,776), Kassala (98,751), El Obeid (90,060), Al-Qadarif (66,465), Atbara (66,116), Kosti (65,257).

In 1980 there were 6 provinces.

CLIMATE. Lying wholly within the tropics, the country has a continental climate and only the Red Sea coast experiences maritime influences. Temperatures are generally high throughout the year, with May and June the hottest months. Winters are virtually cloudless and night temperatures are consequently cool. Summer is the rainy season inland, with amounts increasing from north to south, but the northern areas are virtually a desert region. On the Red Sea coast, most rain falls in winter. Khartoum. Jan. 74°F (23·3°C), July 89°F (31·7°C). Annual rainfall 6″ (157 mm).

CONSTITUTION AND GOVERNMENT. A new Constitution was introduced in 1973 (amended in 1975). Legislative power lies with a National Assembly of 151 members. Executive power lies with the President.

A measure of autonomy has been given to southern Sudan and a People's Assembly of 60 was elected in May 1980. The Assembly is situated at Juba.

The government in Jan. 1983 was composed as follows:

President and Prime Minister and Minister of Defence: Jaafar Mohammed Nemery (re-elected for a third term in April 1983).
First Vice-President, Director of State Security: Maj.-Gen. Umar Mohammed al Tayib. *Second Vice-President:* Lieut.-Gen. Joseph Lagu. *Transport and Communications:* Maj.-Gen. Khalid Hassan Abbas. *Attorney General:* Dr Hassan Abdalla al Turabi. *Finance and Economic Planning:* Ibrahim Munim Mansur. *Education:* Dr Uthman Said Ahmed Ismail. *Prime Minister's Office:* Abu Bakr Mohammed Osman Salih. *Presidential Affairs:* Dr Baha el Din Mohammed Idris. *Energy and Mining:* Dr Muhammad Sharif el Tuhami. *Guidance and National Information:* Dr Mohammed Uthman Abu Saq. *Co-operation, Trade and Supply:* Faroug Ibrahim al Magboul. *Internal Affairs:* Ahmed Abdel Rahman Muhammad. *Foreign Affairs:* Mohammed Mirghani Mubarak. *Adviser to Prime Minister, Minister for Manpower Affairs:* Hayder Muhammad Khabsoun. *President's Office:* Khalid al-Khayr Umar. *Minister and Legal Adviser in President's Office:* Dr Yusuf Mikael Bakhit. *Minister and Adviser in President's Office for Decentralization:* Shaykh Bashir ash-Shaykh. *Minister and Press Adviser to President:* Muhammad Mahjub Sulayman. *Construction and Public Works:* Babkir Ali at-Tawm. *Health:* Dr Ali Muhammad Fadl. *Industry:* Muhammad al-Bashir al-Waqi. *Chairman of the High Council for Religious Affairs:* Dafalla el Haj Yusuf. *Chairman of the National Council for Mass Sports and Youth Welfare:* Ali Muhammad Shummu. There were 5 Ministers of State.

On 9 Dec. 1965 the Constituent Assembly proscribed the Communist Party.

National flag: Three horizontal stripes of red, white, black, with a green triangle based on the hoist.

DEFENCE. Conscription had been legislated but not implemented in 1983.

Army. The Army is organized in 2 armoured, 1 parachute and 7 infantry brigades, with 3 artillery and 1 engineer regiments, and 3 Air Defence brigades. Equipment includes 70 T-54, 53 T-55, 17 T-34 and 20 M-60A3 main battle tanks. Strength (1984) 53,000 (including 3,000 in Air Defence brigades). Paramilitary forces are National Guard (500), Republican Guard (500) and Border Guard (2,500).

Navy. The Navy was established in 1962 with 4 patrol boats built in Yugoslavia and a training mission from the Yugoslav Navy until 1972. There are also 1 larger *ex*-Yugoslav patrol craft, 3 *ex*-Iranian coastal patrol craft, 4 *ex*-Iranian very small coastguard cutters, 2 *ex*-Yugoslav landing craft, 1 small oiler, 1 small survey vessel and 1 water carrier. Personnel in 1984 totalled 2,000 officers and men.

Air Force. The Air Force was built up with Soviet and Chinese assistance, and is now receiving equipment from the USA. Three combat squadrons are equipped with 10 F-5E Tiger II and 2 F-5F fighters, about 8 MiG-21 fighters and 18 J-5 (Chinese-built MiG-17) and J-6 (MiG-19) fighter-bombers. There is 1 transport squadron, with 6 C-130H Hercules and 4 DHC-5D Buffalo turboprop transports; 8 Turbo-Porter light transports; 1 helicopter squadron with 10 BO 105s; 3 BAC 145 jet armed trainers, and some Chinese-built FT-5 (MiG-17) advanced trainers. Personnel total about 3,000.

INTERNATIONAL RELATIONS

Membership. Sudan is a member of UN, OAU, the Arab League and is an ACP state of EEC.

ECONOMY

Planning. The 1978–83, 6-year development plan was published in 1977 and envisaged a total investment of £S2,670m.

Budget. The 1982–83 budget envisages revenue of £S1,300m. and expenditure of £S1,900m.

Currency. The monetary unit is the Sudanese *pound* (£S) divided into 100 *piastres* and 1,000 *milliemes*. Sudanese bank-notes of £S10, £S5, £S1, 50 and 25 *piastres* and Sudanese coins of P. 10, 5, 2; m/ms 10, 5, 2, 1 are in circulation. In March 1984, £1 = £S1·95; US$1 = £S0·77.

Banking. The Bank of Sudan opened in Feb. 1960 with an authorized capital of £S1·5m. as the central bank of the country; it has the sole right to issue currency. Its foreign reserves stood at £S12,631,000m. as at 31 Dec. 1978. All foreign banks were nationalized in 1970.

Weights and Measures. The metric system is in use.

ENERGY AND NATURAL RESOURCES

Oil. Two oil wells in the south-west produce 15,000 bbls per day of high quality oil. An oil refinery is being constructed and 2 oil companies are prospecting for oil and natural gas in the Red Sea area.

Minerals. The following minerals are known to exist in Sudan: gold, graphite, sulphur, chromium-ore (estimate, 9,400m. tonnes in 1979), iron-ore, manganese-ore, copper-ore, zinc-ore, fluorspar, natron, gypsum and anhydrite, magnesite, asbestos, talc, halite, kaolin, white mica, coal, diatomite (kieselguhr), limestone and dolomite, pumice, lead-ore, wollastonite, black sands, vermiculite pyrites.

Gold is being exploited on a small scale at Gabeit and at Abirkateib (in Kassala Province); alluvial gold is occasionally exploited in Southern Fung and Equatoria. Total production of good ores was 31 kg in 1978. Iron-ore was discovered in Red Sea area in 1976.

Manganese mining activities started in the 1950s but this industry did not develop well and in 1979 only 200 tonnes was produced. Processed and scrap white mica have been mined since the late fifties; it went out of production for almost a decade, but started again in 1970 when 170 tonnes were produced; 1979, 1,000 tonnes. A big deposit of vermiculite and a medium-sized deposit of pyrophyllite are known to occur in the Sinkat District. Reserves of metallurgical grade chromite occur in the Ingessana Hills, Blue Nile Province. Huge reserves of chrysotile asbestos are proved in this vicinity and also in Qala El Nahal area, Kassala Province. Deposits of magnesite, with or without talc, are known to occur in the Ingessana Hills and Qala El Nahal areas in addition to other occurrences in the Halaib area, Red Sea Province.

Agriculture. The Sudan is a predominantly agricultural country. Cotton is by far the most important cash crop on which the Sudan depends for earning foreign currency. The two types of cotton grown in the Sudan are: (*a*) long staple sakellaridis and sakel types (derivatives of sakellaridis), grown in Gezira, White Nile, Abdel Magid and private pump schemes; (*b*) short staple, mainly American types, in Equatoria and Nuba Mountains, generally by rain cultivation.

Production (1982) in 1,000 tonnes: Sorghum, 2,100; sugar-cane, 2,529; groundnuts, 800; cotton, 290; millet, 230; wheat, 150; sesame, 200; cotton seed, 300.

One of the largest sugar complexes in the world was opened at Kenana in March 1981. It is capable of processing 330,000 tonnes a year.

Livestock (1982): Cattle, 19·2m.; sheep, 18·5m.; goats, 13·2m.; poultry, 28m.

Forestry. Gum arabic, mainly hashab gum from *Acacia senegal*, is the sole forest produce exported from the Sudan on a major scale. Production (1980) 34,000 tons.

COMMERCE. Total trade for calendar years, in US$1m.:

	1978	1979	1980	1981
Imports[1]	624	736	1,127	1,643
Exports	563	514	689	796

[1] Including government imports.

Total trade between Sudan and UK (British Department of Trade returns, in £1,000 sterling):

	1979	1980	1981	1982	1983
Imports to UK	19,747	13,362	10,889	9,929	18,693
Exports and re-exports from UK	106,403	124,697	118,647	136,636	133,432

Tourism. There were 27,000 visitors in 1977.

COMMUNICATIONS

Roads. In the Northern Sudan there are about 550 km of asphalted roads, other than town roads. The remaining roads are only cleared tracks mostly impassable directly after rain. The El Gedaref to Kassala road (1,190 km) opened in 1980, and the section from Khartoum to Port Sudan was almost complete in 1980. In Upper Nile Province motor traffic is limited mostly to the months Jan.–May. In the other 5 southern provinces there are a number of good gravelled roads with permanent bridges which can be used all the year round, though minor roads become impassable after rain. Private cars (1972) 29,000; commercial vehicles, 21,500.

Railways. The main railway lines run from Khartoum to El Obeid *via* Wad Medani, Sennar Junction, Kosti and El Rahad (701 km); El Rahad to Nyala *via* Abu Zabad, Babanousa and Ed-Daein (698 km); Sennar Junction to Kassala *via* Gedaref (455 km) and to Roseires *via* Singa (220 km); Kassala to Port Sudan *via* Haiya Junction and Sinkat (550 km); Khartoum to Wadi Halfa *via* Shendi, El Dammer, Atbara, Berber and Abu Hamad Junction (924 km); Abu Hamad to Karima (248 km); Atbara to Haiya Junction (271 km); Babanousa to Wau (444 km). The main flow of exports and imports is to and from Port Sudan *via* Atbara and Kassala. The total length of line open for traffic (1982) was 4,786 km. The gauge is 1,067 mm. Several new lines are planned, including a link from Wadi Halfa across the Egyptian border. In 1981–82, the railways carried 1,149m. passenger-km and 1·7m. tonne-km.

Aviation. Sudan Airways is a government-owned airline, with its headquarters in Khartoum, operating domestic and international services. The latter include services to Asmara, Addis Ababa, Aden, Jiddah, Cairo, Athens, Rome, London, Beirut, Nairobi, N'djamena, Tripoli and Entebbe. In 1980 Sudan Airways carried 519,000 passengers and 6·8m. ton-kg of mail and freight.

Shipping. Supplementing the railways are regular river steamer services of the Sudan Railways, between Karima and Dongola, 319 km; from Khartoum to Kosti, 319 km; from Kosti to Juba, 1,436 km, and from Kosti to Gambeila, 1,069 km. Port Sudan is the country's only seaport; it is equipped with 13 berths. A modernization programme began in Feb. 1980.

Post and Broadcasting (1975). There are 213 permanent post and telegraph offices, 24 travelling post and telegraph offices and 372 agencies. There are 27 wireless telegraph and 99 radio-telephone stations, 36 automatic telephone exchanges and 340 telephone call boxes; number of telephones in 1982 was 68,503 (43,923 in Greater Khartoum). Radio receivers (1982) 1·4m. The television service broadcasts for 35 hours per week. There were (1982) 107,000 TV receivers.

Cinemas. In 1975 there were 58, seating capacity 112,000 and also 43 mobile units.

JUSTICE, RELIGION, EDUCATION AND WELFARE

Justice. The judiciary is a separate and independent department of state directly and solely responsible to the President of the Republic. The general administrative supervision and control of the judiciary is vested in the High Judicial Council.

Civil Justice is administered by the courts constituted under the Civil Justice Ordinance, namely the High Court of Justice—consisting of the Court of Appeal and Judges of the High Court, sitting as courts of original jurisdiction—and Province Courts—consisting of the Courts of Province and District Judges. The law administered is 'justice, equity and good conscience' in all cases where there is no special enactment. Procedure is governed by the Civil Justice Ordinance.

Justice in personal matters for the Moslem population is administered by the Mohammedan law courts, which form the Sharia Divisions of the Court of Appeal, High Courts and Kadis Courts; President of the Sharia Division is the Grand Kadi. The religious law of Islam is administered by these courts in the matters of inheritance, marriage, divorce, family relationship and charitable trusts.

Criminal Justice is administered by the courts constituted under the Code of Criminal Procedure, namely major courts, minor courts and magistrates' courts. Serious crimes are tried by major courts, which are composed of a President and 2 members and have the power to pass the death sentence. Major Courts are, as a rule, presided over by a Judge of the High Court appointed to a Provincial Circuit or a Province Judge. There is a right of appeal to the Chief Justice against any decision or order of a Major Court, and all its findings and sentences are subject to confirmation by him.

Lesser crimes are tried by Minor Courts consisting of 3 Magistrates and presided over by a Second Class Magistrate, and by Magistrates' Courts consisting of a single Magistrate or a bench of lay magistrates.

Religion. The population of the 12 northern provinces is almost entirely Moslem (Sunni), the majority of the 6 southern provinces is pagan. There are small Christian communities, with 2 Coptic Bishops, a Greek Orthodox metropolitan, 4 Anglican bishops, 4 Roman Catholic bishops and Greek Evangelical, Evangelical and Maronite congregations.

Education (1980). 5,729 primary schools had 1·4m. pupils; there were 428,703 pupils in secondary schools and 28,985 in tertiary education. In 1979 Khartoum University with 10 faculties had 8,777 students. The Khartoum branch of Cairo University with 4 faculties had about 5,000 students and the Islamic University of Omdurman with 3 faculties had 1,472 students. Juba University, founded in 1975 with 5 faculties had 425 students.

Health. In 1976 the Ministry of Health maintained 151 hospitals, 1,500 dispensaries and dressing stations, 139 health centres and 620 clinics (with together 17,324 beds) and 1,652 doctors.

DIPLOMATIC REPRESENTATIVES

Of Sudan in Great Britain (3 Cleveland Row, London, SW1A 1DD)
Ambassador: Sayed Abdullah el Hassan (accredited 1 Dec. 1983).

Of Great Britain in Sudan (New Aboulela Bldg, Barlaman Ave., Khartoum)
Ambassador: R. A. Fyjis-Walker, CMG, CVO.

Of Sudan in the USA (2210 Massachusetts Ave., NW, Washington, D.C., 20008)
Ambassador: Omer Salih Eissa.

Of the USA in Sudan (Sharia Ali Abdul Latif, Khartoum)
Ambassador: Hume A. Horan.

Of Sudan to the United Nations
Ambassador: Abdel-Rahman Abdalla.

Books of Reference

Sudan Almanac. Khartoum (annual)
al Rahim, M. Abd, *Changing Patterns of Civilian-Military Relations in the Sudan.* Uppsala, 1978
Barnett, T., *The Gezira Scheme: An Illusion of Development.* London, 1977
Daly, M. W., *Sudan.* [Bibliography] Oxford and Santa Barbara, 1983
El Bushra, El.-S., *An Atlas of Khartoum Conurbation.* Khartoum Univ Press, 1976
Holt, P. M., *A Modern History of the Sudan.* New York, 3rd ed. 1979
Lees, F. A., *The Economic and Political Development of the Sudan.* London, 1977
Nimeiri, S., *Evaluation of the Six Year Development Plan 1977-78—1982-83.* Khartoum, 1978
Wai, D. M. (ed.), *The Southern Sudan: The Problem of National Integration.* London, 1973
Wickens, G. E., *The Flora of Jebel Marra.* London, 1977
Woodward, P., *Condominium and Sudanese Nationalism.* London, 1979

SURINAME

Capital: Paramaribo
Population: 385,000 (1982)
GNP per capita: US$2,840 (1980)

HISTORY. At the peace of Breda (1667) between Great Britain and the United Netherlands, Suriname was assigned to the Netherlands in exchange for the colony of New Netherland in North America, and this was confirmed by the treaty of Westminster of Feb. 1674. Since then Suriname has been twice in British possession, 1799–1802 (when it was restored to the Batavian Republic at the peace of Amiens) and 1804–16, when it was returned to the Kingdom of the Netherlands according to the convention of London of 13 Aug. 1814, confirmed at the peace of Paris of 20 Nov. 1815. On 25 Nov. 1975, Suriname gained full independence and was admitted to the UN on 4 Dec. 1975.

AREA AND POPULATION. Suriname is situated on the north coast of South America and bounded on the north by the Atlantic ocean, on the east by the Marowijne River, which separates it from French Guiana, on the west by the Corantijn River, which separates it from Guyana, and on the south by forests and savannas, which separate it from Brazil.

Area, 163,820 sq. km. Census population (1980), 352,041. Estimate (1982) 385,000. The capital, Paramaribo, had (1971 census) 151,500 inhabitants. Annual rate of growth decreased from 4·34% during 1950–64 to 2·3% during 1964–71, mainly through severe migration primarily to the Netherlands. It is estimated that Suriname lost a total of 150,000 persons by migration (1975–80).

Suriname is divided into 9 districts (populations census 1980): Paramaribo (urban district), 67,718; Commewijne,14,082; Coronie, 2,756; Marowijne, 22,583; Nickerie, 34,598; Saramacca, 10,333; Suriname, 164,879; Brokopondo, 20,448 and Para, 14,644.

The official languages are Dutch and English. English is widely spoken next to Hindi, Javanese and Chinese as inter-group communication. A vernacular, called 'Sranan Tongo' or 'Surinamese', is used as a lingua franca. In 1976 the Government announced that Spanish would become the nation's principal working language.

CONSTITUTION AND GOVERNMENT. On 25 Feb. 1980 the Prime Minister, Henck Arron, was ousted in a *coup*. A National Military Council was established. In Feb. 1982 the civilian Prime Minister, Dr Henk Chin-a-Sen, was dismissed by the Military Council. In March there was an attempted *coup* by a right-wing military group but this failed. A 4-man military committee administered government departments from Feb. to April 1982 under the chairmanship of Lieut.-Col. Deysi Bouterse, the army commander and chairman of the National Military Council. In Jan. 1984 Errol Alibux was dismissed as Prime Minister by Lieut.-Col. Bouterse.

Before the 1982 *coup* there was a council of 13 ministers who were responsible to the Legislative Council (*Staten van Suriname*). The Legislative Council (39 members) was elected for a 4-year period by universal adult suffrage.

Flag: Horizontally green, red, green with the red of double width with yellow 5-pointed star in centre of red bar.

DEFENCE. Armed forces of the Republic of Suriname consist of regular local officers and conscripted personnel with a strength of about 5,000 in 1983. At least 1 Defender twin-engined light transport has been delivered to the armed force of Suriname, from a total order for four. Other equipment includes a Cessna 206 liaison aircraft.

INTERNATIONAL RELATIONS

Membership. Suriname is a member of UN, OAS and is an ACP state of the EEC.

ECONOMY

Planning. For 15 years from independence approximately 3,500m. guilders is available from the Netherlands to carry out an extensive social and economic development programme devised by a joint Dutch and Surinamese team of experts. This programme envisaged, the creation of greater employment and the improvement of the living conditions of the people, but by 1980 only a third of the aid had been spent.

Budget. The expenditures and local revenues (derived from import, export and excise duties, taxes on houses and estates, personal imports and some indirect taxes) are as follows (in 1,000 Suriname guilders):

	1976	1977	1978	1979	1980	1981
Revenues	354,600	541,100	623,100	423,200	479,100	491,900
Expenditures	404,900	581,500	650,500	415,300	475,900	539,600

Outstanding loans in 1980: Local, 51·3m.; foreign, 49·4m. Suriname guilders. Public debt in 1980, 100·7m. Suriname guilders.

Currency. Notes ranging from 5 to 1,000 *Suriname guilders* are legal tender. Currency notes of 1·00 and 2·50 guilders are issued by the Government. In March 1984, US$1 = 1·79 Suriname guilders; £1 sterling = 2·68 Suriname guilders.

Banking. The Central Bank of Suriname is a bankers' bank and also a bank of issue; the Surinaamsche Bank, the Algemene Bank Nederland and the Handels-, Krediet- en Industriebank, are commercial banks; the Suriname People's Credit Bank operates under the auspices of the Government; Surinaamse Postspaarbank (postal savings bank); Surinaamse Hypotheekbank NV (mortgage bank); Surinaamse Investerings Mij. NV (investment bank); Agentschap van de Maatschappij tot financiering van het Nationaal Herstel NV (long-term investments); National Development Bank; The Agrarian Bank.

Weights and Measures. The metric system is in force.

NATURAL RESOURCES

Minerals. Bauxite is the most important mineral; it is being mined in the Suriname and Marowijne districts. Fresh deposits have been found in the western areas. The ore is exported mainly to USA, but partly processed locally into alumina and aluminium. Production (1981 in 1,000 tonnes): Bauxite, 4,100; alumina, 1,248; aluminium, 40·5.

Agriculture. Agriculture is restricted to the alluvial coastal zone; cultivated area in 1981, 77,000 hectares. The staple food crop is rice; 55,000 hectares of paddy were planted in 1981, chiefly in the Nickerie, Commewijne, Saramacca and Coronie districts. Principal products (in 1,000 units) in 1981:

Sugar-cane (kg)	135,165	Maize on cob (kg)	408	Orange (pieces)	37,500
Cocoa (kg)	75	Bananas (kg)	38,775	Grapefruit (pieces)	2,300
Coffee (kg)	53	Rum 50% (litres)	949	Coconuts (pieces)	6,526
Paddy (kg)	265,572	Molasses (kg)	3,580	Palm oil (litres)	4,712

Livestock (1982): 51,000 head of cattle, 4,000 sheep, 9,000 goats, 18,000 pigs, 1·15m. poultry.

Forestry. Suriname has great timber resources. Production in 1981 included 244,000 cu. metres of logs, 80,000 cu. metres of sleepers, 19,000 cu. metres of plywood and 6,000 cu. metres of particle board.

Fishery. The fish catch in 1980 amounted to 2,100 tonnes and the shrimp catch, 3,100 tonnes.

INDUSTRY AND TRADE

Industry. In 1981, there were 3 large bauxite plants, 1 alumina and 1 aluminium smelting plants, sugar- and rice-mills, 3 paint factories, 2 fruit-juice plants, 3 shrimp freezing plants, a plywood factory, timber-mills, a milk pasteurization plant, a butter and margarine factory and a number of various medium and small industries. Shortage of skilled personnel inhibits expansion.

Commerce. Imports and exports in calendar years (in 1 m. Suriname guilders):

	1976	1977	1978	1979	1980
Imports	505·2	642·7	681·3	733·5	900·3
Exports	542·4	617·9	702·4	792·7	918·2

Principal exports in 1981 (in 1,000 Suriname guilders): Alumina, 472,400; bauxite, 112,700; aluminium, 87,400; rice, 63,500; citrus fruit, 689; plywood, 10,202; bananas, 12,202; particle board, 739; shrimp, 64,293; fish, 1,769; vegetables, 3,101.

Principal imports in 1979 (in 1,000 Suriname guilders): Raw and auxiliary materials, 195,480; investment goods, 87,300; fuels and lubricants, 64,980; textile yarn and fabrics, 13,140; foodstuffs, cars and motorcycles, 11,340.

Total trade between Suriname and UK (British Department of Trade returns, in £1,000 sterling):

	1979	1980	1981	1982	1983
Imports to UK	16,825	20,181	11,416	7,593	11,584
Exports and re-exports from UK	7,707	8,112	8,074	10,586	8,914

COMMUNICATIONS

Roads. There are 1,335 km of main roads. Two of them lead from Paramaribo to the bauxite centres of Smalkalden (29 km) and Paranam (30 km) and to the airport of Zanderij (49 km). Another main road runs across the districts of Saramacca (71 km) and Coronie (68 km), a fourth across the Commewijne district (41 km) and a fifth in the Marowijne district, from the bauxite centre Moengo to Albina (45 km). The 'East–West connexion' is almost completed, linking the Corantijn and the Marowijne rivers (375 km).

In 1979 there were 25,558 passenger cars, 6,823 trucks, 1,872 buses, 39,519 powered bicycles and 1,831 motor cycles.

Railway. There is a single-track railway, running from Onverwacht to Bronsweg (86 km); part of the track, from Paramaribo to Onverwacht (34 km) has been removed. Another single-track railway runs from Apoera to the Bakhuis Mountains.

Aviation. Regular air services are maintained by KLM, SLM, Aero Cubano and Cruzeiro do Sul. The international airfield at Zanderij is capable of handling all types of planes.

Suriname Airways Ltd provides daily services between all major districts and maintains also a charter service.

In 1975, 1,205 aircraft landed at Zanderij airport with 40,416 passengers and 1,225 tons of incoming mail and freight.

Shipping. The Royal Netherlands Steamship Co. plies between Amsterdam, Rotterdam, Antwerp, Hamburg and Paramaribo, and New York, Baltimore, New Orleans and Paramaribo. Regular sailings are made to Georgetown, Ciudad Bolivar and most Caribbean ports. The Suriname Navigation Co. maintains services from Paramaribo to Georgetown and Cayenne, and once a month to the Caribbean area. A French and an Italian company maintain passenger services to Europe. The Alcoa Steamship Co. has a fortnightly service to New York, Baltimore, Mobile and New Orleans; a Japanese line sails once a month from Hong Kong and Yokohama to Paramaribo; the Boomerang Line maintains a monthly freight and passenger service between Suriname and Australia. In 1981, 1,021 vessels totalling 4·93m. GRT entered Paramaribo.

Post and Broadcasting. Automatic telephone service links most of the districts in the interior. In 1982 there were 27,495 telephones. Wireless telephone connects

Suriname with the Netherlands, USA, Curaçao, Guyana, French Guiana and Trinidad. There are 6 broadcasting and 1 television stations. In 1974 there were 170,000 radios and 36,000 TV sets. Automatic telex was established in 1972.

Cinemas. In 1981 there were 18 cinemas and 1 drive-in cinema.

Newspapers (1982). There is one daily newspaper.

JUSTICE, RELIGION, EDUCATION AND WELFARE

Justice. There is a court of justice, whose members are nominated by the President. There are 3 cantonal courts.

Religion. There is entire religious liberty. At the end of 1971 the various religious bodies were: Hindus, 112,047; Moslems, 74,078; Roman Catholics, 70,175; Moravian Brethren, 51,868; Reformed and Lutheran, 3,911; Confucians, 80; others, 27,228.

Education. During school-year 1979–80 there were 748 schools with a total of 139,516 pupils and 6,950 teachers. There are also a University with faculties of medicine and law, social, technical and economic studies, 5 technical schools and 5 teachers' training colleges.

Schooling is compulsory from 6 to 12 years of age. Primary education is free and is undertaken by the Government in public schools and by the Roman Catholic and Protestant Missions in denominational schools.

Social Security. The Government subsidizes orphanages and other religious or philanthropical institutions, and maintains an almshouse and institutions for delinquent boys and girls. There are 13 modern hospitals in the country, 4 of which are operated by missions, 2 by a private company, 1 by the military forces and 6 by the Government.

DIPLOMATIC REPRESENTATIVES

Of Great Britain in Suriname
Ambassador: W. K. Slatcher, CMG, CVO (resides in Georgetown).

Of Suriname in the USA (2600 Virginia Ave., NW, Washington, D.C. 20037)
Ambassador: Henricus A. F. Heidweiller.

Of the USA in Suriname (Dr Sophie Redmondstraat 129, Paramaribo)
Ambassador: Robert W. Duemling.

Of Suriname to the United Nations
Ambassador: (Vacant).

Books of Reference

Statistical Information: The General Bureau of Statistics in Paramaribo was established on 1 Jan. 1947. Its publications comprise trade statistics, *Suriname in Figures* (including, from 1953, the former *Handelsstatistiek*) and *Statistische Berichten*.

Economische Voorlichting Suriname. Ministry of Economic Affairs, Paramaribo
Annual Report of the Central Bank of Suriname

SWAZILAND

Capital: Mbabane
Population: 585,000 (1982)
GNP per capita: US$680 (1980)

HISTORY. The Swazi migrated into the country to which they have given their name, in the last half of the 18th century. They settled first in what is now southern Swaziland, but moved northwards under their chief, Sobhuza–known also to the Swazi as Somhlolo. Sobhuza died in 1838 and was succeeded by Mswati. The further order of succession has been Mbandzeni and Bhunu, whose son, Sobhuza II, was installed as King of the Swazi nation in 1921 after a long minority.

The independence of the Swazis was guaranteed in the conventions of 1881 and 1884 between the British Government and the Government of the South African Republic. In 1890, soon after the death of Mbandzeni, a provisional government was established representative of the Swazis, the British and the South African Republic Governments. In 1894 the South African Republic was given powers of protection and administration. In 1902, after the conclusion of the Boer War, a special commissioner took charge, and under an order-in-council in 1903 the Governor of the Transvaal administered the territory, through the Special Commissioner. Swaziland became independent on 6 Sept. 1968.

On 25 April 1967 the British Government gave the country internal self-government. It changed the country's status to that of a protected state with the Ngwenyama, Sobhuza II, recognized as King of Swaziland and head of state. King Sobhuza died on 21 Aug. 1982.

AREA AND POPULATION. Swaziland is bounded on the north, west and south by the Transvaal Province, and on the east by Mozambique and Zululand. The area is 6,705 sq. miles (17,400 sq. km).

The country is divided geographically into 4 longitudinal regions running from north to south; 3 of roughly equal width–Highveld (westernmost), Middleveld, Lowveld–and the Lubombo plateau in the east. The mountainous region on the west rises to an altitude of over 6,000 ft (1,800 metres). The Middleveld is mostly between 1,700 and 3,000 ft, while the Lowveld has an average height of not more than 1,000 ft (300 metres). The whole country is now virtually free from malaria.

Population (census 1976), 527,791. Estimate (1982) 585,000. Mbabane, the administrative capital (22,262). The main urban areas with 1971 populations are: Manzini (16,000); Havelock Mine (4,500); Siteki (3,600); Big Bend (2,900); Mhlume (2,200); Nhlangano (1,700) and Pigg's Peak (1,400).

CLIMATE. A temperate climate with two seasons. Nov. to March is the wet season, when temperatures range from mild to hot, with frequent thunderstorms. The cool, dry season from May to Sept. is characterised by clear, bright sunny days. Mbabane. Jan. 68° F (20°C), July 54° F (12·2°C). Annual rainfall 56″ (1,402 mm).

CONSTITUTION AND GOVERNMENT. Britain's protection ended at independence, when a Constitution similar to the 1967 Constitution was brought into force. The general elections (by universal adult franchise) in April 1967 gave the royalist and traditional Imbokodvo National Movement all 24 seats. The Parliament consists of a House of Assembly, with 24 elected and 6 nominated members and the Attorney-General, who has no vote, and a Senate comprising 12 members, 6 of whom are elected by the House of Assembly and 6 appointed by the King. The executive authority is vested in the King and exercised through a Cabinet presided over by the Prime Minister, and consisting of the Prime Minister, the Deputy Prime Minister and up to 8 other ministers. In April 1973 the King assumed supreme power and the Constitution was suspended and in 1976 it was abolished. On 27 Oct. 1978 a general election took place to elect an electoral college of 80 members. This college elected 40 members for the National Assembly. The King nominated 10 additional members.

Regent: Queen Ntombi.
In Dec. 1983, the Cabinet was composed as follows:
Prime Minister: Prince Bhekimpi Dlamini.
Deputy Prime Minister: B. Sibandze. *Home Affairs:* Prince Gabheni Dlamini.
Agriculture and Cooperatives: A. K. Hlophe. *Health:* Dr S. Hynd. *Education:* S.
D. Dlamini. *Finance:* J. L. F. Simelane. *Justice:* P. L. Dlamini. *Power and Tele-*
communications: Dr V. S. Leibrandt. *Commerce, Industry, Mines and Tourism:*
Prince Nqaba Dlamini. *Foreign Affairs:* R. V. Dlamini. *Establishments and Train-*
ing: E. B. Simelane.

National flag. Horizontally 5 unequal stripes of blue, yellow, red, yellow, blue;
in the centre of the red strip an African shield of black and white, behind which are
2 assegais and a staff, all laid horizontally.

Local Government. The country is divided into the 4 districts of Shiselweni,
Lubombo, Manzini and Hhohho. They are administered by District Commissioners.

DEFENCE

Army Air Wing. First military aircraft acquired by Swaziland, in mid-1979, were 2
Israeli-built Arava light twin-turboprop transports with underwing weapon attachments for light attack duties.

INTERNATIONAL RELATIONS

Membership. Swaziland is a member of UN, OAU, the Commonwealth and is an
ACP state of EEC.

ECONOMY

Budget. Revenue and expenditure (in 1,000 emalangeni) for financial years ending
31 March:

	1978–79	1979–80	1981–82
Revenue	87,000	115,000	139,000
Expenditure	169,000	169,000	199,000

Currency. The currency in circulation in Swaziland is the *emalangeni,* but remains
in the rand monetary area. In March 1984, £1=1·77 *emalangeni;* US$1=1·19
emalangeni.

Banking. Barclays Bank International and the Standard Bank Ltd maintain
branches at Mbabane and Manzini; sub-branches and agencies are operated in 17
other places. Bank rates are those in force throughout South Africa and are prescribed by the main South African offices of the 2 banks. The Swaziland Credit and
Savings Bank, now known as The Swazi Bank, a statutory body, was opened in
1965. It specializes in credit for agriculture and low-cost housing. Its head office is
in Mbabane and it has branches or agencies at 3 other places. A fourth bank, The
Bank of Credit and Commerce International opened in Sept. 1978; its head office is
in Manzini and it has a branch in Mbabane.

ENERGY AND NATURAL RESOURCES

Minerals. Swaziland produced a large tonnage of iron ore from the Ngwenya mine
near Mbabane (but mining has now ceased) and asbestos from the Havelock Mine
(38,046 tons in 1977). Coal is mined at Mpaka (150,000 tons in 1980). Small quantities of quarry stone, kaolin, barytes and pyrophyllite are also mined.
     A railway has been built from the Ngwenya hæmatite deposits to Goba, in
Mozambique, chiefly for the transportation of iron ore. The extensive deposits of
low-volatile bituminous coal in the Lowveld are being worked to provide coal for
the railway, sugar-mills and export.

Agriculture. Some 60% of the country, which covers 4,290,944 acres, is reserved
for occupation by the Swazi. The main crops are sugar (employing 13,000 people),

citrus and rice, all of which are grown under irrigation, and cotton, maize (the staple product), sorghum, tobacco and pineapples. It is usually necessary to import maize from South Africa. Sugar, first produced in 1958, and woodpulp and other forest products are the two main agricultural exports.

Livestock (1982): Cattle, 675,000; goats, 330,000; sheep, 40,000; poultry, 620,000.

COMMERCE. By agreement with the Republic of South Africa, Swaziland is united in a customs union with the republic and receives a *pro rata* share of the customs dues collected.

Total exports in 1982 amounted to E332m. The chief items were: Sugar, woodpulp and other forest products, asbestos, iron ore, citrus fruit, meat and meat products. Imports in 1982 were E543m.

Total trade between Swaziland and UK (British Department of Trade returns, in £1,000 sterling):

	1978	1979	1980	1981	1982	1983
Imports to UK	34,021	37,361	30,438	23,884	40,049	23,965
Exports and re-exports from UK	1,580	1,333	691	7,132	7,654	3,536

Tourism. There were 82,000 visitors in 1981.

COMMUNICATIONS

Roads. There is daily (except Sundays) communication by railway motor-buses between Manzini, Mbabane and Breyten; Manzini, Mankayana and Piet Retief. There are 241 km of tarred trunk roads. Total length of roads 2,750 km.

Railways. The 389 km railway of 1,067 mm gauge built in 1962–64 to haul iron ore from Kadake to Maputo in Mozambique for export was (1982) largely out of use as the iron ore is worked out. Part of the route is being used for a new direct line from Koomatipoort to Richards Bay in the Republic of South Africa, while a southern link to the Republic of South Africa was opened in 1978. In 1981 the railway carried 1·2m. tonnes.

Aviation. The country's chief airport is at Matsapa. It is served by Royal Swazi National Airways connecting with Johannesburg, Durban, Lusaka, Nairobi, Mauritius and Salisbury and South African Airways, connecting with Johannesburg and Durban. Lesotho National Airways flies from Matsapa to Maseru.

Post. There were (1980) 55 post offices, 2 telephone-telegraph agencies and 10 telephone agencies. There were, in Jan. 1982, 15,357 telephones in the country.

Cinemas. There were 5 cinemas in 1980 with a total seating capacity of 1,625.

Newspapers. There were in 1983 one daily, one weekly and one monthly newspaper.

JUSTICE, RELIGION, EDUCATION AND WELFARE

Justice. The judiciary is headed by the Chief Justice. A High Court having full jurisdiction and subordinate courts presided over by Magistrates and District Officers are in existence. During 1969 there were 6,624 convictions in subordinate courts and 36 convictions in the High Court.

There is a Court of Appeal with a President and 3 Judges. It deals with appeals from the High Court. There are 16 Swazi courts of first instance, 2 Swazi courts of appeal and a Higher Swazi Court of Appeal. The channel of appeal lies from Swazi Court of first instance to Swazi Court of Appeal, to Higher Swazi Court of Appeal, to the Judicial Commissioner and thence to the High Court of Swaziland.

Religion. In 1975 there were about 95,000 Christians and about 50,000 adults holding traditional beliefs. A large number of churches and missionary societies are established throughout the country and, in addition to evangelism, are doing important work in the fields of education and medicine. In the larger centres there are churches of several denominations—Protestant, Roman Catholics and others.

Education. In 1982 there were 556 schools with 119,913 pupils in primary classes and 24,826 in secondary classes. The Swaziland Agricultural College and University Centre at Luyengo was opened in Oct. 1966. Technical and vocational training classes are run at the Government's Industrial Training Institute and its Staff Training Institute. The Government also operates a police college. There are 2 teacher training colleges. In 1975 Botswana and Swaziland formed a joint university with campuses in each territory.

Health. In 1980 there were 80 doctors and about 1,560 hospital beds.

DIPLOMATIC REPRESENTATIVES

Of Swaziland in Great Britain (58 Pont St., London SW1X 0AE)
High Commissioner: George Mbikwakhe Mamba (accredited 16 Feb. 1978).

Of Great Britain in Swaziland (Allister Miller St., Mbabane)
High Commissioner: Martin Reith.

Of Swaziland in the USA (4301 Connecticut Ave., NW, Washington, D.C., 20008)
Ambassador: Peter H. Mtetwa.

Of the USA in Swaziland (PO Box 199, Mbabane)
Ambassador: Robert H. Phinny.

Of Swaziland to the United Nations
Ambassador: N. M. Malinga.

Books of Reference

The Kingdom of Swaziland. Swaziland Government Information Services, 1968
Post Independence Development Plan. Mbabane, 1969
Grotpeter, J. J., *Historical Dictionary of Swaziland.* Metuchen, 1975
Jones, D., *Aid and Development in Southern Africa.* London, 1977
Kuper, H., *An African Aristocracy.* New ed. London, 1961.—*The Uniform of Colour.* Johannesburg, 1947.—*The Swazi: An Ethnographical Survey.* London, 1952
Matsebula, J. S. M., *A History of Swaziland.* London, 1972
Nyeko, B., *Swaziland.* [Bibliography] Oxford and Santa Barbara, 1982

SWEDEN

Konungariket Sverige

Capital: Stockholm
Population: 8·3m. (1982)
GNP per capita: US$10,021 (1982)

HISTORY. Organized as an independent unified state in the 10th century, Sweden became a constitutional monarchy in 1809. In 1809 she also ceded Finland to Russia. In 1815 German possessions were ceded to Prussia and Sweden was united with Norway, which union lasted until 1905.

AREA AND POPULATION. The first census took place in 1749, and it was repeated at first every third year, and, after 1775, every fifth year. Since 1860 a general census has been taken every 10 years and, in addition, in 1935, 1945, 1965 and 1975.

Latest census figures: 1940, 6,371,432 (annual increase since 1935: 0·38%); 1950, 7,041,829 (1·1% since 1945); 1960, 7,495,316 (0·64% since 1950); 1965, 7,766,424 (1·04% since 1960); 1970, 8,076,903 (1·04% since 1965); 1975, 8,208,544 (1·02% since 1970); 1980, 8,320,438 (1·01% since 1975).

Counties (Län)	Land area: sq. km	Census population 15 Sept. 1980	Estimated population 31 Dec. 1982	Pop. per sq. km 31 Dec. 1982
Stockholm (city) [1]	} 6,488	1,527,330	1,544,454	238
Stockholm (county) [1]				
Uppsala	6,989	243,273	247,068	35
Södermanland	6,061	252,515	251,610	42
Östergötland	10,569	393,141	392,214	37
Jönköping	9,944	303,354	301,439	30
Kronoberg	8,452	173,619	174,021	21
Kalmar	11,166	241,851	240,823	22
Gotland	3,140	55,362	55,897	18
Blekinge	2,941	153,880	152,091	52
Kristianstad	6,089	280,071	280,299	46
Malmöhus	4,939	743,746	744,336	151
Halland	5,454	230,679	234,339	43
Göteborg and Bohus	5,141	711,934	709,838	138
Älvsborg	11,395	425,189	425,110	37
Skaraborg	7,938	269,715	270,613	34
Värmland	17,582	284,477	282,115	16
Örebro	8,515	274,580	273,128	32
Västmanland	6,302	259,789	257,783	41
Kopparberg	28,264	287,250	286,278	10
Gävleborg	18,191	294,165	292,723	16
Västernorrland	21,711	268,385	266,038	12
Jämtland	49,916	135,084	134,865	3
Västerbotten	55,401	243,723	245,055	4
Norrbotten	98,919	267,321	265,347	3
Total	411,506 [2]	8,320,438	8,327,484	20

[1] From Jan. 1968 Stockholm city and Stockholm county have been united in Stockholm county. [2] Total area of Sweden, 449,964 sq. km.

On 31 Dec. 1982 there were 4,117,357 males and 4,210,127 females.

On 31 Dec. 1982 aliens in Sweden numbered 405,475. Of these, 160,040 were Finns, 38,491 Yugoslavs, 26,963 Danes, 13,141 Greeks, 24,864 Norwegians, 12,977 Germans, 4,368 Italians and 3,180 Austrians.

Vital statistics for calendar years:

	Total living births	Of which illegitimate [1]	Stillborn	Marriages	Divorces	Deaths exclusive of still-born
1980	97,064	38,558	436	37,569	19,887	91,800
1981	94,065	38,742	380	37,793	20,198	92,034
1982	92,748	38,915	374	37,051	20,766	90,671

[1] From 1977 children born to women who were single, divorced or widowed.

Immigration: 1980, 39,426; 1981, 32,272; 1982, 30,381. Emigration: 1980, 29,389; 1981, 29,440; 1982, 28,381.

In 1860 the urban population numbered 435,000 (11% of the total population) and on 31 Dec. 1965, 4,177,212 (54%); including other densely populated areas, the urbanized population in 1965 was 77·4%.

On 15 Sept. 1980, population in densely populated areas was 6,910,431 (83·1%).

Population of largest communities, 31 Dec. 1982:

Stockholm	649,686	Halmstad	76,355	Falun	51,116
Göteborg	425,875	Skellefteå	74,152	Solna	49,606
Malmö	230,381	Karlstad	73,810	Täby	49,026
Uppsala	149,300	Kristianstad	69,197	Hässleholm	48,839
Norrköping	118,236	Huddinge	68,517	Trollhättan	48,773
Västerås	117,793	Luleå	66,354	Mölndal	48,289
Örebro	117,367	Botkyrka	66,062	Borlänge	46,766
Linköping	113,993	Växjö	65,450	Sollentuna	46,633
Jönköping	107,134	Nyköping	64,548	Uddevalla	46,053
Helsingborg	102,952	Örnsköldsvik	60,235	Skövde	45,956
Borås	100,715	Haninge	59,665	Kungsbacka	45,176
Sundsvall	94,360	Karlskrona	59,597	Varberg	45,035
Eskilstuna	89,479	Nacka	58,399	Sandviken	41,956
Gävle	87,621	Östersund	55,981	Motala	41,478
Umeå	82,946	Gotland	55,897	Norrtälje	41,469
Södertälje	79,792	Järfälla	54,823	Västervik	40,906
Lund	79,744	Kalmar	53,499		

Befolkningsförändringar (Population Changes). Annual. 3 vols. Statistics Sweden, Stockholm
Folkmängd 31 Dec. (Population). Annual. 3 vols. Statistics Sweden, Stockholm
Historisk statistik för Sverige. I: Befolkning (Population), 1720–1967. 2nd ed. Statistics
Sweden, Stockholm, 1969

CLIMATE. North Sweden suffers from severe winters, with snow lying for 4–7 months. Summers are fine but cool, with long daylight hours. Further south, winters are less cold, summers are warm and rainfall generally well-distributed over the year, though with a slight summer maximum. Stockholm. Jan. 27°F (−2·7°C), July 62°F (16·5°C). Annual rainfall 21·5″ (536 mm).

REIGNING KING. Carl XVI Gustaf, born 30 April 1946, succeeded on the death of his grandfather Gustaf VI Adolf, 15 Sept. 1973, married 19 June 1976 to *Silvia* Renate Sommerlath, born 23 Dec. 1943 (Queen of Sweden). *Daughter* and *Heir Apparent:* Crown Princess Victoria Ingrid Alice Désirée, Duchess of Västergötland, born 14 July 1977; *son:* Prince Carl Philip Edmund Bertil, Duke of Värmland, born 13 May 1979; *daughter:* Princess Madeleine Thérèse Amelie Josephine, Duchess of Hälsingland and Gästrikland, born 10 June 1982.

Sisters of the King. Princess Margaretha, born 31 Oct. 1934, married 30 June 1964 to Mr John Ambler; Princess Birgitta (Princess of Sweden), born 19 Jan. 1937, married 25 May 1961 (civil marriage) and 30 May 1961 (religious ceremony) to Johann Georg, Prince of Hohenzollern; Princess Désirée, born 2 June 1938, married 5 June 1964 to Baron Niclas Silfverschiold; Princess Christina, born 3 Aug. 1943, married 15 June 1974 to Tord Magnuson.

Uncles of the King. Sigvard, Count of Wisborg, born on 7 June 1907; Prince Bertil, Duke of Halland, born on 28 Feb. 1912, married 7 Dec. 1976 to Lilian May Davies, born 30 Aug. 1915 (Princess of Sweden, Duchess of Halland); Carl Johan, Count of Wisborg, born on 31 Oct. 1916.

Aunt of the King. Princess Ingrid (Princess of Sweden), born 28 March 1910, married 24 May 1935 to Frederik, Crown Prince of Denmark (King Frederik IX), died 14 Jan. 1972.

The following is a list of the kings and queens of Sweden, with the dates of their accession from the accession of the House of Vasa:

House of Vasa		House of Pfalz-Zwei-brücken (contd.)		House of Bernadotte	
Gustaf I	1521			Carl XIV Johan	1818
Eric XIV	1560	Carl XII	1697	Oscar I	1844
Johan III	1568	Ulrica Eleonora	1719	Carl XV	1859
Sigismund	1592			Oscar II	1872
Carl IX	1599	House of Hesse		Gustaf V	1907
Gustaf II Adolf	1611	Fredrik I	1720	Gustaf VI Adolf	1950
Christina	1632			Carl XVI Gustaf	1973
		House of Holstein-Gottorp			
House of Pfalz-Zwei-brücken		Adolf Fredrik	1751		
		Gustaf III	1771		
Carl X Gustaf	1654	Gustaf IV Adolf	1792		
Carl XI	1660	Carl XIII	1809		

The royal family of Sweden have a civil list of 10·7m. kronor; this does not include the maintenance of the royal palaces.

CONSTITUTION AND GOVERNMENT. Sweden's present Constitution came into force in 1975 and replaced the 1809 Constitution. Under the present Constitution Sweden is a representative and parliamentary democracy. Parliament (*Riksdag*) is declared to be the central organ of government. The executive power of the country is vested in the Government, which is responsible to Parliament. The King is Head of State, but he does not participate in the government of the country. Since 1971 Parliament has consisted of one chamber. It has 349 members, who are elected for a period of 3 years in direct, general elections.

Every man and woman who has reached the age of 18 years on election-day itself, and who is not under wardship has the right to vote and to stand for election.

The manner of election to the *Riksdag* is proportional. The country is divided into 28 constituencies. In these constituencies 310 members are elected. The remaining 39 seats constitute a nation-wide pool intended to give absolute proportionality to parties that receive at least 4% of the votes. A party receiving less than 4% of the votes in the country is, however, entitled to participate in the distribution of seats in a constituency, if it has obtained at least 12% of the votes cast there.

The *Riksdag*, elected 1982, has 166 Social Democrats, 86 Conservatives, 56 Centre Party, 21 Liberals and 20 Communists.

The Social Democratic Cabinet was composed as follows in Feb. 1984:

Prime Minister: Olof Palme.

Deputy Prime Minister and Minister with special responsibility for Research: Ingvar Carlsson. *Agriculture:* Svante Lundkvist. *Finance:* Kjell-Olof Feldt. *Health and Social Affairs, with special responsibility for the Social and Health Services:* Gertrud Sigurdsen. *Housing:* Hans Gustafsson. *Labour:* Anna-Greta Leijon. *Education and Cultural Affairs:* Lena Hjelm-Wallen. *Industry:* Thage Peterson. *Health and Social Affairs:* Sten Andersson. *Justice:* Sten Wickbom. *Transport and Communications:* Curt Boström. *Foreign Affairs:* Lennart Bodström. *Education, with special responsibility for cultural affairs, the mass media and comprehensive schools:* Bengt Göransson. *Labour, with special responsibility for immigrant and equality affairs:* Anita Gradin. *Industry, with special responsibility for energy questions:* Birgitta Dahl. *Industry, with special responsibility for state-owned enterprises:* Roine Carlsson. *Public Administration:* Bo Holmberg. *Foreign Affairs, with special responsibility for foreign trade:* Mats Hellström. *Defence:* Anders Thunborg.

All the members of the Cabinet are responsible for the acts of the Government.

Public administration in Sweden is characterized by a unique degree of functional decentralization. The Ministries are not really administrative agencies. They prepare bills for the *Riksdag*, issue general directives and make higher appointments, but, as a rule, do not take individual administrative decisions. The routine administrative work is attended to by the central boards *(centrala ämbetsverk)*. Each board's sphere of activity depends partly on its organization which is decided by the appropriations granted by the *Riksdag*. The Government often asks the boards' opinion on proposed measures.

National flag: Blue with a yellow Scandinavian cross.

National anthem: Du gamla, du fria, du fjällhöga nord (words by R. Dybeck, 1844; folk-tune).

The official language is Swedish. The capital is Stockholm.

Regional and Local Government. For national administrative purposes Sweden is divided into 24 counties *(län)*, in each of which the central government is represented by a state county administrative board *(länsstyrelse)*. The governor *(landshövding)*, appointed by the government, is chairman of the board, which in addition to the governor has 14 members elected by the county council.

Local government and the levying of local taxes are based on the fundamental law and are regulated by the local government act and special acts. According to the local government act Sweden is divided into municipalities in which all men and women who have reached the age of 18 on election-day itself, and not under wardship, are entitled to elect the municipal council. These councils are named *kommunfullmäktige*. The number of municipalities has, since 1951, been reduced from about 2,500 to 284. The municipalities deal with a great variety of different tasks such as social welfare, education and culture, public health, town planning, housing etc. Each county, except Gotland, which consists of only one municipality, has a county council *(landsting)* elected by men and women who enjoy local suffrage. The county councils chiefly administer the health services and medical care. The municipalities of Gothenburg and Malmö do not belong to county councils. Ecclesiastical affairs in all parishes with more than 1,000 inhabitants are dealt with by church councils *(kyrkofullmäktige)*; smaller parishes may make the same arrangement. All elections are conducted on a proportional basis.

Elder, N. C. M., *Government in Sweden: The Executive at Work.* Oxford, 1970
Gustafsson, A., *Local Government in Sweden.* Stockholm, 1983
Lewin, L., Jansson, B., and Sörbom, D., *The Swedish Electorate 1887–1968.* Stockholm, 1972
Vinde, P., *Swedish Government Administration.* 2nd rev. ed. Stockholm, 1978

DEFENCE. A Supreme Commander is, under the Government, in command of the three services. He is assisted by the Defence Staff under a chief of staff.

The military forces are recruited on the principle of national service, supplemented by voluntarily enlisted personnel who form the permanent cadres for training purposes, staff duties, etc.

Liability to service commences at the age of 18, and lasts till the end of the 47th year. The period of training for the Army and Navy is 7½-15 months and for the Airforce 8-15 months.

The territorial organization consists of 6 military commands each one under a general officer commanding.

Army. The C.-in-C. of the Royal Swedish Army has at his disposal the Army Staff under a chief of staff. The peace-time Army consists for training purposes of 16 infantry, 3 cavalry, 6 armour, 7 artillery, 5 AA, 3 engineer, 3 signal and 4 Army Service Corps units, most of which are called 'regiments' *(regementen)*.

The Army is organized and equipped with regard to the varying geographical and climatic conditions of the country. The voluntary Home Guard *(Hemvärnet)* with a total strength of more than 100,000 men ready for action within 2 hours, raised during the War continues to be in force.

Sweden's ground forces, total 900,000 men (including the voluntary Home Guard), can be said to consist of an Army which for the most part is on indefinite leave, but which on short notice can be ready for action. One of the basic principles of the Swedish system of mobilization is the local recruitment of as many units as possible. The storage of equipment and supplies is decentralized on more than 3,000 places.

The active personnel of the Army comprises (1983) about 55,000, including 36,000 conscripts doing basic training.

Navy. The C.-in-C. of the Royal Swedish Navy is assisted by the Chief of Naval Staff, the Inspector of the Navy and the Inspector of the Coast Artillery. The Navy is divided into two branches, the Royal Navy and the Royal Coast Artillery. There are 3 Naval Base Areas: those of the southern, eastern and western coasts. The coast artillery defence areas are those of the Stockholm archipelago, Blekinge, Gothenburg, Gotland and Norrland. There are 5 coastal artillery regiments.

There are 12 diesel-powered patrol submarines, 2 old destroyers, 16 fast missile craft, 12 fast missile/torpedo boats, 6 fast torpedo boats, 2 patrol craft 3 minelayers, 9 coastal minelayers, 10 coastal minesweepers, 4 patrol vessels (ex-minesweepers), 18 inshore minesweepers, 30 coastal patrol craft, 2 mine transports, 16 minelaying boats, 3 torpedo recovery vessels, 16 tenders, 4 surveying vessels, 8 icebreakers, 2 oilers, 1 salvage vessel, 9 artillery landing craft, 81 utility landing craft, 54 minor landing craft, 2 sail training ships, 1 supply ship, 2 water carriers and 17 tugs.

Four submarines, 2 missile armed fast attack craft leaders (officially classed as corvettes), 4 coastal minelayers and 6 coastal minesweepers are under construction or projected.

The Naval Air Arm comprises 10 Boeing Vertol 107 helicopters, 10 JetRanger helicopters and 3 Alouette II training helicopters.

The personnel of the navy and coast artillery in 1984 totalled 18,280 officers and men, comprising 3,350 regulars, 2,570 reservists and 12,360 national servicemen (refresher trainees). Additionally 6,250 conscripts train annually.

The Coast Guard operates 130 cutters, patrol boats and service craft and lists 5 aircraft. Personnel in 1984 numbered 570.

Air Force. The C-in-C. of the Royal Swedish Air Force has at his disposal the Air Staff under a chief of staff.

The combat force consists of 3 fighter-interceptor, 3 ground-attack and 3 mixed interceptor/reconnaissance wings (*flottiljer*), each with 2-3 squadrons of 12-15 aircraft, including 3 reconnaissance squadrons (*divisioner*). Total peace-time strength of the combat units is 20 squadrons with nearly 400 first-line aircraft.

Night and all-weather fighters are the Swedish-built Saab J35 Draken, equipping 7 squadrons, and JA37 Viggen, equipping 5 squadrons (3 more Draken squadrons are to convert to JA37s). The ground-attack wings have 5 squadrons of Saab AJ37 Viggens, and there is provision for 5 light ground-attack squadrons of twin-jet Saab-105s (Sk60s), most of which could be withdrawn in wartime from training units. One Sk60 squadron is designated as part of the primary ground attack force. The 3 reconnaissance squadrons have SF37 (photo) and SH37 (maritime, radar) Viggen reconnaissance aircraft; and there are transport, helicopter and other support units. The Sk60A is the Air Force's standard advanced trainer, to which pupils progress after initial training on piston-engined Bulldogs. Other trainers in service include the Sk61 Bulldog, Sk35C Draken and Sk37 Viggen.

Active strength consists of about 9,500 personnel, including 4,500 conscripts.

INTERNATIONAL RELATIONS

Membership. Sweden is a member of UN and EFTA.

ECONOMY

Budget. Revenue and expenditure of the ordinary budget for fiscal years ending 30 June (in 1m. kr.):

	Revenue	Expenditure		Revenue	Expenditure
1977–78	109,286	125,936	1980–81[2]	155,287	215,238
1978–79	116,264	148,376	1981–82[2]	167,131	235,164
1979–80	128,593	170,695	1982–83[1] [2]	191,554	277,866

[1] Preliminary.
[2] By the introduction of a reformed budget system, the current budget and the capital budget have been consolidated.

The preliminary revenue and expenditure (current accounts) for the fiscal year 1 July 1982 to 30 June 1983 was as follows (in 1m. kr.):

Revenue		Expenditure	
Taxes:		Royal Household and residences	27
Taxes on income,		Justice	8,470
capital gains and		Foreign Affairs	6,528
profits	39,534	Defence	19,662
Statutory social		Health and Social Affairs	65,260
security fees	36,032	Communications	13,289
Taxes on property	3,284	Economic Affairs	473
Value-added tax	45,423	Budget	11,979
Other taxes on goods		Education	33,103
and services	35,156	Agriculture	6,520
Total revenue		Commerce	3,511
from taxes	159,429	Labour	16,815
Non-tax revenue	22,459	Housing and Physical	
Capital revenue	57	Planning	19,408
Loan repayment	2,978	Industry	20,138
Computed revenue	6,630	Local Government	3,094
Total revenue	191,554	Parliament and agencies	522
		Interest on National Debt,	
		etc.	48,196
		Unforeseen expenditure	23
		Changed appropriation	
		of short-term credits	848
		Total expenditure	277,866

On 31 Dec. 1982 the national debt amounted to 377,089m. kr.

Riksgäldskontoret (National Debt Office), *årsbok.* Annual. Stockholm, from 1920
Riksskatteverket (National Tax Board), *årsbok.* Annual. Stockholm, from 1971
The Swedish Budget. Ministry of Economic Affairs and Ministry of the Budget, from 1962/63

Currency. The monetary unit is the Swedish *krona,* of 100 *öre.* In March 1984, £1 = 11·46 *krona*; US$1 = 7·78 *krona.*

Gold coins do not exist as a currency. Central banknotes for 5, 10, 50, 100, 1,000 and 10,000 kr. are legal means of payment.

Banking. The Riksbank, or Central Bank of Sweden, belongs entirely to the State and is managed by directors elected for 3 years by the Parliament, except the chairman, who is designated by the Government. The bank is under the guarantee of the Parliament, its capital and reserve capital are fixed by its constitution. Since 1904, only the Riksbank has the right to issue notes. On 31 Dec. 1982 its note circulation amounted to 38,985m. kr.; its gold and foreign-exchange reserves totalled 25,115m. kr.

There are 14 commercial banks. On 31 Dec. 1982 their total deposits amounted to 212,155m. kr.; advances to the public amounted to 201,425m. kr.

On 31 Dec. 1982 there were 160 savings banks; their total deposits amounted to 103,070m. kr.; advances to the public were 71,859m. kr. Co-operative banks had total deposits of 24,695m. kr.; advances to the public were 17,112m. kr.

Sveriges Riksbank, årsbok. Annual. Stockholm, from 1908
Skandinaviska Enskilda Banken, Kvartalskrift. Quarterly Review (in English). Stockholm, from 1920

Weights and Measures. The metric system is obligatory.

ENERGY AND NATURAL RESOURCES

Electricity. Sweden is rich in hydro-power resources. The total electric energy production in 1981 was 103,300m. kwh. About 58% of this energy was produced in hydro-electric plants. Additional electric energy consumption will in the future mainly be covered by nuclear power and conventional thermal power.

Minerals. Sweden is one of the leading exporters of iron ore. The largest deposits are found north of the polar circle in the area of Kiruna and Gällivare-Malmberget. The ore is exported *via* the Norwegian port of Narvik and the Swedish port of Luleå. There are also important resources of iron ore in southern Sweden (Bergslagen). The most important fields are Grängesberg and Stråssa and the ores are shipped *via* the port of Oxelösund. Some of the southern deposits have, in contrast to the fields in North Sweden, a low phosphorus content.

There are also some deposits of copper, lead and zinc ores especially in the Boliden area in the north of Sweden. These ores are often found together with pyrites. Non-ferrous ores, except zinc ores, are used in the Swedish metal industry and barely satisfy domestic needs.

The total production of iron ores amounted to 23·2m. tons in 1981 and exports to 15m. tons. The production of copper ore was 221,384 tons, of lead ore 123,872 tons, of zinc ore 334,354 tons.

There are also deposits of raw materials for aluminium not worked at present. In southern Sweden there are big resources of alum shale, containing oil and uranium.

Agriculture. According to the farm register which is revised annually the following data was provided for 1982. The number of farms in cultivation of more than 2 hectares of arable land, was 116,350; of these there were 71,498 of 2-20 hectares; 41,511 of 20-100 hectares; 3,341 of above 100 hectares. Of the total land area of Sweden (41,161,500 hectares), 2,950,322 [1] hectares were arable land, 351,442[1] hectares cultivated pastures and (1981) 22,742,235 hectares forests.

	Area (1,000 hectares) [1]			Production (1,000 tonnes)		
Chief crops	1980	1981	1982	1980	1981	1982
Wheat	297·2	230·8	293·1	1,193	1,066	1,490
Rye	68·5	52·4	56·8	225	180	211
Barley	694·4	729·3	677·4	2,172	2,452	2,378
Oats	484·1	507·8	509·4	1,567	1,816	1,663
Mixed grain	59·5	64·1	66·3	157	180	180
Peas and vetches	12·0	14·2	20·5	24	30	44
Potatoes	40·0	40·2	39·7	1,084	1,213	1,036
Sugarbeet	52·1	52·5	53·6	2,257	2,484	2,431
Tame hay	707·5	706·8	707·1	4,132	4,326	4,297
Oil seed	177·5	171·1	171·1	326	323	371

Area of rotation meadows for pasture was (in 1,000 hectares[1]): 1980, 191; 1981, 192; 1982, 193.

Total production of milk (in 1,000 tonnes): 1980, 3,481; 1981, 3,514; 1982, 3,652. Butter production in the same years was (in 1,000 tonnes): 66, 64, 69; and cheese, 101, 108.

Livestock (1982): Cattle, 1·9m.; sheep, 430,000; pigs, 2·6m.; poultry, 8·4m.

Number of farm tractors in 1981, 189,654; combines in 1981, 48,990.

The number of pelts produced in 1981–82 was as follows: Fox, 37,514; mink, 1·3m.; others, 7,548.

[1] Figures refer to holdings of more than 2 hectares of arable land.

Forestry. In 1978–82 the forests covered an area of 23·5m. hectares, *i.e.* roughly 57% of the country's land area. Municipal and State ownership accounts for one-fourth of the forests, companies own another fourth, and the remaining half is in private hands. In the felling seasons, 1980–81 and 1981–82 respectively, 47·9m.

and 48·7m. cu. metres (solid volume under bark) of wood were removed from the forests in Sweden. The sawmill, wood pulp and paper industries are all of great importance. The number of sawmills in 1979 was about 2,600, 400 of which were commercial sawmills, with more than 90% of the total production of sawn hard- and soft-wood. In 1982 the total production was about 10·7m. cu. metres. The wood pulp factories total output amounted to 7·5m. tons (including dissolving pulp) (dry weight).

Fisheries. In 1981 the total catch of the sea fisheries was 249,800 tons, live weight, value 560m. kr.

INDUSTRY AND TRADE

Manufacturing. The most important sector of Swedish manufacturing is the production of metals, metal products, machinery and transport equipment, covering almost half of the total value added by manufacturing. Production of high-quality steel is an old Swedish speciality. A large part of this production is exported. The production of ordinary steel is slightly decreasing and is still short of domestic demand. The total production of steel amounted to 4·2m. tons in 1980. There is also a large production of other metals (aluminium, lead, copper) and rolled semi-manufactured goods of these metals.

These basic metal industries are an important basis for the production of more developed metal products, machinery and equipment, which are to a large extent sold on the world market, *i.e.*, hand tools, mining drills, ball-bearings, turbines, pneumatic machinery, refrigerating equipment, machinery for pulp and paper industries, etc., sewing machines, machine tools, office machinery, high-voltage electric machinery, telephone equipment, cars and trucks, ships and aeroplanes.

Another important manufacturing sector is based on Sweden's forest resources. This sector includes saw-mills, plywood factories, joinery industries, pulp- and paper-mills, wallboard and particle board factories, accounting for about 15% of the total value of manufacturing. A fast increasing sector is the chemical industry, especially the petro-chemical branch. Minerals industries include production of building materials, decorative arts products of glass and china.

Industry groups	No. of establishments		Average no. of wage-earners		Sales value of production (gross) in 1m. kr.	
	1980	1981	1980	1981	1980	1981
Mining and quarrying	121	115	10,447	10,116	3,834	3,557
Metal-ore mining	34	31	9,151	8,859	3,324	2,997
Other mining	87	84	1,296	1,257	510	560
Manufacturing	10,152	9,821	601,941	579,003	309,619	329,047
Manufacture of food, beverages and tobacco	956	918	54,209	53,015	41,229	46,052
Textile, wearing apparel and leather industries	826	791	31,595	29,338	7,896	7,823
Manufacture of wood products including furniture	1,734	1,624	56,820	51,666	24,961	23,564
Manufacture of paper and paper products, printing and publishing	1,110	1,080	72,310	70,635	41,742	45,820
Manufacture of chemicals and chemical, petroleum, coal, rubber and plastic products	709	700	44,444	42,401	47,372	50,066
Manufacture of non-metallic mineral products, except products of petroleum and coal	483	458	20,730	18,866	7,999	8,019
Basic metal industries	179	175	47,042	45,080	26,292	25,275

Industry groups	No. of establishments		Average no. of wage-earners		Sales value of production (gross) in 1 m. kr.	
	1980	1981	1980	1981	1980	1981
Manufacture of fabricated metal products, machinery and equipment	4,037	3,960	270,799	264,331	110,869	121,224
Other manufacturing industries	118	115	3,992	3,671	1,259	1,204
Electricity, gas and water	872	850	11,507	11,464	38,706	44,546
Electricity, gas and steam	741	720	10,839	10,827	37,606	43,373
Water works and supply	131	130	668	637	1,100	1,173

Arbetsmarknadsstatistik (Labour Market Statistics). Monthly. National Labour Market Board, Stockholm, from 1963

Arbetsmarknadsstatistisk Årsbok (Year Book of Labour Statistics). Statistics Sweden, Stockholm, from 1973

Carlson, B., *Trade Unions in Sweden.* Stockholm, 1969

Historisk statistik för Sverige, II (Climate, land surveying, agriculture, forestry, fisheries). Statistics Sweden, Stockholm, 1959

Johansson, Ö., *The Gross Domestic Product of Sweden and its Composition 1861–1955.* Stockholm, 1967

Jörberg, L., *A History of Prices in Sweden 1732–1914.* 2 vols. Stockholm, 1972

Jordbruksekonomiska meddelanden (Journal of Agricultural Economics, published monthly by the National Agricultural Market Board). Stockholm, from 1939

Jordbruksstatistisk årsbok (Yearbook of Agricultural Statistics). Statistics Sweden, Stockholm, from 1965

The Swedish Economy. Ministry of Economic Affairs and National Institute of Economic Research. Stockholm, from 1960

Trade Unions. The Swedish Confederation of Trade Unions (LO) had a total membership of 2,160,982 in 1982, including the Municipal Workers' Union with 566,981 members and the Metal Workers' Union with 44,686.

Commerce. The imports and exports of Sweden, unwrought gold and coin not included, have been as follows (in 1 m. kr.):

	1976	1977	1978	1979	1980	1981	1982
Imports	84,000	90,246	92,717	122,952	141,641	146,040	173,525
Exports	80,195	85,678	98,205	118,147	131,002	144,876	167,975

On 1 Jan. 1974 a new Customs procedure for the imports was introduced. This means that during 1974, 1975 and 1976, a great part of the imports were recorded in the statistics with an extra delay of up to 2 weeks as compared to the registration before 1974.

Corrected import values for 1974, 1975 and 1976, adjusted for the effects of the new time-lags, have been calculated in order to facilitate comparisons with earlier years and to show the development of the trade balance.

The adjustments have not been made by commodity and country. Beginning Jan. 1977 the statistics cover the goods which were actually imported and exported from Sweden during the period to which the statistics refer.

Imports and exports by products (in 1 m. kr.):

	Imports		Exports	
	1981	1982	1981	1982
Food and live animals chiefly for food	8,726	10,101	3,127	4,190
Cereals and cereal preparations	620	621	1,001	1,179
Vegetables and fruit	2,843	3,330	245	279
Coffee, tea, cocoa, spices and manufactures thereof	2,008	2,441	275	307
Feeding stuff for animals (not including unmilled cereals)	984	1,083	46	67
Beverages and tobacco	1,041	1,330	118	156
Crude materials, inedible, except fuels	6,617	6,858	16,348	17,695
Hides, skins and furskins, raw	245	300	404	453
Crude rubber (including synthetic and reclaimed)	314	374	66	91
Cork and wood	2,039	1,242	5,478	7,038
Pulp and waste paper	284	312	6,802	6,442
Textile fibres (other than wool tops) and their wastes (not manufactured into yarn or fabric)	203	271	237	299

	Imports		Exports	
	1981	1982	1981	1982
Crude fertilizers and crude minerals (excluding coal, petroleum and precious stones)	885	1,025	270	293
Metalliferous ores and metal scrap	1,651	2,142	2,796	2,722
Mineral fuels, lubricants and related materials	36,048	42,491	6,574	8,996
Coal, coke and briquettes	1,040	1,518	162	176
Petroleum, petroleum products and related materials	34,634	40,117	5,650	8,348
Chemicals and related products, n.e.s.	11,918	15,344	7,904	9,684
Artificial resins and plastic materials, and cellulose esters and ethers	3,444	4,029	2,404	2,707
Manufactured goods classified chiefly by material	22,880	26,728	38,599	43,748
Paper, paperboard, and articles of paper pulp, of paper or of paperboard	1,449	1,732	14,565	16,143
Textile yarn, fabrics, made-up articles, n.e.s., and related products	3,919	4,501	1,918	2,178
Non-metallic mineral manufactures, n.e.s.	2,015	2,314	1,586	1,919
Iron and steel	5,264	6,695	9,114	10,865
Non-ferrous metals	3,425	3,896	3,039	3,393
Manufactures of metal, n.e.s.	4,063	4,461	5,570	6,060
Machinery and transport equipment	39,746	48,196	59,983	70,523
Power generating machinery and equipment	2,882	3,769	3,936	4,551
Machinery specialized for particular industries	4,132	5,075	7,361	8,239
Metal working machinery	1,533	1,474	1,705	1,749
General industrial machinery and equipment, n.e.s. and machine parts, n.e.s.	7,154	8,163	10,978	11,979
Office machines and automatic data processing equipment	3,901	5,010	2,924	3,527
Telecommunications and sound recording and reproducing apparatus and equipment	2,940	3,363	5,210	6,652
Electrical machinery apparatus and appliances, n.e.s., and electrical parts thereof (including non-electrical counterparts, n.e.s., of electrical household type equipment)	6,789	8,738	5,473	7,062
Road vehicles (including air cushion vehicles)	9,022	11,333	18,262	22,260
Other transport equipment	1,394	1,272	4,134	4,505
Miscellaneous manufactured articles	17,656	20,721	9,893	11,034

Principal import and export countries (in 1 m. kr.):

	Imports from		Exports to	
	1981	1982	1981	1982
Belgium-Luxembourg	4,670	5,291	4,582	6,001
Denmark	8,991	10,005	11,244	12,990
Federal Republic of Germany	23,684	29,986	16,371	17,581
Finland	9,705	9,863	9,381	10,919
France	5,627	6,998	7,726	9,522
Italy	4,388	5,407	4,747	5,258
Netherlands	5,548	7,863	6,554	8,361
Norway	8,973	12,426	13,898	17,766
Switzerland	2,814	3,268	2,916	3,160
USSR	2,651	5,005	2,112	2,219
UK	17,481	21,291	14,460	16,861
USA	11,814	14,621	8,884	11,940

Total trade between Sweden and UK (British Department of Trade returns, in £1,000 sterling):

	1979	1980	1981	1982	1983
Imports to UK	1,605,942	1,475,506	1,533,580	1,673,165	2,051,931
Exports and re-exports from UK	1,542,197	1,623,511	1,601,166	1,935,264	2,937,464

Historisk Statistik för Sverige, 3: Utrikeshandel [Foreign Trade], *1732–1970.* Statistics Sweden, Stockholm, 1972
Utrikeshandel, årsstatistik [Foreign Trade, Annual Bulletin]. Statistics Sweden, Stockholm. 5 vols. Statistical Reports, Series H
Utrikeshandel, månadsstatistik [Foreign Trade, Monthly Bulletin]. Statistics Sweden, Stockholm. Statistical Reports, Series H. Dec.
Utrikeshandel, kvartalsstatistik [Foreign Trade, Quarterly Bulletin]. Statistics Sweden, Stockholm. January – December. Exports respectively imports. Statistical Reports, Series H
Utrikeshandel, års statistik [Foreign Trade, Annual]. Official Statistics of Sweden, Statistics Sweden, Stockholm. Imports and exports. Distribution according to the SITC
Utrikeshandel, årsstatistik [Foreign Trade, Annual]. Official Statistics of Sweden, Statistics Sweden, Stockholm. Imports and exports. Commodities according to the CCN.

COMMUNICATIONS

Roads. On 1 Jan. 1982 there were 184,177 km of public roads comprising State-administered roads, 97,871 km, municipal, 17,598 km, private roads with subsidies, 68,708 km, of which 87,136 km were surfaced. Motor vehicles on 31 Dec. 1982 included 2,935,988 passenger cars, 206,738 buses and lorries and 16,796 heavy motor cycles (all in use).

Railways. At the end of 1982 the total length of railways was 12,366 km, of which 11,750 km belonged to the State; 7,606 km were electrified. In 1982 the number of passengers on the railways was 88m.; weight of goods, 40m. tonnes.

Aviation. Commercial air traffic is maintained in (1) Sweden and other parts of the world by Scandinavian Airlines System (SAS), of which AB Aerotransport (ABA = Swedish Air Lines) is the Swedish partner (DDL = Danish Air Lines and DNL = Norwegian Air Lines being the other two); (2) only within Sweden by Linjeflyg AB. Scandinavian Airlines System have a joint paid-up capital of about Sw. kronor 733m. Capitalization of ABA, Sw. kronor 346m., of which 50% is owned by the Government and 50% by private enterprises. Capitalization of Linjeflyg, Sw. kronor 130m., of which 50% is owned by SAS and 50% by ABA.

In scheduled air traffic during 1981 the total number of km flown was 66·5m.; passenger-km, 5,450·6m.; goods, 180·2m. ton-km; mail, 21·6m. ton-km. These figures represent the Swedish share of the SAS traffic (Swedish domestic and three-sevenths of international traffic) and the Linjeflyg traffic.

Shipping. The Swedish mercantile marine consisted on 30 June 1983 of 463 vessels of 3·25m. gross tons (only vessels of at least 100 gross tons, and excluding fishing vessels and tugs). Stockholm and Göteborg, with together 221 vessels of 2·74m. gross tons in June 1983 are the two major home ports for the Swedish mercantile marine.

Vessels entered from and cleared for foreign countries, exclusive of passenger liners and ferries, with cargoes and in ballast, in 1982, are as follows (only vessels of at least a gross tonnage of 75): With cargoes, 25,018 with a gross tonnage of 83·4m.; in ballast, 12,867 with a gross tonnage of 46·1m.

Post and Broadcasting. The length of telegraph circuits in Dec. 1979 was 1,591,000 km. The circuits of the telephone had a length of 28·2m. km at 31 Dec. 1980. On 1 Jan. 1982 there were 6·89m. instruments employed in the telephone service.

Number of combined radio and television reception fees paid at the end of 1982 was 3,236,000, of which 2·82m. included extra fees for colour television. As from 1 April 1978, special sound broadcasting licences were discontinued.

Sveriges Radio AB is a non-commercial semi-governmental corporation, transmitting 3 programmes on long-, medium-, and short-waves and on FM. There are also regional programmes. It also broadcasts 2 TV programmes. Colour programmes are broadcast by PAL system.

The overseas radio-telegraph and radio-telephone services are conducted by the Swedish Telecommunications Administration.

The number of post offices at the end of 1980 was 1,862. For receipts of the post and telecommunication services *see* the section on Economy.

Cinemas (1982). There were 1,252 cinemas.

Newspapers (1981). There were 168 daily newspapers with a total circulation of 4·8m.

JUSTICE, RELIGION, EDUCATION AND WELFARE

Justice. The administration of justice is entirely independent of the Government. The *Justitiekansler*, or Chancellor of Justice (a royal appointment) and the *Justitieombudsmän* (Judicial Commissioners appointed by the Diet), exercise a control over the administration. In 1968 a reform was carried through which meant that the offices of the former *Justitieombudsman* (Ombudsman for civil affairs) and the *Militieombudsman* (Ombudsman for military affairs) were turned into one sole institution with 3 Ombudsmen, each styled *Justitieombudsman*. They exert a general supervision over all courts of law, the civil service, military laws and the military services. In 1982–83 they received altogether 3,846 cases; of these, 133 were instituted on their own initiative and 3,713 on complaints.

Bruzelius, A., and Ginsburg, R. B., *The Swedish Code of Judicial Procedure*. South Hackensack, 1968
Justitieombudsmännens ämbetsberättelse avgiven till Riksdagen. Annual. Stockholm
The Penal Code of Sweden: As Amended 1 Jan. 1972. South Hackensack, 1972
Rowat, D. C., *The Ombudsman: Citizen's Defender*. London, 1965
Rättsstatistisk årsbok (Year Book of Legal Statistics). Statistics Sweden, Stockholm, from 1975

The *Riksåklagaren* (a royal appointment) is the chief public prosecutor.

The kingdom has a Supreme Court of Judicature and is divided into 6 Courts of Appeal districts and 100 district-court divisions (*tingsrätter*). Regarding rent and tribunal cases the kingdom has an Apartment Appeal Court and 12 rent and tenancy tribunals.

Of the district courts 27 also serve as real estate courts and 6 as water rights courts.

These district courts (or courts of first instance) deal with both civil and criminal cases. More serious criminal cases are generally tried by a judge and a jury (*nämnd*) of 4-5 members (lay judges); petty cases are tried by the judge alone. Civil cases are tried as a rule by 3 to 4 judges or in minor cases by 1 judge. Disputes of greater consequence relating to the Marriage Code and the Code relating to Parenthood and Guardianship are tried by a judge and a *nämnd*. When cases concerning real estate are being tried the court consists of 2 qualified lawyers, 1 specialist on technical matters and 2 lay assessors.

In trials by *nämnd* the judge decides the case except when the majority of the *nämnd* (at least 4 members of 5 or 3 members of 4) differs from him, in which case the decision of the *nämnd* prevails. The cases in Courts of Appeal are generally tried by 4 or 5 judges, but the same cases, which are tried with a judge and a *nämnd* in the first instance, are tried by 3 or 4 judges and a *nämnd* of 2-3 members (lay judges). The court consists in cases concerning real estate of a specialist on technical matters instead of one of the judges and in water-right cases of 3 or 4 judges and 1 or 2 specialists on technical water matters.

Those with low incomes can receive free legal aid out of public funds. In criminal cases a suspected person has the right to a defence counsel, paid out of public funds.

The Attorney-General (*Justitiekanslern*) and the Parliamentary Commissioner (*Justitieombudsmannen*) for the Judiciary and Civil Administration supervises the application in the public sector of acts of parliament and regulations. The Attorney-General is the Government's legal adviser and also the Public Prosecutor.

The holders of the office of Parliamentary Commissioner, 4 in number, are appointed by Parliament.

There were 73 penal and correctional institutions for delinquents, with 4,433 male and 177 female inmates on 1 March 1983 (including delinquents in remand prison). Besides, there were 18 institutions with 499 places for children and juveniles in need of care owing to viciousness, maladjustment or delinquency on 31 Dec. 1982; on 31 Dec. 1982, 362 youths were committed to these institutions.

Religion. The overwhelming majority of the population belong to the Evangelical Lutheran Church, which is the established national church. In 1982 there were 13 bishoprics (Uppsala being the metropolitan see) and 2,569 parishes. The clergy are chiefly supported from the parishes and the proceeds of the church lands. The nonconformists mostly still adhere to the national church. The largest denominations, on 1 Jan. 1982, were: Pentecost Movement, 99,233; The Mission Covenant Church of Sweden, 80,003; Salvation Army, 34,589 (1981); Swedish Evangelical Mission, 24,405; Swedish Baptist Church, 20,913 (1981); Orebro Missionary Society, 20,188; Swedish Alliance Missionary Society, 13,195; Holiness Mission, 5,997.

There were also 107,533 Roman Catholics (under a Bishop resident at Stockholm), about 35,000 Orthodox Catholics (1978) and about 15,000 Jews (1978).

Parliament and Convocation (*Kyrkomötet*) decided in 1958 to admit women to ordination as priests.

Murray, R.. *L'église Suédoise. Son Histoire et Son Organisation.* Stockholm, 1970

Education. By the Swedish Higher Educational Act of 1977 a unified educational system was created by integrating institutions which had previously been administered separately. This new *högskola* includes not only traditional university studies but also those of various professional colleges as well as a number of study programmes offered by the secondary school system. One of the goals of the 1977 university reform was to introduce an increased element of professional training into Swedish higher education. A Certificate of Education is awarded on completion of a general study programme. This certificate states the number of courses taken as well as the points and grades obtained on each course in the study programme.

In Dec. 1980 there were, in these new integrated institutions for higher education, *högskola*, 92,000 registered for undergraduate studies at general study programmes, and 70,900 registered at (*a*) separate courses, (*b*) specialized continuation courses, (*c*) local or individual study programmes. The number of registered students at the general study programmes distributed by sector is as follows: Education for technical professions, 22,600; education for social work and economic and administrative professions, 23,900; education for medical and paramedical professions, 20,000; education for the teaching professions, 21,400; and education for information, communication and cultural professions, 4,100. The number of students enrolled for post-graduate studies was 12,300.

In autumn term in the school year 1980–81 there were 666,700 pupils in primary education (grades 1–6 in compulsory comprehensive schools). Secondary education at the lower stage (grades 7–9 in compulsory comprehensive schools) comprised 365,300 pupils. In secondary education at the higher stage (the integrated upper secondary school), there were 241,500 pupils (excluding about 31,000 pupils in the 4-year technical group regarded as third-level education). The folk high schools, 'people's colleges', had 14,000 pupils in courses of more than 15 weeks.

In municipal adult education there were in the school year 1979–80, 152,000 pupils (corresponding to a gross number of 322,000 participants) and in state adult education there were about 23,000 pupils (of which 19,000 taking correspondence courses).

There are also special schools for pupils with visual and hearing handicaps and those who are mentally retarded (about 13,700 pupils in 1980–81).

Goals for Educational Policy in Sweden. OECD, Paris, 1980
Higher Education for Visiting Students.—Series Studying in Sweden.—National Board of Universities and Colleges. Stockholm, 1978
Götberg, B., and Svärd, S., *The Swedish 'Folk High School': Its Background and its Present Situation.*
Marklund, S., *Educational Administration and Educational Development.* Univ. of Stockholm, 1979.—*The Democratization of Education in Sweden.* Univ. of Stockholm, 1980
Marklund, S. and Bergendal, G., *Trends in Swedish Educational Policy.* Stockholm, 1979
Sundqvist, A., *New Rules for Swedish Study Circles.* Stockholm, 1982

Social Welfare. The social security schemes are greatly expanding. Supported by a referendum, the Diet in 1958 and 1959 decided that the national pensions should be increased successively until 1968 and supplementary pensions paid from 1963. These pensions are of invariable value. In 1969 the Diet decided that as from 1 July 1969 an increment to the basic pension was to be paid to persons without supplementary pensions, and this amount is to be successively increased in a 10-year period. The basic and supplementary pensions consist of old-age and family pensions, as well as pensions paid to the disabled. The financing of the supplementary system is based on the current-cost method.

The most important social welfare schemes are described in the conspectus below.

Type of scheme	Introduced	Scope	Principal benefits
Sickness insurance (compulsory–current law, 1962)	1955	All residents	Hospital fees, most private doctors charge the insured person normally 45 kr., district physicians and doctors in hospitals charge the insured person only 40 kr. for full medical treatment, some reimbursement of cost of transportation as well as costs of physiotherapy, convalescent care, etc., medicines at reduced prices or free of charge. During sickness daily allowance 90% of the yearly income in between 6,000 and 145,500 kr. There is generally no maximum benefit period. Dental care is available to all residents from 17 years of age, the maximum payable by the patient being 60% up to 2,500 kr. and 25% thereafter.
Employment injury insurance (compulsory–current law, 1976)	1901	All employed persons	Medical treatment, medicine and medical appliances, hospital care, sickness benefit 100% of the yearly income in between 6,000 and 145,500 kr. (first 90 days covered by sickness insurance), disability annuities, funeral benefit and survivor's pensions.
Unemployment insurance (current law, 1973)	1935	Members of recognized unemployment insurance societies (about 70% of all employees)	110-280 kr. per day subject to tax.
Basic pensions (current law, 1962)			
Old-age	1914	All citizens	Payable from the age of 65 or, at a reduced rate, from the age of 60. 49,054 kr. per annum for married couples, 27,974 kr. for others (including the special increment of 18,518 kr. and 9,259 kr. respectively for those without supplementary pension); about half of them receive municipal housing supplement.
Disability	1914	All citizens	Payable before the age of 65. Full pension 36,839 kr. per annum (including the special increment of 18,124 kr.).
Survivors	1948	All citizens	Widow's pension is payable before the age of 65. The pension is 27,974 kr. (including the special increment of 9,259 kr.) but less for those who have become widows before the age of 50 and have no child below 16. Many of them receive municipal housing supplements.

Type of scheme	Intro- duced	Scope	Principal benefits
Survivors (cont.)			Child pension is payable before the age of 18. The pension amounts to 8,077 kr. (fatherless or motherless) and 12,214 kr. (orphans).
Supplementary pensions (current law, 1962) Old-age	1960	All gainfully occupied persons	Payable from the same age as the basic pension (see above). The pension is in principle 60% of the insured person's average annual earnings during the best 15 years except an amount corresponding to the basic pension and subject to a ceiling.
Disability	1960	All gainfully occupied persons	Payable before the age of 65. Full pension corresponds in principle to supplementary old-age pension.
Survivors	1960	All gainfully occupied persons	Payable to widow and children, before the age of 19, of a deceased person as a certain percentage of the deceased's supplementary pension.
Partial pensions (current law, 1979)	1976	All employees between 60–65 years of age	The pension is payable between 60–65 years of age. The insured must have reduced his working time by 5 hours on an average a week and the part-time work must thereafter comprise at least 17 hours per week. Furthermore the insured must have worked during at least 5 of the last 12 months and achieved a right to supplementary pension for 10 years after the age of 45. The partial pension is paid out by 50% of the loss of income in connection with the change-over to part-time work.
Parents benefit	1974	All resident parents in connection with confinement	Parents cash benefit of 37 kr. a day during 180 days. Employed parents entitled to daily parents cash benefit of 90% of the daily income (in between 6,000–145,500 kr. yearly) for 180 days. Maximum daily parents cash benefit 358 kr.
Special parents benefit	1978	All resident parents	Special parents cash benefit with the same amount as for parents cash benefit for care of each child during 180 days for the parents together until the child reaches 8 years of age or until the end of the child's first school year if that is later.

Type of scheme	Intro-duced	Scope	Principal benefits
Children's allowances	1948	All children below 16	3,300 kr. per annum. From 1 Jan. 1983, an additional allowance will be paid out for the third child with one-half of an allowance and a full allowance for each additional child.
		Children at school 16–18	275 kr. per month during school-courses.

Total social expenditure, including also hygiene, care of the sick and social assistance, amounted to 181,737m. kr. in 1981, representing 31·9% of the GDP.

The Cost and Financing of the Social Services in Sweden, 1974. Stockholm, 1976
Ministry of Health and Social Affairs, *The Evolution of the Swedish Health Insurance.* Stockholm, 1978
Modern Trends in Swedish Pension Systems. Stockholm, 1968
Socialnytt (Official Journal of the National Board of Health and Welfare). Stockholm, from 1968
Faramond, G. de, *La Suède et la qualité de la Vie.* Paris, 1975
Fry, John (ed.), *Limits of the Welfare State: Critical Views on Post-war Sweden.* Farnborough, 1979
Heclo, H., *Modern Social Politics in Britain and Sweden: From Relief to Income Maintenance.* New Haven, 1974
Holgersson, L., *The Evolution of Swedish Social Welfare.* Stockholm, 1975
Lagerström, L., *Pension Systems in Sweden.* Stockholm, 1976.—*Social Security in Sweden.* Stockholm, 1976
Wilson, D., *The Welfare State in Sweden: A Study in Comparative Social Administration.* London, 1979

DIPLOMATIC REPRESENTATIVES

Of Sweden in Great Britain (11 Montagu Place, London, W1H 2AL)
Ambassador: Leif Leifland (accredited on 10 Nov. 1982).

Of Great Britain in Sweden (Skarpögatan 6-8, 115 27 Stockholm)
Ambassador: Sir Donald Murray, KCVO, CMG.

Of Sweden in the USA (600 New Hampshire Avenue., Washington, D.C., 20037)
Ambassador: Count Wilhelm H. F. Wachtmeister.

Of the USA in Sweden (Strandvägen 101, 115 27 Stockholm)
Ambassador: Franklin S. Forsberg.

Of Sweden to the United Nations
Ambassador: Anders Ferm.

Books of Reference

Statistical Information: The Statistics Sweden, (Statistiska, Centralbyrån, S-11581 Stockholm) was founded in 1858, in succession to the Kungl. Tabellkommissionen, which had been set up in 1756. *Director-General:* Sten Johansson. Its Publications include:

Levnadsförhållanden, årsbok (Living Conditions). Annual. From 1975.—*Rapport.* from 1976
Statistisk årsbok för Sverige (Statistical Abstract of Sweden). From 1914
Siffror om Sverige (Sweden). From 1971. Also in English as *Sweden*
Historisk statistik för Sverige (Historical Statistics of Sweden). 1955 ff. (4 vols. to date)
Allmän månadsstatistik (Monthly Digest of Swedish Statistics). From 1963
Statistiska meddelanden (Statistical Reports). From 1963
Ahlmann, H. W. (ed.), *Sverige, Land och Folk.* 3 vols. Stockholm, 1967
Andersson, L., *A History of Sweden.* Stockholm, 1962
Atlas över Sverige. Stockholm, 1953–71. [Publ. in separate parts dealing with population, economics, etc.]
Britten Austin, P., *The Swedes: How They Live and Work.* Newton Abbot, 1970
Courtier, E., *En Suède.* Montreal, 1970
Documentation on Sweden. Stockholm, 1976
Documents on Swedish Foreign Policy, 1973. Stockholm, 1976

Faramond, G. de, *Un Politique du Bien-Être*. Paris, 1972

Fullerton, B., and Williams, A. F., *Scandinavia*. London, 1972

Furer, H. B. (ed.), *The Scandinavians in America 986–1970. A Chronology and Fact Book.* Dobbs Ferry, 1972

Gullberg, I. E., *Swedish–English Dictionary of Technical Terms.—Svensk-Engelsk Fackordbok.* Stockholm, 2nd ed. 1977

Hancock, M. D., *Sweden. The Politics of Post-Industrial Change.* Hinsdale, Ill., 1972

Heilborn, A., *Travel, Study and Research in Sweden.* 6th ed. Stockholm, 1965

Mead, W. R., and Hall, W., *Scandinavia*. London, 1972

Nobel, The Man and His Prizes. Published by the Nobel Foundation. Stockholm, 1950

Nordic Council, *Yearbook of Nordic Statistics.* From 1962 (in English and one Nordic Language)

Nording, R., *Suède Socialiste et Libre Entreprise.* Paris, 1970

Parent, J., *Le Modèle Suédois.* Paris, 1970

Paul, W. W., *The Story of Scandinavia.* Cincinnati, 1971

Scobbie, I., *Sweden*. London, 1972

Stomberg, A. A., *A History of Sweden.* New York, 1970

Scott, F. D., *Sweden: The Nation's History.* Univ. of Minnesota Press, 1977

Tomason, R. F., *Sweden: Prototype of Modern Society.* New York, 1970

Toyne, S. M., *The Scandinavians in History.* Freeport, 1970

Turner, B., *Sweden*. London, 1976

Sveriges statskalender. Published by Vetenskapsakademien. Annual, from 1813

National Library: Kungliga Biblioteket, Stockholm. *Director:* Lars Tynell.

SWITZERLAND

Schweiz—Suisse—Svizzera

Capital: Bern
Population: 6·4m. (1982)
GNP per capita: US$16,440 (1980)

HISTORY. On 1 Aug. 1291 the men of Uri, Schwyz and Unterwalden entered into a defensive league. In 1353 the league included 8 members and in 1513, 13. Various territories were acquired either by single cantons or by several in common, and in 1648 the league became formally independent of the Holy Roman Empire, but no addition was made to the number of cantons till 1798. In that year, under the influence of France, the unified Helvetic Republic was formed. This failed to satisfy the Swiss, and in 1803 Napoleon Bonaparte, in the Act of Mediation, gave a new Constitution, and out of the lands formerly allied or subject increased the number of cantons to 19. In 1815 the perpetual neutrality of Switzerland and the inviolability of her territory were guaranteed by Austria, France, Great Britain, Portugal, Prussia, Russia, Spain and Sweden, and the Federal Pact, which included 3 new cantons, was accepted by the Congress of Vienna. In 1848 a new Constitution was passed. The 22 cantons set up a Federal Government (consisting of a Federal Parliament and a Federal Council) and a Federal Tribunal. This Constitution, in turn, was on 29 May 1874 superseded by the present Constitution. In a national referendum held in Sept. 1978, 69·9% voted in favour of the establishment of a new canton, Jura, which was established on 1 Jan. 1979.

AREA AND POPULATION. Area and population, according to the census held on 1 Dec. 1970 and the census held on 1 Dec. 1980.

Canton	Area (sq. km)	Census population 1 Dec. 1970	Census population 1 Dec. 1980	Pop. per sq. km, 1980
Zürich (Zurich) (1351)	1,729	1,107,788	1,122,839	650
Bern (Berne) (1553)	6,887	983,296	912,022	151
Luzern (Lucerne) (1332)	1,494	289,641	296,159	198
Uri (1291)	1,075	34,091	33,883	31
Schwyz (1291)	908	92,072	97,354	107
Obwalden (Obwald) (1291)	492	24,509	25,865	53
Nidwalden (Nidwald) (1291)	274	25,634	28,617	104
Glarus (Glaris) (1352)	684	38,155	36,718	54
Zug (Zoug) (1352)	239	67,996	75,930	318
Fribourg (Freiburg) (1481)	1,670	180,309	185,246	111
Solothurn (Soleure) (1481)	791	224,133	218,102	276
Basel-Stadt (Bâle-V.) (1501)	37	234,945	203,915	5,485
Basel-Land (Bâle-C.) (1501)	428	204,889	219,822	513
Schaffhausen (Schaffhouse) (1501)	298	72,854	69,413	233
Appenzell A.-Rh. (Rh.-Ext.) (1513)	243	49,023	47,611	196
Appenzell I.-Rh. (Rh.-Int.) (1513)	172	13,124	12,844	75
St Gallen (St Gall) (1803)	2,016	384,475	391,995	195
Graubünden (Grisons) (1803)	7,109	162,086	164,641	23
Aargau (Argovie) (1803)	1,404	433,284	453,442	323
Thurgau (Thurgovie) (1803)	1,006	182,835	183,795	181
Ticino (Tessin) (1803)	2,811	245,458	265,899	95
Vaud (Waadt) (1803)	3,211	511,851	528,747	164
Valais (Wallis) (1815)	5,231	206,563	218,707	42
Neuchâtel (Neuenburg) (1815)	797	169,173	158,368	199
Genève (Genf) (1815)	282	331,599	349,040	1,237
Jura (1979)	...	...	64,986	78
Total	41,288[1]	6,269,783	6,365,960	154

[1] 15,941 sq. miles.

Population (1982 estimate) 6·4m.

The German language is spoken by the majority of inhabitants in 19 of the 25 cantons above (French names given in brackets), the French in 6 (Fribourg, Vaud, Valais, Neuchâtel, Jura and Genève, for which the German names are given in brackets), the Italian in 1 (Ticino). In 1980, 65% spoke German, 18·4% French, 9·8% Italian, 0·8% Romansch and 6% other languages; counting only Swiss nationals, the percentages were 73·5, 20·1, 4·5, 0·9 and 1. On 8 July 1937 Romansch was made the fourth national language; it is spoken mostly in Graubünden.

At the end of 1982 the population figures of the principal towns (and their *'agglomérations'* or conurbations, 1982) were as follows: Zürich, 366,300 (704,500); Basel, 180,500 (363,100); Geneva, 157,400 (338,700); Bern, 145,300 (289,000); Lausanne, 126,600 (225,600); Winterthur, 107,400; St Gallen, 74,500 (87,200); Luzern, 62,400 (156,900); Biel, 84,000.

The number of foreigners resident in Switzerland at 31 Dec. 1982 was 925,826. Of these, 188,554 were in Zürich canton, 103,119 in Vaud and 101,820 in Geneva.

Vital statistics for calendar years:

	Total	Live births Illegitimate	Marriages	Divorces	Still births	Deaths
1979	71,986	3,190	33,987	10,394	412	57,454
1980	73,661	3,496	35,721	10,910	361	59,097
1981	73,747	3,801	31,889	11,131	373	59,763

The excess of emigrants over remigrants was: 1974, 2,087; 1975, 2,967; 1976, 3,873; 1977, 3,510; 1978, 3,209; 1979, 3,129; 1980, 3,339.

CLIMATE. The climate is largely dictated by relief and altitude and includes continental and mountain types. Summers are generally warm, with quite considerable rainfall; winters are fine, with clear, cold air and cloudless skies. Bern. Jan. 32°F (0°C), July, 65°F (18·5°C). Annual rainfall 39·4″ (986 mm).

CONSTITUTION AND GOVERNMENT. Switzerland is a republic. The highest authority is vested in the electorate, *i.e.*, all Swiss citizens of over 20. This electorate—besides electing its representatives to the Parliament—has the voting power on amendments to, or on the revision of, the Constitution. It also takes decisions on laws and international treaties if requested by 30,000 voters or 8 cantons (facultative referendum), and it has the right of initiating constitutional amendments, the support required for such demands being 50,000 voters (popular initiative).

The Federal Government is supreme in matters of peace, war and treaties; it regulates the army, the railway, telecommunication systems, the coining of money, the issue and repayment of bank-notes and the weights and measures of the republic. It also legislates on matters of copyright, bankruptcy, patents, sanitary policy in dangerous epidemics, and it may create and subsidize, besides the Polytechnic School at Zürich and at Lausanne, 2 federal universities and other educational institutions. There has also been entrusted to it the authority to decide concerning public works for the whole or great part of Switzerland, such as those relating to rivers, forests and the construction of national highways and railways. By referendum of 13 Nov. 1898 it is also the authority in the entire spheres of common law. In 1957 the Federation was empowered to legislate on atomic energy matters and in 1961 on the construction of pipelines of petroleum and gas.

National flag: Red with a white couped cross.

National anthem: Trittst im Morgenrot daher (words by Leonard Widmer, 1808–68; tune by Alberik Zwyssig, 1808–54); adopted by the Federal Council in 1962.

The legislative authority is vested in a parliament of 2 chambers, a *Ständerat*, or Council of States, and a *Nationalrat*, or National Council.

The *Ständerat* is composed of 46 members, chosen and paid by the 23 cantons of the Confederation, 2 for each canton. The mode of their election and the term of membership depend entirely on the canton. Three of the cantons are politically divided—Basel into Stadt and Land, Appenzell into Ausser-Rhoden and Inner-Rhoden, and Unterwalden into Obwalden and Nidwalden. Each of these 'half-cantons' sends 1 member to the State Council.

The *Nationalrat*—after the referendum taken on 4 Nov. 1962—consists of 200 National Councillors, directly elected for 4 years, in proportion to the population of the cantons, with the proviso that each canton or half-canton is represented by at least 1 member. The members are paid from federal funds at the rate of 150 francs for each day during the session and a nominal sum of 10,000 francs per annum.

In 1980 the 200 members were distributed among the cantons[1] as follows:

Zürich (Zurich)	35	Appenzell—Outer- and Inner-Rhoden	3
Bern (Berne)	29	St Gallen (St Gall)	12
Luzern (Lucerne)	9	Graubünden (Grisons)	5
Uri	1	Aargau (Argovie)	14
Schwyz	3	Thurgau (Thurgovie)	6
Unterwalden–Upper and Lower	2	Ticino (Tessin)	8
Glarus (Glaris)	1	Vaud (Waadt)	16
Zug (Zoug)	2	Valais (Wallis)	7
Fribourg (Freiburg)	6	Neuchâtel (Neuenburg)	5
Solothurn (Soleure)	7	Geneve (Genf)	11
Basel (Bâle)—town and country	14	Jura	2
Schaffhausen (Schaffhouse)	2		

[1] The name of the canton is given in German, French or Italian, according to the language most spoken in it, and alternative names are given in brackets.

Composition of the National Council in 1983: Social Democrats, 47; Radicals, 54; Christian-Democratic People's Party, 42; Swiss People's Party, 23; Liberals, 8; Independents, 8; National Campaign/Vigilance, 5; Evangelical Party, 3; Progressive Organizations, 3; Environmentalists, 3; Others, 4.

Council of States (1983): Christian Democrats, 18; Radicals, 14; Social Democrats, 6; Swiss People's Party, 5.

A general election takes place by ballot every 4 years. Every citizen of the republic who has entered on his 20th year is entitled to a vote, and any voter, not a clergyman, may be elected a deputy. Laws passed by both chambers may be submitted to direct popular vote, when 50,000 citizens or 8 cantons demand it; the vote can be only 'Yes' or 'No'. This principle, called the *referendum*, is frequently acted on.

Women's suffrage, although advocated by the Federal Council and the Federal Assembly, was on 1 Feb. 1959 rejected, but in a subsequent referendum, held on 7 Feb. 1971, women's suffrage was carried.

The chief executive authority is deputed to the *Bundesrat*, or Federal Council, consisting of 7 members, elected from 7 different cantons for 4 years by the *Vereinigte Bundesversammlung*, *i.e.*, joint sessions of both chambers. The members of this council must not hold any other office in the Confederation or cantons, nor engage in any calling or business. In the Federal Parliament legislation may be introduced either by a member, or by either House, or by the Federal Council (but not by the people). Every citizen who has a vote for the National Council is eligible for becoming a member of the executive.

The President of the Federal Council (called President of the Confederation) and the Vice-President are the first magistrates of the Confederation. Both are elected by the Federal Assembly for 1 calendar year and are not immediately re-eligible to the same offices. The Vice-President, however, may be, and usually is, elected to succeed the outgoing President.

President of the Confederation for 1984: Léon Schlumpf.

The 7 members of the Federal Council—each of whom has a salary of 203,000 francs per annum, while the President has 215,000 francs—act as ministers, or chiefs of the 7 administrative departments of the republic. The city of Berne is the seat of the Federal Council and the central administrative authorities.

The Federal Council was composed as follows in 1984.

Foreign Affairs: Pierre Aubert.
Interior: Alphons Egli.

Justice and Police: Rudolf Friedrich.
Military: Jean-Pascal Delamuraz.
Finance: Otto Stich.
Public Economy: Kurt Furgler.
Transport, Communications and Energy: Léon Schlumpf.

Local Government. Each of the cantons and demi-cantons is sovereign, so far as its independence and legislative powers are not restricted by the federal constitution; all cantonal governments, though different in organization (membership varies from 5 to 11, and terms of office from 1 to 5 years), are based on the principle of sovereignty of the people.

In all cantons a body chosen by universal suffrage, usually called *der Grosse Rat*, or *Kantonsrat*, exercises the functions of a parliament. In all the cantonal constitutions, however, except those of the cantons which have a *Landsgemeinde*, the referendum has a place. By this principle, where it is most fully developed, as in Zürich, all laws and concordats, or agreements with other cantons, and the chief matters of finance, as well as all revisions of the Constitution, must be submitted to the popular vote. In Appenzell, Glarus and Unterwalden the people exercise their powers direct in the *Landsgemeinde, i.e.,* the assembly in the open air of all male citizens of full age. In all the cantons the *popular initiative* for constitutional affairs, as well as for legislation, has been introduced, except in Lucerne, where the *initiative* exists only for constitutional affairs. In most cantons there are districts (*Amtsbezirke*) consisting of a number of communes grouped together, each district having a Prefect (*Regierungsstatthalter*) representing the cantonal government. In the larger communes, for local affairs, there is an Assembly (legislative) and a Council (executive) with a president, maire or syndic, and not less than 4 other members. In the smaller communes there is a council only, with its proper officials.

Basler Handelskammer, *La neutralité suisse*, 1962
Bonjour, E., *Swiss Neutrality*. London, 1946
Huber, H., *How Switzerland is Governed*. Zürich, 1947
Hughes, C., *The Federal Constitution of Switzerland. Translation and Commentary*. Oxford, 1954
Hughes, C. J., *The Parliament of Switzerland*. Hansard Society, 1962
Marx, Dr Paul, *Systematisches Register zu den geltenden Staatsverträgen der schweizerischen Eidgenossenschaft und der Kantone mit dem Auslande*. Zürich, 1918. *Appendix*, 1934
Rappard, W. E., *La Constitution fédérale de la Suisse*. Zürich, 1948.—*Collective Security in Swiss Experience*. London, 1948
Ruck, Erwin, *Schweizerisches Staatsrecht*. Zürich, 1933
Silbernagel-Caloyanni, Alfred, *Suisse: Organisation Politique, Administrative et Judiciaire de la Confédération Helvétique et de Chaque Canton*. Paris, 1936

DEFENCE. There are fortifications in all entrances to the Alps and on the important passes crossing the Alps and the Jura. Large-scale destructions of bridges, tunnels and defiles are prepared for an emergency.

Army. Switzerland depends for defence upon a *national militia*. Service in this force is compulsory and universal, with few exemptions except for physical disability. Those excused or rejected pay certain taxes in lieu. Liability extends from the 20th to the end of the 50th year for soldiers and of the 55th year for officers. The first 12 years are spent in the first line, called the *Auszug*, or *Élite*, the next 10 in the *Landwehr* and 8 in the *Landsturm*. The unarmed *Hilfsdienst* comprises all other males between 20 and 50 whose services can be made available for non-combatant duties of any description.

The initial training of the Swiss militia soldier is carried out in recruits' schools, and the periods are 118 days for infantry, engineers, artillery, etc. The subsequent trainings, called 'repetition courses', are 20 days annually; but after going through 8 courses further attendance is excused for all under the rank of sergeant. The *Landwehr* men are called up for training courses of 13 days every 2 years, and the *Landsturm* men have to undergo a refresher course of 13 days.

The Army is divided into 3 field corps each of 1 armoured and 2 infantry divisions, 11 independent frontier brigades, 3 mountain divisions, and independent redoubt-, fortress- and territorial-brigades, organized in 4 army corps. Strength on mobilization: 580,000, and 400,000 reserves.

The administration of the Swiss Army is partly in the hands of the Cantonal authorities, who can promote officers up to the rank of captain. But the Federal Government is concerned with all general questions and makes all the higher appointments.

In peace-time the Swiss Army has no general; only in time of war the Federal Assembly in joint session of both Houses appoints a general.

The Swiss infantry are armed with the Swiss automatic rifle and with machine-guns, bazookas and mortars. The field artillery is armed with a Q.F. shielded 10·5 Bofors and field howitzers of 10·5 cm calibre. The heavy artillery is armed with guns of 10·5 cm and howitzers of 15 cm calibre. The armoured troops are equipped with the light French AMX, the British Centurion and a modern Swiss tank.

Air Force. The Air Force has 3 flying regiments, with about 300 combat aircraft. The fighter squadrons are equipped with Swiss-built F-5E Tiger IIs (4 squadrons), Mirage IIIS supersonic interceptor/ground-attack (2 squadrons), Mirage IIIRS fighter/reconnaissance (1 squadron), and Hunter interceptor/ground-attack (9 squadrons) aircraft. Bloodhound surface-to-air missile batteries are operational.

Training aircraft are Pilatus P-2 and PC-7 Turbo-Trainer and Vampire; there are also communications and transport aircraft and helicopters. Personnel numbers, 45,000 on mobilization.

INTERNATIONAL RELATIONS

Membership. Switzerland is a member of OECD, EFTA and the Council of Europe.

ECONOMY

Budget. Revenue and expenditure of the Confederation, in 1m. francs, for calendar years:

	1975	1976	1977	1978	1979	1980
Revenue	13,541	14,287	14,026	15,106	15,050	16,460
Expenditure	12,232	15,863	15,493	15,824	16,764	17,532

The public debt, comprising consolidated debt and flowing debt, of the Confederation in 1980 amounted to 14,126m. francs. The floating debt in 1980 was 4,255m. francs.

Schweizerisches Finanz-Jahrbuch. Bern. Annual. From 1899
Staatstechnung der Schweizerischen Eidgenossenschaft. Bern, 1976

Currency. The *franc* of 100 *Rappen* or *centimes* is the monetary unit. On 10 May 1971 there was a revaluation to 0·21759 gramme of fine gold.

The legal gold coins are 20- and 10-franc pieces; cupro-nickel coins are 5, 2, 1 and ½ franc, 20, 10 and 5 centimes; bronze, 2 and 1 centime. Notes are of 1,000, 500, 100, 50, 20, 10 and 5 francs.

On 10 July 1981 the notes in circulation (of francs of nominal value) was as follows: In 1,000 franc notes, 8,685·1m. francs; in 500, 4,201·9m. francs; in 100, 6,687·3m. francs; in 50, 1,058·3m. francs, and in lower denominations 1,195·8m.

In March 1984, £1 = 3·16 *francs*; US$1 = 2·17 *francs*.

Banking. The National Bank, with headquarters divided between Bern and Zürich, opened on 20 June 1907. It has the exclusive right to issue bank-notes. In 1981 the condition of the bank was as follows (in 1m. francs): Gold, 11,903·9, foreign exchange (currency), 25,495; currency in circulation, 23,336·7.

In 1976 there were 1,740 banking institutions with total assets of 347,710·5m. Swiss francs. They included 28 cantonal banks (79,376m. francs), 5 big banks (161,382m.), 225 regional banks (38,138m.), 185 other banks (43,267m.).

On 31 Dec. 1976 the total amount of savings deposits in Swiss banks was 73,903m. francs, with 11·2m. depositors.

National Bank: Bulletin mensuel.—Das schweizerische Bankwesen. Yearly. From 1920

Weights and Measures. The metric system of weights and measures was made compulsory by the federal law on 3 July 1875 and since 1 Jan. 1887 only metric units have been legal. By the federal law of 24 June 1909 the international electric units were also adopted.

ENERGY AND NATURAL RESOURCES

Electricity. The total production of energy amounted to 52,285m. kwh. in 1982; 37,035m. kwh. were generated by hydro-electric plants.

Gas. The production of gas in 1982 was 39·81m. cu. metres.

Minerals. There are 2 salt-mining districts; that in Bex (Vaud) belongs to the canton, but is worked by a private company, and those at Schweizerhalle, Rheinfelden and Ryburg are worked by a joint-stock company formed by the cantons interested. The output of salt of all kinds in 1982 was 361,964 tonnes.

Agriculture. Of the total area of the country of 4,129,315 hectares, about 1,057,794 hectares (25·6%) are unproductive. Of the productive area of 3,071,521 hectares, 1,051,991 hectares are wooded. The agricultural area, in 1980, consisted of 287,283 hectares arable land (including vineyards), 106,406 hectares artificial meadows and 561,311 hectares permanent meadow. In 1980 there were 125,274 farms with a total area of 1,086,060 hectares. The gross value of agricultural products was estimated at 6,409·7m. francs in 1975 and 7,243·1m. francs in 1980.

In 1980, 176,942 hectares were planted with cereals, of which 85,301 hectares were wheat; barley, 46,111; rye, 8,058; potatoes, 23,664; sugar-beet, 13,075; vegetables, 8,196; tobacco, 769. Production, 1981 (in 1,000 tonnes): Potatoes, 1,048; sugar-beet, 900; wheat, 384; barley, 225; rye, 29; tobacco, 1·8. Milk production (in 1,000 tonnes): 1960, 3,112; 1970, 3,204; 1979, 3,671; 1980, 3,679; 1981, 3,680; 1982, 3,687.

The fruit production (in 1,000 tonnes) in 1981 was: Apples, 235; pears, 134; plums, 29; cherries, 28; nuts, 1.

Wine is produced in 18 of the cantons. In 1980 Swiss vineyards (13,736 hectares) yielded 854,804 hectolitres of wine, valued at 349,725 francs.

Livestock (1982): 45,000 horses, 333,000 sheep, 1,944,000 cattle (including about 856,000 milch cows), 2,093,000 pigs, 5,955,600 poultry (1981).

Forestry. Of the forest area of 999,795 hectares, 56,876 were owned by the Federation or the cantons, 636,069 by communes and 306,850 by private persons or companies in 1982. The utilization of timber, in 1981, was 4,385,931 cu. metres, of which 338,419 in state-owned, 2,747,112 in communal and 1,300,400 in private forests.

INDUSTRY AND TRADE

Industry. The chief food producing industries, based on Swiss agriculture, are the manufacture of cheese, butter, sugar and meat. The production in 1982 was (in tonnes): Cheese, 124,900; butter, 32,500; sugar (1981), 120,811. There are 46 breweries, producing in 1978, 4·05m. hectolitres of beer. Tobacco products in 1982: Cigars, 373·08m.; cigarettes, 26,497m.

Among the other industries, the manufacture of textiles, wearing apparel and footwear, chemicals and pharmaceutical products, bricks, glass and cement, the manufacture of basic iron and steel and of other metal products, the production of machinery (including electrical machinery and scientific and optical instruments) and watch and clock making are the most important. In 1981 there were 8,738 factories with 693,243 workers. In 1982, 41,200 were working in textile industries, 45,000 in the manufacture of clothing and footwear, 70,200 in chemical works, 194,700 in the construction industry, 168,600 in manufacture of metal products, 252,000 in the manufacture of machinery and 55,300 in watch and clock making and in the manufacture of jewellery.

Production in 1982 was: Woollen and blended yarn, 15,467 tonnes; woollen and blended cloth, 7,534 metres; footwear (1981), 5·87m. pairs; cement, 4,099,874 tonnes; raw aluminium, 75,256 tonnes; chocolate, 76,605 tonnes, 25·38m. watches and clocks were exported (1981).

Labour. According to the census of industries, 1975, the total working population was reduced to about 2·7m., of which 6·3% were active in agriculture and forestry, 44·7% in manufacture and construction and 48·9% in services. In all non-agricultural sectors there were 288,470 establishments (including 594 being shut down) with 2,537,738 occupied persons, divided in 159,289 occupants and 2,378,449 employees.

The main groups show the following numbers of gainfully occupied persons: Engineering, 254,185; retail trade, 228,751; construction 225,533; metalwork, 175,983; agriculture and forestry, 172,649; transport and postal services, 171,081; catering, 158,500; wholesale trade, 113,197; banking and insurance, 105,106; food processing, 103,306; textiles, 89,660; chemical industry, 68,975; watchmaking, 61,058.

The foreign labour force with permit of temporary residence was 749,378 in Aug. 1982. Of the number recorded 295,699 were Italians, 90,899 Spaniards, 76,802 Frenchmen, 67,297 Germans and 27,918 Austrians.

The Swiss Federal Union of Administrative and Public Service Workers had, in 1981, a membership of 125,151. The Federation of Trade Unions had about 459,150 members.

Commerce. The special commerce, excluding gold (bullion and coins) and silver (coins), was (in 1m. Swiss francs) as follows:

	1976	1977	1978	1979	1980	1981	1982
Imports	36,871	43,026	42,299	48,730	60,859	60,094	58,059
Exports	37,045	42,159	41,779	44,024	49,607	52,821	52,658

The following table, in 1m. francs, shows the distribution of the special trade of Switzerland among the principal countries:

Countries	Imports from				Exports to			
	1979	1980	1981	1982	1979	1980	1981	1982
Federal Rep. of Germany	13,946·5	16,766·3	16,908·4	17,261·9	8,642·6	9,749·8	9,687·4	9,572·5
France	6,273·3	7,461·8	7,428·5	6,657·2	3,845·2	4,547·6	4,751·3	4,729·4
Italy	5,054·9	5,844·6	5,849·3	5,732·8	3,127·2	3,898·8	4,069·9	3,973·4
Netherlands	2,089·3	2,469·6	2,445·2	2,500·7	1,240·9	1,383·7	1,316·5	1,249·9
Belgium–Lux-embourg	2,003·2	2,502·5	2,543·2	2,345·5	1,255·5	1,565·2	1,396·9	1,404·4
UK	3,754·9	5,072·6	3,457·6	3,180·6	3,090·9	3,134·4	3,428·6	3,268·1
Denmark	417·6	508·8	549·4	517·8	532·1	548·4	576·9	614·5
Ireland	114·7	150·9	176·1	197·8	113·5	91·1	134·7	154·0
Greece	...	...	90·9	75·1	...	...	370·4	422·9
EEC Total	33,654·4	40,777·2	39,448·6	38,469·4	21,847·9	24,919·0	25,732·6	25,389·1
Austria	1,830·0	2,184·4	2,262·7	2,153·6	2,010·9	2,271·0	2,263·0	2,141·6
Norway	178·9	229·1	186·3	168·0	373·1	428·9	444·7	439·2
Sweden	1,041·1	1,229·4	1,215·2	1,096·1	933·1	1,024·5	1,052·7	1,033·9
Portugal	127·6	179·4	190·0	168·5	339·7	400·7	476·5	444·6
Finland	274·0	343·5	338·3	319·9	326·3	397·2	454·4	441·8
Iceland	44·3	47·9	37·2	45·5	13·9	15·2	19·9	17·1
EFTA	3,495·9	4,213·7	4,229·7	3,951·6	3,997·0	4,537·5	4,711·2	4,518·2
Spain	490·9	578·8	617·2	655·0	840·8	903·1	1,020·4	1,263·8
Gibraltar, Malta	3·2	2·9	2·6	2·6	23·1	21·9	27·1	20·6
German Dem. Republic	56·4	68·5	79·9	81·6	242·7	220·3	232·9	221·6
Poland	137·7	240·1	103·5	82·4	320·5	287·5	181·4	179·8
Czechoslovakia	165·9	194·0	168·2	185·9	207·5	234·2	227·4	222·4

Countries	Imports from				Exports to			
	1979	1980	1981	1982	1979	1980	1981	1982
Hungary	150·7	166·5	236·3	191·5	285·3	285·5	339·5	335·0
Yugoslavia	154·1	173·5	145·8	141·9	587·9	552·7	567·5	437·2
Greece	77·0	66·3	...	...	294·2	300·4	...	...
Bulgaria	24·9	40·9	40·4	31·9	100·5	119·7	171·1	166·1
Romania	53·9	60·7	53·6	38·2	178·0	133·6	110·4	78·4
USSR	1,296·7	1,607·9	1,728·3	1,683·4	441·2	499·1	402·5	437·2
Turkey	94·4	113·4	141·4	119·2	175·7	265·5	423·5	368·9
Other European countries	4·2	8·4	8·0	10·6	24·3	45·0	25·0	31·1
Europe Total	39,860·3	48,312·8	47,003·5	45,645·2	29,566·6	33,325·0	34,172·5	33,669·4
Egypt	33·5	71·5	70·9	81·8	280·0	306·4	368·8	573·2
Sudan	4·1	4·4	2·2	1·0	49·8	42·2	53·7	48·9
Libya	258·6	516·5	368·2	526·9	89·7	143·6	195·2	175·6
Tunisia	56·0	11·9	13·3	44·2	35·8	46·8	57·7	50·4
Algeria	151·4	67·4	366·6	264·0	231·4	276·2	204·4	152·8
Morocco	28·3	46·1	21·2	23·6	73·7	66·4	78·6	69·7
Ivory Coast	37·9	35·8	48·1	40·9	44·4	41·4	31·0	33·6
Guinea	1·5	0·3	1·0	2·1	9·3	9·4	9·3	7·4
Ghana	42·8	48·9	33·5	27·4	23·5	23·1	31·5	11·3
Nigeria	137·0	356·5	195·3	454·4	263·2	530·5	683·2	517·2
Zaire	21·7	20·9	6·7	15·6	23·6	25·2	29·9	31·3
SW Africa	7·9	11·6	10·8	14·1	19·0	52·6	46·1	40·4
S Africa, Rep. of	142·8	212·2	153·4	154·0	382·7	499·3	669·6	530·3
Zambia	32·4	21·9	43·5	26·0	16·9	14·3	14·7	24·3
Zimbabwe	11·4	8·7	29·6	35·7	3·6	17·4	40·4	36·5
Tanzania	7·6	3·8	6·4	5·3	20·3	29·8	16·5	21·4
Kenya	19·6	33·7	27·1	27·7	38·3	48·1	45·0	38·6
Other African countries	84·5	89·3	91·9	85·1	171·0	237·7	193·5	442·1
Africa Total	1,079·0	1,561·4	1,489·7	1,829·8	1,776·2	2,410·4	2,769·1	2,805·0
Syria	11·4	36·6	18·5	0·7	98·5	85·1	101·5	115·0
Lebanon	34·9	86·8	53·6	70·3	124·3	238·5	330·2	355·5
Israel	196·7	209·5	205·4	303·4	973·0	871·7	452·3	511·8
Iraq	0·3	0·4	0·8	0·2	229·6	354·9	527·2	680·4
Kuwait	24·8	44·6	2·7	6·3	132·5	128·3	200·8	255·8
Iran	79·3	136·8	81·6	148·8	368·0	463·7	464·4	391·1
Saudi Arabia	186·5	257·3	413·0	293·1	951·6	1,042·4	1,181·8	1,544·3
UAE	374·4	673·2	665·9	227·5	154·3	173·1	236·1	333·6
Pakistan	23·2	40·8	51·4	41·9	67·9	64·8	110·1	101·6
India	139·0	127·8	153·1	152·0	214·9	220·8	288·8	345·9
Thailand	107·3	191·9	104·8	102·2	87·2	103·6	144·0	125·7
Malaysia	41·1	52·1	51·1	44·6	52·4	58·1	67·0	95·9
Singapore	47·9	99·9	81·7	84·6	219·1	267·5	315·4	347·0
China	90·7	128·6	153·7	146·3	197·3	233·4	241·7	263·3
Hong Kong	378·9	572·4	610·0	644·6	800·7	934·6	999·0	867·2
Korea, Rep. of	86·0	113·7	170·0	173·2	267·4	122·9	200·6	172·5
Taiwan	107·5	164·1	143·5	155·1	172·1	184·2	110·7	134·5
Japan	1,338·6	1,989·8	2,297·8	2,147·5	1,300·4	1,273·5	1,435·8	1,365·4
Philippines	22·0	30·3	34·7	35·3	75·9	84·4	94·9	103·4
Indonesia	62·6	61·8	65·2	47·5	89·4	103·2	159·5	204·5
Other Asian countries	87·7	154·5	85·0	112·4	236·0	236·5	350·1	430·6
Asia Total	3,440·8	5,172·9	5,443·5	4,937·5	6,812·5	7,245·2	8,011·9	8,745·0
Canada	220·0	339·2	364·2	288·6	384·3	420·4	536·6	518·5
USA	3,048·8	4,104·9	4,475·5	4,153·2	2,992·8	3,552·0	4,129·1	4,095·2
Mexico	65·2	84·6	31·6	37·5	281·2	371·9	526·1	410·0
Guatemala	53·4	58·2	45·9	43·3	57·1	45·7	47·6	29·5
Honduras	29·9	42·4	43·9	40·6	9·7	11·2	10·6	16·8
Costa Rica	44·1	51·9	49·1	43·7	17·0	13·8	10·8	7·9

		Imports from				Exports to		
Countries	1979	1980	1981	1982	1979	1980	1981	1982
Panama	215·9	302·6	273·1	241·8	224·3	226·9	342·5	192·5
Cuba	12·7	21·1	12·4	14·2	43·5	45·9	61·6	35·6
Colombia	56·7	116·2	77·2	65·3	112·1	130·5	137·1	120·7
Venezuela	12·1	15·0	10·6	7·9	200·4	179·6	227·4	242·1
Brazil	210·4	263·6	287·6	282·0	483·8	497·6	451·9	414·3
Uruguay	14·4	20·6	30·9	27·6	30·6	29·1	33·0	28·2
Argentina	115·4	116·4	137·4	113·7	309·0	318·2	323·2	354·9
Chile	13·5	11·1	11·7	20·5	57·6	72·7	76·7	80·1
Bolivia	2·5	2·5	2·3	2·6	28·8	13·5	39·6	10·8
Peru	31·9	44·9	48·4	23·7	74·3	96·0	141·3	99·9
Ecuador	21·8	14·6	15·4	14·8	70·9	66·4	55·0	62·9
Other American countries	93·0	100·6	113·5	94·2	130·5	173·0	205·1	229·8
Australia and Oceania	88·4	110·7	126·7	132·0	361·3	362·6	513·2	489·6

Custom receipts (in 1,000 francs): 1977, 2,920,800; 1978, 2,989,707; 1979, 3,002,117; 1980, 3,170,700; 1981, 3,243,631.

Total trade between Switzerland (including Liechtenstein) and UK for calendar years (British Department of Trade, in £1,000 sterling):

	1979	1980	1981	1982	1983
Imports to UK	2,564,773	2,614,690	1,708,058	1,669,922	2,154,085
Exports and re-exports from UK	2,407,328	3,076,337	1,601,164	1,196,203	1,385,694

Federal Customs Office, *Statistique mensuelle du commerce extérieur de la Suisse.* From 1925.—*Statistique annuelle du commerce extérieur de la Suisse.* 2 vols. From 1840.—*Rapport annuel de la statistique du commerce Suisse.* From 1889

Tourism. Tourism is an important industry. In 1982, overnight stays in hotels and sanatoria were 35,634,000 (31,327,000 by foreign visitors) and in other accommodation 40,723,000.

COMMUNICATIONS

Roads. There are (1982) 66,544 km of main roads, including 1,170 km of 'national roads' for motor cars only. There is a postal autobus service, which, in 1976, carried 53·7m. passengers. Motor vehicles, as at 30 Sept. 1982, numbered 2,998,000, including 2,473,000 private cars, 179,000 trucks, 178,000 motor cycles, 11,000 buses and 157,000 commercial and agricultural vehicles.

Railways. Railway history in Switzerland begins in 1847. In 1982 the length of the general traffic railways was 4,995 km, and of special lines (funiculars etc.), 859 km. The operating receipts of general traffic lines amounted to (1980) 3,373,416,000 francs; operating expenses, 4,101,371,000 francs. Traffic (1981) was 45m. tonnes and 218m. passengers.

There are many privately-owned lines, the most important of which are the Bern–Lotschberg–Simplon (115 km) and Rhaetian (363 km) networks.

Aviation. In 1981 civil aviation on domestic and international routes carried 12,166,842 passengers, 331,391 tonnes of mail, freight and luggage.

The air transport organization Swissair (founded in 1931) in 1982 carried 189,139 tonnes of freight and 7,168,567 passengers. Swissair had a capital of 422m. francs on 15 May 1977. Its fleet consisted of 53 aircraft in Jan. 1983.

Shipping. A merchant marine was created by a decree of the Swiss Government dated 9 April 1941, the place of registry of its vessels being Basel. In 1981 it consisted of 33 vessels with a total of 319,631 GRT. In 1981, 8,277,359 tonnes of goods were handled in the port of Basel.

Post and Broadcasting. In 1981 there were 3,906 post offices. On 1 Jan. 1982 there were 4,954,628 telephones, all integrated in one dial system.

Wireless communication is furnished by 3 main medium-wave stations and 1 short-wave station. There are 3 television studios and more than 100 transmitters.

TV programmes are financed by licence fees and advertisements. Advertisements are limited to 15 minutes each day. All stations are operated by the Federal Post, Telephone and Telegraph (PTT) services. Radio-telegraph circuits are operated by Radio Suisse SA, radio-telephone circuits by the PTT. Radio licences, 1982, 2,337,257; television licences, 2,057,062.

The total expenditure of the PTT in 1982 was 6,429 francs, the total gross receipts 6,562·2m. francs.

Cinemas (1982). There were 466 cinemas with a seating capacity of 149,975.

Newspapers (1980). The number of daily newspapers was estimated to be 126.

JUSTICE, RELIGION, EDUCATION AND WELFARE

Justice. The Federal Tribunal (*Bundes-Gericht*), which sits at Lausanne, consists of 26-28 members, with 11-13 supplementary judges, appointed by the Federal Assembly for 6 years and eligible for re-election; the President and Vice-President serve for 2 years and cannot be re-elected. The President has a salary of 170,000 francs a year, and the other members 158,000 francs. The Tribunal has original and final jurisdiction in suits between the Confederation and cantons; between cantons and cantons; between the Confederation or cantons and corporations or individuals, the value in dispute being not less than 8,000 francs; between parties who refer their case to it, the value in dispute being at least 20,000 francs; in such suits as the constitution or legislation of cantons places within its authority; and in many classes of railway suits. It is a court of appeal against decisions of other federal authorities, and of cantonal authorities applying federal laws. The Tribunal also tries persons accused of treason or other offences against the Confederation. For this purpose it is divided into 4 chambers: Chamber of Accusation, Criminal Chamber (*Cour d'Assises*), Federal Penal Court and Court of Cassation. The jurors who serve in the Assize Courts are elected by the people, and are paid 100 francs a day when serving.

On 3 July 1938 the Swiss electorate accepted a new federal penal code, to take the place of the separate cantonal penal codes. The new code, which abolished capital punishment, came into force on 1 Jan. 1942.

By federal law of 5 Oct. 1950 several articles of the penal code concerning crime against the independence of the state have been amended with a view to reinforcing the security of the State.

Thormann, P., and Overbeck, A. (ed.), *Das Schweizerische Strafgesetzbuch.* Zürich, 1939

Religion. There is complete and absolute liberty of conscience and of creed. No one is bound to pay taxes specially appropriated to defraying the expenses of a creed to which he does not belong. No bishoprics can be created on Swiss territory without the approbation of the Confederation.

According to the census of 1 Dec. 1980 Roman Catholics numbered 3,030,069 (47·6%) of the population; Protestants, 2,822,266 (44·3%) and others, 513,625 (8·1%). In 1960 Protestants were in a majority in 10 of the cantons and Catholics in 12. Of the more populous cantons, Zürich, Bern, Vaud, Neuchâtel and Basel (town and land) were mainly Protestant, while Luzern, Fribourg, Ticino, Valais and the Forest Cantons are mainly Catholic. The Roman Catholics are under 6 Bishops, viz., of Basel (resident at Solothurn), Chur, St Gallen, Lugano, Lausanne–Geneva–Fribourg (resident at Fribourg) and Sitten (Sion), all of them immediately subject to the Holy See. The Old Catholics have a theological faculty at the university of Bern.

Education. Education is administered by the cantons. Before the year 1848 most of the cantons had organized a system of primary schools, and since that year elementary education has steadily advanced. In 1874 it was made obligatory for the whole country (the school age varying in the different cantons) and placed under the civil authority. In some cantons the cost falls almost entirely on the communes, in others it is divided between the canton and communes. In all the cantons primary instruction is free.

In most cantons there are also secondary schools for youths of from 12 to 15, gymnasia, higher schools for girls, teachers' seminaries, commercial and administrative schools, trade schools, art schools, technical schools, schools for the instruction of girls in domestic economy and other subjects, agricultural schools, schools for horticulture, for viticulture, for arboriculture and for dairy management. There are also institutions for the blind, the deaf and dumb and feeble-minded.

There are 7 universities in Switzerland. These universities are organized on the model of those of Germany, governed by a rector and a senate, and divided into 4 faculties of theology, jurisprudence, philosophy and medicine. In 1980–81 the Federal Institute of Technology at Zürich (founded in 1855) had 658 teachers and (1981–82) 7,556 matriculated students; the Federal Institute of Technology at Lausanne, independent of the university since 1946, had 217 teachers and (1981–82) 2,316 students; the St Gall School of Economics and Social Sciences, founded in 1899, had 148 teachers and (1981–82) 2,008 matriculated students.

University statistics in the winter of 1981–82:

	The-ology	Law	Eco-nomics	Medi-cine	Science	Others	Total	Teaching staff (1980–81)
Basel (1460)	191	905	537	1,676	1,167	1,554	6,030	506
Zürich (1523 & 1833)	222	2,529	1,044	3,122	2,071	6,464	15,452	1,618
Bern (1528 & 1834)	224	1,556	488	1,823	1,405	2,312	7,808	810
Genève (1559[1] & 1873[1])	126	986	870	1,498	1,382	5,454	10,316	831
Lausanne (1537[1] & 1890[2])	93	818	717	1,491	780	1,809	5,708	433
Fribourg (1889)	432	635	593	375	471	2,012	4,518	465
Neuchâtel (1866 & 1909)	52	215	237	91	463	926	1,984	215

[1] Founded as an academy.　　　　　　[2] Reorganized as a university.

These numbers are exclusive of 'visitors', but inclusive of women students.

Social Security. The Federal Insurance Law against illness and accident, of 13 June 1911, entitles all Swiss citizens to insurance against illness; foreigners may be admitted to the benefits. Compulsory insurance against illness does not exist as yet, but cantons and communities are entitled to declare insurance obligatory for certain classes or to establish public benefit (sick fund) associations, and to make employers responsible for the payment of the premiums of their employees. In 1980 the 469 societies insuring against illness had 6,811,581 members.

Unemployment insurance is based since 13 June 1976 upon a Constitution amendment which stipulates unemployment insurance as compulsory for all wage-earners.

A federal law was in preparation in 1976. At 30 Sept. 1975 there existed 123 public and private unemployment insurance organizations with a total membership (31 March 1977) of 1,435,577 (53·5% of working population).

Insurance against accident is compulsory for all officials, employees and workmen of all the factories, trades, etc., which are under the federal liability law. The Swiss Accident Insurance Institution commenced operations on 1 April 1918.

On 6 July 1947 a federal law was accepted by a referendum, providing compulsory old age and widows and widowers insurance for the whole population, as from 1 Jan. 1948. In March 1981 the number of normal pensioners was 983,063, the number of interim pensioners, 34,379. On 1 Jan. 1960 the old-age insurance scheme was extended to cover invalidity. In March 1981, 184,174 invalids received a regular annuity and 20,731 invalids an interim annuity.

DIPLOMATIC REPRESENTATIVES

Of Switzerland in Great Britain (16–18 Montagu Place, London, W1H 2BQ)
Ambassador: François-Charles Pictet (accredited 9 Feb. 1984).

Of Great Britain in Switzerland (Thunstrasse 50, 30005 Bern)
Ambassador: John Powell-Jones, CMG.

Of Switzerland in the USA (2900 Cathedral Ave., NW, Washington, D.C., 20008)
Ambassador: Anton Hegner.

Of the USA in Switzerland (Jubilaeumstrasse 93, 3005, Bern)
Ambassador: John D. Lodge.

Books of Reference

Statistical Information: The Bureau fédéral de statistique (Hallwylstr. 15, 3003 Bern) was established in 1860. *Director:* J.-J. Senglet. Its principal publications are:

Annuaire statistique de la Suisse. Bâle. From 1891
Statistique de la Suisse. From 1930
Contributions à la Statistique Suisse. From 1930
Bibliographie Suisse de statistique et d'économie politique. Annual, from 1937

Swiss Confederation
Annuaire; Budget; Message du Budget; Compte d'Etat (annual) *Feuille Fédérale; Recueil des Lois fédérales* (weekly)
Recueil systématique des lois et ordonnances, 1848–1947 (in German, French and Italian). Bern, 1951
Sammlung der Bundes- und Kantonsverfassungen (in German, French and Italian). Bern, 1937

Federal Department of Economics
La vie économique (and supplements). Monthly. From 1928
Législation sociale de la Suisse. Annual, from 1928

Behrendt, R. F. (ed.), *Strukturwandlugen der schweizerischen Wirtschaft und Gesellschaft.* Bern, 1962
Bonjour, E., Offler, H. S., and Potter, G. R., *A Short History of Switzerland.* Oxford, 1952
Dürrenmatt, P., *Schweizer Geschichte.* Zürich, 1963.—*Schweiz.* Zürich, 1962.—*Wir Schweizer und der totale Krieg.* Zürich, 1960
Imhof, E. (ed.), *Atlas der Schweiz.* Bern, 1965 ff.
Riklin, A., *et al, Handbuch der schweizerischen Aussenpolitik.* Bern, 1975
Schwarz, U., *The Eye of the Hurricane: Switzerland in World War Two.* Boulder, 1980
Sorell, W., *The Swiss: A Cultural Panorama of Switzerland.* Indianapolis, 1972. London, 1973
Unser Schweizer Standpunkt 1914, 1939, 1964. Bern, 1964

National Library: Bibliothèque Nationale Suisse, Hallwylstr.15, 3003, Bern. *Director:* F. G. Maier.

SYRIA

al-Jamhouriya al Arabia as-Souriya

Capital: Damascus
Population: 9·84m. (1983)
GNP per capita: US$1,340 (1980)

HISTORY. For the history of Syria from 1920 to 1946 *see* THE STATESMAN'S YEAR-BOOK, 1957, pp. 1408 f. Complete independence was achieved on 12 Apr. 1946. Syria merged with Egypt to form the United Arab Republic from 2 Feb. 1958 until 29 Sept. 1961, when independence was resumed following a *coup* the previous day. Lieut.-Gen. Hafez al-Assad became Prime Minister following the fifth *coup* of that decade on 13 Nov. 1970, and assumed the Presidency on 22 Feb. 1971.

AREA AND POPULATION. Syria is bounded by the Mediterranean and the Lebanese Republic on the west, by Israel and Jordan on the south, by Iraq on the east and by Turkey on the north. The frontier between Syria and Turkey (Nisibim-Jeziret ibn Omar) was settled by the Franco-Turkish agreement of 22 June 1929.

The area of Syria is 185,180 sq. km (71,498 sq. miles), of which 35,000 sq. km have been surveyed. The census of 1981 gave a total population of 9,171,622, showing about 10% less than the estimates. Estimate (1983) 9·84m. The 14 *mohafaza* (administrative districts) with population, 1975, were: City of Damascus, 1,042,000; Damascus, excluding city, 732,000; Aleppo, 1,523,000; Homs, 629,000; Hama (1970), 514,748; Lattakia (1970), 389,552; Deir-el-Zor, 332,000; Idlib, 428,000; Hassakeh, 532,000; Raqqa, 281,000; Sweida, 162,000; Derá, 282,000; Tartous, 348,000; Kunaitra, 19,000.

Principal towns (census 1970), Damascus, 836,668; Aleppo, 639,428; Homs, 215,423; Hama, 137,421; Lattakia, 125,716; Deir-el-Zor, 66,143.

Arabic is the official language.

CLIMATE. The climate is Mediterranean in type, with mild wet winters and dry, hot summers, though there are variations in temperatures and rainfall between the coastal regions and the interior, which even includes desert conditions. The more moutainous parts are subject to snowfall. Damascus. Jan. 45°F (7°C), July 81°F (27°C). Annual rainfall 9″ (225 mm).

CONSTITUTION AND GOVERNMENT. A new Constitution was approved by plebiscite on 12 March 1973 and promulgated on 14 March. It confirmed the Arab Socialist Renaissance *(Ba'ath)* Party, in power since 1963, as the 'leading party in the State and society'. Legislative power is held by a 195-member People's Council, elected for a 4-year term. At the latest elections on 10 Nov. 1981, all seats were won by the National Progressive Front, a coalition of the Ba'ath Party and 4 smaller ones.

President: Lieut.-Gen. Hafez al Assad (re-elected for further 7-year term in 1978).

First Vice-President: Abdul Halim Khaddam *(Political and Foreign Affairs).* *Second Vice-President:* Rifaat al Assad *(Defence and Security). Third Vice-President:* Mohammed Zuhair Mashrqa *(Party Affairs).*

Prime Minister: Dr Abdul Rauf al-Kasm.

National flag: Three horizontal stripes of red, white, black, with 2 green stars on the white stripe.

DEFENCE. Military service is compulsory for a period of 30 months.

Army. The Army is organized into 4 armoured and 2 mechanized infantry divisions, 2 armoured, 4 mechanized, 2 artillery brigades, 5 commando and 1 parachute regiment and 2 surface-to-surface missile regiments and 26 surface-to-air missile batteries. Strength (1984) about 170,000 (including 120,000 conscripts) and reserves 100,000. There are a further 10,000 men in paramilitary forces. Equipment includes 2,200 T-54/-55, 1,100 T-62 and 900 T-72 main battle tanks.

Navy. The Navy includes 2 small frigates, 20 missile boats, 8 torpedo boats, 1 minesweeper, 2 coastal minesweepers, 1 inshore minesweeper, 3 coastal patrol craft and 1 diving ship (all ex-Soviet) and the 3 patrol vessels (ex-French) transferred in 1962 to form the nucleus of the Syrian Navy. Personnel in 1984 totalled 2,500 officers and men.

Air Force. The Air Force, including Air Defence Command, is believed to have about 50,000 personnel and about 450 first-line jet combat aircraft, made up of about 200 MiG-21, 20 MiG-23 and 24 MiG-25 supersonic interceptors, 60 MiG-23, 16 Su-7, 40 Su-22 and 80 MiG-17 fighter-bombers, plus some MiG-25 reconnaissance aircraft. Additional aircraft are being purchased from the USSR with Saudi Arabian aid. Training units have Spanish-built Flamingo piston-engined primary trainers and Czechoslovakian L-29 Delfin jet basic trainers. There are also transport units with Il-76, An-12, An-24/26, C-47, Il-14 and other types, and helicopter units with Soviet-built Ka-25s, Mi-6s, Mi-8s and Mi-24 gunships, and French-built Gazelles. 'Guideline', 'Goa', 'Gainful' and 'Gaskin' surface-to-air missiles are widely deployed in Syria by Air Defence Command, and 'Gammon' long-range surface-to-air missiles in Lebanon.

INTERNATIONAL RELATIONS

Membership. Syria is a member of UN and the Arab League.

ECONOMY

Planning. The total investment envisaged in the fifth 5-year plan (1981–85) £Syr.101,493m.

Budget. The ordinary budget for the calendar year 1983 provides for expenditure of £Syr.18,672m. and development expenditure of £Syr.18,581m.

Currency. The monetary unit is the Syrian *pound*, divided into 100 *piastres*. In March 1984, £1 = £Syr.10; US$1 = £Syr.3·93.

Banking. The Central Bank has the sole right of issuing currency. Other banks were nationalized in March 1963, namely, the Omaya Bank and its subsidiary, the Popular Mortgage Bank; the Orient Arab Bank; the Bank of Syria and Overseas; the Agricultural Bank; the Arab World Bank. Number of branches, 1973: Central Bank of Syria, 9; Commercial Bank of Syria, 22; Industrial Bank, 3; Agricultural Co-operative Bank, 50; Real Estate Bank, 3; Bank of Popular Discount, 27.

Weights and Measures. A decree dated 22 Aug. 1935 makes the use of the metric system legal and obligatory throughout the whole of the country. In outlying districts the former weights and measures may still be in use. They are: 1 *okiya* = 0·47 lb.; 6 *okiyas* = 1 *oke* = 2·82 lb.; 2 *okes* = 1 *rottol* = 5·64 lb.; 200 *okes* = 1 *kantar*.

ENERGY AND NATURAL RESOURCES

Oil. A branch of the Iraq Petroleum Co.'s oil pipeline from Kirkuk crosses Syria between Makaleb in the east and Nahr el Kebir valley in the west. The Iraq Petroleum Co. has constructed a new pipeline from Kirkuk to the small fishing port of Banias (south of Lattakia), which came into use in April 1952; the Trans-Arabian Pipeline Co.'s line to Sidon crosses southern Syria. Another pipeline is being constructed from the Karachouk oilfield *via* Homs to the port of Tartous. Crude oil production (1981) 9m. tonnes. Reserves (1983) 1,521m. bbls.

Gas. Gas reserves (1982) 700,000m. cubic ft.

Minerals. Phosphate deposits have been discovered at two places near al-Shargiya and at Khneifis. Production, 1975, 857,000 tonnes; other minerals were salt,

34,000; natural asphalt, 31,000. There are indications of lead, copper, antimony, nickel, chrome and other minerals widely distributed. Manganese ore was mined before 1914. Sodium chloride and bitumen deposits are being worked. There is abundance of good calcareous building stone and basalt.

Agriculture. Syria is an agricultural country but is moving towards greater industrialization, the bulk of the population being engaged in the cultivation of the soil and in cattle breeding. In 1977 the irrigated area was 531,000 hectares; in 1980, 139,000 hectares under cotton and 1,449,000 hectares were under wheat, 1,587,000 hectares under barley. The total cultivable area was 14·47m. hectares, including 455,000 hectares of forest and 8,631,000 hectares of steppe and pasture.

Yield of principal crops, 1980 (in 1,000 tonnes): Wheat, 2,226; barley, 1,587; cotton (1982), 422; olives, 392; lentils, 83; millet, 19; sugar-beet, 505.

Livestock (1982): Cattle, 810,000; asses, 242,000; sheep, 11m.; goats, 1·1m.; poultry, 15m.

Fishing. The total catch in 1979 was 3,700 tonnes.

INDUSTRY AND TRADE

Industry. The most important industries are flour, oils, soap, cement, tanning, tobacco, textiles, knitwear, glassware, spinning, sugar, margarine, hosiery, footwear and brassware.

Industrial production in 1980 included (in 1,000 tonnes): Woollen fabrics, 1,200; cement, 2,310; sugar, 141; salt, 111; cotton yarn, 25·2; manufactured tobacco, 9·9.

Commerce. Trade in calendar years in £Syr.1m. was as follows:

	1978	1979	1980	1981
Imports	8,935	13,067	16,188	19,781
Exports	4,160	6,453	8,273	8,254

Cotton is one of the chief exports. Others include oil, cereals, live animals and phosphates. Imports include industrial raw materials, machinery, chemicals and electrical equipment.

Total trade between Syria and UK (British Department of Trade returns, in £1,000 sterling):

	1980	1981	1982	1983
Imports to UK	12,241	4,555	25,644	18,859
Exports and re-exports from UK	81,584	85,244	89,535	72,320

Tourism. In 1981, 1,075,100 tourists visited Syria.

COMMUNICATIONS

Roads. In 1980 there were 13,000 km of asphalted roads, 1,300 km of macadam non-asphalted road and 6,000 km of earth roads. The first-class roads are capable of carrying all types of modern motor transport and are usable all the year round, while the second-class roads are usable during the dry season only, i.e., for about 9 months. The Nairn Transport Company operate a trans-desert pullman motor coach service between Damascus and Baghdad. There are also two pullman transport companies (Elkarnak, Syrian, and Jett, Jordanian) operating a joint service between Damascus and Amman. The motor vehicles registered in 1979 were 28,542 motor cycles, 7,420 buses, 66,243 cars and 85,978 goods vehicles.

Railways. In Syria the following railways are open (in addition to those listed under LEBANON (p. 785)): Standard gauge from Aleppo to Meidan-Ekbes (Turkish frontier), 116 km; Aleppo to Tel-Kotchek (Iraq frontier), 523 km; narrow gauge from Damascus to El Hammé, 195 km; Damascus to Dera'a (Jordan frontier), 130 km. Two lines have recently been constructed: a standard gauge from Akari to Tartous, 42 km, and the 755-km Latakia-Aleppo-Kamechli, opened to traffic in 1976 while the standard gauge Homs to Damascus line was opened in 1983, with a branch to Palmyra. Total network 1,533 km, traffic carried (1980) 1·3m. passengers, 2·4m. tonnes.

Aviation. In 1980, 12,557 aircraft arrived at Damascus and Aleppo airports, disembarking 559,430 passengers.

Shipping. The amount of cargo discharged in 1980 was 2·6m. tons and the amount loaded 430,000 tons. Development of the port of Latakia was in progress in 1983 and a new port was under construction at Tartous.

Post and Broadcasting. An automatic telephone system has been installed in Damascus, and most other towns. Number of telephones (1982), 471,127; of these, 154,615 were in Damascus and 72,981 in Aleppo. There were 1·8m. radio sets in 1982 and 387,000 television receivers.

Newspapers. There were (1977) 3 national daily newspapers in Damascus; other dailies and periodicals appear in Hama, Homs, Aleppo and Latakia.

JUSTICE, RELIGION, EDUCATION AND WELFARE

Justice. Syrian law is based on both Islamic and French jurisprudence. There are 2 courts of first instance in each district, one for civil and 1 for criminal cases. There is also a Summary Court in each sub-district, under Justices of the Peace. There is a Court of Appeal in the capital of each governorate, with a Court of Cassation in Damascus.

Religion. The population is composed mainly of Sunni Moslems and there are also Shiites and Ismailis. There are also Druzes and Alawites. Christians include Greek Orthodox, Greek Catholics, Armenian Orthodox, Syrian Orthodox, Armenian Catholics, Protestants, Maronites, Syrian Catholics, Latins, Nestorians and Assyrians. There are also Jews and Yezides.

Education. The Syrian University was founded in 1924, although the faculties of law and of medicine had existed previously. In 1975 there were 3 universities with 94,794 students.

In 1980, state primary schools had 47,657 teachers and 1,407,388 pupils; secondary and intermediate schools, 28,847 teachers and 519,453 pupils; vocational schools, 3,161 teachers and 24,440 pupils; teacher-training colleges, 1,141 teachers and 10,612 students.

Health. In 1977 there were 7,479 hospital beds (1 per 983 persons) in 31 state hospitals, 69 private hospitals and 4 sanatoria.

DIPLOMATIC REPRESENTATIVES

Of Syria in Great Britain (8 Belgrave Sq., London, SW1X 8PH)
Ambassador: Dr Loutof Allah Haydar (accredited 9 Dec. 1982).

Of Great Britain in Syria (Quarter Malki, 11 Mohammed Kurd Ali St., Damascus)
Ambassador: The Hon. Ivor Lucas, CMG.

Of Syria in the USA (2215 Wyoming Ave., NW, Washington, D.C., 20008)
Ambassador: Dr Rafic Jouejati.

Of the USA in Syria (Abu Rumaneh, Al Mansur St., Damascus)
Ambassador: Robert P. Paganelli.

Of Syria to the United Nations
Ambassador: Dia-Allah El-Fattal.

Books of Reference

Statistical Information: There is a Central Statistics Bureau affiliated to the Council of Ministers. Damascus. It publishes a monthly summary and an annual Statistical Abstract (in Arabic and English).

Abd-Allah, U. F., *The Islamic Struggle in Syria.* Berkeley, 1983
Barthélemy, A., *Dictionnaire arabe-français. Dialectes de Syrie.* 4 vols. Paris, 1935–50
Devlin, J. F., *Syria: Modern State in an Ancient Land.* Boulder, 1983
Hourani, A. H., *Syria and Lebanon.* 2nd ed. R. Inst. of Int. Affairs, 1954
Petran, T., *Syria.* London, 1972

UNITED REPUBLIC OF TANZANIA

Capital: Dodoma
Population: 19·73m. (1983)
GNP per capita: US$260 (1980)

HISTORY. German East Africa was occupied by German colonialists from 1884 and placed under the protection of the German Empire in 1891. It was conquered in the First World War and subsequently divided between the British and Belgians. The latter received the territories of Ruanda and Urundi and the British the remainder, except for the Kionga triangle, which went to Portugal. The country was administered as a League of Nations mandate until 1946 and then as a UN trusteeship territory until 9 Dec. 1961.

Tanganyika achieved responsible government in Sept. 1960 and full self-government on 1 May 1961. On 9 Dec. 1961 Tanganyika became a sovereign independent member state of the Commonwealth of Nations. It adopted a republican form of government on 9 Dec. 1962. For history from the end of the 17th century until 1884 *see* THE STATESMAN'S YEAR-BOOK 1982–83, p. 1170.

On 24 June 1963 Zanzibar became an internal self-governing state and on 9 Dec. 1963 she became independent. On 24 June 1963 the Legislative Council was replaced by a National Assembly.

On 12 Jan. 1964 the sultanate was overthrown and the sultan sent into exile by a revolt of the Afro-Shirazi Party leaders who established the People's Republic of Zanzibar.

On 26 April 1964 Tanganyika, Zanzibar and Pemba combined to form the United Republic of Tanganyika and Zanzibar (named Tanzania on 29 Oct.).

AREA AND POPULATION. Tanzania is bounded north-east by Kenya, north by Lake Victoria and Uganda, north-west by Rwanda and Burundi, west by Lake Tanganyika, south-west by Zambia and Malawi and south by Mozambique. Total area 945,050 sq. km (364,886 sq. miles). The census of Aug. 1978 gave 17,551,925 for the United Republic, of which 17,076,270 were counted in mainland Tanzania and 475,655 in Zanzibar. Estimate (1983) 19·73m.

The chief towns (1978 census populations) are Dar es Salaam, the chief port and former capital (757,346), Zanzibar Town (110,669), Mwanza (110,611), Dodoma, the capital (45,703), Tanga (103,409), Arusha (55,281), Mbeya (76,606), Morogoro (61,890), Mtwara (48,510), Tabora (67,392), Iringa (57,182), and Kigoma (50,044).

The populations of the 22 regions were as follows at the 1978 Census:

Arusha	928,478	Mara	723,295	Rukwa	451,897
Dar es Salaam	851,522	Mbeya	1,080,241	Ruvuma	564,113
Dodoma	971,921	Morogoro	939,190	Shinyanga	1,323,482
Iringa	922,801	Mtwara	771,726	Singida	614,030
Kagera	1,009,379	Mwanza	1,443,418	Tabora	818,049
Kigoma	648,950	Pemba	205,850	Tanga	1,088,592
Kilimanjaro	902,394	Pwani	516,949	Zanzibar	273,365
Lindi	527,902				

Kiswahili is the national language.

CLIMATE. The climate is very varied and is controlled very largely by altitude and distance from the sea. There are three climatic zones: the hot and humid coast, the drier central plateau with seasonal variations of temperature, and the semi-temperate mountains. Dodoma. Jan. 75°F (23·9°C), July 67°F (19·4°C). Annual rainfall 23″ (572 mm). Dar es Salaam. Jan. 82°F (27·8°C), July 74°F (23·3°C). Annual rainfall 43″ (1,064 mm).

CONSTITUTION AND GOVERNMENT. An 'interim constitution' was approved by parliament on 5 July 1965 and assented to by the President on 8 July 1965. A new permanent Constitution was approved in April 1977.

The country is a one-party state. The Tanganyika African National Union and the Afro-Shirazi Party in Zanzibar merged into one revolutionary party, *Chama cha Mapinduzi,* in Jan. 1977.

The President of the United Republic is head of state, chairman of the party and commander-in-chief of the armed forces. The vice-president is head of the executive in Zanzibar and vice-chairman of the party; the Prime Minister is also the leader of the National Assembly.

The National Assembly is composed of 111 elected members, 32 Parliament Members from the Zanzibar Revolutionary Council, 20 Nominated Members from Zanzibar, 25 National Members representing regions, 15 National Members representing mass organizations affiliated to the party, 10 Nominated Members from the mainland and 25 regional secretaries who are *ex-officio* members.

In Dec. 1979 a separate Constitution for Zanzibar was approved. Although at present (1981) under the same Constitution as Tanzania, Zanzibar has, in fact, been ruled by decree since 1964.

The Government was in March 1984 composed as follows:

President of the United Republic: Dr Julius K. Nyerere (re-elected for a further 5-year term in Oct. 1980).

Vice-President: Ali Hassan Mwinyi. *Prime Minister:* Cleopa Msuya.

Foreign Affairs: Salim Ahmed Salim. *Defence and National Service:* Abdallah Twalipo. *Home Affairs:* Brig. Muhiddin Kimaryo. *Finance:* Amir Jamal. *Agriculture:* John B. Machunda. *Justice:* Julie Manning. *Industry:* Basil Mramba. *Land, Housing and Urban Development:* Mustafa Nyang'anyi. *Labour and Social Welfare:* Alfred Tandau. *National Education:* Tabitha Siwale. *Trade:* Lt.-Col. Ali S. Mchumo. *Water and Energy:* Al Noor Kassimu. *Mines:* Jackson Makweta. *Communication and Transport:* John W. Malecela. *Information and Culture:* Daudi Mwakawago. *Animal Husbandry:* Herman Kirigini. *Works:* Samuel Sitta. *Health:* Aaron D. Chiduo. *Natural Resources and Tourism:* Ali H. Mwinyi. *Ministers of State:* George Kahama *(President's Office);* Aboud Aboud, Kighoma Malima *(Vice-President's Office);* Pius Ng'wandu, Paul Kimiti, Getrude Mongella *(Prime Minister's Office). Without Portfolio:* Rashid Kawawa, Abdallah Natepe.

National flag: Divided diagonally green, black, blue, with the black strip edged in yellow.

DEFENCE

Army. The Army consists of 8 infantry brigades; 1 tank, 2 artillery, 2 anti-aircraft, 2 mortar, 1 surface-to-air missile, 2 anti-tank and 2 signals battalions. Equipment includes 30 Chinese Type-59 main battle tanks. Strength (1984) 38,500. There is also a Citizen's Militia of 50,000 men.

Navy. There are 11 fast gunboats (7 *ex*-Chinese and 4 *ex*-GDR), 4 fast torpedo boats and 8 coastal patrol craft; Zanzibar operated another 4 coastal patrol craft. Personnel (1983) 700.

Air Force. The Tanzanian People's Defence Force Air Wing was built up initially with the help of Canada, but combat equipment is now being acquired from China. Personnel totalled about 950 in 1983, with about 15 J-7 (MiG-21), 10 J-6 (MiG-19) and 3 J-5 (MiG-17) jet fighters; 1 F28 Fellowship VIP transport; 6 Buffalo twin-engined STOL transports; 3 HS 748 and some An-26 and An-32 turboprop transports; 1 An-2 light transport; 2 Cessna 404 liaison aircraft; 2 Agusta-built Chinook helicopters; 6 Agusta-Bell JetRanger and 2 Bell 47G light helicopters; and Piper Cherokee, Cessna 310, L-39 Albatross and FT-5 (Chinese-built MiG-17) trainers.

INTERNATIONAL RELATIONS

Membership. Tanzania is a member of UN, OAU, the Commonwealth and is an ACP state of EEC.

ECONOMY

Planning. The third 5-year plan starting 1977 envisaged small but actively growing industrial factories to manufacture small parts with the object of improving foreign exchange earnings.

Budget. Revenue and expenditure (in Tanzanian Sh. 1m.) for financial years ending 30 June:

	1977–78	1978–79	1979–80	1980–81	1981–82	1982–83[1]
Revenue	9,556·2	9,523·0	7,270·0	12,296·1	10,460	10,700
Expenditure	9,556·0	12,267·2	9,100·0	14,802·4	13,687	14,144

[1]Estimate.

Import duties in 1978–79 amounted to Sh. 950m. and income tax to Sh. 1,574m. The main items of expenditure for the year 1969–70 were communications, transport and labour (Sh. 278·5m.), education (Sh. 56·2m.) and agriculture, food and co-operatives (Sh. 109·9m.).

Development expenditure, 1982–83 (estimate), was Sh. 4,816m.

Currency. The monetary unit is the *Tanzanian shilling* divided into 100 *cents*. The Tanzanian coinage has denominations of 5, 10, 20, 50 cents, 1 Sh., 5 Sh., 20 Sh. and 1,500 Sh.; notes, 10 Sh., 20 Sh. and 100 Sh. Notes and coins in circulation at the end of Dec. 1978 were Sh. 3,143m. In 1966 the country left the East African Currency Board, establishing its own national currency, the Tanzanian shilling. In March 1984, £1 = Sh. 16·12; US$ = Sh. 12·31.

Banking. On 14 June 1966 the central bank called the Bank of Tanzania, with a government-owned capital of Sh. 20m., began operations.

On 6 Feb. 1967 all commercial banks with the exception of National Co-operative Banks were nationalized and their interests vested in the National Bank of Commerce on the mainland and the Peoples' Bank in Zanzibar.

Weights. Tanzania has adopted the International System of Weights and Measures (SI), which has been introduced progressively since 1969. An important local unit of weight is the frasla (or frasila) = 35 lb. av.

ENERGY AND NATURAL RESOURCES

Electricity. A hydro-electric station on the Pangani River near Tanga has been built; £3m. of its estimated cost of £5·25m. is being provided by the Commonwealth Development Corporation. The second phase of the Kidatu power-station in Morogoro region is nearing completion; total power generated, 200 mw. Kiwira River power project, estimated to cost Sh.55m., has been completed, total capacity 24 mw. The Musoma power-station has also been completed with a capacity of 6 mw. The Mbeya-Iyunga power-station, capacity 12·5 mw, was completed in 1981.

Minerals. The value of mineral exports in 1976 was Sh. 550m. Principal exports, 1977, were (in Sh. 1m.): Diamonds, 181·3; gold, 50·9; salt, 12; gemstones, 1·8. New discoveries of coal and iron ore were made in the south while copper, cobalt, nickel and tin deposits have been found in Western Tanganyika. Gas, at shallow depths, has been found off the coast.

Agriculture. Production of main agricultural crops in 1981 (in 1,000 tons) was: Maize, 750; sisal, 81; cotton, 167; sugar, 1,287; coffee, 68; wheat, 70; tobacco, 21. Production of sisal has been declining since 1967. The Tanganyika Sisal Corporation has embarked on a diversification programme by introducing various new crops. Crops already planned are cardamon, beans, cashew nuts, citrus, cocoa, coconuts, cotton, maize and timber. Cattle ranching, dairying and twine spinning have also been introduced.

Zanzibar provides the greater part of the world's supply of cloves. There are about 40,000 hectares under cloves with about 1·5m. trees; five-sixths of the clove output is produced on Pemba. Cloves and clove oil (distilled from the stems) form more than half Zanzibar's exports. In recent years cloves production has decreased from an average annual figure of 12,000 tons to 4,000 in 1974 but reached 10,000 tons in 1976.

The coconut industry ranks next in importance. There are about 5·5m. bearing trees in both islands. Chillies, cocoa, limes, other tropical fruits and coil tobacco are also cultivated. The chief food crops are rice, bananas, cassava, pulses, maize and sorghum.

Livestock (1982, including Zanzibar): 13·15m. cattle, 3·9m. sheep, 5·9m. goats, 25m. poultry.

Forestry. Total production (1979) 67,000 cu. metres (coniferous 20,000).

Fisheries. A Fisheries Development Co. is catching sardines and tuna for export. In 1976, 400 tons were exported valued at Sh. 3·5m.

INDUSTRY AND TRADE

Industry. Industry is limited and is mainly textiles, food processing, tobacco and brewing.

Commerce. Total trade (in Sh. 1m.):

	1976	1977	1978	1979	1980	1981
Imports	5,350	6,200	8,582	8,941	10,047	10,065
Exports	4,108	4,537	3,514	4,296	4,165	5,248

In 1980, 17% of imports came from UK, 10% from Federal Republic of Germany, 9% from Japan, 6% Iraq, 6% Netherlands, and 6% USA; 18% of exports went to UK, 13% to Federal Republic of Germany, and 10% to Indonesia.

Major export items 1981 (in Sh. 1m.): Coffee, 1,456; cotton, 689; sisal, 291; cloves, 417; tea, 182; tobacco, 165.

Total trade between Tanzania and UK (British Department of Trade returns, in £1,000 sterling):

	1980	1981	1982	1983
Imports to UK	36,501	25,290	19,521	46,525
Exports and re-exports from UK	110,910	83,643	71,985	62,056

Tourism. In 1981 about 91,600 tourists visited Tanzania.

COMMUNICATIONS

Roads. In 1980 there were 45,631 km of roads and 42,900 cars and 52,100 commercial vehicles.

Railways. On 23 Sept. 1977 the independent Tanzanian Railway Corporation was formed following the break-up of the East African Railways administration. The network totals 2,600 km (metre-gauge), excluding the Tan-Zam Railway 969 km in Tanzania (1,067 mm gauge) operated by a separate administration. In 1980, the state railway carried 2.6m. passengers and 1.2m. tonnes of freight.

Aviation. There are 53 aerodromes and landing strips maintained or licensed by Government; of these, 2 are of international standards category (Dar es Salaam and Kilimanjaro) and 18 are suitable for Dakotas. Air Tanzania Corporation provide regular and frequent services to all the more important towns within the territory and to Mozambique, Zambia, Seychelles, Comoro, Rwanda, Burundi and Madagascar.

There is an all-weather landing-ground in Zanzibar and a smaller all-weather landing-ground in Pemba.

Shipping. In 1980 there were 1,296 ships of 3,176,000 NRT.

Post and Broadcasting. In 1982 there were 96,521 telephones. There are 2 broadcasting stations and colour television operates in Zanzibar. In 1979 there were 5,800 television receivers (on Zanzibar only) and 500,000 radio receivers.

Newspapers (1976). There were 2 dailies, 1 Sunday newspaper, 2 fortnightlies and several monthly magazines.

JUSTICE, RELIGION, EDUCATION AND WELFARE

Justice. The Tanzanian Court of Appeal, which in Sept. 1979 replaced the former Court of Appeal for East Africa, comprises a Chief Justice and 4 Judges of Appeal. The High Court sits regularly in all Regions, but there is a District Court in each District (presided over by a Resident Magistrate) which hears appeals from the more than 800 Primary Courts with jurisdiction over customary and Islamic law.

Religion. In 1980 some 44% were Christian, including Roman Catholics under the Archbishops of Dar es Salaam and Tabora, Anglicans under the Archbishop of Tanzania, and Lutherans. Moslems amount to 33%, but reach 66% in the coastal towns; Zanzibar is 96% Moslem and 4% Hindu. Some 23% follow traditional religions.

Education. The educational system has been integrated on non-racial lines. Schools are maintained by the Government, private and agencies, including missions.

In 1981 there were 9,980 primary schools with 3,538,183 pupils.

Technical and vocational education is provided at several secondary and technical schools and at the Dar es Salaam Technical College.

There were, in 1981, 35 colleges of national education, including the college at Chang'ombe for secondary-school teachers, with 14,785 students and (1980) 170 secondary schools with 9,178 pupils. Five technical secondary schools had 3,129 students in 1981.

In 1981, the Dar es Salaam University had a total of 3,650 students. In the 4 years (1972–76) illiteracy was reduced to about 31%. The University of Dar es Salaam, independent since 1970, has faculties of science, law, arts, social sciences, medicine, agriculture, engineering, commerce and management, veterinary science and forestry.

Health. In 1981 there were 599 doctors and 149 hospitals with 21,352 beds.

DIPLOMATIC REPRESENTATIVES

Of Tanzania in Great Britain (43 Hertford St., London, W1)
High Commissioner: Anthony Balthazar Nyakyi (accredited 15 Dec. 1982).

Of Great Britain in Tanzania (Hifadhi Hse., Samora Ave., Dar es Salaam)
High Commissioner: John Sankey, CMG.

Of Tanzania in the USA (2139 R St., NW, Washington, D.C., 20008)
Ambassador: Benjamin Mkapa.

Of the USA in Tanzania (36 Laibon Rd., Dar es Salaam)
Ambassador: David C. Miller, Jr.

Of Tanzania to the United Nations
Ambassador: Paul Milyango Rupia.

Books of Reference

Atlas of Tanganyika. 3rd ed. Dar es Salaam, 1956
Tanganyika Notes and Records. Tanganyika Society, Dar es Salaam. (Twice yearly, from 1936) *The Economic Development of Tanganyika. Report . . . by the International Bank.* Johns Hopkins Univ. Press and OUP, 1961
Ayany, S. G., *A History of Zanzibar.* Nairobi, 1970
Coulson, A., *Tanzania: A Political Economy.* OUP, 1982
Ingle, C. R., *From Village to State in Tanzania.* London, 1973
Mwansasu, B., *Towards Socialism in Tanzania.* Univ. of Toronto Press, 1979
Nellis, J. R., *A Theory of Ideology: The Tanzanian Example.* New York, OUP, 1972
Nyerere, J., *Freedom and Development.* New York, 1976
Resnick, I. N., *The Long Transition: Building Socialism in Tanzania.* New York and London, 1981
Samoff, J., *Tanzania: Local Politics and the Structure of Power.* Univ. of Wisconsin Press, 1975
Yeager, R., *Tanzania: An African Experiment.* Aldershot, 1982
Yu, G. T., *China's African Policy: A Study of Tanzania.* New York, 1975

THAILAND

Prathes Thai, or Muang-Thai

Capital: Bangkok
Population: 48·8m. (1982)
GNP per capita: US$670 (1980)

HISTORY. Until 24 June 1932 Siam was an absolute monarchy. On that date a *coup d'état* was effected and a Provisional Constitution Act was promulgated on 27 June. This was replaced by the constitution of 10 Dec. 1932, which in turn was superseded by new constitutions.

AREA AND POPULATION. The area of Thailand is 514,000 sq. km (198,250 sq. miles) and is bounded west by Burma and the Indian Ocean, east by the Gulf of Thailand, Cambodia and east and north by Laos.

At the census taken in 1979 the registration gave a population of 45,221,625 (22,775,852 males, 22,445,773 females), of whom 30·4% lived in the Central region, 35·2% in the North-East region, 12·5% in the South region, 21·9% in the North region. Estimate (1982) 48,846,927 (24,297,054 females).

Vital statistics, 1979: Birth rate, 25 per 1,000 population; infant mortality, 56; death rate, 5 per thousand live births.

Thailand is divided into 72 provinces. Bangkok Metropolis is the capital (population 1982, 5,468,286). Other towns (1979 estimate) are Chiang Mai (105,230), Nakhon Ratchasima (87,371), Khon Kaen, (80,286), Udon Thani (76,173), Pitsanulok (73,175), Hat Yai (67,117), Songkhla (65,523), Nakhon Si Thammarat (61,049), Nakhon Sawan (55,741).

CLIMATE. The climate is tropical, with high temperatures and humidity. Over most of the country, 3 seasons may be recognized. The rainy season is June to Oct., the cool season from Nov. to Feb. and the hot season is March to May. Rainfall is generally heaviest in the south and lightest in the north east.

Bangkok. Jan. 78°F (25·6°C), July 83°F (28·3°C). Annual rainfall 56″ (1,400 mm).

REIGNING KING. Bhumibol Adulyadej, born 5 Dec. 1927, younger brother of King Ananda Mahidol, who died on 9 June 1946. King Bhumibol married on 28 April 1950 Princess Sirikit, and was crowned 5 May 1950. Children: Princess Ubol Ratana (born 5 April 1951), Crown-Prince Vajiralongkorn (born 28 July 1952, married 3 Jan. 1977 Soamsawali Kitiyakra), Princess Maha Chakri Sirindhorn (born 2 April 1955), Princess Chulabhorn (born 4 July 1957, married 27 Jan. 1982 Virayudth Didyasarin).

CONSTITUTION AND GOVERNMENT. The military government resigned on 14 Oct. 1973 and a new government was formed. New Constitutions were enacted on 7 Oct. 1974 and on 9 Nov. 1977. However on 20 Oct. 1977 a further military *coup* took place in order to return more swiftly to democracy. A new Constitution designed to restore democracy was promulgated in Dec. 1978 and elections took place on 22 April 1979. Elections were held in April 1983.

The cabinet in Aug. 1983 was composed as follows:

Prime Minister: Gen. Prem Tinsulanonda.
Deputy Prime Minister: Gen. Prachuab Soontarangkun; Boontheng Thongsawasdi; Bhichai Rattakul; Adm. Sonthi Boonyachai. *Defence:* Gen. Prem Tinsulanonda. *Finance:* Sommai Hoontrakul. *Foreign Affairs:* Air Chief Marshal Siddhi Savetsila. *Agriculture and Co-operatives:* Narong Wongwan. *Communications:* Samak Sundaravej. *Commerce:* Kosol Krairiksh. *Interior:* Gen. Sitthi

Chirarochana. *Justice:* Phipop Asitirat. *Education:* Chuan Leekpai. *Public Health:* Marut Bunnag. *Industry:* Ob Vasuratna. *Science, Technology and Energy:* Damrong Lathaphipat. *University Affairs:* Preeda Pathanathabutr.

National flag: Five horizontal stripes of red, white, blue, white, red, with the blue of double width.

Local Government. For purposes of administration Thailand is divided into 72 provinces *(changwads)*, each under the control of a *changwad* governor. The *changwads* are subdivided into 576 districts *(amphurs)* and 80 sub-districts *(king amphurs)*, 5,317 communes *(tambons)* and 49,841 villages *(moobans)*. Local legislative and executive bodies with limited powers are being established with functions, procedure and method of election modelled on those of central Assembly.

DEFENCE. Under the Ministry of Defence Organization Act of 1960 the Ministry of Defence has assumed the Supreme Command and the control of the Army, Navy and Air Force with the advice of the Defence Council headed by the Ministry of Defence. The National Defence College, the Armed Forces Staff College and the Military Preparatory School serve the education of officers. Each service has its own C.-in-C., service council, schools of arms and Command and General Staff College.

Under the Military Service Act of 1954 every able-bodied man between the ages of 21 and 30 is liable to serve 2 years with the colours; 7 years in the first reserve; 10 years in the second reserve; 6 years in the third reserve.

Army. The Army is organized in 4 Regions and consists of 1 cavalry, 1 armoured, 7 infantry, 1 special forces, 1 artillery and 1 anti-aircraft divisions; 11 engineer and 8 independent infantry battalions; and 4 reconnaissance companies. Equipment includes 55 M-48A5 main battle tanks. There is also an Army Aviation force. Strength is 160,000, with 500,000 reserves.

Navy. The Fleet includes 4 frigates (1 modern built in Britain, 2 very old *ex*-US, and 1 very old *ex*-US destroyer escort), 2 corvettes (small frigates), 3 fast large attack gunboats, 6 fast missile craft, 4 coastal minesweepers, 6 patrol vessels, 1 mine counter-measures support ship, 20 gunboats, 24 coastal patrol boats, 8 landing ships, 13 landing craft, 40 minor landing craft, 5 minesweeping boats, 3 surveying ships, 3 surveying boats, 40 river patrol craft, 2 transports, 3 oilers, 3 training ships (old frigate, old corvette, old escort minesweeper), 18 coastguard vessels, 2 water carriers and 4 tugs.

Four patrol vessels are under construction and 2 missile-armed corvettes are ordered.

Naval personnel in 1984 totalled 30,000, including the Marine Corps of 20,000. There is a Royal Naval Academy at Paknam.

At the mouth of the Chao Praya River are the Paknam forts. The naval dockyard was reconstructed.

Air Force. The Royal Thai Air Force was reorganized with the assistance of a US Military Air Advisory Group. It has a strength of about 43,100 personnel, and is made up of a headquarters and Combat, Logistics Support, Training and Special Services Groups. The 3 squadrons of 1st Wing form the primary combat element, equipped with 40 F-5A/B/E/F supersonic fighter-bombers, some of the 45 OV-10C Bronco light reconnaissance/attack aircraft, and 18 T-33A/RT-33A and 4 RF-5A armed reconnaissance aircraft acquired from the USA. Six light attack squadrons in 2nd Wing operate the other OV-10Cs, about 20 T-28 armed piston-engined trainers, 16 A-37B light jet attack aircraft and 25 AU-23A Peacemakers, for security duties. There are transport units equipped with a total of about 70 C-130H/H-30 Hercules, DC-8-62F, HS 748, C-123B Provider, C-47 and smaller aircraft, including 20 Australian-built Missionmasters; training units with Airtrainer CT/4 primary trainers built in New Zealand, Italian-built SF.260MTs, T-37 intermediate and T-33A advanced trainers; and large numbers of helicopters for assault and rescue duties. In 1984, delivery will begin of 31 Model 400 and 16

Model 600 Fantrainers, of which the first 6 will be built in Germany, the remainder partially manufactured and assembled in Thailand.

INTERNATIONAL RELATIONS

Planning. The Fifth National Development Plan, 1982–86 envisages a more equal distribution of income between the urban and rural population.

Membership. Thailand is a member of UN, ASEAN and the Colombo Plan.

ECONOMY

Budget. Ordinary expenditures in 1982 (in 1m. baht): Defence, 31,395; agriculture, 13,587; communications, 10,312; education, 32,630; public health, 6,234.

Revenue in 1980 derived from taxes and duties, sales and charges and government enterprises, 114,835m. baht.

In 1980 the national internal debt was 109,780·6m. baht and the external debt totalled 80,508·7m. baht.

Currency. The unit of currency is the *baht*, formerly called in English the *tical*, which is divided into 100 *satang*. Silver coins have gone out of circulation. Only nickel, copper, tin and bronze coins are now minted, in denominations of 1, 5 *baht*, 50, 25, 10 and 5 *satang*. Currency notes, first issued in 1902, now comprise, 5, 10, 20, 100, 500 *baht* notes.

On 31 March 1976 the total amount of notes and coins in circulation was 30,280m. baht.

In March 1984, £1 = 34·08 *baht*; US$1 = 22·99 *baht*.

Banking. In 1942 the Bank of Thailand was established under the Bank of Thailand Act, B.E. 2485 (1942) and began operations on 10 Dec. 1942, with the functions of a central bank. The Bank was organized on similar lines to the Bank of England, having its banking activities entirely separate from the management of the note issue. The Bank also took over the note issue previously performed by the Treasury Department of the Ministry of Finance. Although the entire capital is owned by the Government, the Bank is an independent body. Its gold and foreign-exchange reserves, at the end of Dec. 1973, amounted to US$1,082m.

In Jan. 1966 the Agricultural Bank and the Provincial Bank merged in the Krung Thai Bank (capital 105m. baht, of which 80% is owned by the Government).

Banks incorporated under Thai law include the Bangkok Bank Ltd, the Bangkok Bank of Commerce Ltd, the Bank of Asia for Industry & Commerce Ltd, the Bank of Ayudhya Ltd, Bangkok Metropolitan Bank Ltd, the Laem Thong Bank Ltd, the Siam City Bank Ltd, the Siam Commercial Bank Ltd, First Bangkok City Bank Ltd, Union Bank of Bangkok Ltd and the Wang Lee Chan Bank Ltd. Foreign banks include the Chartered Bank, the Hongkong and Shanghai Banking Corporation, the Mercantile Bank Ltd, Banque de l'Indochine, Bank of Canton Ltd, Bank of China Ltd, Bank of America, N.T. & S.A., the Mitsui Bank Ltd, The Asia Trust Bank Ltd, Bharat Overseas Bank Ltd, The Chase Manhattan Bank, United Malayan Banking Corporation and the Bank of Tokyo Ltd.

The commercial Thai banks had, in 1981, 1,484 branches in Thailand and 12 abroad; only Mae Hongson province has no commercial bank services. The deposits held by commercial banks in June 1981 amounted to 334,884m. baht.

The Government Savings Bank, which was established as an independent organization in 1947, originated in 1913 when the Government Savings Office was established.

Weights and Measures. The metric system was made compulsory by a law promulgated on 17 Dec. 1923. The actual weights and measures prescribed by law are: Units of weight: 1 *standard picul* = 60 kg; 1 *standard catty* (¹/₁₀₀ picul) = 600 grammes; 1 *standard carat* = 20 centigrammes. Units of length: 1 *sen* = 40 metres; 1 *wah* (¹/₂₀ sen) = 2 metres; 1 *sauk* (½ wah) = 0·50 metre; 1 *keup* (½ sauk) = 0·25 metre. Units of square measure: 1 *rai* (1 sq. sen) = 1,600 sq. metres; 1 *ngan* (½ rai) = 400 sq. metres; 1 *sq. wah* (¹/₁₀₀ ngan) = 4 sq. metres. Units of capacity: 1 *standard kwien* =

2,000 litres; 1 *standard ban* (½ kwien) = 1,000 litres; 1 *standard sat* (¹⁄₅₀ ban) = 20 litres; 1 *standard tannan* (¹⁄₂₀ sat) = 1 litre.

Legislation passed in 1940 provided that the calendar year shall coincide with the Christian Year, and that the year of the Buddhist era 2484 shall begin on 1 Jan. 1941. (The New Year's Day was previously 1 April.) The years B.E. 2514–2518 therefore correspond to A.D. 1974 and 1975.

ENERGY AND NATURAL RESOURCES

Electricity. In 1981, steam power accounted for 52% of production (81% of the fuel being imported) and 34% hydro-electric. Only 20% of the population had access to electricity on 31 Dec. 1976.

Oil. Extensive oil and gas exploration in the Gulf of Thailand were producing commercial quantities in Sept. 1981.

Minerals. The mineral resources are extensive and varied, including cassiterite (tin ore), wolfram, scheelite, antimony, coal, copper, gold, iron, lead, manganese, molybdenum, rubies, sapphires, silver, zinc and zircons. By far the most important are tin and wolfram. Ore output in 1978 (in tonnes): Iron, 88,121; manganese, 72,211; tin (1980), 46,526; lead, 39,121; antimony, 6,759; wolfram, 5,815; lignite, 638,942; gypsum, 280,905.

Agriculture. The chief produce of the country is rice, which forms the national food and the staple article of export. The area under paddy is about 18m. acres. With the completion of the Chao Phya dam located near Chainat in 1957 the irrigable area in the Central Plain had by 1962 been extended to about 8,409,000 rai (3,363,600 acres). Additional projects now under construction will bring the irrigable lands to the total of about 11,605,900 rai (4,642,360 acres). Tank irrigation projects which were designed to ensure water supply for upland crop cultivation, especially in the north-eastern part, irrigate 325,418 rai (130,167 acres).

Output of the major crops in 1982 was (in 1,000 tonnes): Paddy (1981), 19,000; maize, 4,200; sugar-cane, 27,000; kenaf, 270; tobacco, 50; tapioca-root, 16,000; soybeans, 150; coconut, 750; mung beans, 275; cotton, 250; groundnuts, 158.

Livestock, 1982 (in 1,000): horses, 21; buffaloes, 6,150; cattle, 4,500; pigs, 3,700; poultry, 63,264.

Forestry. About 60% of the land area of Thailand is under forest. In the north, mixed deciduous forests with teak *(Tectona grandis, Linn.)*, growing in mixture with several other species, predominate. In the north-eastern section hardwood of the *Dipterocarpus* species, especially *Shorea obtusa* and *Pentacme Siamensis, Kurz* exist in most parts. In all other regions of the country tropical evergreen forests are found, with the well-known timber of commerce, Yang (*Dipterocarpus alatus, Roxb* and *Dipterocarpus* spp.) as the outstanding crops. Most of the teak timber exploited in northern Thailand is floated down to Bangkok. Some of them, however, are exported through the Salween into Burma.

About one-third of the teak-forest area is being exploited by the Forest Industry Organization, and the remaining two-thirds is to be worked by timber company lessees and other private enterprises.

Output of main forestry products in 1981 was (in 1,000 tonnes): Teak, 60·9; yang and other woods, 1,807·7; firewood, 638·6; charcoal, 141·5.

Rubber production (in 1,000 tonnes), 1955, 133·3; 1960, 170·8; 1969, 281·8; 1973, 384; 1978, 467; 1979, 531; 1980, 501; 1981, 510; 1982, 540.

Fisheries. In 1981 the catch of sea fish was 1,415,600 tonnes; of freshwater fish, 161,200 tonnes, and (1979) of marine prawns, shrimps and crabs, 116,500 tonnes.

INDUSTRY AND TRADE

Industry. Production of manufactured goods in 1978 included 5,004,490 tonnes of cement, 46,818 tonnes of white cement, 1,584,453 tonnes of sugar, 149·8m. gunny bags, 39,721 tonnes of paper, 23,905 tonnes of cigarettes, 95,363 tonnes of sweetened condensed milk, 15,830 tonnes of evaporated milk, 108·3m. litres of beer, 875m. sq. yd of cotton textiles, 887·2m. sq. yd of man-made textiles, 4,673,432 sheets of plywood and 1,166,614 sq. metres of vinyl tiles.

Trade Unions. The Thai National Trade Union Congress is a member of the International Confederation of Free Trade Unions.

Commerce. The foreign trade (in 1m. baht) was as follows:

	1976	1977	1978	1979	1980	1981
Imports (c.i.f.)	72,877	96,062	108.899	146,161	188,686	216,746
Exports (f.o.b.)	60,797	70,463	83,065	108,179	133,197	153,001

In 1980 the main imports (in 1m. baht): Fuels and lubricants, 58,667; machinery, 43,113; manufactured goods, 28,505; chemicals, 22,385.

In 1980 the main items of export (in 1m. baht): Rice, 19,505; tapioca products, 14,838; rubber, 12,400; tin, 11,347; maize, 7,296; sugar, 2,975; prawns, 1,959; tobacco leaves, 1,376; kenaf and jute, 155; teak and woods, 3.

In 1981 imports from Japan (24%), Saudi Arabia (14%), USA (13%), Singapore (7%). Exports to Japan (14%), USA (13%), Netherlands (12%) and Singapore (8%).

Total trade between Thailand and UK (British Department of Trade returns, in £1,000 sterling):

	1979	1980	1981	1982	1983
Imports to UK	52,188	52,004	56,343	76,529	87,823
Exports and re-exports from UK	94,115	96,926	91,473	104,825	131,833

Tourism. In 1981 2,015,615 foreigners visited Thailand spending 21,000m. baht.

COMMUNICATIONS

Roads. In 1982 the length of highways and provincial roads open to traffic was approximately 44,200 km, of which about 13,226 km (1978) were concrete or asphalt-surfaced. Motor vehicles registered in 1975 included 248,561 passenger cars, 22,079 buses, 178,425 lorries and 456,651 motor cycles.

Railways. In 1982 there were 3,735 km of state railways (metre gauge) open to traffic.

The northern line runs from Bangkok to Chiang Mai (741 km), the extreme northern terminus. The southern line (990 km) runs from Bangkok down the Peninsula to the frontier station of Padang Besar, where it connects with the Malayan railway from Penang, and to Singapore. Another line (214 km) branching off from Haad Yai on the southern line runs along the east coast of the peninsula to Su-gnai Kolok, where it connects with the Malayan railway line. There are branch lines (totalling 190 km) to Song Khla, Nakhon-Si Thammarat, Kan Tang and Tha-Kanon. The extensions of the north-eastern line (264 km) from Nakhon Ratsima (Korat) to Nong Khai (360 km) and from Kaeng Koi to Buayai (250 km) have been completed. The Nakhon Ratsima–Ubol line (311 km) has been completed as far as Ubol Rat Thani. The eastern line (255 km) runs from Makkasan to Aran Pradet on the Kampuchea frontier. The northern and southern railway systems are linked by a railway bridge over the Menam Chao Phya, and both systems terminate in Bangkok. All state railways are under one management and in 1981 carried 78·8m. passengers and 6m. tons of freight.

Aviation. Thai Airways Co. Ltd (TAC), established in 1947, is the sole Thai air transport enterprise, with authorized capital of 300m. baht. The Company operates 11 domestic routes and 3 international routes. On 24 Aug. 1959 Thai Airways and the Scandinavian Airlines System set up a new company, Thai International Airways, to operate the international air services from Thailand. In 1981–82, more than 2m. passengers were carried.

Shipping. In 1978, 2,736 vessels of 11,731,083 NRT entered and 2,521 of 9,888,190 NRT cleared the port of Bangkok.

The port of Bangkok, about 30 km from the mouth of the Chao Phya River, is capable of berthing ocean-going vessels of 10,000 gross tons and 28 ft draught. Bangkok is now a port of entry for Laos, and goods arriving in transit are sent up by rail to Nong Khai and ferried across the river Mekhong to Vientiane.

Post and Broadcasting. In 1974 there were 555 post offices proper, 341 licensed and Amphur post offices and 545 railway-station post offices. In 1967, the length of telegraph lines was 21,203 km. In 1982 there were 529,106 telephones, of which 389,852 were in Bangkok.

In 1981, there were 265 radio stations and 9 television stations.

Cinemas (1978). There were 366 cinemas with a seating capacity of 263,738.

Newspapers (1979). There are 20 daily newspapers in Bangkok, including 3 in English and 7 in Chinese, with a combined circulation of more than 800,000.

JUSTICE, RELIGION, EDUCATION AND WELFARE

Justice. The judicial power is exercised in the name of the King, by *(a)* courts of first instance, *(b)* the court of appeal *(Uthorn)* and *(c)* the Supreme Court *(Dika)*. The King appoints, transfers and dismisses judges, who are independent in conducting trials and giving judgment in accordance with the law.

Courts of first instance are subdivided into 20 magistrates' courts *(Kwaeng)* with limited civil and minor criminal jurisdiction; 85 provincial courts *(Changwad)* with unlimited civil and criminal jurisdiction; the criminal and civil courts with exclusive jurisdiction in Bangkok; the central juvenile courts for persons under 18 years of age in Bangkok.

The court of appeal exercises appellate jurisdiction in civil and criminal cases from all courts of first instance. From it appeals lie to Dika Court on any point of law and, in certain cases, on questions of fact.

The Supreme Court is the supreme tribunal of the land. Besides its normal appellate jurisdiction in civil and criminal matters, it has semi-original jurisdiction over general election petitions. The decisions of Dika Court are final. Every person has the right to present a petition to the Government who will deal with all matters of grievance.

Religion. About 95% of the population are Buddhists, 4% Moslems, 1% Christians, Hindus and others.

Education. Primary education is compulsory for children between the ages of 7–14 and free in local municipal schools. In 1978 there were 7,612,534 students enrolled in 31,966 government schools and 1,119,528 in 2,327 private schools. In 1977 there were 45 teachers' training schools with 4,986 teachers and 115,117 students and 180 government vocational schools with 8,100 teachers and 147,997 students. In 1978 there were 12 universities: Chulalongkorn University (1917), Thammasat University (1934), Universities of Medical Science, Agriculture and Fine Arts; Ramkamhaeng University (1971)—all in Bangkok; Chiengmai University (1964), the Khon Kaen University (1966) in the north-east and Prince of Songkhla University (1968) in the south.

Health. In 1982 there were 434 hospitals and 6,496 health centres throughout the country. In 1982 there were 6,550 physicians, 1,122 dentists and (1977) 2,236 pharmacists.

DIPLOMATIC REPRESENTATIVES

Of Thailand in Great Britain (30 Queen's Gate, London, SW7 5JB)
Ambassador: Phan Wannamethee (accredited 19 Dec. 1977).

Of Great Britain in Thailand (Wireless Rd., Bangkok)
Ambassador: Justin Staples, CMG.

Of Thailand in the USA (2300 Kalorama Rd., NW., Washington, D.C., 20008)
Ambassador: M. R. Kasem S. Kasemsri.

Of the USA in Thailand (95 Wireless Rd., Bangkok)
Ambassador: John Gunther Dean.

Of Thailand to the United Nations
Ambassador: M. L. Birabhongse Kasemsri.

Books of Reference

Thailand into the 80's. Office of the Prime Minister, Bangkok, 1979

Thailand Statistical Yearbook. National Statistical Office, Bangkok

Thailand 1982: Plans, Problems and Prospects. Government's Public Relations Department, Bangkok, 1982

Thailand in Brief. Government's Public Relations Department, Bangkok, 1977

Bibliography of Materials About Thailand in Western Languages. Chulalongkorn University, Bangkok, 1960

Douner, W., *The Five Faces of Thailand.* Hamburg and London, 1978

Haas, M. R., *Thai–English Student's Dictionary.* OUP, 1966

Kirkup, J., *Bangkok.* London, 1968

Morrell, D. and Samudavanija, C., *Political Conflict in Thailand.* Cambridge, Mass., 1981

TOGO

Capital: Lomé
Population: 2·96m. (1983)
GNP per capita: US$410 (1980)

République Togolaise

HISTORY. The Republic of Togo became independent on 27 April 1960, after having been a German protectorate (1894–1914, subsequently divided between the French and the British), a mandate of the League of Nations (20 July 1922) and a trusteeship territory of the United Nations (14 Dec. 1946).

On 28 Oct. 1956 a plebiscite was held to determine the status of the territory. Out of 438,175 registered voters, 313,458 voted for an autonomous republic within the French Union and the end of the trusteeship system. The trusteeship was abolished on the achievement of independence on 27 April 1960.

On 13 Jan. 1963 the President Sylvanus Olympio was murdered by n.c.o.s. of the army. Nicolas Grunitzky, a former prime minister and Olympio's brother-in-law, was appointed President of the Republic and head of government. On 13 Jan. 1967 in a bloodless *coup* the army under Col. Etienne Eyadéma made President Grunitzky 'voluntarily withdraw'. On 14 April 1967 Col. Eyadéma assumed the offices of President and Defence. There was a return to constitutional government in Jan. 1980.

AREA AND POPULATION. Togo is bounded west by Ghana, north by Upper Volta, east by Benin and south by the Bight of Benin. Area, about 56,785 sq. km. The population of Togo in 1970 (census) was 1,953,778; 1983 (estimate) 2,963,000. The capital is Lomé (population, 1979, 247,000), other towns (1977, population) being Sokodé (33,500), Kpalimé (25,500), Atakpamé (21,800), Bassar (17,500), Tsévié (15,900) and Anécho (13,300).

The southern part of Togo is peopled by tribes using several different languages, of which the principal, Ewe and Mina, are languages of the Kwa group. The northern half contains, ethnologically, a totally different population descended largely from Hamitic tribes and speaking a fairly large number of different languages of the Voltaic (Gur) group, of which Dagomba, Tem and Kabre are the most important. French is the official language.

CLIMATE. The tropical climate produces wet seasons from March to July and from Oct. to Nov. in the south. The north has one wet season, from April to July. The heaviest rainfall occurs in the mountains of the west, south-west and centre. Lomé. Jan. 81°F (27·2°C), July 76°F (24·4°C). Annual rainfall 35″ (875 mm).

CONSTITUTION AND GOVERNMENT. Following approval in a referendum on 30 Dec. 1979, a new Constitution came into force on 13 Jan. 1980, when the Third Togolese Republic was proclaimed. It provides for an Executive President, directly elected for a 7-year term, and for a National Assembly of 67 deputies, elected on a regional list system for a 5-year term. Elections were held on 30 Dec. 1979.

All candidates are nominated by the *Rassemblement du peuple togolais*, the sole legal Party since 1969; it is administered by a 33-member Central Committee and a 9-member Political Bureau appointed by the President.

The government in Feb. 1983 was composed as follows:
President, Minister of Defence: Gen. Gnassingbe Eyadéma.
Foreign Affairs and Co-operation: Dr Anani Kuma Akakpo-Ahianyo. *Planning and Administrative Reform:* Koffi Walla. *Interior:* Kpotivi Têvi' Djidjogbé Laclé. *Economy and Finance:* Têtê Têvi Bénissan. *Public Works, Mines, Energy and Water Resources:* Barry Moussa Barque. *Health and Social Affairs:* Hodabalo Bodjona. *Rural Development:* Anani Gassou. *Labour and Civil Service:* Nyandi

Seibou Napo. *Parliamentary Affairs:* Mme. Massa Dagadzi. *Rural Planning:* Samon Korto. *Information, Posts and Telecommunications:* Gbegnon Amegboh. *Youth, Sports and Culture:* Koffi Sama. *First and Second Cycle Education:* Komlan Agbetiafa. *Third and Fourth Cycle Education:* Ayssa Agbetra. *Justice:* Ayivi Mawuko Ajavon. *Commerce and Transport:* Phali Djalla. *Secretaries of State:* Mme. Sophie Meatchi *(Health and Women's Affairs),* Bloua Yao Agbo *(Industry and State Enterprises).*

National flag: Five horizontal stripes of green and yellow, a red quarter with a white star.

Local Government: There are 5 regions (Maritime, Des Plateaux, Du Centre, De La Kara and Des Savanes), each under an inspector appointed by the President; they are divided into 21 *prefectures,* each administered by a district chief assisted by an elected district council.

DEFENCE. Armed forces numbered (1984) about 5,080, all forming part of the Army.

Army. The Army consists of 2 infantry, 1 Presidential Guard commando and 1 para-commando regiments, with artillery and logistic support units. Equipment includes 7 T-34 and 2 T-54/-55 main battle tanks. Strength (1984) 4,000, with a further 750 men in a paramilitary force.

Navy. In 1983 there were 2 British-built coastal patrol craft, 2 defence launches and a naval base at Lomé. Naval personnel, 105 officers and men.

Air Force. An Air Force, established with French assistance, has 6 Brazilian-built EMB-326 Xavante (Aermacchi MB.326) armed jet trainers; 5 Alpha Jet advanced trainers, with strike capability, 1 DC-8, 1 Boeing 727 and 1 twin-turbofan F28 Fellowship for VIP use, 2 turboprop Buffalo transports; 2 Broussard communications aircraft; 5 Magister jet trainers; 1 Puma and 1 Lama helicopter.

INTERNATIONAL RELATIONS

Membership. Togo is a member of UN, OAU and is an ACP state of EEC.

ECONOMY

Planning. The fourth 5-year development plan (1981–85) provides for investment of 368,490m. francs CFA, of which 116,397m. are for rural development, 98,625m. for industrial development and 100,690m. for infrastructure.

Budget. The ordinary budget for 1983 balanced at 75,800m. francs CFA.

Currency. The unit of currency is the *franc* CFA with a parity rate of 50 *francs* CFA to 1 French *franc.* The rate of exchange (March 1984) was 588·75 francs CFA to £1; US$1 = 401·08.

Banking. The bank of issue is the *Banque Centrale des Etats de l'Afrique de l'Ouest.* Seven commercial and 3 development banks are based in Lomé.

ENERGY AND NATURAL RESOURCES

Electricity. Production (1980) 75m. kwh.

Minerals. A Mines Department was set up in 1953 after the discovery of very rich deposits of phosphate and bauxite; mining began in 1961. Output of phosphate rock (1980) 2,895,000 tonnes. Other mineral deposits are limestone, estimated at 200m. tons; iron ore, estimated at 550m. tons with iron content varying between 40% and 55%, and marble estimated at 20m. tonnes.

Agriculture. Inland the country is hilly, rising to 3,600 ft, with streams and waterfalls. There are long stretches of forest and brushwood, while dry plains alternate with arable land. Maize, yams, cassava, plantains, groundnuts, etc., are cultivated; oil palms and dye-woods grow in the forests; but the main commerce is based on coffee, cocoa, palm-oil, palm-kernels, copra, groundnuts, cotton, manioc. There are considerable plantations of oil and cocoa palms, coffee, cacao, kola, cassava and cotton. Production, 1981 (in 1,000 tonnes): Cassava, 470; maize, 137; millet, 107; cottonseed (1980), 30; rice, 25; groundnuts, 20.

Livestock (1982): Cattle, 250,000; sheep, 835,000; swine, 360,000; horses, 3,000; asses, 1,000; goats, 750,000.

INDUSTRY AND TRADE

Industry. There is a cement works (production, 1978; 327,000 tonnes); a second is being built in co-operation with Ghana and Ivory Coast with a capacity of 1·2m. tonnes per annum. An oil refinery of 1m. tonne capacity opened in Lomé in 1978 and a steel mill (20,000 tonne capacity) in 1979. Industry, though small, is developing and there are about 40 medium sized enterprises in the public and private sectors, including textile and food processing plants.

Trade (in 1m. francs CFA):

	1976	1977	1978	1979	1980
Imports	44,420	69,834	85,887	110,208	116,357
Exports	24,914	39,115	53,035	46,432	71,285

In 1980, of the exports, phosphates amounted to 40%, cocoa beans 12% and coffee 8% by value; 20% of exports went to the Netherlands and 15% to France. Of the imports, France supplied 25% and Nigeria, 16%.

Total trade between Togo and UK (British Department of Trade returns, in £1,000 sterling):

	1979	1980	1981	1982	1983
Imports to UK	3,991	7,395	4,981	1,827	2,161
Exports and re-exports from UK	18,773	28,967	21,423	21,881	12,212

Tourism. There were about 117,000 tourists in 1980.

COMMUNICATIONS

Roads. There were, in 1980, 7,450 km of roads, of which 2,513 km were paved. In Dec. 1980 there were 26,067 passenger cars and 14,017 commercial vehicles.

Railways. There are 4 metre-gauge railways connecting Lomé with Anécho (continuing to Cotonou in Benin), Kpalimé, Tabligbo and (*via* Atakpamé) Blitta; total length 525 km. In 1982 the railways carried 16m. tonne-km and 105m. passenger-km.

Aviation: Air services connect Lomé with Paris, Dakar, Abidjan, Douala, Accra, Lagos, Cotonou and Niamey and by internal services with Sokodé, Mango, Dapaong, Atakpamé and Niamtougou.

Shipping. In 1979, 879 vessels landed 1,264,000 tonnes and cleared 323,000 tonnes at Lomé. The merchant marine comprises 7 vessels of 25,714 gross tons. In 1981 some 2·2m. tonnes of phosphate were loaded at the port of Kpémé.

Post and Broadcasting. There were (1972) 39 post offices and 16 postal agencies and (1981), 7,870 telephones. Togo is connected by telegraph and telephone with Ghana, Benin, Abidjan and Dakar, and by wireless telegraphy with Europe and America. There were 5,000 television receivers and 125,000 radio receivers in 1981.

Newspapers. There is 1 daily newspaper (circulation 10,000).

JUSTICE, RELIGION, EDUCATION AND WELFARE

Justice. The Supreme Court and two Appeal Courts are in Lomé, one for criminal cases and one for civil and commercial cases. Each receives appeal from a series of local tribunals.

Religion. In 1980, 28% of the population were Catholics, 17% Moslem (chiefly in the north) and 9% Protestant; while 46% follow animist religions.

Education. In 1980 there were 484,272 pupils and 8,920 teachers in primary schools, 119,801 pupils and 2,855 teachers in secondary schools, 7,793 students and (1978) 326 teachers in technical schools and 300 students and 22 teachers at the teacher-training college. The University of Benin at Lomé (founded in 1970) had 3,700 students in 1980.

Health. In 1977 there were 61 hospitals with 3,438 beds; there were also 128 doctors, 5 dentists, 26 pharmacists, 554 midwives and 880 nursing staff.

DIPLOMATIC REPRESENTATIVES

Of Togo in Great Britain (116 Knightsbridge, London SW1)
Chargé d'Affaires: Abou Yacoubou.

Of Great Britain in Togo
Ambassador: K. F. X. Burns (resides in Accra).

Of Togo in the USA (2208 Massachusetts Ave., NW, Washington, D.C., 20008)
Ambassador: Ellom-Kodjo Schuppius.

Of the USA in Togo (Rue Pelletier Caventou, Lomé)
Ambassador: Howard K. Walker.

Of Togo to the United Nations
Ambassador: Atsu-Koffi Amega.

Books of Reference

Cornevin, R., *Histoire du Togo.* 3rd ed., Paris, 1969
Feuillet, C., *Le Togo en general.* Paris, 1976
Piraux, M., *Le Togo aujourd'hui.* Paris, 1977

TONGA

Friendly Islands

Capital: Nuku'alofa
Population: 98,750 (1983)
GNP per capita: US$520 (1980)

HISTORY. The Kingdom of Tonga attained unity under Taufa'ahau Tupou (George I) who became ruler of his native Ha'apai in 1820, of Vava'u in 1833 and of Tongatapu in 1845. By 1860 the kingdom had become converted to Christianity (George himself having been baptized in 1831). In 1862 the king granted freedom to the people from arbitrary rule of minor chiefs and gave them the right to the allocation of land for their own needs. These institutional changes, together with the establishment of a parliament of chiefs, paved the way towards the democratic constitution under which the kingdom is now governed, and provided a background of stability against which Tonga was able to develop her agricultural economy.

The kingdom continued up to 1899 to be a neutral region in accordance with the Declaration of Berlin, 6 April 1886. By the Anglo-German Agreement of 14 Nov. 1899 subsequently accepted by the USA, the Tonga Islands were left under the Protectorate of Great Britain.

A protectorate was proclaimed on 18 May 1900, and a British Agent and Consul appointed.

AREA AND POPULATION. The kingdom consists of some 169 islands and islets with a total area of 289 sq. miles (748 sq. km; including inland waters), and lies between 15° and 23° 30' S. lat and 173° and 177° W. long., its western boundary being the eastern boundary of Fiji. The islands are split up into the following groups reading from north to south: The Niuas, Vava'u, Ha'apai, Kotu, Nomuka, Otu Tolu and Tongatapu. The 3 main groups, both from historical and administrative significance, are Tongatapu in the south, Ha'apai in the centre and Vava'u in the north. The Tongatapu group was discovered by Tasman in 1643.

The capital is Nuku'alofa on Tongatapu (18,312).

The islands to the east, being mostly of limestone formation, are low lying and with but a few exceptions seldom exceed 100 ft above sea-level. The islands to the west are of a volcanic nature, approximately 11, average between 350 and 3,433 ft in height. After a violent volcanic eruption in Sept. 1946 on the island of Niuafo'ou (Tin Can Island to philatelists, so named because of the method that was used of collecting and delivering mail) the 1,300 inhabitants were evacuated, most of them to Tongatapu and 'Eua, but more than 600 have returned since 1958. It was thought that a new island had been born when an eruption took place on the Metis Shoal on 12 Dec. 1967; during the volcanic activity a small rocky mass reached a maximum elevation of about 50 ft, but by Feb. 1968 the area was once more awash.

Census population (1976) 90,085 (males, 46,036); estimate, 1983, 98,750.

CLIMATE. Generally a healthy climate, though Jan. to March is hot and humid, with temperatures of 90°F (32·2°C). Rainfall amounts are comparatively high, being greatest from Dec. to March.

CONSTITUTION AND GOVERNMENT. Relations between the UK and Tonga have been governed by the 1900 Treaty of Friendship and Protection and several subsequent revisions. For earlier history of this relationship *see* THE STATESMAN'S YEAR-Book, 1970–71. By exchange of letters on 19 May 1970 it was agreed that the UK Government should, as from 4 June 1970, cease to have any responsibility for the external relations of the Kingdom of Tonga.

King: HM King Taufa'ahau Tupou IV, GCVO, GCMG, KBE, born 4 July 1918, succeeded on 16 Dec. 1965 on the death of his mother, Queen Salote Tupou III; his coronation took place on 4 July 1967.

Prime Minister: HRH Prince Tu'ipelehake, KCMG, KBE, younger brother of the King.

National flag: Red with a white quarter bearing a red couped cross.

The present Constitution is almost identical with that granted in 1875 by King George Tupou I. There is a Privy Council, Cabinet, Legislative Assembly and Judiciary. The legislative assembly, which meets annually, is composed of 7 nobles elected by their peers, 7 elected representatives of the people and the Privy Councillors (numbering 8); the King appoints one of the 7 nobles to be the Speaker. The elections are held triennially. In 1960, women voted for the first time.

INTERNATIONAL RELATIONS

Membership. Tonga is a member of the Commonwealth and is an ACP state of EEC.

ECONOMY

Planning. The Third Plan 1975–80 was the kingdom's first attempt at formal, comprehensive indicative planning covering both the public and private sectors. Estimated expenditure for the public sector during the plan period amounted to T$31m. A Fourth Plan, 1980–85, is being implemented.

Budget. Revenue and expenditure in T$1,000:

	1977–78	1978–79	1979–80	1980–81[1]	1981–82[1]
Revenue	8,628	8,722	10,596	12,147	14,744
Expenditure	8,515	8,932	10,538	11,899	14,736

[1] Estimate.

The principal sources of revenue are import dues, income tax, port and service tax, wharfage, philatelic revenue and telephone rentals.

The public debt at 30 June 1980 was T$16,428,909.

Currency. There is a government note issue of *pa'anga* (T$)10, 5, 2, 1 and ½ and coin issue of T$2, T$1 and *seniti* 50, 20, 10, 5, 2 and 1. In Sept. 1974, following devaluation by Australia, the Australian dollar equalled 88 *seniti*. In April 1963 gold coins were issued in denominations of 1, ½ and ¼ *koula* (1 *koula* = T$20) and in July 1967, Coronation Palladium coins of 1, ½ and ¼ *hau* (1 *hau* = T$100). In Nov. 1975, gold coins (T$100, 75, 50 and 25) and silver coins (T$20, 10 and 5) were issued to commemorate the centenary of the Constitution. In July 1978, 2 silver coins (T$2 and T$1) were issued to commemorate the sixtieth birthday of the King. In March 1984, £1 = 1·56 *pa'anga*; US$1 = 1·06 *pa'anga*.

AGRICULTURE. Tongan produce (exports 1977) consists of copra (T$3,931,390); packaged desiccated coconut (T$866,942); bananas (T$401,519); swamp taros (T$246,485).

Livestock (1982): Cattle, 11,000; horses, 15,000; pigs, 80,000; goats, 18,000; poultry, 175,000.

COMMERCE. In 1982, imports were valued at T$41,204,700 while exports and re-exports were T$3,645,598 and T$642,308 respectively.

Main imports (in T$): Food 8,936,148, beverages and tobacco 2,316,709, crude materials 3,128,660, fuel and lubricants 5,714,938, oils and fats 38,575, chemicals 2,646,068, manufactured goods 9,417,568, machinery and transport equipment 6,028,881.

Principal destinations for Tongan exports/re-exports in 1982 were: Australia (T$1,814,386), New Zealand (T$1,643,274), USA (T$354,447), Fiji (T$174,440) and Hawaii (T$52,345). Of 1982 imports (in T$), New Zealand furnished 15,358,975; Australia, 9,675,775; USA, 3,914,705; Fiji, 2,938,194; Singapore, 2,700,893; Japan, 2,509,902; Taiwan, 740,680; China (Mainland), 679,135; UK, 594,797.

Total trade between Tonga and UK (British Department of Trade returns, in £1,000 sterling):

	1980	1981	1982	1983
Imports to UK	9	56	38	25
Exports and re-exports from UK	821	286	764	648

COMMUNICATIONS

Roads. In 1980 there were 2,849 registered motor vehicles.

Aviation. International air service connexions to Tongatapu are now provided by Air Pacific and Polynesian Airlines with 5 flights per week to Auckland, 3 to Fiji, 5 to Western Samoa and 2 to Niue. South Pacific Island Airways provide a service 3 times per week from Pago Pago, American Samoa, TonVava'u in the Northern Group and through to Tongatapu. Internal air service flights are operated daily, except Sundays to 'Eua, Ha'apai and Vava'u island groups.

Shipping. The Union Steamship Co. of New Zealand maintains a fortnightly service New Zealand–Fiji–Samoa–Tonga, and cargo steamers visit the group from time to time for shipments of copra. Shipping cleared at all ports in 1983, 116 cargo vessels, 22 cruise vessels, 6 gas vessels and 18 tankers.

Cruise ships from the following lines call at Vava'u and Nuku'alofa: P & O, Sitmar, Royal Viking. The Shipping Corporation of Polynesia maintains a regular inter-island shipping service between 'Eua, Ha'apai and Vava'u.

Post. The kingdom has its own issue of postage stamps. Telephones numbered 2,608 in 1982.

JUSTICE, RELIGION AND EDUCATION

Justice. Now that British extra-territorial jurisdiction has lapsed British and foreign nationals charged with an offence against the laws of Tonga (the enforcement of which is a responsibility of the Minister of Police) are fully subject to the jurisdiction of the Tongan courts to which they are already subject in all civil matters.

Religion. The Tongans are Christian, the vast majority being adherents of the Wesleyan Church.

Education. The Tongans enjoy free education, free medical attendance and dental treatment. In 1980 there were 97 government and 13 denominational primary schools, with a total of 19,012 pupils. There were 7 government and 65 mission schools and 1 private school at which post-primary education was provided for both boys and girls, with a total roll of 14,881. There was one government teacher-training college with 123 students; 4 government technical and vocational schools with 266 pupils and 6 denominational technical and vocational schools with 367 students. 175 students were undergoing training overseas.

DIPLOMATIC REPRESENTATIVES

Of Tonga in Great Britain (New Zealand Hse., Haymarket, London, SW1Y 4TE)
High Commissioner: Sonatane Tuá Taumoepeau-Tupou (accredited 18 Feb. 1983).

Of Great Britain in Tonga (Nuku'alofa)
High Commissioner: B. Coleman.

Of the USA in Tonga
Ambassador: F. Eckert, Jr (resides in Suva).

Books of Reference

Bain, K. R., *Royal Visit to Tonga: Tonga Government Official Record.* London, 1954.–*The Friendly Islanders.* London, 1967
Churchward, C. M., *Tongan Dictionary.* London, 1959
Luke, Sir Harry, *Queen Salote and Her Kingdom.* London, 1954
Wood, A. H., *A History and Geography of Tonga.* Rev. ed. Nuku'alofa, 1963

TRINIDAD AND TOBAGO

Capital: Port-of-Spain
Population: 1·2m. (1980)
GNP per capita: US$4,370 (1980)

HISTORY. Trinidad was discovered by Columbus in 1498 and colonized by the Spaniards in the 16th century. During the French Revolution a large number of French families settled in the island. In 1797, Great Britain being at war with Spain, Trinidad was occupied by the British and ceded to Great Britain by the Treaty of Amiens in 1802. Trinidad and Tobago were joined in 1889.

Under the Bases Agreement concluded between the governments of the UK and the USA on 27 March 1941, and the concomitant Trinidad–US Bases Lease of 22 April 1941, defence bases were leased to the US Government for 99 years. On 8 Dec. 1960 the US agreed to abandon 21,000 acres of leased land and the US has since given up the remaining territory, except for a small tracking station.

AREA AND POPULATION. Area: Trinidad, 1,864 sq. miles (4,828 sq. km); Tobago, 116 sq. miles (300 sq. km). Population (census 7 April 1970): 931,071 (459,512 males and 471,559 females) (Trinidad, 892,317; Tobago, 38,754). Capital, Port-of-Spain, 62,680; other important towns, San Fernando (36,879) and Arima (11,636). The majority are of African descent (42·83%), the balance being made up of Indians (40·11%), mixed races (14·17%), Chinese (0·86%) and Syrian Lebanese (0·11%). English is spoken generally.

Estimated population in 1980, 1·2m.

Vital statistics (rate per 1,000), 1979: Births, 23·8; deaths, 6·6; infant deaths, 23·9. Proportion of population under 15 years (1979) 36·5%.

Tobago is situated about 21 miles north-east of Trinidad. Main town is Scarborough.

Principal goods shipped from Tobago to Trinidad are copra, cocoa, livestock and poultry, fresh vegetables, coconut oil and coconut fibre.

CLIMATE. A tropical climate whose dry season runs from Jan. to June, with a wet season for the rest of the year. Temperatures are uniformly high the year round. Port-of-Spain. Jan. 78°F (25·6°C), July 79°F (26·1°C). Annual rainfall 65″ (1,631 mm).

CONSTITUTION AND GOVERNMENT. On 31 Aug. 1962 Trinidad and Tobago became an independent member state of the British Commonwealth. A Republican Constitution was adopted on 26 Oct. 1976.

The Constitution provides for a bicameral legislature of a Senate and a House of Representatives. The Senate consists of 31 members, 16 being appointed by the President on the advice of the Prime Minister, 6 on the advice of the Leader of the Opposition and 9 at the discretion of the President.

The voting age in the 1976 election was reduced from 21 to 18 years and ballot boxes were re-introduced in place of the voting machines used in previous elections.

Tobago has a 15-man House of Assembly (with limited powers).

The House of Representatives consists of 36 (34 for Trinidad and 2 for Tobago) elected members and a Speaker elected from outside the House.

The Cabinet consists of the Prime Minister, appointed by the President, and other Ministers, including the Attorney-General.

In Nov. 1981 the People's National Movement held the 27 seats.

President: Ellis Clarke.
Prime Minister and Minister of Finance and Planning: George Chambers.
National flag: Red with a diagonal black strip edged in white.

DEFENCE. The Defence Force has a regular and a reserve infantry battalion and a support battalion equipped with 81mm mortars, and there is also a small air element, equipped with a Cessna 402 light transport, and 2 S-76 and 2 Gazelle helicopters for surveillance, liaison and casualty evacuation. Personnel in 1983 totalled 50.

In 1984 there are 2 Swedish (Karlskrona)-built patrol vessels and 4 British (Vosper, Portsmouth)-built patrol craft. A Commodore is Chief of Defence Staff while a Commander directs the Coast Guard. Personnel strength is 45 officers and 540 ratings.

INTERNATIONAL RELATIONS

Membership. Trinidad and Tobago is a member of UN, the Commonwealth, Caricom and is an ACP state of EEC.

ECONOMY

Budget. The 1982 budget envisaged revenue (in TT$1,000) as 6,800m. and expenditure as 10,100m.

Total external debt at 31 Dec. 1982, US$554·5m.

Currency. The currency is the *Trinidad and Tobago dollar* of 100 *cents*. £1 = TT$3·56; US$1 = TT$2·41 (March 1984).

Banking. Banks operating: Barclays Bank of Trinidad and Tobago Ltd; Royal Bank of Trinidad and Tobago Ltd; Bank of Commerce, Trinidad and Tobago Ltd; Bank of Nova Scotia; Chase Manhattan Bank; Citibank; National Commercial Bank of Trinidad and Tobago; Workers' Bank of Trinidad and Tobago. A Central Bank began operations in Dec. 1964.

Government savings banks are established in 62 offices, with a head office in Port-of-Spain.

ENERGY AND NATURAL RESOURCES

Electricity. In 1982, 2,350m. kwh was generated.

Oil. Oil production is one of Trinidad's leading industries and an important source of revenue. Commercial production began in 1909; production of crude oil in 1982 was 177,000 bbls per day. Trinidad also possesses 3 refineries, with throughput capacity of 151m. bbls annually; crude oil is imported from Venezuela, Indonesia, Ecuador, Nigeria, Brazil, and Saudi Arabia and refined in Trinidad. The 'Pitch Lake' is an important source of asphalt.

Gas. In 1982 production was 558,800m. cu. feet, of which 129,200m. was flared and lost.

Agriculture. Hectares under cultivation and care include (1981): Forest, 229,000; cocoa, 20,000; sugar, 28,000. Sugar production in 1982 was 78,685 (1981: 93,317) tonnes. The territory is still largely dependent on imported food supplies, especially flour, dairy products, meat and rice. Areas have been irrigated for rice, and soil and forest conservation is practised.

Livestock (1982): Cattle, 79,000; sheep, 12,000; goats, 48,000; pigs, 61,000; poultry, 7·6m.

INDUSTRY AND TRADE

Industry. In 1981, 217,989 tonnes of steel were produced at the first integrated steelworks to be constructed in the Caribbean which was opened in 1981. Other manufacturing include ammonia, fertilizers (1982 production, 939,700 tonnes), sugar, cement, paints, plastics and petrochemicals.

Labour. The working population in 1982 was 443,000 and unemployment was about 10%; about 30% of the labour force belong to unions.

Commerce. Exports in 1982 were US$3,057m. of which US$2,707 was mineral fuels and products and chemicals, US$148m. USA took 50% of exports. Imports totalled US$3,518m. of which US$1,161m. was for machinery and transport of which the USA supplied 25% and UK, 9%.

Total trade of Trinidad and Tobago with UK (British Department of Trade returns, in £1,000 sterling):

	1979	1980	1981	1982	1983
Imports to UK	41,243	35,088	37,153	65,154	52,748
Exports and re-exports from UK	104,562	120,270	121,465	158,436	148,811

Tourism. In 1979, 196,060 foreigners visited Trinidad and Tobago spending TT$298·2m.

COMMUNICATIONS

Roads. There were (1984) about 4,000 miles of main and local roads. Motor vehicles registered in 1978 totalled 176,895, including 112,572 private cars, 18,895 hired and rented cars, and 27,399 goods vehicles.

Aviation. The following airlines operate scheduled passenger, mail and freight services. British West Indian Airways, Ltd, Air Canada, PANAM, KLM, Linea Aeropostal Venezolana, Aerolinas Argentinas, Leeward Islands Air Transport, Air France, ASPA, Air India, Caribair, British Airways, American Airlines and Guyana Airways.

Shipping. In 1977 48m. tons of cargo were handled.

Post and Broadcasting. International communications to all parts of the world are provided by Trinidad and Tobago External Telecommunications Co. Ltd (TEXTEL) by means of a satellite earth station and various high quality radio circuits. The marine radio service is also maintained by TEXTEL. Number of post offices (1979), 63; postal agencies, 175; number of telephones (1979), 77,799. Four wireless stations are maintained by the Trinidad Government and 3 by airline companies. There were 500,000 radio and 230,000 television receivers in 1981. A meteorological station is maintained at Piarco airport.

Cinemas (1973). There are 72 cinemas and 4 drive-in cinemas.

Newspapers (1979). There are 2 daily newspapers with a total daily circulation of 179,400, 3 Sunday newspapers with a total circulation of 186,200, 2 evening papers and 5 weekly newspapers.

JUSTICE, RELIGION, EDUCATION AND WELFARE

Justice. The High Court consists of the Chief Justice and not fewer than 10 puisne judges. In criminal cases a judge of the High Court sits with a jury of 12 in cases of treason and murder, and with 9 jurors in other cases. The Court of Appeal consists of the Chief Justice and 3 Justices of Appeal; there is a limited right of appeal from it to the Privy Council. There are 10 High Courts and 28 magistrates' courts.

Religion. In 1970, 18·1% of the population were Anglicans (under the Bishop of Trinidad and Tobago), 35·6% Roman Catholics (under the Archbishop of Port-of-Spain), 4·2% Presbyterians, 24·7% Hindus and 6·3% Moslems.

Education. In 1972–73 there were 476 primary and intermediate schools (government assisted) and (1971–72) 116 secondary schools (47 government and assisted and 69 private).

There were 222,928 pupils on roll in the primary and intermediate schools and 35,302 in the secondary schools (government and assisted). Education in government and assisted secondary schools was made free in 1960. There are also 5 training colleges. Technical and commercial education is provided by 4 government sponsored technical schools.

Health. State medical services are free and in 1972 a National Insurance Scheme was established.

DIPLOMATIC REPRESENTATIVES

Of Trinidad and Tobago in Great Britain (42 Belgrave Sq., London, SW1X 8NT)
High Commissioner: Frank O. Abdullah (accredited 9 March 1983).

Of Great Britain in Trinidad and Tobago (Furness Hse., 90 Independence Sq.,
Port-of-Spain)
High Commissioner: D. N. Lane, CMG.

Of Trinidad and Tobago in the USA (1708 Massachusetts Ave., NW, Washington,
D.C., 20036)
Ambassador: Dr James O'Neil-Lewis.

Of the USA in Trinidad and Tobago (15 Queen's Park West, Port-of-Spain)
Ambassador: Melvin H. Evans.

Of Trinidad and Tobago to the United Nations
Ambassador: D. H. N. Alleyne.

Books of Reference

Statistical Information: The Central Statistical Office, Government of Trinidad and Tobago, 2
Edward St., Port-of-Spain. *Director:* J. Harewood. Publications include *Annual Statistical
Digest, Quarterly Economic Report, Annual Overseas Trade Report, Population and Vital
Statistics Annual Report.*

Report of the Trinidad and Tobago Independence Conference, 1962. (Cmnd. 1757.) HMSO,
1962

Facts on Trinidad and Tobago. Public Relations Division, Prime Minister's Office, Port-of-
Spain, 1978

Immigration Guidelines. Government Printer, Port-of-Spain, 1980

Oil and Energy, Trinidad and Tobago. Government Printer, Port-of-Spain, 1980

Trinidad and Tobago Year Book. Port-of-Spain. Annual (from 1865)

Cooper, St G. C. and Bacon, P. R. (eds.), *The Natural Resources of Trinidad and Tobago.*
London, 1981

Central Library: The Central Library of Trinidad and Tobago, Queen's Park East, Port-of-
Spain. *Acting Librarian:* Mrs L. Hutchinson.

TUNISIA

Al-Djoumhouria Attunusia

Capital: Tunis
Population: 6·95m. (1983)
GNP per capita: US$1,310 (1980)

HISTORY. Tunisia was a French protectorate from 1883 and achieved independence on 20 March 1956. The Constituent Assembly, elected on 25 March 1956, abolished the monarchy (of the Bey of Tunis) on 25 July 1957 and proclaimed a republic.

AREA AND POPULATION. The boundaries are on the north and east the Mediterranean Sea, on the west Algeria and on the south Libya. The area is about 164,150 sq. km (63,362 sq. miles), including that portion of the Sahara which is to the east of the Djerid, extending towards Ghadamès.

At the census of 8 May 1975 there were 5,588,209 inhabitants (2,840,913 males and 2,747,209 females) of whom 49% were urban. Estimate (1983) 6,945,000.

The census populations of the *gouvernorats* were as follows as at 8 May 1975:

Béja	248,770	Kassérine	238,499	Sfax	474,879
Bizerta	343,708	Le Kef	233,155	Sidi Bouzid	218,511
Gabès	255,717	Mahdia	218,217	Siliana	192,668
Gafsa	237,844	Médénine	292,970	Sousse	254,601
Jendouba	299,702	Monastir	223,150	Tunis Nord	944,130
Kairouan	338,477	Nabeul	368,114	Tunis Sud	205,097

Tunis, the capital, had (census, 1975) 550,404 inhabitants: Sfax, 171,297; Sousse, 69,530; Bizerta, 62,856; Djerba, 70,217; Kairouan, a holy city of the Moslems, 54,546; Gafsa, 42,225; Gabès, 40,585; Béja, 39,226.

Vital statistics (1976). Births, 208,728; deaths, 36,912; marriages, 47,940.

The official language is Arabic but the use of French is widespread.

CLIMATE. The climate ranges from warm temperate in the north, where winters are mild and wet and the summers hot and dry, to desert in the south. Tunis. Jan. 48°F (8·9°C), July 78°F (25·6°C). Annual rainfall 16″ (400 mm). Bizerta. Jan. 52°F (11·1°C), July 77°F (25°C). Annual rainfall 25″ (622 mm).

CONSTITUTION AND GOVERNMENT. The Constitution of the republic was promulgated on 1 June 1959. The President and the National Assembly are elected simultaneously by direct universal suffrage for a period of 5 years. The President cannot be re-elected more than 3 times consecutively, however on 18 March 1975 the National Assembly proclaimed Bourguiba 'President for Life'. An amendment to the Constitution in 1969 gives the Prime Minister power to act as President in case of a sudden vacancy of the Presidency.

Elections were held on 1 Nov. 1981, when all 136 seats in the National Assembly were won by the *Front National*, an alliance of the ruling *Parti Socialiste Destourien* (109 seats) and the *Union générale des travailleurs tunisiens* (27 seats).

President of the Republic and Head of Government: Habib Ben Ali Bourguiba (elected 25 July 1957, re-elected 8 Nov. 1959, 8 Nov. 1964, 2 Nov. 1969, Nov. 1974). Declared President for life in 1975.

The Cabinet in Nov. 1983 was composed as follows:

Prime Minister: Mohammed M'Zali.
Special Adviser to the President: Habib Bourguiba, Jr. *Justice:* M'hamed Chaker. *Foreign Affairs:* Beji Caied Essebsi. *Interior:* Idris Guiga. *Defence:* Salaheddine Bali. *Planning:* Ismail Khelil. *Finance:* Salah Ben M'Barkq. *National Economy:*

Rashid Sfar. *Housing:* Moncef Belhaj Amor. *Equipment:* Sadok Ben Jomaq. *Information:* Abderrazak Kefi. *National Education:* Mohamed Frej Chedli. *Higher Education and Scientific Research:* Abdelaziz Ben Dhia. *Agriculture:* Lassaad Ben Osman. *Public Health:* Dr Souad Yacoubi. *Transport and Communications:* Brahim Ktlouaja. *Social Affairs:* Mohamed Ennaceur. *Youth and Sports:* Mohamed Kraiem. *Family and Women's Affairs:* Fathia M'zali. *Minister-Delegate responsible for Prime Minister's Office:* Mongi Kooli. *Minister-Delegate attached to Prime Minister responsible for Civil Service and Administrative Reform:* Mezri Chekir. *Secretary of State for International Co-operation:* Ahmed Ben Arfa. *Secretary of State for Foreign Affairs:* Mahmoud Mestiri.

Local Government. The country is divided into 18 *gouvernorats*, each subdivided into *délégations, communes and imadas.*

Flag: Red with a white circle in the middle, on which is a 5-pointed red star encircled by a red crescent.

DEFENCE. Selective military service is 1 year. Officer-cadets are being trained in France.

Army. The Army consists of 2 combined arms, 1 Sahara and 1 para-commando brigades; 1 armoured reconnaissance, 3 field, 2 anti-aircraft and 1 engineer regiments. Equipment includes 14 M-48 main battle, and 55 AMX-13 and 20 M-41 light tanks. Strength is 23,000. There are also the paramilitary gendarmerie (5,000 men) and National Guard (3,500 men).

Navy. The flotilla consists of 1 frigate (*ex*-US 40-year-old destroyer-escort), 2 fast gunboats (*ex*-Chinese), 2 fast attack craft (British-built in 1977), 2 coastal minesweepers, 4 patrol vessels (French built), 10 coastal patrol boats, 2 protection launches and 1 large tug. Three light corvette type, missile armed fast attack craft are being built in France. In 1984 naval personnel totalled 2,600 officers and ratings.

Air Force. Equipment of the Air Force, acquired from various Western sources, includes 1 squadron of Aermacchi M.B.326K/L jet light attack aircraft (to be supplemented with 6 F-5E Tiger II fighters and 2 F-5Fs); 12 SF.260W piston-engined light trainer/attack aircraft; 1 C-130H turboprop transport, 3 Flamant light transports, 4 S.208 liaison aircraft, 6 SF.260M trainers, 12 T6 Texan advanced trainers, 7 M.B.326B and 4 F-5F jet trainers, 1 Puma, 4 UH-1H, 18 AB.205, 6 Ecureuil and about 12 Alouette II and III helicopters. Personnel, about 2,000.

INTERNATIONAL RELATIONS

Membership. Tunisia is a member of UN, OAU and the Arab League.

ECONOMY

Planning. A sixth development plan (1982–86) envisaged investment of 8,000m. dinars.

Budget (in 1,000 dinars). Budget estimates, 1982, revenue, 1,042,000; expenditure, 954,000.

Currency. On 1 Nov. 1958 a new currency, the *dinar*, divided into 1,000 *millimes*, was established. Note circulation, Aug. 1980, was 910m. *dinars*.

Currency consists of coins of 1, 2, 5, 10, 20, 50, 100 and 500 *millimes*, and notes of 500 *millimes*, 1 *dinar*, 5 and 10 *dinars*. £1 = 1·02 *dinar*; US$1 = 0·71 *dinar* (March 1984).

Banking. The Central Bank of Tunisia is the bank of issue. In 1983 there were 39 banks operating in Tunisia, including 7 off-shore banks. Bank deposits amounted to 2,115m. dinars at 31 Dec. 1982.

Weights and Measures. The metric system of weights and measures has almost entirely taken the place of those of Tunisia, but corn is still sold in *kaffis* and *wibas*.

The *kfiz* (of 16 *wiba*, each of 12 *sa'*) = 16 bushels. The *ounce* = 31·487 grammes. The principal measure of length is the metre.

ENERGY AND NATURAL RESOURCES

Electricity. The electricity, gas and water services, formerly run by a French company, were nationalized on 26 Nov. 1959 and are now run respectively by the Société Tunisienne d'Electricité et du Gaz (STEG) and the Société Nationale d'Exploitation et de Distribution du Eaux (SONEDE).
Electrical energy generated was 3,080m. kwh. in 1983, of which (1980) 2,432m. was produced by STEG.

Oil. Crude oil production (1983) 5,601,000 tonnes.

Gas. Natural gas production (1983) 400m. cu. metres.

Minerals. Mineral production (in 1,000 tonnes) in 1983 (and 1981): Phosphate, 5,450 (4,978); iron ore, 230 (400); lead ore, 8·7 (14); zinc ore, 16 (15).
Processed minerals (in 1,000 tonnes) in 1982: Pig iron, 97; crude steel, 105.

Agriculture. Tunisia may be divided into 5 districts—the north, characterized by its mountainous formation, having large and fertile valleys (*e.g.*, the valley of the Medjerdah and the plains of Mornag, Mateur and Béja); the north-east, with the peninsula of Cap Bon, the soil being specially suited for the cultivation of oranges, lemons and tangerines; the Sahel, where olive trees abound; the centre, the region of high table lands and pastures, and the desert of the south, famous for its oases and gardens, where dates grow in profusion.
Agriculture is the chief industry, and large estates predominate. Of the total area of 15,583,000 hectares, about 9m. hectares are productive, including 2m. under cereals, 3·6m. used as pasturage, 900,000 forests and 1·3m. uncultivated.

Products		1979–80	1980–81	1981–82
Hard wheat		740	800	963
Soft wheat		130	160	180
Barley		300	270	270
Olive oil	(in 1,000 tonnes)	85	145	90
Oranges and lemons		160	220	170
Dates		47	46	53
Wine (in 1,000 hectolitres)		619	619	555

Other products are apricots, pears, apples, peaches, plums, figs, pomegranates, almonds, shaddocks, pistachios, esparto grass, henna and cork.
Livestock (1982): Horses, 52,000; asses, 206,000; mules, 70,000; cattle, 600,000; sheep, 4·5m.; goats, 800,000; camels, 173,000; pigs, 4,000.

Fisheries. In 1980, 6,209 boats with 22,555 men were engaged in fishing. In 1982 the catch amounted to 62,800 tonnes; 1981, 57,500.

INDUSTRY AND TRADE

Industry. Major modern plants include a sugar refinery in Béja (57,700 tonnes in 1975), a cellulose plant in Kassérine (22,000 tonnes in 1976), a petroleum refinery in Bizerta and a steel plant at Menzel Bourguiba. There is a marble work plant and a tyre factory at Mégrine.
In 1972 a phosphoric acid plant opened at Ghannouche with an annual capacity of 120,000 tonnes.
Production, 1977 (in 1,000 tonnes): Refined oil, 1,130; cement, 680; metal castings, 200; steel, 200; rounded bars, 145; paper pulp, 22.

Trade Unions. The Union Générale des Travailleurs Tunisiens won 27 seats in the parliamentary elections (1 Nov. 1981). There are also the Union Tunisienne de l'Industrie, du Commerce et de l'Artisanat (UTICA, the employers' union) and the Union National des Agriculteurs (UNA, farmers' union).

Commerce. The imports and exports for calendar years (in 1,000 dinars) were as follows:

	1976	1977	1978	1979	1980	1981	1982
Imports	656,700	735,000	834,000	1,156,800	1,483,170	1,649,000	1,937,900
Exports	338,300	390,000	440,000	726,700	891,410	1,042,200	1,153,900

Exports to France in 1982 totalled 219·2m. dinars, and imports from France, 520·9m. dinars and exports to USA were valued at 268·8m. dinars and imports from USA were valued at 149·9m. dinars.

Total trade between Tunisia and UK (British Department of Trade returns, in £1,000 sterling):

	1979	1980	1981	1982	1983
Imports to UK	9,084	17,566	22,070	12,628	18,125
Exports and re-exports from UK	24,660	29,872	35,157	38,632	44,559

Tourism. In 1981, 2·2m. tourists visited Tunisia, not counting ships' passengers in transit.

COMMUNICATIONS

Roads. In 1975 there were 16,695 km of roads, of which 10,645 km were main roads.

Number of motor vehicles, 1978, included 115,326 private cars, 84,563 commercial cars, 10,861 motor cycles and 35,598 tractors.

Railways. In 1980 there were 2,152 km of railways (479 km of 1,435 mm gauge and 1,673 km of 1,000 mm gauge), and carried 1,575m. tonne-km and 944m. passenger-km.

Aviation. The national airline is 'Tunis-Air'. The main airport is at Tunis-Carthage. In 1981, 3,515,675 passengers were carried.

Shipping. The main port is Tunis, and its outer port is Tunis-Goulette. These two ports and Sfax, Sousse and Bizerta are directly accessible to ocean going vessels. The port of La Skhirra, in the south, is used for the shipping of Algerian and Tunisian oil.

In 1981, 5,055 ships of 20,422,000 tons entered Tunisian ports.

Post and Broadcasting. There were, in 1981, 188,476 telephones. There were, in 1978, 403 post offices, and 6 wireless transmitting stations. Wireless sets in use in 1976 were 1,124,000. Television began in 1966 and in 1979 there were 255,700 sets.

Cinemas (1976). There were 175 cinemas with a seating capacity of 44,000.

Newspapers. There are 2 Arabic and 3 French daily newspapers.

JUSTICE, RELIGION, EDUCATION AND WELFARE

Justice. There are 51 magistrates' courts, 13 courts of first instance, 3 courts of appeal (in Tunis, Sfax and Sousse) and the High Court in Tunis.

A Personal Status Code was promulgated on 13 Aug. 1956 and applied to Tunisians from 1 Jan. 1957. This raised the status of women, made divorce subject to a court decision, abolished polygamy and decreed a minimum marriage age.

Religion. The constitution recognizes Islam as the state religion. There are about 20,000 Roman Catholics, under the Prelate of Tunis. The Greek Church, the French Protestants and the English Church are also represented.

Education. All education was in 1956 made dependent on the Ministry of National Education. The 208 independent koranic schools have been nationalized and the distinction between religious and public schools has been abolished. All education is free from primary schools to university. A teachers' training college (*école normale supérieure*) was established in 1955. There are also a high school of law, 2 centres of economic studies, 2 schools of engineering, 2 medical schools, a faculty of agriculture and 2 institutes of business administration.

In 1980–81 there were 2,613 primary schools with 26,989 teachers and 1,045,011 pupils; 236 secondary schools with 12,629 teachers and 210,895 pupils; 60,137 students at technical and vocational schools and 4,101 students in teacher-training; higher education mainly at the University of Tunis had 31,887 students and 3,869 teaching staff.

Health. In 1976 there were 268 hospitals (13,145 beds). The registered medical personnel in Tunisia comprised 1,210 doctors (843 Tunisians and 367 foreigners), 313 pharmacists, 176 dentists and 60 veterinaries.

Social Security. A system of social security was set up in 1950 (amended 1963, 1964 and 1970).

DIPLOMATIC REPRESENTATIVES

Of Tunisia in Great Britain (29 Prince's Gate, London, SW7 1QG)
Ambassador: Sadok Bouzayen (accredited 26 Nov. 1981).

Of Great Britain in Tunisia (5 Place de la Victoire, Tunis)
Ambassador and Consul-General: Sir Alexander Stirling, KBE, CMG.

Of Tunisia in the USA (2408 Massachusetts Ave., NW, Washington, D.C., 20008)
Ambassador: Habib Ben Yahia.

Of the USA in Tunisia (144 Ave. de la Liberté, Tunis)
Ambassador: Walter L. Cutler.

Of Tunisia to the United Nations
Ambassador: Taieb Slim.

Books of Reference

Statistical Information: Institut National de la Statistique (27 Rue de Liban, Tunis) was set up in 1947. Its main publications are: *Annuaire statistique de la Tunisie* (latest issue, 1975).

Bannour, A. (ed.), *Economic Yearbook of Tunisia.* 2nd ed. Tunis, 1966
Findlay, Allan M., Findlay, Anne M., and Lawless, R. I., *Tunisia.* [Bibliography] Oxford and Santa Barbara, 1982
Knapp, W., *Tunisia.* London, 1970
Ling, D. L., *Tunisia: From Protectorate to Republic.* Indiana Univ. Press, 1967
Rudebeck, L., *The Tunisian Experience: Party and People.* London, 1970
Sylvester, A., *Tunisia.* London, 1969
Tomkinson, M., *Tunisia: A Holiday Guide.* London and Hammamet, 1984

TURKEY

Türkiye Cumhuriyeti

Capital: Ankara
Population: 47m. (1983)
GNP per capita: US$1,114 (1980)

HISTORY. The Turkish War of Independence (1919–22), following the disintegration of the Ottoman Empire, was led and won by Mustafa Kemal (Atatürk) on behalf of the Grand National Assembly which first met in Ankara on 23 April 1920. On 20 Jan. 1921 the Grand National Assembly voted a constitution which declared that all sovereignty belonged to the people and vested all power, both executive and legislative, in the Grand National Assembly. The name 'Ottoman Empire' was later replaced by 'Turkey'. On 1 Nov. 1922 the Grand National Assembly abolished the office of Sultan and Turkey became a republic on 29 Oct. 1923.

On 27 May 1960 the Turkish Army, directed by a National Unity Committee under the leadership of Gen. Cemal Gürsel, overthrew the government of the Democratic Party. The Grand National Assembly was dissolved and party activities were suspended. Party activities were legally resumed on 12 Jan. 1961. A new constitution was approved in a referendum held on 9 July 1961 and general elections were held the same year.

On 12 Sept. 1980, the Turkish armed forces overthrew the Demirel Government (Justice Party). Parliament was dissolved and all activities of political parties were suspended. The Constituent Assembly was convened in Oct. 1981, and prepared a new Constitution which was enforced after a national referendum on 7 Nov. 1982. New legislation regarding political parties and elections was being prepared in 1983.

AREA AND POPULATION. Turkey is bounded west by the Aegean Sea and by Greece, north by Bulgaria and the Black Sea, east by the USSR and Iran, and south by Iraq, Syria and the Mediterranean.

The area (including lakes) is 779,452 sq. km (300,947 sq. miles). Area in Europe (Trakya), 23,764 sq. km. Area in Asia (Anadolu), 755,855 sq. km; population estimate (1983), 47m.

The census population is given as follows:

	Total		Total		Total
1927	13,648,270	1950	20,947,188	1970	35,605,176
1935	16,158,018	1955	24,064,763	1975	40,347,719
1940	17,820,950	1960	27,754,820	1980	45,217,556
1945	18,790,174	1965	31,391,421		

The Treaty of Peace between the Allied Powers and Turkey, which was signed at Lausanne on 24 July 1923, defined the European frontier of the new Turkey and to some extent her Asiatic frontiers. This treaty was ratified by the Grand National Assembly in Ankara on 23 Aug. 1923 and entered into force 6 Aug. 1924.

The Treaty of Lausanne and the conventions attached to it provided for the demilitarization of zones adjoining the European frontier, the Dardanelles and the Bosphorus, subject to the right to maintain a garrison at Istanbul, for the demilitarization of İmroz, Bozcaada (Tenedos) and Tavşan Islands, as well as the islands in the Sea of Marmara with one exception and for a special administrative regime in İmroz and Bozcaada.

On 10 July 1936 a new Straits Convention was signed at Montreux (ratified on 9 Nov. 1936) to take the place of the 1923 Convention, whereby Turkey obtained the right of re-militarizing the zone of the Straits, and this area was re-occupied by Turkish troops on 21 July 1936. The International Commission of the Straits ceased to function on 30 Sept. 1936.

By an agreement between the Turkish and French Governments concluded at Ankara on 23 June 1939, the Sanjak of Alexandretta (the Hatay) was incorporated in the Turkish Republic.

The population of the provinces, at the census of Oct. 1980, was as follows:

Adana	1,485,743	Erzincan	282,022	Maraş	738,032
Adıyaman	367,595	Erzurum	801,809	Mardin	564,967
Afyonkarahisar	597,516	Eskişehir	543,802	Muğla	438,145
Ağrı	368,009	Gaziantep	808,697	Muş	302,406
Amasya	341,287	Gireşun	480,083	Nevşehir	256,933
Ankara	2,854,689	Gümüşane	275,191	Niğde	512,071
Antalya	748,706	Hakkari	155,463	Ordu	713,535
Artvin	228,997	Hatay	856,271	Rize	361,258
Aydin	652,488	İsparta	350,116	Sakarya	548,747
Balıkesir	853,177	İçel	843,931	Samsun	1,008,113
Bilecik	147,001	İstanbul	4,741,890	Siirt	445,483
Bingöl	228,702	İzmir	1,976,763	Sinop	276,242
Bitlis	257,908	Kars	700,238	Sivas	750,144
Bolu	471,751	Kastamonu	450,946	Tekirdağ	360,742
Burdur	235,009	Kayseri	778,383	Tokat	624,508
Bursa	1,148,492	Kırklareli	283,408	Trabzon	731,045
Çanakkale	391,568	Kırşehir	240,497	Tunceli	157,974
Çankırı	258,436	Kocaeli	596,899	Urfa	602,736
Çorum	571,831	Konya	1,562,139	Uşak	247,224
Denizli	603,338	Kütahya	497,089	Van	468,646
Diyarbakir	778,150	Malatya	606,996	Yozgat	504,433
Edirne	363,286	Manisa	941,941	Zonguldak	954,512
Elâziğ	440,808				

The population of towns of over 100,000 inhabitants, at the census of Oct. 1980, was as follows:

İstanbul	2,772,708	Samsun	198,749	Elaziğ	142,983
Ankara	1,877,755	İzmit	190,423	Denizli	135,373
İzmir	757,854	Erzurum	190,241	Adapazari	130,977
Adana	574,515	Malatya	179,074	İskenderun	124,824
Bursa	445,113	K. Maraş	178,557	Balikesir	124,051
Gaziantep	374,290	Kirikkale	178,401	Tarsus	121,074
Konya	329,139	Kağithane	175,540	Zonguldak	109,044
Eskişehir	309,431	Antalya	173,501	Trabzon	108,403
Kayseri	281,320	Sivas	172,864	Buca	103,105
Diyarbakir	235,617	Bayrampaşa	165,723	Küçükköy	100,406
Mersin	216,308	Urfa	147,488		

The population of Turkey according to 'mother tongue' (1965 census) comprises 28,289,680 Turks, 2,219,502 Kurds, 365,340 Arabs, 57,337 Circassians, 48,143 Greeks, 48,096 Armenians, 33,094 Georgians, 23,715 Lazes and 9,124 Spanish-speaking Jews.

CLIMATE. Coastal regions have a Mediterranean climate, with mild, moist winters and hot, dry summers. The interior plateau has more extreme conditions, with low and irregular rainfall, cold and snowy winters and hot, almost rainless summers. Ankara. Jan. 32°·5F (0·3°C), July 73°F (23°C). Annual rainfall 14·7″ (367 mm). Istanbul. Jan. 41°F (5°C), July 73°F (23°C). Annual rainfall 28·9″ (723 mm). Izmir. Jan. 46°F (8°C), July 81°F (27°C). Annual rainfall 28″ (700 mm).

CONSTITUTION AND GOVERNMENT. The Turkish Grand National Assembly was dissolved on 12 Sept. 1980. The National Security Council took over its functions and powers. On 23 Oct. 1981 a Consultative Assembly was inaugurated. In early 1983 the National Security Council was acting as the upper house and the Consultative Assembly as the lower house.

Religious courts were abolished in 1924, Islam ceased to be the official state religion in 1928, women were given the franchise and western-style surnames were adopted in 1934.

The task of the Consultative Assembly was to prepare a new Constitution to replace that of 1961. The Assembly began its work in Oct. 1981 under the presidency of Sadi Irmak and on 7 Nov. 1982 a national referendum established that 98% of the electorate were in favour of the new Constitution.

Turkish men and women are entitled to vote at the age of 21 and to become deputies at the age of 30 and second members of Senate at the age of 40. Secret ballot was introduced by law on 10 July 1948.

Elections were held on 6 Nov. 1983. Of the 399 seats in the Grand National Assembly the Motherland Party won 211; The Populist Party, 117; The National Democracy Party, 71.

Past Presidents of the Republic: Mustafa Kemal Atatürk (29 Oct. 1923–10 Nov. 1938), İsmet İnönü (11 Nov. 1938–21 May 1950), Celâl Bayar (22 May 1950–27 May 1960), Cemal Gürsel (26 Oct. 1961–27 March 1966), Cevdet Sunay (29 March 1966–28 March 1973), Fahri S. Korutürk (6 April 1973–6 April 1980).

President, Head of National Security Council: Kenan Evren.
The Cabinet appointed 13 Dec. 1983 was composed as follows:
Prime Minister: Turgut Ozal.
Deputy Prime Minister and Minister of State: I. Kaya Erdem. *Justice:* Necat Eldem. *Defence:* Zeki Yavuzturk. *Interior:* Ali Tanriyar. *Foreign Affairs:* Vahit Halefoglu. *Finance and Customs:* Vural Arikan. *Education, Youth and Sports:* Vehbi Dincerler. *Public Works and Housing:* I. Sefa Giray. *Health and Social Welfare:* Mehmet Aydin. *Transportation and Communication:* Veysel Atasoy. *Agriculture, Forestry and Rural Affairs:* H. Husnu Dogan. *Labour and Social Security:* Mustafa Kalemli. *Industry and Commerce:* Cahit Aral. *Energy and Natural Resources:* Cemal Buyukbas. *Culture and Tourism:* M. Mukerrem Tascioglu.
There are 6 Ministers of State.

National flag: A white crescent and star on red.
National anthem: Korkma! Sönmez bu şafaklarda yüzen al sancak (words by Mehmed Akif Ersoy; tune by Zeki Güngör; adopted 12 March 1921).

Local Government. The Constitution of 1921 provided for the administrative division of the country into *Il*, (province, now 67 in number), divided into *Ilçe* (district), subdivided in their turn into *Bucak* (township or commune). At the head of each Il is a Vali representing the Government. Each Il has its own elective council.

The İlçe is regarded as a mere grouping of Bucaks for certain purposes of general administration. The Bucak or commune is an autonomous entity and possesses an elective council charged with the administration of such matters as are not reserved to the State.

According to the municipal law passed in 1930, Turkish women have the right to be electors and to be elected at local and national elections.

DEFENCE. Several bills for the reorganization of the armed forces were passed in June 1961 by the Grand National Assembly. One of these placed all organizations connected with national defence under the authority of the Minister of National Defence. Another created a Supreme Council of National Security, under the chairmanship of the Prime Minister, with the object of co-ordinating the resources of the country in case of war. Besides the Minister of National Defence and the Chief of the General Staff, the heads of economic Ministries are members of this council.

Military service in Army, Air Force and Navy is 18 months for officers and 20 months for other ranks. Men are called up when they reach the age of 20.

Army. The Army consists of 16 infantry divisions (2 mechanized), 6 armoured, 4 mechanized, 11 infantry, 1 parachute and 1 commando brigades; 4 surface-to-surface missile, 8 armoured reconnaissance, 32 artillery and 8 anti-aircraft battalions. Equipment includes 3,000 M-48, 500 M-47 and 77 Leopard main battle tanks. Strength (1984) 470,000 (including 420,000 conscripts), and reserves number 700,000. There is also a paramilitary gendarmerie of 125,000 men.

Navy. The fleet includes 16 diesel-powered submarines (6 new designed in Federal Republic of Germany and 10 old *ex*-US patrol submarines), 13 old *ex*-US destroyers, 4 frigates (2 modern Turkish-built and 2 *ex*-German Navy), 1 large minelayer, 6 coastal minelayers, 1 fast attack gunboat (light corvette type), 13 fast missile craft, 7 fast torpedo boats, 22 coastal minesweepers, 8 patrol vessels, 4 inshore minesweepers, 9 minehunting boats, 20 patrol craft, 3 repair ships, 2 submarine support ships, 1 large training ship, 1 training ship (ex-German support frigate), 5 landing ships, 50 landing craft, 20 minor landing craft, 3 submarine rescue ships, 9 oilers, 10 transports, 2 survey ships, 3 survey boats, 4 boom defence vessels, 3 depot ships, 4 training craft, 3 gate vessels, 25 auxiliary vessels, 14 tugs, 2 tenders, 9 water carriers, and 7 floating docks.

Future construction includes 6 diesel-electric patrol submarines designed in the Federal Republic of Germany, but to be built in Turkey.

The naval bases are at Gölcük in the Gulf of İzmit, at İskenderun, at Taskizak (İstanbul) and at İzmir.

Personnel strength in 1984 totalled 45,000 officers and ratings.

The Coast Guard, formed in July 1982 from the naval wing of the Jandarma, with a rear-admiral as Commander-in-Chief, has 26 patrol vessels, 9 medium patrol craft and 10 coastal patrol cutters, and an initial establishment of 1,000 officers and men.

Air Force. The Air Force is under the control of the General Staff and, operationally, under 6 ATAF. It is organized as 2 tactical air forces, with headquarters at Eskisehir and Diyarbakir, each having a flight of C-47s, UH-1H helicopters, AT-11s and T-33s. Combat aircraft comprise F-104G and F-104S Starfighters in 8 squadrons; RF-104Gs in 1 squadron; RF-5As in 1 squadron; F-4E and RF-4E Phantoms in 8 squadrons; plus Nike-Hercules surface-to-air missile batteries. The 6 transport squadrons are equipped with Transall C-160, C-130 Hercules, Viscount and C-47 aircraft, and UH-IH helicopters. Training types include T-33A, T-37 and T-38 advanced trainers, T-34 basic and T-41 primary trainers and F-5A/Bs for weapons training. Personnel strength is about 53,000, with over 320 combat aircraft. Aircraft on order include the first batch of 40 of a planned total of 160 F-16s.

INTERNATIONAL RELATIONS

Membership. Turkey is a member of UN, OECD, NATO and Council of Europe and an Associate of EEC.

ECONOMY

Planning. The first 5-year development plan, 1963–67, provided for investments of TL68,000m. (at 1965 prices); TL64,000m. were invested, the gross national product increasing at the rate of 6·7% per annum. The second 5-year plan (1968–72) aimed at achieving an annual growth of 7%; external financing amounting to US$1,716m. The third 5-year plan (1973–78) set out to achieve an annual growth of 7·4%. The fourth 5-year plan (1979–83) sets out to achieve an annual growth of 8%.

Budget. Estimates of revenue and expenditure (in TL1,000) for financial years 1 March–28/29 Feb.:

	1978–79	1979–80	1980–81	1981–82
Revenue	247,253,177	372,309,378	706,687,182	1,480,965,037
Expenditure	276,148,529	409,430,671	756,687,182	1,540,965,037

Currency. The Turkish *Lira* (TL) is divided into 100 *kuruş (piastres).* Coins in general circulation are of the following values: 25 and 50 *kuruş,*; 1, 2½ and 5 *Lira.* Bank-notes in circulation are as follows: 5, 10, 20, 50, 100, 500, 1,000 and 5,000 *Lira.* In March 1984, US$1 = 309·50 *Lira*; £1 = 450·13.

Banking. The Turkish banking system is composed of the Central Bank of the Republic of Turkey (Merkez Bankası) and 44 other banks. Thirteen (including the Central Bank) are established by special laws.

The 13 banks established by special laws carry out specialized banking activities beside their general banking transactions. Five of them are state economic enterprises whose capital is owned wholly by the State. They include: Ziraat Bankası (rural credits, capital: TL1,500m.), Sümerbank (textiles, etc., capital: TL2,250m.), Etibank (mining, energy, capital: TL3,250m.), İller Bankası (urban works, capital:

TL2,000m.), İstanbul Emniyet Sandığı (savings bank). Six of them are joint-stock companies; the majority of their share capital is owned by the public sector. They include: the Emlâk Kredi Bankası (housing, capital: TL1,000m.), Denizcilik Bankası (shipping, capital: TL2,000m.), Türkiye Vakıflar Bankası (investments of pious foundations, funds, capital: TL200m.), Türkiye Halk Bankası (small business, capital: TL1,000m.); Türkiye Öğretmenler Bankası (teachers' housing, capital: TL30m.), T. C. Turizm Bankası (tourism, capital: TL1,000m.).

The development banks are: Devlet Yatırım Bankası (investment credits to state economic enterprises, capital: TL1,000m.), Türkiye Sınaî Kalkınma Bankası (investment credit to the private sector, capital: TL328·66m.), Sınaî Yatırım ve Kredi Bankası (industrial medium-term credit, capital: TL40m.).

Of the 31 commercial banks, 5 are foreign banks established in Turkey, and one is a bank whose capital is shared by a foreign bank.

The total credit volume of banks at 31 Dec. 1982 amounted to TL2,703,102m.

Weights and Measures. The metric system came into force on 1 Jan. 1934. On 24 May 1928 the Grand National Assembly made European numerals obligatory as from 1 June 1929.

On 1 March 1917 the Gregorian calendar was introduced into Turkey, to be used side by side with the Hegira calendar, while as from 26 Dec. 1925 it was decided finally to adopt the Gregorian calendar alone.

ENERGY AND NATURAL RESOURCES

Electricity. The potential hydro-electric power in Turkey is estimated at 56,000m. kwh. In 1981 the electrical power plants (hydro-electric or thermal) produced 24,900m. kwh.

Oil. Oil is being produced in Garzan and Raman by the Turkish Petroleum Co. Under the oil law of 14 Oct. 1954 private companies can explore and produce oil. Turkish companies produced 940,000 tons in 1980 and foreign companies 1,376,000 tons. The 3 refineries refined 12m. tons of crude oil in 1975. With a fourth refinery, introduced in 1973, total refining capacity now reaches 24m. tons a year. The oil pipeline Batman–Iskenderun (494 km) was opened on 4 Jan. 1967. Imports (refined locally) in 1983 were 14·3m. tonnes.

Minerals. The Turkish provinces, especially those in Asia, are reported rich in minerals. Turkey is one of the four principal producers of chrome in the world.

Production of principal minerals (in 1,000 tonnes) was:

	1979	1980	1981
Coal	4,051	3,602	3,973
Lignite	11,051	13,639	15,057
Chromite	176	170	208
Copper concentrate	127	101	159
Sulphur	21	23	29
Wolfram concentrates (tonnes)	258	294	293
Phosphate	27	21	43
Alumina	75	137	131

Of the Government organizations producing these ores, Zonguldak coal mines operate under the Turkish State Coal Exploitation; while the copper mines at Murgul and Ergani, the Eastern chromite mines, Keçiborlu sulphur, Emet cole-manite, Küre pyrite and cupriferous pyrite, Keban argentiferous lead mines operate under the Etibank.

Agriculture. The number of people aged 15 and over engaged in agriculture in 1980 was 10,482,856.

In 1982, 27,281,000 hectares were cultivated land, 20,667,000 hectares of its own and 6,614,000 hectares fallow; vineyards, fruit orchards and olive groves occupied 2,892,000 hectares; forest occupied 20,199,000 hectares.

The soil for the most part is very fertile; the principal products are cotton, to-bacco, cereals (especially wheat), figs, silk, olives and olive oil, dried fruits, liquorice root, nuts, almonds, mohair, skins and hides, furs, wool, gums, canary seed, linseed and sesame. The principal tobacco districts are Samsun, Bafra,

Çarsamba, İzmit and İzmir. Two-thirds of the exports of leaf tobacco goes to the USA. The principal centre for silk production is Bursa. The production of olive oil, mainly confined to the Ils of Aydın and Balıkesir, is very important (107,000 tonnes in 1981). Sugar production (refined) in 1982 was 1·05m. tonnes. Agricultural production (in tonnes) in 1982 included 3·5m. grapes, 1·2m. oranges and lemons, 218,000 hazelnuts, 1·6m. apples, 1·32m. olives, 3m. potatoes. Tea production (fresh leaves, 1981) was 210,000 tonnes.

Turkey produced 385 tonnes of flax fibre and 9,800 tonnes of hemp fibre in 1982. Cotton production was 481,000 tonnes in 1982. Agricultural tractors numbered 436,367 in 1980.

Yield (in 1,000 tonnes) of principal crops:

	1978	1979	1980	1981	1982
Wheat	16,700	17,500	16,500	17,000	17,500
Barley	4,750	5,240	5,300	5,900	6,300
Maize	1,300	1,350	1,240	1,200	1,360
Rye	620	620	525	530	420
Tobacco	293	217	234	177	206
Oats	370	370	355	325	330
Rice	190	225	143	198	210

Livestock (1982): 49·60m. sheep, 18,926,000 goats, 15,981,000 cattle, 1·27m. asses, 772,000 horses, 1m. buffaloes.

In 1981 Turkey produced 33·6m. tonnes of wool, 547,000 tonnes of cattle and sheep meat and 256,000 tonnes of poultry.

Forestry. On 8 Feb. 1937 a new forest law was voted, providing for state control of all forests, including those under private ownership. It contains measures for planting, protection against fire, marauders and insects, and lays down penalties for infringement of its clauses. The most wooded Ils are Kastamonu, Aydın, Bursa, Bolu, Trabzon, Konya and Balıkesir. Of the forest land, 10,417,560 hectares belonged to the State in 1951. In 1982 total forest land was 20,199,000 hectares.

Fisheries. On 25 Aug. 1964 Turkey extended her waters in which she has exclusive fishing rights to 12 nautical miles. In 1981, 466,004 tons of sea and fresh water food was produced.

INDUSTRY AND TRADE

Industry. Production in 1982 included 15,777,000 tonnes of cement and 398,000 tonnes of paper. Industrial plants number about 30,000.

In 1981 Turkey produced (in tonnes) 4,203,000 of iron and steel, 10,449,000 of petroleum products, 2,364,000 of crude oil, 2,346,000 of iron ore (1978), 15,057,000 of lignite (clean), 3,973,000 of coal (clean), 208,000 of chrome, 27,300 of copper, 828,000 of boron (1978). There are steel works at Karabük, Ereğli and Iskenderun.

Trade Unions. The trade-union movement began in 1947. There are 4 national confederations (including Türk-İş and Disk) and 6 federations. There are 35 unions affiliated to Türk-İş and 17 employers' federations affiliated to Disk, whose activities were banned on 12 Sept. 1980. In 1979, labour unions totalled 802 and employers' unions, 108.

Employment, 1980: Manufacturing, 2,036,843; construction, 813,838; transport, communications and warehousing, 545,686; mining, 179,127; services, 41,923. There were 157,466 manufacturing firms, 236,995 trading establishments and 580,635 service establishments in 1975.

Commerce. Imports and exports (in US$1m.) for calendar years:

	1979	1980	1981	1982
Imports	5,069	7,909	8,933	8,735
Exports	2,261	2,910	4,703	5,746

Exports (1982) in US$1m.: Cotton, 308; hazelnuts, 240; tobacco, 349; textiles, 1,057; raisins, 101; cereals and pulses, 338.

Imports (1982) in US$1m.: Crude oil, 3,419; machinery, 1,690; chemicals, 843;

transportation equipment, 604; iron and steel, 592; petroleum products, 221; non-ferrous metals, 122; rubber and plastics, 237.

In 1982 (provisional) imports (in US$1m.) from the Middle East and North Africa were 3,678; EEC, 2,466; Iraq, 1,310; Federal Republic of Germany, 1,009; Libya, 920; US, 813. Exports to the Middle East and North Africa, 2,690; EEC, 1,755; Iran, 791; Federal Republic of Germany, 707; Iraq, 610.

Total trade between Turkey and UK (British Department of Trade returns, in £1,000 sterling):

	1979	1980	1981	1982	1983
Imports to UK	67,060	49,243	128,226	207,763	184,976
Exports and re-exports from UK	135,734	147,118	159,849	218,116	244,024

Tourism. A tourist industry is developing. The number of foreign tourists was about 1·4m. in 1982.

COMMUNICATIONS

Roads. Turkey had, in 1982, 60,712 km of national highways, of which (1980) 54,318 were hard surfaced. In 1982 there were registered 1,187,899 motor vehicles, including 746,506 passenger cars and 99,680 buses.

Railways. Total length of railway lines in 1982 was 8,193 km, all state-owned; 202 km electrified. In 1980 railways carried 2·6m. passengers and 1·2m. tonnes of freight.

Aviation. The State Airways Administration, formed in 1938, has been converted into the mixed company Turkish Airlines (Türk Havayollari Anonim Ortaklığı); British Airways became a partner in July 1957. It conducts foreign services to Athens, Beirut, Brussels, Amsterdam, Munich, Rome, Frankfurt, Vienna, London, Paris, Belgrade, Nicosia, Tel-Aviv and Baghdad.

In 1982 Turkish Airlines flew a total of 19,526 flight km. İstanbul or Ankara are connected with all the principal countries by 27 national airlines.

Shipping. In 1982 Turkish Maritime Lines and private companies had a gross tonnage of 2,061,000, with a total of 3,083 ships. The main ports in order of tonnage capacity are: İstanbul, İzmir, Samsun, Mersin, İskenderun and Trabzon.

Ports built or extended since 1950 are İskenderun, Ereğli, Trabzon, Samsun, Mersin, Zonguldak, Giresun, Hopa, Antalya and Bandirma. New facilities have been provided at Haydarpaşa, Salıpazari, Hopa, Yarımca and İzmir.

Post and Broadcasting. Number of telephones in 1982 was 2,104,113; İstanbul, 656,908; Ankara, 385,819.

In 1980 there were 4,283,753 licensed wireless sets. There were 3,348,138 television receivers.

Newspapers. In 1975 there were 2,362 daily newspapers and periodicals in the Turkish language, 2 in Greek, 1 in French, 1 in Armenian and 1 in English. In 1976, 27 dailies were published in Ankara, 40 dailies in İstanbul, 6 dailies in İzmir, 5 dailies in Bursa and 4 dailies in Konya.

JUSTICE, RELIGION, EDUCATION AND WELFARE

Justice. The unified legal system consists of: (1) justices of the peace (single judges with limited but summary penal and civil jurisdiction); (2) courts of first instance (single judges, dealing with cases outside the jurisdiction of (3) and (4)); (3) central criminal courts (a president and 2 judges, dealing with cases where the crime is punishable by imprisonment over 5 years); (4) commercial courts (3 judges); (5) state security courts, to prosecute offences against the integrity of the state (a president and 4 judges, 2 of the latter being military).

The civil and military Courts of Cassation sit at Ankara.

The Council of State is the highest administration tribunal; it consists of 5 chambers. Its 31 judges are nominated from among high-ranking personalities in politics, economy, law, the army, etc.

The Military Court of Cassation in Ankara is the highest military tribunal. The Military Administrative Court deals with the judicial control of administrative acts and deeds concerning military personnel.

The Constitutional Court, set up under the Constitution, can review and annul legislation and try the President of the Republic, Ministers and senior judges. It consists of 15 regular and 5 alternate members.

The Civil Code and the Code of Obligations have been adapted from the corresponding Swiss codes. The Penal Code is largely based upon the Italian Penal Code, and the Code of Civil Procedure closely resembles that of the Canton of Neuchâtel. The Commercial Code is based on the German.

Religion. Freedom of religion is guaranteed by the Constitution. Although Islam is not the official state religion of Turkey, Moslems form 98·2% of the population. The administration of the Moslem religious organizations is in charge of the Presidency of Religious Affairs, attached to the Prime Minister's office. The Turkish Republic is a secular state.

İstanbul is the seat of the Œcumenical Patriarch, who is the head of the Orthodox Church in Turkey. The Armenian Church (Gregorian) is ruled by a Patriarch in İstanbul who is subordinate to the Katholikos of Etchmiadzin, the spiritual head of all Armenians. The Armenian Apostolic Church is ruled by the Patriarch of Cilicia. The Chaldeans (Nestorian Uniats) have a Bishop at Mardin. The Syrian Uniats have a See of Mardin and Amida, but it is united with their Patriarchate of Antioch (residence, Damascus). Greek Uniats (Byzantine Rite) have as their Ordinary in İstanbul, the Titular Bishop of Gratianopolis. The Latins have an Apostolic Delegate in İstanbul and an Archbishop in İzmir, but their Patriarch of İstanbul is titular and non-resident. There is a Grand Rabbi (Hahambaşı) in İstanbul for the Jews, who are nearly all Sephardim.

A law passed in Dec. 1934 forbids the wearing of clerical garb for those other than religious leaders except in places of worship and during divine service. The constitution forbids the political exploitation of religion or any impairment of the secular character of the republic.

In lieu of religious formulae, all citizens take oaths on their honour.

Education. Elementary education is compulsory and co-educational and, in state schools, free. All children from 7 to 12 are to receive primary instruction, which may be given in state schools, schools maintained by communities, or private schools, or, subject to certain tests, at home. The state schools are under the direct control of the Ministry of Education. They include primary schools, secondary or middle schools, and *lycées* or secondary schools of a superior kind. There are also training schools for male and female teachers, and technical schools. In 1979 there were 18 universities and 102 other institutes of higher education; in 1982, a further 8 universities were founded. The important non-Moslem communities in İstanbul maintain their own schools, which, like all 'private' schools, are subject to the supervision of the Ministry of Education.

Literacy of the population of 6 years and over was 10·6% in 1927, 19·2% in 1935, 29% in 1945, 40·9% in 1955, 48·7% in 1965, 49% in 1970, 61·7% in 1975.

Religious instruction in schools, hitherto prohibited, was made optional in elementary and middle schools in May 1948. There are many training schools for Moslem clergy as well as a Faculty of Theology in Ankara.

Statistics for 1981–82	*Number*	*Teachers*	*Students*
Primary schools (state and private)	45,871	210,599	5,864,000
Secondary schools (state and private)	4,252	37,445	1,240,000
High schools (state and private)	1,169	43,173	541,000
Vocational and technical schools	1,900	36,327	531,000
Faculties (university and higher education)	334	22,223	241,000

On 1 Nov. 1928 the Grand National Assembly voted a law for the adoption of Latin characters as from 1 Dec. 1928. The publication of books in Arabic characters was forbidden after 1 Jan. 1929.

Health. Public health is the responsibility of the Ministry of Health and Social Welfare, established in 1920; social insurance for workers comes under the

Workers' Insurance Institution attached to the Ministry of Labour. A law promulgated in 1961 and being implemented from 1963 provides for the nationalization of the health services within 15 years. In 1980, 2·2m. workers and employees were covered by social insurance, including free medical care.

In 1982 there were 30,956 doctors and 96,138 beds in some 630 hospitals.

DIPLOMATIC REPRESENTATIVES

Of Turkey in Great Britain (43 Belgrave Sq., London, SW1X 8PA)
Ambassador: Rahmi Gümrükçüoğlu (accredited 4 Aug. 1981).

Of Great Britain in Turkey (Sehit Ersan Caddesi 46/A, Cankaya, Ankara)
Ambassador: R. M. Russell, CMG.

Of Turkey in the USA (1606–23rd St., NW, Washington, D.C., 20008)
Ambassador: Dr Şükrü Elekdağ.

Of the USA in Turkey (110 Ataturk Blvd., Ankara)
Ambassador: Robert Strausz-Hupe.

Of Turkey to the United Nations
Ambassador: A. Coşkun Kirca.

Books of Reference

Statistical Information: The State Institute of Statistics in Ankara consists of a research bureau and 10 sections dealing with agriculture, education, foreign trade, etc. It published an *Annuaire Statistique/Istatistik Yıllığı* (1928–53) and *Aylık Istatistik Bülteni*, Monthly Bulletin of Statistics.

Almanac: Turkey 1983. 1983
The Turkish Constitution, 1971. Ankara, 1972
Resmi Gazete, Official Gazette. Ankara
Konjonktür. Ministry of Commerce (three times a year, from 1940)
Banque Centrale de la République de Turquie. *Bulletin Mensuel* (from Jan. 1953)
Bulletins of the Chambers of Commerce of Istanbul and Izmir
Dodd, C. H., *The Crisis of Turkish Democracy.* Beverley, 1983
Goodwin, G., *A History of Ottoman Architecture.* London, 1971
Guclu, M., *Turkey.* [Bibliography] Oxford and Santa Barbara, 1981
Hale, W., *The Political and Economic Development of Modern Turkey.* London, 1981
Kazancigil, A. and Ozbudun, E., (eds.) *Atatürk: Founder of a Modern State.* London, 1981
Kinross, Lord, *Atatürk.* London, 1964
Koray, Enver, *Türkiye Tarih Yayınları Bibliografyası 1729–1950 (Bibliography of Historical Works on Turkey).* Ankara, 1952
Kortepeter, C. M., *Ottoman Imperialism During Reformation: Europe and the Caucasus.* London, 1972
Landau, J. M., *Radical Politics in Modern Turkey.* Leiden, 1974
Sezer, D. B., *Turkey's Security Policies.* London, 1981
Tamkoc, M., *The Warrior Diplomats.* Univ. of Utah Press, 1976
Weiker W., *The Modernization of Turkey.* New York, 1981

State Library: MilliKütüphane Müdürlüğü, Ankara.

THE TURKS AND CAICOS ISLANDS

Capital: Grand Turk
Population: 7,436 (1980)

HISTORY. After a long period of rival French and Spanish claims the islands were eventually secured to the British Crown by the appointment in 1766 of a Res:dent British Agent, and became a separate colony in 1973 after association at various times with the colonies of the Bahamas and Jamaica.

AREA AND POPULATION. The Turks and Caicos Islands are geographically part of the Bahamas extremity, of which they form the south-eastern archipelago. There are upwards of 30 small cays; area 192 sq. miles (430 sq. km). Only 6 are inhabited; the largest, Grand Caicos, is 30 miles long by 2 to 3 miles broad. The seat of government is at Grand Turk, 7 miles long by 1·25 broad; 3,146 inhabitants. Population, 1980 census, 7,436; South Caicos, 1,392; Middle Caicos, 371; North Caicos, 1,266; Providenciales, 979; Salt Cay, 282.

Vital statistics (1980): Births, 247; marriages, 32; deaths, 13.

CLIMATE. An equable and healthy climate as a result of regular trade winds, though hurricanes are sometimes experienced. Rainfall on Grand Turk is 21″ (525 mm) but is greater in the Caicos Islands.

CONSTITUTION AND GOVERNMENT. A new Constitution was introduced in Aug. 1976, providing for an Executive Council and a Legislative Council. The Governor retains responsibility for external affairs, internal security, defence and certain other matters. The Executive Council comprises 3 official members: the Chief Secretary, the Financial Secretary and the Attorney-General; a Chief Min:ster and 3 other ministers from among the elected members of the Legislative Council; and is presided over by the Governor. The Legislative Council consists of a Speaker, the 3 official members of the Executive Council, 11 elected members and 2 appointed members.

Governor: C. J. Turner, OBE.

Flag: British Blue Ensign with the shield of the Colony in the fly.

ECONOMY

Budget. 1982–83 revenue US$6,437,000; budgetary aid, US$2,149,000; expenditure, US$8,586,000.

Currency. The currency in circulation is US$.

Banking. In 1980 there were 6 commercial banks operating in the Islands. The Government Savings Bank has 3 branches. Barclays Bank International and the Oxford International Bank and Trust Co. Ltd have offices in Grand Turk with branches in South Caicos, North Caicos and Providenciales.

COMMERCE (1982–83). Exports, US$2,515,119, and imports, US$20,903,776. Principal imports, food, drink, tobacco and clothing. The main exports are crawfish, dried and fresh conch, and conch shells. The catch is processed in three plants operating in South Caicos.

Total trade between Turks and Caicos Islands and UK (British Department of Trade returns, in £1,000 sterling):

	1980	1981	1982	1983
Imports to UK	8	5	5	18
Exports and re-exports from UK	295	973	405	902

TOURISM. Number of hotels and guest houses, 19 (beds 600). Number of visitors, 1982, 13,342.

COMMUNICATIONS

Aviation. There is a 6,335 ft paved airfield on Grand Turk. On South Caicos there is a 6,000 ft paved airstrip under construction and on Providenciales a 7,000 ft paved airstrip. There are small paved and unpaved airstrips on the other 3 inhabited islands. Air Florida Airlines operate a thrice weekly passenger service to Miami. Bahamas Air operate a twice weekly scheduled passenger service to the Bahamas. Air Turks and Caicos operate a twice daily service to the islands and 2 flights a week to Cap Haitien (Haiti). Turks Air Ltd operates a regular weekly cargo service to Miami.

Shipping. Registered shipping (1981), 165 sailing vessels of 2,366 tons and 34 motor vessels of 5,015 tons.

Post and Broadcasting. Air-mail is received and dispatched by Miami twice or thrice weekly. Surface mail from all parts of the world is routed *via* the US arriving at 3 weekly intervals from Miami, Florida. There is no regular outgoing surface mail. Cable & Wireless (West Indies) provide internal and international cable, telephone, telex and telegraph services. There were (1981) 932 telephones. North Caicos and Salt Cay are linked with the Providenciales and Grand Turk exchanges respectively. The Government operates a radio broadcasting service from the Islands to Grand Turk, call sign VSI radio Turks and Caicos, for a total of 106 hours a week on 1,460 KHZ medium wave. Number of receivers, approximately 6,000.

EDUCATION AND WELFARE

Education. Education is free and compulsory up to 15 years of age in the 14 government primary and 3 government secondary schools. There are also 3 private primary schools. Pupils at Turks and Caicos High School, 372; South Caicos and Providenciales, 208; North Caicos Junior High, 91. Expenditure on education 1982–83 was US$1,086,936.

Health. In 1983 there were 4 doctors and 30 hospital beds.

TUVALU

Capital: Funafuti
Population: 7,349 (1979)
GNP per capita: US$570 (1980)

HISTORY. Formerly the Ellice Islands, a British Protectorate since 1892. On the recommendation of a Commissioner, appointed by the British Government, to consider requests that the island group be separated from the Gilbert Islands, a referendum was held in 1974. There was a large majority in favour of separation and this took place in Oct. 1975. Independence was achieved on 1 Oct. 1978.

AREA AND POPULATION. Tuvalu (formerly the Ellice Islands) lie between 5° 30′ and 11° S. lat. and 176° and 180° E. long. and comprise Nanumea, Nanumanga, Niutao, Nui, Vaitupu, Nukufetau, Funafuti (administrative centre), Nukulaelae and Niulakita. Population (census 1979) 7,349. Area approximately 9½ sq. miles (24 sq. km). The population is of a Polynesian race.

CLIMATE. A pleasant but monotonous climate with temperatures averaging 86°F (30°C), though trade winds from the east moderate conditions for much of the year. Funafuti. Jan. 84°F (28·9°C), July 81°F (27·2°C). Annual rainfall 160″ (4,003 mm).

CONSTITUTION AND GOVERNMENT. The Constitution provides for a Prime Minister and 4 other Ministers to be elected from among the 12 elected members of the House of Parliament, for which general elections took place on 8 Sept. 1981. The Cabinet, chaired by the Prime Minister, consists of the 4 ministers and 2 *ex officio* members, the Attorney-General and the Secretary to Government, who are also *ex officio* members of the House of Assembly. Local Government services are provided by an elected Island Council on each of the 8 atolls.

Governor-General: Fiatau Penitala Teo, GCMG, MBE.
Prime Minister: Dr Tomasi Puapua.
Finance: Henry F. Naisali. *Social Services:* Falaile Pilitati. *Commerce and Natural Resources:* Lale Seluka. *Works and Communications:* Metia Tealoi.

National flag: Light blue with the Union Jack in the canton, and 9 gold stars in the fly arranged in the same pattern as the 9 islands.

Local Government. There is a town council on Funafuti and island councils on the 7 other main islands, each consisting of 6 elected members including a president.

INTERNATIONAL RELATIONS

Membership. Tuvalu is a member of the Commonwealth and is an ACP state of EEC.

ECONOMY

Budget. In 1983 the budget envisaged expenditure of $A3·5m.

Currency. The unit of currency is the Australian *dollar* although Tuvaluan coins up to $A1 are in local circulation.

Banking. The Tuvalu National Bank was established at Funafuti in 1980.

NATURAL RESOURCES

Agriculture. Coconut palms are the main crop. Fruit and vegetables are grown for local consumption.

Fisheries. Sea fishing is excellent but is largely unexploited.

INDUSTRY AND TRADE

Industry. The main sources of income are from overseas remittances from Tuvaluans working abroad, philatelic and copra sales, and handicrafts.

Employment. A significant number of the population are employed in the phosphate industry on Nauru. The remainder are engaged in harvesting coconuts and fishing.

Commerce. Commerce is dominated by co-operative societies, the Tuvalu Co-operative Wholesale Society being the main importer. Imports (1981) $124,480.

Total trade between Tuvalu and UK (British Department of Trade returns, in £1,000 sterling):

	1980	1981	1982	1983
Imports to UK	34	6	7	35
Exports and re-exports from UK	362	132	48	55

COMMUNICATIONS

Aviation. Tuvalu is linked to the outside world by Fiji Air which operates twice a week, on Monday and Thursday, and Air Tungaru once a week on Tuesdays.

Shipping. Funafuti is the only port and a deep-water wharf was opened in 1980. Inter-island communication is by ship; a limited service using an amphibious plane came into operation in 1980.

Post and Broadcasting. The Tuvalu Broadcasting Service transmits daily in Tuvaluan and English and all islands have daily radio communication with Funafuti. There were 92 telephones in 1982.

JUSTICE, RELIGION, EDUCATION AND WELFARE

Justice. There is a High Court presided over by the Chief Justice of Fiji. Appeals lie to the Fiji Court of Appeal.

Religion. The majority of the population are Christians mainly Protestant but with small groups of Roman Catholics, Seventh Day Adventists, Jehovah's Witnesses and Bahai's.

Education. In 1980 there was 1 secondary school jointly administered by the Government and the Church. In addition there were 8 primary schools with (1982, inclusive of 300 pupils in community training centres) 1,290 pupils run by Island Councils and subsidized by the central government. In 1979, a maritime school was opened on Amatuku islet. Tuvaluans requiring further education must seek it abroad.

Health. In 1978 there was 1 central hospital with 36 beds situated at Funafuti. There were 3 doctors.

DIPLOMATIC REPRESENTATIVES

Of Great Britain in Tuvalu
High Commissioner: R. A. R. Barltrop CVO. (resides in Suva).

Of Tuvalu in the USA
Ambassador: Ionatana Ionatana (resides in Tuvalu).

UGANDA

Capital: Kampala
Population: 13·22m. (1979)
GNP per capita: US$280 (1980)

HISTORY. Uganda became a British Protectorate in 1894, the province of Buganda being recognized as a native kingdom under its Kabaka. In 1961 Uganda was granted internal self-government with federal status for Buganda.

Uganda became a fully independent member of the Commonwealth on 9 Oct. 1962 after nearly 70 years of British rule. Full sovereign status was granted by the Uganda Independence Act, 1962, and the Constitution is embodied in the Uganda (Independence) Order in Council, 1962. The post of Governor-General was on 9 Oct. 1963 replaced by that of President as head of state, elected by the National Assembly for a 5-year term.

AREA AND POPULATION. Uganda is bounded on the north by Sudan, on east by Kenya, on south by Tanzania and west by Zaïre. Total area 91,343 sq. miles (236,860 sq. km), including 15,217 sq. miles (39,459 sq. km) of swamp and water.

The population of Uganda was 13·22m. (1979 estimate). On 4 Aug. 1972 President Amin announced that he would ask the UK to take responsibility for Asians in Uganda holding British passports. Later that year 27,200 Asians had left Uganda for Britain. The majority of the Africans (1,044,000) are Baganda, the tribe from which the country takes its name.

About 3m. Africans speak Bantu languages; there are a few Congo pygmies living near the Semliki River; the rest of the Africans belong to the Hamitic, Nilotic and Sudanese groups. Ki-Swahili is generally understood in trading centres. The capital is Kampala; the population of greater Kampala (1975), 332,000.

The official language is English.

CLIMATE. Although in equatorial latitudes, the climate is more tropical, because of its elevation, and is characterized the year round by hot sunshine, cool breezes and showers of rain. The wettest months are March to June and there is no dry season. Temperatures vary little over the year. Kampala. Jan. 72°F (22·2°C), July 68°F (20°C). Annual rainfall 45″ (1,125 mm).

CONSTITUTION AND GOVERNMENT. Uganda became a republic on 8 Sept. 1967. Under the 1967 Constitution, the executive authority is vested in the President.

In 1971, Dr A. Milton Obote was overthrown by troops led by Gen. Idi Amin.

In April 1979 a force of the Tanzanian Army and Ugandan exiles advanced into Uganda taking Kampala on 11 April. On 14 April Dr Yusuf Lule was sworn in as President and the country is to be administered, initially, by the Uganda National Liberation Front.

The former Attorney-General, Godfrey Lukongwa Binaisa, QC, was appointed President by the National Consultative Council on 20 June 1979. Dr Lule subsequently left the country. Dr Binaisa was subsequently overthrown in May 1980 by the army. At the elections held on 10–11 Dec. 1980, the Uganda People's Congress was declared to have held 72 of the 124 elective seats in the new Parliament, the Democratic Party 51 seats, and the Uganda Patriotic Movement 1 seat.

President, Minister of Foreign Affairs and Finance: Dr Milton Obote.
Vice-President, Minister of Defence: Paulo Muwanga.
Prime Minister: Otema Alimadi.

National flag: Six horizontal stripes of black, yellow, red, black, yellow, red, in the centre a small white disc bearing a representation of a Balearic Crested Crane.

For administrative purposes Uganda is divided into 10 provinces, subdivided into 38 districts. The provinces are: Busoga, Central, Eastern, Karamoja, Nile, North Buganda, Northern, South Buganda, Southern, Western.

DEFENCE

Army. The Army had a strength of 15,000 in 1984 and was organized in 3 brigades. Equipment includes 10 T-34/-54/-55 and 3 M-4 tanks.

Navy. A small lake patrol was initiated in 1977.

Air Force. The Air Force was formed in 1964 and later underwent rapid expansion with the assistance of Israeli and Czechoslovakian training missions. Prior to the events of 1979 equipment included about 10 MiG-21 and 12 MiG-17 jet fighter-bombers, 2 MiG-15 UTI two-seat trainers, about 5 L-29 Delfin and 8 Israeli-built Magister armed jet trainers, 11 Super Cub liaison aircraft, 5 Piaggio P 149 piston-engined trainers, 6 Swiss-built Bravo primary trainers, 6 Agusta-Bell 205, 2 Agusta-Bell 206 JetRanger and some Mi-8 helicopters. Personnel numbered about 1,000. In addition the Police Air Wing had 1 Twin Otter and 1 Caribou twin-engined STOL transports, 1 Turbo-Beaver and 1 Piper Aztec light transports, and about 7 Bell 205, JetRanger, Bell 212 and Scout helicopters. The status of these aircraft was unknown in early 1984.

INTERNATIONAL RELATIONS

Membership. Uganda is a member of UN, OAU, the Commonwealth and is an ACP state of EEC.

ECONOMY

Budget. The revenue and expenditure (exclusive of loan disbursements) for fiscal years (1 July–30 June) were (in Uganda Sh. 1m.):

	1978–79	1979–80	1980–81	1981–82
Revenue	3,197	3,810	2,835	25,292
Expenditure	5,441	4,224	7,568	21,422

Currency. East African Currency Board notes ceased to be legal tender from 14 Sept. 1967. The monetary unit is the *Uganda shilling* divided into 100 *cents*. In March 1984, £1 = 404 Uganda shillings; US$1 = 269 Uganda shillings.

Banking. The Bank of Uganda was set up on 16 May 1966; its external assets as at 31 Aug. 1967 were £9m. The Uganda Credit and Savings Bank, set up in 1950, was on 9 Oct. 1965 reconstituted as the Uganda Commercial Bank, with its capital fully owned by the Government.

Barclays Bank International has 11 branches and 7 agencies; National & Grindlays Bank Ltd has 12 branches and 12 agencies; the Standard Bank Ltd has 6 branches and 2 agencies; the Bank of Baroda Ltd has 3 branches; the Bank of India Ltd has 2 branches. Other banks operating in Uganda are the Algemene Bank Nederland NV and the Commercial Bank of Africa.

ENERGY AND NATURAL RESOURCES

Electricity. Industrial expansion is based on hydro-electric power provided by the Owen Falls scheme, which has a capacity of 150,000 kwh. Production (1978) 630m. kwh.

Minerals. With the opening of the Kilembe mine in 1956, copper has become Uganda's most valuable mineral export. Production (1978) in tonnes: Blister copper, 600; tin, 120; phosphate rock (1977) 5,000.

Agriculture. In 1983, agriculture was still recovering from the administration of 1971–79. Cotton and coffee are the principal exports, the former being grown entirely and the latter very largely by African farmers. Production (1980) in 1,000 tonnes: Tobacco, 3; coffee, 135·2; cotton lint, 13·3; tea, 1·5; sugar, 1·5.

Livestock (1982): Cattle, 5m.; asses, 16,000; sheep, 1m.; goats, 2·2m.; pigs, 260,000; poultry, 13·4m.

Forestry. Exploitable forests consist almost entirely of hardwoods. Internal consumption is rising. About half of the timber exported goes to the UK and another quarter to Kenya and Tanganyika, from which the bulk of the softwood imports are obtained. Sawn wood production (1977) 24,000 cu. metres.

Fishery. With its 13,600 sq. miles of lakes and many rivers, Uganda possesses one of the largest fresh-water fisheries in the world. In 1978 fish production was 223,800 tonnes. Fish farming (especially carp and tilapia) is a growing industry.

COMMERCE. Trade (in US$1m.):

	1979	1980	1981[1]
Imports	322·1	503·7	400·0
Exports	397·2	319·1	220·0

[1] Estimate.

Total trade between Uganda and UK (British Department of Trade returns, in £1,000 sterling):

	1979	1980	1981	1982	1983
Imports to UK	19,189	30,735	18,186	23,107	29,645
Exports and re-exports from UK	18,881	33,526	24,650	31,272	21,092

COMMUNICATIONS

Roads. There are 3,876 miles of all-weather roads maintained by the Ministry of Works, of which 796 miles are two-lane bitumenized highways, and some 11,230 miles of other roads, maintained by district governments.

Railways. On 26 Aug. 1977 Uganda Railways was formed following break-up of the East African Railways administration. The network totals 1,286 km (metre gauge). In 1980 railways carried 2·3m. passengers and 297,630 tonnes of freight.

Aviation. Entebbe had a first-class international airport which had direct flights to Europe, Rhodesia, Sudan, Kenya, Burundi, Ghana, Ethiopia, Zaïre, Nigeria, USSR, and Rwanda by Sudan Airways, Air Congo, SABENA, Air France, Ethiopian Airlines, Air Zaïre and Aeroflot. The airport was damaged during the 1979 invasion. Eleven other government airfields are used for internal communications.

Posts and Broadcasting. There were 48,884 telephones in use at 1 Jan. 1978. There were 275,000 radio receivers and about 75,000 television sets in 1982

Cinemas. In 1971 there were 16 cinemas with a seating capacity of 8,000.

JUSTICE, RELIGION, EDUCATION AND WELFARE

Justice. The High Court of Uganda, presided over by the Chief Justice and 12 puisne judges, exercises original and appellate jurisdiction throughout Uganda. Subordinate courts, presided over by Chief Magistrates and Magistrates of the first, second and third grade, are established in all areas: jurisdiction varies with the grade of Magistrate. Chief and first-grade Magistrates are professionally qualified; second-and third-grade Magistrates are trained to diploma level at the Law School, Entebbe.

Chief Magistrates exercise supervision over and hear appeals from second- and third-grade courts.

The Court of Appeal for Eastern Africa was re-established on 9 Dec. 1962 as the Court of Appeal for Uganda; it hears appeals from the High Court.

Religion. About 62% of the population are Christian and 6% Moslem.

Education. Education is a joint undertaking by the Government, local authorities and, to some extent, voluntary agencies. The education system is divided into 3 sectors, primary, secondary and post-secondary. The primary course covers 7 years. There were 1·4m. pupils in grant-aided primary schools in 1982. Education at secondary level falls into 4 categories, namely, secondary schools, which are the grammar type of schools with a course extending over 6 years to High School Certificate; technical schools; farm schools; and primary teacher-training colleges. Further education is provided at the Uganda Technical College, the National Teachers' College, the Uganda College of Commerce and Agricultural Colleges.

There are also several Departmental Training Schools for training staff for different departments.

The medical department has 8 such schools for training nurses, midwives, medical assistants, health inspectors, and other medical staff.

University level education is available at Makerere University College and the 2 other constituent Colleges of the University of East Africa; the University College, Nairobi, in Kenya, and the University College, Dar es Salaam, in Tanzania. Uganda students also go to universities and colleges outside East Africa for higher education.

Health. In 1973 there were 300 doctors and over 15,000 hospital beds.

DIPLOMATIC REPRESENTATIVES

Of Uganda in Great Britain (Uganda Hse., Trafalgar Sq., London, WC2N 5DX)
High Commissioner: Shafiq Arain.

Of Great Britain in Uganda (10/12 Obote Ave., Kampala)
High Commissioner: C. McLean, CMG, MBE.

Of Uganda in the USA (5909, 16th St., NW, Washington, D.C., 20011)
Ambassador: John Wycliffe Lwamafa.

Of USA in Uganda
Ambassador: Allen C. Davis.

Of Uganda to the United Nations
Ambassador: Olara Otunnu.

Books of Reference

Atlas of Uganda. Dept. of Lands and Surveys. Kampala, 1962
Collison, R. L., *Uganda.* [Bibliography] Oxford and Santa Barbara, 1981
Gukiina, P. M., *Uganda: A Case Study in African Political Development.* Univ. of Notre Dame Press, 1972
Hills, D., *The White Pumpkin.* New York, 1976
Jørgensen, J. J., *Uganda: A Modern History.* London, 1981
Kitching, A. L., and Blackledge, G. R., *A Luganda–English and English–Luganda Dictionary.* Kampala, 1925
Larimore, A. E., *The Alien Town: Patterns of Settlement in Uganda.* Chicago, 1959
Listowel, J., *Amin.* Irish Univ. Press, 1973
Mamdani, M., *Imperialism and Fascism in Uganda.* London, 1983

UNION OF SOVIET SOCIALIST REPUBLICS

Capital: Moscow
Population: 273·8m. (1984)

Soyuz Sovyetskikh
Sotsialisticheskikh
Respublik

POST-REVOLUTION HISTORY. Up to 12 March 1917 the territory now forming the USSR, together with that of Finland, Poland and certain tracts ceded in 1918 to Turkey, but less the territories then forming part of the German, Austro-Hungarian and Japanese empires–East Prussia, Eastern Galicia, Transcarpathia, Bukovina, South Sakhalin and Kurile Islands–which were acquired during and after the Second World War, was constituted as the Russian Empire. It was governed as an autocracy under the Tsar, with the aid of Ministers responsible to himself and a State Duma with limited legislative powers, elected by provincial assemblies chosen by indirect elections on a restricted franchise.

On 8 March 1917 a revolution broke out. The Duma parties, on 12 March, set up a Provisional Committee of the State Duma, while the factory workmen and the insurgent garrison of Petrograd elected a Council (Soviet) of Workers' and Soldiers' Deputies. Soviets were also elected by the workmen in other towns, in the Army and Navy and, as time went on, by the peasantry. On 15 March 1917 the Tsar abdicated, and the Provisional Committee, by agreement with the Petrograd Soviet, appointed a Provisional Government and, on 14 Sept., proclaimed a republic. However, a political struggle went on between the supporters of the Provisional Government–the Mensheviks and the Socialist-Revolutionaries–and the Bolsheviks, who advocated the assumption of power by the Soviets. When they had won majorities in the Soviets of the principal cities and of the armed forces on several fronts, the Bolsheviks organized an insurrection through a Military-Revolutionary Committee of the Petrograd Soviet. On 7 Nov. 1917 the Committee arrested the Provisional Government and transferred power to the second All-Russian Congress of Soviets. This elected a new government, the Council of People's Commissars, headed by Lenin.

On 25 Jan. 1918 the third All-Russian Congress of Soviets issued a Declaration of Rights of the Toiling and Exploited People, which proclaimed Russia a Republic of Soviets of Workers', Soldiers' and Peasants' Deputies; and on 10 July 1918 the fifth Congress adopted a Constitution for the Russian Soviet Federal Socialist Republic. In the course of the civil war other Soviet Republics were set up in the Ukraine, Belorussia and Transcaucasia. These first entered into treaty relations with the RSFSR and then, in 1922, joined with it in a closely integrated Union.

AREA AND POPULATION. The total area of the Soviet Union in April 1984 was 22·4m. sq. km (8·65m. sq. miles). The census population on 15 Jan. 1970 was 241·7m. (111·4m. males, 130·3m. females; 136m. urban, 105·7m. rural). The census population on 17 Jan. 1979 was 262·4m. (122·3m. males, 140·1m. females, 163·6m. urban, 98·9m. rural). The increase of 27·6m. in urban population between 1970 and 1979 was due to natural increase and 15·6m. rural dwellers becoming part of the urban population resulting from migration because of the development of industry and transport, and increased farm mechanization, and from the the urbanization of large rural centres. Consequently, despite a natural increase of 8·7m. in rural areas, there was a net decrease of 6·9m. over this period. Population at 1 Jan. 1983, 271·2m. (126·9m. males, 144·3m. females; 174·6m. urban; 96·6m. rural).

Regions, towns, streets, factories, schools, etc., named after Stalin were renamed in Nov. 1961 when Stalin's body was removed from the Lenin-Stalin tomb in Red

Square in Moscow. Similarly, in Jan. 1962 towns bearing the names of Molotov, Kaganovich and Malenkov were renamed.

The areas (in 1,000 sq. km) and population (in 1m., in Jan. 1983) of the constituent republics are as follows (capitals in brackets):

Constituent Republics	Area	Population	Constituent Republics	Area	Population
RSFSR (Moscow)	17,075	141·0	Tadzhikistan (Dushanbe)	143	4·2
Ukraine (Kiev)	604	50·5	Kirgizia (Frunze)	199	3·8
Uzbekistan (Tashkent)	447	17·0	Lithuania (Vilnius)	65	3·5
Kazakhstan (Alma-Ata)	2,717	15·5	Armenia (Yerevan)	30	3·2
Belorussia (Minsk)	208	9·8	Turkmenistan (Ashkhabad)	488	3·0
Azerbaijan (Baku)	87	6·4	Latvia (Riga)	64	2·6
Georgia (Tbilisi)	70	5·1	Estonia (Tallinn)	45	1·5
Moldavia (Kishinev)	34	4·1			

Nationalities. The most numerous nationalities at the 1979 census were: 137·4m. Russians, 42·3m. Ukrainians, 12·5m. Uzbeks, 9·5m. Belorussians, 6·6m. Kazakhs, 6·3m. Tatars, 5·5m. Azerbaijanians, 4·1m. Armenians, 3·6m. Georgians, 3m. Moldavians, 2·9m. Tadzhiks, 2·9m. Lithuanians, 2m. Turkmenians, 1·9m. Germans, 1·9m. Kirgiz, 1·8m. Jews, 1·8m. Chuvashes, 1·4m. Latvians, 1·4m. Bashkirs, 1·2m. Mordovians, 1·2m. Poles, 1m. Estonians. The great majority (in each case 73-99%) indicated the language of their nationality as their native tongue; exceptions were the Bashkirs (67%), Germans (57%), Poles (29%) and Jews (14%).

Estimated losses of population in the Second World War, 20m., of which 7m. were military losses.

The following tables show the growth of the population in Russia:

1897 (Russian Empire)	126,900,000	1959 (census)	208,826,650
1913 (Russian Empire)	170,900,000	1970 (census)	241,720,134
1913 (present frontiers)	159,153,000	1979 (census)	262,436,227
1939 (census)	170,557,093		

The following was the population on 1 Jan. 1983 of the larger towns (in 1,000):

Aktyubinsk	218	Dzerzhinsk (Gorky		Komsomolsk-on-	
Alma-Ata	1,023	region)	269	Amur	284
Andizhan	247	Engels	173	Kostroma	264
Angarsk	251	Ferghana	187	Kramatorsk	187
Arkhangelsk	399	Frunze	577	Krasnodar	595
Armavir	167	Gomel	432	Krasnoyarsk	845
Ashkhabad	338	Gorlovka	339	Kremenchug	220
Astrakhan	481	Gorky	1,382	Krivoi Rog	674
Baku	1,638	Grodno	230	Kuibyshev	1,242
Barnaul	561	Grozny	387	Kurgan	334
Belaya Tserkov	171	Irkutsk	582	Kursk	404
Belgorod	268	Ivano-Frankovsk	180	Kustanai	185
Berezniki	190	Ivanovo	474	Kutaisi	207
Biisk	221	Izhevsk	594	Kzyl-Orda	177
Blagoveshchensk	186	Kalinin	433	Leninakan	218
Bobruisk	214	Kaliningrad	374	Leningrad	4,779
Bratsk	231	Kaluga	287	Lipetsk	432
Brest	208	Kamensk-		Lvov	711
Brezhnev	394	Uralski	195	Lyubertsy	165
Bryansk	418	Karaganda	600	Magnitogorsk	419
Bukhara	200	Kaunas	395	Makeyevka	446
Cheboksary	364	Kazan	1,031	Makhachkala	287
Chelyabinsk	1,077	Kemerovo	495	Melitopol	167
Cherepovets	290	Kerch	163	Minsk	1,405
Cherkassy	259	Khabarovsk	560	Mogilev	325
Chernigov	263	Kharkov	1,519	Moscow	8,396
Chernovtzy	232	Kherson	337	Murmansk	405
Chimkent	352	Kiev	2,355	Nalchik	218
Chita	326	Kirov	404	Namangan	256
Djambul	292	Kirovabad		Nikolayev	474
Dneprodzerzhinsk	265	(Azerbaijan)	253	Nizhni Tagil	411
Dnepropetrovsk	1,128	Kirovograd	253	Norilsk	183
Donetsk	1,055	Kishinev	580	Novgorod	210
Dushanbe	530	Klaipeda	188	Novocherkassk	187

Novokuznetsk	564	Ryazan	483	Tomsk	459
Novorossiisk	171	Rybinsk	247	Tselinograd	253
Novosibirsk	1,370	Samarkand	505	Tula	527
Odessa	1,097	Saransk	293	Tyumen	397
Omsk	1,080	Saratov	887	Ufa	1,034
Ordzhonikidze		Semipalatinsk	301	Ulan-Ude	321
(Vladikavkaz)	296	Sevastopol	328	Ulyanovsk	509
Orel	322	Severodvinsk	219	Uralsk	183
Orenburg	505	Shakhty	216	Ust-Kamenogorsk	296
Orsk	259	Simferopol	324	Vilnius	525
Osh	188	Smolensk	321	Vinnitsa	350
Pavlodar	302	Sochi	304	Vitebsk	324
Penza	515	Stavropol	281	Vladimir	320
Perm	1,037	Sterlitamak	233	Vladivostok	584
Petropavlovsk-		Sumgait	214	Volgograd	962
Kamchatski	237	Sumy	248	Vologda	260
Petropavlovsk (North		Sverdlovsk	1,269	Volzhsky	232
Kazakhstan)	219	Syktyvkar	191	Voronezh	831
Petrozavodsk	247	Syzran	171	Voroshilovgrad	485
Podolsk	207	Taganrog	285	Yaroslavl	619
Poltava	290	Tallinn	454	Yerevan	1,095
Prokopyevsk	270	Tambov	286	Yoshkar-Ola	223
Pskov	185	Tashkent	1,944	Zaporozhye	835
Riga	867	Tbilisi	1,125	Zhdanov	516
Rostov-on-Don	977	Temirtau	223	Zhitomir	264
Rovno	205	Togliatti	560	Zlatoust	202
Rubtsovsk	161				

Narodnoe khozyaistvo SSSR, Moscow, annual
Ezhegodnik Bol'shoi Sovetskoi Entsiklopedii, Moscow, annual
Itogi Vsesoyuznoi perepisi naseleniya 1959 goda. SSSR (svodnyi tom), Moscow, 1962
Itogi Vsesoyuznoi perepisi naseleniya 1970 goda, 7 vols. Moscow, 1972–74
Naselenie SSSR: spravochnik, Moscow, 1983
Naselenie SSSR po dannym Vsesoyuznoi perepisi naseleniya 1979 goda, Moscow, 1980
Sovetskii Soyuz. Geograficheskoe opisanie, 22 vols. Moscow, 1966–72
Desfosses, H., *Soviet Population Policy: Conflicts and Restraints*. Oxford, 1981
Kish, G., (ed.), *An Economic Atlas of the Soviet Union*. (2nd ed.), Ann Arbor, 1971
Lorrimer, F., *The Population of the Soviet Union*. Geneva, 1946
Mathieson, R. S., *The Soviet Union: An Economic Geography*. London, 1975
Mellor, R. H., *The Soviet Union and its Geographical Problems*. London, 1982
Wixman, R., *The Peoples of Russia and the USSR*. London, 1984

CLIMATE. The USSR comprises several different climatic regions, ranging from polar conditions in the north, through sub-arctic and humid continental, to sub-tropical and semi-arid conditions in the south. Rainfall amounts are greatest in areas bordering the Baltic, Black Sea, Caspian Sea and eastern coasts of Asiatic Russia. In most cases, there is a summer maximum.

Moscow, Jan. 15°F (−9·4°C), July 65°F (18·3°C). Annual rainfall 25·2″ (630 mm). Arkhangelsk, Jan. 5°F (−15°C), July 57°F (13·9°C). Annual rainfall 20·1″ (503 mm). Leningrad, Jan. 17°F (−8·3°C), July 64°F (17·8°C). Annual rainfall 19·5″ (488 mm). Vladivostok, Jan. 6°F (−14·4°C), July 65°F (18·3°C). Annual rainfall 24″ (599 mm).

CONSTITUTION

Constituent Republics. The Union of Soviet Socialist Republics was formed by the union of the RSFSR, the Ukrainian Soviet Socialist Republic, the Belorussian Soviet Socialist Republic and the Transcaucasian Soviet Socialist Republic; the Treaty of Union was adopted by the first Soviet Congress of the USSR on 30 Dec. 1922. In Oct. 1924 the Uzbek and Turkmen Autonomous Soviet Socialist Republics and in Dec. 1929 the Tadzhik Autonomous Soviet Socialist Republic were declared constituent members of the USSR, becoming Union Republics.

At the 8th Congress of the Soviets, on 5 Dec. 1936, a new constitution of the USSR was adopted. The Transcaucasian Republic was split up into the Armenian Soviet Socialist Republic, the Azerbaijan Soviet Socialist Republic and the Georgian Soviet Socialist Republic, each of which became constituent republics of the Union. At the same time the Kazakh Soviet Socialist Republic and the Kirghiz

Soviet Socialist Republic, previously autonomous republics within the RSFSR, were proclaimed constituent republics of the USSR.

In Sept. 1939 Soviet troops occupied eastern Poland as far as the 'Curzon line', which in 1919 had been drawn on ethnographical grounds as the eastern frontier of Poland, and incorporated it into the Ukrainian and Belorussian Soviet Socialist Republics. In Feb. 1951 some districts of the Drogobych Region of the Ukraine and the Lublin Voivodship of Poland were exchanged.

On 31 March 1940 territory ceded by Finland was joined to that of the Autonomous Soviet Socialist Republic of Karelia to form the Karelo-Finnish Soviet Socialist Republic, which was admitted into the Union as the 12th Union Republic. On 16 July 1956 the Supreme Soviet of the USSR adopted a law altering the status of the Karelo-Finnish Republic from that of a Union (constituent) Republic of the USSR to that of an Autonomous (Karelian) Republic within the RSFSR.

On 2 Aug. 1940 the Moldavian Soviet Socialist Republic was constituted as the 13th Union Republic. It comprised the former Moldavian Autonomous Soviet Socialist Republic and Bessarabia (44,290 sq. km, ceded by Romania on 28 June 1940), except for the districts of Khotin, Akerman and Ismail, which, together with Northern Bukovina (10,440 sq. km), were incorporated in the Ukrainian Soviet Republic. The Soviet-Romanian frontier thus constituted was confirmed by the peace treaty with Romania, signed on 10 Feb. 1947. On 29 June 1945 Ruthenia (Sub-Carpathian Russia, 12,742 sq. km) was by treaty with Czechoslovakia incorporated into the Ukrainian Soviet Socialist Republic.

On 3, 5 and 6 Aug. 1940 Lithuania, Latvia and Estonia were incorporated in the Soviet Union as the 14th, 15th and 16th Union Republics respectively. The change in the status of the Karelo-Finnish Republic reduced the number of Union Republics to 15.

After the defeat of Germany it was agreed by the governments of the UK, the USA and the USSR (by the Potsdam declaration) that part of East Prussia should be embodied in the USSR. The area (11,655 sq. km), which includes the towns of Konigsberg (renamed Kaliningrad), Tilsit (renamed Sovietsk) and Insterburg (renamed Chernyakhovsk), was joined to the RSFSR by decree of 7 April 1946.

By the peace treaty with Finland, signed on 10 Feb. 1947, the province of Petsamo (Pechenga), ceded to Finland on 14 Oct. 1920 and 12 March 1946, was returned to the Soviet Union. On 19 Sept. 1955 the Soviet Union renounced its treaty rights to the naval base of Porkkala-Udd and on 26 Jan. 1956 completed the withdrawal of the forces from Finnish territory.

In 1945, after the defeat of Japan, the southern half of Sakhalin (36,000 sq. km) and the Kurile Islands (10,200 sq. km) were, by agreement with the Allies, incorporated in the USSR. [1]

[1] However, Japan asks for the return of the Etorofu and Kunashiri Islands as not belonging to the Kurile Islands proper. The Soviet Government informed Japan on 27 Jan. 1960 that the Habomai Islands and Shikotan would be handed back to Japan on the withdrawal of the American troops from Japan.

GOVERNMENT. The Soviet Union is a socialist state of the whole people (1977 constitution), the political units of which are the Soviets of People's Deputies. All central and local authority is vested in these Soviets.

The economic foundation of the USSR is the socialist system of economy and the socialist ownership of the means of production. There are two forms of socialist property: (1) state property (property of the whole people); (2) co-operative and collective farm (*kolkhoz*) property (property of individual collective farms and property of co-operative associations). The land, mineral deposits, waters, forests, mills, factories, mines, railways, water and air transport, banks, means of communication, large state-organized agricultural enterprises, such as state farms (*sovkhozy*), machine-repair stations and the like, as well as municipal enterprises and the principal dwelling-house properties in the cities and industrial localities, are state property, but the land occupied by collective farmers is secured to them in perpetuity so long as they use it in accordance with the laws of the country. The members of the *kolkhozy* may have small plots of land attached to their dwellings for their own use. Peasants unwilling to enter a kolkhoz may retain their individual farms, but they are not allowed to employ hired labour. The right of personal property of citizens in their income from work and in their savings, in their dwelling houses and auxiliary household economy, their domestic furniture and utensils and objects of personal use and comfort, as well as the right of inheritance of personal property of citizens, are protected by law. The constitution recognizes the right of all citizens to work, rest, leisure, education, health protection, housing, maintenance in old age, sickness or incapacity, without distinction of sex, race or nationality, and lays down that any direct or indirect restriction of the rights of, or conversely, the establishment of direct or indirect privileges for, citizens on account of their race, or nationality, as well as the advocacy of racial or national exclusiveness, or hatred or contempt, is punishable by law. The franchise is enjoyed by all citizens of the USSR, including members of the Armed Forces, who have reached the age of 18, irrespective of sex, with the exception of the legally certified insane. Candidates for election to the Supreme Soviet of the USSR must be 21 years of age; for all other authorities the minimum age for candidates is 18. A member of any Soviet may be recalled by a decision of a majority of his or her electors if he or she fails to give satisfaction (law on procedure for this, 30 Oct. 1959).

The USSR consists of 15 Union Republics, each inhabited by a major nationality which gives its name to the republic. These are divided into 129 territories and regions, and these again into 3,201 districts and 2,124 towns and 3,936 urban settlements (1 Jan. 1983). Within the villages there are 41,782 rural districts (usually each including a number of villages). The territories and regions also include a number of smaller nationalities, forming their own self-governing units–20 Autonomous Soviet Socialist Republics, 8 Autonomous Regions and 10 Autonomous Areas.

The highest legislative organ is the Supreme Soviet of the USSR. It consists of two chambers with equal legislative rights, elected for a term of 5 years: the Council of the Union and the Council of Nationalities. Each has 750 members. The present Supreme Soviet, the 'Eleventh Convocation', was elected on 4 March 1984.

The Council of the Union is elected by the citizens of the USSR on the basis of constituencies with equal populations (approximately 1 deputy for every 300,000 population). Its Chairman since 1970 has been A. P. Shitikov. The Council of Nationalities is elected by the citizens of the USSR on the basis of national-territorial areas (32 deputies from each Union Republic, 11 from each Autonomous Republic, 5 from each Autonomous Region and 1 from each Autonomous Area). Its Chairman since 1974 has been V. P. Ruben. Plenary sessions of the Supreme Soviet are normally held twice a year for two or three days at a time.

Each chamber elects 17 standing commissions: mandates; legislative proposals; foreign affairs; planning and budget; industry; transport and communications; building and the building materials industry; agriculture; science and technology; consumer goods and trade; utilities and services; health and social security; education and culture; women's work and social conditions and the protection of motherhood and childhood; youth affairs; energy; and conservation and the rational use of natural resources. Membership of the commissions presently embraces 1,210 deputies (80·7% of the total).

Deputies are elected by the voters on the basis of universal, equal and direct suffrage by secret ballot. The only legal political party is the Communist Party of the Soviet Union; non-members are classed as non-party citizens. Candidates are selected at preliminary 'constituency electoral consultation' meetings (selection conferences), to which organizations which have put forward nominations send delegates, who discuss the various nominees. As a consequence, to date, a single candidate has been agreed upon in each constituency, whose name appears on the ballot paper to be endorsed (by non-deletion) or struck out as the voter desires. These procedures are governed by the Law on Elections to the Supreme Soviet of the USSR, adopted in April 1978. At the election on 4 March 1984, 184,006,373 electors voted (99·99% of the total). The Supreme Soviet elected on that day consists of 1,071 Communist and 428 non-party deputies; 492 are women, 522 manual workers in industry and state farms, and 242 collective farmers.

The highest executive and administrative body of state authority in the USSR is the Council of Ministers of the USSR, which is appointed by the USSR Supreme Soviet at a joint sitting of the two chambers. It consists of a Chairman (in effect the Soviet Prime Minister), First Vice-Chairmen and Vice-Chairmen, Ministers of the USSR, and Chairmen of State Committees of the USSR. Chairmen of the Councils of Ministers of the Union Republics are *ex officio* members of the USSR Council of Ministers. The Council of Ministers of the USSR had more than 100 members in 1984, and day-to-day co-ordination of governmental matters is accordingly delegated to a smaller body, the Presidium of the Council of Ministers, which meets approximately every week. The Council of Ministers is responsible and accountable to the Supreme Soviet and is required to report regularly to the Supreme Soviet upon its work. Between sessions of the Supreme Soviet the Council of Ministers is responsible to the Presidium of the USSR Supreme Soviet.

The Presidium of the Supreme Soviet of the USSR is elected from among the deputies at a joint session of both chambers of the Supreme Soviet. It consists of a chairman (in effect the President of the USSR), a first vice-chairman, 15 vice-chairmen (1 from each Union Republic), 21 members and a secretary (39 members in all). The Presidium acts as the supreme state authority between sessions of the Supreme Soviet and is accountable to it for all its actions. The Presidium convenes sessions of the Supreme Soviet and co-ordinates the work of its standing commissions; it interprets the law of the USSR and ratifies and denounces international treaties; it confers medals, orders and other distinctions; it decides matters such as citizenship, amnesties, pardons, martial law and states of emergency; and it appoints the high command of the Soviet Armed forces and Soviet diplomatic representatives. It is empowered to adopt decrees *(ukazy)* and resolutions *(postanovleniya)*.

Soon after the adoption of the 1936 Constitution all the constituent republics of the Union held their Soviet congresses, at which they adopted their own constitutions based in all essentials upon the Constitution of the Union but adapted where necessary to local requirements. In April 1978 the Supreme Soviets of the Union Republics similarly adopted new republican constitutions based upon the new Constitution of the USSR approved by the Supreme Soviet in Oct. 1977. Article 73 of the 1977 Constitution of the USSR reserves to the central government the spheres of war and peace, diplomatic relations, defence, foreign trade, state security, economic planning, education, the basic principles of legislation, and other matters of 'all-Union significance'. The right of the constituent republics to withdraw from the Union is, however, formally recognized in Article 72. Union Republics have their own Supreme Soviets, Presidiums and Councils of Ministers, and exercise a wide range of devolved powers in local matters.

There are 20 Autonomous Republics in the USSR, which are similarly governed by their own Supreme Soviets, Presidiums and Councils of Ministers exercising devolved powers over local matters. Most (16) are in the RSFSR; 2 are in Georgia and 1 each in Azerbaijan and Uzbekistan. Five Autonomous Regions are in the RSFSR, 1 each in Azerbaijan, Georgia, and Tadzhikistan. All 10 Autonomous Areas are in the RSFSR. Elections are held every five years to the Supreme Soviets of Union and Autonomous Republics. At the most recent elections (Feb. 1980), 10,188 deputies were elected; 3,799 (37·3%) were women, 3,476 (34·1%) were non-Party, 3,531 (43·7%) were industrial workers and 1,622 (15·9%) were collective farmers.

Regions and territories, districts, towns and rural areas are similarly governed by their own Soviets, elected for a term of 2½ years. At the most recent elections (June 1982), 2,288,885 deputies were elected to these Soviets; 1,145,591 (50·1%) were women, 1,308,239 (57·2%) were non-Party, 1,013,101 (44·3%) were industrial workers and 570,001 (24·9%) were collective farmers. On 1 Jan. 1983 there were 47,412 rural and urban Soviets in the USSR with 2·3m. deputies and over 3m. voluntary co-opted members participating in the work of their standing committees.

State flag: Red, with sickle and hammer in gold in the upper corner near the staff, and above them a 5-pointed star bordered in gold.

National anthem: Soyuz nerushimy respublik svobodnykh (words by S. Mikhalkov and G. El-Registan; music by A. V. Alexandrov; 1944, revised 1977).

Chairman of the Presidium of the Supreme Soviet of the USSR: K. U. Chernenko.

First Vice-Chairman: Viktor Vasilievich Kuznetsov.

Secretary of the Presidium: Tengiz Menteshashvili.

Chairman of the Council of Ministers of the USSR: Nikolai Aleksandrovich Tikhonov (Oct. 1980).

First Vice-Chairman: I. V. Arkhipov (Dec. 1980).

Minister of Defence: Marshal D. F. Ustinov. *Minister of Foreign Trade:* N. S. Patolichev. *Minister for Foreign Affairs:* A. A. Gromyko.

Constitution (Fundamental Law) of the USSR. Moscow, 1977
Konstitutsiya SSSR. Konstitutsii Soyuznykh Sovetskikh Respublik. Moscow, 1978
Unger, A. L., *Constitutional Development in the USSR.* London, 1981
Ezhegodnik Bol'shoi Sovetskoi Entsiklopedii. Moscow, annual
F. J. M. Feldbrugge, (ed.), *The Constitution of the USSR and the Union Republics.* Alphen aan den Rijn, 1979

Communist Party of the Soviet Union. According to the rules adopted by the 22nd Congress of the Party on 31 Oct. 1961, the Communist Party of the Soviet Union 'unites, on a voluntary basis, the more advanced, politically more conscious section of the working class, collective-farm peasantry and intelligentsia of the USSR', whose principal objects are to build a Communist society by means of gradual transition from Socialism to Communism, to raise the material and cultural level of the people, to organize the defence of the country and to strengthen ties with the workers of other countries.

The Party is built on the territorial-industrial principle. The supreme organ is the Party Congress. Ordinary congresses are convened not less than every 5 years. The Congress elects a Central Committee which meets at least every 6 months, carries on the work of the Party between congresses, and guides the work of central Soviet and public organizations through Party groups within them.

The Central Committee forms a Political Bureau *(Politburo)* to direct the work of the Central Committee between plenary meetings, a Secretariat to direct current work and a Party Control Committee to deal with disciplinary matters; it also elects the General Secretary. Similar rules hold for the regional, territorial and republican levels of the party organization. The 'basis of the Party', the primary Party organization, exists in factories, state and collective farms, units of the Soviet Army and Navy, in villages, offices, educational establishments etc. where there are at least 3 Party members. There were over 425,000 primary Party organizations in 1983.

The Central Committee elected by the 26th Congress in March 1981 consisted of 319 members and 151 candidate (non-voting) members. Of these 39·6% were drawn from the central and regional party apparatus, and 5·7% were workers or peasants.

In March 1984 the Politburo of the Central Committee consisted of the following members: K. U. Chernenko, G. A. Aliev, M. S. Gorbachev, V. V. Grishin, A. A. Gromyko, D. A. Kunaev, G. V. Romanov, N. A. Tikhonov, D. F. Ustinov, V. V. Shcherbitsky, M. S. Solomentsev and V. I. Vorotnikov and the following candidate (non-voting) members: V. M. Chebrikov, P. N. Demichev, V. I. Dolgikh, V. V. Kuznetsov, B. N. Ponomarev, E. A. Shevardnadze.

Secretariat: K. U. Chernenko *(General Secretary);* V. I. Dolgikh; I. V. Kapitonov; E. K. Ligachev; B. N. Ponomarev; M. S. Gorbachev; G. V. Romanov; K. V. Rusakov; N. I. Ryzhkov and M. V. Zimyanin.

Chairman of the Party Control Committee: M. S. Solomentsev.

Chairman of the Central Auditing Commission: G. F. Sizov.

In Jan. 1983 the Communist Party had 18,117,903 members (about 9·3% of the adult population). Of these, 44·1% were classified as workers, 12·4% as collective farmers and 43·5% as office workers; 27·4% were women, and 59·7% were

Russians. The party's youth wing, the Komsomol (All-Union Leninist Communist Union of Youth), had 41·4m. members in 1982. In Dec. 1982, V. M. Mishin was elected First Secretary of its Central Committee.

Istoriya Kommunisticheskoi partii Sovetskogo Soyuza, 6 vols. Moscow, 1964ff.
Istoriya Kommunisticheskoi partii Sovetskogo Soyuza, 6th ed. Moscow, 1982
Rules of the Communist Party of the Soviet Union. Moscow, 1977
KPSS v rezolyutsiyakh i resheniyakh s''ezdov, konferentsii i plenumov TsK, 8th ed., 14 vols. Moscow, 1970–1982
Resolutions and Decisions of the Communist Party of the Soviet Union, ed. R. H. McNeal, 5 vols. Toronto, 1974–82
Spravochnik partiinogo rabotnika. Moscow, annual
Hill, R. and Frank, P., *The Soviet Communist Party.* London, 1981
Schapiro, L. B., *The Communist Party of the Soviet Union.* 2nd ed., London, 1970

DEFENCE. On 25 Feb. 1946 the control of the Soviet Armed Forces was unified under a single Ministry of the Armed Forces. On 25 Feb. 1950 the Defence Ministry was divided into a War Ministry and a Navy Ministry; on 15 March 1953 a single Ministry of Defence was reconstituted.

In 1955 the Air Defence Command and in 1960 the Strategic Rocket Forces were established as the 4th and 5th 'branches' of the armed forces beside the army, navy and air force.

The direction of Party and political work in the Armed Forces is exercised by the Central Committee of the Communist Party of the Soviet Union through the chief political directorate of the Ministry of Defence. The chiefs of the political departments of military commands, fleets and armies must be Party members of 5 years' standing and the chiefs of political departments of divisions and regiments Party members of 3 years' standing. About 90% of the officers are members of the Communist Party or Young Communist League, and 50% have had an engineering and technical education.

Military service begins at the age of 19 (or 18 for graduates of secondary schools). Active service lasts 2 years for privates in the Army and M.V.D. troops, 3 years for n.c.o.s in the Army and M.V.D. troops and for privates and n.c.o.s in the Air Force, 4 years for privates and n.c.o.s in the Coastal Defence, 5 years for ratings in the Navy. Reserve service lasts up to the ages of 35, 45 or 50 years according to fitness, family status and other considerations. Conscientious objection is treated as a criminal offence. Students in places of higher education are freed from military service, but receive military instruction. About half the service personnel have had higher, or 10-year, education and over 80% are members of the Communist Party.

Total strength of the armed forces was over 5m. in 1984, with a probable 25m. reserves and a further 500,000 in paramilitary forces.

The estimated expenditure on defence (in 1m. rubles) for 1961 was 9,255; 1970, 17,900; 1980, 17,100; 1983, 17,050.

Army. The Army is thought to consist of 50 tank, 134 motor rifle, 7 airborne and 15 artillery divisions; 8 air assault brigades; and various independent tank, artillery, missile and engineer units. Equipment includes some 35,000 T-54/-55/-62, 7,500 T-64 and 7,500 T-72/-80 main battle tanks. Strength (1984) 1·8m. (including 1·4m. conscripts).

Navy. The Soviet Fleet is steadily expanding and progressively modernizing under a continuity of policy and technology given by the nearly three decades in office of Admiral of the Fleet of the Soviet Union Sergei Georgiyevich Gorshkov, C.-in-C. of the Soviet Navy and Deputy Minister of Defence. The overall picture is of an unprecedentedly powerful and well-balanced navy, the capacity of which is increasing annually by scientific application and numerical strength.

The principal surface ships of the Soviet Navy are as follows:

Com-pleted	Name	Standard displace-ment Tons	Aircraft	Principal armament	Shaft horse-power	Speed Knots

Aircraft Carriers [1]

1984	Kharkov [2]		13 fixed wing	4 twin SS missile launchers;		
1982	Novorossiisk	39,000	aircraft	4 twin SA missile launchers;	140,000	32
1978	Minsk		20 helicopters	1 twin AS missile launcher;		
1976	Kiev			4 76-mm AA guns		

[1] See Aircraft carriers under construction and projected, successors of *Kiev* class, next page. [2] Scheduled for completion in late 1984.

Battle Cruisers [1]

| 1984 | Leonid Brezhnev | 22,000 | 3 helicopters | 20 single SS missile launchers; 16 SA missile launchers; | 160,000 | 35 |
| 1980 | Kirov | | | 2 AS missile launchers; 2 100-mm guns | | |

[1] The first battle cruisers, and the largest combatant warships, apart from aircraft carriers, to be built for any navy since the Second World War. Main engines comprise 2 nuclear reactors and oil-fired superheat boilers for steam turbines.

Helicopter Carriers

| 1968 | Leningrad | 16,500 | 14 helicopters | 2 twin SA missile launchers; 1 twin AS missile launcher; | 100,000 | 31 |
| 1967 | Moskva | | | 2 twin 57-mm AA guns | | |

Cruisers

| 1982 | Kulakov | 8,500 | 2 helicopters | 2 quadruple SS missile launchers; 8 SA missile launchers; | 94,000 | 33 |
| 1982 | Udaloy [1] | | | 2 single 100-mm guns | | |

[1] Four more light cruisers of the *Udaloy* class are being completed or under construction.

| 1983 | Otchyanny | 8,000 | 1 helicopter | 8 SS missile launchers; 2 SA missile launchers; | 100,000 | 32 |
| 1982 | Sovremenny [1] | | | 4 130-mm guns | | |

[1] Four more light cruisers of the Sovremenny class are under construction.

| 1982 | Slavia | 13,000 | 2 helicopters | 16 SS missiles; SA vertical launchers; AS missile launchers; 100-mm guns | 120,000 | 34 |

Two more heavy cruisers of this Krasina class are under construction.

1979	Tallin					
1978	Tashkent			2 quadruple SS missile launchers;		
1977	Petropavlovsk					
1976	Azov [3]	8,200	1 helicopter	8 twin SA missile launchers;	124,000	34
1975	Kerch			4 76-mm AA guns		
1974	Ochakov					
1973	Nikolaiev					

[3] *Azov*, nominally of this Kara class, is of a modified design, with a different guided missiles system, as trials ship for the armament of subsequent classes of cruisers.

Cruisers

Completed	Name	Standard displacement Tons	Aircraft	Principal armament	Shaft horsepower	Speed Knots
1958	Admiral Senyavin[1]					
1957	Mikhail Kutuzov					
1956	Dimitri Pojarski					
1956	Oktyabrskaya Revolutsiya [3]					
1956	Admiral Lazarev					
1955	Alexandr Suvorov	16,000		12 6-in.; 12 3·9-in.	110,000	32
1954	Admiral Ushakov					
1954	Dzerzhinski [2]					
1953	Alexandr Nevski					
1953	Murmansk					
1953	Zhdanov [1]					
1953	Sverdlov [4]					

[1] *Admiral Senyavin* now has a helicopter pad and hangar ('X' and 'Y' turrets removed), leaving her with only six 6-mm guns, while *Zhdanov* has high deckhouse ('X' turret removed). Each carries twin surface-air missile launchers. Both latterly employed as command and communications ships.

[2] *Dzerzhinski* has only nine 6-in. guns in 3 triple turrets, 'X' turret having been replaced by a twin surface-air missile launcher.

[3] This ship, first named *Molotovsk*, was renamed in 1957.

[4] Of the older cruisers, *Kirov* and *Slava* (ex-*Molotov*) were deleted from the effective list in 1976-77 and *Zheleznyakov* in 1978. *Komsomolets* was latterly used as a training ship.

Capital Support Ship

1977	Berezina [1]	40,000	2 helicopters	Twin SA missile launcher; 4 57-mm guns	54,000	22

[1] Very impressive militarised replenishment ship designed to support the new Soviet aircraft carriers.

Submarines

70(9)[3]	SSBN	Nuclear powered	Ballistic missile armed [1] *q.v.*
15	SSB	Diesel-electric powered	Ballistic missile armed
48	SSGN	Nuclear powered	Cruise (guided) missile armed
18	SSG	Diesel-electric powered	Cruise missile armed
66	SSN	Nuclear powered	Torpedo (only) armed
235[2]	SS	Conventionally (diesel) powered	Conventionally (torpedo) armed

[1] See table. All missile-carrying submarines are also armed with torpedoes.

[2] Including 85 patrol submarines in reserve or used for training only.

[3] Nine reportedly had missile tubes removed for conversion to fleet submarines, SSN (nuclear propelled).

Capital (Strategic) Submarines (SSBN)

Class	No.	Displacement Tons	Missile Tubes (vertical)		Nuclear Reactors	Shaft horsepower	Speed Knots
S [1]	2	30,000	20	SS-NX-20	2	120,000	24
D3	15	13,350	16	SS-N-18	1	60,000	24
D2	4	11,400	16	SS-N-8	1	60,000	25
D1	18	10,000	12	SS-N-8	1	60,000	25
Y	25 (9) [3]	9,300	16	SS-N-6	1	40,000	30
H3	1	5,750	3	SS-N-8	1	25,000	26
H2	5	5,600	3	SS-N-5	1	25,000	26

[1] Sierra, formerly known as Typhoon class. These vessels, of battleship dimensions, are the largest submarines ever built. Launched in Sept. 1980 and Sept. 1982. The vertical missile cylinders are mounted forward of the fin.

Note: All these classes also carry six 21-inch torpedo tubes, except 'S' class, possibly eight.

There are also 14 other missile-armed light-cruiser size leaders, 43 missile-armed destroyers, 38 gun-armed destroyers, (including 13 in reserve), 32 missile-armed frigates, 48 gun-armed frigates, 3 ocean minelayers, 83 missile-armed corvettes, 152 gun-armed corvettes, 145 fleet minesweepers, 90 coastal minesweepers, 42 minehunters, 60 inshore minesweepers, 51 minesweeping boats, 130 fast missile craft, 17 fast torpedo boats, 90 fast anti-submarine boats, 55 patrol craft, 18 hydrofoil missile boats, 30 hydrofoil torpedo boats, 15 hydrofoil gunboats, 30 coastal patrol launches, 95 river patrol boats, 84 major amphibious and auxiliary roll-on roll-off ships, 2 dock landing ships, 30 tank landing ships, 60 medium landing ships, 35 utility landing craft, 70 minor landing craft, 60 intelligence collecting ships, 70 major support ships, 11 space associated ships, 140 survey ships, 64 oceanographic research ships, 6 missile range ships, 3 nuclear powered icebreakers, 60 icebreakers, 20 training ships. 200 fishery protection ships, 28 fleet replenishment ships, 55 oilers, 13 special tankers, 45 salvage vessels, 80 transports, 25 submarine rescue ships, 135 tenders, 10 lifting ships, 15 cable ships, 35 degaussing ships, 110 fleet tugs, 60 hovercraft and thousands of auxiliaries, para-military ships and service craft.

The new construction programme includes another aircraft carrier, considerably larger and reportedly nuclear-powered, 3 very large nuclear powered ballistic missile submarines, 2 nuclear powered cruise missile submarines, 6 nuclear powered torpedo-armed submarines, 3 diesel-electric propelled patrol submarines, 10 guided missile cruisers and large anti-submarine leaders, 3 frigates and 4 corvettes.

In the progressive forward procurement programme more conventionally propelled aircraft carriers of improved 'follow-on' class are envisaged, together with nuclear powered surface ships, conventionally propelled submarines and specialized support ships, to fit into the Soviet global and strategic maritime pattern.

There are 5 shipyards in and near Leningrad; Black Sea yards are at Nikolaiev and Sevastopol, new shipyards are at Molotovsk in the White Sea region and at Komsomolsk on the Amur.

The completion of a through canal system between the Baltic and White Seas, allowing regular traffic *via* the North-East Passage (during the ice-free season), facilitates the navigation of suitable ships between the Baltic and Far East.

Estimated number of personnel in 1984 totalled 500,000, including naval aviation, naval infantry, coastal defence, cadets and apprentices (but excluding 75,000 civilians in administration and new construction). Only 18% of naval personnel are volunteers, *i.e.*, officers and petty officers, the remainder comprising national service men serving 3 years at sea and 2 if ashore.

Air Force. The Soviet Air Force (excluding the strategic bomber force and Voyska PVO air defence force) was believed to have a personnel strength, in 1983, of over 370,000 officers and men. To supplement long-range rocket missiles (estimated at 1,398 emplaced ICBM, 600 MRBM/IRBM), the strategic bomber force has still about 105 Tupolev Tu-95 ('Bear')[1] 4-turboprop bombers, 70 Myasishchev M-4 4-jet bombers and flight-refuelling tankers ('Bison'), 500 twin-jet Tupolev Tu-16 ('Badger'), and 135 supersonic Tupolev Tu-22 ('Blinder') bombers, ECM and reconnaissance aircraft, and at least 150 Tupolev ('Backfire') swing-wing bombers. All types are used also by the Naval Air Force for long-range maritime reconnaissance; the Tu-16, Tu-95, Tu-22 and 'Backfire' can carry air-to-surface guided self-propelled cruise missiles and all 5 types have provision for flight refuelling. A new swing-wing strategic bomber ('Blackjack'), larger and faster than the American B-1, is being flight tested.

The tactical air forces, under local army command in the field, have an estimated total of 6,000 ground attack, air combat, ECM and reconnaissance aircraft, including 2,400 MiG-23/27 ('Flogger') and 800 two-seat Sukhoi Su-24 ('Fencer') supersonic swing-wing aircraft, 200 twin-jet Yakovlev Yak-28 ('Brewer') reconnaissance aircraft, 100 single-jet Sukhoi Su-7B ('Fitter-A'), 800 swing-wing Su-17 ('Fitter-C/D/G/H/J'), and 600 MiG-21 ('Fishbed') fighter-bombers, 500 Su-15 ('Flagon'), 60 MiG-25 ('Foxbat') and some MiG-31 ('Foxhound') interceptors, and an increasing number of new Su-25 ('Frogfoot') twin-engined ground attack aircraft supported by 125 MiG-21 and 170 MiG-25 ('Foxbat') reconnaissance aircraft, and 3,500 helicopters, including very large Mi-26 ('Halo') transports and up to 1,000 heavily-armed Mi-24 ('Hind') assault helicopters, in gunship/transport versions. Electronic warfare duties are performed by a variety of aircraft, including Yak-28s and Mi-8 and Mi-17 helicopters. The Voyska PVO defence forces, organized as a separate service, have an estimated total of 1,250 jet interceptors. A high proportion of the squadrons are equipped with MiG-23 ('Flogger'), Su-15 ('Flagon'), MiG-25 ('Foxbat') and improved MiG-31 ('Foxhound') all-weather interceptors, armed with air-to-air missiles. The twin-jet Yak-28P ('Firebar') and Tu-28P ('Fiddler') make up the balance of the force. Early warning and fighter-control duties are performed by about 10 radar-carrying adaptations of the Tu-114 turboprop transport, redesignated Tu-126 ('Moss'); these are being replaced by a more effective radar-equipped AWACS version ('Mainstay') of the Il-76 transport. Aircraft expected to enter service in 1984/85 include the Su-27 ('Flanker') and MiG-29 ('Fulcann') counter-air fighters, each with potential attack capability. Very large numbers of surface-to-air guided missiles are operational, on some 10,000 launchers, including the new high-performance SA-10 (low-altitude) and SA-12 (high-altitude) with capability against cruise and submarine-launched missiles respectively, the older 'Guild', 'Guideline', 'Goa', 'Gainful' and 'Ganef', the long-range 'Gammon' and the 'Galosh' which is deployed around Moscow on 32 launchers and has anti-missile capability.

Soviet Air Force transport squadrons have 400 An-12 ('Cub') 4-turboprop transports and 50 An-24s ('Coke') and An-26s ('Curl'), with 50 An-22s ('Cock'), and 250 Il-76 ('Candid') heavy four-jet freighters. The very large four-jet An-400 ('Condor') is under development to replace the An-22. Training aircraft include the piston-engined Yak-18 primary trainer, the Czech-built L-29 Delfin and L-39 jet basic trainers and versions of operational types such as MiG-21, MiG-23, MiG-25, MiG-15, Su-7, Su-15, Su-17, Yak-28 and Tu-22.

[1] For convenience Soviet aircraft and missiles are usually referred to by invented English names in non-Soviet military writings.

Naval Air Force. Operating 1,100 fixed-wing aircraft and helicopters, the Soviet Navy has the world's second largest naval air arm. Under the control of the various naval commands, *i.e.*, Baltic, Black Sea and Pacific, the Naval Air Arm has an estimated 220 Tu-16 ('Badger') twin-jet bombers, and 100 'Backfire' swing-wing bombers, able to carry air-to-surface missiles, 40 supersonic twin-jet Tu-22 ('Blinder') maritime reconnaissance aircraft, a small number of Su-17 ('Fitter') shore-based fighters, and 80 Beriev M-12 ('Mail') maritime patrol amphibians. For reconnaissance, anti-submarine and electronic warfare there are about 95 Tu-142 ('Bear') 4-engined bombers, 90 Tu-16s, and a few Tu-22s, plus a small number of Il-20s ('Coot-A') and 60 Il-38s ('May'). The Tu-142 also has an important targeting rôle for ships fitted with anti-shipping missile launchers. Over 250 anti-submarine and missile targeting/guidance helicopters, notably the Ka-27 ('Helix') and Ka-25 ('Hormone'), are carried in naval vessels, including 3 aircraft carriers (which also operate Yak-36 ('Forger') VTOL attack/reconnaissance aircraft) and 2 helicopter carriers. Several hundred transport, flight refuelling tanker ('Badger'), utility and training fixed-wing aircraft and Mi-14 ('Haze') shore-based ASW helicopters are also under Navy control.

Berman, H. J., and Kerner, M. (ed.), *Soviet Military Law and Administration.* 2 vols. Harvard Univ. Press, 1955
Scott, H. F., and Scott, W. F., *The Armed Forces of the USSR.* 2nd ed. Boulder, 1981
Smith, M. J., *The Soviet Navy, 1941–1978: A Guide to Sources in English.* Oxford and Santa Barbara, 1981
Suvorov, V., *The Liberators: The Soviet Army.* London, 1981
Watson, B. W., *Red Navy at Sea.* Boulder, 1982

INTERNATIONAL RELATIONS

Membership. USSR is a member of UN, Comecon and the Warsaw Pact.

ECONOMY

Planning. Planning is based on public ownership in industry and trade, and on mixed public and collective (co-operative) ownership in agriculture. The first plan drawn up by Gosplan (the State Planning Commission) was the 'Goelro' drawn up in 1920. This was to be the basis for the economic development of the country and for the construction of a system of electrical power plants with an aggregate capacity of 1·75m. kw., in the course of 15 years.

For details of Planning 1925–1942 see THE STATESMAN'S YEAR-BOOK, 1981–82 p. 1226.

For details of the fourth 5-year plan, 1946–50, see THE STATESMAN'S YEAR-BOOK, 1952, pp. 1424 f. The 1950 target of the gross output of industry was exceeded by 2%.

On 10 Oct. 1952 the 19th Congress of the Communist Party issued directives for the fifth 5-year plan, 1951–55; for details, see THE STATESMAN'S YEAR-BOOK, 1953, pp. 1435-36. During Sept. and Oct. 1953 the Government issued a number of decrees to stimulate the development of agriculture, the output of consumer goods and the expansion of the home trade. For details of these decrees, see THE STATESMAN'S YEAR-BOOK, 1955, pp. 1448-50.

The directive for the sixth 5-year plan, 1956-60, was adopted by the 20th Congress of the Communist Party on 25 Feb. 1956; for details see THE STATESMAN'S YEAR-BOOK, 1958, p. 1472.

In May 1955 Gosplan was reorganized to consist of 2 state commissions for long-term planning (Gosplan) and for current planning (Gosekonomkomissiya); at the same time a committee was set up to improve the application to industry of advanced science and technology (Gostekhnika).

Between 1954 and 1956 considerable changes were made in planning methods. In March 1954 collective farms were given greater authority over planning their own output, only the quantities required by the State in fixed deliveries being determined beforehand, and voluntary sales by contract. In 1955 they were authorized to make changes in their statutes, which had followed a fixed model since 1935. In 1955-57 over 15,000 industrial establishments in various basic industries, previously controlled by the Union Government, and later a number of entire light industries were turned over to the constituent (Union) Republics. By 1962 they controlled from 95 to 100% of all industrial output.

In 1957 a comprehensive plan for decentralization of management of industry was initiated. Industrial establishments responsible for about 71% of all Soviet industrial output were turned over to Economic Councils set up in 104 (in 1963: 47) economic administrative areas. These in 1962 controlled 73% of all industrial production. The Ministries previously responsible for the industries concerned were either abolished or transformed into purely planning and supervisory bodies. The State Committee for current planning was abolished, and Gosplan was given wider powers.

In consequence of this change a 7-year plan for 1959-65 was adopted by the 21st Congress of the Communist Party in Feb. 1959. Industrial output was to increase by 80%; it was in fact, in 1965, 84% above that of 1959. Capital investments would roughly equal the total for 1917-58: special attention was to be given to mechanization of agriculture and arduous industrial labour, automation and new technological processes, and housing. Diesel or electric traction of railway freight was to rise to 85%. Real incomes were to rise 40%, the 7-hour day (6 hours for miners) became general in 1960 and the 40-hour week in 1961, and introduction of the 35-hour week (30 hours for miners) began in 1964.

In Oct. 1965 the regional and Republic Economic Councils were abolished and also 28 Ministries for various branches of industry (17 Union-Republican, i.e., corresponding to similar Ministries in the Union Republics, and 11 all-Union).

A 20-year plan was adopted by the 22nd Congress of the Communist Party on 31 Oct. 1961, which envisaged a ninefold growth in electricity output and big increases in production of steel, oil, coal, machinery and cement, and also in grain, milk and meat. Two new iron and steel centres were to be developed in Kazakhstan and in Kursk region. A single deepwater system was to link the main inland waterways in the European USSR. Some rivers in northern Asia were to be diverted south for irrigation purposes. A 6-hour day for a 6-day week or 35 hours for a 5-day week were to be achieved by 1970. Housing, water, gas, heating, public urban transport and school meals were to be free by 1980. These and cognate measures were to provide 'the material and technical basis of communism'.

The 23rd Congress of the Communist Party in April 1966 adopted 'directives' for a 5-year plan for 1966-70. Under these, power output was to reach 830,000-850,000m. kwh.; oil, 345-355m. tons; coal, 665-675m. tons; steel, 124-129m. tons; mineral fertilizers, 62-65m. tons; machine-tools, 220,000-230,000; cars, 700,000-800,000; tractors, 600,000-625,000; paper, 5-5·3m. tons; cement, 100-105m. tons; fabrics, 9·5-9·8m. sq. metres; leather footwear, 610-630m. pairs; meat, 5·9-6·2m. tons; butter, 1·2m. tons; sugar, 9·8-10m. tons. The average annual output of grain was to increase 30% over 1964-65. 7,000 km of new railway line, 63,000 km of new motor roads and 35-40 new airports were to be built; marine tonnage was to be increased by 50%.

The 9th Five-Year Plan adopted in 1971 provided for an increase in electric power output to 1,065,000m. kwh.; oil to 496m. tons; gas, 320,000m. cu. metres; steel, 146m. tons; coal, 695m. tons; mineral fertilizers, 90m. tons; tractors, 575,000; passenger cars, 1·26m., and lorries, 750,000. Grain output was to rise to 195m. tons in 1975; meat, approximately 16m. tons; milk, 100m. tons; textiles, 11,000m. sq. metres; leather footwear, 830m. pairs. Average wages were to increase by 22%, incomes of collective farmers 30-35%, and the average of real incomes by 31%. 3,400 miles of new railway tracks were to be built and 3,700 miles electrified, with 17,000 miles of new oil pipelines, and 40% more cargo carried by sea. Over 16m. flats and houses were to be built.

By July 1972, 43,000 industrial plants had been transferred to the new system of decentralized cost-accounting; they produced 94% of total output of Soviet industry and 95% of its total profit. All public establishments in trade and catering and all the state farms have gone over to the new system.

On 29 Oct. 1976, the Supreme Soviet adopted the 10th Five-Year Plan (1976–80). This provided for an increase of industrial output from 104·3% of the 1975 level to 136%, an average annual increase of agricultural output by 16%, freight traffic (all forms) from 105·7% to 132%, state capital investments from 105·1% of the 1975 level in 1976 to 114·6% in 1980, real income per head from 103·7% to 121%, retail commodity turnover from 103·6% to 128·7%. 550m. sq. metres of new housing were to be built. Children in pre-school establishments would increase by 104·4% in 1976 and 125·5% in 1980, pupils in day schools from 108·9% to 148·8%, and students in higher education from 100·4% to 105·4%. Hospital beds were to increase from 102·2% in the first year to 109·7% in the final year.

In 1979 it was decided that from 1981 detailed plans would be drawn up at the outset for each year of a 5-year plan, so that enterprises could spread their potential more rationally over the whole period.

The 11th Five-Year Plan, adopted in 1981, aims to raise living standards. The focus is Siberia and the Soviet Far East, with their large resources of energy and raw materials, and also Central Asia, with its favourable combination of labour resources and raw materials. Virtually no industries will be developed in the European part of the USSR and the plan envisages speeding up the development of labour-intensive branches of agriculture, consumer goods and engineering industries in Central Asia. National income (in the Soviet definition) is to increase by 18% between 1980 and 1985; industrial production is to increase by 26%, capital investment by 5·4%, freight traffic by 19·4%, real incomes by 16·5%, agricultural production by 13%, and retail trade in the state and co-operative sectors by 23% over the same period. Pensions are to be raised and the minimum wage is to be increased to 80 rubles a month, and efforts are to be made to increase state assistance to families with young children and to improve the food and care given to them in schools and pre-school institutions.

In May 1982 the CPSU Central Committee adopted a series of resolutions intended to bring about an improvement in agricultural production more particularly. The resolutions, described as the party's 'food programme', are designed to achieve an expansion in all sectors of production and a reduction in imports from the West by means of a simplified and more decentralised system of management, increased procurement prices for many products, and enhanced bonuses and other incentives.

In July 1983 a limited devolution of authority to enterprise level was introduced in five ministries (heavy and transport machine-building, electro-technical industry, and three republican ministries), initially on an experimental basis, in order to raise the quality and effectiveness of their production. Further measures have sought to reduce absenteeism and improve labour discipline.

Narodnoe khozyaistvo SSSR za 60 let (1917–1977). Moscow, 1977
Narodnoe khozyaistvo SSSR. Moscow, annual
Resheniya partii i pravitel'stva po khozyaistvennym voprosam. Vol. 1ff. Moscow, 1967ff
Ekonomicheskaya entsiklopediya: Politicheskaya ekonomiya. Vol. 1ff. Moscow, 1972ff
Istoriya sotsialisticheskoi ekonomiki SSSR. 7 vols. Moscow, 1976–80
Nove, A., *An Economic History of the USSR.* Rev. ed., Harmondsworth, 1982.—*The Soviet Economic System.* 2nd ed., London, 1980
US Congress, Joint Economic Committee, *The Soviet Economy in a Time of Change,* 2 vols. Washington D.C., 1979
Gregory, P. R. and Stuart, R. C., *Soviet Economic Structure and Performance.* 2nd ed., New York, 1981
Tikhonov, N. A., *Guidelines for the Economic and Social Development of the USSR for 1981–1985 and for the period ending in 1990.* Moscow, 1981

Budget. Revenue and expenditure in 1m. rubles for calendar years:

	1977	1978	1979	1980	1983	1984 [1]
Revenue	247,800	265,800	275,600	302,700	354,106	366,008
Expenditure	242,800	260,200	275,100	294,600	353,905	365,792

[1] Estimate.

The 1984 budget allotted 207,893m. rubles to the national economy, 17,054m. to defence and 118,205m. to social and cultural services.

The social insurance budget, which is controlled by the Central Council for Trade Unions and its affiliated bodies, was 29,476m. rubles in 1977, 31,179m. in 1978, 33,089m. in 1979, 35,296 in 1980 and 37,417m. in 1981.

The national income was assessed (in 1,000m. rubles) at 152·9 in 1961, 289·1 in 1970, 305 in 1971, 313·6 in 1972, 337·8 in 1973, 354 in 1974, 440·6 in 1979, 462·2 in 1980, 482·1 in 1981 and 523·4 in 1982.

Income tax was abolished on 1 Oct. 1961 for earnings up to 60 rubles per month and reduced for earnings between 61 and 70 rubles; in Dec. 1967 further cuts of 25% were made for earnings from 61 to 80 rubles; in 1972 earnings up to 70 rubles were freed of income tax, and taxes on incomes up to 90 rubles were cut by about 33⅓%. Capital investment (1981) was 138,800m. rubles, including 125,200m. by State and co-operative enterprises, 11,900m. by collective farms and 1,700m. by individuals (on housing).

Currency. As from 1 Jan. 1961 the gold content of the *ruble* was raised from 0·222 168 to 0·987 412 gramme. The official exchange rates (March 1984) 1·157 *rubles* = £1; 0·795 *rubles* = US$1.

The gold holdings of the USSR were, in Dec. 1955, estimated at about 200m. fine oz. (US$7,000m.), or about 20% of the world total of monetary gold.

The currency in circulation is: (1) State Bank notes in denominations of 10, 25, 50 and 100 *rubles;* (2) Treasury notes in denominations of 1, 3 and 5 *rubles;* (3) cupro-nickel coins in denominations of 10, 15, 20 and 50 *kopeks* and 1 *ruble;* (4) cupro-zinc coins in denominations of 1, 2, 3 and 5 *kopeks.*

Banking. The State Bank began operations on 16 Nov. 1921. By an edict of 7 April 1959 a number of specialized banks for planned long-term investments, which had existed since 1932, were abolished. The State Bank, in addition to short-term credits, effects long-term investments in agriculture and in individual rural house building. The Bank for Financing Capital Investments (*Stroibank*) covers industry, transport, urban housing schemes and public utilities and individual house-building in towns.

Deposits in 79,706 savings banks were over 165,723m. rubles to the credit of 148m. depositors at 1 Jan. 1982.

Weights and Measures. The metric system has been in use since 1 Jan. 1927.

The Gregorian Calendar was adopted as from 14 Feb. 1918.

ENERGY AND NATURAL RESOURCES

Electricity. There were (1982) 57 fuel-burning power stations of over 1m. kw. capacity, and these account for nearly 80% of the country's electricity.

Hydro-electric stations have been constructed on major rivers. Among them are the Bratsk (4·5m. kw.), completed in 1967 — until recently the world's largest, Ust-Ilimsk, Central Siberia (3·6m. kw.), Krasnoyarsk (6m. kw.) and a 1·26m. kw. station on the River Pechora (Far North). The Sayano-Shushenskaya hydro-power station, part of the Yenisei chain, and already in part operation, will have a 6·4m. kw. capacity when completed in 1983. A 245m. high dam has to be built before completion, in a gorge in the Sayan Range. Another large hydro-electric station is under construction on the River Kureika, Siberia, to provide energy for the mining and metallurgical centre at Norilsk in the Arctic.

Total installed capacity of power stations in 1938 was 8·7m. kw. and 276·7m. kw. in 1981. Industry consumes about 70% of the total electricity. Over 35,000 small rural power stations have been closed in recent years owing to supply from State stations becoming available, but there are still many operating in the countryside. 800 towns and urban settlements were heated by central thermal plants.

The world's first commercial nuclear power station in Obninsk, built in 1954, was followed by the Beloyarsk, Novo-Voronezh, Leningrad, Kursk, Cherno-byl, Armenian and Shevchenko nuclear stations. Soviet nuclear power plants so far have standard slow 1m. kw. reactors, but a 1·5m. kw. reactor has now been designed. A fast reactor is functioning at Shevchenko.

The general design for a nuclear thermal station has been developed, and practical experience in this field has been obtained at the Bilibino nuclear power station in the Arctic, which supplies electricity and heat to the inhabitants on the Chukchi Peninsula.

In 1979 a 500,000 kw. MHD pilot project was started in Ryazan. This first-generation MHD station will have an efficiency of 50% as against 40% in the best thermal power stations and will consume about 20% less fuel. An experimental tidal energy station is working at Kislaya Guba (Murman coast).

Total electricity output in 1982 was 1,367,000 kwh.

The country's integrated power grid is now in operation, covering over 900 power stations, which are handled by a central control panel in Moscow.

A unified power grid ('Mir') with all the Socialist countries of eastern Europe was built up between 1962 and 1967. Total capacity (1972) was 58m. kw.

Oil. In the 1930s practically all Soviet oil came from the Caucasian fields, of which the Baku fields yielded 75-80% and the Grozny and Maikop fields between them 15%. Since then, the distribution has considerably changed. The Ural-Volga area, the 'Second Baku', has 4 large centres in operation, at Samarska Luka (Kuibyshev), Tuimazy (Bashkiria), Ishimbaev (Bashkiria) and Perm, producing nearly 100m. tonnes annually.

A large new oilfield has been developed in the Trans-Volga area of the Saratov region. The Tyumen (West Siberian) complex now accounts for over 50% of the USSR's oil output. In 1982 the USSR extracted 612·6m. tonnes of oil.

The total length of pipeline on 1 Jan. 1939 was 4,212 km, divided as follows: Baku-Batumi, 1,717 km; Grozny-Makhachkala, 150 km; Grozny-Armavir-Tuapse, 618 km; Armavir-Trudovaya, 488 km; Guriev-Orsk, 845 km, and other, 394 km. One pipeline (1,700 km) was completed in 1955, connecting Tuimazy in Bashkiria with the refineries of Omsk. In 1957 the Almetyevsk-Gorky pipeline (580 km) and 479 km of the Stavropol-Moscow pipeline were completed. At the end of 1981 there were 70,800 km of pipeline, through which (in 1981) were conveyed 637·7m. tonnes of oil.

The construction of the 'Druzhba' pipeline of about 5,327 km from the oilfields near Kuibyshev to Poland and the German Democratic Republic (northern branch) and to Czechoslovakia and Hungary (southern branch)–separating in Belorussia–begun in 1960, was completed in 1965. Now a double line, it has an annual throughput of 50m. tonnes.

In 1976 the USSR exported 148·5m. tonnes of crude oil and oil products.

Meyerhoff, A. A., *The Oil and Gas Potential of the Soviet Far East*. Beaconsfield, 1981

Gas. A natural-gas pipeline from Gazli, near Khiva, to Voskresensk, near Moscow (2,750 km), with a planned capacity of 100m. cu. metres per day, began operating in Oct. 1967. Since then it has been extended to Czechoslovakia, where a 1,000 km extension, for transmission of Soviet gas to Austria, Italy and German Democratic Republic and Federal Republic of Germany, is under construction and another to Bulgaria. Another natural-gas pipeline, over 3,000 km from Medvezhye (Tyumen Region) to Moscow, began operating in Oct. 1974. A second pipeline from this region, linking the Urengoi deposit with Petrovsky in the Central European area of the USSR, became operational in 1980, and is to be continued to the southern Ukraine, to a total length of 3,000 km. A gas pipeline starting from Orenburg (Urals), passing across the Volga at Kamyshin, and continuing across the Ukraine *via* Kremenchug and Vinnitsa to Czechoslovakia (2,750 km), reached the Soviet frontier in Jan. 1979. When completed, it is to supply Czechoslovakia, Poland, Bulgaria and Hungary with 14,000m. cu. metres annually and Romania with 1,500m. A unified gas-grid exceeding 124,000 km now exists.

By Dec. 1981 construction work had begun on the 5,000 km Urengoi (West Siberia)-Uzhgorod-West Europe gas pipeline.

Over 50,000 km of long-distance trunk gas pipelines were built and put into service in the 10th Five-Year Plan period, bringing the total to 130,000 km.

Minerals. Mining experts are trained in 6 mining, 3 oil and 1 peat institutes, the mining faculties of 17 higher educational establishments, oil faculties of 2 industrial institutes and a peat faculty at the Belorussian Polytechnical Institute.

The Soviet Union is rich in minerals. Soviet scientists claim that it contains 58% of the world's coal deposits, 58·7% of its oil, 41% of its iron ore, 76·7% of its apatite, 25% of all timber land, 88% of its manganese, 54% of its potassium salts and nearly one-third of its phosphates.

Estimated output (in tonnes) in 1962: Copper, 634,900; zinc, 399,000; lead, 363,000; tungsten, 10,500; antimony, 5,980; silver, 27m. fine oz. Output in 1963: Baryte, 199,500; magnesium, 31,745; aluminium, 961,400; manganese ore (1977), 8·6m.; graphite, 54,000; bauxite, 4·3m.; asbestos, 1·3m.; phosphate rock, 3·7m. (plus 7·4m. apatite); chromite, 1·23m.; gold, 12·5m. fine oz.; molybdenum, 12·5m. lb.; cadmium (1956), 160.

Output of iron and steel in the USSR (in 1m. tonnes):

	Pig-iron	Ingot steel	Rolled steel		Pig-iron	Ingot steel	Rolled steel
1913	4·2	4·2	3·5	1960	46·8	65·3	50·9
1928–29	4·0	4·8	3·9	1965	66·2	91·0	61·7
1932	6·2	5·9	4·4	1970	85·9	115·9	80·6
1940	14·9	18·3	13·1	1979	109·0	149·1	119·0
1946	10·0	13·4	9·6	1980	107·3	147·9	118·3
1950	19·2	27·3	20·9	1981	107·8	148·4	118·2

Coal production (in 1m. tonnes) was 29·1 in 1913, 64·4 in 1932, 165·9 in 1940, 261·1 in 1950, 509 6 in 1960, 624·1 in 1970, 701·3 in 1975, 711 in 1976, 722 in 1977, 724 in 1978, 719 in 1979, 716·4 in 1980, 704 in 1981, 718·1 in 1982.

The main centre of the atomic ore industry is at Ust-Kamenogorsk in the Altai Mountains. Uranium deposits are being worked near Taboshar (south-east of Tashkent), Andizhan (in the Tynya-Muyan Mountains), Slyudianka (near Lake Baikal), on the Kolyma River and in Southern Armenia.

Output of natural gas reached 500·7m. cu. metres in 1982.

Agriculture. The Soviet Union, up to about 1928 predominantly agricultural in character, has become an industrial-agricultural country. Of the gross social product, industry and transport accounted for 42·1% in 1913 and 67·7% in 1981; agriculture for 57·9% in 1913 and 14·1% in 1981. Of the total state land fund of 2,227·5m. hectares, agricultural land in use in 1981 amounted to 1,051·5m., state forests and state reserves to 1,112·2m. hectares. 20% of all gainfully employed in 1981 were engaged in agriculture and forestry (1913, 75%).

The total area under cultivation (including single-owner peasant farms, state farms and collective farms) was (in the same territory) 118·2m. hectares in 1913, 129·7m. in 1933, 146·3m. in 1950, 203m. in 1960, 206·7m. in 1970, 217·9 in 1976, 217·6m. in 1977, 226·9m. in 1978, 226·6m. in 1981.

Collective farms on 1 Nov. 1981 possessed 246·9m. hectares, of which 102·4m. were under crops of various kinds; state farms and other state agricultural undertakings possessed 796·4m. hectares, of which 120·8m. were under crops; manual and clerical workers held 4·1m. hectares as allotments.

In Nov. 1969 the Third Congress of collective farmers adopted a new model constitution, considerably enlarging the planning powers of collective farms and making payments to their members a priority.

Since 1969 conferences of collective farms have elected 2,417 district collective farm councils with 85,000 members, to study and co-ordinate local experience in methods and finance. Processing and other joint agricultural productive establishments in 1980 numbered 9,638.

Produce marketed (after consumption by farms) was, in 1m. tonnes, for the present area of the USSR:

	1950	1960	1970	1980		1950	1960	1970	1980
Grain	38·2	54·1	80·8	81·3	Meat[2] and fats	2·5	6·0	9·4	11·8
Raw Cotton[1]	3·5	4·3	6·9	10·0	Milk and milk				
Sugar-beet	19·7	52·2	71·4	64·4	products	11·4	29·1	48·0	59·4
Potatoes	14·0	13·7	18·1	16·6	Wool	138·0	319·0	395·0	453·0
Other vegetables	4·3	8·0	13·8	20·6	Eggs (1,000m.)	3·5	10·5	22·1	46·5

[1] Seed-cotton unginned.   [2] Slaughter weight.

Since 1954 grain crops have been measured in 'barn crop' (*i.e.*, net quantities delivered to barns) and not in 'gross harvest' or 'biological yield' (*i.e.*, calculated as growing crops) as previously. Average annual crops (in 1m. tonnes): 1909–13, 72·5; 1946–50, 64·8; 1951–55, 88·5; 1956–60, 121·5; 1961–65, 130·3; 1966–70, 167·5; 1971–75, 181·6; 1976–80, 205; 1980, 189·1.

Other produce (in 1m. tonnes) in 1980: Milk, 90·9; sugar-beet, 81; potatoes, 67; vegetables, 27·3; meat (slaughter weight), 15·1; raw cotton, 9·96; sunflower, 4·6; 67,900m. eggs.

In Dec. 1963 collective farms comprised 99·7% of all peasant holdings. In 1980 they produced 90% of all sugar-beet, cotton 66%, milk 38%, marketed grain 50%, meat 32%, potatoes 19%, other vegetables 24%, eggs 7%.

Between 1953 and 1 Jan. 1982 the number of collective farms was reduced, mainly by amalgamation and partly by transformation into state farms, from 93,300 to 26,300, their cultivated area falling from 132m. hectares to 98·9m. The number of state farms rose in the same period from 4,857 to 21,600, their cultivated area from 15·2m. hectares to 120·8m.

State purchases in 1980 (in 1m. tonnes; 1979 figures in brackets): Grain, 69·4 (62·8); sugar-beet, 65·2 (69·3); milk, 57·2 (59); meat (live weight), 15·9 (16·7); cotton, 9·96 (9·2); eggs (1,000m.), 43·1 (41·1).

By 1981 the main field work on state and collective farms and joint inter-farm enterprises (ploughing, sowing of grain, cotton and sugar-beet, and the harvesting of grain and silage crops) was fully mechanized; 90% of sugar-beet pulling and 68% of cotton-picking were mechanized, as was 91% of the milking.

Rural power stations in 1940 had a capacity of 265,000 kw.; in 1976, 2·9m. kw. 99·9% of collective farms and 99·9% of state farms were using electric power in 1973. In 1981 agriculture consumed 113,888m. kwh. of electric power.

Investments in agriculture in 1981 were 23,700m. rubles by the state and 10,400m. by collective farms. Total agricultural output in 1980 was valued at 122,000m. rubles.

In 1913 the total of irrigated land was 4m. hectares; in 1953, 11m.; in 1981, 18m. The total of land drained was 8·4m. hectares in 1956 and 17m. in 1981. In 1975 nearly 85m. hectares were treated from the air against weed, pest and disease.

In 1913, 188,000 tonnes of mineral fertilizers were used; in 1950, 5·3m. tonnes, and in 1981, 84m. On 1 Jan. 1982 there were 2·6m. tractors, 741,000 grain combine harvesters and 1·7m. lorries in the countryside.

An All-Union Academy of Agricultural Sciences, founded in 1929, has regional branches in Siberia and Central Asia and 310 research institutes.

Livestock (1 Jan. 1982), in 1m. head: Cattle, 115·9 (including 43·7 milch cows); pigs, 73·3; sheep, 142·4. Since 1957 the enumeration of livestock has been made on 1 Jan. instead of 1 Oct., *i.e.*, after the winter sales and slaughter for the market.

Percentage of farm production in 1980:

	All grain	Cotton	Sugar-beet	Pota-toes	Other vegetables	Meat	Milk	Eggs	Wool
State	49	34	10	17	43	37	32	61	46
Collective	50	66	90	19	34	32	38	7	32
Private [1]	1	0	0	64	33	31	30	32	22

[1] *i.e.*, household plots of collective farmers.

Forestry. On the 791·6m. hectares of forest land of the USSR, 772·2m. hectares is administered and worked by the State; the remainder, 19·4m. hectares in extent, is granted for use to the peasantry free of charge.

The largest forest areas are 515m. hectares in the Asiatic part of USSR, 51·4m. along the northern seaboard, 25·4m. in the Urals and 17·95m. in the north-west.

On 24 Oct. 1948 a plan was published for planting crop-protecting forest belts, introducing crop rotation with grasses and building of ponds and water reservoirs in the steppe and forest-steppe areas of the European part of the USSR. By the middle of 1952 some 2·6m. hectares had been planted with shelter-belt trees and 13,500 ponds and reservoirs had been built. The planting of the shelter belts in the Kamyshin-Volgograd and Byelgorod-Don areas has in the main been completed. A Volga forest belt has been planted along 1,200 km of railway. Re-afforestation was carried out on 2·5m. hectares of land in 1980.

Fisheries. The fishing catch including whaling (in 1,000 tons): 1913, 1,051; 1940, 1,422; 1960, 3,541; 1980, 9,526.

Blandon, P., *Soviet Forest Industries.* Boulder, 1983
Johnson, D. G., and Brooks, K. M., *The Prospects for Soviet Agriculture in the 1980s.* Bloomington, 1983
Shaffer, H. G., *Soviet Agriculture.* New York, 1977
Symons, L., *Russian Agriculture: A Geographic Survey.* London, 1972
Vasiliev, P., and Kozlovsky, V., *Forest Wealth of the USSR* (in Russian). Moscow, 1959

INDUSTRY AND TRADE

Industry. The organization of industry in the USSR is based on state ownership and control, administered by a separate ministry for each large industry.

Under the successive 5-year plans, large-scale modern industrial works have been constructed, namely: 1st, over 1,500; 2nd, 4,500; 3rd (up to June 1941), 3,000; wartime, 3,500 (apart from reconstruction of destroyed plants); 4th, 6,200; 5th, 3,200; 6th, 2,700; 7th (1959–65), 5,470; 8th (1966–70), 1,870; 9th (1971–75), 2,000; 10th (1976–80), 1,200.

Output of some heavy industries was as follows:

Industry	1913	1950	1960	1970	1980	1983
Iron ore (1m. tonnes)	9·2	39·7	106·2	197·3	244·7	245·0
Oil (1m. tonnes)	9·2	37·9	148·0	353·0	603·2	616·0
Electric power (1,000m. kwh.)	1·9	91·2	292·0	740·9	1,295·0	1,416·0
Coal (1m. tonnes)	29·2	261·1	509·6	624·1	716·4	716·0
Steel (1m. tonnes)	4·2	27·3	65·3	115·9	147·9	153·0
Steam and gas turbines (1,000 kw.)	5·9	2,381·0	9,200·0	16,191·0	20,300·0	15,400·0
Steel pipe (1m. tonnes)	–	2·0	5·8	12·4	18·2	18·7
Diesel locomotives (1,000 h.p.)	–	125·0	1,303·0	3,794·0	3,836·0	3,800·0
Electric locomotives (1,000 h.p.)	–	2,428·0	2,972·0	2,428·0	3,395·0	3,800·0
Lorries and buses (1,000)	–	294·4	384·8	571·9	872·3	865·7
Automobiles (1,000)	–	64·6	138·8	344·2	1,327·0	1,300·0
Tractors (1m. h.p.)	–	5·5	11·4	29·4	47·0	49·3
Sulphuric acid (1m. tonnes)	0·1	2·1	5·4	12·1	23·0	24·7
Excavators (no.)	–	3,540·0	12,290·0	30,800·0	42,000·0	41,800·0
Timber (commercial, 1m. cu. metres) [1]	27·2	161·0	261·5	298·5	277·7	271·0
Cement (1m. tonnes)	1·8	10·2	45·5	95·2	125·0	128·0

[1] Excluding collective farm production.

The process of industrial mechanization and the installation of automatic remote control is being pushed ahead. About 90% of Soviet pig-iron and 87% of the steel is produced in fully automatic furnaces. All hydro-electric plants (in terms of capacity) are fully automatic. Coal production in open-cast mines has been completely mechanized; hydraulic mining is coming into general use. Coal-cutting and underground haulage was over 99% mechanized by the end of 1962 (loading on inclined seams 56%); peat-cutting, 100%, and loading, nearly 80%; timber-cutting, 98%; haulage to loading centres, 93%, and despatch, 97%.

Output in some consumer industries was as follows:

Industry	1913	1950	1960	1970	1980	1983
Cotton fabrics (1m. linear metres)	2,672	3,899	6,387	7,482	8,063	
Woollen fabrics (1m. linear metres)	108	156	342	496	564	11,400
Silk fabrics (1m. linear metres)	43	130	810	1,241	1,632	
Leather footwear (1m. pairs)	60	203	419	679	744	745
Clocks and watches (1m.)	1	8	26	40	67	69
Radio receivers (1m.)	–	1	4	8	9	9
Television sets (1m.)	–	–	2	7	8	9
Refrigerators (1,000)	–	1	530	4,140	5,925	5,700
Paper (1,000 tonnes)	269	1,193	2,334	4,185	5,288	5,700
Meat (slaughter weight, 1m. tonnes) [1]	5	5	9	12	15	16
Butter (1,000 tonnes) [1]	104	336	737	963	1,278	1,500
Granulated sugar (1,000 tonnes)	1,363	2,523	6,360	10,221	10,127	12,400
Canned foods (1m. tins)	116	1,113	4,864	10,678	15,268	17,100

Since 1945 the cotton industry has expanded, especially in the Urals, Central Asia and Siberia. Large mills have been built at Kamyshin, Kherson, Barnaul, Engels, Alma-Ata, Chernigov and Frunze.

Trade Unions and Labour. Trade unions are organized on an industrial basis, all workers, whether manual or brain, in every branch of a given industry being eligible for membership of the same union. Collective farmers may join trade unions.

Since 1933 the trade unions have carried out the functions of the former Labour Commissariat; they control and supervise the application of labour laws, introduce new labour laws for approval by the Government and administer social insurance and factory inspection. Social insurance is non-contributory. The All-Union Congress has met at irregular intervals; the 14th Congress met in 1968, the 15th in 1972 and the 18th in 1982.

In 1944 there were 176 unions. This number was reduced by amalgamation of unions to 22 in 1958, but increased to 30 in 1977. Contributions range from 0·5 to 6% of wages. There are 167 regional and Republican Trades Councils. Membership (1983) 132m.

Chairman, Central Council of Trade Unions: S. Shalayev.

Industrial and clerical workers engaged (1983) in the whole national economy were 116·1m., 51% of them women; a further 13m. were engaged in collective-farm agriculture. The 7-hour day (6 hours for miners underground and other heavy trades) was generally in operation by the end of 1960. The average working week since 1970 has been 39·4 hours and the working day in industry 6·93 hours. The 5-day week (without reduction of total working hours) was introduced in 1967.

New 'Fundamentals of Labour Legislation', intended to codify and extend labour laws adopted in the last 40 years, were adopted by the Supreme Soviet in July 1970. They lay down, *inter alia,* the right to receive wages irrespective of the income of the enterprise concerned; the right to free vocational and advanced technical training; the right to form trade unions without state registration; the right of trade unions to participate in and supervise management and planning, labour legislation, safety regulation and housing, fixing of working conditions and wages, etc. Pensioners in Jan. 1983 numbered 52·4m., including 36m. old age. Average monthly wages in the state sector were 182 rubles in 1983.

Profsoyuzy SSSR. Dokumenty i materialy. 5 vols., Moscow, 1963–74
Sbornik postanovlenii VTsSPS. Moscow, 1960ff, quarterly
Ruble, B. A., *Soviet Trade Unions. Their Development in the 1970s.* CUP, 1981

Commerce. Retail home trade takes three forms–state, co-operative and the free market, *i.e.,* sales by individual collective-farm members and by the collective farms of their surplus products, after having fulfilled their statutory deliveries and made their regular allocations to their members.

In 1981 the consumer co-operative societies had 63m. members and did over 27% of the retail trade of the USSR. They were organized in 5,100 societies, employing about 3m. workers, with 369,000 retail shops, 90,000 catering establishments, 12,700 bakeries and 324 canneries. Their central union is affiliated to the International Co-operative Alliance. Retail trade by the State and co-operatives totalled 305,700m. rubles in 1983; by collective farm markets (agricultural produce), 8,100m. rubles. Total state and co-operative retail trade turnover represented (in comparable prices) an increase of 76% on 1970.

Foreign trade is organized as a state monopoly. Importation and exportation of goods are effected under licences issued by the Ministry for Foreign Trade and its respective departments in pursuance of a plan annually sanctioned by the Government. The right of purchasing goods for importation, and that of selling Soviet exports abroad, is vested in Trade Delegations and representatives of the appropriate state corporations in foreign countries.

There are 29 state import and export organizations, including chartering and tourist corporations (one, Vostokintorg, dealing with Mongolia, Sinkiang and Afghánistán). The Central Union of Consumers' Societies (Tsentrosoyuz) is also authorized to conduct foreign trade operations.

For foreign trade up to 1938 *see* THE STATESMAN'S YEAR-BOOK, 1951, p. 1465. The Central Statistical Department of the USSR estimates that, in comparable prices, the volume of foreign trade in 1940 was less than one-quarter that of 1913, but was in 1981, 48 times as large as in 1913. Exports in 1982 were valued at 63,165m. rubles (34,136m. to the socialist countries), and imports at 56,411m. rubles (30,816m. from the socialist countries).

Russia's imports of machinery and equipment, between 1940 and 1982, rose from 32·4 to 34·4%, ores and concentrates fell from 26·6 to 9·9%, foodstuffs rose from 14·9 to 23·7% and manufactured consumer goods rose from 1·4 to 12·7% by value; exports of fuel and electricity increased from 13·2 to 52·3% and of machinery and equipment from 2 to 12·9% by value over the same period.

Main items of exports in 1982:

Oil and oil products (1m. rubles)	25,382·8	Vegetable oil (1,000 tonnes)	113·9
Iron ore (1m. tonnes)	33·2	Tractors (1m. rubles)	252·1
Iron and rolled metal (1m. rubles)	1,614·9	Motor cars (1,000)	252·4
Paper (1,000 tonnes)	691·2	Clocks and watches (1m.)	21·7
Cotton (1,000 tonnes)	948·8	Grain (1m. rubles)	284·8

Total trade between the USSR and UK for calendar years (British Department of Trade returns, in £1,000 sterling):

	1980	1981	1982	1983
Imports to UK	422,000	426,717	645,135	728,491
Exports and re-exports from UK	449,200	408,254	355,678	445,003

Tourism. Pre-revolutionary Russia was never a country for any but the most hardy and better-off tourists, as the introductory pages of Baedeker's guide made clear. For her subjects, too, touring was no more inviting. Acute shortage of hotels and boarding-houses, poor roads, lack of ordinary services for visitors were among the least of their difficulties. These have not by any means been fully overcome: but very great efforts to meet them have been made.

	1972	1973	1974	1975
Foreign visitors to the USSR	2,316,974	2,909,158	3,446,933	3,690,751
Of whom, from non-Socialist countries	875,395	1,309,979	1,558,522	1,582,741
Soviet visitors abroad	1,973,333	2,082,385	2,224,601	2,450,087
Of whom, to non-Socialist countries	854,792	868,725	893,059	932,119

Within the USSR, tourism by Soviet citizens has been much encouraged by the trade unions, which have developed an extensive network of facilities, particularly for hikers, campers and climbers. These facilities number more than 10,000 tourist camps, 966 tourist 'bases' (supply depots for hiring equipment), and over 6,000 cabins for anglers, hunters and mountaineers. The Central Council of Trade Unions also owns or controls 137 river or seagoing ships, 120 trains and 8,000 motor coaches exclusively for tourist use.

Soviet tourists recorded by this network numbered 40,000 in 1950; 1,997,000 in 1965; 5,041,000 in 1970 and 23,915,000 in 1981.

COMMUNICATIONS

Roads. By 1940 there were over 1·5m. km of constructed roads, of which 143,000 km were suitable for motor traffic. The total length of motor roads in 1982 was 761,000 km. Road freights by lorry amounted to 859m. tonnes in 1940 and 25,900m. tonnes in 1981. Passengers carried were 590m. in 1940 and 43,691m. in 1982. In 1982, 22,200 inter-urban bus routes had a total length of 3,319,000 km.

Railways. The length of railways in Jan. 1983 was 143,300 km (1913: 58,500 km), of which 45,700 km was electrified. Diesel and electric traction now account for almost 100% of all movements, with the electrified network handling 56% of the traffic. In 1979 60% of all freight traffic and 40% of passengers went by rail (1913: 57% and 91% respectively), and railways ran 3,600,000m. tonne-km in 1983.

Operations are centred on 32 regions with headquarters at: Baku, Alma-Ata, Tyndin, Minsk, Irkutsk, Gorki, Khabarovsk, Donetsk, Chita, Tbilisi, Aktyubinsk, Novosibirsk, Kemerovo, Krasnoyarsk, Kuibyshev, Lvov, Kishinev, Moscow, Odessa, Leningrad, Riga, Saratov, Dnepropetrovsk, Sverdlovsk, Yaroslavl, Rostov-on-Don, Tashkent, Tselinograd, Voronezh, Kharkov and Chelyabinsk.

Extensive railway construction is in progress, including routes northwards from Surgut to Urengoi and Nizhe-Vartovskoye, and the great Baikal-Amur Magistral (BAM) project. This is a new main line to the east, sited well to the north of the existing Trans-Siberian route to the Pacific ports of Nakhodka and Vladivostok. It runs from Lena, on the Lena river, to Komsomolsk-on-Amur, 3,145 km distant, and will be double-track and electrified. When open throughout in 1983–84, BAM will become the principal route for export traffic to the eastern ports, easing the very heavy pressure on the Trans-Siberian line, which is only partially electrified and not double-track throughout.

BAM is the most arduous railway building project ever tackled by Soviet engineers, and the greatest drawback to development of the region has been its severe geological and climatic conditions. There is permafrost throughout the area, and winter temperatures fall to –60°C. Construction work has occupied nearly a decade, and has required over 3,200 bridges, tunnels and culverts.

Underground railways have been built in Moscow, Leningrad, Kiev, Tbilisi, Kharkov, Tashkent, Baku, Gorky and Yerevan. Others are under construction at Minsk, Novosibirsk, Omsk, Dnepropetrovsk, Kuibyshev and Sverdlovsk.

Aviation. In 1983 total length of internal airlines in the USSR was approximately 811,000 km; 109m. passengers were carried internally and externally. The Central Asian Airways in some instances provide the only means of communication across the desert and mountainous regions of the local republics. An 8,500-km air service was opened in Feb. 1941 between Moscow and Anadyr (Eastern Siberia), through Archangel, Igarka, Khatanga, Tiksi Bay and Cape Schmidt, *i.e.*, along the entire course of the Northern Sea Route. There are also other Arctic airlines, *e.g.*, Igarka-Gulf of Kozhevnikov; Igarka-Dickson Island; Yakutsk-Tiksi Bay; Yakutsk-Viluisk; Yakutsk-Verkhoiansk.

Direct air services are maintained throughout the year between Moscow and the capitals of all Soviet republics as well as London, New York, Montreal, Tōkyō, Delhi, Rangoon, Belgrade, Peking, Pyongyang, Ulan Bator, Kábul, Tirana, Paris, Warsaw, Prague, Budapest, Bucharest, Sofia, Vienna, Berlin, Helsinki, Stockholm, Copenhagen, Jakarta, Dakar and Gander. Soviet air services reached 87 countries in 1981, and 20 foreign lines have regular services to the USSR, including British Airways, KLM, SAS, Air France, SABENA, Air India, PANAM. The first Soviet airbus, the 350-seater IL-86, began flights on civil aviation routes in 1981. The

120-seater YAK-42 will gradually replace the TU-134 and AN-24 on major shorter routes.

MacDonald, H., *Aeroflot: Soviet Air Transport Since 1923.* London, 1975

Shipping. In 1977 the Soviet mercantile marine comprised 7,000 self-propelled vessels, of which 80% were built between 1957 and 1966. By May 1977 the gross cargo capacity was (including fishing vessels) 20·8m. registered tonnes (16m. tonnes dead-weight).

Freights carried were: In 1913 (present frontiers), 35·1m. tonnes; in 1940, 73·9m. tonnes; and in 1983, 606m. tonnes; 139m. passengers were carried. The Soviet share in world marine tonnage was 2% in 1960 and 6% in 1977. Deep-sea ports are under construction at Vostochny (Far East) and Grigorevsky (Black Sea) with new deep-sea wharves at Ventspils (Latvia), Murmansk and Archangel (for Arctic traffic). Archangel is kept open by icebreakers all the year round from 1979. Foreign freights in 1977 totalled 14% of all Soviet seaborne trade.

The North Sea route affords convenient communication between the European USSR and the Far East along the Soviet coast, for the produce of the basins of the Ob, Yenissei, Lena and Kolyma rivers.

The length of navigable rivers and canals in exploitation was (1983) 138,900 km, of which the length of floatable rivers is 87,000 km. There are several thousand miles of canals and other artificial waterways; among them the Baltic and White Sea Canal (235 km), the Moscow-Volga Canal (130 km). Goods turnover on inland waterways was 28,900m. tonne-km in 1913, 35,900m. in 1940, 45,900m. in 1950 and 262,400m. in 1982; freight carried rose from 35·1m. tonnes in 1913 to 604·5m. tonnes in 1982.

The Volga-Don Shipping Canal was opened for traffic in 1952. The Volga-Don waterway from Volgograd to Rostov is 540 km long, of which the Volga-Don canal comprises 101 km. The canal has transformed the section of the river from Kalach, where the Don is joined by the Volga-Don canal, to Rostov into a deep-water highway suitable for big Volga shipping. The canal links the White, Baltic, Caspian, Azov and Black Seas into a single water transport system. In Oct. 1964 the 2,430-km Baltic-Volga waterway, linking Klaipeda on the Baltic to Kakhovka at the mouth of the Dnieper and suitable for 5,000-tonne vessels, was begun. Reconstruction of the 18th-century Mariinsky canal system in north-west Russia was completed, providing a through waterway from Leningrad to Rybinsk (on the Upper Volga) and cutting the passage of freight from 18 to 2½ days.

At the end of 1977 the longest train ferry route in the world was opened between the Soviet Union and Bulgaria (Ilyichovsk-Varna).

The first section of Vostochny port, in Wrangel Bay on the Pacific coast, is completed. It will be the country's largest deep-sea port.

In 1962 a canal was completed across the Kara-Kum desert in southern Turkmenistan (replacing an earlier project for a more costly scheme across the north of the republic). The canal, from Bussag on the river Amu-Darya to Archnan, northwest of Ashkhabad, through the Murgab oasis, 900 km long, supplies water to an area exceeding 200,000 hectares, suitable for cotton, fruit, vineyards and livestock. An extension to the Caspian (500 km) is under construction: the complete system will irrigate 1m. hectares.

An irrigation canal system (250 miles), bringing water from Kakhovka on the Dnieper to the North Crimea, is nearing completion. Work to divert water from the Pechora and Vychegda rivers (flowing into the White Sea) south to the Volga is in progress. Work has begun on a 300-mile canal which will supply water from the Irtysh to Karaganda in Central Kazakhstan, irrigating over 150,000 acres; the first 37 miles were opened in 1965 and another 45 miles in Dec. 1967. Most of the 11 reservoirs required had been completed by 1 Jan. 1972. Other irrigation canals under construction are Kuibyshev (279 km long, to supply over 100,000 hectares) and Stavropol (481 km, irrigating 200,000 hectares); the second section of the latter went into commission in Nov. 1974, 14 months ahead of schedule. In Sept. 1972 the Saratov Canal (irrigating 1m. hectares) went into commission.

Post and Broadcasting. In Dec. 1982 the number of post, telegraph and telephone offices was 90,883 and of general telephones 26·4m.

The International radio-telecommunications services are operated by the Ministry of Communications of the USSR. The Great Northern Telegraph Co., Ltd, of Denmark, operates cables connecting Denmark with Leningrad, whence connexion is made by means of a trans-Siberian landline with Vladivostok. From the latter place the Great Northern Telegraph Co. owns cables connecting with Japan, China and Hong Kong. Direct radio and telephone communication with India is provided for in an agreement concluded in 1955.

The State Committee for Broadcasting and Television produces 3 programmes in Moscow, broadcasting throughout the Union. In addition the regional radio stations produce 1, 2 or 3 programmes for the republics as well as local programmes for a town or region. The foreign service from Moscow is beamed to all parts of the world, in 64 languages. Chinese has 28½ hours programme time a day. Several republics have their own foreign services. English is broadcast from Moscow, Kiev, Tashkent, Vilnius and Yerevan. There are 117 TV centres in the USSR, several of them producing more than 1 programme. In Moscow there are 4 programmes. Colour programmes are broadcast by the SECAM system. A nationwide system of space telecommunications, consisting of satellites and ground stations, takes TV broadcasts to distant parts of the country.

Number of receivers, Jan. 1980: radio, 66m.; television, 64·3m.

Cinemas and theatres (Jan. 1983). There were 142,000 permanent and 9,400 mobile cinemas. In Jan. 1983 there were 615 theatres, to which 120·9m. visits were made.

Newspapers. In 1982, 8,285 newspapers with a total daily circulation of 176m. copies were published in 57 languages of the USSR.

JUSTICE, RELIGION, EDUCATION AND WELFARE

Justice. The basis of the judicial system is the same throughout the Soviet Union, but the constituent republics have the right to introduce modifications and to make their own rules for the application of the codes of laws. The Supreme Court of the USSR is the chief court and supervising organ for all constituent republics and is elected by the Supreme Soviet of the USSR for 5 years. Supreme Courts of the Union and Autonomous Republics are elected by the Supreme Soviets of these republics, and Territorial, Regional and Area Courts by the respective Soviets, each for a term of 5 years. At the lowest level are the People's Courts, which are elected directly by the population.

Court proceedings are conducted in the local language with full interpreting facilities as required. All cases are heard in public, unless otherwise provided for by law, and the accused is guaranteed the right of defence.

Laws establishing common principles of legislation in various fields are adopted by the Supreme Soviet and are then enacted in more specific form and implemented by subordinate levels of state and judicial authority.

The Law Courts are divided into People's Courts and higher courts. The People's Courts consist of the People's Judge and 2 Assessors, and their function is to examine, as the first instance, most of the civil and criminal cases, except the more important ones, some of which are tried at the Regional Court, and those of the highest importance at the Supreme Court. The Regional Courts supervise the activities of the People's Courts and also act as Courts of Appeal from the decisions of the People's Court. Special chambers of the higher courts deal with offences committed in the Army and the public transport services.

People's Judges and Assessors, who serve on a rota basis, are elected directly by the citizens of each constituency: judges for 5 years, assessors for 2½. Should a judge be found not to perform his duties conscientiously and in accordance with the mandate of the people, he may be recalled by his electors.

The People's Assessors are called upon for duty for 2 weeks in a year. The People's Assessors for the Regional Court must have had at least 2 years' experience in public or trade-union work. The list of Assessors for the Supreme Court is drawn up by the Supreme Soviet of the republic.

The Labour Session of the People's Court supervises the regulations relating to the working conditions and the protection of labour and gives decisions on conflicts arising between managements and employees, or the violation of regulations.

Disputes between State institutions must be referred to an arbitration commission. Disputes between Soviet State institutions and foreign business firms may be referred by agreement to a Foreign Trade Arbitration Commission of the All-Union Chamber of Commerce.

The Procurator-General of the USSR is appointed for 5 years by the Supreme Soviet. All procurators of the republics, autonomous republics and autonomous regions are appointed by the Procurator-General of the USSR for a term of 5 years. The procurators supervise the correct application of the law by all state organs, and have special responsibility for the observance of the law in places of detention. The procurators of the Union republics are subordinate to the Procurator-General of the USSR, whose duty it is to see that acts of all institutions of the USSR are legal, that the law is correctly interpreted and uniformly applied; he has to participate in important cases in the capacity of State Prosecutor.

Capital punishment was abolished on 26 May 1947, but was restored on 12 Jan. 1950 for treason, espionage and sabotage, on 7 May 1954 for certain categories of murder, in Dec. 1958 for terrorism and banditry, on 7 May 1961 for embezzlement of public property, counterfeiting and attack on prison warders and, in particular circumstances, for attacks on the police and public order volunteers and for rape (15 Feb. 1962) and for accepting bribes (20 Feb. 1962).

In view of criminal abuses, extending over many years, discovered in the security system, the powers of administrative trial and exile previously vested in the security authorities (MVD) were abolished in 1953; accelerated procedures for trial on charges of high treason, espionage, wrecking, etc., by the Supreme Court were abolished in 1955; and extensive powers of protection of persons under arrest or serving prison terms were vested in the Procurator-General's Office (1955). Supervisory commissions, composed of representatives of trade unions, youth organizations and local authorities, were set up in 1956 to inspect places of detention.

Further reforms of the civil and criminal codes were decreed on 25 Dec. 1958. Thereby the age of criminal responsibility has been raised from 14 to 16 years; deportation and banishment have been abolished; a presumption of innocence is not accepted, but the burden of proof of guilt has been placed upon the prosecutor. Secret trials and the charge of 'enemy of the people' have been abolished. Articles 70 and 190 of the Criminal Code, which deal with 'anti-Soviet agitation and propaganda' and 'crimes against the system of administration' respectively, have however been widely used against political dissidents in more recent years.

Butler, W. E., *The Soviet Legal System. Selected Contemporary Legislation and Documents.* New York, 1978.—*Soviet Law.* London, 1983
Hazard, J., Butler, W. E. and Maggs, P., *The Soviet Legal System.* 3rd ed., New York, 1977
Simons, W. B., (ed.), *The Soviet Codes of Law.* Alphen aan den Rijn, 1980

Religion. With the Revolution the Orthodox Church lost its position as the dominant religion and all religions were placed on an equal footing. Article 52 of the 1977 Soviet Constitution reads as follows: 'Citizens of the USSR are guaranteed freedom of conscience, that is, the right to profess or not to profess any religion, and to conduct religious worship or atheistic propaganda. Incitement of hostility or hatred on religious grounds is prohibited. In the USSR the church is separated from the state, and school from the church.'

By decree of 2 Feb. 1918 the Orthodox Church was disestablished; its property, together with that of all other denominations, was nationalized. The congregations themselves have to maintain their churches and clergy, regardless of confession or denomination. A minimum of 20 persons may request and receive the use of a church building, free of charge, except for maintenance, insurance, land taxes, etc. About two-thirds of all the churches have been closed since 1917, but about 20,000 churches and 18 religious seminaries were reported to be in operation in 1983. Religious instruction may be given in private, but otherwise only in church classes. The income of religious communities is not subject to taxation. Religious instruction in classes for persons under 18 is forbidden. The state supplies paper and printing facilities to all denominations for producing the Bible, the Koran, prayer books, missals, etc.

Relations between the religious communities of all creeds and the Government are maintained through a Council for Religious Affairs which is attached to the Council of Ministers of the USSR. (*Chairman*, V. A. Kuroyedov).

The Russian Orthodox Church, represented by the Patriarchate of Moscow, had, in 1983, about 30m. regular worshippers. There are still many Old Believers, whose schism from the Orthodox Church dates from the 17th century. The Russian Church is headed by the Patriarch of Moscow and All Russia, assisted by the Holy Synod, which has 7 members–the Patriarch himself and the Metropolitans of Krutitsy and Kolomna (Moscow), Leningrad and Kiev *ex officio*, and 3 bishops alternating for 6 months in order of seniority from the 3 regions forming the Moscow Patriarchate. The Patriarchate of Moscow maintains jurisdiction over a few parishes of Russian Orthodox abroad, at Tehrán, Jerusalem, German Democratic Republic, France (1 archbishop), England, North and South America (2 bishops). There are 19 monasteries and nunneries, and 6 Orthodox academies and seminaries with 10 journals.

After the Russian Orthodox Church the next Christian community in importance are the Armenians; their Catholicos (Patriarch), whose seat is at Etchmiadzin, is head of all the Armenian (Gregorian) communities throughout the world. There is an Armenian Orthodox academy and a seminary.

The Georgian Orthodox Church has its own organization under a Catholicos (Patriarch) who is resident in Tbilisi and who directs the church's seminary in Mtskheta.

Protestantism is represented chiefly by the Evangelical Christian Baptists, with over 512,000 baptized adult members and some 5,000 churches; the Lutherans are concentrated mainly in the Baltic States (350,000 in Estonia, 600,000 in Latvia), the Reformed in the Transcarpathian Region of the Ukraine (70,000). Both Baptists and Lutherans conduct theological courses. The Methodist Church functions in Estonia.

The Roman Catholics are most numerous in Lithuania and the western Ukraine. There are 2 Roman Catholic arch-episcopates and 4 episcopates in Lithuania with 630 churches and a seminary at Kaunas providing a 5-year course. In 1946 some 3·5m. Uniates in the USSR were compelled to withdraw their allegiance to Rome and came under the jurisdiction of the Orthodox Patriarchate in Moscow. In Latvia there are an arch-episcopate and 1 episcopate (Riga and Liepaja) of the Roman Catholic Church.

The Moslems (estimate 30m. members, mainly Sunnis), are divided into 4 administrative regions, 3 of them (Central Asia and Kazakhstan, European Russia and Siberia, Northern Caucasus) headed by a Mufti; the largest (Transcaucasia, with its centre at Baku) by a Sheikh-ul-Islam.

There is a Moslem academy and a madrasah in Central Asia. Several editions of the Koran have appeared in recent years.

There are various Jewish communities, the chief being in Moscow and Kiev. Large synagogues maintain bakeries for producing unleavened bread. There is a Jewish Yeshiva in Moscow (established 1956) and 180 synagogues as well as several dozen minyans. The Central Buddhist Council of the USSR is headed by a Lama with communities in Buryatia, Tuva, Kalmykia and in the national (minority) areas of the Chita and Irkutsk regions.

O religii i tserkvi: sbornik vazhneishikh vyskazivanii klassikov Marksizma-Leninizma, dokumentov KPSS i sovetskogo gosudarstva 2nd ed., Moscow, 1981
Bordeaux, M., *Opium of the People. The Christian Religion in the USSR.* London, 1965.–*Religious Ferment in Russia.* London, 1968
Curtiss, J. S., *The Russian Church and the Soviet State, 1917–50.* New York, 1953
Kochan, L., (ed.), *Jews in Soviet Russia since 1917.* 3rd ed., Oxford, 1977
Kolarz, W., *Religion in the Soviet Union.* London, 1961
Kuroedov, V. A., *Religiya i tserkov' v sovetskom gosudarstve.* Moscow, 1981
Lane, C., *Christian Religion in the Soviet Union.* London, 1978

Education. Education is free and compulsory from 7 to 16/17. Co-education was reintroduced in all schools on 1 Sept. 1954. There are 2 types of general schools–with an 8-year or a 10-year curriculum; the minimum school-leaving age is now 17. Pupils who leave an 8-year school continue their education at either a 10-year school or a vocational training school. A 10-year school pupil may also transfer to vocational school after the 8th year. Vocational school pupils must reach the same standard of general education as those at 10-year general schools, and so stay on at school longer. Instruction is given in more than 100 languages.

In 1982–83 there were 142,000 primary and secondary schools. Pupils in general educational schools numbered 44·3m. (9·1m. of them in the ninth and tenth forms) and the teachers 2·7m. Those at vocational and specialized technical secondary schools numbered 9·8m.

At the end of 1940 labour reserve schools (both vocational and industrial) were organized, admitting applicants from 14 to 17 years of age. From 1959 onwards these and other technical schools were reorganized as town and rural vocational and technical schools, at which pupils stay for a year longer than at general schools, combining completion of general secondary education with vocational training. From 1940 to 1977 inclusive they trained 35m. skilled workers. In 1978, 2·3m. graduated from such schools, including 628,000 for agriculture; 600,000 agricultural mechanics were trained in state and collective farms. Over 4,300 vocational training schools existed in 1981, training 2·17m. boys and girls, all of whom receive a full secondary education. In 1983, 15·5m. children of from 3 to 7 years of age attended kindergartens. Children in boarding schools numbered over 800,000 in 1972–73.

In 1982–83 there were 4,418 technical colleges with 4·5m. students, and 891 universities, institutes and other places of higher education, with 5·3m. students (including 1·6m. taking correspondence or evening courses). Among the 65 university towns are: Moscow, Leningrad, Kharkov, Odessa, Tartu, Kazan, Saratov, Tomsk, Kiev, Sverdlovsk, Tbilisi, Alma-Ata, Tashkent, Minsk, Gorky and Vladivostok.

On 1 Jan. 1983 there were 1·43m. scientific workers in places of higher education, research institutes and Academies of Sciences. There are 33,000 foreign students from 130 countries.

The Academy of Sciences of the USSR had 780 members and corresponding members. Total learned institutions under the USSR Academy of Sciences number 244, with 49,523 scientific staff. Fourteen of the Union Republics have their own Academies of Sciences, with scientific staff numbering 49,079. There are also Siberian, Far Eastern and other branches of the USSR Academy. On 1 Jan. 1981 there were 96,820 post-graduate students in Academy and other higher educational institutions, 59% studying on a part-time basis.

The Academy of Pedagogical Sciences had 14 research institutes with 1,640 staff.

In 1982 over 103m. people were studying at schools, colleges and training or correspondence courses. 110 per 1,000 of the employed population had a higher education (1939, 13; 1959, 33).

Grant, N., *Soviet Education*. 4th ed., Harmondsworth, 1979
Matthews, M., *Education in the Soviet Union*. London, 1982

Health and Social Security. All health services are free of charge although payment is required for medicines; but private practice exists. The health service is administered by the Ministry of Health of the USSR, which supervises the work of the Health Ministries of the Union Republics and the Autonomous Republics.

In 1944 an Academy of Medical Sciences was formed; it has under its direct control 42 research institutes. In all, there were, in 1976, 393 medical research institutions with 70,000 research staff. Smallpox, trachoma and malaria have been virtually eliminated.

In 1981–82, 98 institutes and medical faculties had a total of 383,800 students taking a 6-year course.

In Dec. 1982 there were 23,100 civil hospitals with 3·4m. beds. There were 837,000 infants in day nurseries. 1,071,200 doctors (including dentists) were in the health service. All confinements in towns and 75% in the country were in hospital.

There were 37,000 outpatients' clinics, apart from the 25,800 women's consultation centres and children's clinics.

The death-rate in the USSR in 1982 was 10·1 per 1,000, and the birth rate 18·9 per 1,000. Infant death rate was 27·9 (per 1,000 live births) in 1974, compared with

273 in 1913, 184 in 1940 and 81 in 1950. Average expectation of life, 70 (1913, 32).

Social insurance is administered by the trade unions, through social insurance councils elected in places of work and social insurance sub-committees of factory committees: about 5m. volunteers are engaged in this work. 41·9m. people went to holiday sanatoria or rest homes in 1981. 51·4m. people, including 10·8m. collective farmers, were receiving state pensions in Jan. 1982; of these, 9·5m. were old-age pensioners.

Total number of holiday sanatoria providing toning-up treatment at resorts in 1981 was 2,343, with accommodation for 559,000; in addition, there were 2,669 overnight sanatoria at large plants for treatment of mild disorders without absence from work, accommodating 222,000. There were also 1,204 trade union-managed holiday hotels with a capacity of 382,000, holidays being partly or wholly at trade unions' expense.

State expenditure (in 1m. new rubles) on health services proper, 1960, 4,800; 1970, 9,300; 1975, 11,500; 1980, 14,800; 1981, 15,200.

Between 1950 and 1977 56,748,000 apartments (in towns) and houses (in rural areas) were built. In 1983, 2m. apartments and houses were built. Rents in the USSR have not been increased since 1928 and in 1982 account for about 3% of the expenditure of an average worker's family. By the end of 1982, 80% of all housing had a gas supply installed, 91% had running water, 88% had central heating and 80% of the urban population lived in individual rather than communal apartments. 56% of total housing space is publicly and 44% is privately owned.

DIPLOMATIC REPRESENTATIVES

Of the USSR in Great Britain (13 Kensington Palace Gdns., London, W8 4QX)
Ambassador: Viktor I. Popov.

Of Great Britain in the USSR (Naberezhnaya Morisa Toreza 14, Moscow 72)
Ambassador: Sir Iain Sutherland, KCMG.

Of the USSR in the USA (1125-16th St., NW, Washington, D.C., 20036)
Ambassador: Anatoly F. Dobrynin.

Of the USA in the USSR (Ulitsa Chaikovskogo 19, Moscow)
Ambassador: Arthur A. Hartman.

Of the USSR to the United Nations
Ambassador: Oleg Aleksandrovich Troyanovsky.

Books of Reference

Narodnoye Khozyaistvo SSSR 1922–1982 (National Economy of the USSR). Jubilee Statistical Yearbook. Moscow, 1982
Pravda (Truth). Daily organ of the Central Committee of the Communist Party
Izvestiya (News). Daily organ of the Presidium of the Supreme Soviet of the USSR
Vedomosti Verkhovnovo Soveta. Bulletin of the Supreme Soviet of the USSR in the languages of the 15 republics; published weekly
Sovetskaya Torgovlya. Thrice-weekly publication of the Ministry of Trade of the USSR
Planovoye Khoziaistvo. Monthly. Moscow
Voprosy Torgovli. A monthly journal published by the Ministry of Trade of the USSR
Vneshnaya Torgovlya. Published by the Ministry for Foreign Trade. Monthly. Moscow
Trud. The daily organ of the All-Union Central Council of Trade Unions
Professionalnye Soyuzy. A trade union fortnightly. Moscow
Kommunist. A fortnightly organ of the Communist Party of the Soviet Union
Finansy i Khozyaistvo. A weekly publication of the Ministry for Finance
Bolshaya Sovetskaya Entsiklopedia. 65 vols. Moscow, 1926–47; 2nd ed., 51 vols. Moscow, 1949–58; 3rd ed., Moscow, 1959–78; annual supplement (*Yezhegodnik*)
Soviet Union. A monthly pictorial. Moscow. (In English)
Soviet Import-Export Dictionary (in Russian, with English, etc., terms). Moscow, 1952
Soviet Studies; A Quarterly Review. Ed. R. A. Clarke. Glasgow, quarterly.
The Current Digest of the Soviet Press. Published by Joint Committee on Slavic Studies. Weekly. Washington, D.C.
Baylis, J., and Segal, G., (eds.) *Soviet Strategy.* London, 1981
Beloff, M., *The Foreign Policy of Soviet Russia, 1929–41.* 2 vols. 1947–49.–*Soviet Policy in the Far East.* Oxford, 1953.–*Soviet Policy in Asia, 1944–52.* Oxford, 1953

Brown, A., and Kaser, M., *The Soviet Union Since the Fall of Krushchev*. London, 2nd ed. 1978.—*Soviet Policy for the 1980s*. London, 1982

Byrnes, J. F. (ed.), *After Brezhnev. Sources of Soviet Conduct in the 1980s*. London, 1983

Carr, E. H., *A History of Soviet Russia*. 14 vols. London, 1951–78

Clarke, R. A., and Matko, D. J. I., (eds.), *Soviet Economic Facts 1917–80*. London, 1983

Degras, J. (compiler), *Soviet Documents on Foreign Policy, 1917–41*. 3 vols. London, 1948–52

Deutscher, I., *Trotsky*. 3 vols. OUP, 1954 ff.

Edmonds, R., *Soviet Foreign Policy: the Brezhnev Years*. Oxford, 1983

Falla, P. S., *The Oxford English-Russian Dictionary*. OUP, 1984

Fitzsimmons, T., and others, *USSR; Its People, Its Society, Its Culture*. New Haven, 1960

Galperin, I. R., *New English-Russian Dictionary*. 2 vols. Moscow, 1972

Gruzinov, V. F., *The USSR's Management of Foreign Trade*. London, 1980

Hammond, T. T. (ed.), *Soviet Foreign Relations and World Communism: A Selected Bibliography*. Princeton, 1965

Hough, J. F. and Fainsod, M., *How the Soviet Union is Governed*. Rev. ed. Harvard Univ. Press, 1979

Humphrey, C., *Karl Marx Collective: Economy, Society and Religion in a Siberian Collective Farm*. CUP, 1983

Jones, D. L., *Books in English in the Soviet Union 1917–73: A Bibliography*. London and New York, 1975

Kaiser, R. G., *Russia: The People and the Power*. London, 1976

Kelly, D. R., (ed.), *Soviet Politics in the Brezhnev Era*. London, 1980

Lenin, V. I., *Collected Works*. 45 vols. London, 1960–70

McCauley, M., *The Soviet Union since 1917*. London, 1981

Nove, A., *The Soviet Economic System*. London, 1977

Pares, Sir B., *A History of Russia*. London, 1962

Paxton, J., *Companion to Russian History*. London and New Nork, 1984

Preobrazhensky, A. G., *Etymological Dictionary of the Russian Language*. Columbia Univ. Press, 1951

Riasanovsky, N. V., *A History of Russia*. 3rd ed. OUP, 1977

Shabad, T., and Mote, V.L., *Gateway to Siberian Resources (The BAM)*. New York and London, 1977

Schapiro, L., and Godson, J., *The Soviet Worker*. London, 1981

Slusser, R. M., and Triska, J. F., *A Calendar of Soviet Treaties, 1917–57*. Stanford Univ. Press, 1959

Smirnitsky, A. I. (ed.), *Russko-angliiskii slovar*. 4th ed. Moscow 1959

Stalin, J. V., *Collected Works*. 13 vols. London, 1952–55

Thompson, A., *Russia/USSR: A Selective Annotated Bibliography of Books in English*. Oxford and Santa Barbara, 1979

Treadgold, D. W., *Twentieth Century Russia*. 5th ed. Boston, 1981

Utechin, S. V. (ed.), *Everyman's Concise Encyclopaedia of Russia*. London, 1961

Vernadsky, G., *A History of Russia*. 4th ed. Yale Univ. Press, 1954

Wheeler, M., *The Oxford Russian-English Dictionary*. OUP, 3rd ed., 1984

RUSSIAN SOVIET FEDERAL SOCIALIST REPUBLIC (RSFSR)

Rossiiskaya Sovietskaya Federativnaya Sotsialisticheskaya Respublika

AREA AND POPULATION. The RSFSR occupies over 76% of the total area of the USSR stretching from the Far North to the Black Sea in the south and from the Far East to Kaliningrad in the west. 82·6% of its population in Jan. 1979 were Russians, the rest being 38 national minorities such as the Tatars, Ukrainians, Jews, Mordovians, Chuvashis, Bashkirs, Poles, Germans, Udmurts, Buryats, Mari, Yakuts and Ossetians. The 2 principal cities are Moscow, the capital, with a population (Jan. 1983) of 8·4m. (without suburbs, 8,202,000) and Leningrad, the second capital, 4,779,000 (without suburbs, 4,255,000). Among other important large towns are Gorky, Rostov-on-Don, Volgograd, Sverdlovsk, Novosibirsk, Chelyabinsk, Kazan, Omsk and Kuibyshev. Population, 1982, 141,012,000.

The RSFSR contains great mineral resources: iron ore in the Urals, the Kerch Peninsula and Siberia; coal in the Kuznetz Basin, Eastern Siberia, Urals and the sub-Moscow Basin; oil in the Urals, Azov-Black Sea area, Bashkiria, and West

Siberia. It also has abundant deposits of gold, platinum, copper, zinc, lead, tin and rare metals.

The RSFSR produces about 70% of the total industrial and agricultural output of the Soviet Union. Industrial and office workers averaged 66·2m. in 1981.

CONSTITUTION AND GOVERNMENT. The RSFSR adopted its present constitution at a meeting of the Supreme Soviet in April 1978, following 330,000 town and country meetings in which 25m. citizens took part.

Chairman, Presidium of the Supreme Soviet: M. A. Yasnov.
Chairman, Council of Ministers: V. I. Vorotnikov.
Foreign Minister: F. E. Titov.

The RSFSR consists of:

(1) *Territories:* Altai, Khabarovsk, Krasnodar, Krasnoyarsk, Primorye, Stavropol.

(2) *Regions:* Amur, Archangel, Astrakhan, Belgorod, Briansk, Chelyabinsk, Chita, Gorky, Irkutsk, Ivanovo, Kaluga, Kalinin, Kaliningrad, Kamchatka, Kemerovo, Kirov, Kostroma, Kuibyshev, Kurgan, Kursk, Leningrad, Lipetsk, Magadan, Moscow, Murmansk, Novgorod, Novosibirsk, Omsk, Orel, Orenburg, Penza, Perm, Pskov, Rostov, Ryazan, Sakhalin, Saratov, Smolensk, Sverdlovsk, Tambov, Tomsk, Tula, Tyumen, Ulyanovsk, Vladimir, Volgograd, Vologda, Voronezh, Yaroslavl.

(3) *Autonomous Soviet Republics:* Bashkir, Buryat, Checheno-Ingush, Chuvash, Daghestan, Kabardino-Balkar, Kalmyk, Karelian, Komi, Mari, Mordovian, North Ossetia, Karachayevo-Cherkess, Tartar, Tuva, Udmurt, Yakut.

(4) *Autonomous Regions:* Adygei, Karachai-Circassian, Gorno-Altai, Jewish, Khakass.

(5) *Autonomous Areas:* Aginsky-Buryat, Chukot, Evenki, Khanty-Mansi, Komi-Permyak, Koryak, Nenetz, Taimyr (Dolgano-Nenetz), Ust-Ordynsky-Buryat, Yamalo-Nenetz.

The Supreme Soviet, elected in Feb. 1980, consisted of 975 deputies (1 per 150,000 population); 650 were Communists, 341 women, 591 workers and collective farmers.

On 20 June 1982, 1,139,925 deputies were elected to local authorities; 578,461 (50·7%) were women, 658,241 (57·7%) non-Party and 773,073 (67·8%) industrial workers and collective farmers.

FINANCE. Revenue and expenditure balanced as follows (in 1m. rubles): 1982, 67,205; 1984 (estimate), 88,855. These figures, and those for the other 14 Union Republics, include grants from the Union Budget.

COMMUNICATIONS. Length of railways on 1 Jan. 1982 was 83,311 km, inland waterways, 126,000 km, hard-surface motor roads, 448,200 km.

Newspapers. In 1981 there were 4,436 newspapers, 4,132 of them in Russian. Daily circulation of Russian-language newspapers, 118·8m., other languages, 3m.

EDUCATION. In 1981–82 there were 20·1m. pupils in primary and secondary schools; 3,067,200 students in 499 higher educational establishments (including correspondence students) and 2,587,200 students in 2,509 technical colleges of all kinds (including correspondence students). There were 8·4m. children attending pre-school institutions. There were, on 1 Jan. 1982, 963,400 scientific staff in over 3,000 learned and scientific institutions.

In 1957 a Siberian branch of the Academy of Sciences was organized, in charge of all scientific research institutions from the Urals to the Pacific.

There is an Academy of Municipal Economy (with 5 research institutions and a staff of 437).

HEALTH. Doctors at the end of 1981 numbered 579,900, and hospital beds 1·8m. (133,400 in 1913 and 482,000 in 1940).

BASHKIR AUTONOMOUS SOVIET SOCIALIST REPUBLIC

Area 143,600 sq. km (55,430 sq. miles), population (Jan. 1983) 3·85m. Capital, Ufa. Bashkiria was annexed to Russia in 1557. It was constituted as an Autonomous Soviet Republic on 23 March 1919. Population, census 1979, included 24·3% Bashkirians, 40·3% Russians, 24·5% Tatars, and 3·2% Chuvashes.

280 deputies were elected on 24 Feb. 1980, 109 of them women.

In 1979–80 there were over 5,000 schools with 746,000 pupils. There is a state university and a branch of the USSR Academy of Sciences with 8 learned institutions (511 research workers). There were 126,000 students in technical colleges and higher schools.

In Jan. 1979 there were 11,400 doctors and 46,205 hospital beds.

There are expanding chemical, coal, steel, electrical engineering, timber and paper industries. There were 631 collective farms and 160 state farms in 1977. Crop area was 4,573,000 hectares. Bashkiria is a major oil producer in USSR.

BURIAT AUTONOMOUS SOVIET SOCIALIST REPUBLIC

Area is 351,300 sq. km (135,650 sq. miles). The Buriat Republic, situated to the south of the Yakut Republic, adopted the Soviet system 1 March 1920. This area was penetrated by the Russians in the 17th century and finally annexed from China by the treaties of Nerchinsk (1689) and Kyakhta (1727). The population (Jan. 1981) was 929,000. Capital, Ulan-Udé. The name of the republic was changed from 'Buriat-Mongol' on 7 July 1958. The population (1979 census) includes 23% Buriats and 72% Russians. Population, 1983, 970,000.

170 deputies were elected on 24 Feb. 1980, 59 of them women.

The main industries are coal, timber, building materials, fisheries, sheep and cattle farming. In 1977 there were 100 state and 59 collective farms. Crop area was 888,700 hectares. Gold, molybdenum and wolfram are mined.

In 1979–80 there were over 700 schools with 157,000 pupils, 16 technical colleges with 219,000 students and 2 higher educational institutions with 22,400 students. A branch of the Siberian Department of the Academy of Sciences had 4 learned institutions with 281 research workers.

At the end of 1979 there were 2,700 doctors and (1978) 11,102 hospital beds.

CHECHENO-INGUSH AUTONOMOUS SOVIET SOCIALIST REPUBLIC

Area, 19,300 sq. km (7,350 sq. miles); population (Jan. 1983), 1·19m. Capital, Grozny. After 70 years of almost continuous fighting, the Chechens and Ingushes were conquered by Russia in the late 1850s. In 1918 each nationality separately established its 'National Soviet' within the Terek Autonomous Republic, and in 1920 (after the Civil War) were constituted areas within the Mountain Republic. The Chechens separated out as an Autonomous Region on 30 Nov. 1922 and the Ingushes on 7 July 1924. In Jan. 1934 the two regions were united, and on 5 Dec. 1936 constituted as an Autonomous Republic. This was dissolved in 1944, but reconstituted on 9 Jan. 1957: 232,000 Chechens and Ingushes returned to their homes in the next 2 years. The population (1979 census) includes 52·9% Chechens, 11·7% Ingushes, and 29·1% Russians.

175 deputies were elected on 24 Feb. 1980, 95 of them women.

The republic has one of the major Soviet oilfields: also a number of large engineering works, chemical factories, building materials works and food canneries. There is an expanding timber, woodworking and furniture industry. In 1977–78 there were 100 state and 45 collective farms. Crop area was 460,400 hectares.

There were, in 1979–80, 534 schools with 259,000 pupils, 12 technical colleges with 14,400 students and 2 places of higher education with 12,100 students. In 1977 there were 75 hospitals, 2,900 (1980) doctors and 11,210 hospital beds.

CHUVASH AUTONOMOUS SOVIET SOCIALIST REPUBLIC

Area, 18,300 sq. km (7,064 sq. miles); population (Jan. 1983), 1,312,000. Capital, Cheboksary. The territory was annexed by Russia in the middle of the 16th century. On 24 June 1920 it was constituted as an Autonomous Region, and on 21 April 1925 as an Autonomous Republic. The population (1979 census) includes Chuvashes (68·4%), Russians (26%), Tatars (2·9%) and Mordovians (1·6%). 200 deputies were elected on 24 Feb. 1980, 79 of them women.

Like most of the Autonomous Republics, Chuvashia before 1914 was a region of primitive agriculture with a certain development of the timber industry. Today it has several big railway repair works, an expanding electrical and other engineering industries, building materials, chemicals, textiles and food industries; timber felling and haulage are largely mechanized. In 1977 there were 210 collective farms and 96 state farms. Grain crops account for nearly two-thirds of all sowings and fodder crops for nearly a quarter. Fruit and wine-growing are a developing branch of agriculture. Crop area was 829,300 hectares.

In 1979–80 there were 254,200 pupils at school, 24,500 students at technical colleges and 14,300 students undertaking higher education. There were 2,901 doctors and 13,950 hospital beds.

DAGESTAN AUTONOMOUS SOVIET SOCIALIST REPUBLIC

Area, 50,300 sq. km (19,416 sq. miles); population (Jan. 1983), 1·7m. Capital, Makhachkala. Over 30 nationalities inhabit this republic apart from Russians (11·6% at 1979 census); the most numerous are the Avartsy (25·7%), Dargintsy (15·2%), Lezginy (11·6%), Kumyki (12·4%), Laki (5·1%), Tabasarany (4·4%) and Azerbaidjanis (4%). Annexed from Persia in 1723, Dagestan was constituted an Autonomous Republic on 20 Jan. 1921. 210 deputies were elected on 24 Feb. 1980, 82 of them women.

There are large engineering, oil, chemical, woodworking, textile, food and other light industries. Agriculture is very varied, ranging from wheat to grapes, with sheep farming and cattle breeding; in 1977 there were 311 collective farms and 233 state farms. Crop area was 413,900 hectares. A chain of power stations is under construction in the Sulak River (total capacity 2·5m. kw.).

In 1977–78 there were 1,576 schools with 475,900 pupils, 33,800 technical students (1979–80) and 4 higher education establishments with 23,400 students; and a branch of the USSR Academy of Sciences with 4 learned institutions (373 research workers). Doctors numbered 5,300 and hospital beds 17,300.

KABARDINO-BALKAR AUTONOMOUS SOVIET SOCIALIST REPUBLIC

Area, 12,500 sq. km (4,825 sq. miles); population (Jan. 1983) 702,000. Capital, Nalchik. Kabarda was annexed to Russia in 1557. The republic was constituted on 5 Dec. 1936. Population (1979 census) includes Kabardinians (45·6%), Balkars (9%), Russians (35·1%). 160 deputies were elected on 24 Feb. 1980, 70 of them women.

Main industries are ore-mining, timber, engineering, coal, food processing, timber and light industries, building materials. Grain, livestock breeding, dairy farming and wine-growing are the principal branches of agriculture. There were, in 1977, 54 state and 74 collective farms.

In 1979–80 there were 250 schools with 144,000 pupils, 11,600 students in 11 technical colleges and 8,600 students receiving higher education; 2,500 doctors and 7,530 hospital beds.

KALMYK AUTONOMOUS SOVIET SOCIALIST REPUBLIC

Area, 75,900 sq. km (29,300 sq. miles); population (Jan. 1983), 310,000. Capital, Elista (64,000). The population (1979 census) includes 41·5% Kalmyks, 42·6% Russians, 6·6% Kazakhs, Chechens and Dagestanis.

The Kalmyks migrated from western China to Russia (Nogai Steppe) in the early 17th century. The territory was constituted an Autonomous Region on 4 Nov. 1920, and an Autonomous Republic on 22 Oct. 1935; this was dissolved in 1943. On 9 Jan. 1957 it was reconstituted as an Autonomous Region and on 29 July 1958 as an Autonomous Republic once more.

130 deputies were elected on 24 Feb. 1980, 54 of them women.

Main industries are fishing, canning and building materials. Cattle breeding and irrigated farming (mainly fodder crops) are the principal branches of agriculture. In 1977 there were 90 state and 23 collective farms. Crop area was 831,400 hectares.

In 1979–80 there were 60,500 pupils in 242 schools, 7,902 students in technical colleges and 4,800 in higher education; 858 doctors and 4,355 hospital beds.

KARELIAN AUTONOMOUS SOVIET SOCIALIST REPUBLIC

HISTORY. Before 1917, Karelia (then known as the Olonets Province) was noted chiefly as a place of exile for political and other prisoners.

After the November Revolution of 1917, Karelia formed part of the RSFSR. In June 1920 a Karelian Labour Commune was formed and in July 1923 this was transformed into the Karelian Autonomous Soviet Socialist Republic (one of the autonomous republics of the RSFSR). On 31 March 1940, after the Soviet–Finnish war. practically all the territory (with the exception of a small section in the neighbourhood of the Leningrad area) which had been ceded by Finland to the USSR was added to Karelia and the Karelian Autonomous Republic was transformed into the Karelo-Finnish Soviet Socialist Republic as the 12th republic of the USSR. In 1946, however, the southern part of the republic, including its whole seaboard and the town of Viipuri (Vyborg) and Keksholm, was attached to the RSFSR and in 1956 the republic reverted to ASSR status with the RSFSR.

AREA AND POPULATION. The Karelian Autonomous Republic, capital Petrozavodsk, covers an area of 172,400 sq. km, with a population of 759,000 (Jan. 1983). Karelians represent 11·1% of the population, Russians, 71·3%, Belorussians 8·1%, Ukrainians 3·2%, Finns 2·7% (1979 census).

150 deputies were elected on 24 Feb. 1980, 53 of them women.

NATURAL RESOURCES. Karelia is chiefly noted for its wealth of timber, some 70% of its territory being forest land. It is also rich in other natural resources, having large deposits of diabase, spar, quartz, marble, granite, zinc, lead, silver, copper, molybdenum, tin, baryta, iron ore, etc. Karelia takes first place in the USSR for the production of mica. It has 43,643 lakes, which, as well as its rivers, are rich in fish.

Agriculture. There were 10 collective fisheries and 60 state farms in 1976. Livestock on 1 Jan. 1980 included 93,400 cattle, 40,000 pigs, 100,000 sheep and goats.

INDUSTRY. The republic has 25 large-scale enterprises, such as timber-mills, paper-cellulose works, mica, chemical plants, power stations and furniture factories. Output, 1977: Timber, 12·3m. cu. metres; paper and cellulose, 1,733,700 tonnes; power, 2,796m. kwh.; canned fish, 12·3m. tins.

The construction of the White Sea–Baltic Canal had a powerful influence on the economic development of Karelia. New refrigerating plants, cellulose factories and timber industry equipment began working in 1970.

COMMUNICATIONS. A railway between Petrozavodsk and Suoyarvi connects the capital and the Murmansk Railway with the main railway line Sortavala–Vyborg. A railway line was also laid between Kandalaksha and Kuolayarvi. Length of track, 1,600 km.

EDUCATION. In 1979–80 there were 115,600 pupils in 747 schools. There were 10,200 students in 3 places of higher education and 10,200 in 10 technical colleges.

There are in Petrozavodsk a university (4,028 full-time students, 2,036 taking correspondence courses and 622 evening students in 1971), 2 other higher institutes and a teachers' training college. A branch of the Academy of Sciences was set up in 1949 with 8 learned institutions (349 research workers).

HEALTH. There were over 3,000 doctors in 1980, and 11,600 hospital beds.

KOMI AUTONOMOUS SOVIET SOCIALIST REPUBLIC

Area, 415,900 sq. km (160,540 sq. miles); population (Jan. 1983), 1·18m. Capital, Syktyvkar (176,500). Annexed by the princes of Moscow in the 14th century and occupied by British and American forces in 1918–19, the territory was constituted as an Autonomous Region on 22 Aug. 1921 and as an Autonomous Republic on 5 Dec. 1936. The population (1979 census) includes Komi (25·3%), Russians (56·7%), Ukrainians and Belorussians (10·7%).

180 deputies were elected on 24 Feb. 1980, 59 of them women.

There are large coal, oil, timber, gas, asphalt and building materials industries; light industry is expanding. Livestock breeding (including dairy farming) is the main branch of agriculture. There were 51 state farms in 1977. Crop area, 92,000 hectares.

In 1979–80 there were 189,000 pupils in 789 schools, 12,000 students receiving higher education, 18,400 students in 13 technical colleges; and a branch of the Academy of Sciences with 4 learned institutions (297 research workers).

There were 3,900 doctors and 16,200 hospital beds.

MARI AUTONOMOUS SOVIET SOCIALIST REPUBLIC

Area, 23,200 sq. km (8,955 sq. miles); population (Jan. 1983), 719,000 Capital, Yoshkar-Ola. The Mari people were annexed to Russia, with other peoples of the Kazan Tatar Khanate, when the latter was overthrown in 1552. On 4 Nov. 1920 the territory was constituted as an Autonomous Region, and on 5 Dec. 1936 as an Autonomous Republic. The population (1979 census) includes Mari (43·5%), Tatars (5·8%), Chuvashes (1·1%), Russians (47·5%).

150 deputies were elected on 24 Feb. 1980, 57 of them women.

There are over 300 modern factories. The main industries are metalworking, timber, paper, woodworking and food processing. In 1977 there were 105 collective farms and 72 state farms. Over 69% of cultivated land is grain, but flax, potatoes, fruit and vegetables are also expanding branches of agriculture, as is also livestock farming. 625,300 hectares were under crops.

Estimated reserves of the Pechora coalfield are 262,000m. tons.

In 1979–80 there were 714 schools with 130,100 pupils. Technical colleges and higher education establishments had a total of 33,300 students.
There were 3,000 doctors and 8,500 hospital beds.

MORDOVIAN AUTONOMOUS SOVIET SOCIALIST REPUBLIC

Area, 26,200 sq. km (10,110 sq. miles); population (Jan. 1983), 973,000. Capital, Saransk. By the 13th century the Mordovian tribes had been subjugated by the Russian princes of Ryazan and Nizhni-Novgorod. In 1928 the territory was constituted as a Mordovian Area within the Middle-Volga Territory, on 10 Jan. 1930 as an Autonomous Region and on 20 Dec. 1934 as an Autonomous Republic. The population (1979 census) includes Mordovians (34·2%), Russians (59·7%), Tatars (4·6%)

175 deputies were elected on 24 Feb. 1980, 74 of them women.

The Republic has a wide range of industries: Electrical, timber, cable, building materials, furniture, textile, leather and other light industries. Agriculture is devoted chiefly to grain, sugar-beet, sheep and dairy farming. In 1977 there were 76 state and 275 collective farms.

There were 173,800 children at school, 38,100 students in technical colleges and at the state university and institutes, in 1979–80. There were 2,835 doctors and 12,400 hospital beds.

NORTH OSSETIAN AUTONOMOUS SOVIET SOCIALIST REPUBLIC

Area, 8,000 sq. km (3,088 sq. miles); population (Jan. 1983), 608,000. Capital, Ordzhonikidze (formerly Vladikavkaz). The Ossetians, known to antiquity as Alani (who were also called by their immediate neighbours 'Ossi' or 'Yassi'), were annexed to Russia after the latter's treaty of Kuchuk-Kainardji with Turkey, and in 1784 the key fortress of Vladikavkaz was founded on their territory (given the name of Terek region in 1861). On 4 March 1918 the latter was proclaimed an Autonomous Soviet Republic, and after the Civil War this territory with others was set up as the Mountain Autonomous Republic (20 Jan. 1921), with North Ossetia as the Ossetian (Vladikavkaz) Area within it. On 7 July 1924 the latter was constituted as an Autonomous Region and on 5 Dec. 1936 as an Autonomous Republic. The population (1979 census) comprises chiefly Ossetians (50·5%), Russians (33·9%), Ingushi and other Caucasian nationalities (8·1%).

150 deputies were elected on 24 Feb. 1980, 68 of them women.

The main industries are non-ferrous metals (mining and metallurgy), maize-processing (at the Beslan Works, the largest in Europe) timber and woodworking, textiles, building materials, distilleries and food processing. There is also a prosperous and varied agriculture. In 1977 there were 36 state and 44 collective farms.

There were in 1979–80, 106,700 children in 205 schools, 15,100 students in technical colleges and 18,800 students in 4 higher educational establishments (pedagogical, agriculture, medical and mining-metallurgical institutes). There were over 3,000 doctors and over 7,000 hospital beds.

TATAR AUTONOMOUS SOVIET SOCIALIST REPUBLIC

Area, 68,000 sq. km (26,250 sq. miles); population (Jan. 1983), 3,475,000. Capital, Kazan. From the 10th to the 13th centuries this was the territory of the flourishing Volga-Kama Bulgar State; conquered by the Mongols, it became the seat of the Kazan (Tatar) Khans when the Mongol Empire broke up in the 15th century, and in 1552 was conquered again by Russia. On 27 May 1920 it was constituted as an Autonomous Republic. The population (1979 census) includes Tatars (47·7%), Chuvashes, Mordovians and Udmurts (5·9%), Russians (44%).

250 deputies were elected on 24 Feb. 1980, 97 of them women.

The Republic has highly developed engineering, oil and chemical industries, while timber, building materials, textiles, clothing and food industries are also expanding. The Kama works at Brezhnev plan to produce 400,000 vehicles annually. In 1977, 552 collective and 238 state farms served a total area under crops of 3·8m. hectares.

In 1979–80 there were 3,492 schools with 638,000 pupils, 39 technical colleges with 62,000 students and 12 higher educational establishments with 71,000 students (including a state university). There is a branch of the USSR Academy of Sciences with 5 learned institutions (512 research workers).

Doctors at the end of 1979 numbered 11,000 and hospital beds 40,000.

TUVA AUTONOMOUS SOVIET SOCIALIST REPUBLIC

Area, 170,500 sq. km (65,810 sq. miles); population (Jan. 1983), 274,000. Capital, Kyzyl (71,000). Tuva was incorporated in the USSR as an autonomous region on 13 Oct. 1944 and elevated to an Autonomous Republic on 10 Oct. 1961. It is situated to the north-west of Mongolia, between 50° and 53°N. lat. and between 90° and 100°E. long. It is bounded to the east, west and north by Siberia, and to the south by Mongolia. The Tuvans are a Turkic people, formerly ruled by hereditary or elective tribal chiefs. (For the earlier history of the former Tannu-Tuva Republic, *see* THE STATESMAN'S YEAR-BOOK, 1946, p. 798.) The population (1979 census) includes Tuvans (60·5%) and Russians (36·2%).

130 deputies were elected to its Supreme Soviet on 24 Feb. 1980, 53 of them women.

Tuva is well-watered and has much good pastoral land; 47 hydro-electric stations have been set into operation. The Tuvans are mainly herdsmen and cattle farmers, but, in 1977, 376,000 hectares were under crops. There are deposits of gold, cobalt and asbestos. The main exports are hair, hides and wool, and the imports manufactured goods and iron. There are 60 state farms. Mining, woodworking, garment, leather, food and other industries are rapidly developing.

In 1979–80 there were 194 schools with 71,500 pupils; 5 technical colleges with 4,200 students, and an Institute of Linguistics, Literature and History with 2,700 students; 11 newspapers (2 in Russian). There were 860 doctors and 4,530 hospital beds.

A Soviet steamer-service along the river Yenisei maintains communication with Minussinsk, in Central Siberia. Internal transport is chiefly by lorry and motor coach. There is an air service from Kyzyl to Krasnoyarsk.

UDMURT AUTONOMOUS SOVIET SOCIALIST REPUBLIC

Area, 42,100 sq. km (16,250 sq. miles); population (Jan. 1983), 1,538,000. Capital, Izhevsk. The Udmurts (formerly known as 'Votyaks') were annexed by the Russians in the 15th and 16th centuries. On 4 Nov. 1920 the Votyak Autonomous Region was constituted (the name was changed to Udmurt—used by the people themselves—in 1932), and on 28 Dec. 1934 was raised to the status of an Autonomous Republic. The population (1979 census) includes Udmurts (32·2%), Tatars (6·6%), Russians (58·3%).

200 deputies were elected on 24 Feb. 1980, 78 of them women.

Heavy industry includes the manufacture of locomotives, machine tools and other engineering products, timber and building materials. There are also light industries—clothing, leather, furniture, food, etc.

There were 95 state and 261 collective farms in 1977; crop area 1·4m. hectares.
In 1979–80 there were 513 schools with 252,000 pupils; 5,800 finished technical colleges and 3,800 schools of higher education.
There were over 5,000 doctors and over 16,000 hospital beds.

YAKUT AUTONOMOUS SOVIET SOCIALIST REPUBLIC

The area is 3,103,000 sq. km (1,197,760 sq. miles); population (Jan. 1983), 944,000. Capital, Yakutsk (149,000). The Yakuts were subjugated by the Russians in the 17th century. The territory was constituted an Autonomous Republic on 27 April 1922. The population (1979 census) includes Yakuts (36·9%), other northern peoples (2·2%), Russians (50·4%).

205 deputies were elected on 24 Feb. 1980, 92 of them women.

The principal industries are mining (gold, tin, mica, coal) and livestock-breeding. The Soviet Soyuz-Zoloto Trust and a number of individual prospectors are working the fields. Silver- and lead-bearing ores and coal are worked; large diamond fields have been opened up. Timber and food industries are developing. There was 1 collective farm in 1975 with 82 state farms, with an area under crops of 95,000 hectares. Trapping and breeding of fur-bearing animals (sable, squirrel, silver fox, etc.) are an important source of income. A severe climate and lack of railways are serious obstacles to the economic development of the republic. There are, however, 10,000 km of roads and internal air lines totalling 10,000 km including an air service between Irkutsk and Yakutsk.

In 1979–80 there were 179,800 secondary school pupils, 10,200 technical college students and 6,600 at university and teacher training colleges.

There were 3,094 doctors and 12,700 hospital beds.

ADYGEI AUTONOMOUS REGION

Part of Krasnodar Territory. Area, 7,600 sq. km (2,934 sq. miles); population (Jan. 1983), 413,000. Capital, Maikop (128,000). Established 27 July 1922.

Chief industries are timber, woodworking, food processing; but engineering is rapidly expanding. Cattle breeding predominates in agriculture. There were 39 collective and 26 state farms in 1976.

In 1977–78 there were 267 schools with (1980) 68,900 pupils, 6 technical colleges with (1980) 13,100 students and a pedagogical institute with 4,000 students. Regional newspapers are in Adygei and Russian. There were 1,089 doctors and 5,240 hospital beds.

GORNO-ALTAI AUTONOMOUS REGION

Part of Altai Territory. Area, 92,600 sq. km (35,740 sq. miles); population (Jan. 1983), 177,000. Capital, Gorno-Altaisk (39,000). Established 1 June 1922 as Oirot Autonomous Region; renamed 7 Jan. 1948.

Chief industries are gold, mercury and brown-coal mining, timber, chemicals and dairying. Cattle breeding predominates; pasturages and hay meadows cover over 1m. hectares, but 142,000 hectares are under crops. There were 20 collective and 33 state farms in 1977.

In 1979–80 there were 29,500 school pupils; technical colleges had 4,540 students and 3,539 students were receiving higher education. There were 410 doctors and 2,470 hospital beds.

JEWISH AUTONOMOUS REGION

Part of Khabarovsk Territory. Area, 36,000 sq. km (13,895 sq. miles); population (Jan. 1983), 200,000 (1979 census, Russians, 84·1%; Ukrainians, 6·3%; Jews,

5·4%). Capital, Birobidjan (75,000). Established as Jewish National District in 1928, became an Autonomous Region 7 May 1934.

Chief industries are non-ferrous metallurgy, building materials, timber, engineering, textiles, paper and food processing. There were in 1977, 50 factories, 156,000 hectares under crops, 88,500 cattle and 39,000 pigs. There were 35 state farms and 2 collective farms in 1976.

In 1979–80 there were 31,900 schoolchildren; students in technical colleges numbered 5,500. There are a Yiddish national theatre, a Yiddish newspaper and a Yiddish broadcasting service. Doctors numbered 488 and hospital beds 2,860.

KARACHAYEVO-CHERKESS AUTONOMOUS REGION

Part of Stavropol Territory. Area, 14,300 sq. km (5,442 sq. miles); population (Jan. 1983), 380,000. Capital, Cherkessk (96,000). A Karachai Autonomous Region was established on 26 April 1926 (out of a previously united Karachayevo-Cherkess Autonomous Region created in 1922), and dissolved in 1943. A Cherkess Autonomous Region was established on 30 April 1928. The present Autonomous Region was re-established on 9 Jan. 1957.

Ore-mining, engineering, chemical and woodworking industries have been built up since 1917. There are 70 large factories, and a copper works and sugar factory are under construction. A large irrigation scheme, Kuban-Kalaussi, is being developed, to irrigate 200,000 hectares. Livestock breeding and grain growing predominate in agriculture; crop area in 1977 was 197,900 hectares. There were 14 collective farms and 40 state farms in 1976.

In 1979–80 there were 73,000 pupils in (1977–78) 220 schools, 6 technical colleges (1977–78) with 6,500 students and 2 institutes with 3,300 students; 935 doctors and (1977–78) 3,720 hospital beds.

KHAKASS AUTONOMOUS REGION

Part of Krasnoyarsk Territory. Area, 61,900 sq. km (23,855 sq. miles); population (Jan. 1983), 523,000. Capital, Abakan (143,000). Established 20 Oct. 1930.

Coal- and ore-mining, timber and woodworking industries have been highly developed since 1917. The region is linked by rail with the Trans-Siberian line. Large textile and sugar factories are being built.

In 1979, 619,200 hectares were under crops. Livestock breeding, dairy and vegetable farming are developed. There are 58 state farms.

In 1979–80 there were 70,900 pupils in (1977–78) 363 schools, 7 (1977–78) technical colleges with 9,300 students and 5,800 students in higher educational establishments; 1,170 doctors and 6,800 hospital beds. A Khakass alphabet was created after the Revolution.

Books of Reference

Armstrong, T., *Russian Settlement in the North.* CUP, 1965
Conolly, V., *Beyond the Urals. Economic Developments in Soviet Asia.* London, 1967
Dallin, D. J., *The Rise of Russia in Asia.* New York, 1949.—*Soviet Russia and the Far East.* London, 1949
Kolarz, W., *The Peoples of the Soviet Far East.* London, 1954
Istoriya Sibiri s drevneishikh vremen do nashikh dnei. 5 vols., Leningrad, 1968–69

UKRAINE
Ukrainska Radyanska Sotsialistichna Respublika

HISTORY. The Ukrainian Soviet Socialist Republic was proclaimed on 25 Dec. 1917 and was finally established in Dec. 1919. In Dec. 1920 it concluded a military and economic alliance with the RSFSR and on 30 Dec. 1922 formed, together with the other Soviet Socialist Republics, the Union of Soviet Socialist Republics. On 1 Nov. 1939 Western Ukraine (about 88,000 sq. km) was incorporated in the Ukrainian SSR. On 2 Aug. 1940 Northern Bukovina (about 6,000 sq. km) ceded to the USSR by Romania 28 June 1940, and the Khotin, Akkerman and Izmail provinces of Bessarabia were included in the Ukrainian SSR, and on 29 June 1945 Ruthenia (Sub-Carpathian Russia), about 7,000 sq. km, was also incorporated. From the new territories 2 new regions (provinces) were formed, Chernovitz and Izmail.

AREA AND POPULATION. The Ukraine is in south-west USSR; it has a Black Sea coast and western frontiers with Romania, Hungary, Poland and Czechoslovakia. It is bounded north by Belorussia and otherwise by the RSFSR. In 1938 the Ukrainian SSR covered an area of 445,000 sq. km (171,770 sq. miles); it now covers 603,700 sq. km (231,990 sq. miles).

Population, Jan. 1983, 50,461,000 (in 1979, 73·6% Ukrainians, 21·1% Russians, 1·3% Jews, 0·8% Belorussians).

The principal towns are the capital Kiev, Kharkov, Donetsk, Odessa, Dnepropetrovsk, Lvov, Zaporozhye and Krivoi Rog.

The Ukrainian Soviet Socialist Republic consists of the following regions: Cherkassy, Chernigov, Chernovtzy, Crimea (transferred from the RSFSR on 19 Feb 1954), Dnepropetrovsk, Donetsk, Ivan Franko, Khmelnitsky (formerly Kamenetz-Podolsk), Kharkov, Kherson, Kiev, Kirovograd, Lvov, Nikolayev, Odessa, Poltava, Rovno, Sumy, Ternopol, Vinnitza, Volhynia, Voroshilovgrad, Zakarpatskaya (Transcarpathia), Zaporozhye, Zhitomir.

CONSTITUTION AND GOVERNMENT. The Supreme Soviet, elected on 24 Feb. 1980, consists of 650 deputies (1 per 90,000 population); 447 are Communists and 234 women. A new Constitution, based on that of the USSR, was adopted in April 1978.

At elections to regional district, urban and rural Soviets (19 June 1982), out of 525,500 deputies returned, 258,808 (49·2%) were women, 295,174 (56·2%) non-Party and 378,018 (72·4%) industrial workers and collective farmers.

Chairman, Presidium of the Supreme Soviet: A. F. Vatchenko.
Chairman, Council of Ministers: A. P. Lyashko.
Foreign Minister: G. G. Shevel.
First Secretary, Communist Party: V. V. Shcherbitsky.

FINANCE. Budget estimates (in 1m. rubles), 1982, 24,102; 1984, 27,787.

AGRICULTURE. The Ukraine contains some of the richest land in the USSR. It raises wheat, buckwheat, beet, sunflower, cotton, flax, tobacco, soya, hops, the rubber plant kok-sagyz, fruit and vegetables, and in 1976 provided nearly 20% of the grain production in the USSR and over 62% of the sugar-beet. Nine-tenths of the grain exported from USSR came from the Ukraine. The area under cultivation was 27·9m. hectares in 1913, 27m. in 1939 before the new territories were added, and 34·2m. in 1978.

Output (in 1m. tonnes) in 1979 (1913 figures in tons in brackets): Sugar-beet, 47·1 (9·3); sunflower seed, 2·4 (0·07); flax, 0·014 (0·004); potatoes, 23·9 (8·5); meat and fats, 3·6 (1·1); milk, 22·5 (4·7); wool, 0·028 (0·015); 13,747m. eggs (3,005m.); grain, 50·6m.

On 1 Jan. 1979 there were 25·4m. cattle, 20·7m. pigs, 9·2m. sheep and goats. In 1949 silver-fox breeding farms were started.

On 1 Jan. 1982 there were 2,127 state farms and 7,089 collective farms.

Irrigation networks supplied 1·82m. hectares of land; 2·2m. hectares were drained.

Tractors numbered 408,800 at 1 Jan. 1981 and combine harvesters, 89,900.

INDUSTRY. Coal in the Donets field (25,900 sq. km stretching from Donetsk to Rostov), estimated to contain 60% of the bituminous and anthracite-coal reserves of the USSR, yielded, in 1961, 186·1m. tonnes—about 36% of the USSR production. Large new seams have been found near Novo-Moskovsk (Dnepropetrovsk region), Kharkov, Lugansk (beyond the Don) and on the left bank of the Dnieper. Within the present frontiers of the Ukraine, coal output was 22·8m. tons in 1913, 83·8m. tons in 1940, 78m. tons in 1950 and 217m. tons in 1977.

Combining coal from the Donets field with the iron-ore from the mines in Krivoi Rog has made possible the development of a large ferrous metallurgical industry in the Ukraine. Output of iron ore was 6·9m. tons in 1913, 18·9m. tons in 1940 and 126m. tons in 1977.

Manganese is also available at Nikopol; output in 1976, 6·7m. tons.

Pig-iron output was 2·9m. tons in 1913, 9·6m. tons in 1940, 9·2m. tons in 1950 and 46·4m. tons in 1975. Steel output (within present frontiers) was 2·4m. tons in 1913, 8·9m. in 1940, 8·4m. in 1950 and 53·7m. in 1977.

The Ukraine also contains oil, rich deposits of salt and various important chemicals. Oil output was 1m. tons in 1913 (in present frontiers), 353,000 tons in 1940 and 10·5m. tons in 1977; with 68·7m. cu. metres of natural gas.

The Ukraine has highly developed chemical and machine-construction industries producing one-fifth of the total output of machinery and chemicals in the USSR. 142,000 tractors and 3,500 main-line diesel locomotives were produced in 1979.

In Northern Bukovina there are deposits of gypsum, oil, alabaster, brown coal and timber. Output of mineral fertilizers was 36,000 tons in 1913 and 21·1m. tons in 1981; cement output increased in the same years from 269,000 to 22·5m. tons (in present frontiers in both cases). Paper output in 1977 was 250,000 tons (1913: 26,900).

Consumer goods and food industries are important. Output of cotton fabrics was (in present frontiers) 4·7m. linear metres in 1913, 13·8m. in 1940, 20·6m. in 1950 and 429·4m. in 1975. Granulated sugar output was 1913, 1·1m. tons; 1940, 1·6m. tons; 1950, 1·8m. tons, and 1977, 6·8m. tons. Leather footwear manufactured in 1940 totalled 40·8m. pairs; 1979, 176m.

The number of industrial and office workers at the end of 1950 was 6·9m., and the average in 1981, 20·2m. There were 1,816,000 specialists with a higher education.

During the first 5-year plan (1929–32) the Dnieper power-station was built; destroyed during the War, it was restored during the fourth plan (1946–50). Another large hydro-electric station at Kakhovka began operations during the fifth plan (1951–55). Power output (in 1,000m. kwh.) increased as follows: 1913, 0·5; 1940, 12·4; 1950, 14·7; 1981, 231.

COMMUNICATIONS. The total length of railways of the Ukrainian SSR in 1981 was 22,650 km, the navigable rivers, 3,900 km. Length of hard-surface motor roads was 171,900 km.

Airlines connect Kiev, Lvov, Chernovtsy and Odessa with Crimean and Caucasian spas, Kiev with Tbilisi, Odessa with Riga and Donetsk.

Newspapers (1981). Out of 1,754 newspapers, 1,285 were in Ukrainian. Daily circulation of Ukrainian-language newspapers, 15·5m., other languages, 8m.

RELIGION. Several Christian Churches have their adherents in the Ukraine, the chief being the Orthodox Greek Church and the Catholic Church. The Western Ukraine Uniate Church, which in 1596 had been forced by the Poles to establish unity with the Roman Church, severed this connexion in March 1946 and joined the Orthodox Church. There are also some Protestants as well as Jews and others.

EDUCATION. In 1981–82 the number of pupils in 22,800 primary and secondary schools was 7·5m.; 147 higher educational establishments had 882,900 students, and 726 technical colleges 795,200 students; 2·5m. children were attending 17,400 pre-school institutions.

The Ukrainian Academy of Sciences was established in 1919; in 1980 it had 70 institutions with 13,369 scientific staff. There is an academy of building and architecture. Total scientific staff in 814 learned institutions numbered 185,100.

HEALTH. Doctors numbered 189,400 in 1981, and hospital beds, 636,400.

Books of Reference

Allen, W. E. D., *The Ukraine: A History.* London, 1940
Andrusyshen, C. H. (ed.), *Ukrainian-English Dictionary.* Toronto, 1955
Chamberlin, W. H., *The Ukraine.* New York, 1945
Chirovsky, N. L., *The Ukrainian Economy.* New York, Paris, Toronto, 1965
Hrushevsky, M., *A History of the Ukraine.* New Haven, 1941
Manning, C. A., *Twentieth-century Ukraine.* New York, 1951
Mirchuk, L. (ed.), *Ukraine and its People.* London, 1949
Istoriya Ukrainskoi SSR. 2 vols. Kiev, 1969
Soviet Ukraine. (English ed.) Ukrainian Soviet Encyclopaedia, 1970
Ukraine: A Concise Encyclopaedia. 2 vols. Toronto, 1963–71

BELORUSSIA

Belaruskaya Sovietskaya Sotsialistychnaya Respublika

HISTORY. The Belorussian Soviet Socialist Republic was set up on 1 Jan. 1919. It forms one of the constituent republics of the USSR.

AREA AND POPULATION. Belorussia is situated along the Western Dvina and Dnieper. It is bounded west by Poland, north by Latvia and Lithuania, east by the RSFSR and south by the Ukraine. The area is 207,600 sq. km (80,134 sq. miles). The capital is Minsk. Other important towns are Gomel, Vitebsk, Mogilev, Bobruisk, Grodno and Brest. On 2 Nov. 1939 western Belorussia was incorporated with an area of over 108,000 sq. km and a population of 4·8m. The population (Jan. 1983) was 9,807,000; 79·4% of this population in 1979 (census) were Belorussians, 4·2% Poles, 11·9% Russians, 2·4% Ukrainians and 1·4% Jews.

Belorussia now comprises the following regions: Brest, Gomel, Grodno, Mogilev, Minsk, Vitebsk.

CONSTITUTION AND GOVERNMENT. The Supreme Soviet, elected in 1980, consists of 485 deputies (1 per 20,000 population); 328 are Communists and 180 women. A new Constitution was adopted in April 1978.

At elections to regional, district, urban and rural Soviets (20 June 1982), of 85,394 deputies returned, 42,326 (49·6%) were women, 48,743 (57·1%) non-Party and 58,839 (68·9%) industrial workers and collective farmers.

Chairman, Presidium of the Supreme Soviet: I. E. Poliakov.
Chairman, Council of Ministers: V. I. Brovikov.
Foreign Minister: A. E. Gurinovich
First Secretary, Communist Party: N. Slyunkov.

FINANCE. Budget estimates (in 1m. rubles), 1983, 5,737; 1984, 6,697.

NATURAL RESOURCES. Belorussia is hilly, with a general slope towards the south. It contains large tracts of marsh land, particularly to the south-west, and valuable forest land wooded with oak, elm, maple and white beech: there are over 6,500 peat deposits.

AGRICULTURE. Agriculturally, Belorussia may be divided into three main sections—Northern: growing flax, fodder, grasses and breeding cattle for meat and dairy produce; Central: potato growing and pig breeding; Southern: good natural pasture land, hemp cultivation and cattle breeding for meat and dairy produce. The area under cultivation (in hectares) was 4·5m. in 1913, 5·2m. in 1940 and 6·3m. in 1979. There were 6·8m. cattle, 4·6m. pigs and 540,000 sheep and goats on 1 Jan. 1980.

Output of main agricultural products (in 1,000 tonnes) in 1979 (1913 figures in brackets): Flax, 78 (33); sugar-beet, 1,383 (0); potatoes, 15,253 (4,024); meat, 915 (219); milk, 6·3 (1·4); wool, 1·1 (2·3); grain, 4·6 (2·6); 2,894m. eggs (413m.).

On 1 Jan. 1982 there were 1,772 collective farms and 903 state farms. About 2·5m. hectares of marsh land had been drained for agricultural use, 828,200 of these for crops. This land has been found to be as rich as the soil of the Black Earth Zone, and yields good harvests of grain, fodder, potatoes, kok-sagyz and other crops. In Jan. 1980, 2·6m. hectares were drained and 36,300 hectares of land irrigated. In Jan. 1981 there were 117,200 tractors and 27,400 grain combine harvesters.

INDUSTRY. Industry in this republic was almost completely destroyed during the years 1941–45. By 1956, aggregate industrial output was three times what it had been in 1940. Plants producing tip-lorries, machine-tools and agricultural machinery are prominent.

The republic also contains timber works; a match factory in Borisov; building materials, machine, prefabricated house construction, glass-blowing and other factories; canneries, creameries and other food industries; chemical, textiles, artificial-silk, flax-spinning and leather works.

The automobile and tractor industry produced 89,100 tractors and 32,500 lorries in 1979. Cement output, 33,000 tons in 1913, was 2·17m. tons in 1975. Leather footwear output 9·8m. pairs in 1940, was 41·6m. pairs in 1979. Linen fabrics, 13,000 linear metres in 1913, 68·4m. in 1975; woollens, 37,000 linear metres in 1913, 29m. in 1975.

Particular attention has been paid to the development of the peat industry with a view to making Belorussia as far as possible self-supporting in fuel, and in 1939 local peat provided 67·5% of her total requirements of fuel. The average annual output is about 18m. tonnes.

There are also rich deposits of rock salt. In 1951 the first sugar refinery in Belorussia was opened in Grodno; sugar output in 1979 was 313,900 tonnes.

Output of electricity in 1981, 33,300m. kwh. (508m. in 1940). New power-plants have been built in Baranovichi, Grodno, Molodechno and Lida.

The number of industrial and office workers in 1981 was 4,113,000.

COMMUNICATIONS. In 1981 there were 5,510 km of railways, 47,500 km of motor roads (38,100 km hard-surface) and 3,900 km of navigable waterways.

Newspapers (1981). Of 203 newspapers published 128 were in Belorussian. Daily circulation of Belorussian-language newspapers, 1·6m., other languages, 3·2m.

EDUCATION. In 1981–82 there were 178,800 students in 33 places of higher education and 162,800 students in 136 technical colleges. There were 38,100 scientific personnel in 178 institutions, and 340,000 specialists with a higher education employed in the national economy. The Belorussian Academy of Sciences controlled 32 learned institutions with 5,378 scientific staff. The number of children in primary and secondary schools was 489,000 in 1914–15, and 1·5m. in 1981–82. 511,000 children were attending pre-school institutions in 1981–82.

HEALTH. In 1981 there were 33,500 doctors (900 in 1913, within present frontiers), and 122,500 hospital beds (6,400 in 1913).

Books of Reference

Vakar, N. P., *Belorussia.* Harvard Univ. Press, 1956.—*A Bibliographical Guide to Belorussia.* Harvard Univ. Press, 1956
Istoriya Belorusskoi SSR. 2nd ed. 2 vols. Minsk, 1961

AZERBAIJAN
Azarbaijchan Soviet Sotsialistik Respublikasy

HISTORY. The 'Mussavat' (Nationalist) party, which dominated the National Council or Constituent Assembly of the Tatars, declared the independence of Azerbaijan on 28 May 1918, with a capital, first at Ganja (Elizavetpol) and later at

Baku. On 28 April 1920 Azerbaijan was proclaimed a Soviet Socialist Republic. From 1922, with Georgia and Armenia it formed the Transcaucasian Soviet Federal Socialist Republic. In 1936 it assumed the status of one of the Union Republics of the USSR.

AREA AND POPULATION. Azerbaijan covers an area of 86,600 sq. km (33,430 sq. miles) and has a population (Jan. 1983) of 6,399,000. Its capital is Baku. Other important towns are Kirovabad and Sumgait. Nakhichevan is the capital of the Autonomous Republic of the same name.

Azerbaijan includes the Nakhichevan Autonomous Republic and the Nagorno-Karabakh Autonomous Region. Situated in the eastern area of Transcaucasia, it is protected by mountains in the west and north, washed by the Caspian Sea in the east and bounded by Iran in the south. Its climate is inclined to drought.

In 1979 (census) 78·1% of the population were Azerbaijanis. Other nationalities were Russians (7·9%), Armenians (7·9%) and Daghestanis (3·4%).

CONSTITUTION AND GOVERNMENT. The Supreme Soviet, elected in 1980, consists of 450 deputies (1 per 10,000 population); 312 are Communists and 179 women. A new Constitution was adopted in April 1978.

At elections to the Nagorno-Karabakh regional Soviet and the district, urban and rural Soviets (20 June 1982), of 50,799 deputies returned, 24,432 (48·1%) were women, 28,775 (56·6%) non-Party and 34,059 (67%) industrial workers and collective farmers.

Chairman, Presidium of the Supreme Soviet: K. A. Khalilov.
Chairman, Council of Ministers: G. Seidov.
First Secretary, Communist Party: K. M. Bagirov.

FINANCE (in 1m. rubles). Budget estimates, 1983, 2,428; 1984, 2,551.

AGRICULTURE. The chief agricultural products are grain, cotton, rice, grapes, fruit, vegetables, tobacco and silk. The Mexican rubber plant *grayule* has been acclimatized. A new kind of high-yielding winter wheat has been produced for use in mountainous parts of the republic.

Livestock on 1 Jan. 1979: Cattle, 1·7m.; pigs, 167,000; sheep and goats, 5·3m.

Output of main agricultural products (in 1,000 tonnes) in 1978 (1913 figures in brackets): Cotton, 742 (4); potatoes, 131 (38); tea, 20 (0); meat, 136 (40); milk, 768 (203); wool, 10·2 (4·1); grapes, 1,045; fruit, 217; 691m. eggs (97m.).

Azerbaijan has become an important cotton-growing and sub-tropical base. About 70% of cultivated land is irrigated. On the irrigated land crops of Egyptian and Sea-Island cotton are obtained. Here, too, rice and lucerne are cultivated, and in the mountain valleys there are also orchards, vineyards and silk cultures.

In the south along the coast of the Caspian, where the climate is more moist, there are tea plantations, and citrus fruits and other sub-tropical plants are grown.

In 1941 a scientific research institute for sub-tropical research was opened to develop the culture of sub-tropical plants in Azerbaijan and other parts of Transcaucasia. A forestry research institute was opened in 1949.

There were on 1 Jan. 1982, 601 collective farms, 735 state farms, 35,300 tractors and 4,300 grain combine harvesters.

INDUSTRY. The republic is rich in natural resources: oil, iron, aluminium, copper, lead, zinc, precious metals, sulphur pyrites, limestone and salt. Iron and steel and aluminium works have been built at Sumgait.

The most important industry is the oil industry, especially in the Baku region. The output of oil was 7·7m. tonnes in 1913, 22·2m. tonnes in 1940 and 16·5m. tonnes in 1976. The largest producing area lies along the western shore of the Caspian Sea, north and south of Baku, where the largest refineries are located. Other wells lie west of Baku, and some have been drilled in the Caspian itself, off the Apsheron Peninsula. Baku is connected by a double pipeline with Batum on the Black Sea. All the oilfields have been electrified and are connected with Baku.

Azerbaijan has also copper, chemical, cement and building material, food, timber, salt, textiles and fishing industries. 788,000 tonnes of steel were produced in 1976, 1·4m. tons of cement, 130·4m. linear metres of cotton fabrics, 15·8m. pairs leather footwear, 32·3m. linear metres of silk fabrics, 1·3m. tons of iron ore.

In addition to Baku, other important industrial centres are Kirovabad, Nukha, Stepanakert, Nakhichevan, Lenkoran.

In 1981 electric power output was 14,600m. kwh. Output of gas, which began in 1928 with 176m. cu. metres, was 10,989m. in 1976. Pipelines from Karadag to Baku and Sumgait supply gas fuel for all oil-cracking factories and most engineering works.

Synthetic rubber works (Sumgait), tyre works and a worsted combine (Baku) and a large textile combine (Mingechaur) have been built.

The number of industrial and office workers in 1981 was 1,853,000.

COMMUNICATIONS. Railway lines, apart from narrow gauge, 1,900 km. The first electrical railway (42 km) in the USSR was constructed in Azerbaijan in 1924; in 1949, 27 km was added, and the line now runs Baku-Surakhany-Sabunchi-Buzovny-Baku. The capital is also linked by rail with Tbilisi, Yerevan, Derbent, Julfa and Astara. There were, in 1981, 26,400 km of motor roads (21,300 km hard-surface) and 500 km of inland waterways.

Newspapers (1981). There were 218 newspapers, 141 in the Azerbaijani language (circulation 2·18m.), other languages, 493,000.

EDUCATION. In 1981–82 there were 1·6m. pupils in 4,300 elementary and secondary schools and 150,000 children attending pre-school institutions. There were 76 technical colleges with 78,800 students, 18 higher educational institutions, including a state university at Baku, with 108,600 students (including correspondence students).

The Azerbaijan Academy of Sciences has 28 research institutions with 4,314 research workers. There are 142 learned and scientific institutions, with 21,500 research workers in all.

HEALTH. In 1981 there were 21,400 doctors and 61,200 hospital beds. There were also 619 maternity and infant welfare centres.

NAKHICHEVAN AUTONOMOUS SOVIET SOCIALIST REPUBLIC

Area, 5,500 sq. km (2,120 sq. miles), population (Jan. 1983), 257,000. Capital, Nakhichevan (37,000). This territory, on the borders of Turkey and Iran, forms part of the Azerbaijan SSR although separated from it by the territory of Soviet Armenia. Its population, mainly Azerbaijanis, had a chequered history for 1,500 years under the ancient Persians, Arabs, Seljuk Turks, Mongols, Ottoman Turks and modern Persians before being annexed by Russia in 1828. On 9 Feb. 1924 it was constituted as an Autonomous Republic within Azerbaijan. Its Supreme Soviet, elected 24 Feb. 1980, has 110 members including 52 women.

The republic has silk, clothing, cotton, canning, meat-packing and other factories. Nearly 70% of the people are engaged in agriculture, of which the main branches are cotton and tobacco growing. Fruit and grapes are also produced in increasing quantity. There are 47 collective and 26 state farms. Crop area 37,400 hectares.

In 1977–78 there were 225 (218, 1979–80) primary, 8-year and 11-year schools with 70,800 pupils. There were 1,700 pupils in 4 technical colleges and a pedagogical institute with 2,400 students.

Doctors numbered 503, and hospital beds, 2,378.

NAGORNO-KARABAKH AUTONOMOUS REGION

Area, 4,400 sq. km (1,700 sq. miles); population (Jan. 1983), 168,000. Capital, Stepanakert (33,000). Populated by Armenians (75·9%) and Azerbaijanis (23%), a separate khanate in the 18th century, it was established on 7 July 1923 as an Autonomous Region within Azerbaijan.

Main industries are silk, wine, dairying and building materials. Crop area is 67,200 hectares; cotton, grapes and winter wheat are grown. There are 53 collective and 21 state farms.

In 1979–80 there were 188 schools, 5 technical colleges, a teacher training college and a higher educational institution with 42,000 students; 402 doctors and 1,720 hospital beds.

Books of Reference

Baddeley, J. F., *The Rugged Flanks of Caucasus*. 2 vols. Oxford, 1941
Tutaeff, D., *The Soviet Caucasus*. London, 1942

GEORGIA

Sakartvelos Sabchota Sotsialisturi Respublica

HISTORY. The independence of the Georgian Social Democratic Republic was declared at Tiflis on 26 May 1918 by the National Council, elected by the National Assembly of Georgia on 22 Nov. 1917. The independence of Georgia was recognized by the USSR on 7 May 1920. On 12 Feb. 1921 a rising broke out in Mingrelia, Abkhazia and Adjaria, and Soviet troops invaded the country, which, on 25 Feb. 1921, was proclaimed the Georgian Soviet Socialist Republic. At the first Transcaucasian Soviet Congress, 15 Dec. 1922, Georgia, together with Armenia and Azerbaijan, united to form the Transcaucasian Soviet Federal Socialist Republic, and a federal constitution was adopted and published 10 Jan. 1923. In 1936 the Georgian Soviet Socialist Republic became one of the constituent republics of the USSR and, like other republics of USSR, adopted a new Constitution.

AREA AND POPULATION. Georgia is bounded west by the Black Sea and south by Turkey, Armenia and Azerbaijan. It occupies the whole of the western part of Transcaucasia and covers an area of 69,700 sq. km (26,900 sq. miles). Its population on 1 Jan. 1983 was 5,134,000. The capital is Tbilisi (Tiflis). Other important towns are Kutaisi (207,000), Rustavi (139,000), Batumi (129,000), Sukhumi (122,000), Poti (54,000), Gori (59,000).

Protected from the north by the Caucasian mountains and receiving in the west the warm, moist winds from the Black Sea into which most of its rivers flow, Georgia is outstanding for its fine, warm climate and its natural wealth, variety and beauty. It has the highest snow-capped peaks of the Caucasian mountains. Georgia contains valuable sulphur and other medicinal springs. Georgians, an ancient people, were (1979 census) 68·8% of the population; Armenians 9%; Russians, 7·4%; Azerbaijanis, 5·1%; Ossetians, 3·2%; Abkhazians, 1·7%.

CONSTITUTION AND GOVERNMENT. The Georgian Soviet Socialist Republic includes the Abkhazian ASSR, the Adjarian ASSR and the South Ossetian Autonomous Region.

The Supreme Soviet, elected in 1980, consists of 440 deputies (1 per 10,000 population); 158 are women, 290 Communists. A new Constitution was adopted in April 1978.

At elections to the district, rural and urban Soviets, and that of the South Ossetian region (20 June 1982), of 50,643 deputies returned 25,403 (50·2%) were women, 29,083 (57·4%) non-Party and 34,780 (68·7%) industrial workers and collective farmers.

Chairman, Presidium of the Supreme Soviet: P. G. Gilashvili.
Chairman, Council of Ministers: D. L. Kartvelishvili.
First Secretary, Communist Party: E. A. Shevardnadze.

FINANCE (in 1m. rubles). Budget estimates, 1983, 2,387; 1984, 2,781.

AGRICULTURE. There are 3 main agricultural areas: (1) The moist subtropical area along the Black Sea Coast, where are cultivated tea, citrus fruits (lemons, oranges, mandarins, etc.), the tung tree (which yields special industrial oils), eucalyptus, bamboo, high-quality tobacco; (2) Imeretia (the Kutais region) where the chief cultures are grapes and silk, and (3) Kakhetia, along the Alazani (a tributary of the Kura river), famed for its orchards and wines. Land (in hectares) under cultivation was 748,000 in 1913, 896,000 in 1940, 778,000 in 1961, 800,000 in 1979.

Output of main agricultural products (in 1,000 tonnes) in 1978 (1913 figures in brackets): Sugar-beet, 115 (0); fruit, 811; grapes, 784; tea in leaf, 454; meat, 133 (49); wool, 5·5 (3·4); milk, 631 (222); wine, 19·9m. decalitres; 629m. eggs (119m.).

On 1 Jan. 1982 there were 691 collective farms working over 66% of all agricultural land, 517 state farms working nearly 34% of such land. In the Colchis area 115,000 hectares of extremely rich land have been reclaimed. There are 389,000 hectares of irrigated land. 151,400 hectares of marsh land have been drained. Tractors numbered 24,900 on 1 Jan. 1981; grain combines, 1,500.

Livestock on 1 Jan. 1980: Cattle, 1·5m.; pigs, 940,400; sheep and goats, 2m.

Georgia is rich in forest lands where fine varieties of timber are grown. Area covered by forests, 2·4m. hectares.

INDUSTRY. The most important mining industry of Georgia is the exploitation of the manganese deposits, the richest of which lie in the Chiatura region, where 1·6m. tonnes of ore were produced in 1971. Manganese deposits in Georgia are calculated at 250m. tonnes, distributed over an area of 140 sq. km. The most important coal seams are at Tkvarcheli (deposits estimated at 250m. tonnes) and Tkibuli (deposits of 80m. tonnes). Other important minerals are baryta, the best in the USSR, fire-resisting and other clays, diatomite shale, oil, agate, marble, cement, alabaster, iron and other ores, building stone, arsenic, molybdenum, tungsten and mercury. In 1941 a goldfield was discovered. Output of coal in 1976 was 1·9m. tonnes (625,000 in 1940).

Since the Second World War the Transcaucasian Metallurgical Plant has been built at Rustavi (near Tbilisi) and a motor works at Kutaisi. There are modern factories for processing green tea-leaves, creameries and breweries; Georgia has also textile and silk industries.

In 1977, 784,000 tonnes of pig-iron, 1·5m. tonnes of steel, 1,334,000 tonnes of rolled metal were produced; also 1·7m. tonnes of cement, 748,000 tonnes of mineral fertilizer, 56·7m. linear metres of cotton fabrics, 43·8m. linear metres of silk fabrics, 14·8m. pairs of leather footwear and 46,200 tons of granulated sugar.

Georgia's fast flowing rivers form an abundant source of energy. One of the most powerful stations completed in recent years is Tbilisi (1m. kw.). Power output in 1981 was 15,100m. kwh. (742m. in 1940).

There were 2,014,000 industrial and office workers in 1981.

COMMUNICATIONS. Length of railways in 1981 was 1,420 km. The trunk line leading from Batumi through Tbilisi to Baku on the Caspian Sea has several narrow-gauge branches on Georgian territory to the coalmines of Tkibuli, to the port of Poti, to the manganese mines of Chiatura, to the mineral springs of Borjom and the health resort Bakuriani, to the towns Signakh and Telavi, in Kakhetia, and to the Armenian frontier, across the coalmine district of Alaverdi. The last branch divides in Armenia, going on the one side to Tabriz in Iran, and on the other to Erzerum in Anatolia. A railway line from Akhal-Senaki along the Black Sea coast, through Sukhumi to Tuapse, was completed in 1946. All lines are electrified or work on diesel traction. In 1981 there were 38,200 km of motor roads, 31,600 km of them hard-surfaced.

Newspapers (1981). Out of 141 newspapers, 122 were in Georgian. Daily circulation in Georgian language newspapers, 2·7m., other languages, 500,000.

EDUCATION. In 1981–82 there were 900,000 pupils in 3,800 primary and secondary schools, 53,000 in 90 technical colleges and 87,400 students in 19 higher educational institutions. Tbilisi University has 16,300 students. In towns, 11 years' education is usual. In Abastuman there is an astro-physical observatory. In 1936 a branch of the Academy of Sciences of the USSR was formed in Tbilisi, and in Feb. 1941 a Georgian Academy of Sciences was opened, which in 1980 had 43 institutions with scientific staff totalling 5,617. There were in all 194 research institutions with 25,500 scientific staff.

In 1981, 170,000 children were attending pre-school institutions.

HEALTH. There were 25,200 doctors and 54,300 hospital beds in 1981.

ABKHAZIAN AUTONOMOUS SOVIET SOCIALIST REPUBLIC

Area, 8,600 sq. km (3,320 sq. miles); population (Jan. 1983), 517,000. Capital Sukhumi. This area, the ancient Colchis, included Greek colonies from the 6th century B.C. onwards. From the 2nd century B.C. onwards, it was a prey to many invaders—Romans, Byzantines, Arabs, Ottoman Turks—before accepting a Russian protectorate in 1810. However, from the 4th century A.D. a West Georgian kingdom was established by the Lazi princes in the territory (known to the Romans as 'Lazica') and by the 8th century the prevailing language was Georgian and the name Abkhazia. In March 1921 a congress of local Soviets proclaimed it a Soviet Republic, and its status as an Autonomous Republic, within Georgia, was confirmed on 17 April 1930.

Population (1979 census) Abkhazians, 17·1%, Georgians, 43·9% and Russians, 16·4%.

140 Deputies were elected on 24 Feb. 1980, 57 of them women.

The Abkhazian coast (along the Black Sea) possesses a famous chain of health resorts—Gagra, Sukhumi, Akhali-Antoni, Gulripsha and Gudauta—sheltered by thickly forested mountains.

The republic has coal, electric power, building materials and light industries. In 1976 there were 93 collective farms and 48 state farms; main crops are tobacco, tea, grapes, oranges, tangerines and lemons. Crop area 41,400 hectares.

Livestock, 1 Jan. 1980: 32,500 cattle, 16,200 pigs, 9,200 sheep and goats.

101,500 pupils were attending 460 schools in 1976–77. There were 7 technical colleges with 3,100 students; 6,100 students were receiving higher education (including correspondence courses). A university has been opened in Sukhumi.

There were 152,700 industrial and office workers, and 13,200 specialists with a higher education in the national economy in 1978. Doctors, 1,883; hospital beds, 5,800.

ADJARIAN AUTONOMOUS SOVIET SOCIALIST REPUBLIC

Area, 3,000 sq. km (1,160 sq. miles); population (Jan. 1983), 371,000. Capital, Batumi. After a history similar to that of Abkhazia, it fell under Turkish rule in the 17th century, and was annexed to Russia (rejoining Georgia) after the Berlin Treaty of 1878. On 16 July 1921 the territory was constituted as an Autonomous Republic within the Georgian SSR.

Population (1979 census) Georgians, 80·1%, Russians, 9·8% and Armenians 4·6%.

110 deputies were elected on 24 Feb. 1980, 43 of them women.

The republic specializes in sub-tropical agricultural products. These include tea, mandarines and lemons, grapes, bamboo, eucalyptus, etc. Livestock: 116,000 cattle, 10,000 sheep and goats. In 1976 there were 77 collective farms and 21 state farms.

There are shipyards at Batumi, modern oil-refining plant (the pipeline from the Baku oilfields ends at Batumi), food-processing and canning factories, clothing, building materials, drug factories, etc.

Health resorts are Kobuleti, Tsikhisdziri, Batumi on the coast and Beshumi in the hills. The sub-tropical climate and flora, and the combination of mountains and sea, make this republic (like Abkhazia) a favourite holiday area.

In 1979 there were 76,400 pupils at school, several technical colleges with 3,500 students, a pedagogical institute and several research institutions. 2,000 students were receiving a higher education.

There were (1978) 92,700 industrial and office workers, and 10,500 specialists with a higher education in the national economy. Doctors, 1,097; hospital beds, 3,695.

SOUTH OSSETIAN AUTONOMOUS REGION

This area was populated by Ossetians from across the Caucasus (North Ossetia), driven out by the Mongols in the 13th century. The region was set up within the Georgian SSR on 20 April 1922. Area, 3,900 sq. km (1,505 sq. miles); population (Jan. 1983), 98,000 (1979 census, Ossetians, 66·4% and Georgians, 28·8%). Capital, Tskhinvali (34,000).

Main industries are mining, timber, electrical engineering and building materials. Crop area, chiefly grains, was 21,700 hectares in 1979; other pursuits are sheep-farming (103,500 sheep and goats) and vine-growing. There were 14 collective farms and 13 state farms.

There are a pedagogical institute (2,345 students) and several technical colleges (700 students). In 1976 there were 24,000 pupils in elementary and secondary schools.

There were (1978) 34,900 industrial and office workers, and 3,800 specialists with a higher education in the national economy. Doctors, 401; hospital beds, 1,350.

Books of Reference

Lang, D. M., *A Modern History of Georgia*. London, 1962. — *The Georgians*. London, 1966
Tutaeff, D., *The Soviet Caucasus*. London, 1942
Istoriya Gruzii. 3 vols. Tbilisi, 1962–73

ARMENIA
Haikakan Sovetakan Sotsialistakan Respublika

HISTORY. On 29 Nov. 1920 Armenia was proclaimed a Soviet Socialist Republic. The Armenian Soviet Government, with the Russian Soviet Government, was a party to the Treaty of Kars (March 1921), which confirmed the Turkish possession of the former Government of Kars and of the Surmali District of the Government of Yerevan. From 1922 to 1936 it formed part of the Transcaucasian Soviet Federal Socialist Republic. In 1936 Armenia was proclaimed a constituent republic of the USSR.

AREA AND POPULATION. Armenia covers an area of 29,800 sq. km (11,490 sq. miles). It is bounded in the north by Georgia, in the east by Azerbaijan and in the south and west by Turkey and Iran. It is a very mountainous country with but little forest land, has many turbulent rivers and a highly fertile soil, but subject to drought. In Jan. 1983 the population was 3,219,000. Census (1979)

89·7% of the population were Armenians, the rest are Russians (2·3%), Kurds (1·7%), Azerbaijanians (5·3%). The capital is Yerevan. Other large towns are Leninakan (218,000) and Kirovakan (159,000).

CONSTITUTION AND GOVERNMENT. The Supreme Soviet, elected in 1980, consists of 340 deputies (1 per 5,000 population); 121 are women, 218 Communists. A new Constitution was adopted in April 1978.

At elections to the district, urban and rural Soviets (20 June 1982), of 27,165 deputies returned 13,513 (49·7%) were women, 15,376 (56·6%) non-Party and 18,975 (69·9%) industrial workers and collective farmers.

Chairman, Presidium of the Supreme Soviet: B. E. Sarkisov.
Chairman, Council of Ministers: F. T. Sarkisian.
First Secretary, Communist Party: K. S. Demirchian.

FINANCE. Budget estimates (in 1m. rubles), 1983, 1,625; 1984, 1,773

AGRICULTURE. The chief agricultural area is the valley of the Arax and the area round Yerevan. Here there are considerable cotton plantations as well as orchards and vineyards. Sub-tropical plants, such as almonds and figs, are also grown. Olive groves and pomegranate plantations occupy large areas; experiments are being made to naturalize cork oak. In the mountainous areas the chief pursuit is livestock raising. In 1913 the total cultivated area of Armenia amounted to 346,000 hectares; in 1940, 434,000; in 1965, 400,000; in 1970, 409,000; in 1978, 500,000.

Output of main agricultural products (in 1,000 tonnes) in 1978 (1913 figures in brackets): Wheat, 318 (110); sugar-beet, 162 (0); potatoes, 223 (47); fruit, 157; grapes, 244; meat, 83·5 (19); milk, 495 (129); wool, 5 (2·3); and 440m. eggs (54m.).

Area of irrigated land in Armenia in 1979 was 270,000 hectares.

There were, on 1 Jan. 1982, 280 collective farms, and these together with the 476 state farms tilled 99·9% of the total cultivated area. Livestock included 233,000 pigs, 772,100 cattle and 2·3m. sheep and goats. All the state farms and collective farms had been electrified by the end of 1960. There were 13,000 tractors and 1,500 grain and cotton combines in Jan. 1980.

INDUSTRY. Armenia contains large deposits of copper, zinc, aluminium, molybdenum and other metals. It is also rich in marble, granite, cement and other building materials. The mining of these minerals is becoming more and more important. Among other industries are the chemical, producing chiefly synthetic rubber and fertilizers, and the extraction and processing of building materials such as cement, pumice-stone, tuffs, marble, volcanic basalt and fire-proof clay, ginning- and textile-mills, carpet weaving, food, including wine-making, fruit, meat-canning and creameries. Machine-tool and electrical engineering works have also been established. Among the industrial centres are Yerevan, Leninakan, Alaverdi, Kafan, Kirovakan, Daval, Megri and Oktemberyan. Output of electricity in 1981 was 14,300m. kwh. A chain ('cascade') of 8 hydro-electric stations on the river Razdan, as it falls about 3,300 ft from the mountain lake Sevan to its junction with the Arax, has been completed.

In 1977 there were produced 1,828,000 tons of cement, 416,000 tons of mineral fertilizers, 95·6m. linear metres of cotton fabrics, 18·5m. linear metres of silk fabrics, 11·8m. pairs of leather footwear, 13,900 tons of granulated sugar and 8·9m. decalitres of wine (excluding collective farm output).

There were 1,233,000 industrial and office workers employed in the national economy in 1981.

COMMUNICATIONS. Length of railways in 1981, 750 km; motor roads, 9,700 km (hard surface, 8,100); airlines, 570 km.

Newspapers (1981). Out of 87 newspapers 77 appeared in Armenian. Daily circulation of Armenian-language newspapers, 1·4m., other languages, 124,000.

EDUCATION. In 1981–82 there were 600,000 pupils in 1,535 primary and secondary schools; 66 technical colleges with 49,200 students; 13 higher educational institutions with 58,600 students (including correspondence students). Yerevan houses the Armenian Academy of Sciences, 43 scientific institutes, a medical institute and other technical colleges, and a state university. 31 learned institutions with 2,992 scientific staff are under the Academy of Sciences. Scientific workers totalled 17,700 in 101 institutions in 1978.

In 1981 there were 139,000 children in pre-school institutions.

HEALTH. In 1981 there were 11,100 doctors and 26,600 hospital beds.

Books of Reference

Kurkjian, V., A History of Armenia. New York, 1958
Lang, D.M., Armenia: Cradle of Civilization. London, 1978.—The Armenians. A People in Exile. London, 1981
Missakian, J., A Searchlight on the Armenian Question, 1878–1950. Boston, Mass., 1950
Shaginyan, M., A Journey Through Soviet Armenia. Moscow (English ed., 1954)

MOLDAVIAN SOVIET SOCIALIST REPUBLIC

Respublika Sovietike Sochialiste Moldovenyaske

HISTORY. The Moldavian Soviet Socialist Republic, capital Kishinev, was formed by the union of part of the former Moldavian Autonomous Soviet Socialist Republic (organized 12 Oct. 1924), formerly included in the Ukrainian Soviet Socialist Republic, and the areas of Bessarabia (ceded by Romania to the USSR, 28 June 1940) with a mainly Moldavian population. As from 2 Aug. 1940 the MSSR includes the following regions of the former Moldavian Autonomous Soviet Socialist Republic: Grigoriopol, Dubossarsk, Kamensk, Rybnitz, Slobodzeisk and Tiraspol, and the following districts of Bessarabia: Beltsk, Bendery, Kagulsk, Kishinev, Orgeev and Sorok. The republic, however, is divided not into regions but into 36 rural districts, 21 towns and 40 urban settlements.

AREA AND POPULATION. Moldavia is bounded in the east and south by the Ukraine and on the west by Romania. The area is 33,700 sq. km (13,000 sq. miles). In Jan. 1983 the population was 4,052,000, of whom (1979 census) 63·9% are Moldavians. Others include Ukrainians (14·2%), Russians (12·8%), Gagauzi (3·5%), Jews (2%). Apart from Kishinev, larger towns are Tiraspol (154,000), Beltsy (139,000) and Bendery (114,000).

CONSTITUTION AND GOVERNMENT. The Supreme Soviet, elected in 1980, consists of 380 deputies (1 per 10,000 population); 138 are women, 253 Communists. A new Constitution was adopted in April 1978.

At elections to the district, urban and rural Soviets (20 June 1982), of 37,626 deputies returned, 18,865 (50·1%) were women, 21,286 (56·6%) non-Party and 26,519 (70·5%) industrial workers and collective farmers.

Chairman, Presidium of the Supreme Soviet: I. P. Kalin.
Chairman, Council of Ministers: I. G. Ustiyan.
First Secretary, Communist Party: S. K. Grossu.

FINANCE. Budget estimates (in 1m. rubles), 1983, 1,952; 1984, 2,265.

AGRICULTURE. On 1 Jan. 1982 there were 366 collective farms and 413 state farms. All ploughing and sowing is mechanized. Livestock included (1 Jan. 1979) 1·1m. cattle, 2m. pigs and 1·2m. sheep and goats. There were 50,300 tractors and 3,800 combine harvesters.

Output of main agricultural products (in 1,000 tonnes) in 1978 (1913 figures in tons in brackets): Wheat, 1,288 (526); maize, 1,165 (639); sugar-beet, 2,807 (15), sunflower seeds, 350 (9); potatoes, 335 (119); other vegetables, 1,227; fruit, 929; grapes, 1,377; meat, 253 (53); milk, 1,200 (210); wool, 2·5 (3); 880m. eggs (275m.). Bessarabia has an equable climate and very fertile soil. It contains nearly one quarter of the vineyards of the USSR. Bessarabia is also rich in fish in the south: sturgeon, mackerel, brill.

INDUSTRY. There are canning plants, wine-making plants, woodworking and metallurgical factories, a factory of ferro-concrete building materials, and footwear and textile plants. Moldavia takes third place in the USSR in the production of wine, tobacco and food-canning. Production in 1977 included 28·9m. linear metres of silk fabrics, 16·3m. pairs of leather footwear, 424,100 tons of granulated sugar. 1,525m. tins of preserves and 24·7m. decalitres of wine. Meat and dairy produce are rapidly expanding food industries.

There are lignite, phosphorites, gypsum and valuable building materials.

In 1981 there were 1,557,000 industrial and office workers working in the national economy. Electricity generated (1981) 16,700m. kwh.

COMMUNICATIONS. Length of railways, 1,150 km. There is direct air communication with Leningrad, Moscow, Kiev, Lvov and across the Black Sea. There are 11,200 km of motor roads (9,600 hard surface), and 1,100 km of inland waterways.

Newspapers (1981). There were 183 newspapers, 78 were in Moldavian. Daily circulation of Moldavian-language newspapers, 1,159,000, other languages, 921,000.

EDUCATION. In 1981–82 there were 700,000 pupils in 1,800 primary, secondary and special schools, 59,300 students in 51 technical colleges and 52,600 students in 8 higher educational institutions including the state university. A Moldavian Academy of Sciences was established in 1961: it had 17 research institutions and a scientific staff of 962 in 1979. In all, there are 68 learned institutions with 8,100 scientific staff. In 1981 there were 273,000 children attending pre-school institutions.

HEALTH. Moldavia has 800 medical centres, many district hospitals, a state medical institute and 9 medical schools with over 2,500 students. Doctors in 1981 numbered 13,100; hospital beds, 49,000.

Books of Reference

Zlatova, Y., and Kotelnikov, V., *Across Moldavia* (English ed.). Moscow, 1959
Istoriya Moldavskoi SSR. 2nd ed. 2 vols. Kishinev, 1965–68

ESTONIA
Eesti Nõukogude Sotsialistlik Vabariik

HISTORY. The workers' and soldiers' Soviets in Estonia took over power on 8 Nov. 1917, were overthrown by the German occupying forces in March 1918, and were restored to power as the Germans withdrew in Nov. 1918, establishing the 'Estland Labour Commune'. It was overthrown with the assistance of British naval forces in May 1919, and a democratic republic proclaimed. In March 1934 this regime was, in turn, overthrown by a fascist *coup*.

The secret protocol of the Soviet-German agreement of 23 Aug. 1939 assigned Estonia to the Soviet sphere of interest. An ultimatum (16 June 1940) led to the formation of a government acceptable to the USSR; on 21 July the State Duma proclaimed the establishment of an Estonian Soviet Socialist Republic and applied to join the USSR: on 6 Aug. the Supreme Soviet accepted the application. The incorporation has been accorded *de facto* recognition by the British Government, but not by the US Government, which continues to recognize an Estonian consul-general in New York.

AREA AND POPULATION. Estonia is bounded west and north by the Baltic, east by the RSFSR and south by Latvia. Area, 45,100 sq. km (17,410 sq. miles); population, 1,507,000 (Jan. 1983). Census (1979) 64·7% were Estonians, 27·9% Russians, 2·5% Ukrainians and 1·6% Belorussians. The capital is Tallinn. Other large towns are Tartu (109,000), Pärnu, Narva (78,000). There are 15 districts, 33 towns and 26 urban settlements.

CONSTITUTION AND GOVERNMENT. The Supreme Soviet, elected in 1980, consists of 285 deputies (1 per 10,000 population); 101 are women, 193 Communists. A new Constitution was adopted in April 1978.

At elections to district, urban and rural Soviets (20 June 1982), out of 11,010 deputies returned 5,459 (49·6%) were women, 6,090 (55·3%) non-Party and 7,438 (67·6%) industrial workers and collective farmers.

Chairman, Presidium of the Supreme Soviet: A. F. Riuitel.
Chairman, Council of Ministers: V. I. Klauson.
First Secretary, Communist Party: K. G. Vaino.

FINANCE. Budget estimates (in 1m. rubles), 1983, 1,259; 1984, 1,447.

AGRICULTURE. Agriculture and dairy farming are the chief occupations. Area under cultivation was 697,000 hectares in 1913, 918,000 hectares in 1940 and 954,000 hectares in 1978. There were 143 agricultural and 8 fishery collectives and 158 state farms in 1982 using 19,400 tractors and 3,500 grain combines. 97% of state farms and 70% of collective farms were receiving electric power.

On 1 Jan. 1980 there were 822,000 head of cattle, 150,000 sheep and goats, 1,052,000 pigs and 5·8m. poultry.

Output of main agricultural products (in 1,000 tonnes) in 1979 (1913 figures in brackets): Potatoes, 1,243 (689); grains, 1,052 (428); other vegetables, 109; meat (slaughter weight), 188 (60); milk, 1,138 (415); wool, 0·3 (0·7); 493m. eggs (67m.).

INDUSTRY. Some 22% of the territory is covered by forests which provide good material for its sawmills, furniture, match and pulp industries, as well as wood fuel. Since the end of the war, 80,000 hectares have been afforested. 966,700 hectares of marsh land had been reclaimed by 1977.

Estonia has rich high-quality shale deposits (particularly in the north-east) which are estimated at 3,700m. tons. Shale output was 1·9m. tons in 1940 and 30m. in 1977. A factory for the production of gas from shale and a pipeline (208 km long) from Kohtla-Järve supplies shale gas to Leningrad and Tallinn. Estonian factories are now turning out agricultural and peat-digging machines, complex control and measuring instruments. The 'Volta' factory in Tallinn produces electric motors.

In the neighbourhood of Tallinn, phosphorites have been found, and in 1947 a plant for refining and for the production of super-phosphates was started. Estonia also contains valuable peat deposits, and some of her electrical stations work on peat. There are 350 rural electric stations. Electricity generated (1981) 17,800m. kwh. Output of mineral fertilizers in 1977 was 1·4m. tons; cement, 1·26m. tons; paper, 106,000 tons; cotton fabrics, 196m. linear metres; linen fabrics, 6·1m. linear metres; sawn timber, 733,000 cu. metres; leather footwear, 6·1m. pairs.

In 1981 there were 704,000 industrial and office workers and 62,000 specialists with a higher education engaged in the national economy.

COMMUNICATIONS. Length of railways in 1981, 1,010 km. Estonia has 20 ports, but Tallinn handles four-fifths of the total sea-going transport. Inland waterways total 500 km; motor roads, 27,600 km (hard surface, 25,200 km). Airlines link Tallinn with Moscow, Leningrad, Riga and the Estonian islands.

Newspapers (1981). There were 44 newspapers, 31 of them in Estonian. Daily circulation of Estonian-language newspapers, 1,021,000, other languages, 184,000.

EDUCATION. Estonia has retained an 11-year school curriculum, when it was reduced to 10 years elsewhere in the USSR. In 1981–82 pupils in 600 primary, secondary and special schools numbered 216,000. There were 25,500 students in 6 higher educational establishments, including Tartu (Dorpat) University, founded in 1632, and 23,800 students in 37 technical colleges.

The Estonian Academy of Sciences, founded in 1946, has 24 institutions with 985 scientific staff; in all, 6,000 scientists are working in 72 institutions.

In 1981 there were 84,000 children attending pre-school institutions.

HEALTH. In 1981 there were 6,300 doctors and 18,800 hospital beds.

Books of Reference

Istoriya Estonskoi SSR. 3 vols. Tallin, 1961–74
Küng, A., *A Dream of Freedom.* Cardiff, 1980
Misiuras, R-J., and Taagepera, R., *The Baltic States: Years of Dependence 1940–1980.* Farnborough, 1983
Parming, T., and Jarvesro, E., (eds.) *A Case Study of a Soviet Republic.* Boulder, 1978
Saagpakk, P. F., *Estonian-English Dictionary.* New Haven, 1982
Silvet, J., *Inglise—eestisõnaraamat.* Vadstena, 1949
Varetz, E. F., and Tarmisto, V. Y., *Estoniya.* Moscow, 1967 (in Russian)

LATVIA
Latvijas Padomju Socialistiska Republika

HISTORY. In the part of Latvia unoccupied by the Germans, the Bolsheviks won 72% of the votes in the Constituent Assembly elections (Nov. 1917). Soviet power was proclaimed in Dec. 1917, but was overthrown when the Germans occupied all Latvia (Feb. 1918). Restored when they withdrew (Dec. 1918), it was overthrown once more by combined British naval and German military forces (May–Dec. 1919), and a democratic government set up. This régime was in turn replaced when a fascist *coup* took place in May 1934.

The secret protocol of the Soviet–German agreement of 23 Aug. 1939 assigned Latvia to the Soviet sphere of interest. An ultimatum (16 June 1940) led to the formation of a government acceptable to the USSR; on 21 July a People's Diet proclaimed the establishment of the Latvian Soviet Socialist Republic and applied to join the USSR: whose Supreme Soviet accepted the application on 5 Aug. The incorporation has been accorded *de facto* recognition by the British Government, but not by the US Government, which continues to recognize the Chargé d'Affaires in Washington, D.C.

AREA AND POPULATION. Latvia is bounded north by Estonia and the Baltic Sea, west by the Baltic Sea, south by Lithuania and Belorussia and east by the RSFSR. Latvia has a total area of 63,700 sq. km (25,590 sq. miles). Population, Jan. 1983, 2,569,000, of whom (1979 census) 53·7% are Latvians and 32·8% Russians. There are 26 districts, 56 towns and 36 urban settlements.

The chief town is Riga (the capital); other principal towns are Daugavpils (Dvinsk) (122,000), Liepāja (109,000), Jelgava (Mitau) (69,000) and Ventspils (Windau).

CONSTITUTION AND GOVERNMENT. The Supreme Soviet, elected in 1980, consists of 325 deputies (1 per 10,000 population); 113 are women, 218 Communists. A new Constitution was adopted in April 1978.

At elections to district, urban and rural Soviets (20 June 1982), of 23,369 deputies returned, 11,490 (49·2%) were women, 12,389 (53%) non-Party and 15,609 (66·8%) industrial workers and collective farmers.

Chairman, Presidium of the Supreme Soviet: P. Y. Strautmanis.
Chairman, Council of Ministers: Y. Y. Ruben.
First Secretary, Communist Party: A. E. Voss.

FINANCE. Budget estimates (in 1m. rubles), 1983, 1,862; 1984, 2,154.

AGRICULTURE. Latvia is now no longer mainly an agricultural country. The urban population, 35% of the total in 1939, was 70% in Jan. 1982.

Latvian forest lands, state and private (2·4m. hectares), produced in 1937–38, 3·4m. cu. metres of timber; 1977 output, 3·9m. cu. metres.

Area under cultivation was 1·4m. hectares in 1913, 2m. in 1940, 1·7m. in 1978. 1·8m. hectares of marsh land have been drained (1979).

Cattle breeding and dairy farming are the chief agricultural occupations. Oats, barley, rye, potatoes and flax are the main crops.

After the establishment of the Soviet regime about 960,000 hectares were distributed among the landless peasants or those with very small holdings. On 1 Jan. 1982 there were 243 state farms and 320 collective farms. There were 32,900 tractors and 6,800 grain combine harvesters. By 1 Jan. 1964, all state farms and collective farms were using electric power.

Livestock (1 Jan. 1980): Cattle, 1·4m. (1939: 1·3m.); sheep, 211,000 (1939: 1·5m.); pigs, 1·4m. (1939: 891,500).

Output of main agricultural products (in 1,000 tonnes) in 1979 (1913 figures in brackets): Sugar-beet, 195 (0); potatoes, 1,626 (645); all grains, 1,171 (880); other vegetables, 147; fruit, 35; meat and fats, 250 (122); milk, 1,664 (673); wool, 0·5 (1·4); flax, 4·1 (21); 720m. eggs (136m.).

INDUSTRY. Latvia is the main producer of electric railway passenger cars and long-distance telephone exchanges in the USSR, fourth in output of paper and woollen goods, fifth of sawn timber, sixth of mineral fertilizers.

Industrial output in 1977 (in 1,000 tons) included: Steel, 502; rolled metal, 630; cement, 903; granulated sugar, 271; paper, 169; fish catch, 550; cotton fabrics, 62·8m. linear metres; linen fabrics, 21·3m. linear metres; woollens, 14m. linear metres; silks, 19·9m. linear metres; leather footwear, 10·2m. pairs; radio sets, 2·4m. (no.). Electricity generated (1981) 4,800m. kwh.

Peat deposits extend over 645,000 hectares or about 10% of the total area, and it is estimated that total deposits are 3,000–4,000m. tons; output, 1971, 2·3m. tons. There are also gypsum deposits; amber is frequently found in the coastal districts.

In 1981 industrial and office workers numbered 1,207,000.

COMMUNICATIONS. In 1981 the length of railways was 2,380 km, and motor roads, 23,500 km (hard surface, 17,400 km). Riga is the largest port in the Baltic after Leningrad.

Newspapers (1981). There were 103 newspapers (62 in Lettish). Daily circulation of Lettish-language newspapers, 1·2m., other languages 469,000.

RELIGION. The Latvian Lutheran Church numbered 600,000 members in 1956.

EDUCATION. In 1981–82 there were 900 primary and secondary schools, with a total of 400,000 pupils; 117,000 children attended pre-school institutions. Ten places of higher education had 47,200 students, 55 technical colleges had 41,500 students; there were also 21 music and art schools, 3 teachers' training colleges and an agricultural academy. In 1946 an Academy of Sciences was opened which in 1979 had 16 research institutes with a staff of 1,700 scientific workers; there were over 12,000 scientific workers in 101 research institutions.

HEALTH. There were 11,400 doctors and 34,900 hospital beds in 1981.

Books of Reference

Latvian Academy of Sciences, *Istoriya Latviiskoi SSR.* Riga. 3 vols. 1952–58
Bilmanis, A., *A History of Latvia.* Princeton Univ. Press, 1951
Roze, B. and K., *Latviska–Angliska Vārdnīcā.* Göppingen, 1948
Spekke, A., *History of Latvia.* Stockholm, 1951
Turkina, E., *Angliski–Latviska Vārdnīca.* Riga, 1948.—*Latviešu-Anglu Vārdnīca.* Riga, 1962

LITHUANIA
Lietuvos Tarybu Socialistine Respublika

HISTORY. In 1914–15 the German army occupied the whole of Lithuania. On its withdrawal (Dec. 1918) Soviets were elected in all towns and a Soviet republic was proclaimed. In the summer of 1919 it was overthrown by Polish, German and nationalist Lithuanian forces, and a democratic republic established. In Dec. 1926 this regime was in turn overthrown by a fascist *coup*.

The secret protocol of the Soviet–German frontier treaty of 28 Sept. 1939 assigned the greater part of Lithuania to the Soviet sphere of influence. In Oct. 1939 the province and city of Vilnius (in Polish occupation 1920–39) were ceded by the USSR. An ultimatum (16 June 1940) led to the formation of a government acceptable to the USSR. A people's Diet, elected on 14–15 July, proclaimed the establishment of the Lithuanian Soviet Socialist Republic on 21 July and applied for admission to the USSR, which was effected by decree of the USSR Supreme Soviet on 3 Aug. and included also those parts of Lithuania which had been reserved for inclusion in Germany. This incorporation has been accorded *de facto* recognition by the British Government, but not by the US Government, which continues to recognize a Lithuanian Chargé d'Affaires in Washington, D.C.

AREA AND POPULATION. Lithuania is bounded north by Latvia, east and south by Belorussia, west by Poland, the Kaliningrad area of the RSFSR and the Baltic Sea. The total area of Lithuania is 65,200 sq. km (25,170 sq. miles) and the population (Jan. 1983) 3,506,000, of whom 80% were Lithuanians, 8·6% Russians and 7·7% Poles (1979 census).

The capital is Vilnius (Vilna). Other large towns are Kaunas (Kovno), Klaipeda (Memel), Šiauliai (130,000) and Panėvežys (112,000). There are 44 rural districts, 92 towns and 21 urban settlements.

CONSTITUTION AND GOVERNMENT. The Supreme Soviet, elected in 1980, consists of 350 deputies (1 per 15,000 population); 125 are women, 235 Communists. A new Constitution was adopted in April 1978.

At elections to district, urban and rural Soviets (20 June 1982), of 28,410 deputies returned, 14,140 (49·8%) were women, 16,139 (56·8%) non-Party and 19,291 (67·9%) industrial workers and collective farmers.

Chairman, Presidium of the Supreme Soviet: A. S. Barkauskas.
Chairman, Council of Ministers: R.-B. I. Songeila.
First Secretary, Communist Party: P. P. Griškevičius.

FINANCE. Budget estimates (in 1m. rubles), 1983, 2,704; 1984, 3,237.

AGRICULTURE. Lithuania before 1940 was a mainly agricultural country, but has since been considerably industrialized. The urban population was 23% of the total in 1937 and 59% in Jan. 1978. The resources of the country consist of timber and agricultural produce. Of the total area, 49·1% is arable land, 22·2% meadow and pasture land, 16·3% forests and 12·4% unproductive lands.

Area under cultivation in 1913 was 1·9m.; in 1938, 2·7m.; in 1977, 2·4m. hectares. By 1978 over 2·5m. hectares of swamps had been drained.

Output of main agricultural products (in 1,000 tonnes) in 1978 (1913 figures in brackets): All grains, 2,225 (1,449); sugar-beet, 803 (0); flax, 12 (17); potatoes, 2.313 (1,375); other vegetables, 365; fruit, 153; meat and fats, 463 (159); milk, 2.681 (832); wool, 0·2 (1·5); 943m. eggs (264m.).

On 1 Jan. 1980 there were 2·2m. cattle, 2·6m. pigs, 60,000 sheep and goats.

Forests cover 1,554,000 hectares; 70% of the forests consist of conifers, mostly pines. Peat reserves total 4,000m. cu. metres.

Between 1940 and 1947 about 575,500 hectares (about 1·4m. acres) were distributed among the landless and poor peasant farmers. In 1981 there were 45,900 tractors and 10,300 grain combines serving 741 collective farms and 311 state farms.

INDUSTRY. Heavy engineering, shipbuilding and building material industries are developing. Industrial output included, in 1977: Cement, 2·99m. tons; granulated sugar, 207,100 tons; paper, 124,000 tons; cotton fabrics, 86·3m. linear metres; linens, 19m. linear metres; woollens, 12·4m. linear metres; sawn timber, 1m. cu. metres; leather footwear, 9·4m. pairs; electric power, 11·700m. kwh.

In 1981 there were 1,485,000 industrial and office workers employed in the national economy.

COMMUNICATIONS. Length of railways, 2,030 km. Vilnius has one of the largest airports of the USSR. There are 32,000 km of motor roads (21,700 km hard surface) and 600 km of inland waterways. Klaipeda, as a non-freezing harbour and fishery base, is of national importance.

Newspapers (1981). Of 126 newspapers, 99 were in Lithuanian. Daily circulation of Lithuanian-language newspapers, 1·9m., other languages, 270,000.

RELIGION. In 1956, the Lithuanian Lutheran Church had 215,000 members; Roman Catholics, including those in Estonia and Latvia, numbered 2·5m.

EDUCATION. In 1981–82 there were 600,000 pupils in 2,300 primary, secondary and special schools. The University of Vytautas the Great, at Kaunas, was opened on 16 Feb. 1922. On 15 Jan. 1940 certain faculties were transferred to Vilnius to join the ancient University of Vilnius (founded 1570). In 1981–82 there were 12 higher educational institutions with 71,300 students: in 68 technical colleges of all kinds there were 66,400 students. The Lithuanian Academy of Sciences, founded in 1941, had 11 institutions with a total scientific staff of 1,727; there were 88 scientific institutions with 13,500 research personnel. 160,000 children in 1981 were attending pre-school institutions.

HEALTH. In 1981 there were 13,800 doctors and 41,900 hospital beds.

Books of Reference

Griškevičius, P. P., *Land on the Nemunas*. Moscow, 1977
Jurgela, C. R., *History of the Lithuanian Nation*. New York, 1948
Kantantas, F., *A Lithuanian Bibliography*. Univ. of Alberta Press, 1975
Peteraitis, V., *Lithuanian–English Dictionary*. 2 vols. Chicago, 1960
Vardys, S., (ed.) *Lithuania under the Soviets: Portrait of a Nation, 1940–45*. New York, 1965

SOVIET CENTRAL ASIA

Soviet Central Asia embraces the Kazakh Soviet Socialist Republic, the Uzbek Soviet Socialist Republic, the Turkmen Soviet Socialist Republic, the Tadzhik Soviet Socialist Republic and the Kirghiz Soviet Socialist Republic.

Turkestan (by which name part of this territory was then known) was conquered by the Russians in the 1860s. In 1866 Tashkent was occupied and in 1868 Samarkand, and subsequently further territory was conquered and united with Russian Turkestan. In the 1870s Bokhara was subjugated, the emir, by the agreement of 1873, recognizing the suzerainty of Russia. In the same year Khiva became a vassal state to Russia. Until 1917 Russian Central Asia was divided politically into the Khanate of Khiva, the Emirate of Bokhara and the Governor-Generalship of Turkestan.

In the summer of 1919 the authority of the Soviet Government became definitely established in these regions. The Khan of Khiva was deposed in Feb. 1920, and a People's Soviet Republic was set up, the medieval name of Khorezm being revived. In Aug. 1920 the Emir of Bokhara suffered the same fate, and a similar regime was set up in Bokhara. The former Governor-Generalship of Turkestan was constituted an Autonomous Soviet Socialist Republic within the RSFSR on 11 April 1921.

In the autumn of 1924 the Soviets of the Turkestan, Bokhara and Khiva Republics decided to redistribute the territories of these republics on a nationality basis; at the same time Bokhara and Khiva became Socialist Republics. The redistribution was completed in May 1925, when the new states of Uzbekistan, Turkmenistan and Tadzhikistan were accepted into the USSR as Union Republics. The remaining districts of Turkestan populated by Kazakhs were united with Kazakhstan which was established as an ASSR in 1925 and became a Union Republic in 1936. Kirghizia, until then part of the RSFSR, was established as a Union Republic in 1936.

Books of Reference

Akiner, S., *The Islamic Peoples of the Soviet Union.* London, 1983
Bennigsen, A., and Broxup, M., *The Islamic Threat to the Soviet State.* London, 1983
Nove, A. and Newth, J. A., *The Soviet Middle East.* London, 1967
Rywkin, M., *Moscow's Muslim Challenge.* New York, 1982
Wheeler, G., *The Modern History of Soviet Central Asia.* London, 1964.—*The Peoples of Soviet Central Asia.* London, 1966

KAZAKHSTAN
Kazak Soviettik Sotzialistik Respublikasy

HISTORY. On 26 Aug. 1920 Uralsk, Turgai, Akmolinsk and Semipalatinsk provinces formed the Kirgiz (in 1925 renamed Kazakh) Autonomous Soviet Socialist Republic within the RSFSR. It was made a constituent republic of the USSR on 5 Dec. 1936. To this republic were added the parts of the former Governorship of Turkestan inhabited by a majority of Kazakhs. It consists of the following regions: Aktyubinsk, Alma-Ata, Chimkent, Dzhambul, Dzhezkazgan, East Kazakhstan, Guryev, Karaganda, Kokchetav, Kustanai, Kzyl-Orda, Mangyshlak, North Kazakhstan, Pavlodar, Semipalatinsk, Taldy-Kurgan, Tselinograd, Turgai, Uralsk.

AREA AND POPULATION. Kazakhstan is bounded on the west by the Caspian Sea and the RSFSR, on the east by China, on the north by the RSFSR and on the south by Uzbekistan and Kirghizia. The area of the republic is 2,717,300 sq. km (1,049,155 sq. miles). It is the next in size to the RSFSR, is far larger than all the other Central Asian Soviet Republics combined and stretches nearly 3,000 km from west to east and over 1,500 km from north to south. Population (Jan. 1983) 15,452,000, of whom 55% live in urban areas. The Kazakhs form 36%, Russians 40·8% and Ukrainians 6·1% of the population (1979 census), as a result of the industrialization of the country since 1941 and the opening of virgin lands since 1945. The population includes over 100 nationalities.

The capital is Alma-Ata, formerly Verny; other large towns are Karaganda, Semipalatinsk, Chimkent and Petropavlovsk. In all there are 82 towns, 189 urban settlements and 218 rural districts.

CONSTITUTION AND GOVERNMENT. The Supreme Soviet, elected in 1980, consists of 510 deputies (1 per 20,000 population); 182 are women, 336 Communists. A new Constitution was adopted in April 1978.

At elections to the regional, district, urban and rural Soviets (20 June 1982), out of 128,365 deputies returned, 63,006 (49·1%) were women, 74,480 (58%) non-Party and 87,991 (68·6%) industrial workers and collective farmers.

President, Presidium of the Supreme Soviet: S. N. Imashav.
Chairman, Council of Ministers: B. A. Ashimov.
First Secretary, Communist Party: D. A. Kunayev.

FINANCE. The budget (in 1m. rubles) balanced as follows: 1983, 9,351; 1984, 10,487.

AGRICULTURE. Kazakh agriculture has changed from primarily nomad cattle breeding to production of grain, cotton and other industrial crops. In 1978 the crop area was 35·3m. hectares—over 16% of the total cultivated area of the USSR (1913, 4·2m.; 1940, 6·8m.).

1,827,000 hectares of land have an irrigation network.

The 'Ukrainka' winter wheat has been transformed into a spring wheat suitable for cultivation in Kazakhstan. Tobacco, rubber plants and mustard are also cultivated. Kazakhstan has rich orchards and vineyards; 25,000 hectares were under vines and 101,000 under orchards in 1978. Between 1954 and 1959, over 23m. hectares of virgin and long fallow land were opened up, 544 new state grain farms being organized for the purpose. Grain deliveries to the state were 10·5m. tons in 1960; 2·4m. in 1965; 13·4m. in 1970; 5·1m. in 1975; 8·2m. in 1977; 16,784 in 1978.

Kazakhstan is noted for its livestock, particularly its sheep, from which excellent quality wool is obtained. The Akharomerino is a newly developed crossbreed of merino sheep and the wild Akhar mountain ram. Livestock on 1 Jan. 1979 included 8·01m. cattle, 34·2m. sheep and goats and 2·6m. pigs.

There were, on 1 Jan. 1982, 394 collective farms and 2,098 state farms with 237,400 tractors and 109,700 grain combine harvesters. There were 5,293 rural power stations of 307,800 kwh. capacity.

Output of main agricultural products (in 1m. tonnes) in 1978 (1913 figures in brackets): All grains, 34·5 (2·2); cotton, 0·3 (0·015); sugar-beet, 2·5 (0); potatoes, 1·83 (0·18); other vegetables, 2·29; meat, 1 (0·44); milk, 4·4 (0·85); 3,352m. eggs (233m.); wool, 0·1 (0·04).

INDUSTRY. Kazakhstan is extremely rich in mineral resources. Coal and tungsten in Karaganda (in the centre), oil along the river Emba (in the west), copper, lead and zinc—Kazakhstan contains about one-half of the total deposits of these three metals contained in the USSR—Iceland spar (in the south), nickel and chromium in the Kustanai and Semipalatinsk regions, molybdenum and other minerals.

In 1943 big deposits of manganese were found in Eastern Kazakhstan; new coal seams were also discovered there. In South Kazakhstan new copper and bauxite deposits have been found.

Coal, oil, non-ferrous metallurgy, heavy engineering and chemical industries have brought Kazakhstan to the third place among the industrial republics of the USSR.

Coal output in 1977 was 93·7m. tons; oil, 23·3m. tons; steel, 5·6m. tons; rolled metal, 4·4m. tons; cement, 6·8m. tons; mineral fertilizers, 6·5m. tons; cotton fabrics, 101·2m. linear metres; leather footwear, 31·2m. pairs; woollen fabrics, 16·7m. linear metres; granulated sugar, 120,100 tons. The Leninogorsk and Chimkent lead plants, the Balkhash, Irtysh and Karaskpai copper-smelting works and others supply the country with non-ferrous metals. A meat-packing plant has been built in Semipalatinsk, a fish cannery in Guryev, a chemical plant in Aktyubinsk, a tractor works at Pavlodar, and a superphosphate plant in Dzhambul. The oil industry in Emba and Aktyubinsk yields high-quality aviation oil. Iron ore output in 1977 was 23·4m. tons.

Aviation plays an important part in agriculture. About 14m. hectares were in 1970 treated from the air (destruction of pests, surface feeding of sugar-beet plantations, pollination of orchards, etc.).

Among recent enterprises are a large textile combine at Kustanai, hosiery factories at Djezkazgan, Leninogorsk and Aktyubinsk, a sugar factory at Aksu, meat canneries at Djetygar and Kzyl-Orda.

Electric power output in 1981 was 63,700m. kwh.

There were, in 1981, 6,151,000 industrial and office workers in the national economy.

COMMUNICATIONS

Roads. In 1981 there were 105,900 km of motor roads (79,000 km hard surface).

Railways. A 430-km railway line between the settlements of Mointi and Chu in Kazakhstan to complete the Transkazakh trunk line, connecting Petropavlovsk,

Akmolinsk, Karaganda and Balkhash, was opened in 1953. The new line links the Transkazakh trunk line with the Turkestan–Siberian railway carrying Karaganda coal to South Kazakhstan. The Akmolinsk–Pavlodar railway (438 km), a section of the South Siberian line, was opened in Dec. 1953. Other lines in operation are Dzhambul–Chalaktan, Akmolinsk–Kartaly, Uralsk–Iletsk, Guriev–Kandagach. In 1981 the total length of railways in operation was 14,270 km. Over 600 km of narrow-gauge line and 700 km of broad-gauge line were built in the virgin lands area in 1951-57.

Inland waterways. Total length 5,500 km.

Newspapers (1981). Of 435 newspapers, 159 were in the Kazakh language. Daily circulation of Kazakh-language newspapers, 1·9m., other languages, 3·5m.

EDUCATION. Nearly the whole population is literate. In 1981–82 there were 3·3m. pupils at 8,700 elementary and secondary schools; 238 technical colleges with 270,600 students, 55 higher educational institutions with 267,900 students, and 207 research institutes with 34,700 scientific personnel. The Kazakh Academy of Sciences, founded in 1945, had, in 1980, 31 institutions, the scientific staff of which numbered 4,139. 902,000 children were attending pre-school institutions.

HEALTH. In 1981 there were 49,900 doctors and 199,400 hospital beds.

Books of Reference

Istoriya Kazakhskoi SSR. 2 vols. Alma-Ata, 1957–59
Alampiev, P., *Soviet Kazakhstan.* Moscow, 1958.—*Where Economic Inequality is No More.* Moscow, 1959

TURKMENISTAN

Tiurkmenostan Soviet Sotsialistik Respublikasy

HISTORY. The Turkmen Soviet Socialist Republic was formed on 27 Oct. 1924 and covers the territory of the former Trans-Caspian Region of Turkestan, the Charjiui vilayet of Bokhara and a part of Khiva situated on the right bank of the Oxus. In May 1925 the Turkmen Republic entered the Soviet Union as one of its constituent republics.

AREA AND POPULATION. Turkmenistan is bounded on the north by the Autonomous Kara-Kalpak Republic, a constituent of Uzbekistan, by Iran and Afghánistán on the south, by the Uzbek Republic on the east and the Caspian Sea on the west. The principal Turkmen tribes are the Tekkés of Merv and the Tekkés of the Attok, the Ersaris, Yomuds and Goklans. All speak closely related varieties of a Turkic language (of the south-western group); many are Sunni Mohammedans.

The country passed under Russian control in 1881, after the fall of the Turkoman stronghold of GökTépé. Census (1979) 68·4% of the population were Turkmenians, most of whom were nomads before the First World War. 12·6% are Russians living mostly in urban areas, and 8·5% Uzbeks. There are also Kazakhs (2·9%), Tatars, Ukrainians, Armenians and others.

The area of Turkmenistan is 488,100 sq. km (186,400 sq. miles), and its population in Jan. 1983 was 3,042,000.

There are 5 regions: Chardzhou, Maruy, Ashkhabad, Tashauz and Krasnovodsk, comprising 42 rural districts, 15 towns and 74 urban settlements.

The capital is Ashkhabad (Poltoratsk); other large towns are Chardzhou (152,000), Mary (Merv) (81,000), Nebit-Dag (78,000) and Krasnovodsk (55,000).

CONSTITUTION AND GOVERNMENT. The Supreme Soviet, elected in 1980, consists of 330 deputies (1 per 5,000 population); 107 are women, 224 Communists. A new Constitution was adopted in April 1978.

At elections to regional, district, urban and rural Soviets (20 June 1982), of

23,478 deputies returned, 11,623 (49·5%) were women, 13,317 (56·7%) non-party and 16,312 (69·5%) industrial workers and collective farmers.

Chairman, Presidium of the Supreme Soviet: B. Yazkuliev.
Chairman, Council of Ministers: C. S. Karryev.
First Secretary, Communist Party: M. G. Gapurov.

FINANCE. Budget estimates (in 1m. rubles), 1983, 1,193; 1984, 1,346.

AGRICULTURE. The main occupation of the people is agriculture, based on irrigation. Turkmenistan produces cotton, wool, Astrakhan fur, etc. It is also famous for its carpets, and produces a special breed of Turkoman horses and the famous Karakul sheep.

There were 328 collective farms and 112 state farms in 1982, with 37,100 tractors and 1,100 grain combines. There were 608 rural power stations.

A considerable area is under Egyptian cotton, and from it has been evolved an original Soviet long-fibred cotton.

The main grain grown is maize. Sericulture, fruit and vegetable growing are also important; dates, olives, figs, sesame and other southern plants are grown. There is fishing in the Caspian. 900,000 hectares were under cultivation in 1978 (1913, 318,000; 1940, 411,000).

Between 1958 and 1970 the Kara-Kum Canal was extended to 860 km. In 1971 the fourth section, to reach the Caspian, was begun to reach 1,000 km. By 1978 over 892,000 hectares had been irrigated.

Livestock on 1 Jan. 1980: Cattle, 602,000; pigs, 158,000; sheep and goats, 4·5m.

Output of main agricultural products (in 1,000 tonnes) in 1978 (1913 figures in brackets): Wheat, 281 (113); cotton, 1,215 (69); vegetables, 284; grapes, 63; fruit, 39; meat, 67 (58); milk, 307 (63); wool, 15·3 (9·7); 243m. eggs (18m.).

INDUSTRY. Turkmenistan is rich in minerals, such as ozocerite, oil, coal, sulphur and salt. Industry is being developed, and there are now chemical, tailoring, textile, light, food, agricultural implements, cement and other factories, oil refineries, as well as ore-mining.

In the Kara-Kum Desert deposits of magnesium, minerals and coal have been discovered, as well as some 50 new saltmines. Here a new oil town, Nebit-Dag, has sprung up. On the Kara-Bogaz bay a sulphate industry has been developed. Industrial output in 1977 included 14·8m. tons of oil, 564,000 tons of cement, 23·1m. linear metres of cotton fabrics, 3·5m. pairs of leather footwear. Electric power output was 7,200m. kwh. (in 1981); 62,581m. cu. metres of natural gas were produced.

In 1981 there were 736,000 industrial and office workers in the national economy.

COMMUNICATIONS. Length of motor roads 20,600 km (15,600 km hard surface). Motor communication exists between Ashkhabad and Meshed (Iran).

Length of railways, 2,120 km. The line Chardzhou–Kungrad crosses the Chardzhou and Tashauz regions of Turkmenia and runs across Uzbekistan. Another line connects Chardzhou and Urgench. Inland waterways, 1,300 km.

Airlines connect Leninsk and Tashauz, and Ashkhabad and remote areas in the west, north and east.

Newspapers (1981). Of 68 newspapers, 55 were in the Turkmen language. Daily circulation of Turkmenian-language newspapers, 820,000, other languages, 212,000.

EDUCATION. In 1981–82 there were 1,900 primary and secondary schools with 700,000 pupils, 8 higher educational institutions with 37,100 students, 35 technical colleges with 34,400 students, and 11 music and art schools. The Turkmen Academy of Sciences directs the work of 14 learned institutions with a staff of 972 scientists; there were 58 research institutions in all, with 5,000 research

workers, in 1978. A Turkmenian State University was opened in 1951: in 1973 it had 10,124 students.
In 1981, 132,000 children were attending pre-school institutions.

HEALTH. In 1981 there were 8,500 doctors and 31,600 hospital beds.

Book of Reference

Istoriya Turkmenskoi SSR. 2 vols. Ashkhabad, 1957

UZBEKISTAN
Ozbekiston Soviet Sotsialistik Respublikasy

HISTORY. In Oct. 1917 the Tashkent Soviet assumed authority, and in the following years established its power throughout Turkestan. The semi-independent Khanates of Khiva and Bokhara were first (1920) transformed into People's Republics, then (1923–24) into Soviet Socialist Republics and finally merged in the Uzbek SSR and other republics.

The Uzbek Soviet Socialist Republic was formed on 27 Oct. 1924 from lands formerly included in Turkestan. It includes a large part of the Samarkand region, the southern part of the Syr Darya, Western Ferghana, the western plains of Bukhara, the Kara-Kalpak ASSR and the Uzbek regions of Khorezm. In May 1925 Uzbekistan, by the decision of the Congress of Soviets of the USSR, was accepted as one of the constituent republics of the Soviet Union.

AREA AND POPULATION. Uzbekistan is bordered on the north by the Kazakh Soviet Socialist Republic, on the east by the Kirghiz Soviet Socialist Republic and the Tadzhik Soviet Socialist Republic, on the south by Afghánistán and on the west by the Turkmen Soviet Socialist Republic. The Uzbeks, who form 68·7% (1979 census) of the population, were the ruling race in Central Asia until the arrival of the Russians during the third quarter of the 19th century. The several native states over which Uzbek dynasties formerly ruled were founded in the 15th century upon the ruins of Tamerlane's empire. The Uzbek speak Jagatai Turkish, which is related to Osmanli and Azerbaijan Turkish; many are Sunni Moslems. Russians numbered (census 1979) 10·8%, Tadzhiks, 3·9%, Tatars 4·2%.

The area of Uzbekistan is 447,400 sq. km (172,741 sq. miles). The population in Jan. 1983 was 17,039,000 (42% urban). The country comprises the following regions: Andizhan, Bukhara, Dzhizak, Ferghana, Kashkadar, Khorezm, Namangan, Navoi, Samarkand, Surkhan-Darya, Syr-Darya, Tashkent and the Autonomous Soviet Socialist Republic of Kara Kalpakia. The capital of the Republic is Tashkent; other large towns are Samarkand, Andizhan, Namangan. There are 87 towns, 84 urban settlements and 138 rural districts.

On 19 Sept. 1963 the Supreme Soviet of the USSR confirmed decisions of the Supreme Soviets of Kazakhstan and Uzbekistan, transferring over 40,000 sq. km from the former to the latter to ensure more efficient use of the 'Hungry Steppe'.

CONSTITUTION AND GOVERNMENT. The Supreme Soviet, elected in 1980, consists of 510 deputies (1 per 15,000 population); 178 are women, 346 Communists. A new Constitution was adopted in April 1978.

At elections to the regional, district, urban and rural Soviets (20 June 1982), of 102,699 deputies returned, 50,883 (49·5%) were women, 58,248 (56·7%) non-Party and 71,026 (69·2%) industrial workers and collective farmers.

President, Presidium of the Supreme Soviet: Vacant.
Chairman, Council of Ministers: N. D. Khudaiberdyev.
First Secretary, Communist Party: I. B. Usmankhodjayev.

FINANCE. Budget estimates (in 1m. rubles), 1983, 6,551; 1984, 7,256.

AGRICULTURE. Uzbekistan is a land of intensive farming, based on artificial irrigation. It is the chief cotton-growing area in the USSR and the third in the world. About 3·3m. hectares of collective and state farmland have irrigation networks, totalling 150,000 km in length, and all are in full use.

In 1939 the Ferghana Canal (270 km) was built. During 1940, among the irrigation canals completed were: the North Ferghana Canal (165 km), and Andreyev South Ferghana Canal (108 km) and the first section of the Tashkent Canal (63 km). A canal from the Amu-Darya to Bokhara across the Kzyl-Kum and Ust-Urt deserts (180 km) was completed in 1965. A 200-km canal joining the river Zeravshan with the Kashka Darya at the village of Paruz was completed in Aug. 1955; it is part of the Iski–Angara Canal. The first section (93 km) of a canal irrigating the southern 'Hungry Steppe' was opened in 1960; 500,000 hectares of this desert were under cultivation in 1967.

Agriculture flourishes, particularly in the well-watered, warm, rich oases areas, such as the Ferghana valley, Zeravshan, Tashkent and Khorezm, where cotton, fruit, silk and rice are cultivated. In the higher-lying plains grain is grown; the wide desert and semi-desert area of Western Uzbekistan is mainly given to pasture land and the breeding of the Karakul sheep; there is a Karakul institute at Samarkand.

Orchards occupied 195,000 hectares and the vineyards 70,000 hectares in 1977. The Central Asian Branch of the Scientific Research Institute of Viticulture in Tashkent has produced new frost resistant grapes by crossing the wild Amur grape with Central Asian and European types. In 1982 there were 851 collective farms and 1,012 state farms, with 157,300 tractors and 8,500 cotton picking and grain combines. Ploughing, cotton-sowing and cultivation are completely mechanized; cotton picking over 46%.

Uzbekistan provides 67% of the total cotton, 50% of the total rice and 60% of the total lucerne grown in the USSR. The area under crops was 2,189,000 hectares in 1913, 3,036,000 hectares in 1940 and 3·9m. hectares in 1978.

Livestock on 1 Jan. 1979: 3·23m. cattle, 8·1m. sheep and goats and 368,000 pigs.

Output of main agricultural products (in 1,000 tonnes) in 1978 (1913 figures in tons in brackets): Wheat, 757 (513); maize, 1,052 (39); cotton, 5,763 (517); potatoes, 227 (46); fruit, 124; grapes, 103; meat, 302 (89); milk, 2,073 (231); wool, 28·4 (5·3); 1,397m. eggs (87m.)

Afforestation over an area of 50,000 hectares has been carried out to protect the Bokhara and Karakul oases from the advancing Kzyl-Kum sands and to stop the sand-drifts in a number of districts of Central Ferghana.

INDUSTRY. Of its mineral resources, in addition to oil and coal, copper and building materials and ozocerite deposits are now also exploited. New very rich coal deposits were discovered in 1944 and 1947 near Tashkent.

There are nearly 1,600 factories and mills. They include a factory of agricultural machinery (in Tashkent), a cement factory, a sulphur-mine, an oxygen factory, a paper-mill, a leather factory, textile-mills, clothing factories, iron and steel works, the Chirchik electro-chemical plant, a superphosphate plant in Kokand and oil refineries, coalmines, etc. Output in 1977 included 5·4m. tons of coal, 411,000 tons of steel, 1·4m. tons of oil, 3·54m. tons of cement, 5·9m. tons of mineral fertilizers, 223·1m. linear metres of cotton fabrics, 107m. linear metres of silk fabrics, 27·1m. pairs of leather footwear, 784,000 hectolitres of wine (apart from collective farm output). Gold is being worked at Muruntau, Chadak and Kochbulak.

The Tashkent power station (2m. kw.) was completed in 1971. Power output in 1981 was 35,400m. kwh. (481m. kwh. in 1940). Two natural-gas pipelines (Djai-kak–Tashkent, Ferghana–Kokand) and a third from Bokhara to the Urals are operating. Natural gas output (1976) was 36,100m. cu. metres.

In 1981 there were 4,358,000 industrial and office workers in the national economy.

COMMUNICATIONS. The total length of railway in 1981 was 3,460 km. Branches lead to Karshe-Kitab, Kerki-Termez, Jalal-Abad, Namangan, Andijan and other centres. In 1947–55 a new line was built from Chardzhou to Kungrad.

The Great Uzbek Highway was completed in April 1941. Total length of motor roads in 1981 was 68,600 km (hard surface, 57,500 km). Inland waterways, 1,100 km.

An airline, serving all of Central Asia, is most developed in Uzbekistan.

Newspapers (1981). There were 188 newspapers in the Uzbek language out of a total of 281. Daily circulation of Uzbek-language newspapers, 3·7m., other languages, 1·3m.

EDUCATION. In 1981–82 there were 9,500 elementary and secondary schools with 4·2m. pupils, 43 higher educational establishments with 285,200 students and 227 technical colleges with 244,300 students. Uzbekistan has an Academy of Sciences and 188 research institutes with 33,600 scientific staff, 3,878 of them in 30 institutions of the Uzbek Academy of Sciences. There are universities and medical schools in Tashkent and Samarkand. In 1981, 996,000 children were attending pre-school institutions.

The Uzbek Arabic script was in 1929 replaced by the Latin alphabet which in 1940 was superseded by one based on the Cyrillic alphabet.

HEALTH. In 1981 there were 49,200 doctors and 191,000 hospital beds.

Book of Reference

Istoriya Uzbekskoi SSR. 4 vols. Tashkent, 1967–68

KARA-KALPAK AUTONOMOUS SOVIET SOCIALIST REPUBLIC

Area, 165,600 sq. km (63,920 sq. miles); population (Jan. 1983), 1,009,000. Capital, Nukus (127,000). The Karakalpaks are first mentioned in written records in the 16th century as tributary to Bokhara, and later to the Kazakh Khanate. In the second half of the 19th century, as a result of the Russian conquest of Central Asia, they came under Russian rule. On 11 May 1925 the territory was constituted within the then Kazakh Autonomous Republic (of the Russian Federation) as an Autonomous Region. On 20 March 1932 it became an Autonomous Republic within the Russian Federation, and on 5 Dec. 1936 it became part of the Uzbek SSR. Census (1979) Karakalpaks were 31·1% of population, Uzbeks, 31·5% and Kazakhs, 26·9%.

185 deputies were elected to its Supreme Soviet on 20 Feb. 1980, of whom 68 were women and 118 Communists.

Its manufactures are in the field of light industry—bricks, leather goods, furniture, canning, wine. Output of cotton in 1977 was 371,000 tons (in 1913, 8,000 tons). There were 4,217 tractors. Cattle numbered 308,000 and sheep and goats 621,000. There were 43 collective and 84 state farms. 218,300 industrial and office workers, and 14,800 specialists with a higher education, were employed in the national economy.

In 1979–80 there were 256,400 pupils at schools, 24,718 at technical colleges, and 5,543 at university. There is a branch of the Uzbek Academy of Sciences with 190 scientific staff.

There were 1,878 doctors and 8,920 hospital beds.

TADZHIKISTAN
Respublikai Sovieth Sotsialistii Tojikiston

HISTORY. The Tadzhik Soviet Socialist Republic was formed from those regions of Bokhara and Turkestan where the population consisted mainly of Tadzhiks. It was admitted as a constituent republic of the Soviet Union on 5 Dec. 1929.

AREA AND POPULATION. Tadzhikistan is situated between 39° 40' and 36° 40' N. lat. and 67° 20' and 75° E. long., north of the Oxus (Amu-Darya). On the west and north it is bordered by Uzbekistan and by the Kirghiz Soviet Socialist Republic; on the east by Chinese Turkestan and on the south by Afghánistán. It includes three regions (Leninabad, Kurgan-Tyube and Kulyab) and 41 rural districts, 18 towns and 49 urban settlements, together with the Gorno-Badakhshan Autonomous Region. Its highest mountains are Communism Peak (7,495 metres) and Lenin Peak (7,127 metres). Even the lowest valleys in the Pamirs are not below 3,500 metres above sea-level. The huge mountain glaciers are the source of many rapid rivers—the tributaries of the Amu-Darya, which flows from east to west along the southern border of Tadzhikistan. About 58·8% of the population are Tadzhiks. They speak an Iranian dialect, little different from Persian, and they are considered to be the descendants of the original Aryan population of Turkestan. Unlike the Persians, the Tadzhiks are mostly Sunnis. Of the rest, 22·9% are Uzbeks living in the north-west of the republic. Russians and Ukrainians number 10·4% (1979 census).

The area of the territory is 143,100 sq. km (55,240 sq. miles). Population (Jan. 1983), 4,239,000. The capital is Dushanbe. Other large towns are Leninabad (143,000), Kurgan-Tyube, Kulyab.

CONSTITUTION AND GOVERNMENT. The Supreme Soviet, elected in 1980, consists of 349 deputies (1 per 5,000 population); 123 are women and 238 Communists. A new Constitution was adopted in April 1978.

At elections to the district, urban and rural Soviets and the regional Soviet of Gorno-Badakhshan (20 June 1982), out of 26,627 deputies returned 13,216 (49·6%) were women, 15,227 (57·2%) non-Party and 18,677 (70·1%) industrial workers and collective farmers.

Chairman, Presidium of the Supreme Soviet: M. Kholov.
Chairman, Council of Ministers: K. N. Makhkamov.
First Secretary, Communist Party: R. Nabiyev.

FINANCE. Budget estimates (in 1m. rubles), 1983, 1,370; 1984, 1,512.

AGRICULTURE. The occupations of the population are mainly farming, horticulture and cattle breeding. Area under crops in 1978 was 800,000 hectares (1913, 494,000; 1940, 807,000). Wine production, 1976 was 450,000 hectolitres.

There are 43,000 km of irrigation canals: the irrigation networks cover about 602,000 hectares of land.

Tadzhikistan grows many varieties of fruit, including apricots, figs, olives, pomegranates, a local variety of lemons and oranges, and in the south sugar-cane has been grown. Even on the highest mountain plateaux of the Pamirs, 'the roof of the world', the biological station of Tadzhikistan (3,860 metres above sea-level) has succeeded in raising crops of 60 varieties of barley, 10 varieties of oats, 4 of wheat, as well as vegetables. Eucalyptus and geranium are grown for the perfumery industry. Jute, rice and millet are also grown.

Tadzhikistan contains rich pasture lands, and cattle breeding is a very important branch of its agriculture. Livestock on 1 Jan. 1979: 1·1m. cattle, 2·9m. sheep and goats and 123,000 pigs.

The Gissar sheep is famous in the south for its meat and fat; the Karakul sheep is widely bred for its wool.

There were 158 collective farms (all with electric power) and 255 state farms in 1982, with 31,700 tractors and 1,400 cotton and grain combine harvesters.

Output of main agricultural products (in 1,000 tonnes) in 1978 (1913 figures in tons in brackets): Wheat, 183 (133); maize, 48 (2); cotton, 903 (32); potatoes, 142 (10); other vegetables, 340; fruit, 287; grapes, 175; meat, 92·4 (48); milk, 461 (102); wool, 5·6 (2·1); 337m. eggs (20m.).

INDUSTRY. The original small-scale handicraft industries have been replaced by big industrial enterprises, including mining, engineering, food, textile, clothing and silk factories.

There are rich deposits of brown coal, lead, zinc and oil (in the north of the republic), rare elements, such as uranium, radium, arsenic and bismuth. Asbestos, mica, corundum and emery, lapis lazuli, potassium salts, sulphur and other minerals have been found in other parts of the republic.

Industrial output in 1977 included: 800,000 tons of coal, 274,000 tons of oil, 1·01m. tons of cement, 116m. linear metres of cotton fabrics, 58m. linear metres of silk fabrics; leather footwear, 7·3m. pairs; refrigerators, 134,400.

There are 80 big electrical stations. The hydro-electric Varzob station began to operate in 1954, that at Kairak-Kum on the Syr Darya River was completed in 1957 and 2 more at Murgab in 1964. Output in 1981 was 13,500m. kwh. (in 1940, 62m. kwh.).

Construction of an electro-chemical combine, the largest in the USSR, has begun in the Yavan steppe in south Tadzhikistan, and the 3·2m. kw. power station in the upper reaches of the Vakhsh River was near completion in 1979.

In 1981 there were 973,000 industrial and office workers in the national economy.

COMMUNICATIONS

Roads. There are 17,000 km of motor roads. Of these, 13,800 km are hard surface, including the Osh–Khorog (700 km), Yasui–Bazar–Charm (107 km) and Dushanbe–Khorog in the Pamirs (557 km) roads.

Railways. A railway line between Termez and Dushanbe (258 km) connects the republic with the railway system of the USSR. The mountainous nature of the republic makes ordinary railway construction difficult; accordingly 345 km of narrow gauge railways have been constructed (Kurgan–Tyube–Piandzh and Dushanbe–Kurgan–Tyube, connecting Dushanbe with the cotton-growing Vakhsh valley are particularly important). Length of railways, 1981, 470 km.

Aviation. Dushanbe is connected by air with Moscow, Tashkent, Baku and the regional and district centres of the republic.

Shipping. A steamship line on the Amu-Darya runs between Termez, Sarava and Jilikulam on the river Vakhsh (200 km).

Newspapers (1981). 66 newspapers had a total daily circulation of 1·35m. Of these, 51 with 1,004,000 circulation, were in Tadzhik.

EDUCATION. In 1981–82 there were 3,100 primary and secondary schools with 1·1m. pupils, 10 higher educational institutions with 56,800 students and 38 technical colleges with 40,100 students; the Tadzhik state university had 12,467 students. In 1981, 113,000 children were attending pre-school institutions. In 1951 an Academy of Sciences was established; it has 17 institutions, the scientific staff of which numbers 1,324; there are 61 research institutions in all, with 6,900 scientific personnel. The Pamir research station is the highest altitude meteorological observatory in the world.

In 1940 a new alphabet based on Cyrillic was introduced.

HEALTH. There are 277 hospitals as well as maternity homes, clinics and special institutes to combat tropical diseases. There were 10,000 doctors in 1981 and 41,800 hospital beds.

GORNO-BADAKHSHAN AUTONOMOUS REGION

Comprising the Pamir massif along the borders of Afghánistán and China, the region was set up on 2 Jan. 1925. Area, 63,700 sq. km (24,590 sq. miles); population (Jan. 1983), 140,000 (83% Tadjiks, 11% Kirghiz). Capital, Khorog (14,800).

There were 36,800 pupils in 268 schools in 1977–78 and 170 students in technical colleges, 151 doctors and 1,005 hospital beds.

Mining industries are developed (gold, rock-crystal, mica, coal, salt). Wheat, fruit and fodder crops are grown and cattle and sheep are bred in the western parts. In 1978 there were 65,500 cattle, 347,000 sheep and goats.
In 1976 there were 17 collective farms and 15 state (livestock) farms.

Books of Reference

Academy of Science of Tadzhikistan, *Istoriya Tadzhikskogo Naroda.* 3 vols. Moscow, 1963–65
Chumichev, D. A., *Tadzhikskaya SSR.* Moscow, 1954
Luknitsky, P., *Soviet Tajikistan* [In English]. Moscow, 1954

KIRGHIZIA
Kyrgyz Sovietik Sotsialistik Respublikasy

HISTORY. After the establishment of the Soviet regime in Russia, Kirghizia became part of Soviet Turkestan, which itself became an Autonomous Soviet Socialist Republic within the RSFSR in April 1921. In 1924, when Central Asia was reorganized territorially on a national basis, Kirghizia was separated from Turkestan and formed into an autonomous region within the RSFSR. On 1 Feb. 1926 the Government of the RSFSR transformed Kirghizia into an Autonomous Soviet Socialist Republic within the RSFSR, and finally in Dec. 1936 Kirghizia was proclaimed one of the constituent Soviet Socialist Republics of the USSR.

AREA AND POPULATION. The territory of Kirghizia covers 198,500 sq. km (76,460 sq. miles), and its population in Jan. 1983 was 3,801,000. The republic comprises 3 regions: Issyk-Kul, Naryn and Osh. There are 18 towns, 31 urban settlements and 37 rural districts. Its capital is Frunze (formerly Pishpek). Other large towns are Osh (188,000), Przhevalsk (56,000), Kyzyl-Kia, Tokmak.

Kirghizia is situated on the Tien-Shan mountains and bordered on the east by China, on the west by Kazakhstan and Uzbekistan, on the north by Kazakhstan and in the south by Tadzhikistan. The Kirghizians are of Turkic origin and form 47·9% (1979 census) of the population; the rest are Russians (25·9%), Ukrainians (3·1%), Uzbeks (12·1%) and Tatars (2%).

CONSTITUTION AND GOVERNMENT. The Supreme Soviet, elected in 1980, consists of 350 deputies (1 per 5,000 population); 126 are women, 235 Communists. A new Constitution was adopted in April 1978.

At elections to the regional, district, urban and rural Soviets (20 June 1982), of the 27,875 deputies returned, 13,966 (50·1%) were women, 15,671 non-Party and 19,314 (69·3%) industrial workers and collective farmers.

Chairman, Presidium of the Supreme Soviet: T. Kh. Koshoev.
Chairman, Council of Ministers: A. Duisheev.
First Secretary, Communist Party: T. U. Usubaliev.

FINANCE. Budget estimates (in 1m. rubles), 1983, 1,647; 1984, 1,789.

AGRICULTURE. Kirghizia is famed for its livestock breeding. On 1 Jan. 1979 there were 957,000 cattle, 298,000 pigs, 10m. sheep and goats. Yaks are bred as meat and dairy cattle, and graze on high altitudes unsuitable for other cattle. Crossed with domestic cattle, hybrids are produced much heavier than ordinary Kirghiz cattle and giving twice the yield of milk. The Kirghizian horse is famed for its endurance, but it is of small stature; it has in recent years been crossed with Don, Arab and other breeds.

On 1 Jan. 1982 there were 180 collective and 240 state farms. Area under crops (1978), 1·3m. hectares (1913, 640,000; 1940, 1,056,000). There were 26,300 tractors and 4,400 grain combine harvesters and 1,600 cotton combines in 1980; nearly all collective and state farms received electric power.

Kirghizia raises wheat sufficient for its own use and other grains and fodder, particularly lucerne; also sugar-beet, hemp, kenaf, kendyr, tobacco, medicinal plants and rice. Sericulture, fruit, grapes and vegetables and bee-keeping are major branches of Kirghiz agriculture. Agriculture is highly mechanized; nearly all the area under crops is worked by tractors. In 1977 irrigation networks in collective and state farms covered 933,000 hectares; practically all were in use. A canal in the western Tien-Shan ranges and a reservoir in the Urto-Tokoi mountains are being constructed.

The health resorts of Jety-Oguz (7,200 ft) and Jalal-Abad are famous for their mild alpine climate and mineral springs.

Output of main agricultural products (in 1,000 tonnes) in 1979 (1913 figures in tons in brackets): Wheat, 767 (250); maize, 193 (37); cotton, 208 (28); sugar-beet, 1,418 (0); potatoes, 227 (19); other vegetables, 361; fruit, 177; grapes, 70; meat, 154 (39); milk, 662 (91); wool, 33 (4·7); 416m. eggs (19m.).

INDUSTRY. Kirghizia contains 500 large modern industrial enterprises including sugar refineries, tanneries, cotton and wool-cleansing works, flour-mills, a tobacco factory, food, timber, textile, engineering, metallurgical, oil and mining enterprises.

The output of coal in 1976 was 4·3m. tons; oil, 230,000 tons; silk fabrics, 9·7m. linear metres; cotton fabrics, 64m. linear metres.

Granulated sugar, (1977) 270,000 tons; leather footwear, 10·1m. pairs.

Hydro-electric power stations are being built in the Central Tien-Shans and the cotton-growing districts in the Osh Region, the Chui valley and on the shore of Lake Issyk-Kul. Power output (1981) was 10,400m. kwh.

There were, in 1981, 1,131,000 industrial and office workers in the national economy.

COMMUNICATIONS. In the north a railway runs from Lugovaya through Frunze to Rybachi on Lake Issyk-Kul. Towns in the southern valleys are linked by short lines with the Ursatyevskaya–Andizhan railway in Uzbekistan. Total length of railway is 370 km. Most of the traffic is by road; there were 25,800 km of motor roads (18,000 hard surface) in 1981. A road tunnel through the Tien-Shan mountains at an altitude of 9,600 ft, connecting Frunze and Osh, is being constructed. Inland waterways, 600 km. Airlines link Frunze with Moscow and Tashkent.

Newspapers (1981). Of 109 newspapers with a daily 124m. circulation, 61 with 768,000 circulation are in the Kirghiz language.

EDUCATION. Kirghizia had 1,700 primary, continuation (8-year) and secondary schools with 900,000 pupils in 1981–82; 154,000 children attended 853 preschool institutions. There were also 10 higher educational institutions with 57,600 students, 41 technical and teachers' training colleges with 50,200 students, as well as music and art schools. The Kirghizian Academy of Sciences was established in 1954. In 1980 there were 65 research institutes, 18 of them, with 1,509 scientific staff, operating under its auspices; the others have scientist staffs of 6,225. A university was opened in 1951. It has 13,370 students, 6,268 full-time, 1,054 evening and 6,048 correspondence students taking a full degree course. In Sept. 1940 a new alphabet, based on Cyrillic, was introduced.

HEALTH. In 1981 there were 11,200 doctors and 44,900 hospital beds.

Books of Reference

Istoriya Kirgizskoi SSR. 5 vols. Frunze, 1983 ff.
Ryazantsev, S. N., *Kirghizia.* Moscow, 1951

UNITED ARAB EMIRATES

Population: 1·17m. (1982)
GNP per capita: US$30,070 (1980)

HISTORY. From Sha'am, 35 miles south-west of Ras Musam dam, for nearly 400 miles to Khor al Odeid at the south-eastern end of the peninsula of Qatar, the coast, formerly known as the Trucial Coast, of the Gulf (together with 50 miles of the coast of the Gulf of Oman) belongs to the rulers of the 7 Trucial States. In 1820 these rulers signed a treaty prescribing peace with the British Government. This treaty was followed by further agreements providing for the suppression of the slave trade and by a series of other engagements, of which the most important are the Perpetual Maritime Truce (May 1853) and the Exclusive Agreement (March 1892). Under the latter, the sheikhs, on behalf of themselves, their heirs and successors, undertook that they would on no account enter into any agreement or correspondence with any power other than the British Government, receive foreign agents, cede, sell or give for occupation any part of their territory save to the British Government.

British forces withdrew from the Gulf at the end of 1971 and the treaties whereby Britain had been responsible for the defence and foreign relations of the Trucial States were terminated, being replaced on 2 Dec. 1971 by a treaty of friendship between Britain and the United Arab Emirates. The United Arab Emirates (formed 2 Dec. 1971) consists of the former Trucial States: Abu Dhabi, Dubai, Sharjah, Ajman, Umm al Qawain, Ras al Khaimah (joined in Feb. 1972) and Fujairah. The small state of Kalba was merged with Sharjah in 1952. *See* map in THE STATESMAN'S YEAR-BOOK, 1972-73, The Gulf States of the Middle East.

AREA AND POPULATION. The Emirates are bounded north by the Persian Gulf, east by Oman, south and west by Saudi Arabia, north-west by Qatar. The area of these states is approximately 32,300 sq. miles (92,100 sq. km). The total population at census (1980), 1,040,275 (717,475 male). Estimate (1982) 1,175,000. About one-tenth are nomads.

Population, 1980 census (1982, estimate): Abu Dhabi, 449,000 (516,000); Ajman, 36,100 (42,000); Dubai, 278,000 (296,000); Fujairah, 32,200 (38,000); Ras al Khaimah, 73,700 (83,000); Sharjah, 159,000 (184,000); Umm al Qawain, 12,300 (14,000).

CLIMATE. The country experiences desert conditions, with rainfall both limited and erratic. The period May to Nov. is generally rainless, while the wettest months are Feb. and March. Temperatures are very high in the summer months. Dubai. Jan. 74°F (23·4°C), July 108°F (42·3°C). Annual rainfall 2·4" (60 mm).

GOVERNMENT. The Emirates are a federation, headed by a Supreme Council which is composed of the 7 rulers and which in turn appoints a Council of Ministers. The Council of Ministers drafts legislation and a federal budget; its proposals are submitted to a federal National Council of 40 elected members which may propose amendments but has no executive power.

President: HH Sheikh Zayed bin Sultan al Nahyan, Ruler of Abu Dhabi.

Members of the Supreme Council of Rulers:

HH Sheikh Rashid bin Saeed al-Maktoum, Vice-President and Ruler of Dubai.
HH Sheikh Sultan bin Mohammed al-Qasimi, Ruler of Sharjah.
HH Sheikh Saqr bin Mohammed al-Qasimi, Ruler of Ras al Khaimah.
HH Sheikh Rashid bin Ahmed al-Mualla, Ruler of Umm al Qaiwain.
HH Sheikh Hamad bin Mohammed al Sharqi, Ruler of Fujairah.
HH Sheikh Humaid Rashid bin al-Nuaimi, Ruler of Ajman.

The Council of Ministers formed in July 1983 was:

Prime Minister: H.H. Sheikh Rashid bin Said al-Maktoum.

Deputy Prime Ministers: Sheikh Maktoum bin Rashid al-Maktoum; Sheikh Hamdan bin Muhammad al-Nahayan.

Interior: Sheikh Mubarak bin Muhammad al-Nahayan. *Finance and Industry:* Sheikh Hamdan bin Rashid al-Maktoum. *Defence:* Sheikh Mohammed bin Rashid al-Maktoum. *Information and Culture:* Sheikh Ahmed bin Hamed. *Petroleum and Mineral Resources:* Dr Mana Saaed al-Otaiba. *Economy and Commerce:* Saif al-Jarwan. *Communications:* Muhammad Saeed al-Mualla. *Internal Affairs:* Hammouda bin Ali. *Public Works and Housing:* Muhammad Khalifa al-Kindi. *Education and Youth:* Faraj al-Mazroui. *Without Portfolio:* Ahmed Sultan al-Qassimi. *Planning:* Sheikh Humaid al-Mualla. *Cabinet Affairs:* Saaed al-Ghaith. *Minister of State for Supreme Council Affairs:* Sheikh Abdul Aziz al-Qassimi. *Justice:* Abdulla al-Mazroui. *Islamic Affairs and AWQAF:* Sheikh Mohammed al-Khazraji. *Agriculture and Fisheries:* Saaed al-Raghbani. *Minister of State for Foreign Affairs:* Rashid Abdulla. *Water and Electricity:* Hamad bin Nasir al-Oweis. *Health:* Hamad al-Madfa.

National flag: Three horizontal stripes of green, white, black, with a vertical red strip in the hoist.

DEFENCE

Army. The Army consists of 1 Royal Guard brigade, 5 armoured, 9 infantry, 3 artillery and 3 air defence battalions. Equipment includes 100 AMX-30 and 18 Lion OF-40 Mk 1 main battle tanks. The strength was (1984) 46,000.

Navy. The naval flotilla includes 6 new German-built missile armed fast attack craft, 9 British-built patrol craft and 2 tenders. Personnel in 1984 numbered 1,200 officers and ratings.

The Coast Guard flotilla comprises 13 armed coastal patrol craft, 16 armed small patrol cutters, 26 light launches, 1 amphibious craft, 2 diving tenders, 1 water carrier and 5 tugs.

Air Force. Formation of an air wing in Abu Dhabi, to support land forces, began in 1968 with the purchase of some light STOL transports and helicopters. Expansion has been rapid. Current equipment includes 25 Mirage 5 supersonic fighter-bombers, 3 Mirage 5R tactical reconnaissance aircraft and 2 Mirage 5D 2-seat trainers (to be replaced by Mirage 2000s, with delivery of first 18 to begin in 1986); 4 C-130 Hercules and 4 Buffalo turboprop transports; 4 CASA C-212 Aviocar ECM/elint aircraft; about 40 Gazelle, Alouette III, Puma, Super Puma and Agusta-Bell 205 helicopters; 14 PC-7 Turbo-Trainers and 6 Alpha Jets. On order are 16 Hawk light attack/trainers. Initial personnel were mostly British but considerable assistance is now being received from Arab countries and from Pakistan. The air wing became the Air Force of Abu Dhabi in 1972, in which year 3 JetRanger helicopters were transferred to the air wing of the Union Defence Force, since combined with the Dubai Police Air Wing to form a single component of the United Emirates Air Force. Current equipment of the Dubai Air Wing of the UEAF, bought mainly in Italy, comprises 6 Aermacchi MB 326K jet light attack aircraft, 1 Aeritalia G222 twin-turboprop transport, 1 piston-engined SF.260W armed basic trainer, 5 SF.260TP turboprop trainers, and 2 MB 326L jet trainers, 4 Bell 205A-1, 3 Bell 212 and 6 JetRanger helicopters and 1 Cessna 182 liaison aircraft, plus 2 L-100-30 Hercules transports and a Boeing 720B and a variety of other types for VIP use. Eight Hawks are on order.

INTERNATIONAL RELATIONS

Membership. The UAE is a member of UN and of the Arab League.

External Debt. The UAE (mainly the government of Dubai) borrowed about $205m. on Eurocurrency markets in 1976 and about $850m. in 1977.

ECONOMY

Planning. The first 5-year plan (1981-85) envisages expenditure of UD 13,000m.

Budget. Revenue is principally derived from oil-concession payments. The federal budget (1983) was DH 18,500m.

Currency. The UAE issued its own currency in 1972 based on the *dirham*. 1 UAE *dirham* = 10 *dinar* = 1,000 *fils*. There are notes of 1, 5, 10, 50, 100 and 1,000 *dirham* and coins of 1, 5, 10, 25, 50 and 100 *fils*. Rate of exchange, March 1984: £1 = 5·46 *dirham*; US$1 = 3·673 *dirham*.

Banking. The British Bank of the Middle East has branches in Dubai, Abu Dhabi, Sharjah, Fujairah, Ajman and Ras al Khaimah; the Chartered Bank has branches in Dubai, Sharjah, Abu Dhabi and Al Ain; the National & Grindlays Bank (Ottoman Branch) has branches in Abu Dhabi and Sharjah. The Arab Bank has branches in Ajman, Ras al Khaimah, Sharjah, Abu Dhabi and Dubai; the Citibank has branches in Dubai, Sharjah and Abu Dhabi; the Habib Bank of Pakistan has branches in Abu Dhabi, Dubai and Sharjah and the United Bank Ltd of Pakistan branches in Dubai, Sharjah, Abu Dhabi and Al Ain. Barclays Bank International has branches in Abu Dhabi, Dubai, Ras Al Khaimah and Sharjah. There is also the National Bank of Dubai, formed in 1963 which has a branch in Abu Dhabi and Umm al Qaiwain, and the Bank of Oman Ltd, formed in 1967, which has branches in Ajman, Abu Dhabi and Dubai. The Commercial Bank opened in Dubai in 1969. The Bank Sadarat of Iran has branches in Abu Dhabi, Dubai and Sharjah. The National Bank of Abu Dhabi, formed in 1967, has its head office in Abu Dhabi and a branch office in Dubai.

ENERGY AND NATURAL RESOURCES

Oil. *Abu Dhabi.* Until the end of 1972 production was in the hands of 2 major companies, the Abu Dhabi Petroleum Co. and the Abu Dhabi Marine Area. The Government has acquired a 60% interest in both companies. Ownership in 1976 was as follows: *ADPC*, 60% Government; 9·5% BP; 9·5% Shell; 9·5% CFP; 4·75% Mobil; 2% Partex. *ADMA*, 60% Government; 26·7% BP/Japan Oil Development Co.; 13·3% CFP. A Japanese company, Abu Dhabi Oil Co. (ADOCO) began production from its Mubarraz field in 1973. There are other companies which have concessions in the State: Japan's Middle East Oil; a US consortium led by Pan Ocean Oil and Sunningdale Oils of Canada. A State Petroleum Co., the Abu Dhabi National Oil Co. (ADNOC), was formed in 1971 and began to set up its own tanker fleet known as the Abu Dhabi National Tankers Co. (ADNATCO). At the end of 1972 Abu Dhabi signed a participation agreement which would have given it an immediate 25% interest in the companies, rising to 51% by 1982. Oil production, 1983, 750,000 bbls.

Dubai. In July 1975 Dubai decided to take full control of all foreign oil and gas operations in the State. The companies were to remain however. A Dubai producing group was set up to comprise the foreign interests–US and continental companies. Dubai Petroleum Co. (DPC–a subsidiary of Continental Oil) has a 30% interest in this group; the other members are Dubai Marine Areas (*Compagnie Française des Pétroles*) with 50%; Deutsche Texaco with 10%; Dubai Sun Oil 5%; and Delfzee Dubai Petroleum (Wintershall) 5%. Oil production, 1983, 330,000 bbls.

Sharjah. In Sharjah the concession is given to Crescent Oil, its shareholders are: Ashland Oil, Skelly Oil, Kerr-McGee, Cities Services and Juniper. Other oil concessions have recently been given to the Crystal Oil Co. of USA and the Reserves Oil and Gas Co. Oil production, 1983, 10,000 bbls.

Ajman. An oil concession was awarded to United Refining in 1974.

Umm al Qawain. The concession here was given to US Occidental Petroleum; another was awarded to a consortium led by the US company United Refinery.

Ras al Khaimah. The Dutch oil firm Vitol took over Union's concession in 1973. Shell began prospecting in 1969 but pulled out in 1971. A concession in the same area was awarded to Peninsula Petroleum, a subsidiary of the US California Time Group, in 1973.

Gas. Abu Dhabi has reserves of natural gas, nationalized in 1976. The Abu Dhabi Gas Liquefaction Plant at Das Island (51% ADNOC) has a capacity of 2m. tons LNG, 1m. tons LPG, 220,000 tons of light distillate and 230,000 tons of pelletized sulphur. Gas exports (1980) US$350m.

Agriculture. The fertile Buraimi Oasis, known as Al Ain, is largely in Abu Dhabi territory, but owing to lack of water and good soil there is little agriculture in the rest of UAE. There are 15,000 hectares of cultivated land. However, since the establishment of an agricultural trials station and an agricultural school in Ras al Khaimah the number of gardens under cultivation has more than doubled and there have been remarkable increases in the variety of crops and the length of the agricultural season. An experimental agricultural farm exists in Al Ain which produces vegetables for Abu Dhabi.

Livestock (1982): Cattle, 27,000; camels, 70,000; sheep, 140,000; goats, 400,000.

Fisheries. The industry is still a major employer. Sharjah exports shrimps and prawns; a fishmeal plant is operating in Ras al Khaimah and plants are planned for Ajman and Sharjah.

INDUSTRY AND TRADE

Industry. Main industries in Abu Dhabi relate to the construction industry and to oil and gas extraction; there is also a steel rolling mill. Dubai has a cement factory of 500,000 tons annual capacity, and a dry dock. Twenty companies are now fully operational at the complex in Jebel Ali consisting of a liquefied petroleum gas plant. An aluminium smelter with power station and desalination plant was opened in Feb. 1979. Sharjah has a cement factory and various manufacturing estates. Ras al Khaimah also produces cement and crushed rock.

Commerce. Imports in 1981 for UAE were US$9,823m. Exports and re-exports totalled US$21,792m. Oil exports accounted for 95% of the total.

Total trade between the UAE (excluding Abu Dhabi) and UK (British Department of Trade returns, in £1,000 sterling):

	1979	1980	1981	1982	1983
Imports to UK	143,071	239,519	118,697	82,706	107,574
Exports and re-exports from UK	328,773	287,615	245,388	286,079	254,862

Total trade between Abu Dhabi and UK (British Department of Trade returns, in £1,000 sterling):

	1979	1980	1981	1982	1983
Imports to UK	93,990	246,422	274,651	184,253	202,232
Exports and re-exports from UK	159,426	214,309	246,672	272,889	312,902

Tourism. In 1982 there were 9,836 rooms for tourists.

COMMUNICATIONS

Aviation. International airports at Dubai and Abu Dhabi are served by a large number of major airlines, as well as by Gulf Air partially owned by the Government of the UAE. Abu Dhabi's new airport opened and commenced operations in Jan. 1982. A new international airport was inaugurated at Sharjah in 1979. A Ras al Khaimah international airport was opened early in 1976 although it initially had only one scheduled service by Kuwait Airways. An airstrip exists at Al Ain, in the Buraimi Oasis, and in the oilfields, both onshore and offshore, on Das Island, while construction of a strip at Khor Fakkan is planned.

Abu Dhabi and Dubai are served by Alia, Air France, Air India, British Airways, Egyptair, Iran Air, Kuwait Airways, Middle East Airlines, PIA, KLM, Gulf Air, Czechoslovak Airlines, Hungarian Airlines, Royal Nepal Airlines, Iberia, Turkish

Airlines, Iraqi Airways, Olympic, SABENA, Saudia, Syrian Arab Airlines and TMA. Lufthansa and Singapore Airlines initiated scheduled flights to Dubai in mid-1976, while Sharjah is served by Gulf Air and TMA. A number of cargo airlines also fly regularly to the country's major airports. An air-taxi service, Emirates Air Services, flying between Abu Dhabi and Dubai, began in June 1976.

Shipping. In 1980 Port Rashid was enlarged to 37 berths. Abu Dhabi has dry docks and there are smaller ports at Sharjah and Ras al Khaimah. Jebel Ali is a port and industrial estate 35 km south-west of Dubai city and had (1982) 66 berths.

In 1976, the Government of the UAE joined with Qatar, Bahrain, Saudi Arabia, Kuwait and Iraq in forming the United Arab Shipping Co.

Post and Broadcasting. In 1982 there were 240,167 telephones, of which 71,344 were in Abu Dhabi and 82,158 in Dubai. In Sharjah a new telephone company has been formed and the other Northern States are now linked by telephone. The new Cable and Wireless Station at Jebel Ali in the State of Dubai links the system with the international communication network.

Television stations are at Abu Dhabi and Dubai, with extension of the service well advanced to the rest of the Emirates. Stations for The Voice of the United Arab Emirates began broadcasting in 1972 at Abu Dhabi, Dubai, Ras al Khaimah and Sharjah. Estimated radios (1976) 50,000 and television sets over 16,000.

Newspapers (1982). There are a number of daily and weekly publications mostly in Arabic, but some in English, notably *The Emirates News* of Abu Dhabi, *The Gulf News,* a daily, published in Dubai and the *Khaleej Times* (daily), also published in Dubai.

JUSTICE, RELIGION, EDUCATION AND WELFARE

Justice. UAE subjects and citizens of all Arab and Moslem states are subject to the jurisdiction of the local courts. In the local courts the rules of Islamic law prevail. A new code of law is being produced for Abu Dhabi. In Dubai there is a court run by a *qadi*, while in some of the other States all legal cases are referred immediately to the Ruler or a member of his family, who will refer to a *qadi* only if he cannot settle the matter himself. In Abu Dhabi a professional Jordanian judge presides over the Ruler's Court. The 95th article of the provisional Constitution of 1971 provided for the setting up of a Union Supreme Court and Union Primary Tribunals.

Religion. Nearly all the inhabitants are Moslem of the Sunni and Shi'ite sects.

Education (1982). Primary and secondary education for boys and girls is available in the UAE, and there are now 383 schools with over 113,000 pupils, with a further 379 planned. There are 4 junior colleges and 112 adult education centres, established to eliminate illiteracy. The education system is the same as that followed in Kuwait, and many of the teachers are supplied by the Kuwait, Qatar, Egypt, Jordan and Bahrain education departments. The oil companies in Abu Dhabi operate apprentice training schools and there is also a vocational training institute. A vocational training centre is under construction.

There are trade schools in Sharjah, Dubai and Ras al Khaimah. The UAE university had 3,500 students with 406 lecturers in 1981.

Health. A tuberculosis sanatorium is to be constructed by the State of Kuwait in Sharjah. In 1980 there were more than 20 hospitals (2,972 beds) and over 47 clinics. There were 1,202 doctors.

DIPLOMATIC REPRESENTATIVES

Of the UAE in Great Britain (30 Prince's Gate, London, SW7 1PT)
Ambassador: Mohamed Mahdi Al-Tajir (accredited 15 Nov. 1983).

Of Great Britain in the UAE
Ambassador: H. B. Walker, CMG (at the British Embassy, Abu Dhabi).

Of the UAE in the USA (600 New Hampshire Ave., NW, Washington, D.C., 20037)
Ambassador: Ahmed S. Al-Mokarrab.

Of the USA in the UAE (Sheikh Khalid Bldg., Corniche Rd., Abu Dhabi)
Ambassador: George Quincy Lumden, Jr.

Of the UAE to the United Nations
Ambassador: Fahim Sultan Al-Qasimi.

Books of Reference

Middle East Annual Review. London
United Arab Emirates: A Record of Achievement, 1979–1981. Ministry of Information and Culture. Abu Dhabi, 1981
Abdullah, M.M. *The UAE: A Modern History.* London and New York, 1978
Al-Baharna, H. M., *The Legal Status of the Arabian Gulf States.* Manchester, 1969
Bey, F.H., *From Trucial States to United Arab Emirates.* London, 1982
Busch, B. C., *Britain and the Persian Gulf 1894–1914.* California, 1967
Daniel, John, *Abu Dhabi: A Portrait.* London, 1974
Fenelon, K. G., *The United Arab Emirates: An Economic and Social Survey.* 2nd ed. London, 1973
Hawley, D. F., *Courtesies in the Trucial States.* 1965.—*The Trucial States.* London, 1971
Hopwood, D., *The Arabian Peninsula.* London, 1972
Izzard, M., *The Gulf,* 1980
Khalifa, A. M., *The U.A.E.: Energy Development.* London, 1980
Mann, C., *Abu Dhabi: Birth of an Oil Sheikhdom.* Beirut, 1964
Mallakh, R.S., *The Economic Development of the United Arab Emirates,* London, 1981
Marlowe, J., *The Persian Gulf in the 20th Century.* London, 1962
Miles, S. B., *The Countries and Tribes of the Persian Gulf.* 3rd ed. London, 1966
Mostyn, T., *UAE-A MEED Practical Guide.* London, 1982
Sadiq, M. T. *with* W. P. Snavely, *Bahrain, Qatar and the UAE: Colonial Past, Present Problems and Future Prospects.* Lexington, Mass., 1972
Soffan, L. U., *Women of the United Arab Emirates.* London, 1980
Tomkinson, M., *The United Arab Emirates: An Insight and a Guide.* London and Hammamet, 1975
Zahlan, R. S., *The Origins of the United Arab Emirates.* London, 1978

UNITED KINGDOM OF GREAT BRITAIN AND NORTHERN IRELAND

Capital: London
Population: 55·78m. (1981)
GNP per capita: US$7,920 (1980)

'Great Britain' is a geographical term describing the main island of the British Isles which comprises England, Scotland and Wales (so called to distinguish it from 'Little Britain' or Brittany). By the Act of Union, 1801, Great Britain and Ireland formed a legislative union as the United Kingdom of Great Britain and Ireland. Since the separation of Great Britain and Ireland in 1921 Northern Ireland remained within the Union which is now the United Kingdom of Great Britain and Northern Ireland. The United Kingdom does not include the Channel Islands or the Isle of Man which are direct dependencies of the Crown with their own legislative and taxation systems.

GREAT BRITAIN

AREA AND POPULATION. Area (in sq. km) and population (present on census night) at the census taken 5 April 1981:

Divisions	Area	Total
England	130,357	46,362,836
Wales (incl. Monmouthshire)	20,761	2,791,851
Scotland	78,762	5,130,735
	229,880	54,285,422

Population at the 4 previous decennial censuses:

Divisions	1931	1951	1961	1971
England	37,359,045	41,159,213	43,460,525	46,019,000
Wales	2,158,374	2,598,675	2,644,023	2,731,000
Scotland	4,842,980	5,096,415	5,178,490	5,228,963
Army, Navy and Merchant Seamen abroad	434,532	—	—	—
Total	44,794,931	48,854,303	51,283,038	53,978,963

Population (usually resident) at the census of 1981:

Divisions	Males	Females	Total
England	22,288,395	23,483,561	45,771,956
Wales (incl. Monmouthshire)	1,336,323	1,413,317	2,749,640
Scotland	2,428,472	2,606,843	5,035,315
Great Britain	26,053,190	27,503,721	53,556,911

In 1981 in Wales and Monmouthshire 21,283 persons 3 years of age and upwards were able to speak Welsh only, and 482,276 able to speak Welsh and English (preliminary figures): these totals represent 19% of the total population. In Scotland in 1981, 79,307 of the usually resident population could speak Gaelic (1·3%); 3,113 could read or write Gaelic, but could not speak it.

At the census of 1981, in England and Wales, there were 17,706,492 private households; in Great Britain, 19,500,113.

The age distribution in 1981 of the 'usually resident' population of England and Wales and Scotland was as follows (in 1,000):

Age-group		England and Wales	Scotland	Great Britain
Under	5	2,910	308	3,219
5 and under 10		3,207	344	3,551
10	,, 15	3,846	425	4,271
15	,, 20	4,020	447	4,467
20	,, 25	3,564	394	3,959
25	,, 35	6,931	701	7,632
35	,, 45	5,885	588	6,473
45	,, 55	5,474	575	6,049
55	,, 65	5,410	541	5,951
65	,, 70	2,426	241	2,667
70	,, 75	2,062	204	2,265
75	,, 85	2,280	221	2,501
85 and upwards		507	46	552
Total		48,522	5,035	53,557

At 30 June 1982 the estimated population of Great Britain was 54,772,000. Age and sex distribution: between 0 and 15, 5,621,800 males, 5,334,500 females; 15 and under 65, 17,761,000 males; 15 and under 60, 16,201,200 females; aged 65 and over, 3·25m. males; 60 and over, 6·6m. females.

England and Wales: The census population, (present on census night) of England and Wales 1801 to 1981:

Date of enumeration	Population	Pop. per sq. mile	Date of enumeration	Population	Pop. per sq. mile[1]
1801	8,892,536	152	1891	29,002,525	497
1811	10,164,256	174	1901	32,527,843	558
1821	12,000,236	206	1911	36,070,492	618
1831	13,896,797	238	1921	37,886,699	649
1841	15,914,148	273	1931	39,952,377	685
1851	17,927,609	307	1951	43,757,888	750
1861	20,066,224	344	1961	46,104,548	791
1871	22,712,266	389	1971	48,749,575	323
1881	25,974,439	445	1981	49,154,687	325

[1] Per sq. km from 1971

There is only one other major country in Europe, Netherlands (population density 421 persons per sq. km), more crowded than England and Wales.

The birth places of the 1981 'usually resident' population were: England, 41,552,500; Wales, 2,758,026; Scotland, 752,188; Northern Ireland, 209,042; Ireland, 579,833; Commonwealth, 1,429,407; foreign countries, 1,209,091.

Local authority areas in being from April 1974. Area in sq. km and population estimate 30 June 1982:

ENGLAND Metropolitan counties	Area sq. km	Population	Non-Metropolitan counties—contd.	Area sq. km	Population
Greater London	1,580	6,765,100	Derbyshire	2,631	910,900
Greater Manchester	1,286	2,605,000	Devon	6,715	966,200
Merseyside	652	1,511,000	Dorset	2,654	604,600
South Yorkshire	1,560	1,312,800	Durham	2,436	608,100
Tyne and Wear	540	1,149,600	East Sussex	1,795	670,600
West Midlands	899	2,667,000	Essex	3,674	1,484,100
West Yorkshire	2,039	2,063,100	Gloucestershire	2,638	505,500
			Hampshire	3,772	1,486,300
Non-metropolitan counties			Hereford and Worcester	3,927	638,500
Avon	1,338	930,900	Hertfordshire	1,634	967,500
Bedfordshire	1,235	511,900	Humberside	3,512	855,800
Berkshire	1,256	699,500	Isle of Wight	381	119,000
Buckinghamshire	1,883	580,800	Kent	3,732	1,485,900
Cambridgeshire	3,409	596,600	Lancashire	3,043	1,384,100
Cheshire	2,322	931,900	Leicestershire	2,553	860,700
Cleveland	583	566,900	Lincolnshire	5,885	551,800
Cornwall and Isles of			Norfolk	5,355	704,900
Scilly	3,546	429,600	Northamptonshire	2,367	537,000
Cumbria	6,809	482,500	Northumberland	5,033	299,700
			North Yorkshire	8,317	678,100

Non-Metropolitan counties—contd.	Area sq. km	Population	WALES	Area sq. km	Population
Nottinghamshire	2,164	991,400	Clwyd	2,425	394,500
Oxfordshire	2,611	547,600	Dyfed	5,765	333,500
Shropshire	3,490	380,400	Gwent	1,376	440,200
Somerset	3,458	432,300	Gwynedd	3,868	231,900
Staffordshire	2,716	1,019,000	Mid-Glamorgan	1,019	539,300
Suffolk	3,800	611,200	Powys	5,077	110,500
Surrey	1,655	1,013,900	South Glamorgan	416	389,800
Warwickshire	1,981	477,300	West Glamorgan	815	368,500
West Sussex	2,016	672,500			
Wiltshire	3,481	527,500	Total Wales		2,808,200
Total		46,798,600	Total—England and Wales		49,606,800

County districts with populations of over 90,000 (estimate, 30 June 1982):

ENGLAND			
Allerdale	95,600	East Staffordshire	95,800
Amber Valley	109,100	Elmbridge	111,700
Arun	120,200	Epping Forest	115,100
Ashfield	106,000	Erewash	103,000
Aylesbury Vale	132,700	Exeter	100,500
Barnsley	225,400	Gateshead	211,600
Basildon	154,800	Gedling	104,300
Basingstoke and Deane	132,000	Gillingham	95,200
Bassetlaw	102,700	Gloucester	92,400
Beverley	107,400	Gravesham	95,800
Birmingham	1,017,300	Grimsby	92,200
Blackburn	142,800	Guildford	124,100
Blackpool	147,200	Halton	122,800
Bolton	262,300	Harrogate	140,400
Bournemouth	144,300	Hartlepool	94,000
Bradford	464,700	Havant	115,600
Braintree	113,300	Horsham	105,600
Breckland	97,500	Huntingdon	127,400
Brighton	149,000	Ipswich	120,400
Bristol	399,600	King's Lynn and West Norfolk	121,400
Broadland	98,100	Kingston upon Hull	271,100
Broxtowe	104,300	Kirklees	377,100
Burnley	93,700	Knowsley	172,800
Bury	175,600	Lancaster	126,400
Calderdale	191,800	Langbaurgh	150,200
Cambridge	101,100	Leeds	716,100
Canterbury	123,200	Leicester	282,400
Carlisle	100,900	Liverpool	510,700
Charnwood	140,700	Luton	165,100
Chelmsford	141,000	Macclesfield	147,900
Cherwell	112,700	Maidstone	130,800
Chester	115,800	Manchester	458,600
Chesterfield	96,600	Mansfield	99,200
Chichester	99,300	Mendip	90,300
Chiltern	92,600	Mid-Bedfordshire	105,800
Chorley	91,500	Middlesbrough	149,800
Colchester	138,700	Mid-Sussex	123,300
Coventry	317,400	Milton Keynes	133,900
Crewe and Nantwich	98,500	Newark	104,300
Dacorum	131,100	Newbury	124,900
Darlington	98,700	Newcastle under Lyme	120,000
Derby	215,600	Newcastle upon Tyne	281,000
Doncaster	288,700	New Forest	146,300
Dover	102,800	Northampton	162,200
Dudley	301,100	Northavon	120,100
East Devon	107,800	North Bedfordshire	132,800
East Hampshire	91,600	North-East Derbyshire	97,600
East Hertfordshire	110,700	North Hertfordshire	108,600
Eastleigh	94,000	North Tyneside	197,000
East Lindsey	105,700	North Wiltshire	106,400
		Norwich	126,200

ENGLAND—*contd.*

Nottingham	277,800	Swale	110,300
Nuneaton and Bedworth	113,200	Tameside	216,800
Oldham	220,600	Teignbridge	96,200
Oxford	116,400	Tendring	115,000
Peterborough	137,300	Test Valley	93,900
Plymouth	253,600	Thamesdown	152,500
Poole	121,600	Thanet	122,700
Portsmouth	190,000	Thurrock	126,100
Preston	126,500	Tonbridge and Malling	98,600
Reading	137,700	Torbay	112,600
Reigate and Banstead	116,400	Trafford	219,800
Rochdale	207,100	Tunbridge Wells	98,200
Rochester upon Medway	144,700	Vale of White Horse	104,300
Rotherham	252,900	Vale Royal	111,900
Rushcliffe	92,800	Wakefield	313,400
St Albans	125,600	Walsall	267,200
St Helens	189,600	Warrington	172,200
Salford	245,600	Warwick	115,200
Salisbury	102,800	Waveney	101,000
Sandwell	309,300	Waverley	112,100
Scarborough	101,700	Wealden	120,700
Sedgefield	92,300	Welwyn Hatfield	93,900
Sedgemoor	90,500	West Lancashire	108,100
Sefton	298,700	West Wiltshire	100,500
Sevenoaks	111,700	Wigan	309,200
Sheffield	545,800	Winchester	92,500
Slough	98,200	Windsor and Maidenhead	132,900
Solihull	199,300	Wirral	339,200
Southampton	207,500	Wokingham	119,500
South Bedfordshire	108,200	Wolverhampton	255,400
South Cambridgeshire	110,800	Woodspring	164,200
Southend on Sea	157,600	Worthing	92,900
South Kesteven	98,600	Wrekin	126,200
South Lakeland	95,900	Wychavon	95,500
South Norfolk	96,100	Wycombe	157,600
South Oxfordshire	131,200	Wyre	98,800
South Ribble	97,900	Wyre Forest	92,000
South Staffordshire	98,400	Yeovil	133,700
South Tyneside	160,600	York	102,000
Spelthorne	92,000	**WALES**	
Stafford	116,700	Cardiff	279,800
Staffordshire Moorlands	95,800	Newport	134,100
Stockport	289,400	Ogwr	130,100
Stockton on Tees	172,900	Rhymney Valley	105,200
Stoke on Trent	251,300	Swansea	188,100
Stratford on Avon	101,200	Taff Ely	94,500
Stroud	102,400	Torfaen	90,200
Suffolk Coastal	99,500	Vale of Glamorgan	110,000
Sunderland	299,400	Wrexham Maelor	113,600

The following table shows the distribution of the urban and rural population of England and Wales in 1951, 1961, 1971, and 1981 (preliminary).

		Population		Percentage	
	England and Wales	Urban districts [1]	Rural districts [1]	Urban [1]	Rural
1951	43,757,888	35,335,721	8,422,167	80·8	19·2
1961	46,071,604	36,838,442	9,233,162	80·0	20·0
1971	48,755,000	38,151,000	10,598,000	78·2	21·5
1981	49,011,417	37,686,863	11,324,554	76·9	23·1

[1] As existing at each census.

Conurbations. These are aggregates of local-authority areas with high population densities. In April 1981 there were 6 in England and Wales, with a population of 14·7m. (30% of total population). Their populations were: Greater London, 6·7m.; Tyneside, 0·7m.; W. Yorks., 1·67m.; S.E. Lancs., 2·24m.; Merseyside, 1·13m.; W. Midlands, 2·24m.

Greater London Boroughs. Estimated population on 30 June 1982.

Barking and		Hammersmith		Lambeth	247,700
Dagenham	151,200	and Fulham	149,400	Lewisham	233,600
Barnet	294,800	Haringey	204,600	Merton	166,600
Bexley	217,900	Harrow	198,800	Newham	212,300
Brent	254,000	Havering	242,400	Redbridge	227,800
Bromley	297,900	Hillingdon	232,800	Richmond-on-	
Camden	175,900	Hounslow	204,400	Thames	160,400
Croydon	321,500	Islington	162,900	Southwark	214,600
Ealing	282,000	Kensington and		Sutton	170,100
Enfield	262,100	Chelsea	136,800	Tower Hamlets	144,500
Greenwich	216,000	Kingston upon		Waltham Forest	215,700
Hackney	183,300	Thames	133,700	Wandsworth	258,500
				Westminster	185,700

The City of London (677 acres) is part of the County of Greater London but retains some independent powers. Resident population (1982 estimate) 5,200.

Census of England and Wales, 1961. HMSO. 1961–65
Royal Commission on Local Government in Greater London, Report. HMSO, 1960 (Cmnd. 1164)
Census 1971, England and Wales. HMSO, 1971–75
Census 1971, Great Britain; Advance Analysis. HMSO, 1972
Census 1981, Great Britain. HMSO, 1981–83
Census 1981, England and Wales. HMSO, 1981–83

Scotland: Area 78,762 sq. km, including its islands, 186 in number, and inland water 1,580 sq. km.

Population (including military in the barracks and seamen on board vessels in the harbours) at the dates of each census:

Date of enumeration	Population	Pop. per sq. mile	Date of enumeration	Population	Pop. per sq. mile [1]
1811	1,805,864	60	1901	4,472,103	150
1821	2,091,521	70	1911	4,760,904	160
1831	2,364,386	79	1921	4,882,497	164
1841	2,620,184	88	1931	4,842,980	163
1851	2,888,742	97	1951	5,096,415	171
1861	3,062,294	100	1961	5,179,344	174
1871	3,360,018	113	1971	5,229,963	68
1881	3,735,573	125	1981	5,130,735	66
1891	4,025,647	135			

[1] per sq. km from 1971.

The 1981 population present on census night included 2,466,000 males, 2,664,000 females.

Population of the local authority areas:

Regions	Districts	Area sq.km	Estimated population 1982
Borders		4,662	99,784
	Berwickshire		18,270
	Ettrick and Lauderdale		31,725
	Roxburgh		35,277
	Tweeddale		14,512
Central		2,590	273,391
	Clackmannan		47,855
	Falkirk		144,361
	Stirling		81,175
Dumfries and Galloway		6,475	145,139
	Annandale and Eskdale		35,467
	Nithsdale		56,217
	Stewartry		23,214
	Wigtown		30,241
Fife		1,308	327,362
	Dunfermline		122,898
	Kirkcaldy		142,361
	N.E. Fife		62,103

Regions	Districts	Area sq. km	Estimated population 1982
Grampian		8,550	471,942
	Aberdeen City		203,927
	Banff and Buchan		81,699
	Gordon		62,309
	Kincardine and Deeside		42,482
	Moray		81,525
Highland		26,136	200,150
	Badenoch and Strathspey		12,402
	Caithness		27,380
	Inverness		56,770
	Lochaber		20,422
	Nairn		10,119
	Ross and Cromarty		47,518
	Skye and Lochalsh		11,298
	Sutherland		14,241
Lothian		1,756	738,372
	E. Lothian		80,666
	Edinburgh City		436,936
	Midlothian		82,411
	W. Lothian		138,359
Strathclyde		13,856	2,404,532
	Argyll and Bute		68,834
	Bearsden and Milngavie		39,429
	Clydebank		52,024
	Clydesdale		57,554
	Cumbernauld and Kilsyth		62,031
	Cumnock and Doon Valley		45,260
	Cunninghame		138,707
	Dumbarton		78,648
	E. Kilbride		82,949
	Eastwood		53,572
	Glasgow City		765,915
	Hamilton		108,459
	Inverclyde		100,387
	Kilmarnock and Loudoun		82,154
	Kyle and Carrick		114,565
	Monklands		110,667
	Motherwell		150,037
	Renfrew		206,179
	Strathkelvin		87,161
Tayside		7,668	391,846
	Angus		93,038
	Dundee		179,674
	Perth and Kinross		119,134
Island Authority Areas			
Orkney Islands		974	19,056
Shetland Islands		1,427	27,277
Western Isles		2,901	31,884

Population of cities and large towns:

	Census population				Census population		
	1961	1971	1981		1961	1971	1981
Glasgow	1,055,017	893,790	762,288	Kilmarnock	47,509	48,992	52,080
Edinburgh	468,361	453,025	419,187	Dunfermline	47,151	51,738	52,057
Dundee	182,978	182,930	174,746	Clydebank	49,651	48,170	51,656
Aberdeen	185,390	181,785	190,200	Hamilton	41,928	46,376	51,529
Paisley	95,750	95,067	84,789	Coatbridge	53,825	51,985	50,866
Greenock	74,560	69,171	57,324				

Larger New Towns: East Kilbride, 71,316; Irvine, 55,278.

The birthplaces of the 1981 "usually resident" population were: Scotland, 4,548,708; England, 297,784; Wales, 12,733; Northern Ireland, 33,927; Ireland 27,018; Commonwealth, 48,515; foreign countries, 65,384.

The population of the Central Clydeside conurbation in 1981 was 1,713,287.

At 30 June 1982 the estimated sex distribution of the population in Scotland was: between 0 and 15, 545,400 males, 522,300 females; 15 and 65, 1,663,500 males, 15 and 60, 1,558,300 females; 65 and over, 277,600 males, 60 and over, 598,100 females.

Isle of Man and Channel Islands:

	Area in	Census population		
Islands	*sq. km*	*1961*	*1971*	*1981*
Isle of Man	572	48,151	56,289	64,679
Jersey	116	57,200	69,329	77,000
Guernsey, Herm and Jethou	64			
Alderney	8	47,178	53,734	56,000
Sark, Brechou and Lihou	6			

Vital statistics for England and Wales:

	Estimated home population at 30 June [1]	*Total live births*	*Illegitimate live births*	*Deaths*	*Marriages*	*Divorces, annulments and dissolutions*
1975	49,469,800	603,445	54,891	582,841	380,620	120,522
1976	49,459,200	584,270	53,766	598,516	358,567	126,694
1977	49,440,400	569,259	55,379	575,928	356,954	129,053
1978	49,442,500	596,418	60,637	585,901	368,258	143,667
1979	49,508,200	638,028	69,467	593,019	368,853	138,706
1980	49,603,000	656,234	77,372	581,385	370,022	148,301
1981	49,634,300	634,492	80,983	577,890	351,973	145,713
1982	49,606,800 [2]	625,931	89,857	581,861	342,166	146,698

[1] The population actually in England and Wales.   [2] Provisional.

In 1982 the proportion of male to female births was 1,055 male to 1,000 female; the live birth rate was 12·6 and the death rate 11·7 per 1,000 of the population; infant mortality rate 10·8 per 1,000 of live births. The average age at marriage was 29·8 years for males and 27 years for females.

Vital statistics for Scotland:

	Estimated home population at 30 June [1]	*Total births*	*Illegitimate births*	*Deaths*	*Marriages*	*Divorces, annulments and dissolutions*
1976	5,205,100	64,895	6,025	65,253	37,543	8,692
1977	5,195,000	62,342	5,968	62,294	37,288	8,823
1978	5,179,400	64,295	6,304	65,123	37,814	8,458
1979	5,167,000	68,366	6,960	65,747	37,860	8,837
1980	5,153,000	68,892	7,678	63,299	38,501	10,530
1981	5,149,500	69,054	8,447	63,828	36,237	9,895
1982	5,166,557	66,196	9,395	65,022	34,942	11,288

[1] Includes merchant navy at home and forces stationed in Scotland.

In 1982 the proportion of male to female births was 1,050 male to 1,000 female; the live birth rate was 12·8 and the death rate 12·6 per 1,000 of the population; infant mortality rate, 11 per 1,000 live births. The average age of marriage was 28 years for males and 26 years for females.

Emigration and Immigration. During the last hundred years the UK has most often been an exporter of population. Throughout the period 1881–1931 there was a consistent net loss from migration, though the fifteen years 1931–46 brought a reversal of the trend as a result of immigration from Europe. Since the Second World War the loss has largely continued. However, during the five years 1956–1961, increased immigration particularly from the new Commonwealth and Pakistan, resulted in a net gain. Decreased emigration in 1979 also produced a small net gain.

Since 1964 migration figures have been available from the International Passenger Survey. This is a sample survey conducted by the Office of Population, Censuses and Surveys, covering all the principal air and sea routes between the UK and overseas, except those to and from the Republic of Ireland. For the years 1964–72 the survey shows an average annual net loss for the UK of 63,000. During the decade 1973–1982 the annual net outflow has been reduced to an average of 43,000. Both immigration and emigration have decreased.

The table below, derived from the International Passenger survey, summarizes migration statistics for 1982 (in 1,000):

By country of last or future intended residence		Into UK	Out from UK	Balance
All Countries		201·7	258·9	−57·3
Australia, Canada, New Zealand		20·3	75·1	−54·8
India, Bangladesh, Sri Lanka		17·3	4·7	+12·6
Other Commonwealth		30·2	33·6	− 3·4
EEC		53·8	37·2	+16·6
USA		19·0	29·5	−10·5
South Africa		8·5	26·7	−18·2
Rest of World		52·5	52·1	+ 0·5
By sex/age				
Males	0–14	27·7	27·9	− 0·2
	15–24	25·7	27·9	− 2·2
	25–44	38·5	65·3	−26·9
	45 and over	8·4	13·4	− 4·9
	All ages	100·3	134·5	−34·2
Females	0–14	24·4	24·2	+ 0·1
	15–24	34·2	34·4	− 0·2
	25–44	36·6	51·7	−15·0
	45 and over	6·1	14·1	− 8·0
	All ages	101·3	124·4	−23·1

CLIMATE. The climate is cool temperate oceanic, with mild conditions and rainfall evenly distributed over the year, though the weather is very changeable because of cyclonic influences. In general, temperatures are higher in the west and lower in the east in winter and rather the reverse in summer. Rainfall amounts are greatest in the west, where most of the high ground occurs.

London. Jan. 40°F (4·5°C), July 64°F (18°C). Annual rainfall 24″ (600 mm). Aberdeen. Jan. 39°F (4°C), July 57°F (14°C). Annual rainfall 31·3″ (783 mm). Belfast. Jan. 40°F (4·5°C), July 61°F (16°C). Annual rainfall 34·6″ (865 mm). Birmingham. Jan. 35°F (1·5°C), July 58°F (14·5°C). Annual rainfall 26·5″ (663 mm). Cardiff. Jan. 40°F (4·4°C), July 61°F (16·3°C). Annual rainfall 42·6″ (1,065 mm). Edinburgh. Jan. 38°F (3·5°C), July 58°F (14·5°C). Annual rainfall 26·7″ (668 mm). Glasgow. Jan. 39°F (4°C), July 60°F (15·5°C). Annual rainfall 37·2″ (930 mm). Manchester. Jan. 41°F (5°C), July 62°F (16·5°C). Annual rainfall 34·1″ (853 mm).

QUEEN, HEAD OF THE COMMONWEALTH. Elizabeth II Alexandra Mary, born 21 April 1926 daughter of King George VI and Queen Elizabeth; married on 20 Nov. 1947 Lieut. Philip Mountbatten (formerly Prince Philip of Greece), created Duke of Edinburgh, Earl of Merioneth and Baron Greenwich on the same day and created Prince Philip, Duke of Edinburgh, 22 Feb. 1957; succeeded to the crown on the death of her father, on 6 Feb. 1952. Offspring: *Charles* Philip Arthur George, Prince of Wales (Heir Apparent), born 14 Nov. 1948, married Lady Diana Spencer on 29 July 1981. Offspring: *William* Arthur Philip Louis, born 21 June 1982; Princess *Anne* Elizabeth Alice Louise, born 15 Aug. 1950, married Mark Anthony Peter Phillips on 14 Nov. 1973. Offspring: *Peter* Mark Andrew, born 15 Nov. 1977; *Zara* Anne Elizabeth, born 15 May 1981. Prince *Andrew* Albert Christian Edward, born 19 Feb. 1960; Prince *Edward* Antony Richard Louis, born 10 March 1964.

The Queen Mother: Queen Elizabeth, born 4 Aug. 1900, daughter of the 14th Earl of Strathmore and Kinghorne; married the Duke of York, afterwards King George VI, on 26 April 1923.

Sister of the Queen: Princess Margaret Rose, born 12 Aug. 1930; married Antony Armstrong-Jones (created Earl of Snowdon, 3 Oct. 1961) on 6 May 1960; divorced, 1978. Offspring: *David* Albert Charles (Viscount Linley), born 3 Nov. 1961; Lady *Sarah* Frances Elizabeth Armstrong-Jones, born 1964.

Children of the late Duke of Gloucester (died 10 June 1974): William Henry Andrew Frederick, born 18 Dec. 1941, died 28 Aug. 1972; Richard Alexander Walter George, Duke of Gloucester, born 26 Aug. 1944, married Birgitte van Deurs on 8 July 1972 (offspring: Alexander Patrick Gregers Richard Windsor, Earl of Ulster, born 24 Oct. 1974; Davina Elizabeth Alice Benedikte Windsor, born 19 Nov. 1977; Rose Victoria Birgitte Louise Windsor, born 1 March 1980).

Children of the late Duke of Kent (died 25 Aug. 1942): Edward George Nicholas Patrick, Duke of Kent, born 9 Oct. 1935; married Katharine Worsley on 8 June 1961 (offspring: George Philip Nicholas, Earl of St Andrews, born 26 June 1962; Lady Helen Windsor, born 28 April 1964; Lord Nicholas Charles Edward Jonathan Windsor, born 25 July 1970). Alexandra Helen Elizabeth Olga Christabel, born 25 Dec. 1936; married 24 April 1963, Angus Ogilvy (offspring: James Robert Bruce, born 29 Feb. 1964; Marina Victoria Alexandra, born 31 July 1966). Michael George Charles Franklin, born 4 July 1942; married Marie-Christine von Reibnitz on 30 June 1978 (offspring: Lord *Frederick* Michael George David Louis Windsor, born 6 April 1979; Lady *Gabriela* Marina Alexander Ophelia Windsor, born 23 April 1981).

The Queen's legal title rests on the statute of 12 and 13 Will. III, ch. 3, by which the succession to the Crown of Great Britain and Ireland was settled on the Princess Sophia of Hanover and the 'heirs of her body being Protestants'. By proclamation of 17 July 1917 the royal family became known as the House and Family of Windsor. On 8 Feb. 1960 the Queen issued a declaration varying her confirmatory declaration of 9 April 1952 to the effect that while the Queen and her children should continue to be known as the House of Windsor, her descendants, other than descendants entitled to the style of Royal Highness and the title of Prince or Princess, and female descendants who marry and their descendants should bear the name of Mountbatten-Windsor. For the Royal Style and Titles of Queen Elizabeth *see* Commonwealth section.

By letters patent of 30 Nov. 1917 the titles of Royal Highness and Prince or Princess are restricted to the Sovereign's children, the children of the Sovereign's sons and the eldest living son of the eldest son of the Prince of Wales.

Provision is made for the support of the royal household by the settlement of the Civil List soon after the beginning of each reign. (For historical details, *see* THE STATESMAN'S YEAR-BOOK, 1908, p. 5, and 1935, p. 4). According to the Civil List Act of 1 Jan. 1972 and the Civil List (Increase of Financial Provision) Order 1975, the Civil List of the Queen, after the usual surrender of hereditary revenues, was (1984) £3,850,000.

The Civil List Acts of 1984 provide for an annuity of £116,200 to the Princess Anne; £186,500 to Prince Philip; £334,400 to Queen Elizabeth (the Queen Mother); £113,100 to the Princess Margaret; £20,000 to Prince Andrew; £20,000 to Prince Edward.

Sovereigns of Great Britain, from the Restoration (with dates of accession):

House of Stewart			
Charles II	29 May 1660	George III	25 Oct. 1760
James II	6 Feb. 1685	George IV	29 Jan. 1820
		William IV	26 June 1830
House of Stewart-Orange		Victoria	20 June 1837
William and Mary	13 Feb. 1689		
William III	28 Dec. 1694	*House of Saxe-Coburg and Gotha*	
		Edward VII	22 Jan. 1901
House of Stewart			
Anne	19 March 1702	*House of Windsor*	
		George V	6 May 1910
House of Hanover		Edward VIII	20 Jan. 1936
George I	1 Aug. 1714	George VI	11 Dec. 1936
George II	11 June 1727	Elizabeth II	6 Feb. 1952

CONSTITUTION AND GOVERNMENT. The supreme legislative power is vested in Parliament, which in its present form, as divided into two Houses of

Legislature, the Lords and the Commons, dates from the middle of the 14th century.

Parliament is summoned by the writ of the sovereign issued out of Chancery, by advice of the Privy Council, at least 20 days previous to its assembling. Every session ends with a prorogation, and all Bills which have not been passed during the session then lapse.

A dissolution may occur by the will of the sovereign, or, as is most usual, during the recess, by proclamation, or finally by lapse of time, the statutory limit of the duration of any Parliament being 5 years.

Under the Parliament Acts 1911 (1 and 2 Geo. V, ch. 13) and 1949 (12, 13 and 14 Geo. VI, ch. 103), all Money Bills (so certified by the Speaker of the House of Commons), if not passed by the House of Lords without amendment, may become law without their concurrence on the royal assent being signified within 1 month. Public Bills, other than Money Bills or a Bill extending the maximum duration of Parliament, if passed by the House of Commons in 2 successive sessions, whether of the same Parliament or not, and rejected each time, or not passed, by the House of Lords, may become law without their concurrence on the royal assent being signified, provided that 1 year has elapsed between the second reading in the first session of the House of Commons and the third reading in the second session. All Bills coming under this Act must reach the House of Lords at least 1 month before the end of the session.

The House of Lords consists of: (1) 798 hereditary peers and peeresses sitting by virtue of creation or descent, other than those who have disclaimed their titles for life under the provisions of the Peerage Act, 1963; (2) life peers being *(a)* 21 Lords of Appeal (active and retired), under the Appellate Jurisdiction Act, 1876, as amended; *(b)* (24 Dec. 1983) 352 life peers (including 46 women peers) under the Life Peerages Act, 1958: (3) 2 archbishops and 23 bishops of the Church of England (as long as they hold their sees).

The full House thus consists of 1,196, and the average attendance is about 300; at the end of Dec. 1983 172 peers were on leave of absence and 94 peers (including 7 minors) were without writs of summons.

The House of Commons consists of members (of both sexes) representing constituencies determined by the Parliamentary Boundary Commissions. Persons under 21 years of age, Clergy of the Church of England and of the Scottish Episcopal Church, Ministers of the Church of Scotland, Roman Catholic clergymen, civil servants, members of the regular armed forces, policemen, most judicial officers and other office-holders named in the House of Commons (Disqualification) Act are disqualified from sitting in the House of Commons. No English or Scottish peer can be elected to the House of Commons unless he has disclaimed his title for life under the Peerage Act, 1963, but Irish peers and holders of courtesy titles, who are not members of the House of Lords, are eligible.

In Aug. 1911 provision was first made for the payment of a salary of £400 per annum to members, other than those already in receipt of salaries as officers of the House, as Ministers or as officers of Her Majesty's household. As from 1 Jan. 1984 the salaries of members are £16,106 per annum, with income-tax relief on expenses incurred in the course of parliamentary duties. There is a secretarial allowance of up to £12,000 per annum and a living allowance, for an additional home, of up to £6,163 per annum. Members of the House of Lords are unsalaried but may recover expenses incurred in attending sittings of the House within maxima for each day's attendance of £16 for day subsistence, £40 for night subsistence and £17 for secretarial and research assistance or general office expenses. Additionally, Members of the House who are disabled may recover the extra cost of attending the House incurred by reason of their disablement. In connection with their attendance at the House and for parliamentary duties within the UK Lords may also recover the cost of travelling to and from their main place of residence.

Select Committees consisting of 10–15 Members of all parties exist in order to investigate certain matters.

The Representation of the People Act 1948, abolished the business premises and University franchises, and the only persons entitled to vote at Parliamentary elections are those registered as residents or as service voters. No person may vote in more than one constituency at a general election. Persons may apply on certain grounds to vote by post or by proxy.

All persons over 18 years old and not subject to any legal incapacity to vote and who are either British subjects or citizens of Ireland are entitled to be included in the register of electors for the constituency containing the address at which they were residing on the qualifying date for the register and are entitled to vote at elections held during the period for which the register remains in force. The current register was published in Feb. 1983.

Members of the armed forces, Crown servants employed abroad, and the wives accompanying their husbands, are entitled, if otherwise qualified, to be registered as 'service voters' provided they make a 'service declaration'. To be effective for a particular register, the declaration must be made on or before the qualifying date for that register.

The Representation of the People Act 1969, abolished the occupier's qualification for voting in Local Government elections.

The House of Commons (Redistribution of Seats) Acts 1944, 1949 and 1958, provided for the setting up of Boundary Commissions for England, Wales, Scotland and Northern Ireland. The Commissions are required to make general reports at intervals of not less than 10 and not more than 15 years and to submit reports from time to time with respect to the area comprised in any particular constituency or constituencies where some change appears necessary. Any changes giving effect to reports of the Commissions are to be made by Orders in Council laid before Parliament for approval by resolution of each House. The electorate of the United Kingdom and Northern Ireland in the register used at the election of June 1983 numbered 42,703,019, of whom 35,569,230 were in England, 2,138,384 in Wales, 3,934,220 in Scotland and 1,061,185 in Northern Ireland.

At the general election held in June 1983, 635 members were returned, 523 from England, 72 from Scotland, 38 from Wales and 17 from Northern Ireland. Every constituency returns a single member.

Devolution in Wales and Scotland was decided by referendum on 1 March 1979. In Wales the result was 956,330 against a regional Assembly and 243,048 for. In Scotland 1,230,937 (32·85% of those entitled to vote) voted for an Assembly and 1,153,502 against. However, the Scotland and Wales Acts stated that the relevant Secretary of State must lay order for the repeal of legislation if less than 40% of those entitled to vote voted 'Yes' and the Acts were repealed in June 1979.

The following is a table of the duration of Parliaments called since Nov. 1935.

Reign	When met	When dissolved	Duration (years and days)	
George V, Edward VIII and George VI	26 Nov. 1935	15 June 1945	9	205
George VI	1 Aug. 1945	3 Feb. 1950	4	188
,,	1 Mar. 1950	5 Oct. 1951	1	219
George VI and Elizabeth II	31 Oct. 1951	6 May 1955	3	188
Elizabeth II	7 June 1955	18 Sept. 1959	4	105
,,	20 Oct. 1959	25 Sept. 1964	4	341
,,	27 Oct. 1964	10 Mar. 1966	1	134
,,	18 Apr. 1966	29 May 1970	4	81
,,	29 June 1970	8 Feb. 1974	3	225
,,	12 Mar. 1974	20 Sept. 1974	0	224
,,	22 Oct. 1974	7 April 1979	4	167
,,	9 May 1979	13 May 1983	4	4
,,	15 June 1983	—	—	—

The executive government is vested nominally in the Crown, but practically in a committee of Ministers, called the Cabinet, which is dependent on the support of a majority in the House of Commons.

The head of the Ministry is the Prime Minister, a position first constitutionally recognized, and special precedence accorded to the holder, in 1905. His colleagues in the Ministry are appointed on his recommendation, and he dispenses the greater portion of the patronage of the Crown.

Heads of the Administrations since 1935 (C. = Conservative, L. = Liberal, Lab. = Labour, Nat. = National, Coal. = Coalition, Care. = Caretaker):

S. Baldwin (Nat.)	7 June 1935	H. Macmillan (C.)	10 Jan. 1957
N. Chamberlain (Nat.)	28 May 1937	Sir Alec Douglas-Home (C.)	18 Oct. 1963
W. S. Churchill (Coal.)	10 May 1940	H. Wilson (Lab.)	16 Oct. 1964
W. S. Churchill (Care.)	23 May 1945	E. Heath (C.)	19 June 1970
C. R. Attlee (Lab.)	26 July 1945	H. Wilson (Lab.)	12 Mar. 1974
W. S. Churchill (C.)	26 Oct. 1951	J. Callaghan (Lab.)	5 Apr. 1976
Sir Anthony Eden (C.)	6 Apr. 1955	M. Thatcher (C.)	4 May 1979

In March 1984 the Government consisted of the following members:

(a) MEMBERS OF THE CABINET

1. *Prime Minister and First Lord of the Treasury and Minister for Civil Service:* Rt Hon. Margaret Thatcher, MP, born 1925. (Salary £30,304 per annum.)

2. *Lord President of the Council and Leader of the House of Lords:* Rt Hon. Viscount Whitelaw, CH, MC, born 1918. (£31,680.)

3. *Lord Chancellor:* Rt Hon. The Lord Hailsham, CH, born 1907. (£31,680.)

4. *Secretary of State for Foreign and Commonwealth Affairs:* Rt Hon. Sir Geoffrey Howe, QC, MP, born 1926. (£30,304.)

5. *Secretary of State for the Home Department:* Rt Hon. Leon Brittan, QC, MP, born 1939. (£30,304.)

6. *Chancellor of the Exchequer:* Rt Hon. Nigel Lawson, MP, born 1932. (£30,304.)

7. *Secretary of State for Education and Science:* Rt Hon. Sir Keith Joseph, Bt, MP, born 1918. (£30,304.)

8. *Secretary of State for Northern Ireland:* Rt Hon. James Prior, MP, born 1927. (£30,304.)

9. *Secretary of State for Energy:* Rt Hon. Peter Walker, MBE, MP, born 1932. (£30,304.)

10. *Secretary of State for Defence:* Rt Hon. Michael Heseltine, MP, born 1933. (£30,304.)

11. *Secretary of State for Scotland:* Rt Hon. George Younger, TD, MP, born 1931. (£30,304.)

12. *Secretary of State for Wales:* Rt Hon. Nicholas Edwards, MP, born 1934. (£30,304.)

13. *Secretary of State for the Environment:* Rt Hon. Patrick Jenkin, MP, born 1926. (£30,304.)

14. *Lord Privy Seal and Leader of the House of Commons:* Rt Hon. John Biffen, MP, born 1930. (£30,304.)

15. *Secretary of State for Social Services:* Rt Hon. Norman Fowler, MP, born 1938. (£30,304.)

16. *Secretary of State for Trade and Industry:* Rt Hon. Norman Tebbit, MP, born 1931. (£30,304.)

17. *Chancellor of the Duchy of Lancaster:* Rt Hon. The Lord Cockfield, born 1916. (£31,680.)

18. *Secretary of State for Employment:* Rt Hon. Tom King, MP, born 1933. (£30,304.)

19. *Minister of Agriculture, Fisheries and Food:* Rt Hon. Michael Jopling, MP, born 1930. (£30,304.)

20. *Chief Secretary to the Treasury:* Rt Hon. Peter Rees, QC, MP, born 1926. (£30,304.)

21. *Secretary of State for Transport:* Rt Hon. Nicholas Ridley, MP, born 1929. (£30,304.)

(b) LAW OFFICERS

22. *Attorney-General:* Rt Hon. Sir Michael Havers, QC, MP, born 1923. (£32,224.)

23. *Lord Advocate:* Rt Hon. Lord Mackay, QC, born 1927. (£31,730.)

24. *Solicitor-General:* Sir Patrick Mayhew, QC, MP, born 1929. (£26,364.)

25. *Solicitor-General for Scotland:* Peter Fraser, QC, MP, born 1945. (£22,424.)

(c) MINISTERS NOT IN THE CABINET

26. *Parliamentary Secretary, Treasury (Chief Whip):* Rt Hon. John Wakeham, MP, born 1932. (£25,174.)

27. *Minister of State, Privy Council Office, Minister for the Arts:* Rt Hon. The Earl of Gowrie, born 1939. (£26,670.)

28. *Minister of State, Foreign and Commonwealth Office:* Rt Hon. The Baroness Young, born 1926. (£26,670.)

29. *Minister of State, Foreign and Commonwealth Office, Minister for Overseas Development:* Rt Hon. Timothy Raison, MP, born 1929. (£21,364.)

30. *Minister of State, Foreign and Commonwealth Office:* Malcolm Rifkind, MP, born 1946. (£21,364.)

31. *Minister of State, Foreign and Commonwealth Office:* Richard Luce, MP, born 1936. (£21,364.)

32. *Minister of State, Home Office:* Rt Hon. Douglas Hurd, CBE, MP, born 1930. (£21,364.)

33. *Minister of State, Home Office:* David Waddington, QC, MP, born 1929. (£21,364).

34. *Financial Secretary, Treasury:* John Moore, MP, born 1937. (£21,364.)

35. *Minister of State, Treasury:* Barney Hayhoe, MP, born 1925. (£21,364.)

36. *Minister of State, Treasury:* Ian Stewart, MP, born 1935. (£21,364.)

37. *Minister of State, Northern Ireland Office:* Hon. Adam Butler, MP, born 1931. (£21,364.)

38. *Minister of State, Northern Ireland Office:* The Earl of Mansfield, born 1930. (£26,670.)

39. *Minister of State, Department of Energy:* Rt Hon. Alick Buchanan-Smith, MP, born 1932. (£21,364.)

40. *Minister of State, Ministry of Defence, Armed Forces:* John Stanley, MP, born 1942. (£21,364.)

41. *Minister of State, Ministry of Defence, Defence Procurement:* Geoffrey Pattie, MP, born 1936. (£21,364.)

42. *Minister of State, Scottish Office:* Rt Hon. The Lord Gray, born 1927. (£26,670.)

43. *Minister of State, Welsh Office:* John Stradling Thomas, MP, born 1925. (£21,364.)

44. *Minister of State, Department of the Environment, Minister for Local Government and Environmental Services:* The Lord Bellwin, born 1923. (£26,670.)

45. *Minister of State, Department of the Environment, Minister for Housing and Construction:* Ian Gow, TD, MP, born 1937. (£21,364)

46. *Minister of State, Department of Health and Social Security, Minister for Health:* Rt Hon. Kenneth Clarke, QC, MP, born 1940. (£21,364.)

47. *Minister of State, Department of Health and Social Security, Minister for Social Security:* Dr Rhodes Boyson, MP, born 1925. (£21,364.)

48. *Minister of State, Department of Trade and Industry, Minister for Trade:* Rt Hon. Paul Channon, MP, born 1935. (£21,364.)

49. *Minister of State, Department of Trade and Industry, Minister for Information Technology.* Rt Hon. Kenneth Baker, MP, born 1934. (£21,364.)

50. *Minister of State, Department of Trade and Industry:* Norman Lamont, MP, born 1942. (£21,364.)

51. *Minister of State, Department of Employment:* Hon. Peter Morrison, MP, born 1944. (£21,364.)

52. *Minister of State, Department of Employment:* John Selwyn Gummer, MP, born 1939. (£21,364.)

53. *Minister of State, Ministry of Agriculture, Fisheries and Food:* Rt Hon. The Lord Belstead, born 1932. (£26,670.)

54. *Minister of State, Ministry of Agriculture, Fisheries and Food:* John MacGregor, OBE, MP, born 1937. (£21,364.)

55. *Minister of State, Department of Transport:* Lynda Chalker, MP, born 1942. (£21,364.)

Leader of the Opposition in the House of Commons: Rt Hon. Neil Kinnock, MP, born 1942. (£27,764.)

Leader of the Opposition in the House of Lords: The Lord Cledwyn of Penrhos, born 1916. (£21,450.)

The Constitution of the House of Commons after the general election held on 9 June 1983 was as follows: Conservative, 397; Labour, 209; Alliance 23 (Liberals, 17, SDP, 6); Others, 21.

Craig, F. W. S., *British Electoral Facts 1885–1975.* London, 1976.—*The Most Gracious Speeches to Parliament 1900–1974.* London, 1975
Herman, V., and Att, J. E., *Cabinet Studies.* London, 1976
Jennings, Sir I., *Cabinet Government.* 3rd. ed. CUP, 1959.—*The British Constitution.* 5th ed. CUP, 1966.—*Parliament.* 2nd ed. CUP, 1957.—*Party Politics.* 3 vols. CUP, 1960–62
Jones, J. M., *British Nationality Law.* Rev. ed. London, 1955
King, A. (ed.), *The British Prime Minister.* London, 1969.—*British Members of Parliament.* London, 1974
Laundy, P., *The Office of Speaker.* London, 1964
Lindsay, T. F., *The Conservative Party 1918–1970.* London, 1976
Mackintosh, J. P., *The British Cabinet.* 3rd ed. London, 1977.—*The Government and Politics of Britain.* 4th ed. London, 1977
May, Sir T. E., *Treatise on the Law, Privileges, Proceedings and Usage of Parliament.* 19th ed., London, 1976
Mellors, C., *The British MP.* London, 1982
Pelling, H., *A Short History of the Labour Party.* London, 1976
Rush, M., and Shaw, M., *House of Commons.* London, 1974
Stacey, F., *British Government 1966–1975.* London, 1975
Taylor, E., *The House of Commons at Work.* 7th ed. London, 1967
The Times Guide to the House of Commons, June 1983. London, 1983
Wilding, N., and Laundy, P., *An Encyclopaedia of Parliament.* 4th ed. London, 1972
Young, R., *The British Parliament.* London, 1962

European Parliament: On 7 June 1979 Great Britain elected 81 representatives to the European Parliament, of which 66 came from England, 8 from Scotland and 4 from Wales, each constituency returning a single member by a first past the post system. Northern Ireland returned 3 members by single transferable vote. 13,446,076 votes were cast, on a 33% poll. The seats were won as follows: Conservative 60, Labour 17, Scottish Nationalists 1, Ulster Unionists 1, Democratic Unionists 1, Social, Democratic and Labour Party 1.

Local Government. Local Administration is carried out by four different types of bodies, namely: (i) local branches of some central ministries, such as the Department of Health and Social Security; (ii) local sub-managements of nationalized industries (coal, electricity, gas, public transport and the post office); (iii) specialist authorities such as water authorities; and (iv) the system of *local government* described below. The phrase 'local government' has come to mean that part of the local administration conducted by elected councils.

There are two separate systems: one for England and Wales and one for Scotland, but both systems are financed by a species of tax on property, levied locally, combined with government grants which, in the aggregate, amount to more than the yield of the local tax. This local tax is called 'the rate'. The system of financing local government was the subject of a major review in 1975.

Local Government: England and Wales—*Outside London.* England and Wales have slightly differing systems. Each country has three types of councils namely, county, district and English parish or Welsh Community Councils. In addition, England has some metropolitan county and district councils.

Councillors are elected by their local electors for 4 years. The chairman of the council is one of the councillors elected by the rest. In a district with the status of city or borough his title is mayor, or in a few famous places Lord Mayor. Any parish or community council can by simple resolution adopt the style 'town council' and the status of town for the parish or community. The chairman of the council will be known as the town mayor.

Counties and Districts: There are 47 non-metropolitan counties (of which 8 are in Wales) and 6 metropolitan counties (Greater Manchester, Merseyside, South Yorkshire, Tyne and Wear, West Yorkshire and West Midlands). Within the counties there are 369 districts (36 metropolitan and 333 non-metropolitan, of which 37 are in Wales).

Parishes and Communities: There are some 10,000 parishes within the English districts, of which 7,000 or so have councils. About 300 are former small boroughs or urban districts which became successor parishes. Parishes generally, however, remain comparatively unaffected by reorganization.

In Wales, parishes have been replaced by communities. Unlike England, where many areas are not in any parish, communities have been established for the whole of Wales. There is one for each former parish, county borough, borough or urban district (or part thereof where the former area is divided by a new boundary). There are 1,004 communities altogether, of which 800 or so have councils.

The Local Government Act 1972 laid down the boundaries for all the counties and districts in England and Wales except the English non-metropolitan districts.

Permanent Local Government Boundary Commissions for England and for Wales advise the Secretaries of State on boundaries and electoral arrangements.

A council has only those powers which have been conferred upon it expressly by Act of Parliament, and no more. The relationship between the different types of council is one of specialization, not of hierarchy. The larger do not supervise the smaller; each being, within its own sphere, entitled to make its own decisions. Government sanction, however, is required to borrow money and to sell land below its market value, and certain types of land use are subject to planning control.

Councils are kept within the law by a system of publicly regulated audit, and in the last resort they can be restrained from exceeding their powers by the courts.

Local government functions may be classified into county, district and parish or community functions, but whereas county and district functions are distinct, the parish and community functions are mostly concurrent with those of the districts. Arrangements may, however, be made so that any council may discharge functions of any other as its agent.

The following is the classification of powers given above: *Parish and Community Functions.* Allotments, burial and cremation, halls, meeting places and entertainments, facilities for exercise and recreation, public lavatories, street lighting, off-street vehicle parking, footpaths, the support of local arts and crafts, the encouragement of tourism and the right to be consulted by the district council on planning applications and certain byelaws. *District Functions.* In addition to the Parish and Community functions, aerodromes, civic restaurants, housing, markets, refuse collection, the administration of planning control, the formulation of local plans, sewerage, on behalf of the water authority, museums, the licensing of places of entertainment and refreshment, and the constitutional oversight of parishes and communities. *County Functions.* The formulation of structure plans, traffic, transportation and roads, education, public libraries and museums, youth employment and social services.

There are, in addition, a number of special arrangements. Four district councils in Wales have been designated as library authorities and Welsh district councils have powers in relation to allotments currently with community councils. The county councils in England and Wales separately or jointly appoint the fire and police authorities, and the bodies responsible for national parks. In Metropolitan counties the district not the county councils are responsible for education, social services and libraries.

The total number of local government electors in England and Wales was 37,707,813 in 1983.

Greater London. Since 1965 London has been governed by the Greater London Council covering the whole metropolitan area, and by 32 London Boroughs and the City of London, each with responsibilities in its own area. In the City and the 12 boroughs covering the inner part of Greater London education is the responsibility of the Inner London Education Authority, a special Committee of the GLC but independent of it, while in the 20 outer boroughs the London Borough Council is the education authority. Other functions are divided between the GLC and the boroughs. The main responsibilities of the GLC are strategic planning, major roads, public transport (through the London Transport Executive, which is responsible to it), housing, major parks and open spaces, the fire service, refuse disposal and Thames flood prevention. The boroughs are the primary housing authorities in their own areas, while the GLC is concerned with matters affecting the whole of London. The City has preserved a large measure of independence and has its own powers regarding police, justice, bridges, sanitation, etc. Except in the City the police authority covering the whole of Greater London is the Metropolitan Police, which is responsible direct to the Central Government.

Estimated population of Greater London in June 1982 was 6,795,300, and rateable value at 1 April 1983 was £2,005,252,673. Estimated gross revenue expenditure of the GLC in 1983–84 was £2,937·3m. (including £1,011m. for the ILEA and £745m. for London Transport). Estimated gross capital expenditure, 1983–84 was £489m., including ILEA £17m., London Transport £153m. and £15m. for housing loans. The GLC outstanding debt at 1 April 1983 was £2,403,554,332; ILEA, £191,942,966m.

Scotland. Under the system, which came into effect in 1975, the Scots mainland is divided into 9 regions, and in addition there are the 3 islands areas of Orkney, Shetland and the Western Isles. There is no equivalent to the English metropolitan county. The regions are divided into districts which total 53. All these units have a council consisting of councillors elected for 4 years and a chairman elected by the councillors for 4 years. Community councils have been established under schemes submitted by district and islands councils. These community councils cannot claim public funds as of right, nor do they have powers directly conferred by Statute: consequently they are not local authorities in the sense that Welsh Community Councils are.

As in England and Wales a permanent Local Government Boundary Commission advises the Secretary of State on Local Authority Boundaries and electoral arrangements.

On the mainland, functions are allocated between regional and district authorities, in the same way (with minor exceptions) as they are allocated between English counties on the one hand and English districts and parishes on the other, but the councils of the islands areas, which have no districts, perform both sets of functions.

Despite differences of nomenclature the effect of the reforms of 1972 (England)

and 1973 (Scotland) is to assimilate the systems of mainland Scotland and of England and Wales more closely than has been the case in the past.

The total number of local government electors in Scotland was 3,913,510 in 1982.

Complaints. Under both systems, complaints, by members of the public, of maladministration may be investigated by a Commissioner for Local Administration. Initially a complaint must be referred to him through a councillor, but a direct approach to him is possible if this fails. He can deal only with matters for which there is no other remedy; he reports to the council concerned and may publish his report.

For map of regions *see* THE STATESMAN'S YEAR-BOOK, 1974–75.

Our Changing Democracy: Devolution to Scotland and Wales. HMSO, 1975
Arnold-Baker, C., *The Local Government Act 1972.* London, 1973

DEFENCE. The Defence Council was established on 1 April 1964 under the chairmanship of the Secretary of State for Defence, who is responsible to the Sovereign and Parliament for the defence of the realm. Vested in the Defence Council are the functions of commanding and administering the Armed Forces. The Secretary of State heads the Ministry of Defence as a Department of State. There are 4 subordinate Ministers; 2 Ministers of State and 2 Parliamentary Under Secretaries of State.

Defence Council membership comprises the Secretary of State, 2 Ministers of State, the 2 Parliamentary Under-Secretaries, the Chief of the Defence Staff, the 3 single Service Chiefs of Staff, the Vice-Chief of Defence Staff (Personnel and Logistics), the Chief of Defence Procurement, the Chief Scientific Adviser and the Permanent Under-Secretary of State.

There are 3 Service Boards, each of which enjoys delegated powers for the administration of matters relating to the naval, military and air forces respectively.

Defence policy decision making is a collective Governmental responsibility. Important matters of policy are considered by the full Cabinet or, more frequently, by the Defence and Oversea Policy Committee under the chairmanship of the Prime Minister. Other members of this Committee include the Secretary of State for Defence, the Foreign and Commonwealth Secretary and the Home Secretary.

Logistics Services. Since the inception of a unified Ministry of Defence in 1964, progress has been made in the rationalization of the logistics services of the Royal Navy, the Army and the Royal Air Force. The Air Force Department is responsible for accommodation stores for maintenance and for the initial furnishing of new buildings; the Army Department is the single management authority for the design, development, procurement and inspection of clothing other than certain specialized clothing; the Navy Department has for some time been responsible for ration policy provisioning, procurement, storing and distribution of food to main depots and to Army forward supply depots in BAOR and is responsible for water transport to its tri-service responsibilities. The supply of Naval air stores has been integrated with those of the RAF.

The Procurement Executive. An important development in 1971 was the creation of a Procurement Executive to combine the Defence Procurement responsibilities of the Ministry of Defence and the former Ministry of Aviation Supply.

Service Strengths at 1 April 1983, all ranks, males and females, UK personnel only: Royal Navy and Royal Marines, 72,000; Army, 159,300; Royal Air Force, 89,900; Total, 321,000. The Ministry of Defence employed 209,000 civilians in April 1983.

Defence Budget Estimates: 1982–83, £14,091m.; 1983–84, £15,733m.

Army. Control of the British Army is vested in the Defence Council and is exercised through the Army Board, which consists of 7 civilian and 5 military members. The Secretary of State for Defence is Chairman of the Army Board. The other civilian members are the Ministers of State for the Armed Forces and Defence Procurement and the Parliamentary Under Secretaries of State for the Armed Forces and Defence Procurement; the Chief of Establishments and Research Nuclear; the Deputy Under Secretary of State (Army) (who is the Secretary of the Board) and the Second Permanent Under Secretary of State.

The Military members of the Army Board are the Chief of the General Staff, the Adjutant-General, the Quartermaster-General, the Master-General of the Ordnance and the Vice-Chief of the General Staff. The Chief of the General Staff is the professional head of his Service and the professional adviser to Ministers on the Army aspects of military problems. He is responsible for the fighting efficiency of his Service; for the consideration of all Army aspects of policy planning; for Army advice on the conduct of operations; and for the issuing of such single Service operational orders as may be appropriate resulting from defence policy decisions. He is also responsible for the Territorial Army. The Chief of the General Staff is a member of the Chiefs of Staff Committee which is collectively responsible to HM Government for professional advice on strategy and military operations and on the military implication of defence policy. This advice is tendered to the Secretary of State for Defence by the Chairman of the Chiefs of Staff Committee, the Chief of the Defence Staff. In exercise of his General Staff responsibilities the Chief of the General Staff is assisted by the Vice-Chief of the General Staff. The Adjutant-General is responsible for Army manpower within the policy set up by the General Staff; for recruiting and selection; for the administration and individual training of military personnel; for the discipline of the Army; for pay and allowances and pensions; for Army medical services; for dental and nursing services; for legal services; for the veterinary and remount services; for the Army Cadet Forces; for questions of Army welfare and education including school children overseas; and for resettlement and sports. The Quartermaster-General is responsible for logistic planning for the Army; for the storage, distribution, maintenance, repair and inspection of equipment, stores and ammunition; for development of stores; for supply, transport and accommodation; for the development, production and inspection of clothing; for military movements and transportation; for the Army postal, catering, salvage and fire services; and for questions connected with canteens, institutes and military labour. The Master General of the Ordnance is a member of both the Army Board and of the Procurement Executive Management Board. He is responsible to the Chief of Defence Procurement for the financial and technical management of the approved programme for the procurement of land service equipment for the Armed Services, and to the Army Board for the co-ordination of the Army's total equipment programme. The Chief Scientist (Army) is responsible for providing scientific advice to the Army Board and its members and for ensuring that the Defence Research Programme properly reflects their needs. He is also a member of the Procurement Executive as Director General, Research (B). The Deputy Under-Secretary of State (Army) is responsible for the general co-ordination of Army Board business and, under the Permanent Under-Secretary of State and the Second Permanent Under-Secretary of State, for providing the Board with financial and administrative guidance.

Headquarters United Kingdom Land Forces at Wilton commands all Army units in UK except Ministry of Defence controlled units. The Ministry of Defence retains direct operational control of units in Northern Ireland. Command by HQ United Kingdom Land Forces is exercised through 9 district headquarters. There are 3 major overseas Commands: Land Forces Cyprus, Hong Kong and the British Army of the Rhine. There are also garrisons in Berlin, Gibraltar, Falkland Islands and Belize.

The strength of the Regular Army (less the Brigade of Gurkhas and locally enlisted personnel) on 1 April 1983 was 153,100 men and 6,100 women. Strength of reserve forces were: Regular reserves, 137,700; territorial army, 72,100.

The Territorial Army had a strength of 72,600 (Jan. 1983). Its role is to provide a national reserve for employment on specific tasks at home and overseas and to meet the unexpected when required; and, in particular, to complete the Army Order of Battle of NATO committed forces and to provide certain units for the support of NATO Headquarters, to assist in maintaining a secure UK base in support of forces deployed on the Continent of Europe and to provide a framework for any future expansion of the Reserves. In addition, men who have completed service in the Regular Army normally have some liability to serve in the Regular Reserve. All members of the TA and Regular Reserve may be called out by a Queen's Order in time of emergency or imminent national danger and most of the TA and a large proportion of the Regular Reserve may be called out by a Queen's Order when warlike operations are in preparation or in progress. There is a special reserve force in Northern Ireland, the Ulster Defence Regiment, 7,000 strong, which gives support to the regular army.

Men, women and juniors enlist in the Army for 22 years' active and reserve service. However, under a scheme introduced in May 1981 they are entitled to give 12 months' notice (18 months' for women) to leave active service provided they serve for a minimum of 3 years. Alternatively, they can agree to serve for 6 or 9 years to receive the benefit of higher rates of pay. Those enlisting in certain technical trades must agree to serve for a minimum of 6 years. Recruits under the age of 17½ on reaching the age of 18 are entitled either to confirm their original engagement or to reduce their period of service to 3 years.

Women serve in both the Regular Army and the TA in the Queen Alexandra's Royal Army Nursing Corps, the Ulster Defence Regiment and the Women's Royal Army Corps, the latter's employments including communications, motor transport, clerical and catering duties. Some officers of the Women's Royal Army Corps are employed on the staffs of military headquarters.

Barnett, C., *Britain and her Army 1509–1970.* London, 1970
Blaxford, G., *The Regiments Depart: A History of the British Army 1945–70.* London, 1971
Haswell, J., *The British Army.* London, 1975
Johnson, F. A., *Defence by Ministry: The British Ministry of Defence 1944–1974.* London, 1980
Stanhope, H., *The Soldiers: An Anatomy of the British Army.* London, 1979

Navy. The Royal Navy is a permanent establishment, governed by the Admiralty Board of the Defence Council. The Secretary of State for Defence is Chairman of the Admiralty Board. The naval members and their responsibilities are as follows: The Chief of the Naval Staff and First Sea Lord (professional head of the Royal Navy), assisted by the Vice-Chief of the Naval Staff, responsible for fighting efficiency, policy planning and operations advice; The Chief of Naval Personnel and Second Sea Lord, responsible for the manning of the Fleet, service conditions, training, discipline and welfare; The Controller of the Navy (formerly also Third Sea Lord), responsible for research and development, design, production, inspection, repair and maintenance of ships, their weapons and equipment; The Chief of Fleet Support, known until 1968 as Chief of Naval Supplies and Transport and Vice-Controller (formerly also Fourth Sea Lord), responsible for the provision of naval armament, victualling and medical stores and fuels, and for the movement of transport of persons and material, and superintending Dockyard organization and maintenance of the Fleet. The post of Second Permanent Under-Secretary of State (Royal Navy) (formerly Permanent Secretary) lapsed in 1968 (he was Civil Service head, responsible for general co-ordination of the Admiralty Board business, the interior economy of the Navy department, Navy contracts and the administration of civil staff, and accounting officer for Navy Votes responsible for the control of expenditure and adviser to the Admiralty Board on financial questions). Thus the office of Samuel Pepys, of which the last holder was the 33rd, passed into history.

The following is a summary of the more important units:

Category	1976	1977	1978	1979	1980	1981	1982	1983	1984
Aircraft carriers	3	3	3	3	3	3	3	3	3
Submarines	31	31	30	31	31	32	33	31	32
Destroyers	10	10	11	14	14	15	13	14	15
Frigates	56	56	54	56	55	47	47	46	48

There are also 2 helicopter support ships, 2 assault ships, 2 maintenance ships, 1 ice patrol ship, 12 patrol vessels of corvette size, 12 surveying vessels, 21 minehunters, 15 coastal minesweepers, 2 trawler minesweepers, 1 mine countermeasures support ship, 4 trials ships, 1 submarine tender, 10 patrol boats, 10 mooring, salvage and boom vessels, 10 fleet support and supply ships, 14 fleet oilers, 40 other auxiliaries, 7 logistic landing ships, 60 minor landing craft, 9 fleet tugs, 55 other tugs, and 70 tenders.

In the following table the principal surface warships are grouped in classes, in descending order of modernity.

Com-pleted	Name	Standard displacement Tons	Aircraft	Armament	Shaft horse-power	Speed knots
			Aircraft Carriers			
1982	Illustrious [1]	16,000	5 Sea Harriers;	Twin 'Sea Dart' surface-to-air	112,000	28.0
1980	Invincible [2]		9 Sea King helicopters	missile launchers	(gas)	
1959	Hermes [3]	24,000	Latterly carried; 5 Sea Harriers; 9 Sea King helicopters	2 quadruple 'Seacat' missile launchers	78,000 (steam)	28.0

[1] Sister ship *Ark Royal* scheduled to be completed late 1984/early 1985.

[2] Originally designed as 'Command Cruiser', subsequently re-rated as 'Through-deck Cruiser' (meaning long underdeck hangar with flat-top or near full-length flight deck) and later designated 'Anti-Submarine Cruiser'. Officially listed as anti-submarine warfare carrier in 1980.

[3] Refitted 1980 with 7·5 degree 'ski-jump' ramp for launching Harrier aircraft. Rehabilitated early 1984 as training ship and standby for operational contingency.

Note: For disposals of the large fixed-wing aircraft carriers *Ark Royal* and *Eagle*, the original sister ships of *Hermes* (*Bulwark*, *Albion* and *Centaur*) and the rebuilt *Victorious*; the helicopter cruisers *Blake* and *Tiger*, original sister ship *Lion*, and the other orthodox cruisers *Belfast* (museum ship on the *Thames*), *Ceylon*, *Newfoundland*, *Birmingham*, *Jamaica*, *Superb*, *Kenya*, *Swiftsure*, *Bermuda*, *Mauritius*, *Sheffield* and *Gambia*, see 1983–84 and earlier editions.

Capital (Strategic) Submarines

Class	No.	Displacement (submerged) tons	Missile Tubes (vertical)	Nuclear Reactors	Shaft horse-power	Speed Knots
"R"	4 [1]	8,400	16 Polaris A3	1	15,000	25 dived 20 surface

[1] *Renown*, *Repulse*, *Resolution* and *Revenge* (former battleship names) completed in 1967–69. All also have six 21-in. torpedo tubes.

Other submarines are of the following classes: 'Trafalgar' (nuclear propelled), 2; 'Swiftsure' (nuclear propelled), 6; 'Churchill' (nuclear propelled), 3; 'Valiant' (nuclear propelled), 2; 'Oberon', 13; 'Porpoise', 2.

The destroyers of the Royal Navy are of the following classes: 'Sheffield' (Type 42), 11; 'Bristol' (Type 82), 1; 'County', 3.

Frigates are of the following classes; 'Broadsword' (Type 22), 6; 'Amazon' (Type 21), 6; 'Leander', 24; 'Tribal' (Type 81) from reserve, 3; 'Rothesay', 8; 'Whitby' (Type 12), 1.

Ships under construction or on order include 4 nuclear powered submarines, 1 guided missile armed destroyer, 10 frigates, and 10 mine counter-measures vessels.

The total number of officers and ratings provided for was (in 1,000) 1981–82, 74·3; 1982–83, 70·4; 1983–84, 71·7.

Blackman, R. V. B., *The World's Warships*. London, 1969
Blackman, R. V. B., *Ships of the Royal Navy*. London, 1975
Moore, J. E. (ed.), *Jane's Fighting Ships*. London, annual

Air Force. In May 1912 the Royal Flying Corps first came into existence with military and naval wings, of which the latter became the independent Royal Naval Air Service in July 1914. On 2 Jan. 1918 an Air Ministry was formed, and on 1 April 1918 the Royal Flying Corps and the Royal Naval Air Service were amalgamated, under the Air Ministry, as the Royal Air Force.

In 1937 the units based on aircraft carriers and naval shore stations again passed to the operational and administrative control of the Admiralty, as the Fleet Air Arm. In 1964 control of the RAF became a responsibility of the Ministry of Defence.

The Royal Air Force is administered by the Air Force Board, of which the Secretary of State for Defence is Chairman. The Minister of State for the Armed Forces is Vice-Chairman, and normally acts as Chairman on behalf of the Secretary of State. Other members of the Board are the Under-Secretary of State for the Armed Forces, the Under-Secretary of State for Defence Procurement, the Chief of the Air Staff, Vice-Chief of the Air Staff, Air Member for Personnel, Air Member for Supply and Organization, Controller of Aircraft, Chief Scientist (Royal Air Force), Deputy Under-Secretary of State (Air) and Second Permanent Under-Secretary of State for Administration. The RAF is organized into commands:

Home Commands. Strike and Support Commands. The Air Training Corps and the Air Sections of the Combined Cadet Force are under the administrative control of Support Command and functionally controlled by the Ministry of Defence.

The RAF College, which trains general-duties, engineering, and supply and secretarial graduates for permanent commissions, is at Cranwell. The RAF Staff College is at Bracknell. The Department of Air Warfare is at Cranwell. The RAF Central Flying School is at Leeming. Estimated strength in April 1982, including WRAF and boys, was 91,700.

Strike Command is made up of 3 Groups. Nos 1 and 38 Groups merged in late 1983 to form a new No 1 Group, responsible for the strike/attack, reconnaissance, tanker, battlefield support and transport forces. The Tornado GR1 and Jaguar provide the strike/attack and reconnaissance. Victor and Hercules tanker aircraft are being supplemented by ex-civil VC10s and TriStars converted to air refuelling. Battlefield support forces comprise Harrier GR3s, and Chinook, Puma and Wessex support helicopters. The strategic and tactical transport force comprises VC10s and Hercules, and communications aircraft. No 11 Group controls the air defence forces: Lightning and Phantom supersonic all-weather intercepters, Bloodhound surface-to-air missiles, and ground environment radars, the associated communication systems, and the Ballistic Missile Early Warning System at Fylingdales. No 11 Group also controls the Hawks and Hunters of the Tactical Weapons Units which, in war, would supplement air defence fighters at bases throughout the UK. UK air defence is undergoing major improvements. The Tornado F2 will enter service in late 1984 and will gradually replace the Lightning and some Phantoms. Nimrod AEW3 entered service in 1984, replacing the Shackleton, and in the ground environment, there are new radars and communications systems entering service. No 18 Group is responsible for maritime air operations. ASW is the duty of the Nimrod Mk 2, which also has a capability against surface ships, although Buccaneers provide the main offensive force against a maritime surface threat. No 18 Group also operates Canberras in a multitude of roles, including photo-reconnaissance, target towing and ECM training, as well as Nimrod special-purpose aircraft. Search and rescue units are equipped with Sea King and Wessex helicopters. RAF Regiment short-range air defence squadrons, armed with Rapier, and the field squadrons form part of 1 Group, as does The Queen's Flight, with 3 Andovers and 2 Wessex helicopters. The Military Air Traffic Operations organization also has the status of a Group. Strike Command has NATO commitments, but is available for overseas reinforcement. The training element of RAF Support Command utilizes Bulldog and Chipmunk primary trainers, Jet Provost basic trainers, Hawk advanced trainers, Jetstreams for multi-engine pilot training, twin-jet Dominies for training navigators and other non-pilot aircrew, and Gazelle and Wessex helicopters.

Overseas Commands. Royal Air Force Germany. Small units in Gibraltar, the Falkland Islands, Belize, Cyprus and Hong Kong.

Squadrons of RAF Germany, which form part of NATO's 2nd Allied Tactical Air Force under SACEUR, have Tornado GR1, Harrier and Jaguar attack and reconnaissance aircraft, Phantom fighters, Chinook and Puma Helicopters, Pembroke communications aircraft, and Rapier surface-to-air missile squadrons of the RAF Regiment.

A squadron of Phantom aircraft and a flight of Harriers and Chinooks, together with detachments of Hercules tankers and search and rescue Sea Kings, are based in the Falkland Islands; a squadron of Wessex helicopters is based in Hong Kong.

The Royal Air Force, 1939–45. Vols. I, II, III. HMSO, 1953–54
Taylor J. W. R. (ed.), *Jane's All the World's Aircraft.* London. Annual from 1909

INTERNATIONAL RELATIONS

Membership. The UK is a member of UN, Commonwealth, EEC, OECD, the Council of Europe, NATO and the Colombo Plan.

ECONOMY

Budget. Revenue and expenditure for years ending 31 March, in £ sterling:

Revenue	Estimated in the Budgets	Actual receipts into the Exchequer	More than estimates
1980	51,013,000,000	53,369,000,000	2,256,000,000
1981	65,415,000,000	66,814,000,000	1,399,000,000
1982	75,524,000,000	76,288,000,000	764,000,000
1983	82,895,000,000	83,350,000,000	455,000,000
1984	87,800,000,000	88,700,000,000	900,000,000

The Budget estimate of ordinary revenue for 1984–85 is £98,000m.

Expenditure	Budget and supplementary estimates	Actual payments out of the Exchequer	More than estimates
1980	59,371,000,000	60,753,000,000	1,382,000,000
1981	73,175,000,000	76,728,000,000	3,553,000,000
1982	83,697,000,000	85,425,000,000	1,728,000,000
1983	90,891,000,000	89,041,000,000	−850,000,000
1984	95,600,000,000	97,400,000,000	1,800,000,000

The Budget estimate of ordinary expenditure for 1984–85 is £103,400m.

The imperial revenue in detail for 1983–84 and the expenditure, are given below, as is the budget estimate for 1984–85 (in £1m.):

Sources of revenue	Net receipts 1983–84	Budget estimate 1984–85
Inland Revenue:		
Income	31,300	33,800
Corporation tax	6,000	8,400
Petroleum revenue tax	6,100	6,000
Capital Gains tax	670	710
Development land tax	70	75
Capital transfer tax	610	680
Stamp duties	1,100	860
Total Inland Revenue	45,900	50,500
Customs and Excise:		
Value Added Tax	15,300	18,000
Oil	5,600	6,100
Tobacco	3,800	4,100
Spirits, beer, wine, cider and perry	3,900	4,000
Betting and gaming	630	650
Car tax	700	700
Other excise duties	25	20
Customs duties	1,120	1,230
Agricultural levies	225	200
Total Customs and Excise	31,300	35,000

	Net receipts 1983–84	Budget estimate 1984–85
Customs and Exercise (contd.):		
Vehicle Excise duties	2,020	2,140
National insurance surcharge	1,700	900
Total taxation	80,900	88,500
Miscellaneous receipts:		
Broadcasting receiving licences	750	770
Interest and dividends	430	400
Gas levy	520	510
Oil royalties	1,900	2,000
Other	4,200	5,800
Total	88,700	98,000

The following are the branches of expenditure for year ended 31 March 1984 and the estimates for the year 1984–85 (in £1m.):

	Estimates 1983–84	Estimates 1984–85
Social Security	35,300	37,200
Defence	15,700	17,000
Health and Personal Social Services	14,700	15,400
Education and Science	13,400	13,100
Scotland	6,800	6,900
Industry, Energy, Trade and Employment	6,100	5,600
Transport	4,600	4,400
Law, Order and Protective Services	4,700	4,900
Other Environmental Services	3,800	3,500
Northern Ireland	3,800	4,000
Housing	2,800	2,500
Wales	2,600	2,600
Overseas Services	2,300	2,300
Other Public Services	1,700	1,800
Common Services	1,000	1,100
Agriculture, Fisheries, Food and Forestry	2,100	2,000
Arts and Libraries	600	600
Local authorities	–	700
	120,300	126,200
Gross Debt Interest	15,700	16,000
Total	136,000	142,300

A single graduated income tax came into operation on 6 April 1973, replacing the existing income tax and surtax.

Rates of Personal Tax from 6 April 1984	%
Income between	
£0–£15,400	30
£15,401–£18,200	40
£18,201–£23,100	45
£23,101–£30,600	50
£30,601–£38,100	55
Over £38,100	60

Surcharge on investment income was abolished. Life assurance premium relief for contracts made after 13 March 1984 was abolished.

Under the tax system, the amounts of the personal allowances are adjusted so that they retain their equivalent in relation to earned income.

	1984–85
Personal Allowances	£
Single person }	2,005
Wife's earned income }	
Married man	3,155
Additional allowance	1,150
Dependent relative:	
Single woman claimant	145
Others	100
Housekeeper	100
Relative taking charge of younger brother	
or sister	100
Daughter's services	55
Blind person	360

Deductions of tax under PAYE extend over the full range of unified tax rates and not merely the basic rate. Similarly, assessment on business profits and on other income which was directly assessed to tax, such as rents and interest on bank deposits, are made by reference to the full scale of rates, including where appropriate the investment income surcharge.

The standard rate of 30% is the rate at which tax is deducted from payments of interest, etc., and corresponds under the new corporation tax system, to the tax credit on dividends. Where an individual's total income is such that he is liable on this taxed investment income at rates exceeding 30%, or if his investment income is high enough to make him liable to the surcharge, the higher rate or surcharge liability on this taxed investment income will in general be assessed separately after the end of the tax year.

Corporation Tax. Corporation Tax applies, with certain exceptions, to trades or businesses carried on by bodies corporate or by unincorporated societies or other bodies and this tax came into force from April 1966 replacing Profits Tax. There are reduced rates of Corporation Tax for small companies and for 1984–85 the rate is 45% reducing to 35% by 1986–87. Small companies rates until 1986–87, 30%.

Capital Gains Tax. Gains resulting from the disposal of capital assets (other than British Government and Government guaranteed securities and certain exempted forms of property such as a private car and personal residences) are taxed under the Finance Act 1965. In 1984–85 exemption was granted for all gains made in a financial year which in total did not exceed £5,600 and most trusts on the first £2,800.

Value Added Tax. Value Added Tax was introduced from 1 April 1973 at the rate of 10% on the supply of goods (with certain exceptions) and services. From 18 June 1979 the rate of tax was fixed at 15%.

Kay, J. A. and King, M. A., *The British Tax System.* OUP, 1980

Local Taxation. The rateable value on which rates were leviable in England and Wales on 1 April 1983 was £7,641m. In England and Wales, the average amount of the rates collected per £ of rateable value was £0·34 in 1913–14; and estimated to be 169·9p for 1983–84. In Scotland the rateable value on which rates are leviable on 1 April 1983 was £1,169m. and the average amount per £ of rateable value of the rates was 124·9p. The average domestic water rate was 9p in the £.

Under the Local Government Planning and Land Act 1980, the Government gives general financial assistance to local authorities by means of rate support grants. The Rate Support Grant Supplementary Report (England) 1983–84 deals with the distribution of these grants to local authorities in England only. The grants for 1983–84 contain (i) Block Grant £8,449m., the object of which is to give authorities sufficient grant to put them in a position where they can provide similar standards of service for a similar rate in the £, and (ii) Domestic Grant £686m., which will provide a relief of 18½p for domestic ratepayers except for those in the

Cities of London and Westminster where the relief provided is 35·5p and 26·2p respectively. There is also provision in the 1980 Act for payment of National Parks Supplementary Grant (£5·3m.) to county councils with all or part of a national park in their area, and Transport Supplementary Grant (£450m.) payable to county councils and the Greater London Council. Grants are also payable on revenue expenditure for specific services, including police and housing, and capital expenditure on certain services also attracts grant.

In Scotland, rate support grants are paid under the Local Government (Scotland) Act 1966. The total rate support grant and the amounts of the component parts for the local authority financial year 1984–85, as prescribed in the Rate Support Grant (Scotland) Order 1984 are as follows: total £1,713·2m. comprising needs element £1,486·5m.; resources element £212·4m.; domestic element £14·3m. The domestic element is paid to rating authorities to offset the cost of reducing by 3p in the £ rates payable on domestic properties. A small part of the needs element, £2·3m. in 1984–85, is apportioned among those local authorities incurring extraordinary expenses in connection with developments relating to exploration for or exploitation of offshore petroleum. As in England and Wales capital and revenue grants are also payable on expenditure for certain specified services.

Rates and Rateable Values, 1974–75. HMSO
Rates and Rateable Values in Scotland, 1977–78. HMSO
Estimates, 1982–83. GLC
Analysis of Rateable Values List. GLC, 1977
Report on Rate Support Grant Order 1979. HMSO

Gross National Product:	1946	1960	1970	1980	1982
Expenditure (£1m.)					
Consumers' expenditure	7,273	16,939	31,773	135,738	167,128
Central government final consumption	2,282	4,206	8,961	48,424	60,082
Gross domestic fixed capital formation	925	4,190	9,462	39,411	42,172
Value of physical increase in stocks and work in progress	−126	562	425	−2,706	−1,162
Total domestic expenditure at market prices	10,354	25,897	50,581	220,867	268,220
Exports of goods and services	1,775	5,153	11,533	63,158	73,128
Less Imports of goods and services	−2,083	−5,549	−11,122	−57,913	−67,165
Less Taxes on expenditure	−1,573	−3,378	−8,416	−36,882	−47,082
Subsidies	384	493	884	5,308	5,452
Gross domestic product at factor cost	8,855	22,616	43,460	194,538	232,553
Factor incomes (£1m.)					
Income from employment	5,758	15,174	30,404	136,050	155,133
Income from self-employment [1]	1,126	2,008	3,735	17,581	20,068
Gross trading profits of companies [1]	1,476	3,730	5,935	27,708	33,344
Gross trading surplus of public corporations [1]	20	534	1,447	6,222	9,068
Gross trading surplus of other public enterprises [1]	86	189	151	242	124
Rent [2]	429	1,086	2,833	13,390	16,166

[1] Before providing for depreciation and stock appreciation.
[2] Before providing for depreciation.

	1946	1960	1970	1980	1982
Total domestic income before providing for depreciation and stock appreciation	8,895	22,863	44,837	203,304	236,410
Less Stock appreciation	−125	−122	−1,090	−6,456	−3,907
Residual error	...	−125	−287	−2,310	50
Gross domestic product at factor cost	8,770	22,616	43,460	194,538	232,553
Net property income from abroad	85	233	559	273	1,577
Gross national product	8,855	22,849	44,019	194,265	234,130
Less Capital consumption	...	−2,047	−4,420	−27,223	−33,057
National income	...	20,802	39,599	167,042	201,073

National Economic Development Council. The NEDC (Neddy), which first met in 1962, is the national forum for economic consultation between government, management and unions. It includes leading representatives of the Government, CBI and TUC and also chairmen of nationalized industries and independent members. It meets usually under the chairmanship of the Chancellor of the Exchequer although the Prime Minister takes the chair from time to time. Discussions at the monthly council meetings are normally based on papers, presented by the participating parties, which deal primarily with questions of medium-term national economic performance and prospects, besides seeking to agree on ways of improving industrial efficiency. Council meetings are held in private to encourage the frank exchange of views between members, and discussions are summarized at a press conference taken by the Director-General of the National Economic Development Office (NEDO) following each meeting. The Economic Development Committees (Little Neddies), like the NEDC, bring together representatives of management and unions and officials from Government, who use this neutral meeting place to study the efficiency and prospects of individual industries and sectors and to suggest ways in which these could be improved. The National Economic Development Office (NEDO) provides the professional staff for the NEDC and the EDCs.

Currency. The monetary unit of Great Britain is the *pound sterling.* A gold standard was adopted in 1816, the sovereign or twenty-shilling piece weighing 7·98805 grammes 0·916⅔ fine. Currency notes for £1 and 10s. were first issued by the Treasury in 1914, replacing the circulation of sovereigns. The issue of £1 and 10s. notes was taken over by the Bank of England in 1928. The issue of 10s. notes ceased on the issue of the 50p coin in 1969.

Following the post-war fluctuations in the value of the pound, Great Britain returned to the Gold Standard in 1925 with the pound fixed at the pre-war parity of US$4.8665. But the world financial crisis of 1931 forced the country off the Gold Standard again, and in the following year the Exchange Equalization Account was set up for the purpose of checking undue fluctuations in the exchange value of the pound. With the relative stability of the pound which followed, a 'Sterling Bloc' emerged consisting of most Empire countries and those others who voluntarily pegged their currencies to the pound.

The Bloc was superseded at the outbreak of the Second World War by the 'Sterling Area'. The pound was then fixed at $4.03 and remained at that rate until Sept. 1949, when it was devalued to $2.80. On 18 Nov. 1967 it was further devalued to $2.40. Following the general international currency re-alignment of Dec. 1971, the rate for the pound, in terms of the US$, was fixed at £1 = $2.6057 but in June 1972 the pound was allowed to float. March 1984, £1 = US$1·48.

When the pound was floated in June 1972 measures were also introduced to control payments between the 'Scheduled Territories' (*i.e.*, the UK including the Channel Islands, the Isle of Man and Ireland), and the rest of the Sterling Area as well as the rest of the world. Exchange control restrictions were lifted in Oct. 1979 except for Rhodesia (Zimbabwe) and these were lifted in Dec. 1979.

Coinage. The sovereign (£1) weighs 123·27447 grains, or 7·98805 grammes, 0·916⅔ (or eleven-twelfths) fine, and consequently it contains 113·00159 grains or 7·32238 grammes of fine gold. On 15 Feb. 1971 (Decimalization Day) a decimal currency system was introduced retaining the *pound sterling* as the major unit but now divided into 100 *new pence* instead of 240 old pence. The decimal coins are the £1 (22·5 mm diameter, 9·5 grammes weight); 50p (equilateral curve heptagon, 30 mm diameter, 13·5 grammes); 20p (equilateral curved heptagon 21·4 mm diameter, 5 grammes); 10p (28·5 mm, 11·31 grammes); 5p (23·6 mm, 5·65 grammes); 2p (25·9 mm, 7·12 grammes); 1p (20·3 mm, 3·56 grammes) and ½p which will cease to be issued on 29 March 1984 (17·1 mm, 1·18 grammes). The Decimal Currency Act, 1967 and the Proclamation of 27 Dec. 1968 required that the 50p, 10p and 5p be made of cupro-nickel and the 2p, 1p and ½p of mixed metal; copper, tin and zinc (bronze). The Decimal Currency Act, 1969, provided that the coins of the Queen's Maundy Money should continue to be made in silver to a millesimal fineness of 925.

By Proclamation dated 28 July 1971, which came into force on 30 Aug. 1971, the crown, double-florin, the florin, the shilling and the sixpence are to be treated as coins of the new currency and as being of the denominations respectively of 25, 20, 10, 5 and 2½ new pence. The sixpence was demonetised on 30 June 1980.

The Coinage Act, 1971, specified that the legal tender limits for coins were: Gold coins, for payment of any amount; coins of cupro-nickel and silver of denominations of more than 10p, for payment of any amount not exceeding £10; coins of cupro-nickel and silver of not more than 10p, for payment of any amount not exceeding £5; coins of bronze, for payment of any amount not exceeding 20p.

The value of money issued in the 12 months up to March 1982 was £49m.

UK coins produced in 1980 totalled 1,439·8m., as follows, in millions: 50p 94·035, 25p 11, 10p 93·95, 5p 203, 2p 462·1, 1p 485·4, ½ 184·332.

It is estimated that the following coins were in circulation in the UK at 31 March 1983, in millions: 50p 745, 20p 716, 10p 1,693, 5p 1,963, 2p 2,386, 1p 3,598, ½p 2,549.

Bank-notes. The Bank of England issues notes in denominations of £1, £5, £10, £20 and £50 for the amount of the fiduciary note issue. Under the provisions of the Currency and Bank Notes Act, 1954, which came into force on 22 Feb. 1954, the amount of the fiduciary note issue was fixed at £1,575m., but this figure might be altered by direction of HM Treasury after representations made by the Bank of England.

All Bank of England notes are legal tender in England and Wales, and notes of denominations less than £5 are legal tender in Scotland and Northern Ireland. The banks in Scotland and Northern Ireland have certain note-issuing powers.

The total amount of notes issued at 30 Dec. 1983 was £12,390m., of which £12,386m. were in the hands of other banks and the public and £4m. in the Banking Department of the Bank of England.

Banking. The Bank of England, Threadneedle Street, London, is the Government's banker and the 'banker's bank'. It has the sole right of note issue in England and Wales and manages the National Debt. The Bank operates under royal charters of 1694 and 1946 and the Bank of England Act, 1946. The capital stock has, since 1 March 1946, been held by the Treasury.

The statutory return is published weekly. End-Dec. figures for the past 5 years are as follows (in £1m.):

	Notes in circulation	Notes and coin in Banking Department	Public deposits (government)	Other deposits[1]
1979	10,750	25	26	1,948
1980	10,819	6	36	1,292
1981	11,577	23	45	2,260
1982	12,014	11	109	2,668
1983	12,623	7	51	2,152

[1] Including Special Deposits.

The fiduciary note issue was £12,390m. at 31 Dec. 1983. All the profits of the note issue are passed on to the National Loans Fund.

Official reserves of gold and convertible currencies, SDR and reserve position in the IMF at the end of Dec. 1983 were US$17,817m.

The value of paper debit bank clearings for 1982, £5,771m. Paper credit clearings for 1982, £63m. Automatic direct debits, 1982, £39m.; automatic credit transfers, 1982, £91m.

The following statistics relate to the London clearing banks' groups at mid-Dec. 1983. Total deposits (sterling and currency), £152,434m.; sterling market loans £21,554m.; advances (sterling and currency), £82,530m.; sterling investments £6,077m.

Total net profits from the operations of the main 4 London clearing bank groups in 1983 amounted to £1,075m., of which £269m. in gross dividends, £806m. transferred to reserves.

The clearing banks cover all aspects of banking business in UK including corporate business, and are also actively involved in international banking.

Trustee Savings Banks. Trustee Savings Banks started in Scotland in 1810. They are managed by Boards of Trustees, under the terms of the Trustee Savings Bank Act 1981. There are 4 banks with a network of 1,640 branches throughout the UK and the Channel Islands. The banks are supervised by the TSB Central Board, a statutory body established by the TSB Act 1976.

On 20 Nov. 1983 the funds of all Trustee Savings Banks totalled £6,770m., the total number of accounts exceeded 13m.

National Savings Bank. Statistics for 1981 and 1982:

	Ordinary accounts		Investment accounts	
	1981	1982	1981	1982
Accounts open at 31 Dec.	20,038,438[1]	19,907,123[1]	1,939,304	2,186,267
Amounts—	£1,000	£1,000	£1,000	£1,000
Received	565,693	588,815	1,264,228	1,234,774
Interest credited	81,790	78,913	324,083	382,388
Paid	694,864	684,216	587,719	718,224
Due to depositors at 31 Dec.	1,692,465	1,675,977	2,871,348	3,770,287
Average amount due to each depositor in active accounts	£84·46	£84·19	£1,480·61	£1,724·53

[1] Excluding accounts with balances of less than £1 which have been inactive for 3 years or more.

The amount due to depositors in Ordinary Accounts on 1 Jan. 1984 was approximately £1,774,523,837 and in Investment Accounts £4,381,711,765.

The National Girobank (founded 1968) has 1·33m. customers with balances of £722m.

Bank of England Quarterly Bulletin. Bank of England
Bank of England Annual Report. Bank of England
British Banking and other Financial Institutions. HMSO, 1977
Central Statistical Office, Financial Statistics. HMSO (monthly)
Report of the Committee on the Working of the Monetary System. HMSO, 1959
Report of the Select Committee on Nationalised Industries—The Bank of England. HMSO, 1970
The Royal Mint. 6th ed. HMSO, 1977
Clapham, Sir J. H., *The Bank of England: A History.* 2 vols. CUP, 1944
Craig, J., *The Mint.* Cambridge, 1953
Horne, H. O., *History of Savings Banks.* London, 1947
Sayers, R. H., *The Bank of England 1891–1944.* CUP, 1976

Weights and Measures. Conversion to the metric system was in progress (1978) which will replace the imperial system at present in force.

ENERGY AND NATURAL RESOURCES

Electricity. The electricity industry was vested in the British Electricity Authority on 1 April 1948. Following the re-organization of the electricity supply industry after the passing of the Electricity Act, 1957, the statutory bodies comprising the electricity service in England and Wales are the Electricity Council, the Central Electricity Generating Board and the 12 Area Electricity Boards.

The Electricity Council has functioned from Jan. 1958 as the central council for the supply industry in England and Wales for consultation on, and formulation of, general policy; its main functions are to advise the Secretary of State for Energy on all matters affecting the supply industry, and to promote and assist the maintenance and development by the Central Electricity Generating Board and the Area Boards (known collectively as Electricity Boards) of an efficient, co-ordinated and economical system of electricity supply. The Council can also perform services for the Boards, and, in addition, has certain specific functions, particularly in matters of finance, research and industrial relations.

The Central Electricity Generating Board is responsible for the generation and bulk supply of electricity to the 12 Area Boards in England and Wales. It therefore plans the provision of new generating and transmission capacity, including the siting and construction of new generating stations, both conventional and nuclear, and is responsible for the operation and maintenance of generating stations and the main transmission system.

Area Electricity Boards. Each of the 12 Area Electricity Boards acquires bulk supplies of electricity from the Generating Board and is responsible for distribution networks and sales of electricity to its Area consumers. Thus distribution and utilization of electricity, and also the contracting and sale of appliances side of the industry, are their responsibilities.

The number of power stations owned by the Generating Board in England and Wales on 31 March 1983 was 100 with a total output capacity, of 54,751 mw. Total number of customers in England and Wales on 31 March 1983 was 20,828,334 (on 31 March 1982, 20,663,882).

Electricity sold in England and Wales in 1982–83 amounted to 192,859m. units. Revenue from sales of electricity in 1982–83 was £8,643m. Coal used for electricity generation in 1982–83 amounted to 75·3m. tonnes (77m. tonnes in 1981–82). Total fuel (coal equivalent) used in 1981–82 amounted to 94·9m. tonnes and in 1982–83 to 93·1m. tonnes. Nine nuclear stations of total output capacity 4,480 mw provided 14·1% of total units supplied in 1982–83. Eight of these are gas cooled graphite-moderated stations using natural uranium fuel canned in magnesium alloy (Magnox) and 1 is an advanced gas-cooled station (AGR). With 4 AGR stations under construction, output capacity will reach 10,350 mw by Dec. 1988.

The number of persons employed by the Generating Board, the Electricity Council and Area Boards at the end of March 1983 was 141,385.

The North of Scotland Hydro-Electric Board, established under the Hydro-Electric Development (Scotland) Act 1943, is the nationalized authority responsible not only for generating and transmitting electricity but also for distributing and selling it to over 500,000 consumers.

The Board's district covers a quarter of the land mass of Great Britain and lies generally north and west of a line joining the firths of Clyde and Tay as well as all the island groups extending to the Outer Hebrides, Orkney and Shetland. Over 99% of potential consumers have now been provided with supply. On the mainland the Board operates generating stations with a total installed generating capacity of 3,173 mw consisting of 1,752 mw of hydro power and pumped storage, together with 1,260 mw of steam. Diesel stations with a total installed capacity of 126 mw supply the principal island groups together with 35 mw gas turbine. A 1,320 mw of oil/gas fired thermal plant is now operating at Peterhead.

The main transmission system consists of 5,097 circuit km of 275 kv and 132 kv lines linking the power stations and the bulk supply points serving the distribution networks. The system control centre at Pitlochry co-ordinates the operation of the transmission system and power stations together with the continuous interchange of power with the South of Scotland Electricity Board. The number of staff at the end of the year was 3,920.

The South of Scotland Electricity Board was established in April 1955 by the

Electricity Reorganisation (Scotland) Act 1954, replacing in South Scotland 2 Electricity Boards and 2 Divisions of the British Electricity Authority. The area of Scotland served by the Board lies south of a line from the Firth of Clyde to the Firth of Tay and extends to about 8,000 sq. miles (21,000 sq. km), including the industrial belt of Scotland, with a population of 4m. By special arrangement a small part of North-East England is also supplied. The remainder of Scotland is served by the North of Scotland Hydro-Electric Board.

The Board differs from those established in England and Wales in that its responsibilities cover not only the distribution of electricity and retail sale of electrical appliances but also the generation and transmission of bulk power within South Scotland.

At 31 March 1983 the Board operated 17 generating stations (including 2 nuclear and 7 hydro-electric stations) with a total output capacity of 7,866 mw (total effective capacity however, has been reduced by placing 1,510 mw of plant at 2 stations in storage for an indefinite period). In 1982–83 the Board sold 17,397m. units to more than 1·6m. consumers and had a total revenue of £754m. The number of staff employed at the end of the year was 12,720.

Oil. Production 1982, in 1,000 tons (1981 in brackets): Throughput of crude and process oils, 77,174 (78,336); refinery use, 5,593 (5,494); gases, 1,475 (1,466); naphtha, 3,492 (3,406); motor spirits, 19,134 (17,140); kerosene, 6,308 (6,463); diesel oil, 20,581 (20,411); fuel oil, 15,808 (19,069); lubricating oils, 990 (1,063); bitumen, 1,862 (1,735). Total output of refined products, 70,747 (72,006).

Gas. The British gas industry, nationalized in 1949, was reorganized as the British Gas Corporation on 1 Jan. 1973. Under the terms of the Gas Act 1972, the Corporation has the general duty 'to develop and maintain an efficient, co-ordinated and economical system of gas supply'. The chairman and members of the Corporation are appointed by the Secretary of State for Energy. British Gas explores for and produces natural gas, manufactures substitute natural gas, transmits, distributes and sells gas, and sells, installs and maintains gas appliances.

Gas Council (Exploration) Ltd and Hydrocarbons Great Britain Ltd, wholly owned subsidiaries of British Gas, have been involved in exploration for oil and gas in the Irish Sea, the English Channel and Celtic Sea and, in partnership with oil companies, in the North Sea and onshore. British Gas is a partner in gasfields in the southern North Sea and discovered the Morecambe gasfield in the Irish Sea.

In 1982–83, British Gas sold 16,463m. therms of gas. Conversion to natural gas was completed in 1977. There were 15·34m. domestic customers, who used 8,616m. therms; 83,000 industrial customers, who used 5,605m. therms; and 499,000 commercial customers, who used 2,242m. therms.

The turnover of British Gas in 1982–83 was £5,958m. and the average net assets employed at current cost was £11,657m. The surplus for the year was £663m. before tax. In March 1983, there were 101,000 employees.

Minerals. The number of National Coal Board mines producing coal on 26 March 1983 was 191. Statistics of the coalmining industry (including licensed mines) for recent years are as follows:

	1979–80	1980–81	1981–82	1982–83
Saleable output of coal:				
Total deep-mined (1m. tonnes)	110·3	111·4	110·0	106·2
Opencast (1m. tonnes)	13·0	15·3	14·3	14·7
Average weekly number of wage-earners on colliery books:				
All workers (NCB only)	232,476	229,808	218,519	207,640
Underground workers (NCB only)	184,367	183,631	176,036	167,876
Coal exports:				
Total (1m. tonnes)	2·52	4·84	9·37	7·13

Total stocks of coal on 26 March 1983 amounted to 53·3m. tonnes (28·3m. tonnes distributed, 24·9m. tonnes undistributed). Trading profit made by the NCB for the year ended 26 March 1983 amounted to £123m. Interest payable was

£366m., of which to the Secretary of State for Energy, £330m. There was a Deficit grant of £374m. from the Government for the year ended 26 March 1983.

Production of coke (including coke breeze) amounted in 1982–83 to 3·5m. tonnes.

In 1982–83 inland consumption (in 1,000 tonnes) of coal is estimated to have been 110,440, some of the principal users being: Power stations, 80,803; coke ovens, 10,003; domestic, 8,001; other conversion industries, 2,156; collieries, 533; industry, 7,032.

Ezra, D., *Coal and Energy*. London, 1980

The UK is among the 10 largest steel producing countries in the world. Output in recent years was as follows (in 1,000 tonnes):

	Pig-iron	Crude steel	Home consumption[1]
1978	11,434	20,311	20,530
1979	12,898	21,464	20,160
1980[2]	6,316	11,277	15,990
1981	9,554	15,573	15,650
1982	8,389	13,704	15,120

[1] Finished steel (crude steel equivalent).
[2] 1980 figures affected by 3-month industrial dispute.

Exports of finished steel products were 3·4m. tonnes in 1982 and imports, 3·8m. tonnes.

The industry is divided between the 'public sector' and the 'private sector'.

The British Steel Corporation, which was established by the Iron and Steel Act 1967, took over the 14 largest UK iron and steel making concerns (and their subsidiaries) in July 1967 and merged them into a single publicly owned business. With a turnover of more than £3,231m. and a liquid steel output of 11·7m. tonnes in 1982–83, the British Steel Corporation ranks as one of Britain's major manufacturing industries and is one of the world's largest steel makers. The number of employees at the end of 1983 was 73,000. A substantial part of the British steel industry remains in private ownership and there were in 1983 a number of significant producers in mixed public/private ownership. Although responsible for only 15% of UK crude steel production, companies other than the British Steel Corporation produce much higher proportions of steel in finished form. For some products such as wire rod, reinforcement steel, bright bars, wire, open-die forgings and high speed and tool steels, they cover nearly all UK production. Because of the involvement of these companies in higher value steels it accounts for over a third of the total turnover of the British steel industry but employs a smaller proportion of the total labour force.

Iron Castings. Production of iron castings was 1·5m. tonnes in 1982 (1·6m. tonnes in 1981).

Production of non-ferrous metals in 1982 (in 1,000 tonnes): Refined copper, 134·2 (136·1 in 1981); refined lead, 175·2 (198); tin metal, 13·6 (12·9); virgin aluminium, 240·8 (339·2); slab zinc, 79·3 (81·7).

Agriculture. The total land area of the UK is 24m. hectares, of which 18·72m. (1982) is agricultural.

Distribution of the cultivated area in the UK (in 1,000 hectares):

	1981	1982
Corn crops[1]	3,979	4,030
Green crops[2]	1,014	975
Hops	6	6
Fruit	66	61
Bare fallow	76	55
Rotation grasses including lucerne	1,911	1,859
Permanent pasture	5,103	5,097

[1] Includes wheat, barley, rye and oats.
[2] Green crops include beans, potatoes, turnips and swedes, mangolds, sugar-beet, cabbage, etc., for fodder, vegetables, and all other crops.

The number of workers employed in agriculture, forestry and fishing in the UK was, in June 1982, 345,000; 326,000 were solely engaged in agriculture; there were also (Dec. 1982) 186,400 farmers, partners and directors.

Principal crops in the UK as at June in each year:

	Wheat	Barley	Oats	Beans	Potatoes	Fodder crops	Sugar-beet	Rape for oilseed
				Area (1,000 hectares)				
1978	1,257	2,348	180	55	214	223	209	64
1979	1,371	2,343	136	60	204	204	214	74
1980	1,441	2,330	148	61	206	200	213	92
1981	1,491	2,327	144	58	191	222	210	125
1982	1,663	2,222	129	52	192	166	204	174
				Total product (1,000 tonnes)				
1978	6,610	9,850	705	285	7,330	9,835	7,080	155
1979	7,140	9,550	535	286	6,485	9,049	7,660	198
1980	8,470	10,320	600	251	7,105	8,335	7,380	300
1981	8,710	10,230	620	209	6,215	7,945	7,395	325
1982	10,310	10,960	575	229	6,875	7,565	10,005	581

Livestock in the UK as at June in each year (in 1,000):

	1978	1979	1980	1981	1982
Cattle	13,625	13,543	13,426	13,137	13,242
Sheep	29,686	29,860	31,446	32,091	33,053
Pigs	7,708	7,844	7,815	7,828	8,023
Poultry	137,329	134,700	135,105	132,286	135,363

Forestry. On 31 March 1982 the area of productive woodland in Britain was 1,993,000 hectares of which the Forestry Commission managed 909,000 hectares and the private sector 1,084,000 hectares.

The Forestry Commission employed 7,167 staff in 1982. In addition a further 10,600 were employed in private forestry with an estimated 10,920 engaged in the wood processing industry.

In 1982–83 a total of 4·85m. cu. metres of timber was thinned and felled (3·55m. conifer; 2·69m. by the Forestry Commission).

New Planting (1982–83) 21,500 hectares (9,000, Forestry Commission; 12,500, private woodlands).

James, N. D. G., *A History of English Forestry*. London, 1981

Fisheries. Quantity (in 1,000 tonnes) and value (in £1,000) of fish of British taking landed in Great Britain (excluding salmon and sea-trout):

Quantity	1978	1979	1980	1981	1982
Wet fish	880·6	764·1	679·0	664·6	689·4
Shell fish	64·4	62·5	68·6	62·9	60·0
	945·0	826·6	747·6	727·5	749·4
Value					
Wet fish	219,412	211,892	184,847	188,152	213,108
Shell fish	30,492	35,545	32,245	34,405	38,685
	249,904	247,437	217,092	222,557	251,793

The fishing fleet of England and Wales comprised (1982) 4,228 vessels including 1,755 trawlers and 469 line fishing vessels; the Scottish fleet (1982) 2,233 vessels including 746 trawlers and 877 creel fishing vessels.

INDUSTRY AND TRADE

Industry. Statistics of a cross-section of industrial production are as follows (in 1,000 tonnes):

	1980	1981	1982
Sulphuric acid	3,381	2,889	2,587
Synthetic resins	2,259	2,078	1,691
Cotton single yarn	61	43	42
Wool tops	39	39	37
Woollen yarn	81	72	53
Man-made fibres (rayon, nylon, etc.)	450	395	334
Newsprint	363	113	86
Other paper and board	3,454	3,295	3,168
Fertilizers, phosphate, super phosphate, basic slag and compounds (1,000 tons)	3,350	...	...
Cement	14,805	12,729	12,962
Fabricated aluminium (to consumers)	521	444	455

Engineering. Manufacturers' sales (in £1m.) for 1982 (1981 in brackets): Motor vehicles and engines, 4,785 (4,396); motor vehicle bodies and parts, 3,104 (3,058); boilers and process plant, 1,539 (1,223); constructional steelwork, 1,231 (1,004); mechanical lifting and handling equipment, 1,114 (1,014; refrigerating, space-heating, ventilating and air conditioning equipment, 986 (865); construction and earth-moving equipment, 945 (1,019), wheeled tractors, 884 (915); industrial (including marine) engines, 854 (861).

Electrical Goods. Manufacturers' sales (in £1m.) for 1982 (1981 in brackets): Radio and electronic capital goods, 1,939 (1,754); basic electrical equipment, 2,177 (1,938); electronic data processing equipment, 1,094 (1,011); telephone and telegraph apparatus and equipment, 1,264 (1,124); domestic electrical appliances, 903 (922).

Textile Manufacturers. Production of woven cloth for 1982 (1981 in brackets): cotton (1m. metres), 261 (278); man-made fibres (1m. metres), 205 (230); woven woollen and worsted fabrics (1m. sq. metres), deliveries, 100 (97).

Construction. Total value (in £1m.) of constructional work by all agencies in 1982 was 22,540 (21,547 in 1981), including new work, 12,629 (12,354) of which new housing, 3,920 (3,738). Houses for private developers, 2,899 (2,516). New work (other than housing) for private developers, 5,038 (5,044), for public authorities, 3,671 (3,572).

Annual Abstract of Statistics. HMSO
Chester, Sir N., *The Nationalisation of British Industry, 1945–51.* HMSO, 1976
Kelf-Cohen, R., *British Nationalization: 1945–1973.* New York, 1973
Statistical Summary of the Mineral Industry. HMSO, annual

Labour. The distribution of total manpower in Great Britain was in June 1982 (in 1,000): Total working population, 25,916 (15,664 males, 10,032 females). Total employed in armed forces and women's services, 324. Total in civil employment, 20,771, including agriculture, 326; mining and quarrying, 325; manufacture, 5,667; national and local government service, 1,496; transport and communications, 1,363; construction, 1,024; distributive trades, 2,656; insurance, banking, business, professional and scientific services, 4,960; self-employed, 2,157.

The average monthly numbers (based on claimants in 1,000) of registered unemployed in Great Britain were: 1977, 1,345 (males, 1,004; females, 341); 1978, 1,321 (males, 966; females, 355); 1979, 1,234 (males, 887; females, 347); 1980, 1,591 (males, 1,129; females, 461); 1981, 2,422 (males, 1,773; females, 649); 1982, 2,809 (males, 2,056; females, 753).

Trade Unions. In Dec. 1983 there were 102 unions affiliated to the Trades Union Congress with a total membership of 10,510,157 (including about 3·5m. women). The unions affiliated to the TUC in 1983 ranged in size from the Transport and General Workers' Union, with 1,632,957 members, to the Cloth Pressers' Society with 16 members. Non-manual workers accounted for nearly a third of the total TUC membership.

The TUC's executive body, the General Council, is elected at the annual Congress. It is composed of 51 members made up of 34 members nominated by unions with a membership of over 100,000, entitled to automatic representation in proportion to their size, 11 members elected by and from unions smaller than 100,000 and 6 members elected by Congress as a whole to represent women workers.

The General Secretary is elected by the Congress but is not subject to annual re-election.

The TUC General Council appoints committees, which draw upon the services of specialist departments in preparing policies on economic, education, international, employment, industrial organization, and social questions.

The TUC is affiliated to the International Confederation of Free Trade Unions, the Trade Union Advisory Committee of OECD, the Commonwealth Trade Union Council and the European Trade Union Confederation. The TUC provides a service of trade union education. It provides members to serve, with representatives of employers, on joint committees advising the Government on issues of national importance (e.g., National Economic Development Council and various Royal Commissions) and on the managing boards of such bodies as the Health and Safety Commission; Advisory, Conciliation and Arbitration Service; and Manpower Services Commission.

The following table is a statistical summary relating to trade disputes for recent years:

	No. of workers involved	Working days lost through stoppages
1979	4,583,000	29,474,000
1980	830,000	11,964,000
1981	1,499,000	4,266,000

Lovell, J., and Robert. B. C., *A Short History of the T.U.C.* London, 1968
Pelling, H., *A History of British Trade Unionism.* 2nd ed. London, 1972

Commerce. Value of the imports and exports of merchandise (excluding bullion and specie and foreign merchandise transhipped under bond) of the UK for 6 recent years (in £1,000):

	Total imports	Total exports		Total imports	Total exports
1978	40,969,066	37,362,739	1981	51,163,579	50,995,080
1979	48,467,400	42,803,609	1982	56,940,267	55,538,408
1980	51,650,267	49,510,791	1983	65,993,096	60,533,692

The value of goods imported is generally taken to be that at the port and time of entry, including all incidental expenses (cost, insurance and freight) up to the landing on the quay. For goods consigned for sale, the market value in this country is required and recorded in the returns. For exports, the value at the port of shipment (including the charges of delivering the goods on board) is taken. Imports are entered as from the country whence the goods were consigned to the UK, which may, or may not, be the country whence they were last shipped. Exports are credited to the country of ultimate destination as declared by the exporters.

For details of imports and exports for 1982 and 1983, *see* pp. 1316–20.
Trade according to countries for 1982 and 1983 (in £1,000):

Countries	Imports of merchandise from 1982[1]	1983[1]	Exports of merchandise to 1982[1]	1983[1]
Foreign countries				
Europe and Overseas Possessions—				
Albania	45	240	4,453	2,983
Austria	404,318	438,446	251,032	273,702
Belgium and Luxembourg	2,861,809	3,133,905	2,298,118	2,572,673
Bulgaria	21,009	12,355	46,104	44,577
Czechoslovakia	82,007	101,302	70,105	69,456
Denmark and Faroe Islands	1,344,565	1,528,552	1,099,039	1,161,516
Finland	849,933	995,017	513,558	539,721
France	4,269,103	5,043,118	4,486,458	5,651,521
German Dem. Rep.	133,921	167,625	63,665	60,997
Germany (Fed. Rep. of)	7,414,073	9,667,444	5,414,733	6,063,989
Greece	151,688	164,917	255,281	280,204
Hungary	44,051	53,834	77,446	91,845
Iceland	72,721	66,505	102,714	65,176
Italy	2,745,094	3,188,219	2,022,711	2,292,788
Netherlands	4,474,663	5,097,763	4,653,416	5,440,701
Netherlands Antilles	76,421	97,486	59,359	84,289
Norway	2,023,441	2,820,760	924,651	828,612
Poland	151,737	177,067	133,340	151,721
Portugal, Azores and Madeira	379,949	475,902	430,684	396,988
Romania	51,515	58,865	115,244	82,160
Spain	956,935	1,110,029	870,416	1,128,439
Canary Islands	44,574	56,305	83,508	98,603
Sweden	1,673,165	2,051,931	1,935,264	2,397,464
Switzerland and Liechtenstein	1,669,922	2,154,085	1,196,203	1,385,894
Turkey	207,763	184,976	218,116	244,024
USSR	645,135	728,491	355,678	445,008
EEC	25,252,103	30,098,053	23,117,856	26,516,335
EFTA	7,073,449	9,003,645	5,354,105	5,887,557
Yugoslavia	52,115	83,951	158,881	148,645
Africa—				
Algeria	176,304	157,645	199,234	233,426
Angola	7,368	45,732	25,781	22,847
Burundi	8,737	3,485	1,522	3,155
Cameroon	9,108	52,481	22,462	26,445
Egypt	412,802	79,826	338,645	370,489
Ethiopia	10,833	12,071	27,584	34,092
Ivory Coast	56,097	79,255	28,238	25,591
Liberia	8,213	7,181	14,069	13,877
Libya	342,476	224,050	260,937	274,169
Mali	3,385	3,833	4,403	15,856
Mauritania	5,462	6,044	1,943	1,719
Morocco	60,219	75,602	95,487	99,727
Mozambique	10,611	9,175	14,473	28,618
Rwanda	510	2,919	2,079	2,326
Senegal	14,196	22,333	22,349	13,212
South Africa, Republic of	745,803	764,909	1,192,891	1,109,039
S.W. Africa/Namibia	45,413	62,437	3,973	3,425
Sudan	9,929	18,693	136,636	133,432
Tunisia	12,628	18,126	38,632	44,659
Zaïre	15,801	11,192	20,557	21,129
Asia—				
Afghánistán	20,855	19,837	9,344	10,310
Bahrain	35,459	37,488	152,272	150,264
Burma	5,342	4,726	44,242	21,927
China	193,231	231,417	103,051	159,722
Indonesia	91,704	169,454	212,066	193,642
Iran	225,971	100,545	333,715	629,980
Iraq	79,764	30,334	875,179	400,259
Israel	275,139	314,148	224,362	354,860
Japan	2,657,977	3,355,450	681,463	797,848
Jordan	17,487	28,680	295,274	262,503
Korea (South)	321,691	440,354	167,752	168,942
Kuwait	104,793	67,281	333,247	333,273

[1] Provisional figures.

Countries	Imports of merchandise from 1982[1]	1983[1]	Exports of merchandise to 1982[1]	1983[1]
Asia—(contd.)				
Lebanon	24,237	11,521	67,640	81,435
Pakistan	81.531	80,277	199,178	191,647
Philippines	127.061	160,701	97,908	102,949
Qatar	33.984	10,063	245,390	216,385
Saudi Arabia	1,447.775	897,702	1,361,665	1,478,587
Syria	25.644	18,859	89,535	72,320
Thailand	76.529	87,823	104,825	131,833
America—				
Argentina	58.728	194	37,349	4,472
Bolivia	20.899	14,834	4,943	4,711
Brazil	443.956	560,277	158,837	157,758
Chile	111,206	107,644	56,897	43,520
Colombia	34,502	56,458	50,328	51,023
Costa Rica	15,068	22,299	5,455	11,041
Cuba	17,688	14,010	64,835	45,737
Dominican Republic	5,752	6,662	10,161	11,594
Ecuador	9,288	11,022	60,792	35,008
El Salvador	2,017	425	5,244	7,653
Guatemala	13,476	9,764	8,127	7,440
Haiti	2,615	1,646	3,704	4,171
Honduras (not British)	4,693	7,082	4,659	9,539
Mexico	106,067	160,978	162,946	95,674
Nicaragua	3,282	1,810	4,940	2,367
Panama	9,521	5,341	83,250	42,276
Paraguay	2,790	3,129	16,915	15,263
Peru	92,120	118,414	39,370	32,947
Puerto Rico	33,445	58,804	25,735	35,936
Uruguay	23,107	33,361	13,926	10,763
USA	6,638,250	7,442,671	7,457,114	8,336,979
Venezuela	141,892	183,731	148,666	87,937
Total (including those not specified above)	49,263,388	57,352,440	45,697,731	50,833,257
Commonwealth countries:				
In Europe—				
Cyprus	89,908	87,436	111,882	127,837
Gibraltar	4,229	4,266	29,712	26,495
Malta	42,792	40,852	71,823	71,895
In Africa				
West Africa:				
Gambia	2,031	3,781	10,087	13,261
Ghana	78,438	58,192	66,709	82,234
Nigeria, Federation of	356,802	387,975	1,225,164	798,276
Sierra Leone	14,438	17,710	19,110	13,735
South Africa:				
Botswana	19,140	21,713	5,163	3,250
Lesotho	682	216	1,260	2,080
Malawi	42,478	42,050	20,893	18,183
Swaziland	40,049	23,966	7,654	3,536
Zambia	39,957	50,242	61,248	55,501
Zimbabwe	62,584	68,446	95,019	64,734
East Africa:				
Kenya	104,312	128,454	153,858	111,249
Mauritius	119,450	128,437	20,857	22,499
Tanzania	19,521	46,525	71,985	62,055
Uganda	23,107	29,645	31,272	21,092
Seychelles	696	615	10,086	7,502
St Helena	754	457	7,049	10,343
In Asia—				
Bangladesh	25,558	4,726	58,179	50,979
Hong Kong	872,545	1,178,343	732,489	726,711
India	379,169	366,928	805,321	804,779
Malaysia	185,239	222,673	210,805	248,239
Singapore	245,453	404,122	406,172	469,155
Sri Lanka	42,000	25,189	60,211	70,136

[1] Provisional figures.

Countries	Imports of merchandise from 1982[1]	1983[1]	Exports of merchandise to 1982[1]	1983[1]
In Oceania—				
Australia	493,196	552,642	1,043,615	940,279
Fiji Islands	39,826	46,943	9,088	12,184
Nauru	32	1,421	1,843	1,715
New Zealand	539,137	486,305	323,201	286,054
Papua New Guinea	28,031	28,142	15,911	18,236
Western Samoa	107	156	285	468
In America—				
Bahamas	18,273	24,013	26,364	17,815
Barbados	14,887	11,899	26,886	31,938
Belize	13,326	11,565	10,455	8,726
Bermuda	5,128	4,019	18,222	24,924
Canada	1,439,619	1,522,187	851,703	968,269
Falkland Islands	2,568	4,022	4,150	7,269
Guyana	50,495	42,810	13,145	13,685
Jamaica	92,760	94,036	56,025	116,188
Leeward Islands	12,094	3,852	18,388	20,577
Trinidad and Tobago	65,154	52,748	158,436	148,811
Windward Islands	37,797	39,843	16,961	17,926
Total, Commonwealth countries (including those not specified above)	5,676,846	6,350,589	6,950,180	6,645,160
Ireland	2,000,033	2,290,067	2,890,497	3,055,277
Grand Total	56,940,267	65,993,096	55,538,408	60,533,692

[1] Provisional figures.

Imports and exports for 1982 and 1983 (Great Britain and Northern Ireland) (in £1,000):

Import values c.i.f. Export values f.o.b.	Total imports 1982[1]	1983[1]	Domestic exports 1982[1]	1983[1]
0. Food and Live Animals				
Live animals (excluding zoo animals, dogs and cats)	133,113	170,334	179,076	187,356
Meat and meat preparations	1,370,861	1,313,480	346,028	·496,238
Dairy products and eggs	567,914	629,191	318,557	305,866
Fish and fish preparations	404,249	505,590	162,303	203,617
Cereals and cereal preparations	549,897	595,340	773,863	736,712
Fruit and vegetables	1,608,300	1,718,946	153,757	163,162
Sugar, sugar preparations, honey	429,548	424,436	121,059	144,917
Coffee, tea, cocoa, spices	722,413	800,004	249,880	291,318
Feeding stuff for animals	446,507	523,629	68,244	78,735
Miscellaneous food preparations	181,130	210,385	123,798	140,691
Total of Section 0	6,413,933	6,891,336	2,496,565	2,748,612
1. Beverages and Tobacco				
Beverages	517,531	617,339	1,059,266	1,051,195
Tobacco and tobacco manufactures	319,226	344,743	391,426	434,976
Total of Section 1	836,757	962,083	1,450,692	1,486,172
2. Crude Materials, Inedible, except Fuels				
Hides, skins and furskins, undressed	189,451	184,878	180,479	200,179
Oil seeds, oil nuts and oil kernels	259,586	216,929	7,938	37,841
Crude rubber (including synthetic and reclaimed)	182,907	197,445	122,786	141,667
Wood and cork	673,469	937,988	28,590	24,148
Pulp and waste paper	412,465	428,033	11,602	15,784
Textile fibres and their waste	410,704	475,571	315,042	374,695
Crude fertilizers and crude minerals (excluding fuels)	263,478	285,695	224,582	223,857

[1] Provisional figures.

Import values c.i.f.	Total imports		Domestic exports	
Export values f.o.b.	1982[1]	1983[1]	1982[1]	1983[1]

2. Crude Materials, Inedible, except Fuels—Contd.

	1982[1]	1983[1]	1982[1]	1983[1]
Metalliferous ores and metal scrap	977,530	1,358,103	346,594	444,200
Crude animal and vegetable materials, not elsewhere specified	243,320	279,852	57,341	64,914
Total of Section 2	3,612,910	4,364,493	1,294,953	1,527,285

3. Mineral Fuels, Lubricants and Related Materials

Coal, coke and briquettes	224,382	276,081	330,339	239,437
Petroleum and petroleum products	6,274,079	5,738,044	10,641,634	12,524,959
Gas, natural and manufactured	902,722	1,052,938	221,213	362,115
Total[2] of Section 3	7,401,183	7,067,063	11,193,187	13,126,511

4. Animal and Vegetable Oils and Fats

Fats	316,958	358,811	46,467	59,106

5. Chemicals

Chemical elements and compounds	1,711,635	2,017,606	2,287,128	2,627,096
Dyeing, tanning and colouring materials	197,962	235,064	464,121	568,714
Medicinal and pharmaceutical products	374,592	470,122	977,966	1,074,213
Essential oils and perfume; toilet and cleansing preparations	242,219	305,258	523,999	574,323
Fertilizers, manufactured	127,027	172,546	48,766	69,682
Plastic materials	1,017,735	1,323,445	875,332	980,133
Total[3] of Section 5	4,181,221	5,119,501	6,119,360	6,929,252

6. Manufactured Goods Classified Chiefly by Material

Leather and dressed furs	154,552	183,981	202,149	232,944
Rubber	326,180	419,604	417,855	451,844
Wood and cork (excluding furniture)	436,614	578,767	83,235	85,189
Paper, paperboard	1,678,457	1,906,348	502,867	543,136
Textile yarn, fabrics	1,929,693	2,320,056	1,190,783	1,284,638
Non-metallic mineral manufactures	1,520,408	2,085,501	1,611,113	1,994,994
Iron and steel	1,369,214	1,260,654	1,293,521	1,330,851
Non-ferrous metals	1,495,679	1,975,277	1,244,721	1,614,520
Manufactures of metal, not elsewhere specified	950,357	1,108,937	1,394,900	1,324,047
Total of Section 6	9,861,155	11,840,125	7,941,146	8,862,164

7. Machinery and Transport Equipment

Boilers, engines, motors and power-units	1,482,724	1,569,162	2,809,218	2,472,470
Agricultural and Industrial machinery	3,499,368	3,919,818	5,537,489	5,085,687
Office machinery	2,122,756	3,019,923	1,599,470	2,049,184
Electrical machinery, apparatus, not elsewhere specified	3,766,589	4,723,665	3,010,643	3,281,166
Transport equipment	5,486,084	6,998,124	5,141,026	5,425,152
Total of Section 7	16,357,521	20,230,691	18,097,846	18,313,659

[1] Provisional figures.
[2] Includes electric energy in 1982.
[3] Includes items not specified here.

Import values c.i.f. Export values f.o.b.	Total imports 1982[1]	1983[1]	Domestic exports 1982[1]	1983[1]
8. Miscellaneous Manufactured Articles				
Sanitary, plumbing, heating and lighting fixtures	103,578	126,737	106,934	108,340
Furniture	400,065	490,473	240,898	257,784
Travel goods, handbags and similar articles	108,580	131,104	19,099	19,266
Clothing	1,500,755	1,601,480	840,351	865,394
Footwear	468,490	541,985	115,259	123,428
Scientific instruments; watches and clocks	1,815,226	1,303,670	1,812,333	1,472,374
Miscellaneous manufactured articles, not elsewhere specified	2,286,557	3,522,243	2,022,945	2,967,477
Total of Section 8	6,683,253	7,714,693	5,157,818	5,814,062
9. Commodities and Transactions not Classified According to Kind				
Total of Section 9	1,275,376	1,444,299	1,740,375	1,666,870
Total[2] of all classes	56,940,267	65,993,096	55,538,408	60,533,692

[1] Provisional figures.   [2] Includes items not specified here.

Tourism. There were an estimated 12m. overseas visitors in 1983. Foreign exchange from tourism was more than £4,500m. including fares paid to British air and shipping lines.

COMMUNICATIONS

Roads. Central government responsibility for highways in England rests with the Secretary of State for Transport. His responsibilities are administered by the Department of Transport through a number of Directorates at Headquarters together with 9 Regional Offices. For Welsh and Scottish roads central government responsibility rests with the Secretaries of State for Wales and Scotland respectively.

The Secretary of State is responsible for all trunk roads. Under the local government system introduced in 1974, the responsible authorities for principal roads are the County Councils. District Councils may claim maintenance powers for urban roads which are neither trunk roads nor classified roads. In London responsibility is shared between the Greater London Council and the London Boroughs.

The Secretary of State has powers to provide roads designed for limited classes of motor traffic, and to confirm schemes for the provision of such special roads by local authorities. The former have the status of trunk roads; the latter principal roads. They are generally referred to as motorways. About 2,300 km of motorways in England were open to traffic in 1982 and some 410 km of trunk motorway are either under construction or in preparation.

The design and supervision of the construction of major trunk roads is carried out by firms of consulting engineers and by local authorities which act as the Secretary of State's agents. The Regional Offices ensure that schemes progress in accordance with the Secretary of State's statutory and financial responsibilities. Regional Controllers (Roads and Transportation) are responsible for smaller trunk road schemes and for the maintenance of all trunk roads, including motorways. Local authorities can act as the Secretary of State's agents for construction and maintenance. The work is carried out by them or by contractors on their behalf and the cost borne by Central Government.

Aid to local authorities' transport expenditure is now given through Rate Support Grant and through Transport Supplementary Grant which is paid to County Councils whose expenditure for the year, as accepted by the Secretary of State, exceeds the level determined by a formula prescribed in the Rate Support Grant Report.

Public highways in Great Britain in 1982, excluding lengths of unsurfaced roads (green lanes), totalled 343,320 km (England, 261,183 km; Wales, 32,040 km; Scotland, 50,097 km). There were 12,325 km of all-purpose trunk roads, 2,658 km of trunk and principal motorways, 34,485 km of principal roads (excluding motorways) and 293,850 km of other roads.

At 1 April 1974 there were about 9,000 km of unsurfaced roads (green lanes) in England and 3,000 in Wales.

Motor vehicles for which licences were current under the Vehicles (Excise) Act, 1971, at 31 Dec. 1982, numbered 19·77m., including 15·69m. private cars and private vans, 1·37m. mopeds, scooters and motor cycles, 111,000 public transport vehicles and 1·7m. goods vehicles.

New vehicle registrations in 1982 numbered 2·1m.

Road casualties in Great Britain numbered in 1982, 334,000 including 5,934 killed; in 1981, 325,000 including 5,846 killed.

Railways. The British Railways Board as a public authority owns and manages British Rail, the national rail network, British Rail Engineering Ltd., British Rail Property Board, Sealink UK Ltd., Freightliners Ltd., Transportation Systems and Market Research Ltd. (Transmark), Travellers-Fare and British Rail Investments Ltd. The role of the Board is to determine policies and objectives, establish the organisation to carry them out, monitor performance and take major decisions.

The Group turnover in 1982 was nearly £1,930m. and just under 213,000 staff were employed, of which 161,000 were involved in the railway business.

The management of the railways is the responsibility of the Chief Executive (Railways). He establishes plans and budgets for the achievement of objectives set by the Board, monitors and achieves results against the plans and budgets, and directs the organisation and deployment of manpower resources. He is assisted by other Board members with responsibility for functions such as Engineering, Research, Finance and Planning, Marketing, Operating, Productivity and Personnel.

In 1982, British Rail carried 142m. tonnes of freight and parcels and 630m. passenger journeys were made.

The rail business is split into 5 sectors and directors act on behalf of the Chief Executive (Railways) to control policy. The sectors are InterCity, London and South East Services, Provincial Services, Freight and Parcels. A director is responsible for efficient operation and budgeting within his sector, each of which bears its fair share of the fixed costs of operation, such as signalling and track maintenance. The day-to-day running of the rail network is the responsibility of 5 regional managers to whom local area and station managers report.

		1981	1982
Passenger Receipts and Traffic			
1 Receipts	£m.	1,022·8	924·1
Passenger journeys	m.	718·5	630·1
Passenger miles (estimated)	m.	19,100·0	17,100·0
Freight Train Traffic			
Receipts	£m.	503·7	478·2
Traffic	m. tonnes	154·2	141·9
Net tonne miles (trainload and wagonload)	m.	10,877·0	9,867·0
Locomotives			
Diesel		2,864	2,750
Electric		267	266
Advanced Passenger Trains			
Power cars		6	6
Passenger carriages		30	30
High Speed Tains			
Power cars		181	197
Passenger carriages		664	709
Coaching vehicles		18,268	16,889
Freight vehicles (excluding brake vans)		88,327	71,452
Stations		2,742	2,711
Route open for traffic	miles	10,831	10,706

The London Transport Executive is the authority responsible for the operation of the capital's Underground and bus services. Overall policy and financial control is exercised by the Greater London Council. In Jan. 1983, London Transport had 241 route miles of railway open for traffic and also operated over 19 route miles owned by British Rail. Rolling stock owned: Underground, 4,069 (2,630 motor cars, 1,439 trailer cars); buses, 6,205. Number of train miles run in passenger service (1982) was 29m.; number of bus miles run in passenger service (1982) was 164m. The number of passengers carried in 1982 was: Underground 497m.; buses 1,042m. Average fare per passenger journey (1982): Underground 55·6p; buses 24·3p.

Gross receipts in 1980 for these Boards were: British Railways Board, from 1975 the Railways Act 1974 introduced, *inter alia*, new arrangements for the financial support of the railway passenger system and provided for the reconstruction of the finances of the Board (1981) £1,664·8m.[1]; London Transport Executive, (1982), £537m.[1]; British Transport Docks Board, £131·2m.; National Bus Company, £4,603m.[1]; National Freight Corporation, £417m., and British Waterways Board, £13·1m.[1].

[1] Excludes support grants.

Railway Finances. [Serpell Report] HMSO, London, 1983

Aviation. British Airways Board was set up by the Civil Aviation Act 1971, but is now constituted under the British Airways Board Act 1977. Initially it acted as a holding corporation for the two state airlines British Overseas Airways Corporation (BOAC) and British European Airways Corporation (BEA), but as from 1 April 1974 the business of BOAC and BEA were transferred to and vested in British Airways Board and BOAC and BEA were dissolved. British Airways Board carried on those businesses from that date under the trading name of British Airways.

British Airways is engaged in the provision of air transport services for passengers, cargo and mail worldwide, both on scheduled and charter services. It operates long and short haul international services, as well as an extensive domestic network. In 1982–83, it carried 14·6m. passengers, and at 31 March 1983 it had a fleet of 184 aircraft (including 36 helicopters) and it employed 37,517 personnel.

In addition to British Airways, there were 1982 about 44 independent air transport operators, the principal ones being British Caledonian Airways and British Midland Airways. In recent years there has been a significant expansion of the independent operators.

Pursuant to the Civil Aviation Act 1980, the business and undertaking of British Airways Board was transferred to and vested in a limited liability company, British Airways Plc, with effect from 1 April 1984. Although HM Government will initially hold all the shares in the new company, it is the Government's intention, pursuant to its 'privatization' polices, to introduce private capital into the company at the earliest suitable opportunity.

Following the Civil Aviation Act 1971, the Civil Aviation Authority was established as an independent public body responsible for the economic and safety regulation of British civil aviation. It took over the responsibilities of the former Air Transport Licensing Board and Air Registration Board, and also runs the National Air Traffic Services in conjunction with the Ministry of Defence.

In addition to the public transport operators there are a number of companies engaged in miscellaneous aviation activities such as crop-spraying, aerial survey and photography, and flying instruction.

The operating and traffic statistics of the UK airlines on scheduled services during the calendar year 1982 (and 1981) are as follows: Aircraft km flown, 332m. (360m.); revenue passengers carried, 20·6m. (21.4m.); cargo (freight and mail) carried 263,798 (294,866) tonnes.

Traffic between the UK airports and places abroad in 1982 (and 1981) on all services included 511,375 (495,759) air transport aircraft movements.

There were 7,449 civil aircraft registered in the UK at 31 Dec. 1983.

Shipping. The UK flag merchant fleet in July 1983 totalled 29m. DWT (dry cargo,

12·1m. DWT; tankers 17m. DWT) representing 4·3% of the world fleet. The total number of UK flag ships was 1,260. The number of UK nationality seafarers was about 46,000 as at 30 Nov. 1983.

Capital investment in new tonnage and facilities by British shipping companies 1976–82 (inclusive) was over £2,800m. In 1982 capital expenditure was an estimated £278m. The average age of UK owned and registered tonnage in mid-1983 was 9·1 years.

Total gross earnings by UK owned and registered ships in 1981 amounted to £2,655m. The net contribution to UK balance of payments was £1,044m. and, in addition, there were gross import savings of £449m.

On 30 Nov. 1983, 72 UK flag ships (4·4m. DWT) were laid up out of a world total of 1,689 ships (80·3m. DWT).

GCBS Facts and Figures 1980. 1980
Committee of Inquiry into Shipping. Cmnd 4337. HMSO, 1970

Inland Waterways. There are approximately 2,500 miles of navigable canals and locked river navigations in Great Britain. Of these, the British Waterways Board is responsible for some 300 miles of commercial waterways (maintained for freight traffic) and some 1,100 miles of cruising waterways (maintained for pleasure cruising, fishing and amenity). The Board is also responsible for a further 600 miles of canals, some of which are no longer navigable and whose future is being considered in conjunction with local authorities; a number of these lengths have been restored for cruising or as local amenities. The Board's gross receipts for the year 1982 were £17·8m. The total traffic on their waterways was 4.6m. tonnes.

The most important of the river navigations and canals under other authorities include the rivers Thames, Great Ouse, Nene and Yorkshire Ouse, the Norfolk Broads and the Manchester Ship Canal.

The Port of Manchester was opened to maritime traffic in 1894 by the construction of the Manchester Ship Canal, which is 35¼ miles in length and owned and operated by the Manchester Ship Canal Company. The entrance lock is 80 ft (24·38 metres) wide and the maximum width of other locks within the canal is 65 ft (19·81 metres). Ships up to 28 ft 10 in. (8·78 metres) freshwater draught can navigate to Ince Oil Berth; ships up to 24 ft (7·31 metres) draught can navigate to Manchester docks but within these docks draught is limited to 22 ft (6·70 metres).

The Port of Manchester includes the Queen Elizabeth II Oil Dock at Eastham (separate entrance lock 100 ft wide), the oil docks at Stanlow and a considerable number of public and private wharves and installations along the canal, as well as the container terminal at Ellesmere Port. Total sea-borne and barge traffic in 1983 amounted to 11·6m. tonnes; operating revenue, £23·7m.; operating profit, £1·14m. The total issued capital at 31 Dec. 1983 was £17·2m.

Edwards, L. A., *Inland Waterways of Great Britain and Northern Ireland.* 5th ed. St. Ives, 1972
Farnie, D. A., *The Manchester Ship Canal and the Rise of the Port of Manchester.* Manchester Univ. Press, 1980
Hadfield, C., *British Canals.* 6th ed. Newton Abbot, 1979
McKnight, H., *The Shell Book of Inland Waterways.* Newton Abbot, 1975
Paget-Tomlinson, E. W., *Complete Book of Canal and River Navigations.* Albrighton, 1978

Posts and Telecommunications. In Oct. 1981 the Post Office ceased to control telecommunications services, which became the responsibility of a separate corporation, British Telecom. The Post Office provides: Royal Mail general collection and delivery services, handling more than 40m. letters and parcels a day; Royal Mail Special Services including guaranteed delivery to any UK address overnight (Datapost), locally and to other major towns and cities on the same day (Expresspost) and by facsimile transmission to many UK and overseas centres; International Datapost offers guaranteed swift delivery to 42 countries; postal, National Girobank and many agency services on behalf of government departments at 22,000 post office counters; full banking facilities through National Girobank, a separately managed business within the Corporation. Number of post offices at 31 March 1983 was 22,300; number of posting boxes including those at post offices, over 100,000; staff employed, 176,000 (including 20,700 sub-postmasters employed on an agency basis).

	1979–80 (1m.)	1980–81 (1m.)	1981–82 (1m.)	1982–83 (1m.)
Correspondence (incl. registered items) posted	10,208	9,969	9,883	10,500
Parcels handled	180	172	183	193

Income (1982–83) £2,714m. Profit, £136·5m.

On 31 March 1983 there were 6,303 local exchanges, 271 automanual centres, 409 main network switching centres, 77,000 call offices, 19·5m. exchange connections and 28,882,000 telephone stations. There were 94,000 telex exchange connections and 99,000 datel modems. During the year 17,800m. local telephone calls, 3,603m. trunk calls and 322m. international calls were made.

901,000 inland telegrams and 1·9m. international telegrams were sent.

96,000m. inland telex calls were made and 270m. international telex minutes recorded.

Broadcasting. Radio and television services are provided by the BBC and by the Independent Broadcasting Authority and its programme contractors. The BBC, constituted by Royal Charter until 31 Dec. 1996, has responsibility for providing domestic and external broadcast services, the former financed from the television licence revenue, the latter by Government grant. The domestic services include 2 national television services, 4 national radio network services and an expanding local radio service.

The IBA constituted until 31 Dec. 1996 by the Broadcasting Act 1981 provides an independent television service on a regional basis, with programmes provided by its programme contractors. The 1981 Act provided for the establishment of the fourth television channel and of the Welsh Fourth Channel Authority (WFCA) which provides a Welsh service on that channel in Wales; they started broadcasting in Nov. 1982. The IBA also provides independent local radio services. All these services are financed by the sale of broadcast advertising time.

The BBC's domestic radio services are available on LF, MF and VHF; those of the IBA on MF and VHF. The television services of the 2 authorities BBC1, BBC2, ITV, and Channel 4 are broadcast at UHF in 625-line definition and in colour.

The broadcasting authorities, whose governing bodies are appointed (by HM the Queen in the case of the BBC and by the Home Secretary in the case of the IBA and WFCA) as trustees for the public interest in broadcasting, are independent of government in matters of programme content and are publicly accountable to Parliament for the discharge of their responsibilities.

In 1981 the Broadcasting Complaints Commission was set up to consider and adjudicate upon complaints of unfair or unjust treatment in broadcast programmes or of unwarranted infringement of privacy in or in the making of programmes. The number of broadcast receiving licences in force on 30 Nov. 1982 was 18·41m., including 14·41m. for colour.

25 Years of ITV. London, 1980

Cinemas. In 1983 there were 1,500 screens in 803 cinemas and there were 60m. admissions.

Newspapers. In 1983 there were 11 national dailies.

Benn's Press Directory. Tunbridge Wells, Annual

JUSTICE, RELIGION, EDUCATION AND WELFARE

Justice. *England and Wales.* The legal system of England and Wales, divided into civil and criminal courts has at the head of the superior courts, as the ultimate court of appeal, the House of Lords, which hears each year a number of appeals in civil matters, including a certain number from Scotland and Northern Ireland, as well as some appeals in criminal cases. In order that civil cases may go from the Court of

Appeal to the House of Lords, it is necessary to obtain the leave of either the Court of Appeal or the House itself, although in certain cases an appeal may lie direct to the House of Lords from the decision of the High Court. An appeal can be brought from a decision of the Court of Appeal or the Divisional Court of the Queen's Bench Division of the High Court in a criminal case provided that the Court is satisfied that a point of law 'of general public importance' is involved, and either the Court or the House of Lords is of the opinion that it is desirable in the public interest that a further appeal should be brought. As a judicial body, the House of Lords consists of the Lord Chancellor, the Lords of Appeal in Ordinary, commonly called Law Lords, and such other members of the House as hold or have held high judicial office. The final court of appeal for certain of the Commonwealth countries is the Judicial Committee of the Privy Council which, in addition to Privy Counsellors who are or have held high judicial office in the UK, includes others who are or have been Chief Justices or Judges of the Superior Courts of Commonwealth countries.

Civil Law. The main courts of original civil jurisdiction are the county courts for less important cases, and the High Court for the more important ones.

There are about 300 county courts located throughout the country, grouped in districts, and each presided over by a circuit judge. They have a general jurisdiction to determine all actions founded on contract or tort involving sums of not more than £5,000 and can also deal with other classes of use, such as landlord and tenant, probate, equity and admiralty, up to certain limits. Certain matters, such as actions of libel and slander, are entirely reserved for the High Court. In addition, certain designated county courts have jurisdiction in matrimonial proceedings. Divorce proceedings must now commence in these courts and, subject to being transferred to the High Court upon becoming defended, are determined in the County Court.

The High Court has both appellate and original jurisdiction, covering virtually all civil causes not determined in the county court. The judges of the High Court are attached to one of its 3 divisions: Chancery; Queen's Bench; and Family; each with its separate field of jurisdiction. There are 76 such judges, called puisne judges. For the hearing of cases at first instance, the High Court judges sit singly. Appellate jurisdiction is usually exercised by Divisional Courts consisting of 2 (sometimes 3) judges, though in certain circumstances a judge sitting alone may hear the appeal.

The Restrictive Practices Court was set up in 1956 under the Restrictive Trade Practices Act, and is responsible for deciding whether a restrictive trade agreement is in the public interest. It is presided over by a High Court judge, but laymen sit on the bench also. Another specialist court is the Employment Appeal Tribunal, with similar composition, which hears appeals in employment cases from lower tribunals.

The Court of Appeal (Civil Division) hears appeals in civil actions from the High Court and County Courts and certain special courts such as the Restrictive Practices Court and the Employment Appeal Tribunal. Its President is the Master of the Rolls, aided by 18 Lords Justices of Appeal sitting in 6 or 7 divisions of 2 or 3 judges each.

Civil proceedings are instituted by the aggrieved person, but, as they are a private matter, they are frequently settled by the parties to a dispute through their lawyers before the matter actually comes to court. In some cases, at the instance of either party, a jury may sit to decide questions of fact and award of damages.

Criminal Law. At the base of the system of criminal courts are the lay justices who try the great proportion of minor offenders (over 98% of all criminal cases) as well as undertaking a small proportion of civil work. Magistrates' courts are comprised of 3 lay justices who are unpaid and need not possess legal qualifications (though they undergo a course of training), though they do have the assistance on points of law of a professional clerk to justices. In central London and large cities there exist stipendiary magistrates, paid for their duties. These are professional lawyers and usually sit alone. Exercising summary jurisdiction in petty sessions, justices have power to pass sentences of imprisonment up to, in general, 6 months, and to impose fines up to, in general, £1,000. One of their functions is to examine persons charged with indictable offences and to determine whether they should be committed for trial at the Crown Court. Justices deal each year with about 2m. cases, including thefts, assaults, road traffic infringements, drug abuse, breaches of licensing laws, etc. There are some 22,106 justices who are appointed to the Commission of the Peace by the Lord Chancellor, and some 3,672 justices appointed by the Chancellor of the Duchy of Lancaster; each assisted by advisory committees. Women are eligible to be appointed justices, and the number on the Commission of the Peace is 10,833.

Specially qualified justices sit in juvenile courts to deal with cases involving persons under 17 years of age charged with criminal offences (other than homicide and other grave offences) or brought before the court as being in need of care or control. These courts normally sit with 3 justices, including 1 woman, and are accommodated separately from other courts.

Specially qualified justices also sit in the domestic courts to deal with matrimonial proceedings, custody, guardianship and maintenance of children, affiliation and adoption. These courts normally sit with 3 justices including 1 woman.

Above the magistrates' courts is the Crown Court. This was set up by the Courts Act 1971 to replace quarter sessions and assizes. Unlike quarter sessions and assizes, which were individual courts, the Crown Court is a single court which is capable of sitting anywhere in England and Wales. It has power to deal with all trials on indictment and has inherited the jurisdiction of quarter sessions to hear appeals, proceedings on committal of persons for sentence, and certain original proceedings on civil matters under individual statutes.

The jurisdiction of the Crown Court is exercisable by a High Court judge, a Circuit judge or a Recorder (who is a part-time judge) sitting alone, or, in specified circumstances, with justices of the peace. The Lord Chief Justice has given directions as to the types of case to be allocated to High Court judges (the more serious cases) and to Circuit judges or Recorders respectively.

Appeals from magistrates' courts go either to a Divisional Court of the High Court (when a point of law alone is involved) or to the Crown Court where there is a complete re-hearing. Appeals from the Crown Court in cases tried on indictment lie to the Court of Appeal (Criminal Division). Appeals on questions of law go by right, and appeals on other matters by leave. The Lord Chief Justice or a Lord Justice sits with judges of the High Court to constitute this court.

There remains as a last resort the invocation of the royal prerogative exercised on the advice of the Home Secretary. In 1965 the death penalty was abolished for murder.

All contested criminal trials, except those which come before the magistrates' courts, are tried by a judge and a jury consisting of 12 members. The defence may object, without showing cause, to up to 3 jurors. The prosecution may ask that any number may 'stand by' until the jury panel is exhausted, and only then need to show cause. When these peremptory challenges have been exhausted further challenges may only be made for cause and this rarely happens. The jury decides whether the accused is guilty or not. The judge is responsible for summing up on the facts and explaining the law; he sentences convicted offenders. If, after at least 2 hours of deliberation, a jury is unable to reach a unanimous verdict it may, provided that in a full jury of 12 at least 10 of its members are agreed, bring in a majority verdict. The failure of a jury to agree on a unanimous verdict or to bring in a majority verdict involves the retrial of the case before a new jury.

The Employment Appeal Tribunal. The Employment Appeal Tribunal which is a superior Court of Record with the like powers, rights, privileges and authority of the High Court, was set up in 1976 to hear appeals on questions of fact and law against decisions of industrial tribunals and of the Certification Officer. The appeals are heard by a High Court Judge sitting with 2 members (in exceptional cases 4) appointed for their special knowledge or experience of industrial relations either on the employer or the trade union side, with always an equal number on each side. Industrial tribunals are responsible for deciding questions under Employment Protection (Consolidation) Act, 1978, Equal Pay Act, 1970, Sex Discrimination Act 1975, Employment Protection Act 1975, Employment Act 1980, Race Relations Act, 1976, and Employment Acts 1980 and 1982. The great bulk of their work is concerned with the problems which can arise between employees and their employers. The Certification Officer is responsible for deciding questions under the Trade Union Act 1913, the Trade Union (Amalgamations, etc.) Act 1964, the Trade Union and Labour Relations Act 1974 and the Employment Protection Act 1975.

Military Courts. Offences by persons subject to service law against the system of military law created under the powers of the Army Act, Air Force Act or Naval Discipline Act are dealt with either summarily or by courts-martial. Petitions may be made to the Defence Council. Subsequent appeals lie to a Courts-Martial Appeals Court, and from that court an appeal may lie to the House of Lords.

The Personnel of the Law. All judicial officers except the Lord Chancellor (who is a member of the Cabinet) are independent of Parliament and the Executive. They are all appointed by the Crown on the advice of the Prime Minister or the Lord Chancellor and hold office until retiring age. The legal profession is divided; barristers, who advise on legal problems and conduct cases in court, usually act for the public only through solicitors, who deal directly with the legal business brought to them by the public. Most judicial appointments are made from barristers of long standing. though solicitors are eligible for appointment as Recorders, who may, after 3 years, be appointed Circuit Judges.

Legal Aid. Broadly there are 3 kinds of legal aid. Firstly there is legal advice and assistance, otherwise known as the 'Green Form' scheme. This includes advice and help on any question of English law, both civil and criminal, but does not normally cover any form of representation before a court or tribunal. Since May 1980, however, as an extension of the scheme assistance by way of representation has been available for certain proceedings, chiefly civil, in magistrates' courts. Secondly, under Part I of the Legal Aid Act 1974, there is legal aid for civil court proceedings. Under the provisions of the Act, aid is available to those of low or moderate means either free or subject to a contribution, depending on means. In 1982–83 there were over 733,000 applications for advice and assistance under the Legal Advice and Assistance Scheme and over 184,000 legal aid certificates were issued. The cost of legal aid in civil cases is met from (*a*) contributions from assisted persons; (*b*) the operation of the statutory charge which gives the Law Society a first charge on money or property recovered or preserved for an assisted person to the extent of that person's liability for his own costs; (*c*) costs recovered from opposing parties and (*d*) a grant from the Exchequer. The net cost of civil legal aid to the state in the year 1982–83 amounted to £82·2m. and the cost of the legal advice and assistance scheme was £38·8m. of which £8·3m. was accounted for by assistance by way of representation.

Under Part II of the Legal Aid Act 1974 a court dealing with criminal proceedings may order legal aid to be given if it considers it is desirable in the interests of justice and if it also considers that the defendant (or appellant) requires financial assistance in meeting the costs he may incur. The interests of justice are not statutorily defined but may include, for example, situations where the defendant is in real danger of going to prison or losing his job, where substantial questions of law are to be argued or where the defendant is unable to follow the proceedings and explain his case due to inadequate knowledge of English, mental illness or other mental or physical disability. Legal aid must be granted, subject to means, in the following circumstances: where a person is committed for trial on a charge of murder, where the prosecutor appeals or applies for leave to appeal from the criminal division of the Court of Appeal or the Courts-Martial Appeal Court to the House of Lords, and in certain circumstances where the court is considering depriving a defendant of his liberty.

The costs of legal aid in criminal proceedings are paid by the central government, but courts have power to require legally aided persons to contribute towards the cost of legal aid given to them. The net cost of legal aid in criminal proceedings in the year 1982–83 was £106·4m., £51·2m. of this was for legal aid in the higher courts which is paid for out of the Lord Chancellor's vote and £54·9m. for legal aid in the magistrates' courts which is paid from the legal aid fund.

Under the Parliamentary Commissioner Act, passed 22 March 1967, M.P.s may refer to the Parliamentary Commissioner complaints received from the public regarding improper or inequitable administration in most spheres of central government affairs. Generally, other available remedies (such as legal action) must be exhausted before a complaint can be investigated. If a complaint is found to require a remedy the Parliamentary Commissioner makes a report to Parliament.

Commissions for Local Administration in England and Wales were set up under the Local Government Act 1974. The Commissioners carry out similar functions in relation to local government bodies to those the Parliamentary Commissioner discharges with regard to maladministration in central government.

Police. The authorized establishment of the police force in England and Wales in Dec. 1983 was 121,802: the actual strength was 109,927 men and 11,076 women. In addition there were 15,351 special constables (including 3,588 women). Total police net expenditure (estimated) in England and Wales for 1981–82 was £2,148·8m.

Blom-Cooper, L., and Drewry, G., *Final Appeal: A Study of the House of Lords in its Judicial Capacity.* OUP, 1972
Critchley, T. A., *A History of Police in England and Wales.* Rev. ed. London, 1978

SCOTLAND. The High Court of Justiciary is the supreme criminal court in Scotland and has jurisdiction in all cases of crime committed in any part of Scotland, unless expressly excluded by statute. It consists of the Lord Justice-General, the Lord Justice-Clerk and 19 other judges, who are the same judges as of the Court of Session, the Scottish supreme civil court. The Court, which is presided over by the Lord Justice-General, whom failing, the Lord Justice-Clerk, exercises an appellate jurisdiction as well as one of first instance, sits as business requires in Edinburgh both as a Court of Appeal (the *quorum* being 3 judges) and as a court of first instance and on circuit as a court of first instance. The decisions of the Court in either case are not subject to review by the House of Lords. One judge sitting with a jury of 15 persons can, and usually does, try cases, but 2 or more (with a jury) may do so in important or complex cases. It has a privative jurisdiction over cases of treason, murder, rape, deforcement of messengers and breach of duty by magistrates. It also, in practice, is the only court which tries cases of incest, sodomy and other serious or aggravated crimes against person or property and generally those cases in which a sentence greater than imprisonment for 2 years may be imposed either under statute or common law. Moreover, the Court has inherent power to try and to punish all acts which are plainly criminal though previously unknown and not dealt with by any statute.

The appellate jurisdiction of the High Court of Justiciary extends to all cases tried on indictment, whether in the High Court or the Sheriff Court, and persons so convicted may appeal to the Court against conviction or sentence or both except that there is no appeal against any sentence fixed by law. By such an appeal, a person may bring under review of the High Court of Justiciary any alleged miscarriage of justice including any alleged miscarriage of justice on the basis of the existence and significance of additional evidence which was not heard at the trial and which was not available and could not reasonably have been made available at the trial. It is also a court of review from courts of summary criminal jurisdiction, and on the final determination of any summary prosecution either party may appeal to the Court by way of stated case on questions of law, procedure, etc., but not on questions of fact, except in relation to a miscarriage of justice alleged by the person accused on the basis of the existence and significance of additional evidence which was not heard at the trial and which was not available and could not reasonably have been made available at the trial. A further or complementary form of process of review which can be resorted to by convicted persons in these courts is by Bill of Suspension (and Liberation), but it is of strictly limited application. A prosecutor in cases tried on indictment or under summary criminal procedure may also bring under review a decision in law, prior to final judgment of the case, by way of Bill of Advocation. The Court also hears appeals under the Courts-Martial (Appeals) Act 1951.

The Sheriff Court has an inherent universal criminal jurisdiction (as well as an extensive civil one) limited in general to crimes and offences committed within a sheriffdom (a specifically defined region), which has, however, been curtailed by statute or practice under which the High Court of Justiciary has exclusive jurisdiction in relation to the crimes above-mentioned. This Court is presided over by a Sheriff-Principal or Sheriff, and when trying cases on indictment sits with a jury of 15 persons. His power of awarding punishment involving imprisonment is restricted to 2 years in the maximum, but he may under certain statutory powers remit the prisoner to the High Court for sentence. The Sheriff also exercises a wide summary criminal jurisdiction and when doing so sits without a jury; and he has concurrent jurisdiction with every other court within his sheriffdom in regard to all offences competent for trial in summary courts. The great majority of offences which come before the courts are of a minor nature and, as such, are disposed of in the Sheriff Courts. In cases to be tried on indictment either in the High Court of Justiciary or in the Sheriff Court, the judge may, and in some cases must, before the trial, hold a Preliminary Diet to decide questions of a preliminary nature, whether to the competency or relevancy or otherwise. Any decision at a preliminary diet can be the subject of an appeal to the High Court of Justiciary prior to the trial.

District Courts in each local authority district have jurisdiction in minor offences occurring within the district. These courts are presided over by lay magistrates, known as justices, and have limited powers of fine and imprisonment.

The Court of Session, presided over by the Lord President (the Lord Justice-General in criminal cases), is divided into an Inner House comprising 2 divisions of 4 judges each with mainly appellate function, and an Outer House comprising 13 single judges, sitting individually at first instance; it exercises the highest civil jurisdiction in Scotland, with the House of Lords as a court of appeal.

Police. The police forces in Scotland at the end of 1982 had an authorized establishment of 13,267; the strength was 12,495 men and 719 women. There were 2,736 part-time special constables. The total police net expenditure in Scotland was £209·8m. for 1981–82.

CIVIL JUDICIAL STATISTICS

ENGLAND AND WALES	1980	1981	1982
Appellate Courts			
Judicial Committee of the Privy Council	61	54	62
House of Lords	85	65	71
Court of Appeal	1,488	...	1,686
High Court of Justice (appeals and special cases from inferior courts)	1,360	1,282	1,482
Courts of First Instance			
High Court of Justice:			
Chancery Division[1]	16,328	15,650	17,119
Queen's Bench Division	200,989	182,620	164,396
Family Division[2]	1,100	1,014	1,046
County courts: Divorce	177,415	176,162	181,853
Other	1,756,029	1,916,105	2,119,511
Other courts[3]	6,328	6,345	...
SCOTLAND			
House of Lords (Appeals from Court of Sessions)	4	12	11
Court of Session—General Department	29,459	30,043	31,471
Sheriff's Ordinary Cause	35,757	37,364	35,949
Sheriff's Summary Cause	151,941	131,855	166,127

[1] Including contentious probate, 3rd Patents Court.
[2] Principal registry matters.
[3] From Jan. 1972 certain 'other' courts, namely, the Palatine Chancery Court of Lancaster and Durham were merged with the High Court; the Mayor's and City of London Court became a County Court; Borough Courts of Record were abolished. The figure 6,345 for 1981 represents: Court of Protection, 4,266; Lands Tribunal, 1,262; Employment Appeal Tribunal, 793; Transport Tribunal, 24.

CRIMINAL STATISTICS

ENGLAND AND WALES

	Total number of offenders		Indictable offences[1]	
	1981	1982	1981	1982
Aged 10 and over				
Proceeded against in magistrates' courts[2]	2,293,556	2,221,326	522,597	538,806
Found guilty at magistrates' courts	2,041,651	1,963,600	401,585	407,694
Found guilty at the Crown Court	62,978	67,443	62,977	67,437
Cautioned[3]	153,826	160,482	103,896	111,315
Aged 10 and under 17				
Proceeded against in magistrates' courts[2]	129,709	121,468	94,706	90,169
Found guilty at magistrates' courts	116,972	108,709	85,322	80,447
Found guilty at the Crown Court	1,288	1,309	1,288	1,309
Cautioned[3]	108,237	112,684	87,602	92,907

SCOTLAND

	All Crimes and Offences		Crimes[5]	
	1980	1981	1980	1981
All persons and companies				
Proceeded against in all courts	264,844	246,295	54,374	58,767
Charge proved	246,263	226,095	47,795	51,620
Children (aged 8–15)				
Proceeded against in all courts	1,166	1,042	698	660
Given formal police warning/ referred to reporter	22,344	23,125	17,113	18,402

[1] Includes offences which can be tried either at the Crown Court or at magistrates' courts.

[2] Almost all defendants are initially proceeded against in magistrates' courts.

[3] Offenders who, on admission of guilt, are given an oral caution by or on the instruction of a senior police officer as an alternative to court proceedings. Such cautions are not given for motoring offences.

[4] Young persons under 16 years of age.

[5] Crimes are generally the more serious criminal acts and offences the less serious. 'Crimes' are not equivalent in coverage to 'indictable/triable either way offences'.

Average population in prisons, borstals and detention centres (1982) in England and Wales was 43,707 (convicted 37,951; untried 5,362, and 394 non-criminal prisoners); in Scotland (1982), 4,891 (sentenced, 4,047; remanded, 844 and 3 others).

Criminal Statistics, England and Wales. 1983
Prison Statistics, England and Wales, 1982. HMSO, 1983
Paterson, A., *The Law Lords.* London, 1982

Religion. The Anglican Communion has originated from the Church of England and parallels in its fellowship of autonomous churches the evolution of British influence beyond the seas from colonies to dominions and independent nations. There is no terrestrial head of the Anglican Communion; the Archbishop of Canterbury presides as *primus inter pares* at the decennial meetings of the bishops of the Anglican Communion at the Lambeth Conference.

The Anglican churches, in addition to the Church of England, comprise the churches, councils, and provinces in communion with the see of Canterbury; which are situated in Wales; Ireland; Scotland; United States of America; Canada; Australia; New Zealand; West Indies; Brazil; South Africa; Central Africa; West and East Africa; Jerusalem and the Middle East; South East Asia; Burma; Sri Lanka; Japan; South America; China.

In addition to the dioceses included within the Provinces of Canterbury and York, there are several dioceses overseas over which the Archbishop of Canterbury exercises metropolitical jurisdiction, while Church of England chaplaincies in

North and Central Europe formerly under the jurisdiction of the Bishop of London now form the diocese of Europe.

England and Wales. The established Church of England, which baptizes about 40% of the children born in England (*i.e.* excluding Wales but including the Isle of Man and the Channel Islands), is Protestant Episcopal. Civil disabilities on account of religion do not attach to any class of British subject. Under the Welsh Church Acts, 1914 and 1919, the Church in Wales and Monmouthshire was disestablished as from 1 April 1920, and Wales was formed into a separate Province.

The Queen is, under God, the supreme governor of the Church of England, with the right, regulated by statute, to nominate to the vacant archbishoprics and bishoprics. The Queen, on the advice of the First Lord of the Treasury, also appoints to such deaneries, prebendaries and canonries as are in the gift of the Crown, while a large number of livings and also some canonries are in the gift of the Lord Chancellor.

There are 2 archbishops (at the head of the 2 Provinces of Canterbury and York), and 42 diocesan bishops including the bishop of the diocese of Europe, which is part of the Province of Canterbury. Each archbishop has also his own particular diocese, wherein he exercises episcopal, as in his Province he exercises metropolitan, jurisdiction. In Dec. 1983 there were 69 suffragan and assistant bishops, 39 deans and provosts of cathedrals and 105 archdeacons. The General Synod, in England, consists of a House of Bishops, a House of Clergy and a House of Laity, and has power to frame legislation regarding Church matters. The first two Houses consist of the members of the Convocations of Canterbury and York, each of which consists of the diocesan bishops and elected representatives of the suffragan bishops, 6 for Canterbury province and 3 for York (forming an Upper House), deans, provosts, and archdeacons, and a certain number of proctors elected as the representatives of the inferior clergy, together with, in the case of Canterbury Convocation, representatives of the Universities of Oxford, Cambridge and London and in the case of York a representative for the Universities of Durham and Newcastle; the chaplains in the Forces (forming the Lower House). They are elected by their fellow suffragans. The House of Laity is elected by the lay members of the Deanery Synods. Parochial affairs are managed by annual parochial church meetings and parochial church councils. Every Measure passed by the General Synod must be submitted to the Ecclesiastical Committee, consisting of 15 members of the House of Lords nominated by the Lord Chancellor and 15 members of the House of Commons nominated by the Speaker. This committee reports on each Measure to Parliament, and the Measure receives the Royal Assent and becomes law if each House of Parliament resolves that the Measure be presented to the Queen.

At 31 Dec. 1983 there were 13,530 ecclesiastical parishes, inclusive of the Isle of Man and the Channel Islands. These parishes do not, in many cases, coincide with civil parishes. Owing to the pastoral re-organization, although most parishes have their own churches, not every parish nowadays can have its own incumbent or minister; so that in some areas one or more parishes may be served by a clergyman, who must be in priest's orders, and in these cases he holds the parishes in plurality or as part of a united benefice. In Dec. 1983 there were 7,044 beneficed clergymen excluding dignitaries, 1,323 other clergymen of incumbent status and 1,742 assistant curates working in the parishes.

Private persons possess the right of presentation to over 2,000 benefices; the patronage of the others belongs mainly to the Queen, the bishops and cathedrals, the Lord Chancellor, and the universities of Oxford and Cambridge. In addition to the 10,109 parochial incumbents and assistant curates, there were (1983) 378 dignitaries, 320 non-parochial clergymen working within the diocesan framework and approximately 2,000 non-parochial clergymen outside the framework.

In 1980 there were estimated to be 1·8m. Easter and 1·8m. Christmas Communicants.

Of the 40,434 churches and chapels registered for the solemnization of marriages at 30 June 1983, 16,637 belonged to the Established Church and the Church in

Wales and 23,797 to other religious denominations. Of the 342,166 marriages celebrated in 1982 (351,973 in 1981), 34% were in the Established Church and the Church in Wales, 18% in churches or chapels of other denominations and 48% were civil marriages in a Register Office.

Roman Catholics in England and Wales were 4,242,980 in 1983. There were 5 archdioceses and 16 dioceses, 6,918 clergy and 2,666 parish churches and 1,208 other churches open to the public. Convents, 1,291.

The Unitarians have about 250 places of worship, the Catholic Apostolic Church over 80, the New Jerusalem Church about 75. The Salvation Army, a religious body with a quasi-military organization, carries on both spiritual and social work at home and abroad, and had, in British Territory, 1982, 2,135 officers, 1,042 corps. There were also 38 eventide homes, 13 maternity homes, 2 maternity hospitals, 46 hostels for men, 14 hostels for women and girls, and 9 approved and training schools.

The following is a summary of statistics of certain churches in England and Wales, Channel Islands and Isle of Man:

Denomination	Full members	Ministers in charge	Local and lay preachers
Methodist	487,972	3,506	14,847
Independent Methodist	4,515	151	—
Wesleyan Reform Union	3,455	24	171
United Reform	150,000	1,800	—
Baptist	221,766	1,714	—
Calvinistic Methodist Church of Wales	85,041	230	—
Moravian	4,000	40	—
Society of Friends	18,303	—	—

There are about 354,000 Jews in the UK with about 240 synagogues.

Scotland. The Church of Scotland (established in 1560 at the Reformation and re-established in 1688 as part of the Revolution Settlement) is Presbyterian, the ministers all being of equal rank. There is in each parish a kirk session consisting of the minister and a number of laymen called elders. There are presbyteries (formed by groups of parishes), meeting frequently throughout the year, and these are again grouped in synods, which meet half-yearly and can be appealed to against the decisions of the presbyteries.

The supreme court is the General Assembly, which now consists of some 1,250 members, half clerical and half lay, chosen by the different presbyteries. It meets annually in May (under the presidency of a Moderator appointed by the Assembly, the Sovereign being present or represented by a Lord High Commissioner, appointed by the Queen on the nomination of the Government of the day), and sits for 7 days. Any matters not decided during this period may be left to a Commission which will sit if required.

On 2 Oct. 1929 the Church of Scotland and the United Free Church of Scotland were reunited under the name of The Church of Scotland, and the two bodies met in General Assembly in Edinburgh as one. The united Church had, in Scotland, on 31 Dec. 1981, 1,846 congregations, 953,933 members; 20,138 teachers and 120,138 scholars in attendance in Sunday schools. The Church courts are the General Assembly, 12 synods, 46 presbyteries in Scotland, 1 in England and 2 on the Continent. Income in 1981 was £30,665,558. There are divinity faculties in 4 Scottish universities of Edinburgh, Glasgow, Aberdeen and St Andrews, with 60 professors and lecturers who are mostly ministers of the Church of Scotland.

The Episcopal Church of Scotland is a province of the Anglican Church and is one of the historic Scottish churches. It consists of 7 dioceses. As at 31 Dec. 1983 it had 286 churches and missions, 237 clergy and 69,299 members, of whom 39,585 were communicants.

There are in Scotland some small outstanding Presbyterian bodies and also Baptists, Congregationalists, Methodists and Unitarians.

The Roman Catholic Church which celebrated the centenary of the restoration of the hierarchy in 1978, had in Scotland (1983) 1 cardinal, 1 archbishop and 9 bishops, 1,122 clergy, 476 parishes, and 814,400 adherents.

The proportion of marriages in Scotland according to the rites of the various Churches in 1982 was: Church of Scotland, 39·5%; Roman Catholic, 13·9%; Episcopal, 1·5%; United Free, 0·5%; others, 4·6%; civil, 39·9%.

Bossy, J., *The English Catholic Community, 1570–1850.* London, 1975
Moorman, J. R. H., *A History of the Church in England.* London, 1973

Education. *The Publicly Maintained System of Education England and Wales:* Compulsory schooling begins at the age of 5 and the minimum leaving age for all pupils is 16.[1] No tuition fees are payable in any publicly maintained school (but it is open to parents, if they choose, to pay for their children to attend other schools). The post-school stage, which is voluntary, includes universities, polytechnics and other further education establishments (including those which provide courses for the training of teachers), as well as adult education and the youth service. Financial assistance is generally available to students on higher education courses in the university and non-university sectors and to some students on other courses in further education.

Nursery Education. Children under 5 may be provided for in nursery schools and nursery classes in primary schools. In the public sector no fees are payable. There were (1983) 575 nursery schools accommodating 49,551 children while some 3,764 primary schools contained nursery classes accommodating 198,294 children. Over 80% of all these children attend on a part-time basis. There are also 210,372 children under 5 attending maintained primary schools.

Primary Schools. Children normally begin primary school when they are 5. Nearly half of the 20,482 primary schools take the complete age-range from 5 upwards. About 3,900 take infants only, up to about 7 years; the rest take juniors only, from 7 or 8 on. The great majority of primary schools take both boys and girls. Nearly 13,000 of these schools had between 100 and 300 pupils each; of the remainder, over half had 100 pupils or less.

There are 1,930 primary schools in Wales. In those primary schools (and some secondary schools) which are in the predominantly Welsh-speaking areas, the main language of instruction is Welsh. There are also 'Welsh', or, more accurately, bilingual schools in mainly English-speaking parts of Wales. Generally children transfer from primary to secondary schools at 11.

[1] As a result of the Education (School Leaving Dates) Act 1976, one of the two former leaving dates was amended. This means that pupils whose dates of birth fall between 1 Feb. and 31 Aug. (inclusive) cease to be of compulsory school age on the Friday before the last Monday in May. Some of these pupils will leave school before their 16th birthdays. Pupils whose dates of birth fall between 1 Sept. and 31 Jan. (inclusive) remain of compulsory school age until the end of the Easter term following their 16th birthdays.

Middle Schools. In some areas middle schools have been developed. These cover the age-ranges 8 to 12, 9 to 12, 9 to 13, 10 to 13 or 10 to 14. In Jan. 1982 there were 1,413 middle schools, just one more than in 1981; this stabilizing of numbers comes after a decade of rapid growth (there were only 15 middle schools in 1969).

Secondary Education. In some areas, pupils are still selected at 11 for grammar schools on the basis of ability. The grammar schools, of which there were 185 at Jan. 1982, provide a mainly academic course from age 11 to 18. There were also a small number of technical schools which are the academic equals of grammar schools but can specialize to a greater or lesser extent in technical studies. Modern schools provide a general education up to the minimum school leaving age, though some pupils can, and increasingly do, stay on beyond that age. At Jan. 1982 there were 357 of these schools. There are also a small number of other schools which are various combinations of grammar, technical and modern schools.

All authorities now operate some comprehensive schools to which pupils are admitted without reference to ability or aptitude. In Jan. 1982 there were 3,358 fully comprehensive schools with over 3·15m. pupils, in comparison with 221 such schools with about 210,000 pupils in 1965. With the development of comprehensive education various patterns of secondary school organization have come into operation, of which the main ones are: all through schools with an age-range of 11–18 or 11–16 (with possible transfer to an 11–18 school or to a sixth form college (*i.e.*, 16–19) for further studies); 3-tier systems, which incorporate middle schools with a transfer age of 12, 13 or 14, and corresponding 12–18, 13–18 or 14–18 schools; or a system of junior and senior comprehensive schools, catering for the 11–18 age group with a transfer age of 13 or 14.

Direct Grant Grammar Schools. These schools receive grants direct from the Department of Education and Science for their secondary departments (or 'upper schools') and are independent of local education authorities. With the phasing out of the direct grant system now in its final stages, however, there were (1984) only 10 schools receiving grant in respect of pupils attending them. It is expected that direct grant payments will cease in 1987.

Assisted Places Scheme. In order to give able children a wider range of educational opportunity the government set up, in 1981, the assisted places scheme to give help with tuition fees at independent schools to parents who could not otherwise afford them. In the school year 1983–84, the 223 participating schools offered a total of 5,773 assisted places, 4,752 for entry at age 11, 12 or 13, and 1,021 for entry at sixth form level.

Special Education. Since 1971, when the education of severely mentally handicapped children became the responsibility of the education service, the right to education of all handicapped children has been recognised.

The Education Act 1981, which came into force in April 1983, switched the focus of attention from a child's disability to his special educational needs. The Act restated the Government's policy that no child should be placed in a special school if his needs can be met in an ordinary school.

The majority of handicapped children attend special schools of which there are at present around 1,560 catering for approximately 122,500 pupils. Some 3,200 pupils are educated in hospital schools and around 7,200 in independent schools under arrangements made by local education authorities.

Increasingly, however, handicapped children are being integrated into ordinary schools either in designated classes or on an individual basis. At present around 15,400 pupils with special educational needs are in designated special classes at maintained ordinary schools. Of maintained special schools, 1,038 are day schools and a further 312 have boarding facilities. Attendance is compulsory from 5–16. In addition, local authorities can make special educational provision below the age of 5 for those ascertained as being in need of it and until the age of 18 for those who want it (education from 16–18 may be provided either in a school or in a college of further education). In addition to the provision in ordinary and special schools, authorities make special arrangements for educating children at home, in small groups or in hospitals. About 4,500 pupils are being educated at present otherwise than at school. There are also some establishments which provide further education, P.E. vocational training and for assessment for employment purely for handicapped school leavers. The statistics in this and the preceding paragraph are for England only and are valid at Jan. 1983.

Ancillary Services. Local education authorities may provide registered pupils at any school maintained by them with milk, meals and refreshment and they may make such charges as they think fit for anything they provide. For pupils whose parents are in receipt of supplementary benefit or family income supplement, however, authorities are required to ensure that such provision is made for the pupil at mid-day as appears to them to be requisite and anything which is provided must be free of charge. Authorities are also required to remit the charge for anything they provide for other pupils if having regard to their circumstances, they consider it appropriate to do so. Facilities must also be provided, free of charge, for consuming any meals or other refreshments which pupils bring to school themselves.

Local education authorities also have power to provide milk, meals and refreshment for pupils in non-maintained schools, if they wish to do so, under such terms as may be agreed with the proprietors as long as the cost does not exceed what it would have been if the pupils had been at a school maintained by an authority.

Further and Higher Education (Non-University). In Nov. 1982 there were about 512 institutions in England and Wales providing courses of further education, ranging from shorthand instruction to degree-level, postgraduate work and courses of teacher-training. Course enrolments numbered 592,709 full-time (including 67,094 sandwich students) and 1·32m. part-time and evening; students released by their employers numbered 413,614. There were in addition 4,318 adult education centres (formerly known as evening institutes), and youth clubs which provided mainly part-time courses of non-advanced general education and were attended by 1,534,000 students. At the top end of this range, outside the university sector, are the 30 polytechnics. These are engaged mainly in higher education, offering degrees of a standard comparable to those of universities, professional qualifications and courses in a wide range of disciplines leading to awards of the Business and Technician Education Council. Many other colleges of further education are however involved to a greater or lesser extent in the higher education sector of further education. Most polytechnics and further education colleges cater for a mixture of full and part-time students, and also sandwich students whose periods of study at college alternate with periods of practical training in industry or other employment. The Secretary of State receives advice on the funding and management of advanced further education from the National Advisory Body for Local Authority Higher Education (NAB) whose remit covers almost all non-university provision at this level, most of which is maintained by local education authorities.

Courses were also provided by the Workers' Educational Association (7,375), the University extramural departments (7,460) and the Welsh National Council of YMCAs (60). The total number of students registered at these courses was 332,376.

Education at institutions of further education is not free, but fees are generally low, and are remitted for most students under the age of 18 by the local authority.

The Youth Service. A wide range of facilities for the leisure-time recreation and informal special education of young people primarily of post-school age is provided by local education authorities and voluntary youth organizations. A duty is laid upon local education authorities by the provisions of the 1944 Education Act to secure the adequacy of such facilities for young people in their area; to this end they either provide, maintain and staff youth clubs, centres and other facilities from their own resources or assist voluntary agencies to do so.

Grants to voluntary agencies to help meet the cost of regional and national capital projects and to national voluntary bodies towards their headquarters and training expenses are made by the Government.

Awards to Students. Local education authorities are responsible for making mandatory awards to suitably qualified students taking first-degree and comparable courses, courses of initial teacher-training and certain other advanced level courses. These awards cover fees and maintenance but the maintenance grants are subject to the income of the student and his parents or spouse. In addition scholarships may be available both from universities and other sources. The authorities may also give discretionary awards to students who do not qualify for mandatory awards including those taking non-degree level courses.

In 1981–82 there were 399,318 full value awards current in all, 50% at university and 36,259 were for teacher-training courses. These include awards to students at university departments of education for which responsibility was transferred to local authorities in 1975–76. Lesser value awards, for which the maximum rate of grant payable is below the full cost of the student's fees and maintenance, were also made by the authorities. There were 79,466 such awards taken up in the academic year 1981–82.

The Research Council gave 6,916 new awards in 1983–84 and there were 13,525 current awards in that academic year. The Department gave 1,268 new awards (state studentships and state bursaries) in 1983 and in 1984 awards totalled 2,170.

Teachers. In order to qualify for work in maintained schools, most teachers take a course of professional training. Graduates and holders of some specialist qualifications obtained before 1 Jan. 1970 are regarded as qualified to teach without training, but anyone obtaining these qualifications after that date is obliged to take a training course before being appointed for the first time to a primary school, and since 1 Jan. 1974 before first appointment to a secondary school.

In 1982 there were some 75 non-university institutions (including 23 polytechnics) and 31 university departments of education providing courses of initial teaching in England and Wales.

In Oct. 1981 there were about 30,000 students on initial teacher-training courses.

On 30 Sept. 1983, 417,000 full-time teachers were employed by local education authorities in maintained nursery, primary and secondary schools in England and Wales.

Finance. Total current and capital expenditure on education in England from public funds (excluding university education) is estimated at £10,092m. for 1982–83 as compared with £9,335m. for 1981–82.

Scotland. The statistics on schools relate to education authority and grant-aided schools. From 1974–75 all teachers employed in these schools require to be qualified; figures given are full-time equivalents.

Nursery Education. In Sept. 1981 there were 531 nursery schools and departments, with a total enrolment of 33,350 pupils.

Primary Education. In Sept. 1981 there were 2,520 primary schools and departments and the number on the registers was 498,968.

In Sept. 1981, 24,616 teachers were employed in primary schools and departments.

Secondary Education. In Sept. 1981 there were 461 secondary schools with 415,763 pupils. Of these schools, 376 were all-through comprehensive establishments providing the full range of Scottish Certificate of Education courses and also non-certificate courses. A further 61 schools were comprehensive in intake and provided both non-certificate and certificate courses, the latter however only up to Ordinary grade. Of the remaining 29 schools, these were selective in intake, 20 provided certificate courses only (Ordinary grade and Higher grade) and 4 non-certificate and certificate courses, the latter again not extending beyond Ordinary grade. Pupils who start their secondary education in schools which do not cater for courses beyond Ordinary grade may in the light of their performance, or for other reasons, be transferred at the end of their second or fourth year to schools providing Higher grade courses.

There were 28,918 teachers in secondary schools at Sept. 1981.

Special Schools. In Sept. 1981 there were 324 special schools and departments. The total number of handicapped children under instruction was 11,270, of which 8,394 were mentally handicapped, 917 were physically handicapped, 321 were blind or partially blind and 594 were deaf or partially deaf, and 1,044 were otherwise handicapped.

At Sept. 1981 there were 25 'List D' schools (these establishments correspond to Community Homes in England and Wales) with a total enrolment of 1,134.

Further Education. Centres and colleges for formal further education numbered 187 in 1981–82.

The student population was 206,846, of whom 46,960 attended full-time (advanced courses, 24,538; non-advanced, 22,422) and 159,886 part-time (advanced courses, 27,796; non-advanced, 132,090).

Teacher-Training. In Nov. 1981 there were 4,320 students in 7 colleges of education on pre-service courses of teacher-training.

Finance. Total expenditure on education met from revenue in 1981–82 was £1,289·3m. (excluding university education and loan charges).

Independent Schools. Outside the state system of education there were in England nearly 2,350 independent schools in Jan. 1984, ranging from large 'public' schools to small local ones. There were (Jan. 1983) 510,074 full-time and 13,191 part-time pupils in these schools. In Wales 11,680 full-time pupils attended 72 independent schools. Fees are charged by all these schools, which receive no grant from central government sources. All independent schools in England are required to be registered by the Department and are liable to the inspection by HM Inspector. The term 'public schools' refers to independent schools in membership of the Headmasters' Conference, Governing Bodies Association or the Governing Bodies of Girls' Schools Association. Qualifications under which a school may be represented at the Headmasters' Conference include the measure of independence enjoyed by the governing body and the amount of advanced courses undertaken. Some of these schools are for boarders only, but the majority include non-resident 'day-pupils'. In Scotland there were 95 independent schools, with a total of 16,652 pupils in Sept. 1978. A small number of the Scottish independent schools are of the 'public school' type but they are not known as 'public schools' since in Scotland this term is used to denote education authority (i.e., state) schools.

The earliest of the schools were founded by, and attached to, the medieval churches. Many were founded as 'grammar' (classical) schools in the 16th century, receiving charters from the reigning sovereign. Reformed mainly in the middle of the 19th century, these schools now provide the highest form of English pre-university education. Among the most well-known independent schools are Eton College, founded in 1440 by Henry VI, with 1,250 boys; Winchester College, 1394, founded by William of Wykeham, Bishop of Winchester, 600 boys; Harrow School, founded in 1560 as a grammar school by John Lyon, a yeoman, 740 boys; Charterhouse, 1611, 670 boys. Among the earliest foundations are King's School, Canterbury, founded 600; King's School, Rochester, 604; St Peter's, York, 627.

Universities. In *England* there are 33 traditional degree-giving universities. In addition there are the University of Manchester Institute of Science and Technology; the London and Manchester Business Schools and the Open University. Eight new universities have been established since 1961.

In *Wales* there is 1 university, the University of Wales, with colleges at Aberystwyth, Bangor, Cardiff, Lampeter and Swansea. The Welsh National School of Medicine is a school of the University, and the University of Wales Institute of Science and Technology became a constituent college in Nov. 1967.

In *Scotland* there are 8 universities, Aberdeen, Dundee, Edinburgh, Stirling, Strathclyde, Heriot-Watt, Glasgow and St Andrews. The Carnegie Trust for Scottish Universities (founded, 1901) has a capital (1980) of £7m. and an annual income of £490,000; 50% of the income is devoted to the improvement and expansion of Scottish Universities and 50% to assist students with their fees.

All these universities and colleges are independent, self-governing institutions, although they receive substantial aid from the State (in the case of the Open University by direct grant from the Department of Education and Science, and the traditional universities through the University Grants Committee). The UGC is a committee appointed by the Secretary of State for Education and Science designed to advise the Government on the needs of the universities, and to prepare plans for future development. The members are drawn from education and industry. The Government receives advice on the universities' requirements for central computing facilities from the Computer Board for the Universities and Research Councils whose members are also drawn from the universities and industry.

The Royal College of Art and the Cranfield Institute of Technology are primarily postgraduate institutions which award higher degrees under charters granted in 1967 and 1969 respectively. They receive grants direct from the Department of Education and Science.

The local education authorities have no responsibility for universities.

The Open University received its Royal Charter on 1 June 1969 and is an independent, self-governing institution, awarding its own degrees. It is financed by the

Government through the Department of Education and Science and by the receipt of students' fees.

Tuition is by means of correspondence textbooks, radio and television broadcasts and summer schools. Students can also attend one of 288 local study centres. No formal qualifications are required for entry to undergraduate or associate student courses.

Anyone resident in the UK aged 21 or over may apply. There are 134 undergraduate courses; many are available on a one-off basis to associate students.

In 1983 it had some 65,000 undergraduates, about 29,000 continuing education students and some 700 postgraduate students. The university has 2,900 full-time staff working at its Milton Keynes headquarters and in 13 regional offices throughout the country. There are 5,000 part-time tutors and counsellors.

The University of Buckingham, formerly the University College at Buckingham offers two-year degree courses. The academic year commencing in Jan. and consisting of four ten-week terms. There are three-year courses in European Studies, where an intercalated year is spent abroad. There are four Schools of Studies: Accounting, Business, and Economics; Humanities; Law; and Sciences. A number of postgraduate courses are also offered. In 1983, there were 507 full-time students. Opened in 1976, the University of Buckingham received its Royal Charter in March 1983.

All universities charge fees, but financial help is available to students from several sources.

The universities themselves provide scholarships of various kinds and all local education authorities have a system of awards to help suitable students to attend university.

The amount of aid given generally depends upon the parents' means. The majority of the students at the English and Welsh universities are in receipt of some form of financial assistance.

Awards known as state studentships are offered on a competitive basis by the Department from among candidates considered by the universities and other higher education institutions to be qualified for post-graduate studies in the humanities; similar awards, tenable at universities or other higher education institutions, are offered by the Research Councils to students studying science, mathematics and technology at post-graduate level.

The following table gives the approximate number of professors, lecturers, etc., and students (full-time and sandwich courses) for 1981–82:

University or college	Students	Staff	University or college	Students	Staff
Aston	5,057	617	Reading	5,780	743
Bath	3,614	453	Salford	4,347	502
Birmingham	8,848	1,455	Sheffield	7,907	1,098
Bradford	4,873	574	Southampton	6,200	1,041
Bristol	7,067	1,145	Surrey	3,316	489
Brunel	2,838	356	Sussex	4,469	634
Cambridge	11,663	1,213	Warwick	5,320	640
City	2,776	341	York	3,436	397
Durham	4,813	587			
East Anglia	4,334	506	*Wales*—		
Essex	3,208	340	Aberystwyth U.C.	3,232	444
Exeter	5,055	593	Bangor U.C.	2,983	415
Hull	5,619	587	Cardiff U.C.	5,514	701
Keele	2,881	334	St David's, Lampeter	765	71
Kent	4,197	461	Swansea U.C.	3,887	509
Lancaster	4,612	547	Welsh Nat. School of		
Leeds	10,914	1,367	Medicine	728	274
Leicester	4,855	616	Univ. of Wales Institute of		
Liverpool	8,066	1,160	Science and Technology	2,945	324
London Business School	232	62			
London	40,873	7,899	*Scotland*—		
Loughborough	5,403	620	Aberdeen	5,557	867
Manchester Business School	176	50	Dundee	3,272	532
Manchester	11,325	1,646	Edinburgh	9,898	1,476
Univ. of Manchester Inst. of			Glasgow	9,996	1,458
Science and Technology	4,504	649	Heriot-Watt	3,186	382
Newcastle	7,726	1,114	St Andrews	3,426	387
Nottingham	7,055	944	Stirling	2,743	305
Oxford	11,803	1,989	Strathclyde	6,876	926

Women students are admitted on equal terms with men. Number of women students: England, 88.692; Wales, 8,014; Scotland, 18,661. There are, however, colleges exclusively for female students at Oxford and Cambridge. Total number of full-time or sandwich students at universities listed above: England, 235,187; Wales, 20,054; Scotland, 44,954; total, 300,195.

McIntosh, N. E., Calder, J.A. and Swift, B., *A Degree of Difference.* London, 1976
Perry, W., *Open University: A Personal Account.* Open Univ. Press, 1976
Tunstall, J., *The Open University.* London, 1974

The British Council. The British Council was established in Nov. 1934 and incorporated by Royal Charter in 1940. Its aims are the promotion of an enduring understanding and appreciation of Britain in other countries through cultural, educational and technical co-operation.

The Council's expenditure in 1981–82 amounted to £147·1m. Funds were provided by a grant-in-aid of £34·1m. from the Overseas Information (Foreign and Commonwealth Office) Vote and a contribution of £19·4m. from the Overseas Aid Vote. A further £57·4m. was provided by the Overseas Development Administration to cover the cost of administration of, and the reimbursement of sums expended on technical co-operation schemes. The balance of £36·2m. was derived from Council earnings and from international agencies, overseas governments, etc. for educational services.

The Council is governed by a board consisting of up to 30 members, 2 of whom are nominated by Ministers. There are advisory committees for Scotland and Wales and also advisory committees for the main branches of the Council's work. In Jan. 1983 the Council had staff in 81 countries.

The Council is designated by the British Government to carry out over 30 bilateral cultural agreements, including that with the Soviet Union. The Council's work broadly divides into English language teaching; education and training; the development of university links and interchange; the promotion of wider use and availability of British books and periodicals; the development of personal contacts and the provision of information abroad on British experience and resources in the fields of education, medicine, science, technology and the arts.

The general policy in the field of English language teaching is to advise and assist education authorities overseas, particularly in curriculum and materials development and the training of local teachers of English; courses are provided in Britain and abroad for the further training of English language teaching experts from overseas. In many countries the Council runs its own English teaching centres. The Council acts as a centre for the dissemination of information about British educational thought and practice at all levels and, through its complement of education specialists working overseas, it has become closely involved with the administration of aid on behalf of the Overseas Development Administration. It assists in producing English teaching and other educational television and radio programmes overseas and arranges overseas consultancies and training in TV, radio and the application of media to development both in Britain and overseas. A prominent aspect of its education work is the assistance given in developing countries to the adoption of modern and locally relevant methods of science and mathematics teaching in schools. Following the merger with TETOC in 1982, the Council is responsible for advising ODA on its policies in the fields of technical education, industrial training, agricultural education, public administration and management development. Over 850 lecturers etc., mainly in the field of English language, are working overseas, having been recruited by the British Council on behalf of universities, schools, etc. in over 100 different countries. The Council is concerned to promote closer international academic collaboration through a variety of interchange and linking schemes, and through the provision of information and advice on educational institutions; it also administers the British Government's Technical Co-operation Training Programme and scholarship programmes on behalf of a large number of international organizations, notably UN and EEC. It administers examinations on behalf of a number of British examining boards.

During recent years the Council has collaborated with British educational institutions and firms in designing and implementing a wide range of education projects, for which overseas authorities or multilateral agencies pay the full cost.

The sciences, including medicine, technology and agriculture, form an increasingly important part of Council work. Contacts are built up and information collected and distributed through the specialist departments in London and the qualified scientists serving overseas, who also advise on training in Britain and the provision of experts abroad.

The importance of the arts as a medium for fostering cultural relations is reflected in the Council's encouragement of the appreciation of British achievements in the performing and the visual arts, both by supporting local activity and by sending theatre and ballet companies, orchestras and chamber groups, and exhibitions both of fine arts, crafts and photographs, from Britain on tours overseas. The Council also produces booklets, records and tapes on a wide range of literary and artistic subjects and in addition makes extensive use of films and video cassettes in support of its arts and educational work.

The Council runs, or is associated with, over 100 libraries in the countries in which it is represented. It arranges touring exhibitions of new British books and periodicals (some 80,000 books were exhibited in 269 exhibitions 1982–83). Additional publicity for British books is provided by the publication *British Book News*, and the distribution of specialized book lists. The Council also administers ODA funds (approximately £2·6m. in 1982–83) for the presentation of books to educational institutions in developing countries and the subsidized publication of low-priced books for students under the imprint of the English Language Book Society.

The Council arranges short advisory tours overseas by British experts. In a number of countries it is also the overseas administrative arm of the British Volunteer Programme. It awards scholarships and bursaries and arranges study programmes for some 30,000 visitors a year in Britain. It administers central government funds for youth exchanges with other countries.

In Britain the Council administers the programmes of award schemes for overseas students, meets many students on arrival from overseas, and provides an accommodation service for students from overseas for whom it has a special responsibility. The Council runs offices in Britain, mainly in university cities, for these purposes.

The Council is increasingly called on to administer training schemes and educational services financed by overseas authorities, or by multilateral agencies, on a contractual basis. The Council's specialist courses and summer schools provide advanced study in a number of fields, notably medicine, science, literature and the arts, English language and education. Payment is made by the student, or his parent organization, or by some other sponsor.

The Council produces the following periodicals: *British Medical Bulletin, Media in Education and Development* and *British Book News*. Other publications include the series *Writers and their Work, Notes on Literature, British Education, British Books and Libraries;* a number of booklets including *Higher Education in the United Kingdom, Introducing Wales, How to Live in Britain* and *Statistics of Overseas Students in Britain*. The Council has sponsored two major series of literature recordings, *The Complete Works of Shakespeare* and *The English Poets from Chaucer to Yeats*.

Chairman: Sir Charles Troughton, CBE, MC, TD.
Director-General: Sir John Burgh, KCMG, CB.
Headquarters: 10 Spring Gdns., London, SW1A 2BN.

Arts Council of Great Britain. The Arts Council is an independent organization established by Royal Charter in 1946, and is the principal channel for British Government aid to the arts. The Council's objects are to develop and improve the knowledge, understanding and practice of the arts, to increase their accessibility to the public, and to advise and co-operate with government departments, local authorities and other organizations.

The Council consists of a Chairman and not more than 19 other members who are appointed by the Minister for the Arts, after consultation with the Secretaries of State for Scotland and Wales. The Council is advised by panels and committees concerned with different aspects of the arts. With the approval of the appropriate Minister, the Council appoints committees for Scotland and Wales known respectively as the Scottish Arts Council and the Welsh Arts Council.

The Council receives a grant-in-aid from the Government voted annually by Parliament. The grant-in-aid for 1984–85 is £100m., including £1·4m. for the Housing the Arts Fund.

As well as giving financial help and advice to several hundred artistic organizations from the major opera, dance, drama companies, orchestras and festivals, to the smallest touring theatre and experimental group, the Council encourages such diverse interests as contemporary dance, photography, art films, and helps professional creative writers, dramatists, poets, musicians, composers, artists and photographers by means of bursary and award schemes. The Council provides funds for specialist training courses in the arts, and assists projects for the construction of new buildings, or improvements to existing ones under its 'Housing the Arts' scheme.

A growing proportion of the Council's funds is channelled to the network of regional arts associations which practically covers the whole of England and Wales. The regional arts associations are not branches of the Arts Council, but are autonomous bodies, financed by a combination of Arts Council, local authority and private funds.

The Council mounts art exhibitions at the Hayward and Serpentine and other galleries in London and also in the regions. Other direct promotions include tours of opera and drama companies, of the Council's own films on the arts and of music groups under the Contemporary Music Network scheme. The Council has a library of contemporary British poetry at its headquarters.

Chairman: Sir William Rees-Mogg.
Secretary-General: Luke Rittner.
Headquarters: 105 Piccadilly, London W1V 0AU. *The Scottish Arts Council:* 19–20 Charlotte Sq., Edinburgh, EH2 4DF. *The Welsh Arts Council:* 9 Museum Place, Cardiff, CF1 3NX.

National Insurance. The National Insurance Act, 1946, came into operation on 5 July 1948, repealing the existing schemes of health, pensions and unemployment insurance. This Act, along with later legislation, was consolidated as the National Insurance Act, 1965.

The Social Security Act 1975 introduced, from 6 April 1975, a new system of national insurance contributions to replace the previous system of flat-rate and graduated contributions. Since 6 April 1975, Class 1 contributions have been related to the employee's earnings and are collected with PAYE income tax, instead of by affixing stamps to a card. Class 2 and Class 3 contributions remain flat-rate, but, in addition to Class 2 contributions, those who are self-employed may be liable to pay Class 4 contributions, which for the year 1984–85 will be at the rate of 6·3% on profits or gains between £3,950 and £13,000, which are assessable for income tax under Schedule D. The non-employed and others whose contribution record is not sufficient to give entitlement to benefits are able to pay a Class 3 contribution voluntarily to qualify for a limited range of benefits. Class 2 contributions for 1984–85 are £4·60 a week for men and women. Class 3 contributions are £4·50 a week.

From 6 April 1978 the Social Security Pensions Act 1975 introduced earnings-related retirement, invalidity and widows' pensions. Employee's national insurance contribution liability depends on whether he is in contracted out or not contracted out employment. The not-contracted out employee pays 9% on all earnings up to £250 a week. The employer's rate is 10·45% and a 1·5% surcharge of all earnings. An employee's contracted-out contribution is 9% of the first £34 a week of earnings and 6·85% of earnings between £34 and £250 a week. The employer's contribution is 10·45% (and the 1·5% surcharge) of the first £34 of weekly earnings and 6·35% (and the 1·5% surcharge) of earnings between £34 and £250 a week.

The State supplements the contributions paid by contributors and employers, from general taxation. Contributions (other than the surcharge) and supplement together with interest on investments form the income of the National Insurance Fund from which benefits are paid.

Statutory Sick Pay (SSP). The Social Security and Housing Benefits Act 1982 provides that, from 6 April 1983, employers will be responsible for paying statutory sick pay (SSP) to their employees for up to 8 weeks of sickness absence in a tax year. SSP will replace the employee's entitlement to State sickness benefit which will not be payable as long as any employer's responsibility for SSP remains.

Benefits. The range of benefits are unaffected by the new arrangements from 5 April 1975. The benefits are: (1) Unemployment benefit; (2) Sickness benefit; (3) Invalidity benefit; (4) Maternity benefit; (5) Widow's benefit; (6) Guardian's allowance; (7) Child's special allowance; (8) Retirement pension; (9) Death grant.

Qualification for any benefit depends upon fulfilment of the appropriate contribution conditions employed persons may qualify for or the benefits self-employed may qualify for all except unemployment benefit. Employed persons may qualify for all the benefits; self-employed may qualify for all except unemployment.

Sickness Benefit. From 24 Nov. 1983 the rate is £25·95 a week plus £16 a week for an adult dependant, plus £0·15 for each child for whom child benefit is in payment.

Unemployment Benefit is paid through the local unemployment benefit offices of the Department of Employment. The rate is £27·05 a week plus £16·70 a week for an adult dependant, plus £0·15 for each child for whom child benefit is in payment.

Invalidity Benefit replaces sickness benefit after 168 days of entitlement. It comprises a basic invalidity pension of £32·60 weekly and an invalidity allowance of £7·15 if incapacity began before age 40: £4·60 if incapacity began between 40 and 50 or £2·30 if it began between 50 and 60 (55 for women). Increases are: £19·55 for an adult dependant plus £7·60 for each child for whom child benefit is payable.

Maternity Benefit. For a confinement a woman may receive a maternity grant of £25 and, where 2 or more children are born at the confinement, a further grant of £25 for each additional child who is alive 12 hours after its birth. There are no contribution conditions. The grant is paid on the satisfaction of a simple 'presence in Great Britain' test by the mother. If the woman has been gainfully employed or self-employed, and has paid sufficient full-rate national insurance contributions in the relevant income tax year, she may receive a maternity allowance of £25·95 a week normally payable for 18 weeks commencing 11 weeks before the expected week of confinement, provided she does not work during this period. Maternity allowance may be increased in certain circumstances in respect of dependants in the same way as sickness and unemployment benefits.

Widow's Benefit. On her husband's death a widow normally qualifies for 26 weeks for an allowance of £47·65 a week for herself plus an increase of £7·60 a week for each child for whom child benefit is payable. At the end of the 26 weeks she may qualify for a widowed mother's allowance of £34·05 for herself, and the increases for the children for whom child benefit is payable continue at the same rate as for the first 26 weeks of widowhood. She may also receive her allowance at the personal rate of £34·05 a week if she has living with her a son or daughter who is under 19. The child increase for widow's allowance and widowed mother's allowance is, generally speaking, payable only in respect of a child for whom child benefit is payable.

A widow's pension may be paid to: (i) A widow after the termination of her widow's allowance, if she does not qualify for widowed mother's allowance and was aged 40 or more when her husband died; (ii) A widow after she ceases to be entitled to a widowed mother's allowance if she is then aged 40 or more. The standard rate of this pension is £34·05 a week if the widow was 50 or more when her husband died or when her entitlement to widowed mother's allowance ended. If she was between 40 and 50, however, the standard rates of total pension range in 7% steps from 93% of the full age-50 rate (*i.e.*, £31·67 a week) for the widow who was 49 at that time to 30% (*i.e.*, £10·22 a week) for the widow who was then 40.

Child's Special Allowance. An allowance may be payable for the children of divorced parents where the father has died. It is payable to the mother if she has not remarried and her former husband was contributing, or legally liable to contribute, at least 25p a week towards the children's support in cash or kind or if she took reasonable steps to enforce maintenance and she was entitled to child benefit for the child(ren) when her former husband died or it is her child by her former husband and he was entitled to child benefit for the child(ren) when he died. It is similar to the increases for widow's children and is payable at the same rates.

Guardian's Allowance. A person who is responsible for an orphan child may be entitled to a guardian's allowance of £7·60 a week in addition to the amount of child benefit payable in respect of that child. Normally both the child's parents must be dead but when the child is illegitimate, or the parents were divorced, or one parent is missing, or serving a long sentence of imprisonment, the allowance may, in certain circumstances, be paid on the death of one parent only.

Retirement Pension. In order to receive a retirement pension, men between 65 and 70, and women between 60 and 65 must have retired from regular employment. From 6 April 1979 a woman divorced over the age of 60 must satisfy the retired conditions before a pension is payable. The standard rates of basic pensions are £34·05 a week for a man or woman on his or her own contributions and £20·45 for a married woman through her husband's contributions. Proportionately reduced pensions are payable where contribution records are deficient. For a person who reaches pension age on or after 6 April 1979, additional pension may also be payable. This is based on the earnings on which he or she has paid Class 1 contributions in each complete tax year between April 1978 and pension age. If the person has been a member of a contracted-out occupational pension scheme, that scheme will be responsible for paying the whole or part of the additional pension. An increase of £20·45 a week may be payable for a dependent wife. If she resides with the beneficiary the increase is gradually reduced for earnings over £45 a week. If she does not reside with the beneficiary an increase is not payable if she earns more than £20·45 a week. In addition £7·60 a week may be payable for each child for whom child benefit is payable. In certain circumstances an increase of £20·45 a week may be payable for a woman having care of the pensioner's children. In addition, a man who had paid graduated contributions receives 4·44p per week for every £7·50 of graduated contributions paid, and a woman 4·44p per week for every £9 paid. Although no further graduated contributions have been paid after April 1975, pension already earned will be paid along with the basic pension in the normal way. If, after being awarded a retirement pension, a man under 70 or a woman under 65 earns more than £65 in a calendar week the pension for the next pension week, including any increase for dependants, will be reduced by 5p for every 10p earned between £65 and £69 and by 5p for every 5p earned over £69. If retirement is postponed after minimum pension age increments of basic pension can be earned for periods of deferred retirement. Between 6 April 1975 and 5 April 1979 increments were earned at the rate of one-eighth penny per £1 of the pension rate for every 6 days (excluding Sundays) for which the pension had been foregone. From 6 April 1979 increments are earned at the rate of one-seventh penny per £1 of basic pension for every 6 days (excluding Sundays) for which pension has been foregone. Any days for which another benefit has been paid will not count. These increments must be at least 1% of the pension rate unless the minimum was earned under the arrangements which applied before 6 April 1979. For periods between 6 April 1975 and that date, the rate was one-eighth penny per £1 of the basic pension rate for every 6 days and for periods of deferred retirement before 6 April 1975 increments were based on the number of contributions paid as an employed or self-employed person. At age 70 for a man (65 for a woman) the pension for which a person has qualified may be paid in full whether a person continues in work or not irrespective of the amount of earnings. At the age of 80 an age addition of £0·25 a week is payable. In addition non-contributory pensions are now payable, subject to residence conditions, to persons aged 80 and over who do not qualify for a retirement pension or qualify for one at a low rate. The rates of these pensions, which are financed by Exchequer funds, are £20·45 a week for a single person and £12·25 for a married woman. These amounts do not include the £0·25 age addition.

Death Grant. This is a lump sum paid on the death of an insured person or his close relative. The normal amount of the payment is: For an adult, £30; for a child aged 6 but under 18, £22·50; for a child aged 3 but under 6, £15; for a child under 3, £9. For the death of a person who was within 10 years of pensionable age on 5 July 1948 (*i.e.,* a man over 55 and a woman over 50 on that date) only half the standard amount is payable. No grant is payable for the death of a person who was over the pensionable age on 5 July 1948.

The Industrial Injuries Provisions of the Social Security Act, 1975. The Industrial Injuries Act, which also came into operation on 5 July 1948, with its later amending Acts, was consolidated as the National Insurance (Industrial Injuries) Act, 1965. This legislation was incorporated in the Social Security Act, 1975. The scheme provides a system of insurance against 'personal injury by accident arising out of and in the course of employment' and against certain prescribed diseases and injuries due to the nature of the employment. It takes the place of the Workmen's Compensation Acts and covers persons who are employed earners under the Social Security Act. There are no contribution conditions for the payment of benefit. Three types of benefit are provided:

(1) Disablement benefit. This is payable where, as the result of an industrial accident or prescribed disease, there is a loss of faculty. The loss of faculty will be assessed as a percentage by comparison with a person of the same age and sex whose condition is normal. If the assessment is 20%, or more, benefit will be a pension varying according to the assessment, from £11·12 a week to £55·60 a week. If the assessment is under 20% benefit will normally be a gratuity of an amount not exceeding £3,690. Unemployability supplement plus age additions similar to invalidity allowance, may be payable to a disablement pensioner who, as a result of the relevant loss of faculty is incapable of work and likely to remain permanently so incapable. Increases for dependants at the same rates as for invalidity pension are also payable to a disablement pensioner who is entitled to unemployability supplement. The supplement cannot be paid at the same time as certain other benefits payable under the Social Security Act or out of public funds. Other increases of disablement benefit may be payable *(i)* where the loss of faculty causes special hardship, *i.e.,* it prevents the beneficiary from undertaking his regular job or one of an equivalent standard of earnings; *(ii)* there is a need for constant attendance; *(iii)* there is exceptionally severe disablement and the need for constant attendance is likely to be permanent; or *(iv)* disablement is assessed at less than 100% and the beneficiary is in hospital for treatment for his injury or prescribed disease. Pensions for persons under 18 are at a reduced rate. When injury benefit was abolished for industrial accidents occurring and prescribed diseases commencing on or after 6 April 1983, a common start date was introduced for the payment of disablement benefit 90 days (excluding Sundays) after the date of the relevant accident or onset of the disease.

(2) Death Benefit. On the death of a person as the result of an industrial accident or a prescribed disease, certain dependants may qualify for benefit. Benefit for a widow is a pension normally of £47·65 weekly for the first 26 weeks and thereafter £34·60, depending on such factors as age, entitlement to a child's allowance and permanent incapacity for self-support. If the conditions for pension at the higher rate are not satisfied the widow may receive a pension of £10·22 a week. Child allowances may be payable to the widow, or other person, entitled to child benefit for children of the deceased. For widows, these allowances are usually at the rate of £7·60 a week for each child; for other persons, the rate is £0·15 for each child. An allowance of £1 is payable to a woman having care of a child of the deceased. Benefit for widowers, parents and certain other relatives takes the form of pensions, allowances or gratuities according to the relationship to, and degree of maintenance by, the deceased.

War Pensions. The number of beneficiaries in receipt of war (1914–18) pensions or allowances as at 30 Oct. 1983 was 23,100. The number of beneficiaries in receipt of war (1939–45 and later) pensions or allowances in payment as at 30 Oct. 1983 was 293,400. The expenditure for both wars for 1982–83 was £504m. The expenditure is exclusive of administrative expenses.

National Insurance Fund. At 1 April 1982 the balance of the National Insurance Fund amounted to £4,046,465,000. Income during the period 1 April 1982 to 31 March 1983, consisting of contributions from insured persons and employers, payments from the Exchequer and interest on investments, etc., was £19,393·009m. Payments of benefit in respect of unemployment were £1,499,648,000; sickness, £494,456,000; invalidity, £1,593,181,000; maternity, £153m.; widows, £725m.; guardian's allowance and child's special allowance, £2·2m.; retirement pension, £13,548,856,000; death grants, £16,935,000; injury benefit, £46,469,000; disablement benefits, £343,535,000; death benefit, £51m. Included in these figures are the following estimated amounts of graduated retirement benefit, £252m.; additional component, £90m.; earning related supplement having ceased. Administrative and other payments cost approximately £941,833,000. The balance at 31 March 1981 was £4,023,461,000.

From 1 April 1975 the National Insurance Reserve Fund and the Industrial Injuries Fund were merged with the National Insurance Fund. All basic scheme contributions payable under the 1975 Social Security Act are paid into the single fund out of which the existing range of benefits will continue to be financed. The new national insurance fund will continue to receive a Treasury Supplement set at a level of 13% of total contribution income.

Child Benefit. Child benefit is a tax-free cash allowance for all children. The weekly rate for each child is £6·50 from Nov. 1983. Child benefit is payable for all children under age 16 and for those under age 19 receiving full-time non-advanced education at a college or school. One Parent Benefit. This is a tax-free cash allowance for certain people bringing up children alone. It is payable for the first or only child in the family in addition to child benefit. The weekly rate from Nov. 1983 is £4·05.

Family Income Supplement. Family income supplement is payable to families with at least 1 dependent child where the man or woman is in remunerative work for at least 30 hours a week (24 hours for lone parents), and where the family's normal gross weekly income (but excluding child benefits) is below a prescribed amount. The prescribed amount for a 1-child family is £85·50, this amount being increased by £9·50 for each additional child in the family. The weekly rate of benefit payable is one-half of the difference between the prescribed amount and the family's normal income, subject to a maximum weekly payment of £22 for families with 1 child, increasing by £2 for each additional child. Benefit is usually payable for 52 weeks and is not affected by changes in circumstances. The prescribed amounts are the same for both 1- and 2-parent families.

Attendance allowance. This is a tax-free allowance for severely disabled people, including children aged 2 or over, who require a lot of help from another person. There are 2 rates, the higher rate of £27·20 a week for those who require attention or supervision by day and night, and the lower rate of £18·15 a week for those who need the attendance either by day or night. In addition to the medical requirements a simple test of residence and presence in Great Britain must also be satisfied.

Invalid Care Allowance. May be paid to those under pensionable age who stay at home to care for a person who is receiving attendance allowance or constant attendance allowance. In general married women do not qualify for this benefit. Current rate £20·45 a week, with increases for dependants.

Supplementary Benefit. Under the Supplementary Benefits Act, 1976, as amended by the Social Security Act 1980, benefit is payable to any persons in Great Britain aged 16 years or over (excluding persons at school or college or anyone directly involved in a trade dispute) who are not in full-time remunerative work and who are without resources, or whose resources (including national insurance benefits) need to be supplemented in order to meet their requirements. A person who is excluded from benefit under the normal rules may, nevertheless, receive payments to meet urgent need. The general standards by reference to which supplementary benefit is granted are determined by statutory regulations approved by Parliament. Persons who are dissatisfied with the amount of benefit granted to them may appeal to an independent Appeal Tribunal established under the Act.

During the financial year 1980–81 net payments on supplementary benefit amounted to £2,859m.

Newman, T. S., *Digest of British Social Insurance*. London, 1947 (and supplements, to date)

National Health. The National Health Service in England and Wales started on 5 July 1948 under the National Health Service Act, 1946. There is a separate Act for Scotland and also one for Northern Ireland, where the Health Services are run on similar lines to those in England and Wales.

The National Health Service, which is available to every man, woman and child, is a charge on the national income in the same way as the armed forces and other facilities.

Every person normally resident in this country is entitled to use any complete part of the services, and no insurance qualification is necessary.

Most of the cost of running the service is met from the national exchequer, *i.e.*, from taxes.

Since Sept. 1957 a small weekly National Health Service contribution has been payable by contributors and where applicable by their employers. For convenience this contribution is collected with the National Insurance contribution and for 1982–83 is estimated to be £1,618m. for Great Britain.

Organization. Under the provisions of the Health Service Act 1980, the administration of the National Health Service in England and Wales is organized under a system of regional and district health authorities accountable to the Secretary of State for the Social Services and the Secretary of State for Wales. In Scotland the National Health Service is administered under the National Health Service (Scotland) Act 1978, by 15 Health Boards and a Common Services Agency all accountable to the Secretary of State for Scotland.

There are 192 district health authorities in England responsible for the administration and development of health services in their district. Fourteen regional health authorities, each consisting of a number of health districts, are responsible for allocating resources between the district health authorities in their regions and for monitoring their performance. The regional authorities are responsible for developing strategic plans and priorities and for carrying out certain executive functions.

Services. The National Health Service broadly consists of hospital and specialist services, general medical, dental and ophthalmic services, pharmaceutical services, community health services and school health services. All these services are free of charge except for such things as prescriptions, spectacles, dentures and dental treatment, amenity beds in hospitals and for some of the community services, for which charges are made with certain exemptions.

The total cost of the Health and Personal Social Services (Great Britain) is estimated at £17,483m. for 1982–83 and the estimated net expenditure by the Exchequer (except for the Local Authority Personal Social Services, where the rates and the Exchequer grants are estimated at about £2,341m.) in 1982–83 is £12,651m.

The provisional number of abortions performed in 1982 under the provisions of the Abortion Act, 1967, was 162,797, of which 128,328 related to England and Wales residents. Of these 128,328 abortions, 71,717 (55·9%) were to single women, 40,427 (31·5%) were to married women, and 16,184 (12·6%) were to widowed, divorced or separated women and to women who did not state their marital status.

The number of abortion notifications received in Scotland in 1982 under the provisions of the Abortion Act 1967, was 8,372, of which 8,345 related to Scottish residents. Of these 8,372 notifications, 4,793 (57·3%) were to single women, 2,605

(31·1%) were to married women, and 974 (11·6%) were to widowed, divorced or separated women and to women who did not state their marital status.

In 1977 there were 26,810 general medical practitioners, 13,564 general dental practitioners and 219,900 qualified nurses and midwives. There were (1977) 469,849 allocated hospital beds.

Personal Social Services. Under the Local Authority Social Services Act 1970 and in Scotland the Social Work (Scotland) Act 1968 the welfare and social work services provided by local authorities were made the responsibility of a new local authority department—the Social Services Department in England and Wales, and Social Work Departments in Scotland headed by a Director of Social Work. The social services thus administered include: the fostering, care and adoption of children, welfare services and social workers for the mentally disordered, the disabled and the aged, and accommodation for those needing residential care services. In Scotland the social work departments' functions also include the supervision of persons on probation, of adult offenders and of persons released from penal institutions or subject to fine supervision orders.

The number of persons in residential and temporary accommodation provided by or on behalf of local authorities was as follows:

England and Wales (31 March)	Residential accommodation Adults	Scotland (31 March)	Residential accommodation Adults and Children
1980	136,337	1980	16,810
1981	135,101	1981	16,446
1982	134,152	1982	15,823
1983 [1]	132,748		

[1] Estimate.

England and Wales. Expenditure and income relating to the personal social services administered by local authorities (in £1,000 sterling):

Year ended 31 March	Gross current expenditure	Income from sales, fees and charges	Net current expenditure
1978	1,178,771	189,018	989,753
1979	1,335,252	214,757	1,120,495
1980	1,623,607	247,696	1,375,911
1981	1,997,767	294,710	1,703,057
1982 [1]	2,214,750	327,152	1,887,598

[1] Provisional.

Scotland. The total local authority expenditure for 1980–81 in respect of residential accommodation and welfare services under the Social Work (Scotland) Act, 1968, was £268·3m. Central Government expenditure on social work totalled £10·5m.

Klein, R., *The Politics of the National Health Service.* London, 1983
Watkin, B., *The National Health Service.* London, 1978

DIPLOMATIC REPRESENTATIVES

Of the USA in Great Britain (Grosvenor Sq., London, W1A 1AE)
Ambassador: John J. Louis, Jr.

Of Great Britain in the USA (3100 Massachusetts Ave., Washington, D.C., 20008)
Ambassador: Sir Oliver Wright, GCVO, DSC.

Of Great Britain to the United Nations
Ambassador: Sir John Thomson, KCMG.

Books of Reference

The annual and other publications of the various Public Departments, and the Reports, etc. of Royal Commissions and Parliamentary Committees. (These may be obtained from HM Stationery Office.)
Bickmore, D. P., and Shaw, M. A. (ed.), *The Atlas of Great Britain and Northern Ireland.* OUP, 1963

Burn, D., *The Structure of British Industry.* 2 vols. CUP, 1958
Central Statistical Office. *Annual Abstract of Statistics.* HMSO.—*Monthly Digest of Statistics.* HMSO
Central Office of Information. *Britain: An Official Handbook.* HMSO, annual.
Demangeon, A., *The British Isles.* 3rd ed. London, 1952
Directory of British Associations. Beckenham, annual
Government Statistical Service. *Social Trends.* HMSO.—*Regional Statistics.* HMSO
Halsey, A. H., *Trends in British Society Since 1900.* London, 1972
History of the Second World War. HMSO, 1949 ff.
Jenkin, M., *British Industry and the North Sea.* London, 1981
Kendall, M. G. (ed.), *The Source and Nature of the Statistics of the United Kingdom.* 2 vols. London, 1952–1957
Mitchell, B. R., *Abstract of British Historical Statistics.* OUP, 1962
Oxford History of England. 15 vols. OUP, 1936 ff.
Stamp, L. D., and Beaver, S. H., *The British Isles: A Geographic and Economic Survey.* 4th ed., London, 1954
Woodward, Sir E. L., and Butler, R., *Documents on British Foreign Policy, 1919–39.* HMSO, 1957 ff.

Scotland

Scottish Council (Development and Industry). *Inquiry into the Scottish Economy, 1900–61.* Edinburgh, 1961
Scottish Office. *Scottish Economic Bulletin.* HMSO (quarterly).—*Scottish Abstract of Statistics.* HMSO (annual)
The New Scottish Local Authorities: Organisation and Management Structures. HMSO, 1973
Brand, J., *The National Movement in Scotland.* London, 1978
Campbell, R. H., *The Rise and Fall of Scottish Industry, 1707–1939.* Edinburgh, 1981
Donaldson, G. (ed.) *The Edinburgh History of Scotland.* 4 vols. Edinburgh, 1965–75
Drucker, N. and H. M., *The Scottish Government Year Book.* London, 1980
Grant, E., *Scotland.* [Bibliography] Oxford and Santa Barbara, 1982
Hogg, A., and Hutcheson, A. MacG., *Scotland and Oil.* 2nd ed. Edinburgh, 1975
Johnston, T. L., *Structure and Growth in the Scottish Economy.* London, 1971
Kellas, J. G., *The Scottish Political System.* 2nd ed. CUP, 1975
Meikle, H. W. (ed.), *Scotland: A Description of Scotland and Scottish Life.* London, 1947
Turnock, D., *Patterns of Highland Development.* London, 1970

Wales

Wales: The Way Ahead (Cmnd 3334.) HMSO, 1971
Wales: Employment and the Economy. Cardiff, 1972
Digest of Welsh Statistics. HMSO (annual)
Thomas, B. (ed.), *The Welsh Economy.* Cardiff, 1962
Williams, D., *A History of Modern Wales.* New ed. London, 1977
Williams, G., (ed.) *Social and Cultural Change in Contemporary Wales.* London, 1978

NORTHERN IRELAND

AREA AND POPULATION. Area (revised by the Ordnance Survey Department) and population at the census of 5 April 1981 were as follows:

District	Population 1981	Area (Hectares)
Antrim	44,384	40,527
Ards	57,626	36,779
Armagh	47,618	66,733
Ballymena	54,426	63,384
Ballymoney	22,873	41,687
Banbridge	29,885	44,131
Belfast	295,223	13,017
Carrickfergus	28,458	8,484
Castlereagh	60,757	8,441
Coleraine	46,272	47,763
Cookstown	26,624	51,207
Craigavon	71,202	27,989
Down	52,869	63,835
Dungannon	41,073	76,266
Fermanagh	51,008	169,952
Larne	28,929	33,744

District	Population 1981	Area (Hectares)
Limavady	26,270	58,523
Lisburn	82,091	43,595
Londonderry [1]	83,384	37,258
Magherafelt	30,825	56,186
Moyle	14,252	49,378
Newry and Mourne	72,243	88,589
Newtownabbey	71,631	15,108
North Down	65,849	7,241
Omagh	41,159	112,354
Strabane	35,028	86,090
Northern Ireland	1,481,959	1,348,261

[1] Name changed to Derry in 1984.

Vital statistics for calendar years:

	Marriages	Divorces	Births	Deaths
1978	10,304	599	26,239	16,153
1979	10,214	757	28,178	16,811
1980	9,923	896	28,582	16,835
1981 [1]	9,636	775	27,302	16,256
1982 [1]	8,237 [2]	1,383	27,028	15,918

[1] Provisional. [2] Jan.–Sept.

CONSTITUTION AND GOVERNMENT. The Northern Ireland Constitution Act 1973 as amended by the Northern Ireland Constitution (Amendment) Act 1973 and the Northern Ireland Assembly Act 1973 provide for a Northern Ireland Assembly of 78 members and a Northern Ireland Executive of not more than 11 members (including the Chief Executive Member). The Secretary of State appointed this full number to take office from 1 Jan. 1974. He may also, under the Amendment Act, appoint others to carry out particular functions in the Administration up to a total (including members of the Executive) of 15. This additional number were appointed.

Devolution of legislative and executive responsibility to the Northern Ireland Assembly and the new Administration under Section 2 of the Constitution Act was given effect by the Northern Ireland Constitution (Devolution) Order 1973 from 1 Jan. 1974 ('the appointed day'). On that day, Section 1 of the Northern Ireland (Temporary Provisions) Act 1972 expired and, with it, the power to legislate for Northern Ireland by Order in Council under that Act.

Power to make laws (to be known as Measures) in respect of 'transferred' matters, that is on matters other than those listed in Schedules 2 and 3 to the Constitution Act was vested in the Assembly subject to the overriding power of the UK Parliament to legislate on such matters and subject to Section 17 of the Constitution Act which declares void any provision which discriminates against any person or class of persons on the ground of religious belief or political opinion. The procedure for Measures is set out in the Standing Orders of the Assembly. All Measures require the approval of the Queen in Council before they become law. The first election of Members to the 78 seats in the Northern Ireland Assembly was held in 1973. The state of the parties following the election was: Social Democratic and Labour Party 19; Democratic Unionist Loyalist Coalition 8; Official Unionist 24; Northern Ireland Labour 1; Other Unionist 8; Alliance 8; Vanguard Unionist Coalition 7; Other Loyalist Coalition 2; Other Loyalist 1. Northern Ireland also returns 17 members to the UK House of Commons. In the general election, June 1983, the Official Unionists won 11 seats; Democratic Unionists, 3; Popular Unionist Party, 1; Social Democratic and Labour Party, 1; Sinn Fein, 1.

On 28 May 1974 the Unionist members of the Administration resigned, as a result of which the Secretary of State terminated the appointments of members, and HM the Queen prorogued the Assembly for a period of 4 months (thus preventing it from legislating). Parliament subsequently enacted the Northern Ireland Act 1974 extending the prorogation of the Assembly and providing for its dissolution. The Act also reintroduced the power to legislate for Northern Ireland by Order in Council.

The Assembly was dissolved on 28 March 1975, and an election, provided for under the 1974 Act, of a Constitutional Convention took place on 1 May 1975. The Convention had the purpose of considering what provision for the government of Northern Ireland was likely to command the most wide-spread acceptance throughout the community there. The Convention was dissolved on 5 March 1976. Direct rule continues in being under the terms of the Northern Ireland Act 1974.

In Jan. 1980, the main political parties were invited by the Secretary of State to take part in a Conference with the object of seeking the highest level of agreement on the future government of the Province. In Oct. 1982 elections to the new Assembly of 78 members elected by proportional representation took place. Results were: Official Unionists, 26; Democratic Unionists, 21; Social Democratic and Labour Party, 14; Alliance, 10; Sinn Fein, 5; Independent Unionist, 1; Ulster Popular Unionist Party, 1.

What began ostensibly as a Civil Rights campaign in 1968, escalated into a full-scale offensive designed to overthrow the State. This offensive was originally mounted by an illegal organization, the Irish Republican Army (not to be confused with the legitimate Army of the Republic of Ireland). At times counter-measures have required the services of over 20,000 regular troops, in addition to the Royal Ulster Constabulary, the RUC Reserve and the part-time Ulster Defence Regiment.

Secretary of State for Northern Ireland: Right Hon. James Prior, MP.

Local Government. Northern Ireland has a single-tier system of 26 district councils based on main centres of population.

The district councils are responsible for the provision of a wide range of local services including refuse collection and disposal, street cleansing, litter prevention, consumer protection, environmental health, miscellaneous licensing, the provision and management of recreational and cultural facilities, the promotion of tourist development schemes, the enforcement of building regulations and gas supply. They have in addition both a representative role in which they send forward representatives to sit as members of statutory bodies including the Northern Ireland Housing Council, the Fire Authority and the Area Boards for health and personal social services and education and libraries; and a consultative role under which the Department of Environment (NI) and the Northern Ireland Housing Executive, among others, have an obligation to consult them regarding the provision of the regional services for which these bodies are responsible.

The Government's policy for the future development of the Province is contained in the *Regional Physical Development Strategy 1975–95* which was published in May 1977. Basically the policy advocates that the main town in each District Council area should be developed to fulfil its function as the prime centre in the district and for any other specialized rôles it may have such as an industrial centre, port or tourist resort. The Strategy also recognizes that the smaller towns and villages have an important rôle to play, depending on the availability of services, as locations for smaller scale industries service centres and as dormitory centres for people not wishing to live in the towns where they find employment.

The Regional Strategy provides a framework within which development plans can be prepared for all the districts. Since its adoption of the Strategy the Department has been engaged in formulating the detailed policies and proposals for future communications, the location of industry, housing and major services in the light of anticipated population growth and distribution.

A development plan sets down the broad policies and proposals for the development or other use of land in the area covered by the plan over a period of up to 20 years ahead. Development plans have been published for the Belfast Urban Area, North Down, Londonderry, West Tyrone, East Tyrone, Newry, Limavady, Armagh, East Antrim, Magherafelt, Fermanagh, the North East of the Province which incorporates the Coleraine-Portrush-Portstewart area and Lisburn. A review of the Londonderry area plan has also been published.

FINANCE. There exists a separate Northern Ireland Consolidated Fund from which is met the expenditure of Northern Ireland Departments. Its main sources of revenue are: *(i)* The Northern Ireland attributed share of UK taxes; *(ii)* A non-specific grant in aid of Northern Ireland's revenue, payable by the Secretary of State for Northern Ireland; *(iii)* Rates and other receipts of Northern Ireland Departments.

The general principle underlying the financial arrangements is that Northern Ireland should have parity of taxation and services with Great Britain.

Since the financial year 1981–82 the income of the Northern Ireland Consolidated Fund has been as follows (in £ sterling):

	1981–82	1982–83	1983–84
Attributed share of UK taxes	1,475,213,755[1]	1,607,112,320[2]	1,649,500,000[3]
Payments by UK Government:			
Grant in Aid	585,000,000	630,000,000	725,892,000
Refund of value added tax	18,274,933	18,119,788	18,000,000
Regional and district rates	153,950,000	166,150,000	169,000,000
Other receipts	255,517,656	260,262,632	241,054,000
Total	2,487,956,344	2,681,644,740	2,803,446,000

[1] Including final adjustment for 1979–80.
[2] Including final adjustment for 1980–81.
[3] Provisional.

The public debt at 31 March 1983 was as follows: Northern Ireland 7% Exchequer Stock 1982–84, £20m.; Ulster Savings Certificates, £157,556,000; Ulster Development Bonds, £1,825,800; borrowing from UK Government, £707,663,377; borrowing from Northern Ireland Government Funds, £236,764,098; borrowing from bank, £100,000; borrowing from building societies, £12m.; European Investment Bank Loan, £19,209,386; total, £1,155,118,661.

The above amount of public debt is offset by equal assets in the form of loans from Government to public and local bodies and of cash balances.

ENERGY AND NATURAL RESOURCES

Electricity. The planning, generation and distribution of electricity supplies are the responsibility of the Northern Ireland Electricity Service.

The installed capacity of the system is 2,400 mw largely provided from 4 thermal power-stations.

The total sales of electricity in Northern Ireland in the year ended 31 March 1983 amounted to 4,507m. units supplied to a total of 535,983 consumers.

Water Supplies and Sewerage. The Water Service Division of the Department of the Environment (NI) is responsible for water supply and sewerage. Some 687m. litres (151m. gallons) of water a day are supplied throughout the Province. More than 95% of the population have a mains supply of water and about 90% live in property connected to public sewers.

The Department is also responsible for the conservation and planned development of water resources in Northern Ireland.

Minerals. The output of minerals (in 1,000 tonnes) during 1982 was approximately: Basalt and igneous rock (other than granite), 6,151; grit and conglomerate, 2,524; limestone, 2,609; sand and gravel, 3,665; and other minerals (rocksalt, flint, sandstone, diatomite, granite, chalk, clay and shale), 699.

Agriculture. Estimated gross output in 1982:

	Quantity (1,000)	Value (£m.)			Quantity (1,000)	Value (£m.)
Fat cattle	463	220·6	Grass seed		—	—
Calves	14	2·2	Hay and straw		9	0·4
Store cattle	16	5·5	Fruit	tonnes	12	2·9
Exports of breeding head			Vegetables		37	4·0
livestock	10	1·3	Mushrooms		5	5·5
Fat sheep and lambs	630	20·1	Flowers		—	1·9
Fat pigs	1,126	71·9	Other items		—	43·4
Poultry (tonnes)	54	37·2				
Eggs: for human						
consumption (dozen)	93,167	32·4				
Wool (tonnes)	1,712	1·5	Total receipts			658·7
Milk (litres)	1,301,339	179·7	Value of changes in			
Potatoes	258	18·9	stocks due to volume			+5·5
Oats	5	0·5				
Barley tonnes	79	8·6	Gross output			664·2
Wheat	2	0·2				

Area (in 1,000 hectares) of crops at June census (1981 and 1982):

	1981	1982		1981	1982
Oats	3·4	3·1	Other crops	5·0	8·1
Barley	51·0	47·0	Fruit	2·4	2·3
Other cereals and pulses	1·4	1·6	Grass for mowing	252·8	253·3
Potatoes	12·5	13·9	Grass for grazing	501·2	506·0
Turnips, swedes, kale			Rough grazing (excluding		
and cabbage[1]	0·8	0·7	common land)	197·7	189·1
Vegetables	1·2	1·3			

[1] Stock feeding only.

Livestock (1,000) at June census (1981 and 1982):

	1981	1982		1981	1982
Dairy cows	270	280	Total sheep	1,139	1,234
Beef cows	205	197	Breeding sows	65	70
Total cattle	1,436	1,429	Total pigs	627	640
Breeding ewes	575	626	Total poultry	11,486	10,979

INDUSTRY AND TRADE

Industry. In 1983 (March) employment in manufacturing and construction amounted to 125,450, some 27% of the total workforce. Of this number, 34,050 (27%) were engaged in the engineering and allied industries, which include ship-building and aircraft manufacture. The former predominance of shipbuilding has diminished, and the engineering sector now produces an impressive variety of goods: from textile machinery, air-conditioning plant and oilfield equipment to automobile and aero-engine components, data-processing equipment, and elec-tronic components. The textile industry, with a workforce of 13,950 includes longer established sectors such as spinning and weaving as well as more recently established activities such as the production of carpets, man-made fibres and hosiery. The related clothing and footwear sector employs 13,100 people. Taken together, food, drink and tobacco account for 18,050 jobs, the remainder of the manufacturing sector comprising a multiplicity of activities, such as chemicals, rubber and plastic goods, and furniture accounting for 20,950. The construction industry employs 25,150 people. The Government offers a comprehensive range of incentives to encourage the establishment of new and the expansion of existing industry, including substantial grants towards capital investment, the provision of government-built factories, and grant relief on corporation tax. At 31 March 1983 there were 204 new projects and 158 expansions of existing projects giving employ-ment to 67,229 workers.

Labour. The main source of statistics in Northern Ireland is the census of employment which was conducted annually from 1971 to 1978 and then in 1981. This provides industrial analyses of employees distinguishing between full-time and part-time employees. The census is supplemented by a less detailed quarterly sample enquiry which since 1979 has been used to provide the main mid-year employment estimate. This showed that at March 1983 there were 465,700 jobs for employees in Northern Ireland; of which 250,600 were taken up by males.

Statistics of persons claiming benefit at Social Security Offices are used to compile monthly unemployment figures for Northern Ireland. In 1982 the average number (estimate) of unemployed was 108,300; this represents an average of 19·4% of all employees. The Department of Economic Development provides an all-age guidance and placement service through a network of Jobmarkets situated in the principal towns of Northern Ireland. They maintain registers of persons seeking employment (either full- or part-time) and those already in employment who wish to change their job. In 1982 the number of vacancies filled in Northern Ireland by the Employment Service was 19,280 (adults and young persons), and 18,165 were placed in centres of training.

Assistance is available to employers who transfer key workers temporarily or permanently to Northern Ireland from other countries or within Northern Ireland in connection with the establishment or expansion of an industrial undertaking.

The Department of Economic Development maintains a register of disabled persons who are in the employment field and under the provisions of the Disabled Persons (Employment) Acts (NI) 1945 and 1960, makes efforts to find suitable work for those who are unemployed. Employment rehabilitation courses are provided at the Employment Rehabilitation Unit at Mill Road, Newtownabbey and training courses at various locations are available to assist unemployed disabled persons to readjust themselves to working conditions and to enhance their prospects of obtaining suitable employment. Allowances are paid to persons attending these courses.

Enterprise Ulster is an independent statutory body whose objective as a direct labour organization is to recruit workers from the unemployed register. Work is carried out mainly for public bodies and projects are of a community and amenity nature such as play areas, parks, playing fields, etc. In Sept. 1983, 129 projects were in operation providing employment for 1,160 employees, of whom 58 were employed as part of the Youth Training Programme. There are 12 Government Training Centres in Northern Ireland which provide over 3,000 training places and an annual output of over 5,000 trainees.

The Action for Community Employment Scheme, which came into operation in April 1981, provides temporary employment for long-term unemployed adults by funding projects which are of benefit to the community. In Sept. 1983 some 1,000 such projects were operational, providing employment for 2,700 people.

Government Training Centres contribute to the Youth Training Programme, having up to 2,400 places available for 16–17-year-olds who have been unable to find employment. A special six-month broad based modular course provides basic training in a wide variety of skills and the six-month craft skill courses provide initial apprentice training. The remaining places are reserved for adult trainees.

To supplement the Government Training Centres facilities, arrangements have been made for the use of spare training capacity in industry and commerce to attach people to firms for training courses. By this means a wide variety of training is made available and this has been further supplemented by extensive use of spare capacity in other training agencies and in Colleges of Further Education.

A comprehensive Youth Training Programme has been introduced and when fully operational will cater for the vocational preparation needs of all 16- and 17-year olds whether in employment, in full-time education or unable to find work. All minimum age school leavers who cannot get a job are guaranteed a year's continuous full-time training under the Programme. In 1983–84 a total of almost 14,000 training places are being made available, mainly in Government Training Centres, Further Education Colleges, Work Preparation Units and with employers.

The Department of Economic Development administers a Management Development Programme designed to encourage companies in the private sector in Northern Ireland to develop management structures and to train individual managers in a planned way to a high level of competence. Since the Programme was introduced in Oct. 1982 over 900 managers have been trained in this way.

In the sphere of industrial relations an independent and statutory body entitled The Labour Relations Agency was established under the Industrial Relations (NI) Order 1976 with the general duty to promote the improvement of industrial relations and to encourage the extension, development and, where necessary, the reform of collective bargaining machinery. The Agency is empowered to undertake research and provide an advisory service on industrial relations matters and to act as a forum for discussion of matters of mutual concern to management and unions. It also has a range of specific functions in the industrial relations field, including the settlement of disputes concerning trade-union recognition. The Agency's major role is in relation to the provision of conciliation and arbitration services. This means that, supplementing the procedures within industry for the prevention and settlement of disputes, the Agency plays an important part as an impartial third party in helping the sides to clarify issues in dispute and to settle their differences by agreement. Where conciliation fails, the Agency may arrange, if the parties agree, for independent arbitration by one or more persons appointed by the Agency or by the Industrial Court. Occasionally a settlement is promoted by the appointment of a Court of Inquiry. However, the great majority of industrial disputes are settled without stoppage of work, and Northern Ireland's record of days lost due to industrial disputes bears favourable comparison with that of the rest of the UK.

The Fair Employment Agency for Northern Ireland was established under the Fair Employment (NI) Act 1976, with the duties of promoting equality of opportunity in employments and occupations as between persons of different religious beliefs (including people without any religious belief), of working for the elimination of religious and political discrimination (made unlawful by the Act) in employments and occupations, and of keeping under review patterns and trends of employment and occupations.

The Equal Opportunities Commission for Northern Ireland was established under the Sex Discrimination (NI) Order 1976 with the duties of working towards the elimination of sex discrimination in the fields covered by the Order, of promoting equality of opportunity between men and women generally and of keeping under review the working of the Order and equal pay legislation.

The Department of Economic Development is responsible for the administration of the Health and Safety at Work (NI) Order 1978 which came into force 1 May 1979. Existing statutory provisions including the Factories Act (NI) 1965 and the Office and Shop Premises Act (NI) 1966 together with many new provisions for the health, safety and welfare of persons at work are enforced by the Department's Health and Safety Inspectorate. The 1978 Order extends to all persons at work with the exception of private domestic employment and applies to over 40,000 employment situations. The 1978 Order lays duties on employers, employees, self-employed, manufacturers and suppliers of materials and persons having control of buildings. Employers and self-employed have duties in regard to persons not employed by them but who may be affected by their operations at work. Agricultural provisions are enforced by the Department of Agriculture and some existing statutory provisions under factories and shops legislation continue to be enforced by district councils with some additional duties.

TOURISM. Tourism earns a substantial amount of revenue for Northern Ireland and total spending by some 712,000 visitors in 1982 was 48m.; day excursions provided an additional £20m. Altogether tourism provides over 9,000 permanent jobs and some 3,000 temporary or seasonal jobs. The Northern Ireland Tourist Board plays a major role in promoting the development of tourist traffic in Northern Ireland.

The protection of scenic beauty, scientific and nature interest, and wildlife is fostered under the Amenity Lands Act (NI) 1965 and the Wild Birds Protection Acts (NI) 1931 to 1968 by the Department of the Environment for Northern Ireland, which is advised by the Ulster Countryside Committee, the Nature Reserves Committee and the Wild Birds Advisory Committee. Eight Areas of Outstanding Natural Beauty and 53 Areas of Scientific Interest have been designated, and in these areas special attention is given respectively to the amenity and scientific aspects of planning applications. Country Parks have been established at Crawfordsburn, Redburn and Scrabo, Co. Down, at the Roe Valley and Ness Wood, Co. Londonderry, at Castle Archdale, Co. Fermanagh and at The Birches ('Peatlands') in N. Armagh. The Lagan Valley between Belfast and Lisburn is being administered as Northern Ireland's first Regional Park. Forty-one National Nature Reserves have been declared, and steady progress is being made with the acquisition of further reserves. Ten areas have been designated as Bird Sanctuaries.

The Department is advised by the Historic Monuments Council on the exercise of its powers under the Historic Monuments Act (NI) 1971 in respect of the conservation of historic monuments and the preservation of objects of archaeological or historic interest. At present there are some 153 monuments in State care and over 511 are scheduled. The Department, advised by the Historic Buildings Council, is also responsible for listing buildings of special architectural or historic interest and for designating areas of similar interest the character or appearance of which it is desirable to preserve or enhance. To date some 6,400 buildings have been listed and 19 areas have been designated. Grants are payable by the Department to assist in the repair or maintenance of listed buildings and for schemes of enhancement in conservation areas.

COMMUNICATIONS

Road and Rail. All train services are operated by the Northern Ireland Railways Co. Ltd which is a subsidiary of the Northern Ireland Transport Holding Co. The number of track miles operated is 357; passenger route miles, 210. In 1982–83 railways carried 5·2m. passengers. Most bus services are operated by two other subsidiaries, Ulsterbus Ltd and Citybus Ltd. Ulsterbus runs services outside the Belfast area (except for a few services provided by privately owned bus undertakings) while all the services within the Belfast area are run by Citybus.

The Department of the Environment (NI) administers a licensing system for professional hauliers with the objective of maintaining standards and conditions necessary for the safe operation of vehicles and fair competition between hauliers. The level of services provided and the rates charged by the industry are determined by the normal economic forces of supply and demand. At 31 March 1983 there were 1,532 professional hauliers and 2,692 vehicles licensed to engage in road haulage.

The number of motor vehicles licensed at 31 Dec. 1982 was 462,560, comprising private cars, 403,520; motor cycles, 15,500; hackney vehicles, 2,210; goods vehicles, 18,500; agricultural tractors, 9,220. In addition, there were 13,610 vehicles which were not subject to licence duty.

The Department of the Environment (NI) is responsible for the provision and maintenance of all public roads, bridges and street lighting in the Province, the provision and operation of car parks, and for the operation of the Strangford Ferry. In addition to Headquarters Division the Roads Service of the Department operates through Divisional Offices in Ballymena, Belfast, Coleraine, Craigavon, Downpatrick and Omagh and smaller offices in other centres.

At 1 April 1983 the total mileage of roads was 14,721, graded for administrative purposes as follows: Motorway 77 miles; all purpose trunk, 338 miles; Class I, 1,057 miles; Class II, 1,760 miles; Class III, 2,947 miles; unclassified, 8,542 miles.

Aviation. Northern Ireland Airports Ltd is responsible for the operation of Belfast Airport. A major 4-stage development programme was started in 1977 and the first 2 stages have now been completed, while the design of Stage 3 works is under way. The completion of the programme will leave the airport better equipped to handle traffic growth in the foreseeable future. In 1982, 1·4m. passengers and 19,549 tonnes of freight and mail were handled.

Scheduled passenger services operate between Belfast and 24 domestic airports throughout the UK.

Shipping. Passenger services operate between Belfast and Liverpool and between Larne and (i) Cairnryan and (ii) Stranraer. Conventional cargo services have given way in many cases to container, unit load and drive on/drive off services. The latter type of service now operates between Belfast, Larne and Warrenpoint to various ports in UK.

JUSTICE, RELIGION, EDUCATION AND WELFARE

Justice. The Lord Chancellor has responsibility for the administration of all courts in Northern Ireland through the Northern Ireland Court Service, and is responsible for the appointment of judges and resident magistrates.

The court structure in Northern Ireland has 3 tiers–the Supreme Court of Judicature of Northern Ireland (comprising the Court of Appeal, the High Court and the Crown Court), the County Courts and the Magistrates' Courts. There are 25 Petty Sessions districts which when grouped together for administration purposes form 7 County Court Divisions and 4 Circuits.

The County Court has general civil jurisdiction subject to an upper monetary limit of £5,000. Appeals from the Magistrates' Courts lie to the County Court, while appeals from the County Court lie to the High Court. Circuit Registrars have jurisdiction to deal with most defended actions up to £500 and most undefended actions up to £5,000. They also deal, by an informal arbitration procedure, with small claims whose value does not exceed £300. An appeal from the decision of a Circuit Registrar lies to the High Court.

Police. The police force consists of the Royal Ulster Constabulary, supported by the Royal Ulster Constabulary Reserve, a mainly part-time force.

Religion. The religious professions at the census of 1981 were: Roman Catholics, 414,532; Presbyterians, 339,818; Church of Ireland, 284,253 (including Church of England, 2,503 and Episcopal Church of Scotland, 278); Methodists, 58,731; others and not stated, 387,406.

Education. Education in Northern Ireland is administered centrally by the Department of Education and locally by 5 education and library boards. The Department is concerned with the whole range of education from nursery education through to higher education and continuing education; for sport and recreation; for youth services; for the arts and culture (including libraries) and for community relations and community development. District councils are the main providers of sport, recreation and community facilities and the education and library boards have a responsibility where the facilities are intended primarily for education and youth service activities. The Department assists with grants as far as the district councils are concerned and meets the full cost in relation to education and library boards.

The 5 education and library boards which took over responsibility for the local administration of the education and library services on 1 Oct. 1973 are required to ensure that there are sufficient schools of all kinds to meet the needs of their area. They provide primary and secondary schools, special schools for handicapped pupils and institutions of further education. The boards also make contributions towards the cost of maintaining voluntary schools; award university and other scholarships; meet the tuition fees of the great majority of pupils attending grammar schools; provide milk and meals; free books and transport for pupils; enforce school attendance; regulate the employment of children and young people and secure the provision of recreational and youth service facilities. They are also required to develop a comprehensive and efficient library service for their areas. The following are the statistics for the 1981–82 academic year:

Universities. The Queen's University of Belfast (founded in 1849 as a college of the Queen's University of Ireland and reconstituted as a separate university in 1908) had 109 professors, 232 readers and senior lecturers, 507 lecturers and tutors and 6,376 full-time students.

The New University of Ulster at Coleraine, of which Magee University College, Londonderry, is now an integral part, had 26 professors, 45 readers and senior lecturers, 165 lecturers and demonstrators and 1,862 full-time students.

The Ulster Polytechnic is a central institution providing higher non-university education for the whole of Northern Ireland with a full-time academic staff of 552,

4,554 full-time and 2,636 part-time students on vocational and professional courses and 228 students on specialist teacher-training courses.

Secondary Education. 78 grammar schools with 59,038 pupils and 3,602 full-time teachers; 183 secondary (intermediate) schools with 15,098 pupils and 6,931 full-time teachers.

Primary Education. 1,042 primary schools with 186,998 pupils and 7,954 teachers; 81 nursery schools with 4,279 pupils and 147 teachers.

Further Education. 26 institutions of further education with 1,861 full-time and 1,743 part-time teachers and an enrolment of 14,334 full-time, 12,883 part-time day and 15,856 evening students on vocational courses; and nearly 44,166 students on non-vocational (mostly evening) courses.

Special Educational Treatment. 35 special schools, including hospital schools with 2,805 pupils and 345 teachers.

Teachers. There were 20,840 full-time teachers (8,479 men and 12,361 women) in grant-aided schools and institutions of further education. The minimum general teacher-training course is of 3 years' duration and there were 1,817 students (542 men and 1,275 women) in training; these included students following teacher-training courses at university establishments and at Ulster Polytechnic and Londonderry College of Technology, and the 3 Colleges of Education.

Expenditure. Expenditure by the Department of Education in 1981–82 was £491·4m.

Health and Personal Social Services. Under the provisions of the Health and Personal Social Services (NI) Order 1972, the Department of Health and Social Services is responsible for the provision of integrated health and personal social services in Northern Ireland, designed to promote the physical and mental health of the people of Northern Ireland through the prevention, diagnosis and treatment of illness, and also to promote their social welfare. Four Health and Social Services Boards, Eastern, Northern, Southern and Western, established under the above Order, administer health and personal social services, as the Department directs, within their designated areas.

Social Security. The social security schemes in Northern Ireland are similar to those in force in Great Britain.

National Insurance. During the year ended 31 March 1983 (estimate), £21·8m. sickness benefit was paid to an average of 14,800 persons and £50·7m. unemployment benefit was paid to an average of 36,100 persons. Widows' benefits amounting to £26·5m. were paid to 14,900 persons and retirement pensions totalling £293·5m. were paid to an average of 198,000 persons. Invalidity pensions and allowances totalling £79·7m. were paid to approximately 33,400 persons. Accidents in respect of which claims to benefit are made occur at the rate of 187 per week and £1·1m. industrial injury benefit was paid in 1982–83 to an average of 654 persons. Industrial disablement benefit amounting to £10m. was paid to an average of 4,900 persons. Maternity benefit totalling £6·2m. was paid to approximately 27,700 persons. Receipts, of the Northern Ireland Insurance Fund in the year ended 31 March 1983 were £514·5m. and payments were £528·3m.

Child Benefit. During the year ended 31 March 1983, £139m. was paid to an average of 215,700 families.

Supplementary Benefits. In 1982–83, £240m. was paid to an average of 163,900 persons.

Family Income Supplement. In 1982–83, £9m. was paid to an average of 12,500 persons.

Books of Reference

The annual and other publications of the various Departments and the Reports, etc., of Parliamentary Committees may be obtained from HM Stationery Office, Belfast.

Ulster Year Book, 1983. Belfast, HMSO, 1983
Census of Population Reports, Northern Ireland. Belfast, HMSO, 1981
Annual Abstract of Statistics. Belfast, HMSO
Northern Ireland Development 1970–75. Belfast, HMSO, 1970
Who Makes What in Northern Ireland: A Trade Directory. Belfast, HMSO, 10th ed. 1979
Reports on the Census of Production of Northern Ireland. Belfast, HMSO, 1976
Re-organization of Secondary Education in Northern Ireland. Belfast, HMSO, 1976
The Statutes Revised: Northern Ireland. HMSO, 1982
Bell, G., *The Protestants of Ulster.* London, 1976
Bew, P., Gibbon, P. and Patterson, H., *The State in Northern Ireland, 1921–1972.* New York, 1980
Biggs-Davison, J., *The Hand is Red.* London, 1974
Boal, F. W. and Douglas, J. N. H., *Integration and Division.* London, 1982
Farrell, M., *Northern Ireland: The Orange State.* London, 1976
Flackes, W. D., *Northern Ireland: Political Directory 1968–83.* London, 1983
Heskin, K., *Northern Ireland: A Psychological Analysis.* Dublin, 1980
Hull, R. H., *The Irish Triangle.* Princeton Univ. Press, 1976
Kelly, K., *The Longest War: Northern Ireland and the IRA.* Dingle, Westport and London, 1982
Quekett, Sir A. S., *The Constitution of Northern Ireland.* 3 pts. Belfast, 1928–47
Rose, R., *Northern Ireland: A Time of Choice.* London, 1976
Wallace, M., *British Government in Northern Ireland: From Devolution to Direct Rule.* Newton Abbot, 1982
Watt, D. (ed.), *The Constitution of Northern Ireland.* London, 1981
Winchester, S., *Northern Ireland in Crisis: Reporting the Ulster Troubles.* New York, 1975

ISLE OF MAN

AREA AND POPULATION. Area, 221 sq. miles (572 sq. km); resident population census April 1981, 64,679. The principal towns are Douglas (population, 19,944), Ramsey (5,818), Peel (3,688), Castletown (3,141). Vital statistics, 1982: Births, 724; deaths, 981; marriages, 394. The number of Manx-speaking people was 284 in 1971 (165 in 1961 and 4,657 in 1901), all of whom were bilingual.

CONSTITUTION AND GOVERNMENT. The Isle of Man is administered in accordance with its own laws by the Court of Tynwald, consisting of the Governor, appointed by the Crown; the Legislative Council, composed of the Lord Bishop of Sodor and Man, the Attorney-General (who does not vote) and 8 members selected by the House of Keys, total 10 members; and the House of Keys, a representative assembly of 24 members chosen on adult suffrage with 12 months' residence for 5 years by the 6 'sheadings' or local sub-divisions, and the 4 municipalities. The Island is not bound by Acts of the Imperial Parliament unless specially mentioned in them.

A special relationship exists between the Isle of Man and the European Economic Community providing for free trade and adoption by the Isle of Man of the EEC's external trade policies with third countries. The Island remains free to levy its own system of rates and taxes.

The elections to the House of Keys, Nov. 1981, resulted in the return of 21 Independents and 3 Labour. Number of voters, 47,449.

An Executive Council to advise the Governor on all matters of government was set up under the Isle of Man Constitution Act, 1961. It consists at present of 5 members of the House of Keys and 3 of the Legislative Council.

Lieut.-Governor: Sir Nigel Cecil, KBE, CB (term of office began Sept. 1980).
Government Secretary: P. J. Hulme.
Government Treasurer: W. Dawson.

Flag: Red, with 3 steel-coloured legs armoured and spurred (knees and spurs, yellow) in the centre.

ECONOMY

Budget. Revenue is derived from customs duties, value added tax and from income tax. In 1983–84 the budget allowed for gross revenue and capital expenditure of £135,555,610. Income tax was 20p in the £. No death duties or surtaxes are levied. Company registration tax is levied at a flat rate of £250 on every company incorporated in the Isle of Man which trades and is controlled outside the island. A Land Speculation Tax applies at the same rate as income tax.

The Island currently makes an annual contribution to the UK Government of 2·5% of net 'common purse' receipts (share of customs and excise duties and VAT received by Treasury) towards the cost of defence and other common services provided by the UK Government. That contribution currently amounts to about £965,000.

Currency. Notes to the value of £50, £20, £10, £5, £1 and 50p are issued by the Isle of Man Government. Annual minting of decimal coinage takes place, and in 1973, 1974, 1977 and 1979 and thereafter legal tender gold coins in half sovereign, sovereign, £2 and £5 pieces were issued. Commemorative crowns have also been issued since 1970, and silver and platinum decimal sets have been minted more recently. From 1978 onwards £5, £1, and 20p coins were minted for general circulation. Plastic £1 notes were introduced in 1983.

AGRICULTURE. The principal agricultural produce of the Island consists of oats. wheat, barley, potatoes, grasses, fatstock dairy products. The total area under grass and crops in 1982 was 78,044 acres and of rough grazings, 39,144 acres. The total area under cereals was 10,877 acres, including 1,495 under oats, 701 under wheat and 8,417 under barley or bere. There were also 1,007 acres under turnips and swedes, 770 under potatoes and 63,562 acres of grassland.

Livestock in 1982: 1,004 horses, 34,740 cattle, 125,744 sheep, 4,116 pigs and 87,560 poultry.

TOURISM. In 1981–82 tourism contributed 10% of national income and about 5,000 were employed in the industry during the summer season.

COMMUNICATIONS

Roads. There are 500 miles of good roads. The International TT Motor Cycle Races and cycle races take place annually. Omnibus services operate to all parts of the island.

Number of vehicles (31 March 1983): 27,755 cars, 3,855 goods vehicles and engineering plant, 1,035 agricultural vehicles, 2,852 motor cycles and scooters and 730 taxis and public service vehicles.

Railways. Several novel transport systems operate on the Island during the summer season, including 100-year-old horse-drawn trams, and the Manx Electric Railway, linking Douglas, Ramsey and Snaefell Mountain (2,036 ft). The Isle of Man Steam Railway also operates between Douglas and Port Erin.

Aviation. Ronaldsway Airport handles scheduled services operated by Manx Airlines. Dan-Air, Avair, Genair, Spaceground, Air Ecosse, and Loganair to and from London, Manchester, Belfast, Dublin, Glasgow, Liverpool, Blackpool, etc. Air taxi services also operate.

Shipping. Car ferries of the Isle of Man Steam Packet Co. link the Island with Liverpool throughout the year and similar services operate to Fleetwood, Ardrossan, Dublin and Belfast during the summer season.

Manx Line provides a roll-on roll-off service between Douglas and Heysham. A roll-on roll-off service for commercial vehicles is also operated to Liverpool.

Broadcasting. The first constitutionally licensed commercial radio station in the British Isles, Manx Radio, is operated by Government on medium and VHF wavelengths from Douglas.

Newspapers. In 1982 there were 5 weekly newspapers.

JUSTICE AND EDUCATION

Police. The police force numbered 148 all ranks and 10 cadets in 1982.

Education. Education is compulsory between the ages of 5 and 15. In Jan. 1983 there were 37 primary schools with 5,309 pupils in attendance. The net expenditure on education for 1983–84 amounted to £16·2m.; in addition, capital expenditure of £810,000 was made for school buildings. There are 7 secondary schools, 5 provided by the Board of Education (4,603 registered pupils), 1 direct grant school for girls (310 registered pupils), 1 independent public school for boys (346 registered pupils), 1 college of further education (3,695 full-, part-time and evening pupils).

Books of Reference

Isle of Man Digest of Economic and Social Statistics, 1982–83. Isle of Man Government, 1983
Isle of Man Family Expenditure Survey 1981–82. Isle of Man Government, 1983
A Businessman's Briefing 1982–83. Isle of Man Government 1982
Tynwald Companion 1982. Isle of Man Government, 1982
Manx Tourism 77. Isle of Man Government, 1977
Policy Planning Programme. Isle of Man Government, 1982
A Guide to Industrial and Financial Opportunities. Isle of Man Government, 1983
Kinvig, R. H., *History of the Isle of Man.* Oxford, 1945.—*The Isle of Man: A Social, Cultural and Political History.* Liverpool Univ. Press, 1975
Mais, S. P. B., *Isle of Man.* London, 1954
Solly, M., *Anatomy of a Tax Haven. The Isle of Man and Manx Income Tax,* 2 vols. Douglas, 1980
Stenning, E. H., *Portrait of the Isle of Man.* London, 1958

CHANNEL ISLANDS

AREA. The Channel Islands are situated off the north-west coast of France and are the only portions of the 'Duchy of Normandy' now belonging to the Crown of England, to which they have been attached since the Conquest. They consist of Jersey (28,717 acres), Guernsey (15,654 acres) and the following dependencies of Guernsey–Alderney (1,962), Brechou (74), Great Sark (1,035), Little Sark (239), Herm (320), Jethou (44) and Lihou (38), a total of 48,083 acres, or 75 sq. miles (194 sq. km).

The climate is mild. Total rainfall (1982), Jersey, 1,037·2 mm; Guernsey, 979·5 mm. Temperature registered (1982): highest, Jersey, 28·2°C.; Guernsey, 26·9°C.; lowest, Jersey, −4·2°C.; Guernsey, −2·4°C.

CONSTITUTION. The Lieut.-Governors and Cs.-in-C. of Jersey and Guernsey are the personal representatives of the Sovereign, the Commanders of the Armed Forces of the Crown and the channel of communication between the Crown and the insular governments. They are appointed by the Crown and have a voice but no vote in the Assemblies of the States (the insular legislatures). The Secretaries to the Lieut.-Governors are their staff officers.

The Bailiffs are appointed by the Crown and are Presidents both of the Assembly of the States and of the Royal Courts of Jersey and Guernsey. They have in the States a casting vote.

LANGUAGE. The official languages are French and English, but English is gradually supplanting French. The language commonly used is English, but in the country districts of Jersey and Guernsey and throughout Sark some people also speak a Norman-French dialect; that of Alderney has died out.

TRADE. From 1958 the trade of the Channel Islands with the UK has been regarded as internal trade.

COMMUNICATIONS

Road. Omnibus services operate in all parts of Jersey and Guernsey.

Aviation. Scheduled air services are maintained by Air UK, Jersey European, British Midland, Aurigny Air Services, Dan-Air, Brymon Airways, Guernsey Airlines, NLM City Hopper and other companies between the islands and airports in the UK, Ireland, the Netherlands and France. During the summer months these services are greatly increased, both in the number of airports served and in the frequency of flights.

Shipping. Passenger and cargo steam services between Jersey, Guernsey and England are maintained by British Rail; between Guernsey, Jersey and England and St Malo by the Commodore Shipping Co.; between Guernsey, Jersey, Alderney and France by Condor Ltd (hydrofoil), and between Guernsey, Jersey, Alderney and England and Guernsey and Sark by local companies.

Post and Broadcasting. Postal and overseas telephone and telegraph services are maintained by the respective Postal Administrations of each bailiwick. The local telephone services are maintained by the insular authorities. There were, in 1983, 55,461 subscribers in Jersey and 38,634 in Guernsey.

There is an independent television station in Jersey and local radio stations, BBC Radio Jersey and Guernsey, opened in 1982.

JUSTICE AND RELIGION

Justice. Justice is administered by the Royal Courts of Jersey and Guernsey, each of which consists of the Bailiff and 12 Jurats, the latter being elected by an electoral college. There is an appeal from the Royal Courts to the Courts of Appeal of Jersey and of Guernsey. A final appeal lies to the Privy Council in certain cases. A stipendiary magistrate in each, Jersey and Guernsey, deals with minor civil and criminal cases.

Church. Jersey and Guernsey each constitutes a deanery within the diocese of Winchester. The rectories (12 in Jersey; 10 in Guernsey) are in the gift of the Crown. The Roman Catholic and various Nonconformist Churches are represented.

Books of Reference

Ambrière. F., *Les Iles Anglo-Normandes.* Paris, 1971
Coysh, V., *The Channel Islands: A New Study.* Newton Abbot, 1977
Cruickshank, C., *The German Occupation of the Channel Islands.* London, 1975
Lempière, R., *Portrait of the Channel Islands.* London, 1970.–*History of the Channel Islands.* London, 1974
Lockley, R. M., *The Channel Islands.* London, 1968
Myhill, H., *Introducing the Channel Islands.* London, 1964
Uttley, J., *The Story of the Channel Islands.* London, 1966

JERSEY

POPULATION (census 1980), 76,100. In the year ended 31 Dec. 1982 there were 885 births and 848 deaths. The town is St Helier on the south coast.

CONSTITUTION. The States consist of 12 senators (elected for 6 years, 6 retiring every third year), 12 Constables (triennial) and 29 Deputies (triennial), all elected on universal suffrage by the people.

The island legislature is 'The States of Jersey'. The States comprises the Bailiff, the Lieut.-Governor, 12 Senators, the Constables of the 12 parishes of the island, 29 Deputies, the Dean of Jersey, the Attorney-General and the Solicitor-General. They all have the right to speak in the Assembly, but only the 53 elected members (the Senators, Constables and Deputies) have the right to vote; the Bailiff has a casting vote. General elections for Senators and Deputies are held every third year. Except in specific instances, enactments passed by the States require the sanction of The Queen-in-Council. The Lieut.-Governor has the power of veto on certain forms of legislation.

Flag: White with a red diagonal cross. In the top centre of the flag a shield of the arms of Jersey ensigned with the Plantagenet Crown.

Lieut.-Governor and C.-in-C. of Jersey: Gen. Sir Peter Whiteley, GCB, OBE.
Secretary and ADC to the Lieut.-Governor: Cdr D. M. L. Braybrooke, MVO, RN (Retd).

Bailiff of Jersey and President of the States: Sir Frank Ereaut.
Deputy Bailiff: P. L. Crill, CBE.

ECONOMY

Budget (year ending 31 Dec. 1982). Revenue, £130,074,676; expenditure, £112,535,570; public debt, £349,543. The standard rate of income tax is 20p in the pound. No super-tax or death duties are levied. Parochial rates of moderate amount are payable by owners and occupiers.

Currency. The States issue bank-notes in denominations of £10, £5 and £1.

INDUSTRY AND TRADE

Industry. Principal activities: Tourism; total number of hotel and guesthouse bedrooms (1982), 12,257; expenditure of tourists (1982), £145m. Agriculture, total output (1982), £30·7m.; total exports (1982), £21·8m. Light industry, mainly electrical goods, textiles and clothing. Total exports (1980), £29m. Banking and finance, total bank deposits and balances due to parent companies by deposit-taking institutions (1982), £13,700m.

Commerce (1980). Principal imports: Machinery and transport equipment, £57·3m.; manufactured goods, £43·4m.; food, £40m.; mineral fuels, £21·5m.; chemicals, £15·1m., and miscellaneous, £53·6m. Principal exports (1980): Machinery and transport equipment, £28m.; food, £22·2m; manufactured goods, £15·6m., and miscellaneous, £24·1m.

COMMUNICATIONS

Aviation. The Jersey airport is situated at St Peter. It covers approximately 375 acres. Number of aircraft movements (1982) 23,789; number of passenger arrivals, 673,903.

Shipping (1982). All vessels arriving in Jersey from outside Jersey waters report at St Helier or Gorey on first arrival. There is a harbour of minor importance at St Aubin. Number of commercial vessels entering St Helier, 4,227; number of registered craft (of 15 ft and over), 1,582. Passengers arrived in 1982, 546,929.

EDUCATION (1982). There were 7 States secondary schools and 26 States primary schools; 4,243 pupils attended the primary schools, 4,328 the secondary schools. There were 9 private primary schools with 1,270 pupils and 5 private secondary schools with 955 pupils. Highlands College offers full- and part-time courses to Ordinary and National Certificate and Diploma levels or similar standards and, together with Les Quennevais Adult Community Centre, evening classes in technical and recreational subjects.

Books of Reference

Balleine, G. R., *Biographical Dictionary of Jersey.* London, 1948.–*A History of the Island of Jersey.* London, 1950.—*The Bailiwick of Jersey.* 3rd ed. London, 1970

Bois, F. ce L., *The Constitutional History of Jersey.* Jersey, 1970
Carre, A. L., *English–Jersey Language Vocabulary.* Jersey, 1972
Le Maistre, F., *Dictionnaire Jersiais–Français.* Jersey, 1966
Powell, G. C., *Economic Survey of Jersey.* Jersey, 1971

States of Jersey Library: Royal Square, St Helier. *Librarian:* J. K. Antill, FLA.

GUERNSEY

POPULATION. Census population(1981) 53,313. Births during 1982 were 609; deaths, 644. The town is St Peter Port.

CONSTITUTION. The government of the island is conducted by committees appointed by the States.

The States of Deliberation, the Parliament of Guernsey, is composed of the following members: The Bailiff, who is President *ex officio;* 12 Conseillers; H.M. Procureur and H.M. Comptroller (Law Officers of the Crown), who have a voice but no vote; 33 People's Deputies elected by popular franchise; 10 Douzaine Representatives elected by their Parochial Douzaines; 2 representatives of the States of Alderney.

The States of Election, an electoral college, elects the Jurats and Conseillers. It is composed of the following members: The Bailiff (President *ex officio*); the 12 Jurats or 'Jurés-Justiciers'; the 12 Conseillers; H.M. Procureur and H.M. Comptroller; the 33 People's Deputies; 34 Douzaine Representatives; and (for the election of Conseillers) 4 representatives of the States of Alderney.

Since Jan. 1949 all legislative powers and functions (with minor exceptions) formerly exercised by the Royal Court have been vested in the States of Deliberation. Projets de Loi (Bills) require the sanction of The Queen-in-Council.

Flag: White with a red cross.

Lieut.-Governor and C.-in-C. of Guernsey and its Dependencies: Air Chief Marshal Sir Peter Le Cheminant, GBE, KCB, DFC.
Secretary and ADC to the Lieut.-Governor: Capt. D. P. L. Hodgetts.

Bailiff of Guernsey and President of the States: Sir Charles Frossard.
Deputy Bailiff of Guernsey: G. M. Dorey.

FINANCE (year ending 31 Dec. 1982). Revenue, £60,464,344 (including £1,854,194 for Alderney); expenditure, £51,537,384 (including £1,722,418 for Alderney). States' funded debt less sinking fund provisions, £826,354; note and coin issue, £27,085,783. The standard rate of income tax is 20p in the pound. States and parochial rates are very moderate. No super-tax or death duties are levied.

COMMERCE (1982). Principal imports: Coal, 27,368 tonnes; petrol and oils, 131,422,262 litres. Principal exports: Tomatoes (1982), £18,248,365; flowers and fern, £13,544,868; sweet peppers, £283,517; aubergines, £56,195; other vegetables, £411,852; plants, £469,628.

COMMUNICATIONS

Aviation. The airport in Guernsey, situated at La Villiaze, has a landing area of approximately 124 acres and a tarmac runway of 4,800 ft. In 1982, 176,386 passengers arrived from places outside the Channel Islands.

Shipping. The principal harbour is that of St Peter Port, and there is a harbour at St Sampson's (used mainly for commercial shipping). In 1982 the number of ship tonnes gross entering and leaving Guernsey was 10,404,704. 136,911 passengers arrived from places outside the Channel Islands. Ships registered in Guernsey at 31

Dec. 1982 numbered 818 and 523 fishing vessels. Small craft registered, 4,050. In 1982, 10,280 yachts visited Guernsey.

EDUCATION. There are 2 public schools in the island: Elizabeth College, founded by Queen Elizabeth in 1563, for boys, and the Ladies' College, for girls. The States grammar schools provide for education up to University entrance requirements, and there are numerous modern secondary and primary schools and a College of Further Education. The total number of school children is 9,134. Facilities are available for the study of art, domestic science and many other subjects of a technical nature. There is also a convent school with boarding facilities for girls.

ALDERNEY. Population (census, 1971), 1,686 (1981 estimate, 2,086). The island has an airport. The constitution of the island (reformed 1949) provides for its own popularly elected President and States (12 members), and its own Court. The town is St Anne's.

Flag: White with a red cross with the island badge in the centre.

President of the States: J. Kay-Mouat.
Clerk of the States: W. R. Jones, MA.
Clerk of the Court: P. J. Beer.

SARK. Population (census, 1971), 584 (1978 estimate, 600). The Constitution is a mixture of feudal and popular government with its Chief Pleas (parliament), consisting of 40 tenants and 12 popularly elected deputies, presided over by the Seneschal. The head of the island is the Seigneur. Sark has no income tax. Motor vehicles, except tractors, are not allowed.

Flag: White with a red cross and a red first quarter bearing two gold lions.

The Seigneur: J. M. Beaumont.
Seneschal: H. Carré, MBE.

Books of Reference

Carteret, A. R. de, *The Story of Sark.* London, 1956
Clark, L., *Sark Discovered.* London, 1956
Coysh, V., *Alderney.* Newton Abbot, 1974
Durand, R., *Guernsey, Present and Past.* Guernsey, 1933.—*Guernsey under German Rule.* London, 1946
Hathaway, Sybil, *Dame of Sark: An Autobiography.* London, 1961
Le Huray, C. P., *The Bailiwick of Guernsey.* London, 1952
Marr, L. J., *A History of Guernsey.* Guernsey, 1982
Robinson, G. W. S., *Guernsey.* Newton Abbot, 1977
Wood, A. and M. S., *Islands in Danger.* 2nd ed. London, 1957
Wood, J., *Herm, Our Island Home.* London, 1973

UNITED STATES OF AMERICA

Capital: Washington, D.C.
Population: 226·5m. (1980)
GNP per capita: US$11,360 (1980)

HISTORY. The Declaration of Independence of the 13 states of which the American Union then consisted was adopted by Congress on 4 July 1776. On 30 Nov. 1782 Great Britain acknowledged the independence of the USA, and on 3 Sept. 1783 the treaty of peace was concluded and was ratified by the USA on 14 Jan. 1784.

AREA AND POPULATION. Population of conterminous USA at each census from 1790 to 1950, and for USA including Alaska and Hawaii, from 1960. Residents of Puerto Rico, the Philippine Islands, Guam, American Samoa and the Virgin Islands of the USA, and persons in the military and naval service stationed abroad are not included in the figures of this table. Residents of Indian reservations are excluded prior to 1890.

	White	Negroes [1]	Other races [2]	Total	Decennial increase %
1790	3,172,464 [3]	757,208	—	3,929,672	—
1800	4,306,446	1,002,037	—	5,308,483	35·1
1810	5,862,073	1,377,808	—	7,239,881	36·4
1820	7,866,797	1,771,562	—	9,638,359	33·1
1830	10,537,378	2,328,642	—	12,866,020	33·5
1840	14,195,805	2,873,648	—	17,069,453	32·7
1850	19,553,068	3,638,808	—	23,191,876	35·9
1860	26,922,537	4,441,830	78,954 [4]	31,443,321	35·6
1870 [5]	33,589,377	4,880,009	88,985	38,558,371	22·6
1870 [5]	*34,337,292*	*5,392,172*	*88,985*	*39,818,449*	*26·6*
1880	43,402,970	6,580,793	172,020	50,155,783	30·1
1890	55,101,258	7,488,676	357,780	62,947,714	25·5
1900	66,809,196	8,833,994	351,385	75,994,575	21·0
1910	81,731,957	9,827,763	412,546	91,972,266	21·0
1920	94,820,915	10,463,131	426,574	105,710,620	14·9 [6]
1930	110,286,740 [7]	11,891,143	597,163	122,775,046	16·1 [6]
1940	118,214,870	12,865,518	588,887	131,669,275	7·3
1950	134,942,028	15,042,286	713,047	150,697,361	14·5
1960 [8]	158,831,732	18,871,831	1,619,612	179,323,175	18·5
1970	177,748,975	22,580,289	2,882,662	203,211,926	13·3
1980	188,371,622	26,495,025	11,679,158	226,545,805	11·4

[1] Seventeen southern states (including D.C.) in 1900 had 7,922,969 Negroes (89·7% of the total Negro population); in 1920, 8,912,231 (85·2%); in 1940, 9,904,619 (77%); in 1950, 10,225,407 (68%); in 1960, 11,311,607 (59·9%); in 1970, 11,969,961 (53%); in 1980, 14,048,000 (53%).

[2] 1870: 63,199 Chinese, 55 Japanese and 25,731 Indians; 1880, 105,465 Chinese, 148 Japanese and 66,407 Indians; 1890, 107,488 Chinese, 2,039 Japanese and 248,253 Indians; 1900, 89,863 Chinese, 24,326 Japanese and 237,196 Indians; 1910, 71,531 Chinese, 72,157 Japanese, 265,683 Indians and 3,175 other races; 1920, 61,639 Chinese, 111,010 Japanese, 244,437 Indians and 9,488 other races; 1930, 332,397 Indians, 74,954 Chinese, 138,834 Japanese and 50,978 other races; 1940, 333,969 Indians, 77,504 Chinese, 126,947 Japanese and 50,467 other races; 1950, 343,410 Indians, 141,768 Japanese, 117,629 Chinese, 110,240 other races; 1960, 523,591 Indians, 464,332 Japanese, 237,292 Chinese, 176,310 Filipino, 218,087 other races; 1970, 792,730 Indians, 591,290 Japanese, 435,062 Chinese, 343,060 Filipino, 720,520 other races; 1980, 1,420,400 Indians, 701,000 Japanese, 806,000 Chinese, 774,700 Filipino, 7,977,000 other races.

[3] Made up of Anglo-Scottish, 89·1%; German, 5·6%; Dutch, 2·5%; Irish, 1·9%; French, 0·6%.

[4] 34,933 Chinese and 44,021 Indians.

[5] Enumeration in 1870 incomplete. Figures in italics represent estimated corrected population.

[*Footnotes continued on p. 1366.*]

Total population in 1980 at 226,545,805 comprised 110,053,161 males and 116,492,644 females; 167,050,992 were urban and 59,494,813 were rural. Negroes, 12,519,189 males and 13,975,836 females.

Estimated population, including Alaska and Hawaii, and armed forces overseas, on 1 July 1950, 152,271,000; 1955, 165,931,000; 1960, 180,671,000; 1965, 194,303,000; 1970, 204,878,000; 1975, 215,973,000; 1976, 218,035,000; 1977, 220,239,000; 1978, 222,585,000; 1979, 225,055,000; 1980, 227,658,000; 1981, 229,807,000.

The age distribution by sex of the total population of the US (excluding armed forces overseas, US population abroad and outlying areas) at the 1980 census was as follows:

Age-group	Male	Female	Total
Under 5	8,362,009	7,986,245	16,348,254
5–9	8,539,080	8,160,876	16,699,956
10–14	9,316,221	8,925,908	18,242,129
15–19	10,755,409	10,412,715	21,168,124
20–24	10,663,231	10,655,473	21,318,704
25–34	18,381,903	18,699,936	37,081,839
35–44	12,569,719	13,064,991	25,634,710
45–54	11,008,919	11,790,868	22,799,787
55–59	5,481,863	6,133,391	11,615,254
60–64	4,669,892	5,417,729	10,087,621
65–74	6,756,502	8,824,103	15,580,605
75 and over	3,548,413	6,402,409	9,968,822
Total	110,053,161	116,492,644	226,545,805

The following table includes population statistics, the year in which each of the original 13 states ratified the constitution, and the year when each of the other states was admitted into the Union. Postal abbreviations for the names of the states are shown in brackets. Land area includes land temporarily or partially covered by water, and lakes, etc., of less than 40 acres. (For census population by states and regions in 1940 and 1950 *see* THE STATESMAN'S YEAR-BOOK, 1952, pp. 552 and 553.)

Geographic divisions and states		Land area: sq. miles 1980	Census population 1 April 1970	Census population 1 April 1980	Pop. per sq. mile, 1980
United States		3,539,289	203,235,298	226,545,805	64·0
New England		63,012	11,847,186	12,348,493	196·0
Maine (1820)	(Me.)	30,995	993,663	1,124,660	36·3
New Hampshire (1788)	(N.H.)	8,993	737,681	920,610	102·4
Vermont (1791)	(Vt.)	9,273	444,732	511,456	55·2
Massachusetts (1788)	(Mass.)	7,824	5,689,170	5,737,037	733·3
Rhode Island (1790)	(R.I.)	1,055	949,723	947,154	897·8
Connecticut (1788)	(Conn.)	4,872	3,032,217	3,107,576	637·8
Middle Atlantic		99,733	37,283,339	36,786,790	368·9
New York (1788)	(N.Y.)	47,377	18,241,266	17,558,072	370·6
New Jersey (1787)	(N.J.)	7,468	7,168,164	7,364,823	986·2
Pennsylvania (1787)	(Pa.)	44,888	11,793,909	11,863,895	264·3

[6] Between the 1910 census (15 April 1910) and the 1920 census (1 Jan. 1920), the period covered was 116 months (less than a full decade). Adjusting for this, the exact rate of increase for the decade was 15·4%. Similarly correcting for the 123 months between the 1920 and 1930 censuses, the true rate of increase was 15·7%.

[7] Figures for 1930 have been revised to include Mexicans (1,422,533), who were classified with 'Other Races' in the 1930 census reports.

[8] Figures for 1960 strictly comparable with those given for other years (*i.e.*, excluding Alaska and Hawaii) are: White, 158,454,956; Negroes, 18,860,117; other races, 1,149,163; total, 178,464,236; decennial increase, 18·4%.

Geographic divisions and states		Land area: sq. miles 1980	Census population 1 April 1970	Census population 1 April 1980	Pop. per sq. mile, 1980
East North Central		243,961	40,252,678	41,682,217	170·9
Ohio (1803)	(Oh.)	41,004	10,652,017	10,797,630	263·3
Indiana (1816)	(Ind.)	35,932	5,193,669	5,490,224	152·8
Illinois (1818)	(Ill.)	55,645	11,113,976	11,426,518	205·3
Michigan (1837)	(Mich.)	56,954	8,875,083	9,262,078	162·6
Wisconsin (1848)	(Wis.)	54,426	4,417,933	4,705,767	86·5
West North Central		508,132	16,344,389	17,183,453	33·8
Minnesota (1858)	(Minn.)	79,548	3,805,069	4,075,970	51·2
Iowa (1846)	(Ia.)	55,965	2,825,041	2,913,808	52·1
Missouri (1821)	(Mo.)	68,945	4,677,399	4,916,686	71·3
North Dakota (1889)	(N.D.)	69,300	617,761	652,717	9·4
South Dakota (1889)	(S.D.)	75,952	666,257	690,768	9·1
Nebraska (1867)	(Nebr.)	76,644	1,483,791	1,569,825	20·5
Kansas (1861)	(Kans.)	81,778	2,249,071	2,363,679	28·9
South Atlantic		266,910	30,671,337	36,959,123	138·5
Delaware (1787)	(Del.)	1,932	548,104	594,338	307·6
Maryland (1788)	(Md.)	9,837	3,922,399	4,216,975	428·7
Dist. of Columbia (1791)	(D.C.)	63	756,510	638,333	10,132·3
Virginia (1788)	(Va.)	39,704	4,648,494	5,346,818	134·7
West Virginia (1863)	(W. Va.)	24,119	1,744,237	1,949,644	80·8
North Carolina (1789)	(N.C.)	48,843	5,082,059	5,881,766	120·4
South Carolina (1788)	(S.C.)	30,203	2,590,516	3,121,820	103·4
Georgia (1788)	(Ga.)	58,056	4,589,575	5,463,105	94·1
Florida (1845)	(Fla.)	54,153	6,789,443	9,746,324	180·0
East South Central		178,824	12,804,552	14,666,423	82·0
Kentucky (1792)	(Ky.)	39,669	3,219,311	3,660,777	92·3
Tennessee (1796)	(Tenn.)	41,155	3,924,164	4,591,120	111·6
Alabama (1819)	(Al.)	50,767	3,444,165	3,893,888	76·7
Mississippi (1817)	(Miss.)	47,233	2,216,912	2,520,638	53·4
West South Central		427,271	19,322,458	23,746,816	55·6
Arkansas (1836)	(Ark.)	52,078	1,923,295	2,286,435	43·9
Louisiana (1812)	(La.)	44,521	3,643,180	4,205,900	94·5
Oklahoma (1907)	(Okla.)	68,655	2,559,253	3,025,290	44·1
Texas (1845)	(Tex.)	262,017	11,196,730	14,229,191	54·3
Mountain		855,193	8,283,585	11,372,785	13·3
Montana (1889)	(Mont.)	145,388	694,409	786,690	5·4
Idaho (1890)	(Id.)	82,412	713,008	943,935	11·5
Wyoming (1890)	(Wyo.)	96,989	332,416	469,557	4·8
Colorado (1876)	(Colo.)	103,595	2,207,259	2,889,964	27·9
New Mexico (1912)	(N. Mex.)	121,335	1,016,000	1,302,894	10·7
Arizona (1912)	(Ariz.)	113,508	1,772,482	2,718,215	23·9
Utah (1896)	(Ut.)	82,073	1,059,273	1,461,037	17·8
Nevada (1864)	(Nev.)	109,894	488,738	800,493	7·3
Pacific		896,253	26,525,774	31,799,705	35·5
Washington (1889)	(Wash.)	66,511	3,409,169	4,132,156	62·1
Oregon (1859)	(Oreg.)	96,184	2,091,385	2,633,105	27·4
California (1850)	(Calif.)	156,299	19,953,134	23,667,902	151·4
Alaska (1959)	(Ak.)	570,833	302,173	401,851	0·7
Hawaii (1960)	(Hi.)	6,425	769,913	964,691	150·1

Geographic divisions and states	Land area: sq. miles 1980	Census population 1 April 1970	Census population 1 April 1980	Pop. per sq. mile, 1980
Outlying Territories, total	4,691	4,720,306	3,565,376	760
Puerto Rico (1898)	3,515	2,712,033	3,196,520	909
Virgin Islands (1917)	132	62,438	96,569	731
American Samoa (1900)	77	27,159	32,297	419
Guam (1898)	209	84,996	105,979	507
Northern Marianas (1947)	184	9,640	16,780	91
Trust Territory of the Pacific (1947)	533	81,300	116,149	217
Midway Islands (1867)	2	2,220	453	226
Wake Island (1898)	3	1,647	302	100
Johnston and Sand Islands (1858)	...	1,007	327	...

The 1970 census showed 8,733,770 foreign-born Whites. The 8 countries contributing the largest numbers who were foreign-born were Italy, 1,005,687; Germany, 830,498; Canada, 798,782; Mexico, 746,327; UK, 681,140; Poland, 547,010; USSR, 461,444; Ireland, 250,492.

Increase or decrease of native White, and foreign-born White, population from 1860 to 1970, by decades:

	Native White			Foreign-born White		
	Total	Increase	Per cent increase	Total	Increase or decrease (–)	Per cent. change
1860	22,825,784	5,513,251	31·8	4,096,753	1,856,218	82·8
1870	28,095,665	5,269,881	23·1	5,493,712	1,396,959	34·1
1880	36,843,291	8,747,626	31·1	6,559,679	1,065,967	19·4
1890	45,979,391	9,018,732 [1]	24·5	9,121,867	2,562,188	39·1
1900	56,595,379	10,615,988	23·1	10,213,817	1,091,950	12·0
1910	68,386,412	11,791,033	20·8	13,345,545	3,131,728	30·7
1920	81,108,161	12,721,749	18·6	13,712,754	367,209	2·8
1930	96,303,335	15,195,174	18·7	13,983,405	270,651	2·0
1940	106,795,732	10,492,397	10·9	11,419,138	–2,564,267	–18·3
1950	124,780,860	17,985,128	16·8	10,161,168	–1,257,970	–11·0
1960	149,543,638	24,762,778	19·8	9,293,992	– 867,176	– 8·5
1970	169,385,451	19,841,813	13·3	8,773,770	– 560,222	6·0

[1] Exclusive of population specially enumerated in 1890 in Indian Territory and on Indian reservations.

The population of leading cities (with over 100,000 inhabitants) at the censuses of 1970 and 1980 were as follows:

Cities	1 April 1970	1 April 1980	Cities	1 April 1970	1 April 1980
New York, N.Y.	7,895,563	7,071,639	Boston, Mass.	641,071	562,994
Chicago, Ill.	3,369,357	3,005,072	New Orleans, La.	593,471	557,515
Los Angeles, Calif.	2,811,801	2,966,850	Jacksonville, Fla.	504,265	540,920
Philadelphia, Pa.	1,949,996	1,688,210	Seattle, Wash.	530,831	493,846
Houston, Tex.	1,233,535	1,595,138	Denver, Colo.	514,678	492,365
Detroit, Mich.	1,514,063	1,203,339	Nashville-Davidson, Tenn.	426,029	455,651
Dallas, Tex.	844,401	904,078	St Louis, Mo.	622,236	453,085
San Diego, Calif.	697,471	875,538	Kansas City, Mo.	507,330	448,159
Phoenix, Ariz.	584,303	789,704	El Paso, Tex.	322,261	425,259
Baltimore, Md.	905,787	786,775	Atlanta, Ga.	495,039	425,022
San Antonio, Tex.	645,153	785,880	Pittsburgh, Pa.	520,089	423,938
Indianapolis, Ind.	736,856	700,807	Oklahoma City, Okla.	368,164	403,213
San Francisco, Calif.	715,674	678,974	Cincinnati, Ohio	453,514	385,457
Memphis, Tenn.	623,988	646,356	Fort Worth, Tex.	393,455	385,164
Washington, D.C.	756,668	638,333	Minneapolis, Minn.	434,400	370,951
Milwaukee, Wisc.	717,372	636,212	Portland, Oregon	379,967	366,383
San José, Calif.	459,913	629,442	Honolulu, Hawaii	630,528	365,048
Cleveland, Ohio	750,879	573,822	Long Beach, Calif.	358,879	361,334
Columbus, Ohio	540,025	564,871			

Cities	1 April 1970	1 April 1980
Tulsa, Okla.	330,350	360,919
Buffalo, N.Y.	462,768	357,870
Toledo, Ohio	383,062	354,635
Miami, Fla.	334,859	346,865
Austin, Tex.	253,539	345,496
Oakland, Calif.	361,561	339,337
Albuquerque, N. Mex.	244,501	331,767
Tucson, Ariz.	262,933	330,537
Newark, N.J.	381,930	329,248
Charlotte, N.C.	241,420	314,447
Omaha, Nebr.	346,929	314,255
Louisville, Ky.	361,706	298,451
Birmingham, Ala.	300,910	284,413
Wichita, Kans.	276,554	279,272
Sacramento, Calif.	257,105	275,741
Tampa, Fla.	277,714	271,523
St Paul, Minn.	309,866	270,230
Norfolk, Va.	307,951	266,979
Virginia Beach, Va.	172,106	262,199
Rochester, N.Y.	295,011	241,741
St Petersburg, Fla.	216,159	238,647
Akron, Ohio	275,425	237,177
Corpus Christi, Tex.	204,525	231,999
Jersey City, N.J.	260,350	223,532
Baton Rouge, La.	165,921	219,419
Anaheim, Calif.	166,408	219,311
Richmond, Va.	249,332	219,214
Fresno, Calif.	165,655	218,202
Colorado Springs, Colo.	135,517	215,150
Shreveport, La.	182,064	205,820
Lexington-Fayette, Ky.	108,137	204,165
Santa Ana, Calif.	155,710	203,713
Dayton, Ohio	243,023	203,371
Jackson, Miss.	153,968	202,895
Mobile, Ala.	190,026	200,452
Yonkers, N.Y.	204,297	195,351
Des Moines, Iowa	201,404	191,003
Grand Rapids, Mich.	197,649	181,843
Montgomery, Ala.	133,386	177,857
Knoxville, Tenn.	174,587	175,030
Anchorage, Alaska	48,081	174,431
Lubbock, Tex.	149,101	173,979
Fort Wayne, Ind.	178,269	172,196
Lincoln, Nebr.	149,518	171,932
Spokane, Wash.	170,516	171,300
Riverside, Calif.	140,089	170,876
Madison, Wisc.	171,809	170,616
Huntington Beach, Calif.	115,960	170,505
Syracuse, N.Y.	197,297	170,105
Chattanooga, Tenn.	119,923	169,565
Columbus, Ga.	155,028	169,441
Las Vegas, Nev.	125,787	164,674
Salt Lake City, Utah	175,885	163,033
Worcester, Mass.	176,572	161,799
Warren, Mich.	179,260	161,134
Kansas City, Kans.	168,213	161,087
Arlington, Tex.	90,229	160,113
Flint, Mich.	193,317	159,611
Aurora, Colo.	74,974	158,588
Tacoma, Wash.	154,407	158,501
Little Rock, Ark.	132,483	158,461
Providence, R.I.	179,116	156,804
Greensboro, N.C.	144,076	155,642
Fort Lauderdale, Fla.	139,590	153,279
Mesa, Ariz.	63,049	152,453
Springfield, Mass.	163,905	152,319
Gary, Ind.	175,415	151,953
Raleigh, N.C.	122,830	150,255
Stockton, Calif.	109,963	149,779
Amarillo, Tex.	127,010	149,230
Hialeah, Fla.	102,452	145,254
Newport News, Va.	138,177	144,903
Bridgeport, Conn.	156,542	142,546
Huntsville, Ala.	139,282	142,513
Savannah, Ga.	118,349	141,390
Rockford, Ill.	147,370	139,712
Glendale, Calif.	132,664	139,060
Garland, Tex.	81,437	138,857
Paterson, N.J.	144,824	137,970
Hartford, Conn.	158,017	136,392
Springfield, Mo.	120,096	133,116
Fremont, Calif.	100,869	131,945
Winston-Salem, N.C.	133,683	131,885
Evansville, Ind.	138,764	130,496
Lansing, Mich.	131,403	130,414
Torrance, Calif.	134,968	129,881
Orlando, Fla.	99,006	128,291
New Haven, Conn.	137,707	126,109
Peoria, Ill.	126,963	124,160
Garden Grove, Calif.	121,155	123,307
Hampton, Va.	120,779	122,617
Hollywood, Fla.	106,873	121,323
Erie, Pa.	129,265	119,123
Pasadena, Calif.	112,951	118,550
Beaumont, Tex.	117,548	118,102
San Bernadino, Calif.	106,869	117,490
Macon, Ga.	122,423	116,896
Youngstown, Ohio	140,909	115,436
Topeka, Kans.	125,011	115,266
Chesapeake, Va.	89,580	114,486
Lakewood, Colo.	92,743	112,860
Pasadena, Tex.	89,957	112,560
Independence, Mo.	111,630	111,806
Cedar Rapids, Iowa	110,642	110,243
Irving, Tex.	97,260	109,943
South Bend, Ind.	125,580	109,727
Sterling Heights, Mich.	61,365	108,999
Oxnard, Calif.	71,225	108,195
Ann Arbor, Mich.	100,035	107,966
Tempe, Ariz.	63,550	106,743
Sunnyvale, Calif.	95,976	106,618
Modesto, Calif.	61,712	106,602
Elizabeth, N.J.	112,654	106,201
Eugene, Oregon	79,028	105,624
Bakersfield, Calif.	69,515	105,611
Livonia, Mich.	110,109	104,814
Portsmouth, Va.	110,963	104,577
Allentown, Pa.	109,871	103,758
Berkeley, Calif.	114,091	103,328
Waterbury, Conn.	108,033	103,266
Davenport, Iowa.	98,469	103,264
Concord, Calif.	85,164	103,255
Alexandria, Va.	110,927	103,217
Stamford, Conn.	108,798	102,453
Boise City, Idaho	74,990	102,451
Fullerton, Calif.	85,987	102,034
Albany, N.Y.	115,781	101,727
Pueblo, Colo.	97,774	101,686
Waco, Tex.	95,326	101,261
Columbia, S.C.	113,542	101,208
Durham, N.C.	95,438	100,831
Reno, Nev.	72,863	100,756
Roanoke, Va.	92,115	100,220

Vital Statistics: Vital statistics are based on records of births, deaths, fœtal deaths, marriages and divorces filed with registration officials of states and cities. Figures for the US include Alaska beginning with 1959 and Hawaii beginning with 1960.

Annual collection of mortality records from a national death-registration area was inaugurated in 1900. A national birth-registration area was established in 1915. These areas, which at their inception comprised 10 states and the District of Columbia, expanded gradually until 1933, when both the birth- and death-registration areas covered the entire continental US. Marriage and divorce statistics are compiled from reports furnished by state and local officials. Data on annulments are included in the divorce statistics. The marriage-registration area was established in 1957 with 30 states and 3 other areas. The divorce-registration area was established in 1958 with 14 states and 2 other areas. In Jan. 1980 the marriage-registration area included 42 states and D.C., and the divorce-registration area included 30 states.

	Live births [1]	Deaths [2]	Marriages [3]	Divorces [4]	Maternal deaths [5]	Deaths under 1 year [6]
1900	—	343,217	709,000	56,000	—	—
1910	2,777,000	696,856	948,000	83,000	—	—
1920	2,950,000	1,118,070	1,274,476	170,505	16,320	170,911
1930	2,618,000	1,327,240	1,126,856	195,961	14,915	143,201
1940	2,559,000	1,417,269	1,595,874	264,000	8,876	110,984
1950	3,632,000	1,452,454	1,667,231	385,144	2,960	103,825
1960	4,257,850 [7]	1,711,982	1,523,000	393,000	1,579	110,873
1970	3,731,386 [7]	1,921,031	2,158,802	708,000	803	74,667
1980	3,612,258	1,989,841	2,390,252	1,189,000	334	45,526
1981 [8]	3,646,000	1,987,000	2,438,000	1,219,000	340	42,700
1982 [8]	3,704,000	1,986,000	2,495,000	1,180,000	330	41,700

[1] Figures through 1959 include adjustment for under-registration (the 1959 registered count was 4,244,796); beginning 1960 figures represent number registered.
[2] Excluding fœtal deaths and deaths among the armed forces overseas.
[3] Estimates for all years except 1970.
[4] Includes reported annulments. Estimated for all years.
[5] Deaths for 1979–81 (Ninth Revision, International Classification of Diseases, 1975). Deaths from complications of pregnancy, childbirth and the puerperium. Deaths for 1968–78 were classified according to the Eighth Revision, International Classification of Diseases, adopted, 1965. Deaths for 1958–67 were classified according to the Seventh Revision of the International Lists of Diseases and Causes of Death, those for 1949–57 according to the Sixth Revision and those for 1939–48, according to the Fifth Revision.
[6] Excluding fœtal deaths.   [7] Based on a 50% sample.   [8] Provisional.

The crude birth rate, based on total live-birth estimates per 1,000 total population, fell from 29·5 in 1915 to 18·4 in 1933; it rose to a peak of 26·6 in 1947—its highest for 25 years. This peak reflects demobilization (1945–46), the record marriage rate that followed, and the high levels of employment and income. The decrease in the following 3 years was moderate. In 1951 the rate moved upward and levelled off in 1957 at about 25 per 1,000 population. Since 1957 the crude birth rate has declined every year to 18·4 live births per 1,000 population in 1966. The crude birth rate for 1979 was 15·6. Estimated number of illegitimate births in 1980 was 665,747, a ratio of 184·2 illegitimate births per 1,000 registered live births.

Deaths, excluding fœtal deaths (per 1,000 population), declined from 17·2 in 1900 to 10 in 1946. The death rate has been below 10 per 1,000 since 1947, fluctuating slightly from year to year, mainly under the impact of occurrences of outbreaks of severe respiratory diseases. Since the record low of 9·2 in 1954 the rate has changed only between 9·3 and 9·7. The rate for 1970, 9·5; for 1973, 9·3; for 1974, 9·1; for 1975, 8·8; for 1976, 8·8; for 1977, 8·6; for 1978, 8·7; for 1979, 8·5; 1980, 8·8.

Leading causes of death, 1980, per 100,000 population: Diseases of heart, 336; malignant neoplasms, 183·9; cerebrovascular diseases, 75·1; accidents, 46·7. Suicides in 1980 were 11·9 per 100,000 population; homicides, 10·7.

The marriage rate per 1,000 population for selected years are: 1920, 12; 1932, 7·9; 1946, 16·4; 1951, 10·4; 1961, 8·5; 1969, 10·6; 1970, 10·6; 1971, 10·6; 1975, 10; 1976, 9·9; 1977, 9·9; 1978, 10·3; 1979, 10·4; 1980, 10·6. The divorce rates per 1,000 population for selected years are: 1920, 1·6; 1946, 4·3; 1951, 2·5; 1961, 2·3; 1971, 3·7; 1976, 5; 1977, 5; 1978, 5·1; 1979, 5·3; 1980, 5·2.

Maternal mortality rates (deaths of mothers from conditions associated with deliveries and complications of pregnancy, childbirth and the puerperium) per 100,000 live births, were 1915–19, 727·9 and thereafter declined: 493·9 for 1935–39; 376 for 1940; 207·2 for 1945; 83·3 for 1950; 47 for 1955; 37·1 for 1960; 31·6 for 1965; 21·5 for 1970; 12·8 for 1975; 11·2 for 1977; 9·6 for 1978; 9·6 for 1979; 9·2 for 1980. The 1980 rate for white women was 6·7 and for all other women 19·8. By state, the average maternal mortality rate for 1976–78 was highest for Wyoming (32·9) and lowest for Connecticut (3·7).

The infant mortality rates, per 1,000 live births were: 1915–19, 95·7; 1920–24, 76·7; 1925–29, 69; 1930–34, 60·4; 38·3 in 1945; 29·2 in 1950; 26·4 in 1955; 26 in 1960; 20 in 1970; 16·1 in 1975; 15·2 in 1976; 14·1 in 1977; 13·8 in 1978; 13·1 in 1979. In 1979 the rate for whites was 11·4; for all other, 19·8. In 1980, white, 11, all other, 19·1.

Immigration: The Immigration and Nationality Act, as amended by Public Law 95–412, establishes a worldwide numerical ceiling of 290,000 visas, with a maximum of 20,000 visas available for any one country. The visas are allocated under a system of 7 preference categories, 4 of which are designed to reunite close relatives of US citizens and resident aliens of the US, 2 for skilled and professional workers and 1 for refugees. Visa numbers not used in any of the preference categories are made available to qualified non-preference immigrants. Spouses, children and parents of US citizens are exempt from the numerical limitations.

During the year ended 30 Sept. 1979, 460,348 aliens became permanent residents of the US. Of the total immigrants admitted, 331,747 had obtained visas abroad and entered the US while 128,601 aliens who were already in the US had their status adjusted to that of permanent residents.

Immigrant aliens admitted to US for permanent residence, by country or region of birth.

Country or region of birth	*Immigrants admitted*			
	1976	1977 [1]	1978	1979
All countries	398,613	462,315	601,442	460,348
Europe	72,411	70,000	73,198	60,845
Germany (GDR and FRG)	5,836	6,372	6,739	6,314
Greece	8,417	7,838	7,035	5,090
Italy	8,380	7,500	7,415	6,174
Poland	3,805	4,000	5,050	4,413
Portugal	10,511	9,657	10,445	7,085
Spain	2,254	2,487	2,297	1,933
UK	11,392	12,477	14,245	13,907
Yugoslavia	2,820	2,791	2,621	2,171
Other Europe	18,996	16,868	17,351	13,758
Asia	149,881	157,759	249,776 [1]	189,293
China and Taiwan	18,823	19,764	21,315	24,264
Hong Kong	5,766	5,632	5,158	4,119
India	17,487	18,613	20,753	19,708
Japan	4,258	4,178	4,010	4,048
Korea (North and South)	30,803	30,917	29,288	29,248
Philippines	37,281	39,111	37,216	41,300
Thailand	6,923	3,945	3,574	3,194
Other Asia	28,540	35,599	128,462	63,412
North America	142,307	187,345	220,778	157,579
Canada	7,638	12,688	16,863	13,772
Mexico	57,863	44,079	92,367	52,096
Cuba	29,233	69,708	29,754	15,585
Dominican Republic	12,526	11,655	19,458	17,519
Haiti	5,410	5,441	6,470	6,433
Jamaica	9,026	11,501	19,265	19,714
Trinidad and Tobago	4,839	6,106	5,973	5,225
Other West Indies	5,805	9,600	10,441	9,598
Central America	9,912	16,485	20,153	17,547
Other North America	55	82	34	90

[1] Year ending 30 Sept.

Country or region of birth	1976	Immigrants admitted 1977 [1]	1978	1979
South America	22,699	32,954	41,764	35,344
Colombia	5,742	8,272	11,032	10,637
Ecuador	4,504	5,302	5,732	4,383
Other South America	12,453	19,380	25,000	20,324
Africa	7,723	10,155	11,524	12,838
Australia and New Zealand	1,796	1,986	2,184	1,999
Other countries	1,796	2,106	2,218	2,450

[1] Year ending 30 Sept.

The total number of immigrants admitted from 1820 up to 30 Sept. 1979 was 49,125,313; this included 6,984,909 from Germany (GDR and FRG), and from Italy 5,300,387.

Aliens coming to the US for temporary periods of time are classified as non-immigrants. During the first 9 months of fiscal year 1979, a total of 7,060,082 non-immigrants were admitted. This is exclusive of multiple entry documents and excludes border crossers, crewmen and insular travellers. Tourists, primarily from Mexico, Japan, the UK, the West Indies, Germany (GDR and FRG) and Canada numbered 3,160,963. There were 992,025 aliens expelled during the first 9 months of fiscal year 1979. Of this number, 25,888 were deported and 966,137 were required to depart without formal orders of deportation.

In accordance with the Immigration and Nationality Act, 5,381,106 aliens reported their address in Jan. 1980. Of this total, 4,532,647 were permanent residents and 848,459 were aliens here temporarily. Of the permanent resident aliens who reported the best represented nationalities were the following: Mexico, 992,765; Canada, 301,085; Cuba, 279,100; UK, 273,521; Philippines, 223,743; Italy, 163,700; Germany (GDR and FRG), 147,647. Over 76% of the permanent resident aliens reported their states of residence as: California, 1,261,069; New York, 690,383; Texas, 411,163; Florida, 335,457; Illinois, 256,091; New Jersey, 238,883; Massachusetts, 152,916, and Michigan, 118,588.

In the year ended 30 Sept. 1979, 164,150 persons became US citizens through naturalization; this includes, 132,533 naturalized under the general provisions of 5-year residence in the US, 25,701 spouses and children of US citizens, 5,874 military and 42 who were naturalized under other provisions. Of the total, there were 13,313 former nationals of Cuba, 17,749 of the Philippines, 11,446 of China and Taiwan, 13,406 of Korea, 8,065 of UK, 7,296 of Italy, 8,046 of Mexico and 7,632 of Jamaica.

CLIMATE. For temperature and rainfall figures, see entries on individual states as indicated by regions, below, of mainland USA.

Pacific Coast. The climate varies with latitude, distance from the sea and the effect of relief, ranging from polar conditions in North Alaska through cool to warm temperate climates further south. The extreme south is temperate desert. Rainfall everywhere is moderate. *See* Alaska, California, Oregon, Washington.

Mountain States. Very varied, with relief exerting the main control; very cold in the north in winter, with considerable snowfall. In the south, much higher temperatures and aridity produce desert conditions. Rainfall everywhere is very variable as a result of rain-shadow influences. *See* Arizona, Colorado, Idaho, Montana, Nevada, New Mexico, Utah, Wyoming.

High Plains. A continental climate with a large annual range of temperature and moderate rainfall, mainly in summer, although unreliable. Dust storms are common in summer and blizzards in winter. *See* Nebraska, North Dakota, South Dakota.

Central Plains. A temperate continental climate, with hot summers and cold winters, except in the extreme south. Rainfall is plentiful and comes at all seasons, but there is a summer maximum in western parts. *See* Mississippi, Missouri, Oklahoma, Texas.

Mid-West. Continental, with hot summers and cold winters. Rainfall is moderate, with a summer maximum in most parts. *See* Indiana, Iowa, Kansas.

Great Lakes. Continental, resembling that of the Central Plains, with hot summers but very cold winters because of the freezing of the lakes. Rainfall is moderate with a slight summer maximum. *See* Illinois, Michigan, Minnesota, Ohio, Wisconsin.

Appalachian Mountains. The north is cool temperate with cold winters, the south warm temperate with milder winters. Precipitation is heavy, increasing to the south but evenly distributed over the year. *See* Kentucky, Pennsylvania, Tennessee, West Virginia.

Gulf Coast. Conditions vary from warm temperate to sub-tropical, with plentiful rainfall, decreasing towards the west but evenly distributed over the year. *See* Alabama, Arkansas, Florida, Louisiana.

Atlantic Coast. Temperate maritime climate but with great differences in temperature according to latitude. Rainfall is ample at all seasons; snowfall in the north can be heavy. *See* Delaware, District of Columbia, Georgia, Maryland, New Jersey, New York, North Carolina, South Carolina, Virginia.

New England. Cool temperate, with severe winters and warm summers. Precipitation is well distributed with a slight winter maximum. Snowfall is heavy in winter. *See* Connecticut, Maine, Massachusetts, New Hampshire, Rhode Island, Vermont. *See* also Hawaii and Outlying Territories.

CONSTITUTION AND GOVERNMENT. The form of government of the USA is based on the constitution of 17 Sept. 1787.

By the constitution the government of the nation is composed of three co-ordinate branches, the executive, the legislative and the judicial.

The National Government has authority in matters of general taxation, treaties and other dealings with foreign Powers, foreign and inter-state commerce, bankruptcy, postal service, coinage, weights and measures, patents and copyright, the armed forces (including, to a certain extent, the militia), and crimes against the USA; it has sole legislative authority over the District of Columbia and the possessions of the US.

The 5th article of the constitution provides that Congress may, on a two-thirds vote of both houses, propose amendments to the constitution, or, on the application of the legislatures of two-thirds of all the states, call a convention for proposing amendments, which in either case shall be valid as part of the constitution when ratified by the legislatures of three-fourths of the several states, or by conventions in three-fourths thereof, whichever mode of ratification may be proposed by Congress. Ten amendments (called collectively 'the Bill of Rights') to the constitution were added 15 Dec. 1791; two in 1795 and 1804; a 13th amendment, 6 Dec. 1865, abolishing slavery; a 14th in 1868, including the important 'due process' clause; a 15th, 3 Feb. 1870, establishing equal voting rights for white and coloured; a 16th, 3 Feb. 1913, authorizing the income tax; a 17th, 8 April 1913, providing for popular election of senators; an 18th, 16 Jan. 1919, prohibiting alcoholic liquors; a 19th, 18 Aug. 1920, establishing woman suffrage; a 20th, 23 Jan. 1933, advancing the date of the President's and Vice-President's inauguration and abolishing the 'lame-duck' sessions of Congress; a 21st, 5 Dec. 1933, repealing the 18th amendment; a 22nd, 26 Feb. 1951, limiting a President's tenure of office to 2 terms, or to 2 terms plus 2 years in the case of a Vice-President who has succeeded to the office of a President; a 23rd, 30 March 1961, granting citizens of the District of Columbia the right to vote in national elections; a 24th, 4 Feb. 1964, banning the use of the poll-tax in federal elections; a 25th. 10 Feb. 1967, dealing with Presidential disability and succession; a 26th, 22 June 1970, establishing the right of citizens who are 18 years of age and older to vote.

National flag: Seven red and 6 white alternating stripes, horizontal; with a blue canton, extending down to the lower edge of the 4th red stripe from the top, and displaying 50 white 5-pointed stars, one for each state. The stars have one point directed vertically upward, and they are arranged in 6 rows of 5 each, alternating with 5 rows of 4 each. On the admission of additional states, stars are added, effective on 4 July following the date of admission. Congress, by law of 22 Dec. 1942, has codified 'existing rules and customs' pertaining to the display of the flag, for civilians.

National anthem: The Star-spangled Banner, 'Oh say, can you see by the dawn's early light' (words by F. S. Key, 1814; tune by J. S. Smith; formally adopted by Congress 3 March 1931).

National motto: 'In God we trust'; formally adopted by Congress 30 July 1956.

Presidency. The executive power is vested in a president, who holds office for 4 years, and is elected, together with a vice-president chosen for the same term, by electors from each state, equal to the whole number of senators and representatives to which the state may be entitled in the Congress. The President must be a natural-born citizen, resident in the country for 14 years, and at least 35 years old.

The presidential election is held every fourth (leap) year on the Tuesday after the first Monday in November. Technically, this is an election of presidential electors, not of a president directly; the electors thus chosen meet and give their votes (for the candidate to whom they are pledged, in some states by law, but in most states by custom and prudent politics) at their respective state capitals on the first Monday after the second Wednesday in December next following their election; and the votes of the electors of all the states are opened and counted in the presence of both Houses of Congress on the sixth day of January. The total electorate vote is one for each senator and representative.

If the successful candidate for President dies before taking office the Vice-President-elect becomes President; if no candidate has a majority or if the successful candidate fails to qualify, then, by the 20th amendment, the Vice-President acts as President until a president qualifies. The duties of the Presidency, in absence of the President and Vice-President by reason of death, resignation, removal, inability or failure to qualify, devolve upon the Speaker of the House under legislation enacted 18 July 1947. And in case of absence of a Speaker for like reason, the presidential duties devolve upon the President *pro tem.* of the Senate and successively upon those members of the Cabinet in order of precedence, who have the constitutional qualifications for President.

The presidential term, by the 20th amendment to the constitution, begins at noon on 20 Jan. of the inaugural year. This amendment also installs the newly elected Congress in office on 3 Jan. instead of—as formerly—in the following December. The President's salary is $200,000 per year, plus $50,000 to assist in defraying expenses resulting from official duties. Also he may spend up to $100,000 non-taxable for travel and $20,000 for official entertainment. The office of Vice-President carries a salary of $91,000, plus $10,000 allowance for travel, all taxable.

The President is C.-in-C. of the Army, Navy and Air Force, and of the militia when in the service of the Union. The Vice-President is *ex-officio* President of the Senate, and in the case of 'the removal of the President, or of his death, resignation, or inability to discharge the powers and duties of his office', he becomes the President for the remainder of the term.

President of the United States: Ronald Reagan, of California, born at Tampico, Illinois, in 1911; Governor of California, 1967–75.

At the Presidential election on 4 Nov. 1980 total vote cast, including men and women in the armed services, was 86,513,296, of which Ronald Reagan (R.) received 43,901,812 (50·7%), James Earl Carter (D.) 35,483,820 (41%) and John Anderson 5,719,722 (6·6%). Electoral college votes: Reagan 489; Carter 49; Anderson 0.

PRESIDENTS OF THE USA

Name	From state	Term of service	Born	Died
George Washington	Virginia	1789–97	1732	1799
John Adams	Massachusetts	1797–1801	1735	1826
Thomas Jefferson	Virginia	1801–09	1743	1826
James Madison	Virginia	1809–17	1751	1836
James Monroe	Virginia	1817–25	1759	1831
John Quincy Adams	Massachusetts	1825–29	1767	1848

Name	From state	Term of service	Born	Died
Andrew Jackson	Tennessee	1829–37	1767	1845
Martin Van Buren	New York	1837–41	1782	1862
William H. Harrison	Ohio	Mar.–Apr. 1841	1773	1841
John Tyler	Virginia	1841–45	1790	1862
James K. Polk	Tennessee	1845–49	1795	1849
Zachary Taylor	Louisiana	1849–July 1850	1784	1850
Millard Fillmore	New York	1850–53	1800	1874
Franklin Pierce	New Hampshire	1853–57	1804	1869
James Buchanan	Pennsylvania	1857–61	1791	1868
Abraham Lincoln	Illinois	1861–Apr. 1865	1809	1865
Andrew Johnson	Tennessee	1865–69	1808	1875
Ulysses S. Grant	Illinois	1869–77	1822	1885
Rutherford B. Hayes	Ohio	1877–81	1822	1893
James A. Garfield	Ohio	Mar.–Sept. 1881	1831	1881
Chester A. Arthur	New York	1881–85	1830	1886
Grover Cleveland	New York	1885–89	1837	1908
Benjamin Harrison	Indiana	1889–93	1833	1901
Grover Cleveland	New York	1893–97	1837	1908
William McKinley	Ohio	1897–Sept. 1901	1843	1901
Theodore Roosevelt	New York	1901–09	1858	1919
William H. Taft	Ohio	1909–13	1857	1930
Woodrow Wilson	New Jersey	1913–21	1856	1924
Warren Gamaliel Harding	Ohio	1921–Aug. 1923	1865	1923
Calvin Coolidge	Massachusetts	1923–29	1872	1933
Herbert C. Hoover	California	1929–33	1874	1964
Franklin D. Roosevelt	New York	1933–Apr. 1945	1882	1945
Harry S. Truman	Missouri	1945–53	1884	1972
Dwight D. Eisenhower	New York	1953–61	1890	1969
John F. Kennedy	Massachusetts	1961–Nov. 1963	1917	1963
Lyndon B. Johnson	Texas	1963–69	1908	1973
Richard M. Nixon	California	1969–74	1913	—
Gerald R. Ford	Michigan	1974–77	1913	—
James Earl Carter	Georgia	1977–81	1924	—
Ronald Reagan	California	1981–	1911	—

VICE-PRESIDENTS OF THE USA

Name	From state	Term of service	Born	Died
John Adams	Massachusetts	1789–97	1735	1826
Thomas Jefferson	Virginia	1797–1801	1743	1826
Aaron Burr	New York	1801–05	1756	1836
George Clinton	New York	1805–12 [1]	1739	1812
Elbridge Gerry	Massachusetts	1813–14 [1]	1744	1814
Daniel D. Tompkins	New York	1817–25	1774	1825
John C. Calhoun	South Carolina	1825–32 [1]	1782	1850
Martin Van Buren	New York	1833–37	1782	1862
Richard M. Johnson	Kentucky	1837–41	1780	1850
John Tyler	Virginia	Mar.–Apr. 1841 [1]	1790	1862
George M. Dallas	Pennsylvania	1845–49	1792	1864
Millard Fillmore	New York	1849–50 [1]	1800	1874
William R. King	Alabama	Mar.–Apr. 1853 [1]	1786	1853
John C. Breckinridge	Kentucky	1857–61	1821	1875
Hannibal Hamlin	Maine	1861–65	1809	1891
Andrew Johnson	Tennessee	Mar.–Apr. 1865 [1]	1808	1875
Schuyler Colfax	Indiana	1869–73	1823	1885
Henry Wilson	Massachusetts	1873–75 [1]	1812	1875
William A. Wheeler	New York	1877–81	1819	1887
Chester A. Arthur	New York	Mar.–Sept. 1881 [1]	1830	1886
Thomas A. Hendricks	Indiana	Mar.–Nov. 1885 [1]	1819	1885
Levi P. Morton	New York	1889–93	1824	1920

[1] Position vacant thereafter until commencement of the next presidential term.

1376

Name	From state	Term of service	Born	Died
Adlai Stevenson	Illinois	1893–97	1835	1914
Garret A. Hobart	New Jersey	1897–99 [1]	1844	1899
Theodore Roosevelt	New York	Mar.–Sept. 1901 [1]	1858	1919
Charles W. Fairbanks	Indiana	1905–09	1855	1920
James S. Sherman	New York	1909–12 [1]	1855	1912
Thomas R. Marshall	Indiana	1913–21	1854	1925
Calvin Coolidge	Massachusetts	1921–Aug. 1923 [1]	1872	1933
Charles G. Dawes	Illinois	1925–29	1865	1951
Charles Curtis	Kansas	1929–33	1860	1935
John N. Garner	Texas	1933–41	1868	1967
Henry A. Wallace	Iowa	1941–45	1888	1965
Harry S. Truman	Missouri	1945–Apr. 1945 [1]	1884	1972
Alben W. Barkley	Kentucky	1949–53	1877	1956
Richard M. Nixon	California	1953–61	1913	—
Lyndon B. Johnson	Texas	1961–Nov. 1963 [1]	1908	1973
Hubert H. Humphrey	Minnesota	1965–69	1911	1978
Spiro T. Agnew	Maryland	1969–73	1918	—
Gerald R. Ford	Michigan	1973–74	1913	—
Nelson Rockefeller	New York	1974–77	1908	1979
Walter Mondale	Minnesota	1977–81	1928	—
George Bush	Texas	1981–	1924	—

[1] Position vacant thereafter until commencement of the next presidential term.

Cabinet. The administrative business of the nation has been traditionally vested in several executive departments, the heads of which, unofficially and *ex officio,* formed the President's Cabinet. Beginning with the Interstate Commerce Commission in 1887, however, an increasing amount of executive business has been entrusted to some 60 so-called independent agencies, such as the Veterans Administration, Housing and Home Finance Agency, Tariff Commission, etc.

All heads of departments and of the 60 or more administrative agencies are appointed by the President, but must be confirmed by the Senate.

The Cabinet consisted of the following (March 1984):

1. *Secretary of State* (created 1789). George P. Shultz; businessman, Secretary of Labor, 1969–70, Secretary of the Treasury, 1972–74; born 1920.

2. *Secretary of the Treasury* (1789). Donald Regan, of New York; Chairman of Merrill Lynch and Company, securities; born 1918.

3. *Secretary of Defense* (1947). Caspar Weinberger, Vice-President of the Bechtel Power Corporation; lawyer, former Secretary of Health, Education and Welfare; born 1918.

4. *Attorney-General* (Department of Justice, 1870). Edwin Meese, of California; Lawyer and Special Counsellor to the President; born 1931.

5. *Secretary of the Interior* (1849). William Clark, Lawyer, Justice of California Supreme Court; President's Assistant for National Security Affairs, 1982–83; born, 1930.

6. *Secretary of Agriculture* (1889). John R. Block, of Illinois; farmer; director of the Illinois Farm Bureau; born 1935.

7. *Secretary of Commerce* (1903). Malcolm Baldrige, of Connecticut; manufacturer; born 1922.

8. *Secretary of Labor* (1913). Raymond J. Donovan, of New Jersey; construction company executive; born 1930.

9. *Secretary of Health and Human Services* (1953). Margaret M. Heckler, of Massachusetts; lawyer and congresswoman; born 1931.

10. *Secretary of Housing and Urban Development* (1966). Samuel J. Pierce, of New York; lawyer; born 1922.

11. *Secretary of Transportation* (1967). Elizabeth H. Dole, of North Carolina; lawyer, Federal Trade Commissioner 1973–79, President's public liaison assistant, 1981; born 1936.

12. *Secretary of Energy* (1977). Donald P. Hodel, of Oregon; lawyer, undersecretary at the Department of the Interior 1978–81; born 1935.

13. *Secretary of Education* (1979). Terrel H. Bell, of Utah; Commissioner of Education, Utah, 1976–81; born 1921.

Each of the above Cabinet officers receives an annual salary of $80,100 and holds office during the pleasure of the President.

Congress: The legislative power is vested by the Constitution in a Congress, consisting of a Senate and House of Representatives.

Electorate: By amendments of the constitution, disqualification of voters on the ground of race, colour or sex is forbidden. Accordingly, the electorate consists theoretically of all citizens of both sexes over 18 years of age, but the franchise is not universal. There are requirements of residence varying in the several states as to length from 6 months to 2 years and differing requirements as to registration. In 20 states the ability to read (usually an extract from the constitution) is required—in Alaska the ability to read English; in Hawaii, English or Hawaiian; in Louisiana, English or one's native tongue. In Alabama the voter must take an 'anti-Communist oath' and fill out a questionnaire to the satisfaction of the registrars. In some southern states voters are required to give a reasonable explanation of what they read. In most states convicts are excluded from the franchise, in some states duellists and fraudulent voters.

Legislation designed to discourage the rise of third parties has been adopted in a few states. In Illinois a new party must present a petition signed by at least 25,000 voters, including at least 200 in each of 50 of the 102 counties.

The method of balloting varies greatly. Seventeen states use different ballots for federal, state and local elections. In Delaware and South Carolina the various political parties furnish their own ballot-papers to the voters as he or she enters the polling-booth.

Senate: The Senate consists of 2 members from each state, chosen by popular vote for 6 years, one-third retiring or seeking re-election every 2 years. Senators must be no less than 30 years of age; must have been citizens of the USA for 9 years, and be residents in the states for which they are chosen. The Senate has complete freedom to initiate legislation, except revenue bills (which must originate in the House of Representatives); it may, however, amend or reject any legislation originating in the lower house. The Senate is also entrusted with the power of giving or withholding its 'advice and consent' to the ratification of all treaties initiated by the President with foreign Powers, a two-thirds majority of senators present being required for approval. (However, it has no control over 'international executive agreements' made by the President with foreign governments; such 'agreements', representing an important but very recent development, cover a wide range and are actually more numerous than formal treaties.) It also has the power of confirming or rejecting major appointments to office made by the President, but it has no direct control over the appointment by the President of 'personal representatives' or 'personal envoys' on missions abroad. Members of the Senate constitute a High Court of Impeachment, with power, by a two-thirds vote, to remove from office and disqualify any civil officer of the USA impeached by the House of Representatives, which has the sole power of impeachment.

The Senate has 16 Standing Committees to which all bills are referred for study, revision or rejection. The House of Representatives has 24 such committees. In both Houses each Standing Committee has a chairman and a majority representing the majority party of the whole House; each has numerous sub-committees. The jurisdictions of these Committees correspond largely to those of the appropriate executive departments and agencies. Both Houses also have a few special Committees with limited duration; there were (1984) 4 Joint Committees.

House of Representatives: The House of Representatives consists of 435 members elected every second year. The number of each state's representatives is determined by the decennial census, in the absence of specific Congressional legislation affecting the basis. The states, in 1983, had the following representatives:

Alabama	7	Indiana	10	Nebraska	3	South Carolina	6
Alaska	1	Iowa	6	Nevada	2	South Dakota	1
Arizona	5	Kansas	5	New Hampshire	2	Tennessee	9
Arkansas	4	Kentucky	7	New Jersey	14	Texas	27
California	45	Louisiana	8	New Mexico	3	Utah	3
Colorado	6	Maine	2	New York	34	Vermont	1
Connecticut	6	Maryland	8	North Carolina	11	Virginia	10
Delaware	1	Massachusetts	11	North Dakota	1	Washington	8
Florida	19	Michigan	18	Ohio	21	West Virginia	4
Georgia	10	Minnesota	8	Oklahoma	6	Wisconsin	9
Hawaii	2	Mississippi	5	Oregon	5	Wyoming	1
Idaho	2	Missouri	9	Pennsylvania	23		
Illinois	22	Montana	2	Rhode Island	2		

The Supreme Court decided on 17 Feb. 1964, that the federal constitution requires congressional districts within each state to be substantially equal in population. By almost invariable custom the representative lives in the district from which he is elected.

Representatives must be not less than 25 years of age, citizens of the USA for 7 years and residents in the state from which they are chosen. The District of Columbia, Guam, American Samoa and the Virgin Islands have one non-voting delegate each. The House also admits a 'resident commissioner' from Puerto Rico, who has the right to speak on any subject and to make motions, but not to vote; he is elected in the same manner as the representatives but for a 4-year term. Each of the two Houses of Congress is sole 'judge of the elections, returns and qualifications of its own members'; and each of the Houses may, with the concurrence of two-thirds, expel a member. The period usually termed 'a Congress' in legislative language continues for 2-years, terminating at noon on 3 Jan.

The salary of a senator is $60,662 per annum, with tax-free expense allowance and allowances for travelling expenses and for clerical hire. The salary of the Speaker of the House of Representatives is $90,100 per annum, with a taxable allowance. The salary of a Member of the House is $69,800.

No senator or representative can, during the time for which he is elected, be appointed to any *civil* office under authority of the USA which shall have been created or the emoluments of which shall have been increased during such time; and no person holding *any* office under the USA can be a member of either House during his continuance in office. No religious text may be required as a qualification to any office or public trust under the USA or in any state.

The 98th Congress (1983–84) was constituted (Jan 1983) as follows: Senate, 53 Republicans, 46 Democrats, 1 Independent; House of Representatives, 267 Democrats, 166 Republicans and 3 seats subject to re-election.

Indians: By an Act passed on 2 June 1924 full citizenship was granted to all Indians born in the USA, though those remaining in tribal units were still under special federal jurisdiction. Those remaining in tribal units constitute from one-half to three-fourths of the Indian population. The Indian Reorganization Act of 1934 gave the tribal Indians, at their own option, substantial opportunities to self-government and of self-controlled corporate enterprises empowered to borrow money, buy land, machinery and equipment; these corporations are controlled by democratically elected tribal councils; by 1945 roughly a third of the Indians had taken advantage of this Act. Recently a trend towards releasing Indians from federal supervision has resulted in legislation terminating supervision over specific tribes. Indian lands (1979) amounted to 52,468,000 acres, of which 42,008,000 was tribally owned and 10·01m. in trust allotments. Indian lands are held free of taxes. Total Indian population at the 1980 census was 1,418,195, of which Oklahoma, Arizona, California and New Mexico accounted for 628,400.

State and Local Government: The Union comprises 13 original states, 7 states which were admitted without having been previously organized as territories, and

30 states which had been territories—50 states in all. Each state has its own constitution (which the USA guarantees shall be republican in form), deriving its authority, not from Congress, but from the people of the state. Admission of states into the Union has been granted by special Acts of Congress, either (1) in the form of 'enabling Acts' providing for the drafting and ratification of a state constitution by the people, in which case the territory becomes a state as soon as the conditions are fulfilled, or (2) accepting a constitution already framed, and at once granting admission.

Each state is provided with a legislature of two Houses (except Nebraska, which since 1937 has had a single-chamber legislature), a governor and other executive officials, and a judicial system. Both Houses of the legislature are elective, but the senators (having larger electoral districts usually covering 2 or 3 counties compared with the single county or, in some states, the town, which sends 1 representative to the Lower House) are less numerous than the representatives, while in 38 states their terms are 4 years; in 12 states the term is 2 years. Of the 4-year senates, Illinois, Montana and New Jersey provide for two 4-year terms and one 2-year term in each decade. Terms of the lower houses are usually shorter; in 45 states, 2 years.

Members of both Houses are paid at the same rate, which varies from $200 per biennium (New Hampshire) to $31,000 per year (Michigan). The trend is towards annual sessions of state legislatures; in 1982, 36 were constitutionally required to meet annually (in 1939, only 4), the other 14 holding biennial sessions, 12 in the odd-numbered and 2 in the even-numbered years. Of these 14, 6 met annually in practice by invoking flexible constitutional powers to reconvene at intervals during the biennium.

The Governor has power to summon an extraordinary session, but not to dissolve or adjourn. The duties of the two Houses are similar, but in many states money bills must be introduced first in the Lower House. The Senate sits as a court for the trial of officials impeached by the other House, and often has power to confirm or reject appointments made by the Governor.

State legislatures are competent to deal with all matters not reserved for the federal government by the federal constitution nor specifically prohibited by the federal or state constitutions. Among their powers are the determination of the qualifications for the right of suffrage, and the control of all elections to public office, including elections of members of Congress and electors of President and Vice-President; the criminal law, both in its enactment and in its execution, with unimportant exceptions, and the administration of prisons; the civil law, including all matters pertaining to the possession and transfer of, and succession to, property; marriage and divorce, and all other civil relations; the chartering and control of all manufacturing, trading, transportation and other corporations, subject only to the right of Congress to regulate commerce passing from one state to another; labour; education; charities; licensing; fisheries within state waters, and game laws (apart from the hunting of migratory birds, which is a federal concern under treaties with Canada and Mexico). Taxes on income were left to the states until 1913, when the 16th amendment authorized the imposition of federal taxes on income without regard to apportionment.

The Governor is chosen by direct vote of the people over the whole state. His term of office varies in the several states from 2 to 4 years, and his salary from $35,000 (Arkansas, Delaware, Maine) to $85,000 (New Jersey, New York). His duty is to see to the faithful administration of the law, and he has command of the military forces of the state. He may recommend measures but does not present bills to the legislature. In some states he presents estimates. In all but one of the states (North Carolina) the Governor has a veto upon legislation, which may, however, be overridden by the two Houses, in some states by a simple majority, in others by a three-fifths or two-thirds majority. In some states the Governor, on his death or resignation, is succeeded by a Lieut.-Governor who was elected at the same time and has been presiding over the state Senate. In several states the Speaker of the Lower House succeeds the Governor.

The chief officials by whom the administration of state affairs is carried on (secretaries, treasurers, members of boards of commissioners, etc.) are usually chosen by the people at the general state elections for terms similar to those for which governors hold office.

Local Government. The chief unit of local government is the county, of which there were (1982) 2,992 with definite functions; in addition, Rhode Island has 5 'counties' which have no functions; Alaska does not have 'counties' as such and, since Oct. 1960, there has been no active county government in Connecticut. Louisiana has 64 'parishes'. The counties maintain public order through the sheriff and his deputies, who may, in a crisis, be drawn temporarily from willing citizens; in many states the counties maintain the smaller local highways; other functions are the granting of licences and the apportionment and collection of taxes. In a few states they also manage the schools.

The unit of local government in New England is the rural township, governed directly by the voters, who assemble annually or oftener if necessary, and legislate in local affairs, levy taxes, make appropriations and appoint and instruct the local officials (selectmen, clerk, school-committee, etc.). Townships are grouped to form counties. Where cities exist, the township government is superseded by the city government.

The **District of Columbia,** ceded by the State of Maryland for the purposes of government in 1791, is the seat of the US Government. It includes the city of Washington, and embraces a land area of 61 sq. miles. The Reorganization Plan No. 3 of 1967 instituted a Mayor Council form of government with appointed officers. In 1973 an elected Mayor and elected councillors were introduced; in 1974 they received power to legislate in local matters. Congress retains power to enact legislation and to veto or supersede the Council's acts. Since 1961 citizens have had the right to vote in national elections. On 23 Aug. 1978 the Senate approved a constitutional amendment giving the District full voting representation in Congress. This has still to be ratified.

The **Commonwealth of Puerto Rico, American Samoa, Guam and the Virgin Islands** each have a local legislature, whose acts may be modified or annulled by Congress, though in practice this has seldom been done. Puerto Rico since its attainment of commonwealth status on 25 July 1952, enjoys practically complete self-government, including the election of its governor and other officials. The conduct of foreign relations, however, is still a federal function and federal bureaux and agencies still operate in the island.

General supervision of territorial administration is exercised by the Office of Territories in the Department of Interior.

Congress and the Nation, 4 vols., Congressional Quarterly, Washington, from 1965—*Congressional Ethics,* Rev. ed., 1980.—*Congressional Quarterly Almanac,* annual
Constitution of the US, National and State. 2 vols. [with subsequent amendments]. Dobbs Ferry, 1962
Political profiles. 5 vols. New York, from 1978
Adrian, C. R., *State and Local Government.* 4th ed. New York, 1977
Barone, M. (ed.), *The Almanac of American Politics.* New York and London, Annual
Bone, H. A., *American Politics and the Party System.* 4th ed. New York, 1971
Brenner, P., *The Limits and Possibilities of Congress.* New York, 1983
Corwin, E. S., *Presidential Power and the Constitution.* Cornell Univ. Press, 1976
Egger, R. A., *The President of the United States.* 2nd ed. New York, 1972
Ferguson, J. H., and McHenry, D. E., *Elements of American Government.* 6th ed. New York, 1963.—*The American Federal Government.* 12th ed. New York, 1973.—*The American System of Government.* 12th ed. New York, 1973
Fisher, L., *Presidential Spending Power.* Princeton Univ. Press, 1975
Hardin, C. M., *Presidential Power and Accountability: Towards a New Constitution.* Univ. of Chicago Press, 1974
Kelly, A. H., and Harbison, W. A., *The American Constitution, Its Origin and Development.* 4th ed. New York, 1970
Koenig, L. W., *The Chief Executive.* 3rd ed. New York, 1975
Levine, E. L., *An Introduction to American Government.* 2nd ed. New York, 1974
Maddox, R. W., and Fuquay, R. F., *State and Local Government.* 3rd ed. New York, 1975
Ogg, F. A., and Ray, P. O., *Introduction to American Government.* 12th ed. New York, 1962.—*Essentials of American National Government.* 10th ed. New York, 1969.—*Essentials of American State and Local Government.* 10th ed. New York, 1969

Pritchett, C. H., *The American Constitution.* 2nd ed. New York, 1968.—*The American Constitutional System.* New York, 1977
Ripley, R. B., *American National Government and Public Policy.* New York, 1974
Robinson, J. A., *State Legislative Innovation.* New York, 1973
Scheer, R., *America after Nixon: The Politics of the New World Order.* New York, 1975
Seymour – Ure, C., *The American President: Power and Communication.* London, 1982
Tugwell, R. G., *The Enlargement of the Presidency.* Garden City, N.Y., 1960.—*The Emerging Constitution.* New York, 1974
White, T. H., *The Making of the President.* New York, 1960.—*The Making of the President, 1964.* New York, 1965.—*The Making of the President, 1968.* New York, 1969

DEFENCE. The President is C.-in-C. of the Army, Navy and Air Force.

The National Security Act of 1947 provides for the unification of the Army, Navy and Air Forces under a single Secretary of Defense with cabinet rank. The President is also advised by a National Security Council and the Office of Civil and Defense Mobilization.

The major components of the Department of Defense are the Office of the Secretary of Defense and the Joint Chiefs of Staff, who provide immediate staff assistance and advice to the Secretary; the departments of the Army, Navy and Air Force, each separately organized under a civilian head (not of cabinet rank); and the unified and specified commands.

Army. *Secretary of the Army:* John O. Marsh Jr.

Central Administration. The Secretary of the Army is the head of the Department of the Army. Subject to the authority of the President as C.-in-C. and of the Secretary of Defense, he is responsible for all affairs of the Department.

The Secretary of the Army is assisted by the Under Secretary of the Army, 4 Assistant Secretaries of the Army (Installations, Logistics and Financial Management; Research and Development; Manpower and Reserve Affairs, and Civil Works), the General Counsel, an Administrative Assistant, Chief of Legislative Liaison, Chief of Public Affairs and the Army Staff headed by the Chief of Staff, US Army. The office of the Under Secretary of the Army includes a Deputy Under Secretary (Operations Research).

The Chief of Staff is the principal military adviser of the Secretary of the Army, and performs his duties under the direction of the Secretary of the Army, except as otherwise prescribed by law, by the President or by the Secretary of Defense. He has supervision of all members and organizations of the Army. The Vice Chief of Staff assists and advises the Chief of Staff.

The Army General Staff is the principal element of the Army Staff and includes the offices of the Chief of Staff, Vice Chief of Staff, Director of Staff, the 4 Deputy Chiefs of Staff (Military Operations, Personnel, Logistics, and Research, Development and Acquisition), the Comptroller of the Army, the Assistant Chief of Staff for Intelligence, the Ballistic Missile Defense Program Manager and the Army Reserve Forces Policy Committee. Other elements of the Army Staff are the offices of the Judge Advocate General, Surgeon General, Adjutant General, Inspector General and Auditor General, Chief of Chaplains, Chief, Army Reserve, Chief, National Guard Bureau, and Chief of Engineers.

The Army consists of the Regular Army, the Army National Guard of the US, the Army Reserve and civilian workforce; and all persons appointed to or enlisted into the Army without component; and all persons serving under call or conscription, including members of the National Guard of the States, etc., when in the service of the US.

The strength of the Army was (1984) 780,800 (including some 84,000 women).

The US Army Forces Command, with headquarters at Fort McPherson, Georgia, commands the continental US Armies and all assigned Active Army and US Army Reserve troop units in the continental US, Alaska, Hawaii, Panama, Guam, Johnston Island, the Commonwealth of Puerto Rico, and the Virgin Islands of the USA. The headquarters of the continental US Armies are: First US Army, Fort George G. Meade, Maryland; Fifth US Army, Fort Sam Houston, Texas; Sixth US Army, Presidio of San Francisco, California. The US Army Training and Doctrine Command, with headquarters at Fort Monroe, Virginia, co-ordinates and integrates the total combat development effort of the Army as well as developing, managing and supervising the training of individuals of the US Army and authorized foreign nationals. The US Army Health Services Command, with headquarters at Fort Sam Houston, Texas, provides health services in the continental US for the US Army and provides professional education and training for medical personnel of the US Army and authorized foreign national personnel. The US Army Materiel Development and Readiness Command, with headquarters in Alexandria, Virginia, is responsible for all US Army operations dealing with equipment development, procurement, delivery, supply and maintenance. The US Army Communications Command, with headquarters at Fort Huachuca, Arizona, provides worldwide communication to the Department of the Army and supports the Defense Communications Systems. The US Army Military District of Washington, with headquarters at Fort McNair, Washington, D.C. provides support to the Department of the Army and the Department of Defense at the seat of Government.

Some 35% of the Army is deployed overseas. Two divisions two-thirds of which are located in the USA keep equipment in the Federal Republic of Germany and can be flown there in 48–72 hours. Headquarters of US Seventh and Eighth Armies are in Europe and Korea respectively.

Operational Commands and Weapons. The larger commands are the theater army and the corps. The typical theater army may consist of a variable number of corps; combat forces of armour and infantry; air defense artillery (*Nike-Hercules* and *Hawk* and short-range missile battalions); field artillery and Pershing missile battalions; combat support forces of aviation, engineer and signal elements; and combat service support forces. A typical corps consists of a variable number and mixture of infantry, mechanized infantry, armoured, airmobile, and airborne divisions; one or more separate infantry brigades; one or more armoured cavalry regiments; corps artillery (155-mm howitzer, 8-in. howitzer, 175-mm gun, *Lance* missile battalions); an air defense element of a size commensurate with the hostile air threat (*Nike-Hercules, Hawk* and *Chaparral/Vulcan* battalions), and a target acquisition unit; combat support and combat service support forces.

US Army Divisions have a common base (containing command, aviation divisional artillery, combat, combat support units and combat service support units) and a varying mixture of 'combat manoeuvre battalions' (usually 10 or 11 in number in 3 brigades) to make up airborne, infantry, armoured, mechanized infantry and air-mobile divisions. Divisions can in this way be 'tailored' to fit a variety of strategic or tactical situations. An infantry division, with about 16,900 men, may have 8 infantry battalions, an armoured battalion and a mechanized infantry battalion; a mechanized infantry division, with about 16,600 men, may have 6 mechanized infantry battalions and 4 armoured battalions; an armoured division, with about 16,900 men, may have 5 mechanized infantry battalions and 6 armoured battalions; an airborne division, with 13,000 men, may have 9 infantry (airborne) battalions.

Small arms include the M-16, which fires a 5·56-mm cartridge. The standard general-purpose machine-gun is the M-60 (23 lb.; 550 rounds of 7·63-mm per minute). Infantry weapons also include M-203 grenade launcher attachment for the M16A1 rifle, which fire a 40-mm grenade up to 400 metres, the *Tow* and *Dragon* anti-tank missile system, and the M-72 rocket, a light anti-tank weapon.

Combat vehicles of the US Army are the tank, armoured personnel carrier, armoured reconnaissance airborne assault vehicle and the armoured command and reconnaissance vehicle. The first-line tanks are the XM-1 Abrams tank, M-60A3 with 105-mm main armament. The M-60A2, a version of the M-60 series tank, fires both the *Shillelagh* missile and conventional ammunition. The standard armoured personnel carrier is the M-113A1; it carries a mechanized infantry squad. The M-113A1 is also being utilized as the ground scout vehicle in armoured cavalry regiments, squadrons and in scout platoons of armoured and mechanized infantry battalions. The M-551 'Sheridan' is an armoured reconnaissance airborne assault vehicle in armoured cavalry units and light armour battalions; it fires both

Shillelagh missiles and conventional ammunition. Combat vehicles under development are mechanized infantry combat vehicle and armoured reconnaissance scout vehicle.

The approved calibres of artillery are: light, 105-mm howitzer; medium 155-mm howitzer; the heavy, 175-mm gun and 8-in. howitzer. The 4·2-in. mortars and the 81-mm mortar are used by combat manoeuvre elements. The 90-mm, 106-mm recoilless rifles are being replaced by the *Dragon* and *Tow* anti-tank missile systems which are the primary anti-tank weapons. *Chaparral* and *Vulcan*, forward-area air-defence weapons, provide the capability of low-altitude defence against high-performance aircraft.

The Army has two categories of missiles—surface-to-surface (field artillery) and surface-to-air (air defence artillery). Surface-to-surface missiles are: *Pershing II*, ballistic, nuclear warhead, range about 400 miles operational; *Lance*, guided, nuclear warhead, storable, liquid propellant, operational. Surface-to-air missiles, for air defence, are: *Nike-Hercules*, guided, field or fixed installation, nuclear warhead, operational; *Hawk*, homing type, low-to-mid-altitude, field, operational (an improved system has replaced the basic *Hawk*); *Chaparral*, infra-red homing, low-altitude, forward area, operational (improvements to the basic system are under development); *Redeye*, hand-held, infra-red homing, low-altitude, forward area, operational; *Patriot*, mid-to-high-altitude, replacement for *Hawk* and *Nike-Hercules*, under limited production; *Stinger*, hand-held infra-red homing, low-altitude, forward area, replacement for *Redeye* is under development. Anti-tank missiles are: *Tow*, tube launched, optically tracked, wire guided, anti-armour, forward area, operational; *Hellfire*, terminal homing under development.

The Army employs rotary- and fixed-wing aircraft as organic elements of its ground formations where their use is required on a full-time basis and their immediate and constant availability is essential. The front line commander exploits the benefits of aviation technology to perform traditional land battle tasks in the third dimension. This concept of airmobility for ground formation utilizes aerial vehicles as a highly integrated team to perform all five functions of land combat: reconnaissance, command and control, logistics and that inseparable combination, firepower and manoeuvre.

Enlistment, Terms of Service. Since 1974 the Army has operated a 'zero draft' system making it, in effect, an all-regular force. Terms of service may be 3, 4, 5 or 6 years. Men who enlist incur a 6-year obligation and must serve in the reserve any part of the period not served on active duty.

The Army National Guard is a reserve military component with a dual status and rôle. Enlistment is voluntary. The members are recruited by each state, but are equipped and paid by the federal government. Training is supervised by the active Army (FORSOM), and unit organization parallels that for the active army; training facilities are made available by the USA and each state. As the organized militia of the several states, the District of Columbia, Puerto Rico and the Territory of the Virgin Islands, the Guard may be called into service for local emergencies by the sovereigns in those jurisdictions; and may be called into federal service by the President to thwart invasion or rebellion or to enforce federal law. In its role as a reserve component of the Army, the Guard is subject to the order of the President in the event of national emergency. The Air Guard provide 100% of the air defence of Hawaii.

The Army Reserve is designed to supply qualified and experienced units and individuals in an emergency. US Army Forces Command is charged with the command, support and training supervision of US Army Reserve units. Members are assigned to one of 3 categories: the Ready, Standby or Retired Reserve. A limited number of Ready Reservists is subject to call by the President in case of national emergency without declaration of war by Congress. The Standby Reserve and the Retired Reserve may be called only after declaration of war or national emergency by Congress.

The Army Almanac. Dept. of the Army, Washington, D.C.

Navy. *Secretary of the Navy:* Hon. John H. Lehman, Jr.

The Department of the Navy is administered under the Secretary of Defense by the Secretary of the Navy, assisted by the Under Secretary, the Deputy Under Secretary for Financial Management; 3 Assistant Secretaries, for Shipbuilding and Logistics; for Manpower and Reserve Affairs; and for Research, Engineering and Systems, as well as by the Chief of Naval Operations and the Commandant of the Marine Corps. The 3 divisions of the Department of the Navy are:

Navy Department, comprised of staff offices of the Secretary for Legislative Affairs, Information, the Judge Advocate General, Auditor General, Comptroller Program Appraisal, General Counsel, Naval Research; offices of the Chief of Naval Operations which include the Vice Chief, the Assistant Vice Chief/Director of Naval Administration, 6 Deputy Chiefs and 8 Directors; Naval Inspector General; the Surgeon General; and headquarters of the Chief of Naval Material, Bureau of Medicine and Surgery, and Bureau of Naval Personnel.

The Shore Establishment comprises commands dealing with air, electronic, facilities engineering, sea (including ordnance) and supply systems; and other commands: Naval Telecommunications, Naval Intelligence, Naval Security Group, Oceanography, Naval Education and Training, Naval Reserve, Naval Military Personnel, Civilian Personnel and Data Automation, and Naval Medical, as well as supporting establishment of the Marine Corps and Marine Corps Reserve.

The Operating Forces are the Military Sealift Command, U. S. Naval Forces Europe, the Atlantic and Pacific Fleet including Fleet Marine Forces; operating forces of the Marine Corps, and other Navy forces and commands not otherwise assigned.

Major shore activities include 8 shipyards, 32 air stations and facilities, 2 amphibious bases, 3 submarine bases and 13 naval stations and bases. By agreement dated 2 Sept. 1940, Britain granted leases for naval and air bases in Newfoundland, Bermuda, Bahamas, Jamaica, St Lucia, Trinidad, Antigua and Guyana; but these are not all now active.

Naval appropriations in recent fiscal years: 1979, $41,530m.; 1980, $47,084m.; 1981, $57,834m.; 1982, $68,792m.; 1983, $81,936m.; 1984 (planned) $86,864m.

The active personnel on duty on 1 Jan. 1984 was 572,000 Navy officers and enlisted men, plus 197,000 Marine Corp officers and men.

The following is a tabulated statement of US vessels listed on 31 Dec.:

Category	1976	1977	1978	1979	1980	1981	1982	1983
Multi-purpose aircraft carriers	15	15	15	15	15	15	15	14
ASW and other carriers	5 [1]	5 [1]	5 [1]	5 [1]	5 [1]	4 [1]	5 [1]	5 [1]
Helicopter carriers	9	9	10	11	12	12	25 [2]	25 [2]
Command ships	3 [3]	3 [3]	3 [3]	3 [3]	3 [3]	3 [3]	3 [3]	3 [3]
Nuclear powered submarines	108	109	113	115	118	124	129	135 [7]
Submarines (conventional)	15	15	13	10	10	8	6	6
Battleships	4	4	4	4	4	4	4	4
Cruisers	35 [4]	35 [4]	36 [4]	32 [4]	29 [4]	31 [4]	32 [4]	33 [4]
Destroyers	101 [5]	97 [5]	93 [5]	96 [5]	98 [5]	93 [5]	88 [5]	86 [5]
Frigates	65 [6]	65 [6]	65 [6]	69 [6]	67 [6]	77 [6]	82 [6]	102 [6]

[1] Comprises 1 training carrier and 2 anti-submarine carriers and 2 other Essex class carriers in reserve.

[2] Comprises 5 flat-top hangar/dock heavy amphibious assault ships and 7 lighter flat-top hangar ships and 13 lighter semi-flat-top amphibious transports dock.

[3] Includes 1 Middle East Flagship (converted amphibious transport dock).

[4] Includes 24 frigates (destroyer leaders, DLG) reclassified as cruisers in 1975.

[5] Includes 10 frigates (destroyer leaders, DLG) reclassified as destroyers in 1975. Of the 86 destroyers 41 are classified as DDG.

[6] Includes 65 escort ships reclassified as frigates on 1 July 1975.

[7] Includes 4 Trident (Ohio class) ballistic missile armed very large (see Table) vessels, 31 other ballistic missile submarines and 100 attack submarines.

The table below shows principal surface ships, guns under 3-in. calibre not given:

Multi-Purpose (Former Attack) Aircraft Carriers

Completed	Name	Standard displacement Tons	Aircraft	Principal armament	Shaft horse-power	Speed Knots
1982	Carl Vinson	81,600		3 BPDMS[3] launchers	260,000	
1977	Eisenhower	81,600	90	with Sea Sparrow	(nuclear	33
1975	Nimitz	81,600		missiles	power)	
1968	John F. Kennedy	61,000		3 BPDMS launchers		
1965	America	60,300	85	with NATO Sea Sparrow missiles	280,000	34
1962	Enterprise	75,700	84	3 NATO Sea Sparrow missile launchers	300,000 (nuclear power)	35
1962	Constellation	61,000	85	2 twin Terrier missile launchers	280,000	34
1961	Kitty Hawk	61,000	85	2 BPDMS launchers with Sea Sparrow missiles	280,000	34
1959	Independence	60,000		3 BPDMS launchers		
1957	Ranger	60,000	80 to 75	with Sea Sparrow missiles	280,000	34
1956	Saratoga	59,100	80 to 75	2 BPDMS launchers		
1955	Forrestal	59,100	70	with Sea Sparrow missiles	260,000	33
1950	*Oriskany [1]	33,250	70	2 5-in. guns	150,000	33
1947	Coral Sea [2]	52,500	75	Guided missiles	212,000	33
1945	Midway [2]	51,000	75	Guided missiles 2 BPDMS launchers with Sea Sparrow to be fitted	212,000	33
1944	*Bon Homme Richard [1]	33,100	70	4 5-in. guns	150,000	33

[1] In reserve, Bon Homme Richard CVA, Oriskany CV.
[2] Sister ship Franklin D. Roosevelt was stricken in 1977.
[3] Basic Point Defence Missile System.

Anti-Submarine Support Aircraft Carriers

1944	*Bennington					
1943	*Hornet [1]	33,000	45	4 5-in. guns	150,000	33

[1] Sister ship Intrepid was stricken in 1982 to become a memorial ship at New York City. Shangri La was scrapped in 1983.

Training Carrier

1943	Lexington	32,800	—	Removed	150,000	33

The 'Essex' class originally comprised 24 ships, the Essex, Yorktown, Intrepid, Hornet, Franklin, Lexington, Bunker Hill, Wasp, Ticonderoga, Hancock, Randolph, Bennington, Bon Homme Richard, Shangri-La, Tarawa, Antietam, Boxer, Kearsarge, Lake Champlain, Leyte, Philippine Sea, Princeton, Valley Forge, Oriskany. Only the above 4* now remain in reserve. For dates and other details of the 18 stricken during 1964–81, and of the 'Bogue' class, 'Commencement Bay' class, and other former aircraft carriers, see 1981–82 and earlier editions.

Helicopter Carriers [1] (Amphibious Assault Ships)

1981	Pelileu		26 to 42	2 Sea Sparrow		
1980	Nassau	39,300	helicopters	missile launchers		
1978	Belleau Wood	(full load)	(or V/STOL	(BPDMS);	140,000	24
1977	Saipan		aircraft)	3 5-in. guns		
1976	Tarawa [2]					

[1] According to official statistics eleven of the 12 amphibious transports dock (the other is a command ship) of the Austin class; of 12,000 tons, and the two of the Raleigh class, each with a capacity of six helicopters, are now listed under the generic heading of helicopter carriers.
[2] In many ways these five heavy through deck Hangar ships are equivalent to orthodox large aircraft carriers in other principal navies.

Completed	Name	Standard displacement Tons	Aircraft	Principal armament	Shaft horsepower	Speed Knots

Helicopter Carriers [1] (Amphibious Assault Ships)

Completed	Name	Standard displacement Tons	Aircraft	Principal armament	Shaft horsepower	Speed Knots
1970	Inchon					
1968	New Orleans			2 Sea Sparrow		
1966	Tripoli	18,800	20 to 26 helicopters	missile launchers	23,000	23
1965	Guam [1]	(full load)	(or V/STOL	(BPDMS);		
1963	Guadalcanal		aircraft)	4 3-in. guns		
1962	Okinawa					
1961	Iwojima					

[1] *Guam* was modified in 1971–72 as 'interim' sea control ship and operated Harrier aircraft but reverted to the amphibious role in 1974.

Command Ships [1]

Completed	Name	Standard displacement Tons	Aircraft	Principal armament	Shaft horsepower	Speed Knots
1971	Mount Whitney	19,100	1	2 Sea Sparrow missile launchers;	22,000	23
1970	Blue Ridge	(full load)	helicopter	4 3-in. guns (twin)		

[1] *Northampton*, originally heavy cruiser; and: *Wright*, originally light fleet aircraft carrier, converted into Command Ships were stricken from the Navy List in 1977–78.

The amphibious transport dock *Coronado* has been converted to a command ship to relieve *La Salle* as flagship of the Middle East Force.

Battleships

Completed	Name	Standard displacement Tons	Aircraft	Principal armament	Shaft horsepower	Speed Knots
1944	Missouri [1] Wisconsin [1]			9 16-in.; 20 5-in.		
		45,000		9 16-in.; 12 5m.;	212,000	33
1943	Iowa [1] New Jersey [2]			Tomahawk cruise missile launchers; 4 quadruple launch cannisters		

[1] All laid up in reserve since 1955–58 but reactivation scheduled for recommissioning and modernisation and conversion to cruise missile carrier in 1984 (*Iowa*) followed by *Missouri* and *Wisconsin* in 1986 and 1988 if approved.

[2] Reactivated in 1967 and commissioned 1968–69, reserve 1969 to July 1981. Reactivated Oct. 1981 and recommissioned Dec. 1982 on modernisation and conversion to cruise missile carrier. Began first operational deployment in March 1983.

Cruisers

Completed	Name	Standard displacement Tons	Aircraft	Principal armament	Shaft horsepower	Speed Knots
1984	Yorktown	9,000	2 helicopters	2 octuple 'Harpoon' and 2 twin Standard/ ASROC launchers; 2 5-in.	80,000 (gas)	30
1983	Ticonderoga [1]					
1961	Long Beach	14,200	deck for helicopter	2 quadruple Harpoon and 2 twin Terrier/ Standard; guided missile launchers; 2 5-in.	80,000 (nuclear power)	30
1949	Salem*	17,000	—	9 8-in.; 12 5-in; 20 3-in.	120,000	32
1948	Des Moines					
1946	Albany	13,700	—	2 twin 'Tartar' launchers	120,000	32
1945	Chicago	13,600	—	2 5-in.		

[1] Originally rated as guided missile destroyers. *Ticonderoga*, DDG 47, was redesignated CG47 in 1980 when the new type were reclassified as guided cruisers.

* Sister ship *Newport News* was stricken from the Navy List on 31 July 1978.

Albany and *Chicago* were to have been disposed of in 1980 but in 1981 it was planned to retain these ships in reserve for a minimum of three years and *Oklahoma City* retained for logistic support but she was again listed for disposal in 1983.

For conversions and disposals of other cruisers of the 'Oregon City', 'Baltimore', 'Cleveland' and 'Juneau' classes see 1981–82 and earlier editions.

Cruisers, Former Frigates (Destroyer Leaders)

Completed	Name	Standard displacement Tons	Aircraft	Principal armament	Shaft horsepower	Speed Knots
1980	Arkansas			2 quadruple Harpoon;	80,000	
1978	Mississippi	9,000	2 helicopters	2 twin Standard/	(nuclear	30
1977	Texas			ASROC'; 2 5-in.	power)	
1976	Virginia					
1974	South Carolina	9,560	—	2 quadruple Harpoon;	70,000	
1973	California			2 single Standard;	(nuclear	30
				2 5-in.	power)	
1967	Truxtun	8,200	1 helicopter	2 quadruple Harpoon; 1 twin 'Standard'; 1 5-in.; 2 3-in.	60,000 (nuclear	30
1962	Bainbridge	7,600	—	2 quadruple Harpoon; 2 twin 'Standard'	power)	
1964–67	9 Belknap Class [1]	6,570	—	2 quadruple Harpoon; 1 twin Standard; 1 5-in.	85,000	34
1962–64	9 Leahy Class [2]	5,670	—	2 quadruple Harpoon; 2 twin Standard	85,000	34

[1] The 'Belknap' class comprises *Belknap, Biddle, Fox, Horne, Josephus Daniels, Jouett, Sterett, Wainwright* and *William H. Standley.*

[2] The 'Leahy' class comprises *Dale, England, Gridley, Halsey, Harry E. Yarnell, Leahy, Reeves, Richmond K. Turner* and *Worden.*

The 10 'Coontz' class comprises *Coontz, Dahlgren, Dewey, Farragut, King, Luce, Macdonough, Mahan, Preble* and *William V. Pratt.* They were reclassified from frigates (DLG) to destroyers (DDG) on 1 July 1975 when the later frigates above were reclassified as cruisers. See 1981–82 edition for earlier destroyer leader/frigates.

Capital (Strategic) Submarines

Class	No.	Displacement (submerged) Tons	Missile Tubes (Vertical)	Nuclear Reactors	Shaft Horsepower	Speed Knots
'726'	4	18,700	24 Trident	1	60,000	30 dived / 20 surface
'640'	12	8,500	16 Poseidon	1	15,000	30 dived / 20 surface
'616'	19	8,250	16 Poseidon	1	15,000	30 dived / 21 surface
'608'	4 [1]	7,880	16 Polaris	1	15,000	30 dived / 20 surface
'598'	3 [2]	6,888	16 Polaris	1	15,000	31 dived / 20 surface

Completion:- '726' or 'Ohio' class in 1981–84 (five more to follow in 1985–89); '640' or 'Benjamin Franklin' class 1965–67; '616' or 'Lafayette' class in 1963–64; '608' or 'Ethan Allen' class in 1961–63; '598' or 'George Washington' class in 1959–61. All these ballistic missile armed submarines also have four 21-inch torpedo tubes.

[1] This class reclassified as fleet submarines. *Ethan Allen* (608) stricken in 1983 (target).

[2] Three of this class converted to fleet submarines and two scrapped, *Theodore Roosevelt* (600) and *Abraham Lincoln* (602) both targets.

In addition to the above named principal surface ships there are 135 nuclear-powered submarines (including the ballistic missile armed vessels in the table), 6 conventionally propelled submarines, 86 destroyers, 102 frigates, 21 ocean minesweepers, 4 patrol vessels, 6 hydrofoil missile patrol craft, 1 fast patrol boat, 70 amphibious warfare ships, 65 landing craft, 37 replenishment ships, 100 sealift ships, 125 fleet support ships and auxiliaries, 50 oilers, 100 minor landing craft and 1,090 service craft.

Ships under construction include 9 submarines of 18,700 tons submerged with nuclear propulsion and ballistic missiles, 20 nuclear propelled attack (fleet) submarines of 6,900 tons submerged; the giant nuclear propelled aircraft carrier *Theodore Roosevelt* and 2 sister ships each of 93,400 tons war load; 3 destroyers and 24 guided missile frigates.

Projected new construction includes 11 more 'Ohio' class nuclear propelled deterrent or 'strategic' submarines; 12 more nuclear propelled fleet or 'attack' submarines; 2 more large aircraft carriers; 60 guided missile destroyers and 10 frigates.

Naval Aviation. The official figures given in the total aircraft inventory are: 6,346 flown by the Navy and the Marine Corps of which 5,692 are active and 5,057 are operating. There are 635 naval aircraft in the pipeline.

The US Coast Guard operates under the Department of Transportation in time of peace and as a part of the Navy in time of war or when directed by the President. The act of establishment stated the Coast Guard 'shall be a military service and branch of the armed forces of the United States at all times'. The Coast Guard did operate as part of the Navy during the First and Second World Wars. It also had some units serving in Vietnam. It comprises 250 ships including cutters of destroyer, frigate, corvette and patrol vessel types, powerful icebreakers, and paramilitary auxiliaries and tenders, plus some 2,000 small rescue and utility craft. It also maintains 50 fixed-wing aircraft and 110 helicopters. The Coast Guard missions include maintenance of aids to navigation, enforcement of maritime laws, enforcement of international treaties, environmental protection (especially waterway pollution), commercial vessel safety programmes, recreational boating safety, and search and rescue efforts. In the new construction programme are 12 cutters of frigate size and utility each capable of carrying a helicopter. The strength of personnel on 1 Jan. 1984 was 4,950 officers, 1,430 warrant officers and 31,140 enlisted personnel. A few ships had several women assigned as permanent members of the crew.

Air Force. *Secretary of the Air Force:* Verne Orr.

The Department of the Air Force was activated within the Department of Defense on 18 Sept. 1947, under the terms of the National Security Act of 1947. It is administered by a Secretary of the Air Force, assisted by an Under Secretary and 3 Assistant Secretaries (Research, Development and Logistics; Financial Management; and Manpower, Reserve Affairs and Installations). The USAF, under the administration of the Department of the Air Force, is supervised by a Chief of Staff, who is a member of the Joint Chiefs of Staff. He is assisted by a Vice Chief of Staff, Assistant Vice Chief of Staff, and 5 Deputy Chiefs of Staff (Manpower and Personnel; Programs and Resources; Research, Development and Acquisition; Plans and Operations; and Logistics and Engineering).

The USAF consists of active duty Air Force officers and enlisted personnel, civilian employees, the Air National Guard and the Air Force Reserve. For operational purposes the service is organized into 13 major commands, 15 separate operating agencies and 4 direct reporting units. The Strategic Air Command, equipped with long-range bombers based both in the USA and overseas, and with intercontinental ballistic missiles, is maintained primarily for strategic air operations anywhere on the globe. Tactical Air Command is the Air Force's mobile strike force, able to deploy US general-purpose air forces anywhere in the world for tactical air combat operations. The Military Airlift Command provides air transportation of personnel and cargo for all military services on a worldwide basis; and is also responsible for Air Force audio-visual products, weather service, and aerospace rescue and recovery operations.

The other major commands are the Air Force Systems Command, Air Force Logistics Command, Air Force Communications Command, Electronic Security Command, Air Training Command, Alaskan Air Command, Pacific Air Forces, Space Command, United States Air Forces in Europe, and Air University. The Alaskan, Pacific and European commands conduct, control and co-ordinate offensive and defensive air operations according to tasks assigned by their respective theatre commanders.

The separate operating agencies are the Air Force Accounting and Finance Center, Air Force Audit Agency, Air Force Commissary Service, Air Force Engineering and Services Center, Air Force Inspection and Safety Center, Air Force Intelligence Service, Air Force Office of Security Police, Air Force Manpower and Personnel Center, Air Force Medical Service Center, Air Force Service Information and News Center, Air Force Legal Services Center, Air Force Office of Special Investigations, Air Force Operational Test and Evaluation Center, Air Force Reserve, and Air Reserve Personnel Center. Air Force direct reporting units are the Air Force Academy, Air National Guard, Air Force Technical Applications Center and USAF Historical Research Center.

Of the fighter and interceptor aircraft in service, the F-15 Eagle, F-5 Tiger II, F-16 Fighting Falcon, F-106 Delta Dart, F-111 and F-4 Phantom II fly faster than the speed of sound in level flight and can carry a variety of armament. The E-3 Sentry (AWACS) is a large long-range airborne warning and control aircraft; the EF-111A Raven is a tactical electronics jamming aircraft produced by conversion of the F-111A fighter. The subsonic A-7 Corsair II and the A-10 Thunderbolt II are close-support aircraft. Strategic bombers are the B-52 Stratofortress heavy bomber (to be supplemented by B-1B from mid-80s) and the 'swing-wing' FB-111A. The Strategic Air Command also operates the KC-10A Extender and KC-135 Strato-tanker for aerial refuelling, and the SR-71 Blackbird, U-2, and TR-1 for reconnaissance. Primary transport types include the C-141 StarLifter, C-5 Galaxy, KC-10A Extender and the turboprop-powered C-130 Hercules. Intercontinental ballistic missiles in USAF service are Titan II (to be retired, and replaced with Peacekeeper from mid-80s) and Minuteman II and III.

In August 1983, the Air Force had 591,129 personnel. Total 1983 aircraft strength was 9,427.

INTERNATIONAL RELATIONS

Membership. USA is a member of UN, OAS, NATO, OECD and the Colombo Plan.

ECONOMY

Budget. The budget covers virtually all the programmes of federal government, including those financed through trust funds, such as for social security, Medicare and highway construction. Receipts of the Government include all income from its sovereign or compulsory powers; income from business-type or market-orientated activities of the Government is offset against outlays. Budget receipts and outlays (in $1m.):

Year ending 30 June	Receipts[2]	Outlays[2]	Surplus (+) or deficit (−)
1945	45,216	92,690	−47,474
1950	39,485	42,597	− 3,112
1955	65,469	68,509	− 3,041
1960	92,492	92,223	+ 269
1970	192,807	195,652	− 2,845
1981 [1]	599,272	657,204	−57,932
1982	617,766	728,424	−110,658
1983	600,563	795,917	−195,354

[1] From 1977 the fiscal year changed from a 1 July–30 June basis to a 1 Oct.–30 Sept. basis.
[2] From 1970, revised to include Medicare premiums and collections.

Budget receipts, by source, for fiscal years (in $1m.):

Source	1981 [1]	1982 [1]	1983 [1]
Individual income taxes	285,917	298,111	288,938
Corporation income taxes	61,137	49,207	37,022
Social insurance taxes and contributions	182,720	201,132	209,001
Excise taxes	40,839	36,311	35,300
Estate and gift taxes	6,787	7,991	6,053
Customs	8,083	8,854	8,655
Miscellaneous	13,790	16,161	15,594
Total	599,272	617,766	600,563

[1] From 1977, the fiscal year changed from a 1 July–30 June basis to a 1 Oct.–30 Sept. basis.

Budget outlays, by function, for fiscal years (in $1m.):

Source	1981[1]	1982[1]	1983[1][4]
National defence [2]	159,765	187,397	221,502
International affairs	11,130	9,983	12,091
General science, space, and technology	6,359	7,096	7,636
Energy	10,277	4,844	4,151
Natural resources and environment	13,525	13,086	10,438
Agriculture	5,572	14,808	10,411
Commerce and housing credit	3,946	3,843	431
Transportation	23,381	20,589	19,886
Community and regional development	9,394	7,410	7,347
Education, training, employment and social services	31,402	25,411	23,783
Health	65,982	74,018	78,493
Income security	225,099	248,807	259,286
Veterans benefits and services	22,988	23,973	24,220
Administration of justice	4,698	4,648	4,646
General government	4,614	4,833	5,007
General purpose fiscal assistance	6,856	6,161	6,535
Interest	82,537	100,777	111,117
Allowances [3]	...	...	−4,687
Undistributed offsetting receipts	−30,320	−29,261	−40,777
Total budget outlays	657,204	728,424	761,516

[1] From 1977, the fiscal year changed from a 1 July–30 June basis to a 1 Oct.–30 Sept. basis.
[2] Includes allowances for civilian and military pay raises for the Department of Defense.
[3] Includes allowances for civilian agency pay raises and contingencies.
[4] Estimate.

Budget outlays, by agency, for fiscal years (in $1m.):

Agency	1981[1]	1982[1]	1983[1]
Legislative branch	1,209	1,362	⎫ 2,215
The judiciary	637	705	⎭
Executive Office of the President	96	95	94
Funds appropriated to the President	7,010	6,073	5,417
Agriculture	26,030	36,213	46,372
Commerce	2,226	2,045	1,913
Defence—Military [2]	156,035	182,850	205,012
Defence—Civil	3,148	2,971	2,927
Education [3]	15,089	14,081	14,555
Energy [3]	11,797	7,577	8,348
Health and Human Services	226,987	251,259	274,131
Housing and Urban Development	14,033	14,491	15,312
Interior	4,262	3,922	4,485
Justice	2,682	2,584	2,832
Labour	30,084	30,736	38,176
State	1,897	2,193	2,263
Transportation	22,554	19,917	20,591
Treasury	92,633	110,521	116,787
Environmental Protection Agency	5,232	5,004	4,301
National Aeronautics and Space Administration	5,421	6,026	6,657
Veterans Administration	22,903	23,937	24,805
Other independent agencies:			
Foundation for Education Assistance	...	...	...
Office of Personnel Management	18,089	19,973	21,275
Postal Service	1,343	707	789
Railroad Retirement Board	5,308	5,733	6,236
All other	10,803	6,697	5,991
Allowances [4]	...	...	...
Undistributed offsetting receipts	−30,306	−29,261	−35,566
Total budget outlays	657,204	728,424	795,917

[1] From 1977, the fiscal year changed from a 1 July–30 June basis to a 1 Oct.–30 Sept. basis.
[2] Includes allowances for civilian and military pay raises for the Department of Defense.
[3] The Administration proposed in the 1983 Budget that the Departments of Education and Energy be eliminated and that their programmes be transferred to other agencies. Many of the Education programmes went to the proposed Foundation for Education Assistance.
[4] Includes allowances for civilian agency pay raises and contingencies.

National Debt: Gross federal debt outstanding (in $1m.), and *per capita* debt (in $1) on 30 June to 1970 and then on 30 Sept.:

	Public debt	Per capita [2]		Public debt	Per capita [2]
1919 [1]	25,485	243	1970	382,603	1,867
1920	24,299	228	1980	914,317	4,021
1930 [1]	16,185	132	1981	1,003,941	4,365
1940	50,696	382	1982 [3]	1,137,131	4,900
1950	256,853	1,687	1983 [3]	1,273,505	5,420
1960	290,862	1,610			

[1] On 31 Aug. 1919 gross debt reached its First World War (1914–18) peak of $26,596,702,000, which was the highest ever reached up to 1934; on 31 Dec. 1930 it had declined to $16,026m., the lowest it has been since the First World War. On the 30 Nov. 1941, just preceding Pearl Harbor, debt stood at $61,363,867,932. The highest Second World War debt was $279,764,369,348 on 28 Feb. 1946.

[2] *Per capita* figures, beginning with 1960, have been revised; they are based on the Census Bureau's estimates of the total population of the US, including Alaska and Hawaii.

[3] Estimate.

State and Local Finance: Revenue of the 50 states and all local governments (82,688 in 1982) from their own sources amounted to $416,433m. in fiscal year 1980–81; in addition they received $80,294m. in revenue from fiscal aid, shared revenues and reimbursements from the federal government, bringing total revenue from all sources to $506,728m. Of the revenue from state and local sources, taxes provided $244,514m., of which property taxes (mainly imposed by local governments) yielded $74,969m. or 31% of all tax revenue; and sales taxes, both general sales taxes and selective excises, provided $85,971m. (35%).

State tax revenue totalled $149,738m. in fiscal year 1981. Largest sources of state tax revenue are general sales taxes (imposed during 1980 by 45 states), motor fuel sales taxes (all states), individual income (44 states), motor vehicle and operators' licences (49 states), corporation income (46 states), tobacco products (all states) and alcoholic beverage sales taxes (all states).

General revenue of local units from own sources in fiscal year 1980–81 totalled $145,736m. In addition they received $111,443m. from state and federal aids. Property taxes provided 28% of total general revenue.

Total expenditures of state and local governments were $487,048m. in 1980–81, of which approximately 71% was for current operation. Education took $145,784m. in current and capital expenditure; highways, $34,603m.; welfare (chiefly public assistance), $54,121m., and health and hospitals, $36,101m. Capital outlays (construction, equipment and land purchases) totalled $67,596m.

Gross debt of state and local governments totalled $363,892m. or $1,606 *per capita* at the close of their 1980–81 fiscal year. Total cash and investment assets of state and local governments were $454,393m., about 23% being in cash and deposits, and the remainder in investments, mainly non-governmental securities.

US Bureau of the Census, *Governmental Finances in 1980–81.* Washington, 1982
American Economic Association, *Readings in Fiscal Policy.* Homewood, Ill., 1955
Brookings Institute and National Bureau of Economic Research, *Role of Direct and Indirect Taxes in the Federal Revenue System.* Washington, D.C., 1964

National Income. The Bureau of Economic Analysis of the Department of Commerce prepares detailed estimates on the national income and product of the United States. The principal tables are published monthly in *Survey of Current Business;* the complete set of national income and product tables are published in the *Survey* regularly each July, showing data for recent years. *The National Income and Product Accounts of the United States, 1929–1976: Statistical Tables* (1981) and the July 1982 and July 1983 *Survey* contain complete sets of tables from 1929 through 1982. The conceptual framework and statistical methods underlying the US accounts were described in *National Income, 1954.* Subsequent limited changes were described in *US Income and Output* (1958), and in *Survey of Current Business* (Aug. 1965, Jan. 1976 and Dec. 1980).

These latest figures [1] in $1,000m. for various years are as follows:

	1929[2]	1933[3]	1950	1960	1970	1980	1982
I. Gross National Product	103·4	55·8	286·5	506·5	992·7	2,631·7	3,073·0
(a) Personal consumption expenditures	77·3	45·8	192·0	324·9	612·7	1,668·1	1,991·9
(b) Gross private domestic investment	16·2	1·4	53·8	75·9	144·2	401·9	414·5
(c) Net exports of goods and services	1·1	0·4	2·2	5·5	6·7	23·9	17·4
(d) Government purchases of goods and services	8·8	8·2	38·5	100·3	220·1	537·8	649·2
1. GNP *less* capital consumption allowances with capital consumption adjustment, indirect business tax and non-tax liability, business transfer payments, statistical discrepancy, *plus* subsidies less current surplus of government enterprises, equals:							
2. National Income	84·8	39·9	237·6	415·7	810·7	2,116·6	2,450·4
which, *less* corporate profits with inventory valuation and capital consumption adjustments, contributions for social insurance, wage accruals less disbursements, *plus* government transfer payments to persons, interest paid by government to persons and business less interest received by government, interest paid by consumers, personal dividend income, business transfer payments, equals:							
3. Personal income	85·0	47·0	227·2	402·3	811·1	2,165·3	2,578·6
whereof							
4. Personal tax and non-tax payments take	2·6	1·4	20·6	50·4	115·8	336·1	402·1
leaving							
5. Disposal personal income divided into	82·4	45·6	206·6	352·0	695·3	1,828·9	2,176·5
(e) Personal outlays [4]	79·1	46·5	194·7	332·3	639·5	1,718·7	2,051·1
(f) Personal saving	3·3	−0·9	11·9	19·7	55·8	110·2	125·4
IA. GNP in constant (1972) $s	315·7	222·1	534·8	737·2	1,085·6	1,475·0	1,485·4
(a) Personal consumption expenditures	215·1	170·5	337·3	452·0	672·1	931·8	970·2
(b) Gross private domestic investment	55·8	8·4	93·5	104·7	158·5	208·5	194·5
(c) Net exports of goods and services	3·7	0·4	5·9	7·7	3·9	50·3	28·9
(d) Government purchases of goods and services	41·0	42·9	98·1	172·8	251·1	284·3	291·8
II. National Income composed of	84·8	39·9	237·6	415·7	810·7	2,116·4	2,450·4
Compensation of employees	*51·1*	*29·5*	*154·8*	*294·9*	*612·0*	*1,599·6*	*1,865·7*
(g) Salaries and wages	50·5	29·0	147·0	271·9	548·7	1,356·6	1,568·1
(h) Supplements to wages and salaries	0·6	0·5	7·8	23·0	63·2	243·0	297·6
Proprietors' income [5]	*15·0*	*5·9*	*38·7*	*47·2*	*66·2*	*117·4*	*109·0*
(i) Farm [5]	6·1	2·5	13·7	11·7	14·3	21·8	21·5
(j) Business and professional [5]	8·9	3·3	25·0	35·5	51·9	95·6	87·5
Personal income from rents [6]	*4·9*	*2·2*	*7·1*	*14·5*	*19·7*	*31·5*	*49·8*
Net interest	*4·7*	*4·1*	*3·0*	*11·4*	*41·4*	*192·6*	*261·1*
Corporate profits with inventory valuation and capital consumption adjustments	*9·0*	*−1·7*	*33·9*	*47·6*	*71·4*	*191·7*	*165·9*
(k) Tax liabilities	1·4	0·5	17·9	22·7	34·2	84·8	59·2
(l) Inventory valuation adjustment	0·5	−2·1	−5·0	−0·2	−6·6	−42·9	−8·4
(m) Capital consumption adjustment	−1·4	0·6	−4·0	−2·0	2·5	−16·3	−1·1
(n) Dividends	5·8	2·0	8·8	12·9	22·5	58·6	68·7
(o) Undistributed profits	2·8	−1·6	16·2	14·3	18·8	32·0	37·0

[1] The inclusion of statistics for Alaska and Hawaii beginning in 1960 does not significantly affect the comparability of the data.

[2] Peak year between First and Second World Wars. [3] Low point of the depression.

[4] Includes personal consumption expenditures, interest paid by consumers and personal transfer payments to foreigners (net).

[5] With inventory valuation and capital consumption adjustment.

[6] With capital consumption adjustment.

Currency. Prior to the banking crisis that occurred early in 1933, the monetary system had been on the gold standard for more than 50 years. An Act of 14 March 1900 required the Secretary of the Treasury to maintain at a parity with gold all forms of money issued by the USA. For a description of these, see THE STATESMAN'S YEAR-BOOK, 1934, p. 491.

The old gold dollar had a par value of 49·32d., or $4·8666 to the £ sterling; it contained 25·8 grains (or 1·6718 grammes) of gold 0·900 fine. By the act of 12 May 1933 the President of the USA was given authority to reduce the gold content of the dollar by not more than 50% and by the Gold Reserve Act of 30 Jan. 1934 the minimum reduction which he could make was fixed at 40%; on 31 Jan. 1934 he fixed its value at 59·06%, or 15⁵⁄₂₁ grains of gold 0·900 fine. This was equal to a price for gold of $35 a fine oz. (old price, $20·67183). The President's power to alter the gold content of the dollar to 50% of its value, which was extended by Congress in 1937, 1939 and 1941, was not yet again extended in 1943.

The Par Value Modification Act (Public Law 92–268), enacted on 31 March 1972, authorized and directed the Secretary of the Treasury to take the steps necessary to establish a new par value of the dollar of $1 = 0·818513 gramme of fine gold or $38 per fine troy oz. of gold. The Secretary of the Treasury, pursuant to the statutory directive, proposed the new par value for the US dollar to the International Monetary Fund, which par value became effective on 8 May 1972.

In Public Law 93–110, enacted on 21 Sept. 1973, Congress amended the Par Value Modification Act of 1972, and authorized and directed the Secretary of the Treasury to take the steps necessary to establish a new par value of $1 equals 0·828948 Special Drawing Right or 1/42²⁄₉ of a fine troy ounce of gold. Pursuant to the statutory directive, the Secretary of the Treasury notified the International Monetary Fund that, effective 18 Oct. 1973, the par value of the dollar would be changed from 1/38 to 1/42²⁄₉ a fine troy ounce of gold. Expressed in terms of gold, the new par value of the dollar was 0·736662 gramme of gold per dollar, or $42.2222 per fine troy ounce of gold. Expressed in percentage, the change in the par value of the dollar amounted to a reduction of 10% in the former gold content of the dollar. This is the equivalent to an 11·1% increase in the former dollar price of gold.

The USA, on 1 April 1978, accepted the second amendment to the Articles of Agreement of the International Monetary Fund. The par value of the dollar is no longer defined in terms of the Special Drawing Right and gold, and the USA is not obliged to establish and maintain a par value for the dollar.

At the time of the banking crisis in March 1933 gold payments by banks and the Treasury were suspended by the Government, and an embargo was placed on gold exports. Steps were taken to withdraw from circulation all gold coin and gold certificates and to prohibit the private ownership of all gold certificates, gold bullion and gold coin except for numismatic purposes. Public Law 93–373, 14 Aug. 1974, amended the Par Value Modification Act so as to provide for the termination of all governmental restrictions on private ownership of gold, including gold coins, no later than 31 Dec. 1974.

Currency in the USA for many years has comprised several varieties. Prior to May 1933 the legal tender qualities of the classes varied, but in that month all types of currency were made equally legal tender. Under the Coinage Act of 1965, all coins and currencies of the USA, regardless of when coined or issued, are legal tender for all debts, public and private.

Only one of the eight kinds of notes outstanding is now significant: Federal Reserve notes in denominations of $1, $2, $5, $10, $20, $50 and $100. The issue of (a) $500, $1,000, $5,000 and $10,000 Federal Reserve notes; of (b) silver certificates, and of (c) $100, $5 and $2 US notes have been discontinued, although they are still outstanding. The following issues were stopped many years ago and have been in process of retirement: (1) Federal Reserve Bank notes; (2) National Bank notes; (3) Treasury notes of 1890; (4) fractional currency.

Federal Reserve notes are obligations of the USA and a first lien on the assets of the Federal Reserve Banks, through which they are issued. Each of the 12 banks issues them against the security of an equal volume of collateral.

Gold coins (of the old weight and fineness) were $20, $10, $5 and $2½ pieces called *double eagles, eagles, half-eagles* and *quarter-eagles*. The old eagle weighed 258 grains or 16·7181 grammes 0·900 fine, and therefore contained 232·2 grains or 15·0463 grammes of fine gold. Except for collector's holdings, these are no longer in circulation. The stock of gold bullion held by the Treasury on 31 Aug. 1982 was 264m. fine oz., valued at $11,100m.; stock of silver bullion was 38·7m. fine oz. (excluding 137·5m. fine oz. held for defence stockpile). Estimated stock of domestic coin in circulation on 30 June 1983 was $13,909m., including standard silver dollars and silver and other subsidiary coin.

The silver dollar weighs 412·5 grains or 26·7296 grammes 0·900 fine, and contains 371·25 grains or 24·0566 grammes of fine silver. Subsidiary, 0·900 fine, silver coins contain 347·22 grains of fine silver per dollar. These are the half-dollar, quarter-dollar and dime (one-tenth). Minor coins currently issued are the cupro-nickel 5-cent piece and the bronze 1-cent piece. Pursuant to the Coinage Act of 1965, Congress authorized the minting and issuance of new silver clad half-dollars containing 40% silver and cupro-nickel quarter-dollars and dimes containing no silver. In an amendment to the Coinage Act enacted on 31 Dec. 1970, Congress provided that all coins minted thereafter, including dollar and half-dollar coins, be made of cupro-nickel composition. However, a provision in the 1970 law permitted the coining of 1·500 inch dollar coins containing 40% silver. These dollar coins, which bear the likeness of the late President Eisenhower, are sold at premium price to coin collectors. In Oct. 1978 there was authorization of a new dollar bearing the likeness of suffragette Susan B. Anthony. The new dollars, which are 1·043 inches in diameter and weigh 8·1 grammes, replace the cupro-nickel Eisenhower dollars. In 1981 the Mint began producing 1-cent coins made of 97·6% zinc and 2·4% copper (zinc and copper alloy blanks, barrel electro-plated with copper), pursuant to its authority under 31 USC 317(b) to alter the composition of the alloy of the 1-cent coin. In 1983 it was in the process of phasing out production of bronze cents and will shortly only be producing zinc cents.

On 22 July 1982, the Olympic Commemorative Coin Act authorized the limited issue of not more than 50m. one dollar silver coins and 2m. ten dollar gold coins to commemorate the 1984 Olympics. The coins are to be minted in proof and uncirculated condition. The 1·500 inch dollar coins containing 90% silver will be issued in 1983 and 1984. The 1983 Olympic silver dollar will feature the classic Greek discus thrower, while the 1984 Olympic silver dollar will depict the gateway to the entrance to the Los Angeles Memorial Coliseum. The 1·06 inch 1984 ten dollar gold coin weighs 16·718 grammes of an alloy of 90% gold, 10% copper. It features two Olympic Torch bearers and will be the first US coin to carry the 'W' mint mark of the US. Bullion Depository, West Point, N.Y. The coins are being sold at a premium price with the surcharge above the cost of manufacturing and marketing going to support equally the efforts of the US. Olympic Committee and the Los Angeles Olympic Organizing Committee.

Banking. On 31 Aug. 1983 there were 14,795 domestic banks doing a general deposit business with the public and having aggregate deposits of $1,420,200m.

The Federal Reserve System, established under an Act of 1913, comprises the Board of 7 Governors, the 12 regional Federal Reserve Banks with their 25 branches, the Federal Open Market Committee and the Federal Advisory Council. The 7 members of the Board of Governors are appointed by the President with the consent of the Senate. Each Governor is appointed to a full term of 14 years or an unexpired portion of a term, one term expiring every 2 years. No two may come from the same Federal Reserve District. The Board supervises the Reserve Banks and the issue and retirement of Federal Reserve notes; it designates 3 of the 9 directors of each Reserve Bank and designates the Chairman and Deputy Chairman; it passes on the admission of state banks to the System and has power to correct unsound conditions in State member banks or violations of banking law by them, including, if necessary, disciplinary action to remove officers and directors for unsafe or unsound banking practices or for continuous violations of banking laws; it also authorizes State member bank branches and approves mergers and consolidations if the acquiring, assuming or resulting bank is to be a State member; and it has power to control the expansion of bank holding companies and to require divestment of certain non-banking interests. The 12 members of the Federal Open Market Committee include the 7 members of the Board of Governors and 5 of the 12 Federal Reserve Bank presidents. The latter serve 1-year terms on the Committee in rotation except for the President of the Federal Reserve Bank of New York, who is a permanent member. The Federal Open Market Committee influences credit market conditions, money and bank credit, by buying or selling US Government securities; and it also supervises System operations in foreign currencies for the purpose of helping to safeguard the value of the dollar in international exchange markets and facilitating co-operation and efficiency in the international monetary system. The Board also influences credit conditions through powers to set reserve requirements, to approve discount rates at Federal Reserve Banks, and to fix margin requirements on stock-market credit.

The Reserve Banks hold bank reserves, advance funds to depository institutions, issue Federal Reserve notes, which are the principal form of currency in the US, act as fiscal agent for the Government and afford nation-wide cheque-clearing and fund transfer arrangements. They may issue notes, fully secured; discount paper for depository institutions; increase or reduce the country's supply of reserve funds by buying or selling Government securities and other obligations at the direction of the Federal Open Market Committee. Their capital stock is held by the member banks, but it carries no voting rights except in the election of directors.

Every member bank is required to subscribe to stock in the Reserve Bank of its district in an amount equal to 6% of its paid-up capital and surplus. Only one-half of the par value of the stock is paid in, the other half remaining subject to call by the Board of Governors. However, no call has been made for the second half of the subscription. All depository institutions with certain transaction accounts and time deposits are required to hold reserves with the Federal Reserve.

Beginning in 1968, the Congress passed a number of consumer credit protection acts, the first of which was the Truth in Lending Act (and including the Equal Credit Opportunity Act), Home Mortgage Disclosure Act, Consumer Leasing Act and the Fair Credit Billing Act, for which it has directed the Board to write implementing regulations and assume partial enforcement responsibility. To manage these responsibilities the Board has established a Division of Consumer and Community Affairs. To assist it, the Board consults with a Consumer Advisory Council, established by the Congress as a statutory part of the Federal Reserve System.

The Consumer Advisory Council was established by Congress in 1976 at the suggestion of the Board of Governors. Representing both consumers and creditors, the Council meets several times a year to advise the Board on its implementation of consumer regulations and other consumer related matters.

Another statutory body, the Federal Advisory Council, consists of 12 members (one from each district); it meets in Washington at least four times a year to advise the Board of Governors on general business and financial conditions.

Following the passage of the Monetary Control Act of 1980, the Board of Governors established the Thrift Institutions Advisory Council to provide information and views on the special needs and problems of thrift institutions. The group is comprised of representatives of mutual savings banks, savings and loan associations, and credit unions.

Banks which participate in the federal deposit insurance fund have their deposits insured against loss up to $100,000 for each depositor. The fund is administered by the Federal Deposit Insurance Corporation established in 1933; it obtains resources through annual assessments on participating banks.

All members of the Federal Reserve System are required to insure their deposits through the Corporation, and non-member banks may apply and qualify for insurance. On 31 Dec. 1982, 14,487 commercial banks and 315 mutual savings banks with insured deposits of $1,100,000m. were members of the insurance fund. There were 647 uninsured banks comprising 644 commercial banks and trust companies and 103 mutual savings banks.

There are also banks which operate solely in the field of agricultural credits under the Farm Credit Administration; Federal Home Loan Banks makes advances to financial associations and institutions upon the security of home mortgages.

US Board of Governors of the Federal Reserve System. *The Federal Reserve System Purposes and Functions.* 6th ed., 1974.—*Federal Reserve Bulletin.* Monthly.—*Annual Report.*— *Annual Statistical Digest.*—*The Federal Reserve Act, As Amended Through 1978*
Beckhart, B. H., *Federal Reserve System.* New York, 1972
Chandler, L. V., *Economics of Money and Banking.* 7th ed. New York, 1977
Clifford, A. J., *The Independence of the Federal Reserve System.* Philadelphia, 1965
Horovitz, P. M., *Monetary Policy and the Financial System.* 4th ed. Englewood Cliffs, 1979
Maisel, S. J., *Managing the Dollar.* New York, 1973
Timberlake, R. H., *The Origins of Central Banking in the United States.* Cambridge, Massachusetts, 1978
Young, R. A., *Instruments of Monetary Policy in the United States; the Role of the Federal Reserve System.* Washington, 1973

Weights and Measures. British weights and measures are usually employed, but the old Winchester bushel and wine gallon are used instead of the new or Imperial standards: *Wine gallon* = 0·83268 Imperial gallon; *Bushel* = 0·9690 Imperial bushel. Instead of the British cwt of 112 lb., one of 100 lb. is used; the *short* or *net ton* contains 2,000 lb.; the *long* or *gross ton*, 2,240 lb.

ENERGY AND NATURAL RESOURCES

Minerals. Total value of non-fuel minerals produced in US (including Alaska and Hawaii) in 1982 was estimated at $18,691m. ($25,227m. in 1981). Details are given in the following tables.

Production of metallic minerals (long tons, 2,240 lb.; short tons, 2,000 lb.):

	1981		1982	
		Value		Value
Metallic minerals	Quantity	($1,000)	Quantity	($1,000)
Bauxite (dried equiv.) tonnes	1,510	26,489	732	12,334
Copper (recoverable content), tonnes	1,538,160	2,886,440	1,139,563	1,866,895
Gold (recoverable content), troy oz.	1,379,161	633,918	1,446,905	843,908
Iron ore (usable)[1], 1,000 long tons, gross	72,158	2,914,689	35,751	1,491,705
Lead (recoverable content), tonnes	445,535	358,821	512,425	288,528
Molybdenum (content of concentrate), 1,000 lb.	118,916	945,540	77,789	514,834
Silver (recoverable content), 1,000 troy oz.	40,683	427,921	40,239	319,903
Zinc (recoverable content), tonnes	312,418	306,879	300,274	254,668
Other metals	—	341,303	—	251,225
Total metals	—	8,758,000	—	5,544,000

[1]Excluding by-product iron sinter.

The two world wars and record levels of industrial production have hastened the depletion of once abundant supplies of metal and US is increasingly an importer. US is wholly or almost wholly dependent upon imports for industrial diamonds, bauxite, tin, chromite, nickel, strategic-grade mica and long-fibre asbestos; it imports the bulk of its tantalum, platinum, manganese, mercury, tungsten, cobalt and flake graphite, and substantial quantities of antimony, cadmium, arsenic, fluorspar, zinc and bismuth.

In 1982 precious metals were mined mainly in Idaho, Arizona, Montana, Utah and Nevada (in order of combined output of gold and silver). US output of gold (troy oz.), 1930–39, 31,453,370; 1940–49, 24,171,646; 1950–59, 18,817,241; total 1792–1970, 316,620,436. Output of silver (troy oz.), 1930–39, 466,412,499; 1940–49, 434,656,631; 1950–59, 374,055,521; total 1792–1970, 4,701,429,507.

Statistics of important non-metallic minerals and mineral fuels are:

	1981		1982	
		Value		Value
Non-metallic minerals	Quantity	($1,000)	Quantity	($1,000)
Boron minerals, short tons	1,481,000	435,387	1,234,000	384,597
Cement:				
Portland, 1,000 short tons	68,197	3,515,600	61,080	3,084,439
Masonry, 1,000 short tons	2,738	161,819	2,364	145,172
Clays, 1,000 short tons	44,379	988,845	35,345	825,064
Gypsum, 1,000 short tons	11,497	98,101	10,538	89,131

| | 1981 | | 1982 | |
| | | Value | | Value |
Non-metallic minerals	Quantity	($1,000)	Quantity	($1,000)
Lime, 1,000 short tons	18,856	884,197	14,075	696,207
Phosphate rock, 1,000 tonnes	53,624	1,437,986	37,414	950,326
Potassium salts, 1,000 tonnes (K_2O equivalent)	1,908	328,900	1,784	265,600
Salt (common), 1,000 short tons	38,907	637,568	37,880	671,096
Sand and gravel, 1,000 short tons	719,980	2,260,300	625,500	2,022,900
Stone, 1,000 short tons	873,931	3,275,461	791,360	3,063,413
Sulphur (Frasch-process), 1,000 tonnes	5,910	715,683	3,598	434,660
Other non-metallic minerals	—	1,645,153	—	1,514,395
Total non-metallic minerals	—	16,385,000	—	14,147,000

| | 1979 | | 1980 | |
Mineral fuels				
Coal: Bitum. and lignite, 1,000 short tons	776,000	18,360,000	823,000	20,240,000
Pennsylv. anthracite,[1] 1,000 short tons	5,000	200,000	6,000	270,000
Gas: Natural gas,[2] 1 m. cu. ft	20,471,000	24,120,000	20,376,000	32,670,000
Natural gasoline and cycle products, 1,000 bbls of 42 gallons	...	...	...	...
L.P. gases, 1,000 bbls of 42 gallons				
Petroleum (crude), 1,000 bbls of 42 gallons	3,121,000	39,450,000	3,146,000	66,670,000

[1] Includes a small quantity of anthracite mined in states other than Pennsylvania.
[2] Value at wells.

Minerals Yearbook. Bureau of Mines. Washington, D.C. Annual from 1932–33; continuing the *Mineral Resources of the United States* series (1866–1931); from 1963 in 3 vols. *(Metals, Minerals, Fuels; Area Reports, Domestic; and Area Reports, International)*

Agriculture. Agriculture in the USA is characterized by its ability to adapt to widely varying conditions, and still produce an abundance and variety of agricultural products. From colonial times to about 1920 the major increases in farm production were brought about by adding to the number of farms and the amount of land under cultivation. During this period nearly 320m. acres of virgin forest were converted to crop land or pasture, and extensive areas of grass lands were ploughed. Improvident use of soil and water resources was evident in many areas.

During the next 20 years the number of farms reached a plateau of about 6·5m., and the acreage planted to crops held relatively stable around 330m. acres. The major source of increase in farm output arose from the substitution of power-driven machines for horses and mules. Greater emphasis was placed on development and improvement of land, and the need for conservation of basic agricultural resources was recognized. A successful conservation programme, highly co-ordinated and on a national scale—to prevent further erosion, to restore the native fertility of damaged land and to adjust land uses to production capabilities and needs—has been in operation since early in the 1930s.

Following the Second World War the uptrend in farm output has been greatly accelerated by increased production per acre and per farm animal. These increases are associated with a higher degree of mechanization; greater use of lime and fertilizer; improved varieties, including hybrid maize and grain sorghums; more effective control of insects and disease; improved strains of livestock and poultry; and wider use of good husbandry practices, such as nutritionally balanced feeds, use of superior sites and better housing. During this period land included in farms decreased slowly, crop land harvested declined somewhat more rapidly, but the number of farms declined sharply.

Some significant changes during these transitions are:

All land in farms totalled less than 500m. acres in 1870, rose to a peak of over 1,200m. acres in the 1950s and declined to 1,039m. acres in 1982, even with the addition of the new States of Alaska and Hawaii in 1960. The number of farms declined from 6·35m. in 1940 to 2·4m. in 1982, as the average size of farms doubled. The average size of farms in 1982 was 433 acres, but ranged from a few acres to many thousand acres. In 1978, 215,088 farms (128,254 in 1974) were less than 10 acres; 475,241 (379,543), 10–49 acres; 814,689 (827,884), 50–179 acres; 595,356 (616,098), 180–499 acres; 215,112 (207,297), 500–999 acres; 98,521 (92,712), 1,000–1,999 acres; 63,635 (62,225) 2,000 acres or more.

Farms operated by owners or part-owners, 1978, were 2,165,000 (87% of all farms), by all tenants, 314,000 (13%). The average size of farms in 1978 was 235 acres for full-owners, 792 acres for part-owners and 396 acres for tenants. Farms with white operators numbered 2,398,726, and those with operators who were black or of other races were 79,916. A higher proportion of blacks and operators of other races were tenants and operated a significantly smaller acreage than white operators.

In 1982 (with 1960 figures in parentheses) large-scale, highly mechanized farms with sales of agricultural products totalling $20,000 and over per farm made up 40% (8·6%) of all farms and accounted for 90% (48·3%) of the value of farm products sold. Farms selling between $19,999 and $2,500 worth of products per farm were 39% (44·8%) of all farms and sold 8·2% (43·3%) of all sales. The remaining 21% (46·6%) of all farms sold less than $2,500 worth of products per farm, 1·8% (8·4%) of total sales. Operators in every sales category received off-farm income, but operators selling less than $2,500 per year received 91·7% of their average income of $22,063 from non-farm sources in 1980.

A century ago three-quarters of the total US population was rural, and practically all rural people lived on farms. In April 1980 26% of the population was rural, and 6m. farm residents accounted for 3% of the total population.

Hired farm workers in 1982 averaged about 2·5m., and farm family workers, including operators, about 2·6m. In 1950 there were nearly 10m. farm workers. At that time each farm worker supplied farm products for 15 people; in 1974, 55 people, in 1977, 60 people and in 1982, 76 people.

Cash receipts from farm marketings and government payments (in $1m.):

	Crops	Livestock and livestock products	Government payments	Total
1932	1,996	2,752	—	4,748
1945	9,655	12,008	742	22,405
1950	12,356	16,105	283	28,744
1960	15,259	18,989	702	34,950
1970	20,976	29,563	3,717	54,256
1978	53,711	59,213	3,030	115,954
1979	63,394	68,522	1,375	133,291
1980	69,026	67,405	1,286	137,717
1981	74,920	68,478	1,930	145,328
1982	74,353	70,199	3,490	148,042

Realized gross farm income (including government payments), in $1m., was 139,535 in 1980, compared with 143,466 in 1981; net income of farm operators (only from farm sources), 20,100 (25,100). Farm-mortgage debt, on 1 Jan. 1981, was $84,100m.

US agricultural exports, fiscal year, totalled: 1973–74, $21,608m.; 1974–75, $21,854m.; 1975–76, $22,760m.; 1976–77, $23,974m.; 1977–78, $27,290m.; 1978–79, $31,975m.; 1979–80, $40,481m.; 1980–81, $43,780m.

Total area of farm land under irrigation in 1978 was 50,837,940 acres (302,674 farms).

Federal income taxes paid by farm people was $15m. in 1941, $1,365m. in 1948, $1,182m. in 1967, $3,434m. in 1971, $5,309m. in 1972, $8,364m. in 1973 and $8,277m. in 1974. Total taxes levied on farm real estate were $3,098m. in 1976, $3,039m. in 1977, $3,021m. in 1978, $3,215m. in 1979, $3,450·9m. in 1980 and $3,695·5m. in 1981.

According to census returns and estimates of the Economic Research Service, the acreage and specified values of farms has been as follows (area in 1,000 acres; value in $1,000):

	Farm area [1]	Crop land available for crops	Value, land, bldgs, machinery, livestock	Value of products sold in preceding year
1910	878,798	432,000	41,089,000	...
1930	986,771	480,000	57,815,000	9,609,924
1940	1,060,852	467,000	41,829,000	6,681,581
1950	1,158,566	478,000	99,366,000	22,051,129
1959	1,125,508	448,100	164,200,000	30,492,721
1969	1,063,346	459,048	206,751,000	44,519,658
1978	1,029,695	461,341	5,653,400,000	108,113,519

[1] Acreages are for the preceding year except for 1959.

The areas and production of the principal crops for 3 years were:

	1980			1981			1982		
	Har-vested 1,000 acres	Produc-tion 1,000 bu.	Yield per acre bu.	Har-vested 1,000 acres	Produc-tion 1,000 bu.	Yield per acre bu.	Har-vested 1,000 acres	Produc-tion 1,000 bu.	Yield per acre bu.
Corn for grain	73,061	6,647,543	91	74,700	8,201,598	109·8	73,152	8,397,334	114·8
Oats	8,640	457,593	53	9,415	509,167	54·1	10,561	616,981	58·4
Barley	7,233	358,544	49·6	9,158	479,333	52·3	9,113	522,387	57·3
All wheat	70,984	2,369,666	33·4	81,013	2,798,738	34·5	78,841	2,808,737	35·6
Rice (cwt)	3,295	145,063	4,403	3,792	182,742	4,819	3,252	154,216	4,742
Soybeans for beans	67,856	1,817,097	26·4	66,368	2,000,145	30·1	70,783	2,276,976	32·2
Flaxseed	703	8,128	11·6	617	7,799	12·6	815	11,635	14·3
Cotton lint (bale)	13,215	11,122	404	13,841	15,646	543	9,728	12,010	593
Potatoes (cwt)	1,155	301,006	261	1,237	338,591	274	1,273	349,268	274
Tobacco (lb.)	915	1,772,001	1,936	976	2,063,611	2,114	907	1,982,245	2,183

Wheat. The chief wheat-growing states (1980) were (estimated yield in 1,000 bu.): Kansas. 420,000; Oklahoma, 195,000; N. Dakota, 179,650; Washington, 160,200; Texas, 130,000; Montana, 119,800; Nebraska, 112,100; Colorado, 109,900; Minnesota, 102,556; Idaho, 96,030; Missouri, 89,010; California, 85,500.

Cotton. Leading production, 1980, by state (in 1,000 bales, 480 lb. net weight) was: Texas, 3,305; California, 3,150; Arizona, 1,413; Mississippi, 1,150; Louisiana, 455; Arkansas, 450; Alabama, 275; Oklahoma, 216; Tennessee, 200; Missouri, 178.

Tobacco. Output (1,000 lb.) of the chief tobacco-growing states (92% of the crop) was, in 1980: N. Carolina, 763,665; Kentucky, 409,222; S. Carolina, 125,125; Tennessee, 112,544; Georgia, 110,550; Virginia, 108,919.

Fruit. A wide variety of fruits are grown; the chief products are as follows:

	1980		1981		1982	
	Production 1,000 tons	Value $1,000	Production 1,000 tons	Value $1,000	Production 1,000 tons	Value $1,000
Apples	4,353	821,827	3,877	852,981	4,055	803,723
Citrus Fruit	16,491	1,304,177	15,105	1,866,685	12,113	1,712,712
Grapes	5,576	1,323,152	4,458	1,322,431	6,616	1,349,808

Dairy produce. In 1981, production of milk was 133,000m. lb.; milkfat (1980), 4,692m. lb.; cheese (not including cottage cheese), 4,229m. lb.; butter, 1,228m. lb.; eggs, 69,600m.

Livestock (1982). Cattle, 115·7m.; pigs, 58·69m.; sheep, 12·94m.; goats, 1·39m.; horses, 10·16m.; poultry, 392m.

The value (in $1,000) was:

	1979	1980	1981
Cattle of all kinds	44,697,773	55,831,294	54,359,749
Sheep and lambs	890,970	992,127	904,488
Swine (hogs and pigs) [1]	5,023,454	3,774,920	4,822,265

[1] At 1 Dec. of previous year.

Total value of livestock, excluding poultry and goats and, from 1961, horses and mules (in $1m.) on farms in the USA on 1 Jan. was: 1930, 6,061; 1933 (low point of the agricultural depression), 2,733; 1970, 22,886; 1976, 29,483; 1977, 29,053; 1978, 31,952; 1979, 50,612; 1980, 60,598; 1981, 60,087.

In 1980 the production of shorn wool was 105·4m. lb. from 13·2m. sheep (average 1970–74, 320m. lb. from 18·2m. sheep); of pulled wool, 1m. lb. (1970–74, 10·1m. lb.).

Forestry. In 1977 the US forest lands, including Alaska and Hawaii, capable of producing timber for commercial use, covered 482,485,900 acres (more than one-fifth of the land area), classified as follows: Saw-timber stands, 215,435,700 acres; pole timber stands, 135,609,900 acres; seedling and sapling stands, 115,032,100 acres; non-stocked and other areas, 16,408,200 acres. Ownership of commercial forest land is distributed as follows: Federal government, 99,410,400 acres; state, county, municipal and Indian, 36,311,200 acres; privately owned, 346,764,300 acres, including 115,777,100 acres on farms. Of the saw-timber stand (2,578,940m. bd ft) Douglas fir constitutes 514,317; Southern yellow pine, 321,563; Western yellow (ponderosa and jeffrey) pine, 192,638; other softwoods, 956,890; hardwoods, 593,532. In 1976 growing stock timber removals amounted to 14,229,023,000 cu. ft compared to net annual growth of about 21,664,316,000 cu. ft. Saw-timber removals amounted to 65,176,618,000 bd ft against an annual growth of 74,620,832,000 bd ft. The net area of the 155 national forests and other areas in USA and Puerto Rico administered by the US Department of Agriculture's Forest Service, including commercial and non-commercial forest land, was on 30 Sept. 1982, 190·8m. acres.

Fire takes a heavy annual toll in the forest; total area burned over in 1980 was 5,260,825 acres; 1,486,188,000 acres of land are now under organized fire-protection service. The area planted or seeded in forest and wind barrier nursery stock in the year ending 30 Sept. 1982 was 2,374,794 acres, an increase of 448,250 acres over the previous year.

Land Areas of National Forest System. Forest Service, US Dept. of Agriculture, 1982
Report of the Forest Service, 1982

Fisheries. The main fishing industries are in California (anchovy, tuna and sole); Alaska (notably salmon); Washington (salmon and halibut); Florida (the main source of turtles and sponges); Massachusetts, Maine, North Carolina and Oregon. Total catch, 1981 (preliminary), 5,977m. lb. valued at $2,388m.

Tennessee Valley Authority. Established by Act of Congress, 1933, the TVA is a multiple-purpose federal agency which carries out its duties in an area embracing some 41,000 sq. miles, in 125 counties (aggregate population, about 7·9m.) in the 7 Tennessee River Valley states: Tennessee, Kentucky, Mississippi, Alabama, North Carolina, Georgia and Virginia. In addition, 76 counties outside the Valley are served by TVA power distributors. Its 3 directors are appointed by the President, with the consent of the Senate; headquarters are in Knoxville, Tenn. There were 36,491 employees in Sept. 1983.

In the 1930s and 1940s, the Tennessee Valley offered the world a model of the first effort to develop all resources of a major river valley under one comprehensive programme, the Tennessee Valley Authority. The multipurpose development of the Tennessee River for flood control, navigation, and electric power production was the first big task for TVA. But there were other needs; controlling erosion on the land, introducing better fertilizers and new farming practices, eradicating malaria, demonstrating ways electricity could lighten the burdens in the home and increase production on the farm, and a multitude of potential job-producing enterprises.

In the depression year, 1933, the average *per capita* income in the Valley was $168, compared with the national average of $375. Through the years, TVA has placed a strong emphasis on the economic development of the Valley. An abundant supply of reasonably priced power, combined with a reliable navigation system, has provided a strong incentive for industry to locate in the Valley. By 1980, the region's *per capita* income had multiplied over 44 times to $7,378, while the national average had increased 25 times.

Taming the Tennessee River has had two positive effects on the Valley: flood damages averted by river control now exceed $2,400m.; and a navigable channel system 650 miles long, connecting with the American system of inland waterways, provides a readily accessible transportation system for industry. In 1982, 27m. (estimate) tons of barge-traffic travelled the TVA river system.

Another activity is experimentation in the development and manufacture of chemical fertilizers, accompanied by programmes designed to encourage proper fertilizer use in all parts of the United States and the world. TVA's National Fertilizer Development Center is recognized world-wide for its expertise in fertilizer technology. TVA also works closely with other federal agencies, and with state and local authorities in combating soil erosion, improving forest resources, improving agriculture, and in the development of local industries based on natural resources.

In recent years, attention has focused mainly on TVA's power programme. TVA supplies electric power to 160 local distribution systems serving 2·9m. customers. The power system originated with the water-power development of the Tennessee River, but has become predominantly a coal-fired system as power requirements have outgrown the region's hydro-electric potential. In fiscal year 1983, the TVA system generated 114,331m. kwh. Installed capacity in 1983 was 32·1m. kw, with another 5·2m. kw under construction at TVA's nuclear plants.

Because of the ever-increasing cost of energy in today's world, TVA has focused a good deal of its attention and resources on the research and demonstration of new and alternative energy sources. TVA is playing a lead rôle in the development of atmospheric fluidized bed combustion (AFBC) technology, an innovative process of burning high-sulphur coal cleanly and cheaply. TVA is continuing its research and demonstrations into solar energy, both for residential and commercial uses; energy from wood and waste products, and electric vehicle development. Other TVA activities include demonstration of effective ways of reclaiming strip-mined areas and development of new and improved methods of controlling air and water pollution.

Power operations are financially self-supporting from revenues. In fiscal year 1982 power revenues were $3,981m., and net income $390m. Power facilities are financed from revenues and the sale of revenue bonds and notes, and TVA is repaying appropriations previously invested in power facilities. Other TVA resource development programmes continue to be financed from congressional appropriations, which amount to $122·5m. in 1982–83.

Annual Report of the TVA. Knoxville, 1934 to date
Clapp, G.R., *The TVA; An Approach to the Development of a Region.* Univ. of Chicago Press, 1955
Lilienthal, D. E., *TVA: Democracy on the March.* 20th Anniversary ed. New York and London, 1953
Owen, M., *The Tennessee Valley Authority.* New York, 1973
Tennessee Valley Authority. *A History of the Tennessee Valley Authority.* Knoxville, Tennessee, 1982.—*TVA: The First Twenty Years* (ed. R. C. Martin), Univ. of Tennessee Press, 1956

INDUSTRY AND TRADE

Industry. The following table presents industry statistics of manufactures as reported at various censuses from 1909 to 1977 and from the Annual Survey of Manufactures for years in which no census was taken. The figures for 1958 to 1977 include data for some establishments previously classified as non-manufacturing. The figures for 1939, but not for earlier years, have been revised to exclude data for establishments classified as non-manufacturing in 1954. The figures for 1909–33 were previously revised by the deduction of data for industries excluded from manufacturing during that period.

The statistics for 1958, 1963, 1967, 1972 and 1977 relate to all establishments employing 1 or more persons anytime during the year; for 1950, 1956–57, 1959–62, 1966 and 1968–74 on a representative sample of manufacturing establishments of 1 or more employees; for 1929 through 1939, those reporting products valued at $5,000 or more; and for 1909 and 1919, those reporting products valued at $500 or more. These differences in the minimum size of establishments included in the census affect only very slightly the year-to-year comparability of the figures.

The annual Surveys of Manufactures carry forward the key measures of manufacturing activity which are covered in detail by the Census of Manufactures. The estimate for 1950 is based on reports for approximately 45,000 plants out of a total of more than 260,000 operating manufacturing establishments; those for 1956–57 on about 50,000, and those for 1959–62, 1966 and 1968–74 on about 60,000 out of about 300,000. Included are all large plants and representative samples of the much more numerous small plants. The large plants in the surveys account for approximately two-thirds of the total employment in operating manufacturing establishments in the US.

	Number of establish- ments	Production workers (average for year)	Production workers' wages total ($1,000)	Value added by manufacture [1] ($1,000)
1909	264,810	6,261,736	3,205,213	8,160,075
1919	270,231	8,464,916	9,664,009	23,841,624
1929	206,663	8,369,705	10,884,919	30,591,435
1933	139,325	5,787,611	4,940,146	14,007,540
1939	173,802	7,808,205	8,997,515	24,487,304
1950	260,000	11,778,803	34,600,025	89,749,765
1960	...	12,209,514	55,555,452	163,998,531
1963	306,317	12,232,041	62,093,601	192,082,900
1966	...	13,826,500	78,256,400	250,880,100
1967	305,680	13,955,300	81,393,600	261,983,800
1968	...	14,041,200	87,480,400	285,058,900
1969	...	14,357,800	93,459,600	304,440,700
1970	...	13,528,000	91,609,000	300,227,600
1971	...	12,874,900	93,231,700	314,138,400
1972	312,662	13,526,500	105,494,700	353,974,200
1973	...	14,233,100	118,332,300	405,623,500
1974	...	13,970,900	124,983,200	452,468,400
1975	...	12,567,900	121,427,200	442,485,800
1976	...	13,051,200	137,564,000	511,470,900
1977	350,757	13,691,000	157,163,700	585,165,600
1978	...	14,228,700	176,416,800	657,412,000
1979	...	14,537,800	192,881,500	747,480,500
1980	...	13,900,100	198,164,000	773,831,300
1981	...	13,542,800	212,200,900	837,506,500

[1] For the period 1954–67 value added represents adjusted value added and for earlier years unadjusted value added. Unadjusted is obtained by subtracting cost of materials, supplies and containers, fuel, electricity and contract work from the value of shipments for products manufactured plus receipts for services rendered. Adjusted value added also takes into account value added by merchandizing operations plus net change in finished goods and work-in-process inventories between the beginning and end of the year.

For comparison of broad types of manufacturing, the industries covered by the Census of Manufactures have been divided into 20 general groups according to the *Standard Industrial Classification.*

Code No.	Industry group	Census year	Production workers (average for year)	Production workers' wages, total ($1,000)	Value added by manu- facture [1] ($1,000)
20. Food and kindred products		1979	1,101,400	13,837,600	68,732,900
		1980	1,091,200	14,814,400	75,490,900
		1981	1,068,700	15,707,100	80,794,700
21. Tobacco manufactures		1979	47,700	667,900	5,342,700
		1980	46,600	767,400	6,147,600
		1981	49,100	891,400	6,429,600
22. Textile mill products		1979	732,300	6,941,300	18,154,400
		1980	706,200	7,212,400	18,983,300
		1981	678,500	7,439,000	19,463,200
23. Apparel and related products		1979	1,129,500	7,937,900	21,709,700
		1980	1,129,500	8,503,400	23,425,500
		1981	1,078,600	8,734,400	25,639,900
24. Lumber and wood products		1979	632,200	6,989,900	20,107,000
		1980	581,700	6,719,900	18,029,900
		1981	543,800	6,752,900	17,321,000
25. Furniture and fixtures		1979	397,500	3,814,200	10,998,800
		1980	383,800	3,926,000	11,631,100
		1981	374,100	4,189,100	12,668,700
26. Paper and allied products		1979	509,100	7,635,600	27,136,300
		1980	493,900	8,203,500	29,760,500
		1981	486,800	8,820,400	32,366,700
27. Printing and publishing		1979	698,400	8,760,600	40,004,400
		1980	716,000	9,599,100	44,374,700
		1981	719,700	10,454,000	49,351,600

[1] Figures represent adjusted value added. For definitions see footnote to previous table.

Code No.	Industry group	Census year	Production workers (average for year)	Production workers' wages, total ($1,000)	Value added by manufacture [1] ($1,000)
28. Chemical and allied products		1979	552,000	8,849,900	70,356,000
		1980	544,700	9,482,600	74,384,100
		1981	532,600	10,230,100	80,032,300
29. Petroleum and coal products		1979	106,200	2,188,700	28,847,000
		1980	99,800	2,135,000	24,815,600
		1981	101,000	2,522,100	26,740,300
30. Rubber and plastics products, not elsewhere classified [2]		1979	592,900	6,938,700	23,112,400
		1980	544,400	6,777,300	22,568,700
		1981	541,900	7,392,700	26,005,900
31. Leather and leather products		1979	206,600	1,542,400	4,248,500
		1980	200,500	1,635,300	4,851,200
		1981	196,800	1,766,000	5,230,300
32. Stone, clay and glass products		1979	521,700	7,232,800	24,467,600
		1980	479,700	7,190,300	24,051,000
		1981	462,500	7,568,600	24,853,900
33. Primary and metal industries		1979	952,900	18,184,000	50,882,100
		1980	854,200	17,306,200	47,619,200
		1981	825,900	18,564,100	49,550,600
34. Fabricated metal products [2]		1979	1,286,400	17,552,700	56,892,600
		1980	1,224,000	17,908,500	57,917,100
		1981	1,182,800	19,134,000	61,558,200
35. Machinery (except electrical)		1979	1,640,500	24,305,400	92,527,600
		1980	1,595,700	25,771,300	99,435,400
		1981	1,561,000	27,762,200	111,393,700
36. Electrical machinery [2]		1979	1,337,400	16,592,800	66,476,300
		1980	1,303,000	17,762,600	73,149,500
		1981	1,278,100	19,192,400	79,720,400
37. Transportation equipment [2]		1979	1,383,500	25,199,500	80,387,800
		1980	1,213,000	24,109,000	76,591,800
		1981	1,185,300	26,096,600	82,938,200
38. Instruments and related products [2]		1979	370,800	4,561,700	24,598,100
		1980	370,700	5,021,400	27,913,100
		1981	368,300	5,536,700	31,493,800
39. Miscellaneous manufacturing		1979	338,800	3,147,900	11,934,700
		1980	321,500	3,318,400	12,691,100
		1981	307,500	3,447,100	13,953,500

[1] Figures represent adjusted value added. For definitions see footnote to previous table, p. 1,402.
[2] Figures for 1967 are not comparable to 1972 due to revisions in the Standard Industrial Classification System.

Iron and Steel: Output of the iron and steel industries (in net tons of 2,000 lb.), according to figures supplied by the American Iron and Steel Institute, was:

	Furnaces in blast 31 Dec.	Pig-iron (including ferro-alloys)	Raw steel	Steel by method of production [1]			Basic Oxygen
				Open hearth	Bessemer	Electric [2]	
1932 [3]	44	9,835,227	15,322,901	13,336,210	1,715,925	270,044	...
1939	195	35,677,097	52,798,714	48,409,800	3,358,916	1,029,067	...
1944 [4]	218	62,866,198	89,641,600	80,363,953	5,039,923	4,237,699	...
1950	234	66,400,311	96,336,075	86,262,509	4,534,558	6,039,008	...
1960	114	68,566,384	99,281,601	86,367,506	1,189,196	8,378,743	3,346,156
1970	152	87,933,000	131,514,000	48,022,000	—	20,162,000	63,330,000
1980	...	70,329,000	111,835,000	13,054,000	—	31,166,000	67,617,000
1981	...	75,096,000	120,828,000	13,452,000	—	34,145,000	73,231,000
1982	...	43,309,000	74,577,000	6,110,000	—	23,158,000	45,309,000

[1] The sum of these 4 items should equal the total in the preceding column; any difference appearing is due to the very small production of crucible steel, omitted prior to 1950.
[2] Includes crucible production beginning 1950.
[3] Low point of the depression.
[4] Peak year of war production.

Wholesale price index of iron and steel mill products (1967 = 100) was: 1950, 59·4; 1960, 96·4; 1970, 114·3; 1978, 254·4; 1979, 280·4; 1980, 302·7; 1981, 337·6; 1982, 349·7.

Consumption of ore, 1982, was 60·9m. net tons, of which blast-furnaces took 50·6m. net tons; agglomerating plants, 9·98m. net tons; and steel producing furnaces, 273,000 net tons.

The iron and steel industry in 1982 employed 198,477 wage-earners (compared with 449,888 in 1960), who worked an average of 33·3 hours per week and earned an average of $16·81 per hour: total wages were $5,800m. and total salaries for 90,960 employees were $3,034m.

Annual Statistics Report. American Iron and Steel Institute

Labour. The American labour movement comprises about 203 national and international labour organizations plus a large number of small independent local or single-firm labour organizations. In 1980 total membership was approximately 23·9m., including 1·7m. Canadian workers affiliated with American labour organizations and under 120,000 others outside the USA. The American Federation of Labor (founded 1881 and taking its name in 1886) and the Congress of Industrial Organizations merged into one organization, named the AFL–CIO, in Dec. 1955, representing 16·8m. workers in 1980.

Unaffiliated or independent labour organizations, inter-state in scope, including those organizing coalminers, teamsters and government employees and railroad workers, had an estimated total membership excluding all foreign members (1980) of about 6·8m. Labour organizations represented approximately 20% of the labour force in 1980.

The Labor–Management Relations (Taft–Hartley) Act, 1947, applicable to industries affecting inter-state commerce, prohibits the closed shop, but permits union shop arrangements except where forbidden by state laws. Statutes regulating, restricting or prohibiting closed shop or other types of union security agreements are in effect in 20 states which ban all types of union security agreements (Alabama, Arizona, Arkansas, Florida, Georgia, Iowa, Kansas, Louisiana, Mississippi, Nebraska, Nevada, North Carolina, North Dakota, South Carolina, South Dakota, Tennessee, Texas, Utah, Virginia and Wyoming). Colorado and Wisconsin ban all-union agreements unless a certain percentage of employees have voted for them; in Hawaii an all-union agreement may be entered into unless a majority of employees votes against it. Thirteen states have acts to prevent industrial disputes between public utilities and their employees by means of compulsory arbitration or seizure; however, a number of these laws have been declared unconstitutional in so far as industries in inter-state commerce are concerned. Laws to restrict or regulate picketing or other strike activities have been enacted in over half the states. About one-half of the states also prohibit certain types of strikes, as 'sit down', jurisdictional or sympathy strikes.

The Employee Retirement Income Security Act of 1974 protects the interests of workers and their beneficiaries who are entitled to benefits from employee pension and welfare plans. The law requires disclosure of plan provisions and financial information and establishes standards of conduct for trustees and administrators of welfare and pension plans. It provides funding, participation and vesting requirements for pension plans and makes termination insurance available for most pension plans. The law does not require a company to establish a welfare or pension plan.

Minimum wage laws governing private employers are in operation in 45 jurisdictions: 41 states, the District of Columbia, Guam, Puerto Rico and the Virgin Islands have minimum wage laws and minimum wage rates. As of 1 Aug. 1978, all but one of the laws cover men, women and, usually, minors. The exception covers only women and minors. The minimum wage rate under federal law is $3.35 per hour for employees who are engaged in commerce, in the production of goods for commerce or in certain enterprises which are engaged in commerce as well as federal employees.

A total of 2,568 strikes and lockouts occurred in 1981, involving 1·1m. workers and 24·7m. idle days; the number of idle days was 0·11% of the year's total working time of all workers.

There are 3 federal agencies which provide formal machinery for the adjustment of labour disputes: (1) The Federal Mediation and Conciliation Service, now an independent agency, whose mediation services are available 'in any labor dispute in any industry affecting commerce'; under Executive Order 11491, as amended, to federal agencies and organizations of federal employees involved in negotiation disputes; and in state and local government collective bargaining disputes when adequate dispute resolution machinery is not available to the parties. Its aim is to prevent and minimize work stoppages. (2) The National Mediation Board (1934) provides much the same facilities for the railroad and air-transport industries pursuant to the Railway Labor Act. (3) The National Railroad Adjustment Board (1934) acts as a board of final appeal for grievances arising over the interpretation of existing collective agreements under the Railway Labor Act; its decisions are binding upon both sides and enforceable by the courts.

The National Labor Relations Act, as amended by the Labor–Management Relations (Taft–Hartley) Act, 1947 (*see* THE STATESMAN'S YEAR-BOOK, 1955, p. 617), was amended by the Labor–Management Reporting and Disclosure Act, 1959, and again amended in 1974. The 1959 Act requires extensive reporting and disclosure of certain financial and administrative practices of labour organizations, employers and labour relations consultants. In addition, certain powers are vested in the Secretary of Labor to prevent abuses in the administration of trusteeships by labour organizations, to provide minimum standards and procedures for the election of union officers and to establish rules prescribing minimum standards for determining the adequacy of union procedures for the removal of officers. Other provisions impose a fiduciary responsibility upon union officers and provide for the exclusion of those convicted of certain named felonies from office for specified periods; more stringently regulate secondary boycotts and banning of 'hot' cargo agreements; put limitations upon organizational and recognition picketing and permit States to assert jurisdiction over labour disputes where the National Labor Relations Board declines to act. The Act also contains a 'Bill of Rights' for union members (enforceable directly by them) dealing with such things as equal rights in the nomination and election of union officers, freedom of speech and assembly subject to reasonable union rules, and safeguards against improper disciplinary action.

The Bureau of Labor Statistics estimated that in 1981 the total labour force was 110,812,000 (64·3% of those 16 years and over); the armed forces accounted for 2,142,000 and the civilian labour force for 108·67m., of whom 100,397,000 were employed and 8,273,000—or 7·6%—were unemployed. The following table shows employment by industry group and sex and percentage distribution of the total:

Industry Group	Male	Female	Total	Percentage distribution
Employed (1,000 persons):	57,397	43,000	100,397	100·0
Agriculture, forestry and fisheries	2,824	694	3,519	3·5
Mining	949	170	1,118	1·1
Construction	5,566	494	6,060	6·0
Manufacturing:				
Durable goods	9,798	3,368	13,166	13·1
Non-durable (including not specified)	5,108	3,543	8,651	8·6
Transportation, communication and other				
public utilities	4,875	1,758	6,633	6·6
Wholesale and retail trade	10,907	9,617	20,524	20·4
Finance, insurance and real estate	2,545	3,588	6,133	6·1
Business and repair services	2,794	1,344	4,138	4·1
Personal services	1,075	2,839	3,914	3·9
Entertainment and recreation services	671	436	1,107	1·1
Professional and related services	6,936	13,265	20,201	20·1
Public administration	3,348	1,884	5,233	5·2

Bureau of Labor Statistics, US Dept. of Labor. *Directory of National Unions and Employee Associations in the US.* 1979.—*Brief History of the American Labor Movement.* 1976.— *Analysis of Work Stoppages.* 1979.—*Employment and Earnings.* Monthly

A Guide to Basic Law and Procedures under the National Labor Relations Act, National Labor Relations Board, Washington, D.C., 1976

Brody, D., *Workers in Industrial America: Essays on the Twentieth-century Struggle.* New York, 1980

Commerce. The subjoined table gives the total value of the imports and exports of merchandise by yearly average or by year (in $1m.):

	Exports Total	Exports US mdse.[1]	General imports		Exports[2] Total	Exports[2] US mdse.[1]	General imports[2]
1946–50	11,829	11,673	6,659	1978	143,663	141,126	176,052
1951–55	15,333	15,196	10,832	1979	181,816	178,578	210,285
1956–60	19,204	19,029	13,650	1980	220,783	216,668	245,262
1961–65	24,006	24,707	17,659	1981	233,739	228,961	260,982
1970	43,224	42,590	39,952	1982	212,275	207,158	...

[1] Excludes re-exports.   [2] Includes US Virgin Islands trade with foreign countries.

For a description of how imports and exports are valued, see *Explanation of Statistics of Report FT990, Highlights of US Export and Import Trade,* Bureau of the Census, US Department of Commerce, Washington, D.C., 1946.

The 'most favoured nation' treatment in commerce between Great Britain and US was agreed to for 4 years by the treaty of 1815, was extended for 10 years by the treaty of 1818, and indefinitely (subject to 12 months' notice) by that of 1827.

Imports and exports of gold and silver bullion and specie in calendar years (in $1,000):

	Gold Exports	Gold Imports	Silver Exports	Silver Imports
1932	809,528	363,315	13,850	19,650
1940	4,995	4,749,467	3,674	58,434
1944	959,228	113,836	126,915	23,373
1955	7,257	104,592	8,331	72,932
1960	1,647	335,032	25,789	57,438
1965	1,285,097	101,669	54,061	64,769
1970	36,887	227,472	53,003	58,838
1975	429,278	406,583	104,086	274,106
1980	2,787,431	2,508,520	1,326,878	1,336,009
1981	2,501,337	1,950,555	181,380	842,882

The domestic exports of US produce, including military, and the imports for consumption by economic classes for 3 calendar years were (in $m.):

	Exports (US merchandise) 1980	1981	1982	Imports for consumption 1980	1981	1982
Food and live animals	27,744	30,291	23,950	15,766	15,233	14,453
Crude materials	23,791	20,993	19,248	10,516	11,193	8,585
Machinery and transport equipment	84,628	95,736	87,148	60,558	69,627	73,320
Chemicals	20,740	21,187	19,890	8,593	9,448	9,493
Total	156,903	168,207	150,236	95,433	105,501	105,851

Leading exports of US merchandise are listed below for the calendar year 1982: Special category merchandise is included. Data for major subdivisions of certain classes are also given:

Commodity	$1m.	Commodity	$1m.
Machinery, total	87,148	Chemicals	19,890
Power generating machinery	9,461	Chemical elements and compounds	1,969
Metalworking machinery	1,611	Plastic materials and resins	3,650
Agricultural machines and tractors	2,887	Soybeans	6,240
Office machines	10,207	Cotton	1,955
Telecommunications apparatus	3,864	Textiles and apparel	3,715
Electrical apparatus	11,471	Tobacco and manufactures	2,845
Electrical power machinery and switchgear	3,624	Iron and steel-mill products	2,101
		Non-ferrous base metals and alloys	1,768
Automobiles (and parts)	15,611	Pulp, paper and products	4,068
Aircraft (and parts)	11,775	Coal	5,987
Grains and preparations	14,747	Fruits, nuts and vegetables	2,715
Wheat (and flour)	6,869	Petroleum and products	5,947
Coarse grains	6,420	Firearms of war and ammunition	3,261

Chief imports for 28 commodity classes for consumption for the calendar year 1982:

Commodity	$1m.	Commodity	$1m.
Petroleum and products	59,396	Rubber	735
Petroleum	45,862	Textiles and apparel	10,972
Petroleum products	13,535	Clothing	8,165
Non-ferrous base metals	1,552	Cotton fabrics, woven	489
Copper	988	Machinery, total	38,664
Aluminium	1,336	Electrical apparatus	7,071
Nickel	568	Agricultural machines and tractors	1,242
Bauxite, crude	383	Office machines	4,299
Tin	378	Coffee	2,730
Pulp, paper and products	5,333	Chemicals	9,493
Newsprint	2,749	Chemical elements and compounds	5,605
Wood pulp	1,485	Uranium oxide	...
Fertilizers	963	Plywood	...
Sugar	863	Oils and fats	406
Iron and steel-mill products	9,184	Cocoa (and cacao beans)	323
Cattle, meat and preparations	2,364	Glass and pottery	1,351
Automobiles and parts	29,218	Footwear	3,437
Fish (and shellfish)	3,143	Toys and sports goods	2,698
Fruit, nuts and vegetables	2,816	Furs, undressed	127
Alcoholic beverages	2,513	Telecommunications apparatus	9,051
Wool and other hair	152	Artworks and antiques	2,024
Metal manufactures	4,294	Grains and animal feeds	...
Diamonds (excl. industrial)	1,917		

Total trade beween the USA and the UK for 5 years (British Department of Trade returns, in £1,000 sterling):

	1979	1980	1981	1982	1983
Imports to UK	4,919,882	6,043,774	6,048,305	6,638,250	7,442,671
Exports and re-exports from UK	4,047,158	6,668,342	6,258,157	7,457,114	8,336,979

Imports and exports by continents, areas and selected countries for calendar years (in $1m.):

	General imports		Exports incl. re-exports [1]	
Area and country	1981	1982	1981	1982
Canada	46,414	46,477	39,564	33,720
20 American Republics	32,023	32,513	38,950	30,086
Western Europe	51,865	52,346	65,377	60,054
Western Hemisphere	85,436	84,467	81,667	67,312
Canada	46,414	46,477	39,564	33,720
20 American Republics	32,023	32,513	38,950	30,086
Central American Common Market	1,546	1,467	1,773	1,405
Costa Rica	365	358	373	330
El Salvador	259	319	308	292
Guatemala	349	336	559	390
Honduras	433	365	349	275
Nicaragua	140	90	184	119
Panama	297	255	844	839
Latin American FTA	28,981	29,650	35,260	26,879
Argentina	1,124	1,128	2,192	1,299
Brazil	4,475	4,285	3,798	3,423
Chile	604	666	1,465	925
Colombia	819	801	1,771	1,903
Ecuador	1,021	1,131	854	828
Mexico	13,765	15,986	17,789	11,817
Paraguay	48	39	108	78
Peru	1,224	1,099	1,486	1,117
Uruguay	158	258	163	196
Dominican Republic	926	629	772	664
Haiti	274	310	301	299
Bolivia	177	109	189	99
Venezuela	5,566	4,768	5,445	5,206
Bahamas	1,262	1,050	441	590
Netherlands Antilles	2,626	2,117	499	660
Jamaica	366	294	479	468
Trinidad and Tobago	2,215	1,627	688	894

[1] 'Special category' exports are included in these totals.

Area and country	General imports 1981	General imports 1982	Exports incl. re-exports [1] 1981	Exports incl. re-exports [1] 1982
Europe				
Western Europe	51,855	52,346	65,377	60,054
OECD Countries	51,399	51,966	64,548	59,378
European Economic Community [2]	41,624	42,509	52,363	47,932
Belgium and Luxembourg	2,297	2,396	5,765	5,229
Denmark	850	904	887	732
France	5,851	5,545	7,341	7,110
Germany (Fed. Rep.)	11,379	11,975	10,277	9,291
Ireland	498	556	1,025	983
Italy	5,189	5,301	5,360	4,616
Netherlands	2,366	2,494	8,595	8,604
UK	12,835	13,095	12,439	10,645
Greece	359	242	676	721
Turkey	261	274	789	868
EFTA countries	...	...	...	...
Austria	382	491	484	371
Norway	2,477	1,973	892	950
Portugal	238	283	1,075	838
Sweden	1,714	1,993	1,842	1,689
Switzerland	2,448	2,340	3,022	2,707
Finland	525	414	613	489
Iceland	198	184	71	77
Spain	1,533	1,505	3,397	3,456
Yugoslavia	437	360	648	494
Soviet bloc.	1,555	1,067	4,338	3,610
Poland	365	212	682	295
USSR	348	228	2,431	2,587
Asia [3] [4]	92,395	85,686	65,711	67,477
Near East	18,543	11,812	14,964	15,950
Egypt	397	547	2,159	2,875
Iran	64	585	300	122
Iraq	164	39	914	846
Israel	1,243	1,164	2,521	2,271
Kuwait	86	40	976	941
Lebanon	19	19	296	294
Saudi Arabia	14,391	7,443	7,327	9,026
Japan	37,612	37,744	21,823	20,966
Other Asia	52,524	45,139	38,413	40,912
Bangladesh	85	...	158	...
Hong Kong	5,428	5,540	2,635	2,453
India	1,202	1,404	1,748	1,599
Indonesia	6,022	4,224	1,302	2,025
Korea, Republic of	5,227	5,637	5,116	5,529
Malaysia	2,183	1,885	1,537	1,736
Singapore	2,114	2,195	3,003	3,214
Pakistan	174	165	492	700
Philippines	1,964	1,806	1,787	1,854
Sri Lanka	154	175	91	198
Thailand	946	884	1,170	915
Taiwan (Formosa)	8,049	8,893	4,305	4,367
Vietnam	5	...	10	...
China	1,895	...	3,603	...
Oceania	3,353	3,131	6,436	5,700
Australia	2,465	2,287	5,242	4,535
New Zealand and W. Samoa	718	777	940	900

[1] See note on previous page.
[2] 1981 and 1982 figures include Greece.
[3] Includes Egypt.
[4] Excludes Yemen (Aden) (formerly Southern Yemen), and Bahrain.
[5] Less than one-half of rounded unit.

	General imports		Exports incl. re-exports [1]	
Area and country	1981	1982	1981	1982
Africa [2]	26.674	17,223	8,938	7,396
Algeria	5.038	2,673	717	909
Ethiopia	83	102	62	43
Libya	5.301	512	813	301
Morocco	36	45	429	397
Ghana	246	362	154	116
Liberia	113	91	128	113
Nigeria	9,249	7,045	1,523	1,295
Kenya	52	71	150	98
Zaïre	423	407	141	91
South Africa, Republic of [3]	2,445	1,967	2,912	2,368

[1] See note on p. 1407.
[2] Excludes Egypt.
[3] Includes also South-West Africa (Namibia).

US Department of Commerce, Bureau of Census. Report FT 990, Highlights of US Export and Import Trade

Tourism. In 1982, 21·9m. tourists visited the USA and spent over US$11,290m. They came mainly from Canada (10·4m.), Europe (3·8m.), Mexico (2·6m.) and Asia (2·3m.). Approximately 23·1m. US tourists travelled abroad, mainly to Canada (11m.), Europe (4·1m.), Mexico (3·6m.) and the Caribbean and Central America (2·6m.).

COMMUNICATIONS

Roads. On 31 Dec. 1982 the total US public road[1] mileage, including rural and urban roads, amounted to 3,866,296 miles, of which 3,398,810 miles were surfaced roads. The total mileage cited includes 825,385 miles of rural roads under control of the states, 2,139,790 miles of local roads, 260,565 miles of federal park and forest roads, and 640,556 miles of urban roads and streets. Expenditures for construction and maintenance amounted to $32,288m. in 1982.

By the end of 1982, toll roads, financed by private capital through bond issues and administered by state toll authorities, totalled 4,755 miles (including some under construction) compared with 344 miles in 1940.

Motor vehicles registered in the calendar year 1982 were (Federal Highways Administration) 159,509,825, including 123,697,863 automobiles, 559,197 buses and 35,252,765 trucks.

Inter-city trucks (private and for hire) averaged 502,000m. revenue net ton-miles in 1982. Of the 559,197 buses in service in 1982, 442,133 were school buses. Inter-city service operated a total of 1,140m. bus-miles and carried a total of 390m. revenue passengers in 1982.

There were 43,805 deaths in road accidents in 1982.

[1] Public road mileage excludes that mileage not open to public travel, not maintained by public authority, or not passable by standard four-wheel vehicles. This excluded mileage was reported to the US Federal Highway Administration prior to 1981.

Railways. Railway history in the USA commences in 1828, but the first railway to convey both freight and passengers in regular service (between Baltimore and Ellicott's Mills, Md., 13 miles) dates from 24 May 1830. Mileage rose to 52,922 miles in 1870; to 167,191 miles in 1890, and to a peak of 266,381 miles in 1916, falling thereafter to 261,871 in 1925; 246,739 in 1940 and 222,164 in 1969 (these include some duplication under trackage rights and some mileage operated in Canada by US companies). The ordinary gauge is 4 ft 8½ in. (about 99·6% of total mileage). The USA has about 29% of the world's railway mileage.

In addition to the independent railroad companies, railway service is provided by two federally-assisted organizations, the National Railroad Passenger Corporation (Amtrak), and the Consolidated Rail Corporation (Conrail).

Amtrak was set up on 1 May 1971 to maintain a basic network of inter-city passenger trains with government assistance, and is responsible for almost all non-commuter services with 27,000 miles of route. From 1 Jan. 1983, an Amtrak commuter division took over from Conrail all commuter services not acquired by State or regional agencies.

Conrail is the organization established on 1 April 1976 to run freight services in the industrial north-east formerly operated by the bankrupt Penn Central, Reading, Lehigh Valley, Central of New Jersey, Erie Lackawanna, Lehigh & Hudson railroads, and Pennyslvania-Reading Seashore Lines.

The following table, based on the figures of the Interstate Commerce Commission, shows some railway statistics for 4 calendar years:

	1960	1970	1980 [2]	1982 [1] [2]
Classes I and II Railroads				
Mileage owned (first main tracks)	223,779	204,621	157,078	147,049
Revenue freight originated (1 m. short tons)	1,421	1,572	1,537	1,268
Freight ton-mileage (1 m. ton-miles)	591,550	771,012	932,748	795,004
Passengers carried (1,000)	488,019	289,469	281,503	[3]
Passenger-miles (1 m.)	31,790	10,786	6,557	[3]
Operating revenues ($1 m.)	9,587	12,209	28,708	27,353
Operating expenses ($1 m.)	7,135	9,806	26,761	26,389
Net railway operating income ($1 m.)	1,055	506	1,364	718
Net income after fixed charges ($1 m.)	855	126	2,029	1,417
Class I Railroads:				
Locomotives in service	40,949	27,086	28,240	26,923
Steam locomotives	25,640	—	—	—
Freight-train cars (excluding caboose cars)	1,721,269	1,423,921	1,101,343	1,000,857
Passenger-train cars	57,146	11,177	2,219	1,808
Average number of employees	1,220,784	566,282	458,996	378,906
Average wage per week ($1)	72.59	188.71	474.21	559.37

[1] Class I railroads only. From 1981, Class II railroads were no longer required to file annual reports.
[2] Data for National Railroad Passenger Corporation excluded.
[3] This data has been discontinued.

Aviation. In civil aviation there were, on 31 Dec. 1982, 733,255 certified pilots (including 156,361 student pilots) and 258,971 registered civil aircraft.

Airports on 31 Dec. 1982: Air carrier, 699; general aviation, 15,132. Of these airports, 12,596 were conventional land-based, while 458 were seaplane bases, 2,712 were heliports and 65 stolports (STOL—Short Take-Off and Landing).

Statistics from the Civil Aeronautics Board indicate that for 12 months ended June 1983 on US flag carriers in scheduled international service there were 20·3m. enplanements with 307m. aircraft miles (excluding all-cargo) for a total of 50,658m. revenue passenger-miles. The non-scheduled airlines had a total of 13,025m. revenue passenger-miles internationally and domestically. Domestically US scheduled airlines in 1983 had 284·4m. enplanements with a total of 2,402m. aircraft miles for 219,635m. revenue passenger-miles. (A revenue passenger-mile is one paying passenger carried per mile.)

Shipping. On 1 Sept. 1983 the US merchant marine included 822 sea-going vessels of 1,000 gross tons or over, with aggregate dead-weight tonnage of 25m. This included 302 tankers of 16·7m. DWT.

On 1 Sept. 1983 US merchant ocean-going vessels were employed as follows: Active, 463 of 18m. DWT, of which 184 of 6m. tons were foreign trade, 209 of 11m. tons in domestic trade and 70 of 1·5m. tons in other US agency operations. Inactive vessels totalled 7m. DWT; 105 of 3·8m. DWT privately owned were laid up and 254 of 2·8m. tons were in the National Defense reserve fleet. Of the total vessels in the US fleet, 557 of 25m. DWT were privately owned.

US exports and imports carried on dry cargo and tanker vessels in the year 1982 totalled 676m. long tons, of which 31·2m. long tons or 4·6% were carried in US flag vessels.

Post and Broadcasting. The telephone business is largely in the hands of the American Telephone and Telegraph Company (AT & T) and its telephone operating subsidiaries, which together are known as the Bell System. There are, however, many hundreds of smaller telephone companies having no common ownership affiliation with the Bell companies, but which connect with them for universal service, countrywide and worldwide. In addition, several new entrants have begun to compete with AT & T in the long-distance telephone market. The message telegraph and telex services are in the hands of The Western Union Telegraph Company, and the international record carriers, which compete with the telephone industry in providing leased private lines. Western Union also provides an intercity telephone service.

The number of telephones in service in the USA has increased in the period since 1945 at a much faster rate than has the population. Among principal reasons are the significant increase in the percentage of households with telephone service and the enormous growth in the number of extension telephones.

In marked contrast, the number of public telegrams has decreased by a substantial amount. Telegrams have lost favour due to shifts in user preference to the airmail and to the telephone. The telex services of the telegraph company have also found broad acceptance in place of telegrams for business purposes. The following table contains key data items on a comparative basis for the domestic telephone and message telegraph services:

	1950	1960	1970	1980
All telephone systems:				
Total telephones	43,131,000	74,342,000	120,218,000	180,425,000
Bell System:				
Total telephones	35,343,400	60,735,100	96,561,000	141,674,000
Average daily telephone calls	140,782,000	219,093,000	368,363,000	580,230,000
Local	134,870,000	209,373,000	346,505,000	527,543,000
Long distance	5,912,000	9,720,000	21,858,000	52,687,000
Total plant in service ($1,000)	10,101,522	24,072,499	54,813,202	132,831,794
Total operating revenues ($1,000)	3,271,029	7,958,125	17,094,846	51,203,404
Employees, number	523,251	580,405	772,980	847,768
Western Union Telegraph Co.:				
Public telegrams for year	153,054,000	102,931,000	46,084,000	40,801,398
Total plant ($1,000)	294,451	398,023	1,029,149	2,101,007
Revenue from public telegrams ($1,000)	132,281	160,746	126,739	115,612
Total operating revenues ($1,000)	177,994	262,365	402,456	696,972
Employees, number	40,482	32,655	24,293	12,649

International communication services, providing overseas connexions with all parts of the world, are furnished principally by the American Telephone and Telegraph Company and three telegraph companies. The old submarine cable telegraph systems have all been abandoned in favour of using telegraph circuits derived from voice channels in the newer telephone ocean cables, which have also made inroads on the use of high-frequency radio. More recently, satellite communications facilities have been utilized not only for telephone and telegraph services but for television and data transmission as well.

International overseas telegrams, inbound to and outbound from the continental US, numbered 11·7m. in 1980 (12·5m. in 1978). This service has tended to decline in volume in recent years. It first lost ground to the air-mail and then to the telex and telephone services. For the US and its possessions the volume of international overseas telephone calls has grown enormously with the availability of the excellent voice-transmission qualities provided in the telephone ocean cables and in the satellite radio relays. Whereas international telephone calls were 990,000 in 1955, the last year in which there was no cable service available, there were 149·6m. such calls in 1980.

Postal business for the years ended 30 Sept. included the following items:

	1979	1980	1981	1982
Number of post offices, on 30 June [1]	30,449	30,326	30,242	30,155
Postal revenue ($1,000) [2]	16,106,085	17,142,760	19,133,041	22,599,937
Postal expenses ($1,000) [3]	17,529,303	19,412,587	21,369,139	22,826,217

[1] The US Postal Service was established 1 July 1971. Financial statements prior to that date are those of the Post Office Department. Such statements for 1968–71 have been restated to be in a format and on an accounting principle basis generally consistent with 1972.

[2] Operating revenue excludes government appropriations, operating reimbursements and other income.

[3] Operating expenses are stated net of operating reimbursements and exclude certain costs financed by revenue.

On 1 Jan. 1975 there were in the USA and Territories, 7,068 authorized commercial radio stations, 711 commercial television stations: of non-commercial stations 717 were for radio, 241 for television.

Cinemas. Cinemas increased from 17,003 in 1940 to 20,239 in 1950 and decreased to 42,187 in 1967.

Newspapers. Of the daily newspapers being published in the USA in 1971, 339 were morning papers with a circulation of 26,116,000, and 1,425 were evening papers with a circulation of 36,115,000. The 590 Sunday papers had a total circulation of 49·7m.

JUSTICE, RELIGION, EDUCATION AND WELFARE

Justice. Legal controversies may be decided in two systems of courts: the federal courts, with jurisdiction confined to certain matters enumerated in Article III of the Constitution, and the state courts, with jurisdiction in all other proceedings. The federal courts have jurisdiction exclusive of the state courts in criminal prosecutions for the violation of federal statutes, in civil cases involving the government, in bankruptcy cases and in admiralty proceedings, and have jurisdiction concurrent with the state courts over suits between parties from different states, and certain suits involving questions of federal law.

The highest court is the Supreme Court of the US, which reviews cases from the lower federal courts and certain cases originating in state courts involving questions of federal law. It is the final arbiter of all questions involving federal statutes and the Constitution; and it has the power to invalidate any federal or state law or executive action which it finds repugnant to the Constitution. This court, consisting of 9 justices who receive salaries of $94,700 a year (the Chief Justice, $100,700), meets from Oct. until June every year and disposes of about 4,450 cases, deciding about 380 on their merits. In the remainder of cases it either summarily affirms lower court decisions or declines to review. A few suits, usually brought by state governments, originate in the Supreme Court, but issues of fact are mostly referred to a master.

The US courts of appeals number 12 (in 11 circuits composed of 3 or more states and 1 circuit for the District of Columbia); the 132 circuit judges receive salaries of $77,300 a year. Any party to a suit in a lower federal court usually has a right of appeal to one of these courts. In addition, there are direct appeals to these courts from many federal administrative agencies. In the year ending 30 June 1983, 29,630 appeals were filed in the courts of appeals.

The trial courts in the federal system are the US district courts, of which there are 89 in the 50 states, 1 in the District of Columbia and 1 each in the territories of Puerto Rico, Virgin Islands, Guam and the Northern Marianas. Each state has at least 1 US district court, and 3 states have 4 apiece. Each district court has from 1 to 27 judgeships. There are 515 US district judges ($73,100 a year), who handle about 241,850 civil cases and 48,450 criminal defendants every year.

In addition to these courts of general jurisdiction, there are special federal courts of limited jurisdiction. US Claims Court (6 judges at $77,300 a year) decides claims for money damages against the federal government in a wide variety of matters; the Court of International Trade determines controversies concerning the classification and valuation of imported merchandise.

The judges of all these courts are appointed by the President with the approval of the Senate; to assure their independence, they hold office during good behaviour and cannot have their salaries reduced. This does not apply to the territorial judges, who hold their offices for a term of years. The judges may retire with full pay at the age of 70 years if they have served a period of 10 years, or at 65 if they have 15 years of service, but they are subject to call for such judicial duties as they are willing to undertake. Only 9 US judges up to 1984 have been involved in impeachment proceedings, of whom 3 district judges and 1 commerce judge were convicted and removed from office.

Of the 241,842 civil cases filed in the district courts in the year ending 30 June

1983, about 95,295 arose under various federal statutes (such as labour, social security, tax, patent, securities, antitrust and civil rights laws); 34,210 involved personal injury or property damage claims; 67,276 dealt with contracts; and 8,812 were actions concerning real property.

Of the 35,872 criminal cases filed in the district courts in the year ending 30 June 1983, about 1,900 were charged with alleged infractions of the immigration laws; 3,400, the transport of stolen motor vehicles; about 3,400 larceny and theft; 7,650, embezzlement and fraud; and 7,650 narcotics laws.

Persons convicted of federal crimes are either fined, released on probation under the supervision of the probation officers of the federal courts, confined in prison for a period of up to 6 months and then put on probation (known as split sentencing) or confined in one of the following institutions: 3 for juvenile and youths; 7 for young adults; 7 for intermediate term adults; 7 for short-term adults; 2 for females; 1 hospital and 15 community service centres. In addition, prisoners are confined in centres operated by the National Institutes of Mental Health. In addition, prisoner drug addicts may be committed to US Public Health Service hospitals for treatment. Prisoners confined in institutions operated by the US Bureau of Prisons for the year ending 30 Sept. 1982, numbered 28,133.

The state courts have jurisdiction over all civil and criminal cases arising under state laws, but decisions of the state courts of last resort as to the validity of treaties or of laws of the US, or on other questions arising under the Constitution, are subject to review by the Supreme Court of the US. The state court·systems are generally similar to the federal system, to the extent that they generally have a number of trial courts and intermediate appellate courts, and a single court of last resort. The highest court in each state is usually called the Supreme Court or Court of Appeals with a Chief Justice and Associate Justices, usually elected but sometimes appointed by the Governor with the advice and consent of the State Senate or other advisory body; they usually hold office for a term of years, but in some instances for life or during good behaviour. Their salaries range from $24,000 to $84,584 a year. The lowest tribunals are usually those of Justices of the Peace; many towns and cities have municipal and police courts, with power to commit for trial in criminal matters and to determine misdemeanours for violation of the municipal ordinances; they frequently try civil cases involving limited amounts.

The death penalty is illegal in Alaska, Hawaii, Iowa, Maine, Minnesota, Oregon, West Virginia, Wisconsin and Michigan; in North Dakota it is legal only for treason and first-degree murder committed by a prisoner serving a life sentence for first-degree murder, in Rhode Island only for murder committed by a prisoner serving a life sentence and in Vermont and New York for the murder of a peace officer in the line of duty and for first-degree murder by those who kill while serving a life sentence for murder. The death penalty is legal in 37 states. Until 1982 it had fallen into disuse and had been abolished *de facto* in many states. The US Supreme Court had held the death penalty, as applied in general criminal statutes, to contravene the eighth and fourteenth amendments of the US constitution, as a cruel and unusual punishment when used so irregularly and rarely as to destroy its deterrent value.

In 1967 only 2 persons were executed under civil authority; both for murder. There were no executions 1968–76. In 1977 a convicted murderer requested that he should be executed and after a lengthy legal dispute the sentence was carried out at Utah state prison. Six persons were executed between 1977 and 1982. In Jan. 1983, 1,050 prisoners in 31 states were reported under sentence of death.

The total number of civilian executions carried out in the US from 1930 to 1982 was 3,866.

Federal 'Political' Crimes. Prosecutions for what may be loosely described as 'political' offences, or crimes directed towards the overthrow by violence of the federal government, which were somewhat numerous in the early 1950s, have declined sharply over the last 20 years and are now exceedingly rare.

A Guide to Court Systems. Institute of Judicial Administration. New York, 1960
The United States Courts. Administrative Office of the US Courts, Washington, D.C., 20544
Blumberg, A. S., *Criminal Justice: Issues and Ironies.* 2nd ed. New York, 1973
Huston, L. A., *The Department of Justice.* New York, 1967
Huston, L. A., and others, *Roles of the Attorney General of the United States.* New York, 1968
McCloskey, R. G., *The Modern Supreme Court.* Harvard Univ. Press, 1972
McLauchlan, W. P., *American Legal Processes.* New York, 1977
Walker, S. E., *Popular Justice.* New York, 1980

Religion. *The Yearbook of American and Canadian Churches for 1983,* published by the National Council of the Churches of Christ in the USA, New York, presents the latest figures available from official statisticians of church bodies. The large majority of reports are for the calendar year 1981, or a fiscal year ending 1981. The 1981 reports indicated that there were 138,452,614 members with 339,053 local churches. There were 291,722 clergymen having local congregations. The principal religious bodies (numerically or historically) or groups of religious bodies are shown below:

Denominations	Local churches	Total membership
Summary:		
Protestant bodies	308,049	76,339,453
Roman Catholic Church	24,277	51,207,579
Jews [1]	3,500	5,921,205
Eastern Churches	1,628	3,852,545
Old Catholic, Polish National Catholic and Armenian	407	921,085
Buddhists	60	60,000
Miscellaneous [2]	1,132	150,747
1980 totals	339,053	138,452,614 [3]

Protestant Church Membership	Total membership
Baptist bodies	
Southern Baptist Convention	13,782,644
National Baptist Convention, USA	5,500,000
National Baptist Convention of America, Inc.	2,668,799
National Primitive Baptist Convention	250,000
American Baptist Churches in the USA	1,607,541
American Baptist Association	225,000
Progressive National Baptist Convention	521,692
Conservative Baptist Association of America	225,000
Regular Baptist Churches	300,839
Free Will Baptists	216,848
Baptist Missionary Association of America	228,381
Christian Church (Disciples of Christ)	1,173,135
Christian Churches and Churches of Christ	1,063,254
Church of the Nazarene	492,203
Churches of Christ	1,600,222
The Episcopal Church	2,767,440
Latter-Day Saints:	
Church of Jesus Christ of Latter-Day Saints	3,490,000
Reorganized Church of Jesus Christ of Latter-Day Saints	190,087
Lutheran Bodies:	
Lutheran Church in America	2,921,829
The Lutheran Church-Missouri Synod	2,636,715

[1] Includes Orthodox, Conservative and Reformed bodies.
[2] Includes non-Christian bodies such as Spiritualists, Ethical Culture, Unitarian-Universalists.
[3] Care should be taken in interpreting membership statistics for the US Churches. Some statistics are accurately compiled and others are estimates. Also statistics are not always comparable.

Protestant Church Membership	Total membership
Lutheran Bodies (contd.):	
The American Lutheran Church	2,346,207
Wisconsin Evangelical Lutheran Synod	410,288
Methodist Bodies:	
United Methodist Church	9,519,407
African Methodist Episcopal Church	2,210,000
African Methodist Episcopal Zion Church	1,134,176
Christian Methodist Episcopal Church	786,707
Pentecostal Bodies:	
Assemblies of God	1,788,394
Church of God in Christ, International	200,000
Church of God in Christ	3,709,661
Church of God (Cleveland, Tenn.)	456,797
United Pentecostal Church, International, Inc.	465,000
Presbyterian Bodies: [1]	
United Presbyterian Church in the USA	2,379,249
Presbyterian Church in the US	823,143
Reformed Churches:	
Reformed Church in America	345,762
Christian Reformed Church	215,411
The Salvation Army	414,999
Seventh-day Adventists	588,536
United Church of Christ	1,726,244

[1] In June 1983, these two Presbyterian Bodies merged to form Presbyterian Church (USA).

Yearbook of American and Canadian Churches. Annual, from 1951. New York

Clarke, E. T., The Small Sects in America. Rev. ed. New York, 1949

Johnson, A. W., and Yost, F. H., Separation of Church and State in the United States. Minneapolis and London, 1949

Mead, F. S., Handbook of Denominations in the US. 6th ed. Nashville, 1975

Education. Under the system of government in the USA, elementary and secondary education is committed in the main to the several states. Each of the 50 states and the District of Columbia has a system of free public schools, established by law, with courses covering 12 years plus kindergarten. There are 3 structural patterns in common use; the K8–4 plan, meaning kindergarten plus 8 elementary grades followed by 4 high school grades; the K6–3–3 plan, or kindergarten plus 6 elementary grades followed by a 3-year junior high school and a 3-year senior high school; and the K6–6 plan, kindergarten plus 6 elementary grades followed by a 6-year high school. All plans lead to high-school graduation, usually at age 17 or 18. Vocational education is an integral part of secondary education. In addition, some states have, as part of the free public school system, 2-year colleges in which education is provided at a nominal cost. Each state has delegated a large degree of control of the educational programme to local school districts (numbering 15,858 in autumn 1981), each with a board of education (usually 3 to 9 members) selected locally and serving mostly without pay. The school policies of the local school districts must be in accord with the laws and the regulations of their state Departments of Education. While regulations differ from one jurisdiction to another, in general it may be said that school attendance is compulsory between the ages of 7 to 16.

The Census Bureau estimates that in Nov. 1979 only 1m. or 0·6% of the 170m. persons who were 14 years of age or older were unable to read and write; in 1930 the percentage was 4·8. In 1940 a new category was established—the 'functionally illiterate', meaning those who had completed fewer than 5 years of elementary schooling; for persons 25 years of age or over this percentage was 3 in March 1982 (for the non-white population alone it was 7·4%); it was 0·8% for white and 0·7% for non-whites in the 25–29-year-old group. The Bureau reported that in March 1982 the median years of school completed by all persons 25 years old and over was 12·6, and that 17·7% had completed 4 or more years of college. For the 25–29-year-old group, the median school years completed was 12·8 and 21·7% had completed 4 or more years of college.

In the autumn of 1982, 12,426,000 students (6,031,000 men and 6,394,000 women) were enrolled in 3,280 colleges and universities; 2,505,000 were first-time students. About 26% of the population between the ages of 18 and 24 were enrolled in colleges and universities.

Public elementary and secondary school revenue is supplied from the county and other local sources (about 43% in 1981–82), state sources (48%) and federal sources (about 9%). In 1981–82 expenditure for public elementary and secondary education totalled about $109,400m., including $99,000m. for regular day school programmes, $1,700m. for other programmes, $6,500m. for capital outlay and $2,100m. for interest on school debt. The current expenditure per pupil in average daily attendance was about $2,670. The total cost per pupil, also including capital outlay and interest, amounted to about $2,900. Estimated total expenditures, for private elementary and secondary schools in 1981–82 were $14,200m. In 1981–82 the 3,280 universities and colleges expended $70,339m. from current funds, of which $46,219m. was spent by institutions under public control. The federal government contributed 11·5% of total current-fund revenue; state governments, 30·3%; student tuition and fees, 21·9%; and all other sources, 36·3%.

Vocational education below college grade, including the training of teachers to conduct such education, has been federally aided since 1918. During the school year 1979–80 enrolments in the vocational classes were: Agriculture, 879,000; distributive occupations, 961,000; health occupations, 834,000; home economics, 3,938,000; trade and industry, 3,216,000; technical education, 499,000; office occupations, 3·4m.; other programmes, 2,726,000. Federal support funds were $745,481,000.

Summary of statistics of regular schools (public and private), teachers and pupils in autumn 1982 (compiled by the US National Center for Education Statistics):

Schools by level	Number of schools 1980–81	Teachers autumn 1982	Enrolment autumn 1982
Elementary schools:			
Public	61,069	1,165,000	23,700,000
Private	16,792	187,000	3,600,000
Secondary schools:			
Public	24,362	945,000	15,800,000
Private	5,678	88,000	1,300,000
Higher education:			
Public	1,497	637,000	9,696,000
Private	1,734	233,000	2,730,000
Total	111,132	3,255,000	56,826,000

Most of the private elementary and secondary schools are affiliated with religious denominations. Of the children attending private elementary and secondary schools in 1980–81, 3,138,000 or 63·2% were enrolled in Roman Catholic schools.

During the school year 1980–81 high-school graduates numbered about 3,026,000 (1,485,000 boys and 1,541,000 girls). Institutions of higher education conferred 935,140 bachelor's degrees for the academic year 1980–81, 469,883 to men and 465,257 to women; 295,739 master's degrees, 147,043 to men and 148,696 to women; 32,958 doctorates, 22,711 to men and 10,247 to women; and 71,956 first professional degrees, 52,792 to men and 19,164 to women.

During the academic year, 1981–82, 326,300 foreign students were enrolled in American colleges and universities. The percentages of students coming from various areas in 1981–82 were: South and East Asia, 32·5; Middle East, 22·8; Latin America, 17; Africa, 12·8; Europe, 8·9; North America, 4·7; Oceania, 1·2.

School enrolment, Oct. 1981, embraced 94% of the children who were 5 and 6 years old; 99% of the children aged 7–13 years; 94% of those aged 14–17, 49% of those aged 18 and 19, 32% of those aged 20 and 21, and 16% of those aged 22–24 years.

The US National Center for Education Statistics estimates the total enrolment in the autumn of 1983 at all of the country's elementary, secondary and higher educational institutions (public and private) at 56,675,000 (57,101,000 in the autumn of 1982); this was 24·6% of the total population of the USA as of 1 Sept. 1982.

Enrolment at the elementary and secondary school level is expected to be down by 0·9% in autumn 1983 and total enrolment in the colleges and universities to rise by about 0·2%.

The number of teachers in regular public and private elementary and secondary schools in the autumn of 1983 is expected to decrease slightly to 2,375,000. The average annual salary of the public school teachers was about $20,500 in 1982–83.

Digest of Education Statistics. Annual. Dept. of Education, Washington 20202, D.C. (from 1962)

American Junior Colleges. 6th ed. American Council on Education. Washington, 1963

American Universities and Colleges. 9th ed. American Council on Education. Washington, 1964

Ayer's Directory of Newspapers and Periodicals. Annual, from 1880. Philadelphia

Health and Welfare. Admission to the practice of medicine (for both doctors of medicine and doctors of osteopathic medicine) is controlled in each state by examining boards directly representing the profession and acting with authority conferred by state law. Although there are a number of variations, the usual time now required to complete basic training is 8 years beyond the secondary school with up to 3 years of additional graduate training. Certification as a specialist may require between 3 and 5 more years of graduate training plus experience in practice. In academic year 1981–82 the 141 US schools (15 osteopathic and 126 allopathic) graduated 16,669 physicians. About 30·2% of first-year students were women. In Dec. 1981 the estimated number of active physicians (MD and DO—in all forms of practice) in the US, Puerto Rico and outlying US areas was 467,700 (1 active physician to 504 population). The distribution of physicians throughout the country is uneven, both by state and by urban–rural areas.

In 1981–82 the 60 dental schools graduated 5,371 dentists. Active dentists in Dec. 1982 numbered 132,000 (1 active dentist to 1,766 population).

In academic year 1981–82, there were 1,422 registered nursing programmes in the US and 74,975 graduates. In Dec. 1981 registered nurses employed full- or part-time were 1 to 188 population.

Number of hospitals listed by the American Hospital Association in 1980 was 6,965, with 1,365,000 beds and 38,892,000 admissions during the year; average daily census was 1·06m. Of the total, 359 hospitals with 117,000 beds were operated by the federal government; 1,835 with 212,000 beds by state and local government; 3,339 with 693,000 beds by non-profit organizations (including church groups); 730 with 87,000 beds are proprietary. The categories of non-federal hospitals are 5,904 short-term general and special hospitals with 992,000 beds; 157 non-federal long-term general and special hospitals with 39,000 beds; 534 psychiatric hospitals with 215,000 beds; 11 tuberculosis hospitals with 2,000 beds.

Social welfare legislation was chiefly the province of the various states until the adoption of the Social Security Act of 14 Aug. 1935. This as amended provides for a federal system of old-age, survivors and disability insurance; health insurance for the aged and disabled; supplemental security income for the aged, blind and disabled; federal state unemployment insurance; and federal grants to states for public assistance (medical assistance for the aged and aid to families with dependent children generally) and for maternal and child-health and child-welfare services. The Social Security Administration of the Department of Health and Human Services has responsibility for the programmes—old-age, survivors and disability insurance, supplemental security income and aid to families with dependent children. The Health Care Financing Administration, an agency of the same Department, has federal responsibility for health insurance for the aged and disabled (Medicare) and medical assistance (Medicaid). The Department's Office of Human Development administers human service programmes for such groups as the elderly, children, youth, native Americans and persons with developmental disabilities, and its Public Health Service supports maternal and child-health services. Unemployment insurance is the responsibility of the Department of Labor.

The Social Security Act provides for protection against the cost of medical care through the two-part programme of health insurance for people 65 and over and for certain disabled people under 65, who receive disability insurance payments or who have permanent kidney failure (Medicare). During fiscal year 1982, payments totalling $34,343m. were made under the hospital insurance part of Medicare on behalf of 29·1m. people. During the same period, $14,806m. was paid under the voluntary medical insurance part of Medicare on behalf of 28·4m. people.

In 1982 about 116m. persons worked in employment covered by old-age, survivors and disability insurance.

In Dec. 1982 over 35·8m. beneficiaries were on the rolls, and the average benefit paid to a retired worker (not counting any paid to his dependants) was about $419 per month.

Benefits paid during calendar year 1982 totalled $156,173m., including $17,339m. paid to disabled workers and their dependants.

In Dec. 1982, 10·5m. persons (adults and children) were receiving payments under aid to families with dependent children (average monthly payment, $310 per family). Total payments under aid to families with dependent children were $12,941m. for the calendar year 1982.

In Dec. 1982, about 3·8m. persons were receiving supplementary security income payments, including over 1·5m. persons aged 65 or over; 77,000 blind persons, and over 2·2m. disabled persons. Payments, including supplemental amounts from various states, totalled $9,200m. in 1982.

In 1981, block grants supplanted some categorical grants to states for services. In 1982, federal appropriations for the social services block grant amounted to $2,400m. In addition, 1982 federal appropriations for human services to selected target groups totalled $2,296m. Included in this amount were $1,416m. for children and youth; $729m. for the elderly; $58m. for persons with developmental disabilities; and $28m. for native Americans. During 1982, the public Health Services awarded a total of $373·8m. for maternal and child health services, $316·2m. as block grants to the states and the remaining $57·6m. for special projects of regional and national significance. In addition, approximately $2·6m. was spent for research and $28·3m. for training in the fields of maternal and child health.

Burns, E. M., *Social Security and Public Policy.* New York, 1956 (Repr. 1976).—*Health Services for Tomorrow.* New York, 1973
Friedlander, W. A., *Introduction to Social Welfare.* 4th ed. New York, 1974
Grob, G. N., (ed.), *Social Problems and Social Policy Series.* 51 vols. New York, 1975
Grob, G. N., *et al.*, (eds.), *Mental Illness and Social Policy: The American Experience.* 41 books. New York, 1973

DIPLOMATIC REPRESENTATIVES

Of the United States in Great Britain (Grosvenor Sq., London, W1A 1AE)
Ambassador: Charles H. Price II (accredited 20 Dec. 1983).

Of Great Britain in the USA (3100 Massachusetts Ave., Washington, D.C., 20008)
Ambassador: Sir Oliver Wright, GCMG, GCVO, DSC.

Of the United States to the United Nations
Ambassador: Jeane Kirkpatrick.

Books of Reference

I. STATISTICAL INFORMATION

Within the federal government of the USA, responsibilities for the collection, compilation, analysis and publication of statistics are decentralized among a number of agencies, with specified responsibilities for general-purpose statistics in particular areas. In addition, most agencies of the Government collect statistical data as a by-product of their administrative or operating responsibilities in specific fields. Responsibility for co-ordinating the decentralized statistical activities rests in the Office of Statistical Standards Bureau of the Budget, Washington 25, D.C., as a part of the Executive Office of the President. This Office reviews all proposed collections of statistical data to avoid duplication or overlapping; promotes the use of improved statistical techniques; develops standard definitions and classifications so that the data collected by different agencies are comparable; serves as liaison between federal agencies and international organizations and as an information centre on government statistical programmes. The Division does not itself collect or publish statistics.

The major general-purpose statistical agencies and their principal areas of responsibility are:

(1) Bureau of the Census in the Department of Commerce (A. Ross Eckler, Director). Decennial censuses of population and housing and quinquennial censuses of agriculture, manufactures and business; current statistics on population and the labour force, manufacturing activity and commodity production, retail and wholesale trade and services, foreign trade, and state and local government finances and operations.

(2) Bureau of Labor Statistics in the Department of Labor (Geoffrey H. Moore, Commissioner). Current statistics on employment, earnings, man-hours, labour turnover, industrial accidents, work stoppages, wage rates; collective bargaining agreements; construction, industrial productivity; wholesale prices, retail prices and urban consumers' price indexes; income and expenditures of urban families.

(3) Statistical Reporting Service and Economic Research Service in the Department of Agriculture. Statistics on crop and livestock production and inventories; crop forecasts; food processing and food consumption; farm population, labour and wages; farm management; farm ownership values, transfers; taxation and finance; prices farmers pay and receive; farm income; accidents; studies of land and water uses.

(4) National Center for Health Statistics in the Public Health Service, Department of Health, Education and Welfare (Theodore D. Woolsey, Chief). Current statistics on births, deaths, marriages and divorce.

(5) Bureau of Mines in the Department of the Interior (John F. O'Leary, Director). Statistics on production, consumption and stocks of metals and minerals, and on injuries in mineral industries.

Other agencies in which statistics are an important by-product of regulatory or other administrative functions include: Social Security Administration in the Department of Health, Education and Welfare; Internal Revenue Service in the Treasury Department; Federal Power Commission; Federal Trade Commission; Interstate Commerce Commission, and the Securities and Exchange Commission.

Among the more important statistical publications of a fairly general nature are:

Statistical Abstract of the United States, published by the Bureau of the Census, Department of Commerce. Annual. Important summary statistics on the industrial, social, political and economic organization of the USA, with a representative selection from most of the important statistical publications. *Survey of Current Business,* published by the Office of Business Economics, Department of Commerce. Monthly. Interpretative text and charts reviewing business trends, etc.; official estimates of national income. *Economic Indicators,* prepared by the Council of Economic Advisers and published by the Congressional Joint Committee on the Economic Report. Monthly. Tables and charts presenting current data on the total output of the economy; prices; employment and wages; production and business activity; purchasing power; money, banking and federal finance. *Monthly Labor Review,* published by the Bureau of Labor Statistics, Department of Labor. *Federal Reserve Bulletin,* published by the Board of Governors of the Federal Reserve System. Monthly. Current data on money and banking and selected other economic series. Federal Reserve indexes of industrial production, etc.; international financial statistics. *Treasury Bulletin,* published by the Office of the Secretary, Department of the Treasury. Monthly. Current coverage of federal fiscal statistics; international capital movements. *Minerals Yearbook,* published by the Bureau of Mines, Department of the Interior. Annual. *Agricultural Statistics,* published by the Department of Agriculture. Annual. *Crops and Markets,* published by the Bureau of Agricultural Economics in the Department of Agriculture. Monthly. Crop report and market statistics. *Foreign Agriculture,* published by the Office of Foreign Agriculture Service, Department of Agriculture. Monthly. Foreign agricultural production, foreign government policies relating to agriculture and international trade in agricultural products. *Vital Statistics of the United States,* published by the Public Health Service, US Department of Health, Education and Welfare. Monthly and Annual. Natality and mortality data tabulated by place of occurrence, with supplemental tables for Puerto Rico and the Virgin Islands; and tabulated by place of residence.

An annotated bibliography of about 100 periodical statistical publications is included in *Statistical Services of the United States Government,* a pamphlet issued by the Division of Statistical Standards, Bureau of the Budget, describing the general organization of the statistical system of the USA and the principal types of economic statistics.

II. OTHER OFFICIAL PUBLICATIONS

Guide to the Study of the United States of America. General Reference and Bibliography Division, Library of Congress. 1960.
Historical Statistics of the United States, Colonial Times to 1957: A Statistical Abstract Supplement. Washington, 1960.—*Continuation to 1962 and Revisions,* 1965.
United States Government Manual. Washington. Annual.

The official publications of the USA are issued by the US Government Printing Office and are distributed by the Superintendent of Documents, who issued in 1940 a cumulative *Catalog of the Public Documents of the . . . Congress and of All the Departments of the Government of the United States.* This *Catalog* is kept up to date by *United States Government Publications, Monthly Catalog* with annual index and supplemented by *Price Lists.* Each *Price List* is devoted to a special subject or type of material, *e.g., American History* or *Census.* Useful guides are Schmeckebier, L. F., and Eastin, R. B. (eds.), *Government Publications and Their Use.* 2nd ed., Washington, D.C., 1961; Boyd, A. M., *United States Government Publications.* 3rd ed. New York, 1949, and Leidy, W. P., *Popular Guide to Government Publications.* 2nd ed. New York and London, 1963.

Treaties and other International Acts of the United States of America (Edited by Hunter Miller), 8 vols. Washington, 1929–48. This edition stops in 1863. It may be supplemented by *Treaties, Conventions . . . Between the US and Other Powers, 1776–1937* (Edited by William M. Malloy and others). 4 vols. 1909–38. A new Treaty Series, *US Treaties and Other International Agreements* was started in 1950.

Writings on American History. Washington, annual from 1902 (except 1904–5 and 1941–47).

III. Non-Official Publications

A. Handbooks

National Historical Publications Commission. *Guide to Archives and Manuscripts in the United States,* ed. P. M. Hamer. Yale Univ. Press, 1961

Adams, J. T. (ed.), *Dictionary of American History.* 2nd ed. 7 vols. New York, 1942

Dictionary of American Biography, ed. A. Johnson and D. Malone. 23 vols. New York, 1929–64.—*Concise Dictionary of American Biography.* New York, 1964

Current Biography. New York, annual from 1940; monthly supplements

Handlin, O., and others. *Harvard Guide to American History.* Cambridge, Mass., 1954

Herstein, S. R. and Robbins, N., *United States of America.* [Bibliography] Oxford and Santa Barbara, 1982

Lord, C. L. and E. H., *Historical Atlas of the US.* Rev. ed. New York, 1969

Who's Who in America. Chicago, 1899–1900 to date; monthly Supplement. 1940 to date

B. General History

Barck, Jr, O. T., and Blake, N. M., *Since 1900: A History of the United States.* 5th ed. New York, 1974

Bellot, H. H., *American History and American Historians.* London, 1952, repr. 1974

Billington, R. A., *Westward Expansion.* 4th ed. New York, 1974

Carman, H. J., and others, *A History of the American People.* 3rd ed. 2 vols. New York, 1967

Commager, H. S. (ed.), *Documents of American History.* 8th ed. New York, 1966

Divine, R. A., *Since 1945: Politics and Diplomacy in Recent American History.* New York, 1975

Hicks, J. D., *The American Nation, A History of the United States from 1865.* 5th ed. Boston, 1971

Link, A. S., and Catton, W. B., *American Epoch: A History of the United States Since the 1890s.* 4th ed. New York, 1967

Morison, S. E., *The Oxford History of the American People.* OUP, 1968

Morison, S. E., with Commager, H. S., *The Growth of the American Republic.* 2 vols. 5th ed. OUP, 1962–63

Nicholas, H. G., *The Nature of American Politics.* OUP, 1980

Parkes, H. B., *The United States of America, A History.* 3rd ed. New York, 1968

Scammon, R. N. (ed.), *American Votes: A Handbook of Contemporary American Election Statistics.* Washington, D.C., 1956 to date (biennial)

Schlesinger, A. M., *The Rise of Modern America, 1865–1951.* 4th ed. New York, 1951.—*The Age of Roosevelt.* 4 vols. New York and London, 1957–62.—*A Thousand Days: John F. Kennedy in the White House.* New York and London, 1965

Snowman, D., *America Since 1920.* London, 1978

Watson, R. A., *The Promise and Performance of American Democracy.* 2nd ed. New York, 1975

C. Minorities

Bennett, M. T., *American Immigration Policies: A History.* Washington, D.C., 1963

Burma, J. J., *Spanish-speaking Groups in the US.* Duke University Press, 1954, repr. 1974

Frazier, E. F., *The Negro Family in the United States.* Chicago Univ. Press, 1966

McNickle, D., *The Indian Tribes of the United States.* OUP, 1962.—*Native American Tribalism.* OUP, 1973

Sklare, M., *The Jew in American Society.* New York, 1974

Wissler, Clark, *Indians of the United States.* Rev. ed. New York, 1966

D. Economic History
The Economic History of the United States. 9 vols. New York, 1946 ff.
Bining, A. C., and Cochran, T. C., *The Rise of American Economic Life.* 4th ed. New York, 1963
Dorfman, J., *The Economic Mind in American Civilization.* 5 vols. New York, 1946–59
Faulkner, H. U., *American Economic History.* 8th ed. New York, 1960
Friedman, M., and Schwartz, A. J., *A Monetary History of the United States, 1867–1960.* New York, 1963
Mund, V. A., *Government and Business.* 4th ed. New York, 1965

E. Foreign Relations
Documents on American Foreign Relations. Princeton, from 1948. Annual
The United States in World Affairs. 1931 ff. Council on Foreign Relations. New York, from 1932. Annual
Allison, G., and Szanton. P., *Remaking Foreign Policy: The Organizations Connection.* New York, 1976
Bartlett, R. (ed.), *The Record of American Diplomacy; Documents and Readings in the History of American Foreign Relations.* 4th ed. New York, 1964
Beloff, M., *The United States and the Unity of Europe.* London, 1963, repr. 1976
Connell-Smith, G., *The United States and Latin America.* London, 1975
DeConde, A., *The American Secretary of State.* London, 1963, repr. 1976
Morgan, R., *The United States and West Germany, 1945–73.* OUP, 1975
Schwab, G., (ed.), *United States Foreign Policy at the Crossroads.* Westport, 1982
Smith, R. F., *The United States and Cuba. Business and Diplomacy, 1917–1960.* New York, 1962
Stebbins, R. P., and Adam, E. A., *Documents of American Foreign Relations, 1968–69.* New York, 1972
Vance, C., *Hard Choices: Critical Years in America's Foreign Policy.* New York, 1983
Wilcox, F. O., and Frank, R. A., *The Constitution and the Conduct of Foreign Policy.* New York, 1976

F. National Character
Coan. O. W., *America in Fiction, An Annotated List of Novels.* 5th ed. Stanford Univ. Press, 1967
Curti, M. B., *The Growth of American Thought.* 3rd ed. New York, 1964
Degler, C. N., *Out of Our Past: The Forces That Shaped Modern America.* Rev. ed. New York, 1970
Duigan, P., and Rabushka, A., (eds.), *The United States in the 1980s.* Stanford, 1980

National Library: The Library of Congress. Washington 25, D.C. *Librarian:* Lawrence Quincy Mumford, AB, MA, BS.

STATES AND TERRITORIES

For information as to State and Local Government, see under UNITED STATES, *pp.* 1378–80.

Against the names of the Governors and the Secretaries of State, (D.) stands for Democrat and (R.) for Republican.

Figures for the revenues and expenditures of the various states are those of the Federal Bureau of the Census unless otherwise stated, which takes the original state figures and arranges them on a common pattern so that those of one state can be compared with those of any other.

Official publications of the various states and insular possessions are listed in the *Monthly Check-List of State Publications,* issued by the Library of Congress since 1910. Their character and contents are discussed in J. K. Wilcox's *Manual on the Use of State Publications* (1940). Of great importance bibliographically are the publications of the Historical Records Survey and the American Imprints Inventory, which record local archives, official publications and state imprints. These publications supplement those of state historical societies which usually publish journals and monographs on state and local history. An outstanding source of statistical data is the material issued by the various state planning boards and commissions, to which should be added the annual *Governmental Finances* issued by the US Bureau of the Census.
The Book of the States. Biennial. Council of State Governments, Lexington, 1953 ff.
State Government Finances. Annual. Dept. of Commerce, 1966 ff.

Regionalism
Odum, H. W., *American Regionalism, A Cultural–Historical Approach to National Integration.* New York, 1938
Visher, S. X., *Climatic Atlas of the USA.* Harvard Univ. Press., 1954

A. North-East

Gottman, J., *Megalopolis, the Urbanized North-eastern Seaboard of the US.* New York, 1964

B. The South

Clement, E., *A History of the Old South.* New York, 1949

Ezell, J. S., *The South Since 1865.* New York and London, 1963

Heseltine, W. B., and Smiley, D. L., *The South in American History.* 2nd ed. Englewood Cliffs, 1960

Stephenson, W. H., and Coulter, E. M. (ed.), *A History of the South.* 10 vols. Louisiana State Univ. Press, 1947–67

C. The Middle West

Lynd, R. S. and H. M., *Middletown: A Study in Contemporary American Culture.* New York and London, 1929.—*Middletown in Transition: A Study in Cultural Conflicts.* New York and London, 1937

Nye, R. B., *Midwestern Progressive Politics, 1870–1938.* Michigan State Univ. Press, 1959

D. The West

Fogelson, R. U., *The Fragmented Metropolis: Los Angeles, 1850–1930.* Harvard Univ. Press, 1967

Fuller, G. W., *History of the Pacific Northwest.* 2nd ed. New York, 1938

Johansen, D. O., and Gates, C. M., *Empire of the Columbia: A History of the Pacific North-West,* New York, 1957

Parrish, P. H., *Before the Covered Wagon.* Portland, Oreg., 1931

Quiett, G. C., *They Built the West: An Epic of Rails and Cities.* New York and London, 1934

Scott, H. W., *History of the Oregon Country.* 6 vols. Cambridge, Mass., 1924

Winther, O. O., *The Great Northwest: A History.* 2nd ed., rev. New York, 1950

ALABAMA

HISTORY. Alabama, settled in 1702 as part of the French Province of Louisiana, and ceded to the British in 1763, was organized as a Territory, 1817, and admitted into the Union on 14 Dec. 1819.

AREA AND POPULATION. Alabama is bounded north by Tennessee, east by Georgia, south by Florida and the Gulf of Mexico and west by Mississippi. Area, 51,998 sq. miles, including 1,535 sq. miles of inland water. Census population, 1 April 1980, 3,893,888, an increase of 13·06% over that of 1970. Estimate (1981) 3,917,000. Births, 1982, 60,296 (15·1 per 1,000 population); deaths, 34,957 (9); infant deaths (under 28 days), 556 (9·2 per 1,000 live births); marriages, 47,431 (12·3); divorces, 24,910 (6·8).

Population in 5 census years was:

	White	Negro	Indian	Asiatic	Total	Per sq. mile
1910	1,228,832	908,282	909	70	2,138,093	41·4
1930	1,700,844	944,834	465	105	2,646,248	51·3
1960	2,283,609	980,271	1,726	915	3,266,521	64·0
			All others			
1970	2,533,831	903,467	6,867		3,444,165	66·7
1980	2,872,621	996,335	24,932		3,893,888	74·9

Of the total population in 1980, 49% were male, 61% were urban and 65% were 21 years or older.

The large cities (1980 census) were: Birmingham, 284,413 (metropolitan area, 847,487; Mobile, 200,452 (443,536); Huntsville, 142,513 (308,593); Montgomery (capital), 177,857 (272,687); Tuscaloosa, 75,211 (137,541).

CLIMATE. Birmingham. Jan. 46°F (7·8°C), July 80°F (26·7°C). Annual rainfall 54″ (1,346 mm). Mobile. Jan. 52°F (11·1°C), July 82°F (27·8°C). Annual rainfall 63″ (1,577 mm). Montgomery. Jan. 49°F (9·4°C), July 81°F (27·2°C). Annual rainfall 53″ (1,321 mm). *See* Gulf Coast, p. 1373. The growing season ranges from 190 days (north) to 298 days (south).

CONSTITUTION AND GOVERNMENT. The present constitution dates from 1901; it has had 410 amendments. The legislature consists of a Senate of 35 members and a House of Representatives of 105 members, all elected for 4 years. The Governor and Lieut.-Governor are elected for 4 years.

The state is represented in Congress by 2 senators and 7 representatives. Applicants for registration must take an oath of allegiance to the United States and fill out a questionnaire to the satisfaction of the registrars. In the 1980 presidential election Reagan polled 654,192 votes, Carter, 636,730 and Anderson, 15,844.

Montgomery is the capital.

Governor: George C. Wallace (D.), 1983–86 ($50,000).
Lieut.-Governor: Bill Baxley (D.) ($400 a month plus daily allowances).
Secretary of State: Don Siegelman (D.) ($32,836).

BUDGET. The total receipts for the fiscal year ending 30 Sept. 1981 were $7,431·9m.; total expenditure was $6,896·3m.

The net long-term debt on 30 Sept. 1981 amounted to $906·8m.

Per capita income (1980) was $7,434.

ENERGY AND NATURAL RESOURCES

Minerals. Production of principal minerals (financial year 1982): Coal, about 27·5m. short tons; limestone, 15·2m. short tons. Total (non-fuel) mineral output was valued at $300m.

Agriculture. The number of farms in 1983 was 54,000, covering 12·1m. acres; average farm had 224 acres and was valued at $189,000.

Cash receipts from farm marketings, 1982: Crops, $1,004m.; livestock and products, $1,214m.; and total, $2,218·1m. Principal crops: soybeans, cotton, wheat and peanuts; potatoes, tomatoes, hay and corn are also important. In 1982, poultry accounted for the largest percentage of cash receipts from farm marketings; cattle and calves were second, soybeans third, cotton and cotton seed fourth.

Forestry. Area of national forest lands, Oct. 1983, 644,432 acres; state forest, 147,400; industrial forest, 4,458,000; private non-industrial forest, 16m.; other government-owned forest, 324,200.

INDUSTRY. Alabama is predominantly industrial. In 1981, 6,448 manufacturing establishments employed 364,130 production workers, earning over $5,725m. Pig-iron, 1981, amounted to 2·5m. net tons.

TOURISM. In 1982 about 24m. travelled to or through Alabama from other states. Total income from tourism (including receipts from Alabama holiday-makers) was about $2,700m.

COMMUNICATIONS

Roads. Paved roads of all classes in 1981 totalled 58,920 miles; total highways, 88,020 miles.

Railways. In 1981 the railways had a length of 4,796 miles.

Aviation. In 1981–82 the state had 89 publicly owned and 29 privately owned licensed airfields.

Shipping. The only deep-water port is Mobile, with a large ocean-going trade; imports (1982), 39·6m. tons; exports, 20·2m. tons. The docks can handle 35 ocean-going vessels at once. The 9-ft channel of the Tennessee River traverses North Alabama for 200 miles; a Tennessee-Tombigbee waterway is under construction. The Warrier–Tombigbee Waterway (476 miles) connects the Birmingham industrial area with Mobile and also with the Gulf Intracoastal Waterway; the Chattahoochee River 9-ft channel extends from the Gulf to Phenix City (Alabama). In 1971 a 9-ft channel was completed which connects Montgomery and

Mobile through the Alabama River System. The Alabama State Docks also operates a system of 14 inland docks; there is 1 privately-run inland dock.

JUSTICE, RELIGION, EDUCATION AND WELFARE

Justice. The prison population on 1 Sept. 1983 was 9,370.

From 1 Jan. 1927 to 1 June 1983 there were 155 executions (electrocution): 122 for murder, 25 for rape, 5 for armed robbery, 1 for burglary and 1 for carnal knowledge. Before 1 Jan. 1927, persons executed in Alabama were hanged locally by the sheriffs in the counties of their conviction.

In 39 counties the sale of alcoholic beverage is permitted, and in 28 counties it is prohibited.

Religion. Chief religious bodies (in 1980) are: Southern Baptist Convention (about 1,182,018), Churches of Christ (113,919), United Methodist (about 344,790), Roman Catholic (106,123), African Methodist Episcopal Zion (139,714), Christian Methodist Episcopal (about 53,493) and Assemblies of God (48,610).

Education. In 1982–83 the 1,400 (estimated) public elementary and high schools required 31,548 teachers to teach 718,940 pupils enrolled in grades K-12. In 1982 there were 14 senior public institutions (13 4-year institutions and 1 upper-division college) with 102,065 students and 4,163 faculty members in 1981–82. The 21 junior colleges had 38,858 students and 1,250 teachers, 22 technical schools had 24,743 students and 822 teachers.

Health. In Jan. 1983 there were 139 hospitals (20,998 beds) licensed by the State Board of Health. In 1982–83 hospitals for mental diseases had 2,545 beds. Facilities for the mentally retarded (1 Sept. 1983) had 1,455 cases.

Pensions and Security. In Aug. 1983 Alabama paid supplements (to federal welfare payments) to 13,992 recipients of old-age assistance, receiving an average of $59.76 each; 5,244 permanently and totally disabled, $63.78; 131 blind, $60.54. Combined state–federal aid to dependent children was paid to 54,752 families, average $111.40 per family.

Books of Reference

Alabama Official and Statistical Register. Montgomery. Quadrennial
Alabama Encyclopædia. Vol. I. Northport, 1965
Economic Abstract of Alabama. Center for Business and Economic Research, Univ. of Alabama, 1975
The Deep South in Transformation: A Symposium. Univ. of Alabama Press, 1964
Farmer, H., *The Legislative Process in Alabama.* Univ. of Alabama, 1949

ALASKA

HISTORY. Discovered in 1741 by Vitus Bering, its first settlement, on Kodiak Island, was in 1784. The area known as Russian America with its capital (1806) at Sitka was ruled by a Russo-American fur company and vaguely claimed as a Russian colony. Alaska was purchased by the United States from Russia under the treaty of 30 March 1867 for $7·2m. It was not organized until 1884, when it became a 'district' governed by the code of the state of Oregon. By Act of Congress approved 24 Aug. 1912 Alaska became an incorporated Territory; its first legislature in 1913 granted votes to women, 7 years in advance of the Constitutional Amendment.

Alaska officially became the 49th state of the Union on 3 Jan. 1959.

AREA AND POPULATION. Alaska is bounded north by the Beaufort Sea, west and south by the Pacific and east by Canada. It has the largest area of any state, being more than twice the size of Texas. The gross area (land and water) is 591,004 sq. miles; the land area is 570,833 sq. miles of which 86·6% was in federal ownership in 1978. Census population, 1 April 1980, was 401,851, including military personnel, an increase of 33·5% over 1970. Estimate (1981), 412,000. Births, 1980, were 9,557 (23·8 per 1,000 population); deaths, 1,811 (4·5); infant deaths, 117 (12·3 per 1,000 live births); marriages, 5,361 (13·4); divorces, 3,517 (8·7).

Population in 5 census years was:

	White	Negro	All Others	Total	Per sq. mile
1940	39,170	...	33,354	72,524	0·13
1950	92,808	...	35,835	128,643	0·23
1960	174,649	...	51,518	226,167	0·40
1970	236,767	8,911	54,704	300,382	0·53
1980	309,728	13,643	78,480	401,851	0·70

Of the total population in 1980, 53·01% were male, 64·34% were urban and 68·57% were aged 21 years or over.

The largest city is Anchorage, which had a 1980 census population of 174,430. Other city area populations (1980), Fairbanks, 22,645; Juneau, 19,528; Sitka, 7,803; Ketchikan, 7,198. There are 11 major incorporated boroughs, of which the largest are Anchorage, Fairbanks-North Star (53,983), Kenai Peninsula (25,282), Juneau and Matanuska-Susitna (17,816).

CLIMATE. Anchorage. Jan. 12°F (–11·1°C), July 57°F (13·9°C). Annual rainfall 15″ (371 mm). Fairbanks. Jan. –11°F (–23·9°C), July 60°F (15·6°C). Annual rainfall 12″ (300 mm). Sitka. Jan. 33°F (0·6°C), July 55°F (12·8°C). Annual rainfall 87″ (2,175 mm). See Pacific Coast, p. 1372.

CONSTITUTION AND GOVERNMENT. An important provision of the Enabling Act is that the state has the right to select 103·55m. acres of vacant and unappropriated public lands in order to establish 'a tax basis'; it can open these lands to prospectors for minerals, and the state is to derive the principal advantage in all gains resulting from the discovery of minerals. In addition, certain federally administered lands reserved for conservation of fisheries and wild life have been transferred to the state. Special provision is made for federal control of land for defence in areas of high strategic importance.

The constitution of Alaska was adopted by public vote, 24 April 1956. The state legislature consists of a Senate of 20 members (elected for 4 years) and a House of Representatives of 40 members (elected for 2 years). The state sends 2 senators and 1 representative to Congress. The franchise may be exercised by all citizens over 18 years of age.

The capital is Juneau. A new capital site near Anchorage was chosen in 1976.

In the 1980 presidential election Reagan polled 86,112 votes, Carter 41,842.

Governor: William Sheffield (D.), 1983–86 ($74,196).
Lieut.-Governor: Steve McAlpine (D.) 1983–86 ($69,240).

ECONOMY

Budget. Total state government revenue for the year ended 30 June 1981 (Annual Financial Report figures) was $4,232·2m. ($2,296·1m. from taxation, $314·1.m from federal sources). Total expenditure was $4,824·2m.

In 1976 a Permanent Fund was set up for the deposit of at least 25% of all mineral-related revenue. Cash and investment holdings at 30 June, 1982, $3,176·2m.

General obligation bonds at 30 June 1980, $809m.

Per capita income (1981) was $13,763.

Banking. Annual average assets, $2,418·9m., total deposits $1,932·2m.

ENERGY AND NATURAL RESOURCES

Oil and Gas. Commercial production of crude petroleum began in 1959 and by 1961 had become the most important mineral by value. Production: 1961, 6·3m. bbls (of 42 gallons); 1965, 11m. bbls; 1976, 67m. bbls; 1977, 169m. bbls; 1981, 587m. bbls. Oil comes mainly from Prudhoe Bay, the McArthur River field and several Cook Inlet fields. Natural gas marketed production, 1981, 243,000m. cu. ft. Value of fuel minerals (1980), $9,383m. Alaska receives 90% of all royalties (12·5%) from oil, gas and coal production on federal lands and the full 12·5% royalty for oil and gas production in state lands (coal royalties are being negotiated). Revenue to the state from oil and gas production tax in 1980–81 was $1,170m., from corporate petroleum tax $860·1m. and from royalties $1,491·3m. In 1969, the state conducted a major competitive lease sale for the arctic coastal region where reserves are estimated to be as large as 50,000m. bbls. A further competitive lease sale for the Beaufort Sea was conducted in 1979.

Oil from the Prudhoe Bay arctic field is now carried by the Trans-Alaska pipeline to Prince William Sound on the south coast, where a tanker terminal has been built at Valdez.

Minerals. Value of production, 1981: sand and gravel (46·4m. short tons), $87·5m.; crushed stone (5·4m. short tons), $26·9m.; gold (134,000 troy oz.), $55m.; others, including silver, gemstones, lead, copper, tin, barite and platinum group minerals, $1·6m.

Agriculture. In some parts of the state the climate during the brief spring and summer (about 100 days in major areas and 152 days in the south-eastern coastal area) is suitable for agricultural operations, thanks to the long hours of sunlight, but Alaska is a food-importing area. In 1982 about 2m. acres was farmland; 90% of this was unimproved pasture primarily government leases for grazing of sheep and beef cattle in south-west Alaska. In 1980 (preliminary) there were 8,400 cattle, 1,100 milch cows, 1,800 hogs and 4,300 sheep stock.

Farm income in 1981: $13m. of which $8m. was from crops (mainly hay and potatoes) and $5m. from livestock and dairy products.

There were about 25,000 reindeer in western Alaska in 1980, owned by individual Eskimo herders except for 750 at Nome owned by the Government.

Forestry. In south-eastern Alaska timber fringes the shore of the mainland and all the islands extending inland to a depth of 5 miles. The state's enormous forests could produce an estimated annual sustained yield of 1,500m. bd ft of lumber, nearly twice Alaska's record 1973 cut. Alaska has 2 national forests: the Tongass of 16·9m. acres and the Chugach of 5·9m. acres. An estimated total of 454m. bd ft was cut in 1980 on public lands, of which 453·7m. came from national forests and 33,800 from state forests. Total cut, including timber from private land and land held by the Bureau of Indian Affairs, about 563·7m. bd ft. Alaska has 2 large pulp-mills at Ketchikan and Sitka.

Fisheries. The catch for 1980 was 983·7m. lb. of fish and shellfish having a value to fishermen of $561·8m. This compares with 471m. lb. in 1971 with a value of $85·5m. Salmon remains the highest per unit value species, with a catch in 1980 of 511·7m. lb. valued to the fishermen at $268·5m.

INDUSTRY. Main industries with employment, 1981: Government, 54,800; trade, 31,165; services, 29,491; contract construction, 12,470; manufacturing, 11,655; mining including oil and gas, 7,925.

The major manufacturing industry was food processing, followed by timber industries. Total employment outside agriculture, 175,485. Total wages and salaries, $4,377,697,900.

TOURISM. About 690,000 tourists visited the state in 1982.

COMMUNICATIONS

Roads. Alaska's highway and road system, 1981, totalled 13,699 miles, including marine highway systems, local service roads, borough and city streets, national park, forest and reservation roads and military roads. Registered motor vehicles, 1981, 341,637.

The Alaska Highway extends 1,523 miles from Dawson Creek, British Columbia, to Fairbanks, Alaska. It was built by the US Army in 1942, at a cost of $138m.

The greater portion of it, because it lies in Canada, is maintained by the Canadian Government.

Railways. There is a railway of 111 miles from Skagway to the town of Whitehorse, the White Pass and Yukon route, in the Canadian Yukon region. The government-owned Alaska Railroad runs from Seward to Fairbanks, a distance of 471 miles. This is a freight service with only occasional passenger use. A passenger service operates from Anchorage to Fairbanks via Denali National Park in the tourist season.

Aviation. In 1982 the state had about 1,070 airports, of which about half were publicly owned. Commercial passengers by air from Alaska's largest international airports Anchorage and Fairbanks numbered 1·1m. at Anchorage and 273,512 at Fairbanks. General aviation aircraft in the state per 1,000 population was about ten times the US average.

Shipping. Regular shipping services to and from the US are furnished by 2 steamship and several barge lines operating out of Seattle and other Pacific coast ports. A Canadian company also furnishes a regular service from Vancouver, B.C. Freight handled at the Port of Anchorage, 1981 (short tons): Bulk petroleum, 365,999; vans, flats and containers, 1,154,060; cement and drilling mud, 32,497; vehicles, 39,822; total 1·65m.

A 1,000 nautical-mile ferry system for motor cars and passengers (the 'Alaska Marine Highway') operates from Seattle, Washington and Prince Rupert (British Columbia) to Juneau, Haines (for access to the Alaska Highway) and Skagway. A second system extends throughout the south-central region of Alaska linking the Cook Inlet area with Kodiak Island and Prince William Sound.

JUSTICE, RELIGION, EDUCATION AND WELFARE

Justice. There is no death penalty in Alaska.

Religion. Many religions are represented, including the Russian Orthodox, Roman Catholic, Episcopalian, Presbyterian, Methodist and other denominations.

Education. During 1980–81 there were 85,862 pupils at public schools, 3,900 at private schools. The Bureau of Indian Affairs schools had 2,668 pupils attending schools in the state. The University of Alaska (founded in 1922) had (1978) 4,382 students on the main campus, 3,341 at its branches in Anchorage and Juneau and 13,958 in community colleges. Other colleges had 674 students in 1978.

Health. In 1982 there were 28 acute care hospitals with 1,397 beds, of which 7 were federal public health hospitals; there was 1 mental hospital; there were 24 mental health clinics.

Welfare. Old-age assistance was established under the Federal Social Security Act; in 1982 aid to dependent children covered a monthly average of 6,617 households; payments, an average of $409 per month; aid to the blind and to the disabled was given to a monthly average of 2,170 persons receiving on average $185 per month. An average of 5,492 people per month received Medicaid.

Books of Reference

Statistical Information: Department of Commerce and Economic Development, Division of Economic Enterprise, Pouch EE, Juneau.

Alaska Economic Information. Reporting Service, Division of Economic Enterprise, Juneau 99811. Quarterly
Alaska Economy, The. Division of Economic Enterprise, Juneau. Annual
Look North. Department of Economic Development, Juneau, 1970
Gardey, J., *Alaska: The Sophisticated Wilderness.* London, 1976
Hulley, Clarence C., *Alaska Past and Present.* Portland, Oregon, 1970
Rogers, G. W., *Alaska in Transition: the south-east region.* Johns Hopkins Univ. Press, 1960.—*The Future of Alaska.* Johns Hopkins Univ. Press, 1962
Tourville, M., *Alaska, a Bibliography, 1570–1970.* 1971

State Library: Pouch G, Juneau. *Librarian:* Richard Engen.—Alaska Historical Library, Pouch G, Juneau. *Librarian:* Phyllis de Muth.

ARIZONA

HISTORY. Arizona was settled in 1752, organized as a Territory in 1863 and became a state on 14 Feb. 1912.

AREA AND POPULATION. Arizona is bounded north by Utah, east by New Mexico, south by Mexico, west by California and Nevada. Area, 113,909 sq. miles, including 346·6 sq. miles of inland water. Of the total area (72,680,320 acres) 32,336,577 were owned by the federal government in 1970, including 19,623,000 acres held by the Office of Indian Affairs. Census population on 1 April 1980 (preliminary) was 2,717,866, an increase of 53·4% over 1970. Estimate (1981) 2,794,000. Births, 1982, 52,628; deaths, 21,951; infant deaths (1980), 684; marriages, 31,408; divorces, 20,259.

Population in 5 census years:

	White	Negro	Indian	Chinese	Japanese	Total	Per sq. mile
1910	171,468	2,009	29,201	1,305	371	204,354	1·8
1930	378,551	10,749	43,726	1,110	879	435,573	3·8
1960	1,169,517	43,403	83,387	2,937	1,501	1,302,161	11·3

	White	Negro	All others	Total	Per sq. mile
1970	1,604,498	53,344	117,557	1,775,399	15·6
1980	2,240,033	75,034	402,799	2,717,866	23·9

Of the population in 1980, 1,337,666 were male, 2,278,189 were urban and 1,820,909 were aged 20 and over.

The 1980 (preliminary) census population of Phoenix was 789,704; Tucson, 330,537; Scottsdale, 88,364; Tempe, 106,743; Mesa, 152,453; Glendale, 96,988.

CLIMATE. Phoenix. Jan. 52°F (11·1°C), July 90°F (32·2°C). Annual rainfall 8" (191 mm). Yuma. Jan. 55°F (12·8°C), July 91°F (32·8°C). Annual rainfall 3" (75 mm). *See* Mountain States, p. 1372.

CONSTITUTION AND GOVERNMENT. The state constitution (1910, with now 70 amendments) placed the government under direct control of the people through the Initiative, Referendum and the Recall. The state Senate consists of 30 members, and the House of Representatives of 60, all elected for 2 years. Arizona sends to Congress 2 senators and 5 representatives. In the 1980 presidential election Reagan polled 529,688 votes, Carter 246,843, Anderson 76,952, Clark 18,784 and DeBerry 1,094.

The state capital is Phoenix. The state is divided into 15 counties.

Governor: Bruce Babbitt (D.), 1978– ($50,000).
Secretary of State: Rose Mofford (D.).

BUDGET. General revenues, year ending 30 June 1982 (US Census Bureau figures), were $1,990·9m. (taxation, $1,378·9m. and federal aid, $236·2m.); general expenditures, $2,337·1m. (education, $1,206·7m.; transport $254·3m., and public welfare, $385·9m.).

Per capita income (1981) was $9,693.

NATURAL RESOURCES

Minerals. The mining industries of the state are important, but less so than agriculture and manufacturing. By value the most important mineral produced is copper. Production (1981): Copper (848,750 tons); gold (100,339 troy oz.) and silver (8,055 troy oz.) are both largely recovered from copper ore. Other minerals include sand and gravel (22,679 short tons), zinc (138 tons) and lead (993 tons). Total value of minerals mined in 1981 was $2,565,840.

Agriculture. Arizona, despite its dry climate, is well suited for agriculture along the water-courses and where irrigation is practised on a large scale from great reservoirs constructed by the US as well as by the state government and private interests.

Irrigated area, 1978, 1·2m. acres. The wide pasture lands are favourable for the rearing of cattle and sheep, but numbers are either stationary or declining compared with 1920.

In 1982 Arizona contained 7,000 farms and ranches with 1·16m. acres of crop land, out of a total farm and pastoral area of 38·3m. acres. The average farm was estimated at 5,417 acres. Farming is highly commercialized and mechanized and concentrated largely on cotton picked by machines and by Indian, Mexican and migratory workers.

Area under cotton (1982), 506,600 acres; 1·2m. bales (of 500 lb.) of cotton were harvested.

Cash income, 1982, from crops, $974·9m.; from livestock, $682·4m. Most important cereals are grain sorghums and barley; other crops include oranges, grapefruit and lettuce. On 1 Jan. 1982 there were 1m. all cattle, 79,000 milch cows, 377,000 sheep and (1981) 170,000 swine.

Forestry. The national forests in the state had an area (1980) of 11·27m. acres.

INDUSTRY. Manufacturing establishments (numbering 2,838 in 1981) had 156,674 production workers, earning $2,972·9m.

TOURISM. In 1982 total estimated tourist business in the state was $4,540m.

COMMUNICATIONS

Roads. In 1980 there were 75,200 miles of city and county roads, and 4,596 miles maintained by federal agencies.

Aviation. Airports, 1981, numbered 224, of which 96 were for public use.

JUSTICE, RELIGION, EDUCATION AND WELFARE

Justice. A 'right-to-work' amendment to the constitution, adopted 5 Nov. 1946, makes illegal any concessions to trade-union demands for a 'closed shop'.

The Arizona prisons 30 June 1981 held 5,199. There have been no executions since 1963; from 1930 to 1963 there were 38 executions (lethal gas) all for murder, and all men (28 whites, 10 Negro).

Religion. The leading religious bodies are Roman Catholics and Mormons (Latter Day Saints); others include Methodists, Presbyterians, Baptists and Episcopalians. No recent statistics of membership are available.

Education. School attendance is compulsory between the ages of 8 and 16 years, and instruction is free for pupils from 6 to 21 years of age. The enrolled pupils in 1982–83 in the elementary schools were 343,364 and public high schools had 154,725 pupils. Teachers for both elementary and high schools totalled 27,000. Teachers' salaries averaged $18,000. The state maintains 3 universities at Tucson, Tempe and Flagstaff and 17 junior colleges.

Health. In 1980 there were 79 hospitals reported by the State Department of Health; capacity 11,600 beds. Resident patients in state mental hospitals on 30 June 1980 numbered 631.

Social Security. Old-age assistance (maximum depending on the programme) is given, with federal aid, to needy citizens 65 years of age or older. In June 1980, 2,300 people were receiving general assistance at an average of $105.29 a month; 18,875 families (52,642 recipients), $61.55 per recipient in aid to dependent children; in the supplemental payment programme 1,200 old persons received $86.38 per month; 6 blind, $61.17; 663 totally disabled, $36.44.

Books of Reference

Arizona Statistical Review. 39th ed. Valley National Bank, Phoenix, 1983
Federal Writers' Project. *Arizona: The Grand Canyon State.* 4th ed. New York, 1966
Comeaux, M. L., *Arizona: a Geography.* Boulder, 1981
Goff, J. S., *Arizona Civilization.* 2nd ed. Cave Creek, 1970

Mason, B. B., and Hink, H., *Constitutional Government of Arizona.* 6th ed.Tempe, 1979

State Library: Department of Library, Archives and Public Records, Capitol, Phoenix 85007.
Director: Sharon G. Womack.

ARKANSAS

HISTORY. Arkansas was settled in 1686, made a territory in 1819 and admitted into the Union on 15 June 1836. The name originated with the Quapaw Indian tribe. The constitution, which dates from 1874, has been amended 59 times.

AREA AND POPULATION. Arkansas is bounded north by Missouri, east by Tennessee and Mississippi, south by Louisiana, south-west by Texas and west by Oklahoma. Area, 53,187 sq. miles (1,109 sq. miles being inland water). Census population on 1 April 1980 was 2,286,435, an increase of 18·9% from that of 1970. Estimate (1981) 2,296,000. Births, 1980, were 35,852 (15·4 per 1,000 population); deaths, 18,525 (9·6); infant deaths, 419 (11·7 per 1,000 live births); marriages, 27,673 (11·9); divorces 16,492 (7·1).

Population in 5 census years was:

	White	Negro	Indian	Asiatic	Total	Per sq. mile
1910	1,131,026	442,891	460	72	1,574,449	30·0
1930	1,375,315	478,463	408	296	1,854,482	35·2
1960	1,395,703	388,787	580	1,202	1,786,272	34·0
			All others			
1970	1,565,915	352,445	4,935		1,923,295	37·0
1980	1,890,002	373,768	22,335		2,286,435	43·9

Of the total population in 1980, 48·3% were male, 51·5% were urban, 65·1% were 21 years of age or older.

Little Rock (capital) had a population of 158,461 in 1980; Fort Smith, 71,626; North Little Rock, 64,288; Pine Bluff, 56,636; Fayetteville, 36,608; Hot Springs, 35,781; Jonesboro, 31,530; West Memphis, 28,138. The population of the largest standard metropolitan statistical areas: Little Rock–North Little Rock, 393,774; Fayetteville–Springdale, 178,609; Fort Smith (Arkansas portion), 132,064; Pine Bluff, 90,718.

CLIMATE. Little Rock. Jan. 42°F (5·6°C), July 81°F (27·2°C). Annual rainfall 49" (1,222 mm). *See* Gulf Coast, p. 1373.

GOVERNMENT. The General Assembly consists of a Senate of 35 members elected for 4 years, partially renewed every 2 years, and a House of Representatives of 100 members elected for 2 years. The sessions are biennial and usually limited to 60 days. The Governor and Lieut.-Governor are elected for 2 years. The state is represented in Congress by 2 senators and 4 representatives.

In the 1980 presidential election Reagan polled 402,945 votes, Carter 379,919.

The state is divided into 75 counties; the capital is Little Rock.

Governor: Bill Clinton (D.), 1983–84 ($35,000).
Lieut.-Governor: Winston Bryant (D.) ($14,000).
Secretary of State: Paul Riviere (D.) ($22,500).

FINANCE

Budget. The state's general revenue for the fiscal year 1981 was $3,150·7m., of which taxation furnished $1,551·2m. and federal aid, $912·9m. General expenditure was $2,980m., of which education took $1,193·1m.; highways, $414·6m., and public welfare, $362·6m.

Net long-term debt for the financial year 1981 was $2,296·7m.

Per capita income (1981) was $8,044.

Banking. In 1982 total bank deposits were $10,535·4m.

ENERGY AND NATURAL RESOURCES

Minerals. In 1979 crude petroleum amounted to 18·9m. bbls; natural gas, 132·4m. cu. ft; bromine brine, 234·7m. bbls; crushed stone, 14m. tons; sand and gravel 13·1m. tons. Arkansas produces about 90% of the country's supply of bauxite for aluminium; production 1978, 1·9m. tons dried bauxite equivalent. The state has a large coal area; 224,655 short tons were mined in 1979. Total mineral output in 1979 was valued at $667·9m.

Agriculture. In 1978 (Federal Census Report), 51,773 farms had a total area of 15·1m. acres; average farm was of 292 acres; 7·6m. acres were harvested cropland; 1,685,520 acres were irrigated.

The largest sources of income in 1981 were chickens including broilers ($725·6m.); soybeans ($580·5m.); cattle and calves ($338·7m.); rice ($686·3m.); wheat ($230·7m.) and cotton ($218·6m.). Cash farm income (1981) was $3,436·1m.; from crops, $1,825·1m., and from livestock, $1,611·5m.

Livestock on 1 Jan. 1983 included 1·9m. all cattle, 84,000 milch cows and 585,000 swine.

INDUSTRY. In Aug. 1983 total employment averaged 925,000 (75,800 agricultural, 205,200 manufacturing, 159,900 wholesale and retail trade, 126,400 government). The Arkansas Department of Labor estimated that 166,100 factory production workers earned an average $284.92 per week (40·3 hours). The most important manufacturing group was food and kindred products employing 36,900, followed by electric and electronic equipment (24,300) and lumber and wood products (19,900). Construction employed 33,000.

COMMUNICATIONS

Roads. Total road mileage, 81,837 miles. State-maintained highways (1 Jan. 1983) total 16,104 miles; local county highways, 49,326 miles; city streets, 9,577 miles; federal roads, 1,641 miles; roads not publicly maintained, 5,189 miles. In 1981 there were 1,487,021 registered motor vehicles.

Railways. In 1979 there were in the state 5,308·4 miles of commercial railway.

Aviation. Five air carrier and 9 commuter airlines serve the state; there were, in 1983, 140 airports (86 public-use and 54 private).

Waterways. There are about 1,000 miles of navigable streams including the Kerr-McClellan Channel which bisects the state and gives access to the sea *via* the Mississippi River.

RELIGION, EDUCATION AND WELFARE

Religion. The most numerous religious bodies in the state are Baptist (601,200 members estimated in 1979), Methodist (219,398), Roman Catholic (53,555) and Assembly of God (26,910). Total known membership, all denominations, 976,867.

Education. In the school year 1981–82 elementary and secondary schools had 428,008 enrolled pupils and 22,419 classroom teachers. Average salaries of teachers in elementary and secondary schools was $14,113. Expenditure on elementary and secondary education was $868·8m.

An educational TV network began operating in 1966 with a full 12-hour-day telecasting.

Higher education is provided at 31 institutions: 9 state universities, 1 medical college, 12 private or church colleges, 10 community or junior colleges. Total enrolment in institutions of higher education, 1982–83, was 73,200.

There were (1982–83) 23 vocational-technical schools with 30,420 students, including extension class students. Total expenditure, 1982–83, $55·2m.

Social Welfare. In Oct. 1983, 409,000 persons were drawing old-age assistance at an average amount of $317.85 per month; 22,085 families (43,618 children), $130.43 per family; 44,000 persons were receiving disability benefits at an average of $409.09 per month.

There were 100 licensed hospitals (12,247 beds) in 1983, and 230 licensed nursing homes (22,549 beds).

State prisons in Oct. 1983 had 4,073 inmates (178 per 100,000 population).

Books of Reference

Directory of Arkansas Mineral Producers and Production. Arkansas Geological Commission, Little Rock
Current Employment Developments. Arkansas Employment Security Division, Little Rock
Arkansas State and County Economic Data. Industrial Research and Extension Center, Little Rock
State Government Finances. U.S. Dept. of Commerce, Bureau of the Census.
Agricultural Statistics for Arkansas. U.S. Dept. of Agriculture, Crop Reporting Service, Little Rock, 1982
Ferguson and Atkinson, *Historic Arkansas.* Little Rock, 1966

CALIFORNIA

HISTORY. California, first settled in July 1769, was from its discovery down to 1846 politically associated with Mexico. On 7 July 1846 the American flag was hoisted at Monterey, and a proclamation was issued declaring California to be a portion of the US, and on 2 Feb. 1848, by the treaty of Guadalupe–Hidalgo, the territory was formally ceded by Mexico to the US, and was admitted to the Union 9 Sept. 1850 as the thirty-first state, with boundaries as at present.

AREA AND POPULATION. Area, 158,706 sq. miles (2,407 sq. miles being inland water). In 1983 the federal government owned 45m. acres (45·03% of the land area); in 1975, 546,000 acres were under jurisdiction of the Bureau of Indian Affairs, of which 472,000 acres were tribal. Public lands, vacant in 1975, totalled 15,607,125 acres, practically all either mountains or deserts.

Census population, 1 April 1980, 23,667,902, an increase of 18·5% over 1970, making California the most populous state of the USA (New York: 17,557,288). Estimate (1981) 24,196,000. Births in 1981, 420,418 (17·4 per 1,000 population); deaths, 184,732 (7·6); infant deaths, 4,270 (10·2 per 1,000 live births); marriages, 217,348 (9); divorces, dissolutions and nullities, 140,473 (5·8).

Population in 5 census years was:

	White	Negro	Japanese	Chinese	Total (incl. all others)	Per sq. mile
1910	2,259,672	21,645	41,356	36,248	2,377,549	15·0
1930	5,408,260	81,048	97,456	37,361	5,677,251	35·8
1960	14,455,230	883,861	157,317	95,600	15,717,204	99·0
1970	17,761,032	1,400,143	213,280	170,131	19,953,134	125·7

	White	Negro	All other	Total (incl. all others)	Per sq. mile
1980	18,030,893	1,819,281	3,817,728	23,667,902	149·1

Of the 1980 population 49·3% were male, 91·3% were urban and 67·2% were 21 years old or older.

The largest cities with 1980 census population are:

Los Angeles	2,966,850	Anaheim	219,494	Fremont	131,945
San Diego	875,538	Fresno	217,289	Torrance	129,881
San Francisco	678,974	Santa Ana	204,023	Garden Grove	123,307
San José	629,546	Riverside	170,591	San Bernardino	118,794
Long Beach	361,334	Huntington Beach	170,505	Pasadena	118,550
Oakland	339,337	Stockton	149,779	Oxnard	108,195
Sacramento	275,741	Glendale	139,060		

Urbanized areas (1980 census): Los Angeles–Long Beach, 9,477,926; San Francisco–Oakland, 3,191,913; San Diego, 1,704,352; San José, 1,243,900;

Sacramento, 796,266; San Bernardino–Riverside, 703,316; Oxnard–Ventura–Thousand Oaks, 378,420; Fresno, 331,551.

CLIMATE. Los Angeles. Jan. 55°F (12·8°C), July 70°F (21·1°C). Annual rainfall 15″ (381 mm). Sacramento. Jan. 45°F (7·2°C), July 74°F (23·3°C). Annual rainfall 19″ (472 mm). San Diego. Jan. 55°F (12·8°C), July 69°F (20·6°C). Annual rainfall 10″ (259 mm). San Francisco. Jan. 50°F (10°C), July 59°F (15°C). Annual rainfall 22″ (561 mm). Death Valley. Jan. 52°F (11°C), July 100°F (38°C). Annual rainfall 1·6″ (40 mm). See Pacific Coast, p. 1372.

CONSTITUTION AND GOVERNMENT. The present constitution became effective from 4 July 1879; it has had numerous amendments since 1962. The Senate is composed of 40 members elected for 4 years—half being elected each 2 years—and the Assembly, of 80 members, elected for 2 years. Two-year regular sessions convene in Dec. of each even-numbered year. The Governor and Lieut.-Governor are elected for 4 years.

California is represented in Congress by 2 senators and 45 representatives.

In the 1980 presidential election Reagan polled 4,524,835 votes, Carter 3,083,652 and Anderson 739,832.

The capital is Sacramento. The state is divided into 58 counties.

Governor: George Deukmejian (R.), 1983–86 ($49,100).
Lieut.-Governor: Leo McCarthy (D.), 1983–86 ($42,500).
Secretary of State: March Fong Eu (D.) ($42,500).

BUDGET. For the year ending 30 June 1983 total revenues were $20,479m.; total expenditures were $21,630m. ($10,829m. for education, $7,270m. for health and welfare).

The long-term state debt (general obligation bonds outstanding) was $6,550m. on 30 June 1983.

Per capita personal income (1982) was $12,567.

ENERGY AND NATURAL RESOURCES

Minerals. California is one of the three most important petroleum-producing states of the US (Texas and Louisiana being the other two); crude oil output was estimated at 373m. bbls in 1982. Output of natural gas was 378,000m. cu. ft; of natural gas liquids, (1982) 240m. bbls. Gold output was 6·3m. troy oz. (1981); asbestos, boron minerals, diatomite, tungsten, sand and gravel, salt, magnesium compounds, lead, zinc, copper and iron ore are also produced. The estimated value of all the minerals produced (other than petroleum) was $1,689m. in 1982.

Agriculture. Extending 700 miles from north to south, and intersected by several ranges of mountains, California has almost every variety of climate, from the very wet to the very dry, and from the temperate to the semi-tropical. Of the total surface area (100,313,600 acres), estimates (1971) show 5·9m. acres to be seriously eroded, 35·4m. acres moderately affected and 58·8m. with little or no erosion.

In 1981 there were 80,000 farms, comprising 34m. acres; average farm, 423 acres. Cotton, fruit, poultry and vegetables are important. Cash receipts, 1982, from crops, $8,999m.; from livestock and poultry, $4,381m. Dairy produce, cattle, grapes, cotton, hay, nursery products (in that order) are the main sources of farm income.

Production of cotton lint, 1982, was 3m. bales (480 lb.); other field crops included sugar-beet (4·2m. short tons). Cereal crops include maize, 1·3m. short tons; wheat, 2·4m. short tons, and rice, 1·8m. short tons. Principal crops include wine, table and raisin grapes (5·95m. short tons); peaches (758,500 short tons); pears (320,500 short tons); apricots (110,000 short tons); prunes (125,000 short tons); plums, nectarines, avocados, olives and cherries. Citrus fruit crops were: Oranges, 1·6m. short tons; lemons, 703,000 short tons; grapefruit, 216,000 short tons.

On 1 Jan. 1983 the farm animals were: 940,000 milch cows, 4·9m. all cattle, 920,000 sheep and 160,000 swine.

Forestry. Total forest area in 1975 was 36,549,000 acres, of which 16,299,000 acres was commercial forest. California ranks third to Oregon and Washington in volume of standing timber (278,000m. bd ft); total annual cut is about 2,319m. bd ft (1982). National forest service land in 1982 was 19·6m. acres.

Fishery. California ranks first as a fishing state (by value of fish caught). The catch in 1982 was 824m. lb.; leading species were anchovy, tuna and mackerel.

INDUSTRY. In 1982, manufacturing employed about 2m. The fastest-growing industries were instruments and related products, non-electrical machinery, electric and electronic equipment, transport equipment and fabricated metal products. The aerospace industry is important, as is also food-processing.

COMMUNICATIONS

Roads. In 1982 California had 52,644 miles of roads inside cities and 121,244 miles outside. In 1980 there were about 13·3m. registered cars and over 3·5m. commercial vehicles, leading all states in all items by a wide margin.

Railways. Total mileage of railways, 1 Jan. 1977, was 7,600 miles. There are 2 systems: Amtrack and Southern Pacific Railroad commuter trains. Amtrack carries about 900,000 passengers per year, Southern Pacific about 5m.

Aviation. In 1980 there were 311 public airports and 950 private airstrips.

Shipping. The chief ports are San Francisco and Los Angeles.

JUSTICE, RELIGION, EDUCATION AND WELFARE

Justice. State prisons, 1 Jan. 1982, had 27,159 male and 1,288 female inmates. From 1893 to 1942, 307 inmates were executed by hanging. From 1938 to 1976, 194 inmates were executed by lethal gas. No further death sentences were passed until 1980.

Religion. The Roman Catholic Church, with 2,483,411 adherents in 1954, is much stronger than any other single church; next are the Jewish congregations with an estimated 431,471 members, Methodists, Presbyterians and Baptists. There were 210,000 Episcopalians in 1973.

Education. Full-time attendance at school is compulsory for children from 6 to 16 years of age for a minimum of 175 days per annum, and part-time attendance is required from 16 to 18 years. In autumn 1982 there were 4m. pupils enrolled in elementary and secondary schools. Estimated expenditure on public schools, 1981–82, was $11,675m.

Community Colleges had 1,296,296 students in autumn 1982.

California has two publicly supported higher education systems: the University of California (1868) and the California State University and Colleges. In autumn 1982, the University of California with campuses for resident instruction and research at Berkeley, Los Angeles, San Francisco and 6 other centres, had 129,667 full-time students. California State University and Colleges with campuses at Sacramento, Long Beach, Los Angeles, San Francisco and 15 other cities had 195,571 full-time students. In addition to the 28 publicly supported institutions for higher education there are 117 private colleges and universities which had a total estimated enrolment of 187,962 in the autumn of 1982.

Health. In 1979 there were 608 general hospitals; capacity, 114,400 beds. On 30 June 1980 state hospitals for the mentally disabled had 4,836 patients and state hospitals for the developmentally disabled had 8,522 patients.

Social Security. On 1 Jan. 1974 the federal government (Social Security Administration) assumed responsibility for the Supplemental Security Income/State Supplemental Program which replaced the State Old-Age Security. The SSI/SSP provides financial assistance for needy aged (65 years or older), blind or disabled persons. An individual recipient may own assets up to $1,500; a couple up to $2,250, subject to specific exclusions. There are federal, state and county programmes assisting the aged, the blind, the disabled and needy children. In Dec. 1980, 512,000 families with one or more children were receiving an average of $399 per month per family.

Books of Reference

California Statistical Abstract. 24th ed. Dept. of Finance, Sacramento, 1983
Economic Report of the Governor. Governor's Office, Sacramento, Annual
Arnold, R. K. (ed.), *The California Economy 1947–1980.* Menlo Park, 1961
Crouch, W. E., and others, *California Government and Politics.* 2nd ed. New York, 1960

State Library: The California State Library, Library-Courts Bldg, Sacramento 95814.

COLORADO

HISTORY. Colorado was first settled in 1858, made a Territory in 1861 and admitted into the Union on 1 Aug. 1876.

AREA AND POPULATION. Colorado is bounded north by Wyoming, north-east by Nebraska, east by Kansas, south-east by Oklahoma, south by New Mexico and west by Utah. Area, 104,090 sq. miles (496 sq. miles being inland water). Federal lands, 1974, 23,974,000 acres (36% of the land area).

Census population, 1 April 1980, was 2,889,964, an increase of 680,368 or 30·8% since 1970. Estimated (1982), 3,045,000. Births, 1981, were 52,104 (17·6 per 1,000 population); deaths, 19,360 (6·5); infant deaths, 517 (9·9 per 1,000 live births); marriages, 37,210 (12·5); dissolutions, 19,515 (6·6).

Population in 5 census years was:

	White	Negro	Indian	Asiatic	Total	Per sq. mile
1910	783,415	11,453	1,482	2,674	799,024	7·7
1930	1,018,793	11,828	1,395	3,775	1,035,791	10·0
1950	1,296,653	20,177	1,567	5,870	1,325,089	12·7
1970	2,112,352	66,411	8,836	10,388	2,207,259	21·3
			All others			
1980	2,570,615	101,702	216,517		2,888,834 [1]	27·7

[1] Preliminary.

Of the total population in 1980, 49·6% were male, 80·6% were urban; 68% were aged 20 years or older. Large cities with 1980 census population (and 1982 estimate): Denver, 492,365 (500,600); Colorado Springs, 215,150 (230,553); Aurora, 158,588 (178,665); Lakewood, 112,860 (117,436); Pueblo, 101,686 (99,619); Arvada, 84,576 (91,262); Boulder, 76,685 (80,651); Fort Collins, 65,092 (68,307); Wheat Ridge, 30,293 (54,995); Greeley, 53,006 (54,063); Westminster, 50,211.

CLIMATE. Denver. Jan. 31°F (–0·6°C), July 73°F (22·8°C). Annual rainfall 14″ (358 mm). Pueblo. Jan. 30°F (–1·1°C), July 83°F (28·3°C). Annual rainfall 12″ (312 mm). *See* Mountain States, p. 1372.

CONSTITUTION AND GOVERNMENT. The constitution adopted in 1876 is still in effect with (1982) 78 amendments. The General Assembly consists of a Senate of 35 members elected for 4 years, one-half retiring every 2 years, and of a House of Representatives of 65 members elected for 2 years. Sessions are annual, beginning 1951. The Governor, Lieut.-Governor, Attorney-General and Secretary of State are elected for 4 years. Qualified as electors are all citizens, male and female (except convicted, incarcerated criminals), 18 years of age, who have resided in the state and the precinct for 32 days immediately preceding the election. The state is divided into 63 counties. The state sends to Congress 2 senators and 6 representatives.

In the 1980 presidential election Reagan polled 652,264 votes, Carter 368,009 and Anderson 130,633.
The capital is Denver.

Governor: Richard D. Lamm (D.), 1983–86 ($60,000).
Lieut.-Governor: Nancy Dick (D.), 1983–86 ($32,500).
Secretary of State: Natalie Meyer (R.), 1983–86 ($32,500).

BUDGET. The state's total budget, 1982–83, is $2,816m., of which taxation and other revenue furnish $2,139m. and federal grants $677m. Education takes $1,213m.; health, welfare and rehabilitation, $660m., and highways, $399m. Total state and local taxes *per capita* (1982–83) were $1,011.
The state has no general debt. The net long-term debt (in revenue bond) on 30 June 1982 was $141m.
Per capita personal income (1982) was $11,664.

ENERGY AND NATURAL RESOURCES

Minerals. Colorado has a variety of mineral resources. Among the most important are crude oil, metals and coal. Mineral production in 1982 (estimate) $2,200m. in value. An estimated 28,600 people were employed in extracting petroleum and natural gas in 1983; 6,100 in metals and 4,500 in coal and non-metals.

Agriculture. Farms number about 26,000, with a total area of 35·8m. acres in 1982 (53·3% of the land area); 6,625,600 acres (1982) were harvested crop land; average farm, 1,345 acres (1978). Cash income, 1982, from crops $1,156·6m.; from livestock, $2,012m. In 1978 there were 3,518,166 acres under irrigation.
Production of principal crops in 1982: Maize for grain, 110·4m. bu. (from 830,000 acres); wheat, 87·5m. bu. (3·0m.); hay, 3·7m. tons (1·4m.); dry beans, 2·1m. cwt (170,000); potatoes, 14·2m. cwt (51,400); sugar-beet, 920,000 tons (46,000); oats, barley and sorghums are grown, as well as fruit.
On 1 Jan. 1981 the number of farm animals was: 75,000 milch cows, 3m. all cattle, 750,000 sheep, 290,000 swine. The wool clip in 1981 yielded 8·0m. lb. of wool.

INDUSTRY. In 1983 1,456,000 were employed in non-agricultural sectors, of which 328,000 were in trade; 288,200 in services; 238,800 in government; 185,100 in manufacturing; 80,000 in construction; 82,700 in transport and public utilities; 39,700 in mining; 84,400 in finance, insurance and property. In manufacturing the biggest employers were non-electrical machinery, foods and kindred products, and printing. Value added by manufacturing was $7,580m. (1983 estimate).

TOURISM. In 1983 about 12m. people spent holidays in Colorado, of whom about 2·4% were Colorado residents. Overall expenditure, $1,577m.; $36·3m. of this was from ski-ing holidays.

COMMUNICATIONS

Roads. The state highway system (1983) included 9,232 miles of highway. County roads totalled 56,898, and city streets, 9,352 miles. Total road mileage, 80,483, of which 5,001 miles are unmaintained county and city roads.

Railways. In 1982 there were in the state 3,220 miles of main-track and branch railway.

Aviation. There were (1983) 244 airports in the state. Of these, 69 are publicly owned and open to the public; 26 are privately owned and open to the public; 149 are private and not open to the public.

JUSTICE, RELIGION, EDUCATION AND WELFARE

Justice. At 30 Sept. 1983 there were 3,294 people committed to the State Department of Corrections, inmates of the State Penitentiary, the State Reformatory and other institutions. In 1967 there was 1 execution; since 1930 executions (by lethal gas) numbered 47, including 41 whites, 5 Negroes and 1 other; all were for murder.

Colorado has a Civil Rights Act (1935) forbidding places of public accommodation to discriminate against any persons on the grounds of race, religion, sex, colour or nationality. No religious test may be applied to teachers or students in the public schools, 'nor shall any distinction or classification of pupils be made on account of race or colour'. In 1957 the General Assembly prohibited discrimination in employment of persons in private industry and in 1959 adopted the Fair Housing Act to discourage discrimination in housing. A 1957 Act permits marriages between white persons and Negroes or mulattoes.

Religion. In 1983 the Roman Catholic Church had 439,574 members; the ten main Protestant denominations had 258,970 members; the Jewish community had 42,000 members. Buddhism is among other religions represented.

Education. In autumn 1981 the public elementary and secondary schools had 544,174 pupils and 35,490 teachers and administrators; total instructional salaries averaged $19,577. Enrolments in universities and larger colleges, autumn 1982, were: US Air Force Academy (Colorado Springs), 4,477 students; University of Colorado (Boulder), 22,177; University of Colorado (Denver), 10,720; University of Colorado (Colorado Springs), 5,288; University of Colorado (Medical Center), 1,385; Colorado State University (Fort Collins), 18,909; University of Denver (Denver), 8,099; Colorado School of Mines (Golden), 2,948; University of Northern Colorado (Greeley), 9,671; University of Southern Colorado (Pueblo), 4,950; Western State College (Gunnison), 2,800; Adams State College (Alamosa), 2,007; Metropolitan State College (Denver), 16,596; Colorado College (Colorado Springs), 1,961; Fort Lewis College (Durango), 3,506; Mesa College (Grand Junction), 3,377.

Health. Approved hospitals, 1980, numbered 93 with 12,691 beds. In 1981, there were 23 public mental health centres and clinics with 79,000 patients and 2 public mental hospitals with 7,900.

Social Security. A constitutional amendment, adopted 1956, provides for minimum old age pensions of $100 per month, which may be raised on a cost-of-living basis ($352 for 1982); for a $5m. stabilization fund and for a $10m. medical and health fund for pensioners. Old-age assistance is available to citizens 60 years of age with assets not exceeding $1,000 (excluding home ownership). In 1981–82 an average of 24,200 persons were drawing an average of $105.06 per month.

Books of Reference

Directory of Colorado Manufacturers, 1982. Business Research Division, School of Business, Univ. of Colorado, Boulder, 1982
Economic Outlook Forum, 1982. Colorado Division of Commerce and Development, and the College of Business, Univ. of Colorado, Denver, 1981

State Library: Colorado State Library, State Capitol, Denver, 80203.

CONNECTICUT

HISTORY. Connecticut was first settled in 1634 and has been an organized commonwealth since 1637. In 1629 a written constitution was adopted which, it is claimed, was the first in the history of the world formed under the concept of a social compact. This constitution was confirmed by a charter from Charles II in 1662, and replaced in 1818 by a state constitution, framed that year by a constitutional convention.

AREA AND POPULATION. Connecticut is bounded north by Massachusetts, east by Rhode Island, south by the Atlantic and west by New York. Area, 5,018 sq. miles (147 sq. miles being inland water).

Census population, 1 April 1980, 3,107,576, an increase of 2·5% since 1970. Estimate (1981) 3,134,000. Births (1980) were 34,069 (11 per 1,000 population); deaths, 26,597 (8·5); infant deaths, 343 (10 per 1,000 live births); marriages, 25,761 (8·3); divorces, 11,448.

Population in 5 census years was:

	White	Negro	Indian	Asiatic	Total	Per sq. mile
1910	1,098,897	15,174	152	533	1,114,756	231·3
1930	1,576,700	29,354	162	687	1,606,903	328·0
1960	2,423,816	107,449	923	3,046	2,535,234	517·5
			All others			
1970	2,835,458	181,177	15,074		3,031,709	629·0
1980	2,799,420	217,433	4,533	18,970	3,107,576	634·3

Of the total population in 1980, 1,498,005 persons were male, 2,449,774 persons were urban. Those 19 years old or older numbered 2,228,805.

The chief cities and towns, with census population 1 April 1980, are:

Bridgeport	142,546	New Britain	73,840
Hartford	136,392	Danbury	69,470
New Haven	126,109	Bristol	57,370
Waterbury	103,266	Meriden	57,118
Stamford	102,453	West Haven	53,184
Norwalk	77,767	Milford	50,898

Larger urbanized areas, 1980 census: Hartford, 726,114; Bridgeport, 395,455; New Haven, 417,592; Waterbury, 228,178; Stamford, 198,854.

CLIMATE. New Haven: Jan. 28°F (–2·2°C), July 72°F (22·2°C). Annual rainfall 46″ (1,151 mm). *See* New England, p. 1373.

CONSTITUTION AND GOVERNMENT. The 1818 Constitution was revised in June 1953 effective 1 Jan. 1955. On 30 Dec. 1965 a new constitution went into effect, having been framed by a constitutional convention in the summer of 1965 and approved by the voters in Dec. 1965.

The 1965 Constitution provides for 30 to 50 members of the Senate (instead of 24 to 36) and for 125 to 225 members of the House of Representatives, to be elected from assembly districts, rather than 2 or 1 from each town, as in the former constitution. The convention has added a new provision for a 3-day session following each regular or special session, solely to reconsider bills vetoed by the Governor.

The General Assembly consists of a Senate of 36 members and a House of Representatives of 151 members. Members of each House are elected for the term of 2 years (annual salary $9,500 first year, $7,500 second year; expenses $2,000 and mileage allowance). Legislative sessions are annual. The Governor and Lieut.-Governor are elected for 4 years. All citizens (with necessary exceptions and the usual residential requirements) have the right of suffrage.

Connecticut is one of the original 13 states of the Union. The state is represented in Congress by 2 senators and 6 representatives.

In the 1980 presidential election Reagan polled 677,210 votes, Carter 541,732. The state capital is Hartford.

Governor: William A. O'Neill (D.), 1983–86 ($42,000).
Lieut.-Governor: Joseph J. Fauliso (D.), ($25,000).
Secretary of State: Julia Tashjian (D.) ($25,000).

BUDGET. For the year ending 30 June 1980 (state government figures) general revenues were $2,394,071,891 (taxation, $1,712m., and federal aid, $344·8m.); general expenditures were $2,393,636,000 (education, $636·6m., highways, $157·5m., and public welfare, $598·8m.).

The total net long-term debt on 31 Aug. 1980 was $1,944m.

Per capita income, 1980 federal estimate, was $11,445.

NATURAL RESOURCES

Minerals. The state has some mineral resources: sheet mica, sand, gravel, clays and stone; total production in 1980 was valued at $62·8m.

Agriculture. In 1978 the state had 4,560 farms with a total area of 500,369 acres; average farm was of 110 acres, valued at $2,227 per acre. Total cash income, 1980, was $254·8m., including $97·5m. from crops and $157·3m. from livestock and products (mainly from dairy products and poultry). Principal crops are hay, silage, forest, greenhouse and nursery products, tobacco, potatoes, sweet corn, tomatoes, apples, peaches, pears, vegetables and small fruit.

Livestock (1 Jan. 1980): 108,000 all cattle (value $70·7m.), 5,200 sheep ($387,000), 11,000 swine ($699,000) and 5·8m. poultry ($12m.).

Forestry. The state had (1980) 137,782 acres of state forest land, which is about 4·2% of the total land area.

INDUSTRY. Manufacturing establishments employed 417,560 production workers in Aug. 1980 who earned average weekly wages of $294.47; value added by manufacture (1980), $15,973m. Total non-agricultural employment in Aug. 1980 was 1,386,350. The main industries are transport equipment, non-electrical machinery and fabricated metals.

COMMUNICATIONS

Roads. The state (1 Jan. 1981) maintains 4,035 miles of highways, all surfaced. Motor vehicles registered in 1979 numbered 2,229,000 (licences issued 1980, 1,688,373).

Railways. In 1981 there were 950 miles of railway track.

Aviation. In 1981 there were 61 airports (27 commercial including 5 state-owned, and 34 heliports).

JUSTICE, RELIGION, EDUCATION AND WELFARE

Justice. In 1981 there were no executions; since 1930 there have been 22 executions (19 by electrocution, 3 by hanging), including 19 whites and 3 Negroes, all for murder. The 6 community correctional centres, 1974, had 1,508 inmates; 5 correctional institutions had 1,136 inmates.

The Civil Rights Act makes it a punishable offence to discriminate against any person or persons 'on account of alienage, colour or race' and to hold up to ridicule any persons 'on account of creed, religion, colour, denomination, nationality or race'. Places of public resort are forbidden to discriminate. Insurance companies are forbidden to charge higher premiums to persons 'wholly or partially of African descent'. Schools must be open to all 'without discrimination on account of race or colour'.

Religion. The leading religious denominations (1980) in the state are the Roman Catholic (1·4m. members), United Churches of Christ, Protestant Episcopal, Jewish, Greek Orthodox, Methodist, Baptist, Presbyterian.

Education. Elementary instruction is free for all children between the ages of 4 and 16 years, and compulsory for all children between the ages of 7 and 16 years. In 1979 there were 715 public elementary schools, 170 middle schools and 142 high schools; enrolment was 304,637 (grades 1–6) and 289,120 (grades 7–12). The 17 state vocational technical schools had 527,152 students. Expenditure of the state Board of Education, 1978–79, was $267,154,300 grants in aid; local expenditure, $1,038,344,461. Average salary of teachers in public schools, 1978–79, $14,609.

Connecticut has 47 colleges, of which one state university, 4 state colleges, 5 state technical colleges and 12 regional community colleges are state funded. The University of Connecticut at Storrs, founded 1881, had 1,253 faculty and 22,407 students in 1980–81. Yale University, New Haven, founded in 1701, had 2,088 faculty and 9,626 students. Wesleyan University, Middletown, founded 1831, had

297 faculty and 2,775 students. Trinity College, Hartford, founded 1823, had 145 faculty and 2,007 students. Connecticut College, New London, founded 1915, had 203 faculty and 1,974 students. The University of Hartford, founded 1877, had 305 faculty and 9,836 students. The regional community colleges (2-year course) had 514 faculty and 34,082 students.

Health. Hospitals listed by the American Hospital Association, 1981, numbered 65, with 17,935 beds. The state operated one general hospital, one veterans' hospital, 8 hospitals for the mentally ill (2,450 patients in Jan. 1981), 2 training schools for the mentally retarded (and 12 regional centres), one chronic disease hospital (56 in-patients in Jan. 1981) and a state-aided institution for the blind.

Social Security. Disbursements during the year ending 30 June 1981 amounted to $10,751,924 for old-age assistance, and medical aid to the aged, $5,413,444. The average monthly number of cases, 1980–81, was 4,782. In other areas of welfare, there was an average of 47,096 cases for aid to families with dependent children; 889 cases for such aid where the parent is unemployed; 84 cases for aid to the blind; 6,357 for aid to the disabled; 1,411 for Connecticut Assistance and Medical Aid to the disabled.

Books of Reference

The Register and Manual of Connecticut. Secretary of State. Hartford. Annual
The Structure of Connecticut's State Government. Connecticut Public Expenditure Council. Hartford, 1973
Adams, V. Q., *Connecticut: The Story of Your State Government.* Chester, 1973
Smith, Allen R., *Connecticut, a Thematic Atlas.* Newington, 1974

State Library: Connecticut State Library, Capitol Avenue, Hartford, 06015. *State Librarian:* Clarence R. Walters.

DELAWARE

HISTORY. Delaware, permanently settled in 1638, is one of the original 13 states of the Union, and the first one to ratify the Federal Constitution.

AREA AND POPULATION. Delaware is bounded north by Pennsylvania, north-east by New Jersey, east by Delaware Bay, south and west by Maryland. Area 2,044 sq. miles (112 sq. miles being inland water). Census population, 1 April 1980 was 594,338, an increase of 46,234 or 8·4% since 1970. Estimate (1981), 598,000. Births in 1981, 9,372; deaths, 5,169; infant deaths, 114; marriages, 4,561; divorces, 2,921.

Population in 5 census years was:

	White	Negro	Indian	Asiatic	Total	Per sq. mile
1910	171,102	31,181	5	34	202,322	103·0
1930	205,718	32,602	5	55	238,380	120·5
1960	384,327	60,688	597	410	446,292	224·0

	White	Negro	All others	Total	Per sq. mile
1970	466,459	78,276	3,369	548,104	276·5
1980	488,002	96,157	10,179	594,338	290·8

Of the total population in 1980, 48·4% were male, 70·7% were urban and 65·7% were 21 years old or older.

The 1980 census figures show Wilmington with population of 70,195; Newark, 25,241; Dover, 23,512; Elsmere Town, 6,493; Milford City, 5,356; Seaford City, 5,256.

CLIMATE. Wilmington. Jan. 32°F (0°C), July 75°F (23·9°C). Annual rainfall 43″ (1,076 mm). *See* Atlantic Coast, p. 1373.

CONSTITUTION AND GOVERNMENT. The present constitution (the fourth) dates from 1897, and has had 51 amendments; it was not ratified by the electorate but promulgated by the Constitutional Convention. The General Assembly consists of a Senate of 21 members elected for 4 years and a House of Representatives of 41 members elected for 2 years. The Governor and Lieut.-Governor are elected for 4 years.

With necessary exceptions, all adult citizens, registered as voters, who have resided in the state 1 year, and complied with local residential requirements, have the right to vote; those who have attained the age of 18 since 1900 must be able to read English and to write their names. Citizens resident for 3 months or over may vote for President and Vice-President only.

Delaware is represented in Congress by 2 senators and 1 representative, elected by the voters of the whole state.

In the 1980 presidential election Reagan polled 111,252 votes, Carter 105,754.

The state capital is Dover. Delaware is divided into 3 counties.

Governor: Pierre S. du Pont (R.), 1981–85 ($35,000).
Lieut.-Governor: Michael N. Castle (R.) ($16,600).
Secretary of State: Glenn C. Kenton (R.) ($44,800) (appointed by the Governor).

FINANCE. For the year ending 30 June 1982 general receipts were $1,624·6m., of which federal grants were $182·2m. General expenditure was $1,574·7m.

On 30 June 1982 the total debt was $539·2m.

Per capita income (1981) was $11,279.

ENERGY AND NATURAL RESOURCES

Minerals. The mineral resources of Delaware are not extensive, consisting chiefly of clay products, stone, sand and gravel and magnesium compounds. Value of mineral production in 1980 was $2m.

Agriculture. Delaware is mainly an industrial state, but about 1m. acres is in farms, which in 1981 numbered 4,000; average farm was of 186 acres and all farms were valued (land and buildings) at $1,255m.

Cash income, 1980, from crops and livestock, $333m., of which $237m. was from livestock and products. The chief crops are corn and soybeans.

INDUSTRY. In 1980 manufacturing establishments employed 71,000 people; value added by manufacture, $2,466m., mainly from chemicals, transport equipment and food.

COMMUNICATIONS

Roads. The state in 1981 maintained 4,655 miles of roads and streets and 1,371 miles of federally-aided highways. There were also 594 miles of municipal maintained streets. Vehicles registered in 1981, 443,511.

Railways. In 1981 the state had 290 miles of railway.

Aviation. Delaware had 17 airports, of which 12 were for general use in 1981.

JUSTICE, RELIGION, EDUCATION AND WELFARE

Justice. State prisons, 1 July 1981–30 June 1982, had daily average of 1,434 inmates. The death penalty was illegal from 2 April 1958 to 18 Dec. 1961. Executions since 1930 (by hanging) have totalled 12 (none since 1946).

Religion. Membership, 1979–80: Methodists, 60,489; Roman Catholics, 103,060; Episcopalians, 18,696; Lutherans, 10,000.

Education. The state has free public schools and compulsory school attendance. In Sept. 1981 the elementary and secondary public schools had 95,072 enrolled pupils and 5,458 classroom teachers. Appropriation for public schools (financial year 1982) was about $231·5m. Average salary of classroom teachers (financial year 1981), $19,290. The state supports the University of Delaware at Newark

(1834) which had approximately 870 faculty members and 18,615 students in Sept. 1982, and Delaware State College, Dover (1892), with 144 faculty members and 2,151 students.

Health. In 1981 there were 15 hospitals (4,179 beds) listed by the American Hospital Association. During financial year 1982 patients in mental hospitals numbered 1,963.

Social Security. In 1974 the federal Supplemental Security Income (SSI) programme lessened state responsibility for the aged, blind and disabled. SSI payments in Delaware (1981), \$12·2m. Provisions are also made for the care of dependent children; in 1981 there were 29,000 recipients in 10,300 families (average monthly payment per family, \$227). The total state programme for the year ending 30 June 1980 was \$32m. for the care of dependent children.

Books of Reference

Information: Division of Historical and Cultural Affairs, Hall of Records, Dover.

State Manual, Containing Official List of Officers, Commissions and County Officers. Secretary of State, Dover. Annual
The Delaware Economy, 1939–58. Bureau of Economic & Business Research, Univ. of Delaware, 1961
Topical History of Delaware. Division of Historical and Cultural Affairs. Dover, 1977

DISTRICT OF COLUMBIA

HISTORY. The District of Columbia, organized in 1790, is the seat of the Government of the US, for which the land was ceded by the states of Maryland and Virginia to the US as a site for the national capital. It was established under Acts of Congress in 1790 and 1791. Congress first met in it in 1800 and federal authority over it became vested in 1801. In 1846 the land ceded by Virginia (about 33 sq. miles) was given back.

AREA AND POPULATION. The District forms an enclave on the Potomac River, where the river forms the south-west boundary of Maryland. The area of the District of Columbia is 68·68 sq. miles, 6 sq. miles being inland water.

Census population, 1 April 1980, was 638,333, a decrease of 16% from that of 1970. Estimate (1981) 631,000. Metropolitan statistical area of Washington, D.C.–Md–Va. (1980), 3m. Density of population in the District, 1980, 10,453 per sq. mile. Births, 1980, in the District were 9,257 (14·5 per 1,000 population); resident deaths, 6,982 (10·9); infant deaths, 228 (24·6 per 1,000 live births); marriages, 5,182 (8·1); divorces, 3,473 (5·4).

Population in 5 census years was:

	White	Negro	Indian	Chinese and Japanese	Total	Per sq. mile
1910	236,128	94,446	68	427	331,069	5,517·8
1930	353,981	132,068	40	780	486,869	7,981·5
1960	345,263	411,737	587	3,532	763,956	12,523·9
				All others		
1970	209,272	537,712		9,526	756,510	12,321·0
1980	171,768	448,906		17,659	638,333	10,184·0

CLIMATE. Washington. Jan. 34°F (1·1°C), July 77°F (25°C). Annual rainfall 43″ (1,064 mm). *See* Atlantic Coast, p. 1373.

GOVERNMENT. Local government, from 1 July 1878 until Aug. 1967, was that of a municipal corporation administered by a board of 3 commissioners, of whom 2 were appointed from civil life by the President, and confirmed by the Senate, for a term of 3 years each. The other commissioner was detailed by the President from the Engineer Corps of the Army. Reorganization Plan No. 3 of 1967 submitted by the President to Congress on 1 June 1967 abolished the Commission form of government and instituted a new Mayor Council form of government with officers appointed by the President with the advice and consent of the Senate. On 24 Dec. 1973 the appointed officers were replaced by an elected Mayor and councillors, with full legislative powers in local matters as from 1974. Congress retains the right to legislate, to veto or supersede the Council's acts. The 23rd amendment to the federal constitution (1961) conferred the right to vote in national elections; in the 1980 presidential election Carter polled 130,231 votes, Reagan, 23,313. On 23 Aug. 1978 the Senate approved a constitutional amendment giving the District full voting representation in Congress. In order to become part of the constitution the amendment must be ratified by 38 state legislatures within 7 years. It would give the District 2 senators and a number of representatives according to population.

BUDGET. The District's revenues are derived from a tax on real and personal property, sales taxes, taxes on corporations and companies, licences for conducting various businesses and from federal payments. In financial year 1982 the Council authorized a budget of $1,513,255,700.

The District of Columbia has no bonded debt not covered by its accumulated sinking fund. *Per capita* personal income, 1980, $12,039.

INDUSTRY. The District's main industries (1982) are government service (37%); services (31%); wholesale and retail trade (10%); finance, real estate, insurance, communications, transport and utilities (12%); total employed, 1980, 1,633,000.

TOURISM. About 17m. visitors stay in the District every year and spend about $1,000m.

COMMUNICATIONS

Roads. Within the District are 340 miles of bus routes. There are 1,101 miles of streets maintained by the District; of these, 673 miles are local streets, 262 miles are major arterial roads.

Railways. There is a rapid rail transit system including a town subway system. This coordinates with the bus system and connects with Union railway station and the National Airport. Nine rail lines serve the District.

Aviation. The District is served by 3 general airports; across the Potomac River in Arlington, Va., is National Airport, in Chantilly, Va., is Dulles International Airport and in Maryland is Baltimore—Washington International Airport.

JUSTICE, RELIGION AND EDUCATION

Justice. Since 1958 there have been no executions; from 1930 to 1957 there were 40 executions (electrocution) including 3 whites for murder and 35 Negroes for murder and 2 for rape. The death penalty was declared unconstitutional in the District of Columbia on November 16, 1973

The District's Court system is the Judicial Branch of the District of Columbia. It is the only completely unified court system in the United States, possibly because of the District's unique city-state jurisdiction. Until the District of Columbia Court Reform and Criminal Procedure Act of 1970, the judicial system was almost entirely in the hands of Federal Government. Since that time, the system has been similar in most respects to the autonomous systems of the states.

Religion. The largest churches are the Protestant and Roman Catholic Christian churches; there are also Jewish, Eastern Orthodox and Islamic congregations.

Education. In 1981–82 there were about 90,000 pupils in secondary and elementary schools. Expenditure on public schools, 1982–83, averages $3,530 per pupil. There are also 17,560 pupils in private elementary and secondary schools. Higher education is given through the Consortium of Universities of the Metropolitan Washington Area, which consists of six universities and three colleges:

Georgetown University, founded in 1795 by the Jesuit Order (12,000 students in 1982); George Washington University, non-sectarian founded in 1821 (17,000); Howard University, founded in 1867 (11,000); Catholic University of America, founded in 1887 (7,700; American University (Methodist) founded in 1893 (12,500); University of D.C., founded 1976 (13,500); Gallandet College, founded 1864 (1,000); Mount Vernon College, founded 1875 (500); Trinity College, founded 1897 (1,000). There are four other schools of higher education.

All benefit from such facilities as the 12 museums of the Smithsonian Institution, the Library of Congress, National Archives, and the Legal Libraries of the US Supreme Court and Department of Justice.

Social Security The District government provides primary health care for residents, mainly through its Department of Human Services, (about 6,280 employees). Departmental budget, 1981, $470m. of District, Federal and other funds.

Books of Reference

Statistical Information: The Metropolitan Washington Board of Trade publications.
Reports of the Commissioners of the District of Columbia. Annual. Washington
Federal Writers' Project. *Washington, D.C.: A Guide to the Nation's Capital.* New York

FLORIDA

HISTORY. White men, probably Spaniards but possibly English, saw Florida for the first time in the period 1497–1512. Juan Ponce de Leon sighted Florida on 27 March 1513. Going ashore between 2 and 8 April in the vicinity of what is now St Augustine, he named the land 'Pasqua de Flores' because his landing was 'in the time of the Feast of Flowers'. The first permanent settlement in the entire US was made at St Augustine, 8 Sept. 1565. It was claimed by Spain until 1763, then ceded to England; back to Spain in 1783, and to the US in 1821. Florida became a Territory in 1821 and was admitted into the Union on 3 March 1845.

AREA AND POPULATION. Florida is a peninsula bounded west by the Gulf of Mexico, south by the Straits of Florida, east by the Atlantic, north by Georgia and north-west by Alabama. Area, 58,664 sq. miles, including 4,510 sq. miles of inland water. Census population, 1 April 1980 (preliminary), was 9,739,992, an increase of 43·4% since 1970. Estimate (1981) 10,183,000. Births in 1980 were 131,923; deaths, 106,815; infant deaths, 1,904; marriages, 110,575; divorces, 71,409.

Population in 5 federal census years was:

	White	Negro	All Others	Total	Per Sq. Mile
1940	1,381,986	514,198	1,230	1,897,414	35·0
1950	2,166,051	603,101	2,153	2,771,305	51·1
1960	4,063,881	880,168	7,493	4,952,788	91·5
1970	5,719,343	1,041,651	28,449	6,789,443	125·6
1980	8,178,387	1,342,478	219,127	9,739,992	180·1

Of the population in 1980, 48% of the total were male; 84·3% were urban and 72·4% were 20 years of age or over.

The largest cities in the state (1980 census) are: Jacksonville, 540,898; Miami, 346,931; Tampa, 271,523; St Petersburg, 236,893; Fort Lauderdale, 153,256; Hialeah, 145,254; Orlando, 128,394; Hollywood, 117,188; Miami Beach, 96,298; Clearwater, 85,450; Tallahassee, 81,548; Gainesville, 81,371; West Palm Beach, 62,530; Largo, 58,977; Pensacola, 57,619.

CLIMATE. Jacksonville. Jan. 55°F (12·8°C), July 81°F (27·2°C). Annual rainfall 54″ (1,353 mm). Key West. Jan. 70°F (21·1°C), July 83°F (28·3°C). Annual rainfall 39″ (968 mm). Miami. Jan. 67°F (19·4°C), July 82°F (27·8°C). Annual rainfall 60″ (1,516 mm). Tampa. Jan. 61°F (16·1°C), July 81°F (27·2°C). Annual rainfall 51″ (1,285 mm). *See* Gulf Coast, p. 1373.

CONSTITUTION AND GOVERNMENT. The 1968 Legislature revised the constitution of 1885. The state legislature consists of a Senate of 40 members, elected for 4 years, and House of Representatives with 120 members elected for 2 years. Sessions are held annually, and are limited to 60 days. The Governor is elected for 4 years, and can hold two terms in office. Two senators and 19 representatives are elected to Congress.

In the 1980 presidential election Reagan polled 2,046,951 votes and Carter 1,419,475.

The state capital is Tallahassee. The state is divided into 67 counties.

Governor: Robert Graham (D.), 1983–86 ($69,550).
Lieut.-Governor: Wayne Mixson (D.), 1983–86 ($60,455).
Secretary of State: George Firestone (D.), 1983–86 ($59,385).

FINANCE. There is no state income tax on individuals. For the year ending 30 June 1981 the state had a general revenue of $8,063m. General expenditure was $7,807m., of which education took $3,601·6m.; public welfare, $891·4m.; and highways, $891·4m.

Net long-term debt, 30 June 1981, amounted to $1,940·8m.

Per capita personal income (1981) was $10,165.

NATURAL RESOURCES

Minerals. Chief mineral is phosphate rock, of which marketable production in 1981 was 41·7m. tonnes, leading all states (national production 53·6m. tons). Total value of mineral production, 1981, $1,725·5m.

Agriculture. In 1981, there were 40,000 farms; net income per farm was $21,817. Total value of all farm land and buildings, 1981, $19,600m. There were 847,056 acres in citrus groves and 12·2m. acres of other farms and ranches. Total cash receipts from crops and livestock (1981), $4,144m., of which crops provided $3,114·6m. Oranges, grapefruit, melons and vegetables are important. Other crops are soybeans ($68m.), sugar-cane, tobacco and peanuts. On 1 Jan. 1981 the state had 2·1m. cattle, including 189,000 milch cows, and 257,000 swine.

The national forests area in Sept. 1980 was 1,097,930 acres. There were (1983) 16m. acres of commercial forest.

Fisheries. Florida has extensive fisheries for oysters, shrimp, red snapper, crabs, mackerel and mullet. Catch (1980), 187·4m. lb. valued at $132·8m.

INDUSTRY. In 1980 there were 12,226 manufacturers. They employed 462,728 persons. Value added by manufacture (1977), $9,255·1m. The metal-working, lumber, chemical, woodpulp, food-processing and instruments industries are important.

TOURISM. During 1982 39·3m. tourists visited Florida. They spent $21,500m. making tourism one of the biggest industries in the state. There are 121 state parks, 4 state forests, 1 national park and 4 national forests. The state parks were visited by 15m. people in 1982, 1·3m. of them campers.

COMMUNICATIONS

Roads. The state (1979) had 96,300 miles of road and streets including 8,854 miles of primary federally-aided highways.

In 1980–81, 10·3m. vehicle licence plates were issued.

Railways. In 1979 there were 3,698 miles of railway.

Aviation. In 1982 Florida had 514 airports, including 128 public use airports of which 16 are international, 20 have air carrier service and 10 have scheduled commuter service. There are 3 public and 9 private seaplane bases.

UNITED STATES OF AMERICA

JUSTICE, RELIGION, EDUCATION AND WELFARE

Justice. Since 1968 there have been 2 executions, by electrocution, for murder; from 1930 to 1968 there were 168 executions (electrocution), including 130 for murder, 37 for rape and 1 for kidnapping. State prisons, 30 June 1982, had 26,036 in-mates.

Religion. The main Christian churches are Roman Catholic, Baptist, Methodist, Presbyterian and Episcopalian.

Education. Attendance at school is compulsory between 7 and 16.

In 1981–82 the public elementary and secondary schools had 1,477,938 enrolled pupils. State expenditure on public schools (1981–82) was $4,133·5m. The state maintains 28 community colleges with 357,993 enrolments in 1982.

There are 9 universities in the state system, namely the University of Florida at Gainesville (founded 1853) with 34,061 students in 1982; the Florida State University (founded at Tallahassee in 1857) with 22,116 students; the University of South Florida at Tampa (founded 1960) with 24,978 students; Florida A. & M. University at Tallahassee (founded 1887) with 4,728 students; Florida Atlantic University (founded 1964) at Boca Raton with 8,296 students; the University of West Florida at Pensacola with 5,279 students; the University of Central Florida at Orlando with 13,093 students; the University of North Florida at Jacksonville with 4,998 students; Florida International University at Miami with 11,892 students.

Health. Hospitals, 1983, numbered 263 with 59,048 beds; there were 225 general, 38 special and 1 tuberculosis hospitals.

Social Security. From 1974 aid to the aged, blind and disabled became a federal responsibility. The state continued to give aid to families with dependent children and general assistance. Monthly payments 1981–82: aid to 4,800 blind averaged $188.44; aid to 174,089 dependent children averaged $63.46; aid to 145,000 disabled averaged $181.91; aid to 123,000 aged averaged $149.49.

Books of Reference

Florida Population: Summary of the 1980 Census. Univ. of Florida Press, 1981
Florida Statistical Abstract. Univ. of Florida Press, 1980
Florida Tourist Study. Florida Department of Commerce, Tallahassee. Annual
Historical Florida Economic Data 1970–80. Florida Dept. of Commerce, 1980
Report. Florida Secretary of State. Tallahassee. Biennial
Report of the Comptroller. Tallahassee. Biennial
Dimensions. Bureau of Business and Economic Research, Univ. of Florida, Gainesville. Monthly
Morris, Allen. *The Florida Handbook.* Tallahassee. Biennial
Raisz, E. J., and others, *Atlas of Florida.* Univ. of Florida Press, 1974

State Library: Gray Building, Tallahassee. *Librarian:* Barratt Wilkins.

GEORGIA

HISTORY. Georgia (so named from George II) was founded in 1733 as the 13th original colony; she became the 4th original state.

AREA AND POPULATION. Georgia is bounded north by Tennessee and North Carolina, north-east by South Carolina, east by the Atlantic, south by Florida and west by Alabama. Area, 58,910 sq. miles, of which 854 sq. miles are inland water. Census population, 1 April 1980, was 5,464,265. Estimate (1981), 5,574,000. Births, 1980, were 95,980 (17·5 per 1,000 population); deaths, 43,519 (7·9); infant deaths, 1,208 (12·6 per 1,000 live births); marriages, 69,416 (12·7); divorces and annulments, 33,636 (6·2).

Population in 5 census years was:

	White	Negro	Indian	Asiatic	Total	Per sq. mile
1910	1,431,802	1,176,987	95	237	2,609,121	44·4
1930	1,837,021	1,071,125	43	317	2,908,506	49·7
1960	2,817,223	1,122,596	749	2,004	3,943,116	67·7
			All others			
1970	3,391,242	1,187,149	11,184		4,589,575	79·0
1980	3,948,007	1,465,457	50,801		5,464,265	92·7

Of the 1980 population, 2,641,030 were male, 3,406,171 were urban and those 20 years of age and over numbered 3,601,895.

The largest cities are: Atlanta (capital), with population, 1980 census, of 422,293 (urbanized area, 2,010,368); Columbus, 168,598 (238,593); Savannah, 133,672 (225,581); Macon, 116,044 (251,736); Albany, 74,471 (112,257).

CLIMATE. Atlanta. Jan. 43°F (6·1°C), July 78°F (25·6°C). Annual rainfall 49″ (1,234 mm). *See* Atlantic Coast, p. 1373.

CONSTITUTION AND GOVERNMENT. A new constitution was ratified in the general election of 2 Nov. 1976, proclaimed on 22 Dec. 1976 and became effective 1 Jan. 1977. The General Assembly consists of a Senate of 56 members and a House of Representatives of 180 members, both elected for 2 years. The Governor and Lieut.-Governor are elected for 4 years. Legislative sessions are annual, beginning the 2nd Monday in Jan. and lasting for 40 days.

Georgia was the first state to extend the franchise to all citizens 18 years old and above. The state is represented in Congress by 2 senators and 10 representatives.

Registered voters, 1976, numbered 2,178,623. At the 1980 presidential election Carter polled 890,955 votes, Reagan 654,168 and Anderson 36,055.

The state capital is Atlanta. Georgia is divided into 159 counties.

Governor: Joe F. Harris (D.), 1982–86 ($60,000).
Lieut.-Governor: Zell Miller (D.) ($28,846).
Secretary of State: Max Cleland (D.) ($38,400).

BUDGET. For the fiscal year ending 30 June 1981 general revenue was $5,847,545,000; general expenditure was $5,401,240,000.

On 30 June 1981 total liability was $1,378,211,000.

Estimated *per capita* personal income (1981), was $8,960.

NATURAL RESOURCES

Minerals. Georgia is the leading producer of kaolin. The state ranks first in production of crushed and dimensional granite, second in production of fuller's earth and marble (crushed and dimensional).

Mineral products, 1980, had a value of $771m.

Agriculture. In 1978, 58,648 farms covered 37% of the land area; average farm was of 234 acres. For 1980 cotton output was 86,000 bales (of 480 lb.). Other crops, 1980, included tobacco, 110·5m. lb; corn, 54·6m. bu.; peanuts and pecans 52m. lb. Cash income, 1980, $2,705m: from crops, $1,173·4m.; from livestock, $1,503·3m.

On 1 Jan. 1981 farm animals included 1·9m. all cattle, including 130,000 milch cows and 2·3m. swine.

Forestry. The forested area in 1980 was 25m. acres.

INDUSTRY. In 1980 the state's manufacturing establishments had 452,000 workers; the value added by manufacture was $15,013m., mainly from textiles, transport equipment, food, wood products and paper, chemicals.

TOURISM. In 1979 the tourist industry employed 182,370 earning $1,100m. Tourists spent $2,200m. and tax revenue was $95·9m.

COMMUNICATIONS

Roads. Total road mileage (Dec. 1980) was 134,500 including 88,900 rural and 11,850 primary federal-aided. Motor vehicles registered, 1981, numbered 3,850,000.

Railways. In 1976 there were 5,417 miles of railways.

Aviation. In 1981 there were 125 public and 168 private airports.

Shipping. The principal port is Savannah.

JUSTICE, RELIGION, EDUCATION AND WELFARE

Justice. State prisons, 31 Dec. 1981, had 12,377 inmates. Since 1964 there has been one execution (for murder). From 1924 to 1964 there were 415 executions (electrocution), including 75 whites and 268 Negroes for murder, 3 whites and 63 Negroes for rape and 6 Negroes for armed robbery.

Under a Local Option Act, the sale of alcoholic beverages (not including malt beverages and light wines) is prohibited in more than half the counties.

Religion. An estimated 78% of the population are church members. Of the total population, 74·3% are Protestant, 3·2% are Roman Catholic and 1·5% Jewish.

Education. Since 1945 education has been compulsory; tuition is free for pupils between the ages of 6 and 18 years. In 1980 public elementary and secondary schools had 1m. pupils and 56,200 teachers. Teachers' salaries averaged $15,900 (secondary) and $15,200 (elementary). Integration in public schools is now an accepted practice.

The University of Georgia (Athens) was founded in 1785 and was the first chartered State University in the US. Other institutions of higher learning include Georgia Institute of Technology (Atlanta), Emory University (Atlanta), Agnes Scott College (Decatur), Georgia College (Milledgeville), Georgia State University (Atlanta) and Mercer University (Macon). The Atlanta University Center, devoted primarily to Negro education, includes Clark College and Morris Brown College, co-educational, Morehouse, a liberal arts college for men, Interdenominational Theological Center, a co-educational theological school, and Spelman College, the first liberal arts college for Negro women in the US. Atlanta University serves as the graduate school centre for the complex. Wesleyan College near Macon is the oldest chartered women's college in the US. Total enrolment, 1980, was 184,200 in 76 institutions of higher education.

Health. Hospitals licensed by the Department of Human Resources, 1980, numbered 191 with 31,100 beds. State facilities for the mentally retarded had 1,363 resident patients in 1980; there were 4,527 in mental care hospitals.

Social Security. In Dec. 1980, 71,100 persons were receiving SSI old-age assistance of an average $104 per month; 89,900 families were receiving as aid to dependent children an average of $133 per family; aid to 80,500 disabled persons was $163 monthly.

Books of Reference

Georgia History in Outline. Univ. of Georgia Press, Athens, 1978

Bonner, J. C., and Roberts, L. E., eds., *Studies in Georgia History and Government.* Reprint Company, Spartanburg, 1940 Repr.

Pound, M. B., and Saye, A. B., *Handbook on the Constitution of the U.S. and Georgia.* Univ. of Georgia Press, Athens, 1978

Rowland, A. R., *A Bibliography of the Writings on Georgia History.* Hamden, Conn., 1978

Saye, A. B., *A Constitutional History of Georgia, 1732–1968.* Univ. of Georgia, Athens, Rev. ed., 1970

State Library: Judicial Building, Capital Sq., Atlanta. *State Librarian:* John D. M. Folger.

HAWAII

HISTORY. The Hawaiian Islands, formerly known as the Sandwich Islands, were discovered by Capt. James Cook in Jan. 1778. During the greater part of the 19th century the islands formed an independent kingdom, but in 1893 the reigning Queen, Liliuokalani (died 11 Nov. 1917), was deposed and a provisional government formed; in 1894 a Republic was proclaimed, and in accordance with the request of the people of Hawaii expressed through the Legislature of the Republic, and a resolution of the US Congress of 6 July 1898 (signed 7 July by President McKinley), the islands were on 12 Aug. 1898 formally annexed to the US. On 14 June 1900 the islands were constituted as a Territory of Hawaii.

Statehood was granted to Hawaii on 18 March 1959.

AREA AND POPULATION. The Hawaiian Islands lie in the North Pacific Ocean, between 18° 50′ and 28° 15′ N. lat. and 154° 40′ and 178° 15′ W. long., about 2,090 nautical miles south-west of San Francisco. There are more than 20 islands in the group, of which 7 are inhabited. The land and inland water area of the state is 6,450 sq. miles, with census population, 1 April 1980, of 964,691, an increase of 194,778 or 25·4% since 1970; density was 150 per sq. mile.

The principal islands are Hawaii, 4,038 sq. miles (population, 1980, 92,053); Maui, 729 (62,823); Oahu, 608 (762,534); Kauai, 553 (38,856); Molokai, 261 (6,049); Lanai, 140 (2,119); Niihau, 73 (226); Kahoolawe, 45 (0). The capital Honolulu, on the island of Oahu, had a population in 1980 of 365,048 and Hilo on the island of Hawaii, 43,957.

Figures for racial groups, 1980, are: 318,770 White, 239,748 Japanese, 133,940 Filipinos, 115,500 Hawaiian, 56,285 Chinese, 17,962 Korean, 17,364 Negroes, 65,122 all others. Of the total, approximately 92% were citizens of the US.

Inter-marriage between the races is popular. Of the 11,678 persons married in the calendar year 1979, 38·2% married a wife or husband of a different race. Births, 1981, were 18,230; deaths, 5,269; infant deaths, 178; marriages, 12,218; divorces and annulments, 4,253.

CLIMATE. All the islands have a tropical climate, with an abrupt change in conditions between windward and leeward sides, most marked in rainfall. Temperatures vary little. Honolulu. Jan. 71°F (21·7°C), July 78°F (25·6°C). Annual rainfall 31″ (775 mm).

CONSTITUTION AND GOVERNMENT. The constitution took effect on 21 Aug. 1959.

The Legislature consists of a Senate of 25 members elected for 4 years, and a House of Representatives of 51 members elected for 2 years. The constitution provides for annual meetings of the legislature with 60-day regular sessions. The Governor and Lieut.-Governor are elected for 4 years. The registered voters, 1982, numbered 405,005.

The state sends to Congress 2 senators and 2 representatives.

In the 1980 presidential election Carter polled 135,879 votes, Reagan, 130,112.

Governor: George R. Ariyoshi (D.), 1983–86 ($59,400).

BUDGET. Revenue is derived mainly from taxation of sales and gross receipts, real property, corporate and personal income, and inheritance taxes, licences, public land sales and leases. For the year ending 30 June 1981 state general fund receipts amounted to $1,162·5m.; special fund receipts, $742·6m., and federal grants, $389·8m. State expenditures were $1,940·3m. (education, $580·9m.; highways, $41·1m.; public welfare, $297·8m.; figures include both special and general funds).

Net long-term debt, 31 Dec. 1981, amounted to $2,217·9m.

Estimated *per capita* personal income (1981) was $11,036.

NATURAL RESOURCES

Minerals. Total value of mineral production, 1980, amounted to $59·7m. Cement shipped from plants amounted to 371,000 short tons; stone, 6·87m. short tons.

Agriculture. Farming is highly commercialized, aiming at export to the American market, and highly mechanized. In 1980 there were 4,300 farms with an acreage of 1·97m.

Sugar and pineapples are the staple crops. Income from crop sales, 1981, was $401m., and from livestock, $88m. The sugar crop was valued at $207·4m.; pineapples, $89·7m.; other crops, $104m.

Forestry. Commercial forests totalled 948,000 acres (1982); state lands, 1·4m. acres. Land held by the federal government totalled 296,803 acres.

INDUSTRY AND TRADE

Industry. In 1978 manufacturing establishments employed 23,700 production workers who earned an estimated $285·2m.; value added by manufacture was estimated at $782·9m.

Commerce. In 1980 imports of newsprint, fertilizer, lumber, feed, crude oil and other products from foreign countries such as Saudi Arabia, Indonesia and Japan exceeded $1,842m. In 1980 exports, primarily food and manufactures, amounted to $174·3m. About 68% of Hawaii's overseas trade is with the mainland USA.

Tourism. Tourism is an outstanding factor in Hawaii's economy. Tourist arrivals numbered 109,798 in 1955, and reached 3·93m. in 1981. Tourist expenditures, totalling $55m. in 1955, contributed $3,200m. to the state's economy in 1981.

COMMUNICATIONS

Roads. In 1981 there were 649,350 motor vehicles, and a total of 4,003 miles of highways (including 36 miles of federally assisted highways).

Aviation. There were 10 commercial airports in 1981; passengers arriving from overseas numbered 4·3m., and there were 6·7m. passengers between the islands.

Shipping. Several lines of steamers connect the islands with the mainland USA, Canada, Australia, the Philippines, China and Japan. In 1979, 10,686 inbound vessels entered Hawaiian ports; cargo arriving, 1978, 9m. tons; passengers arriving, 89,305.

Post. There were 728,352 telephones at 31 Dec. 1981.

JUSTICE, RELIGION, EDUCATION AND WELFARE

Justice. There is no capital punishment in Hawaii.

Religion. The residents of Hawaii are mainly Christians, though there are many Buddhists. A sample survey in 1979 showed that 31% were Roman Catholic, 34% Protestant, 12% Buddhist, 2·5% Latter Day Saints.

Education. Education is free, and compulsory for children between the ages of 6 and 18. The language in the schools is English. In 1981–82 there were 230 public schools (162,805 pupils with 8,139 teachers) and 146 private schools (38,039 pupils and 2,308 teachers) ranging from kindergarten through the 12th grade. The University of Hawaii, founded in 1907, had 20,319 day students in 1980; total university and college attendance 1981–82, 52,197.

Social Security. During 1980 the state spent $255·2m., the federal government met 42% of this fund. In 1980 there were 23 non-military hospitals (2,882 beds in 1980) listed by the Department of Health. During 1981 the average number of persons served by major welfare programmes was 72,480.

Books of Reference

Government in Hawaii. Tax Foundation of Hawaii. Honolulu, 1981
Guide to Government in Hawaii. 7th ed. Legislative Reference Bureau. State of Hawaii, Honolulu, 1980
All About Hawaii: Thrum's Hawaiian Annual and Standard Guide. Honolulu, 1875 to date
Current Hawaiiana (quarterly bibliography). Hawaii Library Association, Honolulu
Allen, G. E., *Hawaii's War Years.* 2 vols. Hawaii Univ. Press, 1950–52
Day, A. Grove, *Hawaii and Its People.* New York, 1955.—and Stroven, C., *A Hawaiian Reader.* New York, 1961
Kuykendall, R. S., and Day, A. G., *Hawaii, A History.* Rev. ed. New Jersey, 1961
Mann, A. F., *Hawaii: The Fiftieth State: Government and Economy.* Honolulu, 1960
Morgan, J. R., *Hawaii.* Boulder, 1982
Pukui, M. K., and Elbert, S. H., *Hawaiian–English Dictionary.* Honolulu, 1957
Smith, Branford, *Yankees in Paradise: The New England Impact on Hawaii.* Philadelphia, 1956

IDAHO

HISTORY. Idaho was first permanently settled in 1860, although there was a mission for Indians in 1836 and a Mormon settlement in 1855. It was organized as a Territory in 1863 and admitted into the Union as a state on 3 July 1890.

AREA AND POPULATION. Idaho is bounded north by Canada, east by the Rocky Mountains of Montana and Wyoming, south by Nevada and Utah, west by Oregon and Washington. Area, 83,564 sq. miles, of which 1,153 sq. miles are inland water. In 1970 the federal government owned 33,979,389 acres (64% of the state area). Census population, 1 April 1980, 943,935, an increase of 32·4% since 1970. Estimate (1981) 959,000.

Births, 1982, 19,581 (20·4 per 1,000 population); deaths, 6,924 (7·2); infant deaths, 195 (10 per 1,000 live births); marriages, 14,066 (14·7); divorces, 6,238 (6·5).

Population in 5 census years was:

	White	Negro	Indian	Asiatic	Total	Per sq. mile
1910	319,221	651	3,488	2,234	325,594	3·9
1930	438,840	668	3,638	1,886	445,032	5·4
1960	657,383	1,502	5,231	2,958	667,191	8·1
1970	693,375	3,655	5,413	2,526	713,008	8·5
			All others			
1980	901,641	2,716	39,578		943,935	11·3

Of the total 1980 population, 471,155 were male, 509,702 were urban and those 20 years of age or older 600,470.

The largest cities are Boise (capital) with 1980 census population of 102,160; Pocatello, 46,340; Idaho Falls, 39,734; Lewiston, 27,986; Twin Falls, 26,209; Nampa, 25,112.

CLIMATE. Boise. Jan. 29°F (–1·7°C), July 74°F (23·3°C). Annual rainfall 12″ (303 mm). *See* Mountain States, p. 1372.

CONSTITUTION AND GOVERNMENT. The constitution adopted in 1890 is still in force; it has had 122 amendments. The Legislature consists of a Senate of 35 members and a House of Representatives of 70 members, all the legislators being elected for 2 years. The Governor, Lieut.-Governor and Secretary of State are elected for 4 years. Voters are citizens, over the age of 18 years. The state is represented in Congress by 2 senators and 2 representatives.

In the 1980 presidential election Reagan polled 290,699 votes, Carter 110,192.
The state is divided into 44 counties. The capital is Boise.

Governor: John V. Evans (D.), 1983–86 ($50,000).
Lieut.-Governor: David Leroy (R.), 1983–86 ($14,000).
Secretary of State: Pete Cenarrusa (R.), 1983–86 ($37,500).

BUDGET. For the year ending 30 June 1983 (State Auditor's Office) general revenues were $421·8m. and general expenditures included education, $423·6m., transport, $166m., and health and welfare, $184·4m.

Per capita personal income (1982) was $9,210.

NATURAL RESOURCES

Minerals. Production of the most important minerals (1982): Lead, 38,397 tonnes (1981); silver, 14·8m. troy oz.; zinc, 27,722 tons; copper, 3,074 tons; gold, 24,140 troy oz. (1979). There is some tungsten, antimony and vadium. Non-metallic minerals include phosphate rock, barite, clay, garnet, gypsum, perlite, lime, cement, pumice, sand and gravel and dimension stone. Value of total mineral output was $300m. in 1982.

Agriculture. Agriculture is the leading industry, although a great part of the state is naturally arid. Extensive irrigation works have been carried out, bringing an estimated 3·5m. acres under irrigation; 83 reservoirs have a total capacity of 10·4m. acre-ft, 7·3m. acre-ft of which is primarily used for irrigation.

In 1983 there were 24,400 farms with a total area of 15·1m. acres (28% of the land area); average farm had 619 acres with land and buildings valued at approximately $700 per acre.

In 1983 there were 51 soil conservation districts, managed by local farmers and ranchers, covering most of the state.

Cash receipts from marketings, 1982, was $2,116m. ($1,289m. from crops and $827m. from livestock). The most important crops are potatoes and wheat—potatoes leading all states; in 1982 the production amounted to 91·7m. cwt, cash receipts $363m. Other crops are sugar-beet, alfalfa, barley, field peas, onions and apples. On 1 Jan. 1983 the number of sheep was 429,000; milch cows, 175,000; all cattle, 1·95m.; swine, 105,000 (1 Dec. 1982).

Forestry. In 1982 a total of 20,635,700 acres (37·6% of the state's area) was in forests; 13,540,600 acres of this was commercial (non-reserved) forest. The volume of sawtimber in commercial forests was 139,600m. bd ft. The stumpage value of forest products was about $91m., and an additional $207m. was added by process. Ownership of commercial forests is 70% federal, 6·5% state and local government, 0·5% Indian, 22·3% private. Some 22,900 workers are involved in forestry.

INDUSTRY. In 1980 there were about 1,500 manufacturing establishments and they employed about 48,000 workers; value added by manufacture was $1,931m.

TOURISM. Money spent by travellers in 1982 was about $1,132m. Estimated state and local tax receipts from tourism, $46m. Jobs generated, 25,000 (pay-roll over $300m.).

COMMUNICATIONS

Roads. The state maintained in 1983, 4,951 miles of the total of 67,254 miles of public roads; 715,245 passenger vehicles were registered in 1982.

Railways. The state had (1983) 2,026 miles of railways (including 2 AMTRAK routes) operated by 4 companies and serving all but 2 counties.

Aviation. There were 72 municipally owned airports in 1982.

Shipping. Water transport is provided from the Pacific to the Port of Lewiston, by way of the Columbia and Snake rivers, a distance of 464 miles.

JUSTICE, RELIGION, EDUCATION AND WELFARE

Justice. The death penalty is mandatory for first degree murder, but has been used sparingly. Since 1926 only 3 men (white) have been executed, by hanging (2 in 1951 and 1 in 1957). Execution is by firing squad or lethal injection. The state prison system, 1 Oct. 1983, had 1,095 inmates.

Religion. The leading religious denomination is the Church of Jesus Christ of Latter Day Saints (Mormon Church), with 191,286 adherents; Roman Catholics have 53,104; Methodists, 19,017; Presbyterians, 14,130; Episcopalians, 5,000, and Lutherans, 4,602.

Education. In 1982–83 public elementary schools (grades K to 6) had 115,237 pupils and 5,210 classroom teachers; secondary schools had 90,587 pupils and 4,845 classroom teachers.

Average salary, 1982–83, of elementary and secondary classroom teachers, $17,549. The University of Idaho, founded at Moscow in 1889, had 363 professors in 1982–83 and 8,998 students. There are 9 other institutions of higher education; 5 of them are public institutions with a total enrolment (1982–83) of 23,880 (excluding vocational-technical colleges).

Social Welfare. Old-age assistance is granted to persons 65 years of age. In Aug. 1983, 932 persons were drawing an average of $112.65 per month; 6,907 families with 12,377 children were drawing an average of $242.63 per case (or $91.38 per eligible person); 19 blind persons, $89.47; 546 children were receiving $314.08 per child for foster care.

Health. In Sept. 1983 skilled nursing covered 4,478 beds; intermediate care, 4,624; intermediate care for the mentally retarded 552. Hospitals had 3,416 beds and home health agencies totalled 21.

Books of Reference

Idaho Blue Book. Secretary of State. Boise, 1981–82
Idaho. Idaho First National Bank
Idaho Almanac. Division of Economic and Community Affairs, 1977
Idaho's Yesterdays. State Historical Society. Quarterly

ILLINOIS

HISTORY. Illinois was first discovered by Joliet and Marquette, two French explorers, in 1673, and settled in 1720. In 1763 the country was ceded by the French to the British. In 1783 Great Britain recognized the title of the US to Illinois, which was organized as a Territory in 1809 and admitted into the Union on 3 Dec. 1818.

AREA AND POPULATION. Illinois is bounded north by Wisconsin, northeast by Lake Michigan, east by Indiana, south-east by the Ohio River (forming the boundary with Kentucky), west by the Mississippi River (forming the boundary with Missouri and Iowa). Area, 56,345 sq. miles, of which 700 sq. miles are inland water. Census population, 1980, 11,418,461, an increase of 2·71% since 1970. Estimate (1981), 11,462,000. Births in 1980 were 186,578; deaths, 100,356; infant deaths, 2,693; marriages 110,667; divorces, 50,405.

Population in 5 census years was:

	White	Negro	Indian	All others	Total	Per sq. mile
1910	5,526,962	109,049	188	2,392	5,638,591	100·6
1930	7,295,267	328,972	469	5,946	7,630,654	136·4
1960	9,010,252	1,037,470	4,704	28,732	10,081,158	180·3
				All others		
1970	9,600,381	1,425,674		87,921	11,113,976	199·4
1980	9,225,575	1,675,229		517,657	11,418,461	203·0

Of the total population in 1980, 5,533,525 were male, 9,474,939 persons were urban and 7,743,162 were 20 years of age or older.

The most populous cities with population (1980 census), are:

Chicago	3,005,072
Rockford	139,712
Peoria	124,160
Springfield (cap.)	99,637
Decatur	94,081
Joliet	77,956
Aurora	81,293
Evanston	73,706
Waukegan	67,653
Elgin	63,798

Standard Metropolitan Statistical Area population (1980 census): Chicago, 7,102,378; East St Louis, 565,874; Peoria, 365,864; Rockford, 279,514; Springfield, 176,089; Decatur, 131,375.

CLIMATE. Chicago. Jan. 25°F (–3·9°C), July 73°F (22·8°C). Annual rainfall 33″ (836 mm). *See* Great Lakes, p. 1373

CONSTITUTION AND GOVERNMENT. The present constitution became effective 1 July 1971. The General Assembly consists of a House of Representatives of 177 members, elected for 2 years and a Senate of 59 members who serve 2 terms of 4 years and 1 of 2 years during a decade. Sessions are annual. The Governor and Lieut.-Governor are elected as a team for 4 years; the Comptroller and Secretary of State are elected for 4 years. Electors are citizens 18 years of age, having the usual residential qualifications.

The state is divided into legislative districts, in each of which 1 senator and 3 representatives are chosen; for the election of the latter each elector has 3 votes, of which he may cast 3 for 1 candidate or distribute them equally among no more than 3 candidates.

Illinois is represented in Congress by 2 senators and 22 representatives.

In the 1980 presidential election Reagan polled 2,358,094 votes, Carter 1,981,413.

The capital is Springfield. The state has 102 counties.

Governor: James R. Thompson (R.), 1983–86 ($58,000).
Lieut.-Governor: George Ryan (R.), 1983–86 ($45,500).
Secretary of State: Jim Edgar, 1983–86 ($50,500).

BUDGET. For the year ending 30 June 1981 general revenues were $14,250·2m. and general expenditures were $13,934·3m.

Total net long-term debt, 30 June 1981, was $6,919·6m.

Per capita personal income (1981) was $11,479.

ENERGY AND NATURAL RESOURCES

Minerals. Chief mineral product is coal; 88 operative mines had an output (1981) of 51·7m. tons. Mineral production also included: Crude petroleum, 24m. bbls; fluorspar. Total value of mineral products, 1980, was $2,770m.

Agriculture. In 1980, 105,000 farms had an area of 28·6m. acres; the average farm was 272 acres.

Cash receipts, 1981, from crops, $5,420m.; from livestock and livestock products, $2,225m. Illinois is a large producer of maize and soybeans, the state's leading cash commodities. Output, 1981: maize, 1,453m. bu.; soybeans, 355m. bu; wheat, 92·5m. bu. In Jan. 1980 there were 235,000 milch cows, 2·7m. all cattle, 190,000 sheep and 6·9m. swine (1979). The wool clip in 1979 was 1·3m. lb.

Forestry. National forest area under the US Forest Service administration, 1981, was 262,000 acres. Total forest land, 3·8m. acres.

INDUSTRY AND TRADE

Industry. In 1980, manufacturing establishments employed 1,272,000 workers;

value added by manufacture was $50,543m. Largest industry was machinery (excluding electrical).

Labour. In 1980 there were 4·89m. employees, of whom 1·2m. were in manufacturing, 1·1m. in trade, 944,000 in services, 764,000 in government.

COMMUNICATIONS

Roads. In 1979 there were 7·5m. passenger cars, 1·3m. trucks and buses, 924,372 trailers (1978) and 281,000 motor cycles registered in the state. In 1979 there were 17,604 miles of state administered roads. There were 4,291 miles of interstate or freeway roads.

Railways. There were 1978, 10,672 miles of main line railway.

Shipping. In 1981 the seaport of Chicago handled 31,599,167 short tons of cargo.

Aviation. There were (1981) 98 public and 831 private airports.

JUSTICE, RELIGION, EDUCATION AND WELFARE

Justice. In 1980 there were no executions; since 1930 there have been 90 executions (electrocution), including 58 white men, 1 white woman and 31 Negro men, all for murder. In 1979 the total average daily prison population was 11,211.

A Civil Rights Act (1941), as amended, bans all forms of discrimination by places of public accommodation, including inns, restaurants, retail stores, railroads, aeroplanes, buses, etc., against persons on account of 'race, religion, colour, national ancestry or physical or mental handicap'; another section similarly mentions 'race or colour.'

The Fair Employment Practices Act of 1961, as amended, prohibits discrimination in employment based on race, colour, sex, religion, national origin or ancestry, by employers, employment agencies, labour organizations and others. These principles are embodied in the 1971 constitution.

Religion. Among the larger religious denominations are: Roman Catholic, Jewish, United Presbyterian Church, USA, Lutheran Church in America, Lutheran Church Missouri Synod, American Baptist, Disciples of Christ, and Methodist.

Education. Education is free and compulsory for children between 7 and 16 years of age. In 1980–81 there were 1,011 school districts. Public school elementary enrolments were 1,334,904 pupils and 59,865 teachers; secondary enrolments, 648,554 pupils and 32,373 teachers. Enrolment (1980–81) in non-public schools was 261,466 elementary and 91,690 secondary. Teachers' salaries, 1980–81, averaged $19,519. Total expenditure on public schools, 1979–80, $4,923m. Total enrolment in 158 institutions of higher education (autumn 1981) was 660,000.

Colleges and universities with over 3,000 students:

Founded	Name	Place	Control	Autumn 1980 Enrolment
1851	Northwestern University	Evanston	Methodist	15,793
1857	Illinois State University	Normal	Public	19,000
1867	University of Illinois	Urbana	Public	61,000
1869	Chicago State University [1]	Chicago	Public	7,125
1869	Southern Illinois University	Carbondale	Public	27,255
1870	Loyola University	Chicago	Roman Catholic	14,909
1890	University of Chicago	Chicago	Non-Sect.	8,700
1895	Eastern Illinois University	Charleston	Public	9,600
1895	Northern Illinois University	DeKalb	Public	27,000
1897	Bradley University	Peoria	Non-Sect.	4,893
1898	DePaul University	Chicago	Roman Catholic	12,857
1899	Western Illinois University	Macomb	Public	11,030
1940	Illinois Institute of Technology [2]	Chicago	Non-Sect.	9,200
1945	Roosevelt University	Chicago	Non-Sect.	4,245
1961	Northeastern Illinois University [3]	Chicago	Public	10,061

[1] Formerly Illinois Teachers College (South).
[2] Illinois Institute of Technology formed in 1940 by merger of two older technical schools.
[3] Formerly Illinois Teachers' College (North).

Health. In 1980 hospitals listed by the American Hospital Association numbered 285, with 73,535 beds. In 1980 state institutions for the mentally retarded had 3,791 residents and state hospitals for the mentally ill, 4,368.

Social Security. State-administered Supplemental Security Income (SSI) was paid to 29,800 recipients in 1981; payments totalled $29m. Aid to families with dependent children was paid to 226 families in 1980, average monthly payment per family, $277; total payments. $722m.

Books of Reference

Blue Book of the State of Illinois. Edited by Secretary of State. Springfield. Biennial
Angle, P. M., and Beyer, R. L., *A Handbook of Illinois History.* Illinois State Historical Society, Springfield, 1943
Pease, T. C., *The Story of Illinois.* 3rd ed. Chicago, 1965

The Illinois State Library: Springfield, Il.627567. *State Librarian:* Jim Edgar.

INDIANA

HISTORY. Indiana, first settled in 1732–33, was made a Territory in 1800 and admitted into the Union on 11 Dec. 1816.

AREA AND POPULATION. Indiana is bounded west by Illinois, north by Michigan and Lake Michigan, east by Ohio and south by Kentucky across the Ohio River. Area, 36,185 sq. miles, of which 253 sq. miles are inland water. Census population, 1 April 1980, was 5,490,224, an increase of 294,832 or 5·7% since 1970. Estimate (1981) 5,468,000. In 1982 births were 83,890 (15·3 per 1,000 population); deaths 46,584 (8·5); infant deaths, 951 (11·3 per 1,000 live births); marriages 55,924 (10·2).

Population in 5 census years was:

	White	Negro	Indian	Asiatic	Total	Per sq. mile
1910	2,639,961	60,320	279	316	2,700,876	74·9
1930	3,125,778	111,982	285	458	3,238,503	89·4
1960	4,388,554	269,275	948	2,447	4,662,498	128·9
			All others			
1970	4,820,324	357,464	15,881		5,193,669	143·9
1980	5,004,394	414,785	71,045		5,490,224	152·8

Of the total in 1980, 2,665,805 were male, 3,525,298 were urban and 3,545,431 were 21 years of age or older.

The largest cities with population (census 1980) are: Indianapolis (capital), 711,539; Fort Wayne, 172,196; Gary, 151,953; Evansville, 130,496; South Bend, 109,727; Hammond, 93,714; Muncie, 77,216; Anderson, 64,695; Terre Haute, 61,125.

CLIMATE. Indianopolis. Jan. 29°F (−1·7°C), July 76°F (24·4°C). Annual rainfall 41″ (1,034 mm). *See* The Mid-West, p. 1372.

CONSTITUTION AND GOVERNMENT. The present constitution (the second) dates from 1851; it has had (as of Nov. 1983) 34 amendments. The General Assembly consists of a Senate of 50 members elected for 4 years, and a House of Representatives of 100 members elected for 2 years.

A constitutional amendment of 1970 allows the legislators to set the length and frequency of sessions, which are currently held annually. The Governor and Lieut.-Governor are elected for 4 years. The state is represented in Congress by 2 senators and 10 representatives.

In the 1980 presidential election Reagan polled 1,255,656 votes, Carter 844,197.

The state capital is Indianapolis. The state is divided into 92 counties and 1,008 townships.

Governor: Robert D. Orr (R.), 1981–85 ($48,000 plus expenses).
Lieut.-Governor: John Mutz (R.), 1981–85 ($34,000 plus expenses).
Secretary of State: Edwin Simcox (R.), 1982–86 ($34,000).

BUDGET. In the fiscal year 1980–81 (US Census Bureau figures) total revenues were $5,488·1m. ($1,228·6m. from federal government, $2,808·8m. from taxes), total expenditures were $5,664·2m. ($2,239·3m. for education, $683m. for public welfare and $591·6m. for highways).
Total long-term debt, on 30 June 1982, was $932m.
Per capita personal income (1981) was $9,720.

ENERGY AND NATURAL RESOURCES

Minerals. The state produced 30·9m. short tons of crushed limestone and 161,000 short tons of dimension limestone in 1980; the output of coal was 30·9m. short tons; petroleum, 5m. bbls (of 42 gallons).

Agriculture. Indiana is largely agricultural, about 75% of its total area being in farms. In 1982, 77,200 farms had 16m. acres (average, 211 acres). Cash income, 1982, from crops, $2,439m.; from livestock and products, $1,792m.

The chief crops (1982) were maize (815m. bu.), winter wheat (46·4m. bu.), oats (6·1m. bu.), soybeans (183·2m. bu.), popcorn, rye, barley, hay (alfalfa, clover, timothy), lespedeza seed, mint, clover seed, apples, strawberries, tomatoes, watermelons and tobacco.

The livestock on 1 Jan. 1982 included 1·75m. all cattle, 207,000 milch cows, 138,000 sheep and lambs, 4·1m. swine, 21·9m. chickens. In 1982 the wool clip yielded 852,000 lb. of wool from 124,000 sheep.

Forestry. The national forests area, 9 Sep. 1983, was 188,252 acres; 13 state forests and 2 state nurseries totalled 142,336 acres in July 1983.

INDUSTRY. Manufacturing establishments employed, in 1981, 649,032 workers, earning $13,541·8m. The steel industry is the largest in the country.

COMMUNICATIONS

Roads. In 1981 there were 91,469 miles of highways, roads and streets, of which 66,412 miles were county highways and 11,148 miles state highways. Motor vehicles registered, 1982, 4,342,071.

Railways. In 1980 there were 5,252 miles of mainline railway, 921 miles of secondary track and 3,295 miles of side and yard track.

Aviation. Of airports, 1981, 125 were for public use, 401 were private and 3 were military.

JUSTICE, RELIGION, EDUCATION AND WELFARE

Justice. In 1963–80 there were no executions; in 1981 there was one (electrocution), for murder; since 1930 there have been 2 others (electrocution), both for murder. State correctional institutions, 1 Oct. 1983, had 9,971 inmates.

The Civil Rights Act of 1885 forbids places of public accommodation to bar any persons on grounds not applicable to all citizens alike; no citizen may be disqualified for jury service 'on account of race or colour'. An Act of 1947 makes it an offence to spread religious or racial hatred.

A 1961 Act provided 'all . . . citizens equal opportunity for education, employment and access to public conveniences and accommodations' and created a Civil Rights Commission.

Religion. Religious denominations include Methodists, Roman Catholic, Disciples of Christ, Baptists, Evangelical United Brethren, Presbyterian churches, Society of Friends.

Education. School attendance is compulsory from 7 to 16 years. In 1981–82 public and parochial schools, had 1,123,812 pupils and 49,019 teachers. Teachers' salaries, grades 1–12, averaged $18,645. Total expenditure for public schools, $2,455·9m.

The principal institutions for higher education are (1981–82):

Founded	Institution	Control	Students (full-time)
1801	Vincennes University	State	3,724
1824	Indiana University, Bloomington	State	38,930
1837	De Pauw University, Greencastle	Methodist	2,034
1842	University of Notre Dame	R.C.	5,851
1850	Butler University, Indianapolis	Independent	2,067
1859	Valparaiso University, Valparaiso	Evangelical Lutheran Church	3,555
1870	Indiana State University, Terre Haute	State	10,118
1874	Purdue University, Lafayette	State	33,095
1898	Ball State University, Muncie	State	13,917

Health. Hospitals listed by the Indiana State Board of Health (1981) numbered 120 (23,929 beds). On 30 June 1982, 11 state mental hospitals had 6,512 patients enrolled (4,519 present).

Social Security. Old-age assistance, assistance to the blind and to the disabled were transferred from state to federal programmes in June 1974. In Jan.–June 1983, state supplemental assistance and/or Federal Supplemental Security assistance was paid to an average of 12,164 elderly persons per month (total $7·6m.), 1,175 blind ($1·3m.) and 25,798 disabled ($26·89m.).

Books of Reference

Indiana State Chamber of Commerce. *Here is Your Indiana Government.* 18th ed. Indianapolis, 1977
Martin, J. B., *Indiana: An Interpretation.* New York, 1947

State Library: Indiana State Library, 140 North Senate, Indianapolis 46204. *Director:* C. Ray Ewick.

IOWA

HISTORY. Iowa, first settled in 1788, was made a Territory in 1838 and admitted into the Union on 28 Dec. 1846.

AREA AND POPULATION. Iowa is bounded east by the Mississippi River (forming the boundary with Wisconsin and Illinois), south by Missouri, west by the Missouri River (forming the boundary with Nebraska), north-west by the Big Sioux River (forming the boundary with South Dakota) and north by Minnesota. Area, 56,275 sq. miles, including 310 sq. miles of inland water. Census population, 1 April 1980, 2,913,387, an increase of 3·17% since 1970. Estimate, 1981, 2,899,000. Births, 1982, were 44,716; deaths, 26,852; infant deaths, 453; marriages, 27,189; dissolutions of marriages, 10,869.

Population in 5 census years was:

	White	Negro	Indian	Asiatic	Total	Per sq. mile
1870	1,188,207	5,762	48	3	1,194,020	21·5
1930	2,452,677	17,380	660	222	2,470,939	44·1
1960	2,729,286	25,354	1,708	1,022	2,757,537	49·2
			All others			
1970	2,782,762	32,596	10,010		2,825,368	50·5
1980	2,838,805	41,700	32,882		2,913,387	51·7

At the census of 1980, 1,416,195 were male, 1,624,547 were urban and 1,971,502 were 20 years of age or older.

The largest cities in the state, with their census population in 1980 are: Des

Moines (capital), 191,003; Cedar Rapids, 110,243; Davenport, 103,264; Sioux City, 82,003; Waterloo, 75,985; Dubuque, 62,321; Council Bluffs, 56,449; Iowa City, 50,508; Ames, 45,775; Cedar Falls, 36,322; Clinton, 32,828; Mason City, 30,144; Burlington, 29,529; Fort Dodge, 29,423; Ottumwa, 27,381.

CLIMATE. Cedar Rapids. Jan. 20°F (–6·7°C), July 74°F (23·3°C). Annual rainfall 36″ (903 mm). Des Moines. Jan. 19°F (–7·2°C), July 75°F (23·9°C). Annual rainfall 31″ (773 mm). *See* The Mid-West, p. 1372.

CONSTITUTION AND GOVERNMENT. The constitution of 1857 still exists; it has had 37 amendments. The General Assembly comprises a Senate of 50 and a House of Representatives of 100 members, meeting annually for an unlimited session. Senators are elected for 4 years, half retiring every second year: representatives for 2 years. The Governor and Lieut.-Governor are elected for 4 years. The state is represented in Congress by 2 senators and 6 representatives. Iowa is divided into 99 counties; the capital is Des Moines.

In the 1980 presidential election Reagan polled 676,026 votes, Carter 508,672.

Governor: Terry Branstad (R.), 1983–86 ($60,000).
Lieut.-Governor: Robert Anderson (D.), 1983–86 ($18,000).
Secretary of State: Mary Jane Odell (R.) ($35,600).

BUDGET. For fiscal year 1982 state tax revenue was $1,754·2m. General expenditures were $1,300m. for education, $374·3m. for social services and human resources, and $38·7m. for transport.

On 30 June 1982 the net long-term debt was $857·3m.

Per capita personal income (1982) was $10,532.

ENERGY AND NATURAL RESOURCES

Minerals. The leading products by value are cement (21·8m. tons in 1981) and limestone (22·4m. tons in 1981). Coalfields produced 526,000 tons in 1982. The value of mineral products, 1981, was $243·4m.

Agriculture. Iowa is the wealthiest of the agriculture states, partly because nearly the whole area (95·5%) is arable and included in farms. It has escaped large-scale commercial farming. The average farm (in 1982) was 289 acres.

Cash farm income (1982 estimate) was $10,343m.; from livestock, $6,013m., and from crops, $4,330m. Production of corn grain in 1982 was 1,591m. bu. Red meat production in 1982 totalled 5,680m. lb. On 1 Dec. 1982 livestock included swine, 14·3m. (leading all states); milch cows, 385,000; all cattle, 6·45m., and sheep and lambs, 457,000. The wool clip (1980) yielded 3·8m. lb. of wool.

INDUSTRY. In 1980 manufacturing establishments employed 258,070 people with annual payroll at $4,520·4m., value added by manufacture was $11,570m.

COMMUNICATIONS

Roads. On 1 Jan. 1982 number of miles of streets and highways was 112,323; there were 2·6m. licensed drivers and 2·9m. registered vehicles.

Railways. The state, 1982, had 5,189 miles of track, and 6 Class I railways.

Aviation. Airports (1982), numbered 350, including 133 lighted airports and 92 all-weather runways. There were almost 3,200 private aircraft.

JUSTICE, RELIGION, EDUCATION AND WELFARE

Justice. There is now no capital punishment in Iowa. State prisons, 22 Sept. 1983, had 2,034 inmates.

Religion. Chief religious bodies in 1980 were: Roman Catholic (542,698 members); United Methodists, 258,252; American Lutheran, 200,712 baptised members; United Presbyterians, 85,000; United Church of Christ, 50,679.

Education. School attendance is compulsory for 24 consecutive weeks annually during school age (7–16). In 1982–83 505,407 were attending primary and secondary schools; 50,733 pupils attending non-public schools. Classroom teachers numbered 33,066 with average salary of $18,990. Total expenditure on public schools in 1982–83 was $1,636,128,000. Leading institutions for higher education (1982–83) were:

Founded	Institution	Control	Full-time Professors	Students
1843	Clarke College, Dubuque	Independent	54	896
1847	University of Iowa, Iowa City	State	1,601	29,599
1847	Grinnell College, Grinnell	Independent	105	1,219
1852	Wartburg College, Waverly	American Lutheran	67	1,140
1853	Cornell College, Mount Vernon	Independent	64	961
1858	Iowa State University, Ames	State	1,554	26,020
1876	Univ. of Northern Iowa, Cedar Falls	State	570	11,204
1881	Drake University, Des Moines	Independent	265	6,008
1881	Coe College, Cedar Rapids	Independent	75	1,448
1894	Morningside College, Sioux City	Methodist	72	1,235

Health. In 1982, the state had 137 hospitals (about 20,484 beds). In Oct. 1983 hospitals for mental diseases had 2,022 resident patients.

Social Security. Iowa has a Civil Rights Act (1939) which makes it a misdemeanour for any place of public accommodation to deprive any person of 'full and equal enjoyment' of the facilities it offers the public.

Supplemental security income (SSI) assistance is available for the aged (65 or older), the blind and the disabled. In Aug. 1983, 8,704 elderly persons were drawing an average of $107 per month, 858 blind persons $185 per month, and 14,599 disabled persons $183 per month. Aid to dependent children, established in 1974, was received by 37,961 families representing 107,176 persons at a monthly average of $335 per family.

Books of Reference

Statistical Information: State Departments of Health, Public Instruction and Social Services; State Aeronautics, Commerce and Development Commissions; Crop and Livestock Reporting Services, Des Moines; Iowa Dept. of Transportation, Ames; Geological Survey, Iowa City; Iowa College Aid Commission.

Annual Survey of Manufactures. US Department of Commerce
Government Finance. US Department of Commerce
Official Register. Secretary of State. Des Moines. Biennial
Petersen, W. J., *Iowa History Reference Guide.* Iowa City, 1952

Iowa State Library: Des Moines 50319.

KANSAS

HISTORY. Kansas, settled in 1727, was made a Territory (along with part of Colorado) in 1854, and was admitted into the Union with its present area on 29 Jan. 1861.

AREA AND POPULATION. Kansas is bounded north by Nebraska, east by Missouri, with the Missouri River as boundary in the north-east, south by Oklahoma and west by Colorado. Area, 82,277 sq. miles, including 499 sq. miles of inland water. Census population, 1 April 1980, 2,364,236, an increase of 5·1% since 1970. Estimate (1981) 2,383,000. Vital statistics, 1981: Births, 41,202 (17·2 per 1,000 population); deaths, 21,579 (9); infant deaths, 452 (11 per 1,000 live births); marriages, 26,137 (10·9); divorces 13,484 (5·6).

Population in 5 federal census years was:

	White	Negro	Indian	Asiatic	Total	Per sq. mile
1870	346,377	17,108	914	—	364,399	4·5
1930	1,811,997	66,344	2,454	204	1,880,999	22·9
1960	2,078,666	91,445	5,069	2,271	2,178,611	26·3
			All others			
1970	2,122,068	106,977	17,533		2,249,071	27·5
1980	2,168,221	126,127	69,888		2,364,236	28·8

Of the total population in 1980, 1,156,941 were male, 1,575,899 were urban and those 20 years of age or older numbered 1,620,368.

Cities, with 1980 census population, are Wichita, 279,835; Kansas City, 161,148; Topeka (capital), 115,266; Overland Park, 81,784; Lawrence, 52,738.

CLIMATE. Dodge City. Jan. 29°F (–1·7°C), July 78°F (25·6°C). Annual rainfall 21″ (518 mm). Kansas City. Jan. 30°F (–1·1°C), July 79°F (26·1°C). Annual rainfall 38″ (947 mm). Topeka. Jan. 28°F (–2·2°C), July 78°F (25·6°C). Annual rainfall 35″ (875 mm). Wichita. Jan. 31°F (–0·6°C), July 81°F (27·2°C). Annual rainfall 31″ (777 mm). *See* Mid-West, p. 1372.

CONSTITUTION AND GOVERNMENT. The year 1861 saw the adoption of the present constitution; it has had 78 amendments. The Legislature includes a Senate of 40 members, elected for 4 years, and a House of Representatives of 125 members, elected for 2 years. Sessions are annual. The Governor and Lieut.-Governor are elected for 4 years. The right to vote (with the usual exceptions) is possessed by all citizens. The state is represented in Congress by 2 senators and 5 representatives.

The state was the first (of 42 states) to establish in 1933 a Legislative Council; this is now called the Legislative Coordinating Council and has 7 members.

In the 1980 presidential election Reagan polled 566,812 votes, Carter 326,150.

The capital is Topeka. The state is divided into 105 counties.

Governor: John Carlin (D.), 1983–86 ($45,000).
Lieut.-Governor: Thomas Docking (D.), 1983–86 ($13,500).
Secretary of State: Jack H. Brier (R.) ($27,500).

BUDGET. For the year ending 30 June 1982 (Governor's Budget Report) general revenue fund was $2,641,221,484. General expenditures were $1,333,496,424.

Bonded debt outstanding for 1982 amounted to $316·9m.

Per capita personal income (1981) was $10,824.

ENERGY AND NATURAL RESOURCES

Minerals. Important minerals are coal, petroleum, natural gas, lead and zinc. Value of production (1980), $2,478m.

Agriculture. Kansas is pre-eminently agricultural, but sometimes suffers from lack of rainfall in the west. In 1982, 76,000 farms covered 48·5m. acres; average farm, 638 acres.

Cash income, 1982, from crops was $2,470m.; from livestock and products, $3,305·3m.

Kansas is a great wheat-producing state. Its output in 1982 was 462m. bu. Other crops in 1982 (in bushels) were maize, 140·2m.; sorghum, 207·7m.; soybeans, 47m.; oats, 7·5m.; barley, 2·3m. The state has an extensive livestock industry, comprising, on 1 Jan. 1983, 127,000 milch cows, 5·75m. all cattle, 190,000 sheep and lambs 1·67m. swine. Wool clip (1981), 1,684,000 lb. from 230,000 sheep.

INDUSTRY. Employment distribution (1982): 24·7% in trade; 20·3% in government; 18·8% in services; 18·1% in manufacturing; 6·7% in transport and utilities; 4.3% in finance, insurance and real estate; 4·1% in construction; 2% in mining. Value added by manufacture in 1980 was $7,498m. The slaughtering industry, other food processing, aircraft, the manufacture of transport equipment and petroleum refining are important.

COMMUNICATIONS

Roads. The state in Dec. 1982 had 135,087 miles of roads and streets including 8,916 miles of interstate and other primary and federally-aided highways.

Railways. There were 7,273 miles of railway in Jan. 1982.

Aviation. There were 384 airports and landing strips in 1983, of which 168 were public.

JUSTICE, RELIGION, EDUCATION AND WELFARE

Justice. There were 3,390 prisoners in state institutions, 30 June 1983. The death penalty (by hanging) for murder was abolished in 1907 and restored in 1935; there have been no executions since 1968; executions 1934 to 1968 have been 15 (all for murder).

For the various Civil Rights Acts forbidding racial or political discrimination, *see* THE STATESMAN'S YEAR-BOOK, 1955, p. 666. The 1965 Kansas Act against Discrimination declared that it is the policy of the state to eliminate and prevent discrimination in all employment relations, and to eliminate and prevent discrimination, segregation or separation in all places of public accommodations covered by the Act.

Religion. The most numerous religious bodies are Roman Catholic, Methodists and Disciples of Christ.

Education. In 1982–83 organized school districts had 1,519 elementary and secondary schools which had 407,074 pupils and 26,053 teachers. Average salary of public school teachers, $18,231 (elementary and secondary). There were 20 independent colleges, 20 community colleges, 2 Bible colleges, 1 municipal university.

Kansas has 6 state-supported institutions of higher education: the University of Kansas, Lawrence, founded in 1865; Kansas State University, Manhattan (1863); Emporia State University, Emporia; Pittsburg State University, Pittsburg; Fort Hays State University, Hays and Wichita State University, Wichita. The state also supports a two-year technical school, Kansas Technical Institute, at Salina.

Health. In 1982 the state had 166 hospitals (188,512 beds) listed by the American Hospital Association; hospitals had an average daily occupancy rate of 70·3%.

Social Security. In Dec. 1980, 92,100 persons received state and federal aid under programmes of aid to the aged or disabled and aid to dependent children. Total payments amounted to $114·9m. in 1980.

Books of Reference

Annual Economic Report of the Governor. Topeka
Directory of State Officers, Boards and Commissioners and Interesting Facts Concerning Kansas. Topeka, Biennial
Drury, J. W., *The Government of Kansas.* Lawrence, Univ. of Kansas, 1970
Zornow, W. F., *Kansas: A History of the Jayhawk State.* Norman, Okla., 1957

State Library: Kansas State Library, Topeka.

KENTUCKY

HISTORY. Kentucky, first settled in 1765, was originally part of Virginia; it was admitted into the Union on 1 June 1792 and its first legislature met on 4 June.

AREA AND POPULATION. Kentucky is bounded north by the Ohio River (forming the boundary with Illinois, Indiana and Ohio), north-east by the Big

Sandy River (forming the boundary with West Virginia), east by Virginia, south by Tennessee and west by the Mississippi River (forming the boundary with Missouri). Area, 40,409 sq. miles, of which 740 sq. miles are water. Census population, 1980 3,660,777, an increase of 13·6% since 1970. Estimate (1981) 3,662,000. Births in 1981, 57,212 (15·6 per 1,000 population); deaths, 33,260 (9·1); infant deaths, 563 (9·8 per 1,000 live births); marriages, 32,217 (8·8); divorces, 16,671 (4·6).

Population in 5 census years was:

	White	Negro	All others	Total	Per sq. mile
1930	2,388,364	226,040	185	2,614,589	65·1
1950	2,742,090	201,921	795	2,944,806	73·9
1960	2,820,083	215,949	2,124	3,038,156	76·2
1970	2,981,766	230,793	6,147	3,218,706	81·2
1980	3,379,006	259,477	22,294	3,660,777	92·3

Of the total population in 1980, an estimated 1,789,000 were male, 1,862,183 were urban and 2,359,614 were 21 years old or older.

The principal cities with census population in 1980 are: Louisville, 298,451 (urbanized area, 654,938); Lexington-Fayette, 204,165; Owensboro, 54,450; Covington, 49,563; Bowling Green, 40,450; Paducah, 29,315; Hopkinsville, 27,318; Ashland, 27,064; Frankfort (capital), 25,973.

CLIMATE. Kentucky has a temperate climate. Temperatures are moderate during both winter and summer, precipitation is ample without a pronounced dry season, and there is little snow during the winter. Lexington. Jan. 33°F (0·6°C), July 76°F (24·4°C). Annual rainfall 45″ (1,126 mm). Louisville. Jan. 33°F (0·6°C), July 77°F (25°C). Annual rainfall 43″ (1,077 mm). See Appalachian Mountains, p. 1373.

CONSTITUTION AND GOVERNMENT. The constitution dates from 1891; there had been 3 preceding it. The 1891 constitution was promulgated by convention and provides that amendments be submitted to the electorate for ratification. The General Assembly consists of a Senate of 38 members elected for 4 years, one half retiring every 2 years, and a House of Representatives of 100 members elected for 2 years. A constitutional amendment approved by the voters in Nov. 1979, changes the year in which legislators are elected from odd to even numbered years and establishes an organizational session of the legislature, limited to ten legislative days, in odd-numbered years. The amendment provides for regular sessions limited to 60 legislative days between the first Tuesday after the first Monday of Jan. and 15 April of even numbered years. The Governor and Lieut.-Governor are elected for 4 years. All citizens are (with necessary exceptions) qualified as electors; the voting age was in 1955 reduced from 21 to 18 years. Registered votes, Aug. 1981: 1,819,075. In the 1980 presidential election Reagan polled 635,274 votes, Carter 617,417.

The state is represented in Congress by 2 senators and 7 representatives.

The capital is Frankfort. The state is divided into 120 counties.

Governor: Martha Layne Collins (D.), 1983–86 ($50,000).
Lieut.-Governor: Stephen L. Beshear (D.) ($49,143).
Secretary of State: Droxell R. Davis (D.) ($49,143).

BUDGET. For the fiscal year ending 30 June 1983 revenues received within the five major operating funds amounted to $4,296·4m. Included in this figure are $2,211·9m. General Fund revenues and $844m. Federal Fund revenues. Total expenditures amounted to $4,424·8m. including education and humanities, $1,286·9m.; human resources benefits payments, $590·9m.; and transport, $723·3m.

The general obligation bonded indebtedness on 30 June 1983 was $226m.

Per capita personal income (1982) was $8,934.

ENERGY AND NATURAL RESOURCES

Minerals. The principal mineral product of Kentucky is coal, 150·2m. short tons mined in 1982, value $4,571m. Output of petroleum, 7·3m. bbls (of 42 gallons); natural gas, 51,924m. cu. ft; stone, 29·6m. short tons, value $106m.; clay 591,000 short tons, value $3·1m.; sand and gravel, 4·3m. short tons, value $9m. Total value of non-fuel mineral products in 1982 was $200,786,000. Other minerals include fluorspar, ball clay, lead, zinc, silver, cement, lime, industrial sand and gravel, oil shale and tar sands.

Agriculture. In 1982, 101,000 farms had an area of 14·5m. acres. The average farm was 144 acres.

Cash income, 1982, from crops, $1,630m., and from livestock, $1,274m. The chief crop is tobacco: production, in 1982, 577m. lb., ranking second to N. Carolina in US. Other principal crops include corn, soybeans, wheat, barley, sorghum grain, hay, oats and rye.

Stock-raising is important in Kentucky, which has long been famous for its horses. The livestock in 1982 included 243,000 milch cows, 2·7m. cattle and calves, 23,000 sheep, 920,000 swine.

Forestry. Total forests area, 1978, 12,160,800 acres. Total commercial forest land, 1978, 11,901,900 acres; 92% is privately owned.

INDUSTRY. In 1982 the state's 3,200 manufacturing plants had 186,675 production workers; value added by manufacture in 1981 was $12,000m. The leading manufacturing industries (by employment) are non-electrical machinery, electrical equipment, apparel and other fabric products and foods. Direct foreign investment in manufacturing by foreign investors was $890m. in 1983.

TOURISM. In 1982 tourist expenditure was $2,008m., producing over $125m. in tax revenues and generating 110,770 jobs. The state had (1983) 749 hotels and motels, 198 campgrounds and 43 state parks.

COMMUNICATIONS

Roads. In 1983 the state had over 69,000 miles of federal, state and local roads. There were over 2·4m. motor vehicle registrations in 1982.

Railways. In 1983 there were about 3,300 miles of railway.

Aviation. There are (1983) 117 aircraft landing areas and 2,000 registered aircraft in Kentucky. Seven airports served 5–6m. passengers with scheduled services in 1982.

Shipping. There is an increasing amount of barge traffic on 1,090 miles of navigable rivers. There are 5 river ports, 1 under construction and 3 planned.

JUSTICE, RELIGION, EDUCATION AND WELFARE

Justice. There are 10 correctional institutions.

In 1982–83 the prisons had an average of 4,131 inmates. There has been no execution since 1962. A session of Congress in 1976 limited the death penalty to cases of kidnap and murder.

Total executions, 1911–62, were 162, including 76 whites and 86 Negroes; 144 were for murder, 7 for rape, 6 for criminal offences, 5 for armed robbery.

Religion. The chief religious denominations in 1980 were: Southern Baptists, with 883,096 members, Roman Catholic (365,277), United Methodists (234,536), Christian Churches and Church of Christ (81,222) and Christian (Disciples of Christ) (78,275).

Education. Attendance at school between the ages of 6 and 15 years (inclusive) is compulsory, the normal term being 175 days. In 1982–83, 20,931 teachers were employed in public elementary and 11,306 in secondary schools, in which 434,426 and 215,942 pupils enrolled respectively. Expenditure on elementary and secondary day schools in 1982–83 was about $1,437·4m.; public school classroom teachers' salaries (1982–83) averaged $18,384.

There were also 4,119 teachers working in private elementary and secondary schools with 72,848 students.

The state has 24 universities and senior colleges, 5 junior colleges and 13 community colleges, with a total (autumn 1982) of 134,841 students. Of these universities and colleges, 22 are state-supported, and the remainder are supported privately. The largest of the institutions of higher learning are (autumn 1982): University of Kentucky, with 22,829 students; University of Louisville, 19,744 students; Western Kentucky University, 12,855 students; Eastern Kentucky University, 13,041 students; Murray State University, 7,587 students; Morehead State University, 6,370 students; Northern Kentucky University, 9,339 students. Five of the several privately endowed colleges of standing are Berea College, Berea; Centre College, Danville; Transylvania University, Lexington; Georgetown College, Georgetown; and Bellarmine College, Louisville.

Health. In 1983 the state had 108 licensed general hospitals (15,945 beds), 11 psychiatric hospitals (1,845 beds) and 4 children's hospitals (234 beds).

Welfare. In June 1983 there were 247,275 persons receiving financial assistance; 90,835 of these persons received the Federal Supplemental Security Income (SSI); 35,441 of them were aged, 2,024 blind, 53,370 disabled. The average monthly SSI payment in each group is as follows: $121.75 to aged, $226.78 to blind and $214.99 to disabled. Also, in the all state funded Supplementation programme payments were made in June 1983 to 7,671 persons, of which 4,155 were aged, 105 blind and 3,411 disabled. The average State Supplementation payment was $112.89 to aged, $80.05 to blind and $122.17 to disabled.

In the Aid to Families with Dependent Children Programme as of June 1983, aid was given to 153,307 persons in 57,954 families. The average payment per person was $69.24, per family $183.17.

In addition to money payments, medical assistance, food stamps and social services are available.

Books of Reference

Kentucky 1983 Economic Statistics. 19th ed. Department of Economic Development, Frankfort, 1983

LOUISIANA

HISTORY. Louisiana was first settled in 1699. That part lying east of the Mississippi River was organized in 1804 as the Territory of New Orleans, and admitted into the Union on 30 April 1812. The section west of the river was added very shortly thereafter.

AREA AND POPULATION. Louisiana is bounded north by Arkansas, east by Mississippi, with the Mississippi River forming the boundary in the north-east, south by the Gulf of Mexico and west by Texas, with the Sabine River forming most of the boundary. Area, 52,453 sq. miles, including lakes, rivers and coastal waters inside 3-mile limit; land area, 44,873 sq. miles. Census population, 1 April 1980, 4,205,900, an increase of 15·5% since 1970. Estimate (1981) 4,308,000. Births, 1981, 81,105 (18·8 per 1,000 population); deaths, 35,747 (8·3); infant deaths, 1,112 (13·7 per 1,000 live births); marriages, 44,929; divorces, 17,377.

Population in 5 census years was:

	White	Negro	Indian	Asiatic	Total	Per sq. mile
1910	941,086	713,874	780	648	1,656,388	36·5
1930	1,322,712	776,326	1,536	1,019	2,101,593	46·5
1960	2,211,715	1,039,207	3,587	2,004	3,257,022	72·2
			All others			
1970	2,541,498	1,086,832	12,976		3,641,306	81·1
1980	2,911,243	1,237,263	55,466		4,203,972 [1]	93·5

[1] Preliminary.

Of the 1980 total, 2,039,894 were male, 2,885,535 were urban; those 20 years of age or older numbered 2,699,100.

The largest cities with their 1980 census population are: New Orleans, 557,482; Baton Rouge (capital), 219,486; Shreveport, 205,815; Lafayette, 81,961; Kenner, 66,382.

CLIMATE. New Orleans. Jan. 54°F (12·2°C), July 83°F (28·3°C). Annual rainfall 58" (1,458 mm). *See* Gulf Coast, p. 1373.

CONSTITUTION AND GOVERNMENT. The present constitution dates from 1974.

The Legislature consists of a Senate of 39 members and a House of Representatives of 105 members, both chosen for 4 years. Sessions are annual; a fiscal session is held in odd years. The Governor and Lieut.-Governor are elected for 4 years.

A Governor may serve a second consecutive term. Qualified electors are (with the usual exceptions) all registered citizens with the usual residential qualifications.

In the 1980 presidential election Reagan polled 792,853 votes, Carter 708,453.

The state sends to Congress 2 senators and 8 representatives. Louisiana is divided into 64 parishes (corresponding with the counties of other states).

Governor: Edwin W. Edwards (D.), 1984–88 ($73,440).
Lieut.-Governor: Robert Freeman (D.), 1980–84 ($63,367).
Secretary of State: James Brown (D.), 1984–88 ($60,169).

BUDGET. For the fiscal year ending 30 June 1982 (Louisiana State Budget Office figures) general revenues were $6,091,714,373, of which $1,236,983,444 were federal funds; total expenditures were $6,067,203,315 (education, $2,077,432,518; transport and development, $416,170,800; health, hospitals and public welfare, $1,578,334,592).

Per capita personal income (1982) was $10,231.

ENERGY AND NATURAL RESOURCES

Minerals. The yield in 1981 of crude petroleum was 157·79m. bbls. Rich sulphur mines are found in the state, and wells for the extraction of sulphur by means of hot water and compressed air are in operation; output, 1980, 2·6m. tonnes.

Louisiana is the USA's main salt producer. Output of salt (1980) was 12·6m. short tons valued at $132·2m. Total output of raw, non-fuel minerals in 1981 was valued at $574m.

Agriculture. The state is divided into two parts, the uplands and the alluvial and swamp regions of the coast. A delta occupies about one-third of the total area. Manufacturing is the leading industry, but agriculture is important. In 1978 there were about 35,500 farms with annual average sales of at least $1,000; average farm, 293 acres.

Cash income, 1980, from crops $1,194·8m.; from livestock, $458·1m. Production of sugar-cane was valued at $100·6m.; rice, $214·87m.; sweet potatoes, $23·1m.; soybeans, $557·6m.; pecans, $9·4m.; cotton, $231·1m.

In 1979 the state contained 128,000 milch cows, 1·7m. all cattle, 13,000 sheep and 150,000 swine.

Forestry. Forests, 14·5m. acres, represent 47% of the state's area. Income from manufactured products exceeds $2,500m. annually. In 1982 pulpwood cut, 3,867,994·3 cords; sawtimber cut, 927·4m. bd ft.

INDUSTRY. The manufacturing industries are chiefly those associated with petroleum, chemicals, lumber, food, paper. Investment in manufacturing, 1980–81, about $9,000m.

TOURISM. Travellers spent an estimated $3,300m. in 1982. State tax revenue,

$99·3m. (3% of state tax revenue). New Orleans is the site of the Louisiana World Exposition in 1984.

COMMUNICATIONS

Roads. The state has more than 16,326 miles of public roads. In June 1982, over 4·6m. vehicles were registered in the state.

Railways. In 1980 the railways in the state had a length of about 3,700 miles.

Aviation. There were, 1981, about 240 commercial and private airports.

Shipping. In 1981 New Orleans handled 188·9m. tons of cargo. The Mississippi and other waterways provide 7,500 miles of navigable water.

JUSTICE, RELIGION, EDUCATION AND WELFARE

Justice. Prisons, Oct. 1982, had 9,257 inmates.

Since 1961 there has been 1 execution; total executions by electrocution since 1930 were 136.

Religion. The Roman Catholic Church is the largest denomination in Louisiana, with 1,316,441 members in 1979. The leading Protestant Churches are Southern Baptist, with (1979) 524,566 members; Methodist, (1979) 136,972.

Education. School attendance is compulsory between the ages of 7 and 15, both inclusive. In 1981–82 there were 1,493 public elementary and high schools which had 808,322 pupils with a current expenditure of $2,297 per pupil. Private schools had 157,330. In 1981–82, instructional staff had an average salary of $18,500. There are 16 four-year public colleges and universities and 12 non-public four-year institutions of higher learning. There are 53 state trade and vocational-technical schools. Superior instruction is given in the Louisiana State University system with 56,520 students (1982). Tulane University in New Orleans had 10,400; The Roman Catholic Loyola University in New Orleans had 4,550; Dillard University in New Orleans had 12,000; and the Southern University system, 11,800.

Health. In 1982 the state had 156 licensed hospitals (25,410 beds); 3 mental hospitals cared for 12,381 patients.

Social Security. In Dec. 1982, assistance was being given to 94,264 elderly persons; 64,709 families with dependent children; 4,120 general assistance cases and 635 Vietnamese and Cambodian refugees. Supplemental Security assistance was given to 68,915 blind and physically disabled people. Aid was from state and federal sources.

Books of Reference

Louisiana Almanac. New Orleans, 1979–80
The History and Government of Louisiana. Legislative Council, Baton Rouge, 1975
Louisiana State Agencies Handbook. Public Affairs Research Council of Louisiana. Baton Rouge, 1979
The State of the State: an Economic and Social Report to the Governor. Louisiana State Planning Office, New Orleans, 1978
Statistical Abstract of Louisiana. Division of Business and Economic Research, Univ. of New Orleans, 1977
Davis, E. A., *Louisiana, the Pelican State.* Louisiana State Univ. Press, Baton Rouge, 1975
Hansen, H., (ed.), *Louisiana, a Guide to the State.* Rev. ed. New York, 1971
Kniffen, F. B., *Louisiana, its Land and People.* Louisiana State Univ. Press, Baton Rouge, 1968

State Library: The Louisiana State Library, Baton Rouge, Louisiana. *State Librarian:* Thomas F. Jaques.

MAINE

HISTORY. After a first attempt in 1607, Maine was settled in 1623. From 1652 to 1820 it was part of Massachusetts and was admitted into the Union on 15 March 1820.

AREA AND POPULATION. Maine is bounded west, north and east by Canada, south-east by the Atlantic, south and south-west by New Hampshire. Area, 33,265 sq. miles, of which 2,269 are inland water. Of the state's total area, about 17·2m. acres (87%) are in timber and wood lots. Census population, 1 April 1980 1,125,027, an increase of 13·29% since 1970. Estimate (1981) 1,133,000. In 1980 live births numbered 16,095; deaths, 10,857; infant deaths, 140; marriages, 14,351; divorces 6,239.

Population for 5 census years was:

	White	Negro	Indian	Asiatic	Total	Per sq. mile
1910	739,995	1,363	892	121	742,371	24·8
1930	795,185	1,096	1,012	130	797,423	25·7
1950	910,846	1,221	1,522	185	913,774	29·4
			All others			
1970	985,276	2,800	3,972		992,048	31·0
1980	1,109,850	3,128	12,049		1,125,027	36·3

Of the total population in 1980, 48·5% were male, 40·7% were urban and 60·5% were 21 years or older.

The largest city in the state is Portland with a census population of 61,572 in 1980. Other cities (with population in 1980) are: Lewiston, 40,481; Bangor, 31,643; Auburn, 23,128; South Portland, 22,712; Augusta (capital), 21,819; Biddeford, 19,638; Waterville, 17,779.

CLIMATE. Average maximum temperatures range from 56·3°F in Waterville to 48·3°F in Caribou, but record high (since *c.* 1950) is 103°F. Average minimum ranges from 36·9°F in Rockland to 28·3°F in Greenville, but record low (also in Greenville) is −42°F. Average annual rainfall ranges from 48·85″ in Machias to 36·09″ in Houlton. Average annual snowfall ranges from 118·7″ in Greenville to 59·7″ in Rockland. *See* New England, p. 1373.

CONSTITUTION AND GOVERNMENT. The constitution of 1820 is still in force, but it has been amended 143 times. In 1951, 1965 and 1973 the Legislature approved recodifications of the constitution as arranged by the Chief Justice under special authority.

The Legislature consists of the Senate with 33 members and the House of Representatives with 151 members, both Houses being elected simultaneously for 2 years. Apart from these legislators and the Governor (elected for 4 years), no other state officers are elected. The Justices of the Supreme Judicial Court give their opinion upon important questions of law and upon solemn occasions when required by the Governor, Senate or House of Representatives. The suffrage is possessed by all citizens, 18 years of age; persons under guardianship for reasons of mental illness have no vote. Indians residing on tribal reservations and otherwise qualified have the vote in all county, state and national elections but retain the right to elect their own tribal representative to the legislature.

In the 1980 presidential election Reagan polled 238,522 votes, Carter 220,974 and Anderson 53,327.

The state sends to Congress 2 senators and 2 representatives.

The capital is Augusta. The state is divided into 16 counties.

Governor: Joseph E. Brennan (D.), 1983–86 ($35,000).
Secretary of State: Rodney S. Quinn (D.), 1983–86 ($25,000).

BUDGET. For the financial year ending 30 June 1983 total general revenue was $1,282,798,224 and expenditure was $1,358,474,201.

Total net long-term debt on 30 June 1983 was $3·3m.

Per capita personal income (Dec. 1982) was $9,042.

NATURAL RESOURCES

Minerals. Minerals include sand and gravel, stone, lead, clay, copper, peat, silver and zinc. Mineral output, 1981, was valued at over $38·4m.

Agriculture. In 1982, 7,900 farms occupied 1·56m. acres; the average farm was 197 acres.

Cash receipts, 1982, $427·1m., of which $96·8 came from potatoes; Maine is the third largest producer of potatoes (about 9% of the country's total of 27m. cwt). Other important items include eggs ($93·2m.), dairy products ($106·1m.) and poultry ($26·8m.); these with potatoes provide 76% of receipts. Sweet corn, peas and beans, oats, hay, apples and blueberries are also grown. On 1 Jan. 1982 the farm animals included 59,000 milch cows, 146,000 all other cattle, 15,000 sheep, 9,400 swine.

Forestry. Lumber, wood turnings and pulp are important. In 1981 the cut of softwood was 769,195m. bd ft; hardwood, 150,898m. bd ft, and pulpwood, 3,417,586 cords. Spruce and fir, white pine, hemlock, white and yellow birch, sugar maple, northern white cedar, beech and red oak are the most important species cut. There were (1982) 17,200,000 acres of commercial forest (98% in private ownership). National forests comprise 37,500 acres; other federal, 35,800; state forests, 163,000 acres; municipal, 75,200 acres. Wood products industries are of great economic importance; in 1981 the lumber and wood industries' production was valued at $3,091·8m. (43% of industrial production). There were (1981) 384 primary manufacturers and over 800 secondary.

Fisheries. In 1982, 217,980,000 lb. of fish and shellfish (valued at $102,870,000 were landed; the catch included 22,893,000 lb. of lobsters (valued at $50,776,000). 50·8m. lb. of sardines ($3·3m.); 1·7m. lb. of scallops ($6·8m.); 4·3m. lb. of soft clams ($6·5m.); 15·67m. lb of dabs ($6·3m.).

INDUSTRY. In 1981, 2,246 manufacturing establishments reported 113,571 workers, earning $1,697·8m.; gross value of production, $7,854·1m. (increase of 10·6% from 1980). Leading industry is paper with 44 plants, 18,328 workers and output valued at $2,752·8m. (35% of the state's total manufactures).

TOURISM. There are about 3·5m. visitors annually, generating about $500m. in business.

COMMUNICATIONS

Roads. In 1983 there were 22,098 miles of roads, of which 3,973 miles were state highways and 4,359 miles were state-aided; town streets and miscellaneous, 13,766 miles. In March 1983, 1,725,558 motor vehicles were registered, including 603,291 passenger vehicles, 83,395 commercial vehicles and 38,872 motorcycles.

Railways. In 1983 there were nearly 1,525 miles of mainline railway tracks.

Aviation. Licensed airports, 1983, numbered 104, including 34 commercial public airports, 13 non-commercial and 4 commuter airports; there are 2 military airports, 27 private landing strips and 20 seaplane bases.

JUSTICE, RELIGION, EDUCATION AND WELFARE

Justice. The state's penal system in Sept. 1983 held 411 adults in the State Prison, 212 in the Correctional Center and 209 juveniles in the Youth Center. There is no capital punishment. Inmates serving life sentences are eligible for parole consideration after 15 years, less remission for good conduct, provided they were imprisoned before the passage of a new Criminal Code by the 107th Maine Legislature, which abolished the parole system.

Religion. The largest religious bodies are: Roman Catholic (270,283 members), Baptists (36,808 members) and Congregationalists (40,750 members), and other Christian Churches (34,066 members).

Education. Education is free for pupils from 5 to 21 years of age, and compulsory from 7 to 17. In 1981–82 the 772 public schools (619 elementary, 103 secondary and 50 combined elementary and secondary) had 12,829 staff and 216,313 enrolled pupils. In 1981–82 there were 153 private schools with 1,090 teachers and 15,836 pupils. Public school teachers' salaries, 1981–82, averaged $15,605. Total public expenditure on public elementary and secondary education in 1981–82, $423,510,684.

The state University of Maine, founded in 1865, had (1982–83) 968 professors and 27,768 students at 7 locations; Bowdoin College, founded in 1794 at Brunswick, had 104 professors and 1,379 students; Bates College at Lewiston, 99 professors and 1,452 students; Colby College at Waterville, 121 professors and 1,685 students; Husson College, Bangor, 33 professors and 1,499 students; Westbrook College at Westbrook, 50 professors and 1,036 students; Unity College at Unity, 20 professors and 327 students, and the University of New England (formerly St Francis College) at Biddeford, 29 professors and 725 students.

Health. In 1981 the state had 46 general hospitals (4,523 beds); 3 hospitals for mental diseases, acute and psychiatric care (318 beds); 130 nursing homes (8,591 beds).

Social Security. Supplemental Security Income (SSI) (maximum payment for single person, $314·30 per month) is administered by the Social Security Administration. It became effective on 1 Jan. 1974 and replaces former aid to the aged, blind and disabled, administered by the state with state and federal funds. SSI is supplemented by Medicaid for nursing home patients or hospital patients. State payments for SSI recipients for Jan. 1983 totalled $381,000, covering 19,856 cases. Aid to families with dependent children is granted where one or both parents are disabled or absent and income is insufficient; aid was being granted in Aug. 1983 to 16,952 families (31,123 children) with an average payment per family of $308·33 per month. Total aid under the programme, Aug. 1983, $5·2m. Payments under Maine Medical Assistance programme totalled $202m. for the financial year 1982–83. There is a programme of assistance for catastrophic illness. Child welfare services include basic child protective services, enforcing child support, establishing paternity and finding missing parents, foster home placements, adoptions; services in divorce cases and licensing of foster homes, day care and residential treatment services, and public guardianship. There are also protective services for adults.

Books of Reference

Maine Register, State Year-Book and Legislative Manual. Tower Publishing, Portland. Annual
Federal Writers' Project. *Maine, a Guide 'Down East'.* Courier Gazette, 1970
Banks, R., (ed.), *A History of Maine: a Collection of Readings on the History of Maine 1600–1970.* Kendall/Hunt, 1969
Banks, R., *Maine Becomes A State.* Wesleyan U.P., 1970
Day, C. A., *Farming in Maine, 1060–1940.* Univ. Maine Press, 1963
Rowe, W. H., *Maritime History of Maine.* Norton, New York, 1948

MARYLAND

HISTORY. Maryland, first settled in 1634, was one of the 13 original states.

AREA AND POPULATION. Maryland is bounded north by Pennsylvania, east by Delaware and the Atlantic, south by Virginia and West Virginia, with the Potomac River forming most of the boundary, and west by West Virginia. Chesapeake Bay almost cuts off the eastern end of the state from the rest. Area, 10,460 sq. miles, of which 623 sq. miles are inland water; in addition, water area under Maryland jurisdiction in Chesapeake Bay amounts to 1,726 sq. miles. Census population, 1 April 1980, 4,216,975, an increase since 1970 of 293,078 or 7·5%. Estimate (1981) 4,263,000. In 1980 births were 59,833 (14·2 per 1,000 population); deaths, 34,025 (8·1); infant deaths, 844 (14·1 per 1,000 live births); marriages (1981), 47,128 (11·1); divorces (1981), 17,150 (4).

Population for 5 federal censuses was:

	White	Negro	Indian	Asiatic	Total	Per sq. mile
1920	1,204,737	244,479	32	413	1,449,661	145·8
1930	1,354,226	276,379	50	871	1,631,526	165·0
1960	2,573,919	518,410	1,538	5,700	3,100,689	314·0
			All others			
1970	3,194,888	499,479	28,032		3,922,399	396·6
1980	3,158,838	958,150	99,987		4,216,975	428·7

Of the total population in 1980, 2,042,558 were male, 3,386,026 persons were urban and those 20 years old or older numbered 2,889,816.

The largest city in the state (containing 18·7% of the population of the state) is Baltimore, with 786,775 in 1980; population of metropolitan area, 2,174,023. Maryland residents in the Washington, D.C., metropolitan area total more than 1m.; other cities (1980) are Dundalk (71,293); Towson (51,083); Silver Spring (72.893); Bethesda (62,736), Bowie (33,695), Hagerstown (34,132), Annapolis (capital), 31,740. Incorporated places: Cumberland, 25,933; Cambridge, 11,703; Frederick, 28,086; Gaithersburg, 26,424; Rockville, 43,811.

CLIMATE. Baltimore. Jan. 36°F (2·2°C), July 79°F (26·1°C). Annual rainfall 41″ (1,026 mm). See Atlantic Coast, p. 1373.

CONSTITUTION AND GOVERNMENT. The present constitution dates from 1867; it has had 125 amendments. The General Assembly consists of a Senate of 47, and a House of Delegates of 141 members, both elected for 4 years, as are the Governor and Lieut.-Governor. Voters are citizens who have the usual residential qualifications. At the 1980 presidential election Carter polled 726,161 votes, Reagan 680,606 and Anderson 119,537.

Maryland sends to Congress 2 senators and 8 representatives.

The state capital is Annapolis. The state is divided into 23 counties and Baltimore City.

Governor: Harry R. Hughes (D.), 1983–86 ($60,000).
Lieut.-Governor: J. Joseph Curran (D.), 1983–86 ($52,500).
Secretary of State: Patricia Holtz ($36,000).

BUDGET. For the fiscal year ending 30 June 1982 general revenues were $4,573,766,000 ($2,686,385,000 from taxation). General expenditures, $4,792,849,000, including $934,163,000 for education and $1,362,042,000 for public welfare and health; $666,070,000 for highways.

Total authorized long-term state debt, 30 June 1982 was $3,006,793,000. (Issued and outstanding, $2,207,660,000; authorized but not issued, $799,133,000.)

Per capita personal income (1982) was $12,238.

ENERGY AND NATURAL RESOURCES

Minerals. Value of non-fuel mineral production, 1982, was $171·5m. Sand and gravel (9·7m. short tons) and stone (15·1m. short tons) account for over 62% of the total value. Coal is the leading mineral commodity by value followed by Portland cement, sand and gravel and stone. Output of coal was 3·5m. short tons, valued at about $109m. Natural gas is produced from 2 fields in Garrett County; 56m. cu. ft in 1981. A third gas field in the same county is used for natural gas storage.

Agriculture. Agriculture is an important industry in the state. In 1982 there were approximately 18,000 farms with an area of 2·8m. acres (35% of the land area).

Farm animals, 1 Jan. 1983, were: Milch cows, 120,000; all cattle, 375,000; swine, 200,000 (1982); sheep and lambs, 17,000; chickens (not broilers), 4·4m. (1982). The most important crops, 1981, were: corn for grain, 72·4m. bu.; soybeans, 10·9m. bu.; tobacco, 33m. lb., and hay, 551,000 tons.

Cash receipts from farm marketings, 1981, were $1,061·3m.; from livestock and livestock products, $697·1m., and crops, $364·2m. Dairy products and broilers are important.

INDUSTRY. In 1978 manufactories had 169,700 production workers earning $2,218·8m.; value added by manufacture, $7,739·2m. Chief industries are food and kindred products, primary metal products, electrical and electronic equipment, chemicals and products, transport equipment.

TOURISM. Tourism is one of the state's leading industries. In 1981 tourists spent over $2,700m.

COMMUNICATIONS

Roads. The state highway department maintained, 1 Jan. 1981, 5,243 miles of highways, of which 80 miles were toll roads. The 23 counties maintained 17,073 miles of highways, and the 159 municipalities (including the city of Baltimore) maintained 3,895 miles of streets and alleys. Total mileage, 1 Jan. 1981, of public highways, streets and alleys, 26,211 miles. In 1982, 3m. automobiles were registered.

Railways. Railways, in 1982, had 1,100 miles of line.

Aviation. There were, 1982, 39 commercially licensed airports.

Shipping. In 1982 Baltimore was the fourth largest US seaport in value of trade, fifth in tonnage handled.

JUSTICE, RELIGION, EDUCATION AND WELFARE

Justice. Prisons on 23 Sept. 1983 had 11,382 men and 393 women; the total equalled 275 per 100,000 population, a high rate, which may be explained by the fact that Maryland incarcerates domestic relations law violators in state prisons; state prisons also receive a considerable number of persons committed for misdemeanours by magistrates' courts of the counties as well as from Baltimore's court system.

Since 1930 there have been 68 executions (by lethal gas since 1957; earlier by hanging)—7 whites and 37 Negroes for murder, and 6 whites and 18 Negroes for rape. Last execution was June 1961.

Maryland's prison system has conducted a work-release programme for selected prisoners since 1963. All institutions have academic and vocational training programmes.

In accordance with the 1950 Supreme Court decisions declaring segregation unconstitutional, the University of Maryland and other public and private colleges admitted Negro students in Sept. 1956. Elementary and secondary schools accept the ruling, and gradual integration is under way in all counties under different methods.

Religion. Maryland was the first US state to give religious freedom to all who came within its borders. Present religious affiliations of the population are approximately: Protestant, 32%; Roman Catholic, 24%; Jewish, 10%; remaining 34% is non-related and other faiths.

Education. Education is compulsory from 6 to 16 years of age. In Sept. 1982 the public elementary schools (including kindergartens and secondary schools) had 699,201 pupils. Teachers and principals in the elementary and secondary schools numbered 40,366. Average salary of instructional staff in elementary and secondary schools (1981–82) was $21,899. Current expenditure by local school boards on education, 1982–83, was $2,250m., of which the state's contribution was $900m.

In 1982 there were 34 degree-granting 4-year institutions and 22 2-year colleges. The largest two were the University of Maryland system, with 61,717 students (Sept. 1982) and Towson State College with 14,858 students (Sept. 1982).

Health. In Jan. 1983, 81 hospitals (22,831 beds) were licensed by the State Department of Health and Mental Hygiene.

The Maryland State Department of Health, organized in 1874, was in 1969 made part of the Department of Health and Mental Hygiene which performs its functions through its central office, 23 county health departments and the Baltimore City Health Department. For the financial year 1982 the department's budget was $937,324,169, of which $643,137,961 were general funds and $15,242,957 special funds appropriated by the General Assembly. The balance of the budget, $278,943,251, derives from federal funds.

During financial year 1982 Maryland's programme of medical care for indigent and medically indigent patients covered an average of 354,309 persons. The programme, which covers in-patient and out-patient hospital services, laboratory services, skilled nursing home care, physician services, pharmacy services, dental services and home health services, cost approximately $474·3m.

Social Security. Under the supervision of the Department of Human Resources, local social service departments administer public assistance for needy persons. In June 1983 families with dependent children received $16,917,837 (188,634 recipients, average actual monthly payment $89.69); general public assistance payments were $2,203,077 (18,624 recipients, average actual monthly payments $118.29).

Books of Reference

Statistical Information: Maryland Department of Economic and Community Development, Annapolis, 21401.

Maryland Manual: A Compendium of Legal, Historical and Statistical Information Relating to the State of Maryland. Annapolis. Biennial

DiLisio, J. E., *Maryland.* Boulder, 1982

State Library: Maryland State Library, Annapolis. *Director:* Michael S. Miller.

MASSACHUSETTS

HISTORY. The first permanent settlement within the borders of the present state was made at Plymouth in Dec. 1620, by the Pilgrims from Holland, who were separatists from the English Church, and formed the nucleus of the Plymouth Colony. In 1628 another company of Puritans settled at Salem, forming eventually the Massachusetts Bay Colony. In 1630 Boston was settled. In the struggle which ended in the separation of the American colonies from the mother country, Massachusetts took the foremost part, and on 6 Feb. 1788 became the sixth state to ratify the US constitution.

AREA AND POPULATION. Massachusetts is bounded north by Vermont and New Hampshire, east by the Atlantic, south by Connecticut and Rhode Island and west by New York. Area, 8,284 sq. miles, 460 sq. miles being inland water. The census population 1 April 1980, was 5,737,037, an increase of 47,867 or 0·8% since 1970. Estimate (1981) 5,773,000. Births, 1981 were 73,931 (12·9 per 1,000 population); deaths, 52,814 (9·2 per 1,000); infant deaths, 710 (9·6 per 1,000 live births); marriages, 47,802 (8·3); divorces, 19,502 (3·4).

Population at 4 federal census years was:

	White	Negro	Other	Total	Per sq. mile
1950	4,611,503	73,171	5,840	4,690,514	598·4
1960	5,023,144	111,842	13,592	5,148,578	656·8
1970	5,477,624	175,817	35,729	5,689,170	725·8
1980	5,362,836	221,279	152,922	5,737,037	732·0

Of the total population in 1980, 47·6% were male, 83·8% were urban and 32% were 21 years old or older.

In 1980 the population of the principal towns and cities was:

Boston	562,994	Fall River	92,574	Framingham	65,113
Worcester	161,799	Lowell	92,418	Lawrence	63,175
Springfield	153,319	Quincy	84,743	Waltham	58,200
New Bedford	98,478	Newton	83,622	Medford	58,076
Cambridge	95,322	Lynn	78,471	Weymouth	55,601
Brockton	95,172	Somerville	77,372	Chicopee	55,112

The largest of 10 standard metropolitan statistical areas, 1980 census were: Boston, 2,763,357; Springfield–Chicopee–Holyoke, 530,668; Worcester, 372,940.

CLIMATE. Boston. Jan. 28°F (–2·2°C), July 71°F (21·7°C). Annual rainfall 41″ (1,036 mm). *See* New England, p. 1373.

CONSTITUTION AND GOVERNMENT. The constitution dates from 1780 and has had 116 amendments. The legislative body, styled the General Court of the Commonwealth of Massachusetts, meets annually, and consists of the Senate with 40 members, elected biennially, and the House of Representatives of 160 members, elected for 2 years. The Governor and Lieut.-Governor are elected for 4 years. The state sends 2 senators and 11 representatives to Congress.

At the 1980 presidential election Reagan polled 1,056,223 votes, Carter 1,053,800.

Electors are all citizens 18 years of age or older.

The capital is Boston. The state has 14 counties, 39 cities and 312 towns.

Governor: Michael S. Dukakis (D.), 1983–86 ($40,000).
Lieut.-Governor: John F. Kerry (D.) ($30,000).
Secretary of the Commonwealth: Michael J. Connolly (D.) ($30,000).

BUDGET. For the fiscal year ending 30 June 1983 the total revenue of the state was $8,216,514,068 ($4,992·5m. from taxes and $1,874·1m. from federal aid); general expenditures, $8,107,763,929m. ($558·4m. for education, $593·6m. for highway and transport construction and $1,809·8m. for public welfare).

The net long-term debt on 30 June 1983 amounted to $3,181·6m.

Per capita personal income (1982) was $12,088.

NATURAL RESOURCES

Minerals. There is little mining within the state. Total mineral output in 1982 was valued at $89m., of which most came from sand, gravel and stone.

Agriculture. On 1 Jan. 1980 there were 5,900 farms (11,179 in 1959) with an area of 680,000 acres.

Cash income, 1982, totalled $362·8m.; dairy, $87·9m.; greenhouse and nursery, $92m.; poultry, $27·5m.; vegetables, $39·5m.; tobacco, $15m.; cranberries, $54m.; other fruit, $18·3m.; potatoes, $3·8m.; all other, $24·8m.

Principal 1980 crops include cranberries, 1,185,000 bbls; apples, 2·4m. (42-lb. units); potatoes, 748,000 cwt, and tobacco, 2m. lb. On 1 Jan. 1980 farms in the state had 45,000 milch cows, 103,000 all cattle, 60,000 swine (Dec. 1979), 126,000 turkeys and 1·8m. chickens.

Forestry. State forests cover about 256,000 acres. Total forest land covers about 3m. acres. Commercially important hardwoods are sugar maple, northern red oak and white ash; softwoods are white pine and hemlock. About 240m. bd ft of timber are cut annually.

Fisheries. The 1982 catch amounted to 299·6m. lb. of finfish valued at $108m.; 44·3m. lb. of shellfish ($96m.); including 11·2m. lb. of lobster ($25·6m.).

INDUSTRY. In 1982, 10,694 manufacturing establishments employed an average of 640,044 workers, who earned $12,608·2m.; value added by manufacture (1978) was $18,632m. The 3 most important manufacturing groups, based on employment, were electric and electronic equipment, machinery (except electrical), instruments and related products.

LABOUR. In Aug. 1983 the work force was 3,006,000. Changes in the industrial pattern have caused the loss of jobs in the shoe and textile industries. In 1981 there were 102 work stoppages involving 28,700 workers which resulted in 696,000 man-days idle.

COMMUNICATIONS

Roads. In Dec. 1983 the state had 33,800 miles of roads and streets and in 1982 registered 4m. motor vehicles.

Railways. In 1983 there were 1,310 miles of mainline railway.

Aviation. There were, in 1983, 52 aircraft landing areas for commercial operation, of which 27 were publicly owned.

Shipping. The state has 3 deep-water harbours, the largest of which is Boston (port trade (1981), 20,306,450 short tons). Other ports are Fall River and New Bedford.

JUSTICE, RELIGION, EDUCATION AND WELFARE

Justice. On 9 Sept. 1983 state penal institutions held 4,574 inmates. There have been no executions since 1947.

Religion. The principal religious bodies are the Roman Catholics, Jewish Congregations, Methodists, Episcopalians and Unitarians.

Education. A regulation effective from 1 Sept. 1972 makes school attendance compulsory for ages 6–16. In 1981–82 expenditure by cities and towns on public schools was $3,089m., including $201m. debt retirement and service payments. In 1981–82 there were 61,632 classroom teachers and 941,396 pupils.

Within the state there were (1982) 126 degree-granting institutions of higher learning (including 89 colleges and universities) with (1982–83) 14,274 full-time teaching staff and about 415,320 students. Some leading institutions are:

Year opened	Name and location of universities and colleges	Students 1982
1636	Harvard University, Cambridge [1]	21,252
1793	Williams College, Williamstown [1]	2,006
1821	Amherst College, Amherst [1]	1,561
1837	Mount Holyoke College, South Hadley [2]	1,979
1843	College of the Holy Cross, Worcester [1]	2,511
1852	Tufts University, Medford [1,3]	6,778
1861	Mass. Institute of Technology, Cambridge [1]	9,510
1863	University of Massachusetts, Amherst [1]	26,638
1863	Boston College (RC), Chestnut Hill [1]	14,171
1865	Worcester Polytechnic Institute, Worcester [1]	3,552
1869	Boston University, Boston [1]	28,042
1870	Wellesley College, Wellesley [2]	2,220
1875	Smith College, Northampton [1]	2,971
1879	Radcliffe College, Cambridge [1]	2,435
1885	Springfield College, Springfield [1]	2,511
1887	Clark University, Worcester [1]	3,169
1894	University of Lowell [1]	14,562
1898	Northeastern University, Boston [1,4]	42,406
1899	Simmons College, Boston [2]	2,773
1948	Brandeis University, Waltham [1]	3,580

[1] Co-educational.   [3] Includes Jackson College for women.
[2] For women only.   [4] Includes Forsyth Dental Center School.

Health. In 1980 the state had 186 hospitals (with 39,170 beds); average daily census, 38,799, of which 7,890 patients were in public and private mental hospitals and in 1983 3,446 patients were in institutions for the mentally retarded.

Social Security. The Department of Public Welfare had an appropriation of $1,727m. in 1982 and paid $477m. in aid to families with dependent children (average 110,600 families per month); other main items were general relief (average 22,601 cases), Supplemental Security Income (average 109,300 cases) and Medical Assistance (average 307,200 cases).

Books of Reference

Annual Reports. Massachusetts and US Boards, Commissions, Departments and Divisions, Boston, 1980

Manual for the General Court. By Clerk of the Senate and Clerk of the House of
Representatives, Boston, Mass. Biennial
Levitan, D., and Mariner, E. C., *Your Massachusetts Government.* Boston, Mass., 1980
Higher Education Publications, Washington, D.C., 1983

MICHIGAN

HISTORY. Michigan, first settled by Marquette at Sault Ste Marie in 1668,
became the Territory of Michigan in 1805, with its boundaries greatly enlarged in
1818 and 1834; it was admitted into the Union with its present boundaries on 26
Jan. 1837.

AREA AND POPULATION. Michigan is divided into two by Lake
Michigan. The northern part is bounded south by the lake and by Wisconsin, west
and north by Lake Superior, east by the North Channel of Lake Huron; between
the two latter lakes the Canadian border runs through straits at Sault Ste Marie.
The southern part is bounded west and north by Lake Michigan, east by Lake
Huron, Ontario and Lake Erie, south by Ohio and Indiana. Area, 58,527 sq. miles,
of which 56,954 sq. miles are land area, 1,573 sq. miles are inland water. Census
population, 1 April 1980, 9,262,078, an increase of 380,252 or 4·3% since 1970.
Estimate (1981) 9,204,000. In 1981 births were 140,579; deaths, 75,818; infant
deaths, 1,851; marriages, 85,252; divorces, 43,167.

Population of 5 federal census years was:

	White	Negro	Indian	Asiatic	Total	Per sq. mile
1910	2,785,247	17,115	7,519	292	2,810,173	48·9
1930	4,663,507	169,453	7,080	2,285	4,842,325	84·9
1960	7,085,865	717,581	9,701	10,047	7,823,194	137·2

	White	Negro	All others	Total	Per sq. mile
1970	7,833,474	991,066	50,543	8,875,083	156·2
1980	7,872,241	1,199,023	190,814	9,262,078	162·6

Of the total population in 1980, 4,513,951 were male, 6,547,842 persons were
urban and those 20 years old or older numbered 6,144,925. 162,440 were of Spanish origin.

Population of the chief cities (census of 1 April 1980) was:

Detroit	1,203,339	Dearborn	90,660	Royal Oak	70,893
Grand Rapids	181,843	Westland	84,603	Dearborn Heights	67,706
Warren	161,134	Kalamazoo	79,722	Troy	67,102
Flint	159,611	Taylor	77,568	Wyoming	59,616
Lansing (capital)	130,414	Saginaw	77,508	Farmington Hills	58,056
Sterling Heights	108,999	Pontiac	76,715	Roseville	54,311
Ann Arbor	107,316	St Clair Shores	76,210		
Livonia	104,814	Southfield	75,568		

Larger standard metropolitan areas, 1980 census: Detroit, 4,344,139; Grand
Rapids, 601,106; Flint, 521,541; Lansing, 467,584.

CLIMATE. Detroit. Jan. 25°F (−3·9°C), July 72°F (22·2°C). Annual rainfall 32″
(813 mm). Grand Rapids. Jan. 23°F (−5°C), July 72°F (22·2°C). Annual rainfall
32″ (803 mm). Lansing. Jan. 23°F (−5°C), July 71°F (21·7°C). Annual rainfall 30″
(754 mm). *See* Great Lakes, p. 1373.

CONSTITUTION AND GOVERNMENT. The present constitution was
adopted in April 1963 and became effective on 1 Jan. 1964. The Senate consists of
38 members, elected for 4 years, and the House of Representatives of 110 members,
elected for 2 years. The Governor and Lieut.-Governor are elected for 4 years.
Electors are all citizens over 18 years of age meeting the usual residential requirements. The state sends to Congress 2 senators and 18 representatives.

At the 1980 presidential election Reagan polled 1,915,225 votes, Carter 1,661,532 and Anderson 275,223.

The capital is Lansing. The state is organized in 83 counties.

Governor: James J. Blanchard (D.), 1983–86 ($65,000).
Lieut.-Governor: Martha Griffiths (D.), 1983–86 ($45,000).
Secretary of State: Richard H. Austin (D.), ($60,000).

BUDGET. For the financial year ending 30 Sept. 1982, the general fund revenue was $7,763,766,000 (taxation, $6,508,251,002, and federal aid, $2,577,866,176); total revenue, $10,412,113,599; special revenue funds, $4,000,885,000; general expenditures, $10,011,261,489.

Per capita personal income (1982 estimate) was $11,188.

ENERGY AND NATURAL RESOURCES

Minerals. Most important minerals by value of production are iron ore, petroleum and cement. Output (1982): Iron ore, 6·7m. long tons ($313m.); Portland cement, 3·1m. short tons ($147·3m.); petroleum, 31·6m. bbls ($1,036·3m.); copper, 32,000 short tons ($35·9m.); sand and gravel, 24m. short tons ($72·4m.); stone, 21·7m. short tons ($70·9m.); lime, 680,000 short tons ($32·6m.); natural gas, 143,319m. cu. ft ($460·6m.). Total value of natural salines, $182m. Mineral output in 1982 was valued at $2,475·1m.

Agriculture. The state, formerly agricultural, is now chiefly industrial. In 1982 it contained 65,000 farms with a total area of 11·5m. acres; the average farm was 177 acres. Cash income, 1981, from crops, $1,678·2m.; from livestock and products, $1,111·1m. Principal crops are maize (production, 1981, 273m. bu.), oats (21m. bu.), wheat (41·5m. bu.), sugar-beet (2m. tons); soybeans (29·1m. bu.), hay (3·8m. tons). On 1 Jan. 1982 there were in the state 130,000 sheep, 396,000 milch cows, 1·45m. all cattle, 690,000 swine, 8·1m. chickens and 50,000 turkey breeder hens. In 1981 the wool clip yielded 975,000 lb. of wool.

Forestry. The forests of Michigan consist of 19,373,400 acres, about 52% of total state land area. About 18·9m. acres of this total is commercial forest, 67% of which is privately owned, 19% state forest, 13% national forest and 1% in various public ownerships. Three-fourths of the timber volume is hardwoods, principally hard and soft maples, aspen, oak and elm. Christmas trees are another important forest crop.

Michigan leads in the number of state parks and public campsites. There are 83 state parks and recreation areas, 6 state forests, 5 national forests and 3 national parks. There are 180 state forest campgrounds and 66 state game and wildlife areas.

INDUSTRY. Transport equipment and non-electrical machinery are the most important manufactures. The state ranks first in 19 manufacturing categories; among principal products are motor vehicles and trucks, cement, chemicals, furniture, paper, cereal, baby food and pharmaceuticals. Total labour force, 1982, 4,275,000, of which 871,100 are in manufacturing.

COMMUNICATIONS

Roads. State trunk-line mileage (31 July 1980) totalled, 9,500, all hard surfaced. Passenger car registrations, 18 Sept. 1981, 5,075,091.

Railways. On 1 Jan. 1980 there were 6,153 miles of railway and 383 miles of active car-ferry routes.

Aviation. Airports (1980) numbered 205 licensed airports, 88 certified but not licensed and 23 air carrier airports.

JUSTICE, RELIGION, EDUCATION AND WELFARE

Justice. The 1963 Constitution provides that no person shall be denied the equal protection of the law; nor shall any person be denied the enjoyment of his civil or political rights or be discriminated against in the exercise thereof because of religion, colour or national origin. A Civil Rights Commission was established, and its powers and duties were implemented by legislation in the extra session of 1963. Earlier statutory enactments guaranteeing civil rights in specific areas are as follows. An Act of 1885, last amended in 1956, orders all places of public accommodation and resort, etc., to furnish equal accommodations without discrimination. An Act of 1941, as last amended, forbids the Civil Service in counties with population exceeding 1m. to discriminate against employees or applicants on the ground of political, racial or religious opinions or affiliations. An Act of 1881 incorporated into the school code of 1955 forbids any discrimination in school facilities. An Act of 1893 incorporated in the insurance code of 1956 prohibits insurance companies from discriminating between white and coloured persons.

In 1951 the legislature restored the unique one-man grand jury system abandoned in 1949.

Religion. There were 2,004,288 Roman Catholics in 1979; largest Protestant denominations, Lutherans, 500,000; United Methodists, 278,245; United Presbyterians, 155,864; Episcopalians, 63,873.

Education. Education is compulsory for children from 6 to 16 years of age. The operating expenditure for graded and ungraded public schools for the fiscal year ending 30 June 1982, was $4,311,715,359; total, including capital and debt expenditures, $5,056,640,674. In 1981–82 there were 574 school districts (elementary and secondary schools) with 1,792,334 pupils and 78,447 teachers. Teachers' salaries in 1982 averaged $24,304.

In the autumn of 1981 the public 4-year institutions reported 235,027 students and the non-public institutions reported 67,509 students. The community colleges had an autumn enrolment (1981) of 211,871 students.

Universities and students (1982):

Founded	Name	Students
1817	University of Michigan	35,629
1849	Eastern Michigan University	18,078
1855	Michigan State University	42,730
1884	Ferris State College	11,008
1885	Michigan Technological University	7,640
1868	Wayne State University	29,775
1892	Central Michigan University	17,132
1889	Northern Michigan University	8,377
1903	Western Michigan University	20,580
1946	Lake Superior State College	2,494
1959	Oakland University	11,721
1960	Grand Valley State College	6,366
1965	Saginaw Valley College	4,370

Social Welfare. Old-age assistance is provided for persons 65 years of age or older who have resided in Michigan for one year before application; assets must not exceed various limits. In 1974 federal Supplementary Security Income (SSI) replaced the adults' programme. In 1982 aid was supplied to a monthly average of 730,739 dependent children in 232,939 families at $424·85 per family.

Health. In 1981 the state had 216 hospitals (40,217 beds) licensed by the state and 21 psychiatric hospitals.

In 1957 a programme came into force which provided for free medical care and hospital treatment for certain categories of persons. On 1 Oct. 1966 this programme was superseded by a more comprehensive programme called 'Medicaid' which, with federal support, disbursed in 1981, $1,297·8m. to 480,299 persons.

Books of Reference

Michigan Department of Economic Development. *Publications.* Lansing
Michigan Manual. Dept of State. Lansing. Biennial
Bureau of Business Research, Wayne State University. *Michigan Statistical Abstract.* Detroit, 1983
Bald, F. C., *Michigan in Four Centuries.* 2nd ed. New York, 1961

Blanchard, J. J., *Economic Report of the Governor 1983*. Lansing, 1983
Catton. B., *Michigan—a Bicentennial History*. Norton, New York, 1976
Lewis, F. E., *State and Local Government in Michigan*. Lansing, 1979
Dunbar, W. F., and May, G. S., *Michigan: A History of the Wolverine State*. Grand Rapids, 1980
Sommers, L. (ed.), *Atlas of Michigan*. East Lansing, 1977

State Library Services: Library of Michigan, Lansing 48909. *Interim State Librarian:* Susan M. Haskin.

MINNESOTA

HISTORY. Minnesota, first explored in the 17th century and first settled in the 20 years following the establishment of Fort Snelling (1819), was made a Territory in 1849 (with parts of North and South Dakota), and was admitted into the Union, with its present boundaries, on 11 May 1858.

AREA AND POPULATION. Minnesota is bounded north by Canada, east by Lake Superior and Wisconsin, with the Mississippi River forming the boundary in the south-east, south by Iowa, west by South and North Dakota, with the Red River forming the boundary in the north-west. Area, 84,402 sq. miles, of which 4,854 sq. miles are inland water. Census population, 1 April 1980, 4,075,970, an increase of 7·1% since 1970. Estimate (1981), 4,094,000. Births in 1980, 67,843 (16·6 per 1,000 population); deaths, 33,415 (8·2); infant deaths, 679 (10 per 1,000 live births); marriages, 37,625 (9·2); divorces, 15,274 (3·7).

Population in 5 census years was:

	White	Negro	Indian	Asiatic	Total	Per sq. mile
1910	2,059,227	7,084	9,053	344	2,075,708	25·7
1930	2,542,599	9,445	11,077	832	2,563,953	32·0
1960	3,371,603	22,263	15,496	3,642	3,413,864	42·7

	White	Negro	All others	Total	Per sq. mile
1970	3,736,038	34,868	34,163	3,805,069	47·6
1980	3,935,770	53,344	86,856	4,075,970	51·4

Of the 1980 population, 1,997,826 were male; 2,725,270 were urban; those 21 years of age or older numbered 2,656,947.

The largest cities are Minneapolis, 370,951; St Paul (capital), 270,230 (Minneapolis–St Paul standard metropolitan statistical area, 1,972,208 in 1970); Duluth, 92,811; Bloomington, 81,831; Rochester, 57,890.

CLIMATE. Duluth. Jan. 8°F (–13·3°C), July 63°F (17·2°C). Annual rainfall 29" (719 mm). Minneapolis-St. Paul. Jan. 12°F (–11·1°C), July 71°F (21·7°C). Annual rainfall 26" (656 mm). *See* Great Lakes, p. 1373.

CONSTITUTION AND GOVERNMENT. The present constitution dates from 1858; it has had 94 amendments. The Legislature consists of a Senate of 67 members, elected for 4 years, and a House of Representatives of 134 members, elected for 2 years. The Governor and Lieut.-Governor are elected for 4 years. The state sends to Congress 2 senators and 8 representatives.

In the 1980 presidential election Carter polled 954,173 votes, Reagan 873,268.

The capital is St Paul. There are 87 counties, four containing less than 400 sq. miles, the largest being 6,092 sq. miles.

Governor: Rudy Perpich (D.), 1983–86 ($66,500).
Lieut.-Governor: Marlene Johnson (D.), 1983–86 ($38,000).
Secretary of State: Joan Anderson Growe (DFL.), 1983–86 ($36,000).

BUDGET. The general fund budget for the 1979–81 2-year period was $7,900m.; tax relief $760m., education $2,848m., public welfare $1,112m., transport $683m.

Net long-term debt, 30 June 1980, was $881m.

Per capita personal income (1979) was $8,865.

NATURAL RESOURCES

Minerals. The iron ore and taconite industry is the most important in the USA. Production of usable iron ore in 1981 was 50m. tons, value $2,062m. Other important minerals are sand and gravel, crushed and dimension stone, lime and manganiferous ore. Total value of mineral production, 1981, $2,151·9m.

Agriculture. Agriculture, including processing, is the leading industry. In 1982 there were 103,000 farms with a total area of 30·4m. acres (60% of the land area); the average farm was of 295 acres. Average value of land and buildings (1982) $348,800. Commercial farms in 1978 numbered 102,963; 12% of the farms were operated by tenant-farmers. Cash income, 1981, from crops, $3,520m.; from livestock, $3,390m. In 1981 Minnesota ranked first in oats, wild rice and timothy seed, and second in spring wheat, sugar-beet, red clover seed, non-fat dry milk, cheese, rye, processing sweet corn, turkeys and sunflower seed. Other important products are hay, butter, eggs, sheep, flaxseed, milch cows, milk, corn, barley, swine, cattle for market, soybeans, honey, potatoes, chickens, dry edible beans, and green peas for processing. Of livestock, cattle represents 13·7% of total farm income, swine 11·5% and milk 18·9%. Of crops, corn represents 17·3% and soybeans 14%. On 1 Jan. 1982 the farm animals included 3·88m. all cattle, 905,000 milch cows, 335,000 sheep and lambs, 4·3m. swine, 13·6m. chickens and 567,000 breeder hen turkeys. Turkey production, 1981, 25·7m. In 1981 the wool clip amounted to 2·25m. lb. of wool from 308,000 sheep.

Honey production (1981), 8·2m. lb; beeswax, 188,000 lb. About 95% of US commercial wild rice paddies are in Minnesota. Production from 16,000 acres (1981), 2·3m. lb. of processed wild rice; production from natural stands, 1m. lb.

Forestry. Forests of commercial timber cover 13·69m. acres, of which 53·5% is government-owned. The value of forest products in 1980 was $1,917m.; $770·9m. of this was from pulpwood and $977·3m. from secondary manufacturing. Logging, pulping, saw-mills and associated industries employed 52,294 in 1980.

INDUSTRY. In 1980 manufacturing establishments employed 384,000 workers; value added by manufacture was $14,305m.

TOURISM. Estimates for 1981 give approximately 8·5m. tourists (55% from outside the state), with a total expenditure of $2,256m.

COMMUNICATIONS

Roads. The state highway system (interstate and state trunk highways) covered 12,100 miles in 1981; total highway, road and street mileage, 130,800. In 1981, 2,092,170 passenger automobiles were registered.

Railways. There are 8 Class I railroads operating, with mainline mileage of 7,229 (total track miles, 7,510).

Aviation. Airports in 1980 numbered 593 (141 municipal, 27 privately owned for public use, 387 personal use, 11 public seaplane bases, 14 private, 74 for personal use).

JUSTICE, RELIGION, EDUCATION AND WELFARE

Justice. A Civil Rights Act (1927) forbids places of public resort to exclude persons 'on account of race or colour' and another section forbids insurance companies to discriminate 'between persons of the same class on account of race'. Contractors on public works may have their contracts cancelled if 'in the hiring of common or skilled labour' they are found to have discriminated on the grounds of 'race, creed or colour'. The state's penal reformatory system on 31 June 1971 held 2,144 men and women. There is no death penalty in Minnesota.

Religion. The chief religious bodies are: Lutheran with 1,112,495 members in 1970; Roman Catholic, 1,061,614; Methodist, 213,084. Total membership of all denominations, 3,044,055.

Education. In 1981, there were 51,720 kindergarten students, 318,852 elementary students, and 381,726 secondary students enrolled in 1,631 public schools. There were 6,588 kindergarten students, 51,405 elementary students and 33,084 secondary students enrolled in 553 private schools. There were 44,048 public school classroom teachers and 5,252 private. The average salary for a public classroom teacher was $18,161. Total public school expenditures for 1981 were $2,211m. and total revenues were $2,199m. Of the total revenues, $1,179m. came from State funds and $134m. came from Federal funds. The University of Minnesota at Minneapolis–St Paul, chartered in 1851 and opened in 1869, had a total enrolment in 1981 of 58,705 students. The 18 public community colleges (2-year) had a total enrolment of 34,894. Seven state universities (4-year) had 1981 enrolment of 41,361, State universities are at Bemidji, Mankato, Marshall, Moorhead, St Cloud, Winona, Minneapolis and St Paul.

Health. In 1980 the state had 165 general acute hospitals with 17,601 beds. Patients resident (average daily census) in institutions under the Department of Public Welfare included 1,520 mentally ill, 2,692 mentally retarded and 637 chemically dependent. There are 2 state nursing homes with (1979–80) a 753-bed capacity.

Social Security. On 1 Jan. 1974 the state administered programmes of old age assistance, aid to the disabled, and aid to the blind were given over to federal administration under the Supplemental Security Income (SSI) Programme. For some states, the new maintenance grants were less than under the state administered programmes. These states could establish a supplemental programme to correct the deficiency. The Minnesota Supplemental Aid (MSA) programme was later expanded to cover individuals who were not receiving SSI and to provide one-time payment for certain special needs such as major home repair, replacement of essential basic furniture or appliances, moving expenses and fuel and utility adjustments.

Books of Reference

Statistical Information: Current information is obtainable from the Department of Energy, Planning and Development (480 Cedar Street, St Paul 55101); non-current material from the Reference Library, Minnesota Historical Society, St Paul 55101. Demographic information (current) is available on request from the Office of State Demographer, DEP D, 101 Capitol Square Building, 550 Cedar Street, St Paul 55101.

Legislative Manual. Secretary of State. St Paul. Biennial
Minnesota Statistical Profile. Dept. of Energy, Planning and Development, Biennial
Minnesota Agriculture Statistics. Dept. of Agric., St Paul. Annual
Manufacturers' Directory. Nelson Name Service, Minneapolis, Biennial

MISSISSIPPI

HISTORY. Mississippi, settled in 1716, was organized as a Territory in 1798 and admitted into the Union on 10 Dec. 1817. In 1804 and in 1812 its boundaries were extended, but in March 1817 a part was taken to form the new Territory of Alabama, leaving the boundaries substantially as at present.

AREA AND POPULATION. Mississippi is bounded north by Tennessee, east by Alabama, south by the Gulf of Mexico and Louisiana, west by the Mississippi River forming the boundary with Louisiana and Arkansas. Area, 47,689 sq. miles, 457 sq. miles being inland water. Census population, 1 April 1980, 2,520,638, an increase of 13·6% since 1970. Estimate (1981), 2,531,000. Births, 1982, were 45,537; deaths, 22,776; infant deaths, 682; marriages, 27,584; divorces, 12,861.

Population of 6 federal census years was:

	White	Negro	Indian	Asiatic	Total	Per sq. mile
1910	786,111	1,009,487	1,253	263	1,797,114	38·8
1930	998,077	1,009,718	1,458	568	2,009,821	42·4
1950	1,188,632	986,494	2,502	1,286	2,178,914	46·1
1960	1,257,546	915,743	3,119	1,481	2,178,141	46·1
			All others			
1970	1,393,283	815,770	7,859		2,216,912	46·9
1980	1,615,190	887,206	18,242		2,520,638	53·0

Of the population in 1980, 1,213,878 were male, 1,192,805 were urban and 1,601,157 were 20 years old or older.

The largest city (1980) is Jackson, 202,895. Others are: Biloxi, 49,311; Meridian, 46,577; Hattiesburg, 40,829; Greenville, 40,613; Gulfport, 39,676; Pascagoula, 29,318; Columbus, 27,383; Vicksburg, 25,434; Tupelo, 23,905.

CLIMATE. Jackson.Jan. 47°F (8·3°C), July 82°F (27·8°C). Annual rainfall 49″ (1,221 mm). Vicksburg. Jan. 48°F (8·9°C), July 81°F (27·2°C). Annual rainfall 52″ (1,311 mm). *See* Central Plains, p. 1372.

CONSTITUTION AND GOVERNMENT. The present constitution was adopted in 1890 without ratification by the electorate; it has since had 48 amendments.

The Legislature consists of a Senate (52 members) and a House of Representatives (122 members), both elected for 4 years, as are also the Governor and Lieut.-Governor. Electors are all citizens who have resided in the state 1 year, in the county 1 year, in the election district 6 months next before the election and have been registered according to law. In the 1980 presidential election Reagan polled 441,089 votes, Carter 429,281 and Anderson 12,036.

The state is represented in Congress by 2 senators and 5 representatives.

The capital is Jackson; there are 82 counties.

Governor: William Forrest Winter (D.), 1980–84 ($53,000).
Lieut.-Governor: Bradford Johnson Dye (D.) ($34,000).
Secretary of State: Edwin Lloyd Pittman (D.) ($34,000).

BUDGET. For the fiscal year ending 30 June 1983 the general revenues were $2,590,264,359 (taxation, $1,578,079,761; federal aid, $793,216,611; other state resources, $218,967,987), and general expenditures were $2,679,986,700 ($919,570,469 for education, $313,331,421 for highways and $165,994,011 for public welfare).

On 30 June 1983 the total net long-term debt was $1,121·1m.

Per capita personal income (1980) was $6,580 (lowest in US).

ENERGY AND NATURAL RESOURCES

Minerals. Petroleum and natural gas account for about 90% (by value) of mineral production. Output of petroleum, 1981, was 34,381,093 bbls and of natural gas 229,404,669m. cu. ft. There are 6 oil refineries. Value of oil and gas products sold 1981 was $1,807,679,550.

Agriculture. Agriculture is the leading industry of the state because of the semi-tropical climate and a rich productive soil. In 1983 farms with annual sales of $1,000 or more numbered 51,000 with an area of 14·3m. acres. Average size of farm was 280 acres. This compares with an average farm size of 138 acres in 1960.

Cash income from all crops and livestock during 1982, including government payments, was $2,535·2m. Cash income from crops was $1,488·1m. and from livestock and products, $943·2m. The chief product is cotton, cash income $651·9m. from 1m. acres producing 1·76m. bales of 480 lb. Soybeans (92·3m. bu. from 3·5m. acres), rice, corn, hay, wheat, oats, sorghum, peanuts, pecans, sweet potatoes, peaches, other vegetables, nursery and forest products continue to contribute.

On 1 Jan. 1983 there were 1·8m. head of cattle and calves on Mississippi farms. Milch cows and heifers which had calved totalled 96,000, beef cows and heifers that had calved, 874,000; hogs and pigs, 280,000. Of cash income from livestock and products, 1982, $267·4m. was credited to cattle and calves. Cash income from poultry and eggs totalled $427·7m.; dairy products, $127·3m.; swine, $56·9m.

In 1983 there were 82 soil-conservation districts covering 26,342,406 acres.

Forestry. In 1982 income from forestry amounted to $406m.; output of logs, lumber, etc., was 1,009·5m. bd ft; pulpwood, 4,490,389 cords; stump wood, 27,449 tons; turpentine gum, 313 bbls. There are about 16·5m. acres of forest (55% of the state's area). National forests area, 1983, 1·1m. acres.

INDUSTRY. In 1982 the 1,968 manufacturing establishments employed 220,469 workers, earning $2,981,686,298.

TOURISM. Total receipts, 1982, $1,100m. from about 8m. tourists.

COMMUNICATIONS

Roads. The state in July 1983 maintained 10,175 miles of highways, of which 10,095 miles were paved. In 1982, 1,590,472 cars were registered.

Railways. The state in 1983 had 3,101·14 miles of railway.

Aviation. There were 101 public airports in 1983, 91 of them general. There were also 72 privately owned airfields.

JUSTICE, RELIGION, EDUCATION AND WELFARE

Justice. In 1983 there was 1 execution; from 1955 to 1983 executions (by gas-chamber) totalled 32 (8 whites and 14 Negroes for murder, 9 Negroes for rape and 1 Negro for armed robbery). On 20 Oct. 1983 the state prisons had 5,552 inmates.

Religion. Southern Baptists in Mississippi (1982), 632,000 members; Methodists 200,336; Roman Catholics (1983), 95,276; Negro Baptists about 475,000.

The number of churches relative to the population is the highest in the US (one church per 289 persons; national average, 814).

Education. Attendance at school was compulsory until this was repealed by the Legislature in 1956. The public elementary and secondary schools in 1982–83 had 471,663 pupils and 25,256 classroom teachers.

In 1982–83, teachers' average salary was $14,135. The expenditure per pupil in average daily attendance, 1981–82, was $1,863.

There are 21 universities and senior colleges, of which 8 are state-supported. The University of Mississippi, at Oxford (1844), had, 1983–84, 402 instructors and 9,236 students; Mississippi State University, Starkville, 522 instructors and 12,325 students; Mississippi University for Women, at Columbus, 119 instructors and 2,278 students; University of Southern Mississippi, Hattiesburg, 537 instructors and 11,333 students; Jackson State University, Jackson, 331 instructors and 6,503 students; Delta State University, Cleveland, 167 instructors and 3,438 students; Alcorn State University, Lorman, 140 instructors and 2,555 students; Mississippi Valley State University, Itta Bena, 118 instructors and 2,575 students. State operational expenditure, 1982–83, for higher education was $222·4m.

Junior colleges had (1982–83) 53,682 students and 2,154 instructors. The state appropriation for junior colleges, 1982–83, was $39·6m.

Health. In 1983 the state had 120 acute general hospitals (12,968 beds) listed by the Mississippi Health Care Commission. In 1983, 14 hospitals with facilities for care of the mentally ill had 2,599 beds.

Social Security. Department of Public Welfare figures show (June 1982) 389 persons receiving State Mandatory Supplementation payments amounting to $6,039.86 or an average of $15.53 per case. The state Medicaid commission paid (1981–82) $304m. for medical services, including $34·6m. for drugs, $46·7m. for skilled nursing home care, $75·1m. for hospital services. There were 70,336 persons eligible for Aged Medicaid, 1,981 persons eligible for Blind Medicaid and 59,951 persons eligible for Disabled Medicaid benefits at 30 June 1983. In June 1982 49,668 families with 104,548 dependent children received $4,410,932 in the Aid to Dependent Children programme. The average payment was $88.81 per family or $42.19 per child.

Books of Reference

1980 Census of Population and Housing: Mississippi.
Mississippi Official and Statistical Register. Secretary of State. Jackson. Biennial
Bettersworth, J. K., *Mississippi: A History.* Rev. ed. Austin, Tex., 1964

Mississippi Library Commission: PO Box 10700 Jackson, MS. 39209–0700. *Manager of Information Services:* Sharman B. Smith.

MISSOURI

HISTORY. Missouri, first settled in 1735 at Ste Genevieve, was made a Territory on 1 Oct. 1812, and admitted to the Union on 10 Aug. 1821. In 1837 its boundaries were extended to their present limits.

AREA AND POPULATION. Missouri is bounded north by Iowa, east by the Mississippi River forming the boundary with Illinois and Kentucky, south by Arkansas, south-west by Oklahoma, west by Kansas and Nebraska, with the Missouri River forming the boundary in the north-west. Area, 68,945 sq. miles, 752 sq. miles being water.

Census population, 1 April 1980, 4,916,686, an increase since 1970 of 5·1%. Estimate (1982), 4,951,000. Births, 1981, were 76,758 (15·9 per 1,000 population); deaths, 49,780 (10·1); infant deaths, 971 (12·7 per 1,000 live births); marriages, 54,124 (11·0); divorces, 27,975 (5·7).

Population of 5 federal census years was:

	White	Negro	Indian	Asiatic	Total	Per sq. mile
1910	3,134,932	157,452	313	638	3,293,335	47·9
1930	3,403,876	223,840	578	1,073	3,629,367	52·4
1960	3,922,967	390,853	1,723	3,146	4,319,813	62·5
			All others			
1970	4,177,495	480,172	19,732		4,677,399	67·0
1980	4,345,521	514,276	56,889		4,916,686	71·3

Of the total population in 1980, 2,365,487 were male, 3,350,746 persons were urban and those 18 years of age or older numbered 3,554,203.

The principal cities at the 1980 census (and estimates, 1982) are:

St Louis	453,085 (419,004)	Columbia	62,061 (64,004)
Kansas City	448,159 (436,002)	Florissant	55,372 (56,006)
Springfield	133,116 (137,006)	University City	42,738 (41,007)
Independence	111,806 (111,009)	Joplin	38,893 (39,002)
St Joseph	76,691 (76,008)	St Charles	37,379 (41,004)

Metropolitan areas, 1980: St Louis, 2,356,000; Kansas City, 1,327,000.

CLIMATE. Kansas City. Jan. 30°F (–1·1°C), July 79°F (26·1°C). Annual rainfall 38″ (947 mm). St. Louis. Jan. 32°F (0°C), July 79°F (26·1°C). Annual rainfall 40″ (1,004 mm). *See* Central Plains, p. 1372.

CONSTITUTION AND GOVERNMENT. A new constitution, the fourth, was adopted on 27 Feb. 1945; it has been amended 26 times. The General Assembly consists of a Senate of 34 members elected for 4 years (half for re-election every 2 years), and a House of Representatives of 163 members elected for 2 years. The Governor and Lieut.-Governor are elected for 4 years. Missouri sends to Congress 2 senators and 9 representatives.

Voters (with the usual exceptions) are all citizens and those adult aliens who, within a prescribed period, have applied for citizenship. In the 1980 presidential election Reagan polled 1,074,181, Carter, 931,182 and Anderson 77,920.

Jefferson City is the state capital. The state is divided into 114 counties and the city of St Louis.

Governor: Christopher Bond (R.), 1981–85 ($55,000).
Lieut.-Governor: Kenneth Rothman (D.), 1981–85 ($30,000).
Secretary of State: James C. Kirkpatrick (D.) 1981–85 ($42,500).

BUDGET. For the year 1981 the total revenues from all funds were $4,434·68m. (federal revenue, $1,175·68m., general revenue, $3,793·96m.).

Total outstanding debt, 1981, was $1,335·3m.

Per capita personal income (1981) was $9,876.

NATURAL RESOURCES

Minerals. Principal minerals are lead (ranks first in USA), zinc (ranks second), clays, coal, iron ore, and stone for cement and lime manufacture. Value of production (1981) $870m., a 17·5% decrease from that of 1980.

Agriculture. In 1982 there were (preliminary) 121,000 farms in Missouri covering 32·4m. acres. The average size of farms is 267 acres. Production of principal crops, 1981: Corn, 213·4m. bu.; soybeans, 159·1m. bu.; wheat, 89m. bu.; sorghum grain, 75·2m. bu.; oats, 1·1m. bu.; cotton, 168,000 bales (of 480 lb.). Cash receipts from farming, 1981, $4,179m. Export value of farm produce, $1,318m., to which soybeans contributed $607·8m.

Forestry. Forest land area, 1982, 32·4m. acres.

INDUSTRY. The largest employer in 1982 (preliminary) was manufacturing, in which the transport equipment industry employed 56,009 workers. Other large industries are food and kindred products, electrical equipment and supplies, apparel and related products and non-electrical machinery, leather products, chemicals, paper, metal industries, stone, clay and glass. Retail trade employed 326,375 in 1981, 103,233 of them in eating and drinking places; wholesale trade employed 135,282.

LABOUR. The State Board of Mediation has jurisdiction in labour disputes involving only public utilities. The Prevailing Wage Law (1959) provides that no less than the local hourly rate of wages for work of a similar character shall be paid to any workmen engaged in public works. The Industrial Commission has authority to inspect records and to institute actions for penalties described in the Act. There is a state programme for industrial safety in hand, under the Federal Occupational and Health Act. In June 1983 the estimated number of employed was 2,148,478, and 217,017 were unemployed. The unemployment rate was 9·2% (estimate).

COMMUNICATIONS

Roads. Federal and state highways, Dec. 1981, totalled 118,403 miles. In 1981 there were 3·3m. vehicles licensed in the state, of which 3,741 were private and commercial buses.

Railways. The state has 16 Class I railroads, operating approximately 3,820 miles of main-line track and 1,810 miles of branch-line track.

Aviation. In 1981 there were 118 public airports and 275 private airports.

Shipping. Ten carrier barge lines operate on 1,900 miles of navigable waterways, including the Missouri and Mississippi Rivers. Boat shipping seasons: Missouri River, March–end Nov.; Mississippi River, early March–mid-Dec.

Post and Broadcasting. There were 243 commercial radio stations and 30 TV stations in 1983 (preliminary). The number of telephones in 1980 was 3·87m.

Newspapers. There were (1983) 48 daily and 238 weekly newspapers.

JUSTICE, RELIGION, EDUCATION AND WELFARE

Justice. State prisons in 1981 had an average of 6,489 inmates. Of those committed, 70% are aged 17–29. There have been no executions since 1965 although the death penalty was reinstated in 1978; since 1930 executions (by lethal gas) have totalled 40, including 31 for murder, 6 for rape and 3 for kidnapping. The Missouri Law Enforcement Assistance Council was created in 1969 for law reform.

Religion. Chief religious bodies (1980) are Catholic, with 800,228 members, Southern Baptists (700,053), United Methodists (270,469), Christian Churches

(175,101), Lutheran (157,928), Presbyterian (38,254). Total membership, all denominations, about 2·6m. in 1980.

Education. School attendance is compulsory for children from 7 to 16 years for the full term. In the 1982–83 school year, public schools (kindergarten through grade 12) had 802,841 pupils. Total expenditure for public schools in 1981, $1,759m. Salaries for teachers (kindergarten through grade 12), 1982–83, averaged $18,000. Institutions for higher education include the University of Missouri, founded in 1839 with campuses at Columbia, Rolla, St Louis and Kansas City, with 3,352 accredited teachers and 51,811 students in 1981. Washington University at St Louis, founded in 1857, and St Louis University (1818), are both private universities. Thirteen state colleges had 121,821 students in 1981. Private colleges had (1981) 34,249 students. Church-affiliated colleges (1981) had 28,652 students. Public junior colleges had 42,615 students. There are about 697 secondary and post-secondary institutions offering vocational courses. There were 244,000 students in higher education in autumn 1981.

Health. There were 9 state mental health hospitals and centres and 2 children's psychiatric hospitals in 1983, admitting 23,692 patients.

Social Security. In 1980–81 the number of recipients of medicaid was 321,000. The number of recipients of Aid to Dependent Children was 213,547 with an average monthly payment per family of $213.67 in 1981.

Books of Reference

Annual Survey of Manufactures, U.S. Dept. of Commerce, Bureau of the Census
General Population Characteristics, U.S. Dept. of Commerce, Bureau of the Census
Missouri Final Production Count, Office of Comptroller and Budget Director, Jefferson City
Missouri Corporate Planner, Division of Commerce and Industrial Development, Jefferson City

MONTANA

HISTORY. Montana, first settled in 1809, was made a Territory (out of portions of Idaho and Dakota Territories) in 1864 and was admitted into the Union on 8 Nov. 1889.

AREA AND POPULATION. Montana is bounded north by Canada, east by North and South Dakota, south by Wyoming and west by Idaho and the Bitterroot Range of the Rocky Mountains. Area, 147,138 sq. miles, including 1,551 sq. miles of water, of which the federal government, 1979, owned 27,741,000 acres or 29·7%. US Bureau of Indian Affairs administered 5·26m. acres, of which 2,204,000 were allotted to tribes. Census population, 1 April 1980, 786,690, an increase of 13·3% since 1970. Estimate (1981), 793,000. Births, 1981, were 13,999 (18 per 1,000 population); deaths, 6,709 (8·5); infant deaths, 153 (10·7 per 1,000 live births); marriages, 8,209 (10·4); divorces 5,004 (6·3).

Population in 5 census years was:

	White	Negro	Indian	Asiatic	Total	Per sq. mile
1910	360,580	1,834	10,745	2,870	376,053	2·6
1930	519,898	1,256	14,798	1,239	537,606	3·7
1950	572,038	1,232	16,606	—	591,024	4·1
1970	663,043	1,995	27,130	1,099	694,409	4·7
1980	740,148	1,786	37,270	2,503	786,690	5·3

Of the total population in 1980, 392,625 were male, 416,402 persons (52·9%) were urban. Persons 20 years of age or older numbered 524,836. Median age, 29 years. Households, 283,742.

The largest cities (1980) are Billings, 66,798; Great Falls, 56,725. Others, 1980: Butte-Silver Bow, 37,205; Missoula, 33,388; Helena (capital), 23,938; Bozeman, 21,645; Anaconda-Deer Lodge County, 12,518; Havre, 10,891; Kalispell, 10,648.

CLIMATE. Helena. Jan. 18°F (−7·8°C), July 69°F (20·6°C). Annual rainfall 13" (325 mm). *See* Mountain States, p. 1372.

CONSTITUTION AND GOVERNMENT. A new constitution was ratified by the voters on 6 June 1972, and fully implemented on 1 July 1973; the Senate to consist of 50 senators, elected for 4 years, one half at each biennial election. The 100 members of the House of Representatives are elected for 2 years.

The Governor and Lieut.-Governor are elected for 4 years. Montana sends to Congress 2 senators and 2 representatives.

In the 1980 presidential election Reagan polled 206,814 votes, Carter 118,032.

The capital is Helena. The state is divided into 56 counties.

Governor: Ted Schwinden (D.), 1981–85 ($47,963).
Lieut.-Governor: George Turman (D.), 1981–85 ($34,344).
Secretary of State: Jim Waltermire (R.), 1981–85 ($31,692).

BUDGET. Total state revenues for the year ending 30 June 1981 were $1,269,327,000 ($465m. taxes); total expenditures were $1,096,301,000 ($307·8m. for education, $193m. for highways and $116·8m. for public welfare).

Total net long-term debt on 30 June 1981 was $82,034,000.

Per capita personal income (1981) was $9,412.

ENERGY AND NATURAL RESOURCES

Electricity. Electric power generated in June 1983 was 1,027 gwh., of which 902 gwh. was hydro-electric and 123 gwh. from coal-fired plants; minimal amounts were from oil- and gas-fired plants and 1 gwh. from other sources.

Minerals (1981). Output of crude petroleum, 31m. bbls; copper, 62,485 tonnes; sand and gravel, 6·1m. short tons; phosphate rock, undisclosed; silver, 2·9m. troy oz.; gold, 54,267 troy oz.; zinc, 25 tonnes; natural gas, 56,565m. cu. ft; coal, 33·5m. short tons. Value of total mineral production (1981), $1,894·3m., with petroleum ($1,073·9m.) the first, coal ($407·2m.) the second, copper ($117·3m.) the third and natural gas ($108m.) the fourth most important commodity.

Agriculture. In 1982 there were 24,000 farms and ranches (50,564 in 1935) with an area of 62·1m. acres (47,511,868 acres in 1935). Large-scale farming predominates; in 1982 the average size per farm was 2,588 acres. Income from all farm marketings was $1,483·3m. in 1981 (crops, $854·2m.; livestock, $629m.). Irrigated area harvested in 1981 was 1·73m. acres; non-irrigated, 7·98m. acres.

The chief crops are wheat, amounting in 1981 to 172·8m. bu., ranking sixth in US; barley, 56·7m. bu.; oats, 4·8m. bu.; sugar-beet, hay, potatoes, alfalfa, dry beans, flax and cherries. In 1981 there were 29,000 milch cows, 2·9m. all cattle; 200,000 swine.

The wool clip in 1981 was 5·56m. lb. from 616,000 head of sheep.

Forestry. Total forest area (1977), 22·5m. acres. In 1981 there were 16·8m. acres within 11 national forests.

INDUSTRY. In 1981 manufacturing establishments numbering 612 had 17,264 production workers; value added by manufacture was (1978) $850·6m.

LABOUR (Aug. 1983). Work force, 393,200; total employed, 362,600; total non-agricultural workers, 320,900; agricultural workers, 41,700. Workers employed by major industry group: Mining, 7,000 (average net weekly earnings, $492.78); contract construction, 12,900 ($569.65); manufacturing, 21,000 ($422.75); transport and public utilities, 18,900 ($465.37); wholesale/retail trade, 73,700 ($206.38); finance/insurance/real estate, 13,100 ($207.27); services, 55,300 ($200.63); government, 64,200 (no income figures available). Average weekly earnings for all workers in private non-agricultural industries $281.60. Total unemployed 30,600 (7·8% of the work force in Aug. 1983 as compared to 9·2% nationally for that month).

There were 16 work stoppages in 1980 involving 4,900 workers, with a total of 96,900 man days idle during the year.

COMMUNICATIONS

Roads. In Dec. 1982 the state had 63,151 miles of maintained public roads and streets including 11,733 miles of the federal-aid system. At 26 Oct. 1983 there were 506,080 passenger vehicles, 319,515 trucks and 50,688 motor cycles registered.

Railways. In Dec. 1983 there were 4,314 route miles of railway in the state.

Aviation. There were 126 airports open for public use in Dec. 1983, of which 120 were publicly owned.

JUSTICE, RELIGION, EDUCATION AND WELFARE

Justice. On 1 Nov. 1983 the Montana state prison held 777 inmates and the Women's Correctional Center, 17. Since 1943 there have been no executions; total since 1930 (all by hanging) was 6; 4 whites and 2 Negroes, for murder.

Religion. The leading religious bodies are (1982): Roman Catholic with 131,000 active members; Lutheran, 68,000; Methodist, 25,000 (church estimates).

Education. In Oct. 1982 public elementary and secondary schools had 152,335 pupils. Public elementary and secondary school teachers (9,517 full-time) had an average salary of $19,488. Expenditure on public school education (1982–83) (excluding special education programmes) was $360·9m.; expenditure per pupil was $2,373. The Montana University system consists of the Montana State University, at Bozeman (autumn 1983 enrolment: 11,447 students), the University of Montana, at Missoula, founded in 1895 (9,371), the Montana College of Mineral Science and Technology, at Butte (2,306), Northern Montana College, at Havre (1,859), Eastern Montana College, at Billings (4,424) and Western Montana College, at Dillon (941).

Social Security. In Sept. 1983, 3,569 persons over age 65 were receiving in medical assistance an average of $772.21 per month; 52 blind persons, $579.42; 2,983 totally disabled, $599.85; 6,823 families (12,369 dependent children) receiving in aid-to-dependent children assistance an average of $307.03 per month. Aid was from state and federal sources.

Health. In Aug. 1983 the state had 61 hospitals (3,426 beds) listed by the Montana Board of Health. Four centres for mental disease and development disorders had 962 beds and 841 patients.

Books of Reference

Montana Agricultural Statistics. U.S. Dept. of Agriculture, Montana Crop and Livestock Reporting Service. Biennial from 1946
Montana Employment and Labor Force. Montana Dept. of Labor and Industry. Monthly from 1971
Montana Federal-Aid Road Log. Montana Dept. of Highways and US Dept. of Transportation, Federal Highway Administration. Annual from 1938
Montana Vital Statistics. Montana Dept. of Health and Environmental Sciences. Annually from 1954
Statistical Report. Montana Dept. of Social and Rehabilitation Services. Monthly from 1947
Lang, W, L., and Myers, R. C., *Montana, Our Land and People.* Pruett, 1979
Malone, M. P., and Roeder, R. B., *Montana, A History of Two Centuries.* Univ. of Washington Press, 1976

NEBRASKA

HISTORY. The Nebraska region was first reached by white men from Mexico under the Spanish general Coronado in 1541. It was ceded by France to Spain in

1763, retroceded to France in 1801, and sold by Napoleon to the US as part of the Louisiana Purchase in 1803. Its first settlement was in 1847, and on 30 May 1854 it became a Territory and on 1 March 1867 a state. In 1882 it annexed a small part of Dakota Territory, and in 1908 it received another small tract from South Dakota.

AREA AND POPULATION. Nebraska is bounded north by South Dakota, with the Missouri River forming the boundary in the north-east and the boundary with Iowa and Missouri to the east; south by Kansas, south-west by Colorado and west by Wyoming. Area, 77,355 sq. miles, of which 711 sq. miles are water. Census population, 1980 1,569,825, an increase of 5·7% since 1970. Estimate (1981), 1,577,000. Births, 1981, were 27,164 (17·2 per 1,000 population); deaths, 14,580 (9·2); infant deaths, 268 (9·9 per 1,000 live births); marriages, 14,363 (9·1): divorces, 6,769 (4·3).

Population in 5 census years was:

	White	Negro	Indian	Asiatic	Total	Per sq. mile
1910	1,180,293	7,689	3,502	730	1,192,214	15·5
1920	1,279,219	13,242	2,888	1,023	1,296,372	16·9
1960	1,374,764	29,262	5,545	1,195	1,411,330	18·3
			All others			
1970	1,432,867	39,911	10,715		1,483,791	19·4
1980	1,490,381	48,390	31,054		1,569,825	20·5

Of the total population in 1980, 48·8% were male,62·9% were urban 65·6% were 21 years of age or older. The largest cities in the state are: Omaha, with a census population, 1980, of 313,911; Lincoln (capital), 171,932; Grand Island, 33,180; North Platte, 24,509; Fremont, 23,979; Hastings, 23,045; Bellevue, 21,813; Kearney, 21,158; Norfolk, 19,449.

The Bureau of Indian Affairs, as of 30 June 1981, administered 65,000 acres, of which 22,000 acres were allotted to tribal control.

CLIMATE. Omaha. Jan. 22°F (−5·6°C), July 77°F (25°C). Annual rainfall 29″ (721 mm). See High Plains, p. 1372.

CONSTITUTION AND GOVERNMENT. The present constitution was adopted in 1875; it has been amended 176 times. By an amendment adopted in Nov. 1934 Nebraska has a single-chambered legislature (elected for 4 years) of 49 members—the only state in the Union to have one. The Governor and Lieut.-Governor are elected for 4 years. Amendments adopted in 1912 and 1920 provide for legislation through the initiative and referendum and permit cities of more than 5,000 inhabitants to frame their own charters. A 'right-to-work' amendment adopted 5 Nov. 1946 makes illegal the 'closed shop' demands of trade unions. Nebraska is represented in Congress by 2 senators and 3 representatives.

In the 1980 presidential election Reagan polled 413,338 votes, Carter 164,270 and Anderson 44,024.

The capital is Lincoln. The state has 93 counties.

Governor: Robert Kerrey (D.), 1983–86 ($40,000).
Lieut.-Governor: Donald F. McGinley (D.) ($32,000).
Secretary of State: Allen Beerman (R.) ($32,000).

BUDGET. For the fiscal year ending 30 June 1980 (US Census Bureau figures) the state's revenues were $1,506m. (taxation, $817m. and federal aid, $361m.); general expenditures were $1,341m. ($416m. for education, $265m. for highways and $191m. for public welfare).

The state has a bonded indebtedness limit of $100,000.

Per capita personal income (1981) was $10,366.

ENERGY AND NATURAL RESOURCES

Minerals. The total output of minerals, 1980, was valued at $271·8m., petroleum (6m. bbls) and sand and gravel (12m. tons) being the most important.

Agriculture. Nebraska is one of the most important agricultural states. In 1981 it contained approximately 65,000 farms, with a total area of 48m. acres. The average farm was 734 acres.

In 1980, 7·2m. acres were irrigated and 68,319 irrigation wells were registered. Cash income from crops (1981), $2,855·2m., and from livestock, $3,520·8m. Principal crops, with estimated 1981 yield: Maize, 802·7m. bu. (ranking third in US); wheat, 106·2m. bu.; sorghums for grain, 164·8m. bu.; oats, 15·4m. bu.; soybeans, 82·7m. bu. About 953 farms grow sugar-beet for 5 factories; output, 1981, 1·9m. short tons. On 1 Jan. 1982 the state contained 7·3m. all cattle (ranking third in US), 122,000 milch cows, 225,000 sheep and 4·1m. swine.

Forestry. The area of national forest, 1980, was 352,000 acres.

INDUSTRY. In 1977 there were 1,969 manufacturing establishments. In 1978 61,400 production workers earned $786·5m. and value added by manufacturing was $2,821·8m. The chief industry is meat-packing, employing (1978), 8,200 (7,100 production workers) and value added was $258·3m.

COMMUNICATIONS

Roads. The state-maintained highway system embraced 9,885 miles in 1981; local roads, 96,270 miles. In 1981, 796,790 automobiles were registered.

Railways. In 1981 there were 7,342 miles of railway.

Aviation. Airports (1981) numbered 318, of which 112 were publicly owned.

JUSTICE, RELIGION, EDUCATION AND WELFARE

Justice. A 'Civil Rights Act' revised in 1969 provides that all people are entitled to a 'full and equal enjoyment of the accommodations, advantages, facilities and privileges' of hotels, restaurants, public conveyances, amusement places and other places. The state university is forbidden to discriminate between students 'because of age, sex, color or nationality'. An Act of 1941 declares it to be 'the policy of this state' that no trade union should discriminate, in collective bargaining, 'against any person because of his race or color'.

The state's prisons had, 19 Oct, 1982, 1,484 inmates (94 per 100,000 population). From 1930 to 1962 there were 4 executions (electrocution), 3 white men and 1 American Indian, all for murder, and none since.

Religion. The Roman Catholics had 332,000 members in 1982; Protestant Churches, 667,298; Jews, 7,500 members. Total, all denominations, 1,006,798 (unofficial figures).

Education. School attendance is compulsory for children from 7 to 16 years of age. Public elementary schools, autumn 1981, had 185,940 enrolled pupils.. Teachers' salaries, 1981–82, averaged $16,570. Estimated public school expenditure for year ending 30 Aug. 1981 was $632·6m. Total enrolment in 30 institutions of higher education, autumn 1981, was 93,513 students. The largest institutions were (1981):

Opened	Institution	Students
1867	Peru State College, Peru (State)	818
1869	Univ. of Nebraska, Lincoln (State)	24,786
1878	Creighton Univ., Omaha (RC)	5,766
1883	Midland Lutheran College, Fremont (Lutheran)	875
1887	Nebraska Wesleyan Univ. (Methodist)	1,183
1891	Union College, Lincoln (Seventh Day Adventist)	942
1894	Concordia Teachers' College, Seward (Lutheran)	1,068
1905	Kearney State College, Kearney (State)	7,004
1908	Univ. of Nebraska, Omaha (State)	14,023
1910	Wayne State College, Wayne (State)	2,233
1911	Chadron State College, Chadron (State)	1,909
1923	College of St. Mary	897
1966	Bellevue College, Bellevue (Private)	2,615

The state holds 1·52m. acres of land as a permanent endowment of her schools; permanent public school endowment fund in Aug. 1982 was $71·1m.

Health. In 1982 the state had 113 hospitals and 576 patients in mental hospitals.

Social Security. The administration of public welfare is the responsibility of the County Divisions of Welfare with policy-forming, regulatory, advisory and supervisory functions performed by the State Department of Public Welfare. In 1981 public welfare provided financial aid and/or services as follows: for 6,188 individuals who were aged, blind or disabled, with an average state supplement of $57.02; for 13,731 families with dependent children, with an average payment of $286.34 per family; for about 70,000 individuals who had medical needs, $1,708.91, per individual; for 1,768 children in need of child welfare services; for 3,307 children who were in need of crippled children's services and medical care. The amount of aid is based on need in accordance with State assistance standards; the programme of aid to families with dependent children is limited to a maximum maintenance payment of $293 for 1 child plus $71 for each additional child.

Books of Reference

Agricultural Atlas of Nebraska. Univ. of Nebraska Press, 1977
Climatic Atlas of Nebraska. Univ. of Nebraska Press, 1977
Economic Atlas of Nebraska. Univ. of Nebraska Press, 1977
Nebraska. A Guide to the Cornhusker State. Univ. of Nebraska Press, 1979
Nebraska Statistical Handbook, 1982–83. Nebraska Dept. of Econ. Development, Lincoln
Nebraska Blue-Book. Legislative Council. Lincoln. Biennial
Olson, J. C., *History of Nebraska.* Univ. of Nebraska Press, 1955

State Library: State Law Library, State House, Lincoln. *Librarian:* Larry D. Donelson.

NEVADA

HISTORY. Nevada, first settled in 1851, when it was a part of the Territory of Utah (created 1850), was made a Territory in 1861, enlarged in 1862 by an addition from Utah Territory and admitted into the Union on 31 Oct. 1864 as the 36th state. In 1866 and 1867 the area of the state was significantly enlarged at the expense of the Territories of Utah and Arizona.

AREA AND POPULATION. Nevada is bounded north by Oregon and Idaho, east by Utah, south-east by Arizona, with the Colorado River forming most of the boundary, south and west by California. Area 110,561 sq. miles, 667 sq. miles being water. The federal government in 1973 owned 60,908,872 acres, or 86·5% of the land area. Vacant public lands, 48,340,876 acres. The Bureau of Indian Affairs controlled 1·35m. acres in 1975, of which 1,062,047 acres have been assigned to Indian tribes.

Census population on 1 April 1980, 799,184, an increase of 310,446 or 63·5% since 1970. Estimate (1981) 845,000. Births, 1980, were 13,156 (16·5 per 1,000 population); deaths, 6,408 (8); infant deaths, 157 (12 per 1,000 live births); marriages, 115,411 (144·5 per 1,000 population, largest of any state); divorces, 13,659 (17·1).

Population in 5 census years was:

	White	Negro	Indian	Asiatic and all others	Total	Per sq. mile
1910	74,276	513	5,240	1,846	81,875	0·7
1930	84,515	516	4,871	1,156	91,058	0·8
1960	263,443	13,484	6,681	1,670	285,278	2·6
1970	449,850	27,579	7,329	3,980	488,738	4·4
			All others			
1980	699,377	50,791	49,016		799,184	7·2

Of the total population in 1980, 404,372 were male, 681,682 were urban and 556,021 were 20 years of age or older.

The largest cities are Las Vegas, with population at the 1980 census of 164,674 (1982 estimate, 183,184); Reno, 100,756 (107,607); North Las Vegas, 39,196

(47,543); Sparks, 38,114 (42,604); Carson City, 30,807 (33,929); and Henderson, 20,905 (28,680). Clark County (Las Vegas, North Las Vegas and Henderson) and Washoe County (Reno and Sparks) together had 81% of the total state population in 1980 (82% in 1982).

CLIMATE. Las Vegas. Jan. 44°F (6·7°C), July 85°F (29·4°C). Annual rainfall 4″ (112 mm). Reno. Jan. 32°F (0°C), July 69°F (20·6°C). Annual rainfall 7″ (178 mm). *See* Mountain States, p. 1372.

CONSTITUTION AND GOVERNMENT. The constitution adopted in 1864 is still in force, with over 60 amendments. The Legislature meets biennially (and in special sessions) and consists of a Senate of 20 members elected for 4 years, half their number retiring every 2 years, and an Assembly of 40 members elected for 2 years. The Governor, Lieut.-Governor and Attorney-General are elected for 4 years. Qualified electors are all citizens with the usual residential qualification. Nevada is represented in Congress by 2 senators and 2 representatives. A Supreme Court of 5 members is elected for 4 years on a non-partisan ballot.

In the 1980 presidential election Reagan polled 155,017 votes, Carter 66,466 and Anderson 17,651.

The state capital is Carson City. There are 16 counties, 17 incorporated cities and towns, 44 unincorporated towns and 1 city-county (Carson City).

Governor: Richard Bryan (D.), 1983–86 ($50,000).
Lieut.-Governor: Bob Cashell (D.) ($8,000).
Secretary of State: William D. Swackhammer (D.) ($32,500).

BUDGET. For the fiscal year ending 30 June 1983 estimated state general fund revenues were $352·4m., including federal receipts; general expenditures were $417m. Education followed by human resources and public safety received the largest appropriations.

State bonded indebtedness on 30 June 1983, was $19·1m. The state has no franchise tax, capital stock tax, special intangibles tax, chain stores tax, stock transfer tax, admissions tax, estate tax, gift tax, income taxes or inheritance tax. The sales and use tax and gaming taxes are the largest revenue producers.

Per capita personal income (1982) was $11,981.

ENERGY AND NATURAL RESOURCES

Electricity. Electricity power stations supplied 8,463m. mwh. in 1978. There were about 316,484 private and commercial customers in 1979. There are 8 suppliers of natural gas producing 51,696,121m.cu. ft in 1978.

Minerals. Production, 1981, in order of value was gold, barite, silver, and sand and gravel. Other minerals are gypsum, iron ore, mercury, lime, lithium, petroleum, gemstones, lead, molybdenum, fluorspar, perlite, pumice, clays, talc, salt, tungsten, magnesite, diatonite and zinc. Value of mineral output for 1981, $504m.

Agriculture. In 1982, an estimated 2,900 farms had a farm area of 8·9m. acres (9·2m. in 1960). Farms averaged (1981) 2,871 acres. Area under irrigation (1979) was 1·3m. acres compared with 542,976 acres in 1959.

Gross income, 1981, from crops, livestock and government payments, $249·1m. Cattle, dairy products, hay, potatoes and sheep are the principal commodities in order of cash receipts. Total value of crops produced, $13·2m., of which hay accounted for 17·1%. On 1 Jan. 1982 there were 16,000 milch cows, 359,000 beef cattle, 129,000 sheep and 129 lambs.

Forestry. The area of national forests (1975) under US Forest Service administration was 5,051,938 acres.

INDUSTRY. The main industries are the service industry, especially tourism and legalized gambling, mining and smelting, livestock and irrigated agriculture, chemical manufacturing, and lumber processing. In 1981 there were 843 manufacturing establishments with 20,094 employees, earning $362m.

Gaming industry gross revenue for financial year 1982, $2,627·4m. There were at the same time 1,300 licences in force.

LABOUR. The annual average unemployment for 1982 was 10% of the work force. All industries employed 411,500 workers. Main industries and employees, 1982: Mining, 7,100; contract construction, 22,100; manufacturing, 19,500; transport (except railways), public works and utilities, 24,000; interstate railways, 1,800; hotels, gaming and recreation, 115,000; other service industries, 62,400; retail trade, 70,300; government, 57,700.

COMMUNICATIONS

Roads. Highway mileage (federal, state and local) totalled 49,659 in 1973, of which 16,464 miles were surfaced; motor vehicle registrations at 1 Jan. 1982 numbered 757,609.

Railways. In 1973 there were 1,553 miles of main-line railway. Nevada is served by Southern Pacific, Union Pacific and Western Pacific railways, and Amtrac passenger service for Carlin, Elko, Reno and Sparks.

Aviation. There were (1974) 114 civil airports and heliports (1,307 civil aircraft registered); 16 scheduled airlines operated. During 1982 McCarren International Airport handled 9·5m. passengers and Cannon International Airport handled 2·6m. passengers.

Post. In 1976 there were 11 telephone exchanges with (1980), 787,232 telephones in service.

JUSTICE, RELIGION, EDUCATION AND WELFARE

Justice. Prohibition of marriage between persons of different race was repealed by statute in 1959.

A 1965 Civil Rights Act makes it illegal for persons operating public accommodations, employers of 15 or more employees, labour unions, and employment agencies to discriminate on the basis of race, colour, religion or national origin; a 1971 law makes racial discrimination in the sale or renting of houses illegal. A Commission on Equal Rights of Citizens is charged with enforcing these laws.

Between 1924 and 1967 executions (by lethal gas—the first state to adopt this method, in 1921), numbered 31. Capital punishment was abolished in 1972 and later re-introduced; there was 1 execution (by lethal gas) in 1979.

Religion. Roman Catholics are the most numerous religious group, followed by members of the Church of Jesus Christ of Latter-day Saints (Mormons) and various Protestant churches.

Education. School attendance is compulsory for children from 7 to 17 years of age. In Oct. 1982 the 184 public elementary schools, including kindergartens, had 73,315 pupils; there were 95 secondary public schools, including junior and high schools, with 66,794. Special schools for handicapped pupils had 10,995. There were 3,411 elementary teachers (average salary $21,822), 2,827 secondary teachers with an average salary of $22,740. There were 36 parochial and private schools. The University of Nevada, Reno, had, in 1982, 334 full-time instructors and 9,311 students (regular, non-degree and correspondent), and University of Nevada, Las Vegas, 315 instructors and 11,031 students. Two-year community colleges operate as part of the University of Nevada system in Carson City, Elko and Las Vegas. There were (1982) 23,183 students.

Health. In 1976 the state had 24 hospitals (3,064 beds) and 19 skilled nursing units (1,158 beds).

Social Security. Old-age assistance is granted to all 65 years of age or older who are in need, and have assets not over $750 ($1,500 for married couples); end of fiscal year 1974–75, total expenditure was $6.179,040 at an average of $140 each person per month, for 3,678 people. Families with dependent children received

$7,613,458 at $45.52 monthly average per person. The blind received $328,440 at $170 for 161 people. Nevada is the only state without aid to the permanently and totally disabled.

Books of Reference

Information: Bureau of Business and Economic Research (Univ. of Nevada).

Handbook of the Nevada Legislature, 55th Session, 1969. Legislative Counsel Bureau. Carson City

Legislative Manual, State of Nevada, 55th Session, 1969. Legislative Counsel Bureau. Carson City

Political History of Nevada. Secretary of State. Carson City, 1965

Financing State and Local Government in Nevada. Legislative Counsel Bureau. Carson City 1960

Study of General Fund Revenues of the State of Nevada. Legislative Counsel Bureau. Carson City, 1966

Education, Manpower and Economic Data for Nevada. Nevada Employment Security Dept., Carson City, 1971

Bushnell, E., *The Nevada Constitution: Origin and Growth.* Univ. of Nevada Press, 2nd ed., 1968

Hulse, James W., *The Nevada Adventure, A History.* Univ. of Nevada Press, 2nd ed., 1969

Mack, E. M., and Sawyer, B. W., *Here is Nevada: A History of the State.* Sparks, Nevada, 1965

State Library: Nevada State Library, Carson City. *State Librarian:* Mildred J. Heyer.

NEW HAMPSHIRE

HISTORY. New Hampshire, first settled in 1623, is one of the 13 original states of the Union.

AREA AND POPULATION. New Hampshire is bounded north by Canada, east by Maine and the Atlantic, south by Massachusetts and west by Vermont. Area, 9,279 sq. miles, of which 286 sq. miles are inland water. Census population, 1 April 1980, 920,610, an increase of 24·8% since 1970. Estimate (1981), 936,000. Births, 1980, were 12,330; deaths, 7,190; infant deaths, 101; marriages, 9,049; divorces, 4,471.

Population at 5 federal censuses was:

	White	Negro	Indian	Asiatic	Total	Per sq. mile
1910	429,906	564	34	68	430,572	47·7
1930	464,351	790	64	88	465,293	51·6
1960	604,334	1,903	135	549	606,921	65·2
			All others			
1970	733,106	2,505	2,070		737,681	81·7
1980	910,099	3,990	6,521		920,610	101·9

Of the total population in 1980, 448,462 were male, 480,325 were urban; those 20 years of age or older numbered 625,562.

The largest city of the state is Manchester, with a 1980 census population of 90,757. Other cities are: Nashua, 67,817; Concord (capital), 30,; Portsmouth, 26,214; Dover, 22,265; Keene, 21,385; Rochester, 21,579; Berlin, 13,090; Laconia, 15,579; Claremont, 14,575; Lebanon, 11,052; Somersworth, 10,313.

CLIMATE. Manchester. Jan. 22°F (–5·6°C), July 70°F (21·1°C). Annual rainfall 40″ (1,003 mm). *See* New England, p. 1373.

CONSTITUTION AND GOVERNMENT. While the present constitution dates from 1784, it was extensively revised in 1792 when the state joined the Union. Since 1775 there have been 16 state conventions with 49 amendments adopted to amend the constitution.

The Legislature consists of a Senate of 30 members, elected for 2 years, and a House of Representatives, restricted to between 375 and 400 members, elected for 2 years. The Governor and 5 administrative officers called 'Councillors' are also elected for 2 years.

Electors must be adult citizens, able to read and write, duly registered and not paupers or under sentence for crime. New Hampshire sends to the Federal Congress 2 senators and 2 representatives.

In the 1980 presidential election Reagan polled 221,705 votes, Carter 108,864 and Anderson 49,693.

The capital is Concord. The state is divided into 10 counties.

Governor: John Sununu (R.), 1983–85 ($44,520).
Secretary of State: William M. Gardner (D.) ($31,270).

BUDGET. The state government's general revenue for the fiscal year ending 30 June 1981 (US Census Bureau figures) was $943·9m.; general expenditures, $951·9m.

Net long-term debt, 30 June 1981, was $1,038·8m.

Per capita personal income (1981) was $10,073.

NATURAL RESOURCES

Minerals. Minerals are little worked; they consist mainly of sand and gravel, stone, and clay for building and highway construction. Value of mineral production, 1980. $25m.

Agriculture. In 1982, there were 3,000 farms occupying 1m. acres; average farm was 169 acres. The US Soil Survey estimates that the state has 164,167 acres of excellent soil, 486,615 acres of fair soil, 530,630 of poor soil and 3,843,798 of non-arable soil. Only 636,195 acres (11% of the total area) show moderate erosion.

Cash income, 1981, from crops and livestock, $97m. The chief field crops are hay and vegetables; the chief fruit crop is apples. On 1 Jan. 1975 animals on farms were 40,000 milch cows, 69,000 all cattle, 4,800 sheep, 8,700 swine, 1·8m. poultry, 28,000 turkeys and about 36,225 horses.

Forestry. In 1979 forest land totalled 5m. acres; national forest, 705,000 acres.

INDUSTRY. In 1980, manufacturing establishments employed 107,000 workers, and value added by manufacture was $3,606m.; 54% of manufacturing employment is accounted for in durable goods.

Principal industries are, electrical machinery, non-electrical machinery, metal products, textiles and shoes.

COMMUNICATIONS

Roads. On 1 Jan. 1975 the length of state highways was 4,373 miles, of which the state maintained 4,155 miles and municipalities 218 miles. The length of town roads, urban and rural, totalled 7,918 miles. Motor vehicles registered, 1980, numbered 655,000.

Railways. In 1975 the length of railway in the state was 826 miles.

Aviation. In 1981 there were 15 public and 37 private airports.

JUSTICE, RELIGION, EDUCATION AND WELFARE

Justice. The state prison held 316 persons on 1 Jan. 1980. Since 1930 there has been only one execution (by hanging)—a white man, for murder, in 1939.

Religion. The Roman Catholic Church is the largest single body. The largest Protestant churches are Congregational, Episcopal, Methodist and United Baptist Convention of N.H.

Education. School attendance is compulsory for children from 6 to 14 years of age during the whole school term, or to 16 if their district provides a high school.

Employed illiterate minors between 16 and 21 years of age must attend evening or special classes, if provided by the district.

In 1980 the public elementary and secondary schools enrolled 171,000 pupils. Public school salaries, 1979–80, averaged $13,342. Total expenditure on public schools in 1980 was estimated at $324m.

Total enrolment, 1980, in 25 institutions of higher education was 46,800 students. Dartmouth College, at Hanover was founded in 1769, the University of New Hampshire, at Durham was founded in 1866.

Health. In 1980 the state had 33 hospitals (4,680 beds). On 1 Jan. 1980 mental hospitals had 608 patients, and there were 679 persons in state institutions for the mentally retarded.

Social Security. The Division of Welfare handles public assistance for (1) aged citizens 65 years or over, (2) needy aged aliens, (3) needy blind persons, (4) needy citizens between 18 and 64 years inclusive, who are permanently and totally disabled, (5) needy children under 21 years, (6) Medicaid and the medically needy not eligible for a monthly grant.

In Dec. 1980, 2,100 persons were receiving SSI old-age assistance of an average $87 per month; 3,200 permanently and totally disabled, $166 per month; 8,600 families with dependent children, $271 per month.

Books of Reference

Morrison, L. S., *The Government of New Hampshire.* Concord, 1952
N.H. Register. State Year Book and Legislative Manual. Portland, Maine, 1965
Squires, J. D., *Granite State of the United States.* New York, 1956

NEW JERSEY

HISTORY. New Jersey, first settled in the early 1600s, is one of the 13 original states in the Union.

AREA AND POPULATION. New Jersey is bounded north by New York, east by the Atlantic with Long Island and New York City to the north-east, south by Delaware Bay and west by Pennsylvania. Area (US Bureau of Census), 7,787 sq. miles (319 sq. miles being inland water). Census population, 1 April 1980, 7,364,823, an increase of 2·7% since 1970. Estimate (1981) 7,404,000. Births, 1981, were 96,205 (13·1 per 1,000 population); deaths, 67,053 (9·1); infant deaths, 1,016 (10·6 per 1,000 live births); marriages, 58,010 (7·9); divorces, 27,852 (3·8).

Population at 5 federal censuses was:

	White	Negro	Indian	Asiatic	All others	Total	Per sq. mile
1910	2,445,894	89,760	168	1,345	—	2,537,167	337·7
1930	3,829,663	208,828	213	2,630	122	4,041,334	537·3
1960	5,539,003	514,875	1,699	8,778	2,427	6,066,782	739·5
1970	6,349,908	770,292	4,706	20,537	22,721	7,168,164	953·1
1980	6,127,467	925,066	8,394	103,847	200,048	7,364,823	986·2

Of the population in 1980, 3,533,012 were male, 6,557,377 persons were urban, 5,116,581 were 20 years of age or older.

Census population of the larger cities and towns in 1980 was:

Newark	329,248	Irvington	61,493	Parsippany-	
Jersey City	223,532	Union City	55,593	Troy Hills	49,868
Paterson	137,970	Vineland	53,753	Middleton	62,574
Elizabeth	106,201	Passaic	52,463	Union Township	50,184
Trenton (capital)	92,124	Woodbridge	90,074	Bloomfield	47,792
Camden	84,910	Hamilton	82,801	Atlantic City	40,199
Clifton	74,388	Edison	70,193	Plainfield	45,555
East Orange	77,025	Cherry Hill	68,785	Hoboken	42,460
Bayonne	65,047			Montclair	38,321

Largest urbanized areas (1980) were: Newark, 1,963,000; Jersey City, 555,483; Paterson-Clifton-Passaic, 447,785; Trenton (NJ–Pa.), 305,678.

CLIMATE. Jersey City. Jan. 31°F (–0·6°C), July 75°F (23·9°C). Annual rainfall 41″ (1,025 mm). Trenton. Jan. 32°F (0°C), July 76°F (24·4°C). Annual rainfall 40″ (1,003 mm). *See* Atlantic Coast, p. 1373.

CONSTITUTION AND GOVERNMENT. The legislative power is vested in a Senate and a General Assembly, the members of which are chosen by the people, all citizens (with necessary exceptions) 18 years of age, with the usual residential qualifications, having the right of suffrage. The present constitution, ratified by the registered voters on 4 Nov. 1947, has been amended 27 times. In 1966 the Constitutional Convention proposed, and the people adopted, a new plan providing for a 40-member Senate and an 80-member General Assembly. This plan, as certified by the Apportionment Commission and modified by the courts, provides for 40 legislative districts, with 1 senator and 2 assemblymen elected for each. Assemblymen serve 2 years, senators 4 years, except those elected at the election following each census, who serve for 2 years. The Governor is elected for 4 years.

The state sends to Congress 2 senators and 14 representatives.

In the 1980 presidential election Reagan polled 1,546,557 votes, Carter 1,147,364 and Anderson 234,632.

The capital is Trenton. The state is divided into 21 counties, which are subdivided into 567 municipalities—cities, towns, boroughs, villages and townships.

Governor: Thomas H. Kean (R.), 1982–85 ($85,000).
Secretary of State: Jane Burgio ($60,000).

BUDGET. For the year ending 30 June 1984 (US Census Bureau figures) general revenues were $6,845·3m. (taxation $4,972·3m. and federal aid, $1,872·9m.); general expenditures were $12,250m. (education, $2,191·9m.; highways, $319m., and public welfare, $1,348·7m.).

Total net long-term debt, 30 June 1983, was $3,653·6m.

Per capita personal income (1982) was $12,930.

NATURAL RESOURCES

Minerals. The chief minerals are stone ($57·8m., 1982) and sand and gravel ($45·8m.); others are zinc ($16m.), clay products ($563,000), peat ($1·47m.) and gemstones ($1,000). New Jersey is a leading producer of greensand marl, magnesium compounds and peat. Total value of mineral products, 1982, was $142m.

Agriculture. Livestock raising, market-gardening, fruit-growing, horticulture and forestry are pursued. In 1982, 9,500 farms had a total area of 1·03m. acres; average farm in 1981 had 108 acres valued at $2,366 per acre.

Cash income, 1980, from crops, $248·6, and livestock, $122·3m.

Leading crops are tomatoes (value, $20·58m., 1981), all corn ($45·26m.), peaches ($21·51m.), hay ($27·32m.), blueberries ($18·2m.), soybeans ($29·72m.).

Farm animals on 1 Jan. 1981 included 41,000 milch cows, 100,000 all cattle, 9,700 sheep and lambs and 45,000 swine.

INDUSTRY. In 1982 manufacturing establishments employed 719,630 workers, receiving $15,319·1m. in wages. The principal industries by value are: Chemicals and allied products, construction, electrical and electronic equipment, machinery (except electrical).

COMMUNICATIONS

Roads. In 1980 there were 33,810 miles of roads (municipal, 21,128 miles; state, 2,662 miles; county, 8,398 miles; others, 1,022 miles).

Railways. In 1980, the state had 1,607 route miles of railway.

Aviation. There were (1981) 271 airports, of which 35 were publicly owned.

JUSTICE, RELIGION, EDUCATION AND WELFARE

Justice. State prisons in 1983 had 8,804 inmates. Since 1930 executions (by electrocution) have totalled 74, including 47 whites, 25 Negroes and 2 other races, all for murder. There have been none since 1966. Future executions would be by lethal injection.

The constitution of New Jersey forbids discrimination against any person on account of 'religious principles, race, color, ancestry or national origin'. The state has had, since 1945, a 'fair employment act', *i.e.*, a Civil Rights statute forbidding any employer, public or private (with 6 or more employees), to discriminate against any applicant for work (or to discharge any employee) on the grounds of 'race, creed, color, national origin or ancestry'. Trade unions may not bar Negroes from membership.

Religion. The Roman Catholic population of New Jersey in 1982 was 2·95m. The five largest Protestant sects were United Methodists, 184,000; United Presbyterians, 174,000; Episcopalians, 147,000; Lutherans, 89,000; American Baptists, 74,000. There were 40,000 African Methodists and 4,000 Christian Methodist Episcopalians. The main Jewish sects were Reform (38,000) and Conservative (27,000).

Education. Elementary instruction is compulsory for all from 6 to 16 years of age and free to all from 5 to 20 years of age. In autumn 1981 public elementary schools had 753,348 and secondary schools had 451,370 enrolled pupils; public colleges in autumn 1982 had 321,387 students, including 118,216 in community colleges, and independent colleges had 65,288. The total cost of public schools, 1979–80, $3,520·9m. Average salary of all elementary and secondary classroom teachers in public schools 1982–83 was $21,751.

Rutgers, the State University (founded as Queen's College in 1766) had, in 1982, an opening autumn enrolment of 47,224 full- and part-time students. Princeton (founded in 1746) had 6,121 students in autumn 1983. Fairleigh Dickinson (1941), had 16,796 in 1983; Kean College, 13,340 in 1982; Montclair State College, 14,816 in 1982; Glassboro State College, 9,108 in 1982; Trenton State College, 9,296 in 1982.

Health. In 1981 the state had 132 hospitals (42,193 beds), listed by the American Hospital Association.

Social Security. In the financial year 1982 gross expenditure for all public assistance programmes was $548,392,000. Average monthly total of cases was $338,000 with an average grant per case of $322.

Books of Reference

Legislative District Data Book. Bureau of Government Research. Annual
Manual of the Legislature of New Jersey. Trenton. Annual
Boyd, J. P. (ed.), *Fundamentals and Constitutions of New Jersey, 1664–1954.* Princeton, 1964
Cunningham, J. T., *New Jersey: America's Main Road.* Rev. ed. New York, 1976
League of Women Voters of New Jersey. *New Jersey: Spotlight on Government.* Rutgers Univ. Press, 3rd ed., 1978
Lehne, R., and Rosenthal, A. (eds.), *Politics in New Jersey.* Rev. ed., Rutgers Univ. Press, 1979

State Library: 185 W. State Street, Trenton, N.J. 08625. *State Librarian:* Barbara F. Weaver.

NEW MEXICO

HISTORY. The first European settlement was established in 1598. Until 1771 New Mexico was the Spanish kings' 'Kingdom of New Mexico'. In 1771 it was annexed to the northern province of New Spain. When New Spain won its independence in 1821, it took the name of Republic of Mexico and established New Mexico as its northernmost department. When the war between the US and Mexico was concluded on 2 Feb. 1848 New Mexico was recognized as belonging to the US, and on 9 Sept. 1850 it was made a Territory. Part of the Territory was assigned to Texas; later Utah was formed into a separate Territory; in 1861 another part was transferred to Colorado, and in 1863 Arizona was disjoined, leaving to New Mexico its present area. New Mexico became a state in Jan. 1912.

AREA AND POPULATION. New Mexico is bounded north by Colorado, north-east by Oklahoma, east by Texas, south by Texas and Mexico and west by Arizona. Land area 121,335 sq. miles (258 sq. miles water). Public lands, administered by federal agencies (1975) amounted to 26·7m. acres or 34% of the total area. The Bureau of Indian Affairs held 7·3m. acres; the State of New Mexico held 9·4m. acres; 34·4m. acres were privately owned.

Census population, 1 April 1980, 1,302,894, an increase of 285,839 or 28% since 1970. Estimate (1982) 1,359,000. Vital statistics, 1981: Births, 26,565 (20 per 1,000 population); deaths, 8,668 (6·5); infant deaths, 256 (9·6 per 1,000 live births); marriages (1980), 17,213 (13·2); divorces (1980), 10,426 (8·0).

The population in 5 census years was:

	White	Negro	Indian	Asian and Pacific Islander	Other	Total	Per sq. mile
1910	304,594	1,628	20,573	506		327,301	2·7
1940	492,312	4,672	34,510	324		531,818	4·4
1960	875,763	17,063	56,255	1,942		951,023	7·8
1970	915,815	19,555	72,788	7,842 [1]		1,016,000	8·4
1980	977,587	24,020	106,119	6,825	188,343	1,302,894	10·7

[1] Includes unspecified races, 1970.

Of the 1980 total, 642,157 were male, 939,963 persons were urban; 884,987 were 18 years of age or older.

Before 1930 New Mexico was largely a Spanish-speaking state, but since 1945 an influx of population from other states has reduced the percentage of persons of Spanish origin or descent to 36·6%.

The largest cities are Albuquerque, with population (Census, 1980) 332,336. Santa Fé (capital), 49,160; Las Cruces, 45,086; Roswell, 39,676; Farmington, 31,222.

CLIMATE. Santa Fé. Jan. 29°F (−1·7°C), July 68°F (20°C). Annual rainfall 15″ (366 mm). *See* Mountain States, p. 1372.

CONSTITUTION AND GOVERNMENT. The constitution of 1912 is still in force with 103 amendments. The state Legislature, which meets annually, consists of 42 members of the Senate, elected for 4 years, and 70 members of the House of Representatives, elected for 2 years. The Governor and Lieut.-Governor are elected for 4 years. The state sends to Congress 2 senators and 3 representatives.

In the 1980 presidential election Reagan polled 250,779 votes, Carter 167,826.

The state capital is Santa Fé. For local government the state is divided into 33 counties.

Governor: Toney Anaya (D.), 1983–86 ($60,000).
Lieut.-Governor: Mike Runnells (D.), 1983–86 ($38,500).
Secretary of State: Clara Jones (D.), 1983–86 ($38,500).

BUDGET. For the year ending 30 June 1981 (US Census Bureau figures) general revenues were $2,476·9m. ($1,179m. from taxation and $465·2m. from federal government); general expenditures, $1,936·3m. (education, $888m.; highways, $225·6m., and public welfare, $192·1m.).

Long-term debt on 30 June 1981 was $757·1m.

Per capita personal income (1982) was $9,190.

ENERGY AND NATURAL RESOURCES

Minerals. New Mexico is the country's largest domestic source of uranium, perlite and potassium salts. Production of recoverable U_3O_8 was 12·4m. lb. in 1981;

perlite (1982), 433,000 short tons; potassium salts, 1·5m. tonnes; petroleum, 70·5m. bbls (of 42 gallons); natural gas, 965,447m. cu. ft; natural gas liquids, 42·5m. bbls (of 42 gallons); copper, 59,693 tonnes; coal, 18·1m. short tons market-ed. The value of the total mineral output (1982) was \$5,028m. An average of 26,700 persons were employed monthly in the mining industry in 1982.

Agriculture. New Mexico produces cereals, vegetables, fruit, livestock and cotton. Dry farming and irrigation have proved profitable in periods of high prices. There were 13,500 farms and ranches covering 47·4m. acres in 1981, average farm (or ranch) was valued (land and buildings) at \$481,954 in the 1978 US Census of Agriculture; 3,862 farms and ranches were of 1,000 acres and over.

Cash income, 1982 (preliminary), from crops, \$336·6m., and from livestock products, \$627·1m. Principal crops are wheat (13·3m. bu. from 530,000 acres), hay (1·4m. tons from 320,000 acres) and grain sorghums (14·6m. bu. from 310,000 acres). Farm animals on 1 Jan. 1983 included 58,000 milch cows, 1·5m. all cattle, 610,000 sheep and 38,000 swine. National forest area (1980) covered 9·2m. acres.

INDUSTRY. Average monthly non-agricultural employment during 1982 was 473,900: 34,000 were employed in manufacturing, 125,400 in government. Value added by manufacture, 1980, \$1,067m. Leading manufacturers were primary metals, petroleum and food.

COMMUNICATIONS

Roads. On 1 Jan. 1981 the state had 78,877 miles of road, of which the state main-tained 12,685 miles. Motor vehicle registrations, 1982, 1,349,394.

Railways. In 1981 there were 2,076 miles of railway.

Aviation. There were 78 public-use airports in Dec. 1983.

JUSTICE, RELIGION, EDUCATION AND WELFARE

Justice. The number of state prison inmates, average population 1983 (prelimin-ary), was 2,313, including 409 in juvenile centres; there were also 101 New Mexico prisoners held outside the state. The death penalty (by electrocution formerly, and now by lethal injection) has been imposed on 8 persons since 1933, 6 whites and 2 Negroes, all for murder. The last execution was in 1961.

Since 1949 the denial of employment by reason of race, colour, religion, national origin or ancestry has been forbidden. A law of 1955 prohibits discrimination in public places because of race or colour. An 'equal rights' amendment was added to the constitution in 1972.

Religion. There were (1975) approximately 356,530 Protestant Church members and 315,470 Roman Catholics.

Education. Elementary education is free, and compulsory between 6 and 17 years or high-school graduation age. In 1980–81 the 89 school districts had an estimated enrolment of 262,236 students in public elementary and secondary schools. Pri-vate and parochial schools had 20,319 pupils. There were 14,155 teachers receiv-ing an average salary of \$16,944. Public education expenditure was \$697·5m.

The state-supported 4-year institutes of higher education are (autumn 1982):

	Full-time Faculty	Students
University of New Mexico, Albuquerque	731	23,407
New Mexico State University, Las Cruces	538	12,512
Eastern New Mexico University, Portales	160	3,730
New Mexico Highlands University, Las Vegas	120	2,312
Western New Mexico University, Silver City	67	1,570
New Mexico Institute of Mining and Technology, Sorocco	85	1,362

Health. In 1980 the state had 53 short-term hospitals (4,337 beds).

Social Security. In Dec. 1982, 14,410 persons were receiving federal supplemental security income for the disabled (average $207.66 per month); 9,234 persons were receiving old-age assistance (average $125.32 per month); 458 persons were receiving aid to the blind (average $207.01 per month). In 1981 a monthly average of 55,095 people received aid to families with dependent children (average $69.90 per month).

Books of Reference

New Mexico Business (monthly; annual review in Jan.–Feb. issue). Bureau of Business and Economic Research, Univ. of N.M., Albuquerque
New Mexico Statistical Abstract: 1980. Bureau of Business and Economic Research, Univ. of N.M., Albuquerque, 1980
Muench, D., and Hillerman, T., *New Mexico.* Belding, Portland, Oregon, 1974

NEW YORK STATE

HISTORY. From 1609 to 1664 the region now called New York was claimed by the Dutch; then it came under the rule of the English, who governed the country until the outbreak of the War of Independence. On 20 April 1777 New York adopted a constitution which transformed the colony into an independent state; on 26 July 1788 it ratified the constitution of the US, becoming one of the 13 original states. New York dropped its claim to Vermont after the latter was admitted to the Union in 1791. With the annexation of a small area from Massachusetts in 1853, New York assumed its present boundaries.

AREA AND POPULATION. New York is bounded west and north by Canada with Lake Erie, Lake Ontario and the St Lawrence River forming the boundary; east by Vermont, Massachusetts and Connecticut, south-east by the Atlantic, south by New Jersey and Pennsylvania. Area, 49,108 sq. miles (1,731 sq. miles being water). Census population, 1 April 1980, 17,557,288, a decrease of 3.7% since 1970. Estimate (1981) 17,602,000. Births in 1979 were 234,867; deaths, 162,966; infant deaths, 3,177; marriages, 115,912; divorces, 64,420 (includes all dissolutions).

Population in 5 census years was:

	White	Negro	Indian	Asiatic	Total	Per sq. mile
1910	8,966,845	134,191	6,046	6,532	9,113,614	191·2
1930	12,143,191	412,814	6,973	15,088	12,588,066	262·6
1960	15,287,071	1,417,511	16,491	51,678	16,782,304	350·2
			All others			
1970	15,834,090	2,168,949	233,828		18,236,967	380·3
1980	13,961,106	2,401,842	1,194,340		17,557,288	367·0

Of the 1980 population, 8,338,961 were male, 14,857,202 were urban; those 20 years of age or older numbered 12,232,284. Aliens registered in Jan. 1980 numbered 801,411.

The population of New York City, by boroughs, census of 1 April 1980 was: Manhattan, 1,427,533; Bronx, 1,169,115; Brooklyn, 2,230,936; Queens, 1,891,325; Staten Island, 352,121; total, 7,071,030. The New York metropolitan statistical area had, in 1980, 9,080,777.

Population of other large cities and incorporated places census, April 1980, was:

Buffalo	357,002	Troy	56,614	Auburn	32,548
Rochester	241,509	Binghamton	55,745	Poughkeepsie	29,757
Yonkers	194,557	White Plains	46,999	Watertown	27,861
Syracuse	170,292	Rome	43,826	Lindenhurst	26,919
Albany (capital)	101,767	Hempstead	40,404	Rockville Center	25,405
Utica	75,435	Freeport	38,272	Newburgh	23,438
Niagara Falls	71,344	Jamestown	35,775	Garden City	22,927
New Rochelle	70,345	Valley Stream	35,769	Massapequa Park	19,779
Schenectady	67,877	N. Tonawanda	35,760		
Mount Vernon	66,023	Elmira	35,327		

Other large urbanized areas, census 1980; Buffalo, 1·2m.; Rochester, 970,313; Albany–Schenectady–Troy, 794,298.

CLIMATE. Albany. Jan. 24°F (–4·4°C), July 73°F (22·8°C). Annual rainfall 34″ (855 mm). Buffalo. Jan. 24°F (–4·4°C), July 70°F (21·1°C). Annual rainfall 36″ (905 mm). New York. Jan. 30°F (–1·1°C), July 74°F (23·3°C). Annual rainfall 43″ (1,087 mm). *See* Atlantic Coast, p. 1373.

CONSTITUTION AND GOVERNMENT. The present constitution dates from 1894; a later constitutional convention, 1938, is now legally considered merely to have amended the 1894 constitution, which has now had 93 amendments. The Constitutional Convention of 1967 (4 April through 26 Sept.) was composed of 186 delegates who proposed a new state constitution; however this was rejected by the registered voters on 7 Nov. 1967. The Senate consists of 60 members, and the Assembly of 150 members, both elected every 2 years. The Governor and Lieut.-Governor are elected for 4 years. The right of suffrage resides in every adult who has been a citizen for 90 days, and has the residential qualifications; new voters must establish, by certificates or test, that they have had at least an elementary education.

The state is represented in Congress by 2 senators and 34 representatives.

In the 1980 presidential election Reagan polled 2,893,831 votes, Carter 2,728,372 and Anderson 467,801.

The state capital is Albany. For local government the state is divided into 62 counties, 5 of which constitute the city of New York. New York leads in state parks and recreation areas, covering 252,984 acres in 1979.

Cities are in 3 classes, the first class having each 175,000 or more inhabitants and the third under 50,000. Each is incorporated by charter, under special legislation. The government of New York City is vested in the mayor (Edward Koch), elected for 4 years, and a city council, whose president and members are elected for 4 years. The council has a President and 37 members, each elected from a state senatorial district wholly within the city. The mayor appoints all the heads of departments, except the comptroller, who is elected. Each of the 5 city boroughs (Manhattan, Bronx, Brooklyn, Queens and Richmond) has a president, elected for 4 years. Each borough is also a county bearing the same name except Manhattan borough, which, as a county, is called New York, and Brooklyn, which is Kings County.

Governor: Mario Cuomo (D.), 1983–86 ($85,000).
Lieut.-Governor: Alfred del Bello (D.), 1983–86 ($60,000).
Secretary of State: Gail Schaefer (D.), 1983–86 ($64,400).

BUDGET. The state's general revenues for the financial year ending 31 March 1982 were $16,142m. ($14,959m. from taxes); general expenditures were $16,126m. ($5,298m. for education, $8,049m. for social services, $1,893m. for transport).

Per capita personal income was $10,252 in 1980.

The assessed valuation in 1980 of taxable real property in New York City was $38,056m. The assessed valuation of the state was $86,741m.

ENERGY AND NATURAL RESOURCES

Minerals. Production of principal minerals in 1980: Sand and gravel (22,000 short tons), salt (5,500 short tons), zinc (33,629 tonnes), petroleum (824,296 bbls), natural gas (15,680m. cu. ft). The state is a leading producer of titanium concentrate, talc, abrasive garnet, wollastonite and emery. Quarry products include trap rock, slate, marble, limestone and sandstone. Value of mineral output in 1980 $497·9m.

Agriculture. New York has large agricultural interests. On 1 Jan. 1981 it had 49,000 farms, with a total area of 9·9m. acres; average farm was 202 acres.

Cash income, 1980, from crops and livestock, $2,420m. Dairying, with 18,500 farms, 1981, is an important type of farming with produce at a market value of

$1,520m. Field crops comprise maize, winter wheat, oats and hay. New York (1981) ranks second in US in the production of apples, and maple syrup. Other products are grapes, tart cherries, peaches, pears, plums, strawberries, raspberries, cabbages, onions, potatoes, maple sugar. Estimated farm animals, 1981, included 1·95m. all cattle, 912,000 milch cows, 70,000 sheep, 165,000 swine and 10·6m. chickens.

INDUSTRY. In 1981 manufacturing establishments numbering 31,849 employed 1,439,872 workers whose average weekly earnings were $385. Leading industries were clothing, non-electrical machinery, printing and publishing, electrical equipment, instruments, food and allied products and fabricated metals.

COMMUNICATIONS

Roads. There were (1981) 109,485 miles of municipal and rural roads. The New York State Thruway extends 559 miles from New York City to Buffalo; in 1981 receipts from tolls amounted to $183,289,532. The Northway, a 176-mile toll-free highway, is a connecting road from the Thruway at Albany to the Canadian border at Champlain, Quebec.

Motor vehicle registrations in 1981 were 8·7m., most of which (7m.) were private passenger vehicles.

Railways. There were in 1981, 3,891 miles of Class I railways.

Aviation. There were 471 airports and landing areas in 1981.

Shipping. The canals of the state, combined in 1918 in what is called the Improved Canal System, have a length of 524 miles, of which the Erie or Barge canal has 340 miles. In 1981 the canals carried 807,925 tons of freight.

JUSTICE, RELIGION, EDUCATION AND WELFARE

Justice. The State Human Rights Law was approved 12 March 1945, effective 1 July, 1945. The State Division of Human Rights is charged with the responsibility of enforcing this law. The division may request and utilize the services of all governmental departments and agencies; adopt and promulgate suitable rules and regulations; test, investigate and pass judgment upon complaints alleging discrimination in employment, in places of public accommodation, resort or amusement, education, and in housing, land and commercial space; hold hearings, subpoena witnesses and require the production for examination of papers relating to matters under investigation; grant compensatory damages and require repayment of profits in certain housing cases among other provisions; apply for court injunctions to prevent frustration of orders of the Commissioner.

On 30 Dec. 1981, 25,600 persons were in state prisons.

In 1963–81 there were no executions. Total executions (by electrocution) from 1930 to 1962 were 329 (234 whites, 90 Negroes, 5 other races; all for murder except 2 for kidnapping).

In 1980 murders reported in New York were 2,225; total violent crimes, 179,981. Police strength (sworn officers) in 1980 was 55,222 (27,394 New York City).

Religion. The churches are Roman Catholic, with 6,367,576 members in 1981, Jewish congregations (about 2m. in 1981) and Protestant Episcopal (299,929 in 1980).

Education. Education is compulsory between the ages of 7 and 16. In autumn 1980 the public elementary schools (grades kindergarten to 6) enrolled 1,393,945 children, public secondary schools (grades 7 to 12) had 1,466,626 pupils; classroom teachers numbered 170,694 in public schools. Total expenditure on public schools in 1980–81 was $9,069,092,216. Teachers' salaries, 1980–81, averaged $21,316.

The state's educational system, including public and private schools and secondary institutions, universities, colleges, libraries, museums, etc., constitutes (by legislative act) the 'University of the State of New York', which is governed by a Board of Regents consisting of 15 members appointed by the Legislature. Within the framework of this 'University' was established in 1948 a 'State University' which controls 64 colleges and educational centres, 30 of which are locally operated community colleges. The 'State University' is governed by a board of 16 Trustees, appointed by the Governor with the consent and advice of the Senate.

Higher education in the state is conducted in 248 institutions (628,530 full-time students), of which 163 are under private control and 85 under public control.

In autumn 1980 the 248 institutions of higher education in the state had a total of 1,108,140 degree and non-degree credit students. Among them were:

Founded	Name and place	Teachers	Students
1754	Columbia University, New York	3,965	17,410
1795	Union University, Schenectady and Albany	178	2,071
1824	Rensselaer Polytechnic Institute, Troy	442	6,145
1831	New York University, New York	2,615	45,000
1846	Colgate University, New York	205	2,550
1846	Fordham University, New York	958	14,653
1847	University of the City of New York, New York	12,426	172,683
1848	University of Rochester, Rochester	1,549	11,159
1854	Polytechnic Institute of New York	242	4,583
1856	St Lawrence University, Canton	173	2,375
1857	Cooper Union Institute of Technology, New York	161	872
1861	Vassar College, Poughkeepsie	230	2,364
1863	Manhattan College, New York	291	3,498
1865	Cornell University, Ithaca	1,863	17,866
1870	Syracuse University, Syracuse	1,100	11,819
1948	State University of New York	13,228	372,415

The Saratoga Performing Arts Centre (5,100 seats), a non-profit, tax-exempt organization, which opened in 1966, is the summer residence of the New York City Ballet and the Philadelphia Orchestra—two groups which present special educational programmes for students and teachers.

Health. In 1981 the state had 278 hospitals (67,798 beds), 585 skilled nursing homes (62,435 beds) and 241 other institutions (24,302 beds). In 1980 mental health facilities had 27,309 patients and institutions for the mentally retarded had 18,577 patients.

Social Security. The federal Supplemental Security Income programme covered aid to the needy aged, blind and disabled from 1 Jan. 1975. In the state programme for 1980, $4,543m. was paid in Medicaid to 2,288,000 people; aid to dependent children in 1980 went to 1,248,900 recipients, average benefits $371 per family per month.

Books of Reference

New York Red Book. Albany, 1979–80

Legislative Manual. Department of State, 1980–81

New York State Statistical Yearbook, 1979–80. Albany

Connery, R. and G. B., *Governing New York State: The Rockefeller Years.* Academy of Political Science, New York, 1974

Ellis, D. M., *History of New York State.* Cornell Univ. Press, 1967

Flick, A. (ed.), *History of the State of New York.* Columbia Univ. Press, 1933–37

Lincoln, C., *Constitutional History of New York 1809–1877.* Rochester, 1906

Rosenwhike, I., *Population History of New York City.* Syracuse Univ. Press, 1972

Wolfe, G. R., *New York: A Guide to the Metropolis.* New York Univ. Press, 1975

State Library: The New York State Library, Albany 12230. *State Librarian and Assistant Commissioner for Libraries:* Joseph Shubert.

NORTH CAROLINA

HISTORY. North Carolina, first settled in 1585 by Sir Walter Raleigh and permanently settled in 1663, was one of the 13 original states of the Union.

AREA AND POPULATION. North Carolina is bounded north by Virginia, east by the Atlantic, south by South Carolina, south-west by Georgia and west by Tennessee. Area, 52,669 sq. miles, of which 3,826 sq. miles are inland water. Census population, 1 April 1980, 5,874,429, an increase of 15·5% since 1970. Estimated population (1982), 6,058,154.

Births, 1979, were 83,782 (14·9 per 1,000 population); marriages, 45,064 (8); deaths, 46,640 (8·3); infant deaths, 1,270 (15·2 per 1,000 live births); divorces and annulments, 27,245 (4·9).

Population in 6 census years was:

	White	Negro	Indian	Asiatic	Total	Per sq. mile
1910	1,500,511	697,843	7,851	82	2,206,287	45·3
1930	2,234,958	918,647	16,579	92	3,170,276	64·5
1950	2,983,121	1,047,353	3,742	—	4,061,929	82·7
1960	3,399,285	1,116,021	38,129	2,012	4,556,155	92·2
			All others			
1970	3,901,767	1,126,478	53,814		5,082,059	104·1
1980	4,453,010	1,316,050	105,369		5,874,429	111·5

Of the total population in 1980, 2,852,012 were male, 2,818,794 were urban and 3,976,359 were 20 years old or older; 14·8% were non-white.

Cities (with census population in 1980) are: Charlotte, 310,799; Greensboro, 154,763; Winston-Salem, 131,211; Raleigh (capital), 148,299; Durham (1970), 95,438; High Point, 63,169; Asheville, 57,708; Fayetteville, 59,476.

CLIMATE. Climate varies sharply with altitude; the warmest area is in the south east near Southport and Wilmington; the coldest is Mount Mitchell (6,684 ft). Raleigh. Jan. 42°F (5·6°C), July 79°F (26·1°C). Annual rainfall 46″ (1,158 mm). *See* Atlantic Coast, p. 1373.

CONSTITUTION AND GOVERNMENT. The present constitution dates from 1971 (previous constitution, 1776 and 1868/76); it has had 12 amendments. The General Assembly consists of a Senate of 50 members and a House of Representatives of 120 members; all are elected by districts for 2 years. The Governor and Lieut.-Governor are elected for 4 years. The Governor may succeed himself but has no veto. There are 17 other executive heads of department, 8 elected by the people and 7 appointed by the Governor. All registered citizens with the usual residential qualifications have a vote.

The state is represented in Congress by 2 senators and 11 representatives.

In the presidential election of 1980 Reagan polled 915,018 votes, Carter 875,635 and Anderson 52,800.

The capital is Raleigh, established in 1792.

Governor: James B. Hunt, Jr (D.), 1977–85 ($55,104).
Lieut.-Governor James C. Green (D.) ($45,636).
Secretary of State: Thad Eure (D.) ($45,636).

BUDGET. General revenue for the year ending 30 June 1983 was $2,403·8m. General expenditure was $3,440·7m.

On 30 June 1981 the net total long-term debt amounted to $853·2m.
Per capita personal income (1982) was $9,032.

NATURAL RESOURCES

Minerals. Mining production in 1982 was valued at $275·1m. Principal minerals were stone, sand and gravel, phosphate rock, feldspar, clay, mica, lithium minerals, olivine, kaolin and talc. North Carolina ranked first in the production of mica, feldspar, olivine spodumene and phrophyllite. It is also the leading producer of bricks, making about 13% of the total US production.

Agriculture. In 1981 there were 93,000 farms in North Carolina covering 11·7m. acres; average size of farms was 126 acres and average value $167,400.

The state leads in producing tobacco, sweet potatoes, turkeys and farm forest products. Cash receipts from farming (1981), $4,200m., of which $2,600m. was from crops and $1,600m. from livestock, dairy and poultry products. Value of crop production: flue-cured tobacco, $1,300m.; maize, $380m.; soybeans, $289m.; peanuts, $157m.; sweet potatoes, $64m.; wheat, $54m.; hay, $41m. On 1 Jan. 1981 farms had 1·16m. all cattle, 1·98m. swine and 18·5m. chickens.

Forestry. Commercial forest covered 19·5m. acres (62·6% of land area), in 1983. Main products are hardwood veneer and hardwood plywood.

Fisheries. Commercial fish catch, 1980, amounted to 356m. lb.; value approximately $68·8m. The catch is mainly of menhaden, crabmeat, bay scallops, flounder, croaker, shrimps, sea trout, spots and clams.

INDUSTRY. North Carolina's 9,668 industrial establishments in 1980 had 824,200 production workers. The leading industries are textile goods, manufacture of cigarettes, chemicals, electronics and electrical machinery, processing of food crops and the manufacture of furniture and bricks. In 1982 investment in new and expanded industry was $1,290m.

TOURISM. Total receipts of the travel industry, $3,100m. in 1982.

COMMUNICATIONS

Roads. The state maintained, 1981, 76,032 miles of highways, comprising all rural roads and 4,388 miles of urban streets which are major thoroughfares. In Sept. 1981, 2,989,776 automobiles, 904,708 trucks and 572,550 other vehicles were registered.

Railways. The state in 1983 contained 4,117 miles of railway operating in 91 of the 100 counties. There are 23 Class I, II and III rail companies.

Aviation. In 1981 there were 71 public airports of which 9 are served by major airlines and 5 by commuter airlines.

Shipping. There are 2 ocean ports, Wilmington and Morehead City.

JUSTICE, RELIGION, EDUCATION AND WELFARE

Justice. Total executions 1910–62, 362. Prison population at 8 Oct. 1983, 15,995.

Religion. Leading denominations are the Baptists (48·9% of church membership), Methodists (20·7%), Presbyterians (7·7%), Lutherans (3%) and Roman Catholics (2·7%). Total estimate of all denominations in 1983 was 2·6m.

Education. School attendance is compulsory between 6 and 16.

Public school enrolment, 1982–83, was 1,107,490; elementary and secondary schools numbered 2,005. Instructional staff (1980) consisted of 67,586 classroom teachers and administrators. Expenditure for public schools is 63·3% from state, 23·6% from local and 13·1% from federal sources.

In autumn 1982–83 state-supported colleges and universities included 23 community colleges with 60,730 students; 35 technical institutes with 55,897 students. The 16 senior universities are all part of the University of North Carolina system, the largest campus being at Chapel Hill, where the university was founded in 1789 and first opened in 1792. Its 1982 enrolment was 100,912 undergraduates. The total enrolment of public institutions of higher learning in 1982 was 218,606.

In addition to the state-supported institutions there were 8 private junior colleges with an enrolment of 4,760 and 30 private senior institutions with a total enrolment of 41,904. The total enrolment in private institutions for 1982 was 52,538.

Health. In Oct. 1983 the state had 157 hospitals (32,345 beds).

Social Security. In June 1982 there were 900,070 persons receiving $300·4m. in social security benefits. Of that number 496,020 were retired, receiving $186·67m.; 85.640 were disabled ($34·7m.); 318,410 others received $79m.

Books of Reference

North Carolina Manual. Secretary of State. Raleigh. Biennial
Corbitt, D. L., *The Formation of the North Carolina Counties.* Raleigh, 1969
Lefler, H. T., and Newsome, A. R., *North Carolina: The History of a Southern State.* Univ. of N.C., Chapel Hill, 1963

NORTH DAKOTA

HISTORY. North Dakota was admitted into the Union, with boundaries as at present, on 2 Nov. 1889; previously it had formed part of the Dakota Territory, established 2 March 1861.

AREA AND POPULATION. North Dakota is bounded north by Canada, east by the Red River (forming a boundary with Minnesota), south by South Dakota and west by Montana. Land area, 69,262 sq. miles, and 1,403 sq. miles of water. The Federal Bureau of Indian Affairs administered (1971) 850,000 acres, of which 153,000 acres were assigned to tribes. Census population, 1 April 1980, 652,717, an increase of 34,956 or 5·7% since 1970. Estimate (1981), 658,000. Births in 1982 were 12,654 (19 per 1,000 population); deaths, 5,385 (8·0); infant deaths, 134; marriages, 6,194; divorces, 2,193.

Population at 5 census years was:

	White	Negro	Indian	Asiatic	Total	Per sq. mile
1910	569,855	617	6,486	98	577,056	8·2
1930	671,851	377	8,617	194	680,845	9·7
1960	619,538	777	11,736	274	632,446	9·1
			All others			
1970	599,485	2,494	15,782		617,761	8·9
1980	625,557	2,568	24,692		652,717	9·4

Of the total population in 1980, 328,126 were male, 317,821 were urban and 419,234 were 21 years old or older. Estimated outward migration, 1970–80, 16,983.

The largest cities are Fargo with population (census), 1980, of 61,383; Grand Forks, 43,765; Bismarck (capital), 44,485, and Minot, 32,843.

CLIMATE. Bismarck. Jan. 8°F (–13·3°C), July 71°F (21·1°C). Annual rainfall 16″ (402 mm). Fargo. Jan. 6°F (–14·4°C), July 71°F (21·1°C). Annual rainfall 20″ (503 mm). *See* High Plains, p. 1372.

CONSTITUTION AND GOVERNMENT. The present constitution dates from 1889; it has had 95 amendments. The Legislative Assembly consists of a Senate of 53 members elected for 4 years, and a House of Representatives of 106 members elected for 2 years. The Governor and Lieut.-Governor are elected for 4 years. Qualified electors are (with necessary exceptions) all citizens and civilized Indians. The state sends to Congress 2 senators elected by the voters of the entire state and 1 representative.

In the 1980 presidential election Reagan polled 193,695 votes, Carter 79,189 and Anderson 23,640.

The capital is Bismarck. The state has 53 organized counties.

Governor: Allen I. Olson (R.), 1981–85 ($60,812 plus expenses).
Lieut.-Governor: Ernest Sands (R.), 1981–85 ($12,500 plus expenses).
Secretary of State: Ben Meier (R.), 1981–85 ($43,380 plus expenses).

FINANCE. General revenue of state and local government year ending 30 June 1980, was $1,249m.; general expenditures, $1,201m., taxation provided $553m. and federal aid, $280m.; education took $427m.; highways, $198m., and public welfare, $98m.

Total net long-term debt (local government) on 30 June 1980, $826m.

Per capita personal income (1981) was $10,213.

ENERGY AND NATURAL RESOURCES

Minerals. The mineral resources of North Dakota consist chiefly of oil which was discovered in 1951. Production of crude petroleum in 1982 was 47m. bbls; of natural gas, 56,700m. cu. ft. Output (1981) of lignite coal was 17·9m. short tons. Total value of mineral output, 1980, $880m.

Agriculture. Agriculture is the chief pursuit of the North Dakota population. In 1982 there were 38,000 farms (61,963 in 1954) with an area of 42m. acres (41,876,924 in 1954); the average farm was of 1,097 acres. The greater number of farms are cash-grain or livestock farms with annual sales of $20,000–$39,999.

Cash income, 1982, from crops, $2,156·4m., and from livestock, $589·1m. North Dakota leads in the production of barley, sunflowers, flaxseed and durum. Other important products are wheat, pinto beans, sugar-beet, potatoes, hay, oats, rye and maize.

The state has also an active livestock industry, chiefly cattle raising. On 1 Jan. 1983 the farm animals were: 94,000 milch cows, 2m. all cattle, 220,000 sheep and 210,000 swine. The wool clip yielded (1982), 1·8m. lb. of wool from 193,000 sheep.

Forestry. National forest area, 1977, 422,000 acres, of which 115,000 acres are federally owned or managed.

INDUSTRY. From 1970 to 1982 agricultural employment fell from 51,920 to 51,870; non-agricultural jobs rose from 148,910 to 268,300. Between 1970 and 1982, employment in manufacturing rose from 9,910 to 14,920, in trade from 43,890 to 67,190 and in government from 49,240 to 60,710.

COMMUNICATIONS

Roads. The state highway department maintained, in 1981, 7,220 miles of highway; local authorities, 95,938 miles, and municipal, 3,193 miles.

Car and truck registrations in 1980 numbered 645,441.

Railways. In 1980 there were 5,262 miles of railway.

Aviation. Airports in 1980 numbered 262, of which 107 were publicly owned.

JUSTICE, RELIGION, EDUCATION AND WELFARE

Justice. The state penitentiary, on 24 Jan. 1984, held 424 inmates. Of these, 55 were incarcerated at the North Dakota State Farm. There is no death penalty.

Religion. The leading religious denominations are the Roman Catholics, with 171,185 members in 1975; Combined Lutherans, 216,579; Methodists, 28,880; Presbyterians, 18,636.

Education. School attendance is compulsory between the ages of 7 and 16, or until the 17th birthday if the eighth grade has not been completed. In Oct. 1982 the public elementary schools had 80,704 pupils; secondary schools, 35,907 pupils. State expenditure on public schools, 1980, $427m. Private schools had 9,528 elementary pupils and 3,292 secondary pupils in 1982.

The university at Grand Forks, founded in 1883, had 9,440 students in 1982; the state university of agriculture and applied science, at Fargo, 8,079 students. Total enrolment in the 8 public institutions of higher education, 1982, 35,011.

Health. In 1982 the state had 60 hospitals (5,880 beds), and 79 nursing homes (5,100).

Social Security. In 1980 grants were made to 105,000 people, including 74,000 ret:red workers, 23,000 survivors of workers and 8,000 disabled workers.

Books of Reference

No:th Dakota Growth Indicators, 1981. 19th ed. Economic Development Commission, Bismarck, 1982
North Dakota Blue Book. Secretary of State, Bismarck, 1981
Statistical Abstract of North Dakota, 1983. Bureau of Business and Economic Research, Univ. of North Dakota, 1983
Goodey. R. B. (ed.) *Readings in the Geography of North Dakota.* North Dakota Studies, 1968
Robinson, E. B., *History of North Dakota.* Univ. of Nebraska Press, 1966

OHIO

HISTORY. Ohio, first settled in 1788, unofficially entered the Union on 19 Feb. 1803; entrance was made official, retroactive to 1 March 1803, on 8 Aug. 1953.

AREA AND POPULATION. Ohio is bounded north by Michigan and Lake Erie, east by Pennsylvania, south-east and south by the Ohio River (forming a boundary with West Virginia and Kentucky) and west by Indiana. Area, 41,330 sq. miles, of which 325 sq. miles are inland water. Census population, 1 April 1980 (preliminary), 10,797,419, an increase of 145,402 or 1·4% since 1970. Estimate (1981) 10,781,000. In 1980 births numbered 169,359 (15·7 per 1,000 population); deaths, 97,779 (9); infant deaths, 2,020 (12 per 1,000 live births); marriages, 99,522 (9·2); divorces and annulments, 58,225 (5·4).

Population at 5 census years was:

	White	Negro	Indian	Asiatic	Total	Per sq. mile
1910	4,654,897	111,452	127	645	4,767,121	117·0
1930	6,335,173	309,304	435	1,785	6,646,697	161·6
1960	8,909,698	786,097	1,910	8,692	9,706,397	236·9
			All others			
1970	9,646,997	970,477	34,543		10,652,017	260·0
1980	9,597,266	1,076,734	123,419		10,797,419	263·5

Of the total population in 1980, 5,217,027 were male, 7,914,500 persons were urban. Those 20 years old or older numbered 7,294,471.

Census population of chief cities on 1 April 1980 was:

Cleveland	572,532	Hamilton	62,845	Cuyahoga Falls	43,710
Columbus	561,943	Lakewood	61,921	Mentor	42,065
Cincinnati	383,058	Kettering	61,223	Newark	41,200
Toledo	354,265	Euclid	59,896	Marion	37,040
Akron	236,820	Elyria	57,039	East Cleveland	36,957
Dayton	193,319	Cleveland Heights	55,563	North Olmsted	36,486
Youngstown	115,429	Warren	55,456	Upper Arlington	35,648
Canton	94,632	Mansfield	53,907	Lancaster	34,953
Parma	92,578	Lima	47,381	Garfield Heights	33,380
Lorain	75,339	Middletown	43,719	Zanesville	28,655
Springfield	72,098				

Urbanized areas, 1980 census: Cleveland, 1,895,997; Cincinnati, 1,392,394; Columbus (the capital), 1,088,973; Dayton, 826,891; Akron, 660,233; Toledo, 791,137; Youngstown-Warren, 529,887; Canton, 403,847.

CLIMATE. Cincinnatti. Jan. 33°F (0·6°C), July 78°F (25·6°C). Annual rainfall 39″ (978 mm). Cleveland. Jan. 27°F (−2·8°C), July 71°F (21·1°C). Annual rainfall 35″ (879 mm). Columbus. Jan. 29°F (−1·7°C), July 75°F (23·9°C). Annual rainfall 34″ (850 mm). *See* Great Lakes, p. 1373.

CONSTITUTION AND GOVERNMENT. The question of a general revision of the constitution drafted by an elected convention is submitted to the people every 20 years. The constitution of 1851 had 105 amendments by 1978.

In the 112th General Assembly the Senate consisted of 33 members and the House of Representatives of 99 members. The Senate is elected for 4 years, half each 2 years; the House is elected for 2 years; the Governor, Lieut.-Governor and Secretary of State for 4 years. Qualified as electors are (with necessary exceptions) all citizens 18 years of age who have the usual residential qualifications. Ohio sends 2 senators and 21 representatives to Congress.

In the 1980 presidential election Reagan polled 2,206,545 votes, Carter, 1,752,414.

The capital (since 1816) is Columbus. Ohio is divided into 88 counties.

Governor: Richard Celeste (D.), 1983–86 ($50,000).
Lieut.-Governor: Myrl H. Shoemaker (D.), 1983–86 ($50,000).
Secretary of State: Sherrod Brown (D.), 1983–86 ($50,000).

BUDGET. For the year ending 30 June 1980 (Budget of the State of Ohio) total general revenue was $12,180·3m. and general expenditure was $11,397·4m.

The net long-term debt of the state on 30 June 1980 was $4,014·9m.

Per capita personal income (1980) was $9,462.

ENERGY AND NATURAL RESOURCES

Minerals. Ohio has extensive mineral resources, of which coal is the most important by value: output (1981) 37·4m. short tons. Production of crude petroleum, 14m. bbls; natural gas, 139,000m. cu. ft. Other minerals include stone, clay, sand and gravel. Value of fuel minerals, 1980, $1,828m.; non-fuel, $562·3m.

Agriculture. Ohio is extensively devoted to agriculture. In 1981, 94,000 farms covered 16m. acres; all farms were valued at $28,143m.

Cash income 1980, from crop and livestock and products, $3,746·7m. The most important crops in 1980 were: Maize (440·7m. bu.),wheat (67·1m. bu.), oats (19·4m. bu.), soybeans (135·4m. bu.). The wool clip in 1976 yielded 3·35m. lb. from 423,000 sheep. On 1 Jan. 1981 there were 2m. swine 1·81m. all cattle and 310,000 sheep.

Forestry. State forest area, 1978, 170,000 acres including reclamation area.

INDUSTRY. In 1980, manufacturing employed 1,253,000 workers. The value added by manufacture was $50,176m. The largest industry was manufacturing of non-electrical machinery.

COMMUNICATIONS

Roads. The state (1977) maintained 19,458 miles of highway, including 1,303 miles of interstate highways and 241 miles on the Ohio Turnpike; there were 91,511 miles of country, township, city, park and forest development roads. Total miles of highway maintained by all government agencies (1977) 110,969.

Railways. The railroads had 7,400 route miles of track in 1978.

Aviation. Ohio had (1978) 719 airports and airfields, of which 212 are commercial and 527 private, 130 heliports and 2 seaplane bases. There were 6,600 licensed aeroplanes.

JUSTICE, RELIGION, EDUCATION AND WELFARE

Justice. A Civil Rights Act (1933) forbids inns, restaurants, theatres, retail stores and all other places of public resort to discriminate against citizens on grounds of 'colour or race'; none may be denied the right to serve on juries on the grounds of 'colour or race'; insurance companies are forbidden to discriminate between 'white persons and coloured, wholly or partially of African descent'.

A state Civil Rights Commission (created 1959) has general administrative powers to prevent discrimination because of race, colour, religion, national origin or ancestry in employment, labour organization membership, use of public accommodations and in obtaining 'commercial housing' or 'personal residence'. Ohio has no *de jure* segregation in the public schools.

The state's adult correctional institutions, 30 Oct. 1978, held 8,285 inmates (average daily count). Total executions (by electrocution) since 1930 were 170, all for murder. There have been no executions since 1963. The Department of Rehabilitation and Correction was created in July 1972, and has established probation services in 51 counties where services would otherwise be inadequate or nonexistent.

Religion. Many religious faiths are represented, including (but not limited to) the Baptist, Jewish, Lutheran, Methodist, Presbyterian and Roman Catholic.

Education. School attendance during full term is compulsory for children from 6 to 18 years of age. In 1980 public schools had 2,025,000 enrolled pupils; elementary schools had 54,100 teachers; secondary schools had 45,200 teachers. Teachers' salaries averaged $16,800 (secondary) and $15,700 (elementary). Operating expenditure on elementary and secondary schools for 1980 was $3,839m. The state's universities and colleges had a total enrolment (1980) of 489,100 students; the following had 7,000 or more students, autumn 1977:

Founded	Institutions	Enrolments
1804	Ohio University, Athens (State)	13,021
1809	Miami University, Oxford (State)	14,759
1826	Case Western Reserve University, Cleveland	8,108
1850	University of Dayton (R.C.)	9,620
1870	University of Akron (State)	23,121
1872	Ohio State University, Columbus (State)	51,003
1872	University of Toledo (State)	16,933
1874	University of Cincinnati (State-affiliated)	32,952
1887	Sinclair Community College, Dayton	13,752
1908	Youngstown University (State)	15,696
1910	Bowling Green State University (State)	16,439
1912	Kent State University (State)	19,396
1962	Cuyahoga Community College (Municipal)	27,250
1964	Cleveland State University (State)	17,627
1964	Wright State University (State)	13,067

Health. In 1980 the state had 239 hospitals (63,600 beds) listed by the American Hospital Association. Hospitals for mental diseases had 6,444 patients; state facilities for the mentally retarded had 4,778 resident patients.

Social Security. Public assistance is administered through 4 basic programmes: aid to dependent children, emergency assistance, Medicaid and general relief. Total public assistance expenditures during the year ending 30 June 1978 were $1,322·4m. In 1976–77 the number of persons receiving public assistance averaged 626,100 per month. Under the aid to dependent children programme $429·9m. provided assistance to an average of 526,434 recipients per month. Payments for Medicaid were $603·5m.; for social services, $189m.; for general relief, $78·4m., and emergency assistance, $21·6m. Recipients of general relief averaged 47,923 per month, emergency assistance, 30,585. Recipients of Medicaid during the year, 799,915.

Books of Reference

Official Roster: Federal State, County Officers and Department Information. Secretary of State, Columbus. Biennial
Rosebloom, E. H., and Weisenburger, F. P., *A History of Ohio.* State Arch. and Hist. Soc., Columbus, 1953

OKLAHOMA

HISTORY. An unorganized area in the centre of the present state was thrown open to white settlers on 22 April 1889. The Territory of Oklahoma, organized in

1890 to include this area and other sections, was opened to white settlements by runs or lotteries during the next decade. In 1893 the Territory was enlarged by the addition of the Cherokee Outlet, which fixed part of the present northern boundary. On 16 Nov. 1907 Oklahoma was combined with the remaining part of the Indian Territory and admitted as a state with boundaries substantially as now.

AREA AND POPULATION. Oklahoma is bounded north by Kansas, north-east by Missouri, east by Arkansas, south by Texas (the Red River forming part of the boundary) and, at the western extremity of the 'panhandle', by New Mexico and Colorado. Area 68,782 sq. miles, of which 1,137 sq. miles are water. Census population, 1 April 1980, 3,025,266, an increase of 465,803 or 18% since 1970. Estimate (1981), 3,100,000. Births, 1980, were 52,065; deaths, 28,908; infant deaths 660; marriages, 46,509; divorces, including annulments, 24,226.

The population at 5 federal censuses was:

	White	Negro	Indian	Asiatic	Total	Per sq. mile
1910	1,444,531	137,612	74,825	187	1,657,155	23·9
1930	2,130,778	172,198	92,725	339	2,396,040	34·6
1960	2,107,900	153,084	68,689	1,414	2,328,284	33·8
			All others			
1970	2,280,362	171,892	106,999		2,559,253	37·2
1980	2,597,783	204,658	222,825		3,025,266	43·2

In 1980, 1,476,719 were male, 2,035,082 were urban and those 20 years of age or older numbered 2,052,729. In eastern Oklahoma the US Bureau of Indian Affairs is responsible for 14 Indian tribes, about 97,000 Indians on over 800,000 acres.

The most important cities with population, 1980 are Oklahoma City (capital), 403,213, Tulsa, 360,919; Lawton, 80,054; Norman, 68,020; Enid, 50,363; Midwest City, 49,559.

CLIMATE. Oklahoma City. Jan. 37°F (2·8°C), July 81°F (27·2°C). Annual rainfall 32″ (803 mm). Tulsa. Jan. 37°F (2·8°C), July 82°F (27·8°C). Annual rainfall 37″ (925 mm). *See* Central Plains, p. 1372.

CONSTITUTION AND GOVERNMENT. The present constitution, dating from 1907, provides for amendment by initiative petition and legislative referendum; it has had 106 amendments.

The Legislature consists of a Senate of 48 members, who are elected for 4 years, and a House of Representatives elected for 2 years and consisting of 101 members. The Governor and Lieut.-Governor are elected for 4-year terms; the Governor can only be elected for two terms in succession. Electors are (with necessary exceptions) all citizens 18 years or older, with the usual qualifications.

The state is represented in Congress by 2 senators and 6 representatives.

In the 1980 presidential election Reagan polled 695,570 votes, Carter 402,026, Anderson 38,284 and Clark 13,828.

The capital is Oklahoma City. The state has 77 counties.

Governor: George Nigh (D.), 1983–86 ($70,000).
Lieut.-Governor: Spencer Bernard (D.), 1983–86 ($40,000).
Secretary of State: Jeanette B. Edmondson (D.), 1983–86 ($37,500).

BUDGET. Total revenue for the year ending 30 June 1981 (State Budget Office figures) was $3,982m. General revenue was $1,361m.

Bonded indebtedness for the year ending 30 June 1981, $1,169m.

Per capita personal income (1981) was $9,081.

ENERGY AND NATURAL RESOURCES

Minerals. Resources include petroleum, helium, natural gas, coal (bituminous), cement, granite, gypsum, olivestone, sand, gravel and some copper and silver. Production for 1981 was: Petroleum, 154,057,000 bbls; natural gas, 2,029,667m. cu. ft. In March 1981 there were 82,639 oilwells and 16,994 natural gaswells in production. Total value of mineral production, 1981, $8,677,798.

Agriculture. In 1980 the state had 73,000 farms with a total area of 35m. acres; average farm was 479 acres with an average gross income of $49,569. In 1980, there were 43,792 full-time farmers or ranchers, 25,719 part-owners and 10,019 tenants. Large-scale commercial farming is predominant.

The conservation and development of the renewable natural resources of the state has received close attention by local, county and state governments during the past 40 years. All of the land in the state is within the boundaries of one of the 88 conservation districts. Of the total surface (44m. acres), 92% is under a basic conservation plan prepared by the conservation district with assistance from the Soil Conservation Service. The Oklahoma Conservation Commission reported that good conservation measures by farmers, such as minimum tillage and crop residue management, are helping to conserve moisture and protect crops from erosion. Through Jan. 1980, 125 work plans had been approved for watersheds established in 1946 to aid flood control. In addition, 2,540 flood-prevention dams and 62 multi-purpose dams have been built or approved under this project. In 1981 there were 4 active Resource Conservation and Development Areas covering 16·8m. acres in 31 counties. Plans for 5 other areas covering another 32 counties have been submitted.

A trend of the last 40 years has been the conversion of arable land to grass; cattle and calves rank first in agricultural products, valued, 1981, at $1,460m.; winter wheat is second, at $845m.

Cash income from crops and livestock products 1981, $2,855m. The most valuable crop is winter wheat (production, 1981, 172m. bu.). Other crops (production, 1981) included hay (3·3m. tons), cotton (440,000 bales of 480 lb.), grain sorghums (22m. bu.) and peanuts (189m. lb.). On 1 Jan. 1982 the stock included 111,000 milch cows, 5·8m. all cattle, 105,000 sheep and lambs, 4·2m. farm chickens and 245,000 swine.

Forestry. There are nearly 10m. acres of forest, one half considered commercial. The forest products industry, concentrated in the southeastern counties, employs approximately 7,000 in over 100 manufacturing plants with an estimated combined annual payroll of $75m. Value of shipments of lumber and forest products in 1980 was over $50m.

INDUSTRY. The retail trade and service industries each employed 15% of the working population in 1981. Among other industries the most important by payroll employment (1982) were: mining (103,700); construction (49,300); transport and utilities (67,700); manufacturing (193,700); government (245,000); finance, insurance and property (58,800). In 1982 the civilian non-agricultural labour force averaged 1·2m.

COMMUNICATIONS

Roads. In 1982 there were 12,178 miles of inter-state, federal and state highway open, 81,304 miles of county roads, 15,458 miles of city streets, 487 miles of turnpike and 344 miles of park and forest roads. Motor vehicle registrations, 1980, 2,731,628.

Railways. In 1982 Oklahoma had 5,005 miles of railway operated by 12 companies.

Aviation. Airports, 1982, numbered 288, of which 131 were municipally owned. Seven cities were served by CAB-certificated airlines.

Shipping. The McClellan-Kerr Arkansas Navigation System provides access from east central Oklahoma to New Orleans through the Verdigris, Arkansas and Mississippi rivers. The main ports are Catoosa and Muskogee.

JUSTICE, RELIGION, EDUCATION AND WELFARE

Justice. Penal institutions, Oct. 1981, held 5,122 inmates. There are 9 correction centres and 9 community treatment centres.

The death penalty was suspended in 1966 and re-imposed in 1974. Since 1915 there have been 83 (52 whites, 27 Negroes, 4 other races) executions. Electrocution was replaced (1977) by lethal injection.

Religion. The chief religious bodies in 1980 were Baptists, 674,766; United Methodists, 248,635; Roman Catholics, 122,820; Churches of Christ, about 80,000; Assembly of God, 63,992; Disciples of Christ, 45,070; Presbyterian, 38,605; Lutheran, 33,664; Nazarene, 22,090; Episcopal, 21,500.

Education. In 1981–82 there were 611,246 pupils enrolled in elementary and secondary schools, 38,460 teachers at elementary schools and secondary schools had average salaries of $15,200. Total expenditure on public schools (1980–81), $1,028m.

In 1980–81, there were 3,415 special education units with 65,598 students in class.

The University of Oklahoma (founded at Norman in 1890) had 753 full-time faculty and 20,333 enrolled students in spring 1981; Oklahoma State University of Agriculture and Applied Science (founded in 1890 at Stillwater) had 718 full-time faculty and 20,739 students; Central State University (founded at Edmond in 1890) had 320 full-time faculty and 10,820 students. There are 10 other institutions of higher learning in the state system at the senior level and 14 junior colleges. Total enrolment in institutions of higher education, spring 1981, 154,266.

Health. In 1981 there were 134 hospitals (15,642 beds). In 1981 institutions for the mentally retarded had 1,828 inmates; the schools for deaf and blind had 234 children, 3 schools for delinquents, 862 children, 2 children's homes, 679 children.

Social Security. Public assistance, financial year 1981 was being drawn by 148,435 persons, receiving an average monthly payment of $930. This includes old age assistance, aid to families with dependent children, AFDC emergency, AFDC foster home care, aid to the blind and aid to the disabled. Medical payments were made for 234,393 persons, totalled $317·9m. and averaged $1,356.50 per person. Intermediate care was provided for 26,664 persons at an average of $5,914.05 per person. Non-technical medical care was provided for 10,129 persons at an average of $2,127.96 per person. A total of $29,954,310 was spent for vocational rehabilitation.

Books of Reference

Directory, of Oklahoma. Dept. of Libraries, Oklahoma City
Chronicles of Oklahoma. State Historical Society, Oklahoma City (from 1921)
Statistical Abstract of Oklahoma, 1980. Centres for Economic and Management Research, Univ. of Oklahoma, Norman, 1980
Dale, E. E., and Aldrich, G., *History of Oklahoma.* New York, 1969
McReynolds, Edwin C., *Oklahoma: A History of the Sooner State.* Rev. ed. Univ. of Oklahoma, Norman, 1964
Morgan, H. W., and Morgan, A. H., *Oklahoma: A Bicentennial History.* New York, 1977
Ruth, K., *et al.*, (eds.), *Oklahoma: A Guide to the Sooner State.* Rev. ed. Univ. of Oklahoma, Norman, 1957
Strain, J. W., *Outline of Oklahoma Government.* Central State Univ., Edmond, 1978

State Library: Oklahoma Dept. of Libraries, 200 N.E. 18th Street, Oklahoma City 73105.
State Librarian and State Archivist: Robert L. Clark, Jr.

OREGON

HISTORY. Oregon was first settled in 1811 by the Pacific Fur Co. at Astoria, a provisional government was formed on 5 July 1834; a Territorial government was organized, 14 Aug. 1848, and on 14 Feb. 1859 Oregon was admitted to the Union.

AREA AND POPULATION. Oregon is bounded north by Washington, with the Columbia River forming most of the boundary, east by Idaho, with the Snake

River forming most of the boundary, south by Nevada and California and west by the Pacific. Area, 97,073 sq. miles, 889 sq. miles being inland water. The federal government owned (1976) 32,370,216 acres (52·55% of the state area). Census population, 1 April 1980, 2,633,105, an increase of 541,720 or 26% since 1970. Estimated population (1982), 2,656,185. In 1980 births numbered 43,998 (16·7 per 1,000 population); deaths, 21,793 (8·2); infant deaths 556 (12 per 1,000 live births); marriages, 23,115 (8·8), and divorces, 17,925 (6·8).

Population at 5 federal censuses was:

	White	Negro	Indian	Asiatic	Total	Per sq. mile
1910	655,090	1,492	5,090	11,093	672,765	7·0
1930	938,598	2,234	4,776	8,179	953,786	9·9
1960	1,732,037	18,133	8,026	9,120	1,768,687	18·4
1970	2,032,079	26,308	13,510	13,290	2,091,385	21·7
1980	2,490,610	37,060	27,314	34,775	2,633,105	27·3

Of the total population in 1980, 1,296,566 were male, 1,788,354 persons were urban. Those 18 years and older numbered 1,910,048.

The US Bureau of Indian Affairs (area headquarters in Portland) administers (1976) 742,151·74 acres, of which 597,222·94 acres are held by the US in trust for Indian tribes, and 144,928·8 acres for individual Indians.

The largest towns, according to 1980 census figures, are: Portland, 366,383; Eugene, 105,664; Salem (the capital), 89,233; Corvallis, 40,960; Medford, 39,603; Springfield, 41,621; Beaverton, 31,926; Albany, 26,678. Metropolitan areas (1980): Portland, 1,236,294; Eugene-Springfield, 273,114; Salem, 249,655.

CLIMATE. Portland. Jan. 39°F (3·9°C), July 67°F (19·4°C). Annual rainfall 44″ (1,100 mm). *See* Pacific Coast, p. 1372.

CONSTITUTION AND GOVERNMENT. The present constitution dates from 1859; some 80 items in it have been amended. The Legislative Assembly consists of a Senate of 30 members, elected for 4 years (half their number retiring every 2 years), and a House of 60 representatives, elected for 2 years. The Governor is elected for 4 years. The constitution reserves to the voters the rights of initiative and referendum and recall. In Nov. 1912 suffrage was extended to women.

The state sends to Congress 2 senators and 5 representatives.

In the 1980 presidential election Reagan polled 571,044 votes, Carter 456,890 and Anderson, 112,389.

The capital is Salem. There are 36 counties in the state.

Governor: Victor Atiyeh (R.), 1983–86 ($53,394 plus $1,000 monthly for expenses).

Secretary of State: Norma Paulus (R.) ($45,619).

BUDGET. Oregon has 2-year financial periods. Total resources for the biennium 1981–83 were $13,957,634,165 (federal funds, $1,003m.; individual taxes, $2,123·7m.; business taxes, $1,587·4m.); total expenditures, $10,052,272,033 (education, $2,451·9m.; economic development and consumer services, $2,983·5m.; human resources, $2,398·6m.).

In Feb. 1983 the outstanding bonded debt was $6,000m.

Per capita personal income (1981) was $10,008.

ENERGY AND NATURAL RESOURCES

Electricity. On 1 Jan. 1982 four privately owned utilities, 11 municipally owned utilities, 18 co-operatives and 4 utility districts provided electricity in the state. The privately owned companies provided 73% of the electricity. Hydroelectricity plants (67 in 1983) have an installed capacity of 5m. kw., of which multi-purpose federal projects like the Bonneville Power Administration accounted for 3·5m. kw. The Trojan Nuclear plant has a capacity of 1,080mw., and Boardman coal-fired plant, 530mw.

Minerals. Oregon's mineral resources include gold, silver, nickel copper, lead, mercury, chromite, sand and gravel, stone, clays, lime, silica, diatomite, expansible shale, scoria, pumice and uranium. There is geothermal potential. Value of mineral products, 1981, was $163m.

Agriculture. Oregon, which has an area of 61,557,184 acres, is divided by the Cascade Range into two distinct zones as to climate. West of the Cascade Range there is a good rainfall and almost every variety of crop common to the temperate zone is grown; east of the Range stock-raising and wheat-growing are the principal industries and irrigation is needed for row crops and fruits.

There were, in 1982, 36,000 farms with an acreage of 18·3m. (29·7% of the land area), including (1974) 5·3m. acres of total crop land; average farm size in 1982 was 532 acres; most are family-owned corporate farms.

Cash receipts from crops in 1981–82 amounted to $992·5m., and from livestock and livestock products, $588·4m., of which cattle and calves made $307·4m. Principal crops are hay ($170·3m.), wheat ($297·9m.), potatoes, peppermint, ryegrass seed, pears, onions, snap beans, sweet corn and barley.

Livestock, 1 July 1980: Milch cows, 93,000; cattle and calves, 1·5m.; sheep and lambs, 350,000; swine, 100,000.

Forestry. About 29·8m. acres is forested, almost half of the state. Of this amount, 24·2m. is commercial forest land suitable for timber production; ownership is as follows (acres): US Forestry service, 11·6m. (48%); Forest Industry, 5·5m. (22·8%); Small non-industrial landowners, 3·6m. (14·7%); US Bureau of Land Management, 2·2m. (9%); State of Oregon, 820,000 acres (3·4%) and other owners (city, county, Indian), 496,000 acres (2·1%). Oregon's commercial forest lands provided an estimated 1982 harvest of 5,200m. bd ft of logs, as well as the benefits of recreation, water, grazing, wildlife and fish. Trees vary from the coastal forest of hemlock and spruce to the state's primary species, Douglas-fir, throughout much of western Oregon. In eastern Oregon, ponderosa pine, lodgepole pine and true firs are found. Here, forestry is often combined with livestock grazing to provide an economic operation. Along the Cascade summit and in the mountains of northeast Oregon, alpine species are found.

Production, 1981: plywood, 5,561m. sq. ft (value $991·5m.); Douglas Fir lumber, 3,842m. bd. ft ($948·3m.); Ponderosa Pine lumber, 1,273m. bd. ft ($386m.); pulp and paper, 4·8m. tons ($8·5m.).

Fisheries. All food and shellfish landings in the calendar year 1981 amounted to a value of $58m. The most important are: tuna, crabs, bottom fish, shrimp.

INDUSTRY. Forest products manufacturing is Oregon's leading industry, and provides for 20% of the country's softwood lumber needs, 40% of its plywood and more than 25% of the hardboard. More than one-third of the economy depends directly or indirectly on timber industries; about 78,130 (1981) people are employed. The payroll was $1,600m. and value of production, $3,490m. During 1981, manufacturing employed 203,300, of which 148,500 made durable goods; trade, 253,700, construction, 37,600.

TOURISM. In 1982, 14,391,400 out-of-state tourists visited Oregon; the total income from tourism was estimated to be $1,300m.

COMMUNICATIONS

Roads. The state maintains (1982) 7,555 miles of primary and secondary highways, almost all surfaced; counties maintain 27,697 miles, and cities 6,913 miles; there were 79,167 miles in national parks and federal reservations. Registered motor vehicles, 31 Dec. 1981, totalled 2·3m.

Railways. The state had (1980) 19 common carrier railways with a total mileage of 4,428.

Aviation. In Oct. 1982 there were 4 public-use and 85 personal-use heliports; 5 public-use seaplane bases; 206 personal-use airports; 110 public-use airports including 37 state-owned airports.

Shipping. Portland is a major seaport for large ocean-going vessels and is 101 miles inland from the mouth of the Columbia River. In 1982 the port handled 6·6m. short tons of cargo; main commodities for this and other Columbia River ports are grain and petroleum.

Post and Broadcasting. In Dec. 1982 there were 137 commercial radio stations and 13 educational radio stations. There were 14 commercial television stations and 6 educational television stations. There were also 5 campus limited radio stations and 1 subscription radio station.

Newspapers. In 1982 there were 21 daily newspapers with a circulation of 653,392 and 89 non-daily newspapers.

JUSTICE, RELIGION, EDUCATION AND WELFARE

Justice. There are 3 correctional institutions in Oregon, all in Salem. The Oregon State Penitentiary, on 30 June 1982, held 1,779 males; the Women's Correctional Center had a resident population of 73; and the Oregon Correctional Institution, which is for first offenders, had a population of 926. The Oregon Correctional Division's Release Center in Salem held 323 inmates, 110 inmates were held in Oregon State Hospital wards and 16,174 offenders were on parole or probation.

The sterilization law, originally passed in 1917, was amended in 1967. The amendments changed the number of persons on the Board of Social Protection from 15 to 7 and provided that the Public Defender would automatically represent all persons examined. The basis on which a person would be subject to examination by the Board are: *(a)* if such person would be likely to procreate children having an inherited tendency to mental retardation or mental illness, or *(b)* if such person would be likely to procreate children who would become neglected or dependent because of the person's inability by reason of mental illness or mental retardation to provide adequate care.

Religion. The chief religious bodies are Catholic, Baptist, Lutheran, Methodists, Presbyterian and Mormon.

Education. School attendance is compulsory from 7 to 18 years of age if the twelfth year of school has not been completed; those between the ages of 16 and 18 years, if legally employed, may attend part-time or evening schools. Others may be excused under certain circumstances. In 1981–82 the public elementary schools had 330,810 students and the secondary schools, 148,458. Total expenditure on elementary and secondary education (1980–81) was $1,726·7m.

Leading state-supported institutions of higher education (autumn 1982) included:

	Students
University of Oregon, Eugene	15,467
Oregon Health Sciences University:	1,431
Oregon State University, Corvallis	16,759
Portland State University, Portland	14,541
Western Oregon State College, Monmouth	2,473
Southern Oregon State College, Ashland	4,161
Eastern Oregon State College, La Grande	1,764
Oregon Institute of Technology, Klamath Falls	2,653

Largest of the privately endowed universities are Lewis and Clark College, Portland, with (1982) 3,054 students; University of Portland, 2,872 students; Willamette University, Salem, 1,859 students; Reed College, Portland, 1,122 students, and Linfield College, McMinnville, 1,496 students. There are 13 community colleges and 1 area education district with an estimated enrolment of 293,886 students in 1981–82.

Health. In Oct. 1982 there were 91 licensed hospitals. In Oct. 1979 there were 4 state hospitals for mentally ill and mentally retarded (2 for mentally ill, 1 for mentally retarded and 1 with both programmes). On 30 June 1982 there were 931 mentally ill patients and 1,629 mentally retarded.

Social Security. Old-age assistance is provided for all needy persons 65 years or older who meet certain eligibility requirements. In financial year 1979–80, 3,598 cases per month received average payments of $5.36 cash and $87.54 services. For the same period 98,278 persons in 36,166 families with dependent children received an average $279.74 per month; 552 blind recipients $38.56 cash and $62.52 services; 7,009 disabled $15.94 cash and $41.86 services; 4,501 general assistance cases $134.73 cash and $5.45 services.

Medical assistance and mental health costs averaged $14,494,000 per month.

A system of unemployment benefit payments, financed by employers, with administrative allotments made through a federal agency, started 2 Jan. 1938, and covers about 66,500 employers with average employment in 1979 of 1,024,535. By June 1980, $1,717m. in taxes had been paid into the trust fund plus $297·3m. in interest and reimbursed benefits. About $1,691m. has been paid in benefits which from July 1980 range from $38 to $138 weekly and up to $3,588 per year. About 38,406 state employees, 48,060 school employees, 5,507 community college employees and 18,879 political subdivision employees are participants in the public employees retirement programme. The same employees are covered under the federal old-age, survivors and disability insurance programme. Approximately 31,016 retired employees are receiving monthly benefit cheques.

Books of Reference

Oregon Blue Book. Issued by the Secretary of State. Salem. Biennial
Federal Writers' Project. *Oregon: End of the Trail.* Rev. ed. Portland, 1972
Atkeson, R., *Oregon.* Portland, 1968.—*Oregon Coast.* Portland, 1972
Baldwin, E. M., *Geology of Oregon.* Rev. ed. Dubuque, Iowa, 1976
Carey, C. H., *General History of Oregon, prior to 1861.* 2 vol. (1 vol. reprint, 1971) Portland, 1935
Corning, H. M. (ed.), *Dictionary of Oregon History.* New York, 1956
Dicken, S. N., *Oregon Geography.* 5th ed. Eugene, 1973.—with Dicken, E. F., *Making of Oregon: a Study in Historical Geography.* Portland, 1979
Dodds, G. B., *Oregon: A Bicentennial History.* New York, 1977
Friedman, R., *Oregon for the Curious.* 3rd ed. Portland, 1972
Highsmith, R. M. Jr. (ed.), *Atlas of the Pacific Northwest.* Corvallis, 1973
McArthur, L. A., *Oregon Geographic Names.* 4th ed., rev. and enlarged. Portland, 1974
Patton, Clyde P., *Atlas of Oregon.* Univ. Oregon Press, Eugene, 1976

State Library: The Oregon State Library, Salem. *Librarian:* Marcia Lowell.

PENNSYLVANIA

HISTORY. Pennsylvania, first settled in 1682, is one of the 13 original states in the Union.

AREA AND POPULATION. Pennsylvania is bounded north by New York, east by New Jersey, south by Delaware and Maryland, south-west by West Virginia, west by Ohio and north-west by Lake Erie. Area, 45,308 sq. miles, of which 420 sq. miles are inland water. Census population, 1 April 1980, 11,863,895, an increase of 63,129 or 0·5% since 1970. Estimate (1981) 11,871,000. Births, 1982, 161,561; deaths, 118,450; infant deaths, 1,853; marriages, 93,350; reported divorces, 38,545.

Population at 5 census years was:

	White	Negro	Indian	All others	Total	Per sq. mile
1910	7,467,713	193,919	1,503	1,976	7,665,111	171·0
1930	9,196,007	431,257	523	3,563	9,631,350	213·8
1960	10,454,004	852,750	2,122	10,490	11,319,366	251·5
				All others		
1970	10,745,219	1,015,884		39,663	11,800,766	262·9
1980	10,652,320	1,046,810		164,765	11,863,895	264·3

Of the total population in 1980, 47·9% were male, 69·3% were urban and 68·1% were 21 years of age or older.

The population of the larger cities and townships, 1980 census, was:

Philadelphia	1,688,210	Scranton	88,117	Lancaster	54,725
Pittsburgh	423,938	Reading	78,686	Harrisburg	53,264
Erie	119,123	Bethlehem	70,419	Wilkes-Barre	51,551
Allentown	103,758	Altoona	57,078	York	44,619

Larger urbanized areas, 1980 census: Philadelphia (in Pennsylvania), 3,682,709; Pittsburgh, 2,263,894; Northeast, 640,396, Allentown–Bethlehem–Easton (in Pennsylvania), 551,052; Harrisburg, 446,576.

CLIMATE. Philadelphia. Jan. 32°F (0°C), July 77°F (25°C). Annual rainfall 40″ (1,006 mm). Pittsburgh. Jan. 31°F (–0·6°C), July 74°F (23·3°C). Annual rainfall 37″ (914 mm). *See* Appalachian Mountains, p. 1373.

CONSTITUTION AND GOVERNMENT. The present constitution dates from 1968. The General Assembly consists of a Senate of 50 members chosen for 4 years, one-half being elected biennially, and a House of Representatives of 203 members chosen for 2 years. The Governor and Lieut.-Governor are elected for 4 years. Every citizen 18 years of age, with the usual residential qualifications, may vote. The state sends to Congress 2 senators and 23 representatives.

In the 1980 presidential election Reagan polled 2,261,872 votes, Carter 1,937,540 and Anderson 292,921.

The state capital is Harrisburg. The state is organized in counties (numbering 67), cities, boroughs, townships and school districts.

Governor: Richard Thornburgh (R.), 1979–86 ($75,000).
Lieut.-Governor: William W. Scranton (R.) ($54,500).

BUDGET. Total revenues for the year ending 30 June 1983 were $7,320·7m.; general fund expenditure, $7,604·4m. (education, $3,508·9m.; transport, $155·6m.; public welfare, $2,716·6m.; environment, $112·7m.).

On 30 June 1983 outstanding long-term debt (excluding highway bonds) amounted to $2,577·0m.

Per capita personal income (1982) was $10,955.

ENERGY AND NATURAL RESOURCES

Minerals. Pennsylvania is almost the sole producer of anthracite coal; its output reached a peak of 100,445,299 short tons in 1917 with a labour-force of 156,148 men. Production in 1983: Anthracite, 4·02m. tons, with about 1,700 men; bituminous coal, 71·92m. tons, with about 14,700 men; crude petroleum (1982), 3·72m. bbls; natural gas (1981), 122,454m. cu. ft. Total value of other minerals produced (1981), $316·1m., including $216m. for cement.

Agriculture. Agriculture, market-gardening, fruit-growing, horticulture and forestry are pursued within the state. In 1982 there were 60,000 farms with a total farm area of 8·8m. acres (4·6m. acres in crops); the average farm was 147 acres with average value per acre of $1,279. Cash income, 1982, from crops, $758m., and from livestock, $2,913m.

Pennsylvania ranks ninth in the production of tobacco (25·9m. lb., 1982 value $20·5m.) and leads in mushrooms (273m. lb., value $179·6m.). Other crops are winter wheat (8·21m. bu.), oats (19·77m. bu.), maize (133·6m. bu.), barley (3·74m. bu.) and potatoes (5·76m. cwt). On 1 Jan. 1983 there were on farms: 2·0m. cattle and calves, including 738,000 milch cows, 98,000 sheep, 830,000 swine. Milk production, 1982, was 9,260m. lb. valued at $1,391m., and eggs numbered 4,324m. valued at $281m. Pennsylvania is also a major fruit producing state; in 1982 apples totalled 525m. lb.; peaches, 90m. lb.; tart cherries, 5·5m. lb.; sweet cherries, 600 tons; and grapes, 47,000 tons. Other important items are soybeans (3·2m. bu.), vegetables for processing (116,000 tons), fresh vegetables (2·3m. cwt) and broiler-chickens (114·9m.).

Forestry. In 1982 national forest lands totalled 510,517 acres; state forests, 2,064,533 acres; state parks, 278,930 acres; state game land, 1,250,980 acres; game land leased but not owned by the state, 3,957,438 acres (co-operative and safety-zone programmes).

INDUSTRY. Pennsylvania is third in national production of iron and steel. Output of steel, 1982, 10·9m. net tons.

In 1981, 16,388 manufacturing establishments employed 1,321,109 workers (wages, $25,069m.).

COMMUNICATIONS

Roads. Highways and roads in the state (federal, local and state combined) totalled (1983) 114,949 miles. Registered motor vehicles for 1982 numbered 7,417,311 (including 5,528,626 passenger cars, 1,486,325 trucks, truck-tractors and trailers).

Railways. In 1982, 49 railways operated within the state with a line mileage of about 6,300.

Aviation. There were (1982) 161 commercial airports, 3 public landing strips, 242 heliports, 391 airports for personal use and 16 seaplane bases.

Shipping. Trade at Delaware River ports (1981, short tons) imports, 58·1m., exports, 8·0m. Trade at Erie ports (1981): imports 50,004 short tons, exports 10,730 short tons.

Post and Broadcasting. Broadcasting stations comprised (1982) 41 television stations and 378 radio stations.

Newspapers. There were (1983) 111 daily and 219 weekly newspapers.

JUSTICE, RELIGION, EDUCATION AND WELFARE

Justice. No executions took place in 1963–83; since 1930 there have been 149 executions (electrocution), all for murder.

State prison population, on 31 Dec. 1982, was 10,572.

Religion. The chief religious bodies in 1977 were the Roman Catholic, with 3,717,667 members; Protestant, 3,150,920 (1971); and Jewish, 469,078. The 5 largest Protestant denominations (by communicants) were: Lutheran Church in America, 766,276; United Methodist, 728,915 (1971), United Presbyterian Church in the USA, 573,905 (1971); United Church of Christ, 257,138; Episcopal, 193,399 (1971).

Education. School attendance is compulsory for children 8–17 years of age. In 1982–83 the public kindergartens and elementary schools had 872,629 pupils; public secondary schools had 911,340 pupils. Non-public schools had 288,665 elementary pupils and 112,963 secondary pupils. Average salary, public school professional personnel, men $23,562; women $20,825; for classroom teachers, men $22,058, women $20,542.

Leading senior academic institutions included:

Founded	Institutions	Faculty (Autumn 1982)	Students (Autumn 1982)
1740	University of Pennsylvania (non-sect.)	3,690	22,317
1787	University of Pittsburgh	3,163	35,317
1832	Lafayette College, Easton (Presbyterian)	196	2,398
1842	Villanova University (R.C.)	675	11,720
1846	Bucknell University (Baptist)	230	3,256
1851	St Joseph's College, Philadelphia (R.C.)	325	6,086
1852	California University of Pennsylvania	344	4,528
1855	Pennsylvania State University	3,630	65,091
1855	Millersville University of Pennsylvania	321	6,420
1863	LaSalle College, Philadelphia (R.C.)	414	7,068
1866	Lehigh University, Bethlehem (non-sect.)	442	6,287

Founded	Institutions	Faculty (Autumn 1982)	Students (Autumn 1982)
1871	West Chester University of Pennsylvania	462	9,704
1875	Indiana University of Pennsylvania	691	12,503
1878	Duquesne University, Pittsburgh (R.C.)	508	6,298
1884	Temple University, Philadelphia	2,703	29,643
1885	Bryn Mawr College	159	1,810
1888	University of Scranton (R.C.)	246	4,620
1891	Drexel University, Philadelphia	857	12,339
1900	Carnegie-Mellon University, Philadelphia	860	5,998

Health. In 1982 the state had 235 hospitals (55,537 beds) listed by the State Health Department, excluding federal hospitals and mental institutions.

Social Security. During the year ending 30 June 1982 the monthly average number of cases receiving public assistance was: aid to families with dependent children, 608,591; blind pension, 4,833; general assistance, 197,899.

Payments for medical assistance for the year ending 30 June 1982 totalled $1,932·2m. Under the medical assistance programme payments are made for inpatient hospital care ($637·5m.); care in public institutions (nursing homes, mental institutions and geriatric centres) ($695·5m.); private nursing home care ($276·7m.); other medical care ($322·5m.).

Books of Reference

Pennsylvania Manual. General Services, Bureau of Publications, Harrisburg. Biennial
Pennsylvania's Regions, A Survey of the Commonwealth. State Planning Board. Harrisburg, 1967
Pennsylvania Statistical Abstract. Dept. of Commerce, Harrisburg. Annual
Pennsylvania State Industrial Directory. New York. Annual
Carstens, A. H., *What to See in Pennsylvania.* 2nd ed. Cresco, 1965
Klein, P. S., and Hoogenboom, A., *A History of Pennsylvania.* New York, 1973
League of Women Voters of Pennsylvania, *Key to the Keystone State.* Philadelphia, 1972
Pennsylvania Chamber of Commerce, *Pennsylvania Government Today.* State College, Pa., 1973
Stevens, S. K., *Pennsylvania: Birthplace of a Nation.* New York, 1964.—*Exploring Pennsylvania: Geography History, Civics.* 3rd ed. New York, 1968
Wilkinson, N. B., *Bibliography of Pennsylvania History.* Pa. Historical & Museum Commission. Harrisburg, 1957

RHODE ISLAND

HISTORY The earliest settlers in the region which now forms the state of Rhode Island were colonists from Massachusetts who had been driven forth on account of their non-acceptance of the prevailing religious beliefs. The first of the settlements was made in 1636, settlers of every creed being welcomed. In 1647 a patent was executed for the government of the settlements, and on 8 July 1663 a charter was executed recognizing the settlers as forming a body corporate and politic by the name of the 'English Colony of Rhode Island and Providence Plantations, in New England, in America'. On 29 May 1790 the state accepted the federal constitution and entered the Union as the last of the 13 original states.

AREA AND POPULATION. Rhode Island is bounded north and east by Massachusetts, south by the Atlantic and west by Connecticut. Area, 1,212 sq. miles, of which 158 sq. miles are inland water. Census population, 1 April 1980, 947,154 a decrease of 0·3% since 1970. Estimate (1981), 953,000.

Births, 1981, were 12,430; deaths (excluding foetal deaths), 9,138; infant deaths (1980) 150; marriages (1980) 7,480; divorces (1980) 3,582.

Population of 5 census years was:

	White	Negro	Indian	Asiatic	Total	Per sq. mile
1910	532,492	9,529	284	305	542,610	508·5
1930	677,026	9,913	318	240	687,497	649·3
1960	838,712	18,332	932	1,190	859,488	812·4
1970	914,757	25,338	1,390	5,240	949,723 [1]	905·0
			All other			
1980	896,692	27,584	22,878		947,154	903·0

[1] Through tabulation errors there were 2,998 people unaccounted for, as to race and sex, in 1970.

Of the total population in 1980, 451,251 were male, 824,004 were urban and 665,054 were 20 years of age or older.

The chief cities and their population (census, 1980) are Providence, 156,304; Warwick, 87,127; Cranston, 71,992; Pawtucket, 71,204; East Providence, 59,980; Woonsocket, 45,914; Newport, 29,259; North Kingston (town), 21,938; Middletown (town), 17,216. The Providence–Pawtucket–Warwick Standard Metropolitan Statistical Area had a population of 914,110 in 1970.

CLIMATE. Providence. Jan. 28°F (–2·2°C), July 72°F (22·2°C). Annual rainfall 43″ (1,079 mm). *See* New England, p. 1373.

CONSTITUTION AND GOVERNMENT. The present constitution dates from 1843; it has had 36 amendments. The General Assembly consists of a Senate of 50 members and a House of Representatives of 100 members, both elected for 2 years, as are also the Governor and Lieut.-Governor. Every citizen, 18 years of age, who has resided in the state for 30 days, and is duly registered, is qualified to vote.

Rhode Island sends to Congress 2 senators and 2 representatives.

At the 1980 presidential election Carter polled 198,342 votes, Reagan, 154,793.

The capital is Providence. The state has 5 counties (unique in having no political functions) and 39 cities and towns.

Governor: J. Joseph Garrahy (D.), 1982–84 ($42,500).
Lieut.-Governor: Thomas R. Diluglio (D.), 1982–84 ($30,500).
Secretary of State: Susan Farmer (R.), 1982–84 ($30,500).

BUDGET. For the fiscal year ending 30 June 1982 (Office of the State Controller) total revenues were $1,106·4m. (taxation, $6,645m., and federal aid, $302·3m.); general expenditures were $1,134·5m. (education, $212·3m.; highways, $63m.; and public welfare, $304·2m.).

Total net long-term debt on 30 June 1982 was $214·6m.

Per capita personal income (1981) was $10,466.

NATURAL RESOURCES

Minerals. The small mineral output, mostly stone, sand and gravel, was valued (1980) at $7·5m.

Agriculture. While Rhode Island is predominantly a manufacturing state, agriculture contributed $32·5m. to the general cash income in 1980. In 1978 it had 865 farms with an area of 75,791 acres (11·1% of the total land area), of which 36,632 acres were crop land; the average farm was 98·1 acres, valued (land and buildings) at $72,033.

Fisheries. In 1981 the catch was 80m. lb (live weight) valued at $49m.

INDUSTRY. Total non-agricultural employment in 1981 was 400,500, of which 126,300 were manufacturing, 274,200 non-manufacturing. Manufacturing firms totalled 3,259; average weekly earnings for production workers in manufacturing, $238.26; value added by manufacture (1977), $2,737m. Principal industries are metals and machinery, textiles and jewellery–silverware.

COMMUNICATIONS

Roads. The state had (1 Jan. 1980) 5,758 miles of road, of which 1,313 were state-owned. In 1978, 605,000 motor vehicles were registered.

Railways. In 1977, 6 railways operated 135 line-miles.

Aviation. Of the 12 airports in 1980, 7 were state-owned and 5 privately owned. Theodore Francis Green airport at Warwick, near Providence, is served by 7 airlines, and handled 1,004,464 passengers and 14m. lb. of freight in 1980.

Shipping. Waterborne freight through the Port of Providence (1980) totalled 6·4m. tons.

Broadcasting. There are 22 radio stations and 4 television stations in the state.

JUSTICE, RELIGION, EDUCATION AND WELFARE

Justice. The state's penal institutions, Nov. 1979, had 675 inmates (70 per 100,000 population).

The death penalty is illegal, except that it is mandatory in the case of murder committed by a prisoner serving a life sentence.

Religion. Chief religious bodies are (estimated figures Sept. 1975): Roman Catholic with 597,000 members; Protestant Episcopal (baptized persons), 50,000; Baptist, 22,500; Congregational, 12,000; Methodist, 10,000; Jewish, 24,000.

Education. In 1980–81 the 230 public elementary schools had 4,080 teachers and total enrolment of 68,275 pupils; about 15,000 pupils were enrolled in private and parochial schools. The 68 senior and vocational high schools had 4,134 teachers and 70,967 pupils. Teachers' salaries (1979–80) averaged $13,660. Local expenditure, for schools (including evening schools) in 1980–81 totalled $363·5m.

There are 11 institutions of higher learning in the state, including 1 junior college. The state maintains Rhode Island College, at Providence, with 800 faculty members, and 8,800 full-time students (1980), and the University of Rhode Island, at South Kingstown, with over 850 faculty members and over 14,000 students (including graduate students). Brown University, at Providence, founded in 1764, is now non-sectarian; in 1980 it had over 500 full-time faculty members and full-time students. Providence College, at Providence, founded in 1917 by the Order of Preachers (Dominican), had (1980) 218 professors and 3,800 students. The largest of the other colleges are Bryant College, at Smithfield, with 125 faculty and over 4,800 students, and the Rhode Island School of Design, in Providence, with about 100 faculty and 1,400 students.

Health. In 1982 the state had 24 hospitals (over 7,000 beds), including 4 mental hospitals.

Social Security. In 1980 aid to dependent children was granted to 54,000 children in 18,700 families at an average payment per family of $325 per month, and the state also had a general assistance programme. (All other aid programmes were taken over by the federal government.)

Books of Reference

Rhode Island Manual. Prepared by the Secretary of State. Providence
Providence Journal Almanac: A Reference Book for Rhode Islanders. Providence. Annual
Rhode Island Basic Economic Statistics. Rhode Island Dept. of Economic Development. Providence, 1972

State Library: Rhode Island State Library, State House, Providence 02908. State Librarian: Elliott E. Andrews.

SOUTH CAROLINA

HISTORY. South Carolina, first settled permanently in 1670, was one of the 13 original states of the Union.

AREA AND POPULATION. South Carolina is bounded in the north by North Carolina, east and south-east by the Atlantic, south-west and west by Georgia. Area, 31,113 sq. miles, of which 909 sq. miles are inland water. Census population, 1 April 1980, 3,121,833, an increase of 20·5 since 1970. Estimate (1981) 3,167,000. Births, 1981, were 51,908 (16·6 per 1,000 population); deaths, 25,138 (8·1); infant deaths, 809 (15·6 per 1,000 live births); marriages, 53,915 (17·3); divorces and annulments, 13,595 (4·4).

The population in 5 census years was:

	White	Negro	Indian	Asiatic	Total	Per sq. mile
1910	679,161	835,843	331	65	1,515,400	49·7
1930	944,049	793,681	959	76	1,738,765	56·8
1960	1,551,022	829,291	1,098	946	2,382,594	78·7
			All others			
1970	1,794,432	789,040	3,588		2,587,060	83·2
1980	2,150,507	948,623	22,703		3,121,833	100·3

Of the total population in 1980, 49% were male, 54·1% were urban and 55% were 25 years old or older.

Populations of large towns at the 1980 census (with those of associated metropolitan areas): Columbia (capital), 97,104 (395,775); Charleston, 69,296 (411,582); Greenville, 58,190; Spartanburg, 43,502 (Greenville–Spartanburg, 562,934).

CLIMATE. Columbia. Jan. 47°F (8·3°C), July 81°F (27·2°C). Annual rainfall 45" (1,125 mm). See Atlantic Coast, p. 1373.

CONSTITUTION AND GOVERNMENT. The present constitution dates from 1895, when it went into force without ratification by the electorate. The General Assembly consists of a Senate of 46 members, elected for 4 years (half retiring biennially), and a House of Representatives of 124 members, elected for 2 years. The Governor and Lieut.-Governor are elected for 4 years. Only registered citizens have the right to vote. South Carolina sends to Congress 2 senators and 6 representatives.

At the 1980 presidential election Reagan polled 441,841 votes, Carter 430,385 and Anderson 14,153.

The capital is Columbia.

Governor: Richard Riley (D.), 1983–87 ($60,000).
Secretary of State: John Tucker Campbell (D.), 1983–87 ($50,000).

BUDGET. For the fiscal year ending 30 June 1983 general revenues were $1,969·9m.; general expenditures were $1,936·3m.

On 30 June 1983 the total bonded debt was $600m.

Per capita personal income (1982) was $8,468.

NATURAL RESOURCES

Minerals. Non-metallic minerals are of chief importance: value of mineral output in 1983 (provisional) was $235·5m., chiefly from limestone for cement, clay, stone, sand and gravel. Production of kaolin, vermiculite, scrap mica and fuller's earth is also important.

Agriculture. In 1983 there were 31,000 farms covering a farm area of 5·9m. acres. The average farm was of 190 acres. Of the 33,412 farms of the 1978 census, there were 1,068 of 1,000 acres or more, average farm 188 acres; owners operated 19,339 farms; tenants 3,908. There were 2,044 farms with $100,000 or more in value of sales.

Cash receipts from farm marketing in 1982 amounted to $772m. for crops and $399m. for livestock. Chief crops are tobacco ($218m.), soybeans ($196m.), and wheat ($59m.). Production, 1981: Cotton 164,000 bales; peaches, 420m. lb.; soybeans, 32·5m. bu.; tobacco, 148·6m. lb.; eggs, 1,613m. bu. Livestock on farms, 1982: 700,000 all cattle, 440,000 swine.

Forestry. The forest industry is important; state and private forest land (1981), 12·5m. acres. National forests amounted to 578,724 acres.

INDUSTRY. A monthly average of 360,600 workers were employed in manufacturing in 1983 (preliminary), earning $5,635·5m. Major sectors are textiles (32%), apparel (12%) and chemicals (8·8%).

Tourism is the second largest industry; tourists spent an estimated $2,500m. in 1982.

COMMUNICATIONS

Roads. Total highway mileage in the combined highway system in 1983 was 39,632 miles. Motor vehicle registrations numbered 2m. in 1982.

Railways. In 1983 the length of railway in the state was 2,939 miles.

Aviation. There were, 1983, 72 airports and 1,700 registered aircraft.

Shipping. The state has 3 deep-water ports.

JUSTICE, RELIGION, EDUCATION AND WELFARE

Justice. In Sept. 1983 penal institutions held 9,526 inmates.

Education. In 1982–83 the total public-school enrolment (K-12) was 622,426; there were 360,429 white pupils and 261,997 non-white pupils. The total number of teachers was 31,761; average salary was $16,523.

For higher education the state operates the University of South Carolina, founded at Columbia in 1801, with, 1983, 34,741 enrolled students; Clemson University, founded in 1889, with 12,429 students; The Citadel, at Charleston, with 3,040 students; Winthrop College, Rock Hill, with 4,999 students; Medical University of S. Carolina, at Charleston 2,254 students; S. Carolina State College, at Orangeburg, with 4,123 students, and Francis Marion College, at Florence, with 3,131 students; the College of Charleston has 5,323 students and Lander College, Greenwood, 2,136. There are 16 technical institutions (34,965).

There are also 473 private kindergartens, elementary and high schools with total enrolment (1983) of 51,445 pupils, and 31 private and denominational colleges and junior colleges with (1983) enrolment of 27,503 students.

Health. In 1983 the state had 191 hospitals and nursing homes and 108 intermediate care institutions licensed by the South Carolina Department of Health and Environmental Control.

Social Security. In 1981 there were 46,700 recipients of social security benefits per month. The average monthly expenditure in benefits was $120m.

Books of Reference

Reports of the South Carolina State Development Board. Columbia. Annual
South Carolina Legislative Manual. Columbia. Annual
South Carolina Statistical Abstract, 1982. South Carolina Budget and Control Board, Columbia, 1982

State Library: South Carolina State Library, Columbia.

SOUTH DAKOTA

HISTORY. South Dakota was first visited by Europeans in 1743 when Verendrye planted a lead plate (discovered in 1913) on the site of Fort Pierre, claiming the region for the French crown. Beginning with a trading post in 1794, it was settled from 1857 to 1861 when Dakota Territory was organized. It was admitted into the Union on 2 Nov. 1889.

AREA AND POPULATION. South Dakota is bounded north by North Dakota, east by Minnesota, south-east by the Big Sioux River (forming the boundary with Iowa), south by Nebraska (with the Missouri River forming part of the boundary) and west by Wyoming and Montana. Area, 77,116 sq. miles, of which 1,164 sq. miles are water. Area administered by the Bureau of Indian Affairs, 1980, covered 5m. acres (10% of the state), of which 2·6m. acres were held by tribes. The federal government, 1979, owned 3,492,000 acres or 7·1% of the total.

Census population, 1 April 1980, 690,178, an increase of 3·5% since 1970. Estimate (1981) 686,000. Births, 1982, were 12,839 (18·6 per 1,000 population); deaths, 6,588 (9·5); infant deaths, 131 (10·2 per 1,000 live births); marriages, 8,353 (12·1); divorces, 2,564 (3·7).

Population in 5 federal censuses was:

	White	Negro	Indian	Asiatic	Total	Per sq. mile
1910	563,771	817	19,137	163	583,888	7·6
1930	669,453	646	21,833	101	692,849	9·0
1960	653,098	1,114	25,794	336	680,514	8·9
			All others			
1970	630,333	1,627	34,297		666,257	8·8
1980	638,955	2,144	49,079		690,178	9·0

Of the total population in 1980, 340,370 were male, 320,223 were urban and 441,851 were 21 years of age or older.

Population of the chief cities (census of 1980) was: Sioux Falls, 81,071; Rapid City, 46,340; Aberdeen, 25,973; Watertown, 15,632, Mitchell, 13,917; Brookings, 14,915; Huron, 13,000.

CLIMATE. Rapid City. Jan. 25°F (–3·9°C), July 73°F (22·8°C). Annual rainfall 19″ (474 mm). Sioux Falls. Jan. 14°F (–10°C), July 73°F (22·8°C). Annual rainfall 25″ (625 mm). *See* High Plains, p. 1372.

CONSTITUTION AND GOVERNMENT. Voters are all citizens 18 years of age or older who have complied with certain residential qualifications. The people reserve the right of the initiative and referendum. The Senate has 35 members, and the House of Representatives 70 members, all elected for 2 years; the Governor and Lieut.-Governor are elected for 4 years. The state sends 2 senators and 1 representative to Congress.

In the 1980 presidential election Reagan polled 198,343 votes, Carter 103,855 and Anderson 21,431.

The capital is Pierre (population, 1980, 11,973). The state is divided into 66 organized counties.

Governor: William Janklow (R.), 1983–86 ($49,025).
Lieut.-Governor: Lowell Hansen, 1983–86 ($6,800 plus expense allowance).
Secretary of State: Alice Kundert, 1983–86 ($33,275).

BUDGET. For the fiscal year ending 30 June 1982 general revenues were $584·4m. and expenditures, $564·7m. Taxes and fees from state sources furnished $266·3m. and federal receipts $251·8m.

Per capita personal income (1981) was $8,833.

NATURAL RESOURCES

Minerals. The mineral products include gold (267,392 troy oz. in 1980, second largest yield of all states), sand and gravel (100,000m. short tons), silver (51,000 troy oz.). Mineral products, 1980, were valued at $227·7m., of which gold accounts for $163·8m.

Agriculture. In 1978, 39,665 farms had an acreage of 45m.; the average farm had 1,123 acres. Farm units are large; at the 1978 census there were only 3,850 farms of 50 acres or less, compared with 10,264 exceeding 1,000 acres. 14,475 farms sold produce valued at $40,000 or over.

South Dakota ranks first in the US as producer of oats (133·8m. bu. in 1982) and rye (4·68m. bu.) and second in flaxseed (3·33m. bu.) and hay (8·63m. tons). The other important crops (1982) are sorghum (17·25m. bu.), and sunflower seeds (659·98m. bu.) The farm livestock on 1 Jan. 1983 included 4·06m. cattle, 680,000 sheep, 1·51m. swine. There are about 148,000 bee colonies; honey production (1981) 9·2m. lb.

Forestry. National forest area, 1981, 1,998,000 acres.

INDUSTRY. In 1981, manufacturing establishments numbered 667 and had 24,500 workers who earned $388·6m. Food processing is by far the largest industry with 93 plants employing 7,436 workers and an annual payroll of $152·8m. There are 166 printing and publishing plants employing 2,304 workers with annual payroll of $5·96m. Also significant are dairy, lumber and wood products, and machinery. Metal fabrication and the electronic components industry are rapidly growing.

COMMUNICATIONS

Roads. Total highway mileage was 17,056 in 1981. Registered passenger cars numbered 637,000 in 1981.

Railways. In 1981 there were 2,024·2 miles of railway in operation. The state owns 837·8 miles of track of which 435 miles is operating.

Aviation. In 1981 there were 69 general aviation airports and 9 air carrier airports.

JUSTICE, RELIGION, EDUCATION AND WELFARE

Justice. The State prisons had, in 1980, 635 inmates. The death penalty was illegal from 1915 to 1938; since 1938, one person has been executed, in 1949 (by electrocution), for murder.

Religion. The chief religious bodies are (1970): Lutherans with 162,243 members, Roman Catholics (138,250), Methodist (45,795), Disciples of Christ (22,374), Presbyterian (19,494), Baptist (16,055) and Episcopal (17,268).

Education. Elementary and secondary education are free from 6 to 21 years of age. Between the ages of 8 and 16, attendance is compulsory. In 1981–82 136,481 pupils were attending elementary and high (including parochial) schools (8,124 full-time equivalent classroom teachers).

Teachers' salaries (1981–82) averaged an estimated $14,717. Total expenditure on public schools (1981–82), $346·1m.

The School of Mines at Rapid City, established 1885, had, spring 1983, 2,717 students; the State University at Brookings, 6,820 students; the University of South Dakota, founded at Vermillion in 1882, 5,918 students; Northern State College, 2,596 students; Black Hills State College, 1,973 students; Dakota State College, 1,089 students. The 9 private colleges had 6,163 students. The federal Government maintains Indian schools on its reservations and 2 outside at Flandreau and Pierre.

Health. In 1983 the state Health Department listed 56 licensed hospitals (average size 63 beds).

Social Security. In financial year 1981–82, a monthly average of $319,047 was received by 3,427 aged persons; $26,627, by 138 blind; $637,651, by 4,054 disabled. Mandatory supplement to federal SSI payments were a monthly average of $1,146 to 42 aged; $164 to 3 blind; $2,342 to 65 disabled. An average of $1,418,272 was received by 16,848 recipients of aid to dependent children. An average of $11,459 was received by 165 Asian refugees. Average monthly medical payments of $2,729,329 were made to 6,009 aged; $21,496, to 75 blind; $2,387,475, to 3,236 disabled.

Books of Reference

Governor's Budget Report. South Dakota Bureau of Finance and Management. Annual
South Dakota Historical Collections. 1902–80

South Dakota Legislative Manual. Secretary of State, Pierre, S.D. Biennial
Berg, F. M., *South Dakota: Land of Shining Gold.* Hettinger, 1982
Karolevitz, Robert F., *Challenge: the South Dakota Story.* Sioux Falls, 1975
Milton, John R., *South Dakota; a Bicentennial History.* New York, W. W. Norton, 1977
Schell, H. S., *History of South Dakota.* 3rd ed. Lincoln, Neb., 1975

State Library: South Dakota State Library, State Library Building, Pierre, S.D., 57501. *State Librarian:* Clarence L. Coffindaffer.

TENNESSEE

HISTORY. Tennessee, first settled in 1757, was admitted into the Union on 1 June 1796.

AREA AND POPULATION. Tennessee is bounded north by Kentucky and Virginia, east by North Carolina, south by Georgia, Alabama and Mississippi and west by the Mississippi River (forming the boundary with Arkansas and Missouri). Area, 42,144 sq. miles (989 sq. miles water). Census population, 1 April 1980, 4,591,120, an increase of 665,102 or 16·9% since 1970. Estimate (1981), 4,612,000. Vital statistics, 1981 (provisional): Births, 67,050 (14·5 per 1,000 population); deaths, 40,480 (8·8); infant deaths 846 (12·6 per 1,000 live births); marriages, 60,094 (26·1); divorces, 31,167 (13·5).

Population in 6 census years was:

	White	Negro	Indian	Asiatic	Total	Per sq. mile
1910	1,711,432	473,088	216	53	2,184,789	52·4
1930	2,138,644	477,646	161	105	2,616,556	62·4
1950	2,760,257	530,603	339	334	3,291,718	78·8
1960	2,977,753	586,876	638	1,243	3,567,089	85·4
			All others			
1970	3,293,930	621,261	8,496		3,923,687	95·3
1980	3,835,452	725,942	29,726		4,591,120	111·6

Of the population in 1980, 2,216,600 were male, 2,773,573 were urban and those 21 years of age or older numbered 3,026,398.

The cities, with population, 1980, are Memphis, 646,356; Nashville (capital), 455,651; Knoxville, 175,030; Chattanooga, 169,565; Clarksville, 54,777; Jackson, 49,131; Johnson City, 39,753; Murfreesboro, 32,845; Kingsport, 32,027; Oak Ridge, 27,662. Standard metropolitan areas (1980): Memphis, 810,043; Nashville, 850,505; Knoxville, 476,517; Chattanooga, 320,761; Johnson City–Bristol–Kingsport, 343,041; Clarksville, 83,342.

CLIMATE. Memphis. Jan. 41°F (5°C), July 82°F (27·8°C). Annual rainfall 49″ (1,221 mm). Nashville. Jan. 39°F (3·9°C), July 79°F (26·1°C). Annual rainfall 48″ (1,196 mm). *See* Appalachian Mountains, p. 1373.

CONSTITUTION AND GOVERNMENT. The state has operated under 3 constitutions, the last of which was adopted in 1870 and has been since amended 22 times (first in 1953). Voters at an election may authorize the calling of a convention limited to altering or abolishing one or more specified sections of the constitution. The General Assembly consists of a Senate of 33 members and a House of Representatives of 99 members, senators elected for 4 years and representatives for 2 years. Qualified as electors are all citizens (with the usual residential and age (18) qualifications). Tennessee sends to Congress 2 senators and 9 representatives.

In the 1980 presidential election Reagan polled 787,761 votes, Carter 783,051 and Anderson 35,991.

For the Tennessee Valley Authority *see* pp. 1400–01.

The capital is Nashville. The state is divided into 95 counties.

Governor: Andrew Lamar Alexander (R.), 1983–86 ($68,226).
Secretary of State: Gentry Crowell (D.), ($46,524).

BUDGET. For 1980–81 total revenue was $4,271·2m.; general expenditure, $4,230·9m.
Total net long-term debt on 30 June 1981 amounted to $1,473m.
Per capita personal income (1981) was $8,604.

ENERGY AND NATURAL RESOURCES

Minerals. Total value of mineral production 1980: fuel minerals (mainly coal), $280m.; non-fuel (mainly stone and zinc), $408m.

Agriculture. In 1982, 95,000 farms covered 13m. acres. The average farm was of 141 acres (only a few states had a smaller average) valued, land and buildings, at $972 per acre.
Cash income (1980) from crops was $852·4m.; from livestock, $844·6m. Main crops were cotton and tobacco.
On 1 Jan. 1980 the domestic animals included 200,000 milch cows, 2·3m. all cattle, 12,000 sheep, 1·4m. swine.

Forestry. Forests occupy 13·16m. acres (50% of total land area). The forest industry and industries dependent on it employ about 40,000 workers, earning $150m. per year. Wood products are valued at over $500m. per year. National forest system land (1981) 623,000 acres.

INDUSTRY. The manufacturing industries include iron and steel working, but the most important products are chemicals, including synthetic fibres and allied products, electrical equipment and food. In 1980, manufacturing establishments employed 491,000 workers; value added by manufactures was $16,138m.

TOURISM. 48m. out-of-state tourists spent $1,327m. in 1978. 90m. people travelled through the state in 1977. 8·6% of retail business is generated by tourists and travellers. There are 21,260 retail sales and service enterprises based on the tourist business. There are 146,180 people employed in industries directly connected with tourism.

COMMUNICATIONS

Roads. In 1977 there were 81,932 miles of municipal and rural roads, 38,312 miles of surfaced rural roads and 30,639 miles of unsurfaced rural roads. The state is served by 115 intrastate bus companies and 31 privately owned internal bus services.
Motor-vehicle registrations, 1981, totalled 2,842,452.

Railways. The state had (1975) 3,500 miles of track on 11 railways.

Aviation. The state is served by 11 major airlines. Airports, 1970, numbered 78 public airports and 72 private.

JUSTICE, RELIGION, EDUCATION AND WELFARE

Justice. There has been no execution since 1960; since 1930 there have been 22 whites and 44 Negroes executed (by electrocution) for murder and 5 whites and 22 Negroes for rape. A US Supreme Court ruling prohibits the use of capital punishment under present Tennessee law, except for first degree murder.
Prison population, 1 Jan. 1980, 6,626.
The law prohibiting the inter-marriage of white and Negro was declared unconstitutional by the US Supreme Court in June 1967.

Religion. The leading religious bodies are the Southern Baptists, Methodists and Negro Baptists.

Education. School attendance has been compulsory since 1925 and the employment of children under 16 years of age in workshops, factories or mines is illegal.

In 1980–81 there were 1,733 public schools with a net enrolment of 889,847 pupils. In 1981 49,021 teachers earned an average salary of $15,395·82. Total expenditure for operating county and city public schools (kindergarten to Grade 12) in 1980–81, $1,539·9m. Tennessee has 49 accredited colleges and universities, 18 2-year colleges and 28 vocational schools. The universities include the University of Tennessee, Knoxville (founded 1794), with 29,270 students in 1979; Vanderbilt University, Nashville (1873) with 7,373, Tennessee State University (1912) with 5,396, the University of Tennessee at Chattanooga (1886) with 7,106 and Fisk University (1866) with 1,154.

Health. In 1980 the state had 167 hospitals with 30,900 beds. State facilities for the mentally retarded had 2,174 resident patients; mental hospitals had 3,200 (1 Jan. 1980).

Social Security. In 1980 Tennessee paid $2,233m. to retired workers and their survivors and to disabled workers. Total beneficiaries: 448,000 retired; 169,000 survivors and 122,000 disabled. 354,000 people received $380m. in Medicaid. 56,000 families received aid to dependent children ($85m.). Supplemental Security Income ($198·7m.) was paid to 130,600.

Books of Reference

Tennessee Dept. of Finance and Administration, Annual Report, Annual
Dept. of Education Annual Report for Tennessee, Annual
Tennessee Blue Book. Secretary of State, Nashville

State Library: State Library and Archives, Nashville. *Librarian:* Miss K. Culbertson. *State Historian:* Dr S. Horn.

TEXAS

HISTORY. In 1836 Texas declared its independence of Mexico, and after maintaining an independent existence, as the Republic of Texas, for 10 years, it was on 29 Dec. 1845 received as a state into the American Union. The state's first settlement dates from 1686.

AREA AND POPULATION. Texas is bounded north by Oklahoma, northeast by Arkansas, east by Louisiana, south-east by the Gulf of Mexico, south by Mexico and west by New Mexico. Area, 266,807 sq. miles (including 4,790 sq. miles of inland water). Census population, 1 April 1980 (provisional), 14,228,383, an increase of 27% since 1970. Estimate (1981), 14,766,000. Vital statistics for 1980: Births, 268,717 (18·9 per 1,000 population); deaths, 108,586 (7·6); infant deaths, 3,226 (12 per 1,000 live births); marriages, 187,118 (13·2); divorces, 97,161 (6·8).

Population for 5 census years was:

	White	Negro	Indian	Asiatic	Total	Per sq. mile
1910	3,204,848	690,049	702	943	3,896,542	14·8
1930	4,967,172	854,964	1,001	1,578	5,824,715	22·1
1960	8,374,831	1,187,125	5,750	9,848	9,579,677	36·5
			All others			
1970	9,717,128	1,399,005	80,597		11,196,730	42·7
1980	11,197,663	1,710,250	1,320,470		14,228,383	54·2

Of the population in 1980, 6,998,301 were male, 11,327,159 persons were urban. Those 20 years old and older numbered 9,357,309. A census report, 1980, showed, 2,985,643 persons of Spanish origin.

The largest cities, with census population in 1980, are:

Houston	1,554,992	Amarillo	149,167	Odessa	89,797
Dallas	901,450	Beaumont	118,031	Garland	138,749
San Antonio	783,296	Wichita Falls	93,543	Laredo	91,229
Fort Worth	382,349	Irving	109,575	San Angelo	72,655
El Paso	424,522	Waco	101,267	Galveston	61,601
Austin (capital)	343,390	Arlington	159,117	Midland	70,291
Corpus Christi	230,715	Abilene	98,231	Tyler	70,720
Lubbock	174,157	Pasadena	111,884	Port Arthur	61,106

Larger urbanized areas, 1980: Houston, 2,891,146; Dallas-Fort Worth, 2,964,342; San Antonio, 1,070,245.

CLIMATE. Dallas. Jan. 45°F (7·2°C), July 84°F (28·9°C). Annual rainfall 38″ (945 mm). El Paso. Jan. 44°F (6·7°C), July 81°F (27·2°C). Annual rainfall 9″ (221 mm). Galveston. Jan. 54°F (12·2°C), July 84°F (28·9°C). Annual rainfall 46″ (1,159 mm). Houston. Jan. 52°F (11·1°C), July 83°F (28·3°C). Annual rainfall 48″ (1,200 mm). See Central Plains, p. 1372.

CONSTITUTION AND GOVERNMENT. The present constitution dates from 1876; it has been amended 233 times. The Legislature consists of a Senate of 31 members elected for 4 years (half their number retire every 2 years), and a House of Representatives of 150 members elected for 2 years.

The Governor and Lieut.-Governor are elected for 4 years. Qualified electors are all citizens with the usual residential qualifications. Texas sends to Congress 2 senators and 27 representatives.

In the 1980 presidential election Reagan polled 2,510,705 votes, Carter, 1,881,147.

The capital is Austin. The state has 254 counties.

Governor: Mark White (D.), 1983–86 ($71,400).
Lieut.-Governor: William P. Hobby (D.), 1983–86 ($7,200).
Secretary of State: David Dean (R.) ($42,700).

BUDGET. In the fiscal year ending 31 Aug. 1981 general revenues were $15,252,265,000; general expenditures, $12,910,237,000. Texas has a large revenue derived from the severance tax (*i.e.*, tax on the removal of oil, natural gas and sulphur from the soil or waters of the state).

Net long-term debt, 31 Aug. 1981, was $2,652,136,000.
Per capita personal income (1981) was $10,743.

ENERGY AND NATURAL RESOURCES

Minerals. In 1975 Texas had 31% of proved US crude oil reserves. Production, 1981: Crude petroleum, 945m. bbls. Other mineral products include natural gas (7,010,000 m.c.f.), natural gasoline, butane and propane gases, helium, crude gypsum, granite and sandstone, salt and cement. Total value of mineral products in 1980, $34,710m., of which $32,975 was for fuels.

Agriculture. Texas is one of the most important agricultural states of the Union. In 1982 it had 185,000 farms covering 138m. acres; average farm was of 748 acres valued, land and buildings, at $576 per acre. Large-scale commercial farms, highly mechanized, dominate in Texas; farms of 1,000 acres or more in number far exceed that of any other state. But small-scale farming persists.

Soil erosion is serious in some parts. For some 97,297,000 acres drastic curative treatment has been indicated and for 51,164,000 acres, preventive treatment.

Production, 1981: Cotton, 5,663,000 bales (of 480 lb); maize (128m. bu.), wheat (183m. bu.), oats and barley (13·6m. bu. in 1980), soybeans (11m. bu.), peanuts, oranges, grapefruit, peaches, potatoes, sweet potatoes.

Cash income, 1981, from crops was $4,712m.; from livestock, $5,423m.

The state has a very great livestock industry, leading in the number of all cattle, 13·7m. on 1 Jan. 1981, and sheep, 2·36m.; it also had 320,000 milch cows, and 930,000 swine.

Forestry. There were (1980) 23·3m. acres of forested land.

INDUSTRY. In 1980 manufacturing establishments employed 1m. workers; value added by manufacturing, $47,145m. Chemical industries along the Gulf Coast, such as the production of synthetic rubber and of primary magnesium (from sea-water), are increasingly important.

COMMUNICATIONS

Roads. In 1979 there were 264,900 miles of roads including 199,500 miles of rural roads. Motor registration in 1980, 10·2m.

Railways. The railways (1974) had a total mileage of 19,134 miles, of which 13,303 miles were main lines.

Aviation. In 1981 there were 322 public and 1,109 private airports.

Shipping. The port of Houston, connected by the Houston Ship Channel (50 miles long) with the Gulf of Mexico, is the largest inland cotton market in the world. Cargo handled 1981, 100·9m. tonnes.

JUSTICE, RELIGION, EDUCATION AND WELFARE

Justice. The prison system, Jan. 1980, held 26,522 men and women. Total executions from 1930 have been 300.

Texas has adopted 11 laws governing the activities of trade unions. An Act of 1955 forbids the state's payment of unemployment compensation to workers engaged in certain types of strikes.

Religion. The largest religious bodies are Roman Catholics, Baptists, Methodists, Churches of Christ, Lutherans, Presbyterians and Episcopalians.

Education. School attendance is compulsory from 7 to 17 years of age. In 1965–66 all public schools had completed or begun desegregation.

In autumn 1980 public elementary schools (kindergarten through grade 6) had 2,049,000 enrolled pupils and secondary schools, 851,000 enrolled pupils; in 1982 there were 166,000 classroom teachers. Teachers' salaries, 1982, averaged $17,500. Total public school expenditure, 1980, $5,256m.

The state has 156 institutions of higher learning with an estimated enrolment, Sept. 1981, of 716,000 students. The largest institutions, with faculty numbers and student enrolment, spring 1983, were:

Founded	Institutions	Control	Faculty	Students
1845	Baylor University, Waco	Baptist	587	10,473
1852	St Mary's University, San Antonio	R.C.	187	3,311
1869	Trinity University, San Antonio	Presb.	316	3,103
1873	Texas Christian University, Fort Worth	Christian	422	6,283
1876	Texas A. and M. Univ., College Station	State	2,093	36,127
1876	Prairie View Agr. and Mech. Coll., Prairie View	State	288	4,495
1879	Sam Houston State University	State	486	9,856
1883	University of Texas System (every campus)	State	10,270	114,800
1890	North Texas State University, Denton	State	1,173	18,782
1891	Hardin-Simmons University, Abilene	Baptist	123	1,948
1889	East Texas State University, Commerce	State	401	7,768
1899	South West Texas State University, San Marcos	State	668	16,038
1903	Texas Woman's University, Denton	State	622	7,827
1906	Abilene Christian College, Abilene	Church of Christ	286	4,546
1911	Southern Methodist University, Dallas	Methodist	622	9,150
1923	Stephen F. Austin State University	State	585	11,881
1923	Texas Technical University, Lubbock	State	1,539	23,000
1925	Texas Arts and Industries University, Kingsville	State	202	5,245
1934	University of Houston, Houston	State	3,236 [1]	49,241 [1]
1947	Texas Southern University, Houston	State	453	9,147
1951	Lamar University, Beaumont	State	650	14,600

[1] 1982.

Health. In 1980, the state had 561 hospitals (81,800 beds) listed by the American Hospital Association; on 1 Jan. 1980 mental hospitals had 6,559 resident patients and state institutions for the mentally retarded, 11,178 resident patients (1980).

Social Security. Aid is from state and federal sources. Old-age assistance (SSI) was being granted in Dec. 1980 to 146,800 persons, who received an average of $101 per month; aid was given to 320,000 dependent children (average payment per family, $109 per month).

Books of Reference

Texas Almanac. Dallas. Biennial
MacCorkle, S. A., and Smith, D., *Texas Government.* 7th ed. New York, 1974
Richardson, R. N., *Texas, the Lone Star State.* 3rd ed. New York, 1970

Legislative Reference Library: Box 12488, Capitol Station, Austin, Texas 78811. *Director:* James R. Sanders.

UTAH

HISTORY. Utah, which had been acquired by the US during the Mexican war, was settled by Mormons in 1847, and organized as a Territory on 9 Sept. 1850. It was admitted as a state into the Union on 4 Jan. 1896 with boundaries as at present.

AREA AND POPULATION. Utah is bounded north by Idaho and Wyoming, east by Colorado, south by Arizona and west by Nevada. Area, 84,899 sq. miles, of which 2,826 sq. miles are water. The federal government (1967) owned 35,397,274 acres or 67·1% of the area of the state. The area of unappropriated and unreserved lands was 23,268,250 acres in 1974. The Bureau of Indian Affairs in 1974 administered 3,035,190 acres, all of which were allotted to Indian tribes.

Census population, 1 April 1980, 1,461,037, an increase of 38% since 1970. Estimate (1981), 1,518,000. Births in 1980 were 43,708 (29·9 per 1,000 population); deaths, 8,556 (5·9); infant deaths, 505 (11·5 per 1,000 live births); marriages, 17,074 (11·7); divorces, 7,957 (5·4).

Population at 5 federal censuses was:

	White	Negro	Indian	Asiatic	Total	Per sq. mile
1910	366,583	1,144	3,123	2,501	373,851	4·5
1930	499,967	1,108	2,869	3,903	507,847	6·2
1960	873,828	4,148	6,961	5,207	890,627	10·8
1970	1,031,926	6,617	11,273	6,230	1,059,273	12·9
1980	1,382,550	9,225	19,256	15,076	1,461,037	17·7

Of the total in 1980, 724,501 were male, 1,232,908 persons were urban; 860,304 were 20 years of age or older.

The largest cities are Salt Lake City (capital), with a population (census, 1980) of 162,960; Provo, 74,007; Ogden, 64,444; Bountiful, 32,877; Orem, 52,399; and Logan, 26,844.

CLIMATE. Salt Lake City. Jan. 29°F (–1·7°C), July 77°F (25°C). Annual rainfall 16″ (401 mm). *See* Mountain States, p. 1372.

CONSTITUTION AND GOVERNMENT. Utah adopted its present constitution in 1896 (now with 61 amendments). It sends to Congress 2 senators and 3 representatives.

The Legislature consists of a Senate (in part renewed every 2 years) of 30 members, elected for 4 years, and of a House of Representatives of 75 members elected for 2 years. The Governor is elected for 4 years. The constitution provides for the initiative and referendum. Electors are all citizens, who, not being insane or criminal, have the usual residential qualifications.

The capital is Salt Lake City. There are 29 counties in the state.

In the 1980 presidential election Reagan polled 439,687 votes, Carter 124,266.

Governor: Scott Matheson (D.), 1981–84 ($48,000).
Lieut.-Governor: David S. Monson (R.), 1981–84 ($33,500).
Attorney-General: David L. Wilkinson (R.) ($36,500).

BUDGET. For the year ending 30 June 1981 general revenue was $2,053·4m. while general expenditures were $1,896·4m.
The net long-term debt on 30 June 1981 was about $578m.
Per capita personal income (1981) was $8,307.

ENERGY AND NATURAL RESOURCES

Minerals The principal minerals are: copper, gold, petroleum, lead, silver and zinc. The state also has natural gas, clays, tungsten, molybdenum, uranium and phosphate rock. Total value of mineral production, 1980, $2,000m.

Agriculture. In 1982 Utah had 13,000 farms covering 12m. acres, of which about 2m. acres were crop land and about 300,000 acres pasture. About 1m. acres had irrigation; the average farm was of 953 acres.

Of the total surface area, 9% is severely eroded and only 9·4% is free from erosion; the balance is moderately eroded.

Cash income, 1981, from crops, $142m. and from livestock, $413m. The principal crops (1980) are: Barley, 10·8m. bu.; wheat (spring and winter), 8·9m. bu.; oats, 915,000 bu.; potatoes, 1·1m. cwt; hay (alfalfa, sweet clover and lespedeza), 2m. tons; maize, 1·5m. bu. In 1981 there were 660,000 sheep; 77,000 milch cows; 875,000 all cattle; 58,000 swine. The 1978 wool clip yielded 4·7m. lb. of wool; 936m. lb. of milk were produced; and 1·46m. chickens produced 335m. eggs.

Forestry. Area of national forests, 1981, was 9,129,000 acres, of which 8·05m. acres were under forest service administration.

INDUSTRY. In 1980 manufacturing establishments had 93,000 workers; value added by manufacture was $3,415m. Leading manufactures by value added are primary metals, ordinances and transport, food, fabricated metals and machinery, petroleum products.

COMMUNICATIONS

Roads. The state has about 50,000 miles of highway. In 1980 there were 1,009,000 motor vehicles registered.

Railways. On 1 July 1974 the state had 1,734 miles of railways.

Aviation. In 1981 there were 57 public and 45 private airports.

JUSTICE, RELIGION, EDUCATION AND WELFARE

Justice. The number of inmates of the state prison on 1 Jan. 1980 was 960. Since 1930 total executions have been 14 (13 by shooting, 1 by hanging—the condemned man has choice), all whites, and all for murder.

Religion. Latter-day Saints (Mormons) form about 73% of the church membership of the state, with approximately 829,990 members in 1974; their church is a substantial property-owner. There were (1970) about 50,483 Catholics. Most Protestant denominations are represented.

Education. School attendance is compulsory for children from 6 to 18 years of age. There are 40 school districts. Teachers' salaries, 1980, averaged $14,965. There were (autumn 1980) 333,000 pupils in public elementary and secondary schools. In 1980 estimated public school expenditure was $665m.

The University of Utah (1850) (24,364 students in 1983) is in Salt Lake City; the Utah State University (1890) (11,112 students) is in Logan. The Mormon Church maintains the Brigham Young University at Provo (1875) with 2,700 students. Other colleges include: Westminster College, Salt Lake City, 1,120 students in

1982; Weber State College, Ogden, 10,000; Southern Utah State College, Cedar City, 2,400; College of Eastern Utah, Price, 1,250 in 1982; Snow College, Ephraim, 1,404 in 1982; Dixie College, St George, 2,010; L.D.S. Business College, Salt Lake City, 895. Total higher education students in 14 institutions, 1981, 97,000. A state bond of $70m. was approved in July 1975 for the University of Utah medical centre.

Health. In 1980, the state had 42 hospitals (5,300 beds) listed by the Utah Department of Social Services. Mental hospitals had 317 resident patients on 1 Jan. 1980; state facilities for the mentally retarded had 763.

Social Security. The state department of public welfare provided assistance during Dec. 1980 to 43,700 persons receiving aid to dependent children at an average $314 per family per month; aid to the aged, the blind and disabled is provided from federal funds.

Books of Reference

Compiled Digest of Administrative Reports. Secretary of State, Salt Lake City. Annual
Statistical Abstract of Government in Utah. Utah Foundation, Salt Lake City. Annual
A Statistical Abstract of Utah's Economy. Bureau of Economic and Business Research, Univ. of Utah, 1964
Utah Agricultural Statistics. Dept. of Agriculture, Salt Lake City. Annual
Utah: Facts. Bureau of Economic and Business Research, Univ. of Utah, 1975
Arrington, L., *Great Basin Kingdom: An Economic History of the Latter-Day Saints, 1830–1900.* Cambridge, Mass., 1958

VERMONT

HISTORY. Vermont, first settled in 1724, was admitted into the Union as the fourteenth state on 4 March 1791. The first constitution was adopted by convention at Windsor, 2 July 1777, and established an independent state government.

AREA AND POPULATION. Vermont is bounded north by Canada, east by New Hampshire, south by Massachusetts and west by New York. Area, 9,614 sq. miles, of which 341 sq. miles are inland water. Census population, 1 April 1980 (preliminary), 511,456, an increase of 15% since 1970. Estimate (1981) 516,000. Births, 1982, were 8,028 (15·5 per 1,000 population); deaths, 4,479 (8·6); infant deaths, 75 (9·3 per 1,000 live births); marriages, 5,570 (10·7); divorces, 2,620 (5).

Population at 5 census years was:

	White	Negro	Indian	Asiatic	Total	Per sq. mile
1910	354,298	1,621	26	11	355,956	39·0
1930	358,965	568	36	41	359,611	38·8
1960	389,092	519	57	172	389,881	42·0
1970	442,553	761	229	787	444,732	48·0
1980	506,736	1,135	984	1,355	511,456	55·1

Of the population in 1980, 249,080 were male, 172,735 persons were urban; those 20 years of age or older numbered 343,666. The largest cities are Burlington, with a population in 1980 of 37,712; Rutland, 18,436; Barre, 9,824.

CLIMATE. Burlington. Jan. 17°F (−8·3°C), July 70°F (21·1°C). Annual rainfall 33" (820 mm). *See* New England, p. 1373.

CONSTITUTION AND GOVERNMENT. The constitution was adopted in 1793 and has since been amended. Amendments are proposed by two-thirds vote of the Senate every 4 years, and must be accepted by two sessions of the legislature; they are then submitted to popular vote. The state Legislature, consisting of a Senate of 30 members and a House of Representatives of 150 members (both elected for 2 years), meets in Jan. in odd-numbered years. The Governor and Lieut.-

Governor are elected for 2 years. Electors are all citizens who possess certain residential qualifications and have taken the freeman's oath set forth in the constitution.

The state is divided into 14 counties; there are 251 towns and cities and other minor civil divisions. The state sends to Congress 2 senators and 1 representative, who are elected by the voters of the entire state.

In the 1980 presidential election Reagan polled 94,628 votes, Carter 81,952.

The capital is Montpelier (8,241, census of 1980).

Governor: Richard Snelling (R.), 1983–84 ($50,003).
Lieut.-Governor: Peter Smith (R.) ($22,006).
Secretary of State: James Douglas (R.) ($29,993).

BUDGET. The general revenue for the year ending 30 June 1980 was $711·1m.; general expenditure was $675·9m.

Total net long-term debt, 1 July 1980, was $654,159,000.

Per capita personal income (1980) was $7,827.

NATURAL RESOURCES

Minerals. Stone, chiefly granite, marble and slate, is the leading mineral produced in Vermont, contributing about 60% of the total value of mineral products. Other products include asbestos, talc, peat, sand and gravel. Total value of mineral products, 1981, $51m.

Agriculture. Agriculture is the most important industry. In 1978 the state had 7,273 farms covering 29·6% of the land area; the average farm was of 241 acres. Cash income, 1981, from livestock and products, $365·4m.; from crops, $30·2m. The dairy farms produce about 2,300m. lb. of milk annually. The chief agricultural crops are hay, apples and maple syrup. In 1981 Vermont had 355,000 cattle, 11,000 sheep, 9,000 swine, 425,000 poultry.

Forestry. In 1982 the harvest was 82m. bd ft hardwood and 93m. bd ft softwood saw-logs, and 267,000 cords of pulpwood and boltwood. About 600,000 cords was cut for firewood.

The state is nearly 80% forest, with 12% in public ownership. National forests area (1983), 285,000 acres. State-owned forests, parks, fish and game areas, 250,000 acres; municipally-owned, 38,500 acres.

INDUSTRY. In 1978, manufacturing establishments employed 31,500 production workers who earned $354·2m.; value added by manufacture was $1,382·7m.

COMMUNICATIONS

Roads. The state had 14,000 miles of roads in 1983, including 12,900 miles of rural roads. Motor vehicle registrations, 1983, 500,735.

Railways. There were, in 1983, 756 miles of main line railway, 300 of which was leased by the state to private operators.

Aviation. There were 22 airports in 1983, of which 10 were state operated, 2 municipally owned and 10 privately owned but open to public use.

JUSTICE, RELIGION, EDUCATION AND WELFARE

Justice. In Jan. 1980 there were 411 people in prison. The Vermont State Prison was closed in Aug. 1975 and prisoners transferred to federal prisons and community correction centres.

Religion. The principal denominations are Roman Catholic, United Church of Christ, United Methodist, Protestant Episcopal, Baptist and Unitarian–Universalist.

Education. School attendance during the full school term is compulsory for children from 7 to 16 years of age, unless they have completed the 10th grade or undergo approved home instruction. In 1982–83 the public elementary schools had 48,166 enrolled pupils; the public secondary schools had 43,344 pupils; the 82 private schools had 8,580 pupils. Full-time teachers for public elementary schools numbered 2,941, secondary schools 3,310. Teachers' salaries for 1983 averaged $15,794 (elementary) and $16,747 (secondary).

The University of Vermont (1791) had 8,205 full-time students in autumn 1982; Middlebury College (1800), 1,932 students; Norwich University (1834), 2,308 students (including Vermont College); St Michael's College, 1,721 students; the 5 state colleges, 3,796 students; all other colleges, 3,120.

Health. In Sept. 1983 the state had 16 general hospitals (898 beds), 2 mental hospitals and 1 T.B. hospital. There was 1 federal general hospital with 224 beds.

Social Security. Old-age assistance (SSI) was being granted in 1980 to 2,400 persons, drawing an average of $108 per month; aid to dependent children was being granted to 24,300 persons, drawing an average of $340 per family per month; and aid to the permanently and totally disabled was being granted to 5,200 persons, drawing an average of $192.

Books of Reference

Legislative Directory. Secretary of State, Montpelier. Biennial
Vermont Facts and Figures. Office of Statistical Co-ordination, Montpelier
Vermont Year-Book, formerly *Walton's Register.* Chester. Annual

State Library: Vermont Dept.of Libraries, Montpelier. *State Librarian:* Patricia Klinck.

VIRGINIA

HISTORY. The first English Charter for settlements in America was that granted by James I in 1606 for the planting of colonies in Virginia. The state was one of the 13 original states in the Union. Virginia lost just over one-third of its area when West Virginia was admitted into the Union (1863).

AREA AND POPULATION. Virginia is bounded north-west by West Virginia, north-east by Maryland, east by the Atlantic, south by North Carolina and Tennessee and west by Kentucky. Area, 40,767 sq. miles including 1,063 sq. miles of inland water. Census population, 1 April 1980, 5,346,818, an increase of 695,370 or 14·9% since 1970. Estimate (1981) 5,430,000. In 1982 there were 81,098 births (14·8 per 1,000 population); 41,897 deaths (7·7); 1,046 infant deaths (12·9 per 1,000 live births); 62,099 marriages and 26,138 divorces.

Population for 5 federal census years was:

	White	Negro	Indian	Asiatic	Total	Per sq. mile
1910	1,389,809	671,096	539	168	2,061,612	51·2
1930	1,770,441	650,165	779	466	2,421,851	60·7
1960	3,142,443	816,258	2,155	4,725	3,966,949	99·3
			All others			
1970	3,761,514	861,368	25,612		4,648,494	116·9
1980	4,230,000	1,008,311	108,517		5,346,818	134·7

Of the total population in 1980, 49% were male, 66% were urban and 59% were 21 years of age or older.

The population (census of 1980) of the principal cities was: Norfolk, 266,979; Virginia Beach, 262,199; Richmond, 219,214; Newport News, 144,903; Hampton, 122,617; Portsmouth, 104,577; Alexandria, 103,219; Roanoke, 100,427; Lynchburg, 66,743.

CLIMATE. Average temperatures in Jan. are 41°F in the Tidewater coastal area and 32°F in the Blue Ridge mountains; July averages, 78°F and 68°F respectively.

Precipitation averages 36" in the Shenandoah valley and 44" in the south. Snowfall is 5-10" in the Tidewater and 25-30" in the western mountains. Norfolk. Jan. 41°F (5°C), July 79°F (26·1°C). Annual rainfall 46" (1,145 mm). *See* Atlantic Coast, p. 1373.

CONSTITUTION AND GOVERNMENT. The present constitution dates from 1971.

The General Assembly consists of a Senate of 40 members, elected for 4 years, and a House of Delegates of 100 members, elected for 2 years. The Governor and Lieut.-Governor are elected for 4 years. Qualified as electors are (with few exceptions) all citizens 18 years of age, fulfilling certain residential qualifications, who have registered. The state sends to Congress 2 senators and 10 representatives.

In the 1980 presidential election Reagan polled 989,609 votes, Carter 752,174 and Anderson 95,418.

The state capital is Richmond; the state contains 95 counties and 41 independent cities.

Governor: Charles S. Robb (D.), 1983–86 ($60,000).
Lieut.-Governor: Richard J. Davis (D.) $16,000.
Secretary of the Commonwealth: Laurie Naismith (D.) ($21,400).

BUDGET. General revenue for the year ending 30 June 1982 was $5,919m. (taxation, $3,238·9m., and federal aid, $2,680·2m.); general expenditures, $6,095·4m. ($2,048·9m. for education, $732m. for transport and $383·5m. for public welfare).

Total net long-term debt, 30 June 1982, amounted to $240,089,279.

Per capita personal income (1981) was $10,349.

ENERGY AND NATURAL RESOURCES

Minerals (1981). Coal is the most important mineral, with output of 41,977,807 short tons. Lead and zinc ores, stone, sand and gravel, lime and titanium ore are also produced. Total mineral output was 53m. tons.

Agriculture. In 1978 there were 57,000 farms with an area of 10m. acres; average farm had 175 acres and was valued at $163,918.

Income, 1981, from crops, $733m., and from livestock and livestock products, $911m. The chief crops (1981) are corn, hay and peanuts (330·8m. lb.), tobacco (158m. lb.).

Animals on farms on 1 Jan. 1982 included 170,000 milch cows, 1·85m. all cattle, 170,000 sheep and 640,000 swine (Dec. 1981).

Forestry. National forests, 1981, covered 1,627,000 acres.

INDUSTRY. The manufacture of cigars and cigarettes and of rayon and allied products and the building of ships lead in value of products.

TOURISM. Tourists spend about $3,300m. a year in Virginia, attracted mainly by the state's outstanding scenery, coastline and historical interest.

COMMUNICATIONS

Roads. The state highways system, 31 Dec. 1982, had 61,801 miles of highways, of which 8,958 miles were primary roads. Motor registrations, 1981, 3·7m.

Railways. In 1983 there were 3,693 miles of railways.

Aviation. There were, in 1981, 260 airports, of which 58 were publicly owned.

JUSTICE, RELIGION, EDUCATION AND WELFARE

Justice. Executions (by electrocution) since 1930 totalled 96. Prison population, 31 Dec. 1981, 9,013 in federal and state prisons.

Religion. The principal churches are the Baptist, Methodist, Protestant-Episcopal, Roman Catholic and Presbyterian.

Education. Elementary and secondary instruction is free, and for ages 6–17 attendance is compulsory. No child under 12 may be employed in any mining or manufacturing work.

In 1982 the 140 school districts had, in primary schools, 598,415 pupils and 35,121 teachers and in public high schools, 381,224 pupils and 25,736 teachers. Teachers' salaries (1981–82) averaged $17,009. Total expenditure on education, 1981–82, was $2,533m. The more important institutions for higher education (1982) were:

Founded	Name and place of college	Staff	Students
1693	William and Mary College, Williamsburg (State)	557	6,520
1749	Washington and Lee University, Lexington	174	1,679
1776	Hampden-Sydney College, Hampden-Sydney (Pres.)	64	770
1819	University of Virginia, Charlottesville (State)	1,637	16,420
1832	Randolph-Macon College, Ashland (Methodist)	82	856
1832	University of Richmond, Richmond (Baptist)	325	4,066
1838	Virginia Commonwealth University, Richmond	2,230	18,500
1839	Virginia Military Institute Lexington (State)	133	1,309
1865	Virginia Union University, Richmond	110	1,327
1868	Hampton Institute	242	3,351
1872	Virginia Polytechnic Institute and State University	2,523	21,584
1882	Virginia State College, Petersburg	228	4,564
1910	Radford College (State)	300	5,693
1930	Old Dominion University, Norfolk	622	17,023
1956	George Mason University (State)	750	14,273

Health. In 1980 the state had 136 hospitals (31,200 beds) listed by the American Hospital Association.

Social Security. In 1938 Virginia established a system of old-age assistance under the Federal Security Act; in March 1983 persons in 2,034 cases were drawing an average grant of $202.79; aid to permanently and totally disabled, 1,766 cases, average grant $218.96; aid to dependent children, 164,383 persons, average grant $85.77; general relief, 6,642 persons, average grant $146.62.

Books of Reference

Virginia Facts and Figures. Annual Division of Industrial Development, Richmond. Annual
Dabney, V., *Virginia, the New Dominion.* 1971
Friddell, G., *The Virginia Way.* Burda, 1973
Gottmann, J., *Virginia in our Century.* Charlottesville, 1969
Morton, R. L., *Colonial Virginia.* 2 vols. Univ. Press of Virginia, 1960
Rouse, P. *Virginia: a Pictorial History.* Scribner, 1975
Rubin, L. D., Jr., *Virginia: a Bicentennial History.* Norris, 1977

State Library: Virginia State Library, Richmond 23219. *State Librarian:* Donald Haynes.

WASHINGTON

HISTORY. Washington, formerly part of Oregon, was created a Territory in 1853, and was admitted into the Union as a state on 11 Nov. 1889. Its settlement dates from 1811.

AREA AND POPULATION. Washington is bounded north by Canada, east by Idaho, south by Oregon with the Columbia River forming most of the boundary, and west by the Pacific. Area, 68,139 sq. miles, of which 1,627 sq. miles are inland water. Lands owned by the federal government, 1977, were 12·4m. acres or 29·1% of the total area. Census population, 1 April 1980 (preliminary), 4,130,163, an increase of 730,994 or 21·4% since 1970. Estimated population (1982), 4,265,400. Births, 1980 were 67,518; deaths, 32,304; infant deaths, 143; marriages, 47,836; divorces and annulments, 28,733.

Population in 5 federal census years was:

	White	Negro	Indian	Asiatic and others	Total	Per sq. mile
1910	1,109,111	6,058	10,997	15,824	1,141,990	17·1
1930	1,521,661	6,840	11,253	23,642	1,563,396	23·3
1960	2,751,675	48,738	21,076	31,725	2,853,214	42·8
1970	2,351,055	71,308	33,386	53,420	3,409,169	51·2
1980	3,777,296	105,544	60,771	186,552	4,130,163	62·0

Of the total population in 1980, 2,051,369 were male, 3,037,765 persons were urban; 2,837,607 were 20 years of age or older.

There are 24 Indian reservations, the largest being held by the Yakima tribe. Indian reservations in Sept. 1979 covered 2,496,423 acres, of which 1,996,018 acres were tribal lands and 497,218 acres were held by individuals. Total Indian population, 1980, 60,771.

Leading cities are Seattle, with a population (1980 census) of 491,897; Spokane, 170,993; Tacoma, 158,101; Bellevue, 73,711. Others : Yakima, 49,826; Everett, 54,413; Vancouver, 42,834; Bellingham, 45,794; Bremerton, 36,208; Richland, 33,578; Longview, 31,052; Renton, 30,612; Edmonds, 27,526; Walla Walla, 25,618. Urbanized areas (1980 census): Seattle–Everett, 1,600,944; Tacoma, 482,692; Spokane, 341,058.

CLIMATE. Seattle. Jan. 40°F (4·4°C), July 63°F (17·2°C). Annual rainfall 34″ (848 mm). Spokane. Jan. 27°F (–2·8°C), July 70°F (21·1°C). Annual rainfall 14″ (350 mm). See Pacific Coast, p. 1372.

CONSTITUTION AND GOVERNMENT. The constitution, adopted in 1889, has had 63 amendments. The Legislature consists of a Senate of 49 members elected for 4 years, half their number retiring every 2 years, and a House of Representatives of 98 members, elected for 2 years. The Governor and Lieut.-Governor are elected for 4 years. The state sends 2 senators and 7 representatives to Congress.

Qualified as voters are (with some exceptions) all citizens 18 years of age, having the usual residential qualifications.

In the 1980 presidential election Reagan polled 865,244 votes, Carter 650,193 and Anderson, 185,073.

The capital is Olympia (population, 1980 census, 27,447). The state contains 39 counties.

Governor: John Spellman (R.), 1981–85 ($63,000).
Lieut.-Governor: John A. Cherberg (D.), 1981–85 ($28,600).
Secretary of State: Ralph Munro (R.), 1981–85 ($31,000).

BUDGET. For the 2-year budget period 1981–83 the state's total revenue is (projected) $13,545·2m.; general expenditure is (projected) $13,873·5m. (education, $6,150·7m.; transportation, $706·6m., and human resources, $3,636m.). State revenue in the period 1979–81 was $10,623·7m. and expenditure $10,857·8m.

Total net long-term debt on 30 June 1980 was $627,784,980.

Per capita personal income (1982) was $11,635.

ENERGY AND NATURAL RESOURCES

Electricity. With about 20% of potential water-power resources of US, the state is first in developed and potential hydro-electricity. Electric energy produced in 1982, 99,684m. kw.

Minerals. Mining and quarrying employed about 3,000 in 1981, and the sector is not as important as forestry, agriculture or manufacturing. Uranium is mined but figures are not disclosed; other minerals include sand and gravel, stone, coal and clays.

Agriculture. Agriculture is constantly growing in value because of more intensive and diversified farming and because of the 1m.-acre Columbia Basin Irrigation Project. Irrigated land in farms (1974) amounted to 1,286,412 acres.

In 1980 there were 37,800 farms with an acreage of 17m.; average farm was of 451 acres.

Value of farm production, 1982, was $3,057m. (from field crops, $1,359m.; from speciality products, including flowers, bulbs, Christmas trees, $170m., fruit and vegetables, $621 4m., and from livestock and dairy products, $906·5m.). Wheat, the leading farm commodity, was valued at $555·5m. Cattle and calves were valued at $348m. Other major commodities are milk ($440m.), apples ($297m.).

On 1 Jan. 1980 animals on farms included 195,000 milch cows, 1·58m. all cattle, 65,000 sheep and 126,000 swine.

Forestry. Forests cover about 23m. acres, of which 9m. acres are national forest. In 1982, lumber production was 3,014m. bd ft; plywood, 1,200m. bd ft, and pulp wood (1981) 3,494,000 short tons.

Fisheries. Washington ranks second only to Alaska in the catch of salmon and halibut, and in the production of canned salmon.

INDUSTRY. In 1981 manufacturing employed 301,900 workers, of whom 79,100 were in aerospace and 61,200 in the forest products industry. Gross manufacturing income (1 Oct. 1980–30 Sept. 1981): aerospace, $8,380·6m.; forest products, $6,415·6m., of which paper and pulp made $2,571·4m.; food products, $4,801·4m.; primary metals, $2,728·9m.; refining petroleum, $2,227·2m.

Abundance of electric power has made Washington the leading producer of primary aluminium.

COMMUNICATIONS

Roads. The state (1979) maintained 6,920 miles of highway; the counties, 40,767 miles; municipalities, 9,888 miles. Motor vehicle registrations (1980), 3,566,639.

Railways. The railways had, in 1980, 6,057 miles.

Aviation. There were in 1979, 365 airports, 120 publicly owned. In 1978 Seattle–Tacoma Airport traffic was 8·3m. passengers, 48,000 tons of mail and 185,000 tons of freight and express.

JUSTICE, RELIGION, EDUCATION AND WELFARE

Justice. The average daily adult population in state prisons in Jan. 1982 was 4,674. Since 1963 there have been no executions; total 1930–63 (by hanging) was 47, including 40 whites, 5 Negroes and 2 other races, all for murder, except 1 white for kidnapping.

Religion. Chief religious bodies (1971) are the Roman Catholic (366,087), United Methodist (116,723), Lutheran (98,815), Presbyterian (75,818), Latter-day Saints (66,109), Episcopalian (56,319).

Education. Education is given free to all children between the ages of 5 and 21 years, and is compulsory for children from 8 to 15 years of age. In Oct. 1980 the 1,004 elementary schools had 16,785 classroom teachers and 370,597 pupils, 289 junior high and middle schools and 284 high schools had 14,771 classroom teachers and 369,985 pupils. In 1978–79 the average salary of teaching staff was $17,357. There were 2,629 teachers of handicapped children. The total expenditure on public elementary and secondary schools for the school year 1980–81 was $1,791·6m. In Oct. 1980 an estimated 472 private and parochial elementary and secondary schools had 54,600 elementary and high school pupils.

The University of Washington, founded 1861, at Seattle, had, autumn 1982, 34,769 students, and Washington University at Pullman, founded 1890, for science and agriculture, had 16,829 students. Twenty-seven community colleges had (1981) a total enrolment of 161,244 students (89,263 full-time equivalent).

Health. In 1981 the 2 state hospitals for mental illness had a daily average of 1,204 patients; schools for handicapped children, 1,999 residents in Sept. 1981.

In 1981 the state had 109 licensed general hospitals (13,201 beds), 3 licensed psychiatric hospitals (181 beds) and 3 alcoholism hospitals (174 beds).

Social Security. Old-age assistance is provided for persons 65 years of age or older without adequate resources (and not in need of continuing home care) who are residents of the state. In July 1981, 14,287 people were drawing an average of $130·93 per month; aid to 139,514 children in 52,781 families averaged $333·86 per family monthly; to 500 blind persons, $218·05 per person monthly; to 25,557 totally disabled, $216·59 monthly. 5,057 persons, under foster care, received payments of $366·11 per person. Total unemployment in 1981 averaged 176,000 (9·1% of the population). In June 1980 the unemployment insurance system covered 90·5% of employers (103,391). Benefits ranged from $41 to $150 per week and averaged $117·75 per week.

Books of Reference

Washington State Research Council. *Handbook: A Compendium of Statistical and Explanatory Information about State and Local Government in Washington.* 4th ed. Olympia, 1973.—*The Book of Numbers: A Statistical Handbook on Washington State Government.* Olympia, 1977
Washington (State) Office of Financial Management. *Pocket Data Book 1978*
Avery, M. W., *Washington, a History of the Evergreen State.* Univ. of Wash. Press, 1965.—*Government of Washington State.* Univ. of Wash. Press, revised ed. 1973

State Library: Washington State Library, Olympia. *State Librarian:* Roderick Swartz.

WEST VIRGINIA

HISTORY. In 1862, after the state of Virginia had seceded from the Union, the electors of the western portion ratified an ordinance providing for the formation of a new state, which was admitted into the Union by presidential proclamation on 20 June 1863, under the name of West Virginia. Its constitution was adopted by the voters almost unanimously on 26 March 1863.

AREA AND POPULATION. West Virginia is bounded north by Pennsylvania and Maryland, east and south by Virginia, south-west by the Sandy River (forming the boundary with Kentucky) and west by the Ohio River (forming the boundary with Ohio). Area, 24,282 sq. miles, of which 102 sq. miles are water. Census population, 1 April 1980, 1,949,644, an increase of 11·8% since 1970. Estimate (1981), 1,952,000. Births, 1980, 29,438; deaths, 19,178; infant deaths, 347; marriages, 17,391; divorces, 10,275.

Population in 5 federal census years was:

	White	Negro	Indian	Asiatic	Total	Per sq. mile
1910	1,156,817	64,173	36	93	1,221,119	50·8
1940	1,614,191	114,893	18	103	1,729,205	71·8
1960	1,770,133	89,378	181	419	1,860,421	77·3
1970	1,673,480	67,342	751	1,463	1,744,237	71·8
1980	1,874,751	65,051	1,610	5,194	1,949,644	80·3

Of the total population in 1980, 945,408 were male, 705,319 were urban; those 20 years of age or older numbered 1,319,566.

The 1980 census population of the principal cities was: Huntington, 63,684; Charleston, 63,968. Others: Wheeling, 43,070; Parkersburg, 39,967; Morgantown, 27,605; Weirton, 24,736; Fairmont, 23,863; Clarksburg, 22,371.

CLIMATE. Charleston. Jan. 34°F (1·1°C), July 76°F (24·4°C). Annual rainfall 40″ (1,010 mm). *See* Appalachian Mountains, p. 1373.

CONSTITUTION AND GOVERNMENT. The present constitution was adopted in 1872; it has had 51 amendments.

The Legislature consists of the Senate of 34 members elected for a term of 4 years, one-half being elected biennially, and the House of Delegates of 100 members, elected biennially. The Governor is elected for 4 years and may succeed himself once. Voters are all citizens (with the usual exceptions) 18 years of age and meeting certain residential requirements. The state sends to Congress 2 senators and 4 representatives.

In the 1980 presidential election Carter polled 367,462 votes, Reagan 334,206 and Anderson 31,691.

The state capital is Charleston. There are 55 counties.

Governor: John D. Rockefeller IV (D.), 1981–85 ($50,000).
Secretary of State: A. James Manchin (D.) ($30,000).

FINANCE. Total revenues for the year ending 30 June 1980 were $3,608,262,063 ($1,004m. from general revenue fund, $694m. from federal funds, $324m. from state road fund, $215m. from special revenue fund); general expenditures were $3,638,672,449 (education, $758m.; highways, $646m.; public welfare, $379m.; other governmental costs, $417m.).

Bonds outstanding were $934,658,000 on 30 June 1980.

Estimated *per capita* personal income (1980) was $7,800.

ENERGY AND NATURAL RESOURCES

Minerals. 55% of the state is underlain with mineable coal; 96,408,980 short tons of coal were produced in 1980; coke (oven and bee-hive), 79,518,753 short tons. Petroleum output, 572,058m. bbls; natural gas production was 5,044,988 cu. ft. Salt, sand and gravel, sandstone and limestone are also produced. The total value of mineral output in 1980 was $5,111,274,000.

Agriculture. In 1980 the state had 20,000 farms with an area of 4·2m. acres; average size of farm was 210 acres and valued at $651 per acre. Livestock farming predominates.

Cash income, 1980, from crops was $75·8m.; from government payments, $2·5m., and from livestock and products, $182·2m. Total area of major crops harvested was 722,000 acres, chief crop being hay (595,000 acres); all corn, 96,000 acres. Apples (245m. lb.) and peaches (22m. lb.) are important fruit crops. Livestock on farms, 1 Jan. 1980, included 545,000 cattle, of which 37,000 were milch cows; sheep, 113,000; hogs, 56,000; chickens, 940,000 excluding broilers. Production, 1980, included 21·8m. broilers, 149m. eggs; 2·3m. turkeys.

Forestry. State forests, 1980, covered 79,307 acres; national forests, 1,647,146 gross acres; 75% of the state is woodland.

INDUSTRY. In 1980, 1,730 manufactories had 116,552 production workers who earned $2,167·9m. Value added by manufacture (estimate) was $3,660m. Leading industries are primary and fabricated metals, glass, chemicals, wood products, textiles and apparel, and machinery.

In 1980 average state employment was 757,000 who earned an average wage of $276·26 per week.

The first commercial coal liquefaction plant in the USA is being built near Morgantown with the co-operation of the governments of Federal Republic of Germany and Japan and the Gulf Oil Co.

COMMUNICATIONS

Roads. Total highways in 1980, 37,527 miles (state maintained, 33,436 miles; inter-state, 390 miles; national parks and other roads, 4,091 miles; West Virginia Turnpike, 87 miles). Registered motor vehicles, financial year ending 30 June 1980, numbered 1,140,673.

Railways. In 1980 the state had 3,941 miles of railway, all operated by diesel or electric trains.

Aviation. There were 42 licensed airports in 1980.

Post and Broadcasting. There are 65 AM radio stations, 41 FM radio stations. Television stations number 9 VHF and 3 UHF.

Newspapers. Daily newspapers number 25; weekly newspapers 78.

JUSTICE, RELIGION, EDUCATION AND WELFARE

Justice. The state court system consists of a Supreme Court and 31 circuit courts. The Supreme Court of Appeals, exercising original and appellate jurisdiction, has 5 members elected by the people for 12-year terms. Each circuit court has from 1 to 7 judges (as determined by the Legislature on the basis of population and case-load) chosen by the voters within each circuit for 8-year terms.

Effective on 1 July 1967, the West Virginia Human Rights Act prohibits discrimination in employment and places of public accommodations based on race, religion, colour, national origin or ancestry.

There are 8 penal and correctional institutions which had, on 30 June 1980, 1,590 inmates. In 1965 the State Legislature abolished capital punishment.

Religion. Chief denominations in 1980 were United Methodist (175,000 members, estimate), Baptists (141,000) and Roman Catholics (102,600).

Education. Public school education is free for all from 5 to 21 years of age, and school attendance is compulsory for all between the ages of 7 and 16 (school term, 200 days—180–185 days of actual teaching). The public schools are non-sectarian. During school year 1979–80 elementary schools had 13,574 instructional personnel and 230,120 pupils enrolled; secondary schools, 10,824 and 381,233 respectively. Average minimum salary of instructional personnel (1980–81) was $14,948. Total 1979–80 expenditures for public schools, $775,357,181.

Leading institutions of higher education in 1981:

Founded		Full-time students
1837	Marshall University, Huntington	11,482
	School of Medicine	401
1837	West Liberty State College, West Liberty	2,668
1867	Fairmont State College, Fairmont	5,262
1868	West Virginia University, Morgantown	19,874
	School of Medicine	1,437
1872	Concord College, Athens	2,174
1872	Glenville State College, Glenville	1,920
1872	Shepherd College, Shepherdstown	3,001
1891	West Virginia State College	4,368
1895	West Virginia Institute of Technology, Montgomery	3,343
1895	Bluefield State College, Bluefield	2,340
1901	Potomac State College of West Virginia Univ., Keyser	1,104
1972	West Virginia College of Graduate Studies	3,323
1976	School of Osteopathic Medicine, Lewisburg	231

In addition to the universities and state-supported schools, there are 3 community colleges (8,326 students in 1981), 10 denominational and private institutions of higher education (11,221 students in 1981) and 14 business colleges.

Health. In 1980–81 the state had 66 hospitals and 34 licensed personal care homes, 71 skilled-nursing homes and 6 mental hospitals.

Social Security. The Department of Welfare, originating in the 1930s as the Department of Public Assistance, is both state and federally financed. In the year ending 30 June 1981 day care for 5,288 children per month was provided; aid was given to 24,158 families with dependent children (average award, $173·05 per month); handicapped children's services conducted 134,640 examinations; 65,526 families per month received food stamps.

On 1 Jan. 1974 all blind, aged and disabled services were converted to the Federal Supplemental Security Income programme.

Books of Reference

West Virginia Blue Book. Legislature, Charleston. Annual, since 1916

West Virginia Statistical Handbook, 1974. Bureau of Business Research, W. Va. Univ., Morgantown, 1974

Bibliography of West Virginia. 2 parts. Dept. of Archives and History, Charleston, 1939

West Virginia History. Dept. of Archives and History. Charleston. Quarterly, from 1939

Conley, P., and Doherty, W. T., *West Virginia History.* Charleston, 1974

Davis, C. J., and others, *West Virginia State and Local Government.* West Virginia Univ. Bureau for Government Research, 1963

Shetler, C., *Guide to the Study of West Virginia History.* Morgantown, 1960; *West Virginia Civil War Literature.* Morgantown, 1963

Williams, J. A., *West Virginia: A Bicentennial History.* New York, 1976

State Library: Division of Archives and History, Dept. of Culture and History, Charleston.

WISCONSIN

HISTORY. Wisconsin was settled in 1670 by French traders and missionaries. Originally a part of New France, it was surrendered to the British in 1763 and in 1783, when ceded to the US, became part of the North-west Territory. It was then contained successively in the Territories of Indiana, Illinois and Michigan. In 1836 it became part of the Territory of Wisconsin, which also included the present states of Iowa, Minnesota and parts of the Dakotas. It was admitted into the Union with its present boundaries on 29 May 1848.

AREA AND POPULATION. Wisconsin is bounded north by Lake Superior and the Upper Peninsula of Michigan, east by Lake Michigan, south by Illinois, west by Iowa and Minnesota, with the Mississippi River forming most of the boundary. Area, 56,153 sq. miles, including 1,727 sq. miles of inland water, but excluding any part of the Great Lakes. Census population, 1 April 1980 4,705,335, an increase of 6·5% since 1970. Estimated population (1983), 4,777,901. Births in 1982 were 74,327 (15·6 per 1,000 population); deaths, 40,226 (8·5); infant deaths, 700 (9·4 per 1,000 live births); marriages, 42,146 (8·9); divorces and annulments, 17,327.

Population in 5 census years was:

	White	Negro	All others	Total	Per sq. mile
1910	2,320,555	2,900	10,405	2,333,860	42·2
1930	2,916,255	10,739	12,012	2,939,006	53·7
1960	3,858,903	74,546	18,328	3,951,777	72·2
1970	4,258,959	128,224	30,750	4,417,933	80·8
1980	4,442,598	182,593	80,144	4,705,335	86·4

Of the total population in 1980, 49% were male, 64·2% were urban and 67% were 20 years old or older.

Population of the larger cities, 1980 census, was as follows:

Milwaukee	636,212	Appleton	59,032	Beloit	35,207
Madison	170,616	Oshkosh	49,678	Fond du Lac	35,863
Racine	85,725	La Crosse	48,347	Manitowoc	32,547
Green Bay	87,889	Sheboygan	48,085	Wausau	32,426
Kenosha	77,685	Janesville	51,071	Superior	29,571
West Allis	63,982	Eau Claire	51,509	Brookfield	34,035
Wauwatosa	51,308	Waukesha	50,319		

Population of larger urbanized areas, 1980 census: Milwaukee, 1,207,008; Madison, 213,678; Duluth–Superior (Minn.–Wis.), 132,585; Racine, 118,987; Green Bay, 142,747.

CLIMATE. Milwaukee. Jan. 19°F (–7·2°C), July 70°F (21·1°C). Annual rainfall 29″ (727 mm). *See* Great Lakes, p. 1373.

CONSTITUTION AND GOVERNMENT. The constitution, which dates from 1848, has 126 amendments. The legislative power is vested in a Senate of 33 members (1983 term: 19 Democrats, 14 Republicans), elected for 4 years, one-half elected alternately, and an Assembly of 99 members (1983 term: 58 Democrats, 40 Republicans, 1 vacancy) all elected simultaneously for 2 years. The Governor and Lieut.-Governor are elected for 4 years. All 6 constitutional officers serve 4-year terms.

Wisconsin has universal suffrage for all citizens 18 years of age or over; but, as there is no official list of voters, the size of the electorate is unknown; 1,580,090 voted for Governor in 1982.

Wisconsin is represented in Congress by 2 senators and 9 representatives.

In the 1980 presidential election Reagan polled 1,088,845 votes, Carter 981,584 and Anderson 160,657.

The capital is Madison. The state has 72 counties.

Governor: Anthony S. Earl (D.), 1983–87 ($75,337).
Lieut.-Governor: James T. Flynn (D.), 1983–87 ($41,390).
Secretary of State: Douglas La Follette (D.), 1983–87 ($37,334).

BUDGET. For the year ending 30 June 1983 (Wisconsin Bureau of Financial Operations figures) total revenue for all funds was $9,941,960,925 ($4,091,482,250 from taxation and $1,670,033,959 from federal aid). General expenditure from all funds was $8,591,378,779 ($2,625,291,393 for education, $2,468,425,998 for human resources).

Per capita personal income (1982) was $10,774.

ENERGY AND NATURAL RESOURCES

Electricity. There were, Dec. 1982, 89 hydro-electric power plants (15 of them municipal, 59 private in Wisconsin; 15 private outside the state) operated by public utilities with a total installed capacity of 451,330 kw.; output, 1982, was 2,369,029m. kwh. The 15 outside plants are in Michigan; installed capacity 99,990 kw., output 530,849m. kwh.

Fossil fuel and nuclear plants numbered 26 (4 municipal); the former had a total installed capacity of 6,559,766 kw.; total output, (1982), 21,356,450m. kwh; the 2 nuclear plants had an installed capacity of 1,540,682 kw. and a total output (1982) of 10,130,859m. kwh.

There were also 31 internal combustion reciprocating plants (one in Michigan), with a total installed capacity of 107,025 kw. and a total output of (1982) 3,283m. kwh., and 17 internal combustion turbine plants with a total installed capacity of 1,285,950 kw.; total output was (1982) 189,575m. kwh.

There was a total of 163 plants, with a total installed capacity of 9,944,753 kw. and a total output of (1982) 33,902,964m. kwh.

Minerals. Sand and gravel, crushed stone, lime and taconite (iron ore) are the chief mineral products. Mineral production in 1981 was valued at $166·5m. This value included $50m. for sand and gravel, $43m. for crushed stone and about $17m. for lime. Value of all other minerals including lead, zinc, taconite, natural abrasives, peat, cement, gemstones, dimension stone and clay, $51m.

The large Forest County sulphide deposit (5,000 ft long, about 200 ft wide and over 1,500 ft deep and almost vertical) south of Crandon is estimated at over 77m. tons, averaging 5% zinc, 1% copper and lesser amounts of lead, silver and gold. The company owning the Crandon zinc-copper deposit initiated the process to acquire mine permits in 1982. In 1981, northern Wisconsin was explored for base metal deposits in Price, Forest, Lincoln, Rusk, and Marathon counties.

Agriculture. The total number of farms has declined in the last 47 years, but farms have become larger and more productive. On 1 Jan. 1982 there were 92,000 farms with a total acreage of 18·5m. acres and an average size of 201 acres, compared with 142,000 farms with a total acreage of 22·4m. acres and an average of 158 acres in 1959.

Cash income from products sold by Wisconsin farms in 1982 of $5,168m. was the highest on record, and included $4,019m. from livestock and livestock products and $1,148m. from crops.

Wisconsin ranked first among the states in 1982 in the number of milch cows, milk and butter production, output of American, both Brick and Munster, Italian and Blue Mold Cheese. Production of all cheese accounted for 36·2% of the nation's total. The state also ranked first in bulk whole condensed milk and bulk sweetened skim condensed milk, buttermilk, dry whey, condensed whey and lactose. In crops the state ranked first for snap beans for processing, green peas for canning, all hay, beets for canning, corn for silage, cranberries and cabbage for sauerkraut. Production of the principal field crops in 1982 included: Corn for grain, 362m. bu.; corn for silage, 11·4m. tons; oats, 48·4m. bu.; all hay, 13·2m. tons. Other crops of importance 22·6m. cwt of potatoes, 20·1m. lb. of tobacco, 1·3m. bbls of cranberries, 2·7m. cwt of cabbage, 1·8m. cwt of carrots and the processing crops of 562,120 tons of sweet corn, 60,120 tons of beets for canning, 147,920 tons of green peas and 190,280 tons of snap beans.

Forestry. In June 1983 national forests comprised 1·5m. acres; state forests, 425,615 acres; the county forests, 2·28m. acres. Wisconsin has an estimated 14·4m. acres of forest land (about 41·5% of land area) which consists of private (about 58%) and industrial forest. The production and remanufacture of wood and products is one of the state's most important industries.

INDUSTRY. Wisconsin has much heavy industry, particularly in the Milwaukee area. In 1982 the state ranked thirteenth in manufactured exports; non-electrical machinery was the major industrial group (20% of all manufacturing employment), followed by food processing, fabricated metals, electrical machinery, paper and products, transport equipment, primary metals and printing. Manufacturing establishments in 1982 provided 27% of all employment, 37·3% of all earnings; exports (1981) $4,030m. The total number of establishments was 8,779 in 1982; the biggest concentration is in the south-east.

TOURISM. The tourist-vacation industry ranks among the first three in economic importance. Approximately $6,362m. was spent in 1982 by tourists. The decline of lumbering and mining in the northern section of the state has increased dependency on the recreation industry. The Division of Tourism of the Department of Development spent $562,700 to promote tourism in financial year 1982–83.

COMMUNICATIONS

Roads. The state had on 1 Jan. 1983, 107,929 miles of highway. 74% of all roads in the state have a bituminous (or similar) surface. There are 11,917 miles of state trunk roads and 19,544 miles of county trunk roads.

In the year ending 30 June 1982 Wisconsin registered, 2,437,787 private motor cars.

Railways. On 1 Sept. 1981 the state had 5,160 road-miles of railway.

Aviation. There were, in 1983, 103 publicly operated airports. Sixteen airports were served by 9 national air carriers and 7 by regional air carriers.

Shipping. With the opening of the St Lawrence Seaway in 1959, 14 Wisconsin ports became accessible to ocean-going vessels. Green Bay, Kenosha, Manitowoc, Marinette, Milwaukee, Sheboygan and Superior (one of the world's largest iron-ore and grain ports) have developed foreign waterborne commerce. Cargo is also carried by barge on the river Mississippi. Other ports handle mainly Great Lakes traffic.

JUSTICE, RELIGION, EDUCATION AND WELFARE

Justice. The state's penal, reformatory and correctional system on 30 June 1982 held 4,044 men and 153 women in the 10 institutions for adult and juvenile offenders; the probation and parole system was supervising 18,400 men and 3,468 women. Wisconsin does not impose the death penalty.

Religion. Wisconsin church affiliation, as a percentage of the 1980 population, was estimated at 32·2% Catholic, 20·06% Lutheran, 3·74% Methodist, 10·41% other churches and 32·6% un-affiliated.

Education. All children between the ages of 7 and 16 are required to attend school full-time to the end of the school term in which they become 16 years of age. Children living in a district with a vocational school must attend until 18. In 1982–83 the school grades kindergarten–8 had 493,100 pupils and 30,418 (full-time equivalent) teachers; school grades 9–12 had 344,991 pupils and 17,164 teachers. Grade kindergarten–8 teachers' salaries, 1981–82, averaged $19,387; grade 9–12 teachers, $19,895. Total cost per pupil was $2,823 in 1980–81.

In 1981–82 vocational, technical and adult schools had an enrolment of 515,832, and there were 6,333 faculty members in 1979–80. There is a school for the visually handicapped and a school for the deaf.

The University of Wisconsin, established in 1848, was joined by law in 1971 with the Wisconsin State Universities System to become the University of Wisconsin System with 13 degree granting campuses, 13 two-year campuses in the Center System, and the University Extension. The 26 campuses had, in 1982–83, 5,385 full-time professors and instructors, 475 part-time teachers, and 2,112 (full-time equivalent) teaching assistants. In autumn 1982, 159,868 students enrolled (10,867 at Eau Claire, 4,566 at Green Bay, 8,680 at La Crosse, 42,230 at Madison, 26,122 at Milwaukee, 11,221 at Oshkosh, 5,944 at Parkside, 5,433 at Platteville, 5,334 at River Falls, 9,045 at Stevens Point, 7,563 at Stout, 2,170 at Superior, 10,314 at Whitewater and 10,379 in the Center System freshman-sophomore centres). There are also several independent institutions of higher education. These (with 1982–83 enrolment) include 2 universities (12,696), 21 liberal arts colleges (16,337), 5 technical and professional schools (3,916), and 4 theological seminaries (509).

The total expenditure, 1981–82, for all public education (except capital outlay and debt service) was $3,714m.

The state maintains an educational broadcasting and television service.

Health. In May 1982 the state had 152 general and allied special hospitals (23,709 beds), 21 mental hospitals (2,380 beds), 4 treatment centres for alcoholism (81 beds), 1 rehabilitation centre (96 beds). Patients in state and county mental hospitals and institutions for the mentally retarded in July 1980 averaged 2,812.

Social Security. On 1 Jan. 1974 the US Social Security administration assumed responsibility for financial aid (Supplemental Security Income) to persons 65 years old and over, blind persons and totally disabled persons, who satisfy requirements as to need. Recipients receive a federal payment plus a federally administered state supplementary payment, except for those who reside in a medical institution. In July 1983, there were 61,715 SSI recipients in the state. In Jan. 1984 payment levels increased to $413 for a single individual, $463 for an eligible individual with an ineligible spouse, and $633 for an eligible couple. A special payment level of $511 for an individual and $975 for a couple may be paid with special approval for SSI recipients who are developmentally disabled or chronically mentally ill, living in a non-medical living arrangement not his or her own home. All SSI recipients receive state medical assistance coverage.

Under the Aid to Families with Dependent Children programme, 80,784 families constituting 241,865 persons received an average of $421.38 per family in Aug. 1982; there were then 3,710 county foster care cases, average cost per case of $193.49, and 295 state foster care cases, average $193.62. Medicaid in financial year 1982 cost $876·4m.

Books of Reference

Wisconsin Statistical Abstract. Wis. Dept. of Administration, State Bureau of Planning and Budget, Madison, 1979
Dictionary of Wisconsin Biography. Wis. Historical Society, Madison, 1960
Wisconsin Blue Book. Wis. Legislative Reference Bureau, Madison. Biennial

Current, R. N., *The History of Wisconsin*, Vol. II. State Historical Society of Wisconsin, Madison, 1976
Nesbit, R. C., *Wisconsin, A History*. State Historical Society of Wisconsin, Madison, 1973
Smith, Alice E., *The History of Wisconsin*, Vol. 1. State Historical Society of Wisconsin, Madison, 1973

State Information Agency: Legislative Reference Bureau, State Capitol, Madison, Wis. 53702. *Chief:* Dr H. Rupert Theobald.

WYOMING

HISTORY. Wyoming, first settled in 1834, was admitted into the Union on 10 July 1890. The name originated with the Delaware Indians.

AREA AND POPULATION. Wyoming is bounded north by Montana, east by South Dakota and Nebraska, south by Colorado, south-west by Utah and west by Idaho. Area 97,809 sq. miles, of which 820 sq. miles are water. The Yellowstone National Park occupies about 2,221,733 acres; the Grand Teton National Park has 310,350 acres. The federal government in 1979 owned 28,888,546 acres (46·1% of the total area of the state). The Federal Bureau of Land Management administers 17,546,188 acres.

Census population, 1 April 1980, 469,557, an increase of 41·25% since 1970. Estimate (1981) 492,000. Births in 1980 were 10,546 (22 per 1,000 population); deaths, 3,215 (7); infant deaths, 104 (10 per 1,000 live births); marriages, 6,868; divorces, 4,003.

Population in 5 census years was:

	White	Negro	Indian	Asiatic	Total	Per sq. mile
1910	140,318	2,235	1,486	1,926	145,965	1·5
1930	221,241	1,250	1,845	1,229	225,565	2·3
1960	322,922	2,183	4,020	805	330,066	3·4
			All others			
1970	323,619	2,568	6,229		332,416	3·4
1980	446,488	3,364	19,705		469,557	4·8

Of the total population in 1980, 240,560 were male, 295,898 were urban and those over 21 years of age numbered 295,908.

The largest towns are Cheyenne (capital), with census population in 1980 of 47,283; Casper, 51,016; Laramie, 24,410; Rock Springs, 19,458.

CLIMATE. Cheyenne. Jan. 25°F (−3·9°C), July 66°F (18·9°C). Annual rainfall 15″ (376 mm). Yellowstone Park. Jan. 18°F (−7·8°C), July 61°F (16·1°C). Annual rainfall 18″ (444 mm). *See* Mountain States, p. 1372.

CONSTITUTION AND GOVERNMENT. The constitution, drafted in 1890, has since had 43 amendments. The Legislature consists of a Senate of 30 members elected for 4 years, and a House of Representatives of 64 members elected for 2 years. The Governor is elected for 4 years.

The state sends to Congress 2 senators and 1 representative, elected by the voters of the entire state. The suffrage extends to all citizens, male and female, who have the usual residential qualifications.

In the 1980 presidential election Reagan polled 110,700 votes, Carter 49,427, and Anderson 12,072.

The capital is Cheyenne. The state contains 23 counties.

Governor: Ed Herschler (D.), 1983–86 ($55,000).
Secretary of State: Mrs Thyra Thomson (R.), 1983–86 ($37,500).

BUDGET. In the fiscal year ending 1 July 1983 (State Treasurer's figures) general revenues were $1,651,264,415; general expenditures were $1,238,223,166. Revenue Sharing Funds from federal government, $10·2m.

Per capita personal income (1981) was $11,780.

ENERGY AND NATURAL RESOURCES

Minerals. Wyoming is largely an oil-producing state. In 1982 the output of petroleum was valued at $2,980·6m.; natural gas, $1,132m. Other mining: Coal, $1,113·6m.; trona, $121·6m.; uranium, $45·5m.; other minerals mined include iron ore, feldspar, gypsum, limestone, phosphate, sand, gravel and marble, taconite, bentonite and hematite.

Value of mineral products in 1981 was $4,026·2m.

Agriculture. Wyoming is semi-arid, and agriculture is carried on by irrigation and by dry farming. In 1982 there were 9,100 farms and ranches; total land area 35·3m. acres.

Cash receipts, 1981, from crops, $153m.; from livestock and products, $462·7m. Principal commodities are wheat, cattle and calves, lambs and sheep, sugar-beet, barley, hay and wool. Animals on farms on 1 Jan. 1981 included 12,000 milch cows, 1·4m. all cattle (1982), 1·1m. sheep and lambs (1982) and 33,000 swine.

INDUSTRY AND TRADE

Industry. In 1981–82 there were 570 manufacturing establishments. There were 458 mining establishments. A large portion of the manufacturing in the state is based on natural resources, mainly oil and farm products. Leading industries are food, wood products (except furniture) and machinery (except electrical). Casper is the most industrialized city, with 64 manufacturers and 145 mining companies. There were 3,200 new business incorporations in 1981. The Wyoming Industrial Development Corporation assists in the development of small industries by providing credit. Available capital, $3m.

Labour. Mining is the largest employer in the state with 36,100 workers in 1983. The total civilian labour force for June 1983 was 278,159; non-agricultural, 253,314. The average unemployment rate was 9·6% and average weekly earnings were $320.08 for manufacturing production workers.

Tourism. There are over 5m. tourists annually, mainly sportsmen. The state has the largest elk and pronghorn antelope herds in the world, 11 fish hatcheries and numerous wild game. Receipts from hunters and fishermen in 1981, $12,691,187.

COMMUNICATIONS

Roads. The roads in 1983 comprised 5,670 miles of federal highways, 353 miles of state highways and 917 miles of inter-state highway. There were (1981) 554,264 registered motor vehicles and 11 bus companies.

Railways. The railways, 1983, had a length of 2,070 mainline miles.

Aviation. There were 9 towns with regular scheduled services and 5 towns on jet routes in 1979.

JUSTICE, RELIGION, EDUCATION AND WELFARE

Justice. The state penitentiary in July 1979 held 437 male inmates. There are 2 other state correctional institutions. There have been 14 executions in Wyoming, 8 by hanging and 6 by lethal gas.

Religion. Chief religious bodies are the Roman Catholic (with 45,917 members in 1974), Mormon (28,954 in 1971) and Protestant churches (83,327 in 1974). There were 5,000 members of the Eastern Orthodox Church in 1972.

Education. In 1982–83 public elementary and secondary schools had 101,665 pupils. Enrolment in the parochial elementary and secondary schools was about 4,000. Approximately 7,791 public school teachers earned an average of $20,550. The average total expenditure per pupil for 1980–81 was $2,906.

The University of Wyoming, founded at Laramie in 1887, had in autumn 1982,

10,210 students. There are 2-year colleges at Casper, Riverton, Torrington, Cheyenne, Powell, Rock Springs and Sheridan with 39,650 students in 1981–82.

Social Welfare. In Jan. 1974 the federal government assumed many of the previous state programmes including old age assistance, aid to the blind and disabled. The state administers over $10m. annually in emergency aid and aid to families with dependent children. In 1982 financial year, $7,429,443 was distributed in food stamps. Total state expenditure on public assistance and social services programmes, financial year 1981, $31m.

Health. In 1983 the state had 28 hospitals. There are 33 registered nursing homes.

Books of Reference

News of Big Wyoming. Cheyenne, 1975
Official Directory. Secretary of State. Cheyenne. Biennial
1981 Wyoming Data Handbook. Dept. of Administration and Fiscal Control. Division of Research and Statistics, Cheyenne, 1981
Brown, R. H., *Wyoming: A Geography.* Boulder, 1980
Davis, T. S., *A Study of Wyoming People.* Laramie, 1965
Larsen, T. A., *History of Wyoming.* Rev. ed. Univ. of Nebraska, 1979
Trachsel, H. H., and Wase, R., *The Government and Administration of Wyoming.* New York, 1953

OUTLYING TERRITORIES

Non-Self-Governing Territories: Summaries of Information Transmitted to the Secretary-General of the United Nations. Annual
Coulter, J. W., *The Pacific Dependencies of the United States.* New York, 1957
Perkins, W. T., *The United States and its Dependencies.* Leiden, 1962
Wiens, H. J., *Pacific Island Bastions of the US.* New York and London, 1962

GUAM

HISTORY. Magellan is said to have discovered the island in 1521; it was ceded by Spain to the US by the Treaty of Paris (10 Dec. 1898). The island was captured by the Japanese on 10 Dec. 1941, and retaken by American forces from 21 July 1944. Guam is of great strategic importance; substantial numbers of naval and air force personnel occupy about one-third of the usable land.

AREA AND POPULATION. Guam is the largest and most southern island of the Marianas Archipelago, in 13° 26' N. lat., 144° 43' E. long. The length is 30 miles, the breadth from 4 to 10 miles, and there are about 210 sq. miles (543 sq. km). Agaña, the seat of government is about 8 miles from the anchorage in Apra Harbour. The census on 1 April 1980 showed a population of 105,821, an increase of 20,825 or 25% since 1970; those of Guamanian ancestry numbered about 50,794; foreign-born, 28,572; density was 315 per sq. mile. Estimated population (1981), 110,000. On 1 July 1980 transient residents connected with the military were estimated at 20,000. The Malay strain is predominant. The native language is Chamorro; English is the official language and is taught in all schools.

CLIMATE. Tropical maritime, with little difference in temperatures over the year. Rainfall is copious at all seasons, but is greatest from July to Oct. Agaña. Jan. 81°F (27·2°C), July 81°F (27·2°C). Annual rainfall 93" (2,325 mm).

CONSTITUTION AND GOVERNMENT. Guam's constitutional status is that of an 'unincorporated territory' of the US. Entry of US citizens is unrestricted; foreign nationals are subject to normal regulations. In 1949 the President transferred the administration of the island from the Navy Department (who held it from 1899) to the Interior Department. The transfer was completed by 1 Aug. 1950, on the passage of the Organic Act, which conferred full citizenship on the Guamanians, who had previously been 'nationals' of the US.

The Governor and his staff constitute the executive arm of the government. The Legislature is unicameral; its powers are similar to those of an American state legislature. At the general election of Nov. 1980, the Democratic Party won 10 seats and the Republicans 11. All adults 18 years of age or over are enfranchised. Guam returns one non-voting delegate to the House of Representatives.

Governor: Ricardo Bordallo (D.), 1982–85. ($50,000).
Lieut.-Governor: Joseph F. Ada (R.).

ECONOMY

Budget. At 30 June 1976 total assets were $43m.; federal grants $23·4m., taxes, $15m.: total liabilities were $45m.

Banking. Recent changes in banking law make it possible for foreign banks to operate in Guam; the first to obtain a licence was the First Commercial Bank of Taiwan.

ENERGY AND NATURAL RESOURCES

Water. Supplies are from springs, reservoirs and groundwater; 65% comes from water-bearing limestone in the north. The Navy and Air Force conserve water in reservoirs. The Water Resources Research Centre is at Guam University.

Agriculture. The major products of the island are sweet potatoes, cucumbers, water melons and beans. In 1979 there were 175 full-time and 150 part-time farmers. Livestock (1981) included 2,000 cattle, 14,000 hogs, and 190,000 laying hens. Commercial productions (1979) amounted to 3m. lb. of fruit and vegetables ($1·7m.), 1·2m. doz. eggs. There is an agricultural experimental station at Inarajan.

Fisheries. Fresh fish caught in 1980, 258,645 lb. About 16,000 people are active in inshore fishing, with a catch of 208,131 lb. Offshore fishing produced 26,224 lb., including 16,200 lb. of mackerel. Shrimp farming is being developed.

INDUSTRY AND TRADE

Industry. Guam Economic Development Authority controls three industrial estates: Cabras Island (32 acres); Calvo estate at Tamuning (26 acres); Harmon estate (16 acres). Industries include textile manufacture, cement and petroleum distribution, warehousing, printing, plastics and ship-repair. Other main sources of income are construction and tourism.

Labour. In 1980 45% of employment was in government, 18% in trade, 13% in construction, 12% in services and 3% in manufacturing.

Trade. Guam is the only American territory which has complete 'free trade'; excise duties are levied only upon imports of tobacco, liquid fuel and liquor. In the year ending 31 Dec. 1979 imports were valued at $445·8m. and accounted for 91% of trade.

Tourism. Tourism is developing; there were 1,900 visitors in 1964 and 272,681 in 1979, 190,810 of them from Japan.

COMMUNICATIONS

Roads. There are 419 miles of all-weather roads.
    In 1976 there were 54,156 motor vehicles registered.

Aviation. Five commercial airlines (PANAM, Air Nauru, Japan Air Lines, Northwest Orient and Continental Air Micronesia) serve Guam.

Post and Broadcasting. Overseas telephone and radio dispatch facilities are available. In 1981 there were 27,982 telephones.

There are 4 commercial stations, a commercial television station, a public broadcasting station and a cable television station with 10 channels.

Newspapers. There is 1 daily newspaper and 4 weekly publications (all of which are of military or religious interest only).

JUSTICE, RELIGION, EDUCATION AND WELFARE

Justice. The Organic Act established a District Court with jurisdiction in matters arising under both federal and territorial law; the judge is appointed by the President subject to Senate approval. There is also a Supreme Court and a Superior Court; all judges are locally appointed except the Federal District judge. Misdemeanours are under the jurisdiction of the police court. The Spanish law was superseded in 1933 by 5 civil codes based upon California law.

Religion. About 96% of the Guamanians are Roman Catholics; others are Baptists, Episcopalians, Bahais, Lutherans, Mormons, Presbyterians, Jehovah's Witnesses and members of the Church of Christ and Seventh Day Adventists.

Education. Elementary education is compulsory. There are Chamorro Studies courses and bi-lingual teaching programmes to integrate the Chamorro language and culture into elementary and secondary school courses. There were, Sept. 1980, 28 elementary schools, 5 junior high schools, 3 senior high schools, one vocational-technical school for high school students and adults and 1 school for handicapped children. There were 15,849 elementary school pupils, 5,884 junior high and 4,323 senior high school pupils. Department of Education staff included 1,277 teachers. The Catholic schools system also operates 3 senior high schools, 3 junior high and 5 elementary schools. The Seventh Day Adventist Guam Mission Academy operates a school from grades 1 through 12, serving over 100 students. St John's Episcopal Preparatory School provides education for 200 students between kindergarten and the 9th grade. The University of Guam (an accredited institution) had 10,285 students, 1975–76. There is a vocational technical school for high school pupils and adults.

Health. There is a hospital, 8 nutrition centres, a school health programme and an extensive immunization programme. Emphasis is on disease prevention, health education and nutrition.

Books of Reference

Report (Annual) of the Governor of Guam to the US Department of Interior
Beardsley, C., *Guam Past and Present*. Rutland, Vt, 1964
Carano, P., and Sanchez, P. C., *Complete History of Guam*. Rutland, Vt, 1964

COMMONWEALTH OF PUERTO RICO

HISTORY. Puerto Rico, by the treaty of 10 Dec. 1898 (ratified 11 April 1899), was ceded by Spain to the US. The name was changed from Porto Rico to Puerto Rico by an Act of Congress approved 17 May 1932. Its territorial constitution was determined by the 'Organic Act' of Congress (2 March 1917) known as the 'Jones Act', which ruled until 25 July 1952, when the present constitution of the Commonwealth of Puerto Rico was proclaimed.

AREA AND POPULATION. Puerto Rico is the most easterly of the Greater Antilles and lies between the Dominican Republic and the US Virgin Islands. The island has a land area of 3,459 sq. miles and a population, according to the census of 1980, of 3,196,520, an increase of 484,487 or 17·9% over 1970. Of the population in 1970 about 529,000 were bilingual, Spanish being the mother tongue and (with English) one of the two official languages. Urban population (1980) 2,134,365 (66·8%).

Vital statistics (1980–81): Births, 74,220 (22·9 per 1,000 population); deaths, 21,197 (6·4); deaths under 1 year, 1,325 (18·6 per 1,000 live births).

Chief towns (1980) are: San Juan, 434,849; Bayamón, 196,207; Ponce, 189,046; Carolina, 165,954; Caguas, 117,959; Mayaguez, 96,193; Arecibo, 86,766.

The Puerto Rican island of Vieques, 10 miles to the east, has an area of 51·7 sq. miles and 7,662 inhabitants. The island of Culebra, with 1,265 inhabitants, between Puerto Rico and St Thomas, has a good harbour.

CONSTITUTION AND GOVERNMENT. Puerto Rico has representative government, the franchise being restricted to citizens 18 years of age or over, residence (1 year) and such additional qualifications as may be prescribed by the Legislature of Puerto Rico, but no property qualification may be imposed. Women were enfranchised in 1932 (with a literacy test) and fully in 1936. Puerto Ricans do not vote in the US presidential elections, though individuals living on the mainland are free to do so subject to the local electoral laws. The executive power resides in a Governor, elected directly by the people every 4 years. Fourteen heads of departments form the Governor's advisory council, also designated as his Council of Secretaries. The legislative functions are vested in a Senate, composed of 27 members (2 from each of the 8 senatorial districts and 11 senators at large), and the House of Representatives, composed of 51 members (1 from each of the 40 representative districts and 11 elected at large). Puerto Rico sends to Congress a Resident Commissioner to the US, elected by the people for a term of 4 years, but he has no vote in Congress. Puerto Rican men are subject to conscription in US services.

On 27 Nov. 1953 President Eisenhower sent a message to the General Assembly of the UN stating 'if at any time the Legislative Assembly of Puerto Rico adopts a resolution in favour of more complete or even absolute independence' he 'will immediately thereafter recommend to Congress that such independence be granted'.

For an account of the constitutional developments prior to 1952, see THE STATESMAN'S YEAR-BOOK, 1952, p. 742. The new constitution was drafted by a Puerto Rican Constituent Assembly and approved by the electorate at a referendum on 3 March 1952. It was then submitted to Congress, which struck out Section 20 of Article 11 covering the 'right to work' and the 'right to an adequate standard of living'; the remainder was passed and proclaimed by the Governor on 25 July 1952.

At the election on 4 Nov. 1980 the New Progressive Party (advocates of statehood), headed by Carlos Romero Barceló, polled 759,868 votes (47·2% of the total); the Popular Democratic Party, headed by Rafael Hernández Colon, polled 756,434 votes (47% of the total); the Independence Party (full independence by constitutional means), 87,275 (5·4% of the total); Partido Socialista Puertorriqueño (full independence), 5,225 votes (0·3% of the total).

Governor: Carlos Romero Barceló (New Progressive Party), 1980–84 ($35,000).

ECONOMY

Budget. Receipts and disbursements (US$) in central government fund for the year ending 30 June 1982 were:

Balance, 1 July 1981	16,632,000	Disbursements	3,818,678,000
Receipts	3,878,806,000	Balance, 1 July 1979	76,760,000
Total	3,895,438,000		

Assessed value of property, 30 June 1982, was $8,376·3m., and bonded indebtedness, $1,370m.

The US administers and finances the postal service and maintains air and naval bases. US payments in Puerto Rico, including direct expenditures (mainly military), grants-in-aid and other payments to individuals and to business totalled: 1977–78, $2,563·4m.; 1978–79, $2,814·4m.; 1979–80, $3,176m.; 1980–81, $3,426·5m.; 1981–82, $3,553·6m.; 1982–83, $3,626·3m.

Banking. Banks on 30 June 1983 had total deposits of $12,441·8m. and debits of $24,097·6m. Bank loans were $7,777·9m. This includes 17 commercial banks, 1 savings bank, 2 government banks and 5 trust companies.

NATURAL RESOURCES

Minerals. Production: Cement (1982–83), 0·9m. short tons; stone (1981), 20·5m. short tons, value S96·2m. Total value of mineral production in 1981 was $208m.

Agriculture. In 1974 there were 47 'proportional profit' farms of 22,051 cords (about 22,704 acres) (mostly sugar-cane). The land had been bought from the big corporations by the Land Authority.

Production of raw sugar, 96 degrees basis, 1983 crop year, was 100,000 tons.

Livestock (1982): Cattle, 525,651; pigs, 225,654; goats, 11,500; and poultry, 7·2m.

COMMERCE. In 1982–83 imports amounted to $8,506·7m., of which $5,208·9m. came from US; exports were valued at $8,521·3m., of which $7,117·4m. went to US.

In financial year 1983 the US took: Sugar, 77,658 short tons; tobacco and products, 3,723,427 lb.; rum, 22,931,095 proof gallons.

Puerto Rico is not permitted to levy taxes on imports.

Total trade between Puerto Rico and UK (British Department of Trade returns, in £1,000 sterling):

	1979	1980	1981	1982	1983
Imports to UK	40,807	33,002	29,085	33,445	58,804
Exports and re-exports from UK	18,332	16,970	19,819	25,735	35,936

COMMUNICATIONS

Roads. The Department of Public Works had under maintenance in June 1982, 6,966 miles of paved road. Motor vehicles registered 30 June 1982, 1,172,000.

Shipping. In financial year 1982–83, 7,708 American and foreign vessels of 43,705,246 gross tons entered and cleared Puerto Rico.

Post and Broadcasting. In 1983 there were 107 broadcasting stations and 18 television companies. There were (1983) 700,882 telephones.

Cinemas (1980). Cinemas numbered 151, with annual attendance of 8·4m.

Newspapers (1983). There are 5 main newspapers; 3 have a circulation of about 125,000.

JUSTICE AND EDUCATION

Justice. The Commonwealth judiciary system is headed by a Supreme Court of 7 members, appointed by the Governor, and consists of a Superior Tribunal with 11 sections and 92 superior judges, a District Tribunal with 38 sections and 99 district judges, and 60 municipal judges all appointed by the Governor. The police force (1982) consisted of 10,051 men and women.

Education. Education was made compulsory in 1899, but in 1981, 3·6% of the children still had no access to schooling. The percentage of illiteracy in 1976 was 8·7% of those 10 years of age or older. Total enrolment in public schools, 1982–83, was 708,673. Accredited private schools had 80,199 pupils (1981–82). All instruction below senior high school standard is given in Spanish only.

The University of Puerto Rico, in Río Piedras, 7 miles from San Juan, had 51,273 students in 1982–83 and 3,240 in 4 Regional Colleges. Higher education is also available in the Inter-American University of Puerto Rico (37,741 students in 1982–83), the Catholic University of Puerto Rico (13,048), the Sacred Heart College (7,275) and the Fundacion Educativa Ana G. Méndez (13,048). These and other private colleges and universities had 92,346 students.

Books of Reference

Statistical Information: The area of Economic Research and Evaluation of the Puerto Rico Planning Board publishes: *(a)* annual *Economic Report to the Governor; (b) Statistical Year-book* (since 1940–41); *(c) External Trade Statistics* (annual report); *(d) Economic Bulletin* (monthly); *(e) Reports on national income and balance of payments; (f) Socio-Economic Statistics* (since 1940); *(g) Puerto Rico Monthly Economic Indicators.* In addition there are annual reports by various Departments.

Annual Reports. Governor of Puerto Rico. Washington
Bird, A., *Bibliografía Puertorriqueña, 1930–45.* Social Science Research Centre, Univ. of Puerto Rico. 2 vols. 1946–47
Crampsey, R. A., *Puerto Rico.* Newton Abbot, 1973
Jones, C. F., and Pico, R. (eds.), *Symposium on the Geography of Puerto Rico.* Univ. of P.R. Press, 1955

Commonwealth Library: Univ. of Puerto Rico Library, Rio Piedras. *Librarian:* José Lázaro.

AMERICAN SAMOA

HISTORY. The Samoan Islands were first visited by Europeans in the 18th century; the first recorded visit was in 1722. On 14 July 1889 a treaty between the USA, Germany and Great Britain proclaimed the Samoan islands neutral territory, under a 4-power government consisting of the 3 treaty powers and the local native government. By the Tripartite Treaty of 7 Nov. 1899, ratified 19 Feb. 1900, Great Britain and Germany renounced in favour of the US all rights over the islands of the Samoan group east of 171° long. west of Greenwich, the islands to the west of that meridian being assigned to Germany (now the Independent State of Western Samoa, *see* p. 1595). The islands of Tutuila and Aunu'u were ceded to the US by their High Chiefs on 17 April 1900, and the islands of the Manu'a group on 16 July 1904. Congress accepted the islands under a Joint Resolution approved 20 Feb. 1929. Swain's Island, 210 miles north of the Samoan Islands, was annexed in 1925 and is administered as an integral part of American Samoa.

AREA AND POPULATION. The islands (Tutuila, Aunu'u, Ta'u, Olosega, Ofu and Rose) are approximately 650 miles east-north-east of Fiji. The total area of American Samoa is 76·1 sq. miles (197 sq. km); population, 1980, 32,297, nearly all Polynesians or part-Polynesians. The island's 3 Districts are Eastern (population, 1980, 17,311), Western (13,227) and Manu'a (1,732). There is also Swain's Island, with an area of 1·9 sq. miles and 29 inhabitants (1980), which lies 210 miles to the north west. Rose Island (uninhabited) is 0·4 sq. mile in area. In 1981 there were 1,158 births and 153 deaths.

CLIMATE. A tropical maritime climate with a small annual range of temperature and plentiful rainfall. Pago-Pago. Jan. 83°F (28·3°C), July 80°F (26·7°C). Annual rainfall 194″ (4,850 mm).

CONSTITUTION AND GOVERNMENT. American Samoa is constitutionally an unorganized unincorporated territory of the US administered under the Department of the Interior. Its indigenous inhabitants are US nationals and are classified locally as citizens of American Samoa with certain privileges under local laws not granted to non-indigenous persons. Polynesian customs (not inconsistent with US laws) are respected.

Fagatogo is the seat of the Government.

The islands are organized in 15 counties grouped in 3 districts; these counties and districts correspond to the traditional political units. On 25 Feb. 1948 a bicameral legislature was established, at the request of the Samoans, to have advisory legislative functions. With the adoption of the Constitution of 22 April 1960, and the revised Constitution of 1967, the legislature was vested with limited lawmaking authority. The lower house, or House of Representatives, is composed of 20 members elected by universal adult suffrage and 1 non-voting member for Swain's Island. The upper house, or Senate, is comprised of 18 members elected, in the traditional Samoan manner, in meetings of the chiefs.

Governor: Peter Tali Coleman.
Lieut.-Governor: High Chief Tufele Lia.

ECONOMY

Planning. The first formal Economic Development and Planning Office completed its first year in 1971. Much has been done to promote economic expansion within the Territory and a large amount of outside investment interest has been stimulated.

The Office initiated the first Territorial Comprehensive Plan. This plan when completed will, with periodic updating, provide a guideline to territorial development for the next 20 years. The planning programme was made possible under a Housing and Urban Development '701' grant programme, and Economic Development Administration '302' planning programmes.

The focus will be on physical development and the problems of a rapidly increasing population with severely limited labour resources.

Budget. The chief sources of revenue are annual federal grants from the US, and local revenues from taxes, and duties, and receipts from commercial operations (enterprise and special revenue funds), utilities, rents and leases and liquor sales. During the financial year 1983–84 the Government had a revenue of $76·6m. including local appropriations of $9·5m., federal appropriations of $39·6m. and enterprise funds of $17·5m.

Banking. The American Samoa branch of the Bank of Hawaii and the American Samoa Bank offer all commercial banking services. The Development Bank of American Samoa, government owned, is concerned primarily through loans and guarantees with the economic advancement of the Territory.

ENERGY AND NATURAL RESOURCES

Electricity. Net power generated (financial year 1981) was 72·2m. kwh., of which 23·1m. kwh. was supplied to large power users and 20·2m. kwh. to householders. All the Manu'a islands have electricity.

Agriculture. Of the 48,640 acres of land area, 11,000 acres are suitable for tropical crops; most commercial farms are in the Tafuna plains and west Tutuila. Principal crops are taro, bread-fruit, yams, bananas and coconuts. Local sales (1982): taro, 770,315 lb.; bananas, 1m. lb.; vegetables, 584,143 lb.

Livestock (1981): Pigs, 8,000; goats, 8,000; poultry, 45,000.

INDUSTRY AND TRADE

Industry. Fish canning is important, employing the second largest number of people (after government). Attempts are being made to provide a variety of light industries. Tuna fishing and local inshore fishing are both expanding.

Commerce. In 1982 American Samoa exported goods valued at $186,782,060 and imported goods valued at $119,416,918. Chief exports are canned tuna, watches, pet foods and handicrafts. Chief imports are building materials, fuel oil, food, jewellery, machines and parts, alcoholic beverages and cigarettes.

COMMUNICATIONS

Roads. There are (1983) about 76 miles of paved roads and 16 miles of unpaved within the Federal Aid highway system. There are 21 miles of other unpaved roads. Motor vehicles registered, 1983, 3,657.

Aviation. South Pacific Island Airways and Polynesian Airlines operate daily services between American Samoa and Western Samoa. South Pacific Island Airways also operates between Pago Pago and Honolulu, and between Pago Pago and Tonga. The islands are also served by Air Nauru which operates between Pago Pago, Tahiti and Auckland, and Air Pacific (Fiji and westward). South Pacific and Manu'a Air Transport run local services.

Shipping. The harbour at Pago Pago, which nearly bisects the island of Tutuila, is the only good harbour for large vessels in Samoa. By sea, there is a twice-monthly service between Fiji, New Zealand and Australia and regular service between US, South Pacific ports, Honolulu and Japan.

Post and Broadcasting. A commercial radiogram service is available to all parts of the world through 2 principal trunks, United States and Western Samoa. Commercial phone and telex services are operated to all parts of the world on a 24-hour service. Number of telephones (Sept. 1983), 6,029; telex subscribers, 78.

JUSTICE, EDUCATION AND WELFARE

Justice. Judicial power is vested firstly in a High Court. The trial division has original jurisdiction of all criminal and civil cases. The probate division has jurisdiction of estates, guardianships, trusts and other matters. The land and title division decides cases relating to disputes involving communal land and Matai title court rules on questions and controversy over family titles. The appellate division hears appeals from trial, land and title and probate divisions as well as having original jurisdiction in selected matters. The appellate court is the court of last resort. Two American judges sit with 5 Samoan judges permanently. In addition there are temporary judges or assessors who sit occasionally on cases involving Samoan customs. There is also a District Court with limited jurisdiction and there are 69 village courts.

Education. Education is compulsory between the ages of 6 and 18. The Government (1983) maintains 24 consolidated elementary schools, 5 senior high schools with technical departments, 1 community college, special education classes for the handicapped and 92 Early Childhood Education Centres for pre-school children. Total elementary and secondary enrolment (1983), 8,300; in ECE schools, 1,611; classes for the handicapped, 68; total elementary and secondary classroom teachers, 480. Ten private schools had 2,108 students. Learning is by a variety of media including television.

Health. The Department of Health provides the only curative and preventive medical and dental care in American Samoa. It operates a general hospital (173 beds including 49 bassinets), 3 dispensaries on Tutuila, 4 dispensaries in the Manu'a group, 1 on Aunu'u and 1 on Swain's Island. A $3·5m. tropical medical centre was completed and placed in service in 1968. This now embraces the general hospital as well as preventive health services and out-patient clinics for surgery, obstetrics, gynaecology, emergencies, family practice, internal medicine, paediatrics; there are clinics for treatment of the eye, ear, nose and throat, dental and public health departments.

In 1983 there were 27 doctors, 7 dentists, 2 optometrists, 3 nurse anaesthetists, and 3 physician assistants. Total number of health service employees, 397.

VIRGIN ISLANDS OF THE UNITED STATES

HISTORY. The Virgin Islands of the United States, formerly known as the Danish West Indies, were named and claimed for Spain by Columbus in 1493. They were later settled by Dutch and English planters, invaded by France in the mid-17th century and abandoned by the French c. 1700, by which time Danish influence had been established. St Croix was held by the Knights of Malta between two periods of French rule.

They were purchased by the United States from Denmark for $25m. in a treaty ratified by both nations and proclaimed 31 March 1917. Their value was wholly strategic, inasmuch as they commanded the Anegada Passage from the Atlantic Ocean to the Caribbean Sea and the approach to the Panama Canal. Although the inhabitants were made US citizens in 1927, the islands are, constitutionally, an 'unincorporated territory'.

AREA AND POPULATION. The Virgin Islands group, lying about 40 miles due east of Puerto Rico, comprises the islands of St Thomas (28 sq. miles), St Croix (84 sq. miles), St John (20 sq. miles) and about 50 small islets or cays, mostly uninhabited. The total area of the 3 principal islands is 132 sq. miles, of which the US Government owns 9,599 acres as National Park.

The population, according to the census of 1 April 1980, was 95,591, an increase of 33,123 or 53% since 1970. Population had slowly declined since 1835, when it stood at 43,000, but began to recover in the 1940s. Population of St Croix, 49,013; St Thomas, 44,218; St John, 2,360. About 20–25% are native-born, 35–40% from other Caribbean islands, 10% from mainland USA and 5% from Europe. St Croix has over 40% of Puerto Rican origin or extraction, Spanish speaking. In financial year 1980, live births were 2,552 and deaths, 548.

The capital and only city, Charlotte Amalie, on St Thomas, had a population (1980) of 11,756; there are two towns on St Croix. Christiansted with 2,856 and Frederiksted with 1,054.

CONSTITUTION AND GOVERNMENT. The Organic Act of 22 July 1954 gives the US Department of the Interior full jurisdiction; some limited legislative powers are given to a single-chambered legislature, composed of 15 senators elected for 2 years representing the two legislative districts of St Croix and St Thomas-St John.

The Governor is elected by the islanders. A new Constitution was under consideration in March 1979, but was rejected by the electorate; a further constitutional convention was held in 1980. A new document was submitted to the President of the United States and to Congress; it was approved and submitted to the Virgin Islands electorate and was defeated in a referendum in Nov. 1981.

For administration, there are 13 executive departments, 12 of which are under commissioners and the other, the Department of Law, under an Attorney-General. The US Department of the Interior appoints a Federal Comptroller of government revenue and expenditure.

The franchise is vested in residents who are citizens of the United States, 18 years of age or over. In 1982 there were 30,065 voters, of whom 23,188 participated in the local elections that year.

They do not participate in the US presidential election but they have a nonvoting representative in Congress.

The capital is Charlotte Amalie, on St Thomas Island.

Governor: Juan Luis ($51,000).
Lieut.-Governor: Julio A. Brady ($47,000).

ECONOMY

Budget. Under the 1954 Organic Act finances are provided partly from local revenues—customs, federal income tax, real and personal property tax, trade tax, excise tax, pilotage fees, etc.—and partly from Federal Matching Funds, being the excise taxes collected by the federal government on such Virgin Islands products transported to the mainland as are liable.

Budget for financial year 1983, $252·4m.

Currency and Banking. United States currency became legal tender on 1 July 1934. Banks are the Chase Manhattan Bank; the Bank of Nova Scotia; the First Federal Savings and Loan Association of Puerto Rico; Barclays Bank International; Bank of America; Citibank; First Pennsylvania Bank, Banco Popular de Puerto Rico, and the Royal Bank of Canada.

ENERGY AND NATURAL RESOURCES

Electricity. The Virgin Islands Water and Power Authority provides electric power from generating plants on St Croix and St Thomas; St John is served by power cable and emergency generator.

Water. Large de-salinization plants have been established, but rain-water remains the most reliable source. Every building must have a cistern to provide rain-water for drinking, even in areas served by mains (10 gallons capacity per sq. ft of roof for a single-storey house).

Agriculture. With the phasing out of the sugar-cane industry in St Croix, and the accelerated construction activities carried on in all three islands, the number of farms decreased, but there has recently been a revival of interest in food crops. The government has bought 2,000 acres on St Croix, partly for farming.

Land for fruit, vegetables and animal feed is available on St Croix, and there are tax incentives for development. Sugar has been terminated as a commercial crop and over 4,000 acres of prime land could be utilized for food crops.

Livestock (1983): Cattle, 7,188; goats, 6,724; pigs, 2,469; sheep, 3,018.

Fisheries. There is a fishermen's co-operative with a market at Christiansted. There is a shellfish-farming project at Rust-op-Twist, St Croix.

INDUSTRY AND TRADE

Industry. The main occupations on St Thomas are tourism and government service; on St Croix manufacturing is more important. Manufactures include textiles, pharmaceuticals, rum and fragrances. The Martin Marietta Alumina plant processes bauxite from Africa for refining in mainland USA. The Amerada Hess oil refinery has a capacity of 700,000 bbls per day.

The Virgin Islands offer liberal tax exemptions to persons, firms or companies prepared to invest $50,000 in new industries or in the promotion of tourism.

Commerce. Exports, calendar year 1982, totalled $4,961·1m. and imports $5,261·3m.

Total trade between the US Virgin Islands and UK (financial years, British Department of Trade returns, in £1,000 sterling):

	1979	1980	1981	1982	1983
Imports to UK	851	39	13	137	9,706
Exports and re-exports from UK	3,273	18,518	2,882	27,450	4,981

Tourism. Tourism is the most important business. There were about 1·2m. visitors in 1982 spending $314·8m.

About 586,200 tourists came on cruise ships which made more than 750 calls, mainly at St Thomas which has a good, natural deepwater harbour.

COMMUNICATIONS

Roads. The Virgin Islands have (1983) 660 miles of roads, and 42,898 motor vehicles were registered in 1982.

Aviation. There is a daily cargo and passenger service between St Thomas and St Croix. Hamilton Airport on St Croix can take all aircraft except Concorde. Harry S. Truman Airport on St Thomas takes 727-class aircraft; it is being enlarged (1983) to take larger aircraft. There are air connexions to mainland USA, other Caribbean islands, Latin America and Europe.

Shipping. The whole territory has free port status; there is a container port in St. Croix. There is an hourly boat service between St Thomas and St John.

Post and Broadcasting. All three Virgin Islands have a dial telephone system. In Nov. 1982 there were 48,000 telephones. Direct dialling to Puerto Rico and the mainland is now possible. Worldwide radio telegraph service is also available.

The islands are served by 7 radio stations, 4 television stations and 3 newspapers, 2 of them dailies.

RELIGION AND EDUCATION

Religion. There are churches of the Protestant, Roman Catholic and Jewish faiths in St Thomas and St Croix and Protestant and Roman Catholic churches in St John.

Education. Education is compulsory between the ages of 5½ and 16 years, inclusive. In 1982–83 there were 34 public schools (ranging from kindergarten to high schools); enrolment was 25,568; 27 private schools had 7,030 pupils; the public school budget was $61·9m. In 1982 the College of the Virgin Islands had 2,864 registered students; 810 full-time undergraduates, 1,870 part-time undergraduates and 184 graduate students. The College is part of the United States landgrant network of higher education.

Books of Reference

Evans, L. H., *The Virgin Islands: From Naval Base to New Deal.* Ann Arbor, Mich., 1945
Jarvis, J. A., *The Virgin Islands and Their People.* Philadelphia, 1944
McGuire, J. W., *Geographic Dictionary of the Virgin Islands of the United States.* US Coast and Geodetic Survey. Special Publication No. 103. Washington, 1925
Reid, C. F., *Bibliography of the Virgin Islands of the United States.* New York, 1941

TRUST TERRITORY OF THE PACIFIC ISLANDS

HISTORY. Under the Treaty of Versailles (1919) Japan was appointed mandatory to the former German possessions north of the Equator. In 1946 the US agreed to administer the former Japanese-mandated islands of the Caroline, Marshall and Mariana groups (except Guam) as a Trusteeship for the United Nations; the trusteeship agreement was approved by the Security Council 27 April 1947 and came into effect on 18 July 1947. The Trust Territory was administered by the US Navy until 1951, when all the islands except Tinian and Saipan in the Marianas were transferred to the Secretary of the Interior. In 1962 the Interior Department assumed responsibility for them also. On 17 June 1975 the voters of the Northern Mariana Islands, in a plebiscite observed by the UN, adopted the covenant to establish a Commonwealth of the Northern Mariana Islands in Union with the USA. In April 1976 the US government approved the convenant and separated the administration of the Northern Marianas from that of the rest of the Trust Territory; the group has a constitution and a constitutional government, installed 9 Jan. 1978; population, 1 April 1980, 16,800. The rest of the Trust Territory is divided into 3 entities, each with its own constitution. The Marshall Islands, the Federated States of Micronesia (Yap, Kosrae, Truk and Ponape) and the Republic of Belau are all negotiating a status of free association with the US government. Free association will grant the USA the authority to control military and defence activities in return for federal government assistance and budget supports to the autonomous constitutional governments. Termination of the UN Trusteeship Agreement is contingent upon establishing a political status, either free association or independence, for the islands. Negotiations were proceeding in 1981.

AREA AND POPULATION. The Trust Territory extends from 1° to 22° N. lat. and from 142° to 172° E. long. The area is generally known as Micronesia, or 'land of the small islands' (Guam, Kiribati and Nauru not part of the Trust Territory, are also ethnically and geographically Micronesian); total land area 708 sq. miles; population (1980 census), 116,974, excluding Northern Marianas.

The census population of the 6 administrative districts as of Sept. 1980 was: Truk, 37,742; Ponape, 22,319; Marshall Islands, 31,042; Belau, 12,177; Yap, 8,172; Kosrae, 5,522. Nine different languages are spoken, each with variations; English is used in the schools and is the official language.

CLIMATE. Marked by high temperatures throughout the year and high rainfall. Marshall Islands, Jaluit. Jan. 81°F (27·2°C), July 82°F (27·8°C). Annual rainfall 161" (4,034 mm). Caroline Islands, Ponape. Jan. 80°F (26·7°C), July 79°F (26·1°C). Annual rainfall 194" (4,859 mm).

CONSTITUTION AND GOVERNMENT. Constitutional governments are functioning in the Mariana Islands (1978), the Marshall Islands (1979), the Federated States of Micronesia (1979) and the Republic of Belau (1981). Each of the 4 entities is autonomous from the other 3 but all are still legally under the single Trust Territory system. The citizens are Trust Territory citizens until the termination of the Trusteeship. Majuro is the capital of the Marshall Islands. Kolonia, Ponape, is the capital of the Federated States, Koror is the headquarters of Palau and Saipan is the capital of the Commonwealth of the Northern Marianas, as well as the US administrative headquarters.

High Commissioner: Adrian P. Winkel.

INDUSTRY. Tourism is the main source of income from overseas; industrial development is limited. There is some commercial fishing and agriculture, a coconut-processing plant and a tuna-packing plant.

COMMUNICATIONS

Aviation. The island groups are served by Continental Air Micronesia *via* Honolulu. Internal commuter airlines operate in Ponape, Yap, Marshalls, Belau and the Marianas. There are connexions to international routes at Guam and Hawaii.

JUSTICE, RELIGION, EDUCATION AND WELFARE

Justice. The Trust Territory Code, local constitutions and the Trusteeship Agreement are the foundations for law. Local police are responsible for enforcement. There is a Trust Territory High Court, constitutional courts and lesser courts. Local customs are recognized and protected in legal practice, when not in conflict with higher law.

Religion. Freedom of religion is guaranteed in the Trust Territory Code and all constitutions.

Education. Education is free and compulsory through elementary school (grades 1–8). There are public and private elementary and secondary schools and government post-secondary education.

Health. The public health system, which includes 6 district hospitals as well as other hospitals and clinics in outlying areas, is carried on by a staff consisting chiefly of trained Micronesian medical and dental officers and assistants under senior US doctors.

Books of Reference

Report to the United Nations Trusteeship Council, 1979. Dept. of State, Washington, D.C., 1980
Basic Information. High Commissioner's Office, Saipan

UNINCORPORATED TERRITORIES

Johnston Atoll. Two small islands 1,150 km south-west of Hawaii, administered by the US Air Force. Area, under 1 sq. mile; population, 1978, estimate, 300.

Midway Islands. Two small islands at the western end of the Hawaiian chain, administered by the US Navy. Area, 2 sq. miles; population, 1975, estimate, 2,256.

Wake Island. Three small islands 3,700 km west of Hawaii, administered by the US Air Force. Area, 3 sq. miles; population, 1980 census, 300.

UPPER VOLTA

République de Haute-Volta

Capital: Ouagadougou
Population: 7·29m. (1982)
GNP per capita: US$190 (1980)

HISTORY. A separate colony of Upper Volta was in 1919 carved out of the colony of Upper Senegal and Niger, which had been established in 1904. In 1932 it was abolished and most of its territory transferred to Ivory Coast, with small parts added to French Sudan and Niger, but it was re-constituted with its former borders on 4 Sept. 1947. Upper Volta became an autonomous republic within the French Community on 11 Dec. 1958 and reached full independence on 5 Aug. 1960.

On 3 Jan. 1966 the government of Maurice Yameogo was overthrown by a military *coup* led by Lieut-Col. Sangoulé Lamizana, who assumed the Presidency. Constitutional rule was resumed on 21 June 1970 but suspended from 8 Feb. 1974 until May 1978. In a further *coup* on 25 Nov. 1980, President Lamizana was overthrown and a military regime assumed power.

AREA AND POPULATION. Upper Volta is bounded north and west by Mali, east by Niger, south by Benin, Togo, Ghana and the Ivory Coast. The republic covers an area of 274,122 sq. km; population (census, 1975) 5,638,203. Estimate (1982) 7,285,000. Ouagadougou, the capital (286,453 inhabitants), Bobo-Dioulasso (165,171). The largest cities (estimates 1979) were: Koudougou (44,089, 1982), Ouahigouya (38,374, 1982), Kaya (18,402), Banfora (12,358). The principal ethnic groups are the Mossi (48%), Fulani (10%), Lobi-Dagari (7%), Mandé (7%), Bobo (7%), Sénoufo (6%), Gourounsi (5%), Bissa (5%), Gourmantché (5%).

CLIMATE. A tropical climate with a wet season from May to Nov. and a dry season from Dec. to April. Rainfall decreases from south to north. Ouagadougou. Jan. 76°F (24·4°C), July 83°F (28·3°C). Annual rainfall 36" (894 mm).

CONSTITUTION AND GOVERNMENT. Following the *coup* of 25 Nov. 1980, the 1977 Constitution was suspended and the 57-member National Assembly dissolved. Supreme political power is now vested in a new 12-member People's Salvation Council (CSP), ruling through an appointed Cabinet composed in Jan. 1983 of:

President of CNR, Head of State, Minister of the Interior and Security: Capt. Thomas Sankara.

National Defence and War Veterans: Jean Baptiste Lingani. *Minister of State attached to the Presidency:* Blaise Compaore. *Social Affairs:* Bernadette Pale. *Foreign Affairs:* Arba Diallo. *Planning and Co-operation:* Talata Eugène Dondasse. *Finance:* Damo Justin Barro. *Rural Development:* Seydou Traore. *Higher Education and Scientific Research:* Issa Tiendrebeogo. *National Education, Arts and Culture:* Emmanuel Dadjouari. *Information:* Adama Toure. *State Enterprises:* Henri Zongo. *Justice:* Trin Raymond Poda. *Equipment and Communications:* Philippe Ouedraogo. *Public Health:* Abdoul Salam Kabore. *Commerce, Industrial Development and Mines:* Boubacar Hama. *Labour, Social Security and Civil Service:* Fidele Toe. *Youth and Sport:* Ibrahima Kone. *Environment and Tourism:* Laetare Basile Guissou. *Secretary of State for Interior and Security:* Nongoma Ernest Ouedraogo. *Secretary-General of the Cabinet:* Congo Emmanuel Kabore.

National flag: Three horizontal stripes of black, white, red.
Local government: The country is divided into 25 provinces.

DEFENCE

Army. The Army consists of 3 infantry regiments, 1 reconnaissance squadron and support units. Equipment includes 25 armoured cars. Strength (1984), 3,700 with a further 900 men in paramilitary forces.

Air Force. Creation of a small air arm to support the land forces began, with French assistance, in 1964. Equipment now comprises 2 HS.748 twin-turboprop freighters, 2 C-47s, 2 twin-turboprop Frégates, an Aero Commander 500, 1 Broussard and 2 Reims/Cessna Super Skymasters for transport and liaison duties, and 3 Dauphin and Aloutte III helicopters. Personnel total about 75.

INTERNATIONAL RELATIONS

Membership. Upper Volta is a member of UN, OAU and is an ACP state of the EEC.

ECONOMY

Planning. The Third Development Plan 1977–81 aimed at an 8·4% average annual real growth in GDP.

Budget. Government revenue and expenditure balanced in 1983 at 57,949m. francs CFA.

Currency. The unit of currency is the *franc* CFA with a parity rate of 50 *francs* CFA to 1 French *franc*. In March 1984, £1 = 589 *francs*; US$1 = 401 *francs*.

Banking. The *Banque Centrale des Etats de l'Afrique de l'Ouest* is the bank of issue. The main commercial bank is the *Banque Internationale des Voltas*. In Dec. 1982 the savings banks had deposits of 25,957,000 *francs* CFA.

ENERGY AND NATURAL RESOURCES

Electricity. Production of electricity (1982) was 123m. kwh.

Minerals. There are deposits of manganese near Tambao in the north, but exploitation is limited by existing transport facilities. Magnetite, bauxite, zinc, lead, nickel and phosphates have been found in the same area.

Agriculture. Production (1981–82, in tonnes): Sorghum, 657,986; millet, 442,771; maize, 125,204; groundnuts, 77,667; rice (paddy, 1980), 28,657; cotton, 59,474; sesame, 8,017. Rice and groundnuts are of increasing importance.

Livestock (1982): 2·9m. cattle, 2m. sheep, 3m. goats, 70,000 horses, 200,000 donkeys.

INDUSTRY AND TRADE

Industry. In 1981 gross manufacturing (including energy) was 40,189,000 francs CFA, of which textiles (3,461,000 francs CFA) and metal products (2·28m. francs CFA). In 1972 there were 91 industrial units.

Labour. In 1982 the labour force was 3,503,610 of whom (1979) 2,941,000 were engaged in agriculture, forestry and fishing. There were (1981) 4 trade unions.

Commerce. In 1982 imports totalled 113,708m. francs CFA and exports 18,109m. francs CFA. In 1982 the major exports were cotton (41·9%), almonds (16%) and livestock (14·1%). In 1982 France provided 26·7%, the Ivory Coast 12·4% and USA 6·6% of imports, while the Ivory Coast took 21%, France 14·5%, Federal Republic of Germany 7·4% and UK 6·6% of exports.

Total trade between Upper Volta and UK (British Department of Trade returns, in £1,000 sterling):

	1979	1980	1981	1982	1983
Imports to UK	338	2,819	2,864	1,289	1,514
Exports and re-exports from UK	1,234	1,039	5,311	2,166	3,048

Tourism. There were 50,049 tourists in 1982.

COMMUNICATIONS

Roads. The road system comprises 13,134 km, of which 4,396 km are national, 1,744 km departmental, 2,364 km regional and 1,940 km unclassified roads. In 1982 there were 33,769 vehicles, comprising 16,463 private cars, 419 buses, 14,852 commercial vehicles, 411 special vehicles and 1,123 tractors.

Railway. Ouagadougou is the terminus of the Abidjan-Niger railway, of which 517 km lie in Upper Volta. A 355-km extension to the manganese deposits at Tambao is planned with the first 107-km section to Kaya under construction.

Aviation. Ouagadougou and Bobo-Dioulasso are regularly served by UTA and Air Afrique and in 1982 dealt with 120,684 passengers and 6,778 tonnes of freight. Air Volta operates all internal flights to 47 domestic airports.

Post and Broadcasting. There were, in 1982, some 42 post offices and (1978) 3,564 telephones. There are radio stations at Ouagadougou and Bobo-Dioulasso and (1981) 90,000 receivers. The state television service, Voltavision, broadcasts 3 days a week in Ouagadougou; there were (1981) 5,500 receivers.

Newspapers. 3 daily newspapers are published in Ouagadougou.

JUSTICE, RELIGION, EDUCATION AND WELFARE

Justice. There are courts of first instance at Ouagadougou, Bobo-Dioulasso, Ouahigouya and Fada N'Gourma. The Supreme Court, High Court of Justice and Court of Appeal are all in Ouagadougou.

Religion. The majority of the population (53%) follow animist religions; 36% are Moslem and 11% Christian (mainly Roman Catholic).

Education. There were at 1 Jan. 1983, 251,169 pupils in 1,176 primary schools. In 1981–82 there were 25,283 in secondary schools, and 5,122 in technical schools and (1980) 495 students in teacher-training establishments. The Université d'Ouagadougou had 2,887 students in 1982–83.

Health (1980). There were 5 hospitals, 178 dispensaries with maternity units and 60 maternity units alone, 50 health centres, 131 dispensaries and 99 special dispensaries with a total of 4,587 beds. There were 119 doctors, 14 surgeons, 52 pharmacists, 163 health assistants, 229 midwives and 1,345 nursing personnel.

A 10-year health programme started in 1979, providing for 7,000 village health centres, 515 district health centres, regional and sub-regional medical centres, 10 departmental hospitals, 2 national hospitals and a university centre of health sciences in Ouagadougou.

DIPLOMATIC REPRESENTATIVES

Of Upper Volta in Great Britain
Ambassador: (Vacant).

Of Great Britain in Upper Volta
Ambassador: J. M. Willson (resides in Abidjan).

Of Upper Volta in the USA (2340 Massachusetts Ave., NW, Washington, D.C., 20008)
Chargé d'Affaires: Denis G. Nikiema.

Of the USA in Upper Volta (PO Box 35, Ouagadougou)
Ambassador: Julius W. Walker, Jr.

Of Upper Volta to the United Nations
Ambassador: (Vacant).

URUGUAY

República Oriental
del Uruguay

Capital: Montevideo
Population: 2·9m. (1982)
GNP per capita: US$2,820 (1980)

HISTORY. The Republic of Uruguay, formerly a part of the Spanish Viceroyalty of Río de la Plata and subsequently a province of Brazil, declared its independence 25 Aug. 1825 which was recognized by the treaty between Argentina and Brazil signed at Rio de Janeiro 27 Aug. 1828. The first constitution was adopted 18 July 1830.

AREA AND POPULATION. Uruguay is bounded on the north-east by Brazil, on the south-east by the Atlantic, on the south by the Río de la Plata and on the west by Argentina. The area is 186,926 sq. km (72,172 sq. miles). The following table shows the area and the population of the 19 departments (capitals in brackets) as estimated in May 1975:

Departments	Area sq. km	Population	Pop. per sq. km
Artigas (Artigas)	11,378	57,528	4·6
Canelones (Canelones)	4,752	313,858	54·3
Cerro-Largo (Melo)	14,929	73,204	4·8
Colonia (Colonia)	5,682	110,820	18·5
Durazno (Durazno)	14,315	54,990	3·7
Flores (Trinidad)	4,519	24,684	5·2
Florida (Florida)	12,107	66,092	5·3
Lavalleja (Minas)	12,485	65,240	5·3
Maldonado (Maldonado)	4,111	75,607	14·9
Montevideo (Montevideo City)	664	1,345,858	2,102·4
Paysandú (Paysandú)	13,252	98,735	6·6
Río Negro (Fray Bentos)	8,471	49,816	5·5
Rivera (Rivera)	9,829	79,330	7·8
Rocha (Rocha)	11,089	59,952	5·0
Salto (Salto)	12,603	100,407	7·3
San José (San José)	6,963	88,281	11·4
Soriano (Mercedes)	9,223	80,114	8·4
Tacuarembó (Tacuarembó)	21,015	84,829	3·7
Treinta y Tres (Treinta y Tres)	9,539	45,680	4·5
Total	186,926	2,843,296	15·2

Estimated population in 1981 was 2,991,341. In 1980 Montevideo (the capital) had an estimated population of 1,345,858. Other cities (1975): Salto, 80,000; Paysandú, 80,000; Mercedes, 53,000.

CLIMATE. A warm temperate climate, with mild winters and warm summers. The wettest months are March to June, but there is really no dry season. Montevideo. Jan. 72°F (22·2°C), July 50°F (10°C). Annual rainfall 38″ (950 mm).

CONSTITUTION AND GOVERNMENT. Since 1900 Uruguay has been unique in her constitutional innovations, all designed to protect her from the emergence of a dictatorship. The favourite device of the group known as the 'Batllistas' (a *Colorado* faction) which, until defeated at the 1958 elections, held the majority for over 90 years, has been the collegiate system of government, in which the two largest political parties were represented.

One such pattern lasted from 1917 to 1933, when it was abolished by a dictator who re-established the system of an individual President. Until 1951 Presidents were elected every 4 years and they selected their own Cabinet Ministers (*see* list of Presidents in THE STATESMAN'S YEAR-BOOK, 1956, p. 1493). In 1951, on the initiative of the 'Batllistas', the Constitution was amended: the individual presidency was abolished and the executive power vested in a National Council of Government of 9 members (6 from the majority and 3 from the minority parties).

As a result of a referendum held on 27 Nov. 1966, Uruguay returned to the presidential system. The President appoints a council of 11 Ministers; the Vice-President presides over the Senate and the General Assembly when this takes place. A new Constitution was rejected by referendum in Nov. 1980 and in Nov. 1983 an election took place to elect officials who will renegotiate a new draft Constitution prior to a general election in Nov. 1984.

President: Gregorio C. Alvarez (sworn in for a 3½-year term on 1 Sept. 1981).

The Cabinet in Sept. 1983 was as follows:

Interior: Gen. Hugo Linares Brum. *Foreign Affairs:* Dr Carlos A. Maeso. *Justice:* Dr Julio César Espínola. *Economy and Finance:* Cdr Walter Lusiardo Aznárez. *Transport and Public Works:* Francisco D. Tourreilles. *Public Health:* Luis A. Givogre. *Industry and Energy:* Cdr Juan A. Chiarino Rossi. *National Defence:* Dr Justo M. Alonso Leguisamo. *Agriculture and Fisheries:* Carlos Mattos Moglia. *Education:* Dr Raquel Lombardo de la Betolaza. *Labour and Social Security:* Dr Luis A. Crisci. *Secretary to Presidency:* Dr Angel Mario Scelza.

Parliament was dissolved by Presidential decree on 27 June 1973. A new Constitution was being prepared in 1981 and general elections are due to be held in Nov. 1984.

National flag: Nine horizontal stripes of white and blue, a white canton with the 'Sun of May' in gold.

National anthem: Orientales, la patria ó la tumba (words by Francisco Acuña de Figueroa; music by Francisco José Deballi).

DEFENCE

Army. The Army consists of volunteers who enlist for 1-2 years service. There are 3 cavalry, 5 infantry, 1 artillery and 1 engineer brigades, 1 air defence and 1 parachute battalion. Equipment includes 17 M-24, 29 M-3A1 and 22 M-41 light tanks. Strength was (1984) 22,500, with about 120,000 former regulars as reserve.

Navy. The Navy consists of 3 frigates (*ex*-US old destroyer escorts), 1 corvette (*ex*-US fleet minesweeper), 1 patrol vessel (*ex*-coastal minesweeper), 5 patrol craft, 6 coastal patrol craft, 1 transport, 1 training ship, 1 salvage vessel, 5 minor amphibious craft, 2 oilers and 1 tender. Personnel in 1984: totalled 6,626 officers and ratings including naval infantry (marines) and Coastguard, and the small US-equipped naval air service of 21 aircraft and 3 helicopters.

Air Force. Organized with US aid, the Air Force has about 3,500 personnel and 110 aircraft, including 1 counter-insurgency squadron with 6 IA 58 Pucara, 5 AT-33 armed jet trainers and 5 A-37B light strike aircraft, a reconnaissance and training squadron with 6 T-6Gs, 3 transport squadrons with 4 turboprop FH-227/F.27 Friendships, 6 Brazilian-built EMB-110 Bandeirantes (1 equipped for photographic duties), 5 CASA C-212 Aviocars and 6 Queen Airs, a search and rescue squadron with Cessna U-17A aircraft and light helicopters, and a number of Cessna 182 light aircraft for liaison duties. Basic training types are the T-41 and T-34.

INTERNATIONAL RELATIONS

Membership. Uruguay is a member of UN, OAS and LAIA (formerly LAFTA).

ECONOMY

Budget. The receipts and expenditure of the national accounts as approved by the National Council of Government (UR$1m.):

	1977	1978	1979	1980	1981	1982
Revenue	2,937,583	4,349,819	8,423,600	14,954,800	21,260,000	19,551,900
Expenditure	3,178,197	4,750,533	8,300,700	14,879,900	21,368,600	30,761,400

Now covering a 5-year period the budget is presented during the year following election of each new government; differences in actual annual income and expenditure and amendments to the budget (including new taxes) must be approved by Parliament each year-end; these usually come forward in July each year.

Expenditures in 1981 included: Salaries and social security payments, 68·9%; other current expenditure, 12·4%; subsidies and transfer payments, 4·5%; interests of public debts, 1·9%; and investments, 12·3%. Expenditure on public works is separately financed from specific revenues (*e.g.*, fuel tax). A law inaugurating income tax came into operation on 1 July 1961, but was repealed on 1 March 1974.

Foreign debt outstanding in Dec. 1981 was US$3,129m. Total reserves of the Banco Central in Dec. 1981 were US$840·8m.

Currency. The unit of currency is the *Nuevo Peso* (1,000 old pesos) of 100 *centésimos*. The actual circulating medium consists of paper notes issued by the Central Bank in *Nuevo Peso* denominations of 50, 100, 500 and 1,000 *Nuevo Peso*, and 1, 2, 5 and 10 coins.

In March 1984, US$1 = 47·18 *pesos*; £1 = 70 *pesos*.

Banking. The Bank of the Republic (founded 1896), whose president and directors are appointed by the Government has a paid-up capital of N$1,852m. The Banco Central was inaugurated on 16 May 1967. Note circulation in Dec. 1982 was N$9,810m.

A state-owned National Insurance Bank *(Banco de Seguros del Estado)* has a monopoly of new insurance business of all kinds. The Bank re-insures much of its business in London.

Of the 25 banks in Uruguay the Bank of London and South America (British) has a main office and 16 branch agencies.

Weights and Measures. The metric system was adopted in 1862.

ENERGY AND NATURAL RESOURCES

Electricity. The supply of electricity for light, power and traction has been a State monopoly since 1897. In Jan. 1949 the first hydro-electric plant at the site of the dam of Rincón del Bonete was completed with an installed capacity of 128 megawatts. Another plant at Rincón de Baygorria on the Río Negro came into operation in 1960, with a capacity of 108 megawatts. Palmar hydro-electric dam came into operation in early 1982 with an installed capacity of 330 mw. Salto Grande came into full operation in Dec. 1982 with an installed capacity of 1,890 mw, of which Uruguay is getting one-sixth at present. Power output in Dec. 1982 was 3,471,664 mwh.

Oil. An extension of the ANCAP refining plant, opened at Montevideo on 6 Dec. 1961, gives a capacity of 7,500 cu. metres daily of high-octane petrol and high-grade gas for domestic and industrial use.

Agriculture. Uruguay is primarily a pastoral country. Of the total land area of 46m. acres some 41m. are devoted to farming, of which 90% to livestock and 10% to crops. Some large *estancias* have been divided up into family farms; rural landlordism is much less than elsewhere. Uruguay is said to be the only Latin American country in which agricultural workers have the protection of a minimum-wage law. Animals and animal products constituted 29·3% of the exports in 1982.

There were (1982) 11·3m. cattle, 20m. sheep, 530,000 horses, 450,000 pigs, 12,000 goats and 8m. poultry.

The wool clip in 1981–82 was 81,300 tonnes.

Agricultural products are raised chiefly in the departments of Paysandú, Río Negro, Colonia, San José, Soriano and Florida. The average farm is about 250 acres. The principal crops and their estimated yield (in tonnes) in 2 crop years were as follows:

	1981	1982		1981	1982
Wheat	306,600	387,800	Barley	102,900	85,300
Linseed	21,400	11,000	Maize	180,800	97,300
Oats	65,900	20,600	Rice	330,300	418,900

Uruguay is self-sufficient in rice, with a surplus for export. Three sugar refineries handle cane and (mainly) beet, their total production being approximately 92,000 tonnes, and approaching self-sufficiency.

Wine is produced chiefly in the departments of Montevideo, Canelones and Colonia, about enough for domestic consumption. The country has some 6m. fruit trees, principally peaches, oranges, tangerines and pears.

Forestry. In 1980 roundwood removals were 1,729,000 cu. metres, of which 100,000 cu. metres was softwood.

Fisheries. In 1982, the total catch was 123,200 tonnes. Exports were valued at US$44,137,000.

INDUSTRY AND TRADE

Industry. In 1978 there were nearly 77,000 registered enterprises with 405,000 employees. These cover activities such as meat packing, oil refining, cement manufacture, foodstuffs, beverages, leather and textile maufacture, chemicals, light engineering and transport equipment. There are about 100 textile mills, but with the exception of half a dozen large plants, these are on the whole small.

The development of industry is an important economic policy objective and there is a liberal attitude to foreign investment for industrial promotion.

There are a number of public works programmes including airport modernization, port of Montevideo modernization, highways improvements, Montevideo sewage disposal, power production and transmission and telecommunications.

Trade Unions. Trade unions number about 150,000 members. About 1·05m. (35%) population are classed as gainfully occupied. Unemployment rate (average for the country) was 11·9% in Dec. 1982.

Commerce. The foreign trade (officially stated in US$, with the figure for imports based on the clearance permits granted and that for exports on export licences utilized) was as follows (in US$1,000):

	1976	1977	1978	1979	1980	1981	1982
Imports	587·2	721·0	757	1,206	1,602·5	1,598·9	1,057·9
Exports	546·5	607·5	694	787	1,209·3	1,215·4	975·8

Of the imports in 1982 (in US$1m.) USA, 127·7; Nigeria, 127·7; Brazil, 124·9; Venezuela, 91·1; Middle East, 90·8; Iran, 89·1; Argentina, 80·1; Federal Republic of Germany, 63·2; UK, 26·4. Of the exports in 1982 Brazil took 145·8; Argentina, 109; Federal Republic of Germany, 91·7; USSR, 78·6; USA, 75·5; Iran, 55·1; Egypt, 46·6; UK, 36·7.

Principal imports and exports (in US$1,000):

Imports	1981	1982	Exports	1981	1982
Chemicals	139,300	112,100	Meat and meat products	213,600	170,300
Transport materials	210,600	109,800	Hides, furs and leather		
Fuel and lubricants	447,800	416,000	manufactures	138,300	135,600
Machinery and			Wool and manufactures	331,200	262,600
accessories	291,100	141,500	Vegetable products	185,600	147,300

Total trade between Uruguay and UK (British Department of Trade returns, in £1,000 sterling):

	1979	1980	1981	1982	1983
Imports to UK	13,416	16,884	26,330	23,107	33,361
Exports and re-exports from UK	24,735	26,619	20,103	13,926	10,763

Tourism. There were 480,900 tourists in 1981 spending an estimated US$283m.

COMMUNICATIONS

Roads. The main highways, linking Montevideo with the interior, have a total length of 9,899 km, of which about 5,000 km are paved. Other roads, unpaved, are about 4,726 km. Considerable improvements, financed both internally and by international loans, have been carried out in the last few years.

Registered motor vehicles, 31 Dec. 1978, are estimated at 220,000 passenger cars and 92,150 trucks and buses.

Railways. The 4 principal railway systems, embracing 2,987 km, were all built by British capital amounting to £14,513,000. The Uruguayan Government in 1948 bought these railways for £7·15m., assuming control that year. The East Coast Railway (125·5 km) and 3 minor lines were already controlled by the State under a separate administration. In Oct. 1952 the railways were brought under a single administration and a major programme of track upgrading and rolling stock rehabilitation is being carried out. The total railway system open for traffic was (1980) 3,004 km of 1,435 mm gauge. In 1981 it carried 3·3m. passengers and 1·2m. tonnes of freight. In 1979 the 27 km line between Mercedes and Ombucito was opened, providing a direct route from Montevideo to Fray Bentos, while a link with Argentina across the Salto Grande dam was completed in 1982.

Aviation. Carrasco, 22·5 km from Montevideo, is the most important airport. US, Argentine, Brazilian, Chilean, Dutch, French, Fed. German, Scandinavian and Paraguayan airlines fly to and from Uruguay. The state-operated civil airline PLUNA runs services in the interior of the country and to Brazil, Paraguay and Argentina, and Spain.

Shipping. In 1983 there were 13 merchant vessels and 3 tankers. In 1982, 1,115 vessels cleared Montevideo, 17 being British. River transport (1,270 km) is extensive, its main importance being to link Montevideo with Paysandú and Salto.

Post and Broadcasting. The telegraph lines in operation have a total length of 12,083 km. The telephone system in Montevideo is controlled by the State; small companies operate in the interior. Telephone instruments, 1982, numbered 294,350. There are 1,277 post offices. Uruguay has 85 long-wave and 17 short-wave broadcasting stations. There are about 1m. wireless sets and 440,000 television receivers. There are 4 television stations in Montevideo and 11 in the interior. The State itself operates one of the most powerful sound broadcasting stations in South America. Colour television was inaugurated 1981.

Cinemas (1980). Cinemas numbered 85 with seating capacity of 47,000.

Newspapers (1981). There were 5 daily newspapers in Montevideo with aggregate daily circulation of about 210,000; most of the 25–30 provincial newspapers appear bi-weekly.

JUSTICE, RELIGION, EDUCATION AND WELFARE

Justice. The Ministry of Justice was created in 1977 to be responsible for relations between the Executive Power and the Judiciary and other jurisdictional entities. The Court of Justice is made up by 5 members appointed by the Council of the Nation at the suggestion of the Executive Power, for a period of 5 years. This court has original jurisdiction in constitutional, international and admiralty cases and hears appeals from the appellate courts, of which there are 4, each with 3 judges.

In Montevideo there are also 8 courts for ordinary civil cases, 3 for government *(Juzgado de Hacienda)*, as well as criminal and correctional courts. Each departmental capital has a departmental court; each of the 224 judicial divisions has a justice of peace court. In Sept. 1907 the death penalty was abolished, replaced by penal servitude for a period of 30–40 years.

Religion. State and Church are separated, and there is complete religious liberty. The faith professed by the majority of the inhabitants is Roman Catholic. The archbishop of Montevideo has 10 suffragan bishops in Salto, Melo, Florida, Minas, San José, Canelones, Tacuarembó, Mercedes, Maldonado and Montevideo (Auxiliary Bishop).

Protestants numbered about 10,500 in 1957.

Education. Primary education is obligatory; both primary and superior education are free.

In 1979 there were 1,050 primary public schools with 364,910 pupils and approximately 10,300 teachers; in 1979, 249 secondary schools had 196,462 pupils. There are also evening courses for adults. Illiteracy is now confined largely to the older age groups.

The University of the Republic at Montevideo, inaugurated in 1849, has about 16,200 students; tuition is free to both native-born and foreign students; there are 10 faculties. There are 43 normal schools for males and females, and a college of arts and trades with about 33,000 students. There are also many religious seminaries throughout the Republic with a considerable number of pupils, a school for the blind, 2 for deaf and dumb and a school of domestic science.

Health. Hospital beds, 1981, numbered (estimate) 23,000; physicians numbered 5,600.

DIPLOMATIC REPRESENTATIVES

Of Uruguay in Great Britain (48 Lennox Gdns., London, SW1X 0DL)
Ambassador: Dr Luis M. de Posadas Montero (accredited 6 May 1983).

Of Great Britain in Uruguay (Calle Marco Bruto 1073, Montevideo)
Ambassador: Charles William Wallace, CMG, CVO.

Of Uruguay in the USA (1918 F St., NW, Washington, D.C., 20006)
Ambassador: Alejandro Vegh Villegas.

Of the USA in Uruguay (Calle Lauro Muller 1776, Montevideo)
Ambassador: Thomas Aranda, Jr.

Of Uruguay to the United Nations
Ambassador: Dr Juan Carlos Blanco.

Books of Reference

The official gazette is the *Diario Oficial*
Statistical Reports of the Government. Montevideo. Annual and biennial
Anales de Instruccion Primaria. Montevideo. Quarterly

Arcas, J. A., *Historia del siglo XX uruguayo, 1897–1943.* Montevideo, 1950
De Carlos, M., *La escuela púplica uruguaya.* Montevideo, 1949
Fernández Saldaña, J. M., *Diccionario Uruguayo de Biografias.* Montevideo, 1945
Finch, M.H.J., *A Political Economy of Uruguay Since 1870.* London, 1981
Fitzgibbon, R. H., *Uruguay, Portrait of a Democracy.* New Brunswick, NJ, 1954; London, 1956
Montañés, M. T., *Desarrollo de la agricultura en el Uruguay.* Montevideo, 1948
Pendle, G., *Uruguay.* 3rd. ed. Inst. of Int. Affairs, 1963
Porzecanski, A. C., *Uruguay's Tupamaros.* London and New York, 1973
Salgado, José, *Historia de la Republica O. del Uruguay.* 8 vols. Montevideo, 1943

National Library: Biblioteca Nacional del Uruguay, Guayabo 1793, Montevideo. It publishes *Anuario Bibliográfico Uruguayo.*

VANUATU

Republic of Vanuatu

Capital: Vila
Population: 117,000 (1980)
GNP per capita: US$530 (1980)

HISTORY. The group was administered for some purposes jointly, for others unilaterally, as provided for by Anglo-French Convention of 27 Feb. 1906, ratified 20 Oct. 1906, and a protocol signed at London on 6 Aug. 1911 and ratified on 18 March 1922. On 30 July 1980 the Condominium of the New Hebrides achieved independence and became the Republic of Vanuatu.

AREA AND POPULATION. The Vanuatu group lies roughly 500 miles west of Fiji and 250 miles north-east of New Caledonia. The estimated land area is 5,700 sq. miles (14,760 sq. km). The larger islands of the group are: Espiritu Santo, Malekula, Epi, Pentecost, Aoba, Maewo, Paama, Ambrym, Efate, Erromanga, Tanna and Aneityum. They also claim Matthew and Hunter islands. Population at the census (1979) 112,596. Estimate (1980) 117,000. Vila (the capital) 14,000.

There are 3 active volcanoes, on Tanna, Ambrym and Lopevi, respectively. Earth tremors are of common occurrence.

CLIMATE. The climate is tropical, but moderated by oceanic influences and by trade winds from May to Oct. High humidity occasionally occurs and cyclones are possible. Rainfall ranges from 90″ (2,250 mm) in the south to 155″ (3,875 mm) in the north. Vila. Jan. 80°F (26·7°C), July 72°F (22·2°C). Annual rainfall 84″ (2,103 mm).

CONSTITUTION AND GOVERNMENT. General elections took place in Nov. 1975 to elect a 42-member Representative Assembly, replacing the former advisory council. Further general elections took place in Nov. 1979. A committee system was instituted and the Assembly chose its own President from its own members in 1977. The President replaced the Co-Presidents, who were the Resident Commissioners.

President: (Vacant).

The cabinet in Jan. 1984 was composed as follows:

Prime Minister: Walter Hadye Lini, CBE.
Home Affairs and Deputy Prime Minister: S. Regenvanu. *Foreign Affairs:* D Kalpokas. *Education:* O. Tahi. *Finance:* K. Kalsakau. *Health:* W. Korisa. *Transport, Communications and Public Works:* A. Sande. *Agriculture, Forestry, Fisheries:* J. Hopa. *Lands:* S. Molisa.

Flag: Red over green, with a black triangle in the hoist, the three parts being divided by fimbriations of black and yellow, and in the centre of the black triangle a boar's tusk overlaid by two crossed fern leaves.

Language: The national language is Bislama; English and French are also official languages.

ECONOMY

Planning. A National Development Plan (1982-86) envisages expenditure of US$12m.

Budget. The budget for 1982-83 envisages expenditure of 2,472m. Vatu. The main sources of revenue were import and export duties.

Currency. In 1982 a new currency, the *Vatu* was introduced.

Banking. A Central Bank was established in 1980. Because of the absence of direct taxation, with the exception of an added value tax on sales of sub-divided land, there has been growing interest in Vanuatu as a finance centre and 500 overseas companies are using Vila and have contributed 450m. Vatu in invisible export earnings. There were 8 banks in Vila in 1980. There is a National Development Bank and a Central Bank operated by the government and branches of the Bank of Indochine et de Suez at Vila and Santo. Barclays Bank International has a branch in Vila and Santo. Other overseas banks are: ANZ Bank, Westpac Banking Corporation and Hongkong and Shanghai Bank.

NATURAL RESOURCES

Minerals. The manganese mine, established at Forari on Efate by the Compagnie Française de Phosphates de l'Océanie, closed in 1968 but was reopened in 1970 by Southland Mining of Australia. Manganese exports, all to Japan, 1979, 25m. Vatu.

Agriculture. The main commercial crops are copra, cocoa and coffee. Yams, taro, manioc and bananas are grown for local consumption. A large number of cattle are reared on plantations, and an up-grading programme using pure-bred Charolais, Limousins and Illawarras has begun. A beef industry is developing.

Livestock (1982): Cattle, 100,000; goats, 8,000; pigs, 69,000; poultry, 158,000.

Forestry. An active forestry development programme is in progress and more than 26 plantations of South American hardwoods have been established.

Fisheries. The principal catch is tuna (1980, 10,000 tonnes) mainly exported to USA.

INDUSTRY AND TRADE

Industry. There is no heavy industry but there is increasing activity in light industry. Industries include a saw-mill, a soft drinks factory, meat canneries and a modern abattoir, and a fish-freezing plant. A few indigenous crafts, such as basketry, canoe-building and pottery, are practised. Subsistence fishing is done by the Vanuatuan, and a plant for freezing of tuna and bonito commenced operation in 1957. This plant, which is sited on Santo, freezes and packages for export to Japan and elsewhere, fish caught by Taiwanese and other vessels under contract to the British company running the plant. There are over 300 co-operative societies handling 85% of the distribution of goods in the islands.

Commerce. Imports and exports were (in 1m. Vatu):

	1979	1980	1981	1982
Imports	4,276	4,220	5,123	5,794
Exports	2,851	1,759	2,832	2,199

In 1979 the main exports were: Copra, 39,821 tonnes, 1,505m. NH francs; fish, 7,623 tonnes, 831m. NH francs; beef, 750 tonnes, 135m. NH francs. Australia, France and Japan were the major sources of imports and principal imports were food and drink, manufactured goods and petroleum products.

Tourism. Tourism is a growing industry and in 1980 there were 22,000 visitors to Vanuatu.

COMMUNICATIONS

Roads. There are approximately 1,000 km of roads in Vanuatu, of these about 35 km are sealed, mostly on Efate Island. There were 7,000 registered motor vehicles in Vanuatu (1980)

Aviation. External air services are provided by Air Pacific, Solair and Air Vanuatu. Solair has a weekly service Honiara–Santo–Vila and return. Air Vanuatu has 3 services a week Sydney–Vila–Sydney, UTA (Unions de Transports Aériens) and Air Nauru. Air Pacific has two services a week Nandi–Vila–Honiara–Brisbane, and one Nandi–Vila–Noumea–Brisbane. UTA has daily flights from Noumea, and a weekly flight to Wallis. Air Nauru gives a weekly service Vila–Nauru. Inter-island flights are provided by Air Melanesiae. The principal airports are Bauer Field (for Vila) and Pekoa (for Santo). Seventeen smaller airfields provide an internal network. In 1977 there were 1,001 overseas aircraft arrivals in Vila, carrying 59,141 passengers.

Shipping. Several international shipping lines serve Vanuatu, linking the country with Australia, New Zealand, other Pacific territories notably Hong Kong, Japan, North America and Europe. The chief ports are Vila and Santo. In 1977, 394 vessels arrived including 48 cruise ships carrying 40,412 visitors. 92,340 tons of cargo were exported and 102,867 tons discharged. Small vessels provide frequent inter-island services.

Telecommunications. Internal telephone and telegram services are provided by the Posts and Telecommunications and Radio Departments. There are automatic telephone exchanges at Vila and Santo; rural areas are served by a network of teleradio stations. In 1981 there were 3,000 telephones.

External telephone, telegram and telex services are provided by VANITEL, through their satellite earth station at Vila. There are direct circuits to Noumea, Sydney, Hong Kong and Paris and high quality communications are available on a 24-hour basis to most countries in the world. Air radio facilities are provided. Marine coast station facilities are available at Vila and Santo. Radio New Hebrides operates a service 7 days a week in 3 languages, French, English and Pidgin.

JUSTICE, RELIGION, EDUCATION AND WELFARE

Justice. A study was being made in 1980 which could lead to unification of the judicial system.

Religion. The Presbyterian, Anglican, Roman Catholic, Seven Day Adventists, Church of Christ, Apostolic and Assemblies of God have churches and chapels in Vanuatu.

Education. Primary and secondary education facilities are provided in both English and French. There is one technical training facility in Vila and students undergo higher (university) education either at the University of the South Pacific in Fiji, or University of Papua New Guinea or in France. Teacher training for both English and French language teachers is conducted in Vanuatu.

There were (1980) 115 French language primary and 3 secondary schools and 161 English language primary and 5 secondary schools.

Health. Medical care is provided through a network of 106 hospitals, health centres, clinics and dispensaries administered by the Government with the help of a number of voluntary agencies, and WHO. Public health measures and the control of communicable diseases are the responsibility of the public health administration. Local training schemes are devoted to basic community nurse training at hospitals in Vila, to rural health training and refresher courses at a special training health centre in North Efate, or by attachment to other suitable clinics and health centres, and to training of village sanitarians or health orderlies.

Malaria is still the most serious of the major endemic diseases which also include tuberculosis, leprosy, filariasis and venereal disease. During 1975–76 yaws recurred on some islands and there were epidemic outbreaks of dengue, influenza and gastro-enteritis.

For professional and technical education in medicine, nursing, X-ray, dentistry, laboratory work, health inspection, selected students or suitable in-service staff are awarded scholarships and fellowships for overseas training in Solomon Islands, Papua New Guinea, Fiji, New Zealand, Australia, New Caledonia and other countries.

DIPLOMATIC REPRESENTATIVES

Of Vanuatu in Great Britain
High Commissioner: Barak Teme Sope (accredited 4 June 1981).

Of Great Britain in Vanuatu (Melitco Hse., Rue Pasteur, Vila)
High Commissioner: R. B. Dorman.

Book of Reference

Annual Report. HMSO
Pacific Islands Yearbook. Sydney, 1978

VATICAN CITY STATE

Stato della Città del Vaticano

HISTORY. For many centuries the Popes bore temporal sway over a territory stretching across mid-Italy from sea to sea and comprising some 17,000 sq. miles, with a population finally of over 3m. In 1859–60 and 1870 the Papal States were incorporated with the Italian Kingdom. The consequent dispute between Italy and successive Popes was only settled on 11 Feb. 1929 by three treaties between the Italian Government and the Vatican: (1) A Political Treaty, which recognized the full and independent sovereignty of the Holy See in the city of the Vatican; (2) a Concordat, to regulate the condition of religion and of the Church in Italy; and (3) a Financial Convention, in accordance with which the Holy See received 750m. lire in cash and 1,000m. lire in Italian 5% state bonds. This sum was to be a definitive settlement of all the financial claims of the Holy See against Italy in consequence of the loss of its temporal power in 1870. The treaty and concordat were ratified on 7 June 1929. The treaty has been embodied in the Constitution of the Italian Republic of 1947. A revised Concordat between the Italian Republic and the Holy See was signed on 18 Feb. 1984 and on its ratification, the 1929 Concordat will lapse.

The Vatican City State is governed by a Commission appointed by the Pope. The reason for its existence is to provide an extra-territorial, independent base for the Holy See, the government of the Roman Catholic Church.

In 1930 the issue of Papal coinage was resumed, after a lapse of 60 years. In virtue of a special convention between the Vatican City and the Italian Government (last renewed in 1962), each state allows the currency of the other to circulate in its territory. The Vatican City has, however, given an undertaking that the total value of its coins issued in ordinary years will not exceed 100m. lire, 200m. lire in years of 'Sede vacante' or holy years, or 300m. in the year of the opening of a Council.

AREA AND POPULATION. The area of the Vatican City is 44 hectares (108·7 acres). It includes the Piazza di San Pietro (St Peter's Square), which is to remain normally open to the public and subject to the powers of the Italian police. It has its own railway station (opened Nov. 1932), postal facilities, coins and radio. Twelve buildings in and outside Rome enjoy extra-territorial rights, including the Basilicas of St John Lateran, St Mary Major, St Paul without the Walls and the Pope's summer villa at Castel Gandolfo. On 8 Oct. 1951 extra-territorial rights were also granted to a new Vatican radio station on Italian soil. *Radio Vaticana* is broadcasting an extensive service in 34 languages from transmitters in the Vatican City and in Italy.

The Vatican City has about 1,000 inhabitants.

CONSTITUTION. The Pope exercises the sovereignty and has absolute legislative, executive and judicial powers. The judicial power is delegated to a tribunal in the first instance, to the Sacred Roman Rota in appeal and to the Supreme Tribunal of the Signature in final appeal.

The Pope is elected by the College of Cardinals, meeting in secret conclave. The election is by scrutiny and requires a two-thirds majority.

Name and family	Election	Name and family	Election
Benedict XIV *(Lambertini)*	1740	Pius VI *(Braschi)*	1775
Clement XIII *(Rezzonico)*	1758	Pius VII *(Chiaramonti)*	1800
Clement XIV *(Ganganelli)*	1769	Leo XII *(della Genga)*	1823

Name and family	Election	Name and family	Election
Pius VIII *(Castiglioni)*	1829	Pius XI *(Ratti)*	1922
Gregory XVI *(Cappellari)*	1831	Pius XII *(Pacelli)*	1939
Pius IX *(Mastai-Ferretti)*	1846	John XXIII *(Roncalli)*	1958
Leo XIII *(Pecci)*	1878	Paul VI *(Montini)*	1963
Pius X *(Sarto)*	1903	John Paul I *(Luciani)*	1978
Benedict XV *(della Chiesa)*	1914	John Paul II *(Wojtyla)*	1978

Supreme Pontiff: **John Paul II** (Karol Wojtyla), born at Wadowice near Cracow, Poland, 18 May 1920. Archbishop of Cracow 1964–78, created Cardinal in 1967, elected Pope 16 Oct. 1978, inaugurated 22 Oct. 1978.

Pope John Paul II was the first non-Italian to be elected since Pope Adrian VI (a Dutchman) in 1522.

Secretary of State: Cardinal Agostino Casaroli (appointed May 1979).

Flag: Vertically yellow and white, with on the white the crossed keys and tiara of the Papacy.

ROMAN CATHOLIC CHURCH. The Roman Pontiff (in orders a Bishop, but in jurisdiction held to be by divine right the centre of all Catholic unity, and consequently Pastor and Teacher of all Christians) has for advisers and coadjutors the Sacred College of Cardinals, consisting in Jan. 1984 of 129 Cardinals appointed by him from senior ecclesiastics who are either the bishops of important Sees or the heads of departments at the Holy See. In addition to the College of Cardinals, the Pope has created a ' Synod of Bishops'. This consists of the Patriarchs and certain Metropolitans of the Catholic Church of Oriental Rite, of elected representatives of the national episcopal conferences and religious orders of the world, of the Cardinals in charge of the Roman Congregations and of other persons nominated by the Pope. The Synod meets as and when decided by the Pope; its first session was held in the autumn of 1967 and its sixth General Assembly in Sept.–Oct. 1983.

The central administration of the Roman Catholic Church is carried on by a number of permanent committees called Sacred Congregations, each composed of a number of Cardinals and diocesan bishops (both appointed for 5-year periods), with Consultors and Officials. Besides the Secretariat of State and the Council for Public Affairs of the Church (which deals with external relations) there are now 9 Sacred Congregations, viz.: Doctrine, Oriental Churches, Bishops, the Sacraments and Divine Worship, Clergy, Religious, Catholic Education, Evangelization of the Peoples and Causes of the Saints. There are also 3 Secretariats: for Christian Unity, Non-Christians and Non-Believers; a Prefecture of Economic Affairs, a Prefecture of the Pontifical Household and a Statistical Office. Furthermore, the Roman Curia contains 3 tribunals, the Apostolic Penitentiary, the Supreme Tribunal of the Apostolic Signature and the Sacred Roman Rota; and, lastly, various other councils and commissions dealing with the Laity, Justice and Peace, Women, the Family, the Information and Revision of Canon Law, Social Communications, Migration and Tourism and Culture. The Pontifical Academy of Sciences was revived by Pius XI in 1936 with 70 members.

More than 2,500 Roman Catholic prelates and 99 observer-delegates from 27 other Christian Churches attended the Second Vatican Council which met 11 Oct. 1962 and 8 Dec. 1965. Sixteen Constitutions and Decrees were approved at the Council, and 7 commissions were set up to implement these decisions.

DIPLOMATIC REPRESENTATIVES

In its diplomatic relations with foreign countries the Holy See is represented by the Council for Public Affairs of the Church. It maintains permanent observers to the UN in New York and Geneva and to UNESCO and FAO. The Holy See is a member of IAEA and the Vatican City State is a member of UPU and ITU. It therefore attends as a member those international conferences open to State members of the UN and specialized agencies.

British Ambassador: Sir Mark Heath, KCVO, CMG. *First Secretary:* R. J. Griffiths.

Apostolic Pro-Nuncio in Great Britain: Mgr Bruno Heim, Titular Archbishop of Xanto.

Books of Reference

Acta Apostolicæ Sedis Romanæ. Rome
Annuario Pontificio. Rome. Annual
L'Attivià della Santa Sede. Rome. Annual
The Catholic Directory. London. Annual
Code of Canon Law. London, 1983
The Catholic Directory for Scotland. Glasgow. Annual
Bilan du Monde: Encyclopédie catholique du monde chrétien. Tournai, 1964
Cardinale, Mgr. Igino, *Le Saint-Siège et la diplomatie.* Paris and Rome, 1962.—*The Holy See and the International Order.* Gerrards Cross, 1976
Hales, E. E., *The Catholic Church and the Modern World.* London, 1958
Mayer, F. *et al, The Vatican: Portrait of a State and a Community.* Dublin, 1980
Nichols, P., *The Politics of the Vatican.* London, 1968
Pallenborg, C., *Vatican Finances.* Harmondsworth, 1971
Walsh, M. J., *Vatican City State.* [Bibliography] Oxford and Santa Barbara, 1983

VENEZUELA

Republica de Venezuela

Capital: Caracas
Population: 14·69m. (1982)
GNP per capita: US$4,644 (1982)

HISTORY. Venezuela formed part of the Spanish colony of New Granada until 1821 when it became independent in union with Colombia. A separate, independent republic was formed in 1830.

AREA AND POPULATION. Venezuela is bounded north by the Caribbean, east by Guyana, south by Brazil, south-west and west by Colombia. The official estimate of the area is 912,050 sq. km (352,143 sq. miles); the frontiers with Colombia, Brazil and Guyana extend for 2,972 miles and its Atlantic coastline stretches for some 2,000 miles. Over half the population live in the valleys of Caracas and Valencia (once the capital). There are 20 states, 2 territories, the federal district and the federal dependencies (*i.e.* 72 islands in the Antilles); further states may be created from the territories. Bolívar, the largest state, has an area of 91,868 sq. miles; the other states are far smaller. The federal district embraces 745 sq. miles.

The language of the country is Spanish.

Population according to the 1971 census (estimate (1982) 14·69m.):

State	Capital	Population	State	Capital	Population
Anzcátegui	Barcelona	506,297	Portuguesa	Guanare	297,044
Apure	San Fernando	164,705	Sucre	Cumaná	469,006
Aragua	Maracay	543,170	Táchira	San Cristóbal	511,344
Barinas	Barinas	231,046	Trujillo	Trujillo	381,335
Bolívar	Ciudad Bolívar	391,665	Yaracuy	San Felipe	223,540
Carabobo	Valencia	659,339	Zulia	Maracaibo	1,229,037
Cojedes	San Carlos	94,351	Ter. Amazonas	Puerto Ayacucho	21,696
Falcón	Coro	407,957	Ter. Delta		
Guárico	San Juan	318,905	Amacuro	Tucupita	48,139
Lara	Barquisimeto	671,410	Federal District	Caracas	1,860,637
Mérida	Mérida	347,095	Federal Depen-		
Miranda	Los Teques	856,272	dencies	—	463
Monagas	Maturin	298,239			
Nueva Esparta	La Asunción	118,830	Total		10,721,522

The 1971 census excluded tribal Indians estimated at 31,800, of whom 20,000 are in Ter. Amazonas and 4,000 in Zulia. Excluding illegal immigrants, estimated (1979) at about 3m.

The 1971 population of Caracas was 1,035,499; Maracaibo 651,574; Barquisimeto, 330,815; Valencia, 367,154; Maracay, 255,134; San Cristóbal, 152,239; Ciudad Guyana, 143,540; Cabimas, 122,239; Maturín, 121,662; Baruta, 121,066; Cumaná, 119,751; Ciudad Bolívar, 103,728.

Vital statistics, 1979 (estimate): 484,700 births, 74,950 deaths. Life expectancy (1978) 66 years with 53% of population under 18 years.

CLIMATE. The climate ranges from warm temperate to tropical. Temperatures vary little throughout the year and rainfall is plentiful. The dry season is from Dec. to April. Caracas. Jan. 65°F (18·3°C), July 69°F (20·6°C). Annual rainfall 32″ (833 mm). Ciudad Bolívar. Jan. 79°F (26·1°C), July 81°F (27·2°C). Annual rainfall 41″ (1,016 mm). Maracaibo. Jan. 81°F (27·2°C), July 85°F (29·4°C). Annual rainfall 23″ (577 mm).

CONSTITUTION AND GOVERNMENT. The constitution of 1958 provides for popular election for a term of 5 years of a President, a National Congress, and State and Municipal legislative assemblies, and guarantees the freedom of labour, industry and commerce. Aliens are assured of treatment equal to that extended to nationals.

Congress consists of a Senate and a Chamber of Deputies. At least 2 Senators are elected for each State and for the Federal District. Senators must be Venezuelans by birth and over 30 years of age. Deputies must be native Venezuelans over 21 years of age; there is 1 for every 50,000 inhabitants. The territories, on reaching the population fixed by law, also elect deputies. Voting (by proportional representation) is compulsory for men and women over 18. Owing to the high rate of illiteracy, voting is by coloured ballot cards.

The President must be a Venezuelan by birth and over 30 years of age; he has a qualified power of veto.

The following is a list of presidents since 1941:

	Took Office		Took Office
Gen. Isaias Medina Angarita	6 May 1941	Dr Edgard Sanabria	14 Nov. 1958[3]
Rómulo Betancourt	20 Oct. 1945	Rómulo Betancourt	13 Feb. 1959
Rómulo Gallegos	15 Feb. 1948	Raul Leoni	11 March 1964
Lieut.-Col. Carlos Delgado		Rafael Caldera	11 March 1969
Chalbaud	24 Nov. 1948[4]	Carlos Andrés Pérez	
Dr G. Suárez Flamerich	27 Nov. 1950[2]	Rodríguez	12 March 1974
Col. Marcos Pérez Jiménez.	3 Dec. 1952[1]	Dr Luis Herrera Campíns	12 March 1979
Rear-Adm. Wolfgang		Dr Jaime Lusinchi	2 Feb. 1984
Larrazábal Ugueto	23 Jan. 1958[2][3]		

[1] Deposed.   [2] Resigned.   [3] Provisional.   [4] Assassinated 13 Nov. 1950.

President: Dr Jaime Lusinchi, elected 4 Dec. 1983 with 57% of the votes, assumed office on 2 Feb. 1984.

Foreign Minister: Isidro Morales Paul. *Finance Minister:* Manuel Azpurua.

At the Congressional elections held in Dec. 1978, 88 of the 199 seats in the Chamber of Deputies were won by Acción Democrática, 64 by COPEI (the Social Christians) and 27 by other parties.

The city of Caracas is the capital. The 20 states, autonomous and politically equal, have each a legislative assembly and an elected governor. The states are divided into 156 districts and 613 municipalities. There are also 2 federal territories with 7 departments, and a federal district with 2 departments and 2 parishes. Each district has a municipal council, and each municipio a communal junta. The federal district and the 2 territories are administered by the President of the Republic.

National flag: Three horizontal stripes of yellow, blue, red, with an arc of 7 white stars in the centre, and the national arms in the canton.

National anthem: Gloria al bravo pueblo (1811; words by Vicente Salias, tune by Juan Landaeta).

DEFENCE. All Venezuelans on reaching 18 years of age are liable for 2 years in the Armed Forces.

Army. The Army consists of 1 armoured and 1 Ranger brigades; 1 horsed cavalry, 26 infantry and 5 engineer battalions; and 5 artillery groups. Equipment includes 75 AMX-30 main battle and 40 AMX-13 light tanks. Army aviation comprises 30 helicopters and 2 STOL transports. Strength is 27,500

Navy. Strength includes 3 diesel-powered patrol submarines (2 new built in Federal Republic of Germany and 1 very old *ex*-US submarine), 2 old destroyers (*ex*-US), 8 frigates built in Italy (6 new and 2 old), 6 fast missile-armed patrol craft built in Britain in 1974–75, 1 tank landing ship, 2 medium landing ships, 1 transport landing ship (*ex*-repair ship), 12 minor landing craft, 1 survey ship, 2 survey launches, 2 transports and 9 tugs. Coastal patrol boats operated by the National Guard *(Fuezzas Armadas de Cooperacion)* now number 73.

New construction planned includes 4 corvettes, 2 more submarines from the Federal Republic of Germany, 6 fast attack craft, 6 mine countermeasures vessels, 2 landing ships and 1 survey ship.

There is a naval academy and sail training ship for the training of officer cadets and a school of staff studies and various technical training schools. Personnel in 1984 totalled: 9,000 officers and men including 4,000 of the Marine Corps and pilots and crew of the Naval Air Arm comprising 8 S2E Trackers, 6 Agusta AB-212 shipborne helicopters, 6 Bell 47s helicopters and 10 other light aircraft for various and coastguard duties.

Air Force. Formed in 1920, the Air Force of some 4,500 officers and men is a small, but well-equipped service with a total of about 200 aircraft. There are 6 combat squadrons. One is equipped with 18 F-16A and 6 F-16B Fighting Falcons. Two others have 29 Canadair CF-5A fighter-bombers and 6 two-seat CF-5Ds, and 16 Mirage III/5s respectively. Two bomber squadrons are equipped with 20 modernized Canberra jet-bombers and a single reconnaissance Canberra. Another operational squadron has 15 OV-10E Bronco twin-turboprop counter-insurgency aircraft. A helicopter force consists of more than 40 Bell JetRangers, 212s, 214STs and 412s, UH-1B/D/H Iroquois, Agusta A 109s and Alouette IIIs. Transport units are equipped with 7 C-123 Providers, 5 C-130H Hercules, 6 Aeritalia G222s, 1 HS.748 and 5 C-47s. Communications aircraft are Queen Airs and other types. T-34 Mentors are used for training, together with 20 T-2D Buckeye advanced jet trainers, which have a secondary attack role. A battalion of paratroops comes within Air Force responsibility. There is a staff college and a cadet academy.

National Guard, a volunteer force of some 15,000 under the Ministry of Defence, is broadly responsible for internal security. It includes customs and forestry duties among its tasks.

INTERNATIONAL RELATIONS

Membership. Venezuela is a member of UN, OAS, LAIA (formerly LAFTA), OPEC and the Andean Group.

ECONOMY

Planning. The sixth 5-year plan (1981–85) aims to achieve economic growth but with a reorientation of priorities towards social programmes: Education, housing and public services. There are 5 major projects: Caracas metro, Guri hydro-electric scheme, INOS water supply, major housing schemes and the Corpozulia coal and steel complex. These will cost Bs. 67,000m. over 5 years.

Budget. The revenue and expenditure for calendar years were, in Bs.1m., as follows:

	1977	1978	1979	1980	1981	1982
Revenue	51,179	44,480	50,588	71,508	94,865	82,101
Expenditure	50,694	44,273	51,236	72,868	94,544	86,884

Currency. The *bolívar* (Bs.) is divided into 100 *céntimos*. Gold coins, 100 (*pachanos*), 20 and 10 *bolívars* have been minted but are no longer in circulation; silver coins are 5 (*fuerte*), 2, 1 *bolívars*; nickel, 50 (*real*), 25 (*medio*) and 12·5 *céntimos* (*locha*), coppernickel, 5 *céntimos* (*puya*).

The bank-notes in circulation are 500, 100, 50, 20 and 10 bolívars. The circulation of foreign bank-notes is forbidden.

In March 1984, £ = Bs.6·40; US$1 = 5·90.

Banking. The major banks include: Banco Industrial de Venezuela, Banco de Venezuela, Banco nacional de Descuento, Banco Unión, Banco Mercantil y Agrícola, Banco de los Trabajadores de Venezuela, Banco Provincial SAICA, Banco Latino, Banco de Maracaibo, Banco Unido.

ENERGY AND NATURAL RESOURCES

Oil. The oil-producing region around Maracaibo, covering some 30,000 sq. miles, produces about three-quarters of Venezuelan petroleum. Deposits in the Orinoco region are likely to prove one of the largest heavy oil reserves in the world. Nationalization of the privately owned oil sector in 1976 has proved successful. New distribution channels have been established, with the result that the major transnational companies which took 80% of Venezuela's oil in 1976 handled only 50% in 1980. Crude oil and derivatives production (1982) 1·88m. bbls per day.

Proven reserves in mid-1979 stood at 18,500m. bbls, probable reserves at 15,000m. and possible at 102,000m. However, these are considered conservative estimates and new fields off-shore have estimated reserves of 6,000–40,000m. bbls. The Orinoco tar sands belt has reserves variously estimated at between 700,000m. bbls. and 3,000,000m. bbls.

Gas. Production (1978) 34,842m cu. metres.

Minerals. Bauxite is being exploited in the Guayana region by Bauxien, a state agency. There are important goldmines in the region south-east of Bolívar State, and new deposits have been discovered near El Callao (1959) and Sosa Méndez (1961) in the Guayana region. Output, 1982, amounted to 902 kg. Diamond output, from Amazonas territory, was 687,000 carats in 1977. Manganese deposits, estimated at several million tons, were discovered in 1954. Phosphate-rock deposits (yielding from 64 to 82% tricalcium phosphate) are found in the state of Falcón; reserves of 15m. tons of high-quality rock have been established. The state of Sucre has large sulphur deposits. Coal is worked in the states of Táchira, Aragua and Anzoátegui, production in 1977 being 115,000 tonnes. Coal proven reserves in Zulia (160m. tons) are to be developed to service a new thermal power station in the Maracaibo area. An important nickel deposit (at Loma de Hierro near Tejerías) is estimated to equal 600,000 tons of pure nickel. Saltmines are now worked by the Government on the Araya peninsula; output, 1964, 202,000 tonnes. Asbestos and copper pyrite are being exploited. There were proven reserves (1984) of bauxite totalling 200m. tonnes and production of about 3m. per annum are scheduled from 1986.

Iron ore is exploited in Bolívar State by the Orinoco Mining Co. and Iron Mines of Venezuela, subsidiaries respectively of the US Steel Corp. and the Bethlehem Steel Co. Proven reserves at the end of 1980 were 1,800m. tonnes. National output of iron ore, 1982, 11·7m. tonnes.

Agriculture. Venezuela is divided into 3 distinct zones—the agricultural, the pastoral and the forest zone. In the first are grown coffee, cocoa, sugar-cane, maize, rice, wheat (grown in the Andes), tobacco, cotton, beans, sisal, etc.; the second affords grazing for more than 6m. cattle and numerous horses; and in the third, which covers a very large portion of the country, tropical products, such as caoutchouc, balatá (a gum resembling rubber), tonka beans, dividivi, copaiba, vanilla, growing wild, are worked by the inhabitants. The 1982 livestock estimate showed cattle, 11·5m.; pigs, 2·6m.; goats, 1·4m.; sheep, 351,000; poultry, 44m. Area under cultivation is 5,530,898 acres. Agriculture is the weakest sector of the economy, accounting for only 6% of GDP and employing 16·3% of the national workforce. Over 50% of all farmers are engaged in subsistence agriculture and growth rates in agricultural production have not kept pace with the high population increase. Government has introduced a programme of price support, tax incentives and price increases but cattle farming is at present the only profit opportunity.

Production in tonnes in 1982: Coffee, 59,000; maize, 501,000; rice, 670,000; sugar-cane, 5m.

The coffee plantations number 62,673, covering 543,400 acres with 135m. bushes. The Venezuelan cocoa, from 13,000 plantations, is considered to be of high quality; it is grown chiefly in the states of Sucre and Miranda. The sugar industry has 6 government and 20 privately owned mills.

Forestry. Resources have been barely tapped; 600 species of wood have been identified. Output of roundwood timber, 1977, broadleaved, 8m. cu. metres.

Fisheries. The fishing industry is to be developed by the provision of port and processing facilities, research and training.

Total catch (1977) was 152·2m. tonnes.

INDUSTRY AND TRADE

Industry. Production (1982): Steel, 1·99m. tonnes; aluminium, 273,000; ammonia, 535,000; fertilizers, 630,000; cement, 5·43m.; paper, 481,000; vehicles (units) 155,000.

Industrial development is concentrated in capital intensive areas where it can have a competitive advantage within the Andean Group, whereas in more labour intensive industries, the low labour costs of other member countries gives them an advantage. However, Venezuela currently produces 90% of its requirements of processed food, beverages, tobacco, clothing and textiles.

Labour. The labour force in 1983 was 6m., 19·5% were in agriculture, 18·8% in manufacturing and 9·6% in construction.

Wages are the highest in Latin America, there is a high turnover of labour and a corresponding rate of absenteeism.

45% of the labour force is unionized. The most powerful confederation is the CTV (*Confederacion de Trabajadores de Venezuela*, formed 1947), which is dominated by the Accion Democratica party. Estimated membership, 1·1m., claims 2m. Comprises 68 regional and industrial federations with over 6,000 unions, including: FCV (peasants), 700,000; FETRACONS (construction workers), 1m.; FETRASALUD (health workers), 45,000; FETRAMETAL (metal workers and miners), 32,000; the very important FEDEPETROL (oil workers), 6,000; Federacion Venezolana de Maestros (teachers).

Other confederations are CUTV (*Confederacion Unitaria de Trabajadores Venezolanos*, formed 1963). Estimated membership, 40,000, claims 100,000. Comprises 8 regional and 5 industrial federations in 185 local unions; and, CODESA (*Confederacion de Sindicatos Autonomos de Venezuela*, formed 1964). Estimated membership, 10,000, claims 35,000. Dominated by COPEI party. Comprises 120 local unions, including textile, petrol distribution, public health and education workers' federations.

Commerce. Venezuela's exports and imports (in US$1m.):

	1979	1980	1981	1982
Exports	14,199	19,281	20,100	16,549
Imports	10,837	11,318	12,400	13,200

Main export markets in 1982 were USA, Netherlands Antilles because of its oil refining and transhipment facilities, Canada, Puerto Rico, Italy and Spain.

Principal imports are machinery and equipment, manufactured goods, chemical products, foodstuffs.

The USA supplied 47% of all imports in 1982, followed by Federal Republic of Germany, Japan, Italy and the UK.

Total trade between UK and Venezuela (British Department of Trade returns, in £1,000 sterling):

	1979	1980	1981	1982	1983
Imports to UK	100,823	117,614	124,020	141,892	183,731
Exports and re-exports from UK	137,722	131,684	125,315	148,666	87,937

Tourism. 652,000 tourists visited Venezuela in 1977.

COMMUNICATIONS

Roads. There were, 1983, 61,000 km of road fit for traffic the year round; of these 20,000 km are paved. There are 10,097 km of high-speed 4-lane motorway type. The motorway system runs from Caracas to Puerto Cabello *via* Valencia and will shortly be linked direct with one from La Guaira to Caracas. Venezuela has received two World Bank loans for US$4·5m. and 30m. in connexion with this programme, for improvements of the express-ways in Caracas and for 2 roads in the south-west of the country.

Railways. Plans have existed since 1950 for large-scale railway construction but only the Puerto Cabello to Barquisimeto line (175 km–1,435 mm gauge) has been completed. A metro is under construction in Caracas the first section of which was opened in March 1983.

Aviation. The chief Venezuelan airlines are LAV (Líneas Aéreas Venezolanas), a government-owned concern, and AVENSA (Aerovías Venezolanas). Both operate numerous internal services. VIASA operates international routes in conjunction with KLM. There are also 3 specialist air freight companies. In all there are over 100 commercial aircraft in operation. In addition to Venezuelan international services, a number of US and Latin American and European lines operate services to Venezuela. British Caledonian operates twice-weekly flights between London and Caracas.

Shipping. Foreign vessels are not permitted to engage in the coasting trade, except by special concessions or by contract with the Government. La Guaira, Maracaibo, Puerto Cabello, Puerto Ordaz and Guanta are the chief ports. In Dec. 1978 the merchant fleet had an aggregate gross tonnage of 824,000; this included tankers of 368,000 gross tons.

The principal navigable rivers are the Orinoco and its tributaries Apure and Arauca, from San Fernando to Tucupita through Ciudad Bolívar, Puerto Ordaz and San Félix; San Juan from Carípito to the Gulf of Paria; and Esculante in Lake Maracaibo.

Post and Broadcasting. There were 1,377,630 telephones in 1982; 511,336 were in Caracas. An international telex service operates in the Caracas metropolitan zone. There is a submarine telephone link with USA.

There are 77 radio stations at Caracas, Maracaibo, Maracay and other towns. There are 3 television stations in Caracas (two privately owned), of which 2 cover, with relays, most of the country. In 1979 there were about 1·9m. homes with TV receivers.

Cinemas (1977). There were 563 cinemas and 25 drive-ins.

Newspapers (1976). There were 47 daily newspapers, 32 weeklies and 134 magazines.

JUSTICE, RELIGION AND EDUCATION

Justice. The Supreme Court, which operates in Divisions, each with 5 members, is elected by Congress for 5 years. The country is divided into 20 legal districts. They select their own President and Vice-President. The Federal Procurator-General is appointed for 5 years. There are lower federal courts.

Each state has a Supreme Court with 3 members, a superior court, or superior tribunal, courts of first instance, district courts and municipal courts. In the territories there are civil and military judges of first instance, and also judges in the municipios. Finally, there is an income-tax claims tribunal.

Religion. The Roman Catholic is the prevailing religion, but there is toleration of all others. There are 4 archbishops, 1 at Caracas, who is Primate of Venezuela, 2 at Mérida and 1 at Ciudad Bolívar. There are 19 bishops. In the state primary schools instruction is given only to those children whose parents expressly request it. Protestants number about 20,000.

Education. Elementary instruction is free and, from the age of 7 to 13 (the completion of the primary grade), compulsory. In 1974–75 Venezuela had 11,098 primary schools with (1976–77) 63,198 teachers and a total enrolment of 2,204,000 pupils. In 1976–77 there were 720,000 pupils in secondary schools and the number of students in higher education was 248,000 with 15,972 teaching staff. There were 14 universities. The education budget for 1982 was Bs. 8m.

DIPLOMATIC REPRESENTATIVES

Of Venezuela in Great Britain (1 Cromwell Rd., London SW7)
Ambassador: Néstor Coll (accredited 16 Dec. 1982).

Of Great Britain in Venezuela (Torre Las Mercedes, Avenida La Estancia, Chuao, Caracas 1060)
Ambassador: Hugh M. Carless, CMG.

Of Venezuela in the USA (2445 Massachusetts Ave., NW, Washington, D.C., 20008)
Ambassador: Marcial Perez-Chiriboga.

Of the USA in Venezuela (Avenida Francisco de Miranda and Avenida Principal de la Floresta, Caracas)
Ambassador: George Landau.

Of Venezuela to the United Nations
Ambassador: Dr Alberto Martini-Undaneta.

Books of Reference

Statistical Information: The following are some of the principal publications:
Dirección General de Estadística, Ministerio de Fomento, *Boletín Mensual de Estadística.—Anuario Estadístico de Venezuela, 1978.* Caracas, 1979
Banco Central, *Memoria Annual* and *Boletin Mensual*
Ministerio de Sanidad y Asistencia Social, Dirección de Salud Pública, *Anuario de Epidemiología y Asistencia Social*

Betancourt, R., *Venezuela's Oil.* London, 1978
Bigler, G. E., *Politics and State Capitalism in Venezuela.* Madrid, 1981
Buitrón, A., *Causas y Efectos del Exodo Rural en Venezuela.—Efectos Económicos y Sociales de las Inmigraciones en Venezuela.—Las Inmigraciones en Venezuela.* Pan American Union, Washington, D.C., 1956
Gil Yepes, J. A., *The Challenge of Venezuelan Democracy.* London, 1981
Lieuwen, E., *Venezuela.* Rev. ed. OUP, 1969
Lombard, J., *Venezuelan History: A Comprehensive Working Bibliography.* Boston, 1977.—*Venezuela: The Search for Order, the Dream of Progress.* OUP, 1982
Salazar-Carrillo, J., *Oil in the Economic Development of Venezuela.* New York, 1976
Tugwell, F., *The Politics of Oil in Venezuela.* Stanford Univ. Press, 1975

VIETNAM

Capital: Hanoi
Population: 54m. (1981)
GNP per capita: US$170 (1978)

Công Hòa Xã Hôi Chu Nghĩa
Viêt Nam—The Socialist
Republic of Vietnam

HISTORY. The recorded history of Vietnam can be traced to Tonkin (now known as the northern part of Vietnam) at the beginning of the Christian era. Conquered by the Chinese (Han dynasty) in B.C. 111, the kingdom of Nam-Viet, as it was then called, broke free of Chinese domination in 939, though at many subsequent periods it again became a nominal vassal of the Chinese emperors.

By the end of the 15th century the Vietnamese had conquered most of the kingdom of Champa (in Annam, now known as the central part of Vietnam) and by the end of the 18th had acquired Cochin-China (now known as the southern part of Vietnam), formerly Cambodian territory.

French interest in Vietnam started in the late 16th century with the arrival of French and Portuguese missionaries. The most notable of these was Alexander of Rhodes, who, in the following century, romanized Vietnamese writing. At the end of the 18th century a French bishop and several soldiers of fortune helped to establish the Emperor Gia-Long (with whom Louis XVI had signed a treaty in 1787) as ruler of a unified Vietnam, known then as the Empire of Annam.

An expedition sent by Napoleon III in 1858 to avenge the death of some French missionaries led in 1862 to the cession to France of part of Cochin-China, and thence, by a series of treaties between 1874 and 1884, to the establishment of French protectorates over Tonkin and Annam, and to the formation of the French colony of Cochin-China. By a Sino-French treaty of 1885 the Empire of Annam (including Tonkin) ceased to be tributary to China. Cambodia had become a French protectorate in 1863, and in 1899, after extension of French protection to Laos in 1893, the Indo-Chinese Union was proclaimed.

In 1940 Vietnam was occupied by the Japanese and used as a military base for the invasion of Malaya. During the occupation there was considerable underground activity among nationalist, revolutionary and Communist organizations. In 1941 a nominally nationalist coalition of such organizations, known as the Vietminh League, was founded by the Communists.

On 9 March 1945 the Japanese interned the French authorities and proclaimed the 'independence' of Indo-China. In Aug. 1945 they allowed the Vietminh movement to seize power, dethrone Bao Dai, the Emperor of Annam, and establish a republic known as Vietnam, including Tonkin, Annam and Cochin-China, with Hanoi as capital. In Sept. 1945 the French re-established themselves in Cochin-China and on 6 March 1946, after a cease-fire in the sporadic fighting between the French forces and the Vietminh had been arranged, a preliminary convention was signed in Hanoi between the French High Commissioner and President Ho Chi Minh by which France recognized 'the Democratic Republic of Vietnam' as a 'Free State within the Indo-Chinese Federation'. Subsequent conferences convened in the same year at Dalat and Fontainebleau to draft a definitive agreement broke down chiefly over the question of whether or not Cochin-China should be included in the new republic. On 19 Dec. 1946 Vietminh forces made a surprise attack on Hanoi, the signal for hostilities which were to last for nearly 8 years.

An agreement signed by Emperor Bao Dai on behalf of Vietnam on 8 March 1949 recognized the independence of Vietnam within the French Union, and certain sovereign powers were forthwith transferred to Vietnam. The Paris agreements of 29 Dec. 1954 completed the transfer of sovereignty to Vietnam. Supreme authority in the military field remained with the French until the departure of the last French C.-in-C. in April 1956. Treaties of independence and association were initialled by representatives of the French and Vietnamese governments on 4 June 1954.

An agreement on the cessation of hostilities in Vietnam was reached on 20 July 1954 at the Geneva conference. The agreement was signed on behalf of the C.-in-C. of the French Forces in Indo-China and on behalf of the C.-in-C. of the People's Army of Vietnam. The Government of Vietnam did not sign the agreement.

The final declaration of the Geneva conference (21 July 1954) declared that general elections should take place in July 1956. These did not take place, and Vietnam remained divided until 1976.

In Paris on 27 Jan. 1973 an agreement was signed ending the war in Vietnam. After the US withdrawal, however, hostilities continued between the North and the South until the latter's defeat in 1975. President Thieu resigned on 21 April. Gen. Duong Van Minh surrendered to the Communist forces on 30 April. 150,000–200,000 South Vietnamese fled the country, including the former President Thieu.

For details of the former Republic of Vietnam (South Vietnam), see THE STATESMAN'S YEAR-BOOK, 1975–76. After the collapse of President Thieu's regime the Provisional Revolutionary Government established an administration in Saigon on 6 June 1975 under the presidency of Huynh Tan Phat. A North–South conference on reunification of Nov. 1975 announced that agreement on 'the basic problems' had been reached. A general election was held on 25 April 1976 for a National Assembly representing the whole country. Voting was by universal suffrage of all citizens of 18 or over, except former functionaries of South Vietnam undergoing 're-education'. The unification of North and South Vietnam into the Socialist Republic of Vietnam took place formally on 2 July 1976. After previous US vetoes the new administration of President Carter indicated that it was not opposed to Vietnam's application to join the UN, and Vietnam was admitted unanimously and without a vote on 20 Sept. 1977. In June 1978 Vietnam was admitted to Comecon and in Nov. 1978 signed a 25-year treaty of friendship and co-operation with the USSR. Relations with China correspondingly deteriorated, an especially exacerbating factor being the successful Vietnamese military intervention in Kampuchea. On 17 Feb. 1979 China invaded North Vietnam, but claimed that its troops had all withdrawn by 19 March. Peace negotiations were commenced on 18 April 1979 but broken off by the Chinese on 6 March 1980. The Government announced it had suppressed an armed insurrection in the South in Nov. 1982.

AREA AND POPULATION. The country has a total area of 329,566 sq. km and is divided administratively into 36 provinces and 1 special area. Areas and populations (in 1,000) at the census of Oct. 1979 were as follows:

Province	Sq. km	1979	Province	Sq. km	1979
Lai Chau	17,408	322,077	Gia Lai – Kon Tum	18,480	595,906
Son La	14,656	487,793	Dac Lac	18,300	490,198
Hoang Lien Son	14,125	778,217	Phu Khanh	9,620	1,188,637
Ha Tuyen	13,519	782,453	Lam Dong	10,000	396,657
Cao Bang	} 13,731	{ 479,823	Thuan Hai	11,000	938,255
Lang Son		484,657	Dong Nai	12,130	1,304,799
Bac Thai	8,615	815,105	Song Be	9,500	659,093
Quang Ninh	7,076	750,055	Tay Ninh	4,100	684,006
Vinh Phu	5,187	1,488,348	Long An	5,100	957,264
Ha Bac	4,708	1,662,671	Dong Thap	3,120	1,182,787
Ha Son Binh	6,860	1,537,190	Thanh Pho –		
Hanoi (city)[1]	597	2,570,905	Ho Chi Minh[1]	1,845	3,419,978
Hai Hung	2,526	2,145,662	Tien Giang	2,350	1,264,498
Thai Binh	1,344	1,506,235	Ben Tre	2,400	1,041,838
Hai Phong (city)[1]	1,515	1,279,067	Cuu Long	4,200	1,504,215
Ha Nam Ninh	3,522	2,781,409	An Giang	4,140	1,532,362
Thanh Hoa	11,138	2,532,261	Hau Giang	5,100	2,232,891
Nghe Tinh	22,380	3,111,989	Kien Giang	6,000	994,673
Binh Tri Thien	19,048	1,901,713	Minh Hai	8,000	1,219,595
Quang Nam – Da Nang	11,376	1,529,520	Vung Tau – Con Dao[2]	—	91,160
Nghia Binh	14,700	2,095,354			
				329,466	52,741,766

[1] Autonomous city. [2] Special area

At the census of Oct. 1979 the population was 52,741,766 (25,580,582 male; 19·7% urban).

Population (1981), 54m. (Ho Chi Minh 3·5m.; Hanoi, 2m. (1979); growth rate (1980) 2·9% per annum.

84% of the population are Vietnamese (Kinh). There are also over 60 minority groups thinly spread in the extensive mountainous regions. The largest minorities are (1976 figures in 1,000): Tay (742); Khmer (651); Thai (631); Muong (618); Nung (472); Meo (349); Dao (294). In 1981 0·5m. Vietnamese were living abroad, mainly in USA.

From 1979 to 30 Sept. 1983 37,496 persons emigrated legally. Between Apr. 1975 and Sept. 1983 a further 532,680 'boat people' succeeded in finding refuge abroad. By 1983 more 'boat people' were arriving in countries of first asylum than were leaving under the UN's orderly departure scheme. (For previous details *see* THE STATESMAN'S YEAR-BOOK, 1981–82).

CLIMATE. The humid monsoon climate gives tropical conditions in the south and sub-tropical conditions in the north, though real winter conditions can affect the north when polar air blows south over Asia. In general, there is little variation in temperatures over the year. Hanoi. Jan. 62°F (16·7°C), July 84°F (28·9°C). Annual rainfall 72″ (1,830 mm).

CONSTITUTION AND GOVERNMENT. A new Constitution was adopted in Dec. 1980. It states that Vietnam is a state of proletarian dictatorship and is developing according to Marxism–Leninism.

At the elections for the new National Assembly held on 26 April 1981, 613 candidates stood and 496 were elected. 70% of the candidates were standing for the first time.

Local government authorities are the people's councils, which appoint executive committees. Local elections were held in Ho Chi Minh City and the 38 provinces of the former South Vietnam on 5 May 1977.

The 1980 Constitution replaced the Presidency with the State Council, 'the standing organ of the National Assembly and presidium of the Republic'.

Chairman: Truong Chinh. *Vice-Chairmen:* Nguyen Huu Tho, Le Thanh Nghi, Chu Huy Man, Huynh Tan Phat. The *Prime Minister* is the Chairman of the Council of Ministers, Pham Van Dong.

Chairman of the National Assembly: Nguyen Huu Tho.

All political power stems from the Communist Party of Vietnam (until Dec. 1976 known as the Workers' Party of Vietnam), founded in 1930; it had 1m. members in Dec. 1979 (8·8% workers; 17% women). In April 1984 the Politburo consisted of Le Duan *(First Secretary)*; Truong Chinh; Pham Van Dong; Pham Hung *(Deputy Prime Minister and Minister of the Interior)*; Le Duc Tho; Gen. Van Tien Dung *(Minister of Defence)*; Vo Chi Cong; Gen. Chu Huy Man; To Huu *(First Deputy Prime Minister)*; Vo Van Kiet *(Deputy Prime Minister and Chairman, State Planning Commission)*; Do Muoi *(Deputy Prime Minister)* Le Duc Anh; Nguyen Duc Tam. Candidate members: Nguyen Co Thach *(Foreign Minister)*; Dong Si Nguyen *(Deputy Prime Minister)*. Ministers not in the Politburo include: Vo Nguyen Giap; Tran Quynh; Vu Dinh Lieu; Tran Phuong *(Deputy Prime Ministers)*; Chu Tham Phuc *(Finance)*; Le Khac *(Foreign Trade)*; Le Duc Thinh *(Home Trade)*; Dong Si Nguyen *(Transport)*; Mme. Nguyen Thi Binh *(Education)*; Nguyen Ngoc Triu *(Agriculture)*; Phan Hien *(Justice)*.

There are 2 puppet parties, the Democratic (founded 1944) and the Socialist (1946), which are unified with the trade and youth unions in the Fatherland Front.

National flag: Red, with a yellow 5-pointed star in the centre.
National anthem: 'Tien quan ca' ('The troops are advancing').

DEFENCE. Conscription is for 3 years at age 18.

Army. The Army consists of 1 armoured division, 58 infantry divisions (of varying strengths), 7 engineer and 15 economic construction divisions, 10 marine brigades, 5 field and 4 anti-aircraft artillery brigades, 4 engineer brigades, and 6 independent armoured regiments. Equipment includes some 2,000 main battle and 600 light tanks. Strength was (1984) about 1·2m. Paramilitary forces are Border Defence (60,000) and Militia (1·5m.).

Navy. Before the North Vietnamese victory in 1975 the Navy comprised 3 old coastal escorts, 2 fast missile boats, 28 fast torpedo boats, 22 fast motor gunboats, 34 small patrol boats, 24 landing craft, 4 minesweeping boats, 10 tenders, 100 auxiliaries and 200 armed junks. It also had 10 Mi-4 SAR helicopters.

At least 1 frigate, several other major warships and a considerable number of auxiliaries were captured after the South Vietnamese surrender.

The fleet reportedly includes 4 new *ex*-Soviet escorts, 2 old frigates, 2 old corvettes, 1 minesweeper, 6 old submarine chasers, 8 fast missile boats, 12 fast torpedo boats, 18 fast gunboats, 9 fast patrol craft, 9 landing ships, 7 landing craft, 1 torpedo recovery vessel, 15 riverine craft, 24 minesweeping launches, 1 survey ship, 15 auxiliaries and 100 armed junks; but due to the lack of maintenance, spares and trials it is difficult to accurately assess the operational availability, fitness for sea or steaming capacity of this heterogeneous collection or the availability of trained personnel.

It is estimated that 3 missile craft, 12 torpedo boats, 22 gunboats, 4 minesweepers, 24 patrol craft, 25 coastguard cutters, 100 motor launches are non-operational together with 500 riverine craft, 120 landing craft, 30 monitors, 100 converted amphibious craft, 26 vedettes, 36 auxiliaries and 75 service craft.

In 1984 there were an estimated 4,000 naval personnel regulars, with additional conscripts on three to four year terms.

Air Force. The Air Force, built up with Soviet and Chinese assistance, has about 12,000 personal and 275 combat aircraft (plus many stored), including modern US types captured in war. There are reported to be 2 squadrons of variable-geometry MiG-23s, 3 squadrons of MiG-17s, Su-7s and Su-20s, about 180 MiG-21 interceptors; up to 70 C-130 Hercules, An-2, Li-2, An-24, An-26 and Il-14 transports; and a strong helicopter force with UH-1 Iroquois, Mi-6 and Mi-8 helicopters. 'Guideline', 'Goa' and 'Gainful' missiles are operational in large numbers.

INTERNATIONAL RELATIONS

Membership. Vietnam is a member of UN, Comecon and IMF.

ECONOMY

Planning. Long-term forward planning gives priority to creating self-sufficiency in agriculture before progressing to further industrialization. Targets for the second 5-year plan 1976–80 were not met. Growth in agriculture, 18·7%; industry, 17·3%. The third 5-year plan covers 1981–85. An agreement co-ordinating this plan with the current Soviet plan was signed with the USSR in July 1981.

Curtailment of imports, floods and resistance to new economic measures have contributed to a serious shortage of consumer goods, which it is hoped to correct by stimulating regional industry and utilizing the expertise of former businessmen. (For previous plans *see* THE STATESMAN'S YEAR-BOOK, 1976–77, p. 1473.)

Currency. The monetary unit is the *dong* = 10 *hao*, the *hao* = 10 *xu*. There are coins of 1, 2 and 5 *xu*, 1, 2 and 5 *hao*, 1 *dong*; and notes of 1, 2, 5, 10, 20, 30, 50 and 100 *dong*. In March 1984, £1 = 14·55 *dong*; US$1 = 9·79 *dong* (black market 180 *dong*).

Banking. The bank of issue is the National Bank of Vietnam (founded in 1951). There is also a Bank for Foreign Trade (Vietcombank). In 1980 this bank ceased all transactions with US banks.

ENERGY AND NATURAL RESOURCES

Electricity. In 1980, 368m. kwh. of electricity were produced. A hydro-electric power station with a capacity of 2m. kw. is being built at Hoa-Binh with Soviet assistance.

Minerals. North Vietnam is rich in anthracite, lignite and hard coal: total reserves are estimated at 20,000m. tonnes. Anthracite production in 1975 was 5m. tonnes. Coal production was 5·3m. tonnes in 1980. There are deposits of iron ore, manganese, titanium, chromite, bauxite and a little gold. Chromite production in 1962 was 35,000 tons. Reserves of apatite are some of the biggest in the world. Estimated production of phosphates in 1971, 1·1m. tonnes; salt, 150,000 tonnes. In 1973 and 1974 the former Vietnamese Government awarded concessions for offshore oil exploration but Western companies have pulled out of exploration in Vietnam as uneconomic. There are large limestone deposits in Kien Giang, Chau Doc and Thua Thien provinces. A recent geological survey reported on the prospects of valuable bauxite deposits. There is a small coal-bearing region at Nong-Son.

Agriculture. In 1980, 71% of the population was engaged in agriculture. . In the North in 1975 agricultural co-operatives were reorganized into larger units. (Previously there had been about 18,000 co-operatives, each comprising 200–400 households and averaging 200 hectares of land each.) In 1977 there were 15,200 co-operatives in the North averaging 300–500 hectares (less than 100 hectares in mountain regions) and a workforce of 1,000–2,000. There were 105 state farms employing in all 70,000 workers and with 55,000 hectares arable and 50,000 hectares of pasture. Other crops include maize, sugar-cane, sweet potatoes and cotton. The cultivated area in 1980 was 6·97m. hectares (5·54m. hectares for rice); in 1964, 2·4m. hectares were irrigated.

In the South to redress the disproportionate urbanization of the southern population during the war (40% of the population were living in Ho Chi Minh City by April 1975) resettlement of family units in rural areas began after the Communist take-over. Each family was allotted an average of 5,000 sq. metres of land, a dwelling and agricultural equipment. 1,000 sq. metres of this total are for private plots. Families are grouped by twenties in 'mutual aid and labour cells'. In 1972, 83,300 hectares produced 20,000 tonnes of rubber. In 1977 there were 74 state farms and a few experimental co-operatives.

Production in 1,000 tonnes in 1980: Soybeans (32), tea (21), rubber (45), cereals (13,520), maize (475), oil seed plants (595), tobacco (15·6), potatoes (684). (1979) sweet potatoes (from 380,000 hectares), sorghum (35) from 30,000 hectares), beans (45) from 93,000 hectares), coffee (15).The main crop is rice. Production was some 11·69m. tonnes in 1980, 4·4m. tonnes short of requirements.

Livestock (1982): Cattle 2m.; pigs, 11·4m.; goats, 197,000; poultry, 46·1m.

Animal products, 1980: Eggs, 1,129m., meat, 427,000 tonnes.

Forestry. 1,626,000 cu. metres of timber were produced in 1980.

Fisheries. Fishing is important, especially in Halong Bay. In 1976, 6m. tonnes of sea fish and 180,000 tonnes of freshwater fish were caught (representing only 83% of the planned target.)

INDUSTRY AND TRADE

Industry. Next to mining, food processing and textiles are the most important industries; there is also some machine building. Older industries include cement, cotton and silk manufacture. Local industries and handicrafts account for 50% of production.

Private businesses were taken over in 1978. Foreign firms, principally French, are continuing to function, but all US property has been nationalized. There is little heavy industry. Most industry is concentrated in the Ho-Chi-Minh area.

Production (1980, in 1,000 tonnes) iron, 125; steel, 106; sulphuric acid, 6,700; caustic soda, 4,500; mineral fertilizer, 260; pesticides, 18,400; paper, 54,000; sugar, 94,000, cement, 705. 1,500 tractors were built in 1980, and 62! railway coaches. Footwear production, 200,000 pairs. Beer, 942,000 hectolitres.

Kenaf yarn production was 1,615 tons in 1972.

Labour. Average wage (1984) 200 dong per month. Non-agricultural workforce (1980) 3,587,000, of whom 2,238,000 in industry.

Commerce. USSR and Japan are Vietnam's main trading partners; others are Singapore and Hong Kong. Main exports are coal, farm produce, sea produce and livestock. Imports: technical equipment, industrial raw materials, foodstuffs and medical supplies. The Vietnamese Government recognizes a need for foreign aid and credit for the development of an industrial base. An aid agreement was reached with the USSR in Sept. 1981 for 5 years under which the USSR will participate in 40 construction projects and oil exploration in exchange for foodstuffs. By 1981 Sweden was the only Western country to give any significant aid. In 1982 Vietnam's total indebtedness was estimated at US$3,000m. In 1978 the IMF approved a virtually interest-free loan of US$90m. repayable over 50 years, but in July 1982 refused Vietnam's request for US$150m. in Special Drawing Rights until there are reforms in the economy. Foreign investments are encouraged and guaranteed for 15 years. Profits may be transferred and indemnities paid in the event of nationalization. In the case of foreign firms installed in Vietnam all capital may remain in foreign hands if goods are produced for export only; otherwise the Vietnamese Government will retain 51% of shares.

Trade between Vietnam and UK (British Department of Trade returns, in £1,000 sterling):

	1980	1981	1982	1983
Imports to UK	70	130	133	603
Exports and re-exports from UK	15,203	1,180	876	951

COMMUNICATIONS

Roads. In 1973 there were about 9,500 km of roads in the North. In 1970 there were 20,905 km of roads in the South. Of these, 5,908 km were asphalted.

Railways. 'Project Reunification', the rebuilding of the Hanoi–Ho Chi Minh City railway, is a major part of the new authorities' programme to repair and extend all communications systems and link them with the North. The Da Nang–Hue railway was reopened in 1975. Important sections of railway have been reconstructed rapidly since the cessation of hostilities in 1975. The systems total 2,600 km.

Aviation. Civil Aviation of Vietnam operates internal services from Hanoi to Ho Chi Minh City, Cao Bang, Na Son and Dien Bien, Vinh and Hue, and from Ho Chi Minh City to Ban Me Thuot and Da Nang, Can Tho, Con Son Island and Quan Long. Aeroflot (USSR) operate regular services from Ho Chi Min City to Moscow and from Hanoi to Moscow, Rangoon and Vientiane, Interflug (German Dem. Rep.) to Berlin, Moscow and Dacca and Air France to Paris.

Shipping. The major ports are Haiphong, which can handle ships of 10,000 tons, Ho Chi Minh City and Da Nang, and there are ports at Hong Gai and Haiphong Ben Thuy. There are regular services to Hong Kong, Singapore, Kampuchea and Japan. In 1953 there were 830 km of navigable waterways in the North and, in 1971, 4,783 km in the South.

Cargo is handled by the Vietnam Ocean Shipping Agency; other matters by the Vietnam Foreign Trade Transport Corporation.

Post and Broadcasting. In 1966 there were 1·4m. radios. There were 46,509 telephones in the South in 1974. There were 2m. TV sets in 1980.

Cinemas and theatres. 116 films were produced in 1980 (including 10 full-length). There were 145 theatres.

Newspapers and books. The Party daily is *Nhan Dan* ('The People') circulation, 1984: 300,000. The official daily in the South is *Giai Phong*. Two unofficial dailies, *Cong Giao Va Dan Toc* (Catholic) and *Tin Sang* (independent) are also published. 2,564 books were published in 1980 totalling 90·9m. copies.

JUSTICE, RELIGION, EDUCATION AND WELFARE

Justice. There are the Supreme People's Court, local people's courts and military courts. The president of the Supreme Court is responsible to the National Assembly, as is the Procurator-General, who heads the Supreme People's Office of Supervision and Control.

Religion. Taoism is the traditional religion but Buddhism is widespread. At a Conference for Buddhist Reunification in Nov. 1981, 9 sects adopted a charter for a new Buddhist church under the Council of Sangha. The Hoa Hao sect, associated with Buddhism, claimed 1·5m. adherents in 1976. Caodaism, a synthesis of Christianity, Buddhism and Confucianism founded in 1926, has some 2m. followers. There are some 3m. Roman Catholics headed by Cardinal Trinh Van Can, Archbishop of Hanoi and 13 bishops.

Education. Primary education consists of a 10-year course divided into 3 levels of 4, 3 and 3 years respectively. Numbers of pupils and students in 1980–81: nurseries, 2·66m.; primary schools, 12·1m.; complementary education, 2·19m.; vocational secondary education, 130,000. In 1980–81 there were 92,913 nurseries. There were 11,400 schools and 280 vocational secondary schools, with 357,000 and 13,000 teachers respectively.

In 1980–81 there were 83 institutions of higher education (including 3 universities: (Hanoi, Ho Chi Minh City, Central Highlands University at Ban Me Thuot), 13 industrial colleges, 7 agricultural colleges, 5 economics colleges, 9 teacher-training colleges, 7 medical schools and 3 art schools, in all with 16,000 teachers and 159,000 students. In 1981 there were 5,000 Vietnamese studying in the USSR.

Health. In 1975 there were 1,996 hospitals and dispensaries and 93 sanatoria. There were some 13,300 doctors and dentists in 1980 and 197,000 hospital beds.

DIPLOMATIC REPRESENTATIVES

Of Vietnam in Great Britain (12–14 Victoria Rd, London, W8)
Ambassador: Dang Nghiem Bai (accredited 5 Nov. 1982).

Of Great Britain in Vietnam (16 Pho Ly Thuong Kiet, Hanoi)
Ambassador: M. E. Pike.

Of Vietnam to the United Nations
Ambassador: Hoang Bich Son.

Books of Reference

Chen, J. H.-M., *Vietnam: A Comprehensive Bibliography.* London, 1973
Duiker, W. J., *The Communist Road to Power in Vietnam.* Boulder, 1981
Féray, P.-R., *Le Vietnam au Vingtième Siècle.* Paris, 1979
Goodman, A. E., *The Lost Peace: America's Search for a Negotiated Settlement of the Vietnam War.* Stanford Univ. Press, 1978
Harrison, J. P., *The Endless War: Fifty Years of Struggle in Vietnam.* New York, 1982
Higgins, H., *Vietnam.* 2nd ed. London, 1982
Hodgkin, T., *Vietnam: The Revolutionary Path:* London, 1981
Le Thanh Khoi, *Socialisme et Développement au Vietnam.* Paris, 1978
Le Van Hung, *Vietnamese–English Dictionary.* Paris, 1955
Lewy, G., *America in Vietnam.* OUP, 1979
Leitenberg, M., and Burns, R. D., *War in Vietnam.* 2nd ed. Oxford and Santa Barbara, 1982
Nguyen Tien Hung, C., *Economic Developments of Socialist Vietnam, 1955–80.* New York, 1977
Nguyen Van Canh, *Vietnam under Communism, 1975–1982.* Stanford Univ. Press, 1983
Popkin, S. L., *The Rational Peasant: The Political Economy of Rural Society in Vietnam.* Berkeley, 1979
Viet Tran, *J'ai Choisi l'Exil.* Paris, 1979
Voronin, A. S. and Ognetov, I. A. *Sotsialisticheskaia Respublika V'etnam: Spravochnik.* (2nd ed). Moscow, 1981

BRITISH VIRGIN ISLANDS

Capital: Road Town
Population: 12,034 (1980)

HISTORY. The Virgin Islands were discovered by Colombus on his second voyage in 1493. The British Virgin Islands were first settled by the Dutch in 1648 and taken over in 1666 by a group of English planters.

AREA AND POPULATION. The British Virgin Islands form the eastern extremity of the Greater Antilles and, exclusive of small rocks and reefs, number 36, of which 16 are inhabited. The largest are Tortola (1980 population, 9,322), Virgin Gorda (1,443), Anegada (169) and Jost Van Dyke (136). Other islands in the group have a total population of 82; Marine population, 220; Institutional population, 662. Total area about 59 sq. miles (130 sq. km); population (1980), 12,034. Road Town, on the south-east of Tortola, is a port of entry; population, approximately 3,976.

CLIMATE. A pleasantly healthy sub-tropical climate with summer temperatures lowered by sea breezes. Nights are cool and rainfall averages 50″ (1,250 mm).

CONSTITUTION AND GOVERNMENT. The Governor is responsible for defence and internal security, external affairs, the public service, and the courts. The Executive Council consists of the Governor, 1 *ex-officio* member who is the Attorney-General and 4 ministers in the Legislature. The Legislative Council consists of 1 *ex-officio* member who is the Attorney-General and 9 elected members, one of whom is the Chief Minister and Minister of Finance; the Speaker is elected from outside the Council.

Governor: David Robert Barwick, CBE, QC.
Chief Minister: H. Lavity Stoutt.
Flag: The British Blue Ensign with the arms of the Territory in the fly.

ECONOMY

Planning. The Peebles Hospital extension and the Virgin Gorda primary school have been formally opened, work on Road Town Primary School was completed and it was officially opened on 2 Oct. 1983, and there are continuing Youth and Community Development projects. Work on the Slaney Point Sewerage outfall was completed and it was formally opened on 16 Aug. 1983. Phase II of the West End Harbour Extension Development was also completed and it was officially opened on 22 Sept. 1983, and the new Police Building on Virgin Gorda and the new Administration Building on Jost Van Dyke have been formally opened.

Budget. In 1983 revenue (estimate) was US$17,447,000 Capital expenditure (estimate) was US$16,670,063.

Currency. The unit of currency is the US dollar.

Banking. Barclays Bank International, the First Pennsylvania Bank, the Bank of Nova Scotia and the Chase Manhattan Bank have branches in the islands. There are also a large number of Trust Companies.

INDUSTRY AND TRADE

Industry. Agricultural production is now very limited with the chief products being livestock (including poultry), fish, fruit and vegetables. The export trade is carried on almost entirely with the Virgin Islands of the USA. The main industry is tourism and related activities, notably construction.

Livestock (1982): Cattle, 3,000; pigs, 3,000; sheep, 8,000; goats, 13,000.

Trade. In 1980 imports were US$36m. and exports US$1,087,000.

Tourism. There were 155,715 visitors in 1982.

COMMUNICATIONS

Roads. There were (1983) over 66 miles of roads and 3,000 licensed vehicles.

Aviation. Beef Island Airport, about 16 km from Road Town, is capable of receiving 48-seat turbo-prop aircraft. Air BVI operates internal services and external flights to the USVI, St Kitts, Antigua and Puerto Rico. Also, operating services to the BVI are Coral Air, Crown Air and LIAT.

Shipping. There are services to Europe and the USA, and daily services by motor launches to the US Virgin Islands.

Post and Broadcasting. There were (1983) over 2,000 telephones, and an external telephone service links Tortola with Bermuda and the rest of the world, and cable communications also exist to all parts of the world. Radio ZBVI transmits 10,000 watts and has stand-by transmitting facilities of 1,000 watts. Cable and Wireless, also, operates reception of approximately 7 television channels plus a number of FM stereo broadcasting stations.

RELIGION, EDUCATION AND WELFARE

Religion. There are Anglican, Methodist, Seventh-Day Adventist, Roman Catholic and Baptist Churches in the Territory. The Church of God is also represented.

Education. Primary education is provided in 16 government schools, one with a secondary division, 1 secondary school and 9 private schools. Total number of pupils (Dec. 1980) 2,748.

Secondary education to the GCE level and Caribbean Examination Council level is provided at the B.V.I. High School. Total pupils in Dec. 1980, 791.

In 1983 the total number of teachers in all the schools was 198.

Health. In 1983 there were 10 doctors and more than 50 hospital beds. Expenditure, 1983 was US$1,950,100.

Books of Reference

Dookhan, I., *A History of the British Virgin Islands.* Epping, 1975
Elkan, W., and Morley, R., *Employment in a Tourist Economy, British Virgin Islands*
Harrigan, N., and Varlack, P., *British Virgin Islands: A Chronology*

Library: Public Library, Road Town. *Librarian:* Mrs Verna Penn-Mall, MLS, ALA.

WESTERN SAMOA

Capital: Apia
Population: 156,349 (1981)
GNP per capita: US$350 (1976)

Samoa i Sisifo

HISTORY. Western Samoa, a former German protectorate (1900 to the First World War), was administered by New Zealand from 1920 to 1961, at first under a League of Nations Mandate and since 1946 under a United Nations Trusteeship Agreement. In May 1961 a plebiscite held under the supervision of the United Nations on the basis of universal adult suffrage voted overwhelmingly in favour of independence as from 1 Jan. 1962, on the basis of the Constitution, which a Constitutional Convention had adopted in Aug. 1960. In Oct. 1961 the General Assembly of the United Nations passed a resolution to terminate the trusteeship agreement as from 1 Jan. 1962, on which date Western Samoa became an independent sovereign state.

Under a treaty of friendship signed on 1 Aug. 1962 New Zealand acts, at the request of Western Samoa, as the official channel of communication between the Samoan Government and other governments and international organizations outside the Pacific islands area. Liaison is maintained by the New Zealand High Commissioner in Apia, who is the only diplomatic representative accredited to the Government of Western Samoa.

AREA AND POPULATION. Western Samoa lies between 13° and 15° S. lat. and 171° and 173° W. long. It comprises the two large islands of Savai'i and Upolu, the small islands of Manono and Apolima, and several uninhabited islets lying off the coast. The total land area is 1,093 sq. miles (2,830·8 sq. km), of which 659·4 sq. miles (1,707·8 sq. km) are in Savai'i, and 431·5 sq. miles (1,117·6 sq. km) in Upolu; other islands, 2·1 sq. miles (5·4 sq. km). The islands are of volcanic origin, and the coasts are surrounded by coral reefs. Rugged mountain ranges form the core of both main islands and rise to 3,608 ft in Upolu and 6,094 ft in Savai'i. The large area laid waste by lava-flows in Savai'i is a primary cause of that island supporting less than one-third of the population of the islands despite its greater size than Upolu.

The population at the 1981 census was 156,349, of whom (1976) 109,765 were in Upolu (including Manono and Apolima) and 42,218 in Savai'i. The capital and chief port is Apia in Upolu (population 36,000 in 1981).

CLIMATE. A tropical marine climate, with cooler conditions from May to Nov. and a rainy season from Dec. to April. The rainfall is unevenly distributed, with south and east coasts having the greater quantities. Average annual rainfall is about 100″ (2,500 mm) in the drier areas. Apia. Jan. 80°F (26·7°C), July 78°F (25·6°C). Annual rainfall 112″ (2,800 mm).

CONSTITUTION AND GOVERNMENT. The Constitution provides for a Head of State known as 'Ao o le Malo', which position from 1 Jan. 1962 was held jointly by the representatives of the two royal lines of Tuiaana/Tuiatua and Malietoa. On the death of HH Tupua Tamasese Mea'ole, CBE, on 5 April 1963, HH Malietoa Tanumafili II, CBE, became, as provided by the constitution, the sole Head of State for life. Future Heads of State will be elected by the Legislative Assembly and hold office for 5-year terms.

The executive power is vested in the Head of State, who appoints the Prime Minister and, on the Prime Minister's advice, the 8 Ministers to form the Cabinet which has general direction and control of the executive Government.

The Legislative Assembly has 45 members elected from territorial constituencies on a franchise confined to matais or chiefs (of whom there are about 11,000) and 2 members elected on universal adult suffrage from the individual voters roll, which has replaced the old European roll (approximately 1,350 in 1971). One Member is elected as Speaker.

The Constitution also provides for a Council of Deputies. It may have 3 members.

The official languages are English and Samoan.

Head of State: HH Malietoa Tanumafili II, CBE.
Prime Minister: Tofilau Eti Alesana.
National flag: Red with a blue quarter bearing 5 white stars of the Southern Cross.

INTERNATIONAL RELATIONS

Membership. Western Samoa is a member of UN, the Commonwealth and is an ACP state of EEC.

ECONOMY

Budget. In 1983 budgeted revenue was $WS41·3m.; expenditure, $WS69·2m.

Currency. The Western Samoa currency is the *talà* (dollar). In March 1984, £1 = 1·485; US$1 = 1·581.

Banking. In 1959 the Bank of Western Samoa was established with a capital of $WS500,000, of which $WS275,000 was subscribed by the Bank of New Zealand and $WS225,000 by the Government of Western Samoa. In 1977 the Pacific Commercial Bank was established jointly by Australia's Bank of New South Wales and the Bank of Hawaii.

NATURAL RESOURCES

Agriculture. The main products are coconut oil, cocoa, taro, copra and bananas.

Fisheries. The total catch (1983) was 3,150 tonnes, valued at $WS5·1m.

INDUSTRY AND TRADE

Industry. Some industrial activity is being developed associated with agricultural products and forestry.

Commerce. In 1980, imports were valued at $WS57,438,000 and exports at $WS15,828,000. Principal exports were copra (25,317 tons; $WS8,404,700), cocoa (1,503 tons; $WS3,012,600), taro (86,085 cases, $WS1,048,300), timber (1,287,900 sq. ft; $WS324,400), and bananas (70,427 cases; $WS439,700). Chief imports in 1980 included food and live animals ($WS12,352,100), manufactured goods ($WS13,066,700) and machinery and transport equipment ($WS11,708,500) and mineral fuels, lubricants and other materials ($WS9,561,000).

Total trade between Western Samoa and UK (British Department of Trade returns, in £1,000 sterling):

	1978	1979	1980	1981	1982	1983
Imports to UK	567	837	572	90	107	156
Exports and re-exports from UK	719	619	710	431	285	468

Tourism. There were 42,010 visitors in 1978.

COMMUNICATIONS

Roads (1980). Western Samoa has over 396 km of main roads, 403 km of town and secondary roads and 1,243 km of plantation roads fit for light traffic.

A major road development programme has been under way including an all weather coastal road and a cross-island road, both for Upolu. A rural access roads programme to improve access to plantations is also underway. In 1980 there were 1,583 passenger cars and 2,503 commercial vehicles.

Aviation. Western Samoa is linked by daily air service with American Samoa, which is on the route of the weekly New Zealand–Tahiti and New Zealand–Honolulu air services, with connexions to Fiji, Australia, USA and Europe. There are also services throughout the week to and from Tonga, Fiji, Nauru, the Cook Islands and New Zealand. Internal services link Upolu and Savai'i.

Shipping. Western Samoa is linked to Japan, USA, Europe, Fiji, Australia and New Zealand by regular shipping services. The newly established Pacific Forum Shipping Line has its headquarters in Apia.

Post and Broadcasting. There is a radio communication station at Apia. Radio telephone service connects Western Samoa with American Samoa, Fiji, New Zealand, Australia, Canada, USA and UK. Telephone subscribers numbered 5,857 in 1982.

Cinemas. In 1977 there were 10 cinemas with a seating capacity of 7,168.

Newspapers. In 1983, there were 4 weeklies, circulation 12,000 and 2 monthlies (8,000); all were in Samoan and English.

EDUCATION AND WELFARE

Education. In 1980 there were 158 primary, (including intermediate), 38 secondary, 3 secondary vocational and 5 higher education vocational schools, and 2 teacher-training colleges with a total of 55,025 students.

Health. In 1980 there were 30 hospitals (674 beds) and 34 Samoan doctors.

DIPLOMATIC REPRESENTATIVES

Of Great Britain in Western Samoa
High Commissioner: Sir Richard Stratton, KCMG (resides in Wellington, New Zealand).

Of Western Samoa in the USA and also to the United Nations
Ambassador: Maiava Iulai Toma.

Books of Reference

Statistical Year-Book. Annual
Economic Prospects. 1978
The Economy of Western Samoa. 1968
Clare, B. L., *A Review of Social, Labour and Economic Conditions in Western Samoa.* Apia, 1962, reprinted 1963.—*The Parliament of Western Samoa.* Rev. ed. Apia, 1964
Fox, J. W. (ed.), *Western Samoa.* Univ. of Auckland, 1963
Milner, G. B., *Samoan–English, English–Samoan Dictionary.* OUP, 1965

YEMEN ARAB REPUBLIC

Capital: San'a
Population: 7·7m. (1980)
GNP per capita: US$460 (1980)

al Jamhuriya al Arabiya al Yamaniya

HISTORY. On the death of the Iman Ahmad on 18 Sept. 1962, army officers seized power on 26–27 Sept., declared his son, Saif Al-Islam Al-Badr (Iman Mansur Billah Muhammad), deposed and proclaimed a republic. The republican régime was supported by Egyptian troops, whereas the royalist tribes received aid from Saudi Arabia. On 24 Aug. 1965 President Nasser and King Faisal signed an agreement according to which the two powers are to support a plebiscite to determine the future of the Yemen; a conference of republican and royalist delegates met at Haradh on 23 Nov. 1965, but no plebiscite was agreed upon. At a meeting of the Arab heads of state in Aug. 1967 the President and the King agreed upon disengaging themselves from the civil war in Yemen. At the time there were still about 50,000 Egyptian troops in the country, holding San'a, Ta'iz, Hodeida and the plains, whereas the mountains were in the hands of the royalist tribes. By the end of 1967 the Egyptians had withdrawn.

AREA AND POPULATION. In the north the boundary between the Yemen and Saudi Arabia has been defined by the Treaty of Taif concluded in June 1934. This frontier starts from the sea at a point some 5 or 10 miles north of Maidi and runs due east inland until it reaches the hills some 30 miles from the coast, whence it runs northwards for approximately 50 miles so as to leave the Sa'da Basin within the Yemen. Thence it runs in an easterly and south-easterly direction until it reaches the desert area near Nejran. The area is about 73,300 sq. miles (195,000 sq. km) with a population of 7,701,893, census 1980. There were 1,395,123 citizens working abroad mainly in Saudi Arabia and the United Arab Emirates not included in the census total. The capital is San'a with a population of 277,817.

The most important towns are the port of Hodeida (population, 126,386), and Ta'iz (119,572); other towns are Ibb, Yerim, Dhamar and the ports of Mokha and Loheiya.

CONSTITUTION AND GOVERNMENT. On 31 Oct. 1962, 13 April 1963, 17 April 1964, 9 May 1965 the revolutionary council issued 'interim' constitutions.

In Feb. 1979 fighting started between Yemen Arab Republic and the People's Democratic Republic of Yemen. A ceasefire was established in March and an agreement to unite the 2 countries was reached on 31 March 1979 and discussions to this end continued during 1982.

On 6 Feb. 1978 a 99-man (increased to 159 in 1979) People's Constituent Assembly was established. A General People's Congress met in 1982 composed of 1,000 members (700 elected).

President: Lieut.-Col. Ali Abdullah Saleh.
Prime Minister: Dr Abdel Karim Ali al-Iryani.
National flag: Three horizontal stripes of red, white, black, with a green star in the centre.

DEFENCE. Military service for 3 years is compulsory.

Army. The Army consists of 5 armoured, 1 mechanized, 9 infantry, 1 parachute and 3 artillery brigades, 1 central guard force and 3 anti-aircraft artillery and 2 air defence battalions. Equipment includes 150 T-34, 500 T-54/-55 and 64 M-60 main battle tanks. Strength (1984) 20,000.

Navy. The flotilla consists of 2 fast missile craft, 4 fast attack craft, 4 patrol craft and 4 small but very fast (50-knot) torpedo-boats, 2 inshore minehunters, 12 small coastal patrol boats and 2 landing craft (all 30 *ex*-Soviet). Personnel in 1984 numbered 600 officers and men.

Air Force. Built up with aid from both the USA and USSR, as well as Saudi Arabia, the Air Force is believed to be receiving many new Soviet aircraft. Current equipment includes 20 Su-22 fighter-bombers, 40 MiG-21 fighters, 12 MiG-17s, 14 F-5E/Bs, a total of 11 Il-14, C-47, An-24/26, C-130 Hercules and Skyvan transports, Mi-8 and Agusta-Bell JetRanger and 212 helicopters. Personnel (1983) about 1,500.

INTERNATIONAL RELATIONS

Membership. The Yemen Arab Republic is a member of UN and the Arab League.

ECONOMY

Planning. A development plan (1982–86) envisages expenditure of 27,400m. riyals.

Budget. The budget for 1981–82 had estimated revenue, 5,282m. riyal; estimated expenditure, 8,470m. riyal.

Currency. The currency is the paper *riyal* of 100 rial. In March 1984, 6·84 *riyal* = £1 and 5·05 *riyal* = US$1.

NATURAL RESOURCES

Minerals. The only commercial mineral being exploited is salt and (1981) production was 64,000 tons. Reserves (estimate) 25m. tonnes.

Agriculture. Wherever water-supply allows, and in general throughout the south-western part of the country, millet (*dhurra*) is grown as a subsistence crop. The traditional cultivation of coffee (no longer exported through Mokha) continues but is giving place to that of qat (*cathula edulis*), a narcotic shrub. Cotton (production, 1982, 5,000 tonnes) is grown in the Tihama, the coastal belt, round Bait al Faqih and Zabid (seat of a medieval university). Fruit is plentiful, especially fine grapes from the San'a district.

Livestock (1982): Cattle, 950,000; camels, 107,000; sheep, 3·2m.; goats, 7·5m.; poultry, 3·5m.

Fisheries. Total catch (1980) 17,000 tonnes.

INDUSTRY AND TRADE

Industry. There is very little industry. In 1970 there were over 60 industrial enterprises employing 4,750. The largest is a textile factory at San'a. A cement factory with a capacity of 100,000 tonnes a year exists.

Commerce. Imports totalled 8,500m. riyals in 1980, the largest items being food and live animals. Exports totalled 103m. in 1980.

Total trade between Yemen Arab Republic and UK (British Department of Trade returns, in £1,000 sterling):

	1979	1980	1981	1982	1983
Imports to UK	2,305	469	966	1,340	1,857
Exports and re-exports from UK	49,169	36,428	31,599	52,593	56,315

COMMUNICATIONS

Roads. There were (1981) 19,223 km of roads of which 1,924 are asphalted.

Aviation. There are 3 international airports: San'a, Ta'iz and Hodeida.

Shipping. Hodeida, Mokha, Salif and Loheiya are the 4 main ports.

Post and Broadcasting. There were about 90,350 telephones in 1981. In 1983 there were 25,000 television and 110,000 radio receivers.

EDUCATION AND WELFARE

Education. There were (1980–81) 418,263 pupils at primary schools, 25,037 at intermediate, and 9,895 at higher secondary schools, and 2,450 at teacher-training establishments. In 1980–81 the University of San'a (founded in 1974) had 4,220 students.

Health. In 1983 there were 60 hospitals and health centres with 4,000 beds.

DIPLOMATIC REPRESENTATIVES

Of Yemen Arab Republic in Great Britain (41 South St., London, W1Y 5PD)
Ambassador: Ahmed Daifellah Al-Azeib (accredited 16 Oct. 1982).

Of Great Britain in Yemen Arab Republic (23/25 Qasr al Jumhuri St., San'a)
Ambassador: J. F. Walker, CMG, MBE.

Of Yemen Arab Republic in the USA (600 New Hampshire Ave., NW, Washington, D.C., 20037)
Ambassador: Mohamad A. Al-Eryani.

Of the USA in Yemen Arab Republic (P.O. Box 1088, San'a)
Ambassador: David E. Zweifel.

Of Yemen Arab Republic to the United Nations
Ambassador: Muhammad Abdul Aziz Sallam.

Books of Reference

Bidwell, R., *The Two Yemens.* Boulder and London, 1983
Heyworth-Dunne, G. E., *Al-Yemen. Social, Political and Economic Survey.* Cairo, 1952
Ingrams, H., *The Yemen.* London, 1963
Macro, E., *Yemen and the Western World, 1571–1964.* London, 1967
Peterson, J. E., *Yemen: The Search for a Modern State.* London, 1982
Smith, R., *The Yemens.* [Bibliography] Oxford and Santa Barbara, 1984
Stookey, R. W., *Yemen: The Politics of the Yemen Arab Republic.* Boulder, 1978

THE PEOPLE'S DEMOCRATIC REPUBLIC OF YEMEN

Capital: Aden
Population: 2m. (1981)
GNP per capita: US$420 (1980)

Jumhurijah al-Yemen
al Dimuqratiyah
al Sha'abijah—
Southern Yemen

HISTORY. Between Aug. and Oct. 1967 the 17 sultanates of the Federation of South Arabia (*see* map in the STATESMAN'S YEAR-BOOK, 1965–66) were overrun by the forces of the National Liberation Front (NLF). The rulers were deposed, resigned or fled. At the same time the rival organization of FLOSY (Front for the Liberation of Occupied South Yemen) fought a civil war against NLF and harassed the British forces and civilians in Aden. In Nov. the UAR withdrew its support from FLOSY, and with the backing of the Army the NLF took over throughout the country.

The last British troops left Aden on 29 Nov., and on 30 Nov. the Southern Yemen People's Republic was proclaimed and the name subsequently changed to the People's Democratic Republic of Yemen.

AREA AND POPULATION. The People's Democratic Republic of Yemen is bounded north by Yemen Arab Republic and Saudi Arabia, east by Oman, south by the Gulf of Aden and west by the Yemen Arab Republic. The Republic covers an area of approximately 111,074 sq. miles (287,682 sq. km). The population was (estimate, 1981) 2,030,000. The main towns are Aden (capital) (population, 264,326), including Shaikh Othman (30,000), Mukalla, (100,000) and Maalla (44,626).

The island of **Kamaran** in the Red Sea (area 70 sq. miles) was in British occupation from 1915 to 1967, when the inhabitants opted in favour of remaining with the Republic but Yemen Arab Republic occupied it in 1972.

The island of **Perim** was first occupied by the French in 1738. In 1799 the British took formal possession but evacuated the island the same year. It was re-occupied by the British in Jan. 1851 and was later used as a coaling station. In Nov. 1967 the inhabitants opted in favour of remaining with the Republic.

The island of **Socotra** lying to the east of the Horn of Africa in the Arabian sea (area 1,400 sq. miles) was formerly part of the Sultanate of Qishn and Socotra and became part of the Republic in 1967.

CLIMATE. A desert climate prevails, modified in parts by altitude, which affects temperatures by up to 12°C, as well as rainfall, which is very low in coastal areas. Aden. Jan. 75°F (24°C), July 90°F (32°C). Annual rainfall 1·8″ (46 mm).

CONSTITUTION AND GOVERNMENT

An amended Constitution was approved by the Supreme People's Council on 31 Oct. 1978.

Meetings took place during 1981–83 between President Mohammed and the President Saleh of the Yemen Arabic Republic, to discuss further steps towards unification.

Cabinet at Jan. 1984 was composed as follows:

Secretary General of the Yemen Socialist Party, Chairman of the Presidium of the Supreme People's Council and Prime Minister: Ali Nasser Mohammed. *First Deputy Prime Minister and Minister for Local Government:* Brig. Ali Ahmed Nasser Antar. *Deputy Prime Minister and Minister of Fisheries:* Anis Hassan Yayha. *Deputy Prime Minister:* Ali Abdul Ar-razzaq Ba Dhib. *Defence:* Brig. Saleh Musleh Qassam. *Chairman of the State Security Committee:* Salih Munassanar As-Siyayli. *Foreign Affairs:* Salim Saleh Mohammed. *Interior:* Col. Mohammed Abdullah al-Battani. *Minister of State for the Council of Ministers:* Abdu Aziz Abdul Wali. *Finance:* Mahmood Said Madhi. *Health:* Dr Abdul Aziz Addali. *Constructions:* Haidar Abubaker Al Attas. *Labour and Civil Service:* Nasr Nasser Ali. *Culture and Tourism:* Rashid Mohammed Thabit. *Education:* Hassan Ahmed Asalami. *Communications:* Abdulla Mohammed Aziz. *Agriculture:* Mohammed Suleiman Nasser. *Industry:* Abdul Kader Bagamal. *Justice:* Khaled Fadhal Mansour. *Trade and Supply:* Ahmed Obeid al Fadhli. *Planning:* Dr Farag Bin Ghanem. *Housing:* Ahmed Mohammed Alqatabi.

National flag. Three horizontal stripes of red, white, black, with a blue triangle based on the hoist bearing a red star.

DEFENCE. Military service for 2 years is compulsory.

Army. The Army comprises 1 armoured, 2 mechanized, 9 infantry, 1 artillery, 1 rocket and 1 surface-to-surface missile brigades and 10 artillery battalions. Equipment includes 450 T-54/-55/-62 main battle tanks. Strength (1984) about 22,000.

Navy. The Navy comprises 7 fast missile craft, 2 fast torpedo-boats, 2 fast attack craft, 2 anti-submarine patrol vessels, 1 gunboat, 1 fleet minesweeper, 1 tank landing ship, 3 medium landing ships and 3 minor landing craft, all transferred from the Soviet Navy and 3 *ex*-British inshore minesweepers and 6 very small British-built launches. Personnel in 1984 totalled 1,000 officers and men.

Air Force. Formed in 1967, the Air Force is now equipped mainly with aircraft of Soviet design. It has received about 50 MiG-21 fighters, 35 MiG-17 fighter-bombers, a few Il-28 twin-jet bombers, 30 Su-22 attack aircraft, 15 Mi-24 gunship helicopters, 4 An-24 twin-turboprop transports, about 25 L-39 jet trainers and about 6 Mi-8 and 6 Mi-4 helicopters. Personnel about 3,000.

INTERNATIONAL RELATIONS

Membership. The People's Democratic Republic of Yemen is a member of UN and the Arab League.

ECONOMY

Planning. The revised 5-year plan (1980–85) envisaged expenditure of 425m. dinars.

Budget. The budget of the Republic (in 1m. Yemeni dinars) for 1980–81 envisaged revenue at 86 and expenditure at 96.

Currency. The currency is the South Yemen *dinar* and is divided into 1,000 *fils*. Coins: 50, 25, 5, 1 *fils*; notes: 10, 5 and 1 *dinar*, 500 and 250 *fils*. In March 1984, £1 = 0.509 *dinars*; US$1 = 0·343 *dinars*.

Banking. The leading bank is the National Bank of Yemen. All foreign banks have been nationalized.

ENERGY AND NATURAL RESOURCES

Electricity. Production (1979) 245m. kwh.

Agriculture. Agriculture is the main occupation of the people. This is largely of a subsistence nature, sorghum, sesame and millet being the chief crops, and wheat and barley widely grown at the higher elevations. Of increasing importance, however, are the cash crops which have been developed since the Second World War, by far the most important of which is the Abyan long-staple cotton, now the country's major export.

Owing to paucity of rainfall, cultivation is largely confined to fertile valleys and flood plains on silt, built up and irrigated in the traditional manner. These traditional methods are being augmented and replaced by the use of modern earth moving machinery and pumps. Irrigation schemes with permanent installations are in progress. Production (1982 in 1,000 tonnes): Millet, 60; wheat, 15; cotton lint, 4; cotton seed, 8; sesame, 4; barley, 2.

Livestock (1982): Cattle, 120,000; sheep, 1·01m.; goats, 1·35m.; poultry, 1·58m.

Fisheries. There is a thriving fisheries industry, fish being the Republic's major export after cotton. Catch (1980) 97,000 tonnes.

INDUSTRY AND TRADE

Industry. Light industry is being established and paint, match and textile factories are in production.

Commerce. Trade is mainly transhipment and entrepôt, Aden serving as a centre of distribution to and from neighbouring territories. Transit trade is mainly in cotton piece-goods, grains, coffee, hides and skins, and cheap consumer goods.

In 1980 imports totalled 527m. dinar; exports and re-exports, 269m. dinar.

Total trade between Republic of Yemen and UK (British Department of Trade returns, in £1,000 sterling):

	1979	1980	1981	1982	1983
Imports to UK	2,713	5,685	7,272	26,631	10,627
Exports and re-exports from UK	18,920	25,425	31,480	35,577	36,673

COMMUNICATIONS

Roads. There are 1,150 miles of roads. Registered motor vehicles in 1980 numbered 33,000.

Aviation. Nine airlines operate scheduled services: Alyemda, Air-India, Ethiopian Airlines, Middle East Airlines, Yemen Airlines, Aeroflot, Saudi Airlines, Kuwait Airways, and Air Djibouti.

Shipping. Because of its favourable geographical position and its efficient service to ships, Aden used to be one of the busiest oil-bunkering ports in the world, handling some 550 ships a month.

Post and Broadcasting. The automatic telephone system provided service to about 9,876 subscribers in 1973.

In 1983 there were 150,000 radio and 26,000 television receivers.

Cinemas (1971). There were 19 cinemas with a seating capacity of about 20,000.

JUSTICE, RELIGION, EDUCATION AND WELFARE

Justice. There is a Supreme Court and Magistrates' Courts. In some areas Moslem and local Common Law are administered.

Religion. The majority of the population is Moslem. There are small numbers of Christians and Hindus.

Education. There were (1978, estimate) 281,900 primary school pupils and 39,300 secondary school pupils.

Welfare. There were (1979) 44 hospitals with 2,700 beds and about 250 doctors.

DIPLOMATIC REPRESENTATIVES

Of the People's Democratic Republic of Yemen in Great Britain (57 Cromwell Rd., London, SW7 2ED)

Ambassador: Salah Abdulla Muthana (accredited 22 Nov. 1983).

Of Great Britain in the People's Democratic Republic of Yemen (28 Shara Ho Chi Minh, Khormaksar, Aden)
Ambassador: Peter Williams.

Of the People's Democratic Republic of Yemen to the United Nations
Ambassador: Abdalla Saleh Ashtal.

The US Embassy in Aden was closed on 26 Oct. 1969 and UK acts as the protective power.

Books of Reference

Hickinbotham, Sir T., *Aden.* London, 1959
Ingrams, H., *Arabia and the Isles.* London
Smith, R., *The Yemens.* [Bibliography] Oxford and Santa Barbara, 1984
Stookey, R. W., *South Yemen: A Marxist Republic in Arabia.* Boulder and London, 1982
Thesiger, W., *Arabian Sands.* London, 1959

YUGOSLAVIA

Capital: Belgrade
Population: 22·85m. (1983)
GNP per capita: US$2,620 (1980)

Socijalistička Federativna Republika Jugoslavija— Socialist Federal Republic of Yugoslavia

HISTORY. In 1917 the Yugoslav Committee in London drew up the Pact of Corfu, which proclaimed that all Yugoslavs would unite after the first world war to form a kingdom under the Serbian royal house. The Kingdom of Serbs, Croats and Slovenes was proclaimed on 1 Dec. 1918. In 1929 the name was changed to Yugoslavia. During the Second World War Tito's partisans set up a provisional government (AVNOJ) which was the basis of a Constituent Assembly after the war. On 29 Nov. 1945 Yugoslavia was proclaimed a republic.

The peace treaty with Italy, signed in Paris on 10 Feb. 1947, stipulated the cession to Yugoslavia of the greater part of the Italian province of Venezia Giulia, the commune of Zara and the island of Pelagosa and the adjacent islets.

By an agreement of 10 Nov. 1975 the city of Trieste ('Zone A') was recognized as Italian and the Adriatic coastal portion of the former Free Territory of Trieste ('Zone B') as Yugoslav. A free industrial zone was set up in the Fernetici–Sezana region on both sides of the frontier.

AREA AND POPULATION. Yugoslavia is bounded in the north by Austria and Hungary, north-east by Romania, east by Bulgaria, south by Greece and west by Albania, the Adriatic Sea and Italy. The area is 225,804 sq. km. Population at the 1981 census: 22,427,585. Population by sex at the 1971 census: males, 10,077,282; females, 10,445,690. Estimate (1983) 22·85m.

The federal capital is Belgrade (Beograd). Population (1981) 1,407,073 and of other principal towns (B = Bosnia and Herzegovina; C = Croatia; K = Kosovo; Ma =Macedonia; Mo = Montenegro; Se = Serbia; Sl = Slovenia; V = Vojvodina):

Banja Luka (B)	183,618	Priština (K)	216,040
Bitolj (Ma)	137,835	Prizren (K)	134,526
Čačak (Se)	110,676	Rijeka (C)	193,044
Čakovec (C)	116,825	Šabac (Se)	119,669
Gostivar (Ma)	101,188	Sarajevo (B)	448,500
Kragujevac (Se)	164,823	Skopje (Ma)	506,547
Kraljevo (Se)	121,622	Slavonski Brod (C)	106,400
Kruševac (Se)	132,972	Smederevo (Se)	107,366
Kumanovo (Ma)	126,368	Split (C)	235,922
Leskovac (Se)	159,001	Subotica (V)	154,611
Ljubljana (Sl)	305,211	Tetovo (Ma)	162,414
Maribor (Sl)	185,699	Titograd (Mo)	132,290
Mostar (B)	110,377	Titova Mitrovica (K)	105,323
Niš (Se)	230,711	Tuzla (B)	121,717
Novi Sad (V)	257,685	Uroševac (K)	113,680
Osijek (C)	158,790	Zadar (C)	116,174
Pančevo (V)	123,791	Zagreb (C)	1,174,512
Peć (K)	111,071	Zenica (B)	132,733
Prijedor (B)	108,868	Zrenjanin (V)	139,300

Population (1981 census) by ethnic group was *(i)* the 6 'leading nations': Serbs, 8,140,507; Croats, 4,428,043; Moslems, 1,999,890; Slovenes, 1,753,571; Macedonians, 1,341,598; Montenegrins, 579,043; *(ii)* of the 18 other 'nationalities': Albanians, 1,730,878; Hungarians, 426,867. 1,219,024 persons declared themselves 'Yugoslavs' (i.e. not wanting to be listed with any minority). In 1984 about 600,000 nationals worked abroad.

Vital statistics for calendar years:

	Live births	Still-born	Deaths	Infantile deaths	Marriages	Divorces
1979	380,615	...	190,459	12,241	177,305	21,268
1980	382,120	2,675	197,361	12,012	171,439	22,583

The Yugoslav (*i.e.*, South Slav) languages proper are Slovene, Macedonian and Serbo-Croat, the latter having 2 variants (Serbian and Croatian) which are regarded as constituting one language. There are claims, largely politically-motivated, that Croatian is a separate language and Macedonian a dialect of Bulgarian. Macedonian is and Serbian may be written in the Cyrillic alphabet. There are also substantial Albanian and Hungarian-speaking minorities. Art. 246 of the Constitution lays down that 'The languages of the nations and nationalities and their alphabets shall be equal throughout the territory of Yugoslavia'. In practice Serbo-Croat serves as a *lingua franca* throughout the country.

CLIMATE. Most parts have a central European type of climate, with cold winters and hot summers, but the whole coast experiences a Mediterranean climate with mild, moist winters and hot, brilliantly sunny summers with less than average rainfall. Belgrade. Jan. 29°F (–1·5°C), July 72°F (22°C). Annual rainfall 24·4" (610 mm). Sarajevo. Jan. 31°F (–0·5°C), July 67°F (19·6°C). Annual rainfall 37·3" (932 mm). Šibenik. Jan. 45°F (7°C), July 78°F (25·5°C). Annual rainfall 32·5" (813 mm). Split. Jan. 47°F (8·5°C), July 80°F (26·5°C). Annual rainfall 28·1" (703 mm). Zagreb. Jan. 32°F (0°C), July 72°F (22°C). Annual rainfall 34·6" (865 mm).

CONSTITUTION AND GOVERNMENT. The Constitution passed on 31 Jan. 1946 declared the Federal Republic to be composed of 6 republics: Serbia, Croatia, Slovenia, Bosnia and Herzegovina, Macedonia and Montenegro.

On 13 Jan. 1953 a new Constitution (Fundamental Law) confirmed the management of all public affairs by the workers and their representatives (which was introduced in 1950) as the basis of the entire social, economic and political system of Yugoslavia.

The Constitution promulgated 7 April 1963 changed the name of the country into the Socialist Federal Republic of Yugoslavia, composed of the socialist republics of Bosnia and Herzegovina, Crna Gora (Montenegro), Croatia, Macedonia, Serbia and Slovenia (*i.e.*, now ranking in alphabetical order), and the 2 socialist autonomous provinces of Kosovo and Vojvodina within the framework of Serbia.

Under this Constitution, social self-government was exercised by the representative bodies of communes, districts, autonomous provinces, republics and the Federation and the rights to self-government and distribution of income proclaimed in 1953 were extended to those employed in public services. The former Council of Producers, in which only workers and employees engaged in economic production were represented, was replaced by Councils of Working Communities representing the working people employed in every field of social activity.

All the means of production and all natural resources are social property. Exceptions are peasants' holdings (up to 10 hectares of arable land) and handicrafts. Citizens may be owners of houses and dwellings for personal and family needs.

A new Constitution was proclaimed on 21 Feb. 1974. The political principle of this Constitution is the direct transfer of economic and political decision making power to the working people through the 'assembly system'. An assembly is defined (Art. 132) as 'a body of social self-management and the supreme organ of power within the framework of the rights and duties of its socio-political community'. Assemblies are based upon the work-place or community and take various forms depending upon the nature of employment. Art. 133 states, 'Working people in basic self-managing organizations and communities and in socio-political organizations shall form delegations for the purpose of the direct exercise of their rights, duties and responsibilities and of organized participation in the performance of the functions of the assemblies of the socio-political communities', and Art. 135, 'Candidates for members of delegations of basic self-managing organizations and communities shall be proposed and determined by the working people in these organizations and communities in the Socialist Alliance of the Working People ... or in trade union organizations'. At the apex of the assembly system is the federal legislature, the Assembly of the Socialist Federal Republic of Yugoslavia which has 2 Chambers: the Federal Chamber and the Chamber of Republics and Provinces.

The Federal Chamber consists of 30 delegates of self-managing organizations, communities and socio-political organizations from each Republic, and 20 delegates from each Autonomous Province. The Chamber of Republics and Provinces consists of 12 delegates from each Republican Assembly and of 8 delegates from each Provincial Assembly.

Every citizen over the age of 18 has the suffrage (16 if employed). The last elections were held from Jan. to April 1982.

The State Presidency is elected every 5 years. It has 9 members: 8 representatives of the Republics and Autonomous Provinces, and the President of the Presidium of the League of Communists *ex officio.* The annual President is head of state.

Membership of the state Presidency:

Bosnia and Herzegovina: Branko Mikulić; *Croatia:* Josip Vrhovec; *Macedonia:* Lazar Mojsov; *Montenegro:* Veselin Djuranović *(President until May 1985);* *Serbia:* Gen. Nikola Ljubičić; *Slovenia:* Stane Dolanc; *Kosovo:* Sinan Hasani; *Vojvodina:* Radovan Vlajković. The League of Communists had 2·2m. members in Jan. 1983. It is headed by a Presidium of its Central Committee led by Dragoslav Marković (till June 1984). *Secretary:* Nikola Stojanović (until June 1984). Other members of the Presidium: Dimce Belovski, Jure Bilić, Dušan Dragosavac, Kiro Hadži-Vasilev, Franjo Herljević, Milan Kučan, Petar Matić, Veljko Milatović, Miljan Radović, Mitja Ribičić, Nikola Stojanović, Ali Sukrija, Dobrivoje Vidić. There are also 9 *ex-officio* members.

President of the Assembly of the SFRY: Vojo Srzentić (elected May 1983).

The Federal Executive Council consists of 29 ministers. Members of the Council are elected in conformity with the principle of equal representation of the Republics with corresponding representation of Autonomous Provinces.

The President of the Council is elected by the Chambers of the Assembly of the SFRY at the proposal of the Presidency; Members, at the proposal of the candidate Chairman.

President of the Federal Executive Council (Prime Minister): Milka Planinc. *Vice-Presidents:* Zvone Dragan; Borislav Srebrić; Mijat Suković.

Federal Secretary Defence: Adm. Branko Mamula; *Finance:* Vlado Klemenčič; *Foreign Trade:* Milenko Bojanić; *Justice:* Borislav Krajina; *Information:* Mitko Calovski.

National flag: Three horizontal stripes of blue, white, red, with a large red, yellow-bordered star in the centre.

National anthem: Hej, Slaveni, jošte živi reč naših dedova—O Slavs, our ancestors' words still live.

DEFENCE. Military service for 15 months is compulsory. The General People's Defence Law of 1969 bases Yugoslavia's defence on the principle of a nation in arms ready to wage partisan war against any invader. The partisan Territorial Defence Force number about 3m.

Army. The Army is divided into 7 Military Regions and comprises 8 infantry divisions; 8 independent tank, 17 independent infantry, 1 mountain and 1 airborne brigades; 12 field artillery, 12 anti-aircraft, 6 anti-tank and 3 surface-to-air missile regiments. Equipment includes 1,240 T-34/-54/-55 and 60 M-47 main battle tanks. Strength (1983) 191,000 (including 140,000 conscripts), with a reserve of 500,000.

Navy. The Navy comprises 6 diesel powered patrol submarines, 2 midget (2-man) submarines, 2 new *ex*-Soviet frigates, 16 fast missile boats, 15 fast torpedo boats, 3 patrol vessels, 6 fast attack craft, 4 minehunters, 20 patrol boats, 10 inshore minesweepers, 20 river minesweepers, 1 tank landing ship, 13 minelaying landing craft, 1 survey ship, 1 salvage vessel, 2 headquarters ships, 10 transports, 2 training ships, 18 minor landing craft, 4 ammunition carriers, 6 oilers, 4 water carriers and 12 tugs. Personnel in 1984 totalled: 1,500 officers and 12,500 ratings.

Air Force. The Air Force has about 250 combat aircraft and is organized in 2 Air Corps, with HQ at Zagreb and Zemun. There are 2 fighter divisions equipped primarily with about 125 Russian-built MiG-21s, 2 ground-attack divisions of locally-built Jastreb light jet attack aircraft (being replaced with Super Galeb), and 2 squadrons of Jastreb jet reconnaissance aircraft. Transport units fly Il-14 and An-26 twin-engined aircraft, 4-turboprop An-12s, and a few other types in small numbers, notably Turbo-Porters and Yak-40s, Mystère 50s and Learjets for VIP duties. Training types are the nationally-designed UTVA-75 armed primary trainer, Galeb jet basic trainer and the T-33A jet advanced trainer (being replaced with Super Galeb). A large number of Gazelle, Agusta-Bell 205, Mi-4 and Mi-8 helicopters are in service. 'Guideline' and 'Goa' surface-to-air missiles have been supplied by the USSR. Personnel number 37,000.

INTERNATIONAL RELATIONS

Membership. Yugoslavia is a member of UN and has special relationships with Comecon and OECD.

ECONOMY

Planning. A 5-year plan of economic development for 1981–85 envisages that industrial production should increase by 4·5–5%, and that of agriculture by 4·5%. A long-term Economic Stabilisation Programme was introduced in 1983 to deal with the economic crisis, and laws were passed to ensure the prompt repayment of foreign debts. Foreign indebtedness was US$20,000m. in 1983. Control of some prices and increases in others were introduced in Dec. 1983 in an attempt to control inflation.

Budget. Revenue and expenditure (Federal, Republican, Provincial and Communal) for calendar years (in 1m. dinars):

	1974	1975	1976	1977	1978	1979
Revenue	82,302	107,191	148,824	165,875	168,487	224,500
Expenditure	81,492	106,545	148,204	165,832	168,487	222,356

Revenue for 1979 was composed of 102,028m. dinars in the federal budget, 81,520m. dinars in the republican budgets and in the budgets of the autonomous provinces, and 40,952m. dinars in other budgets.

Main items of distributed resources in 1979 (in 1m. dinars): Defence, 56,319; government, 44,215; investments in economy, 1,063; non-economic investments, 8,523.

Currency. On 26 July 1965 the value of 1 *dinar*, divided into 100 *para*, was fixed at 0·710937 milligrammes of fine gold instead of 2·96224 milligrammes. A new *dinar*, equivalent of 100 old dinars, was introduced on 1 Jan. 1966. There are coins of 0·05, 0·1, 0·2, 0·5 and 1, 2, 5 and 10 *dinars*, and notes of 5, 10, 50, 100, 500 and 1,000 *dinars*. Circulation of notes and coins, as of 31 Dec. 1979, was 91,182m. *dinars*. The *dinar* was devalued by 30% in June 1980 and again by 20% in Oct. 1982. Inflation was 58·4% in 1983. In March 1984, £1 = 182 *dinars*; US$1 = 123 *dinars*.

Banking. The National Bank is the bank of issue. There are also republican National Banks, 115 (in 1980) 'internal banks', 160 'basic banks' and 9 'associated banks'. At 30 June 1982 total credits amounted to 2,108,300m. dinars. Savings deposits totalled 219,420m. dinars in 1982.

Weights and Measures. The metric weights and measures have been in use since

1883. The *wagon* of 10 tonnes is used as a unit of measure for coal, roots and corn. The Gregorian calendar was adopted in 1919.

ENERGY AND NATURAL RESOURCES

Electricity. Generation of electricity in 1981 (and 1982) was 60,366m. kwh. (62,324m.), of which 25,089m. kwh. (23,540m.) was hydro-electric.

Minerals. Yugoslavia has considerable mineral resources, including coal (chiefly brown coal), iron, copper ore, gold, lead, chrome, antimony and cement. The most important iron mines are at Vareš and Ljubija in Bosnia, and there are also considerable siderite and limonite iron ores between Prijedor, Sanski Most and Topusko. Copper ore is exploited chiefly at Bor (Serbia). The principal lead mines are at Trepča and Mežice. Chrome mines are in southern Serbia (Kosovo) and Macedonia (Skopje, Kumanovo). There are 2 antimony mines in western Serbia (Podrinje).

Mining output, in 1,000 tonnes, in 1981 (and 1982): Coal, 384 (389); lignite, 40,958 (43,454); bauxite, 3,249 (3,668); salt, 418 (428); manganese ore, 31 (27); iron ore, 4,794 (5,106); copper ore, 18,337 (19,733); lead and zinc ore, 4,365 (4,252); antimony ore, 67 (63); crude petroleum, 4,375 (4,340); pyrite concentrates, 652 (810); magnesite, 300 (328). In 1979, gold output was 4,323 kg; silver, 162,181 kg.

Agriculture. Yugoslavia, with a total area of 25,580,400 hectares, had a cultivated area of 9·9m. hectares in 1982. In 1984, 85% of the arable land was in private hands, though only 6·5% of the 2·6m. private farms were more than 10 hectares of land. The remainder is worked by collective or state farms.

Area (in hectares) and yield (in 1,000 tonnes) in 1982: Maize, 2·3m. (11,126); wheat, 1·6m. (5,218); barley, 0·3m. (669); rye, 53,000 (84); tobacco, 61,121 (77); hemp, 4,035 (33); sunflower, 138,458 (202); potatoes, 282,000 (2,636).

Livestock, Jan. 1982: 515,000 horses, 5·5m cattle, 7·4m. sheep, 8·4m. pigs.

The 1982 yield of fruit was as follows (in 1,000 tonnes): Apples, 746; pears, 177; grapes, 1,780; plums, 1,028; olives, 5; walnuts, 37; 7·6m. hectolitres of wine were produced.

There were, in 1977, 2,599,552 individual holdings and 856,872 peasant co-operatives. Total agricultural work force, 5·4m.; tractors, (1981) 415,655.

Forestry. The forest areas consist largely of beech, oak and fir. Forest area in 1981: 9,240,000 hectares (2,897,000 in private hands). The gross timber cut in 1981 was 20,438,000 cu. metres.

Fisheries. In 1981 the landings of fish were (in tonnes): salt-water, 44,465; fresh-water, 27,232. The number of fishing craft was 222 motor vessels (9,367 GRT) and 1,014 sailing and rowing vessels.

INDUSTRY AND TRADE

Employment. In Dec. 1982 there were 5·9m. employed in the social sector (*i.e.*, excluding armed forces and self-employed) of whom 2·3m. were in manufacturing and mining, and 1·2m. in the social services. There were 915,000 unemployed in 1983, of whom 694,000 were under 30 and 521,550 were women. There were (1982) 5,485,000 trade union members.

Industry. The majority of industries are situated in the north-west part of the country.

Industrial output (in 1,000 tonnes) in 1982 (and 1981): Pig-iron, 2,703 (2,817); steel, 3,805 (3,976); cement, 9,718 (9,779); sulphuric acid, 1,183 (1,248); fertilizers, 2,314 (2,350); plastics, 409 (483). Fabrics (in 1m. sq. metres): Cotton, 372 (377); woollen, 94 (96). Sugar (1,000 tonnes), 683 (791). Motor cars (in 1,000s), 219 (242).

Commerce. Foreign trade, in 1m. dinars, for calendar years:

	1978	1979	1980	1981	1982
Imports	272,522	382,709	411,257	430,166	557,353
Exports	154,725	185,470	245,086	298,360	428,071

Imports to Yugoslavia, 1982, in 1 m. dinars, from: Federal Republic of Germany, 77,653; USSR, 114,395; Italy, 42,751; Czechoslovakia, 24,895; UK, 19,120. Exports from Yugoslavia, 1982, in 1 m. dinars, to: USSR, 143,112; Federal Republic of Germany, 30,097; Italy, 32,664; Czechoslovakia, 26,166; German Democratic Republic, 11,186.

The main imports (by value) in 1982 were (in 1 m. dinars): Machinery, electrical goods, transport means and parts, 154,984; fuel and lubricants, 143,487; manufactured goods, 83,875; chemical products, 62,232; crude articles, 59,449; food, 28,063. The main exports: Machinery, electrical goods, transport means and parts, 133,178; fuel and lubricants, 7,902; manufactured goods, 94,106; chemical products, 44,848; crude articles, 20,764; foods, 38,519.

In April 1983 a five-year trade and co-operation agreement with the EEC was signed. A trade pact was signed with the USSR in March 1983.

Total trade between Yugoslavia and UK (British Department of Trade returns, in £1,000 sterling):

	1979	1980	1981	1982	1983
Imports to UK	51,331	56,802	42,405	52,115	83,951
Exports and re-exports from UK	173,754	190,503	194,846	158,881	148,645

Tourism. In 1981, 6,616,000 (1982: 5,995,000) tourists visited Yugoslavia.

COMMUNICATIONS

Roads (1982). There were 59,380 km of asphalted roads and 35,895 km of macadamized roads. There were 2,702,628 passenger motor cars and 237,771 trucks and buses in 1982. The north–south highway is being converted to 6-lane motorway.

Railways. In 1982 Yugoslavia had 9,389 km of railway, of which 3,431 km are electrified, and ran 11,265 passenger-km and 26,166m. tonne-km of freight.

Aviation. The national airline, Jugoslovenski Aero Transport (Inex Adria-aviopromet, Panadria and Aviogenex) in 1982 flew on its home and international services, 53·4m. km and carried 4·8m. passengers and 84m. ton-km of freight; international services (without Panadria), 2·3m. passengers and 78·5m. ton-km of freight. The chief airfields are Belgrade, Zagreb, Ljubljana, Sarajevo, Skopje, Dubrovnik, Split, Titograd, Tivat, Pula and Zadar.

Shipping. In 1982 Yugoslavia possessed a total of 460 vessels of 2·5m. gross tons.

In 1982 vessels of 46·4m. net tons entered the ports of Yugoslavia.

In 1982 Yugoslavia had 1,248 river craft with 2,426 passenger capacity. The length of the navigable rivers amounted to 1,673 km, that of canals to 664 km. There are 2 navigable lakes: Skadar (391 sq. km, of which 243 in Yugoslavia) and Ohrid (348 sq. km, of which 230 in Yugoslavia). A Tisza-Danube canal system is under construction.

Pipeline. An oil pipeline runs from Krk to Pančevo.

Post and Broadcasting. There were 3,827 post offices and 2,542,000 telephone subscribers in 1982. *Jugoslovenska Radiotelevizija* consists of almost 250 main, relay and local stations operating on medium-waves and FM. *Radio Koper* also broadcasts commercial programmes in Italian for northern parts of Italy. National and regional TV programmes are broadcast. Advertisements are broadcast for maximum 170 minutes each week. Number of receivers in 1981: radio, 4·9m.; television, 4·6m.

Cinemas (1981). 1,278, seating 425,000

Theatres (1980–81). 397, seating (professional only), 26,805.

Newspapers (1981). There were 27 dailies, 2,980 other newspapers and 1,388 journals. There are no party newspapers but *Borba* and *Politika* enjoy semi-official status.

JUSTICE, RELIGION, EDUCATION AND WELFARE

Justice. There are county tribunals, district courts, supreme courts of the constituent republics and a Supreme Court. There are also self-management courts, including courts of associated labour. In county tribunals and district courts the judicial functions are exercised by professional judges and by lay assessors constituted into collegia. There are no assessors at the supreme courts.

All judges are elected by the socio-political communities in their jurisdiction. The judges exercise their functions in accordance with the legal provisions enacted since the liberation of the country.

The constituent republics enact their own criminal legislation, but offences concerning state security and the administration are dealt with at federal level.

Religion. Religious communities are separate from the State and are free to perform religious affairs. All religious communities recognized by law enjoy the same rights.

Serbia has been traditionally Orthodox and Croatia Roman Catholic. Moslems are found in the south as a result of the Turkish occupation. The 1953 percentage of the denominations was: Orthodox, 41·2%; Roman Catholic, 31·7%; Moslems, 12·3%; Protestants, 0·9%; without religion, 12·6%.

The Serbian Orthodox Church with its seat in Belgrade has 20 bishoprics within the country and 4 abroad, 3 in US and Canada and 1 in Hungary. The Serbian Orthodox Church numbers about 2,000 priests.

The Macedonian Orthodox Church with the Archbishop of Ohrid and Macedonia as its head in Skopje, has 4 bishoprics in the country and 1 abroad (American–Canadian–Australian). The Macedonian Orthodox Church numbers about 300 priests.

The Roman Catholic Church is divided into two provinces: Zagreb with 4 suffragan sees, and Sarajevo with 2 suffragan sees. In addition, the Roman Catholic Church has 4 archbishoprics, 10 independent bishoprics directly connected with the Vatican and 3 Apostolic Administrators. There is a National Conference of Bishops with the Archbishop of Zagreb, Cardinal Franjo Kuharič, at its head. The Roman Catholic Church has about 4,000 priests.

The Moslem Religious Union has 4 republic Superiorates in Sarajevo, Skopje, Titograd and Priština. The highest authority is the supreme synod of the Islamic Religious Community, which elects the Reis-ul-Ulema and the Supreme Islamic Superiorate.

The Moslem religious community has about 2,000 priests.

The Protestant churches covering 4 independent Lutheran Churches, numbering about 150,000 believers, the Reformed Christian Church, numbering about 60,000 believers, include also several much smaller churches of Baptists, Methodists, Adventists, Nazarenes, etc., numbering together about 100,000 believers. The Protestant churches have about 450 priests.

Also there are independent Old Catholic Churches with Synodal Council at Zagreb.

The Jewish religion has about 35 communities making up a common league of Jewish Communities with its seat in Belgrade.

Education. Compulsory general education lasts 8 years, secondary 3–4 years. In 1981–82 there were 12,558 primary schools with 133,590 teachers and 2,803,276 pupils. 440 secondary schools (not including those covered by the reform programme) with 65,054 teachers and 240,507 pupils, 307 primary schools for adults with 30,830 pupils, and 585 secondary schools for adults with 41,575 pupils, 118 technical schools for adults with 6,696 pupils, 5 teacher training schools with 1,943 students.

Primary and secondary schools of ethnic minorities: Albanian, 1,336; Hungarian, 230; Bulgarian, 49; Czech, 13; Slovak, 29; Italian, 45; Romanian, 33; Turkish, 75; Ukrainian, 6.

For higher and specialized education there were 352 faculties, academies and high schools with 24,905 professors and instructors and 386,356 students.

Health. In 1981 there were 33,514 doctors and dentists, and 136,820 hospital beds (10,505 psychiatric).

Health insurance benefits totalled 80,710m. dinars and pensions 150,252m. dinars in 1981.

DIPLOMATIC REPRESENTATIVES

Of Yugoslavia in Great Britain (5 Lexham Gdns., London, W8 5JJ)
Ambassador: Dragi Stamenković.

Of Great Britain in Yugoslavia (46 Generala Ždanova, Belgrade)
Ambassador: K. B. A. Scott, CMG.

Of Yugoslavia in the USA (2410 California St., NW, Washington, D.C., 20008)
Ambassador: Budimir Loncar.

Of the USA in Yugoslavia (50 Kneza Miloša, Belgrade)
Ambassador: David Anderson.

Of Yugoslavia to the United Nations
Ambassador: Ignac Golob.

Books of Reference

Statistical Information: The Federal Statistical Office (Savezni Zavod za Statistiku; Kneza Miloša 20, Belgrade) was founded in Dec. 1944. *Director:* Franta Kornel. It publishes: *Indeks* (from April 1952, with English and French translations); *Statistički bilten* (1950 ff., with English or French translations); *Statistical Yearbook* (from 1954, with English, Russian and French translations); *Statistics of Foreign Trade of the SFR Yugoslavia* (annual, from 1946; half-yearly, from 1951); *Statistical Pocket-book* (from 1955; in 5 eds.: Yugoslav, English, French, Russian, German).

The Assembly of the SFR of Yugoslavia. Belgrade, 1974
The Constitution of the Socialist Federal Republic of Yugoslavia. Belgrade, 1974
Alexander, S., *Church and State in Yugoslavia since 1945.* CUP, 1979
Auty, P., *Yugoslavia.* New York, 1965.—*Tito: A Biography.* London, 1970
Burg, S. L., *Conflict and Cohesion in Socialist Yugoslavia: Political Decision-Making since 1966.* Princeton Univ. Press, 1983
Carter, A., *Democratic Reform in Yugoslavia: The Changing Role of the Party.* Princeton Univ. Press and London, 1982
Dedijer, V., *et al., History of Yugoslavia.* New York, 1974
Denitch, B. D., *The Legitimation of a Revolution: The Yugoslav Case.* Yale Univ. Press, 1976
Djilas, M., *Memoir of a Revolutionary.* New York, 1973
Doder, D. *The Yugoslavs.* New York, 1978
Drvodelić, M., *Croatian or Serbian-English Dictionary.* 4th ed. Zagreb, 1978
Filipović, R., *English-Croatian or Serbian Dictionary.* Zagreb, 1980
Horton, J. J., *Yugoslavia.* [Bibliography] Oxford and Santa Barbara, 1978
Horvat, B., *The Yugoslav Economic System.* White Plains, 1976
Kotnik, J., *Slovensko–angleski slovar.* 4th ed. Ljubljana, 1959
Nord, L., *Nonalignment and Socialism: Yugoslavia's Foreign Policy in Theory and Practice.* Uppsala, 1974
Rusinow, D. I., *The Yugoslav Experiment, 1948–1974.* London, 1977
Ristić, Simić, Popović: *An English–Serbocroatian Dictionary.* 2 vols. Belgrade, 1956
Singleton, F., *Twentieth Century Yugoslavia.* London, 1976.–*The Economy of Yugoslavia.* London, 1982
Sirc, L., *The Yugoslav Economy under Self-Management.* London, 1979
Skerlj, R., *English–Slovene Dictionary.* 4th ed. Ljubljana, 1957
Stojanović, R., (ed.) *The Functioning of the Yugoslav Economy.* New York, 1982
Tito, J. B., *The Essential Tito.* New York, 1970
Wilson, D., *Tito's Yugoslavia.* CUP, 1979

REPUBLICS AND AUTONOMOUS PROVINCES

The Federal Republic of Yugoslavia comprises the 6 republics of Bosnia and Herzegovina, Croatia, Macedonia, Montenegro, Serbia and Slovenia, and the 2 autonomous provinces of Kosovo and Vojvodina within the Republic of Serbia.

Each has its own Constitution, Assembly of 3 Chambers (of Associated Labour; of Communes; Socio-Political) and League of Communists within the League of Communists of Yugoslavia, though the latter is not formally a federal institution.

BOSNIA AND HERZEGOVINA

HISTORY. The country was settled by Slavs in the 7th century, the original clan system evolving between the 12th and 14th centuries into a principality under a *Ban,* during which time the Bogomil Christian heresy became entrenched. Bosnia was conquered by the Turks in 1463, and the majority of the Bogomils were converted to Islam. At the Congress of Berlin (1878) the territory was assigned to Austro-Hungarian administration under nominal Turkish suzerainty. Austria-Hungary's outright annexation in 1908 generated tensions which contributed to the outbreak of the first world war.

AREA AND POPULATION. The republic is bounded in the north and west by Croatia, in the east by Serbia and in the south-east by Montenegro. It is virtually land-locked, having a coastline of only 20 km with no harbours. Its area is 51,129 sq km. The capital is Sarajevo.

Population at the 1981 census: 4,124,008, of whom the predominating ethnic groups were Moslems (1,629,924), Serbs (1,320,644) and Croats (758,136). Population density per sq. km: 80·7. Population by sex at the 1971 census: males, 1,834,600; females, 1,911,511.

Vital statistics:

	Live births	Marriages	Deaths	Growth rate per 1,000
1980	70,928	35,012	26,115	10·9
1981	70,125	36,757	26,079	10·9

ECONOMY

Agriculture. In 1981 the agricultural area was 2·62m. hectares. Yields (in 1,000 tonnes) and areas sown (in 1,000 hectares) of principal crops were: wheat, 275 (127); barley, 62 (43); maize, 690 (246); soya, 1,705 (1,143); potatoes, 363 (53). Livestock in 1982 (1,000 head): horses, 139; cattle, 969; sheep, 1,389; pigs, 686. Timber cut in 1981: 6·7m. cu. metres.

Industry. Production (1981): Electricity, 11,298m. kwh; lignite, 5·78m. tonnes; iron ore, 4·06m. tonnes; pig iron, 1·65m. tonnes; bauxite, 2·24m. tonnes; cement, 692m. tonnes; cotton fabrics, 45m. sq. metres; cars, 21,000.

Employment. Population of working age, 1981, 2,817,074; non-agricultural workforce, 868,000, of whom 716,000 worked in production.

CROATIA

HISTORY. The Croats migrated to their present territory in the 6th century and were converted to Roman Catholicism. Croatia was conquered by Hungary in 1091 and remained under Hungarian domination until after the first world war. During the second world war an independent fascist state was set up.

AREA AND POPULATION. Croatia is bounded in the north by Slovenia and Hungary and in the east by Serbia. It has an extensive Adriatic coastline well provided with ports, and includes the historical areas of Dalmatia, Istria and Slavonia, which no longer have administrative status. The capital is Zagreb. Its area is 56,538 sq. km. Population at the 1981 census was 4,601,469, of whom the predominating ethnic groups were Croats (3,454,661), Serbs (531,502), and Hungarians (25,439). Population density per sq. km: 81·4. Population by sex at the 1971 census: males, 2,139,048; females, 2,287,173.

Vital statistics:

	Live births	Marriages	Deaths	Growth rate per 1,000
1980	68,220	33,310	50,100	4·0
1981	67,137	34,397	52,002	3·3

ECONOMY

Agriculture. In 1981 the agricultural area was 3·25m. hectares. Yields (in 1,000 tonnes) and areas sown (in 1,000 hectares) of principal crops were: wheat, 860 (283); barley, 156 (62); maize, 2,399 (469); sugar beet, 1,202 (24); soya, 5,961 (1,530); potatoes, 742 (84). Livestock in 1982 (1,000 head): horses, 87; cattle, 976; sheep, 725; pigs, 1,897. Timber cut in 1981: 4·98m. cu. metres.

Industry. Production (1981): Electricity, 8,324m. kwh; coal, 258,000 tonnes; crude petroleum, 3·14m. tonnes; steel, 407,000 tonnes; plastics, 200,000 tonnes; cement, 3·8m. tonnes; cotton fabrics, 69m. sq. metres; sugar, 153,000 tonnes.

Employment. Population of working age, 1981: 3,040,368; non-agricultural work-force, 1·46m., of whom 1·19m. worked in production.

MACEDONIA

HISTORY. The Slavs settled in Macedonia since the 6th century, who had been Christianized by Byzantium, were conquered by the non-Slav Bulgars in the 7th century and in the 9th century formed a Macedo-Bulgarian empire, the western part of which survived until Byzantine conquest in 1014. In the 14th century it fell to Serbia, and in 1355 to the Turks. After the Balkan Wars of 1912-13 Turkey was ousted, and Serbia received the greater part of the territory, the rest going to Bulgaria and Greece. In 1918 Yugoslav Macedonia was incorporated into Serbia as 'South Serbia'. Possession of this territory has long been a source of contention between Bulgaria and Yugoslavia.

AREA AND POPULATION. Macedonia is land-locked, and is bounded in the north by Serbia and Kosovo, in the east by Bulgaria, in the south by Greece and in the west by Albania. The capital is Skopje. Its area is 25,713 sq. km. Population at the 1981 census was 1,912,257, of whom the predominating ethnic groups were Macedonians (1,281,195), Albanians (377,726) and Turks (86,691). Population density per sq. km, 74·4. Population by sex at the 1971 census: males, 834,692; females, 812,616.

Vital statistics:

	Live births	Marriages	Deaths	Growth rate per 1,000
1980	39,784	16,145	13,534	13·9
1981	39,958	16,450	13,829	13·6

ECONOMY

Agriculture. In 1981 the agricultural area was 1·32m. hectares. Yields (in 1,000 tonnes) and areas sown (in 1,000 hectares) of principal crops were: wheat, 236 (104); barley, 100 (51); maize, 91 (42); cotton, 898 (1,046); tobacco, 26 (23); Livestock in 1982 (1,000 head): horses, 90; cattle, 371; sheep, 2,162; pigs, 210. Timber cut in 1981: 889,000 cu. metres.

Industry. Production (1981): Electricity, 2,300m. kwh; lignite, 1·03m. tonnes; iron ore, 567,000 tonnes; pig-iron, 244,000 tonnes; steel, 386,000 tonnes; copper ore, 2·29m. tonnes; bauxite, 435,000 tonnes; sulphuric acid, 67,000 tonnes; cement, 655,000 tonnes; cotton fabrics, 50m. sq. metres.

Employment. Population of working age, 1981: 1,214,321; non-agricultural work-force, 442,000, of whom 361,000 worked in production.

MONTENEGRO

HISTORY. Montenegro emerged as a separate entity on the break-up of the Serbian Empire in 1355. It was never effectively subdued by Turkey. It was ruled by Bishop Princes until 1851, when a royal house was founded.

AREA AND POPULATION. Montenegro is a mountainous region which opens to the Adriatic in the south-west. It is bounded in the north-west by Bosnia and Herzegovina, in the north-east by Serbia and in the south-east by Albania. The capital is Titograd. Its area is 13,812, sq. km. Population at the 1981 census was 584,310, of whom the predominating ethnic groups were Montenegrins (400,488), Moslems (78,080) and Albanians (37,735). Population density per sq. km: 42·3. Population by sex at the 1971 census: males, 259,209; females, 270,395.

Vital statistics:

	Live births	Marriages	Deaths	Growth rate per 1,000
1980	10,542	4,429	3,703	11·8
1981	10,632	4,439	3,562	12·1

ECONOMY

Agriculture. In 1981 the agricultural area was 517,000 hectares. Yields (in 1,000 tonnes) and areas sown (in 1,000 hectares) of principal crops were: wheat, 7 (3); barley, 10 (6); maize, 13 (7); potatoes, 41 (6). Livestock in 1982 (1,000 head): horses, 24; cattle, 186; sheep, 482; pigs, 27. Timber cut in 1981: 812,000 cu. metres.

Industry. Production (1981): Electricity, 1,835m. kwh; lignite, 1·45m. tonnes; bauxite, 505,000 tonnes; cement, 164,000 tonnes.

Employment. Population of working age, 1981: 383,122; non-agricultural work-force, 135,000, of whom 107,000 worked in production.

SERBIA

HISTORY. The Serbs received Orthodox Christianity from the Byzantines. They threw off the latter's suzerainty to become a large prosperous medieval state, which was destroyed by the Turks at the Battle of Kosovo in 1389. After revolutions in 1804 and 1815 Serbia won increasing degrees of autonomy from Turkey; complete independence came with the Treaty of Berlin in 1878. Its prince took the title of king in 1881.

AREA AND POPULATION. Serbia is land-locked and is bounded in the north-west by Croatia, in the north by Hungary, in the north-east by Romania, in the east by Bulgaria, in the south by Macedonia and in the west by Albania, Montenegro and Bosnia and Herzegovina. It includes the Autonomous Provinces of Kosovo in the south and Vojvodina in the north, which have substantial Albanian and Hungarian populations respectively. Without these its area is 55,968 sq. km. The capital is Belgrade. Population at the 1981 census was 5,694,464, of whom the predominating ethnic group was Serbs (4,865,283). Population density per sq. km: 101·7. Population by sex at the 1971 census: males, 2,585,625; females, 2,664,740.

Vital statistics:

	Live births	Marriages	Deaths	Growth rate per 1,000
1980	80,916	41,821	52,953	5·0
1981	81,079	42,190	55,476	4·5

ECONOMY

Agriculture. In 1981 the agricultural area was 3·4m. hectares. Yields (in 1,000 tonnes) and areas sown (in 1,000 hectares) of principal crops were: Wheat, 1,112 (404); barley, 100 (54); maize, 2,213 (650); sugar-beet, 321 (10); soya, 6,793 (4,742); potatoes, 590 (68). Livestock in 1982: (in 1,000 head): horses, 73; cattle, 1,665; sheep, 2,007; pigs, 2,730. Timber cut in 1981: 2·68m. cu. metres.

Industry. (1981): Electricity, 24,226m. kwh; coal, 127,000 tonnes; lignite, 21·23m. tonnes; pig-iron, 510,000 tonnes; steel, 498,000 tonnes; copper ore, 16·05m.

tonnes; lorries, 13,480; cars, 181,000; sulphuric acid, 916,000 tonnes; plastics, 45,000 tonnes; cement, 1·04m. tonnes; sugar, 38,000 tonnes; cotton fabrics, 55m. sq. metres; woollens, 29m. sq. metres.

Employment. Population of working age, 1981: 3,742,494; non-agricultural workforce, 1·5m., of whom 1·2m. were in production.

KOSOVO

AREA AND POPULATION. Area: 10,887 sq. km. The capital is Priština. Population at the 1981 census, 1,584,441, of whom the predominating ethnic groups were Albanians (1,226,736), and Serbs (209,498). Population density per sq. km: 145·5. Population by sex at the 1971 census: males, 636,958; females, 606,735.

Vital statistics:

	Live births	Marriages	Deaths	Growth rate per 1,000
1980	53,147	12,666	8,909	28·5
1981	50,463	12,040	9,729	25·5

ECONOMY

Agriculture. The agricultural area in 1981 was 585,000 hectares. Yields (in 1,000 tonnes) and sown areas (in 1,000 hectares) of principal crops were: Wheat, 197 (81); maize, 223 (100); sugar-beet, 79 (2); potatoes, 69 (8). Livestock in 1982 (1,000 head): horses, 42; cattle, 408; sheep, 345; pigs, 63. Timber cut in 1981, 361,000 cu. metres.

Industry. Production (1981): Electricity, 3,354m. kwh; lignite, 6·47m. tonnes; sulphuric acid, 70,000 tonnes; cement, 392,000 tonnes.

Employment. Population of working age, 1981: 882,462; non-agricultural workforce, 188,000, of whom 136,000 worked in production.

VOJVODINA

AREA AND POPULATION. Area: 10,887 sq. km. The capital is Novi Sad. Population at the 1981 census, 2,034,772, of whom the predominating ethnic groups were Serbs (1,107,378) and Hungarians (385,356). Population density per sq. km: 94·6. Population by sex at the 1971 census: males, 951,152; females, 1,001,381.

Vital statistics:

	Live births	Marriages	Deaths	Growth rate per 1,000
1980	28,681	15,679	23,227	2·7
1981	26,407	14,965	22,437	2·0

ECONOMY

Agriculture. The agricultural area in 1981 was 1·8m. hectares. Yields (in 1,000 tonnes) and sown areas (in 1,000 hectares) of principal crops were: Wheat, 1,477 (342); barley, 218 (65); maize, 3,909 (660); sugar-beet, 4,286 (85); soya, 77,837 (38,296); potatoes, 339 (25). Livestock in 1982 (1,000 head): horses, 42; cattle, 323; sheep, 270; pigs, 2,273. Timber cut in 1981: 604,000 cu. metres.

Industry. Production (1981): Electricity, 476m. kwh; crude petroleum, 1·23m. tonnes; sulphuric acid, 53,000 tonnes; plastics, 109,000 tonnes; cement, 1·62m. tonnes.

Employment. Population of working age, 1981: 1,351,492; non-agricultural workforce, 572,000, of whom 469,000 worked in production.

SLOVENIA

HISTORY. The lands originally settled by Slovenes in the 6th century were steadily encroached upon by Germans. Slovenia developed as part of Austria-Hungary and only gained independence in 1918.

AREA AND POPULATION. Slovenia is bounded in the north by Austria, in the north-east by Hungary, in the south-east by Croatia and in the west by Italy. There is a small strip of coast south of Trieste. Its area is 20,251 sq. km. The capital is Ljubljana. Population at the 1981 census: 1,891,864, of whom the predominating ethnic group were Slovene (1,712,445). Population density per sq. km: 93·4. Population by sex at the 1971 census: males, 835,998; females, 891,139.

Vital statistics:

	Live births	Marriages	Deaths	Growth rate per 1,000
1980	29,902	12,377	18,820	5·9
1981	30,706	12,300	19,358	6·0

ECONOMY

Agriculture. In 1981 the agricultural area was 889,000 hectares. Yields (in 1,000 tonnes) and sown areas (in 1,000 hectares) of principal crops were: Wheat, 106 (42); maize, 269 (57); sugar-beet, 162 (3); potatoes, 555 (36). Livestock in 1982 (1,000 head): horses, 17; cattle, 565; sheep, 16; pigs, 544. Timber cut in 1981: 3·38m. cu. metres.

Industry. Production (1981): Electricity, 8,551m. kwh; lignite, 5m. tonnes; steel, 777,000 tonnes; lorries, 3,970; cars, 33,000; sulphuric acid, 132,000 tonnes; sugar, 25,000 tonnes; cement, 1·43m. tonnes; cotton fabrics, 135m. sq. metres; woollens, 28m. sq. metres.

Employment. Population of working age, 1981: 1,176,609; non-agricultural workforce, 802,000, of whom 658,000 worked in production.

ZAÏRE

République du Zaïre

Capital: Kinshasa
Population: 31·94m. (1983)
GNP per capita: US$220 (1980)

HISTORY. Until the middle of the 19th century the territory drained by the Congo River was practically unknown. When Stanley reached the mouth of the Congo in 1877, King Leopold II of the Belgians recognized the immense possibilities of the Congo Basin and took the lead in exploring and exploiting it. The Berlin Conference of 1884–85 recognized King Leopold II as the sovereign head of the Congo Free State.

The annexation of the state to Belgium was provided for by treaty of 28 Nov. 1907, which was approved by the chambers of the Belgian Legislature in Aug. and Sept. and by the King on 18 Oct. 1908. The law of 18 Oct. 1908, called the Colonial Charter (last amended in 1959), provided for the government of the Belgian Congo, until the country became independent on 30 June 1960. The country's name was changed from Congo to Zaïre in Oct. 1971. For subsequent history to 1977 *see* THE STATESMAN'S YEAR-BOOK, 1980–81, p. 1613.

AREA AND POPULATION. Zaïre is bounded north by the Central African Republic, north-east by Sudan, east by Uganda, Rwanda, Burundi and Lake Tanganyika, south by Zambia, south-west by Angola, north-west by Congo. There is a 40-km Atlantic coastline separating Angola's province of Cabinda from the rest of that country.

The area of the republic is estimated at 2,344,885 sq. km (905,365 sq. miles). The population is composed almost entirely of Bantu groups, with minorities of Sudanese (in the north), Nilotes (northeast), Pygmies and Hamites (in the east). In the census (1976) the population was 25,568,640. Estimate (1983) 31,944,000; annual growth rate, 2·9%. In 1982 there were about 325,000 refugees in Zaïre including 215,000 from Angola.

The area (in sq. km) and populations (estimate) at 1 July 1976 of the regions are as follows, together with their capitals:

Region	Sq. km	Population 1981	Chief town	Population 1976
Bandundu	295,658	4,119,524	Bandundu (Banningville)	74,467 [1]
Bas-Zaïre	53,920	1,921,524	Matadi	162,396
Equateur	403,293	3,418,296	Mbandaka (Coquilhatville)	149,118
Haut-Zaïre	503,239	4,541,655	Kisangani (Stanleyville)	339,210
Kasai Occidental	156,967	2,935,036	Kananga (Luluabourg)	704,211
Kasai Oriental	168,216	2,336,951	Mbuji-Mayi (Bakwanga)	382,632
Kinshasa City	9,965	2,338,246	Kinshasa (Leopoldville)	2,443,876
Kivu	256,662	4,713,761	Bukavu (Costermansville)	209,051
Shaba	496,965	3,823,172	Lubumbashi (Elizabethville)	451,332

[1] 1970.

Other large towns: Kikwit, 172,450 in 1976; Likasi (Jadotville), 146,394 in 1970.

French is the only official language, but of more than 200 languages spoken, 4 are recognized as national languages. Of these, Kiswahili is used in the east, Tshiluba in the south, Kikongo in the area between Kinshasa and the coast, while Lingala is spoken widely in and around Kinshasa and along the river; Lingala has become the *lingua franca* after French.

CLIMATE. Because of the size and the relief of the country, the climate is very varied, the central region having an equatorial climate, with year-long high temperatures and rain at all seasons. Elsewhere, depending on position north or south of the Equator, there are well-marked wet and dry seasons. The mountains of the east and south have a temperate mountain climate, with the highest summits having considerable snowfall. Kinshasa. Jan. 79°F (26·1°C), July 73°F (22·8°C). Annual rainfall 45″ (1,125 mm). Kananga. Jan. 76°F (24·4°C), July 74°F (23·3°C). Annual rainfall 62″ (1,584 mm). Kisangani. Jan. 78°F (25·6°C), July 75°F (23·9°C). Annual rainfall 68″ (1,704 mm). Lubumbashi. Jan. 72°F (22·2°C), July 61°F (16·1°C). Annual rainfall 50″ (1,237 mm).

CONSTITUTION AND GOVERNMENT. A new Constitution was promulgated on 15 Feb. 1978 and amended in Nov. 1980. The supreme institution is the sole political party, the *Mouvement Populaire de la Révolution* (MPR), whose leader and President is automatically Head of State, of the National Executive Council and of the National Legislative Council. His nomination by the Political Bureau of the MPR (whose 38 members are all nominated by him) is confirmed for a 7-year term (renewable once) by election by universal adult suffrage (all Zaïreans acquire automatic membership of the MPR at birth).

Former President: Joseph Kasavubu, 1 July 1960–25 Nov. 1965 (deposed in coup).

President: Marshal Mobutu Sésé Séko Kuku Ngbendu wa Zabanga (took office 25 Nov. 1965, elected 1 Nov. 1970 and re-elected 5 Dec. 1977).

The National Executive Council is composed of State Commissioners appointed by the President. In July 1983 it was composed as follows:

First State Commissioner (Prime Minister): Kengo wa Dondo.

Foreign Affairs and Co-operation: Kamanda wa Kamanda. *Territorial Administration:* Munongo Mwenda Mairi. *Justice:* Mozagba Ngbuka. *Information, Culture and Arts:* Kande Dzambulate. *Finance and Budget:* Ngole Iliki. *Planning:* Namwisi ma Nkoy. *State Investments:* Pay Pay wa Syakasighe. *Rural Development and Environment:* Kamitatu Massamba. *Economy, Industry and External Trade:* Nyembo Shabani. *Mines and Energy:* Umba Kyamitala. *Transport and Communications:* Inonga Lokonga Lome. *Lands:* Yoka Mangono. *Labour and Social Security:* Kande Buloba Kasumpata. *Higher Education:* Sampassa Kaweta Nilombe. *Primary and Secondary Education:* Makinda Wata Wata. *Scientific Research:* Bayona ba Meya. *Public Health:* Dr Tshibasu Mubiay. *Social Affairs:* Moata Nkuma Wa Bowango. *Civil Service:* Kilolo Musampa Lubemba. *Posts and Telecommunications:* Mukuku w'Etonda. *Sports and Leisure:* Tshobo I. Ngana. *Tourism:* Ndjoli Balanga. *Public Works and Territorial Development:* Bokana w'Ondangela.

Parliament consists of a unicameral National Legislative Council comprising People's Commissioners (one per 100,000 inhabitants) elected by universal suffrage for a 5-year term. At the latest elections (Sept. 1982) 310 People's Commissioners were elected from a list of 1,409 candidates presented by the MPR.

National flag: Green, with a yellow disc bearing an arm holding a flaming torch.

Local government: Zaïre is composed of the *ville neutre* of Kinshasa (administered by a Governor) and 8 regions, each under a Regional Commissioner and 6 Councillors; all are appointed by the President.

DEFENCE

Army. The Army is divided into 3 Military Regions and comprises 1 division; 1 armoured, 2 infantry, 1 parachute, 1 commando and 1 Presidential Guard brigades. Equipment includes 60 Chinese Type-62 light tanks, and 95 AML-60 and 60 AML-90 armoured cars. Strength (1984) 22,000. There is a paramilitary gendarmerie which is responsible for security and also numbered (1984) about 22,000, organized in 40 battalions.

Navy. The Navy consists of 3 flotillas, 1 coastal, 1 river and 1 lake, comprising 4 fast gunboats (*ex*-Chinese), 7 fast torpedo boats (4 *ex*-Chinese and 3 *ex*-North Korean), and 42 coastal patrol boats including 12 US-built and 29 French-built. Personnel in 1984 numbered 1,500 officers and men including 600 marines.

Air Force. The Air Force has been built up with training assistance from Italy. In 1983 it had a squadron of Mirage 5 supersonic fighters, 20 Reims-Cessna Milirole observation and light attack aircraft, 12 Aermacchi MB.326GB and 6 MB.326K armed jet trainers, 6 C-130 Hercules and 3 DHC-5 Buffalo turboprop transports, 8 C-47 and 2 Caribou transports, 9 Super Frelon, Alouette and Puma helicopters, 20 SIAI-Marchetti SF.260MC basic trainers and a variety of other transport and training aircraft. Personnel, approximately 2,500.

INTERNATIONAL RELATIONS

Membership. Zaïre is a member of UN, OAU and is an ACP state of EEC.

ECONOMY

Budget. Revenue was envisaged at 6,773m. zaïres in 1983, and expenditure, 9,173m.

Currency. The currency unit, is the *zaïre*, divided into 100 *makuta*. Each *likuta* (plural *makuta*) is divided into 100 *sengi*. Bank-notes are issued in the following denominations: 10, 5 and 1 *zaïre*, 50, 20, 10 *makuta*; there are coins of 5 *makuta*, 1 *likuta* and 10 *sengi*. In March 1984, £1 sterling = 47·03 *zaïre*; US$1 = 28·75 *zaïre*.

Banking. The central bank is Banque du Zaïre. A development bank with state backing is the Société Financière de Développement (SOFIDE). Commercial banks operating in Zaïre are Banque de Paris et des Pays-Bas, Banque de Kinshasa, National & Grindlays Bank, Barclays Bank SZPRL, First National City Bank, Union Zaïroise de Banques, Banque Commerciale Zaïroise, Bank du Peuple, Caisse Nationale d'Epargne et de Crédit Immobilier and Banque Internationale pour L'Afrique au Zaïre.

Weights and Measures. The metric system was introduced by law on 17 Aug. 1910.

ENERGY AND NATURAL RESOURCES

Electricity. The installed generating capacity (1978) was 1,692 mw, of which 98% was hydroelectric. Production (1980) 4,360m. kwh. A huge new dam at Inga, on the Zaïre River near Matadi, has a potential capacity of 39,600 mw.

Oil. Offshore oil production began in Nov. 1975; crude production (1982) was 8,384,606 bbls.

Minerals. In 1982 most of Zaïre's foreign exchange was derived from mining of copper (505,385 tonnes), zinc concentrates (64,425 tonnes), cobalt (5,573). The most important mining area is in the region of Shaba (formerly Katanga). The principal mining companies are the State-owned Gécamines; the Zaïre-Japanese Sodimiza; the international Société Minière du Tenke-Fungurume which started production in 1976; and 2 diamond companies, MIBA and British Zaïre Diamond Distributors. Production (1982) 5·7m. metric carats.

Agriculture. In 1979, 75% of the 11·7m. workforce were engaged in agriculture. There were 5·65m. hectares of arable land and 24·8m. hectares of pastures and meadows. The main food crops (1981 production in 1,000 tonnes) are: Cassava, 13,000; plantains, 1,450; sugar-cane, 700; maize, 520; groundnuts, 320; bananas, 317; yams, 300; rice, 250. Cash crops include palm oil, 155; coffee, 75; palm kernels, 65; rubber, 28.

Livestock (1982): Cattle, 1·26m.; sheep, 749,000; goats, 2·9m.; pigs, 764,000; poultry, 16·3m.

Forestry. Equatorial rain forests cover 55% of Zaïre's land surface, and 10·28m. cu. metres of timber were produced in 1980.

Fisheries. The catch for 1980 was 115,000 tonnes, almost entirely from inland waters.

INDUSTRY AND TRADE

Commerce. Imports in 1981 totalled 2,769·4m. zaïres, exports totalled 2,360·9m.

zaïres. In 1981, 47% of the exports (by value) consisted of copper, 16% of cobalt, 15% of coffee and 7% of diamonds. 32% of all exports went to Belgium, 18% to Angola and 14% to the USA, while 15% of imports came from Belgium, 8% from Federal Republic of Germany and 11% from the USA.

Total trade between Zaïre and UK (British Department of Trade returns, in £1,000 sterling):

	1978	1979	1980	1981	1982	1983
Imports to UK	98,471	67,006	52,585	17,986	15,801	11,192
Exports and re-exports from UK	20,658	22,246	27,629	22,452	20,557	21,129

Tourism. There were 18,942 visitors in 1976 spending US$11m.

COMMUNICATIONS

Roads. Of 150,000 km of roads only 20,600 km are of national importance and all roads are earth-surfaced. There were 177,931 motor vehicles registered in Dec. 1975. Of these, 95,978 were cars, 33,505 trucks, 2,989 buses, 9,153 motor cycles, and other types, 36,306.

Railways. The total length of public railways in 1980 was 5,254 km on 4 gauges, 858 km being electrified. The railways carried (1981) 1·4m. passengers and 4·2m. tonnes of freight.

Aviation. There are 4 international airports at Kinshasa (Ndjili), Lumumbashi (Luano), Kisangani and Bukavu. There are another 40 airports with regular scheduled internal services, and over 150 other landing strips.

More than twelve international airlines, including British Caledonian Airways, operate in and out of Kinshasa from Europe, Africa and the USA. The national airline Air Zaïre, operates on all the main internal routes as well as on international routes to Europe and other African cities.

Shipping. The Zaïre River and its tributaries are navigable for about 13,700 km. Regular traffic has been established between Kinshasa and Kisangani as well as Ilebo, on the Lualaba (i.e., the river above Kisangani), on some tributaries and on the lakes. Zaïre has only 40 km of sea coast. The merchant marine in 1981 comprised 34 vessels with a total tonnage of 92,044 GRT. Kinshasa, Matadi and Boma are the main seaports; in 1978, 629,422 tonnes of freight were unloaded and 498,380 loaded.

Post and Broadcasting. In 1970 there were 351 post offices. Length of telegraph lines, 2,459 km. There were 15 broadcasting stations, 161 stations of wireless telegraphy and 206 telegraph offices; telephones numbered 30,284 in 1980. There is a ground satellite communications station outside Kinshasa. In 1979 there were 245,000 radio and 7,700 television receivers.

Cinemas (1974): 91 cinemas had a seating capacity of 23,300.

Newspapers. There are 4 dailies: *Salongo* (mornings) and *Elima* (evenings) in Kinshasa; *Njumbe* in Lumumbashi and *Boyoma* in Kisangani.

JUSTICE, RELIGION, EDUCATION AND WELFARE

Justice. A Justice Department was established in Jan. 1980 to replace the Judicial Council. There is a Supreme Court at Kinshasa, 9 Courts of Appeal and 32 courts of first instance.

Religion. In 1980 there were about 10m. Roman Catholics, 7m. Protestants and 4m. Kimbanguistes, as well as some 200,000 Moslems and 2,000 Jews. The remaining inhabitants adhere to animist beliefs.

Education. In 1977–78 there were 3,818,934 pupils in primary schools, 458,776 in secondary schools, 84,995 in technical schools and 99,904 in teacher-training colleges. In 1971 all Institutes of Higher Education combined to form the National University of Zaïre, which 35,000 students were attending by 1979; in 1981 the National University was divided to form 3 Universities at Kinshasa, Kisangani and Lumumbashi.

Health. In 1979 there were 1,900 doctors, 58 dentists, 414 pharmacists, 3,043 midwives, 14,661 nursing personnel and 942 hospitals and medical centres with 79,244 beds.

DIPLOMATIC REPRESENTATIVES

Of Zaïre in Great Britain (26 Chesham Place, London, SW1X 8HH)
Ambassador: (Vacant).

Of Great Britain in Zaïre (Ave. de l'Equateur, Kinshasa)
Ambassador: Nicholas Bayne.

Of Zaïre in the USA (1800 New Hampshire Ave., NW, Washington, D.C., 20009)
Ambassador: Kasongo Mutuale.

Of the USA in Zaïre (310 Ave. des Aviateurs, Kinshasa)
Ambassador: Peter D. Constable.

Of Zaïre to the United Nations
Ambassador: (Vacant).

Books of Reference

Area Handbook for the Democratic Republic of the Congo (Kinshasa). US Government Printing Office, Washington, 1971
Atlas Général du Congo. Académie Royale, Brussels
Cornevin, R., *Histoire de Congo.* Paris, 1963
Gran, G., *Zaire: The Political Economy of Underdevelopment.* New York, 1979
Slade, R. M., *King Leopold's Congo: Aspects of the Development of Race Relations in the Congo's Independent State.* OUP, 1962

ZAMBIA

Capital: Lusaka
Population: 6·24m. (1982)
GNP per capita: US$560 (1980)

HISTORY. The independent Republic of Zambia (formerly Northern Rhodesia) came into being on 24 Oct. 1964 after 9 months of internal self-government following the dissolution of the Federation of Rhodesia and Nyasaland on 31 Dec. 1963.

By an Order in Council dated 4 May 1911 the two provinces of North-eastern and North-western Rhodesia were amalgamated under the name of Northern Rhodesia, with effect from 17 Aug. 1911.

By an Order in Council dated 20 Feb. 1924, the office of Governor was created, an executive council constituted and provision made for the institution of a legislative council which, since 1945, had an unofficial majority. On 1 April 1924 the British South Africa Company was relieved of the administration of the territory by the Crown.

AREA AND POPULATION. Zambia is bounded by Tanzania in the north, Malawi in the east, Mozambique in the south-east and by Zimbabwe and South West Africa (Namibia) in the south. The area is 290,586 sq. miles (752,620 sq. km). Population (1982 estimate) 6,242,000 of which 40% urban.

The republic is divided into 9 provinces. Their names, headquarters, area (in sq. km) and estimated population in 1980 were as follows:

Province	Headquarters	Area	Population	Province	Headquarters	Area	Population
Copperbelt	Ndola	31,328	1,248,888	Eastern	Chipata	69,106	656,381
Luapula	Mansa	50,567	412,789	Southern	Livingstone	85,283	686,469
Northern	Kasama	147,826	677,894	N.-Western	Solwezi	125,827	301,677
Central	Kabwe	116,290	1,207,713	Western	Mongu	126,386	487,988
(including Lusaka)							

The seat of Government is at Lusaka (population, 1980, 538,469). The other important centres are Livingstone, the old capital (71,987), Ndola (282,439), Luanshya (132,164), Mufulira (149,778), Kitwe (314,794), Chililabombwe (61,928), Kalulushi (59,213) and Chingola on the Copperbelt (145,869); Kabwe, the oldest mining township (143,635); Chipata, centre of a tobacco farming area.

CLIMATE. The climate is tropical, but has three seasons. The cool, dry one is from May to Aug., a hot dry one follows until Nov., when the wet season commences. Frosts may occur in some areas in the cool season. Lusaka. Jan. 70°F (21·1°C), July 61°F (16·1°C). Annual rainfall 33" (836 mm). Livingstone. Jan. 75°F (23·9°C), July 61°F (16·1°C). Annual rainfall 27" (673 mm). Ndola. Jan. 70°F (21·1°C), July 59°F (15°C). Annual rainfall 52" (1,293 mm).

CONSTITUTION AND GOVERNMENT. The Constitution provides for a President, elected in the first instance by the General Conference of the ruling party, the United National Independence Party, and thereafter he is elected by the electorate. On 13 Dec. 1972 President Kaunda signed a new Constitution based on one-party rule.

The single political party is the United National Independence Party. Its full-time executive organ (headed by a Secretary-General) is the Central Committee, whose 24 members are elected by the General Conference of the Party. The Central Committee has precedence over the legislative body, the National Assembly, which is led by the Prime Minister and consists of 125 elected members and up to 10 nominated members, including a cabinet of 18 ministers.

Presidential elections were held in Oct. 1983 and on 30 Oct. President Kaunda was sworn in for a fifth 5-year term.

The Cabinet, as in Dec. 1983, was composed as follows:

President and Commander-in-Chief: Kenneth David Kaunda.
Prime Minister: Nalumino Mundia. *Agriculture and Water Development:* Unia Mwila. *Commerce and Industry:* Leonard Subulwa. *Co-operatives:* Justin Mukando. *Defence:* Clement Mwananshiku. *Finance:* Luke Mwananshiku. *Foreign Affairs:* Prof. Lameck Goma. *General Education and Culture:* Kebby Musokotwane. *Health:* Mark Tambatamba. *Higher Educdtion:* Rajah Kunda. *Home Affairs:* Fredrick Chomba. *Information and Broadcasting:* Cosmas Chibanda. *Labour and Social Services:* Fredrick Hapunda. *Lands and Natural Resources:* Fitzpatrick Chuula. *Legal Affairs and Attorney-General:* Gibson Chigaga. *Mines:* Basil Kabwe. *National Commission for Development Planning:* Dr Henry Meebelo. *National Guidance:* Arnold Simuchimba. *Power, Transport and Communications:* Gen. Kingsley Chinkuli. *Tourism:* Rodger Sakuhuka. *Works and Supply:* Haswell Mwale. *Youth and Sport:* Ben Kakoma.

Flag: Green, with in the fly a panel of 3 vertical strips of dark red, black and orange, and above these a soaring eagle in gold.

The provinces are administered by Central Committee Members for the provinces who are responsible for the overall government and Party administration of their respective areas. The Members are assisted by a Political Secretary and a Permanent Secretary. Each district in all provinces is headed by a District Governor, and these are directly responsible to their respective provincial Political Secretaries.

DEFENCE

Army. The Army consists of 1 armoured regiment and 6 infantry battalions, with supporting artillery, engineer and signals units. Equipment includes some 34 main battle tanks and 130 armoured cars. Strength (1984) 12,500. There are also para-military police units numbering 1,200 men.

Air Force. Creation of the Zambian Air Force was assisted initially by an RAF mission. Equipment acquired in this period and still in use includes 5 twin-engined Caribou and 6 single-engined Beaver transports built in Canada. Training and expansion of the Air Force was next taken over by Italy, with the purchase of 23 Aermacchi M.B.326G armed jet basic trainers (of which 18 remain in service), 8 SIAI-Marchetti SF.260M piston-engined trainers and the 10 surviving Agusta-Bell 47G/205/212/JetRanger helicopters. Twelve J-6 (MiG-19) jet fighter-bombers and some CJ-6 primary trainers have since been acquired from China, a squadron of 16 MiG-21 fighters, 3 Yak-40 light jet transports, some An-26 twin-turboprop transports and 6 Mi-8 helicopters from the Soviet Union, 6 SOKO Jastreb jet light attack aircraft and 6 Galeb jet trainers from Yugoslavia, 5 DHC-5 Buffalo twin-turboprop transports from Canada, 6 C-47s built in the USA, 10 Do 28D Skyservant light transports from Germany, 20 Supporter armed light trainers from Sweden.

INTERNATIONAL RELATIONS

Membership. Zambia is a member of UN, the Commonwealth, OAU and is an ACP state of EEC.

ECONOMY

Planning. The third development plan was finally launched in 1979 and by 1983 K3,500m. had been invested.

Budget. Revenue and expenditure for 1984 (in K1m.): envisaged expenditure of 1,508 and revenue of 1,240.

Currency. Decimal currency was introduced on 16 Jan. 1968. The *Kwacha* (K) is divided into 100 *ngwee* (n). Notes of K20, K10, K5, K2 and K1 are in use. In March 1984, £1 = 2·36 *Kwacha*; US$1 = 1·57 *Kwacha*.

Banking. Barclays Bank International has 25 branches, 6 sub-branches and 17 agencies; Standard Bank has 18 branches and 17 agencies; National & Grindlays, 10 branches and 1 sub-branch; Zambia National Commercial Bank, 10 branches and 1 in London; the post office saving bank has branches throughout the republic.

The Finance Development Corporation (FINDECO) controls the building societies, all insurance companies, one commercial bank and has shares in a second one. The Agricultural Finance Corporation provides loans to farmers, co-operatives, farmers' associations, agricultural societies and such bodies as will further the agricultural industry.

ENERGY AND NATURAL RESOURCES

Electricity. The total installed capacity of hydro and thermal power stations, excluding Zambia's share of Kariba South, amounts to 855 mw and the energy consumption during 1978 amounted to some 5,626·3m. kwh. Zambia exports electricity to Zaïre, Zimbabwe and Angola.

The hydro stations are located at Mbala, Mansa, Kasama, Mulungushi, Lunsemfwa and Victoria Falls, Lusiwasi and Kafue Gorge. Work has started on the Kariba North Project. The thermal stations are located on the Copperbelt. A number of diesel power stations have been installed, mostly in the North-Western and Northern Provinces.

Minerals. The total value of minerals produced in 1982 was:

	Output (1,000 tonnes)	Value (K1,000)		Output (1,000 tonnes)	Value (K1,000)
Copper	584·2	710,636	Coal	603·9	22,346
Zinc	38·9	27,648	Cobalt	2·4	45,257
Lead	14·5	6,050	Other	–	43,227

Agriculture. Although 70% of the population is dependent on agriculture only 10% of GDP is provided by the industry. Principal agricultural products (1982) were maize, 508,328 tonnes; sugar, 117,058 tonnes; cotton, 13,171 tonnes; tobacco, 2,565 tonnes; groundnuts, 810 tonnes.

Livestock (1982): 2,250,000 cattle; 240,000 pigs; 38,000 sheep; 343,000 goats, and 13m. poultry.

INDUSTRY AND TRADE

Industry. In Dec. 1982 there were 34,020 persons employed in agriculture, forestry and fisheries; 60,270 in mining and quarrying; 48,070 in manufacturing; 8,060 in electricity and water; 42,150 in construction and 25,350 in transport and communications.

Commerce. In 1982 imports totalled K773m., exports 985m. Copper exports (1981) totalled 552,000 tons valued at K874m.

Total trade between Zambia and UK (British Department of Trade returns, in £1,000 sterling):

	1980	1981	1982	1983
Imports to UK	94,610	41,398	39,957	50,242
Exports and re-exports from UK	103,941	68,223	61,248	55,501

COMMUNICATIONS

Roads. There were (1982) over 5,583 km of tarred roads.

Railways. Zambia Railways are that part of the old Rhodesia Railways north of the Victoria Falls. In 1980 the total route-km was 1,297 km (1,067 mm gauge). In 1981 the Zambian railways (excluding Tan-Zam) carried 1·7m. passengers and 1·9m. tonnes of freight. The Tan–Zam railway, giving Zambia access to Dar es Salaam, was opened in 1975, comprising 892 km of route in Zambia.

Aviation. There were (1982) 130 airports in Zambia (46 government owned). Lusaka is the principal international airport. Seven foreign airlines use Lusaka.

Post. There were (1982) 13 head post offices and 236 other post offices. On 1 Jan. 1982 there were 32,659 telephones.

Cinemas. In 1971 there were 28 cinemas with a seating capacity of 13,400.

Newspapers. There are 2 national daily papers: *The Times of Zambia* (circulation, 65,000) and *Zambia Daily Mail* (45,000).

JUSTICE, RELIGION, EDUCATION AND WELFARE

Justice. The Judiciary consists of the Supreme Court, the High Court and 4 classes of magistrates' courts; all have civil and criminal jurisdiction.

The Supreme Court hears and determines appeals from the High Court. Its seat is at Lusaka.

The High Court exercises the powers vested in the High Court in England, subject to the High Court ordinance of Zambia. Its sessions are held where occasion requires, mostly at Lusaka and Ndola.

All criminal cases tried by subordinate courts are subject to revision by the High Court.

Religion. Freedom of worship is one of the constitutional rights of Zambian citizens. Minority groups, such as the Asian community, are free to practise the religions of Hinduism and Islam, and the views of the leaders of these communities are respected by the Government. The Lumpa Church was banned in 1965 for security reasons, following considerable loss of life, but the Jehovah's Witnesses are allowed to continue their way of life despite the conflict of authority in their views and the views of politicians.

The Christian faith has largely replaced traditional African religion, and the Christian Churches number about 500,000 members and adherents.

Education. In 1977 the primary school enrolments were 936,817, secondary school enrolments were 83,757 and 3,752 students were enrolled for teacher-training. In 1977 the University of Zambia had 3,111 full-time students. Government expenditure on education in 1981 (estimate) was K132·77m.

Health. In 1978 there were 82 hospitals and over 1,000 children's clinics served by 423 doctors.

DIPLOMATIC REPRESENTATIVES

Of Zambia in Great Britain (2 Palace Gate, London, W8 5LS)
High Commissioner: Lieut.-Gen. Peter D. Zuze (accredited 24 June 1982).

Of Great Britain in Zambia (Independence Ave., Lusaka)
High Commissioner: John R. Johnson, CMG.

Of Zambia in the USA (2419 Massachusetts Ave., NW, Washington, D.C., 20008)
Ambassador: Putteho M. Ngonda.

Of the USA in Zambia (PO Box 31617, Lusaka)
Ambassador: Nicholas Platt.

Of Zambia to the United Nations
Ambassador: Paul Lusaka.

Books of Reference

General Information: The Director, Zambia Information Services, PO Box 50020, Lusaka.

Laws of Zambia. 13 vols. Govt. Printer, Lusaka
Beveridge, A. A., and Oberschall, A. R., *African Businessmen and Development in Zambia.* Princeton Univ. Press, 1980
Bliss, A. M., *Zambia.* [Bibliography] Oxford and Santa Barbara, 1984
Bond, G. C., *The Politics of Change in a Zambian Community.* Univ. of Chicago Press, 1976
Kaunda, Kenneth D., *Zambia Shall be Free.* London, 1962.—*Humanism in Zambia.* Lusaka. 2 vols. 1967 and 1974.—*Zambia's Economic Revolution.* Lusaka, 1968.—*Zambia's Guidelines for the Next Decade.* Lusaka, 1968.—*Letter to my Children.* Lusaka, 1973
Roberts, A., *A History of Zambia.* London, 1977
Sklar, R. L., *Corporate Power in an African State.* Univ. of California Press, 1976

ZIMBABWE

Capital: Harare
Population: 7·5m. (1982)
GNP per capita: US$630 (1980)

HISTORY. Prior to Oct. 1923 Southern Rhodesia, like Northern Rhodesia, was under the administration of the British South Africa Co. In Oct. 1922 Southern Rhodesia voted in favour of responsible government. On 12 Sept. 1923 the country was formally annexed to His Majesty's Dominions, and on 1 Oct. 1923 government was established under a governor, assisted by an executive council, and a legislature, with the status of a self-governing colony. For the history of the period 1961–1979 including the period of unilateral declaration of independence *see* THE STATESMAN'S YEAR-BOOK, 1980–81, pp. 1623–25.

AREA AND POPULATION. Zimbabwe is situated between the northern border of the Transvaal and the Zambezi River and is bordered on the east by Mozambique and on the west by the republic of Botswana. The area is 150,699 sq. miles (390,308 sq. km). The capital is Harare (Salisbury). The total population was (1982 census) 7,532,000.

Population of main urban areas (1982 census): Bindura, 18,000; Bulawayo, 414,000; Masvingo (Fort Victoria) 31,000; Kadoma (Gatooma) 45,000; Gweru (Gwelo) 79,000; Chegutu (Hartley) 20,000; Marondera (Marandellas) 20,000; Kwekwe (Que Que) 48,000; Redcliffe, 22,000; Harare (Salisbury) 656,000; Zvishavane (Shabani) 27,000; Chinhoyi (Sinoia) 24,000; Mutare (Umtali) 70,000; Hwange (Wankie) 39,000; Chitungwiza, 175,000.

Vital statistics (1980): Deaths, 22,431. Many living in remote areas do not register births.

CLIMATE. Though situated in the tropics, conditions are remarkably temperate throughout the year because of altitude, and an inland position keeps humidity low. The warmest weather occurs in the three months before the main rainy season, which starts in Nov. and lasts till March. The cool season is from mid-May to mid-Aug. and, though days are mild and sunny, nights are chilly. Harare. Jan. 69°F (20·6°C), July 57°F (13·9°C). Annual rainfall 33″ (828 mm). Bulawayo. Jan. 71°F (21·7°C), July 57°F (13·9°C). Annual rainfall 24″ (594 mm). Victoria Falls. Jan. 78°F (25·6°C), July 61°F (16·1°C). Annual rainfall 28″ (710 mm).

CONSTITUTION AND GOVERNMENT. At the Commonwealth Conference held in Lusaka in Aug. 1979 agreement was reached for a new Constitutional Conference to be held in London and this took place between 10 Sept. and 15 Dec. 1979 at Lancaster House. It was attended by the various factions in Zimbabwe-Rhodesia, including Abel Muzorewa, Robert Mugabe and Joshua Nkomo, and was chaired by Lord Carrington. It achieved 3 objectives: (*i*) the terms of the Constitution for an independent Zimbabwe; (*ii*) terms for a return to legality: and (*iii*) a ceasefire. Lord Soames became Governor-General of Southern Rhodesia in Dec. 1979 and elections took place in March 1980.

Zimbabwe African National Union (ZANU, PF) won 57 of the 80 black seats, Zimbabwe African People's Party (ZAPU), 20 and United National Council (UANC), 3.

Rhodesia (Southern Rhodesia) became the Republic of Zimbabwe on 18 April 1980.

President: Canaan Banana.

The Cabinet in Feb. 1984 was composed as follows:

Prime Minister and Minister of Defence and Industry and Technology: R. G. Mugabe.
Deputy Prime Minister and Minister of Energy and Water Resources and Development: S. V. Muzenda. *National Supplies:* E. M. Nkala. *Finance, Economic Plan-*

ning and Development: B. T. G. Chidzero. *Trade and Commerce:* R. C. Hove. *Home Affairs:* S. V. Mubako. *Education:* D. B. Mutumbuka. *Community Development and Women's Affairs:* T. R. Nhongo. *Agriculture:* D. R. Norman. *Health:* S. T. Sekeramayi. *Information, Posts and Telecommunications:* N. M. Shamuyarira. *Justice, Legal and Parliamentary Affairs:* E. J. M. Zvobgo. *Youth, Sport and Culture:* S. H. S. Makoni. *Foreign Affairs:* W. M. Mangwende. *Labour, Manpower Planning and Social Welfare:* F. M. M. Shava. *Without Portfolio:* D. Ngwenya, F. J. Masango. *Local Government and Town Planning:* E. C. Chikowore. *Natural Resources and Tourism:* V. F. Chitepo. *Lands, Resettlement and Rural Development:* M. E. Mahachi. *Construction and National Housing:* S. S. Mumbengegwi. *Transport:* H. S. M. Ushewokunze. *Mines:* C. D. Ndlovu. *Ministers of State in the Prime Minister's Office:* T. M. Nyagumbo *(Political Affairs and Provincial Development Co-ordination),* E. R. Kadungure *(Defence),* K. M. Kangai *(Industry and Technology),* J. C. Anderson *(Public Service),* J. L. Nkomo *(Deputy Prime Minister),* E. D. Mnangagwa. *Ministers of State in the Deputy Prime Minister's Office:* O. M. Munyaradzi *(Energy Resources and Development),* C. G. Msipa *(Water Resources and Development).*

National flag: Seven horizontal stripes of green, yellow, red, black, red, yellow and green; on a white black-edged triangle in the hoist a red star surmounted by the Zimbabwe Bird in yellow.

The first municipal elections were held in Nov. 1980.

DEFENCE

Army. The Army consists of 1 armoured and 1 artillery regiments; 35 infantry, 1 commando and 1 parachute battalion; and 7 engineer and 6 signals squadrons. Equipment includes 10 T-34 and 18 T-54 main battle tanks. Strength was (1984) 4,000, and there are a further 10,000 paramilitary police.

Air Force. The Zimbabwe Air Force (regular) has a strength of about 1,300 personnel and 130 aircraft in 8 squadrons, of which 2 are intended primarily for a training role. Headquarters ZAF and New Sarum ZAF station are in Harare; the second main base is at Thornhill, Gweru, with many secondary airfields throughout the country. Equipment includes 1 squadron of Canberra bombers with added underfuselage rocket racks; 1 squadron of Hunter FGA.9 fighter-bombers, supported by Hawk training and light attack aircraft, a transport squadron with 6 turboprop CASA Aviocars, 4 twin-engined Islanders and 12 C-47s; a squadron with 9 Reims/Cessna 337 Lynx attack aircraft; a squadron with 14 SIAI-Marchetti SF.260W Genet and 5 turboprop SF.260TP light attack aircraft and 17 SF.260C Genet trainers; a helicopter liaison/transport squadron with 26 Alouette II/IIIs, a helicopter casualty evacuation/transport squadron with 10 Bell 205s and 2 Bell 412s. One fighter squadron is expected to equip with Chinese-built F-6 (MiG-19) aircraft and another with J-7s (MiG-21s).

INTERNATIONAL RELATIONS

Membership. Zimbabwe is a member of UN, OAU, the Non-Aligned Movement and is an ACP state of EEC.

ECONOMY

Budget. Revenue and expenditure (in Z$1,000) for years ending 30 June:

	1979–80	1980–81	1981–82	1982–83	1983–84
Revenue	675,891	949,109	1,359,115	1,764,503	2,079,000
Ordinary expenditure:					
From revenue and loan funds		1,131,229	1,411,904	1,897,383	2,558,894	2,709,410

Receipts during the year ended 30 June 1983 were (in Z$1,000): Income and profits tax, 792,408; taxes on goods and services, 769,951; miscellaneous taxes and other income, 202,144.

The gross amount of the public debt outstanding in June 1983 was Z$2,652,255,472.

Currency. On 17 Feb. 1970 decimal currency was adopted. The unit of currency is the Zimbabwe *dollar* divided into 100 *cents*. In Sept. 1984, £1 = Z$1·63; US$1 = Z$1·10.

Banking. The Reserve Bank of Zimbabwe is the country's central bank; it became operative when the Bank of Rhodesia and Nyasaland ceased operations on 1 June 1965. It acts as banker to the Government and to the commercial banks and as agent of the Government for important financial operations. It is also the central note-issuing authority and co-ordinates the application of the Government's monetary policy.

The post office savings bank had Z$376·9m. deposits at 31 Jan. 1983.

The 5 commercial banks are Barclays Bank of Zimbabwe Ltd, Grindlays Bank Ltd, Zimbabwe Banking Corporation Ltd, Standard Chartered Bank Zimbabwe Ltd, Bank of Credit and Commerce Zimbabwe (Pvt) Ltd.

Weights and Measures. The metric system is in use but the US short ton is also used.

ENERGY AND NATURAL RESOURCES

Minerals. The total value of all minerals produced in 1982 was Z$383,044,000. Output (in 1,000 tonnes) and value (in Z$1,000):

		Output			Value	
	1980	1981	1982	1980	1981	1982
Asbestos	250·9	247·6	194·4	70,201	91,276	76,634
Gold (1,000 oz.)	367·0	371·0	426·0	144,875	117,380	122,773
Chrome ore	553·0	536·0	431·6	18,447	20,406	19,873
Coal	3,134·0	2,867·0	2,800·0	28,001	29,469	35,834
Copper	27·0	24·6	24·8	35,390	27,900	26,839
Nickel	15·1	13·1	13·3	55,571	51,734	49,753
Iron Ore	1,622·0	1,097·7	837·0	14,815	14,841	13,949
Silver (1,000 oz.)	949·0	857·0	918·0	13,004	5,997	5,271

Agriculture. The most important single food crop in Zimbabwe is maize, the staple food of a large proportion of the population; deliveries to the Grain Marketing Board in 1982 were 1,395,909 tonnes. The export potential for the livestock industry has increased with the possibility of new markets in EEC countries. Milk production by the Dairy Marketing Board in 1981–82 was 150·7m. litres.

The country is suitable for the production of both citrus and deciduous fruits and fruit production is now well established.

In 1981–82 seed cotton production was 155,000 tonnes and irrigated wheat production (1982) was 212,882 tonnes.

Tea is grown in the Inyanga and Chipinge districts and production in 1982 was 9,920 tonnes. Coffee growing is of increasing importance (production, 1981-82, 4,978 tonnes) as is sugar; sugar exports (1982) were valued at about Z$41m. Other crops grown in substantial quantities include small grains (sorghums and millet), soya beans and groundnuts. A wide variety of vegetable crops are also produced.

Tobacco is the most important single product, accounting for over 40% of the value of earnings from agricultural exports. In 1982 tobacco exports accounted for 17% of all Zimbabwean foreign exchange earnings.

Livestock (1982): Cattle, 5·6m.; pigs, 182,000; sheep, 299,000; goats, 899,000.

INDUSTRY AND TRADE

Industry. The manufacturing industry has developed from the service and maintenance operations that initially provided the back-up needed by the mining and agricultural sectors, and it now supplies a comprehensive range of consumer goods and a growing number of capital goods to the local market. A high reputation for quality has been won by many manufacturers, including producers of clothing, footwear, furniture, radio equipment, steel sections, agricultural implements and pharmaceutical products.

The Customs Agreement with the Republic of South Africa was extended in March, 1982 pending further discussion. Zimbabwe has also entered into Trade

Agreements with Zambia, Mozambique, Tanzania, Angola and Swaziland. There is a Customs Union with Botswana. In 1981 agriculture and forestry formed 18% and manufacturing (1983) 25% of the GDP.

Labour. The labour force (1983) was 2·5m.; 991,000 (40%) are employed in the formal sector; 750,000 (30%) are peasant cultivators. The remaining 750,000 are either self-employed in the informal sector or unemployed. Nearly 180,500 new job-seekers entered the employment market this year.

The major development in 1982 concerning employment services in Zimbabwe was that the Ministry of Labour and Social Services established the Department of Employment and Employment Development (DEED). The Department is now pursuing an active employment policy designed to achieve the following objectives: (a) To promote full and gainful employment for every Zimbabwean of working age. (b) To ensure that the worker's capabilities and creativity are utilized to the greatest extent possible in order to maximise production, economic growth and development. (c) To ensure fair employment practices and equal opportunities in the employment market so that every Zimbabwean will have access to employment offices, career counselling, vocational training and promotion, irrespective of race, ethnic group, sex, religion, age, physical handicap and residence (urban, rural, density area, suburb). The major functions of the new Department are: (a) To provide nation-wide job placement services to all Zimbabweans. (b) To provide nation-wide career development programmes. (c) To register and monitor private employment agencies. (d) To promote employment creating programmes and projects.

Commerce. Imports and exports (in Z$1,000):

	1978	1979	1980	1981	1982
Imports	404,239	550,908	809,400	1,017,700	999,000
Exports	612,364	702,302	784,000	959,300	1,118,000

Principal imports in 1981 (in Z$1,000): Machinery and transport equipment, 372,400; petroleum products, 189,056; textiles, 67,394; chemicals, 48,424; steel products, 41,224; insecticides and disinfectants, 18,486; medicines and drugs, 16,216.

Principal exports in 1981 (in Z$1,000): Unmanufactured tobacco, 218,280; gold, 117,380; ferrochrome, 79,517; asbestos, 75,947; cotton lint, 60,299; nickel and nickel alloys, 46,787; raw sugar, 45,908; iron and steel, 42,638; maize, 34,738; copper, 18,317; clothing, 12,308; meat, 4,526.

Total trade between Zimbabwe and UK (British Department of Trade returns, in £1,000 sterling):

	1979	1980	1981	1982	1983
Imports to UK	325	28,632	38,331	62,584	68,445
Exports and re-exports from UK	1,497	16,209	45,314	95,019	64,734

Tourism. In 1981, 327,261 tourists visited Zimbabwe.

COMMUNICATIONS. The Ministry of Transport is responsible for the Government's relations with the National Railways of Zimbabwe and with Air Zimbabwe.

Roads. The Ministry of Transport is responsible for the construction and maintenance of all State roads and bridges, and all bridges outside municipal areas. The Ministry assists and supervises junior road authorities who look after the secondary and tertiary roads. State roads are those connecting all the main centres of population, international routes, major links in the system and main roads serving rural communities. The total length of roads is approximately 85,000 km including surfaced, 12,000; gravel, 46,000; earth, 27,000.

Number of motor vehicles, 1982: Passenger cars, 219,000; commercial vehicles, 17,000; motor cycles, 20,000; trailers, 29,000; tractors, 5,000.

Railways. Zimbabwe is served by the National Railways of Zimbabwe, which connect with the South African Railways to give access to the South African ports; with the Mozambique Railways to give access to the ports of Beira and Maputo;

and with the Zambia railway system. In Sept. 1974 the National Railways of Zimbabwe opened another line from Rutenga to connect with South African Railways at Beitbridge. In 1982 there were 3,394 km (1,067 mm gauge) of railways including 335 km electrified. In 1981–82 National Railways of Zimbabwe carried 13·3m. tons of freight and 1·8m. passengers.

Aviation. Air Zimbabwe operates domestic services and also regular flights to Zambia, Kenya, Malawi, Botswana and South Africa, and to London, Frankfurt and Athens in Europe and also to Perth and Sydney in Australia in association with Qantas. The country is also served by British Airways, Kenya Airways, Ethiopian Airlines, Air Tanzania, Air Malawi, Zambian Airways, Mozambique Airlines, South African Airways, Air India, Air Botswana, the Royal Swazi Airlines, UTA French Airlines, Air Portugal, Swissair and Qantas. In 1981-82, 543,005,887 passenger-km were flown.

Shipping. Zimbabwe outlets to the sea are Maputo and Beira in Mozambique and the South African ports.

Post and Broadcasting. At Dec. 1982 there were 155 full post offices, 29 postal telegraph agencies and 27 postal agencies. In Dec. 1982 there were 242,252 telephones in Zimbabwe served by 97 exchanges; 1,282 telex connexions, served by 2 telex exchanges. Zimbabwe Broadcasting Corporation is an independent statutory body broadcasting general service in English and African service in English, Shona, N'debele and Nyanja and 3 regional commercial services in English on medium- and short-waves. Zimbabwe Television Ltd broadcasts one programme 45 hours a week *via* 7 transmitters. In June 1982 there were 82,000 television and 170,000 radio licences.

JUSTICE, RELIGION, EDUCATION AND WELFARE

Justice. The Supreme Court consists of the Chief Justice, the Judge President and at least one other judge of appeal. The High Court consists of a number of puisne judges. The Supreme Court considers appeals from the High Court and lower courts; the High Court has full jurisdiction, civil and criminal, over all persons and matters within Zimbabwe. The Judge President presides over the Supreme Court in the absence of the Chief Justice. The Courts sit at Harare and Bulawayo, and sittings of the High Court are held at three other principal towns three times a year.

Regional Courts, established in Harare and Bulawayo, are intermediate in jurisdiction between the magistrates' courts and the High Court, and have civil jurisdiction.

The tribal courts and District Commissioners' Courts of colonial days have now been replaced by a system of Primary Courts, comprising village courts and community courts. By 1982, 1,100 village and 50 Community Courts had been established. Village courts are presided over by officers selected for that purpose from the local population. They sit with two assessors, and apply customary law. They are not yet able to exercise criminal jurisdiction, but it is anticipated that this will soon come about.

Community Courts are presided over by a Presiding Officer, who is a Government Officer. They have a limited amount of criminal jurisdiction.

Religion. The largest religious groups are the Anglicans and Roman Catholics. Other denominations include Presbyterians, the Methodist Church in Zimbabwe and the United Methodist Church.

Education. Education is non-racial at all levels and not compulsory.

All primary schools offer free tuition; government secondary schools charge from Z$8–Z$18 per term. All instruction is given in English. There are also over 3,600 private primary schools and over 580 private secondary schools, all of which must be registered by the Ministry of Education.

There are 10 teachers' training colleges, 8 of which are in association with the University of Zimbabwe. In addition, there are 4 special training centres for teacher trainees in the Zimbabwe Integrated National Teacher Education Course.

The University of Zimbabwe provides facilities for higher education. In 1982 the total enrolment of full- and part-time students in the 9 Faculties of Agriculture, Arts, Commerce and Law, Education, Engineering, Medicine, Science, Social Studies and Veterinary Science, was 3,091. Of this 2,580 were full-time students.

Health. In 1983 there were 161 hospitals, 438 static rural clinics and health centres and 24 mobile rural clinics operated by the Ministry of Health. All mission health institutions get 100% government grants-in-aid for recurrent expenditure. There was one medical practitioner for every 7,020 inhabitants in Zimbabwe. There is a medical school attached to the University of Zimbabwe in Harare, four government training schools attached to the 4 central hospitals for training state registered nurses, 14 training schools for medical assistants out of which 11 are administered by missions, and two for training maternity assistants, health assistants/health inspectors.

Social Services. It is a statutory responsibility of the government in many areas to provide: Processing and administration of war pensions and old age pensions; protection of children; administration of remand, probation and correctional institutions; registration and supervision of welfare organisations.

DIPLOMATIC REPRESENTATIVES

Of Zimbabwe in Great Britain (Zimbabwe Hse., 429 Strand, London, WC2R 0SA)
High Commissioner: Dr Herbert M. Murerwa (accredited 1 March 1984).

Of Great Britain in Zimbabwe (Stanley Hse., Stanley Ave., Harare)
High Commissioner: Martin Ewans, CMG.

Of Zimbabwe in the USA (2852 McGill Terr., NW, Washington, D.C., 20008)
Ambassador: Edmund O. Z. Chipamaunga.

Of the USA in Zimbabwe (78 Enterprise Rd., Highlands, Harare)
Ambassador: Robert V. Keeley.

Of Zimbabwe to the United Nations
Ambassador: Dr Elleek Kufakunesu Mashingaidze.

Books of Reference

Statistical Information: The Central Statistical Office, PO Box 8063, Causeway, Harare, Zimbabwe, originated in 1927 as the Southern Rhodesian Government Statistical Bureau. Ten years later its name was changed to Department of Statistics, and in 1948 it assumed its present title when it took over responsibility for certain Northern Rhodesian and Nyasaland statistics (which it relinquished in Dec. 1963 on the dissolution of the Federation). It publishes *Monthly Digest of Statistics.*

Akers, M., *Encyclopaedia Rhodesia.* Harare, 1973
Caute, D., *Under the Skin: The Death of White Rhodesia.* London, 1983
Davies, D. K., *Race Relations in Rhodesia.* London, 1975
Good, R. C., *U.D.I.: The International Politics of the Rhodesian Rebellion.* London, 1973
Keppel-Jones, A., *Rhodes and Rhodesia: The White Conquest of Zimbabwe, 1884–1902.* Univ. of Natal Press, 1983
Linden, I., *The Catholic Church and the Struggle for Zimbabwe.* London, 1980
Martin, D., and Johnson, P., *The Struggle for Zimbabwe.* London, 1981
Meredith, M., *The Past is Another Century: Rhodesia 1890–1979.* London, 1979
Morris-Jones, W. H., (ed.) *From Rhodesia to Zimbabwe.* London, 1980
Murphee, M. W. (ed.), *Education, Race and Employment.* Lichfield, 1975
O'Meara, P., *Rhodesia: Racial Conflict or Co-Existence.* Cornell Univ. Press, 1975
Palley, C., *The Constitutional History and Law of Southern Rhodesia, 1888–1965.* OUP, 1966
Pollak, K. and Pollak, O. B., *Rhodesia/Zimbabwe* [Bibliography] Oxford and Santa Barbara, 1979
Stoneham, C., *Zimbabwe's Inheritance.* London, 1982
Vambe, L., *From Rhodesia to Zimbabwe,* London, 1976
Wiseman, H. and Taylor, A. M., *From Rhodesia to Zimbabwe: The Politics of Transition.* Elmsford, N.Y., 1981

Reference Library: National Archives of Zimbabwe, PO Box 8043, Causeway, Harare.

PLACE AND INTERNATIONAL
ORGANIZATIONS INDEX

PRODUCT INDEX